standard catalog of

IMPORTED CARS
1946-1990

by James M. Flammang

FIRST EDITION

© 1992 BY KRAUSE PUBLICATIONS, INC.

Published by Krause Publications, Inc.
700 E. State St.
Iola, WI 54990
Telephone: 715-445-2214

INTERNATIONAL STANDARD BOOK NUMBER 0-87341-158-7
LIBRARY OF CONGRESS CATALOG NUMBER 90-63914
Printed in the United States of America

ACKNOWLEDGEMENTS

No work of this magnitude could be completed without the help and cooperation of many individuals. In addition to the book staff at Krause Publications, the author wishes to thank the following people and organizations for going out of their way to provide information and assistance.

Representatives of existing imported-car manufacturers who provided information and assistance beyond the call of duty include: Ian Norris (Jaguar); Robert D. Mitchell (BMW); A.B. Shuman (Mercedes-Benz); Eileen McDonnell (Peugeot); Tom Jakobowski (Chrysler); Mitch McCullough and Lisa Dunn (Mitsubishi); Robert C. Austin (Volvo); Gerald Rothman (Abarth); and the public relations staff of Audi.

Collectors and enthusiasts who provided special information about their favorite makes include: Dr. Bert J. Davidson (Facel Vega); Jeff S. Savage (Citroen); Christopher Salyer (Lagonda); K.W. Rockett (Reliant Scimitar); Jim Kaminski (Lamborghini); Art Bayless (Fiat); Thomas Ray (Doretti); Rev. Paul A. Wobus II (DAF); and Dyck Livant (Borgward/Goliath/Lloyd).

Special thanks go to James Wren and Linda Busse of the Motor Vehicle Manufacturers Association, for their assistance in making the best use of the MVMA's outstanding research archives; Ronald Grantz, director of the National Automotive History Collection at the Detroit Public Library; Diane Richmond and the staff of the Science/Technology Department of the Chicago Public Library; and the staffs at the public libraries in Skokie, Niles and Arlington Heights, Illinois.

Also singled out for special appreciation are Terry and Sally Boyce, who offered invaluable research materials and helpful advice, as well as hospitality. Thanks also go to Jack Carew and William Siuru Jr., who helped extensively on photo research. Finally, without the expert editorial and research assistance of Marianne Flammang, this book could not have been completed.

ABOUT THE AUTHOR

James M. Flammang is a full-time freelance writer/editor specializing primarily in automobiles and, to a lesser degree, computers and electronics. He has written extensively about automotive history, technology and trends; exotic and future vehicles; the social/cultural impact of the automobile; and repair/restoration techniques. He also writes regularly about the purchase and ownership of every class of vehicle: new, secondhand, and collectible. His automotive articles have appeared not only in *Old Cars Weekly* and other collector car publications, but also in periodicals as diverse as *Visio, American Heritage,* and *Consumer's Research.* He also wrote the *Standard Catalog of American Cars 1976-86,* and contributed to other Krause catalogs. Two of his books were published by Tab Books, and he is a regular contributor to Consumer Guide publications.

Jim's interest in transportation topics dates back to childhood and encompasses nearly everything that moves and carries passengers or cargo: not only cars and trucks, but also trains, buses and ships. Fascination with foreign automobiles began early, when the first MG TCs and Jaguar XK120s started to trickle into the American market. Though British motorcars have ranked as special favorites, his interest in imports has been by no means confined to sports cars and exotics, but includes the full range of economy models that began to proliferate in the 1950s. Fond memories of favorite imports owned include a Volvo PV544, Renault Dauphine, and Volkswagen Beetle (and microbus). He has also enjoyed many long trips behind the wheels of such minicars as the early Toyota Corona, Opel Kadett, and Honda Civic. Few thrills are as well recalled as his first ride in an XK120, and other journeys in a Citroen, Mark IX Jaguar, and two-cycle Saab. Jim has also reveled in more recent jaunts around a track in a rebuilt MG-B, a Jaguar V-12 convertible, and the popular Mazda Miata roadster. Other memorable moments have been spent in the driver's seat of such beauties as a '48 Skoda and '73 Opel GT, even if the vehicles in question weren't operative at that particular moment.

Forced to name a single favorite, Jim might have to select a car that falls between import and domestic: the little Nash Metropolitan. But his Top Ten list would also have to include two or three Jaguars, an Alfa Romeo or two, several early Citroens (especially the prewar-styled 15), the Sunbeam Alpine, early Porsches, Fiat 124, Pegaso, MG TC, gullwing Mercedes-Benz, Morris Minor.... Better make that a Top Twenty list—or even a Top Fifty.

CONTENTS

FOREWORD

The concept behind Krause Publication's "Standard Catalogs" is to compile massive amounts of information about motor vehicles and present it in a standard format which the enthusiast, collector, industry professional or dealer can use to answer common questions.

Those questions include: What year, make and model is the vehicle? What did it sell for new? How rare is it? What's special about it? Some answers are provided by photos, others by the fact-filled text.

In this catalog, a widely-read automotive historian and writer has gathered facts about cars manufactured worldwide and imported into the United States through the years following World War II: specifically, 1946 to 1990. The format he used to guide his research includes descriptive data; information about standard equipment; vehicle identification code and serial number interpretations; tables giving model codes, body type descriptions, original retail (Port of Entry) price, weight and available production totals; engine specifications; technical information; and significant historical facts.

No claim is made about the catalogs being history textbooks or encyclopedias, though they incorporate elements of both. They are not repair manuals. First and foremost, they are collectors' guides which are larger in size, wider in scope and more deluxe in format than similar books on the market.

The long-range goal of Krause Publications is to make all of these catalogs as nearly perfect as possible. We've been told that they have provided nearly 100,000 automobile and truck enthusiasts with hours of enjoyable reading. This one should be particularly helpful to car buffs searching for future collectibles, as well as people seeking to purchase more recent used cars—or to anyone who wishes to learn about the intriguing variety of vehicles that have been exported to the U.S. through this long and fascinating period.

Other catalogs currently available are: *The Standard Catalog of American Cars 1805-1942; The Standard Catalog of American Cars 1946-1975; The Standard Catalog of American Cars 1976-86;* and *The Standard Catalog of Light-Duty American Trucks 1896-1986;* plus separate Standard Catalogs that cover Chevrolet, Ford, Chrysler, Buick and Cadillac automobiles. For ordering information and current prices write: **Krause Publications, 700 E. State St., Iola, WI 54990.**

INTRODUCTION

The Standard Catalog of Imported Cars 1946-1990 is the fifth multi-make volume in the Krause library of information on collectible and historic vehicles. Taken together, they provide the automobile and light-duty truck collector, enthusiast or hobbyist with a comprehensive guide to facts about thousands of vehicles built from the early days of motoring up to recent years. This information also is beneficial to people in the auto trade and industry, who need a one-stop source of facts on either a single make or the entire spectrum of vehicles.

In the years prior to World War II, automobiles trickled into the U.S. market from European manufacturers. Most were luxury and high-end sports models, aimed at wealthy Americans. After the war, thousands of returning servicemen brought European automobiles back with them, thus triggering the wave of imports that began in the late 1940s. Enthusiasts liked the tight handling and high efficiency that characterized European sports cars—or the economical operation of the little sedans, which were so different from the cars offered by Detroit.

Like many stereotypes, the image of an executive or professor at the wheel of a British roadster—tweed cap on his head, pipe in his mouth—had more than a grain of truth. Avant-garde Americans—those who craved something different during the rising tide of "organization man" conformity—did tend to turn toward imports. And in those early postwar years, import generally meant British: MGs and Jaguars, Astons and Singers, right down to quaint little Austins and Hillmans.

At the same time, the French were taking aim at America with the tiny 4CV sedan. And who could have predicted the phenomenon that would be created by the two little Volkswagen Beetles from Germany, which slipped off the ship in 1949. Within a few years, other European countries joined the fray: Italy with its Alfa Romeo and Fiat, Sweden with the Saab and Volvo, even Czechoslovakia with its Skoda.

Waiting in the wings until the late 1950s and early '60s were the Japanese. Long before the debut of its Civic subcompact, Honda sent over a handful of miniature S-series roadsters with high-winding engines and motorcycle-derived gearboxes. Datsun was ready with its Fair Lady sports car, which led to the Z-car series. Toyota, meanwhile, focused on the burgeoning small-sedan market.

This catalog emphasizes makes that were officially imported when new, as well as some that arrived individually, without benefit of an official importer (in recent years, via the "grey" market). Also included are selected makes that occasionally found their way into the U.S. at a later date—or are of sufficient historical interest to warrant inclusion, even if few ever reached America. Many were little-known at the time, but eventually gained popularity. Others were destined to remain virtually anonymous, slipping out of the market after a few years of minimal sales.

For most makes, the data compiled includes a physical description; list of equipment; original specifications; technical data; production/sales figures; and historical footnotes. Over 1,000 photos illustrate the appearance of various models. Each model year is presented in the same standardized format, except that some years are combined when change within that period was minimal. This allows for easy comparisons between years, makes and models.

Even more than for domestic makes, this was a period of contradictions; indeed, of misinformation. Reliable data were far more elusive and sketchy for European and (later) Asian makes than for domestics. All too often, researching imported makes is like piecing together a jigsaw puzzle in which one-fourth of the pieces are missing—and another fourth form a similar, but not identical, puzzle.

Factory publications were not always reliable. Reports in the trade and popular press sometimes made it sound like a new model had already arrived on U.S. shores, or would be enroute at any moment. In reality, it might not appear for months, or years; or never be exported at all.

Specifications often were announced prematurely, or based upon sketchy or erroneous information. Bits of questionable data were picked up by the press and published as though they were gospel. Specs that were accurate at first often changed by the time the car actually appeared in showrooms across the ocean. For that matter, automakers soon began to produce models specially aimed at the American market, with specifications that differed from those sold elsewhere.

Differences between measuring standards also contributed to the confusion. Engine horsepower ratings, for instance, typically did not specify whether they were based on the DIN standard (commonly used in Europe) or SAE. Metric measurements were not always converted correctly to inches. Translations into English often resulted in dubious facts going into print.

Disparities grew worse yet in the 1970s, when most engines were detuned for the American market, to meet tightening Federal emissions requirements. Dimensions also became questionable when special bumpers and other fixtures were installed to meet U.S. standards.

For exotic makes, in particular, absolute facts didn't really exist at all. Some automakers' products were in a constant state of flux, changing specifications whenever it was deemed appropriate, including right in the middle of a model year. For that matter, many imported makes did not abide by the convention of rigorous model-year changes. For them, the model name or number was the important fact, and the actual year of production secondary, so a 1957 model might differ little (if at all) from a '56. In addition, quite a few limited-production sports and luxury cars ranked almost as one of a kind, with few fixed specifications.

Short of building a time machine, then, and traveling back—armed with tape measure and dynamometer—to the day a given car first rolled off the assembly line, there is often no way to be 100% certain of every last detail.

Every effort has been made to ensure that the information in this catalog is as accurate as possible, within the constraints described above. The author and publisher encourage readers who are experts on a particular make or model to contribute any needed corrections or suggestions for future editions. Before submitting a correction, please be certain your information is correct—and that it is the only correct fact. In a work of this sort, there's always a risk of replacing one incorrect detail with another—or worse yet, substituting a flawed figure for one that's actually correct.

Although this catalog includes most makes and models that were imported in significant number, or arrived at a later date, time and space make it impossible to list every non-domestic car that somehow wound up on American soil. Most manufacturers built a number of models in addition to those listed in these pages, for sale in their home country or elsewhere in the world. If your favorite isn't here, please let us know and we'll consider including it in the next edition. Contact the author or editors in care of: Krause Publications, 700 East State St., Iola, WI 54990.

James M. Flammang
Chicago, Illinois

STANDARD CATALOG
OF IMPORTED CARS
ABBREVIATIONS & EXPLANATIONS

Adj.	Adjustable
A/C or **Air Cond.**	Air conditioning
AM, FM, AM/FM	Radio types
Amp	Ampere (or amplifier, for radio)
Approx.	Approximately
Auto. or **AT**	Automatic (transmission)
Base	Lowest-priced, least-equipped model
Bbl.	Barrel (carburetor): e.g., 2Bbl.
Berl	Berlinetta (sedan body)
BHP, bhp	Brake horsepower
Blk	Black
BMC	British Motor Corporation
BSW	Black sidewall (tire)
Brgm	Brougham
Cabr	Cabriolet, Cabrio (convertible)
Carb	Carburetor
Cass.	Cassette (tape player)
CEO	Chief Executive Officer
CID (cid)	Cubic inch displacement
Cont	Continental
Conv	Convertible
Col.	Column (shift)
Cpe	Coupe (body)
C.R.	Compression ratio
Ctry	Country
cc	Cubic centimeters
Cu. In.	Cubic inch (engine displacement)
Cus	Custom
Cyl.	Cylinder
DeL	Deluxe
Dhd	Drophead (coupe)
DHC	Drophead coupe
Dia.	Diameter
DIN	Deutsche Industrie Normen (German horsepower measurement)
Disp.	Displacement (engine size)
DOHC	Dual-overhead-cam (engine)
Dr.	Door (2-dr.)
Dsl	Diesel (engine)
Ea.	Each
EFI	Electronic fuel injection
"Eight"	Eight-cylinder engine
8-tr.	Eight-track (tape player)
EPA	Environmental Protection Agency
Equip.	Equipment
Est	Estate (car)
Est Wag	Estate wagon (station wagon)
Exc.	Except
F	Forward (3F = 3 forward speeds)
FBk	Fastback
FHC	Fixed-head coupe
FI	Fuel-injected
5-spd	Five-speed (transmission)
Fml	Formal
"Four"	Four-cylinder engine
4x4 or **4WD**	Four-wheel drive
4/5P	Four- or five-passenger
4-dr	Four-door
4-spd	Four-speed (transmission)
Ft.	Foot/feet
Ft.-Lbs.	Foot-pounds (torque)
FWD	Front wheel drive
4V	Four-barrel carburetor
Gal.	Gallon
GBR	Glass belted radial (tire)
GM	General Motors Corp.
GT	Gran Turismo (grand touring)
GTO	Gran Turismo Omologato (homologated)
GW	Gull-wing (doors)
H	Horizontally-opposed (flat) engine
HBk or **Hatch**	Hatchback (body)
H.D.	Heavy duty
HP (hp)	Horsepower
Hr.	Hour
HT	Hardtop (body type)
Hwy	Highway
I	Inline (engine)
I.D.	Identification
In.	Inch(es)
Incl.	Included, including
L	Liter (litre)
Lambo	Lamborghini
Land.	Landau
Lb. or **Lbs.**	Pound(s)
Lbs.-Ft.	Pound-feet (torque)
LHD	Left-hand drive
LBk or **Lift**	Liftback (body)
Limo	Limousine
Ltd.	Limited
LWB	Long-wheelbase
MacPh	MacPherson struts (suspension)
Max.	Maximum
Mk	Mark
mm	Millimeters
MPG, mpg	Miles per gallon
MPH, mph	Miles per hour
N/A	Not available
NC	No charge
NBk	Notchback (body)
No.	Number
O/D or **OD**	Overdrive
OHC	Overhead cam (engine)
OHV	Overhead valve (engine)
OPEC	Organization of Petroleum Exporting Countries
Opt.	Optional, option(s)
Orig	Original
OWL	Outline white letter (tire)
Oz.	Ounce
P	Passenger (e.g., 4P)
Phae or **Phtn**	Phaeton
Pkg.	Package (e.g., option)
PFI	Port (multi-point) fuel injection
P.O.E.	Port of Entry (price)
Prod.	Production
Proto	Prototype
Pwr.	Power
R or **Rev**	Reverse
Rbt	Runabout
Rds or **Rdstr**	Roadster
Reg.	Regular
Remote	Remote control
Req.	Requires
RH	Right hand
RHD	Right-hand drive
Roch.	Rochester (carburetor)
RPM, rpm	Revolutions per minute
RPO	Regular production option
RV	Recreational vehicle

RWL	Raised white letter (tire)	**Temp.**	Temperature
Saloon	British term for sedan (especially luxury or low-production model)	**3S**	Three-seat
		Tonn	Tonneau
S	Seat (e.g., 2S for two-seat)	**Tr**	Touring
SAE	Society of Automotive Engineers	**Trafficators**	Turn signals (mechanical)
SBR	Steel-belted radial (tire)	**Trans.**	Transmission or transverse
SC	Supercharged	**TV**	Television
SCCA	Sports Car Club of America	**2-dr**	Two-door
SCI, SCII	Rolls-Royce Silver Cloud I or II	**2V**	Two-barrel (carburetor venturi)
SE	Special edition	**2WD**	Two-wheel drive
Sed	Sedan	**Unibody**	Integral construction (no separate frame)
"Six"	Six-cylinder engine		
SOHC	Single overhead cam	**U.S.A.**	United States of America
Spd	Speed	**Util**	Utility
Spdstr	Speedster	**V**	Venturi (2V carburetor) or Volt (6V)
Spec	Specification (or Special)	**V-4, V-6, V-8**	Vee-block engines
Spt	Sport	**Vic**	Victoria
Sq. In.	Square inch	**VIN**	Vehicle Identification Number
S/R	Sunroof	**V.P.**	Vice-president
Sta Wag	Station wagon	**W**	Window (e.g., 3W)
Std.	Standard	**w/**	With
S/W	Split-window	**w/o**	Without
SWB	Short-wheelbase	**Wag** or **Wgn**	Wagon
Tach	Tachometer	**WB, wb**	Wheelbase
Targa	Removable roof panel(s)	**WLT**	White-lettered tire
Tax.	Taxable (horsepower)	**WSW**	White sidewall (tire)
TBI	Throttle body (fuel) injection	**WW**	Wire wheels
Turbo or **TC**	Turbocharged		

HOW TO USE THIS CATALOG

APPEARANCE AND EQUIPMENT: Word descriptions identify cars by styling features, trim and (to a lesser extent) interior appointments. Standard equipment lists reflect changes that took place during a given model's lifespan. Equipment descriptions also indicate available engines and transmissions.

I.D. DATA: Information is given about the location of the car's serial number or Vehicle Identification Number (VIN), and/or engine number. In many cases, information is included to help in deciphering the coded numbers.

SPECIFICATIONS CHART: The first column gives series or model numbers. Column two tells number of doors, body style and passenger capacity ('4-dr Sed-5P' means a four-door sedan that carries five passengers). Passenger capacity is normally the maximum; optional bucket or other special seats could reduce that number. In some cases, two figures are given (e.g., '4/5P'). That usually means the car is roomy for four passengers but five can squeeze in, and it may have no "official" maximum. Column three gives engine configuration and displacement (in cubic inches). When more than one engine is available, the smallest or "base" version normally is listed. Column four states the Port of Entry price at the time of the car's importation into the U.S. (normally the lowest figure, if there were separate amounts for East and West coast ports). Through the early years, East coast entry was the most common (or cheapest); but that began to change with the influx of imports from Asia. That figure is equivalent to the list (retail) price of a domestically-built car, not including freight and other extra charges. Prices often changed in the course of a year, especially during periods of high inflation; prices shown were valid at some point—usually the early portion—of the period indicated. Column five gives the car's weight ("shipping," "dry" or "unladen" weight, where available; but for early imports, the figures supplied often were not identified by type, and in some cases only the higher "curb" weight is known). The sixth column gives production totals for the year stated, or refers to explanatory notes below the chart. Statistics on imports tended to be supplied by calendar year rather than model year. 'N/A' means data not available.

ENGINE DATA: Engines are normally listed in size order with smallest displacement first, except where clarity dictates some other sequence. A "base" engine is the basic one offered in each model, for the stated P.O.E. price. "Optional" describes all alternate engines, including those that have a price listed in the specifications chart. Optional engines ordinarily cost extra.

CHASSIS DATA: Major dimensions (wheelbase, overall length, height, width and front/rear tread) are given for each model, along with standard tire size for most. Dimensions sometimes varied within a given year, and many published figures were imprecise.

TECHNICAL DATA: This section includes the basic layout of the car; transmissions that were standard or available; steering, front/rear suspension and brake system type; and body construction. Some listings also include transmission gear ratios and/or standard final drive ratio.

MAJOR OPTIONS: Most listings include only the most significant drivetrain or comfort/convenience options, but some are more detailed. Many options were available only on certain series or body types, or in conjunction with other items. Contents of certain option packages are included (or may be specified in the Appearance/Equipment text).

PERFORMANCE: Top speed, acceleration and fuel-mileage figures are given for selected models. Whenever possible, figures shown come from contemporary publications (issued when the car was new), rather than latter-day histories. A figure identified as "factory" or "claimed" is one that was issued by the automaker or its distributor, rather than based upon an independent test. For some recent models, EPA (Environmental Protection Agency) estimates of fuel mileage are given.

PRODUCTION/SALES: This section gives either supplementary production totals (beyond those listed in the Specifications Chart) or, more likely, sales totals for cars sold by U.S. dealers during a specified year. Many sales figures are approximate, especially in the early years, as little usable data exists on actual numbers of cars imported.

ADDITIONAL MODELS: In some cases, models that were rarely or never imported into the U.S., but are of historical interest, are described in this section.

MANUFACTURER & DISTRIBUTOR: This section lists the official name and location of the manufacturer, and identifies its distributor(s) or importer(s) in the U.S. at the time.

HISTORY: In addition to notes on the rise and fall of sales or production, this block includes significant statistics, performance milestones, design details, major corporate personnel changes, important dates and facts, and comments from contemporary periodicals or advertisements that add flavor to the description of each imported vehicle.

ABARTH

Of all the specialty sports cars produced in Europe during the postwar era, few qualify as "custom" more than the creations of Carlo Abarth. Even though the Abarth company of Turin, Italy issued model and price lists in the 1960s, and had a U.S. distributor, the general notion was that just about any engine that the firm modified could be obtained in any of its specially-created bodies. Initially, that list mainly included small, rear-mounted four-cylinder Fiat engines (enlarged in displacement and power) in either ordinary-looking Fiat bodies or coach built coupes and roadsters. After a time, however, Abarth also turned out bigger four-cylinder engines (up to 2 liters) and even a few sixes; and put its talents to work on Siata chassis as well as Fiats.

Like his contemporaries, Enzo Ferrari and Ferrucio Lamborghini, Abarth started small but developed some stunning sports and racing machines. Unlike those better-known builders, he generally stuck with small but potent powerplants, squeezing out gobs of power from only a few cubic inches.

Growing up in Austria, Karl (the Carlo came later) began with motorcycle racing, serving as both mechanic and test rider in the 1920s. Following an accident in 1930, he turned to sidecar-racing. As war erupted in Europe, Karl Abarth accepted an offer to race under Italian sponsorship, adopting a new first name in the process. A drastic accident in Yugoslavia nearly ended his career, but as the war ended Carlo had recovered and was ready for a new start as his family moved to Merano, Italy. Partly as a result of his prewar popularity with racing notables, Carlo and a partner became agents in Italy for the Porsche design firm, not long before Dr. Ferdinand Porsche was released from detention in France. Payment for that release came from race-car builder Piero Dusio, whom Abarth knew through the famed race driver Tazio Nuvolari, and who was then developing the Cisitalia (also listed in this Catalog). Soon, Abarth and his partner, Rudolf Hruska, were part of the Cisitalia team, working toward the creation not only of the strikingly beautiful Cisitalia sports car, but also a Grand Prix racer. Severe financial troubles with that company led to Abarth's departure in 1949, taking with him (in lieu of severance pay) three complete roadsters and a selection of components. That was sufficient to set up Abarth & Co. at Turin. A scorpion became the car's symbol (for Scorpio, Abarth's astrological sign).

At the 1949 Madrid Grand Prix, a prototype 204 did poorly, causing orders to be cancelled. That led Abarth to focus more on parts (mufflers, valve springs, column-shift conversions) than on complete cars. Nevertheless, the first Abarth limited-production car, a 204 Berlinetta powered by a modified Fiat four-cylinder engine, appeared at the Turin (Italy) auto show in 1950. Like the then-new Porsche, it had a torsion-bar front suspension. Additional prototypes and special editions followed in the early 1950s, but not until 1956 did a true production road car emerge: a 750-cc hop-up of the Fiat 600, which helped establish Abarth's close tie to the Fiat organization. An 850TC model followed. As a rule, Fiat supplied bodyshells (or partly-completed cars), which were then modified by Abarth. In return, Fiat gained plenty of publicity as Fiat-Abarths (or Abarth-Fiats) began to dominate their class in European racing, setting more than a hundred world records. Abarth bodies came from a variety of Italian coachbuilders, including Pininfarina and Bertone.

Abarth developed its own engines during the 1960s, starting with a 1300-cc but reaching all the way to 2.0 liters. A V-12 was even developed, but abandoned as a result of rules changes that set a limit to engine displacement. By 1972, Abarths had achieved more than seven thousand class (or overall) racing victories. Financial troubles loomed in the early years of that decade, as Fiat took over part of the Abarth operation. As late as 1980, Fiat-Abarths were winning World Rally Championships and the company continued to build engines for other Italian manufacturers.

Through the 1960s, at least, a fair number of Abarths entered the U.S., and appeared regularly in directories of imported automobiles. Sadly, rather than for his romantically rounded sports/racing cars or his potently modified Fiat minicar "sleepers," Carlo Abarth became best known in America during the 1950s and '60s for aftermarket exhaust systems, advertised regularly in the enthusiast publications.

Note: Abarths of a given type often varied in appearance and mechanical details; thus, specific examples may vary from the descriptions and data given below.

1950-55 ABARTH

204/205 (MONZA) — FOUR — Wearing a Berlinetta body by Vignale, the first Abarth is a striking example of the Italian automotive art. Jarred only by a trio of solid round "port-holes" at each side of the cowl, the body lines flow gracefully from front to rear. Small round parking lights ride below the single round headlamps, with larger rounded auxiliary lights inboard, alongside the narrow portion of the grille, which is made up of horizontal bars. Fully exposed wheel openings closely follow the roundness of the tires, which ride on handsome wire wheels. The low fastback coupe body has a dramatic wraparound back window and small rear quarter windows. Some examples had twin bumperettes in front (nothing in the center). Beneath its flat hood lid was a 1089-cc Cisitalia four-cylinder engine, hooked to a four-speed gearbox. Depending on the state of tune, the Cisitalia engine was capable of propelling an early Abarth to speeds up to 114 mph.

Note: Like many Abarths, the 204/205 was a non-standard item; specific examples may vary from the descriptions given.

I.D. DATA: Not available.

Model	Body Type & Seating	Engine Type/CID	P.O.E. Price	Weight (lbs.)	Prod. Total
205	2-dr Coupe-2P	I4/66	N/A	1450	N/A

ENGINE DATA: BASE FOUR: Inline, overhead-valve four-cylinder (Cisitalia). **Displacement:** 66.4 cu. in. (1089 cc). **Bore & Stroke:** 2.68 x 2.95 in. (68 x 75 mm). **Compression Ratio:** 10.5:1. **Brake Horsepower:** 75 at 6000 rpm. **Torque:** 80 lbs.-ft. Solid valve lifters. Two Weber one barrel carburetors.

CHASSIS DATA: Wheelbase: 87.2/87.8 in. (right/left). **Overall Length:** 138.7 in. **Height:** 45.3 in. **Width:** 58.3 in. **Front Tread:** 50.4 in. **Rear Tread:** 49.2 in. **Wheel Type:** wire.

TECHNICAL: Layout: front-engine, rear-drive. **Transmission:** four-speed manual. **Suspension (front):** upper/lower trailing arms and torsion bars. **Suspension (rear):** rigid axle with semi-elliptic leaf springs. **Brakes:** front/rear drum.

PERFORMANCE: Top Speed: up to 114 mph.

Manufacturer: Abarth & Co., Turin, Italy.

HISTORY: In 1955, Abarth revealed a curious asymmetrical prototype, aimed at the American racing market. The weirdly-shaped 207-A was an inch taller on the left (driver's) side than on the smaller covered passenger cockpit, with a monstrous tailfin directly behind the driver. All four fenders had sharply fin-like structures, standing well above the body line. Optional fuel tanks were available to allow different capacities for various usages. Riding a Fiat chassis, with an 1100-cc engine rated 66 horsepower, the car was expected to be capable of 116 mph and to sell in the U.S. for about $4000, according to *Motor Trend*. Another 1955 Abarth prototype carried a 120-cid twin-cam four-cylinder engine rated 135 horsepower, said to be capable of 124 mph even with a dry weight of 1,958 pounds.

1956-57 ABARTH

750 — FOUR — Abarth development in the mid-1950s focused on the Fiat 600 chassis and engine, beginning with a pair of luscious Bertone-bodied examples. According to *Automobile Year 1957*, "the Abarth coupe and roadster by Bertone are widely regarded as two of the most beautiful small cars ever built." Each had concealed headlamps (opened via a rotating handle under the facia) and frightfully sharp tailfins. The coupe, weighing in at 1,230 pounds, was capable of 100 mph; the lighter-weight Spyder (1,080 pounds), 95 mph. A single-seat streamliner "750 Record," also by Bertone (from a Scaglione design), appeared at the Turin Show and set many long-distance records in the 500, 750 and 1100-cc classes. Two aluminum-bodied Bertone one-off examples

1956 Abarth 207-A Spyder.

(coupe and roadster) were brought into the U.S. by Monte Carlo Imports in Manhattan Beach, California. Mainly, however, Abarth kept more than a hundred workers busy producing special black-crackle/chromium exhaust systems (with colorful scorpion insignia) and multi-carburetor manifolds for a variety of European engines before turning to serious auto production himself.

1958 ABARTH

ABARTH-FIAT 750 — FOUR — By 1958, Abarth was ready for a full-scale assault of sorts on the American market, which came in two forms: potent Abarth-modified engines in a seemingly innocuous little Fiat 600 two-door sedan, and similarly hot engines in gracefully rounded coupe bodies. The first Fiat-Abarth 750 sold for about $2195 in the U.S. and looked like an ordinary Fiat 600 sedan except for the front grille panel, which displayed an Abarth insignia, red striping on the hood, and red flashing on the bodysides. Those red touches were required by Fiat, so European passersby would be able to distinguish a Fiat-Abarth from the ordinary variety (which had about half the horsepower). As it happened, the original Fiat 600-cc engine was expanded to 747 cc and an output of anywhere from 38 to 47 horsepower. That was enough to deliver a top speed of about 76 mph, and 0-60 acceleration time of less than 20 seconds. Both the bore and the stroke were enlarged, with a new counter-balanced crankshaft added. The cylinder head was modified to accept a Weber carburetor, lighter valves installed, radiator enlarged, and four-branch twin-tailpipe exhaust system mounted. Springs in the clutch also were toughened, while the axle ratio switched from the usual 5.375:1 to 4.55:1. A small tachometer was installed inside. Abarth conversion kits were offered in Europe, as well as the completed vehicles.

ABARTH-FIAT 750 (ZAGATO) — FOUR — In addition to the modified two-door Fiat sedan, Abarth began to turn out a similarly-tweaked engine and chassis with elegant Zagato coupe coachwork. "Not since driving the Moretti coupe," reported one *Motor Trend* test driver in 1958, "have I seen so many people gawk in admiration as I drove by, and not since the first TR-2 arrived have I had so much fun just driving around." The aluminum body had a curved windshield, nearly-square rear quarter windows, graceful tailfins, and deeply recessed headlamps. At the front was the expected large shield-shaped Abarth scorpion insignia, with two horizontal arms spreading outward to the twin bumperettes. Small round pointed parking lights stood directly below the headlamp housings. Mechanical details were similar to the sedan, but performance was considerably quicker, due to the coupe's more streamlined shape and lighter weight. This striking coupe was dubbed the "double bubble," and became Abarth's best-known model.

I.D. DATA: Not available.

Model	Body Type & Seating	Engine Type/CID	P.O.E. Price	Weight (lbs.)	Prod. Total
750	2-dr Sedan-4P	I4/46	2195	1350	N/A
750 Zagato	2-dr Coupe-2P	I4/46	N/A	1200	N/A

ENGINE DATA: BASE FOUR: Inline, overhead-valve four-cylinder. **Displacement:** 45.6 cu. in. (747 cc). **Bore & Stroke:** 2.40 x 2.52 in. (61 x 64 mm). **Compression Ratio:** 9.0:1. **Brake Horsepower:** 41.5 at 5500 rpm. **Torque:** 39.8 lbs.-ft. at 4000 rpm. Solid valve lifters. Type 32 Weber carburetor. **Note:** Other engine horsepower ratings were available.

CHASSIS DATA: Wheelbase: (sed) 78.7 in. **Overall Length:** (sed) 130.5 in. **Height:** (sed) 55.3 in. **Width:** (sed) 54.3 in. **Front Tread:** (sed) 45.3 in. **Rear Tread:** (sed) 45.4 in. **Wheel Type:** disc. **Standard Tires:** (sed) 5.20x12.

TECHNICAL: Layout: rear-engine, rear-drive. **Transmission:** four-speed manual. Overall gear ratios: (1st) 16.5:1; (2nd) 10.0:1; (3rd) 6.50:1; (4th) 4.37:1. **Standard Final Drive Ratio:** 4.37:1 or 4.55:1. **Steering:** worm and sector. **Suspension (front):** independent; transverse leaf springs. **Suspension (rear):** independent; swing arms and coil springs. **Brakes:** front/rear drum. **Body Construction:** steel or aluminum unibody.

MAJOR OPTIONS: Vinyl upholstery ($35).

PERFORMANCE: Top Speed: (sed) 76-80 mph; (cpe) 99 mph. **Acceleration (0-60 mph):** about 19.6 seconds (0-50 mph in 11.8 sec.).; (cpe) 15.6 seconds. **Acceleration (quarter-mile):** (sed) 21.6 sec. (61 mph); (cpe) 20.9 sec. (74.1 mph). **Fuel Mileage:** (sed) 43 mpg at 50 mph (factory claim); (cpe) 29.5 mpg average.

Manufacturer: Abarth & Co., Turin, Italy.

Distributor: Hoffman Motors, New York City.

HISTORY: Abarth-Fiat 750s took both class and overall victories at the Sestriere Rally in Europe. Four out of five entries finished the Sebring (Florida) event, one of them winning the Gran Turismo class. One of those entrants then appeared at the drag races in Santa Ana, California, to win the under-1500cc sports class; and also took second place in its class at the SCCA race at Palm Springs, California.

1959 ABARTH

ABARTH-FIAT 750 — FOUR — By 1959, the hopped-up Abarth-Fiat sedans were arriving in the U.S. in some quantity and attracting considerable attention. In addition to the red/yellow Abarth shield on the front panel and twin tailpipes at the rear, the modified sedans had a "Derivation Abarth 750" insignia on the fender and special hubcaps with three "ears." Otherwise, they looked just like the Fiat 600 sedans on which they were based. The "standard" modified Abarth engine produced 41.5 horsepower (nearly twice that of the stock Fiat four).

ABARTH-FIAT 750 (ZAGATO) — FOUR — Appearance of the Zagato-bodied coupe was similar to that of the original described for 1958. Though similar to the Grand Touring engine used in the sedan, the coupe's version had 9.8:1 compression for a rating of 43 horsepower.

ABARTH-MONZA RECORD — FOUR — Similar in overall profile to the Zagato coupe, the Monza Record (also called Record Monza) had a wraparound back window that approached the horizontal, plus miniature triangular rear quarter windows that provided no visibility at all from the fastback coupe's interior. Like the Zagato coupe, it had deeply recessed headlamps, with round parking lights just below their housings. An Abarth shield was at the center of a horizontal trip strip on the front panel, just below the lid. Twin horizontal wraparound semi-bumpers replaced the regular coupe's vertical bumperettes. The basic engine was a 44-bhp version of the modified Fiat four, with 9.8:1 compression and specially-polished and prepared internal components. An optional Bi-albero GT engine, with twin overhead camshafts, developed 57 horsepower and permitted a top speed of 112.5 mph. That engine was used in team cars at the Sebring (Florida) race in 1959.

1959 Abarth 750 Zagato "Mille Miglia" (Coys of Kensington)

ABARTH-ALLEMANO — FOUR — Special bodies, such as the Allemano convertible, were available in the U.S. with the same engine as the Zagato coupe. The Allemano had a completely different look than other Abarth-Fiats, with protruding front fenders (vaguely reminiscent of the 1950-52 Studebaker) and tall tailfins. Other Spyder and coupe bodies of the late 1950s were even more distinctive, even bizarre, with concealed headlamps that allowed a smoother nose, and tailfins so sharp that they looked ready for battle.

I.D. DATA: Not available.

Model	Body Type & Seating	Engine Type/CID	P.O.E. Price	Weight (lbs.)	Prod. Total
750	2-dr Sedan-4P	I4/46	2106	1305	N/A
750 ZAGATO					
750	2-dr Sedan-4P	I4/46	3460	1250	N/A
MONZA RECORD					
750	2-dr Coupe-2P	I4/46	N/A	N/A	N/A
750 GT	2-dr Coupe-2P	I4/46	4900	1190	N/A
ALLEMANO					
750 Spyder	2-dr Rds-2P	I4/46	N/A	N/A	N/A

ENGINE DATA: BASE FOUR (sedan): Inline, overhead-valve four-cylinder. **Displacement:** 45.6 cu. in. (747 cc). **Bore & Stroke:** 2.40 x 2.52 in. (61 x 64 mm). **Compression Ratio:** 9.0:1. **Brake Horsepower:** 41.5 at 5500 rpm. **Torque:** 39.8 lbs.-ft. at 4000 rpm. Solid valve lifters. Type 32 Weber carburetor.

BASE FOUR (Zagato Coupe; Grand Touring): Same as above, except — **Compression Ratio:** 9.8:1. **Brake Horsepower:** 43 at 6000 rpm. **Torque:** 40 lbs.-ft. at 4000 rpm.

BASE FOUR (Monza Record; Mille Miglia Grand Touring): Same as above, except — **Compression Ratio:** 9.8:1. **Brake Horsepower:** 44 at 6000 rpm.

OPTIONAL FOUR (Special Mille Miglia Grand Touring): Same as above, except — **Compression Ratio:** 9.8:1. **Brake Horsepower:** 46 at 6000 rpm.

OPTIONAL FOUR (Special Grand Touring): Same as above, except — **Compression Ratio:** 9.8:1. **Brake Horsepower:** 47 at 6200 rpm.

OPTIONAL FOUR (Monza Record GT): Inline, dual-overhead-cam four-cylinder. **Compression Ratio:** 9.7:1. **Brake Horsepower:** 57 at 7000 rpm. Two Weber 32 DCL3 two-barrel carburetors.

Note: Some of the higher-powered engines were available only when purchasing the Abarth-Fiat chassis alone (sans body).

CHASSIS DATA: Wheelbase: 78.7 in. **Overall Length:** (sed) 130.5 in.; (cpe) 128 in.; (Monza) 137 in. **Height:** (sed) 55.3 in.; (cpe) 47.2 in. **Width:** (sed) 54.3 in.; (cpe) 54.3 in. **Front Tread:** 45.3 in. **Rear Tread:** 45.4 in. **Wheel Type:** disc. **Standard Tires:** (sed) 5.20x12; (cpe) 5.20x12; (Monza) 5.30x12.

TECHNICAL: Layout: rear-engine, rear-drive. **Transmission:** four-speed manual. Overall sedan gear ratios: (1st) 16.5:1; (2nd) 9.77:1 or 10.0:1; (3rd) 6.49:1; (4th) 4.36:1. Overall coupe gear ratios: (1st) 15.4:1; (2nd) 9.36:1; (3rd) 6.07:1; (4th) 4.08:1. Monza Record twin-cam gear ratios: (1st) 3.385:1; (2nd) 2.055:1; (3rd) 1.333:1; (4th) 0.896:1; (rev) 4.275:1. **Steering:** worm and sector. **Suspension (front):** (cpe) independent, transverse leaf spring. **Suspension (rear):** (cpe) independent, coil springs and swing axles. **Brakes:** hydraulic, front/rear drum. **Body Construction:** steel or aluminum unibody. **Fuel Tank:** (sed) 7.1 gallons; (cpe) 8.2 gallons.

PERFORMANCE: Top Speed: (sed) 80 mph; (cpe) 89-96 mph (factory); (Monza Record dual-cam) 112.5 mph (factory). **Acceleration (0-60 mph):** (sed) about 14.9 seconds. **Acceleration (quarter-mile):** 21.6 sec. (61 mph). **Fuel Mileage:** (sed) about 32 mpg average, or 43 mpg at 50 mph (factory claim).

Manufacturer: Abarth & Co., Turin, Italy.

Distributor: Roosevelt Automobile Co., Inc., Washington, D.C.

HISTORY: Ads in 1959 promoted the fact that two Fiat-Abarth coupes, entered by Franklin D. Roosevelt Jr. (Abarth's importer in the U.S. at the time) in the final event of the season at the Marlboro Raceway a year earlier, took six trophies in one afternoon.

1960 ABARTH

750 (ZAGATO) — FOUR — Production continued of the stylish "double bubble" Zagato coupe, with modified Fiat 600 engine.

750 RECORD MONZA — FOUR — Also available was the aluminum-bodied two-seater coupe with twin-cam engine rated 61 horsepower, capable of 0-60 acceleration in 11.2 seconds.

850 — FOUR — At the 1959 Frankfurt Show, there appeared a new 850 coupe made by Allemano, vaguely resembling an Alfa Romeo Giulietta SS. The engine was offered in 52-bhp or 57-bhp tune, permitting 0-60 mph speeds in the 14-second neighborhood and top speeds that topped 100 mph.

1600 — FOUR — Appearing at the Turin auto show in 1960 was a new Abarth 1600 two-seat roadster with 1587-cc four-cylinder engine, capable of 180 kilometers per hour (112 mph).

2100/2200 — SIX — Another attraction at the 1959 Frankfurt Show was an Abarth based on the Fiat 2100, but delivering 20 more horsepower than the stock engine.

Note: Other Fiat-based models also remained in irregular production; see previous listings for details. Abarth also offered a 595, 695, 1000, 1300, and 2200 coupe/cabriolet. All Abarth models had the distinctive and colorful heart/shield-shaped emblem at the front.

I.D. DATA: Not available.

Model	Body Type & Seating	Engine Type/CID	P.O.E. Price	Weight (lbs.)	Prod. Total
750 ZAGATO					
750 GT	2-dr Coupe-2P	I4/46	2895	1250	N/A
RECORD MONZA					
750	2-dr Coupe-2P	I4/46	4370	1340	N/A
850 (ALLEMANO)					
850	2-dr Coupe-2P	I4/51	2995	1345	N/A
850-S	2-dr Coupe-2P	I4/51	N/A	1345	N/A
1600					
1600	2-dr Rds-2P	I4/97	N/A	2112	N/A
2100					
2100	2-dr Coupe-2P	I6	N/A	N/A	N/A

ENGINE DATA: BASE FOUR (750 Zagato Coupe): Inline, overhead-valve four-cylinder. **Displacement:** 45.6 cu. in. (747 cc). **Bore & Stroke:** 2.40 x 2.52 in. (61 x 64 mm). **Compression Ratio:** up to 9.8:1. **Brake Horsepower:** 43 at 5800 rpm. **Torque:** 40 lbs.-ft. at 4000 rpm. Solid valve lifters. Type 32 IMPE Weber one-barrel carburetor.

Note: As before, the 747-cc engine was available in other states of tune.

BASE FOUR (Record Monza): Inline, dual-overhead-cam four-cylinder. **Displacement:** 45.6 cu. in. (747 cc). **Bore & Stroke:** 2.40 x 2.52 in. (61 x 64 mm). **Brake Horsepower:** 61 at 7000 rpm.

BASE FOUR (850): Inline, overhead-valve four-cylinder. **Displacement:** 50.8 cu. in. (833 cc). **Bore & Stroke:** 2.44 x 2.72 in. (62 x 69 mm). **Brake Horsepower:** 52 or 57.

BASE FOUR (1600): Inline, overhead-cam four-cylinder. **Displacement:** 96.8 cu. in. (1587 cc). **Bore & Stroke:** 3.17 x 3.07 in. (80.5 x 78 mm). **Compression Ratio:** 9.0:1. **Brake Horsepower:** 95 at 6000 rpm. Solid valve lifters. Twin-choke carburetor.

BASE SIX (2100/2200): Inline, overhead-valve six-cylinder with three Weber two-barrel carburetors.

CHASSIS DATA: Wheelbase: (750 cpe) 78.7 in. **Overall Length:** (750 cpe) 128 in. **Height:** (750 cpe) 47.2 in. **Width:** (750 cpe) 54.3 in. **Front Tread:** (750 cpe) 45.3 in. **Rear Tread:** (750 cpe) 45.4 in. **Wheel Type:** pressed steel disc. **Standard Tires:** (750 cpe) 5.20x12; (1600) 155x15.

TECHNICAL: Layout: rear-engine, rear-drive. **Transmission:** four-speed manual. 750 coupe gear ratios: (1st) 3.385:1; (2nd) 2.055:1; (3rd) 1.333:1; (4th) 0.896:1. **Standard Final Drive Ratio:** (750 cpe) 4.554:1. **Steering:** (750 cpe) recirculating ball. **Suspension (front):** (750 cpe) independent, transverse leaf spring. **Suspension (rear):** (750 cpe) independent, coil springs and swing axle. **Brakes:** hydraulic, front/rear drum. **Body Construction:** (750 cpe) aluminum unibody. **Fuel Tank:** (750 cpe) 5 gallons.

PERFORMANCE: Top Speed: (750 cpe) 87-89 mph; (750 Monza) 102 mph; (850 cpe) 100+ mph; (1600) 112 mph; (2100) 100+ mph. **Acceleration (0-60 mph):** (750 cpe) 17.3 sec.; (750 Monza) 11.2 sec.; (850 cpe) 14 sec.; (2100) 12 seconds. **Acceleration (quarter-mile):** (750 cpe) 20.9 sec. (65 mph). **Fuel Mileage:** (750 cpe) 37/48 mpg.

Manufacturer: Abarth & Co., Turin, Italy.

Distributor: DFL Company, Chicago, Illinois.

HISTORY: Both the Fiat-Abarth 750 GT and the 750 Record Monza appeared at the New York Auto Show in spring 1960. Conversion kits also became available (priced at $70) to turn a 750 Abarth-Fiat into an 850. Those kits included a new crankshaft, bearings, pistons, and valves. Another kit, priced at $60, could turn the basic 750 or 850 into an overhead-cam engine.

1961 ABARTH

750 — FOUR — Best known of the Abarth lot continued to be the 750, powered by an enlargement of the Fiat 600 engine. The fastback Fiat-Abarth coupe had tiny triangular rear quarter windows, a slightly wraparound back window (near horizontal), slightly recessed covered headlamps above round parking lights, and the usual Abarth shield up front. Abarth's basic coupe could be obtained with any overhead-valve engine, but not with the twin-cam versions. Five stages of engine tuning were available, with compression as high as 9.8:1, including a competition edition. In addition to the lowest-priced Sestriere, a Scorpione coupe and Riviera roadster also were offered.

750 RECORD MONZA — FOUR — Production continued of the upgraded coupe with twin-cam engine.

850 — FOUR — Abarth coupes with the 833-cc engine also continued in production, available with either pushrod overhead valves or twin overhead cams. The Fiat-Abarth 850 Spyder was a clean-looking roadster with conventional vertical headlamp placement, round parking lights somewhat inboard, a long and subtle bodyside crease just below door-handle level, and vertical taillamps.

1600 — FOUR — An Allemano convertible remained available with the "1600" engine.

2200 — SIX — Abarth's "2200" coupe and convertible were considerably larger than their mates and carried front-mounted engines with conventional suspension design.

Note: Descriptions and data are only partial. With only a few exceptions, most Abarth engines could be obtained in most body styles. Abarth's availability list also included 800 and 1000 models, rated at about 52 and 100 bhp, respectively.

I.D. DATA: Not available.

Model	Body Type & Seating	Engine Type/CID	P.O.E. Price	Weight (lbs.)	Prod. Total
750					
Sestriere	2-dr Coupe-2P	I4/46	2895	N/A	N/A
Scorpione	2-dr Coupe-2P	I4/46	3195	N/A	N/A
Riviera	2-dr Rds-2P	I4/46	3195	N/A	N/A
RECORD MONZA					
750	2-dr Coupe-2P	I4/46	N/A	1340	N/A
850					
850	2-dr Coupe-2P	I4/51	3195	1345	N/A
850 Spyder	2-dr Rds-2P	I4/51	3195	N/A	N/A
1600					
1600	2-dr Rds-2P	I4/97	5490	N/A	N/A
2200					
2200	2-dr Coupe-2P	I6	6500	N/A	N/A
2200	2-dr Conv-2P	I6	N/A	N/A	N/A

ENGINE DATA: BASE FOUR (750): Inline, overhead-valve four-cylinder. **Displacement:** 45.6 cu. in. (747 cc). **Bore & Stroke:** 2.40 x 2.52 in. (61 x 64 mm). **Compression Ratio:** 8.5:1. **Brake Horsepower:** 40 at 6200 rpm. Solid valve lifters.

Note: 747-cc engine was available with compression up to 9.8:1.

OPTIONAL FOUR (750): Same as above, except — **Brake Horsepower:** 52 at 6200 rpm.

OPTIONAL MILLE MIGLIA FOUR (750): Same as above, except — **Brake Horsepower:** 59 at 6400 rpm.

TWIN-CAM FOUR (750 Record Monza): Inline, dual-overhead-cam four-cylinder. **Displacement:** 45.6 cu. in. (747 cc). **Bore & Stroke:** 2.40 x 2.52 in. (61 x 64 mm). **Brake Horsepower:** 74 at 6800 rpm.

BASE FOUR (850): Inline, overhead-valve four-cylinder. **Displacement:** 50.8 cu. in. (833 cc). **Bore & Stroke:** 2.44 x 2.72 in. (62 x 69 mm). **Brake Horsepower:** 59 at 6200 rpm (Super, 64 at 6400).

TWIN-CAM FOUR (850): Inline, dual-overhead-cam four-cylinder. **Displacement:** 50.8 cu. in. (833 cc). **Bore & Stroke:** 2.44 x 2.72 in. (62 x 69 mm). **Brake Horsepower:** 79 at 6800 rpm.

BASE FOUR (1600): Inline, dual-overhead-cam four-cylinder. **Displacement:** 96.8 cu. in. (1587 cc). **Bore & Stroke:** 3.17 x 3.07 in. (80.5 x 78 mm). **Brake Horsepower:** 125.

BASE SIX (2200): Inline, overhead-valve six-cylinder rated 150 bhp at 5000 rpm, with three Weber two-barrel carburetors.

CHASSIS DATA: Wheelbase: (750) 78.7 in. **Overall Length:** (750) 136.5 in. **Height:** (750) 46 in. **Width:** (750) 54.3 in. **Front Tread:** (750) 45.6 in. **Rear Tread:** (750) 45.6 in. **Wheel Type:** pressed steel disc. **Standard Tires:** (750) 5.20x12; (1600) 155x15.

Note: Dimensions above are typical, and could vary considerably among the models.

TECHNICAL: Layout: rear-engine, rear-drive except (2200) front-engine, front-drive. **Transmission:** four-speed manual. **Steering:** worm and sector. **Suspension (front):** independent, upper wishbones and transverse leaf spring (except 2200). **Suspension (rear):** independent, coil springs and swing axles (except 2200). **Body Construction:** aluminum unibody.

PERFORMANCE: Similar to 1960.

Manufacturer: Abarth & Co., Turin, Italy.

Distributor: DFL Company, Chicago, Illinois.

HISTORY: Abarth continued to make multi-carb manifolds, special valves, special exhaust and manifold systems for Fiats and other cars, as well as the complete automobiles. At the Turin (Italy) auto show in November 1960, Abarth promoted a Siata-Abarth 600 and 750 models, with 633 and 753 cc engines.

1962-65 ABARTH

Abarth's Fiat-based selection available through the U.S. distributor in Chicago consisted of 21 models in 1962, ranging in engine size from a 700-cc Twin-Cam Record Monza (Zagato) coupe to seven different 2200-cc models, priced as high as $7940. Also available was a new 1300 Abarth-Simca, based on the Simca 1000 chassis and carrying the first all-Abarth engine. Abarths now used Girling disc brakes.

1962 Abarth 1000 RM.

RECORD MONZA — FOUR — The smallest four-cylinder twin-cam engine was officially offered only in the Record Monza Zagato coupe. The Record Monza could also be obtained with an 800-cc pushrod engine, 850-cc pushrod four (52 or 57 bhp), twin-cam 850, and the 1000-cc engine with either pushrod overhead valves or overhead cam.

ALLEMANO — FOUR — Both a Scorpione coupe and Riviera Spyder (roadster) were available with pushrod versions of the 800, 850 or 1000 cc four-cylinder engines.

ALLEMANO 1600/2200 — FOUR — The Allemano coupe and Spyder could also be obtained with the 1600-cc twin-cam engine. Cabriolet and spyder versions of the Allemano body with 2200-cc pushrod engine were offered.

ELANA/FARINA 2200 — SIX — Six-cylinder power was available in the new Elana or Farina body, in either cabriolet or spyder form.

850 TC — FOUR — Although not included in the U.S. price list for 1962, Abarth also produced a four-seat competition sedan with the 847-cc engine (either 57 or 64 bhp). This continued the Fiat 600 sedan body used on early Abarth models (see previous listings).

1965 Abarth-Simca. (William Siuru Jr.)

1300 ABARTH-SIMCA — FOUR — Unlike the long list of Fiat-based Abarths, this new example rode a Simca 1000 chassis, though the Simca profile was nearly buried beneath the Abarth detailing. Providing the power was an Abarth-created 1288-cc four-cylinder engine, rated 125 bhp. Based on the Simca 1000's four, the 1300 engine had a twin-cam aluminum head with hemispherical combustion chambers, and twin Weber carburetors. An aluminum body was used, with disc brakes on all four magnesium wheels.

2000 GT ABARTH-SIMCA — FOUR — In 1964, an Abarth-Simca 2000 GT debuted, with a 195-bhp 2-liter engine and optional six-speed Abarth gearbox. Competition versions of the 2000 could top 150 mph.

Model Year Note: Descriptions and data in this listing apply to 1962 models (except for the 2000 GT).

I.D. DATA: Not available.

Model	Body Type & Seating	Engine Type/CID	P.O.E. Price	Weight (lbs.)	Prod. Total
RECORD MONZA (ZAGATO)					
700 TC	2-dr Coupe-2P	I4	5695	N/A	Note 1
800	2-dr Coupe-2P	I4	3931	N/A	Note 1
850	2-dr Coupe-2P	I4/52	5735	N/A	Note 1
850	2-dr Coupe-2P	I4/52	4026	N/A	Note 1
1000	2-dr Coupe-2P	I4/60	6450	N/A	Note 1
1000	2-dr Coupe-2P	I4/60	4450	1254	Note 1
ALLEMANO SCORPIONE					
800	2-dr Coupe-2P	I4	3931	N/A	Note 1
850	2-dr Coupe-2P	I4/52	4026	N/A	Note 1
1000	2-dr Coupe-2P	I4/60	2995	N/A	Note 1
ALLEMANO RIVIERA SPYDER					
800	2-dr Rds-2P	I4	3931	N/A	Note 1
850	2-dr Rds-2P	I4/52	4082	N/A	Note 1
1000	2-dr Rds-2P	I4/60	2995	N/A	Note 1
ALLEMANO 1600					
1600	2-dr Coupe-2P	I4/97	5890	N/A	Note 1
1600	2-dr Rds-2P	I4/97	5940	N/A	Note 1

Model	Body Type & Seating	Engine Type/CID	P.O.E. Price	Weight (lbs.)	Prod. Total
2200					
Allemano	2-dr Cabr-2P	I6	7390	N/A	Note 1
Allemano	2-dr Spyder-2P	I6	7540	N/A	Note 1
Elana	2-dr Cabr-2P	I6	7575	N/A	Note 1
Elana	2-dr Spyder-2P	I6	7725	N/A	Note 1
Farina	2-dr Cabr-2P	I6	7790	N/A	Note 1
Farina	2-dr Spyder-2P	I6	7940	N/A	Note 1
SIMCA-ABARTH					
1300	2-dr Coupe-2P	I4/79	N/A	1385	Note 1
2000 GT	2-dr Coupe-2P	I4/119	N/A	N/A	Note 1

Note 1: A total of 3,150 Abarths were produced in 1964.

ENGINE DATA: BASE FOUR (850): Inline, overhead-valve four-cylinder. **Displacement:** 51.7 cu. in. (847 cc). **Bore & Stroke:** 2.46 x 2.72 in. (62.5 x 69.0 mm). **Compression Ratio:** 9.2:1. **Brake Horsepower:** 52 at 6000 rpm. **Torque:** 51.3 lbs.-ft. at 4500 rpm. **Note:** A twin-cam version of the 850 also was available.

TWIN-CAM FOUR (1000): Inline, dual-overhead-cam four-cylinder. **Displacement:** 59.9 cu. in. (982 cc). **Bore & Stroke:** 2.56 x 2.91 in. (65 x 74 mm). **Compression Ratio:** 9.3:1. **Brake Horsepower:** 91 at 7100 rpm. **Torque:** 72.3 lbs.-ft. at 5500 rpm. Two Weber downdraft twin-choke carbs. **Note:** An overhead-valve version of the 1000 also was available.

BASE FOUR (1600): Inline, dual-overhead-cam four-cylinder. **Displacement:** 96.8 cu. in. (1587 cc). **Bore & Stroke:** 3.17 x 3.07 in. (80.5 x 78 mm). **Brake Horsepower:** 125 (est.).

BASE SIX (2200): Inline, overhead-valve six-cylinder rated about 150 bhp at 5000 rpm.

BASE FOUR (Abarth-Simca 1300): Inline, dual-overhead-cam four-cylinder. **Displacement:** 78.6 cu. in. (1288 cc). **Bore & Stroke:** 3.00 x 2.80 in. (76.0 x 71.0 mm). **Compression Ratio:** 10.4:1. **Brake Horsepower:** 125 at 7200 rpm. **Torque:** 96 lbs.-ft. at 6000 rpm. Two two-barrel Weber sidedraft carburetors.

BASE FOUR (Abarth-Simca 2000 GT): Inline, dual overhead-cam four-cylinder. **Displacement:** 119 cu. in. (1946 cc). **Bore & Stroke:** 3.46 x 3.15 in. (88 x 80 mm). **Compression Ratio:** 9.8:1. **Brake Horsepower:** 195 at 7300 rpm. **Torque:** 144 lbs.-ft. at 5300 rpm. Two Weber two-barrel carburetors.

CHASSIS DATA: Wheelbase: (850/1000) 78.7 in.; (1300) 82 in. **Overall Length:** (850) 132 in.; (1000) 137 in.; (1300) 140 in. **Height:** (850) 46.8 in.; (1000) 45 in.; (1300) 58 in. **Width:** (850) 55.9 in.; (1000) 54.7 in.; (1300) 58 in. **Front Tread:** (1300) 49.75 in. **Rear Tread:** (1300) 49 in. **Standard Tires:** (1000) 135x13; (1300) 135x13 or 145x13. **Note:** Dimensions above are typical, and could vary considerably among the models.

TECHNICAL: Layout: rear-engine, rear-drive except (2200) front-engine, front-drive. **Transmission:** four-speed manual. **Steering:** worm and sector. **Suspension (front):** independent, upper wishbones and transverse leaf spring (except 2200). **Suspension (rear):** independent, coil springs and swing axles (except 2200). **Brakes:** hydraulic, front disc, rear drum except (1300) four-wheel disc.

PERFORMANCE: Top Speed: (1000 T.C.) 136 mph; (1300) 143 mph (claimed). **Fuel Mileage:** (1000 T.C.) 26 mpg.

Manufacturer: Abarth & Co., Turin, Italy.

Distributor: DFL Company, Chicago, Illinois.

HISTORY: By 1964, Abarth had also introduced a new two-litre model capable of more than 150 mph. Six-speed gearboxes also became available by 1965, in the OT 1600 model (based on the Fiat 850) with its 154-bhp twin-cam engine. Wearing Dunlop racing tires, that OT 1600 could accelerate through a quarter-mile in less than 15 seconds.

1966 ABARTH

Abarth had its own sales company in the U.S. by the mid-1960s, with a revised series of models available. As before, both coupe and roadsters bodies were offered.

850 TC — FOUR — A twin-cam four-cylinder engine powered the basic Abarth Fiat-based model, offered in three states of tune. Even in basic trim, it produced one horsepower per cubic inch and was capable of 87 mph. Rear disc brakes were optional.

OT 1000 — FOUR — With a 54-horsepower (DIN) four-cylinder engine, this Fiat-based Abarth could handle speeds near 95 mph. The OT 1000 came in Berlina (sedan) form, and as an upright-style coupe or Spider convertible.

1000 BIALBERO — FOUR — This Fiat-based model had a rear-mounted 60-cid twin-cam four-cylinder engine, rated 105 horsepower. The low-slung coupe had a protruding rounded nose and deep-set headlamps, with nearly-flat back window and long rear quarter windows.

1150 — FOUR — The 70-cid four-cylinder engine that powered the 1150 series came in ratings from 55 to 85 bhp.

1300 (SIMCA) — FOUR — A 79-cid four-cylinder engine went into the rear of this Simca-based model.

1600/2000 — FOUR — Two larger engines also were used to power Abarth models, displacing either 97 or 119 cid and producing 155 or 195 horsepower. Abarth's Simca-based 2000 was a stylish fastback coupe similar in appearance to the 1000 Bialbero, with a small oval grille across the nose and deeply-recessed headlamps.

I.D. DATA: Not available.

Model	Body Type & Seating	Engine Type/CID	P.O.E. Price	Weight (lbs.)	Prod. Total
850 TC	2-dr Coupe-2P	I4/52	Note 1	N/A	Note 2
OT 1000					
Berlina	2-dr Sedan-4P	I4/60	Note 1	N/A	Note 2
1000	2-dr Coupe-2P	I4/60	Note 1	N/A	Note 2
Spider	2-dr Conv-2P	I4/60	Note 1	N/A	Note 2
1000 BIALBERO					
1000	2-dr Coupe-2P	I4/60	Note 1	N/A	Note 2
1150					
1150	2-dr Coupe-2P	I4/70	Note 1	N/A	Note 2
1300/2000 (SIMCA)					
1300	2-dr Coupe-2P	I4/79	Note 1	1385	Note 2
2000	2-dr Coupe-2P	I4/119	Note 1	N/A	Note 2

Model	Body Type & Seating	Engine Type/CID	P.O.E. Price	Weight (lbs.)	Prod. Total
1600	2-dr Coupe-2P	I4/97	Note 1	N/A	Note 2

Note 1: Pricing similar to subsequent years; see 1967-69 listing.

Note 2: A total of 1,950 Abarths were produced in 1966.

ENGINE DATA: BASE FOUR (850 TC): Inline, dual-overhead-cam four-cylinder. **Displacement:** 51.7 cu. in. (847 cc). **Bore & Stroke:** 2.46 x 2.72 in. (62.5 x 69 mm). **Compression Ratio:** 9.2:1. **Brake Horsepower:** 52 (DIN) at 5800 rpm. **Torque:** 51 lbs.-ft. (DIN) at 2800 rpm. Solex downdraft carburetor.

Engine Note: A Nurburgring version of the 850 engine was rated 55 bhp (DIN); a Corsa edition, 69 bhp (DIN rating).

BASE FOUR (OT 1000): Inline, overhead-valve four-cylinder. **Displacement:** 59.9 cu. in. (982 cc). **Bore & Stroke:** 2.56 x 2.91 in. (65 x 74 mm). **Compression Ratio:** 9.5:1. **Brake Horsepower:** 54 (DIN) at 5200 rpm. **Torque:** 58 lbs.-ft. at 3500 rpm. Three main bearings. One Solex downdraft carburetor.

BASE FOUR (1000 Bialbero): Inline, dual-overhead-cam four-cylinder. **Displacement:** 59.9 cu. in. (982 cc). **Bore & Stroke:** 2.56 x 2.91 in. (65 x 74 mm). **Compression Ratio:** 10.8:1. **Brake Horsepower:** 105 at 7100 rpm. **Torque:** 72 lbs.-ft. at 5500 rpm. Two Solex two-barrel carburetors.

BASE FOUR (1150): Inline four-cylinder. **Displacement:** 70 cu. in. (1147 cc). **Bore & Stroke:** 2.72 x 3.01 in. (69 x 76.4 mm). **Compression Ratio:** 8.5:1. **Brake Horsepower:** 55 at 5600 rpm. **Torque:** 58 lbs.-ft. at 3500 rpm. Solex one-barrel carburetor.

1150 Engine Note: 1150S engine was rated 58 bhp at 5600 rpm; 1150SS, 65 bhp at 5600; 1150 Corsa, 85 bhp at 6500 (12.0:1 compression and two Weber carburetors).

BASE FOUR (1300): Inline, dual overhead-cam four-cylinder. **Displacement:** 78.6 cu. in. (1288 cc). **Bore & Stroke:** 3.00 x 2.80 in. (76 x 71 mm). **Compression Ratio:** 10.8:1. **Brake Horsepower:** 135 at 7200 rpm. **Torque:** 97 lbs.-ft. at 6000 rpm. Two Weber two-barrel carburetors.

BASE FOUR (1600): Inline, dual overhead-cam four-cylinder. **Displacement:** 96.8 cu. in. (1587 cc). **Bore & Stroke:** 3.17 x 3.07 in. (80.5 x 78 mm). **Compression Ratio:** 9.8:1. **Brake Horsepower:** 155 at 7400 rpm. **Torque:** 113 lbs.-ft. at 5500 rpm. Two Weber two-barrel carburetors.

BASE FOUR (2000): Inline, dual overhead-cam four-cylinder. **Displacement:** 119 cu. in. (1946 cc). **Bore & Stroke:** 3.46 x 3.15 in. (88 x 80 mm). **Compression Ratio:** 9.8:1. **Brake Horsepower:** 195 at 7300 rpm. **Torque:** 144 lbs.-ft. at 5300 rpm. Two Weber two-barrel carburetors.

CHASSIS DATA: Wheelbase: (850/1000) 78.7 in.; (1150) 87 in.; (1300/1600/2000) 82.5 in. **Overall Length:** (850) 129.5 in.; (1000 Bialbero) 137 in.; (OT 1000) 140.75 in.; (1150) 150 in.; (1300/1600/2000) 141 in. **Height:** (850) 55.1 in.; (OT 1000) 53.5 in.; (1000 Bialbero) 46 in.; (1150) 52.5 in.; (1300) 45 in.; (1600/2000) 48 in. **Width:** (850) 54.3 in.; (OT 1000) 55.9 in.; (1000 Bialbero) 55.5 in.; (1150) 58.5 in.; (1300) 58.5 in.; (1600) 56.5 in.; (2000) 58.5 in. **Front Tread:** (850) 45.3 in.; (OT 1000) 45.1 in.; (1000 Bialbero) 48 in.; (1150) 49.3 in.; (1300) 49.7 in.; (1600) 48.8 in.; (2000) 49.7 in. **Rear Tread:** (850) 45.7 in.; (1000) 48 in.; (1150) 49.1 in.; (1300) 49.7 in.; (1600) 48.1 in.; (2000) 49.8 in. **Standard Tires:** (850) 13-in.; (1000 Bialbero) 135x13; (1150) 145x13; (1300) 5.00x13; (1600) 5.25x13; (2000) 5.50x13.

TECHNICAL: Layout: rear-engine, rear-drive. **Transmission:** four-speed manual (five- and six-speed available). **Steering:** worm and sector. **Suspension (front):** independent, lower control arms and transverse leaf spring. **Suspension (rear):** independent, semi-trailing arms and coil springs. **Brakes:** hydraulic, front disc, rear drum; four-wheel disc available.

Manufacturer: Abarth & Co., Turin, Italy.

Distributor: Abarth Sales Corp., Newark, New Jersey.

1967-69 ABARTH

A selection of Fiat-Abarth models was offered in the U.S. for 1967, allegedly for street driving, with 1.0- and 2.0-litre engines. Smaller-engined versions (600 and 700 cc) continued to be listed in the Italian price list.

1000 — FOUR — The 1.0-liter selection included a Fiat-Abarth Berlina Corsa 1000 sedan that was considered to be one of the fastest one-litre cars in the world; 1000 and OT 1000 coupes; 1000 and OT 1000 Spider convertibles with Bertone body; OTS 1000 coupe with 80-bhp engine; and OTR 1000 Coupe Radiale. The latter coupe carried a hemi-head four-cylinder engine rated 90 horsepower. Coupes wore the same body as the Fiat 850 on which they were based.

Sports Car Graphic described the Berlina Corsa as "probably the ugliest car we've seen in many a season," but testers were overwhelmed by its performance in Group 2 sedan racing. "It just plain flies," they reported, "into, through, and even out of a corner." The Berlina's body was based on the old Fiat 600 sedan. A fiberglass front bumper was available, which held a large oil cooler; and the rear decklid was braced open permanently.

OT 1300/124 — FOUR — By the 1968 model year, a 79-cid (1290-cc) four-cylinder engine rated 88 bhp was available for installation in Fiat 124-based coupe bodies.

OT 2000 — FOUR — Abarth's 2.0-liter coupe was the most powerful model available, with a twin-cam four-cylinder hemi-head engine that developed as much as 231 horsepower (just about 2 horsepower per cubic inch).

I.D. DATA: Not available.

Model	Body Type & Seating	Engine Type/CID	P.O.E. Price	Weight (lbs.)	Prod. Total
1000	2-dr Coupe-2P	I4/60	2695	N/A	N/A
OT 1000	2-dr Coupe-2P	I4/60	2795	N/A	N/A
1000	2-dr Spider-2P	I4/60	2995	N/A	N/A
OT 1000	2-dr Spider-2P	I4/60	3195	1610	N/A
OTS 1000	2-dr Coupe-2P	I4/60	2995	1610	N/A
OTR 1000	2-dr Coupe-2P	I4/60	3495	1477	N/A
BERLINA CORSA					
1000	2-dr Sedan-4P	I4/60	4987	Note 1	N/A
OT 1300/124					
1300/124	2-dr Coupe-2P	I4/79	N/A	N/A	N/A
2000					
OT 2000	2-dr Coupe-2P	I4/119	7487	1566	N/A

Note 1: The Berlina Corsa weighed a little over 1,200 pounds.

Price Note: Prices shown are for 1967 models.

ENGINE DATA: BASE FOUR (OT 1000): Inline, overhead-valve four-cylinder. **Displacement:** 60 cu. in. (982 cc). **Bore & Stroke:** 2.56 x 2.91 in. (65 x 74 mm). **Compression Ratio:** 9.8:1. **Brake Horsepower:** 74 at 6150 rpm. **Torque:** 76 lbs.-ft. at 5200 rpm. One Weber downdraft carburetor.

BASE FOUR (OTS 1000): Same as above, except — **Compression Ratio:** 11.5:1. **Brake Horsepower:** 80 at 6400 rpm. **Torque:** 88 lbs.-ft. at 5800 rpm.

BASE FOUR (Berlina Corsa): Same as above, except — **Compression Ratio:** 12.0-12.5:1. **Brake Horsepower:** 95 at 7500 rpm.

BASE FOUR (OTR 1000): Same as above, except hemi head — **Compression Ratio:** 9.8:1. **Brake Horsepower:** 90 at 6500 rpm. **Torque:** 92 lbs.-ft. at 5950 rpm. Two Solex two-barrel carburetors.

BASE FOUR (OT1300/124): Inline, dual overhead-cam four-cylinder. **Displacement:** 78.7 cu. in. (1290 cc). **Bore & Stroke:** 3.39 x 2.19 in. (86 x 55.5 mm). **Compression Ratio:** 10.5:1. **Brake Horsepower:** 88 at 5000 rpm. **Torque:** 94 lbs.-ft. at 5600 rpm. One Solex two-barrel carburetor.

BASE FOUR (OT 2000): Inline, dual overhead-cam four-cylinder (hemi head). **Displacement:** 119 cu. in. (1946 cc). **Bore & Stroke:** 3.46 x 3.15 in. (88 x 80 mm). **Compression Ratio:** 10.5:1. **Brake Horsepower:** about 231 (185 DIN at 7200 rpm). **Torque:** 152 lbs.-ft. (DIN) at 6000 rpm.

CHASSIS DATA: Wheelbase: (OT 1000/1300) 79.8 in. **Overall Length:** (OT 1000/1300 cpe) 142 in.; (1000 Spider) 148.9 in. **Height:** (OT 1000 cpe) 50.1 in.; (OT 1000 Spider) 48.0 in. **Width:** (OT 1000/1300) 59.1 in. **Front Tread:** (1000) 45.1 in. **Rear Tread:** (1000) 48 in. **Standard Tires:** (OT 1000 cpe) 155x13; (OT 1000 Spider) 145x13; (Berlina) 4.50x13; (OT 2000) 5.50x13 front, 6.00x13 rear.

TECHNICAL: Layout: rear-engine, rear-drive. **Transmission:** four- or five-speed manual. **Steering:** worm and sector. **Suspension (front):** independent, lower control arms and transverse leaf spring. **Suspension (rear):** independent, semi-trailing arms, coil springs and anti-roll bar. **Brakes:** hydraulic, front disc, rear drum; four-wheel disc available.

PERFORMANCE: Top Speed: (OTS 1000) 100+ mph; (Berlina Corsa) 115 mph. **Acceleration (0-60 mph):** (OTS 1000) 18.6 sec.; (OT 1000 Spider) 18.1 seconds. **Acceleration (quarter-mile):** (Berlina Corsa) 18+ seconds. **Fuel Mileage:** (OTS 1000) 26+ mpg.

Manufacturer: Abarth & Co., Turin, Italy.

Distributor: Abarth Sales Corp., Newark, New Jersey.

POSTSCRIPT: One of the final Abarth models was the Scorpion SS 1300, available by 1970 and priced at $4495 in the U.S. The wide-track fastback coupe body (with rear quarter windows) had concealed headlamps in a sloping nose, with rectangular parking lights at the ends of a wide but squat "grille" opening, with three additional slots below. Round taillamps sat on the squared-off back panel. The basic 1197-cc Fiat 124 sedan engine was enlarged to 1280 cc and developed 100 (SAE) horsepower at 6200 rpm with 11.5:1 compression and a Weber two-barrel carburetor. The four-speed gearbox came from a Fiat 850. Coil springs and an anti-roll bar were used at both ends. Wheelbase was 80.5 inches, and the Scorpion measured 142 inches overall, standing 42.3 inches tall. Four-wheel disc brakes were installed, with 155SR13 tires. *Road Test* magazine ran a Scorpion through the quarter-mile in 16.83 seconds, hitting 81.81 mph. While praising the car's performance, they noted that it had only one windshield wiper and no front license plate bracket, and door windows rolled down only halfway.

A.C.

Though seldom seen in the U.S. before the emergence of the Ace sports roadster in 1953, the A.C. company traced its roots back as far as 1908. That first A.C., known as the "Sociable," was a single-cylinder three-wheeler. A four-cylinder (and four-wheeled) model joined the original shortly before the outbreak of World War I. A 12-horsepower (R.A.C.rating) model appeared after the war. In 1920, A.C. was offering its first two-passenger sports car, with an L-head Anzani four (1496 cc). Two years later, an A.C. became the first car with a 1500-cc engine to go 100 miles in one hour. An experimental model with an overhead-valve engine reached 105.14 mph on the Brooklands track, driven by British airman Harry Hawker; but that was never built.

Not until 1922 did the company come out with a six-cylinder automobile. That one had a new 2.0-litre overhead-cam engine, which served as the foundation for subsequent powerplants. In fact, that same basic engine went beneath A.C. bonnets for the next four decades. A two-litre A.C., driven by Tom Gillett, broke the 24-hour world record in 1924, averaging 82.59 mph. By 1930, the four-cylinder engine had been abandoned, leaving only the six. While often thought of as a producer of family saloons, A.C. also delivered some sporty tourers, such as the 16/80 and 16/90 roadsters of the late 1930s. By 1939, the two-litre engine in the 16/90 reached 90 hp using a Rootes-type supercharger. During the between-the-war years, A.C. established a reputation in reliability trials and hill climbs.

Located at Thames Ditton (near London), the company had established a fine reputation as the postwar era arrived, though for sedate motorcars, rather antiquated and old-fashioned. Their first postwar model carried the familiar 2.0-litre six, and was known (logically enough) as the "2-Litre." At the 1953 London Motor Show, however, came the introduction of the A.C. that would establish the company's reputation worldwide: the Ace sports roadster. A slight modification of the earlier Tojiero sports racing chassis, it had independent four-wheel suspension (using transverse leaf springs). Under its hood lay the familiar A.C. 2-liter light-alloy six. Until 1955, at any rate, when the option of a Bristol-built six-cylinder engine became available. A year after the debut of the Ace came the Aceca coupe, similar in design but with a solid top. As availability of the Bristol engine threatened to cease in the early 1960s, the American race driver and entrepreneur Carroll Shelby took an interest in the Ace. That interest led to the development of a series of Shelby Cobras, created by stuffing an American V-8 beneath the A.C. Ace bonnet. Among the most famous of 1960s sports cars, the Cobras are also among the most emulated, with a wild variety of replicas hitting the market after the original faded away in 1968. Cobras have even served as the inspiration for the Dodge Viper, a concept vehicle car that toured the auto-show circuit in 1989 and later was tentatively scheduled for actual production sometime in the early 1990s.

Company Note: A.C. originally stood for Auto-Carriers and the firm was known at one time as Acedes, Ltd. Some sources omit the periods, calling the make "AC." Because postwar company literature retained the periods, that form is used in this catalog.

1949 A.C. drophead coupe.

CHASSIS DATA: Wheelbase: 117 in. **Overall Length:** 184 in. **Height:** 61 in. **Width:** 67 in. **Front Tread:** 55 in. **Rear Tread:** 56 in. **Wheel Type:** Dunlop steel disc with chromed caps. **Standard Tires:** 6.70x16.

TECHNICAL: Layout: front-engine, rear-drive. **Transmission:** four-speed manual; floor lever (synchromesh 2nd/3rd/4th). Overall gear ratios: (1st) 15.42:1; (2nd) 9.01:1; (3rd) 6.22:1; (4th) 4.55:1; (rev) 15.42:1. **Standard Final Drive Ratio:** 4.55:1. **Steering:** Bishop cam. **Suspension (front):** rigid axle and semi-elliptic leaf springs. **Suspension (rear):** rigid axle and semi-elliptic leaf springs. **Brakes:** Girling hydraulic front, mechanical rear drum. **Body Construction:** aluminum body over framework of seasoned wood, on steel cruciform box-section frame, underslung at rear. **Fuel Tank:** 13.8 gallons (U.S.).

PERFORMANCE: Top Speed: 84-85 mph. **Acceleration (0-60 mph):** N/A (0-50 in 14.4 sec.). **Acceleration (quarter-mile):** 22.2 sec. **Fuel Mileage:** 24 mpg.

Manufacturer: A.C. Cars, Ltd., Thames Ditton, Surrey, England.

HISTORY: Introduced in July 1947.

1947-52 A.C.

1947 A.C. two-liter sports saloon.

2-LITRE — SIX — By October 1947, the A.C. company was ready with a new model. Beneath a streamlined new saloon body stood the old familiar chassis with a beam-type front axle and overhead-cam, 2.0-litre six-cylinder engine. The saloon arrived first, followed in late 1949 by an open Sports Tourer with body by Buckland. A chromed surround for the saloon's windshield came in late 1948. The braking system switched from hydromechanical to all hydraulic for the 1952 model year, at which time the Sports Tourer added wind-up Perspex windows. Both models had a sloping, curved front end with vertical-bar grille. Semi-integrated headlamps stood alongside the grille, bulging somewhat far forward. Separate running lights were mounted just above the bumper. The curve of the saloon's front fender extended only a short distance into the door (hinged at the rear), but the Tourer brought that line all the way to the back fender and had cut down-style doors with curved upper edge. Tourer windshields folded flat.

I.D. DATA: Serial number is stamped on a plate on the right side of the bulkhead. Starting serial number: L800.

Model	Body Type & Seating	Engine Type/CID	P.O.E. Price	Weight (lbs.)	Prod. Total
2-Litre	2-dr Spt Tourer-5P	I6/121	Note 1	2606	N/A
2-Litre	2-dr Spt Saloon-4/5P	I6/121	Note 1	2849	N.A

Note 1: Price at factory was approximately $2750 (circa 1951).

ENGINE DATA: BASE SIX: Inline, overhead-cam six-cylinder. Light alloy block and head. **Displacement:** 121.4 cu. in. (1991 cc). **Bore & Stroke:** 2.56 x 3.94 in. (65 x 100 mm). **Compression Ratio:** 6.5:1 (Spts Tourer, 6.75:1). **Brake Horsepower:** 74 at 4500 rpm (Spts Tourer, 76 at 4500). Five main bearings. Solid valve lifters. Three SU carburetors. 12-volt electrical.

1953-54 A.C.

1954 A.C. Ace.

ACE — SIX — When A.C. owners Charles and Derek Hurlock saw the hand-built British sports racer, the Tojeiro, they couldn't resist. So they bought the production rights for the chassis from its designer, John Tojeiro, who'd created a number of successful racing sports cars. The two-seater racer, whose body showed a kinship with Ferraris, rode a ladder-type chassis made up of three-inch diameter tubes, plus independent wishbone and leaf spring suspension at both ends. One of them held a race-tuned Lea-Francis engine; the other, a 2-litre Bristol powerplant (which had soon become relevant for the production Ace). Because articulated axle shafts were used and the differential housing was bolted to the parallel steel tubes that made up the car's frame, the design had minimal unsprung weight at the rear axle.

The A.C. folks decided it would be easy enough to build both the chassis and a racy body at their own plant. A prototype Ace was displayed at the London Motor Show in October 1953, just a few months after the purchase had been completed; and the first Aces were delivered in 1954. Changes from the original design included a switch to cam-gear steering, and the raising of the too-low headlamps to a height that met international requirements. As for the old but reliable engine, its cylinder block, crankcase and sump are light alloy, with wet cylinder liners. Also helping to cut weight were Al-Fin brake drums and the aluminum body itself.

Long known for quality, A.C. now offered postwar performance to match. "Exciting performance, thrilling speed, beautiful styling," in the words of the marketing people. A Moss gearbox accepted the power from the 1991-cc six-cylinder engine, which was tweaked up to 85 horsepower. A six-branch manifold, which merged into twin pipes, reduced exhaust back pressure to a minimum. A double roller chain operated the single overhead cam shaft. The twin parallel chassis tubes held the suspension and differential,

while tubular outriggers carried the aluminum body. Tubular shocks went on an angle between the frame and lower wishbones. Open shafts extended from the fixed differential to the drivewheels.

A racy, aggressive-looking front end displayed a large, curvaceous grille opening (shaped like a semicircle) with recessed, wide-spaced crosshatch pattern. Small round parking lights stood below the built-in headlamps on the fender tips. "Your comfort is our first consideration," said the Ace sales brochure, adding that "snug-fitting bucket seats really hold you firm." While on the stark side, the cockpit was fitted with leather upholstery over Dunlopillo filling. Doors held map pockets, and the steering wheel adjusted for length and rake. Standard equipment included Dunlop wire wheels. Bumpers were not standard, but little vertical bumperettes went alongside the grille opening to provide a touch of protection.

2-LITRE — SIX — While the new Ace got most of the attention in 1953, the two-litre saloon continued in production as late as 1958 (while the Sports Tourer lasted only into late 1954).For 1953, a four-door saloon joined the two-door version. Bodies were made of 18-gauge aluminum on seasoned wood framing, with mudguards of 16-gauge aluminum. Foglamps and a radio were available, but not standard. Standard colors for 1953 were Black (with red or beige leather); Birch Gray (red or blue leather); Grey jewelessence (red or blue leather); National Gray (a greenish-gray, with red or beige leather); Blue jewelessence (blue or beige leather); Beige Ponce jewelessence (red leather); or Pacific Green jewelessence (beige leather). The leather upholstery went over Dunlopillo cushioning.

I.D. DATA: Serial number is stamped on a plate on the right side of the bulkhead.

Model	Body Type & Seating	Engine Type/CID	P.O.E. Price	Weight (lbs.)	Prod. Total
Ace	2-dr Roadster-2P	I6/121	3200	1685	Note 1
2-LITRE					
2-Litre	2-dr Spt Tourer-5P	I6/121	N/A	N/A	N/A
2-Litre	2-dr Saloon-4/5P	I6/121	N/A	2964	N/A
2-Litre	4-dr Saloon-4/5P	I6/121	N/A	N/A	N/A

Note 1: Total Ace production from 1953-63 was about 220 units.

Note: All specifications and options listed below are for the Ace roadster; see 1947-52 listing for details on the 2-Litre models.

ENGINE DATA: BASE SIX (Ace): Inline, single-overhead-cam six-cylinder (monobloc). Light alloy (aluminum) block and head, with cast iron cylinder liners. **Displacement:** 121.5 cu. in. (1991 cc). **Bore & Stroke:** 2.56 x 3.94 in. (65 x 100 mm). **Compression Ratio:** 7.5:1. **Brake Horsepower:** 85 at 4500 rpm. **Torque:** 105 lbs.-ft. at 2750 rpm. Five main bearings. Solid valve lifters. Three SU carburetors with automatic easy-starting devices. 12-volt electrical system.

CHASSIS DATA: Wheelbase: 90.0 in. **Overall Length:** 151.5 in. **Height:** 49 in. **Width:** 59.5 in. **Front Tread:** 50 in. **Rear Tread:** 50 in. **Wheel Type:** Dunlop wire with center lock. **Standard Tires:** 5.50x16.

TECHNICAL: Layout: front-engine, rear-drive. **Transmission:** four-speed manual (synchro 2nd/3rd/4th); floor shift lever. Overall gear ratios: (1st) 12.34:1; (2nd) 7.21:1; (3rd) 4.98:1; (4th) 3.64:1; (rev) 12.34:1. **Standard Final Drive Ratio:** 3.64:1 (hypoid spiral bevel). **Steering:** Bishop cam-gear. **Suspension (front):** independent; transverse leaf spring and dual wishbones, with Armstrong telescopic shock absorbers. **Suspension (rear):** independent; transverse leaf spring and dual wishbones, with Armstrong telescopic shock absorbers. **Brakes:** Girling hydraulic, front/rear drum. **Body Construction:** aluminum body on tubular chassis (3-inch steel tubing).

MAJOR OPTIONS: Radiomobile radio. Heater. Fram bypass oil filter. Passenger grab handle. Overrider-type bumpers. Gas tank stone shield. Battery stone shield. Second spare wheel/tire. Duplicate ignition coil. Duplicate fuel pump and feed pipes (for reserve supply). Alternate gear ratios.

PERFORMANCE: Top Speed: 100-103 mph. **Acceleration (0-60 mph):** 11.4 sec. **Acceleration (quarter-mile):** 18 sec. **Fuel Mileage:** approx. 18 mpg.

Manufacturer: A.C. Cars, Ltd., Thames Ditton, Surrey, England.

HISTORY: Introduced in October 1953. In addition to the Ace and 2-Litre, the A.C. company offered a three-wheeler Petite economy Runabout (single front wheel) designed for invalids, powered by a small two-stroke engine. Top speed was 40 mph, with fuel mileage of 60-80 mpg.

1955 A.C.

ACE — SIX — The two-seat roadster continued with little change, except for a horsepower boost from the original 85 up to 90 (accompanied by a rise in compression ratio to 8:1). That didn't match the performance of new Bristol-engined Ace for 1956 (see next listing), but the original A.C. powerplant continued to be sold into 1963. Standard Ace equipment included a telescopic steering column, spring-type steering wheel, adjustable bucket seats, leatherette-covered dashboard with Smith instruments, dual exhaust pipes with individual headers, dual wind-tone horns, and Lucas light/starting system.

ACECA — SIX — A fastback coupe variant of the Ace roadster was designed to satisfy "the requirements of the discerning motorist who requires closed body work," which was first shown in late 1954 and produced for the '55 model year. "Composite steel tube and ash body framing, with aluminum paneling", added the brochure, "gives strength and lightness." Front-end appearance was similar to the Ace, but the car's profile (with small rear side windows) was reminiscent of certain Ferraris, notably the 166 and 212. In fact, the influence of Italian design was greater in the coupe than the roadster. Instead of a rounded back end, as in the roadster, the coupe had squared-off rear fenders that looked almost like tailfins when viewed from the side. The car's name was pronounced "Ay-See-Kuh."

2-LITRE — SIX — Two- and four-door saloons continued in production, along with the sports models; see 1947-52 listing for details.

I.D. DATA: Serial number is in same location as 1953-54.

Model	Body Type & Seating	Engine Type/CID	P.O.E. Price	Weight (lbs.)	Prod. Total
Ace	2-dr Roadster-2P	I6/121	3800	1685	Note 1
Aceca	2-dr Fsbk Cpe-2P	I6/121	4500	1840	Note 2

Note 1: Total Ace production from 1953-63, about 220 units.

Note 2: Total Aceca production from 1955-63, about 150 units.

ENGINE DATA: BASE SIX: Inline, single-overhead-cam six-cylinder. Light alloy (aluminum) block and head. **Displacement:** 121.5 cu. in.(1991 cc). **Bore & Stroke:** 2.56 x 3.94 in. (65 x 100 mm). **Compression Ratio:** 8.0:1. **Brake Horsepower:** 90 at 4500 rpm. **Torque:** 105 lbs.-ft. at 2750 rpm. Five main bearings. Solid valve lifters. Three SU carburetors. 12-volt electrical system.

CHASSIS DATA: Wheelbase: 90.0 in. **Overall Length:** (Ace) 151.5 in.; (Aceca) 153.5 in. **Height:** (Ace) 49 in.; (Aceca) 52 in. **Width:** (Ace) 59.5 in.; (Aceca) 61 in. **Front Tread:** 50 in. **Rear Tread:**50 in. **Wheel Type:** Dunlop center-lock wire. **Standard Tires:** 5.50x16.

TECHNICAL: Layout: front-engine, rear-drive. **Transmission:** four-speed manual; floor shift lever. **Standard Final Drive Ratio:** 3.64:1. **Steering:** Bishop cam-gear. **Suspension (front):** independent; transverse leaf spring and dual wishbones. **Suspension (rear):** independent; transverse leaf spring and dual wishbones. **Brakes:** Girling hydraulic, front/rear Al-fin drum. **Body Construction:** (Ace) aluminum body on tubular chassis; (Aceca) aluminum paneling over composite steel tube and ash body framing, on tubular chassis.

MAJOR OPTIONS: Overdrive.

PERFORMANCE: Top Speed: 102-103 mph. **Acceleration (0-60 mph):** (Ace) 11.4 sec.; (Aceca) 13.4 sec.

Manufacturer: A.C. Cars, Ltd., Thames Ditton, Surrey, England.

HISTORY: Introduced: (Ace) October 1953; (Aceca) October 1954.

1956-57 A.C.

ACE/ACECA — SIX — An electrical overdrive transmission became optional in 1956, and front disc brakes became available a year or so later. Otherwise, the basic Ace roadster and Aceca fastback coupe continued with little change. Standard body colors were black, red, maroon, bright blue, green, off-white, and cream. Leather upholstery came in black, red, maroon, green, beige, grey/blue, or grey. Top and tonneau covers were black, red, beige or grey; and the wheels could be red, silver, or cream.

1956 A.C.

ACE-BRISTOL — SIX — Anyone who wasn't satisfied with the power and performance of the basic Ace or Aceca, or who just didn't fancy the idea of an engine whose design dated back to 1919, now had another choice: a Bristol 2-litre six under the hood. This one wasn't exactly new either, however, but based on the 1933-37 BMW six. Ken Rudd, a British race driver, built the first one and the A.C. factory soon followed suit. Shown in fall 1956, the Bristol-powered models were in production by the following spring. Not only were they more powerful, but more amenable to race-tuning. Appearance was almost identical to the A.C.-engined roadster and coupe.

Availability of this engine came about because the British Bristol company had obtained the design earlier, and built it for other auto makers. Instead of an overhead cam, this one was of overhead-valve design with semi-spherical combustion chamber and a rather long stroke. Three downdraft Solex carburetors supplied the fuel. In standard B-type (100B) form, it produced 105 bhp; but the D-type (100D2) engine rated 120 bhp or more. All used a Bristol four-speed gearbox rather than the A.C. unit. Optional Laycock de Normanville overdrive worked in 2nd/3rd/4th. Because the car's weight increased only slightly, performance got a boost with little loss in fuel mileage. John Bolster, writing in *AutoSport* magazine, declared that for "sheer pleasure of driving, this is one of the best sports cars I have ever driven." That article added that the Ace-Bristol "holds the road at least as well as any Continental car."

ACECA-BRISTOL — SIX — The Bristol six also went beneath the bonnet of fastback coupe models, though the original engine continued to be offered as well.

2-LITRE — SIX — Two- and four-door saloons continued in production, along with the sports models; see 1947-52 listing for details.

I.D. DATA: Serial number is in same location as 1953-54.

Model	Body Type & Seating	Engine Type/CID	P.O.E. Price	Weight (lbs.)	Prod. Total
Ace	2-dr Roadster-2P	I6/121	4495	1685	Note 1
Aceca	2-dr Fsbk Cpe-2P	I6/121	5395	1840	Note 2
ACE/ACECA-BRISTOL					
Ace	2-dr Roadster-2P	I6/121	5549	1685	Note 3
Aceca	2-dr Fsbk Cpe-2P	I6/121	6549	1840	Note 4

Note 1: Total Ace production from 1953-63, about 220 units.

Note 2: Total Aceca production from 1955-63, about 150 units.

Note 3: Total Ace-Bristol production from 1957-64, about 466 units.

Note 4: Total Aceca-Bristol production from 1957-64, about 169 units.

Price Note: Prices shown for 1957 were subject to change.

ENGINE DATA: BASE SIX (Ace/Aceca): Inline, single-overhead-cam six-cylinder. Light alloy (aluminum) block and head. **Displacement:** 121.5 cu. in. (1991 cc). **Bore & Stroke:** 2.56 x3.94 in. (65 x 100 mm). **Compression Ratio:** 8.0:1. **Brake Horsepower:** 90 at 4500 rpm. **Torque:** 110 lbs.-ft. at 2500 rpm. Five main bearings. Solid valve lifters. Three SU carburetors. 12-volt electrical system.

BASE SIX (Ace/Aceca-Bristol): Inline, overhead-valve six-cylinder (B-type). Cast iron block and aluminum head. **Displacement:** 120.2 cu. in. (1971 cc). **Bore & Stroke:** 2.60 x3.78 in. (66 x 96 mm). **Compression Ratio:** 8.5:1. **Brake Horsepower:** 105 at 4750 rpm. **Torque:** 123 lbs.-ft. at 3750 rpm. Four main bearings. Solid valve lifters. Three Solex 32PBI-6 downdraft carburetors. Lucas 12-volt electrical system.

1957 A.C Aceca coupe. (William Siuru Jr.)

OPTIONAL SIX (Ace/Aceca-Bristol): (D-type) Same as above, except — **Compression Ratio:** 9.0:1. **Brake Horsepower:** 120 at 5750 rpm. **Torque:** 122 lbs.-ft. at 4500 rpm.

Note: Higher-powered versions of the D-type (100D2) Bristol engine became available, reaching 130 bhp.

CHASSIS DATA: Wheelbase: 90.0 in. **Overall Length:** (Ace) 151.5 in.; (Aceca) 153.5 in. **Height:** (Ace) 49 in.; (Aceca) 52 in. **Width:** (Ace) 59.5 in.; (Aceca) 61 in. **Front Tread:** 50 in. **Rear Tread:** 50 in. **Wheel Type:** Dunlop center-lock wire. **Standard Tires:** 5.50x16 (Bristol, 5.50x16 Michelin X).

TECHNICAL: Layout: front-engine, rear-drive. **Transmission:** four-speed manual; floor shift lever. Overdrive optional. Bristol overall gear ratios: (1st) 11.42:1; (2nd) 7.13:1; (3rd) 5.05:1; (4th) 3.91:1. **Standard Final Drive Ratio:** 3.64:1 exc.(Bristol) 3.91:1. **Steering:** Bishop cam-gear. **Suspension (front):** independent; transverse leaf spring with dual wishbones. **Suspension (rear):** independent; transverse leaf spring with dual wishbones. **Brakes:** front/rear drum; front discs became available during 1957. **Body Construction:** aluminum body on tubular chassis.

MAJOR OPTIONS: Overdrive. Windshield washer. Front and rear bumpers. Heater. Demisters. Glovebox door (Ace only). Battery shield.

PERFORMANCE: Top Speed: 102-103 mph (115-117 mph with Bristol engine). **Acceleration (0-60 mph):** (Ace) 11.4 sec.; (Aceca) 13.4 sec.; (Ace-Bristol) 9.1 sec.; (Aceca-Bristol) 10.3 sec.; (Bristol D-type) 7-8 seconds. **Acceleration (quarter-mile):** (Bristol) 16 sec. **Fuel Mileage:** (Bristol) 18+ mpg.

Manufacturer: A.C. Cars, Ltd., Thames Ditton, Surrey, England.

Distributor: Michell and Pauli, Los Angeles, California.

HISTORY: Bristol models introduced by April 1956. By this time, about five cars were being produced per week at the Thames Ditton plant.

1958-59 A.C.

1958 A.C. Ace roadster. (Coys of Kensington)

ACE/ACECA — SIX — A horsepower boost brought the basic Ace (and Aceca) up to 102 bhp. During this period the original Moss gearbox was dropped, replaced by Triumph TR3A gears (but inside an A.C. housing). A removable hardtop also became optional for Ace, and it could be ordered with a curved windshield instead of the standard flat glass. Another optional item was a cowl that covered part of the radiator, to cut air drag. That could boost the car's top speed to 120 mph.

1959 A.C. Ace Bristol. (Coys of Kensington)

ACE/ACECA-BRISTOL — SIX — The Bristol engine continued to be available in various states of tune, from the basic 105 horsepower up to as much as 130 bhp.

I.D. DATA: Serial number is in same location as 1953-54.

Model	Body Type & Seating	Engine Type/CID	P.O.E. Price	Weight (lbs)	Prod. Total
Ace	2-dr Roadster-2P	I6/121	4799	1685	Note 1
Aceca	2-dr Fsbk Cpe-2P	I6/121	5699	1840	Note 2
ACE/ACECA-BRISTOL					
Ace	2-dr Roadster-2P	I6/121	5649	1685	Note 3
Aceca	2-dr Fsbk Cpe-2P	I6/121	6649	1840	Note 4

Note 1: Total Ace production from 1953-63, about 220 units.

Note 2: Total Aceca production from 1955-63, about 150 units.

Note 3: Total Ace-Bristol production from 1957-64, about 466 units.

Note 4: Total Aceca-Bristol production from 1957-64, about 169 units.

Price Note: Prices shown were effective in 1959, but basic Ace was listed for as little as $3985 delivered in U.S.

ENGINE DATA: BASE SIX (Ace/Aceca): Light alloy (aluminum) block and head. **Displacement:** 121.5 cu. in. (1991 cc). **Bore & Stroke:** 2.56 x3.94 in. (65 x 100 mm). **Compression Ratio:** 8.0:1 or 9.0:1. **Brake Horsepower:** 90 at 4500 or 102 at 5000 rpm. **Torque:** 110 lbs.-ft. at 2500 rpm. Five main bearings. Solid valve lifters. Three SU carburetors. 12-volt electrical system.

BASE SIX (Ace/Aceca-Bristol): Inline, overhead-valve six-cylinder (B-type). Cast iron block and aluminum head. **Displacement:** 120.2 cu. in. (1971 cc). **Bore & Stroke:** 2.60 x3.78 in. (66 x 96 mm). **Compression Ratio:** 8.5:1 (9.0:1 optional engines). **Brake Horsepower:** 105 at 4750 rpm (optional D-type, 120 at 5750). **Torque:** 123 lbs.-ft. at 3750 rpm (D-type, 122 at 4500). Four main bearings. Solid valve lifters. Three Solex 32PBI-6 downdraft carburetors. Lucas 12-volt electrical system.

Note: Higher-powered versions of the D-type (100D2) Bristol engine reached 130 bhp.

CHASSIS DATA: Same as 1956-57.

TECHNICAL: Layout: front-engine, rear-drive. **Transmission:** four-speed manual; floor shift lever. Overdrive optional. Bristol overall gear ratios: (1st) 11.42:1; (2nd) 7.13:1; (3rd) 5.05:1; (4th) 3.91:1. **Standard Final Drive Ratio:** 3.64:1 exc.(Bristol) 3.91:1. **Steering:** Bishop cam-gear. **Suspension (front):** independent; transverse leaf spring with dual wishbones. **Suspension (rear):** independent; transverse leaf spring with dual wishbones. **Brakes:** front/rear drum; front discs available. **Body Construction:** aluminum body on tubular chassis.

MAJOR OPTIONS: Overdrive. Detachable hardtop (Ace). Curved windshield (Ace). Radiator cowl.

PERFORMANCE: Top Speed: (Aceca-Bristol) 103.8 mph. **Acceleration (0-60 mph):** (Aceca-Bristol) 9.4-9.8 seconds. **Acceleration (quarter-mile):** (Ace-Bristol) est. 16 seconds; (Aceca-Bristol) 17.1 seconds. **Fuel Mileage:** (Aceca-Bristol) 20-25 mpg.

Manufacturer: A.C. Cars, Ltd., Thames Ditton, Surrey, England.

Distributor: Worldwide Import, Inc., Los Angeles, California.

1960-61 A.C.

1960 A.C. Ace Cobra 289. (Coys of Kensington)

ACE/ACECA — SIX — Production of the basic Ace roadster and Aceca fastback coupe continued with little change.

ACE/ACECA-BRISTOL — SIX — Production of the Bristol-powered models continued. But when the Bristol firm announced in 1961 that their next 407 model would carry a Chrysler hemi-head V-8, that meant the venerable six-cylinder engine was about to expire—and that A.C. would have no source for optional powerplants. Before long, however, A.C. offered the 2553-cc six (from British Ford Zephyr) instead. See next listing for details.

GREYHOUND — SIX — From late 1959 to 1963, A.C. also built a 2+2 Greyhound coupe for the home market, on a 10-inch longer wheelbase, powered by either the Bristol or A.C. six-cylinder engine. These were not so successful, and rarely found outside Britain. Greyhounds used a flatter grille than the Aceca, with built-in recessed running lights and a hood airscoop. The 1961 model switched to a revised, narrower grille with a pattern of four horizontal bars, plus a wraparound back window.

I.D. DATA: Serial number is in same location as 1953-54.

Model	Body Type & Seating	Engine Type/CID	P.O.E. Price	Weight (lbs.)	Prod. Total
Ace	2-dr Roadster-2P	I6/121	4799	1685	Note 1
Aceca	2-dr Fsbk Cpe-2P	I6/121	5699	1840	Note 2
ACE/ACECA-BRISTOL					
Ace	2-dr Roadster-2P	I6/121	5699	1685	Note 3
Aceca	2-dr Fsbk Cpe-2P	I6/121	6599	1840	Note 4
GREYHOUND					
	2-dr Saloon-2+2P	I6/120	N/A	2240	N/A

Note 1: Total Ace production from 1953-63, about 220 units.

Note 2: Total Aceca production from 1955-63, about 150 units.

Note 3: Total Ace-Bristol production from 1957-64, about 466 units.

Note 4: Total Aceca-Bristol production from 1957-64, about 169 units.

ENGINE DATA: BASE SIX (Ace/Aceca): Light alloy (aluminum) block and head. **Displacement:** 121.5 cu. in. (1991 cc). **Bore & Stroke:** 2.56 x3.94 in. (65 x 100 mm). **Compression Ratio:** 8.0/9.0:1. **Brake Horsepower:** 90 at 4500 (or 102 at 5000 rpm). **Torque:** 110 lbs.-ft. at 2500 rpm (or 120 at 3000). Five main bearings. Solid valve lifters. Three SU carburetors. 12-volt electrical system.

Note: Greyhound was available with a 105-bhp version of the basic six-cylinder engine.

BASE SIX (Ace/Aceca-Bristol): Inline, overhead-valve six-cylinder (D-type). Cast iron block and aluminum head. **Displacement:** 120.2 cu. in. (1971 cc). **Bore & Stroke:** 2.60 x3.78 in. (66 x 96 mm). **Compression Ratio:** 9.0:1. **Brake Horsepower:** 125 at 5750 rpm. **Torque:** 122 lbs.-ft. at 4500 rpm. Four main bearings. Solid valve lifters. Three Solex 32PBI-6 downdraft carburetors. Lucas 12-volt electrical system.

Note: Higher-powered versions of the D-type (100D2) Bristol engine, with 9.5:1 compression, were available. So was the 105-bhp B-type engine; see 1958-59 listing.

BASE SIX (Greyhound): Same as Bristol above, rated 125 bhp at 5750 rpm with 9.0:1 compression ratio.

CHASSIS DATA: Wheelbase: (Ace/Aceca) 90.0 in.; (Greyhound) 100.0 in. **Overall Length:** (Ace) 151.5 in.; (Aceca) 153.5 in.; (Greyhound) 180 in. **Height:** (Ace) 49 in.; (Aceca) 52 in.; (Greyhound) 53 in. **Width:** (Ace) 59.5 in.; (Aceca) 61 in.; (Greyhound) 65.25 in. **Front Tread:** (Ace/Aceca) 50 in. **Rear Tread:** (Ace/Aceca) 50 in. **Wheel Type:** Dunlop center-lockwire. **Standard Tires:** 5.50x16.

TECHNICAL: Layout: front-engine, rear-drive. **Transmission:** four-speed manual; floor shift lever. Overdrive optional. Bristol overall gear ratios: (1st) 11.42:1; (2nd) 7.13:1; (3rd) 5.05:1; (4th) 3.91:1. **Standard Final Drive Ratio:** 3.64:1 exc. (Bristol) 3.91:1; (Greyhound) 4.1:1. **Steering:** Bishop cam-gear. **Suspension (front):** (Ace/Aceca) independent; transverse leaf spring with dual wishbones; (Greyhound) coil springs. **Suspension (rear):** (Ace/Aceca) independent; transverse leaf spring with dual wishbones; (Greyhound) coil springs. **Brakes:** (Ace/Aceca) front/rear drum; front discs available. **Body Construction:** aluminum body on tubular chassis.

MAJOR OPTIONS: Overdrive. Detachable hardtop (Ace). Curved windshield (Ace). Radiator cowl.

PERFORMANCE: Top Speed: (Aceca-Bristol) 103.8 mph; (Greyhound) 108-120 mph. **Acceleration (0-60 mph):** (Aceca-Bristol) 9.4-9.8 seconds. **Acceleration (quarter-mile):** (Ace-Bristol) est. 16 seconds; (Aceca-Bristol) 17.1 seconds; (Greyhound) 19 sec. **Fuel Mileage:** (Aceca-Bristol) 20-25 mpg.

Manufacturer: A.C. Cars, Ltd., Thames Ditton, Surrey, England.

Distributor: Worldwide Import, Inc., Los Angeles, California.

HISTORY: Bristol-powered A.C. models, according to *Sports Cars Illustrated*, "thoroughly dominated Class E competition in American racing."

ACE/ACECA — SIX — Once the Bristol engine became unavailable, A.C. turned to a Ford Zephyr six as the alternate to the original light-alloy powerplant. Working through a Moss gearbox, the Zephyr six came in a broad range of horsepower ratings, from 90 (SAE) all the way to 170. On the other side of the Atlantic, Carroll Shelby got busy turning the six-cylinder Ace into a V-8 Cobra (see below). The last British versions were built in the spring of 1964, and final editions had a smaller, Cobra-like grille.

SHELBY COBRA — V-8 — Referred to as an A.C. in Britain, the V-8 powered version of the Ace roadster adopted the Cobra name in the U.S.: either Shelby-A.C. Cobra or just Shelby Cobra. It happened because Carroll Shelby, a retired race driver from Texas, wanted to squeeze a lightweight American V-8 into the rakish Ace. Shelby spoke to the Hurlock brothers at A.C., who liked the idea—partly because their supply of Bristol six-cylinder engines was about to evaporate. Prototype No. 1 was built at Thames Ditton, then shipped (sans engine and transmission) to the Shelby shop in Venice, California, early in 1962, where final assembly and testing was accomplished. At this time, Ford (U.S.) was taking a shine to performance/racing, and offered its small-block V-8 plus development help. Thus, the first 75 Cobras had the lightweight Ford 260-cid (4.2-litre) V-8 engine, as in the Ford Fairlane of that day. Then came the 289-cid (4727-cc) V-8, with a basic rating of 271 bhp but capable of up to 370 bhp with race tuning. Ford insisted on the label "Powered By Ford" on the valve cover, below the "COBRA" name. The basic tubular chassis was stiffened somewhat, and Salisbury final drive added, with a limited-slip differential. Four-wheel disc brakes were installed, rather than the rear drums used in the basic Ace. The steering gearbox had to be tilted a bit to fit over the V-8 engine. Appearance wasn't much different from the regular Ace, except that the Shelby needed flared wheelarches to fit over its larger tires. Quite a few other engineering changes took place over the next years. After the 125th car, for instance, rack-and-pinion steering replaced the old cam-gear setup. Cobra's Borg-Warner four-speed gearbox was fully synchronized. Smith instruments were used for early models, after which Stewart-Warner gauges were installed.

I.D. DATA: Serial number for Ace/Aceca is in the same location as prior models.

Model	Body Type & Seating	Engine Type/CID	P.O.E. Price	Weight (lbs.)	Prod. Total
Ace	2-dr Roadster-2P	I6/121	Note 1	1685	Note 2
Aceca	2-dr FBk Cpe-2P	I6/121	N/A	1840	Note 3
A.C. SHELBY COBRA					
	2-dr Roadster-2P	V8/260	5995	2100	75
	2-dr Roadster-2P	V8/289	N/A	2100	51

Note 1: Price for Ace with Zephyr engine was $3890 in U.S.

Note 2: Total Ace production from 1953-63, about 220 units.

Note 3: Total Aceca production from 1955-63, about 150 units.

ENGINE DATA: BASE SIX (Ace/Aceca): Light alloy (aluminum) block and head. **Displacement:** 121.5 cu. in. (1991 cc). **Bore & Stroke:** 2.56 x 3.94 in. (65 x 100 mm). **Compression Ratio:** 9.0:1. **Brake Horsepower:** 102 at 5000 rpm. Five main bearings. Solid valve lifters. Three SU carburetors. 12-volt electrical system.

OPTIONAL SIX (Ace/Aceca): Inline, overhead-valve six-cylinder (Ford Zephyr). Cast iron block and aluminum head. **Displacement:** 155.7 cu. in. (2553 cc). **Bore & Stroke:** 3.25 x 3.13 in. (82.55 x 79.5 mm). **Compression Ratio:** 9.5:1. **Brake Horsepower:** 120 at 5000 rpm (optional: 125 at 5000, 155 at 5500, or 170 at 5500). Four main bearings. Solid valve lifters. Three SU HD6 carburetors. 12-volt electrical system.

BASE V-8 (Shelby Cobra): Overhead-valve V-8. Cast iron block and head. **Displacement:** 260 cu. in. (4261 cc). **Bore & Stroke:** 3.80 x 2.87 in. (96.5 x 73 mm). **Brake Horsepower:** 260 at 5800 rpm. **Torque:** 269 lbs.-ft. at 4800 rpm. Hydraulic valve lifters. Holley carburetors. 12-volt electrical system.

OPTIONAL V-8 (Shelby Cobra): Same as above, except — **Displacement:** 289 cu. in. (4727 cc). **Bore & Stroke:** 4.00 x2.87 in. (101.6 x 72.8 mm). **Brake Horsepower:** 271 at 6000 rpm.

CHASSIS DATA: Wheelbase: 90.0 in. **Overall Length:** 151.5 in. **Height:** (Ace) 49 in.; (Aceca) 52 in. **Width:** (Ace) 58.5 in.; (Shelby) 61 in. **Front Tread:** (Ace) 50 in.; (Shelby) 53.25 in. **Rear Tread:** (Ace) 50 in.; (Shelby) 52.5 in. **Standard Tires:** 5.50 x 16 except (Shelby 260) 6.50/6.75 x 15; (Shelby 289) 7.35 x 15 or 185 x 15.

TECHNICAL: Layout: front-engine, rear-drive. **Transmission:** four-speed manual (synchro); floor shift lever. Overdrive optional. **Steering:** (Ace/Aceca) cam-gear. **Suspension (front):** independent, transverse leaf spring, dual wishbones. **Suspension (rear):** independent, transverse leaf spring, dual wishbones. **Brakes:** front/rear drum; front disc available except (Shelby) front/rear discs. **Body Construction:** aluminum body on tubular chassis.

MAJOR OPTIONS: (Ace/Aceca) similar to 1958-61.

PERFORMANCE: Top Speed: (Ace/Aceca) 102-103 mph; (Shelby) 136-138 mph. **Acceleration (0-60 mph):** (Ace) 11.4 sec.; (Aceca) 13.4 sec.; (Shelby) 5.2-5.5 sec. **Acceleration (quarter-mile):** 13.8-13.9 seconds.

Manufacturer: A.C. Cars, Ltd., Thames Ditton, Surrey, England. and Shelby American Inc., Venice, California.

1962-63 A.C.

1962 A.C. Greyhound two-door saloon. (Sotheby's)

1964-65 A.C.

1965 A.C. Ghia "Willment" Cobra 427. (Coys of Kensington)

SHELBY COBRA (Mark II/III) NOTE: Although originally intended for sale solely in America, Shelby Cobras were marketed in Britain as well as the U.S., starting in 1964. Some had the earlier 260- and 289-cid V-8s; but those with the 427-cid big-block also were available. During 1965, coil springs and wishbones replaced the original transverse leaf springs. Going a step further, the original Ace chassis was abandoned in favor of a special frame with larger-diameter tubes, spaced farther apart. The final Cobra was built in December 1968. Because so much work was done to the car at the Shelby facility in California, Cobras are generally viewed as domestic automobiles, even though their bodies hailed from the United Kingdom. See *Standard Catalog of American Cars (1946-75)* for further details.

1966 A.C.

1966 A.C. Cobra 427.

A.C. 427 — V-8 — Rather than merely import Cobras back from the United States, A.C. turned out its own version of a V-8 roadster, intended more for grand touring than competition. A prototype appeared at the London Motor Show in late 1965, and the car went on sale during 1966. Styling of the new drophead coupe (and subsequent hardtop coupe) was markedly different from the earlier Ace or the current Shelby. A low, flat grille gave a distinctive front-end appearance, with wraparound parking lights below the headlamps. The two-seater body was created by Frua (in Italy), and a 427-cid Ford V-8 provided the power. Appearance was similar to the Maserati Mistral (also done by Frua). Underneath, A.C. used a parallel-tube chassis like that of the updated (Mark III) Shelby Cobra, but longer and designed for softer riding qualities. Either a four-speed manual gearbox or Ford three-speed automatic was available. Disc brakes went on all four wheels, which were center-lock wire (unlike the Cobra's alloy wheels). Construction was a multi-step process, with the engine arriving from Michigan; placed in a chassis in Britain; body added and final assembly undertaken in Italy; then back to Britain for testing and inspection.

A.C. 289 — V-8 — A version powered by a 289-cid also was sold in Europe, with a Mark III chassis (as in 427 Cobras).

I.D. DATA: Not available.

Model	Body Type & Seating	Engine Type/CID	P.O.E. Price	Weight (lbs.)	Prod. Total
A.C. 427					
	2-dr Conv-2P	V8/427	N/A	3155	28
A.C. 289					
	2-dr Roadster-2P	V8/289	N/A	N/A	27

Note: Production totals are for full model run, from 1965-73. Some sources say 29 of the 427 convertibles were built.

ENGINE DATA: BASE V-8 (A.C. 289): Displacement: 289 cu. in. (4727 cc). **Bore & Stroke:** 4.00 x 2.87 in. (101.6 x 72.8 mm). **Compression Ratio:** 10.5:1. **Brake Horsepower:** 271 at 6000 rpm. **Torque:** 312 lbs.-ft. at 3400 rpm. Four-barrel carburetor.

BASE V-8 (A.C. 427): Overhead-valve V-8. Cast iron block and head. **Displacement:** 427 cu. in. (6997 cc). **Bore & Stroke:** 4.24 x 3.78 in. (107.6 x 96 mm). **Compression Ratio:** 11.1:1. **Brake Horsepower:** 425 at 6000 rpm. **Torque:** 480 lbs.-ft. at 3700 rpm. Hydraulic valve lifters. Carter four-barrel carburetors.

CHASSIS DATA: Wheelbase: (289) 90 in.; (427) 96 in. **Overall Length:** (289)166 in.; (427) 174 in. **Height:** (289) 51 in.; (427) 51 in. **Width:** (427) 67 in. **Front Tread:** (427) 54 in. **Rear Tread:** (427) 53 in. **Wheel Type:** center-lock wire. **Standard Tires:** 8.15x15.

TECHNICAL: Layout: front-engine, rear-drive. **Transmission:** four-speed manual or Ford C-6 three-speed automatic. **Steering:** rack and pinion. **Suspension (front):** wishbones and coil springs. **Suspension (rear):** wishbones and coil springs. **Brakes:** front/rear discs. **Body Construction:** aluminum body on tubular chassis.

Manufacturer: A.C. Cars, Ltd., Thames Ditton, Surrey, England; body by Frua (Italy); engines from Ford (U.S.).

1967-73 A.C.

A.C. 428 — V-8 — Production of a British version of the Cobra, with distinctive appearance, continued into 1973, but powered by a 428-cid Ford "Interceptor" V-8 rather than the 427 used for the 1966 model. In addition, a fixed-head fastback coupe joined the earlier drophead coupe.

1969 A.C. 428 fastback.

A.C. 289 — V-8 — Production continued of the 289-cid version; see previous listing for details.

Note: The British 427 and 428, intended for the home market, differed in many respects from the Shelby Cobra sold in the U.S. through 1968 and described in the *Standard Catalog of American Cars (1946-75).*

I.D. DATA: Not available.

Model A.C. 428	Body Type & Seating	Engine Type/CID	P.O.E. Price	Weight (lbs.)	Prod. Total
	2-dr Conv-2P	V8/428	N/A	3155	Note 1
	2-dr Fbk Cpe-2P	V8/428	N/A	3155	Note 2

Note 1: Total production from 1965-73, about 28 convertibles.

Note 2: Total production through 1973, no more than 58 coupes.

ENGINE DATA: BASE V-8 (428): Overhead-valve V-8. Cast iron block and head. **Displacement:** 428 cu. in. (7014 cc). **Bore & Stroke:** 4.13 x 3.98 in. (104.9 x 101 mm). **Compression Ratio:** 10.5:1. **Brake Horsepower:** 345 at 4600 rpm. **Torque:** 462 at 2800 rpm.

CHASSIS DATA: Wheelbase: 96.0 in. **Overall Length:** 174 in. **Height:** 51 in. **Width:** 67 in. **Front Tread:** 55 in. **Rear Tread:** 56 in. **Wheel Type:** center-lock wire. **Standard Tires:** 8.15 x 15 or 205 x 15.

TECHNICAL: Same as 1966.

PERFORMANCE: Top Speed: (428) 140 mph. **Acceleration (0-60 mph):** (428) about 6 seconds.

Manufacturer: A.C. Cars, Ltd., Thames Ditton, Surrey, England.

POSTSCRIPT: Produced only in limited quantity, and priced high, the 427/428 were the final sport offerings from the long-lived A.C. firm. A.C. continued to produce three-wheelers for invalids until 1976, then turned to trailer bodies. Early in the 1980s, a few dozen 3-litre coupes were built, with a mid-engine Ford V-6. The company was bought by Scottish businessman Brian Angliss in 1984, and renamed A.C. (Scotland) Ltd., but folded after producing a handful of automobiles. An Ace for the Eighties even appeared in prototype form at the 1986 British International Motor Show in Birmingham, England. Carroll Shelby and his organization remained active long after the demise of the Cobra, turning out special high-performance models for major domestic automakers, including Shelby Dodge Daytonas in the 1980s.

A great many Cobra replicas have been marketed, some similar to the original, others not. Some used fiberglass bodies, and some carried a 428- or 429-cid Ford V-8. The Cobra "Mk IV" built by Auto Kraft Ltd. was claimed to be an exact replica, using original tooling and equipment. That company operated inside the old Brooklands race course at Weybridge, Surrey in England. The firm began by repairing and restoring "real" Cobras, then obtained permission to use the "Cobra" trademark and ship cars to the U.S., to be sold by Ford dealers. The latest ones had a 305-cid (5.0-litre) V-8 engine, as used in Mustangs, and displayed an appearance identical to the last Cobra 427.

ALFA ROMEO

Origins of the Italian Alfa Romeo, famed for exotic sports machines in the prewar years and popularly-priced sports cars after World War Two, were tied to another name well known in early automotive history: Darracq. Specifically, to the Italian company known as *Societa Anonima Italiana Darracq (SAID),* which imported Darracq cars from France. In 1906, Alessando Darracq operated a garage, intended to furnish the Italian market with taxis. Darracq encountered considerable difficulties in Italy, and in 1909 his garage was taken over by the company ALFA (for *Anonima Lombarda Fabbrica Automobile).* In 1911, a businessman named Ing. (engineer) Nicola Romeo became the owner of that organization, calling the company Anonima Ing. Ni-

cola Romeo. Then, in 1918, the new company reorganized and the name was changed to Alfa Romeo S.p.A., the title by which it earned a lasting reputation.

By 1925, the 22/90 Alfa (RLSS, for Super Sport) had become the first "sporting" model to gain attention, due in part to its two-seat configuration with a long, tapered tail. In the years before the war, Alfa Romeo ranked with Bugatti, Bentley and Mercedes in racing victories. The firm's first great competition success came with the P-2, which won 18 major international races from 1924-30. Pre-war Alfa Monzas for racing carried supercharged 2.3- and 2.6-liter engines, inspired by Vittorio Jano. Six-cylinder models came by 1927, carrying 1.5-liter single-overhead-cam Turismo engines. Then came the Gran Turismo dual-overhead-cam design, some of which were produced with a Rootes-style supercharger. By 1929, the twin-cam engine grew to 1752 cc for a new "1750" model, designed by Jano. That one later fared well in racing, and many "1750" bodies were created by Zagato or Touring. A super-charged "1750" won the 1000-mile Italian Mille Miglia in 1930. A model called 8C 2300 won the Targa Florio and Le Mans 24-Hour events in 1931. Also in that year, a 2336-cc straight eight was produced using the dual-overhead-cam configuration. Arranged as twin fours with separate blocks (but one crankcase), it had a 10-bearing crankshaft. With induction assisted by a Rootes blower, that powerplant developed 138 bhp.

In 1933, Alfa Romeo was absorbed by I.R.I., thus owned by the Italian government. And in the latter half of that decade, production was completely absorbed by supplies to the government of industrial vehicles and airplane motors for the war in Africa. An evolution of the 8C 2300 had become the Tipo B (P3) 2.9-liter Grand Prix Car by 1932. Its engine used two blowers and delivered power to two driveshafts. Over a 16-month period in 1932-33, the P3 won seven Grand Prix events. Then, in 1936, a new 8C 2900 with 2905-cc displacement evolved from the P3 racer. This one had twin superchargers and dual Weber carburetors, producing 180 horsepower. Technical features also included an independent front suspension, hydraulic brakes, and front shock absorbers. Only 30 of them were sold in two years, but it hardly mattered. The Alfa plant was now controlled by the government, devoted to weaponry. Full production went to military contracts as war broke out. Alfa's factory at Milan, Italy was badly damaged by aerial bombing, which destroyed almost half the plant and equipment.

At the end of the war, two big problems emerged: rebuilding of plant and equipment, and reconversion to peacetime production. The company returned triumphantly to motor racing, but in 1948 three of its most famous champions died tragically. After a brief pause for retooling in 1950 (their record year), the Alfetta took part in 11 Gran Prix races, winning all of them. World champions included Juan Manuel Fangio, Nino Farina, and Luigi Faggioli. In 1951, Alfa won the world title once again, with Fangio at the wheel. A year later, Alfa entered the tourist and sporting field with its 1900 model, starting with a sedan version, which became "the family car that wins the races."

With ordinary sedans and the Sprint in production by 1953, the 1900 T.I. sedan made its first triumphant appearance, and Alfas dominated the most important European races. Various versions of the 1900, in fact, earned about 100 national and international prizes. No less sensational was the debut of the Disco Volante ("flying saucer") in world championship races. Alfa retired from factory-sponsored racing after 1953.

In 1954, the 1900 and the t.i. Super were well launched on the market, and joined by the Giulietta Sprint coupe, with a body design by Bertone. That was followed by the Giulietta Berlina (sedan), which was displayed at the Torino (Turin), Italy Motor Show in 1955. Toward the end of 1955, Alfa brought out a roadster (convertible) edition, in the Pinin Farina-designed Spider model; plus the Primavera version of the Super 1900.

Known for a minimal level of annual model change, Alfa Romeo models have tended to last a long while in the marketplace, evolving and improving gradually. Each of the Giuliettas, produced until 1963, was powered by a 1290-cc twin-cam four-cylinder engine that could rev to 7000 rpm. Early in the 1960s, the new Giulia replaced the Giulietta, with a similar suspension and running gear but a 1570-cc engine. Then came the 1600 Duetto Spider, with the same running gear but a Pininfarina body that was not universally adored. One of the many Giulia variants was the lightweight GTA, built with racing "homologation" in mind.

At Montreal's Expo 67 (in 1967), a new Bertone-designed Alfa Romeo called the "Montreal" was shown. That went on sale in 1971, built in small numbers until 1977, powered by a four-cam V-8 engine. In more regular production, a GTV-6 coupe joined the familiar Spider roadster. Through the 1980s, the open-topped Spider continued to attract customers each year, including a lower-priced "Graduate" model named after the 1960s movie of that title, in which Dustin Hoffman had driven an Alfa Romeo convertible. Not until 1991 would a replacement for the long-lived Spider roadster emerge, and even that carried some familiar features, including the uniquely-positioned (nearly horizontal) gearshift lever.

Though imported occasionally before World War Two, and in the early postwar years, Alfa Romeos first became available in the U.S. in significant volume around 1956, after the debut of the Giulietta. Alfa Romeo's offices and factory have remained at Milano (Milan), Italy.

Note: Open Alfa Romeos were known as Spyder or Spider; the latter form is used in this Catalog. In the U.S., they were also variously called roadsters or convertibles, even though they had roll-up windows. Most Alfa Romeo coupes adopted the Sprint designation.

1946-50 ALFA ROMEO

1949 2.5-liter Alfa Romeo Tipo 6C-2500 SS Spider. (Christie's)

6C 2500 — After World War Two, during which Alfa Romeo's prewar manufacturing plant in Portello, Italy (a suburb of Milan) had been bombed, the company soon was ready with its first postwar model: the Tipo 6C 2500. Evolved from the like-named 6C 2500 of 1939-43, produced as a five-seat Turismo sedan, Sport and Super Sport, the car was powered by a twin-cam six-cylinder engine. This new model, which became known as *Freccia d'Oro* (Golden Arrow), would be the last Alfa series built with a separate body and frame. This would also be the last coachbuilt Alfa, availble with bodies from Pinin Farina, Stabilimenti Farina, Boneschi, and Touring. Four body styles were produced: a five-passenger berlina (sedan) that looked like a streamlined hardtop coupe, a two-

21

passenger coupe and cabriolet, and a five-passenger cabriolet (convertible). Though attractive, the bodies were considered bulky by some.

All examples were right-hand drive, with a four-speed transmission and column-mounted gearshift lever. Ordinary models had gearboxes synchronized only on the upper two gear ratios, but the Competizione was fully synchronized. The channel-section frame contained an X-member. Wheelbase was 118 inches, except for the SS model, which measured only 106 inches. The Alfa's front suspension consisted of parallel trailing arms (as used later on cars ranging from the Volkswagen Beetle and Porsche, to Aston Martin) and coil springs. The independent rear suspension used swing axles with longitudinal torsion bars. Tubular hydraulic shocks went all around, and drum brakes were used at front and rear. Space at the center of the dashboard could hold either a radio or gauges.

Under the hood was a cast-iron engine block with seven main bearings, topped by a cast aluminum head with dual-overhead-camshaft configuration. It ran with a chain cam drive to the sprocket, then via spur gears. Displacement was 149 cubic inches (2443 cc). Carburetion came from a single Solex unit in the Turismo, all the way to three sidedraft Weber carbs in the Sport and Super Sport. The Turismo edition produced 87 horsepower at 4600 rpm; the Sport delivered three more horses; and the Super Sport reached 110 bhp. Even farther up the scale were the Corsa 125, whipping out 125 horsepower at 4800 rpm; and topping the list, the Competizione, with 145 bhp at 5500 rpm. A tall, narrow version of the traditional Alfa Romeo grille consisted of short horizontal bars. A wide lower grille contained short vertical bars, extending to the tiny round parking lights.

Note: See description of Second Series (1951-53) for additional details.

I.D. DATA: Chassis number is on front crossmember. Prefix 'S' = Sports; 'SS' = Super Sports. Engine number is on right front of block.

Model	Body Type & Seating	Engine Type/CID	P.O.E. Price	Weight (lbs.)	Prod. Total
6C 2500					
	2-dr Berlina Sed-5P	I6/149	N/A	3410	Note 1
	2-dr Cabr-4/5P	I6/149	N/A	3410	Note 1
SS	2-dr Cpe-2P	I6/149	N/A	3080	Note 1
SS	2-dr Cabriolet-2P	I6/149	N/A	3080	Note 1

Note 1: Calendar-year production of Alfa Romeos broke down as follows: (1947) 486 units; (1948) 451 units; (1949) 414 units. Total 6C 2500 production included 695 Sport (cabriolet and sedan) models, built from 1946-52; 680 'S' Golden Arrow 5/6-passenger sedans, built from 1947-52; 413 Super Sport (SS) models, built from 1947-51; and three Competizione models.

Weight Note: Figures shown are approximate. Competiziones weighed only 1870 pounds.

ENGINE DATA: BASE SIX: Inline, double-overhead-cam six-cylinder. Cast iron block and aluminum head. **Displacement:** 149 cu. in. (2443 cc). Bore & Stroke: 2.83 x 3.94 in. (72 x 100 mm). Compression Ratio: 7.0:1 or 7.5:1. **Brake Horsepower:** (Turismo) 87 at 4600 rpm.; (Sport) 90 at 4600; (Super Sport or GT) 105 at 4800; (Corsa 125) 125 at 4800; (Competizione): 145 at 5500. Seven main bearings. Solid valve lifters. **Carburetors:** (Turismo) one Solex; (Sport) two; (Super Sport) three sidedraft Webers.

CHASSIS DATA: Wheelbase: (SS) 106.0 in.; (others) 118.0 in. **Overall Length:** (sed) 192-194 in.; (cabr) 205 in.; (SS cpe) 180 in.; (SS cabr) 177 in. **Width:** 69-70 in. **Front Tread:** 57.1 in. **Rear Tread:** 57.9 in. **Wheel Type:** perforated steel disc. **Standard Tires:** 6.00x18 or 6.50x17.

TECHNICAL: Layout: front-engine, rear-drive. **Transmission:** four-speed manual, column shift (all synchro on Competizione and late models; others synchronized 3rd/4th). **Standard Final Drive Ratio:** 4.35:1. **Steering:** worm and sector. **Suspension (front):** parallel trailing arms with coil springs. **Suspension (rear):** independent swing axles with longitudinal torsion bars. **Brakes:** hydraulic, front/rear drum. **Body Construction:** separate body on channel-section frame with X-member.

PERFORMANCE: Top Speed: (Sport) 96 mph; (SS) 103 mph; (Competizione) 125 mph.

Manufacturer: Alfa Romeo S.p.A., Milan, Italy.

HISTORY: Though featured in some early issues of *Road & Track,* few of these 6C 2500 Alfas ever reached the U.S., but awareness of their existence helped spark interest that later spilled over into subsequent models that were officially imported.

Prior to 1950, most Alfa Romeos were sold (and used) for competition. Alfa's postwar chronicle of racing successes began as early as 1946 with the International Gran Prix at Geneva; the Circuito di Torino; and the Circuito di Milano. In 1947, according to a later company brochure, that list added the Switzerland Gran Prix, the Europe Gran Prix at Spa in Belgium, the Gran Premio di Italia, and the Coppa Delle 1000 Miglia.

In addition to the 6C 2500, Alfa Romeo produced a handful of Type 158/47 one-seat racing cars, using two blowers to raise output from the 1479-cc eight-cylinder engine as high as 350 bhp at 8500 rpm. They were capable of speeds up to 165 mph. Several prototypes of a 6C 3000 also were created.

Note: Alfa Romeo's new 1900 series was introduced late in 1950; see next listing for complete details.

1951-52 ALFA ROMEO

1951 Alfa Romeo 1900 Berlina.

1900 — FOUR — After achieving a certain recognition, if not great sales success, with the low-production 6C 2500 series, Alfa Romeo issued its first new postwar design. That also happened to employ the company's first unibody construction. Berlina (sedan) bodies were built at the Alfa Romeo facility, while coupe and cabriolet versions came from such renowned coachbuilders as Ghia, Boano, Pinin Farina, Bertone, Castagna, Vignale and, especially, Carrozzeria Touring. Like the 6C 2500, the new 1900 turned to a dual-overhead-cam engine, but this time with four cylinders instead of six. The four-speed (synchronized) manual transmission also evolved from that in the 6C 2500, and would later develop into a five-speed for the Super Sprint. Engine displacement was 114.9 cubic inches (1884 cc), and the initial 1900 version developed 80 horsepower. When the 1900C Sprint coupe and cabriolet debuted during 1951, output was up to 100 bhp at 5500 rpm. The engine had a cast iron block and cast aluminum head, and ran with direct chain-drive camshafts that acted upon inclined valves.

Suspensions differed from the 6C 2500. Up front was an independent suspension using parallel (unequal-length) A-arms, coil springs, and an anti-roll bar. At the rear, the "live" axle was attached by single lower trailing arms (on each side), an upper triangulated link from floorpan to differential housing, and coil springs. Aluminum drum brakes contained cast-iron liners.

This time, Alfa Romeo offered the new model in left-hand drive, aimed toward volume production and priced moderately. The Berlina sedan was introduced first, wearing a steel body. (Most of the coachbuilt coupes and cabriolets had aluminum bodies.) Then came the 1900C Touring coupe and cabriolet. A narrow triangular center grille contained horizontal bars, and was flanked by twin air openings, each with a single horizontal bar across its width. Tiny round parking lights stood below the round headlamps. Full rounded wheel openings were evident. The 1900C Touring Coupe had rear quarter windows. The cabriolet body was done by Pinin Farina.

6C 2500 — Second Series — SIX — Appearance and mechanical details of Alfa Romeo's second series of Sports and Super Sports models, which continued the style initiated before World War II, were similar to the 1946-50 models. They were called the Freccia d'Oro ("Golden Arrow") series. The Sports two-door cabriolet models, intended for touring, was claimed to have a roomy and comfortable body with three front and two rear seats. A streamlined two-door sedan also was available. The Super Sports (SS), which carried a higher-powered version of the dual-overhead-cam engine and rode a shorter wheelbase, was a 2-3 seater, offered in open (cabriolet) or closed coupe form. Each wore a narrow grille made up of horizontal strips, a long hood, split windshield, and double-bar split bumpers. Large parking lights sat inboard of the built-in headlamps. Closed models had small back windows. The luggage compartment could be opened from inside the car, and held a spare wheel on a glider.

In Sports trim, with a single carburetor and 7:1 compression, the 2443-cc six-cylinder engine developed 90 hp at 4600 rpm. Its one-piece cylinder block and crankcase were made of cast iron, topped by a light alloy cylinder head with hemispherical combustion chambers. Seven main bearings were used. Valves were arranged in "V" form, directly operated (without rockers) by the two overhead camshafts.

The four-speed gearbox formed a unit with the engine block, and worked through a single-disc, elastic hub, dry plate clutch. A column gearshift lever stood just under the steering wheel. The differential was mounted as a unit with the chassis, working through floating half-axles. The chassis was a one-piece electric welded sheet steel structure of box form, with a partial light alloy lining. Coil springs were used in the independent front suspension; longitudinal torsion bars at the rear. The Sports model had a wheelbase of 118 inches, while the SS measured only 106 inches. Rudge-type wheels held 6.00x18 tires. Hydraulic drum brakes were used.

The Super Sport's engine, identical in displacement, developed 105 bhp at 4800 rpm, using 7.5:1 compression and three horizontal single-body carburetors. The two SS bodies were designed with an extra-low center of gravity.

Bumpers were fixed on the chassis, independent from the body. Two built-in jacks were mounted near doors. Inside, upholstery came in either cloth or special velvet. Dashboard control knobs were made of plexiglass or ivorite. Standard equipment included twin windshield wipers, a rear-view mirror, ashtrays, sun shades, snap-fobs, and direction indicators. Both interior and body colors could be chosen according to personal taste.

The sedan was described as a "streamlined, slim and elegant car for speedy touring" with space for three up front and two in the rear. Its extra-light all-metal body was made of steel tube and steel section members with aluminum sheet panels. The Sports cabriolet wore an all-metal body of sheet steel with light alloy paneling, with a waterproofed fabric top. Two or three people could sit in front, and seatbacks hinged forward to allow access to the rear seats. Leather upholstery and chromium-plated accessories were standard, and space was provided for a radio. The spring-type steering wheel had a gracefully curved crossbar, and could be either leather or bakelite covered.

I.D. DATA: Chassis number (1900) is on right side of firewall, under the hood. Starting chassis number (1900): 1356/00001; (1900C) 1358/010001. Chassis number (6C 2500) is on front crossmember. Prefix 'S' = Sports; 'SS' = Super Sports. Engine numbers are on right front of block.

Model	Body Type & Seating	Engine Type/CID	P.O.E. Price	Weight (lbs.)	Prod. Total
1900					
Berlina	4-dr Sedan-5/6P	I4/115	N/A	2315	Note 1
1900C					
Sprint	2-dr Coupe-2P	I4/115	N/A	2204	Note 1
Sprint	2-dr Cabr-2 + 2P	I4/115	N/A	2425	Note 1
6C 2500 (Second Series)					
Sports	2-dr Sedan-5/6P	I6/149	Note 2	3307	Note 3
Sports	2-dr Sedan-4/5P	I6/149	Note 2	3329	Note 3
Sports	2-dr Cabr-4/5P	I6/149	Note 2	3351	Note 3
SS	2-dr Cpe-2/3P	I6/149	Note 2	3108	Note 3
SS	2-dr Cabriolet-2/3P	I6/149	Note 2	3086	Note 3

Note 1: Total model 1900 production, over the 1950-58 period, came to 21,304 units (including 949 Sprints and 854 Super Sprints).

Note 2: 6C 2500 price in U.S. was approximately $10,000, with a Pinin Farina body.

Note 3: Calendar year production of 6C 2500 models (1950-52) was about 100 units. See previous listing for breakdown from 1947-52.

1900 Price Note: The 1900 sedan soldin the U.S. for approximately $4500, the coupe and cabriolet for $6000 or more.

ENGINE DATA: BASE FOUR (1900): Inline, dual-overhead-cam four-cylinder. Cast iron block and aluminum head. **Displacement:** 114.9 cu. in. (1884 cc). **Bore & Stroke:** 3.25 x 3.46 in. (82.55 x 88 mm). **Compression Ratio:** 7.5:1 except (1900C) 8.0:1. **Brake Horsepower:** (1900) 80 at 4800 rpm; (1900C) 100 at 5500 rpm. Five main bearings. Solid valve lifters. One carburetor except (1900C) two-barrel. 12-volt electrical system.

BASE SIX (6C 2500): Inline, dual-overhead-cam six-cylinder. Cast iron block and aluminum head. **Displacement:** 149 cu. in. (2443 cc). **Bore & Stroke:** 2.83 x 3.94 in. (72 x 100 mm). **Compression Ratio:** 7.0:1 (Super, 7.0:1). **Brake Horsepower:** (Turismo) 87 at 4600 rpm.; (Sports) 90 at 4600; (Super Sports) 105 at 4800; (Corsa 125) 125 at 4800; (Competizione): 145 at 5500. Seven main bearings. Solid valve lifters. **Carburetors:** (Turismo) one Solex; (Sport) two-barrel; (Super Sport) three sidedraft one-barrel Webers.

CHASSIS DATA: Wheelbase: (1900C cpe) 98.5 in.; (1900 sed) 103.5 in.; (6C 2500 SS) 106.0 in.; (6C 2500) 118.0 in. **Overall Length:** (1900C cpe) 170 in.; (1900 sed) 173.2 in.; (6C 2500 5/6P sed) 192.3 in.; (6C 2500 5P sed) 193.7 in.; (6C 2500 cabr) 204.7 in.; (6C 2500 SS cpe) 180.3 in.; (6C 2500 SS cabr) 177.2 in. **Height:** (1900 sed) 58.7 in.; (6C 2500 5/6P sed) 60.2 in.; (6C 2500 5P sed) 58.7 in.; (6C 2500 cabr) 59.1 in.; (6C 2500 SS cpe) 59.1 in.; (6C 2500 SS cabr) 58.3 in. **Width:** (1900C cpe) 65 in.; (1900 sed) 63 in.; (6C 2500 5/6P sed) 71.7 in.; (6C 2500 5P sed) 70.5 in.; (6C 2500 cabr) 70.9 in.; (6C 2500 SS) 70.1 in. **Front Tread:** (1900) 51.6 in.; (6C 2500) 57.1 in. **Rear Tread:** (1900) 51.6 in.; (6C 2500) 57.9 in. **Wheel Type:** (6C 2500) Rudge. **Standard Tires:** (1900) 5.50x16 Pirelli; (6C 2500) 6.00x18 Pirelli.

TECHNICAL: Layout: front-engine, rear-drive. Transmission: four-speed manual, column shift, fully synchronized. Overall 1900 gear ratios: (1st) 13.45:1; (2nd) 8.98:1; (3rd) 6.11:1; (4th) 4.1:1. Overall 6C 2500 Sport gear ratios: (1st) 16.53:1; (2nd) 10.13:1; (3rd) 6.52:1; (4th) 4.35:1. Overall 6C 2500 Super Sport gear ratios: (1st) 14.9:1; (2nd) 9.18:1; (3rd) 5.81:1; (4th) 3.94:1. **Standard Final Drive Ratio:** (1900) 4.1:1. **Steering:** (1900) globoidal worm and roller; (6C 2500) worm and sector. **Suspension (front):** (1900) independent, parallel unequal-length A-arms (transverse quadrilateral), coil springs and anti-roll bar; (6C 2500) parallel trailing arms with coil springs. **Suspension (rear):** (1900) live axle with single lower trailing arms (each side), upper triangulated link from floorpan to differential housing, and coil springs; (6C 2500) independent swing axles with longitudinal torsion bars. **Brakes:** hydraulic, front/rear drum. **Body Construction:** (1900) unibody; (6C 2500) separate body on channel-section frame with X-member. **Fuel Tank:** (1900) 46 liters (12 gal.); (1900C) 60 liters (16 gal.); (6C 2500) 80 liters (21 U.S. gallons).

PERFORMANCE: Top Speed: (1900 sedan) 93 mph (single-carb); (1900 Sprint cabriolet) 100 mph; (1900 Sprint cpe) 106 mph; (6C 2500 Sports) 96 mph; (6C 2500 Super) 102-103 mph. **Acceleration (0-60 mph):** N/A (6C 2500, 0-50 mph in 10 sec. **Fuel Mileage:** (6C 2500) about 22 mpg.

Manufacturer: Alfa Romeo S.p.A., Milan, Italy.

HISTORY: The 1900 sedan was introduced in fall 1950; the 1900C Sprint coupe, in August 1951. Though the 1900 was not a race car, Piero Taruffi and Felice Bonetto finished fifth and ninth in the first running of the 2178-mile *Carrera Panamericana* (Mexican Road Race) in May 1950, averaging 76.5 and 77.8 mph respectively. That event ran from Juarez, Mexico (on the U.S. border) all the way south to the border between Mexico and Guatemala.

Production of the 6C 2500 ceased in 1952. Alfa Romeo's promotional brochure for the Second Series 6C 2500 began: "The roar of the destroying war has just ceased from the skies but down on the earth a new roar is rising, this is a song of revival and announces that peaceful men are at work again." Now, the brochure continued, "the new Alfa Romeos are fanning out towards the roads of the world, which again will be paved with their victories."

From 1952-60, Alfa built nine Disco Volante ("flying saucer") models based on the 1900 chassis, for racing. They featured smooth, graceful aero lines with bulging front and rear fenders and a stylized variant of the Alfa triangular grille. Three were four-cylinder, the rest sixes. The 1997-cc four produced 158 bhp; the 2995-cc six developd 230 bhp. Both coupe and roadster versions were built. Top speeds reached as high as 159 mph. One example finished second in the 1953 Mille Miglia, driven by Juan Manuel Fangio. Fangio also won the 1953 *Supercortemaggiore* (at Merano).

1953 ALFA ROMEO

1900 — FOUR — Model choices this year included the original 1900 Berlina four-door sedan, the 1900C touring coupe and Pinin Farina cabriolet, and a 1900L Victoria cabriolet (also by Farina) that held four or five passengers. Otherwise, appearance and mechanical details were the same as 1951-52. A larger (1975-cc) dual-overhead-cam engine became available in the Berlina Super.

I.D. DATA: Chassis number is on right side of firewall, under the hood. Engine number is on right front of block. See 1951-52 listing for starting serial numbers.

Model	Body Type & Seating	Engine Type/CID	P.O.E. Price	Weight (lbs.)	Prod. Total
1900					
Berlina	4-dr Sedan-5/6P	I4/115	N/A	2315	Note 1
Super	4-dr Sedan-5/6P	I4/115	N/A	N/A	Note 1
1900C	2-dr Coupe-2P	I4/115	N/A	2204	Note 1
1900C	2-dr Cabr-2+2P	I4/115	N/A	2425	Note 1
1900L	2-dr Cabr-4/5P	I4/115	N/A	2425	Note 1

Note 1: Total model 1900 production, over the 1950-58 period, came to 21,304 units (including 949 Sprints and 854 Super Sprints). Of the 3,477 Alfa Romeos built during 1953, approximately 62 were sold in the U.S.

Price Note: A 1900C coupe cost about $7200 in the U.S. in 1953-54.

ENGINE DATA: BASE FOUR (1900): Inline, dual-overhead cam four-cylinder. Cast iron block and aluminum head. **Displacement:** 114.9 cu. in. (1884 cc). **Bore & Stroke:** 3.25 x 3.46 in. (82.55 x 88 mm). **Compression Ratio:** 7.5:1 except (1900C) 7.75:1. **Brake Horsepower:** (1900) 80 at 4800 rpm; (1900C) 100 at 5500 rpm. Five main bearings. Solid valve lifters. One carburetor except (1900C) two-barrel. 12-volt electrical system.

BASE FOUR (1900 Berlina Super): Inline, dual-overhead-cam four-cylinder. Cast iron block and aluminum head. **Displacement:** 120.5 cu. in. (1975 cc). **Bore & Stroke:** 3.33 x 3.46 in. (84.5 x 88 mm). **Brake Horsepower:** 115 at 5500 rpm. Solid valve lifters.

CHASSIS DATA: Wheelbase: (1900C cpe) 98.5 in.; (1900 sed) 103.5 in. **Overall Length:** (1900C cpe) 170 in.; (1900 sed) 173.2 in. **Height:** (1900C cpe) 53.0 in.; (1900 sed) 58.7 in. Width: (1900C cpe) 65 in.; (1900 sed) 63 in. **Front Tread:** 51.6 in. **Rear Tread:** 51.6 in. **Standard Tires:** (1900/1900L) 165x400; (1900C) 6.00x16.

TECHNICAL: Layout: front-engine, rear-drive. **Transmission:** four-speed manual, column shift. **Steering:** globoidal worm and roller. **Suspension (front):** independent, parallel unequal-length A-arms (transverse quadrilateral), coil springs and anti-roll bar. **Suspension (rear):** live axle with single lower trailing arms (each side), upper triangulated link from floorpan to differential housing, and coil springs. **Brakes:** hydraulic, front/rear drum. **Body Construction:** unibody. **Fuel Tank:** (1900) 46 liters (12 gal.); (1900C) 60 liters (16 gal.).

PERFORMANCE: Top Speed: (1900) 93 mph (single-carb); (1900C cpe) 106 mph; (1900C cabriolet) 100 mph.

Manufacturer: Alfa Romeo S.p.A., Milan, Italy.

1954-55 ALFA ROMEO

GIULIETTA — 750 SERIES — FOUR — Smaller than the 1900 series, the new Giulietta also came in Berlina (four-door sedan) form first, followed by the coupe and roadster models. Except for a handful of Sprint coupes that emerged at the Turin auto show in spring 1954, that is. When Alfa Romeo anticipated expansion of production for the new model, a lottery was held among the company's several hundred shareholders. Winners would receive a brand-new Giulietta. Unfortunately, development of the new model fell well behind schedule. The Italian media claimed fraud and threatened a scandal. Winners were drawn, but no cars existed to give away as prizes. Therefore, a small number of 2+2 Giulietta-based Sprint coupes were produced by Nuccio Bertone Carrozzeria, in time for the Turin show. Initially, only enough were ordered to satisfy lottery winners; but production increased as the car grew popular, ultimately reaching a total of 6,000. Those early Sprint coupes had the traditional-styled Alfa Romeo grille, flanked by an air intake opening on each side, each with a single horizontal bar and containing the parking lights. The trunk was hinged above the back window. By the 1955 model year, the gas cap was moved inside the trunk and a chrome rub rail was added.

The Berlina four-door sedan, on the other hand, was designed by Alfa itself. Its front end differed somewhat, as the twin outer grilles contained a row of vertical bars as well as the single horizontal bar. That sedan was followed in mid-1955 by a two-seat open Spider with roll-up windows and a front end identical to the Sprint coupe, but built by Pinin Farina.

Mechanically, the Giulietta was similar to the 1900, which continued in production. The dual-overhead-cam engine, with aluminum block and head, displaced 1290 cc (78.7 cubic inches) and produced 80 horsepower at 6300 rpm. The front suspension of the unibodied sports car consisted of unequal-length A-arms and coil springs, and the rear featured the same design as the 1900. Brakes, too, were similar to those in the 1900, consisting of aluminum drums with cast-iron liners. Not only was the Giulietta attractive and fun to drive, especially in open Spider form, it was also technically pleasing. See next listing for additional description and technical details.

1954 Alfa Romeo Model 1900 two-door.

1900 — FOUR — Production of the 1900 series continued, with a larger (1975-cc) engine in the Super Sprint (SS), which developed 115 horsepower. A T.I. sedan with twin carburetors and dual exhaust pipes arrived in 1954; a Super Primavera coupe (with the taller sedan profile) in 1955.

I.D. DATA: Giulietta chassis number is on the right side of the firewall and inner side of engine hood. Chassis number for 1900 is on right side of firewall, under the hood. Engine number is on right side of crankcase (Giulietta) or right front of block (1900). Starting serial number: (Giulietta Sprint cpe) 1493/00001; (Giulietta Berlina sedan) 1488/00001; (Giulietta Spider) 1495/00001.

Model	Body Type & Seating	Engine Type/CID	P.O.E. Price	Weight (lbs.)	Prod. Total
GIULIETTA					
Berlina	4-dr Sedan-4P	I4/79	N/A	N/A	Note 1
Sprint	2-dr Coupe-2+2P	I4/79	N/A	N/A	Note 1
Spider	2-dr Roadster-2P	I4/79	N/A	N/A	Note 1
1900/1900C					
Berlina	4-dr Sedan-4P	I4/115	N/A	N/A	Note 2
T.I	4-dr Sedan-4P	I4/120	N/A	N/A	Note 2
SS	2-dr Coupe-2P	I4/120	6100	2615	Note 2
Primavera	2-dr Coupe-5P	I4/120	N/A	N/A	Note 2

Note 1: Total Giulietta production (1954-63) came to 27,142 Sprint models; 17,096 Spiders; plus 1,576 Sprint Speciale and Zagato.

Note 2: Total model 1900 production, over the 1950-58 period, came to 21,304 units (including 949 Sprints and 854 Super Sprints).

Annual Production Note: A total of 3,826 Alfa Romeos were produced in 1954 and 5,919 in 1955.

Price Note: 1900 price in U.S. is approximate.

ENGINE DATA: BASE FOUR (Giulietta): Inline, dual-overhead-cam four-cylinder. Cast iron block and aluminum head. **Displacement:** 78.7 cu. in. (1290 cc). **Bore & Stroke:** 2.91 x 2.95 in. (74 x 75 mm). **Compression Ratio:** (Sprint) 8.0:1. **Brake Horsepower:** (Berlina) 50 at 5200 rpm; (Sprint) 65 at 6000 rpm. Solid valve lifters.

BASE FOUR (1900): Inline, dual-overhead-cam four-cylinder. Cast iron block and aluminum head. **Displacement:** 120.5 cu. in. (1975 cc). **Bore & Stroke:** 3.33 x 3.46 in. (84.5 x 88 mm). **Compression Ratio:** 7.5:1 or 8.0:1. **Brake Horsepower:** (1900) 90 at 5200 rpm; (1900C SS) 115 at 5500 rpm. Solid valve lifters.

Note: The 1900 Berlina sedan, still available in 1954, came with the former (smaller) 1884-cc engine.

CHASSIS DATA: Wheelbase: (Giulietta) 93.7 in.; (Giulietta Spider) 86.6 in.; (1900 cpe) 98.5 in.; (1900 sed) 103.5 in. **Overall Length:** (Giulietta Sprint/Spider) 153 in.; (Giulietta sed) 154 in.; (1900 cpe) 170 in.; (1900 sed) 173 in. **Height:** (Giulietta) 55.3 in.; (Giulietta Sprint) 50.7 in.; (1900 cpe) 53.0 in.; (1900 sed) 58.5 in. **Width:** (Giulietta Sprint/Spider) 60 in.; (Giulietta sed) 61 in.; (1900 cpe) 65 in.; (1900 sed) 62.75 in. **Front Tread:** (Giulietta) 50.25 in.; (1900) 51.5 in. **Rear Tread:** (Giulietta) 50 in.; (1900) 51.5 in. **Standard Tires:** (Giulietta) 155x15; (1900) 6.50x15.

TECHNICAL: Layout: front-engine, rear-drive. **Transmission:** four-speed manual (all synchro). **Steering:** (Giulietta) worm and lever; (1900) globoidal worm and roller. **Suspension (front):** independent with unequal-length A-arms, coil springs and anti-roll bar. **Suspension (rear):** live axle with single lower trailing arms (each side), upper triangulated link from floorpan to differential housing, and coil springs. **Brakes:** (Giulietta) hydraulic, front/rear drum; (1900) Girling hydraulic, front/rear drum. **Body Construction:** unibody.

PERFORMANCE: Top Speed: (Giulietta) 99-103 mph; (Giulietta Veloce) 112 mph; (1900) 100 mph; (1900 SS) 112 mph. **Acceleration (0-60 mph):** (1900) 11 sec.

Manufacturer: Alfa Romeo S.p.A., Milan, Italy.

Distributor: Max Hoffman, New York City.

HISTORY: The Giulietta would be produced for nearly a decade (into 1963) for sale in the U.S., and last as late as 1965 for sale elsewhere. The 1900 series was produced through 1958. Previewing the Giulietta, *Road & Track* described it as a "modern Juliet...a wench to win the heart of any motor-minded Romeo before he even gets out of second gear."

Three special show cars on 1900 chassis were built in 1953-54. Known as *Berlina Aerodinamica Technica* (aero design study), they were done by Carrozzeria Nuccio Bertone and popularly referred to as B.A.T. 5, 7 and 9. These startlingly-shaped, indeed bizarre, vehicles had rounded front ends and giant tailfins, and were intended for experimental use only. All three wound up in the U.S. One of them, a B.A.T. 5, was pictured in *Motor Trend* in 1954. Headlights swung outward from the inner side of the fenders. No chrome decorated the dark grey body. Front wheels were shrouded. A concave side panel let hot air exit from the front brakes and tires.

1956 ALFA ROMEO

1956 Alfa Romeo 2000 sports coupe with Boano body.

GIULIETTA — 750 SERIES — FOUR — A Veloce version became available in 1956, with its engine producing 90 horsepower at 6500 rpm, offered in all three body styles. Top speeds up to 111.8 mph were claimed. The engine had altered cam timing, higher compression (9.1:1 versus the standard 8.5:1), twin Weber carburetors instead of the usual single Solex, and steel-tube exhaust headers. Giulietta's independent front suspension used transverse wishbones and variable-rate giant coil springs. The rigid rear axle connected to frame by upper triangular thrust rod and lower radius rods, with coil springs.

1900 — FOUR — A second series of the 1900C Super Sprint was introduced during 1956, with dual two-barrel carburetors. Otherwise, appearance and mechanical details were similar to prior models.

I.D. DATA: Giulietta chassis number is on the right side of the firewall and inner side of engine hood. Chassis number for 1900 is on right side of firewall, under the hood. Engine number is on right side of crankcase (Giulietta) or right front of block (1900). Starting serial number: (Giulietta Sprint Veloce) 1493E/00001.

Model	Body Type & Seating	Engine Type/CID	P.O.E. Price	Weight (lbs.)	Prod. Total
GIULIETTA					
Berlina	4-dr Sedan-4P	I4/79	N/A	1940	Note 1
Sprint	2-dr Coupe-2 + 2P	I4/79	4070	1764	Note 1
Spider	2-dr Rdstr-2P	I4/79	3135	N/A	Note 1
GIULIETTA VELOCE					
Sprint	2-dr Coupe-2P	I4/79	N/A	N/A	Note 1
Spider	2- dr Rdstr-2P	I4/79	N/A	N/A	Note 1
1900/1900C					
SS	2-dr Coupe-2P	I4/120	6100	2615	Note 2
T.I.	4-dr Sedan-4P	I4/120	N/A	N/A	Note 2
Primavera	2-dr Coupe-5P	I4/120	N/A	N/A	Note 2

Note 1: Total Giulietta production (1954-63) came to 27,142 Sprint models; 17,096 Spiders; plus 1,576 Sprint Speciale and Zagato.

Note 2: Total model 1900 production, over the 1950-58 period, came to 21,304 units (including 949 Sprints and 854 Super Sprints).

Annual Production Note: A total of 11,748 Alfa Romeos were produced in 1956.

Giulietta Price Note: Price at factory was approximately $2070 ($3040 for the Sprint).

1900 Price/Weight Note: Figures shown are approximate. Price at factory was approximately $3700 for the Super and $5136 for the Super Sprint.

ENGINE DATA: BASE FOUR (Giulietta): Inline, dual-overhead-cam four-cylinder. Cast iron block and aluminum head. **Displacement:** 78.7 cu. in. (1290 cc). **Bore & Stroke:** 2.91 x 2.95 in. (74 x 75 mm). **Compression Ratio:** up to 8.5:1. **Brake Horsepower:** (Berlina) 50 at 5200 rpm; (Sprint) 65 at 6000 rpm. Solid valve lifters. One downdraft carburetor.

BASE FOUR (Giulietta Veloce): Same as above, except — **Compression Ratio:** 9.1:1. **Brake Horsepower:** 90 at 6500 rpm. **Torque:** 86.8 lbs.-ft. at 4500 rpm. Two Weber carburetors.

BASE FOUR (1900): Inline, dual-overhead-cam four-cylinder. Cast iron block and aluminum head. **Displacement:** 120.5 cu. in. (1975 cc). **Bore & Stroke:** 3.33 x 3.46 in. (84.5 x 88 mm). **Compression Ratio:** 7.5:1 or 8.0:1. **Brake Horsepower:** (1900) 90 at 5200 rpm; (1900C SS) 115 at 5500 rpm. Solid valve lifters. Two two-barrel carburetors (Super Sprint).

CHASSIS DATA: Wheelbase: (Giulietta) 93.7 in.; (Giulietta Spider) 86.6 in.; (1900 cpe) 98.5 in.; (1900 sed) 103.5 in. **Overall Length:** (Giulietta sed) 154 in.; (Giulietta Sprint/Spider) 153 in.; (1900 cpe) 170 in.; (1900 sed) 173 in. **Height:** (Giulietta) 55.3 in.; (Giulietta Sprint) 50.7 in.; (1900 cpe) 53.0 in.; (1900 sed) 58.5 in. **Width:** (Giulietta Sprint/Spider) 60 in.; (Giulietta sed) 61 in.; (1900 cpe) 65 in.; (1900 sed) 62.75 in. **Front Tread:** (Giulietta) 50.25 in.; (1900) 51.5 in. **Rear Tread:** (Giulietta) 50 in.; (1900) 51.5 in. **Standard Tires:** (Giulietta) 155x15; (1900) 165x400.

TECHNICAL: Layout: front-engine, rear-drive. **Transmission:** four-speed manual (synchro); column lever except (Giulietta Veloce) floor lever. **Steering:** (Giulietta) worm and finger; (1900) globoidal worm and roller. **Suspension (front):** independent with unequal-length A-arms, coil springs and anti-roll bar. **Suspension (rear):** live axle with single lower trailing arms (each side), upper triangulated link from floorpan to differential housing, and coil springs. **Brakes:** (Giulietta) hydraulic, front/rear drum; (1900) Girling hydraulic, front/rear drum. **Body Construction:** unibody.

PERFORMANCE: Top Speed: (Giulietta Berlina) 85 mph; (Giulietta) 103 mph; (Giulietta Veloce) 112 mph; (1900) 100 mph; (1900 SS) 112 mph. **Acceleration (0-60 mph):** (Giulietta Spider Veloce) 11 sec.; (1900) 11 sec. **Fuel Mileage:** (Giulietta) up to 34 mpg.

Manufacturer: Alfa Romeo S.p.A., Milan, Italy.

Distributor: Max Hoffman, New York City.

1957 ALFA ROMEO

1957 Alfa Romeo Giulietta Sprint Spider.

HISTORY: Alfa Romeo's U.S. sales brochure described the Giulietta as the younger sister of the Model 1900, noting that it "recalls the pleasing yet forceful grille motif while retaining the smooth body lines."

GIULIETTA — 750 SERIES — FOUR — A curvy Bertone-created Sprint Speciale version of the Giulietta appeared in 1957, and would continue through 1962. Described with understatement in *World's Great Cars* as "strikingly flamboyant," the SS employed a 100-bhp version of the Giulietta twin-cam engine and was capable of speeds near 125 mph and displayed a long nose and tail. Otherwise, the Giulietta continued with minimal change. Models offered this year, according to the promotional material issued at the Paris Salon of October 1956, included the Berlina four-seat, four-door sedan with 50-bhp engine; the Sprint coupe, rated 65 horsepower; the Sprint Veloce, which had a larger fuel tank than the basic Sprint and a 90-bhp engine; and the open Spider (Spyder) two-seater, with engine specifications similar to the Sprint or Veloce.

1900 — FOUR — Production of the 1900 series continued without major change. An announcement at the Paris Salon of October 1956 noted that three models remained available: the 1900 Super, with 90-bhp engine; the 1900 Primavera; and the 1900C Super Sprint, with an engine rated at 115 horsepower.

I.D. DATA: Giulietta chassis number is on the right side of the firewall and inner side of engine hood. Chassis number for 1900 is on right side of firewall, under the hood. Engine number is on right side of crankcase (Giulietta) or right front of block (1900). Serial number prefix: (Giulietta Sprint Veloce) 1493E; (Giulietta Spider Sports) 1495.

1957 Alfa Romeo Giulietta Sprint coupe.

Model	Body Type & Seating	Engine Type/CID	P.O.E. Price	Weight (lbs.)	Prod. Total
GIULIETTA					
Berlina	4-dr Sedan-4P	I4/79	2799	1940	Note 1
Spider	2-dr Roadster-2P	I4/79	3298	1808	Note 1
Sprint	2-dr Coupe-2 + 2P	I4/79	3784	1874	Note 1
GIULIETTA VELOCE					
Sprint	2-dr Coupe-2 + 2P	I4/79	4194	1830	Note 1
Spider	2-dr Roadster-2P	I4/79	3686	1808	Note 1
GIULIETTA SPRINT SPECIALE					
Sprint	2-dr Coupe-2P	I4/79	N/A	N/A	Note 1
1900					
Super	4-dr Sedan-5/6P	I4/79	N/A	2513	Note 2
Primavera	2-dr Coupe-5P	I4/79	N/A	N/A	Note 2
1900C SUPER SPRINT					
	2-dr Coupe-2P	I4/121	5883	2205	Note 2

Note 1: Total Giulietta production (1954-63) came to 27,142 Sprint models; 17,096 Spiders; plus 1,576 Sprint Speciale and Zagato.

Note 2: Total model 1900 production, over the 1950-58 period, came to 21,304 units (including 949 Sprints and 854 Super Sprints).

Annual Production Note: A total of 16,675 Alfa Romeos were produced in 1957.

ENGINE DATA: BASE FOUR (Giulietta): Inline, dual-overhead-cam four-cylinder. Aluminum block and head. **Displacement:** 78.7 cu. in. (1290 cc). **Bore & Stroke:** 2.91 x 2.95 in. (74 x 75 mm). **Compression Ratio:** (Berlina) 7.5:1; (Sprint) 8.0:1; (Veloce) 9.0:1; (Speciale) 9.7:1. **Brake Horsepower:** (Berlina) 50 at 5200 rpm; (Sprint) 65 at 6000 rpm; (S. Veloce) 90 at 6000 rpm; (Speciale) 100. Solid valve lifters. One carburetor except (Veloce) two-barrel Weber; (Speciale) two Webers.

BASE FOUR (1900): Inline, dual-overhead-cam four-cylinder.Cast iron block and aluminum head. **Displacement:** 120.5 cu.in. (1975 cc). **Bore & Stroke:** 3.33 x 3.46 in. (84.5 x 88 mm).**Compression Ratio:** 7.5:1 or 8.0:1. **Brake Horsepower:** (1900) 90 at 4800 rpm; (1900C SS) 115 at 5500 rpm. Solid valve lifters. Two two-barrel carburetors (Super Sprint).

CHASSIS DATA: Wheelbase: (Giulietta Spider) 86.6 in.; (Giul Sprint) 93.7 in.; (1900C Super Sprint) 98.4 in.; (1900 sed) 103.5 in. **Overall Length:** (Giulietta Spider) 152 in.; (Giul sed) 157.1 in.; (Giul Sprint) 156.7 in.; (1900 Super Sprint) 175.2 in.; (1900 sed) 174.8 in. Height: (Giulietta) 55.3 in.; (Giulietta Sprint) 50.7 in.; (1900 cpe) 53.0 in.; (1900 sed) 58.5 in. **Width:** (Giulietta sed) 61.2 in.; (Giul Sprint) 60.4 in.; (Giul Spider) 62.2 in.; (1900 SS) 65.0 in.; (1900 sed) 63.0 in. **Front Tread:** (Giulietta) 50.6 in.; (1900) 52.2 in. **Rear Tread:** (Giulietta) 50.0 in.; (1900) 52.2 in. **Standard Tires:** (Giulietta) 155x15; (1900) 165x400.

TECHNICAL: Layout: front-engine, rear-drive. **Transmission:** (Giulietta) four-speed manual (all synchro); (1900) four-speed; (1900 SS) five-speed. **Steering:** worm and lever. **Suspension (front):** independent with unequal-length A-arms, coil springs and anti-roll bar. **Suspension (rear):** "live" (rigid) axle with single lower trailing arms (each side), upper triangulated link from floorpan to differential housing, and coil springs. **Brakes:** hydraulic, front/rear drum. **Body Construction:** unibody.

PERFORMANCE: Top Speed: (Giulietta sed) 80-84 mph; (Giul Sprint) 99 mph; (Giul Spider) 96 mph; (Giul Veloce) 112 mph; (Sprint Speciale) 125 mph; (1900 Super) 99 mph. **Acceleration (0-60 mph):** (Speciale) under 10 sec. **Fuel Mileage:** (Giulietta sed) near 30 mpg cruising; (1900) about 24 mpg.

Manufacturer: Alfa Romeo S.p.A., Milan, Italy.

Distributor: Hoffman Motor Car Co., New York City and Beverly Hills; Charles Rezzaghi, San Francisco, California.

HISTORY: Introduced to U.S. market on October 1, 1956. Not until the 1957 model year were Alfa Romeos commonly listed in U.S. price guides.

1958 ALFA ROMEO

1958 Alfa Romeo 1900 Super Sprint Coupe by Touring.

GIULIETTA — 750 SERIES — FOUR — The Giulietta Sprint grille now displayed a latticework pattern, and a floor-mounted gearshift lever replaced the column shift. Both horsepower and compression ratio increased this year. The basic Sprint/Spider engine had 8.5:1 compression and produced 80 horsepower, while the Veloce versions jumped to 9.5:1 compression and 90 bhp. As before, the Spider and Spider Veloce wore a traditional center grille containing both horizontal and vertical strips, set in a solid panel. Small round parking lights sat at the outer ends of twin air intake openings that extended close to the center grille. A split bumper design was used. The Sprint and Sprint Veloce grille shape was similar, but with a much tighter crosshatch pattern. Their round parking lights sat at the outer ends of air-intake openings covered with a larger crosshatch pattern than the center grille. A solid front bumper was used, unlike the Spider's split (two-piece) bumper. A Berlina T.I. sedan with higher-compression engine also became available.

1900 SUPER SPRINT — FOUR — For its final year in the Alfa Romeo lineup, the last 1900-series model continued without significant change, powered by a 115-bhp four-cylinder engine with five-speed manual gearbox.

2000 — SERIES 102 — FOUR — A new Alfa sedan emerged in 1958 as the successor to the 1900, with the same engine and running gear. As was common Alfa Romeo practice, the Berlina four-door sedan arrived first and was factory designed and built, whereas the Spider convertible was created by the firm of Carrozzeria Touring. Appearance was similar to the Giulietta. While attractive and comfortable, however, the 2000 was generally slower. The dual-overhead-camshaft, 1975-cc (120.5-cid) four-cylinder engine, with cast iron block and aluminum head, was similar to that used in the second series 1900. Berlina engines used a single downdraft Solex carburetor and produced 105 horsepower at 5300 rpm. Twin Solex sidedraft carburetors went on Spider versions, which delivered 115 bhp at 5900 rpm. A five-speed, fully-synchronized manual transmission was standard. The suspension, too, was similar to the 1900: unequal-length A-arms with coil springs and anti-roll bar up front, with a rigid axle and coil springs at the rear. Brake drums were made of aluminum with cast-iron liners.

I.D. DATA: Giulietta chassis number is on the right side of the firewall and inner side of engine hood. Chassis number for 1900 and 2000 is on right side of firewall, under the hood. Engine number is on right side of crankcase (Giulietta) or right front of block (1900). Serial number prefix: (Giulietta Sprint) 1493; (Giulietta Spider) 1495; (Giulietta Sprint Veloce) 1493E; (Giulietta Berlina T.I.) 1468; (2000) 10204.

Model	Body Type & Seating	Engine Type/CID	P.O.E. Price	Weight (lbs.)	Prod. Total
GIULIETTA					
Berlina	4-dr Sedan-4P	I4/79	N/A	N/A	Note 1
Spider	2-dr Roadster-2P	I4/79	3298	1873	Note 1
Sprint	2-dr Coupe-2+2P	I4/79	3794	1828	Note 1
GIULIETTA VELOCE					
Spider	2-dr Roadster-2P	I4/79	3686	1873	Note 1
Sprint	2-dr Coupe-2P	I4/79	N/A	N/A	Note 1
GIULIETTA SPRINT SPECIALE					
Sprint	2-dr Coupe-2P	I4/79	N/A	N/A	Note 1
1900 SUPER SPRINT					
	2-dr Coupe-2P	I4/121	5883	2184	Note 2
2000					
Berlina	4-dr Sedan-4P	I4/121	3995	N/A	Note 3
Spider	2-dr Roadster-2P	I4/121	N/A	2695	Note 3

Note 1: Total Giulietta production (1954-63) came to 27,142 Sprint models; 17,096 Spiders; plus 1,576 Sprint Speciale and Zagato.

Note 2: Total model 1900 production, over the 1950-58 period, came to 21,304 units (including 949 Sprints and 854 Super Sprints).

Note 3: Total 2000-series production from 1958-62 exceeded 7,000 units, including 3,443 Spiders and 700 Sprints.

Annual Production Note: A total of 22,199 Alfa Romeos were produced in 1958, of which approximately 2,009 were sold in the U.S.

ENGINE DATA: BASE FOUR (Giulietta): Inline, dual-overhead-cam four-cylinder. Aluminum block and head. **Displacement:** 78.7 cu. in. (1290 cc). **Bore & Stroke:** 2.91 x 2.95 in. (74 x 75 mm). **Compression Ratio:** (Berlina) 7.5:1; (Sprint) 8.5:1; (Veloce) 9.5:1. **Brake Horsepower:** (Berlina) 50 at 5200 rpm; (Sprint) 80 (91 SAE) at 6300 rpm; (Veloce) 90 (103 SAE) at 6000 rpm; (Speciale) 100. Solid valve lifters. One carburetor except (Veloce) two-barrel Weber; (Speciale) two Webers.

BASE FOUR (1900): Inline, dual-overhead-cam four-cylinder.Cast iron block and aluminum head. **Displacement:** 120.5 cu.in. (1975 cc). **Bore & Stroke:** 3.33 x 3.46 in. (84.5 x 88 mm).**Compression Ratio:** 7.5:1 or 8.0:1. **Brake Horsepower:** (1900) 90 at 4800 rpm; (1900C SS) 115 at 5500 rpm. Solid valve lifters. Two two-barrel carburetors (Super Sprint).

BASE FOUR (2000): Inline, dual-overhead-cam four-cylinder.Cast iron block and aluminum head. **Displacement:** 120.5 cu.in. (1975 cc). **Bore & Stroke:** 3.33 x 3.46 in. (84.5 x 88 mm).**Compression Ratio:** (sedan) 7.75:1. **Brake Horsepower:** (sedan) 105 (120 SAE) at 5300 rpm; (rds) 115 (131 SAE) at 5900 rpm.Solid valve lifters. Solex carburetor (35APAIG, sedan; 44PHH, roadster).

CHASSIS DATA: Wheelbase: (Giulietta Spider) 86.6 in.; (Giul Sprint) 93.7 in.; (1900C Super Sprint) 98.4 in.; (2000 sed) 107 in.; (2000 rds) 98.4 in. **Overall Length:** (Giulietta Spider) 152 in.; (Giul sed) 157.1 in.; (Giul Sprint) 156.7 in.; (1900 Super Sprint) 175.2 in.; (2000 sed) 186 in.; (2000 rds) 172 in. **Height:** (Giulietta) 55.3 in.; (Giulietta Sprint) 50.7 in.; (1900 cpe) 53.0 in.; (2000 rds) 53.5 in. **Width:** (Giulietta sed) 61.2 in.; (Giul Sprint) 60.4 in.; (Giul Spider) 62.2 in.; (1900 SS) 65.0 in.; (1900 sed) 63.0 in.; (2000 rds) 65.4 in. **Front Tread:** (Giulietta) 50.6 in.; (1900) 52.2 in. **Rear Tread:** (Giulietta) 50.0 in.; (1900) 52.2 in. **Standard Tires:** (Giulietta) 155x15; (1900) 165x400; (2000) 165x400.

TECHNICAL: Layout: front-engine, rear-drive. **Transmission:** (Giulietta) four-speed manual (all synchro); (1900 SS) five-speed; (2000) five-speed. **Steering:** worm and lever. **Suspension (front):** independent with unequal-length A-arms, coil springs and anti-roll bar. **Suspension (rear):** "live" (rigid) axle with single lower trailing arms (each side), upper triangulated link from floorpan to differential housing, and coil springs. **Brakes:** hydraulic, front/rear drum. **Body Construction:** unibody.

PERFORMANCE: Top Speed: (Giulietta sed) 80-84 mph; (Giul Sprint) 99 mph; (Giul Spider) 96 mph; (Giul Veloce) 112 mph; (Speciale) 125 mph; (1900 Super) 99 mph; (2000) 109 mph. **Acceleration (0-60 mph):** (Giulietta Spider) 13.7 sec.; (Giul cpe) 14.0 sec. **Fuel Mileage:** (Giulietta sed) near 30 mpg cruising; (1900) about 24 mpg.

Manufacturer: Alfa Romeo S.p.A., Milan, Italy.

Distributor: Hoffman Motor Car Co., New York City and Beverly Hills; Charles Rezzaghi, San Francisco, California.

HISTORY: Introduced to U.S. market on October 1, 1957. "When the smart set gathers," said a U.S. advertisement in late 1957, "there's a good chance that they're crowding around for a long look at the exciting new Alfa." Alfa Romeo produced various special models, including the Disco Volante and the Sportiva. Both used a 1997-cc engine that produced up to 158 horsepower.

1959 ALFA ROMEO

GIULIETTA — 750/101 SERIES — FOUR — Production of the original Giulietta 750 series continued with little change, but evolved into the 101 series during 1959. The Spider roadster's wheelbase grew to two inches (to 88.6 inches), and the Sprint coupe received a modified grille and taillamps. More significant were modifications to strengthen engine components, though horsepower did not rise. Styling of the two-seat Spider roadster (convertible) had been done by Pinin Farina, according to the brochure issued at the Paris Show, "following the great success obtained by Giulietta Sprint Coupe in the main world's markets." Its reduced wheelbase was said to produce smoother handling. Three round instruments sat directly ahead of the driver, and there was provision for an optional radio in the center of the fascia plate. The upper part of instrument panel was screened to avoid any disturbances by reflection. A floor lever operated the four-speed manual gearbox. Stated horsepower was 80 at 6000 rpm, and the top speed of the Spider approached 100 mph. A Giulietta t.i. four-door sedan also was produced at this time, with a 65-bhp version of the 1290-cc engine.

2000 SERIES — FOUR — Production of the larger 2000 series continued without major change. The sedan was powered by a 120-bhp version of the 1975-cc engine, while the roadster enjoyed 131 bhp. Top cruising speed for the sedan was 105 mph; for the roadster, at least 111 mph. Each used a five-speed, fully synchronized, manual gearbox and rode 165x400 tires.

Note: The roadster version was sometimes referred to as the "2-Liter" model rather than the 2000.

I.D. DATA: Serial number is located on right side of firewall. Engine number is on right side of crankshaft except (2000 series) at front of block. All Giulietta and 2000 models were considered to be 1959s if sold between October 1, 1958 and September 30, 1959.

Model	Body Type & Seating	Engine Type/CID	P.O.E. Price	Weight (lbs.)	Prod. Total
GIULIETTA (750 Series)					
Berlina	4-dr Sedan-4P	I4/79	N/A	N/A	Note 1
T.I.	4-dr Sedan-4P	I4/79	N/A	N/A	Note 1
Spider	2-dr Roadster-2P	I4/79	3519	1873	Note 1
Super	2-dr Roadster-2P	I4/79	3932	1873	Note 1
Sprint	2-dr Coupe-2+2P	I4/79	3951	1828	Note 1
Veloce	2-dr Coupe-2+2P	I4/79	4342	1828	Note 1
2000 SERIES					
Spider	2-dr Roadster-2P	I4/120	5048	2821	Note 2
Berlina	4-dr Sedan-4/5P	I4/120	5078	2821	Note 2

Note 1: Total Giulietta production (1954-63) came to 27,142 Sprint models; 17,096 Spiders; plus 1,576 Sprint Speciale and Zagato.

Note 2: Total 2000-series production from 1958-62 exceeded 7,000 units, including 3,443 Spiders and 700 Sprints.

Annual Production Note: A total of 32,089 Alfa Romeos were produced in 1959, of which approximately 2,085 were sold in the U.S.

Price Note: Foreign tourists visiting the Paris Auto Show in late 1958 could have purchased a Giulietta four-door sedan for $2118, or a 2000 Spider for $3831. An optional Radiomatic radio added $120 on any model.

Giulietta Model Note: In addition to the early 750 series, the Giulietta became available in a 101 series that included Sprint Speciale and Sprint Zagato models.

ENGINE DATA: BASE FOUR (Giulietta): Inline, dual-overhead-cam four-cylinder. Aluminum block and head. **Displacement:** 78.7 cu. in. (1290 cc). **Bore & Stroke:** 2.91 x 2.95 in. (74 x 75 mm). **Compression Ratio:** 8.0:1; (SS) 9.1:1. **Brake Horsepower:** 91 SAE at 6000 rpm; (Veloce) 103 SAE at 6000 rpm. Five main bearings. Solid valve lifters. One Solex carburetor except (Veloce/Speciale) two Webers.

BASE FOUR (2000): Inline, dual-overhead-cam four-cylinder. Cast iron block and aluminum head. **Displacement:** 120.5 cu. in. (1975 cc). **Bore & Stroke:** 3.33 x 3.46 in. (84.5 x 88 mm). **Compression Ratio:** 8.25:1. **Brake Horsepower:** (sedan) 120 SAE at 5300 rpm; (roadster) 131 SAE at 5800 rpm. Five main bearings. Solid valve lifters. Solex carburetor (35APAIG, sedan; 44PHH, roadster).

CHASSIS DATA: Wheelbase: (Giulietta Spider) 86.6/88.6 in.; (Giul Sprint) 93.5 in.; (2-Liter 2000 rds) 98 in.; (2000 sed) 107 in. **Overall Length:** (Giulietta Spider) 152 in.; (Giul Sprint) 157 in.; (2-Liter 2000 rds) 172 in.; (2000 sed) 185.6 in. **Height:** (Giulietta Spider) 51 in.; (2000) 56.4 in.; (2000 Spider) 53.5 in. **Width:** (Giulietta Spider) 61 in.; (2000 Spider) 65.4 in. **Front Tread:** (Giulietta) 50.5 in.; (2000) 55.1 in. **Rear Tread:** (Giulietta) 50 in.; (2000) 54 in. **Standard Tires:** (Giulietta) 155x15; (2000) 165x400.

TECHNICAL: Layout: front-engine, rear-drive. **Transmission:** (Giulietta) four-speed manual; (2000) five-speed manual; both fully synchronized. **Standard Final Drive Ratio:** (Giul SS) 4.10:1 or 4.55:1. **Steering:** worm and roller. **Suspension (front):** long/short control arms, coil springs and anti-roll bar. **Suspension (rear):** rigid axle with coil springs. **Brakes:** hydraulic, front/rear drum. **Body Construction:** steel unibody.

PERFORMANCE: Top Speed: (Giulietta Sprint/Spider) 100-103 mph; (Giul Veloce) 112 mph; (Giul SS/SZ) 124 mph; (2000) 109 mph; (2000 Spider) 111 mph. **Acceleration (0-60 mph):** (Giul Super Spider) 11.7 sec.; (2000 Spider) 14.2 sec. **Acceleration (quarter-mile):** Giul Super Spider 18.8 sec. (80 mph); (2000 Spider) 19.5 sec. (70 mph).

Manufacturer: Alfa Romeo S.p.A., Milan, Italy.

Distributor: Hoffman Motor Car Co., New York City and Beverly Hills, California.

HISTORY: Introduced to U.S. market on October 1, 1958.

1960 ALFA ROMEO

1960 Alfa Romeo 101 Series Giulietta Spider.

GIULIETTA — 101 SERIES — FOUR — Berlina sedans adopted recessed headlamps and an elongated taillamp cluster for 1960. Otherwise, production continued without major change; see previous listing for details. The Spider roadster had roll-up windows, and a plastic hardtop was optional.

2000 SERIES — FOUR — A Bertone-styled Sprint coupe joined the original 2000 sedan and roadster this year. The 2+2 notchback coupe featured thin 'A' and 'C' pillars and a subdued 'B' pillar, with ample glass for good visibility.

I.D. DATA: Serial number is located on right side of firewall. Engine number is on right side of crankshaft (2000 series, front of block). Starting serial numbers: (Giulietta Spider) 1495-05731; (Super Spider) 1495F-05143; (Sprint) 1493-05303; (Sprint Veloce) 1493E-05898; (2000 Spider) 10204-00032.

Model	Body Type & Seating	Engine Type/CID	P.O.E. Price	Weight (lbs.)	Prod. Total
GIULIETTA SPIDER					
	2-dr Roadster-2P	I4/79	3515	1856	Note 1
Super	2-dr Roadster-2P	I4/79	3885	1890	Note 1

Model	Body Type & Seating	Engine Type/CID	P.O.E. Price	Weight (lbs.)	Prod. Total
GIULIETTA SPRINT					
	2-dr Coupe-2+2P	I4/79	3838	1940	Note 1
Veloce	2-dr Coupe-2+2P	I4/79	4144	1970	Note 1
Speciale	2-dr Coupe-2P	I4/79	N/A	N/A	Note 1
Zagato	2-dr Coupe-2P	I4/79	N/A	N/A	Note 1
2000 SERIES					
Spider	2-dr Roadster-2P	I4/120	5365	2649	Note 2
Berlina	4-dr Sedan-4/5P	I4/120	5028	2958	Note 2
Sprint	2-dr Coupe-2+2P	I4/120	5948	N/A	Note 2

Note 1: Total Giulietta production (1954-63) came to 27,142 Sprint models; 17,096 Spiders; plus 1,576 Sprint Speciale and Zagato.

Note 2: Total 2000-series production from 1958-62 exceeded 7,000 units, including 3,443 Spiders and 700 Sprints.

Annual Production Note: A total of 57,870 Alfa Romeos were produced in 1960. Approximately 1,575 were sold in the U.S. in that year.

Giulietta Model Note: A Berlina four-door sedan remained from the earlier 750 series.

Price Note: Some source lists 1960 prices as $50 higher than amounts shown. The 2000 Spider was listed as low as $4998 this year.

ENGINE DATA: BASE FOUR (Giulietta): Inline, dual-overhead-cam four-cylinder. Aluminum block and head. **Displacement:** 78.7 cu. in. (1290 cc). **Bore & Stroke:** 2.91 x 2.95 in. (74 x 75 mm). **Compression Ratio:** 8.5:1 or 9.5:1. **Brake Horsepower:** 91 SAE at 6000 rpm; (Super/Veloce) 103 SAE at 6000 rpm. Five main bearings. Solid valve lifters. One Solex carburetor except (Super/Veloce) two Webers.

BASE FOUR (2000): Inline, dual-overhead-cam four-cylinder. Cast iron block and aluminum head. **Displacement:** 120.5 cu. in. (1975 cc). **Bore & Stroke:** 3.33 x 3.46 in. (84.5 x 88 mm). **Compression Ratio:** 8.25:1. **Brake Horsepower:** (sedan) 120 SAE at 5300 rpm; (roadster) 131 at 5800. Five main bearings. Solid valve lifters. One Solex carburetor (35APAIG, sedan; 44PHH, roadster).

CHASSIS DATA: Wheelbase: (Giulietta Spider) 88.6 in.; (Giul Sprint) 93.5 in.; (2-Liter 2000 rds) 98 in.; (2000 sed) 107 in. **Overall Length:** (Giulietta Spider) 152 in.; (Giul Sprint) 156.5 in.; (2-Liter 2000 rds) 172 in.; (2000 sed) 185.6 in. **Height:** (Giulietta Spider) 51.8 in. **Width:** (Giulietta Spider) 62.2 in.; (Giul Sprint) 60.2 in.; (2000) 65-67 in. **Front Tread:** (Giulietta) 50.5 in.; (2000) 55.1 in. **Rear Tread:** (Giulietta) 50 in.; (2000) 54 in. **Standard Tires:** (Giulietta) 155x15; (2000) 165x400.

TECHNICAL: Layout: front-engine, rear-drive. **Transmission:** (Giulietta) four-speed manual; (2000) five-speed manual; both fully synchronized. **Standard Final Drive Ratio:** (Giulietta) 4.11:1 or 4.55:1. **Steering:** worm and roller. **Suspension (front):** long/short control arms, coil springs and anti-roll bar. **Suspension (rear):** rigid axle with coil springs. **Brakes:** hydraulic, front/rear drum. **Body Construction:** steel unibody.

PERFORMANCE: Top Speed: (Giulietta Sprint) 103 mph; (Giul Spider) 96 mph; (Giul Super Spider) 118 mph; (2000) 109 mph; (2000 Spider) 126 mph. **Acceleration (0-60 mph):** (Giul Super Spider) 11.7 sec.; (Giul Sprint Veloce) 11.8 sec.; (Giul SZ) under 10 sec. **Acceleration (quarter-mile):** Giul Super Spider 18.8 sec. (80 mph).

Manufacturer: Alfa Romeo S.p.A., Milan, Italy.

Distributor: Hoffman Motor Car Co., New York City and Beverly Hills, California.

HISTORY: Introduced to U.S. market on September 1, 1959. "Italians build such exciting cars," exclaimed Alfa's ads in 1960, which promoted their "flair for great design and the technical superiority born of Italian passion for flawless craftsmanship that has been proved by countless victories on road and track."

1961 ALFA ROMEO

GIULIETTA — 101 SERIES — FOUR — No change was evident in Alfa Romeo's smaller series, again available in Spider (roadster) or Sprint (coupe) form, with either a 90-bhp or 103-bhp version of the 1290-cc four-cylinder engine. The high-performance Sprint Speciale and Sprint Zagato coupes also remained available.

2000 — FOUR — Little change was evident in the larger Alfas, which were powered by 1975-cc engines. The roadster had roll-up windows.

I.D. DATA: Serial number is located on right side of firewall. Engine number is on right side of crankshaft (2000 series, front of block). Starting serial numbers: (Spider) 1495-08083; (Super Spider) 1495F-07508; (Sprint) 1493-20025; (Sprint Veloce) 1493E-11012; (Sprint Speciale) 10120-00001; (2000) 10204-00105.

Model	Body Type & Seating	Engine Type/CID	P.O.E. Price	Weight (lbs.)	Prod. Total
GIULIETTA SPIDER					
	2-dr Roadster-2P	I4/79	3150	1890	Note 1
Super	2-dr Roadster-2P	I4/79	3450	1890	Note 1
GIULIETTA SPRINT					
	2-dr Coupe-2+2P	I4/79	3495	1940	Note 1
Veloce	2-dr Coupe-2+2P	I4/79	3795	1970	Note 1
Speciale	2-dr Coupe-2P	I4/79	5550	N/A	Note 1
Zagato	2-dr Coupe-2P	I4/79	N/A	N/A	Note 1
2000					
Spider	2-dr Roadster-2P	I4/120	3995	2649	Note 2
Sprint	2-dr Coupe-2+2P	I4/120	N/A	N/A	Note 2
Berlina	4-dr Sedan-4/5P	I4/120	N/A	N/A	Note 2

Note 1: Total Giulietta production (1954-63) came to 27,142 Sprint models; 17,096 Spiders; plus 1,576 Sprint Speciale and Zagato.

Note 2: Total 2000-series production from 1958-62 exceeded 7,000 units, including 3,443 Spiders and 700 Sprints.

Annual Production Note: A total of 57,181 Alfa Romeos were produced in 1961.

Price Note: Some sources listed prices considerably higher for the 1961 model year ($3520 for Giulietta Spider, $3890 for the Super, $3843 for the Sprint, $4149 for the Sprint Veloce, and $4650 or $5372 for the 2000 Spider).

ENGINE DATA: BASE FOUR (Giulietta): Inline, dual-overhead-cam four-cylinder. Aluminum block and head. **Displacement:** 78.7 cu. in. (1290 cc). **Bore & Stroke:** 2.91 x 2.95 in. (74 x 75 mm). **Compression Ratio:** 8.5:1 or 9.5:1. **Brake Horsepower:** 91 SAE at 6000 rpm; (Super/Veloce) 103 SAE at 6000 rpm. Five main bearings. Solid valve lifters. One Solex carburetor except (Super/Veloce) two Webers.

BASE FOUR (2000): Inline, dual-overhead-cam four-cylinder. Cast iron block and aluminum head. **Displacement:** 120.5 cu. in. (1975 cc). **Bore & Stroke:** 3.33 x 3.46 in. (84.5 x 88 mm). **Compression Ratio:** 8.25:1. **Brake Horsepower:** (sedan) 120 SAE at 5300 rpm; (roadster) 131 at 5800. Five main bearings. Solid valve lifters. One Solex carburetor (35APAIG, sedan; 44PHH, roadster).

CHASSIS DATA: Wheelbase: (Giulietta Spider) 88.6 in.; (Giul Sprint) 93.5 in.; (2000 rds) 98 in.; (2000 sed) 107 in. **Overall Length:** (Giulietta Spider) 152 in.; (Giul Sprint) 156.5 in.; (2000 rds) 172 in.; (2000 sed) 185.6 in. **Height:** (Giulietta Spider) 52.6 in.; (Giul Sprint) 51.8 in. **Width:** (Giulietta Spider) 62.2 in.; (Giul Sprint) 60.2 in.; (2000) 65-67 in. **Front Tread:** (Giulietta) 50.5 in.; (2000) 55.1 in. **Rear Tread:** (Giulietta) 50 in.; (2000) 54 in. **Standard Tires:** (Giulietta) 155x15; (2000) 165x400.

TECHNICAL: Layout: front-engine, rear-drive. **Transmission:** (Giulietta) four-speed manual; (2000) five-speed manual; both fully synchronized. **Steering:** worm and roller. **Suspension (front):** long/short control arms, coil springs and anti-roll bar. **Suspension (rear):** rigid axle with coil springs. **Brakes:** hydraulic, front/rear drum. **Body Construction:** steel unibody.

PERFORMANCE: Top Speed: (Giulietta Sprint/Spider) 103 mph; (Giul Veloce) 112 mph; (Giul SS/SZ) 124 mph; (2000) 109 mph. **Acceleration (0-60 mph):** (Giul Super Spider) 11.7 sec.; (Giul Spider) 12.8 sec. **Acceleration (quarter-mile):** (Giul Super Spider) 18.8 sec. (80 mph).

Manufacturer: Alfa Romeo S.p.A., Milan, Italy.

Distributor: Hoffman Motor Car Co., New York City and Beverly Hills, California.

HISTORY: Introduced to U.S. market on September 1, 1960.

1962 ALFA ROMEO

GIULIETTA — 101 SERIES — FOUR — Little change was evident in the long-lived Giulietta series, again offered as a roadster or coupe. The Sprint Speciale also was available, but the Zagato dropped out.

GIULIA 1600 — 101 SERIES — FOUR — A new Giulia series, introduced late in 1962, differed little from the Giulietta but carried a larger (1570-cc) engine. That four-cylinder powerplant had an aluminum block and cast-iron cylinder liners, and drove a five-speed all-synchro manual gearbox. The Giulia Spyder and Sprint were slightly bigger than comparable Giulietta models, and also capable of improved performance. See next listing for additional details.

2000 — FOUR — This was the final year for the 2000-series Spider roadster, which continued without change.

2600 — SIX — After years of four-cylinder power, Alfa Romeo turned to six cylinders late in 1962. The new 157.6-cid (2854-cc) engine carried on the familiar dual-overhead-camshaft configuration. With bore/stroke dimensions of 83 x 79.6 mm, it was the first oversquare Alfa engine. Output was 145 horsepower at 5900 rpm.

Appearance was similar to the 2000 series, which faded away during the year. Still, the 2600 displayed a different hood, grille, windshield, deck and body trim. The Spider and Sprint had a horizontal air scoop at the front top of the hood. The convertible had large driving lights below and slightly inboard of the headlights, while the coupe had all four lights in a line, and a larger "full-through" grille was framed by hood and fender lines.

As was typical of Alfa Romeo models, the Berlina four-door sedan was factory-built, whereas Bertone produced the Sprint coupe body and Touring did the Spider convertible. Later would come a Zagato coupe with a rounded, protruding nose. This was the first model to offer four-wheel disc brakes for the 2600, partly because it cost close to twice as much as a Giulietta. Stamped-steel disc wheels were standard (as on all postwar Alfa production models); but Borrani center-lock knock-off wires also were available.

I.D. DATA: Serial number is located on the right side of the firewall, and the inner side of the engine hood. Engine number is on right side of crankshaft except (2000 series) at front of block. Starting serial numbers: (Spider) 1495-09308; (Super Spider) 1495F-10659; (Sprint) 1493-20750 or AR-158901; (Sprint Veloce) 1493E-23900; (Sprint Speciale) 10102-00320; (2000) 10204-01063. Alternate starting serial numbers: (Spider) AR-167006; (Super Spider) AR-167181; (Sprint) AR-158901; (Sprint Veloce) AR-158935.

Model	Body Type & Seating	Engine Type/CID	P.O.E. Price	Weight (lbs.)	Prod. Total
GIULIETTA SPIDER					
	2-dr Roadster-2P	I4/79	3150	1900	Note 1
Super	2-dr Roadster-2P	I4/79	3450	1900	Note 1
GIULIETTA SPRINT					
	2-dr Coupe-2+2P	I4/79	3495	1940	Note 1
Veloce	2-dr Coupe-2+2P	I4/79	3795	1940	Note 1
Speciale	2-dr Coupe-2P	I4/79	5550	1892	Note 1
GIULIA 1600					
Spider	2-dr Roadster-2P	I4/96	3395	N/A	Note 2
Sprint	2-dr Coupe-2+2P	I4/96	3595	N/A	Note 2
2000					
Spider	2-dr Roadster-2P	I4/120	3995	2469	Note 3
2600					
Berlina	4-dr Sedan-4/5P	I6/158	3995	N/A	Note 4
Spider	2-dr Roadster-2P	I6/158	5295	2816	Note 4
Sprint	2-dr Coupe-2+2P	I6/158	5895	2864	Note 4

Note 1: Total Giulietta production (1954-63) came to 27,142 Sprint models; 17,096 Spiders; plus 1,576 Sprint Speciale and Zagato.

Note 2: More than 400,000 Giulias were produced from 1962-79, about one-fourth of which were Spider or Sprint models.

Note 3: Total 2000-series production from 1958-62 neared 7,000 units, including 3,443 Spiders and 700 Sprints.

Note 4: Total 2600-series production from 1962-68 included 2,255 Spiders, 6,999 Sprints, 2,092 sedans, and 105 SZ models.

Annual Production Note: A total of 56,460 Alfa Romeos were produced in 1962.

ENGINE DATA: BASE FOUR (Giulietta): Inline, dual-overhead-cam four-cylinder. Aluminum block and head. **Displacement:** 78.7 cu. in. (1290 cc). **Bore & Stroke:** 2.91 x 2.95 in. (74 x 75 mm). **Compression Ratio:** 8.5:1 or 9.5:1. **Brake Horsepower:** 91 SAE at 6000 rpm; (Super/Veloce) 103 SAE at 6000 rpm. Five main bearings. Solid valve lifters. One Solex carburetor except (Super/Veloce) two Webers.

BASE FOUR (2000): Inline, dual-overhead-cam four-cylinder. Cast iron block and aluminum head. **Displacement:** 120.5 cu. in. (1975 cc). **Bore & Stroke:** 3.33 x 3.46 in. (84.5 x 88 mm). **Compression Ratio:** 8.25:1. **Brake Horsepower:** 131 at 5800 rpm. Five main bearings. Solid valve lifters. One Solex 44PHH carburetor.

BASE FOUR (Giulia): Inline, dual-overhead-cam inline four-cylinder. Aluminum block and head. **Displacement:** 95.8 cu. in. (1570 cc). **Bore & Stroke:** 3.07 x 3.23 in. (78 x 82 mm). **Compression Ratio:** 9.0:1. **Brake Horsepower:** 104 at 6200 rpm. Five main bearings. Solid valve lifters. Solex carburetor. Bosch ignition.

BASE SIX (2600): Inline, dual-overhead-cam six-cylinder. Aluminum block and head. **Displacement:** 157.5 cu. in. (2582 cc). **Bore & Stroke:** 3.27 x 3.13 in. (83 x 79.6 mm). **Compression Ratio:** 9.0:1. **Brake Horsepower:** (sedan) 145 SAE at 5900 rpm; (cpe) 165 at 5900 rpm. **Torque:** (cpe) 140 lbs.-ft. at 4000 rpm. Seven main bearings. Solid valve lifters. Three Solex 44PHH carburetors.

CHASSIS DATA: Wheelbase: (Giulietta Spider) 88.6 in.; (Giul Sprint) 93.5 in.; (Giulia Spider) 88.6 in.; (Giulia Sprint) 92.5 in.; (2000 rds) 98 in.; (2000 sed) 107 in. **Overall Length:** (Giulietta Spider) 152 in.; (Giul Sprint) 156.5 in.; (2000 rds) 172 in.; (2000 sed) 185.6 in. **Height:** (Giulietta Spider) 52.6 in.; (Giul Sprint) 51.8 in. **Width:** (Giulietta Spider) 62.2 in.; (Giul Sprint) 60.2 in.; (2000) 65-67 in. **Front Tread:** (Giulietta) 50.5 in.; (2000) 55.1 in. **Rear Tread:** (Giulietta) 50 in.; (2000) 54 in. **Standard Tires:** (Giulietta) 155x15; (2000) 165x400.

TECHNICAL: Layout: front-engine, rear-drive. **Transmission:** (Giulietta) four-speed manual; (2000/2600) five-speed manual; both fully synchronized. **Steering:** worm and roller. **Suspension (front):** long/short control arms, coil springs and anti-roll bar. **Suspension (rear):** rigid axle with coil springs. **Brakes:** hydraulic, front/rear drum; (2600) front disc, rear drum. **Body Construction:** steel unibody.

PERFORMANCE: Top Speed: (Giulietta Sprint/Spider) 103 mph; (Giulietta Veloce) 112 mph; (Giulietta Sprint Speciale) 124 mph; (2000) 109 mph; (2600) 125-126 mph. **Acceleration (0-60 mph):** (2600) 9.6 sec. **Acceleration (quarter-mile):** (2600 cpe) 16.5 sec. (82 mph).

Manufacturer: Alfa Romeo S.p.A., Milan, Italy.

Distributor: Hoffman Motor Car Co., New York City and Beverly Hills, California.

HISTORY: Introduced to U.S. market on September 1, 1961.

1963 ALFA ROMEO

1963 Alfa Romeo Giulia 1600 Sprint. (Christie's)

GIULIETTA — 101 SERIES — FOUR — This would be the final year for the Giulietta, which was replaced by the slightly larger and more powerful Giulia, with the same basic body design. Only the SS coupe had front disc brakes. As before, the Sprint Veloce and Super Spider used a higher-performance engine with different carburetion. The only notable change this year was the addition of side vents to the roll-up windows.

GIULIA — 101/105 SERIES — FOUR — Introduced late in 1962, the replacement for the Giulietta came in Berlina sedan form with a body produced by Alfa Romeo itself, plus a Sprint coupe done at Bertone (though the complete car was assembled at the Alfa plant). The Sprint GT was designed by Giorgio Giugiaro at Bertone. Unlike the Giulietta Spider, the Giulia's convertible model had a hood airscoop. Taillamps were larger, too. Slight suspension revisions were seen on the Giulia. The front suspension consisted of single lower A-arms and separate upper links. At the rear, a T-shaped device replaced the former triangulated link. All-disc brakes were installed. Dimensions were similar to the Giulietta, with a 92.5-inch wheelbase for the Sprint and 88.6 inches for the Spider. Under the Giulia hood was a 1570-cc four-cylinder engine rated 104 horsepower, hooked to a five-speed manual gearbox.

2600 — SIX — Introduced late in 1962, the 2600 (which replaced the 2000 series) continued without major change for the full model year. Huge round auxiliary lights stood below each headlamp and toward the car's center, giving the appearance of quad headlamps. Appearance features also included a traditional triangular center grille with six horizontal bars, ahead of a crosshatch grille that extended to (and surrounded) the headlamps. Small rectangular parking lights were at the bumper, directly below the center of each headlamp pair. The 2600 Spider's center grille was the same as the Sprint, but in a solid front panel. Two small side grilles had three horizontal bars.

I.D. DATA: Serial number is located on the right side of the firewall, and the inner side of the engine hood. Engine number is on right side of block. Giulietta starting serial numbers: (Spider) 1495-09771 or AR-170180; (Super Spider) 1495F-11039 or AR-171846; (Sprint) 1493-21108 or AR-159014; (Sprint Veloce) AR-159004. Series 2600 starting serial numbers: (Sprint) AR-820116; (Spider) AR-191015. Giulia starting serial numbers: (Sprint) AR-352001; (Spider) AR-372001; (TI) AR-400001.

Model	Body Type & Seating	Engine Type/CID	P.O.E. Price	Weight (lbs.)	Prod. Total
GIULIETTA					
Spider	2-dr Roadster-2P	I4/79	3150	1960	Note 1
Super	2-dr Roadster-2P	I4/79	3450	1960	Note 1
Sprint	2-dr Coupe-2+2P	I4/79	3495	2000	Note 1
Veloce	2-dr Coupe-2+2P	I4/79	3795	2000	Note 1
Speciale	2-dr Coupe-2+2P	I4/79	5550	N/A	Note 1
GIULIA 1600 (101 Series)					
Spider	2-dr Roadster-2P	I4/96	3395	2060	Note 2
Sprint	2-dr Coupe-2+2P	I4/96	3595	2070	Note 2
Speciale	2-dr Coupe-2P	I4/96	N/A	N/A	Note 2
GIULIA 1600 (105 Series)					
T.I	4-dr Sedan-4P	I4/96	N/A	N/A	Note 2
T.I. Super	4-dr Sedan-4P	I4/96	N/A	N/A	Note 2
Sprint GT	2-dr Coupe-2+2P	I4/96	N/A	N/A	Note 2
GTZ	2-dr Coupe-2+2P	I4/96	N/A	N/A	Note 2
2600					
Spider	2-dr Roadster-2P	I6/158	5295	2900	Note 3
Sprint	2-dr Coupe-2P	I6/158	5895	2990	Note 3
Berlina	4-dr Sedan-4/5P	I6/158	N/A	N/A	Note 3

Note 1: Total Giulietta production (1954-63) came to 27,142 Sprint models; 17,096 Spiders; plus 1,576 Sprint Speciale and Zagato.

Note 2: More than 400,000 Giulias were produced from 1962-79, about one-fourth of which were Sprint or Spider models.

Note 3: Total 2600-series production from 1962-68 included 2,255 Spiders, 6,999 Sprints, 2,092 sedans, and 105 SZ models.

Annual Production Note: A total of 85,605 Alfa Romeos were produced in 1963.

Giulia Model Note: Only those models with prices shown were commonly sold in the U.S. at this time.

ENGINE DATA: BASE FOUR (Giulietta): Inline, dual-overhead-cam four-cylinder. Aluminum block and head. **Displacement:** 78.7 cu. in. (1290 cc). **Bore & Stroke:** 2.91 x 2.95 in. (74 x 75 mm). **Compression Ratio:** 8.5:1 or 9.5:1. **Brake Horsepower:** 91 SAE at 6000 rpm; (Super/Veloce) 103 SAE at 6000 rpm; (SS) 114 at 6500. Five main bearings. Solid valve lifters. One Solex carburetor except (Super/Veloce) two Webers.

BASE FOUR (Giulia): Inline, dual-overhead-cam inline four-cylinder. Aluminum block and head. **Displacement:** 95.8 cu. in. (1570 cc). **Bore & Stroke:** 3.07 x 3.23 in. (78 x 82 mm). **Compression Ratio:** 9.0:1. **Brake Horsepower:** 104 at 6200 rpm; (Sprint GT) 122 at 6000. **Torque:** (Sprint GT) 103 lbs.-ft. at 3000 rpm. Five main bearings. Solid valve lifters. Solex carburetor. Bosch ignition.

BASE SIX (2600): Inline, dual-overhead-cam six-cylinder. Aluminum block and head. **Displacement:** 157.5 cu. in. (2582 cc). Bore & Stroke: 3.27 x 3.13 in. (83 x 79.6 mm). **Compression Ratio:** 9.0:1. **Brake Horsepower:** (sedan) 145 SAE at 5900 rpm; (cpe/rds) 165 at 5900 rpm. Seven main bearings. Solid valve lifters. Three Solex 44PHH carburetors.

CHASSIS DATA: Wheelbase: (Giulietta Spider) 88.6 in.; (Giul Sprint) 93.5 in.; (Giulia Spider) 88.6 in.; (Giulia Sprint) 92.5 in.; (2600 rds) 98.5 in.; (2600 sed) 101.7 in. **Overall Length:** (Giulietta Spider) 154 in.; (Giul Sprint) 156.5 in.; (Giulia cpe) 156 in.; (Giulia rds) 154 in.; (2600 rds) 177.2 in.; (2600 cpe) 180.5 in. Height: (Giulietta Spider) 52.6 in.; (Giul Sprint) 51.8 in.; (2600) 53 in. **Width:** (Giulietta Spider) 62.2 in.; (Giul Sprint) 60.2 in. **Front Tread:** (Giulietta) 50.5 in.; (2600) 55.2 in. **Rear Tread:** (Giulietta) 50 in.; (2600) 54.2 in. **Standard Tires:** (Giulietta/Giulia) 155x15; (2600) 165x400.

TECHNICAL: Layout: front-engine, rear-drive. **Transmission:** (Giulietta) four-speed manual except (SS) five-speed; (others) five-speed manual; all fully synchronized. **Steering:** (Giulia) recirculating ball; (others) worm and lever. **Suspension (front):** long/short control arms, coil springs and anti-roll bar. **Suspension (rear):** rigid axle with coil springs. **Brakes:** (Giulietta/Giulia) front/rear drum; (2600) front disc/rear drum. **Body Construction:** steel unibody.

PERFORMANCE: Top Speed: (Giulietta Sprint/Spider) 103 mph; (Giulietta Veloce) 112 mph; (Giulietta Sprint Speciale) 124 mph; (2600) 125 mph. **Acceleration (0-60 mph):** (Giulia) 12.2 sec. or less. **Fuel Mileage:** (Giulietta) about 28 mpg; (Giulietta Super/Veloce) 25-26 mpg.

Manufacturer: Alfa Romeo S.p.A., Milan, Italy.

Distributor: Hoffman Motor Car Co., New York City and Beverly Hills, California.

HISTORY: By 1963, Alfa Romeo had about 151 dealers in the U.S. and ranked 19th in import sales.

1964 ALFA ROMEO

GIULIA — 101/105 SERIES — FOUR — Several new models were found on lists of U.S. imports this year, though they'd been introduced earlier in Europe. This was the first year of general availability in the U.S. of the Giulia T.I. sedan, a rather small car with a somewhat squarish shape. The T.I. had a narrow horizontal grille that flared at the outer edges to go around the larger of the twin headlights. An Alfa emblem was centered in the grille. Rectangular parking lights projected outward and were set between the outer headlamps and the bumper. A square rear deck held horizontal rectangular taillamps. Not much of the T.I.'s appearance was similar to other Alfas except for the forward hood line's slope, and the front fender shape.

This was also the first year for official sales in the U.S. of the Sprint GT coupe, which was longer than the other coupes and had a sculptured crease. It also had larger and flatter rear wheel openings. The GT coupe had a horizontal grille with center emblem. The front fender line swelled above the hood surface, while the rear deck scooped inward at the taillights and license plate. A Giulia SS coupe also became available, displaying a streamlined look that evolved from the former Giulietta Sprint Speciale. Its hood line swept forward and dropped to a narrow horizontal grille and full-width air intake, its windshield had a sharper rake, and the front bumper had a stronger wraparound. A pronounced sculptured crease was evident over the front wheel opening, and the straight-through fender line rose above the rear wheels. That model used a high-performance engine with different carburetion. A series number was mounted on the rear deck of each Giulia.

2600 — SIX — Production of the larger six-cylinder series continued without major change, powered by a 158-cid engine. The 2600 measured 26.5 inches longer than an equivalent Giulia. The rear deck held a series number. Sprints had different rear fender and rear deck styling.

I.D. DATA: Serial number is located on the right side of the firewall, and the inner side of the engine hood. Engine number is on the right side of the block. Giulia starting serial numbers: (Sprint) AR-372300; (Spider) AR-352500; (T.I.) AR-401500. Series 2600 starting serial numbers: (Sprint) AR-820200; (Spider) AR-191100.

Model	Body Type & Seating	Engine Type/CID	P.O.E. Price	Weight (lbs.)	Prod. Total
GIULIA 1600 (101 Series)					
Spider	2-dr Roadster-2P	I4/96	3395	1960	Note 1
Sprint	2-dr Coupe-2+2P	I4/96	3595	2070	Note 1
Veloce	2-dr Roadster-2P	I4/96	N/A	N/A	Note 1
Speciale	2-dr Coupe-2+2P	I4/96	N/A	N/A	Note 1
GIULIA 1600 (105 Series)					
T.I.	4-dr Sedan-5P	I4/96	2995	2205	Note 1
T.I. Super	4-dr Sedan-5P	I4/96	N/A	N/A	Note 1
Sprint GT	2-dr Coupe-2+2P	I4/96	4295	N/A	Note 1
GTZ	2-dr Coupe-2+2P	I4/96	N/A	N/A	Note 1
GTC	2-dr Roadster-2P	I4/96	N/A	N/A	Note 1
2600					
Spider	2-dr Roadster-2P	I6/158	4995	2900	Note 2
Sprint	2-dr Coupe-2+2P	I6/158	5895	2990	Note 2
Berlina	4-dr Sedan-5P	I6/158	4995	2830	Note 2

Note 1: More than 400,000 Giulias were produced from 1962-79, about one-fourth of which were Sprint or Spider models.

Note 2: Total 2600-series production from 1962-68 included 2,255 Spiders, 6,999 Sprints, 2,092 sedans, and 105 SZ models.

Annual Production Note: A total of 65,193 Alfa Romeos were produced in 1964.

Giulia Model Note: Only those models with prices shown were commonly sold in the U.S. at this time.

2600 Price Note: The 2600 Spider was listed as high as $5295 during 1964.

ENGINE DATA: BASE FOUR (Giulia): Dual overhead-cam inline four-cylinder. Aluminum block and head. **Displacement:** 95.8 cu. in. (1570 cc). **Bore & Stroke:** 3.07 x 3.23 in. (78 x 82 mm). **Compression Ratio:** 9.0:1. **Brake Horsepower:** 104 at 6200 rpm; (Sprint GT) 122 at 6000; (SS) 106 at 6500. **Torque:** (Sprint GT) 103 lbs.-ft. at 3000 rpm. Five main bearings. Solid valve lifters. Solex carburetor. Bosch ignition.

BASE SIX (2600): Inline, dual-overhead-cam six-cylinder. Aluminum block and head. **Displacement:** 157.5 cu. in. (2582 cc). **Bore & Stroke:** 3.27 x 3.13 in. (83 x 79.6 mm). **Compression Ratio:** 9.0:1. **Brake Horsepower:** (sedan) 145 SAE at 5900 rpm; (Spider/Sprint) 165 at 5900 rpm. Seven main bearings. Solid valve lifters. Three Solex 44PHH carburetors.

CHASSIS DATA: Wheelbase: (Giulia rds) 88.6 in.; (Giulia cpe) 92.5 in.; (Giulia sed) 99 in.; (2600 rds) 98 in.; (2600 cpe) 101.75 in.; (2600 sed) 107 in. **Overall Length:** (Giulia rds) 154 in.; (Giulia cpe) 156 in.; (Giulia sed) 162 in.; (Giulia Sprint GT) 161 in.; (2600 rds) 177 in.; (2600 cpe) 180.5 in.; (2600 sed) 186 in. **Height:** (Giulia Spider) 53 in.; (Giulia Sprint GT) 52 in.; (2600 cpe) 52.5 in. **Width:** (Giulia Sprint GT) 62 in. **Front Tread:** (Giulia) 50.4 in.; (Giulia Sprint GT) 51.5 in.; (2600) 55.2 in. **Rear Tread:** (Giulia) 50 in.; (2600) 54 in. **Standard Tires:** (Giulia) 155x15; (2600) 165x400.

TECHNICAL: Layout: front-engine, rear-drive. **Transmission:** five-speed manual (fully synchronized). **Steering:** worm and sector. **Suspension (front):** long/short control arms, coil springs and anti-roll bar. **Suspension (rear):** rigid axle with coil springs. **Brakes:** (Giulia) front disc, rear drum; (Giulia 1600 T.I./Sprint GT) front/rear disc; (2600) front/rear disc. **Body Construction:** steel unibody.

PERFORMANCE: Top Speed: (Giulia T.I.) 105 mph; (Giulia Sprint/Spider) 105+ mph; (Giulia Sprint GT) 112 mph; (Giulia Sprint Speciale) 125+ mph; (2600) 125 mph. **Acceleration (0-60 mph):** (Giulia) 12.2 sec. or less; (Giulia Sprint GT) 10.6 sec. **Acceleration (quarter-mile):** (Giulia Sprint GT) 18.5 sec. (81 mph). **Fuel Mileage:** (Giulia T.I.) 31 mpg; (Giulia Sprint GT) 24-27 mpg; (2600) 16+ mpg.

Manufacturer: Alfa Romeo S.p.A., Milan, Italy.

1965 ALFA ROMEO

GIULIA — FOUR — Certain models that had been introduced earlier became available in the U.S. on a regular basis this year. The Spider Veloce roadster (convertible), for one, differed from the standard Spider by virtue of its higher horsepower, using two horizontal twin-choke carburetors instead of the customary single vertical carb. It could be identifed by a "Veloce" name on the decklid, and had a higher top speed than its mates. Available on special order was the T.I. Super, also with more power and a higher top speed, identified by 'SUPER' lettering on the left hood nose, and also on the right rear of the trunk lid. Customers could also order a four-seat GTC convertible, or even a GTA lightweight racer.

2600 — SIX — Available on a more regular basis this year (though still on special order) was the 2600 Berlina four-door sedan, which was 20 inches longer than the T.I. sedan. Headlights stood outside the grille, separated slightly from the inner lights. Three vertical bars were set into dominant horizontal bars of the grille, on each side of a center Alfa emblem. That 2600 also had a very narrow airscoop effect at the lower edge of the grille, a solid front bumper with no dividers, and rear vent windows. The rear bumper displayed more of a wraparound shape. In addition, chrome side moldings extended from behind the headlamps into the middle of the rear door panel.

I.D. DATA: Serial number is located on right side of firewall. Engine number is on right side of block. Giulia starting serial numbers: (T.I. sedan) AR-446000; (T.I. Super sedan) AR-430000; (Spider) AR-373959; (Spider Veloce) AR-379986; (Sprint GT coupe) AR-353225; (SS coupe) AR-380000; (TZ coupe) AR-750000. Series 2600 starting serial numbers: (Berlina sedan) AR-800074; (Spider) AR-191320; (Sprint coupe) AR-820400.

Model	Body Type & Seating	Engine Type/CID	P.O.E. Price	Weight (lbs.)	Prod. Total
GIULIA (101 Series)					
Spider	2-dr Roadster-2P	I4/96	3318	2060	Note 1
Veloce	2-dr Roadster-2P	I4/96	3514	2094	Note 1
Speciale	2-dr Coupe-2+2P	I4/96	4886	2097	Note 1
GIULIA (105 Series)					
T.I	4-dr Sedan-5P	I4/96	2927	2060	Note 1
T.I. Super	4-dr Sedan-5P	I4/96	4595	2060	Note 1
Sprint GT	2-dr Coupe-2+2P	I4/96	4201	2094	Note 1
TZ	2-dr Coupe-2+2P	I4/96	8395	2094	Note 1
GTC	2-dr Roadster-2P	I4/96	N/A	N/A	Note 1
GTA	2-dr Coupe-2+2P	I4/96	N/A	N/A	Note 1
GTV	2-dr Coupe-2P	I4/96	N/A	N/A	Note 1
2600					
Berlina	4-dr Sedan-5P	I6/158	4995	N/A	Note 2
Spider	2-dr Roadster-2+2P	I6/158	4886	2688	Note 2
Sprint	2-dr Coupe-4P	I6/158	5760	2828	Note 2

Note 1: More than 400,000 Giulias were produced from 1962-79, about one-fourth of which were Sprint or Spider models.

Note 2: Total 2600-series production from 1962-68 included 2,255 Spiders, 6,999 Sprints, 2,092 sedans, and 105 SZ models.

Annual Production Note: A total of 61,236 Alfa Romeos were produced in 1965.

Giulia Model Note: Only those models with prices shown were commonly sold in the U.S. at this time.

Price Note: Some sources listed 1965 prices for readily-available models as $68 to $135 higher than figures shown.

ENGINE DATA: BASE FOUR (Giulia): Inline, dual-overhead-cam four-cylinder. Aluminum block and head. **Displacement:** 95.8 cu. in. (1570 cc). **Bore & Stroke:** 3.07 x 3.23 in. (78 x 82 mm). **Compression Ratio:** 9.0:1. **Brake Horsepower:** 104 at 6200 rpm; (Sprint GT) 122 at 6000; (SS) 126 at 6500. **Torque:** (Sprint GT) 103 lbs.-ft. at 3000 rpm. Five main bearings. Solid valve lifters. Solex carburetor; (Veloce/Sprint GT) two Weber carburetors. Bosch Ignition.

BASE SIX (2600): Inline, dual-overhead-cam six-cylinder. Aluminum block and head. **Displacement:** 157.4 cu. in. (2584 cc). **Bore & Stroke:** 3.27 x 3.13 in. (83 x 79.6 mm). **Compression Ratio:** 8.5:1 or 9.0:1. **Brake Horsepower:** (sedan) 145 SAE at 5900 rpm; (Spider/Sprint) 165 at 5900 rpm. Seven main bearings. Solid valve lifters. Two Solex carburetors; (Sprint/Veloce) three Solex 44PHH carburetors.

CHASSIS DATA: Wheelbase: (Giulia rds) 88.6 in.; (Giulia SS) 89 in.; (Giulia cpe) 92.5 in.; (Guilia GT) 93 in.; (Giulia sed) 99 in.; (2600 rds) 98.5 in.; (2600 cpe) 101.75 in.; (2600 sed) 107 in. **Overall Length:** (Giulia sed) 166 in.; (Giulia rds) 153.75 in.; (Giulia GT) 161 in.; (Giulia SS) 162 in.; (2600 rds) 177.25 in.; (2600 cpe) 180.5 in.; (2600 sed) 186 in. **Height:** (Giulia Spider) 52.6 in.; (Giul sed) 56.3 in.; (Giul SS) 50.4 in.; (Giul Sprint GT) 51.8 in.; (2600 rds/cpe) 52.4 in.; (2600 sed) 55.3 in. **Width:** (Giulia Spider) 62.2 in.; (Giulia GT) 62.2 in.; (Giulia sed) 61.4 in.; (Giul SS) 65.4 in.; (2600 cpe) 67.2 in.; (2600 rds) 63 in.; (2600 sed) 66.9 in. **Front Tread:** (Giulia) 50.9 in.; (Giulia sed/Sprint GT) 51.6 in.; (2600) 55.1 in. **Rear Tread:** (Giulia) 50 in.; (2600) 53.9 in. **Standard Tires:** (Giulia) 155x15; (2600) 165x400.

TECHNICAL: Layout: front-engine, rear-drive. **Transmission:** five-speed manual (fully synchronized). **Steering:** worm and roller. **Suspension (front):** long/short control arms, coil springs and anti-roll bar. **Suspension (rear):** rigid axle with trailing lower radius arms, upper A-bracket and coil springs. **Brakes:** front/rear disc. **Body Construction:** steel unibody.

PERFORMANCE: Top Speed: (Giulia T.I.) 105 mph; (Giulia Sprint/Spider) 105+ mph; (Giulia Sprint GT) 112-122 mph; (Giulia Sprint Speciale) 125+ mph; (2600) 125 mph. **Acceleration (0-60 mph):** (Giulia) 12.2 sec. or less.; (Giulia Sprint GT) 10.2 sec. **Acceleration (quarter-mile):** (Giulia Sprint GT) 17.7 sec. (78 mph). **Fuel Mileage:** (Giulia T.I.) 31 mpg; (Giulia Sprint GT) 21-26 mpg; (2600) 16+ mpg.

Manufacturer: Alfa Romeo S.p.A., Milan, Italy.

Distributor: Alfa Romeo, Inc., Newark, New Jersey.

HISTORY: Introduced to U.S. market on September 8, 1964.

1966 ALFA ROMEO

GIULIA — FOUR — Production continued with little change. By this time, the Giulia was completely different in appearance from the initial 101-series. The Sprint Speciale was still built by Bertone. A new Sprint Zagato (called GTZ) fastback coupe featured an independent rear suspension and had an abbreviated Kamm-style tail end.

DUETTO — FOUR — A new small Spider convertible (roadster) appeared at the 1966 Geneva Show, named Duetto. Designed by Pininfarina, it had been inspired by a design exercise of 1959, on the Disco Volante chassis. Styling features included a rounded front and back, headlamps recessed in deep nacelles, and a full-length wide bodyside groove. This appearance would continue on Spiders into the 1970s and '80s, long after the Duetto name disappeared. As the Duetto entered production, bodies were also built by Pininfarina. See next listing for details and specifications.

2600 — SIX — Little change was evident in the six-cylinder Alfa Romeo lineup. Sedan engines produced 148 horsepower; others 165 bhp.

I.D. DATA: Serial number is located on right side of firewall. Engine number is on right side of block. Giulia starting serial numbers: (T.I.) AR-447801; (Spider) AR-374101; (Spider Veloce) AR-390001; (Sprint GT) AR-611401; (Sprint Speciale) AR-380051. Series 2600 starting serial numbers: (Spider) AR-191351; (Sprint) AR-820501.

Model	Body Type & Seating	Engine Type/CID	P.O.E. Price	Weight (lbs.)	Prod. Total
GIULIA 1600					
Spider	2-dr Roadster-2P	I4/96	3318	2060	Note1
Veloce	2-dr Roadster-2P	I4/96	3514	2060	Note 1
Sprint GT	2-dr Coupe-2+2P	I4/96	4201	2060	Note 1
Speciale	2-dr Spt Cpe-2+2P	I4/96	4886	2097	Note 1
T.I.	2-dr Sedan-5/6P	I4/96	2927	2204	Note 1
GTZ	2-dr Coupe-2P	I4/96	N/A	N/A	Note 1
GTC	2-dr Roadster-2P	I4/96	N/A	2293	Note 1
TZ	2-dr Coupe-2P	I4/96	N/A	1411	Note 1
GTA	2-dr Coupe-2+2P	I4/96	N/A	1753	Note 1
2600					
Berlina	4-dr Sedan-5/6P	I6/158	N/A	3043	Note 2
Spider	2-dr Roadster-2+2P	I6/158	4886	2688	Note 2
Sprint	2-dr Coupe-4P	I6/158	5760	2828	Note 2

Note 1: More than 400,000 Giulias were produced from 1962-79, about one-fourth of which were Sprint or Spider models.

Note 2: Total 2600-series production from 1962-68 included 2,255 Spiders, 6,999 Sprints, 2,092 sedans, and 105 SZ models.

Annual Production Note: A total of 59,971 Alfa Romeos were produced in 1966.

Giulia Model Note: Only those models with prices shown were commonly sold in the U.S. at this time.

ENGINE DATA: BASE FOUR (Giulia): Inline, dual-overhead-cam four-cylinder. Aluminum block and head. **Displacement:** 95.8 cu. in. (1570 cc). **Bore & Stroke:** 3.07 x 3.23 (78 x 82 mm). **Compression Ratio:** 9.0:1 except (SS) 9.7:1. **Brake Horsepower:** (T.I./Spider) 106 at 6000 rpm; (Super) 112 at 5500; (Sprint Veloce/Speciale) 126 at 6500; (Sprint GT) 122 at 6000. **Torque:** (T.I.) 101 lbs.-ft. at 4000 rpm; (Super) 110 at 2000; (Sprint Veloce/Speciale) 112 at 4200; (Sprint GT) 111 at 3000. Five main bearings. Solid valve lifters. Solex carburetor; (Veloce) two Weber carburetors.

BASE SIX (2600): Inline, dual-overhead-cam six-cylinder. Aluminum block and head. **Displacement:** 157.7 cu. in. (2584 cc). Bore & Stroke: 3.27 x 3.13 in. 83 x 79.6 mm). **Compression Ratio:** (sedan) 8.5:1; (Sprint/Spider) 9.0:1. **Brake Horsepower:** (sedan) 148 SAE at 5900 rpm.; (Sprint/Spider) 165 at 5900 rpm. **Torque:** (sedan) 170 lbs.-ft. at 3400 rpm; (Sprint/Spider) 159 at 4000. Seven main bearings. Solid valve lifters. Two Solex carburetors; (Sprint/Spider) three two-barrel Solex 44PHH carburetors.

CHASSIS DATA: Wheelbase: (Giulia Spider/Veloce) 88.6 in.; (Giulia SS) 88.6 in.; (Giulia GT) 92.5 in.; (Giulia sed) 98.8 in.; (2600 rds) 98.5 in.; (2600 cpe) 101.6 in.; (2600 sed) 107.1 in. **Overall Length:** (Giulia Spider/Veloce) 153.6 in.; (Giulia GT) 160.6 in.; (Giulia SS) 162.2 in.; (Giulia sed) 163 in.; (2600 cpe) 180.3 in.; (2600 rds) 177.2 in.; (2600 sed) 185 in. **Height:** (Giulia Spider) 52.6 in.; (Giul sed) 56.3 in.; (Giul SS) 50.4 in.; (Giul Sprint GT) 51.8 in.; (2600 rds/cpe) 52.4 in.; (2600 sed) 55.3 in. **Width:** (Giulia Spider) 62.2 in.; (Giulia GT) 62.2 in.; (Giulia sed) 61.4 in.; (Giul SS) 65.4 in.; (2600 cpe) 67.2 in.; (2600 rds) 63 in.; (2600 sed) 66.9 in. **Front Tread:** (Giulia) 50.9 in.; (Giulia sed/Sprint GT) 51.6 in.; (2600) 55.1 in. **Rear Tread:** (Giulia) 50.9 in.; (Giulia Sprint GT) 50.0 in.; (2600) 53.9 in. **Standard Tires:** (Giulia) 155x15; (2600) 165x400.

TECHNICAL: Layout: front-engine, rear-drive. **Transmission:** five-speed manual (all synchro). **Steering:** worm and roller. **Suspension (front):** long/short control arms, coil springs and anti-roll bar. **Suspension (rear):** rigid axle with trailing lower radius arms, upper A-bracket and coil springs. **Brakes:** front/rear disc. **Body Construction:** steel unibody.

PERFORMANCE: Top Speed: (Giulia T.I./Spider) 105 mph; (Sprint GT) 122 mph; (Spider Veloce) 112 mph; (2600 Sprint) 112 mph; (Sprint Speciale) 125 mph; (2600 sed) near 109 mph. **Acceleration (0-60 mph):** (Giulia Sprint GT) 10.2 sec.; (Giulia SS) 11.0 sec. **Acceleration (quarter-mile):** (Giulia SS) 17.8 sec. (78 mph). **Fuel Mileage:** (Giulia T.I.) 31 mpg; (Giul Spider) 26 mpg; (Giul Sprint GT) 25 mpg; (2600 Sprint/Spider) 17 mpg; (Giul Spider Veloce/Sprint Speciale) 20 mpg.

Manufacturer: Alfa Romeo S.p.A., Milan, Italy.

Distributor: Alfa Romeo, Inc., Newark, New Jersey.

1967-68 ALFA ROMEO

GIULIA — FOUR — Production of the Giulia series continued with little change. In addition to the regular models, a GTA racing coupe was available, with a light aluminum body and 133-horsepower engine. The Sprint Speciale 2+2 coupe featured a curved windshield and rear window, along with a low sloping hood.

DUETTO — FOUR — Following introduction during 1966, the new Duetto Spider, intended to phase out the Giulia Spider, continued in full production. Wearing all-new sheetmetal, it used the Giulia Veloce's drivetrain and suspension.

2600 — SIX — Though no longer listed in U.S. directories, the 2600 series remained in production.

I.D. DATA: Serial number is located on right side of firewall. Engine number is on right side of block. Starting serial number: (Giulia Super) 305001; (Giulia GTV) 242001; (Giulia Sprint Speciale) 380101; (Giulia Sprint GTA) 613001; (Duetto) 660001.

Model	Body Type & Seating	Engine Type/CID	P.O.E Price	Weight (lbs.)	Prod. Total
GIULIA					
Super	4-dr Sedan-5P	I4/96	2995	1907	Note 1
T.I.	4-dr Sedan-5P	I4/96	2927	2204	Note 1
Sprint	2-dr GT Cpe-2+2P	I4/96	4200	2094	Note 1
GTA	2-dr Coupe-2+2P	I4/96	7550	1753	Note 1
GTV	2-dr Coupe-2+2P	I4/96	5550	N/A	Note 1
GTZ	2-dr Coupe-2+2P	I4/96	N/A	N/A	Note 1
TZ 2	2-dr Coupe-2+2P	I4/69	N/A	N/A	Note 1
DUETTO 1600					
Spider	2-dr Conv-2P	I4/96	3950	2064	N/A
2600					
Berlina	4-dr Sedan-5P	I6/58	N/A	N/A	Note 2
SZ	2-dr Coupe-4P	I6/58	N/A	N/A	Note 2

Note 1: More than 400,000 Giulias were produced from 1962-79, about one-fourth of which were Sprint or Spider models.

Note 2: Total 2600-series production from 1962-68 included 2,255 Spiders, 6,999 Sprints, 2,092 sedans, and 105 SZ models.

Annual Production Note: A total of 76,831 Alfa Romeos were produced in 1967, followed by 97,220 in 1968.

Model Availability Note: Only those models with prices shown were commonly sold in the U.S. at this time.

ENGINE DATA: BASE FOUR (Giulia): Inline, dual-overhead-cam four-cylinder. Aluminum alloy block and head. **Displacement:** 95.8 cu. in. (1570 cc). **Bore & Stroke:** 3.07 x 3.23 (78 x 82 mm). **Compression Ratio:** 9.0:1; (Duetto/Sprint) 9.7:1. **Brake Horsepower:** (Spider) 106 at 6000 rpm; (Super) 112 at 5500; (Duetto, Sprint Veloce/GTV) 125 at 6500; (GTA) 133 at 6000. **Torque:** (Super) 110 lbs.-ft. at 3000 rpm; (Duetto/Sprint) 115 at 3000 rpm. Five main bearings. Solid valve lifters. Solex carburetor; (Veloce) two Weber carburetors.

BASE SIX (2600): Inline, dual-overhead-cam six-cylinder. Aluminum block and head. **Displacement:** 157.7 cu. in. (2584 cc). **Bore & Stroke:** 3.27 x 3.13 in. 83 x 79.6 mm). **Compression Ratio:** (sedan) 8.5:1; (SZ) 9.0:1. **Brake Horsepower:** (sedan) 148 SAE at 5900 rpm; (SZ) 165 at 5900 rpm. **Torque:** (sedan) 170 lbs.-ft. at 3400 rpm; (SZ) 159 at 4000. Seven main bearings. Solid valve lifters. Two Solex carburetors; (SZ) three two-barrel Solex 44PHH carburetors.

CHASSIS DATA: Wheelbase: (Giulia cpe) 92.5 in.; (Giulia sed) 98.8 in.; (Duetto) 88.6 in.; (2600 cpe) 101.6 in.; (2600 sed) 107.1 in. **Overall Length:** (Giulia cpe) 160.6 in.; (Giulia sed) 163 in.; (Duetto) 167 in.; (GTV) 161 in.; (GTA) 162 in.; (2600 cpe) 180.3 in.; (2600 sed) 185 in. **Height:** (Giulia cpe) 51.2 in.; (Giulia sed) 56.3 in.; (Duetto) 51 in.; (GTV) 52 in.; (GTA) 50 in.; (2600 cpe) 67.2 in.; (2600 sed) 66.9 in. **Width:** (Giulia cpe) 62.2 in.; (Giulia sed) 61.4 in.; (Duetto) 64 in.; (2600 cpe) 67.2 in.; (2600 sed) 66.9 in. **Front Tread:** (Giulia) 51 in.; (Sprint) 51.6 in.; (Duetto) 51 in.; (2600) 55.1 in. **Rear Tread:** (Giulia/Duetto) 50 in.; (2600) 53.9 in. **Standard Tires:** (Giulia) 155x15; (Duetto) 155x15; (2600) 165x400.

TECHNICAL: Layout: front-engine, rear-drive. **Transmission:** five-speed manual (all synchro). **Steering:** worm and roller. **Suspension (front):** long/short control arms, coil springs and anti-roll bar. **Suspension (rear):** rigid axle with trailing lower radius arms, upper A-bracket and coil springs. **Brakes:** front/rear disc. **Body Construction:** steel unibody.

PERFORMANCE: Top Speed: (Giulia Super/Spider) 108 mph; (Giul Sprint GTV) 115 mph; (Duetto) 118 mph; (GTA) 120+ mph; (Duetto Spider) 120+ mph. **Acceleration (0-60 mph):** (Duetto 1600 Spider) 9.6-10.5 sec.; (Giulia Super) 11.5 sec. **Acceleration (quarter-mile):** (Duetto 1600 Spider) 17.7 sec. (78 mph); **Fuel Mileage:** (Giulia Super/Spider) 30+ mpg.

Manufacturer: Alfa Romeo S.p.A., Milan, Italy.
Distributor: Alfa Romeo, Inc., Newark, New Jersey.
HISTORY: Introduced to U.S. market in June 1966.
1968 Model Year Note: Only leftover '67 models were sold in the U.S. during most of 1968, because Alfa Romeos could not yet meet the current federal air pollution standards.

1969-70 ALFA ROMEO

1750 — FOUR — A larger engine went into the Guilia series at this time, changing the name to "1750." The new 1779-cc (108.5-cid) engine produced 132 horsepower. The "Duetto" name didn't last long, as the open-topped Alfa Romeo was now called, simply, "Spider." A Berlina (four-door sedan) styled by Bertone also became available, as did a GT coupe. Standard equipment included a tachometer, reclining seats, all-disc brakes, Roadspeed Pirelli radial tires, heater/defroster, turn signals, roll-up windows, windshield washer, backup lights, leatherette upholstery, and trip odometer. Early in 1969, as the new 1750s arrived, Alfa-Spica mechanical fuel injection replaced carburetors on all models destined for the U.S. market.

GTA 1300 JUNIOR — FOUR — The racing version of the Giulia continued in production, powered by a 1290-cc engine.

I.D. DATA: Serial number is located on right side of firewall. Engine number is on right side of block. Serial number range: (Spider) 1480001 to 1482999; (GT) 1530001 to 1531999; (Berlina) 1555001 to 1556999.

Model	Body Type & Seating	Engine Type/CID	P.O.E. Price	Weight (lbs.)	Prod. Total
SPIDER VELOCE					
1750	2-dr Conv-2P	I4/109	4198	2116	Note 1
GT VELOCE					
1750	2-dr Coupe-4P	I4/109	4446	2138	Note 1
BERLINA					
1750	4-dr Sedan-5P	I4/109	3495	2270	Note 1
GTA 1300 JUNIOR					
	2-dr Coupe-2 + 2P	I4/79	N/A	N/A	Note 1

Note 1: A total of 104,305 Alfa Romeos were produced in 1969, followed by 107,989 in 1970.

Price Note: Prices rose by $100 for the 1970 model year.

ENGINE DATA: BASE FOUR: Inline, dual-overhead-cam four-cylinder. Aluminum block and head. **Displacement:** 108.5 cu. in. (1779 cc). **Bore & Stroke:** 3.15 x 3.48 (80 x 88.5 mm). **Compression Ratio:** 9.0:1. **Brake Horsepower:** 132 at 5500 rpm. **Torque:** 138 lbs.-ft. at 3000 rpm. Five main bearings. Solid valve lifters. Spica mechanical fuel injection.

Note: European engines used two Weber carburetors.

CHASSIS DATA: Wheelbase: (Spider) 88.6 in.; (GT cpe) 92.5 in.; (Berlina) 101.1 in. **Overall Length:** (Spider) 167.3 in.; (GT) 160.6 in.; (Berlina) 172.8 in. **Height:** (Spider) 50.8 in.; (GT) 51.8 in.; (Berlina) 56.3 in. **Width:** (Spider) 64.2 in.; (GT) 62.3 in.; (Berlina) 61.6 in. **Front Tread:** 52.1 in. **Rear Tread:** 50.1 in. **Wheel Type:** 5.5-inch. **Standard Tires:** 165HR14.

Spider Dimension Note: Starting at this time and continuing for many years, some sources listed the convertible's length as 167.3 inches or more, while others claimed it was 162.2 inches or less. The difference is probably related to the car's protruding bumpers.

TECHNICAL: Layout: front-engine, rear-drive. **Transmission:** five-speed manual (all synchro). **Standard Final Drive Ratio:** 4.56:1. **Steering:** worm and roller or recirculating ball. **Suspension (front):** long/short control arms, coil springs and anti-roll bar. **Suspension (rear):** rigid axle with trailing links, upper T-arms and coil springs. **Brakes:** front/rear disc. **Body Construction:** steel unibody except (GTA Jr) aluminum.

MAJOR OPTIONS: Removable hardtop: Spider ($250). Leather steering wheel ($60). AM/FM/shortwave radio ($146). Roll bar: Veloce ($100). Front bumper guards: GT ($20); Veloce ($23). Rear bumper guards: Veloce ($25). Racing mirrors ($7). Metallic paint: Spider/Berlina ($85).

PERFORMANCE: Top Speed: (Spider/GT) 118 mph; (Berlina) 112+ mph. **Acceleration:** (Spider/GT) 9.9 sec.; (Berlina) 11 sec. **Fuel Mileage:** 18-21 mpg average.
Manufacturer: Alfa Romeo S.p.A., Milan, Italy.
Distributor: Alfa Romeo, Inc., Newark, New Jersey.
HISTORY: Introduced to U.S. market on February 18, 1969. As a result of strikes in Italy, importation of 1970 models was delayed.

1971 ALFA ROMEO

1750 — FOUR — Alfa Romeo's Spider convertible adopted a cut-down Kamm-style tail this year, for a new look. The Spider's front end remained completely different from that of the coupe and sedan, highlighted by headlamps recessed in deep nacells and a long sloping nose with small triangular Alfa grille at the center, between the bumper guards. Otherwise, the three body styles continued without great change except for a slight (3 bhp) power increase. New front seats in the GT Veloce offered greater lateral support. By this time, the traditional Alfa triangular grille had shrunk considerably.

Note: A new 2000 series was introduced in Europe at this time, but did not become available in the U.S. until 1972. The new Montreal coupe also entered production in 1971. See next listing for details on both.

I.D. DATA: Serial number is located on right side of firewall. Engine number is on right side of block. Serial number range: (Spider) 1485001 to 1486999; (GT) 1532001 to 1533999; (Berlina) 1557001 to 1557999.

Model	Body Type & Seating	Engine Type/CID	P.O.E. Price	Weight (lbs.)	Prod. Total
SPIDER VELOCE					
1750	2-dr Conv-2 + 2P	I4/109	4595	2167	Note 1
GT VELOCE					
1750	2-dr Coupe-4P	I4/109	4795	2167	Note 1
BERLINA					
1750	4-dr Sedan-5P	I4/109	3795	2321	Note 1

Note 1: A total of 123,309 Alfa Romeos were produced in 1971, including 25,834 series 1750 models.

ENGINE DATA: BASE FOUR: Inline, dual-overhead-cam four-cylinder. Aluminum block and head. **Displacement:** 108.5 cu. in. (1779 cc). **Bore & Stroke:** 3.15 x 3.48 (80 x 88.5 mm). **Compression Ratio:** 9.0:1. **Brake Horsepower:** 135 at 5500 rpm. **Torque:** 137 lbs.-ft. at 2900 rpm. Five main bearings. Solid valve lifters. Spica mechanical fuel injection.

Note: European engines used two Weber carburetors.

CHASSIS DATA: Wheelbase: (Spider) 88.6 in.; (GT cpe) 92.5 in.; (Berlina) 101.1 in. **Overall Length:** (Spider) 167.3 in.; (GT) 160.6 in.; (Berlina) 172.8 in. **Height:** (Spider) 50.8 in.; (GT) 51.8 in.; (Berlina) 56.3 in. **Width:** (Spider) 64.2 in.; (GT) 62.3 in.; (Berlina) 61.6 in. **Front Tread:** 52.1 in. **Rear Tread:** 50.1 in. **Wheel Type:** 5.5-inch. **Standard Tires:** 165HR14.

TECHNICAL: Layout: front-engine, rear-drive. **Transmission:** five-speed manual (all synchro). **Standard Final Drive Ratio:** 4.56:1. **Steering:** worm and roller. **Suspension (front):** long/short control arms, coil springs and anti-roll bar. **Suspension (rear):** rigid axle with trailing lower radius arms, upper A-bracket and coil springs. **Brakes:** power front/rear disc. **Body Construction:** steel unibody.

PERFORMANCE: Top Speed: (Spider/GT) 118 mph; (Berlina) 112+ mph. **Acceleration (0-60 mph):** (Berlina) 11.0 sec. **Acceleration (quarter-mile):** (Berlina) 17.9 sec. (76 mph).
Manufacturer: Alfa Romeo S.p.A., Milan, Italy.
HISTORY: The Junior Z coupe, with Zagato two-seat body and 80-cid twin-cam engine, was available in Europe but not the U.S.

1972 ALFA ROMEO

1972 Alfa Romeo Alfasud four-door Berlina.

2000 — 115 SERIES — FOUR — An increase in bore dimension turned the "1750" series into the "2000" for the 1972 model year. The new engine displaced 1962 cubic centimeters and produced 129 horsepower, using Spica fuel injection. European versions still came with two Weber sidedraft carburetors instead. Following typical Alfa Romeo practice, the Berlina four-door sedan appeared first, wearing the same body as the 1750. That included quad headlamps, exposed wheel lug nuts, and a '2000' badge on the rear end. A GTV coupe followed later in the year, wearing a grille made up of multiple horizontal bars. By 1974, they would be available with an automatic transmission. Other modifications included a new ventilation system and revised instruments. Wheels also were restyled, and a limited-slip differential was available. Standard equipment included a 0-8000 rpm tachometer and 0-140 mph speedometer.

MONTREAL — V-8 — One of the attractions at Expo '67 in Montreal, Canada had been a prototype of a new Montreal fastback coupe, marking Alfa's appearance as a representative of the auto industry. The Bertone-styled coupe was based on the 105-series Giulia, and displayed seven large air slots to the rear of each door, like a mid-engine design. A production version of the Montreal emerged in 1970 with a similar appearance, but a new front end. The four-cam, 2593-cc aluminum-block V-8 engine, with Spica fuel injection, produced 230 horsepower at 6500 rpm. Essentially, it was a detuned version of the T33 racing engine. A ZF five-speed gearbox was installed, with disc brakes all around. The production Montreal displayed the same C-pillar slots as the original show car. Quad headlamps in big openings stood alongside a traditional Alfa shield-shaped center opening, and partly behind a slatted grille. Capable of 0-60 mph acceleration in the eight-second neighborhood, the Montreal could reach a top speed of 132 mph. Never certified for sale in the U.S., the Montreal was promoted only minimally worldwide. A total of 3,925 were built from 1971 to 1975.

I.D. DATA: Serial number is located on right side of firewall. Engine number is on right side of block. Serial number range: (Spider) 1486187 to 1486872; (GT) 3020001 up; (Berlina) 3000001 up.

Model	Body Type & Seating	Engine Type/CID	P.O.E. Price	Weight (lbs.)	Prod. Total
SPIDER VELOCE					
2000	2-dr Roadster-2P	I4/120	5249	2167	Note 1
GT VELOCE					
2000	2-dr Coupe-2 + 2P	I4/120	4948	2167	Note 1
BERLINA					
2000	4-dr Sedan-5P	I4/120	4254	2321	Note 1
MONTREAL					
	2-dr Fbk Cpe-2 + 2P	V8/158	N/A	2830	3925

Note 1: A total of 140,595 Alfa Romeos were produced in 1972, including 50,293 series 2000 models.

Montreal Production Note: Never certified for U.S. sale; figure shown is approximate total for the full run, through 1976. A total of 668 were built in 1971, 2,377 in 1972, 302 in 1973, 205 in 1974, 323 in 1975, and a final 23 units in 1976.

2000 GT Veloce Note: This model was sometimes called "GTV."

1972 Alfa-Romeo Montreal coupe owned by R. Bartel. (John Gunnell)

ENGINE DATA: BASE FOUR (2000): Inline, dual-overhead-cam four-cylinder. Aluminum block and head. **Displacement:** 119.7 cu. in. (1962 cc). **Bore & Stroke:** 3.31 x 3.48 (84 x 88.5 mm). **Compression Ratio:** 9.0:1. **Brake Horsepower:** 129 at 5800 rpm. **Torque:** 132 lbs.-ft. at 3500 rpm. Five main bearings. Solid valve lifters. Spica mechanical fuel injection.

BASE V-8 (Montreal): 90-degree, dual-overhead-cam V-8. Aluminum block and head. **Displacement:** 158.2 cu. in. (2593 cc). **Bore & Stroke:** 3.15 x 2.54 (80 x 64.5 mm). **Compression Ratio:** 9.0:1. **Brake Horsepower:** 230 (SAE gross) at 6500 rpm. **Torque:** 199 lbs.-ft. (SAE gross) at 4750 rpm. Five main bearings. Solid valve lifters. Spica fuel injection.

CHASSIS DATA: Wheelbase: (Spider) 88.6 in.; (GT) 92.5 in.; (Berlina) 101.2 in.; (Montreal) 92.5 in. **Overall Length:** (Spider) 167.9 in.; (GT) 161.4 in.; (Berlina) 172.8 in.; (Montreal) 166.1 in. **Height:** (Spider) 50.8 in.; (GT) 51.8 in.; (Berlina) 56.3 in.; (Montreal) 47.4 in. **Width:** (Spider) 64.1 in.; (GT) 62.2 in.; (Berlina) 61.6 in.; (Montreal) 65.8 in. **Front Tread:** (2000) 52.1 in.; (Montreal) 54.1 in. **Rear Tread:** (2000) 50.2 in.; (Montreal) 52.8 in. **Wheel Type:** steel disc. **Standard Tires:** 165HR14.

TECHNICAL: Layout: front-engine, rear-drive. **Transmission:** five-speed manual; (Montreal) ZF five-speed. Overall 2000 GTV coupe gear ratios: (1st) 15.05:1; (2nd) 9.07:1; (3rd) 6.16:1; (4th) 4.56:1; (5th) 3.60:1. **Standard Final Drive Ratio:** 4.56:1. **Steering:** recirculating ball or worm and lever. **Suspension (front):** long/short control arms, coil springs and anti-roll bar; (Montreal) lower A-arms, upper lateral and trailing links, coil springs and anti-roll bar. **Suspension (rear):** rigid axle with trailing lower radius arms, upper A-bracket and coil springs; (Montreal) live axle, single lower trailing arms, upper T-bar to differential case, and coil springs. **Brakes:** front/rear disc. **Body Construction:** steel unibody.

PERFORMANCE: Top Speed: (2000 cpe) 110 mph; (Montreal) 132 mph. **Acceleration (0-60 mph):** (2000 cpe) 9.6 sec.; (2000 Berlina) 10.7 sec.; (Montreal) 8.0 sec. **Acceleration (quarter-mile):** (2000 cpe) 17.6 sec. (80.5 mph); (2000 Berlina) 18.0 sec. (77.5 mph); (Montreal) 8.0 sec. **Fuel Mileage:** (2000 cpe) near 24 mpg.
Manufacturer: Alfa Romeo S.p.A., Milan, Italy.
HISTORY: A new front-drive Alfasud sedan was introduced in Europe at this time, with an 1186-cc engine.

1973
ALFA ROMEO

2000 — FOUR — Production of the convertible, coupe and sedan (Berlina) models, powered by a 1962-cc four-cylinder engine, continued without major change.

MONTREAL — V-8 — Production of the semi-supercar continued through 1975, without significant change; see 1972 listing for details.

I.D. DATA: Serial number is located on right side of firewall. Engine number is on right side of block. Starting serial number: (Spider) 3041001; (GT) 3021501; (Berlina) 3001001.

Model	Body Type & Seating	Engine Type/CID	P.O.E. Price	Weight (lbs.)	Prod. Total
SPIDER VELOCE					
2000	2-dr Conv-2P	I4/120	5258	2292	Note 1
GT VELOCE					
2000	2-dr Coupe-4P	I4/120	5474	2292	Note 1
BERLINA					
2000	4-dr Sedan-5P	I4/120	4437	2442	Note 1
MONTREAL					
	2-dr Fbk Cpe-2+2P	V8/158	N/A	2830	Note 2

Note 1: A total of 204,902 Alfa Romeos were produced in 1973, including 38,083 series 2000 models.
Note 2: Close to 3,925 Montreal coupes were produced during the full run, 1971-76. A total of 668 were built in 1971, 2,377 in 1972, 302 in 1973, 205 in 1974, 323 in 1975, and a final 23 units in 1976.

ENGINE DATA: BASE FOUR (2000): Inline, dual-overhead-cam four-cylinder. Aluminum block and head. **Displacement:** 119.7 cu. in. (1962 cc). **Bore & Stroke:** 3.31 x 3.48 (84 x 88.5 mm). **Compression Ratio:** 9.0:1. **Brake Horsepower:** 129 at 5800 rpm. **Torque:** 130 lbs.-ft. at 3700 rpm. Five main bearings. Solid valve lifters. Spica mechanical fuel injection.

BASE V-8 (Montreal): 90-degree, dual-overhead-cam V-8. Aluminum block and head. **Displacement:** 158.2 cu. in. (2593 cc). **Bore & Stroke:** 3.15 x 2.54 (80 x 64.5 mm). **Compression Ratio:** 9.0:1. **Brake Horsepower:** 230 (SAE gross) at 6500 rpm. **Torque:** 199 lbs.-ft. (SAE gross) at 4750 rpm. Five main bearings. Solid valve lifters. Spica fuel injection.

CHASSIS DATA: Wheelbase: (Spider) 88.6 in.; (GT) 92.5 in.; (Berlina) 101.1 in.; (Montreal) 92.5 in. **Overall Length:** (Spider) 167.9 in.; (GT) 161.4 in.; (Berlina) 172.7 in.; (Montreal) 166.1 in. **Height:** (Spider) 50.8 in.; (GT) 51.8 in.; (Berlina) 56.3 in.; (Montreal) 47.4 in. **Width:** (Spider) 64.1 in.; (GT) 62.2 in.; (Berlina) 61.6 in.; (Montreal) 65.8 in. **Front Tread:** (2000) 52.1 in.; (Montreal) 54.1 in. **Rear Tread:** (2000) 50.1 in.; (Montreal) 52.8 in. **Standard Tires:** 165HR14.

TECHNICAL: Layout: front-engine, rear-drive. **Transmission:** five-speed manual; (Montreal) ZF five-speed. **Standard Final Drive Ratio:** (2000) 4.56:1. **Steering:** recirculating ball or worm and lever. **Suspension (front):** long/short control arms, coil springs and anti-roll bar; (Montreal) lower A-arms, upper lateral and trailing links, coil springs and anti-roll bar. **Suspension (rear):** rigid axle with trailing lower radius arms, upper A-bracket and coil springs; (Montreal) live axle, single lower trailing arms, upper T-bar to differential case, and coil springs. **Brakes:** front/rear disc. **Body Construction:** steel unibody. **Fuel Tank:** (2000) 14 gal. exc. (Spider) 13.4 gal.

PERFORMANCE: Top Speed: (Montreal) 132 mph. **Acceleration (0-60 mph):** (Montreal) 8.0 sec.

Manufacturer: Alfa Romeo S.p.A., Milan, Italy.

1974
ALFA ROMEO

1974 Alfa Romeo 2000 Spyder Veloce 2+2 open sports car. (Christie's)

2000 — FOUR — This was the final appearance for the Sprint coupe, but the Spider convertible (and Berlina sedan) continued in production. Each model had a sharp price jump this year.

1974 Alfa Romeo Montreal. (William Siuru Jr.)

MONTREAL — V-8 — Production of the luxury Alfa Romeo continued without change.
I.D. DATA: Serial number is located on right side of firewall. Engine number is on right side of block. Starting serial number: (Spider) 3042501; (GT) 3023001; (Berlina) 3002301.

Model	Body Type & Seating	Engine Type/CID	P.O.E. Price	Weight (lbs.)	Prod. Total
SPIDER VELOCE					
2000	2-dr Conv-2P	I4/120	6550	2220	Note 1
GT VELOCE					
2000	2-dr Coupe-4P	I4/120	6450	2181	Note 1
BERLINA					
2000	4-dr Sedan-5P	I4/120	5350	2470	Note 1

Model	Body Type & Seating	Engine Type/CID	P.O.E. Price	Weight (lbs.)	Prod. Total
MONTREAL					
	2-dr Fstbk Cpe-2+2P	V8/158	N/A	2830	Note 2

Note 1: A total of 208,386 Alfa Romeos were produced in 1974, including 19,354 series 2000 models.

Note 2: Close to 3,925 Montreal coupes were produced during the full run, 1971-76. A total of 668 were built in 1971, 2,377 in 1972, 302 in 1973, 205 in 1974, 323 in 1975, and a final 23 units in 1976.

ENGINE DATA: BASE FOUR (2000): Inline, dual-overhead-cam four-cylinder. Aluminum block and head. **Displacement**: 119.7 cu. in. (1962 cc). **Bore & Stroke**: 3.31 x 3.48 (84 x 88.5 mm). **Compression Ratio**: 9.0:1. **Brake Horsepower**: 129 at 5800 rpm. **Torque**: 130 lbs.-ft. at 3700 rpm. Five main bearings. Solid valve lifters. Spica mechanical fuel injection.

BASE V-8 (Montreal): 90-degree, dual-overhead-cam V-8. Aluminum block and head. **Displacement**: 158.2 cu. in. (2593 cc). **Bore & Stroke**: 3.15 x 2.54 (80 x 64.5 mm). **Compression Ratio**: 9.0:1. **Brake Horsepower**: 230 (SAE gross) at 6500 rpm. **Torque**: 199 lbs.-ft. (SAE gross) at 4750 rpm. Five main bearings. Solid valve lifters. Spica fuel injection.

CHASSIS DATA: **Wheelbase**: (Spider) 88.6 in.; (GT) 92.5 in.; (Berlina) 101.2 in.; (Montreal) 92.5 in. **Overall Length**: (Spider) 166.2 in.; (GT) 161.4 in.; (Berlina) 176.7 in.; (Montreal) 166.1 in. **Height**: (Spider) 48.8 in.; (GT) 51.8 in.; (Berlina) 56.3 in.; (Montreal) 47.4 in. Width: (Spider) 64.1 in.; (GT) 62.2 in.; (Berlina) 61.6 in.; (Montreal) 65.8 in. **Front Tread**: (2000) 52.1 in.; (Montreal) 54.1 in. **Rear Tread**: (2000) 50.1 in.; (Montreal) 52.8 in. **Standard Tires**: (2000) 165HR14; (Montreal) 195/70VR14.

TECHNICAL: **Layout**: front-engine, rear-drive. **Transmission**: five-speed manual; (Montreal) ZF five-speed. **Standard Final Drive Ratio**: (2000) 4.56:1. **Steering**: recirculating ball or worm and lever. **Suspension (front)**: long/short control arms, coil springs and anti-roll bar; (Montreal) lower A-arms, upper lateral and trailing links, coil springs and anti-roll bar. **Suspension (rear)**: rigid axle with trailing lower radius arms, upper A-bracket and coil springs; (Montreal) live axle, single lower trailing arms, upper T-bar to differential case, and coil springs. **Brakes**: front/rear disc. **Body Construction**: steel unibody.

PERFORMANCE: **Top Speed**: (Montreal) 132 mph. **Acceleration (0-60 mph)**: (Montreal) 8.0 sec.

Manufacturer: Alfa Romeo S.p.A., Milan, Italy.

HISTORY: "Why drive a car," Alfa Romeo asked during this era, "when you can drive a legend?"

1975 ALFA ROMEO

2000 SPIDER VELOCE — FOUR — Little was new in the familiar Alfa two-seat convertible. Power came from the all-aluminum 1962-cc four-cylinder engine, hooked to a five-speed manual gearbox.

ALFETTA — FOUR — Alfa Romeo's new GT coupe and four-door sedan were promoted for their combination of performance and economy. Each carried the same 1962-cc four-cylinder engine as the Spider convertible. The coupe rode a 94.5-inch wheelbase, four inches than that of the four-door sedan. The five-speed manual gearbox actually served as a transaxle, mounted in the rear (between the back wheels) as a unit with the clutch, flywheel and differential. A De Dion rear axle was used, as compared to the conventional "live" axle found on the 2000 Spider. The Alfetta also turned to rack-and-pinion steering, and came with standard four-wheel power disc brakes. The coupe held four passengers; the sedan could squeeze in one more. Quad round headlamps were installed, with the traditional Alfa triangular grille in the center. Unlike many small sedans, the Alfetta had vent windows.

MONTREAL — V-8 — Production of the fastback coupe, which had begun in 1971, continued through 1975; see 1972 listing for full details.

I.D. DATA: Alfa Romeo's 14-symbol serial number is located on the right side of the firewall and the windshield post. The first two letters indicate manufacturing plant. The next five symbols identify the model ('115.02' = Spider Veloce; '116.29' = Alfetta GT; '116.33' = Alfetta Berlina). All the remaining digits form the sequential serial number.

Model	Body Type & Seating	Engine Type/CID	P.O.E. Price	Weight (lbs.)	Prod. Total
SPIDER VELOCE					
2000	2-dr Conv-2P	I4/120	7250	2320	Note 1
ALFETTA					
GT	2-dr Coupe-4P	I4/120	8195	2310	Note 1
	4-dr Sedan-4/5P	I4/120	6995	2337	Note 1
MONTREAL					
	2-dr Fbk Cpe-2+2P	V8/158	N/A	2830	Note 2

Note 1: A total of 189,682 Alfa Romeos were produced in 1975, including 10,274 series 2000 models. Approximately 5,342 Alfas were sold in the U.S. that year.

Note 2: Close to 3,925 Montreal coupes were produced during the full run, 1971-76. A total of 668 were built in 1971, 2,377 in 1972, 302 in 1973, 205 in 1974, 323 in 1975, and a final 23 units in 1976.

ENGINE DATA: BASE FOUR: Inline, dual-overhead-cam four-cylinder. Aluminum block and head. **Displacement**: 119.7 cu. in. (1962 cc). **Bore & Stroke**: 3.31 x 3.48 (84 x 88.5 mm). **Compression Ratio**: 9.0:1. **Brake Horsepower**: (2000 Spider) 129 at 5800 rpm; (Alfetta) 110 bhp. **Torque**: (2000) 130 lbs.-ft. at 3700 rpm; (Alfetta) 110 at 4500 rpm. Five main bearings. Solid valve lifters. Spica mechanical fuel injection.

CHASSIS DATA: **Wheelbase**: (2000 Spider) 88.6 in.; (Alfetta cpe) 94.5 in.; (Alfetta sed) 98.8 in. **Overall Length**: (2000 Spider) 166.2 in.; (Alfetta cpe) 165 in.; (Alfetta sed) 168 in. **Height**: (2000 Spider) 48.8 in.; (Alfetta cpe) 52.5 in.; (Alfetta sed) 56.5 in. **Width**: (2000 Spider) 64.1 in.; (Alfetta cpe) 65.5 in.; (Alfetta sed) 65.8 in. **Front Tread**: (2000 Spider) 52.1 in.; (Alfetta) 53.5 in. **Rear Tread**: (2000 Spider) 50.1 in.; (Alfetta cpe) 53.5 in.; (Alfetta sed) 53.2 in. **Standard Tires**: (2000 Spider) 165x14; (Alfetta cpe) 185HR14; (Alfetta sed) 165SR14.

TECHNICAL: **Layout**: front-engine, rear-drive. **Transmission**: five-speed manual (rear mounted in Alfetta). **Standard Final Drive Ratio**: (2000 Spider) 4.56:1; (Alfetta) 4.1:1. **Steering**: (2000 Spider) recirculating ball or worm and roller; (Alfetta) rack and pinion. **Suspension (front)**: (2000 Spider) long/short control arms with coil springs and anti-roll bar; (Alfetta) long/short control arms with torsion bars and anti-roll bar. **Suspension (rear)**: (2000 Spider) rigid axle with coil springs and anti-roll bar; (Alfetta) De Dion axle with coil springs and anti-roll bar. **Brakes**: front/rear disc. **Body Construction**: steel unibody. **Fuel Tank**: (2000) 12 gal.; (Alfetta cpe) 14.3 gal.; (Alfetta sed) 13.2 gal.

PERFORMANCE: **Acceleration (0-60 mph)**: (Alfetta) 12.5 sec. **Acceleration (quarter-mile)**: (Alfetta) 18.3 sec. (74.5 mph). **Fuel Mileage**: (Alfetta) 25 mpg EPA highway.

Manufacturer: Alfa Romeo S.p.A., Milan, Italy.

Distributor: Alfa Romeo Inc., Englewood Cliffs, New Jersey.

HISTORY: Introduced to U.S. market in July 1975. The Alfetta was billed as "a new balance of power" and the "world's first truly balanced production car," due to its 50/50 weight distribution. It was named after the old Alfetta 158/159 Grand Prix racing car, and declared one of the year's 10 best by *Road & Track* magazine.

1976 ALFA ROMEO

SPIDER VELOCE — FOUR — Production of the Alfa two-seater convertible, sole remnant of the 2000 series, continued with little change.

ALFETTA — FOUR — Little change was evident in the GT coupe or four-door sedan, introduced for the 1975 model year, except for minor body trim and grille revisions in the sedan. Alfa Romeo called the sedan "the most technically advanced production car in the world." Technical features included a De Dion rear end with five-speed transaxle, rack-and-pinion steering, and power disc brakes. An adjustable steering column was standard.

Note: Final Montreal coupes were produced in 1976; see 1972 listing for details.

I.D. DATA: Alfa Romeo's 14-symbol serial number is located on the right side of the firewall and the windshield post. The first two letters indicate manufacturing plant. The next five symbols identify the model ('11502' = Spider Veloce; '11629' = Alfetta GT; '11633' = Alfetta Berlina). All the remaining digits form the sequential serial number. Starting serial number: (Spider) AR115023048031; (Alfetta GT) AR116290002001; (Alfetta sedan) AR116330002501.

Model	Body Type & Seating	Engine Type/CID	P.O.E. Price	Weight (lbs.)	Prod. Total
SPIDER VELOCE					
2000	2-dr Conv-2P	I4/120	7895	2455	Note 1
ALFETTA					
GT	2-dr Coupe-4P	I4/120	8515	2310	Note 1
Sports	4-dr Spt Sed-4/5P	I4/120	7235	2689	Note 1

Note 1: A total of 201,145 Alfa Romeos were produced in 1976, including 4,530 series 2000 models and 17,472 Alfetta 2000. Approximately 5,283 were sold in the U.S. that year.

ENGINE DATA: BASE FOUR: Inline, dual-overhead-cam four-cylinder. Aluminum block and head. **Displacement**: 119.7 cu. in. (1962 cc). **Bore & Stroke**: 3.31 x 3.48 (84 x 88.5 mm). **Compression Ratio**: 9.0:1. **Brake Horsepower**: 110 at 5500 rpm. **Torque**: 110 lbs.-ft. at 4500 rpm. Five main bearings. Solid valve lifters. Spica mechanical fuel injection.

CHASSIS DATA: **Wheelbase**: (Spider) 88.6 in.; (Alfetta cpe) 94.5 in.; (Alfetta sed) 98.8 in. **Overall Length**: (Spider) 167.9 in.; (Alfetta cpe) 171 in.; (Alfetta sed) 172.4 in. **Height**: (Spider) 50.8 in.; (Alfetta cpe) 52.5 in.; (Alfetta sed) 56.3 in. **Width**: (Spider) 64.1 in.; (Alfetta cpe) 65.5 in.; (Alfetta sed) 63.7 in. **Front Tread**: (Spider) 52.1 in.; (Alfetta) 53.5 in. **Rear Tread**: (Spider) 50.1 in.; (Alfetta) 53.4-53.5 in. **Standard Tires**: (Spider) 165HR14; (Alfetta cpe) 185/70HR14; (Alfetta sed) 165SR14.

TECHNICAL: **Layout**: front-engine, rear-drive. **Transmission**: five-speed manual (rear mounted in Alfetta). **Standard Final Drive Ratio**: (Spider) 4.56:1; (Alfetta) 4.1:1. **Steering**: (Spider) recirculating ball or worm and roller; (Alfetta) rack and pinion. **Suspension (front)**: (2000 Spider) long/short control arms with coil springs and anti-roll bar; (Alfetta) long/short control arms with torsion bars and anti-roll bar. **Suspension (rear)**: (2000 Spider) rigid axle with coil springs and anti-roll bar; (Alfetta) De Dion axle with trailing arms, Watt linkage, coil springs and anti-roll bar. **Brakes**: front/rear disc. **Body Construction**: steel unibody. **Fuel Tank**: (2000 Spider) 12 gal.; (Alfetta) 13.2 gal.

MAJOR OPTIONS: Air conditioning ($595). AM/FM radio with tape player ($200). Cast magnesium alloy wheels ($220). Metallic paint ($145).

Manufacturer: Alfa Romeo S.p.A., Milan, Italy.

Distributor: Alfa Romeo Inc., Englewood Cliffs, New Jersey.

1977 ALFA ROMEO

2000 SPIDER VELOCE — FOUR — Production of the Alfa Romeo two-seat convertible continued with little change, again powered by the 1962-cc four-cylinder engine. Standard equipment included a tachometer, Texalta interior, hand throttle, trip odometer, lighter, two-speed heater, reclining bucket seats, underhood and trunk lights, carpeted trunk, simulated wood steering wheel, and 165HR14 tires on cast magnesium wheels.

ALFETTA — FOUR — Two body styles of the performance-oriented Alfetta series were available again: the Sprint Veloce coupe, and four-door sports sedan. The rear-mounted five-speed transaxle (with De Dion rear end) helped give the car an even 50/50 weight distribution. Standard equipment included an adjustable steering column with padded wheel, reclining seats, tinted glass, and a heated rear window. The sedan added an electric clock and mahogany instrument panel trim. Tires on the coupe were 185/70HR14 size; the sedan wore 165SR14 rubber. The Alfetta was replaced in 1978 by a new four-door called, simply, the Sports Sedan.

I.D. DATA: Alfa Romeo's 14-symbol serial number is located on the right side of the firewall and the windshield post. The first two letters indicate manufacturing plant. The next five symbols identify the model ('115.02' = Spider Veloce; '116.29' = Alfetta GT; '116.33' = Alfetta Berlina sedan). All the remaining digits form the sequential serial number.

Model	Body Type & Seating	Engine Type/CID	P.O.E. Price	Weight (lbs.)	Prod. Total
2000 SPIDER VELOCE					
11502	2-dr Conv-2P	I4/120	8795	2455	Note 1
ALFETTA					
11629	2-dr GT Cpe-4P	I4/120	8895	2710	Note 1
11633	4-dr Spt Sed-4/5P	I4/120	7595	2690	Note 1

Note 1: A total of 201,118 Alfa Romeos were produced in 1977, including 3,566 series 2000 models and 44,192 Alfetta 2000. Approximately 6,712 were sold in the U.S. during that year.

ENGINE DATA: BASE FOUR: Inline, dual-overhead-cam four-cylinder. Aluminum block and head. **Displacement:** 119.7 cu. in. (1962 cc). **Bore & Stroke:** 3.31 x 3.48 (84 x 88.5 mm). **Compression Ratio:** 9.0:1. **Brake Horsepower:** 110 at 5500 rpm. **Torque:** 110 lbs.-ft. at 4500 rpm. Five main bearings. Solid valve lifters. Spica mechanical fuel injection.

CHASSIS DATA: Wheelbase: (Spider) 88.6 in.; (Alfetta) 94.5 in. **Overall Length:** (Spider) 161.6/167.9 in.; (Alfetta cpe) 171 in.; (Alfetta sed) 172.4 in. **Height:** (Spider) 50.8 in.; (Alfetta cpe) 52.4 in.; (Alfetta sed) 56.3 in. **Width:** (Spider) 64.4 in.; (Alfetta cpe) 65.4 in.; (Alfetta sed) 63.7 in. **Front Tread:** (Spider) 52.1 in.; (Alfetta) 53.5 in. **Rear Tread:** (Spider) 50.1 in.; (Alfetta) 53.4 in. **Standard Tires:** (Spider) 165HR14; (Alfetta cpe) 185/70HR14; (Alfetta sed) 165SR14.

TECHNICAL: Layout: front-engine, rear-drive. **Transmission:** five-speed manual (rear mounted in Alfetta). **Standard Final Drive Ratio:** (Spider) 4.56:1; (Alfetta) 4.1:1. **Steering:** (Spider) recirculating ball or worm and roller; (Alfetta) rack and pinion. **Suspension (front):** (2000 Spider) long/short control arms with coil springs and anti-roll bar; (Alfetta) long/short control arms with torsion bars and anti-roll bar. **Suspension (rear):** (2000 Spider) rigid axle with coil springs and anti-roll bar; (Alfetta) De Dion axle with trailing arms, Watt linkage, coil springs and anti-roll bar. **Brakes:** front/rear disc. **Body Construction:** steel unibody. **Fuel Tank:** (2000 Spider) 12 gal.; (Alfetta) 13.2 gal.

MAJOR OPTIONS: Air conditioning: Alfetta ($595). Cast magnesium alloy wheels: Alfetta ($220). Metallic paint ($145).

PERFORMANCE: Top Speed: (Spider) 115 mph; (Alfetta GT cpe) 111 mph; (Alfetta sed) 109 mph. **Acceleration (0-60 mph):** (Spider) 11.4 sec.; (Alfetta sedan) 14.1 sec.; (Alfetta GT) 13.7 sec. **Acceleration (quarter-mile):** (Spider) 18.2 sec. (75 mph); (Alfetta sedan/cpe) 19.2 sec. (71 mph).

Manufacturer: Alfa Romeo S.p.A., Milan, Italy.

Distributor: Alfa Romeo Inc., Englewood Cliffs, New Jersey.

1978 ALFA ROMEO

SPIDER VELOCE — FOUR — Little change was evident in the two-seat convertible, which was one of the few actual open-topped models available in the U.S. at this time. Though almost dropped not long before, continued popularity kept the car on the import list. About 90 percent of the total factory output of 2,000 Spider convertibles, in fact, were exported to the U.S. They were easy to spot on the road, with a large black rubber front bumper ahead of a long nose, and a prominent bodyside depression. Standard equipment included a hydraulic clutch, chrome exhaust, tachometer, reclining bucket seats, chrome mirror, magnesium wheels, trip odometer, and all-synchro five-speed manual gearbox.

1978 Alfa Romeo GTU Sprint Veloce.

SPRINT VELOCE — FOUR — The Alfetta name faded away from the hatchback coupe, which again held a 1962-cc four-cylinder engine, as in the Spider convertible. Standard equipment was similar to the Spider, but also included rocker panel moldings, rubber/chrome beltline moldings, electrically heated rear window, and an electric clock.

SPORTS SEDAN — FOUR — The revised four-door sedan that appeared later in the 1978 model year dropped the Alfetta name. It also became available for the first time with a three-speed automatic transmission instead of the usual five-speed manual gearbox. Other options included a leather interior and a sunroof. Sheetmetal was new from the cowl forward, and taillamps were larger than before. Under the hood again was the same engine that powered the Spider convertible: a 1962-cc four-cylinder unit with aluminum block and cylinder head, producing 111 horsepower in U.S. trim. The front suspension consisted of unequal-length control arms and torsion bars; the De Dion rear included coil springs and a Watts linkage. Standard equipment was similar to the coupe.

I.D. DATA: Alfa Romeo's 14-symbol serial number is located on the right side of the firewall and the windshield post. The first two letters indicate manufacturing plant. The next five symbols identify the model. All the remaining digits form the sequential serial number. Starting serial number: (Spider) AR115410002001; (Sprint) AR116150003001; (Sports sedan) AR116580001011.

Model	Body Type & Seating	Engine Type/CID	P.O.E. Price	Weight (lbs.)	Prod. Total
2000 SPIDER VELOCE					
115.41	2-dr Conv-2P	I4/120	9195	2455	Note 1
SPRINT VELOCE					
116.15	2-dr Coupe-4P	I4/120	8695	2620	Note 1

Model	Body Type & Seating	Engine Type/CID	P.O.E. Price	Weight (lbs.)	Prod. Total
SPORTS SEDAN					
116.58	4-dr Spt Sed-5P	I4/120	7995	2700	Note 1

Note 1: A total of 219,501 Alfa Romeos were produced in 1978, including 3,350 series 2000 models and 33,996 Alfetta 2000. Approximately 6,137 Alfa Romeos were sold in the U.S. that year (3,562 convertibles, 1,663 coupes, and 912 sedans).

Price Note: Sprint price rose to $8895 and sedan to $8345 during the year.

ENGINE DATA: BASE FOUR: Inline, dual-overhead-cam four-cylinder. Aluminum block and head. **Displacement:** 119.7 cu. in. (1962 cc). **Bore & Stroke:** 3.31 x 3.48 (84 x 88.5 mm). **Compression Ratio:** 9.0:1. **Brake Horsepower:** 111 at 5500 rpm. **Torque:** 110 lbs.-ft. at 4500 rpm. Five main bearings. Solid valve lifters. Spica mechanical fuel injection.

CHASSIS DATA: Wheelbase: (Spider) 88.6 in.; (Sprint cpe) 94.5 in.; (sed) 98.8 in. **Overall Length:** (Spider) 167.9 in.; (Sprint cpe) 171 in.; (sed) 172.4 in. **Height:** (Spider) 50.8 in.; (Sprint cpe) 52.5 in.; (sed) 56.3 in. **Width:** (Spider) 64.4 in.; (Sprint cpe) 65.5 in.; (sed) 63.7 in. **Front Tread:** (Spider) 52.1 in.; (Sprint cpe/sed) 53.5 in. **Rear Tread:** (Spider) 50.1 in.; (Sprint cpe/sed) 53.4-53.5 in. **Standard Tires:** (Spider) 165HR14; (Sprint cpe) 185/70HR14; (sed) 165SR14.

TECHNICAL: Layout: front-engine, rear-drive. **Transmission:** five-speed manual. **Standard Final Drive Ratio:** (Spider) 4.56:1; (others) 4.1:1. **Steering:** (Spider) recirculating ball or worm and roller; (others) rack and pinion. **Suspension (front):** (2000 Spider) long/short control arms with coil springs and anti-roll bar; (others) long/short control arms with torsion bars and anti-roll bar. **Suspension (rear):** (2000 Spider) rigid axle with three trailing links, coil springs and anti-roll bar; (others) De Dion axle with two trailing links, Watt linkage, coil springs and anti-roll bar. **Brakes:** power front/rear disc. **Body Construction:** steel unibody. **Fuel Tank:** (Spider) 12.2 gal.; (others) 12.9 gal.

MAJOR OPTIONS: Three-speed automatic trans. (sports sedan). Air conditioning ($595). Magnesium alloy wheels ($250). AM/FM stereo with tape player ($240-$290). Sunroof ($290). Hardtop: Spider ($399). Leather interior: Spider ($300); Sprint ($360); sedan ($390). Metallic paint ($165-$215).

PERFORMANCE: Top Speed: (Spider) 115 mph; (Sprint) 116 mph; (sedan w/auto.) about 110 mph. **Acceleration (0-60 mph):** (Sprint) 10.1 sec.; (sedan w/auto.) 13.3 sec. **Acceleration (quarter-mile):** (Sprint) 17.8 sec. (79.5 mph); (sedan w/auto.) 19.8 sec. (74 mph). **Fuel Mileage:** (Spider) 18/25 mpg EPA; (Sprint cpe) 18/25 mpg EPA, about 21 mpg average; (sedan) 19/25 EPA, about 22.5 mpg average.

Manufacturer: Alfa Romeo S.p.A., Milan, Italy.

Distributor: Alfa Romeo Inc., Englewood Cliffs, New Jersey.

HISTORY: Introduced to U.S. market in January 1978 except (sedan) February 1978.

1979 ALFA ROMEO

SPIDER VELOCE — FOUR — Whopping price jumps were the biggest change this year. Though an aging design, the two-seat convertible continued to attract sports-car customers, and changed little this year. A tiny version of Alfa's traditional triangular grille was nearly hidden behind the bumper during this period. Standard equipment included an electronic tachometer, trip odometer, lighter, hand throttle, two-speed heater, hydraulic clutch, chrome exhaust, windshield washer, tilt steering wheel, magnesium wheels, and reclining bucket seats.

SPRINT VELOCE — FOUR — Alfa's GT coupe continued with little change. While the Spider had dual round recessed headlamps, the Sprint Veloce (and sedan) wore quad headlamps. The coupe's triangular grille contained four horizontal bars and a round emblem. Standard equipment was similar to the Spider, plus rocker panel moldings and an electric rear-window heater.

SPORTS SEDAN — FOUR — Production of the four-door sedan continued without significant change, after revision during the 1978 model year that included larger taillamps and new front-end sheetmetal. The traditional-style triangular grille contained six horizontal bars and a round emblem. Standard equipment included an electric clock, heated rear window, and tinted glass. A three-speed automatic transmission was available instead of the standard five-speed manual gearbox, and included a limited-slip differential and pitch control.

I.D. DATA: Alfa Romeo's 14-symbol serial number is located on the right side of the firewall and the windshield post. The first two letters indicate manufacturing plant. The next five symbols identify the model. All the remaining digits form the sequential serial number. Starting serial number: (Spider) AR115410006001; (Sprint) AR116150005001; (Sedan) AR116580002501; (Sedan w/automatic) AR116582002001.

Model	Body Type & Seating	Engine Type/CID	P.O.E. Price	Weight (lbs.)	Prod. Total
SPIDER VELOCE					
	2-dr Conv-2P	I4/120	11195	2455	Note 1
SPRINT VELOCE					
	2-dr Coupe-4P	I4/120	10495	2620	Note 1
SPORTS SEDAN					
	4-dr Spt Sed-5P	I4/120	9695	2700	Note 1

Note 1: A total of 207,514 Alfa Romeos were produced in 1979, including 3,974 series 2000 models and 37,172 Alfetta 2000. Approximately 4,011 were sold in the U.S. that year (2,901 Veloces and 1,110 sedans).

Price Note: Sedan with automatic transmission cost $10,295.

ENGINE DATA: BASE FOUR: Inline, dual-overhead-cam four-cylinder. Aluminum block and head. **Displacement:** 119.7 cu. in. (1962 cc). **Bore & Stroke:** 3.31 x 3.48 (84 x 88.5 mm). **Compression Ratio:** 9.0:1. **Brake Horsepower:** 111 at 5000 rpm. **Torque:** 122 lbs.-ft. at 4000 rpm. Five main bearings. Solid valve lifters. Spica mechanical fuel injection.

CHASSIS DATA: Wheelbase: (Spider) 88.6 in.; (Sprint cpe) 94.5 in.; (sed) 98.8 in. **Overall Length:** (Spider) 168.8 in.; (Sprint cpe) 171 in.; (sed) 177 in. **Height:** (Spider) 48.8 in.; (Sprint cpe) 52.4 in.; (sed) 56.3 in. **Width:** (Spider) 64.1 in.; (Sprint cpe) 65.4 in.; (sed) 64.6 in. **Front Tread:** (Spider) 52.1 in.; (Sprint cpe/sed) 53.5 in. **Rear Tread:** (Spider) 50.1 in.; (Sprint cpe/sed) 53.4 in. **Standard Tires:** (Spider) 165HR14; (Sprint cpe) 185/70HR14; (sed) 165SR14.

TECHNICAL: Layout: front-engine, rear-drive. **Transmission:** five-speed manual; ZF three-speed automatic optional on sedan. **Standard Final Drive Ratio:** (Spider) 4.56:1; (others) 4.1:1. **Steering:** (Spider) recirculating ball or worm and roller; (others) rack and pinion. **Suspension (front):** (Spider) long/short control arms with coil springs and anti-roll bar; (others) long/short control arms with torsion bars and anti-roll bar. **Suspension (rear):** (Spider) rigid axle with three trailing links, coil springs and anti-roll bar; (others) De Dion triangulated axle with two trailing links, Watt linkage, coil springs and anti-roll bar. **Brakes:** power front/rear disc. **Body Construction:** steel unibody.

MAJOR OPTIONS: Three-speed automatic trans.: sedan ($600). Air conditioning ($645). Alloy wheels ($425); standard on Spider. AM/FM stereo with tape player ($290). Sunroof ($398). Leather interior: Spider ($375); Sprint cpe ($450); sed ($490). Hardtop: Spider ($399). Metallic paint: Spider ($200); others ($250). Magnesium wheels: cpe/sed ($370); 185-size tires: sed ($50).

PERFORMANCE: Similar to 1978.

Manufacturer: Alfa Romeo S.p.A., Milan, Italy.

Distributor: Alfa Romeo Inc., Englewood Cliffs, New Jersey.

HISTORY: Introduced to U.S. market in September 1978 except (Sprint) July 1978.

1980 ALFA ROMEO

1980 Alfa Romeo Sprint Veloce GT "Mille Miglia" coupe.

SPIDER VELOCE — FOUR — Only one model, the Spider convertible, was offered this year, at an increased price. Importation of other models was delayed. New door panels on the Spider had armrests and a map pocket. The grille was restyled, and cushioned bucket seats had new upholstery. Behind the seats was a carpeted luggage shelf. Standard equipment included a tachometer, 165HR14 tires on alloy wheels, hand throttle, trip odometer, two-speed heater, windshield washer, wood-rim steering wheel, carpeted trunk, and reclining bucket seats.

I.D. DATA: Alfa Romeo's 14-symbol serial number is located on the right side of the firewall and the windshield post. The first two letters indicate manufacturing plant. The next five symbols identify the model. All the remaining digits form the sequential serial number. Starting serial number: (Spider) AR115410010001.

Model	Body Type & Seating	Engine Type/CID	P.O.E. Price	Weight (lbs.)	Prod. Total
SPIDER VELOCE					
	2-dr Conv-2P	I4/120	13995	2455	Note 1

Note 1: A total of 219,571 Alfa Romeos were produced in 1980, including 5,018 series 2000 models. Close to 3,000 Alfa Romeos were sold in the U.S. that year (2,539 Veloces and 458 sedans).

Model/Price Note: Initial Spider selling price was $12,415. Some sources continued to list the Sprint Veloce coupe and Sports Sedan as available in the U.S. in 1980, priced at $10,995 and $10,595, respectively; see previous listing for details.

ENGINE DATA: BASE FOUR: Inline, dual-overhead-cam four-cylinder. Aluminum block and head. **Displacement:** 119.7 cu. in. (1962 cc). **Bore & Stroke:** 3.31 x 3.48 (84 x 88.5 mm). **Compression Ratio:** 9.0:1. **Brake Horsepower:** 109.5 at 5500 rpm. **Torque:** 121.7 lbs.-ft. at 4000 rpm. Five main bearings. Solid valve lifters. Spica mechanical fuel injection.

CHASSIS DATA: Wheelbase: (Spider) 88.6 in. **Overall Length:** (Spider) 168.8 in. **Height:** (Spider) 48.8 in. **Width:** (Spider) 64.1 in. **Front Tread:** (Spider) 52.1 in. **Rear Tread:** (Spider) 50.1 in. **Standard Tires:** (Spider) 165HR14.

TECHNICAL: Layout: front-engine, rear-drive. **Transmission:** five-speed manual. **Standard Final Drive Ratio:** (Spider) 4.56:1. **Steering:** (Spider) recirculating ball or worm and roller. **Suspension (front):** (Spider) long/short control arms with coil springs and anti-roll bar. **Suspension (rear):** (Spider) rigid axle with three trailing links, coil springs and anti-roll bar. **Brakes:** power front/rear disc. **Body Construction:** steel unibody.

MAJOR OPTIONS: Leather interior: Spider ($495). Metallic paint: Spider ($200). AM/FM stereo radio w/cassette player: Spider ($455). Removable hardtop: Spider ($421).

Manufacturer: Alfa Romeo S.p.A., Milan, Italy.

Distributor: Alfa Romeo Inc., Englewood Cliffs, New Jersey.

HISTORY: Introduced to U.S. market in May 1980.

1981 ALFA ROMEO

SPIDER — FOUR — Production of the familiar Alfa Romeo convertible continued with no significant change. Standard equipment included a limited-slip differential, deep pile carpeting, digital clock, hydraulic clutch, wood console, woodgrain steering wheel, door panels with map pocket, chrome exhaust, tinted glass, twin electric remote-control mir-

rors, reclining bucket seats, tachometer, trip odometer, power windows, and intermittent wipers. This year, 185/70HR14 tires rode on cast alloy wheels.

GTV-6 — V-6 — In spring 1981 a coupe was back again in Alfa Romeo's U.S. lineup, now called GTV-6 (or GTV6). Appearance was similar to its predecessors, with a steep rear window in its fastback body. Under the hood, however, was a new 60-degree, single-overhead-cam V-6 engine. Displacing 2492 cc, the V-6 had toothed-belt cam drive and a cam for each bank, operating the valves via tappets, pushrods and rocker arms. Standard equipment included leather upholstery, air conditioning, and a tilt steering wheel. The speedometer, formerly at the center of the dashboard, now sat in front of the driver. A twin-disc clutch was used with the five-speed manual gearbox. Standard equipment was similar to the Spider's, but added air conditioning, metallic paint, magnesium wheels, and leather bucket seats.

I.D. DATA: Alfa Romeo's 17-symbol Vehicle Identification Number (VIN) is on the upper left of the instrument panel, visible through the windshield. Symbols 1-3 ('ZAR') identify the country and manufacturer. Symbols 4-8 denote the model ('BA541' = Spider Veloce; 'AA669' = GTV-6). Next comes a check digit. Symbol 10 indicates the model year ('B' = 1981). Symbol 11 identifies the assembly plant ('1' = Milan, Italy). The final six digits form the sequential serial number. Starting serial number: (Spider) ZARBA541⅛s1000000; (GTV-6) ZARAA669-B1001001.

Model	Body Type & Seating	Engine Type/CID	P.O.E. Price	Weight (lbs.)	Prod. Total
SPIDER VELOCE					
BA541	2-dr Conv-2P	I4/120	14895	2548	Note 1
GTV-6					
AA669	2-dr Coupe-4P	V6/152	16983	2823	Note 1

Note 1: A total of 197,287 Alfa Romeos were produced in 1981. About 2,294 were sold in the U.S. (1,579 Spiders, 606 GTV-6, and 109 sedans).

ENGINE DATA: BASE FOUR (Spider): Inline, dual-overhead-cam four-cylinder. Aluminum block and head. **Displacement:** 119.7 cu. in. (1962 cc). **Bore & Stroke:** 3.31 x 3.48 (84 x 88.5 mm). **Compression Ratio:** 9.0:1. **Brake Horsepower:** 111 at 5500 rpm. **Torque:** 116.3 lbs.-ft. at 2500 rpm. Five main bearings. Solid valve lifters. Fuel injection.

BASE V-6 (GTV-6): Single-overhead-cam 60-degree "vee" type six-cylinder. Aluminum block and head. **Displacement:** 152.0 cu. in. (2492 cc). **Bore & Stroke:** 3.46 x 2.69 (88 x 68.3 mm). **Compression Ratio:** 9.0:1. **Brake Horsepower:** 154 (SAE net) at 5500 rpm. **Torque:** 152 lbs.-ft. at 3200 rpm. Four main bearings. Solid valve lifters. Bosch L-Jetronic fuel injection.

CHASSIS DATA: Wheelbase: (Spider) 88.6 in.; (GTV-6) 94.5 in. **Overall Length:** (Spider) 168.8 in.; (GTV-6) 167.7 in. **Height:** (Spider) 48.8 in.; (GTV-6) 52.4 in. **Width:** (Spider) 64.1 in.; (GTV-6) 65.5 in. **Front Tread:** (Spider) 52.1 in.; (GTV-6) 54 in. **Rear Tread:** (Spider) 50.1 in.; (GTV-6) 53.2 in. **Wheel Type:** (GTV-6) light alloy. **Standard Tires:** (Spider) 185/70HR14; (GTV-6) 195/60HR15.

TECHNICAL: Layout: front-engine, rear-drive. **Transmission:** five-speed manual. **Standard Final Drive Ratio:** (Spider) 4.56:1; (GTV-6) 4.1:1. **Steering:** (Spider) recirculating ball or worm and roller; (GTV-6) rack and pinion. **Suspension (front):** (Spider) long/short control arms with coil springs and anti-roll bar; (GTV-6) lower A-arms, upper transverse arms and trailing links, torsion bars and anti-roll bar. **Suspension (rear):** (Spider) rigid axle with coil springs and anti-roll bar; (GTV-6) De Dion rigid axle with angled trailing links, transverse Watt linkage, coil springs and anti-roll bar. **Brakes:** (Spider) front/rear disc; (GTV-6) front/rear disc, inboard rear. **Body Construction:** steel unibody. **Fuel Tank:** (Spider) 12.2 gal.; (GTV-6) 20 gal.

MAJOR OPTIONS: AM/FM stereo with tape player ($455). Leather interior: Spider ($495). Metallic paint ($200).

PERFORMANCE: Top Speed: (GTV-6) 125 mph. **Acceleration (0-60 mph):** (GTV-6) 8.4 sec. **Fuel Mileage:** (Spider) 20 mpg EPA; (GTV-6) 17 mpg EPA.

Manufacturer: Alfa Romeo S.p.A., Milan, Italy.

Distributor: Alfa Romeo Inc., Englewood Cliffs, New Jersey.

1982 ALFA ROMEO

SPIDER VELOCE — FOUR — Alfa Romeos destined for the U.S. market now had Bosch fuel injection. Otherwise, the long-lived two-seater convertible continued with little change. A special edition Spider sold for less and lacked the standard model's dual electric mirrors, leather upholstery, alloy wheels, and power windows. It also had a vinyl top (versus cloth for the standard model). Both came with tinted glass, a windshield antenna, limited-slip differential, deep pile carpeting, reclining bucket seats, woodgrain steering wheel, intermittent wipers, and 195/70HR14 tires on pressed steel wheels.

1982 Alfa Romeo GTV6. (William Siuru Jr.)

GTV-6 — V-6 — Production of the coupe introduced in the U.S. for 1981 continued with no major change. Standard equipment included air conditioning, a quartz clock, electric rear defogger, locking fuel filler door, front spoiler, sport tilt steering wheel, and 195/60HR15 tires on light alloy wheels. A Balocco special edition added sport graphics, red carpeting, black leather upholstery and steering wheel, a manual sunroof, and specially-painted alloy wheels.

I.D. DATA: Alfa Romeo's 17-symbol Vehicle Identification Number (VIN) is on the upper left of the instrument panel, visible through the windshield. Symbols 1-3 ('ZAR') identify the country and manufacturer. Symbols 4-8 denote the model ('BA541' = Spider Veloce; 'AA669' = GTV-6). Next comes a check digit. Symbol 10 indicates the model year ('C' = 1982). Symbol 11 identifies the assembly plant ('1' = Milan, Italy). The final six digits form the sequential serial number.

Model	Body Type & Seating	Engine Type/CID	P.O.E. Price	Weight (lbs.)	Prod. Total
SPIDER VELOCE					
BA541	2-dr Conv-2P	I4/120	14990	2548	Note 1
GTV-6					
AA669	2-dr Coupe-4P	V6/152	17455	2823	Note 1

Note 1: A total of 188,773 Alfa Romeos were produced in 1982. Approximately 2,193 Alfas were sold in the U.S. that year (1,440 Spiders, 726 GTV-6 coupes, and 27 sedans).

Price Note: Spider Veloce special edition cost $13,495; the Balocco special edition GTV-6 sold for $18,105.

ENGINE DATA: BASE FOUR (Spider): Inline, dual-overhead-cam four-cylinder. Aluminum block and head. **Displacement:** 119.7 cu. in. (1962 cc). **Bore & Stroke:** 3.31 x 3.48 (84 x 88.5 mm). **Compression Ratio:** 9.0:1. **Brake Horsepower:** 111 at 5000 rpm. **Torque:** 116.3 lbs.-ft. at 2500 rpm. Five main bearings. Solid valve lifters. Bosch electronic fuel injection.

BASE V-6 (GTV-6): Single-overhead-cam 60-degree "vee" type six-cylinder. Aluminum block and head. **Displacement:** 152.0 cu. in. (2492 cc). **Bore & Stroke:** 3.46 x 2.69 (88 x 68.3 mm). **Compression Ratio:** 9.0:1. **Brake Horsepower:** 154 (SAE net) at 5500 rpm. **Torque:** 152 lbs.-ft. at 3200 rpm. Four main bearings. Solid valve lifters. Bosch L-Jetronic fuel injection.

CHASSIS DATA: Wheelbase: (Spider) 88.6 in.; (GTV-6) 94.5 in. **Overall Length:** (Spider) 168.8 in.; (GTV-6) 167.7 in. **Height:** (Spider) 48.8 in.; (GTV-6) 52.4 in. **Width:** (Spider) 64.1 in.; (GTV-6) 65.5 in. **Front Tread:** (Spider) 52.1 in.; (GTV-6) 54 in. **Rear Tread:** (Spider) 50.1 in.; (GTV-6) 53.2 in. **Wheel Type:** (GTV-6) light alloy. **Standard Tires:** (Spider) 195/70HR14; (GTV-6) 195/60HR15.

TECHNICAL: Layout: front-engine, rear-drive. **Transmission:** five-speed manual. **Standard Final Drive Ratio:** (Spider) 4.56:1; (GTV-6) 3.42:1. **Steering:** (Spider) recirculating ball or worm and roller; (GTV-6) rack and pinion. **Suspension (front):** (Spider) long/short control arms with coil springs and anti-roll bar; (GTV-6) lower A-arms, upper transverse arms and trailing links, torsion bars and anti-roll bar. **Suspension (rear):** (Spider) rigid axle with coil springs and anti-roll bar; (GTV-6) De Dion rigid axle with angled trailing links, transverse Watt linkage, coil springs and anti-roll bar. **Brakes:** (Spider) front/rear disc; (GTV-6) front/rear disc, inboard rear. **Body Construction:** steel unibody. **Fuel Tank:** (Spider) 12.2 gal.; (GTV-6) 20 gal.

MAJOR OPTIONS: Sunroof (GTV-6). Metallic paint ($200).

PERFORMANCE: Top Speed: (GTV-6) 125 mph. **Acceleration (0-60 mph):** (GTV-6) 8.4 sec. **Fuel Mileage:** (Spider) 22 mpg EPA; (GTV-6) 18 mpg EPA.

Manufacturer: Alfa Romeo S.p.A., Milan, Italy.

Distributor: Alfa Romeo Inc., Englewood Cliffs, New Jersey.

1983 ALFA ROMEO

SPIDER — FOUR — Once again, little change was evident in Alfa Romeo's two-seat convertible.

GTV-6 — V-6 — Production of the four-seat coupe continued with little change.

I.D. DATA: Alfa Romeo's 17-symbol Vehicle Identification Number (VIN) is on the upper left of the instrument panel, visible through the windshield. Symbols 1-3 ('ZAR') identify the country and manufacturer. Symbols 4-8 denote the model ('BA541' = Spider Veloce; 'AA669' = GTV-6). Next comes a check digit. Symbol 10 indicates the model year ('D' = 1983). Symbol 11 identifies the assembly plant ('1' = Milan, Italy). The final six digits form the sequential serial number.

Model	Body Type & Seating	Engine Type/CID	P.O.E. Price	Weight (lbs.)	Prod. Total
SPIDER VELOCE					
BA541	2-dr Roadster-2P	I4/120	15495	2548	Note 1
GTV-6					
AA669	2-dr Coupe-4P	V6/152	17995	2823	Note 1

Note 1: A total of 206,926 Alfa Romeos were produced in 1983. Approximately 3,002 were sold in the U.S. during that year.

ENGINE DATA: BASE FOUR (Spider): Inline, dual-overhead-cam four-cylinder. Aluminum block and head. **Displacement:** 119.7 cu. in. (1962 cc). **Bore & Stroke:** 3.31 x 3.48 (84 x 88.5 mm). **Compression Ratio:** 9.0:1. **Brake Horsepower:** 115 at 5500 rpm. **Torque:** 119.4 lbs.-ft. at 2750 rpm. Five main bearings. Solid valve lifters. Bosch electronic fuel injection.

BASE V-6 (GTV-6): Single-overhead-cam 60-degree "vee" type six-cylinder. Aluminum block and head. **Displacement:** 152.0 cu. in. (2492 cc). **Bore & Stroke:** 3.46 x 2.69 (88 x 68.3 mm). **Compression Ratio:** 9.0:1. **Brake Horsepower:** 154 (SAE net) at 5500 rpm. **Torque:** 152 lbs.-ft. at 3200 rpm. Four main bearings. Solid valve lifters. Bosch L-Jetronic fuel injection.

CHASSIS DATA: Wheelbase: (Spider) 88.6 in.; (GTV-6) 94.5 in. **Overall Length:** (Spider) 168.8 in.; (GTV-6) 171.2 in. **Height:** (Spider) 48.8 in.; (GTV-6) 52.4 in. **Width:** (Spider) 64.1 in.; (GTV-6) 65.5 in. **Front Tread:** (Spider) 52.1 in.; (GTV-6) 54 in. **Rear Tread:** (Spider) 50.1 in.; (GTV-6) 53.2 in. **Wheel Type:** (GTV-6) light alloy. **Standard Tires:** (Spider) 185/70HR14; (GTV-6) 195/60HR15.

TECHNICAL: Layout: front-engine, rear-drive. **Transmission:** five-speed manual. **Steering:** (Spider) recirculating ball; (GTV-6) rack and pinion. **Suspension (front):** (Spider) long/short control arms with coil springs and anti-roll bar; (GTV-6) lower A-arms, upper transverse arms and trailing links, torsion bars and anti-roll bar. **Suspension (rear):** (Spider) rigid axle with coil springs and anti-roll bar; (GTV-6) De Dion rigid axle with angled trailing links, transverse Watt linkage, coil springs and anti-roll bar. **Brakes:** (Spider) front/rear disc; (GTV-6) front/rear disc, inboard rear. **Body Construction:** steel unibody. Fuel Tank: (Spider) 12.2 gal.; (GTV-6) 17 gal.

MAJOR OPTIONS: Air conditioning (Spider). Metallic paint (Spider). Sunroof (GTV-6).

PERFORMANCE: Top Speed: (GTV-6) 125 mph. **Acceleration (0-60 mph):** (GTV-6) 8.4 sec. **Fuel Mileage:** (Spider) 23 mpg EPA; (GTV-6) 22 mpg EPA.

Manufacturer: Alfa Romeo S.p.A., Milan, Italy.

Distributor: Alfa Romeo Inc., Englewood Cliffs, New Jersey.

1984 ALFA ROMEO

SPIDER VELOCE — FOUR — Production of the two-seat convertible continued with little change, with appearance still similar to the Duetto introduced in the mid-1960s. This version had an integral air dam and rear spoiler, as well as vent windows. Standard equipment also included Campagnolo "Daytona" alloy wheels, power windows, tinted glass, reclining leather seats, an electronic tachometer, digital clock, and power remote mirrors.

GTV-6 — V-6 — Little change appeared in the four-seat coupe. Standard equipment included air conditioning, tinted glass, power front windows, rear defroster, alloy wheels, an electronic speedometer and tachometer, three-speed intermittent wipers, reclining leather seats, adjustable steering column, and a leather-rimmed steering wheel and gearshift knob.

I.D. DATA: Alfa Romeo's 17-symbol Vehicle Identification Number (VIN) is on the upper left of the instrument panel, visible through the windshield. Symbols 1-3 ('ZAR') identify the country and manufacturer. Symbols 4-8 denote the model ('BA541' = Spider Veloce; 'AA669' = GTV-6). Next comes a check digit. Symbol 10 indicates the model year ('E' = 1984). Symbol 11 identifies the assembly plant ('1' = Milan, Italy). The final six digits form the sequential serial number.

Model	Body Type & Seating	Engine Type/CID	P.O.E. Price	Weight (lbs.)	Prod. Total
SPIDER VELOCE					
BA541	2-dr Roadster-2P	I4/120	16000	2548	Note 1
GTV-6					
AA669	2-dr Coupe-4P	V6/152	19000	2823	Note 1

Note 1: A total of 200,103 Alfa Romeos were produced in 1984. Approximately 3,702 were sold in the U.S. during that year.

ENGINE DATA: BASE FOUR (Spider): Inline, dual-overhead-cam four-cylinder. Aluminum block and head. **Displacement:** 119.7 cu. in. (1962 cc). **Bore & Stroke:** 3.31 x 3.48 (84 x 88.5 mm). **Compression Ratio:** 9.0:1. **Brake Horsepower:** 115 at 5500 rpm. **Torque:** 119.4 lbs.-ft. at 2750 rpm. Five main bearings. Solid valve lifters. Bosch L-Jetronic fuel injection. Bosch digital ignition.

BASE V-6 (GTV-6): Single-overhead-cam 60-degree "vee" type six-cylinder. Aluminum block and head. **Displacement:** 152.0 cu. in. (2492 cc). **Bore & Stroke:** 3.46 x 2.69 (88 x 68.3 mm). **Compression Ratio:** 9.0:1. **Brake Horsepower:** 154 (SAE net) at 5500 rpm. **Torque:** 152 lbs.-ft. at 3200 rpm. Four main bearings. Solid valve lifters. Bosch L-Jetronic fuel injection. Bosch digital ignition.

CHASSIS DATA: Wheelbase: (Spider) 88.6 in.; (GTV-6) 94.5 in. **Overall Length:** (Spider) 168.8 in.; (GTV-6) 171.2 in. **Height:** (Spider) 48.8 in.; (GTV-6) 52.4 in. **Width:** (Spider) 64.1 in.; (GTV-6) 65.5 in. **Front Tread:** (Spider) 52.1 in.; (GTV-6) 54 in. **Rear Tread:** (Spider) 50.1 in.; (GTV-6) 53.2 in. **Wheel Type:** (GTV-6) light alloy. **Standard Tires:** (Spider) 185/70HR14 Michelin XVS; (GTV-6) 195/60HR15 Pirelli P6.

TECHNICAL: Layout: front-engine, rear-drive. **Transmission:** five-speed manual. **Steering:** (Spider) recirculating ball; (GTV-6) rack and pinion. **Suspension (front):** (Spider) long/short control arms with coil springs and anti-roll bar; (GTV-6) lower A-arms, upper transverse arms and trailing links, torsion bars and anti-roll bar. **Suspension (rear):** (Spider) rigid axle with coil springs and anti-roll bar; (GTV-6) De Dion rigid axle with angled trailing links, transverse Watt linkage, coil springs and anti-roll bar. **Brakes:** (Spider) front/rear disc; (GTV-6) front/rear disc, inboard rear. **Body Construction:** steel unibody. **Fuel Tank:** (Spider) 12.2 gal.; (GTV-6) 17 gal.

MAJOR OPTIONS: Air conditioning: Spider ($995). Metallic paint: Spider ($200). Sunroof (GTV-6).

PERFORMANCE: Top Speed: (GTV-6) 125 mph. **Acceleration (0-60 mph):** (GTV-6) 8.4 sec. **Fuel Mileage:** (Spider) 23 mpg EPA; (GTV-6) 21 mpg EPA.

Manufacturer: Alfa Romeo S.p.A., Milan, Italy.

Distributor: Alfa Romeo Inc., Englewood Cliffs, New Jersey.

1985 ALFA ROMEO

SPIDER GRADUATE — FOUR — Nearly two decades after Dustin Hoffman drove an Alfa Romeo in the 1967 movie *The Graduate*, the company came out with a model by that name. It was a lower-priced version of the Spider Veloce. Standard equipment included the 115-bhp, 2.0-liter twin-cam four-cylinder engine, five-speed gearbox with wood gearshift knob, four-wheel disc brakes, tinted glass, intermittent wipers, a hand-finished wood steering wheel, limited-slip differential, and 185/70HR14 Michelin XVS tires on steel sport wheels with stainless steel trim rings. A 'Graduate' insignia went on the rear deck, and side stripes were included.

SPIDER VELOCE — FOUR — Alfa's two-seat convertible had no major changes for 1985, except for new standard wheels and a broader selection of colors for the body and interior. As before, power came from a twin-cam 2.0-liter four-cylinder engine, producing 115 horsepower and hooked to a five-speed (overdrive) manual gearbox. In addition to the "Graduate" equipment, the Veloce included leather-faced seats, power windows, a digital clock, bronze-tinted windshield and side windows, and Campagnola Daytona alloy wheels. A 'Spider 2.0' deck insignia and Spider Veloce script on the bodyside provided identification.

GTV-6 — V-6 — The Alfa four-seat coupe continued with no major change. Under its hood was a 2.5-liter V-6, rated 154 horsepower. Only a five-speed manual gearbox was offered. Standard equipment was similar to the Spider, but included air conditioning, an electric rear-window defroster, leather-wrapped steering wheel, and 195/60HR15 Pirelli P6 radial tires.

I.D. DATA: Alfa Romeo's 17-digit Vehicle Identification Number is on the upper left of the dashboard, visible through the windshield. Symbols 1-3 ('ZAR') indicate country and manufacturer. Symbols 4-8 denote the car line, configuration, and equipment level ('BA541' = Spider; 'AA669' = GTV-6). Next comes a check digit. Symbol ten indicates model year ('F' = 1985). Symbol 11 identifies the assembly plant. The final six digits form the sequential serial number, starting with 000001.

Model	Body Type & Seating	Engine Type/CID	P.O.E. Price	Weight (lbs.)	Prod. Total
SPIDER VELOCE					
BA541	2-dr Conv-2P	I4/120	16500	2548	Note 1
SPIDER GRADUATE					
BA541	2-dr Conv-2P	I4/120	13495	2548	Note 1
GTV-6					
AA669	2-dr Coupe-4P	V6/152	16500	2823	Note 1

Note 1: A total of 157,825 Alfa Romeos were produced in 1985. Approximately 4,502 were sold in the U.S. during that year.

ENGINE DATA: BASE FOUR (Spider, Graduate): Inline, dual-overhead-cam four-cylinder. Aluminum block and head. **Displacement:** 119.7 cu. in. (1962 cc). **Bore & Stroke:** 3.31 x 3.48 (84 x 88.5 mm). **Compression Ratio:** 9.0:1. **Brake Horsepower:** 115 at 5500 rpm. **Torque:** 119 lbs.-ft. at 2750 rpm. Five main bearings. Solid valve lifters. Bosch electronic fuel injection. Bosch ignition.
BASE V-6 (GTV-6): 60-degree, single-overhead-cam V-6. Aluminum block and head. **Displacement:** 152.0 cu. in. (2492 cc). **Bore & Stroke:** 3.46 x 2.69 (88 x 68.3 mm). **Compression Ratio:** 9.0:1. **Brake Horsepower:** 154 at 5500 rpm. **Torque:** 152 lbs.-ft. at 3200 rpm. Four main bearings. Solid valve lifters. Bosch L-Jetronic fuel injection.

CHASSIS DATA: Wheelbase: (conv.) 88.6 in.; (GTV-6) 94.5 in. **Overall Length:** (conv.) 168.8 in.; (GTV-6) 171.2 in. **Height:** (conv.) 48.8 in.; (GTV-6) 52.4 in. **Width:** (conv.) 64.1 in.; (GTV-6) 65.5 in. **Front Tread:** (conv.) 52.1 in.; (GTV-6) 54.0 in. **Rear Tread:** (conv.) 50.1 in.; (GTV-6) 53.2 in. **Wheel Type:** (Graduate) steel; (Spider, GTV-6) alloy. **Standard Tires:** (Spider/Graduate) 185/70HRx14; (GTV-6) 195/60HR15.

TECHNICAL: Layout: front-engine, rear-drive. **Transmission:** five-speed manual. **Standard Final Drive Ratio:** 4.10:1. **Steering:** (Spider) worm and roller; (GTV-6) rack and pinion. **Suspension (front):** (Spider) upper/lower control arms, coil springs and stabilizer bar; (GTV-6) upper/lower control arms, torsion bars and stabilizer bar. **Suspension (rear):** (Spider) rigid axle with coil springs and stabilizer bar; (GTV-6) De Dion axle with Watt linkage, coil springs and stabilizer bar. **Brakes:** front/rear disc. **Body Construction:** steel unibody. **Fuel Tank:** (conv.) 12.2 gal.; (GTV-6) 17.0 gallon.

MAJOR OPTIONS: AM/FM stereo with cassette tape player: Spider/Graduate ($644). Air conditioning: Spider/Graduate ($995). Leather seating (GTV-6). Sliding sunroof (GTV-6). Metallic paint: Spider ($200).

Manufacturer: Alfa Romeo S.p.A., Milan, Italy.

Distributor: Alfa Romeo Inc., Englewood Cliffs, New Jersey.

HISTORY: Introduced to U.S. market in October 1984.

Note: Although the "Graduate" and later "Quadrifoglio" models were variants of the Spider Veloce convertible, they were typically referred to by the single name, not including a "Spider" prefix.

1986 ALFA ROMEO

SPIDER GRADUATE — FOUR — Alfa's "entry level" Spider roadster (convertible) continued with little change, after its debut for 1985. Powerplant was again the 2.0-liter twin-cam four, driving a five-speed (overdrive) manual transmission. Standard equipment included power four-wheel disc brakes, bronze tinted glass, courtesy lights (with delay), underhood and trunk lights, dual power mirrors, hand-finished mahogany steering wheel, intermittent wipers, and tachometer. The body featured a front air dam and rear spoiler, as well as halogen headlamps. Styled steel wheels held 185/70HR14 Michelin XVS tires.

SPIDER VELOCE — FOUR — Mechanically identical to the Graduate, the step-up Spider added leather seating, power windows, a digital clock, and Campagnolo Daytona alloy wheels.

SPIDER QUADRIFOGLIO — FOUR — A new name for an upgraded version of the familiar convertible stood for "Clover Leaf," which happened to serve as the logo for Alfa's racing activities. Equipment was similar to the Veloce, but added such luxuries as air conditioning, an AM/FM stereo radio with cassette player, aerodynamic trim pieces, and 195/60HR15 Pirelli P6 tires on aluminum wheels. It was offered either with or without a Pininfarina hardtop, which included a rear defogger and added $900 to the price.

GTV-6 — V-6 — No significant change was evident in Alfa's 2+2 coupe, which was powered by a 2.5-liter V-6. Standard equipment included power steering, air conditioning, rear defogger, leather steering wheel and gearshift knob, an adjustable steering column, and 195/60VR15 Pirelli P6 tires on alloy wheels.

I.D. DATA: Alfa Romeo's 17-digit Vehicle Identification Number is on the upper left of the dashboard, visible through the windshield. Symbols 1-3 ('ZAR') indicate country and manufacturer. Symbols 4-8 denote the car line, configuration, and equipment level ('BA541' = Spider; 'AA669' = GTV-6). Next comes a check digit. Symbol ten indicates model year ('G' = 1986). Symbol 11 identifies the assembly plant. The final six digits form the sequential serial number.

Model	Body Type & Seating	Engine Type/CID	P.O.E. Price	Weight (lbs.)	Prod. Total
SPIDER VELOCE					
BA541	2-dr Conv-2P	I4/120	16995	2548	Note 1
SPIDER GRADUATE					
BA541	2-dr Conv-2P	I4/120	13995	2548	Note 1
SPIDER QUADRIFOGLIO					
BA541	2-dr Conv-2P	I4/120	20500	2548	Note 1
GTV-6					
AA669	2-dr Coupe-4P	V6/152	16500	2823	Note 1

Note 1: A total of 168,074 Alfa Romeos were produced in 1986. Approximately 8,201 were sold in the U.S. during that year.

Price Note: Quadrifoglio without hardtop cost $19,600.

ENGINE DATA: BASE FOUR (Spider): Inline, dual-overhead-cam four-cylinder. Aluminum block and head. **Displacement:** 119.7 cu. in. (1962 cc). **Bore & Stroke:** 3.31 x 3.48 (84 x 88.5 mm). **Compression Ratio:** 9.0:1. **Brake Horsepower:** 115 at 5500 rpm. **Torque:** 119 lbs.-ft. at 2750 rpm. Five main bearings. Solid valve lifters. Bosch L-Jetronic fuel injection. Bosch digital ignition.

BASE V-6 (GTV-6): 60-degree, single-overhead-cam V-6. Aluminum block and head. **Displacement:** 152.0 cu. in. (2492 cc). **Bore & Stroke:** 3.46 x 2.69 (88 x 68.3 mm). **Compression Ratio:** 9.0:1. **Brake Horsepower:** 154 at 5500 rpm. **Torque:** 152 lbs.-ft. at 3200 rpm. Four main bearings. Solid valve lifters. Bosch L-Jetronic fuel injection. Bosch digital ignition.

CHASSIS DATA: Wheelbase: (Spider) 88.6 in.; (GTV-6) 94.5 in. **Overall Length:** (Spider) 168.8 in.; (GTV-6) 171.2 in. **Height:** (Spider) 48.8 in.; (GTV-6) 52.4 in. **Width:** (Spider) 64.1 in.; (GTV-6) 65.5 in. **Front Tread:** (Spider) 52.1 in.; (GTV-6) 54.0 in. **Rear Tread:** (Spider) 50.1 in.; (GTV-6) 53.2 in. **Wheel Type:** (Graduate) styled steel; (others) alloy. **Standard Tires:** (Spider) 185/70HR14 Michelin XVS; (GTV-6) 195/60VR15 Pirelli P6.

TECHNICAL: Layout: front-engine, rear-drive. **Transmission:** five-speed manual. **Standard Final Drive Ratio:** 4.10:1. **Steering:** (Spider) ZF worm and roller; (GTV-6) rack and pinion. **Suspension (front):** (Spider) upper/lower control arms, coil springs and stabilizer bar; (GTV-6) upper/lower control arms, torsion bars and stabilizer bar. **Suspension (rear):** (Spider) rigid axle with coil springs and stabilizer bar; (GTV-6) De Dion axle with Watt linkage, coil springs and stabilizer bar. **Brakes:** front/rear disc. **Body Construction:** steel unibody. **Fuel Tank:** (Spider) 12.2 gal.; (GTV-6) 17.0 gallon.

MAJOR OPTIONS: AM/FM stereo with tape player ($644). Air conditioning: Spider/Graduate ($995). Metallic paint: Spider/GTV-6 ($200). Reclining leather bucket seats: GTV-6 ($750). Sliding sunroof: GTV-6 ($500).

Manufacturer: Alfa Romeo S.p.A., Milan, Italy.

Distributor: Alfa Romeo Inc., Englewood Cliffs, New Jersey.

HISTORY: Introduced to U.S. market in October 1985.

1987 ALFA ROMEO

SPIDER — FOUR — Offered again in three price levels, the two-seat convertible continued with little change. Base model was the "Graduate;" next, the Spider Veloce; with Quadrifoglio the most luxurious, including standard air conditioning. Appearance and equipment were the same as 1986.

Note: Alfa's GTV-6 2+2 coupe was dropped after 1986.

MILANO — V-6 — A new Alfa Romeo four-door sedan arrived on the U.S. market in June 1986, offered in three price levels: Silver, Gold, and Platinum. Each carried the same 2.5-liter V-6 as the GTV-6 coupe, initially offered only with the five-speed manual gearbox; later, with optional four-speed automatic. Based on the home-market Alfa 90, the new model was intended as a rival to such "yuppie" favorites as the BMW 3-series and Saab 900, joining a rising number of upscale sports sedans. The new sedan rode a 98.8-inch wheelbase and measured 170.5 inches overall. Appearance was similar to the Alfetta sold in the 1970s, but with a more rounded (less angular) look. Standard equipment on the Silver model included power brakes and steering, foglamps (front and rear), headlamp washers, rear defogger, leather-wrapped steering wheel (with tilt/telescope), tachometer, clock, power windows and door locks, dual power mirrors, remote trunk release, passenger vanity mirror, bronze tinted glass, and front/rear lighters. Front sport seats wore cloth upholstery. Steel wheels held 195/60VR14 tires. Milano Gold added a power driver's seat, lighted passenger vanity mirror, power antenna, and alloy wheels. The top-rung Milano Platinum came with Bosch anti-lock braking, a power sunroof, rear-seat headphone jacks, and 195/55VR15 tires.

I.D. DATA: Alfa Romeo's 17-digit Vehicle Identification Number is on the upper left of the dashboard, visible through the windshield. Symbols 1-3 ('ZAR') indicate country and manufacturer. Symbols 4-8 denote the car line, configuration, and equipment level. Next comes a check digit. Symbol ten indicates model year ('H' = 1987). Symbol 11 identifies the assembly plant. The final six digits form the sequential serial number.

Model	Body Type & Seating	Engine Type/CID	P.O.E. Price	Weight (lbs.)	Prod. Total
SPIDER VELOCE					
BA558	2-dr Conv-2P	I4/120	16995	2548	Note 1
SPIDER GRADUATE					
BA564	2-dr Conv-2P	I4/120	13995	2548	Note 1
SPIDER QUADRIFOGLIO					
BA556	2-dr Conv-2P	I4/120	20500	2548	Note 1
MILANO (Silver, Gold, Platinum)					
DA114	4-dr Sed (slvr)-5P	V6/152	12850	2907	Note 1
DA116	4-dr Sed (gold)-5P	V6/152	14500	2907	Note 1
DA136	4-dr Sed (plat)-5P	V6/152	18995	2907	Note 1

Note 1: A total of 192,024 Alfa Romeos were produced in 1987. Approximately 6,320 were sold in the U.S. during that year.

Price Note: Quadrifoglio with manual transmission cost $19,600. Prices rose during the year.

ENGINE DATA: BASE FOUR (Spider): Inline, dual-overhead-cam four-cylinder. Aluminum block and head. **Displacement:** 119.7 cu. in. (1962 cc). **Bore & Stroke:** 3.31 x 3.48 (84 x 88.5 mm). **Compression Ratio:** 9.0:1. **Brake Horsepower:** 115 at 5500 rpm. **Torque:** 119 lbs.-ft. at 2750 rpm. Five main bearings. Solid valve lifters. Port fuel injection.

BASE V-6 (Milano): Single-overhead-cam 60-degree V-6. Aluminum block and head. **Displacement:** 152.0 cu. in. (2492 cc). **Bore & Stroke:** 3.46 x 2.69 (88 x 68.3 mm). **Compression Ratio:** 9.0:1. **Brake Horsepower:** 154 at 5500 rpm. **Torque:** 152 lbs.-ft. at 3200 rpm. Four main bearings. Solid valve lifters. Port fuel injection.

CHASSIS DATA: Wheelbase: (Spider) 88.6 in.; (Milano) 98.8 in. **Overall Length:** (Spider) 168.6 in.; (Milano) 170.5 in. **Height:** (Spider) 48.8 in.; (Milano) 53.1 in. **Width:** (Spider) 64.1 in.; (Milano) 64.2 in. **Front Tread:** (Spider) 52.1 in.; (Milano) 53.9 in. **Rear Tread:** (Spider) 50.1 in.; (Milano) 53.5 in. **Wheel Type:** (Graduate, Milano Silver) steel; (Quadrifoglio) aluminum; (others) alloy. **Standard Tires:** (Spider) 185/70HR14 Michelin XVS; (Quadrifoglio) 195/60HR15 Pirelli P6; (Milano Gold/Silver) 195/60VR14; (Milano Platinum) 195/55VR15.

TECHNICAL: Layout: front-engine, rear-drive. **Transmission:** five-speed manual. **Standard Final Drive Ratio:** 4.10:1. **Steering:** (Spider) worm and roller; (Milano) rack and pinion. **Suspension (front):** (Spider) upper/lower control arms, coil springs and stabilizer bar; (Milano) parallel transverse links with torsion bars. **Suspension (rear):** (Spider) rigid axle with coil springs and stabilizer bar; (Milano) De Dion axle with Watt linkage, coil springs and stabilizer bar. **Brakes:** front/rear disc; ABS on Milano Platinum. **Body Construction:** steel unibody. **Fuel Tank:** (Spider) 12.2 gal.; (Milano) 17.6 gallon.

MAJOR OPTIONS: Air conditioning: Spider/Graduate ($995): Milano ($850). AM/FM stereo with cassette player ($645). Sliding sunroof: Milano Silver/Gold ($795). Leather seats: Milano ($750). Metallic paint: Spider Veloce ($200-$275); Milano ($350).
Manufacturer: Alfa Romeo S.p.A., Milan, Italy.
Distributor: Alfa Romeo Inc., Englewood Cliffs, New Jersey.
HISTORY: Introduced to U.S. market in October 1986 except (Milano) April 1986. In 1987, the Alfa Romeo company was taken over by Fiat.

1988 ALFA ROMEO

SPIDER — FOUR — For yet another year, Alfa's two-seat convertible continued with little change. Once again, it was offered in three price and equipment levels: lowest-priced "Graduate," mid-level Spider Veloce (which added leather sport seats and power windows), and top-ranked Quadrifoglio. The latter came with standard air conditioning and AM/FM stereo with cassette player, larger wheels/tires, and could be purchased with or without a removable hardtop. Powertrain continued as before: the 2.0-liter four, with five-speed manual gearbox.
MILANO — V-6 — Another version of the Milano four-door sedan, introduced for 1987, arrived this year with a larger (3.0-liter) V-6 under its hood, producing 183 horsepower. Offered only with five-speed manual shift, the Verde (green) had standard anti-lock braking, a limited-slip differential, and Recaro cloth seats. The Milano Gold and Platinum models retained the former 2.5-liter V-6, rated 154 horsepower, and could have a new three-speed automatic transmission, built by ZF in Germany. Models with automatic also had a self-leveling suspension. Standard Milano Gold equipment included air conditioning, power brakes/steering, power windows, central locking, heated power mirrors, tilt/telescope steering, leather-wrapped steering wheel, tinted glass, foglamps, velour upholstery, and 195/60VR14 tires on alloy wheels. Milano Platinum added anti-lock braking, a lighted passenger visor mirror, first-aid kit, tool kit, leather/suede upholstery, and 195/55VR15 tires.

I.D. DATA: Alfa Romeo's 17-digit Vehicle Identification Number is on the upper left of the dashboard, visible through the windshield. Symbols 1-3 ('ZAR') indicate country and manufacturer. Symbols 4-8 denote the car line, configuration, and equipment level. Next comes a check digit. Symbol ten indicates model year ('J' = 1988). Symbol 11 identifies the assembly plant. The final six digits form the sequential serial number.

Model	Body Type & Seating	Engine Type/CID	P.O.E. Price	Weight (lbs.)	Prod. Total
SPIDER VELOCE					
BC576	2-dr Conv-2P	I4/120	19000	2558	Note 1
SPIDER GRADUATE					
BA564	2-dr Conv-2P	I4/120	15400	2550	Note 1
SPIDER QUADRIFOGLIO					
BC570	2-dr Conv-2P	I4/120	22000	2558	Note 1
MILANO (Gold, Platinum, Verde)					
DA116	4-dr Sed (gold)-5P	V6/152	17200	2707	Note 1
DB142	4-dr Sed (plat)-5P	V6/152	21000	2707	Note 1
DA124	4-dr Sed (verde)-5P	V6/181	21200	2907	Note 1

Note 1: Approximately 4,476 Alfa Romeos were sold in the U.S. in 1988. Milano Gold price note: Automatic transmission added $700 to price and changed model no. (part of VIN) to DB140. Alfa Romeo prices rose during the year by $380 to $550.

ENGINE DATA: BASE FOUR (Spider): Inline, dual overhead-cam four-cylinder. Aluminum block and head. **Displacement:** 119.7 cu. in. (1962 cc). **Bore & Stroke:** 3.31 x 3.48 (84 x 88.5 mm). **Compression Ratio:** 9.0:1. **Brake Horsepower:** 115 at 5500 rpm. **Torque:** 119 lbs.-ft. at 2750 rpm. Five main bearings. Solid valve lifters. Port fuel injection.
BASE V-6 (Milano Gold/Platinum): Single-overhead-cam, 60-degree V-6. Aluminum block and head. **Displacement:** 152 cu. in. (2492 cc). **Bore & Stroke:** 3.46 x 2.69 (88 x 68.3 mm). **Compression Ratio:** 9.0:1. **Brake Horsepower:** 154 at 5500 rpm. **Torque:** 152 lbs.-ft. at 3200 rpm. Four main bearings. Solid valve lifters. Port fuel injection.
BASE V-6 (Milano Verde): Single-overhead-cam V-6. **Displacement:** 181 cu. in. (2959 cc). **Bore & Stroke:** 3.66 x 2.86 (93x 72.6 mm). **Brake Horsepower:** 183 at 5800 rpm. **Torque:** 181 lbs.-ft. at 3000 rpm. Four main bearings. Port fuel injection.

CHASSIS DATA: Wheelbase: (Spider) 88.6 in.; (Milano) 98.8 in. **Overall Length:** (Spider) 168.6 in.; (Milano) 170.5 in. **Height:** (Spider) 48.8 in.; (Milano) 53.1 in. **Width:** (Spider) 64.1 in.; (Milano) 64.2 in. **Front Tread:** (Spider) 52.1 in.; (Milano) 53.9 in. **Rear Tread:** (Spider) 50.1 in.; (Milano) 53.5 in. **Wheel Type:** (Graduate, Milano Silver) steel; (others) alloy). **Standard Tires:** (Spider) 185/70HR14 Michelin XVS; (Quadrifoglio) 195/60HR15 (Milano Gold) 195/60VR14; (Milano Platinum/Verde) 195/55VR15.

TECHNICAL: Layout: front-engine, rear-drive. **Transmission:** five-speed manual; three-speed automatic available on Milano Gold, standard on Platinum. **Steering:** (Spider) worm and roller; (Milano) rack and pinion. **Suspension (front):** (Spider) upper/lower control arms, coil springs and stabilizer bar; (Milano) parallel transverse links with torsion bars. **Suspension (rear):** (Spider) rigid axle with coil springs and stabilizer bar; (GTV-6) De Dion axle with Watt linkage, coil springs and stabilizer bar. **Brakes:** front/rear disc; ABS on Milano Platinum/Verde. **Body Construction:** steel unibody. **Fuel Tank:** (Spider) 12.2 gal.; (Milano) 17.6 gallon.

MAJOR OPTIONS: AM/FM stereo with cassette player: Graduate ($645). Air conditioning Spider Veloce/Graduate ($995). Power sunroof: Milano ($795). Metallic paint: Veloce/Quadrifoglio ($275); Milano ($350).

PERFORMANCE: Fuel Mileage: (Spider) 21/27 mpg EPA; (Milano Gold/Platinum w/manual) 18/24 mpg EPA.
Manufacturer: Alfa Romeo S.p.A., Milan, Italy.
Distributor: Alfa Romeo Inc., Englewood Cliffs, New Jersey.
HISTORY: Introduced to U.S. market in September 1987.

1989 ALFA ROMEO

1989 Alfa Romeo Spider Veloce.

SPIDER — FOUR — All three versions of the Alfa Romeo convertible (roadster) were unchanged this year.

MILANO — V-6 — Alfa's four-door sedan again came in Gold and Platinum models with the 2.5-liter V-6 engine, while the Verde model carried a 3.0-liter V-6. Little change was evident. Milano Platinum came only with automatic transmission; Verde, only with five-speed manual. Milano Gold could have the automatic as an option.

I.D. DATA: Alfa Romeo's 17-digit Vehicle Identification Number is on the upper left of the dashboard, visible through the windshield. Breakdown is the same as 1988, except model year code changed to 'K' for 1989.

Model	Body Type & Seating	Engine Type/CID	P.O.E. Price	Weight (lbs.)	Prod. Total
SPIDER VELOCE					
BC576	2-dr Conv-2P	I4/120	20200	2548	Note 1
SPIDER GRADUATE					
BA564	2-dr Conv-2P	I4/120	16700	2550	Note 1
SPIDER QUADRIFOGLIO					
BC570	2-dr Conv-2P	I4/120	23400	2548	Note 1
MILANO					
DA116	4-dr Sed (gold)-5P	V6/152	18475	2907	Note 1
DB142	4-dr Sed (plat)-5P	V6/152	22500	2907	Note 1
DA124	4-dr Sed (verde)-5P	V6/181	22700	2907	Note 1

Note 1: Approximately 2,920 Alfa Romeos were sold in the U.S. in 1989.
Milano Gold Price Note: Automatic transmission added $700 to price and changed Model No. prefix to DB.

ENGINE DATA: BASE FOUR (Spider): Inline, dual overhead-cam four-cylinder. Aluminum block and head. **Displacement:** 119.7 cu. in. (1962 cc). **Bore & Stroke:** 3.31 x 3.48 (84 x 88.5 mm). **Compression Ratio:** 9.0:1. **Brake Horsepower:** 115 at 5500 rpm. **Torque:** 119 lbs.-ft. at 2750 rpm. Five main bearings. Solid valve lifters. Port fuel injection.
BASE V-6 (Milano Gold/Platinum): Single-overhead-cam, 60-degree V-6. Aluminum block and head. **Displacement:** 152 cu. in. (2492 cc). **Bore & Stroke:** 3.46 x 2.69 (88 x 68.3 mm). **Compression Ratio:** 9.0:1. **Brake Horsepower:** 154 at 5500 rpm. **Torque:** 152 lbs.-ft. at 3200 rpm. Four main bearings. Solid valve lifters. Port fuel injection.
BASE V-6 (Milano Verde): Single-overhead-cam V-6. **Displacement:** 181 cu. in. (2959 cc). **Bore & Stroke:** 3.66 x 2.86 (93 x 72.6 mm). **Compression Ratio:** 9.5:1. **Brake Horsepower:** 183 at 5800 rpm. **Torque:** 181 lbs.-ft. at 3000 rpm. Four main bearings. Port fuel injection.

CHASSIS DATA: Wheelbase: (Spider) 88.6 in.; (Milano) 98.8 in. **Overall Length:** (Spider) 168.6 in.; (Milano) 170.5 in. **Height:** (Spider) 48.8 in.; (Milano) 53.1 in. **Width:** (Spider) 64.1 in.; (Milano) 64.2 in. **Front Tread:** (Spider) 52.1 in.; (Milano) 53.9 in. **Rear Tread:** (Spider) 50.1 in.; (Milano) 53.5 in. **Wheel Type:** (Graduate, Milano Silver) steel; (others) alloy). **Standard Tires:** (Spider) 185/70HR14 Michelin XVS; (Quadrifoglio) 195/60HR15 (Milano Gold) 195/60VR14; (Milano Platinum/Verde) 195/55VR15.

TECHNICAL: Layout: front-engine, rear-drive. **Transmission:** five-speed manual; three-speed automatic available on Milano Gold, standard on Platinum. **Steering:** (Spider) worm and roller; (Milano) rack and pinion. **Suspension (front):** (Spider) upper/lower control arms, coil springs and stabilizer bar; (Milano) parallel transverse links with torsion bars. **Suspension (rear):** (Spider) rigid axle with coil springs and stabilizer bar; (GTV-6) De Dion axle with Watt linkage, coil springs and stabilizer bar. **Brakes:** front/rear disc; ABS on Milano Platinum/Verde. **Body Construction:** steel unibody. **Fuel Tank:** (Spider) 12.2 gal.; (Milano) 17.6 gallon.

MAJOR OPTIONS: AM/FM stereo with cassette player: Graduate ($645). Air conditioning: Spider Veloce/Graduate ($995). Power sunroof: Milano ($795). Cruise control: Milano ($200). Metallic paint: Veloce/Quadrifoglio ($275); Milano ($350).

PERFORMANCE: Fuel Mileage: (Spider) 21/27 mpg EPA; (Milano Gold/Platinum w/manual) 18/24 mpg EPA; (Milano Verde) 18/25 mpg EPA.
Manufacturer: Alfa Romeo S.p.A., Milan, Italy.
Distributor: Alfa Romeo Inc., Englewood Cliffs, New Jersey.
HISTORY: Introduced to U.S. market in September 1988.

1990 ALFA ROMEO

SPIDER — FOUR — As the 1990 model year opened, only the three versions of Alfa's Spider convertible were officially on sale in the U.S. The Milano was dropped, to make way for the new 164 sedan, scheduled to arrive later in the season. The Spider's four-cylinder engine got a modest horsepower increase this year, as a result of new electronic controls. Otherwise, little change was evident.

I.D. DATA: Alfa Romeo's 17-digit Vehicle Identification Number is on the upper left of the dashboard, visible through the windshield. Breakdown is the same as 1988, except model year code changed to 'L' for 1990.

Model	Body Type & Seating	Engine Type/CID	P.O.E. Price	Weight (lbs.)	Prod. Total
SPIDER VELOCE					
BC558	2-dr Conv-2P	I4/120	20950	2548	N/A
SPIDER GRADUATE					
BA564	2-dr Conv-2P	I4/120	16950	2550	N/A
SPIDER QUADRIFOGLIO					
BC556	2-dr Conv-2P	I4/120	23950	2548	N/A

ENGINE DATA: BASE FOUR: Inline, dual-overhead-cam four-cylinder. Aluminum block and head. **Displacement:** 119.7 cu. in. (1962 cc). **Bore & Stroke:** 3.31 x 3.48 (84 x 88.5 mm). **Compression Ratio:** 9.0:1. **Brake Horsepower:** 120 at 5800 rpm. **Torque:** 117 lbs.-ft. at 2700 rpm. Five main bearings. Solid valve lifters. Port fuel injection.

CHASSIS DATA: Wheelbase: 88.6 in. **Overall Length:** 168.8 in. **Height:** 48.8 in. **Width:** 64.1 in. **Front Tread:** 52.1 in. **Rear Tread:** 50.1 in. **Standard Tires:** 185/70R14 except (Quadrifoglio) 195/60HR15.

TECHNICAL: Layout: front-engine, rear-drive. **Transmission:** five-speed manual. **Steering:** ZF worm and sector. **Suspension (front):** upper/lower control arms with coil springs and stabilizer bar. **Suspension (rear):** rigid axle with coil springs and stabilizer bar. **Brakes:** front/rear disc. **Body Construction:** steel unibody. **Fuel Tank:** 12.2 gal.

MAJOR OPTIONS: AM/FM stereo with cassette player: Graduate ($645). Air conditioning: Veloce/Graduate ($995). Metallic paint ($275).

PERFORMANCE: Fuel Mileage: 23/30 mpg EPA.

Manufacturer: Alfa Romeo S.p.A., Milan, Italy.

Distributor: Alfa Romeo Inc., Englewood Cliffs, New Jersey.

HISTORY: Introduced to U.S. market in September 1989.

POSTSCRIPT: In spring 1990, the new 164 four-door sedan, on a 104.7-inch wheelbase, went on sale as a replacement for the Milano. Using a front-wheel drive layout, it carried the same 3.0-liter V-6 engine as the Milano, rated 182 horsepower (200 bhp in a higher-performance 'S' model). Alfa Romeo's Spider remained in the U.S. lineup far longer than most would have predicted, doubtless a tribute to its Italian styling and overall "feel," including the unique near-horizontal positioning of its gearshift lever. Finally, for the 1991 model year, a restyled Spider was introduced, using the same engine as the original but available with either manual shift or automatic. Neither appearance nor basic structure changed dramatically.

ALLARD

Sydney Allard not only sold motorcars in London during the 1930s, at his family's Ford dealership, he also loved trials racing. Already in 1929, at the age of 19, he was racing three-wheel Morgan Super Sports at the Brookland course, though with minimal success. Following some early tries at rallies and hillclimbs with flathead Ford racing cars, by 1936 he'd built the first Allard Special. In a unique combination (to say the least), its shortened Ford V-8 coupe chassis and running gear held a portion of a GP 57 Bugatti body. The Special performed well in hillclimbs, rallies and trials. Over the next few years, until war broke out, Allard built eleven more, all powered by either a Ford V-8 or Lincoln Zephyr V-12.

After the war, Allard's family kept their Ford dealership running, but Sydney formed the Allard Motor Co. In January of 1946 he announced his first postwar car, a J1 two-seat racer. Again built with a flathead Ford V-8 and transmission, mounted on a special chassis, it would be produced at a new plant in Clapham (not far from central London). Instead of Ford's customary- and antiquated-front suspension, Allard had early on adopted a design by Leslie Bellamy for an independent suspension with split front axle, a conversion of the standard Ford transverse leaf spring setup.

For 1950 he introduced the J2, which became better known and led to strong interest in America. The J2 had an aluminum body, cycle fenders, ladder frame, De Dion rear end, and coil springs in front. Like most Allard products, this one could hold a variety of engines. Most British Allards held a Mercury V-8; a few added Ardun overhead-valve cylinder heads. With a 160-horsepower OHV Cadillac V-8 beneath its bonnet, the J2 could hit 110 mph. Sydney Allard and Tommy Cole drove a Cadillac-powered racer to 3rd place at Le Mans in 1950. Later in the decade, the J2 and subsequent J2X (with tubular frame) won hundreds of races in North America. Allards were offered either complete or "chassis only," shipped to the U.S. without engine or transmission. Some wound up with Cadillac V-8s; others with Chrysler powerplants.

Competition was a motivating force in the Allard firm. In 1952, Sydney won the Monte Carlo event driving a K2. As the more sedate K3 tourer came along a year later, though, sales were down. Allards couldn't compete with the new Jaguar XK120 in modern styling, and the non-racing models weren't quite quick enough. Starting in the mid-1950s, he tried a smaller, more modern Palm Beach model with a four- or six-cylinder engine from British Ford (Consul or Zephyr), but those failed to attract sufficient attention. The company also tried to sell Allards with the twin-cam Jaguar engine, but those fared little better. The final Allards were made in 1959.

1946-49 ALLARD

1947 Allard K.

K1 — V-8 — The postwar K1 was essentially the same as Allard's prewar J1 design, but on a six-inch longer wheelbase. Under the hood was a nearly-stock British 221-cid Ford V-8 rated 85 horsepower. Some examples had a higher-powered 239-cid V-8 from Canadian Mercury, delivering as much as 100 horsepower. The stock transverse-spring front axle was split to become an independent swing axle, in what had already become the traditional Allard style. At the rear was a torque tube with "live" beam axle, held by a transverse leaf spring. The K1 frame, of stamped-steel channel sections, was made for Allard by Thomsons of Wolverton. Steel body panels went over a wood framework.

The car had a rather homemade look, with a squarish grille of vertical bars that appeared to roll down the curvy nose. Front and rear fenders were separate. All K1 examples were right-hand drive. A handful (possibly three) of the 151 K1s built arrived in the U.S., though it was never officially offered for sale in America.

According to *Autocar* magazine, the early postwar Allard had "roadholding and stability which allow an enthusiastic driver to throw it about as he pleases." Describing entry into the driver's seat, *The Motor* noted that one was "immediately impressed by the way in which appearance has been blended with the requirements of the fast driver," including "outstanding forward visibility." As for its potential, they added: "What appear to be impossible speeds can be safely maintained without the slightest sign of skidding."

L/M — V-8 — In addition to the roadsters for which Allard became best known, the company turned out more sedate, four-passenger touring models and drophead coupes. By 1949, they even added a series of "P" saloons (sedans). These, too, were available with a choice of engines. Four-seat Allards had roll-up windows; two-seaters did not. All had suicide (rear-hinged) doors.

Model	Body Type & Seating	Engine Type/CID	P.O.E. Price	Weight (lbs.)	Prod. Total
K1	2-dr Roadster-2P	V8/221	N/A	2460	151
J1	2-dr Roadster-2P	V8/239	N/A	N/A	12
L	2-dr Touring-4P	V8/221	N/A	N/A	191
M	2-dr Dhd Cpe-4P	V8/221	N/A	N/A	500

Note: Production totals are for the full model run of each model.

1947 Allard competition two-seater.

ENGINE DATA: BASE V-8: L-head "vee-type" eight-cylinder. Cast iron block and head. **Displacement:** 221.0 cu. in. (3622 cc). **Bore & Stroke:** 3.06 x 3.75 in. **Compression Ratio:** 6.1:1 or (K1) 7.0:1. **Brake Horsepower:** 85 at 3600 rpm (some 95-bhp). Three main bearings. Solid valve lifters. One downdraft carburetor.

OPTIONAL V-8: L-head "vee-type" eight-cylinder (Canadian Mercury). Cast iron block and head. **Displacement:** 239 cu. in. (3917 cc). **Bore & Stroke:** 3.19 x 3.75 in. (81 x 95.26 mm). **Compression Ratio:** 7.5:1. **Brake Horsepower:** 95 at 3600 rpm (some 100-bhp). Three main bearings. Solid valve lifters.

CHASSIS DATA: Wheelbase: (J) 100.0 in.; (K) 106.0 in.; (four-seat) 112.0 in.. **Overall Length:** 168 in. **Width:** (K) 71 in. **Front Tread:** (K) 56 in. **Rear Tread:** (K) 50 in. **Standard Tires:** 6.25x16.

TECHNICAL: Layout: front-engine, rear-drive. **Transmission:** three-speed manual (synchro 2nd/3rd). **Suspension (front):** split swing axle (independent). **Suspension (rear):** beam axle with torque tube and transverse leaf spring. **Brakes:** Lockheed front/rear drum. **Body Construction:** aluminum body on wood framework, atop stamped-steel channel-section frame.

PERFORMANCE: Top Speed: 92-93 mph. **Acceleration (0-60 mph):** N/A (0-50 in 11.5 sec.). **Acceleration (quarter-mile):** near 20 seconds (done on wet road).

PRODUCTION/SALES: A total of seven Allards were built in 1946; 173 were sold in 1947; 432 sold in 1948, and 265 sold in 1949.

Manufacturer: Allard Motor Co. Ltd., Clapham, London SW4, England.

HISTORY: Among their many racing victories in the early postwar years, Allards won the Lisbon Rally in 1947 and 1949, took five awards in the Alpine Rally (1947 and 1948), won the Team Trophy (and two others) in the 1949 Monte Carlo Rally, and two more in the 1950 Monte Carlo event.

1950-51 ALLARD

1950 Allard J2X.

J2 — V-8 — Although the early postwar Allards were well received in Britain, Sydney Allard also wanted to make stronger inroads into the U.S. market for sporty semi-racers. "Specially designed for the American competition motorist," the updated J2, which helped to achieve that goal, resulted from a trip he took to the U.S. Riding a wheelbase

identical to the original J1 (100 inches), it did well both in the marketplace and on the race courses of the world.

Customers could choose from a variety of engines: a 239-cid Ford V-8, an Ardun conversion (140-bhp), or a Chrysler or Cadillac OHV V-8. Allard's price list noted that this was "to permit the enthusiast to fit his own particular choice of motor, hopped up or otherwise." The J2 was in fact a competition car that also happened to be capable of going out on road touring, available with either left- or right-hand drive. The body had bolt-on rear fenders and cycle-style front fenders, with separate headlamps and tiny round taillamps. Though basic in appearance and engineering, the J2 was quick and displayed an unmistakable race-car look. A small vertical-bar pentagonal grille sat in a curvy protruding nose. The engine-turned instrument panel contained a five-inch speedometer and tachometer, oil and temperature gauge, ammeter and fuel gauge, and fuel switch. Solex racing-type carburetors were used on the standard engine, which used an oil cooler radiator. As the brochure suggested, it had "just about everything for the speed man."

1950-'52 Allard K2.

K2 — V-8 — Sleeker in appearance, less square-looking than the K1, the reworked K2 Sports Two-Seater tourer could be spotted by its trio of Buick-style "portholes" along each side of the small hood, which carried small hood straps and sat far back from the grille. That small pentagonal vertical-bar grille, like that in the J2, replaced the former K1's "waterfall" type grille.

This Allard still used a live rear axle with transverse leaf spring, and a split-type front axle design (with two coil springs rather than the original transverse leaf). Cut-down doors displayed a graceful top curve. The rear end reminded some viewers of the Jaguar XK120. Headlamps sat flush in "clamshell" fenders. Short side bumperettes were used at both front and rear. Though basic, the cockpit was actually less austere than the prior two-seater, similar in design to the four-passenger L/M/P models. A fabric curtain behind the seat gave access to a small luggage area. Leather bucket seats faced a telescopic steering wheel. Rubber bags in the seat cushions were inflatable for a custom fit. The dashboard displayed a tachometer.

Both right- and left-hand drive models were offered. Instrument panels held full gauges. Frame components were stamped by Thomsons of Wolverhampton. Powertrains and axles again came from Ford, though the Allard used a narrower track than Ford. Four engines were available: the 221-cid flathead Ford V-8, a 239-cid Mercury flathead V-8, an Ardun modification of the 221-cid Ford (140-bhp),or a bored-out Mercury engine (266.8 cubic inches) with aluminum heads. Speed equipment, though created by Allard, was based on U.S. components, which simplified servicing in America. A considerable number of K2s found their way to U.S. buyers. Standard equipment included high-compression aluminum cylinder heads, floor gearshift lever, racing-type fly-off handbrake, windshield, and all-weather equipment.

I.D. DATA: Not available.

Model	Body Type & Seating	Engine Type/CID	P.O.E. Price	Weight (lbs.)	Prod. Total
J2	2-dr Roadster-2P	V8/239	3244	Note 1	90
K2	2-dr Roadster-2/3P	V8/221	3094	2780	119
K2	2-dr Spts Sed-5P	V8/221	3325	N/A	N/A

Note 1: J2 chassis weighed 1,950 pounds.

Price Note: Roadster models sold without engine for $2619 (J2) and $2739 (K2). They were also available as chassis only, with or without engine. Purchased separately, a J-Type engine cost $568, body $560, and the chassis assembly $2237. A J2 with Cadillac V-8 was priced at $3995.

ENGINE DATA: BASE V-8 (K2): L-head "vee-type" eight-cylinder. Cast iron block and head. **Displacement:** 220.9 cu. in. (3622 cc). **Bore & Stroke:** 3.06 x 3.75 in. (77.8 x 95.25 mm). **Compression Ratio:** 6.1:1 or 7.0:1. **Brake Horsepower:** 85/90 at 3600 rpm (95 hp optional). Three main bearings. Solid valve lifters. One downdraft carburetor.

BASE V-8 (J2); OPTIONAL (K2): L-head "vee-type" eight-cylinder (Canadian Mercury). Cast iron block and head. **Displacement:** 239 cu. in. (3917 cc). **Bore & Stroke:** 3.19 x 3.75 in. (81 x 95.26 mm). **Compression Ratio:** 7.5:1. **Brake Horsepower:** 95/100 at 3600 rpm. **Torque:** 181 lbs.-ft. at 2000 rpm. Three main bearings. Solid valve lifters.

OPTIONAL V-8: Ford V-8 with Ardun overhead-valve heads (140-bhp).

OPTIONAL V-8 (standard on J-type Competition model): Mercury V-8 bored to 266.8 cid, with aluminum heads. **Displacement:** 266.8 cu. in. (4377 cc). **Bore & Stroke:** 3.31 x 3.87 in. (84 x 98.4 mm). **Brake Horsepower:** 120 at 3800 rpm. Three main bearings. Solid valve lifters.

OPTIONAL V-8 (J2): Overhead-valve "vee" type eight-cylinder (Chrysler). Cast iron block and head. **Displacement:** 331 cu. in. (5420 cc). **Bore & Stroke:** 3.81 x 3.62 in. **Brake Horsepower:** 180 at 4000 rpm. **Torque:** 312 lbs.-ft. at 2000 rpm. Five main bearings. Hydraulic valve lifters.

OPTIONAL V-8 (J2): Overhead-valve "vee" type eight-cylinder (Cadillac). Cast iron block and head. **Displacement:** 331 cu. in. (5420 cc). **Bore & Stroke:** 3.81 x 3.62 in. **Compression Ratio:** 7.5:1. **Brake Horsepower:** 160 at 3800 rpm. **Torque:** 312 lbs.-ft. at 1800 rpm. Five main bearings. Hydraulic valve lifters.

CHASSIS DATA: Wheelbase: (J2) 100.0 in.; (K2) 106.0 in.; (L/M/P) 112.0 in. **Overall Length:** (J2) 148 in.; (K2) 168 in. **Height:** (K2) 62 in. **Width:** (J2) 63 in.; (K2) 71 in. **Front Tread:** 56 in. **Rear Tread:** 52 in. **Wheel Type:** (J2) disc; (K2) bolt-on stamped-steel disc. **Standard Tires:** (J2) 6.00x16; (K2) 6.25x16.

TECHNICAL: Layout: front-engine, rear-drive. **Transmission:** three-speed manual (synchro 2nd/3rd). **Standard Final Drive Ratio:** (J2) 3.54:1; (K2) 3.78:1. **Steering:** Marles. **Suspension (front):** split I-beam swing axles with coil springs (independent). **Suspension (rear):** De Dion axle with quick-change differential and coil springs; (K2) transverse leaf spring. **Brakes:** (J2) Lockheed 12-inch Al-fin front/rear drums. **Body Construction:** aluminum body on stamped-steel channel-section frame. **Fuel Tank:** (J2) 26 gallons with reserve.

PERFORMANCE: Top Speed: (J2 with Cad V-8) 110 mph; some reports as high as 130 mph. **Acceleration (0-60 mph):** N/A (J2 w/Cad V-8, 0-50 mph in 5.5 seconds). **Acceleration (quarter-mile):** (J2 w/Cad V-8) 16.3 sec.

PRODUCTION/SALES: A total of 305 Allards were sold during 1950, and 337 the following year (all models). At least 21 went to U.S. buyers in 1950, and 42 in 1951.

Manufacturer: Allard Motor Co., Ltd., Clapham, London, England.

Distributor: Moss Motors Ltd., Los Angeles, California.

HISTORY: Introduced: (J2) 1949; (K2) 1950. The first K2 sports two-seater arrived in California in March 1950. The Ardun overhead-valve conversion kit for the flathead Ford V-8 engine came from Zora Arkus-Duntov, in New York City. Operating with pushrods and rocker arms, it resulted in an engine similar to early Chrysler hemi V-8s. The Ardun option was abandoned after the first few dozen J2 models. Highly modified Cadillac V-8 Allards reached 250 bhp with twin carburetors, special camshafts and racing heads, able to go from 0-100 mph in as little as 12 seconds.

1952-54 ALLARD

Allard production never reached beyond a few hundred annually, but the company introduced a surprising proliferation of models; not to mention the wide choice of powerplants.

K3 — V-8 — Much tamer than the race-oriented J series, the K3 (like the K2 before it) was the touring model of the Allard line. Introduced in 1952, it had a far different look: much more modern, inside and out. Rounded lines, with three horizontal bars in an unadorned opening, made up the K3's grille. Little ornamentation was evident on the aluminum body, except for a small emblem below the grille that said 'ALLARD' in red.

In fact, the K3 looked something like the American-built Cunningham C2. Once again, this Allard had a small horizontal hood (more of a lid) and no door handles. Small round parking lamps stood below the headlamps. Gauges went in the center of the basic dashboard. As before, it used a split-axle front suspension and a De Dion rear axle. Wheelbase of 100 inches was 6 inches shorter than that of the K2. A choice of four engines was offered: British Ford flathead V-8 (221 cid); Mercury flathead V-8 (239 cid); Chrysler ohv V-8; or, later on, a Jaguar twin-cam six. Standard equipment included the 221-cid (3.6-liter) V-8, luxury leather upholstery, and bench seating for three people sitting abreast. The windshield opened, and the car had an automatic backup light as well as a spacious, lighted, lockable luggage compartment.

1953 Allard K3 convertible.

J2X — V-8 — Allard's competition-type roadster on a 100-inch wheelbase, in either standard or Le Mans form, was available with Chrysler, Lincoln or Mercury engines as well as a Cadillac V-8. Appearance was about the same as the former J2, though the spare tire was now sidemounted (on the right side) rather than in a rear compartment. Suspension was also the same as J2, but front radius rods were now the "leading" rather than "trailing" style. The 'X' in the car's name stood for extended, indicating that the frame was lengthened by six inches to accommodate those rods (though wheelbase was the same 100 inches). The engine moved forward, too. Most J2X models had a Chrysler or Cadillac ohv V-8 engine, but some carried the standard 239-cid (3.9-liter) flathead Mercury V-8. Many examples had the available center-lock, knock-off wire wheels. J2X was largely a racing model, as opposed to the touring J2. At least, that was the intention.

The standard J2X had a custom-built two-seater aluminum body with cycle-style front fenders and aerodynamic windshield. The more costly Le Mans edition had a completely different look, with an aerodynamic body. Following the usual Allard layout, a split front axle was used at the front, with a De Dion rear axle, with coil springs all around. Optional on both bodies were a full-width windshield, wire wheels and disc.

JR (RACING) — V-8 — Allard's racing roadster on a 96-in wheelbase, weighing only 1,900 pounds, was available with Chrysler, Cadillac and Mercury engines.

PALM BEACH — FOUR OR SIX — In an attempt to move into another segment of the market, Allard introduced the shorter (96-inch wheelbase) Palm Beach Roadster. Instead of the usual V-8 engine, it carried a Ford Zephyr six-cylinder (68-horsepower) or Consul four-cylinder (47-horsepower).

MONTE CARLO — V-8 — This two-door saloon on a 100-inch wheelbase came with a standard Ford 239 cu. in. (3.6-liter) V-8 engine, or the option of Chrysler, Cadillac or Lincoln V-8s of up to 210 horsepower. Standard equipment included a split bench front seat, luxury hide upholstery, spare wheel under the hood, and built-in radio antenna.

SAFARI — V-8 — Allard was nothing if not versatile, even offering a two-door station wagon (Estate Car) on a 112-inch wheelbase, with a standard 85-horsepower, 221 cu. in. (3.6-liter) Ford V-8 engine. Like the other Allards, it could be ordered with Lincoln, Chrysler or Cadillac powerplants. "Strikingly modern in design," stated the sales brochure, the Safari "is the perfect combination of a comfortable saloon car with the sleek lines and general roadworthiness of the sports car." Standard equipment included luxury hide upholstery, backup light, hydraulically-operated hood, and built-in radio antenna.

1954 Allard Model K3.

I.D. DATA: Not available.

Model	Body Type & Seating	Engine Type/CID	P.O.E. Price	Weight (lbs.)	Prod. Total
K3 AND J2 SERIES					
K3	2-dr Roadster-3/4P	V8/221	3402	2900	62
J2X	2-dr Roadster-2P	V8/239	3480	2150	83
J2X LeMans	2-dr Roadster-2P	V8/239	N/A	2350	Note 1
JR	2-dr Roadster-3P	V8/331	N/A	1900	7
PALM BEACH					
21C	2-dr Roadster-3P	I4/92	2436	1848	8
65	2-dr Roadster-3P	I6/138	2576	1932	65
MONTE CARLO/SAFARI (P2)					
M. Carlo	2-dr Sedan-5/6P	V8/239	N/A	3200	11
Safari	2-dr Sta Wag-6P	V8/239	N/A	3450	10

Note 1: Production included in J2X figure.

Price Note: Palm Beach prices rose to $2850 and $2995.

ENGINE DATA: BASE FOUR (Palm Beach): Inline, ohv four-cylinder. Cast iron block and head. **Displacement:** 92.0 cu. in. (1508 cc). **Bore & Stroke:** 3.13 x 3.00 in. (79.4 x 76.2 mm). **Compression Ratio:** 6.8:1. **Brake Horsepower:** 47 at 4400 rpm. Solid valve lifters. Zenith downdraft carburetor.

BASE SIX (Palm Beach): Inline, OHV six-cylinder. **Displacement:** 138 cu. in. (2267 cc). **Bore & Stroke:** 3.13 x 3.00 in. (79.4 x 76.2 mm). **Compression Ratio:** 6.8:1. **Brake Horsepower:** 68 at 4000 rpm. Solid valve lifters. Zenith downdraft carburetor.

Note: Later Palm Beach Mark II had a 2553-cc Ford Zodiac engine rated 90 horsepower, with three Zenith carburetors; or a 190-bhp Jaguar six.

OPTIONAL SIX (K3): Inline, dual overhead-cam six-cylinder (Jaguar). Cast iron block and aluminum head. **Displacement:** 210 cu. in. (3442 cc). **Bore & Stroke:** 3.27 x 4.17 in. (83 x 106 mm). **Brake Horsepower:** 160 at 5200 rpm.

BASE V-8 (K3, Safari, Monte Carlo): L-head "vee-type" eight-cylinder. Cast iron block and head. **Displacement:** 221 cu. in. (3622 cc). **Bore & Stroke:** 3.06 x 3.75 in. (77.8 x 95.25 mm). **Compression Ratio:** (Safari/Monte Carlo) 6.1:1; (K3) 7.0:1. **Brake Horsepower:** (Safari/Monte Carlo) 85 at 3500 rpm; (K3) 95 at 3800 rpm. Solid valve lifters. Ford-Chandler-Groves carburetor.

BASE V-8 (J2X); **OPTIONAL** (K3): L-head "vee-type" eight-cylinder (Mercury). Cast iron block and head. **Displacement:** 239 cu. in. (3917 cc). **Bore & Stroke:** 3.19 x 3.75 in. (81 x 95.3 mm). **Compression Ratio:** 7.0:1. **Brake Horsepower:** 95/100 at 3600 rpm (J2X, 140 at 4000). **Torque:** 181 lbs.-ft. at 4000 rpm. Solid valve lifters. Two carburetors.

OPTIONAL V-8 (K3/J2X): Overhead-valve "vee" type eight-cylinder (Chrysler). Cast iron block and head. **Displacement:** 331 cu. in. (5420 cc). **Bore & Stroke:** 3.81 x 3.62 in. **Brake Horsepower:** 180 at 4000 rpm (bhp ranged from 160 to 235, at 4000-4400 rpm). **Torque:** 312 to 330 lbs.-ft. at 2000-2600 rpm. Hydraulic valve lifters.

BASE V-8 (JR); **OPTIONAL** (J2X): Overhead-valve "vee" type eight-cylinder (Cadillac). Cast iron block and head. **Displacement:** 331 cu. in. (5420 cc). **Bore & Stroke:** 3.81 x 3.62 in. **Compression Ratio:** 7.1:1 (up to 8.25:1). **Brake Horsepower:** 210 at 4500 rpm (bhp ranges from 190 to 250). **Torque:** 322-330 lbs.-ft. at 2200-2700 rpm. Hydraulic valve lifters.

CHASSIS DATA: Wheelbase: (Palm Beach, JR) 96 in.; (K3, J2X, Monte Carlo) 100 in.; (Safari/Monte) 112 in. **Overall Length:** (J2X) 155 in.; (K3) 177 in.; (Palm Beach) 132 in.; (Monte) 192 in. **Height:** (J2X) 44.5 in.; (K3) 54 in.; (Safari/Monte) 60 in. **Width:** (J2X) 68 in.; (K3) 66.5 in.; (Palm Beach) 58 in.; (Safari/Monte) 71 in. **Front Tread:** (J2X) 56 in.; (K3) 56 in.; (Palm Beach) 51 in.; (Monte) 56.5 in. **Rear Tread:** (J2X) 52.5 in.; (K3) 58.5 in.; (Palm Beach) 50 in.; (Monte) 58.5 in. **Wheel Type:** steel; Rudge Whitworth knock-off wire wheels optional. **Standard Tires:** (J2X) 6.00x16; (K3) 6.25x16; (Safari/Monte) 6.25x16; (Palm Beach) 6.40x13.

TECHNICAL: Layout: front-engine, rear-drive. **Transmission:** three-speed manual (synchro); four-speed with Jaguar engine. **Standard Final Drive Ratio:** (J2X) 3.27:1; (K3) 3.50:1; (Safari/Monte) 3.78:1; (Palm Beach (4.37:1). **Steering:** (J2X) Marles. **Suspension (front):** split axle with radius rods and coil springs (independent). **Suspension (rear):** De Dion axle with coil springs except (Palm Beach) Zephyr axle with trailing link and coil springs. **Brakes:** Girling hydraulic, front/rear drum; (J2X) inboard rear with Al-Fin drums. **Body Construction:** (K3) aluminum "envelope" body on frame that used two stacked chrome-moly tubes for side rails; (Monte Carlo/Safari) tubular chassis frame.

MAJOR OPTIONS: J2X OPTIONS: Complete Le Mans type body ($280). Full-size windshield with wipers and hood ($123.20). Five fitted wire wheels with hubs and caps ($224). Additional spare tire sidemount ($27.72). Tonneau cover ($31). Oil cooler radiator ($19.27). Set of fitted Dunlop "Road Speed" tires and tubes ($95.35). Luggage carrier ($47.60). Quick-change rear end ($28). Oil temperature gauge ($14). Le Mans type headlamps and stone guards ($36.40). 8000-rpm tachometer ($15.40). Le Mans type racing mirror ($17.92). 40-gallon fuel tank ($56). Cadillac modification and kit ($140). Chrysler modification and kit ($168).

K3 OPTIONS: Set of five fitted Rudge Whitworth knock-off wire wheels, hubs and caps ($224). Cadillac modification and kit ($140). Chrysler modification and kit ($168).

PALM BEACH OPTIONS: Set of fitted wire wheels ($224).

PERFORMANCE: Top Speed: Factory ratings, (K3) 98 mph; (J2X) 120 mph; (Palm Beach) 85 mph. Palm Beach went up to 100 mph w/Zephyr six. **Acceleration (0-60 mph):** (Palm Beach) 22 seconds (factory); (J2X) 7.9 seconds w/modified 320-bhp Chrysler V-8. Runs of 7.2 seconds have been achieved. **Acceleration (0-50 mph):** factory ratings, (J2X) 6.8 sec.; (K3) 8.3 sec.; (Monte) 12.8 sec. **Acceleration (quarter-mile):** (J2X) 16.7 seconds w/modified 320-bhp Chrysler V-8.

PRODUCTION/SALES: A total of 132 Allards were sold during 1952, 123 during 1953, and 44 during 1954 and beyond. Of the 123 sold during 1953, 119 were exported. At least 51 went to U.S. buyers in 1952, plus approximately 62 in 1953, and 15 in 1954.

Manufacturer: Allard Motor Co. Ltd., Clapham, London, England.

POSTSCRIPT: Rumors of a merger between Allard and Chrysler were rampant at this time, including suspicion of a fast, compact, lightweight and low-cost car that would use the Dodge Red Ram V-8 engine and transmission. Although production officially continued through 1959, only about seven additional cars were built after 1954, including the Mark II version of the Palm Beach. *Road & Track* in October 1954 complimented the K3 Allard for its fine acceleration, handling and steering, while complaining about the large turning radius. Fault was also found with the car's clutch and transmission, as well as its flapping top, poor ventilation and wipers, and lack of a heater/defroster.

Most K3 models were sold in the U.S. The first J2X was delivered in London in September 1951; the second, two months later, went to America. The last J2X was built in November, 1954. The J2X earned quite a few race victories in the U.S., driven by such people as Tom Carstens and Bill Pollack. At the 1952 Monte Carlo Rally, an Allard P.1 saloon beat 328 rivals, to bring Britain its first victory in 21 years.

Until his death in 1966, Sydney Allard worked on sunroofs, dragsters and ambulance conversions. Much later, in the early 1980s, production began in Canada of a J2 replica, powered by a Chrysler V-8 engine.

ALPINE

From 1955 through the 1960s, a small company operated by Jean Redele at Dieppe, France, produced a series of fiberglass-bodied two-seat racing/rallying coupes based upon the rear-engine Renault chassis, known as the A108 and A110. Redele's first model, however, was called the Mille Miles, named for its debut at the Italian Mille Miglia race in 1955. A year later, an Alpine took first place in its class at that event. Early Alpines were based upon Renault 4CV mechanical components. By 1957, both coupe and cabriolet versions were available, powered by the slightly larger Dauphine engine: either 845 cc, or bored out to 904 cc.

Painted in French blue, Alpines became strong contenders in rally events through the 1960s. By 1963, the original A108 with its steel-tube structure evolved into the A110, again based up Renault's Dauphine, with a 998-cc engine and central steel backbone chassis. Before long, highly-tuned versions of the 1108-cc four from the Renault R8 were employed. These came in a choice of two body styles: the GT4 coupe with 2+2 seating and an aerodynamic Berlinette two-seater, the latter using a 1255-cc engine. A tightening link with Renault brought even larger powerplants into Alpine chassis, including the all-alloy 1565-cc unit from the Renault 16. Alpines also were produced in Mexico, Brazil and Spain.

By 1971 the company had a far different A310 model ready for road use. Considerably larger and roomier than its predecessors, the A310 retained the traditional Renault rear engine (grown to 1605 cc) with a 2+2 fiberglass body. Initially powered by only four cylinders, the A310 offered an optional V-6 engine by late 1976. Except for a handful of coupes that entered the U.S. via the "gray market," most were sold in Europe. The A310's successor arrived in 1985: a striking GTA coupe. Though initially aimed at the U.S. market, the GTA never managed to cross the Atlantic with official approval. When Chrysler acquired Renault's interest in the dying American Motors in 1987, any attempts to import the French coupe were dashed. Chrysler was readying its TC Maserati for sale in the U.S., and wasn't about to offer two similar models, so the GTA remained in Europe.

Specifications Note: Data shown below is typical; other models were produced, and other Renault engines used. Alpines were not officially imported into the U.S.

1963-70 ALPINE

A110 — FOUR — Replacing the early A108, the A110 coupe used a tubular steel backbone chassis and initially carried a 998-cc engine from the Renault Dauphine, producing 77 horsepower. Before long, a tuned variant of the Renault R8's engine was available, displacing 1108 cc and delivering 87 bhp. Those evolved into higher-powered versions, some Gordini-tuned, offered in both GT4 and Berlinette body styles.

GT4 — FOUR — The four-seat Alpine coupe was powered by a 1108-cc four-cylinder Renault engine, with four-speed manual transmission. The GT4 coupe had a protruding nose (with air intake below), wraparound windshield and back window, front vent wings, and rather large rear quarter windows. 'ALPINE' lettering ran across the rear engine cover.

BERLINETTE — FOUR — The two-seat coupe carried a 1255-cc four-cylinder engine with Gordini cylinder head, hooked to a five-speed manual gearbox. Basic appearance was similar to the GT4 coupe, but the Berlinette's side windows slanted backward, and the rear quarter windows were smaller and triangular in shape. The rear window had a deeper wraparound, while the wraparound windshield displayed a much steeper slant.

I.D. DATA: Not available.

Model	Body Type & Seating	Engine Type/CID	P.O.E. Price	Weight (lbs.)	Prod. Total
GT4	2-dr Coupe-2+2P	I4/68	N/A	1323	Note 1
Berlinette	2-dr Coupe-2P	I4/77	N/A	1202	Note 1

Note 1: A total of 350 Alpine cars were produced in 1964, 113 in 1965, 343 in 1966, 329 in 1967, 358 in 1968, 688 in 1969, and 976 in 1970.

ENGINE DATA: BASE FOUR (GT4): Inline, overhead-valve four-cylinder. Cast iron block and light alloy head. **Displacement:** 67.6 cu. in. (1108 cc). **Bore & Stroke:** 2.76 x 2.83 in. (70 x 72 mm). **Compression Ratio:** 9.5:1. **Brake Horsepower:** 65 (SAE) at 6200 rpm. **Torque:** 67 (SAE) lbs.-ft. at 4000 rpm. Five main bearings. Solid valve lifters. One Weber 32 DIR two-barrel carburetor.

BASE FOUR (Berlinette): Inline, overhead-valve four-cylinder. Cast iron block and light alloy head. **Displacement:** 76.6 cu. in. (1255 cc). **Bore & Stroke:** 2.93 x 2.83 in. (74.5 x 72 mm). **Compression Ratio:** 10.5:1. **Brake Horsepower:** 103 (SAE) at 6750 rpm. **Torque:** 86 (SAE) lbs.-ft. at 5000 rpm. Five main bearings. Solid valve lifters. Two Weber 40 DCOE two-barrel carburetors.

Engine Note: Ratings shown were valid around 1968. Other engine sizes and ratings were available during the period, including a 1296-cc four that produced 120 horsepower, another that delivered 130 bhp, and a 95-bhp version of the 1108-cc engine.

CHASSIS DATA: Wheelbase: (GT4) 89.4 in.; (Berlinette) 82.7 in. **Overall Length:** (GT4) 159.4 in.; (Berlin.) 151.6 in. **Height:** (GT4) 49.2 in.; (Berlin.) 44.5 in. **Width:** (GT4) 59 in.; (Berlin.) 57.1 in. **Front Tread:** (GT4) 49.2 in.; (Berlin.) 51 in. **Rear Tread:** (GT4) 49.2 in.; (Berlin.) 50.2 in. **Standard Tires:** (GT4) 145x15; (Berlin.) 155x15.

TECHNICAL: Layout: rear-engine, rear-drive. **Transmission:** (GT4) four-speed manual; (Berlinette) five-speed manual. **Steering:** rack and pinion. **Suspension (front):** upper/lower control arms, coil springs and anti-roll bar. **Suspension (rear):** independent with swinging semi-axles, trailing radius arms and coil springs. **Brakes:** front/rear disc. **Body Construction:** fiberglass (integral) on steel backbone chassis.

PERFORMANCE: Top Speed: (GT4) about 105 mph; (Berlinette) about 127 mph. **Fuel Mileage:** (GT4) about 29 mpg U.S.; (Berlinette) about 23 mpg U.S.

Manufacturer: Automobiles Alpine, Dieppe, France.

HISTORY: Alpine also produced some examples with twin-cam heads and hemi-heads, as well as single-seat racing cars. Sale of these models continued for a time after the introduction of the restyled A310, including a Berlinette Tour de France coupe powered by a 1289-cc or 1565-cc engine.

1971-85 ALPINE & ALPINE-RENAULT

A310 — FOUR/V-6 — Dramatically low in profile, the stylishly angular French fastback coupe had seating for two up front, and two smaller folks in back. A steel backbone chassis contained independent suspension on all four wheels, and wore a fiberglass body. At the rear was a Renault overhead-valve four-cylinder engine, as in the R16 model, producing 127 horsepower. That was connected to a four-speed (or five-speed) all-synchro manual transaxle. Styling of the A310 was in the aggressive, near-supercar mode, looking at home with Ferraris and Lamborghinis of the day. A bodyside crease ran the full length of the car, which displayed both front vent and rear quarter windows and a large (nearly horizontal) louvered backlight. 'ALPINE RENAULT' block lettering went on the back panel. Headlamps sat behind sloping glass covers. Early models had twin triangular air ducts on the front fender tops, just to the rear of the outer lights. Performance nearly matched the car's appearance, with top speed past 130 mph even with only four cylinders. The V-6 edition, introduced late in 1976, was quicker yet and wore a hanging-back rear spoiler as well as bulging fender flares, for an even more aggressive look. Pirelli tires were larger, and the body dimensions grew somewhat. Larger rectangular mirrors replaced the early rounded units. Developing 150 horsepower, the V-6 was developed jointly by Peugeot, Renault and Volvo, and saw widespread usage in European automobiles.

I.D. DATA: Not available.

Model	Body Type & Seating	Engine Type/CID	P.O.E. Price	Weight (lbs.)	Prod. Total
A310	2-dr Coupe-2+2P	I4/98	N/A	1852	Note 2
A310	2-dr Coupe-2+2P	V6/162	Note 1	2245	Note 2

Note 1: Price in 1984 was about $28,800, or 140,860 Francs at the factory in France.

Note 2: A total of 2,334 four-cylinder models were produced through 1985. A total of 116 A310s were produced in 1971, 589 in 1972, 655 in 1973, 347 in 1974, 1,103 in 1975, 1,216 in 1976, 1,381 in 1979, 1,137 in 1980, 1,261 in 1981, 1,001 in 1982, and 1,127 in 1983.

ENGINE DATA: BASE FOUR: Inline, overhead-valve four-cylinder. Light alloy block and head. **Displacement:** 98 cu. in. (1605 cc). **Bore & Stroke:** 3.07 x 3.31 in. (78 x 84 mm). **Compression Ratio:** 10.2:1. **Brake Horsepower:** 127 DIN (140 SAE) at 6250 rpm. **Torque:** 108 lbs.-ft. (109 SAE) at 5000 rpm. Five main bearings. Solid valve lifters. Two Weber 45 DCOE two-barrel carburetors.

OPTIONAL V-6: 90-degree, single-overhead-cam "vee" type six-cylinder. Light alloy block and head. **Displacement:** 162.5 cu. in. (2664 cc). **Bore & Stroke:** 3.46 x 2.87 in. (88 x 73 mm). **Compression Ratio:** 10.1:1. **Brake Horsepower:** 150 (DIN) at 6000 rpm. **Torque:** 151 lbs.-ft. at 3500 rpm. Four main bearings. Two Solex carburetors (one single-barrel and one two-barrel).

CHASSIS DATA: Wheelbase: 89.4 in. **Overall Length:** (four) 164.6 in.; (V-6) 167.3 in. **Height:** (four) 42.3 in.; (V-6) 45.3 in. **Width:** (four) 63.8 in.; (V-6) 65 in. **Front Tread:** 54.3 in.; (V-6) 55.5 in. **Rear Tread:** (four) 55.5 in.; (V-6) 56.3 in. **Standard Tires:** (four) 165x13 front, 185x13 rear; (V-6) 190/55VR13 front, 220/55VR14 rear.

TECHNICAL: Layout: rear-engine, rear-drive. **Transmission:** four-speed or five-speed manual. **Steering:** rack and pinion. **Suspension (front):** upper/lower control arms, coil springs and anti-roll bar. **Suspension (rear):** upper/lower control arms, coil springs and anti-roll bar. **Brakes:** front disc, rear drum or front/rear disc (front/rear disc on V-6). **Body Construction:** fiberglass body on steel backbone chassis.

PERFORMANCE: Top Speed: (four) 130-134 mph; (V-6) 137-140+ mph. **Acceleration (0-60 mph):** (four) 8.1 sec.; (V-6) about 7.5 sec. **Acceleration (quarter-mile):** (V-6) 15 sec. **Manufacturer:** Automobiles Alpine, Dieppe, France; (later) Regie Nationale des Usines Renault, Boulogne Billancourt, Paris, France.

HISTORY: Financial problems in the 1970s led to the purchase of the Alpine firm by Renault. The GTA coupe debuted in 1984, but didn't become readily available until 1986; see next listing.

1986-90 ALPINE-RENAULT

1986 Alpine Renault.

GTA — V-6 — Though similar in appearance to the former A310, the GTA was designed by Renault engineers rather than by the earlier firm operated by Jean Redele. Export to the U.S. was anticipated from the start, but that was not destined to happen. Larger than the A310, the GTA also used a steel backbone chassis, but in monocoque form, with the fiberglass body panels bonded directly in place rather than mounted separately. As before, the V-6 engine was rear-mounted and drove the rear wheels via a five-speed manual transaxle. Below the integrated front bumper was a spoiler, and the rear spoiler also had a more integrated look. Overall, the aerodynamic GTA had a much better drag coefficient than its predecessor (only 0.28), and looked it. Both normally aspirated and turbocharged versions of the Peugeot-Renault-Volvo V-6 engine were offered, in two different displacements.

I.D. DATA: Not available.

Model	Body Type & Seating	Engine Type/CID	P.O.E. Price	Weight (lbs.)	Prod. Total
GTA	2-dr Coupe-2 + 2P	V6/174	N/A	2540	Note 1

Note 1: A total of 1,256 Alpines were produced in 1986, and 1,216 in 1987.

ENGINE DATA: BASE V-6: 90-degree, single-overhead-cam "vee" type six-cylinder. **Displacement:** 174 cu. in. (2849 cc). **Brake Horsepower:** 160 (DIN) at 5750 rpm. **Torque:** 166 lbs.-ft. at 3500 rpm. Single and twin-choke carburetion.

OPTIONAL TURBOCHARGED V-6: 90-degree, single-overhead-cam "vee" type six-cylinder. **Displacement:** 150 cu. in. (2458 cc). **Brake Horsepower:** 200 (DIN) at 5750 rpm. **Torque:** 214 lbs.-ft. at 2500 rpm. Garrett turbocharger.

CHASSIS DATA: Wheelbase: 92.1 in. **Wheels:** (front) 6-inch; (rear) 8.5-inch light alloy. **Standard Tires:** (front) 195/50VR15; (rear) 255/45VR15.

TECHNICAL: Layout: rear-engine, rear-drive. **Transmission:** five-speed manual. **Steering:** power rack and pinion. **Suspension (front):** upper/lower control arms, coil springs and anti-roll bar. **Suspension (rear):** upper/lower control arms, coil springs and anti-roll bar. **Brakes:** front/rear disc. **Body Construction:** unibody; fiberglass body bonded to steel backbone chassis.

PERFORMANCE: Top Speed: (turbo) 149-155 mph. **Acceleration (0-60 mph):** (turbo) 6.3-6.5 sec. **Acceleration (quarter-mile):** (turbo) 14.5 sec. **Manufacturer:** Regie Nationale des Usines Renault, Boulogne Billancourt, Paris, France. **HISTORY:** Introduced early in 1984, the GTA wasn't generally available until mid-1986.

ALVIS

Long known as a well-engineered, quality motorcar, the Alvis has a history dating back to the years just after World War I. Founded at Coventry, England in 1919 by T.G. John, a one-time naval architect, the company that bore his name got its start by building engines and carburetor castings. With the assistance of G.P.H. de Freville, they soon designed a powerplant for the first Alvis motorcar: the 10/30. (The Alvis name didn't stand for anything, incidentally, but merely had an appealing sound.) Sporting editions evolved early. While the regular 10/30 with its 1.5-liter four-cylinder engine managed 60 mph, a Super Sports displayed the "duck's back" profile that would become an Alvis tradition.

In 1923 came the 12/50 model with overhead-valve four-cylinder engine, one of which won the Junior Car Club's 200-mile race at Brooklands, running at 93.29 mph. Two years later, an experimental front-drive race car fared well in hillclimbs, but the production version launched later in the decade lacked sales appeal even with a 100-mph top speed. The year 1928 brought the first six-cylinder engine, installed the next season in a Silver Eagle model. Like all Alvis motorcars, its body came from a separate coach builder. A variety of companies produced Alvis bodies in the prewar years, including Vandan Plas, H.J. Mulliner, Charlesworth, and Cross & Ellis. During the late 1920s, front-wheel-drive Alvis racing cars (with independent front suspension) made a strong showing on many European courses.

Late in 1931, the new Speed Twenty arrived, carrying a 2.5-liter six-cylinder engine and capable of 90 mph. Longer and lower than prior Alvis models, the Twenty was compared by some to the famed SS1 from Swallow (Jaguar). On the technical side, an all-synchromesh gearbox arrived in 1934, along with independent front suspension, both for the first time on a British car. Two years later, the Speed Twenty engine grew to 2.76-liter displacement, while the company changed its name to Alvis Ltd. Motorcars weren't the firm's sole venture by any means; they also produced aircraft engines and armored vehicles. The Speed Twenty-Five moved up to a 3.57-liter engine, and in 1937 came the announcement of a 4.3-liter powerplant delivering 137 bhp (or up to 170 bhp in racing trim), ready to roll at 100 mph. As late as 1940, a total of 108 automobiles came out of the Alvis factory. During the 1941 "blitz," however, the plant was totally destroyed. Not only machinery, but blueprints and records were lost. Later on, engineers simply proceeded to create new blueprints, little by little, based upon parts removed from cars that were brought into the factory for servicing.

In the first year of peace following the war, 1946, Alvis introduced a new model: the TA14 tourer. Based on the prewar 12/70 series, it was offered with a choice of saloon or drophead coupe body (done by Mulliner or Tickford, respectively). A TB14 sports roadster also emerged, with styling that didn't win universal acclaim. Then, from 1950 to 1954, Alvis produced the better-known 21 series, powered by 3.0-liter six-cylinder engines. The line began with a TA21 tourer, as well as a handful of TB21 sports tourers. Production halted late in 1954 because the Mulliner firm, which had been supplying bodies, changed hands and no longer served that function. By the 1950s, British Alvis owners had already formed a strong bond with their own Alvis club.

Motorcar production shrunk to a trickle during the mid-1950s, with only a TC108/G on the market, wearing a body designed by Graber (of Switzerland). Expanded production resumed during 1958, as a result of an agreement between Alvis and Park Ward. That firm built a pair of two-door bodies based on the Graber design: a closed saloon and a convertible. In 1965, after Alvis was taken over by Rover, a mid-engine V-8 sports car was proposed; but that prospect faded away. Auto production finally ceased in late 1967.

1947-49 ALVIS

1947 Alvis "Fourteen" saloon.

1948 Alvis TA 14 four-door sport sedan. (Christie's)

TA14 — FOUR — Based on the prewar 12/70 series, the TA14 wore a four-door saloon body by H.J. Mulliner, or a drophead coupe body by Tickford. Each had a built-in trunk. The Sports Tourer, added for 1949, adopted separate parking lights and dual carburetors for 1950. *Motor Trend* in 1949 noted that the Fourteen was typically British and small in size, in keeping with the European trend. Though quite popular in Britain (for a small company), few were exported to the U.S.

TB14 — FOUR — Styling of the TB14 Sports Tourer roadster was different from the TA14, with cutdown doors, though both used the same chassis.

I.D. DATA: Chassis serial number is on the top (right front) of the spring housing, and on a plate on the cross member alongside the starting handle guide. Chassis numbering began at 20500. Engine number is on the right side of the block, behind the generator.

Model	Body Type & Seating	Engine Type/CID	P.O.E. Price	Weight (lbs.)	Prod. Total
TA14	4-dr Saloon	I4/115	N/A	3080	3,311
TA14	2-dr Dhd Cpe	I4/115	N/A	N/A	Note 1
TB14	2-dr Roadster-2P	I4/115	N/A	2730	100

Note 1: Production included in saloon total.

Price Note: The TB14 Sports Tourer roadster sold for about $2795 at the factory in its final form.

ENGINE DATA: BASE FOUR: Inline, overhead-valve four-cylinder. **Displacement:** 115.4 cu. in. (1892 cc). **Bore & Stroke:** 2.91 x 4.33 in. (74 x 110 mm). **Compression Ratio:** 6.9:1. **Brake Horsepower:** (TA) 65 at 4000 rpm; (TB) 68 at 4000. Three main bearings. Solid valve lifters. One or two SU carburetors. 12-volt electrical.

CHASSIS DATA: Wheelbase: 108.0 in. **Overall Length:** 174 in. **Height:** 61.8 in. **Width:** 66 in. **Front Tread:** 54 in. **Rear Tread:** 54 in. **Wheel Type:** steel disc. **Standard Tires:** 6.00x16.

TECHNICAL: Layout: front-engine, rear-drive. **Transmission:** four-speed manual (synchro); floor lever. **Standard Final Drive Ratio:** (TA) 4.87:1; (TB) 4.30:1. **Steering:** Marles worm and double roller. **Suspension (front):** semi-elliptic leaf springs. **Suspension (rear):** rigid axle, semi-elliptic leaf springs. **Brakes:** Girling hydromechanical, front/rear drum. **Body Construction:** separate body on wood framework.

PERFORMANCE: Top Speed: 84 mph. **Fuel Mileage:** 24 mpg. **Manufacturer:** Alvis Ltd., Coventry, England.

HISTORY: Introduced: (TA saloon) October 1945; (TA drophead) January 1948; (TA sports tourer) October 1948. The drophead coupe was deleted after the 1949 model year, but the other models continued in production until October 1950.

1950-53 ALVIS

1950 Alvis.

1951 Alvis TA 21 four-door sports saloon. (Christie's)

TA21 — THREE-LITRE — SIX — The Three-Litre Alvis (series 21) rode a new chassis with independent front suspension and carried a six-cylinder engine, rather than the former four. Four-door sedan and two-door drophead coupe body styles were offered (by H.J. Mulliner and Tickford, respectively). Styling was less than modern, with an upright profile and vertical-style grille reminiscent of prewar models. Alvis saloons, in particular, were built to appear traditional and dignified rather than sporty or even up-to-date. The drophead coupe, on the other hand, had a much more modern and sophisticated look, accented by the rakish rear skirts with curved cutouts and two-tone color schemes that became available. Headlamps of each body type were semi-integral, mounted alongside the grille. Front doors were hinged at the rear; back doors at the front. A flat windshield was used. Inside, round gauges flanked a round speedometer in the center of the elegantly-finished hardwood instrument panel. Standard equipment included a heater. Partial rear fender skirts were added for the 1951 model year, along with separate parking lights atop the fenders. The engine added twin SU carburetors during 1952, along with dual exhausts. The same chassis continued in service on subsequent Alvis models. *Auto Age* put Alvis "in a class by itself...of conservative design," yet it was light in weight and "many of the handling characteristics of the sports car have been built into the chassis."

1951 Alvis saloon.

1951 Alvis roadster.

TB21 — SIX — A separate Sports Tourer model was introduced later, powered by a dual-carburetor engine. A V-shaped windshield was added for the 1952 model year.

TC21 — SIX — Successor to the TA21 was introduced in late 1953; see next listing for details.

I.D. DATA: Serial number is stamped atop the chassis frame, above the offside front spring. The prefix indicates model (TA21 or TB21), followed by five digits. That number is also stamped on the side of the engine block, between the generator and fuel pump.

Model	Body Type & Seating	Engine Type/CID	P.O.E. Price	Weight (lbs.)	Prod. Total
TA21	4-dr Saloon-4/5P	I6/183	4250	3250	Note 1
TA21	2-dr Dhd Coupe-4/5P	I6/183	4450	2850	Note 1
TB21	2-dr Spts Tourer	I6/183	N/A	2828	N/A

Note 1: A total of 1,310 TA21 models were produced during the full model run.

ENGINE DATA: BASE SIX: Inline, overhead-valve six-cylinder. Cast iron block and head. **Displacement:** 182.6 cu. in. (2993 cc). **Bore & Stroke:** 3.31 x 3.54 in. (84 x 90 mm). **Compression Ratio:** 7.0:1. **Brake Horsepower:** (TA) 83/93 at 4000 rpm; (TB) 95 at 4000 rpm. Power rose to 103 at 4000 rpm with dual carburetors. Seven main bearings. Solid valve lifters. Solex dual downdraft carburetor or (later) one or two SU carburetors.

CHASSIS DATA: Wheelbase: 111.5 in. **Overall Length:** (TA) 182.5 in.; (TB) 177.2 in. **Height:** (TA) 62.5 in.; (TB) 58.0 in. **Width:** (TA) 66 in.; (TB) 67 in. **Front Tread:** 54.6 in. **Rear Tread:** 54.1 in. **Wheel Type:** Dunlop disc. **Standard Tires:** Dunlop 6.00x15.

TECHNICAL: Layout: front-engine, rear-drive. **Transmission:** four-speed manual (synchro). Overall gear ratios: (1st) 12.15:1; (2nd) 7.89:1; (3rd) 5.44:1; (4th) 4.09:1; (rev) 12.15:1. **Standard Final Drive Ratio:** (TA) 4.09:1; (TB) 3.77:1. **Steering:** Burman-Douglas recirculating ball. **Suspension (front):** independent; wishbones, coil springs and anti-roll bar. **Suspension (rear):** rigid axle, semi-elliptic leaf springs. **Brakes:** Lockheed hydraulic, front/rear drum. **Body Construction:** separate body and frame, with wooden body framework. **Fuel Tank:** 17 U.S. gallons.

PERFORMANCE: Top Speed: 92 mph. **Acceleration (0-60 mph):** 13.4 seconds.

Manufacturer: Alvis Ltd., Coventry, England.

Distributor: Fergus Motors (New York City) and Cavalier Motors Ltd. (Los Angeles).

HISTORY: Introduced: (TA21) March 1950; (TB21) October 1950. The TB21 Sports model was dropped at the end of the 1952 model year.

1954-55 ALVIS

1954 Alvis TC 21-100.

TC21 AND TC21/100 — SIX — The old-fashioned profile of the TA21 got only a mild facelift for this newer model, which also came in either saloon (sedan) or drophead coupe form. Base powerplant was the 85-horsepower version of the 2993-cc six-cylinder engine, while the high-speed TC21/100 got a 100-horsepower variant. Known as the "Grey Lady," the four-door sedan attracted considerable attention during its debut at the 1953 London Motor Show. Unlike its predecessor, the new model sported concealed door hinges and narrower door pillars, plus rear quarter windows that opened for ventilation. Side windows had chromed frames. The TC21/100 also had higher compression ratio, center-lock wire wheels, and a higher (3.77:1) axle ratio. Buyers were guaranteed a car that could hit 100 mph. Biggest drawback to American shoppers was the hefty selling price.

"One of the fastest standard 3-liter saloons in the world," proclaimed the Alvis show brochure of the TC21/100, "yet it sets a new standard for smooth, silent power. Docile in traffic, it will idle smoothly at a mere 10 miles per hour in top gear, accelerating rapidly away whenever opportunity offers." Inside were separately adjustable divided bench-type front seats, upholstered in leather. Garnish rails and window frames were finished with polished walnut. A folding armrest went into the rear seat. The restyled one-piece instrument panel was finished in polished walnut, and a Smith's "air conditioning" unit was standard. Lucas fog and passing lamps stood up front. Whichever engine was installed, the TC21 retained a formal, somewhat old-fashioned appearance for this period. "Grey Lady" script stood at the front of the sedan's hood side. Both sedans had rear fender skirts, a vertical bar grille, and semi-integrated headlamps.

A drophead coupe joined the original sedan during the 1954 model year. Though similar in basic design, the drophead coupe had less of an old-fashioned look. On its hood, toward the firewall on both sides of the car, was a horizontal ventilator.

I.D. DATA: Same as 1950-53.

Model	Body Type & Seating	Engine Type/CID	P.O.E. Price	Weight (lbs.)	Prod. Total
TC21	4-dr Sedan-5P	I6/183	N/A	3250	250
TC21/100	4-dr Sedan-5P	I6/183	4450	3250	475
TC21/100	2-dr Dhd Cpe	I6/183	N/A	N/A	Note 1

Note 1: Included in sedan production total.

ENGINE DATA: BASE SIX: Inline, overhead-valve six-cylinder. **Displacement:** 182.6 cu. in. (2993 cc). **Bore & Stroke:** 3.30 x 3.54 in. (84 x 90 mm). **Compression Ratio:** 8:1. **Brake Horsepower:** (TC21) 93 at 4000 rpm; (TC21/100) 100 at 4000 rpm. Seven main bearings. Solid valve lifters. Two SU carburetors. 12-volt electrical system. Lucas ignition.

CHASSIS DATA: Wheelbase: 111.5 in. **Overall Length:** 182.5 in. **Height:** 63 in. **Width:** 66 in. **Front Tread:** 54.6 in. **Rear Tread:** 54.1 in. **Wheel Type:** (TC21/100) Dunlop center-lock wire wheels with knock-on hubs. **Standard Tires:** 6.00x15 or 6.40x15.

TECHNICAL: Layout: front-engine, rear-drive. **Transmission:** four-speed manual (synchro); floor lever. Overall gear ratios: (1st) 12.15:1; (2nd) 7.89:1; (3rd) 5.44:1; (4th) 4.09:1; (rev) 12.15:1. **Standard Final Drive Ratio:** (TC21/100) 3.77:1; (TC21) 4.09:1. **Steering:** Burman recirculating ball. **Suspension (front):** coil springs and anti-roll bar. **Suspension (rear):** rigid axle, semi-elliptic leaf springs. **Brakes:** hydraulic, front/rear drum. **Body Construction:** separate body and frame.

PERFORMANCE: Top Speed: 101 mph. **Acceleration (0-60 mph):** 16.5 sec. **Fuel Mileage:** 18 mpg (approx.).

Manufacturer: Alvis Ltd., Coventry, England.

HISTORY: Introduced: (TC21 sedan) October 1953; (TC21/100 drophead) March 1954. Production of the sedan continued until early 1956, but the drophead coupe dropped out during 1955.

1956-57 ALVIS

TC108/G — GRABER — SIX — Although the chassis was the same (from the TC21/100), the body was vastly different for this two-door coupe. Designed by Carrosseries Graber (of Switzerland), the four-seat body was built by the Willowbrook firm, in limited quantity. With more modern lines and a 100+ mph top speed, the new Alvis attracted interest; but only a handful came out of the coachworks during this period. Headlamps were now built into the fenders, with small round parking/signal lights below. While the grille retained the same basic shape as before, made up of vertical bars, it displayed a far more modern appearance. Rounded wheel openings were evident at front and rear, as part of the greatly updated coupe profile, which used thin pillars between the front door and rear quarter-window glass. The spare tire was mounted in a tray, below the trunk. For the 1957 model year, a chrome strip was added down the center of the hood.

1956 Alvis three-liter coupe with body by Graber.

I.D. DATA: Same as 1950-53.

Model	Body Type & Seating	Engine Type/CID	P.O.E. Price	Weight (lbs.)	Prod. Total
TC108/G	2-dr Coupe-4P	I6/183	N/A	3085	30

ENGINE DATA: BASE SIX: Inline, overhead-valve six-cylinder. **Displacement:** 182.6 cu. in. (2993 cc). **Bore & Stroke:** 3.30 x 3.54 in. (84 x 90 mm). **Compression Ratio:** 8:1. **Brake Horsepower:** 104 at 4000 rpm. **Torque:** 163 lbs.-ft. at 2500 rpm. Seven main bearings. Solid valve lifters. Two SU H6 carburetors. 12-volt electrical system.

CHASSIS DATA: **Wheelbase:** 111.5 in. **Overall Length:** 189 in. **Height:** 62.5 in. **Width:** 66 in. **Front Tread:** 54.6 in. **Rear Tread:** 54.1 in. **Standard Tires:** 6.40x15.

TECHNICAL: **Layout:** front-engine, rear-drive. **Transmission:** four-speed manual (synchro); floor lever. **Standard Final Drive Ratio:** 3.77:1. **Steering:** Burman recirculating ball. **Suspension (front):** coil springs and anti-roll bar. **Suspension (rear):** rigid axle, semi-elliptic leaf springs. **Brakes:** Lockheed hydraulic, front/rear drum. **Body Construction:** separate body and frame.

PERFORMANCE: **Top Speed:** 100 + mph. **Acceleration (quarter-mile):** 19.8 seconds.

Manufacturer: Alvis Ltd., Coventry, England.

HISTORY: Introduced: October 1955. Production continued into 1958.

1958-62 ALVIS

1959 Alvis TD 21 fixed head coupe with Graber body. (Coys of Kensington)

1960 Alvis TD 21 drophead coupe. (Christie's)

TD21 — SIX — Alvis took advantage of the attractive styling of the low-production Graber design and turned it into a revised 21 series. The new body was built by Park Ward of London, and came in both hardtop coupe (saloon) and convertible form. Front disc brakes became available, as did an automatic transmission. Inside, a tachometer was mounted separately on a walnut dashboard panel. During 1962, the Series II added all-wheel disc brakes; it also had built-in foglights. Final models (in 1963) came with a ZF five-speed manual gearbox instead of the customary four-speed. The six-cylinder engine produced 104 bhp at first, but rose to 115 bhp in 1959.

TC108/G — GRABER — SIX — Production continued into 1958; see previous listing.

I.D. DATA: Serial number is on top of chassis, above the right front spring. Engine number is on the right side of the block.

Model	Body Type & Seating	Engine Type/CID	P.O.E. Price	Weight (lbs.)	Prod. Total
TD21	2-dr Coupe-4P	I6/183	N/A	3285	1,060
TD21	2-dr Conv-4P	I6/183	N/A	N/A	Note 1

1962 Alvis TD-21 coupe.

Note 1: Included in coupe production total.

ENGINE DATA: BASE SIX: In line, overhead-valve six-cylinder. **Displacement:** 182.6 cu. in. (2993 cc). **Bore & Stroke:** 3.30 x 3.54 in. (84 x 90 mm). **Compression Ratio:** 8.5:1. **Brake Horsepower:** 104 at 4000 (later, 115 at 4000). **Torque:** (later model) 152 lbs.-ft. at 2500 rpm. Seven main bearings. Solid valve lifters. Two SU H4 carburetors. 12-volt electrical system.

CHASSIS DATA: **Wheelbase:** 111.5 in. **Overall Length:** 187-189 in. **Height:** 60 in. **Width:** 66-67 in. **Front Tread:** 54.6 in. **Rear Tread:** 54.1 in. **Standard Tires:** 6.00/6.40x15.

TECHNICAL: **Layout:** front-engine, rear-drive. **Transmission:** four-speed manual (synchro); floor lever. **Steering:** Burman recirculating ball. **Suspension (front):** wishbones, coil springs and anti-roll bar. **Suspension (rear):** rigid axle, semi-elliptic leaf springs. **Brakes:** hydraulic, front/rear drum; front disc brakes standard in 1960. **Body Construction:** separate body and frame.

MAJOR OPTIONS: Automatic transmission. Wire wheels.

PERFORMANCE: **Top Speed:** 100-105 mph. **Acceleration (quarter-mile):** 19.4 seconds.

Manufacturer: Alvis Ltd., Coventry, England.

HISTORY: Introduced: September 1958.

1963-65 ALVIS

1964 Alvis TE 21 drophead coupe. (Christie's)

TE21 — SIX — Vertically-stacked quad headlamps replaced the former round single units, but otherwise the Alvis remained similar to the TD21. Engine horsepower rose to 130, however, and the chassis gained some suspension/steering modifications. Either a ZF five-speed manual gearbox or automatic transmission was available.

TD21 — SIX — Production continued into 1963; see previous listing.

I.D. DATA: Similar to 1950-53.

Model	Body Type & Seating	Engine Type/CID	P.O.E. Price	Weight (lbs.)	Prod. Total
TE21	2-dr Coupe-4/5P	I6/183	N/A	3450	350
TE21	2-dr Conv-4P	I6/183	N/A	N/A	Note 1

1963 Alvis TD 21 Series II two-door saloon. (Sotheby's)

Note 1: Included in coupe production total.

ENGINE DATA: BASE SIX: Inline, overhead-valve six-cylinder. **Displacement:** 182.6 cu. in. (2993 cc). **Bore & Stroke:** 3.30 x 3.54 in. (84 x 90 mm). **Compression Ratio:** 8.5:1. **Brake Horsepower:** 130 at 5000 rpm. Seven main bearings. Solid valve lifters. Two SU HD6 carburetors. 12-volt electrical system.

CHASSIS DATA: Wheelbase: 111.5 in. **Overall Length:** 188.5 in. **Height:** 60 in. (conv, 59 in.). **Width:** 66 in. **Front Tread:** 55.6 in. **Rear Tread:** 54.1 in. **Standard Tires:** 6.00/6.40x15.

TECHNICAL: Layout: front-engine, rear-drive. **Transmission:** four-speed or five-speed manual; automatic optional. **Standard Final Drive Ratio:** 3.07:1 or 3.54:1. **Steering:** Burman recirculating ball. **Suspension (front):** wishbones, coil springs and anti-roll bar. **Suspension (rear):** rigid axle and semi-elliptic leaf springs. **Brakes:** hydraulic, front/rear disc. **Body Construction:** separate body and frame.

MAJOR OPTIONS: Automatic transmission.

PERFORMANCE: Top Speed: 112 mph. **Acceleration (quarter-mile):** 18.8 seconds.
Manufacturer: Alvis Ltd., Coventry, England.

1966-67 ALVIS

TF21 — SIX — A new cylinder head added 20 more horsepower to the long-lived six-cylinder engine of the Alvis, and power steering became available. Otherwise, the 21-series continued as before for its final seasons.

TE21 — SIX — Production continued into 1966; see previous listing.

I.D. DATA: Similar to 1950-53.

Model	Body Type & Seating	Engine Type/CID	P.O.E. Price	Weight (lbs.)	Prod. Total
TF21	2-dr Coupe-4P	I6/183	N/A	3475	105
TF21	2-dr Conv-4P	I6/183	N/A	N/A	Note 1

Note 1: Included in coupe production total.

ENGINE DATA: BASE SIX: Inline, overhead-valve six-cylinder. **Displacement:** 182.6 cu. in. (2993 cc). **Bore & Stroke:** 3.30 x 3.54 in. (84 x 90 mm). **Compression Ratio:** 9:1. **Brake Horsepower:** 150 at 4750 rpm. Seven main bearings. Solid valve lifters. Three SU HD6 carburetors. 12-volt electrical system.

CHASSIS DATA: Wheelbase: 111.5 in. **Overall Length:** 189 in. **Height:** (cpe) 60 in.; (conv) 59 in. **Width:** 66 in. **Front Tread:** 55.6 in. **Rear Tread:** 54.1 in. **Standard Tires:** 6.00/6.40x15.

TECHNICAL: Layout: front-engine, rear-drive. **Transmission:** five-speed manual (synchro). **Standard Final Drive Ratio:** 3.22:1 or 3.54:1. **Steering:** Burman recirculating ball. **Suspension (front):** wishbones, coil springs and anti-roll bar. **Suspension (rear):** rigid axle and semi-elliptic leaf springs. **Brakes:** hydraulic, front/rear disc. **Body Construction:** separate body and frame.

MAJOR OPTIONS: Automatic transmission.

PERFORMANCE: Top Speed: 120 mph. **Acceleration (quarter-mile):** 17.8 seconds.

Manufacturer: Alvis Ltd., Coventry, England.

BODY STYLE NOTE: Later model (TD/TE/TF) two-doors were generally referred to as saloons (sedans) in Britain but coupes in the U.S.

AMPHICAR

Although amphibious vehicles for military and scientific applications were nothing new, the idea of an amphibian that could be used as the family car was unique in 1961. Produced by West German engineers and scientists after what the company claimed were some 15 years of re-

search (and $25 million in development costs), the Amphicar was aimed primarily at the American marketplace. The company, in fact, had been organized by a group of prominent American businessmen. Manufactured in West Germany by IWK (Industrie Werke Karlsruhe), under the ownership of the Quandt Group, the vehicle was handled by the Amphicar Corp. of America, in New York City.

"Anyone who can drive an automobile can operate Amphicar either as a car or a boat," claimed the company's fact sheet. To convert it from land to water use, you "simply drive it into the water and switch on the twin screws which provide water propulsion. These propellers are powered by the same engine that provides land drive. For shore landing, rear engine drive and propeller drive may be operated simultaneously. On water, Amphicar has both forward speeds and reverse."

Amphicar evolved from a concept by amphibious-vehicle expert Hans Trippel, who'd been active in the field since 1932 and displayed a prototype at the 1959 Geneva auto show. That one had an Austin engine, but the production Amphicar switched to a powerplant from the Triumph Herald.

The Amphicar's first public appearance in the U.S. was at the Fifth Annual International Automobile Show in New York City, on April 1, 1961 (April Fool's Day, as it happened). Orders were being accepted from that point on, with sale anticipated "soon." Billed as "the sport car that swims," and "the car that's fun to own," Amphicar was an all-new design, not a modification of an existing land automobile.

Unfortunately for its creators, not enough people appeared to crave a car/boat combination. Among various publicity stunts with the vehicle, a team of four soldiers crossed the English Channel in a pair of Amphicars, in 1965.

"As a car," declared *Car and Driver* in 1967, Amphicar "behaves a bit too much like a boat." Moreover, they added, its "steering is vague, the brake pedal requires the strength of Hercules, and the ride is characterized by an uncertain, billowy, wobbling motion." Narrow tires and a high center of gravity didn't help handling. *Car and Driver's* opinion that "the Amphicar is not beautiful," on the other hand, was by no means universally shared. Quite a few Americans fell in love with the little car/boat's look and novelty. While acknowledging Amphicar's shortcomings, Tom McCahill of *Mechanix Illustrated* advised in 1961 that the "guy who owns one of these at any of our thousands of lakes this summer will be the hit of the season."

In addition to general lack of interest, though, the car's body tended to suffer horrendous corrosion (logically enough) when running in salt water. Conforming to tightening regulations for both road and marine operation also became a problem. The manufacturing firm changed its name a couple of times, but continued to build Amphicars in small numbers through 1967, never turning a profit. Of the 800 or so Amphicars built before the firm finally expired in 1968, about 600 came to the U.S.

1961-68 AMPHICAR

770 — FOUR — Amphicar was touted as the only "boat" that didn't require special expensive gasoline-oil or diesel fuel. Customers were further assured that the car's electrically welded, self-supporting steel body would float safely. For water safety, the design used 21.6 inches of freeboard. Inside were two separate turning seats up front, and a bench seat in the rear. The vehicle could hold four people comfortably. In the bow was space for the gasoline tank, spare tire and tools. Navigation lights and all other Coast Guard requirements for a vessel of its size were included. A self-supporting, floating battery had longitudinal and transverse stiffeners, electrically welded.

An extra locking lever sealed each door snugly before hitting the water. The drivetrain converted at the flick of a switch from land to water operation. Front wheels served as rudders of a sort. Braking was done by shifting into reverse and hitting the gas hard. Landing on shore was accomplished by using the pushing force of both rear wheels, either separately or together.

Amphicar's four-cylinder engine came from the Standard Motor Company (Britain), while the gearbox was produced by the Hermes firm in Germany. The engine used inverted valves with pushrods and rocker arms. Spring legs had double-acting hydraulic telescopic shocks. On land, Amphicar's 17-inch steering wheel delivered a turning circle of 32 feet.

Standard equipment included heater, defroster, four-speed synchromesh transmission, spare wheel and tire, turn indicators, twin wipers, safety glass windshield, waterproof upholstery, outside mirror, lighter, tool kit and U.S. Coast Guard approved navigation lights. Safety features included hydraulic duplex brakes and a separate hand brake system for the rear wheels. A protecting bumper went all around the vehicle. The collapsible cabriolet top was easily removable, using a zipper. With the top attached, a panoramic window gave excellent visibility in all directions.

1964 Amphicar.

I.D. DATA: Not available.

Model	Body Type & Seating	Engine Type/CID	P.O.E. Price	Weight (lbs.)	Prod. Total
770	2-dr Conv-4P	I4/70	3395	2292	Note 1

Note 1: About 800 were built, three-fourths of which came to the U.S.

Price Note: Price shown was announced for 1961. Retail price dropped to $2695 in 1964, and back up to $3031 by 1967.

ENGINE DATA: BASE FOUR: Inline, overhead-valve four-cylinder (Triumph). Cast iron block and head. **Displacement:** 70.0 cu. in. (1147 cc). **Bore & Stroke:** 2.72 x 2.99 in. (69.1 x 75.9 mm). **Compression Ratio:** 8.0:1. **Brake Horsepower:** 43 (SAE) at 4750-5000 rpm. **Torque:** 61 lbs.-ft. at 2250 rpm (first announced as 58.25 lbs.-ft. at 2750 rpm). Three main bearings. Solid valve lifters. Single downdraft Solex carburetor. 12-volt electrical system (Lucas battery).

1966 Amphicar.

CHASSIS DATA: Wheelbase: 82.7 in. **Overall Length:** 170.3 in. **Height:** 59.8 in. **Width:** 60.3 in. **Front Tread:** 47.3 in. **Rear Tread:** 49.2 in. **Wheel Type:** steel disc, 5.5x13. **Standard Tires:** 6.40x13.

Note: Dimensions shown are for production model; figures announced at car's debut differed slightly.

TECHNICAL: Layout: rear-engine, rear-drive; two nylon rear propellers. **Transmission:** four-speed manual (all synchromesh) plus reverse on land. **Standard Final Drive Ratio:** 4.72:1. **Steering:** worm and roller (first announced as spindle, with divided knuckles). **Suspension (front):** independent; coil springs and trailing links. **Suspension (rear):** independent; coil springs and trailing links. **Brakes:** hydraulic, front/rear drum; 8.8-inch drum diameter (first announced as 9.05-inch). **Body Construction:** electrically welded, self-supporting steel body/chassis (integral). **Fuel Tank:** 10.8 gallons (later, 13 gallons).

MAJOR OPTIONS: Radio ($63). Anchor ($12.95). Anchor cleats ($10.85). Marine kit: fire extinguisher, floating cushions, flares, paddle ($49.25).

PERFORMANCE: Top Speed: factory announced 90 mph on land (75 mph cruising) and 10 mph on water; later road tests reached no more than 65-75 mph. **Acceleration (0-60 mph):** 43 seconds. **Acceleration (quarter-mile):** 25.2 seconds, reaching 51 mph. **Fuel Mileage:** 32 mpg (approx.); 1.5 gallons per hour on water (factory figures).

Manufacturer: IWK (Industrie Werke Karlesruhe) in West Germany, under the ownership of the Quandt Group; for Amphicar Corp. of America in New York City. Importer: Ranchero Motors, Carlstadt, New Jersey.

HISTORY: Introduced April 1, 1961 at the Fifth International Automobile Show in New York. Also seen at Miami Boat Show in 1961. By 1967 there were 71 Amphicar dealers in the U.S.

ARMSTRONG SIDDELEY

Known also as a British aircraft component manufacturer, Armstrong Siddeley had been building quality motorcars since 1919. The company was created by a merger of two earlier motorcar builders: Armstrong-Whitworth and Siddeley-Deasy (run by John Siddeley). Their first offering, a big Thirty with five-litre six-cylinder engine, carried coachwork done by Armstrong Siddeley itself (a practice that would continue, unlike that of many other luxury-car manufacturers). It sold rather well, to affluent commoners and the royal family alike. Two smaller models followed in the early 1920s: a 2.3-litre six, then a 1.8-liter four. By the mid-1920s, Armstrong was selling 4,000 or so cars annually. Only a few years later, Armstrong Siddeley became one of the first automakers to turn to the Wilson epicyclic gearbox, an early form of semi-automatic transmission using a preselector. In fact, Armstrong Siddeley obtained the rights to that gearbox and formed a separate marketing company to supply it to other manufacturers. Along with the lineup of prewar luxury models, an occasional sporty tourer appeared, and even participated in trials/rally events.

Naturally, Armstrong Siddeley was busy with aircraft engines during World War II, but became one of the first British firms to introduce a truly new car model, just as the war ended. Powered by a 2.0-liter six-cylinder engine, that Sixteen series came in three forms: a Typhoon coupe, Lancaster four-door saloon (sedan), and Hurricane drophead coupe. An increase in bore dimension brought the engine to 2.3-litre displacement in 1949, and a Whitley saloon replaced the Lancaster. A limousine appeared in 1950, powered by the same engine. Better known in America is the Sapphire series, which debuted in 1953 with a 3.4-litre engine as a rival to the Jaguar Mark saloons. By that time, a total of 12,570 Armstrong Siddeleys had been built since the war ended. The final Star Sapphires were built in mid-1960, though aircraft-engine production continued for some years.

1945-48 ARMSTRONG SIDDELEY

SIXTEEN — SIX — Unlike most cars that emerged just after World War II, which were little more than warmed-over examples of models that had sold in the late 1930s, Armstrong Siddeley's trio of 2.0-litre motorcars was fresh. The six-cylinder engine developed 70 horsepower. Three models were available: a two-door fixed-head coupe, two-door drophead coupe, and four-door saloon (sedan). Each had a grille made up of horizontal bars, peaked forward at the center. Built-in headlamps were fairly low in the fenders. Vestigial running boards were evident.

1947 Armstrong Siddeley Typhoon two-door sportsman's saloon.

1947 Armstrong Siddeley Hurricane drophead coupe.

I.D. DATA: A six-digit chassis serial number is stamped on a plate on the front of the scuttle. The first two digits ('16') denote the R.A.C. horsepower rating, followed by a sequential number. A two-letter prefix, starting with 'Z.G.,' changed to 'Z.H.,' etc. with every batch of 1,000 vehicles produced. Starting serial number: 160001. A six-digit engine number with prefix 'E' was stamped on the front mounting bracket boss.

Model	Body Type & Seating	Engine Type/CID	P.O.E. Price	Weight (lbs.)	Prod. Total
Lancaster	4-dr Sedan	I6/121	N/A	3250	Note 1
Typhoon	2-dr Coupe	I6/121	N/A	N/A	Note 1
Hurricane	2-dr Dhd Coupe	I6/121	N/A	N/A	Note 1

Note 1: A total of 12,570 Armstrong Siddeleys were produced from 1945 to 1953. Only one was known to have been sold in the U.S. during 1948.

ENGINE DATA: BASE SIX: Inline, overhead-valve six-cylinder. **Displacement:** 121.4 cu. in. (1991 cc). **Bore & Stroke:** 2.56 x 3.94 in. (65 x 100 mm). **Compression Ratio:** 7.0:1. **Brake Horsepower:** 70 at 4200 rpm. Four main bearings. One downdraft carburetor.

CHASSIS DATA: Wheelbase: 115 in. **Overall Length:** 187.5 in. **Width:** 68 in. **Front Tread:** 54.0 in. **Rear Tread:** 54.5 in. **Standard Tires:** 5.50x17.

TECHNICAL: Layout: front-engine, rear-drive. **Transmission:** four-speed (Wilson preselector gearbox). **Standard Final Drive Ratio:** 5.10:1. **Body Construction:** steel body on steel frame.

Manufacturer: Armstrong Siddeley Motors, Ltd., Coventry, England.

1949-52 ARMSTRONG SIDDELEY

1949 Armstrong Siddeley fixed-head coupe.

1950 Armstrong Siddeley Lancaster four-door light saloon.

1952 Armstrong Siddeley 18 hp Hurricane drophead coupe. (Christie's)

2.3 LITRE — EIGHTEEN — SIX — Armstrong Siddeley's overhead-valve six-cylinder engine grew to 2.3-litre displacement for 1949, as a result of an increase in the bore dimension. Before long, a new Whitley saloon replaced the Lancaster, but the fixed-head and drophead coupes continued in a form similar to that of 1945-48. Though new for 1945, the upright styling still conveyed an old-fashioned, prewar look that included rear-hinged (suicide) doors.

"The new Armstrong Siddeleys have become a familiar sight on the roads," said the early sales catalog. All body styles were designed with special non-drumming construction, with aluminum used wherever practical. Hurricane, the drophead coupe, had a three-position top. In warm weather, its center panel could be furled to give extra ventilation, keeping the top up to extend protection from the sun. Or it could be lowered completely. The rear panel of the top zippered open and shut.

Between-the-axles seating was intended to deliver the greatest comfort. Independently adjustable front seats could be positioned to form a bench seat for three. A slim windshield frame and door pillars ensured maximum visibility, and the well-proportioned rear luggage compartment was completely enclosed. A fingertip's touch operated the preselector gearbox. Features included a reserve fuel switch, adjustable steering column, large locking glovebox, door map pockets, and easy-to-operate built-in jacks. Those jacks were accessible through trap doors in the front compartment. Exterior door hinges were concealed. Overriders were now fitted to the bumpers, and rubber strips to the door sills, to prevent damage.

Inside, soft hide upholstery was deeply cushioned. Wide rear seats had a center folding armrest, able to hold three passengers. Deeply padded side armrests held non-spill ashtrays. Footrests were formed at the back of front seats, and the front compartment had door armrests and recessed handles. The passenger sun visor contained a vanity mirror. An electric clock with light was combined with the rear-view mirror. "Air conditioning" was built in and incorporated a defroster and demister. Fitted suitcases were available.

Typhoon, the two-door sports saloon (fixed-head coupe) also had a slim windscreen frame and door pillars. Its top used special non-drumming construction, with an inside lining of cream leathercloth. Front seats could be positioned to form a bench seat for three, while the rear seat had a folding center armrest. A sunshine roof was one of the features of Lancaster four-door saloon, which had headlininig of cream leather cloth. Later, a Whitley model replaced the Lancaster.

The 2309-cc six-cylinder engine developed 75 horsepower, working through a four-speed preselector gearbox with a control lever on the steering column. That included an automatic centrifugal-type clutch. Front suspension was independent, with torsion bars and wishbones. Standard body colors included black, dark blue or green with gold line on molding; turquoise blue with fawn line on molding; and fawn or grey with white line on molding. Upholstery came in blue, brown, green, or maroon. The Hurricane's soft top came in grey, blue, maroon, or fawn color.

I.D. DATA: Serial numbers same as 1945-48, except that prefix changed from '16' to '18.'

Model	Body Type & Seating	Engine Type/CID	P.O.E. Price	Weight (lbs.)	Prod. Total
Lancaster	4-dr Saloon	I6/140	Note 1	3420	Note 2
Whitley	4-dr Saloon	I6/140	Note 1	3350	Note 2
Typhoon	2-dr Spts Saloon	I6/140	Note 1	3349	Note 2
Hurricane	2-dr Dhd Coupe	I6/140	Note 1	3292	Note 2

Note 1: The Lancaster sold for 995 pounds in Britain; the other two models for 975 pounds (plus purchase tax). That translated to about $2730 in England.

Note 2: A total of 12,570 Armstrong Siddeleys were produced from 1945 to 1953. Only two were known to have been sold in the U.S. during 1949.

Note: A limousine on longer (134-inch) wheelbase was introduced in 1950.

ENGINE DATA: BASE SIX: Inline, overhead-valve six-cylinder. **Displacement:** 140 cu. in. (2309 cc). **Bore & Stroke:** 2.756 x 3.937 in. (70 x 100 mm). **Compression Ratio:** 7.0:1. **Brake Horsepower:** 75 at 4200 rpm. Four main bearings. Hydraulic valve lifters. One downdraft carburetor. 12-volt electrical.

CHASSIS DATA: Wheelbase: 115 in. exc. (limo) 134 in. **Overall Length:** (4-dr saloon) 187.5 in.; (2-dr) 186 in.; (limo) 195 in. **Height:** (4-dr saloon) 63 in.; (2-dr) 61 in. **Width:** 68 in. exc. (limo) 70 in. **Front Tread:** 54.0 in. **Rear Tread:** 54.5 in. **Wheel Type:** bolt-on disc with chromed hubcaps. **Standard Tires:** 5.50x17 except (limo) 7.00x16.

TECHNICAL: Layout: front-engine, rear-drive. **Transmission:** four-speed (Wilson preselector gearbox). Gear ratios: (1st) 18.36; (2nd) 10.66:1; (3rd) 7.22:1; (top) 5.10:1. **Standard Final Drive Ratio:** 5.10:1. **Steering:** Burman recirculatory ball "F" type. **Suspension (front):** independent; wishbones and torsion bars with Luvax Girling hydraulic shock absorbers. **Suspension (rear):** semi-elliptic leaf springs with Luvax Girling hydraulic shock absorbers. **Brakes:** Luvax Girling hydromechanical. **Body Construction:** steel body on steel frame.

Manufacturer: Armstrong Siddeley Motors, Ltd., Coventry, England.

1953-54 ARMSTRONG SIDDELEY

1953 Armstrong Siddeley Sapphire 3.4-liter four-door six-light saloon.

1954 Armstrong Siddeley Sapphire.

2.3-LITRE — EIGHTEEN — SIX — Production of the 2.3-litre models continued into 1953 as the new Sapphire appeared. Standard colors for the Hurricane drophead coupe were black, dark blue, grey, and Langham grey; or two-tones of Langham grey and green, dark blue and black, grey and dark grey, or grey and blue. See previous listing for details.

SAPPHIRE — 346 — SIX — Named for one of the jet aircraft engines produced by the Armstrong Siddeley company, the Sapphire had a considerably larger engine than the former model: 3.4 litres, delivering 120 horsepower. A twin-carburetor version of that engine delivered 150 horsepower. A four-speed gearbox was used, with either column (manual) shift or an electric preselector that employed a control box on the steering column.

Two different bodies were used: a Six Light (six-window) and a Four Light (four-window) saloon. The Four Light Sapphire differed in that it had no windows in the rear quarters, but included built-in cubby (storage) boxes. A traditional-style grille, mildly V-shaped, contained vertical bars. Built-in headlamps stood inboard of the fenders, with large round foglamps below. Front doors were hinged at the rear, "suicide" style; back doors hinged at the front. Both had vent panes. The contour of the front fender extended gracefully downward through the doors, and along the rear fender skirts.

Inside, a wide bench-type front seat was used, and both front and rear seats had a folding center armrest and side armrests. Interiors had space for five or six passengers, with hide upholstery and interior woodwork of burr walnut. Provision was made for a radio. Luggage capacity was an ample 17 cubic feet. Built-in foglamps were standard. Basic equipment also included a heater, front-window vents, ashtrays, map light, two-speed wipers, twin horns, and three grab handles. Standard colors included Silver Grey, Langham Grey, Gazelle Fawn, Sapphire Blue, Dark Blue, Corinthian Green, and Black; or any two-tone combination of those colors. Upholstery came in green, blue, red, brown or beige with cream contrast piping. Carpets were fawn-colored.

Like its predecessors, the Sapphire soon became known for its craftsmanship and engineering. Still, sales never approached those of its primary rival, the Jaguar Mark VII. Sapphire rode a wheelbase six inches shorter than a Mark VII, while performance and price were similar. Small numbers began to arrive in the U.S. during 1953, but it never became any sort of strong seller.

I.D. DATA: A six-digit serial number was stamped atop frame member, alongside the starter; and on a plate on fender valance. The first two digits indicate model ('34); followed by a sequential unit number. Starting serial number: 340001. Engine number (prefix 'E34') is stamped on the crankcase, behind the distributor.

Model	Body Type & Seating	Engine Type/CID	P.O.E. Price	Weight (lbs.)	Prod. Total
SAPPHIRE					
	4-dr Saloon-5/6P	I6/210	4450	3542	Note 1
346	4-dr Saloon-5/6P	I6/210	4250	N/A	Note 1
346	4-dr Lt Saloon-5/6P				

Note 1: A total of 8,187 Sapphires were produced during its full model run, through 1958.

ENGINE DATA: BASE SIX (Sapphire): Inline, overhead-valve six-cylinder. Cast iron block and head. **Displacement:** 209.6 cu. in. (3435 cc). **Bore & Stroke:** 3.54 x 3.54 in. (90 x 90 mm). **Compression Ratio:** 7.0:1 **Brake Horsepower:** 120/125 at 4200 rpm (150/160 at 5000 w/dual carbs). **Torque:** 165 lbs.-ft. at 2000 rpm. One or two Stromberg downdraft carburetors. 12-volt electrical system.

CHASSIS DATA: Wheelbase: 114 in. **Overall Length:** 193 in. **Height:** 63.5 in. **Width:** 72 in. **Front Tread:** 56.6 in. **Rear Tread:** 57.5 in. **Wheel Type:** disc. **Standard Tires:** Dunlop 6.50x16 or 6.70x16.

TECHNICAL: Layout: front-engine, rear-drive. **Transmission:** four-speed; either all-synchro mesh manual shift, or Wilson electric preselector, both with column-mounted control. **Standard Final Drive Ratio:** 4.09:1. **Steering:** Burman recirculating ball. **Suspension (front):** independent; trailing wishbones and coil springs with anti-roll bar. **Suspension (rear):** rigid axle and semi-elliptic leaf springs with anti-roll bar. **Brakes:** Girling hydraulic, front/rear drum. **Body Construction:** steel body on steel frame. **Fuel Tank:** 19.2 U.S. gallons.

MAJOR OPTIONS: Wilson preselector gearbox. Twin carburetors and bucket seats available later.

PERFORMANCE: Top Speed: 87-95 mph (100-103 mph w/twin carb engine). **Acceleration (0-60 mph):** 12.8 seconds (twin carb). **Acceleration (quarter-mile):** 18.6-20 seconds. **Fuel Mileage:** 16.9 mpg (approx.).

Manufacturer: Armstrong Siddeley Motors, Ltd., Coventry, England. **Distributor:** H.L. Arnes, Inc., New York City.

HISTORY: Introduced: October 1952. About 50 Sapphires were reported to have been sold in the U.S. within a few months of its first appearance at the East Coast Port of Entry, in 1953.

1955-57 ARMSTRONG SIDDELEY

1956 Armstrong Siddeley Sapphire 346 Mark II four-door saloon. (Christie's)

SAPPHIRE — 346 — SIX — Production of the 3.4-litre Sapphire continued with little evident change, except that an automatic transmission became available. As before, two versions of the six-cylinder engine, with one or two carburetors, delivering either 125 or 150 horsepower. The sales brochure listed 14 "striking improvements" for the 1955 model year, including more powerful servo-assisted brakes, ultra-violet dashboard lighting, an automatic-on roof light, rear stoneguards added to the mudguards, flashing turn signals, and automatic underhood and trunk lights. Both four-speed manual (column) shift and the electric preselector continued to be available, but the optional "no clutch" model (four-speed automatic), based on Hydra-Matic, was strongly promoted. The sales catalog went so far as to claim that "the NO-CLUTCH Sapphire drives itself--thinks for you in every driving situation." Sapphire body colors included Black, Elephant Grey over Silver Grey, Black over Pearl Grey, Silver Grey, Corinthian Green over Langham Grey, Corinthian Green, Dark Blue over Silver Grey, or Elephant Grey. Automatic-transmission models included wheel rim embellishers, fender mirrors, and a stainless steel exhaust pipe. A limousine version of the Sapphire also became available in 1955, on a 133-inch wheelbase.

Several interesting options became available in 1956, including controlled power steering, adjustable ride control, and power windows. This form of power steering could be shut off, using a dashboard lever. An under-dash knob controlled the damping action of the suspension.

1956 Armstrong Siddeley Sapphire.

SAPPHIRE — 234/236 — FOUR/SIX — Light versions of the Sapphire debuted late in 1955, with two different engine sizes: a 2200-cc four and 2309-cc six. The four was actually a variant of the standard Sapphire engine, with the same bore/stroke dimensions. The six was an updating of the earlier Eighteen engine. The four-cylinder model became known as a family sports car, with surprising performance on the highway, but neither sold well. A Manumatic four-speed transmission was available with the six-cylinder model, permitting shifting without the clutch pedal; touching the gearshift lever caused a centrifugal clutch to disengage. Appearance of the 234/236 models was considerably different from the larger 346, essentially more modern. Headlamps were all the way outboard on the fenders, for one, with small round parking lights below. Though displaying a similar pattern of vertical bars, the center grille curved more gently into the car's hood, whereas the 346 grille met its hood at a sharp corner. Two small side grilles on the smaller models also had a pattern of vertical bars.

I.D. DATA: (Sapphire 346) A six-digit serial number was stamped atop frame member, alongside the starter; and on a plate on fender valance. The first two digits indicate model ('34'); followed by a sequential unit number. Prefix 'A' indicates automatic transmission; 'PS' = preselector; and 'SM' = synchromesh (manual). Starting serial number: (346) 343751; (346 limo) 345000. Engine number (prefix 'E34') is stamped on the crankcase, behind the distributor. (Sapphire 234) Chassis serial number is stamped on frame, alongside front suspension; and on a plate on the fender valance, with the body number. Starting chassis serial no.: 4230001. Engine number (prefix 'E234') is stamped on crankcase, to rear of distributor. (Sapphire 236) Chassis serial number is on a plate on the fender valance, with the body number; and stamped on the frame. Starting chassis number: 230001. Engine number (prefix 'E236') is stamped on the mount.

1957 Armstrong Siddeley Sapphire limousine.

Model	Body Type & Seating	Engine Type/CID	P.O.E. Price	Weight (lbs.)	Prod. Total
SAPPHIRE SIX					
346	4-dr Saloon-5/6P	I6/210	4450	3542	Note 1
346	4-dr Lt Saloon-5/6P	I6/210	N/A	N/A	Note 1
346	4-dr Limousine-7P	I6/210	N/A	N/A	Note 1
SAPPHIRE FOUR/SIX					
234	4-dr Saloon	I4/140	N/A	2964	Note 1
236	4-dr Saloon	I6/141	N/A	3078	Note 1

Note 1: A total of 8,187 Sapphires were produced during its full model run, through 1958.

ENGINE DATA: BASE FOUR (Sapphire 234): Inline, overhead-valve four-cylinder. Cast iron block and head. **Displacement:** 139.7 cu. in. (2290 cc). **Bore & Stroke:** 3.54 x 3.54 in. (90 x 90 mm). **Compression Ratio:** 7.5:1. **Brake Horsepower:** 120 at 5000 rpm. Two SU HD6 carburetors. 12-volt electrical system.

BASE SIX (Sapphire 236): Inline, overhead-valve six-cylinder. Cast iron block and head. **Displacement:** 140.8 cu. in. (2309 cc). **Bore & Stroke:** 2.756 x 3.937 in. (70 x 100 mm). **Compression Ratio:** 7.5:1. **Brake Horsepower:** 85 at 4400 rpm. Stromberg D136 carburetor. 12-volt electrical system.

BASE SIX (Sapphire 346): Inline, overhead-valve six-cylinder. Cast iron block and head. **Displacement:** 209.6 cu. in. (3435 cc). **Bore & Stroke:** 3.54 x 3.54 in. (90 x 90 mm). **Compression Ratio:** 7.0:1. **Brake Horsepower:** 125 at 4700 rpm (150 at 5000 w/dual carbs). One or two Stromberg carburetors. 12-volt electrical system.

CHASSIS DATA: Wheelbase: (234/236) 111 in.; (346) 114 in.; (limo) 133 in. **Overall Length:** (234/236) 180 in.; (346) 193 in.; (limo) 212 in. **Height:** (346) 65.5 in. **Width:** (234/236) 68.5 in.; (346) 72 in. **Front Tread:** (346) 55.1 in. **Rear Tread:** (234/236) 54.3 in.; (346) 57.5 in. **Wheel Type:** disc. **Standard Tires:** (234/236) 6.40x15; (346) Dunlop 6.70x16; (limo) 7.00x16.

TECHNICAL: Layout: front-engine, rear-drive. **Transmission:** (234) four-speed manual. (236) four-speed Manumatic. (346) four-speed; either all-synchromesh manual shift, Wilson electric preselector, or full automatic. Each has column-mounted control. Manual overall gear ratios: 13.54:1, 12.8:1, 8.55:1, 5.81:1 and 4.091:1. Preselector overall gear ratios: 19.473:1, 13.909:1, 8.153:1, 5.564:1, and 4.091:1. Automatic overall gear ratios: 17.609:1, 15.625:1, 10.776:1, 5.932:1, and 4.091:1. **Standard Final Drive Ratio:** (234/236) 4.545:1; (346) 4.091:1; hypoid bevel with semi-floating shafts. **Steering:** Burman recirculating ball. **Suspension (front):** (346) independent; trailing wishbones and coil springs with anti-roll bar. **Suspension (rear):** rigid axle and semi-elliptic leaf springs with anti-roll bar. **Brakes:** (346) Girling hydraulic, front/rear drum; Hydro-Vac assisted. **Body Construction:** steel body on box-section steel frame with cruciform and tubular crossbracing.

MAJOR OPTIONS: (346) Wilson preselector gearbox. Automatic transmission. Twin carburetors. Bucket front seats. Outside fender mirrors. Stainless steel tailpipe. Wheel rim embellishers.

PERFORMANCE: Top Speed: (234) 96.5 mph; (346) 100+ mph w/twin carburetors. **Acceleration (0-60 mph):** N/A but 346 did 0-50 mph in 8.9 sec. (factory). **Acceleration (quarter-mile):** (234) 20.2 seconds; (346) 19.7 seconds.

Manufacturer: Armstrong Siddeley Motors, Ltd., Coventry, England.

HISTORY: Introduced: (234/236) October 1955; (346 automatic) October 1954.

1958-60 ARMSTRONG SIDDELEY

STAR SAPPHIRE — SIX — The two light Sapphires dropped out by 1958, but a luxury model remained, revised and renamed the Star. The new saloon carried a larger engine than before: 3990 cc (243.5 cid). Appearance was similar to the prior 346, but front doors were now hinged at the front (no longer "suicide" style) and bottom edges of the rear fender skirts were angled rather than horizontal. Standard equipment included front disc brakes and power steering. Leather upholstery was used, with polished walnut interior woodwork. An automatic transmission was standard.

SAPPHIRE LIMOUSINE — 346 — SIX — Although the former Sapphire saloon left the lineup, replaced by the new Star, the limousine remained. Riding a 133-inch wheelbase, it carried the earlier (and smaller) 125-horsepower six-cylinder engine. Air conditioning was included in both front and rear compartments. Upholstery was cloth up front, with leather in the back. Also in the rear were an electric clock, grab handles, and rope pulls attached to rear pillars. A four-speed manual gearbox was standard.

I.D. DATA: Serial number was stamped on a plate on a valance, under the hood. Starting serial number: (saloon) 330001; (limo) 370003.

Model	Body Type & Seating	Engine Type/CID	P.O.E. Price	Weight (lbs.)	Prod. Total
STAR SAPPHIRE					
Star	4-dr Saloon-5/6P	I6/243	6950	3920	N/A
LIMOUSINE					
346	4-dr Limousine-7P	I6/210	N/A	4032	N/A

ENGINE DATA: BASE SIX (Star): Inline, overhead-valve six-cylinder. Cast iron block and head. **Displacement:** 243.5 cu. in. (3990 cc). **Bore & Stroke:** 3.82 x 3.54 in. (97 x 90 mm). **Compression Ratio:** 7.5:1. **Brake Horsepower:** 165 at 4250 rpm. **Torque:** 260 lbs.-ft at 2000 rpm. Two Stromberg (or Zenith) carburetors. 12-volt electrical system.

BASE SIX (346 Limousine): Inline, overhead-valve six-cylinder. Cast iron block and head. **Displacement:** 209.6 cu. in. (3435 cc). **Bore & Stroke:** 3.54 x 3.54 in. (90 x 90 mm). **Compression Ratio:** 7.0:1. **Brake Horsepower:** 125 at 4700 rpm. **Torque:** 182 lbs.-ft. at 2000 rpm. Stromberg carburetor.

CHASSIS DATA: Wheelbase: (saloon) 114 in.; (limo) 135 in. **Overall Length:** (saloon) 194 in.; (limo) 212 in. **Height:** (saloon) 62 in.; (limo) 66 in. **Width:** (saloon) 74 in.; (limo) 72 in. **Front Tread:** 57.9 in. **Rear Tread:** 57.5 in. **Standard Tires:** (saloon) 6.70x16; (limo) 7.00x16 or 7.60x15.

TECHNICAL: Layout: front-engine, rear-drive. **Transmission:** (Star) automatic; (limo) four-speed manual. **Standard Final Drive Ratio:** 3.77:1 or 4.09:1. **Steering:** Burman recirculating ball. **Suspension (front):** coil springs. **Suspension (rear):** rigid axle and semi-elliptic leaf springs. **Brakes:** Girling front disc, rear drum. **Body Construction:** steel body on steel frame.

MAJOR OPTIONS: (Star) Controlled power steering. Adjustable ride control.

PERFORMANCE: Top Speed: (Star) 99 mph. **Acceleration (0-60 mph):** N/A (Star, 0-50 mph in 11.3 sec.). **Acceleration (quarter-mile):** (Star) 21 seconds.

Manufacturer: Armstrong Siddeley Motors, Ltd., Coventry, England.

HISTORY: Final Armstrong Siddeley saloons (sedans) were built in 1960.

ARNOLT-BRISTOL

If Chicago imported-car and accessory dealer S.H. Arnolt (nicknamed "Wacky") hadn't also served as vice-president of the Bertone coachbuilding firm in Italy, neither the Arnolt-Bristol roadster nor several other low-production hybrid sports cars might have existed. Arnolt had previ-

ously built a rebodied Arnolt-MG, on a T-series MG chassis. When he attended the London Motor Show in 1952. "Wacky" had another idea in mind and spoke with executives of the Bristol Aeroplane Company about building a wildly different body for their car's chassis. After a visit to the plant, he bought a Bristol 404 platform with running gear and shipped it off to Milan, Italy for a new body. A prototype of the complete car appeared at the London Show in November 1953. Later, the completed vehicles were shipped from Italy to Illinois for sale to eager buyers.

Immodestly billed as "the world's most distinguished sports car," the internationally-created Arnolt-Bristol was designed to blend racing-car speed and agility with flowing Italian design, resulting in a motorcar to tempt the most discriminating connoisseur. "American ingenuity," explained the brochure, "envisioned this dashing sports car. British engineering skill and Italian artistry helped to bring it into being." A 1958 ad for the stripped-down Bolide, in racing trim, promised "a round-the-clock sports car, as much at home at the supermarket or country club as on the race course." Arnolt's multinational operation continued to produce the race-winning sports car for the next eight years.

1954-61 ARNOLT-BRISTOL

1956 Arnolt-Bristol two-liter.

BOLIDE AND DELUXE — SIX OR V-8 — A collection of swoopy curves, led by a pinched-look front end, the Arnolt-Bristol was built mainly in roadster form, along with a mere two fastback coupes. The basic Bolide edition cost $3995 initially (soon raised to $4245), and wore a cut-down windshield with no top at all. An extra $750 bought the DeLuxe version, adding such niceties as bumpers and side curtains. Neither had wind-up windows, but the coupes did. Headlamps were inset into low air openings alongside the minimalist oval center grille. Tiny round parking lamps in recessed nacelles stood farther outward. Round tail lamps were similarly recessed. Deep cushioned "anatomic" bucket seats had armrests alongside, with the interior upholstered in crushed grain Connolly leather "in harmonizing colors." The austere Bolide roadsters were upholstered in synthetic leather. An open parcel compartment was contained in the dashboard, which featured a full complement of gauges including a tachometer/clock.

Whereas the standard Bristol two-liter six-cylinder BS1 sports-racer engine (which descended from the prewar BMW 328 six) delivered a moderate 105 horsepower, the carefully-tuned Arnolt edition reached 130. Brakes and transmission came not from a Bristol 404, but from the earlier 403 model. Because Arnolt-Bristols were essentially hand-built, specifications varied; no two were quite identical. Early models carried steel disc wheels, but center-lock wheels were added later. The company claimed an extremely high power-to-weight ratio of one horsepower for less than 14.7 pounds, for the Competition model.

A total of four roadsters later had a 283 cu. in. Corvette V-8 engine installed, instead of the usual Bristol inline six.

I.D. DATA: Serial number: 404X3000 to 404X3141. Engine number: 205 to 342.

Model	Body Type & Seating	Engine Type/CID	P.O.E. Price	Weight (lbs.)	Prod. Total
DeLuxe	2-dr Roadster-2P	I6/120	4745	2050	135
DeLuxe	2-dr Fbk Cpe-2P	I6/120	5995	N/A	2
Bolide	2-dr Roadster-2P	V8/283	3995	2000	5

Price Note: Prices shown are for 1955 models. Bolide price soon rose to $4245, though a "Competition" model was advertised for $3995; and the open DeLuxe model rose to $4995.

Weight Note: Weights varied, since specs were different for each car.

Production Note: Total shown includes 12 cars that were destroyed in a warehouse fire in Chicago. Coupe production uncertain.

ENGINE DATA: BASE SIX: Inline, overhead-valve six-cylinder (Bristol BS1 Mark II). Cast iron block and aluminum alloy head. **Displacement:** 120.23 cu. in. (1971 cc). **Bore & Stroke:** 2.598 x 3.779 in. (66 x 96 mm). **Compression Ratio:** 9.0:1. **Brake Horsepower:** 130 at 5500 rpm. **Torque:** 128 lbs.-ft. at 5000 rpm. Four main bearings. Solid valve lifters. Three Solex Type 32 B.I. multi-jet downdraft carburetors. Lucas 12-volt electrics.

CHASSIS DATA: Wheelbase: 96.25 in. **Overall Length:** (Rds) 167 in.; (Conv/Cpe) 171.25 in. **Height:** (Rds) 44 in.; (Conv/Cpe) 55.75 in. **Width:** 68 in. **Front Tread:** 51.86 in. **Rear Tread:** 54 in. **Wheel Type:** steel disc (later models, center-lock disc). **Standard Tires:** Michelin 5.50x16.

TECHNICAL: Layout: front-engine, rear-drive. **Transmission:** four-speed manual (synchromesh 2nd, 3rd and 4th). Standard gear ratios: (1st) 11.4:1; (2nd) 7.12:1; (3rd) 5.04:1; (4th) 3.9:1; (rev) 11.27:1. Other ratios were available. **Standard Final Drive Ratio:** 3.9:1 (other ratios available). **Steering:** rack and pinion. **Suspension (front):** twin wishbones with transverse leaf springs. **Suspension (rear):** live axle with radius arms and longitudinal torsion bars. **Brakes:** hydraulic, front/rear drum. **Body Construction:** steel body with aluminum hood and decklid on box-section steel frame, except for five semi-racing models that had aluminum bodies.

MAJOR OPTIONS: Front and rear bumpers (Bolide). Light waterproof top (Bolide). Curved safety glass windshield (Bolide). Windshield wipers (Bolide).

PERFORMANCE: Top Speed: 107-120 mph. **Acceleration (0-60 mph):** about 10 sec. **Acceleration (quarter-mile):** 17.5 seconds, reaching 85 mph. **Fuel Mileage:** 24 mpg at 60 mph (factory).

PRODUCTION/SALES: Incorporated in the total of 142 cars built were five semi-racer versions with aluminum bodies. Approximately 15 Arnolt-Bristols were sold in the U.S. in 1958, and 22 in 1959.

Manufacturer/Distributor: S.H. Arnolt, Inc., Chicago, Illinois. Chassis from Bristol Aeroplane Co. Ltd., Bristol, England. Bodies by Bertone at Turin, Italy.

HISTORY: Arnolt-Bristol started its racing success early, winning the 2-litre class at Watkins Glen, New York. The first-place finisher was driven by S.H. Arnolt himself. Arnolt-Bristols also won their class at the Sebring (Florida) 12 Hour race in both 1955 and 1956, and continued racing success into the 1960s. At the 1955 Sebring event, Arnolt-Bristol's was the only team to finish intact, and earned two trophies for team performance. Arnolt-Bristols took 1st, 3rd and 6th place in their class in the 1960 Sebring race. By late 1955, Arnolt-Bristol had seven dealers in the U.S., in addition to the main outlet in Chicago. One last car was built as late as 1964, using leftover parts from the bin. S.H. Arnolt died in 1960.

Note: Because the Arnolt-Bristol is sometimes considered a domestic automobile, despite its British chassis/drivetrain and Italian-installed body, it is also listed in the *Standard Catalog of American Cars* (1946-75).

ASTON MARTIN

Although the first true Aston Martin automobiles weren't produced in Great Britain until 1919, the name dates back to 1913 and the partnership of Robert Bamford with Lionel Martin, a sportsman and auto enthusiast. Joined in a dealership handling Singer motorcars, the two wanted to build a sophisticated racing car. The resulting "special" vehicle, powered by a 1.4-liter Coventry-Simplex L-head four-cylinder engine and riding a Bugatti-designed 1908 Isotta-Fraschini racing chassis, was named for the Aston Clinton hillclimb. That event, at a site just outside London, had formerly been run by Singer automobiles. Lionel Martin contributed his surname to the second element of the new car's title.

Similarities to Bugatti didn't diminish when the first real production Aston Martins were built in 1919 (not sold until two years later). A Coventry-Simplex engine remained beneath its bonnet, capable of producing speeds beyond 70 mph. Early in the 1920s, Aston broke 10 world records and began to make a strong showing in nearly every type of competition. An Aston nicknamed "Bunny" took five world records at the Brooklands course.

In 1924, the firm was taken over by the Charnwood family, who experienced financial woes within a year or so. Rescue was attempted by two men, "Bert" Bertelli and W.S. Renwick, initiating what would turn into a chain of ownership changes. Then, in 1927, came a new Aston Martin two-seater, built at the Feltham facility in Middlesex, England. Instead of a Coventry-Simplex engine, this one used a new 1.5-liter four with single overhead camshaft. Overall, however, its design was nothing special. By 1930, only 30 of these revised Astons had been built.

As sales began of the low, four-seat International sports model, company ownership wound up in the hands of W. Prudeaux Brune. He didn't last long either, turning over

control in 1932 to Sir Arthur Sutherland. Adopting a 73-bhp engine in 1934, the Aston Martin was capable of reaching 80 mph. One of the most striking models of that era was the two-seat Ulster racer, noteworthy for its cycle-style fenders, long tail, and outside exhaust manifold.

A new 2-liter model with 1949-cc engine came in 1936, wearing either a saloon or sports tourer body. A "Speed" edition won the 1938 Leinster Trophy. A year later, the new "Atom" model began to emerge, designed by Claude Hill on a multi-tube space frame; but the war postponed serious development.

Unlike many British firms that resumed production hurriedly after World War II, Aston Martin couldn't seem to get started. Help this time came in 1947, when industrialist David Brown bought the company, bringing with him some badly-needed funds. Brown, who'd formerly manufactured gears and tractors, also bought the Lagonda company at the same time--a purchase that included access to a new dual-overhead-camshaft six-cylinder engine. Brown's name (actually initials) would carry on for decades in the 'DB' series of Aston Martin sports cars.

Aston's first postwar model was the DB1, based on the Atom design, but no more than 15 were built. Greater success came with the DB2, created in 1949 and placed on sale the next year, with that Lagonda 2580-cc engine under its hood and a new multi-tube chassis below the closed coupe or drophead coupe body. This aero-styled two-seat model was designed by Frank Feeley, formerly of Lagonda. By 1950, Aston was significantly involved in motor racing, which led to offering the higher-powered Vantage engine for an extra 100 Pounds (Sterling). A lightweight version of the DB2 fared well at Le Mans, and won its class at the Italian Mille Miglia race.

Then, in 1951, came the DB3 racer on a tubular chassis with 140-horsepower engine and a De Dion rear end. Later versions carried a larger (2922-cc) edition of the twin-cam engine, producing 162 bhp. The DB3S race car, built in small numbers for "road" use starting in 1953, had a shapelier body on a short wheelbase and could hit 150 mph. The DB3S emerged victorious in eight racing events it entered in 1953.

On the production front, the DB2 led to the DB2-4, which looked similar to its predecessor but offered 2+2 seating and a hatchback rear. By this time, the standard engine was the 2922-cc six. Front disc brakes became available in 1957, with a power booster, as the name changed to DB Mark III (dropping the 2-4 designation). A DBR1 racing car was produced in 1957, but never built for "road" use.

The next production Aston Martin was the DB4, powered by an enlarged (3.7-liter) version of the twin-cam six, churning out some 240 horsepower. That DB4 soon became a logical rival to the Ferraris and Maseratis of the day. Short-wheelbase GT versions were offered with up to 325 horsepower, some of which wore a lightweight Zagato body.

The now-familiar dual-overhead-cam engine grew to 4-liter dimensions by 1963, in the DB5. A four-seat DB6 came next, built through the latter half of the 1960s. That led to the wider (and heavier) DBS, also powered by the 4-liter six.

Six-cylinder power began to fade away after 1969, with the debut of a new 5.3-liter four-cam V-8 engine in the DBS. Subsequent "Vantage" versions of the V-8 could hit speeds of 170 mph. After 25 years under David Brown's stewardship, the company changed hands in 1972, going to Company Developments Ltd.; and then several more times through the 1970s, until it was finally taken over by Ford. The Aston Martin V-8, which dropped the 'DB' designation after Brown's departure, continued in production through the 1980s, in both solid-topped and Volante convertible form. The most recent Aston is the Virage, introduced in 1988-89. In addition to the sporty coupes and convertibles, Aston Martin produced a dramatically opulent Lagonda four-door saloon from 1976 to 1990.

Body Style Note: Closed two-door Aston Martins were generally referred to as saloons (sedans) in Britain, but coupes in the U.S.

1948-49 ASTON MARTIN

1949-'50 2.6-liter Aston-Martin DB Mark II prototype sports coupe. (Christie's)

DB1 — 2-LITRE — FOUR — Development of the "Atom" project that had begun during the war resulted in the low-production DB1, designed by Claude Hill and offered in closed (saloon) or convertible (drophead coupe) form. The car's name stood for the company's new owner (David Brown) and the fact that this was the first model built. It was also called the Two-Litre Sports, by virtue of its two-liter four-cylinder engine, which produced 90 horsepower. A box-section, multi-tube space frame chassis was used, with coil springs all around.

The DB1's standard four-seater convertible body was designed by Frank Feeley, who, while with the Lagonda company, had designed not only the 1930 V-12 models but also the latest 2.6-liter Lagonda sedan. The DB1's three-section grille, with a large center segment flanked by two small outer grilles at the base (all with vertical bars) suggested the shape that would be used on later Aston Martins. The curvaceous bodyside displayed sweeping, sculptured lines from front to rear. Front fenders swept downward into the door, meeting bulging rear fenders. Stylish rear fender skirts left the knock-off wire wheel hubs exposed.

I.D. DATA: Chassis serial number plate is located on the firewall. Prefix 'AMC' is followed by digits indicating year offered on sale ('48' to '50'). Engine number is on right front engine mount. Chassis serial number range: AMC/48/1 to AMC/50/15.

Model	Body Type & Seating	Engine Type/CID	P.O.E. Price	Weight (lbs.)	Prod. Total
DB1	2-dr Conv cpe-4P	I4/120	N/A	2240	13
DB1	2-dr Saloon-4P	I4/120	N/A	N/A	1

Production Note: Some sources indicate that 15 were built, rather than 14.

Body Style Note: Closed two-door Aston Martins were generally referred to as saloons (sedans) in Britain, but coupes in the U.S.

ENGINE DATA: BASE FOUR: Inline, overhead-valve four-cylinder. Cast iron block. **Displacement:** 120.2 cu. in. (1970 cc). **Bore & Stroke:** 3.25 x 3.62 in. (82.55 x 92 mm). **Compression Ratio:** 7.25:1. **Brake Horsepower:** 90 (SAE) at 4750 rpm. Solid valve lifters. Two SU carburetors.

CHASSIS DATA: Wheelbase: 108 in. **Overall Length:** 176 in. **Width:** 67.5 in. **Front Tread:** 54 in. **Rear Tread:** 54 in. **Wheel Type:** wire. **Standard Tires:** 5.75x16.

TECHNICAL: Layout: front-engine, rear-drive. **Transmission:** four-speed manual; column gearshift lever. **Final Drive Ratio:** 4.10:1. **Suspension (front):** independent; coil springs with trailing arms and anti-roll bar. **Suspension (rear):** live axle with coil springs, radius rods and Panhard rod. **Brakes:** front/rear drum. **Body Construction:** separate body on box-section, multi-tube chassis.

PERFORMANCE: Top Speed: 85-95 mph.
Manufacturer: Aston Martin Ltd., Feltham, Middlesex, England.

HISTORY: DB1 was introduced in September 1948 and discontinued by May 1950. The costly-to-build DB1 was far from a profit earner for Aston, but that didn't matter at this time since David Brown had bought the firm more as a lark than as a moneymaker. Because Brown planned to introduce the new Lagonda twin-cam six-cylinder engine into an Aston Martin, the DB1 was considered an interim, temporary model. The low production also makes it one of the rarest and most difficult examples to restore and maintain, especially since the engine was never used in any other model. A special lightweight, two-passenger DB1 sports racer won the 1948 Belgian Spa 24-Hour race, driven by St. John "Jock" Horsfall and Leslie Johnson.

1950-52 ASTON MARTIN

1951 Aston-Martin DB2.

1952 Aston-Martin DB2 lightweight two-seat sports coupe. (Christie's)

DB2 — SIX — This was the first "real" Aston produced under David Brown's stewardship, closer to a competition car than a road automobile. A closed two-door saloon (fastback coupe) arrived first, followed by a drophead coupe. Styled by Frank Feeley, both body styles carried two passengers (the factory claimed three could fit in), and were sleeker and faster than the DB1. The DB2's 2.6-liter, twin-cam six-cylinder engine had been designed by W.O. Bentley, who'd been Lagonda's technical director since 1935. Valves were actuated directly via thimble tappets, eliminating the need for adjustment. Hemispherical combustion chambers were formed into the cylinder head. The initial engine delivered at least 105 horsepower, but a later optional Vantage version, introduced early in 1951, produced up to 125 bhp. The four-speed transmission was built by David Brown Industries and could be ordered with either a floor or column shift lever.

Unlike the prototypes that had been raced in 1949, the production DB2 wore wraparound bumpers front and rear, which extended onto the bodysides. It also carried a reasonable amount of road equipment. The lightweight multi-tube steel chassis evolved from the DB1 design, and carried a handcrafted aluminum-alloy body with a hinged nose/hood/fender section that tilted forward for engine access. The body was moored on Silentbloc mountings. Initial models wore a three-piece grille made up of vertical bars, with air intakes outboard of the license plate to help cool the brakes. During 1951 the grille changed to a one-piece design made up of horizontal bars, similar in overall shape to the early version (wider at bottom in what would become the traditional Aston style). A small airscoop stood ahead of the windshield. Separate parking lights were installed, and the fastback coupe had a small backlight. No trunk lid was included, but there was a hinged cover over the spare tire compartment. Small round protruding taillamps stood just above the back bumper. Early models had twin gas caps below locking filler doors in each rear fender, which opened from inside the car; but only one filler was used in 1951 and later. Inside was a 17-inch spring-spoke steering wheel, map reading light, leather-covered panels, upholstered Dunlopillo seats, and a folding center armrest. Round instruments on an aircraft-styled panel included a tachometer and clock. Luggage went into the space behind the seats. Right-hand drive was standard. Center-lock wire wheels held Dunlop 6.00x16 tires. Windshield washers became standard by 1952. A radio could be installed.

DB3 — SIX — Aston's racing car, produced from 1951 to 1953, carried a more powerful (140-bhp) version of the twin-cam six-cylinder engine. The sport roadster had a shorter (93-inch) wheelbase and used torsion-bar suspension. A De Dion rear axle was used, as well as a new five-speed gearbox.

I.D. DATA: Chassis serial number plate is located on the cowl (right side) and stamped on upper right top frame tube, just ahead of the firewall. Prefix 'LML' is followed by digits indicating year of release for sale. Engine number suffix is identical to serial number, stamped on timing cover or right front engine mount. Prefix 'LB6B' is followed by digits indicating year of release for sale. DB2 chassis serial number range: LML/50/5 to LML/50/406 (early team and development cars were numbered LMA/49/1 to LMA/49/4). DB2 engine number prefixes: LB6B (105-horsepower); LB6E (116-horsepower); LB6V (Vantage 125-horsepower); VB6B (later Vantage); VB6E (export version of VB6B). DB3 chassis serial number range: DB3/1 to DB3/10. DB3 starting engine number: DP/101.

Model	Body Type & Seating	Engine Type/CID	P.O.E. Price	Weight (lbs.)	Prod. Total
DB2	2-dr Dhd Cpe-2/3P	I6/157	6050	2662	97
DB2	2-dr Fbk Cpe-2/3P	I6/157	5950	2500	309
DB3 (RACE CAR)					
DB3	2-dr Spt Rds-2P	I6/157	N/A	2052	10

DB2 Production Note: A total of 409 to 411 DB2 models were built during the full 1950-53 production run, including three Graber drophead coupes. Some sources indicate a smaller number of drophead coupes (as few as 49), but a larger number of fixed-head models produced.

DB2 Price Note: The DB2 closed saloon (coupe) cost 1915 Pounds (Sterling) in Britain; the drophead coupe came to 2043 Pounds. In 1952, the solid-topped model sold for about $5200 in the U.S.

Body Style Note: Closed two-door Aston Martins were generally referred to as saloons (sedans) in Britain, but fastback coupes in the U.S.

ENGINE DATA: BASE SIX (DB2): Inline, dual-overhead-cam six-cylinder. Cast iron block. **Displacement:** 157.5 cu. in. (2580 cc). **Bore & Stroke:** 3.07 x 3.54 in. (78 x 90 mm). **Compression Ratio:** 6.5:1. **Brake Horsepower:** 105-107+ (SAE) at 5000 rpm. **Torque:** 125 lbs.-ft. at 3000 rpm. Four main bearings. Solid valve lifters. Twin variable-jet SU carburetors. Lucas ignition.

OPTIONAL SIX (Vantage): Same as DB2 engine above, but — **Compression Ratio:** 8.16:1. **Brake Horsepower:** 120-125 at 5000 rpm. **Torque:** 144 lbs.-ft. at 3000 rpm.

BASE SIX (DB3): Same as DB2 engine above, but — **Compression Ratio:** 8.16:1. **Brake Horsepower:** 140 at 5200 rpm. Three Weber carburetors.

CHASSIS DATA: Wheelbase: (DB2) 99.25 in.; (DB3) 93 in. **Overall Length:** (DB2) 162.5 in.; (DB3) 159.5 in. **Height:** (DB2) 53.5 in. **Width:** (DB2) 65 in.; (DB3) 61.5 in. **Front Tread:** (DB2) 54 in. **Rear Tread:** (DB2) 54 in. **Wheel Type:** (DB2) Dunlop center-lock wire. **Standard Tires:** (DB2) 6.00x16 (5.75x16 available on early models).

DB3 Tread Note: Maximum DB3 tread was 51 in.

TECHNICAL: Layout: front-engine, rear-drive. **Transmission:** (DB2) four-speed manual (synchro 2nd/3rd/4th); floor or column lever. Standard DB2 overall gear ratios: (1st) 11.03:1 (2nd) 7.48:1; (3rd) 5.02:1; (4th) 3.77:1; (rev) 11.03:1. Optional DB2 overall gear ratios: (1st) 11.03:1; (2nd) 7.05:1; (3r) 4.75:1; (4th) 3.77:1; (rev) 11.03:1. Final Drive Ratio: (DB2) 3.77:1 (4.1:1, 3.67:1 or 3.5:1 available); (DB3) 3.41:1. **Steering:** worm and roller. **Suspension (front):** (DB2) independent with coil springs, trailing links and anti-roll bar; (DB3) torsion bar. **Suspension (rear):** (DB2) independent with live axle, coil springs, radius rods and Panhard rod; (DB3) De Dion axle with torsion bar. **Brakes:** Girling hydraulic, front/rear drum. **Body Construction:** (DB2) aluminum body on multi-tube steel chassis with cruciform bracing.

MAJOR OPTIONS: Close-ratio (racing-type) gearbox. Alternate axle ratios. Vantage engine. Radio. Light bi-metal brake drums.

PERFORMANCE: Top Speed: (DB2) 110-117 mph; (DB2 Vantage) 122-125 mph. **Acceleration (0-60 mph):** (DB2) 12.4 sec. (0-50 mph in 8.6 sec., 0-100 mph in 38.8 sec.); (DB2 Vantage) 10.8 sec. **Acceleration (quarter-mile):** (DB2) 18.5 sec.

Manufacturer: Aston Martin Ltd., Feltham, Middlesex, England.

HISTORY: DB2 was introduced in May 1950 and discontinued in April 1953. DB3 was introduced in September 1951 and discontinued in May 1953. The DB2's American debut took place in 1950, at the British Motor Show in New York City. Ads in U.S. publications for Aston's "Sports Saloon" and "Drophead Coupe" promised "To Delight the Fast Car Enthusiast." The two body styles were described as "luxuriously appointed and immaculately finished." Aston Martin literature issued at the 1952 Paris Salon called DB2 "the race-bred luxury sports car," adding that "speed is built into its every line; exhilaration is there for the most enthusiastic sports driver....The culmination of thirty years of Aston Martin Racing success." A later American ad described the car as "Like a piece of precious sculpture."

Three prototype fastback coupes, styled by Frank Feeley, entered the 1949 Le Mans 24-Hour race. Two had the former DB1 four-cylinder engine, while one was powered by the new Lagonda six. They failed to score, but soon afterward an Aston earned third place overall at the Spa 24-Hour race in Belgium. Aston Martin won its class at the 1951 Le Mans event, also finishing third, fifth, seventh and tenth overall. All five entrants finished the race. Astons also won their class at the 1951 and 1952 Mille Miglia, 1951 International Alpine Trial, and 1951/52 Silverstone International Production Car Race.

Tom McCahill, the famed automotive writer at *Mechanix Illustrated*, praised the Aston's comfort but faulted its steering and handling, noting that "this was no car for one-arm amateur driving." Veteran road-racer Phil Hill, on the other hand, writing in *Motor Trend*, called the DB2's steering "fantastic....the best cornering car I've had." He went so far as to say "I have never driven a car that tracks as straight and as comfortably as the Aston." Hill also claimed the "furnishings are Rolls-Royce-like in character," with chrome "applied over solid brass."

1953-56 ASTON MARTIN

1954 Aston-Martin.

DB2 — SIX — Production of the DB2 continued into spring 1953; see 1950-52 listing for details.

DB2-4 — Mk I/II — SIX — The DB2-4 was a revamping of the original DB2 design to hold four passengers. Revised to a hatchback body, it came with a standard "Vantage" 125-horsepower, high-compression engine, formerly available as an option in the DB2. That helped maintain performance, since the new version was heavier. Starting in mid-1954, a Mark II engine of larger displacement (2922-cc versus 2580-cc) became available, developing 140 horsepower. Once again, the David Brown four-speed manual gearbox was installed.

Ostensibly a four-passenger Aston, the DB2-4 actually qualified as a 2+2; and that only barely, as the back was a mighty tight squeeze, intended for "occasional" use only. Semi-bucket front seats folded forward and inward, giving access to the back seats. The cockpit was plusher than in the two-seat version. Standard equipment included two-speed wipers, trafficators (turn signals), and an octane selector. A radio was optional. Both a convertible (drophead coupe) and hardtop coupe (called saloon in Britain) were

offered again, but the coupe now had a one-piece windshield rather than the former divided glass. The sloping back end now held an outward-hinging panel, incorporating the rear window, which allowed access to the trunk from outside. In short, it was a top-hinged hatchback, something new for a sports model. The roofline displayed a bit of a bulge at the rear, which allowed some headroom for the back-seat passengers. A smaller gas tank rode above the spare tire, and the luggage area grew considerably. The rear seatback folded forward to form a rubber ribbed flat floor, setting the stage for a design that would become commonplace a few decades later. As before, 6.00x16 tires rode Dunlop center-lock quick-change wire wheels. Mark II features included a hood airscoop and side vents for interior ventilation, a fly-off handbrake (next to the gearshift lever), and a gas cap inside the trunk. By this time, flashing turn signals replaced the early semaphore units.

1954 Aston-Martin DB 2/4.

Coupe bodies were built by H.J. Mulliner and Sons at Birmingham, the company well known for creating Rolls-Royce coachwork (and also involved with the new Triumph TR2). For 1955, a notchback coupe was added, built by Tickford (at Newport Pagnell), the firm that had also produced the DB2-4 convertible. This coupe had a conventional hood and front fenders rather than the tilt-forward nose. By 1955, chrome trim was added to the fluted rubber on door sills. The Mk II version also had a chrome trim strip.

DB3S — SIX — Another version of the DB3 racing model was produced from 1953 through 1956, with a high-output version of the 2922-cc twin-cam six-cylinder engine. Using three Weber or Solex carburetors, it delivered either 180 or 210 bhp. Wheelbase of the racing coupe was 87 inches (a foot shorter than the DB2-4). The DB3S was far more streamlined and curvy than the DB3, with upward-bulged fenders front and rear. A total of 19 DB3S sports-racing Astons were built, in addition to the all-out racers.

I.D. DATA: Chassis serial number is located on a plate on the firewall (right side), and stamped atop the right upper frame tube, ahead of the firewall. Engine number, which is identical to the serial number, is stamped on the timing cover and on the firewall plate. DB2-4 chassis serial number range: LML/501 to LML/1065. DB2-4 Mk II chassis serial number range: AM300/1100 to AM300/1299. DB2-4 engine number prefix: VB6E (2.6-liter Vantage); VB6J (2.9-liter). DB3S chassis serial number prefix: DB3S. Engine number prefix: VB6K or (race engine) DP101.

Model	Body Type & Seating	Engine Type/CID	P.O.E. Price	Weight (lbs.)	Prod. Total
DB2 (1953)					
DB2	2-dr Fbk Cpe-2/3P	I6/157	5850	2500	Note 1
DB2	2-dr Dhd Cpe-2/3P	I6/157	6150	2662	Note 1
DB2-4 Mk I (1953-55)					
DB2-4	2-dr Fbk Cpe-2+2P	I6/157	5950	2635	566
DB2-4	2-dr Dhd Cpe-2+2P	I6/157	6295	N/A	N/A
DB2-4 Mk II					
DB2-4	2-dr Fbk Cpe-2+2P	I6/178	5995	N/A	139
DB2-4	2-dr Dhd Cpe-2+2P	I6/178	6295	N/A	24
DB2-4	2-dr Notch Coupe	I6/178	N/A	N/A	34
DB3S					
DB3S	2-dr Coupe-2P	I6/178	Note 2	2052	30

1956 Aston-Martin DB 2/4 Mark II fixed head coupe. (Christie's)

Note 1: See 1950-52 DB2 listing.
Note 2: "Road" version of DB3S racer sold for 3684 Pounds (Sterling) in Britain.
DB2-4 Price Note: Selling prices in England in autumn 1953 were 1925 Pounds (Sterling) for the hardtop coupe and 2025 Pounds (Sterling) for the drophead coupe, not including purchase tax.
DB2-4 Mk II Production Note: Total Mk II production, 199 units (1955-57), including two Spider models built by Touring.
DB3S Production Note: Only 19 DB3S models were production cars; 11 were for racing.

Model Name Note: The DB2-4 was sometimes referred to as D.B.2-4 or DB2/4. A Mark I designation was sometimes (not always) used for the first DB2-4 version.

Body Style Note: Closed two-door Aston Martins were generally referred to as saloons (sedans) in Britain, but fastback coupes in the U.S.

ENGINE DATA: BASE SIX (DB2-4 Mk I, 1953-54): Inline, dual-overhead-camshaft six-cylinder (Vantage). Cast iron block. **Displacement:** 157.4 cu. in. (2580 cc). **Bore & Stroke:** 3.07 x 3.54 in. (78 x 90 mm). **Compression Ratio:** 8.16:1. **Brake Horsepower:** 125 (SAE) at 5000 rpm. **Torque:** 144 lbs.-ft. at 2400 rpm. Four main bearings. Solid valve lifters. Twin variable-jet SU carburetors. 12-volt electrical system.

BASE SIX (DB2-4 Mk II, 1954-57): Inline, dual-overhead-camshaft six-cylinder (Vantage). Cast iron block. **Displacement:** 178 cu. in. (2922 cc). **Bore & Stroke:** 3.27 x 3.54 in. (83 x 90 mm). **Compression Ratio:** 8.2:1. **Brake Horsepower:** 140 (SAE) at 5000 rpm. **Torque:** 178 lbs.-ft. at 3000 rpm. Four main bearings. Solid valve lifters. Twin SU carburetors. 12-volt electrical system.

1956 Aston-Martin DB 2/4.

Note: A 165-bhp version of the Mk II engine, with 8.6:1 compression, also became available.

BASE SIX (DB3S): Inline, dual-overhead-camshaft six-cylinder. Cast iron block. **Displacement:** 178 cu. in. (2922 cc). **Bore & Stroke:** 3.27 x 3.54 in. (83 x 90 mm). **Compression Ratio:** 8.5:1/8.6:1. **Brake Horsepower:** 180 at 5500 rpm (210-220 bhp available). Four main bearings. Solid valve lifters. Three Weber or Solex carburetors.

CHASSIS DATA: Wheelbase: (DB2-4) 99 in.; (DB3S) 87 in. **Overall Length:** (DB2-4) 169.5 in.; (DB3S) 153.8 in. **Height:** (DB2-4) 53.5 in.; (DB3S) 41 in. **Width:** (DB2-4) 65 in.; (DB3S) 58.8 in. **Front Tread:** (DB2-4) 54 in. **Rear Tread:** (DB2-4) 54 in. **Wheel Type:** (DB2-4) Dunlop center-lock quick-change wire. **Standard Tires:** (DB2-4) 6.00x16.

DB3S Tread Note: Widest tread dimension was 49 in.

TECHNICAL: Layout: front-engine, rear-drive. **Transmission:** four-speed manual (2nd/3rd/4th synchro). Overall DB2-4 gear ratios: (1st) 10.9:1; (2nd) 7.38:1; (3rd) 4.96:1; (4th) 3.73:1; (rev) 10.9:1. **Final Drive Ratio:** (DB2-4) 3.73:1. Conversion sets for 4.1:1 and 3.5:1 axle ratios were available. **Steering:** (DB2-4) worm and roller. **Suspension (front):** (DB2-4) independent with coil springs, trailing arms and anti-roll bar; (DB3S) torsion bar. **Suspension (rear):** (DB2-4) independent with live axle, coil springs, radius rods and Panhard rod; (DB3S) De Dion axle with torsion bar. **Brakes:** hydraulic, front/rear drum. **Body Construction:** aluminum body on multi-tube steel chassis with cruciform bracing. **Fuel Tank:** (DB2-4) 20.4 gallon.

MAJOR OPTIONS (DB2-4): Radio. Twin Lucas foglamps. Twin Marchal Rectilux foglamps. Fender mirrors. Al-Fin brake drums. Alternate axle ratios.

PERFORMANCE: Top Speed: (DB2-4 Mk I) 111 mph; (DB2-4 Mk II) 120 mph; (DB3S) 135-150 mph. **Acceleration (0-60 mph):** (DB2-4 Mk I) 12.6 sec.; (DB2-4 Mk II) 11.1 sec.; (DB3S) 6.6 sec. **Acceleration (quarter-mile):** (DB2-4) 18.9 sec.; (DB2-4 Mk II) 17.9 sec. Fuel Mileage: (DB2-4) 20 mpg (approx.).

PRODUCTION/SALES: Approximately 62 Aston Martins were sold in the U.S. in 1953, and 24 in 1954.

Manufacturer: Aston Martin Division of David Brown Corporation Ltd., Feltham, Middlesex, England.

HISTORY: DB2-4 was introduced in October 1953 and discontinued in October 1955. DB2-4 Mk II was introduced in October 1955 and discontinued in August 1957. DB3S was introduced in May 1953 and discontinued in December 1956. Aston Martin promoted the DB2-4 "for speed and comfort on long distance touring." Eventually, the DB3S won 15 international victories, including the Sports Car World Championship.

1957 ASTON MARTIN

DB2-4 — Mk II — SIX — The Mk II version of Aston's 2+2 continued into early 1957; see previous listing for details.

DB Mk III — SIX — Aston's 2922-cc six-cylinder engine gained horsepower in its next incarnation, producing 162 horsepower at 5500 rpm. With optional dual exhausts, output rose to 178 horsepower. Known as the DBA engine, it had a stiffer block, strengthened crankshaft, and larger valves than the prior six-cylinder powerplant. Both a fixed-head and drophead coupe were offered, but the drophead's top had a more upright look than before. The new grille displayed a tight-mesh crosshatch pattern, but carried on the traditional overall shape. Tiny round parking lights stood below the headlamps. Taillamps that had first been used in the Humber Hawk were mounted on slightly restyled Aston fenders. They now ran the full depth of the back fenders. Inside, a new instrument panel designed by Frank Feeley put all gauges in a hooded panel ahead of the driver, instead of toward the center as before. Girling front disc brakes were optional at first, but would soon become standard in the Mk IIIB edition, introduced late in 1957. Three transmis-

sions were available: the standard four-speed manual gearbox, optional Laycock de Normanville overdrive unit (which was quite popular), or a Borg-Warner three-speed automatic. A variety of competition options were available.

Note: This model was often referred to erroneously as the DB2-4 Mk III.

I.D. DATA: Chassis serial number is located on a plate on the firewall (right side), and stamped atop the right upper frame tube, ahead of the firewall. Engine number, which is identical to the serial number, is stamped on the timing cover and on the firewall plate. Chassis serial number range: (DB Mk IIIA/B) AM300/3A/1300 to AM300/3/1850. Engine number prefixes: DBA (162-bhp).

Model	Body Type & Seating	Engine Type/CID	P.O.E. Price	Weight (lbs.)	Prod. Total
DB Mk III					
Mk III	2-dr Fbk Cpe-2+2P	I6/178	6995	2850	Note 1
Mk III	2-dr Dhd Cpe-2+2P	I6/178	N/A	N/A	Note 1

Note 1: A total of 550 DB Mk III versions were produced from 1957 to 1959 (plus one competition model with 214-bhp engine).

Body Style Note: Closed two-door Aston Martins continued to be referred to as saloons (sedans) in Britain, but fastback coupes in the U.S.

ENGINE DATA: BASE SIX (DBA): Inline, dual-overhead-camshaft six-cylinder. Cast iron block. **Displacement:** 178 cu. in. (2922 cc). **Bore & Stroke:** 3.27 x 3.54 in. (83 x 90 mm). **Compression Ratio:** 8.16:1. **Brake Horsepower:** 162 (SAE) at 5500 rpm. **Torque:** 180 lbs.-ft. at 4000 rpm. Four main bearings. Solid valve lifters. Two variable-jet SU carburetors. 12-volt electrical system.

Note: Engine with dual exhausts was rated 178 bhp.

CHASSIS DATA: Wheelbase: 99.0 in. **Overall Length:** 171.5 in. **Height:** 54 in. **Width:** 65 in. **Front Tread:** 54 in. **Rear Tread:** 54 in. **Wheel Type:** wire. **Standard Tires:** 6.00x16.

TECHNICAL: Layout: front-engine, rear-drive. **Transmission:** four-speed manual; overdrive or automatic optional. **Final Drive Ratio:** 3.77:1. **Steering:** worm and roller. **Suspension (front):** independent with coil springs, trailing arms and anti-roll bar. **Suspension (rear):** independent with live axle, coil springs, radius rods and Panhard rod. **Brakes:** hydraulic, front/rear drum; Girling front disc brakes optional. **Body Construction:** aluminum body on multi-tube chassis.

MAJOR OPTIONS: Overdrive. Borg-Warner three-speed automatic transmission. Girling disc brakes. Close-ratio gearbox. Engine oil cooler. Competition clutch and suspension. Oversize (33.6-gallon) fuel tank.

PERFORMANCE: Top Speed: 119-120 mph. **Acceleration (0-60 mph):** 9.3 sec. **Acceleration (quarter-mile):** 17.4 sec.

Manufacturer: Aston Martin Division of David Brown Corporation Ltd., Feltham, Middlesex, England.

Distributor: J.S. Inskip Inc., New York City; S.H. Arnolt Inc., Chicago; British Motor Car Distributors Ltd., San Francisco; and Peter Satori Co. Ltd., Pasadena, California.

HISTORY: DB Mk III introduced March 1957 (in Mk IIIA form); discontinued in July 1959 as Mk IIIB. The "2-4" designation was dropped. Early models of the DB Mk III were intended for export. In addition to the production vehicles described, 14 DBR racing models were built from 1956 to 1960 with the 2922-cc six, producing some 265 bhp at 6500 rpm using 9:1 compressoin and three Weber carburetors.

1958-59 ASTON MARTIN

1958 Aston-Martin DB Mark III drophead coupe. (Christie's)

DB Mk IIIB — SIX — The successor to Aston's DB2-4, introduced early in 1957, continued into 1958-59 as the Mk IIIB; see previous listing for additional details. Front disc brakes were now standard. During the 1958 model year, a DBB engine became available, with higher compression and 18 more horsepower than the earlier DBA. Special engines with even higher power carried three SU or three Weber carburetors, the latter for competition use. The 195-bhp version was known as the DBD. An automatic transmission became available, and brakes had a power booster.

DB4 — SIX — In addition to an all-new body design, the new DB4, which debuted in autumn 1958, got a larger six-cylinder engine and considerably more power. Using twin two-inch SU carburetors, the all-aluminum six-cylinder engine produced 240 horsepower (263 SAE). Every major part was new. The chassis, designed by Harold Beach, was simpler than before but more rigid. Instead of the former multi-tube design, the DB4 used a pressed-steel platform frame. Wheelbase dropped an inch, down to 98, and the rear track changed slightly. Four passengers had a bit more space than before, though the Aston Martin still qualified more as a 2+2 than a full four-seater. A new fully-synchronized four-speed gearbox could have optional overdrive. A Borg-Warner automatic became available later, but few were sold. Dunlop disc brakes were used front and rear, with vacuum servo power assist. The body design, from Carrozzeria Touring in Milan, Italy, displayed that firm's *superleggera* (super light) principles. Aluminum panels went over a latticework array of small tubes. Early versions had a rear-hinged hood, but that would change for 1960. Coachwork was done by Tickford Ltd., a David Brown Company. A convertible version would not arrive until late 1961.

I.D. DATA: Chassis serial number for DB Mk III is located on a plate on the firewall (right side), and stamped atop the right upper frame tube, ahead of the firewall. DB Mk III engine number, which is identical to the serial number, is stamped on the timing cover and on the firewall plate. Chassis serial number for DB4 is stamped on the firewall plate. Suffix 'L' = LHD; 'R' = RHD. DB4 engine number is on the left front of the block, with prefix '370.' Starting serial number: (DB Mk IIIB) AM300/3/140L; (DB4) DB4/101. DB Mk III engine number prefixes: DBA (162-bhp); DBB (180-bhp); DBD (195-bhp); DBC (214-bhp).

Model	Body Type & Seating	Engine Type/CID	P.O.E. Price	Weight (lbs.)	Prod. Total
DB Mk IIIB					
Mk IIIB	2-dr Fbk Cpe-2+2P	I6/178	7550	2800	Note 1
Mk IIIB	2-dr Dhd Cpe-2+2P	I6/178	8190	N/A	Note 1
DB4					
DB4	2-dr Fbk Cpe-4P	I6/224	Note 2	2884	Note 3

Note 1: Total of 550 units produced from 1957 to 1959 (plus one competition model with 214-bhp engine).

Note 2: The early DB4 sold for 2650 Pounds (Sterling) in Britain (about $7475), not including purchase tax, and cost $9870 in the U.S. by 1960.

Note 3: A total of 1,113 DB4 models were built from 1958 to 1963; of that number, 149 (built in 1958-59) had the rear-hinged hood.

Price Note: Figures for DB Mk III were valid in 1959; fastback coupe cost $6995 in 1958.

Body Style Note: Closed two-door Aston Martins continued to be referred to as saloons (sedans) in Britain, but fastback coupes in the U.S.

ENGINE DATA: BASE SIX (DB Mk IIIB): Inline, dual-overhead-camshaft six-cylinder (DBA). Cast iron block. **Displacement:** 178 cu. in. (2922 cc). **Bore & Stroke:** 3.27 x 3.54 in. (83 x 90 mm). **Compression Ratio:** 8.16:1. **Brake Horsepower:** 162 (SAE) at 5500 rpm. **Torque:** 180 lbs.-ft. at 4000 rpm. Four main bearings. Solid valve lifters. Two variable-jet SU carburetors. 12-volt electrical system.

OPTIONAL DBB/DBD SIX (DB Mk IIIB): Same as DBA above, except — **Brake Horsepower:** 180 (SAE) at 5500 rpm (195-202 bhp with triple carburetors). **Torque:** 180 lbs.-ft. at 4000 rpm. Four main bearings. Solid valve lifters. Twin SU carburetors (triple Weber or SU carbs optional). 12-volt electrical system.

BASE SIX (DB4): Inline, dual-overhead-camshaft six-cylinder. Aluminum alloy block and head. **Displacement:** 224 cu. in. (3670 cc). **Bore & Stroke:** 3.62 x 3.62 in. (92 x 92 mm). **Compression Ratio:** 8.25:1. **Brake Horsepower:** 240 at 5500 rpm (263 SAE at 5700 rpm). **Torque:** 240 lbs.-ft. at 4250 rpm. Seven main bearings. Solid valve lifters. Two SU carburetors. 12-volt electrical system.

CHASSIS DATA: Wheelbase: (DB Mk III) 99.0 in.; (DB4) 98.0 in. **Overall Length:** (DB Mk III) 171.5 in.; (DB4) 176.4 in. **Height:** (DB Mk III) 54.25 in.; (DB4) 51.5 in. **Width:** (DB Mk III) 65 in.; (DB4) 66 in. **Front Tread:** 54 in. **Rear Tread:** (DB Mk III) 54 in.; (DB4) 53.5 in. **Wheel Type:** center-lock wire. **Standard Tires:** 6.00x16.

TECHNICAL: Layout: front-engine, rear-drive. **Transmission:** four-speed manual, fully synchronized; overdrive or automatic optional. DB4 overall gear ratios: (1st) 8.82:1; (2nd) 6.16:1; (3rd) 4.42:1; (4th) 3.54:1; (rev) 8.92:1. **Final Drive Ratio:** (DB Mk III) 3.77:1; (DB4) 3.54:1. **Steering:** (DB Mk III) worm and roller; (DB4) rack and pinion. **Suspension (front):** (DB Mk III) independent with coil springs, trailing arms and anti-roll bar; (DB4) upper/lower control arms, coil springs and anti-roll bar. **Suspension (rear):** (DB Mk III) independent with live axle, coil springs, radius rods and Panhard rod; (DB4) live axle with Watt linkage, trailing link and coil springs. **Brakes:** (DB Mk III) front disc, rear drum; (DB4) Dunlop power front/rear disc. **Body Construction:** (DB Mk III) aluminum body on multi-tube steel frame; (DB4) "Superleggera" with aluminum panels over latticework array of small tubes, atop a pressed steel platform frame. **Fuel Tank:** (DB4) 22.8 gallon.

MAJOR OPTIONS (DB4): Laycock de Normanville overdrive. Borg-Warner three-speed automatic transmission. Radio. Fog and spot lamps. Fender mirrors. Whitewall tires. Chrome wheels. Fitted suitcases. Three Weber carburetors. Oil cooler. Powr-Lok differential. Alternate axle ratios.

PERFORMANCE: Top Speed: (DB Mk III DBA) 119-120 mph; (DB Mk III DBD) 124 mph; (DB4) 141 mph. **Acceleration (0-60 mph):** (DB Mk III DBD) 8.2 sec.; (DB4) 8.5 sec. **Acceleration (quarter-mile):** (DB4) 16.8 sec.

PRODUCTION/SALES: The Aston Martin Owners Association has issued DB4 production totals by Series number, as follows (but the Aston company never used such Series designations): Series 1 (149 built); had rear-hinged hood. Series 2 (351 built, starting in January 1960); had front-hinged hood. Series 3 (162 built, starting in April 1961); had only minor changes. Series 4 (260 built, including 30 convertibles, starting in September 1961); had revised grille. Series 5 (185 built, starting in September 1962); had higher roofline. In addition, three GT models were built with a 302-horsepower engine in 1961. Approximately 50 Aston Martins were sold in the U.S. in 1958, and 68 in 1959.

Manufacturer: Aston Martin Lagonda Ltd., Hanworth Park, Feltham, Middlesex, England.

Distributor: J.S. Inskip Inc., New York City; S.H. Arnolt Inc., Chicago; British Motor Car Distributors Ltd., San Francisco; and Peter Satori Co. Ltd., Pasadena, California.

HISTORY: DB Mk IIIB introduced in autumn 1957; DB4 introduced in autumn 1958. The DB Mk III was dropped during 1959. Most assembly work on the new DB4 was performed at the Newport Pagnell plant, which had been modernized. John Wyer was now Aston's general manager. Ads promoted the DB4 as "a companion to the DB Mark 3," adding that it could accelerate to 100 mph and come to a stop "within thirty seconds." An Aston Martin won the 1959 Le Mans race, and the company took the World Manufacturer's Championship. All told, 1959 was a top racing year for Aston, led by the special DBR 1/2. A prototype DB4GT won the production-car race at Silverstone (in Britain) in early 1959.

In 1958, Prince Philip of Britain gave Aston Martin Lagonda his Royal Warrant of Appointment. That bestowed the right to display his coat of arms on the cars, and for company letterheads to read "Motorcar Manufacturers by Appointment to His Royal Highness."

1960-62 ASTON MARTIN

DB4 — SIX — Early in 1960, the DB4 got a front-hinged hood to replace the former rear-hinged version. Overdrive also became available as an option. The body wore a wraparound windshield and had space inside for four adults (or so the literature claimed). In September 1961, the grille was revised and Vantage models got sloping covers over their headlamps. The new optional Vantage engine produced 26 more horsepower than the basic inline twin-cam six. Both 3670-cc engines had hemispherical combustion chambers and a seven-bearing crankshaft. Late in 1961, a four-seat convertible joined the original DB4 fastback coupe. Atop the DB4's unitized platform-type frame was a superstructure of welded tubes, with light alloy body panels. The platform chassis had large box-section side and crossmembers with an integral-mounted bulkhead. Dunlop all-disc brakes with power assist were standard. A choice of three axle rations was

available. Dunlop center-lock wheels held Avon Turbospeed 6.00x16 tires. A DB4 could travel from a standstill to 100 mph and back down to zero in 27.2 seconds, according to the Motor Industry Research Association. Leather upholstery with Chapman Reutter seat fittings, dual exhausts, windshield washers, and a high-capacity heat/vent system were standard.

1961 Aston-Martin DB4 Mark II Superleggera Grand Touring coupe. (Christie's)

1962 3.7-liter Aston-Martin DB4GT Supperleggera coupe. (Christie's)

DB4GT — SIX — A semi-racing model produced in limited quantity, the DB4GT was smaller and lighter than a regular DB4, riding a five-inch shorter wheelbase. Doors were shorter, the cockpit smaller, with no back seat. Built of 18-gauge magnesium alloy panels, the DB4GT's body carried on the graceful lines of the regular DB4, but its more rounded front end held recessed (cowled) headlamps. Only 75 were built in all, plus a few specially made for racing teams.

Under the hood was a new version of the 3.7-liter twin-overhead-cam six with high-lift camshaft, large valves and higher (9.0:1) compression, fed by three dual-choke Weber 45DCOE4 carburetors. The engine produced 331 bhp (SAE), versus 263 for the basic DB4 powerplant. Dual ignition was standard, using twin distributors and two spark plugs per cylinder. A "Powr-Lok" limited-slip differential was included, with a choice of five axle ratios. Standard equipment included a wood-rimmed steering wheel on a column that adjusted for both rake and length, front/rear Girling disc brakes, and 6.00x16 Avon Turbospeed tires on Borrani center-lock wire wheels with light alloy rims. Fully adjustable seats had light alloy tubular frames, contoured to the body. A DB4GT could accelerate from a standstill to 100 mph and brake down to zero in 20 seconds.

1962 3.7-liter Aston-Martin DB4 convertible. (Christie's)

DB4 ZAGATO — SIX — The Zagato company in Italy built this special DB4 fastback coupe, which was even lighter than the GT, thus more competitive in racing. Only about 19 were built in late 1960. Bumpers were available only on special request. Although the body was built and installed in Italy, final assembly and painting took place at Newport Pagnell in England.

I.D. DATA: Chassis serial number for DB4 is stamped on the firewall plate. Suffix 'L' = LHD; 'R' = RHD. DB4 engine number is on the left front of the block, with prefix '370.' Starting serial number: (DB4) continued from 1958-59; (DB4GT) DB4GT/0101.

Model	Body Type & Seating	Engine Type/CID	P.O.E. Price	Weight (lbs.)	Prod. Total
DB4	2-dr Fbk Cpe-4P	I6/224	10500	2884	Note 1
DB4	2-dr Conv Cpe-4P	I6/224	11250	N/A	Note 1
DB4GT	2-dr GT Coupe-2P	I6/224	12500	2706	75
DB4 Zagato	2-dr Fbk Cpe-2P	I6/224	13500	2600	19

Note 1: A total of 1,113 DB4 models were built from 1958 to 1963; see previous listing for breakdown.

Price Note: Prices shown were valid in 1962. In 1960, the basic DB4 coupe sold for $9870.

Body Style Note: Closed two-door Aston Martins continued to be referred to as saloons (sedans) in Britain, but fastback coupes in the U.S.

ENGINE DATA: BASE SIX: Inline, dual-overhead-camshaft six-cylinder. Aluminum alloy block and head. **Displacement:** 224 cu. in. (3670 cc). **Bore & Stroke:** 3.62 x 3.62 in. (92 x 92 mm). **Compression Ratio:** 8.25:1. **Brake Horsepower:** 240 at 5500 rpm (263 SAE at 5700 rpm). **Torque:** 240 lbs.-ft. at 4250 rpm. Seven main bearings. Solid valve lifters. Two SU carburetors. 12-volt electrical system.

OPTIONAL VANTAGE SIX (DB4): Same as above, but 266 bhp at 5750 rpm (available from September 1961).

BASE SIX (DB4GT): Same as above, except — **Compression Ratio:** 9.0:1. **Brake Horsepower:** 302 at 6000 rpm (331 bhp SAE). **Torque:** 240 lbs.-ft. at 5000 rpm. Three dual-choke Weber 45DCOE4 carburetors.

DB4 ZAGATO SIX: Same as above, except — **Compression Ratio:** 9.7:1. **Brake Horsepower:** 314 at 6000 rpm. **Torque:** 278 lbs.-ft. at 5000 rpm.

CHASSIS DATA: Wheelbase: (DB4) 98.0 in.; (DB4GT) 93.0 in. **Overall Length:** (DB4) 176.75 in.; (DB4GT) 171.75 in. **Height:** (DB4/DB4GT) 52 in. **Width:** (DB4/DB4GT) 66 in. **Front Tread:** (DB4/DB4GT) 54 in. **Rear Tread:** (DB4/DB4GT) 53.5 in. **Wheel Type:** (DB4) Dunlop center-lock wire with five-inch rims; (DB4GT) Borrani 5Kx16 center-lock wire with light alloy rims. **Standard Tires:** 6.00x16 Avon Turbospeed.

TECHNICAL: Layout: front-engine, rear-drive. **Transmission:** four-speed manual (fully synchronized); overdrive or automatic optional. DB4GT gear ratios: (1st) 2.49:1; (2nd) 1.74:1; (3rd) 1.25:1; (4th) 1.0:1; (rev) 2.43:1. **Final Drive Ratio:** (DB4) 3.31:1, 3.54:1 or 3.77:1; (DB4GT) 2.93:1, 3.31:1, 3.54:1, 3.77:1 or 4.09:1. **Steering:** rack and pinion. **Suspension (front):** upper/lower control arms, coil springs and anti-roll bar. **Suspension (rear):** live axle with Watt linkage, trailing links and coil springs. **Brakes:** front/rear disc. **Body Construction:** (DB4) aluminum panels over latticework array of small tubes, atop a pressed steel platform frame; (DB4GT) magnesium alloy body panels. **Fuel Tank:** (DB4) 22.8 gallon; (DB4GT) 36 gallon with quick-action filler caps.

MAJOR OPTIONS: Overdrive. Borg-Warner three-speed automatic transmission. Radio. Fog and spot lamps. Fender mirrors. Chrome wheels. Whitewall tires. Fitted suitcases. Three dual-choke Weber carburetors. Oil cooler. Powr-Lok differential. Alternate axle ratios.

PERFORMANCE: Top Speed: (DB4) 141 mph; (DB4GT) 142 mph; (DB4 Zagato) 153 mph. **Acceleration (0-60 mph):** (DB4) 8.5 sec.; (DB4GT) 6.4 sec.; (DB4 Zagato) 6.1 sec. **Acceleration (quarter-mile):** (DB4) 16.8 sec.; (DB4GT) 14.5 sec.

PRODUCTION/SALES: See previous listing for detailed DB4 production breakdown.

Manufacturer: Aston Martin Lagonda Ltd., Hanworth Park, Feltham, Middlesex, England (plant at Newport Pagnell).

HISTORY: DB4 introduced in autumn 1958; DB4GT introduced late in 1959. "In this year of triumphant Aston Martin achievement," said the company's brochure at the October 1959 Paris Show, the "David Brown Aston Martin DB4.G.T." was announced. "Embodying the lessons of ten years of endeavor on the most arduous race circuits of the world," the brochure continued, "this new Gran Touring model is designed to provide for the most critical of high performance car owners a culminating experience of really fast motoring." Evolved from a short-chassis DB4 driven by Stirling Moss in 1959, the DB4GT was described by *Sports Car Graphic* as a "race car in luxury clothing."

1963-64 ASTON MARTIN

1963 Aston-Martin DB4.

DB4 — SIX — Production of the DB4 model continued into 1963; see previous listings for further details.

DB4GT — SIX — Aston's semi-racer also continued officially in production into 1963, though few were built; see previous listing for full data on the DB4GT and the special Zagato edition.

1964 Aston-Martin DB5 — James Bond car.

DB5 — SIX — Even non-enthusiasts soon got to know Aston's DB5, because a special model appeared in the James Bond movie, *Goldfinger.* The familiar inline dual-overhead-cam six-cylinder engine grew to 243.7 cubic inches (3995 cc) in this version, as a result of enlarging the bore by 4 mm. Horsepower now reached 282 (325 bhp with the Vantage option, which became available by fall 1964). Initial versions had a choice of four different transmissions: standard four-speed, four-speed with overdrive, ZF five-speed, or automatic. By mid-1964, the four-speed and overdrive were dropped as the five-speed became standard. Its fifth gear was an overdrive ratio. Both the fixed-head and open bodies were done by Touring in Italy, using the *Superleggera* design principle introduced with the DB4. Headlamps on the hardtop coupe went behind sloping covers, while the convertible's were exposed. A detachable steel hardtop was optional for the convertible.

I.D. DATA: Serial number is located on a plate on the firewall, under the hood. Engine number is identical to the serial number.

Model	Body Type & Seating	Engine Type/CID	P.O.E. Price	Weight (lb.s)	Prod. Total
DB4 (1963)					
DB4	2-dr Fbk Cpe-4P	I6/224	10500	2983	Note 1
DB4	2-dr Conv Cpe-4P	I6/224	11250	N/A	Note 1
DB4GT	2-dr GT Cpe-2P	I6/224	12500	2705	75
DB4 Zagato	2-dr Coupe-2P	I6/224	14250	N/A	19
DB5					
DB5	2-dr Coupe-4P	I6/244	12775	3233	886
DB5	2-dr Conv Cpe-4P	I6/244	13650	N/A	123

Note 1: A total of 1,113 DB4 models were built from 1958 to 1963; see previous listings for breakdown. Some sources put the total as high as 1,187 units.

DB4 Engine Note: Coupe with Vantage engine sold for $11,150.

DB5 Production Note: A total of 1,021 DB5 models were built from 1963 to 1965, plus 12 shooting brakes (see 1965-66 listing).

ENGINE DATA: BASE SIX (DB4): Same as 1960-62.

BASE SIX (DB4GT): Same as 1960-62.

BASE SIX (DB5): Inline, dual-overhead-camshaft six-cylinder. Aluminum alloy block and head. **Displacement:** 243.7 cu. in. (3995 cc). **Bore & Stroke:** 3.78 x 3.62 in. (96 x 92 mm). **Compression Ratio:** 8.9:1. **Brake Horsepower:** 282 at 5500 rpm. **Torque:** 288 lbs.-ft. at 3850 rpm. Seven main bearings. Solid valve lifters. Three SU carburetors. 12-volt electrical system.

OPTIONAL VANTAGE ENGINE (DB5): Same as above, except 325 bhp at 5750 rpm; three twin-choke Weber carburetors (available after fall 1964).

CHASSIS DATA: Wheelbase: (DB4/DB5) 98.0 in.; (DB4GT) 93.0 in. **Overall Length:** (DB4) 176.8 in.; (DB4GT) 172 in.; (DB5) 180 in. **Height:** (DB4/DB4GT) 52 in.; (DB5) 53 in. **Width:** (DB4/DB4GT) 66 in.; (DB5) 66 in. **Front Tread:** (DB4/DB4GT) 54 in.; (DB5) 54 in. **Rear Tread:** (DB4/DB4GT) 53.5 in.; (DB5) 53.5 in. **Wheel Type:** center-lock wire. **Standard Tires:** (DB4) 6.00x16; (DB5) 6.70x15.

TECHNICAL: Layout: front-engine, rear-drive. **Transmission:** four-speed manual; overdrive, five-speed ZF manual or automatic transmission optional. (After mid-1964, five-speed manual gearbox became standard on DB5, with automatic optional.) **Final Drive Ratio:** (DB4) 3.77:1; (DB5) 3.31:1; other ratios available. **Steering:** rack and pinion. **Suspension (front):** upper/lower control arms, coil springs and anti-roll bar. **Suspension (rear):** live axle with Watt linkage, radius rods and coil springs. **Brakes:** front/rear disc. **Body Construction:** *"superleggera"* with aluminum panels over a latticework array of small tubes, atop a pressed steel platform frame. **Fuel Tank:** 22.8 gallon.

MAJOR OPTIONS: ZF five-speed gearbox. Overdrive transmission. Automatic transmission.

PERFORMANCE: Top Speed: (DB5) 141 mph. **Acceleration (0-60 mph):** (DB5) 8.1 sec. **Acceleration (quarter-mile):** (DB5) 16.0 sec.

Manufacturer: Aston Martin Lagonda Ltd. (David Brown Co.), Newport Pagnell, Buckinghamshire, England.

Distributor: Aston Martin Lagonda Inc., King of Prussia, Pennsylvania.

HISTORY: The DB5 was introduced in mid-1963 and remained in production until September 1965.

1965-66 ASTON MARTIN

DB5/VOLANTE — SIX — Production of the DB5 with 3995-cc six-cylinder engine continued into 1965, when it was replaced by the DB6. See previous listing for details. For 1965, the DB5 convertible got quarter bumpers to replace the former full-width design. An extra oil-cooler air intake went below the license plate, and the convertibles took on the "Volante" name (which would remain into the 1980s). An even dozen DB5s were converted to shooting brakes (station wagons) by the Harold Radford firm in London, in 1965.

1966 Aston-Martin DB6 Vantage Superleggera Grand Touring four-seater. (Christie's)

DB6/VOLANTE — SIX — Larger and more plush than its DB5 predecessor, the new DB6 also had less of a sporting image. Wheelbase was 3.75 inches longer, overall length 2 inches greater, but the chassis was otherwise the same as the DB5. The modifications in dimensions allowed more space in the back seat. The suspension configuration was also the same as before, while the Salisbury-type axle took a revised position. A "Powr-Lok" limited-slip differential was now standard. So were chrome wire wheels, air conditioning, and a radio.

No significant change took place in the engine, which again displaced 3995 cc and produced 282 bhp. Body construction was different this time around. Instead of the strictly lightweight *Superleggera* construction, this model combined aluminum body panels with an ordinary steel floor and inner panels. Frontal appearance was similar to the DB5, with a low-mounted air scoop for oil cooling; but from the cowl rearward, considerable change took place. The DB6 roofline was taller; its wraparound windshield higher and more upright. Although the coupe again came in a fastback design, its rear quarter windows now swept upward rather than downward. The former tapered tail disappeared, replaced by a squared-off Kamm-style back end. Doors held quarter windows, and quarter bumpers went on each corner. The Volante convertible arrived about a year after the DB6 fixed-head coupe, with a new power top. Neither the higher-power Vantage engine nor the Borg-Warner automatic transmission cost extra. Power steering became optional for the first time on an Aston. Standard DB6 fittings included electric windows, air conditioning, adjustable shock absorbers, heated rear window, and power antenna.

I.D. DATA: Chassis serial number for DB6 is located on a plate on the right of the cowl, under the hood, mounted horizontally on a ledge. Serial number consists of a 'DB6' prefix followed by the sequential production number, followed by a letter to denote left- or right-hand drive. Engine number is also found on that identification plate, with prefix '400.'

Model	Body Type & Seating	Engine Type/CID	P.O.E. Price	Weight (lbs.)	Prod. Total
DB5 (1965)					
DB5	2-dr Coupe-4P	I6/244	12850	3233	Note 1
Volante	2-dr Conv Cpe-4P	I6/244	13750	N/A	Note 1
DB6					
DB6	2-dr Coupe-4P	I6/244	15400	3250	1321
Volante	2-dr Conv Cpe-4P	I6/244	15400	N/A	140
Radford	Shooting Brake	I6/244	N/A	N/A	6

Note 1: A total of 1,021 DB5 models were built from 1963 to 1965, plus 12 shooting brakes in 1965.

DB6 Production Note: Figures shown for DB6 are for full production run, which ended in November 1970. Shooting brakes (station wagons) were specially built by the Radford firm in London. Some sources put the total considerably higher, at a total of 1,753 units.

ENGINE DATA: BASE SIX (DB5/DB6): Inline, dual-overhead-camshaft six-cylinder. Aluminum alloy block and head. **Displacement:** 243.7 cu. in. (3995 cc). **Bore & Stroke:** 3.78 x 3.62 in. (96 x 92 mm). **Compression Ratio:** 8.9:1. **Brake Horsepower:** 282 at 5500 rpm. **Torque:** 288 lbs.-ft. at 3850 rpm (280 DIN at 4500). Seven main bearings. Solid valve lifters. Three SU carburetors. 12-volt electrical system.

OPTIONAL VANTAGE ENGINE (DB5 Volante, DB6): Same as above, except — **Brake Horsepower:** 325 at 5750 rpm. **Torque:** 290 lbs.-ft. at 4500 rpm. Three twin-choke Weber 45DCOE9 carburetors.

CHASSIS DATA: Wheelbase: (DB5) 98.0 in.; (DB6) 101.75 in. **Overall Length:** (DB5) 180 in.; (DB6) 182 in. **Height:** (DB5) 53 in.; (DB6) 54.5 in. **Width:** (DB5) 66 in.; (DB6) 66 in. **Front Tread:** (DB5) 54 in.; (DB6) 53.5 in. **Rear Tread:** (DB5) 54 in.; (DB6) 53.5 in. **Wheel Type:** chrome wire. **Standard Tires:** (DB5) 6.70x15; (DB6) 6.70x15.

TECHNICAL: Layout: front-engine, rear-drive. **Transmission:** five-speed manual or Borg-Warner automatic. Overall gear ratios: (1st) 10.18:1; (2nd) 6.57:1; (3rd) 4.59:1; (4th) 3.73:1; (5th) 3.11:1; (rev) 12.35:1. (Fifth gear is an 0.83:1 overdrive.) **Final Drive Ratio:** (DB6) 3.73:1. **Steering:** rack and pinion. **Suspension (front):** upper/lower control arms, coil springs and anti-roll bar. **Suspension (rear):** live axle with Watt linkage, radius rods and coil springs. **Brakes:** front/rear disc. **Body Construction:** (DB5) *"superleggera"* with aluminum panels over a latticework array of small tubes, atop a pressed steel plat-

form frame; (DB6) aluminum body panels with steel floor and inner panels. **Fuel Tank:** (DB5) 22.8 gal.; (DB6) 23 gal.

MAJOR OPTIONS: Vantage engine (NC). Automatic transmission (NC). Power steering.

PERFORMANCE: Top Speed: (DB6 w/Vantage engine) 140-148 mph; (European DB6) 150 mph; (European DB6 Vantage) 161 mph; (Volante) 148 mph. **Acceleration (0-60 mph):** (DB6 w/Vantage engine) 6.5-6.7 sec. **Acceleration (quarter-mile):** (DB6) 14.5-15.4 sec. (about 94 mph).

Manufacturer: Aston Martin Lagonda Ltd. (David Brown Co.), Newport Pagnell, Buckinghamshire, England.

Distributor: Aston Martin Lagonda Inc., King of Prussia, Pennsylvania.

HISTORY: DB6 was introduced in late 1965 and remained in production until July 1969, when a Mk II version debuted. By 1966, Aston Martin's fortunes were at a low point. For one thing, the connection with Touring faded away, because that Italian design/coachbuilding company collapsed financially. In addition, demand for costly automobiles was declining in Britain. *Car and Driver* declared a DB6 to be "undoubtedly one of the spectacular cars made--until you try driving it." Without doubt, they continued, it was "one of the most attention grabbing cars on the road," and "everything on the car has been beautifully made." But they went on to fault engine noise, the car's handling on bumpy roads, and the hard steering that "requires the strength of a hairy mammoth to crank it around."

1967-68 ASTON MARTIN

1967 four-liter Aston-Martin DB6 Volante. (Christie's)

DB6/VOLANTE — SIX — Production of the DB6 continued into 1970, concurrent with the new DBS; see previous listing for details.

1968 Aston-Martin DBS. *

DBS — SIX — To mark the appearance of an all-new model, Aston Martin dropped its practice of adding a number to the 'DB' prefix and called this one DBS, though much of its running gear and chassis were shared with the prior DB6. Wheelbase grew by an inch, track width by five inches, body width by six inches, allowing more passenger space inside. Front suspension remained the same as on the DB6, but the rear got a new De Dion axle arrangement. The DBS weighed considerably more than its predecessor, but got no power boost to compensate. Thus, performance dwindled quite a bit.

Styling was by William Towns, who offered designs for both a coupe and a new Lagonda sedan. The latter was not accepted, but the fastback coupe became the DBS. Though similar in basic appearance to the DB6, it displayed a more angular look. Quad headlamps flanked an eggcrate grille made up mainly of horizontal strips, with vertical divider strips. A convertible was not part of the DBS series, and would not return for some years.

Space was available under the DBS hood for a V-8 engine, but that would not arrive until 1969. Powerplants were the same as on the DB6: either the base 282-horsepower dual-overhead-cam six, or a Vantage 325-bhp version. AE-Brico fuel injection was on the option list, but partly because of unreliable performance it found few takers.

I.D. DATA: Chassis and engine serial numbers are located on a plate on the right of the cowl, under the hood.

Model	Body Type & Seating	Engine Type/CID	P.O.E. Price	Weight (lbs.)	Prod. Total
DB6	2-dr Coupe-4P	I6/244	15400	3250	1321
Volante	2-dr Conv Cpe-4P	I6/244	15400	N/A	140
Radford	Shooting Brake	I6/244	N/A	N/A	6
DBS					
DBS	2-dr Fbk Cpe-4P	I6/244	16850	3760	787

DB6 Production Note: Figures shown for DB6 are for full production run, which ended in November 1970. Shooting brakes (station wagons) were specially built by the Radford firm in London.

DBS Production Note: Figure shown is for full production run, through 1973.

ENGINE DATA: BASE SIX (DB6/DBS): Inline, dual-overhead-camshaft six-cylinder. Aluminum alloy block and head. **Displacement:** 243.7 cu. in. (3995 cc). **Bore & Stroke:** 3.78 x 3.62 in. (96 x 92 mm). **Compression Ratio:** 8.9:1. **Brake Horsepower:** 282 at 5500 rpm. **Torque:** 288 lbs.-ft. at 3850 rpm (280 DIN at 4500). Seven main bearings. Solid valve lifters. Three SU carburetors. 12-volt electrical system.

OPTIONAL VANTAGE ENGINE (DB6/DBS): Same as above, except — **Compression Ratio:** 9.4:1. **Brake Horsepower:** 325 at 5750 rpm. **Torque:** 290 lbs.-ft. at 4500 rpm. Three twin-choke Weber carburetors.

CHASSIS DATA: Wheelbase: (DB6) 101.75 in.; (DBS) 102.75 in. **Overall Length:** (DB6) 182 in.; (DBS) 180.5 in. **Height:** (DB6) 54.5 in.; (DBS) 52.25 in. **Width:** (DB6) 66 in.; (DBS) 72 in. **Front Tread:** (DB6) 54 in.; (DBS) 59 in. **Rear Tread:** (DB6) 53.5 in.; (DBS) 59 in. **Wheel Type:** center-lock wire. **Standard Tires:** (DB6) 6.70x15; (DBS) 8.10x15.

TECHNICAL: Layout: front-engine, rear-drive. **Transmission:** ZF five-speed manual or Borg-Warner automatic. **Final Drive Ratio:** 3.73:1 (3.54:1 available). **Steering:** rack and pinion. **Suspension (front):** upper/lower control arms, coil springs and anti-roll bar. **Suspension (rear):** (DB6) live axle with Watt linkage, radius rods and coil springs; (DBS) De Dion axle with Watt linkage, trailing arms and coil springs. **Brakes:** front/rear disc. **Body Construction:** (DB6) aluminum body panels with steel floor and inner panels. **Fuel Tank:** (DB6) 23 gal.; (DBS) 25.2 gal.

MAJOR OPTIONS: Vantage engine (NC). Automatic transmission (NC). Power steering. AE-Brico fuel injection (DBS).

PERFORMANCE: Top Speed: (DB6) 148-162 mph; (DBS) 140 mph. **Acceleration (0-60 mph):** (DB6 w/Vantage engine) 6.5 sec.; (DBS w/Vantage engine) 8.5 sec. **Acceleration (quarter-mile):** (DB6) 14.5-15.0 sec.; (DBS) 16.3 sec. **Fuel Mileage:** 10 mpg (approx.).

Manufacturer: Aston Martin Lagonda Ltd. (David Brown Co.) Newport Pagnell, Buckinghamsire, England.

Distributor: Aston Martin Lagonda Inc., King of Prussia, Pennsylvania.

HISTORY: DBS was introduced in October 1967, and remained in production until 1972, when the 'DB' prefixes were dropped.

1969-71 ASTON MARTIN

DB6/VOLANTE — SIX — Production of the DB6 continued until late 1970; see previous listings for full details. By autumn 1969, a Mark II version appeared with flared wheel arches to surround fatter tires. Otherwise, little change was evident. AE-Brico fuel injection was optional.

DBS — SIX/V-8 — Starting in 1969, the DBS coupe had a choice of two powerplants available: the familiar inline dual-overhead-cam six, or a new light-alloy, 5.3-liter dohc V-8. That V-8 actually had made its first appearance for racing in 1967. The engine was virtually hand-built. Aston ceased issuing horsepower (or performance) data at this time, allowing only that the engine output was "sufficient;" but initial horsepower is estimated to have been at least 350. Later versions topped 400 horsepower. Power steering was now standard. Buyers who didn't want the ZF five-speed manual gearbox got three-speed TorqueFlite instead of the former Borg-Warner automatic. Standard equipment included air conditioning, power brakes and steering, a wood-rimmed dished-spoke steering wheel, and a radio. Seven round dials sat in a shrouded oval panel, ahead of the driver. Tires were larger on the V-8 version: GR70VR15 size, on ventilated cast alloy wheels. Early DBS models had quad round headlamps within a full-width grille.

I.D. DATA: Chassis serial number is located on a plate on the cowl (right side), along with the engine number; or in 1971, on the inner right front fender panel. Starting serial number: (1970) DBS/5494/LC; (1971) DBSV8/10030/LC.

Model	Body Type & Seating	Engine Type/CID	P.O.E. Price	Weight (lbs.)	Prod. Total
DB6 (1969-70)					
DB6	2-dr Coupe-4P	I6/244	N/A	3250	1321
Volante	2-dr Conv Cpe-4P	I6/244	N/A	N/A	140
Radford	Shooting Brake	I6/244	N/A	N/A	6
DBS/V-8					
DBS	2-dr Fbk Cpe-4P	I6/244	17900	3760	Note 1
Vantage	2-dr Fbk Cpe-4P	I6/244	N/A	N/A	70
DBS V-8	2-dr Fbk Cpe-4P	V8/326	N/A	3800	N/A

Note 1: A total of 787 six-cylinder DBS models were built from 1967-73, plus 70 Vantage models.

DB6 Production Note: Figures shown for DB6 are for full production run, which ended in November 1970. Shooting brakes (station wagons) were specially built by the Radford firm in London.

DBS V-8 Note: Models with the V-8 engine were not commonly listed as available in the U.S. until 1971 or 1972.

ENGINE DATA: BASE SIX (DB6/DBS): Inline, dual-overhead-camshaft six-cylinder. Aluminum alloy block and head. **Displacement:** 243.7 cu. in. (3995 cc). **Bore & Stroke:** 3.78 x 3.62 in. (96 x 92 mm). **Compression Ratio:** 8.9:1. **Brake Horsepower:** 282 at 5500 rpm. **Torque:** 288 lbs.-ft. at 3850 rpm (280 DIN at 4500). Seven main bearings. Solid valve lifters. Three SU carburetors. 12-volt electrical system.

OPTIONAL VANTAGE ENGINE (DB6/DBS): Same as above, except — **Compression Ratio:** 9.4:1. **Brake Horsepower:** 325 at 5750 rpm. **Torque:** 290 lbs.-ft. at 4500 rpm. Three twin-choke Weber carburetors.

BASE V-8 (DBS V-8): 90-degree, dual-overhead-camshaft V-8. Light alloy block and head. **Displacement:** 325.9 cu. in. (5340 cc). **Bore & Stroke:** 3.94 x 3.35 in. (100 x 85 mm). **Compression Ratio:** 9.0:1. **Brake Horsepower:** 350 + (estimated). **Torque:** 400 lbs.-ft. at 4000 rpm. Five main bearings. Bosch mechanical fuel injection. 12-volt electrical system.

CHASSIS DATA: Wheelbase: (DB6) 101.75 in.; (DBS) 102.75 in. Overall Length: (DB6) 182 in.; (DBS) 180.5 in. Height: (DB6) 54.5 in.; (DBS) 52.25 in. Width: (DB6) 66 in.; (DBS) 72 in. Front Tread: (DB6) 54 in.; (DBS) 59 in. Rear Tread: (DB6) 53.5 in.; (DBS) 59 in. Wheel Type: (DB6/DBS) center-lock wire; (V-8) five-stud, ventilated cast alloy. Standard Tires: (DB6) 8.15x15; (DBS) 8.10x15; (DBS V-8) GR70VR15 Pirelli Cinturato.

TECHNICAL: Layout: front-engine, rear-drive. Transmission: ZF five-speed manual or three-speed TorqueFlite automatic. DBS V-8 gear ratios: (1st) 2.90:1; (2nd) 1.78:1; (3rd) 1.22:1; (4th) 1.00:1; (5th) 0.845:1. Standard Final Drive Ratio: DBS V-8 3.54:1 w/manual, 3.31:1 w/automatic. Steering: rack and pinion. Suspension (front): upper/lower control arms, coil springs and anti-roll bar. Suspension (rear): (DB6) live axle with Watt linkage, radius rods and coil springs; (DBS) De Dion axle with Watt linkage, trailing arms and coil springs. Brakes: front/rear disc. Body Construction: (DBS) aluminum body panels with steel floor and inner panels, on platform frame.

MAJOR OPTIONS: Vantage engine. Automatic transmission.

PERFORMANCE: Top Speed: (DB6 w/Vantage engine) 148 mph; (DBS) 140 mph; (DBS V-8) about 160 mph. Acceleration (0-60 mph): (DB6 w/Vantage engine) 6.5 sec.; (DBS w/Vantage engine) 8.5 sec. Acceleration (quarter-mile): (DB6) 14.5 sec.; (DBS) 16.3 sec. (DBS V-8) 14.3 sec.
Note: Early factory claims for the European DBS V-8 included a top speed of 170 mph, 0-60 mph in 5.7 seconds, and 0-100 in 12.5 seconds.
Manufacturer: Aston Martin Lagonda Ltd. (David Brown Co.) Newport Pagnell, Buckinghamsire, England.
Distributor: Aston Martin Lagonda Inc., King of Prussia, Pennsylvania.

HISTORY: DB6 Mk II was introduced in July 1969 and remained in production until November 1970. Production of the DBS V-8 began in 1969 and continued until spring 1972, when the 'DB' portion of the name was dropped. Unlike many European makes, which borrowed American V-8 engines in these years, Aston Martin built its own.

1972-76 ASTON MARTIN

VANTAGE — SIX — In 1972, the six-cylinder DBS was restyled and renamed "Aston Martin Vantage." This new version had single headlamps and a narrower grille with a tight crosshatch pattern of black mesh. The 325-horsepower engine became standard. Production ceased in mid-1973, leaving only the V-8 to carry on.

AM V-8 — V-8 — With the departure of David Brown from the Aston Martin company, the 'DB' prefix was dropped, and the V-8 coupe renamed "Aston Martin V-8." At the same time, it got a new single-headlamp nose (replacing the former quad setup) and a narrower black-mesh grille, like the six-cylinder version. In addition, a hood bulge replaced the former scoop. During 1973, fuel injection was abandoned and the V-8 returned to a quartet of Weber carburetors. Later yet, in the 1980s, an improved version of Bosch fuel injection would replace the carburetors.

I.D. DATA: Serial number is on the inner right front fender panel, in the engine compartment. Engine number is on the top of the engine, near the front center. Starting serial number (1972): (DBS V-8) DBSV8/10030/LC (continued from 1971). Later prefix: 'V8', followed by sequential serial number.

Model	Body Type & Seating	Engine Type/CID	P.O.E. Price	Weight (lbs.)	Prod. Total
Vantage	2-dr Fbk Cpe-4P	I6/244	N/A	3760	Note 1
V-8	2-dr Fbk Cpe-4P	V8/326	22000	3800	N/A

Note 1: A total of 787 six-cylinder DBS models (plus Vantage models) were built from 1967-73.
Price Note: Base price for the V-8 coupe rose to $33,950 by 1976.
Production Note: A total of 250 Aston Martins were produced in 1973, 200 in 1974, only 20 in 1975, and 176 in 1976.

ENGINE DATA: BASE SIX (Vantage): Inline, dual-overhead-camshaft six-cylinder. Aluminum alloy block and head. Displacement: 243.7 cu. in. (3995 cc). Bore & Stroke: 3.78 x 3.62 in. (96 x 92 mm). Compression Ratio: 8.9:1. Brake Horsepower: 325 at 5750 rpm. Torque: 290 lbs.-ft. at 4500 rpm. Seven main bearings. Solid valve lifters. Three twin-choke Weber carburetors.

BASE V-8 (V-8): 90-degree, dual-overhead-camshaft V-8. Light alloy block and head. Displacement: 325.9 cu. in. (5340 cc). Bore & Stroke: 3.94 x 3.35 in. (100 x 85 mm). Compression Ratio: 8.3:1/9.0:1. Brake Horsepower: 350+ (estimated gross). Torque: 400 lbs.-ft. at 4000 rpm. Five main bearings. Bosch electronic fuel injection (replaced by four Weber dual-choke carburetors during 1973).

CHASSIS DATA: Wheelbase: 102.75 in. Overall Length: 180.5 in. Height: 52.25 in. Width: 72 in. Front Tread: 59 in. Rear Tread: 59 in. Standard Tires: (Vantage) 8.10x15; (V-8) GR70VR15.

TECHNICAL: Layout: front-engine, rear-drive. Transmission: ZF five-speed manual or three-speed TorqueFlite automatic. Final Drive Ratio: (V-8) 2.88:1. Steering: rack and pinion. Suspension (front): upper/lower control arms, coil springs and anti-roll bar. Suspension (rear): De Dion axle with Watt linkage, trailing arms and coil springs. Brakes: front/rear disc. Body Construction: aluminum body panels with steel floor and inner panels on platform frame. Fuel Tank: (V-8) 25.2 gallon.

MAJOR OPTIONS: Automatic transmission.
PERFORMANCE: Top Speed: (carbureted V-8) 145 mph; (fuel-injected V-8) 136 mph. Acceleration (0-60 mph): (carbureted V-8) 6.2 sec.; (fuel-injected V-8) 0-50 mph in 4.5 sec. Fuel Mileage: under 11 mpg (U.S.).
Manufacturer: Aston Martin Lagonda Ltd., Newport Pagnell, Buckinghamsire, England.
Distributor: Aston Martin Lagonda Inc., King of Prussia, Pennsylvania.

HISTORY: Aston Martin's new Lagonda sedan entered production in 1976; see next listing for details. Production of the six-cylinder DBS halted in July 1973, ending the reign of the twin-cam six. All subsequent Astons carried a V-8 engine. By 1972, David Brown had sold his interest in the company to Company Developments Ltd., so the DBS V-8 was renamed, simply, Aston Martin V-8. For some six months during 1974-75, no Astons at all were built as the company scampered for both funds and managers.

1977-80 ASTON MARTIN

1978 Aston-Martin V-8. (William Siuru Jr.)

V-8 VANTAGE/VOLANTE — V-8 — Horsepower of the V-8 coupe got a boost in 1977, by a claimed 15 percent. In the same year, a Vantage V-8 joined the lineup, wearing a deep front air dam (with cooling slots), blanked grille, large Cibie driving lamps ahead of the grille, rear lip spoiler, and big Pirelli P7 tires. The initial rating of the Vantage engine was an estimated 400 horsepower. It had revised cam profiles, and larger intake valves and carburetors. Vantage models were built only to order, with manual shift. In June 1978, a Volante convertible was added; but not until two years later could it be ordered with the Vantage engine option. Standard V-8 equipment included a front passenger footrest, reclining front bucket seats, contoured rear seat with folding armrest, Sundym glass, power windows, and electrically-heated rear window. Also included in late 1970s models were Coolaire air conditioning and a Blaupunkt electronically-controlled stereo radio with cassette player.

1979 Aston-Martin V-8.

LAGONDA — V-8 — In 1976, a massive four-door saloon joined the Aston Martin coupe, taking the Lagonda nameplate that had not been used since the demise of the Lagonda Rapide. Luxurious and angular in appearance, the saloon carried the same 5340-cc V-8 engine as the sports models, with a three-speed automatic transmission. A version with five-speed manual gearshift also was announced. Styling was an amalgam of sharp edges, with a tapered nose, narrow vertical-bar grille, and large retracting headlamps. Rectangular parking lights stood at outer ends of the nose, with two rectangular auxiliary lights inboard of each (and somewhat recessed). Standard equipment included air conditioning, a fire extinguisher, and a tachometer. An electronic dashboard displayed ribbon-type scales and 16 warning lights, with readouts for average speed, fuel consumption, and inside and outside temperature. Touch switches controlled the automatic transmission. Bucket-type front seats were upholstered in English hide and included vernier reclining adjustments, plus map pockets on the back. Contoured rear seats had a folding armrest. A Philips stereo radio contained a cassette recorder/player. Lagondas were claimed to be capable of 140-mph top speed.

Note: See Lagonda listing in this Catalog for details on earlier Lagonda models.

I.D. DATA: Serial number is on inner right front fender panel, under the hood. Engine number is on top of engine, near front center. Serial number range: (Lagonda) L/13001/R to LOJR 13645 (in 1990).

Model	Body Type & Seating	Engine Type/CID	P.O.E. Price	Weight (lbs.)	Prod. Total
V-8	2-dr Fbk Cpe-4P	V8/326	52250	3800	Note 1
Vantage	2-dr Fbk Cpe-4P	V8/326	55700	3800	Note 1
Volante	2-dr Conv Cpe-4P	V8/326	71835	3950	Note 1
LAGONDA					
	4-dr Saloon-4/5P	V8/326	N/A	4622	Note 2

Note 1: A total of 262 Aston Martins (all models) were built in 1977, 280 in 1978, 266 in 1979, and 203 in 1980. Approximately 39 Volante convertibles were sold in the U.S., in 1980 alone.

Note 2: A total of 645 Lagonda saloons were produced, through January 1990.

V-8 Price Note: V-8 prices shown are for 1979, with five-speed gearbox. Price of the basic V-8 in 1977 was $33,950. Price in 1979 with automatic transmission was $49,850 for the basic V-8 or $69,860 for the convertible.

ENGINE DATA: BASE V-8 (V-8, Lagonda): 90-degree, dual-overhead-camshaft V-8. Light alloy block and head. **Displacement:** 325.9 cu. in. (5340 cc). **Bore & Stroke:** 3.94 x 3.35 in. (100 x 85 mm). **Compression Ratio:** 8.3:1. **Brake Horsepower:** 350+ (estimated). **Torque:** 400 lbs.-ft. at 4000 rpm. Five main bearings. Four Weber dual-choke carburetors.

OPTIONAL VANTAGE V-8 (V-8): Same as above, except 400 bhp (estimated).

CHASSIS DATA: Wheelbase: (V-8) 102.8 in.; (Lagonda) 114.8 in. **Overall Length:** (V-8) 183.8 in.; (Lagonda) 208 in. **Height:** (V-8) 52.5 in.; (Volante) 54 in.; (Lagonda) 53.3 in. **Width:** (V-8) 72 in.; (Lagonda) 72 in. **Front Tread:** (V-8) 59 in.; (Lagonda) 59 in. **Rear Tread:** (V-8) 59 in.; (Lagonda) 59 in. **Wheel Type:** (V-8) cast alloy; (Lagonda) light alloy ventilated. **Standard Tires:** (V-8) GR70x15 or 235/70VR15; (Vantage) 255/60VR15; (Lagonda) GR70VR15.

TECHNICAL: Layout: front-engine, rear-drive. **Transmission:** (V-8) ZF five-speed manual or three-speed TorqueFlite automatic; (Lagonda) three-speed automatic or five-speed manual. **Final Drive Ratio:** (V-8) 3.31:1 or 3.54:1, or 3.07:1 w/automatic; (Lagonda) 3.07:1 w/automatic, 3.54:1 w/five-speed. **Steering:** (V-8) rack and pinion. **Suspension (front):** upper/lower control arms, coil springs and anti-roll bar. **Suspension (rear):** (V-8) De Dion axle with Watt linkage, trailing arms and coil springs; (Lagonda) same, with self-leveling. **Brakes:** front/rear disc. **Body Construction:** (V-8) aluminum body panels over steel superstructure, integral with platform frame; (Lagonda) steel/aluminum body on steel frame. **Fuel Tank:** (V-8) 25.2 gal.; (Lagonda) 33.3 gallon.

MAJOR OPTIONS: Vantage V-8 engine. Automatic transmission (V-8 exc. Vantage).

PERFORMANCE: Top Speed: (carbureted V-8) 145 mph; (Vantage V-8) 170 mph; (Lagonda) 140 mph. **Acceleration (0-60 mph):** (carbureted V-8) 6.2 sec.; (Vantage V-8) 5.4 sec.; (Lagonda) about 7 sec. (factory claim).

Manufacturer: Aston Martin Lagonda Ltd., Newport Pagnell, Buckinghamsire, England. **Distributor:** Aston Martin Lagonda Inc., King of Prussia, Pennsylvania.

HISTORY: Designed by William Towns, the Lagonda saloon was introduced in 1976, at the London Motor Show. During the 1970s, Aston Martin went through several changes in ownership, winding up a decade later in the hands of Ford. A total of seven early Lagondas were produced between 1974 and early 1976, plus one earlier prototype built for David Brown himself in the late 1960s.

1981-86 ASTON MARTIN

1981 Aston-Martin V8 coupe.

V-8 VANTAGE/VOLANTE — V-8 — Production of Aston Martin's coupe and convertible continued through the 1980s without major alterations. Official specifications for horsepower and torque from the two versions of the 5340-cc V-8 engine were not released at this time, but U.S. versions were considerably detuned.

LAGONDA — V-8 — Production of the striking, ultra-posh four-door saloon continued until January 1990, with a restyling in 1987.

I.D. DATA: A 17-symbol Vehicle Identification Number is on upper left of dashboard, visible through the windshield. Symbol one indicates country ('S' = England). The next two symbols identify the company ('CF' = Aston Martin). Symbol four ('C') indicates gross weight category. Symbols 5-6 identify the engine, followed by a symbol for the restraint system. Symbol eight denotes series/body type ('V' = Vantage; 'C' = Volante; 'S' = saloon). Symbol ten is model year ('A' = 1980, 'B' = 1981, 'C' = 1982, 'D' = 1983, etc.). Symbol 11 identifies the assembly plant ('T' = Tickford). Symbol 12 indicates steering-wheel position ('L' = LHD; 'R' = RHD). The final five digits form the sequential serial number.

Model	Body Type & Seating	Engine Type/CID	P.O.E. Price	Weight (lbs.)	Prod. Total
V-8	2-dr Fbk Cpe-4P	V8/326	96000	4100	Note 1
Vantage	2-dr Fbk Cpe-4P	V8/326	101000	N/A	Note 1
Volante	2-dr Conv Cpe-4P	V8/326	115000	N/A	Note 1
LAGONDA					
	4-dr Saloon-4/5P	V8/326	150000	4622	Note 2

Note 1: A total of 149 Aston Martins were produced in 1981, 138 in 1982, 145 in 1983, 170 in 1984, and 180 in 1985.

Note 2: A total of 645 Lagonda saloons were produced, from 1976 through January 1990.

Price Note: Prices shown were valid in 1982, for V-8s with five-speed manual gearbox. Price of the basic V-8 in 1981 was $88,000; Volante, $113,500. A basic coupe or Volante convertible with automatic transmission sold for $2,000 less than figures shown above.

ENGINE DATA: BASE V-8 (V-8, Lagonda): 90-degree, dual-overhead-camshaft V-8. Light alloy block and head. **Displacement:** 325.9 cu. in. (5340 cc). **Bore & Stroke:** 3.94 x 3.35 in. (100 x 85 mm). **Compression Ratio:** 8.0:1/8.3:1. **Brake Horsepower:** (European) about 289 at 5500 rpm; (U.S.) about 263 at 5000 rpm. **Torque:** (European) about 321 lbs.-ft. at 3000 rpm; (U.S.) about 292 at 4500 rpm. Five main bearings. Four Weber dual-choke carburetors or Bosch fuel injection.

OPTIONAL VANTAGE V-8 (V-8): Same as above, except horsepower estimates reached 406 bhp.

CHASSIS DATA: Wheelbase: (V-8) 102.8 in.; (Lagonda) 114.8 in. **Overall Length:** (V-8) 183.8 in.; (Lagonda) 208 in. **Height:** (V-8) 52.5 in.; (Volante) 54 in.; (Lagonda) 51.5 in. **Width:** (V-8) 72 in.; (Lagonda) 72 in. **Front Tread:** (V-8) 59 in.; (Lagonda) 58.3 in. **Rear Tread:** (V-8) 59 in.; (Lagonda) 59.1 in. **Wheel Type:** (V-8) cast alloy. **Standard Tires:** (V-8) GR70x15 or 235/70VR15; (Vantage) 255/60VR15; (Lagonda) 235/70VR15 Avon Turbospeed.

TECHNICAL: Layout: front-engine, rear-drive. **Transmission:** (V-8) ZF five-speed manual or three-speed TorqueFlite automatic; (Lagonda) three-speed TorqueFlite automatic. **Final Drive Ratio:** (V-8) 3.54:1; (Lagonda) 3.06:1. **Steering:** rack and pinion. **Suspension (front):** upper/lower control arms, coil springs and anti-roll bar. **Suspension (rear):** (V-8) De Dion axle with Watt linkage, trailing arms and coil springs; (Lagonda) same, with self-leveling. **Brakes:** front/rear disc. **Body Construction:** (V-8) aluminum body panels over steel superstructure, integral with platform frame; (Lagonda) steel/aluminum body on steel frame. **Fuel Tank:** (V-8) 27.5 gallon.

MAJOR OPTIONS: Vantage V-8 engine. Automatic transmission (V-8 exc. Vantage).

PERFORMANCE: Top Speed: (carbureted V-8) 145 mph; (Vantage V-8) 170 mph; (Lagonda) 140 mph estimated. **Acceleration (0-60 mph):** (carbureted V-8) 6.2 sec.; (Vantage V-8) 5.4 sec.; (Lagonda) just over 8 sec.

Manufacturer: Aston Martin Lagonda Ltd., Newport Pagnell, Buckinghamshire, England. **Distributor:** Aston Martin Lagonda Inc., New Rochelle, New York.

HISTORY: Lagondas did not reach the U.S. until 1984, and the last Lagonda saloon was produced in January 1990. Victor Gauntlett took control of the Aston Martin company in 1984.

1987-88 ASTON MARTIN

V-8 VANTAGE/VOLANTE — V-8 — Production of Aston Martin's coupe and convertible continued into 1988 without major alterations; the Volante convertible remained into the 1989 model year. By this time, the Vantage Volante convertible had a particularly aggressive look with its front air dam, rear spoiler, side skirts, flared wheel arches, and large round auxiliary lights mounted within the front panel's bright surround molding. Its interior displayed burr walnut, hand-stitched Connolly leather, and Wilton carpeting.

VANTAGE ZAGATO — V-8 — Late in the 1980s, the Zagato firm (in Italy) was scheduled to build 50 coupes and 25 convertibles, using special bodies with aero-shaped undertrays. With a modified and more potent Vantage engine, the two-seat Zagato could accelerate from 0-60 mph in 4.7 seconds, according to Fast & Glamorous Cars. Aston Martin announced that it could hit 185 mph. Styling features of the alloy/reinforced-polyester body included a large hood bulge and large rectangular quad headlamps.

LAGONDA — V-8 — Production of the striking, ultra-posh four-door saloon continued until January 1990. A 1987 restyling smoothed the sharp edges to give the car a more rounded, softer appearance than the original, but with a comparable wedge profile. All the aluminum body panels were new in the restyled version. Three rectangular headlamps sat on each side of the vertical-bar grille, replacing the pop-up headlamps on earlier models. Lagonda also added rocker panel skirts and front/rear undertrays. The gas filler moved to the back-window base (formerly on the C-pillar). Interior luxuries included Connolly leather, burled walnut trim, and Wilton carpeting. Eleven hides were used for each car's interior, while 17 hand-rubbed coats of lacquer finished off the bodywork. All-electronic instruments included a vacuum-fluorescent speedometer. A console gearshift operated the three-speed automatic transmission. Few options were available, apart from fitted leather luggage and special paint.

I.D. DATA: A 17-symbol Vehicle Identification Number is on upper left of dashboard, visible through the windshield. See previous listing for breakdown.

Model	Body Type & Seating	Engine Type/CID	P.O.E. Price	Weight (lbs.)	Prod. Total
V-8	2-dr Fbk Cpe-4P	V8/326	127000	4100	Note 1
Vantage	2-dr Fbk Cpe-4P	V8/326	153000	N/A	Note 1
Volante	2-dr Conv Cpe-4P	V8/326	143000	N/A	Note 1
Vantage	2-dr Conv Cpe-4P	V8/326	167500	N/A	Note 1
Zagato	2-dr Coupe-2P	V8/326	N/A	N/A	Note 2
LAGONDA					
	4-dr Saloon-4/5P	V8/326	177500	4622	Note 3

Note 1: A total of 65 Aston Martins (all models) were sold in the U.S. in 1988 alone.

Note 2: A total of 50 Zagato coupe bodies were produced in Italy, late in the 1980s.

Note 3: A total of 645 Lagonda saloons were produced, from 1976 through January 1990.

Price Note: Prices shown were valid in 1988. Prices in 1989 were $183,000 for the Volante, $197,000 for the Vantage Volante, and $197,000 for the Lagonda saloon.

ENGINE DATA: BASE V-8 (V-8, Lagonda): 90-degree, dual-overhead-camshaft V-8. Light alloy block and head. **Displacement:** 325.9 cu. in. (5340 cc). **Bore & Stroke:** 3.94 x 3.35 in. (100 x 85 mm). **Compression Ratio:** 8.0:1/8.3:1. **Brake Horsepower:** (European) about 309 at 5500 rpm. **Torque:** (European) about 320 lbs.-ft. at 4000 rpm. Five main bearings. Four Weber dual-choke carburetors or Bosch fuel injection.

OPTIONAL VANTAGE V-8 (V-8): Same as above, except horsepower reached up to 403 bhp at 6200 rpm, with torque of 390 lbs.-ft. at 5000 rpm. Horsepower was estimated as high as 432 bhp in Zagato.

CHASSIS DATA: Wheelbase: (V-8) 102.8 in.; (Lagonda) 114.6 in. Overall Length: (V-8) 183.8 in.; (Lagonda) 208 in. Height: (V-8) 52.5 in.; (Volante) 54 in.; (Lagonda) 52 in. Width: (V-8) 72 in.; (Lagonda) 71.5 in. Front Tread: (V-8) 59 in.; (Lagonda) 60.2 in. Rear Tread: (V-8) 59 in.; (Lagonda) 61.5 in. Wheel Type: (V-8) cast alloy; (Lagonda) 7Jx16 alloy. Standard Tires: (Vantage) 255/50VR16; (Lagonda) 255/60VR16.

TECHNICAL: Layout: front-engine, rear-drive. Transmission: (V-8) ZF five-speed manual or three-speed TorqueFlite automatic; (Lagonda) three-speed TorqueFlite automatic. Final Drive Ratio: (late Vantage w/manual shift) 3.062:1; (Lagonda) 3.06:1. Steering: rack and pinion. Suspension (front): upper/lower control arms, coil springs and anti-roll bar. Suspension (rear): (V-8) De Dion axle with Watt linkage, trailing arms and coil springs; (Lagonda) same, with self-leveling. Brakes: front/rear disc. Body Construction: (V-8) aluminum body panels with steel floor and inner panels on platform frame; (Lagonda) steel/aluminum body on steel frame. Fuel Tank: (V-8) 27.5 gallon.

PERFORMANCE: Top Speed: (Vantage V-8) 170 mph; (Vantage Zagato) 185 mph; (Lagonda) 140 mph estimated. Acceleration (0-60 mph): (Vantage V-8) 5.4 sec.; (Vantage Volante) 5.2 sec.; (Zagato) 4.7 sec.; (Lagonda) just over 8 sec. Acceleration (quarter-mile): (European Lagonda) 16.6 sec.

Manufacturer: Aston Martin Lagonda Ltd., Newport Pagnell, Buckinghamshire, England.
Distributor: Aston Martin Lagonda Inc., New Rochelle, New York.

HISTORY: The Volante convertible remained available in the U.S. into 1989. The last Lagonda saloon rolled off the assembly line in January 1990. Ford bought a three-quarter interest in the Aston Martin company in September 1987, three years after it had been taken over by Victor Gauntlett, who continued as chairman. A Volante served James Bond well in the movie, *The Living Daylights*, just as earlier Aston Martins had been driven by Sean Connery as he portrayed the famous Ian Fleming character.

1989-90 ASTON MARTIN

1990 Aston-Martin Virage.

VIRAGE — V-8 — At the October 1988 Birmingham (England) International Motor Show came the debut of the new Virage, to replace the former Vantage V-8 model. It was created, in the words of co-designer John Heffernan, as the "evolutionary successor" to the DB-series and the more recent V-8s. Displaying a distinct wedge shape, the Virage's hand-formed aluminum body had uniquely angular styling, curved only in profile, yet conveying a more rounded look than the V-8. Design features included a low cockpit, aero-style flush glass, absence of chrome, and few insignias. New flush rectangular headlamps gave the car a wider look. Exhaust pipes fit into chassis niches. An underbody tray, like that used in the Vantage Zagato, added to the clean, unified appearance, with no pieces hanging loose below. Under the hood was an unusually handsome engine, with plates covering the sparkplug valleys, detailed cam covers atop each cylinder head, and a brass plate on the engine to identify its assembler. Considerable aluminum was used in the Virage's construction, especially in the suspension and brake system, to save weight. The chassis was designed in concert with the Cranfield Institute of Technology Finite Element Analysis Department, a leader in British aerospace technology. Running on no-lead gasoline with a catalytic converter, the Virage was described as "one of the most powerful environmentally-friendly cars in the world." Unlike earlier Astons, it didn't have to be detuned for sale in the U.S., but could be sold in the same form worldwide. Engine design was the work of Callaway Engineering, in Old Lyme, Connecticut, best known for its Twin-Turbo Corvettes.

Interior features included crimson Connolly leather on seats, doors and console, and Wilton carpets. Heated seats had a memory adjustment that also adjusted the outside mirrors (which also were heated).

Note: The Volante convertible coupe and Lagonda saloon remained on sale in the U.S. through 1989; see previous listing for details.

I.D. DATA: A 17-symbol Vehicle Identification Number is on upper left of dashboard, visible through the windshield. See previous listing for details on breakdown.

Model	Body Type & Seating	Engine Type/CID	P.O.E. Price	Weight (lbs.)	Prod. Total
VIRAGE					
	2-dr Coupe-2+2P	V8/326	200000+	3947	N/A

ENGINE DATA: BASE V-8: Dual-overhead-camshaft V-8 (32-valve). Light alloy block and head. Displacement: 325.9 cu. in. (5340 cc). Bore & Stroke: 3.94 x 3.35 in. (100 x 85 mm). Compression Ratio: 9.5:1. Brake Horsepower: 330 at 6000 rpm. Torque: 350 at 4000 rpm. Weber-Marelli fuel injection.

CHASSIS DATA: Wheelbase: 102.8 in. Overall Length: 186.5 in. Height: 52.0 in. Width: 73 in. Front Tread: 59.4 in. Rear Tread: 59.9 in. Wheel Type: 8Jx16 aluminum alloy. Standard Tires: Avon Turbospeed 255/60VR16.

TECHNICAL: Layout: front-engine, rear-drive. Transmission: five-speed manual or three-speed automatic. Final Drive Ratio: 3.062:1. Steering: rack and pinion. Suspension (front): upper/lower control arms, coil springs and anti-roll bar; Bilstein gas shock absorbers. Suspension (rear): De Dion axle with Watt linkage, trailing arms and coil springs; Bilstein gas shock absorbers. Brakes: front/rear disc (vented front, solid rear). Body Construction: aluminum body on box-section steel frame. Fuel Tank: 30.2 gallon.

PERFORMANCE: Top Speed: 155 mph (with automatic). Acceleration (0-60 mph): 6.0 sec. (with automatic).
Manufacturer: Aston Martin Lagonda Ltd., Newport Pagnell, Buckinghamshire, England.
Distributor: Aston Martin Lagonda of North America, Inc., Stamford, Connecticut.

HISTORY: On sale in England in 1989, the Virage did not reach the U.S. marketplace until summer 1990 (and then in minuscule numbers). Even before the Virage went on sale in Britain, the company had 50 orders booked, with sizable deposits paid. In January 1990, the Virage had its U.S. debut at the North American International Auto Show in Detroit, to a fanfare of trumpets and smoke. Lack of detuning, said company chairman Victor Gauntlett, meant Americans now would "know how a *real* Aston Martin feels." Not many Americans, of course, with production so tiny.

Engine experiments began at Callaway in 1987, directed by Tim Good, including conversion of an existing Lagonda V-8 and the manufacture of prototype parts. Final development took place at the Aston facility in England. The original aluminum block was retained, with all-new 16-valve heads. Body design was the work of Ken Greenley and John Heffernan.

Aston Martin returned to motor racing in 1989 with its AMR1, which finished eight of its ten tries, ranking sixth overall in the World Sports-Prototype Championship. The race car was powered by a 6.3-liter version of the Virage engine, which delivered more than 650 bhp.

AUDI

Entering the German auto manufacturing business in 1910, the Audi company compiled an impressive history, remaining independent until the Depression years. August Horch had set up a company under his own name in 1899, leaving a decade later. Compelled by German courts to rename his newly-formed firm, he chose a Latin translation of "Horch." Audi, then, translates to "Listen!" In 1911, Horch himself won the Alpine Rally of the Austrian Automobile Club in an Audi. Early examples wore a narrow, pointed radiator. A 14/50 model, introduced in 1921, had an aluminum cylinder block and four-wheel brakes. A six-cylinder Type M appeared at the International Motor Show in Berlin two years later, and remained in production until 1928. By that time, the figure '1' had become Audi's symbol, acquired during a design contest in 1924.

After purchasing the rights and machinery for the defunct (American) Rickenbacker's engine in 1927, the company began to produce Audis based on that powerplant, sold under the Dresden (six-cylinder) and Zwickau (straight eight) badges. In 1932, Audi joined DKW, Horch, and Wanderer to form the Auto Union group. Much later, that group of four would be recalled in the symbol worn by modern Audi grilles: four interlocking rings. During the 1930s, the Audi badge went on a new front-wheel-drive car with 2-litre Wanderer six-cylinder engine and bodywork. Its engine grew to 2.3 litres in 1935, giving a 110-mph top speed. A rear-drive Audi 920 with 3.2-litre Horch six appeared late in 1938. In addition to production Auto Union models, the years just before World War II brought rear-engined Auto Union Grand Prix cars. Initially designed by Dr. Ferdinand Porsche, they vied with Mercedes-Benz in racing circles.

Through most of the next three decades, however, the interlocking-ring badge would be worn by other cars under the Auto Union banner, and the Audi name soon faded away. After the war, following release from nationalization, Auto Union focused on small two-stroke cars, notably the DKW. Daimler-Benz became a major shareholder by 1956. Then, in 1964, Volkswagen bought Daimler-Benz's share and the Audi nameplate was readied for revival, starting with a 1.7-litre front-wheel-drive European model that had actually been styled and engineered in part by Daimler-Benz, before VW bought in. In 1966, the 80 and Super 90 sedans were introduced, followed in 1968 by the 1.5-litre series 60 and the larger series 100. Then came a merger

with NSU Motorenwerke. By 1970, the first Audis began to make their way to the American market, starting with the Super 90 and the freshly-styled 100LS. For 1973, the Fox arrived on American shores, based upon the European series 80. That evolved into the 4000 series late in the decade.

Technical innovation soon became Audi's forte, with the introduction of a five-cylinder engine in 1976 (powering the 100 series, named "5000" in America), and a turbo-powered five-cylinder by 1980. After decades of focus on front-wheel-drive vehicles, Audi also took an interest in four-wheel-drive, starting with an Iltis 4WD model developed by VW for the German army. Walter Treser, an Audi engineer, then installed the 4WD system in an Audi 80 sedan, paving the way for a production version. That came in March 1980 with the unveiling of the Audi Quattro rally coupe, rated at 320 horsepower. By summer, a roadgoing edition was on the market, producing a more modest 200 horsepower and capable of 135 mph. At least 2,000 Quattros were built each year, enough for rally qualification; and the Quattro concept expanded to other Audi models. Late in 1983 came the Quattro Sport, on a shorter wheelbase, with four valves per cylinder and capable of 300 bhp in standard tune (more than 400 bhp for rallying). Only 200 were built for homologation (qualification) purposes. As is customary, each development was introduced to the European market first, taking longer to arrive in the U.S.

On the American scene, Audi suffered a major burst of bad publicity with charges that the automatic-transmission 5000 series suffered from unintended acceleration. A voluntary recall of all 1978-86 examples for installation of a shift lock device did not quell the accusations, which persisted even after Audi was exonerated by NHTSA in the late 1980s (the instances of sudden acceleration determined to be due to driver error rather than an engineering flaw). Audi introduced a new series of models late in the decade, adopting the numbering system used all along in Europe. Highlight in the high-performance field was the V8 Quattro, which debuted for the 1990 model year.

1970 AUDI

This was the first year of official Audi imports to the U.S., including both the Super 90 and 100LS models. Each had a four-cylinder, overhead-valve engine and front-wheel drive. Automatic transmissions were not available initially.

SUPER 90 — FOUR — Audi's "trademark" was its grille emblem, consisting of four interlocking rings, which symbolized the joining of four different companies back in 1932. That emblem sat in the center of a horizontal bar between the single round headlamps (which bulged forward), ahead of a blacked-out grille pattern. An 'Audi' nameplate went on the front fender, just above the long horizontal bodyside trim molding. Small horizontal taillamps sat in a wraparound housing, just below the trunk lid. The Super 90 rode a 98-inch wheelbase and was powered by a 107.5 cid (1760 cc) four-cylinder engine, delivering 100 horsepower. Two- and four-door sedans were available, along with a station wagon. Standard equipment included a four-speed manual transmission, front disc brakes (with dual hydraulic system), backup lights, wheel trim rings, chrome exhaust tip, a locking gas cap, and side marker lights. Leatherette interiors had a front map pocket, fully reclining front seats with adjustable headrests, three assist grips, dome light, coat hooks, right vanity mirror, front shoulder/lap belts, rear lap belts, two-speed wiper, pneumatic windshield washer, collapsible steering column, deep-dish steering wheel, day/night mirror, padded control knobs, and a padded dashboard. Sedans had a heated rear window. The Super 90 body evolved from the DKW F102, introduced in 1963.

100LS — FOUR — Longer in wheelbase (105.3 inches) than the Super 90, the 100LS was powered by a four-cylinder engine of the same displacement but rated at 115 horsepower. A horizontal trim strip ran the full length of the car, which came in two- and four-door sedan form. Like the Super 90, its grille carried an emblem of four interlocking rings, with quad headlamps at the ends of the horizontal grille trim strip. Standard equipment was similar to the Super 90, but with power brakes and interval windshield wipers (with electric washer). Interior features included a drop-down glovebox, full-width parcel tray, fabric-insert seats, and three-point seatbelts. Front disc brakes were mounted inboard. *Road & Track* called the 100LS "far handsomer with its more recently designed body" than the Super 90, "a pleasant car to look at and...a pleasant car to drive." On the other hand, they determined that "acceleration is only barely adequate for use in normal American traffic conditions."

I.D. DATA: Chassis serial number is located on a plate on top of instrument panel and is also stamped into the crossmember behind the battery (Super 90), or on upper right corner of firewall (100LS). Numbering might also be found on left windshield post, or under the hood at the wheel well. Engine number for early Super 90 is stamped on the block above the fuel pump; for 100LS and later Super 90, at the bellhousing at the left rear of the block. The 10-digit Vehicle Identification Number (VIN) consist of two digits to

indicate the model ('02' = S90 2-dr; '03' = S90 4-dr; '04' = S90 wagon; '80' = 100LS 2-dr; '81' = 100LS 4-dr); followed by a digit that denotes the model year ('0' = 1970). Then comes the sequential serial number. Starting serial number: (Super 90 2-dr) 0201000001; (Super 90 4-dr) 0301000001; (Super 90 wagon) 0401000001; (100LS 2-dr) 8001000001; (100LS 4-dr) 8101000001.

Model	Body Type & Seating	Engine Type/CID	P.O.E. Price	Weight (lbs.)	Prod. Total
SUPER B					
Super 90	2-dr Sedan-5P	I4/107	2995	2205	Note 1
Super 90	4-dr Sedan-5P	I4/107	3095	2235	Note 1
Super 90	2-dr Sta Wag-5P	I4/107	3245	2302	Note 1
100LS					
100LS	2-dr Sedan-5P	I4/107	3695	2325	Note 2
100LS	4-dr Sedan-5P	I4/107	3795	2380	Note 2

Note 1: A total of 1,134 Super 90 models were sold in the U.S. during 1970.

Note 2: A total of 6,557 100LS sedans were sold in the U.S. during 1970.

ENGINE DATA: BASE FOUR (Super 90): Inline, overhead-valve four-cylinder. Cast iron block and light alloy head. **Displacement:** 107.4 cu. in. (1760 cc). **Bore & Stroke:** 3.21 x 3.32 in. (81.5 x 84.4 mm). **Compression Ratio:** 10.2:1. **Brake Horsepower:** 100 (SAE) at 5200 rpm. **Torque:** 116 lbs.-ft. at 3000 rpm. Five main bearings. Solid valve lifters. Solex 32/32DIDTA carburetor.
BASE FOUR (100LS): Same as above, except — **Brake Horsepower:** 115 (SAE) at 5600 rpm. **Torque:** 119 lbs.-ft. at 3200 rpm. Solex 32/32TDID carburetor.

CHASSIS DATA: Wheelbase: (Super 90) 98.0 in.; (100LS) 105.3 in. **Overall Length:** (Super 90) 173.8 in.; (100LS) 182.6 in. **Height:** (Super 90) 57.2 in.; (100LS) 56.1 in. **Width:** (Super 90 sed) 63.7 in.; (Super 90 wag) 64.0 in.; (100LS) 68.1 in. **Front Tread:** (Super 90) 52.8 in.; (100LS) 56 in. **Rear Tread:** (Super 90) 52 in.; (100LS) 56.1 in. **Wheel Type:** disc. **Standard Tires:** (Super 90) 165Sx13; (100LS) 165SR14.

TECHNICAL: Layout: front-engine, front-drive. **Transmission:** four-speed manual (fully synchronized). 100LS gear ratios: (1st) 3.40:1; (2nd) 1.94:1; (3rd) 1.36:1; (4th) 0.966:1. **Standard Final Drive Ratio:** 3.89:1. **Steering:** rack and pinion. **Suspension (front):** (Super 90) wishbones, torsion bars and stabilizer bar; (100LS) coil springs with upper and lower (unequal-length) control arms and stabilizer bar. **Suspension (rear):** torsion crank (rigid) axle with coil springs, trailing arms, Panhard rod, built-in stabilizer bar, and double-action shock absorbers. **Brakes:** front disc, rear drum. **Body Construction:** welded, unitized frame of pressed steel sections. **Fuel Tank:** 15 gallons.

MAJOR OPTIONS: Sliding sunroof ($130-$135). Air conditioning. Tinted glass ($85-$90). Tinted glass w/rear defroster: S90 wagon ($135). Tachometer ($30-$40). Wolfsburg AM radio ($45). Emden AM/FM radio ($85). Rear defogger: S90 wagon ($40). Metallic paint: 100LS ($155). Leatherette upholstery: S90 sedan ($35). Whitewall tires: S90 ($35). Radial whitewall tires: 100LS ($40). Center shifting console (NC).

PERFORMANCE: Top Speed: (Super 90) 101 mph; (100LS) 103-105 mph. **Acceleration (0-60 mph):** (100LS) 13.6 seconds. **Acceleration (quarter-mile):** (100LS) 19.2 seconds (70 mph). **Fuel Mileage:** (100LS) 24-26 mpg.

PRODUCTION/SALES: A total of 309,560 Audis (and NSU models) were sold worldwide during 1970, of which 7,691 Audis were sold in the U.S.

Manufacturer: Audi NSU Auto Union Aktiengesellschaft, Ingolstadt, West Germany.

Distributor: Porsche-Audi, Englewood Cliffs, New Jersey.

1971 AUDI

1971 Audi four-door sedan.

SUPER 90 — FOUR — Appearance and standard equipment were the same as 1970.

100LS — FOUR — Appearance and equipment were the same as 1970.

I.D. DATA: Serial numbers are in same locations as 1970. Starting serial number: (Super 90 2-dr) 0211000001; (Super 90 4-dr) 0311000001; (Super 90 wagon) 0411000001; (100LS) 8111000001.

Model	Body Type & Seating	Engine Type/CID	P.O.E. Price	Weight (lbs.)	Prod. Price
Super 90	2-dr Sedan-5P	I4/107	2995	2117	Note 1
Super 90	4-dr Sedan-5P	I4/107	3095	2147	Note 1
Super 90	2-dr Sta Wag-5P	I4/107	3245	2214	Note 1
100LS					
100LS	2-dr Sedan-5P	I4/107	3495	2315	Note 2
100LS	4-dr Sedan-5P	I4/107	3595	2357	Note 2

Note 1: A total of 2,425 Super 90 models were sold in the U.S. during 1971.

Note 2: A total of 18,179 100LS sedans were sold in the U.S. during 1971.

Price Note: 100LS models with automatic transmission cost $200 more.

ENGINE DATA: Same as 1970.

CHASSIS DATA: Wheelbase: (Super 90) 98.0 in.; (100LS) 105.3 in. **Overall Length:** (Super 90) 173.8 in.; (100LS) 182.6 in. **Height:** (Super 90 sed) 57.2 in.; (100LS) 56.1 in. **Width:** (Super 90) 64.0 in.; (100LS) 68.1 in. **Front Tread:** (Super 90) 52.8 in.; (100LS) 56 in. **Rear Tread:** (Super 90) 52 in.; (100LS) 56.1 in. **Wheel Type:** disc. **Standard Tires:** (Super 90) 165S13; (100LS) 165SR14.

TECHNICAL: Layout: front-engine, front-drive. **Transmission:** four-speed manual (fully synchronized) or (100LS) three-speed automatic. **Standard Final Drive Ratio:** 3.89:1. **Steering:** rack and pinion. **Suspension (front):** (Super 90) wishbones, torsion bars and stabilizer bar; (100LS) coil springs with upper and lower control arms and stabilizer. **Suspension (rear):** torsion crank (rigid) axle with coil springs, trailing arms, Panhard rod, built-in stabilizer bar, and double-action shock absorbers. **Brakes:** front disc, rear drum. **Fuel Tank:** 15.3 gallons.

MAJOR OPTIONS: Automatic transmission: 100LS ($200). Air conditioning. AM radio ($45). AM/FM radio ($85). Rear defogger: S90 wag ($40). Whitewall tires: S90 ($35). Radial whitewall tires: 100LS ($40). Sliding sunroof ($130-135). Tinted glass ($85-90). Tachometer ($30-40). Leatherette upholstery: S90 sedan ($35). Metallic paint: 100LS ($155). Roof ski rack ($35.55). Roof luggage rack ($51.65). Trailer hitch. Child safety seat ($19.95). Fanfare horns. Window vent shades ($11.95). Vinyl gearshift knob ($4.55). Wood gearshift knob ($3.75). Mud flaps ($3.60).

PERFORMANCE: Same as 1970.

PRODUCTION/SALES: A total of 184,706 Audis (all models) were produced during 1971, of which 20,604 were sold in the U.S.

Manufacturer: Audi NSU Auto Union Aktiengesellschaft, Ingolstadt, West Germany.

Distributor: Porsche-Audi, Englewood Cliffs, New Jersey.

HISTORY: In August 1971, the 100GL was unveiled in Europe, a deluxe sedan intended to appeal to enthusiasts.

1972 AUDI

1972 Audi 100 four-door sedans.

SUPER 90 — FOUR — Little change was evident in the smaller Audi for its final season in the U.S. market.

100 — FOUR — A 114.2 cubic-inch four-cylinder engine replaced the former 107.5-cid powerplant. The new engine was rated 91 horsepower, under the new SAE (net) rating system. The 100 series now came in three versions: basic 100, I00LS, and a 100GL that came with a standard automatic transmission. Appearance was similar to earlier models.

I.D. DATA: Serial numbers are in same locations as 1970. Starting serial number: (Super 90 2-dr) 0221000001; (Super 90 4-dr) 0321000001; (Super 90 wagon) 0421000001; (100) 8521000001; (100GL) 8521000001; (100LS 2-dr) 8021000001; (100LS 4-dr) 8121000001.

Model	Body Type & Seating	Engine Type/CD	P.O.E. Price	Weight (lbs.)	Prod. Total
SUPER					
Super 90	2-dr Sedan-5P	I4/107	3085	2117	Note 1
Super 90	4-dr Sedan-5P	I4/107	3194	2147	Note 1
Super 90	2-dr Sta Wag-5P	I4/107	3335	2214	Note 1
100 SERIES					
100	2-dr Sedan-5P	I4/114	3595	2315	Note 2
100	4-dr Sedan-5P	I4/114	3705	2357	Note 2
100LS	2-dr Sedan-5P	I4/114	3745	2315	Note 2
100LS	4-dr Sedan-5P	I4/114	3855	2357	Note 2
100GL	2-dr Sedan-5P	I4/114	4245	2315	Note 2
100GL	4-dr Sedan-5P	I4/114	4355	2357	Note 2

Note 1: A total of 1,928 Super 90 models were sold in the U.S. during 1972 (though only 721 were reported to have been built in Germany that year).

Note 2: A total of 26,703 100 series sedans were sold in the U.S. during 1972. A total of 109,467 100LS and 43,650 100GL sedans were produced that year.

Price Note: 100/100LS models with automatic transmission cost $225 more.

ENGINE DATA: BASE FOUR (Super 90): Inline, overhead-valve four-cylinder. Cast iron block and light alloy head. **Displacement:** 107.4 cu. in. (1760 cc). **Bore & Stroke:** 3.21 x 3.32 in. (81.5 x 84.4 mm). **Compression Ratio:** 8.2:1. **Brake Horsepower:** 90 at 5200 rpm. **Torque:** 105 lbs.-ft. at 3000 rpm. Five main bearings. Solid valve lifters. Two-barrel carburetor.

BASE FOUR (100 Series): Inline, overhead-valve four-cylinder. Cast iron block and light alloy head. **Displacement:** 114.2 cu. in. (1872 cc). **Bore & Stroke:** 3.31 x 3.32 in. (84.0 x 84.4 mm). **Compression Ratio:** 8.2:1. **Brake Horsepower:** 91 (net) at 5200 rpm. **Torque:** 111 lbs.-ft. at 3500 rpm. Five main bearings. Solid valve lifters. Two-barrel carburetor.

CHASSIS DATA: Wheelbase: (Super 90) 98 in.; (100) 105.3 in. **Overall Length:** (Super 90) 174 in.; (100) 182.6 in. **Height:** (Super 90) 57.2 in.; (100) 56.1 in. **Width:** (Super 90) 64 in.; (100) 68.1 in. **Front Tread:** (Super 90) 52.8 in.; (100) 56 in. **Rear Tread:** (Super 90) 52 in.; (100) 56.1 in. **Wheel Type:** steel disc. **Standard Tires:** (Super 90) 165S13; (100) 165SR14.

TECHNICAL: Layout: front-engine, front-drive. **Transmission:** four-speed manual (fully synchronized) or three-speed automatic. **Standard Final Drive Ratio:** (Super 90) 4.11:1; (100LS) 3.89:1; (100GL) 3.91:1. **Steering:** rack and pinion. **Suspension (front):** (Super 90) wishbones, torsion bars and stabilizer bar; (100) coil springs with upper and lower control arms and stabilizer bar. **Suspension (rear):** torsion crank axle with coil springs, built-in stabilizer bar, Panhard rod, and double-action shock absorbers. **Brakes:** front disc, rear drum. **Body Construction:** welded, unitized frame of pressed steel sections.

MAJOR OPTIONS: Automatic transmission: 100/100LS ($225). Other options similar to 1970-71.

PERFORMANCE: Acceleration (0-60 mph): (100LS w/automatic) 13.7 sec. **Acceleration (quarter-mile):** (100LS w/auto.) 19.5 sec. (69 mph). **Fuel Mileage:** (100LS) about 20 mpg.

PRODUCTION/SALES: A total of 240,631 Audis (all models) were produced during 1972, of which 28,631 were sold in the U.S.

Manufacturer: Audi NSU Auto Union Aktiengesellschaft, Ingolstadt, West Germany.

Distributor: Porsche-Audi Division, Volkswagen of America Inc., Englewood Cliffs, New Jersey.

HISTORY: The sports-oriented Audi 80 debuted in Europe during summer 1972, and garnered four "Car of the Year" awards at European shows that year. The 100,000th Audi 100 was produced in October 1972.

1973 AUDI

FOX — SERIES 80 — FOUR — A new Fox (series 80 in Europe) sedan replaced the Super 90 series. As before, the grille contained an emblem of four interlocking rings in the center of a horizontal trim strip, which met the single round headlamp housings. 'Audi' and 'Fox' badges went on the decklid, above rectangular tri-section taillamps. Horizontal bodyside moldings ran the full length of the car. Wheelbase was about the same as the Super 90, measuring 97.2 inches. Under the hood was a 1471-cc four-cylinder engine, rated 75 horsepower (net). A "Silver Fox" limited-edition sedan also was offered.

100 — FOUR — The 100 series changed little this year, except for an improved braking system and high-capacity discharge ignition system. The quad-headlamp front end again displayed the traditional grille emblem of four interlocking rings. Standard equipment included a four-speed manual gearbox, power front disc brakes, locking gas cap, two-speed wiper/washers, outside rear-view mirror, full wheel covers, heater/defroster, heated rear defogger, reclining bucket seats with adjustable headrests, a padded instrument panels, electric clock, front map pockets, and three-point front seatbelts. The 100GL added a three-speed automatic transmission, vinyl roof, tinted glass, corduroy/leatherette seats, and deluxe wheel covers.

I.D. DATA: Serial number is in the same location as 1970-72. Starting serial number: (Fox) 32000001; (100) 8531000001; (100GL) 8531000001; (100LS 2-dr) 8031000001; (100LS 4-dr) 8131000001.

Model	Body Type & Seating	Engine Type/CID	P.O.E. Price	Weight (lbs.)	Prod. Total
FOX					
84	2-dr Sedan-4/5P	I4/90	3399	1925	Note 1
85	4-dr Sedan-4/5P	I4/90	3509	1959	Note 1
100 SERIES					
100	2-dr Sedan-5P	I4/114	3695	2394	Note 2
100	4-dr Sedan-5P	I4/114	3805	2430	Note 2
100LS	2-dr Sedan-5P	I4/114	4150	2447	Note 2
100LS	4-dr Sedan-5P	I4/114	4260	2476	Note 2
100GL	2-dr Sedan-5P	I4/114	4650	2430	Note 2
100GL	4-dr Sedan-5P	I4/114	4760	2476	Note 2

Note 1: A total of 14,919 Audi Fox models were sold in the U.S. during 1973.

Note 2: A total of 31,065 100 series sedans were sold in the U.S. during 1973.

Price Note: During the year, the price of the 100LS four-door rose to $4485.

ENGINE DATA: BASE FOUR (Fox): Inline, overhead-valve four-cylinder. Cast iron block and light alloy head. **Displacement:** 89.7 cu. in. (1471 cc). **Bore & Stroke:** 3.01 x 3.15 in. (76.5 x 80.0 mm). **Compression Ratio:** 8.2:1. **Brake Horsepower:** 75 at 5800 rpm. **Torque:** 81.5 lbs.-ft. at 4000 rpm. Five main bearings. Solid valve lifters. Solex two-barrel carburetor.

BASE FOUR (100 Series): Inline, overhead-valve four-cylinder. Cast iron block and light alloy head. **Displacement:** 114.2 cu. in. (1872 cc). **Bore & Stroke:** 3.31 x 3.32 in. (84.0 x 84.4 mm). **Compression Ratio:** 8.2:1. **Brake Horsepower:** 91 at 5200 rpm. **Torque:** 110 lbs.-ft. at 3500 rpm. Five main bearings. Solid valve lifters. Two-barrel carburetor.

CHASSIS DATA: Wheelbase: (Fox) 97.2 in.; (100LS) 105.3 in. **Overall Length:** (Fox) 171.9 in.; (100) 182.6 in. **Height:** (Fox) 53.9 in.; (100) 56.1 in. **Width:** (Fox) 63 in.; (100) 68.1 in. **Front Tread:** (Fox) 52.7 in.; (100) 56 in. **Rear Tread:** (Fox) 52.6 in.; (100) 56.1 in. **Wheel Type:** steel disc. **Standard Tires:** (Fox) 155SR13; (100) 165SR14.

TECHNICAL: Layout: front-engine, front-drive. **Transmission:** four-speed manual (fully synchronized) or three-speed automatic. Fox manual gear ratios: (1st) 3.45:a; (2nd) 2.06:1; (3rd) 1.37:1; (4th) 0.97:1. **Standard Final Drive Ratio:** (Fox) 4.11:1. **Steering:** rack and pinion. **Suspension (front):** (Fox) MacPherson struts with lower control arms, coil springs and stabilizer bar; (100LS) coil springs with upper and lower control arms and stabilizer bar. **Suspension (rear):** beam axle with coil springs, built-in stabilizer and Panhard rod. **Brakes:** front disc, rear drum. **Body Construction:** steel unibody. **Fuel Tank:** (Fox) 12 gallons; (100) 15.3 gal.

MAJOR OPTIONS: Automatic transmission ($245). Sunroof ($175-$194). Air conditioning ($495). Vinyl roof ($96). Tinted glass ($85). Wolfsburg AM radio ($94). Emden AM/FM radio ($119). Leatherette interior ($50). Tachometer ($47). Metallic paint ($177).

Note: Options listed above are for 100 series (some items were standard on 100GL).

PERFORMANCE: Top Speed: (Fox) 100 mph; (100) 105 mph. **Acceleration (0-60 mph):** (Fox) 12.7 sec.; (100) 12.7-13.9 sec. **Acceleration (quarter-mile):** (Fox) 19.0 sec. (75.5 mph). **Fuel Mileage:** (Fox) about 27 mpg; (100) 20-24 mpg.

PRODUCTION/SALES: A total of 397,914 Audis (all mdoels) were produced during 1973, of which 46,136 were sold in the U.S. (including 152 leftover Super 90 models).

Manfacturer: Auto NSU Union Aktiengesellschaft, Ingolstadt, West Germany.

Distributor: Porsche-Audi Division, Volkswagen of America Inc., Englewood Cliffs, New Jersey.

HISTORY: Introduced: (100 series) September 1, 1972; (Fox) May 31, 1973. *Motor Trend* voted the 100LS "Car of the Year." The millionth Audi (since production resumed in late 1965) was built this year.

1974 AUDI

FOX — FOUR — New in 1973, the Fox changed little for the 1974 model year. Standard equipment included a four-speed manual transmission, front disc brakes, two-speed wiper/washers, lighter and ashtrays, courtesy and trunk lights, clock, day/night mirror, heater/defroster, heated rear defroster, and outside mirror. Energy-absorbing bumpers were installed, front and rear.

100LS — FOUR — The larger Audi shrunk to just one model in the 100 series, available as a two- or four-door sedan. The sales slogan at this time was that "It's a lot of car for the money. It's a lot of miles to the gallon."

I.D. DATA: Fox serial number is on left windshield post and stamped into the upper center of the firewall. 100LS chassis number is on a plate atop the instrument panel, visible through the windshield, and stamped into the upper right corner of the firewall. An identification plate for each model is also found on the right wheel well. Fox engine numbers are stamped on the left of the block, above the fuel pump. 100LS engine numbers are on the left side of the block, at the clutch housing. Audi's 10-digit Vehicle Identification Number (VIN) consist of two digits to indicate the model, followed by a digit for model year; then the sequential serial number. Starting serial number: (Fox) 42000001; (100LS) 41000001.

Model	Body Type & Seating	Engine Type/CID	P.O.E. Price	Weight (lbs.)	Prod. Total
FOX					
84	2-dr Sedan-4/5P	I4/90	3975	1925	Note 1
85	4-dr Sedan-4/5P	I4/90	4110	1969	Note 1
100LS					
80	2-dr Sedan-5P	I4/114	4975	2315	Note 2
81	4-dr Sedan-5P	I4/114	5110	2315	Note 2

Note 1: A total of 26,453 Audi Fox models were sold in the U.S. during 1974.

Note 2: A total of 23,984 100LS sedans were sold in the U.S. during 1974 (out of 56,114 100LS models built that year).

ENGINE DATA: BASE FOUR (Fox): Inline, overhead-valve four-cylinder. Cast iron block and light alloy head. **Displacement:** 89.7 cu. in. (1471 cc). **Bore & Stroke:** 3.01 x 3.15 in. (76.5 x 80.0 mm). **Compression Ratio:** 8.2:1. **Brake Horsepower:** 75 at 6000 rpm. **Torque:** 81.5 lbs.-ft. at 4000 rpm. Five main bearings. Solid valve lifters. Two-barrel carburetor.

BASE FOUR (100LS): Inline, overhead-valve four-cylinder. Cast iron block and light alloy head. **Displacement:** 114.2 cu. in. (1872 cc). **Bore & Stroke:** 3.31 x 3.32 in. (84.0 x 84.4 mm). **Compression Ratio:** 8.2:1. **Brake Horsepower:** 91 at 5200 rpm. **Torque:** 110 lbs.-ft. at 3500 rpm. Five main bearings. Solid valve lifters. Two-barrel carburetors.

CHASSIS DATA: Wheelbase: (Fox) 97.2 in.; (100LS) 105.3 in. **Overall Length:** (Fox) 172 in.; (100LS) 187.2 in. **Height:** (Fox) 53.6 in.; (100LS) 55.7 in. **Width:** (Fox) 64.7 in.; (100LS) 69 in. **Front Tread:** (Fox) 52.7 in.; (100LS) 55.9 in. **Rear Tread:** (Fox) 52.5 in.; (100LS) 56.1 in. **Wheel Type:** steel disc. **Standard Tires:** (Fox) 155SR13; (100LS) 165SR14.

TECHNICAL: Layout: front-engine, front-drive. **Transmission:** four-speed manual (fully synchronized) or three-speed automatic. **Standard Final Drive Ratio:** 4.11:1. **Steering:** rack and pinion. **Suspension (front):** (Fox) MacPherson struts with lower control arms, coil springs and stabilizer bar; (100LS) coil springs with upper and lower control arms and stabilizer bar. **Suspension (rear):** beam axle with coil springs, built-in stabilizer and Panhard rod. **Brakes:** front disc, rear drum. **Body Construction:** steel unibody.

MAJOR OPTIONS: Automatic transmission ($250). Power steering: 100LS ($175). Sunroof ($220). Air conditioning: Fox ($495); others ($545). Vinyl roof: 100LS ($125). Wolfsburg AM radio: Fox ($45); 100LS ($110). Leatherette interior: Fox ($45); 100LS ($50). Tachometer ($65). Tinted glass ($75-$85). Whitewall tires ($45-55).

PERFORMANCE: Top Speed: (Fox) 100 mph; (100LS) 105 mph. **Acceleration (0-60 mph):** (Fox) 12.7 sec.; (100) 12.7-13.9 sec. **Acceleration (quarter-mile):** (Fox) 19.0 sec. (75.5 mph). **Fuel Mileage:** (Fox) 22-25 mpg; (100LS) 18-24 mpg.

PRODUCTION/SALES: A total of 265,134 Audis (all models) were produced during 1974, of which 50,437 were sold in the U.S.

Manufacturer: Audi NSU Auto Union Aktiengesellschaft, Ingolstadt, West Germany.

Distributor: Porsche-Audi Division, Volkswagen of America Inc., Englewood Cliffs, New Jersey.

HISTORY: Introduced: October 1, 1973.

1975 AUDI

FOX — FOUR — A station wagon joined the Fox sedans this year, while the latter got a sharp price hike. Appearance and equipment were similar to 1974, but a 1.6-litre (97-cid) overhead-cam four-cylinder engine with fuel injection replaced the former carbureted 1.5-litre four.

100LS — FOUR — "People buy cars for all kinds of reasons," said the 100LS sales brochure for 1975. "The Audi has all of them." The larger Audis showed a whopping price rise this year, of more than $700. Appearance was similar to 1974. Standard equipment included a fuel-injected engine, front disc brakes, steel-belted radial tires, electric rear window defogger, side window defoggers, vanity mirrors, grab handles, coat hangers, and front/rear ashtrays. The interior was roomy enough for five, claimed to have "just about as much head, leg and shoulder room as a Rolls Royce Silver Shadow." The steering column held a high/low beam control as well as controls for the windshield wiper/washer. African hardwood veneer inlay adorned the dashboard, which also held a quartz clock. Velour-upholstered seats reclined completely.

1975 Audi Fox two-door sedan.

I.D. DATA: Audi's ten-digit serial numbers are in same locations as 1974. First two digits indicate model; digit three is model year; and the final seven digits are the sequential serial number. Starting serial number: (Fox 2-dr) 8452000001; (Fox 4-dr) 8552000001; (Fox wag) 3352900001; (100LS 2-dr) 8051000001; (100LS 4-dr) 8151000001.

Model	Body Type & Seating	Engine Type/CID	P.O.E. Price	Weight (lbs.)	Prod. Price
FOX					
849	2-dr Sedan-4/5P	I4/97	4450	1978	Note 1
850	4-dr Sedan-4/5P	I4/97	4600	2038	Note 1
331	4-dr Sta Wag-4/5P	I4/97	4850	2105	Note 1
100LS					
809	2-dr Sedan-5P	I4/114	5695	2492	Note 2
810	4-dr Sedan-5P	I4/114	5845	2533	Note 2

Note 1: A total of 30,346 Audi Fox models were sold in the U.S. during 1975.

Note 2: A total of 20,334 100LS sedans were sold in the U.S. during 1975.

Price Note: Prices on West Coast were $150 higher. Prices rose during the model year, ranging from $4700 to $6152.

ENGINE DATA: BASE FOUR (Fox): Inline, overhead-cam four-cylinder. Cast iron block and light alloy head. **Displacement:** 97.0 cu. in. (1588 cc). **Bore & Stroke:** 3.13 x 3.15 in. (79.5 x 80.0 mm). **Compression Ratio:** 8.2:1. **Brake Horsepower:** 83 at 5800 rpm (79 bhp in California). **Torque:** 89 lbs.-ft. at 3300 rpm. Five main bearings. Solid valve lifters. Continuous fuel injection.

BASE FOUR (100LS): Inline, overhead-valve four-cylinder. Cast iron block and light alloy head. **Displacement:** 114.2 cu. in. (1871 cc). **Bore & Stroke:** 3.31 x 3.32 in. (84.0 x 84.4 mm). **Compression Ratio:** 8.0:1. **Brake Horsepower:** 95 at 5500 rpm. **Torque:** 104 lbs.-ft. at 3200 rpm. Five main bearings. Solid valve lifters. Fuel injection.

CHASSIS DATA: Wheelbase: (Fox) 97.2 in.; (100LS) 105.3 in. **Overall Length:** (Fox) 172 in.; (100LS) 187.2 in. **Height:** (Fox) 53.6 in.; (100LS) 55.7 in. **Width:** (Fox) 62.7 in.; (100LS) 69 in. **Front Tread:** (Fox) 52.7 in.; (100LS) 55.9 in. **Rear Tread:** (Fox) 52.5 in.; (100LS) 56.1 in. **Wheel Type:** (100LS) 4.5x14 steel. **Standard Tires:** (Fox) 155SR13; (100LS) 165SR14 SBR.

TECHNICAL: Layout: front-engine, front-drive. **Transmission:** four-speed manual (fully synchronized) or three-speed automatic. **Standard Final Drive Ratio:** 4.11:1. **Steering:** rack and pinion. **Suspension (front):** (Fox) MacPherson struts with lower control arms, coil springs and stabilizer bar; (100LS) coil springs with upper and lower control arms and stabilizer bar. **Suspension (rear):** torsion crank axle with coil springs, built-in stabilizer bar, Panhard rod, and double-action shock absorbers. **Brakes:** front disc, rear drum. **Body Construction:** welded, unitized frame of pressed steel sections. **Fuel Tank:** (Fox) 12 gal.; (100LS) 15.3 gallons.

MAJOR OPTIONS: FOX OPTIONS: Automatic transmission ($275). Sunroof. Air conditioning. Alloy wheels. **100LS OPTIONS:** Automatic transmission ($275). Power steering. Sunroof. Air conditioning. AM/FM radio. Radio with cassette player. Tachometer. Metallic paint. Tinted glass. Whitewall tires. Leatherette upholstery.

PERFORMANCE: Similar to 1974.

PRODUCTION/SALES: A total of 203,851 Audis (all models) were produced during 1975, of which 50,680 were sold in the U.S.

Manufacturer: Audi NSU Auto Union Aktiengesellschaft, Ingolstadt, West Germany.

Distributor: Porsche-Audi Division, Volkswagen of America Inc., Englewood Cliffs, New Jersey.

HISTORY: Introduced: September, 1974 except (Fox wagon) January, 1975. "The answer is Audi" was the sales slogan of the period.

1976 AUDI

FOX — FOUR — Little change was evident in the smaller Audi series, which was powered by the fuel-injected 1588-cc four-cylinder engine introduced for 1975.

100LS — FOUR — Power front disc brakes were now mounted inboard rather than outboard, for improved cooling. Otherwise, the larger Audi sedan was the same as in 1975.

I.D. DATA: Fox serial number is on left windshield post and stamped into the upper center of the firewall. 100LS chassis number is on a plate atop the instrument panel (visible through the windshield), and also stamped into the upper right corner of the firewall and/or on right side of crossmember behind engine. An identification plate for each model is also found on the right wheel well. Fox engine numbers are stamped on the left of the block, above the fuel pump. 100LS engine numbers are on the left side of the block, at the clutch housing. First two digits of the VIN indicate model; digit three is model year; and the final seven digits are the sequential serial number. Starting serial number: (Fox 2-dr) 8462000001; (Fox 4-dr) 8562000001; (Fox wag) 3362900001; (100LS 2-dr) 8061000001; (100LS 4-dr) 8161000001.

Model	Body Type & Seating	Engine Type/CID	P.O.E. Price	Weight (lbs.)	Prod. Price
FOX					
849	2-dr Sedan-4/5P	I4/97	5100	2011	Note 1
850	4-dr Sedan-4/5P	I4/97	5250	2060	Note 1
331	4-dr Sta Wag-4/5P	I4/97	5500	2100	Note 1
100LS					
809	2-dr Sedan-5P	I4/114	6950	2489	Note 2
810	4-dr Sedan-5P	I4/114	7100	2531	Note 2

Note 1: A total of 21,763 Audi Fox models were sold in the U.S. during 1976.
Note 2: A total of 11,553 100LS sedans were sold in the U.S. during 1976.

ENGINE DATA: BASE FOUR (Fox): Inline, overhead-cam four-cylinder. Cast iron block and light alloy head. **Displacement:** 97.0 cu. in. (1588 cc). **Bore & Stroke:** 3.13 x 3.15 in. (79.5 x 80.0 mm). **Compression Ratio:** 8.2:1. **Brake Horsepower:** 79 at 5500 rpm. **Torque:** 89 lbs.-ft. at 3300 rpm. Five main bearings. Solid valve lifters. Fuel injection.

BASE FOUR (100LS): Inline, overhead-valve four-cylinder. Cast iron block and light alloy head. **Displacement:** 114.2 cu. in. (1871 cc). **Bore & Stroke:** 3.31 x 3.32 in. (84.0 x 84.4 mm). **Compression Ratio:** 8.0:1. **Brake Horsepower:** 95 at 5500 rpm. **Torque:** 104 lbs.-ft. at 3200 rpm. Five main bearings. Solid valve lifters. Fuel injection.

CHASSIS DATA: Wheelbase: (Fox) 97.2 in.; (100LS) 105.3 in. **Overall Length:** (Fox) 172.0 in.; (100LS) 188.0 in. **Height:** (Fox) 53.7 in.; (100LS) 54.6 in. **Width:** (Fox) 69.1 in. **Front Tread:** (Fox) 52.7 in.; (100LS) 57.0 in. **Rear Tread:** (Fox) 52.5 in.; (100LS) 56.1 in. **Standard Tires:** (Fox) 155SR13; (100LS) 165SR14 SBR.

TECHNICAL: Same as 1975.

MAJOR OPTIONS: Similar to 1975.

PRODUCTION/SALES: A total of 240,286 Audis (all models) were produced during 1976, of which 33,316 were sold in the U.S. (a considerable drop from the 1975 total).
Manufacturer: Audi NSU Auto Union Aktiengesellschaft, Ingolstadt, West Germany.
Distributor: Porsche-Audi Division, Volkswagen of America, Englewood Cliffs, New Jersey.

1977 AUDI

FOX — FOUR — Quad headlamps replaced the single units on the smaller Audi for 1977, in a modified grille panel. Otherwise, the smaller Audi continued as before, powered by a 97-cid (1588 cc) four-cylinder engine. Standard equipment included a four-speed manual transmission, power front disc brakes (dual hydraulic system), heater/defroster, electric rear-window defogger, driver's remote-control mirror, reclining front seats with adjustable headrests, center console, trip odometer, clock, and front vent windows. The station wagon added a leatherette-covered steering wheel.

100LS — FOUR — Little change was evident in the larger Audi for its final season in the lineup. Standard equipment was similar to the Fox, but also included power steering, a side-window defogger, tinted glass, velour interior, deluxe padded steering wheel, trunk carpeting, visor vanity mirror, and a rear center armrest.

I.D. DATA: Audi's ten-digit serial numbers are in the same locations as 1976. First two digits indicate model; digit three is model year; and the final seven digits are the sequential serial number. Starting serial number: (Fox 2-dr) 8472000001; (Fox 4-dr) 8572000001; (Fox wag) 3372900001; (100LS 2-dr) 8071000001; (100LS 4-dr) 8171000001.

Model	Body Type & Seating	Engine Type/CID	P.O.E. Price	Weight (lbs.)	Prod. Total
FOX					
849	2-dr Sedan-4/5P	I4/97	5295	2011	Note 1
850	4-dr Sedan-4/5P	I4/97	5445	2060	Note 1
331	4-dr Sta Wag-4/5P	I4/97	5695	2100	Note 1
100LS					
809	2-dr Sedan-5P	I4/114	7150	2489	Note 2
810	4-dr Sedan-5P	I4/114	7300	2531	Note 2

Note 1: A total of 23,284 Audi Fox models were sold in the U.S. during 1977.
Note 2: A total of 7,671 100LS sedans were sold in the U.S. during 1977.
Price Note: An automatic transmission added $275 to the price of either the Fox or 100LS.

ENGINE DATA: BASE FOUR (Fox): Inline, overhead-cam four-cylinder. Cast iron block and light alloy head. **Displacement:** 97 cu. in. (1588 cc). **Bore & Stroke:** 3.13 x 3.15 in. (79.5 x 80.0 mm). **Compression Ratio:** 8.2:1. **Brake Horsepower:** 79 at 5500 rpm. **Torque:** 89 lbs.-ft. at 3300 rpm. Five main bearings. Solid valve lifters. Fuel injection.

BASE FOUR (100LS): Inline, overhead-valve four-cylinder. Cast iron block and light alloy head. **Displacement:** 114.2 cu. in. (1871 cc). **Bore & Stroke:** 3.31 x 3.32 in. (84.0 x 84.4 mm). **Compression Ratio:** 8.0:1. **Brake Horsepower:** 95 at 5500 rpm. **Torque:** 104 lbs.-ft. at 3200 rpm. Five main bearings. Solid valve lifters. Fuel injection.

CHASSIS DATA: Wheelbase: (Fox) 97.2 in.; (100LS) 105.3 in. **Overall Length:** (Fox) 173.8 in.; (100LS) 187.9 in. **Height:** (Fox) 53.6 in.; (100LS) 54.6 in. **Width:** (Fox) 64.8 in.; (100LS) 69.1 in. **Front Tread:** (Fox) 52.7 in.; (100LS) 57.0 in. **Rear Tread:** (Fox) 52.5 in.; (100LS) 56.1 in. **Standard Tires:** (Fox) 155SR13; (100LS) 165SR14 SBR.

TECHNICAL: Layout: front-engine, front-drive. **Transmission:** four-speed manual (fully synchronized) or three-speed automatic. **Standard Final Drive Ratio:** 4.11:1. **Steering:** rack and pinion. **Suspension (front):** (Fox) MacPherson struts with lower control arms, coil springs and stabilizer bar; (100LS) coil springs with upper and lower control arms and stabilizer bar. **Suspension (rear):** torsion crank axle with coil springs, built-in stabilizer bar, Panhard rod, and double-action shock absorbers. **Brakes:** front disc, rear drum. **Body Construction:** welded, unitized frame of pressed steel sections. **Fuel Tank:** (Fox) 11.9 gal.; (100LS) 15.3 gallons.

MAJOR OPTIONS: Air conditioning: Fox ($445); 100LS ($550). Sunroof: Fox ($220); 100LS ($250). Alloy wheels: Fox ($150). Leatherette interior trim ($50-$60). Tachometer ($65). Metallic paint: Fox ($185); 100LS ($210). Tinted glass: Fox ($50).

PERFORMANCE: Top Speed: (Fox) 103 mph; (100LS) 105 mph. **Acceleration (0-60 mph):** (Fox) 11.5 sec.; (100LS) 12.5 sec. **Fuel Mileage:** (Fox) 24/36 mpg EPA; (100LS) 18/27 mpg EPA.

PRODUCTION/SALES: A total of 321,101 Audis (all models) were produced during 1977, of which 35,849 were sold in the U.S. (including 4,894 of the first 5000 models, described in the next listing).
Manufacturer: Audi NSU Auto Union Aktiengesellschaft, Ingolstadt, West Germany.
Distributor: Porsche-Audi Division, Volkswagen of America, Englewood Cliffs, New Jersey.

HISTORY: Introduced September 1976.

1978 AUDI

1978 Audi Fox four-door sedan.

FOX — FOUR — The smaller Audi continued with minimal change. *Car and Driver* called it the "car that breaks all the rules....not big and yet it fits four to five people and their luggage with space to spare....not expensive and yet it's a ball to drive," and, regardless of its small, economical engine, "one of the quickest sedans going." Standard Fox equipment included power front disc brakes, electric rear defogger, intermittent wiper/washers (with fingertip control), vent windows, a four-speed (all-synchro) manual gearbox, trip odometer, clock, driver's remote-control mirror, visor vanity mirror, and locking glovebox. Interiors had brushed velour trim and reclining front bucket seats. A limited-edition GTI two-door sedan (actually an option package) came with a tachometer and racing-style steering wheel. Automatic transmission was available.

5000 — FIVE — A new 5000 series replaced the former 100LS for 1978, becoming the first production model with a five-cylinder (inline) engine. Developing 103 bhp, the overhead-cam powerplant displaced 130.8 cubic inches (2144 cc). The front end displayed recessed round quad headlamps in twin rectangular panels alongside the rectangular grille, which contained the customary Audi interlocking-ring insignia. Horizontal-style taillamps were used. Standard equipment was similar to the Fox, but added cruise control, tinted glass, adjustable rear headrests, trunk carpeting, remote-control tinted mirror, leatherette-covered steering wheel, rear center armrest, lighter, front/rear assist handles, a dual-tone horn, and chromed tailpipe. Available only as a four-door sedan, the body displayed bright window and bodyside moldings as well as vent wings on both doors and slim triangular rear quarter windows. The 185/70HR14 blackwall radial tires held full wheel covers.

I.D. DATA: Fox ten-digit serial number is on the left windshield post and the upper center of the firewall (or on right front wheel housing). 5000 serial number is on driver's side of instrument panel (visible through the windshield) and on cowl panel in the engine compartment. First two digits indicate model; digit three is model year; and the final seven digits are the sequential serial number. Starting serial number: (Fox 2-dr) 8482000301; (Fox 4-dr) 8582000301; (Fox wag) 3382900001; (5000) 4382000051.

Model	Body Type & Seating	Engine Type/CID	P.O.E. Price	Weight (lbs.)	Prod. Total
FOX					
849	2-dr Sedan-4/5P	I4/97	5895	2011	Note 1
850	4-dr Sedan-4/5P	I4/97	6045	2060	Note 1
331	4-dr Sta Wag-4/5P	I4/97	6345	2100	Note 1
5000					
433	4-dr Sedan-5P	I5/131	8450	2588	Note 2

Note 1: A total of 19,584 Audi Fox models were sold in the U.S. during 1978.

Note 2: A total of 20,761 series 5000 sedans were sold in the U.S. during 1978 (plus 537 leftover 100LS sedans).

Price Note: 5000 price rose to $8780 during the model year; Fox price rose by $59. Option prices also rose somewhat during the model year.

ENGINE DATA: BASE FOUR (Fox): Inline, overhead-cam four-cylinder. Cast iron block and light alloy head. **Displacement:** 97 cu. in. (1588 cc). **Bore & Stroke:** 3.13 x 3.15 in. (79.5 x 80.0 mm). **Compression Ratio:** 8.2:1. **Brake Horsepower:** 78 at 5500 rpm (reduced power in California). **Torque:** 84 lbs.-ft. at 3200 rpm. Five main bearings. Solid valve lifters. Fuel injection.

BASE FIVE (5000): Inline, overhead-cam five-cylinder. Cast iron block and light alloy head. **Displacement:** 130.8 cu. in. (2144 cc). **Bore & Stroke:** 3.13 x 3.40 in. (79.5 x 86.4 mm). **Compression Ratio:** 8.0:1. **Brake Horsepower:** 103 at 5500 rpm (100 bhp in California). **Torque:** 110 lbs.-ft. at 4000 rpm. Six main bearings. Solid valve lifters. Fuel injection.

CHASSIS DATA: Wheelbase: (Fox) 97.2 in.; (5000) 105.7 in. **Overall Length:** (Fox) 173.8 in.; (5000) 189.4 in. **Height:** (Fox) 53.6 in.; (5000) 54.8 in. **Width:** (Fox) 64.8 in.; (5000) 69.4 in. **Front Tread:** (Fox) 52.7 in.; (5000) 57.9 in. **Rear Tread:** (Fox) 52.5 in.; (5000) 56.9 in. **Standard Tires:** (Fox) 155SR13; (5000) 185/70HR14.

TECHNICAL: Layout: front-engine, front-drive. **Transmission:** four-speed manual (fully synchronized) or three-speed automatic. **Standard Final Drive Ratio:** (Fox) 4.11:1; (5000) 3.90:1. **Steering:** rack and pinion. **Suspension (front):** MacPherson struts with coil springs and anti-sway bar. **Suspension (rear):** (Fox) rigid axle with trailing links, Panhard rod, coil springs and anti-sway bar; (5000) rigid axle with trailing arms, coil springs and Panhard rod. **Brakes:** front disc, rear drum. **Body Construction:** steel unibody. **Fuel Tank:** (Fox) 11.9 gal.; (5000) 15.8 gallons.

MAJOR OPTIONS: GTI option package: Fox 2-dr ($295). Automatic transmission: Fox ($275); 5000 ($225). Air conditioning: Fox ($495); 5000 ($595). Sunroof: Fox ($280) Power sunroof: 5000 ($550). Tachometer ($65). Sport shock absorbers: 2-dr Fox ($70). Power package: 5000 ($460). Tinted glass: Fox ($50). AM/FM stereo: Fox ($255); 5000 ($150-$325). Power windows: 5000 ($245). Power door locks: 5000 ($130). Heatable driver's seat: 5000 ($60); left/right seats ($100). Alloy wheels: Fox ($170); 5000 ($215). 175/70SR13 tires: Fox ($60).

PERFORMANCE: Top Speed: (Fox) 103 mph; (5000) 103 mph. **Acceleration (0-60 mph):** (Fox) 12.2-12.8 sec.; (5000) 11.7-12.9 sec. **Acceleration (quarter-mile):** (5000) 19.5 sec. (73 mph). **Fuel Mileage:** (Fox) 20-23 mpg city and 29-37 mpg highway, EPA ratings, or 28 mpg average; (5000) 17-20 mpg.

PRODUCTION/SALES: A total of 340,423 Audis (all models) were produced during 1978, of which 40,882 were sold in the U.S. (including 537 leftover 100LS models).

Manufacturer: Audi NSU Auto Union Aktiengesellschaft, Ingolstadt, West Germany.

Distributor: Porsche-Audi Division, Volkswagen of America, Englewood Cliffs, New Jersey.

HISTORY: Introduced August 1977.

1979 AUDI

FOX — FOUR — For its final year in the Audi lineup, the smaller sedans and wagon continued with little change. "There wasn't, still isn't, an ounce of fat on this Italian design," said *Road & Track,* "that looks small from the outside but is actually very roomy on the inside" and was capable of accelerating to 60 mph in 12.8 seconds. The GTI package was offered again this year, containing an AM/FM stereo radio, sports steering wheel, tachometer and extra gauges, Recaro-type front seats in a black interior, metallic silver paint, and 175SR13 tires. As before, the Fox was powered by a 97-cid (1588-cc) overhead-cam four, delivering 78 horsepower.

5000 — FIVE — A 5000S sedan joined the original base model this year. That luxury model added power windows, tinted glass, air conditioning, AM/FM stereo radio with rear speakers and power antenna, power door/trunk locks, driver's seat height adjustment, 6J14 light alloy wheels, and a rear lighter to the basic 5000 equipment. A five-speed manual gearbox was standard this year, replacing the former four-speed.

I.D. DATA: Audi's ten-digit serial numbers were in same locations as 1978. First two digits indicate model; digit three is model year; and the final seven digits are the sequential serial number. Starting serial number: (Fox 2-dr) 8492000001; (Fox 4-dr) 8592000001; (Fox wag) 3392900001; (5000) 4392000001.

Model	Body Type & Seating	Engine Type/CID	P.O.E. Price	Weight (lbs.)	Prod. Price
FOX					
849	2-dr Sedan-4/5P	I4/97	6295	2011	Note 1
850	4-dr Sedan-4/5P	I4/97	6445	2060	Note 1
331	4-dr Sta Wag-4/5P	I4/97	6745	2100	Note 1
5000					
433	4-dr Sedan-5P	I5/131	8995	2622	Note 2
433	4 dr 'S' Sed-5P	I5/131	10575	2622	Note 2

Note 1: A total of 6,151 Audi Fox models were sold in the U.S. during 1979.

Note 2: A total of 28,276 series 5000 sedans were sold in the U.S. during 1978 (plus 8,282 of the 4000 sedans introduced at mid-year, described in the next section).

Price Note: The 5000 soon rose to $9395 during the model year; the 5000S, to $10,975.

ENGINE DATA: BASE FOUR (Fox): Inline, overhead-cam four-cylinder. Cast iron block and light alloy head. **Displacement:** 97 cu. in. (1588 cc). **Bore & Stroke:** 3.13 x 3.15 in. (79.5 x 80 mm). **Compression Ratio:** 8.2:1. **Brake Horsepower:** 78 at 5500 rpm. **Torque:** 83 lbs.-ft. at 3200 rpm. Five main bearings. Solid valve lifters. Fuel injection.

BASE FIVE (5000): Inline, overhead-cam five-cylinder. Cast iron block and light alloy head. **Displacement:** 130.8 cu. in. (2144 cc). **Bore & Stroke:** 3.13 x 3.40 in. (79.5 x 86.4 mm). **Compression Ratio:** 8.0:1. **Brake Horsepower:** 103 at 5500 rpm (100 bhp in California). **Torque:** 110 lbs.-ft. at 4000 rpm. Six main bearings. Solid valve lifters. Fuel injection.

CHASSIS DATA: Wheelbase: (Fox) 97.2 in.; (5000) 105.7 in. **Overall Length:** (Fox) 173.8 in.; (5000) 189.4 in. **Height:** (Fox) 53.6 in.; (5000) 54.8 in. **Width:** (Fox) 64.8 in.; (5000) 69.4 in. **Front Tread:** (Fox) 52.7 in.; (5000) 57.9 in. **Rear Tread:** (Fox) 52.5 in.; (5000) 56.9 in. **Standard Tires:** (Fox) 155SR13; (5000) 185/70HR14.

TECHNICAL: Layout: front-engine, front-drive. **Transmission:** (Fox) four-speed manual; (5000) five-speed. Three-speed automatic optional. **Standard Final Drive Ratio:** (Fox) 4.11:1; (5000) 3.90:1. **Steering:** rack and pinion. **Suspension (front):** MacPherson struts with coil springs and anti-sway bar. **Suspension (rear):** (Fox) rigid axle with trailing links, Panhard rod, coil springs and anti-sway bar; (5000) torsion crank axle with trailing arms, coil springs and Panhard rod. **Brakes:** front disc, rear drum. **Body Construction:** steel unibody. **Fuel Tank:** (Fox) 11.9 gal.; (5000) 19.8 gallons.

MAJOR OPTIONS: Automatic transmission: Fox ($295); 5000 ($325). GTI package: Fox 2-dr ($630). Air conditioning: Fox ($510); 5000 ($595). Sunroof: Fox ($280). Power sunroof: 5000 ($640). AM/FM stereo: Fox ($265); 5000 ($165-$355). Power antenna: 5000 ($95). Alloy wheels: 5000 ($240). Power package: 5000 ($500). Tinted glass: Fox ($55). Heated front seats: 5000 ($110). Tachometer ($70-$75). Leather trim: 5000 ($595). Leatherette trim: Fox ($55). Vent windows: 5000 ($75). Metallic paint ($185-$245). Whitewall tires: Fox sedan ($75). 175/70SR13 tires: Fox $65).

PERFORMANCE: Similar to 1978.

PRODUCTION/SALES: A total of 413,948 Audis (all models) were produced during 1979, of which 42,709 were sold in the U.S. (including 8,282 series 4000 models).

Manufacturer: Audi NSU Auto Union Aktiengesellschaft, Ingolstadt, West Germany.

Distributor: Porsche-Audi Division, Volkswagen of America, Englewood Cliffs, New Jersey.

1980 AUDI

1980 Audi 5000 turbo four-door sedan.

4000 — FOUR/FIVE — Replacing the former Fox during the 1979 model year, the new 4000 was similar in concept but longer, wider and heavier. Appearance was similar to the larger 5000 series, with recessed quad headlamps, but the horizontal bodyside molding ran lower: at the level of the top of the wheel openings. Only two-door and four-door sedans were offered, with nothing to replace the Fox station wagon. The 97 cubic-inch (1588 cc) overhead-cam four-cylinder engine, with transistorized ignition, produced 78 horsepower. It was essentially the same as that in the departed Fox. A five-speed manual gearbox was standard. Automatic shift, not available initially, later added a hefty $1500 to the car's price, partly because it also included the five-cylinder engine from the 5000 series. Standard equipment included power front disc brakes, carpeting, lighter, passenger assist handle, quartz clock, center console, electric rear defogger, day/night mirror, remote-control outside mirror, visor vanity mirror, leatherette-covered steering wheel, front storage shelf, crushed velour trim, trip odometer, and intermittent wiper/washers. Reclining front bucket seats had adjustable headrests. The 4000's dashboard held a voltmeter, oil temperature gauge, and locking glovebox.

5000 — FIVE — The larger Audi sedans continued with minor changes. A reworked dashboard held new instruments, outside mirrors were electrical, and the vanity mirror was illuminated. Base engine again was a gasoline-powered five-cylinder rated 100 horsepower, but a diesel five also became available. Also new this year was a Turbo sedan. Its engine had the same displacement as the base five, but produced 130 horsepower. Standard equipment on the 5000 sedan included a five-speed manual transmission, power steering and brakes, cruise control, bright window and bodyside moldings, rear center armrest, front and rear assist handles, lighter, tinted glass, twin remote tinted mirrors, full wheel covers, and 185/70HR14 blackwall tires. The 5000S added an AM/FM stereo radio with power antenna, air conditioning, driver's seat height adjustment, 6Jx14 alloy wheels, power windows and door/trunk locks, and front vent windows.

I.D. DATA: Vehicle identification number (VIN) is on a plate atop the instrument panel, visible through the windshield; and also on the ledge in the engine compartment (4000), or stamped into the upper right corner of the firewall (5000). Engine number (4000) is on the left side of the block, below the cylinder head, next to the distributor; (5000) stamped on left side of block, at clutch housing. 5000 models also have an engine code number stamped on the starter end of the block, just below the cylinder head, indicating the exact cylinder bore dimension. Starting serial number: (4000) 81A0000001; (5000) 43A0000001.

Model	Body Type & Seating	Engine Type/CID	P.O.E. Price	Weight (lbs.)	Prod. Total
4000					
811	2-dr Sedan-4/5P	I4/97	7495	2133	Note 1
813	4-dr Sedan-4/5P	I4/97	7685	2178	Note 1
5000					
433	4-dr Sedan-5P	I5/131	10300	2624	Note 2
433	40dr Turbo Sed-5P	I5/131	16480	2963	Note 2
433	4-dr 'S' Sed-5P	I5/131	12240	2624	Note 2

Note 1: A total of 14,681 series 4000 Audis were sold in the U.S. during 1980.

Note 2: A total of 27,802 series 5000 Audis were sold in the U.S. during 1980. Automatic Transmission Note: An automatic transmission added $1500 to price of 4000 series, and included the five-cylinder engine.

Diesel Note: A diesel-engine 5000 sedan cost $11,100; a diesel 5000S was $13,040. Price Note: 4000 prices rose considerably during the model year, to $8650 for the two-door and $8870 for the four-door. Series 5000 prices rose by $300 during the model year (except for the Turbo).

ENGINE DATA: BASE FOUR (4000): Inline, overhead-cam four-cylinder. Cast iron block and aluminum alloy head. **Displacement:** 97 cu. in. (1588 cc). **Bore & Stroke:** 3.13 x 3.15 in. (79.5 x 80 mm). **Compression Ratio:** 8.0:1. **Brake Horsepower:** 78 at 5500 rpm (76 bhp in California). **Torque:** 84 lbs.-ft. at 3200 rpm (83 in California). Five main bearings. Solid valve lifters. Bosch K-Jetronic fuel injection.

BASE FIVE (5000): Inline, overhead-cam five-cylinder. Cast iron block and aluminum alloy head. **Displacement:** 130.8 cu. in. (2144 cc). **Bore & Stroke:** 3.13 x 3.40 in. (79.5 x 86.4 mm). **Compression Ratio:** 8.0:1. **Brake Horsepower:** 100 at 5100 rpm. **Torque:** 110 lbs.-ft. at 4000 rpm. Six main bearings. Solid valve lifters. Fuel injection.

Note: The five-cylinder gas engine was also used later in the 4000 sedans with automatic transmission.

TURBO FIVE (5000): Same as above, except — **Compression Ratio:** 7.0:1. **Brake Horsepower:** 130 at 5400 rpm. **Torque:** 142 lbs.-ft. at 3000 rpm.

DIESEL FIVE (5000): Inline, overhead-cam five-cylinder. **Displacement:** 121.0 cu. in. (1986 cc). **Bore & Stroke:** 3.09 x 3.40 in. (79.5 x 78.5 mm). **Compression Ratio:** 23.0:1. **Brake Horsepower:** 67 at 4800 rpm. **Torque:** 86.4 lbs.-ft. at 3000 rpm.

CHASSIS DATA: Wheelbase: (4000) 99.5 in.; (5000) 105.5 in. **Overall Length:** (4000) 176.6 in.; (5000) 189.5 in. **Height:** (4000) 53.7 in.; (5000) 54.7 in. **Width:** (4000) 66.2 in.; (5000) 69.6 in. **Front Tread:** (4000) 55.1 in.; (5000) 57.9 in. **Rear Tread:** (4000) 55.9 in.; (5000) 56.9 in. **Wheel Type:** (4000) 5Jx13; (5000) 5.5Jx14. **Standard Tires:** (4000) 175/70SR13; (5000) 185/70HR14.

TECHNICAL: Layout: front-engine, front-drive. **Transmission:** five-speed manual (fully synchronized) except (Turbo) three-speed automatic. **Steering:** rack and pinion. **Suspension (front):** MacPherson struts with lower A-arms, coil springs and anti-sway bar. **Suspension (rear):** beam axle with coil springs, Panhard rod and built-in anti-sway bar. **Brakes:** power front disc, rear drum except (5000 Turbo) all disc. **Body Construction:** steel unibody. **Fuel Tank:** (4000) 15.8 gallons; (5000) 19.8 gallons.

MAJOR OPTIONS: Automatic transmission: 4000 ($1500); 5000 ($375). Sliding sunroof: 4000 ($400); 5000 ($690). Air conditioning: 4000 ($575); 5000 ($650). Leather seats: 5000 ($650). Power windows: base 5000 ($290). AM/FM stereo radio: 4000, base 5000 ($385); w/power antenna ($485). AM/FM stereo with tape player: 4000, base 5000 ($525); w/power antenna ($625). Heated front seat: 5000 ($120). Height-adjustable driver's seat: 4000 ($60). Tachometer ($80). Alloy wheels: 4000 ($200); base 5000 ($260).

PERFORMANCE: Top Speed: (4000) 101-104 mph; (5000) 103 mph; (5000 dsl) 93 mph. **Acceleration (0-60 mph):** (4000) 11.5-12.8 seconds; (5000) 11.7 seconds; (5000 dsl) 19.0 sec. **Acceleration (quarter-mile):** (4000) 18.6 seconds (74 mph). **Fuel Mileage:** (4000) average 26-27 mpg, EPA 22/34 mpg; (5000) 17/34 mpg; (5000 dsl) 26/34 mpg.

PRODUCTION/SALES: A total of 346,235 Audis (all models) were produced during 1980, of which 42,483 were sold in the U.S.

Manufacturer: Audi NSU Auto Union AG, Ingolstadt, West Germany.

Distributor: Porsche-Audi Division, Volkswagen of America, Englewood Cliffs, New Jersey.

HISTORY: New 4000 models introduced in U.S. In February 1979; 5000 in September 1979. Production of the Audi Quattro (four-wheel-drive) began this year, with 292 built for sale outside the U.S.

1981 AUDI

1981 Audi 4000 5+5 two-door sedan.

4000 — FOUR/FIVE — Abandoning the 97-cid four-cylinder engine that descended from the Fox, the 4000 for 1981 came with either a larger (105 cubic-inch) four, or with the 100-bhp five-cylinder powerplant, borrowed from the 5000. Four-cylinder models came with a manual gearbox; fives could have automatic. Appearance and standard equipment were similar to 1980. The 5+5 sport sedan, aimed at "the most demanding drivers," included cloth sports bucket seats with a driver's height adjustment, power steering, 175/70SR13 tires on special cast alloy wheels, wide lower bodyside moldings, black window moldings, oil pressure gauge in the console, and a tachometer.

COUPE — FIVE — Added late in the model year was an Audi coupe, which mixed the 4000 chassis with the 5000 drivetrain. Thus, the 99.8-inch wheelbase sedan carried a five-cylinder engine rated 100 bhp, hooked to a five-speed manual gearbox.

5000 — FIVE — As before, the 5000 series came with a choice of three five cylinder engines: standard 100-horsepower, turbocharged 130-bhp, or a smaller-displacement diesel. Appearance and standard equipment were similar to 1980. Audi claimed that the 5000S turbo accelerated from zero to 50 mph in 7.5 seconds. The turbo sport sedan included four-wheel disc brakes and 205/60HR15 tires.

I.D. DATA: Audi's 17-symbol Vehicle identification number (VIN), starting with 'WAU', is on a plate atop the instrument panel, visible through the windshield. It is also on the ledge in the engine compartment (4000), or stamped into the upper right corner of the firewall (5000). Engine number (4000) is on the left side of the block, below the cylinder head, next to the distributor; (5000) stamped on left side of block, at clutch housing. 5000 models also have an engine code number stamped on the starter end of the block, just below the cylinder head, indicating the exact cylinder bore dimension. Symbol five indicates engine type. Symbols 7-8 indicate model: '81' = 4000; '43' = 5000. Tenth symbol is the model year ('B' = 1981). Starting sequential serial number: 000501.

Model	Body Type & Seating	Engine Type/CID	P.O.E. Price	Weight (lbs.)	Prod. Total
4000					
81	2-dr Sedan-4/5P	I4/105	8990	2087	Note 1
81	4-dr Sedan-4/5P	I4/105	9210	2132	Note 1
81	2-dr 5+5 Sed-4/5P	I5/131	11105	2478	Note 1
COUPE					
85	2-dr Coupe-4/5P	I5/131	11875	2510	Note 1
5000					
43	4-dr Sedan-5P	I5/131	11240	2624	Note 2
5000S					
43	4-dr Sedan-5P	I5/131	12840	2624	Note 2
43	4-dr Turbo Sed-5P	I5/131	17650	2963	Note 2

Note 1: A total of 18,941 series 4000 sedans and 2,553 coupes were sold in the U.S. during 1981.

Note 2: A total of 29,323 series 5000 Audis were sold in the U.S. during 1981.

Diesel Engine Note: A diesel engine added $850 to the 5000 and 5000S prices shown. Automatic Transmission Note: An automatic transmission added $405 to prices shown.

ENGINE DATA: BASE FOUR (4000): Inline, overhead-cam four-cylinder. Cast iron block and aluminum alloy head. **Displacement:** 105.0 cu. in. (1715 cc). **Bore & Stroke:** 3.13 x 3.40 in. (79.5 x 86.4 mm). **Compression Ratio:** 8.2:1. **Brake Horsepower:** 74 (SAE) at 5000 rpm. **Torque:** 89.6 lbs.-ft. at 3000 rpm. Five main bearings. Solid valve lifters. Fuel injection.

BASE FIVE (4000 automatic, 5+5, Coupe, 5000): Inline, overhead-cam five-cylinder. Cast iron block and aluminum alloy head. **Displacement:** 130.8 cu. in. (2144 cc). **Bore & Stroke:** 3.13 x 3.40 in. (79.5 x 86.4 mm). **Compression Ratio:** 8.0:1. **Brake Horsepower:** 100 at 5100 rpm. **Torque:** 112 lbs.-ft. at 3000 rpm. Six main bearings. Solid valve lifters. Bosch K-Jetronic fuel injection.

TURBO FIVE (5000): Same as above, except — **Compression Ratio:** 7.0:1. **Brake Horsepower:** 130 at 5400 rpm. **Torque:** 142 lbs.-ft. at 3000 rpm.

DIESEL FIVE (5000): Inline, overhead-cam five-cylinder. **Displacement:** 121.0 cu. in. (1986 cc). **Bore & Stroke:** 3.09 x 3.40 in. (79.5 x 78.5 mm). **Compression Ratio:** 23.0:1. **Brake Horsepower:** 67 at 4800 rpm. **Torque:** 86.4 lbs.-ft. at 3000 rpm. Mechanical fuel injection.

CHASSIS DATA: Wheelbase: (4000) 100.0 in.; (Coupe) 99.8 in.; (5000) 105.5 in. **Overall Length:** (4000) 176.6 in.; (Coupe) 177 in.; (5000) 188.9 in. **Height:** (4000) 53.7 in.; (Coupe) 53.1 in.; (5000) 54.7 in. **Width:** (4000) 66.2 in.; (Coupe) 66.3 in.; (5000) 69.6 in. **Front Tread:** (4000) 55.1 in.; (5000) 57.9 in. **Rear Tread:** (4000) 55.9 in.; (5000) 56.9 in. **Wheel Type:** (4000) 5Jx13; (5000) 5.5Jx14. **Standard Tires:** (4000) 175/70SR13; (4000 automatic, Coupe) 185/60HR14; (5000) 185/70SR14; (Turbo) 205/60HR15.

TECHNICAL: Layout: front-engine, front-drive. **Transmission:** five-speed manual (fully synchronized) or three-speed automatic. **Steering:** rack and pinion. **Suspension (front):** MacPherson struts with lower A-arms, coil springs and anti-sway bar. **Suspension (rear):** beam axle with coil springs, Panhard rod and built-in anti-sway bar. **Brakes:** power front disc, rear drum except (5000 Turbo) all disc. **Body Construction:** steel unibody. **Fuel Tank:** (4000) 15.8 gallons; (5000) 19.8 gallons.

MAJOR OPTIONS: Power steering: 4000 ($390). Sliding sunroof: 4000 ($430); 5000 ($745). Air conditioning: 4000 ($620); 5000 ($700). Leather seats: 5000 ($750-$1080). Power windows: 4000 ($260-$315); 5000 ($325). AM/FM stereo with tape player: 4000, base 5000 ($675). Tachometer ($85). Cruise control: 4000 ($180). Power door locks ($160). Heated mirrors ($175). Heated front seat: 5000 ($130). Height-adjustable driver's seat ($65). Power seats: 5000 ($465). Vent windows: 5000 ($95). Alloy wheels: 4000 ($215/$560); base 5000 ($320).

PERFORMANCE: Top Speed: (4000) 100 mph (factory); (4000 automatic) 105 mph; (4000 5+5) 108 mph; (5000) 107 mph (factory); (5000 Turbo) 113 mph; (5000 Diesel) 93 mph (factory). **Acceleration (0-60 mph):** (4000) 14.0 sec.; (4000 automatic) 12.9 sec.; (5000) 12.5 sec.; (5000 dsl) 18.9 sec.; (5000 Turbo) 9.4-10.6 seconds. **Acceleration (quarter-mile):** (4000 auto.) 19 seconds (72 mph); (5000 Turbo) 17.1 seconds (80 mph). **Fuel Mileage:** (4000) 26/41 mpg; (4000 auto.) about 25 mpg; (4000 5+5) 21/36 mpg (5000) 19/33 mpg; (5000 dsl) 27/43 mpg; (5000 Turbo) about 17 mpg.

PRODUCTION/SALES: A total of 50,817 Audis were sold in the U.S. during 1981.

Manufacturer: Audi NSU Auto Union AG, Ingolstadt, West Germany.

Distributor: Porsche-Audi Division, Volkswagen of America, Englewood Cliffs, New Jersey.

1982 AUDI

4000 — FOUR — Gasoline-powered sedans continued with little change, but the 5+5 sports sedan was dropped, replaced by the fastback Coupe (below) that debuted during the 1981 model year. Sedans added an "Econominder" system to remind manual-shift drivers when to upshift for best gas mileage, along with a vacuum gauge that operated in top gear. Standard 4000 equipment included power front disc brakes, carpeting, clock, electric rear defogger, voltmeter, oil-temperature gauge, locking glovebox, remote mirror, lighter, carpeting, wide bodyside moldings, and 175/70SR13 tires with wheel trim rings. Reclining front bucket seats were upholstered in crushed velour and faced a four-spoke steering wheel. Both a gas and diesel version were available. A new 4000S model added bright trim and grille moldings, alloy wheels, a sport steering wheel, visor vanity mirror, rear head restraints, console, and trip odometer.

COUPE — FIVE — Production continued of this blend of 4000 chassis with 5000 five-cylinder powertrain, with little change. The Coupe rode 185/60HR14 tires and carried a tachometer and rear spoiler.

5000 — FIVE — Little change was evident in the larger Audi series. As before, three engines were offered: normally-aspirated five-cylinder, diesel five, and a turbocharged gas five. Standard equipment for the 5000S included air conditioning, power door locks, tinted glass, trunk carpeting, protective side moldings, cruise control, power steering, power windows, lighted ashtray, center armrest, reclining front seats, and 185/70SR14 tires. The Turbo added a tachometer, and AM/FM stereo with cassette player and automatic antenna.

1982 Audi 4000 4E two-door sedan.

Note: The limited-production Audi Quattro (four-wheel-drive) coupe became available in the U.S. during the 1982 model year; see next listing for details.

I.D. DATA: Audi's 17-symbol Vehicle identification number (VIN), starting with 'WAU', is on a plate atop the instrument panel, visible through the windshield. It is also on the ledge in the engine compartment (4000), or stamped into the upper right corner of the firewall (5000). Engine number (4000) is on the left side of the block, below the cylinder head, next to the distributor; (5000) stamped on left side of block, at clutch housing. 5000 models also have an engine code number stamped on the starter end of the block, just below the cylinder head, indicating the exact cylinder bore dimension. Symbols 6-8 indicate model: '081' = 4000; '085' = 4000 cpe; '043' = 5000. Tenth symbol is the model year ('C' = 1982). Starting sequential serial number: (4000) 000115; (5000) 000501.

Model	Body Type & Seating	Engine Type/CID	P.O.E. Price	Weight (lbs.)	Prod. Total
4000					
811	2-dr Sedan-4/5P	I4/105	9755	2087	Note 1
813	4-dr Dsl Sedan-4/5P	I4/97	10515	2197	Note 1
4000S					
813	4-dr Sedan-5P	I4/105	10865	2132	Note 1
COUPE					
855	2-dr Coupe-4P	I5/131	12370	2243	Note 1
5000					
433	4-dr Dsl Sedan-5P	I5/121	17780	2668	Note 2
433	4-dr S Sedan-5P	I5/131	13665	2624	Note 2
437	4-dr Turbo Sed-5P	I5/131	18490	2919	Note 2

Note 1: A total of 16,336 series 4000 sedans and 4,524 coupes were sold in the U.S. during 1982.
Note 2: A total of 25,094 series 5000 Audis were sold in the U.S. during 1982.
Price Note: An automatic transmission added $405 to prices shown.

ENGINE DATA: BASE FOUR (4000): Inline, overhead-cam four-cylinder. Cast iron block and aluminum alloy head. **Displacement:** 105.0 cu. in. (1715 cc). **Bore & Stroke:** 3.13 x 3.40 in. (79.5 x 86.4 mm). **Compression Ratio:** 8.0:1. **Brake Horsepower:** 74 (SAE) at 5000 rpm. **Torque:** 89.6 lbs.-ft. at 3000 rpm. Five main bearings. Solid valve lifters. Fuel injection.

BASE FIVE (Coupe, 5000S): Inline, overhead-cam five-cylinder. Cast iron block and aluminum alloy head. **Displacement:** 130.8 cu. in. (2144 cc). **Bore & Stroke:** 3.13 x 3.40 in. (79.5 x 86.4 mm). **Compression Ratio:** 8.2:1. **Brake Horsepower:** 100 at 5100 rpm. **Torque:** 112.3 lbs.-ft. at 3000 rpm. Six main bearings. Solid valve lifters. Fuel injection.

DIESEL FOUR (4000): Inline, overhead-cam four-cylinder. Cast iron block and aluminum alloy head. **Displacement:** 97.0 cu. in. (1588 cc). **Bore & Stroke:** 3.01 x 3.40 in. (76.5 x 86.4 mm). **Compression Ratio:** 23.0:1. **Brake Horsepower:** 52 at 4800 rpm. **Torque:** 71.5 lbs.-ft. at 2000 rpm. Five main bearings. Solid valve lifters. Fuel injection.

TURBO FIVE (5000): Same as above, except -- **Compression Ratio:** 7.0:1. **Brake Horsepower:** 130 at 5400 rpm. **Torque:** 142 lbs.-ft. at 3000 rpm.

DIESEL FIVE (5000): Inline, overhead-cam five-cylinder. **Displacement:** 121.0 cu. in. (1986 cc). **Bore & Stroke:** 3.09 x 3.40 in. (79.5 x 78.5 mm). **Compression Ratio:** 23.0:1. **Brake Horsepower:** 67 at 4800 rpm. **Torque:** 86.4 lbs.-ft. at 3000 rpm.

CHASSIS DATA: Wheelbase: (4000) 99.8 in.; (5000) 105.5 in. **Overall Length:** (4000) 176.6 in.; (5000) 188.9 in. **Height:** (4000) 53.7 in.; (5000) 54.7 in. **Width:** (4000) 66.2 in.; (5000) 69.6 in. **Front Tread:** (4000) 55.1 in.; (5000) 57.9 in.; (Turbo) 58.1 in. **Rear Tread:** (4000) 55.9 in.; (5000) 56.9 in.; (Turbo) 57.2 in. **Wheel Type:** (4000) 5Jx13; (5000) 5.5Jx14. **Standard Tires:** (4000) 175/70SR13; (Coupe) 185/60HR14; (5000) 185/70SR14.

TECHNICAL: Layout: front-engine, front-drive. **Transmission:** five-speed manual (fully synchronized) or three-speed automatic except (4000 dsl) four-speed. **Steering:** rack and pinion. **Suspension (front):** MacPherson struts with coil springs and anti-roll bar. **Suspension (rear):** torsion crank axle with Panhard rod, coil springs and anti-roll bar. **Brakes:** power front disc, rear drum exc. (Turbo) four-wheel disc. **Body Construction:** steel unibody. **Fuel Tank:** (4000) 15.8 gallons; (5000) 19.8 gallons.

MAJOR OPTIONS: Power steering: 4000 ($390). Option groups: 4000 ($850-$1125). Sliding sunroof: 4000 ($430); 5000 ($745). Air conditioning: 4000 ($620); 5000 ($700). Leather seats: 5000 ($750-1080). Power windows: 4000 ($260-315); 5000 ($325). AM/FM stereo with tape player ($675). Power seat: 5000 ($465). Heated front seat: 5000 ($130).

PERFORMANCE: Similar to 1981.

PRODUCTION/SALES: A total of 306,581 Audis (all models) were produced during 1982, of which 45,954 were sold in the U.S. Total production included 2,462 Audi Quattros.
Manufacturer: Audi NSU Auto Union AG, Ingolstadt, West Germany.
Distributor: Porsche-Audi Division, Volkswagen of America, Englewood Cliffs, New Jersey.

1983 AUDI

1983 Audi Coupe GT.

4000 — FOUR — A turbocharger was added to Audi's optional diesel engine this year. The 1.6-litre diesel four was also available in the Volkswagen Rabbit and Quantum. Otherwise, little was changed. Diesels could have either the five-speed manual gearbox or a new "E-Mode" three-speed automatic transmisison, introduced during the 1982 model year, which allowed the car to "freewheel" (with fuel flow cut off) when the driver's foot left the accelerator pedal. Models for 1983 included a base two-door sedan with 1.7-litre gasoline four-cylinder engine, and a 4000S with air conditioning, open-up vent windows, height-adjustable driver seats, rear headrests, power steering, cruise control, and wider tires on 5.5x13 light alloy wheels. Standard 4000 equipment included halogen headlamps, front and rear stabilizer bars, 175/70SR13 tires on 5Jx13 wheels, tinted glass, sport steering wheel, tachometer, dual remote mirrors, space-saver spare tire, large front spoiler, wide bodyside moldings, and upshift indicator light. Reclining front bucket seats had crushed velour upholstery.

COUPE — FIVE — Once again, the fastback Coupe rode a 4000 chassis and carried a 131-cid five-cylinder engine from the 5000 series. Standard equipment included a front air dam, rear spoiler, 185/60HR14 tires, sport reclining front bucket seats in tweed cloth, and an oil pressure gauge.

QUATTRO — FIVE — The new Quattro, introduced early in 1982 (as an '83 model) had the same bodyshell as the Coupe but added full-time four-wheel drive, disc brakes on all four wheels, independent rear suspension, and a turbocharged five-cylinder engine with air-to-air intercooler. Both the Coupe and Quattro came with a standard five-speed manual gearbox, but only the Coupe could get the three-speed automatic. Standard Quattro fittings included front/rear spoilers, tinted glass, turbo boost gauge, tachometer, power door locks and antenna, power windows, intermittent wipers, dual remote heated mirrors, lighted visor mirror, cruise control, AM/FM stereo radio with cassette player, and power steering. The 205/60HR15 tires rode 6Jx15 light alloy wheels. A tool kit was included, and the gas tank held 23.8 gallons.

1983 Audi 5000 turbo diesel.

5000 — FIVE — For its final season in the form that emerged in the 1978 model year, Audi's larger series was essentially unchanged. A turbocharger was added to the 2.0-litre optional diesel engine, and the normally-aspirated 5000 diesel was dropped. Both the turbocharged and normally-aspirated gasoline five-cylinder engines continued. A five-speed (overdrive) manual gearbox was standard with the non-turbo engine, but Turbos came only with "E-mode" three-speed automatic.

I.D. DATA: Audi's 17-symbol Vehicle identification number (VIN), starting with 'WAU', is on a plate atop the instrument panel, visible through the windshield. It is also on the ledge in the engine compartment (4000), or stamped into the upper right corner of the firewall (5000). Engine number (4000) is on the left side of the block, below the cylinder head, next to the distributor; (5000) stamped on left side of block, at clutch housing. 5000 models also have an engine code number stamped on the starter end of the block, just below the cylinder head, indicating the exact cylinder bore dimension. Symbols 7-8 indicate model: '81' = 4000; '43' = 5000. Tenth symbol is the model year ('D' = 1983). Starting sequential serial number: 000001.

Model	Body Type & Seating	Engine Type/CID	P.O.E. Price	Weight (lbs.)	Prod. Total
4000					
811	2-dr Sedan-5P	I4/1015	10205	2087	Note 1
4000S					
813	4-dr Sedan-5P	I4/105	11780	2132	Note 1
813	4-dr Dsl Sed-5P	I4/97	12425	2196	Note 1
813	4-dr T Dsl Sed-5P	I4/97	13330	N/A	Note 1
COUPE					
855	2-dr Coupe-4P	I5/131	12680	2243	Note 1
QUATTRO					
857	2-dr Coupe-4P	I5/131	35000	2915	N/A
5000					
43	4-dr 'S' Sedan-5P	I5/131	14355	2624	Note 2
43	4-dr Turbo Sed-5P	I5/131	19425	2919	Note 2
43	4-dr Dsl Sed-5P	I5/121	17780	2919	Note 2

Note 1: A total of 13,804 series 4000 sedans and 3,598 coupes were sold in the U.S. during 1983.

Note 2: A total of 30,532 series 5000 Audis were sold in the U.S. during 1983.

Price Note: An automatic transmission added $425 to price shown for the 4000S, 5000S and Coupe; and $515 to the 4000S Turbo Diesel.

ENGINE DATA: BASE FOUR (4000): Inline, overhead-cam four-cylinder. Cast iron block and aluminum alloy head. **Displacement:** 105.0 cu. in. (1715 cc). **Bore & Stroke:** 3.13 x 3.40 in. (79.5 x 86.4 mm). **Compression Ratio:** 8.2:1. **Brake Horsepower:** 74 (SAE) at 5000 rpm. **Torque:** 89.6 lbs.-ft. at 3000 rpm. Five main bearings. Solid valve lifters. Fuel injection.

DIESEL FOUR (4000): Inline, overhead-cam four-cylinder. Cast iron block and aluminum alloy head. **Displacement:** 97.0 cu. in. (1588 cc). **Bore & Stroke:** 3.01 x 3.40 in. (76.5 x 86.4 mm). **Compression Ratio:** 23.0:1. **Brake Horsepower:** 52 at 4800 rpm. **Torque:** 71.5 lbs.-ft. at 2000 rpm. Five main bearings. Solid valve lifters. Fuel injection.

TURBODIESEL FOUR (4000): Same as diesel above, except — **Brake Horsepower:** 68 at 4500 rpm. **Torque:** 98 lbs.-ft. at 2800 rpm.

BASE FIVE (Coupe, 5000): Inline, overhead-cam five-cylinder. Cast iron block and aluminum alloy head. **Displacement:** 130.8 cu. in. (2144 cc). **Bore & Stroke:** 3.13 x 3.40 in. (79.5 x 86.4 mm). **Compression Ratio:** 8.2:1. **Brake Horsepower:** 100 at 5100 rpm. **Torque:** 112.3 lbs.-ft. at 3000 rpm. Six main bearings. Solid valve lifters. Fuel injection.

TURBO FIVE (Turbo 5000): Same as above, except — **Compression Ratio:** 7.0:1. **Brake Horsepower:** 130 at 5400 rpm. **Torque:** 142 lbs.-ft. at 3000 rpm.

TURBO FIVE (Quattro): Same as above, except — **Compression Ratio:** 7.0:1. **Brake Horsepower:** 160 at 5500 rpm. **Torque:** 170 lbs.-ft. at 3000 rpm.

TURBODIESEL FIVE (5000): Inline, overhead-cam five-cylinder. **Displacement:** 121.0 cu. in. (1986 cc). **Bore & Stroke:** 3.09 x 3.40 in. (79.5 x 78.5 mm). **Compression Ratio:** 23.0:1. **Brake Horsepower:** 84 at 4500 rpm. **Torque:** 127 lbs.-ft. at 2800 rpm.

CHASSIS DATA: Wheelbase: (4000) 99.8 in.; (Quattro) 99.4 in.; (5000) 105.5 in. **Overall Length:** (4000) 176.6 in.; (Coupe) 177.0 in.; (Quattro) 178.2 in.; (5000) 188.9 in. **Height:** (4000) 53.8 in.; (Coupe) 53.1 in.; (Quattro) 52.0 in.; (5000) 54.7 in. **Width:** (4000) 66.2 in.; (Coupe) 66.3 in.; (Quattro) 67.9 in.; (5000) 69.6 in. **Front Tread:** (4000) 55.1 in.; (Quattro) 55.9 in.; (5000) 57.9 in.; (5000 Turbo) 58.1 in. **Rear Tread:** (4000) 55.9 in.; (Quattro) 57.4 in.; (5000) 56.9 in.; (5000 Turbo) 57.2 in. **Standard Tires:** (4000) 175/70SR13; (Coupe) 185/60HR14; (5000) 185/70SR14; (Quattro) 205/60HR15.

TECHNICAL: Layout: front-engine, front-drive except (Quattro) four-wheel-drive. **Transmission:** five-speed manual (fully synchronized) or three-speed automatic. **Steering:** rack and pinion. **Suspension (front):** MacPherson struts with coil springs and anti-roll bar. **Suspension (rear):** torsion crank axle with Panhard rod, coil springs and anti-roll bar except (Quattro) independent coil springs/struts. **Brakes:** power front disc, rear drum except (Turbo/Quattro) four-wheel disc. **Body Construction:** steel unibody. **Fuel Tank:** (4000) 15.8 gallons; (Quattro) 23.8 gallons; (5000) 19.8 gallons.

MAJOR OPTIONS: Air conditioning: 4000/cpe ($725). AM/FM stereo with cassette tape player and automatic antenna cpe ($650); 5000 ($695). Power steering: 4000 ($420). Alloy wheels: 4000 ($250). Power sunroof: 4000 ($475); 5000 ($870); cpe/Quattro ($450). Power windows: 4000, cpe ($300); 4000S ($350). Passenger seat height adjuster: cpe ($75). Power seats: 5000 ($540). Leather trim: cpe ($1620); Quattro ($1500); 5000 ($1300). Heated front seat: cpe ($150). Heated mirrors: 5000 ($205). Rear wiper/washer: cpe, Quattro ($210). Cruise control: 4000 ($210). Metallic paint ($285-$350). Power door locks: 4000/S, cpe ($190). Tachometer ($95); N/A with automatic.

PERFORMANCE: Top Speed: (Coupe) 111 mph; (Quattro) 128 mph; (5000 Turbo) 110 mph. **Acceleration** (0-60 mph): (Coupe) 11.2 seconds; (Quattro) 8.2 seconds; (5000 Turbo) 11.6 seconds. **Acceleration (quarter-mile):** (Coupe) 18.1 seconds (75.5 mph); (Quattro) 16.2 seconds (86.5 mph); (5000 Turbo) 18.4 seconds (75.5 mph). **Fuel Mileage:** (Coupe) about 25 mpg; (Quattro) about 17 mpg; (5000 Turbo) about 19 mpg.

PRODUCTION/SALES: A total of 358,213 Audis (all models) were produced during 1983, of which 47,934 were sold in the U.S. Production included 1,455 Quattros.

Manufacturer: Audi NSU Auto Union AG, Ingolstadt, West Germany.

Distributor: Porsche-Audi Division, Volkswagen of America, Englewood Cliffs, New Jersey.

1984 AUDI

4000S — FOUR — A bigger and more potent engine went under the hoods of Audi's smaller sedans, borrowed from the Volkswagen Rabbit GTI. A new 4000S Quattro sedan (described below) became available. Both the 1.7-liter gasoline four and the diesel engine were dropped, replaced by a 1.8-litre four. Bumpers this year were rated for only 2.5-mph crashes (formerly 5-mph). Standard equipment on all models included air conditioning, power steering, alloy wheels, tachometer, cruise control, electric mirrors, and leather steering wheel. Four-door models also had standard power door locks and windows.

4000S QUATTRO — FIVE — Fascination with the four-wheel-drive concept in the Audi Quattro sports coupe led to a new 4000S Quattro sports sedan. Instead of the 2.1-litre (2144 cc) five-cylinder engine used in other models, the new 4WD Quattro's turbo enjoyed a bore increase to reach 2.2-litre (2226-cc) displacement. The 4WD sedan came with air conditioning, a front air dam, black bumpers, tinted glass, dual heated power mirrors, AM/FM stereo with cassette player, power driver's seat height adjustment, decklid spoiler, leather sport steering wheel, and 195/60HR14 tires on 6Jx14 spoke alloy wheels.

COUPE GT — FIVE — Mechanical changes that included vented front disc brakes, a rear spoiler, close-ratio five-speed gearbox and sport exhaust, plus a new "GT" designation, went on Audi's coupe during the 1983 model year and continued for '84. The coupe also included spoke-style alloy wheels.

QUATTRO — FIVE — The turbo-powered (and expensive) Quattro 4WD continued in limited production.

1984 Audi 5000S sedan.

5000S — FIVE — Introduced as an early 1984 model in the spring of '83, the new larger Audi series was billed as the world's most aerodynamic sedan. The new wedge-profile body had a tall deck in back, a small spoiler up front, and a sloping hood. Rectangular quad headlamps were slightly staggered in their recessed housings, which flanked the customary Audi grille with its center insignia of four interlocking rings. Not only the windshield and back window, but the side windows, were virtually flush-fitting. Even the outside mirrors were integrated into the overall design. A full-width back panel contained the taillamps. Standard equipment included air conditioning, a front air dam, power windows, decklid spoiler, cloth reclining front bucket seats with driver's height adjustment, tachometer, digital clock, and 185/70R14 tires on 6Jx14 alloy wheels.

A Turbo edition and a four-door station wagon joined the original four-door sedan as the full model year began. The wagon displayed a steeply-raked windshield and back window, as well as a big rear spoiler. A locking storage compartment under the carpeted cargo floor could hold two small suitcases. Additional luggage could be stored behind the back seat, hidden by a sliding security cover. Audi's five-cylinder engine added electronic idle controls to its fuel injection system and the valve lifters switched to hydraulic operation. Audi claimed that the intercooled Turbo sedan, offered only with automatic transmission, could accelerate from zero to 60 mph in 10.6 seconds, and reach 124 mph. Turbos came with a sport suspension, digital boost gauge, four-wheel disc brakes, trip computer, and 15-inch alloy wheels.

I.D. DATA: Audi's 17-symbol Vehicle identification number (VIN), starting with 'WAU', is on a plate atop the instrument panel, visible through the windshield. It is also on the ledge in the engine compartment (4000), or stamped into the upper right corner of the firewall (5000). Engine number (4000) is on the left side of the block, below the cylinder head, next to the distributor; (5000) stamped on left side of block, at clutch housing. 5000 models also have an engine code number stamped on the starter end of the block, just below the cylinder head, indicating the exact cylinder bore dimension. Symbols 7-8 indicate model: '81' = 4000S; '85' = coupe; '44' = 5000S. Tenth symbol is the model year ('E' = 1984). Starting sequential serial number: 000001.

Model	Body Type & Seating	Engine Type/CID	P.O.E. Price	Weight (lbs.)	Prod. Total
4000S					
81	2-dr Sedan-5P	I4/109	12390	2146	Note 1
81	4-dr Sedan-5P	I4/109	12980	2215	Note 1
COUPE GT					
85	2-dr Coupe-4P	I5/131	14500	2196	Note 1
4000S QUATTRO					
85	4-dr Sedan-5P	I5/136	16500	2745	Note 1
QUATTRO					
85	2-dr Cpe-4P	I5/131	35000	2132	Note 2
5000S					
44	4-dr Sedan-5P	I5/131	16480	2844	Note 3
44	4-dr Turbo Sed-5P	I5/131	22250	3042	Note 3
44	4-dr Sta Wag-5P	I5/131	17480	2954	Note 3

Note 1: A total of 19,303 series 4000 sedans and 3,585 coupes were sold in the U.S. during 1984.

Note 2: About 50 Quattros were sold in the U.S. during the 1984 model year.

Note 3: A total of 48,318 series 5000 Audis were sold in the U.S. during 1984.

ENGINE DATA: BASE FOUR (4000S): Inline, overhead-cam four-cylinder. Cast iron block and aluminum alloy head. **Displacement:** 109.0 cu. in. (1780 cc). **Bore & Stroke:** 3.19 x 3.40 in. (81 x 86.4 mm). **Compression Ratio:** 8.5:1. **Brake Horsepower:** 85 at 5500 rpm. Torque: 100 lbs.-ft. at 3000 rpm. Five main bearings. Fuel injection.

BASE FIVE (GT Coupe, 5000S): Inline, overhead-cam five-cylinder. Cast iron block and aluminum alloy head. **Displacement:** 130.8 cu. in. (2144 cc). **Bore & Stroke:** 3.13 x 3.40 in. (79.5 x 86.4 mm). **Compression Ratio:** 8.2:1. **Brake Horsepower:** 100 at 5500 rpm. **Torque:** 107 lbs.-ft. at 3000 rpm. Six main bearings. Hydraulic valve lifters. Bosch K-Jetronic fuel injection.

TURBO FIVE (5000S Turbo): Same as above, except — **Compression Ratio:** 8.3:1. **Brake Horsepower:** 140 at 5500 rpm. **Torque:** 149 lbs.-ft. at 2500 rpm.

TURBO FIVE (Quattro): Same as above, except — **Compression Ratio:** 7.0:1. **Brake Horsepower:** 160 at 5500 rpm. **Torque:** 181 lbs.-ft. at 3000 rpm.

BASE FIVE (4000S Quattro): Inline, overhead-cam five-cylinder. Cast iron block and aluminum alloy head. **Displacement:** 136 cu. in. (2226 cc). **Bore & Stroke:** 3.19 x 3.40 in. (81.0 x 86.4 mm). **Compression Ratio:** 8.5:1. **Brake Horsepower:** 115 at 5500 rpm. **Torque:** 126 lbs.-ft. at 3000 rpm. Six main bearings. Hydraulic valve lifters. Bosch KE-Jetronic fuel injection.

CHASSIS DATA: Wheelbase: (4000S/cpe) 99.8 in.; (4000S Quattro) 99.4 in.; (Quattro) 99.5 in.; (5000S) 105.8 in. **Overall Length:** (4000S/Quattro) 176.6 in.; (cpe) 177.0 in.; (Quattro) 178.2 in.; (5000S) 192.7 in. **Height:** (4000S/Quattro) 53.8 in.; (cpe) 53.1 in.; (Quattro) 52.0 in.; (5000S sed) 54.7 in.; (5000S wag) 55.7 in. **Width:** (4000S) 66.2 in.; (4000S Quattro) 66.4 in.; (cpe) 66.3 in.; (Quattro) 67.9 in.; (5000S) 71.4 in. **Front Tread:** (4000S/cpe) 55.1 in.; (4000S Quattro) 55.4 in.; (Quattro) 56.0 in.; (5000S) 58.1 in.; (5000S Turbo) 57.8 in. **Rear Tread:** (4000S/cpe) 55.9 in.; (4000S Quattro) 55.8 in.; (Quattro) 57.4 in.; (5000S) 57.4 in. **Standard Tires:** (4000S) 175/70SR13; (4000S Quattro) 195/60HR14; (5000S) 185/70SR14; (5000S Turbo) 205/60HR15.

TECHNICAL: Layout: front-engine, front-drive except (Quattro) four-wheel-drive. **Transmission:** five-speed manual (fully synchronized) or three-speed automatic. **Steering:** rack and pinion. **Suspension (front):** MacPherson struts with coil springs and anti-roll bar. **Suspension (rear):** beam axle with Panhard rod, coil springs and anti-roll bar except (Quattro) independent coil springs/struts; (4000S Quattro) Chapman struts with lower A-arms and coil springs. **Brakes:** power front disc, rear drum except (Quattro) four-wheel disc. **Body Construction:** steel unibody. **Fuel Tank:** (4000S) 15.8 gal.; (4000S Quattro) 18.5 gal.; (Quattro) 23.8 gal.; (5000S) 21.1 gallons.

MAJOR OPTIONS: Removable sunroof: 4000S/Quattro ($475). Power sunroof: 5000S ($895); 4000S Quattro ($625). AM/FM stereo with cassette tape player ($360). Heated front seats: 5000S ($160). Power front seats with memory: 5000S ($650). Trip computer: 5000S ($190). Rear wiper/washer: cpe ($220). Metallic paint ($310-$350). Leather trim: 5000S ($1025). Leatherette trim: 5000S, cpe ($350).

PERFORMANCE: Top Speed: (4000S Quattro) 116 mph; (5000S) 110 mph; (5000S Turbo) 124 mph. **Acceleration (0-60 mph):** (4000S Quattro) 10.2 sec.; (5000S) 11.8 sec.; (5000S Turbo) 10.6 seconds. **Acceleration (quarter-mile):** (4000S Quattro) 17.3 sec. (76 mph); (5000S) 18.2 seconds (74.5 mph); (5000S Turbo) 17.8 sec. (79 mph). **Fuel Mileage:** (4000S Quattro) about 21 mpg; (5000S) about 21 mpg; (5000S Turbo) about 18 mpg.

PRODUCTION/SALES: A total of 344,733 Audis (all models) were produced during 1984, of which 71,206 were sold in the U.S.

Manufacturer: Audi AG, Ingolstadt, West Germany.

Distributor: Porsche-Audi Division, Volkswagen of America, Troy, Michigan.

HISTORY: New 5000 series introduced in May 1983; 4000 series in October 1983.

1985 AUDI

1985 Audi Quattro turbo.

4000S — FOUR — Only the four-door sedan remained in the 4000 series; the two-door sedan was dropped. Restyled, more rounded bodies displayed new aero hedlamps, integrated (body-color) bumper aprons, and full-width taillamps. A sharp horsepower boost came to the base 1.8-litre four-cylinder engine, now up to 102 bhp. Vented front disc brakes were added, and 60-series rode 14-inch alloy wheels.

4000S QUATTRO — FIVE — The 4WD sports sedan continued with little change.

COUPE GT — FIVE — New aero styling up front, including integrated body-color bumper aprons and aero headlamps, was the major change for the sporty fastback coupe.

QUATTRO — FIVE — A small number of Quattro turbos continued to arrive in the U.S., again with a $35,000 price tag. They received a new instrument panel this year, with digital electronic gauges and a graphic tachometer.

5000S — FIVE — The 2.2-litre five-cylinder engine, introduced in the 4000S Quattro, now went under 5000S hoods, replacing the former 2.1-litre version. The turbocharged five did not increase in displacement.

I.D. DATA: Similar to 1984.

Model	Body Type & Seating	Engine Type/CID	P.O.E. Price	Weight (lbs.)	Prod. Total
4000S					
81	4-dr Sedan-5P	I4/109	13950	2215	Note 1
COUPE GT					
85	2-dr Coupe-4P	I5/136	15250	2196	Note 1
4000S QUATTRO					
85	4-dr Sedan-5P	I5/136	17450	2745	Note 1
QUATTRO					
85	2-dr Cpe-4P	I5/131	35000	2132	N/A

Model	Body Type & Seating	Engine Type/CID	P.O.E. Price	Weight (lbs.)	Prod. Total
5000S					
44	4-dr Sedan-5P	I5/136	17710	2765	Note 2
44	4-dr Turbo Sed-5P	I5/131	23875	2963	Note 2
44	4-dr Sta Wag-5P	I5/136	18920	2624	Note 2

Note 1: A total of 22,345 series 4000 sedans and 3,659 coupes were sold in the U.S. during 1985.

Note 2: A total of 48,057 series 5000 Audis were sold in the U.S. during 1985.

ENGINE DATA: BASE FOUR (4000S): Inline, overhead-cam four-cylinder. Cast iron block and aluminum alloy head. **Displacement:** 109.0 cu. in. (1780 cc). **Bore & Stroke:** 3.19 x 3.40 in. (81 x 86.4 mm). **Compression Ratio:** 10.0:1. **Brake Horsepower:** 102 at 5500 rpm. **Torque:** 105 lbs.-ft. at 3250 rpm. Five main bearings. Fuel injection.

BASE FIVE (4000S Quattro, GT Coupe, 5000S): Inline, overhead-cam five-cylinder. Cast iron block and aluminum alloy head. **Displacement:** 136 cu. in. (2226 cc). **Bore & Stroke:** 3.19 x 3.40 in. (81.0 x 86.4 mm). **Compression Ratio:** 8.5:1. **Brake Horsepower:** 115 at 5500 rpm. **Torque:** 126 lbs.-ft. at 3000 rpm. Six main bearings. Hydraulic valve lifters. Bosch KE-Jetronic fuel injection.

TURBO FIVE (5000S Turbo): Inline, overhead-cam five-cylinder. Cast iron block and aluminum alloy head. **Displacement:** 131 cu. in. (2144 cc). **Bore & Stroke:** 3.13 x 3.40 in. (79.5 x 86.4 mm). **Compression Ratio:** 8.0:1. **Brake Horsepower:** 140 at 5500 rpm. **Torque:** 149 lbs.-ft. at 2500 rpm.

TURBO FIVE (Quattro): Same as 131-cid five above, except -- **Compression Ratio:** 7.0:1. **Brake Horsepower:** 160 at 5500 rpm. **Torque:** 181 lbs.-ft. at 3000 rpm.

CHASSIS DATA: Wheelbase: (4000S/cpe) 99.8 in.; (Quattro) 99.5 in.; (5000S) 105.8 in. **Overall Length:** (4000S/Quattro) 176.6 in.; (cpe) 177.0 in.; (Quattro) 178.2 in.; (5000S) 192.7 in. **Height:** (4000S/Quattro) 53.8 in.; (cpe) 53.1 in.; (Quattro) 52.0 in.; (5000S sed) 54.7 in.; (5000S wag) 55.7 in. **Width:** (4000S) 66.2 in.; (4000S Quattro) 66.4 in.; (cpe) 66.3 in.; (Quattro) 67.9 in.; (5000S) 71.4 in. **Front Tread:** (4000S/cpe) 55.1 in.; (4000S Quattro) 55.4 in.; (Quattro) 56.0 in.; (5000S) 58.1 in.; (5000S Turbo) 57.8 in. **Rear Tread:** (4000S/cpe) 55.9 in.; (Quattro) 57.4 in.; (5000S) 57.8 in. **Standard Tires:** (4000S) 175/70R13; (4000S Quattro) 195/60R14; (Quattro) 185/60H14; (5000S) 185/70SR14; (5000S Turbo) 205/60HR15.

TECHNICAL: Layout: front-engine, front-drive except (Quattro) four-wheel-drive. **Transmission:** five-speed manual (fully synchronized) or three-speed automatic. **Steering:** rack and pinion. **Suspension (front):** MacPherson struts with coil springs and anti-roll bar. **Suspension (rear):** beam axle with Panhard rod, coil springs and anti-roll bar except (Quattro) independent coil springs/struts; (4000S Quattro) Chapman struts with lower A-arms and coil springs. **Brakes:** power front disc, rear drum except (Quattro) four-wheel disc. **Body Construction:** steel unibody. **Fuel Tank:** (4000S/cpe) 15.8 gal.; (4000S Quattro) 18.5 gal.; (Quattro) 23.8 gal.; (5000S) 21.1 gallons.

MAJOR OPTIONS: Similar to 1984.

Manufacturer: Audi AG, Ingolstadt, West Germany.

Distributor: Porsche-Audi Division, Volkswagen of America, Troy, Michigan.

1986 AUDI

1986 Audi 5000S wagon.

4000S — FOUR — Except for an increase in torque output from the standard four-cylinder engine, the basic 4000S sedan continued with little change. A Commemorative Edition added Alcantara leather upholstery, aero alloy wheels, power sunroof, AM/FM stereo radio with cassette player, leather-wrapped steering wheel, and metallic paint.

4000CS QUATTRO — FIVE — The 4000CS Quattro sedan (formerly called 4000S Quattro) remained available, with little change other than new hydraulic mounts for the five-cylinder 136-cid engine.

COUPE GT — FIVE — Sale of the standard Coupe continued, but the Quattro Turbo coupe was dropped this year (at least in the U.S.).

5000S/CS — FIVE — Aero headlamps and fully galvanized sheetmetal body panels were new this year, but otherwise the basic 5000 series continued as before. A larger (136-cid) turbocharged engine went into the 5000CS Turbo sedan, as well as a 5000CS Quattro Turbo four-wheel-drive sedan. The 5000CS had anti-lock braking. Both Turbos came with a standard five-speed manual gearbox this year. A Turbo Quattro could accelerate from 0-60 mph in about 8.3 seconds, with top speed of 132 mph, yet deliver an average of 20 mpg.

I.D. DATA: Similar to 1984.

Model	Body Type & Seating	Engine Type/CID	P.O.E. Price	Weight (lbs.)	Prod. Total
4000S					
813	4-dr Sedan-5P	I4/109	14320	2337	Note 1

Model	Body Type & Seating	Engine Type/CID	P.O.E. Price	Weight (lbs.)	Prod. Total
COUPE GT					
855	2-dr Coupe-4P	I5/136	15555	2507	Note 1
4000CS QUATTRO					
854	4-dr Sedan-5P	I5/136	17800	2824	Note 1
5000S/CS					
443	4-dr Sedan-5P	I5/136	18065	2844	Note 2
447	4-dr Turbo Sed-5P	I5/136	24095	3086	Note 2
445	4-dr Sta Wag-5P	I5/136	19275	2954	Note 2
5000CS TURBO QUATTRO					
4472	4-dr Sedan-5P	I5/136	27975	3351	Note 2
4477	4-dr Sta Wag-5P	I5/136	29185	3437	Note 2

Note 1: A total of 16,437 series 4000 Audis and 2,847 coupes were sold in the U.S. during 1986.

Note 2: A total of 40,513 series 5000 Audis were sold in the U.S. during 1986.

Commemorative Edition Note: Special editions of the 4000S, 4000CS Quattro and GT Coupe with extra equipment became available during the model year, priced at $17,010, $20,365 and $18,525, respectively.

ENGINE DATA: BASE FOUR (4000S): Inline, overhead-cam four-cylinder. Cast iron block and aluminum alloy head. **Displacement:** 109.0 cu. in. (1780 cc). **Bore & Stroke:** 3.19 x 3.40 in. (81 x 86.4 mm). **Compression Ratio:** 10.0:1. **Brake Horsepower:** 102 at 5500 rpm. **Torque:** 111 lbs.-ft. at 3250 rpm. Five main bearings. Fuel injection.

BASE FIVE (GT Coupe, 5000S): Inline, overhead-cam five-cylinder. Cast iron block and aluminum alloy head. **Displacement:** 136 cu. in. (2226 cc). **Bore & Stroke:** 3.19 x 3.40 in. (81.0 x 86.4 mm). **Compression Ratio:** 8.5:1. **Brake Horsepower:** 110 at 5500 rpm. **Torque:** 122 lbs.-ft. at 3000 rpm. Six main bearings. Hydraulic valve lifters. Fuel injection.

BASE FIVE (4000CS Quattro): Same as above, except — **Brake Horsepower:** 115 at 5500 rpm. **Torque:** 126 lbs.-ft. at 3000 rpm.

TURBO FIVE (5000CS Turbo/Quattro): Inline, overhead-cam five-cylinder. Cast iron block and aluminum alloy head. **Displacement:** 136 cu. in. (2226 cc). **Bore & Stroke:** 3.19 x 3.40 in. (81.0 x 86.4 mm). **Compression Ratio:** 7.8:1. **Brake Horsepower:** 158 at 5500 rpm. **Torque:** 166 lbs.-ft. at 3000 rpm.

CHASSIS DATA: Wheelbase: (4000S/cpe) 99.8 in.; (5000S) 105.8 in. **Overall Length:** (4000S) 176.6 in.; (cpe) 177.0 in.; (5000S) 192.7 in. **Height:** (4000S) 53.8 in.; (cpe) 53.1 in.; (5000S sed) 54.7 in.; (5000S wag) 55.7 in. **Width:** (4000S) 66.2 in.; (cpe) 66.3 in.; (5000S) 71.4 in. **Front Tread:** (4000S/cpe) 55.1 in.; (5000S) 57.8 in. **Rear Tread:** (4000S/cpe) 55.9 in.; (5000S) 57.8 in.

TECHNICAL: Layout: front-engine, front-drive except (Quattro) four-wheel-drive. **Transmission:** five-speed manual (fully synchronized) or three-speed automatic. **Steering:** rack and pinion. **Suspension (front):** MacPherson struts with coil springs and anti-roll bar. **Suspension (rear):** torsion beam axle with Panhard rod, coil springs and anti-roll bar. **Brakes:** (4000, Coupe) power front disc, rear drum; (4000CS Quattro, 5000 series) four-wheel disc. **Body Construction:** steel unibody.

MAJOR OPTIONS: Automatic transmission ($475). AM/FM stereo with cassette ($390). Ski rack: 5000S ($95). Anti-lock braking: 5000CS ($995). Removable sunroof: GT cpe ($495). Power tilt/slide sunroof ($695-$975). Leather interior ($950-$1095). Leatherette interior: 4000S/5000S ($95). Trip computer ($210). Heated front seats ($180). Heated front/rear seats: 5000CS Turbo Quattro ($295). Power front seats w/memory: 5000S ($695). Forged alloy wheels: 5000CS Turbo Quattro ($195). Roof rails: 5000S/CS wagon ($200). Power door locks: GT cpe ($200). Power antenna: GT cpe ($95). Rear wiper/washer: GT cpe ($230).

Manufacturer: Audi AG, Ingolstadt, West Germany.

Distributor: Audi of America Inc., Troy, Michigan.

1987 AUDI

4000S — FOUR — For its last official year in the Audi lineup, the 4000 sedan changed little.

4000CS QUATTRO — FIVE — Little was new for the four-wheel drive 4000CS Quattro sedan, except for a displacement and power increase in its five-cylinder engine.

GT COUPE — FIVE — During the 1987 model year, the coupe's five-cylinder engine grew and got a boost to 130 bhp.

5000S/CS — FIVE — Like the other five-cylinder models, the 5000S added horsepower during the model year through a displacement increase. Anti-lock braking was now available on the base sedan and wagon, as well as the 5000CS Turbo Quattro. ABS remained standard on the Turbo Quattro. In response to allegations by safety groups that Audi 5000s with automatic transmissions suffered from unintended acceleration, the company issued a voluntary recall of all 1978-86 models to install an Automatic Shift Lock device. This would prevent shifting from Park to Reverse or Drive unless the brake pedal was pressed down.

I.D. DATA: Similar to 1984.

Model	Body Type & Seating	Engine Type/CID	P.O.E. Price	Weight (lbs.)	Prod. Total
4000S					
81	4-dr Sedan-5P	I4/109	15875	2337	Note 1
COUPE GT					
85	2-dr Coupe-4P	I5/136	17580	2507	Note 1
4000CS QUATTRO					
85	4-dr Sedan-5P	I5/136	19850	2824	Note 1
5000S/CS					
44	4-dr Sedan-5P	I5/136	20060	2844	Note 2
44	4-dr Turbo Sed-5P	I5/136	26640	3086	Note 2
44	4-dr Sta Wag-5P	I5/136	21390	2954	Note 2
5000CS TURBO QUATTRO					
44	4-dr Sedan-5P	I5/136	31250	3351	Note 2
44	4-dr Sta Wag-5P	I5/136	32555	3437	Note 2

Note 1: A total of 11,972 series 4000 Audis and 1,990 coupes were sold in the U.S. during 1987.

Note 2: A total of 26,042 series 5000 Audis were sold in the U.S. during 1987.

ENGINE DATA: BASE FOUR (4000S): Inline, overhead-cam four-cylinder. Cast iron block and aluminum alloy head. **Displacement:** 109.0 cu. in. (1780 cc). **Bore & Stroke:** 3.19 x 3.40 in. (81 x 86.4 mm). **Compression Ratio:** 10.0:1. **Brake Horsepower:** 102 at 5500 rpm. **Torque:** 111 lbs.-ft. at 3250 rpm. Five main bearings. Fuel injection.

BASE FIVE (4000CS, Coupe GT, 5000S): Inline, overhead-cam five-cylinder. Cast iron block and aluminum alloy head. **Displacement:** 136 cu. in. (2226 cc). **Bore & Stroke:** 3.19 x 3.40 in. (81.0 x 86.4 mm). **Compression Ratio:** 8.5:1. **Brake Horsepower:** 110 at 5500 rpm. **Torque:** 122 lbs.-ft. at 3000 rpm. Six main bearings. Hydraulic valve lifters. Fuel injection.

BASE FIVE (later): Inline, overhead-cam five-cylinder. Cast iron block and aluminum alloy head. **Displacement:** 141 cu. in. (2309 cc). **Bore & Stroke:** 3.25 x 3.40 in. (82.5 x 86.4 mm). **Compression Ratio:** 10.0:1. **Brake Horsepower:** 130 at 5700 rpm. **Torque:** 140 lbs.-ft. at 4500 rpm. Six main bearings. Hydraulic valve lifters. Fuel injection.

TURBO FIVE (5000CS Turbo/Quattro): Inline, overhead-cam five-cylinder. Cast iron block and aluminum alloy head. **Displacement:** 136 cu. in. (2226 cc). **Bore & Stroke:** 3.19 x 3.40 in. (81.0 x 86.4 mm). **Compression Ratio:** 7.8:1. **Brake Horsepower:** 158/162 at 5500 rpm. **Torque:** 166/177 lbs.-ft. at 3000 rpm.

CHASSIS DATA: Same as 1986.

TECHNICAL: Same as 1986.

MAJOR OPTIONS: Automatic transmission ($500). Ski rack: 5000S ($95). Anti-lock braking: 5000S/CS. Removable sunroof: GT cpe ($535). Power tilt/slide sunroof ($750-$1055). Trip computer ($250). Heated front seats ($180-$195). AM/FM stereo radio w/cassette ($410). Heated front/rear seats: 5000CS Turbo Quattro ($350). Power front seats w/memory: 5000S ($750). Forged alloy wheels: 5000CS Turbo Quattro ($250). Roof rails: 5000S/CS wagon ($200). Power door locks: GT cpe ($215). Power antenna: GT cpe ($95). Rear wiper/washer: GT cpe ($230).

Manufacturer: Audi AG, Ingolstadt, West Germany.

Distributor: Audi of America Inc., Troy, Michigan.

1988 AUDI

1988 Audi 90 four-door sedan.

80/90 — FOUR/FIVE — Replacing the 4000 series were new model 80 and 90 sedans, adopting the numbering system used for European Audis and powered by larger engines. Wheelbase was slightly longer than the 4000, and appearance was similar to the larger Audis. That meant aero headlamps, flush window glass and door handles, and a steep windshield angle. A Quattro (four-wheel-drive) version also was offered in both series, with a 2.3-litre five-cylinder engine rather than the standard 2.0-litre four. Quattros came only with a five-speed manual gearbox, but two-wheel-drive models could have the three-speed automatic. The standard 90 model was available with either the five-cylinder powerplant and manual shift, or four-cylinder with automatic.

5000S/CS — FIVE — Little change was evident on the senior Audis, which were in their final season before switching to 100/200 (European) nomenclature.

Model	Body Type & Seating	Engine Type/CID	P.O.E. Price	Weight (lbs.)	Prod. Total
80					
89	4-dr Sedan-5P	I4/121	18600	2568	Note 1
89	4-dr 4WD Sed-5P	I5/141	22700	2904	Note 1
90					
89	4-dr Sedan-5P	I4/121	24330	2732	Note 2
89	4-dr 4WD Sed-5P	I5/141	27720	2948	Note 2
5000S/CS					
44	4-dr Sedan-5P	I5/141	22180	2844	Note 3
44	4-dr Turbo Sed-5P	I5/136	30010	3086	Note 3
44	4-dr Sta Wag-5P	I5/141	23620	2930	Note 3
44	4-dr 4WD Sed-5P	I5/141	26490	3307	Note 3
5000CS TURBO QUATTRO					
44	4-dr Sedan-5P	I5/136	33800	3351	Note 3
44	4-dr Sta Wag-5P	I5/136	35250	3437	Note 3

Note 1: A total of 5,702 series 80 Audis were sold in the U.S. during 1988.
Note 2: A total of 6,106 series 90 Audis were sold in the U.S. during 1988.
Note 3: A total of 7,256 series 5000 Audis were sold in the U.S. during 1988.

ENGINE DATA: BASE FOUR (80, 90 w/automatic): Inline, overhead-cam four-cylinder. **Displacement:** 121 cu. in. (1983 cc). **Bore & Stroke:** 3.25 x 3.65 in. (82.5 x 92.8 mm). **Compression Ratio:** 10.5:1. **Brake Horsepower:** 108 at 5300 rpm. **Torque:** 121 lbs.-ft. at 3200 rpm. Five main bearings. Hydraulic valve lifters. Fuel injection.
BASE FIVE (80 Quattro, 90 w/manual, 90 Quattro, 5000S): Inline, overhead-cam five-cylinder. Cast iron block and aluminum head. **Displacement:** 141 cu. in. (2309 cc). **Bore & Stroke:** 3.25 x 3.40 in. (82.5 x 86.4 mm). **Compression Ratio:** 10.0:1. **Brake Horsepower:** 130 at 5700 rpm. **Torque:** 140 lbs.-ft. at 4500 rpm. Fuel injection.
TURBO FIVE (5000CS Turbo/Quattro): Inline, overhead-cam five-cylinder. Cast iron block and aluminum alloy head. **Displacement:** 136 cu. in. (2226 cc). **Bore & Stroke:** 3.19 x 3.40 in. (81.0 x 86.4 mm). **Compression Ratio:** 7.8:1. **Brake Horsepower:** 162 at 5500 rpm. **Torque:** 177 lbs.-ft. at 3000 rpm.

CHASSIS DATA: Wheelbase: (80/90) 100.2 in.; (5000S) 105.8 in. **Overall Length:** (80/90) 176.3 in.; (5000S) 192.7 in. **Height:** (80/90) 55.0 in.; (5000S sed) 54.7 in.; (5000S wag) 55.7 in. **Width:** (80/90) 66.7 in.; (5000S) 71.4 in. **Front Tread:** (80/90) 55.6 in.; (5000S) 57.8 in. **Rear Tread:** (80/90) 56.3 in.; (5000S) 57.8 in.

TECHNICAL: Layout: front-engine, front-drive except (Quattro) four-wheel-drive. **Transmission:** five-speed manual (fully synchronized) or three-speed automatic. **Steering:** rack and pinion. **Brakes:** front/rear disc. **Body Construction:** steel unibody.

MAJOR OPTIONS: Automatic transmission: 80/5000S ($525). Power sunroof: 80 ($795); 5000S ($1125). Anti-lock braking: 80 Quattro, 5000S ($1150). Auto check system: 80 Quattro ($100). Trip computer ($245). Roof rails: wagon ($215). AM/FM stereo radio w/cassette: 80, 5000S ($495). Forged alloy wheels: 5000CS Quattro ($275). Power seat: 90, 5000S ($795). Ski rack ($120). Heated front seats ($225). Heated front/rear seats: 5000CS Quattro ($375).

Manufacturer: Audi AG, Ingolstadt, West Germany.
Distributor: Audi of America Inc., Troy, Michigan.

1989 AUDI

1989 Audi 80 Quattro four-door sedan.

80/90 — FOUR/FIVE — The restyled (and renumbered) smaller Audi series, introduced for 1988, continued with minimal change. As before, the two-wheel-drive model 80 had a four-cylinder engine. This year, all 90 series sedans came with the five-cylinder powerplant; the five had formerly been offered only with manual shift in the 2WD model.

100/200 — FIVE — Like the smaller Audis a year earlier, the senior series switched to the European numbering system. Not much was changed otherwise, except for minor body and interior revisions that included flush-fit door handles and Zebra-wood dashboard paneling that curved into the front of each door. That dashboard displayed a full set of analog gauges. A driver's air bag was standard on the 200, which came with a turbo-charged 2.2-litre five-cylinder engine. The 100 carried a 2.3-litre five (normally aspirated). The "entry level" 100E sedan came only with automatic shift.

Model	Body Type & Seating	Engine Type/CID	P.O.E. Price	Weight (lbs.)	Prod. Total
80					
89	4-dr Sedan-5P	I4/121	19350	2612	Note 1
89	4-dr 4WD Sed-5P	I5/141	23610	2954	Note 1
90					
89	4-dr Sedan-5P	I5/141	25310	2789	Note 2
89	4-dr 4WD Sed-5P	I5/141	28840	2976	Note 2
100					
44	4-dr Sedan-5P	I5/141	27480	2932	Note 3
44	4-dr 'E' Sed-5P	I5/141	24980	2932	Note 3
44	4-dr Sta Wag-5P	I5/141	28960	3042	Note 3
44	4-dr 4WD Sed-5P	I5/141	30805	3306	Note 3
200					
44	4-dr Sedan-5P	I5/136	32455	3086	Note 4
44	4-dr 4WD Sed-5P	I5/136	36355	3351	Note 4
44	4-dr Sta Wag-5P	I5/136	37855	3439	Note 4

Note 1: A total of 4,590 series 80 Audis were sold in the U.S. during 1989.

Note 2: A total of 4,423 series 90 Audis were sold in the U.S. during 1989.

Note 3: A total of 7,722 series 200 Audis were sold in the U.S. during 1989 (plus 2,139 in late 1988).

Note 4: A total of 2,777 series 100 Audis were sold in the U.S. during 1989 (plus 1,167 in late 1988).

ENGINE DATA: BASE FOUR (80): Inline, overhead-cam four-cylinder. Cast iron block and aluminum head. **Displacement:** 121 cu. in. (1983 cc). **Bore & Stroke:** 3.25 x 3.65 in. (82.5 x 92.8 mm). **Compression Ratio:** 10.5:1. **Brake Horsepower:** 108 at 5300 rpm. **Torque:** 121 lbs.-ft. at 3200 rpm. Five main bearings. Hydraulic valve lifters. Fuel injection.
BASE FIVE (80 Quattro, 90, 100): Inline, overhead-cam five-cylinder. Cast iron block and aluminum head. **Displacement:** 141 cu. in. (2309 cc). **Bore & Stroke:** 3.25 x 3.40 in. (82.5 x 86.4 mm). **Compression Ratio:** 10.0:1. **Brake Horsepower:** 130 at 5700 rpm. **Torque:** 140 lbs.-ft. at 4500 rpm. Fuel injection.
BASE TURBO FIVE (200): Inline, overhead-cam five-cylinder. Cast iron block and aluminum alloy head. **Displacement:** 136 cu. in. (2226 cc). **Bore & Stroke:** 3.19 x 3.40 in. (81.0 x 86.4 mm). **Compression Ratio:** 7.8:1. **Brake Horsepower:** 162 at 5500 rpm. **Torque:** 177 lbs.-ft. at 3000 rpm. Six main bearings. Hydraulic valve lifters. Turbocharged and intercooled.

CHASSIS DATA: Wheelbase: (80/90) 100.2 in.; (100/200) 105.8 in. **Overall Length:** (80/90) 176.3 in.; (100/200) 192.7 in. **Height:** (80/90) 55.0 in.; (100/200 sed) 54.7 in.; (100/200 wag) 55.7 in. **Width:** (80/90) 66.7 in.; (100/200) 71.4 in. **Front Tread:** (80/90) 55.6 in.; (100/200) 57.8 in. **Rear Tread:** (80/90) 56.3 in.; (100/200) 57.8 in.

TECHNICAL: Layout: front-engine, front-drive except (Quattro) four-wheel-drive. **Transmission:** five-speed manual (fully synchronized) or three-speed automatic. **Steering:** rack and pinion. **Brakes:** front/rear disc. **Body Construction:** steel unibody.

MAJOR OPTIONS: Similar to 1988.
Manufacturer: Audi AG, Ingolstadt, West Germany.
Distributor: Audi of America Inc., Troy, Michigan.

1990 AUDI

80/90 — FOUR/FIVE — Anti-lock brakes were standard on both 90 models, and optional on the 80 Quattro this year. The 90 Quattro adopted the new 20-valve version of the Audi five-cylinder engine, introduced on the new Coupe Quattro. As before, the two-wheel-drive 80 sedan carried a four-cylinder engine; all the others were five-cylinder.

COUPE QUATTRO — FIVE — The hatchback coupe's modified five-cylinder engine had twin cams and 20 valves, producing 164 horsepower (34 more than the standard five). Built on the same platform as the 80/90 sedans, the coupe also used the same full-time 4WD system as the 80/90 Quattros and came only with a five-speed manual gearbox.

100/200 — FIVE — All 100/200 models had a driver's air bag this year, and the lowest-priced 100E sedan was dropped, along with the 100 station wagon.

1990 Audi V-8 Quattro.

V8 QUATTRO — V-8 — Audi took a big jump in performance for 1990 with the new high-performance sedan. The aluminum 3.6-liter V-8 engine produced 240 horsepower, hooked to a four-speed overdrive automatic transmission with permanent four-wheel drive. Three shift modes were included in the transmission: E (economy); S (sport); and M (manual). Standard features included a driver's air bag, anti-lock braking, cellular phone, leather upholstery, and Bose sound system. Appearance was similar to the 100/200, but body panels (except for the roof and front doors) were not shared. Audi claimed that the V8 was capable of accelerating from zero to 60 mph in 8.7 seconds, and could reach a top speed of 146 mph.

Model	Body Type & Seating	Engine Type/CID	P.O.E. Price	Weight (lbs.)	Prod. Total
80					
8A	4-dr Sedan-5P	I4/121	18900	902612	Note 1
8A	4-dr 4WD Sed-5P	I5/141	22800	2954	Note 1
90					
8A	4-dr Sedan-5P	I5/141	23990	2789	Note 1
8A	4-dr 4WD Sed-5P	I5/141	27500	3042	Note 1
COUPE QUATTRO					
8B	2-dr HB Cpe-5P	I5/141	29750	3174	
100					
44	4-dr Sdan-5P	I5/141	26900	3042	Note 1
44	4-dr 4WD Sed-5P	I5/141	29470	3263	Note 1
200					
44	4-dr Sedan-5P	I5/136	33405	3263	Note 1
44	4-dr 4WD Sed-5P	I5/136	35805	3483	Note 1
44	4-dr Sta Wag-5P	I5/136	36930	3572	Note 1
V8 QUATTRO					
44	4-dr Sedan-5P	V8/217	47450	3946	Note 1

Note 1: A total of 21,106 Audis were sold in the U.S. during 1990.

ENGINE DATA: BASE FOUR (80): Inline, overhead-cam four-cylinder. Cast iron block and aluminum head. **Displacement:** 121 cu. in. (1983 cc). **Bore & Stroke:** 3.25 x 3.65 in. (82.5 x 92.8 mm). **Compression Ratio:** 10.5:1. **Brake Horsepower:** 108 at 5300 rpm. **Torque:** 121 lbs.-ft. at 3200 rpm. Five main bearings. Hydraulic valve lifters. Fuel injection.

BASE FIVE (80 Quattro, 90 2WD, 100): Inline, overhead-cam five-cylinder. Cast iron block and aluminum head. **Displacement:** 141 cu. in. (2309 cc). **Bore & Stroke:** 3.25 x 3.40 in. (82.5 x 86.4 mm). **Compression Ratio:** 10.0:1. **Brake Horsepower:** 130 at 5500 rpm. **Torque:** 140 lbs.-ft. at 4000 rpm. CIS fuel injection.

BASE FIVE (Coupe Quattro, 90 Quattro): Inline, dual-overhead-cam five-cylinder (20-valve). Cast iron block and aluminum head. **Displacement:** 141 cu. in. (2309 cc). **Bore & Stroke:** 3.25 x 3.40 in. (82.5 x 86.4 mm). **Compression Ratio:** 10.3:1. **Brake Horsepower:** 164 at 6000 rpm. **Torque:** 157 lbs.-ft. at 4500 rpm. Hydraulic valve lifters. Fuel injection.

BASE TURBO FIVE (200): Inline, overhead-cam five-cylinder. Cast iron block and aluminum alloy head. **Displacement:** 136 cu. in. (2226 cc). **Bore & Stroke:** 3.19 x 3.40 in. (81.0 x 86.4 mm). **Compression Ratio:** 8.4:1. **Brake Horsepower:** 162 at 5500 rpm. **Torque:** 177 lbs.-ft. at 3000 rpm. Six main bearings. Hydraulic valve lifters. Turbocharged and intercooled.

BASE V-8 (V8 Quattro): Dual-overhead-cam V-8 (32-valve). Aluminum block and heads. **Displacement:** 217 cu. in. (3562 cc). **Bore & Stroke:** 3.19 x 3.40 in. (81.0 x 86.4 mm). **Compression Ratio:** 10.6:1. **Brake Horsepower:** 240 at 5800 rpm. **Torque:** 245 lbs.-ft. at 4000 rpm.

CHASSIS DATA: Wheelbase: (80/90/cpe) 100.4 in.; (100/200) 105.6 in.; (V8) 106.4 in. **Overall Length:** (80/90) 176.3 in.; (cpe) 176.0 in.; (100/200) 192.7 in.; (V8) 191.9 in. **Height:** (80/90) 55.0 in.; (cpe) 54.3 in.; (100/200 sed) 54.7 in.; (100/200 wag) 55.9 in.; (V8) 55.9 in. **Width:** (80/90) 66.7 in.; (cpe) 67.6 in.; (100/200) 71.4 in.; (V8) 71.4 in.

TECHNICAL: Layout: front-engine, front-drive except (Quattro) four-wheel-drive. **Transmission:** five-speed manual (fully synchronized) or three-speed automatic except (V8 Quattro) four-speed automatic. **Steering:** rack and pinion. **Brakes:** front/rear disc. **Body Construction:** steel unibody.

Manufacturer: Audi AG, Ingolstadt, West Germany.
Distributor: Audi of America Inc., Troy, Michigan.

AUSTIN

Like that of most British motorcars, Austin's history goes back to the early days of the automobile. At least back to 1906, to be precise, when the first Austin was sold: the 5-liter model 25/30. Even before that time, Herbert Austin, the company's founder, had produced vehicles for the Wolseley Company. At the turn of the century, his first four-wheeled vehicles were victorious in a 1000-mile trial. Smaller 10, 15 and 20 hp models followed the 25/30, as well as the first Austin "Seven." Quite a few Austins were large in size and power: up to 60 hp in the early years. In 1921 came a new 12-hp model, as the company grew quite successful. A year later, the economical and legendary second-series "Seven," which sold for even less than one of the primitive cyclecars of the day. Known as the "baby" Austin, the tiny four-seater served as the brunt of countless jokes over the years but sold very nicely. By 1929, 100,000 Sevens had been produced, and many were built under license in other countries (including America, as the American Austin (Bantam). In 1931, a modified Austin Seven hit 94 mph at Daytona Beach, Florida.

A 10-hp Austin arrived by 1932, and proved successful through the Depression years. By the time war broke out in 1939, Austin's offerings ranged from the third-generation Seven all the way up to a Twenty-Eight limousine. Several models were produced for military use during World War II, and debuted for private use before the war ended.

Models Twelve and Sixteen (the latter in revised form) continued into 1946 and beyond, but the first new postwar models were the A40 Dorset and Devon of 1947. They replaced the models Eight, Ten and Twelve. Two models re-entered the limousine market in that year: the Sheerline and Princess (first announced for a 3.5-liter powerplant, but produced with a 4-liter instead). Those two displayed the razor-edge styling that was popular among middle- and large-size British passenger cars in the early postwar years. In 1948, a new A70 Hampshire replaced the former Sixteen. Its engine would soon be adapted for the Austin-Healey sports car.

A year later, the A90 Atlantic arrived, serving as something close to a sports car with its 2.6-liter engine and snappy performance. That one drew considerable attention in America as a result of shattering a series of stock-car records at the Indianapolis Speedway. In fact, the production A90 was aimed strictly at the American market.

Far more than most British automakers, in fact, Austin gained quite a following in the U.S. in the early postwar years. By 1948, considerable numbers of the little A40s were arriving at the East Coast Port of Entry. Sales of 8,600 cars came quickly. By 1954, nearly 30,000 Austins (mainly A40s) found American buyers. The compact sedans were practical and economical, with a reputation for durability and passable performance. All that and a low selling price proved hard for the gradually-rising legion of small-car fans to resist.

In 1950 came a sports convertible version of the A40. A fourth edition of the Austin Seven (dubbed A30) debuted in 1951 and soon began to arrive in America, though in smaller numbers than the larger A40 models. Then, in 1953, the A40 took on a more stylish and modern look under the Somerset badge, with appearance similar to that of the Hereford, which had emerged in 1950. The bigger Sheerline was dropped in 1953, but the posh Princess continued. In 1954, the familiar A40 turned into the Cambridge, and added an A50 relative with a larger engine. The A90 badge resumed, but gracing a Westminster model that had little connection to the sporty A90 Atlantic, which had expired earlier. A revised series lineup arrived for 1956, as the A30 became an A35, and the medium-size models turned into A95 and A105. Meanwhile, production had begun of the two-seat Metropolitan, sold under the Nash and Hudson badges (see Metropolitan listing).

A new A40 Farina was announced in 1958. But the big news came in 1959 with the arrival of the fifth "Seven," quickly dubbed the "Mini" as a result of its diminutive dimensions and cute appearance. Quite a few variants of the front-drive Mini appeared, included a Mini-Moke, some surprisingly quick Mini-Coopers, and a Countryman station wagon. Austin's version of the new Morris 1100, also with a transverse-mounted front-drive engine, arrived in 1963 with a "hydrolastic" suspension. As the 1970s neared, the Mini disappeared but Austin continued with its American and Marina models before leaving the U.S. marketplace. In sum, Austin produced a far broader variety of vehicles in the postwar period than Americans were aware of, but only selected ones made it to these shores.

Model Number Note: Published model numbers were sometimes written with a hyphen (A-40), and sometimes without (A40). The hyphen is not used in the following descriptions.

1947-48 AUSTIN

A40 — FOUR — Introduced in Britain for 1947 as the first new postwar Austins, the A40 Devon and Dorset soon began to trickle into American showrooms. Each had concealed running boards, built-in headlamps, rear-opening (front-hinged) doors, and a winged 'A' on the hood. Tiny round parking lights stood below the headlamps. The front fender line continued in a bulge through the lower portion of the doors, all the way to the rear fender. The vertical-style center grille was made up of horizontal strips. For additional details, see 1949 listing.

A125 — SHEERLINE — SIX — See 1949 listing.

I.D. DATA: Serial number is located on right side of chassis, below the generator (except A125, on glovebox lid). Engine number is stamped on right side of block, below the head gasket. Serial number range: 286001 to 325200. Starting engine number: 300301.

Note: A similar numbering system is used on Austins (and other BMC vehicles) into the 1960s. Chassis numbers consist of three letters and one (or two) figures, followed by the serial number. First letter denotes make ('A' = Austin). Second letter indicates engine size ('L' = under 800 cc; 'A' = 800-999 cc; 'G' = 1000-1399 cc; 'H' = 1400-1999 cc; 'B' = 2000-2999 cc; 'D' = 3000-3999 cc). Letter three indicates body type: 'C' = chassis; 'D' = coupe; 'J' = convertible; 'N' = 2-seat Tourer; 'P' = hardtop; 'S' = 4-door saloon (sedan); '2S' = 2-door saloon (sedan); 'T' = 4-seat Tourer; 'U' = pickup; 'V' = van. The next digit indicates series (if any), to denote a major change. An additional prefix letter ('L') indicates left-hand drive. The sequential serial number comes at the end.

1947 Austin 16 four-door sedan.

Engine numbers consist of one or two digits followed by a series of letters and then by the sequential serial number. The first letter denotes engine size ('8' = 803 cc; '9' = 950 cc; '12' = 1200 cc; '15' = 1500 cc; '16' = 1600 cc; '22' = 2200 cc; '25' = 2500 cc; '26' = 2600 cc; '29' = 2900 cc). The next letter indicates make ('A' = Austin). The following letters indicate transmission type ('A' = automatic; 'N' = manual (column) shift; 'M' = Manumatic clutch; 'O' = Borg-Warner overdrive; 'R' = Laycock de Normanville overdrive; 'U' = manual (floor) shift. One or two letters following the serial number identify an engine with oversize bore and/or undersize crankshaft journals.

Model	Body Type & Seating	Engine Type/CID	P.O.E. Price	Weight (lbs.)	Prod. Total
A40	2-dr Dorset Sed-4P	I4/73	1595	2150	Note 1
A40	4-dr Devon Sed-5P	I4/73	1720	2280	Note 1

Note 1: A total of 10,500 A40s were produced during 1947, and 42,500 during 1948.

ENGINE DATA: BASE FOUR: Inline, overhead-valve four-cylinder. Cast iron block and head. Displacement: 73.2 cu. in. (1200 cc). Bore & Stroke: 2.57 x 3.50 in. (65.5 x 88.9 mm). Compression Ratio: 7.2:1. Brake Horsepower: 40 at 4300 rpm. Torque: 59 lbs.-ft. at 2200 rpm. Three main bearings. Solid valve lifters. Single Zenith carburetor. Lucas ignition.

CHASSIS DATA: Wheelbase: 92.5 in. Overall Length: 153 in. Height: 62.5 in. Width: 61 in. Front Tread: 48.5 in. Rear Tread: 49.5 in. Wheel Type: pressed steel disc with chromed hub covers. Standard Tires: 5.25x16.

TECHNICAL: Layout: front-engine, rear-drive. Transmission: four-speed manual (synchro 2nd/3rd/4th). Standard Final Drive Ratio: 5.43:1. Steering: cam gear. Suspension (front): independent; coil springs and wishbones. Suspension (rear): rigid axle, semi-elliptic leaf springs and anti-roll torsion bar. Brakes: Girling hydraulic front, mechanical rear. Body Construction: steel body on pressed steel frame with box-section side and crossmembers.

PERFORMANCE: Top Speed: 71 mph. Acceleration (0-60 mph): N/A (0-50 mph in 20.5 sec). Acceleration (quarter-mile): 24.4 sec.

PRODUCTION/SALES: A total of 42,500 Austin passenger cars were built during 1946, 62,544 during 1947, and 46,000 during 1948. Of the 30,000 A40s built by July 1948, 11,000 went to the U.S. (and only 1,000 remained in Britain). About 8,610 Austins were sold in the U.S. during 1948.

ADDITIONAL MODELS: For the home market, Austin also continued to produce the Eight, Ten, Twelve and Sixteen, with four different engine sizes. A new Sixteen (four-cylinder) and Princess (six-cylinder) arrived by 1948.

Manufacturer: The Austin Motor Co. Ltd., Longbridge, Birmingham, England.

Distributor: The Austin Motor Co. Ltd., New York City.

HISTORY: In September 1947, Austin's chairman L.P. Lord set up the Austin Motor Co. Ltd. in America, and a companion organization in Canada. Cars began to arrive in November 1947; and by August 1948, more than 13,000 had been delivered to the U.S. and Canada. A press release noted that "More British Austins have been sold in the U.S. during 1948 than any other make of imported automobile for a single year." In addition, "Austin was the first British manufacturer to produce a completely new postwar car, new in engine, chassis and styling." Production of the Dorset two-door sedan did not last so long, but the four-door continued with little change into 1951.

In America, it's 'Austin of England,'" declared Austin's export brochure, "and the names of the latest models find their place in the titles of the dealer organizations handling them." Thus, Devon Motors in Santa Ana, California (to take just one example) was picked as the site for the announcement of the new A40 Devon. A photo of Dorset Motor Company in New Jersey revealed a full range of Austins, from the A40 to the big A125 Sheerline. By the end of July, 1948, more than 106,000 Austins had been exported from Britain. And in a single year, more had been sold in America than in the entire world (outside Britain) in 1938-39. In 1938, British automakers had exported only 633 cars in all to North America.

In October 1948, a stock A40 two-door sedan was driven by its owner from Los Angeles to New York in 57 hours, 27 minutes, averaging 53.3 mph for the 3,062-mile trip.

1949 AUSTIN

A40 — DORSET/DEVON/COUNTRYMAN — FOUR — A station wagon joined the original A40 two- and four-door sedans, which otherwise continued with little appearance or mechanical change. Half of the horizontal-bar grille was mounted in the hood, the other half below. A gracefully swooping front fender line extended into the door base. Rear wheels had rounded cutouts in the fenders. Twin taillamps were standard. The 73.2-cid four-cylinder, overhead-valve engine was rated 40 horsepower, hooked to a four-speed manual gearbox with synchromesh on the top three ratios. Dorset was a two-door, window sedan with fixed top; Devon, a four-door with six windows and sliding top. All-steel bodies had rear-opening doors with concealed hinges and running boards.

Leather upholstery was standard, along with a 16-inch spring-spoke steering wheel. Front seats were individually adjustable. Rear seats had side armrests; the Devon sedan added a folding center armrest in back. A hood lock was released from inside the car. Heating/defrosting units were built-in, and each car had provision for a radio. The dashboard held a glovebox on the right and instruments ahead of the driver, in a central control panel. Standard body colors included Burgundy, Portland Gray, Horizon Blue, and Mist Green (each with beige upholstery and fawn carpets); or Black with brown upholstery and carpets.

The Countryman two-door station wagon had similar construction and features, but larger tires (5.00x17 instead of 5.25x16). "You can depend on it!" said the sales brochure, adding that a Countryman was "ideal for farm and estate transport," capable of carrying six people with luggage (or two people with 1,150 pounds of cargo). Two individual front seats were installed, and a single-piece fold-flush back seat, with occasional corner cushions available. A roof ventilator was standard. Door windows were the fully wind-up type. A full-width parcel tray went under the dash. At the rear was a tongue-and-grooved wooden floor, with an interior roof light and a separate spare tire compartment. Two horizontal doors gave access to the load space.

A90 — ATLANTIC — FOUR — Aimed at American customers, the Atlantic first appeared in convertible form, powered by a 2660-cc overhead-valve four-cylinder engine with twin SU carburetors. The four-speed transmission used a column gearshift lever. Either a manual or power top was available, the latter at a higher price. The body was made of steel and aluminum panels. Top speed was close to 95 mph. The streamlined front end held a low, split horizontal grille with horizontal bars in each section, parking lights flanking the grille, and a large spotlight at its center. A flying 'A' upright emblem stood above each of the headlamps, which were mounted somewhat inboard, alongside the hood. A wide trim strip ran back along that hood. This was the first Austin to abandon the upright "radiator" look at the front end. Leather upholstery was standard, and the dashboard was covered in leather. Three people could sit in front, and two more (occasionally) in the rear. A radio was optional. Rear-opening doors concealed the running boards. The initial price of $3975 dropped sharply, to a mere $2795, by the time the car went on sale in America. An A90 Sport Sedan arrived later; see 1951 listing for details.

A125 — SHEERLINE — SIX — Introduced in Britain in 1947, examples of the big six-cylinder Sheerline began to trickle into the U.S. in the late 1940s. The front end held an upright chrome grille made up of vertical bars, separate headlamps, and parking lights mounted on the fenders. Front door held vent windows, and the windshield was split. Like the smaller Austins, the A125 front-fender line extended into the lower portion of the doors, toward the rear fenders. Standard equipment included a radio and heater. A limousine was added late in 1949. Sheerline production continued into 1954.

I.D. DATA: Serial number is located on right side of chassis, below generator; except (Sheerline) on glovebox lid. Engine number is on right side of block, below head gasket. Serial number range: (Devon/Dorset) 325201-421000; (Countryman) 325001 to 427000; (Atlantic) BD2L-35500 or BD1L-176 and up; (Sheerline) 120-up.

Note: Certain specific vehicles with serial numbers in 1949 range were considered 1950 models. See 1947-48 Austin for breakdown of prefix letters and digits.

1949 Austin A135 Princess saloon.

Model	Body Type & Seating	Engine Type/CID	P.O.E. Price	Weight (lbs.)	Prod. Total
A40 DORSET/DEVON					
A40	2-dr Dorset Sed-4P	I4/73	1520	2150	Note 1
A40	4-dr Devon Sed-5P	I4/73	1595	2250	Note 1
A40 COUNTRYMAN					
A40	2-dr Station Wag-6P	I4/73	1995	1900	Note 1
A90 ATLANTIC					
A90	2-dr Conv-4/5P	I4/162	2795	2900	Note 2
A125 SHEERLINE					
A125	4-dr Sedan-6P	I6/243	5800	4500	N/A

Note 1: A total of 90,800 A40s were produced during 1949.

Note 2: A total of 15,000 A90 models were produced during 1949.

Price Note: A90 convertible with hydraulic top had P.O.E. price of $2995. Initial price for the A90 was $3975.

ENGINE DATA: BASE FOUR (A40 Dorset, Devon, Countryman): Inline, overhead-valve four-cylinder. Cast iron block and head. Displacement: 73.2 cu. in. (1200 cc). Bore & Stroke: 2.57 x 3.50 in. (65.5 x 88.9 mm). Compression Ratio: 7.2:1. Brake Horsepower: 40 at 4300 rpm. Torque: 59 lbs.-ft. at 2200 rpm. Three main bearings. Solid valve lifters. Single Zenith carburetor. Lucas ignition.

BASE FOUR (A90 Atlantic): Inline, overhead-valve four-cylinder. Cast iron block and head. Displacement: 162.2 cu. in. (2660 cc). Bore & Stroke: 3.437 x 4.375 in. (87.3 x 111.1 mm). Compression Ratio: 7.5:1. Brake Horsepower: 88 at 4000 rpm. Torque: 140 lbs.-ft. at 2500 rpm. Three main bearings. Solid valve lifters. Twin SU carburetors. Lucas ignition.

BASE SIX (Sheerline): Inline, overhead-valve six-cylinder. Cast iron block and head. Displacement: 243 cu. in. (3993 cc). Bore & Stroke: 3.44 x 4.38 in. Compression Ratio: 6.8:1. Brake Horsepower: 125. Four main bearings. Solid valve lifters. Stromberg carburetor. Lucas ignition.

CHASSIS DATA: Wheelbase: (A40) 92.5 in.; (A90) 96 in.; (A125) 119 in. Overall Length: (A40) 153 in. except Countryman, 157.5 in.; (A90) 177 in.; (A125) 192 in. Height: (A40) 62.5 in.; (A90) 60 in.; (A125) 67 in. Width: (A40) 61 in.; (A90) 70 in.; (A125) 73 in. Front Tread: (A40) 48.5 in.; (Countryman) 49.5 in.; (A90) 53.5 in.; (A125) 58 in. Rear Tread: (A40) 49.5 in.; (Countryman) 50.25 in.; (A90) 55.5 in.; (A125) 60 in. Wheel Type: (A40) pressed steel disc with chromed hubcaps; (A90) steel disc. Standard Tires: (A40) 5.25x16 except Countryman, 5.00x17; (A90); 5.50x16; (A125) 6.50x16. Fuel Tank: (A40) 10.5 U.S. gallons; (A90) 15 gallons; (A125) 19 gallons.

TECHNICAL: Layout: front-engine, rear-drive. Transmission: four-speed manual. A90 convertible gear ratios: (1st) 13.65:1; (2nd) 8.25:1; (3rd) 5.19:1; (4th) 3.667:1. Standard Final Drive Ratio: (A40) 5.43:1 except Countryman, 6.14:1; (A90) 3.667:1; (A125) 4.45:1. Steering: cam gear. Suspension (front): independent; wishbones and coil springs. Suspension (rear): rigid axle, semi-elliptic leaf springs and anti-roll torsion bar. Brakes: Girling hydraulic front, mechanical rear. Body Construction: steel body on pressed steel frame.

PERFORMANCE: Top Speed: (A40) 70+ mph; (A90) 92 mph; (A125) 81 mph. Acceleration (0-60 mph): N/A; 0-50 mph: (A40) 20.6 sec.; (A 90) 11.2 sec.; (A125) 12.4 sec. Acceleration (quarter-mile): (A40) 24.4 sec.; (A90) 20.9 sec.; (A125) 21.9 sec. Fuel Mileage: (A40) 30-35 mpg; (A90) 18-21 mpg; (A125) 15 mpg.

PRODUCTION/SALES: A total of 116,996 Austin passenger cars were produced during 1949. About 3,642 Austins were sold in the U.S. during 1949.

ADDITIONAL MODELS: A135 Princess limousines also were exported occasionally to the U.S., with specifications similar to the A125 Sheerline but six-cylinder engine rated 130 bhp. The A70 also was exported in small numbers (see 1951 listing).

Manufacturer: The Austin Motor Co. Ltd., Longbridge, Birmingham, England.

Distributor: The Austin Motor Co. Ltd., New York City.

HISTORY: In April 1949, an A90 convertible broke 63 stock-car records at the Indianapolis raceway, covering 11,850 miles in seven days and nights "under appalling weather conditions" at an average speed of 70.54 mph. At the time, it was the only European car to hold American stock-car records.

A 1949 brochure from Fergus Motors of New York City explained that: "Austin once again presents its two fine low-upkeep automobiles with their high compression valve-in-head engines insuring sparkling performance at 35 miles per gallon. Modern coachwork and independent front wheel suspension insure room and comfort on the highway and in the city. Models available in a choice of five color combinations with leather upholstery." In addition to the passenger cars, Austin marketed in the U.S. a half-ton panel delivery and pickup, which looked similar to the Countryman station wagon.

1950 AUSTIN

1950 Austin A40 Devon saloon.

A40 — DEVON/COUNTRYMAN — FOUR — The Dorset two-door sedan disappeared, but the Devon four-door sedan and Countryman station wagon continued with little change.

A90 — ATLANTIC — FOUR — The convertible continued with little change. A sport sedan also was produced, but took longer to arrive in U.S. hands; see next listing for details.

A125 — SHEERLINE — SIX — A few six-cylinder Sheerlines continued to be exported; see 1949 listing for details.

I.D. DATA: Serial number is located on right side of chassis, below generator; except (Sheerline) on glovebox lid. Engine number is on right side of block, below head gasket. Serial number range: (Mark 2 Devon) G52A/L-405001 and up; (DeLuxe Devon) G52/L-427001 to 511000; (Countryman) GP2/L-421001 to 490000; (Atlantic) BD2/L-38101 to 62000.

Note: Certain specific DeLuxe Devon vehicles with serial numbers in 1950 range were considered 1951 models. See 1947-48 Austin for breakdown of prefix letters and digits.

Model	Body Type & Seating	Engine Type/CID	P.O.E. Price	Weight (lbs.)	Prod. Total
A40 DEVON					
A40	2-dr Mark 2 Sed-4P	I4/73	1225	2250	Note 1
A40	4-dr Deluxe Sed-5P	I4/73	1539	2250	Note 1
A40 COUNTRYMAN					
A40	2-dr Sta Wag-6P	I4/73	1649	2175	Note 1
A90 ATLANTIC					
A90	2-dr Conv-4/5P	I4/162	2460	2800	12,723

Note 1: A total of 110,000 A40 models were produced during 1950.

Price Note: A90 convertible with hydraulic top and side windows had P.O.E. price of $2634. Some sources indicate lower prices for most models during 1950.

ENGINE DATA: BASE FOUR (A40): Inline, overhead-valve four-cylinder. Cast iron block and head. Displacement: 73.2 cu. in. (1200 cc). Compression Ratio: 7.2:1. Brake Horsepower: 40 at 4300 rpm. Torque: 58 lbs.-ft. at 2400 rpm. Three main bearings. Solid valve lifters. Single Zenith carburetor. Lucas ignition.

BASE FOUR (A90): Inline, overhead-valve four-cylinder. Cast iron block and head. Displacement: 162.2 cu. in. (2660 cc). Bore & Stroke: 3.44 x 4.38 in. (65.5 x 88.9 mm). Compression Ratio: 7.5:1. Brake Horsepower: 88 at 4400 rpm. Torque: 140 lbs.-ft. at 2500 rpm. Three main bearings. Solid valve lifters. Twin SU carburetors. Lucas ignition.

CHASSIS DATA: Wheelbase: (A40) 92.5 in.; (A90) 96 in. Overall Length: (A40) 153 in. except Countryman, 157.5 in.; (A90) 177.1 in. Height: (A40) 62.5 in.; (A90) 60 in. Width: (A40) 61 in.; (A90) 70 in. Front Tread: (A40) 48.5 in.; (A90) 53.5 in. Rear Tread: (A40) 49.5 in.; (A90) 55.5 in. Standard Tires: (A40) 5.25x16 except Countryman, 5.00x17; (A90) 5.50x16.

TECHNICAL: Layout: front-engine, rear-drive. Transmission: four-speed manual. Standard Final Drive Ratio: (A40) 5.14:1 except Countryman, 6.14:1; (A90) 3.667:1. Steering: cam gear. Suspension (front): independent; wishbones and coil springs. Suspension (rear): rigid axle, semi-elliptic leaf springs and anti-roll bar. Brakes: hydraulic front, mechanical rear. Body Construction: steel body on steel frame.

PERFORMANCE: Same as 1949.

PRODUCTION/SALES: A total of 142,723 Austin passenger cars were produced during 1950. About 5,452 Austins were sold in the U.S. during 1950.

Manufacturer: The Austin Motor Co. Ltd., Longbridge, Birmingham, England.

Distributor: The Austin Motor Co. Ltd., New York City.

HISTORY: The model year for U.S. sales began January 1950. At Montlhery, France, an Austin A40 Devon covered 10,000 miles in 10,000 minutes.

1951 AUSTIN

A40 — DELUXE DEVON/COUNTRYMAN — FOUR — A two-door convertible version of the small Austin joined the original four-door sedan, which continued with little change. The Countryman station wagon also continued as before. A Sports version of the A40 debuted with a higher-powered (50 horsepower) engine. Its wide recessed grille, curved at the top, had a pattern of horizontal strips; and all four wheel openings were rounded.

A70 — HEREFORD — FOUR — Small numbers of the mid-range A70, introduced in Britain for the 1949 model year, were exported to the U.S. The Hereford sedan was restyled for 1951, replacing the Hampshire, with side grilles extending outward from the center grille, below the inboard built-in headlamps. Grille sections contained horizontal bars. Front doors contained vent windows, and the windshield was one-piece. Under the Hereford's hood was a 2199-cc four-cylinder engine, rated 68 horsepower.

A90 — ATLANTIC — FOUR — A two-door, four/five-passenger Sport Sedan joined the original Atlantic convertible, also aimed at the American market. Its all-steel body had a fabric-covered top. Gear ratios were lower. Otherwise, appearance and mechanical details were identical to the convertible.

A125 — SHEERLINE — SIX — The biggest Austin continued in limited production with little change.

I.D. DATA: Serial number is located on right side of chassis, below generator; except (Sheerline) on glovebox lid. Engine number is on right side of block, below head gasket. Starting serial number: (DeLuxe Devon) G52/L-511001; (Devon conv) GD2/L-611001; (Countryman) GP2/L-490001; (A70) BS3/L-93642; (A90 conv) BD2/L-62001; (A90 sedan) BE2/L-62001; (A125) DS1/L-7501.

Note: See 1947-48 Austin for breakdown of prefix letters and digits.

Model	Body Type & Seating	Engine Type/CID	P.O.E. Price	Weight (lbs.)	Prod. Total
A40 DELUXE DEVON					
A40	4-dr Sedan-5P	I4/73	1567	2250	Note 1
A40 SPORTS					
A40	2-dr Sport Conv-4P	I4/73	2195	2150	Note 1
A40 COUNTRYMAN					
A40	2-dr Sta Wagon-6P	I4/73	1687	2175	Note 1
A70 HEREFORD					
A70	4-dr Sedan-5/6P	I4/134	2495	2719	N/A
A90 ATLANTIC					
A90	2-dr Conv-4/5P	I4/162	2460	2800	Note 2
A90	2-dr Spt Sedan-4/5P	I4/162	2890	3016	Note 2
A125 SHEERLINE					
A125	4-dr Sedan-6P	I6/243	5465	4256	N/A

Note 1: A total of about 100,000 A40 models were produced during 1951.

Note 2: A total of about 8,000 A90 models were produced during 1951; and about 15,000 convertibles in the full production run.

Price Note: A90 convertible with hydraulic top and side windows had P.O.E. price of $2634. Some sources indicate higher prices for certain models during 1951.

ENGINE DATA: BASE FOUR (A40): Inline, overhead-valve four-cylinder. Cast iron block and head. Displacement: 73.2 cu. in. (1200 cc). Bore & Stroke: 2.57 x 3.50 in. (65.5 x 88.9 mm). Compression Ratio: 7.2:1. Brake Horsepower: 40 at 4300 rpm; (Sports) 50 bhp. Torque: 58 lbs.-ft. at 2400 rpm. Three main bearings. Solid valve lifters. Zenith carburetor (Sports, two SU). Lucas ignition.

BASE FOUR (A70): Inline, overhead-valve four-cylinder. Cast iron block and head. Displacement: 134.1 cu. in. (2199 cc). Bore & Stroke: 3.125 x 4.37 in. (79.4 x 111.1 mm). Compression Ratio: 6.8:1. Brake Horsepower: 68 at 3800 rpm. Torque: 116 lbs.-ft. at 1700 rpm. Solid valve lifters. Zenith carburetor.

BASE FOUR (A90): Same as 1950.

BASE SIX (Sheerline): Inline, overhead-valve six-cylinder. Cast iron block and head. Displacement: 243 cu. in. (3993 cc). Bore & Stroke: 3.43 x 4.37 in. Compression Ratio: 6.8:1. Brake Horsepower: 125. Four main bearings. Solid valve lifters. Stromberg carburetor. Lucas ignition.

CHASSIS DATA: Wheelbase: (A40) 92.5 in.; (A70) 87 in.; (A90) 96 in.; (A125) 119 in. **Overall Length:** (A40) 153.25 in.; (A40 Sports) 159.5 in.; (A40 Countryman) 157.5 in.; (A70) 167.5 in.; (A90) 177.3 in.; (A125) 192 in. **Height:** (A40) 63.8 in.; (A40 Spt) 57 in.; (A90) 61 in. **Width:** (A40) 61.0 in.; (A40 Spt) 61.25 in.; (A70) 69.5 in.; (A90) 70 in.; (A125) 73 in. **Front Tread:** (A40) 48.5 in.; (A70) 54 in.; (A90) 53.5 in. **Rear Tread:** (A40) 49.5 in.; (A70) 56 in.; (A90) 55.5 in. **Standard Tires:** (A40) 5.25x16 except Countryman, 5.00x17; (A70) 5.50x16; (A90) 5.50x16; (A125) 6.50x16.

TECHNICAL: Layout: front-engine, rear-drive. **Transmission:** four-speed manual. A90 convertible overall gear ratios: (1st) 13.65:1; (2nd) 8.25:1; (3rd) 5.19:1; (4th) 3.667:1; (rev) 17.528:1. A90 sedan overall gear ratios: (1st) 15.34:1; (2nd) 9.28:1; (3rd) 5.84:1; (4th) 4.125:1; (rev) 19.93:1. **Standard Final Drive Ratio:** (A40) 5.14:1; (A40 Spts) 4.8:1; (A40 Countryman) 6.14:1; (A70) 4.125:1; (A90 sed) 4.125:1; (A90 conv) 3.667:1; (A125) 4.45:1. **Steering:** cam gear. **Suspension (front):** independent; wishbones and coil springs. **Suspension (rear):** rigid axle, semi-elliptic leaf springs and anti-roll bar. **Brakes:** Girling hydraulic front, mechanical rear; (A70) hydraulic. **Body Construction:** steel body on steel frame.

PERFORMANCE: Top Speed: (A40) 70+ mph; (A40 Spt) 78-80 mph; (A70) 83 mph; (A90) 92 mph; (A125) 81 mph. **Acceleration (0-60 mph):** (A40 Spt) 25.6-30.6 sec.; (0-50 mph) (A40) 20.6 sec.; (A40 Spt) 16.3 sec.; (A 90) 11.2 sec.; (A125) 12.4 sec.) **Acceleration (quarter-mile):** (A40) 24.4 sec.; (A40 Spt) 21.1-23.2 sec.; (A70) 22.1 sec.; (A90) 20.9 sec.; (A125) 21.9 sec. **Fuel Mileage:** (A40) 30-35 mpg; (A90) 18-21 mpg; (A125) 15 mpg.

PRODUCTION/SALES: A total of 121,500 Austin passenger cars were produced during 1951. About 3,800 were sold in the U.S.

Manufacturer: The Austin Motor Co. Ltd., Longbridge, Birmingham, England.

Distributor: The Austin Motor Co. Ltd., New York City.

HISTORY: The 1951 model year for U.S. sales begin in November 1950.

1952 AUSTIN

A40 — SOMERSET/COUNTRYMAN — FOUR — A restyling of the A40 was accompanied by a switch from the Devon to Somerset designation, and a slight horsepower boost. A smaller grille contained horizontal bars, while auxiliary grilles on each side held small vertical bars. As before, the front fender line extended to the rear fenders. A sedan and convertible were offered. The Sports Convertible and Countryman station wagon continued as before. Full hydraulic brakes were added before the 1952 model year began. Sports Convertible ads promised that it was "Engineered for speed...styled for comfort."

A90 — ATLANTIC — FOUR — Production of the Sports Sedan continued as before.

A125 — SHEERLINE — SIX — Production of the larger, six-cylinder Austin continued with little change.

I.D. DATA: Serial number is located on right side of chassis, below generator; except (Sheerline) on glovebox lid. Engine number is on right side of block, below head gasket. Starting serial number: (Somerset sedan) G54/L-657001; (Somerset conv) GD5/L667087; (Somerset spt conv) GD3/L633001; (Countryman) GP4/L-651001; (Atlantic) BE2/L-91600; (Sheerline) DS1-2-7501.

Note: See 1947-48 Austin for breakdown of prefix letters and digits.

Model	Body Type & Seating	Engine Type/CID	P.O.E. Price	Weight (lbs.)	Prod. Total
A40 SOMERSET					
A40	2-dr Conv-4P	I4/73	1945	2220	Note 1
A40	4-dr Sedan-4P	I4/73	1795	2220	Note1
A40 SPORTS					
A40	2-dr Sports Conv-4P	I4/73	2295	2150	Note 1
A40 COUNTRYMAN					
A40	2-dr Sta Wagon-6P	I4/73	1895	2310	Note 1
A90 ATLANTIC					
A90	2-dr Spt Sedan-4P	I4/162	3395	3016	Note 1
A125 SHEERLINE					
A125	4-dr Sedan-6P	I6/243	5685	4256	Note 1

Note 1: A total of about 118,000 Austin passenger cars were produced during 1952; approximately 4,800 were sold in the U.S.

ENGINE DATA: BASE FOUR (A40): Inline, overhead-valve four-cylinder. Cast iron block and head. **Displacement:** 73 cu. in. (1200 cc). **Bore & Stroke:** 2.58 x 3.50 in. (65.6 x 88.9 mm). **Compression Ratio:** 7.2:1. **Brake Horsepower:** 42 at 4300 rpm (50 at 4800 rpm on Sport Convertible). **Torque:** 62 lbs.-ft. at 2200-2400 rpm. Three main bearings. Solid valve lifters. Single Zenith carburetor. Lucas ignition.

BASE FOUR (A90): Same as 1950-51.

BASE SIX (A125): Same as 1950-51.

CHASSIS DATA: Wheelbase: (A40) 92.5 in.; (A90) 96 in.; (A125) 119 in. **Overall Length:** (A40) 159.5 in.; (A90) 177.3 in.; (A125) 192 in. **Height:** (A40) 64 in.; (A40 Spt) 57 in.; (A90) 61 in. **Width:** (A40) 63 in.; (A40 Spt) 61.25 in.; (A90) 70 in.; (A125) 73 in. **Front Tread:** (A40) 48.5 in.; (A90) 53.5 in. **Rear Tread:** (A40) 49.5 in.; (A90) 55.5 in. **Standard Tires:** (A40) 5.25x16 except Countryman, 5.00x17; (A90) 5.50x16; (A125) 6.50x16.

TECHNICAL: Layout: front-engine, rear-drive. **Transmission:** four-speed manual. **Standard Final Drive Ratio:** (A40) 5.28:1 except Sport Conv., 4.8:1 or 5.14:1 and Countryman, 6.14:1; (A70) 4.125:1; (A125) 4.45:1. **Steering:** cam gear. **Suspension (front):** independent; wishbones and coil springs. **Suspension (rear):** rigid axle, semi-elliptic leaf springs and anti-roll bar. **Brakes:** hydraulic front/rear drum. **Body Construction:** steel body on steel frame.

PERFORMANCE: Top Speed: (A40) 68-72 mph; (A40 Spts conv) 78-80 mph. **Acceleration (0-60 mph):** (A40) 29 sec.; (A40 Spts) 25.6-30.6 seconds. **Acceleration (quarter-mile):** (A40 Spts) 21.2-23.2 seconds. **Fuel Mileage:** (A40 Spts) up to 35 mpg.

Manufacturer: The Austin Motor Co. Ltd., Longbridge, Birmingham, England.

Distributor: The Austin Motor Co. Ltd., New York City and Hollywood, California.

HISTORY: Production of the A90 saloon (sedan) continued until September 1952. British Motor Corp. (BMC) was formed in February 1952 by a merger of the Austin and Morris companies.

1953 AUSTIN

A30 — "SEVEN" — FOUR — A modern-day version of the mini-sized Austin Seven sedan, given the A30 designation, was powered by the same overhead-valve engine used in the Morris Minor. All Austins, in fact, carried overhead-valve engines. American ads promised that the A30 would deliver 40 miles per gallon, and that the car "Cuts your operating costs 50%." Standard equipment included a heater. Appearance was similar to the larger A40, but with a smaller center grille made up of horizontal bars, and no auxiliary (side) grilles. Headlamps were mounted farther out on the fenders, and higher up than the A40's. Front doors contained vent windows.

A40 — SOMERSET/COUNTRYMAN — FOUR — Production of the four A40-based models continued with little change, but the Sports Convertible ceased production during 1953. The Somerset convertible had a trim strip along the front of each front fender. Its three-position folding top could be placed in the "Coupe-de-ville" position, for appearance that was "smartly continental." Headlamps on all A40 models were mounted inboard, above the side grilles. The center grille contained horizontal bars plus a single center vertical divider bar. Each A40 model came with a standard heater.

I.D. DATA: Serial number is located on left side sun visor. Engine number is on right side of block, below head gasket. Starting serial number: (A30) AS3/L2401. Vehicles sold on or after November 24, 1952 were considered 1953 models.

Note: See 1947-48 Austin for breakdown of prefix letters and digits.

Model	Body Type & Seating	Engine Type/CID	P.O.E. Price	Weight (lbs.)	Prod. Total
A30 "SEVEN"					
AS3	4-dr Sedan-4P	I4/49	1495	1484	Note 1
A40 SOMERSET					
A40	2-dr Conv-4P	I4/73	1945	2220	Note 1
A40	4-dr Sedan-4P	I4/73	1795	2220	Note 1
A40 SPORTS					
A40	2-dr Sports Conv-4P	I4/73	2295	2150	Note 1
A40 COUNTRYMAN					
A40	2-dr Station Wag-4P	I4/73	1895	2310	Note 1

Note 1: Approximately 3,087 Austins were sold in the U.S. during 1953.

ENGINE DATA: BASE FOUR (A30): Inline, overhead-valve four-cylinder. Cast iron block and head. **Displacement:** 48.8 cu. in. (803 cc). **Bore & Stroke:** 2.28 x 3.00 in. (58 x 76.2 mm). **Compression Ratio:** 7.2:1. **Brake Horsepower:** 30 at 4800 rpm. **Torque:** 40 lbs.-ft. at 2400 rpm. Three main bearings. Solid valve lifters. Zenith carburetor.

BASE FOUR (A40): Inline, overhead-valve four-cylinder. Cast iron block and head. **Displacement:** 73.2 cu. in. (1200 cc). **Bore & Stroke:** 2.58 x 3.50 in. (65.6 x 88.9 mm). **Compression Ratio:** 7.2:1. **Brake Horsepower:** 42 at 4600 rpm (50 at 4800 rpm on Sports Convertible). **Torque:** 58 lbs.-ft. at 2200 rpm (61 at 3000 on Sports Convertible). Three main bearings. Solid valve lifters. Single Zenith carburetor.

CHASSIS DATA: Wheelbase: (A30) 79.5 in.; (A40) 92.5 in. **Overall Length:** (A30) 136.4 in.; (A40) 159.5 in. except Sport Conv., 159.25 in. and Countryman, 159.4 in. **Height:** (A30) 58.25 in.; (A40 Spt) 57 in. **Width:** (A30) 55.25 in.; (Somerset) 63 in.; (A40) 61 in. **Front Tread:** (A30) 45.25 in.; (A40) 48.5 in. **Rear Tread:** (A30) 44.75 in.; (A40) 49.5 in. **Standard Tires:** (A30) 5.20x13; (A40) 5.25x16 except Countryman, 5.00x17.

TECHNICAL: Layout: front-engine, rear-drive. **Transmission:** four-speed manual. A30 overall gear ratios: (1st) 21.03:1; (2nd) 13.32:1; (3rd) 8.64:1; (4th) 5.14:1; (rev) 26.63:1. **Standard Final Drive Ratio:** (A30) 5.14:1; (A40) 5.28:1 except Sport Conv., 4.8:1 or 5.14:1 and Countryman, 6.14:1. **Steering:** cam gear. **Suspension (front):** independent; wishbones and coil springs. **Suspension (rear):** rigid axle, semi-elliptic leaf springs and anti-roll bar. **Brakes:** hydraulic front/rear drum. **Body Construction:** steel body on steel frame (A30, unibody).

PERFORMANCE: Top Speed: (A30) 62 mph; (A40) 68-72 mph; (A40 Spts Conv) 78-80 mph. **Acceleration (0-60 mph):** (A40) 29 sec.; (A40 Spt) 25.6-30.6 sec. **Acceleration (quarter-mile):** (A40) 24.3 sec.; (A40 Spt) 21.2-23.2 seconds. **Fuel Mileage:** (A40) approx. 28 mpg.

HISTORY: The new A30 was seen at the Paris Salon in late 1952. A sales brochure for this tiniest Austin came with a pair of 3-D viewing glasses.

1954 AUSTIN

1954 Austin A40 Somerset.

A30 — "SEVEN" — FOUR — Production of the smallest Austin, on a 79.5-inch wheelbase, continued with little change except that a two-door sedan joined the original four-door.

A40 — SOMERSET/COUNTRYMAN — FOUR — Little change was evident on the A40 series, which again included two Somerset models and a Countryman wagon. Production of the Sports Convertible ceased during 1953.

I.D. DATA: Serial number is located on left side sun visor and/or inside body panel, to left of steering column. Engine number is on right side of block, below head gasket. Serial numbers continued from 1953. Vehicles sold on or after November 23, 1953 were considered 1954 models.

Note: See 1947-48 Austin for breakdown of prefix letters and digits.

Model	Body Type & Seating	Engine Type/CID	P.O.E. Price	Weight (lbs.)	Prod. Total
A30 "SEVEN"					
AS4	2-dr Sedan-4P	I4/49	1450	1484	Note 1
AS4	4-dr Sedan-4P	I4/49	1495	1525	Note 1
A40 SOMERSET					
A40	2-dr Conv-4P	I4/73	1945	2184	Note 1
A40	4-dr Sedan-4P	I4/73	1695	2220	Note 1
A40 COUNTRYMAN					
A40	2-dr Station Wag-4P	I4/73	1895	2310	Note 1

Note 1: Approximately 1,528 Austins were sold in the U.S. during 1954.

Note: Price shown for Somerset sedan included PVC upholstery; sedan with leather upholstery and heater sold for $1795.

ENGINE DATA: BASE FOUR (A30): Same as 1953.
BASE FOUR (A40): Same as 1953.

CHASSIS DATA: Wheelbase: (A30) 79.5 in.; (A40) 92.5 in. **Overall Length:** (A30) 136.4 in.; (A40) 159.5 in. except Countryman, 159.25 in. **Height:** (A30) 58.25 in.; (A40) 64 in. **Width:** (A30) 55.1 in.; (A40) 61-63 in.; (wag) 64.5 in. **Front Tread:** (A30) 45.25 in.; (A40) 48 in. **Rear Tread:** (A30) 44.75 in.; (A40) 50 in. **Standard Tires:** (A30) 5.20x13; (A40) 5.25x16 except Countryman, 5.00x17.

TECHNICAL: Same as 1953.

PERFORMANCE: Top Speed: (A30) 62 mph; (A40) 72 mph. **Acceleration (0-60 mph):** (A40) 29 sec. **Fuel Mileage:** (A40) approx. 28 mpg.
Manufacturer: The Austin Motor Co. Ltd., Birmingham, England.
Distributor: Austin Motor Co. Ltd., New York City or San Francisco.

1955 AUSTIN

1955 Austin Princess saloon.

A50 — CAMBRIDGE — FOUR — Introduction of an all-new Austin produced plenty of excitement in England, with its modernized appearance. A new grille, low and wide with a rounded upper bar, displayed a mesh pattern. Small round parking lights stood directly below the slightly-shrouded headlamps. An insignia was mounted above the grille center. The hood contained an airscoop that fed the standard fresh-air heater. Both front and rear doors held vent wings. Bodyside trim strips dipped down at the rear door. Twin round stacked taillamps stood on each side of the rear panel, somewhat inboard, just above the bumper. Flashing turn signals also were new. Individual front seats were upholstered in leather, the right one adjustable. A huge parcel shelf stood just below the dashboard, along with a locking glovebox. The gas cap also had a lock. Brake and clutch pedals were mounted on the cowl, and the clutch had hydraulic boost available. Under the hood was a 91-cid (1489-cc) four-cylinder overhead-valve engine, rated 50 horsepower. A column lever operated the four-speed gearbox. Almost no parts were interchangeable with the former A40 sedan, but an A40 version of the Cambridge also appeared, carrying the former (smaller) engine.

Note: American publications sometimes used the model name "Cambrian" rather than "Cambridge" for the A50 (and for the subsequent A55).

A90 — WESTMINSTER — SIX — The next version of the A90, which replaced the A70 Hereford, was far different from the Atlantic of the late 1940s and early '50s. This one was similar in appearance to the new A50, with a wide grille, but on a longer (104-inch)

wheelbase and powered by an 85-horsepower, six-cylinder engine. All doors contained vent panes. Like the new A50, it used unibody construction. Also like the A50, the spare tire was on a tray that lowered by use of a cranking handle.

I.D. DATA: Serial number is located on left side sun visor, left door hinge pillar post, and/or right side of chassis below generator. Engine number is on right side of block, below head gasket. Serial numbers for both new models started at 101. Vehicles sold on or after October 25, 1954 were considered 1955 models.

Note: See 1947-48 Austin for breakdown of prefix letters and digits.

Model	Body Type & Seating	Engine Type/CID	P.O.E. Price	Weight (lbs.)	Prod. Total
A50 CAMBRIDGE					
HS5	4-dr Sedan-4P	I4/91	1895	2248	Note 1
A90 WESTMINSTER					
BS4	4-dr Sedan-4P	I6/161	2275	2600	Note 1

Note 1: About 179,600 Austins were produced during 1955, including those not exported to the U.S.

ENGINE DATA: BASE FOUR (A50): Inline, overhead-valve four-cylinder. Cast iron block and head. **Displacement:** 90.9 cu. in. (1489 cc). **Bore & Stroke:** 2.875 x 3.50 in. (73.0 x 88.9 mm). **Compression Ratio:** 7.2:1. **Brake Horsepower:** 50 at 4400 rpm. **Torque:** 74 lbs.-ft. at 2100 rpm. Three main bearings. Solid valve lifters. Single Zenith carburetor.
BASE SIX (A90): Inline, overhead-valve six-cylinder. Cast iron block and head. **Displacement:** 161 cu. in. (2639 cc). **Bore & Stroke:** 3.125 x 3.50 in. (79.4 x 88.9 mm). **Compression Ratio:** 7.3:1. **Brake Horsepower:** 85 at 4000 rpm. Four main bearings. Solid valve lifters. Zenith carburetor.

CHASSIS DATA: Wheelbase: (A50) 99.25 in.; (A90) 103.5 in. **Overall Length:** (A50) 162.25 in.; (A90) 170.25 in. **Height:** (A50) 61.5 in.; (A90) 63.7 in. **Width:** (A50) 61.5 in.; (A90) 64 in. **Front Tread:** (A50) 48.5 in.; (A90) 51.5 in. **Rear Tread:** (A50) 49.0 in.; (A90) 53.5 in. **Standard Tires:** (A50) 5.60x15; (A90) 6.40x15.

TECHNICAL: Layout: front-engine, rear-drive. **Transmission:** four-speed manual. A50 overall gear ratios: (1st) 19.2:1; (2nd) 11.7:1; (3rd) 7.26:1; (4th) 4.88:1. **Standard Final Drive Ratio:** (A50) 4.3:1, or 4.875:1 with overdrive; (A90) 3.9:1. **Steering:** cam gear. **Suspension (front):** independent; wishbones and coil springs. **Suspension (rear):** rigid axle, semi-elliptic leaf springs and anti-roll bar. **Brakes:** hydraulic front/rear drum. **Body Construction:** steel unibody.

PERFORMANCE: Top Speed: (A50) 73.6-75.6 mph; (A90) 85.7-92 mph. **Acceleration (0-60 mph):** (A50) 24.4-28.3 sec. **Acceleration (quarter-mile):** (A50) 23.4-29.2 sec.; (A90) 21 sec. **Fuel Mileage:** (A50) 24-29 mpg.
Manufacturer: The Austin Motor Co. Ltd., Birmingham, England.
Distributor: Austin Motor Co. Ltd., New York City or San Francisco.

HISTORY: The model year began October 25, 1954 for A50 sales in the U.S.

1956 AUSTIN

1956 Austin London taxi.

A50 — CAMBRIDGE — FOUR — Production of the A50 continued with little change. Final models, built at the end of the year, may have the higher-powered engine of the subsequent A55 model.

A90 — WESTMINSTER — SIX — Overdrive was optional on the A90 sedan, which otherwise continued with little change.

I.D. DATA: Serial number is located on left front door hinge pillar post or left side sun visor. Engine number is on right side of block, below head gasket. Serial numbers not available. Vehicles sold on or after October 19, 1955 were considered 1956 models.

Note: See 1947-48 Austin for breakdown of prefix letters and digits.

1956 Austin Princess.

1956 Austin Westminster saloon.

Model	Body Type & Seating	Engine Type/CID	P.O.E. Price	Weight (lbs.)	Prod. Total
A50 CAMBRIDGE					
HS5	4-dr Sedan-5P	I4/91	1895	2200	Note 1
A90 WESTMINSTER					
BS4	2-dr Sedan-5P	I6/161	2275	2912	Note 1

Note 1: Approximately 110,000 Austins were produced during 1956, including those models not exported to the U.S. About 1,600 were sold in the U.S. during 1956.

ENGINE DATA: BASE FOUR (A50): Inline, overhead-valve four-cylinder. Cast iron block and head. **Displacement:** 90.9 cu. in. (1489 cc). **Bore & Stroke:** 2.875 x 3.50 in. (73.0 x 88.9 mm). **Compression Ratio:** 7.2:1 (final models, 8.3:1). **Brake Horsepower:** 50 at 4400 rpm (final models, 51 bhp at 4250). **Torque:** 74 lbs.-ft. at 2100 rpm. Three main bearings. Solid valve lifters. Zenith carburetor.

BASE SIX (A90): Same as 1955.

CHASSIS DATA: Same as 1955.

TECHNICAL: Same as 1955.

PERFORMANCE: Same as 1955.

HISTORY: The model year for A50 sales began October 19, 1955.

1957 AUSTIN

A35 — FOUR — An update of the former A35 "baby" Austin looked similar to its predecessor, but added tiny round pointed parking lights below the headlamps. The grille was again made up of horizontal strips. Door hinges were exposed, and the bulge in the side of the front fender extended into the door, tapering toward the rear. Wheelbase was 79.5 inches, and the 58-cid four-cylinder engine delivered 34 horsepower (four more than the A30). A four-speed gearbox was used. Gas mileage up to 50 mpg was claimed. The all-steel unibody was designed with fully stressed skin. Standard equipment included adjustable front bucket seats, turn signal flashers, twin wipers, and a full-width parcel shelf. The DeLuxe model sold in the U.S. also included a heater/defroster, bumpers, ashtrays, and hinged rear side windows.

A50 — CAMBRIDGE — FOUR — The A50 remained in production during fall 1956, at the start of the 1957 model year; see prior listing for details.

A55 — Mk I CAMBRIDGE — FOUR — Appearance of the new A55 was similar to the A50, but its back window was larger and the car was longer overall. A similar grille was dominated by horizontal strips.

A95 — WESTMINSTER — SIX — Except for a grille revised to display a single horizontal bar, the Westminster continued as before. An automatic transmission was available.

I.D. DATA: Serial number is located on left front door hinge pillar post or on the left side sun visor. Engine number is on right side of block, below head gasket. Serial numbers not available. Vehicles sold on or after October 19, 1956 were considered 1957 models.

Note: See 1947-48 Austin for breakdown of prefix letters and digits.

Model	Body Type & Seating	Engine Type/CID	P.O.E. Price	Weight (lbs.)	Prod. Total
A35					
AS5	2-dr Del Sed-4P	I4/58	1557	1512	Note 1
A55 Mk I CAMBRIDGE					
HS6	4-dr Sedan-5P	I4/91	2019	2200	Note 1
A95 WESTMINSTER					
BS6	4-dr Sedan-5P	I6/161	2340	2912	Note 1

Note 1: Approximately 165,000 Austins were produced during 1957, including those models not exported to the U.S. About 1,500 Austins were sold in the U.S. during 1957.

A50/55 Price Note: Remaining A50 models were priced at $1895 P.O.E.

ENGINE DATA: BASE FOUR (A35): Inline, overhead-valve four-cylinder. Cast iron block and head. **Displacement:** 57.82 cu. in. (948 cc). **Bore & Stroke:** 2.478 x 3.00 in. (62.9 x 76.2 mm). **Compression Ratio:** 8.3:1. **Brake Horsepower:** 34 at 4750 rpm. **Torque:** 50 lbs.-ft. at 2000 rpm. Three main bearings. Solid valve lifters. Zenith carburetor.

BASE FOUR (A55): Inline, overhead-valve four-cylinder. Cast iron block and head. **Displacement:** 90.9 cu. in. (1489 cc). **Bore & Stroke:** 2.875 x 3.50 in. (79.4 x 88.9 mm). **Compression Ratio:** 8.3:1. **Brake Horsepower:** 51 at 4250 rpm. **Torque:** 81 lbs.-ft. at 2000 rpm. Three main bearings. Solid valve lifters. Zenith carburetor.

BASE SIX (A95): Inline, overhead-valve six-cylinder. Cast iron block and head. **Displacement:** 161 cu. in. (2639 cc). **Bore & Stroke:** 3.125 x 3.50 in. **Compression Ratio:** 8.25:1. **Brake Horsepower:** 92 at 4500 rpm. **Torque:** 130 lbs.-ft. at 2000 rpm. Four main bearings. Solid valve lifters. Zenith carburetor.

CHASSIS DATA: Wheelbase: (A35) 79.5 in.; (A55) 99.25 in.; (A95) 105.75 in. **Overall Length:** (A35) 136.4 in.; (A55) 166.9 in.; (A90) 180 in. **Height:** (A35) 59.3 in.; (A55) 60.5 in.; (A95) 62 in. **Width:** (A35) 55.1 in.; (A55) 61.5 in.; (A95) 64 in. **Front Tread:** (A35) 45.3 in.; (A55) 51.5 in.; (A95) 51.5 in. **Rear Tread:** (A35) 44.8 in.; (A55) 51.3 in.; (A95) 51.3 in. **Standard Tires:** (A55) 5.90x13; (A95) 6.40x15.

TECHNICAL: Layout: front-engine, rear-drive. **Transmission:** four-speed manual. **Standard Final Drive Ratio:** (A35) 4.55:1; (A95) 3.9:1. **Steering:** cam gear. **Suspension (front):** independent; wishbones and coil springs. **Suspension (rear):** rigid axle, semi-elliptic leaf springs and anti-roll bar. **Brakes:** hydraulic front/rear drum. **Body Construction:** steel unibody.

PERFORMANCE: Top Speed: (A35) 73.2 mph; (A55) 77.1 mph; (A95) 87.7 mph. **Acceleration (quarter-mile):** (A35) 26.5 sec.; (A55) 24 sec.; (A95) 22.1 sec.

Manufacturer: The Austin Motor Co. Ltd., Longbridge, Birmingham, England.

Distributor: Hambro Automotive Corp., New York City; also distributors in Los Angeles and San Francisco.

ADDITIONAL MODELS: A few A105 DeLuxe sedans may also have been imported, priced at $2650 P.O.E. Austin also continued to produce the big Princess IV four-door saloon for the home market.

HISTORY: The A55 was introduced in February 1957.

1958 AUSTIN

A35 — FOUR — Production of the smallest Austin continued with little change. Standard equipment included turn signals, heater/defroster, overdrive, and disc wheels. Whitewall tires cost $13 extra.

A40 — FOUR — A completely different form of the old A40, which disappeared from the U.S. import list in the mid-1950s, emerged during 1958. Beneath its bonnet was the same little four-cylinder engine as the A35, rated 34 horsepower. This version appeared to be a cross between a two-door sedan and a station wagon, constructed as a sedan but lacking a conventional trunk, and an angled back end. This gave rear passengers more headroom than in an ordinary sedan. The trunk lid opened from the top, not the bottom, like a wagon's tailgate. A slight overhang of the rear roofline added to the car's modern, attractive look. Coachwork was designed by none other than Pinin Farina in Italy. Up front, a large, wide rectangular grille contained a crosshatch pattern. Headlamps and parking lights sat in the same tapered oval housings at the fender tips. Each element of the three-piece wraparound rear bumper could be removed separately. Inside, the back seat folded down for cargo storage. Under the dashboard was a full-length parcel tray, joining the locking glovebox. A short floor-mounted gearshift lever controlled the four-speed transmission. At the top of the rear seatback, a fabric apron could snap into place to separate the trunk area and form a shelf. Side windows were hinged on the DeLuxe model.

A55 — CAMBRIDGE Mk I — FOUR — Production of the A55, which replaced the former A50, continued with little change. Lower in profile than the A50, this version also had smaller wheels. The 51-horsepower engine had a full-flow oil filter. Separate front seats were contoured in design, and allowed three people to sit abreast. A wraparound rear window was used, and back doors had vent panes. The A55's gas filler cap was in an unusual location, alongside the decklid (which had exposed hinges). A Manumatic clutch and overdrive became available during the model year.

I.D. DATA: Serial number is on left front door hinge pillar pose or left sun visor. Engine number is on right side of block, below head gasket.

Note: See 1947-48 Austin for breakdown of prefix letters and digits.

Model	Body Type & Seating	Engine Type/CID	P.O.E. Price	Weight (lbs.)	Prod. Tota.
A35					
AS5	2-dr Sedan-4P	I4/58	1557	1550	Note 1
A40					
A2S6	2-dr Sedan-4P	I4/58	1795	1680	Note 1
A55 CAMBRIDGE Mk I					
HS6	4-dr Sedan-5P	I4/91	2214	2250	Note 1

Note 1: Approximately 175,000 Austins were produced during 1958, including those models not exported to the U.S. About 1,691 Austins were sold in the U.S. during 1958.

ENGINE DATA: BASE FOUR (A35, A40): Inline, overhead-valve four-cylinder. Cast iron block and head. **Displacement:** 57.8 cu. in. (948 cc). **Bore & Stroke:** 2.478 x 3.00 in. (62.9 x 76.2 mm). **Compression Ratio:** 8.3:1. **Brake Horsepower:** 34 at 4750 rpm. **Torque:** 50 lbs.-ft. at 2000 rpm. Three main bearings. Solid valve lifters. Zenith carburetor.

BASE FOUR (A55): Inline, overhead-valve four-cylinder. Cast iron block and head. **Displacement:** 90.9 cu. in. (1489 cc). **Bore & Stroke:** 2.875 x 3.50 in. (73.0 x 88.9 mm). **Compression Ratio:** 8.3:1. **Brake Horsepower:** 51 at 4250 rpm. **Torque:** 91 lbs.-ft. at 2000 rpm. Three main bearings. Solid valve lifters. Zenith carburetor.

CHASSIS DATA: Wheelbase: (A35) 79.5 in.; (A40) 83.5 in.; (A55) 99.25 in. **Overall Length:** (A35) 136.4 in.; (A40) 144.25 in.; (A55) 166.8 in. **Height:** (A35) 55.1 in.; (A40) 56.75 in.; (A55) 60.25 in. **Width:** (A35) 55.1 in.; (A40) 59.5 in.; (A55) 61.6 in. **Front Tread:** (A35) 45.3 in.; (A40) 59.4 in.; (A55) 48.5 in. **Rear Tread:** (A35) 44.8 in.; (A40) 59.4 in.; (A55) 49.0 in. **Standard Tires:** (A35/A40) 5.20x13; (A55) 5.90x13.

TECHNICAL: Layout: front-engine, rear-drive. **Transmission:** four-speed manual (2nd/3rd/4th synchronized); floor lever (A35/40) or column lever (A55). **Standard Final Drive Ratio:** (A35) 4.55:1; (A40) 4.22:1; (A55) 4.3:1. **Steering:** cam gear; (A55) cam and peg. **Suspension (front):** independent; wishbones and coil springs. **Suspension (rear):** rigid axle, semi-elliptic leaf springs and (A55) anti-roll bar. **Brakes:** hydraulic front/rear drum. **Body Construction:** steel unibody.

PERFORMANCE: Top Speed: (A35) 73 mph; (A40) 73 mph; (A55) 77 mph. **Acceleration (0-60 mph):** (A40) 36 sec.; (A55) 27 sec. **Acceleration (quarter-mile):** (A35) 26.5 sec.; (A40) 24.5 sec. (A55) 24 sec. **Fuel Mileage:** (A35) up to 50 mpg; (A40) 35-40 mpg; (A55) 22-35 mpg.

Manufacturer: The Austin Motor Co. Ltd., Longbridge, Birmingham, England.
Distributor: Hambro Automotive Corp., New York City.

1959 AUSTIN

1959 Austin A-35 two-door sedan.

A35 — FOUR — For its final year, the A35 continued with no change.

A40 — FOUR — This was the first full year of the two-door A40, described by some as a blend of car and station wagon. The DeLuxe model had chrome around the windows. Both carried the same engine as the smaller A35 sedan. See previous listing for details.

A55 — CAMBRIDGE Mk I — FOUR — The first Cambridge was dropped at the end of 1958, replaced by the Mark II.

A55 — CAMBRIDGE Mk II — FOUR — Wider than its predecessor (63.5 inches versus 62), the new A55 had a much different, more square look with rather sharp tailfins at the rear. Front fenders reached forward slightly at the top. Styling was by Pinin Farina, who also penned the smaller A40 wagon-styled sedan. Overall, the effect carried the traditional British "razor-edge" profile into the modern era. The bodyside's horizontal crease line met an upward-bent front trim strip in the center of the rear door, continuing all the way back to the vertical taillamps, which came to a point at the tops of the fins. The 1489-cc four-cylinder engine delivered 53 horsepower, able to produce a 0-60 time below 22 seconds. Tall seats held four adults easily, and could squeeze in as many as six. Front and rear doors had vent panes. A floor lever operated the four-speed gearbox, synchronized on the upper three gear ratios.

Note: Some publications referred to the A55 as "Cambrian" rather than "Cambridge," just as they had for the A50 model.

850 — MINI — FOUR — The first Austin Minis were produced during 1959; see next listing for details.

I.D. DATA: Serial number is on left front door hinge pillar post, or left sun visor. Engine number is on right side of block, below head gasket. Starting serial number: (A55 Mk II) 101.

Note: See 1947-48 Austin for breakdown of prefix letters and digits.

Model	Body Type & Seating	Engine Type/CID	P.O.E. Price	Weight (lbs.)	Prod. Total
A35					
AS5	2-dr Sedan-4P	I4/58	1557	1550	Note 1
A40					
A2S6	2-dr Std Sed-4P	I4/58	1795	1596	Note 1
A2S6	2-dr Del Sed-4P	I4/58	1856	1596	Note 1
A55 CAMBRIDGE Mk I					
HS6	4-dr Sedan-4P	I4/91	2199	2200	Note 1
A55 CAMBRIDGE Mk II					
AHS1	4-dr Sedan-4P	I4/91	2198	2283	Note 1

Note 1: Approximately 210,000 Austins were produced during 1959, including those models not exported to the U.S. About 4,433 Austins were sold in the U.S. during 1959.

A55 Price Note: Mark II cost $100 more at West Coast P.O.E.

ENGINE DATA: BASE FOUR (A35, A40): Inline, overhead-valve four-cylinder. Cast iron block and head. **Displacement:** 57.8 cu. in. (948 cc). **Bore & Stroke:** 2.478 x 3.00 in. (62.9 x 76.2 mm). **Compression Ratio:** 8.3:1. **Brake Horsepower:** 34 at 4750 rpm. **Torque:** 50 lbs.-ft. at 2000 rpm. Three main bearings. Solid valve lifters. Zenith carburetor.

BASE FOUR (A55): Inline, overhead-valve four-cylinder. Cast iron block and head. **Displacement:** 90.9 cu. in. (1489 cc). **Bore & Stroke:** 2.875 x 3.50 in. (73.0 x 88.9 mm). **Compression Ratio:** 8.3:1. **Brake Horsepower:** 53 at 4350 rpm. **Torque:** 82.5 lbs.-ft. at 2100 rpm. Three main bearings. Solid valve lifters. SU carburetor.

CHASSIS DATA: Wheelbase: (A35) 79.5 in.; (A40) 83.5 in.; (A55) 99.25 in. **Overall Length:** (A35) 136.4 in.; (A40) 144.25 in.; (A55) 166.9 in.; (A55 Mark II) 178 in. **Height:** (A35) 59.1 in.; (A40) 52.8 in.; (A55 Mk II) 59.8 in. **Width:** (A35) 55.1 in.; (A40) 59.4 in.; (A55 Mk II) 63.5 in. **Front Tread:** (A35) 45.3 in.; (A40) 47.5 in.; (A55 Mk II) 48.9 in. **Rear Tread:** (A35) 44.8 in.; (A40) 47.0 in.; (A55 Mk II) 49.9 in. **Standard Tires:** (A35/A40) 5.20x13; (A55) 5.90x13; (A55 Mk II) 5.90x14.

TECHNICAL: Layout: front-engine, rear-drive. **Transmission:** four-speed manual. **Standard Final Drive Ratio:** (A35/A40) 4.55:1; (A55) 4.31:1 or 4.875:1; (A55 Mk II) 4.55:1. **Steering:** cam gear. **Suspension (front):** independent; wishbones and coil springs. **Suspension (rear):** rigid axle, semi-elliptic leaf springs. **Brakes:** hydraulic front/rear drum. **Body Construction:** steel unibody.

MAJOR OPTIONS: Sunroof: (A55) $55). Electric clock: A55 ($17). Whitewall tires: A35/40 ($25); A55 ($35). Windshield washer: A35/40 ($15).

PERFORMANCE: Top Speed: (A35) 73 mph; (A40) 70-73 mph; (A55 Mk II) 79+ mph. **Acceleration (0-60 mph):** (A55 Mk II) 21.7 sec. **Acceleration (quarter-mile):** (A55 Mk II) 21.7 sec. (60 mph). **Fuel Mileage:** (A35) 38-40 mpg; (A55 Mk II) 20-26 mpg.

HISTORY: The 1959 model year for U.S. sales began October 1, 1958.

1960 AUSTIN

850 — MINI — FOUR — This was the first official year in the U.S. marketplace for the renowned Mini, which became the best-selling Austin in the U.S. in the early 1960s. A transverse-mounted four-cylinder engine provided front-wheel drive via a four-speed gearbox in the engine sump. Performance was surprisingly swift, and the interior was far roomier than it appeared. The Mini was only 120 inches long. Among its many unique features was a rubber cone spring suspension, front and rear. BMC described it as "an entirely new concept in motoring" that "easily out-classes any car anywhere near its price in performance, roominess, comfort and economy. Before long, souped-up Cooper versions appeared to take advantage of the car's light weight and performance potential, as did aftermarket add-ons. A Morris version also was produced, with the same specifications, differing only in grille design. The Austin version of the wide grille had the same rounded upper bar, but a pattern made up of slim horizontal strips. Round parking lights stood directly below the headlamps. Ten-inch tires made the car look even lower and tinier than it was. Standard colors were white, red or black, with gray and black fleck upholstery. Standard equipment included a rear-view mirror, rubber floor mats, driver's sun visor, individual bucket front seats (driver's adjustable), full-width parcel tray, door pockets, rear-seat pockets, storage under rear seat and behind rear backrest, cloth upholstery, washable headliner, and sill finishers. Ventilated disc wheels with four studs held Dunlop 5.20x10 tubeless tires. Rack and pinion steering was used. An accessory group consisted of windshield washers, foam rubber seating, wheel hub disc embellishers, hinged rear-quarter lights, overriders, two sun visors, chromed filler cap, and chromed rear license plate light.

A40 — FOUR — The A40 continued with little change.

A55 — CAMBRIDGE Mk II — FOUR — The revised A55 continued with little change for its first full year in the U.S. market.

A99 — WESTMINSTER — SIX — An occasional example of the big Austin, revised in 1959, appeared in the U.S. Its 2912-cc six-cylinder engine was rated 112 horsepower.

I.D. DATA: Serial number is on left front door hinge pillar post or left sun visor; (850) on left inner wheel arch valance. Engine number is on right side of block, below head gasket. Starting serial number or sequential number: (850) AA2S7L/0107; (A40) 3906; (A55) 316; (A99) BS9/687.

Note: See 1947-48 Austin for breakdown of prefix letters and digits.

Model	Body Type & Seating	Engine Type/CID	P.O.E. Price	Weight (lbs.)	Prod. Price
850 (MINI)					
AA2S	2-dr Sedan-4P	I4/52	1295	1288	Note 1
A40					
A2S6	2-dr Std Sed-4P	I4/58	1795	1596	Note 1
A2S6	2-dr DeL Sed-4P	I4/58	1856	1596	Note 1
A55 CAMBRIDGE Mk II					
AHS1	4-dr Sedan-4P	I4/91	2198	2352	Note 1
A99 WESTMINSTER					
BS9	4-dr Sedan	I6/178	3095	N/A	Note 1

Note 1: Approximately 240,000 Austins were built during 1960.

ENGINE DATA: BASE FOUR (850): Inline, overhead-valve four-cylinder. Cast iron block and head. **Displacement:** 51.7 cu. in. (848 cc). **Bore & Stroke:** 2.478 x 2.687 in. (62.9 x 68.3 mm). **Compression Ratio:** 8.3:1. **Brake Horsepower:** 37 at 5500 rpm. **Torque:** 45 lbs.-ft. at 3450 rpm. Three main bearings. Solid valve lifters. Semi-downdraft SU carburetor (model HS2).

BASE FOUR (A40): Inline, overhead-valve four-cylinder. Cast iron block and head. **Displacement:** 57.8 cu. in. (948 cc). **Bore & Stroke:** 2.478 x 3.00 in. (62.9 x 76.2 mm). **Compression Ratio:** 8.3:1. **Brake Horsepower:** 34 at 4750 rpm. **Torque:** 50 lbs.-ft. at 2000 rpm. Three main bearings. Solid valve lifters. Single Zenith carburetor.

BASE FOUR (A55): Inline, overhead-valve four-cylinder. Cast iron block and head. **Displacement:** 90.9 cu. in. (1489 cc). **Bore & Stroke:** 2.875 x 3.50 in. (73.0 x 88.9 mm). **Compression Ratio:** 8.3:1. **Brake Horsepower:** 53 at 4350 rpm. **Torque:** 83 lbs.-ft. at 2100 rpm. Three main bearings. Solid valve lifters. SU carburetor.

BASE SIX (A99): Inline, overhead-valve six-cylinder. Cast iron block and head. **Displacement:** 177.7 cu. in. (2912 cc). **Bore & Stroke:** 2.875 x 3.50 in. (83.3 x 88.9 mm). **Compression Ratio:** 8.2:1. **Brake Horsepower:** 112 at 4750 rpm. Two SU carburetors.

CHASSIS DATA: Wheelbase: (850) 80.2 in.; (A40) 83.5 in.; (A55) 99.25 in. **Overall Length:** (850) 120 in.; (A40) 144.25 in.; (A55) 178 in. **Height:** (850) 53 in.; (A40) 56.8 in.; (A55) 59 in. **Width:** (850) 55 in.; (A40) 59.4 in.; (A55) 63.5 in. **Front Tread:** (850) 47.8 in.; (A40) 47.5 in.; (A55) 48.9 in. **Rear Tread:** (850) 45.9 in.; (A40) 47 in.; (A55) 49.9 in. **Standard Tires:** (850) 5.20x10; (A40) 5.20x13; (A55) 5.90x14.

TECHNICAL: Layout: front-engine, rear-drive except (Mini) front-drive. **Transmission:** four-speed manual. Mini overall gear ratios: (1st) 13.657:1; (2nd) 8.176:1; (3rd) 5.317:1; (4th) 3.765:1; (rev) 13.657:1. **Standard Final Drive Ratio:** (850) 3.765:1; (A40) 4.55:1; (A55) 4.55:1. **Steering:** (Mini) rack and pinion. **Suspension (front):** coil springs and wishbones except (Mini) rubber with upper/lower suspension arms and ball joints. **Suspension (rear):** rigid axle, semi-elliptic leaf springs except (Mini) independent, rubber with radius arms. **Brakes:** hydraulic, front/rear drum. **Body Construction:** steel unibody.

PERFORMANCE: Top Speed: (850 Mini) 74 mph, factory; (A40) 70-71 mph; (A55) 76 + mph. **Acceleration (0-60 mph):** (850 Mini) 26.5 sec., factory **Acceleration (quarter-mile):** (850 Mini) 23.3 sec., factory; (A40) 24.5 sec.; (A55) 23 sec. **Fuel Mileage:** (850 Mini) 40/50 mpg, factory.

MAJOR OPTIONS: (850 Mini) Heater. Whitewall tires. PVC seating and adjustable passenger seat.

Manufacturer: The Austin Motor Co. Ltd., Longbridge, Birmingham, England.

Distributor: Hambro Automotive Corp., New York City.

1961 AUSTIN

850 — MINI — FOUR — While Austin continued to export some of its larger models to the U.S., the 850 Mini (sometimes referred to as successor to the "Seven") was the only one that sold in significant number. Designed by Alec Issigonis, the Mini continued in its 1959-60 form as a boxy, no-frills subcompact with surprising performance potential. A Cooper series with larger-displacement engine debuted during 1961; see next listing for details.

A40 — FOUR — No change was evident in the Farina-styled A40, but a station wagon joined the original wagon-styled sedan. Both were available in standard or DeLuxe trim.

A55 — CAMBRIDGE Mk II — FOUR — Production of the A55 continued with little change. A floor gearshift lever was standard, with column shift and overdrive optional.

A99 — WESTMINSTER — SIX — Production of the biggest Austin continued with little change, but few reached the U.S. Unlike other models, this one had a three-speed transmission with overdrive and front disc brakes. Wheelbase was 108 inches; overall length, 188 inches. The 178-cid six-cylinder engine was rated 112 horsepower.

I.D. DATA: Serial number is on left door pillar plate or on a plate between the fender well and radiator. An identification number on a plate on the firewall, under the hood, contained the prefix BMC/61 to indicate the model year. Engine number is on right side of block, below head gasket.

Note: See 1947-48 Austin for breakdown of prefix letters and digits.

Model	Body Type & Seating	Engine Type/CID	P.O.E. Price	Weight (lbs.)	Prod. Total
850	2-dr Sedan-4P	I4/52	1295	1320	Note 1
A40					
A40	2-dr Std Sed-4P	I4/58	1795	1596	Note 1
A40	2-dr DeL Sed-4P	I4/58	1856	1596	Note 1
A40	2-dr Std Sta Wag-4P	I4/58	1835	1596	Note 1
A40	2-dr DeL Sta Wag-4P	I4/58	1879	1596	Note 1
A55 CAMBRIDGE Mk II					
AHS1	4-dr Sedan-4P	I4/91	2198	2352	1596
A99 WESTMINSTER					
A99	4-dr Sedan	I6/178	3095	3233	Note 1

Note 1: Approximately 190,000 Austins were produced during 1961, including those models not exported to the U.S.

ENGINE DATA: BASE FOUR (850): Inline, overhead-valve four-cylinder. Cast iron block and head. **Displacement:** 51.7 cu. in. (848 cc). **Bore & Stroke:** 2.48 x 2.69 in. (62.9 x 68.3 mm). **Compression Ratio:** 8.3:1. **Brake Horsepower:** 37 at 5500 rpm. **Torque:** 44 lbs.-ft. at 2900 rpm. Three main bearings. Solid valve lifters. SU carburetor (model HS2).

BASE FOUR (A40): Inline, overhead-valve four-cylinder. Cast iron block and head. **Displacement:** 57.8 cu. in. (948 cc). **Bore & Stroke:** 2.478 x 3.00 in. (62.9 x 76.2 mm). **Compression Ratio:** 8.3:1. **Brake Horsepower:** 34 at 4750 rpm. **Torque:** 50 lbs.-ft. at 2000 rpm. Three main bearings. Solid valve lifters. Single Zenith carburetor.

BASE FOUR (A55): Inline, overhead-valve four-cylinder. Cast iron block and head. **Displacement:** 90.9 cu. in. (1489 cc). **Bore & Stroke:** 2.875 x 3.50 in. (73.0 x 88.9 mm). **Compression Ratio:** 8.3:1. **Brake Horsepower:** 53 at 4350 rpm. **Torque:** 81 lbs.-ft. at 2000 rpm. Three main bearings. Solid valve lifters. SU carburetor.

BASE SIX (A99): Same as 1960.

CHASSIS DATA: Wheelbase: (850) 80 in.; (A40) 83.5 in.; (A55) 99.25 in. **Overall Length:** (850) 120 in.; (A40) 144.25 in.; (A55) 175.4 in. **Height:** (850) 53.5 in.; (A40) 56.8 in.; (A55) 59.8 in. **Width:** (850) 55.5 in.; (A40) 59.4 in.; (A55) 63.5 in. **Front Tread:** (850) 47.4 in.; (A40) 47.5 in.; (A55) 48.6 in. **Rear Tread:** (850) 45.8 in.; (A40) 47.0 in.; (A55) 49.9 in. **Standard Tires:** (850) 5.20x10; (A40) 5.20x13; (A55) 5.90x14; (A99) 7.00x14.

TECHNICAL: Layout: front-engine, rear-drive except (Mini) front-drive. **Transmission:** four-speed manual exc. (A99) 3-speed w/overdrive. **Standard Final Drive Ratio:** (850) 3.77:1; (A40) 4.55:1; (A55) 4.55:1. **Steering:** (Mini) rack and pinion. **Suspension (front):** wishbones and coil springs except (Mini) rubber. **Suspension (rear):** rigid axle, semi-elliptic leaf springs and (A55) stabilizer bar exc. (Mini) rubber. **Brakes:** hydraulic front/rear drum exc. (A99) front disc, rear drum. **Body Construction:** steel unibody.

PERFORMANCE: Top Speed: (850) 73 mph; (A40) near 75 mph; (A55) 76 mph; (A99) near 100 mph. **Fuel Mileage:** (850) 40 mpg; (A99) 20-30 mpg.

Manufacturer/Distributor: Same as 1961.

1962 AUSTIN

850 — MINI — FOUR — Production of the basic 850 Mini with 848-cc engine continued as before, with a specific export model added later. Joining the original two-door sedan was a station wagon version, 10 inches longer overall. Minis had a floor-mounted starter button, manual choke, and sliding door windows. The 850 earned the Dewar Trophy in England for its "advanced development in automotive design."

1962 Austin Mini-Cooper two-door sedan.

MINI COOPER — FOUR — Appearance of the new high-performance Mini was similar to the basic model, except for its "Super" trim package. A larger (997-cc) four-cylinder engine with twin carburetors delivered 55 horsepower, to give a top speed of 85 mph. Standard equipment included front disc brakes, leathercloth seat upholstery, and a 0-100 mph speedometer. Morris also put out a Cooper version, described as having "sports-car specification;" see the Morris listing for additional details.

A40 — FOUR — Production of the A40 continued as before; see previous listing for details. As part of BMC's new policy of standardization, all A40s built after October 1962 had a larger 1098-cc engine; but export to the U.S. disappeared in any case.

A60 — CAMBRIDGE — FOUR — Production of the A55 Cambridge continued, but changed over to the A60 during the 1962 model year. An automatic transmission was optional.

I.D. DATA: Serial number is on left door pillar plate or on a plate between the fender well and radiator. An identification number on a plate on the firewall, under the hood, contained the prefix BMC/62 to indicate the model year. Engine number is on right side of block, below head gasket. Starting serial number: (850) A/2S7L/4036; (Cooper) CA/2S7L/138301.

Note: See 1947-48 Austin for breakdown of prefix letters and digits.

Model	Body Type & Seating	Engine Type/CID	P.O.E. Price	Weight (lbs.)	Prod. Price
850					
A2S7	2-dr Sedan-4P	I4/52	1295	1330	N/A
	2-dr Sta Wag-4P	I4/52	1669	1428	N/A
MINI COOPER					
CA2S7	2-dr Sedan-4P	I4/61	1725	1400	Note 1
A60 CAMBRIDGE					
A60	4-dr Sedan-4P	I4/99	2298	2420	N/A

Note 1: Approximately 9,987 Mini Coopers were produced during the 1962 model year (4,554 of them for export). Total Mini Cooper production for the full model run was 101,242 (not including 'S' models).

ENGINE DATA: BASE FOUR (850): Inline, overhead-valve four-cylinder. Cast iron block and head. **Displacement:** 51.8 cu. in. (848 cc). **Bore & Stroke:** 2.48 x 2.69 in. (62.9 x 68.3 mm). **Compression Ratio:** 8.3:1. **Brake Horsepower:** 37 at 5500 rpm. **Torque:** 44 lbs.-ft. at 2900 rpm. Three main bearings. Solid valve lifters. SU carburetor (model HS2).

BASE FOUR (Mini Cooper): Inline, overhead-valve four-cylinder. Cast iron block and head. **Displacement:** 60.9 cu. in. (997 cc). **Bore & Stroke:** 2.458 x 3.20 in. (62.4 x 81.3 mm). **Compression Ratio:** 9.0:1. **Brake Horsepower:** 55 at 6000 rpm. **Torque:** 54 lbs.-ft. at 3600 rpm. Three main bearings. Solid valve lifters. Two SU H2 carburetors.

BASE FOUR (A60): Inline, overhead-valve four-cylinder. Cast iron block and head. **Displacement:** 98.9 cu. in. (1622 cc). **Bore & Stroke:** 3.00 x 3.50 in. **Compression Ratio:** 8.3:1. **Brake Horsepower:** 61 at 4500 rpm. **Torque:** 90 lbs.-ft. at 2100 rpm. Three main bearings. Solid valve lifters.

CHASSIS DATA: Wheelbase: (850) 80 in.; (A60) 100.25 in. **Overall Length:** (850) 120.5 in.; (850 wag) 130 in.; (A60) 177.5 in. **Height:** (850) 53 in.; (A60) 58.9 in. **Width:** (850) 55.5 in.; (A60) 63.5 in. **Front Tread:** (850) 47.8 in.; (A60) 50.6 in. **Rear Tread:** (850) 45.9 in.; (A60) 51.4 in. **Standard Tires:** (850) 5.20x10; (A40) 5.20x13; (A55/60) 5.90x14.

TECHNICAL: Layout: (Mini) front-engine, front-drive; (others) front-engine, rear-drive. **Transmission:** four-speed manual. Cooper overall gear ratios: (1st) 12.05:1; (2nd) 7.213:1; (3rd) 5.11:1; (4th) 3.765:1. Optional Cooper gear ratios: (1st) 11.03:1; (2nd) 6.598:1; (3rd) 4.674:1. **Standard Final Drive Ratio:** (850) 3.765:1; (A60) 4.3:1. Other ratios available for Cooper. Steering: (Mini) rack and pinion. **Suspension (front):** (850) rubber springs; (Cooper) transverse wishbones and Moulton rubber springs; (A60) wishbones and coil springs. **Suspension (rear):** (850) rubber springs; (Cooper) trailing arms with Moulton rubber springs; (A60) rigid axle, semi-elliptic leaf springs. **Brakes:** hydraulic front/rear drum except (Cooper) front disc, rear drum. **Body Construction:** steel unibody.

MAJOR OPTIONS: (Mini Cooper) Radio. Heater. Competition equipment.

PERFORMANCE: Top Speed: (850) 70 mph; (Cooper) 85 mph; (A40) 70+ mph; (A55) 80+ mph. **Acceleration (0-60 mph):** (850) 29 sec. **Fuel Mileage:** (850) 38-50 mpg.

ADDITIONAL MODELS: The large Princess sedan occasionally made its way to the U.S., priced at $3995 P.O.E.

Manufacturer/Distributor: Same as 1960-61.

HISTORY: The model year for U.S. sales began September 1, 1961. Late arrivals were introduced March 23, 1962. The Mini Cooper was announced in Britain in July 1961, and went on sale in September of that year.

1963 AUSTIN

850 — MINI — FOUR — Production of the basic Mini continued as before, with an 848-cc engine. Greatest attention, however, went to the higher-performance Cooper models.

MINI COOPER — FOUR — Little was changed in appearance or mechanical details of the performance-oriented Mini Cooper, which looked like an ordinary front-drive Mini but carried a bigger (997 cc) four-cylinder engine, rated 55 horsepower. A Cooper was capable of 80-85 mph, but during the model year an even more potent 'S' version would arrive with a 1071-cc engine; see 1964 listing for details.

A60 CAMBRIDGE — FOUR — Production of the A60 continued, as introduced during the 1962 model year. Its wide grille had a tiny crosshatch pattern dominated by horizontal strips, extending around the circular parking lamps at the bottom but narrower at the top, with an insignia in the center. Single rectangular headlamps were used. A station wagon joined the original sedan.

A125 — PRINCESS — SIX — The big Princess sedan was available on special order; see next listing for details.

I.D. DATA: Serial number is on left inner fender panel, under the hood. Engine number is on right side of block, below head gasket. A BMC/63 prefix in the identifying number on a plate on the firewall (under the hood) indicated the 1963 model year. Starting serial number: (850 export/Super) AA2S7L/125538; (Cooper) CA2S7L/138301; (A60) AAHS9L/101; (Princess) VBS2L/101.

Note: See 1947-48 Austin for breakdown of prefix letters and digits.

Model	Body Type & Seating	Engine Type/CID	P.O.E. Price	Weight (lbs.)	Prod. Total
850	2-dr Export Sed-4P	I4/52	1399	1294	Note 1
850	2-dr Super Sed-4P	I4/52	1499	1294	Note 1
850	2-dr Sta Wagon-4P	I4/52	1671	1456	Note 1
MINI COOPER					
	2-dr Sedan-4P	I4/61	1791	1294	Note 2
A60 CAMBRIDGE					
A60	4-dr Sedan-4P	I4/99	2387	2471	Note 1
A60	4-dr Countryman-4P	I4/99	2719	2632	Note 1

Note 1: Approximately 250,000 Austins were produced during 1963, including those models not exported to the U.S.

Note 2: About 11,510 Mini Coopers were produced during the 1963 model year (including Morris models), of which almost half were exported.

ENGINE DATA: BASE FOUR (850): Same as 1962.

BASE FOUR (Mini Cooper): Same as 1962.

BASE FOUR (A60): Inline, overhead-valve four-cylinder. Cast iron block and head. **Displacement:** 99.1 cu. in. (1622 cc). **Bore & Stroke:** 3.00 x 3.50 in. **Compression Ratio:** 8.3:1. **Brake Horsepower:** 61 at 4500 rpm. **Torque:** 90 lbs.-ft. at 2100 rpm. Three main bearings. Solid valve lifters.

CHASSIS DATA: Wheelbase: (850) 80 in.; (A60) 100.25 in. **Overall Length:** (850) 120.5 in.; (850 wag) 130 in.; (A60) 177.5 in. **Height:** (850) 53 in.; (A60) 58.9 in. **Width:** (850) 55.5 in.; (A60) 63.5 in. **Front Tread:** (850) 47.8 in.; (A60) 50.6 in. **Rear Tread:** (850) 45.9 in.; (A60) 51.4 in. **Standard Tires:** (850 Mini) 5.20x10; (Cooper) 145x10; (A60) 5.90x14.

TECHNICAL: Same as 1962.

MAJOR OPTIONS: Automatic transmission: A60 ($220).

PERFORMANCE: Top Speed: (850) 70 mph; (Cooper) 85 mph. **Acceleration (0-60 mph):** (850) 29 sec. **Fuel Mileage:** (850) 38-50 mpg.

HISTORY: The model year for U.S. sales began September 1, 1962.

1964 AUSTIN

850 — FOUR — Little change was evident in the basic Mini, though American interest was shifting strongly to the Cooper versions.

MINI COOPER — FOUR — If the 997-cc Cooper engine of 1962-63 wasn't sufficient, this year brought additional possibilities: a 998-cc version (with the same 55-horsepower rating as the 997 cc) and a selection of 'S' editions. Three 'S' engine sizes were available: 1071 cc (introduced during the 1963 model year); 970 cc (a short-stroke version with domed pistons); and a 1275 cc four, rated 75 horsepower. The 1275-cc version came with a 130-mph speedometer and actual top speed of up to 99 mph. Its original Moulton rubber suspension soon changed to a Hydrolastic system. "The stock Mini is so rational it's irritating," said Car and Driver, lamenting the fact that the basic models had little emotional appeal. Coopers, on the other hand, added a healthy helping of "sheer exuberant performance and fun" to the rational package. "It's the sort of car that'll get you in trouble if you don't control your baser instincts."

Note: In addition to engine-displacement differences, Coopers had a long series of running changes in details; not to mention the availability of both factory and aftermarket competition components. So actual vehicles may vary considerably from the original specifications.

A60 CAMBRIDGE — FOUR — Production of the A60 sedan and station wagon continued with little change for its final year of U.S. availability.

MARK II PRINCESS — SIX — On special order, Americans could still obtain a big six-cylinder Princess sedan.

I.D. DATA: Serial number is on left side inner wheel arch or top of radiator frame except (A60) on firewall. Engine number is on right side of block, below head gasket. A BMC/64 prefix in the identifying number on a plate on the firewall (under the hood) indicated the 1964 model year. Starting serial number: (850 export/Super) AA2S7L/303300; (Cooper) CA2S7L/306200; (Cooper 'S' 1071) CA2S7L/384101; (Cooper 'S' 998) CA2S7L/486096; (A60) AAHS9L/101; (Princess) VBS2L/101.

Note: See 1947-48 Austin for breakdown of prefix letters and digits.

Model	Body Type & Seating	Engine Type/CID	P.O.E. Price	Weight (lbs.)	Prod. Total
850	2-dr Export Sed-4P	I4/52	1462	1294	Note 1
850	2-dr Super Sed-4P	I4/52	1499	1294	Note 1
850	2-dr Sta Wagon-4P	I4/52	1671	1456	Note 1
MINI COOPER					
	2-dr Sedan-4P	I4/61	1824	1294	Note 2
	2-dr 'S' Sed-4P	I4/65	2181	1400	Note 2
A60 CAMBRIDGE					
A60	4-dr Sedan-4P	I4/99	2387	2471	Note 1
A60	4-dr Countryman-4P	I4/99	2719	2632	Note 1
MARK II PRINCESS					
Mark II	4-dr Sedan-6P	I6/238	4985	3416	Note 1

Note 1: Approximately 315,000 Austins were produced during 1964, including those models not exported to the U.S.

Note 2: Coopers came with a variety of engines. Approximately 9,181 Coopers (including Morris models) were produced during the 1964 model year, of which more than half were exported. About 4,342 Cooper 'S' models were produced during the 1964 model year, with less than half exported. Total Austin Cooper 'S' production (all model years) consisted of approximately 489 units with 970-cc engine and 2,133 with 1071-cc engine, with the vast majority carrying the 1275-cc engine.

ENGINE DATA: BASE FOUR (850): Inline, overhead-valve four-cylinder. Cast iron block and head. **Displacement:** 51.8 cu. in. (848 cc). **Bore & Stroke:** 2.48 x 2.69 in. (62.9 x 68.3 mm). **Compression Ratio:** 8.3:1. **Brake Horsepower:** 37 at 5500 rpm. **Torque:** 44 lbs.-ft. at 2900 rpm. Three main bearings. Solid valve lifters. SU carburetor (model HS2).

BASE FOUR (Cooper 997): Inline, overhead-valve four-cylinder. Cast iron block and head. **Displacement:** 60.9 cu. in. (997 cc). **Bore & Stroke:** 2.458 x 3.20 in. (62.4 x 81.3 mm). **Compression Ratio:** 9.1:1. **Brake Horsepower:** 55 at 6000 rpm. **Torque:** 54 lbs.-ft. at 3600 rpm. Three main bearings. Solid valve lifters. Two SU HS2 carburetors.

BASE FOUR (Cooper 998): Same as above, except — **Displacement:** 60.9 cu. in. (998 cc). **Bore & Stroke:** 2.458 x 3.20 in. (64.6 x 76.2 mm). **Compression Ratio:** 9.0:1. **Brake Horsepower:** 55 at 5800 rpm. **Torque:** 57 lbs.-ft. at 3000 rpm.

BASE FOUR (Cooper 'S' 1071): Inline, overhead-valve four-cylinder. Cast iron block and head. **Displacement:** 65.4 cu. in. (1071 cc). **Bore & Stroke:** 2.78 x 2.69 in. (70.6 x 68.3 mm). **Compression Ratio:** 9.0:1. **Brake Horsepower:** 70 at 6000 rpm. **Torque:** 62 lbs.-ft. at 4500 rpm. Three main bearings. Solid valve lifters. Two SU carburetors.

BASE FOUR (Cooper 'S' 970): Same as above, except -- **Displacement:** 59.2 cu. in. (970 cc). **Bore & Stroke:** 2.78 x 2.44 in. (70.6 x 61.9 mm). **Compression Ratio:** 9.75:1. **Brake Horsepower:** 65 at 6500 rpm. **Torque:** 55 lbs.-ft. at 3500 rpm.

BASE FOUR (Cooper 'S' 1275): Same as above, except -- **Displacement:** 77.9 cu. in. (1275 cc). **Bore & Stroke:** 2.78 x 3.20 in. (70.6 x 81.3 mm). **Compression Ratio:** 9.5:1. **Brake Horsepower:** 75 at 5800 rpm. Torque: 79 lbs.-ft. at 3000 rpm.

BASE FOUR (A60): Same as 1963.

BASE SIX (Princess): Inline, overhead-valve six-cylinder. Cast iron block and head. **Displacement:** 238.5 cu. in. **Bore & Stroke:** 3.75 x 3.50 in. **Compression Ratio:** 7.8:1. **Brake Horsepower:** 175 at 4800 rpm.

CHASSIS DATA: Wheelbase: (850) 80 in.; (A60) 96 in.; (Princess) 110 in. **Overall Length:** (850) 120.25 in.; (850 Wag) 129.9 in.; (A60) 174.5 in.; (Princess) 188.5 in. **Height:** (850/Cooper) 53 in.; (A60) 58.9 in. **Width:** (850/Cooper) 55.5 in.; (A60) 63.5 in. **Front Tread:** (850/Cooper) 47.8 in.; (Cooper 'S') 48.5 in.; (A60) 50.6 in. **Rear Tread:** (850/Cooper) 45.9 in.; (Cooper 'S') 48.3 in.; (A60) 51.4 in. **Standard Tires:** (850 Mini) 5.20x10; (Cooper 'S') 5.50x10 or 145x10; (A60) 5.90x14; (Princess) 7.50x13.

TECHNICAL: Layout: (Mini/Cooper) front-engine, front-drive; (A60) rear-drive. **Transmission:** four-speed manual. **Standard Final Drive Ratio:** (850/Cooper) 3.765:1. **Steering:** (Mini/Cooper) rack and pinion; (A60) cam and peg. **Suspension (front):** (Mini/Cooper) rubber springs except (late S 1275) Hydrolastic; (others) wishbones and coil springs. **Suspension (rear):** (Mini/Cooper) rubber springs except (late S 1275) Hydrolastic; (others) rigid axle and semi-elliptic leaf springs. **Brakes:** hydraulic front/rear drum except (Cooper) front disc, rear drum.. **Body Construction:** steel unibody.

MAJOR OPTIONS: Automatic transmission: A60 ($220). Close-ratio gearbox: Cooper 'S'. Auxiliary gas tank: Cooper 'S'.

Note: A broad variety of competition parts were available for the Cooper, from the factory.

PERFORMANCE: Top Speed: (850) 70+ mph; (Cooper 'S') 90-95 mph; (Cooper S 1275) 96-99 mph. **Acceleration (quarter-mile):** (850) 23.7 sec.; (Cooper S 1275) 18.4 sec. **Fuel Mileage:** (850) 45 mpg; (Cooper 'S') 35-40 mpg.

HISTORY: Introduced: (Cooper 998) January 1964; (Cooper 1071) March 1963; (Cooper 970/1275) March 1964. For the home market, a transverse-engine 1800 model was available at this time.

1965 AUSTIN

850 — MINI — FOUR — Little changed in the basic Mini for 1965, except that Hydrolastic suspension replaced the earlier rubber springs.

MINI COOPER 'S' — FOUR — Production of Cooper 'S' models with the 1071-cc engine ceased before the 1965 model year, but the 1275-cc edition continued with little change. A broad variety of other engine choices was available in Britain, but imported Cooper 'S' models usually had the 1275-cc engine at this time.

MARK II PRINCESS — SIX — The Princess sedan was again available on special order, but the smaller A60 sedan no longer was included on lists of Austin imports. See previous listing for details.

I.D. DATA: Serial number is on left inner fender panel or top of radiator frame. Engine number is on right side of block, below head gasket. Serial numbers continued from 1964.

Note: See 1947-48 Austin for breakdown of prefix letters and digits.

Model	Body Type & Seating	Engine Type/CID	P.O.E. Price	Weight (lbs.)	Prod. MINI Total
850	2-dr Export Sed-4P	I4/52	1483	1294	Note 1
COOPER 'S'					
	2-dr Sed-4P	I4/78	2349	1400	Note 1

Note 1: Approximately 310,000 Austins were produced during 1965, including those models not exported to the U.S. A total of approximately 5,352 Cooper 'S' models (including Morris) were produced during the 1965 model year, of which fewer than half were exported. Over the entire model run through 1972, 44,859 Cooper 'S' models were produced.

ENGINE DATA: BASE FOUR (850): Inline, overhead-valve four-cylinder. Cast iron block and head. **Displacement:** 51.8 cu. in. (848 cc). **Bore & Stroke:** 2.48 x 2.69 in. (62.9 x 68.3 mm). **Compression Ratio:** 8.3:1. **Brake Horsepower:** 37 at 5500 rpm. **Torque:** 44 lbs.-ft. at 2900 rpm. Three main bearings. Solid valve lifters. SU carburetor (model HS2).
BASE FOUR (Mini Cooper 'S'): Inline, overhead-valve four-cylinder. Cast iron block and head. **Displacement:** 77.9 cu. in. (1275 cc). **Bore & Stroke:** 2.78 x 3.20 in. (70.6 x 81.3 mm). **Compression Ratio:** 9.5:1. **Brake Horsepower:** 78 at 5800 rpm. **Torque:** 80 lbs.-ft. at 3000 rpm. Three main bearings. Solid valve lifters. Two SU carburetors.

Note: Various other Cooper 'S' engine sizes and horsepower ratings continued to be produced, though not all were imported; see prior listings.

CHASSIS DATA: Wheelbase: (850) 80 in. **Overall Length:** (850) 120.25 in. **Height:** (850) 53 in. **Width:** (850) 55.5 in. **Front Tread:** (850) 47.8 in.; (Cooper) 47.5 in. **Rear Tread:** (850) 45.9 in.; (Cooper) 46.3 in. **Standard Tires:** (850/Mini) 5.20x10; (Cooper) 5.50x10 or 145x10.

TECHNICAL: Layout: front-engine, front-drive. **Transmission:** four-speed manual. **Standard Final Drive Ratio:** 3.765:1. **Steering:** rack and pinion. **Suspension (front):** Hydrolastic. **Suspension (rear):** Hydrolastic. **Brakes:** hydraulic front/rear drum except (Cooper) front disc, rear drum. **Body Construction:** steel unibody.

PERFORMANCE: Top Speed: (850) 70+mph; (Cooper) up to 100 mph. **Fuel Mileage:** (850) 45 mpg; (Cooper) 25-28 mpg.

ADDITIONAL MODELS: Other Austins in production, mainly for sale in Europe, included the A40, A110 Westminster, 1100, and 1800.

HISTORY: The model year for U.S. sales began September 1, 1964.

1966 AUSTIN

850 — FOUR — Production of the basic Mini continued with little change, though fewer found their way to the U.S.

MINI MOKE — FOUR — A Jeep-like utility touring vehicle was added to the Mini lineup, and exported to the U.S. Dimensions and engine details were similar to the basic Mini.

MINI COOPER 'S' — FOUR — As before, the 1275-cc version of the performance-oriented Cooper was most often exported to the U.S., though 998-cc Coopers continued to be produced through 1969.

PRINCESS 'R' — SIX — As before, the big Austin Princess was available on special order.

I.D. DATA: Serial number is located between radiator and fender, or on the firewall. Engine number is on right side of block, below head gasket. Starting serial number: (850) AA2S7/L575100; (Cooper) CA2S7L/549752; (Mini Moke) AAB1L/513101.

Note: See 1947-48 Austin for breakdown of prefix letters and digits.

Model	Body Type & Seating	Engine Type/CID	P.O.E. Price	Weight (lbs.)	Prod. Total
850					
AA2S7	2-dr Sedan-4P	I4/52	1483	1294	N/A
MINI MOKE					
AAB1	2-dr Tourer-4P	I4/52	1270	1204	N/A
MINI COOPER 'S'					
CA2S7	2-dr Sedan-4P	I4/78	2349	1400	Note 1
PRINCESS 'R'					
	4-dr Sedan-5P	I6/238	6765	N/A	N/A

Note 1: Approximately 4,228 Cooper 'S' models (including Morris) were produced during the 1966 model year, nearly three-fourths of which were exported.

ENGINE DATA: BASE FOUR (850/Moke): Inline, overhead-valve four-cylinder. Cast iron block and head. **Displacement:** 51.8 cu. in. (848 cc). **Bore & Stroke:** 2.48 x 2.69 in. (62.9 x 68.3 mm). **Compression Ratio:** 8.3:1. **Brake Horsepower:** 37 at 5500 rpm. **Torque:** 44 lbs.-ft. at 2900 rpm. Three main bearings. Solid valve lifters. SU carburetor (model HS2).
BASE FOUR (Mini Cooper 'S'): Inline, overhead-valve four-cylinder. Cast iron block and head. **Displacement:** 77.9 cu. in. (1275 cc). **Bore & Stroke:** 2.78 x 3.20 in. **Compression Ratio:** 9.5:1. **Brake Horsepower:** 78 at 5800 rpm. **Torque:** 80 lbs.-ft. at 3000 rpm. Three main bearings. Solid valve lifters. Two SU carburetors.

Note: Various other Cooper 'S' engine sizes and horsepower ratings continued to be produced, though not all were imported; see 1964 listing.

CHASSIS DATA: Wheelbase: (850/Moke/Cooper) 80 in.; (Princess) 110 in. **Overall Length:** (850/Cooper) 120.25 in.; (Moke) 120 in.; (Princess) 188 in. **Height:** (850/Cooper) 53 in.; (Moke) 56 in. **Width:** (850) 55.5 in.; (Moke) 51.5 in.; (Cooper) 47.5 in. **Rear Tread:** (850) 46.9 in.; (Moke) 46.8 in.; (Cooper) 46.3 in. **Standard Tires:** (850/Moke) 5.20x10; (Cooper) 145x10; (Princess) 7.50x13.

TECHNICAL: Layout: (Mini/Cooper) front-engine, front-drive. **Transmission:** four-speed manual. **Steering:** (Mini/Cooper) rack and pinion. **Suspension (front):** (Mini/Cooper) wishbones with hydrolastic rubber cone springs. **Suspension (rear):** (Mini/Cooper) independent; trailing arms with hydrolastic rubber cone springs and pitch tension springs. **Brakes:** hydraulic front/rear drum except (Cooper) front disc, rear drum.. **Body Construction:** steel unibody.

PERFORMANCE: Same as 1965.

HISTORY: The model year for U.S. sales began September 1, 1965.

1967 AUSTIN

1967 Austin FX4 diesel London-type limousine taxi. (Christie's)

MINI COOPER 'S' — FOUR — Only the 1275-cc Cooper 'S' was imported into the U.S. in any quantity in this final year of its full official availability, with little change.

I.D. DATA: Serial number is on a plate beetween the fender well and radiator, or on the firewall. Engine number is on right side of block, below head gasket. Starting serial number: CA2S7L/750000.

Note: See 1947-48 Austin for breakdown of prefix letters and digits.

Model	Body Type & Seating	Engine Type/CID	P.O.E. Price	Weight (lbs.)	Prod. Total
MINI COOPER 'S'					
CA2S7	2-dr Sedan-4P	I4/78	2431	1400	Note 1

Note 1: A total of 44,859 Cooper 'S' models were produced during the full model run, through 1972.

ENGINE DATA: BASE FOUR (Cooper 'S'): Inline, overhead-valve four-cylinder. Cast iron block and head. **Displacement:** 77.9 cu. in. (1275 cc). **Bore & Stroke:** 2.78 x 3.20 in. **Compression Ratio:** 9.5:1. **Brake Horsepower:** 78 at 5800 rpm. **Torque:** 80 lbs.-ft. at 3000 rpm. Three main bearings. Solid valve lifters. Two SU carburetors.

Note: Various other Cooper 'S' engine sizes and horsepower ratings continued to be produced, though not all were imported; see 1964 listing.

CHASSIS DATA: Wheelbase: 80 in. **Overall Length:** 120.25 in. **Height:** 53 in. **Width:** 55.5 in. **Front Tread:** 47.5 in. **Rear Tread:** 46.3 in. **Standard Tires:** 145x10.

TECHNICAL: Layout: front-engine, front-drive. **Transmission:** four-speed manual (synchronized 2nd/3rd/4th). **Standard Final Drive Ratio:** 3.44:1. **Steering:** rack and pinion. **Suspension (front):** wishbones with hydrolastic rubber cone springs. **Suspension (rear):** independent; trailing arms with hydrolastic rubber cone springs and pitch tension springs. **Brakes:** front disc, rear drum. **Body Construction:** steel unibody.

PERFORMANCE: Top Speed: (850) 70+ mph; (Cooper) up to 100 mph. **Acceleration (0-60 mph):** (Cooper 1275) 11.5 seconds. **Acceleration (quarter-mile):** (Cooper 1275) 18.4 seconds. **Fuel Mileage:** (850) 45 mpg; (Cooper) 25-28 mpg.

HISTORY: The model year for U.S. sales began September 1, 1966.

1968-69 AUSTIN

1969 Austin Mini-Cooper S two-door sedan.

AMERICA — FOUR — A larger Austin came to America for 1968, with a name designating its destination and billed as "the perfect second car." This two-door sedan rode a 93-inch wheelbase and measured 147 inches overall. A transverse-mounted four-cylinder engine produced 58 horsepower. The grille contained a pattern of four thick horizontal elements, with a round insignia in its center and 'AUSTIN AMERICA' block lettering along the center of the upper bar. Outer edges of the grille came to a point below the single round headlamps, which stood above rectangular amber parking lights. At the rear of the sharply-slanted back end were vertical-style taillamps. Austin's automatic transmission lever selected any of the four speeds, to allow for manual shifting between gears. The company claimed that it was the "lowest-priced car anywhere with a fully automatic transmission." The America's sales brochure also repeated a statement by Road & Track that this model was produced by the same people who'd done the Mini, "the single most outstanding production car design executed since World War II" and this example was "the biggest bargain in today's imported-car market." Front doors had wind-down windows and hinged vent windows. Rear side windows hinged outward. Standard equipment included a heater, twin front bucket seats with adjustable head restraints, full-width rear bench seat, twin sun visors, lighted side markers (front and rear), inside and outside mirrors, and full carpeting. Standard body colors included Damask Red, Glacier White, Bermuda Blue, Bronze Yellow, Pale Primrose, British Racing Green, Antelope, and Faun Brown.

I.D. DATA: Serial number is on the lock platform under the hood, or on the firewall. A 13-symbol Vehicle Identification Number was used starting with the 1969 model year; see 1970 listing for breakdown. Starting serial number: (America) A/A2SAU101M.

Model	Body Type & Seating	Engine Type/CID	P.O.E. Price	Weight (lbs.)	Prod. Total
AMERICA					
	2-dr Sedan-4P	I4/78	1845	1852	Note 1

Note 1: Approximately 16,391 Austins were sold in the U.S. during 1969.
Price Note: The America with manual transmission cost $1799 in 1968.

ENGINE DATA: BASE FOUR: Inline, overhead-valve four-cylinder; transverse mounted. Cast iron block and head. **Displacement:** 77.9 cu. in. (1275 cc). **Bore & Stroke:** 2.78 x 3.20 in. **Compression Ratio:** 8.8:1. **Brake Horsepower:** 58 at 5250 rpm. **Torque:** 69 lbs.-ft. at 3000 rpm. Three main bearings. Solid valve lifters. One SU carburetor. 12-volt electrical.

CHASSIS DATA: Wheelbase: 93.5 in. **Overall Length:** 146.75 in. **Height:** 53.0 in. **Width:** 60.38 in. **Front Tread:** 51.5 in. **Rear Tread:** 50.88 in. **Wheel Type:** ventilated disc. **Standard Tires:** Dunlop 5.95x12.

TECHNICAL: Layout: front-engine, front-drive. **Transmission:** (1968) four-speed manual, all-synchromesh; floor lever. Four-speed automatic optional. Manual overall gear ratios: (1st) 12.89:1; (2nd) 8.10:1; (3rd) 5.23:1; (4th) 3.65:1; (rev) 12.93:1. Automatic overall gear ratios: (1st) 10.12:1; (2nd) 6.96:1; (3rd) 5.49:1; (4th) 3.76:1; 10.12:1. **Standard Final Drive Ratio:** (manual) 3.65:1; (automatic) 3.76:1. **Steering:** rack and pinion. **Suspension (front):** independent; uenqual-length levers and "Hydrolastic" displacers, with swivel axles mounted on ball joints. **Suspension (rear):** independent with trailing arms and "Hydrolastic" displacers, auxiliary springs and anti-roll bar. **Brakes:** front disc, rear drum. **Body Construction:** steel unibody.

MAJOR OPTIONS: Automatic transmission. Radio. Front grille guard. Rear deck guard. Rubber mats. Electric clock. Locking gas cap. Convenience kit (front rubber floor mats, door scuff plates, doorsill protection plates, lighter and walnut gearshift handle).

PERFORMANCE: Top Speed: 79 mph. **Fuel Mileage:** 30 mpg average.
Manufacturer: British Leyland Corp., London, England.
Distributor: British Leyland Motors Inc., Leonia, New Jersey.

HISTORY: Introduced: May 1968. Austin's 850 Mini and Cooper 'S' disappeared from the U.S. market this year, though they continued into the 1970s in Britain. More than four million Minis were produced altogether.

1970 AUSTIN

AMERICA — FOUR — Production of the front-drive Austin America continued with little change. Standard equipment included a padded steering wheel, deluxe wheel covers, heater/defroster, two-speed wiper/washer, front disc brakes, three-point front safety belts, washable Ambia vinyl upholstery, front bucket seats, backup lights, courtesy lights, outside mirror, and six-ply tires.

I.D. DATA: Serial number is on the firewall under the hood, on the left side of the dashboard, visible through the windshield, or on the left door post (inside car). A 13-symbol VIN was used on all British Leyland vehicles beginning with the 1969 model year. Symbol one indicates make ('A' = Austin). Symbol two indicates engine type. Symbols three and four indicates model (2S = two-door sedan); Symbol five is Series. Symbol six denotes a car to U.S. specification. Symbol eight denotes year ('A' = 1970). That is followed by the sequential serial number and then by a letter that denotes assembly plant. Starting serial number: AA2SDUA/101.

Model	Body Type & Seating	Engine Type/CID	P.O.E. Price	Weight (lbs.)	Prod. Total
AMERICA					
	2-dr Sedan-4P	I4/78	1815	1924	Note 1

Note 1: Approximately 13,634 Austins were sold in the U.S. during 1970.
Price Note: An automatic-transmission America was priced at $1949.
ENGINE DATA: Same as 1968-69.
CHASSIS DATA: Same as 1968-69.
TECHNICAL: Same as 1968-69.
MAJOR OPTIONS: Accessory group (aluminum scuff plates, aluminum threshold plates, walnut T-shift handle or crested knob, lighter, and crested rubber mats). Grille guard ($21.95). Rear guard ($18.95). Rubber mats ($12.95). Motorola AM radio ($51 plus installation kit). Center console with lighted shift quadrant and Jensen speaker ($49.95). Kienzie electric clock. "America" key fob ($1.75). Locking gas cap ($6.95). Whitewall tires ($33).

PERFORMANCE: Top Speed: 85 mph. **Acceleration (0-60 mph):** 17.5-18 seconds. **Fuel Mileage:** 30 mpg.
Manufacturer/Distributor: Same as 1968-69.

1971-72 AUSTIN

1971 Austin America.

AMERICA — FOUR — Promoted as "the big little car," the America got a new grille design for 1971, containing two horizontal strips across its center, with an Austin badge on the upper bar and 'America' insignia on the right (passenger) side. Single headlamps stood above amber rectangular parking lamps. The front-wheel-drive layout again used a transverse-mounted front engine. A unique no-springs, no-shocks liquid suspension was designed to cut down bounce, pitch and roll. That sealed system was said to be "virtually maintenance free." Rack-and-pinion steering was said to be "borrowed from our Jaguar and MG." Front disc brakes were used and a special brake-pressure limiting valve helped keep the rear wheels from locking in a panic stop. Inside were deep vinyl seats, deep pile carpeting, a woodgrain dashboard, special no-slip covering on the steering wheel, and front armrests. New side moldings had rubber inserts. A separate compartment for the spare tire was below the trunk. Standard equipment included twin bucket front seats with adjustable head restraints, rear bench seat, full-width package shelf under the dash (except with air conditioning), padded dual sun visors, front door storage pockets, lighted side markers (front and rear), windshield washers, no-glare padded dash, and a manual choke. Because the wheels were mounted at extreme corners of the frame (like the former Mini), the interior was quite roomy. Engine, transmission and suspension were mounted on a rubber-insulated sub-frame to help reduce noise. Body colors included Glacier White, Wild Moss, Bronze Yellow, Teal Blue, Bedouin, Blaze, Racing Green, and Limeflower. Interiors came in Autumn Leaf or Navy, depending on the body color.

I.D. DATA: Serial number is on the left side of the dashboard, visible through the windshield; and on the left door post. See explanation of VIN symbols in 1970 listing. Starting serial number: AA2SDUB101.

Model	Body Type & Seating	Engine Type/CID	P.O.E. Price	Weight (lbs.)	Prod. Total
AMERICA					
AA2S	2-dr Sedan-4P	I4/78	1985	1924	Note 1

Note 1: Approximately 6,550 Austins were sold in the U.S. during 1971. Although imports halted during 1972, about 1,010 were sold in that year.

Price Note: An automatic-transmission America was priced at $2135.

ENGINE DATA: BASE FOUR: Inline, overhead-valve four-cylinder; transverse mounted. Cast iron block and head. **Displacement:** 77.9 cu. in. (1275 cc). **Bore & Stroke:** 2.78 x 3.20 in. **Compression Ratio:** 8.8:1. **Brake Horsepower:** 58 at 5250 rpm. **Torque:** 69 lbs.-ft. at 3000 rpm. Three main bearings. Solid valve lifters. One SU carburetor. 12-volt electrical.

CHASSIS DATA: **Wheelbase:** 93.5 in. **Overall Length:** 146.75 in. **Height:** 53.0 in. **Width:** 60.38 in. **Front Tread:** 51.5 in. **Rear Tread:** 50.88 in. **Wheel Type:** ventilated disc. **Standard Tires:** Dunlop 5.95x12.

TECHNICAL: **Layout:** front-engine, front-drive. **Transmission:** four-speed manual, all-synchromesh; floor lever. Four-speed automatic optional. **Standard Final Drive Ratio:** (manual) 3.65:1; (automatic) 3.76:1. **Steering:** rack and pinion. **Suspension (front):** independent; unequal-length levers and "Hydrolastic" displacers, with swivel axles mounted on ball joints. **Suspension (rear):** independent with trailing arms and "Hydrolastic displacers, auxiliary springs and anti-roll bar. **Brakes:** front disc, rear drum. **Body Construction:** steel unibody.

MAJOR OPTIONS: Automatic transmission ($150). Air conditioning ($335 plus installation). Convenience kit: front rubber floor mats, door scuff plates, doorsill protector plates, lighter, and walnut gearshift knob ($26.95). Motorola AM radio ($51 plus $17 for installation kit). Whitewall tires ($33). Luggage rack ($29.95). Front grille guard ($17.95). Rear deck guard ($19.95). Rubber mats ($19.95). Electric clock ($19.95 plus mtg bracket). Cigarette lighter ($3.95). Walnut gearshift handle. Tinted glass ($38). Key fob ($1.75).

PERFORMANCE: **Top Speed:** 85 mph (cruising in 60s). **Fuel Mileage:** up to 30 mpg.

Manufacturer: British Leyland Corp., Longbridge, Birmingham, England.

Distributor: British Leyland Motors, Inc., Leonia, New Jersey.

HISTORY: Model year for U.S. sales began October 1, 1970.

1973-74 AUSTIN

1974 Austin Marina four-door.

MARINA — FOUR — Following the demise of the America, yet another Austin model made a final stab at the American marketplace. The Marina's sales brochure emphasized the new Austin's heritage, noting that it came from the "people who build Jaguar, MG, Triumph and Land Rover." Disc brakes and the standard four-speed all-synchro transmission were developed by Triumph. Handling was said to derive from Jaguar: "well-bred handling that a man understands and a woman appreciates." Rack-and-pinion steering likewise came from Jag, delivering a 31-foot turning circle. Land Rover contributed the chassis, with 96-inch wheelbase. Offered in two-door GT coupe and four-door sedan form, with manual or automatic shift, the Marina held a "race-toughened" engine from MG: actually, a single-carb version of the MGB's 1800-cc four. Torsion bar suspension was used.

The car's "lean, clean, aerodynamic lines reflect the classic English appearance of uncluttered good looks," said the corporate brochure. Separate 'Austin' lettering stood on top of the hood, at the front, on driver's side. Single headlamps were recessed into a blackout front panel, alongside a simple grille consisting of a wide rectangular bright frame. Inside that frame, two red rectangles flanked a center insignia. Standard equipment included tinted glass, padded sun visors (vanity mirror on passenger side), reclining vinyl front bucket seats, vinyl bench rear seat with pull-down armrest, automatic retracting rear seatbelts, inertia-type front seatbelts, automatic trunk light, cigarette lighter, ashtrays, lockable glovebox with parcel shelves, and cut-pile molded carpets. Nine body colors were available: Damask Red, Glacier White, Blaze, Lime Flower, Teal Blue, Green Mallard, Harvest Gold, Midnight Blue, and Black Tulip. Interiors came in Black, Autumn Leaf or Geranium, depending on body color. The two-door GT added a tachometer, pinstripes, and walnut-finished instrument panel.

I.D. DATA: Serial number is on the left door trim post, visible through windshield and on a plate attached to the left door post. Engine number is on a plate attached to right side of block. See explanation of VIN symbols in 1970 listing. Starting serial number (1973): (four-door) AH4SDD101; (two-door) AH2DDD101. Starting serial number (1974): (four-door) AH4SDE101; (GT) AH2DDE102.

Model	Body Type & Seating	Engine Type/CID	P.O.E. Price	Weight (lbs.)	Prod. Total
MARINA					
	2-dr GT Sedan-4P	I4/110	2675	2156	N/A
	4-dr Sedan-4P	I4/110	2625	2193	N/A

ENGINE DATA: BASE FOUR: Inline, overhead-valve four-cylinder. Cast iron block and head. **Displacement:** 109.7 cu. in. (1798 cc). **Bore & Stroke:** 3.16 x 3.50 in. (80.3 x 88.9 mm). **Compression Ratio:** 8.0:1. **Brake Horsepower:** 68.5 (SAE) at 5000 rpm. **Torque:** 87 lbs.-ft. (SAE) at 2750 rpm. Three main bearings. Solid valve lifters. One SU HIF 6 carburetor. 12-volt electrical.

CHASSIS DATA: **Wheelbase:** 96.0 in. **Overall Length:** (2-dr) 166.12 in.; (4-dr) 169.12 in. **Height:** (2-dr) 55.1 in.; (4-dr) 55.98 in. **Width:** (2-dr) 64.61 in.; (4-dr) 64.81 in. **Front Tread:** 52.0 in. **Rear Tread:** 52.0 in. **Wheel Type:** pressed steel. **Standard Tires:** 155x13 radial.

TECHNICAL: **Layout:** front-engine, rear-drive. **Transmission:** four-speed manual, all-synchromesh; floor lever. Three-speed Borg-Warner Model 35 automatic optional. **Standard Final Drive Ratio:** (manual) 3.636:1. **Steering:** rack and pinion. **Suspension (front):** independent; torsion bars with lever shock absorbers. **Suspension (rear):** semi-elliptic leaf springs. **Brakes:** front disc, rear drum, power-assisted. **Body Construction:** pressed steel unibody.

MAJOR OPTIONS: Automatic transmission ($195). Air conditioning ($340). AM, AM/FM or AM/FM stereo radio. Whitewall tires ($30). Electrically-heated rear window ($36). Wheel trim rims. Rubber floor mats. Front mud flaps. Wood- or leather-covered gearshift knob.

PERFORMANCE: **Top Speed:** 97 mph. **Acceleration (0-60 mph):** 14 sec. **Fuel Mileage:** 22-28 mpg (average).

Manufacturer: British Leyland Motors Corp., Longbridge, Birmingham, England.

Importer: British Leyland Motors, Inc., Leonia, New Jersey.

HISTORY: Introduced: February 22, 1973.

1975 AUSTIN

MARINA — FOUR — This was the final year for Austins in America. At the front of the hood, on the driver's side, 'Marina' script replaced the former 'Austin' lettering. The price was later cut as low as $2499.

I.D. DATA: Serial number is in the same location as 1973-74. Starting serial number: (four-door) AH4SDF100M; (GT) AH2DDF101M.

Model	Body Type & Seating	Engine Type/CID	P.O.E. Price	Weight (lbs.)	Prod. Total
MARINA					
	2-dr GT Sedan-4P	I4/110	3150	2156	N/A
	4-dr Sedan-4P	I4/110	3100	2193	N/A

ENGINE DATA: Same as 1973-74.

CHASSIS DATA: Same as 1973-74.

TECHNICAL: Same as 1973-74.

MAJOR OPTIONS: Similar to 1973-74.

PERFORMANCE: Similar to 1973-74.

POSTSCRIPT: Austins continued in production in Britain after exports to America ceased, though most models were also sold under other nameplates. That had been the case ever since the formation of British Motor Corporation (BMC). Rather than abandon the Austin name, the parent company decided in 1982 to transform BL Cars Ltd. (British Leyland) into the Austin Rover Group Ltd.

AUSTIN-HEALEY

As its name suggests, the renowned Austin-Healey sports car was the product of two very different companies. During the late 1940s, Austin became known to American motorists as a major British producer of quaint little sedans, long popular in England and gaining surprising favor on the west side of the Atlantic. Donald Healey's operation was far smaller (see separate Healey listing). It evolved from his experience in the 1930s as a racer and engineer, and his role as technical director at the Triumph organization, as well as that of a low-volume manufacturer. After the war, Healey had begun to build sports cars powered by Riley engines in his shop at Warwick (most notably, the Silverstone). In 1952, British Motor Corporation (which produced the Austin) held a competition for a design of a new sports car, which would use components from Austin vehicles. Healey's "Hundred" won the competition, receiving an award at the 1952 Earl's Court (London) motor show. Before production began at Longbridge, Birmingham, the car was renamed Austin-Healey by Leonard Lord, head of BMC.

The new sports car went into production in spring 1953, selling in Britain for 1323 pounds (Sterling). Within a few months, the price was cut by 100 pounds. Powerplant was the 2660-cc four from the Austin A90 Atlantic, rated 90 horsepower. Because sales of that model had never reached the anticipated level, plenty of engines happened to be on hand to slip beneath the bonnet of the sports car's hood. Austin-Healeys soon became popular in America, as a result of their reasonable price and attractive appearance, coupled with a tough and well-proven engine. Servicing was available at Austin dealers throughout the U.S. The same basic body and chassis was used for the next decade and a half, through the big Austin-Healey's final season in 1967. A six-cylinder edition debuted in 1956, followed by 2+2 variants of the original two-seater; and a bigger six-cylinder powerplant for the 3000 series. Meanwhile, in 1958, the small Sprite version appeared as a complement to the big Healeys. That one attracted its own legion of fans in original "bugeye" form and, to a lesser extent, the restyled Mark II/III/IV versions. MG put out its own version of the Sprite (called Midget), but the big Austin-Healeys were in a class by themselves.

Engine Note: Publicized horsepower/torque values (and other specifications) for Austin-Healeys, especially the later models, were even less uniform than for most other European makes. Thus, figures in U.S. trade and consumer publications may vary slightly from those shown below.

1953-54 AUSTIN-HEALEY

1954 Austin-Healey 100/4 roadster.

"100" (BN1) — FOUR — Austin-Healey's "envelope" style two-seater body, with beautifully smooth and flowing lines, was welded to the frame. A shell-shaped grille was made up of thin vertical bars. Small round parking lights stood directly below the built-in round headlamps. At the rear were tiny round taillamps, just above the bumper. The lid on the full trunk had exposed hinges. Full wheel openings were used at both front and rear. Beneath the bonnet, the 2660-cc Austin A90 Atlantic engine was rated 90 horsepower at 4000 rpm. The transmission also came from the Austin A90, but with its 1st gear eliminated. Instead, a Laycock de Normanville overdrive unit was added, which operated in each gear. Overdrive activated at 40 mph when the switch was turned on.

Though rather shallow, the trunk did hold a modest amount of luggage. Standard equipment for full weather protection included a heater, disappearing top and "Perspex" detachable side curtains (no wind-up windows). Outer fender sections were easy to remove from the body, which included a fold-back adjustable one-piece windshield. Ground clearance was minimal, especially with the car's low-riding exhaust system, which often led to problems. The instrument panel held a 6000-rpm tachometer and 120-mph speedometer, and the steering wheel was adjustable. Bucket seats were provided for driver and passenger, the latter shaped to hold the rider in position through hard cornering. The gas filler nozzle was inside the trunk.

American enthusiasts loved the new sports roadster. "It's Really That Good," trumpeted the headline on the *Motor Trend* road test in November 1953. One of the magazine's editors noted that it was "light and short, making it easy for both the sports car enthusiast and the housewife to drive," with handling "good enough for even the most ardent driver." The brochure distributed at 1953 motor shows announced that Austin-Healey was for "the enthusiast who wants quality," targeting "the skilled driver who wishes to practice the exciting art of fast motoring."

1954 Austin-Healey 100/4. (Coys of Kensington)

I.D. DATA: An identification plate is attached to the right front door pillar. The chassis number consists of three letters and one (or two) figures, followed by the serial number. First letter denotes make ('H' = Healey). Second letter indicates engine size ('B' = 2000-2999 cc. Letter three indicates body type: 'J' = convertible; 'N' = 2-seat Tourer. The next digit indicates series (if any), to denote a major change. An additional prefix letter ('L') indicates left-hand drive. This numbering system is used on Austin-Healeys (and other BMC vehicles) into the 1960s.

The engine number is stamped on a pad on the right side of the block, above the oil filter, just below No. 1 spark plug. It consists of one or two digits followed by a series of letters and then by the sequential serial number. The first letter denotes engine size ('26' = 2600 cc). The next letter indicates make ('A' = Austin). The following letters indicates transmission type ('R' = Laycock de Normanville overdrive; 'U' = manual (floor) shift. One or two letters following the serial number may identify an engine with oversize bore and/or undersize crankshaft journals.

Starting chassis serial number: 133134. Engine number prefix: 1B.

Model	Body Type & Seating	Engine Type/CID	P.O.E. Price	Weight (lbs.)	Prod. Total
100 (BN1)	2-dr Spt Rdstr-2P	I4/162	2985	2015	10,688

Production Note: Production shown is for entire model run, through fall 1955.

Weight Note: At introduction time, the factory announced weights of 1,900 pounds (dry) and 2,176 pounds (curb, but without fuel).

ENGINE DATA: BASE FOUR: Inline, overhead-valve four-cylinder (BN1). Cast iron block and head. **Displacement:** 162.2 cu. in. (2660 cc). **Bore & Stroke:** 3.4375 x 4.375 in. (87.3 x 111.1 mm). **Compression Ratio:** 7.5:1. **Brake Horsepower:** 90 at 4000 rpm. **Torque:** 144 lbs.-ft. at 2000 rpm. Three main bearings. Solid valve lifters. Two SU H4 carburetors. 12-volt electrical system (two 6-volt batteries).

CHASSIS DATA: **Wheelbase:** 90 in. **Overall Length:** 151.5 in. **Height:** 49 in. **Width:** 60 in. **Front Tread:** 48.8 in. **Rear Tread:** 49.5 in. **Wheel Type:** wire-spoke knock-on (centerlock). **Standard Tires:** 5.90x15 (or 6.00x15).

TECHNICAL: **Layout:** front-engine, rear-drive. **Transmission:** three-speed manual (floor lever) with overdrive on 2nd and 3rd gears. Overall gear ratios without overdrive: (1st) 9.28:1; (2nd) 5.85:1; (3rd) 4.125:1; (rev) 20.53:1. Ratios with overdrive engaged: (1st) 7.00:1; (2nd) 4.42:1; (3rd) 3.12:1. **Standard Final Drive Ratio:** 4.125:1 (3.66:1 without overdrive). **Steering:** Burman cam and lever. **Suspension (front):** coil springs and anti-roll (torsion) bar. **Suspension (rear):** rigid axle with semi-elliptic leaf springs and anti-sway (track) bar. **Brakes:** Girling hydraulic, front/rear drum. **Body Construction:** steel body panels welded to frame (early test cars had all-aluminum panels).

MAJOR OPTIONS: Overdrive. Higher axle ratio. Alfin brake drums.

PERFORMANCE: **Top Speed:** 103-111 mph. **Acceleration (0-60 mph):** 10.5 seconds (0-80 mph in 18 seconds). **Acceleration (quarter-mile):** 17.5-18.5 seconds. **Fuel Mileage:** up to 25 mpg (factory).

PRODUCTION/SALES: More than half of all Austin-Healeys were shipped to the United States. Approximately 2,003 found U.S. customers during 1954 alone.

Manufacturer: The Austin Motor Co. Ltd., Longbridge, Birmingham, England; associated with Donald Healey Motor Co. Ltd., Warwick, England.

Distributor: Austin Motor Co. Ltd., New York or San Francisco.

HISTORY: "It's fast! It's dependable! It's record-breaking!" So read the sales brochure at the London Motor Show in October 1953, pointing out that 142.636-mph speed over a measured mile that a modified Austin-Healey 100, driven by none other than Donald Healey, eked out at the Bonneville Salt Flats in Utah. The brochure (and subsequent ads) further pointed to the hundred "Class D" records the car had broken, for both speed and endurance. Another Austin-Healey, modified for high altitude, averaged 122.03 mph over a 2,000-mile run. And a stock model averaged 104.3 mph for 24 straight hours.

The prototype appeared at the London Motor Show in late 1952, and production began in spring 1953. Two examples were hastily assembled to appear at the International Motor Sports Show in New York City that year. Bodies were later built by Richard and Alan Jensen at their West Bromwich facility, from a design by Donald Healey (but modified a bit by the Tickford firm). U.S. customers planning to travel abroad were advised that they could purchase an Austin-Healey at home but accept delivery in England.

Because the basic engine had fairly modest compression (7.5:1), considerable modification was possible to boost its output. In fact, the Austin company provided such a kit on special order. Gaining 15 percent more power was reasonable by boosting the compression ratio, installing a special camshaft, and modifying the carburetion and ignition.

1955 AUSTIN-HEALEY

PERFORMANCE: Top Speed: 106-111 mph (100M, 109-118 mph; 100S, 126+ mph). **Acceleration (0-60 mph):** 10.5 seconds; (100M) 9.6 sec.; (100S) 7.8 sec.. **Acceleration (quarter-mile):** 17.5-18.5 seconds. **Fuel Mileage:** 25 mpg average (factory).

Manufacturer: The Austin Motor Co. Ltd., Longbridge, Birmingham, England.

Distributor: Austin of England, New York or San Francisco.

HISTORY: A 100S placed third at the Sebring 12-Hour Race in 1954. And a streamlined evolution of that car, carrying a 224-bhp supercharged engine, hit 192 mph on the Bonneville Salt Flats.

1955 Austin-Healey 100/4 BN1 roadster. (Christie's)

"100" (BN1/BN2) — FOUR — Except for the substitution of a four-speed gearbox (with manually-activated overdrive) for the original three-speed in the BN2 evolution, which arrived late in 1955, the basic Austin-Healey continued as before. Standard equipment included overdrive, heater, defroster, twin carburetors, and knock-on wire wheels. *Motor Trend* noted that the Austin-Healey delivered "pool table flat cornering (and) stable four-foot roadability." Development of peak torque at only 2,000 rpm also gave it swift acceleration through the gears, while tight steering (2.5 turns lock-to-lock) enhanced its handling powers. An almost even weight distribution (49/51) also helped performance.

1955 Austin-Healey 100/4. (Coy's of Kensington)

100M — FOUR — Arriving late in 1955, a higher-powered version of the basic roadster, with Le Mans engine modification kit, developed 110 horsepower rather than the usual 90. See next listing for further details.

100S (AHS) — FOUR — A racing 100S (S = Sebring) was developed by the Healey firm rather than Austin. Its stripped-down aluminum body wore no bumpers, and the much-modified engine with Weslake cylinder head developed 132 horsepower. Disc brakes were used all around. Only 50 were built during 1955.

I.D. DATA: Serial number and engine number are in same location as 1953-54. Starting serial number: (BN2) 228047; (100S) 3501.

Model	Body Type & Seating	Engine Type/CID	P.O.E. Price	Weight (lbs.)	Prod. Total
100 (BN1)	2-dr Spt Rdstr-2P	I4/162	2985	2150	10,688
100 (BN2)	2-dr Spt Rdstr-2P	I4/162	2985	2168	3,924
100M (BN2)	2-dr Spt Rdstr-2P	I4/162	3275	2170	1,159
100S	2-dr Spt Rdstr-2P	I4/162	4995	1960	50

Note: Production totals include the entire BN2 run, through summer 1956. The original BN1 continued in production into 1955.

ENGINE DATA: BASE FOUR: Inline, overhead-valve four-cylinder. Cast iron block and head. **Displacement:** 162.2 cu. in. (2660 cc). **Bore & Stroke:** 3.4375 x 4.375 in. (87.3 x 111.1 mm). **Compression Ratio:** 7.5:1 except (100M) 8.1:1; (100S) 8.3:1. **Brake Horsepower:** 90 at 4000 rpm except (100M) 110 at 4500; (100S) 132 at 4700. **Torque:** 150 lbs.-ft. at 2000 rpm except (100M) 150 at 2200; (100S) 168 at 2500. Three main bearings. Solid valve lifters. Two SU H4 carburetors. 12-volt electrical.

CHASSIS DATA: Wheelbase: 90 in. **Overall Length:** 151.5 in. except (100S) 148 in. **Height:** 49 in. **Width:** 60 in. **Front Tread:** 48.8 in. **Rear Tread:** 49.5 in. **Wheel Type:** wire-spoke knock-on (center-lock). **Standard Tires:** 5.90x15 except (100S) 5.50x15.

TECHNICAL: Layout: front-engine, rear-drive. **Transmission:** (BN2) four-speed manual (floor lever) with manual overdrive. **Standard Final Drive Ratio:** 3.667:1 (100S, 2.92:1). **Steering:** Burman cam and lever. **Suspension (front):** coil springs and anti-roll (torsion) bar. **Suspension (rear):** rigid axle with semi-elliptic leaf springs and anti-sway (track) bar. **Brakes:** Girling hydraulic, front/rear drum except (100S) disc brakes. **Body Construction:** steel body welded to frame except (100S) lightweight aluminum body.

1956-57 AUSTIN-HEALEY

1956 Austin-Healey 100/4 BN2 roadster. (Sportscar)

"100" (BN2) — FOUR — Production of the four-cylinder roadster continued into 1956, in BN2 form with the four-speed gearbox; see previous listing for additional details.

100M (BN2) — FOUR — A separate price was quoted in 1956 for the version with a Le Mans modification kit, which boosted horsepower to 110 and torque to 154 pound-feet. That kit consisted of 8:1 compression pistons, a high-lift camshaft, different carburetors and intake manifold, modified distributor, louvered hood (with strap), and a racing roll bar.

100-6 (BN4) — SIX — The new six-cylinder Austin-Healey debuted by September 1956, riding a slightly longer wheelbase. Two tiny back seats were added, suitable for children. Other modifications went into the cockpit, grille, and trim elements. The 2639-cc BMC C-series engine was rated 102 horsepower; but since the car itself gained several hundred pounds, performance slipped down a hair. Displacement was actually a tad smaller than the earlier four-cylinder powerplant. This was the four-port version of the engine; a six-port edition of the cylinder head would come later. A four-speed gearbox was standard, with overdrive optional. In addition to the engine change, the second-generation Austin-Healey had a new hood with an airscoop, plus a new horizontal oval-shaped grille, which almost came to a point at its outer ends and was dominated by horizontal bars (with three vertical-bar separators). A winged insignia stood just to the rear of the grille, ahead of the hood. Weatherproofing improvements included the addition of a fixed windshield and the use of rubber channels in its pillars to mate with rubber flanges on the side curtains. The folding top had a larger plastic back window. Doors now had locking outside handles. Inside was a padded dashboard, with an armrest between the two front seats. As before, the steering column was adjustable. The car's battery was mounted in the trunk, along with the spare tire, leaving little room for luggage. The gas filler nozzle was no longer inside the trunk, but mounted on the rear deck.

1957 Austin-Healey 100-6.

I.D. DATA: Serial number and engine number are in same location as 1953-55. Starting serial number: 50769. Engine prefix (100-6): C26.

Model	Body Type & Seating	Engine Type/CID	P.O.E. Price	Weight (lbs.)	Prod. Total
FOUR-CYLINDER					
100 (BN2)	2-dr Spt Rds-2P	I4/162	2985	2200	Note 1
100M (BN2)	2-dr LeMans Rds-2P	I4/162	3275	2200	Note 1
SIX-CYLINDER					
100-6 (BN4)	2-dr Spt Rds-2 + 2P	I6/161	3195	2436	10,826

Note 1: See 1955 listing for complete production figures.

100-6 Production Note: Figure shown is for complete run of the BN4 version, from August 1956 to March 1959.

ENGINE DATA: BASE FOUR (100): Inline, overhead-valve four-cylinder. Cast iron block and head. **Displacement:** 162.2 cu. in. (2660 cc). **Bore & Stroke:** 3.4375 x 4.375 in. (87.3 x 111.1 mm). **Compression Ratio:** 7.5:1 except (100M) 8:1. **Brake Horsepower:** 90 at 4000 rpm except (100M) 110 at 4500. **Torque:** 150 lbs.-ft. at 2000 rpm except (100M) 150 at 2200. Three main bearings. Solid valve lifters. Two SU H4 carburetors. 12-volt electrical.

BASE SIX (100-6): Inline, ohv six-cylinder (four-port head). Cast iron block and head. **Displacement:** 161 cu. in. (2639 cc). **Bore & Stroke:** 3.125 x 3.50 in. (79.4 x 88.9 mm). **Compression Ratio:** 8.26:1. **Brake Horsepower:** 102 at 4600 rpm. **Torque:** 142 lbs.-ft. at 2400 rpm. Four main bearings. Solid valve lifters. Two SU H4 carburetors. 12-volt electrical.

CHASSIS DATA: Wheelbase: (100) 90 in.; (100-6) 92 in. **Overall Length:** (100) 151 in.; (100-6) 157.5 in. **Height:** 49 in. **Width:** (100) 60 in.; (100-6) 60.5 in. **Front Tread:** (100) 49 in.; (100-6) 48.8 in. **Rear Tread:** (100) 50.8 in.; (100-6) 50 in. **Wheel Type:** ventilated press steel disc (knock-on wire wheels available). **Standard Tires:** 5.90x15.

TECHNICAL: Layout: front-engine, rear-drive. **Transmission:** four-speed manual with overdrive (floor lever). **Standard Final Drive Ratio:** 3.91:1. **Steering:** cam and lever. **Suspension (front):** coil springs and anti-roll (torsion) bar. **Suspension (rear):** rigid axle with semi-elliptical leaf springs and anti-sway (track) bar. **Brakes:** Girling hydraulic, front/rear drum. **Body Construction:** steel body welded to frame.

PERFORMANCE: Top Speed: (100-6) 104 mph. **Acceleration (0-60 mph):** (100) 10.5 sec.; (100M Le Mans) 8.2 sec.; (100-6) 12.9 sec. **Acceleration (quarter-mile):** (100) 17.5 sec.; (100M Le Mans) 16.0 sec.; (100-6) 18.9 sec.

PRODUCTION/SALES: A total of 57,352 six-cylinder Austin-Healeys were built, from 1956 to 1967.

Manufacturer: The Austin Motor Co. Ltd., Longbridge, Birmingham, England.

Distributor: Hambro Automotive Corp,, New York City.

HISTORY: "Rarin' to go," read the ads for the new Austin-Healey 100-Six, "either in competition or just for a family holiday spin." The "maneuverability and eager response of this powerful, road-hugging thoroughbred is so fast and sure you'll wonder if it's reading your mind." The six-cylinder model was introduced in August 1956. In the fall of 1957, Austin-Healey assembly shifted to the MG plant at Abingdon, and the six-port engine rated 117 horsepower was added (see next listing).

1958 AUSTIN-HEALEY

1958 Austin-Healey 100-6 roadster.

SPRITE — FOUR — A completely different Austin-Healey emerged in 1958, considerably smaller in size as well as power. Affectionately called the "bugeye" Sprite in the U.S. ("frogeye" in Britain) because of its protruding headlamps atop the hood, the tiny two-seater used components from the little Austin A35 sedan. A lightweight steel unibody (just 2,460 pounds at the curb) combined with the 948-cc BMC A-series four-cylinder engine, rated 43 horsepower, to deliver good performance, complemented by direct (tight) steering. The car's rack-and-pinion steering, brakes and rear axle stemmed from the Morris Minor. A rather small oval grille contained a tight crosshatch mesh, surrounded by a heavy bright molding. A small round emblem stood just to the rear of the grille. For engine access, the entire front end (including fenders) hinged upward. No external trunk access was provided, but seats folded down to gain entry into the storage space. The cockpit was basic but nicely finished, holding a leather-covered dashboard and leather upholstery. A tachometer was optional, and a detachable hardtop became available before long.

100-6 (BN4/BN6) — SIX — While production continued of the four-port engine, a new six-port version brought a leap from the original 102 up to 117 horsepower. The increase resulted from the new cylinder head with six separate ports for intake and exhaust, mated to a new cast aluminum intake manifold. Carburetor throats and the valves themselves also grew larger this time around. A two-seater body (BN6) also became available again, offered along with the 2 + 2 version (BN4). Bodily changes were minimal, including the fact that the back half of the plastic window in the car's side curtain now slid forward instead of toward the rear. Two models were available. The standard model came with disc wheels, and only two options: a heater and tonneau cover. The deluxe model included wire wheels, turn signals, heater, telescopic steering column, tonneau cover, and overdrive. A hardtop was optional.

I.D. DATA: Serial number is located on right side of firewall except (Sprite) left side of front fender well. Engine number is on left side of block except (Sprite) top right side of block. Serial number: (Sprite) H-AN5-501 to H-AN5-50116. Engine prefix: (100-6 BN6) 26D.

Model	Body Type & Seating	Engine Type/CID	P.O.E. Price	Weight (lbs.)	Prod. Total
SPRITE					
AN5	2-dr Roadster-2P	I4/58	1795	1316	8,279
100-6					
BN4	2-dr Spt Rds-2 + 2P	I6/161	2919	2436	Note 1
BN4	2-dr DeL Rds-2 + 2P	I6/161	3195	2436	Note 1
BN6	2-dr Spt rds-2P	I6/161	3087	2436	Note 2
BN6	2-dr DeL Rds-2P	I6/161	3389	2436	Note 2

Note 1: Total BN4 production from 1956-59 was 10,826 units.

Note 2: Total BN6 production through 1959 was 4,150 units.

ENGINE DATA: BASE FOUR (Sprite): Inline, overhead-valve four-cylinder. Cast iron block and head. **Displacement:** 57.8 cu. in. (948 cc). **Bore & Stroke:** 2.478 x 3.00 in. (62.9 x 76.2 mm). **Compression Ratio:** 8.3:1. **Brake Horsepower:** 42.5 at 5000 rpm. **Torque:** 52 lbs.-ft. at 3300 rpm. Three main bearings. Solid valve lifters. Two SU H1 carburetors. 12-volt electrical.

BASE SIX (early 100-6): Inline, ohv six-cylinder (four-port head). Cast iron block and head. **Displacement:** 161 cu. in. (2639 cc). **Bore & Stroke:** 3.125 x 3.50 in. (79.4 x 88.9 mm). **Compression Ratio:** 8.25:1. **Brake Horsepower:** 102 at 4600 rpm. **Torque:** 142 lbs.-ft. at 2400 rpm. Four main bearings. Solid valve lifters. Two SU H4 carburetors. 12-volt electrical.

BASE SIX (100-6) Inline, overhead-valve six-cylinder (six-port). Cast iron block and head. **Displacement:** 161 cu. in. (2639 cc). **Bore & Stroke:** 3.125 x 3.50 in. (79.4 x 88.9 mm). **Compression Ratio:** 8.7:1. **Brake Horsepower:** 117 at 4750 rpm. **Torque:** 150 lbs.-ft. at 3000 rpm. Four main bearings. Solid valve lifters. Two SU HD6 carburetors. 12-volt electrical.

CHASSIS DATA: Wheelbase: (Sprite) 80 in.; (100) 92 in. **Overall Length:** (Sprite) 132.6 in.; (100) 157.5 in. **Height:** (Sprite) 49.8 in.; (100) 49 in. **Width:** (Sprite) 53 in.; (100) 60.5 in. **Front Tread:** (Sprite) 45.8 in.; (100) 48.8 in. **Rear Tread:** (Sprite) 44.8 in.; (100) 50.0 in. **Wheel Type:** (Sprite) disc; (100 std) disc; (100 DeL) wire. **Standard Tires:** (Sprite) 5.20x13 or 145SR13; (100) 5.90x15.

TECHNICAL: Layout: front-engine, rear-drive. **Transmission:** four-speed manual (floor lever). Sprite overall gear ratios: (1st) 15.3:1; (2nd) 10.0:1; (3rd) 5.96:1; (4th) 4.22:1. 100-6 gear ratios: (1st) 3.08:1; (2nd) 1.91:1; (3rd) 1.33:1; (4th) 1:1; (overdrive) 0.78:1. **Standard Final Drive Ratio:** (Sprite) 4.22:1; (100-6) 4.10:1. **Steering:** (Sprite) rack and pinion; (100) cam and lever. **Suspension (front):** (Sprite) upper/lower A-arms with coil springs; (100) wishbones with coil springs. **Suspension (rear):** (Sprite) double trailing links with quarter-elliptic leaf springs and lever-type shock absorbers; (100) rigid axle, semi-elliptic leaf springs. **Brakes:** hydraulic, front/rear drum. **Body Construction:** (Sprite) unibody; (100) separate body and frame.

MAJOR OPTIONS: (Sprite) Heater ($55.75). Tachometer ($13.75). Windshield washer ($6.25). Tonneau cover ($19.95). (100-6) Hardtop ($239). Heater ($55); but included in DeLuxe model.

PERFORMANCE: Top Speed: (Sprite) 83 mph; (100) 104 mph. **Acceleration (0-60 mph):** (Sprite) 20.2-20.9 sec.; (100) 10.2-11.6 sec. **Acceleration (quarter-mile):** (Sprite) 21.6-22.5 sec.; (100) 17-18.2 sec. (75-76 mph). **Fuel Mileage:** (Sprite) 27.5 mpg overall; (100) 27 mpg.

PRODUCTION/SALES: A total of 129,354 Sprites were produced from 1958 to 1971 (not including the similar MG Midget). Approximately 5,446 Austin-Healeys were sold in the U.S. in 1958.

Manufacturer: The Austin Motor Co. Ltd., Longbridge, Birmingham, England.

Distributor: Hambro Automotive Corp,, New York City; also two distributors in California.

HISTORY: The Healey organization was commissioned by BMC chairman Sir Leonard Lord to design the Sprite as a "back to basics" companion to the latest MG. Production began in mid-1958. The name had been used before the war on a Riley model. Sprite was the first British sports car to use unibody construction.

1959-60 AUSTIN-HEALEY

SPRITE — FOUR — Production of the tiny two-seater continued with little change.

100-6 (BN4/BN6) — SIX — Production of the first six-cylinder Austin-Healey continued into 1959, until it was replaced by the new 3000.

3000 (BN7/BT7) — SIX — In spring of 1959, the engine of the "Big Healey" grew to 2912-cc displacement, hence the new designation. Front disc brakes also were added. The new engine developed 124 bhp (seven more than before), able to deliver a top speed around 115 mph. Power would grow in jumps over the next eight years of the car's life, eventually reaching 148 bhp. Two body styles were available: a two-seater BN7 and a BT7 with 2 + 2 capacity. While carrying on the same oval shape as its predecessor, the 3000's grille switched to vertical bars for its pattern. As before, small round parking lights stood directly below the round headlamps, and the hood carried an airscoop with vertical-bar pattern at its leading edge. Pointed round taillamps were just above the back bumper, with smaller round lenses higher up on the deck. As before, the trunk lid had exposed hinges. Both standard and DeLuxe models were available.

1959 Austin-Healey "Bugeye" Sprite roadster.

1960 Austin-Healey "Bugeye" Sprite roadster.

I.D. DATA: Serial number is located on right side of firewall except (Sprite) left side of front fender well. Engine number is on left side of block except (Sprite) top right side of block. Starting serial number: (Sprite) see prior listing; (3000) 101. Starting engine number: (3000) 29D-U-H101.

Model	Body Type & Seating	Engine Type/CID	P.O.E. Price	Weight (lbs.)	Prod. Total
SPRITE					
AN5	2-dr Roadster-2P	I4/58	1795	1316	Note 1
100-6					
BN4	2-dr Spt Rds-2 + 2P	I6/161	2919	2436	Note 2
BN4	2-dr DeL Rds-2 + 2P	I6/161	3195	2436	Note 2
BN6	2-dr Spt Rds-2P	I6/161	3087	2436	Note 2
BN6	2-dr DeL Rds-2P	I6/161	3389	2436	Note 2
3000 (Mk I)					
BN7	2-dr DeL Rdstr-2P	I6/178	3371	2465	2,825
BT7	2-dr Spt Rdstr-2 + 2P	I6/178	3051	2465	10,825
BT7	2-dr DeL Rdstr-2 + 2P	I6/178	3371	2465	Note 3

Note 1: A total of 21,566 Sprites were produced in 1959, and 18,665 in 1960.

Note 2: See previous listing.

Note 3: Included in basic BT7 total. Both production figures shown are for full model run of the Mk I, from 1959 to 1961.

ENGINE DATA: BASE FOUR (Sprite): Inline, overhead-valve four-cylinder. Cast iron block and head. **Displacement:** 57.8 cu. in. (948 cc). **Bore & Stroke:** 2.478 x 3.00 in. (62.9 x 76.2 mm). **Compression Ratio:** 8.3:1. **Brake Horsepower:** 42.5 at 5000 rpm. **Torque:** 52 lbs.-ft. at 3300 rpm. Three main bearings. Solid valve lifters. Two SU H1 carburetors. 12-volt electrical.

BASE SIX (100-6) Inline, overhead-valve six-cylinder (six-port). Cast iron block and head. **Displacement:** 161 cu. in. (2639 cc). **Bore & Stroke:** 3.125 x 3.50 in. (79.4 x 88.9 mm). **Compression Ratio:** 8.7:1. **Brake Horsepower:** 117 at 4750 rpm. **Torque:** 150 lbs.-ft. at 3000 rpm. Four main bearings. Solid valve lifters. Two SU HD6 carburetors. 12-volt electrical.

BASE SIX (3000): Inline, overhead-valve six-cylinder. Cast iron block and head. **Displacement:** 177.7 cu. in. (2912 cc). **Bore & Stroke:** 3.282 x 3.50 in. (83.3 x 88.9 mm). **Compression Ratio:** 9.1:1. **Brake Horsepower:** 124 at 4600 rpm. **Torque:** 162 lbs.-ft. at 2700 rpm. Four main bearings. Solid valve lifters. Two SU HD6 carburetors. 12-volt electrical.

CHASSIS DATA: Wheelbase: (Sprite) 80 in.; (100/3000) 92 in. **Overall Length:** (Sprite) 132.6 in.; (100/3000) 157.5 in. **Height:** (Sprite) 49.8 in.; (100/3000) 49 in. **Width:** (Sprite) 53 in.; (100/3000) 60.5 in. **Front Tread:** (Sprite) 45.8 in.; (100/3000) 48.75 in. **Rear Tread:** (Sprite) 44.8 in.; (100/3000) 50 in. **Standard Tires:** (Sprite) 5.20x13; (100) 5.90x15; (3000) 5.90x15.

TECHNICAL: Layout: front-engine, rear-drive. **Transmission:** four-speed manual (floor lever). **Standard Final Drive Ratio:** (Sprite) 4.22:1; (100-6) 4.10:1; (3000) 3.91:1. **Steering:** (Sprite) rack and pinion; (100/3000) cam and peg. **Suspension (front):** (Sprite) upper/lower A-arms with coil springs; (100/3000) wishbones with coil springs. **Suspension (rear):** (Sprite) double trailing links with quarter-elliptic leaf springs; (100/3000) rigid axle, semi-elliptic leaf springs. **Brakes:** hydraulic, front/rear drum except (3000) front disc, rear drum. **Body Construction:** (Sprite) unibody; (100/3000) separate body and frame.

MAJOR OPTIONS: (3000) Overdrive.

PERFORMANCE: Top Speed: 85 mph; (3000) 112-115 mph. **Acceleration (0-60 mph):** (3000) 9.8-11.4 sec. **Acceleration (quarter-mile):** (3000) 17.9 sec.

PRODUCTION/SALES: Approximately 16,564 Austin-Healeys were sold in the U.S. during 1959.

HISTORY: Introduced: (3000) spring 1959. K.N. Rudd (Engineers) Ltd. in England marketed a modification kit with three SU carburetors on a special intake manifold, to give the 3000 a considerable horsepower/torque boost.

1961 AUSTIN-HEALEY

1961 Austin-Healey 3000 Mark I roadster. (Sotheby's)

SPRITE — FOUR — Production of the original Sprite continued into 1961, when it was replaced by the Mk II version.

SPRITE Mk II — FOUR — The second-generation Sprite had a restyled body that gave it a more ordinary appearance. The squared-off front end held a rectangular grille with crosshatch mesh pattern. Rectangular parking lights (with rounded top edges) stood below the conventional fender-mounted round headlamps; the distinctive "bugeye" headlamps were gone. Fenders now bolted in position, and the rear-hinged hood raised by itself in the ordinary fashion, leaving the fenders stable. The back end, too, displayed an ordinary appearance with a standard lockable trunk lid. Under the hood was the same 948-cc four-cylinder engine, with a modest horsepower increase resulting in a rise in compression ratio (from 8.3:1 to 9:1). Other engine modifications included a revised intake-valve opening, bigger intake valves, double valve springs, and larger-throat SU carburetors. A close-ratio four-speed gearbox was installed, along with front disc brakes. Also improved was the weatherproofing of the folding top, using a metal-back overlap joint along the windshield top, along with sliding plastic side windows. Inside, bucket seats were upholstered in plastic. The new MG Midget (see MG listing) was no more than a "badge-engineered" version of the same car, and usually sold better than Sprite.

3000 — SIX — Production of the original 3000 continued into 1961, when it was replaced by the Mk II version.

3000 Mk II — SIX — Little change was evident on the 3000's body in its second generation, but the engine added eight horsepower as a result of the addition of an extra carburetor. Performance showed little, if any, improvement. The gearshift linkage also was modified, but the triple-carb setup lasted only one year. As before, both two-seater and 2 + 2 versions were available.

I.D. DATA: Serial number is located on right side of firewall except (Sprite) left side of front fender well. Engine number is on left side of block except (Sprite) top right side of block. Serial number range: (Sprite Mk II) H-AN6-101 to 24731. Starting serial number: (3000) 101; (3000 Mk II) 13751.

Model	Body Type & Seating	Engine Type/CID	P.O.E. Price	Weight (lbs.)	Prod. Total
SPRITE					
AN5	2-dr Roadster-2P	I4/58	1795	1316	Note 1
SPRITE Mk II					
AN6	2-dr Roadster-2P	I4/58	1868	1450	10,059
3000					
BN7	2-dr DeL Rdstr-2P	I6/178	3371	2465	Note 2
BT7	2-dr Spe Rdstr-2 + 2P	I6/178	3051	2465	Note 2
BT7	2-dr DeL Rdstr-2 + 2P	I6/178	3371	2465	Note 2
3000 Mk II					
BN7	2-dr DeL Rdstr-2P	I6/178	3371	2465	355
BT7	2-dr Spt Rdstr-2 + 2P	I6/178	3051	2465	5,096
BT7	2-dr DeL Rdstr-2 + 2P	I6/178	3371	2465	Note 3

Note 1: Included in Sprite Mk II figure.

Note 2: See previous listing.

Note 3: Included in basic BT7 total; 3000 Mk II production figures shown are for the full model run, 1961-62.

ENGINE DATA: BASE FOUR (Sprite): Same as 1958-60.

BASE FOUR (Sprite MK II): Inline, overhead-valve four-cylinder. Cast iron block and head. **Displacement:** 57.8 cu. in. (948 cc). **Bore & Stroke:** 2.478 x 3.00 in. (62.9 x 76.2 mm). **Compression Ratio:** 9.0:1. **Brake Horsepower:** 46 at 5500 rpm. **Torque:** 53 lbs.-ft. at 2750 rpm. Three main bearings. Solid valve lifters. Two SU HS2 carburetors. 12-volt electrical.

BASE SIX (3000): Same as 1959-60.

BASE SIX (3000 Mk II): Inline, overhead-valve six-cylinder. Cast iron block and head. **Displacement:** 177.7 cu. in. (2912 cc). **Bore & Stroke:** 3.282 x 3.50 in. (83.3 x 88.9 mm). **Compression Ratio:** 9.0:1. **Brake Horsepower:** 132 at 4750 rpm. **Torque:** 167 lbs.-ft. at 3000 rpm. Four main bearings. Solid valve lifters. Three SU HS4 carburetors. 12-volt electrical.

CHASSIS DATA: Wheelbase: (Sprite) 80 in.; (3000) 92 in. **Overall Length:** (Sprite) 132.6 in.; (Sprite Mk II) 137.25 in.; (3000) 157.5 in. **Height:** (Sprite) 49.8 in.; (3000) 49 in. **Width:** (Sprite) 53 in.; (3000) 60.5 in. **Front Tread:** (Sprite) 45.8 in.; (3000) 48.75 in. **Rear Tread:** (Sprite) 44.8 in.; (3000) 50 in. **Standard Tires:** (Sprite) 5.20x13; (3000) 5.90x15.

TECHNICAL: Layout: front-engine, rear-drive. **Transmission:** four-speed manual. **Standard Final Drive Ratio:** (Sprite Mk II) 4.22:1 (3000) 3.91:1. **Steering:** (Sprite) rack and pinion; (3000) cam and peg. **Suspension (front):** (Sprite) upper/lower A-arms with coil springs; (100/3000) wishbones with coil springs. **Suspension (rear):** (Sprite) double trailing links with quarter-elliptic leaf springs; (3000) rigid axle, semi-elliptic leaf springs. **Brankes:** hydraulic, front disc, rear drum. **Body Construction:** (Sprite) unibody; (100/3000) separate body and frame.

PERFORMANCE: Top Speed: (Sprite Mk II) 86 mph; (3000 Mk II) 115 mph. **Acceleration (0-60 mph):** (Sprite Mk II) 19.3 sec.; (3000 Mk II) 9.8-10.8 sec. **Acceleration (quarter-mile):** (Sprite Mk II) 21.4 sec.; (3000 Mk II) 17.4 sec.

PRODUCTION/SALES: Approximately 8,935 Austin-Healeys were sold in the U.S. during 1961.

1962 AUSTIN-HEALEY

1962 Austin-Healey 3000.

SPRITE Mk II — FOUR — For most of the year, the Sprite continued as before in its restyled, square-look form. In the fall, however, the original 948-cc four-cylinder engine was replaced by a 1098-cc version.

3000 Mk II ROADSTER (BN7/BT7) and CONVERTIBLE (BJ7) — SIX — The "3000 Mark II" name continued as in 1961, but during 1962 the big Healey got a restyling that brought a curved windshield and wind-up windows. For that reason, it was now branded a "convertible" rather than a roadster. With that change came a slight horsepower boost. The triple-carb setup was abandoned, replaced by dual SU H6 units that actually produced a modest swiftening of acceleration times. DeLuxe models had such extras as wire wheels, adjustable steering column, and a tonneau cover.

I.D. DATA: Serial number is located on right side of firewall except (Sprite) left side of front fender well. Serial number range: (early Mk II Sprite) H-AN6-101 to 24731; (1098-cc Sprite) H-AN7-24732 to 38828. Starting serial number: (3000 rds, two-seat) HBNMK/13751; (3000 rds, four-seat) HBTMK/13751; (3000 BJ7 conv) HBJ7L/17551. Engine number is on left side of block except (Sprite) top right side of block. Engine number prefix: (3000 Mk II) 29E; (BJ7) 29F.

Model	Body Type & Seating	Engine Type/CID	P.O.E. Price	Weight (lbs.)	Prod. Total
SPRITE Mk II					
AN7	2-dr Roadster-2P	I4/58	1868	1460	12,041
3000 Mk II					
BN7	2-dr DeL Rds-2P	I6/178	3420	2465	Note 1
BT7	2-dr Roadster-2+2P	I6/178	3120	2465	Note 1
BT7	2-dr DeL Rds-2+2P	I6/178	3438	2465	Note 1
BJ7	2-dr Conv-2+2P	I6/178	3231	2380	6,113
BJ7	2-dr DeL Conv-2+2P	I6/178	3535	2380	Note 2

Note 1: See previous listing.
Note 2: Included in basic total. Figure shown is for full BJ7 production run, 1962-64.

ENGINE DATA: BASE FOUR (Sprite): Inline, overhead-valve four-cylinder. Cast iron block and head. **Displacement:** 57.8 cu. in. (948 cc). **Bore & Stroke:** 2.478 x 3.00 in. (62.9 x 76.2 mm). **Compression Ratio:** 9.0:1. **Brake Horsepower:** 46 at 5500 rpm. **Torque:** 53 lbs.-ft. at 2750 rpm. Three main bearings. Solid valve lifters. Two SU HS2 carburetors. 12-volt electrical.

BASE FOUR (late Sprite): Inline, overhead-valve four-cylinder. Cast iron block and head. **Displacement:** 67 cu. in. (1098 cc). **Bore & Stroke:** 2.543 x 3.296 in. (64.6 x 83.7 mm). **Compression Ratio:** 8.9:1. **Brake Horsepower:** 56 at 5500 rpm. Three main bearings. Solid valve lifters. Two SU carburetors. 12-volt electrical.

BASE SIX (3000 Mk II): Inline, overhead-valve six-cylinder. Cast iron block and head. **Displacement:** 177.7 cu. in. (2912 cc). **Bore & Stroke:** 3.282 x 3.50 in. (83.3 x 88.9 mm). **Compression Ratio:** 9.0:1. **Brake Horsepower:** 132 at 4750 rpm (BJ7, 134 at 4750). **Torque:** 167 lbs.-ft. at 3000 rpm (BJ7, 167 at 2700). Four main bearings. Solid valve lifters. Three SU HS4 carburetors (BJ7, two SU H6 carburetors). 12-volt electrical.

CHASSIS DATA: Wheelbase: (Sprite) 80 in.; (3000) 92 in. **Overall Length:** (Sprite) 137.25 in.; (3000) 157.5 in. **Height:** (Sprite) 49.75 in.; (3000) 49 in. **Width:** (Sprite) 53 in.; (3000) 60-60.5 in. **Front Tread:** (Sprite) 45.75 in.; (3000) 48.75 in. **Rear Tread:** (3000) 50 in. **Standard Tires:** (Sprite) 5.20x13; (3000) 5.90x15.

TECHNICAL: Layout: front-engine, rear-drive. **Transmission:** four-speed manual (floor lever). **Standard Final Drive Ratio:** (Sprite) 4.22:1; (3000) 3.91:1. **Steering:** (Sprite) rack and pinion; (3000) cam and peg. **Suspension (front):** (Sprite) upper/lower A-arms with coil springs; (100/3000) wishbones with coil springs. **Suspension (rear):** (Sprite) double trailing links with quarter-elliptic leaf springs; (3000) rigid axle, semi-elliptic leaf springs. **Brakes:** hydraulic, front disc, rear drum. **Body Construction:** (Sprite) unibody; (100/3000) separate body and frame.

MAJOR OPTIONS: Hardtop: 3000 ($95).

PERFORMANCE: Top Speed: (Sprite) 88 mph. **Acceleration (0-60 mph):** (Sprite) 16.8 sec.; (3000 conv) 10.3 sec. **Acceleration (quarter-mile):** (Sprite) 21 sec.; (3000 conv) 17.1 sec.

PRODUCTION/SALES: Approximately 10,019 Austin-Healeys were sold in the U.S. during 1962.

HISTORY: The 1962 model year for U.S. sales began June 15, 1961 except (Sprite) July 1, 1961.

1963 AUSTIN-HEALEY

1963 Austin-Healey 3000 Mark II convertible. (Sotheby's)

SPRITE Mk II — FOUR — Production of the Sprite with larger (1098-cc) engine continued with little change into 1963-64.

3000 Mk II CONVERTIBLE (BJ7) — SIX — Production of the "Big Healey" convertible with roll-up windows continued with little change into 1963-64.

I.D. DATA: Serial number is located on right side of firewall except (Sprite) left side of front fender well. Starting serial number: (Sprite) H-AN7L-24732; (3000) see prior listing. Engine number is on left side of block except (Sprite) top right side of block.

Model	Body & Seating	Engine Type/CID	P.O.E. Price	Weight (lbs.)	Prod. Total
SPRITE Mk II					
AN7	2-dr Roadster-2P	I4/67	1875	1450	8,852
3000 Mk II					
BJ7	2-dr Spt Conv-2+2+	I6/178	3231	2380	Note 1
BJ7	2-dr Spt Conv-2+2P	I6/178	3535	2380	Note 1

Note 1: See previous listing.

ENGINE DATA: Same as 1962.
CHASSIS DATA: Same as 1962.
TECHNICAL: Same as 1962.
PERFORMANCE: Same as 1962.
PRODUCTION/SALES: Approximately 8,348 Austin-Healeys were sold in the U.S. during 1963.

HISTORY: The 1963 model year for U.S. sales began September 1, 1962. An S/S version of the Sprite was described in Hot Rod magazine in 1963. Produced by the Donald Healey Motor Co., it used the 948-cc engine with three-quarter Healey cam and Sebring cylinder head.

1964 AUSTIN-HEALEY

1964 Austin-Healey 3000 Mark II convertible.

SPRITE Mk II — FOUR — Production of the Sprite with 1098-cc engine continued with little change into 1964.

SPRITE Mk III — FOUR — While the engine's size stayed the same in Sprite's next incarnation, horsepower rose from 56 to 59. As for appearance, this version had roll-up windows and hinged "butterfly" vent panes at the windows. Wheels were new, and the cockpit took on additional amenities with a restyled fascia and parcel shelf, and angled instrument dials. Otherwise, appearance was similar to the Mark II, with large vertical taillamps and a rectangular mesh grille. Sprites had locking doors and trunk, the latter with 11.5 cubic-foot cargo capacity and a spare tire that lay flat. At chassis level, the rear suspension switched to semi-elliptic leaf springs. Sprite's soft top with collapsible frame could be removed completely. A chrome frame held the curved windshield. Wraparound front/rear bumpers held standard overriders. The company described the car as "A winner on--or off--the track. Economical. Fast. Fun." Standard colors included Tartan Red, Riviera Blue, Old English White, Dove Grey, British Racing Green, and Black.

3000 Mk II (BJ7) — SIX — Production of the "Big Healey" convertible with roll-up windows continued with little change into 1964.

3000 Mk III (BJ8) — SIX — In its final (Mark III) form, the six-cylinder Healey added more luxurious interior appointments including a wood fascia and a center console between the front seats. Engine output got a final boost, too, to 150 horsepower. Later in 1964, a "phase two" version got some chassis modifications, including a switch to radius arms at the rear axle. This was the quickest of the Big Healeys, with a top speed around 120 mph. Standard equipment included an adjustable steering wheel, heater, windshield washers, four-speed manual transmission (with overdrive), and front disc brakes.

I.D. DATA: Serial number is located on right side of firewall except (Sprite) left side of front fender well. Serial number range: (Sprite Mk II) H-AN7-24732 to 38828; (Sprite Mk III) H-AN8-38829 to 64734. Starting serial number: (3000 Mk II) HBJ7L/17751; (3000 Mk III) HBJ8/25315. Engine number is on left side of block except (Sprite) top right side of block. Engine number prefix: (3000 Mk III) 29K.

Model	Body Type & Seating	Engine Type/CID	P.O.E. Price	Weight (lbs.)	Prod. Total
SPRITE Mk II					
AN7	2-dr Roadster-2P	I4/67	1875	1450	Note 1
SPRITE Mk III					
AN8	2-dr Conv-2P	I4/67	1888	1566	11,157
3000 Mk II					
BJ7	2-dr Spt Conv-2 + 2P	I6/178	3535	2380	Note 2
3000 Mk III					
BJ8	2-dr Spt Conv-2 + 2P	I6/178	3565	2380	Note 3

Note 1: Included in Sprite Mk III total for 1964.
Note 2: See previous listing.
Note 3: A total of 17,712 Mark III Healeys were produced from 1964 to the end of 1967 (1,390 in original form and 16,322 "phase two").

ENGINE DATA: BASE FOUR (Sprite Mk II): Same as 1962-63.
BASE FOUR (Sprite Mk III): Inline, overhead-valve four-cylinder. Cast iron block and head. **Displacement:** 67 cu. in. (1098 cc). **Bore & Stroke:** 2.543 x 3.296 in. (64.58 x 83.72 mm). **Compression Ratio:** 9.0:1. **Brake Horsepower:** 59 at 5750 rpm. **Torque:** 62 lbs.-ft. at 3250 rpm. Three main bearings. Solid valve lifters. Two SU HS2 semi-downdraft carburetors. 12-volt electrical.
BASE SIX (3000 Mk III): Inline, overhead-valve six-cylinder. Cast iron block and head. **Displacement:** 177.7 cu. in. (2912 cc). **Bore & Stroke:** 3.282 x 3.50 in. (83.7 x 88.9 mm). **Compression Ratio:** 9.1:1. **Brake Horsepower:** 150 at 5250 rpm. **Torque:** 173 lbs.-ft. at 3000 rpm. Five main bearings. Solid valve lifters. Two SU carburetors. 12-volt electrical.

CHASSIS DATA: Wheelbase: (Sprite) 80 in.; (3000) 92 in. **Overall Length:** (Sprite Mk III) 136 in.; (3000) 157.5 in. **Height:** (Sprite Mk III) 49.5 in.; (3000) 49 in. **Width:** (Sprite) 53 in.; (3000) 60 in. **Front Tread:** (Sprite) 45.75 in.; (3000) 48.75 in. **Rear Tread:** (Sprite) 44.75 in.; (3000) 48.75 in. **Wheel Type:** (Sprite) four-lug pressed steel ventilated disc. **Standard Tires:** (Sprite) 5.20x13; (3000) 5.90x15.

TECHNICAL: Layout: front-engine, rear-drive. **Transmission:** four-speed manual. Sprite gear ratios: (1st) 3.20:1; (2nd) 1.916:1; (3rd) 1.357:1; (4th) 1.00:1. **Standard Final Drive Ratio:** (Sprite) 4.22:1; (3000) 3.91:1 or 3.55:1. **Steering:** (Sprite) rack and pinion; (3000) cam and peg. **Suspension (front):** (Sprite) wishbones, coil springs and lever-type shock absorbers; (3000) wishbones with coil springs. **Suspension (rear):** (Sprite) semi-elliptic leaf springs with lever-type shock absorbers and radius arms; (3000) rigid axle, semi-elliptic leaf springs. **Brakes:** front disc, rear drum. **Body Construction:** (Sprite) steel unibody; (3000) separate body and frame.

MAJOR OPTIONS: (Sprite) Heater. Tonneau cover. Whitewall tires.

PERFORMANCE: Top Speed: (Sprite Mk III) 101 mph; (3000 Mk III) 110-120 mph. **Acceleration (0-60 mph):** (Sprite Mk III) 12.3 sec.; (3000 Mk III) 9.5 sec. **Acceleration (quarter-mile):** (Sprite Mk III) 18.8 sec.; (3000 Mk III) 17 sec.

PRODUCTION/SALES: Approximately 8,397 Austin-Healeys were sold in the U.S. during 1964.

HISTORY: The 3000-series Austin-Healeys did well in competition, especially rallies, taking wins in Alpine events in 1961 and '62; the Liege-Rome-Liege runs in 1960 and '64; and the Austrian Alpine rally of 1964. The 1964 model year for U.S. sales began September 1, 1963.

1965 AUSTIN-HEALEY

1965 Austin-Healey Mark III convertible.

SPRITE Mk III — FOUR — Production continued with little change.
3000 Mk III — SIX — Production of the "phase two" version continued with little change.
I.D. DATA: See 1964 listing.

Model	Body Type & Seating	Engine Type/CID	P.O.E. Price	Weight (lbs.)	Prod. Total
SPRITE Mk III					
AN8	2-dr Conv-2P	I4/67	1888	1566	8,882
3000 Mk III					
BJ8	2-dr Spt Conv-2 + 2P	I6/178	3565	2380	Note 1

Note 1: A total of 17,712 Mark III Healeys were produced from 1964 to the end of 1967 (1,390 in original form and 16,322 "phase two").
ENGINE DATA: Same as 1964.
CHASSIS DATA: Same as 1964.
TECHNICAL: Same as 1964.
PERFORMANCE: Same as 1964.
HISTORY: The 1965 model year for U.S. sales began September 1, 1964.

1966-67 AUSTIN-HEALEY

SPRITE Mk III — FOUR — Production of the Mark III continued into 1966, then was replaced by the Mark IV.

SPRITE Mk IV — FOUR — With the Mark IV version, introduced late in 1966, Sprite got a larger (1275-cc) four-cylinder engine, with a boost to 65 horsepower. That engine was essentially a detuned version of BMC's Mini-Cooper 'S' powerplant, sufficient to give the Sprite a top speed around 95 mph.

3000 Mk III — SIX — This would be the final two-year season for the Big Healey, which continued with little change. Standard equipment included a heater, power brakes, and overdrive transmission.

1966 Austin-Healey 3000 Mark III convertible. (Christie's)

1967 Austin-Healey 3000 Mark III convertible.

I.D. DATA: Serial number is located on right side of fire wall except (Sprite) on left front fender well. Starting serial number: (3000) HBJ8L/33000 (for model year 1967); (Sprite Mk IV) H-AN9-52390 (55400 for model year 1967).

Model	Body Type & Seating	Engine Type/CID	P.O.E. Price	Weight (lbs.)	Prod. Total
SPRITE					
Mk III	2-dr Conv-2P	I4/67	1888	1566	Note 1
Mk IV	2-dr Conv-2P	I4/78	1995	1512	Note 1
3000					
Mark III	2-dr Conv-2 + 2P	I6/178	3565	2380	Note 2

Note 1: A total of 7,024 Sprites were produced in 1966, and 6,895 in 1967.

Note 2: A total of 16,322 "phase two" models were produced from 1964 to 1967.

Price Note: $3000 price is for 1966; raised to $3628 in 1967.

ENGINE DATA: BASE FOUR (Sprite Mk III): Inline, overhead-valve four-cylinder. Cast iron block and head. **Displacement:** 67 cu. in. (1098 cc). **Bore & Stroke:** 2.543 x 3.296 in. (64.58 x 83.72 mm). **Compression Ratio:** 9.0:1. **Brake Horsepower:** 59 at 5750 rpm. Torque: 62 lbs.-ft. at 3250 rpm. Three main bearings. Solid valve lifters. Two SU carburetors. 12-volt electrical.

BASE FOUR (Sprite Mark IV): Inline, overhead-valve four-cylinder. Cast iron block and head. **Displacement:** 77.9 cu. in. (1275 cc). **Bore & Stroke:** 2.78 x 3.20 in. (70.6 x 81.3 mm). **Compression Ratio:** 9.0:1. **Brake Horsepower:** 65 at 6000 rpm. **Torque:** 72 lbs.-ft. at 3000 rpm. Three main bearings. Solid valve lifters. Two SU carburetors. 12-volt electrical.

BASE SIX (3000): Inline, overhead-valve six-cylinder. Cast iron block and head. **Displacement:** 177.7 cu. in. (2912 cc). **Bore & Stroke:** 3.282 x 3.50 in. (83.7 x 88.9 mm). **Compression Ratio:** 9.1:1. **Brake Horsepower:** 150 at 5250 rpm. **Torque:** 173 lbs.-ft. at 3000 rpm. Four main bearings. Solid valve lifters. Two SU carburetors. 12-volt electrical.

CHASSIS DATA: Wheelbase: (Sprite) 80 in.; (3000) 92 in. **Overall Length:** (Sprite) 137.6 in.; (3000) 157.5 in. **Height:** (Sprite) 47.25 in.; (3000) 50 in. **Width:** (Sprite) 55 in.; (3000) 61 in. **Front Tread:** (Sprite) 45.75 in.; (3000) 48.75 in. **Rear Tread:** (Sprite) 44.75 in.; (3000) 50 in. **Standard Tires:** (Sprite) 5.20x13; (3000) 5.90x15.

TECHNICAL: Layout: front-engine, rear-drive. **Transmission:** four-speed manual (floor lever). **Standard Final Drive Ratio:** (Sprite) 4.22:1 or 3.91:1; (3000) 3.55:1 or 3.91:1. **Steering:** (Sprite) rack and pinion; (3000) cam and peg. **Suspension (front):** (Sprite) wishbones, coil springs and lever-type shock absorbers; (3000) wishbones with coil springs. **Suspension (rear):** (Sprite) semi-elliptic leaf springs with lever-type shock absorbers and radius arms; (3000) rigid axle, semi-elliptic leaf springs. **Brakes:** front disc, rear drum. **Body Construction:** (Sprite) steel unibody; (3000) separate body and frame.

MAJOR OPTIONS: Air conditioning: 3000 ($385).

PERFORMANCE: Top Speed: (Sprite Mk IV) 96 mph. **Acceleration (0-60 mph):** (Sprite Mk IV) 12.3 sec. **Acceleration (quarter-mile):** (Sprite Mk IV) 18.8-19.1 sec.

HISTORY: The 1967 model year for U.S. sales began Sept. 1, 1966.

1968-70 AUSTIN-HEALEY

1969 Austin-Healey Sprite.

SPRITE Mk IV — FOUR — For its final three years on the U.S. market, the little Sprite got a new negative-ground electrical system, a safety-type dashboard, and an exhaust emission system. In 1969, new side safety marker lights were added to the cowl on imported models. Final models were called, simply, Austin Sprites, as the "Healey" name was dropped.

I.D. DATA: Serial number is on right side of firewall. Starting serial number (1968): H-AN9U72494 (U.S.).

Model	Body Type & Seating	Engine Type/CID	P.O.E. Price	Weight (lbs.)	Prod. Total
SPRITE					
Mk IV	2-dr Conv-2P	I4/78	2050	1502	Note 1

Note 1: A total of 7,049 Sprites were produced in 1968, 6,133 in 1969, and 1,280 in 1970. Imports to the U.S. ceased in 1970, but an additional 1,022 Sprits were built in 1971.

ENGINE DATA: Same as 1966-67.

CHASSIS DATA: Same as 1966-67.

TECHNICAL: Same as 1966-67.

MAJOR OPTIONS: Hardtop ($169). Front anti-roll bar. Wire wheels. Oil cooler.

PERFORMANCE: Same as 1966-67 Sprite.

PRODUCTION/SALES: A total of 129,354 Sprites were produced in all, starting in 1958 (79,338 of them in the restyled form, starting with the Mark II).

HISTORY: In 1968, the British Leyland company was formed. The nearly-identical MG Midget, which generally sold more strongly than the Sprite, continued in production through 1977; see the MG listing for details.

BENTLEY

Walter Owen Bentley (known as "W.O."), a British engineer, apprenticed in railway work before joining one of his brothers as agent for the French D.F.P. automobile. To boost that car's image, they raced it at the Brooklands course. Serving in the navy during the First World War, W.O. designed rotary aircraft engines. He also became an advocate of aluminum-alloy pistons, informing Ernest Hives (of Rolls-Royce) of the benefits of that material.

After the war ended, in 1919, Bentley joined with two men, F.T. Burgess and Harry Varley, to build a sporting motorcar. A prototype chassis appeared at the London Motor Show that year. Two years later, another prototype raced at Brooklands. Production was underway in 1922 at Cricklewood, a facility right in London, named Bentley Motors. Their first offering was powered by a 3.0-liter, overhead-cam engine that had four valves per cylinder (increasingly common today, but not so in the 1920s). The design also made considerable use of aluminum. Developing at least 65 horsepower, the result was capable of speeds approaching 80 mph. Early models had brakes only on the front wheels, but that was changed in 1924. Three racing models won the team prize at the 1923 Tourist Trophy Race, and another took fourth place at Le Mans. A year later, a Bentley won the 24-hour race at Le Mans. A stock Bentley even raced at Indianapolis in 1922, finishing 20th. Race drivers in the early days became known as the "Bentley Boys."

In 1925, a larger (6.5-liter) six was announced, with the intention of luring away Rolls-Royce customers. That attempt didn't get far, but evolved into the Speed Six chassis, whose engine developed 160 bhp to produce speeds of 90 mph. Racing versions won the Le Mans event from 1927 through 1930. Financial ills led to the takeover of the company by race driver Woolf Barnato, in 1926. A year later, a 4.5-liter model debuted.

Probably the most famous model of them all was the "Blower" Bentley, introduced in 1929, using a 4.5-liter engine redesigned by Amherst Villiers. Bentley himself didn't wholly approve, but allowed enough "blown" models to be built to qualify for "production" racing.

Throughout their history, Bentleys wore distinctive radiators, but their bodies came from varied sources. The early Vanden Plas open four-seater was among the best-known, particularly notable with its British Racing Green paint.

Financial woes loomed again in 1931 as the Depression took its toll, following failure of a big 8.0-liter model to capture Rolls-Royce buyers--and comparable failure of a four-cylinder model half that size. Receivership led to a squabble in the courts, after which the Bentley organization was purchased by Rolls-Royce Ltd. That old-line firm also took on the services of W.O. Bentley, but as an advisor and tester and not for design work. By that time, Bentleys had taken five Le Mans victories.

The first Bentley produced under Rolls ownership came in 1933: a 3.7-liter (actually called 3-1/2) "Silent Sports Car." Powered by a modified Rolls-Royce 20/25 engine and transmission, the Bentley rode an all-new chassis and wore various coachbuilt bodies. Though capable of racing on occasion, these 1930s Bentleys were hardly competition models, but ranked as gentlemen's motorcars. Engine size grew to 4-1/4 liters (actually 4257 cc) in 1936, and an "overdrive" top gear was added later for easier cruising.

All told, 2,432 prewar Bentleys were built under Rolls-Royce stewardship, at a facility in Derby. More than half had the larger engine, offered in 1936-39. The short-lived Mark V added independent front suspension, but production was halted by the outbreak of war.

Following World War II, production resumed in a new plant at Crewe, England, where aircraft engines had been built during the war. Bentley's Mark VI was the first car to be produced at that facility. The standard model wore a body shared with the Rolls-Royce Silver Dawn, but a variety of custom bodies became available from a selection of coachbuilders.

Differences between the Bentley and Rolls-Royce grew slighter in the postwar years, typically amounting to little more than the appearance of the grille. One big exception, however, was the Bentley R-Type Continental, a rakish two-door fastback that was capable of up to 120 mph. When introduced, the Continental was the fastest four-seat saloon in the world. Early examples carried a 4566-cc F-head engine (overhead intake valves, side exhausts), but dimensions grew later to 4.9 liters. A total of 208 Continentals were produced from 1952-55, most of them with lightweight bodies by H.J. Mulliner. Far more R-Type saloons were produced: a total of 2,320, with restyled bodies but far less dramatic than the Continental.

The next generation of conventional saloons (sedans) consisted of the Rolls-Royce Silver Cloud and the S-Series Bentley, powered by a 4.9-liter six-cylinder F-head engine. By that time, an automatic transmission was standard. S-Series Continentals also continued on sale, including both coupes and convertibles. Late in 1959, a new light-alloy 6230-cc V-8 engine replaced the familiar F-head six for the S2/S3 Series. A T-Series Bentley arrived in 1965, with self-leveling suspension and all-disc brakes; joined by a Corniche edition in the early 1970s. W.O. Bentley died in 1971.

Bentleys, according to a company brochure, "have a distinctly different heritage" from Rolls-Royce throughout their history "and have attracted a distinctly different type of driver." Early in the 1980s, the Mulsanne saloon was revamped to revive Bentley's sporting image. Powered by a turbocharged 6750-cc V-8 that developed about 300 horsepower, the big (and expensive) saloon was known as the Mulsanne Turbo. By 1985, the car cost more than 60,000 Pounds (Sterling) in Britain. And when it arrived in the U.S. as the Bentley Turbo R, the price tag read $149,500. Even so, a few affluent Americans liked the idea of an ultra-posh 2-1/2 ton sedan that could accelerate to 60 mph in less than seven seconds and reach speeds of 135 mph or more. Besides, the sticker price on a Bentley Continental convertible was a lot higher than that.

Engine Note: Traditionally, horsepower figures never were quoted for either Bentley or Rolls-Royce engines. Therefore, all figures given in the listings below are estimates.

1946-1951 BENTLEY

MARK VI — SIX — Styling of the first postwar Bentley was shared with the Rolls-Royce Silver Dawn. Upright in profile, similar to the prewar Mark V Park Ward model, the basic four-door saloon (sedan) wore a typical Bentley grille made up of vertical bars, with inboard headlamps alongside. Round parking lights sat below the headlamps, with a large round auxiliary driving light mounted in the center, ahead of the grille, above the bumper. Neither front nor rear fenders were faired into the bodyside, but retained a separate look. A one-piece flat windshield was used. Early examples had large wheel covers with raised centers; later versions were more flat. This was the first Bentley offered with a standard saloon body, built by Pressed Steel Company but assembled at the Bentley factory.

Under the hood was a new F-head, 4257-cc six-cylinder engine with overhead intake valves (operated via pushrods and enclosed rocker arms) and side exhaust valves. The

engine had seven crankshaft bearings and an aluminum cylinder head. Left-hand-drive models had a column lever for the four-speed manual transmission; right-hand-drive Bentleys kept the floor lever. The front suspension consisted of coil springs and wishbones, with long semi-elliptic springs at the rear. Hydraulic rear shock absorbers were controlled by a lever on the steering column head. Stepping on a pedal delivered chassis lubricant to the steering and suspension components. Hydraulic brakes were used in the front, mechanical brakes at the rear. Disc wheels held 6.50x16 India super tires.

Five passengers fit into the standard Sports Saloon. Wheelbase was 120 inches, and the basic model measured 192 inches overall. Standard Bentley equipment included head, side and center lamps; twin stop and tail lamps; a map reading lamp; clock; ammeter, oil gauge, and fuel gauge; directional indicators; dual horns with grilles; lighter; heater and demister; radio; front and back bumpers; side jacking system; and a mascot in the radiator cap. A standard tool kit contained clips to secure the tools. A backup light was incorporated into the rear license plate box. Pleated upholstery was added in 1949. Standard body and upholstery colors by 1949 included: Black, with brown furniture hide; Maroon, with maroon or tan hide; Dark Blue, with dark blue hide; Pearl Metallic, with light blue hide; Metallic Grey, with grey hide; and Two-Tone Grey, with light blue hide. A 1951 list did not include Maroon but added Velvet Green with grey furniture hide, and the Dark Blue version came with beige hide.

Engine bore was increased in May 1951, to 4566-cc displacement, increasing horsepower by at least 18. Side cowl vents also were added.

1947 Bentley Mark VI. (Coys of Kensington)

1949 Bentley Mark VI. (Coys of Kensington)

1950-'52 Bentley fixed-head coupe. (William Siuru Jr.)

1951 Bentley 4.5-liter Mark VI four-passenger drophead coupe. (Christie's)

1951 Bentley 4.5-liter Mark VI four-door sports saloon. (Christie's)

MARK VI (CUSTOM BODIES): Most Bentleys had bodies from custom coachbuilders rather than the standard body installed at the Bentley plant. The four-door Sport Saloon with coachwork by H.J. Mulliner and Co. Ltd. was a four-seater with no-draft ventilation for front and rear seats. It also had very light front pillars "presenting a minimum obstruction to driving vision." History of the Mulliner firm dated back to 1760. H.J. Mulliner had become interested in building bodies for motorcars as early as 1896, forming a branch of the family business right at the turn of the century.

A Drophead Foursome coupe with coachwork by Park Ward & Co. Ltd. had a power-operated folding top, wide doors, and sliding bucket-type front seats with folding backrests. Founded in 1919, Park Ward specialized in drophead coachwork.

The two-door Sports Saloon with coachwork by James Young Ltd. seated five and had a ventilation system controllable from the front seat, plus swiveling ventilators to doors and quarters. James Young had entered the business as a coachbuilder in 1865.

In addition to the custom models listed below, Mark VI Bentleys could be obtained with coachwork by Abbott (drophead or fixed-head coupe); Facel-Metallon (fixed-head coupe); Franay (sedanca or drophead coupe); Graber (coupe); Radford (Countryman); Windovers (two-door saloon); and Worlaufen (drophead coupe).

1951 Bentley Mark VI Special roadster. (Christie's)

I.D. DATA: Serial number plate is located on the left side of the firewall, under the hood. Prefix 'B' is followed by 'L' to indicate left-hand drive. A suffix indicates the series. Engine number is on the left side of the crankcase at lower front, or (later) in upper front corner of left side of crankcase. Prefix 'B' is followed by letters to indicate series. Starting serial number: B-1-AJ.

Model	Body Type & Seating	Engine Type/CID	P.O.E. Price	Weight (lbs.)	Prod. Total
MARK VI (Standard)					
Mk VI	4-dr Spt Saloon-5P	I6/260	9900	4075	Note 1
H.J. Mulliner					
	2-dr Spt Saloon-4P	I6/260	15200	4000	Note 2
	4-dr Spt Saloon-4P	I6/260	15200	4000	Note 2
	4-dr Saloon	I6/260	14185	4000	Note 2
	2-dr Dhd Coupe-4P	I6/260	N/A	N/A	Note 2
Park Ward					
Foursome	2-dr Dhd Cpe	I6/260	14600	4000	Note 3
	2-dr Coupe	I6/260	14150	4000	Note 3
	Saloon	I6/260	N/A	N/A	Note 3

Model	Body Type & Seating	Engine Type/CID	P.O.E. Price	Weight (lbs.)	Prod. Total
Gurney Nutting					
Sedanca	2-dr Coupe	I6/260	N/A	N/A	N/A
James Young					
Clubman	2-dr Coupe	I6/260	N/A	N/A	Note 4
	2-dr Spt Saloon-5P	I6/260	14235	4000	Note 4
	4-dr Spt Saloon-5P	I6/260	N/A	N/A	Note 4
Freestone & Webb					
	2-dr Coupe	I6/260	N/A	N/A	Note 5
	4-dr Saloon	I6/260	N/A	N/A	Note 5
Hooper					
Sedanca	2-dr Coupe	I6/260	N/A	N/A	Note 6
	2-dr Coupe	I6/260	N/A	N/A	Note 6
	4-dr Saloon	I6/260	N/A	N/A	Note 6

Note 1: A total of 4,946 Mark VI Bentley chassis were produced from 1946-52, according to the Rolls-Royce company. Other sources put the total as high as 5,201 (including 1,201 with the larger 4566-cc engine).

Note 2: A total of 301 examples had coachwork by H.J. Mulliner.

Note 3: A total of 167 examples had coachwork by Park Ward.

Note 4: A total of 209 examples had coachwork by James Young.

Note 5: A total of 103 examples had coachwork by Freestone & Webb.

Note 6: A total of 61 examples had coachwork by Hooper and Co.

Weight Note: Figures shown are approximate.

Price Note: Figures shown were valid at the end of the Mark VI model run. Basic saloon cost 2595 Pounds (Sterling) in Britain, in 1949; H.J. Mulliner saloon, 3415 Pounds; Park Ward Foursome drophead coupe, 3485 Pounds; Gurney Nutting sedanca, 3900 Pounds; James Young 2-dr, 3585 Pounds; and James Young 4-dr, 3550 Pounds. Those prices did not include purchase tax. Prices for export as of August, 1951 came to 3800 Pounds for the Mulliner saloon, 3805 for the Park Ward Foursome, and 3735 for the 2-dr James Young saloon. A Bentley Mark VI chassis alone sold for 1985 Pounds (Sterling) in Britain.

ENGINE DATA: BASE SIX (1946 through early 1951): Inline, F-head six-cylinder. Cast iron block and aluminum head. **Displacement:** 260 cu. in. (4257 cc). **Bore & Stroke:** 3.50 x 4.50 in. (88.9 x 114.3 mm). **Compression Ratio:** 6.4:1. **Brake Horsepower:** 126-132 (estimated). Seven main bearings. Solid valve lifters. Two horizontal SU expanding-type carburetors. Lucas ignition. 12-volt electrical system.

BASE SIX (starting July 1951): Same as above, except — **Displacement:** 278.5 cu. in. (4566 cc). **Bore & Stroke:** 3.62 x 4.50 in. (92.1 x 114.3 mm). **Brake Horsepower:** 150 (estimated).

CHASSIS DATA: Wheelbase 120 in. **Overall Length:** 192 in. **Height:** 68.0 in. **Width:** 70.0 in. **Front Tread:** 56 in. **Rear Tread:** 58.5 in. **Wheel Type:** steel disc. **Standard Tires:** 6.50x16.

Note: Dimensions of custom bodies vary.

TECHNICAL: Layout: front-engine, rear-drive. **Transmission:** four-speed manual, column or floor lever (synchro 2nd/3rd/4th). Overall gear ratios: (1st) 11.113:1; (2nd) 7.52:1; (3rd) 5.001:1; (4th) 3.727:1; (rev) 11.767:1. **Standard Final Drive Ratio:** 3.73:1. **Steering:** cam and roller follower. **Suspension (front):** wishbones and coil springs. **Suspension (rear):** rigid axle with semi-elliptic leaf springs. **Brakes:** hydraulic front, mechanical rear (servo-assisted). **Body Construction:** steel body on steel frame (standard model); custom bodies may have aluminum body paneling.

PERFORMANCE: Top Speed: (4257-cc) 94+ mph; (4566-cc) 102 mph. **Acceleration (0-60 mph):** N/A (0-50 mph in 11-12 sec.). **Acceleration (quarter-mile):** 20.4 sec. **Fuel Mileage:** about 16 mpg.

PRODUCTION/SALES: Approximately four Bentleys were sold in the U.S. in 1948, eight in 1949, 18 in 1950, and a dozen in 1951.

Manufacturer: Bentley Motors (1931) Ltd., Crewe, Cheshire, England.

HISTORY: One of Bentley's promotional brochures for the later Mark VI carried an introduction by Wing Commander T.H. Wisdom. "I like the look of the car," he declared, "and the fact that five can sit comfortably inside with their feet on a flat floor is more important than mere sleek lines." Wisdom also noted that "Gear changing is like drawing a knife through butter," concluding with the opinion that a "Bentley is that delightful combination, a...town carriage that captivates by its effortless high performance on the open road." No left-hand-drive models were built until March, 1949.

1952-54 BENTLEY

1952 Bentley 4.5-liter Mark VI four-door saloon. (Christie's)

MARK VI — SIX — Production of the first postwar Bentley continued into 1952, with the larger (4566-cc) engine. See previous listing for details.

1953 R-Type Bentley Standard four-door saloon. (Christie's)

R TYPE — SIX — Bentley's next standard model rode a longer chassis, measuring 8 inches longer overall than the Mark VI. Body lines had a greater sweep at the rear than on the Mark VI. Trunk capacity grew larger, with a top-hinged lid rather than the former bottom-hinged structure. Bentleys displayed the customary winged "B" radiator mascot. Inboard headlamps were only partially built into the front fenders, not so much different from the Mark VI series.

A four-speed automatic transmission became available in January 1953, first on the left-hand-drive saloon; then, later that year, on the RHD saloon as well. Soon, automatic became standard on all LHD models. It used a fluid coupling with two primary epicyclic geartrains and hydraulic servo units. A third geartrain provided reverse. Adoption of an automatic choke eliminated the former manual choke and throttle controls. Bentley's chassis consisted of a box frame strengthened by cruciform bracing member, ensured great rigidity. A centralized lubrication system was standard. A ride-control lever on the steering columns altered the damping action of the rear shock absorbers. As before, front brakes were hydraulic, rears mechanical (assisted by a mechanically-operated servo). A central bar was added to the car's grille early in 1953. The new chassis was welded, not riveted together.

Standard fittings on Bentley's own Sports Saloon included a radio, hot and cold air ventilation and demisting, and electrically-operated demisting for the rear window. A flashlight mounted on the dashboard plugged into a socket on the instrument panel. Small tools were individually housed in rubber in a tray under the driver's seat. Leather upholstery came in pleated and bolster style. The radio control box pulled forward to form a picnic table, and the front compartment had foot-operated ventilators. The radio's antenna folded flush with the top of the windshield when not in use. A sunshine roof was made standard. Rear doors had a generous wrapover to prevent passengers' clothes from coming into contact with the rear fender. Body colors included Black, Tudor Grey, Shell Grey, Midnight Blue, Velvet Green, Lugano Blue, Donegal Green, Maroon, or Two-tone Grey. Leather upholstery came in brown, tan, beige, light blue, grey, or red.

1953 R-Type Bentley 4.5-liter coupe with body by Abbott. (Christie's)

R TYPE (CUSTOM BODIES): Most Bentleys had bodies from custom coachbuilders rather than the standard Sports Saloon body built at the Bentley plant. The four-door saloon by Hooper and Co. seated four or five: two on separately adjustable bucket front seats, and two or three on the rear seat, which had a wide folding armrest. Two folding tables were built into the backs of the bucket seats. Ashtrays and interior lighting were included. The body had a curved windshield. Specially-designed front fenders flowed to the rear of the car and had detachable covers over the rear wheels, fitting flush with the bodysides. A large luggage compartment at the rear was fitted with a door hinged at the top. The export model was 208 inches long.

Park Ward's two-door drophead coupe was available in Four-Light or Two-Light configuration, as a fixed-head or drophead coupe, all with four-seat accommodation. Each had a new high fender line and curved windshield. Coachwork was all metal. The Melloroid top of the Four-Light drophead coupe raised and lowered electrically. The rear compartment of the Two-Light could be converted to increase the size of the luggage space.

Bucket-type front seats held two people and tipped forward to give access to the rear seat. Bolster-type leather upholstery had plain cushions. Comfort features included two interior lights, adjustable armrests in the front seats, slit pockets on each door, a heater under the passenger seat, and a radio with two speakers (one behind the instrument board, the other behind the rear seat). Paint and interior finish was available to the customer's choice. Overall lengths ranged from 204 to 212 inches.

James Young's four-door, four/five-seat Sports Saloon had a curved windshield plus the new high fender line. Rear fenders with deep valances made detachable wheel covers unnecessary. The front bench seat had two center armrests. Armrests for the rear seat were fitted with a locker. Interiors were trimmed in pleated and bolster style, with plain cushions and leather. Features included slit pockets and lockers with sliding shutters in the front doors. The radio played through a speaker in the center of the instrument panel. Three roof lamps were included. The trunk's alligator-style lid was self-propping. Paint and upholstery were to customer's choice.

H.J. Mulliner's four-door Six-Light Saloon featured semi-razor-edge styling and special narrow-section front pillars. Two bucket-type front seats could be adjusted independently, and armrests were installed in each door. The rear seat was fitted with a folding armrest. Upholstery came in leather or cloth, as desired. Two interior lights and a radio were standard. Polished wooden tables were recessed into the backs of front seats. An extra-large boot at the rear had a top hinge, and was spring-balanced.

Various other special bodies were available, as noted in the table below. The coupes built by Abbott were sometimes referred to as "Continentals," and displayed similar lines, but were not mounted on the authentic Continental chassis.

1954 R-Type Bentley Continental sports saloon. (Christie's)

1954 R-type Bentley Continental.

CONTINENTAL — R TYPE — SIX — A striking two-door fastback design brought back both the look and the performance for which prewar Bentleys had been famed. Although the "Continental" designation was adopted by many marques over the years, Bentley's version really was something special--probably the best-remembered and desirable of the postwar models. Viewed from the front, appearance differed little from the ordinary R-Type saloon: an upright vertical-bar grille flanked by inboard, semi-built-in headlamps. In profile, the fastback rear end (with rear quarter windows) and the blending of the front-fender line all the way back to the rear fenders gave the Continental a memorable appearance. Fender skirts added to the clean lines, and fender-mounted mirrors helped enhance the sporting look. Windows were low and large, and the windshield was curved. Standard equipment included a tachometer. Leather upholstery covered front bucket seats and a bench rear seat. Continentals had a close-ratio version of the Bentley four-speed manual gearbox, with 8.22:1 first gear and either a floor- or column-mounted shift lever.

Powered by more potent versions of the Bentley F-head six, the Continental fastback was capable of speeds up to 120 mph. When introduced, in fact, it ranked as the fastest four-seat saloon in the world. Initial examples carried a 4566-cc version of the F-head engine (overhead intake valves, side exhausts). By 1954, for series D/E, the engine grew to 4887 cc. A total of 208 R-Type Continentals were produced, and all except 16 had the distinctive fastback body built by H.J. Mulliner. Officially named a "Sports Saloon," it was commonly referred to as a fastback coupe.

I.D. DATE: Serial number plate is on left side of firewall, under the hood. Prefix 'B' indicates basic R type; 'BC' denotes Continental. Letter 'L' ahead of the series suffix indicates left-hand drive. Engine number is on upper front corner or left side of crankcase. Starting serial number: (R Type) B-2-RT; (Continental) BC-1-A.

Model	Body Type & Seating	Engine Type/CID	P.O.E. Price	Weight (lbs.)	Prod. Total
R TYPE (base)	4-dr Saloon-5P	I6/278	10735	4170	Note 1
H.J. Mulliner					
	2-dr Dhd Cpe	I6/278	N/A	N/A	Note 2
	4-dr Saloon	I6/278	N/A	N/A	Note 2
Park Ward					
	2-dr Dhd Cpe	I6/278	N/A	N/A	Note 3
	2-dr Coupe	I6/278	N/A	N/A	Note 3
	2-dr Saloon	I6/278	N/A	N/A	Note 3

Model	Body Type & Seating	Engine Type/CID	P.O.E. Price	Weight (lbs.)	Prod. Total
James Young					
	4-dr Spt Saloon	I6/278	N/A	N/A	Note 4
	2-dr Coupe	I6/278	N/A	N/A	Note 4
Sedanca	2-dr Coupe	I6/278	N/A	N/A	Note 4
Hooper					
	2-dr Saloon	I6/278	N/A	N/A	Note 5
	4-dr Saloon	I6/278	N/A	N/A	Note 5
Sedanca	2-dr Coupe	I6/278	N/A	N/A	Note 5
Abbott					
	2-dr Coupe	I6/278	N/A	N/A	16
Frankdale					
	4-dr Saloon	I6/278	N/A	N/A	N/A
Freestone & Webb					
	4-dr Saloon	I6/278	N/A	N/A	29
Franay					
	2-dr Coupe	I6/278	N/A	N/A	2
Graber					
	Saloon	I6/278	N/A	N/A	7
Radford Countryman	4-dr Saloon	I6/278	N/A	N/A	20
CONTINENTAL R TYPE					
Mulliner	2-dr Fbk Cpe-4P	I6/278	17350	1705	193
Park Ward	2-dr Coupe	I6/278	N/A	N/A	2
Park Ward	2-dr Dhd Cpe	I6/278	N/A	N/A	4
Farina	2-dr Coupe	I6/278	N/A	N/A	1
Franay	2-dr Coupe	I6/278	N/A	N/A	5
Graber	2-dr Coupe	I6/278	N/A	N/A	3
Bertone	2-dr Saloon	I6/278	N/A	N/A	N/A

Note 1: A total of 2,320 R-Type models were built, from 1952-55, most of which wore the basic Bentley Sports Saloon body.

Note 2: A total of 67 R-Types were built with H.J. Mulliner bodies; second and third saloon listings are all-metal body.

Note 3: A total of 50 R-Types were built with Park Ward bodies.

Note 4: A total of 69 R-Types were built with James Young bodies.

Note 5: A total of 41 R-Types were built with Hooper bodies.

Export Price Note: Prices of export models as of October 1953 were as follows (in Pounds Sterling, exclusive of purchase tax): chassis alone, 2270/2440; Mulliner Continental 4890; Sports Saloon by Bentley, 3100; 2-door Sports Saloon by Park Ward, 4185; Drophead coupe by Park Ward, 4280; 4-door saloon by H.J. Mulliner, 4190; 4-door saloon by Hooper and Co., 4505; 4-door saloon by James Young, 4455 Pounds.

Production Note: Figures shown are for the full 1952-55 period during which the R Series was produced.

Continental Production Note: Of the 208 R-Series Continentals produced, 43 were left-hand-drive.

Continental Model Note: Though commonly described as a fastback coupe, the Mulliner Continental's official title was "Sports Saloon."

ENGINE DATA: BASE SIX (Mark VI, R-Type, Continental R-Type A-C Series): Inline, F-head six-cylinder (overhead intake valves, side exhausts). Cast iron block and aluminum head. **Displacement:** 278.5 cu. in. (4566 cc). **Bore & Stroke:** 3.62 x 4.50 in. (92 x 114 mm). **Compression Ratio:** (Mk VI, early R-Type) 6.4:1; (later R-Type) 6.75:1; (Cont.) 7.25:1. **Brake Horsepower:** (R-Type) 150 at 4500 rpm estimated; (Continental) 153-160 at 4500 rpm estimated. Seven main bearings. Solid valve lifters. Two SU carburetors. 12-volt electrical system.

BASE SIX (Continental R-Type, D-E Series): Same as above, except — **Displacement:** 298 cu. in. (4887 cc). **Bore & Stroke:** 3.75 x 4.50 in. (95 x 114 mm). **Brake Horsepower:** 178 (estimated).

CHASSIS DATA: Wheelbase: 120 in. **Overall Length:** (base R-Type) 200 in.; (Continental) 207 in. **Height:** (R-Type) 66 in.; (Cont.) 63 in. **Width:** (R-Type) 70 in.; (Cont.) 71.5 in. **Front Tread:** 56.76 in. **Rear Tread:** 58.6 in. **Wheel Type:** disc. **Standard Tires:** 6.50x16.

Note: Dimensions of custom bodies vary.

TECHNICAL: Layout: front-engine, rear-drive. **Transmission:** four-speed manual (2nd/3rd/4th synchro); floor or column lever. Overall R-Type gear ratios: (1st) 11.11:1; (2nd) 7.52:1; (3rd) 5.00:1; (4th) 3.73:1; (rev) 11.76:1. Overall Continental gear ratios: (1st) 8.22:1; (2nd) 4.75:1; (3rd) 3.74:1; (4th) 3.07:1. Four-speed automatic transmission optional on LHD cars for export (later standard). Automatic overall gear ratios: (1st) 14.23:1; (2nd) 9.82:1; (3rd) 5.40:1; (4th) 3.73:1; (rev) 16.04:1. **Standard Final Drive Ratio:** (R-Type) 3.727:1; (Continental) 3.07:1. **Steering:** cam and roller follower. **Suspension (front):** wishbones and coil springs. **Suspension (rear):** rigid axle with semi-elliptic leaf springs, enclosed in leather gaiters. **Brakes:** hydraulic front, mechanical rear (servo-assisted). **Body Construction:** steel body on steel box frame with cruciform bracing; custom bodies may have aluminum body panels.

MAJOR OPTIONS: Automatic transmission: R-Type saloon (70 Pounds Sterling in U.K.).

PERFORMANCE: Top Speed: (R-Type) 100-105 mph; (Continental) 115-120 mph. **Acceleration (0-60 mph):** (R-Type) 11-13.5 sec.; (Continental) (0-50 mph in 9.3 sec.). **Acceleration (quarter-mile):** (R-Type) 19.7 sec.; (Cont.) 18.5-19.5 sec. **Fuel Mileage:** 16-21 mpg (Imperial); (Continental) about 16 mpg (U.S.).

PRODUCTION/SALES: Approximately 27 Bentleys were sold in the U.S. in 1952, 44 in 1953, and 35 in 1954.

Manufacturer: Bentley Motors (1931) Ltd., Crewe, Cheshire, England.

HISTORY: Production of the R Series began in 1952 and continued into 1955, when it was replaced by the restyled S Series. Bentley was referred to as the "Silent Sports Car" in sales brochures. "When judged from outward appearances only," said the company brochure in autumn 1953, "the Bentley has the air of a thoroughbred. And on first acquaintance, even before one has actually entered the car, it creates the impression that it must go well and possess that extra something that the others lack." Bentley promoted the Continental as "one of the fastest four-seater saloon cars in the world," adding that it "is capable, with complete safety and absolute comfort, of speeds up to 120 m.p.h." The new automatic transmission was produced by Bentley, under license from General Motors, a modification of GM's Hydra-matic.

Auto Sport Review magazine called the early Continental a "stem-to-stern thoroughbred that runs likes a bullet without losing an iota of its traditional good manners." Only about one per month was expected to be produced, for export only. First deliveries, according to the magazine, were expected in summer 1952 and "will be made only to responsible buyers proved capable of handling that potent type of machine."

1955-58 BENTLEY

1955 Bentley S1. (Coys of Kensington)

1956 Bentley S1 Continental fastback. (Coys of Kensington)

S (S1) SERIES — SIX — Appearance of the standard steel four-door saloon body changed considerably with the S Series. Up front, the grille and inboard headlamps were similar to the previous R Series. Change was most dramatic along the bodysides. Instead of the prewar-style separate-fendered look, the front fender line now flowed gradually into the doors, and the tail adopted a tapered profile comparable to the Continental. Wheelbase grew to 123 inches; overall length reached 212 inches. Except for the grille differences, styling was similar to the Rolls-Royce Silver Cloud I.

Engine dimensions were identical to the prior F-head six, but the 4.9-liter block was new and stronger. Compression was higher, valves larger. Power steering became optional on export models in March 1956, and was standard across the board by September 1958. Top speed was still over 100 mph, even though the car was heavier. New 8.20x15 tires replaced the former 16-inchers. Hydraulic front brakes continued in use up front, with mechanical brakes at rear wheels. An override control allowed manual selection of gears on the four-speed automatic transmission.

Both single body colors and two-tones were available. Single colors included Black, Black Pearl, Midnight Blue, Velvet Green, Maroon, and Lugano Blue. Two-tone combinations included Shell Grey and Tudor Grey; Sage Green and Smoke Green; Sand and Sable; Shell Grey and Black Pearl; Shell Grey and Velvet Green. Seating was adequate for five or six people. English hide upholstery came in tan, red, blue, brown, beige, grey, and green. Fitted pile carpets were in matching colors. Woodwork was done in walnut veneer or solid mahogany. Standard folding center armrests went into front and rear seats. Standard equipment included vanity mirrors, lighters, two-speed wipers and washers, and a map reading light. A two-position ride control switch on the steering column varied the shock absorber setting. A picnic tray and ashtray pulled out from under the fascia panel. Twin foglamps incorporated flashing filaments for direction indicators.

After 1957, a total of 35 long-wheelbase Bentley S1 chassis were produced, measuring 127 inches axle-to-axle (four inches longer than usual). Air conditioning became available on S1 models in 1958, followed by power windows.

1957 Bentley S1 Continental. (Christie's)

1955 Bentley R-Type Continental. (Coys of Kensington)

CONTINENTAL — S1 SERIES — SIX — Even though the S Series grew three inches in wheelbase compared to the R Type, the H.J. Mulliner coachbuilding company modified its Continental fastback coupe to fit the new chassis. Not only the chassis, but the steering and suspension were redesigned. Early Mulliner examples had a slightly more streamlined appearance than the original R-Type Continentals, typically wearing slightly finned rear fenders. These special lightweight versions of the S Series saloon were claimed to offer "really striking acceleration and handling characteristics." A Park Ward sports saloon and drophead coupe also were available, similar in design but differing in top construction and number of windows. The drophead coupe had only single side windows, while the sports saloon also contained rear quarter windows. Those Park Ward models lacked the dramatic fastback look of the Mulliner version. Each four-seat two-door was capable of speeds up to 120 mph, powered by the same 4887-cc engine as the S Series but with higher compression (7.25:1 initially, increased to 8.0:1 in mid-1958). Electrically-controlled rear shock dampers could be set to "hard" for a more rigid ride. An automatic transmission was now standard. Air conditioning became available in 1958, followed by power windows.

Styling of the aluminum body was said to be particularly suited to a two-color scheme. Bucket-type front seats were "anatomically" designed to grip the body and had folding center armrests. Squabs adjusted for rake, and to three positions. Rear seat cushions could be hinged upward against the back of the seat, leaving a large platform area for extra luggage. H.J. Mulliner produced a Flying Spur saloon on the Continental chassis after 1957.

1958 Bentley S1 Standard sedan.

I.D. DATA: Serial number is under the hood, on the left side of the firewall. A 'B' prefix denotes the S1; 'BC' indicates the Continental. Each is followed by a chassis series letter ('L' = LHD). Engine number is on upper front corner of the left side of the crankcase (farther back on models with power steering). Starting serial number: (S1) B-2-AN or B-1-AP; (Continental) BC1-102 AF; (LWB S1) ALB 1-36.

Model	Body Type & Seating	Engine Type/CID	P.O.E. Price	Weight (lbs.)	Prod. Total
S (S1) SERIES					
(base)	4-dr Saloon-5/6P	I6/298	12000	4325	Note 1
LWB	4-dr Saloon	I6/298	N/A	N/A	Note 1
H.J. Mulliner					
	4-dr Saloon	I6/298	N/A	N/A	31
	4-dr Limousine	I6/298	N/A	N/A	5
Park Ward					
	2-dr Coupe	I6/298	N/A	N/A	Note 2

96

Model	Body Type & Seating	Engine Type/CID	P.O.E. Price	Weight (lbs.)	Prod. Total
James Young					
	2-dr Saloon	I6/298	N/A	N/A	Note 2
Hooper					
	4-dr Saloon	I6/298	N/A	N/A	6
Freestone & Webb					
	4-dr Saloon	I6/298	N/A	N/A	Note 2
Graber					
	2-dr Dhd Cpe	I6/298	N/A	N/A	Note 2

1958 Bentley S1 four-door saloon. (Christie's)

CONTINENTAL S1 SERIES

Mulliner	2-dr Fbk Cpe-4P	I6/298	N/A	3875	Note 3
Mulliner	2-dr Dhd Cpe	I6/298	N/A	N/A	Note 3
Mulliner	2-dr Spt Saloon	I6/298	18000	N/A	Note 3
Park Ward	2-dr Dhd Cpe 2-dr	I6/298	18605	N/A	Note 3
Park Ward	Spt Saloon	I6/298	N/A	N/A	Note 3
James Young	Saloon	I6/298	N/A	N/A	Note 3
Hooper	Saloon	I6/298	N/A	N/A	Note 3
Graber	2-dr Dhd Coupe	I6/298	N/A	N/A	Note 3
Franay	2-dr Coupe	I6/298	N/A	N/A	Note 3

CONTINENTAL S1 SERIES (after 1957)
H.J. Mulliner

Flying Spur	4-dr Saloon	I6/298	N/A	N/A	Note 3

Note 1: A total of 3,107 S1-Series models were built from 1955-59, according to the Rolls-Royce company, most of which wore the basic Bentley Sports Saloon body. An additional 35 long-wheelbase (127-inch) chassis were produced after 1957, a dozen of which went to coachbuilders.

Note 2: Only 145 of the 123-inch wheelbase S1 Bentleys carried a coachbuilt body (including those enumerated above).

Note 3: A total of 431 S1-Series Continentals were produced from 1955-59.

Price Note: Price at the factory in 1957 was $10,050 for the base model, $13,500 for the Continental. Price of the base model in the U.S. rose to $13,695 by the end of the S1 model run.

ENGINE DATA: BASE SIX: Inline, F-head six-cylinder (overhead intake valves, side exhausts). Cast iron block and aluminum head. **Displacement:** 298.2 cu. in. (4887 cc). **Bore & Stroke:** 3.75 x 4.50 in. (95 x 114 mm). **Compression Ratio:** 6.6:1 (Continental, 7.25 or 8.0:1). **Brake Horsepower:** (S1) 178 estimated. Seven main bearings. Solid valve lifters. Two SU carburetors. 12-volt electrical system.

CHASSIS DATA: Wheelbase: 123 in. **Overall Length:** (base S1) 212 in.; (Mulliner Continental) 212 in.; (Park Ward Continental) 210.5 in. **Height:** (S1) 64.25 in.; (Cont.) 62 in. **Width:** (S1) 74.75 in.; (Cont.) 71.5-72 in. **Front Tread:** 58 in. **Rear Tread:** 60 in. **Wheel Type:** five-stud steel disc. **Standard Tires:** 8.20x15.

Note: Dimensions of custom bodies vary.

TECHNICAL: Layout: front-engine, rear-drive. **Transmission:** four-speed automatic. Overall S1 gear ratios: (1st) 13.06:1; (2nd) 9.00:1; (3rd) 4.96:1; (4th) 3.42:1; (rev) 14.72:1. Overall Continental gear ratios: (1st) 11.17:1; (2nd) 7.69:1; (3rd) 4.25:1; (4th) 2.92:1; (rev) 12.59:1. **Standard Final Drive Ratio:** (S1) 3.42:1; (Continental) 2.92:1. **Steering:** cam and roller follower (power assist available). **Suspension (front):** unequal-length wishbones and coil springs; anti-roll rod on Continental. **Suspension (rear):** rigid axle with semi-elliptic leaf springs, Z-type anti-roll bar and electrically-controlled piston-type shock absorbers. **Brakes:** hydraulic front, mechanical rear (servo-assisted). **Body Construction:** steel body on steel box-section frame with cruciform bracing; custom bodies may have aluminum body panels.

MAJOR OPTIONS: Manual transmission (early models only). Power steering (standard by late 1958).

PERFORMANCE: Top Speed: (S1) about 103 mph; (Continental) 119 mph. **Acceleration (0-60 mph):** N/A (S1, 0-50 mph in 9.2 sec.; Continental, 9.3 sec.). **Acceleration (quarter-mile):** (S1) 18.9 sec.; (Cont.) 18.8 sec.

PRODUCTION/SALES: Approximately 31 Bentleys were sold in the U.S. in 1955, 85 in 1956, 150 in 1957, and 97 in 1958.

Manufacturer: Bentley Motors (1931) Ltd., Crewe, Cheshire, England.

Distributor: J.S. Inskip Inc., New York City; Peter Satori Ltd., Pasadena, Calif.; British Motor Car Distributors Ltd., San Francisco; and Overseas Motor Corp., Fort Worth, Texas.

HISTORY: Production of the S1 Series began in 1955 and continued into 1959, when it was replaced by the S2. *The Autocar* magazine said: "The latest Bentley model offers a degree of safety, comfort and performance that is beyond the experience and perhaps even the imagination of the majority of the world's motorists." Power steering was so popular that Bentley even converted 50 earlier models, before it became an official option, in response to customer demands. Bentley's brochure for the Continental noted that "the graceful lines of the Mulliner coachwork were arrived at by wind tunnel testing, with the rear mud guards forming fins to stabilize the car at high speed."

Special models offered during the mid-1950s included the Bentley Countryman, priced at $11,791 in the U.S. in late 1955. Extra features included a built-in bed, tape dictating machine, and space for cocktail accoutrements. Provision was made to plug in an electric kettle, to have a nice cup of tea; and to take a wash and use an electric shaver. Rolls-Royce has its own version of the Countryman, higher in price, based on the 1956 Silver Cloud.

1959 Bentley S1 Continental "Standard Steel" Flying Spur four-door saloon. (Christie's)

S2 SERIES — V-8 — In autumn 1959, an all-aluminum 6230-cc (380-cid) V-8 engine replaced six-cylinder power in the Bentley saloon series. The engine's cylinders contained steel wet liners. Appearance was unchanged from the S2 Series, nearly identical to the Rolls-Royce Silver Cloud II, which also got V-8 power. The only difference inside was new ventilation ducts. Performance got a major boost, with top speed reaching 113 mph and 0-60 mph acceleration time quickening to 10.9 seconds. Engine problems in early examples led to a series of modifications, including a major redesign during 1961. Power steering was standard. Optional air-conditioning units required the use of tinted glass. Air-conditioned Bentleys also were painted either silver or off-white. The number of custom coachbuilders working with the Bentley chassis declined by the 1960s.

1960 Bentley S2 four-door sport sedan. (Christie's)

1961 Bentley S2 Continental Flying Spur four-door sedan. (Christie's)

CONTINENTAL — S2 SERIES — V-8 — Acceleration got a boost with the debut of the V-8 engine in the Continental chassis, but top speed slipped downward because of the unchanged axle ratio. As with the regular S2 Series, the number of custom coachbuilders declined by the 1960s. The short list included the four-door Flying Spur saloon, done by H.J. Mulliner.

I.D. DATA: Serial number plate is under the hood, on the left side of the firewall. A 'B' prefix denotes the S2; 'BC' indicates the Continental. Engine number is on upper front corner of the left side of the crankcase.

97

Model	Body Type & Seating	Engine Type/CID	P.O.E. Price	Weight (lbs.)	Prod. Total
S2 SERIES					
(base)	4-dr Saloon-5/6P	V8/380	14595	4424	Note 1
LWB	4-dr Saloon	V8/380	N/A	N/A	Note 1
H.J. Mulliner					
	2-dr Dhd Cpe	V8/380	N/A	N/A	15
Park Ward					
	2-dr Dhd Cpe	V8/380	N/A	N/A	Note 1
James Young					
	4-dr Limousine	V8/380	N/A	N/A	5
Radford					
Countryman	4-dr Saloon	V8/380	N/A	N/A	Note 1
CONTINENTAL S2 SERIES					
H.J. Mulliner					
	2-dr Saloon	V8/380	N/A	N/A	Note 2
Flying Spur	4-dr Saloon	V8/380	N/A	N/A	Note 2
Park Ward					
	2-dr Dhd Cpe	V8/380	N/A	N/A	Note 2
James Young					
	4-dr Saloon	V8/380	N/A	N/A	Note 2

Note 1: A total of 2,310 S2-Series models were built from 1959-62, according to the Rolls-Royce company, most of which wore the basic Bentley Sports Saloon body. Other sources put the total as low as 1,865 units, plus an additional 57 long-wheelbase (127-inch) chassis. In addition to the custom-built S2 models noted above, a few were built by the Franay, Freestone & Webb, and Graber companies.

Note 2: A total of 388 S2-Series Continentals were produced from 1959-62. Probably no more than 105 were sold in the U.S.

ENGINE DATA: BASE V-8: 90-degree, overhead-valve "vee" type eight-cylinder. Cast aluminum block and head. **Displacement:** 380 cu. in. (6230 cc). **Bore & Stroke:** 4.10 x 3.60 in. (104.1 x 91.5 mm). **Compression Ratio:** 8.0:1. **Brake Horsepower:** 200 (estimated). Five main bearings. Hydraulic valve lifters. Two SU diaphragm-type carburetors. 12-volt electrical system.

CHASSIS DATA: Wheelbase: 123 in. except (LWB) 127 in. **Overall Length:** (base S2) 211.75 in.; (LWB S2) 215.75 in.; (Continental) 212-212.5 in. **Height:** (S2) 64 in.; (Cont.) 61 in. **Width:** (S2) 74.75 in.; (Cont.) 71.75-73.5 in. **Front Tread:** 58.5 in. **Rear Tread:** 60 in. **Wheel Type:** five-stud steel disc. **Standard Tires:** (S2) 8.20x15; (Cont.) 8.00x15.

Note: Dimensions of custom bodies vary.

TECHNICAL: Layout: front-engine, rear-drive. **Transmission:** four-speed automatic. Overall S2 gear ratios: (1st) 11.75:1; (2nd) 8.10:1; (3rd) 4.46:1; (4th) 3.08:1; (rev) 13.25:1. Overall Continental gear ratios: (1st) 11.17:1; (2nd) 7.69:1; (3rd) 4.25:1; (4th) 2.92:1; (rev) 12.57:1. **Standard Final Drive Ratio:** (S2) 3.08:1; (Continental) 2.92:1. **Steering:** cam and roller (power assisted). **Suspension (front):** unequal-length wishbones and coil springs, with anti-roll torsion bar. **Suspension (rear):** rigid axle with semi-elliptic leaf springs, single radius rod and electrically-controlled shock absorbers. **Brakes:** hydraulic front, mechanical rear (servo-assisted). **Body Construction:** steel body on steel box-section frame with cruciform bracing; custom bodies may have aluminum body panels. **Fuel Tank:** 21.6 gallons (U.S.).

PERFORMANCE: Top Speed: (S2) 113 mph; (Continental) 113 mph. **Acceleration (0-60 mph):** (S2) 10.9 sec. **Acceleration (quarter-mile):** (Cont.) 18.6 sec.

Manufacturer: Bentley Motors (1931) Ltd., Crewe, Cheshire, England.

HISTORY: Production of the S2 Series began in late 1959 and continued into 1962, when it was replaced by the S3 Series.

1962-1965 BENTLEY

1962 Bentley S2 Continental. (Coys of Kensington)

S3 SERIES — V-8 — Introduced in autumn 1962, the final versions of the S Series enjoyed a rise in power because of larger carburetors and increased compression (up from 8.0:1 to 9.0:1). Interiors grew more spacious, and front seats were separately adjustable. As for appearance, a lowered radiator produced an altered hood line, sloping slightly downward. More noticeable were the new inboard quad (side-by-side) headlamps, in oval housings. As usual, the S3 was nearly identical to the Rolls-Royce Silver Cloud III, except for the Bentley's rounded vertical-bar grille. Top speed rose slightly, to about 115 mph. Power-steering units gave a greater degree of assist, for lighter steering. Standard

equipment included a four-speed automatic transmission, power brakes, radio and heater. Air conditioning also was available.

Custom coachbuilders continued to ply their trade on the Bentley chassis, though in smaller numbers than before. H.J. Mulliner produced only one drophead coupe in the S3 Series, while Park Ward created a slab-sided fixed-head and drophead coupe with slanted quad headlamps and sharp tailfins.

1963 Bentley S3 Continental Flying Spur. (Coys of Kensington)

CONTINENTAL — S3 SERIES — V-8 — By this time, differences between the Continental and the regular S3 Series were minimal. Even their rear-axle ratios became identical, but a running change in the Continental's ratio produced an increase in top speed to about 117 mph. Custom bodies continued, produced by H.J. Mulliner, Park Ward and James Young. This would be the final version of the Continental.

I.D. DATA: Serial number plate is under the hood, on the left side of the firewall. A 'B' prefix denotes the S3; 'BC' indicates the Continental. Engine number is on upper front corner of the left side of the crankcase.

Model	Body Type & Seating	Engine Type/CID	P.O.E. Price	Weight (lbs.)	Prod. Total
S3 SERIES					
(base)	4-dr Saloon-5/6P	V8/380	16355	4659	Note 1
LWB	4-dr Saloon-5/6P	V8/380	N/A	N/A	Note 1
H.J. Mulliner					
	2-dr Coupe	V8/380	N/A	N/A	Note 1
	2-dr Dhd Cpe	V8/380	N/A	N/A	Note 1
Park Ward					
	2-dr Coupe	V8/380	N/A	N/A	Note 1
	2-dr Dhd Cpe	V8/380	N/A	N/A	Note 1
James Young					
LWB	4-dr Limousine	V8/380	N/A	N/A	Note 1
CONTINENTAL S3 SERIES					
H.J. Mulliner-Park Ward					
	2-dr Coupe	V8/380	N/A	N/A	Note 2
	2-dr Dhd Cpe	V8/380	N/A	N/A	Note 2
Flying Spur	4-dr Saloon	V8/380	N/A	N/A	Note 2
James Young					
	2-dr Coupe	V8/380	N/A	N/A	Note 2
	4-dr Saloon	V8/380	N/A	N/A	Note 2

Note 1: A total of 1,630 S3-Series models were built from 1962-65, according to the Rolls-Royce company, most of which wore the basic Bentley Sports Saloon body. Other sources put the total at only 1,286 units, plus an additional 32 long-wheelbase (127-inch) chassis.

Note 2: A total of 312 S3-Series Continentals were produced from 1962-65.

ENGINE DATA: BASE V-8: 90-degree, overhead-valve "vee" type eight-cylinder. Cast aluminum block and head. **Displacement:** 380 cu. in. (6230 cc). **Bore & Stroke:** 4.10 x 3.60 in. (104.1 x 91.5 mm). **Compression Ratio:** 9.0:1. **Brake Horsepower:** 200+ (estimated). Five main bearings. Hydraulic valve lifters. Two SU diaphragm-type carburetors. 12-volt electrical system.

CHASSIS DATA: Wheelbase: 123 in. except (LWB) 127 in. **Overall Length:** (base S3) 211.75 in.; (LWB S3) 215.75 in.; (Continental) 212-212.6 in. **Height:** 64 in. **Width:** (S3) 74.75 in.; (Cont.) 73 in. **Front Tread:** 58.5 in. **Rear Tread:** 60 in. **Wheel Type:** five-stud steel disc. **Standard Tires:** (S3) 8.20x15; (Cont.) 8.00x15.

Note: Dimensions of custom bodies vary.

TECHNICAL: Layout: front-engine, rear-drive. **Transmission:** four-speed automatic. **Standard Final Drive Ratio:** (S3) 3.08:1; (Continental) 3.08:1. **Steering:** cam and roller (power assisted). **Suspension (front):** unequal-length wishbones and coil springs, with anti-roll torsion bar. **Suspension (rear):** rigid axle with semi-elliptic leaf springs, single radius rod and electrically-controlled shock absorbers. **Brakes:** hydraulic front, hydraulic/mechanical rear (servo-assisted). **Body Construction:** steel body on steel box-section frame with cruciform bracing; custom bodies may have aluminum body panels. **Fuel Tank:** (S3) 22.5 gal. (U.S.); (Continental) 21.6 gallon.

PERFORMANCE: Top Speed: (S3) 115 mph; (Continental) 113-117 mph. **Fuel Mileage:** (Cont.) under 12 mpg.

Manufacturer: Bentley Motors (1931) Ltd., Crewe, Cheshire, England.

Distributor: Rolls-Royce Inc., New York City.

HISTORY: Production of the S3 Series began in late 1962 and continued until September 1965, when it was replaced by the T Series.

1966-76 BENTLEY

T (T1) SERIES — V-8 — A new T-Series Bentley was introduced in October 1965, to replace the decade-old S-Series design. Instead of the traditional separate body and frame, the new Bentley employed unit construction. That signaled the end of true cus-

tom bodies from outside coachbuilders. Variants were produced by James Young and Mulliner-Park Ward, but the coachbuilders had to work with the original saloon structure. The new Bentley's wheelbase was 3.5 inches shorter than the S Series, and the basic saloon measured 8 inches shorter overall. Height and width also shrunk. In profile, the T Series had a more squared-off, straight-up-and-down look. Quad headlamps sat alongside the dignified vertical-bar grille, which, as usual, was the main distinguishing feature between the Bentley and the new Rolls-Royce Silver Shadow. Tires grew from 8.45x15 to 235/70HR15 (radial) in 1974, requiring the addition of flares to the wheel arches.

Mechanical features included a new hydraulic-leveling system, which worked in conjunction with the regular coil-spring suspension at front and rear. Four-wheel disc brakes now were standard. So were power steering and power windows, and an automatic transmission. Initial models used the same four-speed automatic as the S Series; but export Bentleys adopted a GM 400 three-speed unit, which became standard on all models in 1968. New cylinder heads went on the 6230-cc V-8 engine, otherwise continued from the S Series; that change moved the spark plug position to above the manifolds. An alternator replaced the DC generator in mid-1968. Air conditioning became standard during 1969, and the front height-control setup was abandoned. Engine displacement grew to 6750 cc (412 cid) in 1970, and central door locking became available. Other running changes included a switch to radial tires and the addition of speed control, both in 1972. Tightening U.S. emissions standards affected Bentleys in the early 1970s, dropping the V-8s compression ratio down to 7.3:1 by 1975. Late in that year, Lucas electronic ignition became standard.

1968 Bentley T1. (Coys of Kensington)

I.D. DATA: Serial number is on left side of cowl, under the hood. The number consists of three letters, followed by four digits. Letter one indicates model ('S' = standard; 'C' = coachbuilt; 'D' = drophead). Letter two indicates make ('B' = Bentley). Letter three indicates right-hand or left-hand drive ('H' = RHD; 'X' = LHD). On later North American models, the third letter denotes the year ('A' = 1972; 'B' = 1973; 'C' = 1974; 'D' = 1975; 'E' = 1976). Serial number range (1966-67): 1000-5999; (1968-69) 6000-8999.

Model	Body Type & Seating	Engine Type/CID	P.O.E. Price	Weight (lbs.)	Prod. Total
(T1) SERIES (base)	4-dr Saloon-5/6P	V8/380	19550	4636	Note 1
H.J. Mulliner-Park Ward					
	2-dr Coupe	V8/380	29000	N/A	98
	2-dr Conv Cpe	V8/380	31400	N/A	41
James Young					
	2-dr Saloon	V8/380	N/A	N/A	15

Note 1: A total of 1,852 T1-Series models were built from 1965-77, according to the Rolls-Royce company, most of which wore the basic Bentley body. Other sources put the total at only 1,712 units.

Base Saloon Price Note: Figure shown for base saloon was valid in 1966. It dropped to $19,450 by 1968, but rose to $23,600 in 1971; $25,000 in 1972; and $27,700 in 1973.

Mulliner-Park Ward Price Note: Figures shown were valid in 1969-70, but rose to $32,000 and $34,000 (respectively) in 1971. By 1973, prices rose to $39,100 for the coupe and $41,900 for the convertible. By that time, they were referred to as "Corniche" models (see next listing).

Production Note: Figures shown for Mulliner-Park Ward custom models cover the 1966-70 period; the James Young version was built in 1966-67. A total of 146 Bentleys were produced during 1973, 120 in 1974, 115 in 1975, and 100 in 1976.

ENGINE DATA: BASE V-8 (1965-70): 90-degree, overhead-valve "vee" type eight-cylinder. Cast aluminum block and head. **Displacement:** 380 cu. in. (6230 cc). **Bore & Stroke:** 4.10 x 3.60 in. (104.1 x 91.5 mm). **Compression Ratio:** 9.0:1. **Brake Horsepower:** 200 (estimated). Five main bearings. Hydraulic valve lifters. Two SU HD8 horizontal carburetors.

BASE V-8 (1970-76): 90-degree, overhead-valve "vee" type eight-cylinder. Cast aluminum block and head. **Displacement:** 412 cu. in. (6750 cc). **Bore & Stroke:** 4.10 x 3.90 in. (104.1 x 99 mm). **Compression Ratio:** 9.0:1 (8.0:1 later; 7.3:1 in 1975). **Brake Horsepower:** 220 (estimated). Five main bearings. Hydraulic valve lifters. Two SU carburetors.

CHASSIS DATA: Wheelbase: 119.5 in. **Overall Length:** 203.5 in. **Height:** 59.75 in. **Width:** 71 in. **Front Tread:** 57.5 in. **Rear Tread:** 57.5 in. **Wheel Type:** disc. **Standard Tires:** (early) 8.45x15; (later) 205x15; (1974-76) 235/70HR15.

TECHNICAL: Layout: front-engine, rear-drive. **Transmission:** four-speed automatic. Gear ratios: (1st) 3.82:1; (2nd) 2.63:1; (3rd) 1.45:1; (4th) 1.00:1; (rev) 4.30:1. Export models and others built after 1967 had GM 400 three-speed automatic. **Standard Final Drive Ratio:** 3.08:1. **Steering:** recirculating ball (variable power assisted). **Suspension (front):** wishbones and coil springs, with automatic leveling (early models). **Suspension (rear):** independent, semi-trailing arms with coil springs and automatic leveling. **Brakes:** hydraulic, front/rear disc. **Body Construction:** steel unibody with front and rear auxiliary frames. **Fuel Tank:** 28.8 gallons (U.S.).

PERFORMANCE: Top Speed: about 120 mph. **Acceleration (0-60 mph):** under 11 sec. (1960s model).

Manufacturer: Bentley Motors (1931) Ltd., Crewe, Cheshire, England.

Distributor: Rolls-Royce Inc., Paramus, New Jersey.

HISTORY: Production of the T1 Series began in late 1965 and continued until 1977, when it was replaced by the T2 Series. The "Corniche" designation for Rolls/Bentley coupes and convertibles was first adopted in 1971. The Rolls-Royce company faced bankruptcy in 1971, and underwent a restructuring.

1977-80 BENTLEY

T2 SERIES — V-8 — As the Rolls-Royce Silver Shadow I evolved into the Shadow II, so too did the Bentley develop into a second T Series. Rack-and-pinion steering replaced the former recirculating-ball setup. Dual-level automatic air conditioning and cruise control became standard. The engine added a new dual exhaust system and new carburetors. Home-market versions added a front air dam and headlamp wipers, but neither item was included on examples destined for the U.S. For that reason, appearance differed little from the prior T1 Series. Inside, the central console was larger and the instrument panel was restyled, using large round gauges below a wide raised hump.

CORNICHE — V-8 — Bentley coupes and convertibles were produced under the "Corniche" name, but in far fewer numbers than the Rolls-Royce versions, introduced in 1971. As before, technical details were identical to the regular T Series. The difference was the special body, produced by Mulliner-Park Ward. Corniches were named for a road that runs between Nice, France and Monte Carlo, along the Mediterranean Sea.

I.D. DATA: Serial number is on left side of cowl, under the hood. The number consists of three letters, followed by four digits. Letter one indicates model ('S' = standard; 'C' = coachbuilt; 'D' = drophead). Letter two indicates make ('B' = Bentley). On North American models, the third letter denotes the year ('F' = 1977; 'G' = 1978; 'K' = 1979; 'L' = 1980).

Model	Body Type & Seating	Engine Type/CID	P.O.E. Price	Weight (lbs.)	Prod. Total
T2 SERIES (base)	4-dr Saloon-5/6P	V8/412	84800	N/A	Note 1
CORNICHE					
	2-dr Coupe	V8/412	138800	N/A	53
	2-dr Conv Cpe	V8/412	147900	N/A	45

Note 1: A total of 568 T2-Series models were built from 1977-81, according to the Rolls-Royce company.

Base Saloon Price Note: Figure shown for base saloon was valid in 1980.

Corniche Price Note: Figures shown were valid in 1980, but rose to $145,740 and $155,295 (respectively) in 1981, as the new Mulsanne emerged.

ENGINE DATA: BASE V-8: 90-degree, overhead-valve "vee" type eight-cylinder. Cast aluminum block and head. **Displacement:** 412 cu. in. (6750 cc). **Bore & Stroke:** 4.10 x 3.90 in. (104.1 x 99 mm). **Brake Horsepower:** 220 (estimated). Five main bearings. Hydraulic valve lifters. Two carburetors.

CHASSIS DATA: Wheelbase: 119.5 in. **Overall Length:** 203.5 in. **Height:** 59.75 in. **Width:** 71 in. **Front Tread:** 57.5 in. **Rear Tread:** 57.5 in. **Wheel Type:** disc. **Standard Tires:** 235/70HR15.

TECHNICAL: Layout: front-engine, rear-drive. **Transmission:** three-speed automatic. **Steering:** rack and pinion (variable power assisted). **Suspension (front):** wishbones and coil springs. **Suspension (rear):** independent, semi-trailing arms with coil springs and automatic leveling. **Brakes:** hydraulic, front/rear disc. **Body Construction:** steel unibody with front and rear auxiliary frames.

PERFORMANCE: Top Speed: (European T2) 118 mph. **Fuel Mileage:** almost 12 mpg (U.S.).

Manufacturer: Bentley Motors (1931) Ltd. (Rolls-Royce Motors Ltd.), Crewe, Cheshire, England.

Distributor: Rolls-Royce Motors Inc., Paramus, New Jersey.

HISTORY: Production of the T2 Series began in 1977 and continued through 1980.

1981-84 BENTLEY

MULSANNE — V-8 — Introduced in Europe in October 1980, the new Bentley series didn't arrive in the U.S. until about June 1981. Styling was modified considerably, giving less of an upright and angular appearance. Mechanically identical to the new Rolls-Royce Silver Spirit (and altered little from the prior T Series), the Mulsanne differed mainly in its grille design, as had been the case for much of the postwar period. Bentley's version, as usual, was made up of vertical bars. A bodyside trim strip ran the full length of the car. Large wraparound rectangular parking lights and taillamps were installed. Headlamps were now faired into the front fenders. Veneered door cappings no longer were used inside. Wheelbase was 120.5 inches, and the new model was about two inches wider and an inch lower than the T Series. Standard equipment included Connolly leather upholstery, Wilton carpeting, a walnut burl instrument panel, and dual-level air conditioning.

MULSANNE TURBO — V-8 — A turbocharger was installed on V-8 Bentley saloons to help revive the car's performance image, which had languished somewhat since the demise of the Continental. With the extra power, a 2-1/2 ton Bentley could reach 60 mph in a startling 6.7 seconds. The Turbo's grille shell was painted body color instead of the customary chrome. When placed on sale in the U.S., the performance model adopted the name "Turbo R" (see next listing).

CORNICHE — V-8 — Convertibles continued in production under the "Corniche" name, just as they were for the Rolls-Royce side of the "family."

I.D. DATA: A 17-symbol Vehicle Identification Number is on the upper left of the dashboard, visible through the windshield. Symbol one is the letter 'S'. Symbol two ('C') identifies the company. Symbol three denotes make ('B' = Bentley). Symbol four is the letter 'Z'. Symbol five gives the body type ('S' = short-wheelbase four-door; 'D' = Corniche conv.). Symbol ten indicates year built ('A' = 1980, 'B' = 1981, etc.). Symbol 11 identifies the assembly plant ('C' = Crewe). Symbol 12 indicates steering-wheel position ('H' = RHD; 'X' = LHD). Symbols 13-17 form the sequential serial number.

Model	Body Type & Seating	Engine Type/CID	P.O.E. Price	Weight (lbs.)	Prod. Total
MULSANNE					
	4-dr Saloon-5P	V8/412	110370	4950	N/A
MULSANNE TURBO					
	4-dr Saloon-5P	V8/412	N/A	5052	N/A

Model	Body Type & Seating	Engine Type/CID	P.O.E. Price	Weight (lbs.)	Prod. Total
CORNICHE					
	2-dr Conv Cpe-4P	V8/412	161950	5204	N/A

Saloon Price Note: Figure shown for base saloon was valid in 1982. A lower-priced version emerged by 1984, priced at $97,950; and the former model, priced at $108,390, was then known as the 'L' type.

Corniche Price Note: Figure shown was valid in 1982. Price fell to $155,470 in 1984.

ENGINE DATA: BASE V-8: 90-degree, overhead-valve "vee" type eight-cylinder. Cast aluminum block and head. **Displacement:** 412 cu. in. (6750 cc). **Bore & Stroke:** 4.10 x 3.90 in. (104.1 x 99 mm). **Compression Ratio:** 9.0:1 (8.0:1 in U.S.). **Brake Horsepower:** 220 (estimated). Five main bearings. Hydraulic valve lifters. Two SU carburetors except (Corniche) Solex four-barrel. U.S. models had Bosch K-Jetronic fuel injection.

BASE V-8 (Mulsanne Turbo): Same as above, except — **Compression Ratio:** 8.0:1. **Brake Horsepower:** 300 (estimated). Solex four-barrel carburetor.

CHASSIS DATA: Wheelbase: 120.5 in.; (Corniche) 120.1 in. **Overall Length:** 209 in.; (Corniche) 204.6 in. **Height:** 58.7 in.; (Corniche) 60 in. **Width:** 74.4 in.; (Corniche) 71.6 in. **Front Tread:** 60.6 in.; (Corniche) 60 in. **Rear Tread:** 60.6 in. **Wheel Type:** disc. **Standard Tires:** 235/70HR15.

TECHNICAL: Layout: front-engine, rear-drive. **Transmission:** three-speed automatic. Overall gear ratios: (1st) 7.7:1; (2nd) 4.62:1; (3rd) 3.08:1. **Standard Final Drive Ratio:** 3.08:1. **Steering:** rack and pinion (variable power assisted). **Suspension (front):** lower wishbones, coil springs and anti-roll bar. **Suspension (rear):** independent, trailing arms with coil springs, auxiliary gas springs, anti-roll bar and automatic leveling. **Brakes:** hydraulic, front/rear disc. **Body Construction:** steel unibody.

PERFORMANCE: Top Speed: (Mulsanne, European) 118 mph; (Turbo) 135 mph. **Acceleration (0-60 mph):** (Turbo) 6.7 sec. **Fuel Mileage:** about 13 mpg.

Manufacturer: Bentley Motors Ltd. (Rolls-Royce Motors Ltd.), Crewe, Cheshire, England.

Distributor: Rolls-Royce Motors Inc., Lyndhurst, New Jersey.

HISTORY: Production of the Mulsanne began in 1980. The Mulsanne Turbo went into production in 1982. The Bentley Eight and Continental were introduced in 1984; see next listing for details. During the mid-1980s, about 30 Bentleys were imported to the U.S. each year.

1985-90 BENTLEY

EIGHT — V-8 — Bentley's lineup expanded with the arrival of the Bentley Eight and the Continental convertible. The late 1980s "Eight" wore a distinctive mesh grille instead of the usual vertical-bar style, said to be "reminiscent of the great racing machines of the 'twenties." Amber wraparound park/signal lights stood alongside the quad round headlamps, which sat in blackout mountings. Interiors were trimmed in straight-grain walnut veneer, with leather upholstery and Wilton carpeting. On the mechanical side, anti-lock braking soon became standard, and alloy wheels were used. By 1987, all Bentley engines were fuel-injected.

MULSANNE S — V-8 — Wearing a conventional bright-shelled Bentley-style vertical-bar grille, the Mulsanne saloon included such performance-oriented features as a front air dam and a tachometer. Its instrument panel and waist rails were formed of straight-grain walnut veneer, with a full center console. Technical features were otherwise identical to the Bentley Eight. Standard equipment included bi-level air conditioning, leather upholstery, and lambswool carpeting. Power front seats in late models were heated, and included a four-position memory and power lumbar support. A driver's-side airbag also became standard.

1990 Bentley Turbo R.

TURBO R — V-8 — The original Mulsanne Turbo evolved into the Turbo R for sale in the U.S., billed as the "ultimate luxury sporting saloon." An electronically-controlled, intercooled Garrett AiResearch turbocharger helped produced 0-60 mph acceleration in less than 7 seconds, 0-100 mph in under 20 seconds, and a top speed beyond 135 mph. A Turbo R could accelerate from 50-70 mph in 4 seconds, with virtually no turbo lag. The cockpit-style interior blended performance extras and luxurious fittings. Those included sports-style seats in hand-cut, hand-stitched Connolly leather, Wilton wool carpeting, and a full set of analog instruments (including tachometer and 170-mph speedometer) in a rich, hand-rubbed burr walnut veneer facia. Standard equipment included bi-level automatic air conditioning that automatically compensated for the sun's heat, a four-position memory seat, sensor for icy road conditions, and fold-down tables. Luxury touches even included an ashtray that emptied automatically. Unlike other Bentley models, the Turbo R had no chromed surround as part of its vertical-bar grille; instead, its

outer edges were body-colored. Appearance features also included a deep front air dam, flared rocker panels, and rear skirts. The power steering had less power-assist than former models. Estimates of the engine's output ranged from about 297 to 325 horsepower, torque from 450 to 487 pound-feet.

1990 Bentley Continental convertible.

CONTINENTAL — V-8 — Convertibles took on a new name (formerly Corniche) in 1984. Bodies were hand-crafted by Mulliner Park Ward. Features included luxury sports-style seats, a power top, and automatic bi-level air conditioning. Instead of the larger wraparound park/signal lights used on other models, the convertible used small amber units at fender tips.

I.D. DATA: A 17-symbol Vehicle Identification Number is on the upper left of the dashboard, visible through the windshield. Symbol one is the letter 'S'. Symbol two ('C') identifies the company. Symbol three denotes make ('B' = Bentley). Symbol four is the letter 'Z'. Symbol five gives the body type ('S' = short-wheelbase four-door; 'D' = Corniche conv.). Symbol ten indicates year built ('F' = 1985, 'G' = 1986, 'H' = 1987, etc.). Symbol 11 identifies the assembly plant ('C' = Crewe). Symbol 12 indicates steering-wheel position ('H' = RHD; 'X' = LHD). Symbols 13-17 form the sequential serial number.

Model	Body Type & Seating	Engine Type/CID	P.O.E. Price	Weight (lbs.)	Prod. Total
EIGHT					
	4-dr Saloon-4/5P	V8/412	108700	5120	N/A
MULSANNE S					
S	4-dr Saloon-4/5P	V8/412	118900	5120	N/A
TURBO R					
	4-dr Saloon-4/5P	V8/412	149500	5270	N/A
CONTINENTAL					
	2-dr Conv Cpe	V8/412	204800	5340	N/A

Price Note: Figures shown were valid in 1989. In 1990 they rose to $114,100 for the Eight, $133,200 for the Mulsanne S, $167,400 for the Turbo R, and $215,000 for the Continental.

ENGINE DATA: BASE V-8: 90-degree, overhead-valve "vee" type eight-cylinder. Cast aluminum block and head. **Displacement:** 412 cu. in. (6750 cc). **Bore & Stroke:** 4.10 x 3.90 in. (104.1 x 99 mm). **Compression Ratio:** 8.0:1. **Brake Horsepower:** 220 (estimated). Five main bearings. Hydraulic valve lifters. Two carburetors, or Bosch MK-Motronic port fuel injection.

BASE V-8 (Turbo R): Same as above, except Garrett AiResearch turbocharged (with intercooler). **Brake Horsepower:** 297 + at 3800 rpm (estimated). **Torque:** up to 487 lbs.-ft. at 2400 rpm (estimated). Bosch MK-Motronic port fuel injection.

CHASSIS DATA: Wheelbase: 120.5 in. **Overall Length:** (Mulsanne) 207.8 in.; (Turbo) 207.4 in.; (Continental) 207.5 in. **Height:** 58.5-58.7 in.; (Cont.) 59.8 in. **Width:** 79 in.; (Cont.) 77.1 in. **Front Tread:** 61 in. **Rear Tread:** 61 in. **Wheel Type:** disc; (Turbo) 7Jx15 aluminum alloy. **Standard Tires:** (Mulsanne) 235/70VR15; (early Turbo) 275/55VR15 Pirelli P7; (later Turbo) 255/65R15 Avon.

TECHNICAL: Layout: front-engine, rear-drive. **Transmission:** three-speed automatic. **Standard Final Drive Ratio:** (Mulsanne) 3.07:1; (Turbo) 2.69:1. **Steering:** rack and pinion (variable power assisted). **Suspension (front):** upper levers, lower wishbones, coil springs and anti-roll bar (Turbo). **Suspension (rear):** independent, semi-trailing arms with coil springs, auxiliary gas springs, Panhard rod, and automatic leveling. **Brakes:** hydraulic, front/rear disc with anti-locking. **Body Construction:** steel unibody; aluminum doors, hood and deck. **Fuel Tank:** 28.5 gallon.

MAJOR OPTIONS: Cocktail cabinet (for console). Trunk-mounted refrigerator.

PERFORMANCE: Top Speed: (Turbo) 135+ mph. **Acceleration (0-60 mph):** (Turbo) 6.7 sec. **Acceleration (quarter-mile):** (Turbo) 15.7 sec. **Fuel Mileage:** (Eight) 9 mpg EPA, barely over 7 mpg in test.

Manufacturer: Rolls-Royce Motor Cars Ltd., Crewe, Cheshire, England.

Distributor: Rolls-Royce Motor Cars Inc., Lyndhurst, New Jersey.

HISTORY: The Turbo R was introduced in Europe in 1985, and came to the U.S. late in 1988. The Bentley Eight went into production in 1984 and entered the U.S. market in late 1986, the Mulsanne S in late 1987. Continentals began production in 1984. Each model described was still on sale in 1990. Promotional material for the Turbo R announced that it "will out-accelerate most high-performance cars currently on the road," and was the "fastest four-door production car on earth." Only four or five per week were to be built for the U.S. market. A turbocharged production Bentley won the British one-hour endurance distance title in 1987, breaking 15 other major records. Traveling over 140 mph, it beat the Lamborghini Countach's record by eight miles.

BERKELEY

Designed by Lawrence Bond (who penned the Bond mini-car a few years earlier, in 1949), the Berkeley took the sports car concept down to its tiniest dimensions. Bond's objective was to create a sporty car that was cheap to buy and run, but performed with enough spirit to appeal to en-

thusiasts. He did his work at the request of Charles Panter of the Berkeley Coachwork Company, a builder of trailers in Britain. Because that firm was already accustomed to working with fiberglass, that material seemed logical for the Berkeley. So Bond developed an alloy-reinforced fiberglass tub, which was bonded to a steel chassis.

Berkeley's initial appearance was at the London Motor Show in the fall of 1956. A modest number of Berkeleys found their way to the U.S., especially to California. Because a Berkeley cost just about as much as some ordinary-size sports cars, such as the Austin-Healey Sprite, sales never reached a sizable figure.

Ads in 1958 promised "vivid acceleration" and "boundless capacity for fun," along with 60-mpg economy. A Berkeley, they said, "generally requites the sportsman's love for a fine machine." In that year (1958), a larger engine was available; and it grew larger yet for 1959-60, the final years for the Berkeley. After attempting to produce one more model, the Bandit (designed by John Tojeiro) in 1961, the Berkeley company returned to the manufacture of trailers.

1956-57 BERKELEY

1957 Berkeley.

328 — TWO — For its first two years on the market, the miniature Berkeley sports car was powered by either an Anzani or Excelsior engine. The latter, known as the "Talisman Twin," was similar in displacement but of different bore/stroke dimensions. Either engine was mounted ahead of the front axle. A gate-style gearshift lever moved in a progressive (forward-and-back) pattern like that of a motorcycle, with neutral positions between gears as well as a main neutral.

To give an indication of the car's tiny size and weight, the fender tops reached only to a 25-inch height, and one man could lift the back end off the ground. A tiny rumble seat for (small) children could be mounted in the space ordinarily filled by the spare tire, which could be moved into the dashboard parcel area instead. Berkeleys had fully independent suspension at all four wheels. Standard fittings included a 120-mph speedometer, fuel gauge and ammeter (but no temperature gauge). Seats had no conventional adjustment, and no provision was made for a heater.

A crosshatch-patterned oval grille stood below the crease at the front of the nose. A round ornament was ahead of the near-horizontal hood. Headlamps were recessed deeply into long nacelles.

I.D. DATA: Serial number plate is located on left side of firewall, in the engine compartment.

Model	Body Type & Seating	Engine Type/CID	P.O.E. Price	Weight (lbs.)	Prod. Total
328	2-dr Roadster-2P	l2/20	1600	616	Note 1

Note 1: About 3,000 Berkeleys were sold by 1960.

Price Note: Price at Port of Entry is approximate. Initial price was equivalent to $1064 (at the factory in England).

ENGINE DATA: ANZANI TWO: Vertical, air cooled two-cylinder. **Displacement:** 19.64 cu. in. (322 cc). **Bore & Stroke:** 2.36 x 2.24 in. (60 x 57 mm). **Compression Ratio:** 8.5:1. **Brake Horsepower:** 18 at 5000 rpm. Amal carburetor. Dual exhausts.

EXCELSIOR TWO: Vertical, air cooled two-cylinder (two-stroke). **Displacement:** 20 cu. in. (328 cc). **Bore & Stroke:** 2.28 x 2.44 in. (58 x 62 mm). **Compression Ratio:** 7.4:1. (8.2:1 optional). **Brake Horsepower:** 18 at 5000 rpm. **Torque:** 21.6 lbs.-ft. at 3000 rpm. Amal carburetor. Dual exhausts.

CHASSIS DATA: Wheelbase: 70 in. **Overall Length:** 123 in. **Height:** 41 in. **Width:** 50 in. **Front Tread:** 44 in. **Rear Tread:** 44 in. **Standard Tires:** 5.20x12 Michelin.

TECHNICAL: Layout: front-engine (transversely mounted), front-drive. **Transmission:** three-speed motorcycle-type with chain drive to three-plate disc clutch. **Standard Final Drive Ratio:** 5.27:1 (by duplex chain and steel sprocket). **Steering:** Burman worm and nut. **Suspension (front):** independent; twin wishbones with combined coil springs and shocks. **Suspension (rear):** independent; swinging axles with combined coil springs and shocks. **Brakes:** Girling front/rear drum. **Body Construction:** unitized three-piece design; body and frame of resin bonded, molded fiberglass with aluminum bulkheads and three crossmembers. Steel subframe for drivetrain and suspension.

MAJOR OPTIONS: Detachable hardtop.

PERFORMANCE: Top Speed: 60-70 mph. **Acceleration (0-60 mph):** N/A (0-50 mph in about 30.6 seconds). **Fuel Mileage:** 60 mpg (factory).

Manufacturer: Berkeley Ltd., Biggleswade, Bedfordshire, England (a manufacturer of house trailers).

1958-59 BERKELEY

1958 Berkeley sports car. (William Siuru Jr.)

328 — TWO — Although production in England switched over to a larger three-cylinder engine during 1957, two-cylinder Berkeleys were still arriving in the U.S. after that time. Home-market models had nicely faired-in headlamps, but because of certain state laws in the U.S., some imported Berkeleys arrived with tackily tacked-on headlamps.

SPORTS 500 — THREE — After an early run with two-cylinder power, the tiny Berkeley added another cylinder to create the Sports model, with a 492-cc powerplant and 30 horsepower. A hardtop coupe also joined the original roadster body. A Siba Dynastart combined starter and generator was used in the 12-volt electrical system. An ammeter replaced the former ignition-warning light. Unique, thinly-upholstered seat cushions rested on wide rubber bands that adjusted easily to the rider's weight. Sliding windows were added to the side curtains by 1959. Road testers at the time praised the tiny sports car's handling, noting that virtually no roll was evident in turns, yet the ride was quite comfortable.

A longer-wheelbase (78-inch) Foursome version, 131 inches overall, carried the same powerplant but was able to squeeze in four passengers.

I.D. DATA: Serial number plate is located on left side of firewall, in engine compartment.

Model	Body Type & Seating	Engine Type/CID	P.O.E. Price	Weight (lbs.)	Prod. Total
328	2-dr Roadster-2P	l2/20	1695	616	Note 1
500	2-dr Roadster-2P	l3/30	1745	725	Note 1
500	2-dr Coupe-2P	l3/30	1850	N/A	Note 1

Note 1: Approximately 551 Berkeleys were imported and sold in the U.S. during 1958, while 361 found customers in 1959.

ENGINE DATA: BASE TWO (328): Vertical, air cooled two-cylinder (Excelsior two-stroke). **Displacement:** 20 cu. in. (328 cc). **Bore & Stroke:** 2.28 x 2.44 in. (58 x 62 mm). **Compression Ratio:** 7.4:1. **Brake Horsepower:** 18 at 5000 rpm. **Torque:** 21.4 lbs.-ft. at 3000 rpm. Amal carburetor.

BASE THREE (500): Vertical, air cooled three-cylinder (Excelsior two-stroke). **Displacement:** 30 cu. in. (492 cc). **Bore & Stroke:** 2.28 x 2.44 in. (58 x 62 mm). **Compression Ratio:** 7.5:1. **Brake Horsepower:** 30 at 5500 rpm. Torque: 35.4 lbs.-ft. at 3500 rpm. Three Amal carburetors.

CHASSIS DATA: Wheelbase: 70 in. except (Foursome) 78 in. **Overall Length:** 122.5 in. except (Foursome) 131 in. **Height:** 43.5 in. **Width:** 50 in. except (Foursome) 54 in. **Front Tread:** 44 in. **Rear Tread:** 44 in. **Standard Tires:** 5.20x12 Michelin.

TECHNICAL: Layout: front-engine (transversely mounted), front-drive. **Transmission:** three-speed motorcycle-type with chain drive to three-plate disc clutch; column shift. **Standard Final Drive Ratio:** 4.64:1 or 5.1:1 (by duplex chain and steel sprocket). **Steering:** Burman worm and nut. **Suspension (front):** independent; wishbones with combined coil springs and shocks. **Suspension (rear):** independent; swinging axles with combined coil springs and shocks. **Brakes:** Girling front/rear drum. **Body Construction:** unitized three-piece design; body and frame of resin bonded molded glass fibre with aluminum bulkheads and crossmembers.

PERFORMANCE: Top Speed: 65-75 mph. **Acceleration (0-60 mph):** N/A (0-50 mph in 31-39 seconds with two-cylinder; in 14.4 seconds with three-cylinder). **Acceleration (quarter-mile):** (two-cylinder) 27.9 seconds, reaching 46.4 mph; (three-cylinder) 22.4 seconds. **Fuel Mileage:** 50-65 mpg.

Manufacturer: Berkeley Ltd., Biggleswade, Bedfordshire, England.

Distributor: Berkeley of America, Inc., New Haven, Connecticut. Three other U.S. distributors in Pensacola, Florida; Hollywood, Calif.; and Lubbock, Texas.

HISTORY: A Berkeley won its class at the 1959 Mille Miglia, and also at the Monza 12-Hour Race, beating Abarths in the process.

1960 BERKELEY

1960 Berkeley roadster.

QB95 — TWO — Only a bit bigger dimensionally than in its first incarnation, the British Berkeley for 1960 carried a considerably bigger powerplant with double the original horsepower and a four-stroke design. The bigger Berkeley was introduced in England during 1959, but as is often the case with imports, took a bit longer to arrive in the U.S.

"Docile, easily handled...for town use, the QB95 becomes a really fast and safe sports car when opened up on clear roads." That's how the company described the 1960 Berkeley for its appearance at the 1959 Turin (Italy) auto show. American advertisements promoted it as "The world's lowest-priced all-sports car."

Appearance actually changed somewhat for the minicar's final season. The tiny roadster now sported a square grille with six horizontal bars, and a sizable hood bulge. Rear tires protruded outward past the rear fenders. A pair of pointed round parking lights on each side stood below the slightly curved headlamps (recessed only at the bottom). Fenders rolled sharply inward below the parking lamps, leaving a large gap alongside the nose section.

Deep well sprung bucket-type seats were upholstered in Vynide. Other features included a locking trunk lid, one-piece curved windshield, and Hardura plastic carpets. Standard equipment included a large parcel tray, door pockets, side screens, aluminum alloy wheel discs, and a tool kit. Body colors were red, light blue, dark green, Old English white, and yellow. Upholstery came in either red or light brown.

QB105 — TWO — For its final attempt at sales success, in 1960, Berkeley added 10 horsepower to the 692-cc two-cylinder engine, via a compression boost to 8.0:1, and put that engine in the smaller (original size) chassis. Both engines were available in the shorter-wheelbase chassis, without the ample trunk space, as indicated by the lack of 'Q' prefix in the model number.

I.D. DATA: Serial number plate is located on left side of firewall, in engine compartment. Starting serial (motor) number (1960 models): 5841.

Model	Body Type & Seating	Engine Type/CID	P.O.E. Price	Weight (lbs.)	Prod. Total
B95	2-dr Roadster-2P	I2/42	1595	784	Note 1
B105	2-dr Roadster-2P	I2/42	N/A	784	Note 1
QB95	2-dr Roadster-2P	I2/42	1795	840	Note 1
QB105	2-dr Roadster-2P	I2/42	N/A	840	Note 1

Note 1: A total of about 3,000 Berkeleys were sold by 1960.
Price Note: The B95 was listed for $1632 on the West Coast in 1960.

ENGINE DATA: BASE TWO: Vertical, overhead-valve, air cooled two-cylinder (Royal Enfield). **Displacement:** 42.34 cu. in. (692 cc). **Bore & Stroke:** 2.76 x 3.54 in. (70 x 90 mm). **Compression Ratio:** (B/QB95) 7.25:1; (B/QB105) 8.0:1. **Brake Horsepower:** (B/QB95) 40 at 5500 rpm; (B/QB105) 50 at 6250. **Torque:** (B/QB95) 43 lbs.-ft. Amal monobloc carburetor.

CHASSIS DATA: Wheelbase: (B) 70 in.; (QB) 78 in. **Overall Length:** (B) 127.5 in.; (QB) 133.5 in. **Height:** 46 in. (ground clearance, 5.5 in.). **Width:** (B) 50 in.; (QB) 54 in. **Front Tread:** 46.25 in. **Rear Tread:** 46 in. **Standard Tires:** 5.20x12 Michelin.

TECHNICAL: Layout: front-engine (transversely mounted), front-drive. **Transmission:** four-speed Albion gearbox (floor shift); cable-actuated, multi-plate Albion clutch. Overall gear ratios: (1st) 13.7:1, (2nd) 8.62:1, (3rd) 5.95:1, (top) 4.31:1; and (rev) 14.05:1. **Standard Final Drive Ratio:** 2.23:1 (by duplex chain and steel sprocket). **Steering:** Burman worm and nut (right- or left-hand drive). **Suspension (front):** independent; unequal-length wishbones with combined coil springs and shocks. **Suspension (rear):** independent; swinging arms with combined coil springs and shocks. **Body Construction:** unitized three-piece design; body and frame of resin bonded molded glass fibre with aluminum bulkheads and crossmembers.

MAJOR OPTIONS: Hardtop. Tachometer. Overriders.

PERFORMANCE: Top Speed: (B/QB95) 85 mph, though the factory claimed top speed of 95 and 105 mph for the two models, equivalent to their model numbers. **Acceleration (0-60 mph):** 14 sec. (factory). **Fuel Mileage:** 50 mpg (at 50 mph).

Manufacturer: Berkeley Ltd., Biggleswade, Bedfordshire, England.
Distributor: Berkeley Motor Cars Ltd., Los Angeles, California.

BIZZARRINI

As the Fifties drew to a close, Giotto Bizzarrini was a Ferrari engineer, having served an earlier stint with Alfa Romeo. Late in 1961, he left Ferrari along with several other unhappy engineers. While the rest of the group joined forces and formed their own company (ATS), Bizzarrini went off on his own. Before long, he became involved with another developing Italian supercar, Lamborghini, and also took on work for the new Iso company. The latter would soon evolve into cars that bore his own name. Bizzarrini designed a V-12 car for Lamborghini, and a chassis for Iso. With a pressed steel platform, all-independent coil-spring suspension and De Dion rear axle, plus a Corvette 327 V-8 under the hood, that chassis served as the foundation for his own creation as well as a support for the four-seat Iso Rivolta coupe. A shorter-wheelbase version of the Rivolta chassis wound up below the two-seat Iso Grifo, which appeared in prototype form at the same time as Bizzarrini's own model, in November 1963 at the Turin (Italy) Motor Show. In fact, the Bizzarrini was identified at the time as an Iso A3C "competition coupe." Both carried a 327-cid Corvette V-8 rated at 365 hp, and both wore bodies styled by Giorgio Giugiaro (of Bertone). Giotto Bizzarrini then negotiated permission to produce a variant of the Grifo under his own name.

That soon-to-be Bizzarrini finished 14th at the 1964 Le Mans 24 Hour race, averaging 106.75 mph and winning the GT class. A class victory came again the following year, as the car finished 9th overall. Like the production version to come, the race car had an aluminum body with twin-slot grille and headlamps recessed behind sloping plastic covers. Iso's version had exposed headlamps and a steel body. Early Bizzarrinis had bodies built by Piero Drogo, but the BBM company took over the coachwork chore after the originals displayed problems. By 1966, a smaller edition known as the GT Europa was also in the works, with a fiberglass body and 1.9-liter Opel four-cylinder engine.

1965-69 BIZZARRINI

GT STRADA 5300 — V-8 — Named after the Italian word for "street," followed by the approximate cubic-centimeter displacement of its American-built V-8 engine, the striking Bizzarrini coupe had a chassis from Iso and a body built by BBM (in Modena), from the Bertone design. The hand-assembled coupe presented an extremely low profile with nearly-horizontal back window and full wheel openings. Doors contained vent wings. Headlamps stood far behind plastic covers. A thin bright bumper stretched between the headlamps, just below the twin side-by-side grille openings. An air-intake opening was below the bumper. The car's front engine, mounted rather far back, had a small forward-hinged lid-style hood for access. Grilled engine cooling vents were evident just behind the front wheel wells. Riding a 96.4-inch wheelbase, the low-slung coupe had disc brakes all around, coil springs at each wheel, and a De Dion rear axle. Cast alloy wheels held 6.00x15 tires up front, and 7.00x15 rubber out back. A four-speed Muncie manual gearbox fed power from the nearly-stock 327-cid Corvette V-8 to the rear wheels, giving the GT a top speed of at least 145 mph and the capability of accelerating to 60 mph in about 6.4 seconds. A 7.5-gallon fuel tank was mounted in each sill, with another 20-gallon tank behind the seats to produce a 35-gallon capacity. Early examples used a 365-bhp version of the Corvette V-8 with solid lifters, but the standard engine then switched to a hydraulic-lifter edition rated 350 bhp. While some of the gauges were mounted on the left, others stretched all across the dashboard, with the speedometer and tachometer far to the right.

GT AMERICA — V-8 — For sale in the U.S., the car was known as the "GT America." Both a standard version with single Holley four-barrel carburetor and a competition edition with four Weber carbs were available. The latter cost an extra thousand or so above the $10,500 base price. A chrome rub strip provided the only bump protection up front, though the rear carried a split bumper. *Road & Track* described their semi-competition Bizzarrini, the first one to arrive in the U.S., as "one of the cars we'd most like to be seen in, and it was a pleasure to look up at XKE's." In addition, they found that "handling borders on the fantastic for a road car." Car and Driver called the GT America version "the lustiest, most evil looking apparition ever to wear license plates," adding that it "can be almost sinfully enjoyable as a fun car but as transportation it's a bad second to an arthritic horse." Testers wondered about the car's claimed "dry" weight of 2,375 pounds,

when the actual test vehicle weighed in at 3,020 pounds with only six gallons of gas in the tanks, and found that the claimed five-inch ground clearance was actually closer to three. The 46-foot turning circle drew no raves, either.

1966 Bizzarrini 5300 GT Strada Series I. (Coys of Kensington)*

1967 Bizzarrini 5300 GT Strada.

I.D. DATA: Not available.

Model	Body Type & Seating	Engine Type/CID	P.O.E. Price	Weight (lbs.)	Prod. Total
GT STRADA 5300/GT AMERICA					
Strada	2-dr Coupe-2P	V8/327	N/A	Note 1	Note 2
America	2-dr Coupe-2P	V8/327	10500	Note 1	Note 2

Note 1: Estimates of Bizzarrini weight ranged from an announced 2,375 pounds (dry) to 3,020 pounds at the curb.

Note 2: Probably no more than 100 Bizzarrinis were built, though one source suggests a total of 149 examples. A total of 30 cars were built during 1966 alone.

ENGINE DATA: BASE V-8 (early): Overhead-valve V-8. Cast iron block and head. **Displacement:** 327 cu. in. (5354 cc). **Bore & Stroke:** 4.00 x 3.25 in. (101.6 x 82.6 mm). **Compression Ratio:** 10.2:1. **Brake Horsepower:** 365 (SAE) at 6000 rpm. **Torque:** 377 (SAE) at 3500 rpm. Five main bearings. Solid valve lifters. One Holley four-barrel carburetor.

BASE V-8 (later): Same as above, except — **Compression Ratio:** 11.0:1. **Brake Horsepower:** 350 at 5800 rpm. **Torque:** 360 lbs.-ft. at 3600 rpm. Hydraulic valve lifters.

BASE V-8 (Competition): Same as above, except — **Brake Horsepower:** 400 at 6000 rpm. **Torque:** 375 lbs.-ft. at 3600 rpm. Solid valve lifters. Four Weber 45 DOEC 12 carburetors.

CHASSIS DATA: Wheelbase: 96.4 in. **Overall Length:** 172-173.6 in. **Height:** 43.0-43.7 in. **Width:** 68 in. **Front Tread:** 55 in. **Rear Tread:** 56 in. **Wheel Type:** Campagnolo knock-off magnesium-alloy. **Standard Tires:** Dunlop R7 (front) 6.00x15; (rear) 7.00x15. Later models used 185HR15 (front) and 225HR15 (rear) Dunlop SP tires.

TECHNICAL: Layout: front-engine, rear-drive. **Transmission:** four-speed manual. Gear ratios: (1st) 2.54:1; (2nd) 1.92:1; (3rd) 1.51:1; (4th) 1.00:1; (rev) 3.36:1. Alternate gear ratios: (1st) 2.20:1; (2nd) 1.64:1; (3rd) 1.27:1; (4th) 1.00:1. **Standard Final Drive Ratio:** 2.88:1, 3.07:1 or 3.31:1 (later, 3.48:1 available). **Steering:** Burman recirculing ball. **Suspension (front):** wishbones, coil springs and anti-roll bar. **Suspension (rear):** De Dion axle with twin trailing radius arms, transverse Watt linkage and coil springs. **Brakes:** Campagnolo front/rear disc (rear inboard). **Body Construction:** fiberglass body panels on pressed steel platform frame (earliest models were aluminum-bodied). **Fuel Tank:** 35 gallons in three tanks.

MAJOR OPTIONS: Competition options included a higher-powered V-8 engine, Plexiglass back window, 43-gallon fuel capacity, 7-inch front wheel rims, 9-inch rear wheel rims, a selection of tires, thicker brake pads, and thinner fiberglass body panels (with larger wheel openings).

PERFORMANCE: Top Speed: 134-145+ mph (factory claimed 160 mph and more). **Acceleration (0-60 mph):** 6.4 seconds. **Acceleration (quarter-mile):** 14.6-14.7 seconds (92-101 mph). **Fuel Mileage:** 11-16 mpg (U.S.).

Manufacturer: Prototipi Bizzarrini Srl, Livorno, Italy.

Distributor: Foreign Cars of Rockland, Nyack, New York.

HISTORY: Prototype was introduced at Turin Motor Show in November 1963, and production began in 1965. Although the GT Strada remained in production (more or less) for half a dozen years, Bizzarrini himself soon lost interest and focused on smaller cars. Late in 1965, he announced production of a "Grifo Baby" with Fiat-Osca 1500-cc engine and five-speed gearbox: a shrunken version of the Iso Grifo, with either metal or plastic bodies. It had all-independent suspension and front disc brakes. By 1967, that evolved into the 128-mph GT Europa 1900, with 1.9-liter Opel engine, which first appeared at the Turin Auto Show in 1966. Fewer than a dozen of those were produced, and the company shut its door in 1969.

BMW

While BMWs of recent years have become almost synonymous with upscale driving pleasure, the famed German company took some time to develop that reputation after World War II. Before the war, the Bayerische Motoren Werke, headquartered at Munich, produced some legendary sports cars wearing the familiar round blue/white emblem. Through the early postwar era, however, the company became much better known in the U.S. for its motorcycles than for automobiles. That BMW emblem, incidentally, is an artist's conception of a whirring airplane propeller, displayed in the state colors of Bavaria. BMW, as it happens, was a major supplier of aircraft engines during the 1930s (and during the war).

Earlier than that, the company's reputation had been well established in the aircraft and motorcycle fields. As early as 1919, a two-cylinder BMW engine, originally intended for industrial use, went into Victoria motorcycles. By 1923, BMW showed its own motorcycle, called the R-32, at the Paris show. Then came a single-cylinder R-39, in 1925. In that same year, R-37 sport models debuted, and BMW bikes began to win races, including the German Grand Prix.

Like the history of so many international automakers, then, BMW's past reaches back to the early years of the century: specifically, to the early teens. During World War I, BMW was an aviation engine supplier, having been founded by Karl Friedrich Rapp in 1913, at Munich. Rapp supplied engines to a company run by Gustav Otto (son of Nikolaus Otto, who'd invented the four-stroke internal-combustion engine). Upon getting a subcontract to produce V-12 aero engines, the Rapp plant became Bayerische Motoren Werke GmbH in 1916; then, two years later, switched to BMW AG.

Instead of a single organization, however, the modern BMW operation evolved from a group of separate companies. Most important was Dixi, an assembler of British Austin Sevens (under license) in Germany. In 1928, BMW acquired the Eisenach operation and took over the Dixi plant, marketing those Austins under the BMW badge. A sedan

produced in 1930 featured four-wheel disc brakes, but in general these Austin/BMW 3/15s were nothing to get excited about. One exception was the 3/15 Wartburg roadster, built in 1930-31 with an 18-horsepower engine, which achieved many race wins.

After the Austin licensing expired, BMW developed its own 3/20 series, built from 1932-34 with 788-cc engines. In 1933, what might be considered the first true BMW automobile appeared, called the Type 303. Powered by an 1182-cc six-cylinder engine, and built on a tubular space frame, it displayed the first "twin-kidney" grille—a trademark of sorts that has appeared on each BMW since that time, in one form or another. A year later, the final Austin-based BMW left the factory, and the new 315 had a larger (1490-cc) engine. In 1935 came the debut of the 319, whose engine displaced 1911 cc; plus sporty 315/1 and 319/1 roadsters with low-slung doors, folding windshields, and triple-carbureted engines. Those were followed the next year by the popular 326.

BMW's best-known prewar model, the rakish two-seat Type 328 roadster with its cutaway doors, also appeared in 1936, making its debut (to victory) at the Nurburgring race that year. With induction via three Solex carburetors, the 328's overhead-cam 1971-cc engine (with rather complex cross pushrods) produced 80 horsepower--enough for a top speed near 95 mph. The streamlined body rode a tubular chassis, and the 328 featured independent front suspension and hydraulic brakes. A stylish 328 coupe featured blended-in fenders and a graceful rear-fender/deck shape. *Auto Sport Review* claimed years later (after the war) that those 328s were guaranteed to hit 102 mph, and sold for about $2200 in the U.S. Prewar BMWs also were sold in Britain, as the Frazer Nash-BMW.

By the time war broke out, BMW was rivaling the established German manufacturers, including Daimler-Benz, not only in production but in competition. Few cars, in fact, rivaled the 328 BMW (and the Frazer-Nash BMW) of the 1930s. A 328 won the two-liter class at Le Mans. Five special lightweight versions with 135-bhp engines were built for the 1940 Mille Miglia, which was won at an average speed of 103 mph, hitting 134 mph on the straights. Only 461 Type 328s were built through 1940, some of which were still racing in the 1950s. That was far below production of the 326 sedan and cabriolet, of which 6,973 were produced from 1936-41.

Early models had been built in Thuringia, which is farther to the north than Munich. Because the Bavarian landscape includes flatlands, long straight roads and (down south) the Alps, such diverse terrain likely helped produce BMW's reputation for all-purpose performance.

Postwar production at Munich did not begin until 1952, after a dispute with the East German firm of Eisenach, which issued a "BMW" automobile of its own. Only after legal action did that company rename its offerings EMW. BMW's first postwar motorcycle, the R-24, arrived in 1948. A 513 prototype automobile was built in 1949-50, powered by a 20-bhp air-cooled engine. Meanwhile, the prewar BMW six-cylinder engine and related technology crossed the English Channel to find a home in the new British-built Bristol (listed separately in this Catalog).

The first "western" BMW automobile was the 501 sedan, powered by the same 1971-cc six-cylinder engine as prewar models. In 1954, a new 2580-cc overhead-valve aluminum V-8 engine, producing 100 horsepower, went under the hood of the sedan, renamed 502. A larger (3168-cc) V-8 powered the stylish 503 cabriolet and coupe later in the decade, as well as the renowned 507 sports car. Riding a shorter wheelbase, the 507 carried a 150-horsepower version of the V-8 and wore a body designed by Count Albrecht Graf Goertz. Torsion bars made up its suspension, front and rear, while the chassis (a shortened version of

the 501/502/503 design) consisted of tubular and box-section elements. Offered as an open roadster, or with a hardtop, the 507 could dash from zero to 60 mph in about 11 seconds, and hit 135 miles per hour. A high price tag helped keep production low, with only 253 built in the late 1950s. All big BMWs of that day emitted a characteristic whistle when running at highway speeds, quite distinct in the front seat.

Sales of that level could hardly keep BMW afloat. What helped most was the manufacture of the little egg-shaped Isetta, built under license from its Italian creator. That evolved into a slightly larger 600, and then into the more conventional 700 design. Nevertheless, financial difficulties late in the 1950s threatened a takeover by Daimler-Benz. That didn't happen, but BMW needed to move in another direction. The big sedans and sports cars sold only in small numbers, and minicars couldn't save the company either. Expansion to conventional-sized vehicles was especially essential, since market surveys revealed that people didn't consider the Isetta and 600 as real BMWs—even if they knew the cars' origins.

The answer came with the first compact-size sedan: the 1500, which debuted in 1962. That led to a succession of similarly-numbered sedans through the 1960s, the digits describing the engine's approximate displacement in cubic centimeters. Early in the 1960s, too, BMW vehicles were winning some racing, rallying and hillclimb victories, largely on the part of privately-owned cars (though sometimes supported by the factory). Before too long, the original sedans were joined by some "T.I." *(Touring Internationale)* editions with even more of a sporting flavor, led by the 1800ti.

In November 1974, after a long legal battle with Hoffman Motors (the early importer), BMW of North America Inc. was formed, as a wholly-owned subsidiary of the German parent company. Even after BMWs began to earn a reputation among enthusiasts, a survey in the U.S. showed that many people thought BMW stood for British Motor Works. The Bavaria editions of the 2.8 and 3.0 sedans, exported after 1971, were the first BMWs to sell strongly in the U.S. During the 1970s, BMW's reputation for quality and performance grew as the 3-Series was introduced as a successor to the 2000 series. That led to a larger 6-Series coupe, a revised 5-Series, and the luxury line of 7-Series sedans. Then, in 1978, BMW announced its M1 supercar, designed by Giugiaro (at Lamborghini) on a multi-tubular chassis with a 24-valve, 3.5-liter variants of the BMW racing six-cylinder engine. Developing 277 horsepower in its standard form, that engine helped send a roadworthy M1 from zero to 60 mph in about 5.5 seconds, or all the way to 162 miles per hour.

Most recent of the BMW entrants has been the 8-Series (850i) coupe, powered by a V-12 engine. During the 1970s and '80s, rising numbers of upscale young professionals became loyal "Bimmer" owners. As the number of "yuppies" grew late in the 1980s, that nickname took on both favorable and derisive connotations—but few disagreed on the merits of the BMW automobiles that remained among their favorites.

Minicar Note: See separate listing for BMW's Isetta, 600 and 700 minicars, produced from 1955-65.

Model Availability Note: For the 1961-75 period, when BMW had not yet become a major force in the U.S. market, many of the models listed below were not officially available in the U.S. They are included here because (1) some were brought in as "grey market" cars, and can thus be assessed for collector value; (2) they are of notable historical interest; and/or (3) they soon evolved into a BMW model that *did* reach U.S. shores.

Model Numbering Note: Models with a letter suffix sometimes included a space between the numerical and letter portions (e.g., 3200 CS). For the sake of clarity, those spaces are omitted in this Catalog (e.g., 3200CS). Suffixes for performance-oriented models such as 'ti' were occasionally capitalized (TI) or included periods (T.I.).

Seating Note: Passenger-capacity figures shown are maximum. Smaller BMW two-door sedans (1500, 1800, etc.) were allegedly five-seat; but the fifth passenger may have a tight squeeze.

1952-53 BMW

501 — SIX — At the April 1951 Internationale Automobil-Ausstellung in Frankfurt, Germany, BMW had exactly one automobile on its display stand: a prototype of the 501. A year later, in autumn 1952, the first production examples were ready for delivery. Early engineering work had been done by Alfred Boning. BMW decided to base its first postwar model on the prewar Type 326, both mechanically and in styling. Furthermore, the new car would be offered first with a 2.0-liter six-cylinder engine (from the prewar 326); then later with a V-8.

Soon nicknamed the "Baroque Angel," the 501 drew praise for its curvaceous design from none other than Pinin Farina. Front doors were hinged at the front, rear doors at the rear ("suicide" style), with rear quarter windows installed. The 'B' pillar slanted slightly backwards. The split-grille front end consisted of two separate grilles, one on each side of a trim strip that extended down from the hood ornament, which also met the trim strip that ran along the hood center. Grilles were mostly made up of vertical bars, with five horizontal-bar separators. Inboard headlamps each stood above a separate, smaller grille with crosshatch pattern. Long parking lamp housings stood atop the front fenders. Black was the only color available. In addition to the four-door sedan, some coupe and cabriolet bodies were built. The first 2,000 bodies were produced by Karosseriewerk Baur (at Stuttgart). Later ones came from the Munich plant. The car itself was built at the Munich facility, which had never before been used for cars.

Power came from a 1971-cc overhead-valve six-cylinder engine, producing 65 horsepower at 4400 rpm (15 bhp more than the prewar model). The engine and clutch hooked to a four-speed gearbox via a short shaft, with the gearbox mounted below the front seat. A rather complex linkage connected the transmission with the column-mounted gearshift lever. Unlike prewar models, which used leaf springs, the 501 rode a suspension made up of longitudinal torsion bars. It used a box-section/tubular chassis and four-wheel drum brakes.

I.D. DATA: Chassis and engine number are stamped on a plate in the left side of the engine compartment, at the firewall. Starting chassis serial number: 40001.

Model	Body Type & Seating	Engine Type/CID	P.O.E. Price	Weight (lbs.)	Prod. Total
501	4-dr Sedan-6P	I6/120	Note 1	2955	Note 2

Note 1: Price in Germany was 15,150 Deutsch Marks (about $3636). Price is U.S. was reported to be approximately $4500.

Note 2: A total of 1,706 Type 501s were produced in 1952-53, followed in 1954-55 by 2,251 Type 501A and 1,371 Type 501B. A total of 49 BMWs were built in 1952, 1,645 in 1953, and 3,471 in 1954.

Weight Note: Figure shown is "curb" weight.

Body Style Note: Coupe and cabriolet versions of the 501 also were offered, with custom-built bodies.

ENGINE DATA: Inline, overhead-valve six-cylinder. Cast iron block and head. **Displacement:** 120.2 cu. in. (1971 cc). **Bore & Stroke:** 2.57 x 3.74 in. (66 x 96 mm). **Compression Ratio:** 6.8:1. **Brake Horsepower:** 65 (DIN) at 4400 rpm. **Torque:** 88 lbs.-ft. at 2000 rpm. Four main bearings. Solid valve lifters. One Solex 30 PAAJ two-barrel carburetor.

CHASSIS DATA: **Wheelbase:** 111.6 in. **Overall Length:** 186.2 in. **Height:** 60.2 in. **Width:** 70.1 in. **Front Tread:** 52.0 in. **Rear Tread:** 55.4 in. **Wheel Type:** 16x4E. **Standard Tires:** 5.50x16.

TECHNICAL: **Layout:** front-engine, rear-drive. **Transmission:** four-speed manual; column lever **Standard Final Drive Ratio:** 4.225:1. **Steering:** bevel gear (pinion and sector). **Suspension (front):** dual A-arms with torsion bars. **Suspension (rear):** rigid "Banjo" axle with torsion bars, two diagonal lateral links and central longitudinal arm (triangular shaped). **Brakes:** hydraulic, front/rear drum. **Body Construction:** separate body on box-section chassis with transverse tubing (ladder-type frame).

PERFORMANCE: **Top Speed:** 84-86 mph. **Fuel Mileage:** 23-28 mpg.

PRODUCTION/SALES: A total of 1,645 BMWs were produced in calendar year 1953, of which 362 were exported.

Manufacturer: Bayerische Motoren Werke AG, Munich, West Germany.

HISTORY: The Type 501 was produced in 1952-53, then replaced by the 501A and 501B for 1954-55. In May 1950, two prototypes for the Type 501 were shown to management: a coupe (with Auteurieth body) and a sedan (done at Munich). Pinin Farina also submitted another possibility, later on, based on his design for the Alfa Romeo 1900 sedan. At this time, Eisenach in East Germany built a car called the BMW. But their model name soon was changed to EMW, to avoid confusion in countries that sold both.

Motor Trend in 1953 pointed out the similarity of the 501's profile to the English Bristol, which was no surprise since the postwar Bristol had its origins in earlier BMWs. The magazine described technical details of the 501 as "a delicacy for the connoisseur." A 501 was the fastest touring car at the 500-kilometer Nurburgring Endurance Trial in 1953, and received the 1953 Golden Wreath award as the most beautiful saloon (sedan).

1954 BMW

1954 BMW Type 501.

501A/B — SERIES 2 — SIX — Two modifications of the BMW 501 four-door sedan replaced the original in 1954-55: the deluxe 501A, and the cheaper (less-equipped) standard 501B. Both carried a more potent, 72-horsepower version of the original's six-cylinder engine.

502 — V-8 — The planned-for V-8 engine finally arrived under a BMW hood in 1954, making its first appearance at the Geneva Salon in the spring of that year. The official debut came in July, as BMW's first postwar V-8 (and the first postwar German V-8). The 502 came in three body styles: four-door sedan, two-door coupe, and two-door cabriolet, each on a 111.6-inch wheelbase. Appearance was similar to the 501, but with foglamps built into lower front fenders, and more chrome trim. A long strip just below the beltline began halfway back on the hood side, and ran beneath the side windows. Front vent wings were installed. The decklid held a 'V-8' emblem. Inside the roomy interior was soft cloth upholstery. Trunk space remained marginal. Later models would add full wheel covers. The 90-degree, overhead-valve V-8 displaced 2580 cc and had an aluminum block and cylinder heads (first one on a mass-produced engine). Output was 100 horsepower at 4800 rpm. Cylinders contained wet liners. As before, a four-speed manual gearbox with column-mounted gearshift lever sent power to the rear wheels. Top speed reached 99 mph, considerably faster than the six-cylinder model. Gearing differed slightly from the 501, with a "longer" ratio in first gear. Wheels held 6.40Sx15L tires.

I.D. DATA: Type 501 chassis and engine number plate is on the firewall, in left side of engine compartment. Type 502 serial number is stamped on first crossmember, below the radiator. Engine number is stamped on the upper right front of the block. Starting serial number: (501A) 42501; (501B) 50100; (502) 60100.

Model	Body Type & Seating	Engine Type/CID	P.O.E. Price	Weight (lbs.)	Prod. Total
501A	4-dr Sedan-6P	I6/120	N/A	N/A	Note 1
501B	4-dr Sedan-6P	I6/120	N/A	2750	Note 1
502/2.6	4-dr Sedan-6P	V8/157	N/A	3175	Note 1

Note 1: A total of 2,251 Type 501A and 1,371 Type 501B models were produced in 1954-55. Total Type 502 production (all years) came to 5,955 units.

Price Note: The 501's price was cut twice in Germany during 1954. The selling price in Germany for the 501A was 14,180 Marks; for the 501B, 12,650 Marks (about $2845). Price of the 502 was 17,800 Marks (about $4238).

Body Style Note: Coupe and cabriolet versions of the 501 and 502 also were offered, with custom-built bodies.

ENGINE DATA: BASE SIX (501A/B): Inline, overhead-valve six-cylinder. Cast iron block and head. **Displacement:** 120.2 cu. in. (1971 cc). **Bore & Stroke:** 2.59 x 3.77 in. (66 x 96 mm). **Compression Ratio:** 6.8:1. **Brake Horsepower:** 72 DIN at 4400 rpm. **Torque:** 88 lbs.-ft. at 2500 rpm. Four main bearings. Solid valve lifters. One Solex two-barrel carburetor. 12-volt electrical system.
BASE V-8 (502): 90-degree, overhead-valve V-8. Aluminum block and heads. **Displacement:** 157.4 cu. in. (2580 cc). **Bore & Stroke:** 2.91 x 2.95 in. (74 x 75 mm). **Compression Ratio:** 7.0:1. **Brake Horsepower:** 100 (DIN) at 4800 rpm. Five main bearings. One Solex 30 PAAJ two-barrel carburetor.

CHASSIS DATA: **Wheelbase:** 111.6 in. **Overall Length:** 186.2 in. **Height:** 60.2 in. **Width:** 70.1 in. **Front Tread:** (501) 52.0 in.; (502) 52.4 in. **Rear Tread:** (501) 55.4 in.; (502) 55.7 in. **Wheel Type:** (502) 15x4.5K. **Standard Tires:** (501) 5.50x16; (502) 6.40Sx15L.

TECHNICAL: **Layout:** front-engine, rear-drive. **Transmission:** four-speed manual (all-synchro); column shift. Overall 501A/B gear ratios: (1st) 17.6:1; (2nd) 10.0:1; (3rd) 6.3:1; (4th) 4.2:1; (rev) 22.8:1. **Standard Final Drive Ratio:** 4.225:1. **Steering:** pinion and segment (bevel gear). **Suspension (front):** dual A-arms with torsion bars. **Suspension (rear):** rigid axle with torsion bars. **Brakes:** hydraulic, front/rear drum. **Body Construction:** separate body on box-section steel frame.

PERFORMANCE: **Top Speed:** (501A) 87-90 mph; (502 V-8) 99 mph. **Fuel Mileage:** about 19 mpg reported (factory claimed 24-28 mpg).

PRODUCTION/SALES: Of the 3,770 BMWs produced during 1954, a total of 528 were exported.

Manufacturer: Bayerische Motoren Werke AG, Munich, West Germany.
Distributor: none yet in U.S.

HISTORY: Production of the Type 502 began early in 1954 and continued into 1961. The V-8 engine was announced at the Geneva Show in March 1954.

1955 BMW

501A/B, 501/3 — SIX — Production of the next series of the six-cylinder four-door sedan began in April 1955, replacing the 501A/B. As before, not only a four-door sedan but a two-door coupe and cabriolet were produced, with bodies from Baur (in Stuttgart) and

Autenrieth (in Darmstadt). Appearance was similar to the original. Inside, the instrument panels retained the prewar look. Under the hood, however, the six-cylinder engine grew to 2077 cc, as a result of a 2-mm bore increase. The 501/3 was sometimes referred to as the 501 *Sechszylinder* (six-cylinder).

501 — V-8 — Joining the 502 in April 1955 was a V-8 powered version of the original Type 501, with a smaller back window and lacking the 502's bodyside chrome. Later (starting in 1958), this plainer model would be called the BMW 2.6. The engine had a bit less power than the 502, producing 95 horsepower at 4800 rpm.

502 (2.6) — V-8 — Production of the Type 502 with a 2.6-liter V-8 continued with little change.

502 (3.2) — V-8 — Initially called the Type 502 3.2-liter (or 502/3.2), the next V-8 BMW had a larger engine: 3168 cc versus 2580 for the original. This came as a result of an 8-mm increase in the bore dimension. In September 1955, a wraparound back window was added to the 502 sedan. This model was generally referred to as, simply, the BMW 3.2.

1955 BMW 502 convertible.

Body Style Note: Four-passenger coupe version of the 501 (and 502) continued to be built by Autenrieth. The convertible was an official BMW model, but also built by Autenrieth. The Baur company also produced 501/502 coupes and convertibles, which displayed a more graceful profile and steeper windshield than the Autenrieth editions. Both of these were considered official BMW models.

I.D. DATA: Type 501 chassis and engine number plate is on the firewall, in left side of engine compartment. Type 502 serial number is stamped on first crossmember, below the radiator. Engine number is stamped on the upper right front of the block. Starting serial number: (501/3) 45002; (501 V-8) 52001; (502 Series 2) 60501.

Model	Body Type & Seating	Engine Type/CID	P.O.E. Price	Weight (lbs.)	Prod. Total
501A	4-dr Sedan-6P	I6/120	N/A	N/A	Note 4
501B	4-dr Sedan-6P	I6/120	Note 1	2750	Note 4
501/3	4-dr Sedan-6P	I6/127	Note 2	2955	Note 4
501	4-dr Sedan-6P	V8/157	N/A	N/A	Note 4
502/2.6	4-dr Sedan-6P	V8/157	N/A	3175	Note 4
502/3.2	4-dr Sedan-6P	V8/193	Note 3	3240	Note 4

Note 1: A 501B sedan sold for about $3800-4300 in the U.S., and about $2845 at the factory.

Note 2: Price in Germany for the 501/3 sedan was 12,500 Marks; for the cabriolet, 7,950 Marks.

Note 3: Price in Germany for the 502/3.2 sedan was 17,850 Marks.

Note 4: A total of 4,567 full-size BMWs were sold in 1955. A total of 4,645 Type 501/3 models and 2,582 Type 502/3.2 were produced through the end of their respective model runs. See previous listings for breakdowns of other models.

Body Style Note: Coupe and cabriolet versions of the 501 and 502 also were offered, with custom-built bodies.

1955 BMW.

ENGINE DATA: BASE SIX (501A/B): Inline, overhead-valve six-cylinder. Cast iron block and head. **Displacement:** 120.2 cu. in. (1971 cc). **Bore & Stroke:** 2.59 x 3.77 in. (66 x 96 mm). **Compression Ratio:** 6.8:1. **Brake Horsepower:** 65/72 at 4400 rpm. **Torque:** 88 lbs.-ft. at 2500 rpm. Four main bearings. Solid valve lifters. One Solex two-barrel carburetor. 12-volt electrical system.

BASE SIX (501/3): Inline, overhead-valve six-cylinder. Cast iron block and head. **Displacement:** 126.7 cu. in. (2077 cc). **Bore & Stroke:** 2.68 x 3.77 in. (68 x 96 mm). **Compression Ratio:** 7.0:1. **Brake Horsepower:** 72 at 4500 rpm. **Torque:** 94 lbs.-ft. at 2500 rpm. Four main bearings. Solid valve lifters. One Solex 32 PAJTA two-barrel carburetor.

BASE V-8 (501, 502/2.6): 90-degree, overhead-valve V-8. Aluminum block and heads. **Displacement:** 157.4 cu. in. (2580 cc). **Bore & Stroke:** 2.91 x 2.95 in. (74 x 75 mm). **Compression Ratio:** 7.0:1. **Brake Horsepower:** (501) 95 DIN at 4800 rpm; (502) 100 DIN at 4800 rpm. Five main bearings. One Solex 30 PAAJ two-barrel carburetor.

BASE V-8 (502/3.2): 90-degree, overhead-valve V-8. Aluminum block and heads. **Displacement:** 193.2 cu. in. (3168 cc). **Bore & Stroke:** 3.23 x 2.95 in. (82 x 75 mm). **Compression Ratio:** 7.2:1. **Brake Horsepower:** 120 (DIN) at 4800 rpm. Five main bearings. One Zenith 32 NDIX two-barrel carburetor.

CHASSIS DATA: Wheelbase: 111.6 in. **Overall Length:** 186.2 in. **Height:** 60.2 in. **Width:** 70.1 in. **Front Tread:** (501/3) 52.0 in.; (502) 52.4 in. **Rear Tread:** (501/3) 55.4 in.; (502) 55.7 in. **Wheel Type:** (501/3) 16x4E or 15x4.5K; (502) 15x4.5K. **Standard Tires:** (501/3) 5.50x16 or 6.40x15; (502) 6.40Sx15L.

TECHNICAL: Layout: front-engine, rear-drive. **Transmission:** four-speed manual (all-synchro); column shift. **Steering:** bevel-gear. **Suspension (front):** dual A-arms with torsion bars. **Suspension (rear):** rigid axle with torsion bars. **Brakes:** hydraulic, front/rear drum. **Body Construction:** separate body on box-section steel frame.

PERFORMANCE: Top Speed: (501/3) 90 mph; (502/3.2) 105 mph.

PRODUCTION/SALES: Of the 17,478 BMWs (all models) produced during 1955, a total of 1,872 were exported.

Manufacturer: Bayerische Motoren Werke AG, Munich, West Germany.

Distributor: Hoffman Motors Corp., New York City.

HISTORY: Production of the 501/3 began in April 1955 and continued into 1958. The 502/3.2 V-8 sedan first appeared at the IAA (Frankfurt) Show in 1955, intended to rival the Mercedes 300. By 1958, it would be called, simply, the BMW 3.2 sedan, and remain in production till 1961. A 505 Pullman State limousine prototype (on stretched 502 chassis) appeared at the 1955 Frankfurt Show. Only two were built, each long and tall, with rich wood on the inside and central partition glass. Bodies were built by Ghia-Aigle, in Switzerland.

Motorsport magazine's tester was "jolted by this sheer magnificence of detail" when trying the 501B, which was supposedly the "cheaper" version of the 501A. "Not a fireball on acceleration," the report admitted, but the car offered "excellent roadability."

Note: See separate listing for BMW's Isetta minicar.

1956 BMW

501/3 — SIX — Production of the third-series 501 continued with little change; see previous listing for details.

501 — V-8 — Production of the V-8 powered 501 continued with little change; see previous listing for details.

502 (2.6/3.2) — V-8 — Production of the 502 series continued with little change, with either a 2.6-liter or 3.2-liter V-8 engine.

503 — V-8 — Joining the original series of four-door sedans were a sporty new close-coupled (2 + 2) coupe and cabriolet (convertible), powered by a 140-horsepower 'S' version of the 3168-cc V-8 engine. Wheelbase was the same as the initial sedans (111.6 inches), so the 503's profile featured a long hood and deck. Though it wore a light alloy (aluminum) body, the coupe and cabriolet were as heavy as a sedan with the 3.2-liter V-8. Designed by Count Albrecht Goertz (a German-American), the 503 had vent windows and quarter windows, plus shrouded headlamps on the fenders, just above round parking lamps. A round BMW emblem stood above the two-unit grille, both segments with vertical bars. Those twin grilles sat in a protruding nose, alongside two side grilles that extended outward to meet the parking lamps. Twin round taillamps were mounted on each side of the rear panel, positioned low on the fenders. Marker lenses went at the front end of front fenders. A bodyside trim strip ran straight from headlamp to rear end, then swept upward at an angle near the rear fender tip.

The 3.2-liter V-8 delivered its 140 bhp at 4800 rpm, using twin Zenith carburetors. Like the closely-related 501/502, the 503's gearbox was located under the seat (though that would change late in 1957).

507 — V-8 — Of all the early postwar BMWs, the 507 has earned the most prominent place in automotive history, as a leading example of "classic" sports-car style and technology. Even sportier in nature than the 503, the two-seat roadster rode a considerably shorter wheelbase (only 97.6 inches, versus 111.6 inches for the 503). Overall length was 172.4 inches. Like the 503's, this graceful body was designed by Count Albrecht Goertz. As the story goes, BMW's U.S. importer, Max Hoffman, encouraged Goertz in the effort--and later claimed he'd actually designed it himself. Under the 507's hood was a 150-horsepower version of the 3168-cc V-8 engine. Depending on rear-axle gearing, this was enough for top speeds of 124 to 136 mph. Or so the factory claimed, at any rate; early road tests estimated the lower figure. Angled air-intake grilles stood on each cowl, with a round BMW emblem at their rear (an arrangement not unlike that of the then-new gullwing Mercedes 300SL). Instead of the customary narrow "twin-kidney" grille, the front end displayed two wide separated openings, each with horizontal strips and vertical dividers. Tiny round parking lamps sat below the headlamps, and the hood showed a slight bulge, with a round BMW emblem ahead of it. The optional removable hardtop almost looked like a permanent part of the car. Priced at 26,500 Deutsch Marks (about $6200) in Germany, the 507 sold for just under $9000 in the U.S., which was too high a price to bring significant sales. A cheaper version was rumored for the future, but never came to pass.

I.D. DATA: Type 501 chassis and engine number plate is on the firewall, in left side of engine compartment. Type 502 serial number is stamped on first crossmember, below the radiator. Type 503/507 serial number is stamped next to the right front suspension component, or on a plate on the left rear side (near the battery). Engine number is stamped on the upper right front of the block. Starting serial number: (501/3) 46220; (501 V-0) 53070; (502/2.6 Series 2) 60860; (502/3.2 Series 1) 62001; (503) 69001; (507) 70001.

Model	Body Type & Seating	Engine Type/CID	P.O.E. Price	Weight (lbs.)	Prod. Total
501/3	4-dr Sedan-6P	I6/127	N/A	2955	Note 1
501	4-dr Sedan-6P	V8/157	N/A	N/A	Note 1
502/2.6	4-dr Sedan-6P	V8/157	7300	3175	Note 1
502/3.2	4-dr Sedan-6P	V8/193	N/A	3240	Note 1
503	2-dr Cpe-2 + 2P	V8/193	Note 2	3310	Note 3
503	2-dr Cabr-2 + 2P	V8/193	Note 2	3310	Note 3
507	2-dr Rds-2P	V8/193	8988	2935	Note 4

Note 1: A total of 4,645 Type 501/3 models and 2,582 Type 502/3.2 were produced through the end of their respective model runs.

Note 2: Price of the 503 in Germany was 29,500 Deutsch Marks (coupe or cabriolet).

Note 3: A total of 412 (possibly 413) Type 503 coupes and cabriolets were produced during their full model run.

Note 4: A total of 253 Type 507s were produced during the full model run (including two prototypes).

Price Note: 502/2.6 price is approximate, and included radio and heater.

Weight Note: 503/507 figures shown are "curb" weight. Data sheet issued at the October 1955 Paris Show gave figures of 1460 kg (3219 pounds) for the 503, and 1170 kg (2579 pounds) for the 507.

Body Style Note: Coupe and cabriolet versions of the 501 and 502 remained available, with custom-built bodies by Autenrieth and Baur.

ENGINE DATA: BASE SIX (501/3): Inline, overhead-valve six-cylinder. Cast iron block and head. **Displacement:** 126.7 cu. in. (2077 cc). **Bore & Stroke:** 2.68 x 3.77 in. (68 x 96 mm). **Compression Ratio:** 7.0:1. **Brake Horsepower:** 72 DIN at 4500 rpm. Four main bearings. Solid valve lifters. One two-barrel Solex carburetor.

BASE V-8 (501, 502/2.6): 90-degree, overhead-valve V-8. Aluminum block and heads. **Displacement:** 157.4 cu. in. (2580 cc). **Bore & Stroke:** 2.91 x 2.95 in. (74 x 75 mm). **Compression Ratio:** 7.0:1. **Brake Horsepower:** 95-105 DIN at 4800 rpm. **Torque:** up to 132 lbs.-ft. at 2500 rpm. Five main bearings. One Solex 30 PAAJ two-barrel carburetor.

BASE V-8 (502/3.2, 503, 507): 90-degree, overhead-valve V-8. Aluminum block and heads. **Displacement:** 193.2 cu. in. (3168 cc). **Bore & Stroke:** 3.23 x 2.95 in. (82 x 75 mm). **Compression Ratio:** (502/3.2) 7.2:1 (503) 7.5:1; (507) 7.8:1. **Brake Horsepower:** (502/3.2) 120 DIN at 4800 rpm; (503) 140 DIN at 4800 rpm; (507) 150-155 DIN at 5000 rpm. **Torque:** (507) 174 lbs.-ft. at 4000 rpm. Five main bearings. One Zenith 32 NDIX two-barrel carburetor (502/3.2). Two Zenith 32 NDIX two-barrel carburetors (503/507).

CHASSIS DATA: Wheelbase: 111.6 in. except (507) 97.6 in. **Overall Length:** 186.2 in. except (503) 187.0 in.; (507) 172.4 in. **Height:** 60.2 in. except (503) 56.7 in.; (507) 51.2 in. **Width:** 70.1 in. except (503) 67.3 in.; (507) 65.0 in. **Front Tread:** (501/3) 52.0 in.; (502) 52.4 in.; (503) 55.1 in.; (507) 56.9 in. **Rear Tread:** (501/3) 55.4 in.; (502) 55.7 in.; (503) 55.9 in.; (507) 56.1 in. **Wheel Type:** (501/3) 16x4E or 15x4.5K; (502) 15x4.5K; (503/507) 16x4.5E. **Standard Tires:** (501/3) 5.50x16 or 6.40x15; (502) 6.40Sx15L; (503/507) 6.00Hx16 racing type.

TECHNICAL: Layout: front-engine, rear-drive. **Transmission:** four-speed manual. Standard 502 V-8 gear ratios: (1st) 4.41:1 (2nd) 2.35:1; (3rd) 1.49:1; (rth) 1.0:1. Standard 503 gear ratios: (1st) 3.54:1; (2nd) 2.202:1; (3rd) 1.395:1; (4th) 1.00:1; (rev) 5.03:1. Overall 507 gear ratios: (1st) 12.5:1; (2nd) 7.66:1; (3rd) 5.03:1; (4th) 3.70:1. **Standard Final Drive Ratio:** (502) 4.23:1; (503) 3.9:1 or 3.42:1; (507) 3.70:1, 3.42:1 or 3.9:1. **Steering:** bevel-gear (pinion and sector). **Suspension (front):** dual A-arms with torsion bars. **Suspension (rear):** rigid axle with torsion bars. **Brakes:** hydraulic, front/rear drum. **Body Construction:** (503/507) aluminum body on steel frame.

Transmission Note: A five-speed gearbox was announced for the 507 at the Paris Show in October 1955, with gear ratios as follows: (1st) 3.09:1; (2nd) 2.023:1; (3rd) 1.5:1; (4th) 1.205:1; (5th) 1.00:1; (rev) 2.205:1. Production models used a four-speed.

PERFORMANCE: Top Speed: (502) 103 mph estimated; (503) 118 mph; (507) 124 mph estimated (factory claimed 136 + mph). **Acceleration (0-60 mph):** (502) 13.7 sec.; (507) 8.8 sec. **Acceleration (quarter-mile):** (507) 16.5 sec. (84 mph). **Fuel Mileage:** (502) 22 mpg average.

PRODUCTION/SALES: Of the 35,483 BMWs (all models) produced during 1956, a total of 3,030 were exported.

Manufacturer: Bayerische Motoren Werke AG, Munich, West Germany.

Distributor: Hoffman Motors Corp., New York City.

HISTORY: The 503 was introduced in September 1955, at the Frankfurt Show, and went on sale by June 1956; production continued until February 1960. Sale of the Type 507 sports car began in November 1956 (after appearance at the Paris Show in fall 1955); production ended in May 1959. *Road & Track* described 507 styling as a "fortuitous combination of all-out racing beastliness and the true grace of postwar Italian design." Early rumors of a 200 + bhp version of the 507 proved unfounded, as did talk of a low-priced edition.

Note: See separate listing for BMW's Isetta minicar.

1957-58 BMW

1957 BMW 507 owned by John M. Kessler of Richmond, Va.

501/3 — SIX — Production of the third-series 501 continued with little change; see 1955 listing for details.

501 — V-8 — Production of the V-8 powered 501 continued with little change; see 1955 listing for details.

502 (2.6/3.2) — V-8 — Production of the 502 series continued, with either a 2.6-liter or 3.2-liter V-8 engine. This year, however, a 3.2-Liter Super was introduced, with a more potent (140 bhp) version of the V-8 powerplant, using twin carburetors and higher compression.

503 — V-8 — In September of 1957, the 503 coupe and convertible switched to a gearbox just behind the engine, so a floor shift became practical. Otherwise, production continued with little change; see previous listing for details.

507 — V-8 — Production of BMW's two-seat sports car continued with little change; see previous listing for details. Front disc brakes became available during 1958.

I.D. DATA: Type 501 chassis and engine number plate is on the firewall, in left side of engine compartment. Type 502 serial number is stamped on first crossmember, below the radiator. Type 503/507 serial number is stamped next to the right front suspension component, or on a plate on the left rear side (near the battery). Engine number is stamped on the upper right front of the block. Starting serial number: (501/3) 47550; (501 V-8) 54650; (502/2.6 Series 2) 61750; (502/3.2 Series 1) 63670; (503/507) continued from 1956.

1958 BMW 507 convertible owned by L. Jack Ruscilli. (John Gunnell)

Model	Body Type & Seating	Engine Type/CID	P.O.E. Price	Weight (lbs.)	Prod. Total
501/3	4-dr Sedan-6P	I6/127	N/A	2955	Note 1
501	4-dr Sedan-6P	V8/157	N/A	N/A	Note 1
502/2.6	4-dr Sedan-6P	V8/157	N/A	3175	Note 1
502/3.2	4-dr Sedan-6P	V8/193	N/A	3240	Note 1
502/3.2 Super	4-dr Sedan-6P	V8/193	N/A	3310	Note 2
503	2-dr Cpe-2 + 2P	V8/193	N/A	3310	Note 3
503	2-dr Cabr-2 + 2P	V8/193	N/A	3310	Note 4
507	2-dr Rds-2P	V8/193	8988	2935	Note 4

Note 1: A total of 40,371 BMWs were produced during calendar year 1957, of which 13,311 were exported. During that year, 1,701 full-size BMWs were sold. A total of 50,256 BMWs were produced during 1958, of which 8,886 were exported. See previous listings for 501/502 production totals.

Note 2: A total of 1,158 502 3.2 Supers were produced during the full model run. Price in Germany was 19,750 Deutsch Marks.

Note 3: A total of 412 (possibly 413) Type 503 coupes and cabriolets were produced during their full model run.

Note 4: A total of 253 Type 507s were produced during the full model run (including two prototypes).

Weight Note: Figures shown are "curb" weight. Some sources give lower amounts.

Body Style Note: Coupe and cabriolet versions of the 501 and 502 remained available, with custom-built bodies by Autenrieth and Baur.

ENGINE DATA: BASE SIX (501/3): Inline, overhead-valve six-cylinder. Cast iron block and head. **Displacement:** 126.7 cu. in. (2077 cc). **Bore & Stroke:** 2.68 x 3.77 in. (68 x 96 mm). **Compression Ratio:** 7.0:1. **Brake Horsepower:** 72 DIN at 4500 rpm. Four main bearings. Solid valve lifters. One Solex carburetor.

BASE V-8 (501, 502/2.6): 90-degree, overhead-valve V-8. Aluminum block and heads. **Displacement:** 157.4 cu. in. (2580 cc). **Bore & Stroke:** 2.91 x 2.95 in. (74 x 75 mm). **Compression Ratio:** 7.0:1. **Brake Horsepower:** 95-105 DIN at 4800 rpm. **Torque:** up to 132 lbs.-ft. at 2500 rpm. Five main bearings. One Solex 30 PAAJ two-barrel carburetor.

BASE V-8 (502/3.2, 503, 507): 90-degree, overhead-valve V-8. Aluminum block and heads. **Displacement:** 193.2 cu. in. (3168 cc). **Bore & Stroke:** 3.23 x 2.95 in. (82 x 75 mm). **Compression Ratio:** (502/3.2) 7.2:1; (3.2 Super, 503) 7.5:1; (507) 7.8:1. **Brake Horsepower:** (502) 120 DIN at 4800 rpm; (3.2 Super, 503) 140 DIN at 4800 rpm; (507) 150-155 DIN at 5000 rpm. **Torque:** (507) 174 lbs.-ft. at 4000 rpm. Five main bearings. One Zenith 32 NDIX two-barrel carburetor (502/3.2). Two Zenith 32 NDIX or 36 NDIX two-barrel carburetors (3.2 Super/503/507).

CHASSIS DATA: Wheelbase: 111.6 in. except (507) 97.6 in. **Overall Length:** 186.2 in. except (503) 187.0 in.; (507) 172.4 in. **Height:** 60.2 in. except (503) 56.7 in.; (507) 51.2 in. **Width:** 70.1 in. except (503) 67.3 in.; (507) 65.0 in. **Front Tread:** (501/3) 52.0 in.; (502) 52.4 in.; (503) 55.1 in.; (507) 56.9 in. **Rear Tread:** (501/3) 55.4 in.; (502) 55.7 in.; (503) 55.9 in.; (507) 56.1 in. **Wheel Type:** steel disc; (501/3) 16x4E or 15x4.5K; (502) 15x4.5K; (503/507) 16x4.5E. **Standard Tires:** (501/3) 5.50x16 or 6.40x15; (502) 6.40Sx15L; (502 3.2 Super) 6.50/6.70Hx15L; (503/507) 6.00Hx16 racing type.

TECHNICAL: Layout: front-engine, rear-drive. **Transmission:** four-speed manual; column shift except (503/507) floor lever. Overall 507 gear ratios: (1st) 12.5:1; (2nd) 7.66:1; (3rd) 5.03:1; (4th) 3.70:1. **Standard Final Drive Ratio:** (507) 3.70:1, 3.42:1, 3.89:1, 3.90:1, or 4.2:1. **Steering:** pinion and sector (bevel-gear). **Suspension (front):** dual A-arms with torsion bars. **Suspension (rear):** rigid axle with torsion bars. **Brakes:** hydraulic, front/rear drum; (507) Alfin drums. **Body Construction:** (503) aluminum body on steel frame; (507) aluminum body on tubular steel frame with crossmembers. **Fuel Tank:** (507) 18.5 gallon.

1958 BMW Type 503. (Coys of Kensington)

MAJOR OPTIONS: Rudge-Whitworth alloy wheels (507). Removable hardtop (507). Right-hand mirror (507). Disc brakes (507).

Note: Some sources indicate that a metal tonneau cover may have been available for the 507 roadster.

PERFORMANCE: Top Speed: (502 3.2 Super) 110 mph; (503) 118 mph; (507) 124-137 mph. **Acceleration (0-60 mph):** (507) 8.8 sec. (some sources reported times as long as 11 sec.). **Acceleration (quarter-mile):** (507) 16.5 sec. (84 mph). **Fuel Mileage:** (507) average 22-24 mpg.

Manufacturer: Bayerische Motoren Werke AG, Munich, West Germany.

Distributor: Hoffman Motors Corp., New York City.

HISTORY: Introduced in spring 1957, the 3.2 Super remained in production into 1961. All except three 507s produced in the full model run wore a body from Karosserteentwarf Graf Goertz.

"Both technically and style-wise," said *Motor Trend*, the 507 was "one of the most desirable sportscars to come along in recent years....Designed purely as a road machine, no effort is spared to make the BMW 507 as close to perfection as possible." *Sports Cars Illustrated* claimed a BMW 507 could accelerate from 0-60 mph in 7 seconds, with its engine producing 205 bhp at 5700 rpm; but the output of the standard model was far lower.

Note: See separate listing for BMW's Isetta and 600 minicars.

1959-60 BMW

501 — V-8 — Production of the 501 four-door sedan with 2.6-liter V-8 engine ceased after 1958, but it remained available in the U.S. into 1959.

Note: The six-cylinder 501 model no longer was available.

502 — V-8 — Production of the 502 sedan with 3.2-liter V-8 continued with little change, except that power steering became available. Both the standard and Super versions were offered, the latter with additional power. By this time, the car was often referred to as the BMW 3.2, omitting the 502 prefix. Front disc brakes became available in 1960 (standard on the Super).

503 — V-8 — BMW's sporty coupe and cabriolet continued with little change into 1959, which would be their final year of production.

507 — V-8 — This would also be the final year of production for the famous BMW sports roadster, which continued with little change.

I.D. DATA: Type 501 chassis and engine number plate is on the firewall, in left side of engine compartment. Type 502 serial number is stamped on first crossmember, below the radiator. Type 503/507 serial number is stamped next to the right front suspension component, or on a plate on the left rear side (near the battery). Engine number is stamped on the upper right front of the block.

Model	Body Type & Seating	Engine Type/CID	P.O.E. Price	Weight (lbs.)	Prod. Total
501	4-dr Sedan-6P	V8/157	5000	N/A	Note 1
502/2.6	4-dr Sedan-6P	V8/157	5600	3175	Note 1
502/3.2	4-dr Sedan-6P	V8/193	6000	3240	Note 1
502/3.2 Super	4-dr Sedan-6P	V8/193	6600	3310	Note 2
503	2-dr Cpe-2 + 2P	V8/193	N/A	3310	Note 3
503	2-dr Cabr-2 + 2P	V8/193	11900	3310	Note 3
507	2-Rds-2P	V8/193	10500	2935	Note 4

Note 1: A total of 42,524 BMWs were produced during calendar year 1959, of which 14,444 were exported. A total of 53,279 BMWs were produced during 1960, of which 22,837 were exported. See previous listings for 501/502 production totals.

Note 2: A total of 1,158 502 3.2 Supers were produced during the full model run. Price in Germany was 21,240 Deutsch Marks in 1960.

Note 3: A total of 412 (possibly 413) Type 503 coupes and cabriolets were produced during their full model run.

Note 4: A total of 253 Type 507s were produced during the full model run (including two prototypes).

Weight Note: Figures shown are "curb" weight. Some sources give lower amounts.

Body Style Note: Coupe and cabriolet versions of the 501 and 502 remained available, with custom-built bodies by Autenrieth and Baur.

ENGINE DATA: BASE V-8 (501, 502/2.6): 90-degree, overhead-valve V-8. Aluminum block and heads. **Displacement:** 157.4 cu. in. (2580 cc). **Bore & Stroke:** 2.91 x 2.95 in. (74 x 75 mm). **Compression Ratio:** 7.0:1. **Brake Horsepower:** 95-105 at 4800 rpm. Five main bearings. One Solex 30 PAAJ two-barrel carburetor.

BASE V-8 (502/3.2, 503, 507): 90-degree, overhead-valve V-8. Aluminum block and heads. **Displacement:** 193.2 cu. in. (3168 cc). **Bore & Stroke:** 3.23 x 2.95 in. (82 x 75 mm). **Compression Ratio:** (502) 7.2:1; (3.2 Super, 503) 7.5:1; (507) 7.8:1. **Brake Horsepower:**

(502) 120 DIN at 4800 rpm; (3.2 Super, 503) 140 DIN at 4800 rpm; (507) 150-155 DIN at 5000 rpm. **Torque:** (507) 174 lbs.-ft. at 4000 rpm. Five main bearings. One Zenith 32 NDIX two-barrel carburetor (502/3.2). Two Zenith 32 NDIX or 36 NDIX two-barrel carburetors (3.2 Super/503/507).

Note: In U.S. listings, the 502 V-8 was rated 140 bhp at 4800 rpm, the 503 V-8 as 162 bhp at 4800 rpm.

CHASSIS DATA: Wheelbase: 111.6 in. except (507) 97.6 in. **Overall Length:** 186.2 in. except (503) 187.0 in.; (507) 172.4 in. **Height:** 60.2 in. except (503) 56.7 in.; (507) 51.2 in. **Width:** 70.1 in. except (503) 67.3 in.; (507) 65.0 in. **Front Tread:** (501/3) 52.0 in.; (502) 52.4 in.; (503) 55.1 in.; (507) 56.9 in. **Rear Tread:** (501/3) 55.4 in.; (502) 55.7 in.; (503) 55.9 in.; (507) 56.1 in. **Wheel Type:** steel disc; (501/3) 16x4E or 15x4.5K; (502) 15x4.5K; (503/507) 16x4.5E. **Standard Tires:** (501/3) 5.50x16 or 6.40x15; (502) 6.40Sx15L; (502 3.2 Super) 6.50/6.70Hx15L; (503/507) 6.00Hx16 racing type.

TECHNICAL: Layout: front-engine, rear-drive. **Transmission:** four-speed manual; column shift except (503/507) floor lever. **Standard Final Drive Ratio:** (502) 3.9:1; (503) 3.9:1; (507) 3.70:1, 3.42:1, 3.89:1, 3.90:1, or 4.2:1. **Steering:** pinion and sector (bevel-gear). **Suspension (front):** dual A-arms with torsion bars. **Suspension (rear):** rigid axle with torsion bars. **Brakes:** hydraulic, front/rear drum; (507) front disc, rear drum available. **Body Construction:** (503) aluminum body on steel frame; (507) aluminum body on tubular steel frame with crossmembers. **Fuel Tank:** (507) 18.5 gallon.

MAJOR OPTIONS: Similar to 1958.

PERFORMANCE: Top Speed: (3.2 Super) 110 mph; (503) 118 mph; (507) 124-136 mph. **Acceleration (0-60 mph):** (507) 8.8 sec. **Acceleration (quarter-mile):** (507) 16.5 sec. (84 mph). **Fuel Mileage:** (507) average 22-24 mpg.

Manufacturer: Bayerische Motoren Werke AG, Munich, West Germany.

Distributor: Hoffman Motors Corp., New York City.

HISTORY: Production of the 501 ended after 1958, the 503 and 507 after 1959, though each would remain on some lists of available models in the U.S. as late as 1961. The 502 and (502) 3.2 remained in production into 1961, when they were replaced by the similar 2600 and 3200 series.

Note: See separate listing for BMW's Isetta, 600 and 700 minicars, produced from 1955-65.

1961 BMW

1961 BMW 3200CS Bertone coupe.

502/2.6, 3.2 — V-8 — This would be the final year of production for the descendants of BMW's 501/502 series, which continued with little change. Both standard and Super versions of the 3168-cc V-8 engine were available. After 1961, the 502 and (502) 3.2 were replaced by the similar 2600 and 3200 series.

2600 — V-8 — New for 1961 was the replacement for the 502 2.6-liter and the 501 V-8 (which had been called the BMW 2.6 in its final era, from fall 1958 onward). Little changed, actually, except for added horsepower and the adoption of front disc brakes as standard. Round taillamp housings were considerably shorter, and body-colored. The standard engine produced 100 horsepower at 4800 rpm, but a 2600L (Luxus) version delivered 110 bhp.

3200 — V-8 — Introduced in September 1961 as the successor to the 3.2 series, this would be the last of the big BMW sedans, before the company turned solidly toward the compact-car segment of the market. Both 3200L (Luxus) and 3200S (Super) versions were produced, the latter with twin carburetors and 160 horsepower, versus 140 bhp for the 3200L's 3168-cc V-8 engine.

I.D. DATA: Type 502 serial number is stamped on first crossmember, below the radiator. Engine number is stamped on the upper right front of the block.

Model	Body Type & Seating	Engine Type/CID	P.O.E. Price	Weight (lbs.)	Prod. Total
502/2.6	4-dr Sedan-6P	V8/157	5600	N/A	Note 1
502/3.2	4-dr Sedan-6P	V8/193	6200	N/A	Note 1
502/3.2 Super	4-dr Sedan-6P	V8/193	6700	3310	Note 2
2600	4-dr Sedan-6P	V8/157	N/A	3175	Note 3
2600L	4-dr Sedan-6P	V8/157	N/A	N/A	Note 3
3200L	4-dr Sedan-6P	V8/193	N/A	3240	Note 4
3200S	4-dr Sedan-6P	V8/193	N/A	3285	Note 5

Note 1: See prior listings for production details on Type 502.

Note 2: A total of 1,158 502 3.2 Supers were produced during the full model run.

Note 3: A total of 1,639 basic Model 2600 BMWs were produced from 1961-63, priced at 16,240 Deutsch Marks in Germany (18,240 Marks for the 2600L).

Note 4: A total of 416 Model 3200L BMWs were produced during the full model run, priced at 19,650 Marks in Germany.

Note 5: A total of 1,027 Model 3200S BMWs were produced during the full model run, priced at 21,240 Marks in Germany (about $5310).

Weight Note: Figures shown are "curb" weight.

ENGINE DATA: BASE V-8 (502/2.6): 90-degree, overhead-valve V-8. Aluminum block and heads. **Displacement:** 157.4 cu. in. (2580 cc). **Bore & Stroke:** 2.91 x 2.95 in. (74 x 75 mm). **Compression Ratio:** 7.0:1. **Brake Horsepower:** 100 at 4800 rpm. Five main bearings. Solid valve lifters. One Solex 30 PAAJ two-barrel carburetor.

BASE V-8 (2600): Same 2580-cc V-8 as above, except — **Brake Horsepower:** (2600) 100 hp at 4800 rpm; (2600L) 110 hp at 4900 rpm. One Zenith 32 NDIX two-barrel carburetor.

BASE V-8 (502/3.2): 90-degree, overhead-valve V-8. Aluminum block and heads. **Displacement:** 193.2 cu. in. (3168 cc). **Bore & Stroke:** 3.23 x 2.95 in. (82 x 75 mm). **Compression Ratio:** 7.2:1 or 7.5:1. **Brake Horsepower:** (3.2) 120 at 4800 rpm; (3.2 Super) 140 at 4800 rpm. Five main bearings. Solid valve lifters. One Zenith 32 NDIX two-barrel carburetor (3.2). Two Zenith 32 NDIX or 36 NDIX two-barrel carburetors (3.2 Super).
BASE V-8 (3200): Same as 3168-cc V-8 above, except — **Compression Ratio:** (3200L) 7.8:1; (3200S) 9.0:1. **Brake Horsepower:** (3200L) 140 hp at 5400 rpm; (3200S) 160 at 5600 rpm. One Zenith 36 NDIX carburetor (3200L); two Zenith carburetors (3200S).
CHASSIS DATA: Wheelbase: 111.6 in. **Overall Length:** 186.2 in. **Height:** 60.2 in. **Width:** 70.1 in. **Front Tread:** 52.4 in. **Rear Tread:** 55.7 in. **Wheel Type:** 15x4.5K steel disc. **Standard Tires:** (502, 2600) 6.40Sx15L; (3.2 Super, 3200S) 6.50/6.70Hx15L; (3200L) 6.40Sx15L.
TECHNICAL: Layout: front-engine, rear-drive. **Transmission:** four-speed manual; column shift. **Steering:** pinion and sector (bevel-gear). **Suspension (front):** dual A-arms with torsion bars. **Suspension (rear):** rigid axle with torsion bars. **Brakes:** (502) hydraulic, front/rear drum; (2600/3200) front disc, rear drum. **Body Construction:** separate body and frame.
PERFORMANCE: Top Speed: (3.2 Super) 110 mph; (2600) 100 mph; (2600L) 103 mph; (3200L) 109 mph; (3200S) 118 mph. **Acceleration (0-60 mph):** N/A (3200S, 0-62 mph in under 14 sec.).
PRODUCTION/SALES: A total of 52,943 BMWs were produced during calendar year 1961, of which 23,058 were exported.
Manufacturer: Bayerische Motoren Werke AG, Munich, West Germany.
Distributor: Hoffman Motors Corp., New York City.
HISTORY: The 2600 and 3200 were produced from 1961 to 1963.
Note: BMW still produced the Isetta 300 and the 700 minicar; see separate listing for details.

1962 BMW

1962 BMW 1500 four-door sedan.

1500 — FOUR — Finally, BMW was ready with the first of its "New Class" models, which were destined to give the faltering company a fresh start. This new four-door sedan was definitely larger than the little 700 (listed separately in this Catalog), but considerably smaller than the big BMWs.

Up front was a tiny version of BMW's already-traditional "kidney" grille, each element made up of vertical strips. Single round headlamps were contained in full-width side grilles with horizontal bars. A round BMW emblem stood at the hood front. Curious integral parking lights wrapped around just below the fender crease, where it met the hood. At the rear were tri-section taillamps, with a BMW emblem and '1500' nameplate on the left of the back panel. Front and rear doors held vent wings. Inside was a simple painted dash. The front end angled forward at the top, showing a profile that would make BMWs easy to spot over the next three decades. Seating was sufficient for five passengers, though more comfortable in back for four.

Under the hood was a new 1.5-liter, single-overhead-cam four-cylinder engine that produced 80 horsepower. The new BMW used unibody construction, as well as a MacPherson strut front suspension. Front disc brakes were standard (rear drums). A four-speed manual gearbox was installed.

2600 — V-8 — Production of the 2600 sedan, introduced in 1961, continued with little change.

3200 — V-8 — The original 3200S and 3200L, introduced in 1961, were joined this year by a new 3200CS (Coupe Sport), intended as a belated successor to the Type 503 of the late 1950s. The Bertone-styled coupe rode a long V-8 chassis, thus serving as the last of the big V-8 BMWs. That engine produced 160 horsepower, as in the 3200S. The body displayed a sizable expanse of glass and a low beltline. A character line ran along each bodyside at mid-height, all the way from headlamp to deck, taking a bit of an upturn at the rear edge of the quarter window (a feature that would become customary on subsequent BMW coupes). At the center of the front end was the customary small two-section "kidney" grille, but alongside that were two wide horizontal-bar grilles. Rectangular parking lights sat below the round headlamps. A round BMW emblem was almost horizontal, just above the grille. On the rear panel was a '3200 CS' nameplate, along with round taillamps. Front vent windows were installed, as well as rather large quarter windows. The passenger compartment itself was rather long.

I.D. DATA: Model 1500 serial number is stamped on upper right of firewall, inside the engine compartment. The 1500 engine number is on left rear of block. A model data plate is on right wall of engine compartment.

Model	Body Type & Seating	Engine Type/CID	P.O.E. Price	Weight (lbs.)	Prod. Total
1500	4-dr Sedan-4/5P	I4/91	N/A	2340	Note 1
2600	4-dr Sedan-6P	V8/157	N/A	3175	Note 2
2600L	4-dr Sean-6P	V8/157	N/A	N/A	Note 2

Model	Body Type & Seating	Engine Type/CID	P.O.E. Price	Weight (lbs.)	Prod. Total
3200L	4-dr Sedan-6P	V8/193	N/A	3240	Note 3
3200S	4-dr Sedan-6P	V8/193	N/A	3285	Note 4
3200CS	2-dr Coupe-5P	V8/193	N/A	3310	Note 5

Note 1: A total of 23,807 Model 1500 BMWs were produced during the full model run, priced at 8,500 to 9,485 Marks in Germany (about $2125 initially).

Note 2: A total of 1,639 basic Model 2600 BMWs were produced from 1961-63.

Note 3: A total of 416 Model 3200L BMWs were produced during the full model run.

Note 4: A total of 1,027 Model 3200S BMWs were produced during the full model run.

Note 5: A total of 603 Model 3200CS BMWs were produced during the full model run, initially priced in Germany at 29,850 Marks.

Weight Note: Figures shown are "curb" weight.

ENGINE DATA: BASE FOUR (1500): Inline, single-overhead-cam four-cylinder. Cast iron block and aluminum head. **Displacement:** 91.4 cu. in. (1499 cc). **Bore & Stroke:** 3.23 x 2.80 in. (82 x 71 mm). **Compression Ratio:** 8.8:1. **Brake Horsepower:** 80 at 5700 rpm (90 SAE at 5900 rpm). **Torque:** 87 lbs.-ft. at 3000 rpm. Five main bearings. Solid valve lifters. One Solex 34 PICB single-barrel carburetor.
BASE V-8 (2600): 90-degree, overhead-valve V-8. Aluminum block and heads. **Displacement:** 157.4 cu. in. (2580 cc). **Bore & Stroke:** 2.91 x 2.95 in. (74 x 75 mm). **Compression Ratio:** 7.0:1. **Brake Horsepower:** 100 at 4800 rpm except (2600L) 110 at 4900 rpm. Five main bearings. Solid valve lifters. One Zenith 32 NDIX two-barrel carburetor.
BASE V-8 (3200): 90-degree, overhead-valve V-8. Aluminum block and heads. **Displacement:** 193.2 cu. in. (3168 cc). **Bore & Stroke:** 3.23 x 2.95 in. (82 x 75 mm). **Compression Ratio:** (3200L) 7.8:1; (3200S/CS) 9.0:1. **Brake Horsepower:** (3200L) 140 hp at 5400 rpm; (3200S/CS) 160 at 5600 rpm. Five main bearings. Solid valve lifters. One Zenith 36 NDIX carburetor (3200L); two Zenith carburetors (3200S/CS).
CHASSIS DATA: Wheelbase: (1500) 100.4 in.; (2600/3200) 111.6 in. **Overall Length:** (1500) 177.2 in.; (2600/3200) 186.2 in.; (3200CS) 190.2 in. **Height:** (1500) 57.1 in.; (2600/3200) 60.2 in.; (3200CS) 57.5 in. **Width:** (1500) 67.3 in.; (2600/3200) 70.1 in.; (3200CS) 67.7 in. **Front Tread:** (1500) 52.0 in.; (2600/3200) 52.4 in. **Rear Tread:** (1500) 53.8 in.; (2600/3200) 55.7 in. **Wheel Type:** (1500) 14x4.5J; (2600/3200) 15x4.5K; (3200CS) 15x5J. **Standard Tires:** (1500) 6.00x14; (2600, 3200L) 6.40Sx15L; (3200S) 6.50/6.70Hx15L; (3200CS) 7.00Hx15L.
TECHNICAL: Layout: front-engine, rear-drive. **Transmission:** four-speed manual; column shift except (1500) floor shift. **Steering:** (1500) worm and roller; (2600/3200) bevel gear. **Suspension (front):** (1500) MacPherson struts with coil springs; (2600/3200) dual A-arms with torsion bars. **Suspension (rear):** (1500) rigid axle with semi-trailing arms and coil springs; (2600/3200) rigid axle with torsion bars. **Brakes:** front disc, rear drum. **Body Construction:** (1500) steel unibody; (2600/3200) separate body and frame.
PERFORMANCE: Top Speed: (1500) 92 mph; (2600) 100 mph; (2600L) 103 mph; (3200L) 109 mph; (3200S) 118 mph; (3200CS) 124 mph. **Acceleration (0-60 mph):** (1500) 14.0 sec. **Acceleration (quarter-mile):** (1500) 19.4 sec.
PRODUCTION/SALES: A total of 53,527 BMWs were produced during calendar year 1962, of which 23,022 were exported.
Manufacturer: Bayerische Motoren Werke AG, Munich, West Germany.
Distributor: Hoffman Motors Corp., New York City.
HISTORY: The 1500 sedan was produced from 1962 to 1964, and led to a long series of larger-engined models. A smaller-engined (1.3-liter) prototype for the 1500 had begun in 1957, but was abandoned. The 1500's debut came at the Frankfurt Show in September 1961. Even with strong demand from the public, however, it took a year or so to get production rolling. Early examples had their troubles, too, notably gearbox and rear-axle woes. The debut of the limited-production 3200CS coupe came at the 1961 IAA (Frankfurt) Show. Production of the 3200CS began in February 1962 and continued into 1965. A convertible prototype of the 3200CS was built, but abandoned.
Note: See separate listing for the BMW 700 minicar.

1963 BMW

1963 BMW Luxus "Limousine." (William Siuru Jr.)

1500 — FOUR — Production of BMW's first "New Class" sedan continued with little change.

1800 — FOUR — Another four-door sedan joined the BMW lineup, debuting at the Frankfurt show in September 1963. Appearance was similar to the 1500, except for the addition of a chromed rocker-panel trim strip, but the engine was larger (as suggested by the model number). The sohc four-cylinder engine produced 90 horsepower, working either with the standard four-speed manual gearbox or an optional three-speed automatic transmission.

2600 — V-8 — Only the 2600L version remained for this final year of the short-lived 2600 series.

3200 — V-8 — This would be the final year for the full-size, larger-engined sedan, which continued with little change. The 3200CS coupe would last into 1965.

I.D. DATA: 1500/1800 chassis serial number is stamped on upper right of firewall. Engine number is on left rear of block. A model data plate is on right wall of engine compartment.

Model	Body Type & Seating	Engine Type/CID	P.O.E. Price	Weight (lbs.)	Prod. Total
1500	4-dr Sedan-5P	I4/91	N/A	2340	Note 1
1800	4-dr Sedan-5P	I4/108	N/A	2405	Note 2
2600L	4-dr Sedan-6P	V8/157	N/A	N/A	Note 3
3200L	4-dr Sedan-6P	V8/193	N/A	3240	Note 4
3200S	4-dr Sedan-6P	V8/193	N/A	3285	Note 5
3200CS	2-dr Sedan-6P	V8/193	N/A	3310	Note 6

Note 1: A total of 23,807 Model 1500 BMWs were produced during the full model run.

Note 2: A total of 102,090 Model 1800 BMWs were produced during the full model run, initially priced in Germany at 9,985 Marks.

Note 3: A total of 1,639 Model 2600 BMWs were produced from 1961-63.

Note 4: A total of 416 Model 3200L BMWs were produced during the full model run.

Note 5: A total of 1,027 Model 3200S BMWs were produced during the full model run.

Note 6: A total of 603 Model 3200CS BMWs were produced during the full model run.

Weight Note: Figures shown are "curb" weight.

ENGINE DATA: BASE FOUR (1500): Inline, single-overhead-cam four-cylinder. Cast iron block and aluminum head. **Displacement:** 91.4 cu. in. (1499 cc). **Bore & Stroke:** 3.23 x 2.80 in. (82 x 71 mm). **Compression Ratio:** 8.8:1. **Brake Horsepower:** 80 at 5700 rpm (90 SAE at 5900 rpm). **Torque:** 87 lbs.-ft. at 3000 rpm. Five main bearings. Solid valve lifters. One Solex 34 PICB single-barrel carburetor.

BASE FOUR (1800): Inline, single-overhead-cam four-cylinder. Cast iron block and aluminum head. **Displacement:** 108 cu. in. (1773 cc). **Bore & Stroke:** 3.31 x 3.15 in. (84 x 80 mm). **Compression Ratio:** 8.6:1. **Brake Horsepower:** 90 at 5250 rpm (102 SAE at 5800 rpm, in U.S.). **Torque:** 105.6 lbs.-ft. (SAE) at 3000 rpm. Five main bearings. Solid valve lifters. One Solex 36-40 PDSI single-barrel carburetor.

BASE V-8 (2600L): 90-degree, overhead-valve V-8. Aluminum block and heads. **Displacement:** 157.4 cu. in. (2580 cc). **Bore & Stroke:** 2.91 x 2.95 in. (74 x 75 mm). **Compression Ratio:** 7.0:1. **Brake Horsepower:** 110 at 4900 rpm. Five main bearings. Solid valve lifters. One Zenith 32 NDIX two-barrel carburetor.

BASE V-8 (3200): 90-degree, overhead-valve V-8. Aluminum block and heads. **Displacement:** 193.2 cu. in. (3168 cc). **Bore & Stroke:** 3.23 x 2.95 in. (82 x 75 mm). **Compression Ratio:** (3200L) 7.8:1; (3200S/CS) 9.0:1. **Brake Horsepower:** (3200L) 140 hp at 5400 rpm; (3200S/CS) 160 at 5600 rpm. Five main bearings. Solid valve lifters. One Zenith 36 NDIX carburetor (3200L); two Zenith carburetors (3200S/CS).

CHASSIS DATA: Wheelbase: (1500/1800) 100.4 in.; (2600/3200) 111.6 in. **Overall Length:** (1500/1800) 177.2 in.; (2600/3200) 186.2 in.; (3200CS) 190.2 in. **Height:** (1500/1800) 57.1 in.; (2600/3200) 60.2 in.; (3200CS) 57.5 in. **Width:** (1500/1800) 67.3 in.; (2600/3200) 70.1 in.; (3200CS) 67.7 in. **Front Tread:** (1500/1800) 52.0 in.; (2600/3200) 52.4 in. **Rear Tread:** (1500/1800) 53.8 in.; (2600/3200) 55.7 in. **Wheel Type:** (1500/1800) 14x4.5J; (2600/3200) 15x4.5K; (3200CS) 15x5J. **Standard Tires:** (1500) 6.00x14; (1800) 6.00Sx14; (2600, 3200L) 6.40Sx15L; (3200S) 6.50/6.70Hx15L; (3200CS) 7.00Hx15L.

TECHNICAL: Layout: front-engine, rear-drive. **Transmission:** four-speed manual; (1500/1800) floor shift, (2600/3200) column shift. Three-speed automatic available on 1800. **Standard Final Drive Ratio:** (1500) 4.38:1. **Steering:** (1500/1800) worm and roller; (2600/3200) bevel gear. **Suspension (front):** (1500/1800) MacPherson struts with coil springs; (2600/3200) dual A-arms with torsion bars. **Suspension (rear):** (1500/1800) rigid axle with semi-trailing arms and coil springs; (2600/3200) rigid axle with torsion bars. **Brakes:** front disc, rear drum. **Body Construction:** (1500/1800) steel unibody; (2600/3200) separate body and frame.

PERFORMANCE: Top Speed: (1500) 92 mph; (1800) 100 mph; (2600L) 103 mph; (3200L) 109 mph; (3200S) 118 mph; (3200CS) 124 mph. **Acceleration (0-60 mph):** (1500) 14.0 sec. **Acceleration (quarter-mile):** (1500) 19.4 sec. **Fuel Mileage:** 26-34 mpg.

PRODUCTION/SALES: A total of 57,880 BMWs were produced during calendar year 1963, of which 26,864 were exported.

Manufacturer: Bayerische Motoren Werke AG, Munich, West Germany.

Distributor: Hoffman Motors Corp., New York City.

HISTORY: Production of the 1800 began in late 1963 and continued into 1968. It turned out to be considerably more popular than the 1500. BMWs in general were not considered trouble-free by U.S. customers at this time, and service wasn't the finest. On the other side of the Atlantic, however, BMW's 1500 was named Car of the Year by *Hobby* (a German magazine).

Note: See separate listing for the BMW 700 minicar.

1964 BMW

1964 BMW 3200 coupe. (William Siuru Jr.)

1500 — FOUR — Production on the first "New Class" BMW continued with little change, for what would be its final season.

1600 — FOUR — Another four-door sedan was introduced in March 1964, with a larger engine than the 1500. A 2-mm increase in bore diameter added 74 cubic centimeters, and 3 extra horsepower. Dimensions were identical to the 1500/1800, and appearance was identical to the 1500 from which it evolved. The only difference was the '1600' badge on its rear panel.

Note: The 1600 was not listed as available in the U.S. until the version introduced for 1966.

1800 — FOUR — A "hotter" version of the 1800 became available early in 1964, setting the stage for future sporty editions with extra performance. Offered only with the four-speed manual gearbox, the 1800ti (sometimes capitalized as 1800 TI, for *Turismo Internationale*) had the same engine as the regular 1800, but two carburetors gave it an output of 110 horsepower versus the 90 bhp rating of the standard engine. Appearance differed little between the 1800 and 1800ti except for a 'TI' label below the '1800' on the back panel.

In addition to the basic 1800ti, about 200 1800ti/SA *(sportausfuhrung)* models were sold only to licensed racers. That version had a much higher (10.5:1) compression ratio and two Weber carburetors, rated 130 horsepower (DIN). It came with a five-speed gearbox and could travel 119 mph. Both the front and rear suspension had anti-roll bars. The model designation was sometimes capitalized as 1800TI/SA.

3200CS — V-8 — Production of the V-8 coupe continued with little change.

I.D. DATA: 1500/1800 chassis serial number is stamped on upper right of firewall. Engine number is on left rear of block. A model data plate is on right wall of engine compartment.

Model	Body Type & Seating	Engine Type/CID	P.O.E. Price	Weight (lbs.)	Prod. Total
1500	4-dr Sedan-5P	I4/91	2995	2315	Note 1
1600	4-dr Sedan-5P	I4/96	N/A	2405	Note 2
1800	4-dr Sedan-5P	I4/108	3298	2359	Note 3
1800ti	4-dr Sedan-5P	I4/108	3530	2470	Note 4
1800ti/SA	4-dr Sedan-5P	I4/108	N/A	N/A	Note 4
3200CS	2-dr Coupe-5P	V8/193	10995	3310	Note 5

Note 1: A total of 23,807 Model 1500 BMWs were produced during the full model run.

Note 2: A total of 9,728 Model 1600 BMWs were produced during the full model run, into early 1966. Price in Germany was 9,485 Deutsch Marks.

Note 3: A total of 102,090 Model 1800 BMWs were produced during the full model run.

Note 4: A total of 19,663 Model 1800ti BMWs were produced during the full model run, 1964-66 (including about 200 race-ready 1800ti/SA models).

Note 5: A total of 603 Model 3200CS BMWs were produced during the full model run.

Model Note: Some U.S. directories still continued to list the 3200S sedan, priced at $7485, even though production ceased in 1963.

Weight Note: Figures shown are "curb" weight.

ENGINE DATA: BASE FOUR (1500): Inline, single-overhead-cam four-cylinder. Cast iron block and aluminum head. **Displacement:** 91.4 cu. in. (1499 cc). **Bore & Stroke:** 3.23 x 2.80 in. (82 x 71 mm). **Compression Ratio:** 8.8:1. **Brake Horsepower:** 80 at 5700 rpm (90 SAE at 5900 rpm). **Torque:** 87 lbs.-ft. at 3000 rpm (90 SAE at 3200 rpm). Five main bearings. Solid valve lifters. One Solex 34 PICB single-barrel carburetor.

BASE FOUR (1600): Inline, single-overhead-cam four-cylinder. Cast iron block and aluminum head. **Displacement:** 96 cu. in. (1573 cc). **Bore & Stroke:** 3.31 x 2.80 in. (84 x 71 mm). **Compression Ratio:** 8.6:1. **Brake Horsepower:** 83 DIN at 5500 rpm (96 SAE at 5700 rpm). **Torque:** 91.2 lbs.-ft. (SAE) at 3000 rpm. Five main bearings. Solid valve lifters. One Solex 36-40 PDSI single-barrel carburetor.

BASE FOUR (1800): Inline, single-overhead-cam four-cylinder. Cast iron block and aluminum head. **Displacement:** 108 cu. in. (1773 cc). **Bore & Stroke:** 3.31 x 3.15 in. (84 x 80 mm). **Compression Ratio:** 8.6:1. **Brake Horsepower:** 90 at 5250 rpm (102 SAE at 5800 rpm). **Torque:** 101 lbs.-ft. SAE at 3000 rpm. Five main bearings. Solid valve lifters. One Solex 36-40 PDSI single-barrel carburetor.

BASE FOUR (1800ti): Same as 1773-cc four above, except — **Compression Ratio:** 9.5:1. **Brake Horsepower:** 110 at 5850 rpm (124 SAE at 6000 rpm). **Torque:** 109.2 lbs.-ft. (SAE) at 4000 rpm. Two Solex 40 PHH carburetors.

BASE FOUR (1800ti/SA): Same as 1773-cc four above, except — **Compression Ratio:** 10.5:1. **Brake Horsepower:** 130 (DIN) at 6100 rpm. **Torque:** 106 lbs.-ft. at 5250 rpm. Two Weber carburetors.

BASE V-8 (3200CS): 90-degree, overhead-valve V-8. Aluminum block and heads. **Displacement:** 193.2 cu. in. (3168 cc). **Bore & Stroke:** 3.23 x 2.95 in. (82 x 75 mm). **Compression Ratio:** 9.0:1. **Brake Horsepower:** 160 DIN at 5600 rpm (185 SAE at 5600 rpm). **Torque:** 177 lbs.-ft. (DIN) at 3600 rpm. Five main bearings. Solid valve lifters. Two Zenith carburetors.

CHASSIS DATA: Wheelbase: (1500/1600/1800) 100.4 in.; (3200CS) 111.6 in. **Overall Length:** (1500/1600/1800) 177.2 in.; (3200CS) 190.2 in. **Height:** (1500/1600/1800) 57.1 in.; (3200CS) 57.5 in. **Width:** (1500/1600/1800) 67.3 in.; (3200CS) 67.7 in. **Front Tread:** (1500/1600/1800) 52.0 in.; (1800ti) 52.4 in.; (3200CS) 52.4 in. **Rear Tread:** (1500/1600/1800) 53.8 in.; (1800ti) 54.2 in.; (3200CS) 55.7 in. **Wheel Type:** (1500/1600/1800) 14x4.5J; (1800ti) 14x5JK; (3200CS) 15x5J. **Standard Tires:** (1500) 6.00x14; (1600/1800) 6.00Sx14; (3200CS) 7.00Hx15L.

TECHNICAL: Layout: front-engine, rear-drive. **Transmission:** four-speed manual; floor shift. Five-speed manual on 1800ti/SA. Three-speed automatic available on 1800. **Standard Final Drive Ratio:** (1500) 4.38:1; (1800) 4.22:1. **Steering:** (1500/1600/1800) worm and roller; (3200CS) bevel gear. **Suspension (front):** (1500/1600/1800) MacPherson struts with coil springs; (3200CS) dual A-arms with torsion bars. **Suspension (rear):** (1500/1600/1800) rigid axle with semi-trailing arms and coil springs; (3200CS) rigid axle with torsion bars. **Brakes:** front disc, rear drum. **Body Construction:** (1500/1600/1800) steel unibody; (3200CS) separate body and frame. **Fuel Tank:** (1500) 11 gal.; (1800) 11 gal.

PERFORMANCE: Top Speed: (1500) 92 mph; (1600) 96 mph; (1800) 100 mph; (1800ti) 105-109 mph; (1800ti/SA) 119 mph; (3200CS) 124 mph.

PRODUCTION/SALES: A total of 61,766 BMWs were produced during calendar year 1964, of which 27,742 were exported.

Manufacturer: Bayerische Motoren Werke AG, Munich, West Germany.

Distributor: Hoffman Motors Corp., New York City.

HISTORY: The 1600 was produced from 1964 to 1966, sold in Europe. The 1800ti was produced from February 1964 to 1966, and available in the U.S. This was the final year for the 1500 sedan.

Note: See separate listing for the BMW 700 minicar.

1965 BMW

1965 BMW 2000C coupe.

1600 — FOUR — Production of the four-door sedan with 1573-cc engine, not listed for sale in American directories, continued with little change.

1800 — FOUR — Production of the 1800 sedans continued with little change, in standard, 1800ti, and 1800ti/SA form.

2000 — FOUR — Yet another enlargement of the basic overhead-cam four-cylinder engine emerged in 1965, in a coupe riding the same 100.4-inch wheelbase as the 1500/1800 sedans. Two sporty versions were introduced: the 2000C, with a 100-bhp 1990-cc engine and single Solex carburetor, available with either a four-speed manual gearbox or ZF three-speed automatic; and the 2000CS, with 120 horsepower, twin carburetors, and four-speed only. The pillarless coupe body was designed by Wilhelm Hofmeister, based on the regular "New Class" chassis. It was built by Karmann, at the Osnabruck plant in northern Germany. Though graceful enough in profile, some considered the 2000 coupe's front end a bit odd, though it was similar to the larger Bertone-styled 3200CS from the windshield back. That similarity would continue on many subsequent coupes.

The unique front end held a tall, narrow version of the usual "kidney" grille, plus a series of vertical slots along the top of the bumpers. Wraparound headlamp units contained rectangular headlamps and round secondary lamps all in one unit, which wrapped around as turn signals. No side grilles were installed. The headlamps stood just below the trim strips that ran around the whole car. Rear quarter windows came to a point at the rear, looking somewhat pentagon-shaped, with a round BMW emblem to the rear of the window near its base. A round BMW emblem went ahead of the hood, sitting horizontally, and on the decklid. Horizontal taillamps were used.

3200CS — V-8 — Production of the larger coupe with V-8 engine continued for one more year, with little change.

I.D. DATA: 1500/1800/2000 chassis serial number is stamped on upper right of firewall. Engine number is on left rear of block. A model data plate is on right wall of engine compartment.

Model	Body Type & Seating	Engine Type/CID	P.O.E. Price	Weight (lbs.)	Prod. Total
1600	4-dr Sedan-5P	I4/96	N/A	2405	Note 1
1800	4-dr Sedan-5P	I4/108	3298	2405	Note 2
1800ti	4-dr Sedan-5P	I4/108	3530	2470	Note 3
1800ti/SA	4-dr Sedan-5P	I4/108	N/A	N/A	Note 3
2000C	2-dr Coupe-2 + 2P	I4/121	N/A	2645	Note 4
2000CS	2-dr Coupe-2 + 2P	I4/121	N/A	N/A	Note 5
3200CS	2-dr Coupe-5P	V8/193	10995	3310	Note 6

Note 1: A total of 9,728 Model 1600 BMWs were produced during the full model run, into early 1966. Price in Germany was 9,485 Deutsch Marks.

Note 2: A total of 102,090 Model 1800 BMWs were produced during the full model run.

Note 3: A total of 19,663 Model 1800ti BMWs were produced during the full model run, 1964-66 (including about 200 race-ready 1800ti/SA models).

Note 4: A total of 2,837 Model 2000C BMWs were produced during the full model run, into 1969. Price in Germany was 16,905 Deutsch Marks.

Note 5: A total of 8,883 Model 2000CS BMWs were produced during the full model run, into 1969. Price in Germany was 17,500 Deutsch Marks.

Note 6: A total of 603 Model 3200CS BMWs were produced during the full model run.

Model Note: Some U.S. directories still continued to list the 3200S sedan, priced at $7485, even though production ceased in 1963.

Weight Note: Figures shown are "curb" weight.

ENGINE DATA: BASE FOUR (1600): Inline, single-overhead-cam four-cylinder. Cast iron block and aluminum head. **Displacement:** 96 cu. in. (1573 cc). **Bore & Stroke:** 3.31 x 2.80 in. (84 x 71 mm). **Compression Ratio:** 8.6:1. **Brake Horsepower:** 83 DIN at 5500 rpm (96 SAE at 5700 rpm). **Torque:** 91.2 lbs.-ft. (SAE) at 3000 rpm. Five main bearings. Solid valve lifters. One Solex 36-40 PDSI single-barrel carburetor.

BASE FOUR (1800): Inline, single-overhead-cam four-cylinder. Cast iron block and aluminum head. **Displacement:** 108 cu. in. (1773 cc). **Bore & Stroke:** 3.31 x 3.15 in. (84 x 80 mm). **Compression Ratio:** 8.6:1. **Brake Horsepower:** 90 at 5250 rpm (102 SAE at 5800 rpm). **Torque:** 101 lbs.-ft. SAE at 3000 rpm. Five main bearings. Solid valve lifters. One Solex 36-40 PDSI single-barrel carburetor.

BASE FOUR (1800ti): Same as 1773-cc four above, except — **Compression Ratio:** 9.5:1. **Brake Horsepower:** 110 DIN at 5850 rpm (124 SAE at 6000 rpm). Two Solex 40 PHH carburetors.

BASE FOUR (1800ti/SA): Same as 1773-cc four above, except — **Compression Ratio:** 10.5:1. **Brake Horsepower:** 130 (DIN) at 6100 rpm. **Torque:** 106 lbs.-ft. at 5250 rpm. Two Weber carburetors.

BASE FOUR (2000C): Inline, single-overhead-cam four-cylinder. Cast iron block and aluminum head. **Displacement:** 121.4 cu. in. (1990 cc). **Bore & Stroke:** 3.50 x 3.15 in. (89 x 80 mm). **Compression Ratio:** 8.5:1. **Brake Horsepower:** 100 DIN at 5500 rpm (113 SAE at 6000 rpm). **Torque:** 115.7 lbs.-ft. (SAE) at 3000 rpm. Five main bearings. Solid valve lifters. One Solex 40 PDSI single-barrel carburetor.

BASE FOUR (2000CS): Same as 1990-cc four above, except — **Compression Ratio:** 9.3:1. **Brake Horsepower:** 120 DIN at 5500 rpm (135 SAE at 5800 rpm). **Torque:** 123 (SAE) at 3600 rpm. Two Solex 40 PHH two-barrel carburetors.

BASE V-8 (3200CS): 90-degree, overhead-valve V-8. Aluminum block and heads. **Displacement:** 193.2 cu. in. (3168 cc). **Bore & Stroke:** 3.23 x 2.95 in. (82 x 75 mm). **Compression Ratio:** 9.0:1. **Brake Horsepower:** 160 DIN at 5600 rpm (185 SAE at 5600 rpm). **Torque:** 177 lbs.-ft. (DIN) at 3600 rpm. Five main bearings. Solid valve lifters. Two Zenith carburetors.

CHASSIS DATA: Wheelbase: (1600/1800/2000) 100.4 in.; (3200CS) 111.6 in. **Overall Length:** (1600/1800) 177.2 in.; (2000) 178.3 in.; (3200CS) 190.2 in. **Height:** (1600/1800) 57.1 in.; (2000) 53.5 in.; (3200CS) 57.5 in. **Width:** (1600/1800) 67.3 in.; (2000) 65.9 in.; (3200CS) 67.7 in. **Front Tread:** (1600/1800) 52.0 in.; (1800ti/2000) 52.4 in.; (3200CS) 67.7 in. **Rear Tread:** (1600/1800) 53.8 in.; (1800ti/2000) 54.2 in.; (3200CS) 55.7 in. **Wheel Type:** (1600/1800) 14x4.5J; (1800ti) 14x5JK; (2000) 14x5.5J; (3200CS) 15x5J. **Standard Tires:** (1600/1800) 6.00Sx14; (2000C) 6.95/175Sx14; (2000CS) 6.95/175Hx14; (3200CS) 7.00Hx15L.

TECHNICAL: Layout: front-engine, rear-drive. **Transmission:** four-speed manual; floor shift. Five-speed manual on 1800ti/SA. Three-speed automatic available on 1800/2000C. **Standard Final Drive Ratio:** (1800) 4.22:1. **Steering:** (1600/1800/2000) worm and roller; (3200CS) bevel gear. **Suspension (front):** (1600/1800/2000) MacPherson struts with coil springs; (3200CS) dual A-arms with torsion bars. **Suspension (rear):** (1600/1800/2000) rigid axle with semi-trailing arms and coil springs; (3200CS) rigid axle with torsion bars. **Brakes:** front disc, rear drum. **Body Construction:** (1600/1800/2000) steel unibody; (3200CS) separate body and frame. **Fuel Tank:** (1800) 11 gal.

PERFORMANCE: Top Speed: (1600) 96 mph; (1800) 100 mph; (1800ti) 105-109 mph; (1800ti/SA) 119 mph; (2000C) 104 mph; (2000CS) 115 mph; (3200CS) 124 mph. **Acceleration (0-60 mph):** (2000CS) 9.8 sec. **Acceleration (quarter-mile):** (2000CS) 17.7 sec. (80 mph).

PRODUCTION/SALES: A total of 67,709 BMWs were produced during calendar year 1965, of which 28,984 were exported.

Manufacturer: Bayerische Motoren Werke AG, Munich, West Germany.

Distributor: Hoffman Motors Corp., New York City.

HISTORY: Both the 2000C and 2000CS were produced from 1965 to 1969. The 2000C's debut came in June 1965. The dual-carb 2000CS turned out to be the more popular of the two.

Note: See separate listing for the BMW 700 minicar, which ceased production in 1965.

1966-67 BMW

1967 BMW 2000C.

1600, 1600-2 — FOUR — If any single model could be said to trigger BMW's ultimate popularity in the U.S., it might be the 1600-2 sedan, introduced in March 1966. Engineered like the "New Class" four-door sedans, it was smaller in size, powered by an 85-horsepower, 1.6-liter overhead-cam engine that delivered fairly snappy performance. The '2' suffix stood for two-door. Wheelbase was two inches shorter than the four-door sedans. Styling features included round headlamps at the ends of horizontal-bar side grilles, in a typical angled-forward front end with wraparound park/signal lamps. Foglamps were optional. Round taillamps were used, with a BMW emblem and '1600' legend to the right of the back panel. In 1967, the 1600-2 designation changed to 1602 in Europe, but two-doors were called 1600 in the U.S.

In September 1967, a convertible (actually a conversion by the Baur company) was added to the 1600 lineup, but only seldom exported from Germany. Also added was a 1600ti version, which was sold in Europe but did not come to the U.S. market. It had higher compression and twin carburetors, and came with either a four-speed or five-speed manual transmission.

1800 — FOUR — Production of the 1800 sedans continued into 1966 with little change, in standard, 1800ti, and race-oriented 1800ti/SA form.

2000 — FOUR — Wearing an entirely different front end than the 2000C/CS coupe, the new four-door sedan carried the same 1990-cc engine, rated 100 bhp. Rectangular headlamps were lower than those on the coupe, integrated into grilles made up of horizontal strips, flanking the customary "kidney" grilles of vertical strips. A trim strip ran along the bodyside and fenders, continuing across the front of the hood. Wraparound park/signal lamps stood just below the body trim strip. Horizontal taillamps were taller than the coupe's, with three sections (one clear). Either the standard four-speed manual gearbox or optional ZF three-speed automatic was available.

2000ti/tilux — FOUR — In addition to the basic 2000 sedan, BMW offered a more potent 'ti' version with twin carburetors, available only with manual shift. Early examples of the 2000ti had the same appearance as the 1800, with round headlamps and taillamps. Later 'TI-lux' (subsequently called 'tilux') editions were revised in appearance.

2000C/CS — FOUR — Production of the 2000 coupes continued with little change; see previous listing for details.

I.D. DATA: Chassis serial number is stamped on upper right of firewall. Engine number is on left rear of crankcase. A model data plate is on right wall of engine compartment.

Model	Body Type & Seating	Engine Type/CID	P.O.E. Price	Weight (lbs.)	Prod. Total
1600-2	2-dr Sedan-5P	I4/96	2477	2070	Note 1
1600ti	2-dr Sedan-5P	I4/96	N/A	2115	Note 2
1600	4-dr Sedan-5P	I4/96	2895	2405	Note 3
1800	4-dr Sedan-5P	I4/108	3225	2405	Note 4
1800ti	4-dr Sedan-5P	I4/108	3520	2470	Note 5
1800ti/SA	4-dr Sedan-5P	I4/108	4474	N/A	Note 5
2000	4-dr Sedan-5P	I4/121	3780	2580	Note 6
2000ti	4-dr Sedan-5P	I4/121	3890	2530	Note 7
2000tilux	4-dr Sedan-5P	I4/121	N/A	N/A	Note 7
2000C	2-dr Coupe-2+2P	I4/121	4985	2645	Note 8
2000CS	2-dr Coupe-2+2P	I4/121	4985	N/A	Note 9

Note 1: A total of 277,320 Model 1600-2 BMWs were produced during the full model run.

Note 2: The 1600ti was not imported into the U.S.

Note 3: A total of 9,728 Model 1600 BMWs were produced during the full model run, into early 1966.

Note 4: A total of 102,090 Model 1800 BMWs were produced during the full model run.

Note 5: A total of 19,663 Model 1800ti BMWs were produced during the full model run, 1964-66.

Note 6: A total of 120,495 Model 2000 sedans were produced during the full model run. Price in Germany was 11,475 Marks.

Note 7: A total of 17,440 Model 2000ti/tilux sedans were produced during the full model run. Price of the 2000ti in Germany was 12,750 Marks.

Note 8: A total of 2,837 Model 2000C coupes were produced during the full model run, into 1969.

Note 9: A total of 8,883 Model 2000CS coupes were produced during the full model run, into 1969.

Price Note: A 2000 sedan with automatic cost $3990. The 2000C price shown included automatic transmission.

Weight Note: Figures shown are "curb" weight.

ENGINE DATA: BASE FOUR (1600, 1600-2): Inline, single-overhead-cam four-cylinder. Cast iron block and aluminum head. **Displacement:** 96 cu. in. (1573 cc). **Bore & Stroke:** 3.31 x 2.80 in. (84 x 71 mm). **Compression Ratio:** 8.6:1. **Brake Horsepower:** (1600) 83 at 5500 rpm; (1600-2) 85 at 5700 rpm (94-96 SAE at 5700 rpm). **Torque:** 91.2 lbs.-ft. (SAE) at 3000 rpm. Five main bearings. Solid valve lifters. One Solex 36-40 PDSI single-barrel carburetor (1600) or one Solex 38 PDSI carburetor (1600-2).

BASE FOUR (1600ti): Same as 1573-cc four above, except — **Brake Horsepower:** 105 at 6000 rpm. Two Solex 40 PHH two-barrel carbutetors.

BASE FOUR (1800): Inline, single-overhead-cam four-cylinder. Cast iron block and aluminum head. **Displacement:** 108 cu. in. (1773 cc). **Bore & Stroke:** 3.31 x 3.15 in. (84 x 80 mm). **Compression Ratio:** 8.6:1. **Brake Horsepower:** 90 at 5250 rpm (102 SAE at 5800 rpm). **Torque:** 105.6 lbs.-ft. (SAE) at 3000 rpm. Five main bearings. Solid valve lifters. One Solex 36-40 PDSI single-barrel carburetor.

BASE FOUR (1800ti): Same as 1773-cc four above, except — **Compression Ratio:** 9.5:1. **Brake Horsepower:** 110 at 5850 rpm (124 SAE at 6000 rpm). Two carburetors.

BASE FOUR (1800ti/SA): Same as 1773-cc four above, except — **Compression Ratio:** 10.5:1. **Brake Horsepower:** 130. Two Weber carburetors.

BASE FOUR (2000, 2000C): Inline, single-overhead-cam four-cylinder. Cast iron block and aluminum head. **Displacement:** 121.4 cu. in. (1990 cc). **Bore & Stroke:** 3.50 x 3.15 in. (89 x 80 mm). **Compression Ratio:** 8.5:1. **Brake Horsepower:** (2000) 100 DIN at 5500 rpm (113 SAE at 5500 rpm); (2000C) 135 SAE at 5500 rpm. **Torque:** (2000) 115 lbs.-ft. SAE at 3000 rpm; (2000C) 123 lbs.-ft. SAE at 3600 rpm. Five main bearings. Solid valve lifters. One Solex 40 PDSI single-barrel carburetor.

BASE FOUR (2000ti/tilux, 2000CS): Same as 1990-cc four above, except — **Compression Ratio:** 9.3:1. **Brake Horsepower:** 120 DIN at 5500 rpm (135 SAE at 5800 rpm). **Torque:** 122.9 lbs.-ft. SAE at 3600 rpm. Two Solex 40 PHH two-barrel carburetors.

CHASSIS DATA: Wheelbase: (1600-2) 98.4 in.; (1600/1800/2000) 100.4 in. **Overall Length:** (1600-2) 166.5 in.; (1600/1800/2000) 177.2 in.; (2000 cpe) 178.3 in. **Height:** (1600-2) 55.5 in.; (1600/1800/2000) 57.1 in.; (2000 cpe) 53.5 in. **Width:** (1600-2) 62.6 in.; (1600/1800/2000) 67.3 in.; (2000 cpe) 65.9 in. **Front Tread:** (1600-2) 52.4 in.; (1600/1800) 52.0 in.; (1800ti, 2000) 52.4 in.; **Rear Tread:** (1600-2) 52.4 in.; (1600/1800) 53.8 in.; (1800ti, 2000) 54.2 in. **Wheel Type:** (1600/1800) 14x4.5J; (1600-2) 13x4.5J; (1800ti) 14x5JK; (2000) 14x5J; (2000ti, 2000 cpe) 14x5.5J. **Standard Tires:** (1600/1800) 6.00Sx14; (1600-2) 165SR13; (2000) 6.45/1655x14 or 165SR14; (2000C) 6.95/175Sx14; (2000CS) 6.95/175Hx14.

TECHNICAL: Layout: front-engine, rear-drive. **Transmission:** four-speed manual; floor shift. Five-speed manual on 1800ti/SA. Three-speed automatic available on 1800, 2000 and 2000C. **Standard Final Drive Ratio:** (1800) 4.22:1; (2000CS) 3.89:1. **Steering:** worm and roller. **Suspension (front):** MacPherson struts with coil springs. **Suspension (rear):** rigid axle with semi-trailing arms and coil springs. **Brakes:** front disc, rear drum. **Body Construction:** steel unibody. **Fuel Tank:** (1800) 11 gal.

PERFORMANCE: Top Speed: (1600) 96 mph; (1600-2) 100 mph; (1600ti) 109 mph; (1800) 100 mph; (1800ti) 105-109 mph; (1800ti/SA) 119 mph; (2000, 2000C) 104 mph; (2000ti) 111 mph; (2000CS) 115 mph. **Acceleration (0-60 mph):** (1600) 11.6 sec. **Acceleration (quarter-mile):** (1600) 18.2 sec. **Fuel Mileage:** (1600) 22-25 mpg; (1800) about 21 mpg; (2000CS) about 21 mpg.

PRODUCTION/SALES: Of the 74,076 BMWs produced in calendar year 1966, a total of 27,120 were exported and 1,253 were sold in the U.S. Of the 87,816 BMWs produced in 1967, a total of 38,698 were exported and 4,564 sold in the U.S.

Manufacturer: Bayerische Motoren Werke AG, Munich, West Germany.

Distributor: Hoffman Motors Corp., New York City.

HISTORY: The 1600-2 coupe was produced from March 1966 into 1971. *Road & Track* gave the 1600-2 a highly favorable review, helping to establish its reputation in the U.S. The 1600ti (not imported to the U.S.) was produced only from September 1967 through 1968. The 2000 sedan was produced from 1966 to 1972; the 2000ti/tilux only to 1970.

BMW took over the Glas company in 1966, and produced a version of their sports coupe with a BMW 1.6-liter drivetrain as the 1600 GT. See Glas listing for details.

1968 BMW

1600 — FOUR — Production of the two-door sedan with 1573-cc engine continued with little change, except for the addition of side-window defrosters. A cabriolet (convertible) also was produced, but seldom seen outside Germany. Neither was the 1600ti sedan.

1800 — FOUR — A new engine went under the hood of the 1800 sedan in 1968. Appearance was similar to the former model, but with a partially blacked-out grille. The rear-end treatment was the same as the 2000 sedan. Inside was a new dashboard with hooded instrument cluster. The new engine was created by mixing the block from the 2000 with the crankshaft out of the 1600. Displacement shrunk slightly from the former 1800 (to 1766 cc), but the design was considerably more oversquare. Output was identical, at 90 horsepower, but the new engine was claimed to "rev" more freely. Both the four-speed manual and three-speed automatic transmission were available. A split (two-circuit) braking system was added.

2000 — FOUR — Production of the 2.0-liter sedan, in standard, 2000ti and 2000tilux versions, continued with little change; see previous listing for details.

2000C/CS — FOUR — Production of the 2000 coupes continued with little change; see previous listings for details.

2002 — FOUR — A new two-door sedan emerged this year, with the 2.0-liter engine. BMW believed it would have been too tough to modify the 1600ti to meet new U.S. emission standards, so they turned to a bigger engine that added 15 horsepower, with only moderate weight increase. This soon became BMW's best seller, priced under $3000 in the U.S. A BMW emblem and '2002' designation went on the right of the back panel.

BMW's twin-carb, performance-oriented 2002ti never came to the U.S. at all, because of emission regulations. In European trim, it had front and rear anti-roll bars and a four- or five-speed gearbox, and a '2002 ti' plate on the driver's side of the grille. The 2002ti engine produced 120 horsepower.

2500 — SIX — BMW returned to the big-car side of the business with two new six-cylinder sedans, powered by a 2.5- or 2.8-liter engine. Somewhat rounded in appearaance, the four-door sedan displayed quad round headlamps at the ends of the horizontal-bar side grilles. At the center was the customary "kidney" grilles, made up of vertical strips. Side marker lenses went at leading edges of front fenders. Three-section horizontal taillamps were used, with a '2500' script on the right side of the decklid. Wheelbase was 106 inches, and the sedan measured 185 inches overall. The 2494-cc engine developed 150 horsepower. An ample tool kit contained spare parts. These were the first production BMW cars with all-disc brakes. Either a four-speed manual or ZF three-speed automatic transmission was available.

1968 BMW 2800 four-door sedan.

2800 — SIX — This was the same sedan as the new 2500, but with a 2.8-liter six-cylinder engine and '2800' badge on the grille. A self-leveling rear suspension and limited-slip differential were standard at first, but not after 1971.

2800CS — SIX — A six-cylinder coupe debuted along with the 2500/2800 sedans, using much of the same body structure and chassis (including rear suspension) as the 2000CS coupe. Its front track was wider than the 2000CS, however, with larger tires and wheels. The front suspension was identical to that of the new 2500/2800 sedans, while power came from the 170-horsepower six installed in the 2800. These coupes were built at the Karmann plant in Osnabruck, and would be replaced by the 3.0CS model in 1971. More aggressive in appearance than the 2000CS, the six-cylinder coupe had quad round headlamps in blackout side grilles. Four small horizontal trim strips stood on the cowl, just below the long bodyside trim molding. Side marker lenses were at the leading edges of front fenders. A three-speed automatic transmission was available.

I.D. DATA: Chassis serial number is stamped at rear of engine compartment. Model data plate is also at rear of engine compartment, on right side. Engine number is on left rear of crankcase.

Model	Body Type & Seating	Engine Type/CID	P.O.E. Price	Weight (lbs.)	Prod. Total
1600	2-dr Sedan-5P	I4/96	2497	2070	Note 1
1600ti	2-dr Sedan-4P	I4/96	N/A	2115	Note 1
1600	2-dr Cabr-4P	I4/96	N/A	N/A	Note 1
1800	4-dr Sedan-5P	I4/108	3225	2490	Note 2
2000	4-dr Sedan-5P	I4/121	3780	2535	Note 3
2000ti	4-dr Sedan-5P	I4/121	4165	2491	Note 4
2000tilux	4-dr Sedan-5P	I4/121	N/A	N/A	Note 4
2000C	2-dr Coupe-2+2P	I4/121	N/A	2645	Note 5
2000CS	2-dr Coupe-2+2P	I4/121	N/A	N/A	Note 6
2002	2-dr Sedan-5P	I4/121	N/A	2073	Note 7
2002ti	2-dr Sedan-5P	I4/121	N/A	2185	Note 8
2500	4-dr Sedan-5P	I6/152	N/A	3000	Note 9
2800	4-dr Sedan-5P	I6/170	N/A	3000	Note 10
2800CS	2-dr Coupe-4P	I6/170	8022	2985	Note 11

Note 1: A total of 277,320 Model 1600 BMWs were produced during the full model run.

Note 2: A total of 39,020 Model 1800 BMWs were produced during the full model run.

Note 3: A total of 120,495 Model 2000 sedans were produced during the full model run.

Note 4: A total of 17,440 Model 2000ti/tilux sedans were produced during the full model run. Price of the 2000ti in Germany was 12,750 Marks.

Note 5: A total of 2,837 Model 2000C coupes were produced during the full model run, into 1969.

Note 6: A total of 8,883 Model 2000CS coupes were produced during the full model run, into 1969.

Note 7: A total of 339,084 Model 2002 coupes were produced during the full model run.

Note 8: A total of 16,448 Model 2002ti coupes were produced during the full model run (but not imported to the U.S.). Price in Germany was 10,990 Deutsch Marks.

Note 9: A total of 93,363 Model 2500 sedans were produced during the full model run.

Note 10: A total of 39,056 Model 2800 sedans were produced during the full model run.

Note 11: A total of 9,399 Model 2800CS coupes were produced during the full model run (of which 1,167 were exported to the U.S.).

ENGINE DATA: BASE FOUR (1600): Inline, single-overhead-cam four-cylinder. Cast iron block and aluminum head. **Displacement:** 96 cu. in. (1573 cc). **Bore & Stroke:** 3.31 x 2.80 in. (84 x 71 mm). **Compression Ratio:** 8.6:1. **Brake Horsepower:** 85 DIN at 5700 rpm (96 SAE at 5800 rpm). **Torque:** 91 lbs.-ft. at 3000 rpm. Five main bearings. Solid valve lifters. One Solex 38 PDSI carburetor.

BASE FOUR (1600ti): Same as 1573-cc four above, except — **Brake Horsepower**: 105 at 6000 rpm. Two Solex 40 PHH two-barrel carburetors.

BASE FOUR (1800): Inline, single-overhead-cam four-cylinder. Cast iron block and aluminum head. **Displacement**: 107.7 cu. in. (1766 cc). **Bore & Stroke**: 3.50 x 2.80 in. (89 x 71 mm). **Compression Ratio**: 8.6:1. **Brake Horsepower**: 90 at 5250 rpm (102 SAE at 5800 rpm). **Torque**: 105.6 lbs.-ft. (SAE) at 3000 rpm. Five main bearings. Solid valve lifters. One Solex 36-40 PDSI single-barrel carburetor.

BASE FOUR (2000, 2000C, 2002): Inline, single-overhead-cam four-cylinder. Cast iron block and aluminum head. **Displacement**: 121.4 cu. in. (1990 cc). **Bore & Stroke**: 3.50 x 3.15 in. (89 x 80 mm). **Compression Ratio**: 8.5:1. **Brake Horsepower**: 100 DIN at 5500 rpm (113-114 SAE at 5550-6000 rpm). **Torque**: 115.7 lbs.-ft. (SAE) at 3000 rpm. Five main bearings. Solid valve lifters. One Solex 40 PDSI single-barrel carburetor.

BASE FOUR (2000ti/tilux, 2002ti,2000CS): Same as 1990-cc four above, except — **Compression Ratio**: 9.3:1. **Brake Horsepower**: 120 DIN at 5500 rpm (135 SAE at 5800 rpm). **Torque**: 123 lbs.-ft. (SAE) at 3000 rpm. Two Solex 40 PHH two-barrel carburetors.

BASE SIX (2500): Inline, single-overhead-cam six-cylinder. Cast iron block and aluminum head. **Displacement**: 152.1 cu. in. (2494 cc). **Bore & Stroke**: 3.39 x 2.82 in. (86 x 71.6 mm). **Compression Ratio**: 9.0:1. **Brake Horsepower**: 150 DIN (170 SAE) at 6000 rpm. **Torque**: 154.8 lbs.-ft. (SAE) at 3700 rpm. Seven main bearings. Solid valve lifters. Two Zenith 35/40 INAT two-barrel carburetors.

BASE SIX (2800, 2800CS): Inline, single-overhead-cam six-cylinder. Cast iron block and aluminum head. **Displacement**: 170.1 cu. in. (2788 cc). **Bore & Stroke**: 3.39 x 3.15 in. (86 x 80 mm). **Compression Ratio**: 9.0:1. **Brake Horsepower**: 170 (192 SAE) at 6000 rpm. **Torque**: 173.6 lbs.-ft. (SAE) at 3700 rpm. Seven main bearings. Solid valve lifters. Two Zenith 35/40 INAT two-barrel carburetors.

CHASSIS DATA: Wheelbase: (1600/2002) 98.4 in.; (1800/2000) 100.4 in.; (2500/2800) 106.0 in.; (2800CS) 103.3 in. **Overall Length**: (1600/2002) 166.5 in.; (1800/2000) 177.2 in.; (2000 cpe) 178.3 in.; (2500/2800) 185.0 in.; (2800CS) 183.5 in. **Height**: (1600, 2002) 55.5 in.; (1800/2000) 57.1 in.; (2000 cpe) 53.5 in.; (2500/2800) 57.1 in.; (2800CS) 53.9 in. **Width**: (1600/2002) 62.6 in.; (1800/2000) 67.3 in.; (2000 cpe) 65.9 in.; (2500/2800) 68.9 in.; (2800CS) 65.7 in. **Front Tread**: (1600/2002) 52.4 in.; (1800/2000) 52.4 in.; (2002ti) 52.8 in.; (2500/2800/2800CS) 56.9 in. **Rear Tread**: (1600/2002) 52.4 in.; (1800) 54.2 in.; (2000) 54.2 in.; (2002ti) 52.8 in.; (2500/2800) 57.6 in.; (2800CS) 55.2 in. **Wheel Type**: (1600) 13x4.5J; (1800) 14x5J; (2000) 14x5J; (2000ti, 2000 cpe) 14x5.5J; (2002) 13x4.5J; (2002ti) 13x5J; (2500/2800) 14x6J. **Standard Tires**: (1600) 165SR13; (1800) 6.45/1655x14; (2000) 6.45/1655x14 or 165SR14; (2000C) 6.95/175Sx14; (2000CS) 6.95/175Hx14; (2002) 165SR13; (2002ti) 165HR13; (2500) 175HRx14; (2800) 195/70HR14; (2800CS) 175HR14 or 195/70HR14.

TECHNICAL: Layout: front-engine, rear-drive. **Transmission**: four-speed manual; floor shift. Three-speed automatic available on most models. **Steering**: worm and roller (power assist available on 2500/2800). **Suspension (front)**: MacPherson struts with coil springs. **Suspension (rear)**: rigid axle with semi-trailing arms and coil springs. **Brakes**: front disc, rear drum except (2500/2800 sedan) four-wheel disc. **Body Construction**: steel unibody.

PERFORMANCE: Top Speed: (1600) 100 mph; (1800) 103 mph; (2000, 2000C) 104 mph; (2000ti) 111 mph; (2000CS) 115 mph; (2002ti) 115 mph; (2500) 118 mph; (2800) 124 mph; (2800CS) 128 mph. **Acceleration (0-60 mph)**: (2002) 10.0-11.3 sec.; (2000CS) 9.8 sec. **Acceleration (quarter-mile)**: (2002) 17.4 sec. (78.9 mph); (2000CS) 17.7 sec. (80 mph). **Fuel Mileage**: (2002) 22-27 mpg.

PRODUCTION/SALES: Of the 116,547 BMWs produced in calendar year 1968, a total of 42,246 were exported and 8,172 were sold in the U.S.

Manufacturer: Bayerische Motoren Werke AG, Munich, West Germany.

Distributor: Hoffman Motors Corp., New York City.

HISTORY: The revised model 1800 was produced from August 1968 to 1972. The 2500 sedan was produced from 1968-77. The 2800CS coupe was built from 1968-71; the 2800 (and later Bavaria version) from 1968-74. The impressive increase in American sales at this time may be attributed to the introduction of the 2002, after 1968. Production of the performance-oriented 2002ti ceased in 1971. Six-cylinder sedans, developed under engineering director Bernhard Osswald, were not available in North America after 1971. They were similar in size to the "New Generation" Mercedes-Benz models, introduced early in 1968.

1969-70 BMW

1600 — FOUR — Production of the two-door BMW with 1573-cc engine continued with little change. Several options were required on U.S. models, including power brakes, bumper guards, a chromed exhaust tip, and Skai upholstery.

1800 — FOUR — Production of the 1.8-liter sedan, introduced a year earlier, continued with little change.

2000 — FOUR — A 2000tii four-door sedan became available late in 1969 with Kugelfischer mechanical fuel injection. Otherwise, it was similar to the earlier 2000ti/tilux. The 2.0-liter engine produced 130 horsepower and was the first fuel-injected BMW.

2000C/CS — FOUR — Production of this pair of four-cylinder coupes halted in 1969.

2002 — FOUR — Production of the 2002 and 2002ti coupes continued with little change. Several options were mandatory on U.S. models, including a tachometer, radial tires, Skai upholstery, and reclining front seats.

2500/2800 — SIX — Production of both six-cylinder sedans continued with little change, as did the 2800CS coupe. See previous listing for details. All were now available in the U.S. A heated back window was standard on the 2800, but a $40 option on the 2500. The 2800 included a rear leveling control and anti-roll bar, plus a limited-slip differential.

I.D. DATA: Chassis serial number is stamped at rear of engine compartment. Model data plate is also at rear of engine compartment, on right side. Engine number is on left rear of crankcase. Starting serial number for 1969 models: (1600) 1562200; (2002) 1660700. Serial number range for 1970 models: (1600) 1569787 to 1571875; (2002) 1666901 to 1676325 or 2530001 to 2532125; (2500) 2120274 to 2120750 or 2150609 to 2150999; (2800) 2420084 to 2420680 or 2460118 to 2460838; (2800CS) 227001 to 2270420 or 228001 to 2280425.

Model	Body Type & Seating	Engine Type/CID	P.O.E. Price	Weight (lbs.)	Prod. Total
1600	2-dr Sedan-5P	I4/96	2727	2073	Note 1
1600	2-dr Cabr-4P	I4/96	N/A	N/A	Note 1
1800	4-dr Sedan-5P	I4/108	N/A	2490	Note 1
2000	4-dr Sedan-5P	I4/121	N/A	2535	Note 1
2000tilux	4-dr Sedan-5P	I4/121	4140	N/A	Note 1
2000tii	4-dr Sedan-5P	I4/121	N/A	2580	Note 2
2000C	2-dr Coupe-2+2P	I4/121	N/A	2645	Note 1
2000CS	2-dr Coupe-2+2P	I4/121	N/A	N/A	Note 1
2002	2-dr Sedan-5P	I4/121	2982	2073	Note 1
2002ti	2-dr Sedan-5P	I4/121	N/A	2185	Note 1
2500	4-dr Sedan-5P	I6/152	5284	2866	Note 1
2800	4-dr Sedan-5P	I6/170	6284	2866	Note 1
2800CS	2-dr Coupe-4p	I6/170	7480	N/A	Note 1

Note 1: See previous listing for complete production breakdown.

Note 2: A total of 1,922 Model 2000tii BMWs were produced during the full model run.

Price Note: Prices shown were valid during the 1969 model year. Initial prices that year were slightly lower, ranging from $2597 for the 1600 to $7150 for the 2800CS. An automatic transmission added $295 to prices of 2000/2002 models, and $240 to 2500/2800 series. Prices in 1970 ranged from $3015 to $8453.

ENGINE DATA: BASE FOUR (1600): Inline, single-overhead-cam four-cylinder. Cast iron block and aluminum head. **Displacement**: 96 cu. in. (1573 cc). **Bore & Stroke**: 3.31 x 2.80 in. (84 x 71 mm). **Compression Ratio**: 8.6:1. **Brake Horsepower**: 85 at 5700 rpm (96 SAE at 5800 rpm). **Torque**: 91 lbs.-ft. SAE at 3000 rpm. Five main bearings. Solid valve lifters. One Solex 38 PDSI carburetor.

BASE FOUR (1800): Inline, single-overhead-cam four-cylinder. Cast iron block and aluminum head. **Displacement**: 107.7 cu. in. (1766 cc). **Bore & Stroke**: 3.50 x 2.80 in. (89 x 71 mm). **Compression Ratio**: 8.6:1. **Brake Horsepower**: 90 at 5250 rpm (102 SAE at 5800 rpm). **Torque**: 105.6 lbs.-ft. (SAE) at 3000 rpm. Five main bearings. Solid valve lifters. One Solex 36-40 PDSI single-barrel carburetor.

BASE FOUR (2000C, 2002): Inline, single-overhead-cam four-cylinder. Cast iron block and aluminum head. **Displacement**: 121.4 cu. in. (1990 cc). **Bore & Stroke**: 3.50 x 3.15 in. (89 x 80 mm). **Compression Ratio**: 8.5:1. **Brake Horsepower**: 100 DIN at 5500 rpm (113-114 SAE at 5550-6000 rpm). **Torque**: 115.7 lbs.-ft. (SAE) at 3000 rpm. Five main bearings. Solid valve lifters. One Solex 40 PDSI single-barrel carburetor.

BASE FOUR (2000tilux, 2002ti, 2000CS): Same as 1990-cc four above, except — **Compression Ratio**: 9.3:1. **Brake Horsepower**: 120 DIN at 5500 rpm (135 SAE at 5800 rpm). **Torque**: 123 lbs.-ft. (SAE) at 3000-3600 rpm). Two Solex 40 PHH twin-barrel carburetors.

BASE FOUR (2000tii): Same as 1990-cc four above, except — **Compression Ratio**: 10.3:1. **Brake Horsepower**: 130 DIN (up to 147 SAE) at 5800 rpm. **Torque**: 130 lbs.-ft. at 3000 rpm. Kugelfischer mechanical fuel injection.

BASE SIX (2500): Inline, single-overhead-cam six-cylinder. Cast iron block and aluminum head. **Displacement**: 152.1 cu. in. (2494 cc). **Bore & Stroke**: 3.39 x 2.82 in. (86 x 71.6 mm). **Compression Ratio**: 9.0:1. **Brake Horsepower**: 150 DIN (170 SAE) at 6000 rpm. **Torque**: 154.8 lbs.-ft. (176 SAE) at 3700 rpm. Seven main bearings. Solid valve lifters. Two Zenith 35/40 INAT two-barrel carburetors.

BASE SIX (2800, 2800CS): Inline, single-overhead-cam six-cylinder. Cast iron block and aluminum head. **Displacement**: 170.1 cu. in. (2788 cc). **Bore & Stroke**: 3.39 x 3.15 in. (86 x 80 mm). **Compression Ratio**: 9.0:1. **Brake Horsepower**: 170 (192 SAE) at 6000 rpm. **Torque**: 173.6 lbs.-ft. (SAE) at 3700 rpm. Seven main bearings. Solid valve lifters. Two Zenith 35/40 INAT two-barrel carburetors.

CHASSIS DATA: Wheelbase: (1600/2002) 98.4 in.; (1800/2000) 100.4 in.; (2500/2800) 106.0 in.; (2800CS) 103.3 in. **Overall Length**: (1600/2002) 166.5 in.; (1800/2000) 177.2 in.; (2000 cpe) 178.3 in.; (2500/2800) 185.0 in.; (2800CS) 183.5 in. **Height**: (1600/2002) 55.5 in.; (1800/2000) 57.1 in.; (2000 cpe) 53.5 in.; (2500/2800) 57.1 in.; (2800CS) 53.9 in. **Width**: (1600/2002) 62.6 in.; (1800/2000) 67.3 in.; (2000 cpe) 65.9 in.; (2500/2800) 68.9 in.; (2800CS) 65.7 in. **Front Tread**: (1600/2002) 52.4 in.; (1800/2000) 52.4 in.; (2002ti) 52.8 in.; (2500/2800/2800CS) 56.9 in. **Rear Tread**: (1600/2002) 52.4 in.; (1800/2000) 54.2 in.; (2002ti) 52.8 in.; (2500/2800) 57.6 in.; (2800CS) 55.2 in. **Wheel Type**: (1600) 13x4.5J; (1800) 14x5J; (2000) 14x5J; (2000 cpe) 14x5.5J; (2002) 13x4.5J; (2002ti) 13x5J; (2500/2800) 14x6J. **Standard Tires**: (1600) 165SR13 or 6.00x13; (1800) 6.45/1655x14; (2000) 6.45x14 or 165SR14; (2000C) 6.95/175Sx14; (2000CS) 6.95/175Hx14; (2002) 165SR13 or 6.00x13; (2002ti) 165HR13; (2000tii) 175HR14; (2500) 175HRx14; (2800) 175HR14, DR70HR14 or 195/70HR14; (2800CS) 175HR14 or 195/70HR14.

TECHNICAL: Layout: front-engine, rear-drive. **Transmission**: four-speed manual; floor shift. Three-speed automatic available on most models. **Standard Final Drive Ratio**: (1600) 4.11:1; (2000) 4.11:1; (2002) 3.64:1; (2500/2800) 3.54:1. **Steering**: worm and roller (power assist available on 2500/2800). **Suspension (front)**: MacPherson struts with coil springs. **Suspension (rear)**: rigid axle with semi-trailing arms and coil springs. **Brakes**: front disc, rear drum except (2500/2800 sedan) four-wheel disc. **Body Construction**: steel unibody. **Fuel Tank**: (1600) 12 gal.; (2000/2002) 12 gal.; (2500) 19.8 gal.; (2800CS) 14.5 gal.

MAJOR OPTIONS: Automatic transmission. Air conditioning. Power steering: 2500/2800 ($190). Heated rear window ($40). Sliding steel sunroof: 1600/2002 ($135); 2000/2500/2800 ($220). AM radio ($70). Blaupunkt AM/FM radio ($140-$185). Leather upholstery: 2000/2500/2800 ($330). Tinted glass ($65-$75). Metallic paint ($65-$100).

PERFORMANCE Top Speed: (1600) 100-102 mph; (1800) 103 mph; (2000) 105 mph; (2000C) 104 mph; (2000CS) 115 mph; (2002ti) 115 mph; (2500) 118 mph; (2800) 124 mph; (2800CS) 128 mph. **Acceleration (0-60 mph)**: (1600) 11.4 sec.; (2000) 11 sec.; (2000CS) 9.8 sec.; (2002) 9.8 sec.; (2500) 9.8-10.0 sec.; (2800) 9 sec.; (2800CS) 8.7 sec. **Acceleration (quarter-mile)**: (2002) 18.5 sec. (77.2 mph); (2000CS) 17.7 sec. (80 mph); (2500) 17.3 sec.; (2800) 16.8 sec. (83.3 mph); (2800CS) 17.6 sec. (85.6 mph). **Fuel Mileage**: (2800) 19.7 mpg average; (2800CS) 20 mpg average.

PRODUCTION/SALES: Of the 147,841 BMWs produced in calendar year 1969, a total of 54,209 were exported. Of the 161,165 BMWs produced in 1970, 66,099 were exported and 14,574 were sold in the U.S.

Manufacturer: Bayerische Motoren Werke AG, Munich, West Germany.

Distributor: Hoffman Motors Corp., New York City and Los Angeles.

HISTORY: The 1969 models debuted in the U.S. on September 1, 1968. The fuel-injected 2000 tii was produced from 1969 to 1972.

Modesty was not BMW's forte. Ads claimed that "BMW is the best sports sedan in the world...a practical family sedan that's a mind-bending joy to drive." Besides that, "driving one will give you a real kick—right in the small of your back, every time you tromp down on its accelerator." As for the bigger 2500/2800, BMW ads insisted: "We didn't design the new larger BMW as an alternative to existing cars, but as a car to which there is no existing alternative."

1971 BMW

1600 — FOUR — A facelifted 1600 two-door, introduced in April 1971, added chrome/rubber bodyside trim (at the lower body crease), rubber bumper strips, and interior modifications. Also new this year was a two-door Touring hatchback, with a concave hatch. It was slightly lower and shorter than an ordinary two-door model. Dimensions were identical to the 1800 Touring model (below).

1800/1802 — FOUR — Body changes took place in the 1800 sedan in April 1971. They included the addition of rectangular headlamps (smoothly integrated in grille) and wider taillamps (from the 2000). Taillamps were now horizontal instead of vertical, wrapping slightly around fenders. Also, the BMW emblem and '1800' designation moved to the right side of the back panel (formerly on left).

A two-door 1802 sedan (and 1800 Touring hatchback) also were added this year, filling the gap between the 1600 and 2002 models. Like the 1600, the new sedan had a fresh bumper design with rubber strip, and a chrome/rubber trim strip between wheel openings (in line witn bumpers). Only the four-speed manual gearbox was available.

2000 — FOUR — Two new 2.0-liter models emerged in 1971: a Touring two-door hatchback, and 2000tii Touring hatchback. Though not the most graceful BMW design, these became the best-selling examples of the Touring hatchbacks. Round headlamps stood at the ends of blackout side grilles with two horizontal bright bars, alongside a blackout "kidney" grille. Large standard driving lights were inboard, near the center grille. 'Touring' script went on the back panel, above the model designation. Round taillamps were installed. Alloy wheels were optional. Rear seatbacks folded down. The 2000 engine produced 100 bhp; the 2000tii (with mechanical fuel injection), 130 bhp. Either a four-speed manual or three-speed automatic transmission was available in the 2000 Touring, while the 2000tii came with a four- or five-speed manual gearbox.

2002 — FOUR — A facelift this year gave European versions a blackout "kidney" grille; blackout side grilles with two horizontal bright strips; round headlamps at ends of side grilles; wraparound park/signal lamps just below the horizontal bodyside trim strip; and round taillamps. A 2002 Cabriolet was added to the lineup. Also new: a 2002tii sedan with fuel injection, available in North America through 1974. Similar in appearance to the facelifted 2002 series, it had rubber bumper inserts, and a chrome/rubber trim strip between the wheel openings, at bumper height. North American versions had side clearance lights.

2500 — SIX — Chrome trim was added to the bodysides for 1971, and side grilles were blacked-out. Otherwise, the 2.5-liter six-cylinder sedan continued with little change.

2800/CS, 2.8 BAVARIA — SIX — Production of the 2800 sedan and 2800CS coupe continued with little change. Aimed at the U.S. market, the 2.8 Bavaria was equipped similar to the 2500 to keep the price down. *Road & Track* referred to the Bavaria as a "detrimmmed 2500."

3.0S — SIX — A larger six-cylinder engine debuted in 1971, in the 3.0S four-door sedan. Power steering and air conditioning were optional. Round quad headlamps stood at ends of blackout side grilles. At the center was the customary "kidney" grille, also blacked-out. The 2985-cc overhead-cam six produced 180 horsepower (170 in the U.S.).

Also debuting in Europe at this time was the 3.0Si, with a more powerful (200-bhp) engine. It would not reach the U.S. until 1976, with a lower (176-bhp) power rating and Bosch L-Jetronic fuel injection.

1971-'75 BMW 3.0 CSi. (William Siuru Jr.)

3.0CS — SIX — The new 2985-cc engine also went into a two-door coupe, successor to the 2800CS, introduced at the April 1971 Geneva Salon. It would arrive in the U.S. for the 1972 model year, nearly identical in appearance to the 2800CS. The North American version had side clearance lights and reflectors, plus standard leather upholstery (optional in Europe). Four-wheel ventilated disc brakes were standard. Either a Getrag four-speed manual or Borg-Warner three-speed automatic transmission was available.

Also introduced in 1971 for European consumption was the 3.0CSi coupe, with Bosch D-Jetronic fuel injection and a 200-bhp rating. Another variant of the 3.0CS was the 3.0CSL coupe, which wore a lighter body and rode wider wheels. Early versions used a carbureted engine, but all were fuel injected after mid-1972. This was a race-oriented model, intended to provide homologation for the BMW company. A 3.0CSL could accelerate to 62 mph in about seven seconds. European versions had no front bumper, but U.S. examples wore one. Standard features also included Plexiglass rear quarter windows and a fiberglass rear bumper. Only a four-speed manual gearbox was available.

I.D. DATA: Chassis serial number is stamped at rear of engine compartment. Model data plate is also at rear of engine compartment, on right side. Engine number is on left rear of crankcase. Serial number range: (1600) 1571876 to 1573162; (2002) 1676326 to 1680000 or 2570001 to 2575394; (2800) 2420681 to 2420708 or 2460839 to 2460862; (2800CS) 2270421 to 2270641 or 2280426 to 2280526.

Model	Body Type & Seating	Engine Type/CID	P.O.E. Price	Weight (lbs.)	Prod. Total
1600	2-dr Sedan-5P	I4/96	3015	2073	Note 1
1600	2-dr Cabr-4P	I4/96	N/A	N/A	Note 1
1600 Touring	2-dr Hatch-5P	I4/96	N/A	N/A	Note 1
1800	4-dr Sedan-5P	I4/108	N/A	2490	N/A
1800 Touring	2-dr Hatch-5P	I4/108	N/A	N/A	Note 2
1802	2-dr Sedan-5P	I4/108	N/A	N/A	Note 3
2000	4-dr Sedan-5P	I4/121	N/A	2535	N/A
2000tii	4-dr Sedan-5P	I4/121	N/A	2580	Note 4
2000 Touring	2-dr Hatch-5P	I4/121	N/A	2270	Note 5
2000tii Tr	2-dr Hatch-5P	I4/121	N/A	2315	Note 6
2002	2-dr Hatch-5P	I4/121	3275	2073	N/A
2002	2-dr Cabr-4P	I4/121	N/A	N/A	Note 7
2002ti	2-dr Sedan-5P	I4/121	N/A	2185	N/A
2002tii	2-dr Sedan-5P	I4/121	N/A	2225	Note 8
2500	4-dr Sedan-5P	I6/152	5753	2866	N/A
2800	4-dr Sedan-5P	I6/170	6779	2866	N/A
2800CS	2-dr Coupe-4P	I6/170	8089	2932	N/A
2.8 Bavaria	4-dr Sedan-5P	I6/170	4987	N/A	N/A
3.0S	4-dr Sedan-5P	I6/182	N/A	3090	Note 9
3.0Si	4-dr Sedan-5P	I6/182	N/A	3130	Note 10
3.0CS	2-dr Coupe-4P	I6/182	N/A	3085	Note 11
3.0CSi	2-dr Coupe-4P	I6/182	N/A	2800	Note 12
3.0CSL	2-dr Coupe-4P	I6/182	N/A	N/A	Note 13

Note 1: A total of 277,320 Model 1600 BMWs were produced during the full model run.
Note 2: A total of 3,099 Touring 1800 BMWs were produced during the full model run.
Note 3: A total of 83,351 Model 1802 BMWs were produced during the full model run.
Note 4: A total of 1,922 Model 2000tii BMWs were produced during the full model run.
Note 5: A total of 5,705 Model 2000 Touring BMWs were produced during the full model run.
Note 6: A total of 5,783 Model 2000tii Touring BMWs were produced during the full model run.
Note 7: A total of 4,199 Model 2002 Cabriolets were produced during the full model run.
Note 8: A total of 38,703 Model 2002tii BMWs were produced during the full model run.
Note 9: A total of 32,567 Model 3.0S BMWs were produced during the full model run.
Note 10: A total of 20,310 Model 3.0Si BMWs were produced during the full model run.
Note 11: A total of 11,063 Model 3.0CS BMWs were produced during the full model run.
Note 12: A total of 8,199 Model 3.0CSi BMWs were produced during the full model run.
Note 13: A total of 1,039 Model 3.0CSL BMWs were produced during the full model run.
Production Note: See previous listings for additonal breakdowns.

ENGINE DATA: BASE FOUR (1600): Inline, single-overhead-cam four-cylinder. Cast iron block and aluminum head. **Displacement:** 96 cu. in. (1573 cc). **Bore & Stroke:** 3.31 x 2.80 in. (84 x 71 mm). **Compression Ratio:** 8.6:1. **Brake Horsepower:** 85 at 5700 rpm (96 SAE at 5800 rpm). **Torque:** 91 lbs.-ft. SAE at 3000 rpm. Five main bearings. Solid valve lifters. One Solex 38 PDSI carburetor.

BASE FOUR (1800, 1802): Inline, single-overhead-cam four-cylinder. Cast iron block and aluminum head. **Displacement:** 107.7 cu. in. (1766 cc). **Bore & Stroke:** 3.50 x 2.80 in. (89 x 71 mm). **Compression Ratio:** 8.6:1. **Brake Horsepower:** 90 DIN at 5250 rpm (102 SAED at 5800 rpm). **Torque:** 105.6 lbs.-ft. (SAE) at 3000 rpm. Five main bearings. Solid valve lifters. One Solex 36-40 (or 40) PDSI single-barrel carburetor.

BASE FOUR (2000, 2002): Inline, single-overhead-cam four-cylinder. Cast iron block and aluminum head. **Displacement:** 121.4 cu. in. (1990 cc). **Bore & Stroke:** 3.50 x 3.15 in. (89 x 80 mm). **Compression Ratio:** 8.5:1. **Brake Horsepower:** 100 DIN at 5500 rpm (113-114 SAE at 5550-6000 rpm). **Torque:** 115.7 lbs.-ft. SAE at 3000 rpm. Five main bearings. Solid valve lifters. One Solex 40 PDSI single-barrel carburetor.

BASE FOUR (2002ti): Same as 1990-cc four above, except — **Brake Horsepower:** 120 DIN at 5500 rpm (135 SAE at 5800 rpm). **Torque:** 123 lbs.-ft. (SAE) at 3000 rpm. Two Solex 40 PHH twin-barrel carburetors.

BASE FOUR (2000tii, 2002tii): Same as 1990-cc four above, except — **Compression Ratio:** 10.3:1. **Brake Horsepower:** 130 DIN (up to 147 SAE) at 5800 rpm. **Torque:** 130 lbs.-ft. at 3000 rpm. Kugelfischer mechanical fuel injection.

BASE SIX (2500): Inline, single-overhead-cam six-cylinder. Cast iron block and aluminum head. **Displacement:** 152.1 cu. in. (2494 cc). **Bore & Stroke:** 3.39 x 2.82 in. (86 x 71.6 mm). **Compression Ratio:** 9.0:1. **Brake Horsepower:** 150 DIN (170 SAE) at 6000 rpm. **Torque:** 154.8 lbs.-ft. at 3700 rpm. Seven main bearings. Solid valve lifters. Two Zenith 35/40 INAT two-barrel carburetors.

BASE SIX (2800, 2800CS, 2.8 Bavaria): Inline, single-overhead-cam six-cylinder. Cast iron block and aluminum head. **Displacement:** 170.1 cu. in. (2788 cc). **Bore & Stroke:** 3.39 x 3.15 in. (86 x 80 mm). **Compression Ratio:** 9.0:1. **Brake Horsepower:** 170 (192 SAE) at 6000 rpm. **Torque:** 173.6 lbs.-ft. (200 SAE) at 3700 rpm. Seven main bearings. Solid valve lifters. Two Zenith 35/40 INAT two-barrel carburetors.

BASE SIX (3.0S, 3.0CS): Inline, single-overhead-cam six-cylinder. Cast iron block and aluminum head. **Displacement:** 182.1 cu. in. (2985 cc). **Bore & Stroke:** 3.50 x 3.15 in. (89 x 80 mm). **Compression Ratio:** 8.0:1 (9.0:1 in Europe). **Brake Horsepower:** 170 SAE at 5800 rpm (180 at 6000 in Europe). Seven main bearings. Solid valve lifters. Two Zenith 35/40 INAT two-barrel carburetors.

BASE SIX (3.0Si, 3.0CSi): Same as 2985-cc six above, except — **Brake Horsepower:** 200 at 5500 rpm. Bosch fuel injection.

CHASSIS DATA: Wheelbase: (1600/1802, 1800/2000 Touring, 2002) 98.4 in.; (1800/2000) 100.4 in.; (2500/2800) 106.0 in.; (2800CS/3.0CS) 103.3 in.; (3.0S) 106.0 in. **Overall Length:** (1600/1802/2002) 166.5 in.; (1800/2000/2000tii Tr) 161.8 in.; (1800/2000) 177.2 in.; (2500/2800) 185.0 in.; (2800CS/3.0CS) 183.5 in.; (3.0S) 195.0 in., but 185.0 in Europe. **Height:** (1600/1802/2002) 55.5 in.; (1800 Tr) 53.5 in.; (1800/2000) 57.1 in.; (2000 Touring) 54.3 in.; (2002 cabr) 53.5 in.; (2500/2800/3.0S) 57.1 in.; (2800CS/3.0CS) 53.9 in. **Width:** (1600/1802, 1800/2000 Tr, 2002) 62.6 in.; (1800/2000) 67.3 in.; (2500/2800/3.0S) 68.9 in.; (2800CS/3.0CS) 65.7 in.; 3.0CSL) 68.1 in. **Front Tread:** (1600/1800/2000/2002) 52.4 in.; (2000tii, 2002ti/tii) 52.8 in.; (2500/2800/2800CS/3.0S/3.0CS) 56.9 in. **Rear Tread:** (1600/1802, 1800/2000 Tr, 2002) 52.4 in.; (1800/2000) 54.2 in.; (2000tii/2002ti/2002tii) 52.8 in.; (2500/2800/3.0S) 57.6 in.; (2800CS/3.0CS) 55.2 in. **Wheel Type:** (1600) 13x4.5J; (1800) 14x5J; (1802) 13x4.5J); (1800ti) 14x5JK; (2000) 14x5J; (2000 Touring) 13x4.5; (2000tii Tr) 13x5; (2002) 13x4.5J; (2002ti/2002tii) 13x5J; (2500/2800) 14x6J; (3.0S) 14x6; (3.0CS) 14x6J. **Standard Tires:** (1600) 165SR13 or 6.00x13; (1800) 6.45/165x14; (1802) 165JR13; (2000) 6.45x14 or 165SR14; (2000 Touring) 165SR13; (2000tii Tr) 165HR13; (2002) 165SR13 or 6.00x13; (2002ti/2002tii) 165HR13; (2000tii) 175HR14; (2500) 175HRx14; (2800) 195/70HR14; (2800CS) 175HR14 or 195/70HR14; (3.0S) 175HR14 in U.S.; (3.0CS) 195/70VRx14.

TECHNICAL: Layout: front-engine, rear-drive. **Transmission:** four-speed manual; floor shift. Four- or five-speed on 2002tii. Three-speed automatic available on most models. **Standard Final Drive Ratio:** (1600) 4.11:1; (2000) 4.11:1; (2500/2800) 3.54:1; (3.0S) 3.45:1 in Europe, 3.64:1 in U.S. **Steering:** worm and roller (power assist available on 2500/2800/3.0S). **Suspension (front):** MacPherson struts with coil springs. **Suspension (rear):** rigid axle with semi-trailing arms and coil springs. **Brakes:** front disc, rear drum except (2500/2800/3.0S) four-wheel disc. **Body Construction:** steel unibody. **Fuel Tank:** (1600) 12 gal.; (2000/2002) 12 gal.; (2500) 19.8 gal.; (2800CS) 14.5 gal.

MAJOR OPTIONS: Automatic transmission: 2500 ($365); 2800 ($364). Air conditioning. Power steering. Power brakes: 1600/2002 ($45 mandatory option).

PERFORMANCE: Top Speed: (1600) 100 mph; (1800) 103 mph; (1802) 104 mph; (1800 Touring) 102 mph; (2000 Touring) 107 mph; (2000tii Touring) 118 mph; (2002ti) 115 mph; (2002tii) 118 mph; (2002 cabr) 107 mph; (2500) 118 mph; (2800) 124 mph; (2800CS) 128 mph; (3.0S) 127 mph; (European 3.0Si) 130 mph; (European 3.0CS) 132 mph; (Euro 3.0CSi) 136 mph. **Acceleration (0-60 mph):** (2002tii) 9.8 sec.; (2.8 Bavaria) 9.3 sec. **Acceleration (quarter-mile):** (2002tii) 17.3 sec.; (2.8 Bavaria) 16.8 sec. **Fuel Mileage:** (2002tii) near 23 mpg; (2.8 Bavaria) 18 mpg.

PRODUCTION/SALES: Of the 164,701 BMWs produced in calendar year 1971, a total of 78,350 were exported and 19,826 were sold in the U.S.

Manufacturer: Bayerische Motoren Werke AG, Munich, West Germany.
Distributor: Hoffman Motors Corp., New York City.

HISTORY: The 1971 models were introduced in the U.S. on September 21, 1970. This was a year of considerable model additions and shuffling. The 1600 was produced from 1971-75; the 1600 Touring from 1971-72; the 1802 from 1971-75; the 1800 Touring from 1971-74; the 2000 Touring from 1971-74; the 2000 tii Touring from 1971-74; 2002 Cabriolet from 1971-75; 2002tii from 1971-75; 3.0S from 1971-77 (to U.S. in 1973; the 3.0Si from 1971-77 (to U.S. in 1976); the 3.0CS from 1971-75; the 3.0CSi from 1971-75; and the 3.0CSL from 1971-75. The Bavaria sedans were the first BMWs to sell well in the U.S., partly because they were priced lower. Most U.S. models in the 1970s were air conditioned.

1972 BMW

1972 BMW 520 four-door sedan.

2000 — FOUR — Production of the basic 2000 sedan and the 2000tii continued into 1972 with little change.

2002 — FOUR — Production of the two-door 2.0-liter model would continue into 1976. The 2002 Cabriolet, available from 1971-75, had a solid Targa-style roof bar.

2800 — SIX — The 2500 sedan dropped out of the North American market, but the 2800 continued with little change, sometimes referred to as the BMW 2.8.

3.0S — SIX — Production of the 3.0-liter sedan for the European market continued with little change. A fuel-injected 3.0Si version was not exported to the U.S. The 3.0 Bavaria became available in the U.S. for the 1972 model year, replacing the 2.8 Bavaria. Priced lower than comparable models, it carried less standard equipment.

3.0CS — SIX — Production of the 3.0-liter coupe continued with little change, in both 3.0CS and 3.0CSi forms. Late in 1972, the limited-production 3.0CSL enjoyed a bore increase to 3003 cc (183.2 cid). That CSL engine produced 200 bhp for racing purposes, mounted in a lightweight body.

1600/1800/2500 Note: These models remained in production but were no longer officially exported to the U.S. market; see previous listings for specifications and details. Production of the 1600 and 1802 two-doors continued into 1975; the 1800 Touring into 1974; and the 2500 into 1977. This was the final year for the 1600 Touring and the 1800 four-door sedan.

I.D. DATA: A seven-digit serial number is on a plate attached to the the steering column, on a plate attached to right fender (inside engine compartment), and stamped into the firewall on the right edge. The number consists of a three-digit prefix that identifies the model, followed by a four-digit sequential number. Engine number is on the left side of the block, at the upper edge of the starter mounting. Starting serial number: (2002) 2575395 or 2532126; (2002tii) 2760001; (Bavaria) 3100001 or 3130001.

Model	Body Type &Seating	Engine Type/CID	P.O.E. Price	Weight (lbs.)	Prod. Total
2000	4-dr Sedan-5P	I4/121	N/A	2535	Note 1
2000tii	4-dr Sedan-5P	I4/121	N/A	2580	Note 1
2002	2-dr Sedan-5P	I4/121	3571	2073	Note 1
2002	2-dr Cabr-4P	I4/121	N/A	N/A	Note 1
2002tii	2-dr Sedan-5P	I4/121	4286	2073	Note 1
2000 Touring	2-dr Hatch-5P	I4/121	N/A	2270	Note 1
2000tii Tr	2-dr Hatch-5P	I4/121	N/A	2225	Note 1
2800 (2.8)	4-dr Sedan-5P	I6/170	N/A	2866	Note 1
3.0S	4-dr Sedan-5P	I6/182	N/A	3090	Note 1
Bavaria	4-dr Sedan-5P	I6/182	5555	2866	Note 1
3.0CS	2-dr Coupe-4P	I6/182	8712	3046	Note 1
3.0CSi	2-dr Coupe-4P	I6/182	N/A	N/A	Note 1

Note 1: See previous listing for model-by-model breakdowns.

Price Note: A 2002 with automatic transmission sold for $3905; Bavaria with automatic, $5936; 3.0CS with automatic, $9111.

ENGINE DATA: BASE FOUR (2000, 2002): Inline, single-overhead-cam four-cylinder. Cast iron block and aluminum head. **Displacement:** 121.4 cu. in. (1990 cc). **Bore & Stroke:** 3.50 x 3.15 in. (89 x 80 mm). **Compression Ratio:** 8.5:1. **Brake Horsepower:** 100 at 5500 rpm (113 SAE at 5800 rpm). **Torque:** 116 lbs.-ft. SAE at 3000 rpm. Five main bearings. Solid valve lifters. One Solex 40 PDSI single-barrel carburetor.
BASE FOUR (2002tii): Same as 1990-cc four above, except — **Compression Ratio:** 10.3:1. **Brake Horsepower:** 125 at 5500 rpm. **Torque:** 127 lbs.-ft. at 4000 rpm. Kugelfischer mechanical fuel injection.
BASE SIX (2800): Inline, single-overhead-cam six-cylinder. Cast iron block and aluminum head. **Displacement:** 170.1 cu. in. (2788 cc). **Bore & Stroke:** 3.39 x 3.15 in. (86 x 80 mm). **Compression Ratio:** 9.0:1. **Brake Horsepower:** 170 (192 SAE) at 6000 rpm. **Torque:** 154.8 (173.6 SAE) lbs.-ft. at 3700 rpm. Seven main bearings. Solid valve lifters. Two Zenith 35/40 INAT two-barrel carburetors.
BASE SIX (3.0S, 3.0CS): Inline, single-overhead-cam six-cylinder. Cast iron block and aluminum head. **Displacement:** 182.1 cu. in. (2985 cc). **Bore & Stroke:** 3.50 x 3.15 in. (89 x 80 mm). **Compression Ratio:** 8.0:1 (9.0:1 in Europe). **Brake Horsepower:** 190 SAE at 5800 rpm (180 DIN at 6000 in Europe). **Torque:** up to 185 lbs.-ft. at 3500 rpm. Seven main bearings. Solid valve lifters. Two Zenith 35/40 INAT two-barrel carburetors.
BASE SIX (3.0CSi): Same as 2985-cc six above, except — **Brake Horsepower:** 200 at 5500 rpm. Bosch D-Jetronic fuel injection.

CHASSIS DATA: Wheelbase: (2002) 98.4 in.; (2000) 100.4 in.; (2800) 106.0 in.; (3.0CS) 103.3 in.; (3.0S) 106.0 in. **Overall Length:** (2002) 166.5 in.; (2000/2000tii Tr) 161.8 in.; (2000) 177.2 in.; (2800) 185.0 in.; (3.0CS) 183.5 in. (3.0S) 195.0 in., but 185.0 in Europe. **Height:** (2002) 55.5 in.; (2000) 57.1 in.; (2000 Touring) 54.3 in.; (2800/3.0S) 57.1 in.; (3.0CS) 53.9 in. **Width:** (2000 Tr, 2002) 62.6 in.; (2000) 67.3 in.; (2800/3.0S) 68.9 in.; (3.0CS) 65.7 in. **Front Tread:** (2000/2002) 52.4 in.; (2000tii, 2002/tii) 52.8 in.; (2800/3.0S/3.0CS) 56.9 in. **Rear Tread:** (2000 Tr, 2002) 52.4 in.; (2000) 54.2 in.; (2000tii/2002tii) 52.8 in.; (2800/3.0S) 57.6 in.; (3.0CS) 55.2 in. **Standard Tires:** (2000) 6.45x14 or 165SR14; (2000 Touring) 165SR13; (2000tii Tr) 165HR13; (2002) 165SR13 or 6.00x13; (2002tii) 165HR13; (2000tii) 175HR14; (2800) 195/70HR14; (3.0S) 175HR14 in U.S.; (3.0CS) 195/70VRx14.

TECHNICAL: Layout: front-engine, rear-drive. **Transmission:** four-speed manual; floor shift. Four- or five-speed on 2002tii. Three-speed automatic available on most models. **Steering:** worm and roller (power assist available on 2800/3.0S). **Suspension (front):** MacPherson struts with coil springs. **Suspension (rear):** rigid axle with semi-trailing arms and coil springs. **Brakes:** front disc, rear drum except (2800/3.0S) four-wheel disc. **Body Construction:** steel unibody.

MAJOR OPTIONS: Automatic transmission: 2002 ($334); Bavaria ($381). Air conditioning. Power steering.

PERFORMANCE: Top Speed: (2000 Touring) 107 mph; (2000tii Touring) 118 mph; (2002tii) 118 mph; (2800) 124 mph; (3.0S) 127 mph; (European 3.0CS) 132 mph; (Euro 3.0CSi) 136 mph. **Acceleration (0-60 mph):** (2002tii) under 10 seconds.

PRODUCTION/SALES: Of the 182,858 BMWs produced in calendar year 1972, a total of 89,406 were exported.

ADDITIONAL MODELS: BMW's experimental 2002 Turbo coupe emerged in 1972, designed by Paul Bracq at the BMW studios and shown at the Olympic games that year. The ultra-low, color-impregnated fiberglass body (red and orange) featured gullwing doors. Safety features included telescopic energy-absorbing front and rear ends, a wide rollbar, and radar that warned if the car ahead was too close. The single-cam turbocharged, mid-mounted 1990-cc engine produced about 200 hp with Kugelfischer mechanical fuel injection. Rack-and-pinion steering was used. The Turbo rode a 94.5-inch wheelbase and measured 163.6 inches overall, standing only 43.3 inches tall. Top speed was estimated at 155 mph, and only two were built.

A new 520 four-door sedan debuted in September 1972, which was not exported to the U.S. Powered by a 2.0-liter engine, it was intended as a replacement for the "New Class" series, measuring 4.7 inches longer overall. Wheelbase was 103.8 inches; overall length 181.9 inches. This was the first new model built at BMW's Dingolfing plant, and used a new numbering system that soon would become standard. Its ergonomically-oriented interior included no-glare instruments and easy-to-reach controls. The four-cylinder engine produced 115 bhp at 5800 rpm, using twin Stromberg carburetors. A 520i version also was introduced, rated 125 bhp and offered only with four-speed manual shift. Late in 1977, a six-cylinder version would become available. A total of 467,112 5-Series models were produced from 1972 to the end of 1978.

Manufacturer: Bayerische Motoren Werke AG, Munich, West Germany.

Distributor: Hoffman Motors Corp., New York City.

1973 BMW

1973 BMW 3.0 CSL. (William Siuru Jr.)

2002 — FOUR — Starting in September 1973, the 2002tii switched to rectangular head-lamps and got restyled wheels. The North American model added impact bumpers. In 1973, the North American version of the 2002 got a revised cylinder head and new two-barrel carburetor, producing 98 horsepower.

2002 TURBO — FOUR — Following the debut of the experimental safety 2002 Turbo coupe in 1972, a production model became available in 1973-74, but never was exported to the U.S. Its debut came at the 1973 Frankfurt Show, and the white-bodied Turbo was easy to spot with its fender flares, colorful striping, and lack of front bumper. Early models had 'turbo 2002' in reverse script on the deep front spoiler, but that was criticized by some observers as too aggressive and soon was removed. A Turbo could accelerate to 100 kph (62 mph) in about eight seconds, but response of the turbo engine was considered somewhat sluggish overall. The 1990-cc engine produced 170 bhp at 5800 rpm. The fuel tank held 18.5 U.S. gallons (5.3 more than a standard 2002). Options include a five-speed gearbox and six-inch alloy wheels.

2800 — SIX — Production of the 2.8-liter six-cylinder sedan continued with little change.

3.0S — SIX — Production of the 3.0-liter six-cylinder sedan and Bavaria continued with little change. The 3.0S became available in the U.S. this year, joining the Bavaria. Standard 3.0S equipment included an upholstered steering wheel, air conditioning, leather upholstery, power windows, wood interior trim, and Becker stereo radio. The lower-priced Bavaria lacked such extras. A fuel-injected 3.0Si version was not sold in the U.S. at this time.

3.0CS — SIX — Production of the 3.0-liter six-cylinder coupes continued with little change. Leather upholstery was a mandatory option on the 3.0CS coupe. Standard equipment included tinted glass, magnesium wheels, and a torsion-bar stabilizer.

From 1973 on, various aero add-ons were available for the race-oriented 3.0CSL, including a fin-style winged rear deck spoiler, air dividers on front fenders, and a rear roof spoiler. Stroke of the 3.0CSL engine was lengthened during 1973, to 3153-cc displacement and a rating of 206 horsepower using Bosch D-Jetronic fuel injection.

1600/1800/2000/2500 Note: These models remained in production but were no longer officially exported to the U.S. market; see previous listings for specifications and details. Production of the 1600 and 1802 two-doors continued into 1975; the 1800 Touring and 2000/tii Touring into 1974; and the 2500 into 1977.

I.D. DATA: A seven-digit serial number is on a plate attached to the the steering column, on a plate attached to right fender (inside engine compartment), and stamped into the firewall on the right edge. The number consists of a three-digit prefix that identifies the model, followed by a four-digit sequential number. Engine number is on the left side of the block, at the upper edge of the starter mounting. Serial number range: (2002) 258238 to 2593704; (2002tii) 2762631 to 2764521; (Bavaria) 3103965 to 3106942 or 3132599 to 3135384; (3.0S) 3106942 up; (3.0CS) 2240391 to 2240975; (3.0S w/automatic) 3135384 up; (3.0CS w/automatic) 2250319 to 2250738.

Model	Body Type &Seating	Engine Type/CID	P.O.E. Price	Weight (lbs.)	Prod. Total
2002	2-dr Sedan-5P	I4/121	4498	2073	Note 1
2002	2-dr Cabr-4P	I4/121	N/A	N/A	Note 1
2002tii	2-dr Sedan-5P	I4/121	5233	2080	Note 1
2002 Turbo	2-dr Sedan-4P	I4/121	6660	2380	Note 2
2800	4-dr Sedan-5P	I6/170	5284	N/A	Note 1
3.0S	4-dr Sedan-5P	I6/182	10628	3050	Note 1
Bavaria	4-dr Sedan-5P	I6/182	7545	N/A	Note 1
3.0CS	2-dr Coupe-4P	I6/182	10634	3070	Note 1
3.0CSi	2-dr Coupe-4P	I6/182	N/A	N/A	Note 1

Note 1: See 1971 and earlier listings for model-by-model breakdowns.

Note 2: A total of 1,672 2002 Turbo sedans were produced, priced in Germany at 18,720 Deutsch Marks. Price shown in this listing is approximate.

Price Note: Model 2002 with automatic sold for $4810; Bavaria with automatic, $7772; 3.0S with automatic, $10,872; 3.0CS with automatic, $11,034.

ENGINE DATA: BASE FOUR (2002): Inline, single-overhead-cam four-cylinder. Cast iron block and aluminum head. **Displacement:** 121.4 cu. in. (1990 cc). **Bore & Stroke:** 3.50 x 3.15 in. (89 x 80 mm). **Compression Ratio:** 8.3:1. **Brake Horsepower:** 98 (SAE) at 5500 rpm. **Torque:** 106 lbs.-ft. (SAE) at 3500 rpm. Five main bearings. Solid valve lifters. One Solex 32/32 DIDTA or 40 DIPTA carburetor.

BASE FOUR (2002tii): Same as 1990-cc four above, except — **Compression Ratio:** 9.0:1. **Brake Horsepower:** 125 (SAE) at 5500 rpm. **Torque:** 127 lbs.-ft. (SAE) at 4000 rpm. Kugelfischer mechanical fuel injection.

BASE FOUR (2002 Turbo): Same as 1990-cc four above, except — **Brake Horsepower:** 170 DIN at 5800 rpm. Kugelfischer mechanical fuel injection.

BASE SIX (2800): Inline, single-overhead-cam six-cylinder. Cast iron block and aluminum head. **Displacement:** 170.1 cu. in. (2788 cc). **Bore & Stroke:** 3.39 x 3.15 in. (86 x 80 mm). **Compression Ratio:** 9.0:1. **Brake Horsepower:** 170 (192 SAE) at 6000 rpm. **Torque:** 154.8 (173.6 SAE) lbs.-ft. at 3700 rpm. Seven main bearings. Solid valve lifters. Two Zenith 35/40 INAT two-barrel carburetors.

BASE SIX (3.0S, 3.0CS): Inline, single-overhead-cam six-cylinder. Cast iron block and aluminum head. **Displacement:** 182.1 cu. in. (2985 cc). **Bore & Stroke:** 3.50 x 3.15 in. (89 x 80 mm). **Compression Ratio:** 8.3:1 (9.0:1 in Europe). **Brake Horsepower:** 170 at 5800 rpm (180 DIN at 6000 in Europe). **Torque:** 185 lbs.-ft. at 3500 rpm. Seven main bearings. Solid valve lifters. Two Zenith 35/40 INAT two-barrel carburetors.

BASE SIX (3.0CSi): Same as 2985-cc six above, except — **Brake Horsepower:** 200 at 5500 rpm. Bosch D-Jetronic fuel injection.

CHASSIS DATA: Wheelbase: (2002) 98.4 in.; (2800) 106.0 in.; (3.0CS) 103.3 in.; (3.0S) 106.0 in. **Overall Length:** (2002) 166.5 in.; (2800) 185.0 in.; (3.0CS) 183.5 in.; (3.0S) 195.0 in. **Height:** (2002) 55.5 in.; (2800/3.0S) 57.1 in.; (3.0CS) 53.9 in. **Width:** (2002) 62.6 in.; (2800/3.0S) 68.9 in.; (3.0CS) 65.7 in. **Front Tread:** (2002) 52.8 in.; (2002tii) 52.8 in.; (2800/3.0S/3.0CS) 56.9 in. **Rear Tread:** (2002) 52.8 in.; (2002tii) 52.8 in.; (2800/3.0S) 57.6 in.; (3.0CS) 55.2 in. **Standard Tires:** (2002) 165SR13; (2002tii) 165HR13; (2002 Turbo) 185/70HR13; (2800) 195/70HR14; (3.0S) 195/70VR14; (Bavaria) 175HR14; (3.0CS) 195/70VRx14.

TECHNICAL: Layout: front-engine, rear-drive except (2002 Turbo) mid-engine, rear-drive. **Transmission:** four-speed manual; floor shift. Five-speed manual standard on 2002tii, available on 2002 Turbo. Three-speed automatic available on most models. **Steering:** worm and roller. **Suspension (front):** MacPherson struts with coil springs. **Suspension (rear):** rigid axle with semi-trailing arms and coil springs. **Brakes:** front disc, rear drum except (2800/3.0S) four-wheel disc. **Body Construction:** steel unibody.

MAJOR OPTIONS: Automatic transmission. Air conditioning: Bavaria ($733); 3.0CS ($710). Limited-slip differential: 3.0S ($163). Power steering: Bavaria ($273). Manual sunroof ($190-$315). Electric sunroof ($275-$410). Power windows: Bav ($286). Tinted glass: 2002 ($63); Bav ($75). Leather upholstery ($520-$650). Rear headrests: Bav ($47). Tachometer: 2002 ($50 mandatory option). Blaupunkt Frankfurt radio ($155) except 3.0S. Magnesium wheels: 2002 ($238); 2002tii ($200); Bav ($295). Michelin XAS radial tires: 2002 ($30); Bav/3.0CS ($54). Metallic paint ($185-$238). Decklid toolbox: Bav ($52).

PERFORMANCE: Top Speed: (2002) 105 mph; (2002tii) 118 mph; (2800) 124 mph; (3.0S) 121-127 mph; (3.0CS) 124 mph; (European 3.0CS) 132 mph; (Euro 3.0CSi) 136 mph; (2002 Turbo) 130 mph. **Acceleration (0-60 mph):** (2002) about 12.8 sec.; (2002tii) 9.9 sec.; (3.0S) 9.4 sec.; (3.0CS) 9.5-10.0 sec. **Acceleration (quarter-mile):** (3.0CS) 17.2 sec. (82.5 mph). **Fuel Mileage:** (2002) about 20 mpg; (3.0S) about 18 mpg; (3.0CS) 17 mpg.

PRODUCTION/SALES: Of the 197,446 BMWs produced in calendar year 1973, a total of 98,423 were exported.

ADDITIONAL MODELS: Starting in 1973, a 525 sedan became available, styled like the 520/520i but powered by the 2494-cc six-cylinder engine. Output was 145 horsepower at 6000 rpm, and both the four-speed manual and three-speed automatic transmissions were available.

Manufacturer: Bayerische Motoren Werke AG, Munich, West Germany.

Distributor: Hoffman Motors Corp., New York City.

HISTORY: The 1973 models were introduced in the U.S. on January 1, 1973. A BMW won the Touring Car class at Le Mans this year, for BMW Motorsport. But activity nearly halted for 1974, with BMW supporting private racers only.

1974 BMW

2002 — FOUR — A special version of the 2002 coupe was offered in the U.S. from 1974-76, meeting new U.S. regulations for 5-mph bumper impact. Rubber-faced aluminum bumpers included shock-absorbing hydraulic struts, adding 9.5 inches to overall length and 200 pounds to the car's weight. New five-inch wheels had different styling, with eight slots around the rim and a recessed hub with center emblem.

2002 TURBO — FOUR — This was the second and final year for the limited-production turbocharged two-door sedan.

2800 — SIX — Production of the 2.8-liter sedan continued with little change.

3.0S — SIX — Production of the 3.0-liter sedan continued with little change. By this time, the 3.0S designation was used on the North American version. Standard equipment on 3.0S models in the U.S. included power steering, air conditioning, leather upholstery, front and rear headrests, tinted glass, power windows, an upholstered steering wheel, wood interior trim, and a three-speaker stereo radio with automatic antenna. The Bavaria sedan with Skai upholstery offered less equipment and a lower price tag. The fuel-injected 3.0Si was not yet available in the U.S., but soon would enter the market.

3.0CS — SIX — Production of the 3.0-liter coupe continued with little change. The 3.0CSL racing coupe also remained in production, with a 3153-cc engine producing 206 bhp.

1600/1800/2000/2500 Note: These models remained in production but were no longer officially exported to the U.S. market; see previous listings for specifications and details. Production of the 1600 and 1802 two-doors continued into 1975, and the 2500 into 1977. This was the final year for the 1800 Touring and 2000 Touring.

I.D. DATA: A seven-digit serial number is on a plate attached to the the steering column, on a plate attached to right fender (inside engine compartment), and stamped into the firewall on the right edge. The number consists of a three-digit prefix that identifies the model, followed by a four-digit sequential number. Engine number is on the left side of the block, at the upper edge of the starter mounting. Starting serial number: (2002) 4220001; (2002 w/automatic) 4280001; (2002tii) 2780001; (Bavaria) 2100001; (Bavaria w/automatic) 3280001; (3.0S w/automatic) 3180001; (3.0CS) 4310001; (3.0CS w/automatic) 4335001.

Model	Body Type &Seating	Engine Type/CID	P.O.E. Price	Weight (lbs.)	Prod. Total
2002	2-dr Sedan-5P	I4/121	4975	2317	Note 1
2002	2-dr Cabr-4P	I4/121	N/A	N/A	Note 1
2002tii	2-dr Sedan-5P	I4/121	5702	2350	Note 1
2002 Turbo	2-dr Sedan-5P	I4/121	6600	N/A	Note 1
2800	4-dr Sedan-5P	I6/170	N/A	N/A	Note 1
3.0S	4-dr Sedan-5P	I6/182	11633	3263	Note 1
Bavaria	4-dr Sedan-5P	I6/182	8468	3097	Note 1
3.0CS	2-dr Coupe-4P	I6/182	11739	3108	Note 1
3.0CSi	2-dr Coupe-4P	I6/182	N/A	N/A	Note 1

Note 1: See earlier listings for model-by-model breakdowns.

Price Note: A 2002 with automatic transmission sold for $5315; 3.0S with automatic, $11,899; Bavaria with automatic, $8716; 3.0CS with automatic, $12,174. Prices shown were valid during the 1973 model year, but initial announced amounts were slightly lower, ranging from $4798 for the 2002 to $11,639 for the 3.0CS. Price for the 2002 Turbo is approximate.

ENGINE DATA: BASE FOUR (2002): Inline, single-overhead-cam four-cylinder. Cast iron block and aluminum head. **Displacement:** 121.4 cu. in. (1990 cc). **Bore & Stroke:** 3.50 x 3.15 in. (89 x 80 mm). **Compression Ratio:** 8.3:1. **Brake Horsepower:** 98 (SAE) at 5500 rpm. Torque: 106 lbs.-ft. (SAE) at 3500 rpm. Five main bearings. Solid valve lifters. One Solex 32/32 DIDTA or 40 DIPTA carburetor.

BASE FOUR (2002tii): Same as 1990-cc four above, except — **Compression Ratio:** 9.0:1. **Brake Horsepower:** 125 at 5500 rpm. **Torque:** 127 lbs.-ft. at 4000 rpm. Kugelfischer mechanical fuel injection.

BASE FOUR (2002 Turbo): Same as 1990-cc four above, except — **Brake Horsepower:** 170 DIN at 5800 rpm. Kugelfischer mechanical fuel injection.

BASE SIX (2800): Inline, single-overhead-cam six-cylinder. Cast iron block and aluminum head. **Displacement:** 170.1 cu. in. (2788 cc). **Bore & Stroke:** 3.39 x 3.15 in. (86 x 80 mm). **Compression Ratio:** 9.0:1. **Brake Horsepower:** 170 (192 SAE) at 6000 rpm. **Torque:** 154.8 (173.6 SAE) lbs.-ft. at 3700 rpm. Seven main bearings. Solid valve lifters. Two Zenith 35/40 INAT two-barrel carburetors.

BASE SIX (3.0S, 3.0CS): Inline, single-overhead-cam six-cylinder. Cast iron block and aluminum head. **Displacement:** 182.1 cu. in. (2985 cc). **Bore & Stroke:** 3.50 x 3.15 in. (89 x 80 mm). **Compression Ratio:** 8.3:1 (9.0:1 in Europe). **Brake Horsepower:** 170 SAE at 5800 rpm (180 DIN at 6000 in Europe). **Torque:** 185 lbs.-ft. (SAE) at 3500 rpm. Seven main bearings. Solid valve lifters. Two Zenith 35/40 INAT two-barrel carburetors.

BASE SIX (3.0CSi): Same as 2985-cc six above, except — **Brake Horsepower:** 200 at 5500 rpm. Bosch fuel injection.

CHASSIS DATA: Wheelbase: (2002) 98.4 in.; (2800) 106.0 in.; (3.0CS) 103.3 in.; (3.0S) 106.0 in. **Overall Length:** (2002) 166.5/176.0 in.; (2800) 185.0 in.; (3.0CS) 183.5 in.; (3.0S) 195.0 in. **Height:** (2002) 55.5 in.; (2800/3.0S) 57.1 in.; (3.0CS) 53.9 in. **Width:** (2002) 62.6 in.; (2800/3.0S) 68.9 in.; (3.0CS) 65.7 in. **Front Tread:** (2002) 52.8 in.; (2002tii) 52.8 in.; (2800/3.0S/3.0CS) 56.9 in. **Rear Tread:** (2002) 52.8 in.; (2002tii) 52.8 in.; (2800/3.0S) 57.6 in.; (3.0CS) 55.2 in. **Standard Tires:** (2002) 165SR13; (2002tii) 165HR13; (2002 Turbo) 185/70HR13; (2800) 195/70HR14; (3.0S) 195/70VR14; (Bavaria) 175HR14; (3.0CS) 195/70VRx14.

TECHNICAL: Layout: front-engine, rear-drive except (2002 Turbo) mid-engine, rear-drive. **Transmission:** four-speed manual; floor shift. Five-speed manual standard on 2002tii, available on 2002 Turbo. Three-speed automatic available on most models. **Steering:** worm and roller. **Suspension (front):** MacPherson struts with coil springs. **Suspension (rear):** rigid axle with semi-trailing arms and coil springs. **Brakes:** front disc, rear drum except (2800/3.0S) four-wheel disc. **Body Construction:** steel unibody. **Fuel Tank:** (2002) 13 gal.; (3.0CS) 19 gal.; (3.0S) 20.6 gal.

MAJOR OPTIONS: Similar to 1973.

PERFORMANCE: Top Speed: (2002) 105 mph; (2002tii) 118 mph; (2800) 124 mph; (3.0S) 121-127 mph; (3.0CS) 124 mph; (European 3.0CS) 132 mph; (Euro 3.0CSi) 136 mph; (2002 Turbo) 130 mph. **Acceleration (0-60 mph):** (2002) 12.8 sec.; (2002tii) 9.5-9.9 sec.; (3.0S) 9.4 sec.; (3.0CS) 9.5 sec. **Acceleration (quarter-mile):** (2002tii) 17.7 sec. **Fuel Mileage:** (2002) near 30 mpg reported.

PRODUCTION/SALES: Of the 188,965 BMWs produced in calendar year 1974, a total of 98,689 were exported.

ADDITIONAL MODELS: Introduced at mid-year 1974, a new 2.5CS coupe was intended as a response to the European energy crisis, but did not last long. Carrying less equipment than the 3.0CS, it also carried the smaller (2.5-liter) six-cylinder engine. Even so, the European edition could accelerate to 100 kph (62 mph) in less than 10 seconds, while delivering impressive gas mileage. The coupe had steel disc wheels and fixed rear quarter windows, and lacked power steering. The 2494-cc engine produced 150 bhp at 6000 rpm, using twin Zenith 32/40 INAT two-barrel carburetors. Both the four-speed manual and three-speed automatic transmissions were available. Top speed was 124 mph, and only 844 were built in all.

A 3.3L also was introduced during the 1974 model year, as the first long-wheelbase model with the enlarged (3.3-liter) six-cylinder engine. This new "flagship" of the BMW fleet had a longer wheelbase and roomier interior. Automatic transmission was standard, but a four speed manual gearbox was available too. The 3295-cc engine produced 190 bhp at 5500 rpm, using twin Zenith carburetors. Later, at the end of 1976, a fuel-injected 3.3Li (with shorter stroke, actually displacing 3.2 liters) would replace the 3.3L. A total of 3,022 3.3L models were built.

Another 5-Series model that never was exported to North America was the 518 sedan, introduced in June 1974. Like the 2.5CS, it was another response to the oil crisis, but this one hung on after the crisis abated. Though designated as a 5-Series vehicle, it carried a 1.8-liter four-cylinder engine that produced 90 bhp at 5500 rpm, with a single Solex carburetor. Only four-speed manual shift was available.

Manufacturer: Bayerische Motoren Werke AG, Munich, West Germany.

Distributor: BMW of North America Inc., Connecticut.

HISTORY: The 1974 models were introduced in the U.S. in October 1973. By summer 1974, BMW had a proving ground just outside Munich. Before that, they'd used ordinary roads for testing. By this time, too, the U.S. was BMW's top export market.

1975 BMW

1975 BMW 2002. (William Siuru Jr.)

320i — FOUR — The subcompact 320i sedan was not yet officially available in the U.S., but introduced in Europe at this time along with the smaller-engined 316/318 (see "Additional Models" at end of this listing). Produced from 1975-77, the carbureted 320 sedan never would reach the U.S. market, but the fuel-injected 320i did for the 1977 model year. Styling features included quad round headlamps, blackout "kidney" and side grilles, '320' designation on grille and decklid, and horizontal wraparound taillamps. The hood opened all the way across to the fenders, as on many other BMW models. The carbureted 1990-cc engine produced 109 bhp at 6000 rpm; the fuel-injected 320i rated 125 bhp at 5700 rpm. When the U.S. version arrived, however, power would be down to 110 bhp at 5800 rpm (105 bhp in California).

2002 — FOUR — BMW's smallest model came only in two-door form and continued with little change.

2800 — SIX — Production of the 2800 sedan continued with little change, but was not listed in U.S. directories at this time.

3.0S/Si — SIX — This popular compact four-door sedan continued with little change for the European market in 3.0S (carbureted) form. The fuel-injected 3.0Si sedan became available in the U.S. at this time, billed as the car "for those who deny themselves nothing." See next listing for details.

3.0CS — SIX — Production of the 3.0-liter coupe series continued with little change, but these models were not listed in U.S. directories at this time. This was the final year for the racing CSL coupe.

530i — SIX — BMW's compact four-door sedan emerged this year as the first model aimed strictly at North American sales. For that reason, it entered the U.S. market immediately, rather than later as was common with other models (many of which never arrived in North America at all). The 530i would remain in production into 1978. Serving as replacement for the Bavaria, in both size and price, the 530i was intended to fill the niche between the 2002/320i and the 3.0Si. *Road & Track* managed to accelerate a 530i from zero to 60 mph in 10.2 seconds, and achieved 19 mpg. *Motor Trend* hit sixty in 9.7 seconds, and approached 21 mpg. Most North American 5-Series sedans had vinyl or leather upholstery, whereas cloth was standard in Europe. These early models had a hood bulge. A special version of the 3.0-liter six was installed, to give Americans performance comparable to a European 528, even with the added weight of safety/emissions gear. Working with a thermal reactor emissions-control system, it ran on leaded gas. The SAE horsepower rating of the 2985-cc powerplant was 176 at 5500 rpm, using Bosch L-Jetronic fuel injection. Either a Getrag four-speed manual or three-speed automatic transmission was available.

1600/1800/2500 Note: These models remained in production but were no longer officially exported to the U.S. market; see previous listings for specifications and details. Production of the 1600 and 1802 two-doors ended after 1975, while the 2500 continued into 1977.

I.D. DATA: A seven-digit serial number is on a plate attached to the the steering column, on a plate attached to right fender (inside engine compartment), and stamped into the firewall on the right edge. The number consists of a three-digit prefix that identifies the model, followed by a four-digit sequential number. Engine number is on the left side of the block, at the upper edge of the starter mounting. Starting serial number: (2002) 2360001; (2002 w/automatic) 2380001; (530i) 5000001; (530i w/automatic) 5020001; (3.0Si) 3170001; (3.0Si w/automatic) 3190001.

Model	Body Type & Seating	Engine Type/CID	P.O.E. Price	Weight (lbs.)	Prod. Total
320i	2-dr Sedan-5P	I4/121	N/A	2380	Note 1
2002	2-dr Sedan-5P	I4/121	5940	2383	Note 1
2002	2-dr Cabr-4P	I4/121	N/A	N/A	Note 1
2002tii	2-dr Sedan-5P	I4/121	N/A	N/A	Note 1
2800	4-dr Sedan-5P	I6/170	N/A	N/A	Note 1
3.0S	4-dr Sedan-5P	I6/182	N/A	3263	Note 1
3.0Si	4-dr Sedan-5P	I6/182	13752	3300	Note 1
3.0CS	2-dr Coupe-4P	I6/182	N/A	N/A	Note 1
3.0CSi	2-dr Coupe-4P	I6/182	N/A	N/A	Note 1
530i	4-dr Sedan-5P	I6/182	9097	3190	Note 1

Note 1: As many as 221,298 BMWs were produced in 1975, of which 106,135 were exported.

Model Availability Note: Models shown with prices were officially imported into the U.S.

Automatic Transmission Note: A 2002 with automatic transmission sold for $6355; a 3.0Si with automatic, $14,123; and a 530i with automatic, $9495.

ENGINE DATA: BASE FOUR (320): Inline, overhead-cam four-cylinder. Cast iron block and aluminum head. **Displacement:** 121.3 cu. in. (1990 cc). **Bore & Stroke:** 3.50 x 3.15 in. (89 x 80 mm). **Brake Horsepower:** 109 at 6000 rpm. Five main bearings. Solid valve lifters. One Solex 32/32 DIDIA carburetor.

BASE FOUR (320i): Same as 1990-cc four above, except with Bosch K-Jetronic fuel injection. **Brake Horsepower:** 125 at 5700 rpm (110 at 5800 in eventual U.S. trim).

BASE FOUR (2002): Inline, overhead-cam four-cylinder. Cast iron block and aluminum head. **Displacement:** 121.3 cu. in. (1990 cc). **Bore & Stroke:** 3.50 x 3.15 in. (89 x 80 mm). **Compression Ratio:** 8.1:1. **Brake Horsepower:** 98 at 5500 rpm. **Torque:** 106 lbs.-ft. at 3500 rpm. Five main bearings. Solid valve lifters. One Solex carburetor.

BASE FOUR (2002tii): Same as 1990-cc four above, except — **Compression Ratio:** 9.0:1. **Brake Horsepower:** 125 at 5500 rpm. **Torque:** 127 lbs.-ft. at 4000 rpm. Kugelfischer mechanical fuel injection.

BASE SIX (2800): Inline, single-overhead-cam six-cylinder. Cast iron block and aluminum head. **Displacement:** 170.1 cu. in. (2788 cc). **Bore & Stroke:** 3.39 x 3.15 in. (86 x 80 mm). **Compression Ratio:** 9.0:1. **Brake Horsepower:** 170 (192 SAE) at 6000 rpm. **Torque:** 154.8 (173.6 SAE) lbs.-ft. at 3700 rpm. Seven main bearings. Solid valve lifters. Two Zenith 35/40 INAT two-barrel carburetors.

BASE SIX (3.0S, 3.0CS): Inline, overhead-cam six-cylinder. Cast iron block and aluminum head. **Displacement:** 182.0 cu. in. (2985 cc). **Bore & Stroke:** 3.50 x 3.15 in. (89 x 80 mm). **Compression Ratio:** 8.1:1. **Brake Horsepower:** 170 at 5800 rpm. Seven main bearings. Solid valve lifters. Two Zenith 35/40 INAT two-barrel carburetors.

BASE SIX (3.0Si, 530i): Same as 2985-cc six above, except — **Brake Horsepower:** 176 at 5500 rpm. **Torque:** 185/188 lbs.-ft. at 4500 rpm. Bosch L-Jetronic fuel injection.

BASE SIX (3.0CSi): Same as 2985-cc six above, except — **Brake Horsepower:** 200 at 5500 rpm. **Torque:** 200 lbs.-ft at 4000 rpm. Bosch fuel injection.

CHASSIS DATA: Wheelbase: (320) 100.9 in.; (2002) 98.4 in.; (2800/3.0S) 106.0 in.; (3.0CS) 103.3 in.; (530i) 103.8 in. **Overall Length:** (320) 171.5 in.; (2002) 176.0 in.; (3.0S) 195.0 in.; (530i) 189.9 in. **Height:** (320) 54.3 in.; (2002) 55.5 in.; (3.0Si) 57.1 in.; (530i) 56.0 in. **Width:** (320) 63.4 in.; (2002) 62.6 in.; (3.0Si) 68.9 in.; (530i) 67.2 in. **Front Tread:** (320) 53.7 in.; (320i) 54.6 in.; (2002) 52.8 In.; (3.0Si) 58.3 in.; (530i) 56.0 in. **Rear Tread:** (320) 54.2 in.; (320i) 55.1 in.; (2002) 52.8 in.; (3.0Si) 57.6 in.; (530i) 57.5 in. **Standard Tires:** (320) 165SR13; (320i) 185/70HR13; (2002) 165SR13; (3.0Si) 195/70VR14; (530i) 195/70HR14.

TECHNICAL: Layout: front-engine, rear-drive. **Transmission:** four-speed manual except (320) four- or five-speed manual. Three-speed automatic available on most models. **Standard Final Drive Ratio:** (530i) 3.64:1. **Steering:** worm and roller except (320) rack and pinion. **Suspension (front):** MacPherson struts with coil springs. **Suspension (rear):** independent, semi-trailing arms with coil springs. **Brakes:** front disc, rear drum except (2800/3.0S/530i) four-wheel disc. **Body Construction:** steel unibody. **Fuel Tank:** (530i) 18.5 gal.

MAJOR OPTIONS: Air conditioning: 530 ($814). Alloy wheels. Sunroof. Leather upholstery ($715). Tool kit: 530i ($62).

PERFORMANCE: Top Speed: (European 320i) 112 mph; (2002tii) 118 mph; (2800) 124 mph; (3.0S) 127 mph; (European 3.0CS) 132 mph; (Euro 3.0CSi) 136 mph; (530i) 120 mph. **Acceleration (0-60 mph):** (2002) 10.3 sec.; (2002tii) under 10 sec.; (3.0S w/manual) 10.9 sec.; (530i w/manual) 9.7 sec. **Acceleration (quarter-mile):** (530i) 17.9 sec. (82.5 mph). **Fuel Mileage:** (2002) about 24.5 mpg; (3.0Si) about 18.4 mpg; (530i) about 19-20 mpg.

PRODUCTION/SALES: A total of 19,419 BMWs were sold in the U.S. in 1975.

ADDITIONAL MODELS: BMW's new 3-Series debuted in Europe late in the 1975 model year, but would not arrive in the U.S. (as the 320i) for a year and a half, as a 1977 model. Roomier in back than the former "02" models, the 3-Series two-door had a softer ride that was criticized by some enthusiasts. Among the changes was a switch to rack-and-pinion (a "first" for postwar BMWs). The 3-Series displayed a raised center hood section and had an upgraded heat/vent system. The 316 and 318 versions introduced at this time never reached North America at all. Each displayed a wedge-shaped profile, and was larger and heavier than the "02" models they replaced. Single round headlamps were used, whereas bigger-engine models had quad headlamps. Front panels contained a blackout "kidney" grille and side grilles. Vertical parking lamps stood outboard of headlamps, with horizontal taillamps at the rear. Soon after introduction, a ribbed black trim plate was added between the taillamps. The 1573-cc engine in the 316 produced 90 horsepower at 6000 rpm, using a single Solex carburetor, and was available with either a four- or five-speed manual gearbox. Front disc/rear drum brakes were installed. Wheelbase was 100.9 inches; overall length, 171.5 inches. Tires were 165SR13 size, and the car could reach 100 mph. The 318 engine displaced 1766 cc and produced 98 bhp at 5800 rpm, and was available with a three-speed automatic transmission. Top speed was 104 mph.

Also debuting in Europe this year was the 1502 two-door sedan, which appeared in January 1975 and would remain in production into 1977, selling rather well. Somewhat plain in appearance, it wore less trim than other models, even lacking chrome trim along the hood/deck opening line. The interior was comparably plain. The 1573-cc four-cylinder engine had lower compression and horsepower, for use with regular gas. It produced 75 bhp at 5800 rpm, using a single Solex carburetor and four-speed manual gearbox. A total of 72,635 were produced.

A 2.8-liter version of the 2500 four-door sedan, designated 2.8L, debuted in 1975 and was produced into 1977. Dimensions and details were similar to the 2500, and to the 2800/Bavaria. Wheelbase was 109.9 inches; overall length, 188.9 inches. A total of 5,036 were produced, priced at 25,530 Deutsch Marks in Germany. Top speed in Europe was 121 mph.

Europeans also got a new 528 four-door sedan in early 1975, with a larger engine than the 525 model. Wood-trimmed doors and dashboard and similar luxuries set it apart from other 5-Series models. The 2788-cc engine produced 165 bhp at 5800 rpm.

Manufacturer: Bayerische Motoren Werke AG, Munich, West Germany.

Distributor: BMW of North America, Montvale, New Jersey.

HISTORY: For six years in a row, the *Car and Driver* Readers Choice Poll named BMW's 2002 "Best Sports Sedan." At this time, BMW chose to abandon the pillarless coupe design for U.S. models rather than modify it to meet U.S. regulations. After 1974, the 2800 was dropped in Europe, replaced by the 3.0S. The fuel-injected engine of the 3.0Si, said BMW's ads, "never fails to astound even the experts with its smooth, turbine-like performance."

1976 BMW

320i — FOUR — The 320i was not officially imported at this time, but would become available for the 1977 model year. See previous and later listings for details.

2002 — FOUR — BMW's two-door sedan (sometimes called a coupe) came with a 2.0-liter four-cylinder engine and either standard four-speed manual gearbox or three-speed automatic. Suspension was independent on all four wheels. Technical changes this year included dual hemispherical combustion chambers in the 2.0-liter engine, and the elimination of the catalytic converter. The 2002 was BMW's most popular U.S. model.

2800 — SIX — Production of the 2800 sedan continued, though it was not necessarily included on lists of models available in the U.S.

3.0Si — SIX — This was BMW's most costly and luxurious model available in the U.S. The six-cylinder drivetrain, with four-speed manual gearbox or three-speed automatic, was identical to that of the smaller 530i, and the body design was similar to the former Bavaria models. With Bosch electronic fuel injection, the engine produced 176 bhp (SAE) at 5500 rpm. Standard equipment included power steering and air conditioning.

530i — SIX — Like other BMW models, the 530i four-door sedan had a narrow two-section grille and four round headlamps in a blacked-out front panel. The engine and transmissions were the same as those used in the 3.0Si. Standard equipment included power steering and air conditioning.

630CS — SIX — Introduced in spring 1976, the new 630CS was not officially imported immediately, but would become available in the 1977 model year, with a 3.0-liter engine. This was the first of the 6-Series Grand Touring coupes, larger and heavier than their predecessors but with similarly long hood, short deck, and tall greenhouse. In this form, however, a modern wedge profile was prominent, with low beltline and ample glass area. Earlier CS coupes had no roof pillar; the 6-Series had a black-finished pillar, but one that was subdued rather than obvious. The hood had a raised center section. Like the 3/5 Series, the 6-Series used "Cockpit Design" with ergonomics in mind. That meant large, no-glare instruments; a wraparound control center; stalk-mounted controls; and a Check Control panel to display system data (with Push Test bar to check fluid levels and light operation). New speed-sensitive power steering was installed, with less boost above a certain engine rpm. The two-door coupe had 2+2 seating. Standard equipment included variable-boost power steering.

2500 Note: The 2500 sedan remained in production into 1977, but was no longer officially exported to the U.S. market; see previous listings for specifications and details.

I.D. DATA: A seven-digit serial number is on a plate attached to the steering column, on a plate attached to right fender (inside engine compartment), and stamped into the firewall on the right edge. The number consists of a three-digit prefix that identifies the model, followed by a four-digit sequential number. Engine number is on the left side of the block, at the upper edge of the starter mounting. Starting serial number: (2002) 2370001; (2002 w/automatic) 2390001; (530i) 5010001; (530i w/automatic) 5030001; (3.0Si) 5040001; (3.0Si w/automatic) 5050001.

Model	Body Type & Seating	Engine Type/CID	P.O.E. Price	Weight (lbs.)	Prod. Total
320i	2-dr sedan-5P	I4/121	N/A	N/A	Note 1
2002	2-dr Sedan-5P	I4/121	6570	2383	Note 1
2002A	2-dr Sedan-5P	I4/121	6855	2403	Note 1
2800	4-dr Sedan-5P	I6/170	N/A	N/A	Note 1
3.0Si	4-dr Sedan-5P	I6/182	14640	3300	Note 2
530i	4-dr Sedan-5P	I6/182	10590	3190	Note 1
630CS	2-dr Coupe-2+2P	I6/182	N/A	3195	Note 1

Note 1: A total of 275,022 BMWs were produced in 1976, of which 139,602 were exported (some sources say 267,618 produced).

Note 2: A total of 20,310 Model 3.0Si sedans were produced during the full model run.

Model Availability Note: Models shown with prices were officially imported into the U.S. and readily available.

Automatic Transmission Note: A 2002 with automatic transmission sold for $6855; a 3.0Si with automatic, $14,990; and a 530i with automatic, $10,940.

ENGINE DATA: BASE FOUR (320): Inline, overhead-cam four-cylinder. Cast iron block and aluminum head. **Displacement:** 121.3 cu. in. (1990 cc). **Bore & Stroke:** 3.50 x 3.15 in. (89 x 80 mm). **Brake Horsepower:** 109 at 6000 rpm. Five main bearings. Solid valve lifters. One Solex 32/32 DIDIA carburetor.

BASE FOUR (320i): Same as 1990-cc four above, except with Bosch K-Jetronic fuel injection. **Brake Horsepower:** 125 at 5700 rpm (110 at 5800 in eventual U.S. trim).

BASE FOUR (2002): Inline, overhead-cam four-cylinder. Cast iron block and aluminum head. **Displacement:** 121.3 cu. in. (1990 cc). **Bore & Stroke:** 3.50 x 3.15 in. (89 x 80 mm). **Compression Ratio:** 8.1:1. **Brake Horsepower:** 98 at 5500 rpm. **Torque:** 106 lbs.-ft. at 3500 rpm. Five main bearings. One Solex 32 DIPTA two-barrel carburetor.

BASE SIX (2800): Inline, overhead-cam six-cylinder. Cast iron block and aluminum head. **Displacement:** 170.1 cu. in. (2788 cc). **Bore & Stroke:** 3.39 x 3.15 in. (86 x 80 mm). **Compression Ratio:** 9.0:1. **Brake Horsepower:** 170 (192 SAE) at 6000 rpm. Seven main bearings. Two carburetors.

BASE SIX (3.0Si, 530i): Inline, overhead-cam six-cylinder. Cast iron block and light alloy head. **Displacement:** 182.0 cu. in. (2985 cc). **Bore & Stroke:** 3.50 x 3.15 in. (89 x 80 mm). **Compression Ratio:** 8.1:1. **Brake Horsepower:** 176 at 5500 rpm. **Torque:** 185/188 lbs.-ft. at 4500 rpm. Seven main bearings. Bosch L-Jetronic fuel injection.

BASE SIX (630CS): Same as 2985-cc six above, but with Solex 4A1 four-barrel carburetor, rated 185 bhp at 5800 rpm. (Not available in U.S.).

CHASSIS DATA: Wheelbase: (2002) 98.4 in.; (320i) 100.9 in.; (3.0Si) 106.0 in.; (530i) 103.8 in; (630CS) 103.4 in. **Overall Length:** (2002) 176.0 in.; (3.0Si) 195.0 in.; (530i) 190.0 in.; (630CS) 187.2 in. **Height:** (2002) 55.5 in.; (3.0Si) 57.1 in.; (530i) 56.0 in.; (630CS) 53.7 in. **Width:** (2002) 62.6 in.; (3.0Si) 68.9 in.; (530i) 67.2 in.; (630CS) 67.9 in. **Front Tread:** (2002) 52.8 in.; (3.0Si) 58.3 in.; (530i) 55.9 in.; (630CS) 56.0 in. **Rear Tread:** (2002) 52.8 in.; (3.0Si) 57.6 in.; (530i) 57.5 in.; (630CS) 58.5 in. **Standard Tires:** (2002) 165SR13; (3.0Si) 195/70HR14; (530i) 195/70HR14.

TECHNICAL: Layout: front-engine, rear-drive. **Transmission:** four-speed manual. **Steering:** (320i) rack and pinion; (630CS) recirculating ball; (others) worm and roller. **Suspension (front):** MacPherson struts with coil springs. **Suspension (rear):** independent, semi-trailing arms with coil springs. **Brakes:** (320i/2002) front disc, rear drum; (3.0S/530i/630CS) front/rear disc. **Body Construction:** steel unibody.

MAJOR OPTIONS: Electric sunroof: 2002 ($407); 3.0Si/530i ($447). Manual sunroof: 2002 ($276); 3.0Si/530i ($342). Alloy wheels: 2002 ($323); 530i ($398). Limited-slip differential ($239). Power windows: 530i ($413). Rear headrests:530i ($71). Rear-seat heat outlets: 530i ($40). Leather upholstery: 2002/530i ($757).

PERFORMANCE: Top Speed: (European 320i) 112 mph; (2800) 124 mph; (530i) 120 mph. **Acceleration (0-60 mph):** (2002) 10.3 sec.; (530i w/manual) 9.7 sec. **Acceleration (quarter-mile):** (530i) 17.9 sec. (82.5 mph). **Fuel Mileage:** (530i) about 19-20 mpg.

PRODUCTION/SALES: A total of 26,509 BMWs were sold in the U.S. in 1976.

Manufacturer: Bayerische Motoren Werke AG, Munich, West Germany.

Distributor: BMW of North America, Montvale, New Jersey.

HISTORY: The 1976 models were introduced to U.S. market in September 1975. Rumors began by this time of a V-12 mid-engine coupe, which never materialized. Production of the 633CSi coupe began during 1976; see next listing for details.

1977 BMW

320i — FOUR — Replacing the 2002 series in the U.S. market, the 320i two-door had a fuel-injected version of the familiar 2.0-liter four-cylinder engine. As BMW advertised, it needed no catalytic converter to meet U.S. emissions standards. The 320i had four-wheel independent suspension with MacPherson struts and eccentrically-mounted coil springs in front, plus semi-trailing arms with coil springs at the rear. Inside, all instruments were curved toward the driver, illuminated with orange light at night. Unlike its 2002 predecessor, the new 320i had no chrome beltline trim strip. Its overall profile was more rounded, with a longer hood and shorter deck. Wheelbase was 2.5 inches longer. New ZF rack-and-pinion steering demanded less effort than earlier models. Standard equipment included a four-speed manual gearbox, tinted glass, electric rear defroster, clock, pop-out rear window, intermittent two-speed wiper/washer, tachometer, and reclining front bucket seats with adjustable headrests and cloth or leatherette upholstery.

1977 BMW 530i four-door sedan. (William Siuru Jr.)

530i — SIX — Like other 5-Series models, the 530i sedan sold in the U.S. got a facelift this year. It included a restyled grille, wider taillamps, right-side-mounted fuel filler door, and narrow raised hood section. Fuel-tank capacity shrunk, too. Standard equipment included air conditioning, a power driver's mirror, adjustable steering wheel, and six-way driver's seat.

630CSi — SIX — The 630CSi was a two-door coupe with the same powertrain as the 530i sedan, now available in the U.S. market with a fuel-injected six-cylinder engine. Both drivetrain and chassis were similar to the 530i sedan, with a body built by Karmann. Styling was by Paul Bracq. Though the car had a substantial 'B' pillar to help meet new U.S. roof-crush requirements, it was covered with patterned black plastic for subtlety. Quad round headlamps were installed, with amber park/signal lights and large wraparound taillamps. Either a Getrag four-speed manual or a three-speed automatic transmission was available. The suspension contained front and rear anti-roll bars. See 1976 listing for additional details. A carbureted 630CS coupe remained available in Europe.

633CSi — SIX — The 633CSi with fuel injection was not officially imported at this time, but would be in the 1978 model year; see that listing for complete data.

2500/2800/3.0Si Note: The 2500 sedan remained in production into 1977, while the 2800 and 3.0Si ended their production lives after 1976. These models were no longer officially exported to the U.S. market; see previous listings for specifications and details.

I.D. DATA: BMW's seven-digit serial number is on the steering column. The first three numbers indicate model and transmission type, and whether it is a 49-state or California-certified car. That is followed by a four-digit sequential serial number. Starting serial number: (320i) 5420001; (320i w/auto.) 5470001; (530i) 5070001; (530i w/auto.) 5090001; (630CSi) 5505001; (630CSi w/auto.) 5515001.

Model	Body Type & Seating	Engine Type/CID	P.O.E. Price	Weight (lbs.)	Prod. Total
320i	2-dr Sedan-5P	I4/121	7990	2650	Note 1
530i	4-dr Sedan-5P	I6/182	12495	3440	Note 1
630CS	2-dr Coupe-2+2P	I6/182	N/A	N/A	Note 1
630CSi	2-dr Coupe-2+2P	I6/182	23600	3360	Note 1
633CSi	2-dr Coupe-2+2P	I6/196	N/A	N/A	Note 1

Note 1: A total of 290,236 BMWs were produced in 1977, of which 144,486 were exported (some sources say 284,471 produced).

Model Availability Note: Models shown with prices were officially imported into the U.S.

Automatic Transmission Note: A 320i with automatic sold for $8340; a 530i with automatic cost $12890.

ENGINE DATA: BASE FOUR (320i): Inline, overhead-cam four-cylinder. Cast iron block and light alloy head. **Displacement:** 121.3 cu. in. (1990 cc). **Bore & Stroke:** 3.50 x 3.15 in. (89 x 80 mm). **Compression Ratio:** 8.1:1. **Brake Horsepower:** 110 at 5800 rpm (105 bhp in California). **Torque:** 112 lbs.-ft. at 3750 rpm (108.5 in California). Five main bearings. Bosch K-Jetronic fuel injection.

BASE SIX (530i, 630CSi): Inline, overhead-cam six-cylinder. Cast iron block and light alloy head. **Displacement:** 182.0 cu. in. (2985 cc). **Bore & Stroke:** 3.50 x 3.15 in. (89 x 80 mm). **Compression Ratio:** 8.1:1. **Brake Horsepower:** 176 at 5500 rpm. **Torque:** 185 lbs.-ft. at 4500 rpm. Seven main bearings. Bosch L-Jetronic fuel injection.

CHASSIS DATA: Wheelbase: (320i) 100.9 in.; (530i) 103.8 in.; (630CSi) 103.4 in. **Overall Length:** (320i) 177.5 in.; (530i) 190.0 in.; (630CSi) 192.7 in. **Height:** (320i) 54.3 in.; (530i) 55.9 in.; (630CSi) 53.7 in. **Width:** (320i) 63.4 in.; (530i) 67.2 in.; (630CSi) 67.9 in. **Front Tread:** (320i) 54.6 in.; (530i) 55.9 in.; (630CSi) 56.0 in. **Rear Tread:** (320i) 55.1 in.; (530i) 57.5 in.l (630CSi) 58.5 in. **Wheel type:** steel sport. **Standard Tires:** (320i) 185/70HR13; (530i/630CSi) 195/70HR14.

TECHNICAL: Layout: front-engine, rear-drive. **Transmission:** four-speed manual. Standard 320i gear ratios: (1st) 3.764:1; (2nd) 2.022:1; (3rd) 1.32:1; (4th) 1.0:1; (rev) 4.096:1. **Standard Final Drive Ratio:** (320i) 3.64:1. **Steering:** (320i) rack and pinion; (530i) worm and roller; (630CSi) recirculating ball. **Suspension (front):** MacPherson struts with coil springs. **Suspension (rear):** independent, semi-trailing arms with coil springs. **Brakes:** (320i) front disc, rear drum; (530i/630CSi) front/rear disc. **Body Construction:** steel unibody. **Fuel Tank** (630CSi) 16.4 gal.

MAJOR OPTIONS: Air cond.: 320i ($550). Lexus group (electric sunroof, power windows, light alloy wheels and leather upholstery): 530i ($1550). Recaro sport seats: 320i ($300). Sport steering wheel: 320i ($40). Becker Mexico radio (630CSi). Metallic paint: 320i ($255); 530i ($325). Sunroof: 320i ($310); 530i ($370). Light alloy wheels: 320i ($225).

PERFORMANCE: Top Speed: (320i) 100-105 mph; (530i) 120+ mph. **Acceleration (0-60 mph):** (320i) 10.4-12.3 sec.; (530i) 9 sec.; (630CSi) 11.0 sec. **Acceleration (quarter-mile):** (320i) 18.2 sec. (74.2-76.0 mph); (630CSi) 17.3 sec. (79 mph). **Fuel Mileage:** (320i) up to 20 mpg (EPA 18 city, 25 highway); (630CSi) about 16 mpg.

PRODUCTION/SALES: A total of 28,776 BMWs were sold in the U.S. in 1977.

ADDITIONAL MODELS: A European successor to the 528 sedan debuted in August 1977, as the fuel-injected 528i. About a year-and-a-half later (for the 1979 model year), it would join the U.S. import list, replacing the 530i. Like other 5-Series models, the 528 got revised wheels at this time (lacking hubcaps or wheel covers). Its only identifying mark was the rear badge. In European trim, the engine produced 176 bhp; as a U.S. model, the rating would be 169 bhp.

Also introduced in Europe were two variants of the 3-Series: a 320-6 with 2.0-liter engine and four-barrel carburetor, and a 323i with fuel-injected 2.3-liter engine. These were the only 3-Series models with all-disc brakes.

Europeans also got an earlier experience with the new luxury 7-Series, offered initially as a 728 (with 2788-cc six) and 730 (with 2985-cc six-cylinder engine). Styling was related to the recently-introduced 6-Series coupes. Among other features, the trunk held an upright spare tire (for the first time). European versions had two different headlamp sizes in a quad setup. These sedans had a unique twin A-arm front suspension (but still MacPherson struts). Anti-skid braking was available. The carbureted 728 engine produced 170 bhp at 5800 rpm; the 730 was rated 184 bhp in Europe. For the 1978 model year, a 733i edition with larger (3210-cc) engine would become available in the U.S.

Manufacturer: Bayerische Motoren Werke AG, Munich, West Germany.
Distributor: BMW of North America, Montvale, New Jersey.

HISTORY: The 1977 models were introduced to the U.S. market in November 1976. The 630CSi became available in March 1977. BMW described the newly-arrived 320i as "successor to the car that started a cult," referring to its predecessors, the 1600 and 2002. Ads noted earlier comments on the 2002, including a *Car and Driver* appraisal in 1972 that had called it "the essence of motoring truth." A 1968 *Car and Driver* report had described the 2002 as "one of modern civilization's all-time best ways of getting somewhere sitting down." BMW's ad theme at this time was: "You Drive a BMW. It does not drive you."

1978 BMW

1978 BMW 635 CSi coupe.

320i — FOUR — BMW's smallest model continued with little change, in two-door sedan form with a 2.0-liter four-cylinder engine.

528i — SIX — The 528i was not officially imported at this time, but would be in the 1979 model year. See that listing for complete data.

530i — SIX — Production of the four-door sedan with 3.0-liter six-cylinder continued with no major change.

630CSi — SIX — The 630CSi started out the model year, but was replaced by a larger-engined version, the 633CSi. See previous listing for 630CSi details.

633CSi — SIX — BMW's stylish two-door coupe adopted a larger engine during the 1978 model year, growing from 3.0 to 3.2 liters. Though rated 200 bhp in Europe, the U.S. version came through with 177 bhp at 5500 rpm, but torque gained 11 pounds-feet. That gave a top speed of 124 mph, versus 133 mph for the European coupe.

635CSi — SIX — Europeans could go a step further in performance with a 3.5-liter version of BMW's large sporty coupe, which debuted in mid-1978. The engine block was the same as that used on the new M1, but with a single-cam cylinder head (12-valve) instead of dual cams. A five-speed manual gearbox was standard. Appearance features included body striping, a deep front spoiler and small rear spoiler (on the deck), and 6.5-inch Mahle-BBS alloy wheels. Anti-skid braking was available. The 3453-cc engine produced 218 horsepower at 5200 rpm, using Bosch L-Jetronic fuel injection. Years later, the 635CSi would also become a U.S. model.

733i — SIX — A new four-door luxury sedan joined the BMW lineup, marking the first appearance of the 3.2-liter engine in the U.S. market. The 3210-cc engine produced 177 bhp in U.S. trim (versus 197 bhp in Europe). Intended as a rival to the Mercedes S-Series, the 733i was packed with comfort and safety features. Longer/wider than prior models, it offered more head/leg room, and had seats "tuned" to the springs/shocks. Rear seats were electrically adjustable. On the dash were an electronic speedometer and tachometer. Improved ZF recirculating-ball steering was installed, along with faster-acting, hydraulically-boosted 11-inch all-disc brakes. The strut-type front suspension had progressive anti-dive; the rear offered full anti-lift action. U.S. versions of the 733i sedan had quad headlamps. Standard 733i equipment included central door and trunk locking, power steering (variable-assist), hydraulic power brakes, power windows, remote outside mirror, adjustable driver's seat (for height and seat angle). North American versions also included air conditioning, tinted glass, stereo AM/FM radio with cassette, and electric-powered sunroof.

M1 — SIX — BMW turned to the supercar market with its M1, which debuted at the October 1978 Paris Salon. Produced by BMW Motorsport through the Baur company (at Stuttgart), the two-door coupe originated at Lamborghini, where most of the engineering and development work was done. Because of financial problems, however, Lamborghini couldn't complete the job. Styling came from Giugiaro, at Ital Design. Except for the tiny "kidney" grille, little about the fiberglass-bodied car looked much like BMW. The mid-mounted dual-overhead-cam, 3453-cc six-cylinder engine was rated 277 horsepower at 6500 rpm in "road" trim, using four valves per cylinder and Kugelfischer mechanical fuel injection. A ZF five-speed transaxle stood behind the engine. A multi-tubular steel frame was used. Three M1 versions were produced: a "road" edition created for race homologation purposes (400 were needed before permission could be granted for racing); Group 4 versions rated 470-500 bhp; and a single Group 5 example, with turbocharged engine churning out a claimed 850 horsepower. In Procar events, Formula One drivers and others raced each other in M1s, as an event before Grand Prix races.

I.D. DATA: BMW's seven-digit serial number is on the steering column or atop the dashboard. Chassis number is on right inner fender support or heater bulkhead. Engine number is on left rear of the block, above the starter. A data plate is on right inner fender panel, or on firewall. The first three numbers indicate model and transmission type, and whether the engine is a 49-state or California-certified. A four-digit sequential serial number follows. Starting serial number: (320i) 54350001; (320i w/auto.) 5475001; (530i) 5380001; (530i w/auto.) 5390001; (633CSi) 5525001; (633CSi w/auto.) 5535001; (733i) 5775001; (733i w/auto.) 5785001.

Model	Body Type & Seating	Engine Type/CID	P.O.E. Price	Weight (lbs.)	Prod. Total
320i	2-dr Sedan-5P	I4/121	9315	2650	Note 1
528i	4-dr Sedan-5P	I6/170	N/A	N/A	Note 1
530i	4-dr Sedan-5P	I6/182	14840	3440	Note 1
630CSi	2-dr Coupe-2 + 2P	I6/182	N/A	N/A	Note 1
633CSi	2-dr Coupe-2 + 2P	I6/196	24870	3360	Note 1
635CSi	2-dr Coupe-2 + 2P	I6/211	N/A	3350	Note 1
733i	4-dr Sedan-5P	I6/196	21365	3800	Note 1
M1	2-dr Coupe-2P	I6/211	N/A	2865	Note 2

Note 1: A total of 320,853 BMWs were produced in 1978, of which 164,131 were exported (some sources say 311,793 produced).

Note 2: A total of 456 M1s were built through 1981, priced at 100,000 Deutsch Marks (about $55,000).

Model Availability Note: Models shown with prices were officially imported into the U.S.

ENGINE DATA: BASE FOUR (320i): Inline, overhead-cam four-cylinder. Cast iron block and aluminum head. **Displacement:** 121.3 cu. in. (1990 cc). **Bore & Stroke:** 3.50 x 3.15 in. (89 x 80 mm). **Compression Ratio:** 8.1:1. **Brake Horsepower:** 110 at 5800 rpm. **Torque:** 112 lbs.-ft. at 3750 rpm. Five main bearings. Bosch K-Jetronic fuel injection.

BASE SIX (530i, 630CSi): Inline, overhead-cam six-cylinder. Cast iron block and aluminum head. **Displacement:** 182.0 cu. in. (2985 cc). **Bore & Stroke:** 3.50 x 3.15 in. (89 x 80 mm). **Compression Ratio:** 8.1:1. **Brake Horsepower:** 176 at 5500 rpm. **Torque:** 185/188 lbs.-ft. at 4500 rpm. Seven main bearings. Bosch L-Jetronic fuel injection.

BASE SIX (633CSi, 733i): Inline, overhead-cam six-cylinder. Cast iron block and aluminum head. **Displacement:** 195.8 cu. in. (3210 cc). **Bore & Stroke:** 3.50 x 3.39 in. (88.9 x 86.1 mm). **Compression Ratio:** 8.0:1. **Brake Horsepower:** 177 at 5500 rpm. **Torque:** 196 lbs.-ft. at 4000 rpm. Seven main bearings. Bosch L-Jetronic fuel injection.

BASE SIX (635CSi): Inline, overhead-cam six-cylinder. Cast iron block and aluminum head. **Displacement:** 210.6 cu. in. (3453 cc). **Bore & Stroke:** 3.68 x 3.31 in. (93.4 x 84 mm). **Brake Horsepower:** 218 (DIN) at 5200 rpm. Seven main bearings. Bosch L-Jetronic fuel injection.

BASE SIX (M1): Inline, dual-overhead-cam six-cylinder. **Displacement:** 210.6 cu. in. (3453 cc). **Bore & Stroke:** 3.68 x 3.31 in. (93.4 x 84 mm). **Brake Horsepower:** 277 (DIN) at 65000 rpm. Seven main bearings. Kugelfischer mechanical fuel injection.

CHASSIS DATA: Wheelbase: (320i) 100.9 in.; (530i) 103.8 in.; (633CSi) 103.4 in.; (733i) 110.0 in.; (M1) 100.8 in. **Overall Length:** (320i) 177.5 in.; (530i) 190.0 in.; (633CSi) 192.7 in.; (733i) 197.4 in.; (M1) 171.7 in. **Height:** (320i) 54.3 in.; (530i) 55.9 in.; (633CSi) 53.7 in.; (733i) 56.3 in.; (M1) 44.9 in. **Width:** (320i) 63.4 in.; (530i) 67.2 in.; (633CSi) 67.9 in.; (733i) 70.9 in.; (M1) 71.8 in. **Front Tread:** (320i) 54.6 in.; (530i) 55.9 in.; (633CSi) 56.0 in.; (733i) 59.1 in.; (M1) 61.0 in. **Rear Tread:** (320i) 55.1 in.; (530i) 57.5 in.l (633CSi) 58.5 in.; (733i) 59.1 in.; (M1) 62.0 in. **Standard Tires:** (320i) 185/70HR13; (530i) 195/70HR14; (633CSi) 195/70VR14; (733i) 205/70HR14; (M1) 205/55VR16 front, 225/50VR16 rear.

TECHNICAL: Layout: front-engine, rear-drive except (M1) mid-engine. **Transmission:** four-speed manual; three-speed automatic available. **Steering:** (320i, M1) rack and pinion; (5-series) worm and roller; (6/7-series) power recirculating ball. **Suspension (front):** MacPherson struts with coil springs except (M1) dual A-arms with coil springs. **Suspension (rear):** independent, semi-trailing arms with coil springs except (M1) dual A-arms with coil springs. **Brakes:** (320i) front disc, rear drum; (others) front/rear disc. **Body Construction:** steel unibody.

MAJOR OPTIONS: Automatic transmission. Sunroof. Alloy wheels. AM/FM stereo. Leather upholstery.

PERFORMANCE: Top Speed: (320i) 100+ mph; (530i) 120+ mph; (633CSi) 124 mph; (733i) 120 mph; (European 635CSi) 140 mph; (M1) 162 mph. **Acceleration (0-60 mph):** (320i) 10.4 sec.; (530i) 9 sec.; (633CSi) 8.4 sec.; (M1) about 5.5 sec. **Acceleration (quarter-mile):** (633CSi) 16.8 sec. (84.5 mph).

PRODUCTION/SALES: A total of 31,439 BMWs were sold in the U.S. in 1978.
Manufacturer: Bayerische Motoren Werken AG, Munich, West Germany.
Distributor: BMW of North America, Montvale, New Jersey.
HISTORY: The 1978 models were introduced to the U.S. market in October 1977.

1979 BMW

1979 BMW 633 CSi coupe.

320i — FOUR — Little was new for BMW's smallest model, the two-door 320i. The single-overhead-cam 2.0-liter four delivered 110 horsepower, to either a four-speed manual gearbox or three-speed automatic.

528i — SIX — A 2.8-liter six powered the newest version of BMW's smallest four-door model, now available in the U.S. to replace the 3.0-liter 530i sedan. The engine added a three-way catalyst converter and Lambda oxygen sensor, and produced seven fewer

horsepower than its predecessor. Performance and fuel mileage were improved, and the 528i ran on no-lead gasoline. *Road & Track* managed to accelerate a 528i to 60 mph in 8.2 seconds, and average 22 mpg (versus 19 mpg for the 530i). Otherwise, appearance and mechanical details changed little. Standard equipment included air conditioning, center door locking, all-disc brakes, and four-wheel independent suspension.

633CSi — SIX — After its debut as a mid-year model in 1978, the 6-series coupe, with larger (3.2-liter) engine than its 630CSi predecessor, continued without major change. Standard equipment in the U.S. included air conditioning, power brakes, and power steering.

733i — SIX — Production of the luxury four-door sedan with 3.2-liter six-cylinder engine continued with little change. Either a four-speed manual gearbox or ZF three-speed automatic was available. Standard equipment in the U.S. included air conditioning, power brakes, and power steering.

I.D. DATA: BMW's seven-digit serial number is on the dashboard near the 'A' pillar, or on the steering column. Chassis number is on right inner fender support or heater bulkhead. Engine number is on left rear of the block, above the starter. A data plate is on right inner fender support panel, or on right side of firewall. The first three numbers indicate model and transmission type, and whether the engine is a 49-state or California-certified. A four-digit sequential serial number follows. Starting serial number: (320i) 5447215; (320i w/auto.) 5479548; (528i) 5330001; (528i w/auto.) 5340001; (633CSi) 5525134; (633CSi w/auto.) 5535181; (733i) 5775217; (733i w/auto.) 5785854.

Note: Serial numbers for California-certified BMWs may differ.

Model	Body Type & Seating	Engine Type/CID	P.O.E. Price	Weight (lbs.)	Prod. Total
320i	2-dr Sedan-5P	I4/121	9735	2530	Note 1
528i	4-dr Sedan-5P	I6/170	15505	3320	Note 1
633CSi	2-dr Coupe-4P	I6/196	26770	3430	Note 1
733i	4-dr Sedan-5P	I6/196	23575	3770	Note 1

Note 1: A total of 328,281 BMWs were produced in 1979.

Price Note: During the model year, prices rose to $10,520 for the 320i, $17,395 for the 528i, $29,265 for the 633CSi, and $25,800 for the 733i.

ENGINE DATA: BASE FOUR (320i): Inline, overhead-cam four-cylinder. Cast iron block and aluminum head. **Displacement:** 121.3 cu. in. (1990 cc). **Bore & Stroke:** 3.50 x 3.15 in. (89 x 80 mm). **Compression Ratio:** 8.1:1. **Brake Horsepower:** 110 at 5800 rpm. **Torque:** 112 lbs.-ft. at 3750 rpm. Five main bearings. Bosch K-Jetronic fuel injection.

BASE SIX (528i): Inline, overhead-cam six-cylinder. Cast iron block and aluminum head. **Displacement:** 170.1 cu. in. (2788 cc). **Bore & Stroke:** 3.39 x 3.15 in. (86 x 80 mm). **Compression Ratio:** 8.2:1. **Brake Horsepower:** 169 at 5500 rpm. **Torque:** 170 lbs.-ft. at 4500 rpm. Seven main bearings. Bosch L-Jetronic fuel injection.

BASE SIX (633CSi, 733i): Inline, overhead-cam six-cylinder. Cast iron block and aluminum head. **Displacement:** 195.8 cu. in. (3210 cc). **Bore & Stroke:** 3.50 x 3.39 in. (88.9 x 86.1 mm). **Compression Ratio:** 8.0:1. **Brake Horsepower:** 177 at 5500 rpm. **Torque:** 196 lbs.-ft. at 4000 rpm. Seven main bearings. Bosch electronic fuel injection.

CHASSIS DATA: Wheelbase: (320i) 100.9 in.; (528i) 103.8 in.; (633CSi) 103.4 in.; (733i) 110.0 in. **Overall Length:** (320i) 177.5 in.; (528i) 190.0 in.; (633CSi) 192.7 in.; (733i) 197.4 in. **Height:** (320i) 54.3 in.; (528i) 55.9 in.; (633CSi) 53.7 in.; (733i) 56.3 in. **Width:** (320i) 63.4 in.; (528i) 67.2 in.; (633CSi) 67.9 in.; (733i) 70.9 in. **Front Tread:** (320i) 54.6 in.; (528i) 56.0 in.; (633CSi) 56.0 in.; (733i) 59.1 in. **Rear Tread:** (320i) 55.1 in.; (528i) 57.9 in.; (633CSi) 58.5 in.; (733i) 59.1 in. **Standard Tires:** (320i) 185/70SR13; (528i) 195/70HR14; (633CSi) 195/70VR14; (733i) 205/70HR14.

TECHNICAL: Layout: front-engine, rear-drive. **Transmission:** four-speed manual; three-speed automatic available. **Standard Final Drive Ratio:** (320i) 3.64:1; (others) 3.45:1. **Steering:** (320i) rack and pinion; (528i) worm and roller; (633CSi/733i) power recirculating ball. **Suspension (front):** MacPherson struts with coil springs. **Suspension (rear):** independent, semi-trailing arms with coil springs. **Brakes:** (320i) front disc, rear drum; (others) front/rear disc. **Body Construction:** steel unibody.

MAJOR OPTIONS: Automatic transmission: 320i ($430-$515); 528i/633CSi ($530-$630). Automatic trans. and cruise control: 733i ($530-$900). Limited-slip differential: 528i/633CSi ($330). Luxus Sport group: 320i ($875). Luxus Touring group: 320i ($1325). Touring group: 320i ($1045). Electric sunroof: 528i ($555). Manual sunroof: 320i ($450). Alloy wheels: 320i ($400); 528i ($475). AM/FM stereo with cassette player: 528i ($495). Leather upholstery: 528i ($890). Metallic paint: 320i ($340); 528i ($415).

PERFORMANCE: Top Speed: (320i) 100-110 mph; (528i) 122-125 mph; (633CSi) 124 mph; (733i) 118 mph. **Acceleration (0-60 mph):** (320i) 10.4 sec.; (633CSi) 8.4 sec. **Acceleration (quarter-mile):** (528i) 16.6 sec.; (633CSi) 16.8 sec. (84.5 mph). **Fuel Mileage:** (528i) 17 mpg EPA.

PRODUCTION/SALES: A total of 34,520 BMWs were sold in the U.S. in 1979.

ADDITIONAL MODELS: The M1 super coupe continued in production into 1981; see 1978 listing for details. The home-market 732i sedan was claimed to be the world's first production car with Digital Motor Electronics. New this year in Europe was the 735i sedan, with 3453-cc engine producing 218 bhp. The 735i would not enter the U.S. market until 1985.

Manufacturer: Bayerische Motoren Werke AG, Munich, West Germany.

Distributor: BMW of North America, Montvale, New Jersey.

HISTORY: The 1979 models were introduced to U.S. market in October 1978.

1980 BMW

320i — FOUR — A smaller four-cylinder engine went into BMW's smallest two-door model. The new engine displaced 1766 cubic centimeters, versus 1990 cc for its predecessor, and produced 100 horsepower. A five-speed manual gearbox was now standard.

528i — SIX — The four-door sedan's 2.8-liter engine had a Lambda-sond emission control system with three-way catalytic converter and oxygen sensor. Standard equipment in the U.S. included a five-speed manual gearbox, power steering, radio, and air conditioning.

633CSi — SIX — Little change was evident in the 3.2-liter coupe, which came with a four-speed manual transmission, power steering, radio, and air conditioning.

733i — SIX — Once again, little change was evident in BMW's most luxurious four-door sedan.

I.D. DATA: BMW's seven-digit serial number is on the left side of the dashboard near the 'A' pillar, except (528i and 733i) on the steering column. Chassis number is on right inner fender support or heater bulkhead. Engine number is on left rear of the block, above the starter. A data plate is on right inner fender support panel, or on firewall. The first three numbers indicate model and transmission type, and whether the engine is a 49-state or California-certified. A four-digit sequential serial number follows. Starting serial number: (320i) 7150000; (320i w/auto.) 7180000; (528i) 6780001; (528i w/auto.) 6790001; (633CSi) 5555001; (633CSi w/auto.) 5560001; (733i) 7350000; (733i w/auto.) 7360000.

1980 3.5-liter BMW MI mid-engined sports coupe. (Christie's)

Model	Body Type & Seating	Engine Type/CID	P.O.E. Price	Weight (lbs.)	Prod. Total
320i	2-dr Sedan-5P	I4/108	11810	2301	Note 1
528i	4-dr Sedan-5P	I6/170	20150	3059	Note 1
633CSi	2-dr Coupe-4P	I6/196	32825	3319	Note 1
733i	4-dr Sedan-5P	I6/196	28945	3434	Note 1

Note 1: A total of 330,087 BMWs were produced in 1980.

Weight Note: Some sources listed higher amounts at this time, up to 2530 pounds for the 320i, 3320 pounds for the 528i, 3430 pounds for the 633CSi, and 3770 pounds for the 733i.

ENGINE DATA: BASE FOUR (320i): Inline, overhead-cam four-cylinder. Cast iron block and aluminum head. **Displacement:** 107.7 cu. in. (1766 cc). **Bore & Stroke:** 3.50 x 2.79 in. (89 x 70.9 mm). **Compression Ratio:** 8.8:1. **Brake Horsepower:** 101 at 5800 rpm. **Torque:** 100 lbs.-ft. at 4500 rpm. Five main bearings. Bosch K-Jetronic fuel injection.

BASE SIX (528i): Inline, overhead-cam six-cylinder. Cast iron block and aluminum head. **Displacement:** 170.1 cu. in. (2788 cc). **Bore & Stroke:** 3.39 x 3.15 in. (86 x 80 mm). **Compression Ratio:** 8.2:1. **Brake Horsepower:** 169 at 5500 rpm. **Torque:** 170 lbs.-ft. at 4500 rpm. Seven main bearings. Bosch L-Jetronic fuel injection.

BASE SIX (633CSi, 733i): Inline, overhead-cam six-cylinder. Cast iron block and aluminum head. **Displacement:** 195.8 cu. in. (3210 cc). **Bore & Stroke:** 3.50 x 3.39 in. (88.9 x 86.1 mm). **Compression Ratio:** 8.0:1. **Brake Horsepower:** 174 at 5200 rpm. **Torque:** 188 lbs.-ft. at 4200 rpm. Seven main bearings. Bosch L-Jeteronic fuel injection.

CHASSIS DATA: Wheelbase: (320i) 100.9 in.; (528i) 103.8 in.; (633CSi) 103.4 in.; (733i) 110.0 in. **Overall Length:** (320i) 177.5 in.; (528i) 190.0 in.; (633CSi) 192.7 in.; (733i) 197.4 in. **Height:** (320i) 54.3 in.; (528i) 55.9 in.; (633CSi) 53.7 in.; (733i) 56.3 in. **Width:** (320i) 63.4 in.; (528i) 67.2 in.; (633CSi) 67.9 in.; (733i) 70.9 in. **Front Tread:** (320i) 54.6 in.; (528i) 56.0 in.; (633CSi) 56.0 in.; (733i) 59.1 in. **Rear Tread:** (320i) 55.1 in.; (530i) 57.9 in.; (633CSi) 58.5 in.; (733i) 59.1 in. **Standard Tires:** (320i) 185/70x13; (530i) 195/70HR14; (633CSi) 195/70VR14; (733i) 205/70HR14.

TECHNICAL: Layout: front-engine, rear-drive. **Transmission:** (320i/528i) five-speed manual; (633CSi/733i) four-speed manual; three-speed automatic available. **Steering:** (320i) rack and pinion; (528i) worm and roller; (633CSi/733i) power recirculating ball. **Suspension (front):** MacPherson struts with coil springs. **Suspension (rear):** independent, semi-trailing arms with coil springs. **Brakes:** (320i) front disc, rear drum; (others) front/rear disc. **Body Construction:** steel unibody.

MAJOR OPTIONS: Automatic transmission: 320i ($575); others ($705). 'S' package: 320i ($2475). Luxus Touring group: 320i ($1590). Leather upholstery (528i). Sunroof. Alloy wheels (320i).

PERFORMANCE: Top Speed: (320i) 105 mph; (633CSi) 124 mph; (733i) 118 mph. **Acceleration (0-60 mph):** (633CSi) 8.4 sec. **Acceleration (quarter-mile):** (320i) 17.1 sec.; (633CSi) 16.8 sec. (84.5 mph); (733i) 16.3 sec. **Fuel Mileage:** (320i) 25 mpg EPA; (733i) 16 mpg EPA.

PRODUCTION/SALES: A total of 37,017 BMWs were sold in the U.S. in 1980 (including 25,786 320i models).

ADDITIONAL MODELS: The M1 super coupe continued in production into 1981; see 1978 listing for details. BMW began to produce a turbocharged 745i sedan this year, with 3210-cc engine delivering 252 horsepower.

Manufacturer: Bayerische Motoren Werke AG, Munich, West Germany.

Distributor: BMW of North America, Montvale, New Jersey.

1981 BMW

320i — FOUR — Little change was evident in BMW's smallest sedan. Power came from a 108-cid (1.8-liter) four-cylinder engine, hooked to a five-speed manual gearbox. A three-speed automatic was optional. Standard equipment included power brakes, tinted glass, reclining front bucket seats, trip odometer, power remote driver's mirror, center console, tachometer, digital clock, intermittent wipers, carpeting, and electric rear-window defroster. Either cloth or leatherette upholstery was available.

528i — SIX — Production of the enthusiast-oriented four-door sedan, powered by a 2788-cc six-cylinder engine driving a five-speed manual gearbox, continued with little change. Standard equipment was similar to the 320i, but included air conditioning, an AM/FM stereo radio with cassette player, four-wheel disc brakes, fold-down center armrests, power steering, power windows, central locking, and a digital clock.

633CSi — SIX — BMW's coupe, on a 103.4-inch wheelbase, was powered by a 3.2-liter six-cylinder engine rated 174 horsepower. Either a new five-speed manual gearbox or optional three-speed automatic was available. Standard equipment was similar to the 528i, adding leather upholstery, BBS Mahle light-alloy wheels, and an electric sunroof.

1981 BMW 733i luxury sedan.

733i — SIX — BMW's top-rung sedan, riding a 110-inch wheelbase, carried the same 3.2-liter six-cylinder engine as the 633CSi coupe. Equipment was also similar, with the addition of rear headrests. A five-speed manual gearbox became standard, with automatic available.

I.D. DATA: A 17-symbol Vehicle Identification Number is on the upper left of the dashboard, visible through the windshield; or on steering column. Symbols 1-3 ('WBA') indicate manufacturer, make and type. Symbols 4-5 denote car line and series. Symbol six (a digit) denotes the body type. Symbol seven identifies the engine. The eighth symbol indicates the restraint system, followed by a check digit. Symbol ten indicates model year ('B' = 1981). Symbol 11 identifies the assembly plant. The final six digits form the sequential serial number. Engine number is on left of block, at upper edge of starter mounting.

Model	Body Type & Seating	Engine Type/CID	P.O.E. Price	Weight (lbs.)	Prod. Total
320i	2-dr Sedan-5P	I4/108	12895	2285	Note 1
528i	4-dr Sedan-5P	I6/170	21995	3022	Note 1
633CSi	2-dr Coupe-4P	I6/196	35910	3222	Note 1
733i	4-dr Sedan-5P	I6/196	31980	3328	Note 1

Note 1: A total of 337,757 BMWs were produced in 1981.
Weight Note: Some sources listed higher weights, from 2500 pounds for the 320i to 3590 pounds for the 733i.
ENGINE DATA: BASE FOUR (320i): Inline, overhead-cam four-cylinder. Cast iron block and light alloy head. **Displacement:** 108 cu. in. (1766 cc). **Bore & Stroke:** 3.50 x 2.80 in. (89 x 71 mm). **Compression Ratio:** 8.8:1. **Brake Horsepower:** 101 at 5800 rpm. **Torque:** 100 lbs.-ft. at 4500 rpm. Five main bearings. Bosch K-Jetronic fuel injection.
BASE SIX (528i): Inline, overhead-cam six-cylinder. Cast iron block and light alloy head. **Displacement:** 170.1 cu. in. (2788 cc). **Bore & Stroke:** 3.39 x 3.15 in. (86 x 80 mm). **Compression Ratio:** 8.2:1. **Brake Horsepower:** 169 at 5500 rpm. **Torque:** 170 lbs.-ft. at 4500 rpm. Seven main bearings. Bosch L-Jetronic fuel injection.
BASE SIX (633CSi, 733i): Inline, overhead-cam six-cylinder. Cast iron block and light alloy head. **Displacement:** 196 cu. in. (3210 cc). **Bore & Stroke:** 3.50 x 3.39 in. (89 x 86 mm). **Compression Ratio:** 8.0:1. **Brake Horsepower:** 174 at 5200 rpm. **Torque:** 188 lbs.-ft. at 4200 rpm. Seven main bearings. Bosch L-Jetronic fuel injection.

CHASSIS DATA: Wheelbase: (320i) 100.9 in.; ; (528i) 103.8 in.; (633CSi) 103.4 in.; (733i) 110.0 in. **Overall Length:** (320i) 177.5 in.; (528i) 190.9 in.; (633CSi) 193.8 in.; (733i) 197.4 in. **Height:** (320i) 54.3 in.; (528i) 55.9 in.; (633CSi) 53.7 in.; (733i) 56.3 in. **Width:** (320i) 63.4 in.; (528i) 67.2 in.; (633CSi) 67.9 in.; (733i) 70.9 in. **Front Tread:** (320i) 54.6 in.; (528i) 56.0 in.; (633CSi) 56.0 in.; (733i) 59.1 in. **Rear Tread:** (320i) 55.0 in.; (528i) 57.9 in.; (633CSi) 58.5 in.; (733i) 59.7 in. **Standard Tires:** (320i) 185/70SR13; (528i) 195/70HR14; (633CSi) 195/70HR14; (733i) 205/70HR14.

TECHNICAL: Layout: front-engine, rear-drive. **Transmission:** five-speed (overdrive) manual; three-speed automatic available. **Standard Final Drive Ratio:** (320i) 3.91:1; (320i w/automatic) 3.64:1; (528i/633CSi/733i) 3.45:1. **Steering:** (320i) rack and pinion; (others) recirculating ball with variable power assist. **Suspension (front):** (320i/528i) MacPherson struts with coil springs and anti-roll bar; (633CSi) double-pivot MacPherson struts with lower lateral links, drag struts, coil springs and anti-roll bar. **Suspension (rear):** (320i/528e/633CSi) independent, semi-trailing arms with coil springs and anti-roll bar; (733i) independent, semi-trailing arms with coil springs. **Brakes:** front/rear disc except (320i) front disc, rear drum. **Body Construction:** steel unibody.

MAJOR OPTIONS: Automatic transmission: 320i ($620); others ($775). Luxus touring group: 320i ($1685). 'S' package: 320i ($2620). Sunroof: 320i ($555). On-board computer: 733i ($635). Leather upholstery: 528i ($1030). Limited-slip differential: 5/6/7-series ($390). Alloy wheels ($500). Metallic paint ($420).

PRODUCTION/SALES: A total of 41,761 BMWs were sold in the U.S. during 1981 (31,902 Model 320i, 6,267 Model 528i, 1,138 Model 633CSi, and 2,454 Model 733i).

ADDITIONAL MODELS: This was the final year of production for the M1 super coupe; see 1978 listing for details.
Manufacturer: Bayerische Motoren Werke AG, Munich, West Germany.
Distributor: BMW of North America, Inc.
HISTORY: The 1981 models were introduced in the U.S. in December 1980. A second-generation 5-series was introduced in Europe in 1981, and would enter the U.S. market for the 1982 model year.

1982 BMW

320i — FOUR — Not much changed in BMW's smallest model. A 108-cid (1.8-liter) four-cylinder engine again provided the power, hooked to a five-speed manual gearbox. A three-speed automatic was optional. Standard equipment included power brakes, tinted glass, reclining front bucket seats, trip odometer, intermittent wipers, full carpeting (including trunk), electric rear-window defroster, and a tool kit.

1982 BMW 528e four-door sedan.

528e — SIX — A new version of the 5-series was introduced this year, replacing the 528i. Drivetrain was BMW's 164-cid (2.7-liter) "eta" six-cylinder engine, rated 121 horsepower and hooked to a standard five-speed manual gearbox. Standard equipment included power steering and four-wheel disc brakes, air conditioning, tinted glass, electric rear-window defroster, AM/FM stereo with cassette player, digital clock, power windows, central locking, power mirror, foglamps, intermittent wipers, cruise control, power sliding sunroof, light-alloy wheels, a fuel economy indicator, and "active check control" warning light panel. Metallic paint was available at no extra cost.

633CSi — SIX — Little changed this year, the BMW coupe rode a 103.4-inch wheelbase. A 3.2-liter six-cylinder engine rated 181 bhp drove either the standard five-speed manual gearbox or optional three-speed automatic. Standard equipment included air conditioning, power sunroof, electric rear-window defroster, AM/FM stereo with cassette player, leather upholstery, power four-wheel disc brakes and steering, power windows, and central door locking. Also standard: an adjustable steering column, remote driver's mirror, driver's seat tilt/height adjustment, tinted glass, intermittent wipers, rear headrests, and light-alloy wheels.

733i — SIX — BMW's top-rung sedan, on a 110-inch wheelbase, had the same drivetrain and equipment as the shorter 633CSi coupe. Little was changed this year.

I.D. DATA: A 17-symbol Vehicle Identification Number is on the upper left of the dashboard, visible through the windshield; or on steering column. Symbols 1-3 ('WBA') indicate manufacturer, make and type. Symbols 4-5 denote car line and series ('AG' = 320i; 'DK' = 528e; 'EB' = 633CSi; 'FF' = 733i). Symbol six (a digit) denotes the body type. Symbol seven identifies the engine. The eighth symbol indicates the restraint system, followed by a check digit. Symbol ten indicates model year ('C' = 1982). Symbol 11 identifies the assembly plant. The final six digits are the sequential serial number. Engine number is on left of block, at upper edge of starter mounting.

Model	Body Type & Seating	Engine Type/CID	P.O.E. Price	Weight (lbs.)	Prod. Total
320i	2-dr Sedan-5P	I4/108	13290	2500	Note 1
528e	4-dr Sedan-5P	I6/164	23325	2960	Note 1
633CSi	2-dr Coupe-4P	I6/196	36995	3340	Note 1
733i	4-dr Sedan-5P	I6/196	33315	3440	Note 1

Note 1: A total of 362,607 BMWs were produced in 1982.
Automatic Transmission Note: Automatic added $620 to the 320i price, and $775 to other models.

ENGINE DATA: BASE FOUR (320i): Inline, overhead-cam four-cylinder. Cast iron block and light alloy head. **Displacement:** 108 cu. in. (1766 cc). **Bore & Stroke:** 3.50 x 2.80 in. (89 x 71 mm). **Compression Ratio:** 8.8:1. **Brake Horsepower:** 101 at 5800 rpm. **Torque:** 100 lbs.-ft. at 4500 rpm. Five main bearings. Bosch fuel injection.
BASE SIX (528e): Inline, overhead-cam six-cylinder ("eta"). Cast iron block and light alloy head. **Displacement:** 164 cu. in. (2693 cc). **Bore & Stroke:** 3.31 x 3.19 in. (84 x 81 mm). **Compression Ratio:** 9.0:1. **Brake Horsepower:** 121 at 4250 rpm. **Torque:** 170 lbs.-ft. at 3250 rpm. Seven main bearings. Bosch fuel injection.
BASE SIX (633CSi, 733i): Inline, overhead-cam six-cylinder. Cast iron block and light alloy head. **Displacement:** 196 cu. in. (3210 cc). **Bore & Stroke:** 3.50 x 3.39 in. (89 x 86 mm). **Compression Ratio:** 8.8:1. **Brake Horsepower:** 181 at 6000 rpm. **Torque:** 195 lbs.-ft. at 4000 rpm. Seven main bearings. Bosch fuel injection.

CHASSIS DATA: Wheelbase: (320i) 100.9 in.; (528e) 103.3 in.; (633CSi) 103.4 in.; (733i) 110.0 in. **Overall Length:** (320i) 177.5 in.; (528e) 189.0 in.; (633CSi) 193.8 in.; (733i) 197.4 in. **Height:** (320i) 54.3 in.; (528e) 55.7 in.; (633CSi) 53.7 in.; (733i) 56.3 in. **Width:** (320i) 63.4 in.; (528e) 66.9 in.; (633CSi) 67.9 in.; (733i) 70.9 in. **Front Tread:** (320i) 54.6 in.; (528e) 56.3 in.; (633CSi) 56.0 in.; (733i) 59.1 in. **Rear Tread:** (320i) 55.0 in.; (528e) 57.9 in.; (633CSi) 58.5 in.; (733i) 59.7 in.

TECHNICAL: Layout: front-engine, rear-drive. **Transmission:** five-speed (overdrive) manual; three-speed automatic available. **Standard Final Drive Ratio:** (320i) 3.91:1; (528e) 2.93:1; (633CSi) 3.25:1; (733i) 3.45:1. **Steering:** (320i) rack and pinion; (others) recirculating ball with variable power assist. **Suspension (front):** (320i) MacPherson struts with coil springs and anti-roll bar; (528e) double-pivot struts with coil springs and anti-roll bar; (633CSi/733i) double-pivot MacPherson struts with lower lateral links, drag struts, coil springs and anti-roll bar. **Suspension (rear):** (320i/528e/633CSi) independent, semi-trailing arms with coil springs and anti-roll bar; (733i) independent, semi-trailing arms with coil springs. **Brakes:** front/rear disc except (320i) front disc, rear drum. **Body Construction:** steel unibody.

MAJOR OPTIONS: Luxus touring group (air cond., AM/FM stereo w/cassette, foglamps): 320i ($1685). 'S' package (special alloy wheels, manual sunroof, Recaro front seats, sport steering wheel, limited-slip differential, sport susp., AM/FM stereo w/cassette, foglamps, power remote right mirror, front air dam, halogen high-beam headlamps, and deluxe tool kit): 320i ($2620). Three-speed automatic transmission ($775) except on 320i ($620). Limited-slip differential ($390); N/A on 320i. Leather upholstery: 528e ($1090). Sliding steel sunroof: 320i ($555). Power sunroof: 528e ($745). On-board computer: 733i ($635). Cruise control: 633CSi w/auto trans. ($310). Metallic paint: 320i ($420). Light alloy wheels: 320i ($500).

PRODUCTION/SALES: A total of 52,393 BMWs were sold in the U.S. during 1982.
Manufacturer: Bayerische Motoren Werke AG, Munich, West Germany.
Distributor: BMW of North America, Inc.
HISTORY: The 1982 models were introduced in the U.S. in December 1981. In the European market, only the 635CSi coupe with a larger engine remained available after 1982. The 633CSi remained in the U.S. lineup through 1984, however, when it, too, was replaced by the 635CSi. The second-generation 3-series debuted in Europe this year.

1983 BMW

320i — FOUR — Production of the 320i (BMW's best seller) halted before the 1983 model year began, but sales of leftover models continued until the replacement 318i arrived, as an early '84 model. See previous listing for additional details.

318i — FOUR — Introduced in the U.S. late in the model year, the replacement for the 320i was similar in appearance but presented a more aerodynamic profile (and reduced air drag) with its sloped hood, front spoiler, and taller deck. Chassis dimensions were slightly smaller, while the interior grew a bit in length. The familiar 1.8-liter four-cylinder engine switched from mechanical fuel injection to Bosch L-Jetronic injection. Coupled with a taller (3.64:1) final drive ratio, it earned higher gas mileage ratings. Both the five-speed (overdrive) manual gearbox and three-speed automatic were offered. Standard equipment included the manual transmission, power brakes and steering, air conditioning, dual power remote-control mirrors, intermittent wipers, time-delay courtesy light, electric antenna, full carpeting , electric rear-window defroster, and foglamps. Reclining front bucket seats came with either cloth or leatherette upholstery, and had adjustable lumbar support. On the dashboard were a tachometer, trip odometer, service interval indicator, fuel economy gauge, and digital clock. Light alloy wheels held 195/60HR14 tires.

528e — SIX — Production of the revised 5-series sedan, introduced for 1982, continued with no change. Drivetrain was again the 121-horsepower, 164-cid (2.7-liter) "eta" six-cylinder engine, with standard five-speed manual gearbox. Standard equipment was the same as 1982.

533i — SIX — A second 5-series model was introduced, powered by the larger (3.2-liter) six-cylinder engine, as in the 633CSi coupe. Like other BMW models, the front end displayed quad round headlamps and the traditional-style two-section center grille. Standard equipment included a five-speed (overdrive) manual transmission, power steering and four-wheel disc brakes, telescopic steering column, leather upholstery, air conditioning, tinted glass, electric rear-window defroster, AM/FM stereo with cassette player, power windows, driver's seat tilt/height adjustment, central door locking, power mirrors, foglamps, intermittent wipers, cruise control, electric sliding steel sunroof, and 200/60x390 tires on light alloy wheels. Dashboard gear included an on-board trip computer that calculated gas mileage, estimated time of arrival, and miles before refueling; plus a digital clock and tachometer.

633CSi — SIX — BMW's coupe, which again carried a 3.2-liter six-cylinder engine rated 181 horsepower, got a front-end facelift in the form of a restyled nose. Chassis modifications focused on a reworked front suspension, similar to that of the 7-series. Standard equipment was similar to the 533i, with a center console, rear bucket seats, front spoiler, and 205/70x14 tires.

733i — SIX — A modest facelift was the major change for BMW's best sedan, which carried the same drivetrain and equipment as the 633CSi coupe. An electronic-tuning AM/FM stereo radio with cassette player was standard, and the four-spoke steering wheel was leather-wrapped.

I.D. DATA: A 17-symbol Vehicle Identification Number is on the upper left of the dashboard, visible through the windshield; or on steering column. Symbols 1-3 ('WBA') indicate manufacturer, make and type. Symbols 4-5 denote car line and series ('AG' = 320i; 'AK' = 318i; 'DK' = 528e; 'DB' = 533i; 'EB' = 633CSi; 'FF' = 733i). Symbol six (a digit) denotes the body type. Symbol seven identifies the engine. The eighth symbol indicates the restraint system, followed by a check digit. Symbol ten indicates model year ('D' = 1983). Symbol 11 identifies the assembly plant. The final six digits are the sequential serial number. Engine number is on left of block, at upper edge of starter mounting.

Model	Body Type & Seating	Engine Type/CID	P.O.E. Price	Weight (lbs.)	Prod. Total
320i	2-dr Sedan-5P	I4/108	13290	2500	Note 1
318i	2-dr Sedan-5P	I4/108	16430	N/A	Note 1
528e	4-dr Sedan-5P	I6/164	23985	2953	Note 1
533i	4-dr Sedan-5P	I6/196	28985	3125	Note 1
633CSi	2-dr Coupe-4P	I6/196	39120	3350	Note 1
733i	4-dr Sedan-5P	I6/196	34300	3440	Note 1

Note 1: A total of 407,507 BMWs were produced in 1983.

ENGINE DATA: BASE FOUR (320i): Inline, overhead-cam four-cylinder. Cast iron block and light alloy head. **Displacement:** 108 cu. in. (1766 cc). **Bore & Stroke:** 3.50 x 2.80 in. (89 x 71 mm). **Compression Ratio:** 8.8:1. **Brake Horsepower:** 101 at 5800 rpm. **Torque:** 100 lbs.-ft. at 4500 rpm. Five main bearings. Bosch K-Jetronic fuel injection.

BASE FOUR (318i): Same as above, but with Bosch L-Jetronic fuel injection. **Compression Ratio:** 9.3:1. **Brake Horsepower:** 101 at 5800 rpm. **Torque:** 103 lbs.-ft. at 4500 rpm.

BASE SIX (528e): Inline, overhead-cam six-cylinder ("eta"). Cast iron block and light alloy head. **Displacement:** 164 cu. in. (2693 cc). **Bore & Stroke:** 3.31 x 3.19 in. (84 x 81 mm). **Compression Ratio:** 9.0:1. **Brake Horsepower:** 121 at 4250 rpm. **Torque:** 170 lbs.-ft. at 3250 rpm. Seven main bearings. Bosch L-Jetronic fuel injection.

BASE SIX (533i, 633CSi, 733i): Inline, overhead-cam six-cylinder. Cast iron block and light alloy head. **Displacement:** 196 cu. in. (3210 cc). **Bore & Stroke:** 3.50 x 3.39 in. (89 x 86 mm). **Compression Ratio:** 8.8:1. **Brake Horsepower:** 181 at 6000 rpm. **Torque:** 195 lbs.-ft. at 4000 rpm. Seven main bearings. Electronic (port) fuel injection.

CHASSIS DATA: Wheelbase: (320i) 100.9 in.; ; (318i) 101.2 in.; (528e/533i) 103.3 in.; (633CSi) 103.4 in.; (733i) 110.0 in. **Overall Length:** (320i) 177.5 in.; (318i) 176.8 in.; (528e/533i) 189.0 in.; (633CSi) 193.8 in.; (733i) 197.4 in. **Height:** (320i) 54.3 in.; (318i) 54.3 in.; (528e/533i) 55.7 in.; (633CSi) 53.7 in.; (733i) 56.3 in. **Width:** (320i) 63.4 in.; (318i) 64.8 in.; (528e/533i) 66.0 in.; (633CSi) 67.9 in.; (733i) 70.9 in. **Front Tread:** (320i) 54.6 in.; (318i) 55.4 in.; (528e/533i) 56.3 in.; (633CSi) 56.0 in.; (733i) 59.1 in. **Rear Tread:** (320i) 55.0 in.; (318i) 55.7 in.; (528e/533i) 57.9 in.; (633CSi) 58.5 in.; (733i) 59.7 in. **Standard Tires:** (318i) 195/60HR14; (528e) 195/70x14; (533i) 200/60x390; (633CSi) 205/70x14.

TECHNICAL: Layout: front-engine, rear-drive. **Transmission:** five-speed (overdrive) manual; three-speed automatic available. **Standard Final Drive Ratio:** (318i) 3.64:1; (528e/533i) 2.93:1; (633CSi) 3.25:1. **Steering:** (320i/318i) power rack-and-pinion; (5/6/7-series) recirculating ball with variable power assist. **Suspension (front):** (318i) MacPherson struts with lower control arms, coil springs and anti-roll bar; (5/6/7-series) MacPherson struts with lower lateral links, coil springs and anti-roll bar. **Suspension (rear):** (318i/733i) independent, semi-trailing arms with coil springs; (528e/533i/633CSi) independent, semi-trailing arms with coil springs and anti-roll bar. **Brakes:** front/rear disc except (318i) front disc, rear drum. **Body Construction:** steel unibody. **Fuel Tank:** (318i) 14.5 gal.; (5/6-series) 16.6 gal.; (733i) 22.5 gallon.

MAJOR OPTIONS: Three-speed automatic transmission: 318i ($495). Automatic trans.; 5/6/7-series ($775). Leather upholstery: 528e ($1090). Limited-slip differential: 5/6/7-series ($390). On-board computer: 528e ($595). Power door locks: 318i ($195). Power windows: 318i ($335). Tinted glass: 318i. AM/FM stereo radio w/cassette player: 318i ($505). Sunroof: 318i ($520).

Note: See 1982 listing for 320i options.

PRODUCTION/SALES: A total of 59,242 BMWs were sold in the U.S. during 1983.
Manufacturer: Bayerische Motoren Werke AG, Munich, West Germany.
Distributor: BMW of North America, Inc.
HISTORY: The 1983 models were introduced in the U.S. in November 1982, except (318i) May 1983.

1984 BMW

1984 BMW 528e four-door sedan. (BMW of North America Inc.)

318i — FOUR — Production of the reworked 3-series two-door sedan continued with little change, after introduction in May 1983. A 1.8-liter four-cylinder engine provided the power, to either a five-speed manual gearbox or optional three-speed automatic. Standard equipment and appearance were the same as 1983.

325e — SIX — A larger (2.7-liter) engine with six cylinders became available in the 3-series, joining the original four. Standard transmission was a five-speed (overdrive) manual gearbox, with a four-speed automatic optional (versus three speeds on the 318i). Four-wheel disc brakes were installed, while the 318i kept rear drums; and the rear suspension added a stabilizer bar. Standard equipment included power brakes and steering, air conditioning, sunroof, power windows, central door locking, AM/FM stereo with cassette player, dual power remote-control mirrors, intermittent wipers, time-delay courtesy light, electric antenna, full carpeting, electric rear-window defroster, leather-wrapped steering wheel and gearshift knob, and foglamps. Reclining front bucket seats came with cloth or leather upholstery, On the dashboard were a tachometer, trip odometer, service interval indicator, fuel economy gauge, and digital clock.

528e — SIX — Little was new in the mid-range four-door sedan, introduced for the 1982 model year. As before, a 121-horsepower, 164-cid (2.7-liter) "eta" six-cylinder engine came with the standard five-speed manual gearbox, or could have an optional four-speed automatic. Standard equipment included power steering and four-wheel disc brakes, telescopic steering column, air conditioning, tinted glass, electric rear-window defroster, AM/FM stereo with cassette player, power windows, driver's seat tilt/height adjustment, central door locking, power mirrors, foglamps, intermittent wipers, cruise control, electric sliding steel sunroof, and light alloy wheels. Dashboard gear included an on-board trip computer, digital clock, and tachometer. Metallic paint was available at no extra cost. Light alloy wheels held 195/70HR tires.

533i — SIX — A larger (3.2-liter) six-cylinder engine again powered the alternate 5-series sedan. Standard equipment was the same as in the 528e, along with leather upholstery, an on-board trip computer, and 200/60VR390 Michelin TRX tires.

633CSi — SIX — Drivetrain details were the same for BMW's coupe as in the 533i sedan: a 181-horsepower, 3.2-liter six-cylinder engine and either five-speed manual or four-speed automatic transmission. Standard equipment was similar to the 533i, but 205/70VR TRX tires were used.

733i — SIX — BMW's biggest sedan carried 205/70HR tires, but otherwise had drivetrain specifications similar to the 533i/633CSi. No major changes were seen this year.

I.D. DATA: A 17-symbol Vehicle Identification Number is on the upper left of the dashboard, visible through the windshield; or on steering column. Symbols 1-3 ('WBA') indicate manufacturer, make and type. Symbols 4-5 denote car line and series ('AB' = 325e; 'AK' = 318i; 'DK' = 528e; 'DB' = 533i; 'EB' = 633CSi; 'FF' = 733i). Symbol six (a digit) denotes the body type. Symbol seven identifies the engine. The eighth symbol indicates the restraint system, followed by a check digit. Symbol ten indicates model year ('E' = 1984). Symbol 11 identifies the assembly plant. The final six digits are the sequential serial number. Engine number is on left of block, at upper edge of starter mounting.

Model	Body Type & Seating	Engine Type/CID	P.O.E. Price	Weight (lbs.)	Prod. Total
318i	2-dr Sedan-5P	I4/108	16430	2360	Note 1
325e	2-dr Sedan-5P	I6/164	19700	2654	Note 1
528e	4-dr Sedan-5P	I6/164	24565	2953	Note 1
533i	4-dr Sedan-5P	I6/196	30305	3134	Note 1
633CSi	2-dr Coupe-4P	I6/196	40705	3350	Note 1
733i	4-dr Sedan-5P	I6/196	36335	3440	Note 1

Note 1: A total of 412,447 BMWs were produced in 1984.

ENGINE DATA: BASE FOUR (318i): Inline, overhead-cam four-cylinder. Cast iron block and light alloy head. **Displacement:** 108 cu. in. (1766 cc). **Bore & Stroke:** 3.50 x 2.80 in. (89 x 71 mm). **Compression Ratio:** 9.3:1. **Brake Horsepower:** 101 at 5800 rpm. **Torque:** 103 lbs.-ft. at 4500 rpm. Five main bearings. Bosch L-Jetronic fuel injection.

BASE SIX (325e, 528e): Inline, overhead-cam six-cylinder ("eta"). Cast iron block and light alloy head. **Displacement:** 164 cu. in. (2693 cc). **Bore & Stroke:** 3.31 x 3.19 in. (84 x 81 mm). **Compression Ratio:** 9.0:1. **Brake Horsepower:** 121 at 4250 rpm. **Torque:** 170 lbs.-ft. at 3250 rpm. Seven main bearings. Bosch electronic (port) fuel injection.

BASE SIX (533i, 633CSi, 733i): Inline, overhead-cam six-cylinder. Cast iron block and light alloy head. **Displacement:** 196 cu. in. (3210 cc). **Bore & Stroke:** 3.50 x 3.39 in. (89 x 86 mm). **Compression Ratio:** 8.8:1. **Brake Horsepower:** 181 at 6000 rpm. **Torque:** 195 lbs.-ft. at 4000 rpm. Seven main bearings. Bosch electronic (port) fuel injection.

CHASSIS DATA: Wheelbase: (318i/325e) 101.2 in.; (528e/533i) 103.3 in.; (633CSi) 103.4 in.; (733i) 110.0 in. **Overall Length:** (318i/325e) 176.8 in.; (528e/533i) 189.0 in.; (633CSi) 193.8 in.; (733i) 197.4 in. **Height:** (318i/325e) 54.3 in.; (528e/533i) 55.7 in.; (633CSi) 53.7 in.; (733i) 56.3 in. **Width:** (318i/325e) 64.8 in.; (528e/533i) 66.0 in.; (633CSi) 67.9 in.; (733i) 70.9 in. **Front Tread:** (318i/325e) 55.4 in.; (528e/533i) 56.3 in.; (633CSi) 56.0 in.; (733i) 59.1 in. **Rear Tread:** (318i/325e) 55.7 in.; (528e/533i) 57.9 in.; (633CSi) 58.5 in.; (733i) 59.7 in. **Standard Tires:** (318i/325e) 195/60HR14; (528e) 195/70HR; (533i) 200/60VR390 Michelin TRX (633CSi) 205/70VR TRX; (733i) 205/70HR.

TECHNICAL: Layout: front-engine, rear-drive. **Transmission:** five-speed (overdrive) manual; three-speed automatic available on 318i, four-speed automatic on other models. **Standard Final Drive Ratio:** (318i w/auto.) 3.64:1; (325e) 2.79:1; (528e/533i) 2.93:1; (633CSi/733i) 3.25:1. **Steering:** (318i/325e) power rack-and-pinion; (5/6/7-series) power recirculating ball. **Suspension (front):** (318i/325e) MacPherson struts with lower control arms, coil springs and anti-roll bar; (5/6/7-series) MacPherson struts with lower lateral links, coil springs and anti-roll bar. **Suspension (rear):** (318i/733i) independent, semi-trailing arms with coil springs; (325e/528e/533i/633CSi) independent, semi-trailing arms with coil springs and anti-roll bar. **Brakes:** front/rear disc except (318i) front disc, rear drum. **Body Construction:** steel unibody. **Fuel Tank:** (318i/325e) 15.3 gal.; (5/6-series) 16.6 gal.; (733i) 22.5 gallon.

MAJOR OPTIONS: Three-speed automatic transmission: 318i ($495). Four-speed automatic trans.: 325e ($595); 5/6/7-series ($795). Luxus package: 318i ($770). Manual sunroof: 318i ($520). Leather upholstery: 3-series/528e ($1090). Limited-slip differential ($370-$390). On-board computer: 528e ($595). TRX wheels/tires: 733i ($850). Rear headrests: 733I ($175). AM/FM stereo radio w/cassette player: 318i ($505). Metalic paint: 3-series ($420).

PRODUCTION/SALES: A total of 70,897 BMWs were sold in the U.S. during 1984.

Manufacturer: Bayerische Motoren Werke AG, Munich, West Germany.

Distributor: BMW of North America, Inc., Montvale, New Jersey.

HISTORY: The 1984 models were introduced in the U.S. in November 1983, except (325e) in spring 1984.

1985 BMW

318i — FOUR — A four-door sedan joined the original two-door in the basic 3-series. Power again came from the 1.8-liter four-cylinder engine, hooked to either a five-speed manual gearbox or a new four-speed automatic (replacing the three-speed). Otherwise, standard equipment and appearance were similar to 1983-84. All 318i models had air conditioning, foglamps, tinted glass, power mirrors, an electric rear-window defroster, power windows, and an electronic tachometer.

325e — SIX — Like the four-cylinder version of the 3-series, the six-cylinder edition now came in both two- and four-door sedan bodies. As before, the engine was a 2.7-liter six, with either five-speed manual or four-speed automatic transmission. Appearance and equipment were similar to 1984. An AM/FM stereo radio with cassette player and four speakers was standard. Two-doors had front sport seats and a leather-wrapped steering wheel. A two-position electric sunroof was standard.

528e — SIX — Production of the basic 5-series sedan continued with the 121-horsepower, 164-cid (2.7-liter) "eta" six-cylinder engine. Standard equipment included air conditioning, a heated driver's door lock, heated power mirrors, tilt steering, power windows, and metallic paint.

524td — SIX — Turbodiesel power became available for the 5-series sedan this year. The new turbocharged engine displaced 2.4 liters and produced 114 horsepower. Appearance and equipment were similar to the 528e, with a standard automatic transmission.

535i — SIX — Replacing the former 533i sedan, the revised version carried a larger (3.4-liter) six-cylinder engine, producing 182 horsepower. Anti-lock braking was another new addition.

635CSi — SIX — Anti-lock braking was the major change in BMW's six-cylinder coupe, along with the substitution of a larger (3.4-liter) engine. Thus, the model number for the version available in the U.S. changed from 633CSi to 635CSi.

735i — SIX — BMW's modification of the 733i sedan gained the larger (3.4-liter) six-cylinder engine and anti-lock braking. It had been available in Europe since 1979.

I.D. DATA: A 17-symbol Vehicle Identification Number is on the upper left of the dashboard, visible through the windshield; or on steering column. Symbols 1-3 ('WBA') indicate manufacturer, make and type. Symbols 4-5 denote car line and series ('AK' = 318i 2-dr; 'AC' = 318i 4-dr; 'AE' = 325e 2-dr; 'AB' = 325e 4-dr; 'DK' = 528e; 'DC' = 535i; 'DB' = 524td; 'EC' = 635CSi; 'FH' = 735i). Symbol six (a digit) denotes the body type. Symbol seven identifies the engine. The eighth symbol indicates the restraint system, followed by a check digit. Symbol ten indicates model year ('F' = 1985). Symbol 11 identifies the assembly plant. The final six digits are the sequential serial number, starting with 000001. Engine number is on left of block, at upper edge of starter mounting.

Model	Body Type & Seating	Engine Type/CID	P.O.E. Price	Weight (lbs.)	Prod. Total
318i	2-dr Sedan-5P	I4/108	16430	2395	Note 1
318i	4-dr Sedan-5P	I4/108	16925	2450	Note 1
325e	2-dr Sedan-5P	I6/164	20970	2710	Note 1
325e	4-dr Sedan-5P	I6/164	21105	2765	Note 1
528e	4-dr Sedan-5P	I6/164	24565	3055	Note 1
524td	4-dr Sedan-5P	I6/149	24560	3240	Note 1
535i	4-dr Sedan-5P	I6/209	30760	3230	Note 1
635CSi	2-dr Coupe-4P	I6/209	41315	3380	Note 1
735i	4-dr Sedan-5P	I6/209	36880	3503	Note 1

Note 1: A total of 87,832 BMWs were sold in the U.S. during 1985.

ENGINE DATA: BASE FOUR (318i): Inline, overhead-cam four-cylinder. Cast iron block and light alloy head. **Displacement:** 108 cu. in. (1766 cc). **Bore & Stroke:** 3.50 x 2.80 in. (89 x 71 mm). **Compression Ratio:** 9.3:1. **Brake Horsepower:** 101 at 5800 rpm. **Torque:** 103 lbs.-ft. at 4500 rpm. Five main bearings. Bosch electronic fuel injection.

BASE SIX (325e, 528e): Inline, overhead-cam six-cylinder ("eta"). Cast iron block and light alloy head. **Displacement:** 164 cu. in. (2693 cc). **Bore & Stroke:** 3.31 x 3.19 in. (84 x 81 mm). **Compression Ratio:** 9.0:1. **Brake Horsepower:** 121 at 4250 rpm. **Torque:** 170 lbs.-ft. at 3250 rpm. Seven main bearings. Bosch electronic (port) fuel injection.

BASE TURBODIESEL SIX (524td): Inline, overhead-cam six-cylinder. Cast iron block and light alloy head. **Displacement:** 149 cu. in. (2443 cc). **Bore & Stroke:** 3.15 x 3.19 in. (80 x 81 mm). **Compression Ratio:** 22.0:1. **Brake Horsepower:** 114 at 4800 rpm. **Torque:** 155 lbs.-ft. at 2400 rpm. Seven main bearings. Electronic fuel injection.

BASE SIX (535i, 635CSi, 735i): Inline, overhead-cam six-cylinder. Cast iron block and light alloy head. **Displacement:** 209 cu. in. (3430 cc). **Bore & Stroke:** 3.62 x 3.39 in. (89 x 86 mm). **Compression Ratio:** 8.0:1. **Brake Horsepower:** 182 at 5400 rpm. **Torque:** 214 lbs.-ft. at 4000 rpm. Seven main bearings. Bosch electronic (port) fuel injection.

CHASSIS DATA: Wheelbase: (318i/325e) 101.2 in.; (528e/535i) 103.3 in.; (635CSi) 103.5 in.; (735i) 110.0 in. **Overall Length:** (318i/325e) 176.8 in.; (528e/535i) 189.0 in.; (635CSi) 193.8 in.; (735i) 197.4 in. **Height:** (318i/325e) 54.3 in.; (528e/535i) 55.7 in.; (635CSi) 53.7 in.; (735i) 56.3 in. **Width:** (318i/325e) 64.8 in.; (528e/535i) 66.0 in.; (635CSi) 67.9 in.; (735i) 70.9 in. **Front Tread:** (318i/325e) 55.4 in.; (528e/535i) 56.3 in.; (635CSi) 56.0 in.; (735i) 59.1 in. **Rear Tread:** (318i/325e) 55.7 in.; (528e/535i/635CSi) 57.5 in.; (735i) 59.7 in. **Standard Tires:** (318i/325e) 195/60HR14; (528e) 195/70HR14; (535i) 200/60VR390 Michelin TRX (635CSi) 220/55VR390; (735i) 205/70VR14.

TECHNICAL: Layout: front-engine, rear-drive. **Transmission:** five-speed (overdrive) manual; three-speed automatic available on 318i, four-speed automatic on other models. **Standard Final Drive Ratio:** (318i manual) 3.90:1; (318i auto.) 3.64:1; (325e) 2.79:1; (528e/535i) 2.93:1; (524td) 3.25:1; (635CSi/735i) 3.25:1. **Steering:** (318i/325e) power rack-and-pinion; (5/6/7-series) power recirculating ball. **Suspension (front):** (318i/325e) MacPherson struts with lower control arms, coil springs and anti-roll bar; (5/6/7-series) MacPherson struts with lower lateral links, coil springs and anti-roll bar. **Suspension (rear):** independent, semi-trailing arms with coil springs and anti-roll bar (except 318i). **Brakes:** front/rear disc except (318i) front disc, rear drum. **Body Construction:** steel unibody. **Fuel Tank:** (5/6-series) 16.6 gal.; (735i) 22.5 gallon.

MAJOR OPTIONS: Three-speed automatic transmission: 318i ($495). Four-speed automatic trans.: 325e ($595); 5/6/7-series ($795). Manual sunroof: 318i ($520). Leather upholstery: 325e ($790); 528e ($1090). Limited-slip differential ($370-$390). Cruise control: 318i ($240). TRX wheels/tires: 735i ($850). Rear headrests: 735i ($175). AM/FM stereo radio w/cassette player: 318i ($505). Metalic paint: 3-series ($420).

Note: Option prices shown above are approximate.

Manufacturer: Bayerische Motoren Werke AG, Munich, West Germany.

Distributor: BMW of North America, Inc., Montvale, New Jersey.

HISTORY: The 1985 models were introduced in the U.S. in November 1984. A 325iX with four-wheel-drive debuted in Europe at this time, but would not arrive in the U.S. market until 1988.

1986 BMW

325/e/es — SIX — Only the six-cylinder version of the 3-series was imported this year. In addition to a basic 325, sold in two- or four-door form at prices near the former 318i, BMW offered a more luxurious 325e four-door. An enthusiast's edition of the two-door also was available, named 325es. Anti-lock braking was now standard on all BMW models. A tri-mode electronic control was added to the available four-speed automatic transmission. It could be used in economy or sport mode, with shift points altered accordingly; or any of three lower gears could be held by selecting the third position. Stereo systems added anti-theft circuitry that made them inoperative if removed from the car. Standard features on the 325e included leather upholstery, an electric sunroof, trip computer, and cruise control. The 325es added such extras as sport front seats, heavy-duty suspension, limited-slip differential, and front and rear spoilers. All versions were powered by the 2.7-liter "eta" six, rated 121 horsepower. A five-speed manual gearbox remained standard.

528e — SIX — Anti-lock braking was added to the basic 5-series sedan, after debuting a year earlier on upper models. Stereo systems added anti-theft circuitry. A driver-selectable shift control was included in the optional four-speed automatic, as in the 3-series. As before, power came from the 164-cid (2.7-liter) "eta" six-cylinder engine.

524td — SIX — Like the 528e, BMW's Turbodiesel sedan added anti-lock braking this year, along with anti-theft protection for the stereo and selectable-shift for the available automatic transmission. Under the hood again was the 2.4-liter turbocharged diesel engine, rated 114 horsepower.

535i — SIX — Changes were minimal on the top-ranked 5-series sedan, except for the selectable-shift provision on the optional automatic transmission.

635CSi — SIX — Power front seats added an electronic memory this year, and the back window added a sun shade. Otherwise, little was new in BMW's coupe. As in other BMWs, the available automatic transmission added a selectable-shift control.

735i — SIX — Not much was new on the basic 735i sedan, but BMW introduced a luxury version called, logically, Luxus (or L7). That one came with silver-grey leather upholstery, on the dashboard and door panels as well as the seats. Also installed was a driver's-side airbag, making this BMW the first in the U.S. to get such protection. Also new: the selectable-shift control (with automatic), electronic front-seat memory and sun shade, as described for the 635CSi coupe; plus a heated driver's seat. As before, power came from the same 3.4-liter six-cylinder engine used on the 535i and 635CSi.

I.D. DATA: A 17-symbol Vehicle Identification Number is on the upper left of the dashboard, visible through the windshield; or on steering column. Symbols 1-3 ('WBA') indicate manufacturer, make and type. Symbols 4-5 denote car line and series ('AB' = 325/es 2-dr; 'AE' = 325/e 4-dr; 'DK' = 528e; 'DC' = 535i; 'DB' = 524td; 'EC' = 635CSi; 'FH' = 735i; 'FG' = L7). Symbol six (a digit) denotes the body type. Symbol seven identifies the engine. The eighth symbol indicates the restraint system, followed by a check digit. Symbol ten indicates model year ('G' = 1986). Symbol 11 identifies the assembly plant. The final six digits are the sequential serial number, starting with 000001. Engine number is on left of block, above the starter.

Model	Body Type & Seating	Engine Type/CID	P.O.E. Price	Weight (lbs.)	Prod. Total
325	2-dr Sedan-5P	I6/164	19560	2723	Note 1
325es	2-dr Sedan-5P	I6/164	21950	2778	Note 1
325	4-dr Sedan-5P	I6/164	20055	2767	Note 1
325e	4-dr Sedan-5P	I6/164	22650	2789	Note 1
528e	4-dr Sedan-5P	I6/164	26280	3075	Note 1
524td	4-dr Sedan-5P	I6/149	25560	3320	Note 1
535i	4-dr Sedan-5P	I6/209	31175	3250	Note 1
635CSi	2-dr Coupe-4P	I6/209	41965	3380	Note 1
735i	4-dr Sedan-5P	I6/209	38280	3540	Note 1
L7	4-dr Sedan-5P	I6/209	42920	3585	Note 1

Note 1: A total of 96,759 BMWs were sold in the U.S. during 1986.

ENGINE DATA: BASE SIX (325/e/es, 528e): Inline, overhead-cam six-cylinder ("eta"). Cast iron block and light alloy head. **Displacement:** 164 cu. in. (2693 cc). **Bore & Stroke:** 3.31 x 3.19 in. (84 x 81 mm). **Compression Ratio:** 9.0:1. **Brake Horsepower:** 121 at 4250 rpm. **Torque:** 170 lbs.-ft. at 3250 rpm. Seven main bearings. Electronic (port) fuel injection.

BASE TURBODIESEL SIX (524td): Inline, overhead-cam six-cylinder. Cast iron block and light alloy head. **Displacement:** 149 cu. in. (2443 cc). **Bore & Stroke:** 3.15 x 3.19 in. (80 x 81 mm). **Compression Ratio:** 22.0:1. **Brake Horsepower:** 114 at 4800 rpm. **Torque:** 155 lbs.-ft. at 2400 rpm. Seven main bearings. Electronic fuel injection.

BASE SIX (535i, 635CSi, 735i, L7): Inline, overhead-cam six-cylinder. Cast iron block and light alloy head. **Displacement:** 209 cu. in. (3430 cc). **Bore & Stroke:** 3.62 x 3.39 in. (89 x 86 mm). **Compression Ratio:** 8.0:1. **Brake Horsepower:** 182 at 5400 rpm. **Torque:** 214 lbs.-ft. at 4000 rpm. Seven main bearings. Electronic (port) fuel injection.

CHASSIS DATA: Wheelbase: (3-series) 101.2 in.; (528e/535i) 103.3 in.; (635CSi) 103.5 in.; (735i) 110.0 in. Overall Length: (3-series) 176.8 in.; (528e/535i) 189.0 in.; (635CSi) 193.8 in.; (735i) 197.4 in. Height: (3-series) 54.3 in.; (528e/535i) 55.7 in.; (635CSi) 53.7 in.; (735i) 56.3 in. Width: (3-series) 64.8 in.; (528e/535i) 66.0 in.; (635CSi) 67.9 in.; (735i) 70.9 in. Front Tread: (3-series) 55.4 in.; (528e/535i) 56.3 in.; (635CSi) 56.0 in.; (735i) 59.1 in. Rear Tread: (3-series) 55.7 in.; (528e/535i/635CSi) 57.5 in.; (735i) 59.7 in. Standard Tires: (3-series) 195/60HR14; (528e) 195/70HR14; (535i) 200/60VR390 Michelin TRX (635CSi) 220/55VR390; (735i) 205/70VR14.

TECHNICAL: Layout: front-engine, rear-drive. Transmission: five-speed (overdrive) manual; four-speed automatic available. Standard Final Drive Ratio: (3-series) 2.79:1; (528e/535i) 2.93:1; (524td) 3.25:1; (635CSi/735i) 3.25:1. Steering: (3-series) power rack-and-pinion; (5/6/7-series) power recirculating ball. Suspension (front): (3-series) MacPherson struts with lower control arms, coil springs and anti-roll bar; (5/6/7-series) MacPherson struts with lower lateral links, coil springs and anti-roll bar. Suspension (rear): independent, semi-trailing arms with coil springs and anti-roll bar. Brakes: front/rear disc. Body Construction: steel unibody. Fuel Tank: (3-series) 14.5 gal.; (5/6-series) 16.6 gal.; (735i) 22.5 gallon.

MAJOR OPTIONS: Four-speed automatic trans.: 3-series ($595); 5/6/7-series ($795). Leather upholstery: 325es ($790); 528e ($1090). Heated seat: 735i ($200). Special sound system: 325e/es, 524td, L7 ($225). Limited-slip differential ($370-$390). TRX wheels/tires: 735i ($850).
Manufacturer: Bayerische Motoren Werke AG, Munich, West Germany.
Distributor: BMW of North America, Inc., Montvale, New Jersey.
HISTORY: The 1986 models were introduced in the U.S. in November 1985. The 535i, 635CSi, 735i and L7 warranted a guzzler tax.
  A sporty M3 two-door with twin-cam engine, developed by BMW Motorsport, became available in Europe this year but would not arrive in the U.S. until 1988. A restyled 7-series sedan debuted in Europe in 1986, as did a BMW-built 3-series convertible. Both would arrive in the U.S. later.

1987 BMW

1987 BMW 325i convertible (BMW of North America Inc.)

325/e/es/i/iC/iS — SIX — After starting the new season as a carryover, the 3-series broadened considerably. A 325iC convertible joined the two- and four-door sedans late in the model year. So did a new 325iS two-door and 325i four-door. The 325e luxury sedan and 325es enthusiast's two-door also continued, making a total of seven versions. All were powered by the familiar 2.7-liter overhead-cam "eta" six, except for the 325i/iS and the convertible, which carried a 2.5-liter six. Standard 325 equipment included a five-speed manual gearbox, power steering and four-wheel disc brakes (with anti-locking), halogen foglamps, power mirrors and windows, center door locking, air conditioning, AM/FM stereo with cassette and anti-theft, a two-way manual sunroof, and cloth or leatherette upholstery. Alloy wheels held 195/65HR14 tires. The 325e added leather upholstery, leather-covered steering wheel and gearshift knob, adjustable rear head restraints, folding rear center armrest, cruise control, an on-board computer, and power sunroof. The 325es two-door included a front spoiler with integrated foglamps, rear spoiler, sport seats, sport suspension, limited-slip differential, M-Technic steering wheel, and map lights.

528e — SIX — Changes were minimal in BMW's 5-series sedan, as powered by a gas engine. The 524td turbodiesel faded out of the lineup this year; see previous listing for details.

535i/iS — SIX — Little was new in the upper 5-series, except for the addition of a new 535iS model that included a front air dam, rear spoiler, M-Technic leather-wrapped steering wheel, and eight-way sport seats. The 535iS was capable of 130+ mph and could accelerate from a standstill to 60 mph in less than 7.5 seconds.

635CSi — SIX — Appearance and equipment for BMW's long-lived six-cylinder coupe were similar to 1986.

L6/M6 — SIX — Two new versions of the BMW coupe body were introduced this year, with two different engines. The L6 came with a 3.4-liter (209-cid) single-cam six, the M6 with a 3.5-liter (211-cid) twin-overhead-cam engine. Standard equipment on the L6 included a four-speed automatic transmission, power four-wheel disc brakes (anti-locking), power steering, automatic air conditioning with separate rear system, cruise control, intermittent wipers, front spoiler, foglamps, heated windshield-washer jets, power windows and mirrors, heated driver's door lock, central locking (including trunk), eight-way power front seats with three-position memory, a time-delay courtesy light, telescoping steering column, tinted glass, and tachometer. Also standard: a rear defogger, power two-way sunroof, rear sunshade, and AM/FM stereo radio with cassette player, equalizer and anti-theft circuitry. Hand-stitched Nappa leather was used on seats,

lower dashboard, console, and doors. Forged alloy wheels held 220/55VR390 tires. The M6 coupe added the 24-valve engine, five-speed manual gearbox, sport suspension, limited-slip differential, and 245/45VR415 Michelin TRX tires.

1987 BMW 735i four-door sedan. (BMW of North America Inc.)

735i — SIX — A new 7-series sedan was anticipated, but otherwise the former model continued with little change, in basic and posh L7 editions. The latter included an all-leather interior, two-stage heated front seats, driver's airbag, and 220/55VR390 TRX tires on aluminum wheels.

I.D. DATA: A 17-symbol Vehicle Identification Number is on the upper left of the dashboard, visible through the windshield; or on steering column. Symbols 1-3 ('WBA') indicate manufacturer, make and type. Symbols 4-5 denote car line and series ('AB' = 325/es 2-dr; 'AE' = 325/e 4-dr; 'AA' = 325iS 2-dr; 'AD' = 325i 4-dr; 'BB' = 325i conv.; 'DK' = 528e; 'DC' = 535i/iS; 'EC' = 635CSi/L6; 'EE' = M6; 'FH' = 735i; 'FG' = L7). Symbol six (a digit) denotes the body type. Symbol seven identifies the engine. The eighth symbol indicates the restraint system, followed by a check digit. Symbol ten indicates model year ('H' = 1987). Symbol 11 identifies the assembly plant. The final six digits are the sequential serial number, starting with 000001. Engine number is on left of block, above the starter.

Model	Body Type & Seating	Engine Type/CID	P.O.E. Price	Weight (lbs.)	Prod. Total
325	2-dr Sedan-5P	I6/164	21475	2723	Note 1
325	4-dr Sedan-5P	I6/164	22015	2767	Note 1
325es	2-dr Sedan-5P	I6/164	24370	2778	Note 1
325e	4-dr Sedan-5P	I6/164	25150	2789	Note 1
325iS	2-dr Sedan-5P	I6/152	26990	2813	Note 1
325i	4-dr Sedan-5P	I6/152	26990	2850	Note 1
325iC	2-dr Conv-4P	I6/152	28875	3015	Note 1
528e	4-dr Sedan-5P	I6/164	28330	3075	Note 1
535i	4-dr Sedan-5P	I6/209	33600	3250	Note 1
535iS	4-dr Sedan-5P	I6/209	35200	3250	Note 1
635CSi	2-dr Coupe-4P	I6/209	46965	3380	Note 1
L6	2-dr Coupe-4P	I6/209	49500	3490	Note 1
M6	2-dr Coupe-4P	I6/211	55950	3570	Note 1
735i	4-dr Sedan-5P	I6/209	42475	3585	Note 1
L7	4-dr Sedan-5P	I6/209	46675	3585	Note 1

Note 1: A total of 87,839 BMWs were sold in the U.S. during 1987.

ENGINE DATA: BASE SIX (325/e/es, 528e): Inline, overhead-cam six-cylinder ("eta"). Cast iron block and light alloy head. Displacement: 164 cu. in. (2693 cc). Bore & Stroke: 3.31 x 3.19 in. (84 x 81 mm). Compression Ratio: 9.0:1. Brake Horsepower: 121 at 4250 rpm. Torque: 170 lbs.-ft. at 3250 rpm. Seven main bearings. Electronic (port) fuel injection.

BASE SIX (325i/iS, 325iC conv.): Inline, overhead-cam six-cylinder. Cast iron block and light alloy head. Displacement: 152 cu. in. (2495 cc). Bore & Stroke: 3.31 x 2.95 in. (84 x 75 mm). Compression Ratio: 8.8:1. Brake Horsepower: 168 at 5800 rpm. Torque: 164 lbs.-ft. at 4300 rpm. Electronic (port) fuel injection.

BASE SIX (535i/iS, 635CSi, L6, L7, 735i): Inline, overhead-cam six-cylinder. Cast iron block and light alloy head. Displacement: 209 cu. in. (3430 cc). Bore & Stroke: 3.62 x 3.39 in. (89 x 86 mm). Compression Ratio: 8.0:1. Brake Horsepower: 182 at 5400 rpm. Torque: 214 lbs.-ft. at 4000 rpm. Seven main bearings. Electronic (port) fuel injection.

BASE SIX (M6): Inline, dual-overhead-cam six-cylinder. Cast iron block and light alloy head. Displacement: 211 cu. in. (3453 cc). Bore & Stroke: 3.68 x 3.31 in. (93 x 84 mm). Compression Ratio: 9.8:1. Brake Horsepower: 256 at 6500 rpm. Torque: 243 lbs.-ft. at 4500 rpm. Seven main bearings. Electronic (port) fuel injection.

CHASSIS DATA: Wheelbase: (3-series) 101.2 in.; (528/535) 103.3 in.; (6-series) 103.5 in.; (735i) 110.0 in. Overall Length: (3-series) 176.8 in.; (528/535) 189.0 in.; (6-series) 193.8 in.; (735i) 197.4 in. Height: (3-series) 54.3 in.; (528/535) 55.7 in.; (6-series) 53.7 in.; (735i) 56.3 in. Width: (3-series) 64.8 in.; (528/535) 66.0 in.; (6-series) 67.9 in.; (735i) 70.9 in. Front Tread: (3-series) 55.4 in.; (528/535) 56.3 in.; (6-series) 56.0 in.; (735i) 59.1 in. Rear Tread: (3-series) 55.7 in.; (528/535) 57.5 in.; (6-series) 57.5 in.; (735i) 59.7 in. Standard Tires: (3-series) 195/65HR14; (528e) 195/70HR14; (535i) 200/60VR390 Michelin TRX; (635CSi/L6/L7) 220/55VR390; (M6) 245/45VR415; (735i) 205/70VR14.

TECHNICAL: Layout: front-engine, rear-drive. Transmission: five-speed (overdrive) manual; four-speed automatic available. Automatic standard on L6. Standard Final Drive Ratio: (3-series) 2.79:1; (528e/535i) 2.93:1; (635CSi/735i) 3.25:1. Steering: (3-series) power rack-and-pinion; (5/6/7-series) power recirculating ball. Suspension (front): (3-series) MacPherson struts with lower control arms, coil springs and anti-roll bar; (5/6/7-series) MacPherson struts with lower lateral links, coil springs and anti-roll bar. Suspension (rear): independent, semi-trailing arms with coil springs and anti-roll bar. Brakes: front/rear disc. Body Construction: steel unibody. Fuel Tank: (3-series) 14.5 gal.; (5/6-series) 16.6 gal.; (735i) 22.5 gallon.

MAJOR OPTIONS: Four-speed automatic trans.: 3-series ($595); 528e ($595); 535i, 6/7-series ($795). Leather upholstery: 325es ($850); 528e ($1090). Limited-slip differential: 325e ($370); 535i ($390). Uprated sound system: 3-series/528e ($225); N/A on base 325. Heated front seats: 735i ($200). TRX wheels/tires: 735i ($850). Metallic paint: 3-series ($335).
Manufacturer: Bayerische Motoren Werke AG, Munich, West Germany.
Distributor: BMW of North America, Inc., Montvale, New Jersey.
HISTORY: The 1987 models were introduced in the U.S. in September 1986, except (535) November 1986.

1988 BMW

1988 BMW 3-Series touring. (William Siuru Jr.)

325/i/iC/iS/iX — SIX — Joining the already-extensive selection of 3-series models was a new four-wheel-drive 325iX, intended to rival the Audi Quattro. The full-time 4WD system sent 37 percent of output to the front wheels, 63 percent to the rear. To help increase traction, front and center differentials locked automatically when wheelspin was detected. Only a two-door was offered with 4WD, carrying the same 2.5-liter engine as the 325i/iS sedans and the convertible. Base models continued with the 2.7-liter "eta" six, which got a boost to 127 bhp. The 325i/iS versions included cruise control, leather upholstery, an on-board computer, and premium sound system with equalizer. The 325iS and convertible contained sports seats. A limited-slip differential went into the 325iS.

M3 — FOUR — A high-performance version of the 3-series two-door arrived this season, powered by a twin-overhead-cam 2.3-liter four-cylinder engine, with four valves per cylinder. The engine was rated 192 horsepower. Standard equipment was similar to the regular 3-series, but included sport front seats with adjustable thigh support, a specially-contoured rear seat, Motorsport steering wheel, 8000-rpm tachometer, oil temperature gauge, uprated suspension, and 205/55VR15 tires. The M3 was developed by BMW Motorsport.

528e/535i/535iS — SIX — Changes were minimal in BMW's 5-series sedans, powered by a 2.7-liter six (528e), which gained six horsepower; or a 3.4-liter six (535i/iS). Standard 528e equipment included a five-speed manual gearbox, power brakes and steering, ABS, automatic air conditioning, power windows, central locking (including trunk), cruise control, tilt/slide power sunroof, power mirrors, heated driver's door lock, eight-way power front seats, and cloth or leatherette upholstery. The 535i added leather upholstery and steering wheel trim, plus Michelin TRX 200/60VR390 tires. The 535iS included aero body trim, a sport suspension, and sport leather seats.

M5 — SIX — A new high-performance version of the 5-series shared engines with the M6 coupe, introduced a year earlier. That was a twin-cam 3.5-liter six, rated 256 horsepower. Equipment was similar to the regular 5-series, but included a deep front air dam with foglamps, limited-slip differential, blackout body trim, decklid spoiler, leather seats and door panels (as well as dashboard and console), ten-way power sport seats, velour trunk trim, and 225/50VR16 tires. This sport/luxury four-door was built by BMW Motorsport GmbH. European editions were rated 315 horsepower.

635CSi/M6 — SIX — BMW's coupes both were potent this year. The 635CSi gained 26 horsepower (now 208 bhp) by adopting the engine from the 735i sedan. As introduced for 1987, the M6 coupe used a 3.5-liter (211-cid) twin-overhead-cam engine rated 256 horsepower. Otherwise, appearance and equipment were similar to 1987. An upgraded L6 was expected, but did not make the lineup this year.

735i — SIX — Introduced as an early '88 model, the revised 735i sedan went on sale in the U.S. in spring 1987, powered by a more potent version of the 3.4-liter six-cylinder engine, producing 208 horsepower. For the 1988 model year, a vacuum power brake booster replaced the original hydraulic unit, and the driver's seat added a power lumbar support adjustor. A four-speed overdrive automatic transmission was standard, but a five-speed manual gearbox was available as a credit option. Luxuries were bountiful. Standard 735i equipment included a driver's airbag, automatic climate control air conditioning (separate right/left controls), eight-way power front seats (three-position driver's memory), heated power mirrors, heated driver's door lock, AM/FM stereo with cassette and equalizer, leather-wrapped steering wheel, velour carpeting, and full leather interior with Bubinga wood trim. Intermittent wipers had speed-sensitive contact pressure and wiping speed, a heated wiper "parking" area, and heated washer jets. Cast alloy wheels held 225/60VR15 tires. The new 7-series used electronic systems to control anti-lock braking, anti-spin control, and shock-absorber adjustment. A longer-wheelbase 735iL version joined the original in summer 1987, wearing the larger body (from the new 750iL) but powered by the 735's six-cylinder engine.

750iL — V-12 — A larger 12-cylinder BMW sedan became available for the 1988 model year. The "750" portion of its name stood for the 5.0-liter overhead-cam aluminum engine, while "L" denoted the longer (116-inch) wheelbase, 4.5 inches longer than the 735i. This was BMW's first V-12, rated 296 horsepower and putting out 332 lbs.-ft. of torque. Each cylinder bank had its own electronic management system. Only the four-speed overdrive automatic transmission was available, with electronic shift controls. "Drive-by-wire" electronic throttle control eliminated the customary mechanical linkage between gas pedal and throttle. Standard equipment included a hydraulic-leveling rear suspension and heated front seats. Speed was limited electronically to 155 mph.

I.D. DATA: A 17-symbol Vehicle Identification Number on the upper left of the dashboard is visible through the windshield. Symbols 1-3 ('WBA') indicate manufacturer, make and type. Symbols 4-5 denote car line and series ('AB' = 325/iX 2-dr; 'AE' = 325 4-dr; 'AA' = 325iS 2-dr; 'AD' = 325i 4-dr; 'AK' = M3; 'BB' = 325i conv.; 'DK' = 528e; 'DC' = 535i/iS, M5; 'EC' = 635CSi; 'EE' = M6; 'GB' = 735i; 'GC' = 735iL/750iL). Symbol six (a digit) denotes the body type. Symbol seven identifies the engine. The eighth symbol indicates the restraint system, followed by a check digit. Symbol ten indicates model year ('J' = 1988). Symbol 11 identifies the assembly plant. The final six digits are the sequential serial number, starting with 000001.

Model	Body Type & Seating	Engine Type/CID	P.O.E. Price	Weight (lbs.)	Prod. Total
325	2-dr Sedan-5P	I6/164	23750	2765	Note 1
325	4-dr Sedan-5P	I6/164	24400	2809	Note 1
325iS	2-dr Sedan-5P	I6/152	28400	2865	Note 1
325i	4-dr Sedan-5P	I6/152	28400	2895	Note 1
325iC	2-dr Conv-4P	I6/152	32500	3055	Note 1
325iX	2-dr Sedan-5P	I6/152	32800	3010	Note 1
M3	2-dr Sedan-5P	I4/140	34000	2735	Note 1
528e	4-dr Sedan-5P	I6/164	31500	3100	Note 1
535i	4-dr Sedan-5P	I6/209	36000	3270	Note 1
535iS	4-dr Sedan-5P	I6/209	36900	3270	Note 1
M5	4-dr Sedan-5P	I6/211	46500	3420	Note 1
635CSi	2-dr Coupe-4P	I6/209	46000	3530	Note 1
M6	2-dr Coupe-4P	I6/211	55950	3570	Note 1
735i	4-dr Sedan-5P	I6/209	53000	3835	Note 1
735iL	4-dr Sedan-5P	I6/209	58000	4015	Note 1
750iL	4-dr Sedan-5P	V12/304	67000	4235	Note 1

Note 1: A total of 73,359 BMWs were sold in the U.S. during 1988.

ENGINE DATA: BASE FOUR (M3): Inline, dual-overhead-cam four-cylinder. Cast iron block and light alloy head. **Displacement:** 140 cu. in. (2302 cc). **Bore & Stroke:** 3.68 x 3.31 in. (93 x 84 mm). **Compression Ratio:** 10.5:1. **Brake Horsepower:** 192 at 6750 rpm. **Torque:** 170 lbs.-ft. at 4750 rpm. Electronic (port) fuel injection.

BASE SIX (325, 528e): Inline, overhead-cam six-cylinder ("eta"). Cast iron block and light alloy head. **Displacement:** 164 cu. in. (2693 cc). **Bore & Stroke:** 3.31 x 3.19 in. (84 x 81 mm). **Compression Ratio:** 8.5:1. **Brake Horsepower:** 127 at 4800 rpm. **Torque:** 170 lbs.-ft. at 3200 rpm. Seven main bearings. Electronic (port) fuel injection.

BASE SIX (325i/iS/iX, 325iC conv.): Inline, overhead-cam six-cylinder. Cast iron block and light alloy head. **Displacement:** 152 cu. in. (2495 cc). **Bore & Stroke:** 3.31 x 2.95 in. (84 x 75 mm). **Compression Ratio:** 8.8:1. **Brake Horsepower:** 168 at 5800 rpm. **Torque:** 164 lbs.-ft. at 4300 rpm. Electronic (port) fuel injection.

BASE SIX (535i): Inline, overhead-cam six-cylinder. Cast iron block and light alloy head. **Displacement:** 209 cu. in. (3430 cc). **Bore & Stroke:** 3.62 x 3.39 in. (89 x 86 mm). **Compression Ratio:** 8.0:1. **Brake Horsepower:** 182 at 5400 rpm. **Torque:** 214 lbs.-ft. at 4000 rpm. Seven main bearings. Electronic (port) fuel injection.

BASE SIX (635CSi, 735i): Same as 3.4-liter six above, except — **Compression Ratio:** 9.0:1. **Brake Horsepower:** 208 at 5700 rpm. **Torque:** 225 lbs.-ft. at 4000 rpm.

BASE SIX (M5, M6): Inline, dual-overhead-cam six-cylinder. Cast iron block and light alloy head. **Displacement:** 211 cu. in. (3453 cc). **Bore & Stroke:** 3.68 x 3.31 in. (93 x 84 mm). **Compression Ratio:** 9.8:1. **Brake Horsepower:** 256 at 6500 rpm. **Torque:** 243 lbs.-ft. at 4500 rpm. Seven main bearings. Electronic (port) fuel injection.

BASE V-12 (750iL): Overhead-cam vee-type 12-cylinder. Aluminum block and heads. **Displacement:** 304 cu. in. (4988 cc). **Bore & Stroke:** 3.31 x 2.95 in. (84 x 75 mm). **Compression Ratio:** 8.8:1. **Brake Horsepower:** 296-300 at 5200 rpm. **Torque:** 332 lbs.-ft. at 4100 rpm. Electronic (port) fuel injection.

CHASSIS DATA: Wheelbase: (3-series) 101.2 in.; (M3) 101.0 in.; (5-series) 103.3 in.; (6-series) 103.5 in.; (735i) 111.5 in.; (750iL) 116.0 in. **Overall Length:** (3-series) 175.6 in.; (325iC conv.) 175.2 in.; (M3) 171.1 in.; (5-series) 189.0 in.; (6-series) 193.8 in.; (735i) 193.3 in.; (750iL) 197.8 in. **Height:** (3-series) 54.3 in.; (325i conv.) 53.9 in.; (M3) 53.9 in.; (5-series) 55.7 in.; (6-series) 53.7 in.; (735i) 55.6 in.; (750iL) 55.1 in. **Width:** (3-series) 64.8 in.; (M3) 66.1 in.; (5-series) 66.0 in.; (6-series) 67.9 in.; (735i/750iL) 72.6 in. **Front Tread:** (3-series) 55.4 in.; (M3) 55.6 in.; (5/6-series) 56.3 in.; (735i) 60.1 in.; (750iL) 60.2 in. **Rear Tread:** (3-series) 55.7 in.; (M3) 56.1 in.; (5/6-series) 57.5 in.; (735i) 61.0 in.; (750iL) 61.3 in. **Standard Tires:** (3-series) 195/65HR14; (M3) 205/55VR15; (528e) 195/70HR14; (535i) 200/60VR390 Michelin TRX; (M5) 225/50VR16; (635CSi/L6) 220/55VR390; (M6) 245/45VR415 Michelin TRX; (735i/750iL) 225/60VR15.

TECHNICAL: Layout: front-engine, rear-drive. **Transmission:** five-speed (overdrive) manual standard, except (735i/750iL) four-speed automatic standard. Automatic optional on other models. **Steering:** (3-series) power rack-and-pinion; (5/6/7-series) power recirculating ball. **Brakes:** front/rear disc (anti-locking). **Body Construction:** steel unibody. **Fuel Tank:** (3-series) 14.5 or 16.4 gal.; (5/6-series) 16.6 gal.; (735i) 21.5 gal.; (750iL) 24 gallon.

MAJOR OPTIONS: Four-speed automatic trans.: 3-series ($645); 528e ($645); 635CSi, 535i/iS ($795). Leather upholstery: 528e ($1090). Limited-slip differential: 325 ($370); 5/6/7-series ($390). Heated driver's seat: M5, 6/7-series ($200). Heated front seats: 325iC conv., M5, 735i ($200). Hard top: 325iC conv. ($3500). Metallic paint: 3-series ($375).

ADDITIONAL MODELS: A Z1 roadster with two-seat plastic body on a steel monocoque chassis was introduced in Europe. Developed by BMW Technik GmbH, the Z1 had a mid-mounted 2494-cc six-cylinder engine rated 170 bhp, vertical-retracting doors, and a Z-arm rear axle.

Manufacturer: Bayerische Motoren Werke AG, Munich, West Germany.

Distributor: BMW of North America, Inc., Woodcliff Lake, New Jersey.

HISTORY: The 1988 models were introduced in the U.S. in October 1987, except (M5, 735i) February 1987; (M3) July 1987; (735iL) May 1988. Most BMW models (except the 3-series) were subject to the gas guzzler tax.

1989 BMW

1989 BMW 535i four-door sedan. (BMW of North America Inc.)

325 — SIX — New body-color bumpers shortened all 3-series models (except the convertible) by 5.4 inches this year. Instead of the former 2.7-liter "eta" engine, all 325 models now carried the smaller 2.5-liter six, rated 168 horsepower. Except for a switch to V-rated tires, appearance and equipment was similar to 1988. Both a two-door and four-door version of the four-wheel-drive 325iX were offered this year, with either manual or automatic transmission. A thinner center brake lamp was installed on the convertible.

M3 — FOUR — Little change was evident on the high-performance version of the 3-series, except for a change from a roof-mounted radio antenna to a windshield version. The 16-valve four-cylinder engine was again rated 192 horsepower. The M3 was now the only 3-series model that did not have an optional automatic transmission.

525i/535i — SIX — A total restyling hit the 5-series this year, the first significant change since its debut in 1975. Only the powertrains were carried over from 1988: the 168-horsepower, 2.5-liter inline six (in the 525i) and the 208-bhp, 3.4-liter six (in the 535i). Appearance was similar to the larger 7-series. Wheelbase was 5.4 inches longer than before (at 108.7 inches), but overall length shrunk by 3.2 inches. The new body measured two extra inches in width, and added close to 300 pounds. Both models came with a standard five-speed manual gearbox, with four-speed automatic optional. An M5 version was introduced in Europe, but not yet available in the U.S. Standard 525i equipment included power steering/brakes, air conditioning with individual temperature controls, leather power front bucket seats, power windows and locks, heated power mirrors, foglamps, tachometer, tinted glass, front/rear reading lights, power sunroof, and 205/65VR15 tires on alloy wheels. The 535i added a driver's airbag, leather-wrapped steering wheel, automatic climate control, and 225/60VR15 tires.

1989 BMW 635CSi two-door sport coupe. (BMW of North America Inc.)

635CSi/M6 — SIX — Both versions of the BMW coupes were carryovers with minimal change. The M6 was actually not produced this year, but leftovers continued on sale. Joining the option list, for installation by dealers, was a CD player (actually a changer). The 635CSi again was powered by the 208-horsepower, 3.5-liter six, as adopted in 1988. This year, it borrowed reworked Servotronic power steering from the 7-series. Standard transmission was the four-speed automatic with driver-selectable economy, sport and manual-shift models. A five-speed manual gearbox was offered at no extra cost. The M6 coupe, built by BMW Motorsport, came only with manual shift and the 256-bhp, 3.5-liter twin-cam six. It featured wider wheels/tires, larger-diameter brakes, a firmer sports suspension, and small decklid spoiler.

735i — SIX — Both the 735i and longer 735iL added infrared remote control to their standard central door-lock system, and received a modified version of the ZF Servotronic power steering that responded to road speed (rather than engine speed). Final drive switched from 3.64:1 to 3.91:1, to boost acceleration. The standard four-speed automatic now had two modes (Economy and Manual) rather than three. Dealers could install a trunk-mounted CD changer.

750iL — V-12 — The 12-cylinder sedan, on 116-inch wheelbase, added an infrared remote control for the door-lock system and modified Servotronic power steering, as in the 735 series. Standard equipment was similar to the 735, but added an anti-theft warning device, Elmwood trim, additional leather trim, a cellular phone, and forged alloy wheels. Heated front seats were standard, as was a trunk-mounted compact-disc changer/player.

I.D. DATA: A 17-symbol Vehicle Identification Number on the upper left of the dashboard is visible through the windshield. Symbols 1-3 ('WB') indicate manufacturer, make and type. Symbols 4-5 denote car line and series ('AB' = 325iX 2-dr; 'AE' = 325iX 4-dr; 'AA' = 325i/iS 2-dr; 'AD' = 325i 4-dr; 'AK' = M3; 'BB' = 325i conv.; 'HC' = M3; 'HD' = 535i; 'EC' = 635CSi; 'EE' = M6; 'GB' = 735i; 'GC' = 735iL/750iL). Symbol six (a digit) denotes the body type. Symbol seven identifies the engine. The eighth symbol ('3') indicates the restraint system, followed by a check digit. Symbol ten indicates model year ('K' = 1989). Symbol 11 identifies the assembly plant. The final six digits are the sequential serial number, starting with 000001.

Model	Body Type & Seating	Engine Type/CID	P.O.E. Price	Weight (lbs.)	Prod. Total
325i	2-dr Sedan-5P	I6/152	24650	2811	Note 1
325i	4-dr Sedan-5P	I6/152	25450	2855	Note 1
325iS	2-dr Sedan-5P	I6/152	28950	2844	Note 1
325iX	2-dr Sedan-5P	I6/152	29950	3010	Note 1
325iX	4-dr Sedan-5P	I6/152	30750	3054	Note 1
325iC	2-dr Conv-4P	I6/152	33850	3055	Note 1
M3	2-dr Sedan-5P	I4/140	34950	2865	Note 1
525i	4-dr Sedan-5P	I6/152	37000	3395	Note 1
535i	4-dr Sedan-5P	I6/209	43600	3530	Note 1
635CSi	2-dr Coupe-4P	I6/209	47000	3530	Note 1
M6	2-dr Coupe-4P	I6/211	55950	3570	Note 1
735i	4-dr Sedan-5P	I6/209	54000	3835	Note 1
735iL	4-dr Sedan-5P	I6/209	58000	4015	Note 1
750iL	4-dr Seand-5P	V12/304	70000	4235	Note 1

Note 1: A total of 64,881 BMWs were sold in the U.S. during 1989.

ENGINE DATA: BASE FOUR (M3): Inline, dual-overhead-cam four-cylinder. Cast iron block and light alloy head. **Displacement:** 140 cu. in. (2302 cc). **Bore & Stroke:** 3.68 x 3.31 in. (93 x 84 mm). **Compression Ratio:** 10.5:1. **Brake Horsepower:** 192 at 6750 rpm. **Torque:** 170 lbs.-ft. at 4750 rpm. Electronic (port) fuel injection.

BASE SIX (325 series, 525i): Inline, overhead-cam six-cylinder. Cast iron block and light alloy head. **Displacement:** 152 cu. in. (2495 cc). **Bore & Stroke:** 3.31 x 2.95 in. (84 x 75 mm). **Compression Ratio:** 8.8:1. **Brake Horsepower:** 168 at 5800 rpm. **Torque:** 164 lbs.-ft. at 4300 rpm. Electronic (port) fuel injection.

BASE SIX (535i, 635CSi, 735i): Inline, overhead-cam six-cylinder. Cast iron block and light alloy head. **Displacement:** 209 cu. in. (3430 cc). **Bore & Stroke:** 3.62 x 3.39 in. (89 x 86 mm). **Compression Ratio:** 9.0:1. **Brake Horsepower:** 208 at 5700 rpm. **Torque:** 225 lbs.-ft. at 4000 rpm. Seven main bearings. Electronic (port) fuel injection.

BASE SIX (M6): Inline, dual-overhead-cam six-cylinder. Cast iron block and light alloy head. **Displacement:** 211 cu. in. (3453 cc). **Compression Ratio:** 9.8:1. **Bore & Stroke:** 3.68 x 3.31 in. (93 x 84 mm). **Brake Horsepower:** 256 at 6500 rpm. **Torque:** 243 lbs.-ft. at 4500 rpm. Seven main bearings. Electronic (port) fuel injection.

BASE V-12 (750iL): Overhead-cam vee-type 12-cylinder. Aluminum block and heads. **Displacement:** 304 cu. in. (4988 cc). **Bore & Stroke:** 3.31 x 2.95 in. (84 x 75 mm). **Compression Ratio:** 8.8:1. **Brake Horsepower:** 300 at 5200 rpm. **Torque:** 332 lbs.-ft. at 4100 rpm. Electronic (port) fuel injection.

CHASSIS DATA: Wheelbase: (3-series) 101.2 in.; (M3) 101.0 in.; (5-series) 108.7 in.; (6-series) 103.3 in.; (735i) 111.5 in.; (735iL/750iL) 116.0 in. **Overall Length:** (3-series) 170.2 in.; (325i conv.) 175.2 in.; (M3) 171.1 in.; (5-series) 185.8 in.; (6-series) 189.6 in.; (735i) 193.3 in.; (735iL/750iL) 197.8 in. **Height:** (3-series) 54.3 in.; (325i conv.) 53.9 in.; (M3) 53.9 in.; (5-series) 55.6 in.; (6-series) 53.7 in.; (735i) 55.6 in.; (735iL/750iL) 55.1 in. **Width:** (3-series) 64.8 in.; (M3) 66.1 in.; (5-series) 68.9 in.; (6-series) 67.9 in.; (7-series) 72.6 in. **Front Tread:** (3-series) 55.4 in.; (M3) 55.6 in.; (5-series) 57.7 in.; (6-series) 56.3 in.; (735i) 60.1 in.; (735iL/750iL) 60.2 in. **Rear Tread:** (3-series) 55.7 in.; (M3) 56.1 in.; (5-series) 58.5 in.; (6-series) 57.5 in.; (735i) 61.0 in.; (735iL/750iL) 61.3 in. **Standard Tires:** (3-series) 195/65VR14; (M3) 205/55VR15; (525i) 205/65VR15; (535i) 225/60VR15; 220/55VR390; (M6) 245/45VR415 Michelin TRX; (735i/750iL) 225/60VR15.

TECHNICAL: Layout: front-engine, rear-drive. **Transmission:** five-speed (overdrive) manual standard, except (735i/750iL) four-speed automatic standard. Automatic optional on other models. **Steering:** (3-series) power rack-and-pinion; (5/6/7-series) power recirculating ball. **Brakes:** front/rear disc (anti-locking). **Body Construction:** steel unibody. **Fuel Tank:** (3-series) 16.4 gal.; (5-series) 21.1 gal.; (735i) 21.5 gal.; (735iL/750iL) 24.0 gallon.

MAJOR OPTIONS: Four-speed automatic trans.: 3-series ($645); Compact-disc changer: 5/6/7-series ($775). Metallic paint: 3-series ($375). Limited-slip differential: 3-series ($370); 5/6/7-series ($390). Heated front seats: 325iX, conv. ($200); 5/6/7-series ($200). Hardtop: 325i conv. ($3500).

Manufacturer: Bayerische Motoren Werke AG, Munich, West Germany.

Distributor: BMW of North America, Inc., Woodcliff Lake, New Jersey.

HISTORY: The 1989 models were introduced in the U.S. in September 1988. All 5/6/7-series BMWs (except the 525i) were subject to the Federal gas guzzler tax. Ads for the 735i this year trumpeted a statement by *AutoWeek* magazine that "the BMW 735i is a luxury sedan that will embarrass most sports cars." *Motor Trend* had asserted that it was "a driver's car first and foremost," in which "the hedonist will find no shortage of genuine leather and real wood trim."

1990 BMW

1990 BMW 325i convertible.

325 — SIX — A driver's-side airbag became standard in all 3-series models this year. A compact-disc changer and remote-control central locking became optional. Newly optional for the 325i and 4WD 325iX included leather upholstery, a power sunroof, and premium eight-speaker sound system. Only the 325i and 325iX came in four-door form. All models were powered by the 2.5-liter six, rated 168 horsepower.

M3 — FOUR — Not much changed in the high-performance two-door sedan. As before, its 16-valve four-cylinder engine was rated 192 horsepower and came only with manual shift.

525i/535i — SIX — A driver's airbag became standard on the 525i, which was again powered by the 168-bhp, 2.5-liter six. Traction control (called Automatic Stability Control) joined the 535i option list during the model year. That model carried the the 208-bhp, 3.4-liter six, and added wood trim and more leather to its interior. A cellular phone became optional in both models this year, as did a trunk-mounted compact-disc changer. The optional remote-control central-locking system activated a burglar alarm as the door locked. An automatic transmission was a no-cost option on the 535i.

735i — SIX — Traction control was a new option on the short (111.5-inch wheelbase) 735i and longer (116-inch) 735iL. The Automatic Stability Control system used the car's anti-lock brake sensors (at rear wheels) to detect wheel slippage and limit power as needed. Otherwise, little change was evident. As before, power came from the 3.4-liter six, with either five-speed manual or four-speed automatic transmission.

750iL — V-12 — The traction control that became optional on the 735 series was now standard on BMW's 12-cylinder sedan, which rode the 116-inch wheelbase. Little other change appeared this year.

6-series Note: The 6-series BMW was dropped after 1989.

I.D. DATA: A 17-symbol Vehicle Identification Number on the upper left of the dashboard is visible through the windshield. Symbols 1-3 ('WB) indicate manufacturer, make and type. Symbols 4-5 denote car line and series ('AB' = 325iX 2-dr; 'AE' = 325iX 4-dr; 'AA' = 325i/iS 2-dr; 'AD' = 325i 4-dr; 'AK' = M3; 'BB' = 325i conv.; 'HC' = 525i; 'HD' = 535i; 'GB' = 735i; 'GC' = 735iL/750iL). Symbol six (a digit) denotes the body type. Symbol seven identifies the engine. The eighth symbol ('3') indicates the restraint system, followed by a check digit. Symbol ten indicates model year ('L' = 1990). Symbol 11 identifies the assembly plant. The final six digits are the sequential serial number, starting with 000001.

Model	Body Type & Seating	Engine Type/CID	P.O.E. Price	Weight (lbs.)	Prod. Total
325i	2-dr Sedan-5P	I6/152	24650	2811	Note 1
325i	4-dr Sedan-5P	I6/152	25450	2855	Note 1
325iS	2-dr Sedan-5P	I6/152	28950	2844	Note 1
325iX	2-dr Sedan-5P	I6/152	29950	3010	Note 1
325iX	4-dr Sedan-5P	I6/152	30750	3050	Note 1
325iC	2-dr Conv-4P	I6/152	33850	3055	Note 1
M3	2-dr Sedan-5P	I4/140	34950	2865	Note 1
525i	4-dr Sedan-5P	I6/152	33200	3440	Note 1
535i	4-dr Sedan-5P	I6/209	41500	3570	Note 1
735i	4-dr Sedan-5P	I6/209	49000	3880	Note 1
735iL	4-dr Sedan-5P	I6/209	53000	4015	Note 1
750iL	4 dr Sedan-5P	V12/304	70000	4235	Note 1

Note 1: A total of 63,646 BMWs were sold in the U.S. during 1990.

ENGINE DATA: BASE FOUR (M3): Inline, dual-overhead-cam four-cylinder. Cast iron block and light alloy head. **Displacement:** 140 cu. in. (2302 cc). **Bore & Stroke:** 3.68 x 3.31 in. (93 x 84 mm). **Compression Ratio:** 10.5:1. **Brake Horsepower:** 192 at 6750 rpm. **Torque:** 170 lbs.-ft. at 4750 rpm. Electronic (port) fuel injection.

BASE SIX (325 series, 525i): Inline, overhead-cam six-cylinder. Cast iron block and light alloy head. **Displacement:** 152 cu. in. (2495 cc). **Bore & Stroke:** 3.31 x 2.95 in. (84 x 81 mm). **Compression Ratio:** 8.8:1. **Brake Horsepower:** 168 at 5800 rpm. **Torque:** 164 lbs.-ft. at 4300 rpm. Electronic (port) fuel injection.

BASE SIX (535i, 735i): Inline, overhead-cam six-cylinder. Cast iron block and light alloy head. **Displacement:** 209 cu. in. (3430 cc). **Bore & Stroke:** 3.62 x 3.39 in. (89 x 86 mm). **Compression Ratio:** 9.0:1. **Brake Horsepower:** 208 at 5700 rpm. **Torque:** 225 lbs.-ft. at 4000 rpm. Seven main bearings. Electronic (port) fuel injection.

BASE V-12 (750iL): Overhead-cam vee-type 12-cylinder. Aluminum block and heads. **Displacement:** 304 cu. in. (4988 cc). **Bore & Stroke:** 3.31 x 2.95 in. (84 x 75 mm). **Compression Ratio:** 8.8:1. **Brake Horsepower:** 296 at 5200 rpm. **Torque:** 332 lbs.-ft. at 4100 rpm. Electronic (port) fuel injection.

CHASSIS DATA: Wheelbase: (3-series) 101.2 in.; (M3) 101.0 in.; (5-series) 108.7 in.; (735i) 111.5 in.; (735iL/750iL) 116.0 in. **Overall Length:** (3-series) 170.3 in.; (325i conv.) 175.2 in.; (M3) 171.1 in.; (5-series) 185.8 in.; (735i) 193.3 in.; (735iL/750iL) 197.8 in. **Height:** (3-series) 54.3 in.; (325i conv.) 53.9 in.; (325iX) 55.1 in.; (M3) 53.9 in.; (5-series) 55.6 in.; (735i) 55.6 in.; (735iL/750iL) 55.1 in. **Width:** (3-series) 64.8 in.; (325iX) 65.4 in.; (M3) 66.1 in.; (5-series) 68.9 in.; (7-series) 72.6 in. **Front Tread:** (3-series) 55.4 in.; (325iX) 55.9 in.; (M3) 55.6 in.; (5-series) 57.7 in.; (735i) 60.1 in.; (735iL/750iL) 60.2 in. **Rear Tread:** (3-series) 55.7 in.; (325iX) 55.7 in.; (M3) 56.1 in.; (5-series) 58.5 in.; (735i) 61.0 in.; (735iL/750iL) 61.3 in.

TECHNICAL: Layout: front-engine, rear-drive except (325iX) four-wheel drive. **Transmission:** five-speed (overdrive) manual standard, except (735i/750iL) four-speed automatic standard. Automatic optional on other models. **Steering:** (3-series) power rack-and-pinion; (5/7-series) power recirculating ball. **Brakes:** front/rear disc (anti-locking). **Body Construction:** steel unibody. **Fuel Tank:** (3-series) 16.4 gal.; (M3) 14.5 gal.; (5-series) 21.1 gal.; (735i) 21.5 gal.; (735iL/750iL) 24.0 gallon.

MAJOR OPTIONS: Four-speed automatic trans.: 3-series, 525i ($700). Metallic paint: 3-series ($375). Leather upholstery: 325 ($895); 525i ($1100). Power sunroof: 325i/iX ($225). Glass sunroof: 325iS, 5-series ($495). Limited-slip differential: 325i/525i, 7-series ($400); Cross-spoke alloy wheels: 325i conv. ($500). Heated front seats: 3/5-series, 735i/iL ($250). Heated rear seats: 750iL ($250). Roll-up rear sunshade: 735iL ($140). Premium sound system: 325iS/iX ($250). Compact-disc changer: 3/5-series, 735i/iL ($780). Cellular phone: 735i/iL ($1205). Ski sack: 325iS, 7-series ($160). Remote alarm system: 3/5-series, 735i ($515).

Manufacturer: Bayerische Motoren Werke AG, Munich, West Germany.
Distributor: BMW of North America, Inc., Woodcliff Lake, New Jersey.
HISTORY: Introduced in U.S. October 1989. Later in 1990, a new 318iS entry-level model appeared, powered by a 1.8-liter four-cylinder engine rated 134 horsepower, available only with five-speed manual shift. Also later in the year, the new 850i V-12 coupe arrived, with four-speed automatic or six-speed manual shift, to replace the abandoned 6-series.

BMW ISETTA, 600 & 700

Though largely eclipsed by their bigger brethren, BMW's minicars have attracted a fair share of attention on their own--both when new and from later enthusiasts and collectors of specialty models. Still, not everyone is even aware that the Isetta came from the BMW factory, or that it was a German make. Actually it wasn't, at first. Neither the concept nor the reality had its origins at BMW. The Isetta's predecessor had been developed by the Iso Works, in Italy, from which BMW purchased the production rights. Designed by Renzo Rivolta (later responsible for the far larger Iso Rivolta), the minicar actually had sold poorly in Italy, but caught on right away in Germany. As fortune had it, the minicar happened to arrive at an appropriate moment: in the midst of a boom in little cars, which were becoming almost trendy. For German production, the original two-cylinder, two-stroke engine was replaced by a single-

cylinder unit, derived from BMW█████████. The Isetta debuted at the 1955 Fr█████ the huge BMW 505 Pullman limous███████ went into production). Nicknamed ██████ rolling egg), the Isetta saw extensive █████ postal service during the 1950s. They ███████ but enthusiastic following in the U.S.

To expand the sales appeal of minicars, ████ a four-passenger Model 600 starting in 195█. ██wasn't enough to forestall the company's sagging f█████es, so a more conventional Model 700 came in 1959. The last variant of that model was produced in 1965, while Isettas remained in production until 1962. Isettas also were built in Britain from 1957-63, and a Brazilian version remained available into 1965.

BMW Isetta

1955-56 BMW ISETTA

ISETTA 250 — ONE-CYLINDER — Before the single-door, single-cylinder Isetta minicar arrived in the U.S., it enjoyed a notable debut in Europe, powered by a smaller engine than the U.S. versions would offer. Power came from a 247-cc BMW R25 motorcycle engine. BMW engines were four-stroke, single-cylinder design, as opposed to the smaller two-stroke twin-cylinder engine used in the original Italian (Iso) model. The entire drivetrain fit between, and ahead of, the car's narrowly-spaced back wheels. Some export models had one back wheel and high front impact bars, aimed at countries that taxed three-wheelers at a lower rate. Early models used friction-type shock absorbers, while later examples switched to hydraulic units.

Though overall appearance of the Iso and Isetta were similar, changes were sufficiently extensive that no parts would interchange between the two. The Isetta's steering wheel moved forward along with the front-opening door, which served as the sole entrance into the car. The initial version, produced through March 1957, had a wraparound rear window, folding sunroof, and small triangular side windows at the front. BMW's blue/white round emblem appeared on the door and the gas filler cap. Headlamps were mounted separately, alongside the door, whereas the Italian Iso's lights had been farther down, installed at the front of large "fender" nacelles. At the rear were separate round taillamps and a center stoplight, plus vertical tubular bumper guards over the thin horizontal bumper. The front end also displayed tubular guards, gracefully curved in shape.

Though supposedly able to seat three people, at least in initial form, an Isetta was a tight enough fit for two. Starting in October 1956, a facelifted second version displayed two-section sliding side windows and a more modest back-window wraparound. See next listing for details on the Model 300, which was powered by a larger (298-cc) engine.

I.D. DATA: Serial number is on right front wheel housing, inside of car. Starting serial number: (250) 400001.

Model	Body Type & Seating	Engine Type/CID	P.O.E. Price	Weight (lbs.)	Prod. Total
250	1-dr Coupe-2P	I1/15	Note 1	795	Note 2

Note 1: Price in Germany was 2,580 Deutsch Marks.
Note 2: A total of 74,312 Model 250 Isettas were produced over the full model run (12,922 built in the first full year).

ENGINE DATA: BASE ONE: Overhead-valve one-cylinder (two-stroke, air-cooled). Cast iron block. **Displacement:** 15.1 cu. in. (247 cc). **Bore & Stroke:** 2.68 x 2.68 in. (68 x 68 mm). **Compression Ratio:** 6.8:1. **Brake Horsepower:** 12 at 5800 rpm. Solid valve lifters. Bing one-barrel carburetor.

Wheelbase: 58 in. **Overall Length:** 90.0 in. **Height:** 52.8 in. **Width:** 54.3 [...] **[...]:** 47.2 in. **Rear Tread:** 20.5 in. **Wheel Type:** 10x3 steel disc. **Standard** [...]0x10.

[...]: Models built after October 1956 were 92.7 inches long.

TECHNICAL: Layout: rear-engine, rear-drive. **Transmission:** four-speed manual. **Steering:** spindle (worm and nut). **Suspension (front):** leading arms with coil springs. **Suspension (rear):** rigid axle with quarter-elliptic leaf springs. **Brakes:** front/rear drum. **Body Construction:** pressed steel body on welded tubing.

PERFORMANCE: Top Speed: up to 53 mph claimed. **Fuel Mileage:** about 43 mpg overall.

Manufacturer: Bayerische Motoren Werke AG, Munich, West Germany. Earlier models built at the Iso Works in Milan, Italy.

HISTORY: The Model 250 Isetta entered production in Germany early in 1955 and remained in the BMW lineup into 1962. The Model 300, with a larger (298-cc) engine, was introduced in 1956 and also remained in production into 1962; see next listing for details. *Motor Trend* reported on the forthcoming Isetta (still built at the Iso Works in Milan, Italy) in November 1954, expressing surprise at the ample legroom and convenient pedal placement, as well as gas mileage of 37.9 mpg in traffic (51.7 mpg on the highway, for 44.5 mpg overall). On the other hand, they began the report by asking such questions as "Do you mind other people laughing *at* you, as well as *with* you?" Already in late 1954, two Americans named Joe Haines and L. Novak were bringing examples into the U.S.

The initial Iso version went on sale in Italy late in 1953. According to *Auto Sport Review,* it had a claimed fuel mileage of 70 mpg and 55-mph top speed with the 9.5-bhp, 198-cc two-stroke engine. Plans were made to produce 50 per day.

1957 BMW ISETTA

1957 BMW Isetta 300.

ISETTA 300 — ONE-CYLINDER — Isettas began to arrive in the U.S. for the 1957 model year, after appearing earlier in Europe. For 1957, fixed-window and sliding-window models were priced identically at $1048. The U.S. price would not change through 1960. This Isetta was longer than the initial Model 250, and had a 298-cc single-cylinder engine rather than the original 247-cc version. Engine output rose by only one horsepower. A sunroof and heater were included on examples sold in the U.S.

I.D. DATA: Serial number is on right wheel housing, inside of car. Engine number is on crankshaft housing, or upper right of timing cover. Model year was determined by date of first registration or certificate of origin.

Model	Body Type & Seating	Engine Type/CID	P.O.E. Price	Weight (lbs.)	Prod. Total
300	1-dr Coupe-2P	I1/18	1048	770	Note 1

Note 1: A total of 87,416 Model 300 Isettas were produced during the full model run, through 1962.

Price Note: Fixed-window and sliding-window models were priced identically. Price of the Model 300 in Germany was 2,886 Deutsch Marks.

ENGINE DATA: BASE ONE: Overhead-valve one-cylinder (air cooled). **Displacement:** 18.2 cu. in. (298 cc). **Bore & Stroke:** 2.83 x 2.87 in. (72 x 73 mm). **Compression Ratio:** 6.8:1. **Brake Horsepower:** 13 at 5200 rpm. **Torque:** 14 lbs.-ft. at 4200 rpm. One Bing carburetor. 12-volt electrical system.

CHASSIS DATA: Wheelbase: 59.1 in. **Overall Length:** 92.7 in. **Height:** 52.8 in. **Width:** 54.3 in. **Front Tread:** 47.2 in. **Rear Tread:** 20.5 in. **Wheel Type:** 10x3 steel disc. **Standard Tires:** 4.80x10.

TECHNICAL: Layout: rear-engine, rear-drive. **Transmission:** four-speed manual (chain/sprocket drive). **Steering:** spindle (worm and nut). **Suspension (front):** leading arms with coil springs. **Suspension (rear):** rigid axle with quarter-elliptic leaf springs. **Brakes:** front/rear drum. **Body Construction:** pressed steel body on welded tubing. **Fuel Tank:** 3.4 gallon (plus reserve).

MAJOR OPTIONS: Mudflap/fender guards. Wheel trim rings. Sunvisors. Pedal pads. Passenger assist grip. Exhaust tip. Steering and gearshift boots. Whitewall tires.

PERFORMANCE: Top Speed: 50-53 mph. **Fuel Mileage:** 40-45 mpg (city).

Manufacturer: Bayerische Motoren Werke AG, Munich, West Germany.

HISTORY: The Model 600 debuted late in 1957; see next listing for details. Production of Isettas also began in England during 1957. The smaller-engined Model 250 also remained in production until 1962, but only the 300 was officially imported into the U.S.

1958 BMW ISETTA/600

1958 BMW Isetta 300.

ISETTA 300 — ONE-CYLINDER — Production of the Model 300 Isetta continued without change; see previous listings for details. Standard equipment included tubular vertical bumpers and aluminum hubcaps.

600 — TWO-CYLINDER — Intended to fill the gap between the miniature Isetta and BMW's luxury models, the 600 wasn't much larger than an Isetta but had a larger (two-cylinder) engine and a door on the right side for access to the back seat. Therefore, it held four passengers, versus two in the Isetta. Though short on the outside, the 600 was rather roomy inside. As on the Isetta, the front (nose) door was the only way to enter the front seat. The 582-cc, horizontally-opposed two-cylinder engine, mounted behind the rear axle, developed 19.5 horsepower, which was good enough for about 62 mph. It was actually a detuned version of one of BMW's air-cooled motorcycle engines (the R50, but with a larger bore), and made the car more suitable for highway travel rather than strictly inner-city operation. In appearance, the 600 resembled the Isetta up front, and the comparably-sized Fiat 600 at the rear. It rode a ladder-type chassis. Instead of the Isetta's narrowly-spaced rear wheels, the 600 had a more conventional layout with rear tread only 2.3 inches narrower than the front dimension. A new semi-trailing arm rear suspension later became standard on BMWs. Headlamps sat alongside the front door, as on the Isetta. A '600' nameplate stood on the rear, below the engine's air-intake grille slots.

I.D. DATA: Isetta serial number is on right wheel housing, inside of car; engine number is on crankshaft housing or upper right of timing cover. 600 serial number is on side wall of engine compartment; engine number is stamped on upper right of timing cover. Model year was determined by date of first registration or certificate of origin.

Model	Body Type & Seating	Engine Type/CID	P.O.E. Price	Weight (lbs.)	Prod. Total
ISETTA					
300	1-dr Coupe-2P	I1/18	1048	770	Note 1
600					
600	2-dr Sedan-4P	H2/35	1398	1166	Note 2

Note 1: A total of 87,416 Model 300 Isettas were produced during the full model run.

Note 2: At least 34,318 Model 600 sedans were produced during the full model run.

600 Price Note: A sunroof cost $89 more. Price in Germany was 3,985 Deutsch Marks.

Weight Note: Figures shown were listed for U.S. models. Curb weight of 600 sedan in Germany was 1215 pounds.

ENGINE DATA: BASE ONE (Isetta 300): Overhead-valve one-cylinder (air cooled). **Displacement:** 18.2 cu. in. (298 cc). **Bore & Stroke:** 2.83 x 2.87 in. (72 x 73 mm). **Compression Ratio:** 7.0:1. **Brake Horsepower:** 13 at 5800 rpm. **Torque:** 14 lbs.-ft. at 4200 rpm. One Bing carburetor. 12-volt electrical system.
BASE TWO (600): Horizontally-opposed, overhead-valve two-cylinder (air cooled). **Displacement:** 35.5 cu. in. (582 cc). **Bore & Stroke:** 2.91 x 2.67 in. (74 x 68 mm). **Compression Ratio:** 6.8:1. **Brake Horsepower:** 19.5 at 4000 rpm (26 SAE at 4500 rpm). **Torque:** 29 lbs.-ft. at 2500 rpm. Solid valve lifters. One Zenith 28KLP1 one-barrel carburetor.

CHASSIS DATA: Wheelbase: (Isetta 300) 59.1 in.; (600) 66.9 in. **Overall Length:** (300) 92.7 in.; (600) 114.2 in. **Height:** (300) 52.8 in.; (600) 54.1 in. **Width:** (300) 54.3 in.; (600) 55.1 in. **Front Tread:** (300) 47.2 in.; (600) 48.0 in. **Rear Tread:** (300) 20.5 in.; (600) 45.7 in. **Wheel Type:** (300) 10x3 steel disc; (600) 10x3.5 steel disc. **Standard Tires:** (300) 4.80x10; (600) 5.20x10.

TECHNICAL: Layout: rear-engine, rear-drive. **Transmission:** four-speed manual. **Steering:** spindle. **Suspension (front):** leading arms with coil springs. **Suspension (rear):** (300) rigid axle with quarter-elliptic leaf springs; (600) semi-trailing arms with coil springs. **Brakes:** front/rear drum. **Body Construction:** (300) pressed steel body on welded-tube frame.

MAJOR OPTIONS: Roof luggage carrier ($35). Tow bar ($35). Windshield washer ($20). Heater ($24). Defroster ($15).

PERFORMANCE: Top Speed: (Isetta 300) 50-53 mph; (600) 62-68 mph. **Acceleration (0-60 mph):** N/A (Isetta, 0-30 mph in 10 sec.; 0-50 mph in 52 sec.). **Acceleration (quarter-mile)** (Isetta 300) 27.7 sec. **Fuel Mileage:** (Isetta 300) 44-62 mpg; (600) up to 58 mpg (factory claim).

PRODUCTION/SALES: As many as 3,925 Isettas were sold in the U.S. during 1958.
Manufacturer: Bayerische Motoren Werke AG, Munich, West Germany.
Distributor: Hoffman Motors Corp., New York City.
HISTORY: Debut of the Model 600 took place in August 1957, and the first examples were delivered a few months later. Production continued only through 1959, as the Model 700 emerged.

"There is very little to go wrong with the Isetta," reported *Road & Track* in 1958, "and repairs should be both simple and cheap." European Isettas could have the smaller (247-cc) engine. U.S. sales weren't helped by a ruling in California that Isettas couldn't enter that state's freeway system.

1959 BMW Isetta 300.

ISETTA 300 — ONE-CYLINDER — Production of the Model 300 Isetta continued without change; see 1955-57 listings for details.

600 — TWO-CYLINDER — Production of the Model 600 mini-sedan continued through 1959, as it was replaced by the Model 700. This model was sometimes referred to in the U.S. as the Isetta 600. A heater was standard; Saxomat automatic clutch and sunroof available.

700 — TWO-CYLINDER — Larger than the Model 600, the new 700 looked more like a regular car, comparable to any of several European (and Asian) subcompacts that would emerge in the 1960s. Nevertheless, it was mechanically similar to the 600, though its two-cylinder engine was larger in displacement and produced more horsepower (30 bhp). The 700 chassis was essentially a "stretch" of the 600's layout. A two-door coupe (designed by Giovanni Michelotti) arrived first, with production starting in August 1959. Late that year, a two-door sedan joined. Starting in September 1960, a 700 Sport convertible also became available.

The 700 coupe displayed a stubby profile with short cockpit and rear quarter windows. Wraparound parking lamps stood below ordinary round headlamps. A round BMW emblem sat at the center of the front panel. Two conventional doors were installed, and rear fenders were modestly finned. The 700 sedan had unusually thin front seatbacks to give more rear legroom. The dashboard held two round dials (speedometer and clock) ahead of the driver. A floor gearshift lever operated the four-speed transmission. As in the 600, an air-cooled two-cylinder engine sat behind the rear wheels. Suspension was similar to the 600, but with larger wheelbase and tread dimensions. This was the first BMW with steel unibody construction. The 700 sedan had ample luggage space under the front hood.

I.D. DATA: Isetta serial number is on right wheel housing, inside of car; engine number is on crankshaft housing or upper right of timing cover. 600 serial number is on side wall of engine compartment; engine number is stamped on upper right of timing cover. 700 serial number is stamped on firewall, in luggage compartment; engine number is stamped on top of engine, ahead of carburetor.

Model	Body Type & Seating	Engine Type/CID	P.O.E. Price	Weight (lbs.)	Prod. Total
ISETTA					
300	1-dr Coupe-2P	I1/18	1048	770	Note 1
600					
600	2-dr Sedan-4P	H2/35	1398	1166	Note 2
700					
700	2-dr Coupe-4P	H2/42	1898	1389	Note 3
700	2-dr Sedan-4/5P	H2/42	1648	N/A	Note 3

Note 1: A total of 87,416 Model 300 Isettas were produced during the full model run.
Note 2: At least 34,318 Model 600 sedans were produced during the full model run.
Note 3: A total of 188,000 Model 700s were produced during the full model run, through December 1965. Breakdown of the initial model came to 23,892 coupes and 55,707 sedans. A total of 3,127 700s were sold in the United States.

700 Price Note: Price of 700 coupe in Germany was 5,500 Marks; of the sedan, 4,760 Marks.

ENGINE DATA: BASE ONE (Isetta 300): Overhead-valve one-cylinder (air cooled). **Displacement:** 18.2 cu. in. (298 cc). **Bore & Stroke:** 2.83 x 2.87 in. (72 x 73 mm). **Compression Ratio:** 7.0:1. **Brake Horsepower:** 13 at 5200 rpm. **Torque:** 14 lbs.-ft. at 4200 rpm. One Bing carburetor. 12-volt electrical system.
BASE TWO (600): Horizontally-opposed, overhead-valve two-cylinder (air cooled). **Displacement:** 35.5 cu. in. (582 cc). **Bore & Stroke:** 2.91 x 2.67 in. (74 x 68 mm). **Compression Ratio:** 6.8:1. **Brake Horsepower:** 19.5 at 4000 rpm. **Torque:** 29 lbs.-ft. at 2500 rpm. Solid valve lifters. One Zenith 28KLP1 one-barrel carburetor.
BASE TWO (700): Horizontally-opposed, overhead-valve two-cylinder (air cooled). Aluminum block and heads. **Displacement:** 42.5 cu. in. (697 cc). **Bore & Stroke:** 3.07 x 2.87 in. (78 x 73 mm). **Compression Ratio:** 7.5:1. **Brake Horsepower:** 30 at 5000 rpm (35 SAE at 5200 rpm). **Torque:** 32.5 lbs.-ft. at 3200 rpm (37 SAE at 3400 rpm). Solid valve lifters. One Solex 34PCI one-barrel carburetor.
CHASSIS DATA: Wheelbase: (Isetta 300) 59.1 in.; (600) 66.9 in.; (700) 83.5 in. **Overall Length:** (300) 92.7 in.; (600) 114.2 in.; (700) 139.4 in. **Height:** (300) 52.8 in.; (600) 54.1 in.; (700 cpe) 50.0 in.; (700 sed) 53.0 in. **Width:** (300) 54.3 in.; (600) 55.1 in.; (700) 58.3 in. **Front Tread:** (300) 47.2 in.; (600) 48.0 in.; (700) 50.0 in. **Rear Tread:** (300) 20.5 in.; (600) 45.7 in.; (700) 47.2 in. **Wheel Type:** (300) 10x3 steel disc, (600) 10x3.5 steel disc; (700) 12x3.5. **Standard Tires:** (300) 4.80x10; (600) 5.20x10; (700) 5.20x12.

1960 BMW Isetta 600 two-door "Limousine."

TECHNICAL: Layout: rear-engine, rear-drive. **Transmission:** four-speed manual. **Standard Final Drive Ratio:** (600/700) 5.43:1. **Steering:** (300/600) spindle; (700) rack and pinion. **Suspension (front):** leading arms with coil springs. **Suspension (rear):** (300) rigid axle with quarter-elliptic leaf springs; (600/700) semi-trailing arms with coil springs. **Brakes:** front/rear drum. **Body Construction:** (300/600) steel body and frame; (700) steel unibody.

MAJOR OPTIONS: Saxomat automatic clutch: 600 ($95); also available on 700. Sunroof: 600 ($89).

PERFORMANCE: Top Speed: (600) 62-68 mph; (700 cpe) 78 mph; (700 sed) 74 mph. **Fuel Mileage:** (600) up to 58 mpg (factory claim).

PRODUCTION/SALES: Approximately 2,586 Isettas were sold in the U.S. during 1959.
Manufacturer: Bayerische Motoren Werke AG, Munich, West Germany.
Distributor: Hoffman Motors Corp., New York City.
HISTORY: Various proposals were offered for the design of the new 700 coupe, including one from Wolfgang Denzel (BMW's distributor in Austria). The two-door sedan remained in production through 1962. Because BMW was facing financial difficulty at this time, with rumors of takeovers, they relied strongly on the 700 to turn things around.

ISETTA 300 — ONE-CYLINDER — Production of the Model 300 Isetta continued with little change, though 1962; see 1955-57 listings for details.

700 — TWO-CYLINDER — In 1961, a Luxus sedan joined the original 700 two-door sedan; but it did not appear on lists of models available in the U.S. until later. New in 1960 was a 700 Sport coupe, followed by a cabriolet that was built by Baur (at Stuttgart). The twin-carbureted engine developed 40 horsepower, and the chassis featured a rear anti-roll bar. The 700 coupe had 'coupe' script at the rear of rear fenders, but otherwise looked like a regular LS model. The 700 Sport made a strong showing on the race course, and the Italian design looked especially appealing in cabriolet form. Inside, however, its tiny rear bench seat was cramped.

Model 600 Note: Production of the 600 mini-sedan ceased in 1959, but it remained on lists of models available in the U.S. as late as 1962. See previous listings for full information.

I.D. DATA: Isetta serial number is on right wheel housing, inside of car; engine number is on crankshaft housing or upper right of timing cover. Model 700 serial number is stamped on firewall, in luggage compartment; engine number is stamped on top of engine, ahead of carburetor.

Model	Body Type & Seating	Engine Type/CID	P.O.E. Price	Weight (lbs.)	Prod. Total
ISETTA					
300	1-dr Coupe-2P	I1/18	1048	770	Note 1
700					
700	2-dr Coupe-4P	H2/42	1898	1389	Note 2
700	2-dr Sedan-4/5P	H2/42	1648	N/A	Note 2
700	2-dr Spt Cpe-4P	H2/42	1998	1435	Note 3
Baur	2-dr Conv-4P	H2/42	N/A	N/A	Note 3

Note 1: A total of 87,416 Model 300 Isettas were produced during the full model run, through 1962.

Note 2: A total of 188,000 Model 700s were produced during the full model run, through December 1965.

Note 3: A total of 11,139 Model 700 Sport coupes were produced during the full model run (plus 2,592 cabriolets).

600 Price Note: The Model 600 sedan continued to be listed in U.S. directories, priced at $1398 ($1487 with sunroof).

ENGINE DATA: BASE ONE (Isetta 300): Overhead-valve one-cylinder (air cooled). **Displacement:** 18.2 cu. in. (298 cc). **Bore & Stroke:** 2.83 x 2.87 in. (72 x 73 mm). **Compression Ratio:** 7.0:1. **Brake Horsepower:** 13 at 5200 rpm. **Torque:** 14 lbs.-ft. at 4200 rpm. One Bing carburetor. 12-volt electrical system.

BASE TWO (700): Horizontally-opposed, overhead-valve two-cylinder (air cooled). Aluminum block and heads. **Displacement:** 42.5 cu. in. (697 cc). **Bore & Stroke:** 3.07 x 2.87 in. (78 x 73 mm). **Compression Ratio:** 7.5:1. **Brake Horsepower:** 30 at 5000 rpm (35 SAE at 5200 rpm). **Torque:** 37 lbs.-ft. (SAE) at 3400 rpm. Solid valve lifters. One Solex 34PCI one-barrel carburetor.

BASE TWO (700 Sport): Same as above, except — **Brake Horsepower:** 40 hp at 5700 rpm. Two Solex 34 PCI single-barrel carburetors.

700 Sport Engine Note: A factory-designed performance kit could boost output of the twin-carburetor engine as high as 55 bhp, with 9.5:1 compression.

CHASSIS DATA: Wheelbase: (Isetta 300) 59.1 in.; (700) 83.5 in. **Overall Length:** (300) 92.7 in.; (700) 139.4 in. **Height:** (300) 52.8 in.; (700 cpe/Sport) 50.0 in.; (700 sed) 53.0 in. **Width:** (300) 54.3 in.; (700) 58.3 in. **Front Tread:** (300) 47.2 in.; (700) 50.0 in. **Rear Tread:** (300) 20.5 in.; (700) 47.2 in. **Wheel Type:** (300) 10x3 steel disc; (700) 12x3.5. **Standard Tires:** (300) 4.80x10; (700) 5.20x12.

TECHNICAL: Layout: rear-engine, rear-drive. **Transmission:** four-speed manual. **Standard Final Drive Ratio:** (700) 5.43:1. **Steering:** (300) spindle; (700) rack and pinion. **Suspension (front):** leading arms with coil springs. **Suspension (rear):** (300) rigid axle with quarter-elliptic leaf springs; (700) semi-trailing arms with swing axles and coil springs. **Brakes:** front/rear drum. **Body Construction:** (300) steel body and frame; (700) steel unibody.

MAJOR OPTIONS: Automatic clutch: 700 ($95). Sunroof: 700 sedan ($89).

PERFORMANCE: Top Speed: (700 cpe) 78 mph; (700 sed) 74 mph; (700 Sport) 84+ mph. **Acceleration (0-60 mph):** (700 Sport w/48-bhp engine) 14.8 sec. **Acceleration (quarter-mile):** (700 Sport w/48-bhp engine) 19.6 sec. (68 mph). **Fuel Mileage:** (700) about 40 mpg.

Manufacturer: Bayerische Motoren Werke AG, Munich, West Germany.

Distributor: Hoffman Motors Corp., New York City.

HISTORY: A 700LS coupe and sedan, on a longer wheelbase, was introduced in 1961; see next listing for details. BMW announced an experimental racing 700RS in 1961, with a small-tube space frame and four-cam version of the 697-cc engine, producing 78 horsepower.

1963-65 BMW 700

700 — TWO-CYLINDER — For 1963, the 700 Sport changed its designation to 700CS and got slightly wider tires. Joining the Luxus, introduced earlier, was a new 700LS two-door sedan, which debuted in March 1963. This one rode a stretched wheelbase (89.8 inches) and was longer overall, which gave more rear passenger space. The 700LS had less equipment (and a lower price tag) than the Luxus. Appearance was similar to the basic 700. Lacking a front grille, the 700LS had little of the traditional BMW look, except for a round emblem on the front panel. A 700LS coupe debuted in 1964, but few were built. Both the 700CS and 700LS coupe had a 40-bhp, dual-carburetor version of the 697-cc engine, while sedan engines produced 10 fewer horsepower.

I.D. DATA: Model 700 serial number is stamped on firewall, in luggage compartment; engine number is stamped on top of engine, ahead of carburetor.

Model	Body Type & Seating	Engine Type/CID	P.O.E. Price	Weight (lbs.)	Prod. Total
700					
	2-dr Coupe-4P	H2/42	1798	1390	Note 1
Baur	2-dr Conv-4P	H2/42	2345	N/A	Note 2
CS	2-dr Spt Cpe-4P	H2/42	1998	1435	Note 2
Luxus	2-dr Sedan-4/5P	H2/42	1648	N/A	Note 3
Luxus LS	2-dr Sedan-4/5P	H2/42	1785	1500	Note 3
Luxus LS	2-dr Coupe-4/P	H2/42	N/A	1520	Note 3

Note 1: A total of 188,000 Model 700s were produced during the full model run, through December 1965.

Note 2: A total of 11,139 Model 700 Sport/CS coupes were produced during the full model run (plus 2,592 cabriolets).

Note 3: A total of 93,061 Model 700LS sedans were produced, and 1,730 LS coupes.

ENGINE DATA: BASE TWO (700): Horizontally-opposed, overhead-valve two-cylinder (air cooled). Aluminum block and heads. **Displacement:** 42.5 cu. in. (697 cc). **Bore & Stroke:** 3.07 x 2.87 in. (78 x 73 mm). **Compression Ratio:** 7.5:1. **Brake Horsepower:** 32 at 5000 rpm (35 SAE at 5000 rpm). **Torque:** 37 lbs.-ft. (SAE) at 3400 rpm. Solid valve lifters. One Solex 34PCI single-barrel carburetor.

BASE TWO (700CS): Same as above, except — **Brake Horsepower:** 40 hp at 5700 rpm. Two Solex 34 PCI single-barrel carburetors.

CHASSIS DATA: Wheelbase: (700) 83.5 in.; (700LS) 89.8 in. **Overall Length:** (700) 139.4 in.; (700LS) 152.0 in. **Height:** (700 cpe) 50.0 in.; (700 sed) 53.0 in.; (700LS sed) 53.5 in.; (700LS cpe) 51.2 in. **Width:** 58.3 in. **Front Tread:** 50.0 in. **Rear Tread:** 47.2 in. **Wheel Type:** 12x3.5 steel disc. **Standard Tires:** (700) 5.20x12; (700CS) 5.50 x 12.

TECHNICAL: Layout: rear-engine, rear-drive. **Transmission:** four-speed manual. **Standard Final Drive Ratio:** (700) 5.43:1. **Steering:** rack and pinion. **Suspension (front):** leading arms with coil springs. **Suspension (rear):** semi-trailing arms with swing axles and coil springs. **Brakes:** front/rear drum. **Body Construction:** steel unibody.

PERFORMANCE: Top Speed: (700 cpe) 78 mph; (700 sed) 74 mph; (700CS cpe) 84+ mph; (700LS cpe) 84 mph. **Fuel Mileage:** (700) about 40 mpg.

Manufacturer: Bayerische Motoren Werke AG, Munich, West Germany.

Distributor: Hoffman Motors Corp., New York City.

HISTORY: Production of the 700CS continued into 1964. The 700LS lasted into 1965.

BOND

Three-wheeled vehicles, and minicars in general, never quite caught on in the U.S. One company that tried briefly to grab a slight foothold in that market was the Bond works, of Great Britain, where three-wheelers gained quite a following in the 1950s. The first Bond minicar was produced in 1949, designed by Laurie Bond (also connected with the Berkeley sports car; see that listing in this Catalog). Production of the Mark B/C/D editions did not begin until 1953, and continued into 1958. Mark E and F versions followed in the 1958-61 period. Later in the 1960s, two versions of a new 250 series were produced, with either one- or two-cylinder engines mounted in the rear. Bond also turned to four-wheeled vehicles, but by that time the marque had long since been forgotten even by those few Americans who'd taken an interest at the time of its inception.

Note: See A.C. and Reliant listings for additional examples of British three-wheeler manufacture.

1953-58 BOND

1954 Bond Minicar Mark C three-wheeler.

MARK B/C/D -- ONE -- A single-cylinder, two-stroke Villiers motorcycle engine provided all the power that this lightweight three-wheeler needed, according to the company. That meant no more than 9 horsepower, from an engine that displaced a mere 12 cubic inches (197 cc). Initial versions were smaller yet: only 122 cc. Mounted as a unit with the three-speed manual gearbox, the little engine drove the front wheel via a roller chain (motorcycle style) and multi-plate clutch. A dashboard-mounted gearshift was used. With independent suspension on all three wheels (single front wheel), and a steering wheel that could turn the car 180 degrees in a nine-foot turning circle, no reverse gear was deemed necessary at first. A reversible model became available in 1957. Those early models relied on low-pressure tires to provide riding comfort, as the rear suspension was rigidly mounted. Three adults could squeeze across the bench seat, with ample space for luggage. Children, at least, might be able to climb into the back of the "family" versions, which were promoted as four-passenger models.

Essentially a convertible, the Bond came with a soft top and side screens. With light-footed driving, a Bond was said to be capable of gas mileage from 85 to 100 mpg, with a cruising speed around 45 mph. Removing four bolts and two cables allowed the entire engine/transmission unit to drop out for quick servicing.

Several improvements emerged by the time the Mark D arrived in 1957. Deluxe models had pushbutton starters (others had to be started manually, from the driver's seat). A 12-volt coil ignition replaced the original magneto. Two reasonably strong men could lift a Bond off the ground, as it weighed around 500 pounds. Then again, two men could lift the front end of a Volkswagen Beetle, too.

I.D. DATA: Not available.

Model	Body Type & Seating	Engine Type/CID	P.O.E. Price	Weight (lbs.)	Prod. Total
Mark C	2-dr Rds-2/3P	I1/12	Note 1	490	N/A
Mark C	2-dr Family Rds-4P	I1/12	Note 1	510	N/A

Note 1: Price in U.S. was estimated to be $950 in 1954.

ENGINE DATA: BASE ONE: One-cylinder, two-stroke (air cooled). **Displacement:** 12 cu. in. (197 cc). **Bore & Stroke:** 2.32 x 2.83 in. (59 x 72 mm). **Compression Ratio:** 7.25:1 to 8.0:1. **Brake Horsepower:** 8.4/9 at 4000-4500 rpm.

Note: Early engines were only 122 cc. Later models (after 1958) could have a 246-cc Villiers engine and four-speed transmission.

CHASSIS DATA: Wheelbase: 66 in. typical. **Overall Length:** 104-109.5 in. (up to 120 in. available). **Height:** 48-50 in. **Width:** 49.5-57 in. **Front Tread:** single wheel. **Rear Tread:** 51.5-53 in. **Standard Tires:** 4.00x8.

TECHNICAL: Layout: front-engine, front-drive (chain). **Transmission:** three-speed manual; dashboard shift lever. **Steering:** worm and sector. **Suspension (front):** trailing arm with coil spring. **Suspension (rear):** independent, trailing arms with rubber in torsion. **Brakes:** mechanical drum. **Body Construction:** aluminum/steel unibody. **Fuel Tank:** 3 gallon.

PERFORMANCE: Top Speed: 45-55 mph. **Acceleration (0-60 mph):** N/A (0-50 mph in 30 sec.). **Fuel Mileage:** about 85-90 mpg.

Manufacturer: Sharp's Commercials Ltd., Bond MiniCar Works, Preston, Lancashire, England; (later) Bond Cars Ltd.

HISTORY: The Bond company also produced a mini-truck version with similar specifications. A Bond finished the Monte Carlo Rally (Glasgow, Scotland to Monaco) in 3.5 days. In later years, Bond turned to four-wheeled vehicles, starting in 1963 with an Equipe GT40 fastback coupe, powered by a 70-cid (1147-cc) Triumph Herald engine. Final three-wheelers in the mid-1960s used components from the Hillman Imp. A total of 1,500 Bond vehicles were produced in 1964.

BORGWARD

Although the history of the Borgward name on automobiles dates back only to 1939, the year that war erupted in Europe, automotive engineer Carl (Karl) F. Borgward began to manufacture car parts in the early 1920s. After acquiring a partnership in Bremer Reifen Industrie, he formed the Bremen Radiator Works Borgward & Co. By 1931, he'd taken over both the Goliath and Hansa companies, merging the trio into Goliath-Borgward & Co., to turn out commercial vehicles. Production of Hansas began in 1934 with the 1100, expanding to include 1700 and 2000 models. The first Borgward, model 2300, was a six-cylinder variant of the Hansa 1700.

By 1948, the company was back in the automobile business and the corporate name soon changed to Carl F. Borgward GmbH, again located in Bremen, West Germany; but the first postwar vehicles carried the Borgward Hansa badge. At the Geneva auto show in 1949 came the debut of the Borgward Hansa 1500, which was the first German car to enter production after the war. That was followed by the 1800 and the six-cylinder 2400. Claimed to have a top speed near 100 mph, the six-cylinder model was eventually offered with Hansamatic transmission. In 1950, a streamlined edition of the 1500 set a dozen international class records at the Montlhery race course, and a year later its engine went under production-car hoods. Model 1500 sport-racers also entered the grueling Carrera Panamericana road race in the early 1950s.

Few Hansas were seen in the U.S., but the subsequent Isabella, which entered production late in 1954, gained a sizable following in America over the next seven years. In essence, the Isabella was a unibodied version of the Hansa 1500. A racing edition won its class at the 1955 Mille Miglia. In the following year, racing editions carried a twin-cam engine with four valves per cylinder. The same company produced the front-drive Goliath and Lloyd (described elsewhere in this Catalog). Among other technical advances, modern Borgwards had independent suspen-

sion on all four wheels. A microbus also was built during the mid-1950s.

Financial woes caused Borgward to abandon racing by 1958, but auto production continued until 1961, when bankruptcy was declared. When Carl Borgward had retired a few months earlier, unable to meet loan payments, some 19,000 automobiles remained in stock, unsold. Tooling for the Isabella was purchased by a Mexican company, which continued to build the economy sedan until 1966, and turned out a handful of related limousines as late as 1970.

1949-54 BORGWARD

1949 Borgward two-door sedan.

1950 Borgward Hansa 1500 sport cabriolet.

HANSA 1500 — FOUR — The Borgward Hansa 1500 debuted in 1949 as the first postwar German automobile on the market. Powerplant was a 91 cubic-inch four-cylinder engine. All Borgward Hansas carried the customary diamond-shaped grille center, half of which extended upward into the hood area. Headlamps were mounted low on the fenders, not far above the bumper. Separate parking lights were mounted in long housings atop the fenders. In addition to the basic sedan, a Sports Cabriolet and station wagon were built.

HANSA 1800 — FOUR — Available with either a gasoline or diesel engine under the hood, the 1800 appeared in 1952 and looked similar to the 1500.

HANSA 2400 — SIX — The six-cylinder Hansa emerged in 1952. Two body styles were offered by 1954: the fastback sedan, which had a distinctive profile, and the Pullman (with trunk). This was Germany's first production automobile with an optional automatic transmission.

ISABELLA — FOUR — The more familiar Isabella debuted in October 1954; see next listing for details.

I.D. DATA: Not available.

Model	Body Type & Seating	Engine Type/CID	P.O.E Price	Weight (lbs.)	Prod. Total
1500	2-dr Sedan-5P	I4/91	2500	2450	Note 1
1500	2-dr Conv-5P	I4/91	3650	N/A	Note 1
1800	4-dr Sedan-5P	I4/107	N/A	N/A	Note 1
2400	4-dr Sedan-P	I6/143	3120	3175	Note 1

Note 1: Almost 10,000 Borgwards (all models) were built in 1949 (1,108 in prewar style); 26,000 in 1950; 38,000 during 1952; 43,000 in 1953; and 60,451 in 1954. A total of 1,148 Hansa 1500s were built in 1949, 8,744 in 1950, 8,618 in 1951, and 2,739 in 1952. A total of 1,059 model 2400s were built, as late as 1958.

1954 Borgward Hansa 2400.

ENGINE DATA: BASE FOUR (1500): Inline, overhead-valve four-cylinder. **Displacement:** 91.4 cu. in. (1498 cc). **Bore & Stroke:** 2.83 x 3.62 in. (72 x 92 mm). **Compression Ratio:** 6.3:1. **Brake Horsepower:** (early) 48-52; (later) 66 at 4400 rpm. Solid valve lifters. Two Solex carburetors.

Note: Sports Cabriolet engine developed 80 bhp at 5200 rpm, with 8.5:1 compression.

BASE FOUR (1800): Inline, overhead-valve four-cylinder. **Displacement:** 107.2 cu. in. (1757 cc). **Bore & Stroke:** 3.07 x 3.62 in. (72 x 92 mm). **Compression Ratio:** 6.4:1. **Brake Horsepower:** 60 at 4200 rpm. Solid valve lifters.

DIESEL FOUR (1800): Same dimensions as gas four, but rated 42 horsepower at 3400 rpm, with 19.8:1 compression.

BASE FOUR (2400): Inline, overhead-valve six-cylinder. **Displacement:** 142.6 cu. in. (2337 cc). **Bore & Stroke:** 3.07 x 3.21 in. (78 x 82 mm). **Compression Ratio:** 6.9:1. **Brake Horsepower:** 82 at 4200 rpm. Solid valve lifters.

CHASSIS DATA: Wheelbase: (1500) 96 in.; (1800) 102.4 in.; (2400) 102 in.; (2400 Pullman) 111.0 in. **Overall Length:** (1500) 164.0 in.; (1800) 175.2 in.; (2400) 175.6 in.; (2400 Pullman) 183.0 in. **Height:** (1500) 54.3 in.; (1800) 61.4 in.; (2400) 58.8 in. **Width:** (1500) 63.8 in.; (1800) 63.8 in.; (2400) 70.1 in. **Front Tread:** (1500) 49.5 in.; (1800) 49.2 in.; (2400) 53.5 in. **Rear Tread:** (1500) 51.2 in.; (1800) 51.2 in.; (2400) 55.9 in. **Standard Tires:** (1500) 5.90x15; (1800) 5.90/6.40x15; (2400) 6.40/6.70x15.

TECHNICAL: Layout: front-engine, rear-drive. **Transmission:** four-speed manual; floor or column shift (a few were three-speed). **Suspension (front):** long/short control arms, coil springs. **Suspension (rear):** independent swing axle, semi-elliptic leaf or coil springs. **Brakes:** hydraulic, front/rear drum. **Body Construction:** steel body on steel frame.

MAJOR OPTIONS: Automatic transmission: 2400 ($240).

PERFORMANCE: Top Speed: (1500) 75 mph; (1800) 85 mph; (Spt Cabr) 100 mph; (2400) 93 mph; (Pullman) 87 mph.

Manufacturer: Carl F.W. Borgward GmbH, Bremen, West Germany.

HISTORY: A 100-bhp Borgward "Supersport" coupe, able to travel nearly 145 mph, lost the 1953 Carrera Panamericana race but earned plenty of attention for the company. In 1954, a fastback two-seat coupe emerged with an 80-hp variant of that 1500-cc engine, able to go 0-60 mph in 15 seconds and hit 105 mph. Below its striking body profile was torsion-bar rear suspension.

1955 BORGWARD

ISABELLA — FOUR — Evolved from the company's success in the 1500-cc racing class with the Hansa 1500, the Isabella became quite a popular small car in the United States during the 1950s. A 1493-cc engine rated 60 horsepower sat under the alligator-style hood. Independent suspension with coil springs was used on all four wheels. Front wheels were suspended on triangular swinging arms and coil springs, with stabilizers and telescopic shock absorbers. Isabella's steering system used three tie rods, for easier track adjustment. A column-mounted gearshift lever selected from four forward speeds. Though officially a four-passenger vehicle, the company claimed that six could squeeze in when necessary. Three round gauges stood on the dashboard. The factory claimed a top speed of 82-83 mph.

Like all Borgward automobiles, the medium-size compact Isabella displayed a diamond-shape emblem on its grille, with horizontal bars emanating outward from the points of the diamond center. Small round parking lamps stood below the round headlamps. Separate 'BORGWARD' letters stood above the grille.

HANSA 1500/1800/2400 — These earlier models continued in production after the Isabella appeared, but were rare in the U.S. See previous listing for details.

I.D. DATA: Serial number is located on top of the right fender well, under the hood. Engine number is on upper left side of block, near the front.

Model	Body Type & Seating	Engine Type/CID	P.O.E. Price	Weight (lbs.)	Prod. Total
Isabella	2-dr Sedan-4P	I4/91	2350	2161	Note 1

Note 1: A total of about 110,000 Borgwards (all models) were produced during 1955. A total of 11,150 Isabellas had been built in late 1954, and two in every five went to the United States during 1955, when 24,658 were built.

ENGINE DATA: BASE FOUR: Inline, overhead-valve four-cylinder. Cast iron block and alloy head. **Displacement:** 91.1 cu. in. (1493 cc). **Bore & Stroke:** 2.95 x 3.33 in. (75 x 84.5 mm). **Compression Ratio:** 6.8:1. **Brake Horsepower:** 60 at 4700 rpm. **Torque:** 79.6 lbs.-ft. at 2500 rpm. Three main bearings. Solid valve lifters. One Solex downdraft carburetor.

CHASSIS DATA: Wheelbase: 102.4 in. **Overall Length:** 173 in. **Height:** 57.75 in. **Width:** 67.2 in. **Front Tread:** 52.6 in. **Rear Tread:** 53.6 in. **Standard Tires:** 5.90x13.

TECHNICAL: Layout: front-engine, rear-drive. **Transmission:** four-speed manual. Gear ratios: (1st) 4.18:1; (2nd) 2.32:1; (3rd) 1.47:1; (4th) 1.00:1; (rev) 4.4:1. **Standard Final Drive Ratio:** 3.90:1 (hypoid gear). **Steering:** Gemmer cam-and-roller. **Suspension (front):** long/short control arms, coil springs. **Suspension (rear):** independent swing axle, coil springs. **Brakes:** hydraulic, front/rear drum. **Body Construction:** steel unibody.

PERFORMANCE: Top Speed: 82-85 mph (factory). **Fuel Mileage:** 28-33 mpg (factory).
Manufacturer: Carl F.W. Borgward GmbH, Bremen, West Germany.
HISTORY: The new Isabella appeared at the International Motor Show in London, in October 1954. During the 1955 model year, the first examples were making their way to the U.S. Race versions of the engine, with fuel injection, soon reached as high as 115 horsepower before factory-authorized racing was abandoned in 1958.

1956 BORGWARD

ISABELLA — FOUR — In addition to the basic Isabella, the 1956 lineup included a Touring Sport (TS) model with a reclining seat and tuned dual-carburetor engine, rated 75 horsepower. The TS had lights on the fenders. Both a sedan and station wagon were available. The wagon had thin rear roof posts. With the rear seat folded, its load space was close to five feet long. Standard wagon equipment included turn signals, heater/fresh air system, front/rear armrests, clock, lighter, and an emergency plug-in light. Turning circle was 36 feet.

In a 1956 *Motorsport* test of the TS model, John Bentley described the car as "well finished, and with more of an American made look than most foreign cars." He managed to accelerate from zero to 60 mph in 14.8 seconds. Another road test of the station wagon, with less-powerful four-cylinder engine, yielded far slower figures.

I.D. DATA: Serial number is located under the hood, atop the right fender well. Engine number is on upper left side of block, near the front.

Model	Body Type & Seating	Engine Type/CID	P.O.E. Price	Weight (lbs.)	Prod. Total
	2-dr Sedan-5P	I4/91	2350	2161	Note 1
	2-dr Station Wag-5P	I4/91	2475	2402	Note 1
TS	2-dr TS Sedan-5P	I4/91	2640	2204	Note 1

Note 1: A total of 17,692 Isabellas were produced in 1956 (plus 3,301 wagons).

ENGINE DATA: BASE FOUR: Inline, overhead-valve four-cylinder. Cast iron block and alloy head. **Displacement:** 91.1 cu. in. (1493 cc). **Bore & Stroke:** 2.95 x 3.33 in. (75 x 84.5 mm). **Compression Ratio:** 6.8:1 (TS, 8.2:1). **Brake Horsepower:** 60 (DIN) at 4700 rpm; (TS) 75 (DIN) at 5200 rpm. **Torque:** (TS) 82.3 lbs.-ft. at 2500 rpm. Three main bearings. Solid valve lifters. One downdraft Solex carburetor.

CHASSIS DATA: Wheelbase: 102.4 in. **Overall Length:** 172.8 in. **Height:** 57.7 in. **Width:** 67.1 in. **Front Tread:** 52.5 in. (TS, 53.7 in.). **Rear Tread:** 53.5 in. **Standard Tires:** 5.90x13.

TECHNICAL: Layout: front-engine, rear-drive. **Transmission:** four-speed manual. Gear ratios: (1st) 3.86:1; (2nd) 2.15:1; (3rd) 1.36:1; (4th) 1.00:1; (rev) 4.06:1. Wagon gear ratios: (1st) 4.18:1; (2nd) 2.32:1; (3rd) 1.47:1; (4th) 1.0:1. **Standard Final Drive Ratio:** 3.90:1. **Steering:** Gemmer cam-and-roller. **Suspension (front):** long/short control arms, coil springs. **Suspension (rear):** independent swing axle, coil springs. **Brakes:** hydraulic, front/rear drum. **Body Construction:** steel unibody.

MAJOR OPTIONS: Radio ($75). Sport Touring engine (about $200). Sunroof.

PERFORMANCE: Top Speed: 82-83 mph; (TS) 90+ mph. **Acceleration (0-60 mph):** (TS sedan) 16-20 seconds; (wagon) 22.9 sec. **Acceleration (quarter-mile):** (wagon) 23.3 sec., reaching 61.8 mph; (TS sed) 19.8 sec.

Manufacturer: Carl F.W. Borgward GmbH, Bremen, West Germany.

HISTORY: Introduced October 1, 1955. TS appeared at the Frankfurt auto show in September 1955.

1957 BORGWARD

1957 Borgward Isabella coupe.

ISABELLA — A sunroof was available for the Isabella two-door sedan, which was otherwise unchanged. The Touring Sport (TS) model again included a reclining seat and higher-horsepower engine. 'Borgward' script was on the cowl, above a full-length horizontal trim strip. At the grille, a horizontal bar extended outward from the diamond points. Bright shrouded moldings encircled each headlamp. Small pointed parking lamps were below the headlamps. Protruding taillamps stood at upper rear corners of fenders.

1957 Borgward Kombi station wagon.

I.D. DATA: Serial number is atop the right fender well, under the hood. Engine number is on upper left side of block, near the front.

Model	Body Type & Seating	Engine Type/CID	P.O.E. Price	Weight (lbs.)	Prod. Total
	2-dr Sedan-5P	I4/91	2495	2161	Note 1
	2-dr Station Wag-5P	I4/91	2685	2402	Note 1
TS	2-dr Touring Spt-5P	I4/91	2845	2204	Note 1
TS	2-dr Conv Cpe	I4/91	3695	2235	Note 1
TS	2-dr Spt Coupe	I4/91	3695	2235	Note 1

Note 1: A total of 23,258 Isabellas were produced in 1957 (plus 7,226 wagons).
ENGINE DATA: Same as 1956.
CHASSIS DATA: Same as 1956.
TECHNICAL: Same as 1956.
MAJOR OPTIONS: Sliding roof: sedan and TS ($180).
PERFORMANCE: Similar to 1956.
HISTORY: Introduced October 1, 1956.

1958 BORGWARD

1958 Borgward Isabella coupe. (William Siuru Jr.)

ISABELLA — FOUR — A coupe joined the original sedan and Combi station wagon this year. Not much changed this year in Isabella's appearance otherwise, but the TS (Touring Sport) engine added a new dual-throat Solex carburetor. Rear springs were stiffer than before. A TS model was easy to identify, with parking lights atop the fenders and a single-width body molding that didn't appear on the base sedan. The TS also included assist straps, armrests, door pockets, a clock and a lighter in its standard-equipment list. Inside, reclining seats could convert into beds.

As usual, the Isabella's grille was easy to spot with its huge diamond in the center, and its unusually wide entry doors. Upholstery was foam rubber over springs. Dashboards contained a speedometer, gas gauge, temperature gauge, and indicator lights for ignition and oil pressure. The coupe had the same front end as other Isabellas but a shorter cockpit, with small rear quarter windows along the deck. A downswept trim line stood out on each bodyside. Coupe ads noted that "You can always depend on Borgward," highlighting the car's engineering qualities.

I.D. DATA: Serial number is under the hood, atop the right fender well. Engine number is on upper left side of block, near the front.

Model	Body Type & Seating	Engine Type/CID	P.O.E. Price	Weight (lbs.)	Prod. Total
	2-dr Sedan-5P	I4/91	2495	2200	Note 1
	2-dr Station Wag-5P	I4/91	2685	2253	Note 1
TS	2-dr Touring Spt-5P	I4/91	2845	2200	Note 1
TS	2-dr Spt Coupe	I4/91	3750	2420	Note 1

Note 1: Approximately 6,561 Borgwards were sold in the U.S. in 1958, out of 22,634 Isabellas built (plus 7,255 wagons).

ENGINE DATA: BASE FOUR: Inline, overhead-valve four-cylinder. Cast iron block and alloy head. **Displacement:** 91.1 cu. in. (1493 cc). **Bore & Stroke:** 2.95 x 3.33 in. (75 x 84.5 mm). **Compression Ratio:** 7.0:1 (TS, 8.2:1). **Brake Horsepower:** 66 at 4700 rpm (TS, 82 at 5800). **Torque:** 79.5 lbs.-ft. (TS, 83.5 lbs.-ft.). Three main bearings. Solid valve lifters. Solex 32PJCB carburetor (TS, 32PAITA dual-throat "Stage" carburetor).
CHASSIS DATA: Wheelbase: 102.4 in. Overall Length: 173 in. Height: (sed) 57.6 in.; (cpe) 53.1 in.; (wag) 59.8 in. Width: 67.0-69.7 in. Front Tread: 52.75 in. Rear Tread: 53.5 in. Standard Tires: 5.90x13 exc. (wagon) 6.40x13.
TECHNICAL: Layout: front-engine, rear-drive. Transmission: four-speed manual, column shift; all synchro. Gear ratios: (1st) 3.86:1; (2nd) 2.15:1; (3rd) 1.36:1; (4th) 1.0:1; (rev) 4.06:1. Standard Final Drive Ratio: 3.90:1. Steering: roller segment. Suspension (front): long/short control arms, coil springs. Suspension (rear): swinging axle, coil springs. Brakes: hydraulic, front/rear drum. Body Construction: steel unibody. Fuel Tank: 12.7 gallon.
MAJOR OPTIONS: Sliding sunroof: sedan and TS ($180).
PERFORMANCE: Top Speed: 80 mph; (TS) 95 mph. Acceleration (0-60 mph): (TS) 16 sec.; (cpe) 18.1 sec.
Manufacturer: Carl F.W. Borgward GmbH, Bremen, West Germany.
Distributor: Fergus Imported Cars, Inc., New York City; or Earle C. Anthony, Inc., Los Angeles.
HISTORY: Introduced October 1, 1957.

1959-60 BORGWARD

1959 Borgward Kombi.

1960 Borgward Isabella two-door sedan.

ISABELLA — FOUR — Sedans now had single-unit taillamps, and grille bars enclosed the diamond-shape grille emblem. Otherwise, little change was evident. Isabella upholstery was leathercloth. New this year was the SR sedan. Later in arriving was a new TS DeLuxe sedan, which turned out to be similar in appearance to the Borgwards that would be produced in Mexico, some years after the German company collapsed. A 100-horsepower limousine became available by 1960.
I.D. DATA: Chassis serial number and identification plate are located under the hood, top the right (passenger) fender well. Engine number is on upper left side of block, near the front.

1960 Borgward Isabella coupes.

Model	Body Type & Seating	Engine Type/CID	P.O.E. Price	Weight (lbs.)	Prod. Total
	2-dr Sedan-6P	I4/91	2495	2200	Note 1
	2-dr SR Sed-6P	I4/91	2675	2200	Note 1
	2-dr Combi Wag-5P	I4/91	2685	2253	Note 1
TS	2-dr Spt Sed-6P	I4/91	2845	2200	Note 1
TS	2-dr DeL Sed-6P	I4/91	3035	2200	Note 1
TS	2-dr Spt Cpe-2P	I4/91	3750	2420	Note 1

Note 1: Approximately 38,000 Borgwards (29,782 Isabellas) were built in 1959, and about 7,629 were sold in the U.S. A total of 28,878 Isabellas were built in 1960 (plus 7,219 wagons).

ENGINE DATA: Same as 1958.

CHASSIS DATA: Same as 1958.

TECHNICAL: Same as 1958.

MAJOR OPTIONS: Sunroof. Tailfins (coupe).

Manufactuer & Distributor: Same as 1958.

HISTORY: Introduced: (1959) October 1, 1958. With an optional speed kit installed on the engine, a Borgward TS sedan set a class record (Class E Touring Sports) at the Bonneville salt flats, averaging 93.56 mph, with a best one-way speed of 97.139 mph. After that accomplishment, the same car went through a 5,000-mile cross-country trek.

1961 BORGWARD

ISABELLA — FOUR — This was the final outing for the coupe, sedan and wagon from Bremen, Germany. Borgward, said one ad, "caters to your taste for luxury...at a price within your means." In its report on the Isabella, *Motor Trend* called the coupe a "plush personal car with an eye for economy." In fact, the magazine compared the coupe's design to that of the original Ford Thunderbird, noting its long deck and short cockpit with small rear quarter windows. A body crease sloped downward through the door, onto the quarter panel, to meet the coupe's bulging back fenders. Inside were reclining semi-bucket seats.

I.D. DATA: Serial number is atop the right fender well. Engine number is on upper left side of block, near the front.

Model	Body Type & Seating	Engine Type/CID	P.O.E. Price	Weight (lbs.)	Total Prod.
	2-dr Sedan-6P	I4/91	2250	2315	Note 1
	2-dr Combi Wag-5P	I4/91	2450	2657	Note 1
TS	2-dr Spt Sed-6P	I4/91	2580	2359	Note 1
TS	2-dr DeL Sed-6P	I4/91	2760	2359	Note 1
TS	2-dr Spt Cpe-2P	I4/91	3550	2425	Note 1

Note 1: A total of 7,395 Isabellas were built in 1961 (plus 2,205 wagons). In all, 202,862 Isabellas had been built since 1954 (including small trucks).

ENGINE DATA: BASE FOUR: Inline, overhead-valve four-cylinder. Cast iron block and alloy head. **Displacement:** 91.1 cu. in. (1493 cc). **Bore & Stroke:** 2.95 x 3.33 in. (75 x 84.5 mm). **Compression Ratio:** 7.0:1 (TS, 8.2:1). **Brake Horsepower:** 66 at 4800 rpm (TS, 82 at 5800). **Torque:** 80 lbs.-ft. at 2500 rpm (TS, 83.8 at 3000). Three main bearings. Solid valve lifters.

CHASSIS DATA: Wheelbase: 102.4 in. Overall Length: 172.8 in. Height: 57.8 in. Width: 67 in. Front Tread: 52.5 in. Rear Tread: 53.5 in. Standard Tires: 5.90x13.

TECHNICAL: Layout: front-engine, rear-drive. Transmission: four-speed manual (column shift); all synchro. Standard Final Drive Ratio: 3.90:1. Steering: Gemmer cam-and-roller. Suspension (front): long/short control arms, coil springs. Suspension (rear): independent swing axle, coil springs. Brakes: hydraulic, front/rear drum. Body Construction: steel unibody.

PERFORMANCE: Top Speed: 81 mph; (cpe) 95 mph. Acceleration (0-60 mph): (cpe) 19.4 sec.

Manufacturer: Carl F.W. Borgward GmbH, Bremen, West Germany.

Distributor: Borgward Motors Corp., Boston, Massachusetts.

BRISTOL

Both before and after World War II, the Bristol Aeroplane Company of Britain had a connection with BMW in Germany. When business slipped after wartime military contracts had been fulfilled, and plant facilities thus became available for other purposes, Bristol turned to automobiles. To help in that effort, Bristol just happened to have on hand a set of plans for prewar BMWs, along with several examples of same. They also managed to acquire the services of former BMW engineer Dr. Fritz Fiedler. Part of the credit for putting Bristol into this favorable position goes to H.J. Aldington of Frazer-Nash (also listed in this Catalog), who arranged to get Fiedler a work permit. Frazer-Nash had been the distributor of BMW motorcars in Britain before the war and used the same engine as Bristol for its postwar vehicles.

Bristol's goal was to build a "high-speed luxury motorcar for the connoisseur, a powerful, elegant model worthy of the 'Bristol' reputation." The first prototypes were completed by late 1946, using bodywork by Pinin Farina (including the traditional BMW "twin-kidney" grille). In the Type 401 sales brochure, an unnamed "eminent motoring authority" was quoted as having named Bristol "one of the great cars of our time." That car's Continental styling was promoted strongly, along with its strong performance, "feather-light steering" and roadholding ability. BMW-derived engines were used until 1961, when they were replaced by Chrysler V-8s. Though not imported in large numbers to the U.S., and basically built to order, Bristols gained quite a following in Britain as high-performance luxury motorcars.

1947-48 BRISTOL

1947 two-liter 400 Bristol saloon.

400 — SIX — The first coupe that Bristol put on the market, introduced at the 1947 Geneva (Switzerland) Salon, bore a strong resemblance to the prewar BMW 327 (as built by the Autenrieth company). Even the grille came in the traditional BMW "twin-kidney" style. Underneath, the 400's box-section chassis also was based on prewar BMW principles. Set on a 114-inch wheelbase, it used steel floor members to maintain structural rigidity. By no means modern in styling, the 400 was also heavy and expensive, but nicely built.

The six-cylinder engine, too, evolved from the 2.0-liter six that had been used in BMW's 328 sports car before World War II. It had the same "cross-pushrod" valve configuration, as well as hemispherical combustion chambers. Power output was 80 horsepower (later raised to 85). Though styled like a coupe, the body style was referred to as a "saloon" in Britain.

1948 Bristol 400. (Coys of Kensington)

I.D. DATA: Not available.

Model	Body Type & Seating	Engine Type/CID	P.O.E. Price	Weight (lbs.)	Prod. Total
400	2-dr Saloon-4P	I6/120	N/A	2537	700

Note: Production includes those 400s built in 1949.

ENGINE DATA: BASE SIX: Inline, overhead-valve six-cylinder (Bristol 85A). Cast iron block and aluminum head. **Displacement:** 120.3 cu. in. (1971 cc). **Bore & Stroke:** 2.60 x 3.78 in. (66 x 96 mm). **Compression Ratio:** 7.5:1. **Brake Horsepower:** 80 at 4200 rpm. **Torque:** 96 lbs.-ft. at 3000 rpm. Four main bearings. Solid valve lifters. Three SU carburetors. 12 volt electrics.

CHASSIS DATA: Wheelbase: 114 in. **Overall Length:** 183 in. **Height:** 59 in. **Width:** 64 in. **Front Tread:** 52 in. **Rear Tread:** 54 in. **Wheel Type:** 4x16. **Standard Tires:** 5.50x16 Dunlop.

TECHNICAL: Layout: front-engine, rear-drive. **Transmission:** four-speed manual (synchromesh 2nd/3rd/4th. Gear ratios: (1st) 4.3:1; (2nd) 2.17:1; (3rd) 1.3:1; (4th) 1:1; (rev) 3.44:1. **Standard Final Drive Ratio:** 3.44:1. **Steering:** rack and pinion. **Suspension (front):** independent; transverse leaf spring with upper wishbones. **Suspension (rear):** rigid (live) axle with lateral links, A-bracket and longitudinal torsion bars. **Brakes:** Lockheed hydraulic; front/rear drum. **Body Construction:** aluminum alloy body panels on steel frame.

PERFORMANCE: Top Speed: 95 mph. **Acceleration (0-60 mph):** N/A (0-50 in 10.3 seconds). **Acceleration (quarter-mile):** 19.7 seconds.

Manufacturer: Bristol Aeroplane Company Ltd., Filton, Bristol, England.

HISTORY: Introduced in 1946. A Type 400 took first place in the Touring category at the 1948 Belgian Circuit de la Sarthe race, and first in the 2-liter class at the Polish Rally.

1949-52 BRISTOL

1949 Bristol.

400 — SIX — The first Bristol automobile continued in production through late 1949, but had earlier been augmented by the 401.

401 — SIX — In addition to offering five more horsepower than the former model 400, the 401 had a more streamlined look, befitting the manufacturer of aircraft components. The new body was produced by Carrozzeria Touring (in Italy), using the new *superleggera* construction method of aluminum body panels on a multi-tube framework. Headlamps were right alongside the grille, which was again in typical "twin-kidney" style. Round foglights stood farther out on the fenders, and a round Bristol badge went above the grille's center. The split windshield was "vee" shaped. The four/five-passenger fastback body even boasted pushbutton door opening (like the 1946-48 Lincoln Zephyr). Ordinary door handles, according to the sales brochures, presented a "potential threat to clothing." Hidden knobs inside the car controlled the "thief-proof" hood and gas cap cover. At the rear, small rectangular taillamps stood just above the bumper.

1951 Bristol 401 saloon. (Sotheby's)

Under the hood was the same BMW-based 2.0-liter inline six-cylinder engine with aluminum cylinder head, hemispherical combustion chambers and inclined overhead valves, hooked to a four-speed gearbox. That combination was strong enough to allow Bristols to run in Rally events. In ten "top-class" races during 1949, a Bristol invariably ranked in the top four spots. A thermostat now controlled the engine's water temperature.

Bristols were available with either right- or left-hand drive. Lockheed hydraulic brakes were used, along with a cable-operated "fly-off" hand brake for the rear wheels. A foot pedal operated the "one-shot" chassis lubrication system. Telescopic shock absorbers were used. The spare tire mounted in a separate bin below the trunk floor. Standard equipment included a radio and a touring kit with spare parts.

402 — SIX — Joining the 401 fastback saloon was a small number of 402 convertibles, wearing a body modified by a number of designers (including Pinin Farina). Actual body construction was done at the Bristol plant, and wasn't the most graceful of open-top designs. On the plus side, the soft top folded away completely to produce a clean profile.

1952 Bristol 401 sports saloon.

I.D. DATA: Not available.

Model	Body Type & Seating	Engine Type/CID	P.O.E. Price	Weight (lbs.)	Total Prod.
400	2-dr Saloon-4P	I6/120	N/A	2537	700
401	2-dr Saloon-4/5P	I6/120	6950	2672	650
402	2-dr Conv-4P	I6/120	N/A	N/A	24

Note: Production totals shown are for all years in which each model was produced (1947-49 for model 400 and 1949-53 for model 401). Only one saloon was known to have been sold in the U.S. during 1951, and none in 1952.

ENGINE DATA: BASE SIX: Inline, overhead-valve six-cylinder (Bristol Type 85C). Cast iron block and aluminum head. **Displacement:** 120.3 cu. in. (1971 cc). **Bore & Stroke:** 2.60 x 3.78 in. (66 x 96 mm). **Compression Ratio:** 7.5:1. **Brake Horsepower:** 85 at 4500 rpm. **Torque:** 107 lbs.-ft. at 3500 rpm. Four main bearings. Solid valve lifters. Three Solex downdraft carburetors. 12-volt electrics.

Note: Some 400 models had the earlier 85A engine (see 1947-48 listing).

CHASSIS DATA: Wheelbase: 114 in. **Overall Length:** 190 in. **Height:** 60 in. **Width:** 67 in. **Front Tread:** 51.75 in. **Rear Tread:** 54 in. **Wheel Type:** 4.5J16 bolt-on "easy clean" disc. **Standard Tires:** 5.50x16 Dunlop or 5.75x16 Michelin X.

TECHNICAL: Layout: front-engine, rear-drive. **Transmission:** four-speed manual (floor lever). Overall gear ratios: (1st) 16.77:1; (2nd) 8.37:1; (3rd) 5.51:1; (4th) 3.9:1; (rev) 13.43:1. (Note: later models, starting with chassis no. 1006, had gearbox as in model 403). **Standard Final Drive Ratio:** 3.90:1 (semi-floating rear axle). **Steering:** rack and pinion (left or right hand). **Suspension (front):** independent; transverse leaf spring with upper wishbones. **Suspension (rear):** rigid (live) axle with lateral links, A-bracket and

longitudinal torsion bars. **Brakes:** Lockheed hydraulic, front/rear drum. **Body Construction:** aluminum alloy body panels on oval-tube steel frame; box-section chassis had four crossmembers and integral rear floor structure. **Fuel Tank:** 18-gallon (plus 2-gallon reserve).

PERFORMANCE: Top Speed: 100 mph (factory claim); 93-96 mph in independent tests. **Acceleration (0-60 mph):** 14.1 to 17.8 seconds. **Acceleration (quarter-mile):** 19.9 seconds. **Fuel Mileage:** about 22.7 mpg in hard driving.

Manufacturer: Bristol Aeroplane Company Ltd., Filton, Bristol, England.

HISTORY: Introduced: (401/402) 1949. In 1949, Bristols took third place overall at the Monte Carlo Rally; second in the Sicilian Targa Florio road race; and first in the touring category of the Tuscany Cup.

1953 BRISTOL

1953 Bristol 403 saloon. (Sotheby's)

401/402 — SIX — Production of the 401 saloon and 402 convertible continued into 1953; see preceding listing for details.

403 — SIX — Similar in appearance and engineering to the former 401, and with the same basic BMW-evolved engine under its hood, the 403 had 15 more horsepower to work with, largely as a result of a revised camshaft profile. The grille was again typical BMW "kidney" style, but with bright vertical bars instead of the former dark-colored bars. In addition, the model badges on hood sides and the trunk lid switched from yellow to red. Otherwise, little change was evident. Only the two-door saloon body (generally referred to as a coupe in the U.S.) was offered. An anti-roll bar was added to the front suspension. Bristols now used a Borg-Warner four-speed gearbox with much different gear ratios, as introduced on final 401 models. Light aluminum brake drums were carefully balanced. Some late examples adopted a shorter gearshift lever with remote linkage.

As noted by *Automobile Topics* magazine, the new 403, just like its predecessors, was sold as "a product for the connoisseur....Certainly, it is not an average automobile." A polished walnut dashboard held a tachometer and full gauge complement, plus ignition and fuel reserve warning lights and two large glove compartments. Crushed grain leather upholstered the bucket seats. Standard equipment included a heater and windshield washer.

404 — SIX — While the Type 403 continued the earlier 401 look, the new 404 (which appeared late in the year) was completely different: smoother and more modern in design. The two-seat fastback coupe design soon became known as the "Businessman's Express," as a result of its quick acceleration and top speed beyond 110 mph. Considerably smaller than its companion, the 404 rode a 96-inch wheelbase. Powerplant was the same BMW-derived inline six, but with higher compression and five additional horsepower. Alfin front brake drums were made of light aluminum. An optional 100C engine, delivering 125 horsepower, was available for competition use. A sales brochure for the sport coupe noted that the 404 "combines the performance of a competition car with the docility and dignity of a town carriage."

This body was built by Bristol, using steel and light alloy panels over a steel and laminated ash (wooden) framework. A dark recessed mesh pattern made the 404's grille look almost like a plain hole in the front of the car. Headlamps moved to the conventional location in fenders, as opposed to the narrow-set installation in the 401/402/403. Small round amber parking lamps went below the headlamps, and the hood sported a scoop. At the rear were small tailfins and round taillamps: two red, two amber. Foglamps were optional. British versions had a central spotlight, while export Bristols often substituted twin auxiliary lamps above the front bumper. The left front fender held an opening for the spare tire, while a matching hatch on the right fender covered the battery and electrical parts. Standard equipment included a heater and windshield washer.

Brochures promoting a drophead two-seater coupe version of the 404 were distributed at the London Motor Show in fall 1953, but no more than one example (built by E.D. Abbott) was produced.

I.D. DATA: (404) starting chassis serial number: 404/2001.

Model	Body Type & Seating	Engine Type/CID	P.O.E. Price	Weight (lbs.)	Total Prod.
403	2-dr Saloon-4/5P	I6/120	5600	2670	300
404	2-dr Coupe-2 + 2P	I6/120	8000	2262	40

Price Note: 404 price is approximate; 403 amount as given in U.S. pricing guide, which listed 404 as only $6370.

Production Note: Production totals shown are for all years in which each model was produced (1953-55 for model 403 and 1953-56 for model 404). Approximately six Bristols were sold in the U.S. in 1953.

ENGINE DATA: BASE SIX (Type 403): Inline, overhead-valve six-cylinder (Bristol Type 100A). Cast iron block and aluminum head. **Displacement:** 120.3 cu. in. (1971 cc). **Bore & Stroke:** 2.60 x 3.78 in. (66 x 96 mm). **Compression Ratio:** 7.5:1. **Brake Horsepower:** 100 at 5000 rpm. **Torque:** 117 lbs.-ft. at 3500 rpm. Four main bearings. Solid valve lifters. Three Solex carburetors. 12-volt electrical.

Note: Final few Type 403s had 100B2 engine, as used in Type 405.

BASE 100B SIX (Type 404): Same as above, but — **Compression Ratio:** 8.5:1. **Brake Horsepower:** 105 at 5000 rpm. **Torque:** 123 lbs.-ft. at 3750 rpm.

OPTIONAL 100C SIX (Type 404): Same as above, but — **Brake Horsepower:** 125 at 5500 rpm.

CHASSIS DATA: Wheelbase: (403) 114 in.; (404) 96.25 in. **Overall Length:** (403) 190 in.; (404) 171.25 in. **Height:** (403) 60 in.; (404) 55.5 in. **Width:** (403) 67 in.; (404) 68 in. **Front Tread:** (403) 51.75 in.; (404) 52.4 in. **Rear Tread:** (403) 54 in.; (404) 54 in. **Wheel Type:** 4.5J16 bolt-on disc. **Standard Tires:** 5.75x16 Dunlop or Michelin X.

TECHNICAL: Layout: front-engine, rear-drive. **Transmission:** four-speed manual (floor lever). **Gear ratios:** (1st, freewheeling) 3.61:1; (2nd) 1.83:1; (3rd) 1.29:1; (4th) 1.0:1; (rev) 2.89:1. **Standard Final Drive Ratio:** 3.90:1 (spiral bevel). **Steering:** rack and pinion (left or right hand). **Suspension (front):** independent; transverse leaf spring with upper wishbones and anti-roll torsion bar. **Suspension (rear):** rigid (live) axle with lateral links, A-bracket and longitudinal torsion bars. **Brakes:** Lockheed hydraulic, front/rear drum (Alfin front or front/rear drums). **Body Construction:** aluminum alloy body panels on oval-tube steel frame; box-section chassis had four cross-members and integral rear floor structure.

MAJOR OPTIONS: Foglamps (404).

PERFORMANCE: Top Speed: (403) about 100 mph; (404) 110-115 mph. **Acceleration (0-60 mph):** (403) about 15 seconds; (404) about 12.3 to 13.5 seconds. **Fuel Mileage:** (403) 20-21 mpg; (404) about 18 mpg.

Manufacturer: Bristol Aeroplane Company Ltd., Filton, Bristol, England.

HISTORY: Introduced: (403) May 1953; (404) October 1953.

1954-57 BRISTOL

1954 Bristol 404. (Coys of Kensington.)

1954 Bristol Type 404 convertible.

403/404 — SIX — Production of the 403 saloon continued into 1955, and of the 404 into 1956; see preceding listing for details.

405 — SIX — A four-door saloon version of the 404 debuted in 1954, on the longer (114-inch) wheelbase of the former 401/402/403, and remained in production into 1958. Front-end appearance was the same as the 404, but the notchback body was a bit more rounded than prior Bristols, with a little more glass area. Both front and rear doors had vent windows. A Laycock de Normanville (electrical) overdrive was now standard, working only on fourth gear. Noting the car's "sleek lines (and) wondrous collection of unusual features," *Motor Trend* called the 405 "a deluxe sedan with true sports car performance and handling."

A heater with demister and a windshield washer were standard. So were leather upholstery with armrests, sliding front bucket seats with rake adjustment, four-inch speedometer and tachometer, and a map reading light. A folding center armrest gave space for a fifth passenger in the rear. As before, the spare tire fit into a compartment inside the left fender, just to the rear of the front tire; and the battery into a matching compartment on the opposite side. The final saloons had front disc brakes and Bristol 110 engines (as used in the Type 406).

In addition to the saloon, a two-door drophead coupe was offered, built by E.D. Abbott Ltd. (of Farnham). Its top, when folded, fit flush into a compartment. Side windows held ventipanes.

Ten body colors were offered, including: Reef Blue, Hungarian Green, Copper Beech, Peach Brown, Torch Red, Midnight Blue, Deep Grey, Ash Grey, Off White, and Black. Those were matched by nine choices of upholstery color.

1955 Bristol 405 drophead coupe.

1956 Bristol 405 drophead coupe. (Sotheby's)

I.D. DATA: Not available.

Model	Body Type & Seating	Engine Type/CID	P.O.E. Price	Weight (lbs.)	Prod. Total
403	2-dr Saloon-4/5P	I6/120	5600	2670	300
404	2-dr Coupe-2 + 2P	I6/120	6370	2262	40
405	4-dr Saloon-4/5P	I6/120	6090	2660	297
405	2-dr Dhd Cpe-4P	I6/120	N/A	2782	43

Price Note: Prices shown were listed in U.S. pricing guides in late 1950s. Other sources state that the 405 Saloon sold for at least $7000 in the U.S. Price at the British factory for the 405 was $5880.

Production Note: Production totals shown are for all years in which each model was produced (1953-55 for model 403, 1953-56 for model 404, and 1954-58 for Type 405).

1956 Bristol 405 saloon.

ENGINE DATA: BASE SIX (Type 403): Same as 1953.
BASE 100B SIX (Type 404): Same as 1953.
BASE 100B2 SIX (Type 405): Same as Type 404 engine, except final models had engine as in Type 406.
OPTIONAL 100C SIX (Type 404): Same as 1953.

CHASSIS DATA: Wheelbase: (403/405) 114 in.; (404) 96.25 in. **Overall Length:** (403) 190 in.; (404) 171.25 in.; (405) 189.25 in. **Height:** (403) 60 in.; (404) 55.5 in.; (405) 57.5 in. **Width:** (403) 67 in.; (404/405) 68 in. **Front Tread:** (403) 51.75 in.; (404/405) 52.4 in. **Rear Tread:** 54 in. **Wheel Type:** 4.5J16 bolt-on disc. **Standard Tires:** (403/404); 5.75x16 Dunlop or Michelin X; (405) 5.75x16 Dunlop or 6.00x16 Michelin.

TECHNICAL: Layout: front-engine, rear-drive. **Transmission:** four-speed manual (floor lever). Gear ratios for Type 403/404: (1st, freewheeling) 3.61:1; (2nd) 1.83:1; (3rd) 1.29:1; (4th) 1.0:1; (rev) 2.89:1. Gear ratios for Type 405: same with addition of 0.78:1 overdrive. **Standard Final Drive Ratio:** (403/404) 3.90:1; (405) 4.22:1. **Steering:** rack and pinion (left or right hand). **Suspension (front):** independent; transverse leaf spring with upper wishbones and anti-roll torsion bar. **Suspension (rear):** rigid (live) axle with lateral links, A-bracket and longitudinal torsion bars. **Brakes:** Lockheed hydraulic, front/rear drum (Alfin front or front/rear drums); Dunlop front disc brakes on final 405 models. **Body Construction:** (403/404) aluminum alloy body panels on steel frame; (405) aluminum alloy panels on steel and laminated ash frame.

MAJOR OPTIONS: Radio. Fitted suitcases (drophead).

PERFORMANCE: Top Speed: (404) 110 mph; (405) 105 mph. **Acceleration (0-60 mph):** (405) 14 seconds (estimated).
Manufacturer: Bristol Aeroplane Company Ltd., Filton, Bristol, England.

HISTORY: Introduced: (403) May 1953; (404) October 1953; (405) 1954.

1958-60 BRISTOL

405 — SIX — Production of the 405 saloon continued into 1958; see preceding listing for details.

406 — SIX — After several years of offering a short-wheelbase coupe and a long-wheelbase saloon (sedan), Bristol switched to a long-wheelbase two-door coupe in 1958. This would be the last Bristol with a BMW-derived inline six under its hood, but enlarged to 135 cu. in. (2.2-liter) displacement this time around. Instead of the former fastback coupe, this would be a notchback, with a more modern and conventional appearance. Tailfins were less pronounced, and the twin taillamps on each side of the back panel were mounted in a diagonal pattern. Backup lights stood alongside the license plate. Quarter windows were considerably larger than in the 404. Although the basic grille shape was similar to the 404/405, it used a brighter pattern of horizontal bars and the nose itself had less of a frontal bulge. Round parking lights were below the fender-mounted single headlamps. The new body weighed considerably more than its predecessor, though peaking at a lower speed. The six-cylinder powerplant drove a four-speed manual gearbox with overdrive. Suspension was similar to prior models, except that a Watt linkage was now used to position the rear axle. Disc brakes were now standard on all four wheels. The body was taller than before, the interior roomier, front/rear track (tread) dimensions larger. As before, too, front fender compartments held the spare tire, battery, and windshield-washer fluid container.

Half a dozen special 406 models had lightweight coupe bodies built by Zagato, and specially-tuned engines that delivered 130 horsepower. Though quite startling in appearance, these were capable of hitting 125 mph.

I.D. DATA: Not available.

Model	Body Type & Seating	Engine Type/CID	P.O.E. Price	Weight (lbs.)	Prod. Total
405	4-dr Saloon-4P	I6/120	N/A	2672	297
405	2-dr Dhd Cpe-4P	I6/120	N/A	2782	43
406	2-dr Coupe-4P	I6/135	Note 1	3009	292
406	2-dr Zagato-4P	I6/135	N/A	2469	6

Note 1: Price at the factory for Type 406 was $8386.

Production Note: Production totals shown are for all years in which each model was produced (1954-58 for Type 405 and 1958-61 for Type 406).

ENGINE DATA: BASE SIX: Inline, overhead-valve six-cylinder (Bristol Type 110). Cast iron block and aluminum head. **Displacement:** 135.2 cu. in. (2216 cc). **Bore & Stroke:** 2.72 x 3.94 in. (69 x 100 mm). **Compression Ratio:** 8.5:1. **Brake Horsepower:** 105 at 4700 rpm. **Torque:** 129 lbs.-ft. at 3000 rpm. Four main bearings. Solid valve lifters. Three Solex carburetors. 12-volt electrics.

OPTIONAL SIX (Zagato specials): Same as above, but -- **Compression Ratio:** 9.0:1. **Brake Horsepower:** 130 at 5750 rpm.

CHASSIS DATA: Wheelbase: 114 in. **Overall Length:** (405) 189.25 in.; (406) 196 in.; (406 Zagato, 185 in.). **Height:** (405) 57.5 in.; (406) 60 in.; (406 Zagato, 55 in.). **Width:** 68 in. (Zagato, 63 in.). **Front Tread:** (405) 52.4 in.; (406) 53 in. **Rear Tread:** (405) 54 in.; (406) 56 in. **Standard Tires:** (405) 5.75x16 Dunlop or 6.00x16 Michelin; (406) 5.75/6.00x16 Dunlop or Michelin or 6.00H16 Dunlop.

TECHNICAL: Layout: front-engine, rear-drive. **Transmission:** four-speed manual (floor lever); hypoid bevel final drive. Gear ratios: (1st, freewheeling) 3.61:1; (2nd) 1.83:1; (3rd) 1.29:1; (4th) 1.0:1; (overdrive) 0.78:1; (rev) 2.89:1. **Standard Final Drive Ratio:** (405) 4.22:1; (406) 4.27:1. **Steering:** rack and pinion. **Suspension (front):** independent; transverse leaf spring with upper wishbones and anti-roll torsion bar. **Suspension (rear):** (405) rigid axle with lateral links, A-bracket and longitudinal torsion bars; (406) rigid axle with lateral links, Watt linkage, torque link and longitudinal torsion bars. **Brakes:** front/rear disc (11.25-inch). **Body Construction:** (405) aluminum alloy panels on steel and laminated ash frame; (406) aluminum body panels on steel frame.

PERFORMANCE: Top Speed: (405) about 105 mph; (406 Zagato) about 125 mph.
Manufacturer: Bristol Aeroplane Company Ltd., Filton, Bristol, England.

HISTORY: Introduced: (405) 1954; (406) 1958. In 1960, the company merged with Hawker Siddeley, with the car division to be called Bristol Cars Ltd.

1961-62 BRISTOL

406 — SIX — Production of the six-cylinder 406 coupe continued into 1961; see preceding listing for details.

407 — V-8 — For the first time, Bristol abandoned its six-cylinder powerplant and turned instead to Canada for a Chrysler "hemi" V-8, of 313 cubic-inch displacement and rated 250 horsepower. The new powerplant, built by Chrysler to meet Bristol's requirements, drove a modified three-speed TorqueFlite automatic. Instead of Chrysler's usual hydraulic valve lifters, this engine had solid lifters. And the displacement itself was unavailable anywhere else in the Chrysler lineup. At long last, too, the old transverse-spring front suspension was abandoned, replaced by a modern arrangement of dual control arms and coil springs. The advantage of replacing the former rack-and-pinion steering with a cam-and-roller setup is less evident, but was required with the big and heavy V-8 under the hood. The enormous horsepower boost made this the fastest (if heaviest) Bristol yet. Though similar in appearance to the 406, the 407 got a lower hoodline with little of the bulge that marked earlier models. A large shield insignia decorated the dark-patterned grille insert, which had a round emblem above it.

I.D. DATA: Not available.

Model	Body Type & Seating	Engine Type/CID	P.O.E. Price	Weight (lbs.)	Prod. Total
406	2-dr Coupe-4P	I6/135	N/A	3009	292
406	2-dr Zagato-4P	I6/135	N/A	2469	6
407	2-dr Coupe-4P	V8/313	N/A	3585	300

Note: Production totals shown are for all years in which each model was produced (1958-61 for Type 406 and 1961-63 for Type 407).

ENGINE DATA: BASE SIX (406): See 1958-60.

BASE V-8 (407): Overhead-valve V-8 (Chrysler Canada). Cast iron block and head. **Displacement:** 313 cu. in. (5130 cc). **Bore & Stroke:** 3.88 x 3.31 in. (98.5 x 84.1 mm). **Compression Ratio:** 9.0:1. **Brake Horsepower:** 250 at 4400 rpm. **Torque:** 340 lbs.-ft. at 2800 rpm. Five main bearings. Solid valve lifters. Carter four-barrel carburetor. 12-volt electrical.

CHASSIS DATA: Wheelbase: 114 in. **Overall Length:** (406) 196 in.; (407) 199 in. **Height:** 60 in. **Width:** 68 in. **Front Tread:** 53 in. **Rear Tread:** (406) 56 in.; (407) 54.5 in. **Wheel Size:** (407) 5K16. **Standard Tires:** (406) 5.75/6.00x16 Dunlop or Michelin or 6.00H16 Dunlop; (407) 6.00H16 Dunlop.

TECHNICAL: Layout: front-engine, rear-drive. **Transmission:** (406) four-speed manual; (407) three-speed TorqueFlite automatic. **Standard Final Drive Ratio:** (406) 4.27:1; (407) 3.31:1 or optional 3.07:1. **Steering:** (406) rack and pinion; (407) Marles cam and roller. **Suspension (front):** (406) transverse leaf spring with upper wishbones and anti-roll torsion bar; (407) unequal-length wishbones with coil springs and anti-roll torsion bar. **Suspension (rear):** rigid (live) axle with lateral links, Watt linkage, Torque link and longitudinal torsion bars. **Brakes:** front/rear disc (11.25-inch). **Body Construction:** aluminum body panels on steel frame.

PERFORMANCE: Top Speed: (406) about 105 mph; (407) 122 mph. **Acceleration (0-60 mph):** (407) 9.9 seconds. **Acceleration (quarter-mile):** (407) 17.4 seconds.

Manufacturer: Bristol Cars Ltd., Filton, Bristol, England.

HISTORY: Introduced: (406) 1958; (407) 1961. Bristol had designed an alternate six-cylinder engine to replace the aging BMW derivation, but for cost reasons chose to adopt the Chrysler V-8 instead. During the run of the 407, the Bristol company was sold to Anthony Crook and Sir George White.

1963-64 BRISTOL

407 — V-8 — Production of the 407 coupe continued into 1963; see preceding listing for details.

408 — V-8 — Styling took a notable turn as Bristol's 408 coupe replaced the 407. Basic construction was unchanged, but the 407 displayed an entirely different grille: wide rectangular in shape, with horizontal bars and inset driving lights. The grille also tapered forward slightly at the top, giving the car a much more angular appearance. Rounded rectangular park/signal lights stood below the single round headlamps in flat panels at the fronts of the fenders. A flat hood extended all the way to the grille, rather than looking more like a short lid as in prior models. Two bodyside trim strips were now used instead of one, but the lower strip ran only part of the distance, stopping halfway back on the door. The roofline, too, was flatter than before. Single tall taillamps now resided along the rear edges of the quarter panels, just below little vestiges of tailfins. On the mechanical side, Armstrong Selectaride adjustable telescopic shock absorbers were now installed at the rear.

I.D. DATA: Not available.

Model	Body Type & Seating	Engine Type/CID	P.O.E. Price	Weight (lbs.)	Prod. Total
407	2-dr Coupe-4P	V8/313	N/A	3585	300
408	2-dr Coupe-4P	V8/313	12000	3585	300

Note: Price and production totals for Type 408 are approximate. Production totals shown are for all years in which each model was produced (1961-63 for Type 407 and 1963-65 for Type 408).

ENGINE DATA: BASE V-8: Same as Type 407 (1961-62).

Note: Final examples of Type 408 (called Mark 2) used the 318-cid V-8 as in Type 409.

CHASSIS DATA: Wheelbase: 114 in. **Overall Length:** (407) 199 in.; (408) 193.5 in. **Height:** (407) 60 in.; (408) 59 in. **Width:** 68 in. **Front Tread:** 53 in. **Rear Tread:** 54.5 in. **Wheel Size:** 5K16. **Standard Tires:** 6.00H16 Dunlop.

TECHNICAL: Layout: front-engine, rear-drive. **Transmission:** three-speed TorqueFlite automatic. **Standard Final Drive Ratio:** 3.31:1 or (optional) 3.07:1. **Steering:** (407) Marles cam and roller; (408) Marles worm. **Suspension (front):** unequal-length wishbones

1965-66 BRISTOL

408 — V-8 — Production of the 408 coupe continued into 1965; see preceding listing for full details.

409 — V-8 — Appearance changed little from the 408 model, but under the hood was a slightly larger Canadian Chrysler V-8 now a familiar (to Americans) 318 cubic inches rather than the former 313. Neither horsepower nor torque got a boost, but reported performance was stronger, with Bristols able to hit 130 mph and break nine seconds in a 0-60 mph sprint. Improved weight distribution, with this larger engine setting farther back in the chassis than its predecessor, may have made a difference. A revised Torque-Flite transmission (now in a lighter weight alloy housing) allowed holding in second gear, for quicker acceleration. Axle ratio changed too, to a standard 3.07:1. Revised springs gave a softer ride. Four-wheel disc brakes continued, but the new ones were supplied by Girling, not Dunlop. A Mark 2 edition of the 409, with power steering, emerged in the fall of 1966.

I.D. DATA: Not available.

Model	Body Type & Seating	Engine Type/CID	P.O.E. Price	Weight (lbs.)	Prod. Total
408	2-dr Coupe-4P	V8/313	12000	3585	300
409	2-dr Coupe-4P	V8/318	Note 1	3527	300

Note 1: Price at the factory for Type 409 was $11,261.

Note: Price and production totals are approximate. Production totals shown are for all years in which each model was produced (1963-65 for Type 408 and 1965-67 for Type 409).

ENGINE DATA: BASE V-8: Overhead-valve V-8 (Chrysler Canada). Cast iron block and head. **Displacement:** 318 cu. in. (5211 cc). **Bore & Stroke:** 3.91 x 3.31 in. (99.3 x 84.1 mm). **Compression Ratio:** 9.0:1. **Brake Horsepower:** 250 at 4400 rpm. **Torque:** 340 lbs.-ft. at 2800 rpm. Five main bearings. Solid valve lifters. Carter four-barrel carburetor. 12-volt electrical.

CHASSIS DATA: Wheelbase: 114 in. **Overall Length:** 193.5 in. **Height:** 59 in. **Width:** 68 in. **Front Tread:** (408) 53 in.; (409) 54 in. **Rear Tread:** 54.5 in. **Wheel size:** 5K16. **Standard Tires:** 6.00H16 Dunlop.

TECHNICAL: Layout: front-engine, rear-drive. **Transmission:** three-speed TorqueFlite automatic. **Standard Final Drive Ratio:** 3.07:1; hypoid bevel final drive. **Steering:** Marles worm (power assisted on Mark 2). **Suspension (front):** unequal-length wishbones with coil springs and anti-roll torsion bar. **Suspension (rear):** rigid (live) axle with lateral links, Watt linkage, Torque link and longitudinal torsion bars. **Brakes:** Girling power-assisted front/rear disc. **Body Construction:** aluminum body panels on steel frame.

PERFORMANCE: Top Speed: (409) 130 mph. **Acceleration (0-60 mph):** (409) 8.8 seconds. **Acceleration (quarter-mile):** (409) 17 seconds.

Manufacturer: Bristol Cars Ltd., Filton, Bristol, England.

HISTORY: Introduced: (408) 1963; (409) 1965; (409 Mark 2) fall 1965.

1967-68 BRISTOL

409 — V-8 — Production of the 409 coupe continued into 1967; see preceding listing for full details.

410 — V-8 — Appearance was similar to the 409 model, except that headlamps were now recessed somewhat, no longer sharing a flat panel with the rectangular park/signal lights below. Air conditioning was now optional, and acrylic body paint replaced the former enamel. Both bodyside trim strips extended nearly the full car length, and met each other at both the front and rear. Instead of the former American-oriented pushbutton controls for the Chrysler TorqueFlite transmission, a floor lever was used. As before, Girling disc brakes were installed on all four wheels, but the 410's system had two separate circuits for "fail-safe" operation. Suspension modifications improved the Bristol's handling, but retained the former basic layout of front coil springs and rear torsion bars. A drop in tire size from 16-inch to 15-inch diameter also helped handling. Power steering was standard (as on the Mark 2 version of the 409).

I.D. DATA: Not available.

Model	Body Type & Seating	Engine Type/CID	P.O.E. Price	Weight (lbs.)	Prod. Total
409	2-dr Coupe-4P	V8/318	N/A	3527	300
410	2-dr Coupe-4P	V8/318	Note 1	3525	300

Note 1: Price of Type 410 at the factory was $11,094.

Production Note: Production totals shown are approximate, and for all years in which each model was produced (1965-67 for Type 409 and 1967-69 for the 410).

ENGINE DATA: BASE V-8: Same as 1965-66 models.

CHASSIS DATA: Same as 1965-66 models, except -- **Rear Tread:** (410) 55 in. **Wheel size:** 5K15. **Standard Tires:** 6.70H15 Avon Turbospeed.

TECHNICAL/PERFORMANCE: Same as 1965-66 models.

MAJOR OPTIONS: Air conditioning.

HISTORY: Introduced: (409 Mark 2) fall 1965; (410) 1967.

1969-76 BRISTOL

1970 Bristol 411 two-door coupe. (Sotheby's)

410 — V-8 — Production of the 410 coupe continued into 1969; see preceding listing for full details.

411 — V-8 — Although similar in appearance to the prior 410 model, the 411 changed in a few details; and subsequent editions would change even more in appearance. Only a short upper bodyside trim strip was used, extending from the front wheel opening barely halfway along the door. Another tiny strip at the same level ran only a few inches, above the rear wheel. Farther down, twin bright strips reached between the front and rear wheels. Both windshield and backlight rake angles became slightly steeper in this version. Vertical taillamps were similar to prior models, but squared off at the top and bottom rather than rounded. As before, backup lights stood alongside the license plate.

Except for suspension and drivetrain modification over the years since the 400 was introduced, the basic box-section platform and squarish body (evolved from a prewar BMW design) had changed remarkably little. Under the hood, though, came yet another major change: a switch from the 318-cid Chrysler hemi V-8 to a 383-cid Chrysler wedge-head engine. The bigger engine added plenty of horsepower and torque, quickening 0-60 mph acceleration time to seven seconds and boosting top speed to near 140 mph. As usual, the big V-8 drove a Chrysler TorqueFlite three-speed automatic transmission. Radial tires were now standard, in 185VR15 size.

While the 411 designation remained through 1976, no less than six variants were sold. A Mark 2 version arrived in late 1970, with wider wheels and a self-leveling rear suspension. Then, in 1972, the Mark 3 edition sported four big (seven-inch) round headlamps, each pair mounted side by side, instead of the former combinations of headlamps and large driving lamps. The full-width oval grille opening, with a dark squarish insert, encompassed all those headlamps. Amber park/signal light lenses were down in the bumper. Instead of a trim strip along the upper bodyside, a narrow paint stripe ran from the leading edge of the front fender to halfway back along the door. Four exhaust outlets emerged from the back end. Next, in 1974, came yet another version: the Mark 4, with a 400-cid Chrysler V-8 (and much lower compression ratio) and a restyled rear end. Finally came a short-lived Mark 5, with little change evident.

I.D. DATA: Not available.

Model	Body Type & Seating	Engine Type/CID	P.O.E. Price	Weight (lbs.)	Total Prod.
410	2-dr Coupe-4P	V8/318	N/A	3525	300
411	2-dr Coupe-4P	V8/383	Note 1	3726	600

Note 1: Price for Type 411 was 6028 British pounds (Sterling).

Note: Figures shown are for Mark 1 version of the Type 411. Weight rose to 3775 pounds for the Mark 4. Production totals shown are for all years in which each model was produced (1967-69 for Type 410 and 1969-76 for the 411).

ENGINE DATA: BASE V-8 (through Mark 3): Overhead-valve V-8 (Chrysler Canada). Cast iron block and head. **Displacement:** 383 cu. in. (6277 cc). **Bore & Stroke:** 4.25 x 3.37 in. (107.9 x 85.7 mm). **Compression Ratio:** 10.0:1. **Brake Horsepower:** 335 (SAE gross) at 5200 rpm. **Torque:** 425 lbs.-ft. at 3400 rpm. Five main bearings. Carter four-barrel carburetor. 12-volt electrics.
BASE V-8 (Mark 4): Same as above, except -- **Displacement:** 400 cu. in. (6556 cc). **Bore & Stroke:** 4.34 x 3.375 in. **Compression Ratio:** 8.2:1. **Brake Horsepower:** 264 (SAE net) at 4800 rpm. **Torque:** 335 lbs.-ft. at 3600 rpm.

CHASSIS DATA: Wheelbase: 114 in. **Overall Length:** (410) 193.5 in.; (411) 193 in.; (411 Mark 3) 194 in.; (411 Mark 4) 194.5 in. **Height:** (410) 59 in.; (411) 57.5 in. **Width:** 68 in. **Front Tread:** 54 in. except (411 Mark 2) 54.5 in. **Rear Tread:** 55 in. except (411 Mark 3) 55.25 in. **Wheel Size:** 5K15. **Standard Tires:** (410) 6.70H15 Avon Turbospeed; (411) 185VR15 Avon Radial.

TECHNICAL: Layout: front-engine, rear-drive. **Transmission:** three-speed TorqueFlite automatic. **Standard Final Drive Ratio:** 3.07:1; hypoid bevel final drive. **Steering:** (410) Marles worm, power-assisted; (411) ZF, power-assisted. **Suspension (front):** unequal-length wishbones with coil springs and anti-roll torsion bar. **Suspension (rear):** rigid (live) axle with lateral links, Watt linkage, torque link and longitudinal torsion bars; Mark 2 added Armstrong automatic hydraulic self-leveling system. **Brakes:** Girling power-assisted front/rear disc. **Body Construction:** aluminum body panels on steel frame.

PERFORMANCE: Top Speed: (411) 138-143 mph. **Acceleration (0-60 mph):** (411) 7.0 seconds.

Manufacturer: Bristol Cars Ltd., Filton, Bristol, England.

HISTORY: Introduced: (410) 1967; (411 Mark 1) 1969.

BRISTOL POSTSCRIPT: The Bristol organization returned to the automotive marketplace in 1978, at least for the home market, announcing a 603 series saloon. Two versions were powered by Chrysler V-8 engines (5211 or 5900 cc). Far different In appearance than the former models, the two-door coupe had quad headlamps and a welded steel body (with aluminum panels) atop a platform-style steel frame. According to a *Motor Trend* report, the modernized Bristol was claimed to run from 0-60 mph in 7.6 seconds and hit a hundred in 19 seconds. A Type 412 also was developed, with a design by Zagato.

BUGATTI

Not every enthusiast is aware that the fabled Bugatti did not quite disappear from the automotive scene after World War II erupted. During the war, the Bugatti plant at Molsheim had been occupied by German forces, and not returned to the family for a time after the 1946 Allied victory. Over the next few years, however, Ettore Bugatti and his son Roland first developed a Type 73 race/touring car powered by a 1.5-liter overhead-cam engine (built in their Paris facility). And a few years after Ettore's death in August 1947, about 20 updated versions of the famed Type 57 were produced at the old Molsheim plant, under the direction of Pierre Marco. The original Type 57 had been powered by a twin-cam 3.3-liter straight eight, rated 140 horsepower, and came in a variety of body styles.

Bugatti had a long racing history, of course, dating back to 1907. During the 1920s, Bugattis managed to emerge victorious in most of the major European road races, scoring more than 4,400 wins by the time war broke out in 1939. Bugatti bodies were known by their distinctive horseshoe-shaped radiators; their chassis by reversed quarter-elliptic rear springs. The Type 57S, wearing a lower body on a shortened chassis, had been designed by Ettore Bugatti's son Jean, and won the LeMans 24-Hour events in both 1937 and 1939. Most potent of the lot, the supercharged 57SC churned out 200 horsepower. Of the 750 Type 57s built before the war, only 40 or so were either the 57S or 57SC edition.

Soon after the war ended, and before Ettore died in 1947, Bugatti produced a 1.5-liter Type 77 race/touring car. Then, in 1951, a handful of modern-styled Type 101s (described below) were built, on the prewar Type 57 chassis.

Even after the Type 101 faded away in 1951, the Bugatti badge didn't quite evaporate. Rumors persisted that a 101 would be built in significant numbers, perhaps in both two-door and four-door form. In the mid-1950s, a Model 251 Grand Prix Bugatti appeared, powered by a crossie-mounted eight-cylinder engine, but its race record was poor. In 1957, *Road & Track* reported that another Bugatti "may see the light of day at last," though it remained in the model stage. That one would have been a four-cylinder, with grille and wheels the only connection to past glories. Even a 16-cylinder Bugatti was proposed. By 1963, Automobiles Bugatti had been purchased by another familiar old name, Hispano-Suiza, which by this time was building diesel and aircraft engines. Before long, the firm was absorbed by a nationalized French organization to build airplane components.

Much later, in 1990, renderings of a Bugatti for the Nineties began to appear, updating the renowned Royale sedan of the early 1930s to modern aerodynamic design, amid speculation about possible production as early as 1992.

1949-51 BUGATTI

TYPE 101 — EIGHT — Though mounted on a chassis from the sporty prewar Type 57, with an inline eight-cylinder 3.3-liter engine under its hood, the briefly-appearing Type 101 wore a completely different, streamlined modern body. Most notable of its styling features was the familiar horseshoe-shape grille, albeit in slightly curved form. Head-

lamps were inboard, alongside the grille, with small round parking lamps on fender tips and separate running lamps above the bumper. The body was provided by Gangloff. Instead of the standard four-speed manual gearbox, a Cotal electromagnetic transmission was announced as available. The Type 101 appeared at the 1951 Paris Salon, with a reported tentative price of about three million francs. Though handsome in physique, and carrying one of the most noted names in the world, it didn't draw enough attention to warrant real production.

1951 Bugatti.

I.D. DATA: Not available.

Model	Body Type & Seating	Engine Type/CID	P.O.E. Price	Weight (lbs.)	Prod. Total
101	2-dr Coupe-4P	I8/199	N/A	3200	Note 1
101	2-dr Cabriolet-4P	I8/199	N/A	3200	Note 1

Note 1: Probably no more than six to ten examples were built, though some sources report production as high as 20 units.

ENGINE DATA: BASE EIGHT: Inline, dual-overhead-cam eight-cylinder. Monobloc design with non-detachable head. **Displacement:** 198.7 cu. in. (3257 cc). **Bore & Stroke:** 2.83 x 3.93 in. (72 x 100 mm). **Compression Ratio:** 6.5:1. **Brake Horsepower:** 135 at 5500 rpm (188 at 5200 with supercharger). Six main bearings. Solid valve lifters. One downdraft Weber carburetor. Delco ignition. Supercharger available.

1951 Bugatti Type 101.

CHASSIS DATA: Wheelbase: 130 in. **Front Tread:** 53 in. **Rear Tread:** 53 in. **Wheel Type:** wire. **Standard Tires:** 6.00x17.

TECHNICAL: Layout: front-engine, rear-drive. **Transmission:** four-speed manual with twin-plate clutch, or Cotal electromagnetic. **Standard Final Drive Ratio:** 4.18:1 (spiral bevel axle). **Steering:** worm and nut. **Suspension (front):** semi-elliptic leaf springs. **Suspension (rear):** reverse quarter-elliptic leaf springs. **Brakes:** hydraulic. **Body Construction:** separate steel body and frame.

MAJOR OPTIONS: Supercharger.

Manufacturer: Automobiles Bugatti, Molsheim and Paris, France.

CISITALIA

Credit for the existence of one of the most gracefully artistic automotive designs of all time, the short-lived Cisitalia, goes to a wealthy Italian salesman, Piero Dusio. Before World War II broke out, Dusio, a one-time professional soccer star, had built up an impressive business manufacturing sporting goods: the *Consorzio Industriale Sportivo Italia.* The Dusio empire also was involved in hotels, banking and textiles.

Because Dusio also took an interest in auto racing, and had driven race cars himself before the war, the company turned to automotive pursuits after the war ended. His first Fiat-based single-seat racing cars, powered by 1100-cc Fiat engines tweaked to 60-plus horsepower, easily took top honors in their class, piloted by some of the top Italian drivers. About 50 were built, from a design by Dante Giacosa with engineering by Dr. Giovanni Savonuzzi. By spring 1946, the first production prototype of the D46 *monoposto* racing car was ready, and a new auto manufacturing company had been formed: Cisitalia SpA. Dusio himself drove the lead car in its first outing, on the Valentino Circuit (near Turin, Italy) in September 1946, where Cisitalias took the top three positions. By 1947, a total of 31 racing Cisitalias had been sold, and the make took second, third and fourth place at that year's Mille Miglia. Aluminum-bodied two-seat racing Cisitalias came in coupe and roadster form, highlighted by sizable tailfins and rear fender skirts.

Turning away from strict racing models, Savonuzzi prepared a design for a streamlined low-slung coupe. Prototype bodies were built by Vignale and by Pinin Farina. One of the Farina renderings became the first road-going Cisitalia, the renowned 202 fastback coupe, which later went on permanent display at New York's Museum of Modern Art as one of the top ten automotive designs of all time. Despite its small size, performance was brisk. A low center of gravity combined with good weight distribution to produce excellent handling.

Meanwhile, Dusio turned to Grand Prix (Formula One) cars, in concert with Dr. Ferdinand Porsche. That venture proved disastrous financially, and the Cisitalia firm sunk into bankruptcy not long after the Grand Prix model went on display at the Turin auto show, in February 1949. Dusio sold his interest in the firm to Automotores Argentinos in Buenos Aires, and went to South America himself to attempt to raise capital for further automotive ventures. The needed financing didn't arrive, but back in Italy, Dusio's son Carlo managed by 1952 to produce a handful of roadgoing coupes with a bigger (2.8-liter) engine. Over the next decade, the Cisitalia firm hung on, sporadically producing a few more Fiat-based bodies and vehicles, ending with a variant of the tiny Fiat 600 as late as 1965.

1947-1952 CISITALIA

202 GRAN SPORT — FOUR — Only a few cars can serve as models of simplicity and tastefulness. Displaying a luscious, gracefully curved profile, the roadgoing Cisitalia that went on limited sale in the U.S. had an oval-shaped recessed grille made up of vertical bars, round headlamps set into panels, a split windshield, and shapely rear quarter windows. Doors blended neatly into the body shape, which had no sharp edges to interrupt

the flow from nose to tail. *Motor Trend* noted a few years after the Cisitalia's debut that its body formed a single unit "marked by curves and indentations," with grille and windows shaped to "delineate the outline of the hood, top and body." The hood curved smoothly downward, below the front fender tops, for superior visibility. A few of those fenders held portholes, an evident concession to the more baroque styling tastes of the time.

"For the light sports car enthusiast who desires the finest," read the 1949 ad from Fergus Motors in New York City, "the Cisitalia Gran Sport and Sports Convertible completely fills the bill. This Farina-bodied beauty rolls at better than 103 mph. Its braking and road holding characteristics cannot be equalled." An open cabriolet later joined the original coupe, priced some $2000 higher.

In addition to the basic 202, Cisitalia produced a Mille Miglia model, plus a Spyder Sport Special and an open Nuvolari. For even more stunning performance, a supercharged Offy-Cisitalia coupe was produced by the Pesco Products Division of the Borg-Warner Corp., powered by a 91 cubic-inch Meyer-Drake Offenhauser four-cylinder engine.

1948 Cisitalia.

1949 Cisitalia Tipo 202. (Coys of Kensington)

1950 Cisitalia.

I.D. DATA: Not available.

Model	Body Type & Seating	Engine Type/CID	P.O.E. Price	Weight (lbs.)	Prod. Total
GRAN SPORT					
202	2-dr Spt Cpe-2P	I4/66	5000	1750	153
202	2-dr Spt Conv-2P	I4/66	7000	N/A	17

Price Note: Prices and weight shown are approximate. Some sources estimated starting price in U.S. at close to $7000.

ENGINE DATA: BASE FOUR (202): Inline, overhead-valve four-cylinder (Fiat-based). Cast iron block and aluminum head. **Displacement:** 66.4 cu. in. (1089 cc). **Bore & Stroke:** 2.68 x 2.95 in. (68 x 75 mm). **Compression Ratio:** 7.5:1. **Brake Horsepower:** 55-60 at 5500 rpm. Three main bearings. Solid valve lifters. One or two Weber downdraft carburetors. Magneto ignition. 12-volt electrical.

CHASSIS DATA: Wheelbase: 94.5 in. **Overall Length:** 147.4 in. **Width:** 55.6 in. **Front Tread:** 49.1 in. **Rear Tread:** 49.1 in. **Wheel Type:** center-lock wire. **Standard Tires:** 5.00x15 or 5.50x15.

TECHNICAL: Layout: front-engine, rear-drive. **Transmission:** four-speed manual (silent third and fourth); floor lever. Special Sport overall gear ratios: (1st) 14.31:1; (2nd) 9.97:1; (3rd) 4.33:1; (4th) 3.67:1. Mille Miglia overall ratios: (1st) 11.05:1; (2nd) 6.04:1; (3rd) 3.96:1; (4th) 3.25:1. **Standard Final Drive Ratio:** 4.10:1; (Spec Spt) 3.67:1; (Mille Miglia) 3.25:1. **Steering:** worm and sector. **Suspension (front):** independent; lower A-arms with transverse leaf spring and telescopic shock absorbers. **Suspension (rear):** rigid axle, semi-elliptic leaf springs. **Brakes:** hydraulic, front/rear drum. **Body Construction:** aluminum body on steel frame (space-frame chassis).

PERFORMANCE: Top Speed: 100-103+ mph (Mille Miglia, 117 mph). **Acceleration (0-60 mph):** N/A (Spec Spt, 0-50 in 11.5 sec.). **Fuel Mileage:** about 22 mpg.

Manufacturer: Automobili Cisitalia, Peschiera 251, Turin, Italy.

Distributor: Guy Vincent, New York City.

POSTCRIPT: American auto magazines in early 1953 eagerly described the details of the next Cisitalia, before its anticipated appearance at the World Motor Sports Show in New York. Sometimes designated 202D, the next-generation Cisitalia also was designed by Pinin Farina, but powered by a 2.8-liter four rated 155 bhp. Top speed was expected to be 145+ mph, with an anticipated price in the U.S. of around $8500.

CITROEN

As early as 1913, Andre Citroen was in the gear-making business. Following a stint as chief engineer at the Mors company, Citroen founded a firm in France under his own name in 1919. Production of the first automobile by the Andre Citroen Motor Company, the Type A (with 1.3-liter four-cylinder engine) began in that year. Designed by Jules Salomon and capable of 40-mph speeds, the Type A used a three-speed gearbox. Within two years, production reached 10,000 units. By that time, too, Citroens were being assembled in London as well as in France.

Citroen took over the Clement-Bayard company in 1922, and began to produce both an improved Type B (grown to 1.5-liter displacement) and a Cloverleaf model with a little 855-cc engine. Larger cars became the focal point in the mid-1920s, led by the 1538-cc model with its flat radiator, four-wheel brakes, and semi-elliptic suspension. This was the first model also built at Slough, in Britain, rather than in London. Production of such British equivalents to the French Citroen would continue into the mid-1960s. Another highlight of the mid-1920s was the debut of the all-steel (Budd) body in Citroen cars.

Six-cylinder power arrived in 1929, in the C6 model. A shorter version carried a four-cylinder engine. Three years later came the 2.5-liter 8CV, with a synchromesh gearbox and box-type chassis. One of those 8CV models, known as *Petite Rosalie,* managed to travel 187,500 miles at an average of 58 mph, setting 43 world records.

As time passed, Citroen became known for innovative styling and ingenious technology. Citroen's badge, consisting of two inverted V's, was meant to represent twin gears, commemorating the company's foundation in the gear business.

Citroen's most famous and unique prewar model, the *Traction Avant* (front-drive) arrived in 1934, with a 1301-cc four-cylinder engine beneath its hood. Known as the 7CV, or simply "Seven," it was noteworthy not only for front-wheel drive, but for positioning the wheels far out at the car's corners, front and rear; and for placing the gearbox ahead of the engine. Construction of the low-slung four-door sedan was special, too. A subframe bolted to the monocoque steel bodyshell held the torsion-bar front suspension, engine and gearbox. Though rather anemic in acceleration, the early *Traction Avant* could top 60 mph on the highway. Before long, these rakishly low sedans be-

came the favorites of European gangsters, both in real life and in films. Production of larger-engined variants of this model (including a six-cylinder edition) would continue through the mid-1950s, with amazingly little change from its original form, either in mechanical construction or appearance.

Even with production hitting 1,000 units per week, the Citroen firm faced bankruptcy in 1934, and had to be rescued by Michelin interests, at the instigation of the French government. Andre Citroen died in 1935, after losing the company he'd founded. Through the mid-1930s, the Traction Avant's engine grew to 1628 cc, then 1911 cc (which came to be the most popular version). A more potent 15CV model arrived in 1938, powered by a 2855-cc six-cylinder engine and riding a 121.5-inch wheelbase. World War II soon interrupted production, however. Following the war, the revived *Traction Avant,* known as the 11 Legere (or 11 Normale in its longer-wheelbase variation) became the first car to use Michelin X radial tires. By the time production halted in 1957, over 750,000 of the slightly homely (in the romantic French manner, that is), intriguingly unforgettable sedans had been built, including over 50,000 with the "Fifteen" six-cylinder engines. Few motorcars of any kind have been so easy to spot, whether on a real-life road or traveling along a movie screen. Equivalents also were produced in England, from 1945 to 1955.

Meanwhile, in 1948, Citroen had turned to a completely different type of motorcar: the even homelier 2CV, designed and constructed for rugged running on European roads. Responding to a perceived interest in strictly utilitarian automobiles, Citroen turned out a vehicle that's seldom been exceeded in all-out practicality, with a homespun personality all its own. Some 300 prototypes had actually been built shortly before the eruption of World War II, with hammock-like seats, in response to a market research study that revealed significant interest in a basic, low-cost automobile. Like the larger *Traction Avant* series, the 2CV enjoyed an unusually long life, still produced in the 1970s, and selling more than five million copies in all. Initially powered by an air-cooled 375-cc, horizontally-opposed two-cylinder engine, the 2CV had coil springs all around. By 1955, a larger 425-cc engine was available. The 2CV had a homemade appearance, with separate headlamps and front-wheel drive. A less-crude-looking but similiarly simple Citroen, called the Ami-6, went on sale in the early 1960s.

Enhancing its reputation for hard-to-ignore automobiles even further, Citroen turned to the aerodynamically streamlined, "ahead of its time" DS19 sedan in 1955. This one had such advanced features as a self-leveling hydropneumatic suspension, power-assisted disc brakes, and semi-automatic gearbox. Detachable steel panels were mounted on its monocoque body structure, which contained front and rear "crumple zones." The DS19 had a drag coefficient of only 0.38, a small figure indeed for its day. Power came from a 1911-cc four-cylinder engine, as used in the *Traction Avant.*

By 1966, after Citroen had taken over the declining Panhard firm (after a decade-long affiliation), the DS19 got a new 1985-cc four, while the lower-priced ID19 kept the former 1911-cc version. At the same time, a more powerful DS21 edition emerged with a short-stroke, 2175-cc engine. A joint venture by Citroen and Maserati resulted in the SM of 1970: a Grand Touring coupe with four-cam 180-horsepower, 2670-cc V-6 engine, capable of close to 140 mph. That turned out to be the last Citroen model officially sold in the U.S., though the Citroen company remained a significant force in the world market. Models produced during the 1970s for sale elsewhere in the world included a smaller GS (introduced in 1970) with an air-cooled flat four-cylinder engine; a limited-production Birotor Wankel version of the GS; and an evolution of the D-Series, the

DS23, with a fuel-injected 2347-cc engine. By 1976, the 2CV's engine had grown to 602 cc, developing 29 horsepower. In 1974, Citroen was taken over by the Peugeot company, and a new CX was announced to replace the long-lived D-Series, of which some 1-1/4 million had been sold. Additional Citroen models entered the world marketplace during the 1980s, but none was exported to the U.S. As the 1990s began, rumors of future Citroens for sale in America popped up sporadically, but no definite announcements were made.

1945-48 CITROEN

11 LEGERE/NORMALE — TRACTION AVANT — FOUR — Decidedly "avant-garde" in appearance when introduced in 1934, the *Traction Avant* resumed production after World War II with little change from its prewar origin. The "no-nonsense" design was noted for wheels far out at each corner, an unusually low center of gravity for a sedan, and front-wheel drive. Torsion-bar suspension was used. The 1911-cc engine developed 56 horsepower, driving a three-speed manual transmission. Styling features of the long and low-looking sedan included rear-hinged front doors ("suicide" style), front-hinged rear doors, separate fender-mounted headlamps, and a twin inverted 'V' pattern (Citroen's symbol) in the angled vertical-bar grille. Separate fenders were installed, but no running boards. Seats were upholstered in cloth. During 1947, the hood added louvers. Appearance of the two models was similar, but the Normale rode a longer wheelbase.

Note: Equivalents of the 11 Legere and 11 Normale were produced in England, known as the "Light Fifteen" and "Big Fifteen." A smaller-engined "Seven" also was produced, but few (if any) were exported to the U.S.

15 (FIFTEEN) — SIX — A six-cylinder version of the prewar-styled four-door sedan also was available, starting in 1948. The 2867-cc engine produced 77 horsepower.

I.D. DATA: Serial number is stamped on a firewall plate. Engine number is stamped on the left front upper edge of the block.

Model	Body Type & Seating	Engine Type/CID	P.O.E. Price	Weight (lbs.)	Prod. Total
TRACTION AVANT					
11 Legere	4-dr Sedan-4P	I4/117	N/A	N/A	Note 1
11 Normale	4-dr Sedan-4P	I4/117	N/A	N/A	Note 1
15	4-dr Sedan-4P	I6/175	N/A	N/A	Note 1

Note 1: A total of 12,654 Citroens were produced in 1946, 22,879 in 1947, and 34,164 in 1948.

ENGINE DATA: BASE FOUR (11 Legere/Normale): Inline, overhead-valve four-cylinder. Cast iron block. **Displacement:** 116.6 cu. in. (1911 cc). **Bore & Stroke:** 3.07 x 3.94 in. (78 x 100 mm). **Compression Ratio:** 6.5:1. **Brake Horsepower:** 56 at 4000 rpm. Three main bearings. Solid valve lifters. Solex carburetor. 6-volt electrical system.

BASE SIX (Fifteen): Inline, overhead-valve six-cylinder. Cast iron block. **Displacement:** 174.9 cu. in. (2867 cc). **Bore & Stroke:** 3.07 x 3.94 in. (78 x 100 mm). **Compression Ratio:** 6.5:1. **Brake Horsepower:** 77 at 3000 rpm. Five main bearings. Solid valve lifters. Solex inverted carburetor. 6-volt electrical system.

CHASSIS DATA: Wheelbase: (11 Legere) 114.5 in.; (11 Normale, 15) 119 in. **Overall Length:** (11 Legere) 176 in.; (11 Normale, 15) 187 in. **Height:** 61 in. **Width:** (11 Legere) 66 in.; (11 Normale, 15) 70 in. **Rear Tread:** (11 Legere) 54 in.; (11 Normale, 15) 58 in. **Wheel Type:** disc. **Standard Tires:** (11) 165x400 Michelin Pilote; (15 Six) 185x400 Michelin Pilote.

TECHNICAL: Layout: front-engine, front-drive. **Transmission:** three-speed manual. **Steering:** rack and pinion. **Suspension (front):** torsion bar. **Suspension (rear):** torsion bar. **Brakes:** Lockheed hydraulic, front/rear drum. **Body Construction:** steel monocoque.

PERFORMANCE: Top Speed: (11 Legere) 71 mph; (15 Six) 81 mph.
Manufacturer: S.A. Andre Citroen, Paris, France.

1949-1954 CITROEN

1949 Citroen 2CV four-door sedan.

2CV — SERIES TA — TWO — No other car built in the world looked even similar to Citroen's down-to-basics, utilitarian sedan, which became available in 1949. In profile, the four-door sedan (with "suicide" front doors) displayed a single, continuous curve, broken only by the flat windshield, vaguely suggesting a lengthened version of Volkswagen's Beetle. Separate headlamps were mounted atop the fender, alongside the front hood. A tapered grille displayed a large oval center emblem with the familiar twin inverted 'V' pattern. A canvas fabric top rolled open along the roof, making the 2CV a sedan with an unusually large sunroof--virtually a convertible. Four adults fit inside, on thinly-padded (but comfortable) seats. *Motor Trend* in 1954 described the 2CV design as "gawky but efficient."

Power came from an air-cooled, 375-cc, horizontally-opposed two-cylinder engine, with integral three-speed (plus overdrive) transaxle driving the front wheels. The rear end of the engine mount rested upon a transverse central frame member, which also held the rack-and-pinion steering, and served as a pivot point for the front suspension. Some observers noted that the simplicity of the 2CV suggested a kinship with the old Model T Ford. Among the cost-cutting measures used in the 2CV's construction was a no-distributor ignition system, employing contact points on the engine fan.

11 LEGERE/NORMALE — TRACTION AVANT — FOUR — Production of the prewar-styled four-door sedans continued with little change. By 1950, it was announced that a four-speed Cotal electromagnetic transmission would be available. Starting late in 1953, the big sedans became available in grey or blue as well as the traditional black. *Motor Trend* noted in 1954 that this bigger Citroen sedan was "essentially unchanged in 19 years," and that a nine-passenger family model was being revived.

Note: *Traction Avant* models were sometimes referred to as 11BL and 11B. Equivalents of the 11 Legere and 11 Normale were produced in England into 1955, known as the "Light Fifteen" and "Big Fifteen."

15 (FIFTEEN) — SIX — Production of the six-cylinder version of the prewar-styled sedan continued into 1955.

1950 Citroen.

1949 Citroen 11CV Legere.

1952 Citroen Model 15 four-door sedan.

1953 Citroen 11CV sedan.

1954 Citroen 15-Six Familiale nine-passenger sedan.

I.D. DATA: Serial number is stamped on a firewall plate. 2CV engine number is stamped on the upper rear edge of the crankcase, ahead of the flywheel. Four-cylinder engine number plate is on right side of block, behind the exhaust manifold. Six-cylinder engine number is stamped on the left front upper edge of the block.

Model	Body Type & Seating	Engine Type/CID	P.O.E. Price	Weight (lbs.)	Prod. Total
2CV	4-dr Sedan-4P	H2/23	Note 1	1120	Note 2
TRACTION AVANT					
11 Legere	4-dr Sedan-4P	I4/117	2275	2250	Note 2
11 Normale	4-dr Sedan-4P	I4/117	2475	2450	Note 2
15	4-dr Sedan-4P	I6/175	2975	2850	Note 2

Note 1: Price in France was 228,000 Francs (under $1000).
Note 2: A total of 49,424 Citroens were produced in 1949, 64,761 in 1950, 78,188 in 1951, 88,626 in 1952, 102,168 in 1953, and 102,758 in 1954.
Price Note: Traction Avant prices above were valid in 1954.
Weight Note: Figures shown are approximate.

ENGINE DATA: BASE TWO (2CV): Horizontally-opposed, overhead-valve two-cylinder (air cooled). Cast iron block and aluminum heads. **Displacement:** 22.9 cu. in. (375 cc). **Bore & Stroke:** 2.44 x 2.44 in. (62 x 62 mm). **Compression Ratio:** 6.2:1. **Brake Horsepower:** 9 at 3500 rpm. Two main bearings. Solid valve lifters. One carburetor. 6-volt electrical system.

BASE FOUR (Eleven): Inline, overhead-valve four-cylinder. Cast iron block. **Displacement:** 116.6 cu. in. (1911 cc). **Bore & Stroke:** 3.07 x 3.94 in. (78 x 100 mm). **Compression Ratio:** 6.5:1. **Brake Horsepower:** 56 at 4000 rpm. Five main bearings. Solid valve lifters. Solex carburetor. 6-volt electrical system.

BASE SIX (Fifteen): Inline, overhead-valve six-cylinder. Cast iron block. **Displacement:** 174.9 cu. in. (2867 cc). **Bore & Stroke:** 3.07 x 3.94 in. (78 x 100 mm). **Compression Ratio:** 6.5:1. **Brake Horsepower:** 77 at 3000 rpm. Five main bearings. Solid valve lifters. Solex inverted carburetor. 6-volt electrical system.

CHASSIS DATA: Wheelbase: (2CV) 94.4 in.; (11 Legere) 114.5 in.; (11 Normale, 15) 119 in. **Overall Length:** (2CV) 149 in.; (11 Legere) 176 in.; (11 Normale, 15) 187 in. **Height:** (2CV) 63 in.; (11/15) 61 in. **Width:** (2CV) 58 in.; (11 Legere) 66 in.; (11 Normale, 15) 70 in. **Front Tread:** (2CV) 49.6 in. **Rear Tread:** (2CV) 49.6 in.; (11 Legere) 54 in.; (11 Normale, 15) 58 in. **Wheel Type:** disc. **Standard Tires:** (2CV) 125x400 or 5.00x16; (11) 165x400 Michelin Pilote; (15 Six) 185x400.

TECHNICAL: Layout: front-engine, front-drive. **Transmission:** (2CV) three-speed (plus overdrive) manual; (11/15) three-speed manual. **Standard Final Drive Ratio:** (2CV) 3.83:1. **Steering:** rack and pinion. **Suspension (front):** (2CV) coil springs; (11/15) torsion bar. **Suspension (rear):** (2CV) coil springs; (11/15) torsion bar. **Brakes:** (2CV) hydraulic, front/rear drum; (11/15) Lockheed hydraulic, front/rear drum. **Body Construction:** (2CV) steel body on platform chassis; (11/15) steel monocoque.

PERFORMANCE: Top Speed: (2CV) about 37 mph claimed initially; (11 Legere) 73 mph; (15 Six) 80 mph.

PRODUCTION/SALES: Approximately 10 Citroens were sold in the U.S. in 1949, followed by 13 in 1950, only five in 1951, 11 in 1952, and 40 in 1953.

Manufacturer: S.A. Andre Citroen, Paris, France.

HISTORY: On sale by October 1949, the 2CV was the first new Citroen introduced after World War II, by a company that was viewed as virtually an institution in France.

1955-56 CITROEN

2CV — TWO — Branded the ugliest car at London's Earl's Court Motor Show, the 2CV changed little during the mid-1950s except for a larger 25.9 cid (425-cc) air-cooled engine that produced 12 horsepower. Produced mainly for sale in France's agricultural districts, where ruggedness was its primary virtue, the car was also a big hit among other types of motorists. Though the back-to-basics 2CV wasn't catching on in the U.S., eager customers in France had to wait two years to buy one. An automatic centrifugal clutch allowed two-pedal operation in traffic, with overdrive on the all-synchro three-speed (four with overdrive) manual gearbox. An L-shaped gearshift handle protruded from the dashboard. Intriguing features included a fabric top that rolled back as a vast sunroof; doors that slid off their hinges; seats that could be removed; and front fenders that could be replaced in one minute. Instead of using conventional upholstery springs, the seats rested on heavy "rubber bands" (rubber strips). The engine sat ahead of the front wheels, with an oil cooler above, inboard brakes behind, and the gearbox to the rear of the differential. The suspension consisted of torsion bars and big shock absorbers all around, with leading arms in front and trailing arms at the rear. Special rods signaled the rear wheels as soon as the front wheels hit a bump. Headlamps adjusted by turning a knob inside the car, and windshield wipers could be operated by hand (otherwise, via the speedometer gear). A built-in jacking system was included. The only instruments were a speedometer and ammeter. A parcel shelf was mounted below the cowl. The 2CV's flat windshield and down-sloping hood allowed good forward visibility, but vision was somewhat limited toward the rear. Not only the doors, but the rear seats and decklid could be removed in minutes, to convert the 2CV into a light truck of sorts.

DS19 — FOUR — No vehicle has ever looked remotely like the Citroen introduced in 1955—the first new full-size model since 1934. 'DS' stood for *Derivation Special,* signifying the car's extensive use of hydropneumatic power. Front-wheel drive was just about the only similarity between the dramatic new DS19 sedan and either the 2CV or the prewar-styled *Traction Avant* 11/15 sedans. Even decades later, the streamlined, aerodynamic DS19 looked futuristic, not dated. Accenting the sleek profile was a reinforced plastic roof and a wraparound windshield with thin corner pillars. Windows had neither supports nor frames. Wheelbase was 123 inches, and the car measured 189 inches overall. The difference between the front and rear tread dimensions was nearly eight inches. Michelin 165x400 X-type tires rode knock-on wheels. Disc brakes were installed in front, drums at the rear, with independent front and rear systems. The 1911-cc four-cylinder engine produced 75 horsepower and 101 pound-feet of torque. The engine had an aluminum head with hemispherical combustion chambers, and two-barrel Weber carburetion.

A central hydraulic system provided power assist for gearshifting, rack-and-pinion steering, brakes, and more. A fingertip selector lever for the four-speed hydraulic gearshift was mounted under the steering wheel. No clutch pedal was installed. The driver simply selected a gear, and the DS 19 declutched and reengaged automatically (hydraulically) in accord with throttle position. The clutch operated from a lower-pressure hydraulic pump in the water pump.

Among the most commented-upon mechanical features of the DS19 was its hydropneumatic (air-oil) suspension, which had each wheel independently suspended on a chamber of compressed air, altering the hydraulic pressure to keep the car level. This was said to be the first use of air-oil suspension in a production car, and the first time a central hydraulic system was employed. A dashboard knob could set the ride height at 6.5, 9.5 or 12 inches. That allowed tire-changing without a jack. The suspension consisted of two suspension arms and one hydropneumatic unit with shock absorber for each front wheel, along with an anti-roll bar and leveling device. At the rear was one suspension arm and one hydropneumatic suspension unit (with shock) for each wheel, as well as the leveling device. Citroen ads described it as "the only suspension that actually floats you on air over the road." All these power assists ran mainly on reservoir pressure; the pump was said to operate only 10 percent of the time. The five-seat monoshell body road a platform with side members of welded sheet steel. No driveshaft tunnel impaired roominess on the flat floor. Six could squeeze inside without great discomfort. The car's spare tire was mounted under the hood.

Styling features included a low, sloping hood; flat, streamlined rear end; low center of gravity; and flashing directional signals mounted atop the plastic roof. The DS19's grille consisted of a simple air-intake opening, low on the front (just above the bumper), with no patterned insert. Another air-intake went below the bumper. Parking lights stood far outboard on front fenders, below the single round headlamps. Body colors included: Black with black roof; Pink Grey with turquoise blue roof; Dark Purple with champagne roof; Champagne with dark purple roof; or Spring Green with champagne roof. Safety was a major focus. Inside was a safety "no-spoke" Life-Guard steering wheel (the only "spoke" being an extension of the steering column) and safety dashboard. Heating came from two separate radiators, to both the front and rear compartments. Wipers included twin two windshield washers. Seats were upholstered in nylon jersey, offered in bright colors to complement the chosen "fashion-right color combinations."

1955 Citroen DS19 four-door sedan.

11/15 — TRACTION AVANT — FOUR/SIX — The prewar-styled 11-series sedans also remained in production as late as 1957, the 15-series into 1955. In fact, the DS19's hydropneumatic suspension was first tried out (and sold) on the six-cylinder 15 sedan in 1954, though at the rear only. See previous listing for further details on these models, which adopted the DS19 engine as it became available.

I.D. DATA: Chassis serial number plate is on right side of firewall; attached (riveted) tag indicates year of sale. DS19 serial number may also be on right front side frame member. 2CV engine number is stamped on upper rear edge of crankcase, ahead of the flywheel. DS19 engine number is on left side of block. Starting serial number: (DS19) 9/560001.

Model 2CV	Body Type & Seating	Engine Type/CID	P.O.E. Price	Weight (lbs.)	Prod. Total
	2-dr Sedan-4P	H2/26	1195	1120	Note 1
DS19					
	4-dr Sedan-5P	I4/117	3295	2475	Note 1
TRACTION AVANT					
11	4-dr Sedan-4P	I4/117	2400	2464	Note 1
15	4-dr Sedan-4P	I6/175	N/A	2850	Note 1

Note 1: A total of 122,442 Citroens were produced in 1955, and 129,900 in 1956.
Price Note: DS19 price was valid in late 1956.
Weight Note: DS19 figure shown is announced curb weight.
Model Number Note: Some Citroen company literature used a hyphen in the model designation (DS-19); other printed material did not. A space was sometimes positioned between the elements of the number (DS 19).

ENGINE DATA: BASE TWO (2CV): Horizontally-opposed, air-cooled two-cylinder. Cast iron block and aluminum head. **Displacement:** 25.9 cu. in. (425 cc). **Bore & Stroke:** 2.60 x 2.44 in. (66 x 62 mm). **Compression Ratio:** 7.0:1. **Brake Horsepower:** 12 at 4000 rpm. Solid valve lifters. Solex 28CBI carburetor.
BASE FOUR (DS19, final Eleven models): Inline, overhead-valve four-cylinder. Cast iron block and aluminum head. **Displacement:** 116.6 cu. in. (1911 cc). **Bore & Stroke:** 3.07 x 3.94 in. (78 x 100 mm). **Compression Ratio:** 7.5:1. **Brake Horsepower:** 75 at 4500 rpm. **Torque:** 101 lbs.-ft. Three main bearings. Solid valve lifters. Weber dual-throat carburetor. 6-volt electrical system.
BASE SIX (Fifteen): Inline, overhead-valve six-cylinder. Cast iron block. **Displacement:** 174.9 cu. in. (2867 cc). **Bore & Stroke:** 3.07 x 3.94 in. (78 x 100 mm). **Compression Ratio:** 6.5:1. **Brake Horsepower:** 77 at 3000 rpm. Five main bearings. Solid valve lifters. Solex inverted carburetor. 6-volt electrical system.

CHASSIS DATA: Wheelbase: (2CV) 94.4 in.; (11) 114.5 in.; (15) 121.5 in.; (DS19) 123 in. **Overall Length:** (2CV) 149 in.; (11) 175 in.; (DS19) 189 in. **Height:** (2CV) 63 in.; (11) 60 in.; (DS19) 58 in. **Width:** (2CV) 58 in.; (11) 65.25 in.; (DS19) 70.5 in. **Front Tread:** (2CV) 49.6 in.; (11) 54 in.; (DS19) 59 in. **Rear Tread:** (2CV) 49.6 in.; (11) 52.25 in.; (DS19) 51.25 in. **Standard Tires:** (2CV) 125x400; (11) 165x400; (DS19) Michelin 'X' 165x400 (or 6.50x15.75).

TECHNICAL: Layout: front-engine, front-drive. **Transmission:** (2CV) four-speed manual; (11/15) three-speed manual; (DS19) four-speed manual with automatic clutch action. DS19 gear ratios: (1st) 3.55:1; (2nd) 1.89:1; (3rd) 1.23:1; (4th) 0.85:1; (rev) 3.80:1. **Standard Final Drive Ratio:** (DS19) 3.89:1. **Steering:** (2CV, 11/15) rack and pinion; (DS19) power rack and pinion. **Suspension (front):** (2CV) leading arms joined to longitudinal springs; (11/15) torsion bar; (DS19) independent, hydropneumatic with parallel control arms, anti-roll bar and leveling device. **Suspension (rear):** (2CV) trailing arms joined to longitudinal springs; (11/15) torsion bar; (DS19) hydropneumatic with trailing arms and leveling device. **Brakes:** (2CV) hydraulic, front/rear drum; (DS19) front disc, rear drum, power assisted. **Body Construction:** (2CV) unitized steel body on platform frame; (11/15) steel monocoque; (DS19) steel monoshell body/chassis. **Fuel Tank:** (DS19) 17 gallon.

MAJOR OPTIONS: Radio (DS19). Whitewall tires (DS19).

PERFORMANCE: Top Speed: (2CV) 45-55 mph; (11) 72-75 mph; (DS19) 90 mph (factory). **Acceleration (0-60 mph):** (2CV) N/A (0-30 mph in about 12 sec.; (15) 21 sec.; (DS19) 18.4 sec. **Acceleration (quarter-mile):** (DS19) 21.4 sec. (64 mph). **Fuel Mileage:** (2CV) 35+ mpg in the city; (DS19) up to 30 mpg (factory).

Manufacturer: S.A. Andre Citroen, Paris, France.
Distributor: Citroen Cars Corp., New York City and Beverly Hills, California.

HISTORY: Appearing at the Paris Show in October 1955, the DS19 was promoted the first new Citroen in 23 years (except for the 2CV). The DS19 also appeared at the International Automobile Show at New York's Coliseum in spring 1956. Ads described the streamlined new model as "distinctively French....so unmistakably Citroen....combining the performance of the sports car with the luxury of the limousine." In addition to receiving "the safest car in the world," buyers would get "Chic Parisienne elegance wedded to the road-hugging power of a Monte Carlo performer." The DS19 was described in a press release as "the dream car of tomorrow, on the road today." Ads intended to attract potential dealers claimed the DS19 would deliver "more sales power than any imported car you have ever known!" They described the car as a "4-door sports car sedan," touting its "Self-Level Ride."

Motor Trend called the 2CV the "freshest concept in motoring," noting that it was the "most-wanted car" in France. Though "painfully ugly but appealing," they added, it displayed a body "nearly free from any compound curves." *The Autocar* (in England) named it "undoubtedly the most original design since the Model T Ford."

"Visibility is remarkable," said *Motorsport* magazine of the DS19 in 1956, "with large windows, thin pillars, and sloping hood." *Auto Age* described the new Citroen as "Studebaker-ish in appearance."

The first U.S. Citroen showroom was located at 300 Park Avenue, in New York City. The new DS19 was promoted as the first "American-type automatic car to be produced in Europe." Sales focused first on the New York and Los Angeles areas. A lower-cost ID19 variant of the DS19 was introduced in France at the end of 1955, and came to the U.S. for the 1957 model year. Citroen established a connection with Panhard in 1955, and would take over the latter company a decade later.

1957 CITROEN

2CV — TWO — Production of the back-to-basics 2CV sedan continued with little change. As before, an L-shaped gearshift lever selected from four speeds, with an emergency brake handle below.

DS19 — FOUR — Production of the futuristic DS19 sedan continued with little change. Standard equipment included the automatic clutch and gearshift operation, power disc brakes, and power steering, operated by a central hydraulic system that also controlled the hydropneumatic suspension.

ID19 — FOUR — Customers who didn't need (or want) all the hydraulically-assisted goodies on Citroen's futuristic DS19 sedan had another choice this year: a lower-priced model that dispensed with those extras, and had a little less power. Initially, at least, that customer could save some $900 by doing without the power gearshift, clutch, steering and brakes. Both models used the "Citmatic" air-oil suspension that "actually floats you on air over the road," however, and the "Citro-Safe" spokeless steering wheel. 'ID' stood for *Idee Depouille*, or "idea despoiled" (meaning the "stripped" or "base" model), according to Citroen expert Jeff S. Savage. See next listing for additional details.

I.D. DATA: Serial number plate is located on right upper side of firewall. 2CV engine number is stamped on upper rear edge of crankcase, ahead of the flywheel. DS19/ID19 engine number is on lower left of block. Starting serial number: (ID19) 200001.

1957 Citroen DS19.

Model	Body Type & Seating	Engine Type/CID	P.O.E. Price	Weight (lbs.)	Prod. Total
2CV	2-dr Sedan-4P	H2/26	1298	1125	Note 1
DS19	4-dr Sedan-5P	I4/117	3495	2475	Note 1
ID19	4-dr Sedan-5P	I4/117	2595	2475	Note 1

Note 1: A total of 139,706 Citroens were produced in 1957.

ENGINE DATA: BASE TWO (2CV): Horizontally-opposed, air-cooled two-cylinder. Cast iron block and aluminum heads. **Displacement:** 25.9 cu. in. (425 cc). **Bore & Stroke:** 2.60 x 2.44 in. (66 x 62 mm). **Compression Ratio:** 7.0:1. **Brake Horsepower:** 12 at 3500 rpm. Solid valve lifters. Solex 28CBI carburetor.
BASE FOUR (DS19/ID19): Inline, overhead-valve four-cylinder. Cast iron block and aluminum head. **Displacement:** 116.6 cu. in. (1911 cc). **Bore & Stroke:** 3.07 x 3.94 in. (78 x 100 mm). **Compression Ratio:** 7.5:1. **Brake Horsepower:** (ID19) 70 at 4500 rpm; (DS19) 75 at 4500 rpm. **Torque:** 97.6 lbs.-ft. at 2500 rpm. Three main bearings. Solid valve lifters. One single-barrel carburetor (ID19); Weber dual-throat carburetor (DS19).

CHASSIS DATA: Wheelbase: (2CV) 94.4 in.; (DS19/ID19) 123 in. **Overall Length:** (2CV) 149 in.; (DS19/ID19) 189 in. **Height:** (2CV) 63 in.; (DS19/ID19) 58 in. **Width:** (2CV) 58 in.; (DS19/ID19) 70.5 in. **Front Tread:** (2CV) 49.6 in.; (DS19/ID19) 59 in. **Rear Tread:** (2CV) 49.6 in.; (DS19/ID19) 51.25 in. **Standard Tires:** (2CV) 125x400; (DS19/ID19) 165x400.

TECHNICAL: Layout: front-engine, front-drive. **Transmission:** four-speed manual. **Steering:** rack and pinion. **Suspension (front):** (2CV) leading arms joined to longitudinal springs; (DS19/ID19) hydropneumatic with parallel control arms. **Suspension (rear):** (2CV) trailing arms joined to longitudinal springs; (DS19/ID19) hydropneumatic with trailing arms. **Brakes:** (2CV) hydraulic, front/rear drum; (DS19/ID19) front disc, rear drum. **Body Construction:** (2CV) unitized steel body on platform frame; (DS19/ID19) monoshell body/chassis.

PERFORMANCE: Top Speed: (2CV) 48-55 mph; (DS19) 90 mph (factory). **Acceleration (0-60 mph):** (2CV) N/A (0-30 mph in about 12 sec.; (DS19) 18.4 sec. **Acceleration (quarter-mile):** (DS19) 21.4 sec. (64 mph). **Fuel Mileage:** (2CV) 35+ mpg in the city, near 43 mpg average; (DS19) up to 30 mpg (factory).

Manufacturer: S.A. Andre Citroen, Paris, France.
Distributor: Citroen Cars Corp., New York City and Beverly Hills, California.

HISTORY: The 1957 models were introduced in the U.S. on October 1, 1956; the ID19 debuted later. "This glimpse of Citroen's new, revolutionary DS 19, "said a late 1956 ad that pictured only the very tip of the car's front end, "is merely a hint of the unparalleled Citroen features, that places a DS19 years ahead, as the most advanced expression of automotive engineering." Other ads quoted Jim Whipple of *Car Life* as saying it's "ten years ahead of its time," and Pete Molson of *Motor Trend* advising that three carloads of evaluators were "left babbling in wonderment." Whipple further stated that the DS19 bore "a marked resemblance to the sketches of dream cars." John Bond of *Road & Track* noted that a DS19 "drives boldly off the beaten path and never feels the bumps."

1958 CITROEN

2CV — TWO — American customers weren't exactly thronging to the Citroen dealerships for a chance at a 2CV, as Europeans had done, but the down-to-basics sunroofed sedan remained on the list of U.S. imports into the 1960s, attracting a small following. Although *Motor Trend* noted that the car had "difficulty staying with traffic" they further exclaimed that "Repairs (were) almost unheard-of; car is trouble-free and near indestructible." A 2CV could hit 60 mph (maybe) and get 50-mpg economy on regular gasoline.

DS19 — FOUR — Production of the deluxe Citroen sedan, with automatic clutch, semi-automatic gearshifting, power disc brakes, and power steering, continued with little change. Even though rear wheels appeared fully enclosed, a tire could be changed easily by removing a total of only two bolts: one from the fender, and another from the wheel. Front seats folded back to form a bed.

1958 Citroen DS19.

145

ID19 — FOUR — The lower-cost version of Citroen's modern sedan also continued with little change, powered by a lower-powered version of the 1911-cc four-cylinder engine. The ID19 lacked the servo-assisted brakes, clutch, gearshift and accessories of the DS19, but had the same air-oil suspension. A lever near the floor, to the driver's left, adjusted ground clearance from 6.5 to 11.5 inches. *Road & Track* testers preferred the ID19's conventional clutch and brake pedals and "good 4-speed column shift" over the DS19's hydraulically-assisted operation, which had small pedals on the floor. Appearance was nearly identical to the DS19.

I.D. DATA: Serial number plate is located on right upper side of firewall. 2CV engine number is stamped on upper rear edge of crankcase, ahead of the flywheel. DS19/ID19 engine number is on lower left of block.

Model	Body Type & Seating	Engine Type/CID	P.O.E. Price	Weight (lbs.)	Prod. Total
2CV	2-dr Sedan-4P	H2/26	1298	1125	Note 1
ID19	4-dr Sedan-5P	I4/117	2695	2475	Note 1
DS19	4-dr Sedan-5P	I4/117	3495	2475	Note 1

Note 1: A total of 178,858 Citroens were produced in 1958.

Price Note: ID19 price rose to $2835.

ENGINE DATA: BASE TWO (2CV): Horizontally-opposed, air-cooled two-cylinder. Cast iron block and aluminum heads. **Displacement:** 25.9 cu. in. (425 cc). **Bore & Stroke:** 2.60 x 2.44 in. (66 x 62 mm). **Compression Ratio:** 7.0:1. **Brake Horsepower:** 12 at 3500 rpm. Torque: 17 lbs.-ft. at 3000 rpm. Solid valve lifters. Solex 28CBI carburetor.

BASE FOUR (ID19/DS19): Inline, overhead-valve four-cylinder. Cast iron block and aluminum head. **Displacement:** 116.6 cu. in. (1911 cc). **Bore & Stroke:** 3.07 x 3.94 in. (78 x 100 mm). **Compression Ratio:** 7.5:1. **Brake Horsepower:** (ID19) 66 at 4000 rpm; (DS19) 75 at 4500 rpm. **Torque:** (ID19) 97.6 lbs.-ft. at 2500 rpm; (DS19) 101.3 lbs.-ft. at 3000 rpm. Three main bearings. Solid valve lifters. One single-barrel carburetor (ID19); Weber dual-throat carburetor (DS19).

CHASSIS DATA: Wheelbase: (2CV) 94.4 in.; (DS19/ID19) 123 in. **Overall Length:** (2CV) 149 in.; (DS19/ID19) 189 in. **Height:** (2CV) 63 in.; (DS19/ID19) 58 in. **Width:** (2CV) 58 in.; (DS19/ID19) 70.5 in. **Front Tread:** (2CV) 49.6 in.; (DS19/ID19) 59 in. **Rear Tread:** (2CV) 49.6 in.; (DS19/ID19) 51.25 in. **Standard Tires:** (2CV) 125x400; (DS19/ID19) 165x400.

TECHNICAL: Layout: front-engine, front-drive. **Transmission:** four-speed manual. ID19 gear ratios: (1st) 3.54:1; (2nd) 1.79:1; (3rd) 1.23:1; (4th) 0.85:1. **Standard Final Drive Ratio:** (ID19) 3.31:1. **Steering:** rack and pinion. **Suspension (front):** (2CV) leading arms joined to longitudinal springs; (DS19/ID19) hydropneumatic with parallel control arms. **Suspension (rear):** (2CV) trailing arms joined to longitudinal springs; (DS19/ID19) hydropneumatic with trailing arms. **Brakes:** (2CV) hydraulic, front/rear drum; (DS19/ID19) front disc, rear drum. **Body Construction:** (2CV) unitized steel body on platform frame; (DS19) monoshell body/chassis.

MAJOR OPTIONS: Radio ($89).

PERFORMANCE: Top Speed: (2CV) 55 mph; (ID19/DS19) 87-90 mph. **Acceleration (0-60 mph):** (2CV) N/A (0-30 mph in about 12 sec.; (ID19) 19.1-19.2 sec.; (DS19) 18.4 sec. **Acceleration (quarter-mile):** (ID19) 21.4-22.2 sec. (62.5-64 mph); (DS19) 21.4 sec. (64 mph). **Fuel Mileage:** (2CV) 35+ mpg in the city; (ID19) 22-29 mpg average; (DS19) up to 30 mpg (factory).

PRODUCTION/SALES: Approximately 1,145 Citroens were sold in the U.S. in 1958.

Manufacturer: S.A. Andre Citroen, Paris, France.

Distributor: Citroen Cars Corp., New York City and Beverly Hills, California.

HISTORY: The 1958 models were introduced in the U.S. on October 1, 1957. By 1958, Citroen had more than 100 dealers in the U.S. (5000 in the world). "Drive a sports car," said the DS19/ID19 ads in 1958, "and take the family along too." Ads also quoted *Road & Track* on the car's suspension: "On every kind of surface traversible by four wheels, it absorbs shock and maintains stability to a degree never achieved before." Citroen claimed it was the "World's Safest Production Car....Economically European, Automatically American."

1959 CITROEN

2CV — TWO — Production of the basic sedan continued with little change, and the car remained on lists of models available in the U.S. Appearance had changed little since its debut. The hoodline sloped sharply down to a slatted air intake, which displayed a double inverted 'V' insignia. On hood sides was a tapering row of louvers, above the wide fenders. Separate headlamps sat quite high. Front and back doors were hinged at the center post. A fold-back fabric top (sunroof) was standard. The body had no rear deck at all; just straight-down fastback design. Rear wheels were fully enclosed by fenders. The 12-bhp, two-cylinder engine produced a top speed around 55 mph, with 45-55 mpg economy. As before, the four-speed manual transmission worked with a combination of centrifugal and manual clutch.

1959 Citroen DS19 four-door sedan.

DS19/ID19 — FOUR — In addition to the standard DS19 sedan, a luxury version entered production this year, intended to be chauffeur-driven. Behind the glass divison window, the rear compartment was like a mobile office, with radio, radio-telephone, desk, electric clock, and a microphone to talk to the driver. Otherwise, changes were minimal this year, limited only to minor details.

A station wagon joined the lower-cost ID-19 series this year, in France, but took longer to reach the American market; see 1961 listing for further details. For cargo-carrying, seats folded down to create a big flat area. The tailgate swung down under the rear floor for loading cargo; that meant near ground level, after lowering the suspension. The wagon could hold three people in front, and carry an 1100-pound load. Its hydropneumatic suspension was tougher than that used on the sedan.

I.D. DATA: Serial number plate is located on right upper side of firewall. 2CV engine number is stamped on upper rear edge of crankcase, ahead of the flywheel. DS19/ID19 engine number is on lower left of block.

Model	Body Type & Seating	Engine Type/CID	P.O.E. Price	Weight (lbs.)	Prod. Total
2CV	2-dr Sedan-4P	H2/26	1298	1125	Note 1
ID19	4-dr Sedan-5P	I4/117	2833	2475	Note 1
DS19	4-dr Sedan-5P	I4/117	3333	2475	Note 1

Note 1: A total of 213,162 Citroens were produced in 1959.

Price Note: Some directories listed the DS19 as low as $3195 at this time; the ID19 as low as $2795.

ENGINE DATA: BASE TWO (2CV): Horizontally-opposed, air-cooled two-cylinder. Cast iron block and aluminum heads. **Displacement:** 25.9 cu. in. (425 cc). **Bore & Stroke:** 2.60 x 2.44 in. (66 x 62 mm). **Compression Ratio:** 7.0:1. **Brake Horsepower:** 12 at 3500 rpm. **Torque:** 17 lbs.-ft. at 3000 rpm. Solid valve lifters. Solex 28CBI carburetor. 6-volt electrical system.

BASE FOUR (ID19/DS19): Inline, overhead-valve four-cylinder. Cast iron block and aluminum head. **Displacement:** 116.6 cu. in. (1911 cc). **Bore & Stroke:** 3.07 x 3.94 in. (78 x 100 mm). **Compression Ratio:** 7.5:1. **Brake Horsepower:** (ID19) 66 at 4000 rpm; (DS19) 75 at 4500 rpm. **Torque:** (ID19) 97.6 lbs.-ft. at 2500 rpm; (DS19) 101.3 lbs.-ft. at 3000 rpm. Three main bearings. Solid valve lifters. One single-barrel carburetor (ID19); Weber dual-throat carburetor (DS19).

CHASSIS DATA: Wheelbase: (2CV) 94.4 in.; (DS19/ID19) 123 in. **Overall Length:** (2CV) 149 in.; (DS19/ID19) 189 in. **Height:** (2CV) 63 in.; (DS19/ID19) 58 in. **Width:** (2CV) 58 in.; (DS19/ID19) 70.5 in. **Front Tread:** (2CV) 49.6 in.; (DS19/ID19) 59 in. **Rear Tread:** (2CV) 49.6 in.; (DS19/ID19) 51.25 in. **Standard Tires:** (2CV) 125x400 or 5.20x15; (ID19/DS19) 165x400 or 5.90x15.

TECHNICAL: Layout: front-engine, front-drive. **Transmission:** four-speed manual (automatic clutch and gear-engagement on DS19). **Steering:** rack and pinion. **Suspension (front):** (2CV) leading arms joined to longitudinal springs; (DS19/ID19) hydropneumatic with parallel control arms. **Suspension (rear):** (2CV) trailing arms joined to longitudinal springs; (DS19/ID19) hydropneumatic with trailing arms. **Brakes:** (2CV) front/rear drum; (DS19/ID19) front disc, rear drum. **Body Construction:** (2CV) unitized steel body on platform frame; (DS19) monoshell body/chassis. **Fuel Tank:** (2CV) 5 gal.; (DS19) 17 gal.

MAJOR OPTIONS: Automatic clutch (2CV/ID19).

PERFORMANCE: Top Speed: (2CV) about 55 mph; (DS19) 85-90 mph. **Acceleration (0-60 mph):** (2CV) N/A (0-30 mph in about 12 sec.; (ID19/DS19) 20 sec. or less. **Acceleration (quarter-mile):** (ID19) 21.4-22.2 sec. (62.5-64 mph); (DS19) 21.4 sec. (64 mph). **Fuel Mileage:** (2CV) up to 45-55 mpg; (ID19/DS19) 22-24 mpg average.

PRODUCTION/SALES: Approximately 2,364 Citroens were sold in the U.S. during 1959.

Manufacturer: S.A. Andre Citroen, Paris, France.

Distributor: Citroen Cars Corp., New York City and Beverly Hills, California.

HISTORY: The 1959 models were introduced in the U.S. on October 1, 1958. A DS19 sedan won the 1959 Monte Carlo Rally. *Sports Cars Illustrated* noted that the DS19's "automatic level-compensators keep the car horizontal at all times, even upon sudden braking."

1960 CITROEN

DS19/ID19 — FOUR — Production of the DS19 deluxe sedan continued with little change. Two levels of the ID19 sedan were available, Luxe and Confort, plus an eight-passenger station wagon.

AMI-6 — TWO — A new Ami sedan debuted in 1960 to replace the 2CV, but took a while to enter the U.S. marketplace. The Ami had a more conventional appearance than the 2CV, with quad headlamps and round parking lamps below. Its most unique feature was the unusual scoop-down hood. Power came from an air-cooled two-cylinder engine, as in the 2CV but larger in displacement (602 cc).

Note: The 2CV remained in production into the 1960s and beyond, but was no longer included on most lists of models exported to the U.S. Some examples arrived as late as 1967, however.

I.D. DATA: Serial number is located on right upper side of firewall. DS19/ID19 engine number is on lower left of block. 1960 models should have AC60 stamped on the identity plate affixed to right side of engine, under the hood.

Model	Body Type & Seating	Engine Type/CID	P.O.E. Price	Weight (lbs.)	Prod. Total
ID19					
Luxe	4-dr Sedan-5P	I4/117	2545	2450	Note 1
Confort	4-dr Sedan-5P	I4/117	2695	2475	Note 1
DS19					
	4-dr Sedan-5P	I4/117	3245	2475	Note 1
AMI-6					
	4-dr Sedan-4P	H2/37	N/A	N/A	Note 1

Note 1: A total of 231,736 Citroens were produced in 1960.

ENGINE DATA: BASE TWO (Ami-6): Horizontally-opposed, air-cooled two-cylinder. Cast iron block and aluminum heads. **Displacement:** 36.6 cu. in. (602 cc). **Bore & Stroke:** 2.91 x 2.76 in. (74 x 70 mm). **Compression Ratio:** 7.75:1. **Brake Horsepower:** 25.5 at 4700 rpm. **Torque:** 29.6 lbs.-ft. at 3000 rpm. Solid valve lifters. Solex carburetor.

BASE FOUR (ID19/DS19): Inline, overhead-valve four-cylinder. Cast iron block and aluminum head. **Displacement:** 116.6 cu. in. (1911 cc). **Bore & Stroke:** 3.07 x 3.94 in. (78 x 100 mm). **Compression Ratio:** 7.5:1. **Brake Horsepower:** (ID19) 66 at 4000 rpm; (DS19) 75 at 4500 rpm. **Torque:** (ID19) 97.6 lbs.-ft. at 2500 rpm; (DS19) 101.3 lbs.-ft. at 3000 rpm. Three main bearings. Solid valve lifters. One single-barrel carburetor (ID19); Weber dual-throat carburetor (DS19).

CHASSIS DATA: Wheelbase: (Ami-6) 94.5 in.; (DS19/ID19) 123 in. **Overall Length:** (Ami-6) 155 in.; (DS19/ID19) 189 in. **Height:** (Ami-6) 58.5 in.; (DS19/ID19) 58 in. **Width:** (Ami-6) 60 in.; (DS19/ID19) 70.5 in. **Front Tread:** (Ami-6) 49.6 in.; (DS19/ID19) 59 in. **Rear Tread:** (Ami-6) 48.1 in.; (DS19/ID19) 51.25 in. **Standard Tires:** (ID19/DS19) 165x400.

TECHNICAL: Layout: front-engine, front-drive. **Transmission:** four-speed manual (automatic clutch and gear-engagement on DS19). **Steering:** rack and pinion. **Suspension (front):** (DS19/ID19) hydropneumatic with parallel control arms; (Ami-6) independent with helical spring interconnection. **Suspension (rear):** (DS19/ID19) hydropneumatic with trailing arms; (Ami-6) independent with helical spring interconnection. **Brakes:** (DS19/ID19) front disc, rear drum. **Body Construction:** (DS19/ID19) monoshell body/chassis; (Ami-6) on platform chassis. **Fuel Tank:** (DS19) 17.5 gal.

PERFORMANCE: Top Speed: (DS19) 85-90 mph. **Acceleration (0-60 mph):** (ID19/DS19) 20 sec. or less. **Acceleration (quarter-mile):** (ID19) 21.4-22.2 sec. (62.5-64 mph); (DS19) 21.4 sec. (64 mph). **Fuel Mileage:** (ID19/DS19) 22-24 mpg average.

Manufacturer: S.A. Andre Citroen, Paris, France.

Distributor: Citroen Cars Corp., New York City and Beverly Hills, California.

HISTORY: The ID19 station wagon began to arrive in the U.S. market during 1960; see next listing for details.

1961 CITROEN

DS19/ID19 — FOUR — The ID19 station wagon was now readily available in the U.S. market, offered in both Luxe and Confort trim, along with the sedan. Wagons could seat eight passengers, including two on facing jump seats in the rear. A roof-mounted luggage rack was standard equipment. Two versions of the deluxe DS19 were available: a regular sedan and Prestige limousine. The Prestige edition had a luxury interior with leather bench front seat, walnut trim in the rear, deep pile carpeting, and a sliding glass partition. The DS19 again came with an automatic clutch, Citromatic power-shifted four-speed gearbox, power brakes, and power steering—all accessories controlled by hydraulic pressure from a central tank. It had a button where the brake pedal otherwise would be, and the gearshift protruded out of the dashboard. Both models retained the hydropneumatic suspension, by which road clearance could be varied from 6.5 to 11.2 inches. The ID-Luxe was considered the "value leader," with non-reclining seats, no armrests, plain hubcaps, and a fiberglass roof. The other ID19 model had all those extras, with a steel top. As before, a 116.6-cid (1911-cc) engine provided the power: up to 83+ bhp in the DS19, but reduced (as usual) in the ID19 with its single-throat carburetor. All models now had air intakes in front fenders (though barely discernible). A special DS19 convertible with custom body by Henri Chapron also was available at this time. Produced in limited quantity, the convertibles did not necessarily appear in lists of available models.

AMI-6 — TWO — Production continued of the replacement for the 2CV, but it was not necessarily listed in American directories of imported models. See 1962 listing for complete description.

I.D. DATA: Serial number is located on right upper side of firewall. A 1961 model should have 'AC61' stamped on the identity plate. Engine number is on lower left of block.

Model	Body Type & Seating	Engine Type/CID	P.O.E. Price	Weight (lbs.)	Prod. Total
ID19					
Luxe	4-dr Sedan-5P	I4/117	2545	2475	Note 1
Luxe	4-dr Sta Wag-6/8P	I4/117	3195	2850	Note 1
Confort	4-dr Sedan-5P	I4/117	2745	2475	Note 1
Confort	4-dr Sta Wag-6/8P	I4/117	3395	2850	Note 1
DS19					
	4-dr Sedan-5P	I4/117	3245	2475	Note 1
Chapron	2-dr Conv-4P	I4/117	Note 2	N/A	Note 1
Prestige	4-dr Limo-5P	I4/117	3795	2775	Note 1
AMI-6					
	4-dr Sedan-4P	H2/37	N/A	1420	Note 1

1961 Citroen Ami-6 four-door.

Note 1: A total of 250,662 Citroens were produced during 1961.

Note 2: Price of the Chapron-bodied convertible was about $5600.

Price Note: Some sources listed prices as $2345 or $2695 for the ID19 Luxe sedan, $2913 for the ID19 Confort, $3470 for the DS19, and $3895 for the Prestige sedan.

ENGINE DATA: BASE TWO (Ami-6): Horizontally-opposed, air-cooled two-cylinder. Cast iron block and aluminum heads. **Displacement:** 36.6 cu. in. (602 cc). **Bore & Stroke:** 2.91 x 2.76 in. (74 x 70 mm). **Compression Ratio:** 7.25:1. **Brake Horsepower:** 25.5 at 4700 rpm. **Torque:** 29.6 lbs.-ft. at 3000 rpm. Solid valve lifters. Solex carburetor.

BASE FOUR (ID19/DS19): Inline, overhead-valve four-cylinder. Cast iron block and aluminum head. **Displacement:** 116.6 cu. in. (1911 cc). **Bore & Stroke:** 3.07 x 3.94 in. (78 x 100 mm). **Compression Ratio:** (ID19) 7.5:1; (DS19) 8.5:1. **Brake Horsepower:** (ID19) 70 at 4500 rpm; (DS19) 83-85 at 4500 rpm. **Torque:** (ID19) 97.6 lbs.-ft. at 2500 rpm; (DS19) 105 lbs.-ft. at 3500 rpm. Three main bearings. Solid valve lifters. One Solex single-barrel carburetor (ID19); Weber dual-throat carburetor (DS19).

CHASSIS DATA: Wheelbase: (Ami-6) 94.5 in.; (DS19/ID19) 123 in. **Overall Length:** (Ami-6) 155 in.; (DS19/ID19) 189 in.; (ID19 wagon) 196 in. **Height:** (Ami-6) 58.5 in.; (DS19/ID19) 58 in.; (ID19 wagon) 60 in. **Width:** (Ami-6) 60 in.; (DS19/ID19) 70.5 in. **Front Tread:** (Ami-6) 49.6 in.; (DS19/ID19) 59 in. **Rear Tread:** (Ami-6) 48.1 in.; (DS19/ID19) 51.25 in. **Standard Tires:** (ID19/DS19) 165x400.

TECHNICAL: Layout: front-engine, front-drive. **Transmission:** four-speed manual (automatic clutch and gear-engagement on DS19). **Standard Final Drive Ratio:** (ID19 wagon) 3.80:1. **Steering:** rack-and-pinion. **Suspension (front):** (ID19/DS19) hydropneumatic with parallel control arms; (Ami-6) independent, with helical spring interconnection. **Suspension (rear):** (ID19/DS19) hydropneumatic with trailing arms; (Ami-6) independent, with helical spring interconnection. **Brakes:** front inboard disc, rear drum. **Body Construction:** (ID19/DS19) steel monoshell. **Fuel Tank:** (DS19) 17.5 gal.

PERFORMANCE: Top Speed: (ID19) 90 mph; (DS19) 95 mph. **Acceleration (0-60 mph):** (ID19/DS19) 20 sec. or less; (ID19 wagon) 21.2 sec. **Acceleration (quarter-mile):** (ID19) 21.4-22.2 sec. (62.5-64 mph); (DS19) 21.4 sec. (64 mph). **Fuel Mileage:** (ID19 wagon) 24-28 mpg.

Manufacturer: S.A. Andre Citroen, Paris, France.

Distributor: Citroen Cars Corp., New York City and Beverly Hills, California.

HISTORY: Some American publications continued to report on the 2CV, even though it was no longer generally available in the U.S. (though still produced through the 1960s). *Motor Trend* in April 1961 noted that the 2CV "will never win any beauty contests, and for this reason has never achieved great success in this country." Nevertheless, they added, it came "very close to being the ultimate utility vehicle—cheap to buy and operate, nearly indestructible, easy to drive, and completely functional." Among the 2CV's virtues, it offered "extraordinary traction."

Motor Trend described the ID19/DS19 as offering "one of the most amazingly comfortable rides on the road." They praised its all-independent, self-leveling suspension for "soaking up bumps with uncanny ease." Having described the original DS19 in 1956 as "five years ahead of its time," they felt the updated version was "still a most radical car."

1962 CITROEN

AMI-6 — TWO — Production of the 2CV's replacement continued, but still was not listed in most American directories of imported models even though it was available from Citroen dealers. The 602-cc two-cylinder engine drove a four-speed all-synchro manual transmission. Standard equipment included a heater and defrosters, fresh-air diffusers, electric wipers, armrests, interior light, and contour-fitting foam rubber upholstery. Standard body colors were April Blue, Ice, Jade-Cream, and Pastel Grey. The unusual front end with its dip-down hood had quad round headlamps and a small oval split grille made up of horizontal bars. Styling features included a back-slanted rear window, plus concave segments along the bodysides that began just ahead of the front doors.

ID19/DS19 — FOUR — Production of the now-familiar Citroen sedans (and wagons) continued with little change. The ID19 sedan came in three trim levels this year. Standard ID19 equipment included Citroen's air-oil suspension with self-level ride and power jacking system, heater/defroster, clock, stainless steel wheel covers, stainless steel trim, windshield washers, trunk and courtesy lights, folding center armrest, and Michelin 'X' safety tires. Confort (also called Comfort) and Luxe models added reclining bed seats. The ID19 station wagon included an aluminum luggage rack. The DS19 model added Citromatic drive, power disc brakes, power steering, a dimming rear-view mirror, dual horns, and a trip odometer. Adjustable reclining seats were upholstered in nylon and rhovenyl jersey, in a wide range of colors, with Dunlopillo carpeting. Citroen literature referred to the hydropneumatic assists as "a host of mechanical slaves who take all that's tiresome out of driving."

I.D. DATA: Serial number is located on right upper side of firewall. Engine number is on lower left of block. A 1962 model should have an identification tag stamped 'AC62' mounted adjacent to the serial number under the hood.

Model	Body Type & Seating	Engine Type/CID	P.O.E. Price	Weight (lbs.)	Prod. Total
AMI-6					
	4-dr Sedan-4P	H2/37	N/A	1420	Note 1
ID19					
Normale	4-dr Sedan-5P	I4/117	2495	2475	Note 1
Luxe	4-dr Sedan-5P	I4/117	2695	2475	Note 1
Luxe	4-dr Sta Wag-8P	I4/117	3195	2850	Note 1
Confort	4-dr Sedan-5P	I4/117	2838	2475	Note 1
Confort	4-dr Sta Wag-8P	I4/117	3345	2850	Note 1
DS19					
Super 83	4-dr Sedan-5P	I4/117	3395	2475	Note 1

Note 1: A total of 308,925 Citroens were produced during 1962.

2CV Note: Even though most directories no longer included the 2CV, Citroen in the U.S. listed its price as $1295 in November 1961.

ENGINE DATA: BASE TWO (Ami-6): Horizontally-opposed, air-cooled two-cylinder. Cast iron block and aluminum heads. **Displacement:** 36.6 cu. in. (602 cc). **Bore & Stroke:** 2.91 x 2.76 in. (74 x 70 mm). **Compression Ratio:** 7.25:1. **Brake Horsepower:** 25.5 at 4700 rpm. **Torque:** 29.6 lbs.-ft. at 3000 rpm. Solid valve lifters. Solex carburetor.

BASE FOUR (ID19/DS19): Inline, overhead-valve four-cylinder. Cast iron block and aluminum head. **Displacement:** 116.6 cu. in. (1911 cc). **Bore & Stroke:** 3.07 x 3.94 in. (78 x 100 mm). **Compression Ratio:** (ID19) 7.5:1; (DS19) 8.5:1. **Brake Horsepower:** (ID19) 70 at 4500 rpm; (DS19) 83-85 at 4500 rpm. **Torque:** (ID19) 97.6 lbs.-ft. at 2500 rpm; (DS19) 105 lbs.-ft. at 3500 rpm. Three main bearings. Solid valve lifters. One Solex 34 single-barrel carburetor (ID19); Weber 24/32 DDC dual-throat carburetor (DS19).

CHASSIS DATA: Wheelbase: (Ami-6) 94.5 in.; (DS19/ID19) 123 in. **Overall Length:** (Ami-6) 155 in.; (DS19/ID19) 189 in.; (ID19 wagon) 196 in. **Height:** (Ami-6) 58.5 in.; (DS19/ID19) 58 in.; (ID19 wagon) 59 in. **Width:** (Ami-6) 60 in.; (DS19/ID19) 70.5 in. **Front Tread:** (Ami-6) 49.6 in.; (DS19/ID19) 59 in. **Rear Tread:** (Ami-6) 48.1 in.; (DS19/ID19) 51.25 in. **Standard Tires:** (ID19/DS19) Michelin 'X' 165x400.

TECHNICAL: Layout: front-engine, front-drive. **Transmission:** four-speed manual (automatic clutch and gear-engagement on DS19). Overall ID19 gear ratios: (1st) 13.8:1; (2nd) 7.35:1; (3rd) 4.78:1; (4th) 3.30:1. **Standard Final Drive Ratio:** 8x31. **Steering:** rack-and-pinion. **Suspension (front):** (Ami-6) independent, with helical spring interconnection; (ID19/DS19) hydropneumatic with parallel control arms and anti-roll bar. **Suspension (rear):** (Ami-6) independent, with helical spring interconnection; (ID19/DS19) hydropneumatic with trailing arms and anti-roll bar. **Brakes:** front inboard disc, rear drum. **Body Construction:** (Ami-6) steel body on reinforced steel platform with plastic top; (ID19/DS19) steel monoshell. **Fuel Tank:** (Ami-6) 6.5 gal.; (DS19) 17.5 gal.

MAJOR OPTIONS: Heavy-duty heater with rear-window defroster: DS19 Super 83, ID19 Confort sedan ($75).

PERFORMANCE: Top Speed: (Ami-6) 70 mph (factory); (ID19) 90+ mph (factory); (DS19) 95+ mph (factory). **Acceleration (0-60 mph):** (ID19/DS19) 20 sec. or less; (ID19 wagon) 21.2 sec. **Acceleration (quarter-mile):** (ID19) 21.4-22.2 sec. (62.5-64 mph);

(DS19) 21.4 sec. (64 mph). **Fuel Mileage:** (Ami-6) 40-45 mpg; (ID19 wagon) 24-28 mpg; (ID19) up to 35 mpg claimed; (DS19) up to 32 mpg claimed.

Manufacturer: S.A. Andre Citroen, Paris, France.

Distributor: Citroen Cars Corp., New York City and Beverly Hills, California.

1963 CITROEN

AMI-6 — TWO — This year, the two-cylinder four-door sedan was finally listed as readily available in the U.S. With its sharply back-slanted rear window and slight rear roof overhang, the body appeared to lean backward. The front fender line came forward at its top, to meet flange frame headlamps. A pronounced hood nose lip dipped down and forward at the center, forming a shallow 'U' shape that reached from above the headlamps nearly to the top of the grille. That grille was a small horizontal oval with horizontal bars over a vertical-bar background. A two-bar bumper and license plate stood ahead of the grille, with parking lights beneath the dual headlamps. Sculptured lines ran along the bodysides, creating a long recessed section. No rear wheel openings were evident. The Ami-6 had a steel body and reinforced fiberglass top.

ID19/DS19 — FOUR — Little change was evident in Citroen's larger models. The ID19 Luxe had a white translucent fiberglass top, while the Confort had a steel top. This would be the last year for the lowest-priced Luxe sedan. Late in the 1963 model year, a DS19 Aero Super convertible became available.

I.D. DATA: Serial number is located on right upper side of firewall. Engine number is on lower left of block. A 1963 model should have an identification tag stamped 'AC63' mounted adjacent to the serial number under the hood.

Model	Body Type & Seating	Engine Type/CID	P.O.E. Price	Weight (lbs.)	Prod. Total
AMI-6					
	4-dr Sedan-4P	H2/37	1595	1420	Note 1
ID19					
Normale	4-dr Sedan-5P	I4/117	2545	2475	Note 1
Luxe	4-dr Sedan-5P	I4/117	2745	2475	Note 1
Luxe	4-dr Sta Wag-8P	I4/117	3525	2800	Note 1
Confort	4-dr Sedan-5P	I4/117	2963	2620	Note 1
Confort	4-dr Sta Wag-7P	I4/117	3695	2800	Note 1
Confort	2-dr Conv	I4/117	5195	2705	Note 1
DS19					
Super 83	4-dr Sedan-5P	I4/117	3245	2620	Note 1
Super 83	2-dr Conv	I4/117	5295	2720	Note 1
Aero Super	4-dr Sedan-5P	I4/117	3795	2640	Note 1
Aero Super	2-dr Conv-4P	I4/117	5660	2740	Note 1

Note 1: A total of 351,321 Citroens were produced during 1963.

Convertible Note: Convertibles on DS/ID chassis were built by Chapron, on special order only, in limited quantity each year.

ENGINE DATA: BASE TWO (Ami-6): Horizontally-opposed, air-cooled two-cylinder. Cast iron block and aluminum heads. **Displacement:** 36.6 cu. in. (602 cc). **Bore & Stroke:** 2.91 x 2.76 in. (74 x 70 mm). **Compression Ratio:** 7.25:1. **Brake Horsepower:** 25.5 at 4700 rpm. **Torque:** 29.6 lbs.-ft. at 3000 rpm. Solid valve lifters. Solex carburetor.

BASE FOUR (ID19/DS19): Inline, overhead-valve four-cylinder. Cast iron block and aluminum head. **Displacement:** 116.6 cu. in. (1911 cc). **Bore & Stroke:** 3.07 x 3.94 in. (78 x 100 mm). **Compression Ratio:** (ID19) 7.5:1; (DS19) 8.5:1. **Brake Horsepower:** (ID19) 70 at 4500 rpm; (DS19) 83-85 at 4500 rpm. **Torque:** (ID19) 97.6 lbs.-ft. at 2500 rpm; (DS19) 105 lbs.-ft. at 3500 rpm. Three main bearings. Solid valve lifters. One Solex 34 single-barrel carburetor (ID19); Weber 24/32 DDC dual-throat carburetor (DS19).

CHASSIS DATA: Wheelbase: (Ami-6) 94.5 in.; (DS19/ID19) 123 in. **Overall Length:** (Ami-6) 155 in.; (DS19/ID19) 189 in.; (ID19 wagon) 196 in. **Height:** (Ami-6) 58.5 in.; (DS19/ID19) 58 in.; (ID19 wagon) 59 in. **Width:** (Ami-6) 60 in.; (DS19/ID19) 70.5 in. **Front Tread:** (Ami-6) 49.6 in.; (DS19/ID19) 59 in. **Rear Tread:** (Ami-6) 48.1 in.; (DS19/ID19) 51.25 in. **Standard Tires:** (ID19/DS19) Michelin 'X' 165x400.

TECHNICAL: Layout: front-engine, front-drive. **Transmission:** four-speed manual (automatic clutch and gear-engagement on DS19). Overall ID19 gear ratios: (1st) 13.8:1; (2nd) 7.35:1; (3rd) 4.78:1; (4th) 3.30:1. **Standard Final Drive Ratio:** 8x31. **Steering:** rack-and-pinion. **Suspension (front):** (Ami-6) independent, with helical spring interconnection; (ID19/DS19) hydropneumatic with parallel control arms and anti-roll bar. **Suspension (rear):** (Ami-6) independent, with helical spring interconnection; (ID19/DS19) hydropneumatic with trailing arms and anti-roll bar. **Brakes:** front inboard disc, rear drum. **Body Construction:** (Ami-6) steel body on reinforced steel platform with plastic top; (ID19/DS19) steel monoshell. **Fuel Tank:** (Ami-6) 6.5 gal.; (DS19) 17.5 gal.

MAJOR OPTIONS: Heavy-duty heater with rear-window defroster: DS19 Super 83, ID19 Confort sedan ($75).

PERFORMANCE: Top Speed: (Ami-6) 70 mph (factory); (ID19) 90+ mph (factory); (DS19) 95+ mph (factory). **Acceleration (0-60 mph):** (ID19/DS19) 20 sec. or less; (ID19 wagon) 21.2 sec. **Acceleration (quarter-mile):** (ID19) 21.4-22.2 sec. (62.5-64 mph); (DS19) 21.4 sec. (64 mph). **Fuel Mileage:** (Ami-6) 40-45 mpg; (ID19 wagon) 24-28 mpg; (ID19) up to 35 mpg claimed; (DS19) up to 32 mpg claimed.

PRODUCTION/SALES: Approximately 2,000 Citroens were sold in the U.S. during 1963.

Manufacturer: S.A. Andre Citroen, Paris, France.

Distributor: Citroen Cars Corp., New York City and Beverly Hills, California.

HISTORY: Citroen DS19s finished second, fourth, fifth, seventh and tenth overall at the Monte Carlo rally.

1964 CITROEN

AMI-6 — TWO — Production of the two-cylinder Citroen continued with little change; see previous listing for details.

ID19/DS19 — FOUR — Production of the larger Citroens continued with little change, except for a modified model lineup. The lower-priced ID19 had standard power brakes and steering. The DS19 came in Grande Route and Aero Super trim, as a sedan or a convertible. Grande Route versions had the conventional all-synchro four-speed manual gearbox, as on the ID19, while the Aero Super retained the automatic clutch/gearshifting system. As before, a three-position lever adjusted ride height with the hydropneumatic suspension.

I.D. DATA: Serial number is located on right upper side of firewall. Engine number is on lower left of block. A 1964 model should have an identification tag stamped 'AC64' mounted adjacent to the serial number under the hood.

Model	Body Type & Seating	Engine Type/CID	P.O.E. Price	Weight (lbs.)	Prod. Total
AMI-6					
	4-dr Sedan-4P	H2/37	1595	1420	Note 1
ID19					
Super	4-dr Sedan-5P	I4/117	3245	2620	Note 1
Super	2-dr Conv-2P	I4/117	5445	2800	Note 1
DeLuxe	4-dr Sta Wag-8P	I4/117	3475	2800	Note 1
Confort	4-dr Sta Wag-7P	I4/117	3645	2800	Note 1
DS19					
Grande Rte	4-dr Sedan-5P	I4/117	3450	2620	Note 1
Grande Rte	2-dr Conv-2P	I4/117	5595	2800	Note 1
Aero Super	4-dr Sedan-5P	I4/117	3645	2800	Note 1
Aero Super	2-dr Conv-4P	I4/117	5595	2800	Note 1

Note 1: A total of 368,532 Citroens were produced during 1964.

Convertible Note: Convertibles on DS/ID chassis were built by Chapron, on special order only, in limited quantity each year.

ENGINE DATA: BASE TWO (Ami-6): Horizontally-opposed, air-cooled two-cylinder. Cast iron block and aluminum heads. **Displacement:** 36.6 cu. in. (602 cc). **Bore & Stroke:** 2.91 x 2.76 in. (74 x 70 mm). **Compression Ratio:** 7.25:1. **Brake Horsepower:** 25.5 at 4700 rpm. **Torque:** 29.6 lbs.-ft. at 3000 rpm. Solid valve lifters. Solex carburetor.

BASE FOUR (ID19/DS19): Inline, overhead-valve four-cylinder. Cast iron block and aluminum head. **Displacement:** 116.6 cu. in. (1911 cc). **Bore & Stroke:** 3.07 x 3.94 in. (78 x 100 mm). **Compression Ratio:** (ID19) 7.5:1; (DS19) 8.5:1. **Brake Horsepower:** (ID19) 70 at 4500 rpm; (DS19) 83 at 4500 rpm. **Torque:** (ID19) 97.6 lbs.-ft. at 2500 rpm; (DS19) 105 lbs.-ft. at 3500 rpm. Three main bearings. Solid valve lifters. One Solex 34 single-barrel carburetor (ID19); Weber 24/32 DDC dual-throat carburetor (DS19).

CHASSIS DATA: Wheelbase: (Ami-6) 94.5 in.; (DS19/ID19) 123 in. **Overall Length:** (Ami-6) 155 in.; (DS19/ID19) 190.5 in.; (ID19 wagon) 197.5 in. **Height:** (Ami-6) 58.5 in.; (DS19/ID19) 58 in.; (ID19 wagon) 59 in. **Width:** (Ami-6) 60 in.; (DS19/ID19) 70.5 in. **Front Tread:** (Ami-6) 49.6 in.; (DS19/ID19) 59 in. **Rear Tread:** (Ami-6) 48.1 in.; (DS19/ID19) 51.25 in. **Standard Tires:** (ID19/DS19) Michelin 'X' 165x400.

TECHNICAL: Layout: front-engine, front-drive. **Transmission:** four-speed manual (automatic clutch and gear-engagement on DS19 Aero Super). Overall ID19 gear ratios: (1st) 13.8:1; (2nd) 7.33:1; (3rd) 4.77:1; (4th) 3.31:1. **Standard Final Drive Ratio:** (Ami-6) 3.63:1; (DS19) 3.89:1. **Steering:** rack-and-pinion. **Suspension (front):** (Ami-6) independent, with helical spring interconnection; (ID19/DS19) hydropneumatic with parallel control arms and anti-roll bar. **Suspension (rear):** (Ami-6) independent, with helical spring interconnection; (ID19/DS19) hydropneumatic with trailing arms and anti-roll bar. **Brakes:** front inboard disc, rear drum. **Body Construction:** (Ami-6) steel body on reinforced steel platform with plastic top; (ID19/DS19) steel monoshell on box-section steel frame. **Fuel Tank:** (Ami-6) 6.5 gal.; (DS19) 17.2 gal.

PERFORMANCE: Top Speed: (Ami-6) 70 mph (factory); (ID19) 90+ mph (factory); (DS19) 95+ mph (factory). **Acceleration (0-60 mph):** (DS19) 17.7 sec. **Acceleration (quarter-mile):** (DS19) 21.3 sec. (65.5 mph). **Fuel Mileage:** (Ami-6) 40-45 mpg; (ID19 wagon) 24-28 mpg; (ID19) up to 35 mpg claimed; (DS19) 24-32 mpg.

Manufacturer: S.A. Andre Citroen, Paris, France.

Distributor: Citroen Cars Corp., New York City and Beverly Hills, California.

HISTORY: *Car and Driver* advised readers that a DS19's "interior comfort is beyond description," with "more living space than in any American four-door sedan except the Checker." Upholstery quality and reclining-seat shapes were described as "pure bliss," while handling rated as "simply fantastic." Performance, on the other hand, was called "train-like, in that it starts very slowly but seems to go faster and faster as maximum velocity is approached." Acceleration, in fact, was the only cause for complaint, ranking "definitely below American minimum requirements." By this time, Citroen had about 170 dealers in the U.S.

1965 CITROEN

AMI-6 — TWO — Production of the two-cylinder Citroen continued with little change; see 1963 listing for details.

ID19/DS19 — FOUR — DS19 convertibles were now available on special order, rather than part of the regular U.S. lineup. This year the ID19 added five horsepower and got a restyled dashboard. Joining the Grande Route and Aero Super in the DS19 selection was a new Pallas, which had a more luxurious interior with new fabric designs (leather upholstery available), as well as stainless steel body trim and wheel covers. The Pallas also had integrated dual foglamps. All models had a four-speed manual (all-synchro) transmission except the DS19 Aero Super, which retained the Citromatic clutchless system with synchromesh only on the top three ratios, automatically activated.

I.D. DATA: Serial number is located on right upper side of firewall. Engine number is on lower left of block. A 1965 model should have an 'AC65' serial-number prefix on an identification tag adjacent to the identifying plate on the firewall.

Model	Body Type & Seating	Engine Type/CID	P.O.E. Price	Weight (lbs.)	Prod. Total
AMI-6					
	4-dr Sedan-4P	H2/37	1595	1420	Note 1
ID19					
Luxe	4-dr Sedan-5P	I4/117	2695	2620	Note 1
Super	4-dr Sedan-5P	I4/117	2885	N/A	Note 1
Luxe	4-dr Sta Wag-8P	I4/117	3525	2800	Note 1
Confort	4-dr Sta Wag-7P	I4/117	3520	2800	Note 1
DS19 GRANDE ROUTE					
	4-dr Sedan-5P	I4/117	3395	2640	Note 1
Pallas	4-dr Sedan-5P	I4/117	3695	N/A	Note 1
DS19 AERO SUPER					
	4-dr Sedan-5P	I4/117	3510	2640	Note 1
Pallas	4-dr Sedan-5P	I4/117	3810	N/A	Note 1

Note 1: A total of 401,439 Citroens were produced during 1965.

Convertible Note: The DS19 Grande Route and Aero Super convertibles were available on special order, priced at $5595.

ENGINE DATA: BASE TWO (Ami-6): Horizontally-opposed, air-cooled two-cylinder. Cast iron block and aluminum heads. **Displacement:** 36.6 cu. in. (602 cc). **Bore & Stroke:** 2.91 x 2.76 in. (74 x 70 mm). **Compression Ratio:** 7.25:1. **Brake Horsepower:** 25.5 at 4700 rpm. **Torque:** 29.6 lbs.-ft. at 3000 rpm. Solid lifters. Solex carburetor.

BASE FOUR (ID19/DS19): Inline, overhead-valve four-cylinder. Cast iron block and aluminum head. **Displacement:** 116.6 cu. in. (1911 cc). **Bore & Stroke:** 3.07 x 3.94 in. (78 x 100 mm). **Compression Ratio:** (DS19) 8.5:1. **Brake Horsepower:** (ID19) 75 at 4500 rpm; (DS19) 83 at 4500 rpm. **Torque:** (DS19) 105 lbs.-ft. at 3500 rpm. Three main bearings. Solid valve lifters. One carburetor (ID19); Weber 24/32 DDC dual-throat carburetor (DS19).

CHASSIS DATA: Wheelbase: (Ami-6) 94.5 in.; (DS19/ID19) 123 in. **Overall Length:** (Ami-6) 155 in.; (DS19/ID19) 190.5 in.; (ID19 wagon) 197.5 in. **Height:** (Ami-6) 58.5 in.; (DS19/ID19) 58 in.; (ID19 wagon) 59 in. **Width:** (Ami-6) 60 in.; (DS19/ID19) 70.5 in. **Front Tread:** (Ami-6) 49.6 in.; (DS19/ID19) 59 in. **Rear Tread:** (Ami-6) 48.1 in.; (DS19/ID19) 51.25 in. **Standard Tires:** (ID19/DS19) 165x400.

TECHNICAL: Layout: front-engine, front-drive. **Transmission:** four-speed manual (automatic clutch and gear-engagement on DS19 Aero Super). **Standard Final Drive Ratio:** (Ami-6) 3.63:1; (DS19) 3.87:1. **Steering:** rack-and-pinion. **Suspension (front):** (Ami-6) independent, with helical spring interconnection with parallel control arms and anti-roll bar. **Suspension (rear):** (Ami-6) independent, with helical spring interconnection; (ID19/DS19) hydropneumatic with trailing arms and anti-roll bar. **Brakes:** front inboard disc, rear drum. **Body Construction:** (Ami-6) steel body on reinforced steel platform with plastic top; (ID19/DS19) steel monoshell on box-section steel frame. **Fuel Tank:** (Ami-6) 6.5 gal.; (DS19) 17 gal.

PERFORMANCE: Top Speed: (Ami-6) 70 mph (factory); (ID19) 90+ mph (factory); (DS19) 95+ mph (factory). **Acceleration (0-60 mph):** (DS19) 17.7 sec. **Acceleration (quarter-mile):** (DS19) 21.3 sec. (65.5 mph). **Fuel Mileage:** (Ami-6) 40-45 mpg; (ID19 wagon) 24-28 mpg; (ID19) up to 35 mpg claimed; (DS19) 24-32 mpg.

Manufacturer: S.A. Andre Citroen, Paris, France.

Distributor: Citroen Cars Corp., New York City and Beverly Hills, California.

HISTORY: Citroen expert Jeff S. Savage advises that "Pallas" simply meant luxury, being derived from the French word for Palace. It was not intended to honor "Pallas," the ancient Greek goddess of widsom.

1966-67 CITROEN

AMI-6 — TWO — Little change was evident on the smaller Citroen sedan, still available in the American market as a successor to the 2CV. For 1966, a station wagon version also was offered. By 1968, the Ami-6 would be dropped from the U.S. lineup.

ID19/DS19 — FOUR — The ID19 station wagon no longer was offered in the U.S. Otherwise, the ID19 and deluxe DS19 continued as before, except that the DS19 adopted a slightly larger engine: 1985 cc, with five main bearings, producing 90 horsepower. The ID19 came in two trim levels (Luxe and Super); the DS19 in four (Grande Route and Aero Super, plus a posh Pallas variant of each. These Citroens still featured an air-oil suspension. Citromatic was standard on the Aero Super and Super Pallas.

DS21/D21 — FOUR — A new model with larger (2175-cc) four-cylinder engine debuted this year, similar in appearance to the DS19 but with quad round headlamps positioned diagonally. The engine produced 109 horsepower. Otherwise, dimensions and mechanical details were nearly identical to the DS19. The DS21 came in station wagon (D21) as well as sedan form, in two trim levels. Luxurious Pallas versions of the sedan also were offered, at $300 extra. Citromatic was standard on the Aero Super and Super Pallas. A convertible also was available at this time, described in *Business Week* magazine as "turtle-style."

1967 Citroen DS21 sedan.

I.D. DATA: Chassis serial number is located on right upper side of firewall, and right front frame member. Engine number is on lower left of block or (DS19/DS21) at front of block.

Model	Body Type & Seating	Engine Type/CID	P.O.E. Price	Weight (lbs.)	Prod. Total
AMI-6					
	4-dr Sedan-4P	H2/37	1703	1420	Note 1
	4-dr Sta Wagon	H2/37	1809	1420	Note 1
ID19					
Luxe	4-dr Sedan-5P	I4/117	2669	2668	Note 1
Super	4-dr Sedan-5P	I4/117	2769	2668	Note 1
DS19					
Grande Rte	4-dr Sedan-5P	I4/121	3305	2855	Note 1
Aero Super	4-dr Sedan-5P	I4/121	3399	2755	Note 1

Model	Body Type & Seating	Engine Type/CID	P.O.E. Price	Weight (lbs.)	Prod. Total
DS19 PALLAS					
Grande Rte	4-dr Sedan-5P	I4/121	3605	N/A	Note 1
Aero Super	4-dr Sedan-5P	I4/121	3699	N/A	Note 1
DS21/D21					
Grande Rte	4-dr Sedan-5P	I4/133	3584	2855	Note 1
Aero Super	4-dr Sedan-5P	I4/133	3679	2855	Note 1
Chapron	2-dr Conv Cpe 4P	I4/133	5872	2900	Note 1
Luxe	4-dr Sta Wag-8P	I4/133	3584	2800	Note 1
Confort	4-dr Sta Wag-7P	I4/133	3722	2800	Note 1
DS21 PALLAS					
Grande Rte	4-dr Sedan-5P	I4/133	3884	2855	Note 1
Aero Super	4-dr Sedan-5P	I4/133	3979	2855	Note 1

Note 1: A total of 451,875 Citroens were produced during 1966, and 419,245 in 1967.

Price Note: Figures shown were valid in 1966. In 1967, the ID19 Super was known as the Grand Luxe.

Station Wagon Price Note: Prices shown were for 109-bhp engine; wagons with 90-bhp engine cost $279 less.

Convertible Note: As in prior years with the DS19 series, the limited-production DS21 convertible wore a body custom-built by Chapron.

ENGINE DATA: BASE TWO (Ami-6): Horizontally-opposed, air-cooled two-cylinder. Cast iron block and aluminum heads. **Displacement:** 36.6 cu. in. (602 cc). **Bore & Stroke:** 2.91 x 2.76 in. (74 x 70 mm). **Compression Ratio:** 7.25:1. **Brake Horsepower:** 25.5 at 4700 rpm. **Torque:** 29.6 lbs.-ft. at 3000 rpm. Solid valve lifters. Solex carburetor.

BASE FOUR (ID19): Inline, overhead-valve four-cylinder. Cast iron block and aluminum head. **Displacement:** 116.6 cu. in. (1911 cc). **Bore & Stroke:** 3.07 x 3.94 in. (78 x 100 mm). **Compression Ratio:** 8.0:1. **Brake Horsepower:** 81 at 4750 rpm. **Torque:** 104 lbs.-ft. at 3500 rpm. Three main bearings. Solid valve lifters.

BASE FOUR (DS19): Inline, overhead-valve four-cylinder. Cast iron block and aluminum head. **Displacement:** 121.1 cu. in. (1985 cc). **Bore & Stroke:** 3.39 x 3.37 in. (86 x 85 mm). **Compression Ratio:** 8.5:1. **Brake Horsepower:** 90 at 5250 rpm. **Torque:** 110 lbs.-ft. at 3500 rpm. Five main bearings. Solid valve lifters.

BASE FOUR (DS21): Inline, overhead-valve four-cylinder. Cast iron block and aluminum head. **Displacement:** 132.7 cu. in. (2175 cc). **Bore & Stroke:** 3.54 x 3.37 in. (90 x 85.5 mm). **Compression Ratio:** 8.75:1. **Brake Horsepower:** 109 at 5500 rpm. **Torque:** 128 lbs.-ft. at 3000 rpm. Five main bearings. Solid valve lifters. Weber two-barrel carburetor.

CHASSIS DATA: Wheelbase: (Ami-6) 94.5 in.; (DS/ID) 123 in. **Overall Length:** (Ami-6) 155 in.; (DS/ID) 190.5 in.; (DS21 wagon) 196.5 in. **Height:** (Ami-6) 58.5 in.; (DS/ID) 58 in. **Width:** (Ami-6) 60 in.; (DS/ID) 70.5 in. **Front Tread:** (Ami-6) 49.6 in.; (DS/ID) 59 in. **Rear Tread:** (Ami-6) 48.1 in.; (DS/ID) 51.25 in. **Standard Tires:** (ID19) 180x380; (DS19) 165x400; (DS21) 180x380 Michelin XAS.

TECHNICAL: Layout: front-engine, front-drive. **Transmission:** four-speed manual (automatic clutch and gear-engagement on DS19/21 Aero Super/Pallas). **Standard Final Drive Ratio:** (DS19) 3.87:1 (DS21) 4.38:1. **Steering:** rack-and-pinion. **Suspension (front):** (Ami-6) independent, with helical spring interconnection; (ID/DS) hydropneumatic with parallel control arms and anti-roll bar. **Suspension (rear):** (Ami-6) independent, with helical spring interconnection; (ID/DS) hydropneumatic with trailing arms and anti-roll bar. **Brakes:** front inboard disc, rear drum. **Body Construction:** (Ami-6) steel body on reinforced steel platform with plastic top; (ID/DS) steel monoshell on box-section steel frame. **Fuel Tank:** (Ami-6) 6.5 gal.; (DS19) 17 gal.

PERFORMANCE: Top Speed: (Ami-6) 70 mph (factory); (ID19) 90+ mph (factory); (DS19) 95+ mph (factory); (DS21) up to 110 mph. **Acceleration (0-60 mph):** (DS19) 17.7 sec. **Acceleration (quarter-mile):** (DS19) 21.3 sec. (65.5 mph). **Fuel Mileage:** (Ami-6) 40-45 mpg; (ID19 wagon) 24-28 mpg; (ID19) up to 35 mpg claimed; (DS19) 24-32 mpg.

Manufacturer: S.A. Andre Citroen, Paris, France.

Distributor: Citroen Cars Corp., New York City and Beverly Hills, California.

HISTORY: *Popular Imported Cars* in 1967 advised that the DS21's "ride is positively superb," and the car was "still ahead of its time." Comparable praise was not given to the car's tiny brake button, said to be barely bigger than a half-dollar.

1968 CITROEN

ID19 — FOUR — By this time, the original 1911-cc engine was gone, as was the DS19 designation. This year's ID19 had the 1985-cc four-cylinder engine, rated 84 horsepower. Citromatic was not included. Two trim levels were offered: Luxe and Grande Route.

DS21/D21 — FOUR — The DS21 sedan and D21 station wagon enjoyed a front-end restyling at this time, with quad round headlamps mounted in a recessed, tapered housing. Outer headlamps sat farther back than their inner mates. Swiveling headlamps were available in Europe, but not on the American version. The DS21 retained the familiar air-oil suspension with adjustable road clearance and built-in power jacking. Either Citromatic or a conventional four-speed transmission was available.

I.D. DATA: Chassis serial number is located on the firewall. Engine number is at the front of the block.

Model	Body Type & Seating	Engine Type/CID	P.O.E. Price	Weight (lbs.)	Prod. Total
ID19					
Luxe	4-dr Sedan-5P	I4/121	2898	2855	Note 1
Grande Rte	4-dr Sedan-5P	I4/121	3060	2855	Note 1
DS21/D21					
Grande Rte	4-dr Sedan-5P	I4/133	3798	2855	Note 1
Aero Super	4-dr Sedan-5P	I4/133	3798	2855	Note 1
Luxe	4-dr Sta Wag-7/8P	I4/133	3683	2900	Note 1
Confort	4-dr Sta Wag-7/9P	I4/133	3927	2900	Note 1
DS21 PALLAS					
Grande Rte	4-dr Sedan-5P	I4/133	4056	2890	Note 1
Aero Super	4-dr Sedan-5P	I4/133	4056	2890	Note 1

Note 1: A total of 384,040 Citroens were produced during 1968.

ENGINE DATA: BASE FOUR (ID19): Inline, overhead-valve four-cylinder. Cast iron block and aluminum head. **Displacement:** 121.1 cu. in. (1985 cc). **Bore & Stroke:** 3.39 x 3.37 in. (86 x 85 mm). **Compression Ratio:** 8.0:1. **Brake Horsepower:** 84 at 5250 rpm. **Torque:** 106 lbs.-ft. at 3000 rpm. Five main bearings. Solid valve lifters.

BASE FOUR (DS21): Inline, overhead-valve four-cylinder. Cast iron block and aluminum head. **Displacement:** 132.7 cu. in. (2175 cc). **Bore & Stroke:** 3.54 x 3.37 in. (90 x 85.5 mm). **Compression Ratio:** 8.75:1. **Brake Horsepower:** 109 at 5500 rpm. **Torque:** 128 lbs.-ft. at 3000 rpm. Five main bearings. Solid valve lifters.

CHASSIS DATA: Wheelbase: 123 in. **Overall Length:** 190.5 in. except (wagon) 196.5 in. **Height:** 58 in. **Width:** 70.5 in. **Front Tread:** 59 in. **Rear Tread:** 51 in. **Standard Tires:** (DS21) 180x380.

TECHNICAL: Layout: front-engine, front-drive. **Transmission:** four-speed manual (or Citromatic gearchange). **Standard Final Drive Ratio:** (DS21) 4.38:1. **Steering:** rack-and-pinion. **Suspension (front):** hydropneumatic with parallel control arms. **Suspension (rear):** hydropneumatic with trailing arms. **Brakes:** front disc, rear drum. **Body Construction:** steel monoshell.

PERFORMANCE: Top Speed: (ID19) 101 mph; (DS21) up to 110 mph (115 mph advertised); (D21 wagon) 105 mph. **Fuel Mileage:** (ID19) 25-30 mpg; (DS21) 21-27 mpg; (D21 wagon) 23-26 mpg.

Manufacturer: S.A. Andre Citroen, Paris, France.

Distributor: Citroen Cars Corp., New York City and Beverly Hills, California.

HISTORY: Citroen took over the Maserati company in the late 1960s, which resulted in development of the SM coupe for the early 1970s. Another derivative of the 2CV, called the Dyane, was now available in Europe with a 602-cc (or 425-cc) engine.

1969 CITROEN

ID19 — FOUR — A sculptured front end with quad headlamps went on the ID19 sedan at this time, giving the still-streamlined French car a new hood and fender profile. The hydropneumatic suspension remained standard, with adjustable road clearance. The four-cylinder engine was now rated 91 horsepower (up by seven).

DS21/D21 — FOUR — Little change was evident in the most costly Citroen series, except that the 132.7-cid (2175-cc) engine was now rated 117 horsepower (up from 109 bhp). Citromatic was now a no-charge option.

I.D. DATA: Chassis serial number is located on the firewall. Engine number is at the front of the block.

ID19

Model	Body Type & Seating	Engine Type/CID	P.O.E. Price	Weight (lbs.)	Prod. Total
Luxe	4-dr Sedan-5P	I4/121	2990	2855	Note 1
Grande Rte	4-dr Sedan-5P	I4/121	3165	2855	Note 1
DS21/D21					
Grande Rte	4-dr Sedan-5P	I4/133	3913	2855	Note 1
Aero Super	4-dr Sedan-5P	I4/133	3913	N/A	Note 1
Luxe D21	4-dr Sta Wagon	I4/133	3616	2950	Note 1
Luxe D19	4-dr Sta Wag-7/8P	I4/133	3835	2950	Note 1
Confort	4-dr Sta Wag-7/9P	I4/133	4077	2950	Note 1
DS21 PALLAS					
Grande Rte	4-dr Sedan-5P	I4/133	4170	2900	Note 1
Aero Super	4-dr Sedan-5P	I4/133	4170	N/A	Note 1

Note 1: A total of 425,508 Citroens were produced in 1969.

ENGINE DATA: BASE FOUR (ID19): Inline, overhead-valve four-cylinder. Cast iron block and aluminum head. **Displacement:** 121.1 cu. in. (1985 cc). **Bore & Stroke:** 3.39 x 3.37 in. (86 x 85 mm). **Compression Ratio:** 8.0:1. **Brake Horsepower:** 91 at 5750 rpm. Five main bearings. Solid valve lifters.

BASE FOUR (DS21): Inline, overhead-valve four-cylinder. Cast iron block and aluminum head. **Displacement:** 132.7 cu. in. (2175 cc). **Bore & Stroke:** 3.54 x 3.37 in. (90 x 85.5 mm). **Compression Ratio:** 8.75:1. **Brake Horsepower:** 117 at 5750 rpm. **Torque:** 125 lbs.-ft. at 4000 rpm. Five main bearings. Solid valve lifters.

CHASSIS DATA: Wheelbase: 123 in. **Overall Length:** 190.5 in. except (wagon) 196.5 in. **Height:** 58 in. **Width:** 70.5 in. **Front Tread:** 59 in. **Rear Tread:** 51 in. **Standard Tires:** (DS21) 180x380 Michelin XAS.

TECHNICAL: Layout: front-engine, front-drive. **Transmission:** four-speed manual. **Standard Final Drive Ratio:** (DS21) 4.38:1. **Steering:** rack-and-pinion. **Suspension (front):** hydropneumatic with parallel control arms. **Suspension (rear):** hydropneumatic with trailing arms. **Brakes:** front disc, rear drum. **Body Construction:** steel monoshell. **Fuel Tank:** 17 gal.

PERFORMANCE: Top Speed: 105 mph advertised. **Fuel Mileage:** (ID19) 25-30 mpg; (DS21) 21-27 mpg; (D21 wagon) 23-26 mpg.

Manufacturer: S.A. Andre Citroen, Paris, France.

Distributor: Citroen Cars Corp., New York City and Beverly Hills, California.

HISTORY: "The Citroen DS21 may not be a *goddess* to the eye of every beholder," said *Road Test* magazine in 1969, "but it has the charm of the ugly duckling with heart of gold. It most certainly is not a look-alike but by golly it sure makes sense."

1970 CITROEN

ID19 — FOUR — Production of the original futuristic Citroen sedan, changed remarkably little since its mid-1950s debut, halted in 1970. It was replaced by the new D Special.

D SPECIAL — FOUR — Equivalent to the long-lived ID19, the new D Special was the lower-priced Citroen offering but came with some of the familiar features, notably the hydropneumatic suspension with its constant-level ride and adjustable road clearance. Appearance was virtually identical to the more deluxe DS21, both featuring quad round recessed headlamps. Under the hood was the 1985-cc four-cylinder engine, producing 91 horsepower and 106 pound-feet of torque. Standard equipment included reclining bucket seats, vinyl upholstery, a folding rear center armrest, clock, and rear defroster.

DS21/D21 — FOUR — In addition to the new D Special, the D-Series sedan again came in DS21 and DS21 Pallas form. Citroen promoted the freshly-restyled "sophisticated aerodynamic design" of the D-Series as offering "even cleaner, swifter lines for front end, hoods and fenders." The new instrument panel contained a tachometer. A "Leather-Tex" interior was available as a no-cost option to replace the standard fabric and padded

vinyl interior. Leather upholstery was optional on the Pallas. Under DS21 hoods was the 2175-cc engine, producing 117 horsepower. Both a conventional four-speed (all-synchro) manual gearbox and new "Quick-Action" Citromatic-Drive were available. Citromatic was standard on the Pallas Aero Super. Standard equipment included reclining bucket seats, heater/defroster, rear-window defroster, folding rear center armrest, clock, lighter, and two-speed wiper/washers. Options included factory-installed air conditioning, AM or AM/FM radio, roof antenna, and a folding front center armrest.

1970 Citroen DS21 station wagon.

I.D. DATA: Chassis serial number is located on the firewall. Engine number is at the front of the block.

Model	Body Type & Seating	Engine Type/CID	P.O.E. Price	Weight (lbs.)	Prod. Total
ID19/D SPECIAL					
Grande Rte	4-dr Sedan-5P	I4/121	3375	2855	Note 1
DS21/D21					
Aero Super	4-dr Sedan-5P	I4/133	4066	2855	Note 1
Luxe	4-dr Sta Wag-7/9P	I4/133	3934	2950	Note 1
Confort	4-dr Sta Wag-7/9P	I4/133	4175	2950	Note 1
DS21 PALLAS					
Aero Super	4-dr Sedan-5P	I4/133	4329	2855	Note 1
Grande Rte	4-dr Sedan-5P	I4/133	4329	2900	Note 1

Note 1: A total of 471,078 Citroens were produced in 1970.

Price Note: The DS21 Confort wagon with Citromatic cost $4335.

ENGINE DATA: BASE FOUR (ID19, D Special): Inline, overhead-valve four-cylinder. Cast iron block and aluminum head. **Displacement:** 121.1 cu. in. (1985 cc). **Bore & Stroke:** 3.39 x 3.37 in. (86 x 85 mm). **Compression Ratio:** 8.0:1. **Brake Horsepower:** 91 at 5750 rpm. **Torque:** 106 lbs.-ft. at 3000 rpm. Five main bearings. Solid valve lifters. One Solex 34PBIC carburetor.

BASE FOUR (DS21): Inline, overhead-valve four-cylinder. Cast iron block and aluminum head. **Displacement:** 132.7 cu. in. (2175 cc). **Bore & Stroke:** 3.54 x 3.37 in. (90 x 85.5 mm). **Compression Ratio:** 8.75:1. **Brake Horsepower:** 117 at 5750 rpm. **Torque:** 126 lbs.-ft. at 3000-3500 rpm. Five main bearings. Solid valve lifters. Weber 28x36 DDE two-barrel carburetor.

CHASSIS DATA: Wheelbase: 123 in. **Overall Length:** 190.5 in. except (wagon) 196.5 in. **Height:** 58 in. **Width:** 70.5 in. **Front Tread:** 59 in. **Rear Tread:** 51 in. **Standard Tires:** 180x380.

TECHNICAL: Layout: front-engine, front-drive. **Transmission:** four-speed manual (Citromatic available on DS21). **Standard Final Drive Ratio:** 4.375:1. **Steering:** rack-and-pinion. **Suspension (front):** hydropneumatic with parallel control arms and anti-roll bar. **Suspension (rear):** hydropneumatic with trailing arms and anti-roll bar. **Brakes:** front disc, rear drum. **Body Construction:** steel monoshell (unibody). **Fuel Tank:** 17 gal.

MAJOR OPTIONS: Air conditioning (about $550). AM radio. AM/FM radio. Roof antenna. High heater ($20). Full leather interior: Pallas ($371). Folding front center armrest. Nine-position seat height adjuster (D Special). Tinted glass. "Leather-Tex" upholstery.

PERFORMANCE: Top Speed: (D Special) 100+ mph (factory); (DS21 sedan) about 110 mph. **Acceleration (0-60 mph):** (DS21) about 12.5 sec.; (D Special) about 14 sec. **Fuel Mileage:** (D Special) up to 30 mpg claimed; (DS21) 25-27 mpg claimed.

ADDITIONAL MODELS: Citroen also marketed a Mehari Surf N' Sun utility vehicle at this time, priced at $1795 in the U.S. The four-seat Jeep-like vehicle (comparable to Volkswagen's "Thing") had front-wheel drive, a folding rear seat, and Michelin safety tires. Wearing a plastic body and fully removable top, it resembled no other Citroen model. The two-cylinder, 37-cid engine produced 33 horsepower.

Manufacturer: S.A. Andre Citroen, Paris, France.

Distributor: Citroen Cars Corp., New York City or Englewood, New Jersey.

1971-72 CITROEN

D SPECIAL (DS20) — FOUR — Production of the lower-cost Citroen, introduced in 1970, continued with little change. It was known as either the DS20 or D Special.

DS21/D21 — FOUR — Production of the deluxe sedan and wagon continued with little change. Citromatic was standard on the Pallas.

SM — V-6 — A stylish new high-performance two-door model joined for 1971, blending Citroen's famous air-oil suspension system with a Maserati engine. The 2670-cc (163-cid) V-6 produced 180 horsepower (SAE). The dramatic fastback coupe body had a nearly-horizontal back window tapering to a squared-off rear end, small rear fender skirts, and large rear quarter windows. Quad round headlamps were recessed and separated by large vertical dividers. Front/rear disc brakes included an anti-locking device. Air conditioning and a radio were standard, as was a five-speed manual gearbox.

I.D. DATA: Chassis serial number is located on the firewall, on left door post, and on a shelf protruding from the center of the instrument panel, visible through the windshield. Engine number is at the front of the block.

1972 Citroen DS21 convertible.

Model	Body Type & Seating	Engine Type/CID	P.O.E. Price	Weight (lbs.)	Prod. Total
D SPECIAL					
DS20	4-dr Sedan-5P	I4/121	3550	2778	Note 1
DS21					
Aero Super	4-dr Sedan-5P	I4/133	4394	2855	Note 1
D21	4-dr Sta Wag-7/9P	I4/133	4483	3087	Note 1
DS21 PALLAS					
Aero Super	4-dr Sedan-5P	I4/133	4644	2855	Note 1
Grand Rte	4-dr Sedan-5P	I4/133	4644	2855	Note 1
SM MASERATI					
SM	2-dr Coupe-2 + 2P	V6/163	11700	3198	Note 2

Note 1: A total of 578,328 Citroens were produced in 1971, and 648,956 in 1972.

Note 2: A total of 868 Citroen-Maserati SMs were produced in 1970, 4,988 in 1971, and 4,036 in 1972.

D-Series Price Note: D-Series figures shown were valid in 1971. Prices in 1972 rose to $3750 for the D Special, $4665 for the DS21 sedan, $5065 for the DS21 Pallas sedan, and $4890 for the station wagon.

SM Price Note: Figure shown was valid in 1972.

ENGINE DATA: BASE FOUR (D Special): Inline, overhead-valve four-cylinder. Cast iron block and aluminum head. **Displacement:** 121.1 cu. in. (1985 cc). **Bore & Stroke:** 3.39 x 3.37 in. (86 x 85 mm). **Compression Ratio:** 8.0:1. **Brake Horsepower:** 91 at 5750 rpm. **Torque:** 106 lbs.-ft. at 3000 rpm. Five main bearings. Solid valve lifters. One Solex 34PBIC carburetor.

D Special Engine Note: Output in 1972 was listed as 98 bhp (SAE gross) at 5750 rpm, and 110 lbs.-ft. at 3000 rpm, with 8.75:1 compression.

BASE FOUR (DS21): Inline, overhead-valve four-cylinder. Cast iron block and aluminum head. **Displacement:** 132.7 cu. in. (2175 cc). **Bore & Stroke:** 3.54 x 3.37 in. (90 x 85.5 mm). **Compression Ratio:** 8.75:1. **Brake Horsepower:** 115-117 at 5750 rpm. **Torque:** 128 lbs.-ft. at 3000-3500 rpm. Five main bearings. Solid valve lifters. Weber 28x36 DDE two-barrel carburetor.

BASE V-6 (SM): 90-degree, dual-overhead-cam V-6. Aluminum block and heads. **Displacement:** 162.9 cu. in. (2670 cc). **Bore & Stroke:** 3.42 x 2.95 in. (87 x 75 mm). **Compression Ratio:** 9.0:1. **Brake Horsepower:** 180 (SAE) at 6250 rpm **Torque:** 172 lbs.-ft. at 4000 rpm. Four main bearings. Solid valve lifters. Three Weber 42 DCNF carburetors.

CHASSIS DATA: Wheelbase: (D-Series) 123 in.; (SM) 116.1 in. **Overall Length:** (D-Series) 190.5 in. except (wagon) 196.5 in.; (SM) 193.6 in. **Height:** (D-Series) 58 in.; (wag) 60.2 in.; (SM) 52.1 in. **Width:** (D-Series) 70.5 in.; (SM) 72.3 in. **Front Tread:** (D-Series) 59 in.; (wag) 59.6 in.; (SM) 60.1 in. **Rear Tread:** (D-Series) 51.2 in.; (wag) 51.8 in.; (SM) 52.2 in. **Standard Tires:** (D-Series) 180x380; (SM) 195/70VR15.

TECHNICAL: Layout: front-engine, front-drive. **Transmission:** (D-Series) four-speed manual (Citromatic available on DS21); (SM) five-speed manual with floor lever. SM gear ratios: (1st) 2.92:1; (2nd) 1.94:1; (3rd) 1.32:1; (4th) 0.97:1; (5th) 0.76:1; (rev) 3.15:1. **Standard Final Drive Ratio:** (DS21) 4.375:1; (SM) 4.375:1. **Steering:** rack-and-pinion. **Suspension (front):** hydropneumatic with parallel control arms and anti-roll bar. **Suspension (rear):** hydropneumatic with trailing arms and anti-roll bar. **Brakes:** (D-Series) front disc, rear drum; (SM) all-disc. **Body Construction:** (D-Series) steel monoshell (unibody); (SM) platform chassis with lateral box members. **Fuel Tank:** D-Series) 17 gal.; (SM) 24 gal.

MAJOR OPTIONS (D-Series): Citromatic transmission: wagon ($150). Air conditioning. Leather interior: DS21 Pallas ($412). Tinted glass ($95). Tinted windshield ($49). Air horn ($32). Roof antenna w/speakers ($32). Seat-height adjuster ($17). Front center armrest: DS21 Pallas; leather ($40); jersey ($26).

PERFORMANCE: Top Speed: (D Special) 100+ mph (factory); (SM) about 137 mph in European trim, 140 mph advertised in U.S. **Acceleration (0-60 mph):** (SM) 8.5 sec. **Acceleration (quarter-mile):** (SM) 16 sec. **Fuel Mileage:** (D Special) up to 30 mpg claimed; (DS21) 25-27 mpg claimed.

ADDITIONAL MODELS: Production of the Chapron-built DS21 convertible continued into the 1970's, in very limited numbers.

Manufacturer: S.A. Andre Citroen, Paris, France.

Distributor: Citroen Cars Corp., Englewood, New Jersey.

HISTORY: Production of the smaller GS Citroen, with air-cooled twin-cam four-cylinder engine, began in 1971; but that model did not enter the U.S. import market. Its 1015-cc engine produced 55 bhp (DIN), for a top speed around 75 mph.

Driving an SM in Europe, reported the editors of Petersen's '71 *Import Car Buyer's Guide,* "was like being in another world--a world of speed, comfort and safety never felt before on any other other car we have driven!"

Though the D-Series would not be available in the U.S. after 1972, it remained in production for sale elsewhere. By 1975, at least 1.25 million had been built. The 2CV also remained in production, through the 1970s and well into the 1980s, soon becoming the world's oldest car model apart from the Volkswagen Beetle.

SM — V-6 — The long-lived D-Series left the U.S. marketplace after 1972, leaving only the Citroen-Maserati SM (and that not for long). The SM got a larger engine in 1973, displacing 2965 cc, giving an extra 10 horsepower. That was available with automatic, while the smaller (2670-cc) V-6 was used in manual-gearbox examples. In addition to the standard two-door coupe, nine SM convertibles and nine four-doors were produced, wearing Chapron-styled bodies. Standard SM equipment included an electric rear defroster, adjustable front bucket seats with adjustable backrest, center and side armrests, tachometer, clock, two-speed wiper/washers, power windows, adjustable steering wheel, tinted glass, leather interior, and AM/FM stereo radio. Michelin 205/70 XWX radial racing tires were standard.

1973 Citroen SM coupe.

I.D. DATA: Not available.

Model	Body Type & Seating	Engine Type/CID	P.O.E. Price	Weight (lbs.)	Prod. Total
SM (MASERATI)					
	2-dr Coupe-4P	V6/181	13350	3263	Note 1

Note 1: A total of 2,619 Citroen-Maserati SMs were produced in 1973, 273 in 1974, and one last example in 1975. Another 135 were built for Citroen by Ligier in 1974-75.

Price Note: Price shown is for 1973; rose to $13,500 ($13,800 with automatic transmission) in 1974.

ENGINE DATA: BASE V-6 (SM with manual shift): 90-degree, dual-overhead-cam V-6. Aluminum block and heads. **Displacement:** 162.9 cu. in. (2670 cc). **Bore & Stroke:** 3.42 x 2.95 in. (87 x 75 mm). **Compression Ratio:** 9.0:1. **Brake Horsepower:** 180 (SAE) at 6250 rpm **Torque:** 172 lbs.-ft. at 4000 rpm. Four main bearings. Solid valve lifters. Three Weber 42 DCNF carburetors.

BASE V-6 (SM with automatic): 90-degree, dual-overhead-cam V-6. Aluminum block and heads. **Displacement:** 180.9 cu. in. (2965 cc). **Bore & Stroke:** 3.61 x 2.95 in. (91.6 x 75 mm). **Compression Ratio:** 9.0:1. **Brake Horsepower:** 190 (SAE) at 6000 rpm. **Torque:** 187 lbs.-ft. at 3000 rpm. Four main bearings. Solid valve lifters. Three Weber two-barrel carburetors.

CHASSIS DATA: Wheelbase: 116.1 in. **Overall Length:** 193.4 in. **Height:** 52.1 in. **Width:** 72.3 in. **Front Tread:** 60 in. **Rear Tread:** 52.3 in. **Standard Tires:** 205/70VR15.

TECHNICAL: Layout: front-engine, front-drive. **Transmission:** five-speed manual, or automatic. **Standard Final Drive Ratio:** 4.375:1. **Steering:** rack-and-pinion. **Body Construction:** on platform frame. **Fuel Tank:** 24 gal.

MAJOR OPTIONS: Air conditioning ($520). Automatic transmission ($300-$375). Sunroof ($500). Bodyside moldings ($90).

PERFORMANCE: Top Speed: up to 140 mph reported with manual shift, 128 mph with automatic.

PRODUCTION/SALES: A total of 2,037 Citroen-Maserati SM coupes were sold in the U.S., out of 12,920 produced.

Manufacturer: S.A. Andre Citroen, Paris, France.

Distributor: Citroen Cars Corp., Englewood, New Jersey.

HISTORY: Citroen began production of a new CX2000 four-door sedan in 1973, but that model never entered the U.S. market. Peugeot took over Citroen (from Michelin) by 1976, dropping the Maserati connection in the process. For 1976, a 2CV Special was introduced in Europe, with specifications similar to the original 1948 model. That meant round headlamps (instead of square), no chrome, and no third side windows. It came only in yellow, whereas the original '48 was only painted grey. Citroen remained a major force in the world marketplace into the 1980s and '90s, but no longer exported cars to the U.S. after the mid-1970s. Early in the 1990s, however, rumors began to circulate about a possible rebirth of the marque in the imported-car ranks.

CONNAUGHT

Known mainly for race cars, the British Connaught engineering company produced a handful of sports roadsters

in the late 1940s and early '50s. Each was powered by a 1767-cc Lea-Francis four-cylinder engine, tuned to deliver as much as 140 horsepower (twice the output of the original 70-bhp powerplant). The sports/racer debuted at the Silverstone course in June 1949, and the first roadgoing model appeared in the following year. As reported in *Motor Trend* late in 1950, Connaughts were said to be "hand finished, one at a time." The magazine called the roadster a "thoroughbred machine." Connaughts were created by Rodney Clarke, well known as a race driver and Bugatti owner. Early examples were raced by Clarke himself, along with Kenneth McAlpine. Final Connaughts were for racing only. By 1957 even that end of the business was abandoned, though the very last car wasn't completed until two years later.

1948-54 CONNAUGHT

L2/L3 — FOUR — Like many low-production sports cars, the Connaught was available with a choice of engine tunes, from the basic 98 horsepower all the way up to 140 bhp. Leaf springs were used at both front and rear on early models. Later examples switched to a torsion-bar front suspension. The aluminum body rode a tubular steel frame. A typical example had faired-in headlamps and a small horizontal oval grille, with a trim strip extending back along the hood from the grille's center. The entire front end (hood, fenders, etc.) hinged forward for engine access. A handful of Connaughts wore cycle fenders.

I.D. DATA: Not available.

Model	Body Type & Seating	Engine Type/CID	P.O.E. Price	Weight (lbs.)	Prod. Total
	2-dr Rds-2P	I4/108	N/A	2165	Note 1

1953 Connaught "A" Type. (Coys of Kensington)

Note 1: Approximately 27 Connaughts were produced from 1949-53.

ENGINE DATA: BASE FOUR: Inline, overhead-valve four-cylinder (modified Lea-Francis). **Displacement:** 107.8 cu. in. (1767 cc). **Bore & Stroke:** 2.95 x 3.94 in. (75 x 100 mm). **Compression Ratio:** 8.5:1/9.5:1. **Brake Horsepower:** 98 at 5500 rpm or 102+ at 5000 rpm. Three main bearings. Solid valve lifters. Two SU carburetors (minimum).

Note: The Lea-Francis engine was available in various states of tune, producing up to 140 bhp (using four horizontal Amal carburetors).

CHASSIS DATA: Wheelbase: 99 in. **Overall Length:** 147 in. **Width:** 59.5 in. **Max. Tread:** 52.5 in. **Standard Tires:** 6.00x16.

TECHNICAL: Layout: front-engine, rear-drive. **Standard Final Drive Ratio:** 4.55:1. **Suspension (front):** semi-elliptic leaf springs or (later) wishbones and torsion bar. **Suspension (rear):** rigid axle with semi-elliptic leaf springs. **Brakes:** hydraulic, front/rear drum. **Body Construction:** aluminum alloy body on tubular steel frame.

PERFORMANCE: Top Speed: 122+ mph.
Manufacturer: Connaught Engineering (Continental Cars Ltd)., Send, Surrey, England.

DAF

As competition increased in the market for small imported cars during the late 1950s, new entrants needed a gimmick. While some of those gimmicks proved frivolous, others were wholly practical. Thus, the Dutch-built DAF was the first small car to come with an automatic transmission as standard equipment. Not an ordinary automatic, either, but an ingenious belt-driven "Variomatic" with an "infinite" range of ratios.

Power reached the rear wheels via a centrifugal clutch and two pairs of variable-diameter pulleys, each operated by a V-belt. A combination of engine vacuum and centrifugal weights determined the working diameter of the drive pulleys. At the other end of the system, spring and belt tension set the diameter of each driven pulley. The result: an infinite range of drive ratios, from 20:1 for startup all the way to 4.4:1, using no gears at all and no clutch pedal. "Shift to DAF-- you'll never shift again," read the promotional sheet a couple of years after the car's appearance in the United States market. The multi-purpose unit also functioned as a maxi-grip differential for positive traction, and provided vacuum for engine braking and overdrive. Belt problems with the automatic transmission were the subject of early rumors, but the company denied that the belts (though exposed to air, mud and dirt) would prove troublesome.

Independent suspension at all four wheels also put the DAF a step ahead of many cars of its era. So did the elimination of the need for chassis lubrication, and the use of rack-and-pinion steering.

Company history began with the two van Doorne brothers: Hubert Jozef, who'd operated an engineering firm from the late 1920s on, and Wim, who served as the businessman of the pair. After production of military equipment ended following World War II, the company turned to commercial vehicles. What led to the DAF automobile was the invention by Hubert of an infinitely-variable, belt-driven automatic transmission, soon to be called Variomatic. Rigorous testing of the device included treks across deserts and hauling of trailers up mountainsides. Early in 1958, the prototype appeared at the Amsterdam auto show. A year later, in March 1959, production began of the model 600. By 1962, some 60,000 cars had been sold. In the mid-1960s, the Variomatic system found its way into military vehicles, and drove a racing car. Although modestly popular in the U.S. for a decade, the little DAF automobile faded away in the late 1960s. Production continued a while longer, however, and the little cars continued to trickle into America as late as 1973. By 1971, Hub van Doorne had begun to develop yet another transmission, this one fully automatic. In 1975, the company was taken over by Volvo and the DAF name disappeared.

1959-61 DAF

600 — TWO — Large enough to hold four grownups and a youngster (or so the company claimed), the initial DAF model was promoted as the "first family car to combine classic European beauty and craftsmanship with fully automatic driving at no extra cost." Not every observer would call the car beautiful, or "sculptured," but it was distinctive. Most notable was the front view, as the hood sloped downward sharply at the front, so its leading edge was about at the level of the bottom of the headlights. That leading edge continued outward, over the headlights, giving them a shrouded appearance. A

'daf' script was mounted in the center of the hood. Farther down was a horizontal grille with angled upper corners and a very tight crosshatch mesh pattern.

An air-cooled, flat two-cylinder engine mounted in the front delivered 22 horsepower. Aluminum cylinders held steel sleeve inserts. A central chassis backbone held a front leaf spring at the forward end and a fork for coil springs at the rear. Standard equipment included a heater, defroster, directional signals, safety-type steering wheel, and sunvisors. Two separate contoured front seats adjusted independently and had adjustable backrests. No greasing was needed, for the life of the car; no surprise since there were no lubrication points at all. As for economy, the company claimed up to 40 miles per gallon, along with a top cruising speed of 57 mph. Space was available for 12.5 cubic feet of luggage.

1960 DAF two-door.

I.D. DATA: Starting serial number (1960): LP003-004802.

Model	Body Type & Seating	Engine Type/CID	P.O.E. Price	Weight (lbs.)	Prod. Total
Standard	2-dr Sedan-4P	H2/36	1499	1390	N/A
Deluxe	2-dr Sedan-4P	H2/36	1599	1390	N/A

Price Note: Prices shown are for 1960 models; initial price in 1959 was $1390. For 1961, prices dropped to $1395 and $1645.

ENGINE DATA: BASE TWO: Horizontally opposed, overhead-valve, air cooled two-cylinder. Aluminum crankcase and cylinders; steel sleeve inserts. **Displacement:** 36 cu. in. (590 cc). **Bore & Stroke:** 3.0 x 2.5 in. (76 x 65 mm). **Compression Ratio:** 7.1:1. **Brake Horsepower:** 22 (SAE) at 4000 rpm. Two main bearings. Solid valve lifters. One carburetor. 6-volt electrical system.

CHASSIS DATA: Wheelbase: 81 in. **Overall Length:** 142 in. **Height:** 54.5 in. **Width:** 57 in. **Front Tread:** 46.5 in. **Rear Tread:** 46.5 in. **Wheel Type:** three-lug mounting. **Standard Tires:** 5.20x12.

TECHNICAL: Layout: front-engine, rear-drive. **Transmission:** infinitely variable automatic, belt-driven (4.4:1 to 20:1 ratio) **Steering:** rack and pinion (28-foot turning circle). **Suspension (front):** independent; transverse leaf spring, with hydraulic shock absorbers serving as swivels. **Suspension (rear):** independent swinging half axle; pivoting V-shaped control arms (triangular guides) and coil springs. **Brakes:** drum; 7-inch diameter. **Body Construction:** press sheet steel unibody with box-section main girder. **Fuel Tank:** 7.5 gallon.

PERFORMANCE: Top Speed: 57 mph (factory; cruising). **Fuel Mileage:** approx. 40 mpg (factory).

Manufacturer: Van Doorne's Automobielfabriek (DAF), Eindhoven, Holland (the Netherlands).

HISTORY: Introduced in spring 1959; prototype at the Amsterdam Automobile Show in early 1958. DAF was the first strictly-Dutch car built in Holland since the luxurious Spijker (Spyker), last produced in the 1920s. A DAF competed on the Lime Rock, Connecticut race course soon after the cars began to arrive in the U.S.

1962-64 DAF

600 — TWO — Sales of the 600 model continued for a time after the 750 and DAFfodil were introduced.

750 — TWO — "More pep...more power...without loss in economy" was the promise of the revised DAF, which gained a more powerful air-cooled two-cylinder engine producing 30 horsepower. As before, belt drive offered a continuously-variable drive ratio; but those ratio limits changed to 3.9:1 and 16.4:1. Two pulley pairs were connected together with V-belts, sending power independently to each rear wheel. Engine vacuum varied the effective diameter of the drive pulleys. As load dropped, the drive pulley grew in diameter. An automatic two-stage centrifugal clutch was attached to the engine flywheel, with a Bosch starter/generator/ignition unit mounted on the front of the crankshaft.

Like the 600, the 750's hood dropped down sharply at the front, between single round headlamps, with 'daf' script in its center. The tightly mesh-patterned grille also was similar to the 600, with round parking lights alongside (below the headlamps). The horizontally-opposed engine now displaced 746 cubic centimeters, able to deliver a top cruising speed of 70 mph. Standard and Deluxe models were offered, the former finished in greyish-blue with chrome-plated side stripes, as well as an ivory-colored grille

and bumpers. Standard equipment included a heater/defroster. The Deluxe came with two-tone upholstery, in a choice of seven body colors. Its trim included chrome-plated side strips, window frames, hubcaps, grille and bumpers.

Promotional material from DAF's factory-owned East Coast distributor noted that the 750 "offers big-car conveniences, roominess and riding qualities without the excessive bulk that 'goes along for the ride' on larger automobiles," adding that its thriftiness could only be described by the cliche that it "pays for itself." They further emphasized the car's "jack-rabbit acceleration" and "dual traction ensuring that you go in snow," along with its "picture window" visibility. The sales brochure continued to push the car's automatic-shifting capabilities, advising that "Even you can drive a DAF!"

DAFFODIL — TWO — Though similar in construction to the 750, the DAFfodil was slightly longer and heavier, with a different front-end appearance. The dip-down hood was the same, but a heavy twin-bar horizontal crossbar divided the DAFfodil's wider grille, which was made up of thin horizontal strips. Parking lights were mounted along that crossbar, which extended to wrap around the front of the fenders. The usual 'daf' script stood at the front of the hood. Standard equipment included a heater/defroster and windshield washer. With its "massive new grille," DAFfodil, according to the sales brochure, was "THE car for both young and old 'moderns' with an eye for style."

1962 DAF Daffodil.

I.D. DATA: Not available.

Model	Body Type & Seating	Engine Type/CID	P.O.E. Price	Weight (lbs.)	Prod. Total
600					
Standard	2-dr Sedan-4P	H2/36	1150	1390	Note 1
DeLuxe	2-dr Sedan-4P	H2/36	1225	1390	Note 1
750					
Standard	2-dr Sedan-4P	H2/45	1320	1320	Note 1
DeLuxe	2-dr Sedan-4P	H2/45	1455	1460	Note 1
DAFfodil					
DeLuxe	2-dr Sedan-4P	H2/45	1550	1470	Note 1

Note 1: A total of 29,748 DAFs were built in 1964 alone.
Price Note: Prices shown are for 1962 models.

ENGINE DATA: BASE TWO (750): Horizontally opposed, overhead-valve, air cooled two-cylinder. Aluminum crankcase and cylinders; steel sleeve inserts. **Displacement:** 45.5 cu. in. (746 cc). **Bore & Stroke:** 3.37 x 2.56 in. (85.5 x 65 mm). **Compression Ratio:** 7.1:1. **Brake Horsepower:** 30 at 4000 rpm. **Torque:** 41.95 lbs.-ft. at 2800 rpm. Two main bearings. Solid valve lifters. Solex 34PBI carburetor. 6-volt electrical system.

CHASSIS DATA: **Wheelbase:** 81 in. **Overall Length:** 142 in. **Height:** 54.3 in. **Width:** 57 in. **Front Tread:** 46.5 in. **Rear Tread:** 46.5 in. **Wheel Type:** pressed steel disc. **Standard Tires:** 5.20x12.

TECHNICAL: **Layout:** front-engine, rear-drive. **Transmission:** infinitely- variable automatic, belt-driven (3.9:1 to 16.4:1 ratio). **Steering:** rack-and-pinion. **Suspension (front):** independent; transverse leaf spring, with hydraulic shock absorbers serving as swivels. **Suspension (rear):** independent; swinging half shafts with torque rods and coil springs. **Brakes:** front/rear drum. **Body construction:** steel unibody. **Fuel Tank:** 7.5 gallons.

MAJOR OPTIONS: Sunroof ($90). Two-tone paint and whitewall tires ($40). Radio ($65).

PERFORMANCE: **Top Speed:** (750) to 70 mph (cruising). **Fuel economy:** 32-40 mpg (approx.).

Manufacturer: Van Doorne Automobielfabriek (DAF), Eindhoven, Holland (the Netherlands).

Distributor: Eastern Cars of Holland, Inc., Brooklyn, New York.

1965-66 DAF

AMERICAN — TWO — Appearance of the two-cylinder minicar with infinitely-variable transmission didn't change much for 1965, but its U.S. name switched from 750 to American. The DAFfodil name continued elsewhere. A floor lever had no settings other than "Drive" and "Reverse" for the Variomatic transmission.

I.D. DATA: Not available.

Model	Body Type & Seating	Engine Type/CID	P.O.E. Price	Weight (lbs.)	Prod. Total
AMERICAN					
Special	2-dr Sedan-4P	H2/45	1489	1460	Note 1
DeLuxe	2-dr Sedan-4P	H2/45	1598	1460	Note 1
DeL Extra	2-dr Sedan-4P	H2/45	1695	N/A	Note 1

Note 1: A total of 33,475 DAFs were built in 1966 alone.

ENGINE DATA: BASE TWO: Horizontally opposed, overhead-valve, air cooled two-cylinder. Aluminum crankcase and cylinders; steel sleeve inserts. **Displacement:** 45.5 cu. in. (746 cc). **Bore & Stroke:** 3.37 x 2.56 in. (85.5 x 65 mm). **Compression Ratio:** 7.5:1. **Brake Horsepower:** 30 (SAE) at 4400 rpm. **Torque:** 42 lbs.-ft. at 2800 rpm. Two main bearings. Solid valve lifters. One Solex 34 PICS downdraft carburetor. 6-volt electrical system.

CHASSIS DATA: **Wheelbase:** 80.7 in. **Overall Length:** 142 in. **Height:** 54.5 in. **Width:** 56.7 in. **Front Tread:** 46.5 in. **Rear Tread:** 46.5 in. **Wheel Type:** pressed steel disc (13-inch). **Standard Tires:** 145x13.

TECHNICAL: **Layout:** front-engine, rear-drive. **Transmission:** infinitely- variable automatic, belt-driven (3.9:1 to 16.4:1 ratio). **Steering:** rack-and-pinion. **Suspension (front):** independent; transverse leaf spring, with hydraulic shock absorbers serving as swivels. **Suspension (rear):** independent; swinging half shafts with torque rods and coil springs. **Brakes:** front/rear drum. **Body Construction:** steel unibody. **Fuel Tank:** 8.5 gallons.

MAJOR OPTIONS: Sunroof.

PERFORMANCE: **Top Speed:** about 75 mph (cruising). **Acceleration (0-60 mph):** N/A (0-50 in 19 seconds). **Acceleration (quarter-mile):** 24.7 sec. **Fuel Mileage:** about 42 mpg.

Manufacturer: Van Doorne Automobielfabriek (DAF), Eindhoven, Holland (the Netherlands).

HISTORY: During this period, DAF also produced a two-door Combiwagon as well as pickup and panel trucks.

1967-73 DAF

1968 DAF 55 coupe.

1972 DAF two-door.

AMERICAN — TWO — Sales of the American continued as the higher-powered model 44 was introduced.

44 — TWO — The next edition of the Dutch-built DAF got a stronger two-cylinder engine, now rated 40 horsepower, along with a more modern and attractive body. With the change in appearance, however, the car became somewhat less distinctive, similar to various other European compacts. The loss of its dip-down hood, in particular, changed the car's profile. The new body had rectangular park/signal lights alongside a tightly crosshatch-patterned grille (with a small grille section added below the bumper). Horizontal trim strips were used above the grille, below the hood front. Though still slightly shrouded, the headlamps no longer had a unique appearance.

55 — FOUR — An even greater change occurred with the next model, introduced in Holland in 1967. This one had a conventional inline four-cylinder engine, rated 50 horsepower, though hooked to the same Variomatic transmission as the earlier two-strokes.

I.D. DATA: Not available.

Model	Body Type & Seating	Engine Type/CID	P.O.E. Price	Weight (lbs.)	Prod. Total
44	2-dr Sedan-4/5P	H2/51	1795	1598	Note 1
55	2-dr Sedan-4/5P	I4/68	N/A	1720	Note 1

Note 1: A total of 72,000 DAFs were built in 1970 alone.

ENGINE DATA: BASE TWO (44): Horizontally opposed, overhead-valve, air cooled two-cylinder. Aluminum crankcase and cylinders; steel sleeve inserts. **Displacement:** 51.5 cu. in. (844 cc). **Bore & Stroke:** 3.37 x 2.90 in. (85.5 x 73.5 mm). **Compression Ratio:** 7.5:1. **Brake Horsepower:** 40 at 4500 rpm. **Torque:** 51 lbs.-ft. at 2400 rpm. Two main bearings. Solid valve lifters. One Solex 40 PICS downdraft carburetor. 6-volt electrical system.

BASE FOUR (55): Inline, overhead-valve four-cylinder. Cast iron block and aluminum head. **Displacement:** 67.6 cu. in. (1108 cc). **Bore & Stroke:** 2.76 x 2.83 in. (70 x 72 mm). **Compression Ratio:** 8.5:1. **Brake Horsepower:** 50 at 5000 rpm. **Torque:** 62 lbs.-ft. at 3000 rpm. Five main bearings. Solex 32 EHSA sidedraft carburetor.

CHASSIS DATA: Wheelbase: 88.6 in. **Overall Length:** 151.6 in. **Height:** 54.3 in. **Width:** 60.6 in. **Front Tread:** 50.4 in. **Rear Tread:** 49.2 in. **Wheel Type:** pressed steel disc. **Standard Tires:** 135x14 (5.65x14).

TECHNICAL: Layout: front-engine, rear-drive. **Transmission:** infinitely- variable automatic, belt-driven. **Steering:** rack-and-pinion. **Suspension (front):** independent; transverse leaf spring, with hydraulic shock absorbers serving as swivels. **Suspension (rear):** independent; swinging half shafts with torque rods and coil springs. **Brakes:** front/rear drum. **Body Construction:** steel unibody.

MAJOR OPTIONS: Sunroof.

PERFORMANCE: Top Speed: (44) about 76 mph; (55) 85 mph. **Acceleration (0-60 mph):** N/A (Model 44 did 0-50 in 15 sec.; 55 in 12 sec.). **Fuel Mileage:** (44) 30-38 mpg.

Manufacturer: Same as 1965-66.

HISTORY: Introduced: (44) October 1966 at Paris Auto Show; (55) 1967. In addition to the models described above, DAF produced a model 30, 31 and 33.

DAIHATSU

From the time of its formation in Japan, the Daihatsu company took some 80 years to send a product to the U.S. market. Founded as an engine manufacturer in 1907, the company that would become Daihatsu turned to three-wheel motorized tricycles by 1930. Military 4WD vehicles followed later in that decade, but postwar production resumed with the three-wheelers (which retained handlebar-type steering) as the company name changed to Daihatsu Kabushiki Kaisha. By 1958, the company was producing its first three-wheeled automobile, a four-door called the Bee, powered by a two-cylinder engine. A four-cylinder Compagno arrived in 1963, available as a coupe, sedan or station wagon. Toyota took over the company in 1968, after which several Toyota-based models adopted the Daihatsu nameplate. Daihatsus were on sale in Europe by 1966, but took far longer to cross the Atlantic. A front-drive Max Cuore arrived in 1978, as did a larger-engined Charade with three-cylinder engine. By the time the first subcompact Daihatsu Charades arrived in the U.S. in the late 1980s, following a 1985 aero restyling, the company had already begun to establish a strong reputation in the four-wheel-drive field. Those early models evolved to the 4WD Rocky of the 1990s, sold along with the Charades.

1988-90 DAIHATSU

CHARADE — THREE/FOUR — Daihatsu made its first appearance in the U.S. market for the 1988 model year, and then only in western and southern states. Voluntary limitation of imports from Japan kept the allotment down to 11,500 Charades for 1988, and 17,000 in 1989. The initial model was a two-door hatchback powered by a 1.0-liter three-cylinder engine. An optional 1.3-liter four-cylinder engine came later, during 1989, as did a three-speed automatic transmission option to replace the standard five-speed manual gearbox. Standard equipment in 1988 included power brakes, reclining cloth front bucket seats, a folding rear seat, tinted windshield, remote fuel-filler door and liftgate releases, rear defogger, intermittent wipers, and a trip odometer. The CLS added power mirrors, a digital clock, bodyside moldings, front mud guards, sport front seats, a rear

wiper/washer, and tachometer. The CSX included air conditioning and AM/FM stereo with cassette player. A longer four-door sedan joined the original hatchback for 1990 (with the four-cylinder engine), as did the Rocky 4WD sport-utility vehicle.

1989 Daihatsu. (Gary Peacock)

1989 Daihatsu Charade CLX.

I.D. DATA: Vehicle Identification Number is atop the instrument panel, visible through the windshield. Starting serial number (1988): JD1FG()()0()J4000001.

Model	Body Type & Seating	Engine Type/CID	P.O.E. Price	Weight (lbs.)	Prod. Total
CHARADE (1988)					
CLS	2-dr Hatch-4P	I3/61	6397	1775	Note 1
CLX	2-dr Hatch-4P	I3/61	7650	1840	Note 1
CSX	2-dr Hatch-4P	I3/61	9232	1850	Note 1
CHARADE (1989)					
CES	2-dr Hatch-4P	I3/61	6197	1760	Note 1
CLS	2-dr Hatch-4P	I3/61	6697	1775	Note 1
CLX	2-dr Hatch-4P	I3/61	7497	1770	Note 1
CHARADE (1990)					
SE	2-dr Hatch-4P	I3/61	6497	1825	Note 1
SX	2-dr Hatch-4P	I3/61	6997	1835	Note 1
SE4	4-dr Sedan-4P	I4/79	7997	2045	Note 1
SX4	4-dr Sedan-4P	I4/79	8697	2055	Note 1

Note 1: A total of 11,460 Daihatsu Charades were sold in the U.S. during 1988, and 15,118 in 1989.

Price Note: A four-cylinder engine added $550 to the hatchback price in 1990.

1990 Daihatsu Charade four-door sedan.

ENGINE DATA: BASE THREE (1988-90): Inline, overhead-cam three-cylinder. Cast iron block and light alloy head. **Displacement:** 60.6 cu. in. (993 cc). **Bore & Stroke:** 2.99 x 2.87 in. (76 x 73 mm). **Compression Ratio:** 9.5:1. **Brake Horsepower:** 53 at 5200 rpm. **Torque:** 58 lbs.-ft. at 3600 rpm. Four main bearings. Multi-point fuel injection.

OPTIONAL FOUR (1989-90): Inline, overhead-cam four-cylinder. **Displacement:** 79 cu. in. (1295 cc). **Bore & Stroke:** 2.99 x 2.81 in. (76 x 71.4 mm). **Compression Ratio:** 9.5:1. **Brake Horsepower:** 80 at 6000 rpm. **Torque:** 74 lbs.-ft. at 4400 rpm. Multi-point fuel injection.

Note: Four-cylinder engine was standard in 1990 sedan.

CHASSIS DATA: Wheelbase: 92.1 in. **Overall Length:** (hatch) 144.9 in.; (sedan) 159.6 in. **Height:** 54.5 in. **Width:** 63.6 in. **Front Tread:** 54.5 in. **Rear Tread:** 53.7 in. **Wheel Type:** (CLS/CLX) steel disc; (CSX) alloy. **Standard Tires:** (CLS) 145/80R13; (CLX) 15580R13; (CSX) 165/70R13.

TECHNICAL: Layout: front-engine, front-drive. **Transmission:** five-speed manual. **Steering:** rack and pinion. **Suspension (front):** MacPherson struts with coil springs. **Suspension (rear):** rigid axle with coil springs. **Brakes:** power front disc, rear drum. **Body Construction:** steel unibody. **Fuel Tank:** 10.6 gallon.

MAJOR OPTIONS: Air conditioning. Automatic transmission. Power steering. Stereo tape player.

Manufacturer: Daihatsu Kogyo Co. Ltd. (part of Toyota Group), Osaka, Japan.

Distributor: Daihatsu America Inc., Los Alamitos, California.

HISTORY: Even as the 1990s began, the Charade remained available only in selected parts of the country. Far more attention went to the Rocky 4WD sport-utility vehicle with its 1.6-liter, 16-valve engine and removable hardtop. Even so, Charade ranked 27th out of 39 subcompacts in U.S. sales in 1989.

DAIMLER

Perhaps best known for stately and dignified motorcars in the early postwar years, including limousines built for the British royal family, the Daimler has a long and notable history that reaches back to the earliest motorcars. Gottlieb Daimler, a German, was one of the early developers of the internal combustion engine for automotive use. As early as 1888, Frederick Simms purchased the rights to that engine, intended for marine applications in Great Britain. Horseless carriages followed in 1896, leading to a broad line of Daimler horseless carriages, built at the Coventry plant. Among the early achievements was the production of the first British-built four-cylinder automobile, in 1899. Over the next 15 years, until World War I broke out, Daimler issued more than 40 different models. Royal patronage began at the turn of the century. King Edward VII, an early motoring fan, took a particular liking to Daimlers. Many engineers who went on to careers at other firms learned their trade at the Daimler works. In 1910, Daimler was purchased by Birmingham Small Arms Company (BSA), a name that would later establish itself in the motorcycle arena.

By the 1920s, Daimler had a long-established reputation for quiet, elegant and refined motorcars. In addition to four- and six-cylinder models, the company turned out a Double-Six chassis in the late 1920s, carrying a low-slung Park Ward body and powered by a 150-bhp, 7-liter V-12 with sleeve valves. Other, smaller-displacement V-12s also used the sleeve-valve configuration. Daimler was among the first automaker to adopt the Wilson self-shifting transmission, with preselector and fluid coupling, making it standard in 1932. A year earlier, Lanchester had joined with Daimler, to produce lower-priced family cars as a complement to the posh limousines and saloons. Sleeve valves gave way to overhead-valve powerplants by 1936, including a series of straight eight. A few examples in the 1930s were of a more sporting nature, some wearing rather dramatic coachwork.

A simpler model lineup emerged after World War II, starting with the expected saloons (sedans) and limousines, powered by six-cylinder and (until 1953) straight

156

eight engines. Then came something completely different, in both name and appearance: the Conquest roadster. Rakish and tailfinned, wearing cutdown doors, the Conquest served as a startling companion to the sedate Daimler models. Late in the 1950s, a full-fledged Daimler SP250 sports car appeared, with V-8 power. In 1960, Jaguar took over the Daimler form. The SP250 lasted through 1964, and the last true Daimler disappeared in 1967. All subsequent Daimlers were essentially badge-engineered versions of the Jaguar XJ6, XJ12, or Mk X. Except in Britain, the Daimler name departed after 1983.

Note: Through 1955, smaller models with four- and six-cylinder engines were produced by Daimler under the Lanchester name; see that listing in this Catalog.

1946-1950 DAIMLER

1948 Daimler 2.5-liter saloon.

1949 Daimler.

DB18 — SIX — Wheelbase was 114 inches for the smallest Daimler saloon and drophead coupe models. Powerplant was a 154-cid (2522 cc) six-cylinder, overhead-valve engine. The standard hydraulically-operated transmission worked through a fluid coupling, with preselector epicyclic gearbox and overdrive top gear, giving four speeds forward and one reverse. Its selector quadrant was beneath the steering wheel. Independent front suspensions consisted of coil springs and links, with hydraulic shocks. At the rear were long semi-elliptic leaf springs. Separate headlamps and a one-piece flat windshield were used on both the four-door saloon and the open coupe. Front doors were hinged at the rear. Both front and rear saloon doors had vent windows. The nearly-upright vee-shaped grille was similar to that used on late prewar models. A special Royal Empress version of the 2.5-litre (DB18) saloon was announced in 1950, described as "custom built for the connoisseur," with a razor-edge design. Powerplant was the 85-horsepower version of the six-cylinder engine, as in the Special Sports. Two separately adjustable bucket seats were in front, while the bench rear seat had a folding center armrest, permitting comfortable seating for four. Interior extras included two cubbyholes in the instrument board, lighter, ashtrays, two electric roof lamps, sun visors, two veneered and polished tables in the back of the front bucket seats, radio under the instrument board, heater under the dash, lambskin rug in the rear, and carpeted front floor with felt underlays throughout. An electrically-operated back blind was controlled from the front seat. Custom coachwork was done by Hooper of London. Small tools were carried in a tool roll in the lower part of the luggage boot.

HISTORY: Promoting "The Finest Line for '49," Fergus Motors in New York City focused on Daimler's royal heritage: "By appointment Motor Car Manufacturers to His Majesty the King, the Daimler Company is known the world over for its supreme Town and Country Limousines, Touring Convertibles and its new 'Sports Special.' There are no finer automobiles built." Production of the DB18 ended during 1950, when it was replaced by the similarly-dimensioned Consort saloon; see next listing. Production of larger Daimlers continued into 1953.

1950 Daimler.

SPECIAL SPORTS — SIX — A drophead coupe (convertible) with more powerful six-cylinder engine joined the DB18 six in 1948. Identical in displacement to the DB18 six, it delivered 85 horsepower. Each half of the split bench-type front seat was separately adjustable. The seatback folded down for access to the rear, making it appear to be a two-seater; but the rear held a single bucket-type seat with armrest. The car's folding top was spring-assisted for lowering, and seats were trimmed in leather. Interior appointments included polished walnut woodwork, a radio and heater, leatherette-covered sun visors, lighter and ashtrays, and carpeting with felt underlays. The custom body was built by Barkers of Coventry. Daimler's hydraulic transmission with preselector gearbox was standard. Below the trunk was a separate space for the spare tire.

DE27 — SIX — Many different bodies were offered on the middle-size Daimler, with a 138-inch wheelbase and larger (249.7 cid) six-cylinder engine. They included a close-coupled and touring limousine by Hooper; a Hooper-bodied saloon; Four and Six Light models by Hooper; saloon, Six Light limousine and close-coupled limousine by Windover; limousine by Barkers; and saloon and close-coupled limo by Freestone & Webb.

DE36 — EIGHT — The largest Daimler, riding a 147-inch wheelbase and powered by a straight eight engine, also came with a wide selection of bodies. They included saloons and limousines by Hooper, Windover, Barkers, and Freestone & Webb.

I.D. DATA: Serial number for DB18 is stamped on a plate on top of chassis, just below firewall; and on a firewall plate. Serial number for DE27/DE36 is stamped on plate attached to chassis, ahead of the firewall. Starting serial no.: (DB18) 50040; (Spec Spts) 53750; (DE27) 51040; (DE36 w/LHD) 51750; (DE36 w/RHD) 51150. Engine number of DB18 is stamped at the front of the block, below the manifold. Engine number of DE27/DE36 is on the fuel pump boss, and on a plate attached to firewall.

Model	Body Type & Seating	Engine Type/CID	P.O.E. Price	Weight (lbs.)	Prod. Total
DB18 SERIES					
DB18	4-dr Saloon	I6/154	N/A	3705	Note 1
DB18	2-dr Dhd Coupe	I6/154	N/A	3705	Note 1
Hooper	4-dr Empress	I6/154	N/A	N/A	Note 1
SPECIAL SPORTS					
	2-dr Dhd Coupe	I6/154	N/A	3534	Note 1
DE27 SERIES					
DE27	4-dr Saloon	I6/250	N/A	5671	Note 1
DE27	4-dr Limo	I6/250	N/A	5671	Note 1
DE36 SERIES					
DE36	4-dr Saloon	I8/333	N/A	6013	Note 1
DE36	4-dr Limo	I8/333	N/A	6013	Note 1

Note 1: Only five Daimlers were known to have been sold in the U.S. during 1950.
Body Note: DE27 and DE36 were offered in a wide variety of body styles by various coachbuilders.
Weight Note: Weights shown above are approximate.

ENGINE DATA: BASE SIX (DB18): Inline, overhead-valve six-cylinder. **Displacement:** 153.8 cu. in. (2522 cc). **Bore & Stroke:** 2.74 x 4.35 in. (69.6 x 110.5 mm). **Compression Ratio:** 7.0:1. **Brake Horsepower:** 70 at 4200 rpm. Four main bearings. Solid valve lifters. One SU carburetor.
BASE SIX (Special Sports): Same as above, except — **Brake Horsepower:** 85 at 4200 rpm. Two SU carburetors.
BASE SIX (DE27): Inline, overhead-valve six-cylinder. **Displacement:** 249.7 cu. in. (4095 cc). **Bore & Stroke:** 3.35 x 4.72 in. (85.1 x 120 mm). **Compression Ratio:** 6.3:1. **Brake Horsepower:** 110 at 3600 rpm. Four main bearings. Solid valve lifters. Two SU carburetors.
BASE EIGHT (DE36): Inline, overhead-valve eight-cylinder. **Displacement:** 333.0 cu. in. (5460 cc). **Bore & Stroke:** 3.35 x 4.72 in. (85.1 x 120 mm). **Compression Ratio:** 6.3:1. **Brake Horsepower:** 150 at 3600 rpm. Five main bearings. Solid valve lifters. Two SU carburetors.

CHASSIS DATA: Wheelbase: (DB18) 114 in.; (Spec Spts) 114 in.; (DE27) 138.4 in.; (DE36) 147 in. **Overall Length:** (DB18) 180 in.; (Spts) 187 in.; (Empress) 192 in.; (DE27) 213.5 in.; (DE36) 222 in. **Height:** (DB18) 63 in.; (Spts) 61 in.; (DE27) 72 in.; (DE36) 72 in. **Width:** (DB18) 64.5 in.; (Spts) 64.5 in.; (Empress) 66.75 in.; (DE27) 73.5 in.; (DE36) 73.5 in. **Front Tread:** (DB18) 52 in.; (Spts) 52 in.; (DE27) 60 in.; (DE36) 60 in. **Rear Tread:** (DB18) 52 in.; (Spts) 52 in.; (DE27) 63 in.; (DE36) 63 in. **Wheel Type:** bolt-on disc. **Standard Tires:** (DB18) 6.00x16; (DE27) 8.00x17; (DE36) 8.00x17.

TECHNICAL: Layout: front-engine, rear-drive. **Transmission:** four-speed manual with preselector; (Spec Spts) overdrive on top gear. Preselector w/overdrive gear ratios: (1st) 3.00:1; (2nd) 1.64:1; (3rd) 1.1:1; (4th) 0.73:1; (rev) 3.16:1. **Standard Final Drive Ratio:** (DB18) 4.37:1; (Spec Spts) 3.55:1; (DE27) 4.72:1; (DE36) 4.09:1; (Empress) 4.857:1. **Steering:** worm and double roller. **Suspension (front):** coil springs. **Suspension (rear):** rigid axle with semi-elliptic leaf springs. **Brakes:** Daimler-Girling hydromechanical drum. **Body Construction:** steel body on steel frame (underslung box section, cruciform braced).

PERFORMANCE: Top Speed: (DB18) 76 mph; (Spec Spts) 86 mph; (DE27/36) 85 mph. **Acceleration (0-60 mph):** N/A (DB18, 0-50 mph in 17.9 sec.; Spts, 0-50 in 16.1 sec.; DE36, 0-50 in 14.5 sec.). **Acceleration (quarter-mile):** (DB18) 25.2 sec.; (Spts) 22.7 sec.; (DE27/36) 23.7 sec.

Manufacturer: The Daimler Company Ltd., Coventry, England.
Distributor/Dealer: Fergus Motors, New York City.

1951 DAIMLER

1951 Daimler DB 18 Special Sports. (Coys of Kensington)

DB18 CONSORT — SIX — Slightly more modern in appearance, the replacement for the earlier DB18 had a curved radiator grille with thick center divider bar, and semi-built-in (inboard) headlamps. Small parking lights sat atop the front fenders. Only a saloon was produced, powered by the 70-bhp, 154-cid (2522 cc) overhead-valve six-cylinder engine.

SPECIAL SPORTS — SIX — Production of the 85-bhp convertible (drophead coupe) continued with no significant change.

DE27 — SIX — Production of the 138-inch wheelbase saloons and limousines continued with no change.

DE36 — EIGHT — Production of 147-inch wheelbase saloons and limousines also continued without change.

I.D. DATA: Serial number for DB18 is stamped on a plate on top of chassis, just below firewall; and on a firewall plate. Serial number for DE27/DE36 is stamped on plate attached to chassis, ahead of the firewall. Starting serial no.: (DB18 Consort) 55000. Engine number of DB18 is stamped at the front of the block, below the manifold. Engine number of DE27/DE36 is on the fuel pump boss, and on a plate attached to firewall.

Model	Body Type & Seating	Engine Type/CID	P.O.E. Price	Weight (lbs.)	Prod. Total
DB18					
Consort	4-dr Saloon	I6/154	N/A	3620	Note 1
SPECIAL SPORTS					
	2-dr Dhd Coupe	I6/154	N/A	3534	Note 1
DE27 SERIES					
DE27	4-dr Saloon	I6/250	N/A	5671	Note 1
DE27	4-dr Limo	I6/250	N/A	5671	Note 1
DE36 SERIES					
DE36	4-dr Saloon	I8/333	N/A	6013	Note 1
DE36	4-dr Limo	I8/333	N/A	6013	Note 1

Note 1: 19 Daimlers were known to have been sold in the U.S. during 1951. **Body Note:** DE27 and DE36 were offered in a wide variety of body styles by various coachbuilders.

Weight Note: Weights shown above are approximate.

Model/Price Note: A Royal 8 convertible coupe, said to be the longest convertible in the world (at 20 feet overall) was offered for sale in the U.S. at $13,025.

ENGINE DATA: BASE SIX (DB18 Consort): Inline, overhead-valve six-cylinder. **Displacement:** 153.8 cu. in. (2522 cc). **Bore & Stroke:** 2.74 x 4.35 in. (69.6 x 110.5 mm). **Compression Ratio:** 7.0:1. **Brake Horsepower:** 70 at 4200 rpm. Four main bearings. Solid valve lifters. One SU carburetor.
BASE SIX (Special Sports): Same as above, except — **Brake Horsepower:** 85 at 4200 rpm. Two SU carburetors.
BASE SIX (DE27): Same as 1946-50.
BASE EIGHT (DE36): Same as 1946-50.

CHASSIS DATA: Wheelbase: (DB18) 114 in.; (Spec Spts) 114 in.; (DE27) 138.4 in.; (DE36) 147 in. **Overall Length:** (DB18) 180 in.; (Spts) 187 in.; (DE27) 213.5 in.; (DE36) 222 in. **Height:** (DB18) 63 in.; (Spts) 61 in.; (DE27) 72 in.; (DE36) 72 in. **Width:** (DB18) 65.5 in.; (Spts) 64.5 in.; (DE27) 73.5 in.; (DE36) 73.5 in. **Front Tread:** (DB18) 52 in.; (Spts) 52 in.; (DE27) 60 in.; (DE36) 60 in. **Rear Tread:** (DB18) 52 in.; (Spts) 52 in.; (DE27) 63 in.; (DE36) 63 in. **Wheel Type:** bolt-on disc. **Standard Tires:** (DB18) 6.00x16; (DE27) 8.00x17; (DE36) 8.00x17.

TECHNICAL: Layout: front-engine, rear-drive. **Transmission:** four-speed manual with preselector. **Standard Final Drive Ratio:** (DB18 Consort) 4.30:1; (Spec Spts) 3.55:1 or 4.86:1; (DE27) 4.72:1; (DE36) 4.09:1. **Steering:** worm and double roller. **Suspension (front):** coil springs. **Suspension (rear):** rigid axle with semi-elliptic leaf springs. **Brakes:** Daimler-Girling hydromechanical drum. **Body Construction:** steel body on steel frame (underslung box section, cruciform braced).

PERFORMANCE: Top Speed: (DB18 Consort) near 82 mph; (Spec Spts) 86 mph; (DE27/36) 85 mph. **Acceleration (0-60 mph):** N/A (DB18, 0-50 mph in 16.9 sec.; Spts, 0-50 in 16.1 sec.; DE36, 0-50 in 14.5 sec. **Acceleration (quarter-mile):** (DB18) 24.3 sec.; (Spts) 22.7 sec.; (DE27/36) 23.7 sec.
Manufacturer: The Daimler Company Ltd., Coventry, England.
Distributor/Dealer: Fergus Motors, New York City.
HISTORY: Consort was introduced in June 1950.

157

1952 DAIMLER

1952 Daimler convertible.

1952 Daimler Conquest saloon. (JC)

DB18 CONSORT — SIX — Production of the six-cylinder Consort, on a 114-inch wheelbase, continued with no significant change.

SPECIAL SPORTS — SIX — Production continued of the higher-powered convertible model, with little change.

REGENCY — 3 LITRE — SIX — Late in 1951, a new six-passenger saloon (sedan) model was announced, featuring a more modern appearance than its mates, without their separate-fender design. Instead, the front fender bulge extended toward the rear, through both doors, to flow into the rear fender bulge. Front-end appearance was similar to the Consort, however, with a curved windshield, slightly curved upright-style grille and semi-built-in (inboard) headlamps, plus small parking lights atop the fenders. Large foglamps were mounted below the headlamps. Front and rear doors had vent windows and concealed hinges. Under the bonnet was a new 90-horsepower, 180 cubic-inch (2952 cc) overhead-valve engine with twin horizontal SU carburetors. As in other models, the fluid transmission used a finger-touch preselector. On the dashboard was a reserve fuel control. Each half of the split bench front seat was separately adjustable. The 18-inch diameter spring-spoked steering wheel sat on an adjustable column. A heater with demisters was built-in. Standard colors were: Black with brown, red or green leather; Blue with blue leather; Light Grey with blue or red leather; Dark Green with green leather; Light Green with beige leather and green piping; Maroon with red leather; Fawn with green leather and beige piping. Daimler described the new model as "serene yet strong, majestic yet sedate, swift without violence." Unfortunately, only a handful of Mark I prototypes were built, but the chassis was used for the Empress series (below) and the Regency name emerged again in 1954, as the Mark II.

EMPRESS — Mk II — SIX — The 3-litre chassis intended for the Regency (above) saw more extensive use as the foundation for a series of special models with Hooper Empress bodies, built in late 1952 and early '53.

DE36 — EIGHT — Production of the straight eight saloon and limousine continued without significant change. What *Motor Trend* described as the "most magnificent of Daimlers" was the $26,000 Gold Star package, owned by Lady Norah Docker. *Auto Sport Review* described a one-off coupe built in 1952 by Hooper & Company for Daimler's board chairman, Sir Bornard Docker. Painted in two-tone metallic blue, its bodysides displayed a "quatrefoil" (four-leaf clover) pattern. Inside was blue leather, with such amenities as a cocktail bar and picnic gear. The car was offered for sale to any overseas buyer for $15,000.

I.D. DATA: Serial number for Consort and Regency is stamped on a plate on top of chassis, just below firewall; and on a firewall plate. Serial number for DE36 is stamped on plate attached to chassis, ahead of the firewall. Starting serial no.: (Regency) 80000; (Empress, LHD); 82400; (Empress, RHD) 82000. Engine number of Consort/Regency is stamped at the front of the block, below the manifold. Engine number of DE36 is on the fuel pump boss, and on a plate attached to firewall.

Model	Body Type & Seating	Engine Type/CID	P.O.E. Price	Weight (lbs.)	Prod. Total
DB18					
Consort	4-dr Saloon-4P	I6/154	4650	3440	Note 1
SPECIAL SPORTS					
Special	2-dr Spt Conv-4P	I6/154	4950	3520	Note 1
REGENCY					
Mk I	4-dr Saloon-6P	I6/180	N/A	4032	Note 1
DE36					
DE36	2-dr Dhd Cpe-5P	I8/333	15000	5910	Note 1
DE36	4-dr Limousine-8P	I8/333	17000	5910	Note 1

Note 1: Approximately 11 Daimlers were known to have been sold in the U.S. during 1952.

Body Note: DE36 chassis came with a wide variety of custom bodies.

ENGINE DATA: BASE SIX (DB18 Consort): Inline, overhead-valve six-cylinder. **Displacement:** 153.8 cu. in. (2522 cc). **Bore & Stroke:** 2.74 x 4.35 in. (69.6 x 110.5 mm). **Compression Ratio:** 7.0:1. **Brake Horsepower:** 70 at 4200 rpm. Four main bearings. Solid valve lifters. One SU carburetor.

BASE SIX (Special Sports): Same as above, except -- **Brake Horsepower:** 85 at 4200 rpm. Two SU carburetors.

BASE SIX (Regency): Inline, overhead-valve six-cylinder. **Displacement:** 180.0 cu. in. (2952 cc). **Bore & Stroke:** 3.00 x 4.25 in. (76.2 x 107.95 mm). **Compression Ratio:** 6.7:1. **Brake Horsepower:** 90 at 4100 rpm. Four main bearings. Solid valve lifters. Two SU carburetors.

BASE EIGHT (DE36): Inline, overhead-valve eight-cylinder. **Displacement:** 333.0 cu. in. (5460 cc). **Bore & Stroke:** 3.35 x 4.72 in. (85.1 x 120 mm). **Compression Ratio:** 6.3:1. **Brake Horsepower:** 150 at 3600 rpm. Five main bearings. Solid valve lifters. Two SU carburetors.

CHASSIS DATA: Wheelbase: (Consort) 114 in.; (Spec Spts) 114 in.; (Regency) 114 in.; (DE36) 147 in. **Overall Length:** (Consort) 180 in.; (Regency) 191 in.; (DE36) 222 in. **Height:** (Consort) 63 in.; (Spts) 62 in.; (Regency) 65 in.; (DE36) 72 in. **Width:** (Consort) 64.5 in.; (Spts) 64.5 in.; (Regency) 71 in.; (DE36) 73.5 in. **Front Tread:** (Consort) 52 in.; (Spts) 52 in.; (Regency) 56 in.; (DE36) 60 in. **Rear Tread:** (Consort) 52 in.; (Spts) 52 in.; (Regency) 57 in.; (DE36) 63 in. **Wheel Type:** bolt-on disc. **Standard Tires:** (Consort) 6.00x16; (Regency) 6.50x16; (DE36) 8.00x17.

TECHNICAL: Layout: front-engine, rear-drive. **Transmission:** four-speed manual with preselector. Regency overall gear ratios: (1st) 17.54:1; (2nd) 9.98:1; (3rd) 6.71:1; (4th) 4.30:1; (rev) 23.2:1. **Standard Final Drive Ratio:** (Consort) 4.30:1; (Spec Spts) 4.86:1; (Regency) 4.30:1; (DE36) 4.09:1. **Steering:** worm and double roller; (Regency) Marles cam and roller. **Suspension (front):** coil springs; (Regency) coil springs with torsional stabilizer bar. **Suspension (rear):** rigid axle with semi-elliptic leaf springs. **Brakes:** Daimler-Girling hydromechanical drum. **Body Construction:** steel body on steel frame (underslung box section, cruciform braced).

PERFORMANCE: Top Speed: (Consort) near 82 mph; (Spec Spts) 86 mph; (DE36) 85 mph. **Acceleration (0-60 mph):** N/A (Consort, 0-50 mph in 16.9 sec.; Spts, 0-50 in 16.1 sec.; DE36, 0-50 in 14.5 sec.). **Acceleration (quarter-mile):** (Consort) 24.3 sec.; (Spts) 22.7 sec.; (DE36) 23.7 sec.

Manufacturer: The Daimler Company Ltd., Coventry, England.

Distributor/Dealer: Fergus Motors, New York City.

HISTORY: Regency was introduced in October 1951.

1953 DAIMLER

1953 Daimler six-cylinder Special Sports "Silver Flash" two-door sport coupe. (Christie's)

CONQUEST — SIX — Even the name suggested something different about the newest Daimler model, straying away from the marque's sedate image. Not until the roadster version arrived for 1954, however, would the extent of the change be evident. Only the saloon debuted at first, priced at 1066 pounds (Sterling), which just happened to be the date of the Norman Conquest. The announcement also happened to be timed to coincide with the Coronation of Queen Elizabeth II, in 1952. The saloon maintained traditional Daimler styling, but brought up to date with headlamps mounted in the fenders and a fenderline that faded away at the back of the front door. The six-window body design had front and rear vent windows. A new six-cylinder engine (slightly smaller than other Daimler models) was installed, rated 75 horsepower. The independent front suspension used laminated torsion bars, unlike the other models with coil springs. Automatic chassis lubrication was standard.

DB18 CONSORT — SIX — Production of the six-cylinder Consort, on a 114-inch wheelbase, ended early in the 1953 model year; see previous listing for details.

REGENCY/EMPRESS — 3 LITRE — SIX — Production of the special model based on the Regency, with a 100-bhp engine, continued into 1953.

Note: Some publications used the Regency name during 1953 to describe the 3-litre models, but it was not officially employed until the Mk II version of 1954.

DE36 — EIGHT — Production of the straight eight saloon and limousine continued into 1953 (its final year) without significant change.

I.D. DATA: Serial number for Regency is stamped on a plate on top of chassis, just below firewall; and on a firewall plate. Serial number for Conquest and DE36 is stamped on plate attached to chassis, ahead of the firewall. Starting serial no.: (Conquest) 82500; Engine number of Regency is stamped at the front of the block, below the manifold. Engine number of Conquest and DE36 is on the fuel pump boss, and on a plate attached to firewall.

Model	Body Type & Seating	Engine Type/CID	P.O.E. Price	Weight (lbs.)	Prod. Total
CONQUEST					
Mk I	4-dr Saloon-4P	I6/149	N/A	3100	Note 1
REGENCY/EMPRESS 3-LITRE					
Mk I	4-dr Saloon-6P	I6/180	N/A	3810	Note 1
Mk II	2-dr Dhd Cpe	I6/180	N/A	4020	Note 1
DE36					
DE36	4-dr Limo-8P	I8/333	17000	5910	Note 1

Note 1: Approximately five Daimlers were known to have been sold in the U.S. during 1953.

Price Note: Approximate prices at the factory in England were $4750 for the Conquest, $6100 for the 3-litre saloon, $6900 for the 3-litre drophead coupe (convertible), and $11,800 for the DE36.

Body Note: DE36 chassis came with a wide variety of custom bodies.

ENGINE DATA: BASE SIX (Conquest): Inline, overhead-valve six-cylinder. **Displacement:** 149.3 cu. in. (2433 cc). **Bore & Stroke:** 3.00 x 3.50 in. (76.2 x 88.9 mm). **Compression Ratio:** 6.6:1. **Brake Horsepower:** 75 at 4000 rpm. **Torque:** 124 lbs.-ft. at 2000 rpm. Four main bearings. Solid valve lifters. One carburetor.

BASE SIX (3-Litre): Inline, overhead-valve six-cylinder. **Displacement:** 180.0 cu. in. (2952 cc). **Bore & Stroke:** 3.00 x 4.25 in. (76.2 x 107.95 mm). **Compression Ratio:** 6.7:1. **Brake Horsepower:** 90 at 4100 rpm. **Torque:** 148 lbs.-ft. at 1600 rpm. Four main bearings. Solid valve lifters. Two SU carburetors.

BASE SIX (3-Litre conv): Same as above, except — **Compression Ratio:** 7.5:1. **Brake Horsepower:** 100 at 4400 rpm.

BASE EIGHT (DE36): Inline, overhead-valve eight-cylinder. **Displacement:** 333.0 cu. in. (5460 cc). **Bore & Stroke:** 3.35 x 4.72 in. (85.1 x 120 mm). **Compression Ratio:** 6.3:1. **Brake Horsepower:** 150 at 3600 rpm. **Torque:** 253 lbs.-ft. at 1200 rpm. Five main bearings. Solid valve lifters. Two SU carburetors.

CHASSIS DATA: Wheelbase: (Conquest) 104 in.; (3-Litre) 114 in.; (DE36) 147 in. **Overall Length:** (Conquest) 177 in.; (3-Litre) 191 in.; (DE36) 222 in. **Height:** (Conquest) 65 in.; (3-Litre) 60 in.; (3-Litre conv) 60 in.; (DE36) 72 in. **Width:** (Conquest) 65.5 in.; (3-Litre) 71 in.; (DE36) 73.5 in. **Front Tread:** (Conquest) 52 in.; (3-Litre) 56 in.; (DE36) 60 in. **Rear Tread:** (Conquest) 52 in.; (3-Litre) 57 in.; (DE36) 63 in. **Wheel Type:** bolt-on disc. **Standard Tires:** (Conquest) 6.70x15; (3-Litre) 6.50x16; (DE36) 8.00x17.

TECHNICAL: Layout: front-engine, rear-drive. **Transmission:** four-speed manual with preselector. **Standard Final Drive Ratio:** (Conquest) 4.56:1; (3-Litre) 4.30:1; (DE36) 4.09:1. **Steering:** worm and double roller; (3-Litre) Marles cam and roller. **Suspension (front):** coil springs; (3-Litre) coil springs with torsional stabilizer bar; (Conquest) laminated torsion bars. **Suspension (rear):** rigid axle with semi-elliptic leaf springs. **Brakes:** Daimler-Girling hydromechanical drum. **Body Construction:** steel body on steel frame (underslung box section, cruciform braced).

PERFORMANCE: Top Speed: (Conquest) 81 mph; (3-Litre) 81 mph; (3-Litre conv) 84 mph; (DE36) 84 mph. **Acceleration (0-60 mph):** N/A (Conquest, 0-50 mph in 16.3 sec.; (DE36, 0-50 in 14.5 sec.). **Acceleration (quarter-mile):** (Conquest) 23.2 sec.; (DE36) 23.7 sec. **Fuel Mileage:** (Conquest) about 20 mpg; (3-Litre) 14-15 mpg; (DE36) about 9 mpg.

Manufacturer: The Daimler Company Ltd., Coventry, England.

HISTORY: Conquest saloon was introduced in spring 1953. The dramatic Conquest roadster (see next listing) appeared at the London Motor Show in October 1953.

upholstery; and Powder Blue with red upholstery. The roadster had a folding top and side curtains, a leather-covered instrument panel, chromed fittings, leather seat upholstery, and full-width door pockets. Foglamps were available, mounted on the front fender apron. Top speed squeezed past 100 mph, as another difference from the customary Daimlers of the day.

Production of the far more sedate Conquest four-door saloon continued with little change. A drophead coupe was added in 1954, with power top and adjustable steering column. Unlike the roadster, it had conventional squared-off doors. Actually, all three Conquest bodies looked similar from the front, with fender-mounted headlamps and curved upright-style grille.

REGENCY/EMPRESS — Mk II — SIX — The revived (and revised) Regency had a 107-horsepower, 3468-cc six-cylinder engine. Appearance was similar to the Conquest saloon, but on the longer (114-inch) wheelbase with long hood. A Hooper Empress body was introduced first, followed by ordinary saloons.

I.D. DATA: Serial number is stamped on plate attached to chassis, ahead of the firewall. Engine number is on the fuel pump boss, and on a plate attached to firewall.

Model	Body Type & Seating	Engine Type/CID	P.O.E. Price	Weight (lbs.)	Prod. Total
CONQUEST					
Mk I	2-dr Rds-2P	I6/149	N/A	2926	N/A
Mk I	4-dr Saloon-5P	I6/149	4400	3126	N/A
MK I	2-dr Dhd Cpe	I6/149	N/A		N/A
REGENCY					
Mk II	4-dr Saloon	I6/211	N/A	3990	N/A
Mk II	4-dr Empress Saloon	I6/211	N/A	N/A	N/A

ENGINE DATA: BASE SIX (Conquest): Inline, overhead-valve six-cylinder. **Displacement:** 149.3 cu. in. (2433 cc). **Bore & Stroke:** 3.00 x 3.50 in. (76.2 x 88.9 mm). **Compression Ratio:** 6.6:1. **Brake Horsepower:** 75 at 4000 rpm. **Torque:** 124 lbs.-ft. at 2000 rpm. Four main bearings. Solid valve lifters. One carburetor.

BASE SIX (Conquest roadster): Same as above, except — **Compression Ratio:** 7.75:1. **Brake Horsepower:** 100 at 4600 rpm. Two SU carburetors.

BASE SIX (Regency): Inline, overhead-valve six-cylinder. **Displacement:** 211.5 cu. in. (3468 cc). **Bore & Stroke:** 3.25 x 4.25 in. (82.55 x 107.95 mm). **Compression Ratio:** 6.5:1. **Brake Horsepower:** 107 at 4000 rpm. Four main bearings. Solid valve lifters. Two SU carburetors.

CHASSIS DATA: Wheelbase: (Conquest) 104 in.; (Regency) 114 in. **Overall Length:** (Conquest) 177 in.; (Regency) 191 in. **Height:** (Conquest) 65 in.; (Conquest rds) 55 in.; (Regency) 65 in.; (Regency conv) 60 in. **Width:** (Conquest) 65.5 in.; (Conquest rds) 66 in.; (Regency) 71 in. **Front Tread:** (Conquest) 52 in.; (Regency) 56 in. **Rear Tread:** (Conquest) 52 in.; (Regency) 57 in. **Wheel Type:** bolt-on disc. **Standard Tires:** (Conquest) 6.70x15; (Conquest rds) 6.00x15; (Regency) 6.50x16.

TECHNICAL: Layout: front-engine, rear-drive. **Transmission:** four-speed manual with preselector. Conquest roadster overall gear ratios: (1st) 14.32:1; (2nd) 8.24:1; (3rd) 5.48:1; (4th) 3.73:1; (rev) 19.43:1. **Standard Final Drive Ratio:** (Conquest) 4.56:1; (Conquest rds) 3.73:1; (Regency) 4.30:1. **Steering:** (Conquest) cam gear; (Regency) Marles cam and roller. **Suspension (front):** (Conquest) laminated torsion bars; (Regency) coil springs with torsional stabilizer bar. **Suspension (rear):** (Conquest) rigid axle with semi-elliptic leaf springs. **Brakes:** Daimler-Girling hydromechanical drum. **Body Construction:** steel body on steel frame (underslung box section, cruciform braced).

PERFORMANCE: Top Speed: (Conquest) 82 mph; (Conquest rds) 100 mph; (Regency) 82 mph. **Acceleration (0-60 mph):** (Conquest) 20.4 sec.; (Conquest rds, 0-50 mph in 10.6 sec.). **Acceleration (quarter-mile):** (Conquest) 23.2 sec.; (Conquest rds) 20.3 sec.; (Regency) 21 sec.

Manufacturer: The Daimler Company Ltd., Coventry, England.

HISTORY: *Motor Trend* reported that the Conquest roadster was designed and built in just six weeks. Part of Daimler's purpose for introducing the roadster was to attempt to capture a few U.S. sales.

1954 DAIMLER

1954 Daimler Conquest four-door.

CONQUEST — SIX — Described as "an entirely new concept in motoring," the new roadster had conventional Daimler styling up front, but a sharply wraparound windshield, cutdown doors, cutaway rear-fender openings, long rear end, and tailfins that had a tacked-on appearance. A "high-speed" 2.5-litre six-cylinder engine rated 100-bhp provided the power, hooked to the usual Daimler transmission with fluid flywheel and preselector gearbox. The two-seater was intended to appeal to younger, more sport-minded customers, whereas Daimlers in general were targeted at the affluent elderly. Like other Daimlers, the roadster used the familiar Daimler preselector gearbox. The desired gear was selected in advanced by moving a small lever on the steering column. Then, as the clutch pedal was depressed, the gears shifted automatically. Standard roadster colors were: Red with cream upholstery; Ivory with red upholstery; Silver with blue

1955 DAIMLER

1955 Daimler convertible.

CONQUEST — SIX — A Century model joined the basic Conquest saloon, powered by the same 100-bhp version of the 2433-cc six-cylinder engine as the Conquest roadster. The drophead coupe (with conventional doors rather than the roadster's cutdown design) also continued. A fixed-head variant of the roadster also became available later.

Instrument panels had inlaid woodwork. The upright curved vertical-bar grille had a broad, bright surround molding. Built-in headlamps stood at fender tips, with parking lights in long housings atop fenders. As before, the roadster had a sharply wraparound windshield with thin framework, and prominent tailfins.

REGENCY — Mk II — SIX — Both 3.5- and 4.5-litre versions of the Regency were announced, but only the smaller engine actually went into production. Appearance was similar to the Conquest saloon, but on a longer wheelbase.

REGINA — SIX — Daimler's new full-scale limo measured more than 18 feet long (possibly the longest in the world at that time), but was powered by a six-cylinder engine. The Regina came in both sedan (limo) and Sportsman models, with most bodies custom made. Stately and huge, it featured squared-off lines. Coil springs were used in front, semi-elliptic leaf springs at the rear.

SPORTSMAN — SIX — The Sportsman saloon was similar to other Daimler models up front, but sported prominent tailfins like those of the Conquest, and carried a more powerful engine than the Regina's. It rode a 114-inch wheelbase. Early Sportsman models had the 4.5-liter engine, but later ones (starting in 1956) turned to the 3.5-litre six.

I.D. DATA: Serial number is stamped on plate attached to chassis, ahead of the firewall. Engine number is on the fuel pump boss, and on a plate attached to firewall.

Model	Body Type & Seating	Engine Type/CID	P.O.E. Price	Weight (lbs.)	Prod. Total
CONQUEST					
Mk I	2-dr Rds-2P	I6/149	N/A	2926	N/A
Mk I	4-dr Saloon-5P	I6/149	4400	3040	N/A
	2-dr Dhd Cpe	I6/149	N/A	N/A	N/A
Century	4-dr Saloon	I6/149	N/A	2840	N/A
REGENCY					
Mk II	4-dr Saloon	I6/211	N/A	3976	N/A
REGINA					
	4-dr Limo-7P	I6/281	N/A	4144	N/A
SPORTSMAN					
	4-dr Saloon	I6/281	N/A	N/A	N/A

Price Note: Approximate prices at the factory in England were $3000 for the Conquest, $3316 for the Conquest Century, $4608 for the Regency, and $12,321 for the Regina.

ENGINE DATA: BASE SIX (Conquest): Inline, overhead-valve six-cylinder. **Displacement:** 149.3 cu. in. (2433 cc). **Bore & Stroke:** 3.00 x 3.50 in. (76.2 x 88.9 mm). **Compression Ratio:** 7.0:1. **Brake Horsepower:** 75 at 4000 rpm. **Torque:** 124 lbs.-ft. at 2000 rpm. Four main bearings. Solid valve lifters. One carburetor.

BASE SIX (Conquest Century/roadster): Same as above, except — **Compression Ratio:** 7.75:1. **Brake Horsepower:** 100 at 4400 rpm. Two SU carburetors.

BASE SIX (Regency): Inline, overhead-valve six-cylinder. **Displacement:** 211.5 cu. in. (3468 cc). **Bore & Stroke:** 3.25 x 4.25 in. (82.55 x 107.95 mm). **Compression Ratio:** 6.5:1. **Brake Horsepower:** 107 at 4000 rpm. Four main bearings. Solid valve lifters. Two SU carburetors.

BASE SIX (Regina): Inline, overhead-valve six-cylinder. **Displacement:** 281.5 cu. in. (4617 cc). **Bore & Stroke:** 3.77 x 4.25 in. (95.25 x 107.95 mm). **Compression Ratio:** 6.5:1. **Brake Horsepower:** 130 at 3600 rpm. Solid valve lifters. Two SU carburetors.

BASE SIX (Sportsman): Same as 4617-cc engine above, except — **Compression Ratio:** 7:1. **Brake Horsepower:** 167 at 3800 rpm.

CHASSIS DATA: Wheelbase: (Conquest) 104 in.; (Regency/Sportsman) 114 in.; (Regina) 130 in. **Overall Length:** (Conquest) 178 in.; (Regency) 191 in.; (Sportsman) 196 in.; (Regina) 217 in. **Height:** (Conquest) 65 in.; (Conquest rds) 55 in.; (Regency) 62.7 in. **Width:** (Conquest) 65.5 in.; (Conquest rds) 66 in.; (Regency) 71 in.; (Sportsman) 70.5 in.; (Regina) 76.5 in. **Front Tread:** (Conquest) 52 in.; (Regency) 56 in. **Rear Tread:** (Conquest) 52 in.; (Regency) 57 in. **Wheel Type:** bolt-on disc. **Standard Tires:** (Conquest) 6.70x15; (Conquest rds) 6.00x15; (Regency) 6.50x16; (Regina) 7.50x16.

TECHNICAL: Layout: front-engine, rear-drive. **Transmission:** four-speed manual with preselector. Conquest roadster overall gear ratios: (1st) 14.32:1; (2nd) 8.24:1; (3rd) 5.48:1; (4th) 3.73:1; (rev) 19.43:1. **Standard Final Drive Ratio:** (Conquest) 4.56:1; (Regency) 4.30:1. **Steering:** (Conquest) cam gear; (Regency) Marles cam and roller. **Suspension (front):** (Conquest) laminated torsion bars; (Regency) coil springs with torsional stabilizer bar. **Suspension (rear):** rigid axle with semi-elliptic leaf springs. **Brakes:** Daimler-Girling hydromechanical drum. **Body Construction:** steel body on steel frame (underslung box section, cruciform braced).

PERFORMANCE: Top Speed: (Conquest) 81 mph; (Conquest rds) 100 mph; (Regency) 82 mph. **Acceleration (0-60 mph):** (Conquest) 20.4 sec.; (Conquest rds, 0-50 mph in 10.6 sec.). **Acceleration (quarter-mile):** (Conquest) 23.2 sec.; (Conquest rds) 20.3 sec.; (Regency) 21 sec.

Manufacturer: The Daimler Company Ltd., Coventry, England.

HISTORY: Dramatic it may have been, but the Conquest roadster lasted for less than two seasons or so in the Daimler lineup, dropped before the 1956 model year began.

1956-59 DAIMLER

CONQUEST — SIX — The dramatic roadster was dropped after 1955, but Daimler offered a drophead coupe with similar profile into 1957. Both 75- and 100-bhp versions of the 2.5-litre six-cylinder engine were available. A third passenger could sit in back, sideways, while front passengers had bucket seats. Standard equipment included a leather-covered instrument panel with tachometer, and leather upholstery.

CONQUEST/CENTURY — Mk II — SIX — The new six-window four-door saloons were similar in appearance to the prior Conquest models, with built-in headlamps and a fender line that continued into the front door. Foglamps were now mounted on the bumper bar, however, and chrome air intakes installed. Powerplant remained the 2.5-litre inline six. Standard Century equipment included leather upholstery, a polished burr walnut instrument panel, and an automatic front-suspension/steering lubrication system that operates when the engine was switched on. Production of the basic Conquest ceased during 1956, but the Century continued into 1957.

104 — SIX — Replacing the Regency Mk II was a new 3.5-litre saloon with a more prosaic nameplate, but similar in appearance and mechanicals. Introduced along with the basic 104 was a special "Ladies' model," with burr walnut facia, power windows, and other extras.

REGINA/SPORTSMAN — SIX — The Regina seven-passenger limousine and Sportsman saloon continued to be available in 1956; see previous listing for details.

1956 Daimler Conquest roadster.

4.5-LITRE — SIX — A four-door saloon was also offered with the 4.5-litre (281.5 cid) six-cylinder engine.

DK400 — SIX — The replacement for the Regina limousine rode a 130-inch wheelbase and measured 217 inches overall. Powerplant was a 4.5-litre (281.5 cid) six, rated 167 horsepower. Eight-seat bodies had three occasional seats and a sliding division window. The seven-seaters had two occasional seats and a drop-style division window. Some examples had custom-built bodies.

I.D. DATA: Serial number is stamped on plate attached to chassis, ahead of the firewall. Engine number is on the fuel pump boss, and on a plate attached to firewall.

Model	Body Type & Seating	Engine Type/CID	P.O.E. Price	Weight (lbs.)	Prod. Total
CONQUEST					
	2-dr Dhd Cpe-3P	I6/149	Note 1	3150	N/A
	4-dr Saloon	I6/149	Note 1	3024	N/A
Century	4-dr Saloon	I6/149	Note 1	2774	N/A
104					
	4-dr Saloon	I6/211	Note 1	4144	N/A
4.5-LITRE/DK400					
	4-dr Saloon	I6/281	Note 1	4144	N/A
DK400	4-dr Limo-7/8P	I6/281	Note 1	4560	N/A

Note 1: Factory prices in 1956 were about $2985 for the Conquest saloon, $3282 for the Conquest Century, $5278 for the 104, $6420 for the 4.5-litre, and $7820 for the DK400 limousine.

ENGINE DATA: BASE SIX (Conquest): Inline, overhead-valve six-cylinder. **Displacement:** 149.3 cu. in. (2433 cc). **Bore & Stroke:** 3.00 x 3.50 in. (76.2 x 88.9 mm). **Compression Ratio:** 7.0:1. **Brake Horsepower:** 75 at 4000 rpm. **Torque:** 124 lbs.-ft. at 2000 rpm. Four main bearings. Solid valve lifters. One carburetor.

BASE SIX (Conquest Century/Drophead): Same as above, except — **Compression Ratio:** 7.75:1. **Brake Horsepower:** 100 at 4400 rpm. **Torque:** 130 lbs.-ft. at 2500 rpm. Two SU carburetors.

BASE SIX (104): Inline, overhead-valve six-cylinder. **Displacement:** 211.5 cu. in. (3468 cc). **Bore & Stroke:** 3.25 x 4.25 in. (82.55 x 107.95 mm). **Compression Ratio:** 7.6:1. **Brake Horsepower:** 137 at 4000 rpm. **Torque:** 191 lbs.-ft. at 2000 rpm. Four main bearings. Solid valve lifters. Two SU carburetors.

BASE SIX (4.5-litre/DK400): Inline, overhead-valve six-cylinder. **Displacement:** 281.5 cu. in. (4617 cc). **Bore & Stroke:** 3.77 x 4.25 in. (95.25 x 107.95 mm). **Compression Ratio:** 7.0:1. **Brake Horsepower:** 167 at 3800 rpm. **Torque:** 260 lbs.-ft. at 2800 rpm. Solid valve lifters. Two SU carburetors.

CHASSIS DATA: Wheelbase: (Conquest/Century) 104 in.; (104) 114 in.; (4.5-liter) 123 in.; (DK400) 130 in. **Overall Length:** (Conquest) 178 in.; (104) 196 in.; (DK400) 217 in. **Height:** (Conquest) 65 in.; (104/4.5-liter) 62.8 in.; (DK400) 69.8 in. **Width:** (Conquest) 65.5 in.; (104) 70.5 in.; (DK400) 77 in. **Wheel Type:** bolt-on disc. **Standard Tires:** (Conquest/Century) 6.70x15; (104) 6.50x16; (DK400) 7.50x16.

TECHNICAL: Layout: front-engine, rear-drive. **Transmission:** four-speed manual with preselector. **Standard Final Drive Ratio:** (Conquest) 4.56:1; (104) 3.92:1; (DK400) 4.27:1. **Steering:** (Conquest) cam gear. **Suspension (front):** (Conquest) laminated torsion bars; (104/DK400) coil springs. **Suspension (rear):** rigid axle with semi-elliptic leaf springs. **Brakes:** front/rear drum. **Body Construction:** steel body on steel frame.

PERFORMANCE: Top Speed: (Conquest) 81-88 mph; (Conquest Century) 90+mph; (104) 100+mph; (DK400) 100 mph. **Acceleration (0-60 mph):** (Conquest) 20.4 sec. **Acceleration (quarter-mile):** (Conquest) 23.2 sec.; (Century) 21.8 sec.; (104) 21 sec.; (DK400) 20.9 sec.

Manufacturer: The Daimler Company Ltd., Coventry, England.

HISTORY: An automatic transmission became available for the first time for the 1957 model year, but the traditional preselector gearbox and fluid transmission also remained available. Otherwise, changes were minimal through 1959. The new SP250 sports car was announced during 1959; see next listing for details.

1960-64 DAIMLER

SP250 — V-8 — To the surprise of many, Daimler veered from its traditional big saloons (sedans) and limousines at the end of the 1950s, turning instead to a two-seat sports car. To a large degree, the SP250 was an evolution of the earlier Conquest roadster. But it probably wouldn't have taken place if not for the development of a new V-8 engine by Edward Turner, a BSA motorcycle designer who'd become Daimler's managing director in 1957. Appearing at the New York Auto Show in spring 1959 (suggesting the car's major target market of American sports-car fans), the two-seater was named Dart. Because Dodge happened to be introducing its new compact of that name around that time, threats of legal action caused Daimler to adopt the SP250 badge.

The compact 2548-cc (153 cid) V-8 used a motorcycle-related valve configuration and hemispherical combustion chambers, producing 140 horsepower at 5800 rpm. It was also far torquier than any other Daimler engine. Front suspension parts and the four-speed manual gearbox also were similar to those in the Triumph TR3A. At the rear was a rigid axle with semi-elliptic leaf springs. Both overdrive and automatic were optional, and four-wheel Girling disc brakes handled stopping.

"Nimble as a kitten in town traffic, yet the highway is the true domain of the SP.250. With the exhilaration of its power, you get the confidence of feather light handling, posi-

tive disc braking and impeccable cornering." That's how Daimler described the SP250, with its fluted wide-oval grille and flaunting rear fins.

Standard colors were Jet Black, Royal Red, Racing Green, and Ivory. Upholstery was tan leather. Wind-up side windows were installed, while the quickly-erected fabric top had transparent quarter windows. The cockpit held two or three people. Adjustable front bucket-type seats wore real hide trim. The padded control panel contained large, quickly-read instruments. A short, rapid-shift type gear lever handled the four-speed transmission, which was synchronized on the top three ratios (with provision for optional overdrive). Standard equipment included a tachometer, ashtray, lockable glovebox, and full-width front bumper.

Styling features of the low front end included a distinctive "V" as part of the grille, set in front of its crosshatch (eggcrate) pattern. Front fenders had a swooping shape, with the domed hood tapering down between the headlamps. Sculptured lines were evident on rear fenders, which had pronounced fins. Not everyone adored the appearance of the fiberglass body (a first for Daimler), which sat upon a separate steel chassis, similar to the TR3A. In addition to its distinctive look—which some declared homely—early bodies were prone to overflexing. Nevertheless, the car was fast, capable of 120 mph and able to hit 60 mph in close to 10 seconds.

I.D. DATA: Serial number is located on the right front chassis crossmember.

Starting serial number: (LHD) 100011; (RHD) 100571.

Model	Body Type & Seating	Engine Type/CID	P.O.E. Price	Weight (lbs.)	Prod. Total
	2-dr Rds-2/3P	V8/153	3900	2090	2,648

Price Note: U.S. price soon fell to $3702 (or $4075 for a hardtop model); but later rose to $3995 and $4245, respectively.

Weight Note: Weight shown is "dry" amount.

ENGINE DATA: BASE V-8: Overhead-valve V-8. Cast iron block and aluminum-alloy head (hemispherical). **Displacement:** 152.6 cu. in. (2548 cc). **Bore & Stroke:** 3.00 x 2.75 in. (76.2 x 69.8 mm). **Compression Ratio:** 8.2:1. **Brake Horsepower:** 140 at 5800 rpm. **Torque:** 155 lbs.-ft. at 3600 rpm. Five main bearings. Solid valve lifters. Two SU HD6 carburetors.

CHASSIS DATA: Wheelbase: 92 in. **Overall Length:** 160.5 in. **Height:** 50.25 in. **Width:** 60.5 in. **Front Tread:** 50 in. **Rear Tread:** 48 in. **Wheel Type:** pressed steel disc. **Standard Tires:** 5.90x15 (5.50x15 optional).

TECHNICAL: Layout: front-engine, rear-drive. **Transmission:** four-speed manual (synchro on 2nd, 3rd and 4th). **Overall gear ratios:** (1st) 10.49:1; (2nd) 6.24:1; (3rd) 4.41:1; (4th) 3.48:1. Overdrive or automatic available. **Standard Final Drive Ratio:** 3.58:1 (hypoid bevel axle). **Steering:** cam-type. **Suspension (front):** long/short control arms with coil springs. **Suspension (rear):** rigid axle and semi-elliptic leaf springs. **Brakes:** Girling front/rear discs. **Body Construction:** fiberglass body on steel frame. **Fuel Tank:** 14 (U.S.) gallons.

MAJOR OPTIONS: Detachable hardtop. Overdrive. Borg-Warner automatic transmission. Knock-on wire wheels (five for $100). Ace discs (four) for bolt-on standard steel wheels. Whitewall tires (five for $50). Adjustable steering column. Leather-covered steering wheel. Front bumper. Rear bumper (in place of standard twin overriders). Tonneau cover. Reserve gas tank and switch. Heater and demister. Adjustable steering column. Cigar lighter. Windshield washers. Exhaust pipe finishers. Foglamps. Pass lamps. Badge bar. Fan cowl (for tropical conditions). Two safety belts. Trickle charger socket. Radio and antenna. Fender mirrors.

PERFORMANCE: Top Speed: 120-123 mph. **Acceleration (0-60 mph):** 9.7-11 sec. (0-100 mph in 28.9 seconds). **Acceleration (quarter-mile):** 17.8-18.2 sec.

ADDITIONAL MODELS: Although most of the focus went on the new sports car, Daimler also produced Majestic saloons and limousines through the early 1960s. The first Majestic saloon, introduced in 1958, rode a short (114-inch) wheelbase and carried a 3.8-litre six-cylinder engine. The Majestic Major, which continued in production until 1967, moved up to a 4561-cc V-8, delivering 220 horsepower; and in 1961, to a 138-inch wheelbase. After the Jaguar takeover, Daimler also introduced a small saloon using the Jaguar Mk II body and the SP250 V-8 engine. See next listing for further details on both.

Manufacturer: The Daimler Company Ltd., Coventry, England.

Distributor: The Daimler Corp., Baltimore, Maryland.

HISTORY: In 1960, the Daimler company was taken over by Jaguar. Introduced in spring 1959, the SP250 went on sale in October 1959. Two-seater sales never approached anticipated levels, and the SP250 never turned a profit. A restyle was proposed, but abandoned.

SP250 POSTSCRIPT: Two improved SP250 versions were built, with little appearance change. In 1961, the "B-Specification" was phased in, with standard equipment that was formerly optional (heater, bumpers, adjustable steering column). It also had a stiffer body. A subsequent "C-Spec" two years later added a standard heater and trickle-charger socket. A small number of later models had a fixed hardtop.

1965-67 DAIMLER

1966 Daimler V8 2.5-liter saloon. (Sotheby's)

250 — 2.5 LITRE — V-8—The combination of Jaguar Mk II body and Daimler SP250 V-8 engine continued in production until 1969. Appearance was similar to the Jaguar, except for the grille.

MAJESTIC MAJOR — V-8 — Production of the last "true" Daimler continued into 1967, on a 114-inch wheelbase with 4561-cc V-8 engine. Appearance was similar to earlier Daimler saloons, with a curved upright grille made up of vertical bars and a six-window body design.

SOVEREIGN — SIX — This was the first of the Jaguar-based Daimlers, which continued in production into the 1980s. Appearance was nearly identical to the Jaguar 420 four-door saloon, except for the Daimler-style grille pattern. Engine was the Jaguar twin-cam 4235-cc inline six, delivering 245 horsepower.

I.D. DATA: Not available.

Model	Body Type & Seating	Engine Type/CID	P.O.E. Price	Weight (lbs.)	Prod. Total
250	4-dr Saloon	V8/153	N/A	3078	N/A
Majestic	4-dr Saloon	V8/278	N/A	3990	N/A
Sovereign	4-dr Saloon	I6/258	N/A	3420	N/A

ENGINE DATA: BASE V-8 (250): Overhead-valve V-8. Cast iron block and aluminum-alloy head (hemispherical). **Displacement:** 152.6 cu. in. (2548 cc). **Bore & Stroke:** 3.00 x 2.75 in. (76.2 x 69.8 mm). **Compression Ratio:** 8.2:1. **Brake Horsepower:** 140 at 5800 rpm. **Torque:** 155 lbs.-ft. at 3600 rpm. Five main bearings. Solid valve lifters. Two SU carburetors.

BASE V-8 (Majestic): Overhead-valve V-8. **Displacement:** 278.2 cu. in. (4561 cc). **Bore & Stroke:** 3.75 x 3.15 in. (95.25 x 80 mm). **Compression Ratio:** 8.0:1. **Brake Horsepower:** 220 at 5600 rpm. Two SU carburetors.

BASE SIX (Sovereign): Inline, dual overhead cam six-cylinder. **Displacement:** 258.3 cu. in. (4235 cc). **Bore & Stroke:** 3.62 x 4.17 in. (92.07 x 106 mm). **Compression Ratio:** 8.0:1. **Brake Horsepower:** 245 at 5500 rpm. Two SU carburetors.

CHASSIS DATA: Wheelbase: (250) 107.5 in.; (Majestic) 138 in.; (Sovereign) 107.5 in. **Overall Length:** (250) 180.75 in.; (Majestic) 226 in.; (Sovereign) 187.75 in. **Width:** (250) 66.75 in.; (Majestic) 73.25 in.; (Sovereign) 66.75 in. **Standard Tires:** (250) 6.40x15; (Majestic) 7.00x16; (Sovereign) 185x15.

TECHNICAL: Layout: front-engine, rear-drive. **Transmission:** four-speed manual or Borg-Warner automatic. **Standard Final Drive Ratio:** (250) 4.27:1; (Majestic) 3.77:1; (Sovereign) 3.77:1 or 3.54:1. **Suspension (front):** coil springs. **Suspension (rear):** (250) cantilever; (Majestic) rigid axle and semi-elliptic leaf springs; (Sovereign) coil springs.

PERFORMANCE: Top Speed: (250) 112 mph; (Majestic) 113 mph; (Sovereign) 117 mph. **Acceleration (quarter-mile):** (250) 19.5 sec.; (Majestic) 18.2 sec.; (Sovereign) 17 sec.

Manufacturer: British Leyland Motor Corp.

Distributor: British Leyland Motors Inc., Leonia, New Jersey.

POSTSCRIPT: For the balance of Daimler's existence, Jaguar bodies and engines were used: both the dual-overhead-cam inline six and the V-12, under the Sovereign nameplate. Early Sovereigns were virtually identical to the 420 Jaguar, except for the addition of a traditional-style Daimler grille. From 1969 to 1973, Daimler also offered a smaller saloon called Sovereign 2, based on the Jaguar XJ6 with the 2.8-litre engine. Starting in 1968, a new limousine on a 141-inch wheelbase was essentially a stretch of the Jaguar Mk X, with razor-edge body shaping by the Vanden Plas company. Sovereigns starting in 1973 adopted the Double Six designation, as in prewar years; but apart from the grille, they differed little from the Jaguar XJ12 of the time. Both two-door and four-door models were offered in the 1970s. See Jaguar listing for additional details on the chassis and engines of these badge-engineered Daimlers.

DATSUN/NISSAN

Though unseen on American roads, some prewar Datsuns that appeared in picture stories were said to resemble scaled-down '33 Fords. That may not be too surprising, since the company began automobile production in 1933 and has a history going farther back yet. Not until 1958 did the first tiny Datsun sedans begin to trickle onto U.S. shores, but the company had been busy in Japan both before and after World War II.

Back in 1911, an American-trained engineer, Masujiro Hashimoto, formed Kwaishinsha Motors to build the first Japanese car. "DAT" stood for initials of three men who provided capital: Kenjiro Den, Rokuro Aoyama and Meitaro Takeuchi. It also happened to mean (in rough translation) "very fast" or, possibly, "fast rabbit." By 1918, the new firm was producing a small two-seater sports car called Datson (for son of DAT). Partly because "son" sounded similar to a Japanese expression that meant "to lose money," the name later changed to Datsun. In 1933, the original Kwaishinsha Motors became Nissan Motor Company Ltd., with public shares offered. Two years later, an assembly line was running at the Yokohama plant and cars were being exported. One of the first was an Austin Seven, built under license from the British firm (not unlike the American Austin/Bantam and German Dixi).

After the war, the factory lay in ruins but was hastily rebuilt by occupation forces in 1946, mainly to build trucks.

A year later, Austin-licensed cars again were rolling off the line, (kin to the contemporary Devon and Somerset). Only 1,594 cars were built by all Japanese companies in 1950, but Datsun alone produced about 2,400 in 1952, and the rising activity even included an interest in competition events. A Datsun Sports roadster debuted in 1952, powered by an 860-cc four-cylinder engine with a three-speed "crash box" transmission and leaf springs all around. The body style, with separate headlamps, rear-hinged doors and fold-down windshield, resembled a topless Model A Ford. An American publication noted that the 1954 sedan "runs reliably if not with tremendous verve," with an engine sound not unlike that of the American Model A. After occupation forces withdrew in 1955, Nissan was ready with its own design for a Datsun 110 sedan. Production of passenger cars reached 13,354 in that year. The sedan soon was joined by a station wagon, a K110 convertible, and a 120 pickup truck. Datsun passenger cars of the mid-1950s still had a crude appearance with exposed door hinges and a split windshield with side-mounted directional indicators. The L-head four produced just 25 horsepower. A "Thrift" four-door sedan was even more boxlike and trucklike in appearance than the DeLuxe model, with an upright back window and rear-hinged front doors.

Few would have imagined when a trickle of Datsuns began to roll into the U.S. for sale in 1958, that this was the start of a full-fledged invasion. The early 210-series and Bluebird mini sedans appealed to only a modest number of Americans, but interest grew considerably when the first sports cars appeared on U.S. shores. The Fair Lady led to the Sports 1500 and 1600, which in turn headed toward the renowned Z-cars of 1970 and beyond. An expanding selection of subcompact and compact sedans and station wagons served as the bread-and-butter for Nissan's sales in the U.S., but the sports cars (and the early performance-oriented 510 sedans) got most of the attention. By the end of the 1970s, more than half a million Datsuns annually were finding American customers.

Model Introduction Note: Partly because Datsuns, like other Japanese cars, appeared first on the West Coast, they often took longer to reach eastern customers and to be listed in the contemporary guidebooks. Whenever possible in the descriptions below, new models are listed (or mentioned) in the year when they first became available somewhere in the U.S.

Model Number Note: Most sources have included the 'L' (meaning left-hand drive) as part of the prefix but some do not. Especially in later years, the prefix letters were often omitted, calling one of the sedan models (for example), simply, "510" rather than "PL510." Some factory material, on the other hand, even added extra suffixes to the already long model numbers. Certain sources have used hyphens in model numbers (SPL-310, 240-Z, etc.), especially for the early years, but they are omitted in this Catalog. An 'S' prefix designates the sports (roadster) models.

gas cap. Little chrome was used on the body, which had fully exposed round wheel openings. Vinyl was used for the upholstery and headliner. Steel handgrips fitted to front doors made them easy to shut. Pedals (including a hydraulic-actuated clutch) were suspended style. Whitewall tires were standard at the start on U.S. imports. Under the hood was a 60.2 cubic-inch (988 cc) overhead-valve four-cylinder engine rated 37 horsepower. A column lever operated the four-speed gearbox, synchronized on the upper three ratios. Standard equipment included a tool kit, lift-out underhood work light (with cord), glovebox, ashtrays, and flashing turn signals.

FAIR LADY — SPL211 (S211) — FOUR — Descended from the early 1950s Datsun sports roadster, the late '50s version, introduced in 1959, wore a fiberglass-reinforced plastic body. Soon, that was replaced by the more modern Fair Lady with a larger (Bluebird) engine. That one proved to be a forerunner of the well-known Z-cars of 1970 and beyond.

PL310 — BLUEBIRD — FOUR — A totally restyled sedan was introduced in California during 1959, but took longer to go on sale elsewhere; see next listing for details.

1959 Datsun 1000 four-door sedan.

I.D. DATA: Serial number is on a plate on the inner left fender well. A prefix gives the model year, with a sequential number at the end. Engine number is low on the block, on a protruding boss.

Model	Body Type & Seating	Engine Type/CID	P.O.E. Price	Weight (lbs.)	Prod. Total
1000					
PL210	4-dr Sedan-4P	I4/60	1799	2035	Note 1
FAIR LADY					
SPL211	2-dr Rds-4P	I4/60	N/A	N/A	Note 1

Note 1: A total of 52 Datsuns were sold in the U.S. in 1958, jumping to 1,290 in 1959.

Model Note: Initial sedan model was called either "PL210" or "1000." Prefix 'S' indicates sports model; letter 'L' denotes left-hand drive.

Weight Note: Gross sedan weight was 2,519 pounds.

ENGINE DATA: BASE FOUR: Inline, overhead-valve four-cylinder (Model C). **Displacement:** 60.2 cu. in. (988 cc). **Bore & Stroke:** 2.875 x 2.323 in. (73 x 59 mm). **Compression Ratio:** 7.0:1 (7.5:1 for U.S. import). **Brake Horsepower:** 34 at 4400 rpm (37 at 4600 for U.S. import). **Torque:** 48 lbs.-ft. at 2400 rpm (49.2 at 2400 for U.S. import). Solid valve lifters. Hitachi (Solex-type) carburetor. 12-volt electrical.

Note: Lower compression and horsepower values above were announced by Datsun/Nissan prior to export to U.S.

CHASSIS DATA: Wheelbase: 87.4 in. Overall Length: 151.97 in. Height: 60.43 in. Width: 57.72 in. Front Tread: 46.06 in. Rear Tread: 46.46 in. Wheel Type: steel disc. Standard Tires: 5.00x15.

TECHNICAL: Layout: front-engine, rear-drive. Transmission: four-speed manual. Gear ratios: (1st) 4.94:1; (2nd) 3.01:1; (3rd) 1.73:1; (4th) 1.00:1; (rev) 6.46:1. **Standard Final Drive Ratio:** 5.57:1 (5.13:1 optional). **Steering:** worm and roller. **Suspension (front):** rigid axle with semi-elliptic leaf springs. **Suspension (rear):** rigid axle with semi-elliptic leaf springs and stabilizer bar. **Brakes:** hydraulic drum. **Body Construction:** steel body on pressed steel box-section frame. **Fuel Tank:** 8.6 gallons (U.S.).

PERFORMANCE: Top Speed: 70 mph (factory). Acceleration (0-60 mph): (1000 sed) 46 seconds. Acceleration (quarter-mile): (1000 sed) 25 seconds (50 mph). **Fuel Mileage:** 25-35 mpg.

ADDITIONAL MODELS: Datsun also produced 211 and 221 sedans on longer wheelbases (92 and 96 inches, respectively), along with mini pickup trucks.

Manufacturer: Nissan Motor Co., Ltd., Tokyo, Japan.

Distributor: Luby-Datsun Ltd., Forest Hills, New York; and Woolverton Motors, North Hollywood, California.

HISTORY: *Mechanix Illustrated's Small Car Guide* described the first Datsun as an "agile little car with lots of thoughtful touches, and a solid feel about it," praising its "thoughtful attention to detail" as well as its roadholding and steering with nearly no body lean. *Business Week* predicted that "the Japanese auto industry isn't likely to carve out a big slice of the U.S. market for itself." Datsun vehicles were displayed at the Imported Car Show in Los Angeles in 1958, and a 210 won the Australian "Mobilgas Trial" rally. The Bluebird 1000 was announced in July 1959, as was a Bluebird 1200.

1958-59 DATSUN

1000 (PL210) — FOUR — Squarish in appearance, with its door hinges exposed, the little Datsun four-door sedan had front-hinged doors, front and rear vent windows, and rode an 87.4 inch wheelbase. A glance at the car's upright profile (somewhat softened by rounded corners) makes it easy to see why Datsuns were popular as taxis in Japan. *Motor Trend* described the first arrivals as "perky," adding that the sedan was "engineered for ruggedness, economy and low manufacturing cost," but featured "functional simplicity rather than austerity." The grille was made up of thick horizontal bars, with 'DATSUN' nameplate on the top bar. Round parking lights stood directly below the single headlamps. A cowl vent sat ahead of the one-piece curved windshield. The gas cap was mounted high up, atop the rear fender. Small chains tethered the radiator cap and

1960 DATSUN

1000 (PL210) — FOUR — Production and sale of the upright-profile sedan continued, but was eclipsed by the more modern Bluebird.

BLUEBIRD — PL310 — FOUR — A totally restyled sedan was introduced in California during 1959, but took longer to go on sale elsewhere. Slightly longer in wheelbase than

the earlier 210-series sedan, the Bluebird also had a larger engine of 72.5 cubic-inch displacement, producing 48 horsepower. Not only a four-door sedan, but a two-door station wagon and a pickup truck were available. A new grille was made up of thin horizontal strips, with vertical dividers. Round parking lights stood below the single round headlamps. The new body had concealed door hinges and a longer rear deck than the former 210-series. A horizontal bodyside trim strip extended most of the car's length, with 'Bluebird' script at the cowl.

FAIR LADY — SPL212 — FOUR — Early in 1960 came the debut of the SPL212 Fair Lady sports roadster, a four-seater with a much sleeker look than the earlier sports models. Side curtains were used, with no roll-up windows. Front-end appearance was identical to the Bluebird sedan. Coil springs replaced the former semi-elliptic leafs up front, but *Motor Trend* complained about the car's hard ride on bumpy roads. Much more rounded than later sports cars, the 212 had full rounded wheel openings, a swooping-down bodyside trim strip, and an oval grille. Round parking lights sat directly below the single headlamps.

Model Note: In its early years on the U.S. market, Datsun did not promote its numerical model designations; most advertisements and road tests referred to the Bluebird and Fair Lady names alone.

I.D. DATA: Serial number is on a plate on the inner left fender well. A prefix gives the model year, with a sequential number at the end. Engine number is low on the block, on a protruding boss.

Model	Body Type & Seating	Engine Type/CID	P.O.E. Price	Weight (lbs.)	Prod. Total
1000					
PL210	4-dr Sedan-4P	I4/60	1616	2035	Note 1
BLUEBIRD					
PL310	4-dr Sedan-4P	I4/72	1616	1918	Note 1
PL310	2-dr Sta Wag-4P	I4/72	1818	2026	Note 1
FAIR LADY					
SPL212	2-dr Spt Rds-4P	I4/72	1996	1985	Note 1

Note 1: A total of 1,169 passenger cars were exported to the U.S. and Canada during 1960, and 1,640 Datsun vehicles (including trucks) were sold in the U.S.

Price Note: Fair Lady price was effective in 1961.

ENGINE DATA: BASE FOUR (PL210): Inline, overhead-valve four-cylinder (Model C). **Displacement:** 60.2 cu. in. (988 cc). **Bore & Stroke:** 2.875 x 2.323 in. (73 x 59 mm). **Compression Ratio:** 7.5:1. **Brake Horsepower:** 37 at 4600 rpm. **Torque:** 48 lbs.-ft. at 2400 rpm. Solid valve lifters. Hitachi (Solex-type) carburetor. 12-volt electrical.

BASE FOUR (Bluebird/Fair Lady): Inline, overhead-valve four-cylinder (Model E). **Displacement:** 72.5 cu. in. (1189 cc). **Bore & Stroke:** 2.875 x 2.796 in. (73 x 71 mm). **Compression Ratio:** 7.5:1. **Brake Horsepower:** 48 (SAE) at 4800 rpm. **Torque:** 60.7 lbs.-ft. at 2400 rpm. Solid valve lifters. One-barrel carburetor. 12-volt electrical.

CHASSIS DATA: Wheelbase: (210) 87.4 in.; (310) 89.8 in. **Overall Length:** (210) 152.7 in.; (310) 153.9 in. **Height:** (210) 60.4 in.; (310) 57.5 in.; (Fair Lady) 153.9 in. **Width:** (210) 57.7 in.; (310) 58.9 in.; (Fair Lady) 58.9 in. **Front Tread:** (210) 46.06 in.; (310) 47.6 in. **Rear Tread:** (210) 46.46 in.; (310) 47 in. **Wheel Type:** steel disc. **Standard Tires:** (210) 5.00x15; (310) 5.60x13; (Fair Lady) 5.20x14.

TECHNICAL: Layout: front-engine, rear-drive. **Transmission:** (210) four-speed manual; (310) three-speed; (Fair Lady) four-speed. **Standard Final Drive Ratio:** (210) 5.57:1 or 5.13:1; (310) 4.63:1. **Steering:** worm and roller. **Suspension (front):** (210) rigid axle with semi-elliptic leaf springs; (310) wishbones and coil springs. **Suspension (rear):** rigid axle with semi-elliptic leaf springs and stabilizer bar. **Brakes:** hydraulic drum. **Body Construction:** steel body on pressed steel box-section frame. **Fuel Tank:** (210) 8.6 gallons; (310) 8.2 gallons.

PERFORMANCE: Top Speed: (210) 70 mph (factory); (310) 77-85 mph; (Fair Lady) 82 mph. **Acceleration (0-60 mph):** (310) 27.5 sec. **Fuel Mileage:** (310) 19-23 mpg.

ADDITIONAL MODELS: Datsun also produced a Bluebird-based pickup truck that sold for $1588 in the U.S.

Manufacturer: Nissan Motor Co., Ltd., Tokyo, Japan.

Distributor: Nissan Motor Corp. U.S.A., Newark, New Jersey and Gardena, California.

HISTORY: Bluebird models took longer to become available in the eastern U.S., and to be listed in American price guides. Nissan Motor Corp. U.S.A. was formed in October 1960.

1961 DATSUN

BLUEBIRD — PL311 — FOUR — Datsun's common practice in the early years on the U.S. market was to upgrade a model by adding a single digit to its model number: thus, 310 turned into 311. Datsun promoted the sedan and wagon's "full-length safety frame," noting that it weighed hundreds of pounds more than other leading imports. The 72-cid four-cylinder engine grew from 48 to 60 bhp during 1961. A column lever operated the three-speed gearbox. Bluebird's grille was made up of horizontal strips with three vertical dividers.

FAIR LADY — SPL213 — FOUR — Upgrading of the S(PL)211 led to a more potent version of the roadster, with a 60-bhp engine. Side curtains were used, rather than roll-up windows, and a snap-on tonneau cover was included. A bodyside trim strip reached forward in an arc ahead of the front wheel opening, serving as a separator for two-tone color combinations. The grille consisted of horizontal strips with a center divider bar. Round parking lights sat below the single round headlamps. The hood was little more than a lid. Standard equipment included a four-speed gearbox (floor lever), whitewall tires, "vinyl leather" upholstery, carpeting, glovebox, dual-tone horn, and lighter. Datsun's sales brochure promised that the "pleasure of driving is possible not only for you, but for three other members of your family also."

Note: Certain U.S. buyer's guides continued to feature the earlier (PL210 series) Datsun sedan models for some time after the Bluebird series became available.

I.D. DATA: Serial number is on a plate on the inner left fender well. A prefix gives the model year, with a sequential number at the end. Engine number is low on the block, on a protruding boss.

Model	Body Type & Seating	Engine Type/CID	P.O.E. Price	Weight (lbs.)	Prod. Total
BLUEBIRD					
PL311	4-dr Sedan-4P	I4/72	1616	1918	Note 1
PL311	2-dr Sta Wag-4P	I4/72	1818	N/A	Note 1
FAIR LADY					
SPL213	2-dr Spt Rds-4P	I4/72	1996	1950	Note 1

Note 1: A total of 76,667 Datsun passenger cars were produced during 1961, and 1,436 vehicles (including trucks) were sold in the U.S. A total of 1,241 passenger cars were exported to the U.S. and Canada.

ENGINE DATA: BASE FOUR (early Bluebird): Inline, overhead-valve four-cylinder (Model E). **Displacement:** 72.5 cu. in. (1189 cc). **Bore & Stroke:** 2.875 x 2.796 in. (73 x 71 mm). **Compression Ratio:** 7.5:1. **Brake Horsepower:** 48 (SAE) at 4800 rpm. **Torque:** 60.7 lbs.-ft. at 2400 rpm. Solid valve lifters. One-barrel carburetor. 12-volt electrical.

BASE FOUR (late Bluebird, Fair Lady): Same as above, except — **Compression Ratio:** 8.2:1. **Brake Horsepower:** 60 at 5000 rpm. **Torque:** 67.3 lbs.-ft. at 3600 rpm. Two-barrel carburetor.

CHASSIS DATA: Wheelbase: (Bluebird) 89.8 in.; (Fair Lady) 87.4 in. **Overall Length:** (Bluebird) 153.9 in.; (Fair) 158.5 in. **Height:** (Bluebird) 57.5 in.; (Fair) 54.3 in. **Width:** (Bluebird) 58.9 in.; (Fair) 58.9 in. **Front Tread:** (Bluebird) 47.6 in.; (Fair) 46.1 in. **Rear Tread:** (Bluebird) 47 in.; (Fair) 46.6 in. **Wheel Type:** steel disc. **Standard Tires:** (Bluebird) 5.60x13; (Fair) 5.20x14.

TECHNICAL: Layout: front-engine, rear-drive. **Transmission:** (Bluebird) three-speed; (Fair Lady) four-speed. **Standard Final Drive Ratio:** 4.63:1. **Steering:** cam and lever. **Suspension (front):** (Bluebird) wishbones and coil springs; (Fair Lady) transverse double link and torsion bars. **Suspension (rear):** rigid axle with semi-elliptic leaf springs and stabilizer bar. **Brakes:** hydraulic drum. **Body Construction:** steel body on pressed steel box-section frame. **Fuel Tank:** (Bluebird) 8.2 gallons.

MAJOR OPTIONS: Radio ($65). Heater.

PERFORMANCE: Top Speed: (Bluebird) 75 mph; (Fair Lady) 82 mph. **Acceleration (0-60 mph):** (Bluebird) 27.5 sec. **Fuel Mileage:** (Bluebird) tests achieved 28-32 mpg, while factory claims reached 38 mpg.

ADDITIONAL MODELS: Datsun also produced a Bluebird-based pickup truck that sold for $1588 in the U.S.

Manufacturer: Nissan Motor Co., Ltd., Tokyo, Japan.

Distributor: Nissan Motor Corp. U.S.A., Newark, New Jersey and Gardena, California.

HISTORY: "Go Datsun and you go American!" That's how Nissan promoted its cars in 1961, referring to the "delightfully roomy, smart looking Datsun Bluebird." Another ad's theme was: "You'll never guess the price!" Yet another advised readers to "Make a date with a Datsun." In October 1961, the upcoming 1500 Sports (SP310) debuted at the Tokyo Motor Show with a larger (1488 cc) engine. By 1961, Datsun had 60 dealers in the U.S. Datsun's small pickup trucks gained a considerable following during the early 1960s.

1962-63 DATSUN

BLUEBIRD — PL312 — FOUR — A minor grille modification was the major change for the next Bluebird, adding a row of four "holes" above the former insert (consisting of horizontal strips with three vertical dividers). A long bodyside trim strip again stood just below door-handle level. Round parking lights were below the headlamps as before, but now touched the grille. An all-synchro column controlled the three-speed gearbox. As in earlier models, the 72-cid engine had sturdy brackets on the valve cover for hoisting, as well as a built-in lamp under the hood. Datsun ads for 1962 said (rather cryptically) that "the proof is in your hands!" This sedan was "bigger, heavier, roomier, more powerful, faster, more economical, safer, more comfortable, stronger" than other economy imports (up to 594 pounds heavier).

SPORTS 1500 — SPL310 — FOUR — The 200-series roadster (see previous listing) gave way to a restyled 300-series, with a larger and more powerful engine and roll-up windows. Round parking lights sat below the single round headlamps (slightly recessed in nacelles), but inboard, just above the bumper. The crosshatch grille had wide "holes" and angled sides that followed the line of the hood front, which contained 'DATSUN' block letters. The revised roadster had a lower, more square, slab-sided profile than the former Fair Lady, with a horizontal bodyside trim strip that stretched the full length of the car. Four round taillamps were stacked two on each side, with a tiny round lens above each stack. A radio and heater were standard. Early models had a single-passenger back seat. Ads promised "Datsun dash...excitement, verve" in this "beauty from the East," with a "rear jump-seat for a full size passenger." That extra seat was dropped later. A second carburetor was added in 1963, for more horsepower.

I.D. DATA: Serial number is on the firewall under the hood. Each serial number is preceded by a model designation. Engine numbers are stamped on the right top edge of the block (preceded by the engine model code). A vehicle identification plate that includes both numbers and other data is attached to the hood ledge or firewall.

Model	Body Type & Seating	Engine Type/CID	P.O.E. Price	Weight (lbs.)	Prod. Total
BLUEBIRD					
PL312	4-dr Sedan-4/5P	I4/72	1616	N/A	Note 1
PL312	4-dr Sta Wag-4/5P	I4/72	1916	N/A	Note 1
1500					
SPL310	2-dr Spt Conv-3P	I4/91	1996	N/A	Note 1

Note 1: A total of 89,003 Datsun passenger cars were produced during 1962, and 118,558 in 1963. During 1962, 2,629 vehicles (including trucks) were sold in the U.S., followed by 4,707 in 1963. A total of 6,905 Sports 1500 convertibles were built.

ENGINE DATA: BASE FOUR (PL312): Inline, overhead-valve four-cylinder (Model E1). Cast iron block. **Displacement:** 72.5 cu. in. (1299 cc). **Bore & Stroke:** 2.875 x 2.80 in. (73 x 71 mm). **Compression Ratio:** 8.2:1. **Brake Horsepower:** 60 at 5000 rpm. **Torque:** 67 lbs.-ft. at 3600 rpm. Three main bearings. Solid valve lifters. Nikki one-barrel carburetor. 12-volt electrical.

BASE FOUR (SPL310): Inline, overhead-valve four-cylinder (Model G). Cast iron block. **Displacement:** 90.8 cu. in. (1488 cc). **Bore & Stroke:** 3.15 x 2.91 in. (80 x 74 mm). **Compression Ratio:** 9.0:1. **Brake Horsepower:** 85 at 5600 rpm (77 bhp with single carburetor). **Torque:** 92 lbs.-ft. at 4400 rpm (87 at 3600 with single carburetor). Solid valve lifters. One or two Hitachi (SU-type) one-barrel carburetors. 12-volt electrical.

CHASSIS DATA: Wheelbase: (Bluebird) 93.8 in.; (SPL310) 89.8 in. **Overall Length:** (Bluebird) 157.5 in.; (SPL310) 155.6 in. **Height:** (Bluebird) 57 in. (SPL310) 50.2 in. **Width:** (Bluebird) 59 in.; (SPL310) 58.9 in. **Front Tread:** (Bluebird) 47.6 in.; (SPL310) 47.8 in. **Rear Tread:** (Bluebird) 47 in.; (SPL310) 47.1 in. **Standard Tires:** (Bluebird) 5.60x13; (SPL310) 5.60x13.

TECHNICAL: Layout: front-engine, rear-drive. **Transmission:** (Bluebird) three-speed or four-speed manual; (SPL310) four-speed manual. **Standard Final Drive Ratio:** (Bluebird) 4.11:1 or 4.375:1; (SPL310) 3.89:1. **Steering:** (SPL310) cam and lever. **Suspension (front):** wishbones and coil springs. **Suspension (rear):** rigid axle with semi-elliptic leaf springs. **Brakes:** front/rear drum. **Body Construction:** (Bluebird) steel unibody; (SPL310) steel body on box-type ladder frame.

PERFORMANCE: Top Speed: (Bluebird) 75 mph; (SPL310) 87-95 mph. **Acceleration (0-60 mph):** (Bluebird) 28 seconds; (SPL310) 15.5 seconds. **Fuel Mileage:** (Bluebird) 28-32 mpg.

ADDITIONAL MODELS: Datsun also produced for the U.S. market a pickup truck and 4WD Patrol.

Manufacturer: Nissan Motor Co. Ltd., Tokyo, Japan.

Distributor: Nissan Motor Co. U.S.A., Newark, New Jersey; Houston, Texas; and Gardena, California.

HISTORY: "As pretty a car as you'll find in the small-import field" was the opinion of *Mechanix Illustrated* in its appraisal of the Bluebird for the Small Car Guide.

1964 DATSUN

PL410 — FOUR — Datsun's subcompact sedan moved from single to quad headlamps as it went from 300- to 400-series designation, with a narrower grille between the pairs. That grille had a wide eggcrate pattern and a round insignia in its center. A surround molding reached around each headlamp pair and continued toward the center to serve as an upper and lower bar for the grille. Under the hood was a 60-horsepower four-cylinder engine, with four-speed manual transmission.

SPORTS 1500 — SPL310 — FOUR — Production of the two-seater roadster sometimes referred to as the "1500," continued with little change. Standard equipment included a tachometer, radio, four-speed gearbox, race-type steering wheel, tonneau cover, whitewall tires, electric wiper/washers, and roll-up windows.

I.D. DATA: Serial number is on the firewall under the hood. Each serial number is preceded by a model designation. Engine numbers are stamped on the right top edge of the block (preceded by the engine model code). A vehicle identification plate that includes both numbers and other data is attached to the hood ledge or firewall.

Model	Body Type & Seating	Engine Type/CID	P.O.E. Price	Weight (lbs.)	Prod. Total
PL410	4-dr Sedan-5P	I4/72	1616	1980	Note 1
PL410	4-dr Sta Wag-5P	I4/72	1816	N/A	Note 1
1500					
SPL310	2-dr Spt Conv-2P	I4/91	2465	199	Note 1

Note 1: A total of 168,674 Datsun passenger cars were produced during 1964, and 10,315 vehicles (including trucks) were sold in the U.S.

ENGINE DATA: BASE FOUR (PL410): Inline, overhead-valve four-cylinder (Model E1). Cast iron block. **Displacement:** 72.5 cu. in. (1299 cc). **Bore & Stroke:** 2.875 x 2.80 in. (73 x 71 mm). **Compression Ratio:** 8.2:1. **Brake Horsepower:** 60 at 5000 rpm. **Torque:** 67 lbs.-ft. at 3600 rpm. Three main bearings. Solid valve lifters. Nikki one-barrel carburetor. 12-volt electrical.
BASE FOUR (SPL310): Inline, overhead-valve four-cylinder (Model G). Cast iron block. **Displacement:** 90.8 cu. in. (1488 cc). **Bore & Stroke:** 3.15 x 2.91 in. (80 x 74 mm). **Compression Ratio:** 9.0:1. **Brake Horsepower:** 85 at 5600 rpm (77 bhp with single carburetor). **Torque:** 92 lbs.-ft. at 4400 rpm (87 at 3600 with single carburetor). Solid valve lifters. Hitachi one-barrel carburetor(s). 12-volt electrical.

CHASSIS DATA: Wheelbase: (410) 93.8 in.; (SPL310) 89.8 in. **Overall Length:** (410) 157.5 in.; (SPL310) 155.6 in. **Height:** (410) 57 in. (SPL310) 50.2 in. **Width:** (410) 59 in.; (SPL310) 58.9 in. **Front Tread:** (410) 47.6 in.; (SPL310) 47.8 in. **Rear Tread:** (410) 47 in.; (SPL310) 47.1 in. **Standard Tires:** (410) 5.60x13; (SPL310) 5.60x13.

TECHNICAL: Layout: front-engine, rear-drive. **Transmission:** (410) three-speed or four-speed manual; (SPL310) four-speed manual. **SPL310 gear ratios:** (1st) 3.515:1; (2nd) 2.41:1; (3rd) 1.328:1; (4th) 1.00:1. **Standard Final Drive Ratio:** (410) 4.11:1 or 4.375:1; (SPL310) 3.89:1. **Steering:** (SPL310) cam and lever. **Suspension (front):** wishbones and coil springs. **Suspension (rear):** rigid axle with semi-elliptic leaf springs. **Brakes:** front/rear drum. **Body Construction:** (410) steel unibody; (SPL310) steel body on box-type ladder frame.

PERFORMANCE: Top Speed: (SPL310) 87-95 mph. **Acceleration (0-60 mph):** (SPL310) 15.5 sec. **Acceleration (quarter-mile):** (SPL310) 20.2 seconds (66 mph).

ADDITIONAL MODELS: Datsun also produced for the U.S. market a pickup truck and 4WD Patrol, and a Cedric sedan.

Manufacturer: Nissan Motor Co. Ltd., Tokyo, Japan.

Distributor: Nissan Motor Co. U.S.A., Newark, New Jersey and Gardena, California.

1965 DATSUN

PL410 — FOUR — A restyled grille with a much tighter crosshatch pattern was the major change for Datsun's subcompact sedan. As before, it stretched between quad headlamps, with a surround molding encompassing both the headlamps and the grille. The former round insignia at the grille's center was replaced by a rectangular 'D' emblem. Rectangular parking/signal lights again were mounted below each headlamp pair. Power was again provided by a 72-cid four-cylinder engine, rated at 60 horsepower, through a four-speed manual gearbox.

SPORTS 1500 — SPL310 — FOUR — Production of the two-seater roadster, often referred to as the "1500," continued with little change but was superseded during the model year by the "1600" (SPL311) with a larger engine; see next listing.

I.D. DATA: Serial number is on the firewall under the hood. Each serial number is preceded by a model designation. Engine numbers are stamped on the right top edge of the block (preceded by the engine model code). A vehicle identification plate that includes both numbers and other data is attached to the hood ledge or firewall.

Model	Body Type & Seating	Engine Type/CID	P.O.E. Price	Weight (lbs.)	Prod. Total
PL410	4-dr Sedan-5P	I4/72	1696	1947	Note 1
PL410	4-dr Sta Wag-5P	I4/72	1896	2112	Note 1
1500					
SPL310	2-dr Spt Conv-2P	I4/91	2465	1940	Note 1

Note 1: A total of 216,858 Datsun passenger cars were produced during 1965, and 18,714 vehicles (including trucks) were sold in the U.S.

ENGINE DATA: BASE FOUR (PL410): Inline, overhead-valve four-cylinder (Model E1). Cast iron block. **Displacement:** 72.5 cu. in. (1299 cc). **Bore & Stroke:** 2.875 x 2.80 in. (73 x 71 mm). **Compression Ratio:** 8.2:1. **Brake Horsepower:** 60 at 5000 rpm. **Torque:** 67 lbs.-ft. at 3600 rpm. Three main bearings. Solid valve lifters. Nikki one-barrel carburetor.
BASE FOUR (SPL310): Inline, overhead-valve four-cylinder (Model G). Cast iron block. **Displacement:** 90.8 cu. in. (1488 cc). **Bore & Stroke:** 3.15 x 2.91 in. (80 x 74 mm). **Compression Ratio:** 9.0:1. **Brake Horsepower:** 85 at 5600 rpm (77 bhp with single carburetor). **Torque:** 92 lbs.-ft. at 4400 rpm (87 at 3600 with single carburetor). Solid valve lifters. One or two Hitachi one-barrel carburetors.

CHASSIS DATA: Wheelbase: (410) 93.8 in.; (SPL310) 89.8 in. **Overall Length:** (410) 157.5 in.; (SPL310) 155.6 in. **Height:** (410) 57 in. (SPL310) 50.2 in. **Width:** (410) 59 in.; (SPL310) 58.9 in. **Front Tread:** (410) 47.6 in.; (SPL310) 47.8 in. **Rear Tread:** (410) 47 in.; (SPL310) 47.1 in. **Standard Tires:** (410) 5.60x13; (SPL310) 5.60x13.

TECHNICAL: Layout: front-engine, rear-drive. **Transmission:** (410) three-speed or four-speed manual; (SPL310) four-speed manual. **Standard Final Drive Ratio:** (410) 4.11:1 or 4.375:1; (SPL310) 3.89:1. **Steering:** (SPL310) cam and lever. **Suspension (front):** wishbones and coil springs. **Suspension (rear):** rigid axle with semi-elliptic leaf springs. **Brakes:** front/rear drum. **Body Construction:** (410) steel unibody; (SPL310) steel body on box-type ladder frame.

ADDITIONAL MODELS: Datsun also produced for the U.S. market a pickup truck and 4WD Patrol. Also available was a Deluxe Cedric four-door sedan on a 103.5-inch wheelbase, with a 95-bhp, 114.7-cid four-cylinder engine, priced at $2585.

Manufacturer: Nissan Motor Co. Ltd., Tokyo, Japan.

Distributor: Nissan Motor Co. U.S.A., Newark, New Jersey and Gardena, California.

HISTORY: A CSP311 two-seater with larger (1595 cc) 96-bhp Model R engine appeared at the Tokyo Auto Show in September 1964, but production did not begin until March 1965. Styling, which was quite similar to the SPL310, was partly done by Albrecht Goertz (later to work on Datsun's Z-car). In May 1965, a modified SPL311, slightly shorter and taller, emerged with that engine; see next listing for details.

1966 DATSUN

PL411 — FOUR — Not much change was evident in Datsun's sedan series, which changed from 410 to 411 designation. A four-door station wagon also continued to be available.

SPORTS 1600 (SPL311) — FOUR — Introduced during the 1965 model year, the upgraded two-seater had a 97.3 cubic-inch (1595 cc) four-cylinder engine, producing 96 horsepower and 103 pound-feet of torque. Appearance was similar to the prior SPL310. Headlamps were recessed, with park/signal lights below and somewhat inboard. The rectangular grille was made up of three horizontal strips, with no center insignia. On each front fender was a small reflector lens, just to the rear of the headlamp. A horizontal bodyside trim strip ran from the front wheel opening to the rear fender tip, with 'Fair Lady' script and '1600' model designation at its forward end. Two round (stacked) lamps stood on each side of the rear panel, with a small reflector lens above each pair. A 'DATSUN' nameplate also went on that back pane, on the driver's side.

Note: The modified two-seater was commonly referred to in the U.S. as the "1600" rather than by its official (and longer) "SP" model number.

I.D. DATA: Serial number is on the firewall under the hood. Each serial number is preceded by a model designation. Engine numbers are stamped on the right top edge of the block (preceded by the engine model code). A vehicle identification plate that includes both numbers and other data is attached to the hood ledge or firewall.

Model	Body Type & Seating	Engine Type/CID	P.O.E. Price	Weight (lbs.)	Prod. Total
PL411	4-dr Sedan-5P	I4/79	1666	1951	Note 1
PL411	4-dr Sta Wag-5P	I4/79	1860	2116	Note 1
1600					
SPL311	2-dr Spt Conv-2P	I4/97	2546	2028	Note 1

Note 1: During 1966, a total of 253,046 Datsun passenger cars were produced, and 29,239 vehicles (including trucks) were sold in the U.S. A total of 5,388 SPL311 roadsters were sold in their first partial year (1965), and 6,125 more in 1966.

ENGINE DATA: BASE FOUR (PL411): Inline, overhead-valve four-cylinder (Model J). Cast iron block. **Displacement:** 79.3 cu. in. (1299 cc). **Bore & Stroke:** 2.87 x 3.06 in. (73 x 77.6 mm). **Compression Ratio:** 8.2:1. **Brake Horsepower:** 67 at 5200 rpm. **Torque:** 77 lbs.-ft. at 2800 rpm. Three main bearings. Solid valve lifters. Two-barrel carburetor. 12-volt electrical.

BASE FOUR (1600): Inline, overhead-valve four-cylinder (Model R). Cast iron block. **Displacement:** 97.3 cu. in. (1595 cc). **Bore & Stroke:** 3.43 x 2.63 in. (87.2 x 66.8 mm). **Compression Ratio:** 9.0:1. **Brake Horsepower:** 96 at 6000 rpm. **Torque:** 103 lbs.-ft. at 4000 rpm. Three (later five) main bearings. Solid valve lifters. Two Hitachi SU-type carburetors. 12-volt electrical.

CHASSIS DATA: Wheelbase: (411) 93.7 in.; (SPL311) 89.8 in. **Overall Length:** (411) 157.3 in.; (SPL311) 155.7 in. **Height:** (411) 56.3 in.; (SPL311) 51.4 in. **Width:** (411) 58.7 in.; (SPL311) 58.9 in. **Front Tread:** (411) 47.5 in.; (SPL311) 47.8 in. **Rear Tread:** (411) 47.2 in.; (SPL311) 47.1 in. **Standard Tires:** (411) 5.60x13; (SPL311) 5.60x14.

TECHNICAL: Layout: front-engine, rear-drive. **Transmission:** four-speed manual. SPL311 gear ratios: (1st) 3.38:1; (2nd) 2.01:1; (3rd) 1.31:1; (4th) 1.00:1; (rev) 3.36:1. **Standard Final Drive Ratio:** (411) 4.11:1; (SPL311) 3.88:1. **Steering:** (411) recirculating ball; (SPL311) cam and roller. **Suspension (front):** wishbones and coil springs, with stabilizer bar. **Suspension (rear):** rigid axle with semi-elliptic leaf springs. **Brakes:** (PL411) front/rear drum; (SPL311) front disc, rear drum. **Body Construction:** (411) steel unibody; (SPL311) steel body on box-type ladder frame. **Fuel Tank:** (411) 10.8 gal.; (SPL311) 11.4 gal.

PERFORMANCE: Top Speed: (PL411) 87 mph; (SPL311) 100-106 mph. **Acceleration (0-60 mph):** (PL411) 20 sec.; (SPL311) 13-13.5 seconds. **Acceleration (quarter-mile):** (SPL311) 19.3 sec. (71 mph). **Fuel Mileage:** (411) 26-33 mpg; (SPL311) 19-23 mpg (some testers got as much as 26-32 mpg).

ADDITIONAL MODELS: Datsun also produced a PL520 pickup truck, which sold in the U.S. for $1655, and a 4WD Patrol for $2641 or $2932.

Manufacturer: Nissan Motor Co. Ltd., Tokyo, Japan.

Distributor: Nissan Motor Co. U.S.A., Secaucus, New Jersey and Gardena, California.

HISTORY: Model year began August 1965 except (SPL311) May 1965. A specially-built model won the 14th East African Safari Rally in 1966. Nissan merged with Prince Motors, which not only had another line of cars in production, but a good test-track. While noting that the 311 roadster was "a little shy on power," *Car and Driver* called it "one of today's best buys."

1967 DATSUN

PL411/RL411 — FOUR — Two engines were available this year under Datsun's sedan and station wagon hoods: either the 79 cubic-inch four (PL411) or a 97.3-cid version (RL411) with twin carburetors, rated 96 horsepower. Standard equipment included a vinyl interior, heater, whitewall tires, carpeting, under-hood trouble light, courtesy light, full wheel covers, and four-speed all-synchro gearbox (either column or floor lever). The RL411 Sport Sedan was advertised as the most powerful of the economy imports. In addition to the increased power, the RL411 included more than 50 items of extra equipment including front disc brakes. Options included a Borg-Warner three-speed automatic transmission. Both models shared the same body, with quad headlamps contained within a surround molding that served as the upper and lower bar for the horizontal-style grille. The station wagon's rear seat folded flat.

1600 (SPL311) — FOUR — Datsun's two-seat roadster (with roll-up windows) continued with little change, powered by the 97.3-cid four-cylinder engine and the all-synchro four-speed gearbox. Standard equipment included deeply-padded, vinyl-upholstered seats, radio, heater/defroster, whitewall tires, carpeting, inside and outside mirrors, electric clock, glovebox, locking floor console, and front disc brakes.

I.D. DATA: Serial number is on the firewall under the hood. Each serial number is preceded by a model designation. Starting serial number: (PL411 sed) PL411-030000; (PL411 wag) PL411-810000; (RL411 sed) RL411-000001; (RL411 wag) RL411-800001; (1600) SPL311-01280. Engine numbers are stamped on the right top edge of the block (preceded by the engine model code). A vehicle identification plate that includes both numbers and other data is attached to the hood ledge or firewall.

Model	Body Type & Seating	Engine Type/CID	P.O.E. Price	Weight (lbs.)	Prod. Total
PL411	4-dr Sedan-5P	I4/79	1666	1951	Note 1
PL411	4-dr Sta Wag-5P	I4/79	1866	2116	Note 1
RL411	4-dr Sedan-5P	I4/97	1846	1984	Note 1
RL411	4-dr Sta Wag-5P	I4/97	2046	2028	Note 1
1600					
SPL311	2-dr Spt Conv-2P	I4/97	2546	2028	Note 1

Note 1: A total of 352,045 Datsun passenger cars were produced during 1967, and 45,496 vehicles (including trucks) were sold in the U.S.

ENGINE DATA: BASE FOUR (PL411): Inline, overhead-valve four-cylinder (Model J). Cast iron block. **Displacement:** 79.3 cu. in. (1299 cc). **Bore & Stroke:** 2.87 x 3.06 in. (73 x 77.6 mm). **Compression Ratio:** 8.2:1. **Brake Horsepower:** 67 at 5200 rpm. **Torque:** 77 lbs.-ft. at 2800 rpm. Three main bearings. Solid valve lifters. Two-barrel carburetor. 12-volt electrical.

BASE FOUR (RL411, SPL311): Inline, overhead-valve four-cylinder (Model R). Cast iron block. **Displacement:** 97.3 cu. in. (1595 cc). **Bore & Stroke:** 3.43 x 2.63 in. (87.2 x 66.8 mm). **Compression Ratio:** 9.0:1. **Brake Horsepower:** 96 at 5600 rpm. **Torque:** 103 lbs.-ft. at 4000 rpm. Three (or five) main bearings. Solid valve lifters. Two Hitachi SU-type carburetors. 12-volt electrical.

CHASSIS DATA: Wheelbase: (411) 93.7 in.; (SPL311) 89.8 in. **Overall Length:** (411) 157.3 in.; (SPL311) 155.7 in. **Height:** (411) 56.3 in.; (SPL311) 51.4 in. **Width:** (411) 58.7 in.; (SPL311) 58.9 in. **Front Tread:** (411) 47.5 in.; (SPL311) 50 in. **Rear Tread:** (411) 47.2 in.; (SPL311) 47 in. **Standard Tires:** (411) 5.60x13; (SPL311) 5.60x14.

TECHNICAL: Layout: front-engine, rear-drive. **Transmission:** four-speed manual. SPL311 gear ratios: (1st) 3.38:1; (2nd) 2.01:1; (3rd) 1.31:1; (4th) 1.00:1; (rev) 3.36:1. **Standard Final Drive Ratio:** (411) 4.11:1; (SPL311) 3.88:1. **Steering:** (411) recirculating ball; (SPL311) cam and roller. **Suspension (front):** wishbones and coil springs, with stabilizer bar. **Suspension (rear):** rigid axle with semi-elliptic leaf springs. **Brakes:** (PL411) front/rear drum; (RL411/SPL311) front disc, rear drum. **Body Construction:** (411) steel unibody; (SPL311) steel body on box-type ladder frame. **Fuel Tank:** (SPL311) 11.4 gal.

MAJOR OPTIONS: Borg-Warner three-speed automatic transmission: 411 ($150).

PERFORMANCE: Top Speed: (PL411) 87 mph; (SPL311) 100-106 mph. **Acceleration (0-60 mph):** (PL411) 20 sec.; (RL411) 14 sec. (factory); (SPL311) 13-13.5 sec. **Acceleration (quarter-mile):** (SPL311) 19.3 sec. (71 mph). **Fuel Mileage:** (411) 26-33 mpg; (SPL311) 19-23 mpg (some testers reported 26-32 mpg).

ADDITIONAL MODELS: Datsun also produced a PL520 pickup truck, which sold in the U.S. for $1666.

Manufacturer: Nissan Motor Co. Ltd., Tokyo, Japan.

Distributor: Nissan Motor Co. U.S.A., Secaucus, New Jersey and Gardena, California.

HISTORY: Model year began September, 1966.

1968 DATSUN

PL510 — FOUR — Even though the new 510 series (initially called "Datsun/2") sedan and station wagon didn't look like anything special, it soon established a reputation for surprising performance, both on the road and the race course. Under the hood was the same overhead-cam, 97.3 cubic-inch four-cylinder engine as the SPL311 two-seater, with a four-speed manual gearbox. An automatic transmission was available. Mechanical features included an independent front and rear suspension, with coil springs and anti-sway bars at both ends. Dimensions were larger and appearance more squarish than the 411 (which it replaced), with a long bodyside crease. Quad headlamps flanked a rectangular grille made up of horizontal strips, with rectangular center emblem. Rectangular parking lights went below each headlamp pair. Dimensions were larger than the 410 series which it replaced. Standard equipment included radial tires, reclining bucket seats, windshield washer, lighter, undercoating, whitewall tires, vinyl floormats, and opening rear side windows. The 510 was designed for easy repair, with plenty of space around the engine.

1600 (SPL311) — FOUR — The basic two-seater continued with little change, powered by the 97.3-cid four-cylinder engine and four-speed gearbox.

1968 Datsun 2000 roadster.

2000 (SRL311) — FOUR — Joining the small-engined two-seat convertible was a new version with a bigger overhead-cam powerplant: 120.9 cubic inches (1982 cc), producing 135 horsepower. Sending the power to the rear wheels was a five-speed manual gearbox. Appearance was similar to the 1600 model, but slightly lower. Round park/signal lights stood below and inboard of the slightly recessed, round headlamps. The grille consisted of an opening that tapered inward at the ends and held two horizontal bars with an insignia in the center. Above the grille stood 'DATSUN' block letters, while the hood contained an airscoop. A '2000' model designation went on the cowl, just to the rear of the front wheels, below the bodyside trim strip. Above that strip were additional 'DATSUN' letters. The car's all-weather top looked a bit tall when raised. Like its less-powerful brother, this one became commonly known in the U.S. by the engine size designation ("2000") rather than the official "SRL311" name.

I.D. DATA: Serial number is on the firewall under the hood. Each serial number is preceded by a model designation. Engine numbers are stamped on the right top edge of the block (preceded by the engine model code). A vehicle identification plate that includes both numbers and other data is attached to the hood ledge or firewall.

Model	Body Type & Seating	Engine Type/CID	P.O.E. Price	Weight (lbs.)	Prod. Total
510					
PL510	4-dr Sedan-5P	I4/97	1996	2017	Note 1
WPL510	4-dr Sta Wag-5P	I4/97	2196	2072	Note 1
1600					
SPL311	2-dr Spt Conv-2P	I4/97	2766	1984	Note 1
2000					
SRL311	2-dr Spt Conv-2P	I4/121	2998	2006	Note 1

Note 1: A total of 571,614 Datsun passenger cars were produced during 1968, and 58,467 vehicles (including trucks) were sold in the U.S.

ENGINE DATA: BASE FOUR (510): Inline, overhead-cam four-cylinder (Model L16). Cast iron block and aluminum head. **Displacement:** 97.3 cu. in. (1595 cc). **Bore & Stroke:** 3.27 x 2.90 in. (83 x 73.7 mm). **Compression Ratio:** 8.5:1. **Brake Horsepower:** 96 at 5600 rpm. **Torque:** 99.8 lbs.-ft. at 3600 rpm. Solid valve lifters. Hitachi two-barrel carburetor. 12-volt electrical.

BASE FOUR (1600): Inline, overhead-valve four-cylinder (Model R). Cast iron block. **Displacement:** 97.3 cu. in. (1595 cc). **Bore & Stroke:** 3.43 x 2.63 in. (87.2 x 66.8 mm). **Compression Ratio:** 9.0:1. **Brake Horsepower:** 96 at 6000 rpm. **Torque:** 103 lbs.-ft. at 4000 rpm. Five main bearings. Solid valve lifters. Two Hitachi SU-type carburetors.

BASE FOUR (2000): Inline, overhead-cam four-cylinder (Model U20). Cast iron block and aluminum head. **Displacement:** 120.9 cu. in. (1982 cc). **Bore & Stroke:** 3.43 x 3.27 in. (87.2 x 83 mm). **Compression Ratio:** 9.5:1. **Brake Horsepower:** 135 at 6000 rpm. **Torque:** 132 lbs.-ft. at 4400 rpm. Five main bearings. Solid valve lifters. Two SU-type carburetors. 12-volt electrical.

CHASSIS DATA: Wheelbase: (510) 95.3 in.; (1600/2000) 89.8 in. **Overall Length:** (510) 162.2 in.; (510 wag) 163.2 in.; (1600/2000) 155.7 in. **Height:** (510) 55.1 in.; (1600/2000) 51.6 in. **Width:** (510) 61.4 in.; (1600/2000) 58.9 in. **Front Tread:** (510) 50.4 in; (510 wag) 50.2 in.; (1600/2000) 50.2 in. **Rear Tread:** (510) 50.4 in.; (510 wag) 49.6 in.; (1600/2000) 47.2 in. **Standard Tires:** (510) 5.60x13; (1600/2000) 5.60x14.

TECHNICAL: Layout: front-engine, rear-drive. **Transmission:** four-speed manual except (2000) five-speed. **Standard Final Drive Ratio:** (510) 3.70:1; (510 wag) 3.889:1; (1600) 3.89:1; (2000) 3.70:1. **Steering:** (1600/2000) cam and peg; (510) recirculating ball. **Suspension (front):** (510) MacPherson struts with coil springs; (1600/2000) wishbones and coil springs. **Suspension (rear):** (510 sed) independent, semi-trailing arms and coil springs; (510 wag/1600/2000) rigid axle with semi-elliptic leaf springs. **Brakes:** front disc, rear drum. **Body Construction:** (1600/2000) steel body on box-type ladder frame; (510) steel unibody. **Fuel Tank:** (510) 12.1 gal.; (1600/2000) 11.4 gal.

MAJOR OPTIONS: Automatic transmission (510). Air conditioning.

PERFORMANCE: Top Speed: (510) 98-100 mph; (1600) 103 mph; (2000) 108-118 mph. **Acceleration (0-60 mph):** (510) 12.7-14.6 sec.; (1600) 13.3 sec.; (2000) 8.4-10.3 sec. **Acceleration (quarter-mile):** (510) 19.7 sec. and 67.5 mph; (2000) 17.6 sec. and 80.5 mph. **Fuel Mileage:** (510) about 25 mpg; (1600/2000) about 22 mpg.

ADDITIONAL MODELS: Datsun also produced a PL520 pickup truck, which sold in the U.S. for $1766.

Manufacturer: Nissan Motor Co. Ltd., Tokyo, Japan.

Distributor: Nissan Motor Co. U.S.A., Secaucus, New Jersey.

HISTORY: Model year began November 1, 1967. Robert Link, Nissan's senior vice-president in the U.S., noted that the 510 "marked the end of all the ridiculous talk that Japanese cars were made of melted down beer cans" and turned Datsun/Nissan into "a household name." In 1968, a 510 won the East African Rally. Popularity in racing led to availability of many competition parts from the aftermarket.

1969 DATSUN

PL510 — FOUR — Production of Datsun's subcompact four-door sedan, powered by a 97-cid OHC four, continued with little change after the 1968 restyling, except for a grille modification and the addition of a two-door model. Each had quad headlamps alongside a rectangular grille with a single horizontal bar above horizontal strips, and center 'D' insignia. An automatic transmission was available on the four-door and station wagon models.

1600 (SPL311) — FOUR — Little changed in the 1595-cc version of Datsun's two-seater.

2000 (SRL311) — FOUR — For its second year in the lineup, the larger-engined sports car displayed no change. Under its hood was a 121-cid (1982 cc) four-cylinder engine delivering 135 horsepower, hooked to a five-speed gearbox with overdrive top gear.

I.D. DATA: Serial number is on the firewall under the hood. Each serial number is preceded by a model designation. Starting serial number: (510 2-dr) PL510-016385; (510 4-dr) PL510-009001; (510 wag) PL510-805001; (1600) SPL311-18001; (2000) SRL311-01400. Engine numbers are stamped on the right top edge of the block (preceded by the engine model code). A vehicle identification plate that includes both numbers and other data is attached to the hood ledge or firewall.

Model	Body Type & Seating	Engine Type/CID	P.O.E. Price	Weight (lbs.)	Prod. Total
PL510	2-dr Sedan-5P	I4/97	1896	2039	Note 1
PL510	4-dr Sedan-5P	I4/97	1996	2041	Note 1
PL510	4-dr Sta Wag-5P	I4/97	2226	2127	Note 1
1600					
SPL311	2-dr Spt Conv-2P	I4/97	2766	1984	Note 1
2000					
SRL311	2-dr Spt Conv-2P	I4/121	3096	2006	Note 1

Note 1: A total of 697,691 Datsun passenger cars were produced during 1969, of which 60,872 (plus 30,236 trucks) were sold in the U.S.

ENGINE DATA: BASE FOUR (510): Inline, overhead-cam four-cylinder (Model L16). Cast iron block and aluminum head. **Displacement:** 97.3 cu. in. (1595 cc). **Bore & Stroke:** 3.27 x 2.90 in. (83 x 73.7 mm). **Compression Ratio:** 8.5:1. **Brake Horsepower:** 96 at 5600 rpm. **Torque:** 99.8 lbs.-ft. at 3600 rpm. Solid valve lifters. Hitachi two-barrel carburetor.

BASE FOUR (1600): Inline, overhead-valve four-cylinder (Model R). Cast iron block. **Displacement:** 97.3 cu. in. (1595 cc). **Bore & Stroke:** 3.43 x 2.63 in. (87.2 x 66.8 mm). **Compression Ratio:** 9.0:1. **Brake Horsepower:** 96 at 6000 rpm. **Torque:** 103 lbs.-ft. at 4000 rpm. Solid valve lifters. Two Hitachi SU-type carburetors.

BASE FOUR (2000): Inline, overhead-cam four-cylinder (Model U20). Cast iron block and aluminum head. **Displacement:** 120.9 cu. in. (1982 cc). **Bore & Stroke:** 3.43 x 3.27 in. (87.2 x 83 mm). **Compression Ratio:** 9.5:1. **Brake Horsepower:** 135 at 6000 rpm. **Torque:** 132 lbs.-ft. at 4400 rpm. Five main bearings. Solid valve lifters. Two SU-type carburetors.

Note: The high-performance 2000 (SRL311) engine was rated 150 bhp at 6000 rpm and 138 lbs.-ft. at 4800 rpm, with two Solex-type carburetors.

CHASSIS DATA: Wheelbase: (510) 95.3 in.; (1600/2000) 89.8 in. **Overall Length:** (510 2-dr) 160.2 in.; (510 4-dr) 162.2 in.; (510 wag) 163.2 in.; (1600/2000) 155.7 in. **Height:** (510) 55.1 in.; (510 wag) 56.5 in.; (1600/2000) 52.2 in. **Width:** (510) 61.4 in.; (1600/2000) 58.9 in. **Front Tread:** (510) 50.4 in; (510 wag) 50.2 in.; (1600/2000) 50.2 in. **Rear Tread:** (510) 50.4 in.; (510 wag) 49.6 in.; (1600/2000) 47.2 in. **Standard Tires:** (510) 5.60x13; (510 wag) 5.60x14; (1600/2000) 5.60x14.

TECHNICAL: Layout: front-engine, rear-drive. **Transmission:** four-speed manual except (2000) five-speed. 510 gear ratios: (1st) 3.65:1; (2nd) 2.17:1; (3rd) 1.42:1; (4th) 1.00:1. Model 2000 gear ratios: (1st) 2.957:1; (2nd) 1.858:1; (3rd) 1.311:1; (4th) 1.00:1; (5th) 0.852:1. **Standard Final Drive Ratio:** (510) 3.90:1; (510 wag) 3.89:1; (1600) 3.89:1; (2000) 3.70:1. **Steering:** (1600/2000) cam and peg; (510) recirculating ball. **Suspension (front):** (510) MacPherson struts with coil springs; (1600/2000) wishbones and coil springs. **Suspension (rear):** (510 sed) independent, semi-trailing arms and coil springs; (1600/2000) rigid axle with semi-elliptic leaf springs. **Brakes:** front disc, rear drum. **Body Construction:** (1600/2000) steel body on box-type ladder frame; (510) steel unibody. **Fuel Tank:** (510) 12.1 gal.; (1600/2000) 11.4 gal.

MAJOR OPTIONS: Automatic transmission (510). Air conditioning.

PERFORMANCE: Top Speed: (510) 100 mph; (1600) 103 mph; (2000) 108+ mph. **Acceleration (0-60 mph):** (510) 12.7-14.6 sec.; (1600) 13.3 sec.; (2000) 8.4-9.3 sec. **Acceleration (quarter-mile):** (510 w/auto.) 20.9 sec. and 67.8 mph. **Fuel Mileage:** (510) about 25 mpg; (1600/2000) about 22 mpg.

ADDITIONAL MODELS: Datsun also produced a PL521 pickup truck, which sold in the U.S. for $1796; and the Nissan Patrol, which cost $2815 (soft top) or $3120 (hard top).

Manufacturer: Nissan Motor Co. Ltd., Tokyo, Japan.

Distributor: Nissan Motor Co. U.S.A., Secaucus, New Jersey and Gardena, California.

HISTORY: Model year began September 1, 1968. *Road Test* magazine noted that the 510 sedan "is wooing the non-enthusiast American buyers out of the domestic showrooms."

1970 DATSUN

PL510 — FOUR — Production of Datsun's subcompact four-door sedan, powered by a 97-cid OHC four, continued with little change. Standard equipment included front disc brakes, a four-speed manual gearbox, vinyl upholstery, a three-speed heater/defroster, windshield washers, twin padded sun visors, front bucket seats, lighter and ashtrays, whitewall tires, and backup lights. Sedans had independent front/rear suspensions; the wagon did not. Wagons had a locking tailgate. A three-speed automatic transmission was optional.

1600 (SPL311) — FOUR — Although quickly eclipsed by the new "Z" car, availability of the earlier sports model with 510-based engine continued into 1970. Standard equipment included front disc brakes, radio, heater/defroster, vinyl bucket seats, clock, roll-up windows, tachometer and trip odometer, padded racing-style steering wheel, tonneau cover, carpeting, whitewall tires, backup lights, and windshield washers.

2000 (SRL311) — FOUR — Availability of the larger-engined carryover sports model also continued into 1970. Standard equipment was similar to the 1600 series.

1970 Datsun 240Z.

240Z — SIX — Billed by Nissan U.S.A. as a "personalized two passenger fastback" whose "sleek, low lines are complemented by a roomy luxurious interior," the 240Z fastback coupe, first of the famed Z-cars, was the next step in the progression that began with the Fair Lady roadsters a decade earlier. The 2.4-liter (2393 cc) single-overhead-cam six-cylinder engine, delivering at least 150 bhp, allowed speeds as high as 125 mph (or so claimed the company, somewhat optimistically). An all-synchro four-speed manual transmission handled the shifting chores. Four-wheel independent suspension, consisting of coil springs and MacPherson struts, was said to be "designed to meet the requirements of all world markets." The all-steel unibody rode a 90.7-inch wheelbase, with front disc and rear drum brakes. As for the interior, added the company, a "flow-through draft-free fresh air system combined with an aerodynamic shape make the car a quiet experience to drive." Oil pressure, water temperature, fuel and ammeter gauges were recessed in a padded and formed dash. A large speedometer with trip odometer, and a tachometer, sat directly ahead of the driver. Deep cushioned vinyl bucket seats with built-in headrests adjusted horizontally and vertically, and reclined up to 10 degrees. Standard 240Z equipment included radial tires, a radio, clock, steering lock, collapsible steering wheel, three anchor seatbelts, backup lights, a wood steering wheel and gearshift knob, front/rear bumper overriders, console box, door armrest, driver footrest, glovebox with lock, windshield and rear-window drip moldings, and coat hangers.

Distinctive recessed headlamps were set deeply into nacelles, far back from the 240Z's protruding nose. Rectangular parking lights sat under the headlamps, below the bumper. Front fenders held reflector lenses, just to the rear of the headlamps. The low, wide grille had a pattern of subtle horizontal bars, while the hood had a moderately-sized bulge. A small round insignia went above the grille. Tiny rear quarter windows were used. Three-section taillamps were mounted in rectangular housings. The new coupe would be "Datsun's answer to the high performance personal car market," developed with the guidance of considerable market research. Designed as a world-class car from the start, it was not one more Japanese model to be altered for export. "We think Datsun has a real winner," said Ron Wakefield of *Road & Track*. That magazine further predicted that "Datsun will establish a market of its own, one which will force other makers to come up with entirely new models to gain a share in it."

I.D. DATA: Serial number is on the firewall under the hood, and/or on the top left of the instrument panel, visible through the windshield. Each serial number is preceded by a model designation. Starting serial number: (PL510) 095010; (PL510 wag) 842001; (1600) 27001; (2000) 07500; (240Z) HLS30-0001. Engine numbers are stamped on the right top edge of the block (preceded by the engine model code). A vehicle identification plate that includes both numbers and other data is attached to the hood ledge or firewall; or to the right front strut housing (240Z).

Model	Body Type & Seating	Engine Type/CID	P.O.E. Price	Weight (lbs.)	Prod. Total
510					
PL510	2-dr Sedan-5P	I4/97	1935	2039	Note 1
PL510	4-dr Sedan-5P	I4/97	2035	2041	Note 1
PL510	4-dr Sta Wag-5P	I4/97	2265	2127	Note 1
1600					
1600	2-dr Conv-2P	I4/97	2766	1984	Note 1
2000					
2000	2-dr Conv-2P	I4/121	3096	2006	Note 1
240Z					
240Z	2-dr Cpe-2P	I6/146	3526	2300	Note 2

Note 1: A total of 899,008 Datsun passenger cars were produced during 1970, of which 104,067 (plus 50,954 trucks) were sold in the U.S.

Note 2: A total of 16,215 240Z coupes were exported to the U.S. in 1970.

ENGINE DATA: BASE FOUR (510): Inline, overhead-cam four-cylinder (Model L16). Cast iron block and aluminum head. **Displacement:** 97.3 cu. in. (1595 cc). **Bore & Stroke:** 3.27 x 2.90 in. (83 x 73.7 mm). **Compression Ratio:** 8.5:1. **Brake Horsepower:** 96 at 5600 rpm. **Torque:** 99.8 lbs.-ft. at 3600 rpm. Solid valve lifters. Hitachi two-barrel carburetor. 12-volt electrical.

BASE FOUR (1600): Same as 510 above, except -- **Compression Ratio:** 9.0:1. **Brake Horsepower:** 96 at 6000 rpm. **Torque:** 103 lbs.-ft. at 4000 rpm. Two Hitachi SU-type carburetors.

BASE FOUR (2000): Inline, overhead-cam four-cylinder (Model U20). Cast iron block and aluminum head. **Displacement:** 120.9 cu. in. (1982 cc). **Bore & Stroke:** 3.43 x 3.27 in. (87.2 x 83 mm). **Compression Ratio:** 9.5:1. **Brake Horsepower:** 135 at 6000 rpm. **Torque:** 132 lbs.-ft. at 4400 rpm. Five main bearings. Solid valve lifters. Two SU-type carburetors. 12-volt electrical.

Note: The high-performance 2000 (SRL311) engine was rated 150 bhp at 6000 rpm and 138 lbs.-ft. at 4800 rpm, with Solex-type carburetion.

BASE SIX (240Z): Inline, overhead-cam six-cylinder (Model L24). Cast iron block and aluminum head. **Displacement:** 146 cu. in. (2393 cc). **Bore & Stroke:** 3.27 x 2.90 in. (83 x 73.7 mm). **Compression Ratio:** 9.0:1. **Brake Horsepower:** 151 at 5600 rpm. **Torque:** 145.7 lbs.-ft. at 4400 rpm. Seven main bearings. Solid valve lifters. Two Hitachi SU-type carburetors. 12-volt electrical.

CHASSIS DATA: Wheelbase: (510) 95.3 in.; (1600/2000) 89.8 in.; (240Z) 90.7 in. **Overall Length:** (510 2-dr) 160.2 in.; (510 4-dr) 162.2 in.; (510 wag) 163.2 in.; (1600/2000) 155.7 in.; (240Z) 162.8 in. **Height:** (510) 55.1 in.; (510 wag) 56.5 in.; (1600/2000) 52.2 in.; (240Z) 50.6 in. **Width:** (510) 61.4 in.; (1600/2000) 58.9 in.; (240Z) 64.1 in. **Front Tread:** (510) 50.4 in; (510 wag) 52.0 in.; (1600/2000) 50.2 in.; (240Z) 53.3 in. **Rear Tread:** (510) 50.4 in.; (510 wag) 49.6 in.; (1600/2000) 50.2 in.; (240Z) 53.0 in. **Standard Tires:** (510) 5.60x13; (510 wag) 5.60x14; (1600/2000) 5.60x14; (240Z) 175x14.

TECHNICAL: Layout: front-engine, rear-drive. **Transmission:** four-speed manual except (2000) five-speed. **Standard Final Drive Ratio:** (510) 3.9:1; (1600) 3.89:1; (2000) 3.7:1; (240Z) 3.36:1. **Steering:** (1600/2000) cam and peg; (510) recirculating ball; (240Z) rack and pinion. **Suspension (front):** (510/240Z) MacPherson struts with coil springs; (1600/2000) wishbones and coil springs. **Suspension (rear):** (510 sed) independent, semi-trailing arms and coil springs; (1600/2000) rigid axle with semi-elliptic leaf springs; (240Z) "Chapman" struts with coil springs and lower wishbones. **Brakes:** front disc, rear drum. **Body Construction:** (1600/2000) steel body on box-type ladder frame; (510/240Z) steel unibody. **Fuel Tank:** (510) 12.1 gal.; (1600/2000) 11.4 gal.; (240Z) 15.9 gal.

MAJOR OPTIONS: Automatic transmission: 510 ($190). Manual AM radio: 510 ($39.50). Pushbutton AM radio: 510 ($59.95). Two-speaker stereo system ($102). Console: 510 ($37.50). Clock: 510 ($20). Wood-rimmed steering wheel ($36.66). Walnut gearshift knob ($3.75). Trunk lid rack ($26.95); N/A on 510. Lighter ($3.56).

PERFORMANCE: Top Speed: (510) 100 mph; (1600) 103 mph; (2000) 118 mph; (240Z) 115-122 mph. **Acceleration (0-60 mph):** (510) 14.6 sec.; (1600) 13.3 sec.; (2000) 9.3 sec.; (240Z) 7.5-8.7 seconds. **Acceleration (quarter-mile):** (240Z) 17.7 seconds. **Fuel Mileage:** (510) about 25 mpg; (1600/2000) about 22 mpg; (240Z) about 19 mpg.

ADDITIONAL MODELS: Datsun also produced a PL521 pickup truck, which sold in the U.S. for $1875.

Manufacturer: Nissan Motor Co. Ltd., Tokyo, Japan.

Distributor: Nissan Motor Co. U.S.A., Secaucus, New Jersey.

HISTORY: Model year began September 15, 1969. By the late 1960s, the likely market was seen as evident for a GT-type sports car with fine roadholding/handling, performance, economy, comfort, and style. In keeping with that perception, Nissan designed the 240Z with a long hood, dramatic fastback roofline, open-up rear hatch, full instrumentation, and ample amenities (AM/FM, reclining seats, rear defogger, flow-thru ventilation). By 1969, a Competition department had already been established at Nissan America. Both the 240Z and the 510 sedan were raced in the U.S. (under Brock Racing Enterprises in the west and Bob Sharp in the east). Datsun publications described modifications for both models, using factory parts; and the aftermarket quickly provided its share of components. In November 1970, a 240Z took seventh place at the Royal Automobile Club (RAC) Rally in Great Britain. Home-market 240Z coupes had a smaller (2000 cc) Model L20 engine.

1971 DATSUN

PL510 — FOUR — Little change was evident in Datsun's two-door and four-door sedan and four-door wagon, introduced in 1968. Powertrain again was the 97-cid OHC four, with four-speed manual or three-speed automatic transmission.

240Z — SIX — Only the "Z" car remained in Datsun's sports car lineup, little changed this year. The former 1600 (SPL311) and 2000 (SRL311) were dropped.

1971 Datsun 240Z.

I.D. DATA: Serial number is on the top left of the instrument panel, visible through the windshield; and/or on the firewall, under the hood. Each serial number is preceded by a model designation. Starting serial number: (PL510 2-dr) 154707; (PL510 4-dr) 154943; (PL510 wag) 869270; (240Z) HLS30-03013. Engine numbers are stamped on the right top edge of the block (preceded by the engine model code). A vehicle identification plate that includes both numbers and other data is attached to the hood ledge or firewall (510); or to the right front strut housing (240Z).

Model	Body Type & Seating	Engine Type/CID	P.O.E. Price	Weight (lbs.)	Prod. Total
PL510	2-dr Sedan-5P	I4/97	1990	2050	Note 1
PL510	4-dr Sedan-5P	I4/97	2120	2094	Note 1
PL510	4-dr Sta Wag-5P	I4/97	2350	2127	Note 1
				2127	
240Z					
240Z	2-dr Cpe-2P	I6/146	3596	2300	Note 2

Note 1: A total of 1,101,506 Datsun passenger cars were produced during 1971, of which 188,030 (not including trucks) were sold in the U.S.

Note 2: A total of 33,684 240Z coupes were exported to the U.S. in 1971.

ENGINE DATA: Same as 1970.

CHASSIS DATA: Wheelbase: (510) 95.3 in.; (240Z) 90.7 in. **Overall Length:** (510 2-dr) 160.2 in.; (510 4-dr) 162.2 in.; (510 wag) 163.2 in.; (240Z) 162.8 in. **Height:** (510) 55.9 in.; (510 wag) 56.5 in.; (240Z) 50.6 in. **Width:** (510) 61.4 in.; (240Z) 64.1 in. **Front Tread:** (510) 50 in.; (510 wag) 50.2 in.; (240Z) 53.3 in. **Rear Tread:** (510) 50 in.; (510 wag) 49.6 in.; (240Z) 53.0 in. **Standard Tires:** (510) 5.60x13; (240Z) 175x14.

TECHNICAL: Layout: front-engine, rear-drive. **Transmission:** four-speed manual. **Standard Final Drive Ratio:** (510) 3.90:1; (240Z) 3.36:1. **Steering:** (510) recirculating ball; (240Z) rack and pinion. **Suspension (front):** (510/240Z) MacPherson struts with coil springs. **Suspension (rear):** (510 sed) independent, semi-trailing arms and coil springs; (240Z) Chapman struts and coil springs with lower wishbones. **Brakes:** front disc, rear drum. **Body Construction:** steel unibody. **Fuel Tank:** (510) 12.1 gal.; (240Z) 15.9 gal.

MAJOR OPTIONS: Automatic transmission: 510 ($170). Air conditioning: 510 ($295); 240Z ($325). Manual AM radio ($39.50). Pushbutton AM radio ($59.95). AM/FM radio ($98.50). AM/FM stereo with 8-track player: 510 ($110). Console: 510 ($37.50). Tachometer: 510 ($58.32). Electric clock: 510 ($20). Wood-rimmed steering wheel ($38.88). Walnut gearshift knob ($3.75). Vinyl gearshift knob ($4.95). Luggage rack: 240Z ($12.95); 510 wag ($59.95). Mag-style hubcaps: 510 ($38.50). Trailer hitch: 510 ($16.95). Footrest: 240Z ($12.95). Center armrest: 240Z ($9.95). Lighter: 510 ($3.57).

PERFORMANCE: Top Speed: (510) 100 mph; (240Z) 115-122 mph. **Acceleration (0-60 mph):** (510) 14.6 sec.; (240Z) 7.5-8.7 seconds. **Acceleration (quarter-mile):** (240Z) 17.7 seconds. **Fuel Mileage:** (510) about 25 mpg; (240Z) about 19 mpg.

ADDITIONAL MODELS: Datsun also produced a PL521 pickup truck, which sold in the U.S. for $1966; and a new subcompact LB110 series, for $1736 and $1866.

Manufacturer: Nissan Motor Co. Ltd., Tokyo, Japan.

Distributor: Nissan Motor Co. U.S.A., Secaucus, New Jersey.

HISTORY: Model year began September 1, 1970. In January 1971 a 240Z placed fifth (overall) in the Monte Carlo Rally. Then in April, they took the first and second spot in the 19th East African Safari Rally (a race in which 72 of the 91 entrants didn't even finish). *Car and Driver* named 240Z the "Car of the Year." A 510 sedan won the SCCA Trans-Am series this year (and again in 1972).

SUBCOMPACT SEDAN NOTE: Due to their minimal historical value and collectibility, smaller subcompact Datsuns and Nissans, starting with the LB110 (1200) series that debuted in 1971, are not described in detail in this Catalog.

1972 DATSUN

PL510 — FOUR — Little change was evident in Datsun's larger two-door and four-door subcompacts, again offered in sedan and wagon form with the 97-cid OHC four. Prices took a substantial hike. Either a four-speed manual or three-speed automatic transmission was available.

240Z — SIX — Production of the first-generation "Z" car continued with little change other than a price rise and a slight drop in compression ratio. Late in the year, however, a change in emissions equipment would cut back on 240Z performance.

I.D. DATA: Serial number is on the top left of the instrument panel, visible through the windshield; and on the firewall, under the hood. Each serial number is preceded by a model designation. Starting serial number: (PL510 2-dr) 295003; (PL510 4-dr) 295579; (PL510 wag) 927564; (240Z) HLS30-46001. Engine numbers are stamped on the right top edge of the block (preceded by the engine model code). A vehicle identification plate that includes both numbers and other data is attached to the hood ledge or firewall (510); or to the right front strut housing (240Z).

Model	Body Type & Seating	Engine Type/CID	P.O.E. Price	Weight (lbs.)	Prod. Total
510					
PL510	2-dr Sedan-5P	I4/97	2306	2039	Note 1
PL510	4-dr Sedan-5P	I4/97	2456	2041	Note 1
PL510	4-dr Sta Wag-5P	I4/97	2656	2127	Note 1
240Z					
240Z	2-dr Cpe-2P	I6/146	4106	2300	Note 2

Note 1: A total of 1,352,251 Datsun passenger cars were produced during 1972, of which 192,710 were sold in the U.S. A total of 268,666 Datsun vehicles (including trucks) were sold.

Note 2: A total of 52,628 240Zs were exported to the U.S. in 1972.

ENGINE DATA: Same as 1970-71.

CHASSIS DATA: Same as 1971.

TECHNICAL: Same as 1971.

MAJOR OPTIONS: Similar to 1971.

PERFORMANCE: **Top Speed**: (510) 100 mph; (240Z) 115-122 mph. **Acceleration (0-60 mph)**: (510) 14.6 sec.; (240Z) 7.5-8.7 seconds. **Acceleration (quarter-mile)**: (240Z) 17.7 seconds. **Fuel Mileage**: (510) about 25 mpg; (240Z) about 19 mpg.

ADDITIONAL MODELS: Datsun also produced PL521 and PL620 pickup trucks, which sold in the U.S. for $2236; and the subcompact LB110 series, which cost $1976 (two-door sedan) and $2116 (coupe).

Manufacturer: Nissan Motor Co. Ltd., Tokyo, Japan.

Distributor: Nissan Motor Co. U.S.A., Secaucus, New Jersey.

HISTORY: Model year began September 1, 1971.

1973 DATSUN

510 — FOUR — Only the two-door sedan remained in the 510 series, continued with little change, and powered again by the 97-cid OHC four. Either a four-speed manual or three-speed automatic transmission was available.

610 — FOUR — A larger series (sedan, two-door hardtop and station wagon) joined the Datsun lineup as top-of-the-line offerings, aiming to mix luxury with economy. Standard features included a woodgrain instrument panel and steering wheel, reclining buckets, full carpeting, power front disc brakes, and electric rear defogger. "Datsun 1800" script on rear fenders identified the 610 series engine.

240Z — SIX — For its fourth and final season, the first-generation "Z" car continued with little change except for the emissions modifications that emerged in late 1972.

I.D. DATA: Serial number is on the top left of the instrument panel, visible through the windshield; and on the firewall, under the hood. Each serial number is preceded by a model designation. Starting serial number: (PL510 2-dr) 423000; (PL610 sed) 015434; (PL610 HT) 015201; (PL610 wag) 801501; (240Z) HLS30-120107. Engine numbers are stamped on the right top edge of the block (preceded by the engine model code). A vehicle identification plate that includes both numbers and other data is attached to the hood ledge or firewall; or to the right front strut housing (240Z).

Note: A few specific examples of PL610 models had serial numbers lower than those listed above.

Model	Body Type & Seating	Engine Type/CID	P.O.E. Price	Weight (lbs.)	Prod. Total
510					
PL510	2-dr Sedan-5P	I4/97	2306	2105	Note 1
610					
PL610	2-dr HT-5P	I4/108	3145	2293	Note 1
PL610	4-dr Sedan-5P	I4/108	2995	2271	Note 1
PL610	4-dr Sta Wag-5P	I4/108	3195	2392	Note 1
240Z					
240Z	2-dr Cpe-2P	I6/146	4695	2350	Note 1

Note 1: A total of 1,487,360 Datsun passenger cars were produced during 1973, of which 231,191 were sold in the U.S. A total of 45,588 240Z coupes were exported to the U.S. in 1973.

ENGINE DATA: BASE FOUR (510): Inline, overhead-cam four-cylinder (Model L16). Cast iron block and aluminum head. **Displacement**: 97.3 cu. in. (1595 cc). **Bore & Stroke**: 3.27 x 2.90 in. (83 x 73.7 mm). **Compression Ratio**: 8.5:1. **Brake Horsepower**: 96 (SAE) at 5600 rpm. **Torque**: 99.8 lbs.-ft. at 3600 rpm. Solid valve lifters. Hitachi two-barrel carburetor.

BASE FOUR (610): Inline, overhead-cam four-cylinder (Model L18). Cast iron block and aluminum head. **Displacement**: 108.0 cu. in. (1770 cc). **Bore & Stroke**: 3.35 x 3.07 in. (85.1 x 84 mm). **Compression Ratio**: 8.5:1. **Brake Horsepower**: 105 (SAE) at 6000 rpm. **Torque**: 108 lbs.-ft. at 3600 rpm. Solid valve lifters. Two-barrel carburetor.

BASE SIX (240Z): Inline, overhead-cam six-cylinder (Model L24). Cast iron block and aluminum head. **Displacement**: 146 cu. in. (2393 cc). **Bore & Stroke**: 3.27 x 2.90 in. (83 x 73.7 mm). **Compression Ratio**: 8.8:1. **Brake Horsepower**: 151 (SAE) at 5600 rpm. **Torque**: 145.7 lbs.-ft. at 4400 rpm. Seven main bearings. Solid valve lifters. Two Hitachi SU-type carburetors.

CHASSIS DATA: **Wheelbase**: (510) 95.3 in.; (610) 98.4 in.; (240Z) 90.7 in. **Overall Length**: (510) 165.4 in.; (610) 172 in.; (610 wag) 174.5 in.; (240Z) 165.2 in. **Height**: (510) 55.9 in.; (610) 54.5-55.7 in.; (240Z) 50.5 in. **Width**: (510) 61.4 in.; (610) 63 in.; (240Z) 64.1 in. **Front Tread**: (510) 50 in.; (610) 51.6 in.; (240Z) 53.3 in. **Rear Tread**: (510) 50 in.; (610) 52 in.; (240Z) 53.0 in. **Standard Tires**: (510) 5.60x13; (610) 6.45x13; (240Z) 175x14.

TECHNICAL: **Layout**: front-engine, rear-drive. **Transmission**: four-speed manual. **Standard Final Drive Ratio**: (510) 3.70:1; (610) 3.70:1; (610 wag) 3.89:1; (240Z) 3.36:1. **Steering**: (510) recirculating ball; (240Z) rack and pinion. **Suspension (front)**: (510/240Z) MacPherson struts with coil springs. **Suspension (rear)**: (510) independent, semi-trailing arms and coil springs; (240Z) Chapman struts with lower wishbones and coil springs. **Brakes**: front disc, rear drum. **Body Construction**: steel unibody. **Fuel Tank**: (510) 11.9 gal.; (610) 14.5 gal.; (610 wag) 13.8 gal.; (240Z) 15.9 gal.

MAJOR OPTIONS: Automatic transmission (PL510/610). Air conditioning. Chrome wheels (240Z).

PERFORMANCE: **Top Speed**: (510) 100 mph; (240Z) 115-122 mph. **Acceleration (0-60 mph)**: (510) 14.6 sec.; (240Z) 10.1 seconds. **Fuel Mileage**: (510) about 25 mpg; (240Z) about 19 mpg.

PRODUCTION/SALES: U.S. sales for calendar year 1973 included: (model 510) 30,688; (610) 75,511; (240Z) 46,282; (260Z) 6,274; (trucks) 87,816.

ADDITIONAL MODELS: Datsun also produced a PL620 pickup truck, which sold in the U.S. for $2575; and the subcompact LB110 series, which cost $2195 (two-door sedan) and $2395 (coupe).

Manufacturer: Nissan Motor Co. Ltd., Tokyo, Japan.

Distributor: Nissan Motor Co. U.S.A., Carson, California.

HISTORY: Model year began October 24, 1972 except (PL610) November 15, 1972.

1974 DATSUN

610 — FOUR — Introduced for 1973, the 610 series took a larger four-cylinder engine this year (119 cid), abandoning its former 108-cid four to the new 710 series.

710 — FOUR — The new series, arriving later in the model year, had the same engine displacement as the prior year's 610, and came in sedan, two-door hardtop, and station wagon form. Dimensions were smaller than the 610 series.

260Z — SIX — After four years on the market, the 240Z was replaced by a 260Z with larger six-cylinder engine. Joining the basic two-seater coupe at mid-year (May 1974) was a 2+2 version, nearly a foot longer. In addition to a larger (2565 cc) engine, the 260Z had transistorized ignition, an electromagnetic fuel pump, new protruding 5-mph bumpers, and a built-in chin spoiler. Both the four-speed manual gearbox and automatic were available. The new model lasted only one year before replacement by the 280Z.

I.D. DATA: Serial number is on the top left of the instrument panel, visible through the windshield; and on the firewall, under the hood. Each serial number is preceded by a model designation. Starting serial number: (610 sed) HL610-000001; (610 wag) HL610-800001; (710 sed) JHL710-000001; (710 cpe) KJHL710-000001; (710 wag) WHL710-800001; (260Z) RLS30-000001. Engine numbers are stamped on the right top edge of the block (preceded by the engine model code). A vehicle identification plate that includes both numbers and other data is attached to the hood ledge or firewall; or to the right front strut housing (260Z).

Model	Body Type & Seating	Engine Type/CID	P.O.E. Price	Weight (lbs.)	Prod. Total
610					
HL610	2-dr HT-5P	I4/119	3669	2313	Note 1
HL610	4-dr Sedan-5P	I4/119	3549	2338	Note 1
HL610	4-dr Sta Wag-5P	I4/119	3879	2475	Note 1
710					
JHL710	2-dr Sedan-5P	I4/108	3039	2214	Note 1
JHL710	4-dr Sedan-5P	I4/108	3139	2236	Note 1
KJHL710	2-dr HT-5P	I4/108	3259	2214	Note 1
WHL710	4-dr Sta Wag-5P	I4/108	3499	2377	Note 1
260Z					
260Z	2-dr Cpe-2P	I6/157	5289	2404	Note 2
260Z	2-dr Cpe-2+2P	I6/157	6089	2669	Note 2

Note 1: A total of 1,255,669 Datsun passenger cars were produced during 1974, of which 185,155 were sold in the U.S.

Note 2: A total of 40,172 260Z two-seat coupes were exported to the U.S. in 1974, plus 9,499 2+2 models.

Price Note: Early announced prices were lower than those shown above.

ENGINE DATA: BASE FOUR (710): Inline, overhead-cam four-cylinder (Model L18). Cast iron block and aluminum head. **Displacement**: 108.0 cu. in. (1770 cc). **Bore & Stroke**: 3.35 x 3.07 in. (85.1 x 84 mm). **Compression Ratio**: 8.5:1. **Brake Horsepower**: 105 (SAE) at 6000 rpm. **Torque**: 108 lbs.-ft. at 3600 rpm. Solid valve lifters. Two-barrel carburetor.

BASE FOUR (610): Inline, overhead-cam four-cylinder (Model L20B). Cast iron block and aluminum head. **Displacement**: 119.1 cu. in. (1952 cc). **Bore & Stroke**: 3.35 x 3.39 in. (85.1 x 86.1 mm). **Compression Ratio**: 8.5:1. **Brake Horsepower**: 110 (SAE) at 5600 rpm. **Torque**: 112 lbs.-ft. at 3600 rpm. Solid valve lifters. Two-barrel carburetor.

BASE SIX (260Z): Inline, overhead-cam six-cylinder (Model L26). Cast iron block and aluminum head. **Displacement**: 156.52 cu. in. (2565 cc). **Bore & Stroke**: 3.27 x 3.11 in. (83 x 79 mm). **Compression Ratio**: 8.8:1. **Brake Horsepower**: 162 (SAE) at 5600 rpm (139 at 5200 in California). **Torque**: 154 lbs.-ft. at 4400 rpm (137 at 4400 in California). Seven main bearings. Solid valve lifters. Two SU-type carburetors.

CHASSIS DATA: **Wheelbase**: (710) 96.5 in.; (610) 98.4 in.; (260Z) 90.7 in.; (260Z 2+2) 102.6 in. **Overall Length**: (710 cpe) 169.3 in.; (710 sed) 170.9 in.; (610) 174-174.2 in.; (610 wag) 176.2 in.; (260Z) 169.1 in.; (260Z 2+2) 173.2 in. **Height**: (710) 55.5 in.; (610) 54.5-55.7 in.; (260Z) 50.6 in. **Width**: (710) 62.2 in.; (610) 63 in.; (260Z) 64.1 in.; (260Z 2+2) 65.0 in. **Front Tread**: (710) 51.6 in; (610) 51.6 in.; (260Z) 53.3 in. **Rear Tread**: (710) 52.4 in.; (610) 52 in.; (260Z) 53.0 in. **Standard Tires**: (610/710) 6.45x13; (260Z) 175HR14.

TECHNICAL: **Layout**: front-engine, rear-drive. **Transmission**: four-speed manual. 260Z gear ratios: (1st) 3.59:1; (2nd) 2.25:1; (3rd) 1.42:1; (4th) 1.00:1. **Standard Final Drive Ratio**: (710) 3.89:1; (610) 3.70:1; (610 wag) 3.90:1; (260Z) 3.36:1 w/manual shift, 3.54:1 w/automatic. **Steering**: (260Z) rack and pinion. **Suspension (front)**: (260Z) MacPherson struts with coil springs. **Suspension (rear)**: (260Z) Chapman struts with lower wishbones and coil springs. **Brakes**: front disc, rear drum. **Body Construction**: steel unibody. **Fuel Tank**: (710) 13.2 gal.; (610) 14.5 gal.; (610 wag) 13.7 gal.; (260Z) 15.8 gal.

MAJOR OPTIONS: Automatic transmission: 710 ($245); 610 ($255); 260Z ($275). Air conditioning ($375-$400). Chrome wheels (240Z). Radio (standard on 260Z).

PRODUCTION/SALES: Calendar year sales in U.S. included: (610) 32,916; (710) 33,366; (240Z) 821; (260Z) 44,507; (trucks) 60,118.

ADDITIONAL MODELS: Datsun also produced a PL620 pickup truck, which sold in the U.S. for $3019; and a new subcompact LB210 series, priced at $2629 and up.

Manufacturer: Nissan Motor Co. Ltd., Tokyo, Japan.

Distributor: Nissan Motor Co. U.S.A., Carson, California.

HISTORY: Model year began November 1, 1973 except (710) January 1, 1974.

1975 DATSUN

610 — FOUR — Production of the 610 series continued with little change. Both the 610 and 710 now had the same size (119-cid) four-cylinder engine.

710 — FOUR — Little change was evident in the 710 series of sedans, coupe and wagon.

260Z — SIX — After introduction late in the 1974 model year, the 260Z was destined to last only for part of the 1975 season before being replaced by the third version of the "Z" car.

280Z — SIX — Appearance of the late-arriving 280Z differed little from the short-lived 260Z, but the six-cylinder inline engine grew to 2753 cc (168 cubic inches) and used Bosch L-Jetronic fuel injection. Tires grew too, to 195/70HR14 size.

I.D. DATA: Serial number is on the top left of the instrument panel, visible through the windshield; and on the firewall, under the hood. Each serial number is preceded by a model designation. Starting serial number: (610 sed) HL610-040001; (610 wag) HL610-840001; (710 sed) JHL710-038001; (710 cpe) JKHL710-025001; (710 wag) JHL710-840001; (260Z) RLS30-060001; (260Z 2+2) GRLS30-015001; (280Z) HLS30-200001; (280Z 2+2) GHLS30-000001. Engine numbers are stamped on the right top edge of the block (preceded by the engine model code). A vehicle identification plate that includes both numbers and other data is attached to the hood ledge or firewall; or to the right front strut housing (260Z/280Z).

Model	Body Type & Seating	Engine Type/CID	P.O.E. Price	Weight (lbs.)	Prod. Total
610					
HL610	2-dr HT-5P	I4/119	4169	2465	Note 1
HL610	4-dr Sedan-5P	I4/119	4029	2472	Note 1
HL610	4-dr Sta Wag-5P	I4/119	4389	2625	Note 1
710					
JHL710	2-dr Sedan-5P	I4/119	3469	2377	Note 1
JHL710	4-dr Sedan-5P	I4/119	3589	2399	Note 1
JHL710	2-dr HT-5P	I4/119	3729	2397	Note 1
JHL710	4-dr Sta Wag-5P	I4/119	3949	2512	Note 1
260Z					
260Z	2-dr Cpe-2P	I6/157	5665	2613	Note 2
260Z	2-dr Cpe-2+2P	I6/157	6465	2803	Note 2
280Z					
280Z	2-dr Cpe-2P	I6/168	6284	2755	Note 2
280Z	2-dr Cpe-2+2P	I6/168	7084	2925	Note 2

Note 1: A total of 1,532,731 Datsun passenger cars were produced during 1975, of which 259,842 were sold in the U.S.

Note 2: Total Z-car production for the 1975 model year was nearly 72,000, of which 55,000 were exported. A total of 40,216 260Z/280Z two-seat coupes were exported to the U.S. in 1975, plus 11,592 2+2 models.

ENGINE DATA: BASE FOUR (610/710): Inline, overhead-cam four-cylinder (Model L20B). Cast iron block and aluminum head. **Displacement:** 119.1 cu. in. (1952 cc). **Bore & Stroke:** 3.35 x 3.39 in. (85.1 x 86.1 mm). **Compression Ratio:** 8.5:1. **Brake Horsepower:** 100 (SAE) at 5600 rpm (610, 110 bhp). **Torque:** 100 lbs.-ft. at 3600 rpm (610, 112 lbs.-ft.). Solid valve lifters. Two-barrel carburetor.

BASE SIX (260Z): Inline, overhead-cam six-cylinder (Model L26). Cast iron block and aluminum head. **Displacement:** 156.52 cu. in. (2565 cc). **Bore & Stroke:** 3.27 x 3.11 in. (83 x 79 mm). **Compression Ratio:** 8.8:1. **Brake Horsepower:** 162 (SAE) at 5600 rpm. **Torque:** 154 lbs.-ft. at 4400 rpm. Seven main bearings. Solid valve lifters. Two SU-type carburetors.

BASE SIX (280Z): Inline, overhead-cam six-cylinder (Model L28). Cast iron block and aluminum head. **Displacement:** 168 cu. in. (2753 cc). **Bore & Stroke:** 3.39 x 3.11 in. (86.1 x 79 mm). **Compression Ratio:** 8.3:1. **Brake Horsepower:** 149 at 5600 rpm. **Torque:** 163 lbs.-ft. at 4400 rpm. Seven main bearings. Solid valve lifters. Bosch L-Jetronic fuel injection.

CHASSIS DATA: Wheelbase: (710) 96.5 in.; (610) 98.4 in.; (280Z) 90.7 in.; (280Z 2+2) 102.6 in. **Overall Length:** (710) 171.7 in.; (710 wag) 173 in.; (610) 174.8-177 in.; (280Z) 173.2 in.; (280Z 2+2) 185.4 in. **Height:** (710) 55.5-55.9 in.; (610) 54.5-56.1 in.; (280Z) 51 in.; (280Z 2+2) 51.2 in. **Width:** (710) 62.2 in.; (610) 63 in.; (280Z) 64.2 in.; (280Z 2+2) 65.0 in. **Front Tread:** (710) 51.6 in; (610) 51.6 in.; (280Z) 53.3 in. **Rear Tread:** (710) 52.4 in.; (610) 52 in.; (280Z) 53.0 in. **Standard Tires:** (610) 165SR13; (710) 6.45x13; (260Z) 175HR14; (280Z) 195/70HR14.

TECHNICAL: Layout: front-engine, rear-drive. **Transmission:** four-speed manual. **Standard Final Drive Ratio:** (710/610) 3.70:1; (280Z) 3.54:1. **Steering:** (260/280Z) rack and pinion. **Suspension (front):** (260/280Z) MacPherson struts with coil springs. **Suspension (rear):** (260/280Z) Chapman struts with lower wishbones and coil springs. **Brakes:** power front disc, rear drum. **Body Construction:** steel unibody. Fuel Tank: (710) 13.2 gal.; (610) 14.5 gal.; (610 wag) 13.7 gal.; (280Z) 17.2 gal.

MAJOR OPTIONS: Automatic transmission: 710/610 ($255); 280Z ($290). Air conditioning. Radio (standard on 260/280Z).

PERFORMANCE: Acceleration (0-60 mph): (280Z) 9.4-11 seconds. **Acceleration (quarter-mile):** (280Z) 17-17.3 seconds. **Fuel Mileage:** (280Z) about 19-20 mpg.

ADDITIONAL MODELS: Datsun also produced a PL620 pickup truck, which sold in the U.S. for $3359 (short-bed) or $3529; and the subcompact LB210 series, priced at $2979 and up.

Manufacturer: Nissan Motor Co. Ltd., Tokyo, Japan.

Distributor: Nissan Motor Co. U.S.A., Carson, California.

HISTORY: Model year began January 1975 except (280Z) March 1975.

1976 DATSUN

610/710 — FOUR — Production of both series continued with little change. Both the 610 and 710 were powered by the same size (119-cid) four-cylinder engine.

280Z — SIX — Little change was evident on the third version of the "Z" car, introduced during the 1975 model year. Both two-seat and 2+2 hatchback coupes were available, the latter longer in wheelbase.

I.D. DATA: Serial number is on the top left of the instrument panel, visible through the windshield; and on the firewall, under the hood. Each serial number is preceded by a model designation. Starting serial number: (610 sed) HL610-070001; (610 wag) HL610-880001; (710 sed) JHL710-070001; (710 cpe) JKHL710-040001; (710 wag) JHL710-890001; (280Z) HLS30-270001; (280Z 2+2) GHLS30-030001. Engine numbers are stamped on the right top edge of the block (preceded by the engine model code). A vehicle identification plate that includes both numbers and other data is attached to the hood ledge or firewall; or to the right front strut housing (280Z).

Model	Body Type & Seating	Engine Type/CID	P.O.E. Price	Weight (lbs.)	Prod. Total
610					
HL610	2-dr HT-5P	I4/119	4349	2388	Note 1
HL610	4-dr Sedan-5P	I4/119	4209	2395	Note 1
HL610	4-dr Sta Wag-5P	I4/119	4569	2550	Note 1
710					
JHL710	2-dr Sedan-5P	I4/119	3614	2299	Note 1
JHL710	4-dr Sedan-5P	I4/119	3749	2321	Note 1
JKHL710	2-dr HT-5P	I4/119	3874	2318	Note 1
JHL710	4-dr Sta Wag-5P	I4/119	4109	2439	Note 1
280Z					
280Z	2-dr Hatch Cpe-2P	I6/168	6594	2588	Note 2
280Z	2-dr Cpe-2+2P	I6/168	7394	2748	Note 2

Note 1: A total of 1,610,319 Datsun passenger cars were produced during 1976, of which 270,103 were sold in the U.S.

Note 2: A total of 45,766 280Z two-seat coupes were exported to the U.S. in 1976, plus 13,792 2+2 models.

ENGINE DATA: BASE FOUR (610/710): Inline, overhead-cam four-cylinder (Model L20B). Cast iron block and aluminum head. **Displacement:** 119.1 cu. in. (1952 cc). **Bore & Stroke:** 3.25 x 3.39 in. (85.1 x 86.1 mm). **Compression Ratio:** 8.5:1. **Brake Horsepower:** 100 (SAE) at 56 rpm (610, 112 bhp). **Torque:** 100 lbs.-ft. at 3600 rpm (610, 108 lb-ft). Solid valve lifters. Two-barrel carburetor.

BASE SIX (280Z): Inline, overhead-cam six-cylinder (Model L28). Cast iron block and aluminum head. **Displacement:** 168 cu. in. (2753 cc). **Bore & Stroke:** 3.39 x 3.11 in. (86.1 x 79 mm). **Compression Ratio:** 8.3:1. **Brake Horsepower:** 149 (170 gross) at 5600 rpm. **Torque:** 163 lbs.-ft. (177 gross) at 4400 rpm. Seven main bearings. Solid valve lifters. Bosch L-Jetronic fuel injection.

CHASSIS DATA: Wheelbase: (710) 96.5 in.; (610) 98.4 in.; (280Z) 90.7 in.; (280Z 2+2) 102.6 in. **Overall Length:** (710) 171.7 in.; (710 wag) 173 in.; (610) 174.8-177 in.; (280Z) 173.2 in.; (280Z 2+2) 185.4 in. **Height:** (710) 55.5-55.9 in.; (610) 54.5-56.1 in.; (280Z) 51 in.; (280Z 2+2) 51.2 in. **Width:** (710) 62.2 in.; (610) 63 in.; (280Z) 64.2 in.; (280Z 2+2) 65.0 in. **Front Tread:** (710) 51.6 in.; (610) 51.6 in.; (280Z) 53.3 in. **Rear Tread:** (710) 52.4 in.; (610) 52 in.; (280Z) 53.0 in. **Standard Tires:** (610) 165SR13; (710) 6.45x13; (280Z) 195/70HR14.

TECHNICAL: Layout: front-engine, rear-drive. **Transmission:** four-speed manual. **Standard Final Drive Ratio:** (710/610) 3.70:1; (280Z) 3.54:1. **Steering:** (280Z) rack and pinion. **Suspension (front):** (280Z) MacPherson struts with coil springs and anti-sway bar. **Suspension (rear):** (280Z) Chapman struts with lower wishbones and coil springs. **Brakes:** power front disc, rear drum. **Body Construction:** steel unibody. **Fuel Tank:** (710) 13.2 gal.; (610) 14.5 gal.; (610 wag) 13.7 gal.; (280Z) 17.2 gal.

MAJOR OPTIONS: Automatic transmission: 710/610 ($265); 280Z ($300). Air conditioning: 710/610 ($455); 280Z ($485). Radio (standard on 280Z).

PERFORMANCE: Acceleration (0-60 mph): (280Z) 9.4-11 seconds. **Acceleration (quarter-mile):** (280Z) 17-17.3 seconds. **Fuel Mileage:** (280Z) about 19-20 mpg (22 mpg highway).

ADDITIONAL MODELS: Datson also produced a PL620 pickup truck, which sold in the U.S. for $3499 (short-bed) or $3669; and the subcompact B210 series, priced at $2844 (for the new "Honeybee" model) and up. Also new this year was an F10 series, which arrived late in the season to become the lowest-priced Datsun. The F10 came in two-door hatchback and sportwagon form.

Manufacturer: Nissan Motor Co. Ltd., Tokyo, Japan.

Distributor: Nissan Motor Corp. U.S.A., Carson, California.

HISTORY: Model year began October 1975.

1977 DATSUN

710 — FOUR — Production of the 710 sedans, hard top coupe and station wagon continued with little change; but the 610 series was dropped.

810 — SIX — Datsun added a new luxury model this year, which would lead the line up for the next decade. Instead of the four-cylinder engine customary in sedans and wagons, the 810 carried a 240Z six-cylinder powerplant. Round quad headlamps were mounted in square housings, above amber rectangular parking lights. The rectangular grille was made up of thin vertical strips, with a wider center bar. Ads promoted the tilt steering wheel, six-way adjustable driver's seat and stereo radio, as well as the 240Z-based powerplant.

200SX — FOUR — Another new addition was the two-door sport coupe, also destined to remain in the Datsun lineup (upgraded periodically) into the 1990s. This first version had hardtop styling and a hatchback body, with single headlamps. Under the hood was the same engine as the 710 sedan, a 119-cid four. The crossbar-style grille, with vertical center insignia and wide eggcrate pattern, contained park/signal lights at its lower corners. Standard equipment included an AM/FM stereo radio, steel-belted radial tires, tachometer, electric rear defogger, reclining bucket seats, electric clock, tinted glass, and power brakes.

280Z — SIX — New features for the "Z" car included "mag" wheel covers, a five-speed manual gearbox, and collapsible spare tire. As for appearance, simulated hood vents replaced the former fender access ports. As before, both two-seat and 2+2 hatchback coupes were available, the latter longer in wheelbase.

I.D.DATA: Serial number is on the top left of the instrument panel, visible through the windshield; and on the firewall, under the hood. Each serial number is preceded by a model designation. Starting serial number: (710 sed) JHL710-108001; (710 cpe) JKHL710-060001; (710 wag) JHL710-920001; (810 sed) HLG810-000001; (810 wag) WHLD810-800001; (200SX)HLS10-100001; (280Z) HLS30-350003; (280Z 2+2) GHLS30-

060003. Engine numbers are stamped on the right top edge of the block (preceded by the engine model code). A vehicle identification plate that includes both numbers and other data is attached to the hood ledge or firewall; or to the right front strut housing(280Z).

Model	Body Type & Seating	Engine Type/CID	P.O.E. Price	Weight (lbs.)	Prod. Total
710					
JHL710	2-dr Sedan-5P	I4/119	3824	2307	Note 1
JHL710	4-dr Sedan-5P	I4/119	3959	2329	Note 1
JKHL710	2-dr HT-5P	I4/119	4084	2336	Note 1
JHL710	4-dr Sta Wag-5P	I4/119	4319	2443	Note 1
810					
HLG810	4-dr Sedan-5P	I6/146	5099	2617	Note 1
WHLD810	4-dr Sta Wag-5P	I6/146	5499	2775	Note 1
200SX					
HLS10	2-dr Coupe-4P	I4/119	4399	2320	Note 1
280Z					
HLS30	2-dr Hatch Cpe-2P	I6/168	6999	2628	Note 2
GHLS30	2-dr Cpe-2+2P	I6/168	8314	2870	Note 2

Note 1: A total of 1,615,866 Datsun passenger cars were produced during 1977, while 488,217 vehicles (including trucks) were sold in the U.S.

Note 2: A total of 54,954 280Z two-seat coupes were exported to the U.S. in 1977, plus 16,065 2 + 2 models.

ENGINE DATA: BASE FOUR (710,200SX): Inline, overhead-cam four-cylinder (Model L20B). Cast iron block and aluminum head. **Displacement:** 119.1 cu. in. (1952 cc). **Bore & Stroke:** 3.35x3.39 in. (85.1 x 86.1 mm). **Compression Ratio:** 8.5:1. **Brake Horsepower:** 97 at 5600 rpm. **Torque:** 102 lbs.-ft. at 3200 rpm. Solid valve lifters. Two-barrel carburetor.

BASE SIX (280Z): Inline, overhead-cam six-cylinder (Model L28). Cast iron block and aluminum head. **Displacement:** 168 cu. in. (2753 cc). **Bore & Stroke:** 3.39 x 3.11 in. (86.1 x 79 mm). **Compression Ratio:** 8.3:1. **Brake Horsepower:** 149 (170 gross) at 5600 rpm. **Torque:** 163 lbs.-ft. (177 gross) at 4400 rpm. Seven main bearings. Solid valve lifters. Bosch L-Jetronic fuel injection.

BASE SIX(810): Inline, overhead-cam six-cylinder (Model L24). Cast iron block and aluminum head. **Displacement:** 146 cu. in. (2393 cc). **Bore & Stroke:** 3.27 x 2.90 in. (83 x 73.7 mm). **Compression Ratio:** 8.6:1. **Brake Horsepower:** 154 (SAE gross) at 5200 rpm. **Torque:** 127 lbs.-ft. (gross) at 4400 rpm. Seven main bearings. Solid valve lifters. Electronic fuel injection.

CHASSIS DATA: Wheelbase: (710) 96. 5 in.; (810) 104.3 in.; (200SX) 92 in.; (280Z) 90.7 in.; (280Z 2 + 2) 102.6 in. **Overall Length:** (710) 171.1 in.; (710 wag) 173.2 in.; (810 sed) 183.5 in.; (810 wag) 185.6 in.; (200SX) 170 in.; (280Z) 173.4 in.; (280Z 2 + 2) 185.6 in. **Height:** (710) 54.5-56.1 in.; (810 sed) 54.5 in.; (810 wag) 56.1 in.; (200SX) 51.2 in.; (280Z) 51 in.; (280Z 2 + 2) 51.4 in. **Width:** (710) 62.2in.; (810) 64.2 in.; (200SX) 63 in.; (280Z) 64.2 in.; (280Z 2 + 2) 65.0 in. **Front Tread:** (710) 51.6 in.; (810) 53.1 in.; (200SX) 50.4 in.; (280Z) 53.3 in. **Rear Tread:** (710) 52.4 in.; (810 sed) 52.7 in.; (810 wag) 53.2 in.; (200SX) 49.8 in.; (280Z) 53.0 in. **Standard Tires:** (710) 6.45 x 13; (810) 185/70HR14; (200SX) 175/70HR13; (280Z) 195/70HR14.

TECHNICAL: Layout: front-engine, rear-drive. **Transmission:** four-speed manual except (200SX) five-speed. **Standard Final Drive Ratio:** (710) 3.70: 1; (810) 3.55:1; (200SX) 3.89:1; (280Z) 3.55:1. **Steering:** (710/810/200SX) recirculating ball; (280Z) rack and pinion. **Suspension (front):** (810/200SX/280Z) MacPherson struts with coil springs and anti-sway bar. **Suspension (rear):** (810) semi-trailing arms with coil springs; (200SX) rigid axle with semi-elliptic leaf springs; (280Z) Chapman struts with lower wishbones and coil springs. **Brakes:** power front disc, rear drum. **Body Construction:** steel unibody. **Fuel Tank:** (710) 13.2 gal.; (810 sed) 15.6 gal.; (810 wag) 14.6 gal.; (200SX) 15.8 gal.; (280Z) 17.2 gal.

MAJOR OPTIONS: Automatic transmission: 710/810 ($275); 200SX ($185); 280Z ($320). Air conditioning. Radio (standard on 260/280Z).

PERFORMANCE: Acceleration (0-60 mph): (810) 12.1 seconds; (200SX) 14.5 sec.; (280Z) 9.4-11 sec. **Acceleration (quarter-mile):** (810) 18 seconds; (200SX) 20.8 sec.; (280Z) 17-17.3 sec. **Fuel Mileage:** (280Z) about 19-20 mpg (22 mpg highway).

PRODUCTION/SALES: Total Z-car production from 1970 through 1977 was 411, 461.

ADDITIONAL MODELS: Datsun also produced a 620 series pickup truck, which sold in the U.S. for $3779 and up; the subcompact B210 series, priced at $3099 and up; and the smaller F10 series, priced at $3649 (wagon) or $3999 (hatchback).

Manufacturer: Nissan Motor Co. Ltd., Tokyo, Japan.

Distributor: Nissan Motor Corp. U.S.A., Carson, California.

HISTORY: Model year began October 1976 except (200SX/710/810) February 1977.

1978 DATSUN

810 — SIX — Datsun's luxury sedan and wagon continued into their second season with little change. Powerplant was again a smaller version of the 240Z six-cylinder engine. *Car and Driver* described it as, mechanically, "a four-door 280Z." Power steering was now standard. Other standard equipment included an AM/FM stereo radio, tinted glass, tilt steering column, and six-way driver's seat. Air conditioning was optional.

200SX — FOUR — The two-door sport coupe continued with little change, powered by a 119 cid (1952 cc) four-cylinder engine. *Car and Driver* spoke for many in describing the stylish sport coupe as "the poorman's Z-car." Although the basic structure evolved from the little B210 subcompact, the engine came from the departed 710 series. A five-speed manual gearbox was standard; three-speed automatic optional.

280Z — SIX — Little was new in the "Z" car, but a "ZX" version would be arriving at the end of the model year. One new body color was available (light blue). An AM/FM stereo radio was standard.

I.D. DATA: Serial number is on the top left of the instrument panel, visible through the windshield; and on the firewall, under the hood. Each serial number is preceded by a model designation. Starting serial number: (810 sed) HLG810-100001; (810 wag) WHLD810-820001; (200SX) HLS10-140301; (280Z)HLS30-420001; (280Z 2 + 2) GHLS30-110001. Engine numbers are stamped on the right top edge of the block (preceded by the engine model code). A vehicle identification plate that includes both numbers and other data is attached to the hood ledge or firewall; or on the lefthood ledge panel at the rear of the strut housing (280Z).

Model	Body Type & Seating	Engine Type/CID	P.O.E. Price	Weight (lbs.)	Prod. Total
810					
HLG810	4-dr Sedan 5-P	I6/146	6208	2549	Note 1
WHLD810	4-dr Sta Wag-5P	I6/146	6538	2757	Note 1
200SX					
HLS10	2-dr Coupe-4P	I4/119	4988	2323	Note 1
280Z					
HLS30	2-dr Hatch Cpe-2P	I6/168	7968	2628	Note 1
GHLS30	2-dr Cpe-2 + 2P	I6/168	9278	2870	Note 1

Note 1: A total of 1,733,132 Datsun passenger cars were produced during 1978, of which about 339,364 were sold in the U.S.

Price Note: Prices rose during the model year to $7258 and $7618 for the 810; $5758 for the 200SX; and $8878 and $10,328 for the 280Z.

ENGINE DATA: BASE FOUR(200SX): Inline, overhead-cam four-cylinder (Model L20B). Cast iron block and aluminum head. **Displacement:** 119.1 cu. in. (1952 cc). **Bore & Stroke:** 3.35 x 3.39 in. (85.1 x 86.1 mm). **Compression Ratio:** 8.5:1. **Brake Horsepower:** 97 at 5600 rpm (lower in California). **Torque:** 102 lbs.-ft. at 3200 rpm. Solid valve lifters. Two-barrel carburetor.

BASE SIX (280Z): Inline, overhead-cam six-cylinder (Model L28). Cast iron block and aluminum head. **Displacement:** 168 cu. in. (2753 cc). **Bore & Stroke:** 3.39 x 3.11 in. (86.1 x 79 mm). **Compression Ratio:** 8.3:1. **Brake Horsepower:** 149 (170 gross) at 5600 rpm. **Torque:** 163 lbs.-ft. (177 gross) at 4400 rpm. Seven main bearings. Solid valve lifters. Bosch L-Jetronic fuel injection.

BASE SIX (810): Inline, overhead-cam six-cylinder (Model L24). Cast iron block and aluminum head. **Displacement:** 146 cu. in. (2393 cc). **Bore & Stroke:** 3.27 x 2.90 in. (83 x 73.7 mm). **Compression Ratio:** 8.6:1. **Brake Horsepower:** 154 (gross) at 5600 rpm. **Torque:** 155 lbs.-ft. (gross) at 4400 rpm. Seven main bearings. Solid valve lifters. Electronic fuel injection.

CHASSIS DATA: Wheelbase: (810) 104.3 in.; (200SX) 92 in.; (280Z) 90.7 in.; (280Z 2 + 2) 102.6 in. **Overall Length:** (810 sed) 183.5 in.; (810 wag) 185.6 in.; (200SX) 170 in.; (280Z) 173.4 in.; (280Z 2 + 2) 185.6 in. **Height:** (810 sed) 54.9 in.; (810 wag) 55.9 in.; (200SX) 51.2 in.; (280Z) 51 in.; (280Z 2 + 2) 51.4 in. **Width:** (810) 64.8 in.; (200SX) 63 in.; (280Z) 64.2 in.; (280Z 2 + 2) 65.0 in. **Front Tread:** (810) 53 in.; (200SX) 50.2 in.; (280Z) 53.3 in. **Rear Tread:** (810) 53 in.; (200SX) 49.8 in.; (280Z) 53.0 in. **Standard Tires:** (810) 185/70HR14; (200SX) 175/70HR13; (280Z) 195/70HR14.

TECHNICAL: Layout: front-engine, rear-drive. **Transmission:** (810) four-speed manual; (200SX/280Z) five-speed. **Steering:** (810/200SX) recirculating ball; (280Z) rack and pinion. **Suspension (front):** MacPherson struts with coil springs and anti-sway bar. **Suspension (rear):** (810) independent, semi-trailing arms and coil springs; (200SX) rigid axle with semi-elliptic leaf springs; (280Z) Chapman struts with coil springs and anti-sway bar. **Brakes:** power front disc, rear drum. **Body Construction:** steel unibody. **Fuel Tank:** (810 sed) 15.6 gal.; (810 wag) 14.6 gal.; (200SX) 15.8 gal.; (280Z) 17.2 gal.

MAJOR OPTIONS: Automatic transmission. Air conditioning.

PERFORMANCE: Acceleration (0-60 mph): (280Z) 9.4 seconds. **Acceleration (quarter-mile):** (280Z) 17.3 seconds. **Fuel Mileage:** (280Z) EPA 16-17 mpg city, 21-23 mpg highway; (200SX) EPA 23-24 mpg city, 28-33 mpg highway; (280Z) EPA 17-18 mpg city, 23-27 mpg highway.

ADDITIONAL MODELS: Datsun revived the 510 nameplate this year, in a sedan that resembled the original of the 1960s and early '70s. It served as a replacement for the abandoned 710, shorter in wheel base and powered by the 2-liter (119-cid) four-cylinder engine. Hatchback and station wagon versions also were marketed. Datsun also continued to produce a 620 series pickup truck, which sold in the U.S. for $4398 and up; the subcompact B210 series, priced at $3488 and up; and the smaller F10 series, priced at $4318 (wagon) or $4638 (hatchback).

Manufacturer: Nissan Motor Co. Ltd., Tokyo, Japan.

Distributor: Nissan Motor Corp. U.S.A., Carson, California.

HISTORY: Model year began in October 1977.

1979 DATSUN

1979 Datsun 210 five-door wagon.

810 — SIX — A two-door hardtop sport coupe with five-speed gearbox joined the original four-door sedan and station wagon this year. Powerplant was again a smaller version of the 240Z six-cylinder engine. Front-end appearance was modified, with a switch to quad rectangular headlamps. The cross hatch grille pattern and hood ornament also were new.

200SX — FOUR — Datsun's two-door sport coupe continued with little change, except with a new black rockerpanel. The 1952-cc OHC four cylinder engine continued to provide the power, through either the standard five-speed manual gearbox or optional three-speed automatic. Standard equipment included power front disc brakes, whitewall radial tires, tachometer, tinted glass, remote trunk opener, rear defroster, and an electric remote-control driver's mirror.

280 ZX — SIX — Publicity for the latest Datsun sports coupe noted that it included "many engineering improvements (plus) all the handling and performance expected from a 'Z' car with a new body design and all-new luxury interior." Appearance was actually quite similar to the 280Z, even though all the body panels were new. Rear quarter windows were considerably longer, coming to a sharp point at the rear. The distinctive headlamp look remained. An integral front spoiler helped cooling. By this time, the original sports-car demeanor was giving way to plushness and comfort, and the ZX actually rode more like a luxury sedan than a traditional sportscar. Aerodynamic qualities had improved, however, from a drag coefficient of 0.467 for the original 240 Z to 0. 385 in this version. Stopping power also got a boost with new four-wheel disc brakes. Standard equipment included an AM/FM stereo radio, air conditioning, cut-pile carpeting, remote hatch release, and power mirrors. A new Grand Luxury option package, standard on the 2+2, included a central warning system that ended with an "OK" notice.

I.D. DATA: Serial number is on the top left of the instrument panel, visible through the windshield; and on the firewall, under the hood. Each serial number is preceded by a model designation. Starting serial number: (810 sed) HLG810-200011; (810 cpe) KHLG810-200011; (810 wag) WHLD810-839001; (200SX) HLS10-181641; (280ZX) HS130-100001; (280ZX 2+2) HGS130-100001. Engine numbers are stamped on the right top edge of the block (preceded by the engine model code). A vehicle identification plate that includes both numbers and other data is attached to the hood ledge or firewall; or on the right side of the firewall, behind the battery (280ZX).

Model	Body Type & Seating	P.O.E. Price	Weight (lbs.)	P.O.E. Price	Prod. Total
810					
KHLG810	2-dr HT Cpe-5P	I6/146	8279	2684	Note 1
HLG810	4-dr Sedan-5P	I6/146	8129	2637	Note 1
WHLD810	4-dr Sta Wag-4P	I6/146	8529	2815	Note 1
200SX					
HLS10	2-dr Coupe-4P	I4/119	6229	2268	Note1
280ZX					
HS130	2-dr Hatch Cpe-2P	I6/168	9899	2596	Note 1
HGS130	2-dr Cpe- 2+2P	I6/168	11599	2862	Note 1

Note 1: A total of 1,738,946 Datsun passenger cars were produced during 1979, of which about 472,252 were sold in the U.S. A total of 71,893 Z-cars were sold world wide.

ENGINE DATA: BASE FOUR(200SX): Inline, overhead-cam four-cylinder (Model L20B). Cast iron block and aluminum head. **Displacement:** 119.1 cu. in. (1952 cc). **Bore & Stroke:** 3.35 x 3.39 in. (85.1 x 86.1 mm). **Compression Ratio:** 8.5:1. **Brake Horsepower:** 92 at 5600 rpm. **Torque:** 107 lbs.-ft. at 3200 rpm. Solid valve lifters. Two-barrel carburetor.

BASE SIX (280ZX): Inline, overhead-cam six-cylinder (Model L28). Cast iron block and aluminum head. **Displacement:** 168 cu. in. (2753 cc). **Bore & Stroke:** 3.39 x 3.11 in. (86.1 x 79 mm). **Compression Ratio:** 8.3:1. **Brake Horsepower:** 135 at 5200 rpm (132 bhp in California). **Torque:** 144 lbs.-ft. at 4400 rpm. Seven main bearings. Solid valve lifters. Bosch L-Jetronic fuel injection.

BASE SIX (810): Inline, overhead-cam six-cylinder (Model L24). Cast iron block and aluminum head. **Displacement:** 146 cu. in. (2393 cc). **Bore & Stroke:** 3.27 x 2.90 in. (83 x 73.7 mm). **Compression Ratio:** 8.9:1 (8.6:1 in California). **Brake Horsepower:** 120 at 5200 rpm. **Torque:**1 25 lbs.-ft. at 4400 rpm. Seven main bearings. Solid valve lifters. Electronic fuel injection.

CHASSIS DATA: Wheelbase: (810) 104.3 in.; (200SX) 92.1 in.; (280ZX) 91.3 in.; (280ZX 2+2) 99.2 in. **Overall Length:** (810 sed) 183.9 in.; (810 wag) 186 in.; (200SX) 170.2 in.; (280ZX) 174 in.; (280ZX 2+2) 181.9 in. **Height:** (810 cpe) 54.5 in.; (810 sed) 54.9 in.; (810 wag) 56.1 in.; (200SX) 51.2 in.; (280ZX) 51 in.; (280ZX 2+2) 51.4 in. **Width:** (810) 64.8 in.; (200SX) 63 in.; (280ZX) 66.5 in. **Front Tread:** (810) 53 in.; (200SX) 50.2 in.; (280ZX) 54.5 in. **Rear Tread:** (810) 53 in.; (200SX) 49.8 in.; (280ZX) 54.3 in. **Standard Tires:** (810) 185/70SR14; (200SX) 175/70SR13; (280ZX) 195/70HR14.

TECHNICAL: Layout: front-engine, rear-drive. **Transmission:** (810 sed/wag) four-speed manual; (200SX/280ZX, 810 cpe) five-speed. 280ZX gear ratios: (1st) 3.321:1; (2nd) 2.077:1; (3rd) 1.308:1; (4th) 1.00:1; (5th) 0.864:1. **Standard Final Drive Ratio:** (810) 3.55:1; (200SX) 3.89:1; (280ZX) 3.55:1. **Steering:** (810/200SX) recirculating ball; (280ZX) rack and pinion. **Suspension (front):** MacPherson struts with coil springs and anti-sway bar. **Suspension (rear):** (810 cpe/sed) independent, semi-trailing arms and coil springs; (200SX, 810 wagon) rigid axle with semi-elliptic leaf springs; (280ZX) semi-trailing arms with coil springs and anti-sway bar. **Brakes:** powerfront disc, rear drum except (280ZX) four-wheel disc. **Body Construction:** steel unibody. Fuel Tank: (810 sed) 15.9 gal.; (810 wag) 14.5 gal.; (200SX) 15.9 gal.; (280ZX) 21.1 gal.

MAJOR OPTIONS: Automatic transmission: 810HT ($260); 810 sed/wag ($390); 200SX ($250); 280ZX ($295). Air conditioning.

PERFORMANCE: Top Speed: (280ZX) 124mph w/manual, 112mph w/automatic. **Acceleration (0-60mph):** (280ZX) 9.2 seconds. **Acceleration (quarter-mile):** (810) 18.7 seconds. **Fuel Mileage:** (810) EPA 16-17 mpg city, 21-23 mpg highway; (200SX) EPA23-24 mpg city, 28-33 mpg highway.

ADDITIONAL MODELS: A new 310 series replaced the subcompact F10. Datsun also continued to produce the 620 series pickup truck (in short, long and king cab versions), which sold in the U.S. for $4739 and up; the subcompact 210 series, priced at $3899 and up; and the smaller 510 series, priced at $5079 and up.

Manufacturer: Nissan Motor Co. Ltd., Tokyo, Japan.

Distributor: Nissan Motor Corp. U.S.A., Carson, California.

HISTORY: Model year began in October 1978. *MotorTrend* named the 280ZX its "Import Car of the Year" for 1979.

1980 DATSUN

810 — SIX — Little change was evident in Datsun' stop-of-the-line sedan, hardtop coupe and station wagon.The engine was a smaller-displacement version of the inlines ix used in the 280ZX. A five-speed gear box was standard in the two-door version; four-speed in the others, with three-speed automatic optional on all three. New options included halogen head lamps and cruise control. Power steering was standard.

200SX — FOUR — After only a short time in Datsun's line up, the sport coupe got a major reworking for 1980: more than six inches longer and three inches wider than the original, with improved visibility and interior space. Both a notch back and hatchback body style were now available, in either standard (DeLuxe) or Sport Luxury (SL) trim. A refined edition of the 1952-cc OHC four-cylinder engine, with fuel injection, delivered 100 horsepower. Both a five-speed manual gearbox and optional three-speed automatic were available.

280 ZX — SIX — Changes were few on the two-seat (or 2+2) sport scoupe, which enjoyed are styling for 1979. Both base and GL (Grand Luxury) models were available this year; GL only for the 2+2. A new warning system checked functions at each start up, giving an" OK" signal if all was well. A T-bar roof, optional on the GL two-seater, consisted of twin tinted-glass panels that could be stored in the luggage compartment. As before, a five-speed manual gearbox was standard; three-speed automatic optional. Power steering, cruise control, radio, cloth upholstery and air conditioning were standard on the GL.

I.D.DATA: Serial number is on the top left of the instrument panel, visible through the windshield; and on the firewall, under the hood. Each serial number is preceded by a model designation. Starting serial number: (810 sed) HLG810-220001; (810 cpe) KHLG810-020001; (810 wag) WHLD810-880001; (200SX) PS110-000001; (200SX hatch) KPS110-000001; (280ZX) HS130-190001; (280ZX 2+2) HGS130-150001. Engine numbers are stamped on the right top edge of the block (preceded by the engine model code). A vehicle identification plate that includes both numbers and other data is attached to the hood ledge or firewall; or on the right side of the firewall, behind the battery (280ZX).

1980 Datsun 810 four-door station wagon.

Model	Body Type & Seating	Engine Type/CID	P.O.E. Price	Weight (lbs.)	Prod. Total
810					
KHLG810	2-dr HTCpe-5P	I6/146	8279	2839	Note 1
HLG810	4-dr Sedan-5P	I6/146	8129	2839	Note 1
WHLD810	4-dr Sta Wag-5P	I6/146	8529	2931	Note 1
200SX					
PS110	2-dr Coupe-4P	I4/119	6389	2615	Note 1
PS110	2-dr SL Cpe-4P	I4/119	7139	2615	Note 1
KPS110	2-dr Hatch-4P	I4/119	6589	2635	Note 1
KPS110	2-dr SL Hatch-4P	I4/119	7389	2635	Note 1
280ZX					
HS130	2-dr Hatch Cpe-2P	I6/168	9899	2786	Note 1
HS130	2-dr GL Hatch-2P	I6/168	12238	2786	Note 1
HGS130	2-dr GL Cpe-2+2P	I6/168	13153	2941	Note 1

Note 1: A total of 1,940,615 Datsun passenger cars were produced during 1980, of which 516, 890 were sold in the U.S.

280ZX Price Note: The 10th anniversary edition sold for $13,850.

ENGINE DATA: BASE FOUR (200SX): Inline, overhead-cam four-cylinder (Model Z20E). Cast iron block and aluminum head. **Displacement:** 119.1 cu. in. (1952 cc). **Bore & Stroke:** 3.35 x 3. 39in. (85.1 x 86.1mm). **Compression Ratio:** 8.5:1. **Brake Horsepower:** 100 at 5200 rpm. **Torque:** 112 lbs.-ft. at 3200 rpm. Solid valve lifters. Electronic fuel injection.

BASE SIX (280ZX): Inline, overhead-cam six-cylinder (Model L28). Cast iron block and aluminum head. **Displacement:**168 cu. in. (2753 cc). **Bore & Stroke:**3.39x3.11 in. (86.1 x 79mm). **Compression Ratio:** 8.3:1. **Brake Horsepower:** 132 at 5200 rpm. **Torque:** 144 lbs.-ft. at 4000 rpm. Seven main bearings. Solid valve lifters. Bosch L-Jetronic fuel injection.

BASE SIX (810): Inline, overhead-cam six-cylinder (Model L24). Cast iron block and aluminum head. **Displacement:** 146 cu. in. (2393c c). **Bore & Stroke:** 3.27x2.90in. (83 x 73.7mm). **Compression Ratio:** 8.9:1. **Brake Horsepower:** 120 at 5200 rpm. **Torque:** 125lbs.-ft. at 4400 rpm. Seven main bearings. Solid valve lifters. Electronic fuel injection.

CHASSIS DATA: Wheelbase: (810) 104.3 in.; (200SX) 94.5 in.; (280ZX) 91.3 in.; (280ZX 2+2) 99.2 in. **Overall Length:** (810 sed) 183.9 in.; (810 wag) 186 in.; (200SX) 176.4 in.; (280ZX) 174 in.; (280ZX 2+2) 181.9 in. **Height:** (810 sed) 54.9 in.; (810 wag) 56.1 in.; (200SX) 51.6 in.; (280ZX) 51 in.; (280ZX 2+2) 51.4 in. **Width:** (810) 64.8 in.; (200SX) 66.1 in.; (280ZX) 66.5 in. **Front Tread:** (810) 53 in.; (200SX) 53 in.; (280ZX) 54.5 in.; (280ZX 2+2) 54.9 in. **Rear Tread:** (810) 53 in.; (200SX) 53 in.; (280ZX) 54.3 in.; (280ZX 2+2) 54.7 in. **Standard Tires:** (810) 185/70 HR14; (200SX) 185/70 SR14; (280ZX) 195/70 HR14.

TECHNICAL: Layout: front-engine, rear-drive. **Transmission:** five-speed manual except (810 sed/wag) four-speed manual. **Standard Final Drive Ratio:** (810) 3.55:1; (200SX) 3.70:1; (280ZX) 3.36:1. **Steering:** (810/200SX) recirculating ball; (280SX) rack and pinion. **Suspension (front):** Mac Pherson struts with coil springs and anti-sway bar. **Suspension (rear):** (810) independent, semi-trailing arms and coil springs; (200SX) rigid axle with coil springs; (280ZX) semi-trailing arms with coil springs and anti-sway bar. **Brakes:** power front disc, rear drum except (280ZX) four-wheel disc. **Body Construction:** steel unibody. **Fuel Tank:** (810 sed) 15.9 gal.; (810 wag) 14.5 gal.; (200 SX) 14 or 15.9 gal.; (280 ZX) 21.1 gal.

MAJOR OPTIONS: Automatic transmission: 810HT ($260); 810 ed/wag ($390); 200SX ($250); 280ZX ($295). Air conditioning. T-top (280ZX). Leather seats (280ZX).

PERFORMANCE: Top Speed: (280 ZX) 124 mph w/manual, 112 mphw/automatic. **Acceleration (0-60mph):** (200SX) 13 sec.; (280ZX) 9.2 seconds. **Acceleration (quarter-mile):** (810) 18.7 seconds. **Fuel Mileage:** (810) EPA 16-17 mpg city, 21-23 mpg highway; (200SX) about 25 mpg city,38 mpg highway; (280ZX) about 21 mpg average.

PRODUCTION/SALES: A total of 628,136 Datsun vehicles (including trucks) were sold in the U.S. during 1980. Sales totals included: (200SX) 92,514; (810) 9,440; (280ZX) 71,533. Biggest seller was the subcompact 210 at 180,324 units.

ADDITIONAL MODELS: Datsun also produced a new 720 series pickup truck (in short, long and kingcab versions), which sold in the U.S. for $4839 and up; the subcompact 210 series, priced at $3899 and up; the 310 series, starting at $4739; and the 510 series, priced at $5339 and up.

Manufacturer: Nissan Motor Co. Ltd., Tokyo, Japan.

Distributor: Nissan Motor Corp. U.S.A., Gardena, California.

HISTORY: "Some people drive it for a living. Some people live to drive it." So read the ads for the "legendary Datsun Z-car," touting its decade of SCCA champion ship victories. To mark the 10th anniversary of the Z-car, a "Limited Edition" 280ZX appeared at the Chicago Auto Show in February 1980. Special features included gold/black paint/tape treatment (badge sand alloy wheels in gold color), a T-bar roof with tinted glass panels, headlamp washers, automatic climate control, and Goodyear Wing foot tires. Code-name: ZX10. Only 3,000 were built, with the code name 'ZX10,' and priced at $13,850. Each had an engraved dash board plaque.

1981 DATSUN

810 — SIX — Datsun's biggest models got a full-scale revamping this year, with new squarish wedge styling and deeper window glass. Deluxe 810 sedans and wagons came with a five-speed manual gearbox, while the new Maxima designation went on the upscale models, available only with three-speed automatic. Rack-and-pinion steering replaced the former recirculating-ball system. Maxima sedans had disc brakes all around, as opposed to the usual front discs and rear drums. Maximas also carried a long list of standard comfort/convenience equipment. Both trim levels had a vocal warning system, with a soft female voice advising the driver to "please turn out the lights." Power plant was the 2.4-liter (146-cid) with electronic fuel injection.

200SX — FOUR — Little change was evident in the sport coupe and hatchback, which, though stylish, were closely related to the 510 in basic chassis and drive train construction. They carried a fuel-injected version of the 510's 119-cid four-cylinder engine, hooked to either a five-speed manual or optional three-speed automatic transmission. The Sports Luxury (SL) package included cloth bucket seats (with driver's thigh support adjustment), AM/FM stereo radio, warning light display, and intermittent wipers.

280ZX — SIX — Though unchanged in size, the 280ZX six-cylinder engine got a compression horsepower boost this year, to 8.8:1 and 145 bhp (a jump of 13). The two-seater came in base and GL trim; the 2+2 in GL level only. Standard equipment and options remained the same, including an available T-top. Early in 1981, a 280ZX Turbo toured the auto shows and went on sale to the public, initially only in the two-seater model. The Garrett AiResearch turbo charger delivered a 7.3 psi boost. Output of the engine was 180 horsepower, with 7.4:1 compression. The turbo was capable of 0-60 mph in 7.1 seconds, and the quarter-mile in 15.4 seconds, reaching 89 mph.

I.D. DATA: Datsun's 17-symbol Vehicle Identification Number (VIN) is on the top left of the instrument panel, visible through the wind shield. Engine numbers are stamped on the right top edge of the block (preceded by the engine model code). A vehicle identification plate that includes both numbers and other data is attached to the hood ledge or firewall; or on the right side of the firewall, behind the battery (280ZX).

Model	Body Type & Seating	Engine Type/CID	P.O.E. Price	Weight (lbs.)	Prod. Total
810					
UO1	4-dr Sedan-5P	I6/146	7979	2740	Note 1
UO1	4-dr Sta Wag-5P	I6/146	8329	2845	Note 1
MAXIMA					
U01	4-dr Sedan-5P	I6/146	10379	2800	Note 1
U05	4-dr Sta Wag-5P	I6/146	10879	2905	Note 1
200SX					
S06	2-dr Coupe-4P	I4/119	7389	2610	Note 1
S04	2-dr Hatch-4P	I4/119	7589	2635	Note 1
280ZX					
Z04	2-dr Hatch Cpe-2P	I6/168	11299	2780	Note 1
Z04	2-dr GL Hatch-2P	I6/168	13949	2840	Note 1
Z06	2-dr GL Hatch-2+2	I6/168	14949	2935	Note 1
Z04	2-dr Turbo GL-2P	I6/168	16999	2938	Note 1

Note 1: A total of 1,864,251 Datsun passenger cars were produced during 1981, of which 464,806 were sold in the U.S.

Price Note: Early announced prices were $400 to $900 lower than those shown above, which were effective during the model year.

ENGINE DATA: BASE FOUR (200SX): Inline, overhead-cam four-cylinder (Model Z20E). Cast iron block and aluminum head. **Displacement:** 119.1 cu.in. (1952 cc). **Bore & Stroke:** 3.35 x 3.39 in. (85.1 x 86.1 mm). **Compression Ratio:** 8.5:1. **Brake Horsepower:** 100 at 5200 rpm. **Torque:** 112 lbs.-ft. at 3200 rpm. Solid valve lifters. Electronic fuel injection.

BASE SIX (280ZX): Inline, overhead-cam six-cylinder (Model L28E). Cast iron block and aluminum head. **Displacement:** 168 cu.in. (2753 cc). **Bore & Stroke:** 3.39 x 3.11 in. (86.1x79 mm). **Compression Ratio:** 8.8:1. **Brake Horsepower:** 145 at 5200 rpm. **Torque:** 156 lbs.-ft. at 4000 rpm. Seven main bearings. Solid valve lifters. Bosch L-Jetronic fuel injection.

BASE SIX (280ZX Turbo): Same as 280ZX six above, except — **Compression Ratio:** 7.4:1. **Brake Horsepower:** 180 at 5600 rpm. **Torque:** 202 lbs.-ft. at 2800 rpm.

BASE SIX (810/Maxima): In line, overhead-cam six-cylinder (Model L24). Cast iron block and aluminum head. **Displacement:** 146 cu. in. (2393 cc). Bore & Stroke: 3.27 x 2.90 in. (83 x 73.7 mm). Compression Ratio: 8.9:1. Brake Horsepower: 120 at 5200 rpm. Torque: 134 lbs.-ft. at 2800 rpm. Seven main bearings. Solid valve lifters. Electronic fuel injection.

Note: A diesel engine became available for the 810/Maxima at mid-year; see next listing for details.

CHASSIS DATA: Wheelbase: (810/Maxima) 103.4 in.; (200SX) 94.5 in.; (280ZX) 91.3 in.; (280ZX 2+2) 99.5 in. **Overall Length:** (810 sed) 183.9 in. (810 wag) 186 in. (200SX) 176.4 in.; (280ZX) 174 in.; (280ZX 2+2) 181.9 in. **Height:** (810 sed) 54.9 in.; (810 wag) 56.1 in.; (200SX) 51.6 in.; (280ZX) 51 in.; (280ZX 2+2) 51.4 in. **Width:** (810) 64.8 in.; (200SX) 66.1 in.; (280ZX) 66.5 in. **Front Tread:** (810) 53 in.;(200SX) 53 in.; (280ZX) 54.5 in.; (280ZX 2+2) 54.9 in. **Rear Tread:** (810) 53 in.; (200SX) 53 in.; (280ZX) 54.3 in.; (280ZX 2+2) 54.7 in. **Standard Tires:** (810) 185/70 HR14; (200SX) 185/70 SR14; (280ZX) 195/70 HR14 or 205/70 HR14; (280ZX Turbo) 205/60x15.

TECHNICAL: Layout: front-engine, rear-drive. **Transmission:** five-speed manual except (Maxima) three-speed automatic. **Standard Final Drive Ratio:** (810/Maxima) 3.55:1; (200SX) 3.70:1; (280ZX) 3.90:1. **Steering:** (810/Maxima) rack and pinion; (200SX) recirculating ball; (280ZX) rack and pinion. **Suspension (front):** MacPherson struts with coil springs and anti-sway bar. **Suspension (rear):** (810/Maxima) semi-trailing arms and coil springs with anti-sway bar; (200SX) rigid axle with coil springs and anti-sway bar; (280ZX) independent, semi-trailing arms with coil springs and anti-sway bar. **Brakes:** (200SX) power front disc, rear drum; (Maxima and 280ZX) four-wheel disc. **Body Construction:** steel unibody. **Fuel Tank:** (810/Maxima) 15.9 or 16.4 gal.; (200SX) 14 or 15.9 gal.; (280ZX) 21.1 ga l.

MAJOR OPTIONS: Automatic transmission: 200SX ($250); 280ZX ($295). Power steering: 200SX ($190). Air conditioning: 200SX ($580); 810 ($600); 280ZX ($635). GL package: 280ZX ($1804). SL package: 200SX ($1050-$1100). Lift-off glass sun roof: 200SX ($249). T-bar roof: 280ZX ($700). Alloy wheels: 200SX ($250).

PERFORMANCE: Top Speed: (280ZX) 124 mph w/manual, 112 mph w/automatic. **Acceleration (0-60 mph):** (200SX) 13 seconds; (280ZX Turbo) 7.1 seconds. **Acceleration (quarter-mile):** (810) 18.7 seconds (280ZX Turbo) 15.4 seconds (89 mph). **Fuel Mileage:** (200SX) about 25 mpg (EPA, 28 mpg).

PRODUCTION/SALES: A total of 584,490 Datsun vehicles (including trucks) were sold in the U.S. during 1981. Sales totals included: (200SX) 76,024; (810/Maxima) 35,495; (280ZX) 63,791.

ADDITIONAL MODELS: Datsun also produced a 720 series pickup truck (in short, long and king cab versions), which sold in the U.S. for $5999 and up; the sub compact 210 series, priced at $4599 and up; the 310 series, starting at $5489; and the 510 series, priced at $6439 and up.

Manufacturer: Nissan Motor Co. Ltd., Tokyo, Japan.

Distributor: Nissan Motor Corp. U.S.A., Gardena, California.

HISTORY: Construction began in 1981 of an assembly plant at Smyrna, Tennessee, to produce Datsuns (Nissans) in the U.S.

1982 DATSUN/NISSAN

1982 Datsun two-door.

MAXIMA — SIX — The former 810 designation was gone, with all of the top-line sedans and wagons now called Maximas. Few features were new, except for quartz-halogen head lamps, a different fabric for the velour upholstery, and revised instrument graphics. A five-speed manual gear box was now standard on both gas-and diesel-engine models, while the three-speed automatic (with lockup torque converter) became an option on sedans. Automatic was standard on the wagon. The 168-cid diesel had become available during the 1981 model year, and was expected to be offered in all states later in 1982. The vocal warning system got a bigger vocabulary this year, including phrases for a key left in the ignition, door ajar, and low fuel supply.

200SX — FOUR — A 2-liter four-cylinder engine replaced the former 2.0-liter in the face lifted 200SX. The sport coupe and hatchback also received a front-end restyling including new soft, body-color urethane bumpers, a checkered-pattern grille, 'B' pillar louvers, and a modified hood and taillamps. The new fuel-injected power plant measured 133 cubic inches and delivered 102 horsepower. Two equipment levels were offered: De-Luxe and Sport Luxury (SL). The optional three-speed automatic transmission included a lockup torque converter, while the SL package included a vocal warning system.

280ZX — SIX — Turbo power was available this year in both the 2+2 and the two-seater, having debuted only on the shorter Z-car during 1981. Turbo models could have either the five-speed manual gear box or the original three-speed automatic. All models added a NACA-style hood scoop, as introduced on the Turbo. Urethane body-color bumpers were new, and the grille took a slightly modified shape. Taillamps also earned a modest restyling, and body side moldings blended into the profile a little more smoothly this year. Power steering was now standard, as was a voice warning system.

I.D. DATA: Datsun's 17-symbol Vehicle Identification Number (VIN) is on the top left of the instrument panel, visible through the windshield. Engine numbers are stamped on the right top edge of the block (preceded by the engine model code). A vehicle identification plate that includes both numbers and other data is attached to the hood ledge or firewall; or on the right side of the firewall, behind the battery (280ZX).

Model	Body Type & Seating	Engine Type/CID	P.O.E. Price	Weight (lbs.)	Prod. Total
MAXIMA:					
UO1	4-dr Sedan-5P	I6/146	11049	2796	Note1
UO5	4-dr Sta Wag-5P	I6/146	11859	2897	Note1
200SX					
S06	2-dr Coupe-4P	I4/133	7739	2576	Note 1
SO4	2-dr Hatch-4P	I4/133	7939	2603	Note 1
280ZX					
Z04	2-dr Hatch Cpe-2P	I6/168	14499	2796	Note 1
Z06	2-dr Hatch-2+2P	I6/168	15499	2891	Note 1
Z04	2-dr Turbo-2P	I6/168	17299	N/A	Note 1
Z06	2-dr Turbo-2+2P	I6/168	18299	3007	Note 1

Note 1: A total of 1,815,792 Datsun/Nissan passenger cars were produced during 1982, of which about 470,246 were sold in the U.S.

Diesel Note: A Maxima sedan with diesel engine cost $11,419; the diesel wagon, $12,229.

Price Note: Early announced prices for 1982 were lower than shown above (similar to 1981).

ENGINE DATA: BASE FOUR (200SX): Inline, overhead-cam four-cylinder (Model Z20E). Cast iron block and aluminum head. **Displacement**: 133.4 cu. in. (2181 cc). **Bore & Stroke**: 3.43 x 3.62 in. (87.1 x 91.9 mm). **Compression Ratio**: 8.5:1. **Brake Horsepower**: 102 at 5200 rpm. **Torque**: 129 lbs.-ft. at 2800 rpm. Solid valve lifters. Electronic fuel injection.

BASE SIX (280ZX): Inline, overhead-cam six-cylinder (Model L28E). Cast iron block and aluminum head. **Displacement**: 168 cu. in. (2753 cc). **Bore & Stroke**: 3.39 x 3.11 in. (86.1 x 79 mm). **Compression Ratio**: 8.8:1 (8.6:1 in California). **Brake Horsepower**: 145 at 5200 rpm. **Torque**: 156 lbs.-ft. at 4000 rpm. Seven main bearings. Solid valve lifters. Bosch L-Jetronic fuel injection.

BASE SIX (280ZX Turbo): Same as 280ZX six above, except — **Compression Ratio**: 7.4:1. **Brake Horsepower**: 180 at 5600 rpm. **Torque**: 202 lbs.-ft. at 2800 rpm.

BASE SIX (Maxima): Inline, overhead-cam six-cylinder (Model L24). Cast iron block and aluminum head. **Displacement**: 146 cu. in. (2393 cc). **Bore & Stroke**: 3.27 x 2.90 in. (83 x 73.7 mm). **Compression Ratio**: 8.9:1. **Brake Horsepower**: 120 at 5200 rpm. **Torque**: 134 lbs.-ft. at 2800 rpm. Seven main bearings. Solid valve lifters. Electronic fuel injection.

DIESEL SIX (Maxima): **Displacement**: 168 cu. in. (2753 cc). **Bore & Stroke**: 3.39 x 3.11 in. (86.1 x 79 mm). **Brake Horsepower**: 80 at 4600 rpm. **Torque**: 120 lbs.-ft. at 5200 rpm.

CHASSIS DATA: **Wheelbase**: (Maxima) 103.4 in.; (200SX) 94.5 in.; (280ZX) 91.3 in.; (280ZX2+2) 99.5 in. **Overall Length**: (Maxima sed) 183.3 in.; (Maxima wag) 186.8 in.; (200SX) 176.4 in.; (280ZX) 174 in.; (280ZX2+2) 181.9 in. **Height**: (Maxima sed) 54.5 in.; (Maxima wag) 55.7 in.; (200SX) 51.6 in.; (280ZX) 51 in.; (280ZX2+2) 51.4 in. **Width**: (Maxima) 64.6 in.; (200SX) 66.1 in.; (280ZX) 66.5 in. **Front Tread**: (Maxima) 54.3 in.; (200SX) 53 in.; (280ZX) 54.5 in.; (280ZX2+2) 54.9 in. **Rear Tread**: (Maxima) 53.5 in.; (200SX) 53 in.; (280ZX) 54.3 in.; (280ZX2+2) 54.7 in. **Standard Tires**: (Maxima) 185/70 HR14; (200SX) 185/70 SR14; (280ZX) 195/70 HR14 or 205/70 HR14; (280ZXTurbo) 205/60 R15.

TECHNICAL: **Layout**: front-engine, rear-drive. **Transmission**: five-speed manual except (Maxima wag) three-speed automatic. **Standard Final Drive Ratio**: (Maxima) 3.54:1; (200SX) 3.70:1; (280ZX) 3.90:1. **Steering**: (Maxima) rack and pinion; (200SX) recirculating ball; (280ZX) rack and pinion. **Suspension** (front): MacPherson struts with coil springs and anti-sway bar. **Suspension (rear)**: (Maxima) semi-trailing arms and coil springs with anti-sway bar; (200SX) rigid axle with coil springs and anti-sway bar; (280ZX) independent, semi-trailing arms with coil springs and anti-sway bar. **Brakes**: (200SX) power front disc, rear drum; (Maxima and 280ZX) four-wheel disc. **Body Construction**: steel unibody. **Fuel Tank**: (Maxima) 15.9 or 16.4 gal.; (200SX) 14 or 15.9 gal.; (280ZX) 21.1 gal.

MAJOR OPTIONS: Automatic transmission: 200SX ($330); 280ZX ($300). Air conditioning: 200SX ($620); Maxima ($600); 280ZX ($650). GL package: 280ZX ($2000). SL package: 200SX ($1350-$1570). T-bar roof: 280ZX ($750). Leather seats: 280ZX ($350-$450).

PRODUCTION/SALES: A total of 578,173 Datsun/Nissan vehicles (including trucks) were sold in the U.S. during 1982. Sales totals included: (200SX) 48,559; (Maxima) 54,187; (280ZX) 57,260.

ADDITIONAL MODELS: Datsun/Nissan also produced a series of pickup trucks with two-wheel and four-wheel drive; the subcompact 210 series; a new front-drive Sentra; the 310 series; and a new front-drive Stanza series.

Manufacturer: Nissan Motor Co. Ltd., Tokyo, Japan.

Distributor: Nissan Motor Corp. U.S.A., Gardena, California.

HISTORY: Model year began in September 1981. The first model to switch from the Datsun to Nissan name was the new-for-1982 front-drive Stanza, which replaced the rear-drive 510. Later in the model year, Nissan's front-drive Sentra replaced the rear-drive 210.

1983 DATSUN/NISSAN

MAXIMA — SIX — A few body modifications were evident on the luxury sedan and wagon, including slight grille and taillamp revisions. Accent models were added to bumpers, wheelwells, and the hood front. A four-speed overdrive automatic transmission replaced the former three-speed. A four-link rear suspension became standard on the station wagon (but the sedan remained independent, with semi-trailing arms). Leather interior trim was optional.

200SX — FOUR — Power steering and a stereo radio became standard on all sport coupe models, but little changed otherwise.

280ZX — SIX — Not much was new in Datsun's sports car series, except for a softening of shock-absorber rates and an increase in tire width. Turbo models used Bridgestone Potenza 60-series radials; others rode on 70-series Goodyear Eagle GTs. A new option package included leather upholstery, automatic temperature control, bronze-tinted glass, electric mirror defoggers, and digital instruments.

I.D.DATA: Datsun/Nissan's 17-symbol Vehicle Identification Number (VIN) is on the top left of the instrument panel, visible through the windshield. Engine numbers are stamped on the right top edge of the block (preceded by the engine model code). A vehicle identification plate that includes both numbers and other data is attached to the hood ledge or firewall; or on the right side of the firewall, behind the battery (280ZX).

Model	Body Type & Seating	Engine Type/CID	P.O.E. Price	Weight (lbs.)	Prod. Total
MAXIMA					
U01	4-dr Sedan-5P	I6/146	10869	2880	Note 1
U05	4-dr Sta Wag-5P	I6/146	12159	3095	Note 1
200SX					
S06	2-dr Coupe-4P	I4/133	7999	2585	Note 1
S04	2-dr Hatch-4P	I4/133	8199	2610	Note 1
280ZX					
Z04	2-dr Hatch Cpe-2P	I6/168	14799	2860	Note 1
Z06	2-dr Hatch-2+2P	I6/168	15799	2958	Note 1
Z04	2-dr Turbo-2P	I6/168	17599	2972	Note 1
Z06	2-dr Turbo-2+2P	I6/168	18599	3081	Note 1

Note 1: A total of 1,858,782 Datsun/Nissan passenger cars were produced during 1983, of which about 521,902 were sold in the U.S.

Diesel Note: A Maxima sedan with diesel engine cost $11,719; the diesel wagon, $12,529.

ENGINE DATA: BASE FOUR (200SX): Inline, overhead-cam four-cylinder (Model Z22). Cast iron block. **Displacement**: 133.4 cu. in. (2181 cc). **Bore & Stroke**: 3.43 x 3.62 in. (87.1 x 91.9 mm). **Compression Ratio**: 8.5:1. **Brake Horsepower**: 102 at 5200 rpm. **Torque**: 129 lbs.-ft. at 2800 rpm. Solid valve lifters. Electronic fuel injection.

BASE SIX (280ZX): Inline, overhead-cam six-cylinder (Model L28). Cast iron block and aluminum head. **Displacement**: 168 cu. in. (2753 cc). **Bore & Stroke**: 3.39 x 3.11 in. (86.1 x 79 mm). **Compression Ratio**: 8.8:1 (8.6:1 in California). **Brake Horsepower**: 145 at 5200 rpm. **Torque**: 156 lbs.-ft. at 4000 rpm. Seven main bearings. Solid valve lifters. Bosch L-Jetronic fuel injection.

BASE SIX (280ZX Turbo): Same as 280ZX six above, except — **Compression Ratio**: 7.4:1. **Brake Horsepower**: 180 at 5600 rpm. **Torque**: 202 lbs.-ft. at 2800 rpm.

BASE SIX (Maxima): Inline, overhead-cam six-cylinder (Model L24). Cast iron block and aluminum head. **Displacement**: 146 cu. in. (2393 cc). **Bore & Stroke**: 3.27 x 2.90 in. (83 x 73.7 mm). **Compression Ratio**: 8.9:1. **Brake Horsepower**: 120 at 5200 rpm. **Torque**: 134 lbs.-ft. at 2800 rpm. Seven main bearings. Solid valve lifters. Electronic fuel injection.

DIESEL SIX (Maxima): **Displacement**: 168 cu. in. (2753 cc). **Bore & Stroke**: 3.39 x 3.11 in. (86.1 x 79 mm). **Brake Horsepower**: 80 at 4600 rpm. **Torque**: 120 lbs.-ft. at 5200 rpm.

CHASSIS DATA: **Wheelbase**: (Maxima) 103.4 in.; (200SX) 94.5 in.; (280ZX) 91.3 in.; (280ZX 2+2) 99.2 in. **Overall Length**: (Maxima sed) 183.3 in.; (Maxima wag) 186.8 in.; (200SX) 176.2 in.; (280ZX) 174 in.; (280ZX 2+2) 181.9 in. **Height**: (Maxima sed) 54.5 in.; (Maxima wag) 55.7 in.; (200SX) 51.6 in.; (280ZX) 51 in. **Width**: (Maxima sed) 65.2 in.; (Maxima wag) 64.6 in.; (200SX) 66.1 in.; (280ZX) 66.5 in. **Front Tread**: (Maxima sed) 54.7 in.; (Maxima wag) 54.3 in.; (200SX) 53 in.; (280ZX) 54.9 in. **Rear Tread**: (Maxima sed) 53.9 in.; (Maxima wag) 53.5 in.; (200SX) 53.7 in.; (280ZX) 54.7 in. **Standard Tires**: (Maxima) 185/70 HR14; (200SX) 185/70 SR14; (280ZX) 205/70 HR14; (280ZX Turbo) 205/60x15.

TECHNICAL: **Layout**: front-engine, rear-drive. **Transmission**: five-speed manual except (Maxima wag) three-speed automatic. **Standard Final Drive Ratio**: (Maxima) 3.55:1; (Maxima w/4-spd auto.) 3.36:1; (200SX) 3.55:1; (200SX w/auto.) 3.70:1; (280ZX) 3.90:1 or 3.55:1. **Steering**: (Maxima) rack and pinion; (200SX) recirculating ball; (280ZX) rack and pinion. **Suspension (front)**: MacPherson struts with coil springs and anti-sway bar. **Suspension (rear)**: (Maxima sed) semi-trailing arms and coil springs with anti-sway bar; (Maxima wag) rigid axle with four trailing links, coil springs and anti-sway bar; (200SX) rigid axle with coil springs and anti-sway bar; (280ZX) independent, semi-trailing arms with coil springs and anti-sway bar. **Brakes**: power front disc, rear drum except (Maxima sed,280ZX) four-wheel disc. **Body Construction**: steel unibody. **Fuel Tank**: (Maxima) 15.9 or 16.4 gal.; (200SX) 14 or 15.9 gal.; (280ZX) 21.1 gal.

MAJOR OPTIONS: Automatic transmission (200SX, 280ZX). Four-speed automatic transmission: Maxima sed ($500). Air conditioning: 200SX ($640); 280ZX ($650). SL package: 200SX ($1190). T-bar roof: 280ZX ($800). Power sun roof: Maxima sed ($480). Leather seats: 280ZX ($500-$600). Leather pkg.: Maxima sed ($800).

PERFORMANCE: **Top Speed**: (200SX) 108 mph; (280ZX) 124 mph. **Acceleration (0-60mph)**: (200SX) 11.5 seconds; (280ZX) 9.7 sec. **Acceleration (quarter-mile)**: (200SX) 18.3 seconds and 75.5 mph; (280ZX) 17.2 sec. and 79.5 mph.

PRODUCTION/SALES: A total of 647,542 imported Datsun/Nissan vehicles (including trucks) were sold in the U.S. during 1983. Sales totals included: (200SX) 31,158; (Maxima) 76,209; (280ZX/300ZX) 71,144.

ADDITIONAL MODELS: Datsun/Nissan continued to produce a series of pickup trucks with two-wheel and four-wheel drive; the subcompact front-drive Sentra; and the front-drive Stanza series. Now this year (actually introduced in mid-year 1982) was the Pulsar, a replacement for the 310. The first version offered was the NX coupe, with pop-up headlamps and a rear profile similar to Ford's EXP. Later Pulsars, introduced during 1983, took ordinary two- and four-door hatchback form. Pulsars rode a 95-inch wheelbase and were powered by a 1.6-liter four-cylinder engine.

Manufacturer: Nissan Motor Co. Ltd., Tokyo, Japan.

Distributor: Nissan Motor Corp. U.S.A., Gardena, California.

HISTORY: Model year began in November 1982.

1984 NISSAN

Marque Note: By 1984, all models had switched from the Datsun to Nissan name.

MAXIMA — SIX — Except for a name change from Datsun to Nissan, changes were minimal this year for the top-of-the-line, rear-drive sedan and station wagon. The diesel-engine option was dropped. Audible wear sensors were installed on the front brake pads. Bodyside moldings grew wider, bumpers added bright accents, and the hood ornament added the Maxima name. A 125-mph speedometer was standard, and the right-hand outside mirror was now convex-shaped for a wider view.

200SX — FOUR — The notchback and hatchback sport coupe were carried over for the first part of the 1984 model year, then replaced in the spring by a new pair with smaller engines and an aero-styled front end with retracting headlamps. Still rear-wheel-drive, the new platform carried a standard 2.0-liter overhead-cam four-cylinder engine, rated 102 horsepower. Two trim levels were offered: Deluxe and XE. Standard equipment included power steering and brakes, five-speed manual gearbox, a digital AM/FM stereo radio, bucket seats, tilt steering, and twin side mirrors. The XE added power windows and mirrors, and cruise control. A Turbo edition, offered only as a hatchback, carried a 1.8-liter turbocharged four, on a modified chassis with independent rear suspension and four-wheel disc brakes. Digital instruments were optional on the Turbo and XE. A four-speed overdrive automatic transmission also was optional.

Note: See previous listing for details on early '84 200SX.

300ZX — V-6 — The fully restyled sports car not only looked a lot different, with aerodynamic touches, but switched from the customary inline six-cylinder engine to V-6 power (first time on a Japanese car). Only the two-seater came with the option of turbo power. Standard engine on both was a 3.0-liter V-6 producing 160 horsepower. The turbo engine delivered 200 bhp. Appearance differed considerably from the former 280ZX: much more angular, with deeply recessed, rectangular retracting (semi-concealed) headlamps above rectangular park/signal lights in a sharp, low nose. The smaller windshield had a steep rake, and the front bumper took on an integrated appearance. Large triangular quarter windows reached far back on the bodyside, coming to a point near the rear of the car. Turbos added a front spoiler. Both models were hatchbacks. A Nissan five-speed manual gearbox was standard for the non-aspirated models; Borg-Warner five-speed for the Turbo; and four-speed overdrive automatic (electronically-controlled) optional. Turbo models also had adjustable shock absorbers.

I.D. DATA: Nissan's 17-symbol Vehicle Identification Number (VIN) is on the top left of the instrument panel, visible through the windshield. Engine numbers are stamped on the right top edge of the block (preceded by the engine model code) except (200SX) on left rear edge of block, next to bell housing; and (300ZX) on right rear edge of right cylinder bank. A vehicle identification plate that includes both numbers and other data is attached to the hood ledge or firewall; or on the front of the left strut housing (300ZX).

Model	Body Type & Seating	Engine Type/CID	P.O.E. Price	Weight (lbs.)	Prod. Price
MAXIMA					
U01	4-dr Sedan-5P	I6/146	11399	2791	Note 1
U05	4-dr Sta Wag-5P	I6/146	12799	2951	Note 1
200SX					
S24	2-dr Coupe-4P	I4/120	8499	2291	Note 1
S26	2-dr Hatch-4P	I4/120	8699	2346	Note 1
S24	2-dr XE Cpe-4P	I4/120	9699	N/A	Note 1
S26	2-dr XE Hatch-4P	I4/120	9999	N/A	Note 1
S26	2-dr Turbo-4P	I4/110	N/A	N/A	Note 1
300ZX					
Z14	2-dr GL Coupe-2P	V6/181	15799	2783	Note 1
Z16	2-dr GL Cpe-2+2P	V6/181	16999	2867	Note 1
Z14	2-dr Turbo Cpe-2P	V6/181	18199	2924	Note 1

Note 1: A total of 1,846,407 Nissan passenger cars were produced during 1984, of which about 485,298 were sold in the U.S.

ENGINE DATA: BASE FOUR (late 200SX): Inline, overhead-cam four-cylinder. Cast iron block. **Displacement:** 120.4 cu. in. (1974 cc). **Bore & Stroke:** 3.33 x 3.46 in. (84.6 x 88 mm). **Compression Ratio:** 8.5:1. **Brake Horsepower:** 102 at 5200 rpm. **Torque:** 116 lbs.-ft. at 3200 rpm. Solid valve lifters. Electronic fuel injection.

TURBO FOUR (200SX): Inline, overhead-cam four-cylinder. **Displacement:** 110.3 cu. in. (1809 cc). **Bore & Stroke:** 3.27 x 3.29 in. (83 x 84 mm). **Compression Ratio:** 8.0:1. **Brake Horsepower:** 120 at 5200 rpm. **Torque:** 134 lbs.-ft. at 3200 rpm. Solid valve lifters. Electronic fuel injection.

BASE V-6 (300ZX): Overhead-cam V-6. Cast iron block. **Displacement:** 180.6 cu. in. (2960 cc). **Bore & Stroke:** 3.43 x 3.27 in. (87.1 x 83 mm). **Compression Ratio:** 9.0:1. **Brake Horsepower:** 160 at 5200 rpm. **Torque:** 174 lbs.-ft. at 4000 rpm. Hydraulic valve lifters. Electronic fuel injection.

BASE V-6 (300ZX Turbo): Same as 300ZX V-6 above, except — **Compression Ratio:** 7.8:1. **Brake Horsepower:** 200 at 5200 rpm. **Torque:** 227 lbs.-ft. at 3600 rpm.

BASE SIX (Maxima): Inline, overhead-cam six-cylinder. Cast iron block and aluminum head. **Displacement:** 146 cu. in. (2393 cc). **Bore & Stroke:** 3.27 x 2.90 in. (83 x 73.7 mm). **Compression Ratio:** 8.9:1. **Brake Horsepower:** 120 at 5200 rpm. **Torque:** 134 lbs.-ft. at 2800 rpm.

CHASSIS DATA: Wheelbase: (Maxima) 103.4 in.; (200SX) 95.5 in.; (300ZX) 91.3 in.; (300ZX 2+2) 99.2 in. **Overall Length:** (Maxima) 183.3 in.; (200SX) 174.4 in.; (300ZX) 170.7 in.; (300ZX 2+2) 178.5 in. **Height:** (Maxima sed) 54.5 in.; (Maxima wag) 55.7 in.; (200SX) 52.4 in.; (300ZX) 49.7 in. **Width:** (Maxima) 65.2 in.; (200SX) 65.4 in.; (300ZX) 67.9 in. **Front Tread:** (Maxima sed) 54.7 in.; (Maxima wag) 54.3 in.; (200SX) 54.3 in.; (300ZX) 55.7 in. **Rear Tread:** (Maxima sed) 53.9 in.; (Maxima wag) 53.5 in.; (200SX) 53.5 in.; (200SX Turbo) 56.1 in.; (300ZX) 56.5 in. **Standard Tires:** (Maxima) 185/70SR14; (200SX) 185/70SR14; (200SX Turbo) 195/60HR15; (300ZX) P215/60R15.

TECHNICAL: Layout: front-engine, rear-drive. **Transmission:** five-speed manual except (Maxima wag) four-speed automatic. **Standard Final Drive Ratio:** (Maxima) 3.54:1; (Maxima w/4-spd auto) 3.70:1; (200SX) 3.70:1; (200SX w/auto.) 3.89:1; (200SX Turbo) 3.90:1; (300ZX) 3.70:1; (300ZX Turbo) 3.54:1. **Steering:** (Maxima) rack and pinion; (200SX) recirculating ball; (300ZX) rack and pinion. **Suspension (front):** MacPherson struts with coil springs and anti-sway bar. **Suspension (rear):** (Maxima sed) semi-trailing arms and coil springs with anti-sway bar; (Maxima wag) rigid axle with four trailing links, coil springs and anti-sway bar; (200SX) rigid axle with coil springs and anti-sway bar; (200SX Turbo and 300ZX) semi-trailing arms, coil springs and anti-sway bar. **Brakes:** (200SX) power front disc, rear drum; (Maxima, 200SX Turbo and 300ZX) four-wheel disc. **Body Construction:** steel unibody. **Fuel Tank:** (Maxima) 15.9 or 16.4 gal.; (200SX) 14.5 gal.; (300ZX) 19 gal.

MAJOR OPTIONS: Four-speed automatic transmission: Maxima sed ($500); 200SX/300ZX (N/A). Air conditioning. Power sunroof: Maxima sed ($480). Leather pkg.; Maxima sed ($800).

PRODUCTION/SALES: A total of 593,860 imported Nissan vehicles (including trucks) were sold in the U.S. during 1984. Sales totals included: (200SX) 63,466; (Maxima) 68,209; (280ZX/300ZX) 73,101; (Pulsar NX) 37,284.

ADDITIONAL MODELS: Nissan continued to produce a series of pickup trucks with two-wheel and four-wheel drive; the subcompact front-drive Sentra; the Pulsar NX coupe; and the front-drive Stanza series.

Manufacturer: Nissan Motor Co. Ltd., Tokyo, Japan.

Distributor: Nissan Motor Corp. U.S.A., Gardena, California.

HISTORY: Model year began in October 1983 except (200SX) introduced in February 1984.

1985-86 NISSAN

MAXIMA — V-6 — An all-new, fully restyled sedan and wagon switched from rear-drive to front-wheel drive this year, and from inline six to V-6 power. The 3.0-liter V-6, as used in the 300ZX sports car, was transverse mounted under Maxima hoods. Sedans came in GL and SE trim; the wagon in GL only. GL models had a standard four-speed overdrive automatic transmission with lockup torque converter, while the SE came with a five-speed manual and driver-adjustable shock absorbers. Keyless entry was standard, along with an AM/FM stereo radio and cassette player that included a graphic equalizer and six speakers. Independent suspension was used at all four wheels. Little changed for the 1986 model year, except for the addition of a theft-deterrent system.

200SX — FOUR — Little change was evident in the notchback and sport coupe after their 1984 restyle. Both non-aspirated and turbo power were available. Hatchbacks added a new rear spoiler for the 1986 model year, and the model name for the base 200SX changed from Deluxe to E series.

1985 Nissan Maxima GL sedan.

1985 Nissan 300 ZX Turbo.

300ZX — V-6 — Changes were modest in the second season for the revised Nissan sports car. New two-tone combinations for the Turbo model included black with gold and dark blue metallic over pewter. Two-tone models also had body-color bumpers and accent stripes. All Turbos came with blackout moldings and smoked taillamp lenses. Standard equipment now included locking T-bar roof panels. For the 1986 model year, all models added flared fenders, rocker panel extensions, and body-color bumpers. Deleting the T-bar roof also created a new base model for 1986, while Turbo coupes switched to larger (16-inch) tires and lost their hood scoop.

I.D. DATA: Nissan's 17-symbol Vehicle Identification Number (VIN) is on the top left of the instrument panel, visible through the windshield. Other identification locations are similar to 1984.

Note: Prices and other data below are for 1985 models.

Model	Body Type & Seating	Engine Type/CID	P.O.E. Price	Weight (lbs.)	Prod. Total
MAXIMA					
U11	4-dr Sedan-5P	V6/181	13499	3060	Note 1
U11	4-dr GL Sedan-5P	V6/181	13499	3095	Note 1
U15	4-dr GL Wag-5P	V6/181	14399	3296	Note 1

1985 Nissan 200SX Turbo hatchback.

200SX					
S24	2-dr Coupe-4P	I4/120	8999	2469	Note 1
S26	2-dr Hatch-4P	I4/120	10249	2623	Note 1
S24	2-dr XE Cpe-4P	I4/120	9199	2546	Note 1
S26	2-dr XE Hatch-4P	I4/120	10749	2712	Note 1
S26	2-dr Turbo Hatch-4P	I4/120	12349	2767	Note 1
300ZX					
Z14	2-dr Coupe-2P	V6/181	17199	3071	Note 1
Z16	2-dr Coupe-2+2P	V6/181	18399	3139	Note 1
Z14	2-dr Turbo Cpe-2P	V6/181	19699	3139	Note 1

Note 1: A total of 1,864,701 Nissan passenger cars were produced during 1985, of which about 535,372 were sold in the U.S. A total of 1,769,484 were produced during 1986.

1986 Nissan SX XE. (Desiree Sikowski-Nelson)

ENGINE DATA: BASE FOUR (200SX): Inline, overhead-cam four-cylinder. Cast iron block. **Displacement:** 120.4 cu. in. (1974 cc). **Bore & Stroke:** 3.33 x 3.46 in. (84.6 x 88 mm). **Compression Ratio:** 8.5:1. **Brake Horsepower:** 102 at 5200 rpm. **Torque:** 116 lbs.-ft. at 3200 rpm. Solid valve lifters. Electronic fuel injection.

TURBO FOUR (200SX): Inline, overhead-cam four-cylinder. **Displacement:** 110.3 cu. in. (1809 cc). **Bore & Stroke:** 3.27 x 3.29 in. (83 x 84 mm). **Compression Ratio:** 8.0:1. **Brake Horsepower:** 120 at 5200 rpm. **Torque:** 134 lbs.-ft. at 3200 rpm. Solid valve lifters. Electronic fuel injection.

BASE V-6 (300ZX): Overhead-cam V-6. Cast iron block. **Displacement:** 180.6 cu. in. (2960 cc). **Bore & Stroke:** 3.43 x 3.27 in. (87.1 x 83 mm). **Compression Ratio:** 9.0:1. **Brake Horsepower:** 160 at 5200 rpm. **Torque:** 174 lbs.-ft. at 4000 rpm. Hydraulic valve lifters. Electronic fuel injection.

BASE V-6 (300ZX Turbo): Same as 300ZX V-6 above, except — **Compression Ratio:** 7.8:1. **Brake Horsepower:** 200 at 5200 rpm. **Torque:** 227 lbs.-ft. at 3600 rpm.

BASE V-6 (Maxima): Same as 300ZX engine above, except — **Brake Horsepower:** 152 at 5200 rpm. **Torque:** 167 lbs.-ft. at 3600 rpm.

CHASSIS DATA: Wheelbase: (Maxima) 100.4 in.; (200SX) 95.5 in.; (300ZX) 91.3 in.; (300ZX 2 + 2) 99.2 in. **Overall Length:** (Maxima sed) 181.7 in.; (Maxima wag) 184.6 in.; (200SX) 174.4 in.; (300ZX) 170.7 in.; (300ZX 2 + 2) 178.5 in. **Height:** (Maxima sed) 55.1 in.; (Maxima wag) 56.1 in.; (200SX) 52.4 in.; (300ZX) 49.7 in. **Width:** (Maxima) 66.5 in.; (200SX) 65.4 in.; (300ZX) 67.9 in. **Front Tread:** (Maxima sed) 57.5 in.; (Maxima wag) 57.3 in.; (200SX) 54.3 in.; (300ZX) 55.7 in. **Rear Tread:** (Maxima sed) 57.1 in.; (Maxima wag) 56.9 in.; (200SX) 53.5 in.; (200SX Turbo) 56.1 in.; (300ZX) 56.5 in. **Standard Tires:** (Maxima) P195/60HR15; (200SX) 185/70SR14; (200SX Turbo) 195/60HR15; (300ZX) P215/60R15 (except 1986 Turbo, 16-inch).

TECHNICAL: Layout: front-engine, rear-drive except (Maxima) front-drive. **Transmission:** five-speed manual except (Maxima GL) four-speed automatic. **Steering:** rack and pinion. **Suspension (front):** MacPherson struts with coil springs and anti-sway bar. **Suspension (rear):** (Maxima sed) MacPherson struts and coil springs with anti-sway bar; (200SX) rigid axle with coil springs and anti-sway bar; (200SX Turbo and 300ZX) semi-trailing arms,coil springs and anti-sway bar. **Brakes:** power front/rear disc except (200SX non-turbo) front disc, rear drum. **Body Construction:** steel unibody. **Fuel Tank:** (Maxima) 15.9 gal.; (200SX) 14.5 gal.; (300ZX) 19 gal.

MAJOR OPTIONS: Air conditioning: 200SX ($675). Electronics pkg.: Maxima ($600). Digital instruments pkg.: 200SX ($950 $1400). Power sunroof: Maxima GL ($500). Sunroof: 200SX Turbo ($280). Leather pkg.; Maxima GL ($600).

PRODUCTION/SALES: A total of 680,629 imported Nissan vehicles (including trucks) were sold in the U.S. during 1984. Sales totals included: (200SX) 65,792; (Maxima) 79,051; (300ZX) 67,409; (Pulsar NX) 49,816.

ADDITIONAL MODELS: Nissan continued to produce a series of pickup trucks with two-wheel and four-wheel drive; the subcompact front-drive Sentra; the Pulsar NX coupe; and the front-drive Stanza series.

Manufacturer: Nissan Motor Co. Ltd., Tokyo, Japan.

Distributor: Nissan Motor Corp. U.S.A., Gardena, California.

HISTORY: Model year began in September 1984 except (Maxima) October 1984.

1987-88 NISSAN

MAXIMA — V-6 — Nissan's top-line sedan and wagon gained a minor facelift in spring 1986, for release as an early 1987 model. A new GXE series replaced the former GL. Sporty SE models could now get the four-speed overdrive automatic transmission instead of the standard five-speed manual. Motorized automatic front seat belts became standard for 1987, as did rear shoulder belts. Powerplant remained the transverse-mounted 3.0-liter V-6 engine. For 1988, Maxima added an optional Sonar Suspension that could sense road conditions ahead and alter shock-absorber damping as needed.

200SX — FOUR/V-6 — Appearance and rear-wheel-drive layout remained similar to prior models, but Nissan's sport coupe moved up to V-6 power for 1987. A four-cylinder engine remained standard in the XE series (notchback and hatchback), but the SE hatch-back came with a 3.0-liter, 160-horsepower V-6 and 205/60R15 tires on alloy wheels. The turbo four was dropped. Each model added a new hood, bumpers, body-colored spoilers (front and rear), and restyled taillamps. Only wheel appearance changed for the 1988 model year, when the SE hatchback added a four-spoke leather-wrapped steering wheel.

1988 Nissan Pulsar NX SE.

300ZX — V-6 — Modest restyling was evident both front and rear on the Nissan sports car for 1987, still available with either two-seat or 2 + 2 configuration. Up front, the hood, air dam and bumper were integrated to reduce the frontal area, with auxiliary driving lights moved under the bumper. Taillamps now stretched full-width across the back end. New wheels had a brushed alloy finish (turbos, charcoal finish). A new turbocharger was installed, but didn't affect power output. Each engine gained five horsepower for the 1988 model year, and the Turbo got new alloy wheels as standard equipment, with a bright silver finish. Compression on the Turbo V-6 also got a boost for 1988, to 8.3:1.

I.D. DATA: Nissan's 17-symbol Vehicle Identification Number (VIN) is on the top left of the instrument panel, visible through the windshield. Other identification locations are similar to 1984.

Note: Prices and other data below are for 1987 models.

Model	Body Type & Seating	Engine Type/CID	P.O.E. Price	Weight (lbs.)	Prod. Price
MAXIMA					
U11	4-dr GXE Sedan-5P	V6/181	16099	3040	Note 1
U11	4-dr SE Sedan-5P	V6/181	16099	3120	Note 1
U15	4-dr GXE Wagon-5P	V6/181	16999	3280	Note 1
200SX					
S24	2-dr XE Cpe-4P	I4/120	10849	2645	Note 1
S26	2-dr XE Hatch-4P	I4/120	11199	2734	Note 1
S26	2-dr SE Hatch-4P	V6/181	14499	2976	Note 1
300ZX					
Z14	2-dr Coupe-2P	V6/181	18499	3139	Note 1
Z16	2-dr Coupe-2 + 2P	V6/181	20649	3265	Note 1
Z14	2-dr Turbo Cpe-2P	V6/181	21399	3265	Note 1

Note 1: A total of 1,803,924 Nissan passenger cars were produced during 1987.

Price Note: Maxima SE and 200SX prices shown above are for manual-transmission models; the Maxima SE with automatic cost $16,849; while automatic added $650 to the 200SX prices.

ENGINE DATA: BASE FOUR (200SX XE): Inline, overhead-cam four-cylinder. Cast iron block. **Displacement:** 120.4 cu. in. (1974 cc). **Bore & Stroke:** 3.33 x 3.46 in. (84.6 x 88 mm). **Compression Ratio:** 8.5:1. **Brake Horsepower:** 102 at 5200 rpm. **Torque:** 116 lbs.-ft. at 3200 rpm. Solid valve lifters. Electronic fuel injection.

BASE V-6 (200SX SE, 300ZX): Overhead-cam V-6. Cast iron block. **Displacement:** 180.6 cu. in. (2960 cc). **Bore & Stroke:** 3.43 x 3.27 in. (87.1 x 83 mm). **Compression Ratio:** 9.0:1. **Brake Horsepower:** 160 at 5200 rpm. **Torque:** 174 lbs.-ft. at 4000 rpm. Hydraulic valve lifters. Electronic fuel injection.

BASE V-6 (300ZX Turbo): Same as 300ZX V-6 above, except — **Compression Ratio:** 7.8:1 (8.3:1 in 1988). **Brake Horsepower:** 200 at 5200 rpm. **Torque:** 227 lbs.-ft. at 3600 rpm.

BASE V-6 (Maxima): Same as 300ZX engine above, except — **Brake Horsepower:** 152 at 5200 rpm. **Torque:** 167 lbs.-ft. at 3600 rpm.

CHASSIS DATA: Wheelbase: (Maxima) 100.4 in.; (200SX) 95.5 in.; (300ZX) 91.3 in.; (300ZX 2 + 2) 99.2 in. **Overall Length:** (Maxima sed) 181.5 in.; (Maxima wag) 184.8 in.; (200SX) 174.4 in.; (300ZX) 170.7 in.; (300ZX 2 + 2) 178.5 in. **Height:** (Maxima) 55.1 in.; (200SX) 50.4 in.; (300ZX) 49.7 in. **Width:** (Maxima) 66.5 in.; (200SX) 65.0 in.; (300ZX) 67.9 in. **Front Tread:** (Maxima sed) 57.5 in.; (Maxima wag) 57.3 in.; (200SX) 54.7 in.; (300ZX) 55.7 in. **Rear Tread:** (Maxima sed) 57.1 in.; (Maxima wag) 56.9 in.; (200SX) 56.1 in.; (300ZX) 56.5 in. **Standard Tires:** (Maxima) P195/60HR15; (200SX XE) 195/60R15; (200SX SE) 205/60R15; (300ZX) P215/60R15.

TECHNICAL: Layout: front-engine, rear-drive except (Maxima) front-drive. **Transmission:** five-speed manual except (Maxima GXE) four-speed automatic. **Steering:** rack and pinion. **Suspension (front):** MacPherson struts with coil springs and anti-sway bar. **Suspension (rear):** (Maxima) MacPherson struts and coil springs with anti-sway bar; (200SX and 300ZX) semi-trailing arms, coil springs and anti-sway bar. **Brakes:** power front/rear disc. **Body Construction:** steel unibody.

MAJOR OPTIONS: Four-speed automatic trans.: 300ZX ($650). Air conditioning: 200SX ($770). Power equipment pkg.: 200SX SE ($1800-$2000). Electronics pkg.: Maxima GXE sed ($700); 300ZX ($1400). Power glass sunroof: Maxima GXE ($700). Front air dam: Maxima SE ($255). Leather pkg.: Maxima GXE sed ($700); 300ZX ($1100-$1200). Leather/electronics pkg.: 300ZX ($2350-$2450).

ADDITIONAL MODELS: Nissan joined the 4WD generation in full with a new Pathfinder sport-utility vehicle, and the Pulsar NX got a major restyling for 1987. Nissan also continued to produce a series of pickup trucks with two-wheel and four-wheel drive; the subcompact front-drive Sentra; and the front-drive Stanza series. A Nissan van also joined the lineup during 1987.

Manufacturer: Nissan Motor Co. Ltd., Tokyo, Japan.

Distributor: Nissan Motor Corp. U.S.A., Gardena, California.

1989-90 NISSAN

1989 Nissan Sentra Standard two-door sedan.

MAXIMA — V-6 — Appearance changed dramatically for 1989, with a new aero restyle that removed the former squarish, boxy look from Nissan's top-of-the-line sedan. No more station wagons were produced. The newest edition rode a 104.3-inch wheelbase (four inches longer than before), and measured six inches longer overall. Powerplant remained the 3.0-liter V-6, as in the 300ZX but transverse-mounted here, now rated 160 horsepower. Two trim levels were available: luxury GXE (with four-speed automatic) or sporty SE (with either the automatic or a five-speed gearbox). GXE models came with front disc, rear drum brakes; but the SE had discs all around and the option of an anti-lock system. Also optional: an electronics package that included Sonar Suspension and a new head-up instrument display that projected the speedometer reading into the car's windshield. Few changes appeared for the 1990 model year, except for some modifications in option packages. SE models also had new standard cloth upholstery.

240SX — FOUR — A completely new sport coupe, again offered as either a notchback or hatchback, replaced the former 200SX for 1989. The new model designation indicated its engine size: a 2.4-liter overhead-cam four. Still rear-wheel-drive, the pair rode a longer (97.4-inch) wheelbase and had four-wheel disc brakes (anti-lock braking optional on the SE hatchback). The 12-valve engine (three valves per cylinder) delivered 140 horsepower. No V-6 option was offered. Either a five-speed manual gearbox or four-speed automatic was available. At the rear, a new multi-link independent suspension replaced the former configuration. Optional only on the XE notchback coupe was a head-up instrument display, which projected the speedometer's reading into the lower left corner of the windshield, visible without taking one's eyes away from the road. Little changed for the 1990 model year, apart from making a power antenna standard. In addition, the sport package available only on the SE in 1989 became available for both models in 1990. It included a sport suspension, alloy wheels, cruise control, and front/rear spoilers.

1990 Nissan 300ZX Turbo.

300ZX — V-6 — Arriving in spring 1989 (as an early 1990 model) was an all-new generation of the Z-car, with a massive power boost. The all-new, twin-overhead-cam (24-valve) 3.0-liter V-6 engine, featuring variable valve timing and distributorless ignition, produced 222 horsepower. A few months later, a 2 + 2 edition joined the original two-seater; and for the 1990 model year, a 300ZX Turbo arrived with twin turbochargers churning out 300 horsepower (280 bhp with automatic). The Turbo V-6 had separate intercoolers for each bank (each cooled by both oil and water), Turbos could be identified by intercooler inlets on the front air dam and a rear spoiler, as well as their Z-rated tires. They also had four-wheel steering, whereby the rear wheels turned slightly in the opposite direction from the fronts as the steering wheel moved, but then switched to the same direction for the remainder of the turn. All 300ZX models had anti-lock braking.

I.D. DATA: Nissan's 17-symbol Vehicle Identification Number (VIN) is on the top left of the instrument panel, visible through the windshield. Other identification locations are similar to 1984.

Note: 240SX prices and other data below are for 1989 models; Maxima and 300ZX, for 1990.

Model	Body Type & Seating	Engine Type/CID	P.O.E. Price	Weight (lbs.)	Prod. Total
MAXIMA					
	4-dr GXE Sedan-5P	V6/181	17699	3193	Note 1
	4-dr SE Sedan-5P	V6/181	18749	N/A	Note 1

Model	Body Type & Seating	Engine Type/CID	P.O.E. Price	Weight (lbs.)	Prod. Total
240SX					
	2-dr Cpe-4P	I4/146	12999	2657	Note 1
	2-dr SE Hatch-4P	I4/146	13199	2690	Note 1
300ZX					
	2-dr GS Hatch-2P	V6/181	27300	3219	Note 1
	2-dr GS Hatch-2 + P	V6/181	28500	3313	Note 1
	2-dr Turbo Cpe-2P	V6/181	33000	3414	Note 1

Note 1: A total of 405,147 Nissan passenger cars were sold in the U.S. during 1989.

Price Note: Prices shown are for models with manual shift (except Maxima GXE). Automatic transmissions added $930 to the price of a Maxima SE, $830 to the 240SX, and $800 to the 300ZX.

ENGINE DATA: BASE FOUR (240SX): Inline, overhead-cam four-cylinder (12-valve). Cast iron block. **Displacement:** 146 cu. in. **Bore & Stroke:** 3.50 x 3.78 in. (88.9 x 96 mm). **Compression Ratio:** 8.6:1. **Brake Horsepower:** 140 at 5600 rpm. **Torque:** 152 lbs.-ft. at 4400 rpm. Electronic fuel injection.

BASE V-6 (300ZX): Twin-overhead-cam V-6 (24-valve). Cast iron block and aluminum heads. **Displacement:** 180.6 cu. in. (2960 cc). **Bore & Stroke:** 3.43 x 3.27 in. (87 x 83 mm). **Compression Ratio:** 10.5:1. **Brake Horsepower:** 222 at 6400 rpm. **Torque:** 198 lbs.-ft. at 4800 rpm. Hydraulic valve lifters. Sequential fuel injection.

BASE V-6 (300ZX Turbo): Same as 300ZX V-6 above, except — **Compression Ratio:** 8.5:1. **Brake Horsepower:** 300 at 6400 rpm (280 bhp with automatic). **Torque:** 283 lbs.-ft. at 3600 rpm.

BASE V-6 (Maxima): Overhead-cam V-6. Cast iron block. **Displacement:** 180.6 cu. in. (2960 cc). **Bore & Stroke:** 3.43 x 3.27 in. (87 x 83 mm). **Compression Ratio:** 9.0:1. **Brake Horsepower:** 160 at 5200 rpm. **Torque:** 181 lbs.-ft. at 3200 rpm. Hydraulic valve lifters. Electronic fuel injection.

1990 Infiniti Q45 touring sedan.

CHASSIS DATA: Wheelbase: (Maxima) 104.3 in.; (240SX) 97.4 in.; (300ZX) 96.5 in.; (300ZX 2+2) 101.2 in. **Overall Length:** (Maxima) 187.6 in.; (240SX) 178.0 in.; (300ZX) 169.5 in.; (300ZX 2+2) 178.0 in. **Height:** (Maxima) 55.1 in.; (240SX) 50.8 in.; (300ZX) 49.2-49.4 in. **Width:** (Maxima) 69.3 in.; (240SX) 66.5 in.; (300ZX) 70.5 in.; (300ZX 2+2) 70.9 in. **Front Tread:** (Maxima) 59.4 in.; (240SX) 57.7 in.; (300ZX) 58.9 in. **Rear Tread:** (Maxima) 58.7 in.; (240SX) 57.5 in.; (300ZX) 60.4 in.; (300ZX Turbo) 61.2 in. **Standard Tires:** (Maxima) 195/60R16; (240SX) 195/60R15; (300ZX) 225/50VR16; (300ZX Turbo) 245/45ZR16 at rear.

TECHNICAL: Layout: front-engine, rear-drive except (Maxima) front-drive. **Transmission:** five-speed manual except (Maxima GXE) four-speed automatic. **Steering:** rack and pinion. **Suspension (front):** Maxima, 240SX) MacPherson struts with coil springs and anti-sway bar; (300ZX) multi-link with coil springs and anti-sway bar. **Suspension (rear):** (Maxima) MacPherson struts and coil springs with anti-sway bar; (240SX and 300ZX) multi-link with coil springs and anti-sway bar. **Brakes:** power front/rear disc except (Maxima GXE) front disc, rear drum; (300ZX) front/rear disc with anti-locking. **Body Construction:** steel unibody.

MAJOR OPTIONS: Anti-lock braking: 240SX SE ($1400). Air conditioning: 240SX ($795). Power convenience pkg.: 240SX ($799-$999). Sport pkg.: 240SX SE ($799). Electronics pkg.: 300ZX ($900-$1600). Power glass sunroof: 240SX XE ($800). Removable glass sunroof: 240SX SE ($450). Leather pkg.; 300ZX ($1000-1200). Nissan-Bose auto system: 300ZX GS ($700).

ADDITIONAL MODELS: Nissan continued to produce the Pathfinder sport-utility vehicle, a new Axxess minivan, the Pulsar NX, a series of pickup trucks, the subcompact front-drive Sentra (best seller in the U.S. market for Nissan), and the front-drive Stanza series.

Nissan's luxury Infiniti line entered the U.S. market for 1990, to rival Toyota's Lexus. Two models were offered: an "entry level" M30 coupe with 3.0-liter V-6 engine, and a posh Q45 sedan powered by a 4.5-liter V-8.

Manufacturer: Nissan Motor Co. Ltd., Tokyo, Japan.

Distributor: Nissan Motor Corp. U.S.A., Gardena, California.

DELAGE

Hardly the best remembered of the elegant French motorcars, the Delage has often been submerged by the more popular--and closely related--Delahaye. Although the marque gained considerable recognition in the prewar years, not every enthusiast is aware that it continued to exist for a time in the postwar period (albeit diminished in form and stature). Although less popular with coachbuilders than the Delahaye (also listed in this Catalog), which was produced by the same company, the Delage retained

an excellent reputation for performance. Whereas the pre-war Delage D8-120 was famed for its four-liter inline eight-cylinder engine, postwar examples stuck with six-cylinder power.

Company history reached back to 1905, when Louis Delage and a colleague joined forces to handle engineering work for other companies and, at the same time, produce a motorcar design of their own. The two-seater result was powered by a De Dion-Bouton engine, offered in large (1059 cc) or small (496 cc) displacement. A taste of racing success led to the adoption of a powerplant of in-between dimensions. Beginning in 1909, four-cylinder engines were produced according to Delage's own requirements, half in their own facility, rather than purchased from outside suppliers. Other mechanical components also were built by Delage, but bodies came from elsewhere. Six-cylinder power arrived in 1913. Type CO and then DE/DI-series Delages emerged after World War I, with more than 14,000 of the latter sold through 1928. Racing also became a part of the Delage philosophy in the 1920s, with victories scored in French, Spanish, British and Italian Grand Prix events. In the late 1920s, in fact, Delage's 1.5-liter racer was deemed virtually unbeatable in its class.

At the 1929 Paris Salon there appeared the Delage that would become the best known: the D8, powered by a 4-liter straight eight and carrying coachwork by such body-builders as Chapron and Saoutchik. Designed in the French *grand routier* (touring) tradition, the D8 was handsome and appealing. With the Depression getting underway, however, it could not find enough buyers to earn a profit. More than 4,300 of the D8 and the six-cylinder D6 were sold by 1933, but that wasn't enough to stave off financial ruin. In the aftermath of receivership in 1935, the company was taken over by Delahaye after the intervention of a middleman. Apart from the grille design, the subsequent cars would be, essentially, Delahayes. Thus, the D8-120 that debuted in 1938 simply added two cylinders to the basic Delahaye 135-series six-cylinder engine. In at least one of its body styles, the D8-120 resembled an Auburn boattail speedster, with a boattail back end and outside exhaust pipes. Only the six-cylinder Delage resumed production after World War II, generally with less flamboyant bodies than their striking predecessors. Few were sold, with the last example produced in 1953.

1946-53 DELAGE

1948 Delage coupe.

1948 Delage convertible.

D6 — SIX — Appearance of the postwar Delage was similar to the Delahaye, except for the grille. The Delahaye sales catalog pictured a two-door cabriolet, four-door Berline, and 7/8-passenger limousine that were otherwise difficult to distinguish from the Delahayes on other pages. The Delage grille was upright rectangular in shape, made up of vertical bars, and flanked by inboard headlamps. Small rectangular parking lights stood below the headlamps, with auxiliary running lights separately mounted above the bumper. Some examples had porthole-like trim along the cowl, or thin horizontal strips. The limousine had large rear quarter windows, while the Berline sedan had blank quarters. All were shown with a split windshield. As with Delahayes, however, actual bodies could differ considerably from those in the catalog, being produced by a variety of companies. Although its six-cylinder engine was some 30 cubic inches smaller in displacement than the Delahaye, the two shared most mechanical details, including suspension, transmission (four-speed manual or Cotal electromagnetic), and even the engine's valve arrangement.

I.D. DATA: Not available.

Model	Body Type & Seating	Engine Type/CID	P.O.E. Price	Weight (lbs.)	Prod. Total
D6	2-dr Cabr-4/5P	I6/178	N/A	3697	Note 1
D6	4-dr Berline-4/5P	I6/178	N/A	N/A	Note 1
D6	4-dr Limo-7/8P	I6/178	N/A	N/A	Note 1

Note 1: Separate production totals were not issued for Delage; see Delahaye listing for combined figures.

Price Note: Chassis price at the factory in France (final models) was about $2,716.

Weight Note: Weight shown is for Chapron body, at the curb. Typical weight was about 3,640 pounds, but some topped two tons.

1951 Delage Berline three-liter.

1954 Delage three-liter convertible.

ENGINE DATA: BASE SIX: Inline, overhead-valve six-cylinder. **Displacement:** 178 cu. in. (2920 cc). **Bore & Stroke:** 3.27 x 3.55 in. (83 x 90 mm). **Compression Ratio:** 6.5:1 or 7.5:1. **Brake Horsepower:** 90 at 3800 rpm (100 hp optional). **Torque:** 134 lbs.-ft. at 2300 rpm. Four main bearings. Solid valve lifters. One or three carburetors. 12-volt.

CHASSIS DATA: Wheelbase: 124 in.; (limo) 129.9 in. **Overall Length:** 192-195 in. (typical). **Height:** 61 in. (typical). **Width:** 67 in. **Front Tread:** 54 in. **Rear Tread:** 57 in. **Wheel Type:** disc. **Standard Tires:** 5.50/6.00x17 (6.50x17 optional).

TECHNICAL: Layout: front-engine, rear-drive. **Transmission:** four-speed manual; Cotal electromagnetic (preselector) available. **Steering:** worm and nut. **Suspension (front):** independent; transverse leaf springs. **Suspension (rear):** rigid axle with semi-elliptic leaf springs. **Brakes:** Lockheed hydraulic, front/rear drum (earlier, mechanical). **Body Construction:** aluminum body on pressed-rail steel frame.

MAJOR OPTIONS: Cotal transmission.

PERFORMANCE: Top Speed: 80-84 mph. **Acceleration (0-60 mph):** 17.6 seconds. **Fuel Mileage:** about 15 mpg.

Manufacturer: S.A. des Automobiles Delahaye, Paris, France.

HISTORY: Although Delages were still listed in American buying guides as late as 1955, the last chassis were built in 1953.

DELAHAYE

Emile Delahaye created the first of the French motorcars to bear his name in 1895, displaying it at the Paris Salon. His creations appeared often at racing events of the late 1890s. By 1903, two years after poor health forced Emile's departure, the company was turning out a seven-liter twin-overhead-cam four-cylinder marine engine, one of which set a water speed record. Early production also included both commercial vehicles and passenger cars. Around 1908, two-cylinder Delahaye taxis were dashing around New York City. For most of the period up to World War I, Delahaye was known for four-cylinder models in various sizes, along with such occasional variants as a V-6. By that time, some 1,500 cars per year were emerging from the plant. In the years following that war, Delahaye largely pursued the manufacture of cars aimed at the middle-class.

Designer Jean Francois joined the firm in 1935 to help create the sporting model for which Delahaye became best known: the Type 135, rival to such exotica as Bugatti and Delage. Its 3.5-liter, overhead-valve six-cylinder engine developed 120 horsepower, while customers less avid for speed might be satisfied with a 3.2-liter version and a mere 110 bhp. Delahayes of that day turned away from ordinary manual gearboxes and toward the Wilson preselector; then to the Cotal transmission, which used epicyclic gearing, an electrical gearshift and electromagnetic clutches.

In 1935, Delahaye merged with another famous French firm, the Delage (listed separately in this Catalog). Delahaye never built bodies for its cars, but turned that chore over to a succession of coachbuilders. The basic 135 chassis carried bodywork by Chapron, LeTourner et Marchand, Figoni Falaschi, and--perhaps most familiar in photographs and to enthusiasts--the flamboyantly baroque Sahoutchik bodies.

Six-cylinder power was used for Delahaye sports cars, starting with the 1934 Coupe des Alpes. With a 3.25-liter, overhead-valve engine under its hood and either a four-speed manual or Cotal electric transmission, that one was capable of about 100 mph. In 1936 came the 3.5-liter Competition (also known as 135M), whose engine was rated 105 or 115 bhp. The 135MS, which won the 1938 Le Mans event, reached up to 130 bhp at 4200 rpm. Type 145 used the same chassis as the 135 but a 4.5-liter V-12 engine, rated about 250 horsepower, capable of both long-distance and Grand Prix racing. Type 165 was the roadgoing version of the 145, with a detuned V-12 engine. Following an appearance at the 1938 Paris Salon, only a handful of V-12 chassis were built (and no eights at all).

In 1939, the British Auto Racing Club staged a race to see what was the fastest European car, at the Brooklands track and also over a mountain road. A Delahaye handled

Brooklands at almost 120 mph, finishing second to Alfa; but Delahaye won through the mountains.

Type 135 was back again after the Second World War, joined by a 4.5-liter Type 175 in 1948. With hydraulic brakes at the ready, its engine delivered as much as 185 horsepower. Other models included the longer-wheelbase 178/180, and for a short time the smaller Type 134 (with 2.2-liter engine). The left-hand-drive Type 180 Berline limousine actually was targeted at American customers.

A more modern body went on the Type 235 in 1951, with a 152-horsepower, 3.5-liter six providing the power for speeds of 100 mph and beyond. That was the only model available through the company's final years, replacing the 135. Coachwork was done by Antem and Le-Tourner et Marchand. As before, Delahaye wasn't only a producer of automobile chassis, but delivered a line of trucks and even a substantial number of jeep-like vehicles in the early 1950s. Delahaye passenger cars faded away in 1954 as the firm was taken over by Hotchkiss, and the trucks lasted only until 1956. As with many expensive makes of that early postwar era in Europe, part of the reason for its failure was cited as rising taxes.

1947-1950 DELAHAYE

1947 Delahaye.

135/135M/135MS/148L — SIX — Most of the Delahaye chassis built in the years immediately after World War II carried the 3557-cc six-cylinder engine, on essentially the same chassis as in the prewar 135-series. A four-speed manual gearbox was available, but quite a few used the Cotal unit instead. The Cotal transmission was an electromagnetic gearbox with frictional fluid clutch, which offered a claimed 99.5 percent efficiency in 4th gear (96.5 percent in lower gears). A small lever in a notched gated at the left of the steering column selected the gears, much like the "Electric Hand" used by Hudson in the 1930s, and in the 1936-37 Cord. A separate gearbox, operated by a floor lever, provided reverse gearing. Use of the clutch pedal was essential only when starting out and stopping. Bodies came from a variety of coachbuilders, including Henri Chapron, Figoni et Falaschi, and others. Type 135 was the basic model with single carburetor; suffix 'M' indicated a trio of Solex carburetors; and suffix 'MS' meant a competition model with the triple-carb engine. For that reason, horsepower ratings ranged from 95 to 130.

Because bodies came from a variety of coachbuilders, appearances varied. A close-coupled 135M coupe by Guillere, for instance, done in 1947, had an upright profile and a tall upright rounded mesh grille that reached below the bumper, with single vertical divider bar; plus separately-mounted headlamps and a rear-mounted spare tire. The upright tapered oval grille of the Figoni et Falaschi convertible coupe was made up of vertical bars, flanked by inboard, low-mounted built-in Marchal headlamps and, just below and to the side, tiny parking lights. Its fenders were devoid of lights. The striking Chapron-built convertible, featured in many photos of the marque, was an amalgation of startling curves (including the door edges), with enclosed front and rear wheels and broad brightwork at the fender fronts.

Even though such a variety of body types was available from other suppliers, pictures in the later Delahaye sales catalog displayed coupes, cabriolets and Berline four-door sedans of identical front-end appearance. Each had an upright tapered oval grille made up of horizontal bars, with a center vertical bar. Inboard headlamps were built-in, alongside the grille, with running lamps below and small round parking lights low on the fender tips. Type 135M was illustrated as a cabriolet (also available as a fixed-head coupe), while the 135MS was shown as a fixed-head (solid-top) coupe but also offered as a cabriolet. Type 148L was a Berline sedan. All had nearly full wheel openings, front and rear. Type 135M was illustrated with a flat (one-piece) windshield; other models with two split windshield. Typical standard equipment included Marchal headlamps, separate running lights, a 170-km/hr speedometer, 4000- or 4500-tachometer, mechanical clock, electric windshield wipers, door storage pockets, and dashboard-mounted rear-view mirror.

1948 Delahaye 3.5-liter Type 135 four-passenger drophead coupe. (Christie's)

175/178/180 — SIX — A larger (4.5-liter) six-cylinder engine powered the 175 series, introduced in 1948. Instead of the mechanical brakes that were standard on the 135 series, these examples had hydraulic brakes. Horsepower ratings ran between 140 and 185, depending on the compression ratio and carburetion setup. A Dubonnet front suspension consisted of enclosed coil springs, while a De Dion axle with semi-elliptic leaf springs brought up the rear. Appearance, as shown in the Delahaye sales catalog, was similar to the 135 series (above), even though various body types were available. Type 175 was displayed as a cabriolet with enclosed rear wheels, but also offered as a solid-top coupe. Type 178 was a four-door Berline sedan with rear-hinged ("suicide") front doors but front-hinged back doors, and open rear wheels. Type 180 limousines were similar, but added rear quarter windows and rear fender skirting. Each was illustrated with a split (two-piece) windshield.

134 — FOUR — A four-cylinder Delahaye also was produced early in the postwar period.

Note: Factory literature sometimes used a space between the basic model number and its letter suffix, if any (e.g., 135M).

I.D. DATA: Not available.

Model	Body Type & Seating	Engine Type/CID	P.O.E. Price	Weight (lbs.)	Prod. Total
134	2-dr Conv Cpe	I4/131	N/A	N/A	Note 1
135	2-dr Cabr/Cpe-4/5P	I6/217	N/A	N/A	Note 1
135M	2-dr Cabr/Cpe-4/5P	I6/217	N/A	N/A	Note 1
135MS	2-dr Cabr/Cpe-4/5P	I6/217	5000	3086	Note 1
148L	4-dr Berline-5/6P	I6/217	N/A	N/A	Note 1
175	2-dr Cabr/Cpe-5/6P	I6/272	N/A	N/A	Note 1
178	4-dr Berline-6P	I6/272	N/A	N/A	Note 1
180	4-dr Limo-8P	I6/272	N/A	N/A	Note 1

Note 1: A total of 483 Delahayes and Delages were sold (worldwide) during 1950. Roughly 200 of the 135 series were thought to be produced between 1935 and 1950. **Price Note:** Prices varied widely depending on the body; figure shown was quoted in 1951, but a Chapron fixed-head coupe, in shortened wheelbase, was said to cost over $15,000 in the U.S.

Weight Note: Weights also varied widely, though the company instruction book quoted a figure of 2,688 pounds for a complete car. A Pennock convertible from 1949 actually tipped the scales at 3,740 pounds, ready to roll.

Body Note: All Delahayes had bodies from other coachbuilders, so body types varied. Two-door models came as closed coupe or cabriolet.

ENGINE DATA: BASE FOUR (134): Inline, overhead-valve four-cylinder. **Displacement:** 131.0 cu. in. **Bore & Stroke:** 3.15 x 4.21 in. **Brake Horsepower:** 55. Five main bearings. Solid valve lifters.

BASE SIX (135): Inline, overhead-valve six-cylinder. **Displacement:** 217.0 cu. in. (3557 cc). **Bore & Stroke:** 3.30 x 4.21 in. (84 x 107 mm). **Compression Ratio:** (135M) 7.1:1. **Brake Horsepower:** 95 or 115. Four main bearings. Solid valve lifters. One carburetor except (135M) three Solex 40 FIL downdraft carburetors. 12-volt electrical. Coil ignition.

BASE SIX (135MS): Same as above, except — **Compression Ratio:** 8.3:1. **Brake Horsepower:** 130 at 3800 rpm (160 hp for racing).

BASE SIX (175/178/180): Inline, overhead-valve six-cylinder. **Displacement:** 271.6 cu. in. (4453 cc). **Bore & Stroke:** 3.70 x 4.21 in. (94 x 107 mm). **Brake Horsepower:** 125-185. Seven main bearings. Solid valve lifters. One or three carburetors. 12-volt electrical.

CHASSIS DATA: Wheelbase: (134/135/175) 116 in.; (148/178) 124 in.; (180) 131 in. **Overall Length:** (135) 178.2 in. **Height:** (135) 60.5 in. **Width:** (135) 69 in. **Front Tread:** (135) 53.8 in.; (175/178/180) 56.5 in. **Rear Tread:** (134) 57.0 in.; (135) 58.1 in.; (175/178/180) 59.6 in. **Wheel Type:** steel disc, Rudge knock-off, or center-lock wire. **Standard Tires:** (134) 5.50x17; (135) 6.00x17; (148/175/178) 6.00x17; (180) 7.00x18.

Note: Dimensions above are typical, since custom-built bodies varied considerably.

TECHNICAL: Layout: front-engine, rear-drive. **Transmission:** four-speed manual (synchro) or optional Cotal electric; column gearshift lever. Overall gear ratios (135M/MS with Cotal): (1st) 11.83:1; (2nd) 7.59:1; (3rd) 5.60:1; (4th) 3.42:1. **Standard Final Drive Ratio:** (135) 3.42:1. **Steering:** (135) worm and nut. **Suspension (front):** (135) independent, transverse leaf spring and control arms; (175/178/180) independent, Dubonnet with enclosed coil springs; **Suspension (rear):** (135) rigid axle with semi-elliptic leaf springs; (175/178/180) semi-elliptical leaf springs with De Dion axle. **Brakes:** (135) Bendix servo-mechanical, front/rear drum; (175/178/180) hydraulic, front/rear drum. **Body Construction:** separate body and frame.

MAJOR OPTIONS: Cotal transmission.

PERFORMANCE: Top Speed: (135M Cabr) 86 mph; (135MS Cabr) 93-105 mph.; (175) 95-102 mph; (175S) 106 mph; (178/180) 86-90 mph. **Acceleration (0-60 mph):** (135MS) 13.7 sec. (0-50 in 11 sec.). **Fuel Mileage:** (135MS) 22-24 mpg.

Manufacturer: Automobiles Delahaye, 10 Rue Du Banquier, Paris, France.

HISTORY: Production of the four-cylinder Type 134 ceased in 1948. Sales slipped to just 77 cars in 1951 (including those of the related Delage), as the Type 235 was introduced and the 4.5-liter versions disappeared; see next listing.

The number of Delahayes imported into the U.S. was small enough that specific examples were sometimes featured in American magazines. A Paris Salon model built in 1946 and later featured in *Motor Trend* was powered by 3.3-liter 201.4 cid competition six-cylinder engine, rated 140 bhp. Its top speed approached 110 mph. A low (48-inch tall) fixed-head two-seater coupe built by Chapron in 1950, on a shorter 103-inch wheelbase, was reminiscent of the prewar Type 57 Bugatti. Profiled in *Motorsport* magazine, the dramatic coupe, with vast hood length, rakishly rounded "suicide" doors, full rounded wheel openings over wire wheels, and 200-horsepower V-12 engine, was sold in the eastern U.S. and claimed to be capable of 120 mph. Other custom Delahayes, such as the four-seat 135M convertible by Pennock (imported by D. Cameron Peck of Chicago in 1949) were not quite as dramatic in appearance, as revealed in that car's profile in *Modern Motor Car*. Each, however, was undeniably elegant.

1951 Delahaye limousine 148L.

135/135M/135MS/148L — SIX — Production of the 135/148 series chassis continued, but was eclipsed by the modernized version known as Type 235.

1952 Delahaye 235 two-door drophead coupe.

235 — SIX — For its final years, Delahaye focused on one chassis/engine design, varying only in wheelbase and power. As before, the Delahaye company produced only the chassis. Elegant custom bodies were done by such firms as Chapron, LeTourner & Marchand, and Vanden Plas. The 3.5-liter engine was similar to that of the long-established 135M and 135MS (prewar and postwar), with higher compression, three carburetors and a special cam. Performance was said to rival that of the former 4.5-liter models. A single-carburetor version also was available.

More modern (and less flamboyant body styles were featured, with modification most evident in the grille and front end of such examples as the late Type 235 Chapron sports convertible. Wide oval grilles had a broad crosshatch pattern that consisted of only three horizontal bars and four vertical bars, plus a vertical center bar extending to the surround molding. Headlamps were in the conventional 1950s position, high on the fender tips. Large round parking lights went below the headlamps. Porthole-like trim elements stood at the cowl. Other examples had a large oval grille with three horizontal bars and a single center vertical bar. Two-tone color schemes could make the front and rear fenders a different color from body.

1953 Delahaye 253M Chapron.

I.D. DATA: Not available.

Model	Body Type & Seating	Engine Type/CID	P.O.E. Price	Weight (lbs.)	Prod. Total
TYPE 135/148					
135	2-dr Cabr/Cpe-4/5P	I6/217	N/A	N/A	Note 1

Model	Body Type & Seating	Engine Type/CID	P.O.E. Price	Weight (lbs.)	Prod. Total
135M	2-dr Cabr/Cpe-4/5P	I6/217	N/A	N/A	Note 1
135M	4-dr Spts Sed-4/5P	I6/217	N/A	3600	Note 1
135MS	2-dr Spts Sed-4/5P	I6/217	N/A	3400	Note 1
148L	4-dr Berline-5/6P	I6/217	N/A	3827	Note 1

TYPE 235

235	2-dr Cabr/Cpe-4/5P	I6/217	N/A	3276	Note 1

Note 1: A total of 77 Delahayes and Delages were sold (worldwide) during 1951, but only three in 1953; so the continued availability of all models shown above was largely theoretical.

Body Note: All Delahayes had bodies from other coachbuilders, so body types varied. Two-door models came as closed coupe or cabriolet.

Price Note: Base price at the factory in 1953 was $7100.

1954 Delahaye 235M two-door drophead coupe. (Coys of Kensington)

1954 Delahaye 235.

ENGINE DATA: BASE SIX (135, 148): Inline, overhead-valve six-cylinder. **Displacement:** 217.0 cu. in. (3557 cc). **Bore & Stroke:** 3.31 x 4.21 in. (84 x 107 mm). **Compression Ratio:** (135M) 7.58:1. **Brake Horsepower:** 90-94 at 3200 rpm; (135M) 115 at 3300. **Torque:** 174 lbs.-ft. at 2200 rpm. Four main bearings. Solid valve lifters. One carburetor except (135M) three Solex downdraft carburetors. 12-volt electrical. Coil ignition.

BASE SIX (135MS): Same as above, except — **Compression Ratio:** 8.0:1. **Brake Horsepower:** 130 at 4000 rpm.

BASE SIX (235): Same as above, except — **Compression Ratio:** 8.0:1. **Brake Horsepower:** 152 at 4200 rpm.

CHASSIS DATA: Wheelbase: (135/235) 116 in.; (148) 124 in. **Overall Length:** (135) 178.2 in.; (235) 187.5 in. **Height:** 59-63 in. **Width:** (135) 69 in. **Rear Tread:** 54 in. **Front Tread:** 57.8 in. **Wheel Type:** steel disc or center-lock wire. **Standard Tires:** 6.00x17.

Note: Dimensions above are typical; custom-built bodies varied considerably.

TECHNICAL: Layout: front-engine, rear-drive. **Transmission:** four-speed manual (synchro) or optional Cotal electric; column gearshift lever. Overall gear ratios (135MS): (1st) 11.83:1; (2nd) 7.59:1; (3rd) 5.60:1; (4th) 3.42:1. **Standard Final Drive Ratio:** (135) 3.42:1; (235) 4.17:1. **Steering:** (135) worm and nut. **Suspension (front):** independent; transverse leaf springs and control arms. **Suspension (rear):** rigid axle with semi-elliptic leaf springs. **Brakes:** Bendix or Lockheed hydraulic, front/rear drum. **Body Construction:** separate aluminum body on pressed rail steel frame.

MAJOR OPTIONS: Cotal transmission.

PERFORMANCE: Top Speed: (135) 88 mph; (135M) 93 mph; (135MS) 99 mph; (235) 110-115 mph. **Acceleration (0-60 mph):** (235) 11.5 seconds. **Fuel Mileage:** 13-14 mpg.

Manufacturer: S.A. des Automobiles Delahaye, Paris, France.

HISTORY: Last of the Delahaye passenger cars was produced in 1954.

180

DELLOW

Fanciers of the traditional in British racing sports cars in the 1950s could skip the Triumphs and MGs and turn instead to the little-known Dellow. Evolved from a series of 1172-cc "trials" racers dating back to 1947, the production Dellows performed as nicely on the road as on the hillclimb or track, able to travel normally at 70-mph speeds. The car's name derived from the company owners, Dellingpole and Lowe. An A-shaped tubular chassis on the trials car used quarter-elliptic leaf springs for the suspension, later switching to coil springs. Bodies were made of alloy, and a two-way handbrake controlled each rear wheel independently. Early Dellow buyers couldn't simply show up and make a purchase, but had to provide their own parts, which were then reconditioned. By 1950, components were coming off Ford shelves. A Wade supercharger became a desirable option. In 1952, a longer four-seater Mark III version was offered. Two years later came a Mark V, which used coil springs up front and served as the final true trials machine. Except for the Mark IV, which didn't go beyond prototype form, all Dellows were powered by a Ford Ten (or 100E) engine. By 1956, the company name had changed from Dellow Motors Ltd. to Dellow Engineering Ltd. The final model, a Mark VI, used a full-width fiberglass body with split windshield and all-weather protection. The marque disappeared in 1959, a victim in part of a desire to produce a more sophisticated automobile (namely, the Mark VI) rather than stick to the original scheme.

1949-50 DELLOW

1950 Dellow.

Mk I — FOUR — The first Dellow two-seater, in production for not much more than a year, rode an 84-inch wheelbase and carried a 31-horsepower engine. Early Dellows had a definite prewar appearance, with separate headlamps and an upright grille split into two oval side-by-side sections. Official export to the U.S. did not begin until 1954.

I.D. DATA: Not available.

Model	Body Type & Seating	Engine Type/CID	P.O.E. Price	Weight (lbs.)	Prod. Total
Mk I	2-dr Roadster-2P	I4/71	N/A	1540	N/A

ENGINE DATA: BASE FOUR: Inline, L-head four-cylinder. **Displacement:** 71.55 cu. in. (1172 cc). **Bore & Stroke:** 2.50 x 3.64 in. (63.5 x 92.5 mm). **Compression Ratio:** 6.16:1 to 7.6:1. **Brake Horsepower:** 31 at 4200 rpm. Solid valve lifters. SU carburetor.

CHASSIS DATA: Wheelbase: 84 in. **Overall Length:** 136 in. **Width:** 52.5 or 55 in. **Front Tread:** 45.0 in. **Rear Tread:** 45.0 in. **Wheel Type:** disc. **Standard Tires:** 4.50x17.

TECHNICAL: Layout: front-engine, rear-drive. **Transmission:** three-speed manual. **Standard Final Drive Ratio:** 5.5:1. **Suspension (front):** transverse leaf spring. **Suspension (rear):** quarter-elliptic leaf springs. **Brakes:** mechanical, front/rear drum. **Body Construction:** aluminum alloy body on tubular frame.

Manufacturer: Dellow Motors Ltd., Birmingham, England.

1951-53 DELLOW

1951 Dellow Mark I open sports two-seater. (Christie's)

Mk II — FOUR — The "A" version of the Mk II Dellow debuted in mid-1951, followed by a "B" edition in 1953. Appearance was similar to the Mk I, which was discontinued as its successor arrived, but the new wheelbase was slightly shorter and 16-inch tires were used. The rear suspension now consisted of coil springs. *The Motor* (in England) described a Mark II Dellow as a "sporting marque with an excellent competition record."

Mk III — FOUR — Dellow also introduced a four-seater variant, on a longer (94.5-inch) wheelbase, with bodywork by Radpanels Ltd. Other specifications were similar to the two-seater.

I.D. DATA: Not available.

Model	Body Type & Seating	Engine Type/CID	P.O.E. Price	Weight (lbs.)	Prod. Total
Mk II	2-dr Roadster-2P	I4/71	N/A	1290	N/A
Mk III	2-dr Roadster-4P	I4/71	N/A	1400	N/A

Price Note: Prices in England in 1953 were 448 pounds (Sterling) for the Mark II and 498 for the Mark III.

ENGINE DATA: BASE FOUR: Inline, L-head four-cylinder. **Displacement:** 71.55 cu. in. (1172 cc). **Bore & Stroke:** 2.50 x 3.64 in. (63.5 x 92.5 mm). **Compression Ratio:** 6.16:1 to 7.6:1. **Brake Horsepower:** 31 at 4200 rpm. Solid valve lifters. SU or Zenith carburetor.

CHASSIS DATA: Wheelbase: (II) 82.5 in.; (III) 94.5 in. **Overall Length:** (II) 136 in.; (III) 150 in. **Height:** 52.5 in. **Width:** (II) 52.5 in.; (III) 55/57 in. **Front Tread:** 45.0 in. **Rear Tread:** 45.0 in. **Wheel Type:** disc. **Standard Tires:** 5.00x16 or 5.50x16.

TECHNICAL: Layout: front-engine, rear-drive. **Transmission:** three-speed manual. **Standard Final Drive Ratio:** 5.5:1. **Suspension (front):** transverse leaf spring. **Suspension (rear):** coil springs. **Brakes:** Girling mechanical, front/rear drum. **Body Construction:** aluminum alloy body on tubular frame.

MAJOR OPTIONS: Marshall-Nordec supercharger.

Manufacturer: Dellow Motors Ltd., Alvechurch, Birmingham, England.

HISTORY: Dellow also produced a Mark IV prototype powered by a larger (1508-cc) engine at this time.

1954-55 DELLOW

1954 Dellow Mark II sports.

Mk IIC — FOUR — The next version of the original design carried a stronger engine but otherwise looked similar to the Mk IIA/B. The first Mk II Dellow arrived in America during 1954, according to *Motorsport* magazine, winding up in the hands of an employee of Republic Aviation. "Dellow is a driver's car," they added, noting that it delivered "somewhat the same sort of enjoyment that the first ride in the old MG-TC provided," while "handling and roadability was much like the Morgan... Cornering at quite high speeds is phenomenally flat and precise." " Unlike the early British models, most exports had the same tire sizes at front and rear, as well as left-hand drive. The entire hood lifted off the car, while the flat windshield could fold down. Standard equipment included two spare tires that mounted on the back end. Leather upholstery was used for the non-adjustable seats, which had a bench-type backrest. Among the available colors was British Racing Green.

Mk III — FOUR — The four-seater continued in production into 1954; see previous listing for details.

Mk V — FOUR — While the original Dellow carried on with an upright grille, this new edition was much more rounded in appearance, with an oval grille (made up of horizontal bars) at its nose. Faired-in front fenders that appeared almost cycle-style when viewed from the front added to its race-car look. Headlamps again were separately mounted, and the squarish doors were hinged at the front. The rear end now extended backward almost horizontally, however, and was thus unable to carry a pair of spare tires like its vertical-rear predecessor. Under the hood, Mk V Dellows carried the more potent 36-horsepower version of the British Ford engine, with 7.6:1 compression. "It's really a man's car," declared *Motor Trend*, one that "doesn't give a hoot for styling trophies." Summarizing its good points, the magazine added that a Dellow is "really a small hairy beast that is at its best charging thru woods, over hills, and across swamps." As for its size and amenities, "driving a Dellow is more like wearing a car than sitting inside one." A vast choice of body colors was available. Semi-bucket seats had a solid (single) backrest and were non-adjustable, but upholstered in leather. Turn signal lights were standard. Mechanical brakes were used, along with a three-speed floor gearshift. Unlike the Mk II models, this one's instrument panel held a tachometer along with the speedometer. The canvas top held a plexiglas wraparound back window.

I.D. DATA: Not available.

Model	Body Type & Seating	Engine Type/CID	P.O.E. Price	Weight (lbs.)	Prod. Total
Mk IIC	2-dr Roadster-2P	I4/71	1650	1288	N/A
Mk V	2-dr Roadster-2P	I4/71	2050	1300	N/A

ENGINE DATA: BASE FOUR: Inline, L-head four-cylinder. **Displacement:** 71.55 cu. in. (1172 cc). **Bore & Stroke:** 2.50 x 3.64 in. (63.5 x 92.5 mm). **Compression Ratio:** 7.0:1 (7.6:1 and 7.8:1 optional). Mk V engine had 7.6:1 compression. **Brake Horsepower:** 31 at 4200 rpm (or 36 at 4400). Solid valve lifters. Two SU semi-downdraft carburetors.

CHASSIS DATA: Wheelbase: (Mk II) 82.5 in.; (Mk V) 84 in. **Overall Length:** (Mk II) 136 in.; (Mk V) 140 in. **Height:** (Mk II) 51 in.; (Mk V) 54 in. **Width:** (Mk II) 55 in.; (Mk V) 54 in. **Front Tread:** 45.0 in. **Rear Tread:** 45.0 in. **Wheel Type:** disc. **Standard Tires:** (Mk II) (front) 4.75x16; (rear) 4.75 or 5.50x16.

TECHNICAL: Layout: front-engine, rear-drive. **Transmission:** three-speed manual. **Standard Final Drive Ratio:** (Mk II) 5.5:1; (Mk V) 4.72:1 or 5.5:1. **Steering: Suspension (front):** (Mk II) transverse leaf spring with stabilizer bar; (Mk V) coil springs. **Suspension (rear):** coil springs with stabilizer bar. **Brakes:** mechanical, front/rear drum. **Body Construction:** aluminum alloy body on tubular frame. **Fuel Tank:** (Mk II) 18 U.S. gallons.

MAJOR OPTIONS: Roots-type supercharger (with single SU carburetor).

PERFORMANCE: Top Speed: (Mk II) 70-80 mph; (Mk V) 89 mph. **Acceleration (0-60 mph):** (Mk II) 13.7 seconds; (Mk V) 0-50 mph in 13.3 seconds. **Fuel Mileage:** (Mk II) 30-35 mpg.

PRODUCTION/SALES: From mid-1955 to mid-1956, about a dozen Dellows were brought into the U.S.

Manufacturer: Dellow Motors Ltd., Alvechurch, Birmingham, England.

Distributor: London Motors, Edgemere, Long Island, New York.

HISTORY: Introduced: (Mk IIC) mid-1954; (Mk V) mid-1954. One of the first Dellows imported to the U.S., driven by Alec Tarpinian (its importer) came close to winning the 1.5-litre class hillclimb at Manchester, New Hampshire.

1956-59 DELLOW

Mk IIC — FOUR — Production continued into 1957; see previous listing for details. U.S. price in 1957 was $1900.

Mk IIE — FOUR — The final version of the original Dellow design changed little in appearance. The 36-horsepower four-cylinder engine was standard.

Mk V — FOUR — Production continued as before; see previous listing for details. U.S. price in 1957 was $2135.

Mk VI — FOUR — A full-width body was used on the last Dellow roadster, which rode much smaller (13-inch) wheels than its predecessors on a longer wheelbase. Both modified (Stage 1) and unmodified Ford four-cylinder engines were offered.

I.D. DATA: Not available.

Model	Body Type & Seating	Engine Type/CID	P.O.E. Price	Weight (lbs.)	Prod. Total
Mk IIE	2-dr Roadster-2P	I4/71	N/A	N/A	N/A
Mk VI	2-dr Roadster-2P	I4/71	2050	1300	N/A

ENGINE DATA: BASE FOUR: Inline, L-head four-cylinder. **Displacement:** 71.55 cu. in. (1172 cc). **Bore & Stroke:** 2.50 x 3.64 in. (63.5 x 92.5 mm). **Compression Ratio:** 7.0:1. **Brake Horsepower:** 36 at 4400 rpm. Solid valve lifters. Solex or SU carburetors.

CHASSIS DATA: Wheelbase: (Mk IIE) 85 in.; (Mk VI) 90 in. **Overall Length:** (Mk IIE) 136 in.; (Mk VI) 142 in. **Width:** (Mk IIE) 55 in.; (Mk VI) 57 in. **Front Tread:** (Mk IIE) 45.0 in.; (Mk VI) 47.5 in. **Rear Tread:** (Mk IIE) 45.0 in. (Mk V) 47.5 in. **Standard Tires:** (Mk IIE) (front) 4.75x16; (rear) 4.75 or 5.50x16. (Mk VI) 5.90x13.

TECHNICAL: Layout: front-engine, rear-drive. **Transmission:** three-speed manual. **Standard Final Drive Ratio:** (Mk VI) 4.429:1. **Steering: Suspension (front):** (Mk IIE) transverse leaf spring with stabilizer bar; (Mk VI) coil springs. **Suspension (rear):** (Mk IIE) coil springs with stabilizer bar; (Mk VI) semi-elliptic leaf springs. **Brakes:** mechanical, front/rear drum. **Body Construction:** aluminum alloy body on tubular frame.

Manufacturer: Dellow Engineering Ltd., Alvechurch, Birmingham, England.

Distributor: London Motors, Edgemere, Long Island, New York; and Light Car Motors, Los Angeles, California.

DELOREAN

Built in Northern Ireland, the highly-publicized (but short-lived) stainless-steel DeLorean sports car was the brainchild of one man, who'd established an impressive track record in the American auto industry. John Z. DeLorean, the son of a Detroit autoworker, attended Lawrence Institute of Technology and received a degree in mechanical engineering. In 1952, after earning his masters degree in automotive engineering from the Chrysler Institute, DeLorean went to work as Packard's head of research and development. His brilliant career at General Motors began four years later, starting in Pontiac's advanced engineering department. DeLorean played major roles in creating the innovative 1961 Tempest and its overhead-cam six-cylinder engine, as well as the first Pontiac GTO.

DeLorean went on to become general manager of Pontiac and brought such cars as the Firebird, Trans Am, and 1969 Grand Prix into existence. In 1969, as general manager of Chevrolet, he turned to development of the Vega subcompact. Three years later, he was promoted to vice-president in charge of GM's domestic car and truck group. Nevertheless, DeLorean left GM in 1973 and set out to build his own company—and an elite car bearing his personal stamp. Early in 1974, he formed the John Z. DeLorean Corporation, followed by the DeLorean Motor Car Company as a subsidiary. Then began a series of complicated financial maneuvers to raise capital, and to establish production capability. DeLorean attracted millions of dollars from investors, including comedian Johnny Carson. The search for a factory location took DeLorean to Western Europe, Puerto Rico and finally, in 1978, to Northern Ireland. There, the British Government offered to provide loans and tax breaks, in hopes of generating jobs in an impoverished section of West Belfast.

Initial conceptions began to evolve around 1973. A non-operable mockup of the DMC-12 was produced by Giorgetto Giugiaro's Ital Design studios in July 1975. The first running prototype appeared in October 1976, powered by a 2.8-liter Citroen four that quickly proved unacceptable. The production 2.8-liter overhead-cam V-6 had been used successfully in Peugeots, Renaults and Volvos. Delivery of production models was promised for June 1979, amid ample publicity. Not until April 1981, however, was production actually underway. Most of the 345 U.S. dealers had no cars to sell until July of that year. Sticker price for the 1981 version rose a bit above the $25,000 projection and, by 1982, climbed close to $30,000. Critics faulted both the design and performance. With sales sluggish, dealer asking prices soon fell. The 1982 model incorporated a number of significant detail improvements.

Weak sales weren't the only problem. Before long, a tangled web of fancy corporate footwork came to light. During winter 1982, the British House of Commons became concerned about protecting its $138 million investment. Investigation focused on misdealings and the company was placed in receivership. A search for a takeover buyer proved unsuccessful. On October 18, 1982, the British Government announced it would close the business. According to the Receiver's Office, in addition to its own debt, over $70 million was owed to other creditors. Mere hours later, John DeLorean was arrested by U.S. Justice Department and F.B.I. officers at the Los Angeles airport, charged with nine counts of racketeering and drug trafficking. According to the Justice Department, the 57-year-old automaker—in an effort to salvage his foundering company—had become involved in a scheme to import 220 pounds of cocaine.

After release on $10 million bond, DeLorean was arraigned on November 8, 1982. He pleaded not guilty, with his attorneys reporting they would seek dismissal on grounds that the wide publicity surrounding the case was attributable to misconduct by government officials. DeLorean was eventually found innocent of drug charges and, after a four-year series of court actions, acquitted in December 1986 of criminal fraud charges. Nevertheless, he agreed to pay creditors $9.4 million (far less than the $80 million claim made by the British government).

Note: Because DeLoreans were often perceived as American cars, ignoring their Irish manufacture, this make is also listed in the *Standard Catalog of American Cars*.

1981-82 DELOREAN

DeLoreans were built in 1981 and 1982.

SERIES DMC-12 — V-6 — Born of high hopes, raised amid controversy, the sleek, sophisticated sports/luxury car featured a slim front-end treatment, gullwing doors, fastback roof, and kammback tail. Former Pontiac engineer Bill Collins developed the unique chassis, which used independent front and rear suspension and a full-length backbone frame that bolted directly to the body. The overhead-cam, 2850-cc Vv6 engine with Bosch fuel injection was mounted at the rear, with power transmitted via a Renault five-speed manual transaxle. An automatic transmission was optional. Coachwork was fiberglass-reinforced plastic, clad in stainless steel.

1982 DeLorean DMC 12 gullwing sports coupe. (Christie's)

Styling highlights also included quad rectangular quartz headlamps, an integral front spoiler, and turbine wheels. Lavish interior appointments centered on glove leather upholstery. The original, projected list price was set at $25,000, but that rose by the time the car appeared. A five-year, 50,000-mile warranty came with each DeLorean sold. Standard equipment included counterbalanced gullwing doors, air conditioning, power windows, adjustable steering wheel, multi-speaker stereo system, electric door mirrors, tinted glass, and an electric locking system.

DeLoreans drew attention wherever they were seen, but problems surfaced quickly. Early troubles included electrical system failures, creaking of fiberglass body panels (under the stainless steel outer skin), loose-fitting control knobs and buttons, and a body that was nearly impossible to keep clean. Although the company claimed a 0-60 mph acceleration time of 8.5 seconds, and 130 mph top speed, others have declared DeLorean's performance "sluggish" and "uninspiring."

I.D. DATA: Serial number range was SCED-T26-T8-BD000500 to SCED-T26-T8-DD02014.

Model	Body Type & Seating	Engine Type/CID	P.O.E. Price	Weight (lbs.)	Prod. Total
DELOREAN					
DMC-12	2-dr Spt Cpe-2P	V6/174	26175	2712	Note 1

Note 1: A total of 7,409 DeLoreans were produced in 1981, and 1,333 in 1982. Approximately 4,000 were shipped to the United States during two years of production.

Price Note: The list price rose to $29,825 for 1982. However, sluggish sales prompted reduction in dealer asking prices to about $18,500 for 1981 models, and $21,900 for 1982s.

ENGINE DATA: BASE V-6 (Peugeot/Renault/Volvo): 90-degree, dual-overhead-camshaft V-6. Aluminum block and heads. **Displacement:** 174 cu. in. (2850 cc). **Bore & Stroke:** 3.58 x 2.87 in. (91 x 73 mm). **Compression Ratio:** 8.8:1. **Brake Horsepower:** 130 (SAE) at 5500 rpm. **Torque:** 166 lbs.-ft. at 3000 rpm. Four main bearings. Bosch K-Jetronic fuel injection.

CHASSIS DATA: Wheelbase: 95 in. **Overall Length:** 168 in. **Height:** 46 in. **Width:** 73 in. **Front Tread:** 65.4 in. **Rear Tread:** 62.7 in. **Wheel Type:** (front) 6x14; (rear) 8x15. **Standard Tires:** Goodyear NCT SBR; (front) 195/60HR14; (rear) 235/60HR15.

TECHNICAL: Layout: rear-engine, rear-drive. **Transmission:** five-speed manual (all synchro). Gear ratios: (1st) 3.36:1; (2nd) 2.06:1; (3rd) 1.38:1; (4th) 1.06:1; (5th) 0.82:1; (rev) 3.18:1. Three-speed automatic transmission optional. **Standard Final Drive Ratio:** 3.44:1. **Steering:** rack and pinion. **Suspension (front):** unequal-length upper/lower control arms with coil springs and anti-sway bar. **Suspension (rear):** independent with diagonal trailing radius arms, upper/lower links and coil springs. **Brakes:** power vented front/rear disc. **Body Construction:** stainless steel-clad plastic. **Fuel Tank:** 16 gallon.

PERFORMANCE: Top Speed: 130 mph (factory claim). **Acceleration (0-60 mph):** 8.5 sec. (factory claim). **Fuel Mileage:** about 24 mpg.

Manufacturer: DeLorean Motor Company, Antrim, Northern Ireland.

Distributor: DeLorean Motor Co., New York City.

DENZEL

Except for the Steyr, Austria has not been known as a major manufacturer of automobiles. For a short time in the late 1950s, however, Wolfgang Denzel, who'd won the 1954 Alpine rally in his virtually home-built racer, produced a two-seater sports car with the intention of courting American 1300-cc racing enthusiasts. As early as 1948, Denzel had built four-seat sports cars based on Jeep-like Volkswagen chassis, sold under the WD name. He also marketed conversion equipment for the VW Beetle.

Although based largely on Volkswagen components, the ultimate design veered somewhat away from VW (as did the Porsche in its early years). Like many other specialty companies, Denzel offered its cars built largely to meet customer specifications rather than as never-changing models. Declaring it "the best-performing 1300-cc car on the road," ready for both street and competition use, *Road & Track* called the Denzel "one of the best all-around dual-purpose machines we have ever found." Though "no pace setter in appearance," declared *Sports Cars Illustrated* in 1958, commenting on the WD's Porsche/VW basis, "a certain aplomb in manner and demeanour tells one that here is something to go racing in." Not cheap when new, it's a rare race/touring roadster today.

1957-60 DENZEL

1954 Denzel WD International 1300.

1300 SUPER — FOUR — The secret to the Denzel's surprising performance was its combination of substantial horsepower (65 DIN) and low weight: only 1,415 pounds. Appearing like a slightly taller, chubby-looking Porsche, the Denzel wore headlamps mounted slightly inboard, flanked by tiny round parking lights. Taillamps were deeply inset. A 2/3 and 1/3 split bench seat with chrome tube framing held two (possibly three) people in a somewhat austere interior. Luggage space was virtually nonexistent, but the roadster body had wind-up windows. A padded dashboard held a tachometer and gauges, while a manual spark lever stood directly above the handbrake. The VW-based engine had roller bearings and a rather radical camshaft profile. Many of the transmissions supplied were non-synchronized "crash boxes." A coupe body was added later.

1500 SUPER — FOUR — Similar to the 1300, this higher-powered edition carried a 1488 cc engine and developed 85 horsepower.

I.D. DATA: Not available.

Model	Body Type & Seating	Engine Type/CID	P.O.E. Price	Weight (lbs.)	Prod. Total
1300	2-dr Roadster-2/3P	H4/78	4695	1415	N/A
1300	2-dr Coupe-2P	H4/78	N/A	1415	N/A
1500	2-dr Roadster-2/3P	H4/78	N/A	N/A	N/A

1957 Denzel WD 1300 Super Series.

ENGINE DATA: BASE FOUR (1300): Horizontally-opposed, overhead-valve four-cylinder (air cooled). **Displacement:** 78.1 cu. in. (1281 cc). **Bore & Stroke:** 3.07 x 2.64 in. (78 x 67 mm). **Compression Ratio:** 8.5:1 (9.9:1 optional). **Brake Horsepower:** 65 (DIN) or 71.5 (SAE) at 5400 rpm. **Torque:** 71 lbs.-ft. at 4400 rpm. Solex 40 PII carburetors (dual-throat Webers optional).

BASE FOUR (1500): Same as above, except -- **Displacement:** 91.8 cu. in. (1488 cc). **Bore & Stroke:** 3.15 x 2.91 in. (80 x 74 mm). **Compression Ratio:** 8.7:1. **Brake Horsepower:** 85 (DIN) at 5400 rpm. **Torque:** 83 lbs.-ft. at 4500 rpm. Two Weber carburetors.

CHASSIS DATA: Wheelbase: 82.7 in. **Overall Length:** 141 in. **Height:** 47.5 in. **Width:** 64.5 in. **Front Tread:** 51.6 in. **Rear Tread:** 51.6 in. **Wheel Type:** aluminum. **Standard Tires:** 5.25x15 Pirelli (Semperit tires for racing).

TECHNICAL: Layout: rear-engine, rear-drive. **Transmission:** four-speed manual. Various gear ratios available, many without synchromesh. **Standard Final Drive Ratio:** 3.76:1 or 4.37:1. **Suspension (front):** torsion bars and trailing link. **Suspension (rear):** swing axle, torsion bars and trailing links. **Brakes:** front/rear drum (Alfin) with hydraulic front booster. **Body Construction:** aluminum body on chassis of round and rectangular tubing. **Fuel Tank:** 13.5 gallon.

PERFORMANCE: Top Speed: (1300) 99+ mph, with estimates as high as 110 mph. **Acceleration (0-60 mph):** (1300) 12.3 to 13.7 seconds. **Acceleration (quarter-mile):** (1300) 17.7-18.0 seconds (77.7 mph). **Fuel Mileage:** 28-34 mpg.

Manufacturer: Wolfgang Denzel, Vienna, Austria.

Distributor: Hannig and Olbrich, North Hollywood, California; or Globe Automotive Imports, Montgomery, New York.

HISTORY: Wolfgang Denzel himself drove to victory in the 1954 Alpine Rally. Further rally wins followed, including the Alpine two years later.

DEUTSCH-BONNET (D.B.)

Hardly the best known of the Fifties sports cars, the French-built Deutsch-Bonnet (D.B.) trickled into the U.S. market for a time, into the early '60s. Created by designer Rene Bonnet, the company's first postwar racing model debuted in 1947; but the seed was sown before the war. The company name stemmed from Bonnet's prewar partnership with Charles Deutsch, which dated back to 1932 and would last until the early 1960s. A champion in 750-cc race events, Bonnet's racing career began in 1932 with rally competition. He and Deutsch built a competition 2-liter racer from the remains of a wrecked prewar Citroen 11CV (Traction Avant). Their first DB1 model was completed in 1938, followed by a smaller DB2 edition. Numbered successors continued after the war, with a DB4 in 1945 and then a 2-liter DB5, all built for race purposes. Before the Automobiles Deutsch & Bonnet company was formed in 1947, they'd also turned out a DB7 open-wheeler.

Bonnet helped to make the Panhard company famous in racing circles, by using their engine in his race car. One of those appeared at the 1949 Paris Salon, and about 15 were built. Bonnet won his class at Le Mans three times, Sebring twice, and the Mille Miglia four times.

By 1952, Bonnet entered a speedster into the 12-hour race at Sebring, Florida, powered by a horizontally-opposed two-cylinder, air-cooled engine. Driven by Steve Lansing and Ward Morehouse it took home a victory in Class H. Later at Montlhery, France, an open two-seater (called the Biplace Le Mans) with an engine displacing only 45.37 cubic inches averaged 110.61 mph for a 3-hour stretch, and managed a 200-mile run at an average speed of 113.71 mph.

What Bonnet really wanted, however, was to produce a GT touring vehicle. That dream came true at the 1952 Paris Motor Show, when the first non-racing models were displayed. Several of the handmade steel-bodied examples were sold, for hefty prices; and they improved each year. Engines ranged from 610 to 1300 cubic centimeters in displacement, and some could be fitted with a supercharger. By 1954-55, Bonnet turned to plastic bodies, after displaying one at the 1953 Paris Salon, with coachwork by Chausson. Tiny in size, the little sports cars from Deutsch & Bonnet delivered plenty of performance, powered by 750 and 850 cc two-cylinder engines. They cost more than $3,000 at the factory in 1955, but by 1958 could be purchased for $3,595 P.O.E. in the United States.

In 1962, Deutsch and Bonnet parted after a disagreement, but Bonnet continued to build cars under his name alone, including the Renault-engined Djet. Two years later, he sold his interest to Matra Sports, which offered a Matra-Bonnet Djet until 1968.

1954 Deutsch Bonnet Grand Turisme.

1955-56 DEUTSCH-BONNET

1956 Deutsch Bonnet.

GRAND TOURISME/HBR 750/1100/1300 — TWO — Quite a selection of models and body styles was available by 1955, including a two- or four-seat Grand Tourisme and the standard type HBR Luxe (also two- or four-seat). In addition to the basic 750 two-cylinder engine, a Type 1100 and 1300 were offered (both supercharged). Another model, the Biplace Le Mans, was for competition only. Most examples were custom-built on a Dyna-Panhard chassis. Typical models of this period had a very sleek, modern look with downward-sloping nose and hidden headlamps; a low, wide grille opening; hardtop-style rear quarter windows; and stood less than 50 inches tall.

I.D. DATA: Not available.

Model	Body Type & Seating	Engine Type/CID	P.O.E. Price	Weight (lbs.)	Prod. Total
750	2-dr Coupe-4P	H2/45	Note 1	1303	N/A
1100	2-dr Coupe-4P	H2/67	Note 1	1340	N/A
1300	2-dr Coupe-4P	H2/79	Note 1	1340	N/A

Note 1: Type 750 cost $3,280 at the factory in France circa 1955; others cost $3,490 to $4,290.

Body Note: Roadster bodies also were available.

ENGINE DATA: BASE TWO (750): Horizontally opposed, overhead-valve two-cylinder. **Displacement:** 45.37 cu. in. (743.8 cc). **Bore & Stroke:** 3.13 x 2.95 in. (79.5 x 74.9 mm). **Brake Horsepower:** 46 at 5500 rpm. 12-volt electrical.

BASE TWO (1100): Same as above, except 1100 cc and supercharged — **Brake Horsepower:** 60 at 5500 rpm.

BASE TWO (1300): Same as above, except 1300 cc and supercharged — **Brake Horsepower:** 65 at 5500 rpm.

TECHNICAL: Layout: front-engine, front-drive. **Transmission:** four-speed manual. **Suspension (front):** transverse leaf spring. **Suspension (rear):** torsion bars. **Brakes:** Satmo Record hydraulic front/rear drum. **Body Construction:** fiberglass monocoque on tubular beam chassis.

PERFORMANCE: Top Speed: (750) 90 mph; (1100) 96 mph; (1300) 98 mph.

Manufacturer: Automobiles Deutsch & Bonnet, Champigny Sur Marne (Seine), France.

1953-54 DEUTSCH-BONNET

MILLE MILES — TWO — A four-seat closed coupe was announced in 1953, and featured in *CARS* magazine. It had a low grille opening with horizontal bar, squared-off front and rear wheel opening, split windshield, and three portholes at the side of the cowl. Weighing just 1,320 pounds, the coupe (actually called a sports sedan) contained a 65-horsepower two-cylinder engine and did 112.7 mph in a record-setting run.

1957 DEUTSCH-BONNET

D.B. 750/850 — TWO — Styling features of the fiberglass-bodied coupes (and roadsters) included a wraparound windshield, large windows, and wide doors. Two-tone paint jobs were typical. Inside the four-seat cockpit were bucket-type front seats and a small back seat. The driver faced a Bonnet (Italian-style) steering wheel and controlled a four-speed gearbox. Headlamps were electrically-controlled. Both 750 and 850 cc two-cylinder engines were availble, developing 47 or 51 horsepower in standard form. Those outputs could be boosted to 54 or 60 bhp. In touring trim, the D.B. was capable of about 90 mph; or more than 100 mph when modified. While conceding the car's flaws, *Road & Track* called it "one of the most interesting machines we have ever tested." One of those flaws was the transverse shift pattern (offset by 90 degrees from the normal layout) for the cable-actuated shift linkage. That was to be changed before significant numbers were imported. In addition, only second and third gears were synchronized; third was direct drive, while fourth was an overdrive ratio.

I.D. DATA: Not available.

Model	Body Type & Seating	Engine Type/CID	P.O.E. Price	Weight (lbs.)	Prod. Total
750	2-dr Coupe-4P	H2/45	N/A	1320	N/A
850	2-dr Coupe-4P	H2/52	3850	1320	N/A

Body Note: Roadster bodies also were produced.

ENGINE DATA: BASE TWO (750): Horizontally opposed, overhead-valve two-cylinder. **Displacement:** 45.37 cu. in. (743.8 cc). **Bore & Stroke:** 3.13 x 2.95 in. (79.5 x 74.9 mm). **Compression Ratio:** 7.8:1. **Brake Horsepower:** 47. Solex two-barrel carburetor.

BASE TWO (850): Horizontally opposed, overhead-valve two-cylinder. **Displacement:** 51.9 cu. in. (851 cc). **Bore & Stroke:** 3.35 x 2.95 in. (85.1 x 74.9 mm). **Compression Ratio:** 7.5:1. **Brake Horsepower:** 51 at 5700 rpm. **Torque:** 47 lbs.-ft. at 3500 rpm. Solex two-barrel carburetor.

Note: Modified engines produced up to 60 bhp at 5600 rpm.

CHASSIS DATA: Wheelbase: 83.9 in. **Front Tread:** 48 in. **Rear Tread:** 48 in. **Standard Tires:** 145x400.

TECHNICAL: Layout: front-engine, front-drive. **Transmission:** four-speed manual. Overall gear ratios: (1st) 13.9:1; (2nd) 7.75:1; (3rd) 5.15:1; (4th) 3.88:1. Alternate gear ratios: (1st) 16.5:1; (2nd) 9.20:1; (3rd) 6.15:1; (4th) 4.71:1. **Steering:** rack and pinion. **Suspension (front):** transverse leaf spring. **Suspension (rear):** semi-independent torsion bars. **Brakes:** hydraulic front/rear drum. **Body Construction:** fiberglass monocoque on tubular beam chassis. **Fuel Tank:** 16.6 gallons.

PERFORMANCE: Top Speed: 88-90 mph (110+ when modified). **Acceleration (0-60 mph):** 21.3 seconds (as little as 18 in French tests). **Acceleration (quarter-mile):** 21.5 seconds.

Manufacturer: Automobiles Deutsch & Bonnet, Champigny Sur Marne (Seine), France.

Distributor: Owens European Motors, San Francisco, California.

HISTORY: By 1957, about 200 D.B. models had been sold; but *Road & Track* estimated that there were no more than three or four in the U.S.

1958-59 DEUTSCH-BONNET

D.B. 850 — TWO — Deutsch-Bonnet advertised only the 850-cc version of its sports coupe when announcing the new model. They promoted the Class H Sports-Production coupe as "The safest sports car in the world." As before, a prestressed fiberglass unibody rode a tubular central beam steel chassis. Deeply recessed headlamps sat in long nacelles, with small park/signal lights below, on the front panel. A wide grille slot stood low on that front panel. Air intake openings on the cowl were split by the long horizontal trim strip that ran from the front wheel opening to the car's rear fender tip. Squared-off wheel openings were evident, front and rear; and the 2+2 body had rear quarter windows. Special D.B. U-joints and front-wheel drive were said to assure unequalled cornering. Powerplant was the Panhard-based, 851-cc air-cooled flat twin, with hydraulic tappets. Its crankshaft was mounted in roller bearings. A new Zenith carburetor and Sirocco-type fan added a few horsepower over the previous version. A dual-purpose engine cooling turbine supplied the heater/defroster. Wheels had independent suspension. At the rear was five cubic feet of luggage space, with a separate spare wheel compartment. Among the options was a transparent plexiglass sunroof, with inside zipper cover to keep the sun's ray in check when desired. *Sports Cars Illustrated* expressed admiration for the Deutsch-Bonnet's unforgettable sight and sound, especially in racing trim.

I.D. DATA: Not available.

Model	Body Type & Seating	Engine Type/CID	P.O.E. Price	Weight (lbs.)	Prod. Total
850	2-dr Coupe-4P	H2/52	3595	1320	N/A

ENGINE DATA: BASE TWO (850): Horizontally opposed, overhead-valve two-cylinder. **Displacement:** 51.9 cu. in. (851 cc). **Bore & Stroke:** 3.35 x 2.95 in. (85.1 x 74.9 mm). **Compression Ratio:** 8.0:1. **Brake Horsepower:** 56 at 5700 rpm. **Torque:** 50.6 lbs.-ft. at 4000 rpm. Zenith two-barrel carburetor.

CHASSIS DATA: Wheelbase: 85 in. **Overall Length:** 160 in. **Height:** 50 in. **Width:** 63 in. **Front Tread:** 49 in. **Rear Tread:** 49 in. **Standard Tires:** 145x400.

TECHNICAL: Layout: front-engine, front-drive. **Transmission:** three or four-speed manual. Overall gear ratios: (1st) 15.6:1; (2nd) 8.7:1; (3rd) 5.8:1; (4th) overdrive. **Standard Final Drive Ratio:** 5.8:1 (other ratios available). **Steering:** rack and pinion. **Suspension (front):** transverse leaf spring. **Suspension (rear):** torsion bars. **Brakes:** hydraulic front/rear drum. **Body Construction:** fiberglass monocoque on tubular beam chassis. **Fuel Tank:** 15.6 gallons.

OPTIONS: Transparent sunroof with inside zipper cover. Al-Fin competition brakes. Wood racing steering wheel. Reinforced rims. Le Mans 750-cc Class H modified cylinder kit (9:1 compression). Electric clock. Fog or driving lamps. Special transmission ratios. Michelin X tires.

PERFORMANCE: Top Speed: 95-105 mph (factory claimed 100 mph in ads). **Fuel Mileage:** 35 mpg (factory).

Manufacturer: Automobiles Deutsch-Bonnet, Champigny Sur Marne (Seine), France.

Distributor: D.B. Automobiles, Broomall, Pennsylvania or Sherman Oaks, California.

HISTORY: In racing, Deutsch-Bonnet had Index and Class victories at Le Mans, France (1954/55/56); the Italian Mille Miglia (1952 through 1957); Sebring, Florida (1952/53/56); and the Irish Tourist Trophy (1954/55).

1960-61 DEUTSCH-BONNET

D.B. 850 — TWO — A new Le Mans open sports model joined the coupe by 1960, also based on the Panhard 851-cc engine. Otherwise, production continued as before. A 750-cc cylinder kit was available to reduce displacement for racing.

I.D. DATA: Not available.

Model	Body Type & Seating	Engine Type/CID	P.O.E. Price	Weight (lbs.)	Prod. Total
850	2-dr Coupe-4P	H2/52	3295		N/A
850	2-dr Rds-4P	H2/52	N/A		N/A

ENGINE DATA: BASE TWO (850): Same as 1958-59.

CHASSIS DATA: Same as 1958-59.

TECHNICAL: Same as 1958-59.

OPTIONS: Similar to 1958-59.

PERFORMANCE: Top Speed: 95-105 mph (up to 115 mph in modified form).

Manufacturer: Automobiles Deutsch-Bonnet, Champigny Sur Marne (Seine), France.

Distributor: World Wide Import Inc., Los Angeles, California.

DKW

Like so many European makes, the German DKW had a long history before it became known to Americans. During World War I, J.S. Rasmussen, a manufacturer of boiler fittings, turned to the production of steam-powered vehicles under the Dampf-Kraft-Wagen name. A few years later, he was involved with electric automobiles, powered bicycles and DKW motorcycles, which came to be called "Das Kleine Wunder" (the little wonder). By 1927, the company had become the world's larger manufacturer of motorcycles. A year later came the first gasoline-powered cars, using a two-stroke engine. In 1932, Auto Union GbmH was formed in what later became East Germany, made up of DKW, Horch, and Wanderer. Although some rear-wheel-drive models were built, the organization became best known for front-drive autos, and for famed racing vehicles.

After the war, two entirely different successors to the prewar DKW emerged by 1949: one in East Germany, the other produced by a revived Auto Union company in Dusseldorf, Ingolstadt, West Germany. "DKW is Here Again," proclaimed the banner at the 1949 Technical Exposition in Hanover, but only a motorcycle and commercial van were evident. A two-cylinder engine and commercial vehicles came first from the postwar Auto Union firm, starting in summer 1950. Those were followed by a three-cylinder version based upon a prototype that had been created before the war. The model 4CV came in closed coupe and cabriolet form, powered by a 690-cc engine. *Motor Trend* in 1954 called the "Sonderklasse" DKW "one of the most promising small European cars ever to blossom forth," adding that "seldom has there been a car with a more interesting background." During the 1950s, DKWs with two-stroke engines gained a fair following in the U.S. and elsewhere; but like many others, it didn't last. Production of the familiar two-stroke cars ended in 1960 as the company went into new hands, and the make expired totally by 1966.

1954-55 DKW

1954 DKW Auto Union Sonderklasse.

MEISTERKLASSE (4CV) — TWO — Seldom seen in the U.S. but popular in Europe in the early 1950s, the two-cylinder Auto Union-DKW sedan was the first model produced by the company in its postwar reincarnation.

SONDERKLASSE 3-6 — THREE — A prototype of the three-cylinder DKW appeared at the Frankfurt Motor Show in 1952, with a Sport Coupe body. Early examples had a horizontal-bar grille and split windshield, but the overall body silhouette was less distinctive than that of later models that were imported to the U.S., with their notably sloping hoods. "Suicide" doors were hinged at the rear as in some prewar domestic automobiles. First offered with a three-speed gearbox (with overdrive), DKW later switched to a four-speed, with an unusual "H" shift pattern. Bucket seats were used in front, but a bench seat in back. The convertible top was padded, and trunk lids had decorative bars.

I.D. DATA: Not available.

Model	Body Type & Seating	Engine Type/CID	P.O.E. Price	Weight (lbs.)	Prod. Total
4CV	2-dr Sedan-4P	I2/43	N/A	1750	Note 1
4CV	2-dr Conv-4P	I2/43	N/A	1870	Note 1
4CV	2-dr Sta Wag-4P	I2/43	N/A	2075	Note 1
3-6	2-dr Sedan-4P	I3/55	N/A	1873	Note 1
3-6	2-dr Conv-4P	I3/55	N/A	N/A	Note 1
3-6	2-dr Conv-2P	I3/55	N/A	N/A	Note 1

Note 1: In 1954, over 33,000 Sonderklasse (three-cylinder) and 2,900 two-cylinder DKWs were built.

ENGINE DATA: BASE TWO (Meisterklasse): Inline, valveless two-cylinder (two-stroke). Cast iron block and light alloy head. **Displacement:** 42.7 cu. in. (690 cc). **Bore & Stroke:** 2.99 x 2.99 in. **Compression Ratio:** 6.5:1. **Brake Horsepower:** 23 at 4500 rpm. No valve lifters. 6-volt electrical.

BASE THREE (Sonderklasse 3-6): Inline, valveless three-cylinder (two-stroke). **Displacement:** 54.9 cu. in. (896 cc). **Bore & Stroke:** 2.80 x 2.99 in. **Compression Ratio:** 6.5:1. **Brake Horsepower:** 35 at 4000 rpm. Four main bearings. No valve lifters. 6-volt electrical.

CHASSIS DATA: Wheelbase: 92 in. exc. (wag) 96 in. **Overall Length:** 163.8 exc. (wag) 166 in. **Height:** 56.5 in. exc. (wag) 62 in. **Width:** 62.4 in. **Front Tread:** 49 in. **Rear Tread:** 49 in. **Standard Tires:** 5.00x16 or 5.60x15.

TECHNICAL: Layout: front-engine, front-drive. **Transmission:** ZF three-speed manual (four-speed on export models), column shift; free wheeling. **Suspension (front):** transverse leaf spring. **Suspension (rear):** rigid axle and transverse leaf spring. **Brakes:** hydraulic, front/rear drum. **Body Construction:** steel body on steel frame.

PERFORMANCE: Top Speed: (3-6) 72 mph. **Acceleration (0-60 mph):** (3-6) 25 seconds. **Fuel Mileage:** about 35 mpg (45 mpg for two-cylinder).

PRODUCTION/SALES: By 1952, about 25,000 of the two-cylinder DKWs were being produced yearly, with predictions of 2,000 cars per month in 1954 (nearly one-third intended for export).

Manufacturer: Auto Union GmbH, Dusseldorf, West Germany.

HISTORY: In 1954, DKW won the European championship for production touring cars, finishing far ahead of its competitor.

1956-57 DKW

3-6 — THREE — As DKW models began to reach the U.S. in significant number, the former horizontal-bar grille switched to the more familiar oval grille with tight crosshatch mesh pattern, and the distinctively curved DKW body silhouette (somewhat reminiscent of a Morris Minor) that lasted until 1961. The deluxe hardtop featured Auto Union's familiar four-ring grille insignia, while the standard version lacked the rings. The rear portion of the Three-Six was slightly more curved than in prior models, for improved appearance and streamlining; and also to allow greater luggage space.

The water cooled three-cylinder, two-cycle engine stood well ahead of the front axle. For lubrication, gasoline and oil had to be mixed in the fuel tank. A four-speed manual gearbox worked through a single dry-plate clutch, driving the front wheels. Most DKWs had two-door bodies, but a four-door, added by 1956, rode a longer wheelbase, as did the station wagon. The four-door had vent windows at the rear, and bench-type front seats.

One of the coupe models was a true hardtop coupe, with no "B" pillar. The other, called Coupe DeLuxe, did have side pillars and was available with an optional sliding fabric sunroof. Though small in size (at least by American standards), the DKW had a claimed capacity of five passengers (up to six for the four-door). The front passenger seat folded and tilted forward, while the backrest of the driver's seat was modified by 1956 to fold slightly sideways and to the front. Sedans and station wagons began to arrive in America in the mid-1950s, but the two-seat and four-seat convertibles were less common. Upholstery came in two colors to match the available two-tone body paint.

Early DKWs had semaphore-style directional signals, but flashers went on the later Three-Six, with a switch on the thick steering column. A control lever there also operated the light switch. An optional Saxomat magnetic clutch operated with a flyweight and vacuum, eliminating the clutch pedal.

I.D. DATA: Serial number plate is to the right of the battery. Engine number is on lower right side of block.

Model	Body Type & Seating	Engine Type/CID	P.O.E. Price	Weight (lbs.)	Prod. Total
3-6	2-dr Sedan-5P	I3/55	1995	1973	Note 1
3-6	4-dr Touring Sed-5P	I3/55	2395	2072	Note 1
3-6	2-dr HT Coupe-5P	I3/55	2195	1973	Note 1
3-6	2-dr Station Wag-5P	I3/55	2495	2149	Note 1
3-6	2-dr DeL Cpe-5P	I3/55	N/A	N/A	Note 1
3-6	2-dr Conv Cpe-2P	I3/55	2895	1912	Note 1
3-6	2-dr Conv Cpe-4P	I3/55	2695	1912	Note 1

Note 1: Approximately 2,000 DKWs were sold in the U.S. in 1957.

ENGINE DATA: BASE THREE: Inline, valveless three-cylinder (two-stroke). **Displacement:** 54.8 cu. in. (896 cc). **Bore & Stroke:** 2.80 x 2.99 in. (71 x 76 mm). **Compression Ratio:** 7.0:1. **Brake Horsepower:** 42 at 4200 rpm. **Torque:** 55 lbs.-ft. at 2250 rpm. Four main bearings. No valve lifters. Solex downdraft carburetor.

CHASSIS DATA: Wheelbase: 92 in. except (4-dr and wagon) 96.5 in. **Overall Length:** 166 in. except (4-dr) 170 in.; (wag) 164 in. **Height:** 57.5-58.5 in. **Width:** 66 in. except (wag) 64 in. **Front Tread:** 50 in. **Rear Tread:** 53 in. **Standard Tires:** 5.60x15.

TECHNICAL: Layout: front-engine, front-drive. **Transmission:** four-speed manual (synchronized 2nd/3rd/4th), column shift; freewheeling (final drive within gearbox). **Standard Final Drive Ratio:** 4.72:1. **Steering:** rack and pinion. **Suspension (front):** top transverse leaf spring; lower transverse control arms. **Suspension (rear):** rigid tubular "floating" axle and transverse leaf spring. **Brakes:** duplex hydraulic, front/rear drum. **Body Construction:** steel body on box-section girder steel frame. **Fuel Tank:** 12 gallon (U.S.).

MAJOR OPTIONS: Saxomat automatic clutch ($100).

PERFORMANCE: Top Speed: near 80 mph. **Acceleration (0-60 mph):** 30.9 seconds (factory claimed 0-49 mph in 18 seconds). **Acceleration (quarter-mile):** 25.3 sec. (54.5 mph). **Fuel Mileage:** up to 35 mpg (factory claimed 30 mpg average).

Manufacturer: Auto Union GmbH, Dusseldorf, West Germany.

HISTORY: DKW models were seen at the New York Auto Show in April, 1956. A brochure issued at that show noted that "DKW automobiles are famous not only as fast touring cars for long distance traveling, but also for their sports successes all over the world." A plastic-bodied 3-6 Monza coupe was seen at Stuttgart in May 1957, appearing far sleeker than the usual DKWs. A California company, Flintridge Motors, began production of a four-seater sports car based on the DKW hardtop coupe, with bodies prepared by Woodill, to sell for $3195. Auto Union/DKW itself also produced a business panel truck and eight-passenger bus that were sold in the U.S.

1958 DKW

1958 DKW 3/6 Monza sport coupe.

3-6 — THREE — Appearance of the standard three-cylinder DKW was the same as in 1957. Improvements included fingertip-contact steering, stronger shock absorbers, progressive rear springs, and a quieter exhaust system. New color combinations were available. Powerplant remained the 896-cc two-stroke engine. The front passenger seat of two-door models folded forward, for easy entry into the rear. A lever below the dashboard put the four-speed transmission into freewheeling. A fuel-to-oil ratio of 40:1 was required for proper lubrication. The "3-6" (or "3=6") designation was meant to remind customers that three cylinders could be considered the equivalent of six, because a two-cycle engine delivered a power stroke from each cylinder with every revolution of the crankshaft. Ads promised "Sports car performance--pleasure car styling," noting that the engine contained only seven moving parts. Other ads explained that the "secret is 2-cycle performance...adding a new dimension of safety." Beginning this year, hardtop coupe doors were hinged at the front rather than the rear.

The optional Saxomat clutch allowed "two-pedal" driving. It would disengage as engine speed fell to a certain minimum, then re-engage as the engine speeded up. "It is child's play to start from a standstill on a hill," promised the company. "The left foot holds the brakes, the right foot is on the accelerator."

AUTO UNION 1000 — THREE — A deluxe version of the DKW with larger-displacement engine, taking the Auto Union name, began to arrive in America during 1958. Major identifying feature was the presence of the Auto Union symbol on the grille: four intertwined rings. The deluxe version had a smooth trunk lid while the DKW car carried ribbing on that lid. A two-seat roadster also appeared, described as being for the "fast motorist."

1958 DKW Auto Union 1000 Special coupe.

I.D. DATA: Serial number plate is on right side of firewall, under the hood. Engine number is on right side of block, near the front, above one inch below the head gasket.

Model	Body Type & Seating	Engine Type/CID	P.O.E. Price	Weight (lbs.)	Prod. Total
3-6	2-dr Sedan-5P	I3/55	1995	1973	Note 1
3-6	4-dr Touring Sed 5P	I3/55	2395	2072	Note 1
3-6	2-dr HT Coupe-5P	I3/55	2195	1973	Note 1
3-6	2-dr Station Wag-5P	I3/55	2495	2149	Note 1
AUTO UNION 1000					
1000	2-dr DeLuxe Cpe-2P	I3/60	2495	1973	Note 1
1000	2-dr Roadster-2P	I3/60	N/A	N/A	Note 1

Note 1: Approximately 3,138 DKWs were sold in the U.S. in 1958.

ENGINE DATA: BASE THREE (900): Inline, valveless three-cylinder (two-stroke). **Displacement:** 54.7 cu. in. (896 cc). **Bore & Stroke:** 2.80 x 2.99 in. (71 x 76 mm). **Compression Ratio:** 7.0:1. **Brake Horsepower:** 40 (45 SAE) at 4250 rpm. Four main bearings. No valve lifters. 6-volt electrical.

BASE THREE (1000): Same as above, except -- **Displacement:** 59.8 cu. in. (980 cc). **Bore & Stroke:** 2.92 x 2.99 in. (74 x 76 mm). **Compression Ratio:** 7.25:1 (rds, 8.0:1). **Brake Horsepower:** 50 (SAE) at 4550 rpm (rds, 56 at 4500).

CHASSIS DATA: Wheelbase: 92 in. except (4-dr and wagon) 96 in. **Overall Length:** 166 in. except (4-dr sed) 170 in.; (wag) 164 in.; (spt cpe) 163 in. **Height:** 57 in. except (4-dr) 58.5 in.; (wag) 61.5 in. **Width:** 66 in. except (4-dr) 64 in. **Front Tread:** 50 in. **Rear Tread:** 53 in. **Standard Tires:** 5.60x15.

TECHNICAL: Layout: front-engine, front-drive. **Transmission:** four-speed manual; column shift; freewheeling (final drive within gearbox). **Standard Final Drive Ratio:** 4.32:1. **Steering:** rack and pinion. **Suspension (front):** top transverse leaf spring; lower transverse control arms. **Suspension (rear):** rigid tubular axle, transverse leaf spring. **Brakes:** duplex hydraulic, front/rear drum. **Body Construction:** steel body on steel frame.

MAJOR OPTIONS: Saxomat automatic clutch. Mile-O-Meter.

PERFORMANCE: Top Speed: 80-85 mph. **Acceleration (0-60 mph):** 25.5 sec. **Fuel Mileage:** 25-40 mpg.

Manufacturer: Auto Union GmbH, Ingolstadt, Dusseldorf, West Germany.

Distributor: Peter Satori Co, Ltd., Pasadena, California; and Germanic Auto Distributors, Inc., New Haven, Connecticut.

HISTORY: Introduced on October 1, 1957.

1959 DKW

1959 DKW F11 two-door. (William Siuru Jr.)

3-6 — THREE — Neither appearance nor price of the basic DKW series changed significantly this year, but the 3-6 designation was not always used.

1000 — THREE — As before, the 1000 Series used a larger three-cylinder engine, delivering 50 horsepower (56 in the sport coupe). Standard equipment included a heater, clock, radiator blind, two-speed wipers, door mirror, lighter, bumper overriders, and two-tone paint. Appearance of the 1000SP Sports Coupe differed considerably from the smaller-engined models. A wide grille with tight mesh pattern extended almost full-width, just above the bumper. The hood held a scoop, and round taillamps brought up the rear, set below narrow tailfins. One reviewer compared the Sport Coupe's appearance to "a T-bird shrunk in the rain."

I.D. DATA: Serial number plate is on right side of firewall, under the hood. Engine number is on right front end of block.

Model	Body Type & Seating	Engine Type/CID	P.O.E. Price	Weight (lbs.)	Prod. Total
3-6	2-dr Sedan-5P	I3/55	1995	1973	Note 1
3-6	4-dr Touring Sed-5P	I3/55	2395	2072	Note 1
3-6	2-dr HT Coupe-5P	I3/55	2195	1973	Note 1
3-6	2-dr Station Wag-5P	I3/55	2495	2149	Note 1
1000	2-dr Spt Cpe-2 + 2P	I3/60	2760	1980	Note 1
1000	2-dr Del HT-5P	I3/60	N/A	N/A	Note 1

Note 1: Approximately 2,268 DKWs were sold in the U.S. in 1959.

ENGINE DATA: BASE THREE (900): Inline, valveless three-cylinder (two-stroke). **Displacement:** 54.7 cu. in. (896 cc). **Bore & Stroke:** 2.80 x 2.99 in. (71 x 76 mm). **Compression Ratio:** 7.0:1. **Brake Horsepower:** 45 (SAE) at 4250 rpm. Four main bearings. No valve lifters. Solex 40ICB downdraft carburetor.

BASE THREE (1000): Same as above, except -- **Displacement:** 59.8 cu. in. (980 cc). **Bore & Stroke:** 2.92 x 2.99 in. (74 x 76 mm). **Compression Ratio:** 8.0:1. **Brake Horsepower:** 50 (SAE) at 4250 rpm exc. (spt cpe) 56 bhp. **Torque:** (spt cpe) 65 lbs.-ft. at 3000 rpm.

CHASSIS DATA: Wheelbase: 92 in. except (4-dr and wagon) 96 in.; (1000 HT) 92.5 in.; (spt cpe) 96.5 in. **Overall Length:** 166 in. except (4-dr) 170 in.; (1000 spt cpe) 163 in. **Height:** 57.7 in. exc. (4-dr sed) 58.5 in.; (1000 HT) 57 in.; (1000 spt cpe) 52 in.; and (wag) 61.5 in. **Width:** 66 in. except (4-dr sed) 64 in. **Front Tread:** 50 in. **Rear Tread:** 53 in. **Standard Tires:** 5.50/5.60x15.

TECHNICAL: Layout: front-engine, front-drive. **Transmission:** four-speed manual (synchro 2nd/3rd/4th), column shift; freewheeling (final drive within gearbox). **Standard Final Drive Ratio:** 4.72:1; (spt cpe) 4.37:1. **Steering:** rack and pinion. **Suspension (front):** transverse leaf spring with wishbones. **Suspension (rear):** floating axle with progressive transverse leaf spring. **Brakes:** duplex hydraulic, front/rear drum. **Body Construction:** steel body on box-section steel frame with crossmembers.

MAJOR OPTIONS: Saxomat automatic clutch. Sunroof (except station wagon). Radio. Grille guards. Whitewall tires. Windshield washers.

PERFORMANCE: Top Speed: 80 mph; (spt cpe) 89 mph. **Acceleration (0-60 mph):** (spt cpe) 14.8 seconds. **Fuel Mileage:** up to 35 mpg.

Manufacturer: Auto Union GmbH, Dusseldorf, West Germany.

Distributor: DKW American.

HISTORY: Introduced on October 1, 1958. A 1000SP Sport Coupe served as pace car for the Sebring (Florida) race.

1960 DKW

1960 DKW Junior.

750 — THREE — A new 750 model, with smaller engine and restyled body, joined the DKW lineup for 1960. Overall dimensions were smaller too, and the new model had completely different styling. Angled "eyebrows" reached over the single round head-lamps. At the ends of the nearly full-width grille, crosshatch-patterned, were round parking/signal lights. Rear ends had a pointed tip, like tiny tailfins. The compact two-door sedan had a wraparound back window.

AU1000 — THREE — Six versions of the 1000 series, with larger three-cylinder engine, were offered for 1960. Three horsepower ratings were available. Appearance was similar to 1959. As before, the hardtop coupe looked much different from the sedans and station wagon, with a full-width grille similar to that of the new 750 and tailfinned rear quarters. The coupe also had a wraparound windshield with nearly vertical A-pillar.

I.D. DATA: Serial number plate is on right side of firewall, under the hood. Engine number is on right front end of block. Suffix 'A' indicates 1960.

Model	Body Type & Seating	Engine Type/CID	P.O.E. Price	Weight (lbs.)	Prod. Total
750	2-dr Sedan-4P	I3/45	1665	1550	N/A
1000	2-dr Sedan-5P	I3/55	1995	1975	N/A
AU1000S	4-dr Sedan-5P	I3/55	2283	2075	N/A
AU1000	2-dr HT Coupe-5P	I3/55	2158	2005	N/A
AU1000S	2-dr HT Coupe-5P	I3/55	N/A	2005	N/A
AU1000SP	2-dr HT Coupe-5P	I3/55	N/A	1980	N/A
AU1000	2-dr Station Wag-5P	I3/55	2321	2150	N/A

ENGINE DATA: BASE THREE (750): Inline, valveless three-cylinder (two-stroke). **Displacement:** 45.2 cu. in. (741 cc). **Bore & Stroke:** 2.68 x 2.68 in. (68 x 68 mm). **Compression Ratio:** 8.0 or 8.25:1. **Brake Horsepower:** 39 at 4400 rpm (34 DIN at 4300). **Torque:** 47 lbs.-ft. at 2500 rpm. Four main bearings. No valve lifters.

BASE THREE (1000). Inline, valveless three-cylinder (two-stroke). **Displacement:** 59.7 cu. in. (980 cc). **Bore & Stroke:** 2.92 x 2.99 in. (74 x 76 mm). **Compression Ratio:** 7.0:1 except (AU1000SP) 8.0:1. **Brake Horsepower:** 50 or 57 at 4500 rpm exc. (AU1000SP) 62 bhp. **Torque:** 57 lbs.-ft. at 2750 rpm. Four main bearings. No valve lifters.

CHASSIS DATA: Wheelbase: (750) 85.6 in.; (1000) 92 in. except (4-dr and wagon) 96 in. **Overall Length:** (750) 155.5 in.; (1000) 166 in. except (4-dr) 170 in. **Height:** (750) 54.6 in. **Front Tread:** (750) 46.5 in.; (1000) 50 in. **Rear Tread:** (750) 47.3 in.; (1000) 53 in. **Standard Tires:** (750) 5.20x12; (1000) 5.60x15.

TECHNICAL: Layout: front-engine, front-drive. **Transmission:** four-speed manual; column shift; freewheeling (final drive within gearbox). **Standard Final Drive Ratio:** (750) 3.88:1; (1000) 4.72:1. **Steering:** rack and pinion. **Suspension (front):** (750) torsion bars; (1000) transverse leaf spring and wishbones. **Suspension (rear):** (750) rigid axle, trailing arms and track rod; (1000) floating axle and progressive transverse leaf spring. **Brakes:** duplex hydraulic, front/rear drum. **Body Construction:** steel body on steel frame.

MAJOR OPTIONS: Similar to 1959.

PERFORMANCE: Top Speed: (750) 70.5 mph. **Acceleration (0-60 mph):** (750) 28.4 seconds. **Acceleration (quarter-mile):** (750) 22.9 seconds (55.4 mph).

Manufacturer: Auto Union GmbH, Dusseldorf, West Germany.

Distributor: Mercedes Benz Sales, Inc., South Bend, Indiana.

HISTORY: Introduced October 1, 1959.

1961 DKW

750 — THREE — Completely different in appearance from its curvy 1000-series companions, with a more modern and squared-off body, the 750 continued with little change after its introduction in 1960. Standard equipment included a heater. The three-cylinder, two-stroke engine developed 39 horsepower and the car held four passengers. The 750 was later called "Junior."

AU1000 — THREE — Unchanged in appearance, continuing the mid-1950s profile, the 1000 series came in a variety of coupe, sedan and station wagon models.

I.D. DATA: Serial number plate is on right side of firewall, under the hood, near the hinge. Engine number is on right front end of block. Suffix 'B' indicates 1961.

Model	Body Type & Seating	Engine Type/CID	P.O.E. Price	Weight (lbs.)	Prod. Total
750	2-dr Sedan-4P	I3/45	1695	1480	Note 1
AU1000	2-dr Sedan-4P	I3/60	1995	1892	Note 1
AU1000	4-dr Sedan-5P	I3/60	2526	1971	Note 1
AU1000S	2-dr HT Coupe-4P	I3/60	2301	1923	Note 1
AU1000SP	2-dr Spt Cpe-2P	I3/60	3925	2039	Note 1
AU1000	2-dr Station Wag-4P	I3/60	2321	2029	Note 1
AU1000	2-dr Coupe-4P	I3/60	2158	N/A	Note 1
AU1000	2-dr Cr Cntry Wag-4P	I3/60	2805	2387	Note 1

Note 1: More than 2,000 DKWs were sold in the U.S. during 1961.

ENGINE DATA: BASE THREE (750): Inline, valveless three-cylinder (two-stroke). **Displacement:** 45.2 cu. in. (741 cc). **Bore & Stroke:** 2.68 x 2.68 in. (68 x 68 mm). **Compression Ratio:** 8.0:1. **Brake Horsepower:** 39 at 4400 rpm. **Torque:** 47 lbs.-ft. at 2500 rpm. Four main bearings.

BASE THREE (AU1000): Inline, valveless three-cylinder (two-stroke). **Displacement:** 59.86 cu. in. (981 cc). **Bore & Stroke:** 2.91 x 2.99 in. (74 x 76 mm). **Compression Ratio:** 7.0 or 7.25:1 except (AU1000SP) 8.0:1. **Brake Horsepower:** 50 at 4500 rpm except (AU1000S) 57 bhp; (AU1000SP) 62 bhp. **Torque:** 61 lbs.-ft. at 2250 rpm exc. (AU1000SP) 69 at 3500. Four main bearings.

CHASSIS DATA: Wheelbase: (750) 85.6 in.; (1000 4-dr) 96.5 in.; (other 1000) 92.5 in. **Overall Length:** (750) 156.1 in.; (1000 4-dr) 170.25 in.; (1000 wag) 165.75 in.; (other 1000) 166.3 in. **Height:** (750) 55 in.; (1000) 57.7 in.; (1000 4-dr) 58.5 in.; (1000 wag) 61.5 in.; (1000SP) 52 in. **Width:** (750) 62 in.; (1000) 66-66.7 in. **Front Tread:** (750) 46 in.; (1000) 50.8 in. **Rear Tread:** (750) 47 in.; (1000) 53.1 in. **Standard Tires:** (750) 5.20x12; (1000) 5.60x15; (AU1000SP) 155Mx15.

TECHNICAL: Layout: front-engine, front-drive. **Transmission:** four-speed manual, column shift; all synchro. **Steering:** rack and pinion. **Suspension (front):** (750) torsion bars; (1000) transverse leaf spring and wishbones. **Suspension (rear):** (750) torsion bars; (1000) floating axle with progressive transverse leaf spring. **Brakes:** hydraulic, front/rear drum. **Body Construction:** steel body on steel frame.

PERFORMANCE: Top Speed: (750) 72 mph; (1000) 79.5 mph cruising; (spt cpe) 90 mph. **Fuel Mileage:** (750) to 35 mph; (1000) 27.4 mpg average.

Manufacturer: Auto Union GmbH, Dusseldorf, West Germany.

Distributor: Mercedes-Benz Sales, South Bend, Indiana.

HISTORY: DKW also produced a Bronco four-wheel-drive Cross Country vehicle that sold for $2775. Advertisements noted that each Auto Union-DKW car "bears a proud heritage. Remember the 200 mph, 660 horsepower Auto Union racers of the thirties. ....Some of their records still stand." The ads further explained that the current DKW "made its mark in racing through DKW Formula Junior successes at Sebring, Riverside and many other circuits in the USA and Europe."

1962 DKW

1962 DKW 1000 SP convertible.

JUNIOR DELUXE — THREE — Evolved from the former 750, the new Junior took a slightly larger two-stroke engine: 796 cc, but still rated the same 39 horsepower. Torque got a boost, however, from 47 to 52 pound-feet. Little changed in appearance from the 750, the Junior had torsion bars up front and laminated transverse torsion bar at the rear. Front brakes were inboard. A dark woodgrain dashboard contained a hooded instrument cluster. Along the bodyside stood a long trim strip at the beltline. Rear quarter windows were fixed in position. The hood dropped down at the front between shrouded single headlamps. Round parking lamps sat at the ends of the grille, which displayed a wide crosshatch pattern with curved top bar. Top speed with the little engine was 70 mph. By this time, the need to premix oil and gasoline was fading away, replaced by an automatic system that injected oil at the carburetor.

AU1000 — THREE — The larger-engined DKW continued with little change.

I.D. DATA: Serial number plate is on right side of firewall, under the hood. Engine number is on right front end of block. Suffix 'C' indicates 1962.

Model	Body Type & Seating	Engine Type/CID	P.O.E. Price	Weight (lbs.)	Prod. Total
Junior	2-dr Sedan-4P	I3/48	1595	1540	Note 1
AU1000	2-dr Sedan-4P	I3/60	1995	1892	Note 1
AU1000S	4-dr Sedan-5P	I3/60	2526	1971	Note 1
AU1000S	2-dr HT Coupe-4P	I3/60	2301	1923	Note 1
AU1000SP	2-dr Spt Cpe-2P	I3/60	3925	2039	Note 1
AU1000	2-dr Station Wag-4P	I3/60	2321	2029	Note 1

Note 1: Just over 1,000 DKWs were sold in the U.S. during 1962.

ENGINE DATA: BASE THREE (Junior): Inline, valveless three-cylinder (two-stroke). **Displacement:** 48.5 cu. in. (796 cc). **Bore & Stroke:** 2.775 x 2.68 in. (70.5 x 68 mm). **Compression Ratio:** 7.0:1 or 7.25:1. **Brake Horsepower:** 39 at 4300 rpm. **Torque:** 52.4 lbs.-ft. at 2500 rpm. Four main bearings.

BASE THREE (AU1000): Inline, valveless three-cylinder (two-stroke). **Displacement:** 59.86 cu. in. (981 cc). **Bore & Stroke:** 2.91 x 2.99 in. (74 x 76 mm). **Compression Ratio:** 7.25:1 except (AU1000SP) 8.0:1. **Brake Horsepower:** 57 at 4500 rpm except (spt cpe) 62 bhp. **Torque:** 62.9 lbs.-ft. at 2250 rpm. Four main bearings.

CHASSIS DATA: Wheelbase: (Junior) 85.6 in.; (AU1000 4-dr) 96.5 in.; (other AU1000) 92 in. **Overall Length:** (Jr) 156 in.; (AU1000 4-dr) 170.3 in.; (AU1000 wag) 164.2 in.; (other AU1000) 165 in. **Height:** (Jr) 56.7 in.; (AU) 57.7 in. **Width:** (Jr) 60.6 in. **Front Tread:** (Jr) 47.2 in.; (AU) 51 in. **Rear Tread:** (Jr) 47.7 in.; (AU) 54 in. **Standard Tires:** (Jr) 5.50x13; (AU) 5.60x15; (AU spt cpe) 155Mx15.

TECHNICAL: Layout: front-engine, front-drive. **Transmission:** four-speed manual; column shift. **Standard Final Drive Ratio:** (Junior) 4.12:1; (1000) 4.72:1. **Steering:** rack and pinion. **Suspension (front):** (Jr) torsion bars; (1000) transverse leaf spring and wishbones. **Suspension (rear):** (Jr) transverse torsion bar; (1000) floating axle, transverse leaf spring. **Brakes:** duplex hydraulic, front/rear drum; (Jr) inboard front. **Body Construction:** steel body on steel frame. **Fuel Tank:** (Jr) 9.5 gallon.

MAJOR OPTIONS: Saxomat automatic clutch ($75). Whitewall tires.

PERFORMANCE: Top Speed: (Junior) 70 mph. **Acceleration (0-60 mph):** (Jr) 27 seconds. **Fuel Mileage:** (Jr) 23-30 mpg.

Manufacturer: Auto Union GmbH, Dusseldorf, West Germany.

Distributor: Mercedes-Benz Sales, Inc., South Bend, Indiana or DKW American, Inc., New York City.

1963 DKW

JUNIOR DELUXE — THREE — Little change was evident on the smaller-engined DKW.

100 — THREE — The larger-engined DKW, with styling from the 1950s, continued with little change.

I.D. DATA: Serial number plate is on right side of firewall, under the hood. Engine number is on right front end of block. Suffix 'D' indicates 1963.

Model	Body Type & Seating	Engine Type/CID	P.O.E. Price	Weight (lbs.)	Prod. Total
Junior	2-dr Sedan-4P	I3/48	1595	1565	Note 1
1000S	2-dr HT Coupe-4P	I3/60	1995	2050	Note 1
1000	2-dr Station Wag-4P	I3/60	2095	2336	Note 1

Note 1: About 651 DKWs were sold in the United States during 1963.
ENGINE DATA: BASE THREE (Junior): Inline, valveless three-cylinder (two-stroke). **Displacement:** 48.5 cu. in. (796 cc). **Bore & Stroke:** 2.775 x 2.68 in. (70.5 x 68 mm). **Compression Ratio:** 7.0:1 or 7.25:1. **Brake Horsepower:** 39 at 4000 rpm. **Torque:** 55.6 lbs.-ft. at 2500 rpm. Four main bearings.
BASE THREE (1000): Inline, valveless three-cylinder (two-stroke). **Displacement:** 59.86 cu. in. (981 cc). **Bore & Stroke:** 2.91 x 2.99 in. (74 x 76 mm). **Compression Ratio:** 7.25:1. **Brake Horsepower:** 57 at 4500 rpm; (wag) 50 at 4500 rpm. **Torque:** 62.9 lbs.-ft. at 2250 rpm. Four main bearings.

CHASSIS DATA: Wheelbase: (Junior) 86 in.; (1000 cpe) 92 in.; (1000 wag) 96 in. **Overall Length:** (Jr) 156.2 in.; (1000 cpe) 166.3 in.; (1000 wag) 165.7 in. **Height:** (Jr) 56.7 in.; (1000) 57.7 in. **Front Tread:** (Jr) 47.2 in.; (1000) 51 in. **Rear Tread:** (Jr) 47.7 in.; (1000) 54 in. **Standard Tires:** (Jr) 5.50x13; (1000) 5.60x15.

TECHNICAL: Layout: front-engine, front-drive. **Transmission:** four-speed manual; column shift; freewheeling (final drive within gearbox). **Standard Final Drive Ratio:** (Jr) 4.12:1; (1000) 4.72:1. **Steering:** rack and pinion. **Suspension (front):** (Jr) torsion bars; (1000) transverse leaf spring and wishbones. **Suspension (rear):** (Jr) torsion bar; (1000) floating axle, transverse leaf spring. **Brakes:** hydraulic, front/rear drum. **Body Construction:** steel body and frame.
PERFORMANCE: Similar to 1962.
Manufacturer: Auto Union GmbH, Dusseldorf, West Germany.
Distributor: Mercedes-Benz Sales, Inc.

1964-65 DKW

F11 — THREE — Two new front-drive models made the DKW lineup for 1964-65, the marque's final stab at the marketplace. The F11 carried a 48 cubic-inch version of the familiar three-cylinder, two-stroke engine.

F12 — THREE — Displacement grew to 899 cubic centimeters for the larger-engined version of the new DKW series. Automatic oil injection was used for the two-stroke, three-cylinder engine. The F12 had a pronounced slant to its front fenders, with single headlamps above rectangular parking lights. A trim strip ran along the beltline, with sculptured framing around wheel openings and rocker panels. 'Auto Union' script went on the nose of the hood, with 'DKW' and the model designation on the back panel. A traditional Auto Union badge with four interlocking circles decorated the horizontal-slat grille. Large vertical taillamps were pointed at the top, to match the upward tapering of the finned rear quarter panels. Both a sedan and a two-seater roadster were offered.

I.D. DATA: Serial number plate is on cowl, near battery, under the hood. Suffix 'E' indicates 1964; 'F' indicates 1965. Engine number is on right side of block.

Model	Body Type & Seating	Engine Type/CID	P.O.E. Price	Weight (lbs.)	Prod. Total
F11	2-dr Sedan-5P	I3/48	1775	1543	N/A
F12	2-dr Sedan-5P	I3/60	1895	1620	N/A
F12	2-dr Roadster-2P	I3/60	2175	1620	N/A

Note: Prices dropped by $30 in 1965.

ENGINE DATA: BASE THREE: Inline, valveless three-cylinder (two-stroke). **Displacement:** 54.3 cu. in. (889 cc). **Bore & Stroke:** 2.93 x 2.68 in. (74.5 x 68 mm). **Compression Ratio:** 7.25:1. **Brake Horsepower:** (F11) 39 at 4000 rpm; (F12) 45 at 4300; (F12 rds) 51 at 4500. **Torque:** (F12) 57.9 lbs.-ft. at 2250 rpm. Four main bearings. 6-volt electrical.

CHASSIS DATA: Wheelbase: 88.6 in. **Overall Length:** 156.3 in. **Height:** (F12 sed) 55.7 in.; (F12 rds) 54.7 in. **Rear Tread:** (rds) 50 in. **Standard Tires:** 5.50x13.

TECHNICAL: Layout: front-engine, front-drive. **Transmission:** four-speed manual; column shift (freewheeling on roadster); all synchromesh. **Standard Final Drive Ratio:** 4.13:1. **Steering:** rack and pinion. **Suspension (front):** adjustable torsion bars. **Suspension (rear):** laminated torsion bar. **Brakes:** front/rear drum except (F12 roadster) front disc, rear drum. **Body Construction:** steel body and frame.
MAJOR OPTIONS: Radio ($61). Whitewall tires ($21).

PERFORMANCE: Top Speed: (F11) 74 mph cruising; (F12 sed) 78 mph; (F12 rds) 85 mph. **Fuel Mileage:** (F11) about 32.5 mpg; (F12 sed) 30.2 mpg; (F12 rds) 25.6 mpg.
Manufacturer: Auto Union GmbH, Dusseldorf, West Germany.

DE TOMASO

Born in Buenos Aires, the son of an Argentian government official, Alejandro de Tomaso showed more interest in auto racing than in managing the family fortune. Amid the anti-Peron political turmoil in his home country, Alejandro fled to Italy in 1955, and began to drive OSCA race cars for the Maserati brothers. Armed with an urge to build cars on his own, he founded De Tomaso Automobili S.p.A. in 1959, with only modest capital. Within two years, he'd built half a dozen Formula 1 race cars, two with OSCA engines. Work began on a roadgoing automobile in 1963, culminating in the Vallelunga, which used a four-cylinder Ford powerplant and backbone-style chassis. With cooperation of the Ford company (and guided by Carroll Shelby), he then developed the V8-powered Mangusta, from a design by Giorgio Giugiaro at the Ghia studio. By that time, De Tomaso had become president of the Ghia design firm, as a result of a purchase of that company by Rowan Industries (a New Jersey operation with ties to De Tomaso's wealthy American-born wife).

Next came the better-known Pantera. While Mangustas had sold in limited numbers in America, the Pantera was to be built with direct Ford distribution in mind. Ford needed a supercar to replace the GT40, and something distinctive for its Lincoln-Mercury dealers to spotlight on the showroom floor. To that end, Ford agreed to supply engines and helped with financing. In a twist of fate, Lee Iacocca became chairman of De Tomaso, as a majority interest in the Italian company had been acquired by Ford in 1970. Panteras were marketed through Lincoln-Mercury dealers, and carried a regular Ford warranty. By 1972, a year after the Pantera went on the market, Alejandro sold his interest in the project, but kept the De Tomaso Automobili name. By 1974, Ford was also ready to quit, partly because of new and tougher U.S. governmental regulations that would have been difficult or impossible for the Pantera to meet without massive structural and powertrain changes. The 1973-74 oil crisis didn't help sales, either. After Ford's departure, Panteras remained in limited production for the European market all the way through the 1970s and '80s. During the 1980s, in fact, they began to trickle back into the U.S. through the efforts of a new independent distributor.

Meanwhile, Alejandro de Tomaso had kept busy with other projects. As early as 1969, he'd turned out a handful of V6-engined Mustelas, followed by the four-door Deauville and the two-door Longchamp, both of which remained in production into the 1980s. In 1976, he took control of Maserati, purchasing the interest obtained by Peugeot as a result of its takeover of the Citroen operation. Production of Maseratis and Innocentis (another acquisition), along with a hundred or so De Tomasos each year, helped make De Tomaso the fifth largest Italian auto producer by the early 1980s.

1963-65 DE TOMASO

VALLELUNGA — FOUR — The first De Tomaso production model, named for an Italian race course, was a Ghia-bodied, open two-seater. Power came from a 1.5-litre British Ford Cortina four-cylinder engine, mounted amidships. Rated at 105 bhp in standard trim, the engine produced 135 horsepower for competition. The backbone-style chassis had a subframe built onto the front to contain the suspension, which consisted of fully independent unequal-length A-arms with an anti-roll bar. At the rear, the engine formed part of the chassis, bolted to the main unit via small triangular attachments that formed part of the transmission housing. In effect, reported *Autosport* in 1965, "the rear suspension is supported almost totally...by the gearbox." That gearbox was a modified Volkswagen five-speed unit. The rear suspension used a single wide lower A-arm, upper links and twin radius rods, with coil springs and an anti-roll bar. The coupe sat low to the ground, with a low nose and roofline, full round wheel openings, and triangular rear quarter windows. Bodies were made of fiberglass, with a massive rear window that lifted for engine access and a rather large lid at the front. Headlamps sat far back in long half-circle nacelles with clear covers. Round taillamps stood at the outer ends of the back panel.

The Vallelunga first appeared at the Turin (Italy) auto show in 1963. Then came one or two alloy-bodied closed prototypes, with bodies built by Fissore. No more than 52 were built in all.

189

1967-70
DE TOMASO

1970 DeTomaso Pantera.

MANGUSTA — V-8 — De Tomaso's first truly serious stab at a production model, named for the mongoose, was a striking sight, almost sculptured in appearance. Either two or four headlamps (depending on the country of destination) rode inside the full-width opening that contained the tight-mesh grille insert, with a small center insignia. Front doors opened outward and had pushbutton locks and vent windows. Three air-intake openings stood to the rear of the small quarter window on one side. Huge twin gullwing-opening engine access covers ran from the back of the doors all the way to the taillamps. Each one contained half of the vast (nearly flat) back window. Horizontal rectangular taillamps sat at the ends of the rear panel, while four exhaust outlet pipes peered upward from nearly ground level. A horizontal body crease ran the full length of the car, past the full wheel openings and large cast-alloy eight-spoke wheels. Styled by Giorgio Giugiaro for the Carrozzeria Ghia studio, the low-slung, aggressively muscular coupe carried a mid-mounted, small-block (302 cid) Ford V-8 engine, in virtually stock form. A five-speed ZF manual transaxle sent the power to the rear wheels of what was, essentially, a detuned race car. The steel backbone chassis consisted mainly of a rectangular tube that ran between the seats. Subframes held the wishbone/coil-spring suspension units and a rack-and-pinion steering mechanism. Aluminum was used for the hood and deck, but most other body panels were made of steel. Seating was provided for two, with virtually no luggage space. Electric windows went only halfway down into the doors. Air conditioning and leather upholstery were standard, an AM/FM radio optional ($185). The dashboard contained seven black dials with luminescent needles, a 300-kph speedometer and an 8000-rpm tachometer. The spare tire fit over the transaxle.

A top speed of 155 mph was claimed, though *Sports Car Graphic* was unable in its early testing to get the Mangusta beyond 111 mph, as the V-8 wouldn't reach past 5100 rpm. *Road & Track* managed 118 mph, while *Car and Driver* estimated the maximum at 128 mph.

Mangustas were exempt from U.S. safety standards until 1971, and didn't even contain seatbelts. A plaque in each trunk, noting that exemption, was signed by Alejandro de Tomaso himself. *Road & Track* complained that a car of this sort "should have been more intelligently designed with regard to crash safety." They took special note of the section of soft fabric and foam rubber that stretched over a sharp metal edge on the dashboard. As for visibility, *Car and Driver* warned that the car's "rear quarters are completely blind."

I.D. DATA: Serial number (for 1969) is on a small identification strip attached to right side member of engine subframe; (1970) on right rear chassis frame, to rear of engine; (1971) on a small plate attached to the right-hand engine support frame.

Model	Body Type & Seating	Engine Type/CID	P.O.E.. Price	Weight (lbs.)	Prod. Total
Mangusta	2-dr Coupe-2P	V8/302	11150	2915	400

Price Note: Later price was $11,500 in U.S.

Weight Note: Approximate figure is shown. Various sources estimated Mangusta weight at 2,600 to 3,120 pounds.

Production Note: Amount shown is approximate. A total of 300 De Tomaso cars were built during 1969 alone. Importer Kjell Qvale told *Car and Driver* that he'd brought in 130 from fall 1968 to fall 1969 (about half of the total production), and expected to receive more.

ENGINE DATA: BASE V-8: Overhead-valve V-8 (Ford). Cast iron block and head. **Displacement:** 302 cu. in. (4950 cc). **Bore & Stroke:** 4.00 x 3.00 in. (101.6 x 76.2 mm). **Compression Ratio:** 10.0:1. **Brake Horsepower:** 230 at 4800 rpm. **Torque:** 310 lbs.-ft. at 2800 rpm. Five main bearings. Hydraulic valve lifters. One Autolite four-barrel carburetor. 12-volt electrical system.

Engine Note: European Mangustas were produced with a modified 289-cid (4727 cc) Ford V-8, rated 305 bhp.

CHASSIS DATA: Wheelbase: 98.4 in. **Overall Length:** 168.3 in. **Height:** 43.3 in. **Width:** 72.0 in. **Front Tread:** 54.9 in. **Rear Tread:** 57.1 in. **Wheel Type:** cast magnesium, 7- and 8-inch x 15. **Standard Tires:** Dunlop SP 185HR15 (front) and 225HR15 (rear).

TECHNICAL: Layout: mid-engine, rear-drive. **Transmission:** ZF five-speed manual transaxle. Gear ratios: (1st) 2.42:1; (2nd) 1.47:1; (3rd) 1.09:1; (4th) 0.958:1; (5th) 0.846:1. **Standard Final Drive Ratio:** 4.22:1. **Steering:** rack and pinion. **Suspension (front):** unequal-length tubular wishbones, coil springs and anti-roll bar. **Suspension (rear):** wide-base unequal-length wishbones, trailing arms, coil springs and anti-roll bar. **Brakes:** Girling front/rear disc, power-assisted. **Body Construction:** steel (some aluminum) panels on unit steel backbone chassis.

PERFORMANCE: Top Speed: 155 mph (claimed); road testers put the maximum at 111-128 mph. **Acceleration (0-60 mph):** 6.3-7.4 seconds. **Acceleration (quarter-mile):** 15.0-17.5 seconds (90-94 mph). **Fuel Mileage:** 14-17 mpg average.

Manufacturer: De Tomaso Automobili S.p.A., Modena, Italy.

Distributor: British Motor Car Distributors, San Francisco, California.

HISTORY: Introduced in November 1966, the prototype Ghia Mangusta first appeared at the Turin (Italy) Auto Show. Significant production did not really begin until fall 1968 and continued until 1972, after the Pantera was introduced.

Sports Car Graphic praised the Mangusta's profile as "about the most beautiful production automobile anywhere....more a work of art than an automobile," with "flawless" Ghia coachwork. Beyond its comfort and quietness on the highway, though, they noted an abundance of irritating problems on its early test car, ranging from a sticky throttle cable to poor rear visibility, as well as "all over the road" handling. Other observers blamed the latter flaw on the backbone chassis, as well as the car's excessive weight at the back end.

"There are other cars we would rather be seen in," declared *Car and Driver* after testing the Mangusta, proclaiming that the car's "Greek-like simplicity and beauty of its shape are stunning....the most beautiful car in the world." In sum, they felt that "As a car the Mangusta has character, but it is hardly what you would call gentle on either mind or body." *Road & Track* said the Mangusta "acted like a magnet for passers-by," attracting more attention than any car they'd ever tested.

1971-72
DE TOMASO

1971 DeTomaso Pantera. (William Siuru Jr.)

MANGUSTA — V-8 — Production of the Mangusta continued into 1971-72; see previous listing for details.

PANTERA — L — V-8 — While production of the Mangusta barely reached a hundred or so per year, the similarly mid-engined Pantera established De Tomaso's presence in the automotive world, and especially in the American marketplace. During its initial four-year run, at least 5,233 were sold in the U.S. Styling followed the same theme as the Mangusta's, but the new body (built by Vignale) was part of a unitized pressed-steel structure. Styling fell into the hands of Tom Tjaarda, an American working for the Ghia studio in Italy. The low, wedge-profile coupe had full wheel openings, small rear quarter windows (with horizontal grillework to the rear), and vent windows on doors. Concealed headlamps rode the low, pointed nose. Below the nose crease was a low, wide rectangular grille opening, with larger rectangular parking lights alongside, plus a matching opening far below (near ground level). The mid-engine design still put most of the weight on the rear of the car, but far less drastically than in the Mangusta. Mounted amidships was a high-output edition of Ford's "Cleveland" 351 cubic-inch (5763 cc) V-8, hooked to the five-speed ZF transaxle. In initial form, the engine produced 310 horsepower (330 in European trim). Top speeds reached 160 mph in Europe, but U.S. buyers had to be satisfied with 140 mph or so. An interior more spacious than the Mangusta even included air conditioning, considered essential to capture American customers. A one-piece engine access lid replaced the Mangusta's twin-gullwing design. Unlike the Mangusta, the Pantera had two luggage areas (front and rear), the front holding a collapsible spare tire. The dashboard held a 200-mph speedometer and 8000-rpm tachometer.

Note: An emission-controlled V-8 with lower compression ratio became standard in 1972; see 1973-74 listing for specifications.

I.D. DATA: Serial number is on a plate attached to top left side of dashboard panel. Starting number (1971): THPNLD 01285.

Model	Body Type & Seating	Engine Type/CID	P.O.E. Price	Weight (lbs.)	Prod. Total
PANTERA					
L	2-dr Coupe-2P	V8/351	9000	2860	Note 1

Note 1: Lincoln-Mercury claims to have sold 6,091 Panteras in the U.S. from 1971-74. Other sources put that total as low as 5,233. Because of limited production and dock strikes, only 130 were sold in the first year, followed by 1,552 in 1972. According to industry sources, a total of 1,033 De Tomaso cars were built in 1971, and 2,718 in 1972.

Price Note: Selling price with mandatory options (air conditioning and alloy wheels) was $9800.

Weight Note: Sources list curb weight from 2,860 to 3,155 pounds.

ENGINE DATA: BASE V-8: Overhead-valve V-8 (Ford). Cast iron block and head. **Displacement:** 351 cu. in. (5763 cc). **Bore & Stroke:** 4.00 x 3.50 in. (101.6 x 89 mm). **Compression Ratio:** 11.0:1. **Brake Horsepower:** 310 (SAE) at 5400 rpm. **Torque:** 380 lbs.-ft. (SAE) at 3400 rpm. Five main bearings. Hydraulic valve lifters. One Autolite four-barrel carburetor. 12-volt electrical system.

Engine Note: European Panteras were rated at 330 bhp (GTS, 350 bhp).

CHASSIS DATA: Wheelbase: 98.4 in. **Overall Length:** 167.4 in. **Height:** 44.1 in. **Width:** 71.3 in. **Front Tread:** 57.0 in. **Rear Tread:** 57.5 in. **Wheel Type:** Campagnolo magnesium alloy; (front) 15x7, (rear) 15x8. **Standard Tires:** (front) 185/70VR15; (rear) 215/70VR15.

1972 DeTomaso Pantera. (William Siuru Jr.)

TECHNICAL: Layout: mid-engine, rear-drive. **Transmission:** ZF five-speed manual transaxle. Early gear ratios: (1st) 2.42:1; (2nd) 1.47:1; (3rd) 1.09:1; (4th) 0.958:1; (5th) 0.846:1. Later gear ratios: (1st) 2.42:1; (2nd) 1.47:1; (3rd) 1.09:1; (4th) 0.846:1; (5th) 0.705:1; (rev) 2.865:1. **Standard Final Drive Ratio:** 4.22:1. **Steering:** rack and pinion. **Suspension (front):** upper/lower (unequal-length) wishbones, coil springs and anti-roll bar. **Suspension (rear):** upper/lower (unequal-length) wishbones, coil springs and anti-roll bar. **Brakes:** front/rear disc, vacuum-assisted. **Body Construction:** steel unibody (steel and aluminum body panels). **Fuel Tank:** 21.0 gallons.

MAJOR OPTIONS: Air conditioning ($500). Campagnolo magnesium alloy wheels ($300). AM radio. AM/FM stereo radio. Note: Alloy wheels and air conditioning were mandatory options.

PERFORMANCE: Top Speed: (early) about 129 mph; (later) 140-150 mph with revised gearing. European Panteras were capable of as much as 162 mph. **Acceleration (0-60 mph):** 5.5-6.8 seconds. **Acceleration (quarter-mile):** 14.0-14.5 seconds (94.5-99.4 mph). **Fuel Mileage:** near 14 mpg average.

Manufacturer: De Tomaso Automobili S.p.A., Modena, Italy.

Distributor: De Tomaso of America, Livonia, Michigan; and Lincoln-Mercury Division, Ford Motor Company, Dearborn, Michigan.

HISTORY: The Pantera appeared at the New York Auto Show in March 1970. Electrical woes and engine overheating plagued quite a few Panteras when new (and later). *Road & Track* found the Pantera much noisier than the Mangusta, partly due to the short mufflers in an Abarth exhaust system. From the start, Ford intended to phase out Pantera production by 1974, when federal regulations were scheduled to change. De Tomaso also produced a Deuville four-door luxury sedan with the Ford 351-cid V-8.

1973-74 DE TOMASO

Foreground — 1974 DeTomaso Pantera "L"; background — 1971 Pantera. (William Siuru Jr.)

PANTERA II — V-8 — Improvements made in response to certain complaints made about the early Panteras were undertaken largely by Ford rather than De Tomaso. Output from the 351 cubic-inch V-8 now came to 266 bhp (SAE net), as a result of tightened emissions regulations and reduced compression ratio. New bumpers added nine inches to the car's overall length, and about 50 pounds to its weight. Up front, a steel bar covered with polyurethane was mounted on two horizontal shock-absorber units. At the rear, a black/chrome steel bar replaced the former, rather flimsy split bumpers. Air conditioning was improved. Disc brakes were now vented rather than solid, and the rear discs were larger. *Car and Driver* still wasn't nearly as happy with the Pantera's comfort and handling as with its profile, noting that "while all of its beholders were ardently wishing that they were in the driver's seat, the driver was usually wishing, with equal fervor, that he was not."

I.D. DATA: Serial number is in same location as 1971-72.

Model	Body Type & Seating	Engine Type/CID	P.O.E. Price	Weight (lbs.)	Prod. Total
PANTERA II					
L	2-dr Coupe-2P	V8/351	10295	3202	Note 1

Note 1: Lincoln-Mercury claims to have sold 6,091 Panteras in the U.S. from 1971-74. Other sources put that total as low as 5,233. A total of 1,831 were sold in 1973, 1,230 in 1974, and 490 leftovers during early 1975. Only 196 De Tomaso cars were built in 1974.

ENGINE DATA: BASE V-8: Overhead-valve V-8 (Ford). Cast iron block and head. **Displacement:** 351 cu. in. (5763 cc). **Bore & Stroke:** 4.00 x 3.50 in. (101.6 x 89 mm). **Compression Ratio:** 8.5:1. **Brake Horsepower:** 266 (SAE net) at 5400 rpm. **Torque:** 301 lbs.-ft. (SAE net) at 3600 rpm. Five main bearings. Hydraulic valve lifters. One four-barrel carburetor. 12-volt electrical system.

CHASSIS DATA: Wheelbase: 99.0 in. **Overall Length:** 176.0 in. **Height:** 44.0 in. **Width:** 71.3 in. **Front Tread:** 57.0 in. **Rear Tread:** 57.5 in. **Wheel Type:** Campagnolo cast magnesium, 7- and 8-inch wide. **Standard Tires:** (front) C60V15; (rear) H60V15.

TECHNICAL: Layout: mid-engine, rear-drive. **Transmission:** ZF five-speed manual transaxle. Gear ratios: (1st) 2.23:1; (2nd) 1.47:1; (3rd) 1.04:1; (4th) 0.85:1; (5th) 0.71:1. **Standard Final Drive Ratio:** 4.22:1. **Steering:** rack and pinion. **Suspension (front):** unequal-length wishbones, coil springs and anti-roll bar. **Suspension (rear):** unequal-length wishbones, coil springs and anti-roll bar. **Brakes:** front/rear vented disc. **Body Construction:** steel unibody (steel and aluminum body panels). **Fuel Tank:** 21.0 gallons.

MAJOR OPTIONS: Air conditioning. AM/FM radio.

PERFORMANCE: Top Speed: 140 mph (estimated). **Acceleration (0-60 mph):** 6.1 seconds. **Acceleration (quarter-mile):** 14.5 seconds (98.2 mph). **Fuel Mileage:** 8-11 mpg average.

Manufacturer: De Tomaso Automobili S.p.A., Modena, Italy.

Distributor: De Tomaso of America, Livonia, Michigan; and Lincoln-Mercury Division, Ford Motor Company, Dearborn, Michigan.

HISTORY: Pantera production for the American market halted in 1974, but leftovers were sold in early 1975. In 1973, De Tomaso began production of the Longchamp, a two-door version of the Deauville. A convertible Deauville was added later. A "special edition" GTS version of the Pantera was introduced in Europe in 1975, with huge 'PANTERA GTS' lettering across the rocker panels, black body moldings, and riveted-on fender flares.

1975-80 DE TOMASO

PANTERA — V-8 — After Ford halted its sale in the U.S., production of the Pantera continued through the 1970s with minimal change, but for the European markets only. Roughly 25 per year were built, powered by a 351-cid V-8 from Ford of Australia, rated at 330 or 350 bhp. A (base) Pantera L, with the 330-bhp V-8, managed 162 mph and a 6.1-second 0-60 time. The GTS model, with front and rear spoilers and 350-bhp, had a claimed top speed of 174 mph. Panteras were especially popular among German enthusiasts. A total of 133 De Tomaso automobiles (Panteras, Longchamps, Deauvilles) were produced during 1975; 62 in 1976; 53 in 1977; 48 in 1978; 38 in 1979; and 37 in 1980.

1981-89 DE TOMASO

1982 DeTomaso Pantera coupe.

PANTERA — V-8 — In 1981, Panteras were reintroduced in the U.S. on a limited scale, marketed by the Panteramerica company in Santa Monica, California; and later by Stauffer Classics, Ltd., in Blue Mounds, Wisconsin. Like the European versions of the late 1970s, these later Panteras came with a Ford of Australia engine (and a price tag that grew steadily to the $60,000 neighborhood). Panteras remained available through the 1980s. GT5 and GT5-S editions took the basic clean lines of the original and tacked on aerodynamic doodads (ground-effects spoilers, a rear wing, etc.), and engines were rated as high as 350 bhp. The GT5, introduced in 1982, had wider wheels than the L and GTS. The GT5-S appeared two years later. Panteras of the 1980s, at least in European form, were capable of 170-mph top speeds and could accelerate from 0-60 mph in 5.5 seconds. American editions had leather upholstery in the two-seat cockpit, with burled wood accents around the gauges. Large vented disc brakes were fed by front and rear air scoops. Most examples sold in the U.S. had the GT5/S trim, including a tall wing spoiler on the decklid. Each had to be modified by the distributor to meet federal standards for emissions and bumper testing.

I.D. DATA: Not available.

Model	Body Type & Seating	Engine Type/CID	P.O.E. Price	Weight. (lbs.)	Prod. Total
PANTERA					
GT5	2-dr Coupe-2P	V8/351	55000	3250	Note 1

Note 1: A total of 77 De Tomaso automobiles (all models) were produced during 1981; 83 in 1982; 77 in 1983; and 71 in 1984.

Price Note: Figure shown was valid in mid-1980s.

ENGINE DATA: BASE V-8: Overhead-valve V-8 (Ford of Australia). Cast iron block and head. **Displacement:** 351 cu. in. (5763 cc). **Bore & Stroke:** 4.00 x 3.50 in. (101.6 x 89 mm). **Compression Ratio:** 8.5:1. **Brake Horsepower:** 350 (SAE) at 6000 rpm. **Torque:** 333 lbs.-ft. (SAE) at 38 rpm. Five main bearings. Hydraulic valve lifters. One Holley four-barrel carburetor. 12-volt electrical system.

Note: 250- and 300-bhp versions also available.

CHASSIS DATA: Wheelbase: 98.8 in. **Overall Length:** 168.1 in. **Height:** 43.3 in. **Width:** 77.6 in. **Front Tread:** 59.4 in. **Rear Tread:** 62.2 in. **Wheel Type:** Campagnolo cast alloy, 10- and 13-inch wide. **Standard Tires:** Pirelli P7 (front) 285/40VR15; (rear) 345/35VR15.

1983 DeTomaso Longchamps GTS.

TECHNICAL: Layout: mid-engine, rear-drive. **Transmission:** ZF five-speed manual transaxle. **Standard Final Drive Ratio:** 2.95:1. **Steering:** rack and pinion. **Suspension (front):** unequal-length wishbones, coil springs and anit-roll bar. **Suspension (rear):** unequal-length wishbones, coil springs and anti-roll bar. **Brakes:** front/rear vented disc, vacuum assisted. **Body Construction:** steel unibody. **Fuel Tank:** 21.1 gallons.
PERFORMANCE: Top Speed: about 147 mph. **Acceleration (0-60 mph):** 5.5 seconds (est). Acceleration (quarter-mile): 14.0 seconds (est.), reaching 99.5 mph.
Manufacturer: De Tomaso Automobili S.p.A., Modena, Italy.
Distributor: Panteramerica, Santa Monica, California; (later) Stauffer Classics Ltd., Blue Mounds, Wisconsin.

DODGE (imports)

Importation of Mitsubishi-built subcompacts, to be marketed under the Dodge name, began in 1971 with the Colt. Plymouth's Arrow also was a Mitsubishi product, but smaller. A Colt GT coupe was added in 1973. Restyling of the body came in 1974, and a slightly smaller version emerged in 1977. Joining the Colt the following year was a sporty Challenger coupe (also marketed as the Plymouth Sapporo).

Colts switched to front-wheel drive for 1979. Plymouth sold equivalent versions as the Champ. By 1983, a single Colt series was marketed by both Dodge and Plymouth dealers. A year later, the tall Colt Vista station wagon (minivan-like in appearance) joined the basic Colt series, and a new Conquest coupe replaced the Challenger. Aero restyling arrived for 1985, and the mid-1980s even brought a turbocharged engine for performance fans. Colts continue to attract subcompact customers for Dodge into the 1990s.

Note: The listings below cover representative model years, rather than every year from 1971 to 1990.

1971-73 DODGE

COLT — FOUR — The first generation of Dodge imports from Japan came in hardtop coupe form as well as pillared coupe, sedan and station wagon body styles. Each rode a 95.3-inch wheelbase. Power came from a 1597-cc overhead-cam four-cylinder engine, initially rated 100 horsepower (dropped to 83 bhp in 1972). A four-speed manual gearbox was standard; three-speed automatic optional. Styling features included quad round headlamps. Standard equipment included an adjustable steering column, variable-ratio steering system, front disc (rear drum) brakes, flow-through ventilation, and vinyl reclining buckets seats (except coupe). Air conditioning was optional. A GT hardtop coupe was added for 1973, with high-visibility paint, rally striping, reclining bucket seats, soft-rim sports steering wheel, center console (with storage bin), and whitewall tires on sport wheels.

1971 Dodge Colt four-door sedan.

1972 Dodge Colt two-door hardtop.

1972 Dodge Colt station wagon.

I.D. DATA: A 13-symbol Vehicle Identification Number is located on the upper left on the instrument panel. The first seven symbols identify the model, model year, transmission and trim; followed by a six-digit sequential serial number. Engine model number is on lower left of block. Engine serial number is stamped on a pad at the upper right front, next to the exhaust manifold.

Model	Body Type & Seating	Engine Type/CID	P.O.E. Price	Weight (lbs.)	Prod. Total
COLT (1973 models)					
6L21	2-dr Coupe-4P	I4/97	2264	2010	Note 1
6H23	2-dr HT Cpe-4P	I4/97	2497	2055	Note 1
6H41	4-dr Sedan-4P	I4/97	2437	2045	Note 1
6P23	2-dr GT HT Cpe-4P	I4/97	2578	2055	Note 1
6H45	2-dr Sta Wag-4P	I4/97	2675	2150	Note 1

Note 1: A total of 28,381 Colts were sold in the U.S. during 1971, 34,057 in 1972, and 35,523 in 1973.

Price Note: Prices in 1971 were $1924 for the coupe, $2074 for the hardtop coupe, $1995 for the sedan, and $2225 for the station wagon.

ENGINE DATA: BASE FOUR: Inline, overhead-cam four-cylinder. Cast iron block and light alloy head. **Displacement:** 97.5 cu. in. (1597 cc). **Bore & Stroke:** 3.03 x 3.39 in. (76.9 x 86 mm). **Compression Ratio:** 8.5:1. **Brake Horsepower:** 100 at 6300 rpm. **Torque:** 101 lbs.-ft. at 4000 rpm. Five main bearings. Solid valve lifters. Two-barrel carburetor.

Engine Note: 1972-73 engine was rated 83 bhp at 5600 rpm and 89 lbs.-ft. at 3600 rpm.

CHASSIS DATA: Wheelbase: 95.3 in. **Overall Length:** 163.4 in. exc. (wagon) 164.0 in. **Height:** (HT/cpe) 54.1 in.; (sed) 55.3 in.; (wag) 56.7 in. **Width:** 61.4-61.8 in. **Front Tread:** 50.6 in. **Rear Tread:** 50.6 in. **Wheel Type:** disc. **Standard Tires:** 6.00x13.

Dimension Note: Early models were slightly smaller in overall length and height.

TECHNICAL: Layout: front-engine, rear-drive. **Transmission:** four-speed manual; automatic available. **Standard Final Drive Ratio:** 3.89:1. **Steering:** recirculating ball. **Suspension (front):** MacPherson struts with coil springs. **Suspension (rear):** rigid axle with semi-elliptic leaf springs. **Brakes:** front disc, rear drum. **Body Construction:** steel unibody.

1973 Dodge Colt two-door hardtop.

MAJOR OPTIONS: Automatic transmission ($183). Air conditioning ($346). AM radio ($61). Tinted glass ($34). Whitewall tires ($33).
Note: Option prices above were valid in 1971. Air conditioning cost $369 in 1973.
PERFORMANCE: Top Speed: 90+ mph. **Acceleration (0-60 mph):** under 14 sec. **Fuel Mileage:** up to 30 mpg.
Manufacturer: Mitsubishi Motors Corp. (Mitsubishi Heavy Industries), Tokyo, Japan.
Distributor: Dodge Division, Chrysler Corp.

1974-76 DODGE

1974 Dodge Colt station wagon.

COLT — FOUR — Though similar in overall appearance, the next-generation Colt had only two headlamps. Parking lights were mounted within the grille, while twin-lens amber side marker lights went at the front of the fenders. As before, a 1597-cc four-cylinder engine provided the power, with rear-wheel drive. An optional 2.0-liter engine also became available (standard in the GT coupe). Bumpers were modified for 1975. Also new for 1975-76 was a Carousel hardtop, painted blue and white. Colts were part of the Galant series in Japan. The larger engine became known as "Silent Shaft" because of its internal counterbalancing shaft.

I.D. DATA: A 13-symbol Vehicle Identification Number is located on the upper left on the instrument panel. The first seven symbols identify the model, model year, transmission and trim; followed by a six-digit sequential serial number. Engine model number is on lower left of block. Engine serial number is stamped on a pad at the upper right front, next to the exhaust manifold.

Model	Body Type & Seating	Engine Type/CID	P.O.E. Price	Weight (lbs.)	Prod. Total
COLT (1976 models)					
6M21	2-dr Coupe-4P	I4/97	3175	2185	Note 1
6S23	2-dr HT Cpe-4P	I4/97	3748	2230	Note 1
6H41	4-dr Sedan-4P	I4/97	3341	2185	Note 1
6P23	2-dr GT HT Cpe-4P	I4/122	3748	2195	Note 1
6H45	2-dr Sta Wag-4P	I4/97	3646	2325	Note 1

Note 1: A total of 42,925 Colts were sold in the U.S. during 1974, 60,356 in 1975, and 48,542 in 1976.
Price Note: Prices in 1974 were $2585 for the coupe, $2830 for the hardtop coupe, $2816 for the sedan, $3015 for the GT coupe, and up to $3271 for the station wagon.

ENGINE DATA: BASE FOUR: Inline, overhead-cam four-cylinder. Cast iron block and light alloy head. **Displacement:** 97.5 cu. in. (1597 cc). **Bore & Stroke:** 3.03 x 3.39 in. (76.9 x 86 mm). **Compression Ratio:** 8.5:1. **Brake Horsepower:** 83 at 5500 rpm. **Torque:** 89 lbs.-ft. at 3500 rpm. Five main bearings. Solid valve lifters. Two-barrel carburetor.
Engine Note: Published ratings for the 1597-cc four varied from 79-83 bhp and 81-89 lbs.-ft. of torque.
BASE FOUR (GT): OPTIONAL (other models): Inline, overhead-cam four-cylinder. Cast iron block and light alloy head. **Displacement:** 121.7 cu. in. (1995 cc). **Bore & Stroke:** 3.31 x 3.54 in. (84.1 x 89.9 mm). **Compression Ratio:** 8.5:1. **Brake Horsepower:** 96 at 5500 rpm. **Torque:** 109 lbs.-ft. at 3500 rpm. Five main bearings. Solid valve lifters. Two-barrel carburetor.
Engine Note: Published ratings for the larger engine varied from 89-96 bhp and 105-109 lbs.-ft. of torque.

1975 Dodge Colt four-door sedan.

CHASSIS DATA: Wheelbase: 95.3 in. **Overall Length:** 171.1 in. exc. (wagon) 172.1 in. **Height:** 55.3 in. exc. (wag) 55.7 in. **Width:** 63.6 exc. (wag) 62.8 in. **Front Tread:** 51.8 in. **Rear Tread:** 51.2 in. **Wheel Type:** disc. **Standard Tires:** (cpe) 6.00x13; (hardtop) A78x13; (GT) BR70x13; (sed/wag) 165SR13.
TECHNICAL: Layout: front-engine, rear-drive. **Transmission:** four-speed manual; automatic available. **Standard Final Drive Ratio:** 3.89:1. **Steering:** recirculating ball. **Suspension (front):** MacPherson struts with coil springs. **Suspension (rear):** rigid axle with semi-elliptic leaf springs. **Brakes:** front disc, rear drum. **Body Construction:** steel unibody.

MAJOR OPTIONS: Automatic transmission: GT/Carousel ($157); others ($250). Air conditioning ($412).
PERFORMANCE: Fuel Mileage (EPA): (cpe) 24 mpg city, 37 mpg highway; (wagon) 20 mpg city, 33 mpg highway.
Manufacturer: Mitsubishi Motors Corp. (Mitsubishi Heavy Industries), Tokyo, Japan.
Distributor: Dodge Division, Chrysler Corp.

1977 DODGE

COLT — FOUR — For 1977, a smaller version of the Colt joined the former lineup, with the same rear-drive layout. This one was known as the Lancer series in Japan, and called "Mileage Makers" in the U.S. They came in coupe and sedan body styles. Engines were the same as in the prior model, a standard 1.6-liter and available 2.0-liter four. This year, the "Silent Shaft" configuration was available in the 1.6-liter engine. That engine was standard in the luxury Carousel and GT hardtop coupes, which had a five-speed gearbox instead of the usual four-speed. The 2.0-liter four was optional in both hardtop coupes and the station wagon. Appearance was similar to the former Colt, but with a new cross-hatch grille pattern. All Colts now had an electric rear-window defroster. A "Freeway Cruise" M/M sedan package included the "Silent Shaft" engine and five-speed gearbox, plus a tachometer, gauges, velour seats with adjustable lumbar support, and maroon/white body. An optional Estate package for the station wagon included woodgrain body panels and adjustable lumbar reclining seats.

I.D. DATA: A 13-symbol Vehicle Identification Number is located on the upper left on the instrument panel. The first seven symbols identify the model, model year, transmission and trim; followed by a six-digit sequential serial number. Engine model number is on lower left of block. Engine serial number is stamped on a pad at the upper right front, next to the exhaust manifold.

Model	Body Type & Seating	Engine Type/CID	P.O.E. Price	Weight (lbs.)	Prod. Total
COLT M/M					
6M21	2-dr Coupe-4P	I4/97	2999	1980	Note 1
6H21	2-dr Cust Cpe-4P	I4/97	3341	2000	Note 1
6H41	4-dr Sedan-4P	I4/97	3422	2065	Note 1
COLT					
6S23	2-dr HT Cpe-4P	I4/97	4041	2185	Note 1
6P23	2-dr GT HT Cpe-4P	I4/97	3988	2185	Note 1
6H45	2-dr Sta Wag-4P	I4/97	3981	2285	Note 1

Note 1: A total of 70,876 Colts were sold in the U.S. during 1977 (plus 3,238 new Challenger/Sapporos; see next listing).
Model Note: The 6S23 hardtop coupe was known as the "Carousel."

ENGINE DATA: BASE FOUR: Inline, overhead-cam four-cylinder. Cast iron block and light alloy head. **Displacement:** 97.5 cu. in. (1597 cc). **Bore & Stroke:** 3.03 x 3.39 in. (76.9 x 86 mm). **Compression Ratio:** 8.5:1. **Brake Horsepower:** 83 at 5500 rpm. **Torque:** 89 lbs.-ft. at 3500 rpm. Five main bearings. Solid valve lifters. Two-barrel carburetor.
Note: "Silent Shaft" version of the 1597-cc four was standard in the hardtop coupes.
OPTIONAL FOUR (Carousel/GT hardtop coupes, station wagon): Inline, overhead-cam four-cylinder. Cast iron block and light alloy head. **Displacement:** 121.7 cu. in. (1995 cc). **Bore & Stroke:** 3.31 x 3.54 in. (84.1 x 89.9 mm). **Compression Ratio:** 8.5:1. **Brake Horsepower:** 96 at 5500 rpm. **Torque:** 109 lbs.-ft. at 3500 rpm. Five main bearings. Solid valve lifters. Two-barrel carburetor.

CHASSIS DATA: Wheelbase: (M/M) 92.1 in.; (others) 95.3 in. **Overall Length:** (M/M) 162.6 in.; (hardtop) 171.1 in.; (wagon) 172.1 in. **Height:** (M/M) 53.5 in.; (hardtop) 54.4 in.; (wag) 55.7 in. **Width:** (M/M) 60.4 in.; (hardtop) 63.6 in.; (wag) 62.8 in. **Front Tread:** (M/M) 51.2 in.; (others) 51.8 in. **Rear Tread:** (M/M) 50 in.; (others) 51.2 in. **Wheel Type:** disc. **Standard Tires:** (M/M) 6.00x13; (others) 165SR13.

TECHNICAL: Layout: front-engine, rear-drive. **Transmission:** (M/M, wagon) four-speed manual; (HT coupe) five-speed manual; automatic available. **Steering:** recirculating ball. **Suspension (front):** MacPherson struts with coil springs. **Suspension (rear):** rigid axle with semi-elliptic leaf springs. **Brakes:** front disc, rear drum. **Body Construction:** steel unibody.

MAJOR OPTIONS: 1995-cc engine: Carousel/GT HT coupe ($182); wagon ($231). Five-speed trans.: wagon ($93). Automatic transmission: GT/Carousel ($177); others ($270). Air conditioning ($395). Freeway cruise pkg.: M/M sedan ($361). Estate wagon pkg. ($260). Red/White Special pkg.: M/M Cust cpe ($177). Vinyl top ($92). Luggage rack: wagon ($68). Tape stripes: M/M cpe ($34); N/A on Red/White. AM radio ($69). AM/FM radio: MM sedan, wagon, GT ($137). Wheel trim rings ($34) Whitewall tires ($48).

Manufacturer: Mitsubishi Motors Corp. (Mitsubishi Heavy Industries), Tokyo, Japan.
Distributor: Dodge Division, Chrysler Corp.

1978 DODGE

1979 Dodge Colt station wagon.

COLT — FOUR — This would be the final year of the rear-drive Colt, which continued with little change except for a new MCA-Jet lean-combustion system in the 1597-cc four-cylinder engine. More air was pumped into each cylinder to produce more thorough burning of the fuel, with the goal of reducing emissions without loss of power. Mitsubishi's "Silent Shaft" engines contained twin rotating shafts to minimize noise and vibration. This year's Colt station wagon rode a 99-inch wheelbase, similar to that of the new Challenger sport coupe, and was available with the larger (2.6-liter) engine.

CHALLENGER — FOUR — A sporty rear-drive coupe, also produced by Mitsubishi, became available in the U.S. this year. A somewhat angular profile was decorated by side-window louvers, large taillamps, and a wrapover rear window. Dual outside mirrors were body-colored. Quad rectangular headlamps were installed, with a split horizontal-bar grille. Race-style aluminum wheels were standard. The front suspension consisted of MacPherson struts with coil springs. Under the hood of initial models was the standard 1597-cc "Silent Shaft" Colt engine; but a 156-cid (2.6-liter) engine became optional, and later standard. A five-speed manual gearbox was standard, with automatic optional. A basic Challenger option package included the 2.6-liter engine, all-disc brakes, power steering, and raised-white-letter tires. A Premium option package added an AM/FM stereo radio with eight-track tape player, intermittent wipers, and power windows.

I.D. DATA: A 13-symbol Vehicle Identification Number is located on the upper left on the instrument panel. The first seven symbols identify the model, model year, transmission and trim; followed by a six-digit sequential serial number. Engine serial number is stamped on a pad at the upper right front, next to the exhaust manifold. Engine model number is stamped near the serial number.

1979 Dodge Challenger coupe.

Model	Body Type & Seating	Engine Type/CID	P.O.E. Price	Weight (lbs.)	Prod. Total
COLT M/M					
6M21	2-dr Coupe-4P	I4/97	3354	2050	Note 1
6H21	2-dr Cust Cpe-4P	I4/97	3734	2065	Note 1
6H45	4-dr Sedan-4P	I4/97	3832	2110	Note 1
COLT					
6H45	2-dr Sta Wag-4P	I4/97	4680	2460	Note 1
CHALLENGER					
2H29	2-dr Spt Cpe-2 + 2P	I4/97	5665	2435	Note 2

Note 1: A total of 42,909 Colts were sold in the U.S. during 1978 (plus 3,134 early '79 models).
Note 2: A total of 30,427 Challengers (and Plymouth Sapporos) were sold in the U.S. during 1978.

ENGINE DATA: BASE FOUR (Colt, Challenger): Inline, overhead-cam four-cylinder. Cast iron block and light alloy head. **Displacement:** 97.5 cu. in. (1597 cc). **Bore & Stroke:** 3.03 x 3.39 in. (76.9 x 86 mm). **Compression Ratio:** 8.5:1. **Brake Horsepower:** 77 at 5200 rpm. **Torque:** 87 lbs.-ft. at 3000 rpm. Five main bearings. Solid valve lifters. Two-barrel carburetor.

OPTIONAL FOUR (Colt wagon, Challenger): Inline, overhead-cam four-cylinder. Cast iron block and light alloy head. **Displacement:** 155.9 cu. in. (2555 cc). **Bore & Stroke:** 3.59 x 3.86 in. (91.1 x 98 mm). **Compression Ratio:** 8.2:1. **Brake Horsepower:** 105 at 5000 rpm. **Torque:** 139 lbs.-ft. at 2500 rpm. Five main bearings. Solid valve lifters.

CHASSIS DATA: Wheelbase: (M/M) 92.1 in.; (Colt wag) 99.0 in.; (Challenger) 99.6 in. **Overall Length:** (M/M) 162.6 in.; (Colt wag) 179.3 in.; (Challenger) 180 in. **Height:** (M/M) 53.5 in.; (Colt wag) 52.4 in.; (Challenger) 52.8 in. **Width:** (M/M) 60.4 in.; (Colt wag) 65.2 in.; (Challenger) 65.9 in. **Front Tread:** (M/M) 51.2 in.; (Colt wag) 53.9 in.; (Challenger) 53.9 in. **Rear Tread:** (M/M) 50 in.; (Colt wag) 53.3 in.; (Challenger) 53.3 in. **Wheel Type:** disc. **Standard Tires:** (M/M) 6.00x13.

TECHNICAL: Layout: front-engine, rear-drive. **Transmission:** (M/M) four-speed manual; (Colt wag, Challenger) five-speed manual; three-speed automatic available. **Steering:** recirculating ball. **Suspension (front):** MacPherson struts with coil springs. **Suspension (rear):** rigid axle with semi-elliptic leaf springs. **Brakes:** front disc, rear drum. **Body Construction:** steel unibody.

MAJOR OPTIONS: Automatic transmission. Power steering: Colt w/2.6-liter engine ($176). Air conditioning: Colt ($493); Challenger ($471). Basic pkg.: Challenger ($591). Premium pkg.: Challenger ($486). Red/White Special pkg.: Colt ($195). Estate wagon pkg.: Colt ($341). Vinyl top (Colt/Challenger). Luggage rack (wagon).

Manufacturer: Mitsubishi Motors Corp. (Mitsubishi Heavy Industries), Tokyo, Japan.
Distributor: Dodge Division, Chrysler Corp.

1979-84 DODGE

COLT (FWD) — FOUR — An all-new front-wheel-drive Colt hatchback became available for 1979, powered by a 1.4-liter four-cylinder engine. Colt's familiar 1.6-liter four was optional. Wheelbase of the new model was 90.6 inches. Marketing of the Mitsubishi-built subcompact continued through 1982 under separate Dodge (Colt) and Plymouth (Champ) banners. After that time, it became just plain Colt, sold by both Dodge and Plymouth dealers. Many examples during this period had the curious Twin-Stick dual-range manual transmission, with eight forward speeds. A turbocharged 1.6-liter four joined in 1984, powering the GTS Turbo. A four-door hatchback joined the original two-door hatchback in 1982.

COLT (RWD) — FOUR — Rear-drive Colts were carried over for 1979, available in coupe, sedan and station wagon form with the standard 1.6-liter MCA-Jet "Silent Shaft" four-cylinder engine and four-speed manual gearbox. The 2.6-liter four was optional. Wagons came with a five-speed, and automatic was available on all models except for the base-engined wagon. The rear-drive coupe and sedan faded away after 1979, while the wagon lingered into 1980.

CHALLENGER — FOUR — Production of the sporty rear-drive coupe continued into 1983. A variant also was marketed as the Plymouth Sapporo. A 2.6-liter four-cylinder "balancer" engine was available in 1979 to replace the standard 1.6-liter four (from the Colt). By 1980, the 2.6-liter became the standard powerplant. Restyling in 1981 caused Challenger to look more like the Sapporo. A "Technica" performance package became available for 1983, featuring silver paint, a black hood and body trim, digital speedometer, and graphic tachometer display. It also included a six-function Electronic Voice Alert system that issued vocal warnings that the door was open, key in ignition, etc. A Road Wheel package for late models included cast aluminum wheels and all-disc brakes.

1981 Dodge Challenger coupe.

I.D. DATA: A 13-symbol or 17-symbol Vehicle Identification Number is located on the upper left of the instrument panel.

Model	Body Type & Seating	Engine Type/CID	P.O.E. Price	Weight (lbs.)	Prod. Total
COLT FWD (1979 models)					
4M24	2-dr Hatch-4P	I4/86	4425	1730	Note 1
4H24	2-dr Cust Hatch-4P	I4/86	4743	1775	Note 1
COLT RWD (1979 models)					
6M21	2-dr Coupe-4P	I4/97	3984	1945	Note 1
6H41	4-dr Sedan-4P	I4/97	4490	2020	Note 1
6H45	2-dr Sta Wag-4P	I4/97	5591	2445	Note 1
COLT FWD (1984 models)					
E24	2-dr E Hatch-4P	I4/86	5095	1865	Note 1
E28	4-dr E Hatch-4P	I4/86	5639	1951	Note 1
E34	2-dr DL Hatch-4P	I4/86	5893	1880	Note 1
E38	4-dr DL Hatch-4P	I4/86	6029	2025	Note 1

Model	Body Type & Seating	Engine Type/CID	P.O.E. Price	Weight (lbs.)	Prod. Total
CHALLENGER (1979 model)					
2H29	2-dr Spt Cpe-2 + 2P	I4/97	6487	2410	Note 2
CHALLENGER (1983 model)					
D43	2-dr Spt Cpe-2 + 2P	I4/156	8323	2620	Note 2

Note 1: A total of 60,521 Colts (plus 29,215 wagons) were sold in the U.S. during 1979; 83,711 (plus 6,734 wagons) in 1980; 84,144 (plus 3878 wagons) in 1981; 52,355 two-door and 22,675 four-door hatchbacks in 1982; 46,479 two-door and 27,192 four-door hatchbacks in 1983; and 44,724 two-door and 19,657 four-door hatchbacks in 1984.

Note 2: A total of 26,488 Challengers (and Plymouth Sapporos) were sold in the U.S. during 1979, 23,187 in 1980, 26,016 in 1981, 27,196 in 1982, 23,937 in 1983, and 836 leftovers in 1984.

1981 Dodge Colt.

ENGINE DATA: BASE FOUR (Colt hatchback): Inline, overhead-cam four-cylinder. Cast iron block and light alloy head. **Displacement:** 86.0 cu. in. (1410 cc). **Bore & Stroke:** 2.91 x 3.23 in. (74 x 82 mm). **Compression Ratio:** 8.8:1. **Brake Horsepower:** 64-70 at 5000-5200 rpm. **Torque:** 78 lbs.-ft. at 3000 rpm. Five main bearings. Solid valve lifters. Two-barrel carburetor.

BASE FOUR (Colt, early Challenger): Inline, overhead-cam four-cylinder. Cast iron block and light alloy head. **Displacement:** 97.5 cu. in. (1597 cc). **Bore & Stroke:** 3.03 x 3.39 in. (76.9 x 86 mm). **Compression Ratio:** 8.5:1. **Brake Horsepower:** 72-80 at 5000-5200 rpm. **Torque:** 85-87 lbs.-ft. at 3000 rpm. Five main bearings. Solid valve lifters. Two-barrel carburetor.

OPTIONAL TURBO FOUR (1984 only): Same as 1.6-liter four above, except — 102 bhp with fuel injection.

BASE FOUR (1980-83 Challenger): OPTIONAL (Colt station wagon): Inline, overhead-cam four-cylinder. Cast iron block and light alloy head. **Displacement:** 155.9 cu. in. (2555 cc). **Bore & Stroke:** 3.59 x 3.86 in. (91.1 x 98 mm). **Compression Ratio:** 8.2:1. **Brake Horsepower:** (1979) 105 at 5000 rpm; (1983) 100 at 5000 rpm. **Torque:** (1979) 139 lbs.-ft. at 2500 rpm; (1983) 137 at 2500 rpm. Five main bearings. Solid valve lifters. Two-barrel carburetor.

1982 Dodge Colt four-door sedan.

1982 Dodge Challenger.

CHASSIS DATA: Wheelbase: (Colt 2-dr hatch) 90.6 in.; (Colt cpe/sed) 92.1 in.; (Colt 4-dr hatch) 93.7 in.; (Colt wag) 99 in.; (Challenger) 99.6 in. **Overall Length:** (Colt 2-dr hatch) 156.9 in.; (Colt 4-dr hatch) 161.0 in.; (Colt cpe/sed) 162.5 in.; (Colt wag) 179.3 in.; (Challenger) 180.0 in. **Height:** (Colt hatch) 50.0 in.; (Colt cpe/sed) 52.8 in.; (Colt wag) 52.4 in.; (Challenger) 52.8 in. **Width:** (Colt hatch) 62.4-62.6 in.; (Colt cpe/sed) 60.4 in.; (Colt wag) 65.2 in.; (Challenger) 65.9 in. **Front Tread:** (Colt hatch) 53.9 in.; (Colt cpe/sed) 51.2 in.; (Colt wag) 53.9 in.; (Challenger) 54.1 in. **Rear Tread:** (Colt hatch) 52.8 in.; (Colt cpe/sed) 50 in.; (Colt wag) 53.3 in.; (Challenger) 53.3 in.

1983 Dodge Colt.

TECHNICAL: Layout: (Colt hatchback) front-engine, front-drive; (other Colts, Challenger) front-engine, rear-drive. **Transmission:** (Colt) Twin-Stick (early) or four-speed (late) manual; (Challenger) five-speed; automatic available. **Steering:** (Colt) rack and pinion; (Challenger) recirculating ball. **Suspension (front):** MacPherson struts with coil springs and anti-roll bar. **Suspension (rear):** (Colt) independent with trailing arms and coil springs; (Challenger) rigid axle with coil springs. **Brakes:** front disc, rear drum. **Body Construction:** steel unibody.

1984 Dodge Colt Vista.

1984 Dodge Conquest.

MAJOR OPTIONS: Automatic transmission. Cruise control. Air conditioning. AM/FM stereo radio with cassette player.

ADDITIONAL MODELS: Dodge also began to offer a new Mitsubishi-built Colt Vista station wagon in 1984, with Twin-Stick transmission on the early models. Power came from a 2.0-liter (122-cid) four-cylinder engine, producing 88 horsepower. The Colt Vista looked more like a small minivan than a customary station wagon.
Replacing the Challenger in the 1984 Dodge lineup was the Conquest sport coupe, with a turbocharged 2.6-liter "Silent Shaft" four-cylinder engine producing 145 horsepower. This was mechanically identical to the Mitsubishi Starion, with slight restyling. Conquests lacked the simulated hood scoop seen on the early Starion, and had a different front bumper and air dam appearance. Early models came only with five-speed manual shift. Wheelbase was 95.9 inches, length 173.2 inches overall, and the Conquest stood 52.2 inches high. See next listing for additional details.
Manufacturer: Mitsubishi Motors Corp. (Mitsubishi Heavy Industries), Tokyo, Japan.
Distributor: Dodge Division, Chrysler Corp.

195

1985-88 DODGE

Model	Body Type & Seating	Engine Type/CID	P.O.E. Price	Weight (lbs.)	Prod. Total
COLT (1985 models)					
E	2-dr Hatch-4P	I4/90	5372	1876	Note 1
E	4-dr Hatch-4P	I4/90	6029	1967	Note 1
DL	2-dr Hatch-4P	I4/90	6492	1984	Note 1
DL	4-dr Sedan-4P	I4/90	6177	1876	Note 1
Premier	4-dr Sedan-4P	I4/90	7409	1989	Note 1
COLT VISTA (1985 models)					
	4-dr Sta Wag-7P	I4/122	8721	2535	Note 2
4WD	4-dr Sta Wag-7P	I4/122	9809	2545	Note 2
CONQUEST (1985 model)					
	2-dr Hatch-4P	I4/156	12564	2820	N/A

Note 1: A total of 38,262 two-door and 6,428 four-door Colt hatchbacks were sold in the U.S. during 1985; 48,487 two-door and 78 leftover four-doors in 1986; 37,943 two-doors and 678 wagons in 1987; and 43,319 two-doors and 10,525 wagons in 1988.

Note 2: A total of 15,270 Colt Vistas were sold in the U.S. during 1985, 23,611 in 1986, 35,096 in 1987, and 29,380 in 1988.

Price Note: Colt prices in 1988 ranged from $5899 to $8943; Colt Vistas sold for $11,122 and $12,405; and the Conquest (now considered part of the Chrysler lineup) was priced at $18,155.

1985 Dodge Conquest.

1986 Dodge Conquest.

1988 Dodge Colt Premier five-door.

COLT — FOUR — An aerodynamic restyling hit the Mitsubishi-built Dodge/Plymouth Colt for 1985, and the car rode a new platform with independent rear suspension. Two-door and four-door hatchbacks were available, along with a four-door sedan. The base two-door came with a four-speed manual gearbox; others, the five-speed. The Twin-Stick transmission was dropped. A 1.6-liter turbocharged engine was optional in the GTS two-door and the upscale Premier sedan, while others were powered by a carbureted 1.5-liter four that delivered 68 horsepower. The four-door was dropped in 1986. A 1987 appearance restyling included new fenders, grille, full-width hood, and flush aero head-lamps. A new DL wagon arrived for 1988, with a fuel-injected version of the 1.5-liter engine, now fuel injected for 75 horsepower.

COLT VISTA — FOUR — Introduced in 1984, the minivan-like station wagon from Mitsubishi took a five-speed manual gearbox as standard in 1985, replacing the initial Twin-Stick unit. A variant with full-time four-wheel-drive became available in mid-1985, and added "shift-on-the-fly" in the following year. The Colt Vista's 2.0-liter engine added hydraulic lifters in 1985, and adopted fuel injection in late 1987 to add eight horsepower. The three-seat wagons held seven passengers. A 1988 restyling included aero headlamps and a new grille.

CONQUEST — FOUR — Production of the sporty rear-drive coupe, introduced for 1984, continued into 1989. It was a close relative of the Mitsubishi Starion, with a turbocharged 2.6-liter four-cylinder engine. Turbocharger bearings adopted water cooling for 1984, and power windows and cruise control became standard. Options included a 100-watt stereo system with steering-wheel remote control.

I.D. DATA: A 17-symbol Vehicle Identification Number is located on the upper left of the instrument panel.

1988 Dodge Colt Vista.

Note: Specifications below are for 1985 models.

ENGINE DATA: BASE FOUR (Colt): Inline, overhead-cam four-cylinder. Cast iron block and light alloy head. **Displacement:** 89.6 cu. in. (1468 cc). **Bore & Stroke:** 2.97 x 3.23 in. (75.5 x 82 mm). **Compression Ratio:** 9.4:1. **Brake Horsepower:** 68 at 5500 rpm. **Torque:** 82 lbs.-ft. at 3500 rpm. Five main bearings. Solid valve lifters. Two-barrel carburetor.
OPTIONAL TURBO FOUR (Colt GTS, Premier): Inline, overhead-cam four-cylinder. Cast iron block and light alloy head. **Displacement:** 97.4 cu. in. (1597 cc). **Bore & Stroke:** 3.03 x 3.39 in. (76.9 x 86 mm). **Compression Ratio:** 7.6:1. **Brake Horsepower:** 102 at 5500 rpm. **Torque:** 122 lbs.-ft. at 3000 rpm. Five main bearings. Solid valve lifters. Fuel injection.
BASE FOUR (Colt Vista): Inline, overhead-cam four-cylinder. Cast iron block and light alloy head. **Displacement:** 122 cu. in. (1997 cc). **Bore & Stroke:** 3.35 x 3.46 in. (85 x 88 mm). **Compression Ratio:** 8.5:1. **Brake Horsepower:** 88 at 5000 rpm. **Torque:** 108 lbs.-ft. at 3600 rpm. Five main bearings. Hydraulic valve lifters. Two-barrel carburetor.
BASE TURBOCHARGED FOUR (Conquest): Inline, overhead-cam four-cylinder. Cast iron block and light alloy head. **Displacement:** 155.9 cu. in. (2555 cc). **Bore & Stroke:** 3.59 x 3.86 in. (91.1 x 98 mm). **Compression Ratio:** 7.0:1. **Brake Horsepower:** 145 at 5000 rpm. **Torque:** 185 lbs.-ft. at 2500 rpm. Five main bearings. Fuel injection.

CHASSIS DATA: Wheelbase: (Colt) 93.7 in.; (Colt Vista) 103.3 in.; (Conquest) 95.9 in. **Overall Length:** (Colt hatch) 157.3 in.; (Colt sedan) 167.3 in.; (Colt Vista) 174.6 in.; (Conquest) 173.2 in. **Height:** (Colt) 53.6 in.; (Colt Vista) 59.8 in.; (Conquest) 51.8 in. **Width:** (Colt) 63.8 in.; (Colt Vista) 64.6 in.; (Conquest) 66.3 in. **Front Tread:** (Colt) 54.7 in.; (Colt Vista) 55.5 in.; (Conquest) 54.9 in. **Rear Tread:** (Colt) 52.8 in.; (Colt Vista) 54.1 in.; (Conquest) 54.1 in.

TECHNICAL: Layout: (Colt/Vista) front-engine, front-drive; (Conquest) front-engine, rear-drive. **Transmission:** (Colt) four- or five-speed manual; (others) five-speed; automatic available. **Steering:** (Colt/Vista) rack and pinion; (Conquest) recirculating ball. **Suspension (front):** MacPherson struts with coil springs and anti-roll bar. **Suspension (rear):** (Colt/Vista) independent with trailing arms and coil springs; (Conquest) independent with MacPherson struts, trailing arms, coil springs and anti-roll bar. **Brakes:** front disc, rear drum except (Conquest) front/rear disc. **Body Construction:** steel unibody.
Manufacturer: Mitsubishi Motors Corp. (Mitsubishi Heavy Industries), Tokyo, Japan.
Distributor: Dodge Division, Chrysler Corp.

1986 Dodge Colt Vista.

1989-90 DODGE

COLT — FOUR — While the Colt four-door station wagon continued in its former form, the two-door hatchback was all new for 1989. More rounded in appearance, the new hatchback was longer, wider and taller than its predecessor. Not only was a Plymouth version offered, but equivalent cars were marketed under the Eagle and Mitsubishi badges: as the Eagle Summit (four-door sedan) and Mitsubishi Mirage (hatchback and sedan). This time, too, the Colt station wagon was available with optional four-wheel-drive, powered by a larger (1.8-liter) engine, with 87 horsepower. Base engine was the same 1.5-liter four that powered the 1985-88 Colts, now rated 81 horsepower with fuel injection. A turbocharged 1.6-liter four was optional again, under the hood of the sporty GT hatchback, with output boosted to 135 bhp. It was dropped after 1989, but a non-turbo version of the twin-cam 1.6-liter four became available. The GT included a sport suspension, tachometer, and aero body panels. Base Colts came with a four-speed manual gearbox; others had the five-speed, or optional three-speed (or four-speed) automatic.

1989 Dodge Colt Vista.

COLT VISTA — FOUR — The Mitsubishi-built station wagon continued with little change, except for the availability of permanent four-wheel-drive in 1990. Power came from a fuel-injected 2.0-liter four, rated 96 horsepower, hooked to either a five-speed manual or three-speed automatic transmission.

I.D. DATA: A 17-symbol Vehicle Identification Number is located on the upper left of the instrument panel.

Model	Body Type & Seating	Engine Type/CID	P.O.E. Price	Weight (lbs.)	Prod. Total
COLT (1989)					
	2-dr Hatch-4/5P	I4/90	6477	2194	Note 1
E	2-dr Hatch-4/5P	I4/90	7279	2205	Note 1
GT	2-dr Hatch-4/5P	I4/90	8620	2238	Note 1
DL	4-dr Sta Wag-4/5P	I4/90	9316	2271	Note 1
DL 4WD	4-dr Sta Wag-4/5P	I4/110	11145	2568	Note 1
COLT VISTA (1989)					
	4-dr Sta Wag-7P	I4/122	11518	2634	Note 2
4WD	4-dr Sta Wag-7P	I4/122	12828	2955	Note 2

Note 1: A total of 48,001 two-door Colt hatchbacks and 8,443 Colt station wagons were sold in the U.S. during 1989.
Note 2: A total of 12,910 Colt Vistas were sold in the U.S. during 1989.

1990 Dodge Colt Vista.

Note: Specifications below are for 1989 models.
ENGINE DATA: BASE FOUR (Colt): Inline, overhead-cam four-cylinder. Cast iron block and light alloy head. **Displacement:** 89.6 cu. in. (1468 cc). **Bore & Stroke:** 2.97 x 3.23 in. (75.5 x 82 mm). **Compression Ratio:** 9.4:1. **Brake Horsepower:** 81 at 5500 rpm. **Torque:** 91 lbs.-ft. at 3000 rpm. Five main bearings. Solid valve lifters. Port fuel injection.
OPTIONAL TURBOCHARGED FOUR (1989 Colt GT): Inline, dual-overhead-cam four-cylinder (16-valve). Cast iron block and light alloy head. **Displacement:** 97.4 cu. in. (1597 cc). **Bore & Stroke:** 3.03 x 3.39 in. (76.9 x 86 mm). **Compression Ratio:** 8.0:1. **Brake Horsepower:** 135 at 6000 rpm. **Torque:** 141 lbs.-ft. at 3000 rpm. Five main bearings. Solid valve lifters. Port fuel injection.

OPTIONAL FOUR (1990 Colt): Inline, dual-overhead-cam four-cylinder. Cast iron block and light alloy head. **Displacement:** 97 cu. in. (1597 cc). **Bore & Stroke:** 3.03 x 3.39 in. (76.9 x 86 mm). **Compression Ratio:** 9.2:1. **Brake Horsepower:** 113 at 6500 rpm. **Torque:** 99 lbs.-ft. at 5000 rpm. Port fuel injection.
BASE FOUR (Colt 4WD): Inline, overhead-cam four-cylinder. **Displacement:** 107.1 cu. in. (1754 cc). **Bore & Stroke:** 3.17 x 3.39 in. (80.5 x 86 mm). **Compression Ratio:** 9.0:1. **Brake Horsepower:** 87 at 5000 rpm. **Torque:** 102 lbs.-ft. at 3000 rpm. Port fuel injection.
BASE FOUR (Colt Vista): Inline, overhead-cam four-cylinder. Cast iron block and light alloy head. **Displacement:** 122 cu. in. (1997 cc). **Bore & Stroke:** 3.35 x 3.46 in. (85 x 88 mm). **Compression Ratio:** 8.5:1. **Brake Horsepower:** 96 at 5000 rpm. **Torque:** 113 lbs.-ft. at 3500 rpm. Five main bearings. Hydraulic valve lifters. Port fuel injection.

CHASSIS DATA: Wheelbase: (Colt hatch) 93.9 in.; (Colt wagon) 93.7 in.; (Colt Vista) 103.3 in. **Overall Length:** (Colt hatch) 158.7 in.; (Colt wagon) 169.3 in.; (Colt Vista) 174.6 in. **Height:** (Colt hatch) 54.1 in.; (Colt wagon) 55.9 in.; (Colt Vista) 57.3 in.; (Colt Vista 4WD) 59.4 in. **Width:** (Colt hatch) 65.5 in.; (Colt wagon) 64.4 in.; (Colt Vista) 64.6 in. **Front Tread:** (Colt hatch) 56.3 in.; (Colt wag) 55.5 in.; (Colt Vista) 55.5 in.; (Colt Vista 4WD) 55.3 in. **Rear Tread:** (Colt hatch) 56.3 in.; (Colt wag) 52.8 in.; (Colt 4WD wag) 53.5 in.; (Colt Vista 4WD) 54.5 in.

TECHNICAL: Layout: front-engine, front-drive. **Transmission:** (Colt) four- or five-speed manual; (others) five-speed; automatic available. **Steering:** rack and pinion. **Suspension (front):** MacPherson struts with coil springs and anti-roll bar. **Suspension (rear):** independent with trailing arms and coil springs. **Brakes:** front disc, rear drum. **Body Construction:** steel unibody.

Manufacturer: Mitsubishi Motors Corp. (Mitsubishi Heavy Industries), Tokyo, Japan.
Distributor: Dodge Division, Chrysler Corp.

(SWALLOW) DORETTI

After William Lyons, head of the Swallow Coachbuilding Company, founded SS Cars Ltd. (Jaguar's predecessor) in 1935, Swallow finished the decade as a producer of side-cars. Following World War II, Swallow went under new ownership, turning to aircraft work while its sidecar operation was taken over by another company, Tube Investments Ltd. Success of the Triumph TR2 sports car, following its 1952 debut, prompted Swallow to make a stab at that market--especially at the American customers for sports roadsters. Thus, the Doretti (named as a variant of Dorothy, who was a daughter of Triumph's American importer) was announced in January 1954. Though differing considerably in appearance from the TR2, it carried a conventional Triumph engine, gearbox and front suspension. About 260 were built in 1953-55 (including one or two coupes) but sales never took off, partly because of the car's high price. Experts disagreed on the Doretti's merits, some claiming that it was heavier and slower than a TR2, others (especially in America) insisting it was quicker. A serious injury to company head Sir John Black, while he was at the wheel of a Doretti, also helped to trigger the car's demise. In 1956, the company was sold to another producer of sidecars, and the limited-production roadsters soon were forgotten.

1954-55 (SWALLOW) DORETTI

DORETTI — FOUR — Sitting atop a box-section tubular steel chassis, the two-seat roadster's flat-sided twin-skin body consisted of steel inner panels and doors and an aluminum alloy outer shell. The conventional body styling included fully rounded wheel openings and a lid-type front-hinged hood. The rectangular grille opening, slightly rounded at the top, contained five horizontal bars with a bright surround molding. Small round parking lights stood directly below the headlamps. A horizontal bodyside trim crease ran along the cowl and into the door (extending near the trailing edge). Doors taller than those on the TR2 eliminated the "wind whipping" typical of that model. A four-speed manual gearbox was standard, with hydraulic clutch; overdrive (operating on fourth gear only) optional. The 121.5-cid Triumph TR2 engine produced 90 horsepower. Inside was leather upholstery, carpeting, and a laminated wood/punched aluminum steering wheel. Symmetrical instruments and controls were mounted in the center of the dashboard, but the speedometer sat ahead of the passenger. Dashboard crash padding covered with

197

1954 Doretti sports car.

laced-on leather continued over the door tops. A removable strapped-in suitcase on a shelf behind the seats matched the seat upholstery and could hold at least a change of clothing. Standard equipment included side curtains, a tonneau cover, and heater. Most examples shipped to the U.S. had wire wheels rather than the standard disc wheels. For competition use, aero-type screens could replace the detachable windshield. Bumper overriders were added for 1955.

I.D. DATA: Chassis serial number is stamped on a plate under the hood, ahead of the dashboard. Engine number is stamped on a boss on the block, behind the ignition coil. Starting serial number: 1001. Ending serial number (1955): 1293.

Model	Body Type & Seating	Engine Type/CID	P.O.E. Price	Weight (lbs.)	Prod. Total
	2-dr Rds-2P	I4/121	3295	1860	Note 1

Note 1: About 260 Dorettis were produced through 1955 (followed by about 16 built after the factory closed, as late as 1958), though some sources claim the total was barely over 100. The total included one or two solid-top coupes.

Price Note: Initial P.O.E. price (shown) was later cut to $2980 with wire wheels, or $2905 with disc wheels.

Weight Note: Dry weight shown; curb weight was 2,155 pounds.

ENGINE DATA: BASE FOUR: Inline, overhead-valve four-cylinder (Triumph TR2). Cast iron block. **Displacement:** 121.5 cu. in. (1991 cc). **Bore & Stroke:** 3.27 x 3.62 in. (83 x 92 mm). **Compression Ratio:** 8.5:1. **Brake Horsepower:** 90 at 4800 rpm. Three main bearings. Solid valve lifters. Twin SU carburetors.

CHASSIS DATA: Wheelbase: 95 in. **Overall Length:** 156 in. **Height:** 48.5 in. **Width:** 61 in. **Max. Tread:** 48 in. **Wheel Type:** disc with hubcaps, or wire wheels. **Standard Tires:** 5.50x15.

TECHNICAL: Layout: front-engine, rear-drive. **Transmission:** four-speed manual (overdrive optional); floor lever. **Standard Final Drive Ratio:** 3.7:1. **Suspension (front):** independent; wishbones and coil springs. **Suspension (rear):** rigid axle with semi-elliptic leaf springs. **Brakes:** Lockheed hydraulic, front/rear drum. **Body Construction:** aluminum body (steel inner panels) on box-section tubular steel frame.

MAJOR OPTIONS: Overdrive ($154).

PERFORMANCE: Top Speed: 100 + mph (75-90 mph touring speed). **Acceleration (0-60 mph):** 13.7 seconds. **Acceleration (quarter-mile):** 19.2 seconds (72 mph).

Manufacturer: Swallow Coachbuilding Co. Ltd. (a subsidiary of Tube Investments Group), Walsall, Staffordshire, England.

Distributor: Standard-Triumph Motor Co. Ltd., New York City; Cal-Sales Inc., Gardena, California; and Southeastern Motors Inc., Hollywood, Florida.

HISTORY: Triumph ads in U.S. publications during 1954 also advised readers to see and test drive the fabulous new Doretti. An American sales brochure promised "elegance without peer..... A hand-finished car, in the aristocratic tradition." Walt Woron of *Motor Trend* noted in 1954 that few cars tested by that magazine had "created as much interest or drawn so much attention as the new Doretti," adding that the car, "above all, is *fun* to drive."

DUAL-GHIA

The Italian-bodied Dual-Ghia came to America in two different categories: as a largely domestic model from 1956-58, then as a full-fledged import for 1960-63. Closely pat-

terned on the Dodge Firearrow concept car of 1953, the first Dual-Ghia used a modified Dodge chassis and drivetrain, with body added in Italy by Carrozzeria Ghia. A total of 104 were built (all convertibles, except for two hardtops), plus 13 prototypes. See *Standard Catalog of American Cars* (1946-75) for details.

1955-'58 Dual Ghia Firebomb convertible.

1960-63 DUAL-GHIA

L6.4 — V-8 — Although the initial Dual-Ghia (built from 1956-58) had been popular with movie stars, sales were modest, with barely more than a hundred built. A second version appeared at the Paris auto show in fall 1960, based on a Virgil Exner design called "Dart." This time, full production went to Italy as the original Dual-Ghia's creator, Gene Casaroll, sold both design and manufacturing rights to the Carrozzeria Ghia company in Torino. Casaroll's Dual Motors, having expanded from Detroit to Port Washington, New York, supplied components for the second-generation model, but otherwise served only as its sales agent in the U.S. Instead of a convertible, as offered in the first version, the revised Dual-Ghia came only as a hardtop coupe.

As before, Dual-Ghia blended an American drivetrain with Italian coachwork, creating a car that was mostly hand built. Both the appearance of the Dual-Ghia and its powerplant differed considerably from the first version. Up front was a wide rectangular grille with rounded corners and recessed crosshatch pattern. That pattern and a single horizontal bar continued outward in a pair of side grilles, which held small round park/signal lights. At the outer ends were single round headlamps. Above each headlamp, the fender had a bulge at the outside, which tapered back toward the windshield. A huge wraparound window appeared at the rear, with a slim pillar on each side, providing an almost semi-fastback profile (with conventional trunk lid). Recessed taillamps stood at the rear fender tips, with four additional round lamps down on the back panel. The luxurious passenger compartment also got a total restyle, including a console that dropped down to meet the transmission hump and floor gearshift lever.

Wheelbase of the hardtop was 115 inches, and the car weighed an even two tons. Under the hood was a Chrysler 383 cubic-inch V-8, rated 335 horsepower, hooked to TorqueFlite automatic. Suspension components also came from Chrysler, with torsion bars in front and semi-elliptic leaf springs at the back end. Thus, servicing would be available at any Chrysler dealer.

This Dual-Ghia cost nearly twice as much as its predecessor. Frank Sinatra bought the first one to roll out of Italy, but that didn't help sales reach the hoped-for goal of five cars per month. Only 26 were built in all.

I.D. DATA: Not available.

Model	Body Type & Seating	Engine Type/CID	P.O.E. Price	Weight (lbs.)	Prod. Total
L6.4	2-dr HT Cpe-5P	V8/383	15000	4000	26

ENGINE DATA: BASE V-8: Overhead valve V-8 (Chrysler). Cast iron block and head. **Displacement:** 383 cu. in. **Bore & Stroke:** 4.25 x 3.38 in. **Brake Horsepower:** 335 at 4600 rpm. **Torque:** 410 lbs.-ft. at 2400 rpm. Five main bearings. Hydraulic valve lifters. Four-barrel carburetor. 12-volt electrical.

CHASSIS DATA: Wheelbase: 115 in. **Overall Length:** 210 in. **Height:** 52 in. **Width:** 75 in.

TECHNICAL: Layout: front-engine, rear-drive. **Transmission:** TorqueFlite three-speed automatic. **Standard Final Drive Ratio:** 3.23:1. **Steering:** full-time power assist. **Suspension (front):** torsion bars. **Suspension (rear):** semi-elliptic leaf springs.

Manufacturer: Carrozzeria Ghia, Torino, Italy.

Distributor: Dual Motors, Detroit, Michigan and Port Washington, New York.

HISTORY: Introduced in fall 1960 at Paris auto show.

ELVA

Doesn't look Latin at all, but the name of this British-built sports car had a Spanish origin. Builder Frank Nichols took it from *Elle va,* meaning "she goes." And that's exactly what the Elva did, on the track or on the street, starting in the late 1950s.

Nichols, a race driver who'd handled Ford Special and Lotus cars on the track, finished the first Elva sports-racer early in 1955, built from scratch without blueprints and sold immediately. Power was supplied by a 1072-cc Ford engine with overhead-valve conversion, while the car's suspension came from a Standard. Observers took an interest in the race car at its first outing, and Nichols quickly formed Elva Engineering Co. Ltd. to produce duplicates, dubbed Mark 1. A subsequent Mark 1B switched to a wishbone-style front suspension, and the next Mark 2 carried a De Dion rear end. A Coventry Climax engine replaced the original Ford along the way. Racing success of one example in the U.S. led to American interest in the Elva, which soon became available on a fairly regular basis. Most of the firm's output in the early years, in fact, went to the western side of the Atlantic, helping Elva to finance a larger plant and turn out most of the parts for subsequent cars on its own.

Elva's first streetable car, the Courier, arrived in 1958, a result of advice from the car's American importer. Production of the race models continued, but Couriers powered by a 1489-cc BMC four-cylinder engine accounted for the majority of the company's output. And most of those left Britain. About 400 were produced by late 1961. Unfortunately for Elva's balance sheet, that American importer went to prison without paying for all the cars he'd accepted. After the original company folded, a second one was formed to continue turning out race cars. Then, production of the Courier resumed under the auspices of Trojan Ltd., which was best known for three-wheeled vehicles. The Mark III edition appeared late in 1962, followed by a Mark IV which switched to independent rear suspension. Frank Nichols assumed consultant duties with Trojan until 1965, when a new coupe with BMW powerplant was announced. Only a handful of prototypes were built, but Couriers remained in (minimal) production up to 1969, controlled by yet another company.

1958-61 ELVA

COURIER — Mk I/II — FOUR — A "boulevard" sports car, the new Courier could be driven on the street but readied for racing on the weekends. Courier had a standard BMC engine (as in the MGA), transmission and rear axle. Though plain, this roadgoing Elva's interior wasn't exactly stark, with leather bucket seats. The streamlined two-seat fiberglass body had a full-width windshield and wraparound bumpers. 'Courier' script and a round insignia sat ahead of the hood lid. A simple air intake stood between the bumper segments and served as the rudimentary grille. No door handles were evident on the body, which had squared-off rear wheel openings and rounded openings up front. Instead of a space frame, as used on Elva's racing cars, the Courier had a ladder-type frame. Front suspension came from the Triumph 10, with Woodhead-Monroe coil springs and Armstrong shocks all around. *Road & Track* described the Courier's ride as "definitely firm." More expensive than an MGA, the Courier weighed more than 400 pounds less. With its BMC B-series engine (as in MGA) mounted low and far to the rear, the Courier had a 50/50 weight distribution and a low hood. Ground clearance was less than four inches, but a high rear end allowed a reasonable amount of luggage space. The rear end and four-speed gearbox also came from the MGA. Inside was a canted steering column. "Despite its scalding performance," reported *Sports Cars Illustrated* in its annual sports-car directory, "the Elva is perfectly suited to normal every-day driving." Its engine "is lightly stressed and therefore non-temperamental."

By 1959, a Courier with larger (1588-cc) MGA engine became available. Couriers were produced mainly for export. Not until 1960 did it become available in the home market, in kit or assembled form.

1961 Elva Courier.

(COMPETITION) MARK 3 — FOUR — Elva also continued to produce a sports-racing model for competition purposes, based on the 1100-cc Climax engine as driven by Archie Scott-Brown, which set a new class record at Brands Hatch and won several American events. This model had a definite race-car look with cutdown, wraparound windshield that flowed into tiny door windows with curved upper edges, and a huge hump at the back (behind the driver). Viewed as a rival to Lotus, its long, streamlined body had a small, unadorned grille opening at the end of a long protruding nose. Front suspension was made up of Triumph TR components, while the rear was a De Dion unit, with coil springs all around. The aluminum body rode a light tubular space frame. Under the hood, a Coventry Climax engine produced 83 bhp at 6800 rpm. Steering operated with just over one turn lock-to-lock. Top speed was about 130 mph.

(COMPETITION) MARK 4 — FOUR — For this next racing version, Elva dropped the De Dion axle and switched to a fully independent rear suspension with swing axle, coil springs and transverse radius arms. The body was now aluminum rather than fiberglass, and the Coventry Climax engine sat farther back than in the prior version.

I.D. DATA: Not available.

Model	Body Type & Seating	Engine Type/CID	P.O.E. Price	Weight (lbs.)	Prod. Total
COURIER					
Mk I	2-dr Rds-2P	I4/91	2785	1410	Note 1
Mk II	2-dr Rds-2P	I4/97	2895	1410	Note 1
COMPETITION					
Mk 3	2-dr Rds-2P	I4/67	N/A	N/A	N/A
Mk 4	2-dr Rds-2P	I4/67	5985	860	N/A

Note 1: By late 1961, about 400 Couriers had been produced.

Price Note: Figure shown was effective in 1959.

Weight Note: Courier curb weights are shown; various sources list much higher dry weights, of 1750 pounds or more.

ENGINE DATA: BASE FOUR (Courier Mk I): Inline, overhead-valve four-cylinder (BMC B-series). Cast iron block and head. **Displacement:** 90.8 cu. in. (1489 cc). **Bore & Stroke:** 2.88 x 3.50 in. (73 x 88.9 mm). **Compression Ratio:** 8.3:1. **Brake Horsepower:** 72 at 5500 rpm. **Torque:** 77.4 lbs.-ft. at 3500 rpm. Three main bearings. Solid valve lifters. Two SU carburetors.

OPTIONAL FOUR (Courier Mk II): Inline, overhead-valve four-cylinder. Cast iron block and head. **Displacement:** 96.9 cu. in. (1588 cc). **Bore & Stroke:** 2.97 x 3.50 in. (75.4 x 88.9 mm). **Compression Ratio:** 8.3:1. **Brake Horsepower:** 77 at 5500 rpm. Solid valve lifters. Two SU carburetors.

BASE FOUR (Mk 3/4 Competition): Inline, overhead-cam four-cylinder (Coventry Climax). **Displacement:** 67.0 cu. in. (1098 cc). **Bore & Stroke:** 2.85 x 2.63 in. (72.4 x 66.6 mm). **Compression Ratio:** 9.8:1. **Brake Horsepower:** 83 at 6800 rpm. **Torque:** 72 lbs.-ft. at 4750 rpm. Solid valve lifters. Two SU carburetors.

CHASSIS DATA: Wheelbase: (Courier) 90.0 in.; (Mk 3) 85.5 in. **Overall Length:** (Courier) 154 in. **Height:** (Courier) 46 in. **Width:** (Courier) 59.5 in. **Front Tread:** (Courier) 50.3 in. **Rear Tread:** (Courier) 50 in. **Standard Tires:** (Courier) 5.20x14; (Mk 3) 4.50/5.25x15.

TECHNICAL: Layout: front-engine, rear-drive. **Transmission:** four-speed manual. Courier gear ratios: (1st) 3.64:1; (2nd) 2.21:1; (3rd) 1.37:1; (4th) 1.00:1. Mk 3 overall gear ratios: (1st) 13.2:1; (2nd) 8.6:1; (3rd) 5.6:1; (4th) 4.6:1. **Standard Final Drive Ratio:** (Courier) 3.73:1; (Mk 3) 4.6:1. **Steering:** rack and pinion. **Suspension (front):** (Courier) independent, twin tubular wishbones and Armstrong coil spring/shock struts; (Mk 3) coil springs. **Suspension (rear):** (Courier) rigid axle with twin parallel trailing arms, track bar, and leaf springs; (Mk 3) De Dion axle; (Mk 4) fully independent with swing axle and coil springs. **Brakes:** (Courier) Lockheed front/rear drum. **Body Construction:** (Courier) fiberglass body on ladder-type chassis of large-diameter steel tubes; (Mk 3) aluminum body on tubular space frame. **Fuel Tank:** (Courier) 12 gallon; (Mk 3) 7.2 gallon.

PERFORMANCE: Top Speed: (Courier) 97-105 mph; (Mk 3) about 130 mph. **Acceleration (0-60 mph):** (Courier) 9.0-12.4 seconds. **Acceleration (quarter-mile):** (Courier) 18.2 sec. (75 mph) to 19.9 sec. (81 mph). **Fuel Mileage:** (Courier) 24-29 mpg.

Manufacturer: Elva Engineering Co. Ltd. (Elva Cars), Bexhill-on-Sea, Sussex, England.

Distributor: Continental Motors Ltd., Washington, DC or Southwestern Motors, San Diego, California.

HISTORY: Couriers proved popular in the U.S., and sales were first limited to export only. Even before the Courier arrived, the Elva name was said to be "better known in the U.S. than in Europe," according to *Sportscar Quarterly.* Quite a few Couriers wound up on race courses, including one driven by Mark Donohue, who later became a racing champion at Indy and elsewhere. A Mk 5 competition model replaced the Mk 4 in 1959. In 1961, Elva's managing director announced that the company had built 140 front-engine Formula Junior single-seaters, with BMC or Auto Union engines. About 80 of those were exported to U.S. Financial woes led to the formation of a new firm, Elva Cars Ltd., in 1961.

1962-66 ELVA

COURIER Mk III — FOUR — Both the Mk III and later Mark IV had front disc brakes. Power came from BMC's 1622-cc four-cylinder engine. Both a fixed-head coupe with reverse-angled back window and an open two-seater were offered. Both were available (in England) in kit form.

COURIER Mk IV — FOUR — The final Courier version had an independent rear suspension, with inboard rear disc brakes added in 1963. Roomier inside, it was available with magnesium wheels. Power came from a 1.5-liter Ford Cortina GT or 1.8-liter MG engine. The T Type Spyder (roadster) wore a low, tightly-crosshatched, wide oval grille and recessed headlamps. Exposed front hinges were used for the hood. 'Elva' script sat on the right of the decklid panel, above one of the small protruding taillamps (which stood just above the bumper). The roadster also had wind-up windows. Some testers complained about difficulty in erecting the soft top, as well as the extreme offset of the car's pedals.

I.D. DATA: Not available.

Model	Body Type & Seating	Engine Type/CID	P.O.E. Price	Weight (lbs.)	Prod. Total
COURIER					
Mk III	2-dr Rds-2P	I4/99	Note 1	Note 2	N/A
Mk III	2-dr Cpe-2P	I4/99	Note 1	Note 2	N/A
Mk IV	2-dr Rds-2P	I4/91	N/A	Note 2	N/A
Mk IV	2-dr Cpe-2P	I4/91	N/A	Note 2	N/A
Mk IV	2-dr Cpe-2P	I4/110	N/A	Note 2	N/A

Note 1: The open sports model sold for 701 pounds (Sterling) in 1962; the coupe for 723 pounds (Sterling).

Note 2: Couriers weighed approximately 1710 pounds.

ENGINE DATA: BASE FOUR (Courier Mk III): Inline, overhead-valve four-cylinder (BMC). **Displacement:** 98.9 cu. in. (1622 cc). **Bore & Stroke:** 3.00 x 3.50 in. (76.2 x 88.9 mm). **Compression Ratio:** 8.9:1. **Brake Horsepower:** 90 at 5000 rpm. **Torque:** 105 lbs.-ft. at 3000 rpm. Solid valve lifters. Two SU carburetors.

BASE FOUR (Courier Mk IV): Inline, overhead-valve four-cylinder (BMC). Cast iron block and head. **Displacement:** 110 cu. in. (1798 cc). **Bore & Stroke:** 3.16 x 3.50 in. (80 x 88.9 mm). **Compression Ratio:** 8.8:1. **Brake Horsepower:** 98 (SAE) at 5400 rpm. **Torque:** 110 lbs.-ft. (SAE) at 3000 rpm. Three main bearings. Solid valve lifters. Two SU carburetors.

OPTIONAL FOUR (Courier Mk IV): Inline, overhead-valve four-cylinder (Ford). **Displacement:** 91.4 cu. in. (1498 cc). **Bore & Stroke:** 3.19 x 2.86 in. (81 x 73 mm). **Compression Ratio:** 9.0:1. **Brake Horsepower:** 83.5 (78 SAE) at 5200 rpm. **Torque:** 97 lbs.-ft. (SAE) at 3600 rpm. Five main bearings. Solid valve lifters. One Weber two-barrel carburetor.

Note: A tuned Ford-Cosworth engine also was available.

CHASSIS DATA: Wheelbase: 90.0 in. **Overall Length:** (Mk III) 154 in.; (Mk IV) 149.5 in. **Height:** (Mk IV) 45.5 in. **Width:** (Mk III) 59.5 in.; (Mk IV) 61 in. **Front Tread:** (Mk IV) 50.5 in. **Rear Tread:** (Mk IV) 49 in. **Standard Tires:** 5.60x13.

TECHNICAL: Layout: front-engine, rear-drive. **Transmission:** four-speed manual. Ford-engine gear ratios: (1st) 3.54:1; (2nd) 2.39:1; (3rd) 1.41:1; (4th) 1.00:1. BMC-engine gear ratios: (1st) 3.64:1; (2nd) 2.27:1; (3rd) 1.37:1; (4th) 1.00:1. **Standard Final Drive Ratio:** (Mk IV) 3.70:1, 3.90:1 or 3.91:1. **Steering:** rack and pinion. **Suspension (front):** wishbones and coil springs with anti-roll bar. **Suspension (rear):** rigid axle with leaf springs; wishbone/coil-spring independent suspension available on Mk IV. **Brakes:** front disc, rear drum; four-wheel discs available on Mk IV. **Body Construction:** fiberglass body on ladder-type chassis of large-diameter steel tubes.

PERFORMANCE: Top Speed: (Mk III) 105 mph; (Mk IV) to 107 mph. **Acceleration (0-60 mph):** 8 seconds (claimed). **Fuel Mileage:** (Mk IV) about 21 mpg.

Manufacturer: Trojan Ltd., Croydon, Surrey, England.

HISTORY: An ad for the Mark III noted that it "Goes to 105 m.p.h... eagerly, sleekly, safely." *Popular Imported Cars* recommended a Mk IV Courier for those who "yearn for the days when sports cars lived up to their name as suntan specials with wire wheels, hot acceleration, steering you had to pay attention to all the time and a pleasant exhaust boom."

POSTSCRIPT: Trojan Ltd. took over Courier production in 1962, leaving Frank Nichols free to focus his efforts on race cars. These included a Mk 6, Mk 7 (available with Cosworth-Ford engines), and Mk 8 (with engines from 1.0 to 2.0 liters, the latter from BMW and Porsche). The 160XS was a roadgoing version of the Mk 8 racer, but only three were built in 1964. The GT160 prototype had hidden headlamps and a 185-bhp engine. By 1964, Trojan controlled all Elva production. Elva was taken over by Ken Sheppard Customized Sports Cars Ltd. in 1965, but no significant vehicle production took place after that time. "Despite successes in SCCA production racing," said *Car and Driver* of the Mk IV Elva Courier in 1966, the "MG-engined sports car hasn't caught on beyond a small claque of devotees." Most Couriers, they speculated, were owned by amateur race drivers. Elva remained on American lists of imported cars into 1967, though regular production ceased a year earlier. One final firm bought up all the remaining Elva parts in 1969, but no further cars were built. By 1973, the Elva name was gone for good.

FACEL VEGA

Although the first Facel Vega automobile didn't emerge until 1954, Jean Daninos had begun the French firm of Forges et Ateliers de Construction d'Eure et de Loire SA (Facel Metallon, for short) sixteen years earlier, in Paris. For the brief time before war broke out, it produced machine tools for the aircraft industry (including combustion chambers for Rolls-Royce engines). Under German occupation during the war, it turned out automobile gas generators. As the postwar years began, the metal-forming company broadened into office and home furniture and other products, as well as bodies for Panhard, Simca, Ford Comete (of France), Delahaye and Bentley automobiles.

Daninos was eager to expand into the automobile industry, hoping to help revive France's prewar eminence in GT motorcar production. At the 1950 Paris motor show, in fact, Facel showed some of its own designs. Later, when Panhard happened to cancel a proposed new model, its tentative spot on the factory floor was vacant, ready for Facel's own creation. The first Vega debuted at the Paris Salon in July 1954, with a DeSoto Firedome V-8 under its hood, and was on sale by the end of that year. (The full Facel Vega name wasn't commonly used until 1956). Its tubular chassis, with channel-and box-section reinforcements, had been designed by Lance Macklin, but the body was the responsibility mainly of Daninos himself. Facels became known for excellent workmanship as well as creative design. Nearly all were exported from France, since high-powered vehicles suffered high taxes in that country. Observers at the time viewed Facel as a rival to two very different Continentals: the stylish Bentley and the Lincoln. *Motor Trend* noted early on that the car has "as much show-stopping quality as the Continental (and maybe more), is finished in the impressive Rolls-Royce style, performs with the agility of the hottest American cars, and handles as well as an Austin-Healey."

Facel Vegas became especially popular in the United States as well as in Europe by 1956, when the commonly-used name changed to FVS (Facel Vega Sport). The list of Facel owners has included celebrities from the entertainment world, such as Corinne Calvet, Ava Gardner, Tony Curtis, and Ringo Starr; such political figures as the Shah of Iran and Prince Charles of Belgium; and racing driver Stirling Moss. Power came from a series of Chrysler V-8 engines, which grew in displacement and horsepower. Meanwhile, a handful of convertibles had been built and a much larger quantity of Excellence four-door hardtops, but both suffered from body rigidity troubles. A smaller Facellia, introduced in the fall of 1959, never came close to the hoped-for sales levels. For 1962 came the Facel II, the swiftest of the lot; but that wasn't enough to save the faltering company, which went into receivership later that year. A Facel III, powered by a Volvo engine, came out the following year. Then, after the SFERMA organization (a subsidiary of Sud-Aviation) had taken over in a one-year bid to save the Facel firm, came a Healey-powered FV6. Official bankruptcy followed in 1965. All told, as many as 3,000 Facel Vegas may have been built, more than half of them the smaller Facellias. Experts differ sharply on total output and model breakdown, however, with some insisting that the total was closer to 2,000.

Note: Because so many versions of the Chyrsler V-8 were used to power Facel Vegas, specifications may vary from those shown below.

1954 Facel Vega.

VEGA (FV) — V-8 — The first Vega's body was an expanded version of the 2+2 hardtop the company had done earlier for the Ford Comete. Modified to produce 180 horsepower, the 276 cu. in. (4.5-liter) DeSoto "hemi" V-8 drove a two-speed PowerFlite automatic transmission. A four-speed manual gearbox was offered, but cost considerably more.

At the center of the front end was a square grille with crosshatch pattern, accompanied by twin rounded side grilles (also crosshatched) that stood high up on the front panel. Large housings at the leading edges of front fenders held single round headlamps on top, with parking/signal lamps down toward the bumper. Atop the tapered hood stood a small scoop. The pillarless body profile (with rear quarter windows) showed fully rounded wheel openings and a long deck, with a rather short cockpit. Horizontal taillamps sat atop the ends of the rear fenders, which angled outward at the base.

Stainless steel trim was abundant, and the interior was plush leather, with a vast complement of controls. Up front, separate seats had folding armrests on their inner sides. Facel Vega was one of the first cars to put a console over the gearbox, with controls that resembled those in an airplane. A large round speedometer and tachometer flanked the steering wheel, with other functions indicated by half a dozen small round gauges. Occasional seats in the rear had side and center armrests. Fold-down rear seatbacks formed a luggage platform, and allowed access to the trunk from inside the car (but there was also a trunk lid). Beneath the carpeted luggage area sat the spare tire. Doors held pivoting vent windows. Standard equipment included two-speed AutoLite windshield wipers and Mopar-type heating/demisting system with fresh air intake. The 22-gallon fuel tank had two filler caps.

FV1 — V-8 — Not long after the first Facel Vega's debut, a larger "Typhoon" engine arrived, displacing 291 cubic inches (4.8 liters) and delivering 200 horsepower. Later in 1955, it grew to 250 horsepower in the FV2 version.

I.D. DATA: Serial number is at the center of the firewall, under the hood. Engine number is at the top center of the block.

Model	Body Type & Seating	Engine Type/CID	P.O.E. Price	Weight (lbs.)	Prod. Total
FV	2-dr HT Cpe-4P	V8/276	7000	3584	47
FV1	2-dr HT Cpe-4P	V8/291	N/A	3584	Note 1

Note 1: Included in FV total. About six special convertible models also were produced around 1955.

ENGINE DATA: BASE V-8 (FV): Overhead-valve "hemi" V-8 (DeSoto). Cast iron block and head. **Displacement:** 276.2 cu. in. (4528 cc). **Bore & Stroke:** 3.62 x 3.34 in. (92.2 x 84.9 mm). **Compression Ratio:** 7.5:1. **Brake Horsepower:** 180 at 4500 rpm. Five main bearings. Hydraulic valve lifters. Ball and Ball two-barrel downdraft carburetor. 6-volt electrical system.

Note: An early announcement from Facel specified a 170-horsepower rating for the first engine.

BASE V-8 (FV1): Overhead-valve "hemi" V-8 (DeSoto). Cast iron block and head. **Displacement:** 291 cu. in. (4768 cc). **Bore & Stroke:** 3.72 x 3.80 in. (94.5 x 96.5 mm). **Compression Ratio:** 7.5:1 (later, 8.5:1). **Brake Horsepower:** 200 at 4400 rpm (later, 250 at 4600). **Torque:** 255 lbs.-ft. at 2000 rpm. Five main bearings. Hydraulic valve lifters. Four-barrel carburetor.

CHASSIS DATA: Wheelbase: 103.5 in. **Overall Length:** 179 in. **Height:** 52 in. **Width:** 69 in. **Front Tread:** 54 in. **Rear Tread:** 54.5 in. **Wheel Type:** bolt-on wire (slotted steel or center-lock wire wheels available). **Standard Tires:** Michelin 7.10x15.

TECHNICAL: Layout: front-engine, rear-drive. **Transmission:** two-speed PowerFlite or Pont-a-Mousson four-speed manual (fully synchronized). **Manual gear ratios:** (1st) 3.45:1; (2nd) 1.96:1; (3rd) 1.37:1; (4th) 1:1. **Standard Final Drive Ratio:** 2.93:1 or 3.31:1 (Salisbury hypoid final drive). **Steering:** Gemmer cam and roller. **Suspension (front):** upper/lower A-arms, coil springs and anti-roll bar. **Suspension (rear):** rigid (live) axle with semi-elliptic leaf springs. **Brakes:** front/rear drum (aluminum). **Body Construction:** steel body welded to tubular steel chassis, with tubular and channel-section cross-bracing. **Fuel Tank:** 22 (Imperial) gallons.

MAJOR OPTIONS: Radio (short/medium/long wave). Power (electric) windows.

PERFORMANCE: Top Speed: (w/3.31 axle) 107 mph; (w/2.93 axle) 120 mph. **Acceleration (0-60 mph):** 10.5 seconds.

Manufacturer: Forges et Ateliers de Construction d'Eure et de Loire (Facel) S.A., Paris, France.

Distributor: Charles Hornburg (west coast); Max Hoffman (New York City).

HISTORY: Prototype was seen at the Facel plant in July 1954, then at the autumn Paris Salon. The car went on sale late that year.

1956-57 FACEL VEGA

1957 Facel Vega FVS two-door sport sedan. (Christie's)

FVS (FV2/FV2B) — V-8 — For 1956, the French luxury coupe was called FVS (Facel Vega Sport) and moved from the initial 291 cubic-inch (4.8-liter) V-8 to a 250-bhp version; then to a 330 cu. in. (5.4-liter) Chrysler V-8 for the FV2B edition. *Motor Trend* referred to the combination of French styling and American power as "Ameripean," noting that the design was unmistakably foreign, but the big wraparound windshield was strictly American.

Appearance was similar to the initial model. Up front was a squarish center grille with crosshatch pattern, flanked by two high side grilles (each with crosshatch pattern and a single vertical bar). The hood held a scoop. Stacked front lamps were used (head- lamps on top), as well as a wraparound windshield with kicked-back A-pillar. Taillamps stood at the rounded rear fender tips, while dual exhaust tips exited from the bumper. A trim strip down the center of the taillamps extended down to the back bumper. Swing-out rear quarter windows looked like those of a regular hardtop coupe when the windows were closed. Stainless steel rocker panel moldings on the bodysides extended up into the doors. Full wheel openings exposed the tires. 'FACEL VEGA' block letters identified the car at both front and rear.

Power brakes and steering became standard by 1957. Leather upholstery was standard, and the rear seatback folded flat to accommodate fitted luggage. A permanently-installed tool box sat above the gas tank in the trunk, with molded cutouts for the tools. Facel Vega's four-speed manual gearbox, available in lieu of the Chrysler automatic, was synchronized in all ratios (including reverse).

I.D. DATA: Serial number is at the center of the firewall, under the hood.

Model	Body Type & Seating	Engine Type/CID	P.O.E. Price	Weight (lbs.)	Prod. Total
FVS	2-dr HT Cpe-4P	V8/330	7500	3500	225

Production Note: FVS production was 107 in calendar year 1956, then 118 in 1957.

ENGINE DATA: BASE V-8 (FV2): Overhead-valve "hemi" V-8 (DeSoto). Cast iron block and head. **Displacement:** 291 cu. in. (4768 cc). **Bore & Stroke:** 3.72 x 3.80 in. (94.5 x 96.5 mm). **Compression Ratio:** 8.5:1. **Brake Horsepower:** 250 at 4600 rpm. Five main bearings. Hydraulic valve lifters. Four-barrel carburetor.
BASE V-8 (FV2B): Overhead-valve "hemi" V-8 (Chrysler). Cast iron block and head. **Displacement:** 330 cu. in. (5407 cc). **Bore & Stroke:** 3.72 x 3.80 in. (94.5 x 96.5 mm). **Compression Ratio:** 8.5:1. **Brake Horsepower:** 255 at 4400 rpm. Five main bearings. Hydraulic valve lifters. Carter four-barrel carburetor. 12-volt electrical.

CHASSIS DATA: Wheelbase: 103.5 in. **Overall Length:** 179 in. **Height:** 52 in. **Width:** 69 in. **Front Tread:** 54 in. **Rear Tread:** 54 in. **Standard Tires:** 6.70x15.

TECHNICAL: Layout: front-engine, rear-drive. **Transmission:** two-speed PowerFlite or Pont-a-Mousson four-speed manual (fully synchronized). **Standard Final Drive Ratio:** 2.93:1 or 3.31:1 (Salisbury hypoid final drive). **Steering:** Gemmer cam and roller. **Suspension (front):** upper/lower A-arms, coil springs and anti-roll bar. **Suspension (rear):** rigid (live) axle with semi-elliptic leaf springs. **Brakes:** front/rear drum. **Body Construction:** steel body welded to tubular steel chassis.

MAJOR OPTIONS: Power steering. Automatic transmission. Fitted luggage set ($600).

PRODUCTION/SALES: A total of 842 FV (and later HK) coupes were produced during the full model run.

PERFORMANCE: Top Speed: (w/2.93:1 axle) about 128 mph; (w/3.31:1 axle) about 112 mph.

Manufacturer: Forges et Ateliers de Construction d'Eure et de Loire (Facel) S.A., Paris, France.

Distributor: Charles Hornburg (west coast); Max Hoffman (New York City).

HISTORY: A new Excellence four-door hardtop sedan was displayed at the Paris Motor Show in late 1957; see next listing.

1958 FACEL VEGA

FVS (FV3/FV4) — V-8 — Facel Vega's coupe grew slightly longer in wheelbase for 1958, while the engine reached 354 cu. in. (5.8-liter) displacement in its FV4 mode. Alternate FV3 editions with smaller (276- or 301-cid) engines also were offered. Four-wheel disc brakes became available this year. Other improvements included the use of stainless steel for bumpers and body trim. Standard radios included twin speakers and a remote-control antenna. Leather upholstery was standard.

EXCELLENCE — V-8 — Joining the original hardtop coupe for the 1958 model year was a four-door hardtop sedan with pillarless design. Front-end appearance was similar to the coupe, with a center grille and two high side grilles. Front doors were hinged at the

front, back doors at the rear, like the Lincoln Continentals that would arrive in the early 1960s. Stacked lamps (with the headlamps on top) were used, along with the usual wrap-around windshield and pointed (but not tall) tailfins. Taillamps were farther down, in a nacelle that extended along the rear fender. Leather upholstery was standard.

I.D. DATA: Serial number is at the center of the firewall, under the hood.

Model	Body Type & Seating	Engine Type/CID	P.O.E. Price	Weight (lbs.)	Prod. Total
FVS	2-dr HT Cpe-4P	V8/354	5515	3528	156
Excellence	4-dr HT Sed-5P	V8/392	12800	N/A	22

Production Note: FVS production includes early HK models (see 1959 listing).

ENGINE DATA: BASE V-8 (FV3): Overhead-valve "hemi" V-8. Cast iron block and head. **Displacement:** 276.1 cu. in. (4527 cc). **Bore & Stroke:** 3.75 x 3.13 in. (95.25 x 79.5 mm). **Compression Ratio:** 8.0:1. **Brake Horsepower:** 200 at 4400 rpm. Five main bearings. Hydraulic valve lifters.
BASE V-8 (FV3B): Same as above, except -- **Displacement:** 301.3 cu. in. (4940 cc). **Bore & Stroke:** 3.91 x 3.13 in. (99.35 x 79.5 mm). **Compression Ratio:** 8.5:1. **Brake Horsepower:** 253 at 4600 rpm.
BASE V-8 (FV4): Overhead-valve "hemi" V-8 (Chrysler). Cast iron block and head. **Displacement:** 354 cu. in. (5801 cc). **Bore & Stroke:** 3.94 x 3.63 in. (100 x 92.2 mm). **Compression Ratio:** 9.25:1. **Brake Horsepower:** 325 at 4600 rpm. **Torque:** 430 lbs.-ft. at 2800 rpm. Five main bearings. Hydraulic valve lifters. Four-barrel carburetor. 12-volt electrical.
BASE V-8 (Excellence): Same as above, except -- **Displacement:** 392 cu. in. (6430 cc). **Bore & Stroke:** 4.00 x 3.90 in. (101.6 x 99.1 mm). **Compression Ratio:** 9.25:1. **Brake Horsepower:** 360 at 5200 rpm.

CHASSIS DATA: Wheelbase: (cpe) 105 in.; (sed) 124.8 in. **Overall Length:** (cpe) 179 in.; (sed) 206.7 in. **Height:** (cpe) 53 in.; (sed) 54.5 in. **Width:** (cpe) 70.8 in.; (sed) 72 in. **Front Tread:** 56 in. **Rear Tread:** 57 in. **Standard Tires:** (cpe) 6.70x15; (sed) 7.60x15.

TECHNICAL: Layout: front-engine, rear-drive. **Transmission:** three-speed TorqueFlite or Pont-a-Mousson four-speed manual (fully synchronized). **Standard Final Drive Ratio:** 3.31:1 or 2.93:1 (Salisbury hypoid final drive). **Steering:** Gemmer cam and roller. **Suspension (front):** upper/lower A-arms, coil springs and anti-roll bar. **Suspension (rear):** rigid (live) axle with semi-elliptic leaf springs. **Brakes:** front/rear drum (discs available). **Body Construction:** steel body welded to tubular steel chassis.

MAJOR OPTIONS: Similar to 1956-57.

PRODUCTION/SALES: A total of 152 Excellence saloons were produced during its full model run. Total FV/HK production was 842 units. Approximately 56 Facel Vegas went to U.S. buyers during 1958.

PERFORMANCE: Top Speed: (cpe) 126-134+ mph; (sed) 118-126 mph. **Acceleration (0-60 mph):** (cpe) 9.5 seconds.

Manufacturer: Forges et Ateliers de Construction d'Eure et de Loire S.A., Paris, France.

Distributor: Charles H. Hornburg Jr. (Los Angeles); Hoffman Motor Company (New York City).

HISTORY: During the 1958 model year, the FV series evolved into the HK500; see next listing.

1959 FACEL VEGA

HK500 — V-8 — Appearance of the new HK500 was similar to the former FVS, on the same 105-inch wheelbase, with what appeared to be stacked quad headlamps up front. Actually, it was again a combination of headlamps on top and auxiliary lights below. The body had a slightly less rounded look than the first models. At first, the powerplant was the same as the final FVS: Chrysler's 354 cu. in. V-8, delivering 325 horsepower. Before long, that engine was augmented by Chrysler's 383 cu. in. wedge V-8, with twin four-barrel Carter carburetors helping to churn up 360 horsepower. A 360-cid V-8 also was offered.

Tom McCahill, ace auto writer for *Mechanix Illustrated,* called the HK500 "sexier than the Place Pigalle and throatier than a Russian basso," adding that it served as a "remarkable and wonderfully satisfying road companion."

EXCELLENCE — V-8 — Facel's limited-production hardtop four-door sedan continued in its previous form, with various engines available including a 360-cid V-8.

I.D. DATA: Serial number is at center of firewall, under the hood.

Model	Body Type & Seating	Engine Type/CID	P.O.E. Price	Weight (lbs.)	Prod. Total
HK500	2 dr HT Cpe-4P	V8/354	9650	3885	190
Excellence	4-dr HT Sed-5P	V8/354	12800	4230	42

Production Note: Figures shown are for calendar year 1959.

ENGINE DATA: BASE V-8 (early HK500/Excellence): Overhead-valve V-8 (Chrysler). Cast iron block and head. **Displacement:** 354 cu. in. (5801 cc). **Bore & Stroke:** 3.94 x 3.63 in. (100 x 92 mm). **Compression Ratio:** 9.25:1. **Brake Horsepower:** 325 at 4600 rpm. **Torque:** 430 lbs.-ft. at 2800 rpm. Five main bearings. Hydraulic valve lifters. Four-barrel carburetor. 12-volt electrical.
BASE V-8 (late HK500/Excellence): Overhead-valve V-8 (Chrysler). Cast iron block and head. **Displacement:** 383 cu. in. (6279 cc). **Bore & Stroke:** 4.25 x 3.38 in. (107.95 x 85.85 mm). **Compression Ratio:** 10.0:1. **Brake Horsepower:** 325 at 4600 rpm (or 360 at 5200). **Torque:** 460 lbs.-ft. at 2800 rpm (or 398 at 3600). Five main bearings. Hydraulic valve lifters. Two four-barrel Carter carburetors. 12-volt electrical.

OPTIONAL V-8 (HK500/Excellence): Same as above, except -- **Displacement:** 360 cu. in. (5907 cc). **Bore & Stroke:** 4.12 x 3.38 in. (104.65 x 85.85 mm). **Compression Ratio:** 10.0:1. **Brake Horsepower:** 360 at 5200 rpm.

CHASSIS DATA: Wheelbase: (HK500) 104.7 in.; (sed) 124.8 in. **Overall Length:** (HK500) 181.1 in.; (sed) 206.7 in. **Height:** (HK500) 53 in.; (sed) 54 in. **Width:** (HK500) 70.8 in.; (sed) 72 in. **Front Tread:** 55.9 in. **Rear Tread:** 57.1 in. **Standard Tires:** (HK500) 6.70x15; (sed) 7.60x15.

TECHNICAL: Layout: front-engine, rear-drive. **Transmission:** three-speed TorqueFlite or Pont-a-Mousson four-speed manual. **Standard Drive Ratio:** 3.30:1. **Steering:** cam and roller. **Suspension (front):** upper/lower A-arms, coil springs and anti-roll bar. **Suspension (rear):** rigid (live) axle with semi-elliptic leaf springs. **Brakes:** front/rear drum (Dunlop discs optional). **Body Construction:** steel body welded to tubular steel chassis. **Fuel Tank:** (cpe) 27 gallons; (sed) 34 gallons.

MAJOR OPTIONS: Similar to 1956-57.

PRODUCTION/SALES: Total HK500 production (all years) was no greater than 490 units, including one specially-built convertible. Total Excellence production for its entire model run was 152 units. Approximately 41 Facel Vegas went to U.S. customers during 1959.

PERFORMANCE: Top Speed: (HK500) 140+ mph.; (Excellence) 125 mph. **Acceleration (0-60 mph):** (HK500) 8.4 seconds (0-100 in 18 seconds); (Excellence) 8.5 seconds. **Acceleration (quarter-mile):** (HK500) 16.3 seconds. **Fuel Mileage:** about 14 mpg.

Manufacturer: Forges et Ateliers de Construction d'Eure et de Loire S.A., Paris, France.

Distributor: Charles H. Hornburg Jr. (Los Angeles); Hoffman Motor Company (New York City).

HISTORY: A smaller Facellia model was introduced in late 1959; see next listing for details.

1960 FACEL VEGA

1960 Facel Vega HK500.

FACELLIA — F2 — FOUR — In the fall of 1959, Facel tried another tack by introducing a small convertible with a four-cylinder engine. Its price was considerably lower than the V-8 Facel Vegas, and the wheelbase nine inches shorter. The goal was to lure customers who might otherwise choose an MG-B or a TR-series Triumph.

"Born yesterday, a classic today," trumpeted the ads. Facellia, they proclaimed, was for "the man who wants everything in an automobile: the high performance of a sports car, the luxuries and conveniences of a touring car." Early reports were favorable. Unfortunately, its engine, designed by Westlake Engineering in Britain but built by Pont-a-Mousson (which also built the Facel Vega manual gearboxes) proved unreliable. Burned pistons turned out to be a major problem. By the time remedies were discovered, the damage had already been done and sales never recovered.

Styling was similar to the bigger Facels, with a center grille plus twin side grilles. This center grille was more square than its big brothers, however, and side grilles a bit lower. All three had tighter crosshatch patterns than on the bigger Facels. Single round headlamps stood above round fog lights, in the same slightly hooded housing behind a plastic "bubble" screen. That aerodynamic styling touch was said to boost top speed by about 5 mph. Parking lamps extended down into bumper cutouts. No hood scoop was used. Suspension and steering also were similar to those in the big Facels. Dunlop disc brakes were used on all four wheels. A removable lift-off hardtop was optional. Inside, seats had a futuristic appearance. Leather was used on seats, doors, and over the padding on the instrument panel. The speedometer, tachometer and clock sat ahead of the driver, with other gauges in a separate console.

HK500 — V-8 — While Facel Vega pinned high hopes on the new and smaller Facellia, the big Chrysler powered coupe continued in production. Four-wheel disc brakes became standard during the 1960 model year.

EXCELLENCE — V-8 — Production of the four-door hardtop sedan continued as before.

I.D. DATA: Serial numbers are at the center of the firewall, under the hood.

Model	Body Type & Seating	Engine Type/CID	P.O.E. Price	Weight (lbs.)	Prod. Total
Facellia	2-dr Coupe-3P	I4/100	3995	2465	Note 1
Facellia	2-dr Conv-3P	I4/100	N/A	N/A	Note 1
HK500	2-dr HT Cpe-4P	V8/383	8550	N/A	202
Excellence	2-dr HT Sed-5P	V8/383	2800	N/A	43

Note 1: Total Facellia production for the 1960 calendar year was 335.

ENGINE DATA: BASE FOUR (Facellia): Inline, dual overhead-cam four-cylinder. Cast iron block and aluminum head. **Displacement:** 100.5 cu. in. (1647 cc). **Bore & Stroke:** 3.23 x 3.07 in. (82 x 78 mm). **Compression Ratio:** 9.4:1. **Brake Horsepower:** 115 at 6400 rpm. **Torque:** 105.5 lbs.-ft. at 4100 rpm. Five main bearings. Solex carburetor (later, two Webers). 12-volt electrical. **BASE V-8 (HK500/Excellence):** Overhead-valve V-8 (Chrysler). Cast iron block and head. **Displacement:** 383 cu. in. (6279 cc). **Bore & Stroke:** 4.25 x 3.38 in. (107.95 x 85.85 mm). **Compression Ratio:** 10.0:1. **Brake Horsepower:** 330/335 at 4600 rpm (or 365 at 5200). **Torque:** 425 or 460 lbs.-ft. at 2800 rpm. Five main bearings. Hydraulic valve lifters. Two four-barrel carburetors. 12-volt electrical.

CHASSIS DATA: Wheelbase: (Facellia) 96.4 in.; (HK500) 105 in.; (sed) 124.8 in. **Overall Length:** (Facellia) 164 in.; (HK500) 180.7 in.; (sed) 206.7 in. **Height:** (Facellia) 51.2 in.; (HK500) 53.5 in.; (sed) 54 in. **Width:** (Facellia) 61.4 in.; (HK500) 70.9 in.; (sed) 72 in. **Front Tread:** (Facellia) 51.2 in.; (HK500) 55.9 in.; (sed) 55.9 in. **Rear Tread:** (Facellia) 50.4 in.; (HK500) 57.1 in.; (sed) 57.1 in. **Standard Tires:** (Facellia) 5.90x14; (HK500) 6.70x15; (sed) 7.10x15.

TECHNICAL: Layout: front-engine, rear-drive. **Transmission:** three-speed TorqueFlite or Pont-a-Mousson four-speed manual; (Facellia) four-speed manual. Overall Facellia gear ratios: (1st) 14.1:1; (2nd) 8.03:1; (3rd) 5.25:1; (4th) 4.10:1. **Standard Final Drive Ratio:** (Facellia) 4.10:1; (Excellence) 3.31:1. **Steering:** cam and roller. **Suspension (front):** upper/lower A-arms, coil springs and anti-roll bar. **Suspension (rear):** rigid (live) axle with semi-elliptic leaf springs. **Brakes:** front/rear drum; discs brakes standard on HK500 later in model year, available on Facellia. **Body Construction:** (Facellia) steel unibody; (others) steel body welded to tubular steel chassis.

PRODUCTION/SALES: Total HK500 production (all years) was no greater than 490 units, including one specially-built convertible. Total Excellence production for its entire model run was 152 units. A total of 598 Facellia (and subsequent Facel III) coupes were built in all, plus 48 2+2 models and 1,181 convertibles, according to French sources.

PERFORMANCE: Top Speed: (Facellia) 114 mph; (HK500) 146+ mph w/2.93:1 axle. **Acceleration (0-60 mph):** (Facellia) 13.7 seconds; (HK500) 8.4-9.7 seconds; (Excellence) 8.8-9.8 seconds. **Acceleration (quarter-mile):** (Facellia) 18.9 seconds (70 mph); (HK500) 17 seconds; (Excellence) 18.3 seconds. **Fuel Mileage:** (Facellia) 20-24 mpg; (HK500) 13-16 mpg; (Excellence) 10-12 mpg.

Manufacturer: Forges et Ateliers de Construction d'Eure et de Loire S.A., Paris, France.

Distributor: Charles H. Hornburg Jr. (Los Angeles); Hoffman Motor Car Co. (New York City).

HISTORY: Packard fans in 1960 suggested that Studebaker-Packard buy a hundred or more Excellence sedans and fit them with leftover Packard V-8s. Nothing came of this proposal, according to Richard Langworth, as Studebaker-Packard was busy marketing Mercedes-Benz cars at the time.

1961 FACEL VEGA

FACELLIA — F2 — FOUR — Production of the smaller Facel continued in its 1960 form.

HK500 — V-8 — Production of the Facel Vega continued for one more season, until it was replaced by the Facel II. *Motor Trend* in 1961 noted that it "has captured the hearts of a great many Americans of discriminating taste on the basis of its svelte, commanding appearance alone." Pleated leather upholstery was just one of its attractions.

EXCELLENCE — V-8 — A revised Excellence would arrive for 1962, but for the time being the former version continued as before.

I.D. DATA: Serial numbers are at the center of the firewall, under the hood.

Model	Body Type & Seating	Engine Type/CID	P.O.E. Price	Weight (lbs.)	Prod. Total
Facellia	2-dr Coupe-3P	I4/100	4470	2465	Note 1
Facellia	2-dr Conv-3P	I4/100	N/A	N/A	Note 1
HK500	2-dr HT Cpe-4P	V8/383	9420	N/A	Note 2
Excellence	4-dr HT Sed-5P	V8/383	12981	N/A	20

Note 1: Total Facellia production for calendar year 1961 was 352 units.

Note 2: A total of 66 HK500 (and Facel II) models were built during calendar year 1961.

ENGINE DATA: Same as 1960.

CHASSIS DATA: Same as 1960.

TECHNICAL: Same as 1960.

PERFORMANCE: Same as 1960.

1962 FACEL VEGA

FACELLIA — F2/F2S — FOUR — The smaller Facel continued in production through 1963; see 1960 listing for details. The F2S engine had higher compression and horsepower, using two sidedraft Weber carburetors.

1962 Facel Vega II coupe.

FACEL II — V-8 — For the second time, the large Facel Vega got a restyling and a new name. Appearance was similar up front, but a lower center grille was more square than the former upright rectangle. The crosshatch pattern was similar, though, with a horizontal bar across each of the side grilles. Quad Marchal headlamps were vertically stacked in oval housings, with two tiny amber lights between each pair. At the rear, smaller lenses sat atop the fenders, with no trim strip running through them (as in prior models). Larger round taillamps were just above the back bumper, and 'Facel II' script decorated the decklid. Wheelbase was the same as the prior HK500 (105 inches), and seating was the same 2 + 2 configuration. While windshields on earlier models had an extreme wraparound, the Facel II's was more subdued, curved at the top and sides. Quarter windows had a more angular shape. Glass for the back window was larger than before, curving at the top and sides, with a steeper rake. The car's roofline was also a tad flatter, and C-pillars were slimmer. All told, the Facel II displayed a more squared-off profile with more aerodynamic appearance.

Chrysler's 383-cid V-8 provided the power, rated 355 horsepower with TorqueFlite or 390 with the standard Pont-a-Mousson four-speed manual gearbox. Disc brakes were used all around. Power steering was standard with the automatic transmission, but optional with manual. As had been traditional all along, the instrument panel had an aircraft-style look. Automatic transmissions no longer used Chrysler's pushbutton controls.

EXCELLENCE — V-8 — The revised Excellence four-door sedan continued for another two years, ending its production life early in 1964. Standard equipment included automatic transmission plus power steering and brakes.

I.D. DATA: Serial numbers were at the center of the firewall, under the hood.

Model	Body Type & Seating	Engine Type/CID	P.O.E. Price	Weight (lbs.)	Prod. Total
Facellia	2-dr Coupe-3P	I4/100	5195	2465	Note 1
Facellia	2-dr Conv-3P	I4/100	4860	N/A	Note 1
Facel II	2-dr HT Cpe-4P	V8/383	9420	3640	91
Excellence	4-dr HT Sed-5P	V8/383	12981	N/A	11

Note 1: Total Facellia production for calendar year 1962 was 346 units.

ENGINE DATA: BASE FOUR (Facellia F2): Inline, dual overhead-cam four-cylinder. Cast iron block and aluminum head. **Displacement:** 100.5 cu. in. (1647 cc). **Bore & Stroke:** 3.23 x 3.07 in. (82 x 78 mm). **Compression Ratio:** 9.4:1. **Brake Horsepower:** 115 at 6400 rpm. **Torque:** 105.5 lbs.-ft. at 4100 rpm. Five main bearings. Solex downdraft carburetor. 12-volt electrical.
BASE FOUR (Facellia F2S): Same as above, except -- **Compression Ratio:** 9.6:1. **Brake Horsepower:** 126 (131 SAE) at 6400 rpm. Two Weber sidedraft carburetors.
BASE V-8 (Facel II, Excellence): Overhead-valve V-8 (Chrysler). Cast iron block and head. **Displacement:** 383 cu. in. (6279 cc). **Bore & Stroke:** 4.25 x 3.38 in. (107.95 x 85.85 mm). **Compression Ratio:** 10.0:1. **Brake Horsepower:** 355 at 4800 rpm (390 at 5400 with manual gearbox). Five main bearings. Hydraulic valve lifters. One four-barrel Carter carburetor (two with manual gearbox). 12-volt electrical.

CHASSIS DATA: Wheelbase: (Facellia) 96.4 in.; (Facel II) 105 in.; (sed) 124.8 in. **Overall Length:** (Facellia) 164 in.; (Facel II) 180.7 in.; (sed) 206.7 in. **Height:** (Facellia) 51 in.; (sed) 54 in. **Width:** (Facellia) 61.4 in.; (Facel II) 70.9 in.; (sed) 70.9 in. **Front Tread:** (Facellia) 51.2 in.; (Facel II) 55.9 in.; (sed) 55.9 in. **Rear Tread:** (Facellia) 50.4 in.; (Facel II) 57.1 in.; (sed) 57.9 in. **Standard Tires:** (Facellia) 5.90x14; (sed) 7.60x15.

TECHNICAL: Layout: front-engine, rear-drive. **Transmission:** three-speed TorqueFlite or Pont-a-Mousson four-speed manual; (Facellia) four-speed manual. **Standard Final Drive Ratio:** (Facellia) 4.10:1; (Excellence) 3.31:1. **Steering:** cam and roller. **Suspension (front):** upper/lower A-arms, coil springs and anti-roll bar. **Suspension (rear):** rigid (live) axle with semi-elliptic leaf springs. **Brakes:** (Facellia/Facel II) front/rear discs. **Body Construction:** (Facellia) steel unibody; (others) steel body welded to tubular steel chassis.

MAJOR OPTIONS: Automatic transmission (Facel II).

PERFORMANCE: Top Speed: (Facellia) 114 mph; (Facel II) 150 mph. **Acceleration (0-60 mph):** (Facellia) 13.7 sec.; (Facellia F2S) 11.2 seconds; (Facel II) 8.3 seconds. **Acceleration (quarter-mile):** (Facellia) 18.9 sec. (70 mph); (Facellia F2S) 16 seconds (73 mph). **Fuel Mileage:** (Facellia) 20-24 mpg.

Manufacturer: Forges et Ateliers de Construction d'Eure de Loire S.A., Paris, France.

Distributor: Charles H. Hornburg Jr. (Los Angeles); Hoffman Motor Car Co. (New York City).

HISTORY: Though considered by some to be the best of the Facels, a high selling price kept the II from helping the faltering company.

1963-64 FACEL VEGA

FACELLIA — F2/F2S — FOUR — The smaller Facel continued in production through 1963; see previous listings for details.

FACEL II — V-8 — Introduced for 1962, the large Chrysler-powered coupe continued in minimal production into 1964; see previous listing for details.

EXCELLENCE — V-8 — Facel's four-door sedan ended its production life in 1963; see previous listings for details.

FACEL III — FOUR — Introduced in spring 1963, the Facel III was powered by a Volvo four-cylinder engine rated 108 horsepower.

FACEL 6 — SIX — In a final desperate move to save the flagging company, then under management by another organization, a version with BMC's 3.0-liter six-cylinder engine (similar to that used in the Austin-Healey 3000, but with a smaller bore) was introduced. The 2860-cc engine developed 150 horsepower.

I.D. DATA: Serial numbers are at the center of the firewall, under the hood.

Model	Body Type & Seating	Engine Type/CID	P.O.E. Price	Weight (lbs.)	Prod. Total
Facellia	2-dr Coupe-3P	I4/100	5195	2465	Note 1
Facellia	2-dr Conv-3P	I4/100	N/A	N/A	Note 1
Facel II	2-dr HT Cpe-4P	V8/383	1550	3640	Note 2
Excellence	4-dr HT Sed-5P	V8/383	N/A	N/A	Note 3
Facel III	2-dr HT Cpe-4P	I4/108	I4/108	N/A	Note 4
Facel 6	2-dr HT Cpe-4P	I6/172	I6/172	N/A	26

Note 1: Total Facellia (and Facel III) production was 477 units for calendar year 1963.

Note 2: Total Facel II was production was 25 units for calendar year 1963, followed by 20 more in 1964.

Note 3: Total Excellence production was 9 units for calendar year 1963, followed by 5 more in 1964.

Note 4: Total Facel III (and FV6) production for calendar year 1964 was 349 units.

ENGINE DATA: BASE FOUR (Facellia F2): Inline, dual overhead-cam four-cylinder. Cast iron block and aluminum head. **Displacement:** 100.5 cu. in. (1647 cc). **Bore & Stroke:** 3.23 x 3.07 in. (82 x 78 mm). **Compression Ratio:** 9.4:1. **Brake Horsepower:** 115 at 6400 rpm. **Torque:** 105.5 lbs.-ft. at 4100 rpm. Five main bearings. Solex downdraft carburetor. 12-volt electrical.
BASE FOUR (Facellia F2S): Same as above, except -- **Compression Ratio:** 9.6:1. **Brake Horsepower:** 126 (131 SAE) at 6400 rpm. Two Weber sidedraft carburetors.
BASE FOUR (Facel III): Inline, overhead-valve four-cylinder (Volvo). **Displacement:** 108 cu. in. (1780 cc). **Bore & Stroke:** 3.31 x 3.15 in. (84.1 x 80 mm). **Compression Ratio:** 10.0:1. **Brake Horsepower:** 108 at 5000 rpm.
BASE SIX (Facel 6): Inline, overhead-valve six-cylinder (BMC). **Displacement:** 172 cu. in. (2860 cc). **Bore & Stroke:** 3.25 x 3.50 in. (82.55 x 88.9 mm). **Compression Ratio:** 9.0:1. **Brake Horsepower:** 150 at 5250 rpm.
BASE V-8 (Facel II, Excellence): Overhead-valve V-8 (Chrysler). Cast iron block and head. **Displacement:** 383 cu. in. (6279 cc). **Bore & Stroke:** 4.25 x 3.38 in. (107.95 x 85.85 mm). **Compression Ratio:** 10.0:1. **Brake Horsepower:** 355 at 4800 rpm (390 at 5400 with manual gearbox). Five main bearings. Hydraulic valve lifters. One four-barrel Carter carburetor (two with manual gearbox). 12-volt electrical.

CHASSIS DATA: Wheelbase: (Facellia) 96.5 in.; (Facel II) 105 in.; (Facel 6) 96.5 in.; (sed) 124.8 in. **Overall Length:** (Facellia) 164 in.; (Facel II) 180.7 in.; (Facel 6) 164 in.; (sed) 206.1 in. **Height:** (Facellia) 50 in.; (Facel II) 51 in.; (sed) 54 in. **Width:** (Facellia) 62.2 in.; (Facel II) 70.9 in.; (Facel III) 62.2 in.; (Facel 6) 62.2 in.; (sed) 72 in. **Front Tread:** (Facellia) 51.2 in.; (Facel II) 55.9 in.; (Facel III) 51.2 in.; (Facel 6) 51.2 in.; (sed) 55.9 in. **Rear Tread:** (Facellia) 50.4 in.; (Facel II) 57.1 in.; (Facel III) 50.4 in.; (Facel 6) 50.4 in.; (sed) 57.9 in. **Standard Tires:** (Facellia) 5.90x14; (sed) 7.60x15.

TECHNICAL: Layout: front-engine, rear-drive. **Transmission:** three-speed TorqueFlite or Pont-a-Mousson four-speed manual; (Facellia) four-speed manual. **Standard Final Drive Ratio:** (Facellia) 4.10:1; (Facel II) 2.93:1. **Steering:** cam and roller. **Suspension (front):** upper/lower A-arms, coil springs and anti-roll bar. **Suspension (rear):** rigid (live) axle with semi-elliptic leaf springs. **Brakes:** (Facellia/Facel II) front/rear discs. **Body Construction:** (Facellia) steel unibody; (others) steel body welded to tubular steel chassis.

MAJOR OPTIONS: Automatic transmission (Facel II).

PERFORMANCE: Top Speed: (Facel II) 150 mph; (others) 100-120 mph.. **Acceleration (0-60 mph):** (Facellia) 13.7 sec.; (Facellia F2S) 11.2 sec.; (Facel II) 8.3 seconds; (others) 10.5-12.5 seconds. **Acceleration (quarter-mile):** (Facellia) 18.9 sec. (70 mph); (Facellia F2S) 16 sec. (73 mph). **Fuel Mileage:** (Facellia) 20-24 mpg.

Manufacturer: Forges et Ateliers de Construction d'Eure et de Loire S.A., Paris, France.

Distributor: Charles H. Hornburg Jr. (Los Angeles); Hoffman Motor Car Co. (New York City).

HISTORY: The Volvo-powered Facel III was introduced in spring 1963, followed the next year by the BMC-powered Facel 6. Another BMC engine was considered, but it was too late to save the Facel name or company. The last Facel Vega automobile was produced in September 1964. Liquidation came early in 1965.

FAIRTHORPE

One might imagine that a company which produced cars named Atom and Electron would have been a pioneer in electrically-powered automobiles, perhaps ahead of their time for the energy crises that would arrive in the 1970s. Not so. Instead, the British firm established in 1954 by Air Vice-Marshal D.C.T. Bennett was simply one more rival in the gasoline-powered minicar market of the 1950s and '60s, but also a pioneer of sorts in fiberglass body construction. Fairthorpe Ltd. had first been engaged in the aircraft industry. Bennett's first car, the Atom, was powered by a choice of BSA motorcycle engines, mounted in the rear. Next came the front-engined Atomata, with a 650-cc BSA engine. Though fairly swift, those early models were

somewhat crudely constructed and did not catch on in the home market; but the Electron of 1956 fared better. By 1957, Fairthorpe had a distributor in the U.S. for that open two-seater, which carried a 1098-cc Coventry Climax four-cylinder engine, and for the less-costly Atom. Next came an Electron Minor, which later adopted a Triumph Spitfire engine. Fairthorpe's limited-production, high-speed (130-mph) Zeta arrived during 1959, powered by a Ford Zephyr engine. Two changes of plant location occurred during the early 1960s. By 1964, the Electron was using an 1147-cc Triumph Herald engine; and four years later, the larger Spitfire powerplant. Fairthorpe also turned out a 1.6-liter Rockette model with Triumph Vitesse engine during the early 1960s. That one evolved into the TX1 and TXGT. Stepping even farther into the performance arena, the company created a TX-S and then the ultimate in 1969: a sleek 130-mph TX-SS coupe with fuel injection. Well before that time, the Fairthorpe name had slipped away from American import-car listings, though production continued in England as late as 1978.

1955-57 FAIRTHORPE

1957 Fairthorpe Electron.

ATOM — Mk I/II — ONE — Of the three Atom models offered, two had single-cylinder motorcycle engines; one had a twin. The single-cylinder models were rated either 11 or 17 horsepower, offering top speeds of 45 or 55 mph. Early examples had a wholly unadorned front end with headlamps mounted separately, halfway back on the "hood" and far off to the side. Later versions had built-in headlamps, though the front ends remained untrimmed. Lightweight bodies (900 pounds or less, total) were built of fiberglass, with both front and rear wheels partly enclosed.

ATOM — Mk III — TWO — The twin-cylinder Atom rated 35-40 horsepower, and was said to be capable of top speeds as high as 80 mph.

ATOM — Mk IIA — ONE — Available by 1956 was a fourth version of the Atom, with a 15-horsepower rotary-valve (two-stroke) engine and 55-mph top speed.

ELECTRON — FOUR — Fairthorpe's lightweight, economical two-seat sports car, introduced during 1956, was claimed to have a 116-mph top speed as a result of its excellent power-to-weight ratio, coupled with easy handling. Its four-cylinder, water-cooled Coventry Climax engine developed up to 84 horsepower. The fiberglass body had seven-inch ground clearance, recessed headlamps, a curved windshield, rounded wheel openings, and exposed door hinges. A very low oval grille opening contained only a single vertical bar, with large air intake "gills at the cowl.

I.D. DATA: Not available.

Model	Body Type & Seating	Engine Type/CID	P.O.E. Price	Weight (lbs.)	Prod. Total
ATOM					
Mk I	2-dr Coupe-2P	1/15	Note 1	860	N/A
Mk II	2-dr Coupe-2P	1/21	Note 1	892	N/A
Mk IIA	2-dr Coupe-2P	12/19	Note 1	892	N/A
Mk III	2-dr Coupe-2P	12/39	1395	900	N/A
ELECTRON					
	2-dr Rds-2P	14/67	2850	995	N/A

Note 1: Price at factory in England was approximately $725 for the Mk I, $774 for Mk II, and $815 for Mk IIA (also $880 for Atom Mk III, and $1960 for the Electron). P.O.E. prices were effective in 1957.

Body Type Note: Some Atoms sold in U.S. were drophead coupes.

ENGINE DATA: BASE ONE (Atom Mk I): Overhead-valve one-cylinder (air cooled). Cast iron block. **Displacement:** 15.1 cu. in. (249 cc). **Bore & Stroke:** 2.48 x 3.15 in. (63 x 80 mm). **Compression Ratio:** 6.5:1. **Brake Horsepower:** 11 at 5400 rpm. **Torque:** 13.5 lbs.-ft. at 3700 rpm. One Amal carburetor. 6-volt electrical system.
BASE ONE (Atom Mk II): Same as above, except — **Displacement:** 21.25 cu. in. (348 cc). **Bore & Stroke:** 2.80 x 3.46 in. (71 x 88 mm). **Brake Horsepower:** 17 at 5500 rpm. 12-volt electrical system.

BASE TWO (Atom Mk IIA): Rotary-valve two-cylinder. **Displacement:** 19.5 cu. in. (322 cc). **Bore & Stroke:** 2.36 x 2.24 in. (60 x 57 mm). **Compression Ratio:** 6.5:1. **Brake Horsepower:** 15 at 4800/5600 rpm. One Amal carburetor. 12-volt electrical system.
BASE TWO (Atom Mk III): Overhead-valve two-cylinder. **Displacement:** 39.4 cu. in. (646 cc). **Bore & Stroke:** 2.75 x 3.30 in. (70 x 84 mm). **Compression Ratio:** 6.5:1. **Brake Horsepower:** 35 at 5700 rpm. **Torque:** 36 lbs.-ft. at 3750 rpm. One Amal carburetor. 12-volt electrical system.
BASE FOUR (Electron): Inline, overhead-cam four-cylinder (Coventry Climax). Cast iron block. **Displacement:** 67 cu. in. (1098 cc). **Bore & Stroke:** 2.85 x 2.62 in. (72.4 x 66.6 mm). **Compression Ratio:** 9.8:1. **Brake Horsepower:** 71/84. Two carburetors. One Amal carburetor.

CHASSIS DATA: Wheelbase: (Atom) 89 in.; (Electron) 82 in. **Overall Length:** (Atom) 132 in.; (Electron) 144 in. **Height:** (Atom) 54 in.; (Electron) 46 in. **Width:** (Atom) 61 in.; (Electron) 60 in. **Tread:** (Atom) 48 in.; (Electron) 48 in. **Standard Tires:** (Atom) 5.20x13; (Electron) 5.20x15.

TECHNICAL: Layout: (Atom) rear-engine, rear-drive; (Electron) front-engine, rear-drive. **Transmission:** (Atom) three-speed manual; (Electron) four-speed manual. **Suspension (front):** swing axles with coil springs. **Suspension (rear):** swing axles with coil springs. **Brakes:** hydraulic, front/rear drum. **Body Construction:** fiberglass body (no chassis).

PERFORMANCE: Top Speed: (Atom Mk I) 45 mph; (Atom Mk II/IIA) 55 mph; (Atom Mk III) 75-80 mph; (Electron) 110-116 mph. **Fuel Mileage:** (Atom) 50-60 mpg.

Manufacturer: Fairthorpe Ltd., Chalfon St. Peter, Buckinghamshire, England.

Distributor: Paul Pollard & Associates, Los Angeles, California.

HISTORY: "Fairthorpe Ltd.," according to a letter from the company soon after it entered automobile production, had "achieved a very low total weight for what is in effect a reasonably spacious car. The economy of running and of first cost is a unique achievement, and the features of independent four-wheel suspension, and of the plastic body are additional attractions." Both Atom and Electron models were available in the U.S. by 1957.

1958 FAIRTHORPE

ATOMATA — TWO — Wearing a restyled body, six inches lower than its Atom predecessor, the new Atomata nevertheless still presented a rather crude appearance. The sharply fastback coupe styling included fenders that extended far beyond the deck to form gigantic square fins, as well as exposed door hinges. A two-cylinder front-mounted BSA 650-cc engine provided 35 horsepower, working through a four-speed gearbox. The two-seat coupe's interior allowed space for one or two additional (small) people behind the front seat. The chassisless design, on an 81-inch wheelbase, featured a body made of reinforced plastic.

ELECTRON MINOR — FOUR — A new, smaller two-seat sports car joined the original Electron, this one powered by a Standard Ten four-cylinder engine rated 38 horsepower. Top speed was 90 mph; gas mileage, as high as 55 mpg.

ELECTRON — Mk II — FOUR — Essentially unchanged except for the addition of front disc brakes, the two-seat roadster came with a standard 1098-cc (67-cid) Coventry Climax engine. Its 84-bhp output was sufficient to propel an Electron to speeds of 120 mph, yet deliver up to 33 mpg. Three optional engines were available: a 1.5-liter Coventry Climax FPF, rated 141 bhp; a 1.5-liter Butterworth, rated 145 bhp; and a modified 1172-cc Ford.

I.D. DATA: Not available.

Model	Body Type & Seating	Engine Type/CID	P.O.E. Price	Weight (lbs.)	Prod. Total
ATOMATA					
	2-dr Coupe-2 + 2P	12/39	N/A	895	N/A
ELECTRON MINOR					
	2-dr Rds-2P	14/58	N/A	980	N/A
ELECTRON					
Mk II	2-dr Rds-2P	14/67	N/A	1150	N/A

ENGINE DATA: BASE TWO (Atomata): Overhead-valve two-cylinder (air-cooled BSA). Cast iron block. **Displacement:** 39.4 cu. in. (646 cc). **Bore & Stroke:** 2.76 x 2.31 in. (70 x 84 mm). **Compression Ratio:** 6.5:1. **Brake Horsepower:** 35 at 5700 rpm. **Torque:** 36 lbs.-ft. at 3750 rpm. One Amal carburetor. 12-volt electrical system.
BASE FOUR (Electron Minor): Inline, overhead-valve four-cylinder (Standard Ten). Cast iron block. **Displacement:** 57.8 cu. in. (948 cc). **Bore & Stroke:** 2.47 x 2.99 in. (63 x 76 mm). **Compression Ratio:** 8.25:1. **Brake Horsepower:** 38 at 5000 rpm. **Torque:** 49 lbs.-ft. at 5000 rpm. One Solex carburetor.
BASE FOUR (Electron Mk II): Inline, overhead-cam four-cylinder (Coventry Climax). Cast iron block. **Displacement:** 67 cu. in. (1098 cc). **Bore & Stroke:** 2.85 x 2.62 in. (72.4 x 66.6 mm). **Compression Ratio:** 9.8:1. **Brake Horsepower:** 84 at 6900 rpm. **Torque:** 67 lbs.-ft. at 4750 rpm. Two SU carburetors.

Note: A 71-bhp version of the Electron also remained available.

CHASSIS DATA: Wheelbase: (Atomata) 81 in.; (Electron Minor) 81 in.; (Electron Mk II) 82 in. **Overall Length:** (Atomata) 129 in.; (Electron Minor) 120 in.; (Electron Mk II) 144 in. **Height:** (Atomata) 48 in.; (Electron Minor) 46 in.; (Electron Mk II) 46 in. **Width:** (Atomata) 60 in.; (Electron Minor) 58 in.; (Electron Mk II) 60 in. **Tread:** (Atomata) 49 in.; (Electron Minor) 49 in.; (Electron Mk II) 48 in. **Standard Tires:** (Atomata) 5.20x13; (Electron Minor) 5.20x13; (Electron) 5.60x15.

TECHNICAL: Layout: front-engine, rear-drive. **Transmission:** four-speed manual. **Standard Final Drive Ratio:** (Atomata) 4.55:1; (Electron Minor) 4.55:1; (Electron Mk II) 4.44:1. **Suspension (front):** independent; wishbones and coil springs. **Suspension (rear):** trailing wishbones with coil springs. **Brakes:** hydraulic, front/rear drum except (Electron Mk II) Girling front disc, rear drum. **Body Construction:** fiberglass body (no chassis).

PERFORMANCE: Top Speed: (Atomata) 80 mph; (Electron Minor) 90 mph; (Electron Mk II) 120-125 mph. **Fuel Mileage:** (Atomata) 50 mpg; (Electron Minor) 45-55 mpg; (Electron Mk II) 33 mpg.

Manufacturer: Fairthorpe Ltd., Chalfon St. Peter, Buckinghamshire, England.

1959 FAIRTHORPE

ATOMATA — TWO — Fairthorpe's fastback coupe continued with minimal change.

ELECTRON MINOR — FOUR — No significant changes were evident in Fairthorpe's smaller two-seat sports car.

ELECTRON — Mk III — FOUR — Compression got a boost in the 1098-cc Coventry Climax engine, from 9.8:1 to 10.5:1. That raised output from 84 to 93 bhp. The Electron was capable of 120-mph top speed.

I.D. DATA: Not available.

Model	Body Type & Seating	Engine Type/CID	P.O.E. Price	Weight (lbs.)	Prod. Total
ATOMATA					
	2-dr Coupe-2 + 2P	I2/39	Note 1	925	N/A
ELECTRON MINOR					
	2-dr Rds-2P	I4/58	Note 1	945	N/A
ELECTRON					
Mk III	2-dr Rds-2P	I4/67	Note 1	1210	N/A

Note 1: Price at the factory in England was about $1205 for the Atomata, $1355 for the Electron Minor, and $2175 for the Mark III Electron.

Model Note: Fairthorpe models were available either fully assembled, or in kit form.

ENGINE DATA: BASE TWO (Atomata): Overhead-valve two-cylinder (air-cooled BSA). Cast iron block. **Displacement:** 39.4 cu. in. (646 cc). **Bore & Stroke:** 2.76 x 3.31 in. (70 x 84 mm). **Compression Ratio:** 6.5:1. **Brake Horsepower:** 35 at 5700 rpm. **Torque:** 36.1 lbs.-ft. at 3750 rpm. One Amal carburetor.

BASE FOUR (Electron Minor): Inline, overhead-valve four-cylinder (Standard Ten). Cast iron block. **Displacement:** 57.8 cu. in. (948 cc). **Bore & Stroke:** 2.47 x 2.99 in. (63 x 76 mm). **Compression Ratio:** 8.25:1. **Brake Horsepower:** 38 at 5000 rpm. **Torque:** 49 lbs.-ft. at 2800 rpm. One Solex carburetor.

BASE FOUR (Electron Mk III): Inline, overhead-cam four-cylinder (Coventry Climax). Cast iron block. **Displacement:** 67 cu. in. (1098 cc). **Bore & Stroke:** 2.84 x 2.62 in. (72.4 x 66.6 mm). **Compression Ratio:** 10.5:1. **Brake Horsepower:** 93 at 6800 rpm. **Torque:** 67 lbs.-ft. at 4750 rpm. Two SU carburetors.

Note: Electron Mk III could also have an optional 1.5-liter Coventry Climax FPF engine (141 bhp), or a 1.5-liter Butterworth (145 bhp).

CHASSIS DATA: Wheelbase: (Atomata/Minor) 81 in.; (Electron Mk III) 82 in. **Overall Length:** (Atomata) 129 in.; (Electron Minor) 132 in.; (Electron Mk II) 144 in. **Height:** (Atomata) 48 in.; (Electron Minor) 46 in.; (Electron Mm III) 46 in. **Width:** (Atomata) 57 in.; (Electron Minor) 58 in.; (Electron Mk III) 60 in. **Tread:** (Atomata/Minor) 49 in.; (Electron Mk III) 48 in. **Standard Tires:** (Atomata) 5.20x13; (Electron Minor) 5.60x13; (Electron Mk III) 5.60x15.

TECHNICAL: Layout: front-engine, rear-drive. **Transmission:** four-speed manual. Overall Atomata/Minor gear ratios: (1st) 19.45:1; (2nd) 11.2:1; (3rd) 6.62:1; (4th) 4.55:1. Overall Electron gear ratios: (1st) 13.85:1; (2nd) 8.2:1; (3rd) 5.43:1; (4th) 4.1:1. **Standard Final Drive Ratio:** (Atomata) 4.55:1; (Electron Minor) 4.55:1.; (Electron Mk III) 4.44:1. **Suspension (front):** independent; wishbones and coil springs. **Suspension (rear):** trailing wishbones with coil springs. **Brakes:** hydraulic, front/rear drum except (Electron Mk III) Girling front disc, rear drum. **Body Construction:** fiberglass body (no chassis). **Fuel Tank:** (Atomata) 7.2 gal.; (Minor) 9.6 gal.; (Mk III) 12 gallons.

PERFORMANCE: Top Speed: (Atomata) 80 mph; (Electron Minor) about 83 mph; (Electron Mk III) 120 mph. **Fuel Mileage:** (Atomata) 50-60 mpg; (Electron Minor) 45-55 mpg; (Electron Mk III) 40-45 mpg.

Manufacturer: Fairthorpe Ltd., Chalfon St. Peter, Buckinghamshire, England.

Distributor: Martin M. Fuss, Tucson, Arizona; Town and Track, Detroit, Michigan; and Bob Martin Auto Sales, Delmar, New York.

1960-62 FAIRTHORPE

ATOMATA — TWO — Fairthorpe's two-cylinder fastback coupe continued with minimal change.

ELECTRON MINOR — FOUR — No significant changes were evident in Fairthorpe's smaller two-seat sports car.

ELECTRON — Mk III — FOUR — Little change was seen in the four-cylinder Electron roadster.

ZETA — SUPER SPORTS — SIX — After several years of two- and four-cylinder power, Fairthorpe turned out a six-cylinder coupe model, using a Ford Zephyr engine that developed 137 horsepower. Zeta's front end had a large, unadorned grille opening, split into two sections (one above the other). Round headlamps sat back from the nose in nacelles, with tiny round parking lights inboard and below.

ELECTRINA — FOUR — A Fairthorpe sedan was announced during 1960, with the same 948-cc engine as the Electron Minor; but it never gained the popularity of the roadsters or coupes.

1962 Fairthorpe Zeta.

I.D. DATA: Not available.

Model	Body Type & Seating	Engine Type/CID	P.O.E. Price	Weight (lbs.)	Prod. Total
ATOMATA					
	2-dr Coupe-2 + 2P	I2/39	Note 1	880	N/A
ELECTRON MINOR					
	2-dr Rds-2P	I4/58	Note 1	895	N/A
ELECTRON					
Mk III	2-dr Rds-2P	I4/67	Note 1	1150	N/A
ZETA SUPER SPORTS					
Zeta	2-dr Coupe-2P	I6/136	N/A	1475	N/A
ELECTRINA					
	2-dr Sedan	I4/58	N/A	995	N/A

Note 1: Price at the factory in England (circa 1960) was about $1265 for the Atomata, $1430 for the Electron Minor, and $2268 for the Mark III Electron. **Model Note:** Fairthorpe models were available either fully assembled, or in kit form.

ENGINE DATA: BASE TWO (Atomata): Same as 1959.

BASE FOUR (Electron Minor, Electrina): Inline, overhead-valve four-cylinder (Standard Ten). Cast iron block. **Displacement:** 57.8 cu. in. (948 cc). **Bore & Stroke:** 2.47 x 2.99 in. (63 x 76 mm). **Compression Ratio:** 8.5:1. **Brake Horsepower:** 45 at 4800 rpm. **Torque:** 49 lbs.-ft. at 3000 rpm. Two SU carburetors.

BASE FOUR (Electron Mk III): Inline, overhead-cam four-cylinder (Coventry Climax). Cast iron block. **Displacement:** 67 cu. in. (1098 cc). **Bore & Stroke:** 2.84 x 2.62 in. (72.4 x 66.6 mm). **Compression Ratio:** 10.5:1. **Brake Horsepower:** 93 at 7000 rpm. **Torque:** 71 lbs.-ft. at 5000 rpm. Two SU carburetors.

Note: Electron Mk III could also have an optional 1.5-liter Coventry Climax FPF engine (141 bhp), or a 1.5-liter Butterworth (145 bhp).

BASE SIX (Zeta): Inline, overhead-valve six-cylinder. Cast iron block. **Displacement:** 135.7 cu. in. (2553 cc). **Bore & Stroke:** 3.15 x 3.15 in. (82.5 x 79.5 mm). **Compression Ratio:** 9.0:1. **Brake Horsepower:** 137 at 5500 rpm. **Torque:** 160 lbs.-ft. at 3200 rpm. Six Amal carburetors.

Note: Zeta was also available with a single Zenith carburetor (90 bhp) or with three SU carburetors.

CHASSIS DATA: Wheelbase: (Atomata/Minor/Electrina) 81 in.; (Electron Mk III) 82 in.; (Zeta) 85.5 in. **Overall Length:** (Atomata) 129 in.; (Electron Minor) 132 in.; (Electrina) 134 in.; (Electron Mk III) 138 in.; (Zeta) 140 in. **Height:** (Atomata) 48 in.; (Electron Minor) 46 in.; (Electron Mk III) 46 in.; (Zeta) 46 in. **Width:** (Atomata) 60 in.; (Electron Minor/Electrina) 58 in.; (Electron Mk III) 58 in.; (Zeta) 58 in. **Tread:** (Atomata/Minor/Electrina) 49 in.; (Electron Mk III) 48 in. **Standard Tires:** (Atomata) 5.20x13; (Electron Minor/Electrina) 5.60x13; (Electron Mk III) 5.60x15; (Zeta) 155.15.

TECHNICAL: Layout: front-engine, rear-drive. **Transmission:** four-speed manual. **Suspension (front):** independent; coil springs. **Suspension (rear):** trailing wishbones with coil springs. **Brakes:** hydraulic, front/rear drum except (Electron Mk III) Girling front disc, rear drum. **Body Construction:** fiberglass body (no chassis). **Fuel Tank:** (Atomata) 7.2 gal.; (Minor) 9.6 gal.; (Mk III) 12 gallons.

PERFORMANCE: Top Speed: (Atomata) 75-80 mph; (Electron Minor) 83-90 mph; (Electron Mk III) 116 mph; (Zeta) 130 mph. **Fuel Mileage:** (Atomata) 55-65 mpg; (Electron Minor) 45-55 mpg; (Electron Mk III) 30-40 mpg; (Zeta) 25 mpg.

Manufacturer: Fairthorpe Ltd., Chalfon St. Peter, Buckinghamshire, England.

Distributor: Martin M. Fuss, Tucson, Arizona; Town and Track, Detroit, Michigan; and Bob Martin Auto Sales, Delmar, New York.

HISTORY: Production of the Atomata ceased in 1960; the Electron Minor in 1963; Zeta in 1965.

POSTSCRIPT: Fairthorpes remained in production into the 1970s, but interest in the U.S. faded away early in the 1960s. A plastic-bodied Electron EM III roadster on a tubular ladder frame, introduced in 1963, carried an 1147-cc Triumph Herald engine delivering 63 or (later) 67 horsepower. Mk IV through VI editions of the Electron carried a 1296-cc powerplant, rated at 75 bhp. From 1962 to 1965, a Rockette sports model was produced, with 88-inch wheelbase and a 1596-cc Vitesse six-cylinder engine. That Rockette evolved into the TXGT coupe of 1967-68, with 1998-cc six-cylinder engine rated at either 95 or 104 bhp. Another fixed-head coupe, the TX-S, arrived in 1969, with a 112-bhp version of the 1998-cc six and top speed of 115 mph. Perhaps the ultimate Fairthorpe, the 140-horsepower TX-SS coupe, was produced in 1969. TX-series Fairthorpes had a more conventional appearance than earlier models, more like a boulevard sports car than a racer or a prototype. The TX-SS had back-slanted door and rear quarter windows and a sharply fastback rear end.

FERRARI

Born in 1898 near Modena, Italy, Enzo Ferrari was driving a car by the time he hit his teens, and racing them by 1919. After joining Alfa Romeo as a test driver in 1920, he placed second in that year's Targa Florio event. In 1929, he left Alfa and founded the Scuderia Ferrari racing team, building and racing modified Alfa Romeos. Enzo's own racing days were over by 1931, but as every sports-car fan knows, he was destined to contribute far more to the field in later years than most people who'd sat behind the wheel for a time. During these Depression years came the debut of the famed "prancing horse" emblem that would later decorate a long succession of Ferrari race and road vehicles.

By 1940, his company became Societa Auto-Avio Costruzioni Ferrari, turning out a straight-eight 815 (not named Ferrari) but World War II prevented automotive development. After peace returned, Ferrari was assisted by Enrico Nardi in realizing his dream of building sports/racing cars of his own design. Setting up shop at Maranello (near Modena), he soon produced his first car, using a 1500-cc V-12 engine designed by Gioacchino Colombo. Essentially handcrafted — like all early Ferraris — these first road-racing models, announced late in 1946, were known as Tipo (Type) 125C. Their first race took place at Piacenza, in May 1947. Only three cars were built in 1947, followed by nine in 1948, rising to a whopping 30 in 1949. The original engine was bored out to 1902 cc displacement to create a Type 159; then enlarged again to become the 1995-cc Type 166 Sport. A variant of that one, known as the Type 166 Inter, was the first roadgoing Ferrari. On the race circuit, Ferrari would take eight Mille Miglia victories, starting in 1948, commemorated by an 'MM' designation on later models of the original chassis.

By 1950-51, the Type 166 evolved into 195 Inter and 212 Inter and Export models, the latter on a shorter wheelbase. Engineer Colombo was replaced by Aurelio Lampredi, who had his own ideas on V-12 design. The 212 engine displaced 2562 cc and produced as much as 170 horsepower. Ferrari's first big-engine model arrived in 1951: the Type 340 America, with a 4101-cc Lampredi-derived V-12 producing 220 horsepower. Capable of some 137 mph in basic form, modifications of the 340 were raced in the U.S. as the 340 Mexico and 340 MM. Even larger engines hit the race courses under factory auspices by 1953, starting with the Type 375 and its 4523-cc V-12, and the 4954-cc verison that produced about 344 horsepower and could hit 60 mph in seven seconds, to say nothing of top speeds beyond 160 mph. By this time, Ferraris had won the 24-Hour Le Mans, Spa and Turin races, as well as Grand Prix events in Luxembourg, Switzerland, Belgium, Sweden, Holland, and Britain. Luigi Chinetti, who would become Ferrari's distributor in the U.S., held the one-hour, 200-kilometer and 100-mile records at the Montlhery track, which he consumed at speeds past 126 mph.

At the 1953 Paris Salon came the debut of the first of Ferrari's 250 series: the 250 Europa, using the Lampredi V-12 and riding a 110-inch wheelbase. A 250 GT Europa soon followed, on a 102-inch wheelbase; and a 94.5-inch version would emerge at the end of the decade. A 410 Superamerica appeared in 1956, with a 4962-cc V-12 beneath its hood. Taking note of the importance of the American market, Ferrari introduced a "California" convertible for 1959, based on the 250 chassis. Not until 1960 and the 250 GT 2+2 did Ferrari acknowledge the need for rear seats

(albeit tiny ones) by some of its customers. That was followed by a 330 GT version with a larger V-12 engine and, in 1967, a 365 GT 2+2. In 1960, the company changed its name to Societa per Azioni Esercizo Fabriche Automobili e Corse Ferrari. Ford made a bid to take over the Ferrari operation early in the 1960s, but that attempt was unsuccessful.

A 400 Superamerica was offered through the early 1960s, followed by the 500 Superfast at mid-decade. Starting in 1963, Ferrari had a mid-engine model suitable for street driving, though the 250 LM was intended mainly for competition. At the same time, roadgoing Ferraris were represented by the new 275 GTB and GTS, which introduced all-independent suspension and a five-speed gearbox as a unit with the rear differential (forming a transaxle). Also in the mid-1960s, the 275 GTB chassis and 330 GT 2+2 engine resulted in a new 330 GTC coupe, while the four-seat 330 series itself evolved into a 365 GT 2+2.

Enzo Ferrari's only son, Dino, had died at the age of 24 in 1956, a tragedy that resulted in the naming of a succession of models for him. The Dino 206 GT was introduced in 1967, followed by the Dino 246 GT two years later. Early Dinos differed from other Ferraris in two major ways: they were powered by mid-mounted V-6 engines rather than the usual V-12s, and they lacked any Ferrari identification. Also new in the late 1960s was the 365 GTB/4, with four-cam V-12, which soon became popular known as the "Daytona." An open 365 GTS/4 Spider convertible also emerged.

One more Dino model appeared in 1973: the 308 GT4, with a mid-mounted V-8 engine (a first for road Ferraris) instead of the former V-6. Then came another type of engine: a horizontally-opposed (flat) 12-cylinder, introduced in the 365 GT4 BB that evolved into the 512 BB. These were known as "boxer" engines, because of the back-and-forth motion of the pistons. Meanwhile, the 365 GT4 2+2 evolved into the four-seat 400i and, in the mid-1980s, the 412i with a larger V-12 engine. On the V-8 front, a new 308 GTB arrived in 1975, followed by a Targa-topped 308 GTS two years later. Early 308 models wore fiberglass bodies rather than the usual steel, but that experiment was abandoned after 1977. Those models lasted into the late 1980s, turning to four-cam (Quattrovalvole) engine configuration and then to a larger 328 version. The 1980s also brought Ferrari's Mondial (world) series, with four-cam V-8 power, on a longer wheelbase than the 308.

Though it seems to have been around forever, the dramatically-styled Testarossa (which repeated a name used on Ferrari race cars in the 1950s) didn't debut until 1985, a year after the race-oriented GTO coupe with its four-cam V-8. As if Ferrari's offerings through the years weren't "super" enough, the company announced its startling F40 coupe in 1987. Rival to the Porsche 959 supercar, the F40 was to be produced in limited number, with a top speed that edged past 200 mph and 0-60 mph acceleration well under four seconds. After considerable difficulty, Ferrari managed to certify the F40 for U.S. sale, but only a few hundred wealthy folk would ever be able to sit behind the wheel, after paying a price that soon soared to the half-million-dollar mark and beyond. On a more modest (for Ferrari) level, the 328 evolved into a 348 and the Mondial to a 't' version before the decade ended. Those and the Testarossa remained in production into the 1990s.

Ferrari Model Numbering Note: Ferraris were normally called Tipo (Type), followed by a numerical designation: sometimes logical, sometimes not. Until recent years, model numbers indicated displacement in cubic centimeters (rounded-off) of each cylinder. Thus, the displacement of each cylinder in the Type 166 was equal to 166.25 cc. After the mid-1950s, the figures generally stood for total

number of liters, but there were many exceptions to the rule. Letters in the model number had varied meanings: A 'C' (Corsa, or race) suffix went on the first racing cars, but 'C' later stood for Competizione on one-seat racers. An 'I' (Inter) designation went on sports/race models. At first, odd numbers in the three-digit designation were used for "road" models, even numbers for competition versions; but that separation soon became ambiguous as dual-purpose models emerged. A 'GT' designation stands for Gran Turismo (Grand Touring). 'GTO' identifies a GT omologato (homologated, or sanctioned for racing). The 'GTB' suffix designates a berlinetta (coupe), while 'GTS' identifies an open model: either a Targa roof or full convertible (Spider, or Spyder). A '/4' suffix indicates a Ferrari with four-cam engine, while 'i' identifies a fuel-injected engine. The "Superamerica" models were sometimes identifed as "Super America" or "SuperAmerica."

Model Availability and Specification Note: Especially in the early years, Ferraris were basically custom built, by no means mass produced. Specifications varied, too, among examples under the same general designation. Therefore, dimensions of a specific car may vary from those shown below, which are typical rather than absolute. Engines also varied considerably, not only in horsepower and torque ratings but in displacement. Listed in these pages are the best-known sizes and ratings, but a large number of variants also were produced, especially for racing purposes.

1947-50 FERRARI

TYPE 166 SPORTS — V-12 — An evolution of the original Type 125 with its 1500-cc V-12 engine, this was the racing model that in effect started the whole Ferrari myth and mystique. No more than two of the compact notchback coupes were built, powered by a 1995-cc enlargement of the V-12. In its racing debut (as an open model) in April 1948, the car won the Targa Florio road race in Sicily, driven by Clemente Biondetti. A month later, Biondetti won the Mille Miglia in the same car, which then wore an Allemano coupe body.

TYPE 166 INTER — V-12 — Ferrari's first road car established the company's design theme for the next decade. Though a close relative to Ferrari racers, the 166 Inter wasn't really as fast as it looked. Powered by the 1995-cc "Colombo" V-12, initially producing 110 horsepower, the car was basically handbuilt, a sign that Ferrari wasn't yet enthused about road cars.

With alternate compression ratios and carburetion, the 60-degree V-12 could produce as much as 150 horsepower, and the basic engine design would last into the 1960s. Each bank used a chain-driven camshaft, actuating inclined valves via rocker arms and finger followers. Each valve was closed with twin hairpin springs. The Inter (and Sport) engine had one twin-choke Weber carburetor, while the more potent 'MM' made use of triple twin-choke Webers. Both block and heads were made of aluminum alloy, with cast-iron cylinder liners and a seven-bearing (six-throw) crankshaft. The 166 MM engine (which won the 1949 Le Mans race) had needle rod bearings. Some examples had compression ratios high enough to run on alcohol fuel.

Various wheelbases were used, ranging from 86.6 inches (in the MM barchetta coupe) to 103.1 inches, with a tubular steel ladder-type chassis that used oval-section main tubes and round-section cross tubes. Independent front suspension used a transverse leaf spring. A "live" (rigid) axle with semi-elliptic leaf springs brought up the rear. Lever-action Houdaille hydraulic shock absorbers were installed (except on the first few examples). Hydraulic brakes had aluminum drums with cast-iron liners. All models were right-hand drive, with worm and peg steering. An unsynchronized five-speed gearbox worked through a single dry-plate clutch. Later 166 MM models had transmissions synchronized in third and fourth gears. Like most Ferraris that would come in subsequent years, Type 166 Inters wore center-lock (knock-off) Borrani wire wheels.

Bodies were supplied by Vignale, Allemano, Bertone, Ghia, Pinin Farina, Stabilimenti Farina, and other coachbuilders, in a variety of styles (as would be true of Ferraris generally through the 1950s, in particular). Best known may have been the roadster by Carrozzeria Touring, which had a bodyside crease line that ran from the top of the front fender across the top of the rear fender, curving down toward the back end. Though known as a barchetta (little boat), it wasn't given that name in Ferrari literature. After a time, its basic design found its way onto the AC Ace and Cobra.

Another body style, the berlinetta coupe by Touring, displayed rear quarter windows, the same type of bodyside crease, and a crosshatch (eggcrate) grille of rounded rectangular shape. It had small round parking lights alongside the grille, aired-in headlamps set back slightly from the grille, a scoop at the front of the hood, and no bumpers. The final 166 model was the Spyder Corsa, a two-seat open racer with cycle fenders, separate headlamps, and a body-colored grille.

TYPE 195 — V-12 — Similar to the 166 Inter in style, chassis and dimensions, the 195 (introduced in 1950) had a larger engine that displaced 2341 cc, a result of enlarging the bore by 5 millimeters. The 195 (road) version produced 130 horsepower using a single Weber carburetor, while the competition Sport engine reached 160 bhp or more via triple Webers. Top speed of the 195 Inter was about 110 mph. A variety of coachbuilt body styles were offered again, as two-seat touring or sports-racer berlinettas (coupes) and convertibles. The majority were done by Pinin Farina or Vignale. Only some two dozen were produced during the brief model run.

TYPE 212 — V-12 — An even larger engine went into the 212 Inter (road) and Export (racing), which were otherwise similar to the 166/195 series. This version of the V-12 was bored to 68 mm, for a displacement of 2562 cc. Horsepower ratings were no more potent than the smaller 195 engine, but top speed reached as high as 120 mph (140 mph in the Export version) . One Weber carburetor produced 130 horsepower or more, while a trio of Webers was good for 150 bhp or better. Remaining in production longer than the 195 (as late as 1953), at least two dozen Export models were produced, and about 80 of the 212 Inters. While the 212 earned more attention than the smaller-engine 195 from American fans, the 340 America (which debuted in 1951) would get even more.

Model Note: 166/195/212 models came with a wide variety of custom bodies, so specifications varied.

I.D. DATA: Not available.

Model	Body Type & Seating	Engine Type/CID	P.O.E. Price	Weight (lbs.)	Prod. Total
TYPE 166 SPORTS (1947-48)					
166	2-dr Coupe	V12/122	N/A	N/A	2
TYPE 166 (1948-51)					
166 Inter	2-dr Coupe-2P	V12/122	N/A	2000	Note 1
166 Inter	2-dr Conv Cpe-2P	V12/122	N/A	2000	Note 1
166 MM	2-dr Coupt-2P	V12/122	N/A	2000	Note 1
166 MM	2-dr Conv Cpe-2P	V12/122	N/A	2000	Note 1
TYPE 195 (1950-51)					
195 Inter	2-dr Coupe-2P	V12/143	N/A	2100	Note 2
195 Inter	2-dr Conv Cpe-2P	V12/143	N/A	2100	Note 2
195 Sport	2-dr Coupe-2P	V12/143	N/A	N/A	Note 2
TYPE 212 (1950-53)					
212 Inter	2-dr Coupe-2P	V12/156	Note 3	2100	Note 4
212 Inter	2-dr Conv Cpe-2P	V12/156	Note 3	2100	Note 4
212 Export	2-dr Coupe-2P	V12/156	Note 3	N/A	Note 4

Note 1: A total of 37 (possibly 38) Type 166 Inter models were produced, through 1953; plus about 32 Type 166 MM (including 12 coupes).

Note 2: Approximately 25 Type 195 models were produced, in 1950-51.

Note 3: A Type 212 Ferrari sold for approximately $9500 in the early 1950s.

Note 4: Approximately 80 Type 212 Inters were produced through 1953, plus as many as 26 Type 212 Export models.

Weight Note: Figures shown are approximate (or averages).

ENGINE DATA: BASE V-12 (Type 166): 60-degree, single-overhead-cam, "vee" type 12-cylinder. Aluminum alloy block and heads (cast-iron cylinder liners). **Displacement:** 122 cu. in. (1995 cc). **Bore & Stroke:** 2.36 x 2.31 in. (60 x 58.8 mm). **Compression Ratio:** 7.5:1/8.0:1. **Brake Horsepower:** 110 at 6000 rpm (up to 150 bhp depending on compression and carburetion). Seven main bearings. One or three twin-choke Weber 32 DCF carburetors.

Sport/MM Engine Note: The 166 Sport engine, with a single carburetor, produced 90 horsepoewr at 5600 rpm. The triple-carbureted 166 MM engine was rated 140/160 bhp at 6600/7200 rpm.

BASE V-12 (Type 195): 60-degree, single-overhead-cam, "vee" type 12-cylinder. Aluminum alloy block and heads (cast-iron cylinder liners). **Displacement:** 142.8 cu. in. (2341 cc). **Bore & Stroke:** 2.56 x 2.31 in. (65 x 58.8 mm). **Compression Ratio:** 7.5:1. **Brake Horsepower:** (Inter) 130 at 6000 rpm; (Sport) 160-180 at 6000 rpm. Seven main bearings. One twin-choke Weber carburetor (Inter) or three twin-choke Webers (Sport).

BASE V-12 (Type 212): 60-degree, single-overhead-cam, "vee" type 12-cylinder. Aluminum alloy block and head (cast-iron cylinder liners). **Displacement:** 156.3 cu. in. (2562 cc). **Bore & Stroke:** 2.68 x 2.31 in. (68 x 58.8 mm). **Compression Ratio:** 8.0:1. **Brake Horsepower:** (Inter) 130-140 at 6000 rpm; (Export) 150-170 at 6500 rpm. Seven main bearings. One twin-choke Weber carburetor (Inter) or three twin-choke 36 DCF Webers (Export).

CHASSIS DATA: Wheelbase: (166 Inter) 98.4 in. or 103.1 in.; (166 MM barchetta, 195 Sport) 86.6 in.; (166 MM cpe, 212 Export) 88.6 in.; (166 Sport) 95.3 in. (195/212 Inter) 98.5 in. **Overall Length:** (166 Inter) 146-156 in. typical. **Height:** (166 Inter) 50 in. typical. **Width:** (166 Inter) 60 in. typical. **Front Tread:** 49.8 in. **Rear Tread:** 49.2 in. **Wheel Type:** Borrani center-lock wire. **Standard Tires:** (166 Inter) 5.90x15 or 5.50x15.

TECHNICAL: Layout: front-engine, rear-drive. **Transmission:** five-speed manual (non-synchro on early 166 models). **Steering:** worm and peg (right-hand drive). **Suspension (front):** unequal-length A-arms with transverse leaf springs. **Suspension (rear):** rigid axle with parallel trailing arms and semi-elliptic leaf springs. **Brakes:** hydraulic, front/rear drum. **Body Construction:** separate body on tubular steel ladder-type frame.

PERFORMANCE: Top Speed: (166 Inter) 112-120 mph; (195) about 110 mph; (212 Inter) about 120 mph; (212 Export) 140 mph.

PRODUCTION/SALES: Only about three Ferraris were sold in the U.S. during 1950.

Manufacturer: Societa Auto-Avio Costruzioni Ferrari, Maranello (Modena), Italy.

HISTORY: Briggs Cunningham is said to have imported the first Ferrari into the U.S., a 1949 Spider. Ferrari's 340 America debuted at the Paris Salon in October 1950; see next listing for details.

1951-53 FERRARI

1951 Ferrari.

1952 Ferrari 2.5-liter Tipo 212 Inter 2+2. (Christie's)

TYPE 166 — V-12 — Production of the 166 Inter continued into 1951; see previous listing for details.

TYPE 195/212 — V-12 — Production of the 195/212 Inter models continued into 1951 and 1953, respectively; see previous listing for details. Ghia and Pinin Farina bodies were seen at the Paris Salon in 1952, notable for being the first left-hand-drive models. Later Vignale and Farina bodies had a curved one-piece windshield, while bodies from Touring Carrozzeria kept their two-piece "vee" windshield.

TYPE 340 AMERICA — V-12 — Though small in numbers produced (only 22 in all, from 1951-55) and oriented toward racing, the 340 America led off a succession of evolutionary Ferraris based on the 166/195/212 chassis, but powered by the larger long-block V-12 engine, as designed by Aurelio Lampredi. The 4101-cc engine had first seen racing use in 1950, initially displacing 3.3 liters but later enlarged to 4.1 and 4.5 liters. Like the Colombo V-12, it had two inclined valves per cylinders and hairpin-type springs, but bore centers were spaced farther apart to permit larger displacement. Also, roller cam followers were used instead of the plain finger-type, and intake valve ports were separate rather than "siamesed." Because the block was 42.1 inches long (five more than the Colombo engine), these were known as "long-block" twelves. Output was 220 horsepower in its initial form, using three twin-choke Weber carburetors and 8.0:1 compression. The all-out racing version was called the 340 Mexico, with a coupe body styled by Michelotti. Wheelbase of that one was a longer 102.4 inches, and its engine produced 280 bhp.

A single-disc clutch sent power to the five-speed gearbox. Chassis construction was similar to the prior models, though larger. Custom bodies, especially the berlinetta coupe by Vignale, featured an extremely long hood and short deck, and rode a 95.3-inch wheelbase. In addition to closed coupes, some seven examples wore barchetta bodies by Touring, and several of those went to U.S. buyers.

TYPE 342 AMERICA — V-12 — Just three months after the debut of the 340 America at the Paris Salon, in October 1950, a longer variant designed for grand touring appeared at the Brussels show. Only six were built, with the same engine as the 340 but reduced in horsepower, working through a fully-synchronized four-speed transmission instead of the non-synchro five-speed. Its track dimensions were larger, and the rear-axle heavier in construction. A complete 342 America arrived at the Turin show in spring 1951, sporting left-hand drive. In its minimal production, the 342 replaced the roadgoing 340 after 1952, but both were built concurrently for competition.

TYPE 375 AMERICA — V-12 — Twice as many 375 Americas left the Ferrari plant as 342 Americas, but the total was still only a dozen, starting in 1953. Wheelbase was longer than that of the 340/342, at 110.2 inches (same as the new 250 Europa, introduced for 1954), and the engine was larger. The 4523-cc V-12 produced 300 horsepower in touring trim, and 340 bhp for competition purposes. While the 250 would be aimed at the European market, the 375 (as its name suggested) would be targeted at Americans, who were presumed to prefer bigger powerplants. In addition to the basic model, a 375 Mille Miglia sports-racing version was offered on a 102.3-inch wheelbase. Roadster and berlinetta bodies were styled by Pinin Farina.

1953 Ferrari 340 MM.

Model Note: 166/195/212 and 340 models came with a wide variety of custom bodies, so specifications varied. See previous listing for details on the 166 MM, 195 Sport, and 212 Export racing models.

I.D. DATA: Not available.

Model	Body Type & Seating	Engine Type/CID	P.O.E. Price	Weight (lbs.)	Prod. Total
TYPE 166/195/212					
166 Inter	2-dr Coupe-2P	V12/122	N/A	2000	Note 1
166 Inter	2-dr Conv Cpe-2P	V12/122	N/A	2000	Note 1
195 Inter	2-dr Coupe-2P	V12/143	N/A	2100	Note 2
195 Inter	2-dr Conv Cpe-2P	V12/143	N/A	2100	Note 2
212 Inter	2-dr Coupe-2P	V12/156	11000	2100	Note 3
212 Inter	2-dr Conv Cpe-2P	V12/156	N/A	2100	Note 3

Model	Body Type & Seating	Engine Type/CID	P.O.E. Price	Weight (lbs.)	Prod. Total
TYPE 340/342/375 AMERICA					
340	2-dr Coupe-2P	V12/250	N/A	1980	Note 4
340	2-dr Conv Cpe-2P	V12/250	N/A	1980	Note 4
340 Mexico	2-dr Coupe-2P	V12/250	16000	1980	Note 4
342	2-dr Coupe-2P	V12/250	11600	2640	Note 5
342	2-dr Conv Cpe-2P	V12/250	N/A	2650	Note 5
375	2-dr Coupe-2P	V12/276	N/A	2530	Note 6
375	Conv Cpe-2P	V12/276	N/A	2530	Note 6

Note 1: As many as 38 Type 166 Inter models were produced, through the full model run.

Note 2: Approximately 25 Type 195 models were produced, through 1951.

Note 3: Approximately 80 Type 212 Inters were produced, through 1953.

Note 4: About 22 Type 340 Americas were produced from 1951-55.

Note 5: About six Type 342 Americas were produced, through 1953.

Note 6: At least 12 Type 375 Americas were produced, through 1955.

Price/Weight Note: Figures are approximate (or averages).

ENGINE DATA: BASE V-12 (166): Same as 1947-50.

BASE V-12 (195): Same as 1947-50.

BASE V-12 (212): Same as 1947-50.

BASE V-12 (340/342 America): 60-degree, single-overhead-cam, "vee" type 12-cylinder (Lampredi). Aluminum alloy block and heads. **Displacement:** 250 cu. in. (4101 cc). **Bore & Stroke:** 3.15 x 2.68 in. (80 x 68 mm). **Compression Ratio:** 8.0:1. **Brake Horsepower:** (340) 220 at 6600 rpm; (342) 200 at 5000 rpm. **Torque:** (342) 268 lbs.-ft. at 3000 rpm. Seven main bearings. Three twin-choke Weber carburetors.

Note: Type 340 Mexico engine was rated 280 bhp at 6600 rpm, and 228 lbs.-ft. at 4500 rpm.

BASE V-12 (375 America): 60-degree, single-overhead-cam, "vee" type 12-cylinder. Aluminum alloy block and heads. **Displacement:** 276 cu. in. (4523 cc). **Bore & Stroke:** 3.31 x 2.68 in. (84 x 68 mm). **Compression Ratio:** 8.4:1. **Brake Horsepower:** 300 at 6300 rpm (340 at 7000 for competition). Seven main bearings. Three Weber 40 DCZ 3 carburetors.

CHASSIS DATA: Wheelbase: (166 Inter) 98.4 in. or 103.1 in.; (195/212 Inter) 98.5 or 102.4 in.; in.; (340 America) 95.3 in.; (340 Mexico) 96 or 102.4 in.; (342) 104.3 in.; (375) 110.2 in. **Overall Length:** (166/195/212) 146-156 in. typical; (340/342) 170 in. average. **Height:** (166/195/212) 50-54 in. typical; (342) 56 in. typical; (340 Mexico) 54 in. **Width:** (166/195/212) 60 in. typical. **Front Tread:** (166/195/212) 49.8-50.0 in.; (340) 50 in.; (342) 52.2 in. **Rear Tread:** (166/195/212) 49.2 in.; (340) 49.2 in.; (342) 52 in. **Standard Tires:** (212 Inter) 6.40x15; (340 Mexico) 6.00x16 front, 6.50x16 rear.

TECHNICAL: Layout: front-engine, rear-drive. **Transmission:** (342/375) four-speed all-synchro manual; (others) five-speed manual (non-synchro). **Steering:** worm and peg. **Suspension (front):** unequal-length A-arms with transverse leaf springs. **Suspension (rear):** rigid axle with parallel trailing arms and semi-elliptic leaf springs. **Brakes:** hydraulic, front/rear drum. **Body Construction:** separate body on tubular steel ladder-type frame.

PERFORMANCE: Top Speed: (166 Inter) 112-120 mph; (195) about 110 mph; (212) 120-124 mph; (340/342/375) 120-149 mph; (340 Mexico) 174 mph claimed. **Acceleration (0-60 mph):** (340 Mexico) just over 6 sec.

ADDITIONAL MODELS: At least 31 Type 250 MM (for Mille Miglia) coupes and spiders, serving as racing versions of the forthcoming 250 Europa, were built in 1952-53. Their 2953-cc V-12 engines producing 240 bhp at 7200 rpm, on 9.0:1 compression. The 250 MM rode a 94.5-inch wheelbase, and could hit 158 mph. An all-synchro four-speed gearbox was used. Tests achieved 0-60 mph acceleration times as quick as 6.1 seconds, and a 14.4-second quarter-mile time.

In 1953-54, no more than 18 Type 375 MM racers were built and sold with a 4523-cc V-12 producing 340 bhp at 7000 rpm. Riding a 104-inch wheelbase, the 375 MM could hit 180 mph. Ferrari also built Type 340 MM race cars for the 1953 season, with up to 300 bhp from their 4.1-liter engines.

Manufacturer: Societa Auto-Avio Costruzioni Ferrari, Maranello (Modena), Italy.

Distributor: Luigi Chinetti, New York City; or Ernie McAfee, Hollywood, California.

HISTORY: The 340 America debuted at the Paris Salon in October 1950, with an open Touring body styled like the original 166 barchetta. Other bodies came from Ghia and Vignale, but Pinin Farina was fast becoming Ferrari's favorite. The 340 Mexico adopted that name because it was designed for the Carrera Panamericana race in that country.

The 250 Europa debuted at the Paris Salon in October 1953; see next listing for details. Ferrari's 212 scored a long list of race victories. In 1951, Pagnibon and Barraquet won the first Tour de France; Vittorio Marzotto and Piero Taruffi took first and second spots in the Tour of Sicily; and Piero Scotti earned a third at the Mille Miglia. Piero Taruffi and Luigi Chinetti won the Mexican Carrera Panamericana, where another Ferrari came in second.

1954-55 FERRARI

1954 Ferrari Model 250 Europa.

TYPE 375 AMERICA — V-12 — Production of this evolution of the 340/342 "America" continued as late as 1955; see previous listing for details. Added for 1954 was a 375 Plus racing roadster for the factory team, with a 4954-cc engine producing 344 horsepower at 6500 rpm. That car won the 1954 Le Mans and Carrera Panamericana races.

TYPE 250 EUROPA — V-12 — No more than 21 of these final evolutions of the Type 166 platform were produced in 1953-55, powered by a smaller (2963-cc) version of the Lampredi V-12 engine. No other Ferrari 250 model used that engine, which was rated at least 200 horsepower, and could deliver speeds up to 135 mph (depending on gearing). An all-synchro four-speed transmission was used.

Both the 250 Europa and the 375 America, with the same chassis and wheelbase, were at the 1953 Paris show, ranking as the largest Ferraris of that era--and the company's first serious stab at roadgoing production GT cars. As usual, various Italian coachbuilders supplied custom bodies, but most were a Pinin Farina design: a high-waisted, smooth-lined, semi-fastback 2+2 coupe, of which 22 were built (Europas and Americas). At least one two-seat cabriolet and four coupes came from Vignale. Nearly all Europas, which rode a 110.2-inch wheelbase, were sold in the U.S.

TYPE 250 GT — V-12 — While the 250 Europa was produced in minimal quantity, the other 250-series model introduced in 1954 was destined to reach far greater numbers over nearly a decade. About 2,500 were built, in fact (including 104 California Spider convertibles and 350 Lussos), making this Ferrari's first real production model. All versions rode the familiar large-diameter ladder-type tubular frame with 102.3-inch wheelbase, except for the eventual California, GTB and GTO, which measured only 94.5 inches. This early model became known as the "long-wheelbase" 250 GT, to distinguish it from a shorter version produced from 1959-64, even though it was considerably shorter than the 250 Europa. Instead of a transverse leaf spring, coil springs were installed up front. A rigid axle went at the rear, a new "Colombo" 2953-cc V-12 engine (evolved from the 250 MM race powerplant) under the hood. Horsepower started at 220, but rose as high as 300 before the series came to a halt in 1962 (the short-wheelbase version would remain into 1964). Drum brakes were installed until 1959, when discs became standard. Top speeds started at about 124-130 mph, but rose over the years to 155 mph or so. Zero-to-sixty acceleration times ran 8 seconds or less.

As was customary, all bodies were designed and built by Italian coachbuilders, mainly Pinin Farina and, to a lesser extent, Vignale. Nearly all were closed coupes, either fastback or semi-fastback. Notable examples included the Pinin Farina coupes built from 1958-60, and the handsome Berlinetta Lusso of 1962-64. The GTO was Ferrari's race/ride version. Some competition models also were built, with five-speed gearboxes rather than the usual four-speed.

I.D. DATA: All 250 Europas and 375 Americas had odd serial numbers. 'EU' in the serial number indicated an Europa; 'AL' was the America *Lungo* (long wheelbase).

Model	Body Type & Seating	Engine Type/CID	P.O.E. Price	Weight (lbs.)	Prod. Total
TYPE 375 AMERICA					
375	2-dr Coupe-2P	V12/276	N/A	2530	Note 1
375	2-dr Conv Cpe-2P	V12/276	N/A	2530	Note 1
TYPE 250 EUROPA					
250 Europa	2-dr Coupe-2+2P	V12/181	13890	2560	Note 2
250 Europa	2-dr Cabr-2P	V12/181	N/A	2560	Note 2
TYPE 250 GT					
250 GT	2-dr Coupe-2P	V12/180	N/A	N/A	Note 3

Note 1: At least 12 Type 375 Americas were produced, through 1955.

Note 2: At least 17 Type 250 Europas were produced in 1953-54.

Note 3: Approximately 2,500 Type 250 GTs were produced over the full model run, through 1962, including 36 Europas.

Body Style Note: Like most early Ferraris, the 250 GT came in a wide variety of body styles, open and closed, from different coachbuilders.

Weight Note: Figures shown are approximate (or averages).

ENGINE DATA: BASE V-12 (375 America): 60-degree, single-overhead-cam, "vee" type 12-cylinder. Aluminum alloy block and heads. **Displacement:** 276 cu. in. (4523 cc). **Bore & Stroke:** 3.31 x 2.68 in. (84 x 68 mm). **Compression Ratio:** 8.4:1. **Brake Horsepower:** 300 at 6300 rpm (340 at 7000 for competition). Seven main bearings. Three Weber 40 DCZ 3 carburetors.

BASE V-12 (250 Europa): 60-degree, single-overhead-cam, "vee" type 12-cylinder (Lampredi). Aluminum alloy block and heads. **Displacement:** 181 cu. in. (2963 cc). **Bore & Stroke:** 2.68 x 2.68 in. (68 x 68 mm). **Compression Ratio:** 8.0:1. **Brake Horsepower:** 200 at 6000-7000 rpm. Seven main bearings.

BASE V-12 (250 GT): 60-degree, single-overhead-cam, "vee" type 12-cylinder (Colombo). Aluminum alloy block and heads (cast-iron cylinder liners). **Displacement:** 180 cu. in. (2953 cc). **Bore & Stroke:** 2.87 x 2.31 in. (73 x 58.8 mm). **Compression Ratio:** 8.0:1-9.0:1. **Brake Horsepower:** 200-220 at 6600-7000 rpm. Seven main bearings. Three Weber 36 DCZ3 carburetors.

CHASSIS DATA: Wheelbase: (375) 110.2 in.; (250 Europa) 104 or 110.2 in.; (250 GT) 102.3 in. **Overall Length:** (340/342) 170 in. typical; (250 Europa) 170 in. typical, with some examples as short as 144 in.; (250 GT) 175 in. typical. **Height:** (250 Europa) 48 in. typical. **Width:** (250 Europa) 60 in. typical. **Front Tread:** (250 Europa) 50.7 in. **Rear Tread:** (250 Europa) 51.5 in.

TECHNICAL: Layout: front-engine, rear-drive. **Transmission:** four-speed all-synchro manual. **Steering:** worm and peg. **Suspension (front):** (375, 250 Europa) unequal-length A-arms with transverse leaf springs; (250 GT) upper/lower A-arms with coil springs. **Suspension (rear):** rigid axle with parallel trailing arms and semi-elliptic leaf springs. **Brakes:** hydraulic, front/rear drum. **Body Construction:** separate body on tubular steel ladder-type frame.

PERFORMANCE: Top Speed: (375 America) 155-161 mph reported; (250 Europa) 115-135 mph; (250 GT) 124-155 mph. **Acceleration (0-60 mph):** (250 Europa) 7.0 sec.

ADDITIONAL MODELS: Racing Ferraris of this period included the 750 Monza and 121 LM.

Manufacturer: Societa Auto-Avio Costruzioni Ferrari, Maranello (Modena), Italy.

Distributor: Luigi Chinetti, New York City; or Ernie McAfee, Hollywood, California.

HISTORY: Ferrari's replacement for the 375 America, the 410 Superamerica, appeared at the Paris Salon in September 1955; see next listing for details.

1956-59 FERRARI

TYPE 250 GT — V-12 — Production of the 250 GT, in a variety of body types from separate coachbuilders, continued into the early 1960s; see previous listing for details. A short-wheelbase version joined in 1959, for the '60 model year; see next listing. While early examples had a tiny rear seat, later ones were strictly two-seaters, with a luggage shelf behind the seats.

Many variants of the 250 GT appeared in the mid-1950s, starting with a Farina berlinetta coupe at the Paris Salon in late 1955. The Geneva show in March 1956 brought another body. Then in 1957, body production was taken over by Scaglietti (at Modena). By that time, the berlinetta (which had an aluminum body) was approved as production GT car. Also announced in 1956 was a Pinin Farina-styled notchback coupe, built at Carrozzeria Boano. Later versions had a higher roofline, called "Ellena" or "high-roof" 250 GT coupe. One touring cabriolet by Farina was at Geneva in 1957, and went into production that year.

1956 Ferrari 250 GT Pininfarina Series 1 Berlinetta.

A Farina-built replacement for the Boana/Ellena, called the "PF coupe," was built through 1960 on the 250 GT chassis. The notchback design had a more angular look. A Series II cabriolet was built by Farina through 1962. The sportier open roadster called the Spyder California was built by Scaglietti into early 1960. It featured wind-up windows, and a special chassis with extra bracing. In 1959, Ferrari introduced its first fresh-air heating system, and a twin-disc clutch replaced single-disc. At the end of the decade, too, front disc brakes replaced the former drum brakes.

TYPE 410 SUPERAMERICA — V-12 — Production totals were modest for this aggressively-styled replacement for the 375 America, which was phased out of the lineup. Only 38 were built in all, in three series, from 1956-59. Fast and powerful, built on a new chassis, a 410 was capable of speeds up to 165 mph in peak tune. Brakes were larger than before, torque output greater. Most bodies came from Pinin Farina, in open or closed form. Coil springs formed the front suspension, as in the 250 GT. Wheelbase was 110.2 inches initially, but shrunk to 102.3 inches by 1958. The ladder-type frame was made up of oval-section main tubes and round cross-tubes. The Lampredi V-12 was bored out by 4 mm to reach 4962-cc displacement, retaining the former 68-mm stroke. Horsepower was 340 at first, then boosted to 360 bhp and even 400 bhp. Compression was only 8.5:1. A multi-disc clutch sent power to the four-speed gearbox. As many as eight axle ratios were available, from 3.11:1 to 3.66:1.

Appearance was similar to the PF coupe (Boano/Ellena) on the smaller (250 GT) chassis. The first complete 410 Superamerica with Pinin Farina coupe body appeared at the Brussels Salon, in January 1956. Nine Series I coupes were similar to that Brussels show car, while one wore a finned Ghia body. Also produced were a coupe and cabriolet by Boano. In Series II, eight Farina bodies were built, plus two specials: a chrome-laden, two-tone example by Scaglietti; and a 4.9 Superfast coupe by Farina, known as Superfast II, lacking the Series I's tailfins. Series III appeared at the 1958 Paris show. Under its hood, spark plugs were now outboard of heads, as on the racing 250 Testa Rossa (formerly within the engine's "vee"). Compression was raised to 9.0:1, horsepower to 360. Drum brake diameter was enlarged, and the gearbox got a conventional H-gate shift pattern. Curved headlamp covers matched restyled front fenderlines, though the final few cars had exposed headlamps. Louvered metal panels were installed where rear quarter windows had been on the prototype.

I.D. DATA: Not available.

Model	Body Type & Seating	Engine Type/CID	P.O.E. Price	Weight (lbs.)	Prod. Total
TYPE 250 GT					
250 GT	2-dr Coupe-2P	V12/180	12500	2650	Note 1
California	2-dr Conv-2P	V12/180	14000	2420	Note 1
TYPE 410 SUPERAMERICA					
410	2-dr Coupe-2P	V12/303	16800	2400	Note 2

Note 1: Approximately 2,500 Type 250 GTs were produced over the full model run; see previous listing for breakdown details.

Note 2: A total of 15 Series I models were built in 1957, eight Series II (1958), and 15 Series III (1959).

Body Style Note: As usual, Ferraris came in a wide variety of body styles, open and closed, from different coachbuilders.

Price Note: A 250 GT coupe was priced at $12,800 at the 1956 New York Auto Show; the advertised price was down to $12,000 by 1959.

Weight Note: Figures shown are approximate (or averages).

ENGINE DATA: BASE V-12 (250 GT): 60-degree, single-overhead-cam, "vee" type 12-cylinder (Colombo). Aluminum alloy block and heads (cast-iron cylinder liners). **Displacement:** 180 cu. in. (2953 cc). **Bore & Stroke:** 2.87 x 2.31 in. (73 x 58.8 mm). **Compression Ratio:** 8.5:1. **Brake Horsepower:** 220-260 at 7000 rpm (240 bhp in 1958-59). **Torque:** 195 lbs.-ft. at 5000 rpm. (in 1959). Seven main bearings. Three Weber two-barrel carburetors.

BASE V-12 (410 Superamerica): 60-degree, single-overhead-cam, "vee" type 12-cylinder (Lambredi). Aluminum alloy block and heads. **Displacement:** 302.7 cu. in. (4962 cc). **Bore & Stroke:** 3.46 x 2.68 in. (88 x 68 mm). **Compression Ratio:** 8.5:1. **Brake Horsepower:** (Series I) 340 at 6000 rpm; (Series II) 360 at 7000 rpm; (Series III) 400 at 6200/6500 rpm. **Torque:** (Series I) 311 lbs.-ft. at 5000 rpm; (Series III) 340 lbs.-ft. at 4700 rpm. Seven main bearings. Three or six Weber two-barrel carburetors.

CHASSIS DATA: Wheelbase: (250 GT) 102.3 in.; (410 Series I) 110.2 in.; (410 Series II/III) 102.3 in. **Overall Length:** (250 GT) 175.5 in. typical; (410 Series II/III) about 185-188 in. **Height:** (250 GT) 54 in.; (410) 54 in. **Width:** (250 GT) 66 in.; (410) 68 in. **Front Tread:** (250 GT) 53.3 in.; (410) 57.3-57.5 in. **Rear Tread:** (250 GT) 53.1 in.; (410) 57.1 in. **Standard Tires:** (250 GT) 6.00x16; (410) 6.50x16.

TECHNICAL: Layout: front-engine, rear-drive. **Transmission:** four-speed all-synchro manual. **Steering:** worm and peg. **Suspension (front):** upper/lower A-arms with coil springs. **Suspension (rear):** rigid axle with parallel trailing arms and semi-elliptic leaf springs. **Brakes:** hydraulic, front/rear drum. **Body Construction:** separate body on tubular steel ladder-type frame.

1958 Ferrari 250 GT Berlinetta Tour de France.

PERFORMANCE: Top Speed: (250 GT) 126-157 mph depending on gearing; (410) 135-165 mph. **Acceleration (0-60 mph):** (250 GT) 7.0-8.0 sec. typical (but as little as 5.9 sec. reported). **Acceleration (quarter-mile):** (250 GT) as little as 16.1 sec. reported. **Fuel Mileage** (410) about 11 mpg.

PRODUCTION/SALES: Approximately 39 Ferraris were sold in the U.S. during 1958, and 61 in 1959.

1959 Ferrari Type 410 Superamerica two-seater sports coupe. (Christie's)

ADDITIONAL MODELS: The curvaceous Type 250 Testa Rossa racing model was produced from 1958-61, powered by a 2953-cc V-12 that produced 300 bhp at 7200 rpm, using 9.8:1 compression and six Weber carburetors. Wheelbase was 92.5 inches. A total of 33 were built, capable of 167-mph top speeds. Price at the factory was about $12,900 in 1958.

A 4.9 Superfast coupe could be obtained in Italy for about $16,000, powered by a 380-bhp, 4962-cc V-12 with 9.0:1 compression and three Weber carburetors. Testing by *Sports Cars Illustrated* yielded 0-60 mph acceleration in 5.6 seconds (versus 5.9 for a 250 GT), and a quarter-mile time of 13.9 seconds. A 4.9 Superfast was advertised for sale in the U.S. at $18,500 in 1958.

Manufacturer: Societa Auto-Avio Costruzioni Ferrari, Maranello (Modena), Italy.

Distributor: Luigi Chinetti Motors Inc., New York City; and Ernie McAfee Engineering Co., Los Angeles or Ferrari Representatives, Hollywood, California.

HISTORY: The short-wheelbase 250 GT appeared at the Paris Salon in October 1959; see next listing for details. At the 1956 Paris show, a new one-off "Superfast" fastback displayed a futuristic look with tapered snout, recessed headlamps (behind clear plastic covers), tall tailfins, and the short (102.3-inch) wheelbase. The 250 GT "California" debuted in the U.S. at the Los Angeles International Auto Show in 1959, described by Pinin Farina as "summing up all the experience of sports." Promotional material noted that it combined "traditional Ferrari elegance and comfort with eminent sports car performance." According to *Classic Sports Cars,* the idea for this open version of the 250 GT came from John von Neumann, Ferrari's agent in Los Angeles.

1960-62 FERRARI

TYPE 250 GT (LWB) — V-12 — Production of the long-wheelbase 250 GT (described in 1954-55 listing) continued into 1962. New for the 1960 model year, and continuing into 1964, was a short-wheelbase version. Tubular telescopic shocks replaced lever hydraulics in 1960, and overdrive was added to the all-synchro four-speed transmission.

TYPE 250 GT (SWB) — V-12 — This was a companion to the "interim" 250 GT berlinetta, which debuted early in 1959. Designed by Pinin Farina (whose name changed to Pininfarina in 1961), the short-wheelbase body was built by Scaglietti as a race/ride two-seater with new rounded contours and a more aggressive look. Wheelbase was nearly eight

inches shorter than the LWB edition, at 94.5 inches. The standard steel body had aluminum doors, hood, and trunklid. Some competition bodies were all-aluminum. Under the hood was the Colombo V-12 design, with spark plugs now outside of the heads and new coil-type valve springs replacing the former hairpin-type. The 2953-cc engine produced as much as 280 horsepower at 7000 rpm. Six axle ratios were offered, from 3.44:1 to 4.57:1. Brakes were disc all around. Top speeds reached as high as 150 mph, and a 250 GT SWB could accelerated from zero to 60 mph in seven seconds or less. Borrani center-lock wire wheels were standard.

During 1959, a Spyder California (with Scaglietti body) had debuted on the SWB chassis to replace the LWB Spyder, which was similar in appearance. The SWB berlinetta (coupe), on the other hand, did not resemble its LWB predecessors. Several differences were evident between the two. Front-fender air outlets, for one, had three vertical bars on the LWB, two on the SWB (though some of each series had none at all). Short-wheelbase Spyders had a horizontal ridge between their taillamps; long-wheelbase 250 GTs did not. Both versions had headlamps behind clear plastic covers. Late in 1962 at the Paris show debuted the attractive 250 GT/L, later known as Berlinetta Lusso (luxury), created by Pininfarina and built by Scaglietti. Its front end was similar to the SWB model, while the Kamm-style tail resembled that of the 250 GTO racing coupe, with round taillamps. Overall, the new fastback profile had a thin-pillar roofline, with aluminum hood, doors, and trunklid. At the center of the dashboard was a large speed-ometer and tachometer, with five gauges ahead of the steering wheel. Lusso was the final 250 GT version.

Pre-production 1960 Ferrari 250 GTE 2+2.

TYPE 250 GTE/GT 2+2 — V-12 — Not only a short-wheelbase variant of the 250 GT, but a new 2+2-seat version, was available by 1960. This was the first four-passenger Ferrari, even if the two in back faced a mighty tight squeeze. All former 2+2s (bodied by Touring, Ghia, or Vignale) in the early 1950s were one-offs, not production models. Wheelbase was 102.3 inches (same as the 250 GT LWB), but the engine, pedals, seat and front floorboard were moved forward to create the rear-seat area. Initially named 250 GTE, the notchback coupe had coil springs in the front suspension and twin headlamps. Body design and construction of the body were by Pininfarina. Minor appearance revisions in 1962 brought a name change to 250 GT 2+2. Before long, it would evolve into the 330 GT America, and 330 GT 2+2. The 2953-cc V-12 (similar to that used in other roadgoing 250 models) produced 240 horsepower, working through a four-speed (plus overdrive) gearbox.

TYPE 400 SUPERAMERICA — V-12 — This final evolution of the America/Superamerica series wore custom bodywork styled and built by Pininfarina. Most were coupes. Wheelbases started at 95.3 inches, then grew to 102.3 inches as Series II. Mechanical details were similar to the former 410. Under the hood was a new version of the Colombo V-12, displacing 3967 cc and producing a claimed 400 bhp initially with its 9.8:1 compression. The Lampredi V-12 engine was abandoned at this time. A single dry-plate clutch replaced the multi-disc unit. Laycock de Normanville electric overdrive was included with the all-synchro four-speed gearbox. Koni telescopic shocks replaced the earlier lever-type units. Borrani center-lock wire wheels were standard.

The 400 Superamerica prototype appeared at the 1959 Turin show, wearing a boxy body with squarish grille, wraparound windshield, and quad headlamps. The production model at the Brussels show in January 1960 was considerably different, with its Farina-styled cabriolet body. A few production cabrios came with a lift-off steel top. Series II was inspired by the Superfast II seen at the 1960 Turin show, which Pininfarina said he'd created with wind tunnel help. Its fastback body was tapered at each end, with retracting headlamps and partly-skirted back wheels. In winter 1961-62 a hood scoop was added, skirts dropped, and headlamps exposed (with clear plastic lenses), to create the PF Coupe Aerodinamico. That body was used for all later 400s.

Note: Starting with the 400 Superamerica, model numbers indicated total engine displacement in deciliters (unit of 10 liters), rather than the number of cubic centimeters per cylinder as before.

1960 Ferrari 250 GT Nembo. (Coys of Kensington)

1962 Ferrari 400 Superamerica. (Coys of Kensington)

I.D. DATA: All 250 GT SWB models had odd (touring) serial numbers.

Model	Body Type & Seating	Engine Type/CID	P.O.E. Price	Weight (lbs.)	Prod. Total
TYPE 250 GT					
250 GT LWB	2-dr Coupe-2P	V12/180	12600	N/A	Note 1
250 GT SWB	2-dr Coupe-2P	V12/180	N/A	N/A	Note 2
California	2-dr Conv-2P	V12/180	13600	N/A	Note 2
TYPE 250 GT 2+2					
250 GT	2-dr Coupe-2+2P	V12/180	12600	2820	Note 3
TYPE 400 SUPERAMERICA					
400	2-dr Coupe-2P	V12/242	N/A	2860	Note 4

Note 1: Approximately 2,500 Type 250 GTs (long-wheelbase) were produced over the full model run; see 1954-55 listing for breakdown details.

Note 2: Production of the 250 GT SWB over the full model run (through 1964) included 175 Berlinettas, 57 Spyder Californias (into early 1963 only), and 350 Berlinetta Lussos.

Note 3: A total of 950 Type 250 GT 2+2s were produced from 1960-63.

Note 4: As many as 54 Type 400 Superamericas were produced from 1960-64, including six cabrios (in 1960), 29 Series I coupes, and 19 Series II coupes.

Body Style Note: As usual, Ferraris came in a wide variety of body styles, open and closed, from different coachbuilders.

Weight Note: Figures shown are approximate (or averages).

ENGINE DATA: BASE V-12 (250 GT): 60-degree, single-overhead-cam, "vee" type 12-cylinder (Colombo). Aluminum alloy block and heads. **Displacement:** 180 cu. in. (2953 cc). **Bore & Stroke:** 2.87 x 2.31 in. (73 x 58.8 mm). **Compression Ratio:** 9.2:1. **Brake Horsepower:** (250 GT SWB, 250 GT 2+2) 240 at 7000 rpm; (racing 250 GT SWB) 280 at 7000 rpm. Seven main bearings. Three twin-choke Weber carburetors.
BASE V-12 (400 Superamerica): 60-degree, single-overhead-cam, "vee" type 12-cylinder (Colombo). Aluminum alloy block and heads. **Displacement:** 242 cu. in. (3967 cc). **Bore & Stroke:** 3.03 x 2.80 in. (77 x 71 mm). **Compression Ratio:** 9.8:1 (later, 8.8:1). **Brake Horsepower:** 400 at 6750 rpm (later, 340 at 7000 rpm). Seven main bearings. Three Weber 46 DCF carburetors.

CHASSIS DATA: Wheelbase: (250 GT LWB) 102.3 in.; (250 GT SWB) 94.5 in.; (250 GT 2+2) 102.3 in.; (400 Series I) 95.3 in.; (400 Series II/III) 102.3 in. **Overall Length:** (250 GT LWB) 185 in. typical; (250 GT SWB) 174 in. typical; (250 GT 2+2) 185 in. typical. **Height:** (250 GT LWB) 53 in. typical; (250 GT SWB) 48 in.; (250 GT 2+2) 51.5 in. **Width:** (250 GT LWB) 67 in. typical; (250 GT SWB) 64 in.; (250 GT 2+2) 65-67.3 in. **Front Tread:** (250 GT SWB/2+2) 53.3 in. **Rear Tread:** (250 GT SWB) 53.1 in.; (250 GT 2+2) 54.7 in.

1962-'64 Ferrari 250 GT Berlinetta Lusso.

TECHNICAL: Layout: front-engine, rear-drive. **Transmission:** four-speed all-synchro manual (plus overdrive in 250 GT 2+2 and 400 Superamerica). **Steering:** worm and peg. **Suspension (front):** upper/lower A-arms with coil springs. **Suspension (rear):** rigid axle with parallel trailing arms and semi-elliptic leaf springs. **Brakes:** front/rear disc. **Body Construction:** separate body on tubular steel ladder-type frame.

PERFORMANCE: Top Speed: (250 GT LWB) 124-155 mph; (250 GT SWB) 140-156 mph; (250 GT 2+2) 115+ mph; (400) 140-160+ mph. **Acceleration (0-60 mph):** (250 GT LWB) 7.0-8.0 sec.; (250 GT SWB) about 6.5-7.0 sec.; (250 GT 2+2) 8.0 sec. **Acceleration (quarter-mile):** (250 GT 2+2) 16.3 sec.

ADDITIONAL MODELS: Ferrari produced a 250 GTO racing car through 1964, after its debut in February 1962. The 2953-cc V-12 produced 280 bhp at 7500 rpm, using 9.8:1 compression and six Weber carburetors. This was the final front-engine race version. GTO stood for *Gran Turismo Omologato*, meaning homologated (sanctioned) for racing. Top speed of the coupe was 176 mph, and a total of 38 or 39 were built on a 102.4-inch wheelbase. The 250 GTO wore no bumpers and had no cockpit insulation. Sliding plastic side windows were used, along with a plastic back window. The engine even lacked an air filter.

Manufacturer: Automobili Ferrari S.p.A. SEFAC, Maranello (Modena), Italy.

Distributor: Luigi Chinetti Motors Inc., New York City.

HISTORY: Ferrari's Type 500 Superfast, produced from 1964-66, evolved from the Superfast II show car that appeared at the Turin show in 1960; and the subsequent Superfast III show car at the 1962 Geneva Salon.
From 1956-60, Ferrari took 1-2-3 victories at the Tour de France. In 1961, Ferraris earned 1-2-3-4 positions, with 250 GT berlinettas. Ads promoted the Spyder California as a car that could be "driven in normal daily use, or raced."
A 2+2 Ferrari was used as the course marshal's car at the Le Mans in 1960, and formal announcement of the new 250 GTE came at the Paris show in October of that year. It was phased out in late 1963, to be replaced by the 330 GT series.

1963 FERRARI

TYPE 250 LM — V-12 — Ferrari's first mid-engined roadgoing GT model was derived from the 250P racing prototype that emerged in March 1963. Ferrari wanted to qualify for production racing at this time, and the 250 LM served as its justification attempt. With optimum gearing, it could reach speeds of 170 mph and beyond. Most bodies were closed coupes, built by Scaglietti, but a few open race roadsters also were produced. In all, no more than 40 were built in both the 250 LM and 275 LM configuration, from 1963-65. The Colombo-derived V-12 engine sat behind the driver. Except for the first example, all were 3.3-liter size, producing 320 horsepower. The multi-tube chassis, similar to that used on race cars, had coil springs with tubular A-arms all around, with a 95-inch wheelbase. Four-wheel disc brakes were installed (inboard at the rear). A multi-disc clutch was mounted on the flywheel between engine and transaxle (later versions put the clutch behind the transaxle). The non-synchro five-speed had all-indirect gearing, which helped allow a low engine position. The Berlinetta body was created by Pininfarina. Its windshield and side windows would go on the Series II 250 GTO. Both had a "flying buttress" roof, with sloping sail panels alongside a vertical back window. Though mainly for racing, this was the first mid-engine Ferrari that could be street-driven. It looked like no other Ferrari, with a low grille below the front-end crease and headlamps behind clear covers. Radiator, oil cooler and oil reservoir were all in nose. All 250/275 LMs were right-hand drive, with a bare minimum of passenger space. Still, they had full road gear, including lights, horn, and spare tire, with weight down to 1874 pounds.

TYPE 250 GT (SWB) — V-12 — Production of the short-wheelbase 250 GT continued through 1964; see previous listing for details.

TYPE 250 GT 2+2 — V-12 — Production of Ferrari's 2+2 continued with little change; see previous listing for details.

TYPE 400 SUPERAMERICA — V-12 — Production of the big-engine Ferrari continued with little change.

I.D. DATA: Not available.

Model	Body Type & Seating	Engine Type/CID	P.O.E. Price	Weight (lbs.)	Prod. Total
TYPE 250 GT					
250 GT SWB	2-dr Coupe-2P	V12/180	12950	N/A	Note 1
California	2-dr Conv-2P	V12/180	12950	N/A	Note 1
TYPE 250 GT 2+2					
250 GT	2-dr Coupe-2+2P	V12/180	12900	2820	Note 2
TYPE 250 LM					
250 LM	2-dr Coupe-2P	V12/180	N/A	1874	Note 3
TYPE 400 SUPERAMERICA					
400	2-dr Coupe-2P	V12/242	N/A	2860	Note 4

Note 1: Production of the 250 GT SWB over the full model run (through 1964) included 175 Berlinettas, 57 Spyder Californias, and 350 Berlinetta Lussos.

Note 2: A total of 950 Type 250 GT 2+2s were produced from 1960-63.

Note 3: Between 35 and 40 Type 250/275 LM racing coupes were produced in 1963-65.

Note 4: As many as 54 Type 400 Superamericas were produced from 1960-64, including six cabrios (in 1960), 29 Series I coupes, and 19 Series II coupes.

Body Style Note: As usual, Ferraris came in a wide variety of body styles, open and closed, from different coachbuilders.

Weight Note: Figures shown are approximate (or averages).

ENGINE DATA: BASE V-12 (250 GT): 60-degree, single-overhead-cam, "vee" type 12-cylinder (Colombo). Aluminum alloy block and heads. **Displacement:** 180 cu. in. (2953 cc). **Bore & Stroke:** 2.87 x 2.31 in. (73 x 58.8 mm). **Compression Ratio:** (250 GT 2+2) 8.8:1. **Brake Horsepower:** (250 GT 2+2) 240 at 7000 rpm; (250 GT SWB) 280 at 7000 rpm. Seven main bearings. Three twin-choke Weber carburetors.
BASE V-12 (initial 250 LM): 60-degree, single-overhead-cam, "vee" type 12-cylinder (Colombo). Aluminum alloy block and heads. **Displacement:** 180 cu. in. (2953 cc). **Bore & Stroke:** 2.87 x 2.31 in. (73 x 58.8 mm). **Compression Ratio:** 9.7:1. **Brake Horsepower:** 300 at 7500 rpm. Seven main bearings. Six 38 DCN Weber carburetors.

Note: All subsequent 250 LMs had a 3286-cc engine; see next listing.

BASE V-12 (400 Superamerica): 60-degree, single-overhead-cam, "vee" type 12-cylinder (Colombo). Aluminum alloy block and heads. **Displacement:** 242 cu. in. (3967 cc). **Bore & Stroke:** 3.03 x 2.80 in. (77 x 71 mm). **Compression Ratio:** 9.8:1/8.8:1. **Brake Horsepower:** 400 at 6750 rpm or 340 at 7000 rpm. Seven main bearings. Three Weber 46DCF carburetors (340 bhp).

CHASSIS DATA: Wheelbase: (250 GT SWB) 94.5 in.; (250 GT 2+2) 102.3 in.; (250 LM) 94.5 in.; (400 Series I) 95.3 in.; (400 Series II/III) 102.3 in. **Overall Length:** (250 GT SWB) 174 in. average; (250 GT 2+2) 183.6 in. average; (250 LM) 161 in.; (400) 172 in. average. **Height:** (250 GT SWB) 48 in.; (250 GT 2+2) 55.4 in.; (400) 51.5 in. **Width:** (250 GT SWB) 64 in.; (250 GT 2+2) 67.3 in.; (400) 66 in. **Front Tread:** (250 GT SWB) 55 in.; (250 GT 2+2) 53.3 in.; (250 LM) 53.1 in. **Rear Tread:** (250 GT SWB) 54.5 in.; (250 GT 2+2) 54.9 in.; (250 LM) 52.7 in. **Standard Tires:** (250 GT SWB) 185x15.

TECHNICAL: Layout: front-engine, rear-drive except (250 LM) mid-engine, rear-drive. **Transmission:** four-speed all-synchro manual (plus overdrive in 250 GT 2+2 and 400 Superamerica) except (250 LM) non-synchro, all-indirect five-speed manual. **Steering:** worm and peg. **Suspension (front):** upper/lower A-arms with coil springs. **Suspension (rear):** rigid axle with parallel trailing arms and semi-elliptic leaf springs except (250 LM) upper/lower A-arms with coil springs. **Brakes:** front/rear disc. **Body Construction:** separate body on tubular steel ladder-type frame.

PERFORMANCE: Top Speed: (250 GT) 124-155 mph; (250 LM) 160 mph (factory claimed 183 mph); (400) 140-160+ mph. **Acceleration (0-60 mph):** (250 GT SWB) about 6.5-7.0 sec.; (250 LM) 6.5 sec. estimated; (250 GT 2+2) 8.0 sec.

ADDITIONAL MODELS: Production of the 250 GTO racing coupe continued until 1964.

Manufacturer: Automobili Ferrari S.p.A. SEFAC, Maranello (Modena), Italy.

Distributor: Luigi Chinetti Motors, New York City.

HISTORY: Ferrari's experiments with mid-engine race cars dated from 1960. The 250P used a race version of the 3.0-liter V12 with six DCN Weber carbs, from the front-engine Testa Rossa. Its chassis came from V-6/V-8 Dino mid-engine racers. A 250P soon broke the lap record at Monza, driven by John Surtees. In November 1963, the 250 LM (for Le Mans) closed version appeared at the Paris Salon. The first one came to the U.S. in late 1963, raced by the North American Racing Team of Luigi Chinetti (Ferrari's U.S. distributor). After a lack of significant success, it caught fire at Sebring and was destroyed.

After phase-out of the 250 GT 2 + 2 in late 1963 came 50 "interim" models with a new Type 209 4.0-liter engine, many displaying an "America" rear nameplate. Those became known as the 330 America.

1964-65 FERRARI

TYPE 250 LM/275 LM — V-12 — When a 250 LM entered the Le Mans race in April 1964, its engine was larger than the original: 3286 cc rather than 2953 cc, the result of a 4-mm bore increase. That accounted for the unofficial name change to 275 LM, but Ferrari did not use that designation for homologation purposes. During 1964, this car took first and second spots at the 12 Hours of Reins race; second in the Tourist Trophy; first at Elkhart Lake; first at Mont Tremblant; and 1-2 at the Coppa Inter-Europa. It won 10 major races in all, and finished second in six. After 1964, all racing was under private auspices.

TYPE 250 GT (SWB) — V-12 — Production of the short-wheelbase 250 GT halted in 1964.

1965 Ferrari 275 GTB Berlinetta coupe.

TYPE 275 GTB/GTS — V-12 — Both fastback berlinetta coupe (GTB) and open Spider (GTS) versions of the new 275 series debuted at the Paris Salon in October 1964, and would continue through 1966. The coupe was intended as a sports/racer, while the GTS convertible was meant for touring. Each rode a 94.5-inch wheelbase on a multi-tube chassis, and carried a Colombo-derived 3286-cc (200.5-cid) V-12. That engine produced 260 horsepower in the Spider, or 280 bhp in the berlinetta. The GTB engine could have three or six Weber carburetors. Instead of a separate gearbox, the five-speed transmission was part of a unit with the final drive, forming a rear transaxle. A thin propeller shaft rode in center bearings. Fully-independent suspension consisted of unequal-length A-arms and coil springs, front and rear. Disc brakes were installed all around. Not the most popular Ferrari design, the 275 displayed a long hood and short deck. Pininfarina did the styling of the Spider and produced the body, which was evolved from the 330 GT 2 + 2. Coupe bodies were built by Scaglietti, from a Pininfarina design, which replaced the 250 GT Berlinetta Lusso. More rounded in appearance than the convertible, the berlinetta coupe could have either a steel body (with aluminum hood, doors, and trunk lid) or one made fully of aluminum. Standard Campagnolo alloy disc wheels went on all models, with Borrani wires optional.

At the 1965 Frankfurt show, the Series II GTS lost its chrome headlamp surrounds and left-door vent wing, while adding external trunk hinges and a hood bulge (over the carburetors). Then, at that year's Paris show, the GTB on display had a lower and longer nose and larger back window. Those changes allow division of the Series I and II into "short-nose" and "long-nose" versions.

1964 Ferrari 330 GT 2 + 2 Series I. (Coys of Kensington)

TYPE 330 GT 2 + 2 — V-12 — Replacing the 250 GT 2 + 2, the new four-passenger coupe was evolved from the 330 America. Not everyone attending the January 1964 press conference that announced its birth was impressed by the Pininfarina design, an opinion shared by a number of people once the new model entered the market. Some disliked the bulbous styling, with quad round headlamps in tapered oval housings. Outboard of the wide crosshatch grille were round amber park lights. Examples built from 1965 on wore two headlamps, with modified side vents and a new protruding nose.

Wheelbase was 104.2 inches. Beneath the hood was a 3967-cc (242-cid) V-12 engine, producing 300 horsepower. A five-speed manual gearbox was standard by 1965, but '64 models used a four-speed with overdrive. Koni adjustable shocks augmented the rear semi-elliptic leafs. Separate braking systems were installed for front and rear. Alloy wheels became standard in 1965, with center-lock Borrani wires optional at extra cost (instead of standard as in early models). About a thousand were produced over the full model run, through 1968, in addition to the 50 Type 330 GTE Americas built in 1963.

TYPE 400 SUPERAMERICA — V-12 — Production of this model, introduced in 1960, continued to 1966; see previous listings for details.

TYPE 500 SUPERFAST — V-12 — Similar to the 400 Superamerica, the new Superfast (which evolved from the Superfast II show car seen at the Turin event in 1960) was longer and heavier than the 400, with a bigger and more powerful engine. Wheelbase was 104.3 inches; overall length around 190 inches. Power came from a 4962-cc (303-cid) V-12, producing 400 horsepower. Bore and stroke were identical to the 410 Superamerica. The rather unique engine was a long-block like the Lampredi, but had removable heads (like the Colombo design) with pressed-in cylinder liners. Dunlop disc brakes went on all four wheels. Appearance was similar to the 400, but with exposed headlamps and a squared-off tail (Kamm-style). Bodies were built by Pininfarina. Borrani wire wheels held 205/15 tires. A total of about 37 were built, in Series I and II, through early 1967.

Note: Some directories continued to list the 250 GT 2 + 2 coupe, though production ceased after 1963; see previous listing for details.

I.D. DATA: Not available.

Model	Body Type & Seating	Engine Type/CID	P.O.E. Price	Weight (lbs.)	Prod. Total
TYPE 250 GT					
250 GT SWB	2-dr Coupe-2P	V12/180	12950	2540	Note 1
TYPE 250 LM (275 LM)					
250 LM	2-dr Coupe-2P	V12/200	N/A	1874	Note 2
275 GTB/GTS					
275 GTB	2-dr Coupe-2P	V12/200	13900	2550	Note 3
275 GTS	2-dr Conv Cpe-2P	V12/200	14500	2750	Note 4
330 GT 2 + 2					
330 GT	2-dr Coupe-2 + 2P	V12/242	14200	3040	Note 5
TYPE 400 SUPERAMERICA					
400	2-dr Coupe-2P	V12/242	17800	2860	Note 6
TYPE 500 SUPERFAST					
500	2-dr Coupe-2P	V12/303	24400	3200	Note 7

Note 1: Production of the 250 GT SWB over the full model run (through 1964) included 175 Berlinettas, 57 Spyder Californias, and 350 Berlinetta Lussos.

Note 2: Between 35 and 40 Type 250/275 LM racing coupes were produced in 1963-65.

Note 3: About 450 Type 275 GTB coupes were produced in all (250 Series I and 200 Series II), through 1967.

Note 4: About 200 Type 275 GTS convertibles were produced, through 1966.

Note 5: About 1,000 Type 330 GT 2 + 2s were produced from 1964-68.

Note 6: As many as 54 Type 400 Superamericas were produced from 1960-64, including six cabrios (in 1960), 29 Series I coupes, and 19 Series II coupes.

Note 7: About 37 500 Superfast coupes (25 Series I and 12 Series II) were produced from 1964-67.

Body Style Note: As usual, Ferraris came in a variety of body styles, open and closed, from different coachbuilders.

Weight Note: Figures shown are approximate (or averages).

ENGINE DATA: BASE V-12 (250 GT): 60-degree, single-overhead-cam, "vee" type 12-cylinder (Colombo). Aluminum alloy block and heads. **Displacement:** 180 cu. in. (2953 cc). **Bore & Stroke:** 2.87 x 2.31 in. (73 x 58.8 mm). **Compression Ratio:** 9.2:1. **Brake Horsepower:** 280 at 7000 rpm. Seven main bearings. Three twin-choke Weber carburetors.

BASE V-12 (250/275 LM): 60-degree, single-overhead-cam, "vee" type 12-cylinder. Aluminum alloy block and heads. **Displacement:** 200.5 cu. in. (3286 cc). **Bore & Stroke:** 3.03 x 2.31 in. (77 x 58.8 mm). **Compression Ratio:** 9.7:1. **Brake Horsepower:** 320-330 at 7000-7500 rpm. Seven main bearings. Six 38 DCN Weber carburetors.

BASE V-12 (275 GTB/GTS): 60-degree, single-overhead-cam, "vee" type 12-cylinder. Aluminum alloy block and heads. **Displacement:** 200.5 cu. in. (3286 cc). **Bore & Stroke:** 3.03 x 2.31 in. (77 x 58.8 mm). **Compression Ratio:** 9.2:1. **Brake Horsepower:** (GTS) 260 at 7000/7500 rpm; (GTB) 280 at 7000/7500 rpm. Seven main bearings. Three Weber 40 DCZ/6 carburetors (six-carb setup available).

BASE V-12 (330 GT 2 + 2): 60-degree, single-overhead-cam, "vee" type 12-cylinder. Aluminum alloy block and heads. **Displacement:** 242 cu. in. (3967 cc). **Bore & Stroke:** 3.03 x 2.80 in. (77 x 71 mm). **Compression Ratio:** 8.8:1. **Brake Horsepower:** 300 at 6000/6600 rpm. Seven main bearings. Three Weber 40 DCZ/6 carburetors.

BASE V-12 (400 Superamerica): 60-degree, single-overhead-cam, "vee" type 12-cylinder (Colombo). Aluminum alloy block and heads. **Displacement:** 242 cu. in. (3967 cc). **Bore & Stroke:** 3.03 x 2.80 in. (77 x 71 mm). **Compression Ratio:** 8.8:1. **Brake Horsepower:** 340 at 7000 rpm. Seven main bearings. Three Weber 46 DCF carburetors.

BASE V-12 (500 Superfast): 60-degree, single-overhead-cam, "vee" type 12-cylinder. Aluminum alloy block and heads. **Displacement:** 302.7 cu. in. (4962 cc). **Bore & Stroke:** 3.46 x 2.68 in. (88 x 68 mm). **Compression Ratio:** 8.8:1. **Brake Horsepower:** 400 at 6500 rpm. Seven main bearings. Three Weber 40 DCZ/6 carburetors.

CHASSIS DATA: Wheelbase: (250 GT SWB) 94.5 in.; (250/275 LM) 94.5 in.; (275 GTB/GTS) 94.5 in.; (330 GT 2 + 2) 104.2 in.; (400 Series II/III) 102.3 in.; (500) 104.3 in. **Overall Length:** (250 GT SWB) 174 in. average; (250/275 LM) 161 in.; (275 GTB/GTS) 171.3 in.; (330 GT 2 + 2) 189.4-190.5 in.; (400) 172 in.; (500) 190-194 in. **Height:** (250 GT SWB) 48 in.; (275 GTB) 49 in.; (275 GTS) 51.5 in.; (330 GT 2 + 2) 53 in.; (400) 51.5 in.; (500) 52.4 in. **Width:** (250 GT SWB) 64 in.; (275 GTB) 67 in.; (275 GTS) 66 in.; (330 GT 2 + 2) 70.5 in.; (400) 66 in.; (500) 71 in. **Front Tread:** (250 GT) 55 in.; (250/275 LM) 53.1 in.; (275 GTB/GTS) 54.2 in.; (330 GT 2 + 2) 55.2 in.; (500) 55 in. **Rear Tread:** (250 GT) 54.5 in.; (250/275 LM) 52.9 in.; (275 GTB/GTS) 54.8 in.; (330 GT 2 + 2) 54.7 in.; (500) 54.5 in. **Standard Tires:** (250 GT) 185x15; (275 GTB) 205x14; (275 GTS) 195x14; (500) 205x15.

TECHNICAL: Layout: front-engine, rear-drive except (250/275 LM) mid-engine, rear-drive. **Transmission:** four-speed all-synchro manual (plus overdrive in 250 GT 2 + 2 and 400 Superamerica) except (250/275 LM) non-synchro, all-indirect five-speed manual; (275 GTB/GTS) five-speed manual rear transaxle; (330 GT 2 + 2) four-speed w/overdrive or five-speed. **Steering:** worm and roller. **Suspension (front):** upper/lower A-arms with coil springs. **Suspension (rear):** rigid axle with parallel trailing arms and semi-elliptic leaf springs except (250/275 LM, 275 GTB/GTS) upper/lower A-arms with coil springs. **Brakes:** front/rear disc. **Body Construction:** separate body on tubular steel ladder-type frame. **Fuel Tank:** (275 GTB) 21.4 gal.; (330 GT) 19.8 gal.

PERFORMANCE: Top Speed: (250 GT) 124-155 mph; (250 LM) 160 mph typical (137-183 mph); (275 GTB) 148 mph; (275 GTS) 143 mph; (330 GT 2+2) 115-125 mph; (400) 140-160+ mph. **Acceleration (0-60 mph):** (250 GT SWB) about 6.5-7.0 sec.; (250/275 LM) 6.5 sec. estimated; (275 GTB) 7.5 sec. or less.

Manufacturer: Automobili Ferrari S.p.A. SEFAC, Maranello (Modena), Italy.

Distributor: Luigi Chinetti Motors, New York City.

HISTORY: Development of the 500 Superfast began with a series of show cars. Following the Superfast II show car of 1960, a Superfast III had appeared at the March 1962 Geneva Salon. That one wore slimmer roof pillars, and had a thermostatically-controlled radiator cover, hidden headlamps, and partial rear skirts. Then came Superfast IV, with the same look but four exposed headlamps. That model would later be sold in the U.S. Late in 1962 came the production Series II Superamerica, on a 102.3-inch wheelbase, lacking the former hood scoop but showing a bulge over the carburetors. That led to the 500 Superfast, seen at Geneva in March 1964.

1966 FERRARI

1966 Ferrari 275 GTB.

TYPE 275 GTB/GTS — V-12 — Production of the basic 275-series coupes and convertible continued with little change, except that after the January 1966 Brussels show a closed torque tube replaced the original open driveshaft. With its more powerful engine, the berlinetta coupe could exceed 167 mph, while the Spider convertible was capable of speeds beyond 149 mph. (As always, speeds varied with axle gearing.) Coupes had light cast alloy wheels, while convertibles wore wire wheels with alloy rims. In autumn 1966, a twin-cam head was added to the 275's engine, turning it into the 275 GTB/4 (below). Meanwhile, a special competition 275 GTB/C berlinetta, introduced in spring 1966, had a lightweight aluminum body, Plexiglas windows, dry-sump lubrication, plus special camshafts, carburetors, pistons, and valves.

TYPE 275 GTB/4 — V-12 — The addition of new twin-cam cylinder heads to the 3.3-liter 275 GTB engine in late 1966 produced the GTB/4, rated 300 horsepower (DIN). Introduced at the Paris show that year, the GTB/4 berlinetta coupe became the first roadgoing Ferrari with a dual-overhead-camshaft engine. Appearance was similar to the basic 275 series. Whereas the basic GTB had a thin "rope drive" propeller shaft, the GTB/4 put the engine, propeller shaft cover, transmission and differential into a single bolted-together unit. The GTB/4 was capable of 155 mph speeds. Approximately 280 were produced, plus ten 275 GTS/4 NART Spyder convertibles built in 1967. All of the open models were sold in the U.S.

TYPE 330 GT 2+2 — V-12 — A five-speed gearbox had replaced the early four-speed (with overdrive) in 1965, matching other Ferrari models. Otherwise, the four-place Ferrari coupe continued with little change. Top speed of the Pininfarina-styled coupe was advertised as 152.2 mph.

TYPE 330 GTC/GTS — V-12 — Except for a larger engine, the new 330 coupe and convertible were similar to the 275 series. As styled by Pininfarina, the new coupe body was somewhat subdued, less rakish than other Ferraris, mixing the 275 GTB chassis and 330 GT 2+2 engine. In essence, it was a blend of 275 GTB chassis and 330 GT 2+2 engine. A small oval horizontal grille stood at the end of a pointed, tapered snout, with twin bumperettes alongside the grille. Exposed headlamps sat above small lower nacelles. Horizontal ribs went on sail panels, and vent wings were installed. Three air-intake slots sat on the rear of front fenders, behind the tops of front wheels. Identifying model script was evident on the rear deck, and a Ferrari insignia was ahead of the hood.

Debuting at the Geneva show in March 1966, the 330 GTC (Gran Turismo Coupe) had a front-mounted 3967-cc V-12 engine rated 300 horsepower at 7000 rpm and a five-speed rear transaxle, plus all-independent suspension and all-disc brakes. Wheelbase was 94.5 inches, and the car measured 173.2 inches overall. As on late examples of the 275 GTB, the driveshaft passed through a torque tube. Air conditioning was optional. A 330 GTS convertible joined the coupe at the October 1966 Paris show. With a top speed claimed to be 150 mph, the 330 GTC could accelerate to 60 mph in about seven seconds and run the quarter-mile in under 15 seconds. Options included a hardtop for the convertible, and Campagnolo alloy wheels.

TYPE 400 SUPERAMERICA — V-12 — This would be the final year for the 400.

TYPE 500 SUPERFAST — V-12 — Also in its final season, the Series II Superfast switched to a five-speed gearbox and had suspended pedals and new engine mounts. As for appearance, a trio of air outlets replaced the 11 small cowl louvers found on Series I models. Advertised top speed of the Pininfarina-styled coupe was 173.9 mph, and it was reported to hit 104 mph in second gear.

I.D. DATA: Not available.

Model	Body Type & Seating	Engine Type/CID	P.O.E. Price	Weight (lbs.)	Prod. Total
275 GTB/GTS					
275 GTB	2-dr Coupe-2P	V12/200	13900	2425	Note 1
275 GTS	2-dr Conv Cpe-2P	V12/200	14500	2536	Note 2
275 GTB/4	2-dr Coupe-2P	V12/200	N/A	N/A	Note 3
330 GT 2+2					
330 GT	2-dr Coupe-2+2P	V12/242	14200	3040	Note 4
330 GTC/GTS					
330 GTC	2-dr Coupe-2P	V12/242	N/A	N/A	Note 5
330 GTS	2-dr Conv Cpe-2P	V12/242	N/A	N/A	Note 6
TYPE 400 SUPERAMERICA					
400	2-dr Coupe-2P	V12/242	N/A	2860	Note 7
TYPE 500 SUPERFAST					
500	2-dr Coupe-2P	V12/303	29300	3087	Note 8

Note 1: About 450 Type 275 GTB coupes were produced in all (250 Series I and 200 Series II), through 1967.

Note 2: About 200 Type 275 GTS convertibles were produced, through 1966.

Note 3: About 280 Type 275 GTB/4 coupes were produced in 1966-67 (plus 10 special spyder convertibles).

Note 4: About 1,000 Type 330 GT 2+2s were produced from 1964-68.

Note 5: About 600 Type 330 GTC coupes were produced, through 1968.

Note 6: About 100 Type 330 GTS convertibles were produced, through 1968.

Note 7: As many as 54 Type 400 Superamericas were produced from 1960-64, including six cabrios (in 1960), 29 Series I coupes, and 19 Series II coupes.

Note 8: About 37 Type 500 Superfast coupes (25 Series I and 12 Series II) were produced from 1964-67.

Body Style Note: As usual, Ferraris came in a variety of body styles, open and closed, from different coachbuilders.

Price Note: The 500 Superfast was listed for as little as $24,400 in the U.S.

Weight Note: Figures shown are approximate (or averages).

Production Note: A total of 700 Ferraris were built in 1966.

1966-'70 Ferrari 330 GTC.

ENGINE DATA: BASE V-12 (275 GTB/GTS): 60-degree, single-overhead-cam, "vee" type 12-cylinder. Aluminum alloy block and heads. **Displacement:** 200.5 cu. in. (3286 cc). **Bore & Stroke:** 3.03 x 2.31 in. (77 x 58.8 mm). **Compression Ratio:** 9.2:1. **Brake Horsepower:** (GTS) 260 DIN at 7600 rpm (280 SAE at 7500 rpm); (GTB) 280 DIN (310 SAE) at 7500 rpm. **Torque:** 217 lbs.-ft. at 5000 rpm. Seven main bearings. Three Weber 40 DCZ/6 carburetors (six-carb setup available in 320-bhp competition engine).

BASE V-12 (275 GTB/4): 60-degree, dual-overhead-cam, "vee" type 12-cylinder. Aluminum alloy block and heads. **Displacement:** 200.5 cu. in. (3286 cc). **Bore & Stroke:** 3.03 x 2.31 in. (77 x 58.8 mm). **Compression Ratio:** 9.2:1. **Brake Horsepower:** 300 at 8000 rpm. Seven main bearings. Six Weber 40 DCN 17 carburetors.

BASE V-12 (330 GT 2+2): 60-degree, single-overhead-cam, "vee" type 12-cylinder. Aluminum alloy block and heads. **Displacement:** 242 cu. in. (3967 cc). **Bore & Stroke:** 3.03 x 2.80 in. (77 x 71 mm). **Compression Ratio:** 8.8:1. **Brake Horsepower:** 300 at 6600/7000 rpm. **Torque:** 288 lbs. ft. (241 DIN) at 5000 rpm. Seven main bearings. Three Weber 40 DCZ/6 carburetors.

BASE V-12 (330 GTC/GTS): 60-degree, single-overhead-cam, "vee" type 12-cylinder (Colombo). Aluminum alloy block and heads. **Displacement:** 242 cu. in. (3967 cc). **Bore & Stroke:** 3.03 x 2.80 in. (77 x 71 mm). **Compression Ratio:** 8.8:1. **Brake Horsepower:** 300 at 7000 rpm. Seven main bearings. Three Weber two-barrel carburetors.

BASE V-12 (400 Superamerica): 60-degree, single-overhead-cam, "vee" type 12-cylinder (Colombo). Aluminum alloy block and heads. **Displacement:** 242 cu. in. (3967 cc). **Bore & Stroke:** 3.03 x 2.80 in. (77 x 71 mm). **Compression Ratio:** 8.8:1. **Brake Horsepower:** 340 at 7000 rpm. Seven main bearings.

BASE V-12 (500 Superfast): 60-degree, single-overhead-cam, "vee" type 12-cylinder. Aluminum alloy block and heads. **Displacement:** 302.7 cu. in. (4962 cc). **Bore & Stroke:** 3.46 x 2.68 in. (88 x 68 mm). **Compression Ratio:** 8.8:1. **Brake Horsepower:** 400 (DIN) at 6500 rpm. **Torque:** 351 lbs.-ft. (DIN) at 4750 rpm. Seven main bearings. Six Weber 40 DCZ/6 two-barrel carburetors.

CHASSIS DATA: Wheelbase: (275 GTB/GTS) 94.5 in.; (330 GT 2+2) 104.2 in.; (330 GTC/GTS) 94.5 in.; (400 Series II/III) 102.3 in.; (500) 104.3 in. **Overall Length:** (275 GTB) 170.3 in.; (275 GTS) 171.3 in.; (330 GT 2+2) 189.4-190.5 in.; (330 GTC/GTS) 173.2 in.; (400) 172 in.; (500) 189.8 in. **Height:** (275 GTB) 49 in.; (275 GTS) 49.2 in.; (330 GT 2+2) 53.5 in.; (330 GTC) 51.2 in.; (330 GTS) 49.2 in.; (400) 51.5 in.; (500) 50.4 in. **Width:** (275 GTB) 67.9 in.; (275 GTS) 65.9 in.; (330 GT 2+2) 69 in.; (330 GTC) 65.75 in.; (330 GTS) 65.9 in.; (400) 66 in.; (500) 70.1 in. **Front Tread:** (275 GTB/GTS) 54.3 in.; (275 GTB/4) 55.2 in.; (330 GT 2+2) 55 in.; (330 GTC/GTS) 55.2 in.; (500) 55 in. **Rear Tread:** (275 GTB/GTS) 54.7 in.; (275 GTB/4) 55.8 in.; (330 GT 2+2) 54.7 in.; (330 GTC/GTS) 55.8 in.; (500) 54.7 in. **Standard Tires:** (275 GTB) 205x14; (275 GTS) 185x14; (330 GT 2+2) 205x15; (330 GTC/GTS) 205x14; (500) 205x15.

TECHNICAL: Layout: front-engine, rear-drive. **Transmission:** (400) four-speed all-synchro manual plus overdrive; (330 GT 2+2, 500) five-speed manual; (275 GTB/GTS, 330 GTC/GTS) five-speed manual in rear transaxle. **Standard Final Drive Ratio:** (275 GTB) 3.30:1 or 3.555:1; (330 GT 2+2) 4.25:1; (500) 3.778:1. **Steering:** worm and roller. **Suspension (front):** upper/lower A-arms with coil springs. **Suspension (rear):** (330 GT 2+2, 400) rigid axle with parallel trailing arms and semi-elliptic leaf springs; (275 GTB/GTS, 330 GTC/GTS) upper/lower A-arms with coil springs. **Brakes:** front/rear disc. **Body Construction:** separate body on tubular steel ladder-type frame.

MAJOR OPTIONS: Limited-slip differential. Competition engine (275 GTB). 195x14 tires (275 GTB). Various gearbox ratios (275 series).

PERFORMANCE: Top Speed: (275 GTB) 152 mph; (275 GTS) about 144 mph; (275 GTB/4) 155 mph; (330 GT 2+2) as much as 151 mph; (330 GTC) 145-150 mph; (400) 140-160+ mph; (500) up to 174 mph. **Acceleration (0-60 mph):** (275 GTB) 5.9-7.5 sec.; (275 GTS) 6.5 sec.; (330 GTC) 7.0 sec.; (330 GT 2+2) 8.0 sec. **Acceleration (quarter-mile):** (275 GTS) 14.0 sec. (95 mph); (330 GTC) 14.6-14.9 sec. (about 95 mph); (330 GT 2+2) 16.0 sec. (102 mph).

Manufacturer: Automobili Ferrari S.p.A. SEFAC, Maranello (Modena), Italy.

Distributor: Luigi Chinetti Motors, New York City.

HISTORY: Paul Frere, writing about the 330 GTC in *The Motor* (Britain) in 1966, was most surprised by "the silence of the engine," though its handling was unchanged, as "close to being as neutral as one could want." Frere was pleased by "the solidness with which it changes direction, particularly in S-bends, where it tracks with about the same precision as a modern race car."

1967 FERRARI

1967 Ferrari 330 GTC.

DINO 206 GT — V-6 — Something different from Ferrari had appeared at the 1965 Paris Salon: a Dino 206S Speciale coupe, styled by Pininfarina with a mid-engine twin-cam, 2.0-liter V-6. That show car's Ferrari-designed engine was nonfunctional, and led to a Dino Berlinetta GT at the 1966 Turin show. The production version, introduced at the next year's Turin event, would carry the first transverse-mounted mid-engine offered by Ferrari. It was also Ferrari's first attempt at introducing a secondary marque, since the Dino carried no Ferrari name or prancing-horse insignia on its body. The all-alloy engine was built by Fiat, and the Dino (named for Enzo Ferrari's deceased son) was aimed at Formula Two racing. Anyone in doubt about the car's origin, however, had only to listen to the V-6's exhaust snarl to be convinced that this was indeed a Ferrari. The low, curvaceous body, built by Scaglietti to Pininfarina specifications, had its headlamps deeply set back into front-fender nacelles, with a tiny grille opening in the short, sloping protruding nose. Alongside the grille were long wraparound bumperettes. Most examples had covered headlamps. A bulged look was evident above front wheels; and to some extent, at the rears as well. A trio of small slots sat on each side of the hood, near the front. An upright back window stood between twin "flying buttress" roof extensions. Front vent wings and trapezoidal rear quarter windows were installed. Wheelbase was 90 inches, and the Dino measured 165 inches long. With its race-inspired 1987-cc V-6 rated 180 horsepower (DIN), a Dino was capable of 140 mph. The five-speed gearbox was mounted in the rear transaxle. Produced until late 1969 in this original form, most Dinos were sold in Europe.

TYPE 275 GTB/4 — V-12 — Production of the twin-cam 3286-cc coupe and convertible continued with little change, into 1968.

TYPE 330 GT 2+2 — V-12 — Ferrari's 2+2 coupe continued with little change, but was soon to be replaced by the new 365 GT 2+2.

TYPE 330 GTC/GTS — V-12 — Introduced a year earlier, the 3967-cc 2+2 coupe and convertible continued with little change, into 1970.

TYPE 365 GT 2+2 — V-12 — Replacing the 330 GT 2+2, the larger-engined fastback coupe appeared at the 1967 Paris Salon, ready to become Ferrari's biggest and poshest model yet. Riding a 104.2-inch wheelbase, the Superfast-style coupe, styled by Pininfarina, measured 196 inches long and weighed close to two tons at the curb. The low, rounded nose displayed an elliptical eggcrate-patterned grille (similar to that of the 330 GTC), with headlamps in lower nacelles. Parking lights were built into bumperettes, and a Ferrari emblem stood ahead of the hood. European models had clear plastic headlamp covers contoured to fender shape. 'Ferrari' lettering went on the decklid. Slim 'A' and 'B' pillars, large tapered rear quarter windows, front vent wings, and flush door handles helped complete the car's look. A Kamm-type tail contained three round taillamps in each housing on the rear panel.

Standard Cromodora alloy disc wheels could be replaced by optional Borrani wires, and starting in 1968 the five-spoke wheels from the Daytona would become standard. Other standard equipment included power brakes/steering, power windows, air conditioning, pleated leather upholstery, full carpeting, and a radio. Needle-type gauges sat ahead of the driver, with controls in a center console. As usual, this Ferrari rode a multitube steel frame, and had all-independent suspension. This Ferrari's self-leveling rear suspension, a "first" for the marque, had been developed in concert with Koni. The 4390-cc Colombo-derived V-12 developed 320 horsepower (DIN) using three downdraft carburetors, driving a five-speed gearbox. A 365 GT 2+2 could accelerate to 60 mph in just over seven seconds. Production continued into 1971, with about 800 built in all. During its three-year life, this model accounted for half of Ferrari production.

I.D. DATA: Not available.

Model	Body Type & Seating	Engine Type/CID	P.O.E. Price	Weight (lbs.)	Prod. Total
206 DINO GT					
206 Dino	2-dr Coupe-2P	V6/121	N/A	1980	Note 1
275 GTB/4					
275 GTB/4	2-dr Coupe-2P	V12/200	N/A	2425	Note 2
330 GT 2+2					
330 GT	2-dr Coupe-2+2P	V12/242	14200	3040	Note 3
330 GTC/GTS					
330 GTC	2-dr Coupe-2P	V12/242	14200	2867	Note 4
330 GTS	2-dr Conv Cpe-2P	V12/242	14200	2640	Note 5
365 GT 2+2					
365 GT	2-dr Coupe-2+2P	V12/268	N/A	3500	Note 6

Note 1: As many as 150 Type 206 Dino GT coupes were produced from 1967-69.
Note 2: About 280 Type 275 GTB/4 coupes were produced in 1966-67 (plus 10 special spyder convertibles).
Note 3: About 1,000 Type 330 GT 2+2s were produced from 1964-68.
Note 4: About 600 Type 330 GTC coupes were produced, through 1968.
Note 5: About 100 Type 330 GTS convertibles were produced, through 1968.
Note 6: About 800 Type 365 GT 2+2 coupes were produced from 1967-71.
Weight Note: Figures shown are approximate (or averages).
Production Note: A total of 706 Ferraris were built in 1967.

ENGINE DATA: **BASE V-6** (206 Dino GT): 65-degree, dual-overhead-cam, "vee" type six-cylinder. Silumin alloy block and heads. **Displacement:** 121 cu. in. (1987 cc). **Bore & Stroke:** 3.39 x 2.24 in. (86 x 57 mm). **Compression Ratio:** 9.7:1. **Brake Horsepower:** 180 (DIN) at 8000 rpm. **Torque:** 138 lbs.-ft. (DIN) at 6500 rpm. Four main bearings. Three Weber two-barrel carburetors.

BASE V-12 (275 GTB/4): 60-degree, dual-overhead-cam, "vee" type 12-cylinder. Aluminum alloy block and heads. **Displacement:** 200.5 cu. in. (3286 cc). **Bore & Stroke:** 3.03 x 2.31 in. (77 x 58.8 mm). **Compression Ratio:** 9.2:1. **Brake Horsepower:** 300 at 8000 rpm. Seven main bearings. Six Weber two-barrel carburetors.

BASE V-12 (330 GT 2+2, 330 GTC/GTS): 60-degree, single-overhead-cam, "vee" type 12-cylinder. Aluminum alloy block and heads. **Displacement:** 242 cu. in. (3967 cc). **Bore & Stroke:** 3.03 x 2.80 in. (77 x 71 mm). **Compression Ratio:** 8.8:1. **Brake Horsepower:** 300 DIN (345 SAE) at 7000 rpm. Seven main bearings. Three Weber two-barrel carburetors.

BASE V-12 (365 GT 2+2): 60-degree, single-overhead-cam, "vee" type 12-cylinder (Colombo). Aluminum alloy block and heads. **Displacement:** 268 cu. in. (4390 cc). **Bore & Stroke:** 3.19 x 2.80 in. (81 x 71 mm). **Compression Ratio:** 8.8:1. **Brake Horsepower:** 320 at 6600 rpm. Seven main bearings. Three Weber carburetors.

CHASSIS DATA: Wheelbase: (206 Dino GT) 90.0 in.; (275 GTB/4) 94.5 in.; (330 GT 2+2) 104.2 in.; (330 GTC/GTS) 94.5 in.; (365 GT 2+2) 104.2 in. **Overall Length:** (206 Dino GT) 165 in.; (275 GTB/4) 173.6 in.; (330 GT 2+2) 189.4 in.; (330 GTC/GTS) 173.2 in.; (365 GT 2+2) 196 in. **Height:** (206 Dino GT) 43.9 in.; (275 GTB/4) 50.8 in.; (330 GT 2+2) 52 in.; (330 GTC) 51.2 in.; (330 GTS) 49.2 in.; (365 GT 2+2) 53 in. **Width:** (206 Dino GT) 66.9 in.; (275 GTB/4) 68.9 in.; (330 GT 2+2) 69 in.; (330 GTC) 65.75 in.; (330 GTS) 65.9 in.; (365 GT 2+2) 70.5 in. **Front Tread:** (206 Dino GT) 56.1 in.; (275 GTB/4) 55.2 in.; (330 GT 2+2) 55.3 in.; (330 GTC/GTS) 55.2 in.; (365 GT 2+2) 56.6 in. **Rear Tread:** (206 Dino GT) 55.1 in.; (275 GTB/4) 55.8 in.; (330 GT 2+2) 55.0 in.; (330 GTC/GTS) 55.8 in.; (365 GT 2+2) 57.8 in. **Standard Tires:** (206 Dino GT) 185x14; (275 GTB/4) 205x14; (330 GT 2+2) 205x15; (330 GTC/GTS) 205x14; (365 GT 2+2) 205x15.

TECHNICAL: Layout: front-engine, rear-drive except (Dino) mid-engine, rear-drive. **Transmission:** (330 GT 2+2) five-speed manual; (206 Dino GT, 275 GTB/4, 330 GTC/GTS, 365 GT 2+2) five-speed manual in rear transaxle. **Steering:** worm and roller. **Suspension (front):** upper/lower A-arms with coil springs. **Suspension (rear):** (330 GT 2+2) rigid axle with parallel trailing arms and semi-elliptic leaf springs; (206 Dino GT, 275 GTB/4, 330 GTC/GTS, 365 GT 2+2) upper/lower A-arms with coil springs. **Brakes:** front/rear disc. **Body Construction:** separate body on tubular steel ladder-type frame.

PERFORMANCE: Top Speed: (206 Dino GT) 142 mph; (275 GTB/4) 165+ mph; (330 GT 2+2) as high as 150+ mph; (330 GTC) 145-150 mph; (365 GT 2+2) 140-145+ mph. **Acceleration (0-60 mph):** (206 Dino GT) about 7.1 sec.; (330 GTC) 7.0 sec.; (365 GT 2+2) 7.1 sec. **Acceleration (quarter-mile):** (330 GTC) 14.6-14.9 sec. (about 95 mph).

Manufacturer: Automobili Ferrari S.p.A. SEFAC, Maranello (Modena), Italy.
Distributor: Luigi Chinetti Motors, New York City.

1968 FERRARI

DINO 206 GT — V-6 — Dino production in this form continued with little change, into 1969.

275 GTB/4 — V-12 — Production of the twin-cam version of the 275 series continued into early 1968.

TYPE 330 GT 2+2 — V-12 — This was the final year for the four-seat Ferrari with 3967-cc V-12, which was replaced by the 365 GT 2+2 series.

TYPE 330 GTC/GTS — V-12 — This was the final year for the coupe and convertible with 3967-cc V-12 engine.

TYPE 365 GTC/GTS — V-12 — Starting in 1968, a larger engine went into the former 330 GTC/GTS, resulting in a model number change. A 4-mm bore increase (to 81 mm) boosted displacement of the V-12 to 4390 cc (267.8 cid), developing 320 horsepower at 6600 rpm. Production would continue into 1970.

TYPE 365 GT 2+2 — V-12 — Introduced in 1967, the 2+2 coupe with 4390-cc V-12 engine would remain in production into 1971.

TYPE 365 GTB/4 "DAYTONA" — V-12 — One of Ferrari's most popular models debuted at the Paris Salon in 1968, soon acquiring the "Daytona" nickname. This would be the final front-engine, two-seat production Ferrari. Pininfarina designed the fastback coupe, but bodies were built by Scaglietti. Layout and chassis were essentially that of the former 275 GTB/4, with 94.5-inch wheelbase, but power came from the new 4390-cc V-12 engine. Using 8.8:1 compression and six Weber carburetors, that twin-cam engine produced 352 horsepower. A five-speed manual transaxle was mounted in the rear. Early models had full-width plastic headlamp covers. That layout was illegal in the U.S., so imported versions had hidden headlamps. From 1970 onward, all Daytonas wore concealed headlamps. A small blackout eggcrate rectangular grille was flanked by rubber-tipped bumperettes. Wraparound amber park/signal lights were installed. The smooth, frill-free shape displayed a horizontal bodyside crease just below the level of the top of the wheel wells. Bumperettes at the rear were black-tipped, to match the front units. Two round taillamps were mounted on each side. Aluminum was used for the doors, hood, and trunklid. Cromodora five-spoke light alloy wheels were standard.

Ranking as Ferrari's most costly production model up to that time, the Daytona was also the fastest, capable of hitting 174 mph. It could run the quarter-mile in 13.8 seconds, reaching 107.5 mph, and accelerate to 60 mph in 5.9 seconds. More than 1,400 examples would be produced over the full model run, which began in 1969 and continued into 1974. Most were closed coupes, but about 127 Spider convertibles were built. A handful of racing berlinetta coupes had all-aluminum bodies, with engines producing up to 405 bhp.

1968 Ferrari 275 GTB/4. (Coys of Kensington)

I.D. DATA: Not available.

Model	Body Type & Seating	Engine Type/CID	P.O.E. Price	Weight (lbs.)	Prod. Total
206 DINO GT					
206 Dino	2-dr Coupe-2P	V6/121	N/A	1980	Note 1
275 GTB/4					
275 GTB/4	2-dr Coupe-2P	V12/200	14900	2315	Note 2
330 GT 2 + 2					
330 GT	2-dr Coupe-2 + 2P	V12/242	14900	3040	Note 3
330 GTC/GTS					
330 GTC	2-dr Coupe-2P	V12/242	14900	2866	Note 4
330 GTS	2-dr Conv Cpe-2P	V12/242	14900	2646	Note 5
365 GTC/GTS					
365 GTC	2-dr Coupe-2P	V12/268	N/A	N/A	Note 6
365 GTS	2-dr Conv Cpe-2P	V12/268	N/A	N/A	Note 7
365 GT 2 + 2					
365 GT	2-dr Coupe-2 + 2P	V12/268	N/A	3500	Note 8
365 GTB/4 "DAYTONA"					
365 GTB/4	2-dr Coupe-2P	V12/268	N/A	3600	Note 9

Note 1: As many as 150 Type 206 Dino GT coupes were produced from 1967-69.

Note 2: About 200 Type 275 GTB/4 coupes were produced from 1966 into early 1968 (plus 10 special spyder convertibles).

Note 3: About 1,000 Type 330 GT 2 + 2s were produced from 1964-68.

Note 4: About 600 Type 330 GTC coupes were produced, through 1968.

Note 5: About 100 Type 330 GTS convertibles were produced, through 1968.

Note 6: Between 150 and 200 Type 365 GTC coupes were produced, through 1970.

Note 7: About 20 Type 365 GTS convertibles were produced, through 1970.

Note 8: About 800 Type 365 GT 2 + 2 coupes were produced from 1967-71.

Note 9: About 1,285 Type 365 GTB/4 coupes (not including convertibles) were produced from 1968-74.

Weight Note: Figures shown are approximate (or averages).

ENGINE DATA: BASE V-6 (206 Dino GT): 65-degree, dual-overhead-cam "vee" type six-cylinder. Silumin alloy block and heads. **Displacement:** 121 cu. in. (1987 cc). **Bore & Stroke:** 3.39 x 2.24 in. (86 x 57 mm). **Compression Ratio:** 9.7:1. **Brake Horsepower:** 180 (DIN) at 8000 rpm. **Torque:** 138 lbs.-ft. (DIN) at 6500 rpm. Four main bearings. Three Weber 40 DCN/4 two-barrel carburetors.

BASE V-12 (275 GTB/4): 60-degree, dual-overhead-cam "vee" type 12-cylinder. Aluminum alloy block and heads. **Displacement:** 200.5 cu. in. (3286 cc). **Bore & Stroke:** 3.03 x 2.31 in. (77 x 58.8 mm). **Compression Ratio:** 9.2:1. **Brake Horsepower:** 300 (DIN) at 8000 rpm. **Torque:** 217 lbs.-ft. at 6000 rpm. Seven main bearings. Six Weber two-barrel carburetors.

BASE V-12 (330 GT 2 + 2, 330 GTC/GTS): 60-degree, single-overhead-cam "vee" type 12-cylinder. Aluminum alloy block and heads. **Displacement:** 242 cu. in. (3967 cc). **Bore & Stroke:** 3.03 x 2.80 in. (77 x 71 mm). **Compression Ratio:** 8.8:1. **Brake Horsepower:** 300 DIN (345 SAE) at 7000 rpm. **Torque:** 241 lbs.-ft. at 5000 rpm. Seven main bearings. Three Weber DCZ/6 or 40 DFI two-barrel carburetors.

BASE V-12 (365 GTC/GTS, 365 GT 2 + 2): 60-degree, single-overhead-cam "vee" type 12-cylinder (Colombo). Aluminum alloy block and heads. **Displacement:** 268 cu. in. (4390 cc). **Bore & Stroke:** 3.19 x 2.80 in. (81 x 71 mm). **Brake Horsepower:** 320 (DIN) at 6600 rpm. **Torque:** 268 lbs.-ft. at 5000 rpm. Seven main bearings. Three Weber carburetors.

BASE V-12 (365 GTB/4): 60-degree, dual-overhead-cam "vee" type 12-cylinder. Aluminum alloy block and heads. **Displacement:** 268 cu. in. (4390 cc). **Bore & Stroke:** 3.19 x 2.80 in. (81 x 71 mm). **Compression Ratio:** 8.8:1. **Brake Horsepower:** 352 at 7500 rpm. **Torque:** 365 lbs.-ft. at 5500 rpm. Seven main bearings. Six Weber 40 DCN 20 twin-choke carburetors.

CHASSIS DATA: Wheelbase: (206 Dino GT) 90.0 in.; (275 GTB/4) 94.5 in.; (330 GT 2 + 2) 104.2 in.; (330 GTC/GTS) 94.5 in.; (365 GT 2 + 2) 104.2 in.; (365 GTC/GTS) 94.5 in.; (365 GTB/4) 94.5 in. **Overall Length:** (206 Dino GT) 165 in.; (275 GTB/4) 173.6 in.; (330 GT 2 + 2) 189.4 in.; (330 GTC) 176 in.; (330 GTS) 174.4 in.; (365 GT 2 + 2) 196 in.; (365 GTC/GTS) 176 in.; (365 GTB/4) 174 in. **Height:** (206 Dino GT) 43.9 in.; (275 GTB/4) 47.2 in.; (330 GT 2 + 2) 52 in.; (330 GTC) 51.2 in.; (330 GTS) 49.2 in.; (365 GT 2 + 2) 53 in.; (365 GTC/GTS) 51.2 in.; (365 GTB/4) 49.0 in. **Width:** (206 Dino GT) 66.9 in.; (275 GTB/4) 67.9 in.; (330 GT 2 + 2) 69 in.; (330 GTC) 65.8 in.; (330 GTS) 65.9 in.; (365 GT 2 + 2) 70.5 in.; (365 GTC/GTS) 65.7 in.; (365 GTB/4) 69.3 in. **Front Tread:** (206 Dino GT) 56.1 in.; (275 GTB/4) 55.2 in.; (330 GT 2 + 2) 55.3 in.; (330 GTC/GTS) 55.2 in.; (365 GT 2 + 2) 56.6 in.; (365 GTC/GTS) 55.2 in.; (365 GTB/4) 56.7 in. **Rear Tread:** (206 Dino GT) 55.1 in.; (275 GTB/4) 55.8 in.; (330 GT 2 + 2) 55 in.; (330 GTC/GTS) 55.8 in.; (365 GT 2 + 2) 57.8 in.; (365 GTC/GTS) 55.8 in.; (365 GTB/4) 56.1 in. **Standard Tires:** (206 Dino GT) 185x14; (330 GTC/GTS) 205x14; (365 GT 2 + 2) 205x15; (365 GTC/GTS) 215x15; (365 GTB/4) 215x15.

TECHNICAL: Layout: front-engine, rear-drive except (Dino) mid-engine, rear-drive. **Transmission:** (206 Dino GT) five-speed manual; (275 GTB/4, 330 GTC/GTS, 330 GT 2 + 2, 365 GTC/GTS, 365 GTB/4) five-speed manual in rear transaxle. **Standard Final Drive Ratio:** (206 Dino GT) 3.41:1; (275 GTB/4) 3.55:1; (330 GT) 4.25:1 (330 GTS) 3.44:1; (365 GT 2 + 2) 4.25:1. **Steering:** (Dino) rack and pinion; (275/330 GTB/4) worm and roller; (365 GT 2 + 2) recirculating ball. **Suspension (front):** upper/lower A-arms with coil springs. **Suspension (rear):** (330 GT 2 + 2) rigid axle with parallel trailing arms and semi-elliptic leaf springs; (206 Dino GT, 275 GTB/GTS, 330 GTC/GTS, 365 GT 2 + 2, 365 GTC/GTS, 365 GTB/4) upper/lower A-arms with coil springs. **Brakes:** front/rear disc. **Body Construction:** separate body on tubular steel ladder-type frame.

216

MAJOR OPTIONS: Air conditioning (330 GTC/GTS). Wire wheels (330 GTC/GTS, 365 GT 2 + 2).

PERFORMANCE: Top Speed: (206 Dino GT) 142-146 mph; (275 GTB/4) 166 mph; (330 GT 2 + 2) 115-125 mph; (330 GTC) 145-152 mph; (330 GTS) 149 mph; (365 GT 2 + 2) 140-152 mph; (365 GTB/4) 174 mph. **Acceleration (0-60 mph):** (206 Dino GT) about 7.1 sec.; (330 GTC) 7.0 sec.; (365 GT 2 + 2) 7.1 sec.; (365 GTB/4) 5.9 sec. **Acceleration (quarter-mile):** (330 GTC) 14.6-14.9 sec. (about 95 mph).

Manufacturer: Ferrari S.p.A. SEFAC, Maranello (Modena), Italy.

Distributor: Luigi Chinetti Motors, New York City and Greenwich, Connecticut.

1969 Ferrari Dino 206 GT. (Coys of Kensington)

DINO 206 GT — V-6 — This would be the final year for the original Dino, as the 246 GT version emerged.

DINO 246 GT — V-6 — Appearance of the second version of the Dino was nearly identical to the first, with significant changes only beneath the hood. This edition carried a larger and more reliable 2418-cc (148-cid) V-6 with a cast iron block instead of the former Silumin alloy. Both bore and stroke were larger than the former engine, so this one developed as much as 195 (DIN) horsepower using 9.0:1 compression. The prototype appeared early in 1969, and production began later that year. Like the prior Dino, it had a tubular steel chassis, fully independent suspension, and front/rear disc brakes. Wheelbase grew 2.1 inches, however, now measuring 92.1 inches. Bodies were built by Scaglietti, while the transverse-mounted engines came from Fiat (but had been designed at Ferrari). Some engine components were manufactured at the Ferrari facility. As before, the extremely low fastback profile featured bulged front fenders, and the car wore no Ferrari name or insignia. Center-lock knock-off Cromodora alloy wheels were standard. Starting in mid-1970, however, five-bolt Campagnolo wheels were installed on most models destined for the U.S. market. On the dashboard, eight instruments sat in an elliptical binnacle just ahead of the driver. Top speed was around 140 mph, and this Dino could accelerate to 60 mph in about eight seconds. Production continued into 1973.

TYPE 365 GTC/GTS, GTC/4 — V-12 — Production of the coupe and convertible with 4390-cc engine continued with little change, into 1970. That was replaced by a 365 GTC/4, which continued into 1972, riding a 98.4-inch wheelbase and capable of speeds as high as 163 mph. Examples destined for the U.S. had large side lights and air conditioning.

TYPE 365 GT 2 + 2 — V-12 — Production of the four-seat Ferrari with 4390-cc V-12 continued into 1971, with little change. Standard equipment included air conditioning, power steering, power windows, and an AM/FM radio.

TYPE 365 GTB/4, 365 GTS/4 "DAYTONA" — V-12 — A Spider convertible (GTS/4) joined the original coupe at the 1969 Frankfurt auto show. Otherwise, the popular "Daytona" continued with little change. Starting in mid-1971, however, the "Daytona" adopted retracting headlamps.

I.D. DATA: Not available.

Model	Body Type & Seating	Engine Type/CID	P.O.E. Price	Weight (lbs.)	Prod. Total
206 DINO GT					
206 Dino	2-dr Coupe-2P	V6/121	13400	1980	Note 1
246 DINO GT					
246 Dino	2-dr Coupe-2P	V6/148	N/A	2380	Note 2
365 GTC/GTS					
365 GTC	2-dr Coupe-2P	V12/268	N/A	N/A	Note 3
365 GTS	2-dr Conv Cpe-2P	V12/268	N/A	N/A	Note 4
365 GT 2 + 2					
365 GT	2-dr Coupe-2 + 2P	V12/268	18900	3487	Note 5
365 GTB/4 "DAYTONA"					
365 GTB/4	2-dr Coupe-2P	V12/268	19700	3600	Note 6
365 GTS/4	2-dr Conv Cpe-2P	V12/268	N/A	N/A	Note 7
365 GTC/4 (1971)					
365 GTC/4	2-dr Coupe-2P	V12/268	N/A	N/A	Note 3

Note 1: As many as 150 Type 206 Dino GT coupes were produced from 1967-69.

Note 2: About 2,732 Type 246 Dino GT coupes were produced from 1969-73.

Note 3: Between 150 and 200 Type 365 GTC coupes were produced, through 1970; followed by about 500 Type 365 GTC/4, through 1972.

Note 4: About 20 Type 365 GTS convertibles were produced, through 1970.

Note 5: About 800 Type 365 GT 2 + 2 coupes were produced from 1967-71.

Note 6: About 1,285 Type 365 GTB/4 coupes were produced from 1968-74.

Note 7: About 127 Type 365 GTS/4 convertibles were produced from 1969-74.

1970 Ferrari 365 GTB/4 Daytona. (Coys of Kensington)

Price Note: Figures shown were valid during 1969. The 365 GT 2 + 2 sold for $21,700 in 1970; the 365 GTB/4 "Daytona" coupe listed for $20,500 in 1970-71.

Weight Note: Figures shown are approximate (or averages).

Production Note: Approximately 730 Ferraris were built in 1969, followed by 850 in 1970, and 1,246 in 1971 (including 832 Dinos and 326 Type 365 GT/GTB).

ENGINE DATA: BASE V-6 (206 Dino GT): 65-degree, dual-overhead-cam "vee" type six-cylinder. Light alloy (Silumin) block and heads. **Displacement:** 121 cu. in. (1987 cc). **Bore & Stroke:** 3.39 x 2.24 in. (86 x 57 mm). **Compression Ratio:** 9.3:1. **Brake Horsepower:** 180 (DIN) at 8000 rpm. **Torque:** 138 lbs.-ft. at 6500 rpm. Four main bearings. Three Weber 40 DCN/4 two-barrel carburetors.

BASE V-6 (246 Dino GT): 65-degree, dual-overhead-cam "vee" type six-cylinder. Cast iron block and light alloy heads. **Displacement:** 148 cu. in. (2418 cc). **Bore & Stroke:** 3.64 x 2.36 in. (92.5 x 60 mm). **Compression Ratio:** 9.0:1. **Brake Horsepower:** 195 (DIN) at 7600 rpm. **Torque:** 167 lbs.-ft. at 5500 rpm. Four main bearings. Three Weber 40 DCNF/6 or 40 DCNF/7 carburetors.

BASE V-12 (365 GTC/GTS, 365 GT 2 + 2): 60-degree, single-overhead-cam "vee" type 12-cylinder (Colombo). Aluminum alloy block and heads. **Displacement:** 268 cu. in. (4390 cc). **Bore & Stroke:** 3.19 x 2.80 in. (81 x 71 mm). **Compression Ratio:** 8.8:1. **Brake Horsepower:** 320 (DIN) at 6600 rpm. **Torque:** 268 lbs.-ft. at 5000 rpm. Seven main bearings. Three Weber 40 DFI carburetors.

BASE V-12 (365 GTB/4, GTS/4): 60-degree, dual-overhead-cam "vee" type 12-cylinder. Aluminum alloy block and heads. **Displacement:** 268 cu. in. (4390 cc). **Bore & Stroke:** 3.19 x 2.80 in. (81 x 71 mm). **Compression Ratio:** 8.8:1. **Brake Horsepower:** 352 at 7500 rpm. **Torque:** 319 lbs.-ft. DIN (365 SAE) at 5000-5500 rpm. Seven main bearings. Six Weber 40 CDN2A or DCN20 twin-choke carburetors.

BASE V-12 (365 GTC/4): Same as dual-overhead-cam 4390-cc V-12 above, except — **Brake Horsepower:** 320-340 at 6200-6800 rpm. **Torque:** 312-318 lbs.-ft. at 4000-4600 rpm.

1971 Ferrari 246 Dino GT. (Coys of Kensington)

CHASSIS DATA: Wheelbase: (206 Dino GT) 90.0 in.; (246 Dino GT) 92.1 in.; (365 GT 2 + 2) 104.3 in.; (365 GTC/GTS) 94.5 in. **Overall Length:** (206 Dino GT) 165 in.; (246 Dino GT) 163.4 in.; (365 GT 2 + 2) 195 in.; (365 GTC/GTS) 174-176 in.; (365 GTC/4) 179.9 in.; (365 GTB/4) 171-174 in. **Height:** (206/246 Dino GT) 43.9 in.; (365 GT 2 + 2) 53 in.; (365 GTC/GTS) 50.5 in.; (365 GTC/4) 50 in.; (365 GTB/4) 49 in. **Width:** (206/246 Dino GT) 66.9 in.; (365 GT 2 + 2) 70 in.; (365 GTC/GTS) 65.5 in.; (365 GTC/4) 70.1 in.; (365 GTB/4) 68-70 in. **Front Tread:** (206/246 Dino GT) 56.1 in.; (365 GT 2 + 2) 56.6 in.; (365 GTC/GTS) 55.2 in.; (365 GTC/4) 57.9 in.; (365 GTB/4) 56.7 in. **Rear Tread:** (206 Dino GT) 55.1 in.; (246 Dino GT) 56.3 in.; (365 GT 2 + 2) 56.6 in.; (365 GTC/GTS) 55.8 in.; (365 GTC/4) 57.9 in.; (365 GTB/4) 56.1 in. **Standard Tires:** (206 Dino GT)185x14; (246 Dino GT) 205x14; (365 GTB/4, GTS/4) 215/70x15.

TECHNICAL: Layout: front-engine, rear-drive except (Dino) mid-engine, rear-drive. **Transmission:** five-speed manual in rear transaxle. **Standard Final Drive Ratio:** (Dino 246 GT) 3.62:1. **Steering:** (Dino 206/246) rack and pinion; (365 365 GTB/4) worm and roller; (365 GT 2 + 2) recirculating ball. **Suspension (front):** unequal-length A-arms with coil springs (anti-roll bar on 206/246 Dino, 365 GTB/4, 365 GTS/4). **Suspension (rear):** (365 GTC/GTS) unequal-length A-arms with coil springs; (365 GT 2 + 2) unequal-length A-arms with coil springs and hydropneumatic self-leveling; (206/246 Dino, 365 GTB/GTS) unequal-length A-arms with coil springs and anti-roll bar. **Brakes:** front/rear disc. **Body Construction:** separate body on tubular steel frame.

MAJOR OPTIONS: Air conditioning: GTB/4 ($800). AM/FM radio: GTB/4 $320.

PERFORMANCE: Top Speed: (206 Dino GT) 142-146 mph; (246 Dino GT) 140-146 mph; (365 GT 2 + 2) 140-152 mph; (365 GTB/4) 174-180 mph. **Acceleration (0-60 mph):** (206 Dino GT) about 7.1 sec.; (246 Dino GT) 8.0 sec.; (365 GT 2 + 2) 7.1 sec.; (365 GTB/4) 5.9 sec.

Manufacturer: Ferrari S.p.A. SEFAC, Maranello (Modena), Italy.
Distributor: Luigi Chinetti Motors, Greenwich, Connecticut.
HISTORY: Fiat used the same 2418-cc V-6 engine installed in the Dino 246 GT in its own front-engined Fiat Dino. The relationship was no surprise, since Fiat bought a controlling interest in Ferrari in 1969.

1972 FERRARI

1972 Ferrari 365 GTC/4. (Coys of Kensington)

DINO 246 GT/GTS — V-6 — A Targa-topped 246 GTS joined the original model this year, wearing a lift-off roof panel above the cockpit. Instead of the coupe's small rear quarter windows, the GTS had metal panels with three small louvers.

TYPE 365 GTB/4, 365 GTS/4 "DAYTONA" — V-12 — Production of the two "Daytona" models continued into 1974; see previous listings for additional details.

TYPE 365 GTC/4 — V-12 — Introduced in 1971, this two-seater coupe with 4390-cc engine continued into 1972 before being replaced by the 365 GT4.

365 GT4 2 + 2 — V-12 — A new four-seat Ferrari became available this year, debuting at the October 1972 Paris show as successor to the 365 GT 2 + 2 (which actually ceased production more than a year earlier). Displaying a pillared notchback coupe profile, it also replaced the 365 GTC/4. Wheelbase was two inches longer than the 365 GT 2 + 2, but this model was markedly shorter overall and weighed considerably more. Interior dimensions were noticeably wider. A 268-cid (4390-cc) four-cam V-12 with six horizontal carburetors provided the power: 320 horsepower at 6200 rpm, hooked to a five-speed manual gearbox. Chassis layout, suspension, brakes and steering were similar to the GTC/4. Five-spoke Cromodora alloy wheels were standard, as were air conditioning, power steering and power brakes. Not typical Ferrari in appearance, the 365 GT4 had a body by Scaglietti and was never certified for sale in the U.S.

I.D. DATA: Not available.

Model	Body Type & Seating	Engine Type/CID	P.O.E. Price	Weight (lbs.)	Prod. Total
246 DINO					
GT	2-dr Coupe-2P	V6/148	14500	2380	Note 1
GTS	2-dr Targa Cpe-2P	V6/148	N/A	N/A	Note 2
365 GTB/4 "DAYTONA"					
365 GTB/4	2-dr Coupe-2P		N/A	3530	Note 3
365 GTS/4	2-dr Conv Cpe-2P	V12/268	N/A	N/A	Note 4
365 GTC/4					
365 GTC/4	2-dr Coupe-2P	V12/268	27500	3197	Note 5
365 GT4 2 + 2					
365 GT4	2-dr Coupe-2 + 2P	V12/268	N/A	4000	Note 6

Note 1: About 2,800 Type 246 Dino GT coupes were produced from 1969-1973.
Note 2: About 1,200 Type 246 Dino GTS Targa coupes were produced from 1972-73.
Note 3: About 1,285 Type 365 GTB/4 coupes were produced from 1968-74.
Note 4: About 127 Type 365 GTS/4 convertibles were produced from 1969-74.
Note 5: Approximately 500 Type 365 GTC/4 coupes were produced in 1971-72.
Note 6: A total of 470 Type 365 GT4 2 + 2 coupes (sometimes called sedans) were produced from 1972-75.

Price Note: 246 Dino GT price is approximate.

Weight Note: Figures shown are approximate (or averages).

Production Note: A total of 1,843 Ferraris (330 of them 365 GT/GTB) were built in 1972.

ENGINE DATA: BASE V-6 (246 Dino GT): 65-degree, dual-overhead-cam "vee" type six-cylinder. Cast iron block and light alloy heads. **Displacement:** 148 cu. in. (2418 cc). **Bore & Stroke:** 3.64 x 2.36 in. (92.5 x 60 mm). **Compression Ratio:** 9.0:1. **Brake Horsepower:** 195 lbs.-ft. (DIN) at 5500 rpm. Four main bearings. Three Weber 40 DCNF 13 two-barrel carburetors.

BASE V-12 (365 GTB/4, GTS/4): 60-degree, dual-overhead-cam, "vee" type 12-cylinder. Aluminum alloy block and heads. **Displacement:** 267.8 cu. in. (4390 cc). **Bore & Stroke:** 3.19 x 2.80 in. (81 x 71 mm). **Compression Ratio:** 8.8:1. **Brake Horsepower:** 352 (DIN) at 7500 rpm. **Torque:** 319 lbs.-ft. at 5000 rpm. Seven main bearings. Six Weber 40 DCN-20 twin-choke carburetors.

BASE V-12 (365 GT4 2 + 2, GTC/4): Same as 4390-cc V-12 above, except — **Brake Horsepower:** (GT4) 320 at 6200 and 320-340 DIN at 6200-6800 rpm. **Torque:** 312/319 lbs.-ft. at 4600 rpm. Seven main bearings. Six Weber twin-choke carburetors.

CHASSIS DATA: Wheelbase: (246 Dino GT) 92.1 in.; (365 GTB/4, GTS/4) 94.5 in.; (365 GT4) 106.3 in.; (365 GTC/4) 98.4 in. **Overall Length:** (246 Dino GT) 163.4 in.; (365 GT4) 174 in.; (365 GT4 2 + 2) 189.4 in.; (365 GTC/4) 179.9 in. **Height:** (246 Dino GT) 43.9 in.; (365 GTB/4) 49.8 in.; (365 GT4 2 + 2) 51.6 in.; (365 GTC/4) in. **Width:** (246 Dino GT) 66.9 in.; (365 GTB/4) 69.3 in.; (365 GT4 2 + 2) 70.7 in.; (365 GTC/4) 70.1 in. **Front Tread:** (246 Dino GT) 56.1 in.; (365 GTB/4) 56.7 in.; (365 GT4 2 + 2) 57.9 in.; (365 GTC/4) 57.9 in. **Rear Tread:** (246 Dino GT) 56.3 in.; (365 GTB/4) 56.1 in.; (365 GT4 2 + 2) 59.1 in.; (365 GTC/4) 57.9 in. **Standard Tires:** (246 Dino GT) 205x14; (365 GTB/4, GTS/4, GTC/4) 215/70x15; (365 GT4 2 + 2) 215/7OVR 15.

TECHNICAL: Layout: (Dino) mid-engine, rear-drive; (365 series) front-engine, rear-drive. **Transmission:** (Dino, 365 GTB/4, 365 GTS/4) five-speed manual in rear transaxle; (365 GT4) five-speed manual. **Standard Final Drive Ratio:** (365 GTB/4) 3.30:1. **Steering:** (Dino) rack and pinion; (365 GTB/4) worm and roller; (365 GTC/4) recirculating ball. **Suspension (front):** unequal-length A-arms with coil springs with anti-roll bar. **Suspension (rear):** (246 Dino, 365 GTB/4, 365 GTS/4) unequal-length A-arms with coil springs and anti-roll bar; (365 GT4 2+2) unequal-length A-arms with coil springs, anti-roll bar and hydraulic self-leveling. **Brakes:** front/rear disc. **Body Construction:** separate body on tubular steel frame.

PERFORMANCE: Top Speed: (246 Dino GT) 140-146 mph; (365 GTB/4) 174 mph; (365 GT4 2+2) about 145 mph; (365 GTC/4) 152-163 mph. **Acceleration (0-60 mph):** (246 Dino GT) 7.9-8.0 sec.; (365 GTB/4) 5.9 sec.; (365 GTC/4) 7.3 sec. **Acceleration (quarter-mile):** (246 Dino GT) 15.25-15.9 sec. (87-92 mph); (365 GTB/4) under 14 sec.; (365 GTC/4) 15.7 sec. (91 mph).

Manufacturer: Ferrari S.p.A. SEFAC, Maranello (Modena), Italy.

Distributor: Luigi Chinetti Motors, Greenwich, Connecticut.

HISTORY: Testing the Dino 246 coupe, *Road & Track* advised readers that its engine was "noisy in the extreme. The sounds are exciting to be sure: busy tappets, whining cam chains and transfer drive, a raucous exhaust system.... Even on a slow run to the corner drugstore, the Dino seems to be working, snarling, racing. The exhaust note at low speeds gives away its 6-cylinder configuration, but as the engine climbs into its effective rev range...it takes on the characteristic Ferrari sounds despite having only half the number of cylinders." *Motor Trend* called the Dino "pleasurably sensual."

1973 FERRARI

1973 Ferrari Dino 246 GT. (Coys of Kensington)

DINO 246 GT/GTS — V-6 — This would be the final year for the V-6 Dino, which was replaced by the 308 with V-8 power.

DINO 308 GT4 — V-8 — Introduced at the autumn 1973 Paris Salon, the next Dino was Ferrari's first V-8 powered road machine and the first four-seater with a mid-engine layout. It would be produced until the end of the decade. The twin-cam, 2927-cc Ferrari-built V-8 engine with four Weber carburetors initally produced 205 horsepower, though later announcements indicated as much as 240 bhp (255 bhp in European trim). A similar engine would soon go into the Type 308 (and later 328) models. A toothed-belt cam drive replaced the usual chain arrangement.

Instead of the customary Pininfarina design, this Dino came from the pens of Bertone, and bore little resemblance to its 246 Dino predecessor. In fact, the 2+2 coupe body was rather plain and unmemorable. Hidden headlamps were installed, with amber rectangular parking lights inset in the black bumper. Air intakes stood aft of tapered rear quarter windows. A horizontal bodyside trim strip could separate two-tone paint jobs, and the "flying buttress" roofline gave this Dino a semi-fastback look. Wheelbase was 100.4 inches, and the 308 GT4 could top 150 mph (at least in European form). As with the two prior Dinos, no Ferrari emblems were evident (until after 1975, that is, when the familiar "prancing horse" went on the nose, wheel hubs, and steering wheel).

TYPE 365 GTB/4, GTS/4 "DAYTONA" — V-12 — Production of the popular "Daytona" would continue into 1974; see previous listings for additional details.

365 GT4 2+2 — V-12 — Production of the 4390-cc four-seater continued into 1975; see previous listings for additional details.

Note: Some American directories for 1973 continued to list the 365 GTC/4 coupe, priced at $26,800; see previous listing for details.

I.D. DATA: Not available.

Model	Body Type & Seating	Engine Type/CID	P.O.E. Price	Weight (lbs.)	Prod. Total
246 DINO					
GT	2-dr Coupe-2P	V6/148	13900	2380	Note 1
GTS	2-dr Targa Cpe-2P	V6/148	14500	2426	Note 2
DINO 308 GT4					
308 GT4	2-dr Coupe-2+2P	V8/179	N/A	2930	N/A
365 GTB/4 "DAYTONA"					
365 GTB/4	2-dr Coupe-2P	V12/268	23940	3600	Note 3
365 GTS/4	2-dr Conv Cpe-2P	V12/268	25810	N/A	Note 4
365 GT4 2+2					
365 GT4	2-dr Coupe-2+2P	V12/268	N/A	4000	Note 5

Note 1: About 2,800 Type 246 Dino GT coupes were produced from 1969-73.

Note 2: About 1,200 Type 246 Dino GTS Targa coupes were produced from 1972-73.

Note 3: About 1,285 Type 365 GTB/4 coupes were produced from 1968-74.

Note 4: About 127 Type 365 GTS/4 convertibles were produced from 1969-74.

Note 5: A total of 470 Type 365 GT4 2+2 coupes (sometimes called sedans) were produced from 1972-75.

Weight Note: Figures shown are approximate (or averages).

Production Note: A total of 1,772 Ferraris (including 1,164 Dinos and 584 series 365) were built in 1973.

ENGINE DATA: BASE V-6 (246 Dino GT): 65-degree, dual-overhead-cam "vee" type six-cylinder. Cast iron block and light alloy heads. **Displacement:** 148 cu. in. (2418 cc). **Bore & Stroke:** 3.64 x 2.36 in. (92.5 x 60 mm). **Compression Ratio:** 9.0:1. **Brake Horsepower:** 195 (DIN) at 7600 rpm. **Torque:** 167 lbs.-ft. at 5500 rpm. Four main bearings. Three Weber 40 DCNF 13 carburetors.

BASE V-8 (Dino 308 GT4): 90-degree, dual-overhead-cam "vee" type eight-cylinder. Light alloy block and heads. **Displacement:** 179 cu. in. (2927 cc). **Bore & Stroke:** 3.19 x 2.80 in. (81 x 71 mm). **Compression Ratio:** 8.8:1. **Brake Horsepower:** 205 at 6600 rpm (possibly as high as 240 bhp available). **Torque:** 209 lbs.-ft. at 5000 rpm. Five main bearings. Four Weber 40 DCNF carburetors.

Note: European Dino 308 GT4 V-8 produced 255 bhp.

BASE V-12 (365 GTB/4, GTS/4): 60-degree, dual-overhead-cam "vee" type 12-cylinder. Aluminum alloy block and heads. **Displacement:** 267.8 cu. in. (4390 cc). **Bore & Stroke:** 3.19 x 2.80 in. (81 x 71 mm). **Compression Ratio:** 8.8:1. **Brake Horsepower:** 352 (DIN) at 7500 rpm. **Torque:** 319 lbs.-ft. DIN (365 SAE) at 5000 rpm. Seven main bearings. Six Weber twin-choke carburetors.

BASE V-12 (365 GT4 2+2): 60-degree, dual-overhead-cam "vee" type 12-cylinder. Aluminum alloy block and heads. **Displacement:** 267.8 cu. in. (4390 cc). **Bore & Stroke:** 3.19 x 2.80 in. (81 x 71 mm). **Compression Ratio:** 8.8:1. **Brake Horsepower:** 320 at 6200 rpm. **Torque:** 319 lbs.-ft. at 4600 rpm. Seven main bearings. Six Weber twin-choke carburetors.

CHASSIS DATA: Wheelbase: (246 Dino GT) 92.1 in.; (Dino 308 GT4) 100.4 in.; (365 GTB/4, GTS/4) 94.5 in.; (365 GT4) 106.3 in. **Overall Length:** (246 Dino GT) 165 in.; (Dino 308 GT4) 174 in.; (365 GT4 2+2) 189.4 in. **Height:** (246 Dino GT) 43.9 in.; (Dino 308 GT4) 46.5 in.; (365 GTB/4) 49.8 in.; (365 GT4 2+2) 51.6 in. **Width:** (246 Dino GT) 66.9 in.; (Dino 308 GT4) 70.9 in.; (365 GTB/4) 69.3 in.; (365 GT4 2+2) 70.7 in. **Front Tread:** (246 Dino GT) 56.1 in.; (Dino 308 GT4) 57.9 in.; (365 GTB/4) 56.7 in.; (365 GT4 2+2) 57.9 in. **Rear Tread:** (246 Dino GT) 56.3 in.; (Dino 308 GT4) 57.5 in.; (365 GTB/4) 56.1 in.; (365 GT4 2+2) 59.1 in. **Standard Tires:** (246 Dino GT) 205/70VR14; (Dino 308 GT4) 205/70VR14; (365 GTB/4, GTS/4) 215/70x15; (365 GT4 2+2) 215/70VR15.

TECHNICAL: Layout: (Dino) mid-engine, rear-drive; (365 series) front-engine, rear-drive. **Transmission:** (Dino, 365 GTB/4, 365 GTS/4) five-speed manual in rear transaxle; (365 GT4) five-speed manual. **Steering:** (Dino) rack and pinion; (365 GTB/4) worm and roller; (365 GT4 2+2) recirculating ball. **Suspension (front):** unequal-length A-arms with coil springs with anti-roll bar. **Suspension (rear):** (246/308 Dino, 365 GTB/4, 365 GTS/4) unequal-length A-arms with coil springs and anti-roll bar; (365 GT4 2+2) unequal-length A-arms with coil springs, anti-roll bar and hydraulic self-leveling. **Brakes:** front/rear disc. **Body Construction:** separate body on tubular steel frame.

PERFORMANCE: Top Speed: (246 Dino GT) 140 mph; (European Dino 308 GT4) 150+ mph; (365 GTB/4) 170+ mph; (365 GT4 2+2) 145-152 mph. **Acceleration (0-60 mph):** (246 Dino GT) 8.0 sec.; (European Dino 308 GT4) 6.4 sec.; (365 GTB/4) 5.9 sec.

Manufacturer: Ferrari S.p.A. SEFAC, Maranello (Modena), Italy.

Distributor: Luigi Chinetti Motors, Greenwich, Connecticut; Chinetti-Garthwaite Imports Inc., Rosemont, Pennsylvania; or Modern Classic Motors, Reno, Nevada.

1974 FERRARI

1974 Ferrari 365 GT4BB. (Coys of Kensington)

DINO 308 GT4 — V-8 — Introduced late in 1973, the replacement for the Dino 246 GT continued with little change; see previous listing for further details.

TYPE 365 GTB/4, 365 GTS/4 "DAYTONA" — V-12 — This would be the final year of production for the popular "Daytona" duo.

TYPE 365 GT4 2+2 — V-12 — Introduced in 1972, the four-seat 365-series coupe continued with little change, into 1975.

TYPE 365 GT4 BB — FLAT-12 — The 'BB' designation of Ferrari's new model of 1974 stood for "berlinetta boxer," to describe not only the coupe body but its horizontally-opposed (flat) 12-cylinder engine, whose pistons might be envisioned as prizefighters on opposite sides, jabbing and backing away from each other. Replacing the front-engine "Daytona" series, the BB carried its new 4390-cc twin-cam engine behind the cockpit, ahead of rear axle. The mid-engine Twelve, with toothed-belt camshaft drive and four triple-barrel Weber carburetors, produced 344 horsepower (DIN) and 302 pound-feet of torque. As usual, the body wore steel body panels but carried an aluminum hood, doors and engine cover. New fiberglass lower panels were painted in matte black. Wheelbase was 98.4 inches. The entire front end hinged forward as a unit, as did the rear-hinged rear section. The long, tapered-forward nose held the radiator, spare tire, and minimal luggage. Hidden headlamps were used. Slight bulges were evident over the front wheels, and the profile displayed a "flying buttress" roofline. Three taillamps stood on each side of the back panel. Pininfarina was responsible for the styling, while Scaglietti built the bodies. The multi-tube chassis used square and rectangular sections instead of round and oval. Three axle ratios were available: 3.90:1, 3.75:1, and 3.46:1.

With an achieved top speed of 175 mph, *Road & Track* in 1975 called the 365 GT4 BB "the fastest road car we've ever tested." As for acceleration, the coupe could hit sixty in 7.2 seconds and run the quarter-mile in 15.5 seconds, reaching 102.5 mph, though noting that the "Boxer is surprisingly heavy." They further explained that "1st gear is very tall and the clutch in our test car slipped badly," so test times might have been swifter yet. Before long, this "boxer" would lead to the 512 BB/BBi.

Note: Some American directories continued to list the Dino 246 GT coupe and GTS convertible, selling for $14,990 and $15,795 respectively, though production halted after 1973; and the 365 GTC coupe at $28,220, which also had ceased production.

I.D. DATA: Not available.

Model	Body Type & Seating	Engine Type/CID	P.O.E. Price	Weight (lbs.)	Prod. Total
DINO 308 GT4					
308 GT4	2-dr Coupe-2 + 2P	V8/179	N/A	2930	N/A
365 GTB/4 "DAYTONA"					
365 GTB/4	2-dr Coupe-2P	V12/268	N/A	3600	Note 1
365 GTS/4	2-dr Conv Cpe-2P	V12/268	N/A	N/A	Note 2
365 GT4 2 + 2					
365 GT4	2-dr Coupe-2 + 2P	V12/268	N/A	4000	Note 3
365 GT4 BB					
365 GT4 BB	2-dr Coupe-2P	H12/268	N/A	3420	Note 4

Note 1: About 1,285 Type 365 GTB/4 coupes were produced from 1968-74.
Note 2: About 127 Type 365 GTS/4 convertibles were produced from 1969-74.
Note 3: A total of 470 Type 365 GT4 2 + 2 coupes (sometimes called sedans) were produced from 1972-75.
Note 4: About 400 Type 365 GT4 BB coupes were produced, from 1974-76.
Weight Note: Figures shown are approximate (or averages).
Production Note: A total of 1,436 Ferraris (316 Dinos, 764 Dino 308s, 127 365 GT/GT4, and 229 BB) were built in 1974.

ENGINE DATA: BASE V-8 (Dino 308 GT4): 90-degree, dual-overhead-cam "vee" type eight-cylinder. Light alloy block and heads. Displacement: 179 cu. in. (2927 cc). Bore & Stroke: 3.19 x 2.80 in. (81 x 71 mm). Compression Ratio: 8.8:1. Brake Horsepower: 205 at 6600 rpm (possibly as high as 240 bhp available). Torque: 209 lbs.-ft. at 5000 rpm. Five main bearings. Four Weber 40 DCNF carburetors.
Note: European 308 GT4 V-8 produced 255 bhp.
BASE V-12 (365 GTB/4, GTS/4): 60-degree, dual-overhead-cam "vee" type 12-cylinder. Aluminum alloy block and heads. Displacement: 267.8 cu. in. (4390 cc). Bore & Stroke: 3.19 x 2.80 in. (81 x 71 mm). Compression Ratio: 8.8:1. Brake Horsepower: 352 (DIN) at 7500 rpm. Torque: 319 lbs.-ft. DIN (365 SAE) at 5000 rpm. Seven main bearings. Six Weber 40 DCN-20 twin-choke carburetors.
BASE V-12 (365 GT4 2 + 2): Same as 4390-cc V-12 engine above, except — Brake Horsepower: 320 at 6200 rpm. Torque: 319 lbs.-ft. at 4600 rpm. Six Weber twin-choke carburetors.
BASE FLAT 12 (365 GT4 BB): Horizontally-opposed, dual-overhead-cam 12-cylinder. Aluminum alloy block and heads. Displacement: 267.8 cu. in. (4390 cc). Bore & Stroke: 3.19 x 2.80 in. (81 x 71 mm). Compression Ratio: 8.8:1. Brake Horsepower: 344 (DIN) at 7000 rpm. Torque: 302 lbs.-ft. at 3900 rpm. Seven main bearings. Four Weber triple-barrel carburetors.

CHASSIS DATA: Wheelbase: (Dino 308 GT4) 100.4 in.; (365 GTB/4, GTS/4) 94.5 in.; (365 GT4 2 + 2) 106.3 in.; (365 GT4 BB) 98.4 in. Overall Length: (Dino 308 GT4) 170.1 in.; (365 GTB/4) 174 in.; (365 GT4 2 + 2) 189.4 in.; (365 GT4 BB) 171.6 in. Height: (Dino 308 GT4) 46.5 in.; (365 GTB/4) 49.8 in.; (365 GT4 2 + 2) 51.6 in.; (365 GT4 BB) 44.1 in. Width: (Dino 308 GT4) 70.9 in.; (365 GTB/4) 69.3 in.; (365 GT4 2 + 2) 70.7 in.; (365 GT4 BB) 70.9 in. Front Tread: (Dino 308 GT4) 57.9 in.; (365 GTB/4) 56.7 in.; (365 GT4 2 + 2) 59.1 in.; (365 GT4 BB) 59.1 in. Rear Tread: (Dino 308 GT4) 57.9 in.; (365 GTB/4) 57.5 in.; (365 GT4 2 + 2) 57.9 in.; (365 GT4 BB) 59.8 in. Standard Tires: (Dino 308 GT4) 205/70VR14; (365 GTB/4, GTS/4) 215/70VR15; (365 GT4 2 + 2) 215/70VR15; (365 GT4 BB) 215/70VR15.

TECHNICAL: Layout: (Dino, 365 GT4 BB) mid-engine, rear-drive; (others) front-engine, rear-drive. Transmission: (Dino, 365 GT4 BB, 365 GTB/4, 365 GTS/4) five-speed manual in rear transaxle; (365 GT4 2 + 2) five-speed manual. Steering: (Dino, BB) rack and pinion; (365 GTB/4) worm and roller; (365 GT4 2 + 2) recirculating ball. Suspension (front): unequal-length A-arms with coil springs and anti-roll bar. Suspension (rear): (308 Dino, 365 GTB/4, 365 GTS/4) unequal-length A-arms with coil springs and anti-roll bar; (365 GT4 BB) unequal-length A-arms with twin coil springs and anti-roll bar; (365 GT4 2 + 2) unequal-length A-arms with coil springs, anti-roll bar and hydraulic self-leveling. Brakes: front/rear disc. Body Construction: separate body on tubular steel frame.

PERFORMANCE: Top Speed: (European Dino 308 GT4) 150-155 mph; (365 GTB/4) 170 + mph; (365 GT4 2 + 2) about 145 mph; (365 GT4 BB) 175-188 mph. Acceleration (0-60 mph): (European Dino 308 GT4) 6.4 sec.; (365 GTB/4) 5.9 sec.; (365 GT4 BB) 7.2 sec. Acceleration (quarter-mile): (365 GT4 BB) 15.5 sec. (102.5 mph).
Manufacturer: Ferrari S.p.A. SEFAC, Maranello (Modena), Italy.
Distributor: Luigi Chinetti Motors, Greenwich, Connecticut.
HISTORY: The new 'BB' wasn't the first horizontally-opposed powerplant to come from Ferrari. A dozen 1.5-liter flat engines had been built in 1964 for Formula One purposes. The term "boxer" had been used earlier when referring to Volkswagen and Porsche engines, and other versions used in Grand Prix and sports/racing vehicles. Ferrari's first roadgoing prototype, however, appeared at the Turin show in 1971. Production of the 365 GT4 BB began late in 1973, as a '74 model.
Road & Track in 1974 called the 308 GT4 "a worthy addition to the long line of great GT cars from Ferrari." The new 365 GT4 BB "boxer" was described in the magazine as a "dying breed."

1975 FERRARI

DINO 308 GT4 — V-8 — The Bertone-bodied eight-cylinder Dino continued with little change; see 1973-74 listings for additional details.
TYPE 308 GTB — V-8 — A new Ferrari debuted at the Paris show in autumn 1975, to replace the Dino 246 (which had gone out of production by 1974). Bodies were built by Scaglietti, from a Pininfarina design. Rather than steel or aluminum, these early 308 GTB bodies were made of fiberglass; though construction would soon change to steel. A wide eggcrate grille stood below the bumper, with Ferrari's prancing horse insignia in its center. Large amber-over-clear park/signal lights went alongside the grille. Hidden headlamps and flared wheel-arches were used, with a "flying buttress" fastback roofline and a low, squared-off nose. Most distinctive of the body's features, though, were the large concave air-intake scoops that ran back from the center of each door, tapering outward as they entered the quarter-panel inlet opening. Four large round taillamps (two red, two amber) went in the Kamm-style tail. Mechanical details were similar to the 246 and 308 Dinos, with unequal-length A-arms and coil springs forming the suspension at each wheel. Wheelbase was 92.1 inches, as on the Dino 246. Power came from a four-cam 2927-cc (179-cid) V-12 with four Weber carburetors, producing 240 horsepower via 8.8:1 compression and hooked to a five-speed all-synchro transaxle.

TYPE 365 GT4 BB — FLAT-12 — Production of the "boxer" coupe with horizontally-opposed engine continued with little change.

I.D. DATA: Not available.

Model	Body Type & Seating	Engine Type/CID	P.O.E. Price	Weight (lbs.)	Prod. Total
DINO 308 GT4					
308 GT4	2-dr Coupe-2 + 2P	V8/179	22550	2930	N/A
308 GTB					
308 GTB	2-dr Coupe-2P	V8/179	28500	3085	Note 1
365 GT4 BB					
365 GTB BB	2-dr Coupe-2P	H12/268	N/A	3420	Note 2

Note 1: About 3,665 Type 308 GTB (and 208 GTB) coupes were produced from 1975-80.
Note 2: About 400 Type 365 GT4 BB coupes were produced, from 1974-76.
Weight Note: Figures shown are approximate (or averages).
Production Note: A total of 1,337 Ferraris (1,211 of them 308s) were built in 1975.

ENGINE DATA: BASE V-8 (Dino 308 GT4, 308 GTB): 90-degree, dual-overhead-cam "vee" type eight-cylinder. Light alloy block and heads. Displacement: 178.6 cu. in. (2927 cc). Bore & Stroke: 3.19 x 2.79 in. (81 x 71 mm). Compression Ratio: 8.8:1. Brake Horsepower: 240 at 6600 rpm. Torque: 195 lbs.-ft. at 5000 rpm. Five main bearings. Four Weber 40 DCNF two-barrel carburetors.
BASE FLAT-12 (365 GT4 BB): Horizontally-opposed, dual-overhead-cam 12-cylinder. Aluminum alloy block and heads. Displacement: 267.8 cu. in. (4390 cc). Bore & Stroke: 3.19 x 2.80 in. (81 x 71 mm). Compression Ratio: 8.8:1. Brake Horsepower: 344 (DIN) at 7000 rpm. Torque: 302 lbs.-ft. at 3900 rpm. Seven main bearings. Four Weber triple-barrel carburetors.

CHASSIS DATA: Wheelbase: (Dino 308 GT4) 100.4 in.; (308 GTB) 92.1 in.; (365 GT4 BB) 98.4 in. Overall Length: (Dino 308 GT4) 176.7 in.; (308 GTB) 166.5 in.; (365 GT4 BB) 171.6 in. Height: (Dino 308 GT4) 47.6 in.; (308 GTB) 44.1 in.; (365 GT4 BB) 44.1 in. Width: (Dino 308 GT4) 71 in.; (308 GTB) 67.75 in.; (365 GT4 BB) 70.9 in. Front Tread: (Dino 308 GT4) 57.9 in.; (308 GTB) 57.9 in.; (365 GT4 BB) 57.9 in. Rear Tread: (Dino 308 GT4) 57.9 in.; (308 GTB) 57.5 in.; (365 GT4 BB) 59.8 in. Standard Tires: (Dino 308 GT4) 205/70VR14; (308 GTB) 205/70VR14 Michelin XWX; (365 GT4 BB) 215/70VR15.

TECHNICAL: Layout: mid-engine, rear-drive. Transmission: five-speed manual in rear transaxle. 308 GTB gear ratios: (1st) 3.58:1; (2nd) 2.37:1; (3rd) 1.69:1; (4th) 1.24:1; (5th) 0.95:1. Standard Final Drive Ratio: (308 GTB) 3.71:1 or 4.06:1. Steering: rack and pinion. Suspension (front): unequal-length A-arms with coil springs and anti-roll bar. Suspension (rear): (Dino 308, 308 GTB) unequal-length A-arms with coil springs and anti-roll bar; (365 GT4 BB) unequal-length A-arms with twin coil springs and anti-roll bar. Brakes: front/rear disc. Body Construction: separate body (fiberglass on 308 GTB) on tubular steel frame.

PERFORMANCE: Top Speed: (European Dino 308 GT4) 150 + mph; (308 GTB) up to 150 mph estimated; (365 GT4 BB) 175 mph. Acceleration (0-60 mph): (European Dino 308 GT4) 6.4 sec.; (308 GTB) 8.2 sec.; (365 GT4 BB) 7.2 sec. Acceleration (quarter-mile): (308 GTB) 17.0 sec. (90.8 mph); (365 GT4 BB) 15.5 sec. (102.5 mph).
ADDITIONAL MODELS: A detuned variant of the Dino 308 GT4 was produced for the home market starting in 1975, as the Type 208 GTB, powered by a 1991-cc engine that produced 170 horsepower.
Manufacturer: Ferrari S.p.A. SEFAC, Maranello (Modena), Italy.
Distributor: Chinetti-Garthwaite Imports, Paoli, Pennsylvania; and Modern Classic Motors, Reno, Nevada.
HISTORY: By this time, Ferrari had 40 dealers in the U.S.

1976-79 FERRARI

1976 Ferrari 308 GTB Koenig Turbo. (Coys of Kensington)

DINO 308 GT4 — V-8 — Production of the last Dino model, with V-8 power, continued into 1979. Standard equipment on U.S. models included air conditioning, power windows, power antenna, leather steering wheel, limited-slip differential, rear defroster, and tinted glass.

TYPE 308 GTB/GTS — V-8 — At the 1977 Frankfurt show, a Targa-roofed Spider GTS joined the original closed coupe. Its removable roof section mounted above the cockpit, and could be stored behind the seats. Vertical louvers went on the rear quarter window area. After a brief flirtation with fiberglass on the first Type 308 models, Ferrari turned to steel for the remainder of the model run. Approximately 300 were to be built in 'glass, for sale in the U.S. Standard GTB equipment included air conditioning, power windows, power antenna, tinted glass, and a rear-window defroster.

1976 Ferrari 365 GTB Boxer coupe.

TYPE 365 GT4 BB — FLAT-12 — Introduced in 1974, the flat-engined "boxer" model ceased production in 1976, replaced by the 512 BB.

TYPE 400i — V-12 — Ferrari's four-seat replacement for the 365 GT4 2+2 debuted at the 1976 Paris show, with a three-speed Turbo Hydra-Matic transmission. With manual shift, it was called the 400i; with automatic, the 400i A. Engine stroke was increased to 78 mm, for displacement of 4823 cc (294 cubic inches), fed by Bosch fuel injection. Horsepower grew by 20, to 340 at 6500 rpm. Body changed included restyled taillamps, a modest front lip spoiler, and wheel lug nuts (replacing the former knock-off hubs). Front seats slid forward for access to the rear. A new four-speaker radio included a tape player. The 400i never was certified for sale in the U.S., though occasional examples crept in via the "grey market."

1978 Ferrari BB 512. (Coys of Kensington)

TYPE 512 BB — FLAT-12 — Ferrari's successor to the 365 GT4 BB entered production about two months before its actual debut at the October 1976 Paris show. Appearance was similar to the 365 GT4 BB, with the addition of a small front chin spoiler and NACA ducts (on lower bodysides ahead of back wheels). Four taillamps were installed, versus six on the 365 GT4 BB. The 4942-cc (302-cid) V-12 engine had an extra millimeter of bore and 7-mm greater stroke, producing up to 360 horsepower (DIN).

I.D. DATA: Ferrari's Vehicle Identification Number is embossed on a metal plate attached to steering column, and stamped in right frame member to rear of engine (under the hood). A prefix identifying the model is followed by a five-digit sequential production number.

Model	Body Type & Seating	Engine Type/CID	P.O.E. Price	Weight (lbs.)	Prod. Total
DINO 308 GT4					
308 GT4	2-dr Coupe-2+2P	V8/179	23875	2930	N/A
308 GTB/GTS					
308 GTB	2-dr Coupe-2P	V8/179	28580	3160	Note 1
308 GTS	2-dr Targa Cpe-2P	V8/179	N/A	3225	Note 1
365 GT4 BB					
365 GT4 BB	2-dr Coupe-2P	H12/268	N/A	3420	Note 2
400i					
400i	2-dr Coupe-2+2P	V12/294	N/A	N/A	N/A
512 BB					
512 BB	2-dr Coupe-2P	H12/302	85000	N/A	N/A

Note 1: About 3,665 Type 308 GTB/GTS (and 208 GTB) coupes were produced from 1975-80.
Note 2: About 400 Type 365 GT4 BB coupes were produced, from 1974-76.
Weight Note: Figures shown are approximate (or averages).
Price Note: Figures shown were valid in 1977, except for the 512 BB in 1978. In 1979, the Dino 308 GT4 sold for $35,652; the 308 GTB for $40,290; the 308 GTS for $36,010.
Production Note: A total of 1,427 Ferraris were built in 1976, followed by 1,798 in 1977, 1,939 in 1978, and 2,308 in 1979.

ENGINE DATA: BASE V-8 (Dino 308 GT4, 308 GTB/GTS): 90-degree, dual-overhead-cam "vee" type eight-cylinder. Light alloy block and heads. **Displacement:** 178.6 cu. in. (2927 cc). **Bore & Stroke:** 3.19 x 2.79 in. (81 x 71 mm). **Compression Ratio:** 8.8:1. **Brake Horsepower:** 240 at 6600 rpm (later, 205 bhp). **Torque:** 195 lbs.-ft. at 5000 rpm (later, 181 lbs.-ft.). Five main bearings. Four Weber 40 DCNF two-barrel carburetors.
BASE FLAT-12 (365 GT4 BB): Horizontally-opposed, dual-overhead-cam 12-cylinder. Aluminum alloy block and heads. **Displacement:** 267.8 cu. in. (4390 cc). **Bore & Stroke:** 3.19 x 2.80 in. (81 x 71 mm). **Compression Ratio:** 8.8:1. **Brake Horsepower:** 344 (DIN) at 7000 rpm. **Torque:** 302 lbs.-ft. at 3900 rpm. Seven main bearings. Four Weber triple-barrel carburetors.

BASE V-12 (400i): 60-degree, dual-overhead-cam "vee" type 12-cylinder. Aluminum alloy block and heads. **Displacement:** 294.2 cu. in. (4823 cc). **Bore & Stroke:** 3.19 x 3.07 in. (81 x 78 mm). **Compression Ratio:** 8.8:1. **Brake Horsepower:** 325-340 at 6000-6500 rpm. **Torque:** 347 lbs.-ft. at 3600 rpm. Seven main bearings. Bosch fuel injection.
BASE FLAT-12 (512 BB): Horizontally-opposed, dual-overhead-cam 12-cylinder. Aluminum alloy block and heads. **Displacement:** 302 cu. in. (4942 cc). **Bore & Stroke:** 3.23 x 3.07 in. (82 x 78 mm). **Compression Ratio:** 9.2:1. **Brake Horsepower:** 360 (DIN) at 6200 rpm. **Torque:** 333 lbs.-ft. at 4600 rpm. Seven main bearings. Four Weber triple-barrel carburetors.

CHASSIS DATA: Wheelbase: (Dino 308 GT4) 100.4 in.; (308 GTB/GTS) 92.1 in.; (365 GT4 BB) 98.4 in.; (400i) 106.3 in.; (512 BB) 98.4 in. **Overall Length:** (Dino 308 GT4) 176.7 in.; (308 GTB/GTS) 172.4 in.; (365 GT4 BB) 171.6 in.; (400i) 189.4 in.; (512 BB) 173.2 in. **Height:** (Dino 308 GT4) 47.6 in.; (308 GTB/GTS) 44.1 in.; (365 GT4 BB) 44.1 in.; (400i) 51.6 in.; (512 BB) 44.1 in. **Width:** (Dino 308 GT4) 70.5 in.; (308 GTB/GTS) 67.7 in.; (365 GT4 BB) 70.9 in.; (400i) 70.9 in.; (512 BB) 72 in. **Front Tread:** (Dino 308 GT4) 57.8 in.; (308 GTB/GTS) 57.9 in.; (365 GT4 BB) 59.1 in.; (400i) 57.9 in.; (512 BB) 59.1 in. **Rear Tread:** (Dino 308 GT4) 57.8 in.; (308 GTB/GTS) 57.9 in.; (365 GT4 BB) 59.8 in.; (400i) 59.1 in.; (512 BB) 61.5 in. **Standard Tires:** (Dino 308 GT4) 205/70VR14; (308 GTB/GTS) 205/70VR14; (365 GT4 BB) 215/70VR15; (400i) 215/70VR15; (512 BB) 215/70VR15 front, 225/70VR15 rear.

TECHNICAL: Layout: (Dino, 308 GTB/GTS, 365 GT4 BB, 512 BB) mid-engine, rear-drive; (400i) front-engine, rear-drive. **Transmission:** (Dino, 365 GT4 BB, 308 GTB/GTS, 512 BB) five-speed manual in rear transaxle; (400i) five-speed manual or three-speed automatic. **Standard Final Drive Ratio:** (308) 3.70:1. **Steering:** (308) rack and pinion; (400i) recirculating ball; (512) worm and roller. **Suspension (front):** unequal-length A-arms with coil springs and anti-roll bar. **Suspension (rear):** (308 Dino, 308 GTB/GTS) unequal-length A-arms with coil springs and anti-roll bar; (365 GT4 BB, 512 BB) unequal-length A-arms with twin coil springs and anti-roll bar; (400i) unequal-length A-arms with coil springs, anti-roll bar and hydraulic self-leveling. **Brakes:** front/rear disc. **Body Construction:** separate body on tubular steel frame. **Fuel Tank:** (308 GTB) 18.5 gallon.

MAJOR OPTIONS: Leather upholstery: Dino 308 GT4 ($640). Leather/velour upholstery: GT4 ($540). Metallic paint ($320). Special colors ($140). Front spoiler: GT4 ($200). 7.5-inch star wheels: GT4 ($650).
Note: Option prices shown above were valid in 1977.

PERFORMANCE: Top Speed: (European Dino 308 GT4) 150+ mph; (308 GTB) 147 mph claimed; (365 GT4 BB) 175 mph; (512 BB) 188 mph (est). **Acceleration (0-60 mph):** (European Dino 308 GT4) 6.4 sec.; (308 GTB) 8.2 sec.; (308 GTS) 7.3 sec.; (365 GT4 BB) 7.2 sec.; (512 BB) 5.5 sec. **Acceleration (quarter-mile):** (308 GTB) 14.6 sec. claimed; (365 GT4 BB) 15.5 sec. (102.5 mph); (512 BB) 14.2 sec. (103.5 mph).

PRODUCTION/SALES: Approximately 617 Ferraris were sold in the U.S. during 1978, and at least 656 in 1979.

Manufacturer: Ferrari S.p.A. SEFAC, Maranello (Modena), Italy.
Distributor: Chinetti-Garthwaite Imports, Paoli, Pennsylvania.

HISTORY: *Road & Track* called the 512 BB "the best all-round sports and GT car we've tested." Their test car had been privately "Federalized," since none were officially certified for sale in the U.S. "If you are fond of admiring stares," said *Car and Driver* in their 1976 Buyers Guide, "the Dino 308 GT4 coupe will suit you nicely."
   "There is no alternative," said Ferrari ads in 1977 Auto Show programs that featured the 308 GTS and its fiberglass body. "It's a forgiving car," they added, "so you don't have to be a racing driver to drive one." Readers were advised to consult their dealers to discuss "the Ferrari mystique."

1980 FERRARI

1980 Ferrari 308 GTSi. (Coys of Kensington)

MONDIAL 8 — V-8 — Debuting at the Geneva (Switzerland) auto show in March 1980, Ferrari's Mondial (which means "world") borrowed its name from that used on four-cylinder sports racers of the early 1950s. Replacing the Bertone-styled Dino 308 GT4, this new Mondial carried the same transverse four-cam mid-mounted 2927-cc (179-cid) engine, producing 205 horsepower. Pininfarina did the styling this time, giving the car a more modern look and a more posh feel. Wheelbase grew by four inches, to 104.2 inches. Front and rear tread widths also were larger. Upholstery was crafted in British Connolly leather, while the leather-rimmed steering wheel adjusted for reach and rake. Standard equipment included air conditioning, central door locking, remote-control mirrors, and a power antenna. A power sunroof soon became optional. Styling features included hidden headlamps, a rather short nose, and a long rear section--a combination that some observers thought lacking in proportion. Full-width grooves went across the hood area. A low horizontal-bar grille contained a prancing horse emblem in its center and wide amber-over-clear park/signal lights alongside. Grilled air intakes stood to the rear of the doors. At the rear were round taillamps.

TYPE 308 GTB/GTS — V-8 — This would be the final year for the carbureted-engine version of the 308 solid-top coupe and Targa coupe, which continued with little change.

TYPE 400i — V-12 — Production of Ferrari's four-seater, not certified for U.S. sale, continued with little change.

TYPE 512 BB — FLAT-12 — Production of the 4942-cc "boxer" engine coupe continued with little change; see previous listings for further details.

Note: Although production of the Dino 308 GT4 had ceased, it was still listed in some U.S. directories in 1980-81 (including 1980 Auto Show advertisements), selling for $39,998.

I.D. DATA: Ferrari's Vehicle Identification Number is embossed on a metal plate attached to steering column, and stamped in right frame member to rear of engine (under the hood). A prefix identifying the model is followed by a five-digit sequential production number.

Model	Body Type & Seating	Engine Type/CID	P.O.E. Price	Weight (lbs.)	Prod. Total
MONDIAL 8					
Mondial 8	2-dr Coupe-2 + 2P	V8/179	N/A	3400	Note 1
308 GTB/GTS					
308 GTB	2-dr Coupe-2P	V8/179	40576	3160	Note 2
308 GTS	2-dr Targa Cpe-2P	V8/179	44912	3225	Note 2
400i					
400i	2-dr Coupe-2 + 2P	V12/294	N/A	N/A	N/A
512 BB					
512 BB	2-dr Coupe-2P	H12/302	N/A	N/A	N/A

Note 1: About 2,500 Mondials were produced from 1980-85.
Note 2: About 3,665 Type 308 GTB/GTS (and 208 GTB) coupes were produced from 1975-80.
Production Note: Approximately 2,381 Ferraris were built in 1980 (455 Type 400/512, and 1,926 Type 308).

ENGINE DATA: BASE V-8 (Mondial, 308 GTB/GTS): 90-degree, dual-overhead-cam, "vee" type eight-cylinder. Light alloy block and heads. **Displacement:** 178.6 cu. in. (2927 cc). **Bore & Stroke:** 3.19 x 2.795 in. (81 x 71 mm). **Compression Ratio:** 8.8:1. **Brake Horsepower:** 205 at 6600 rpm. **Torque:** 181 lbs.-ft. at 5000 rpm. Five main bearings. Four Weber two-barrel carburetors.

BASE V-12 (400i): 60-degree, dual-overhead-cam "vee" type 12-cylinder. Aluminum alloy block and heads. **Displacement:** 294.2 cu. in. (4823 cc). **Bore & Stroke:** 3.19 x 3.07 in. (81 x 78 mm). **Compression Ratio:** 8.8:1. **Brake Horsepower:** 325-340 at 6500 rpm. **Torque:** 347 lbs.-ft. at 3600 rpm. Seven main bearings. Bosch fuel injection.

BASE FLAT-12 (512 BB): Horizontally-opposed, dual-overhead-cam 12-cylinder. Aluminum alloy block and heads. **Displacement:** 302 cu. in. (4942 cc). **Bore & Stroke:** 3.23 x 3.07 in. (82 x 78 mm). **Compression Ratio:** 9.2:1. **Brake Horsepower:** 360 (DIN) at 6200 rpm. Torque: 333 lbs.-ft. at 4600 rpm. Seven main bearings. Four Weber triple-barrel carburetors.

CHASSIS DATA: Wheelbase: (Mondial) 104.2 in.; (308 GTB/GTS) 92.1 in.; (400i) 106.3 in.; (512 BB) 98.4 in. **Overall Length:** (Mondial) 182.7 in.; (308 GTB/GTS) 172.4 in.; (400i) 189.4 in.; (512 BB) 173.2 in. **Height:** (Mondial) 49.6 in.; (308 GTB/GTS) 44.1 in.; (400i) 51.6 in.; (512 BB) 44.1 in. **Width:** (Mondial) 70.5 in.; (308 GTB/GTS) 67.7 in.; (400i) 70.9 in.; (512 BB) 72 in. **Front Tread:** (Mondial) 58.9 in.; (308 GTB/GTS) 57.9 in.; (400i) 57.9 in.; (512 BB) 59.1 in. **Rear Tread:** (Mondial) 59.8 in.; (308 GTB/GTS) 57.9 in.; (400i) 59.1 in.; (512 BB) 61.4 in. **Standard Tires:** (Mondial) 240/55VR390; (308 GTB/GTS) 205/70VR14; (400i) 215/70VR15; (512 BB) 215/70VR15 front, 225/70VR15 rear.

TECHNICAL: Layout: (Mondial, 208 GTB/GTS, 512 BB) mid-engine, rear-drive; (400i) front-engine, rear-drive. **Transmission:** (Mondial, 308 GTB/GTS, 512 BB) five-speed manual in rear transaxle; (400i) five-speed manual or three-speed automatic. Type 308 gear ratios: (1st) 3.23:1; (2nd) 2.10:1; (3rd) 1.52:1; (4th) 1.12:1; (5th) 0.86:1; (rev) 2.92:1. **Steering:** (Mondial/308) rack and pinion; (512) worm and roller. **Suspension (front):** unequal-length A-arms with coil springs and anti-roll bar. **Suspension (rear):** (Mondial, 308 GTB/GTS) unequal-length A-arms with coil springs and anti-roll bar; (512 BB) unequal-length A-arms with twin coil springs and anti-roll bar; (400i) unequal-length A-arms with coil springs, anti-roll bar and hydraulic self-leveling. **Brakes:** front/rear disc. **Body Construction:** separate body on tubular steel frame. **Fuel Tank:** (308 GTB/GTS) 18.5 gal.

PERFORMANCE: Top Speed: (Mondial) near 150 mph; (308 GTB) 147 mph claimed; (512 BB) 188 mph (est). **Acceleration (0-60 mph):** (308 GTB) 8.2 sec.; (308 GTS) 7.3 sec.; (512 BB) 5.5 sec. **Acceleration (quarter-mile):** (308 GTB) 14.6 sec. claimed; (512 BB) 14.2 sec. (103.5 mph).

PRODUCTION/SALES: Approximately 779 Ferraris were sold in the U.S. during 1980.
Manufacturer: Ferrari S.p.A. SEFAC, Maranello (Modena), Italy.
Distributor: Ferrari North America (Division of Fiat Motors of North America Inc.), Montvale, New Jersey.
HISTORY: "What can be conceived can be created" was the headline of Ferrari's ads in Auto Show programs for 1980, which spotlighted the 308 series. Sales of the new Mondial never reached impressive levels, partly due to the car's relatively tame (for Ferrari) appearance.

1981 FERRARI

MONDIAL 8 — V-8 — Bosch K-Jetronic fuel injection replaced the former quarter of carburetors on the V-8 Mondial, introduced in 1980. Horsepower and torque were unchanged.

TYPE 308i GTB/GTS — V-8 — Like the Mondial, the 308 series switched from carburetion to Bosch K-Jetronic fuel injection, adding the letter 'i' to its nomenclature.

TYPE 400i — V-12 — Production of the "family" Ferrari continued with little change.

TYPE 512 BB/BBi — FLAT-12 — Late in 1981, the "boxer" engine switched from carburetion to Bosch K-Jetronic fuel injection. Horsepower dropped to 340 (DIN), torque to 333 pound-feet.

I.D. DATA: Ferrari's 17-symbol Vehicle Identification Number is embossed on a metal plate attached to steering column, and stamped in right frame member to rear of engine (under the hood). Symbol one ('Z') indicates Italy. The next two symbols identify the make ('FF' = Ferrari; 'FD' or 'DF' = Dino). Symbol four indicates engine type; symbol five is restraint system; symbols six and seven denote model ('01' = 308 GTBi; '02' = 308 GTSi; '03' = 308 GTB; '04' = 308 GTS). Next is a market designator ('A' = North America), followed by a check digit. Symbol 10 indicates model year ('B' = 1981). Symbol 11 ('0') is the assembly plant. Last comes the six-digit sequential production number.

Model	Body Type & Seating	Engine Type/CID	P.O.E. Price	Weight (lbs.)	Prod. Total
MONDIAL 8					
Mondial 8	2-dr Coupe-2 + 2P	V8/179	N/A	3400	Note 1
308i GTB/GTS					
308i GTB	2-dr Coupe-2P	V8/179	47440	3085	Note 2
308i GTS	2-dr Targa Cpe-2P	V8/179	52640	N/A	Note 2
400i					
400i	2-dr Coupe-2 + 2P	V12/294	N/A	N/A	Note 2
512 BB					
512 BB	2-dr Coupe-2P	H12/302	N/A	N/A	Note 2

Note 1: About 2,500 Mondials were produced from 1980-85.
Note 2: A total of 2,566 Ferraris (all models) were built in 1981.
Price Note: Figures shown were for 1980 models sold in 1981.

ENGINE DATA: BASE V-8 (Mondial, 308i GTB/GTS): 90-degree, dual-overhead-cam, "vee" type eight-cylinder. Light alloy block and heads. **Displacement:** 178.6 cu. in. (2927 cc). **Bore & Stroke:** 3.19 x 2.795 in. (81 x 71 mm). **Compression Ratio:** 8.8:1. **Brake Horsepower:** 205 at 6600 rpm. **Torque:** 181 lbs.-ft. at 5000 rpm. Five main bearings. Bosch K-Jetronic fuel injection.

BASE V-12 (400i): 60-degree, dual-overhead-cam "vee" type 12-cylinder. Aluminum alloy block and heads. **Displacement:** 294.2 cu. in. (4823 cc). **Bore & Stroke:** 3.19 x 3.07 in. (81 x 78 mm). **Compression Ratio:** 8.8:1. **Brake Horsepower:** 310-340 at 6500 rpm. **Torque:** 347 lbs.-ft. at 3600 rpm. Seven main bearings. Bosch fuel injection.

BASE FLAT-12 (512 BB): Horizontally-opposed, dual-overhead-cam 12-cylinder. Aluminum alloy block and heads. **Displacement:** 302 cu. in. (4942 cc). **Bore & Stroke:** 3.23 x 3.07 in. (82 x 78 mm). **Compression Ratio:** 9.2:1. **Brake Horsepower:** 360 (DIN) at 6200 rpm. **Torque:** 333 lbs.-ft. at 4600 rpm. Seven main bearings. Four Weber triple-barrel carburetors.

Note: Late in the year, the 512 BB switched to Bosch K-Jetronic fuel injection to become the 512 BBi. Horsepower dropped to 340 at 6000 rpm, torque to 333 at 4200 rpm.

CHASSIS DATA: Wheelbase: (Mondial) 104.2 in.; (308i GTB/GTS) 92.1 in.; (400i) 106.3 in.; (512 BB) 98.4 in. **Overall Length:** (Mondial) 182.7 in.; (308i GTB/GTS) 174.2 in.; (400i) 189.4 in.; (512 BB) 173.2 in. **Height:** (Mondial) 49.6 in.; (308i GTB/GTS) 44.1 in.; (400i) 51.6 in.; (512 BB) 44.1 in. **Width:** (Mondial) 70.5 in.; (308i GTB/GTS) 67.7 in.; (400i) 70.9 in.; (512 BB) 72 in. **Front Tread:** (Mondial) 58.9 in.; (308i GTB/GTS) 57.9 in.; (400i) 57.9 in.; (512 BB) 59.1 in. **Rear Tread:** (Mondial) 59.8 in.; (308i GTB/GTS) 57.8 in.; (400i) 59.1 in.; (512 BB) 61.9 in. **Standard Tires:** (Mondial) 240/55VR390; (308i GTB/GTS) 220/55VR390.

TECHNICAL: Layout: (Mondial, 308i GTB/GTS, 512 BB) mid-engine, rear-drive; (400i) front-engine, rear-drive. **Transmission:** (Mondial, 308i GTB/GTS, 512 BB) five-speed manual in rear transaxle; (400i) five-speed manual or three-speed automatic. **Standard Final Drive Ratio:** (308i) 3.71:1. **Steering:** (Mondial/308i) rack and pinion; (512) recirculating ball; (512) worm and roller. **Suspension (front):** unequal-length A-arms with coil springs and anti-roll bar. **Suspension (rear):** (Mondial, 308i GTB/GTS, 512 BB) unequal-length A-arms with coil springs and anti-roll bar; (512 BB) unequal-length A-arms with twin coil springs and anti-roll bar; (400i) unequal-length A-arms with coil springs, anti-roll bar and hydraulic self-leveling. **Brakes:** front/rear disc. **Body Construction:** separate body on tubular steel frame. **Fuel Tank:** (308i) 18.5 gal.

PERFORMANCE: Top Speed: (Mondial) 137 mph; (400i) 149 mph; (512 BB) 174-188 mph (est). **Acceleration (quarter-mile):** (308i GTB) 15.4 sec.; (512 BB) 14.2 sec. (103.5 mph).

PRODUCTION/SALES: Approximately 904 Ferraris were sold in the U.S. during 1981.
Manufacturer: Ferrari S.p.A. SEFAC, Maranello (Modena), Italy.
Distributor: Fiat Motors of North America Inc., Montvale, New Jersey.
HISTORY: The home-market Ferrari 208 added a KKK turbocharger at this time.

1982-83 FERRARI

1982 Ferrari Mondial 8 2 + 2 GT.

MONDIAL 8 — V-8 — Late in 1982, Ferrari's Mondial got a 32-valve Quattrovalvole engine (as did the 308), to replace the former 16-valve V-8. The new engine produced 230 horsepower. In 1983, a true cabriolet (not a Targa-top) became available, serving as the first open roadgoing Ferrari since the 1969 Daytona.

TYPE 308i GTB/GTS — Production of the 308 series continued into 1982, but was phased out by the Quattrovalvole version.

TYPE 308 GTB/GTS QUATTROVALVOLE — V-8 — Like the Mondial (above), the 308 series switched to a 32-valve version of the 179-cid (2927-cc) engine in 1982. At the same time, a small spoiler was added at the rear of the roof, and body-color bumpers (formerly matte black) were integrated into lower-body fairings. Transverse louvers also were inserted between the headlamps.

TYPE 400i — V-12 — Production of the four-seat Ferrari continued with little change, powered by the front-mounted 4823-cc V-12 engine.

TYPE 512 BBi — FLAT-12 — The fuel-injected version of the "boxer," introduced in 1981, continued with little change into 1985.

I.D. DATA: Ferrari's 17-symbol Vehicle Identification Number is embossed on a metal plate attached to steering column, and stamped in right frame member to rear of engine (under the hood). Symbol one ('Z') indicates Italy. The next two symbols identify the make ('FF' = Ferrari; 'FD' or 'DF' = Dino). Symbol four indicates engine type; symbol five is restraint system; symbols six and seven denote model ('01' = 308 GTBi; '02' = 308 GTSi; '03' = 308 GTB; '04' = 308 GTS; '08' = Mondial). Next is a market designator ('A' = North America), followed by a check digit. Symbol 10 indicates model year ('C' = 1982; 'D' = 1983). Symbol 11 ('0') is the assembly plant. Last comes the six-digit sequential production number.

Model	Body Type & Seating	Engine Type/CID	P.O.E. Price	Weight (lbs.)	Prod. Total
MONDIAL 8					
Mondial 8	2-dr Coupe-2+2P	V8/179	63939	3500	Note 1
Mondial 8	2-dr Cabr-2+2P	V8/179	N/A	N/A	Note 1
308i GTB/GTS					
308i GTB	2-dr Coupe-2P	V8/179	51930	3311	Note 2
308i GTS	2-dr Targa Cpe-2P	V8/179	58550	N/A	Note 2
308 QUATTROVALVOLE					
308 GTB	2-dr Coupe-2P	V8/179	N/A	N/A	Note 2
308 GTS	2-dr Targa Cpe-2P	V8/179	N/A	N/A	Note 2
400i					
400i	2-dr Coupe-2+2P	V12/294	N/A	3965	Note 2
512 BBi					
512 BBi	2-dr Coupe-2P	H12/302	N/A	3305	Note 2

Note 1: About 2,500 Mondials were produced from 1980-85.

Note 2: A total of 2,223 Ferraris (553 Type 400/512 and 1,670 Type 208/308/Mondial) were produced in 1982; followed by 2,366 (650 Type 400/512, 1,267 Type 208/308 and 449 Mondials) in 1983.

ENGINE DATA: BASE V-8 (early Mondial, 308i GTB/GTS): 90-degree, dual-overhead-cam, "vee" type eight-cylinder. Light alloy block and heads. **Displacement:** 178.6 cu. in. (2927 cc). **Bore & Stroke:** 3.19 x 2.80 in. (81 x 71 mm). **Compression Ratio:** 8.8:1. **Brake Horsepower:** 205 (SAE) at 6600 rpm. **Torque:** 181 (SAE) lbs.-ft. at 5000 rpm. Five main bearings. Bosch K-Jetronic fuel injection.

BASE V-8 (late Mondial, 308 GTB/GTS Quattrovalvole): 90-degree, dual-overhead-cam, "vee" type eight-cylinder (32-valve). Light alloy block and heads. **Displacement:** 178.6 cu. in. (2927 cc). **Bore & Stroke:** 3.19 x 2.80 in. (81 x 71 mm). **Compression Ratio:** 8.6:1. **Brake Horsepower:** 230 at 6800 rpm. **Torque:** 188 lbs.-ft. at 5500 rpm. Five main bearings. Bosch K-Jetronic fuel injection.

BASE V-12 (400i): 60-degree, dual-overhead-cam, "vee" type 12-cylinder. Aluminum alloy block and heads. **Displacement:** 294.2 cu. in. (4823 cc). **Bore & Stroke:** 3.19 x 3.07 in. (81 x 78 mm). **Compression Ratio:** 8.8:1. **Brake Horsepower:** 310 at 6400 rpm. **Torque:** 347 lbs.-ft. at 3600 rpm. Seven main bearings. Bosch K-Jetronic fuel injection.

BASE FLAT-12 (512 BBi): Horizontally-opposed, dual-overhead-cam 12-cylinder. Aluminum alloy block and heads. **Displacement:** 302 cu. in. (4942 cc). **Bore & Stroke:** 3.23 x 3.07 in. (82 x 78 mm). **Compression Ratio:** 9.2:1. **Brake Horsepower:** 340 (DIN) at 6000 rpm. **Torque:** 333 lbs.-ft. at 4200 rpm. Seven main bearings. Bosch K-Jetronic fuel injection.

CHASSIS DATA: Wheelbase: (Mondial) 104.3 in.; (308 GTB/GTS) 92.1 in.; (400i) 106.3 in.; (512 BBi) 98.4 in. **Overall Length:** (Mondial) 182.7 in.; (308 GTB/GTS) 174.2 in.; (400i) 189.4 in.; (512 BBi) 173.2 in. **Height:** (Mondial) 49.6 in.; (308 GTB) 44.1 in.; (400i) 51.6 in.; (512 BBi) 44.1 in. **Width:** (Mondial) 70.5 in.; (308 GTB/GTS) 67.7 in.; (400i) 70.9 in.; (512 BBi) 72 in. **Front Tread:** (Mondial) 58.9 in.; (308 GTB/GTS) 57.8 in.; (400i) 57.9 in.; (512 BBi) 59.1 in. **Rear Tread:** (Mondial) 59.8 in.; (308 GTB/GTS) 57.8 in.; (400i) 59.1 in.; (512 BBi) 61.9 in. **Standard Tires:** (Mondial) 240/55VR390; (308 GTB/GTS) 205/70VR14; (400i) 240/55VR415; (512 BBi) 180/TR415 front, 210/TR415 rear.

TECHNICAL: Layout: (Mondial, 308 GTB/GTS, 512 BBi) mid-engine, rear-drive; (400i) front-engine, rear-drive. **Transmission:** (Mondial, 308 GTB/GTS, 512 BBi) five-speed manual in rear transaxle; (400i) five-speed manual or three-speed automatic. **Standard Final Drive Ratio:** (Mondial/308i) 3.71:1; (400i w/manual) 4.30:1; (400i A) 3.25:1; (512) 3.21:1. **Steering:** (Mondial/308/512) rack and pinion; (400i) recirculating ball. **Suspension (front):** unequal-length A-arms with coil springs and anti-roll bar. **Suspension (rear):** (Mondial, 308 GTB/GTS) unequal-length A-arms with coil springs and anti-roll bar; (512 BBi) unequal-length A-arms with twin coil springs and anti-roll bar; (400i) unequal-length A-arms with coil springs, anti-roll bar and hydraulic self-leveling. **Brakes:** front/rear disc. **Body Construction:** separate body on tubular steel frame.

PERFORMANCE: Top Speed: (Mondial) 137 mph in U.S. trim; (308 GTB) 147 mph in U.S.; (400i w/manual) 152 mph; (400i A) 149 mph; (512 BBi) 174 mph. **Acceleration (quarter-mile):** (Mondial) 16.5 sec. in U.S. trim; (308) 15.4 sec. in U.S. trim; (400i w/manual) 15.8 sec.; (400i A) 16.4 sec.; (512 BBi) 14.2 sec. (103.5 mph).

PRODUCTION/SALES: Approximately 686 Ferraris were sold in the U.S. during 1982.

ADDITIONAL MODELS: A 208 GTB coupe and GTS Spider also remained in production for the home market, with 1991-cc V-8 rated 155 bhp (DIN).

Manufacturer: Ferrari S.p.A. SEFAC, Maranello (Modena), Italy.

Distributor: Fiat Motors of North America Inc., Montvale, New Jersey.

1984 FERRARI

MONDIAL QUATTROVALVOLE — V-8 — Mondial coupe and cabriolet production with the 32-valve engine continued with little change, into 1985; see previous listing for details. Standard equipment included leather upholstery, power windows, reclining bucket seats, metallic paint, heated rear window, tinted glass, central door locking, air conditioning, and light alloy wheels.

GTO — V-8 — A new limited-production sports-racing Ferrari debuted in 1984, and would remain in the lineup only into 1987, with just 200 built in all. Appearance was similar to the 308/328 coupe, down to the fender bulges and "flag-style" door mirrors, though the GTO rode a longer (96.5-inch) wheelbase. Large spoilers were installed at front and rear. Four driving lamps stood at the ends of the low blackout rectangular grille. The four-cam, 2855-cc (174-cid) V-8 engine, with four valves per cylinder and twin IHI intercooled turbochargers, was longitudinally mounted and delivered 400 horsepower. That engine actually had been developed for Lancia rally cars, as both Ferrari and Lancia were part of the Fiat empire at this time. A twin-disc clutch sent power to the five-speed manual gearbox in the rear transaxle, which used a 2.90:1 final drive ratio. Claimed top speed was 190 mph. A GTO could accelerate to 60 mph in five seconds, and run the quarter-mile in 14.1, hitting 113 mph. Like other Ferrari models of the 1970s and '80s, the GTO was never certified for sale in the U.S., though a handful arrived in American via the "gray market." A road equipment package included power windows, air conditioning, and an AM/FM radio with cassette player.

TYPE 308 QUATTROVALVOLE GTB/GTS — V-8 — Production of the 32-valve version of the 308 closed and Targa-roof coupes continued with little change. Standard equipment included leather upholstery, power windows, tinted glass, light alloy wheels, and a heated rear window.

TYPE 400i — V-12 — Production of Ferrari's four-seater continued with little change. As before, it was available with either manual or automatic transmission. Standard equipment included central door locking, power windows, and air conditioning.

TYPE 512 BBi — FLAT-12 — Ferrari's "boxer" coupe continued into 1985 without change, but soon would be eclipsed by the new Testarossa. Standard equipment included air conditioning, central door locking, and power windows.

I.D. DATA: Ferrari's 17-symbol Vehicle Identification Number is embossed on a metal plate attached to steering column. Symbol one ('Z') indicates Italy. The next two symbols identify the make ('FF' = Ferrari). Symbol four indicates engine type; symbol five is restraint system; symbols six and seven denote model ('08' = Mondial; '12' = 308 GTB Quattrovalvole; '13' = 308 GTS Quattrovalvole; '14' = Mondial Quattrovalvole; '15' = Mondial cabriolet). Next is a market designator ('A' = North America), followed by a check digit. Symbol 10 indicates model year ('E' = 1984). Symbol 11 ('0') is the assembly plant. Last comes the six-digit sequential production number.

Model	Body Type & Seating	Engine Type/CID	P.O.E. Price	Weight (lbs.)	Prod. Total
MONDIAL QUATTROVALVOLE					
Mondial	2-dr Coupe-2+2P	V8/179	59500	3285	Note 1
Mondial	2-dr Cabr-2+2P	V8/179	65000	3440	Note 1
GTO					
GTO	2-dr Coupe-2P	V8/174	83400	2555	Note 2
308 QUATTROVALVOLE					
GTB Berl	2-dr Coupe-2P	V8/179	54300	3190	N/A
GTS Spider	2-dr Targa Cpe-2P	V8/179	59500	3230	N/A
400i					
400i	2-dr Coupe-2+2P	V12/294	N/A	4009	N/A
512 BBi					
512 BBi	2-dr Coupe-2P	H12/302	N/A	3305	N/A

Note 1: About 2,500 Mondials were produced from 1980-85.

Note 2: A total of 200 GTOs were produced from 1984-87, for race homologation purposes; never certified for U.S. sale.

Price Note: U.S. prices included $1450 gas guzzler tax.

Production Note: A total of 2,841 Ferraris were produced in 1984, including 453 Type 400/512, 1,286 Type 208/308, 636 Mondials, 40 GTOs, and 26 early Testarossas.

ENGINE DATA: BASE V-8 (Mondial, 308 GTB/GTS Quattrovalvole): 90-degree, dual-overhead-cam "vee" type eight-cylinder (32-valve). Light alloy block and heads. **Displacement:** 178.6 cu. in. (2927 cc). **Bore & Stroke:** 3.19 x 2.79 in. (81 x 71 mm). **Compression Ratio:** 8.6:1. **Brake Horsepower:** 235 (SAE) at 6800 rpm. **Torque:** 188 lbs.-ft. at 5500 rpm. Five main bearings. Bosch K-Jetronic fuel injection with Lambda control.

Note: European Mondial/308 engine was rated 240 bhp (DIN) with 9.2:1 compression.

BASE V-8 (GTO): 90-degree, dual-overhead-cam "vee" type eight-cylinder. Twin IHI turbochargers with separate intercoolers. **Displacement:** 174 cu. in. (2855 cc). **Bore & Stroke:** 3.15 x 2.79 in. (80 x 71 mm). **Compression Ratio:** 7.6:1. **Brake Horsepower:** 394-400 at 7000 rpm. **Torque:** 366 lbs.-ft. at 3800 rpm. Weber-Marelli electronic fuel injection.

BASE V-12 (400i): 60-degree, dual-overhead-cam "vee" type 12-cylinder. Light alloy block and heads. **Displacement:** 294.2 cu. in. (4823 cc). **Bore & Stroke:** 3.19 x 3.07 in. (81 x 78 mm). **Compression Ratio:** 8.8:1. **Brake Horsepower:** 310-315 at 6400 rpm. **Torque:** 304 lbs.-ft. at 4200 rpm. Seven main bearings. Bosch K-Jetronic fuel injection.

BASE FLAT-12 (512 BBi): Horizontally-opposed, dual-overhead-cam 12-cylinder. Light alloy block and heads. **Displacement:** 302 cu. in. (4942 cc). **Bore & Stroke:** 3.23 x 3.07 in. (82 x 78 mm). **Compression Ratio:** 9.2:1. **Brake Horsepower:** 340 (DIN) at 6000 rpm. **Torque:** 333 lbs.-ft. at 4200 rpm. Seven main bearings. Bosch K-Jetronic fuel injection.

CHASSIS DATA: Wheelbase: (Mondial) 104.3 in.; (GTO) 96.5 in.; (308 GTB/GTS) 92.1 in.; (400i) 106.3 in.; (512 BBi) 98.4 in. **Overall Length:** (Mondial) 182.7 in.; (GTO) 168.9 in.; (308 GTB/GTS) 174.2 in.; (400i) 189.4 in.; (512 BBi) 173.2 in. **Height:** (Mondial) 49.6 in.; (GTO) 44.1 in.; (308 GTB) 44.1 in.; (400i) 51.6 in.; (512 BBi) 44.1 in. **Width:** (Mondial) 70.5 in.; (GTO) 75.2 in.; (308 GTB/GTS) 67.7 in.; (400i) 70.9 in.; (512 BBi) 72 in. **Front Tread:** (Mondial) 58.9 in.; (GTO) 61.4 in.; (308 GTB/GTS) 57.9 in.; (400i) 57.9 in.; (512 BBi) 59.1 in. **Rear Tread:** (Mondial) 59.8 in.; (GTO) 61.5 in.; (308 GTB/GTS) 57.9 in.; (400i) 59.1 in.; (512 BBi) 61.9 in. **Standard Tires:** (Mondial) 240/55VR390; (GTO) 225/50VR16 front, 265/50VR16 rear; (308 GTB/GTS) Goodyear NCT 205/55VR16 front, 225/50VR16 rear; (400i) 240/55VR415; (512 BBi) 180/TR415 front, 210/TR415 rear.

TECHNICAL: Layout: (Mondial, GTO, 308 GTB/GTS, 512 BBi) mid-engine, rear-drive; (400i) front-engine, rear-drive. **Transmission:** (Mondial, GTO, 308 GTB/GTS, 512 BBi) five-speed manual in rear transaxle; (400i) five-speed manual or three-speed automatic. Type 308 gear ratios: (1st) 3.419:1; (2nd) 2.353:1; (3rd) 1.693:1; (4th) 1.244:1; (5th) 0.919:1. **Steering:** rack and pinion except (400i) recirculating ball. **Suspension (front):** unequal-length A-arms with coil springs and anti-roll bar. **Suspension (rear):** (Mondial, GTO, 308 GTB/GTS) unequal-length A-arms with coil springs and anti-roll bar; (512 BBi) unequal-length A-arms with twin coil springs and anti-roll bar; (400i) unequal-length A-arms with coil springs, anti-roll bar and hydraulic self-leveling. **Brakes:** front/rear disc. **Body Construction:** separate body on tubular steel frame.

PERFORMANCE: Top Speed: (European Mondial) 139 mph; (GTO) 189.5 mph; (European 308 GTB) 158 mph; (400i w//manual) 152 mph; (400i A) 146 mph; (512 BBi) 174 mph. **Acceleration (quarter-mile):** (308) about 15.4 sec.; (Mondial) about 16.5 sec.; (GTO) 14.1 sec. (113 mph) but 12.7 sec. claimed; (400i w/manual) 14.8 sec.; (400i w/auto.) 15.6 sec.; (512 BBi) 14.2 sec. (103.5 mph).

MAJOR OPTIONS: Front spoiler (308). Metallic paint (308). Dual air conditioning (400i). Power sunroof (Mondial).

ADDITIONAL MODELS: The 1991-cc V-8 engine in the 208 GTB/GTS turbo, available in Europe, produced 220 horsepower.

Manufacturer: Ferrari S.p.A. SEFAC, Maranello (Modena), Italy.

Distributor: Fiat Motors of North America, Montvale, New Jersey.

HISTORY: The GTO designation reached back to the late 1950s, when Ferrari dominated GT racing with its 250 berlinetta coupes and California Spyder roadsters; and to the more potent (and quicker) 250 GTO that had debuted in 1962, with only 42 copies built. Ferrari's Testarossa debuted late in 1984 at the Paris show; see next listing for details.

1985-86 FERRARI

1986 2.8 liter twin-turbocharged Ferrari 288GTO Berlinetta. (Christie's)

MONDIAL QUATTROVALVOLE — V-8 — The Mondial with 32-valve, 2927-cc engine ceased production in 1985, replaced by the 3.2 Mondial (below).

3.2 MONDIAL — V-8 — A larger (3.2-liter) V-8 engine went into the next Mondial generation, which added Marelli Multiplex electronic ignition to replace the prior Digiplex system. Otherwise, appearance and mechanical details were similar to the former Mondial coupe and cabriolet. Mondial styling features included hidden headlamps, horizontal hood vents, five side louvers, round taillamps (red and amber), and four round exhaust pipes set in a black lower rear panel.

GTO — V-8 — Introduced in 1984, the limited-production GTO sports-racer continued with little change into 1987; see previous listing for further details.

TESTAROSSA — FLAT-12 — By the time the decade of the '80s ended, it seemed as though the Testarossa had been in the Ferrari lineup forever, because it had gained so much attention from enthusiasts and the general public alike. The dramatic two-seater coupe, introduced late in 1984 at the Paris auto show as successor to the Boxer Berlinetta (BB), soon began almost to make Ferrari a household word in America. Reviving the legendary Testa Rossa ("redhead") name of a late-1950s Ferrari sports/racer, so called because of its red cam covers, the new Testarossa was aimed squarely at the U.S. market and engineered to meet U.S. safety and emissions standards. Pininfarina designed and built the dramatically sensuous body, whose shape was honed in a wind tunnel, focusing mainly on front/rear downforce. Though mainly aluminum, steel was used for the roof and doors. Most startling of its styling features were the six huge, long horizontal strakes (ribs) on each bodyside, which led from the door fronts into air scoops just ahead of the rear wheels. Those fed air to twin radiators behind the cockpit. Those strakes weren't added solely for looks, though they certainly attracted plenty of attention. In some countries, the large air openings had to be covered in some way. As a practical matter, too, rear-mounted radiators allowed more luggage space up front. With a rear tread dimension nearly six inches wider than the front, the Testarossa displayed a broad and brawny back end, highlighted by monstrous rear tires. Horizontal rear slats and four round exhaust pipes completed the rear-end picture.

An improved BB-style horizontally-opposed 12-cylinder engine had new 24-valve heads, with four valves per cylinder. Compression dropped slightly, to 8.7:1, while Bosch K-Jetronic fuel injection and Marelli Multiplex ignition continued from the prior BB model. The 4942-cc (302-cid) engine produced 380 horsepower (SAE) and 354 pound-feet of torque, sending that power to a five-speed transaxle via an enlarged twin-disc clutch. Suspension details were similar to the 512 BBi: unequal-length A-arms, coil springs and anti-roll bar up front, with twin coil springs at the rear. Wheelbase was two inches longer than the 512 BBi, at 100.4 inches. A Testarossa not only could approach 180 mph, but was capable of accelerating to 60 mph in 5.3 seconds, and blasting through the quarter-mile in 13.6 seconds or less, hitting 105 mph at the end. Driver and passenger did not lack for comfort, either, with fine leather upholstery inside. In addition to luggage space in the nose, special fitted luggage went into the area behind the seats, ahead of the engine.

TYPE 328 GTB/GTS — V-8 — A larger engine went into the 3-series Ferrari, changing its name from 308 to 328. Also used in the modified Mondial, the 3185-cc V-8 produced 260 horsepower and 213 pound-feet of torque. As before, Bosch K-Jetronic fuel injection and Marelli electronic ignition were used, but the latter adopted a new Multiplex system. Wheelbase grew fractionally, to 92.5 inches. Bumpers were now body-colored, and integrated into the underfairing. Tailpipes and rear foglamps also had a more integrated look. Revised, smoother-surfaced wheels retained their five-pointed star pattern.

TYPE 400i — V-12 — The "family" Ferrari continued into 1985, but was replaced by the 412i (below) with a larger engine.

TYPE 412i — V-12 — An increase of one millimeter in bore dimension enlarged the four-seat Ferrari's engine to 4942 cc (302 cid), changing the name from 400i to 412i. Compression rose to 9.6:1. With new Bosch K-Jetronic fuel injection, the engine produced 340 horsepower. Marelli Microplex electronic ignition was used, and a twin-disc clutch replaced the single-disc unit. New this year was Bosch anti-lock braking. A self-leveling rear suspension and limited-slip differential were standard. Styling features included sharply tapered rear side windows with black edging, long horizontal bodyside creases, and black accents on the rocker-panel bottoms and enlarged, twin-slotted front spoiler. Bumpers changed to body-color, and the back end was slightly taller. Above the low horizontal grille was Ferrari's prancing horse emblem. A gently-sloped hood wore horizontal vents, and concealed (pop-up) headlamps continued from the prior model. Four round taillamps were used (two red, two amber), along with a '412' badge and another prancing horse. Inside, flush-mounted controls replaced the original toggle switches. The 412i debuted at the Geneva Motor Show in early 1985. Still not certified for U.S. sale, the 412i remained a rarity in America.

TYPE 512 BBi — FLAT-12 — Production of the original 'BB' ended in 1985, replaced by the Testarossa (above).

I.D. DATA: Ferrari's 17-symbol Vehicle Identification Number is embossed on a metal plate attached to steering column. Symbol one ('Z') indicates Italy. The next two symbols identify the make ('FF' = Ferrari). Symbol four indicates engine type; symbol five is restraint system. Symbols six and seven denote model ('08' = Mondial; '12' = 308 GTB Quattrovalvole; '13' = 308 GTS Quattrovalvole; '14' = Mondial Quattrovalvole; '15' = Mondial cabriolet; '17' = Testarossa; '18' = 308 conv; '19 = 328 GTB; '20' = 328 GTS; '21' = 3.2 Mondial; '26' = 3.2 Mondial cabriolet; '29' = 328 conv). Next is a market designator ('A' = North America), followed by a check digit. Symbol 10 indicates model year ('F' = 1984; 'G' = 1986). Symbol 11 ('0') is the assembly plant. Last comes the six-digit sequential production number.

Model	Body Type & Seating	Engine Type/CID	P.O.E. Price	Weight (lbs.)	Prod. Total
MONDIAL QUATTROVALVOLE					
Mondial	2-dr Coupe-2+2P	V8/179	59500	3400	Note 1
Mondial	2-dr Cabr-2+2P	V8/179	65000	N/A	Note 1
3.2 MONDIAL					
3.2	2-dr Coupe-2+2P	V8/194	N/A	N/A	N/A
3.2	2-dr Cabr-2+2P	V8/194	N/A	N/A	N/A
GTO					
GTO	2-dr Coupe-2P	V8/174	83400	2555	Note 2
TESTAROSSA					
	2-dr Coupe-2P	H12/302	N/A	3660	N/A
328					
GTB	2-dr Coupe-2P	V8/194	N/A	N/A	N/A
GTS	2-dr Targa Cpe-2P	V8/194	N/A	N/A	N/A
400i					
400i	2-dr Coupe-2+2P	V12/294	N/A	N/A	N/A
412i					
412i	2-dr Coupe-2+2P	V12/302	N/A	4009	N/A
512 BBi					
512 BBi	2-dr Coupe-2P	H12/302	N/A	N/A	N/A

Note 1: About 2,500 Mondials were produced from 1980-85.

Note 2: A total of 200 GTOs were produced from 1984-87, for race homologation purposes; never certified for U.S. sale.

ENGINE DATA: BASE V-8 (Mondial Quattrovalvole): 90-degree, dual-overhead-cam "vee" type eight-cylinder (32-valve). Light alloy block and heads. **Displacement:** 178.6 cu. in. (2927 cc). **Bore & Stroke:** 3.19 x 2.79 in. (81 x 71 mm). **Compression Ratio:** 8.6:1. Brake Horsepower: 230 (SAE) at 6800 rpm. **Torque:** 188 lbs.-ft. at 5500 rpm. Five main bearings. Bosch K-Jetronic fuel injection.

BASE V-8 (3.2 Mondial, 328): 90-degree, dual-overhead-cam "vee" type eight-cylinder (32-valve). Light alloy block and heads. **Displacement:** 194.4 cu. in. (3185 cc). **Bore & Stroke:** 3.27 x 2.90 in. (83 x 73.6 mm). **Compression Ratio:** 9.2:1. **Brake Horsepower:** 260 at 7000 rpm. **Torque:** 213 lbs.-ft. at 5500 rpm. Five main bearings. Bosch K-Jetronic fuel injection.

BASE V-8 (GTO): 90-degree, dual-overhead-cam "vee" type eight-cylinder. Twin IHI turbochargers with separate intercoolers. Light alloy block and heads. **Displacement:** 174 cu. in. (2855 cc). **Bore & Stroke:** 3.15 x 2.79 in. (80 x 71 mm). **Compression Ratio:** 7.6:1. **Brake Horsepower:** 400 at 7000 rpm. **Torque:** 366 lbs.-ft. at 3800 rpm. Five main bearings. Weber-Marelli electronic fuel injection.

BASE FLAT-12 (Testarossa): Horizontally-opposed, dual-overhead-cam 12-cylinder (48-valve). Light alloy block and heads. **Displacement:** 302 cu. in. (4942 cc). **Bore & Stroke:** 3.23 x 3.07 in. (82 x 78 mm). **Compression Ratio:** 8.7:1. **Brake Horsepower:** 380 (SAE) at 5750 rpm. **Torque:** 354 lbs.-ft. at 4500 rpm. Seven main bearings. Bosch K-Jetronic fuel injection.

BASE V-12 (400i): 60-degree, dual-overhead-cam, "vee" type 12-cylinder. Light alloy block and heads. **Displacement:** 294.2 cu. in. (4823 cc). **Bore & Stroke:** 3.19 x 3.07 in. (81 x 78 mm). **Compression Ratio:** 8.8:1. **Brake Horsepower:** 340 at 6500 rpm. **Torque:** 347 lbs.-ft. at 3600 rpm. Seven main bearings. Bosch K-Jetronic fuel injection.

BASE V-12 (412i): 60-degree, dual-overhead-cam, "vee" type 12-cylinder. Light alloy block and heads. **Displacement:** 302 cu. in. (4942 cc). **Bore & Stroke:** 3.23 x 3.07 in. (82 x 78 mm). **Compression Ratio:** 9.6:1. **Brake Horsepower:** 340 at 6000 rpm. **Torque:** 333 lbs.-ft. at 4200 rpm. Seven main bearings. Bosch K-Jetronic fuel injection.

BASE FLAT-12 (512 BBi): Horizontally-opposed, dual-overhead-cam 12-cylinder. Light alloy block and heads. **Displacement:** 302 cu. in. (4942 cc). **Bore & Stroke:** 3.23 x 3.07 in. (82 x 78 mm). **Compression Ratio:** 9.2:1. **Brake Horsepower:** 340 (DIN) at 6000 rpm. **Torque:** 333 lbs.-ft. at 4200 rpm. Seven main bearings. Bosch K-Jetronic fuel injection.

CHASSIS DATA: Wheelbase: (Mondial) 104.2 in.; (GTO) 96.5 in.; (Testarossa) 100.4 in.; (328) 92.5 in.; (400i/412i) 106.3 in.; (512 BBi) 98.4 in. **Overall Length:** (Mondial) 178.5 in.; (GTO) 168.9 in.; (Testa) 176.6 in.; (328) 168.7 in.; (400i/412i) 189.4 in.; (512 BBi) 173.2 in. **Height:** (Mondial) 49.6 in.; (GTO) 44.1 in.; (Testa) 44.5 in.; (328) 40.1 in.; (400i/412i) 51.6 in.; (512 BBi) 44.1 in. **Width:** (Mondial) 70.5 in.; (GTO) 75.2 in.; (Testa) 77.8 in.; (328) 68.1 in.; (400i/412i) 70.9 in.; (512 BBi) 72 in. **Front Tread:** (Mondial) 58.9 in.; (GTO) 61.4 in.; (Testa) 59.8 in.; (328) 58.0 in.; (400i/412i) 57.9 in.; (512 BBi) 59.1 in. **Rear Tread:** (Mondial) 59.7 in.; (GTO) 61.5 in.; (Testa) 65.4 in.; (328) 57.8 in.; (400i/412i) 59.1 in.; (512 BBi) 61.9 in. **Standard Tires:** (Mondial) 240/55VR390; (GTO) 225/50VR16 front, 265/50VR16 rear; (Testa) 225/50VR16 front, 255/50VR16 rear; (400i) 240/55VR415; (412i) 240/55VR16; (512 BBi) 180/TR415 front, 210TR415 rear.

TECHNICAL: Layout: (Mondial, GTO, Testarossa, 328, 512 BBi) mid-engine, rear-drive; (400i/412i) front-engine, rear-drive. **Transmission:** (Mondial, GTO, Testarossa, 328, 512 BBi) five-speed manual in rear transaxle; (400i/412i) five-speed manual or three-speed automatic. **Steering:** rack and pinion except (400i/412i) recirculating ball. **Suspension (front):** unequal-length A-arms with coil springs and anti-roll bar. **Suspension (rear):** (Mondial, GTO, 328) unequal-length A-arms with coil springs and anti-roll bar; (Testarossa, 512 BBi) unequal-length A-arms with twin coil springs and anti-roll bar; (400i/412i) unequal-length A-arms with coil springs, anti-roll bar and hydraulic self-leveling. **Brakes:** front/rear disc; anti-lock on 412i. **Body Construction:** separate body on tubular steel frame; (Testarossa) aluminum body with steel roof and doors.

PERFORMANCE: Top Speed: (3.2 Mondial Cabr) 145 mph; (GTO) near 190 mph; (Testarossa) 180+ mph; (412i) 147-155+ mph. **Acceleration (0-60 mph):** (3.2 Mondial) 7.4 sec.; (3.2 Mondial Cabr) 7.1 sec.; (GTO) 5.0 sec.; (Testarossa) 5.3 sec.; (412i w/manual) 6.7 sec. **Acceleration (quarter-mile):** (Mondial) 15.0 sec.; (Mondial Cabr) 15.3 sec. (94 mph); (GTO) 12.7-14.1 sec. (up to 113 mph); (Testarossa) 13.3-13.6 sec. (105-107 mph); (412i) 15.0 sec. (96.5 mph).

PRODUCTION/SALES: Approximately 771 Ferraris were sold in the U.S. during 1986.

Manufacturer: Ferrari S.p.A. SEFAC, Maranello (Modena), Italy.

Distributor: Ferrari of North America, Hasbrouck Heights, New Jersey.

1987-88 FERRARI

3.2 MONDIAL — V-8 — Production of the Mondial coupe and cabriolet, which switched to a larger engine in 1985, continued with little change.

1988 Ferrari Testarossa.

GTO — V-8 — Final examples of the limited-production sports-racer were produced in 1987; see previous listings for additional details.

TESTAROSSA — FLAT-12 — Production of the popular and flamboyant Testarossa continued with little change; see previous listing for full details.

F40 — V-8 — Wealthy Americans (and others) could hardly wait for a crack at Ferrari's new supercar when it appeared in Europe in 1987. They would have to wait several years, until the first U.S.-certified versions became available. Even then, availability would be so limited that only a few fortunate folks were able to get their hands on one, even if they had the $400,000-plus that it took to seal the deal. Trying to squeeze into an F40 was more than the average person might manage anyway, to say nothing of driving this virtual race car, with its surprisingly stark interior. Form-fitting bucket seats were tolerable only if your own form happened to be trim and tight, unless you ordered one of the two alternate sizes available.

Towering above the F40's tail was a tall rear aerofoil. Apart from that, the F40 displayed some resemblance to the *Evoluzione,* GTO, and 308/328, but with a host of unique differences in its wide body. Wheels and tires, for one, were nearly Indy-car size. The body was packed full of air scoops, grids, and louvers. Drag coefficient was an unremarkable 0.34, but the car's main goal was to achieve maximum downforce. Wheelbase, at 94.5 inches, was identical to the GTO, while the F40 measured two inches shorter overall than a Testarossa. Nose and tail sections were hinged. Apart from rudimentary air conditioning, the F40 offered few driver/passenger comforts. The stark cockpit contained no carpeting, no door panels, no radio--not even windup windows. Only sliding Plexiglas panes were installed, useful for little more than passing through tollbooths. Seats were upholstered in day-glo-orange Nomex and came in three sizes, with four-point safety harnesses. A spongelike safety fuel bladder held 31.7 gallons. Atop a steel-tube space-frame chassis was a body made up of composite materials reinforced with carbon-fiber and Kevlar. Composites also were used in outer body panels. Suspension layout was conventional, with unequal-length A-arms and coil springs (concentric with shocks) and anti-roll bar. Three-position ride-height control, included in early models, automatically dropped the car by 20 mm at speed, but it could be raised to 20 mm above the normal position by touching a switch. The five-speed gearbox was in the rear transaxle, with 2.73:1 final drive ratio. Rack-and-pinion steering had no power assist. Vented, cross-drilled disc brakes used aluminum centers and cast-iron outer segments.

F40 power came from a detuned *Evoluzione* V-8 with twin IHI turbos with air-to-air Behr intercoolers and four valves per cylinder. The 2936-cc (179-cid) powerplant produced 471 horsepower (SAE) at 7000 rpm, and 426 pound-feet of torque. An optional kit was announced that would supposedly boost output to a shocking 671 bhp. Electronics controlled the turbo wastegate, ignition, and port fuel injection, using a Weber-Marelli IAW engine management system. Compression was only 7.8:1, while the turbos delivered boost up to 16 psi. Pirelli "P Zero" tires (245/40ZR17 front and 335/35ZR17 rear) rode five-spoke Speedline modular wheels. Claimed top speed was 201 mph, and estimates of 0-60 mph acceleration reached as low as 3.0 seconds. A F40 was expected to accelerate to 124 mph in just 12.4 seconds.

TYPE 328 GTB/GTS — V-8 — Production of the successor to the 308 series, introduced in 1985, continued with little change.

TYPE 412i — V-12 — Production of the "family" Ferrari four-seater, with enlarged engine as introduced in 1985, continued with little change.

I.D. DATA: Ferrari's 17-symbol Vehicle Identification Number is embossed on a metal plate attached to steering column. Breakdown is similar to 1985-86.

Model	Body Type & Seating	Engine Type/CID	P.O.E. Price	Weight (lbs.)	Prod. Total
3.2 MONDIAL					
3.2	2-dr Coupe-2 + 2P	V8/194	76400	N/A	N/A
3.2	2-dr Cabr-2 + 2P	V8/194	83900	N/A	N/A
GTO					
GTO	2-dr Coupe-2P	V8/174	N/A	2555	Note 1
TESTAROSSA					
	2-dr Coupe-2P	H12/302	134000	3660	N/A
F40					
	2-dr Coupe-2P	V8/179	200000	2425	Note 2
328					
GTB	2-dr Coupe-2P	V8/194	71900	N/A	N/A
GTS	2-dr Targa Cpe-2P	V8/194	77900	N/A	N/A
412i					
412i	2-dr Coupe-2 + 2P	V12/302	N/A	N/A	N/A

Note 1: A total of 200 GTOs were produced from 1984-87, for race homologation purposes; never certified for U.S. sale.
Note 2: Announced F40 production was 400 units, and the supercar remained in production into the 1990s.
Price Note: Figures shown were valid in 1988; F40 price was tentative, as its value rose sharply by the time it became available for U.S. sale.

ENGINE DATA: BASE V-8 (3.2 Mondial, 328): 90-degree, dual-overhead-cam "vee" type eight-cylinder (32-valve). Light alloy block and heads. **Displacement:** 194.4 cu. in. (3185 cc). **Bore & Stroke:** 3.27 x 2.90 in. (83 x 73.6 mm). **Compression Ratio:** 9.2:1. **Brake Horsepower:** 260 at 7000 rpm. **Torque:** 213 lbs.-ft. at 5500 rpm. Five main bearings. Bosch K-Jetronic fuel injection.

BASE V-8 (GTO): 90-degree, dual-overhead-cam "vee" type eight-cylinder. Twin IHI turbochargers with separate intercoolers. Light alloy block and heads. **Displacement:** 174 cu. in. (2855 cc). **Bore & Stroke:** 3.15 x 2.79 in. (80 x 71 mm). **Compression Ratio:** 7.6:1. **Brake Horsepower:** 400 at 7000 rpm. **Torque:** 366 lbs.-ft. at 3800 rpm. Five main bearings. Weber-Marelli electronic fuel injection.

BASE FLAT-12 (Testarossa): Horizontally-opposed, dual-overhead-cam 12-cylinder (48-valve). Light alloy block and heads. **Displacement:** 302 cu. in. (4942 cc). **Bore & Stroke:** 3.23 x 3.07 in. (82 x 78 mm). **Compression Ratio:** 8.7:1. **Brake Horsepower:** 380 (SAE) at 5750 rpm. **Torque:** 354 lbs.-ft. at 4500 rpm. Seven main bearings. Bosch K-Jetronic fuel injection.

BASE V-8 (F40): 90-degree, dual-overhead-cam, "vee" type eight-cylinder (32-valve). Two IHI turbochargers with Behr intercoolers. **Displacement:** 179 cu. in. (2936 cc). **Bore & Stroke:** 3.23 x 2.74 in. (82 x 69.5 mm). **Compression Ratio:** 7.8:1. **Brake Horsepower:** 471 (SAE) at 7000 rpm. **Torque:** 426 lbs.-ft. at 4000 rpm. Five main bearings. Weber-Marelli engine management.

BASE V-12 (412i): 60-degree, dual-overhead-cam, "vee" type 12-cylinder. Light alloy block and heads. **Displacement:** 302 cu. in. (4942 cc). **Bore & Stroke:** 3.23 x 3.07 in. (82 x 78 mm). **Compression Ratio:** 9.6:1. **Brake Horsepower:** 340 at 6000 rpm. **Torque:** 333 lbs.-ft. at 4200 rpm. Seven main bearings. Bosch K-Jetronic fuel injection.

CHASSIS DATA: Wheelbase: (Mondial) 104.2 in.; (Testarossa) 100.4 in.; (F40) 96.5 in.; (328) 92.5 in.; (412i) 106.3 in. **Overall Length:** (Mondial) 178.5 in.; (GTO) 168.9 in.; (Testa) 176.6 in.; (F40) 174.4 in.; (328) 168.7 in.; (412i) 189.4 in. **Height:** (Mondial) 48.6 in.; (GTO) 44.1 in.; (Testa) 44.5 in.; (F40) 44.5 in.; (328) 40.1 in.; (412i) 51.7 in. **Width:** (Mondial) 70.6 in.; (GTO) 75.2 in.; (Testa) 77.8 in.; (F40) 78.0 in.; (328) 68.1 in.; (412i) 70.8 in. **Front Tread:** (Mondial) 58.8 in.; (GTO) 61.4 in.; (Testa) 59.8 in.; (F40) 62.8 in.; (328) 58.0 in.; (412i) 58.1 in. **Rear Tread:** (Mondial) 59.4 in.; (GTO) 61.5 in.; (Testa) 65.4 in.; (F40) 63.4 in.; (328) 57.8 in.; (412i) 59.4 in. **Standard Tires:** (Mondial) 240/55VR390; (GTO) 225/50VR16 front, 265/50VR16 rear; (Testa) 225/50VR16 front, 255/50VR16 rear; (F40) Pirelli "P Zero" 245/40ZR17 front, 335/35ZR17 rear; (412i) 240/55VR16.

TECHNICAL: Layout: (Mondial, GTO, Testarossa, F40, 328) mid-engine, rear-drive; (412i) front-engine, rear-drive. **Transmission:** (Mondial, GTO, Testarossa, 328) five-speed manual in rear transaxle; (412i) five-speed manual or three-speed automatic. **Steering:** rack and pinion except (412i) recirculating ball. **Suspension (front):** unequal-length A-arms with coil springs and anti-roll bar. **Suspension (rear):** (Mondial, GTO, 328) unequal-length A-arms with coil springs and anti-roll bar; (Testarossa) unequal-length A-arms with twin coil springs and anti-roll bar; (412i) unequal-length A-arms with coil springs, anti-roll bar and hydraulic self-leveling. **Brakes:** front/rear disc; anti-lock on 412i. **Body Construction:** separate body on tubular steel frame; (Testarossa) aluminum body with steel roof and doors; (F40) composite body on steel-tube space frame.

PERFORMANCE: Top Speed: (Mondial Cabr) 145 mph; (GTO) near 190 mph; (Testarossa) 180+ mph; (F40) 201 mph claimed; (412i) 147-155+ mph. **Acceleration (0-60 mph):** (Mondial) 7.4 sec.; (Mondial Cabr) 7.1 sec.; (GTO) 5.0 sec.; (Testarossa) 5.3 sec.; (F40) 3.0 sec. (412i w/manual) 6.7 sec. **Acceleration (quarter-mile):** (Mondial) 15.0 sec.; (Mondial Cabr) 15.3 sec. (94 mph); (GTO) 12.7-14.1 sec. (up to 113 mph); (Testarossa) 13.3-13.6 sec. (105-107 mph); (412i) 15.0 sec. (96.5 mph).

PRODUCTION/SALES: Approximately 1,054 Ferraris were sold in the U.S. during 1987, and 805 in 1989.
Manufacturer: Ferrari S.p.A. SEFAC, Maranello (Modena), Italy.
Distributor: Ferrari North America, Hasbrouck Heights, New Jersey.

HISTORY: Enzo Ferrari had announced in June 1986 that he wanted to produce "a car reminiscent of the original 250 LM," to mark Ferrari's 40th anniversary. Pininfarina general manager Leonardo Fioravanti said the forthcoming F40 would "recover the spirit of some of the Ferrari cars of the past" and "give our customers the possibility of driving objects that are very similar to the racing cars." First shown at Maranello on July 21, 1987, the F40 was like a roadgoing version of the GTO *Evoluzione,* and a response to the Porsche 959. Supposedly, it would be available to "qualified" customers only. Announced production, to begin in 1988, was expected to be about 400 units total, starting at around $187,000. By the time certification for U.S. sale came, the list price rose near $400,000, and actual examples in Europe were allegedly trading for figures approaching a million dollars.

1989-90 FERRARI

1990 Ferrari F40. (Coys of Kensington)

MONDIAL t — V-8 — A larger (3405-cc) engine went into the Mondial for the 1990s: a longitudinally-mounted 32-valve V-8 with a totally different block configuration from its predecessor. The same engine was installed in the new 348 series (below). Only the Mondial's five-speed gearbox was transverse-mounted. The new powerplant produced up to 300 horsepower, permitting 0-60 mph acceleration in about 6.5 seconds and a top speed of around 158 mph. The revised engine/gearbox layout, which allowed the driveline to be lowered by about five inches, not only improved handling but eased servicing since the twin-disc clutch was now mounted at the end of the car. Even though the engine compression was 10.4:1, it ran on 95-octane no-lead fuel, supplied through new Bosch Motronic 2.5 fuel injection. For the first time on a Ferrari, a three-position switch offered a soft, medium or hard ride. Anti-lock brakes were standard. As for appearance,

the wheel-arches were less flared than on the prior Mondial, and bodyside air intakes had a less diagonal shape at the rear. Flush-type, body-colored door handles were installed. As in its predecessor, the sloping nose held horizontal vents and pop-up rectangular headlamps. At the rear were the familiar four round taillamps and four exhaust pipe outlets. In short, the body changes were minimal. Mechanically, this was the first Ferrari with power rack-and-pinion steering. Inside, automatic air conditioning could be adjusted separately for the driver and passenger. A restyled instrument panel contained five round gauges ahead of the driver. As before, the Cabriolet was a "true" convertible, not a Targa-topped coupe.

TESTAROSSA — FLAT-12 — Production of the dramatic Testarossa continued with little change.

F40 — V-8 — By the time the F40 supercar was certified for U.S. sale, it had grown into a major legend, and was drawing prices in the legendary league, well above its official selling price.

348 — V-8 — Though similar in appearance to its 328 predecessor, the new 348 series ranked as all-new, with styling cues borrowed from the larger Testarossa. Foremost among those was a set of horizontal strakes on each bodyside, plus additional grillework on the rear end and over the mid-engine. Styling, as before, was by Pininfarina. A sharply-sloped nose contained hidden headlamps, and the "flying buttress" fastback roofline continued from the 308/328. Wheelbase grew by four inches over the 328. With back wheels mounted well to the rear, the car displayed minimal rear overhang. Width grew considerably, and dropping the engine by five inches lowered the 348's center of gravity for improved handling. Introduced at the Frankfurt show in September 1989, the 348 carried the same 3.4-liter engine as the new Mondial t, introduced a few months earlier. The new powerplant delivered some 40 more horsepower than its predecessor, and was mounted longitudinally rather than crosswise (as in the 328). The 348 used monocoque (unibody) construction rather than the typical Ferrari separate body and frame. Both the closed coupe and Targa-roofed version were offered.

412i Note: Only a handful of final 412i models were produced during 1989, as that model disappeared from the Ferrari lineup; see previous listings for details.

I.D. DATA: Ferrari's 17-symbol Vehicle Identification Number is embossed on a metal plate attached to steering column. Breakdown is similar to 1985-86.

Model	Body Type & Seating	Engine Type/CID	P.O.E. Price	Weight (lbs.)	Prod. Total
MONDIAL t					
tb	2-dr Coupe-2+2P	V8/208	N/A	3440	N/A
ts	2-dr Cabr-2+2P	V8/208	N/A	3462	N/A
TESTAROSSA					
	2-dr Coupe-2P	H12/302	161600	3660	N/A
F40					
	2-dr Coupe-2P	V8/179	Note 1	2425	Note 2
348					
GTB	2-dr Coupe-2P	V8/208	N/A	3170	N/A
GTS	2-dr Targa Cpe-2P	V8/208	N/A	3170	N/A

Note 1: Official F40 list price in the U.S. rose far past $300,000 by the time it became available for sale, and reached $423,250 by early 1991; but cars were reported to be changing hands for considerably more.

Note 2: Announced F40 production was 400 units, and the supercar remained in production into the 1990s.

Price Note: Figures shown were valid in 1990.

ENGINE DATA: BASE V-8 (Mondial t, 348): Dual-overhead-cam, "vee" type eight-cylinder (32-valve). **Displacement:** 208 cu. in. (3405 cc). **Bore & Stroke:** 3.35 x 2.95 in. (85 x 75 mm). **Compression Ratio:** 10.4:1. **Brake Horsepower:** 296-300 at 7200 rpm. **Torque:** 238 lbs.-ft. at 4200 rpm. Five main bearings. Bosch Motronic 2.5 port fuel injection.
BASE FLAT-12 (Testarossa): Horizontally-opposed, dual-overhead-cam 12-cylinder (48-valve). Light alloy block and heads. **Displacement:** 302 cu. in. (4942 cc). **Bore & Stroke:** 3.23 x 3.07 in. (82 x 78 mm). **Compression Ratio:** 8.7:1. **Brake Horsepower:** 380 (SAE) at 5750 rpm. **Torque:** 354 lbs.-ft. at 4500 rpm. Seven main bearings. Bosch K-Jetronic fuel injection.
BASE V-8 (F40): 90-degree, dual-overhead-cam, "vee" type eight-cylinder (32-valve). Two IHI turbochargers with Behr intercoolers. **Displacement:** 179 cu. in. (2936 cc). **Bore & Stroke:** 3.23 x 2.74 in. (82 x 69.5 mm). **Compression Ratio:** 7.8:1. **Brake Horsepower:** 471 (SAE) at 7000 rpm. **Torque:** 426 lbs.-ft. at 4000 rpm. Five main bearings. Weber-Marelli engine management.

CHASSIS DATA: Wheelbase: (Mondial) 104.3 in.; (Testarossa) 100.4 in.; (F40) 94.5 in.; (348) 96.5 in. **Overall Length:** (Mondial) 178.5 in.; (Testa) 176.6 in.; (F40) 174.4 in.; (348) 166.7 in. **Height:** (Mondial cpe) 48.6 in.; (Testa) 44.5 in.; (F40) 44.5 in.; (348) 46.1 in. **Width:** (Mondial) 70.6 in.; (Testa) 77.8 in.; (F40) 78.0 in.; (348) 74.6 in. **Front Tread:** (Mondial) 59.8 in.; (Testa) 59.8 in.; (F40) 62.8 in.; (348) 59.2 in. **Rear Tread:** (Mondial) 61.4 in.; (Testa) 65.4 in.; (F40) 63.4 in.; (348) 62.2 in. **Standard Tires:** (Testa) 225/50VR16 front, 255/50VR16 rear; (F40) Pirelli "P Zero" 245/40ZR17 front, 335/35ZR17 rear.

TECHNICAL: Layout: mid-engine, rear-drive. **Transmission:** five-speed manual in rear transaxle. **Steering:** rack and pinion. **Suspension (front):** unequal-length A-arms with coil springs and anti-roll bar. **Suspension (rear):** (Mondial, F40, 348) unequal-length A-arms with coil springs and anti-roll bar; (Testarossa) unequal-length A-arms with twin coil springs and anti-roll bar. **Brakes:** front/rear disc; anti-locking on 348 and Mondial. **Body Construction:** separate body on tubular steel frame except (348) unibody; (Testarossa) aluminum body with steel roof and doors; (F40) composite body on steel-tube space frame.

PERFORMANCE: Top Speed: (Mondial) 158 mph; (Testarossa) 180 mph; (F40) 201 mph claimed. **Acceleration (0-60 mph):** (Mondial) 6.5 sec.; (Testarossa) 5.3 sec.; (F40) 3.0 sec. estimated. **Acceleration (quarter-mile):** (Testarossa) 13.6 sec. (105 mph).

Manufacturer: Ferrari S.p.A. SEFAC, Maranello (Modena), Italy.
Distributor: Ferrari North America, Hasbrouck Heights, New Jersey.

HISTORY: The Mondial t became available in the U.S. late in 1989; the 348 entered production late in 1989 and was on sale in 1990. The F40 became available in the U.S. during 1990. All models shown in this listing continued in production into the early 1990s.

FIAT

Fiat S.p.A., which during the postwar period became the biggest industrial firm in Italy and one of the largest in the world, has a history dating back to its founding in 1899 by Giovanni Agnelli. The first Fiat had tiller steering, chain drive, and a rear-mounted two-cylinder engine. Early in the century, Fiat (Societa Anonimo Fabbrica Italiana di Automobili Torino) became known for its racing cars as well as for production models. Popular examples of the latter included a four-cylinder model 501, introduced in 1919; the overhead-cam 509, in 1924; the 503, which debuted in 1926; the 514, which appeared in 1929; and the 508 Balilla sports car and sedan, introduced in 1932. The Balilla Sports had a 995-cc four-cylinder engine rated 36 horsepower. Early racing successes included a victory at the Targa Florio and French Grand Prix in 1907. Felix Navarro drove a Fiat 477 miles at 70 mph in the 1907 Dieppe event. By that time, Fiat had introduced a six-cylinder model with an 11-liter engine. A V-12 was offered in the early 1920s, on a 152-inch wheelbase chassis. Fiat also debuted a supercharged Grand Prix racer with a twin-cam, 120-cid eight-cylinder engine producing 150 horsepower.

At one time, Fiats were produced in the U.S.: from 1910 to 1918, in a plant at Poughkeepsie, New York. Most familiar of the prewar Fiats to North American eyes, however, may have been the tiny two-seater 500 Topolino (which translates to "little mouse" and was often referred to as "Mickey Mouse"). It appeared in 1936, powered by a 570-cc L-head four-cylinder engine mounted forward of the radiator, in coupe and convertible form. A streamlined 1500 debuted a year earlier, with six-cylinder power.

Known mainly as a producer of little cars with two- and four-cylinder engines, both front- and rear-drive, Fiat also offered V-8 power in the early postwar period. The 8V, serving as the first postwar sports car, appeared at the Geneva show in 1952 with a 2-liter V-8 beneath its hood and a tubular chassis below. That one gained a fiberglass body in 1954, just as Chevrolet's 'glass Corvette was getting underway. Unibody construction emerged in the revised 1100, which debuted in 1953. Although a trickle of Fiats entered the U.S. in the late 1940s and early 1950s, regular importation did not begin until 1957, with the 500, 600, 1100 and 1200 models. Also emerging at that time was the race-oriented Fiat-Abarth (or Abarth-Fiat), listed separately in this Catalog. Fiat made an early stab at the near-sports-car market with its 1100 TV roadster in the mid-to-late 1950s. Starting in 1959, though, the 1200 and 1500 enjoyed greater success with their attractive Pininfarina styling and larger engines (an OSCA-designed twin-cam in the latter model).

A new 2100 sedan and station wagon with six-cylinder power arrived in 1960. A revised 1500 Spider roadster arrived in the U.S. during 1963, replacing the 1200. By 1965, European customers could get another form of Fiat: the little 850 sedan (joined by a fastback coupe and Sport convertible), but that series would not enter the American market until 1967. Also in that year came the debut of the new 124 series. Produced initially as a sedan and wagon, the 124 became most known in Spider convertible (styled by Pininfarina) and sport coupe form, earning considerable popularity in the U.S. The early sporty 124s carried 1438-cc twin-cam engines, but displacements later grew as large as 1756 cc, as five-speed transmissions became standard. Final examples of the 124 Spider, in the late 1970s and early '80s, had a 1995-cc version of the twin-cam powerplant.

Meanwhile, for 1972 a new front-wheel-drive 128 series had become available, followed a year later by a 128SL sport coupe. By that time, automatic transmissions were offered on some 124 models. Fiat turned to mid-engine powertrains in mid-1973 with the debut of the Bertone-bodied X1/9, which was actually part of the 128 series and intended as a replacement for the 850. The little 850 was gone by that time, but the lineup of the mid-1970s also included the 124 Spider, 128, and 131. The two-seat X1/9 models first came with a 1290-cc engine, but by 1979 grew to 1498-cc displacement.

No less notable was the early 1970s installation of Ferrari's V-6 Dino engine into a Fiat Dino model, offered in both Spider and coupe form, styled by Pininfarina and Bertone (respectively). The connection between the two companies was no surprise, since Fiat acquired a half interest in the Ferrari operation in 1969.

A new Brava sedan with 1756-cc engine (than 1995-cc) joined the group in mid-1978, and a new Strada with 1498-cc four the next year. Fiat kept stabbing at the U.S. marketplace into the early 1980s, but sagging sales finally compelled this old-line automaker to abandon the fight. By 1984, the former Spider 2000 wore a Pininfarina badge and the X1/9 adopted the Bertone nameplate rather than being marketed as Fiats. The Spider disappeared by 1986, but X1/9 coupes remained available in the U.S. through the decade. Production of other models has continued for markets elsewhere in the world, and Fiats are assembled in a number of countries in addition to their native Italy. In 1986, Fiat took over Alfa Romeo and remains one of the major forces in the world market, even if products under its own name no longer reach U.S. motorists.

Model Note: A wide variety of additional Fiat models were available in Europe and other markets over the years. This Catalog emphasizes those that were exported to the U.S., or were of special historic interest.

Engine Specification Note: During the early years of serious importation of Fiats into the U.S., a complex and bewildering maze of horsepower and torque ratings were announced and published. Most were DIN (European) ratings, some were SAE; but seldom was the distinction noted. Part of the confusion, as always, results from the fact that changes which occurred on European models often took a year or longer to debut in the U.S., while information about those changes did not necessarily arrive at the same time.

1946 Fiat 500 coupe.

1947-52 FIAT

500 — FOUR — The prewar-styled two-seat, two-door sedan with separate headlamps and "suicide" doors was announced in 1946 and available by mid-1948, under the 500B designation. The early postwar 500 was a streamlined all-metal sedan with wide doors, and turn signals on front pillars. The spare wheel was outside, recessed into the tail. Inside, two independent adjustable seats had folding backrests, for access to ample interior luggage space. Standard equipment included an electric windshield wiper and inside visors. Leather upholstery was available on request. What was described as a "convertible" had a quick-acting sliding roof made of colored weatherproof material.

The four-cylinder, 570-cc side-valve engine with detachable aluminum head produced 13 horsepower. The carburetor was fitted with starting device, while the four-speed gearbox had a silent third gear and synchronized third and fourth. A short, rigid frame contained deep, lightened side members. Wheelbase was 78.75 inches. Independent front suspension consisted of a transverse semi-elliptic spring. Semi-elliptic springs with hydraulic shock absorbers brought up the rear. Worm and worm wheel steering was installed. Disc wheels held 4x15 extra-low-pressure tires. An inspection lamp was optional.

Top speed was 53 mph, and the 500 was claimed to deliver more than 47 mpg. Available in 1949 was a more modern version of the 500, with built-in headlamps and a rectangular grille made up of five horizontal bars.

1948 Fiat Topolino station wagon.

1949 Fiat 500C station wagon.

1950 Fiat 1100 E sedan.

1100 — FOUR — The early 1100B four-door sedan, available from 1947 on, had a prewar look with separate headlamps and a narrow grille made up of numerous horizontal bars. Both front and rear doors were hinged at the center post. With both doors open, no center pillar was evident. The four-passenger body featured a downswept hood with what the company claimed were "new aerodynamic lines." It was called "a brilliant, economical car with smart acceleration."

Upholstery came in cloth or optional leather. Armchair front seats adjusted independently. The squab (back) of the rear seat could be pulled forward to gain access to inside luggage space. All doors had wind-up windows. Standard equipment included chrome-plated bumpers, electric double-arm windshield wiper, driving mirror, stoplight, directional indicators recessed into pillars, interior lighting, clock, two adjustable inside sunvisors, map pockets on doors, and spare wheel recessed into the tail (on the outside).

The 1100's light, stiff frame was braced by a central X-girder, and lower than the level of the transmission shaft. Independent front suspension of the oscillating quadrilateral type used oil-immersed springs and hydraulic shock absorbers enclosed in vertical casings. At the rear were semi-elliptic springs with a transverse stabilizer bar. Worm and worm wheel steering included a separate drag link to each wheel. Under the hood was a 1089-cc overhead-valve four-cylinder engine, rated 32 horsepower. The phosphor-manganese block was cast in one piece with the base chamber, while the aluminum head had inserted valve seats. An inverted carburetor included a starting device and adjustable economiser. A dashboard control operated the starter. A single-plate clutch sent power to the four-speed gearbox, which had silent third and synchro third/fourth gears. Brake drums were aluminum. Disc wheels held 5.00x15 tires. The 1100's wheelbase measured 95.4 inches.

Appearance of the long-wheelbase 1100BL sedan added by 1949 was similar, but it had rear quarter windows (six-window style). An aero-styled 1100S two-door sports coupe, also available in 1949, had a narrow grille made up of vertical bars, as well as twin side grilles that contained four horizontal bars. It had a split windshield and no rear quarter windows. An 1100E four-door sedan, introduced in 1950, was similar in appearance to earlier sedans but its grille was made up of both thin and thick horizontal bars, and it featured a protruding trunk. The 1100ES sports coupe added in 1951 had large rear quarter windows, front vent wings, and a wide horizontal-bar grille.

Fiat's 1100E was described as "the classic model 1100, technically improved," offering four or six seats. The four-seat, four-door sedan had a column-mounted gearshift, twin wipers, disappearing directional indicators, and new chromed bumpers. Stoplights were mounted on rear fenders. Cloth-upholstered, armchair-type front seats adjusted independently. Adjustable sunvisors and door map pockets were included. The 1100EL sedan could seat six (or seven) and had no center pillars, but included vent panes for ventilation. The spare wheel was recessed into the tail, and included a wheel cover. Wheelbase was 95.25 inches for the 1100E, 106 inches for the 1100EL. The 1100E's overhead-valve, four-cylinder engine produced 35 horsepower (30 bhp in the 1100EL). The upper three gears in the four-speed transmission were synchronized.

1951 Fiat 1400 Berlina.

1400 — FOUR — Introduced in 1950, the Model 1400 sedan and cabriolet (convertible) coupe had a boxier profile than earlier Fiats, with built-in headlamps and a wide grille with horizontal bars and thin vertical dividers. Four passengers could be seated comfortably; six if required. The 1395-cc four-cylinder engine, with aluminum head, produced about 45 horsepower. A 1400 could deliver 22 miles per gallon (U.S.) or hit speeds beyond 75 mph, according to Fiat. Independent front suspension included a stabilizing crossbar. The rear suspension used a helical spring and longitudinal leaf. A radio was standard in the cabriolet, optional in the sedan. These Fiats wore a checkerboard-style grille and one-piece windshield.

1500 — SIX — Fiat's six-cylinder model bore a vague resemblance to a 1937 Chevrolet, with its separate headlamps and a grille made up of horizontal bars. The overhead-valve, 1493-cc engine produced 45 horsepower. Its block was cast in one piece with the base chamber, in phosphor-manganese iron, with a detachable cylinder head. A four-speed gearbox was standard, with a single-plate clutch. Wheelbase was 110 inches. The 1500E version available in 1950 switched to a column gearshift, with the spare tire contained in an extended trunk.

I.D. DATA: Model 500 chassis serial number is on the upper right of the front frame crossmember; an identification plate is on the rear wall of the hood, to the right, near the fuel filler plug. Model 1100/1500 chassis number is stamped on right side member, adjacent to the engine suspension buffer bracket; an identification plate is on the right side rear wall of the engine compartment. Model 1400 chassis number is stamped below the identification plate on the right rear wall of the engine compartment. Model 500 engine number is stamped at the front of the block, near the cylinder head. Model 1100 engine number is stamped on the right front of the block, near the cylinder head, and on the fuel pump flange. Model 1400 engine number is stamped on a block cast on the front of the block, near the head. Model 1500 engine number is stamped on right front of block, near cylinder head flange.

Model	Body Type & Seating	Engine Type/CID	P.O.E. Price	Weight (lbs.)	Prod. Total
500					
	2-dr Sedan-2P	I4/35	N/A	N/A	Note 1
1100					
1100B	4-dr Sedan-4P	I4/66	N/A	N/A	Note 1
1100BL	4-dr Sedan-4P	I4/66	N/A	N/A	Note 1
1100E	4-dr Sedan-4P	I4/66	N/A	2068	Note 1
1100EL	4-dr Sedan-6P	I4/66	N/A	N/A	Note 1
1100S	2-dr Spt Cpe	I4/66	N/A	N/A	Note 1
1100ES	2-dr Spt Cpe-4P	I4/66	N/A	N/A	Note 1
1400					
	4-dr Sedan-4/6P	I4/85	N/A	2409	Note 1
	2-dr Cabr-4/6P	I4/85	N/A	N/A	Note 1
1500					
	4-dr Sedan	I6/91	N/A	N/A	Note 1
	4-dr Conv Cpe	I6/91	N/A	N/A	Note 1

Note 1: Approximately 46 Fiats were sold in the U.S. during 1948, followed by 60 in 1949, 45 in 1950, 13 in 1951, and 19 in 1952.

ENGINE DATA: BASE FOUR (500): Inline, side-valve four-cylinder. Cast iron block and aluminum head. **Displacement:** 34.8 cu. in. (570 cc). **Bore & Stroke:** 2.05 x 2.64 in. (52 x 67 mm). **Compression Ratio:** 6.5:1. **Brake Horsepower:** 13 at 4000 rpm (later, 16-17 at 4400 rpm). Two main bearings. Solid valve lifters. One downdraft carburetor with starting device. Battery and coil ignition (12-volt).

BASE FOUR (1100): Inline, overhead-valve four-cylinder. Phosphor-manganese block and aluminum head. **Displacement:** 66.5 cu. in. (1089 cc). **Bore & Stroke:** 2.68 x 2.95 in. (68 x 75 mm). **Brake Horsepower:** (early 1100) 32 at 4000 rpm; (later 1100E) 35 at 4400 rpm; (later 1100EL) 30 at 4400 rpm. Three main bearings. Solid valve lifters. Inverted carburetor with starting device and adjustable economiser.

BASE FOUR (1400): Inline, overhead-valve four-cylinder. Cast iron block and aluminum head. **Displacement:** 85.1 cu. in. (1395 cc). **Bore & Stroke:** 3.23 x 2.60 in. (82 x 66 mm). **Compression Ratio:** 6.7:1. **Brake Horsepower:** 45 at 4400 rpm. Three main bearings. Solid valve lifters. One downdraft carburetor.

BASE SIX (1500): Inline, overhead-valve six-cylinder. Phosphor-manganese iron block and detachable head. **Displacement:** 91.1 cu. in. (1493 cc). **Bore & Stroke:** 2.56 x 2.95 in. (65 x 75 mm). **Compression Ratio:** 5.8:1. **Brake Horsepower:** 45 at 4000 rpm. Four main bearings. Solid valve lifters. One carburetor.

CHASSIS DATA: Wheelbase: (500) 78.75 in.; (1100) 95.4 in.; (1100E) 95.25 in.; (1100EL) 106 in.; (1400) 104.2 in.; (1500) 110 in. **Overall Length:** (500) 128 in.; (1100) 161.5 in.; (1400) 167 in.; (1500) 177 in. **Height:** (500) 54.1 in.; (1100) 59.1 in.; (1400) 61.1 in. **Width:** (500) 50.6 in.; (1100) 59.3 in.; (1400) 65.1 in.; (1500) 63 in. **Front Tread:** (500) 43.5 in.; (1100E) 48.5 in.; (1100EL) 51.75 in.; (1400) 51.4 in.; (1500) 51.25 in. **Rear Tread:** (500) 42.5 in.; (1100E) 48.25 in.; (1100EL) 53.75 in.; (1400) 52.0 in.; (1500) 52.75 in. **Standard Tires:** (500) 4x15 or 4.25x15; (1100) 5.00x15; (1100E) 5.25x15; (1400) 6.00x14; (1500) 5.50x15.

TECHNICAL: Layout: front-engine, rear-drive. **Transmission:** four-speed manual. **Steering:** (500/1100) worm and worm wheel; (1500) worm and roller. **Suspension (front):** (500) independent, transverse semi-elliptic spring; (1100) independent oscillating quadrilateral type with oil-immersed springs and hydraulic shocks enclosed in vertical casings; (1400) independent with stabilizing cross bar. **Suspension (rear):** (500/1500) rigid axle with semi-elliptic leaf springs; (1100) rigid axle with semi-elliptic leaf springs and stabilizer bar; (1400) helical springs and quarter-elliptic longitudinal leaf springs, with torsion rod. **Brakes:** hydraulic, front/rear drum.

PERFORMANCE: Top Speed: (500) 53 mph claimed; (1400) 75+ mph claimed. **Fuel Mileage:** (500) 47+ mpg claimed; (1400) 22 mpg claimed.

Manufacturer: Fiat S.p.A., Turin, Italy.

HISTORY: The 500B (with separate headlamps) was introduced in 1948; the more modern 500C with built-in headlamps a year later. Production of the 1100 and 1500 began in 1947, while the 1400 debuted in 1950. The 1500 was produced only into 1950, but other models continued well into the decade. Originally created in 1936, the 500 was popular in Europe, Mexico and elsewhere in the world because it was compact, reliable and economical.

1953-56 FIAT

1954 Fiat V-8 sports.

500 — FOUR — A station wagon with all-steel body joined the original 500 two-door sedan in 1953, with a wide grille made up of thick and thin horizontal bars. Parking lights stood atop the front fenders, and taillamps protruded at the rear. Production continued into early 1955, but a completely different 500 with two-cylinder power soon would emerge.

600 — FOUR — A new 600 series debuted early in 1955. The two-door sedan had rear-hinged doors, a grille made up of three chrome bars, and a trim strip that ran from each headlamp almost to the rear edge of the door. Though similar in size to the 500, the new model carried four passengers and had luggage space behind the rear seats as well as under the hood. A rear-mounted four-cylinder engine produced 21.5 horsepower. Independent suspension was installed at all four wheels, and unibody construction was used. This was Italy's first small rear-engine, four-passenger car.

By 1956, a new four-door Multipla station wagon was available on the 600 chassis. Styled more like a minivan than a conventional wagon, it had a fastback rear end and a grille made up of vertical bars. A "convertible" (actually sunroof) model also became available in 1956.

1100 — FOUR — The new 1100/103 model for 1953 was said by *Auto Sport Review* to resemble the Ford Consul, with "a touch of Hillman Minx in the grille." It descended from a long line of econocars, dating to 1937 and the Balilla. In that year, the Balilla engine grew from the original 995 cc with three-speed transmission to 1089 cc with four-speed, in a semi-streamlined body. That became an extremely popular model, though less known in the U.S. than the Topolino.

This new 1100 had the same 1089-cc engine, boosted to 36 horsepower, plus a new counterbalanced crankshaft and modified carburetion. Top speed was over 70 mph, with quicker acceleration. Construction was now unibodied, cutting weight by 220 pounds. Seating was provided for four, though the new model was shorter than the former 1100. Appearance was on the boxy side, but with curves, including a curved one-piece windshield. New front coil springs and flat rear leaf springs were installed. Up front was a horizontal-bar grille made up of thick and thin elements; at the rear, vertical-style taillamps. A 103F station wagon joined the original four-door sedan in 1954, lacking the foglamp at the center of the grille that had been added to deluxe series 103 TV (*Turismo Veloce*, or fast tourer) sedans. The TV versions had a more potent engine, adding about 10 mph to top speeds. The 1100 TV came in two-tone colors, with full-length bodyside trim strip. A second trim strip ran lower, across the doors and onto the cowl. Sedan front doors were rear-hinged ("suicide" style).

In 1956, a new 103E series consisted of the basic sedan, TV sedan, and station wagon. The grille was made up of concave vertical bars with a center foglamp. A divided mesh-style grille went on the 1100/103E TV sports roadster. Parking lights were fender-mounted.

1400 — FOUR — Production of the 1400 sedan and convertible continued through the 1950s, but it received less attention than other Fiat models. The 1400A sedan, introduced in 1954, had a larger rear window and modified parking lights. Two years later, the 1400B had a foglamps in the center of its grille. A diesel engine also was available.

8V — V-8 — "Built for speed" and "designed by the wind." That's how Fiat described its new V-8 fastback coupe, for its appearance at the Turin show in April 1953. With a claimed top speed of about 124 mph, the two-seat coupe had fully independent suspension. Most of the fastback bodies were built by Fiat, and most had staggered seating in a narrow cockpit. Some bodies were created by Ghia and Zagato. The aerodynamic 8V design was developed by Rappi (formerly at Isotta Fraschini), using wind-tunnel testing.

An integral body was welded to tubular frame members that consisted of two sheet shells (inner and outer), welded together to form the box-shaped stressed members. Metallic paint was used to finish the body. Bumpers, grille and moldings were polished stainless light alloy (with rubber on the bumpers). Doors contained sliding windows, and the car had a curved windshield and small rear quarter windows. Inboard headlamps stood as part of the oval grille opening, which contained a set of vertical bars. Auxiliary headlamps were mounted in the fenders, in the customary location. Atop the hood was a prominent airscoop. Bulged rear fenders contained small taillamps. Upholstery and interior were finished in imitation leather, and the roof was covered with head/noise insulating material. The spare tire fit inside the car. Instruments included a tachometer, speedometer, clock, fuel gauge, and oil pressure gauge. Separate headlamps were said to comply with ISO international regulations.

The 70-degree V-8 displaced 1996 cc and produced 110 horsepower, using two twin-body Weber carburetors. A four-speed gearbox was synchronized in the upper three gears, and worked through a single-plate dry clutch. Transverse wishbones and coil reaction springs, front and rear, were enclosed in casings, with telescopic shocks and transverse stabilizer bar. Borrani wire-spoke wheels used Whitworth locknuts and held 165x400 tires. Wheelbase was 94.5 inches, and the 8V measured less than 50 inches high (loaded).

1900 — FOUR — Fiat also introduced a 1900 sedan with modern slab-sided body and eggcrate grille, which used a fluid coupling between the engine and clutch. The 1901-cc four developed up to 60 bhp at 3700 rpm. The 1900A, introduced in 1954, wore a vertical-bar grille that also contained one or two thick horizontal bars.

I.D. DATA: Model 500 chassis serial number is on the upper right of the front frame crossmember; an identification plate is on the rear wall of the hood, to the right, near the fuel filler plug. Model 600 chassis number is stamped on the bulkhead, to the left of the identification plate on the top of that bulkhead. Model 1100 chassis number is stamped on right side of rear wall in engine compartment, adjacent to the identification plate. Model 144 chassis number is stamped below the identification plate on the right rear wall of the engine compartment. Model 500 engine number is stamped at the front of the block, near the cylinder head. Model 600 engine number is stamped on rear wall of block, above the timing cover. Model 1100 engine number is stamped on the right front of the block, near the cylinder head, and on the fuel pump flange. Model 1400 engine number is stamped on a block cast on the front of the block, near the head.

Model	Body Type & Seating	Engine Type/CID	P.O.E. Price	Weight (lbs.)	Prod. Total
500					
	2-dr Sedan-2P	I4/35	N/A	1260	Note 1
	2-dr Sta Wag-4P	I4/35	N/A	N/A	Note 1
600					
	2-dr Sedan-4P	I4/39	N/A	1344	Note 1
Sunroof	2-dr Conv-4P	I4/39	N/A	N/A	Note 1
600 MULTIPLA					
	2-dr Sta Wagon	I4/39	N/A	N/A	Note 1
1100					
103	4-dr Sedan-4P	I4/66	N/A	N/A	Note 1
103E	4-dr Sedan-4P	I4/66	N/A	N/A	Note 1
103E TV	4-dr Sedan-4P	I4/66	N/A	1808	Note 1
103F	4-dr Sta Wag-4P	I4/66	N/A	1874	Note 1
103E TV	2-dr Spt Rds-2P	I4/66	N/A	N/A	Note 1
1400					
	4-dr Sedan-4/6P	I4/85	N/A	2500	Note 1
	2-dr Cabr-4/6P	I4/85	N/A	N/A	Note 1
1900					
	4-dr Sedan	I4/116	N/A	2535	Note 1
8V					
	2-dr Coupe-2P	V8/122	N/A	2050	Note 2

Note 1: A total of 131,324 Fiats were produced during 1953, 163, 484 in 1954, 217,937 in 1955, and 261,956 in 1956.

Note 2: A total of 114 Model 8V Fiats were produced.

Weight Note: Figures shown are approximate.

ENGINE DATA: BASE FOUR (500): Inline, side-valve four-cylinder. Cast iron block and aluminum head. **Displacement:** 34.8 cu. in. (570 cc). **Bore & Stroke:** 2.05 x 2.64 in. (52 x 67 mm). **Compression Ratio:** 6.5:1. **Brake Horsepower:** 13 at 4000 rpm (later, 16-17 at 4400 rpm). Two main bearings. Solid valve lifters. One downdraft carburetor w/starting device. 12-volt battery/coil ignition.

BASE FOUR (600): Inline, overhead-valve four-cylinder. Aluminum block and head. **Displacement:** 38.6 cu. in. (633 cc). **Bore & Stroke:** 2.36 x 2.20 in. (60 x 56 mm). **Compression Ratio:** 7.5:1. **Brake Horsepower:** 21.5 at 4600 rpm. Three main bearings. Solid valve lifters. One carburetor.

BASE FOUR (1100): Inline, overhead-valve four-cylinder. Cast iron (phosphor-manganese) block and aluminum head. **Displacement:** 66.5 cu. in. (1089 cc). **Bore & Stroke:** 2.68 x 2.95 in. (68 x 75 mm). **Compression Ratio:** 6.7:1/7.0:1. **Brake Horsepower:** (1100/103) 36 at 4400 rpm; (103E) 40 at 4400 rpm. Three main bearings. Solid valve lifters. One downdraft carburetor.

BASE FOUR (1100 TV): Same as 1089-cc four above, except — **Compression Ratio:** 7.5:1. **Brake Horsepower:** 49 at 5200 rpm.

BASE FOUR (1400): Inline, overhead-valve four-cylinder. Cast iron block and aluminum head. **Displacement:** 85.1 cu. in. (1395 cc). **Bore & Stroke:** 3.23 x 2.60 in. (82 x 66 mm). **Compression Ratio:** 6.7:1. **Brake Horsepower:** 45 at 4400 rpm. Three main bearings. Solid valve lifters. One downdraft carburetor.

BASE FOUR (1900): Inline, overhead-valve four-cylinder. Cast iron block and aluminum head. **Displacement:** 115.9 cu. in. (1901 cc). **Bore & Stroke:** 3.20 x 3.50 in. (82 x 90 mm). **Compression Ratio:** 6.7:1. **Brake Horsepower:** 58-60 at 3700 rpm. Three main bearings. Solid valve lifters.

Note: 1900A had a 70-bhp engine.

BASE V-8 (8V): 70-degree, overhead-valve "vee" type eight-cylinder. **Displacement:** 121.8 cu. in. (1996 cc). **Bore & Stroke:** 2.83 x 2.41 in. (72 x 61.3 mm). **Compression Ratio:** 8.5:1. **Brake Horsepower:** 110 at 6000 rpm. Two twin-body Weber carburetors.

CHASSIS DATA: Wheelbase: (500) 78.75 in.; (600) 78.75 in.; (1100) 92.1 in.; (1400) 104.2 in.; (1900) 104 in.; (8V) 94.5 in. **Overall Length:** (500) 128 in.; (600) 129 in.; (600 Multipla) 139 in.; (1100 sed) 148.6 in.; (1400) 167 in.; (1900) 155 in.; (8V) 160 in. **Height:** (500) 54.1 in.; (600) 55.3 in.; (600 Multipla) 62.3 in.; (1100 sed) 58 in.; (1400) 61.1 in.; (1900) 60 in.; (8V) about 49.5 in. **Width:** (500) 50.6 in.; (600) 54.3 in.; (600 Multipla) 57.1 in.; (1100 sed) 57.4 in.; (1400) 65.1 in.; (1900) 65 in.; (8V) 59 in. **Front Tread:** (500) 43.5 in.; (600) 45.3 in.; (600 Multipla) 48.3 in.; (1100 sed) 48.4 in.; (1400) 51.4 in.; (1900) 52 in.; (8V) 50.75 in. **Rear Tread:** (500) 42.5 in.; (600) 45.5 in.; (1100) 47.8 in.; (1400) 52.0 in.; (1900) 52 in.; (8V) 50.75 in. **Standard Tires:** (500) 4x15 or 4x25x15; (600) 5.20x12; (1100 sed) 5.20x14; (1100 wag) 5.60x14; (1400) 6.00x14; (1900) 6.40x14; (8V) 165x400.

TECHNICAL: Layout: front-engine, rear-drive except (600) rear-engine, rear-drive. **Transmission:** four-speed manual. 8V gear ratios: (1st) 2.695:1; (2nd) 1.768:1; (3rd) 1.257:1; (4th) 1.00:1. **Steering:** (500) worm and sector; (600) worm and segment; (600 Multipla, 1100) worm and roller; (1900) worm and roller. **Suspension (front):** (500) independent, transverse semi-elliptic spring; (600) A-arms with transverse leaf spring; (1100) swing arms with coil springs and torsion rod; (1400) independent with stabilizing cross bar; (1900) radius arms and coil springs; (8V) transverse wishbones and coil reaction springs enclosed in casing, with telescopic shocks and transverse stabilizer bar. **Suspension (rear):** (500/1100) rigid axle with semi-elliptic leaf springs; (600) radius arms with coil springs; (1400) helical spring and longitudinal leaf; (1900) coil springs and small longitudinal leaf springs with transverse torque rod; (8V) transverse wishbones and coil reaction springs enclosed in casing, with telescopic shocks and transverse stabilizer bar. **Brakes:** hydraulic, front/rear drum. **Body Construction:** (600/1100) steel unibody; (8V) on tubular chassis.

PERFORMANCE: Top Speed: (500) 53 mph claimed; (600) 60 mph; (1100 TV) 80-84 mph; (1400) 75+ mph claimed; (1900) 84 mph claimed; (8V) 124 mph. **Acceleration (0-60 mph):** (1100 TV) near 26 sec. **Fuel Mileage:** (500) 47+ mpg claimed; (1400) 22 mpg claimed.

Manufacturer: Fiat S.p.A., Turin, Italy.

HISTORY: Fiat's 8V appeared at European auto shows in spring 1952, and won the Italian sports car championship in 1956. Among other special models, Fiat produced a custom Ghia coupe with projectile-shaped round taillamps and front fenders. The 1900 could have a *Superleggera* hardtop coupe body by Touring, while Zagato did a coupe body on the 1100 chassis and Castagna created an 1100 Spyder. A Jeep-like four-wheel-drive Campagnola utility vehicle also was built early in the 1950s. The 8V did not last long, disappearing by 1955, having been produced largely for racing.

1957 FIAT

500 — TWO — Fiat's reworked smallest model had a rear-mounted, air cooled two-cylinder engine and integral transaxle. A "live" rear axle was used, with independent suspension consisting of single wishbones and coil springs. Riding a 72.4-inch wheelbase, the two-door sunroofed sedan was similar in general appearance to the larger 600. The minicar had no grille, but displayed a large emblem in its front panel. The four-speed transmission was unsynchronized, thus requiring double-clutching to run through the gears. Seats consisted of fabric pads on rubber strips. Rear quarter windows were fixed, but doors contained vent wings. Those doors were rear-hinged ("suicide" style).

600 — FOUR — A rear-mounted 633-cc four-cylinder engine provided the power for the 600 sedan and the larger Multipla station wagon. The transmission and differential were installed as a unit with the engine, with final drive to twin swing axles. Round parking lights stood below single round headlamps in the sedan, with a round emblem in the center of the front panel and outreaching horizontal trim strips on each side of that emblem. Both models had fully independent suspensions. Water temperature was controlled by thermostatic adjustment of airflow to the engine compartment in the sedan, and by a conventional thermostat in the Multipla. The four/five-seat Multipla was considered a "sleeper-type" station wagon, while another version sat six passengers. The Multipla driver sat directly above the front wheel, not unlike a Volkswagen Microbus, but Fiat's wagon had a less boxy profile with its slantback rear end and angled front end. Though it looked considerably bigger than the sedan, the Multipla rode the same 600 chassis. The sedan came with a sunroof, sometimes described as a "convertible."

1100 — FOUR — Following the usual pattern of numbering Fiat models, the 1100 series had a 1089-cc four-cylinder engine, offered in separate ratings for the standard and 1100 TV (Turismo Veloce) series. The four-speed manual transmission had a column-mounted gearshift lever. Front doors of the sedan opened from the front ("suicide" style), rear doors from the rear (both attached to the narrow center post). A vertical-bar grille contained a long horizontal divider bar and large center foglamp, though later models had no such unit (sometimes referred to as a "spinner"). Tiny round parking lights stood at tips of the grille's divider bar, below the headlamps. The 1100 TV convertible had small lights on the fenders rather than below the headlamps. Convertible styling features included a split recessed grille, roll-up windows, and wraparound windshield. The adjustable steering wheel had a recessed hub.

I.D. DATA: Chassis serial number is under the hood on the left side of the firewall except (1100) on right side of firewall; and on right side of body frame. Engine type and serial number are stamped on the block. Model 500 engine number is stamped on a pad cast to the left of the rear end of the crankcase support. Model 600 engine number is stamped at the front of the engine, above the timing chain cover. Model 1100 engine number is stamped on a pad to upper right of block, near the head and above the generator; or below the hood hinges. Engine series: (600 sedan) 100.000; (600 Multipla) 100.008.

Model	Body Type & Seating	Engine Type/CID	P.O.E. Price	Weight (lbs.)	Prod. Total
500					
	2-dr Sedan-4P	I2/29	N/A	N/A	Note 1
600					
	2-dr Sedan-4P	I4/39	1298	1230	Note 1
Sunroof	2-dr Conv-4P	I4/39	1360	N/A	Note 1
600 MULTIPLA					
	4-dr Sta Wag-4/5P	I4/39	1598	N/A	Note 1
	4-dr Sta Wag-6P	I4/39	1598	N/A	Note 1
1100					
	4-dr Sedan-4P	I4/66	1655	1835	Note 1
	4-dr Sta Wag-4P	I4/66	2069	N/A	Note 1
1100 TV					
	4-dr Sedan-4P	I4/66	2035	1880	Note 1
	2-dr Conv-2P	I4/66	2498	N/A	Note 1

Note 1: A total of 290,385 Fiats (all models) were produced during 1957.

ENGINE DATA: BASE TWO (500): Vertical, overhead-valve two-cylinder (air cooled). Aluminum block and head. **Displacement:** 29.2 cu. in. (479 cc). **Bore & Stroke:** 2.59 x 2.75 in. (66 x 70 mm). **Compression Ratio:** 7.0:1. **Brake Horsepower:** 15 at 4000 rpm. Solid valve lifters. One-barrel carburetor.

Note: Initial examples of the new 500 series were rated only 13 horsepower; subsequent versions were rated 15 bhp, then (in 1958) 16.5 bhp.

BASE FOUR (600): Inline, overhead-valve four-cylinder. Aluminum block and head. **Displacement:** 38.6 cu. in. (633 cc). **Bore & Stroke:** 2.36 x 2.20 in. (60 x 56 mm). **Compression Ratio:** 7.0:1/7.5:1. **Brake Horsepower:** 22 at 4600 rpm (28.5 SAE at 4900 rpm). **Torque:** 28.9 lbs.-ft. at 3000 rpm. Three main bearings. Solid valve lifters. One Weber carburetor.

BASE FOUR (1100): Inline, overhead-valve four-cylinder. Cast iron block and aluminum head. **Displacement:** 66.5 cu. in. (1089 cc). **Bore & Stroke:** 2.68 x 2.95 in. (68 x 75 mm). **Compression Ratio:** 7.0:1 except (TV) 8.0:1. **Brake Horsepower:** 40 at 4400 rpm except (TV) 53 at 5200 rpm. **Torque:** 52.4 lbs.-ft. at 3200 rpm. Three main bearings. Solid valve lifters. Weber dual-choke carburetor.

CHASSIS DATA: Wheelbase: (500) 72.4 in.; (600) 78.75 in.; (1100) 92.1 in. **Overall Length:** (500) 116 in.; (600 sedan/conv) 130.5 in.; (600 Multipla) 140.8 in.; (1100 sedan) 148.6 in.; (1100 wagon) 147.6 in.; (1100 conv) 150.4 in. **Height:** (500) 52.2 in.; (600 sedan/conv) 55.3 in.; (600 Multipla) 62.3 in.; (1100 sedan) 58.6 in. **Width:** (500) 52 in.; (600 sedan/conv) 54.3 in.; (600 Multipla) 57.0 in.; (1100 sedan) 57.3 in.; (1100 conv) 57.9 in. **Front Tread:** (500) 44.1 in.; (600 sedan/conv) 45.3 in.; (600 Multipla) 48.3 in. **Rear Tread:** (500) 44.7 in.; (600 sedan/conv) 45.5 in.; (600 Multipla) 45.5 in.; (1100) 47.75 in. **Standard Tires:** (500) 4.88x12; (600) 5.20x12; (1100) 5.20x14 except wagon, 5.60x14.

TECHNICAL: Layout: (500/600) rear-engine, rear-drive; (1100) front-engine, rear-drive. **Transmission:** (500) four-speed manual, constant-mesh; (600/1100) four-speed manual (2/3/4 synchro). **Standard Final Drive Ratio:** (500) 5.125:1; (600) 5.38:1; (600 Multipla) 6.43:1; (1100) 4.30:1. **Steering:** (500) worm and sector; (600) worm and segment; (600 Multipla, 1100) worm and roller. **Suspension (front):** (500) A-arms with coil springs; (600) A-arms with transverse leaf spring; (600 Multipla) A-arms with coil springs; (1100) transverse swinging radius arms with coil springs and anti-roll bar. **Suspension (rear):** (500) single A-arms with coil springs; (600) radius arms with coil springs; (1100) rigid axle with semi-elliptic leaf springs and anti-roll bar. **Brakes:** hydraulic, front/rear drum. **Body Construction:** steel unibody.

PERFORMANCE: Top Speed: (500) 53+ mph; (600) 60 mph; (600 Multipla) near 59 mph; (1100 sed) 70-75 mph; (1100 TV sed) 85 mph; (1100 conv) 90 mph. **Acceleration (0-60 mph):** (600) 54 sec.; (1100 sed) 29.5 sec.; (Model 500 did 0-40 in 18-19 sec.). **Acceleration (quarter-mile):** (600) 26.1 sec.; (600 Multipla) 27.3 sec.; (1100 sed) 23.1 sec. (73.7 mph). **Fuel Mileage:** (500) 52 mpg claimed; (Multipla) 40 mpg average; (1100) 28 mpg average.

ADDITIONAL MODELS: A revised 1900B came in hardtop coupe and sedan form, with a more powerful engine (80 bhp) than its 1900A predecessor. It retained the former fluid coupling, and could hit 90 mph.

Manufacturer: Fiat S.p.A., Turin, Italy.

Distributor: Hoffman Motors Corp., New York City and Beverly Hills, California; or Witkin-Wolf Inc., Los Angeles.

HISTORY: By the mid-1950s, half the new cars sold in Italy were Fiat 600s, according to *Motor Trend*. The 500 was introduced (actually reintroduced, since its history dated back to the 1936 Topolino 500) in an attempt to capture the attention of Italians who rode bicycles and motor scooters.

1958 FIAT

1958 Fiat 600.

500 — TWO — Little change was evident in the two-cylinder sedan, which came with a sunroof.

600 — FOUR — Production of the smallest four-cylinder model continued with little change. The rear seat could fold out as a luggage platform.

1100 — 103D — FOUR — The 1100-series sedan, wagon and roadster with 1089-cc engine took on a few significant changes, starting with the fact that the engine added three horsepower. A Solex carburetor replaced the former Weber unit. The station wagon was called the "Familiare." The four-door sedan still had rear-hinged front doors. Headlamps were bigger, a restyled grille deleted the former center auxiliary light, and bumpers were new. Inside, the driver faced larger pedals and a new black steering wheel, and a black cowl stood above the ribbon-style speedometer. The rear backrest was now fixed. Until the revised series arrived, the former 1100 (and 1100 TV) remained available.

1200 — FOUR — A larger (1221-cc) four-cylinder engine powered the new 1200 Gran Luce series, offered in sedan and Sportsman Roadster (convertible) form. The convertible was intended as a replacement for the 1100 TV two-seater, and a restyled roadster would arrive in 1959. Revolving seats permitted easy entry into the two-seater. All doors on the 1200 sedan opened forward (were front-hinged), and it wore a new honeycomb grille. Trunk hinges were concealed. In essence, the sedan was a facelifted 1100, with a revised roof, slim roof pillars, and longer rear end.

1958 Fiat Multipla.

I.D. DATA: Chassis serial number is under the hood on the left side of the firewall except (1100) on right side of firewall; and on right side of body frame. Engine type and serial number are stamped on the block. Model 500 engine number is stamped on a pad cast to the left of the rear end of the crankcase support. Model 600 engine number is stamped at the front of the engine, above the timing chain cover. Model 1100 engine number is stamped on a pad to upper right of block, near the head and above the generator; or below the hood hinges.

Model	Body Type & Seating	Engine Type/CID	P.O.E. Price	Weight (lbs.)	Prod. Total
500					
	2-dr Sedan-4P	I2/29	1098	N/A	Note 1
600					
	2-dr Sedan-4P	I4/39	1298	1230	Note 1
Sunroof	2-dr Conv-4P	I4/39	1360	N/A	Note 1
600 MULTIPLA					
	4-dr Sta Wag-4/5P	I4/39	1598	N/A	Note 1
	4-dr Sta Wag-6P	I4/39	1598	N/A	Note 1
1100					
	4-dr Sedan-4P	I4/66	1683	1835	Note 1
Familiare	4-dr Sta Wag-4P	I4/66	2069	N/A	Note 1
1100 TV					
	4-dr Sedan-4P	I4/66	2035	1880	Note 1
	2-dr Conv-2P	I4/66	2498	N/A	Note 1
1200					
	4-dr Sedan-4P	I4/75	2253	1880	Note 1
TV	2-dr Conv-2P	I4/75	2498	N/A	Note 1

Note 1: A total of 333,715 Fiats (all models) were produced during 1958.

ENGINE DATA: BASE TWO (500): Vertical inline, overhead-valve two-cylinder. Aluminum block and head. **Displacement:** 29.2 cu. in. (479 cc). **Bore & Stroke:** 2.59 x 2.75 in. (66 x 70 mm). **Compression Ratio:** 7.0:1. **Brake Horsepower:** 16.5 at 4400 rpm. **Torque:** 20 lbs.-ft. at 3500 rpm. Solid valve lifters. One-barrel carburetor.

BASE FOUR (600): Inline, overhead-valve four-cylinder. Aluminum block and head. **Displacement:** 38.6 cu. in. (633 cc). **Bore & Stroke:** 2.36 x 2.20 in. (60 x 56 mm). **Compression Ratio:** 7.5:1. **Brake Horsepower:** 22 at 4600 rpm (28.5 SAE at 4900 rpm). **Torque:** 28.9 lbs.-ft. at 3000 rpm. Three main bearings. Solid valve lifters. One Weber carburetor.

BASE FOUR (1100): Inline, overhead-valve four-cylinder. Cast iron block and aluminum head. **Displacement:** 66.5 cu. in. (1089 cc). **Bore & Stroke:** 2.68 x 2.95 in. (68 x 75 mm). **Compression Ratio:** 7.0:1 except (TV) 8.0:1. **Brake Horsepower:** 43 at 4800 rpm except (TV) 53 at 5200 rpm. **Torque:** 52.4 lbs.-ft. at 3200 rpm. Three main bearings. Solid valve lifters. Solex dual-choke carburetor.

BASE FOUR (1200): Inline, overhead-valve four-cylinder. Cast iron block and aluminum head. **Displacement:** 74.5 cu. in. (1221 cc). **Bore & Stroke:** 2.83 x 2.95 in. (71.9 x 75 mm). **Compression Ratio:** 8.0:1. **Brake Horsepower:** 55 (60 SAE) at 5300 rpm. **Torque:** 60 lbs.-ft. at 3000 rpm. Three main bearings. Solid valve lifters. Weber dual-choke carburetor.

CHASSIS DATA: Wheelbase: (500) 72.4 in.; (600) 78.75 in.; (1100) 92.1 in.; (1200) 92.1 in. **Overall Length:** (500) 116 in.; (600 sedan/conv) 130.5 in.; (600 Multipla) 140.8 in.; (1100 sedan) 154.3 in.; (1100 wagon) 147.6 in.; (1100 conv) 150.4 in.; (1200 sed) 154.3 in.; (1200 conv) 152.6 in. **Height:** (500) 52.2 in.; (600 sedan/conv) 55.3 in.; (600 Multipla) 62.3 in.; (1100 sedan) 58.6 in.; (1200 sed) 59 in. **Width:** (500) 52 in.; (600 sedan/conv) 54.3 in.; (600 Multipla) 57.0 in.; (1100 sedan) 57.3 in.; (1100 conv) 57.9 in.; (1200 sed) 57.4 in.; (1200 conv) 57.9 in. **Front Tread:** (500) 44.1 in.; (600 sedan/conv) 45.3 in.; (600 Multipla) 48.3 in.; (1100) 48.4 in. **Rear Tread:** (500) 44.7 in.; (600 sedan/conv) 45.5 in.; (600 Multipla) 45.5 in.; (1100) 47.75 in. **Standard Tires:** (500) 4.88x12; (600) 5.20x12; (1100/1200) 5.20x14 except wagon, 5.60x14.

TECHNICAL: Layout: (500/600) rear-engine, rear-drive; (1100) front-engine, rear-drive. **Transmission:** (500) four-speed manual, constant-mesh; (600/1100/1200) four-speed manual (2/3/4 synchro). **Standard Final Drive Ratio:** (500) 5.125:1; (600) 5.38:1; (600 Multipla) 6.43:1; (1100) 4.30:1. **Steering:** (500) worm and sector; (600) worm and segment; (600 Multipla, 1100, 1200) worm and roller. **Suspension (front):** (500) A-arms with coil springs; (600) A-arms with transverse leaf spring; (600 Multipla) A-arms with coil springs; (1100/1200) transverse A-arms with coil springs and anti-roll bar. **Suspension (rear):** (500) single A-arms with coil springs; (600) radius arms with coil springs; (1100/1200) rigid axle with semi-elliptic leaf springs and anti-roll bar. **Brakes:** hydraulic, front/rear drum. **Body Construction:** steel unibody.

PERFORMANCE: Top Speed: (500) 53+ mph; (600) 60 mph; (1100 sed) 70 mph; (1100 TV sed) 85 mph; (1100 conv) 90 mph; (1200 TV conv) 89 mph. **Acceleration (0-60 mph):** (600) 54.0 sec.; (1200 TV conv) 18.8 sec. **Acceleration (quarter-mile):** (600) 26.1 sec.; (1200 TV conv) 21.0 sec. (62 mph). **Fuel Mileage:** (500) 52 mpg claimed; (Multipla) 40 mpg average; (1100) 28 mpg average.

PRODUCTION/SALES: Approximately 21,156 Fiats were sold in the U.S. during 1958.

Manufacturer: Fiat S.p.A., Turin, Italy.

Distributor: Fiat Motor Co., New York City; or Hoffman Motors Corp., New York City and Beverly Hills, California.

HISTORY: The 1958 models were introduced to the U.S. market on November 1, 1957. Some Fiat 600 two-door sedans were being turned into swift Fiat-Abarth 750s in the late 1950s; see Abarth listing for details.

1959 FIAT

1959 Fiat 500 two-door sedan.

500 — TWO — Production of the rear-drive two-door continued without major change. The 479-cc engine drove a four-speed gearbox, and a 500 could hit 56 mph or achieve up to 52 mpg. A sunroof was standard. What was described as a "Nuova" convertible was actually the sedan with a top that rolled back all the way. Joining the original sedan a tiny-looking, two-passenger Bianchina coupe with special body. The "Jolly" sedan was sometimes referred to as a "beach buggy." It had basket-weave seats and fully open sides, and was described by *Road & Track* as akin to a modern "surrey with the fringe on top." Ghia designed and built the Jolly body. A Sport 500 also was announced, with a larger, higher-compression engine and more horsepower.

600 — FOUR — The 600's rear-mounted engine got a power increase during the 1959 model year (see next listing for data). Otherwise, little change was evident. As before, doors were rear-hinged.

1100 — FOUR — Unlike 1957 and early '58 models, this year's 1100 had no foglamp in the center of the front grille. Otherwise, the series continued with little change.

1200 — FOUR — Production of the 1221-cc sedan continued with little change. Unlike the 1100 series, the 1200 "Full Light" sedan had front-hinged front doors. Roll-up windows remained standard on the two-seat convertible, which adopted a restyled Pininfarina body that offered a sleeker look than the older 1100/1200 TV series. Its rectangular mesh-patterned grille had angled sides. Both the convertible and sedan were powered by the same 60-bhp (SAE) engine. The sedan had a column-mounted gearshift for its four-speed gearbox; the two-seater, a floor lever.

1500 (1500S) — FOUR — new OSCA-designed twin-cam engine became available in the restyled 1200 two-seater body, creating the 1500 convertible (later referred to as 1500S). Built by Fiat, the 1491-cc engine had "square" dimensions (78-mm bore and 78-mm stroke) and produced 90 horsepower (SAE). Except for larger tires, appearance was similar to the 1200 convertible (which remained available into 1963); but on the inside the 1500 held an aluminum-spoked, wood-rimmed Nardi steering wheel and 8000-rpm tachometer.

I.D. DATA: Chassis serial number is under the hood on the left side of the engine-compartment firewall (500/600); on right side of firewall; and on right side of body frame. Engine type and serial number are stamped on the block. Model 500 engine number is stamped on a pad cast to the left of the rear end of the crankcase support. Model 600 engine number is stamped at the front of the engine, above the timing chain cover. Model 1100 engine number is stamped on a pad to upper right of block, near the head and above the generator; or below the hood hinges. Model 1200 engine number is stamped on the right front end of the block, near the cylinder head flange. Model 1500 engine number is stamped on a pad on the block, and on the identification plate.

Model	Body Type & Seating	Engine Type/CID	P.O.E. Price	Weight (lbs.)	Prod. Total
500					
	2-dr Sedan-4P	I2/29	1098	1070	Note 1
	2-dr Spt Sed-4P	I2/30	1228	1070	Note 1
Bianchina	2-dr Coupe-2P	I2/29	1298	N/A	Note 1
Bianchina	2-dr Spt Cpe-2P	I2/30	1428	N/A	Note 1
Jolly	2-dr Sedan-4P	I2/29	1760	N/A	Note 1
600					
	2-dr Sedan-4P	I4/39	1398	1323	Note 1
Sunroof	2-dr S/R Sed-4P	I4/39	1460	1323	Note 1
600 MULTIPLA					
	4-dr Sta Wag-4/5P	I4/39	1658	1654	Note 1
	4-dr Sta Wag-6P	I4/39	1658	1654	Note 1
1100					
	4-dr Sedan-4/5P	I4/66	1743	1940	Note 1
	4-dr Sta Wag-5P	I4/66	2129	1985	Note 1
1200					
	4-dr Sedan-4/5P	I4/75	1998	2051	Note 1
Spider	2-dr Conv-2P	I4/75	2619	2051	Note 1
1500 (1500S)					
Spider	2-dr Conv-2P	I4/91	N/A	2117	Note 1

Note 1: A total of 412,682 Fiats (all models) were produced during 1959.

ENGINE DATA: BASE TWO (500): Vertical inline, overhead-valve two-cylinder. Aluminum block and head. **Displacement:** 29.2 cu. in. (479 cc). **Bore & Stroke:** 2.59 x 2.75 in. (66 x 70 mm). **Compression Ratio:** 7.0:1. **Brake Horsepower:** 16.5 at 4400 rpm (21 SAE at 4000 rpm). **Torque:** 20 lbs.-ft. at 2700 rpm. Solid valve lifters. Single-barrel carburetor.

BASE TWO (500 Sport): Same as above, but — **Displacement:** 30.5 cu. in. (499 cc). **Bore & Stroke:** 2.65 x 2.75 in. (67.4 x 70 mm). **Compression Ratio:** 8.6:1. **Brake Horsepower:** 21 (25 SAE at 4800 rmp).

BASE FOUR (600): Inline, overhead-valve four-cylinder. Cast iron block and aluminum head. **Displacement:** 38.6 cu. in. (633 cc). **Bore & Stroke:** 2.36 x 2.20 in. (60 x 56 mm). **Compression Ratio:** 7.5:1. **Brake Horsepower:** 22 at 4600 rpm (28.5 SAE at 4900 rpm). **Torque:** 30 lbs.-ft. at 2800 rpm. Three main bearings. Solid valve lifters. One Weber carburetor.

BASE FOUR (1100): Inline, overhead-valve four-cylinder. Cast iron block and aluminum head. **Displacement:** 66.5 cu. in. (1089 cc). **Bore & Stroke:** 2.68 x 2.95 in. (68 x 75 mm). **Compression Ratio:** 7.0:1. **Brake Horsepower:** 43 at 4800 rpm. **Torque:** 52.4 lbs.-ft. at 3200 rpm. Three main bearings. Solid valve lifters. Weber dual-choke carburetor.

BASE FOUR (1200): Inline, overhead-valve four-cylinder. Cast iron block and aluminum head. **Displacement:** 74.5 cu. in. (1221 cc). **Bore & Stroke:** 2.83 x 2.95 in. (71.9 x 75 mm). **Compression Ratio:** 8.0:1. **Brake Horsepower:** 55 (60 SAE) at 5300 rpm. **Torque:** 60 lbs.-ft. at 3000 rpm. Three main bearings. Solid valve lifters. Weber dual-choke carburetor.

BASE FOUR (1500): Inline, dual-overhead-cam four-cylinder. Cast iron block and aluminum head. **Displacement:** 91 cu. in. (1491 cc). **Bore & Stroke:** 3.07 x 3.07 in. (78 x 78 mm). **Compression Ratio:** 8.6:1. **Brake Horsepower:** 90 (SAE) at 6000 rpm. **Torque:** 84 lbs.-ft. at 3600 rpm. Five main bearings. Solid valve lifters. Weber dual-choke carburetor.

CHASSIS DATA: Wheelbase: (500) 72.4 in.; (600) 78.75 in.; (1100) 92.1 in.; (1200) 92.1 in.; (1500) 92.1 in. **Overall Length:** (500) 116.9 in.; (600 sed) 130.5 in.; (600 Multipla) 140.8 in.; (1100 sedan) 154.3 in.; (1100 wagon) 147.6 in.; (1200/1500 conv) 158.7 in. **Height:** (500) 52.0 in.; (600 sed) 55.3 in.; (600 Multipla) 62.3 in.; (1100 sedan) 58.6 in.; (1100 wagon) 59 in.; (1200 sed) 57.8 in.; (1200/1500 conv) 51.1 in. **Width:** (500) 52 in.; (600 sed) 54.3 in.; (600 Multipla) 57.0 in.; (1100 sedan) 57.3 in.; (1100 wagon) 57.5 in.; (1200 sed) 57.4 in.; (1200/1500 conv) 59.8 in. **Front Tread:** (500) 44.1 in.; (600 sed) 45.3 in.; (600 Multipla) 48.3 in.; (1100) 48.6 in.; (1200/1500) 48.7 in. **Rear Tread:** (500) 44.7 in.; (600 sed) 45.7 in.; (600 Multipla) 45.5 in.; (1100) 47.8 in.; (1200) 47.9 in.; (1500) 47.8 in. **Standard Tires:** (500) 4.90x12 or 125x12; (600) 5.20x12; (1100/1200) 5.20x14 except wagon, 5.60x14; (1500) 15-inch.

TECHNICAL: Layout: (500/600) rear-engine, rear-drive; (1100/1200/1500) front-engine, rear-drive. **Transmission:** (500) four-speed manual, constant-mesh; (600/1100) four-speed manual (2/3/4 synchro); (1200/1500) four-speed manual. **Standard Final Drive Ratio:** (500) 5.125:1; (600) 5.38:1; (600 Multipla) 6.43:1; (1100/1200) 4.30:1. **Steering:** (500) worm and sector; (600) worm and segment; (600 Multipla, 1100/1200/1500) worm and roller. **Suspension (front):** (500) A-arms with coil springs; (600) A-arms with transverse leaf spring; (600 Multipla) A-arms with coil springs; (1100/1200/1500) transverse A-arms with coil springs and anti-roll bar. **Suspension (rear):** (500) single A-arms with coil springs; (600) radius arms with coil springs; (1100/1200/1500) rigid axle with semi-elliptic leaf springs and anti-roll bar. **Brakes:** hydraulic, front/rear drum. **Body Construction:** steel unibody.

PERFORMANCE: Top Speed: (500) 53-56 mph; (500 Spt) 66 mph; (600) 60 mph; (1100 sed) 70-75 mph; (1200 sed) 84 mph. **Acceleration (0-60 mph):** (500 Spt) 37.2 sec.; (600) 54.0 sec.; (1200 sed) 20.0 sec. **Acceleration (quarter-mile):** (500 Spt) 25.0 sec. (52 mph); (600) 26.1 sec.; (1200 sed) 21.1 sec. (62 mph). **Fuel Mileage:** (500) 52 mpg claimed; (Multipla) 40 mpg average; (1100) 28 mpg average.

PRODUCTION/SALES: Approximately 38,468 Fiats were sold in the U.S. during 1959.

ADDITIONAL MODELS: A new 1800 sedan and station wagon emerged in 1959 for the home market, powered by a 1795-cc six-cylinder engine and featuring angled-forward front fenders (not unlike the 1957-59 Plymouth).

Manfacturer: Fiat S.p.A., Turin, Italy.

Distributor: Fiat Motor Co. Inc., New York City; or Hoffman Motors Corp., New York City and Beverly Hills, California.

HISTORY: The 1959 models were introduced to the U.S. market on October 1, 1958.

1960 FIAT

1960 Fiat 600D. (William Siuru Jr.)

500 — TWO — Parking lights were now mounted under headlamps, with a flared chrome trim, but little other change was evident in the two-cylinder Fiats. The Sport model had a larger (499-cc) engine with higher compression and four extra horsepower. What were described as "convertible" models had a full roll-back roof.

600 — FOUR — All three body styles (sedan, sunroof sedan, and Multipla wagon) continued with little change. Two-tone paint was available on the sedan. As usual, what was sometimes called the "convertible" was actually a sunroofed sedan. A power boost had occurred during 1959.

1100 — FOUR — Production of the 1089-cc Fiats continued with little change, except that four horizontal bars were mounted on the grille, ahead of its narrowly-spaced vertical bars.

1200 — FOUR — Production of the 1221-cc series continued with little change. The sedan was referred to in ads as the "Full Light." The 1221-cc engine gained three horsepower in 1960, though the increase took longer to appear on U.S. models.

1500 (1500S) — FOUR — Introduced in 1959, the Spider roadster with OSCA-designed twin-cam engine continued with little change, wearing the same Pininfarina-styled body as the 1200 two-seater.

2100 — SIX — Fiat's new six-cylinder sedan was notable for its angled-forward front fenders and finned rear fenders, far different in appearance from other models commonly imported into the U.S. at this time. Front suspension consisted of torsion bars with ball joints. Reclining seats were standard, and the four-speed transmission was fully synchronized. Styling features included quad headlamps, a sharp-edged roofline, wraparound horizontal-bar grille, and wraparound front/rear bumpers.

I.D. DATA: Chassis serial number is under the hood on the left side of the engine-compartment firewall (500/600) or on right side of firewall; and on right side of body frame. Engine type and serial number are stamped on the block. Model 500 engine number is stamped on a pad cast to the left of the rear end of the crankcase support. Model 600 engine number is stamped at the front of the engine, above the timing chain cover. Model 1100 engine number is stamped on a pad to upper right of block, near the head and above the generator; or below the hood hinges. Model 1200 engine number is stamped on the right front end of the block, near the cylinder head flange. Model 1500 engine number is stamped on a pad on the block, and on the identification plate. Serial number range: (500 Spt) 047816 to 082523; (500 conv) 059704 to 088550; (500 Bianchina Spt) 013440 to 014308; (500 Bianchina) 011518 to 013139; (600) 522318 to 688092; (600 sunroof) 551562 to 681617; (1100) 503325 to 588802; (1100 DeL) 553261 to 588420; (1200 sed) 533708 to 588079; (2100) 000001 to 006850.

Model	Body Type & Seating	Engine Type/CID	P.O.E. Price	Weight (lbs.)	Prod. Total
500					
	2-dr Sedan-4P	I2/29	1098	1100	Note 1
	2-dr Spt Sed-4P	I2/30	1228	1125	Note 1
Bianchina	2-dr Coupe-2P	I2/29	1298	1100	Note 1
Bianchina	2-dr Spt Cpe-2P	I2/30	1428	1125	Note 1
Jolly	2-dr Sedan-4P	I2/29	1760	1050	Note 1
600					
	2-dr Sedan-4P	I4/39	1398	1334	Note 1
Sunroof	2-dr S/R Sedan-4P	I4/39	1460	1334	Note 1
Jolly	2-dr Sedan-4P	I4/39	1906	1250	Note 1
600 MULTIPLA					
	4-dr Sta Wag-4/5P	I4/39	1658	1653	Note 1
	4-dr Sta Wag-6P	I4/39	1658	1653	Note 1
1100					
	4-dr Sedan-5P	I4/66	1659	1940	Note 1
Deluxe	4-dr Sedan-5P	I4/66	1782	2018	Note 1
	4-dr Sta Wag-5P	I4/66	2129	1985	Note 1
1200					
	4-dr Sedan-4P	I4/75	1998	2069	Note 1
Spider	2-dr Conv-2P	I4/75	2619	2030	Note 1
1500 (1500S)					
Spider	2-dr Conv-2P	I4/91	3298	2117	Note 1
2100					
	4-dr Sedan-5P	I6/125	2798	2679	Note 1
	4-dr Sta Wag-5P	I6/125	3058	2888	Note 1

Note 1: A total of 500,527 Fiats (all models) were produced during 1960.

Price Note: Some announced prices were higher during the year, including $1743 for the 1100 sedan; $1880 for the 1100 Deluxe; $1998 for the 1100 wagon; $2812 for the 1200 Spider; $3730 for the 1500 Spider; up to $3192 for the 2100 sedan; and up to $3498 for the 2100 wagon.

ENGINE DATA: BASE TWO (500): Vertical inline, overhead-valve two-cylinder. Aluminum block and head. **Displacement:** 29.2 cu. in. (479 cc). **Bore & Stroke:** 2.59 x 2.75 in. (66 x 70 mm). **Compression Ratio:** 7.0:1. **Brake Horsepower:** 16.5 at 4400 rpm (21 SAE at 4000 rpm). **Torque:** 20 lbs.-ft. at 2700 rpm. Solid valve lifters. One single-barrel carburetor.

BASE TWO (500 Sport): Same as above, but — **Displacement:** 30.5 cu. in. (499 cc). **Bore & Stroke:** 2.65 x 2.75 in. (67.4 x 70 mm). **Compression Ratio:** 8.6:1. **Brake Horsepower:** 21 (25 SAE at 4800 rpm).

BASE FOUR (600): Inline, overhead-valve four-cylinder. Cast iron block and aluminum head. **Displacement:** 38.6 cu. in. (633 cc). **Bore & Stroke:** 2.36 x 2.20 in. (60 x 56 mm). **Compression Ratio:** 7.5:1. **Brake Horsepower:** 28.5 (SAE) at 4600 rpm. **Torque:** 30 lbs.-ft. at 2700 rpm. Three main bearings. Solid valve lifters. One Weber carburetor.

BASE FOUR (1100): Inline, overhead-valve four-cylinder. Cast iron block and aluminum head. **Displacement:** 66.5 cu. in. (1089 cc). **Bore & Stroke:** 2.68 x 2.95 in. (68 x 75 mm). **Compression Ratio:** 7.0:1. **Brake Horsepower:** 48 (SAE) at 4800 rpm. **Torque:** 52 lbs.-ft. at 3200 rpm. Three main bearings. Solid valve lifters. Weber dual-choke carburetor.

Note: A variant of the 1100 engine with 7.85:1 compression produced 55 bhp at 5200 rpm.

BASE FOUR (1200): Inline, overhead-valve four-cylinder. Cast iron block and aluminum head. **Displacement:** 74.5 cu. in. (1221 cc). **Bore & Stroke:** 2.83 x 2.95 in. (71.9 x 75 mm). **Compression Ratio:** 8.25:1. **Brake Horsepower:** 55-58 (60-63 SAE) at 5300 rpm. **Torque:** 61 lbs.-ft. at 3000 rpm. Three main bearings. Solid valve lifters. Weber dual-choke carburetor.

BASE FOUR (1500): Inline, dual-overhead-cam four-cylinder. Cast iron block and aluminum head. **Displacement:** 91 cu. in. (1491 cc). **Bore & Stroke:** 3.07 x 3.07 in. (78 x 78 mm). **Compression Ratio:** 8.6:1. **Brake Horsepower:** 90 (SAE) at 6000 rpm. **Torque:** 84 lbs.-ft. at 3600 rpm. Five main bearings. Solid valve lifters. Weber dual-choke carburetor.

BASE SIX (2100): Inline, overhead-valve six-cylinder. Cast iron block and aluminum head. **Displacement:** 125.4 cu. in. (2054 cc). **Bore & Stroke:** 3.03 x 2.89 in. (77 x 73.5 mm). **Compression ratio:** 8.8:1. **Brake Horsepower:** 90/95 (SAE) at 5000 rpm. Solid valve lifters.

CHASSIS DATA: Wheelbase: (500) 72.4 in.; (600) 78.75 in.; (1100) 92.1 in.; (1200) 92.1 in.; (1500) 92.1 in.; (2100) 104.3 in. **Overall Length:** (500) 116.9 in.; (600 sedan) 130.5 in.; (600 Multipla) 140.8 in.; (1100 sedan) 154.3 in.; (1100 wagon) 147.6 in.; (1200 sed) 154.3 in.; (1200/1500 conv) 158.7 in.; (1500) 158.7 in.; (2100) 175.8 in. **Height:** (500) 52.0 in.; (600 sedan) 55.3 in.; (600 Multipla) 62.3 in.; (1100 sedan) 58.6 in.; (1100 wagon) 59 in.; (1200 sed) 58.5 in.; (1200/1500 conv) 51.1 in.; (2100) 57.9 in. **Width:** (500) 52 in.; (600 sedan) 54.3 in.; (600 Multipla) 57.0 in.; (1100 sedan) 57.3 in.; (1100 wagon) 57.5 in.; (1200 sed) 57.4 in.; (1200/1500 conv) 59.8 in.; (2100) 63.6 in. **Front Tread:** (500) 44.1 in.; (600 sedan) 45.3 in.; (600 Multipla) 48.3 in.; (1100) 48.6 in.; (1200) 48.7 in.; (1500) 48.7 in.; (2100) 52.8 in. **Rear Tread:** (500) 44.7 in.; (600 sedan) 45.7 in.; (600 Multipla) 45.5 in.; (1100) 47.9 in.; (1200) 47.9 in.; (1500) 47.8 in.; (2100) 51.5 in. **Standard Tires:** (500) 4.90x12 or 125x12; (600) 5.20x12; (1100/1200) 5.20x14 except wagon, 5.60x14; (2100) 5.90x14; (1500) 15-inch.

TECHNICAL: Layout: (500/600) rear-engine, rear-drive; (1100/1200/1500/2100) front-engine, rear-drive. **Transmission:** four-speed manual. **Steering:** (500) worm and sector; (600) worm and segment; (600 Multipla, 1100/1200/1500) worm and roller. **Suspension (front):** (500) A-arms with coil springs; (600) A-arms with transverse leaf spring; (600 Multipla) A-arms with coil springs; (1100/1200) transverse A-arms with coil springs and anti-roll bar; (1500) swinging arms, coil springs and anti-roll bar. **Suspension (rear):** (500) single A-arms with coil springs; (600) radius arms with coil springs; (1100/1200/1500/2100) rigid axle with semi-elliptic leaf springs and anti-roll bar. **Brakes:** hydraulic, front/rear drum. **Body Construction:** steel unibody.

PERFORMANCE: Top Speed: (500) about 59 mph; (500 Sport) 65 mph; (600) about 60 mph; (1100 sed) 75-81 mph; (1200 sed) 87 mph; (1500) 105 mph; (2100) 93 mph. **Acceleration (0-60 mph):** (600) 54.0 sec.; (1500) 10.6 sec.; (2100) 14.5 sec. **Acceleration (quarter-mile):** (600) 26.1 sec.; (1500) 18.5 sec. (77 mph); (2100) 19.7 sec. (69 mph). **Fuel Mileage:** (500) 40-50 mpg; (600 Multipla) 40 mpg average; (1100) 28 mpg average; (1500) 22-26 mpg.

PRODUCTION/SALES: Approximately 20,773 Fiats were sold in the U.S. during 1960.

ADDITIONAL MODELS: Fiat also produced an 1800 six-cylinder series, with 109.7-cid engine, on the same wheelbase as the 2100. This was sometimes (not always) listed in directories of models available in the U.S. Appearance was similar to the 2100, but with single headlamps and a rectangular grille.

Manufacturer: Fiat S.p.A., Turin, Italy.

Distributor: Fiat Motor Co. Inc., New York City; or Hoffman Motors Corp., New York City and Beverly Hills, California.

HISTORY: The 1960 models were introduced to the U.S. market on October 1, 1959. A larger engine (797-cc) went into the 600 at this time, turning it into a 600D; but that took a bit of time to reach the American market.

1961 FIAT

1961 Fiat 1500 four-door.

500 — TWO — Production of the rear-engine two-cylinder Fiats continued with little change. As before, a sunroof was standard. This was the last year the 500 series was commonly imported into the U.S. A Sport model with higher compression was rated 25 horsepower (four more than the standard engine). The "Jolly" sedan with wicker seats was sometimes referred to as a "beach buggy."

600 — FOUR — All three body styles (sedan, sunroof sedan, and Multipla wagon) continued with little change. The sunroofed model was sometimes referred to as a "convertible." Both conventional and "sleeper" versions of the Multipla were offered.

1100 — FOUR — Production of the 1089-cc Fiats continued with little change. Reclining seats and retracting rear assist handles were standard. Rear-hinged ("suicide") front doors remained. The Deluxe had a second-color trim strip extending from the front of the front door, all the way back to the taillamp, a mesh-patterned grille, and round parking lights. Two versions of the engine were offered, rated either 48 or 55 bhp, with 7.0:1 or 7.85:1 compression.

1200 — FOUR — Production of the 1221-cc series continued with little change. Except for the engine, the "Full Light" sedan was similar to the 1100 in layout, but had larger windows and thin pillars. Unlike the 1100 sedan, however, this model had front-hinged front doors. The 1200 Spider had vent wings, plus a mesh-patterned grille with angled sides, and looked similar to the 1500 roadster.

1500 (1500S) — FOUR — Production of the Pininfarina-styled 1491-cc Spider two-seat roadster continued with little change. The hood contained an airscoop. Examples built from late 1960 onward had front disc brakes.

2100 — SIX — Production of the six-cylinder sedan and station wagon continued with little change. Power came from a 2054-cc engine, hooked to a four-speed gearbox with column gearshift lever. Reclining seats and a rear defroster were standard. Styling features included a back-slanted grille.

I.D. DATA: Chassis serial number is under the hood on the left side of the engine-compartment firewall (500/600) or on right side of firewall; and on right side of body frame. Engine type and serial number are stamped on the block. Model 500 engine number is stamped on a pad cast to the left of the rear end of the crankcase support. Model 600 engine number is stamped at the front of the engine, above the timing chain cover. Model 1100 engine number is stamped on a pad to upper right of block, near the head and above the generator; or below the hood hinges. Model 1200 engine number is stamped on the right front end of the block, near the cylinder head flange. Model 1500 engine number is stamped on a pad on the block, and on the identification plate. Starting serial number: (500 spt sed) 082524; (500 sunroof) 088551; (500 Bianchina Spt) 014309; (500 Bianchina) 013140; (600) 688093; (600 sunroof) 681618; (1100) 588803; (1100 DeL) 588421; (1200 sed) 588080; (1200 Spider) 000187; (1500 Spider) 000383; (2100 sedan) 006851.

Model	Body Type & Seating	Engine Type/CID	P.O.E. Price	Weight (lbs.)	Prod. Total
500					
	2-dr Sedan-4P	I2/29	998	1100	Note 1
	2-dr Spt Sed-4P	I2/30	998	1125	Note 1
Bianchina	2-dr DeL Cpe-2P	I2/29	998	1100	Note 1
Bianchina	2-dr Spt Cpe-2P	I2/30	998	1125	Note 1
Jolly	2-dr Sedan-4P	I2/29	1760	1050	Note 1
600					
	2-dr Sedan-4P	I4/39	1198	1334	Note 1
Sunroof	2-dr Sedan-4P	I4/39	1198	1334	Note 1
Jolly	2-dr Sedan-4P	I4/39	1906	1250	Note 1
600 MULTIPLA					
	4-dr Sta Wag-4/5P	I4/39	1198	1653	Note 1
	4-dr Sta Wag-6P	I4/39	1198	1653	Note 1
1100					
	4-dr Sedan-5P	I4/66	1385	1940	Note 1
Deluxe	4-dr Sedan-5P	I4/66	1485	2018	Note 1
	4-dr Sta Wag-5P	I4/66	1398	1985	Note 1

Model	Body Type & Seating	Engine Type/CID	P.O.E. Price	Weight (lbs.)	Prod. Total
1200					
	4-dr Sedan-5P	I4/75	1648	2069	Note 1
Spider	2-dr Conv-2P	I4/75	2595	2030	Note 1
1500 (1500S)					
Spider	2-dr Conv-2P	I4/91	3298	2117	Note 1
2100					
	4-dr Sedan-5/6P	I6/125	2598	2679	Note 1
	4-dr Sta Wag-5/6P	I6/125	2658	2888	Note 1

Note 1: A total of 566,284 Fiats (all models) were produced during 1961.

Price Note: Higher figures were listed in the course of the year, including $1134 for the 500 Sport sedan; $1398 for the 600 sedan; up to $1693 for the 600 Multipla; up to $1694 for the 1100 sedan; up to $1818 for the 1100 Deluxe; up to $1945 for the 1100 wagon; up to $2025 for the 1200 sedan; up to $2685 for the 1200 Spider; up to $3333 for the 1500 Spider; $2833 for the 2100 sedan; and $3058 for the 2100 wagon.

ENGINE DATA: BASE TWO (500): Vertical, inline overhead-valve two-cylinder. Aluminum block and head. **Displacement:** 29.2 cu. in. (479 cc). **Bore & Stroke:** 2.59 x 2.75 in. (66 x 70 mm). **Compression Ratio:** 7.0:1. **Brake Horsepower:** 21 (SAE) at 4000 rpm. **Torque:** 20 lbs.-ft. at 3500 rpm. Solid valve lifters. One carburetor.

BASE TWO (500 Sport): Same as above, but — **Displacement:** 30.5 cu. in. (499 cc). **Bore & Stroke:** 2.65 x 2.75 in. (67.4 x 70 mm). **Compression Ratio:** 8.6:1. **Brake Horsepower:** 21 (25 SAE at 4800 rpm).

BASE FOUR (600): Inline, overhead-valve four-cylinder. Cast iron block and aluminum head. **Displacement:** 38.6 cu. in. (633 cc). **Bore & Stroke:** 2.36 x 2.20 in. (60 x 56 mm). **Compression Ratio:** 7.5:1. **Brake Horsepower:** 28.5 (SAE) at 4900 rpm. **Torque:** 28.9 lbs.-ft. at 3000 rpm. Three main bearings. Solid valve lifters. One Weber carburetor.

BASE FOUR (1100): Inline, overhead-valve four-cylinder. Cast iron block and aluminum head. **Displacement:** 66.5 cu. in. (1089 cc). **Bore & Stroke:** 2.68 x 2.95 in. (68 x 75 mm). **Compression Ratio:** 7.0:1. **Brake Horsepower:** 48 (SAE) at 4800 rpm. **Torque:** 52 lbs.-ft. at 3200 rpm. Three main bearings. Solid valve lifters. Weber dual-choke carburetor.

Note: A variant of the 1100 engine had 7.85:1 compression and was rated 55 bhp at 5200 rpm.

BASE FOUR (1200): Inline, overhead-valve four-cylinder. Cast iron block and aluminum head. **Displacement:** 74.5 cu. in. (1225 cc). **Bore & Stroke:** 2.83 x 2.95 in. (71.9 x 75 mm). **Compression Ratio:** 8.25:1. **Brake Horsepower:** 63 (SAE) at 5300 rpm. **Torque:** 60 lbs.-ft. at 3000 rpm. Three main bearings. Solid valve lifters. Weber dual-choke carburetor.

BASE FOUR (1500): Inline, dual-overhead-cam four-cylinder. Cast iron block and aluminum head. **Displacement:** 91 cu. in. (1491 cc). **Bore & Stroke:** 3.07 x 3.07 in. (78 x 78 mm). **Compression Ratio:** 8.6:1. **Brake Horsepower:** 90 (SAE) at 6000 rpm. **Torque:** 84 lbs.-ft. at 3600 rpm. Five main bearings. Solid valve lifters. Weber dual-choke carburetor.

BASE SIX (2100): Inline, overhead-valve six-cylinder. Cast iron block and aluminum head. **Displacement:** 125.4 cu. in. (2054 cc). **Bore & Stroke:** 3.03 x 2.89 in. (77 x 73.5 mm). **Compression Ratio:** 8.8:1. **Brake Horsepower:** 90/95 (SAE) at 5000 rpm. Solid valve lifters.

CHASSIS DATA: Wheelbase: (500) 72.4 in.; (600) 78.75 in.; (1100) 92.1 in.; (1200) 92.1 in.; (1500) 92.1 in.; (2100) 104.3 in. **Overall Length:** (500) 117 in.; (600 sedan) 130.5 in.; (600 Multipla) 140.8 in.; (1100 sedan) 154.3 in.; (1100 wagon) 147.6 in.; (1200 sed) 154.3 in.; (1200 conv) 152.6 in.; (1500) 158.7 in.; (2100) 175.8 in. **Height:** (500) 52.2 in.; (600 sedan) 55.3 in.; (600 Multipla) 62.3 in.; (1100 sedan) 58.6 in.; (1200 sed) 57.8 in.; (1200 conv) 51.2 in.; (1500) 51.2 in.; (2100) 57.9 in. **Width:** (500) 52 in.; (600 sedan) 54.3 in.; (600 Multipla) 57.0 in.; (1100 sedan) 57.4 in.; (1200 sed) 57.4 in.; (1200 conv) 57.9 in.; (1500) 60 in.; (2100) 63.6 in. **Front Tread:** (500) 44.1 in.; (600 sedan) 45.3 in.; (600 Multipla) 48.3 in.; (1100) 48.6 in.; (1200) 48.6 in.; (1500) 48.6 in.; (2100) 52.75 in. **Rear Tread:** (500) 44.5 in.; (600 sedan) 45.5 in.; (600 Multipla) 45.5 in.; (1100) 47.9 in.; (1200) 47.9 in.; (1500) 47.8 in.; (2100) 51.4 in. **Standard Tires:** (500) 4.90x12 or 125x12; (600) 5.20x12; (1100/1200) 5.20x14 except wagon, 5.60x14; (1500) 155x15; (2100) 5.90x14 or 6.40x14.

TECHNICAL: Layout: (500/600) rear-engine, rear-drive; (1100/1200/1500/2100) front-engine, rear-drive. **Transmission:** four-speed manual. **Steering:** (500) worm and sector; (600) worm and segment; (600 Multipla, 1100/1500) worm and roller. **Suspension (front):** (500) A-arms with coil springs; (600) A-arms with transverse leaf spring; (600 Multipla) A-arms with coil springs; (1100/1200) transverse A-arms with coil springs and anti-roll bar; (1500) swinging arms, coil springs and anti-roll bar; (2100) wishbones with adjustable torsion bars and anti-roll bar. **Suspension (rear):** (500) single A-arms with coil springs; (600) radius arms with coil springs; (1100/1200/1500/2100) rigid axle with semi-elliptic leaf springs and anti-roll bar. **Brakes:** hydraulic, front/rear drum except (late 1500) front disc, rear drum. **Body Construction:** steel unibody.

PERFORMANCE: Top Speed: (500) about 59 mph; (500 Sport) 65 mph; (600) 60 mph; (1100) 77-81 mph; (1200) 87 mph; (1500) 105 mph; (2100) 87-93 mph. **Acceleration (0-60 mph):** (600) 54.0 sec.; (1100) 23 sec.; (1200) 20.5 sec. **Acceleration (quarter-mile):** (600) 26.1 sec. **Fuel Mileage:** (500) 40-50 mpg; (600 Multipla) 40 mpg average; (1100) 28 mpg average; (1200) 23-29 mpg; (2100) 21 mpg average.

PRODUCTION/SALES: Approximately 11,839 Fiats were sold in the U.S. during 1961.

ADDITIONAL MODELS: A 2300 six-cylinder sedan became available in Europe, as did a Ghia-bodied coupe capable of 120 mph. Series 1500 sedans and other models were marketed elsewhere in the world, though not ordinarily sent to the U.S.

Distributor: Fiat Motor Co. Inc. or Hoffman Motors Corp., New York City and Beverly Hills, California.

HISTORY: The 1961 models were introduced to the U.S. market on October 1, 1960. Late in 1961, Fiat elected to limit the number of models to be exported to the U.S., retaining only the 600D, 1100, and 1200 convertible. A modified 500D also became available, with 499-cc engine and slightly more power than the original, but was not ordinarily imported into the U.S.

1962 Fiat 1200 roadster.

1200 — FOUR — Production of the 1221-cc Spider roadster continued with little change.

I.D. DATA: Chassis serial number is under the hood on the left side of the engine-compartment firewall (600D) or on right side of firewall (1100/1200); and on right side of body frame. Engine type and serial number are stamped on the block. Model 600D engine number is stamped at the front of the engine, above the timing chain cover. Model 1100 engine number is stamped on a pad to upper right of block, near the head and above the generator; or below the hood hinges. Model 1200 engine number is stamped on the right front end of the block, near the cylinder head flange.

Model	Body Type & Seating	Engine Type/CID	P.O.E. Price	Weight (lbs.)	Prod. Total
600D					
	2-dr Sedan-4P	I4/47	1249	1331	Note 1
1100					
Export	4-dr Sedan-5P	I4/66	1498	2017	Note 1
Special	4-dr Sedan-5P	I4/66	1698	2050	Note 1
1200					
Spider	2-dr Conv-2P	I4/75	2595	2030	Note 1

Note 1: A total of 748,608 Fiats (all models) were produced during 1962.

ENGINE DATA: BASE FOUR (600D): Inline, overhead-valve four-cylinder. Cast iron block and aluminum head. **Displacement:** 46.8 cu. in. (767 cc). **Bore & Stroke:** 2.44 x 2.50 in. (62 x 63.5 mm). **Compression Ratio:** 7.5:1. **Brake Horsepower:** 32 (SAE) at 4800 rpm. **Torque:** 36 lbs.-ft. at 3000 rpm. Three main bearings. Solid valve lifters. One Weber single-barrel carburetor.

BASE FOUR (1100): Inline, overhead-valve four-cylinder (103H). Cast iron block and aluminum head. **Displacement:** 66.5 cu. in. (1089 cc). **Bore & Stroke:** 2.68 x 2.95 in. (68 x 75 mm). **Compression Ratio:** (Special) 7.85:1. **Brake Horsepower:** (Special) 55 (SAE) at 5200 rpm. **Torque:** (Special) 52.8 lbs.-ft. at 3500 rpm. Three main bearings. Solid valve lifters. Weber dual-choke carburetor.

BASE FOUR (1200): Inline, overhead-valve four-cylinder. Cast iron block and aluminum head. **Displacement:** 74.5 cu. in. (1221 cc). **Bore & Stroke:** 2.83 x 2.95 in. (71.9 x 75 mm). **Compression Ratio:** 8.25:1. **Brake Horsepower:** 63 (SAE) at 5300 rpm. **Torque:** 60 lbs.-ft. at 3000 rpm. Three main bearings. Solid valve lifters. Weber dual-choke carburetor.

CHASSIS DATA: Wheelbase: (600D) 78.75 in.; (1100/1200) 92.1 in. **Overall Length:** (600D) 131.5 in.; (1100 sedan) 154 in.; (1200 conv) 158.7 in. **Height:** (600D sedan) 55.3 in.; (1100 sedan) 58.6 in.; (1100 Special) 58.3 in.; (1200 conv) 51.2 in. **Width:** (600D sedan) 54.3 in.; (1100 sedan) 57.3 in.; (1100 Special) 58 in.; (1200 conv) 57.9 in. **Front Tread:** (600D) 45.3 in.; (1100/1200) 48.6 in. **Rear Tread:** (600D) 45.7 in.; (1100/1200) 47.8 in. **Standard Tires:** (600D) 5.20x12; (1100/1200) 5.20x14.

TECHNICAL: Layout: (600D) rear-engine, rear-drive; (1100/1200) front-engine, rear-drive. **Transmission:** four-speed manual. **Steering:** (600D) worm and segment; (1100) worm and roller. **Suspension (front):** (600D) lower arms with transverse leaf spring; (1100) transverse A-arms with coil springs and anti-roll bar. **Suspension (rear):** (600D) radius arms with coil springs; (1100) rigid axle with semi-elliptic leaf springs and anti-roll bar. **Brakes:** hydraulic, front/rear drum. **Body Construction:** steel unibody.

PERFORMANCE: Top Speed: (600D) 65-70 mph; (1100 Special) 80 mph; (1200) 87-90 mph. **Acceleration (0-60 mph):** (1100 Special) 32 sec.; (600D) 0-50 mph in 21 sec. **Fuel Mileage:** (600D) 40-55 mpg; (1200) about 29 mpg.

PRODUCTION/SALES: Approximately 9,762 Fiats were sold in the U.S. during 1962.

ADDITIONAL MODELS: Fiat introduced a 1600S two-seat sports car in 1962, replacing the 1500S (which continued in production for a time). Like its predecessor, the 1600S carried a dual-overhead-cam four, but displacement grew to 1568 cc (95.7-cid) and it delivered 90 horsepower (100 SAE) at 6000 rpm. Torque output was 98 pound-feet at 4000 rpm. This model was not included in most lists of imported models at this time.

Manufacturer: Fiat S.p.A., Turin, Italy.

Distributor: Fiat Motor Co. Inc., New York City; and Hoffman Motors Corp., New York City.

HISTORY: The 1962 models were introduced to the U.S. market on October 1, 1961 except (600D and 1100 Special) June 1, 1961.

1962 FIAT

1963 FIAT

600D — FOUR — Only the sedan was available in 1962, with a larger and more powerful engine. The 767-cc four had higher compression and horsepower (now 32 bhp), while the car itself gained better ventilation. The starter was now ignition-key activated, rather than using a control on the floor tunnel. As before, a sunroof version was available, with roll-back fabric top. Unlike the former 600, the 600D had front vent wings.

1100 — FOUR — Only the sedan, in two versions, was available this year. The four-cylinder engine produced 55 horsepower for the 1100 "Special," which was similar to the 1200 sedan that had been imported in 1958-59 and wore front-hinged front doors. The regular 1100 retained its rear-hinged "suicide" doors. The Special also had a wraparound rear window and thin rear pillars. Up front was a crosshatch grille with small round parking lights alongside. Chrome trim strips ran from the hood front about one-third of the way back to the windshield.

600D — FOUR — Production of the rear-drive sedan with 767-cc engine continued with little change.

1100/1100D — FOUR — A "Special" sedan and a new 1100D sedan were offered this year. The 1100D had a larger (1221-cc) engine, as in the 1200 series, but no horsepower increase over the smaller powerplant. The 1100D wore a restyled rectangular grille with rectangular Fiat emblem at upper center, and contained bucket seats. Its front doors were now front-hinged. The 1100D lacked the former sculpted trim line that ran from the lower front fenders along the doors, but displayed a notable full-length bodyside chrome

strip. Its front bumper dividers were shorter and thicker than the prior style, parking lights were rectangular (formerly round), while the rear window reached higher up into the car's roofline. The gas cap was now installed in the left rear fender.

1200 — FOUR — Production of the 1221-cc Spider roadster continued with little change.

I.D. DATA: Chassis serial number is under the hood on the left side of the engine-compartment firewall (600D) or on right side of firewall (1100/1200); and on right side of body frame. Engine type and serial number are stamped on the block. Model 600D engine number is stamped at the front of the engine, above the timing chain cover. Model 1100 engine number is stamped on a pad to upper right of block, near the head and above the generator; or below the hood hinges. Model 1200 engine number is stamped on the right front end of the block, near the cylinder head flange. Serial number range: (600D) 1062603 to 1399742; (1100D) 1020001 to 1034342; (1100 Special) 830435 up; (1200) 012091 up.

Model	Body Type & Seating	Engine Type/CID	P.O.E. Price	Weight (lbs.)	Prod. Total
600D					
	2-dr Sedan-4P	I4/47	1249	1334	Note 1
1100					
Special	4-dr Sedan-4/5P	I4/66	1498	2050	Note 1
1100D	4-dr Sedan-4/5P	I4/75	1498	1975	Note 1
1200					
Spider	2-dr Conv-2P	I4/75	2595	2030	Note 1

Note 1: A total of 909,887 Fiats (all models) were produced during 1963.

ENGINE DATA: BASE FOUR (600D): Inline, overhead-valve four-cylinder. Cast iron block and aluminum head. **Displacement:** 46.8 cu. in. (767 cc). **Bore & Stroke:** 2.44 x 2.50 in. (62 x 63.5 mm). **Compression Ratio:** 7.5:1. **Brake Horsepower:** 32 (SAE) at 4800 rpm. **Torque:** 36 lbs.-ft. at 3000 rpm. Three main bearings. Solid valve lifters. One Weber 281CD or Solex C28PIB-2 single-barrel carburetor.

BASE FOUR (1100): Inline, overhead-valve four-cylinder (103H). Cast iron block and aluminum head. **Displacement:** 66.5 cu. in. (1089 cc). **Bore & Stroke:** 2.68 x 2.95 in. (68 x 75 mm). **Compression Ratio:** 7.85:1. **Brake Horsepower:** 55 (SAE) at 5200 rpm. **Torque:** 52 lbs.-ft. at 3200 rpm. Three main bearings. Solid valve lifters. Weber or Solex two-barrel carburetor.

BASE FOUR (1100D, 1200): Inline, overhead-valve four-cylinder. Cast iron block and aluminum head. **Displacement:** 74.5 cu. in. (1221 cc). **Bore & Stroke:** 2.83 x 2.95 in. (71.9 x 75 mm). **Compression Ratio:** (1100D) 8.0:1; (1200) 8.25:1. **Brake Horsepower:** (1100D) 55 SAE at 5000 rpm; (1200) 63 SAE at 5600 rpm. **Torque:** (1100D) 56 lbs.-ft. at 2500 rpm; (1200) 60 lbs.-ft. at 3000 rpm. Three main bearings. Solid valve lifters. Weber two-barrel carburetor.

CHASSIS DATA: Wheelbase: (600D) 78.5 in.; (1100) 92.1 in.; (1200) 92.1 in. **Overall Length:** (600D) 131.5 in.; (1100) 154 in.; (1200 conv) 158.7 in. **Height:** (600D) 55.3 in.; (1100) 58.6 in.; (1200 conv) 51.2 in. **Width:** (600D) 54.3 in.; (1100 sedan) 57.3 in.; (1200 conv) 57.9 in. **Front Tread:** (600D) 45.3 in.; (1100) 48.6 in.; (1200) 48.6 in. **Rear Tread:** (600D) 45.7 in.; (1100) 47.8 in.; (1200) 47.8 in. **Standard Tires:** (600D) 5.20x12; (1100/1200) 5.20x14.

TECHNICAL: Layout: (600D) rear-engine, rear-drive; (1100/1200) front-engine, rear-drive. **Transmission:** four-speed manual. **Steering:** (600D) screw and sector; (1100/1200) worm and roller. **Suspension (front):** (600D) transverse leaf spring with lower arms; (1100/1200) transverse wishbones with coil springs and anti-roll bar. **Suspension (rear):** (600D) semi-trailing arms with coil springs; (1100/1200) rigid axle with semi-elliptic leaf springs and anti-roll bar. **Brakes:** (600D/1100) front/rear drum; (1200) front disc, rear drum. **Body Construction:** steel unibody.

PERFORMANCE: Top Speed: (600D) 70 mph; (1100D) 80+ mph; (1200) 87-90 mph. **Fuel Mileage:** (600D) 40-55 mpg; (1100D) 29-35 mpg; (1200) about 29 mpg.

PRODUCTION/SALES: Approximately 10,805 Fiats were sold in the U.S. during 1963.

ADDITIONAL MODELS: Production of the 1600S two-seater continued, though it was not included is most lists of imported models. During the 1963 model year, it added rear disc brakes and quad headlamps.

Manufacturer: Fiat S.p.A., Turin, Italy.

Distributor: Fiat Motor Company Inc. and Hoffman Motors Corp., New York City.

HISTORY: The 1963 models were introduced to the U.S. market on October 1, 1962 except (1100 Special) July 15, 1962 and (1100D) January 1, 1963. A new 1500 Spider convertible debuted in the U.S. as a 1963.5 model; see next listing for details.

1964 FIAT

1964 Fiat Pininfarina coupe.

600D — FOUR — Production of the rear-drive sedan with 767-cc engine continued with little change, except that the bodyside moldings now started at the headlamp rims.

1100D — FOUR — Only the 1100D sedan remained of the 1100 series, powered by a 1221-cc engine. Standard equipment included a four-speed manual gearbox, heater, electric wipers, windshield washers, bumper guards, roll-down windows, whitewall tires, and full-length bodyside moldings. Upright in profile, the four-door sedan had a rectangular grille with crosshatch pattern, and rectangular parking lights below single round headlamps.

1500 — FOUR — A new version of the Spider convertible emerged this year, replacing the 1200, with a larger (1481-cc) four-cylinder engine beneath its hood. With 80 horsepower at hand, a Spider was said to be capable of 100 mph. This engine was derived from Fiat's six-cylinder version, as used in the 2100 sedan. Pininfarina was responsible for the styling, which differed considerably from the 1200: lower and longer in appearance, and wearing a low hood without an airscoop. Design features included a low, wide eggcrate-pattern grille with center Fiat insignia, and round parking lights below the single round headlamps. Front bumper dividers wrapped around the front of the horizontal element. Vertical taillamps were installed. Standard equipment included front disc brakes, roll-up windows, Pirelli Cinturato tires, a clock, heater/defroster, padded dashboard, and a racing-style steering wheel. The four-speed manual gearbox was synchronized on all except first gear.

I.D. DATA: Chassis serial number is under the hood on the left side of the engine-compartment firewall (600D) or on right side of firewall (1100D/1500); and/or on right side of body frame. Engine type and serial number are stamped on the block. Model 600D engine number is stamped at the front of the engine, above the timing chain cover. Model 1500 engine number is stamped on the block, and on the identification plate. Starting serial number: (600D) 1399743; (1100D) 1034343; (1500) 025001.

Model	Body Type & Seating	Engine Type/CID	P.O.E. Price	Weight (lbs.)	Prod. Total
600D					
	2-dr Sedan-4P	I4/47	1262	1330	Note 1
1100D					
	4-dr Sedan-4/5P	I4/75	1655	1975	Note 1
1500					
Spider	2-dr Conv-2P	I4/90	2895	2117	Note 1

Note 1: A total of 881,702 Fiats (all models) were produced during 1964.

Price Note: Figure shown for 1500 Spider was advertised as it entered the U.S. market; price was listed later as low as $2639.

ENGINE DATA: BASE FOUR (600D): Inline, overhead-valve four-cylinder. Cast iron block and aluminum head. **Displacement:** 46.8 cu. in. (767 cc). **Bore & Stroke:** 2.44 x 2.50 in. (62 x 63.5 mm). **Compression Ratio:** 7.5:1. **Brake Horsepower:** 32 (SAE) at 4800 rpm. **Torque:** 36 lbs.-ft. at 3000 rpm. Three main bearings. Solid valve lifters. One Weber 281CD or Solex C28PIB-2 single-barrel carburetor.

BASE FOUR (1100D): Inline, overhead-valve four-cylinder. Cast iron block and aluminum head. **Displacement:** 74.5 cu. in. (1221 cc). **Bore & Stroke:** 2.83 x 2.95 in. (71.9 x 75 mm). **Compression Ratio:** 8.0:1. **Brake Horsepower:** 55 (SAE) at 5000 rpm. **Torque:** 56 lbs.-ft. at 2500 rpm. Three main bearings. Solid valve lifters.

BASE FOUR (1500): Inline, overhead-valve four-cylinder. Cast iron block and aluminum head. **Displacement:** 90.4 cu. in. (1481 cc). **Bore & Stroke:** 3.03 x 3.13 in. (77 x 79.5 mm). **Compression Ratio:** 8.8:1. **Brake Horsepower:** 80 (SAE) at 5200 rpm. **Torque:** 86.8 lbs.-ft. at 3200 rpm. Three main bearings. Solid valve lifters. Weber 28-36 DCD 19 (or Solex) two-barrel carburetor.

CHASSIS DATA: Wheelbase: (600D) 78.5 in.; (1100D) 92.1 in.; (1500) 92.1 in. **Overall Length:** (600D) 131.5 in.; (1100D) 154 in.; (1500) 160.8 in. **Height:** (600D) 55.3 in.; (1100D) 58.6 in.; (1500) 51 in. **Width: (600D)** 54.3 in.; (1100D) 57.3 in.; (1500) 59.8 in. **Front Tread:** (600D) 45.3 in.; (1100D) 48.6 in.; (1500) 48.5 in. **Rear Tread:** (600D) 45.7 in.; (1100D) 47.9 in.; (1500) 48.5 in. **Standard Tires:** (600D) 5.20x12; (1100D) 5.20x14; (1500) 145x14.

TECHNICAL: Layout: (600D) rear-engine, rear-drive; (1100D/1500) front-engine, rear-drive. **Transmission:** (600D/1100D) four-speed manual; (1500) four-speed manual (floor lever). **Steering:** (600D) screw and sector; (1100D/1500) worm and roller. **Suspension (front):** (600D) transverse leaf spring with lower arms; (1100D/1500) transverse A-arms with coil springs and anti-roll bar. **Suspension (rear):** (600D) semi-trailing arms with coil springs; (1100D/1500) rigid axle with semi-elliptic leaf springs and anti-roll bar. **Brakes:** (600D/1100D) front/rear drum; (1500) front disc, rear drum. **Body Construction:** steel unibody.

PERFORMANCE: Top Speed: (600D) 70 mph; (1100D) 80+ mph; (1500) 100+ mph claimed. **Acceleration (0-60 mph):** (1500) 13.0-14.7 sec. **Acceleration:** (1500) 19.2-20.1 sec. (about 70 mph). **Fuel Mileage:** (600D) 40-55 mpg; (1100D) 29-35 mpg; (1500) about 25 mpg.

PRODUCTION/SALES: Approximately 8,988 Fiats were sold in the U.S. during 1964.

ADDITIONAL MODELS: Fiat continued to produce the 1600S sports car, introduced in 1962, though it was not included in lists of models imported into the U.S. at this time. Other models offered in the home market included the 500D coupe, 1300 sedan, 1500 sedan, 1800B sedan, and 2300 six-cylinder coupe/sedan.

Manufacturer: Fiat S.p.A., Turin, Italy.

Distributor: Fiat Motor Company Inc., New York City.

HISTORY: The 1964 models were introduced to the U.S. market on September 1, 1963. Ads for the new 1500 roadster promised "superb Italian styling in the spirit of sport."

1965 FIAT

600D — FOUR — Except for the substitution of front-hinged front doors for the traditional "suicide" style doors, production of Fiat's rear-drive sedan with 767-cc engine continued with little change.

1100D — FOUR — A four-door station wagon joined the original 1100D sedan this year. Both were powered by a 1221-cc four-cylinder engine, with four-speed gearbox. The 1100D had aluminum-finned brake drums, rubber-padded bumper guards, and trunk and underhood lights.

1500 — FOUR — For its second year in the lineup, the 1500 Spider two-seat convertible continued with little change. These early examples displayed a curious hole in the rocker panel, below the door; but that would disappear after 1965. As before, the 1481-cc engine produced 80 horsepower. A tachometer replaced the former clock on the instrument panel. During the model year, a five-speed (fully synchronized) manual gearbox became available.

I.D. DATA: Chassis serial number is under the hood on the left side of the engine-compartment firewall (600D) or on right side of firewall (1100D/1500); and/or on right side of body frame. Engine type and serial number are stamped on the block. Model 600D engine number is stamped at the front of the engine, above the timing chain cover. Model 1500 engine number is stamped on the block, and on the identification plate. Starting serial number: (600D) 1821001; (1100D sedan) 1188877 or 1146535; (1100D wagon) 1263910; (1500) 028217.

Model	Body Type & Seating	Engine Type/CID	P.O.E. Price	Weight (lbs.)	Prod. Total
600D					
	2-dr Sedan-4P	I4/47	1262	1275	Note 1
1100D					
1100D	4-dr Sedan-4/5P	I4/75	1595	1896	Note 1
1100D	4-dr Sta Wag-5P	I4/75	1759	1971	Note 1
1500					
Spider	2-dr Conv-2P	I4/90	2639	2040	Note 1

Note 1: A total of 957,941 Fiats (all models) were produced during 1965.

ENGINE DATA: BASE FOUR (600D): Inline, overhead-valve four-cylinder. Cast iron block and aluminum head. **Displacement:** 46.8 cu. in. (767 cc). **Bore & Stroke:** 2.44 x 2.50 in. (62 x 63.5 mm). **Compression Ratio:** 7.5:1. **Brake Horsepower:** 32 (SAE) at 4800 rpm. **Torque:** 38 lbs.-ft. at 3000 rpm. Three main bearings. Solid valve lifters. One Weber 281CD or Solex C28PIB-2 single-barrel carburetor.

BASE FOUR (1100D): Inline, overhead-valve four-cylinder. Cast iron block and aluminum head. **Displacement:** 74.5 cu. in. (1221 cc). **Bore & Stroke:** 2.83 x 2.95 in. (71.9 x 75 mm). **Compression Ratio:** 8.0:1. **Brake Horsepower:** 55 (SAE) at 5000 rpm. **Torque:** 62 lbs.-ft. at 2500 rpm. Three main bearings. Solid valve lifters.

BASE FOUR (1500): Inline, overhead-valve four-cylinder. Cast iron block and aluminum head. **Displacement:** 90.4 cu. in. (1481 cc). **Bore & Stroke:** 3.03 x 3.13 in. (77 x 79.5 mm). **Compression Ratio:** 8.8:1. **Brake Horsepower:** 80 (SAE) at 5200 rpm. **Torque:** 86.8 lbs.-ft. at 3200 rpm. Three main bearings. Solid valve lifters. Weber two-barrel carburetor.

CHASSIS DATA: Wheelbase: (600D) 78.5 in.; (1100D) 92.1 in.; (1500) 92.1 in. **Overall Length:** (600D) 130.5 in.; (1100D sedan) 154 in.; (1100D wagon) 154.1 in.; (1500) 160.8 in. **Height:** (600D) 55.3 in.; (1100D sedan) 57.8 in.; (1100D wagon) 58.5 in.; (1500) 51 in. **Width:** (600D) 54.3 in.; (1100D sedan) 57.3 in.; (1100D wagon) 57.5 in.; (1500) 59.8 in. **Front Tread:** (600D) 45.3 in.; (1100D) 48.6 in.; (1500) 48.5 in. **Rear Tread:** (600D) 45.7 in.; (1100D) 47.9 in.; (1500) 48.5 in. **Standard Tires:** (600D) 5.20x12; (1100D sedan) 5.20x14; (1100D wagon) 5.60x14; (1500) 145x14.

TECHNICAL: Layout: (600D) rear-engine, rear-drive; (1100D/1500) front-engine, rear-drive. **Transmission:** (600D/1100D) four-speed manual; (1500) four-speed manual (floor lever); (late 1500) five-speed manual. **Steering:** (600D) screw and sector; (1100/1500) worm and roller. **Suspension (front):** (600D) transverse leaf spring with lower arms; (1100D/1500) transverse A-arms with coil springs and anti-roll bar. **Suspension (rear):** (600D) radius arms with coil springs; (1100D/1500) rigid axle with semi-elliptic leaf springs and anti-roll bar. **Brakes:** (600D/1100D) front/rear drum; (1500) front disc, rear drum. **Body Construction:** steel unibody.

PERFORMANCE: Top Speed: (600D) 70 mph; (1100D) 80+ mph; (1500) 100+ mph claimed. **Fuel Mileage:** (600D) 40-55 mpg; (1100D) 29-35 mpg; (1500) about 25 mpg.

PRODUCTION/SALES: Approximately 8,194 Fiats were sold in the U.S. during 1965.

ADDITIONAL MODELS: In addition to the 1500 sports car, Fiat produced a 1600S two-seater with 1568-cc (95.7-cid) twin-cam engine that produced 90 horsepower at 6000 rpm, and 98 pound-feet of torque. The 1600S now had all-disc brakes and a five-speed manual gearbox, and wore quad headlamps.

Manufacturer: Fiat S.p.A., Turin, Italy.

Distributor: Fiat Motor Company Inc., New York City.

HISTORY: Fiat's 1500 Spider was introduced to the U.S. market on September 1, 1964; the 1100D sedan on August 15, 1964. The new 850 sedan was now available in Europe, but would not reach the U.S. market until the 1967 model year. Trade advertisements promoted the broad range offered by Fiat's four models: a lowest-priced two-door sedan, a four-door luxury-economy car, a lowest-priced four-door family wagon, and the Pininfarina deluxe sports car. *Car and Driver* described the 1500 sports car as a "civilized two-seater" with an engine "always willing to rev (and) a lovely crisp exhaust note."

1966 FIAT

1966 Fiat Dino Spider roadster.

600D — FOUR — For yet another year, production of Fiat's little rear-drive sedan with 767-cc engine continued with minimal change.

1100D — FOUR — A new 1100R series with 1089-cc engine soon would replace the 1100D, but the latter continued for one more season without change. As before, power came from a 1221-cc four-cylinder engine, with four-speed gearbox.

1500 — FOUR — Fiat's two-seat convertible got a slight power boost this year (three extra horsepower), with a rise in compression to 9.0:1. Otherwise, production continued with little change. This year's grille insignia, however, was a small round one instead of the former rectangular shape. A five-speed manual gearbox was now standard.

I.D. DATA: Chassis serial number is under the hood on the left side of the engine-compartment firewall (600D) or on right side of firewall (1100D/1500); and/or on right side of body frame. Engine type and serial number are stamped on the block. Model 600D engine number is stamped at the front of the engine, above the timing chain cover. Model 1500 engine number is stamped on the block, and on the identification plate. Starting serial number: (600D) 1895844; (1100D sedan) 1188877; (1100D wagon) 1305850; (1500) 040181.

Model	Body Type & Seating	Engine Type/CID	P.O.E. Price	Weight (lbs.)	Prod. Total
600D					
	2-dr Sedan-4P	I4/47	1237	1275	Note 1
1100D					
1100D	4-dr Sedan-4/5P	I4/75	1564	1896	Note 1
1100D	4-dr Sta Wag-5P	I4/75	1724	1971	Note 1
1500					
Spider	2-dr Conv-2P	I4/90	2585	2040	Note 1

Note 1: A total of 1,110,701 Fiats (all models) were produced during 1966.

ENGINE DATA: BASE FOUR (600D): Inline, overhead-valve four-cylinder. Cast iron block and aluminum head. **Displacement:** 46.8 cu. in. (767 cc). **Bore & Stroke:** 2.44 x 2.50 in. (62 x 63.5 mm). **Compression Ratio:** 7.5:1. **Brake Horsepower:** 32 (SAE) at 4800 rpm. **Torque:** 38 lbs.-ft. at 3000 rpm. Three main bearings. Solid valve lifters. One Weber or Solex single-barrel carburetor.

BASE FOUR (1100D): Inline, overhead-valve four-cylinder. Cast iron block and aluminum head. **Displacement:** 74.5 cu. in. (1221 cc). **Bore & Stroke:** 2.83 x 2.95 in. (71.9 x 75 mm). **Compression Ratio:** 8.0:1. **Brake Horsepower:** 55 (SAE) at 5000 rpm. **Torque:** 62 lbs.-ft. at 2500 rpm. Three main bearings. Solid valve lifters. Weber or Solex carburetor.

BASE FOUR (1500): Inline, overhead-valve four-cylinder. Cast iron block and aluminum head. **Displacement:** 90.4 cu. in. (1481 cc). **Bore & Stroke:** 3.03 x 3.13 in. (77 x 79.5 mm). **Compression Ratio:** 9.0:1. **Brake Horsepower:** 83 (SAE) at 5400 rpm. **Torque:** 88 lbs.-ft. at 3200 rpm. Three main bearings. Solid valve lifters. Weber 34DCMD4 two-barrel carburetor.

CHASSIS DATA: Wheelbase: (600D) 78.5 in.; (1100D) 92.1 in.; (1500) 92.1 in. **Overall Length:** (600D) 130.5 in.; (1100D sedan) 154 in.; (1100D wagon) 154.1 in.; (1500) 160.8 in. **Height:** (600D) 55.3 in.; (1100D sedan) 57.8 in.; (1100D wagon) 58.5 in.; (1500) 51 in. **Width:** (600D) 54.3 in.; (1100D sedan) 57.4 in.; (1100D wagon) 57.5 in.; (1500) 59.8 in. **Front Tread:** (600D) 45.3 in.; (1100D) 48.6 in.; (1500) 48.5 in. **Rear Tread:** (600D) 45.7 in.; (1100D) 47.9 in.; (1500) 48.5 in. **Standard Tires:** (600D) 5.20x12; (1100D sedan) 5.20x14; (1100D wagon) 5.60x14; (1500) 145x14.

TECHNICAL: Layout: (600D) rear-engine, rear-drive; (1100D/1500) front-engine, rear-drive. **Transmission:** (600D/1100D) four-speed manual; (1500) five-speed manual. **Standard Final Drive Ratio:** (600D) 4.30:1; (1100D) 4.30:1; (1500) 3.90:1. **Steering:** (600D) worm and sector; (1100D/1500) worm and roller. **Suspension (front):** (600D) transverse leaf spring, lower arms and anti-roll bar; (1100D/1500) A-arms with coil springs and anti-roll bar. **Suspension (rear):** (600D) semi-trailing arms with coil springs and anti-roll bar; (1100D/1500) rigid axle with semi-elliptic leaf springs and anti-roll bar. **Brakes:** (600D/1100D) front/rear drum; (1500) front disc, rear drum. **Body Construction:** steel unibody.

PERFORMANCE: Top Speed: (600D) 65-68 mph; (1100D) 80 mph; (1500) 100+ mph claimed. **Fuel Mileage:** (600D) 41 mpg average; (1100D) 36 mpg average; (1500) 26 mpg average.

ADDITIONAL MODELS: Fiat also continued to produce the tiny two-cylinder 500D, a 1600S two-seater (similar to the 1500, with 1568-cc twin-cam engine), a 1300 sedan, and a six-cylinder 2300 series. These models were not ordinarily imported at this time. Fiat's Dino Spider and coupe with V-6 engines were introduced in Europe by 1967, and expected to reach American customers eventually. See 1969 listing for further details.

Manufacturer: Fiat S.p.A., Turin, Italy.

Distributor: Fiat Motor Company Inc., New York City.

HISTORY: Fiat's 1500 Spider for 1966 was introduced to the U.S. market on June 1, 1965; other models on September 1, 1965.

1967 FIAT

600D — FOUR — Production of the economical 600-series sedan continued with little change. Standard equipment included leatherette upholstery, whitewall tires, heater/defroster, and folding rear seats.

850 — FOUR — Fiat introduced a sporty duo this year to the U.S. market. Both the two-seater Sport convertible and the fastback sport coupe (which debuted first) rode a 79.8-inch wheelbase and carried a 52-horsepower, 843-cc (51-cid) four-cylinder engine mounted in the rear. The new coupe had been available in Europe since 1965. Styling was done by Bertone. Air-intake louvers filled its engine cover, which followed the fastback roofline. Large round taillamps stood on the back panel. Fully independent suspensions used transverse springing up front, coil springs with semi-trailing arms at the rear. Standard equipment included a 100-mph speedometer, tachometer, front disc brakes, and front bucket seats with vinyl leatherette upholstery.

124 — FOUR — A new front-drive Fiat four-door sedan arrived in the U.S. for 1967, powered by a 1197-cc (73-cid) four-cylinder engine. Single round headlamps were inset into the ends of a wide rectangular horizontal-bar grille, with Fiat insignia in its center. Disc brakes were used on all four wheels. The 124 rode a 95.3-inch wheelbase. Early examples had small front bumper guards; later versions were taller. Pleated vinyl upholstery and a padded dashboard were standard. A station wagon also became available soon after the sedan.

1100R — FOUR — Production of the 1100-series sedan and station wagon continued in modestly modified form, with a 1089-cc engine that produced 53 horsepower. A horizontal Solex two-barrel carburetor replaced the former Weber downdraft unit. This 'R' series, replacing the former 1100D, added such safety features as a collapsible steering column, and carried front disc brakes. Styling features included a tight-mesh rectangular grille with center insignia, full-length bodyside trim crease, and sculpted creases around the wheel arches and along the rocker area. Wheels and tires were smaller, windshield and windows larger, and the rear suspension was revised. The four-speed gearbox had a floor lever. Leatherette upholstery and whitewall tires were standard, as were a locking glovebox and full-width parcel shelf, but front seats no longer reclined.

1500 — FOUR — Little change was evident in Fiat's two-seat sports car, again powered by a 1481-cc four-cylinder engine.

I.D. DATA: Model 600D chassis serial number is on the left side of the firewall. Model 850 chassis serial number is on left wall of engine compartment. Model 124 chassis serial number and engine type are on a plate on right side of firewall, with chassis number stamped alongside. Model 1100R and 1500 chassis serial number is on right side of firewall, and on right side of body frame. Model 600D engine number is stamped at the front of the engine, above the timing chain cover. Model 850 engine number is visible between the engine pulleys. Model 124 engine number is on a tag near the dipstick, in left front of engine compartment. Model 1100R engine number is stamped on a pad to upper right of block, near the head and above the generator; or below the hood hinges. Model 1500 engine number is stamped on the right front end of the block, near the cylinder head flange. Starting serial number: (600D) 2060001; (850 cpe) 066884; (850 conv) 0013001; (1100R sed) 1430071; (1100R wag) 1445841; (124 sed) 003054; (1500 Spider) 044031.

Model	Body Type & Seating	Engine Type/CID	P.O.E. Price	Weight (lbs.)	Prod. Total
600D					
	2-dr Sedan-4P	I4/47	1237	1305	Note 1
850					
	2-dr Fbk Cpe-2+2P	I4/51	1795	1560	Note 1
Spider	2-dr Conv-2P	I4/51	1998	N/A	Note 1
124					
	4-dr Sedan-5P	I4/73	1798	1808	Note 1
	4-dr Sta Wag-5P	I4/73	1998	N/A	Note 1
1100R					
	4-dr Sedan-5P	I4/66	1564	1820	Note 1
	4-dr Sta Wag-5P	I4/66	1724	1910	Note 1
1500					
Spider	2-dr Conv-2P	I4/90	2585	2040	Note 1

Note 1: A total of 1,233,892 Fiats (all models) were produced during 1967.

ENGINE DATA: BASE FOUR (600D): Inline, overhead-valve four-cylinder. Cast iron block and aluminum head. **Displacement:** 46.8 cu. in. (767 cc). **Bore & Stroke:** 2.44 x 2.50 in. (62 x 63.5 mm). **Compression Ratio:** 7.5:1. **Brake Horsepower:** 32 (SAE) at 4800 rpm. **Torque:** 40 lbs.-ft. at 2800 rpm. Three main bearings. Solid valve lifters. One Weber or Solex single-barrel carburetor.

BASE FOUR (850): Inline, overhead-valve four-cylinder. Cast iron block and aluminum head. **Displacement:** 51.4 cu. in. (843 cc). **Bore & Stroke:** 2.56 x 2.50 in. (65 x 63.5 mm). **Compression Ratio:** 9.3:1. **Brake Horsepower:** 52 (SAE) at 6400 rpm. **Torque:** 46 lbs.-ft. at 4000 rpm. Three main bearings. Solid valve lifters. One Weber two-barrel carburetor.

BASE FOUR (124): Inline, overhead-valve four-cylinder. Cast iron block and aluminum head. **Displacement:** 73 cu. in. (1197 cc). **Bore & Stroke:** 2.87 x 2.81 in. (73 x 71.5 mm). **Compression Ratio:** 8.8:1. **Brake Horsepower:** 65 (SAE) at 5600 rpm. **Torque:** 69 lbs.-ft. at 3800 rpm. Five main bearings. Solid valve lifters. Two-barrel carburetor.

BASE FOUR (1100R): Inline, overhead-valve four-cylinder. Cast iron block and aluminum head. **Displacement:** 66.5 cu. in. (1089 cc). **Bore & Stroke:** 2.68 x 2.95 in. (68 x 75 mm). **Compression Ratio:** 8.1:1. **Brake Horsepower:** 53 (SAE) at 5000 rpm. **Torque:** 57 lbs.-ft. at 3200 rpm. Three main bearings. Solid valve lifters. Solex sidedraft two-barrel carburetor.

BASE FOUR (1500): Inline, overhead-valve four-cylinder. Cast iron block and aluminum head. **Displacement:** 90.4 cu. in. (1481 cc). **Bore & Stroke:** 3.03 x 3.13 in. (77 x 79.5 mm). **Compression Ratio:** 9.0:1. **Brake Horsepower:** 83 (SAE) at 5400 rpm. **Torque:** 88 lbs.-ft. at 3200 rpm. Three main bearings. Solid valve lifters. Weber two-barrel carburetor.

CHASSIS DATA: Wheelbase: (600D) 78.7 in.; (850) 79.8 in.; (124) 95.3 in.; (1100R) 92.2 in.; (1500) 92.1 in. **Overall Length:** (600D) 129.7 in.; (850) 142 in.; (124) 158.7 in.; (1100R sedan) 156.1 in.; (1100R wagon) 153.8 in.; (1500) 160.8 in. **Height:** (600D) 55.3 in.; (850) 51.2 in.; (124) 53.7 in.; (1100R sedan) 54.5 in.; (1100R wagon) 57.5 in.; (1500) 50.8 in. **Width:** (600D) 54.3 in.; (850) 59 in.; (124) 64.0 in.; (1100R sedan) 57.7 in.; (1100R wagon) 57.5 in.; (1500) 59.8 in. **Front Tread:** (600D) 45.3 in.; (850) 45.6 in.; (124) 52.4 in.; (1100R) 48.5 in.; (1500) 51 in. **Rear Tread:** (600D) 45.7 in.; (850) 47.7 in.; (124) 51.2 in.; (1100R) 47.9 in.; (1500) 48.5 in. **Standard Tires:** (600D) 5.20x12; (850) 5.20x13; (124) 6.15x13 or 155Sx13; (1100R) 155x13 or 6.15x13; (1500) 145x14.

TECHNICAL: Layout: (600D) rear-engine, rear-drive; (124/1100R/1500) front-engine, rear-drive. **Transmission:** (600D/1100R) four-speed manual (2/3/4 synchro); (850) four-speed manual (all synchro); (124) four-speed manual; (1500) five-speed manual. **Steering:** (600D/850) worm and sector; (124/1100R/1500) worm and roller. **Suspension (front):** (600D) A-arms with transverse leaf spring, lower arms and anti-roll bar; (850) upper A-arms with transverse leaf-spring lower arms and anti-roll bar; (124) A-arms with coil springs and anti-roll bar; (1100R) swinging transverse A-arms with coil springs and anti-roll bar; (1500) A-arms with coil springs and anti-roll bar. **Suspension (rear):** (600D) oblique semi-trailing arms with coil springs and anti-roll bar; (850) semi-trailing arms with coil springs and anti-roll bar; (124) rigid axle with radius rods, Panhard rod, coil springs and anti-roll bar; (1100R) rigid axle with semi-elliptic leaf springs; (1500) rigid axle with semi-elliptic leaf springs and anti-roll bar. **Brakes:** (600D) front/rear drum; (850/1100R/1500) front disc, rear drum; (124) front/rear disc. **Body Construction:** steel unibody.

PERFORMANCE: Top Speed: (600D) about 70 mph; (850) 85-87 mph; (124) 87-90 mph; (1100R) 81 mph; (1500) 100+ mph. **Acceleration (0-60 mph):** (850 cpe) near 18 sec.; (124) 14.6 sec.; **Acceleration (quarter-mile):** (850 cpe) 22 sec.; (124) 19.5 sec. (67 mph). **Fuel Mileage:** (850 cpe) about 33 mpg average.

PRODUCTION/SALES: Approximately 15,933 Fiats were sold in the U.S. during 1967.

Manufacturer: Fiat S.p.A., Turin, Italy.
Distributor: Fiat Motor Company Inc., New York City; or Fiat-Roosevelt Motors Inc., Englewood Cliffs, New Jersey.

HISTORY: The 1967 Fiat models were introduced in the U.S. on September 1, 1966, except the 1100R, which debuted in April 1966. "Driving the (850) coupe around town is sheer pleasure," said *Sports Car Graphic* in October 1966. "Extremely maneuverable, it snakes through traffic and parks effortlessly." Fiat 124 advertising at this time featured a lion behind the wheel, advising readers to "Get that king-of-the-road feeling with Fiat." European and American auto writers voted the 124 their "1967 Car of the Year." This would be the final year of U.S. availability for the rear-drive 600D sedan, the 1100R series, and the 1500 convertible.

1968 FIAT

850 — FOUR — Joining the original 850 fastback coupe and two-seat convertible this year was a new two-door sedan. Styling was considerably different than the coupe and Spider, with a vertical front panel that held a wide insignia and single round headlamps. The Spider had recessed headlamps and a much more curvaceous profile, while the fastback coupe had a vertical-panel front end and squared-off back end with four round taillamps. A slightly smaller (817-cid) engine was installed in U.S. models at this time.

124 — FOUR — Four body styles made up the 124 series this year: a two-door sport coupe, two-seat Spider convertible (replacing the 1500 sports car), four-door sedan, and station wagon. The Spider's single round headlamps were partly recessed; the coupe's were not. Four-wheel disc brakes were standard, with an anti-locking device. Designed by Pininfarina, the Spider convertible would remain in the Fiat lineup into the 1980s, though its engine size increased in later years. The Sport Coupe and Spider carried a 1438-cc engine with twin cams, whereas the sedan and wagon made do with an overhead-valve 1197-cc four. Spiders displayed a low, wide grille with large park/signal lights alongside, below single, partly-recessed headlamps. A five-speed gearbox was standard on the Spider, versus four speeds on other models.

I.D. DATA: Model 850 chassis serial number is on left wall of engine compartment. Model 124 chassis serial number and engine type are on a plate on right side of firewall, with chassis number stamped alongside. Model 850 engine number is visible between the engine pulleys. Model 124 engine number is on a tag near the dipstick, in left front of engine compartment. Starting serial number: (850 cpe) 147146; (850 Spider) 21097; (850 sedan) 867880; (124 sed) 00362093; (124 wag) 0353000; (124 cpe) 0034514; (124 conv) 0005619.

Model	Body Type & Seating	Engine Type/CID	P.O.E. Price	Weight (lbs.)	Prod. Total
850					
	2-dr Sedan-4//5P	I4/50	1427	1427	Note 1
	2-dr Fbk Cpe-2+2P	I4/50	1875	1535	Note 1
Spider	2-dr Conv-2P	I4/50	2085	1540	Note 1
124					
	4-dr Sedan-5P	I4/73	1922	1825	Note 1
	4-dr Sta Wag-5P	I4/73	2127	1945	Note 1
	2-dr Spt Cpe-4P	I4/88	2878	2020	Note 1
Spider	2-dr Conv-2P	I4/88	3181	2010	Note 1

Note 1: A total of 1,301,751 Fiats (all models) were produced during 1968.

ENGINE DATA: BASE FOUR (850): Inline, overhead-valve four-cylinder. Cast iron block and aluminum head. **Displacement:** 49.9 cu. in. (817 cc). **Bore & Stroke:** 2.51 x 2.50 in. (64 x 63.5 mm). **Compression Ratio:** (sedan) 8.9:1; (cpe/conv) 10:1. **Brake Horsepower:** (sedan) 42 SAE at 5300 rpm; (cpe/conv) 52-54 SAE at 6400 rpm. **Torque:** (sedan) 44 lbs.-ft. at 3600 rpm; (cpe/conv) 45.6 lbs.-ft. at 4000 rpm. Three main bearings. Solid valve lifters. One Weber two-barrel carburetor (cpe/conv).

BASE FOUR (124 sedan/wagon): Inline, overhead-valve four-cylinder. Cast iron block and aluminum head. **Displacement:** 73 cu. in. (1197 cc). **Bore & Stroke:** 2.87 x 2.81 in. (73 x 71.5 mm). **Compression Ratio:** 8.8:1. **Brake Horsepower:** 65 (SAE) at 5600 rpm. **Torque:** 69 lbs.-ft. at 3800 rpm. Five main bearings. Solid valve lifters. Solex two-barrel carburetor.

BASE FOUR (124 coupe/convertible): Inline, dual-overhead-cam four-cylinder. Cast iron block and aluminum head. **Displacement:** 87.75 cu. in. (1438 cc). **Bore & Stroke:** 3.15 x 2.81 in. (80 x 71.5 mm). **Compression Ratio:** 8.9:1. **Brake Horsepower:** 96 (SAE) at 6500 rpm. **Torque:** 82.5 lbs.-ft. at 4000 rpm. Five main bearings. Solid valve lifters. One Weber two-barrel carburetor.

CHASSIS DATA: Wheelbase: (850) 79.8 in.; (124 cpe/sed/wagon) 95.3 in.; (124 conv) 89.8 in. **Overall Length:** (850 cpe) 142.5 in.; (850 conv) 148.9 in.; (850 sedan) 140.8 in.; (124 cpe) 162 in.; (124 sedan) 158.7 in.; (124 sta wag) 158.7 in.; (124 conv) 156.3 in. **Height:** (850 cpe) 51.2 in.; (850 conv) 48 in.; (850 sedan) 54.5 in.; (124 cpe) 51.3 in.; (124 sedan) 55.9 in.; (124 sta wag) 56.7 in.; (124 conv) 49.2 in. **Width:** (850 cpe) 59.1 in.; (850 conv) 59 in.; (850 sedan) 56.1 in.; (124 cpe) 65.7 in.; (124 sedan/wagon) 65 in.; (124 conv) 63.5 in. **Front Tread:** (850 cpe/conv) 45.6 in.; (850 sedan) 45.1 in.; (124 cpe) 53 in.; (124 sedan/wagon) 52.4 in.; (124 conv) 53.1 in. **Rear Tread:** (850 cpe/conv) 47.7 in.; (850 sedan) 47.7 in.; (124 cpe) 51.8 in.; (124 sedan/wagon) 51.2 in.; (124 conv) 51.9 in. **Standard Tires:** (850 cpe) 5.50x13; (850 sed) 5.50x12; (850 conv) 5.50x12; (124 cpe) 6.50x13; (124 sed) 6.15x13; (124 wagon) 5.60x13; (124 conv) 6.50x13.

TECHNICAL: Layout: (850) rear-engine, rear-drive; (124) front-engine, rear-drive. **Transmission:** (850) four-speed manual; (124) four-speed manual; (124 Spider) five-speed manual; automatic available on 850 sedan. 124 Spider gear ratios: (1st) 3.75:1; (2nd) 2.30:1; (3rd) 1.49:1; (4th) 1.00:1; (5th) 0.91:1. **Standard Final Drive Ratio:** (124 Spider) 4.10:1. **Steering:** (850) screw and sector; (124) worm and roller. **Suspension (front):** (850) A-arms with transverse leaf-spring lower arms and anti-roll bar; (124) A-arms with coil springs and anti-roll bar. **Suspension (rear):** (850) semi-trailing arms with coil springs and anti-roll bar; (124) rigid axle with coil springs and anti-roll bar. **Brakes:** (850 sed) front/rear drum (850 cpe/conv) front disc, rear drum; (124) front/rear disc. **Body Construction:** steel unibody.

PERFORMANCE: Top Speed: (124 Spider) 104 mph. **Acceleration (0-60 mph):** (124 Spider) 10.1 sec. **Acceleration (quarter-mile):** (124 Spider) 17.5 sec. (77 mph). **Fuel Mileage:** (124 Spider) 22-25 mpg.

PRODUCTION/SALES: Approximately 30,521 Fiats were sold in the U.S. during 1968.
ADDITIONAL MODELS: Fiat's Dino Spider and coupe with V-6 engines were available in Europe; see 1969 listing for further details.

Manufacturer: Fiat S.p.A., Turin, Italy.
Distributor: Fiat Motor Company Inc., New York City; or Fiat-Roosevelt Motors Inc., Englewood Cliffs, New Jersey.
HISTORY: The 1968 Fiat models were introduced in the U.S. on September 16, 1967.

1969 FIAT

850 — FOUR — Production of the 850 sedan, fastback coupe and two-seat convertible continued with minor change. New coupe bucket seats had integral headrests. Rear quarter panels had a more pronounced "kickup." See previous listing for additional details.

124 — FOUR — Little was new on the four body styles that made up the 124 series; see previous listing for full details.

I.D. DATA: Model 850 chassis serial number is on left wall of engine compartment. Model 124 chassis serial number and engine type are on a plate on right side of firewall, with chassis number stamped alongside. Model 850 engine number is visible between the engine pulleys. Model 124 engine number is on a tag near the dipstick, in left front of engine compartment. Starting serial number: (850 cpe) 203339; (850 Spider) 38383; (124 sedan) 490920; (124 cpe) 66280; (124 wagon) 49321; (124 conv) 10554.

Model	Body Type & Seating	Engine Type/CID	P.O.E. Price	Weight (lbs.)	Prod. Total
850					
	2-dr Sedan-4/5P	I4/50	1466	1448	Note 1
	2-dr Fbk Cpe-2+2P	I4/50	1952	1597	Note 1
Spider	2-dr Conv-2P	I4/50	2135	1575	Note 1
124					
	4-dr Sedan-5P	I4/73	1965	1897	Note 1
	4-dr Sta Wag-5P	I4/73	2216	2004	Note 1
	2-dr Spt Cpe-4P	I4/88	2934	2087	Note 1
Spider	2-dr Conv-2P	I4/88	3239	2012	Note 1

Note 1: A total of 1,219,161 Fiats (all models) were produced during 1969.
Hardtop Price Note: A hardtop added $225 to the price of the 124 Spider convertible.

ENGINE DATA: BASE FOUR (850): Inline, overhead-valve four-cylinder. Cast iron block and aluminum head. **Displacement:** 49.9 cu. in. (817 cc). **Bore & Stroke:** 2.51 x 2.50 in. (64 x 63.5 mm). **Compression Ratio:** (sedan) 9.5:1; (cpe/conv) 10:1. **Brake Horsepower:** (sedan) 42 SAE at 5300 rpm; (cpe/conv) 52 SAE at 6400 rpm. **Torque:** (sedan) 44 lbs.-ft. at 3600 rpm; (cpe/conv) 45.6 lbs.-ft. at 4000 rpm. Three main bearings. Solid valve lifters. One Weber two-barrel carburetor (cpe/conv).

BASE FOUR (124 sedan/wagon): Inline, overhead-valve four-cylinder. Cast iron block and aluminum head. **Displacement:** 73 cu. in. (1197 cc). **Bore & Stroke:** 2.87 x 2.81 in. (73 x 71.5 mm). **Compression Ratio:** 8.8:1. **Brake Horsepower:** 65 (SAE) at 5600 rpm. **Torque:** 69 lbs.-ft. at 3800 rpm. Five main bearings. Solid valve lifters. One Solex two-barrel carburetor.

BASE FOUR (124 coupe/convertible): Inline, dual-overhead-cam four-cylinder. Cast iron block and aluminum head. **Displacement:** 87.75 cu. in. (1438 cc). **Bore & Stroke:** 3.15 x 2.81 in. (80 x 71.5 mm). **Compression Ratio:** 8.9:1. **Brake Horsepower:** 96 (SAE) at 6500 rpm. **Torque:** 82.5 lbs.-ft. at 4000 rpm. Five main bearings. Solid valve lifters. One Weber two-barrel carburetor.

CHASSIS DATA: Wheelbase: (850) 79.8 in.; (124 cpe/sed/wagon) 95.3 in.; (124 conv) 89.8 in. **Overall Length:** (850 cpe) 143.8 in.; (850 conv) 150.5 in.; (850 sedan) 140.8 in.; (124 cpe) 162 in.; (124 sedan) 158.7 in.; (124 sta wag) 158.7 in.; (124 conv) 156.3 in. **Height:** (850 cpe) 53.2 in.; (850 conv) 48 in.; (850 sedan) 54.5 in.; (124 cpe) 51.3 in.; (124 sedan) 53.7 in.; (124 sta wag) 56.7 in.; (124 conv) 49.2 in. **Width:** (850 cpe) 59.1 in.; (850 conv) 59 in.; (850 sedan) 56.1 in.; (124 cpe) 65.7 in.; (124 sedan/wagon) 64 in.; (124 conv) 63.5 in. **Front Tread:** (850 cpe/conv) 46.1 in.; (850 sedan) 45.1 in.; (124 cpe) 53 in.; (124 sedan/wagon) 52.4 in.; (124 conv) 53.1 in. **Rear Tread:** (850 cpe/conv) 48.1 in.; (850 sedan) 47.7 in.; (124 cpe) 51.2 in.; (124 sedan/wagon) 51.2 in.; (124 conv) 51.9 in. **Standard Tires:** (850 cpe) 5.50x13; (850 sed) 5.50x12; (850 conv) 5.50x12; (124 cpe) 165x13; (124 sed) 6.15x13 or 155x13; (124 wagon) 6.15x13; (124 conv) 165x13.

TECHNICAL: Layout: (850) rear-engine, rear-drive; (124) front-engine, rear-drive. **Transmission:** (850) four-speed manual; (124) four-speed manual; (124 Spider) five-speed manual; automatic available on 850 sedan. 124 sedan gear ratios: (1st) 3.75:1; (2nd) 2.30:1; (3rd) 1.49:1; (4th) 1.00:1. 124 Spider gear ratios: (1st) 3.42:1; (2nd) 2.10:1; (3rd) 1.36:1; (4th) 1.00:1; (5th) 0.912:1. **Standard Final Drive Ratio:** (850 sed) 4.63:1; (850 cpe/conv) 4.875:1; (124 sed) 4.30:1; (124 cpe/conv) 4.10:1. **Steering:** (850) screw and sector; (124) worm and roller. **Suspension (front):** (850) A-arms with transverse leaf-spring lower arms and anti-roll bar; (124) A-arms with coil springs and anti-roll bar. **Suspension (rear):** (850) semi-trailing arms with coil springs and anti-roll bar; (124) rigid axle with coil springs and anti-roll bar. **Brakes:** (850 sed) front/rear drum; (850 cpe/conv) front disc, rear drum; (124) front/rear disc. **Body Construction:** steel unibody.

PERFORMANCE: Top Speed: (850 sed) 75 mph; (850 cpe) 86 mph; (850 conv) 90 mph; (124 sed) 87 mph; (124 cpe) 106 mph; (124 conv) 109 mph. **Acceleration (0-60 mph):** (850 sed) 26 sec.; (850 cpe/conv) 20 sec.; (124 sed) 19.5 sec.; (124 cpe) 10.3 sec.; (124 conv) 12.2 sec. **Acceleration (quarter-mile):** (124 sed) 20.2 sec. (65.1 mph).

PRODUCTION/SALES: Approximately 21,496 Fiats were sold in the U.S. during 1969.

ADDITIONAL MODELS: By 1969, the Fiat Dino Spider and coupe were rumored to be available soon in the U.S., but Fiat had difficulty meeting exhaust emissions requirements. Initial Dinos, introduced in 1966-67, were powered by a 65-degree, 1987-cc (121.25-cid) V-6 engine rated 160 bhp (DIN) at 7200 rpm with 9.0:1 compression. Torque output was 127 pound-feet (DIN) at 6000 rpm, and fuel entered via three Weber 40 DCN carburetors. The four-seat coupe displayed a sleek, curvy fastback profile with large rear quarter windows, front vent wings, and 185HR14 tires on turbine-style wheels. Up front were quad round headlamps and a mesh grille. Wheelbase was 100.4 inches, and the coupe measured 177.4 inches overall in length, 66.8 inches wide, and stood 51.8 inches tall. A five-speed manual gearbox and 4.875:1 final drive were standard. Early Dinos had a coil-spring front suspension, semi-elliptic twin-leaf springs at the rear, worm and roller steering, and all-disc brakes. Top speed was 124 mph. The Dino Spider convertible, with a tiny back seat, rode a shorter (89.8-inch) wheelbase and measured 161.8 inches overall, standing 50 inches high. Appearance differed considerably from the coupe, with bulged front fender, a slightly pointed nose, and squared-off rear end. Top speed of the convertible was 131 mph. A coupe could accelerate in about 8.5 seconds, the convertible in about 7 seconds.

In 1969, as Fiat took over a large share of the Ferrari operation, a larger V-6 engine became available for the Dino 2400. The 2418-cc (147.5-cid) V-6 produced 170 bhp (DIN) at 7200 rpm, and 159 pound-feet of torque at 4600 rpm. The rear suspension switched to wishbones, semi-axles and coil springs, and ER70VR14 tires were installed. Dino production continued into the early 1970s.

Manufacturer: Fiat S.p.A., Turin, Italy.

Distributor: Fiat Motor Company Inc., New York City; or Fiat-Roosevelt Motors Inc., Englewood Cliffs, New Jersey.

1970 FIAT

850 — FOUR — Little appeared to be new on the 850 sedan, fastback coupe and two-seat convertible, except for reshaped (now oblong) side safety lights on the rear fenders of the coupe. Engine output for the coupe and convertible grew to 58 horsepower, from a 903-cc engine; the sedan carried a smaller engine that delivered 42 bhp. The Sport Coupe had forward-protruding headlamps, plus four round taillamps in a chopped-look rear panel. A metal hardtop was available for the Sport Spider convertible, billed as a "beginner's car." Standard coupe/convertible equipment included a tachometer, full carpeting, all-vinyl interior, and body-contoured adjustable-locking bucket seats.

A "Sport Racer" hardtop coupe with tiny rear side windows was offered this year, however, styled by Nuccio Bertone, who "gives a shape to speed." Sport Racer "wet-look" body colors included Racing Red, Positano Yellow, Veridian Green, French Blue, and Canguro Orange. Appearance of the Sport Racer was similar to the convertible up front, with slightly-bulged inset headlamps. Inside, the dash held a 120-mph speedometer and 8000-rpm tachometer.

124 — FOUR — Production of all four 124 body styles continued with little change. "Special" sedan and wagon models offered increased horsepower and radial tires, adopting a detuned version of the 1.4-liter engine formerly used only in the sport coupe and Spider convertible. The Sport Coupe and Spider had a more powerful, twin-overhead-cam version of the 1438-cc engine. A new sedan front end contained quad headlamps, with parking lights integrated into the bumper. Door handles were now recessed, while bodies displayed chrome window frame and rubber bumper guards. The Sport Coupe also had quad headlamps as well as restyled taillamps, while the Spider kept its single-headlamp front end. The coupe rear end was more squared-off than the Spider's.

I.D. DATA: Model 850 chassis serial number is on left wall of engine compartment. Model 124 chassis serial number and engine type are on a plate on right side of firewall, with chassis number stamped alongside. Model 850 engine number is visible between the engine pulleys. Model 124 engine number is on a tag near the dipstick, in left front of engine compartment. Starting serial number: (850 cpe) 0292437; (850 Spider) 0067118 or 0067183; (850 sedan) 1376417; (124 sedan) 0658588; (124 wagon) 0658908; (124 conv) 0021861.

Model	Body Type & Seating	Engine Type/CID	P.O.E. Price	Weight (lbs.)	Prod. Total
850					
	2-dr Sedan-4/5P	I4/50	1504	1480	Note 1
Sport	2-dr Fbk Cpe-2 + 2P	I4/55	1998	1577	Note 1
Spider	2-dr Conv-2P	I4/55	2168	1555	Note 1
Racer	2-dr HT Cpe-2P	I4/55	2471	1631	Note 1
124					
Special	4-dr Sedan-5P	I4/88	2015	1962	Note 1
Special	4-dr Sta Wag-5P	I4/88	2273	2084	Note 1
	2-dr Spt Cpe-4P	I4/88	3001	2160	Note 1
Spider	2-dr Conv-2P	I4/88	3304	2085	Note 1

Note 1: A total of 1,418,929 Fiats (all models) were produced during 1970.

Hardtop Price Note: A metal hardtop added $224 to the price of either the 850 or 124 Spider convertible.

ENGINE DATA: BASE FOUR (850 sedan): Inline, overhead-valve four-cylinder. Cast iron block and aluminum head. **Displacement:** 49.9 cu. in. (817 cc). **Bore & Stroke:** 2.52 x 2.50 in. (64 x 63.5 mm). **Compression Ratio:** 9.5:1. **Brake Horsepower:** 42 (SAE) at 5300 rpm. **Torque:** 44 lbs.-ft. at 3600 rpm. Three main bearings. Solid valve lifters. One Weber single-barrel carburetor.

BASE FOUR (850 coupe/convertible): Inline, overhead-valve four-cylinder. Cast iron block and aluminum head. **Displacement:** 55.1 cu. in. (903 cc). **Bore & Stroke:** 2.56 x 2.68 in. (65 x 68 mm). **Compression Ratio:** 9.5:1. **Brake Horsepower:** 58 (SAE) at 6400 rpm. **Torque:** 47.7 lbs.-ft. at 4000 rpm. Three main bearings. Solid valve lifters. One Weber two-barrel carburetor.

BASE FOUR (124 sedan/wagon): Inline, overhead-valve four-cylinder. Cast iron block and aluminum head. **Displacement:** 87.75 cu. in. (1438 cc). **Bore & Stroke:** 3.15 x 2.81 in. (80 x 71.5 mm). **Compression Ratio:** 8.9:1. **Brake Horsepower:** 76 (SAE) at 5400 rpm. **Torque:** 81 lbs.-ft. at 3300 rpm. Five main bearings. Solid valve lifters. One Weber two-barrel carburetor.

BASE FOUR (124 coupe/conv): Inline, dual-overhead-cam four-cylinder. Cast iron block and aluminum head. **Displacement:** 87.75 cu. in. (1438 cc). **Bore & Stroke:** 3.15 x 2.81 in. (80 x 71.5 mm). **Compression Ratio:** 9.0:1. **Brake Horsepower:** 96 (SAE) at 6500 rpm. **Torque:** 82.5 lbs.-ft. at 4000 rpm. Five main bearings. Solid valve lifters. One Weber two-barrel carburetor.

CHASSIS DATA: Wheelbase: (850) 79.8 in.; (124 cpe/sed/wagon) 95.3 in.; (124 conv) 89.8 in. **Overall Length:** (850 sedan) 140.8 in.; (850 cpe) 142 in.; (850 racer) 148 in.; (850 conv) 148 in.; (124 cpe) 163 in.; (124 sedan/wagon) 159.5 in.; (124 conv) 156 in. **Height:** (850 sedan) 54.5 in.; (850 cpe) 51 in.; (850 conv) 48 in.; (850 racer) 47.4 in.; (124 cpe) 51.3 in.; (124 sedan) 53.75 in.; (124 sta wag) 56.7 in.; (124 conv) 49 in. **Width:** (850 sedan) 57.0 in.; (850 cpe) 59.1 in.; (850 conv) 59 in.; (124 cpe) 65.7 in.; (124 sedan) 63.4 in.; (124 wagon) 64 in.; (124 conv) 63.5 in. **Front Tread:** (850 sedan) 45.1 in.; (850 cpe/conv) 46.1 in.; (124 cpe) 53 in.; (124 sedan/wagon) 52.4 in.; (124 conv) 53.2 in. **Rear Tread:** (850 sedan) 47.9 in.; (850 cpe/conv) 48.1 in.; (124 cpe) 53 in.; (124 sedan/wagon) 51.2 in.; (124 conv) 51.9 in. **Standard Tires:** (850 sed) 145SR13; (850 cpe/conv) 155SR13; (124 cpe) 165x13; (124 sed) 155x13; (124 wagon) 165x13; (124 conv) 165x13.

TECHNICAL: Layout: (850) rear-engine, rear-drive; (124) front-engine, rear-drive. **Transmission:** (850) four-speed manual; (124) four-speed manual; (124 Spider) five-speed manual; automatic available on 850 sedan. Standard 850 cpe/conv gear ratios: (1st) 3.63:1; (2nd) 2.05:1; (3rd) 1.40:1; (4th) 0.96:1; (rev) 3.61:1. **Standard Final Drive Ratio:** (850 sed) 4.62:1; (other 850) 4.87:1; (124 sed) 4.30:1; (124 wag/conv) 4.10:1; (124 spt cpe) 4.44:1. **Steering:** (850) worm and helical gear; (124) worm and roller. **Suspension (front):** (850) upper swinging arms with transverse leaf spring and anti-roll bar; (124) wishbone A-arms with coil springs and anti-roll bar. **Suspension (rear):** (850) semi-trailing arms with coil springs and anti-roll bar; (124) rigid axle with coil springs and anti-roll bar or transverse rod. **Brakes:** (850 sed) front/rear drum; (other 850) front disc, rear drum; (124) front/rear disc. **Body Construction:** steel unibody.

PERFORMANCE: Top Speed: (850 sedan) 70+ mph claimed; (850 cpe/conv) 90+ mph claimed; (850 Racer) 93+ mph; (124 sed/wag) 93 mph; (124 cpe/conv) 106 mph. **Acceleration (0-60 mph):** (850 sed) about 22 sec.; (850 cpe) about 21 sec.; (850 conv) about 20 sec.; (850 Racer) 16.1 sec.; (124 sed) about 19 sec.; (124 wag) about 20 sec. **Acceleration (quarter-mile):** (850 Racer) 20.1 sec. (65.9 mph). **Fuel Mileage:** (850 sedan) about 35 mpg claimed; (850 cpe/conv) 30 mpg; (850 Racer) about 32 mpg.

PRODUCTION/SALES: Approximately 36,096 Fiats were sold in the U.S. during 1970.

ADDITIONAL MODELS: The Dino Spider and coupe continued in production; see 1969 listing for details.

Manufacturer: Fiat S.p.A., Turin, Italy.

Distributor: Fiat Motor Company Inc., New York City; or Fiat-Roosevelt Motors Inc., Englewood Cliffs, New Jersey.

HISTORY: Fiat adopted a new corporate logo at this time, with block letters printed in reverse (white on black) on slanted square blocks. Fiat's 850 Sport Racer was promoted "for the love of moving—around the block or coast to coast." Some testers weren't enthusiastic about the 850's fuel filler, located in the engine compartment above exhaust pipes.

1971 FIAT

850 — FOUR — Production of Fiat's smallest series available in the U.S. continued with little change. As before, a larger (55-cid) engine powered the coupe and Spider convertible.

124 — FOUR — Little change was evident on any of the four models in the 124 series, except that the sport coupe and Spider convertible could be ordered with a larger (1.6-liter) twin-cam engine instead of the usual 1.4-liter version. The 124 sport coupe came with all-disc brakes, electronic tachometer, reclining bucket seats, and lighted engine compartment. An automatic transmission was available for the 124 sedan and station wagon; a five-speed manual gearbox for the sport coupe.

I.D. DATA: Model 850 chassis serial number is on left wall of engine compartment. Model 124 chassis serial number and engine type are on a plate on right side of firewall, with chassis number stamped alongside. Model 850 engine number is visible between the engine pulleys. Model 124 engine number is on a tag near the dipstick, in left front of engine compartment. Starting serial number: (850 cpe) 0340091; (850 Spider) 0090090; (850 sedan) 1569637; (850 HT racer) 0089992; (124 sedan) 0826844; (124 wagon) 0700636; (124 conv) 0033950.

Model	Body Type & Seating	Engine Type/CID	P.O.E. Price	Weight (lbs.)	Prod. Total
850					
	2-dr Sedan-4/5P	I4/50	1555	1512	Note 1
	2-dr Fbk Cpe-2 + 2P	I4/55	2059	1590	Note 1
Spider	2-dr Conv-2P	I4/55	2294	1590	Note 1
Racer	2-dr HT Cpe	I4/55	2619	1622	Note 1
124					
Special	4-dr Sedan-5P	I4/88	2081	1995	Note 1
Special	4-dr Sta Wag-5P	I4/88	2345	2084	Note 1
	2-dr Spt Cpe-4P	I4/88	3086	2178	Note 1
Spider	2-dr Conv-2P	I4/88	3382	2046	Note 1

Note 1: A total of 1,371,729 Fiats (all models) were produced during 1971, including 56,094 Type 124 Sport 1600s and 1,544 Dinos.

Price Note: 124 sport coupe and Spider convertible with optional 1608-cc engine were priced at $3255 and $3482 (respectively). A removable hardtop added $125 to the Spider prices.

ENGINE DATA: BASE FOUR (850 sedan): Inline, overhead-valve four-cylinder. Cast iron block and aluminum head. **Displacement:** 49.9 cu. in. (817 cc). **Bore & Stroke:** 2.52 x 2.50 in. (64 x 63.5 mm). **Compression Ratio:** 9.5:1. **Brake Horsepower:** 42 (SAE) at 5300 rpm. Torque: 44 lbs.-ft. at 3600 rpm. Three main bearings. Solid valve lifters. One Weber single-barrel carburetor.

BASE FOUR (850 coupe/convertible): Inline, overhead-valve four-cylinder. Cast iron block and aluminum head. **Displacement:** 55.1 cu. in. (903 cc). **Bore & Stroke:** 2.56 x 2.68 in. (65 x 68 mm). **Compression Ratio:** 9.5:1. **Brake Horsepower:** 58 (SAE) at 6500 rpm. **Torque:** 51 lbs.-ft. at 4000 rpm. Three main bearings. Solid valve lifters. One Weber two-barrel carburetor.

BASE FOUR (124 sedan/wagon): Inline, overhead-valve four-cylinder. Cast iron block and aluminum head. **Displacement:** 87.75 cu. in. (1438 cc). **Bore & Stroke:** 3.15 x 2.81 in. (80 x 71.5 mm). **Compression Ratio:** 9.0:1. **Brake Horsepower:** 76 (SAE) at 5400 rpm. **Torque:** 81 lbs.-ft. at 3300 rpm. Five main bearings. Solid valve lifters. One Weber two-barrel carburetor.

BASE FOUR (124 coupe/convertible): Inline, dual-overhead-cam four-cylinder. Cast iron block and aluminum head. **Displacement:** 87.75 cu. in. (1438 cc). **Bore & Stroke:** 3.15 x 2.81 in. (80 x 71.5 mm). **Compression Ratio:** 9.0:1. **Brake Horsepower:** 96 (SAE) at 6500 rpm. **Torque:** 82.5 lbs.-ft. at 4000 rpm. Five main bearings. Solid valve lifters. One Weber two-barrel carburetor.

OPTIONAL FOUR (124 coupe/convertible): Inline, dual-overhead-cam four-cylinder. Cast iron block and aluminum head. **Displacement:** 98.1 cu. in. (1608 cc). **Bore & Stroke:** 3.15 x 3.15 in. (80 x 80 mm). **Compression Ratio:** 8.5:1. **Brake Horsepower:** 104 (SAE) at 6000 rpm. **Torque:** 94 lbs.-ft. at 4200 rpm. Five main bearings. Solid valve lifters. Weber two-barrel carburetor.

CHASSIS DATA: Wheelbase: (850) 79.8 in.; (124 cpe/sed/wagon) 95.3 in.; (124 conv) 89.8 in. **Overall Length:** (850 cpe) 143.8 in.; (850 conv) 150.5 in.; (850 sedan) 140.8 in.; (124 cpe) 163.5 in.; (124 sedan) 159.1 in.; (124 wagon) 159.5 in.; (124 conv) 156.3 in. **Height:** (850 cpe) 53.2 in.; (850 conv) 48 in.; (850 racer) 47.4 in.; (850 sedan) 54.5 in.; (124 cpe) 52.8 in.; (124 sedan) 55.9 in.; (124 sta wag) 56.7 in.; (124 conv) 49.2 in. **Width:** (850 cpe) 59.1 in.; (850 conv) 59 in.; (850 sedan) 56.1 in.; (124 cpe) 65.7 in.; (124 sedan) 63.4 in.; (124 wagon) 64 in.; (124 conv) 63.5 in. **Front Tread:** (850 cpe/conv) 46.1 in.; (850 sedan) 45.1 in.; (124 cpe) 53 in.; (124 sedan/wagon) 52.4 in.; (124 conv) 53.2 in. **Rear Tread:** (850 cpe/conv) 48.1 in.; (850 sedan) 47.7 in.; (124 cpe) 51.8 in.; (124 sedan/wagon) 51.2 in.; (124 conv) 51.8 in. **Standard Tires:** (850 cpe) 155SR13; (850 sed) 145SR13; (850 conv) 155x13; (124 cpe) 165HR13; (124 sed) 155SR13; (124 wagon) 165SR13; (124 conv) 165HR13.

TECHNICAL: Layout: (850) rear-engine, rear-drive; (124) front-engine, rear-drive. **Transmission:** (850) four-speed manual; (124) four-speed manual; (124 Spider) five-speed manual; automatic available on 124 sedan/wagon and 850 sedan. **Steering:** (850) screw and sector; (124) worm and roller. **Suspension (front):** (850) A-arms with transverse leaf-spring lower arms and anti-roll bar; (124) A-arms with coil springs and anti-roll bar. **Suspension (rear):** (850) semi-trailing arms with coil springs and anti-roll bar; (124) rigid axle with coil springs and anti-roll bar. **Brakes:** (850 sedan) front/rear drum; (850 cpe/conv) front disc, rear drum; (124) front/rear disc. **Body Construction:** steel unibody.

PRODUCTION/SALES: Approximately 45,469 Fiats were sold in the U.S. during 1971.

ADDITIONAL MODELS: The Dino Spider and coupe continued in production; see 1969 listing for details.

Manufacturer: Fiat S.p.A., Turin, Italy.

Distributor: Fiat Motor Company Inc., New York City; or Fiat-Roosevelt Motors Inc., Englewood Cliffs, New Jersey.

HISTORY: Fiat's 1971 models were introduced in the U.S. in November and December 1970. A new front-drive Fiat 128 debuted late in the 1971 model year, selling for $1831; see next listing for details. By this time, Fiat had 639 dealers in the U.S.

1972 FIAT

850 — FOUR — Only the Bertone-styled Spider convertible was left of the 850 series for the 1972 model year. Bumper overriders were added and fenders modified to meet U.S. headlamp regulations. Five bright new body colors were offered. Inside, controls had English-language markings, the steering wheel was now covered with padded vinyl, and an aluminum finish replaced the former woodgrain dashboard.

128 — FOUR — A new front-wheel-drive Fiat emerged late in the 1971 model year. Upright in appearance, the two-door and four-door sedans and two-door station wagon carried an 1116-cc four-cylinder engine that produced 49 horsepower. A four-speed manual gearbox was standard.

124 — FOUR — Production of the larger rear-drive Fiat series continued with little change. As before, a sedan and station wagon were accompanied by a sport coupe and the Pininfarina-styled Spider convertible. The latter two models carried a larger (98-cid) four-cylinder engine. An automatic transmission was available. Both sport models had a wood-rim steering wheel, wood-faced instrument panel, and full gauges including an electronic tachometer.

I.D. DATA: Fiat's serial number is on the dashboard, visible through the windshield. Model 850 number contains 14 symbols: six symbols to identify series and body style, a seventh to indicate engine, followed by the sequential serial number. Model 128 number contains 11 or 12 symbols: four or five to identify series and body style, followed by a seven-digit sequential serial number. Model 124 number contains 11, 12 or 13 symbols: four or five to indicate series and body style, a sixth (on wagons only) to denote engine type, followed by a seven-digit sequential production number. Starting serial number: (850 Spider) 0110006; (128) 0682801 or 0728924; (124 sedan) 1040465; (124 wagon) 1007317; (124 spt cpe) 0181442; (124 conv) 0047032.

Model	Body Type & Seating	Engine Type/CID	P.O.E. Price	Weight (lbs.)	Prod. Total
850					
Spider	2-dr Conv-2P	I4/55	2424	1580	Note 1
128					
	2-dr Sedan-4/5P	I4/68	1992	1735	Note 1
	4-dr Sedan-4/5P	I4/68	2089	1755	Note 1
	2-dr Sta Wag-4/5P	I4/68	2255	1805	Note 1
124					
Special	4-dr Sedan-5P	I4/88	2305	1983	Note 1
	4-dr Sta Wag-5P	I4/88	2535	2045	Note 1
	2-dr Spt Cpe-4P	I4/98	3378	2167	Note 1
Spider	2-dr Conv-2P	I4/98	3644	2047	Note 1

Note 1: A total of 1,368,216 Fiats (all models) were produced during 1972, including 28,139 Type 124 Sport 1600s and 455 Dinos.

1972 Fiat 128 two-door station wagon.

ENGINE DATA: BASE FOUR (850): Inline, overhead-valve four-cylinder. Cast iron block and aluminum head. **Displacement:** 55.1 cu. in. (903 cc). **Bore & Stroke:** 2.56 x 2.68 in. (65 x 68 mm). **Compression Ratio:** 9.5:1. **Brake Horsepower:** 48 (SAE) at 6500 rpm. **Torque:** 51 lbs.-ft. at 4000 rpm. Three main bearings. Solid valve lifters. One Weber two-barrel carburetor.

BASE FOUR (128): Inline, overhead-cam four-cylinder. Cast iron block and aluminum head. **Displacement:** 68.1 cu. in. (1116 cc). **Bore & Stroke:** 3.15 x 2.19 in. (80 x 55.5 mm). **Compression Ratio:** 8.5:1. **Brake Horsepower:** 49 (SAE) at 6000 rpm. **Torque:** 58 lbs.-ft. at 3600 rpm. Three main bearings. Solid valve lifters. One Weber or Solex carburetor.

BASE FOUR (124 sedan/wagon): Inline, overhead-valve four-cylinder. Cast iron block and aluminum head. **Displacement:** 87.75 cu. in. (1438 cc). **Bore & Stroke:** 3.15 x 2.81 in. (80 x 71.5 mm). **Compression Ratio:** 9.0:1. **Brake Horsepower:** 68 (SAE) at 5400 rpm. **Torque:** 81 lbs.-ft. at 3300 rpm. Five main bearings. Solid valve lifters. One Weber two-barrel carburetor.

BASE FOUR (124 coupe/convertible): Inline, dual-overhead-cam four-cylinder. Cast iron block and aluminum head. **Displacement:** 98.1 cu. in. (1608 cc). **Bore & Stroke:** 3.15 x 3.15 in. (80 x 80 mm). **Compression Ratio:** 8.5:1. **Brake Horsepower:** 90 (SAE) at 6600 rpm. **Torque:** 96 lbs.-ft. at 4000 rpm. Five main bearings. Solid valve lifters. Weber two-barrel carburetor.

CHASSIS DATA: Wheelbase: (850) 79.8 in.; (128) 96.4 in.; (124 cpe/sed/wag) 95.3 in.; (124 conv) 89.8 in. **Overall Length:** (850) 150.5 in.; (128 sedan) 151.8 in.; (128 wagon) 152 in.; (124 cpe) 163.5 in.; (124 sedan) 159.1 in.; (124 wagon) 159.3 in.; (124 conv) 156.3 in. **Height:** (850) 48 in.; (128) 56.4 in.; (124 cpe) 52.8 in.; (124 sedan) 55.9 in.; (124 sta wag) 56.7 in.; (124 conv) 49.2 in. **Width:** (850) 59 in.; (128) 62.6 in.; (124 cpe) 65.7 in.; (124 sedan) 63.4 in.; (124 wagon) 64 in.; (124 conv) 63.5 in. **Front Tread:** (850) 46.1 in.; (128) 51.2 in.; (124 cpe) 53 in.; (124 sedan/wagon) 52.4 in.; (124 conv) 53 in. **Rear Tread:** (850) 48.1 in.; (128) 51.7 in.; (124 cpe) 51.8 in.; (124 sedan/wagon) 51.2 in.; (124 conv) 51.8 in. **Standard Tires:** (850) 155SR13; (128) 145SR13; (124 cpe) 165HR13; (124 sed) 155SR13; (124 wagon) 165SR13; (124 conv) 165HR13.

TECHNICAL: Layout: (850) rear-engine, rear-drive; (128) front-engine, front-drive; (124) front-engine, rear-drive. **Transmission:** (850/128) four-speed manual; (124 sed/wag) four-speed manual; (124 cpe/conv) five-speed manual; automatic available on 124. **Steering:** (850) screw and sector; (128) rack and pinion; (124) worm and roller. **Suspension (front):** (850) A-arms with transverse leaf-spring lower arms and anti-roll bar; (128) MacPherson struts with coil springs and anti-roll bar; (124) A-arms with coil springs and anti-roll bar. **Suspension (rear):** (850) semi-trailing arms with coil springs and anti-roll bar; (128) independent with wide wishbone and transverse leaf spring; (124) rigid axle with coil springs and anti-roll bar. **Brakes:** (850/128) front disc, rear drum; (124) front/rear disc. **Body Construction:** steel unibody.

MAJOR OPTIONS: Automatic transmission: 124 sedan/wagon ($199).

PRODUCTION/SALES: Approximately 58,375 Fiats were sold in the U.S. during 1972, including 12,455 Type 850s and 26,443 124s.

ADDITIONAL MODELS: The Dino Spider and coupe continued in production; see 1969 listing for details.

Manufacturer: Fiat S.p.A., Turin, Italy.

Distributor: Fiat Motor Company Inc. or Fiat-Roosevelt Motors Inc., Englewood Cliffs, New Jersey.

HISTORY: Fiat's 1972 models were introduced in the U.S. on November 1, 1971. The 128 was developed by the Fiat Styling Center with computer and wind-tunnel assistance. Fiat operated a special organization at this time, with the goal of developing engines to meet U.S. and European emissions standards. An SL 1300 coupe version of the 128 with larger engine debuted in 1972; see next listing for details.

1973 FIAT

850 — FOUR — Production of the Spider convertible continued with little change. This would be its final year on the U.S. market.

128 — FOUR — Production of the front-drive Fiats, introduced to the U.S. late in 1971, continued with little change. New this year was an SL 1300 coupe on a nine-inch shorter wheelbase, with a larger (79-cid) engine. Styled by Fiat, the 128 SL 1300 was more than four inches lower than the sedan, with a large rear-quarter "kickup" and thick rear roof pillars.

124 — FOUR — Fiat's front-engine, rear-drive series continued with little change, with four body styles available again.

I.D. DATA: Fiat's serial number is on the dashboard, visible through the windshield. Model 850 number contains 14 symbols: six symbols to identify series and body style, a seventh to indicate engine, followed by the sequential serial number. Model 128 number contains 11 or 12 symbols: four or five to identify series and body style, followed by a seven-digit sequential serial number. Model 124 number contains 11 or 13 symbols: four or five to indicate series and body style, a sixth to denote engine type, followed by a seven-digit sequential production number. Starting serial number: (850) 0123905; (128 2-dr) 1119701; (128 4-dr) 1133272; (128 coupe) 0057027; (128 wagon) 1139447; (124 sedan) 1240167; (124 wagon) 1240221; (124 spt cpe) 0206905; (124 conv) 0059592.

Model	Body Type & Seating	Engine Type/CID	P.O.E. Price	Weight (lbs.)	Prod. Total
850					
Spider	2-dr Conv-2P	I4/55	2739	1595	Note 1
128					
	2-dr Sedan-4/5P	I4/68	2195	1760	Note 1
SL 1300	2-dr Coupe-4P	I4/79	2795	1800	Note 1
	4-dr Sedan-4/5P	I4/68	2299	1795	Note 1
	2-dr Sta Wag-4/5P	I4/68	2444	1835	Note 1
124					
Special	4-dr Sedan-5P	I4/88	2539	2038	Note 1
	4-dr Sta Wag-5P	I4/88	2795	2095	Note 1
	2-dr Spt Cpe-4P	I4/98	3674	2187	Note 1
Spider	2-dr Conv-2P	I4/98	3988	2077	Note 1

Note 1: A total of 1,390,251 Fiats (all models) were produced during 1973, including 3,628 Type 850 Spiders, 23,492 124 Sport 1600s, 31,222 124 Sport 1800s, and 9,052 early X1/9 coupes.

ENGINE DATA: BASE FOUR (850): Inline, overhead-valve four-cylinder. Cast iron block and aluminum head. **Displacement:** 55.1 cu. in. (903 cc). **Bore & Stroke:** 2.56 x 2.68 in. (65 x 68 mm). **Compression Ratio:** 8.5:1. **Brake Horsepower:** 48 (SAE) at 6400 rpm. **Torque:** 45 lbs.-ft. at 4000 rpm. Three main bearings. Solid valve lifters. One Weber two-barrel carburetor.

BASE FOUR (128): Inline, overhead-cam four-cylinder. Cast iron block and aluminum head. **Displacement:** 68.1 cu. in. (1116 cc). **Bore & Stroke:** 3.15 x 2.19 in. (80 x 55.5 mm). **Compression Ratio:** 8.5:1. **Brake Horsepower:** 49 (SAE) at 6400 rpm. **Torque:** 50 lbs.-ft. at 3600 rpm. Three main bearings. Solid valve lifters. One Weber 32 ICEV carburetor.

BASE FOUR (128SL): Inline, overhead-cam four-cylinder. Cast iron block and aluminum head. **Displacement:** 78.7 cu. in. (1290 cc). **Bore & Stroke:** 3.39 x 2.19 in. (86 x 55.5 mm). **Compression Ratio:** 8.5:1. **Brake Horsepower:** 51 (SAE) at 5600 rpm. **Torque:** 62 lbs.-ft. at 3000 rpm. Three main bearings. Solid valve lifters. One Weber 32 ICAI carburetor.

BASE FOUR (124 sedan/wagon): Inline, overhead-valve four-cylinder. Cast iron block and aluminum head. **Displacement:** 87.75 cu. in. (1438 cc). **Bore & Stroke:** 3.15 x 2.81 in. (80 x 71.5 mm). **Compression Ratio:** 8.5:1. **Brake Horsepower:** 68 (SAE) at 5400 rpm. **Torque:** 77.5 lbs.-ft. at 3600 rpm. Five main bearings. Solid valve lifters. One Weber 32 DCOF two-barrel carburetor.

BASE FOUR (124 coupe/convertible): Inline, dual-overhead-cam four-cylinder. Cast iron block and aluminum head. **Displacement:** 98.1 cu. in. (1608 cc). **Bore & Stroke:** 3.15 x 3.15 in. (80 x 80 mm). **Compression Ratio:** 8.5:1. **Brake Horsepower:** 90 (SAE) at 6600 rpm. **Torque:** 87 lbs.-ft. at 3600 rpm. Five main bearings. Solid valve lifters. Weber two-barrel carburetor.

CHASSIS DATA: Wheelbase: (850) 79.8 in.; (128) 96.4 in.; (128SL cpe) 87.5 in.; (124 cpe/sed/wagon) 95.3 in.; (124 conv) 89.8 in. **Overall Length:** (850) 153 in.; (128 sedan/wagon) 154.2 in.; (128SL cpe) 151.8 in.; (124 cpe) 165.3 in.; (124 sedan) 162.2 in.; (124 wagon) 162.2 in.; (124 conv) 159.5 in. **Height:** (850) 48 in.; (128) 56 in.; (128SL cpe) 51.6 in.; (124 cpe) 52.8 in.; (124 sedan) 55.9 in.; (124 sta wag) 56.7 in.; (124 conv) 49.2 in. **Width:** (850) 59.0 in.; (128) 62.2 in.; (128SL cpe) 61.4 in.; (124 cpe) 65.7 in.; (124 sedan) 63.4 in.; (124 wagon) 64 in.; (124 conv) 63.5 in. **Front Tread:** (850) 46.1 in.; (128) 51.2 in.; (128SL cpe) 52.2 in.; (124 cpe) 53 in.; (124 sedan/wagon) 52.4 in.; (124 conv) 53.0 in. **Rear Tread:** (850) 48.1 in.; (128) 51.7 in.; (128SL cpe) 52.5 in.; (124 cpe) 51.8 in.; (124 sedan/wagon) 51.2 in.; (124 conv) 51.8 in. **Standard Tires:** (850) 155SR13; (128) 145SR13; (124 cpe) 165HR13; (124 sed) 155SR13; (124 wagon) 165SR13; (124 conv) 165HR13.

TECHNICAL: Layout: (850) rear-engine, rear-drive; (128) front-engine, front-drive; (124) front-engine, rear-drive. **Transmission:** (850/128) four-speed manual; (124 sed/wag) four-speed manual; (124 cpe/conv) five-speed manual; automatic available on 124 sedan/wagon. Model 850 gear ratios: (1st) 3.64:1; (2nd) 2.06:1; (3rd) 1.41:1; (4th) 0.96:1. Model 128 gear ratios: (1st) 3.58:1; (2nd) 2.24:1; (3rd) 1.45:1; (4th) 1.04:1. Model 124 Spider gear ratios: (1st) 3.80:1; (2nd) 2.18:1; (3rd) 1.41:1; (4th) 1.00:1; (5th) 0.91:1. **Standard Final Drive Ratio:** (850) 4.88:1; (128) 4.07:1; (128 SL) 4.25:1; (124) 4.10:1. **Steering:** (850) screw and sector; (128) rack and pinion; (124) worm and roller. **Suspension (front):** (850) A-arms with transverse leaf-spring lower arms and anti-roll bar; (128) MacPherson struts with coil springs and anti-roll bar; (124) A-arms with coil springs and anti-roll bar. **Suspension (rear):** (850) semi-trailing arms with coil springs and anti-roll bar; (128) independent with wide wishbones and transverse leaf spring; (124) rigid axle with coil springs and anti-roll bar. **Brakes:** (850/128) front disc, rear drum; (124) front/rear disc. **Body Construction:** steel unibody.

MAJOR OPTIONS: Automatic transmission: 124 sedan/wagon ($215).

PERFORMANCE: Top Speed: (128 SL) 87.5 mph. **Acceleration (0-60 mph):** (128 SL) 15.2 sec. **Acceleration (quarter-mile):** (128 SL) 20.5 sec. (68 mph). **Fuel Mileage:** (128 SL) 29 mpg average.

PRODUCTION/SALES: Approximately 58,447 Fiats were sold in the U.S. during 1973, including 8,190 Model 850s and 27,341 124s.

Manufacturer: Fiat S.p.A., Turin, Italy.

Distributor: Fiat Motor Company Inc. or Fiat-Roosevelt Motors Inc., Englewood Cliffs, New Jersey.

HISTORY: During 1973, a new X1/9 Targa-roofed, mid-engine sports car joined the Fiat lineup; see next listing for details. Not everyone cared for the styling of the 128 SL 1300 coupe, including testers at *Road & Track*, through they admitted it had "a certain 'funky' look that may be popular in some quarters, judging from admiring looks (they) got while driving it."

1974 FIAT

1974 Fiat 850 Sport Spider.

128 — FOUR — Production of the front-drive Fiats continued with little change, except that all models now carried a 1290-cc (78.7-cid) four-cylinder engine. Models sold in the U.S. wore energy-absorbing safety bumpers.

X1/9 — FOUR — A new mid-engine Fiat sport coupe with Targa roof entered the U.S. market during 1973, as part of the 128 sedan series. Rather angular and dramatically wedge-shaped in appearance, the X1/9 carried the same four-cylinder engine as the 128 sedan.

124 — FOUR — Once again, four body styles were available in the rear-drive 124 series, with two different engines. This time, those engines grew in displacement, to 97-cid for the sedan and station wagon and 107-cid for the coupe and Spider convertible.

I.D. DATA: Fiat's serial number is on the dashboard, visible through the windshield; and stamped on body rib or bulkhead. Model 128 serial number contains 11 or 12 symbols: four or five to identify series and body style, followed by a seven-digit sequential serial number. Model 124 number contains 11 or 13 symbols: four or five to indicate series and body style, a sixth to denote engine type, followed by a seven-digit sequential production number. Starting serial number: (128 sedan) 128A-1458268; (128SL coupe) 128AC-134471; (128 wagon) 128AF-1458268; (X1/9) 128AS-2564; (124 sedan) 124CS1-71650; (124 wagon) 124AF1-1358304; (124 spt cpe) 124CC1-240100; (124 conv) 124CS1-71650. An identification plate is on the engine-compartment wall (front trunk of X1/9). Engine number is on a pad on the block.

Model	Body Type & Seating	Engine Type/CID	P.O.E. Price	Weight (lbs.)	Prod. Total
128					
	2-dr Sedan-4/5P	I4/79	2445	1890	Note 1
SL	2-dr Coupe-4P	I4/79	2890	1901	Note 1
	4-dr Sedan-4/5P	I4/79	2560	1920	Note 1
	2-dr Sta Wag-4/5P	I4/79	2737	1960	Note 1
X1/9					
	2-dr Targa Cpe-2P	I4/79	3917	1933	Note 1
124					
Special	4-dr Sedan-5P	I4/97	2795	2199	Note 1
	4-dr Sta Wag-5P	I4/97	3186	2248	Note 1
	2-dr Spt Cpe-4P	I4/107	4095	2298	Note 1
Spider	2-dr Conv-2P	I4/107	4395	2128	Note 1

Note 1: A total of 1,205,754 Fiats (all models) were produced during 1974, including 20,620 X1/9 coupes.

Price Note: Higher prices were listed during the course of the year, ranging from $2684 for the 128 two-door sedan to $4658 for the 124 Spider convertible.

ENGINE DATA: BASE FOUR (128, X1/9): Inline, overhead-cam four-cylinder. Cast iron block and aluminum head. **Displacement:** 78.7 cu. in. (1290 cc). **Bore & Stroke:** 3.39 x 2.19 in. (86 x 55.5 mm). **Compression Ratio:** 8.5:1. **Brake Horsepower:** 66.5 (SAE) at 6200 rpm. **Torque:** 68 lbs.-ft. at 3600 rpm. Five main bearings. Solid valve lifters. One Solex two-barrel carburetor.

BASE FOUR (124 sedan/wagon): Inline, overhead-valve four-cylinder. Cast iron block and aluminum head. **Displacement:** 97.2 cu. in. (1593 cc). **Bore & Stroke:** 3.15 x 3.12 in. (80 x 79.2 mm). **Compression Ratio:** 8.0:1. **Brake Horsepower:** 78 (SAE) at 6000 rpm. **Torque:** 85 lbs.-ft. at 3600 rpm. Five main bearings. Solid valve lifters. One two-barrel carburetor.

BASE FOUR (124 coupe/convertible): Inline, dual-overhead-cam four-cylinder. Cast iron block and aluminum head. **Displacement:** 107.1 cu. in. (1756 cc). **Bore & Stroke:** 3.31 x 3.12 in. (84 x 79.2 mm). **Compression Ratio:** 8.0:1. **Brake Horsepower:** 92.5 (SAE) at 6200 rpm. **Torque:** 92 lbs.-ft. at 3000 rpm. Five main bearings. Solid valve lifters. One two-barrel carburetor.

CHASSIS DATA: Wheelbase: (128) 96.4 in.; (128SL cpe) 87.5 in.; (X1/9) 86.7 in.; (124 cpe/sed/wagon) 95.3 in.; (124 conv) 89.8 in. **Overall Length:** (128 sedan/wagon) 157.2 in.; (128SL cpe) 154.5 in.; (X1/9) 153.5 in.; (124 cpe) 169.8 in.; (124 sedan) 165.6 in.; (124 wagon) 164.8 in.; (124 conv) 160.5 in. **Height:** (128) 55.9 in.; (128SL cpe) 51.6 in.; (X1/9) 46.1 in.; (124 cpe) 52.8 in.; (124 sedan) 55.9 in.; (124 sta wag) 56.7 in.; (124 conv) 49.2 in. **Width:** (128) 63.9 in.; (128SL cpe) 61.4 in.; (X1/9) 61.8 in.; (124 cpe) 65.8 in.; (124 sedan) 64.9 in.; (124 wagon) 64.9 in.; (124 conv) 63.5 in. **Front Tread:** (128) 51.3 in.; (128SL cpe) 52.2 in.; (X1/9) 52.5 in.; (124 cpe) 53 in.; (124 sedan/wagon) 52.4 in.; (124 conv) 53 in. **Rear Tread:** (128) 51.7 in.; (128SL cpe) 52.5 in.; (X1/9) 52.9 in.; (124 cpe) 51.8 in.; (124 sedan/wagon) 51.2 in.; (124 conv) 51.8 in. **Standard Tires:** (128) 145SR13; (X1/9) 145HR13; (124 cpe) 165SR13; (124 sed) 155SR13; (124 wagon) 165SR13; (124 conv) 165SR13.

TECHNICAL: Layout: (128) front-engine, front-drive; (X1/9) mid-engine, rear-drive; (124) front-engine, rear-drive. **Transmission:** (124 sed/wag) four-speed manual; (128, X1/9) four-speed manual; (124 cpe/conv) five-speed manual; automatic available on 124 sedan/wagon. **Steering:** (128, X1/9) rack and pinion; (124) worm and roller. **Suspension (front):** (128) MacPherson struts with coil springs and anti-roll bar; (X1/9) MacPherson struts with coil springs; (124) A-arms with coil springs and anti-roll bar. **Suspension (rear):** (128) independent with wide wishbone and transverse leaf spring; (X1/9) independent with lower wishbones, transverse control bar and struts/coil springs. (124) rigid axle with coil springs and anti-roll bar. **Brakes:** (128) front disc, rear drum; (X1/9, 124) front/rear disc. **Body Construction:** steel unibody.

MAJOR OPTIONS: Automatic transmission: 124 sedan/wagon ($247).

PRODUCTION/SALES: Approximately 72,129 Fiats were sold in the U.S. during 1974, including 32,709 Model 124s and 10,397 X1/9 coupes.

Manufacturer: Fiat S.p.A., Turin, Italy.

Distributor: Fiat Motor Company Inc. or Fiat-Roosevelt Motors Inc., Englewood Cliffs, New Jersey.

HISTORY: The 1974 models were introduced to the U.S. market on November 15, 1973.

1975 FIAT

128 — FOUR — Production of the front-drive Fiat series continued with little change.

131 — FOUR — A new rear-drive sedan/wagon series became available this year, powered by a 1756-cc (107-cid) four-cylinder engine with five-speed manual gearbox. Quad round headlamps stood alongside the rectangular, horizontal-bar grille.

124 — FOUR — Both a Spider convertible and a sport coupe were offered again in the 124 series, each powered by a 1756-cc (107-cid) engine. Because of the emergence of the new 131 series, the 124 sedan and station wagon were dropped. Bumpers were revised, displaying a less massive look than those used in 1974.

X1/9 — FOUR — Fiat's mid-engine sport coupe with Targa roof continued with little change, apart from revised bumpers to comply with U.S. regulations.

I.D. DATA: Fiat's serial number is on the dashboard, visible through the windshield; and stamped on a body rib or bulkhead. A prefix consisting of four to seven symbols is followed by a sequential serial number, which also identifies the model year. An identification plate is on engine-compartment wall (front trunk of X1/9). Engine number is on a pad on the block.

Model	Body Type & Seating	Engine Type/CID	P.O.E. Price	Weight (lbs.)	Prod. Total
128					
	2-dr Sedan-4/5P	I4/79	2741	1950	Note 1
	4-dr Sedan-4/5P	I4/79	3049	1980	Note 1
SL	2-dr Coupe-4P	I4/79	3357	1980	Note 1
	2-dr Sta Wag-4/5P	I4/79	3207	1985	Note 1
131					
	2-dr Sedan-4/5P	I4/107	3958	2460	Note 1
	4-dr Sedan-4/5P	I4/107	4092	2460	Note 1
	4-dr Sta Wag-4/5P	I4/107	4420	2510	Note 1
124					
	2-dr Spt Cpe-4P	I4/107	4687	2370	Note 1
Spider	2-dr Conv-2P	I4/107	5129	2320	Note 1
X1/9					
	2-dr Targa Cpe-2P	I4/79	4608	2085	Note 1

Note 1: A total of 1,006,600 Fiats (all models) were produced during 1975, including 23,263 Model 124 Sports and 17,360 X1/9 coupes.

ENGINE DATA: BASE FOUR (128, X1/9): Inline, overhead-cam four-cylinder. Cast iron block and aluminum head. **Displacement:** 78.7 cu. in. (1290 cc). **Bore & Stroke:** 3.39 x 2.19 in. (86 x 55.5 mm). **Compression Ratio:** 8.5:1. **Brake Horsepower:** (128) 62 (SAE) at 6000 rpm; (X1/9) 61 at 5800 rpm. **Torque:** 67 lbs.-ft. (SAE) at 4000 rpm. Five main bearings. Solid valve lifters. Two-barrel carburetor.

BASE FOUR (131, 124): Inline, overhead-cam four-cylinder. Cast iron block and aluminum head. **Displacement:** 107 cu. in. (1756 cc). **Bore & Stroke:** 3.31 x 3.12 in. (84 x 79.2 mm). **Compression Ratio:** 8.0:1. **Brake Horsepower:** 86 (SAE) at 6200 rpm. **Torque:** 90 lbs.-ft. (SAE) at 2800 rpm. Five main bearings. Solid valve lifters. Two-barrel carburetor.

CHASSIS DATA: Wheelbase: (128 cpe) 87.5 in.; (128 sed) 96.4 in.; (131) 98 in.; (124 cpe) 95.3 in.; (124 Spider) 89.7 in.; (X1/9) 86.7 in. **Overall Length:** (128 cpe) 156.4 in.; (128 sed) 158.6 in.; (131) 171.7 in.; (124 cpe) 172.4 in.; (124 Spider) 163.1 in.; (X1/9) 158.5 in. **Height:** (128 cpe) 51.6 in.; (128 sed) 55.9 in.; (131 sed) 53.7 in.; (131 wag) 53.3 in.; (124 cpe) 52.7 in.; (124 Spider) 49.2 in.; (X1/9) 46.1 in. **Width:** (128 cpe) 61.4 in.; (128 sed) 62.6 in.; (131) 64.6 in.; (124 cpe) 66.7 in.; (124 Spider) 63.5 in.; (X1/9) 61.8 in. **Front Tread:** (128 cpe) 52.2 in.; (128 sed/wag) 51.3 in.; (131) 54.1 in.; (124 cpe) 53 in.; (124 Spider) 53.2 in.; (X1/9) 52.5 in. **Rear Tread:** (128 cpe) 52.5 in.; (128 sed) 51.8 in.; (128 wag) 51.6 in.; (131) 51.9 in.; (124 cpe) 51.8 in.; (124 Spider) 52.0 in.; (X1/9) 52.9 in. **Standard Tires:** (128) 145SR13; (131) 160SR13; (124 cpe/conv) 165HR13; (X1/9) 145HR13.

TECHNICAL: Layout: (128) front-engine, front-drive; (131, Spider) front-engine, rear-drive; (X1/9) mid-engine, rear-drive. **Transmission:** (128, X1/9) four-speed manual; (124, 131) five-speed manual; automatic available. **Steering:** (128/131) rack and pinion; (X1/9) rack and pinion; (124) worm and roller. **Suspension (front):** (128/131) MacPherson struts with coil springs and anti-roll bar; (124 Spider) upper/lower A-arms with coil springs and anti-roll bar; (X1/9) MacPherson struts with lower lateral links, compliance struts and coil springs. **Suspension (rear):** (128) independent with wide wishbone and transverse leaf spring; (131) rigid axle with Panhard rod and coil springs; (124 Spider) rigid axle with trailing arms, Panhard rod and coil springs; (X1/9) MacPherson struts with lower A-arms, trailing links and coil springs. **Brakes:** (128, 131) front disc, rear drum; (Spider, X1/9) front/rear disc. **Body Construction:** steel unibody.

MAJOR OPTIONS: Automatic transmission: 131 ($265).

PERFORMANCE: Acceleration (0-60 mph): (X1/9) 14.7 sec. **Fuel Mileage:** (X1/9) about 29 mpg.

PRODUCTION/SALES: A total of 100,511 Fiats were sold in the U.S. during 1975, including 32,238 Model 124s and 15,832 X1/9 coupes.

Manufacturer: Fiat S.p.A., Turin, Italy.

Distributor: Fiat Distributors, Englewood Cliffs, New Jersey.

1976 FIAT

128 — FOUR — Production of the front-drive Fiat series continued with little change. Power came from a 1290-cc four-cylinder engine. Interiors held vinyl seats and door panels, while bumpers were made of aluminum and rubber.

131 — FOUR — Production of the rear-drive sedan/wagon series, introduced during the 1975 model year, continued with little change, powered by a 1756-cc (107-cid) four-cylinder engine. Air conditioning and an automatic transmission were optional; a five-speed gearbox, tachometer, rear defroster and tinted glass were standard.

SPIDER 124 — FOUR — The closed coupe was gone, leaving only the open convertible as the last remaining model in the 124 series. As before, power came from a 1756-cc (107-cid) engine.

X1/9 — FOUR — Though mounted in the middle, the Targa-topped sport coupe's engine was the same as that used in the 128 series. Little change was evident this year.

I.D. DATA: Fiat's serial number is on the dashboard, visible through the windshield; and on a body rib or bulkhead. A prefix consisting of four to seven symbols is followed by a sequential serial number, which also identifies the model year. Starting serial number: (128 sedan) 128A1-1973215; (128 hatch) 128AC-219095; (128 wagon) 128AF1-1971374; (131 two-door sedan) 131A3-86857; (131 four-door sedan) 131A3-86883; (131 wagon) 131AF2-4024185; (Spider) 124CS1-99909; (X1/9) 128AS-40659. An identification plate is on the engine-compartment wall (front trunk of X1/9). Engine number is on a pad on the block.

Model	Body Type & Seating	Engine Type/CID	P.O.E. Price	Weight (lbs.)	Prod. Total
128					
	2-dr Sedan-4/5P	I4/79	2998	1890	Note 1
Custom	2-dr Sedan-4/5P	I4/79	3222	1890	Note 1
Custom	4-dr Sedan-4/5P	I4/79	3380	1930	Note 1
3P Sport	2-dr Hatch Cpe-4P	I4/79	3768	1915	Note 1
	2-dr Sta Wag-4/5P	I4/79	3552	1985	Note 1
131					
131A3	2-dr Sedan-4/5P	I4/107	4286	2350	Note 1
131A3	4-dr Sedan-4/5P	I4/107	4431	2375	Note 1
131AF2	4-dr Sta Wag-4/5P	I4/107	4815	2425	Note 1
SPORT SPIDER 124					
124CS	2-dr Conv-2P	I4/107	5759	2180	Note 1
X1/9					
128AS	2-dr Targa Cpe-2P	I4/79	4947	1970	Note 1

Note 1: A total of 1,098,182 Fiats (all models) were produced during 1976, including 11,820 Sport 124s and 15,783 X1/9 coupes.

ENGINE DATA: BASE FOUR (128, X1/9): Inline, overhead-cam four-cylinder. Cast iron block and aluminum head. **Displacement:** 78.7 cu. in. (1290 cc). **Bore & Stroke:** 3.39 x 2.19 in. (86 x 55.5 mm). **Compression Ratio:** 8.5:1. **Brake Horsepower:** (128) 62 (SAE) at 6000 rpm; (X1/9) 61 at 5800 rpm. **Torque:** 67 lbs.-ft. (SAE) at 4000 rpm. Five main bearings. Solid valve lifters. Weber two-barrel carburetor.

BASE FOUR (131, Spider 124): Inline, overhead-cam four-cylinder. Cast iron block and aluminum head. **Displacement:** 107 cu. in. (1756 cc). **Bore & Stroke:** 3.31 x 3.12 in. (84.0 x 79.2 mm). **Compression Ratio:** 8.0:1. **Brake Horsepower:** 86 (SAE) at 6200 rpm. **Torque:** 90 lbs.-ft. (SAE) at 2800 rpm. Five main bearings. Solid valve lifters. Weber two-barrel carburetor.

CHASSIS DATA: Wheelbase: (128 cpe) 87.5 in.; (128 sed) 96.4 in.; (131) 98 in.; (Spider) 89.7 in.; (X1/9) 86.7 in. **Overall Length:** (128 cpe) 156.4 in.; (128 sed) 158.6 in.; (128 wag) 159.2 in.; (131) 171.7 in.; (Spider) 163.1 in.; (X1/9) 156.2 in. **Height:** (128 cpe) 51.2 in.; (128 sed) 55.9 in.; (131) 53.7 in.; (Spider) 49.2 in.; (X1/9) 46.1 in. **Width:** (128 cpe) 61.4 in.; (128 sed) 62.6 in.; (131) 64.6 in.; (Spider) 63.5 in.; (X1/9) 61.8 in. **Front Tread:** (128 cpe) 52.2 in.; (128 sed) 51.3 in.; (131) 54.1 in.; (Spider) 53.2 in.; (X1/9) 53.3 in. **Rear Tread:** (128 cpe) 52.5 in.; (128 sed) 51.8 in.; (128 wagon) 51.6 in.; (131) 51.9 in.; (Spider) 52.0 in.; (X1/9) 53.6 in. **Standard Tires:** (128) 145SR13; (131) 160SR13; (Spider) 165HR13; (X1/9) 145HR13.

TECHNICAL: Layout: (128) front-engine, front-drive; (131, Spider) front-engine, rear-drive; (X1/9) mid-engine, rear-drive. **Transmission:** (128, X1/9) four-speed manual; (131, Spider 124) five-speed manual; automatic available. **Steering:** (128/131) rack and pinion; (X1/9) rack and pinion; (Spider) worm and roller. **Suspension (front):** (128/131) MacPherson struts with coil springs and anti-roll bar; (Spider) upper/lower A-arms with coil springs and anti-roll bar; (X1/9) MacPherson struts with lower lateral links, compliance struts and coil springs. **Suspension (rear):** (128) wide wishbone with transverse leaf spring; (131) rigid axle Panhard rod and coil springs; (Spider) rigid axle with trailing arms, Panhard rod and coil springs; (X1/9) struts with lower A-arms, trailing links and coil springs. **Brakes:** (128, 131) front disc, rear drum; (Spider, X1/9) front/rear disc. **Body Construction:** steel unibody.

MAJOR OPTIONS: Automatic transmission: 131 ($265). Air conditioning: 131, X1/9 ($420). AM/FM stereo radio. Metallic paint. Rear defroster: 128 sed ($20).

PRODUCTION/SALES: A total of 61,540 Fiats were sold in the U.S. during 1976, including 11,721 124s and 10,647 X1/9 coupes.

Manufacturer: Fiat S.p.A., Turin, Italy.

Distributor: Fiat Distributors, Englewood Cliffs, New Jersey.

HISTORY: Fiat's 1976 models were introduced in the U.S. in October 1975. Advertising for the 128 promised "A lot of car. Not a lot of money."

1977 FIAT

128 — FOUR — Except for a few minor cosmetic modifications, nothing was new on Fiat's front-drive series, offered in four different body styles. Standard equipment included a four-speed manual transmission, reclining bucket seats, and power front disc brakes. Power came from a 1290-cc (78.7-cid) four-cylinder engine.

131 — FOUR — Little change was evident in Fiat's rear-drive sedan series, offered as a two- and four-door sedan, or a station wagon. Under its hood was a 1756-cc (107-cid) four-cylinder engine. The two-door was sometimes called a coupe rather than a sedan.

SPORT SPIDER 124 — FOUR — Production of the open sports car, the only remaining example of Fiat's 124 series, continued with little change. Power came from a 1756-cc (107-cid) engine. Standard equipment included a sport steering wheel, tachometer, and 165HR13 tires on steel disc wheels.

X1/9 — FOUR — Though mounted in the middle, the Targa-topped sport coupe's engine was the same as that used in the 128 series. Little change was evident this year. Standard equipment included a tachometer, sport steering wheel, vinyl upholstery, and 145HR13 tires on mag-style wheels. The coupe's front bumper protruded well ahead of the car.

I.D. DATA: Fiat's serial number is on the dashboard, visible through the windshield; and on a body rib or bulkhead. A prefix consisting of four to seven symbols is followed by a sequential serial number, which also identifies the model year. Starting serial number: (128 sedan) 128A1-0227722; (128 hatch) 128AC-0286709; (128 wagon) 128AF1-0227722; (131 sedan) 131A4-0265525; (131 wagon) 131AF2-4097360; (Spider) 124CS1-0113343; (X1/9) 128AS-0057030. An identification plate is on the engine-compartment wall (front trunk of X1/9). Engine number is on a pad on the block.

Model	Body Type & Seating	Engine Type/CID	P.O.E. Price	Weight (lbs.)	Prod. Total
128					
	2-dr Sedan-4/5P	I4/79	2998	1890	Note 1
Custom	2-dr Sedan-4/5P	I4/79	3282	1890	Note 1
Custom	4-dr Sedan-4/5P	I4/79	3442	1930	Note 1
3P Custom	2-dr Hatch Cpe-4P	I4/79	3828	1915	Note 1
	2-dr Sta Wag-4/5P	I4/79	3591	1985	Note 1
131					
131A3	2-dr Sedan-4/5P	I4/107	4396	2350	Note 1
131A3	4-dr Sedan-4/5P	I4/107	4564	2375	Note 1
131AF2	4-dr Sta Wag-4/5P	I4/107	4948	2425	Note 1
SPORT SPIDER 124					
124CS	2-dr Conv-2P	I4/107	6115	2180	Note 1
X1/9					
128AS	2-dr Targo Cpe-2P	I4/79	5195	1955	Note 1

Note 1: A total of 1,057,261 Fiats (all models) were produced during 1977, including 14,008 Spider 124s and 18,450 X1/9 coupes.

ENGINE DATA: BASE FOUR (128, X1/9): Inline, overhead-cam four-cylinder. Cast iron block and aluminum head. **Displacement:** 78.7 cu. in. (1290 cc). **Bore & Stroke:** 3.39 x 2.19 in. (86 x 55.5 mm). **Compression Ratio:** 8.5:1. **Brake Horsepower:** (128) 62 (SAE) at 6000 rpm; (X1/9) 61.5 at 5800 rpm. **Torque:** 67 lbs.-ft. (SAE) at 4000 rpm. Five main bearings. Solid valve lifters. Two-barrel carburetor.

BASE FOUR (131, Spider 124): Inline, overhead-cam four-cylinder. Cast iron block and aluminum head. **Displacement:** 107 cu. in. (1756 cc). **Bore & Stroke:** 3.31 x 3.12 in. (84 x 79.2 mm). **Compression Ratio:** 8.0:1. **Brake Horsepower:** 86 (SAE) at 6200 rpm. **Torque:** 90 lbs.-ft. (SAE) at 2800 rpm. Five main bearings. Solid valve lifters. Two-barrel carburetor.

CHASSIS DATA: Wheelbase: (128 hatch) 87.5 in.; (128 sed) 96.4 in.; (131) 98.0 in.; (Spider) 89.7 in.; (X1/9) 86.7 in. **Overall Length:** (128 hatch) 156.4 in.; (128 sed) 158.6 in.; (128 wag) 159.2 in.; (131) 171.7 in.; (Spider) 163.0 in.; (X1/9) 158.5 in. **Height:** (128 hatch) 51.2 in.; (128 sed) 55.9 in.; (131 sed) 53.7 in.; (131 wag) 53.3 in.; (Spider) 49.2 in.; (X1/9) 46.1 in. **Width:** (128 hatch) 61.4 in.; (128 sed) 62.6 in.; (131) 64.6 in.; (Spider) 63.5 in.; (X1/9) 61.8 in. **Front Tread:** (128 hatch) 52.2 in.; (128 sed) 51.3 in.; (131) 54.1 in.; (Spider) 53.2 in.; (X1/9) 52.5 in. **Rear Tread:** (128 hatch) 52.5 in.; (128 sed) 51.8 in.; (128 wag) 51.6 in.; (131) 51.9 in.; (Spider) 52.0 in.; (X1/9) 52.9 in. **Standard Tires:** (128) 145SR13; (131) 160SR13/165SR13; (Spider) 165HR13; (X1/9) 145HR13.

TECHNICAL: Layout: (128) front-engine, front-drive; (131, Spider) front-engine, rear-drive; (X1/9) mid-engine, rear-drive. **Transmission:** (128, X1/9) four-speed manual; (131, Spider) five-speed manual; automatic available. **Steering:** (128/131) rack and pinion; (X1/9) rack and pinion; (Spider) worm and roller. **Suspension (front):** (128/131) MacPherson struts with coil springs; (Spider) upper/lower A-arms with coil springs and anti-roll bar; (X1/9) MacPherson struts with lower lateral links, compliance struts and coil springs. **Suspension (rear):** (128) wide wishbone with transverse leaf spring; (131) rigid axle with trailing arms, transverse rod and coil springs; (Spider) rigid axle with trailing arms, Panhard rod and coil springs; (X1/9) struts with lower A-arms, trailing links and coil springs. **Brakes:** (128, 131) front disc, rear drum; (Spider, X1/9) front/rear disc. **Body Construction:** steel unibody.

MAJOR OPTIONS: Automatic transmission ($265). Air conditioning ($420). AM/FM stereo radio.

PRODUCTION/SALES: A total of 63,479 Fiats were sold in the U.S. during 1977, including 12,935 Model 124s and 10,976 X1/9 coupes.

Manufacturer: Fiat S.p.A., Turin, Italy.

Distributor: Fiat Motors of North America, Montvale, New Jersey.

HISTORY: Fiat's 1977 models were introduced in the U.S. in November 1976 except (X1/9 and 124) August 1976 and (128 coupe) January 1977. Advertisements this year compared the price of a X1/9 coupe with those of the similarly mid-engined Maserati Merak and Lamborghini Urraco. For the home market, Fiat introduced a 126 de Ville mini-sedan, called "luxury in a small package," as well as a new 132 "flagship" series and a revised 127 series.

1978 FIAT

128 — FOUR — Slight styling modifications were the only change for Fiat's front-drive series, which returned in hatchback coupe and sedan form. The station wagon was dropped, as a result of poor sales.

131 — FOUR — Fiat's rear-drive sedan series continued with little change, with a 1756-cc engine under its hood.

BRAVA — FOUR — A new Brava series overtook the 131 at mid-year, initially powered by the same 1756-cc four-cylinder engine; but at mid-year, Bravas became available with the new twin-cam 2.0-liter four, also used in the Spider 2000.

SPIDER 124 — FOUR — This would be the final year for 1.8-liter power under the convertible's hood. Fiat's Spider had a wood-trimmed instrument panel, all-disc brakes, and five-speed manual gearbox. At mid-year, a 2.0-liter twin-cam four-cylinder engine became available, changing the Spider's designation to "2000."

X1/9 — FOUR — Production of the mid-engine sport coupe, with 1.3-liter engine (as in the 128 sedan), continued with little change. Radio antennas now sat against the right windshield pillar.

1978 Fiat 128 four-door sedan.

I.D. DATA: Fiat's serial number is on the dashboard, visible through the windshield; and on a body rib or bulkhead. A prefix consisting of four to seven symbols is followed by a sequential serial number, which also identifies the model year. Starting serial number: (128 sedan) 128A1-2468403; (128 hatch) 128AC-319079; (131 sedan) 131A-331279; (131 wagon) 131AF2-4140698; (Brava sedan) 131A3-0373783; (Brava wagon) 131AF2-4213737; (Spider) 124CS1-126166; (X1/9) 128AS-74001. An identification plate is on the engine-compartment wall (front trunk of X1/9). Engine number is on a pad on the block.

Model	Body Type & Seating	Engine Type/CID	P.O.E. Price	Weight (lbs.)	Prod. Total
128					
128A1	2-dr Sedan-4/5P	I4/79	3295	1890	Note 1
128A1	4-dr Sedan-4/5P	I4/79	3695	1930	Note 1
128AC	2-dr Spt Hatch-4P	I4/79	3898	1915	Note 1
131					
131A	2-dr Sedan-4/5P	I4/107	4498	2350	Note 1
131A	4-dr Sedan-4/5P	I4/107	4698	2375	Note 1
131AF	4-dr Sta Wag-4/5P	I4/107	5048	2425	Note 1
BRAVA					
	2-dr Sedan-4/5P	I4/107	4548	N/A	Note 1
Super	2-dr Sedan-4/5P	I4/107	4795	2350	Note 1
Super	4-dr Sedan-4/5P	I4/107	4995	2375	Note 1
Super	4-dr Sta Wag-4/5P	I4/107	5409	2425	Note 1
SPIDER 124					
124CS	2-dr Conv-2P	I4/107	6495	2180	Note 1
X1/9					
128AS	2-dr Targa Cpe-2P	I4/79	5700	1955	Note 1

Note 1: A total of 1,104,0026 Fiats (all models) were produced during 1978, including 16,079 Spider 124s and 19,240 X1/9 coupes.

Price Note: Some initial announced prices were lower than those shown above, ranging from $3050 for the 128 two-door sedan to $5195 for the X1/9 coupe and $6299 for the Spider 124.

ENGINE DATA: BASE FOUR (128, X1/9): Inline, overhead-cam four-cylinder. Cast iron block and aluminum head. **Displacement:** 78.7 cu. in. (1290 cc). **Bore & Stroke:** 3.39 x 2.19 in. (86 x 55.5 mm). **Compression Ratio:** 8.5:1. **Brake Horsepower:** (128) 62 (SAE) at 6000 rpm; (X1/9) 61.5 bhp. **Torque:** 67 lbs.-ft. (SAE) at 4000 rpm. Five main bearings. Solid valve lifters. Two-barrel carburetor.

BASE FOUR (131, Brava, Spider 124): Inline, dual-overhead-cam four-cylinder. Cast iron block and aluminum head. **Displacement:** 107 cu. in. (1756 cc). **Bore & Stroke:** 3.31 x 3.12 in. (84 x 79.2 mm). **Compression Ratio:** 8.0:1. **Brake Horsepower:** 86 (SAE) at 6200 rpm. **Torque:** 90 lbs.-ft. (SAE) at 2800 rpm. Five main bearings. Solid valve lifters. Two-barrel carburetor.

BASE FOUR (late Brava, 2000): Inline, dual-overhead-cam four-cylinder. Cast iron block and aluminum head. **Displacement:** 121.7 cu. in. (1995 cc). **Bore & Stroke:** 3.31 x 3.54 in. (84 x 90 mm). **Compression Ratio:** 8.1:1. **Brake Horsepower:** 86 (SAE) at 5100 rpm. **Torque:** 100-104 lbs.-ft. (SAE) at 3000 rpm. Five main bearings. Solid valve lifters. Two-barrel carburetor.

CHASSIS DATA: Wheelbase: (128 hatch) 87.5 in.; (128 sed) 96.4 in.; (131) 98.0 in.; (Brava) 98.0 in.; (Spider) 89.7 in.; (X1/9) 86.7 in. **Overall Length:** (128 hatch) 156.4 in.; (128 sed) 158.6 in.; (131) 172.4 in.; (Brava) 172.4 in.; (Spider) 163.0 in.; (X1/9) 158.5 in. **Height:** (128 hatch) 51.2 in.; (128 sed) 55.9 in.; (131 sed) 53.5 in.; (131 wag) 55.1 in.; (Brava sed) 54.4 in.; (Brava wag) 54.7 in.; (Spider) 49.2 in.; (X1/9) 46.1 in. **Width:** (128 hatch) 61.4 in.; (128 sed) 62.6 in.; (131) 64.6 in.; (Brava) 65.0 in.; (Spider) 63.5 in.; (X1/9) 61.8 in. **Front Tread:** (128 hatch) 52.2 in.; (128 sed) 51.3 in.; (131) 54.1 in.; (Brava) 54.2 in.; (Spider) 53.2 in.; (X1/9) 52.5 in. **Rear Tread:** (128 hatch) 51.5 in.; (128 sed) 51.8 in.; (131) 51.9 in.; (Brava) 51.9 in.; (Spider) 52.0 in.; (X1/9) 52.9 in. **Standard Tires:** (128) 145SR13; (131) 160SR13; (Brava) 160SR13; (Spider) 165HR13; (X1/9) 145HR13.

TECHNICAL: Layout: (128) front-engine, front-drive; (131, Brava, Spider) front-engine, rear-drive; (X1/9) mid-engine, rear-drive. **Transmission:** (128, X1/9) four-speed manual; (131, Brava, Spider) five-speed manual; three-speed automatic available on 131/Brava. **Steering:** (128, 131, Brava, X1/9) rack and pinion; (Spider) worm and roller. **Suspension (front):** (Brava) MacPherson struts with coil springs and anti-roll bar; (Spider) upper/lower A-arms with coil springs and anti-roll bar; (X1/9) MacPherson struts with lower lateral links, compliance struts and coil springs. **Suspension (rear):** (Brava) four-link rigid axle with Panhard rod and coil springs; (Spider) rigid axle with trailing arms, Panhard rod and coil springs; (X1/9) struts with lower A-arms, trailing links and coil springs. **Brakes:** (128/131/Brava) front disc, rear drum; (Spider, X1/9) front/rear disc. **Body Construction:** steel unibody.

MAJOR OPTIONS: Automatic transmission. Bertone package (X1/9). Rally Sport package (128). AM/FM stereo radio. Air conditioning.

PRODUCTION/SALES: A total of 60,435 Fiats were sold in the U.S. during 1978, including 15,417 124 Spiders and 10,817 X1/9 coupes.

Manufacturer: Fiat S.p.A., Turin, Italy.

Distributor: Fiat Motors of North America, Montvale, New Jersey.

HISTORY: Fiat's 1978 models were introduced in the U.S. in September 1977. Fiat's fortunes were sinking in the American market in the late 1970s, as a result of imperfect quality control and lack of adequate parts/service, as well as the emergence of strong Japanese competitors. In an attempt to improve its image, the company introduced a new owner's program at this time, called "Because We Care." They also offered a two-year, 24,000-mile warranty.

"The worst thing you can say about the X1/9," declared *Road & Track,* "is that it may not have enough power for some." That lack would be remedied for 1979 with a larger (1498-cc) engine. By this time, the U.S. had 650 Fiat dealers. Spider ads pushed the fact that convertibles no longer were produced in the U.S.

1979 FIAT

128 — FOUR — This was the final year for the 128 series, offered in sedan and hatchback form. Actually, production halted in 1978, but it remained on sale into 1979.

STRADA — FOUR — Fiat introduced this new front-drive hatchback sedan with all-independent suspension during the 1979 model year. Two- and four-door hatchbacks were powered by a 1.5-liter four-cylinder engine, with either a five-speed manual gearbox or optional automatic transmission. Single round headlamps were recessed into openings along the full-width, wraparound grille. Styling features included round door-handle openings. Stradas rode a 96.4-inch wheelbase and were more aero-shaped than the 128. The standard two-door came in dark blue, light blue, or white. Custom models were offered in additional colors, and included tinted glass, reclining front bucket seats, and a carpeted cargo area. A $385 Luxury Package for the Custom added woven cloth upholstery, a digital clock, and fold-down rear seats. This model was called the Ritmo in the home market.

BRAVA — FOUR — Fiat's rear-drive replacement for the 131, introduced late in 1978, came in two-door and four-door sedan form, along with a station wagon. Power now came from a 2.0-liter twin-cam four-cylinder engine, identical to that in the Spider 2000 convertible, instead of the initial 1.8-liter unit. Horsepower was the same as before, but torque got a big boost. Either a five-speed manual gearbox or optional GM three-speed automatic was available. Instruments were regrouped at this time, and seats grew wider. Velour upholstery was available for sedans, but wagons wore vinyl and came with a standard luggage rack.

SPIDER 2000 — FOUR — Fiat's open sports car got a performance boost during the prior model year with a new twin-cam 2.0-liter four-cylinder engine, replacing the former 1.8-liter powerplant. Torque grew considerably, though horsepower remained the same. An improved interior included carpeting, bucket seats, and new trim, plus restyled instrument panel and steering wheel. A remote-control left mirror was standard. Appearance changes included a restyled hood, front lip-type spoiler, and larger taillamps. Steel wheels came from the Brava. New body colors and trim options were offered, and a three-speed automatic transmission was available.

X1/9 — FOUR — Engine displacement jumped from 1.3 to 1.5 liters this year, in Fiat's mid-engine sports coupe with its Targa roof. That change cut 0-60 mph acceleration time by about two seconds, according to Fiat. New bucket seats offered better support, and the dashboard held a rearranged instrument grouping. Only a five-speed manual gearbox was available.

I.D. DATA: Fiat's serial number is on the dashboard, visible through the windshield; and on a body rib or bulkhead. A prefix consisting of four to seven symbols is followed by a sequential serial number, which also identifies the model year. Starting serial number: (128 sedan) 128A1-2604627; (128 hatch) 128AC-322016; (Strada) 138A2-2030524; (Brava sedan) 131A4-425154; (Brava wagon) 131AF3-4257818; (Spider 2000) 124CS2-142649; (X1/9) 128AS-98100. An identification plate is on the engine-compartment wall (front trunk of X1/9). Engine number is on a pad on the block.

Model	Body Type & Seating	Engine Type/CID	P.O.E. Price	Weight (lbs.)	Prod. Total
128					
128A1	2-dr Sedan-4/5P	I4/79	3445	1890	Note 1
128A1	4-dr Sedan-4/5P	I4/79	3775	1930	Note 1
128AC	2-dr Spt Hatch-4P	I4/79	4295	1915	Note 1
STRADA					
138A	2-dr Hatch-4/5P	I4/91	4296	2000	Note 1
138A Cust	2-dr Hatch-4/5P	I4/91	4790	1965	Note 1
138A Cust	4-dr Hatch-4/5P	I4/91	4840	2000	Note 1
BRAVA					
131A4	2-dr Sedan-4/5P	I4/122	5290	2375	Note 1
131A4	4-dr Sedan-4/5P	I4/122	5490	2410	Note 1
131AF	4-dr Sta Wag-4/5P	I4/122	5790	2340	Note 1
SPIDER 2000					
124CS	2-dr Conv-2P	I4/122	7090	2240	Note 1
X1/9					
128AS	2-dr Targa Cpe-2P	I4/91	6290	2040	Note 1

Note 1: A total of 1,081,473 Fiats (all models) were produced during 1979, including 18,536 Spiders and 20,083 X1/9 coupes.

Price Note: Some prices rose during the year, reaching $7515 for the Spider 2000 and $7115 for the X1/9 coupe.

ENGINE DATA: BASE FOUR (128): Inline, overhead-cam four-cylinder. Cast iron block and aluminum head. **Displacement:** 78.7 cu. in. (1290 cc). **Bore & Stroke:** 3.39 x 2.19 in. (86 x 55.5 mm). **Compression Ratio:** 8.5:1. **Brake Horsepower:** 62 (SAE) at 6000 rpm. **Torque:** 67 lbs.-ft. (SAE) at 4000 rpm. Five main bearings. Solid valve lifters. Two-barrel carburetor.

BASE FOUR (Strada, X1/9): Inline, overhead-cam four-cylinder. Cast iron block and aluminum head. **Displacement:** 91.4 cu. in. (1498 cc). **Bore & Stroke:** 3.40 x 2.52 in. (86.4 x 63.9 mm). **Compression Ratio:** 8.5:1. **Brake Horsepower:** (Strada) 69 (SAE) at 5100 rpm; (X1/9) 67 at 5250 rpm. **Torque:** (Strada) 77 lbs.-ft. (SAE) at 2500 rpm; (X1/9) 76 lbs.-ft. at 3000 rpm. Five main bearings. Solid valve lifters. Two-barrel carburetor.

BASE FOUR (Brava, 2000): Inline, dual-overhead-cam four-cylinder. Cast iron block and aluminum head. **Displacement:** 121.7 cu. in. (1995 cc). **Bore & Stroke:** 3.31 x 3.54 in. (84 x 90 mm). **Compression Ratio:** 8.1:1. **Brake Horsepower:** 86 (SAE) at 5100 rpm. **Torque:** 100-104 lbs.-ft. (SAE) at 3000 rpm. Five main bearings. Solid valve lifters. Two-barrel carburetor.

CHASSIS DATA: Wheelbase: (128 hatch) 87.5 in.; (128 sed) 96.4 in.; (Strada) 96.4 in.; (Brava) 98.0 in.; (2000) 89.7 in.; (X1/9) 86.7 in. **Overall Length:** (128 hatch) 156.4 in.; (128 sed) 158.6 in.; (Strada) 161.0 in.; (Brava) 172.4 in.; (2000) 163.0 in.; (X1/9) 156.2 in. **Height:** (128 hatch) 51.2 in.; (128 sed) 55.9 in.; (Strada) 53.0 in.; (Brava sed) 54.4 in.; (Brava wag) 54.7 in.; (2000) 48.2 in.; (X1/9) 46.1 in. **Width:** (128 hatch) 61.4 in.; (128 sed) 62.6 in.; (Strada) 64.9 in.; (Brava) 65.0 in.; (2000) 63.5 in.; (X1/9) 61.8 in. **Front Tread:** (128 hatch) 52.2 in.; (128 sed) 51.3 in.; (Strada) 55.1 in.; (Brava) 54.2 in.; (2000) 53.2 in.; (X1/9) 52.5 in. **Rear Tread:** (128 hatch) 51.5 in.; (128 sed) 51.8 in.; (Strada) 55.5 in.; (Brava) 51.9 in.; (2000) 52.0 in.; (X1/9) 52.9 in. **Standard Tires:** (128) 145SR13; (Strada) 145SR13; (Brava) 165SR13; (2000) 165SR13; (X1/9) 165/70SR13.

TECHNICAL: Layout: (128, Strada) front-engine, front-drive; (Brava, 2000) front-engine, rear-drive; (X1/9) mid-engine, rear-drive. **Transmission:** (128) four-speed manual; (others) five-speed manual; three-speed automatic available on Strada/Brava/Spider. **Standard Final Drive Ratio:** (Brava) 3.58:1; (Spider) 3.90:1. **Steering:** (Strada, Brava, X1/9) rack and pinion; (2000) worm and roller. **Suspension (front):** (Strada, Brava) MacPherson struts with coil springs and anti-roll bar; (2000) upper/lower A-arms with coil springs and anti-roll bar; (X1/9) MacPherson struts with lower lateral links, compliance struts and coil springs. **Suspension (rear):** (Strada) Chapman struts with lower A-arms and transverse leaf springs; (Brava) four-link rigid axle with Panhard rod and coil springs; (2000) rigid axle with trailing arms, Panhard rod and coil springs; (X1/9) reaction struts with lower A-arms, trailing links and coil springs. **Brakes:** (Strada/Brava) front disc, rear drum; (Spider 2000, X1/9) front/rear disc. **Body Construction:** steel unibody.

MAJOR OPTIONS: Three-speed automatic transmission: Brava/Spider ($345-$390). Luxury package: Strada ($385). Air conditioning: Brava ($499). Power steering ($225-$285). Sunroof ($347). Power windows ($165). AM/FM stereo radio. Metallic paint ($80-$180).

Note: Not all options were offered on all models.

PRODUCTION/SALES: A total of 58,934 Fiats were sold in the U.S. during 1979, including 14,572 Spider 2000 and 9,347 X1/9 coupes.

Manufacturer: Fiat S.p.A., Turin, Italy.

Distributor: Fiat Motors of North America Inc., Montvale, New Jersey.

HISTORY: Fiat's 1979 models were introduced in the U.S. in October 1978 except (X1/9) November 1978 and (Strada) February 1979. Ads noted the Strada's "flair that could only be Italian," calling it "another Italian work of art." Fiat's sales brochure promoted a statement by *Car and Driver* that the X1/9 was "an up-to-the-minute sports car bursting with old-style fun" that "feels like a junior Ferrari." The magazine added that the Targa-top mid-engine coupe "has cornered the ultra-sophisticated branch of the small sports car market."

1980 FIAT

1980 Fiat Panda two-door sedan.

STRADA — FOUR — Introduced during the 1979 model year, Fiat's front-drive hatchbacks entered their second season with various small changes evident. Wheels were new. So were seat fabrics and color-coordinated seatbelts. On the dashboard was a new 80-mph speedometer. Serving as replacements for the 128, these subcompacts rode a 96.4-inch wheelbase. Options included remote-control mirrors, a sunroof, alloy wheels, whitewall tires, and expanded instrumentation (including a tachometer).

BRAVA — FOUR — The station wagon was dropped this year from Fiat's rear-drive lineup, which replaced the earlier 131 series during 1978. The 2.0-liter engine was available either carbureted or with fuel injection (injection standard in California). Adding fuel injection gave the engine a boost from 80 to 102 horsepower. Brava speedometers now read only to 80 mph. Bumper aprons grew larger this year, and wheels got a restyling. Joining the option list were power windows and door locks. Air conditioning was standard, as were power steering, tilt steering wheel, and reclining front bucket seats. Leather upholstery was optional.

SPIDER 2000 — FOUR — The convertible's 2.0-liter engine, identical to that used in the Brava sedan, was available either carbureted or with fuel injection this year. Otherwise, the long-lived Fiat sports car was a carryover with little change except for a padded three-spoke steering wheel. A five-speed gearbox was standard, three-speed automatic optional. Standard equipment included tinted glass, woodgrain dashboard, electronic tachometer, two-speed/intermittent wiper/washer, expanded-vinyl trimmed seats, passenger visor vanity mirror, and a quartz clock. Power windows, luggage rack, light alloy wheels, AM/FM radio and leather upholstery were optional.

X1/9 — FOUR — Performance matched the Targa-topped coupe's dramatic wedge styling with the 1.5-liter overhead-cam engine that had been adopted in 1979. That was the same engine used in the Strada hatchback sedan. Steel wheels were new for 1980, and restyled interiors were color-keyed, with digital clock standard. Dashboards held an 80-mph speedometer, and a remote-control driver's mirror was standard. Otherwise, little was changed. A five-speed manual gearbox was standard, as added for 1979. Standard equipment included tinted glass, electric rear defroster, two-speed wiper/washers, passenger vanity mirror, padded sports steering wheel, electronic tachometer, and remote-control driver's mirror. Light alloy wheels were optional, as were air conditioning and power windows.

I.D. DATA: Fiat's serial number is on the dashboard, visible through the windshield; and on a body rib or bulkhead. A prefix consisting of four to seven symbols is followed by a sequential serial number, which also identifies the model year. Starting serial number: (Strada) 138A2-02212790 or 138A00-01250001; (Brava) 131A4-553552 or 131A00-06620001; (Spider 2000) 124CS2-157654 or 124CS0-00171001; (X1/9) 128ASI-0012100. An identification plate is on the engine-compartment wall (front trunk of X1/9). Engine number is on a pad on the block.

Model	Body Type & Seating	Engine Type/CID	P.O.E. Price	Weight (lbs.)	Prod. Total
STRADA					
138	2-dr Hatch-4/5P	I4/91	4881	2025	Note 1
138 Custom	2-dr Hatch-4/5P	I4/91	5304	2025	Note 1
138 Custom	4-dr Hatch-4/5P	I4/91	5457	2060	Note 1
BRAVA					
131	2-dr Sedan-4/5P	I4/122	7458	2435	Note 1
131	4-dr Sedan-4/5P	I4/122	7658	2470	Note 1
SPIDER 2000					
124	2-dr Conv-2P	I4/122	8795	2290	Note 1
X1/9					
128	2-dr Targa Cpe-2P	I4/91	8190	2060	Note 1

Note 1: A total of 995,455 Fiats (all models) were produced during 1980, including 14,821 Spiders and 14,993 X1/9 coupes.

Price Note: Figures shown were for carbureted engines; Fiats with fuel-injected engines cost $195 more.

ENGINE DATA: BASE FOUR (Strada, X1/9): Inline, overhead-cam four-cylinder. Cast iron block and aluminum head. **Displacement:** 91.4 cu. in. (1498 cc). **Bore & Stroke:** 3.40 x 2.52 in. (86.4 x 63.9 mm). **Compression Ratio:** 8.5:1. **Brake Horsepower:** (Strada) 65 (SAE) at 5100 rpm; (X1/9) 66 at 5250 rpm. **Torque:** (Strada) 76 lbs.-ft. (SAE) at 2500 rpm; (X1/9) 76 lbs.-ft. at 3000 rpm. Five main bearings. Solid valve lifters. Two-barrel carburetor.

BASE FOUR (Brava, 2000): Inline, dual-overhead-cam four-cylinder. Cast iron block and aluminum head. **Displacement:** 121.7 cu. in. (1995 cc). **Bore & Stroke:** 3.31 x 3.54 in. (84 x 90 mm). **Compression Ratio:** 8.1:1 (8.6:1 in California). **Brake Horsepower:** 80 at 5000 rpm (carbureted); 102 at 5500 rpm (fuel-injected). **Torque:** 100 lbs.-ft. at 3000 rpm (carbureted); 110 lbs.-ft. at 3000 rpm (fuel-injected). Five main bearings. Solid valve lifters. Two-barrel carburetor or optional fuel injection (standard in California).

CHASSIS DATA: Wheelbase: (Strada) 96.4 in.; (Brava) 98.0 in.; (2000) 89.7 in.; (X1/9) 86.7 in. **Overall Length:** (Strada) 161.0 in.; (Brava) 172.4 in.; (2000) 163.0 in.; (X1/9) 156.2 in. **Height:** (Strada) 53.0 in.; (Brava) 54.4 in.; (2000) 48.2 in.; (X1/9) 46.5 in. **Width:** (Strada) 64.9 in.; (Brava) 65.0 in.; (2000) 63.5 in.; (X1/9) 61.8 in. **Front Tread:** (Strada) 55.1 in.; (Brava) 54.2 in.; (2000) 53.2 in.; (X1/9) 53.3 in. **Rear Tread:** (Strada) 55.5 in.; (Brava) 51.9 in.; (2000) 52.0 in.; (X1/9) 53.6 in. **Standard Tires:** (Strada) 145SR13; (Brava) 165SR7013; (2000) 165SR13; (X1/9) 165/70SR13.

TECHNICAL: Layout: (Strada) front-engine, front-drive; (Brava, 2000) front-engine, rear-drive; (X1/9) mid-engine, rear-drive. **Transmission:** five-speed manual; three-speed automatic available on Strada/Brava. **Steering:** (Strada, Brava, X1/9) rack and pinion; (2000) worm and roller. **Suspension (front):** (Strada, Brava) MacPherson struts with coil springs and anti-roll bar; (2000) upper/lower A-arms with coil springs and anti-roll bar; (X1/9) MacPherson struts with lower lateral links, compliance struts and coil springs. **Suspension (rear):** (Strada) Chapman struts with lower A-arms and transverse leaf springs; (Brava) four-link rigid axle with Panhard rod and coil springs; (2000) rigid axle with trailing arms, Panhard rod and coil springs; (X1/9) reaction struts with lower A-arms, trailing links and coil springs. **Brakes:** (Strada/Brava) front disc, rear drum; (Spider 2000, X1/9) front/rear disc. **Body Construction:** steel unibody.

MAJOR OPTIONS: Automatic transmission: Strada Custom ($395); Brava ($499); Spider 2000 ($495). Air conditioning: Strada ($555); X1/9 ($695). Sunroof: Strada Custom ($350); Brava ($400). Tinted glass ($45). Rear defroster: base Strada ($55). AM/FM radio: Strada Custom ($122). AM/FM stereo radio ($315); N/A on Strada. AM/FM stereo radio w/cassette player ($399); N/A on Strada. Roof rack: Strada ($99). Reclining bucket seats: base Strada ($45). Cloth trim: Strada Custom ($40); Brava ($55). Leather upholstery. Power windows: 2000 ($265).

PERFORMANCE: Acceleration (0-60 mph): (Strada) about 13 sec. **Fuel Mileage:** (Strada) 30 mpg average.

PRODUCTION/SALES: A total of 37,184 Fiats were sold in the U.S. during 1980, including 9,733 Spider 2000 and 7,628 X1/9 coupes.

Manufacturer: Fiat S.p.A., Turin, Italy.

Distributor: Fiat Motors of North America Inc., Montvale, New Jersey.

HISTORY: Fiat's 1980 models were introduced in the U.S. in October 1979. Strada was billed as "the lively European economy car;" the Spider 2000 as "a classic European convertible."

1981 FIAT

STRADA — FOUR — Little was new in Fiat's front-drive model, which was powered by a 1.5-liter four-cylinder engine. Adding fuel injection to that engine, however, delivered a boost of 10 horsepower more. Standard equipment included power brakes, fold-down rear seats, a sports steering wheel, visor vanity mirror, styled steel wheels, and bodyside moldings. Custom models added a rear defroster, tinted glass, clock, console, open-up rear side windows, tachometer, and wheel trim rings.

BRAVA — FOUR — A modest appearance change for Fiat's rear-drive notchback sedans included a switch from round to rectangular headlamps and a revised grille pattern. Tail-lamps and the trunk lid also got a restyle. Electronic fuel injection was now standard on the 2.0-liter four-cylinder engine, again available either with a five-speed manual gearbox or three-speed automatic.

SPIDER 2000 — FOUR — An available turbocharged engine was the big news for the Fiat sports car. Actually, the turbocharger was added in the U.S. to the standard twin-cam four-cylinder engine, the conversion becoming available during the 1981 model year. Fuel injection was now standard, rather than an extra-cost option as on the 1980 model's engine. Standard equipment included tinted glass, clock, intermittent wipers, styled steel wheels, a front air dam, and front vent wings. Interiors contained reclining bucket seats with expanded-vinyl upholstery, a tachometer, padded sports steering wheel, and passenger vanity mirror. Styling features included two hood bulges and a black eggcrate-pattern grille.

X1/9 — FOUR — Fuel injection became standard in the mid-engine sports car's engine this year, boosting output by 10 horsepower. Only a five-speed manual gearbox was available. A Targa roof with removable roof section was standard. Also standard: tinted glass, console, carpeting, electric rear defroster, remote driver's mirror, tachometer, padded sports steering wheel, LED digital clock, remote trunk and engine-compartment releases, and styled steel rally wheels.

I.D. DATA: Fiat's new 17-symbol Vehicle Identification Number is on the upper left of the dashboard, visible through the windshield. The first four symbols indicate manufacturer, make and vehicle type; symbol five indicates body type; symbol six denotes model; symbol seven is the restraint system; symbol eight identifies the engine, followed by a check digit; symbol ten indicates model year; symbol eleven identifies the assembly plant. The final six digits make up the sequential serial number. Starting serial number: (Strada) ZFAD()()0A()B()499646 or 138A00-02420236; (Brava) ZFAC()()0B()728952 or 131A00-00691654; (Spider 2000) ZFAAS()0B()B179231 or 124CS0-00164089; (X1/9) ZFABS()0A()B138650 or 128ASO-00129793.

Model	Body Type & Seating	Engine Type/CID	P.O.E. Price	Weight (lbs.)	Prod. Total
STRADA					
138	2-dr Hatch-4/5P	I4/91	5689	2025	Note 1
138 Custom	2-dr Hatch-4/5P	I4/91	6147	2025	Note 1
138 Custom	4-dr Hatch-4/5P	I4/91	6357	2060	Note 1
BRAVA					
131	2-dr Sedan-4/5P	I4/122	8190	2435	Note 1
131	4-dr Sedan-4/5P	I4/122	8390	2470	Note 1

Model	Body Type & Seating	Engine Type/CID	P.O.E. Price	Weight (lbs.)	Prod. Total
SPIDER 2000					
124	2-dr Conv-2P	I4/122	9899	2290	Note 1
124	2-dr Turbo Conv-2P	I4/122	N/A	N/A	Note 1
X1/9					
128	2-dr Targa Cpe-2P	I4/91	8997	2060	Note 1

Note 1: A total of 876,985 Fiats (all models) were produced during 1981.

ENGINE DATA: BASE FOUR (Strada, X1/9): Inline, overhead-cam four-cylinder. Cast iron block and aluminum head. **Displacement:** 91.4 cu. in. (1498 cc). **Bore & Stroke:** 3.40 x 2.52 in. (86.4 x 63.9 mm). **Compression Ratio:** 8.5:1. **Brake Horsepower:** 75 (SAE) at 5500 rpm. **Torque:** 79 lbs.-ft. (SAE) at 3000 rpm. Five main bearings. Solid valve lifters. Electronic fuel injection.

BASE FOUR (Brava, 2000): Inline, dual-overhead-cam four-cylinder. Cast iron block and aluminum head. **Displacement:** 121.7 cu. in. (1995 cc). **Bore & Stroke:** 3.31 x 3.54 in. (84 x 90 mm). **Compression Ratio:** 8.1:1. **Brake Horsepower:** 102 (SAE) at 5500 rpm. **Torque:** 110 lbs.-ft. (SAE) at 3000 rpm. Five main bearings. Solid valve lifters. Electronic fuel injection.

BASE FOUR (Spider 2000 Turbo): Same as 1995-cc four above, except with turbocharger — **Brake Horsepower:** 120 at 6000 rpm. **Torque:** 130 lbs.-ft. at 3600 rpm.

CHASSIS DATA: Wheelbase: (Strada) 96.4 in.; (Brava) 98.0 in.; (2000) 89.7 in.; (X1/9) 86.7 in. **Overall Length:** (Strada) 161.0 in.; (Brava) 172.4 in.; (2000) 163.0 in.; (X1/9) 156.2 in. **Height:** (Strada) 55.1 in.; (Brava) 54.4 in.; (2000) 48.2 in.; (X1/9) 46.5 in. **Width:** (Strada) 64.9 in.; (Brava) 65.0 in.; (2000) 63.5 in.; (X1/9) 61.8 in. **Front Tread:** (Strada) 55.1 in.; (Brava) 54.2 in.; (2000) 53.2 in.; (X1/9) 53.3 in. **Rear Tread:** (Strada) 55.5 in.; (Brava) 51.9 in.; (2000) 52.0 in.; (X1/9) 53.6 in. **Standard Tires:** (Strada) 145SR13; (Brava) 165SR13; (2000) 165SR13; (2000 Turbo) 185/60x14; (X1/9) 165/70SR13.

TECHNICAL: Layout: (Strada) front-engine, front-drive; (Brava, 2000) front-engine, rear-drive; (X1/9) mid-engine, rear-drive. **Transmission:** five-speed manual; three-speed automatic available on Strada/Brava. **Standard Final Drive Ratio:** (Strada) 3.59:1; (2000) 3.90:1 w/5-speed; (X1/9) 4.08:1. **Steering:** (Strada, Brava, X1/9) rack and pinion; (2000) worm and roller. **Suspension (front):** (Strada, Brava) MacPherson struts with coil springs and anti-roll bar; (2000) upper/lower A-arms with coil springs and anti-roll bar; (X1/9) MacPherson struts with lower lateral links, compliance struts and coil springs. **Suspension (rear):** (Strada) Chapman struts with lower A-arms and transverse leaf springs; (Brava) four-link rigid axle with Panhard rod and coil springs; (2000) rigid axle with trailing arms, Panhard rod and coil springs; (X1/9) reaction struts with lower A-arms, trailing links and coil springs. **Brakes:** (Strada) front disc, rear drum; (Brava, 2000, X1/9) front/rear disc. **Body Construction:** steel unibody. **Fuel Tank:** (Strada) 12.1 gal.; (2000) 11.4 gal.; (X1/9) 12.1 gallon.

MAJOR OPTIONS: Automatic transmission: Strada Custom ($426); Brava ($515); Spider 2000 ($520). Air conditioning: Strada ($598); X1/9 ($695). Sunroof: Strada Custom ($375). Tinted glass: base Strada ($48). Rear defroster: base Strada ($59). Rear wiper/washer: Strada Custom ($70). Reclining bucket seats: base Strada ($45). Cloth upholstery: Strada Custom ($45). Leather upholstery: 2000 ($415). Power windows: 2000, X1/9 ($278). Remote-control mirrors: Strada Custom ($160). Alloy wheels: Strada Custom ($550); 2000, X1/9 ($485). Alloy wheels w/low-profile tires: 2000 ($550). Metallic paint: Strada Custom ($160); 2000 ($232); X1/9 ($179).

PERFORMANCE: Acceleration (0-60 mph): (Strada) about 12.1 sec.; (Brava) 11.6 sec.; (2000 Spider) 9.8 sec.; (X1/9) 11.6 sec. **Fuel Mileage:** (Strada) up to 33 mpg average; (Brava) about 25 mpg average; (Spider 2000) 28 mpg average; (X1/9) 30 mpg average.

PRODUCTION/SALES: Approximately 32,185 Fiats were sold in the U.S. during 1981, including 11,574 Spider 2000 and 6,343 X1/9 coupes.

Manufacturer: Fiat S.p.A., Turin, Italy.

Distributor: Fiat Motors of North America Inc., Montvale, New Jersey.

HISTORY: Fiat's 1981 models were introduced in the U.S. in November 1980. This would be the final year of availability in the U.S. for the Brava.

1982 FIAT

1982 Fiat X1/9.

STRADA — FOUR — Little change was evident in the Strada front-drive hatchbacks, which were the only Fiat sedans available in the U.S. this year. As before, they carried the same engine as the X1/9 sports car. Standard equipment was similar to 1981.

SPIDER 2000 — FOUR — Little was new in Fiat's rear-drive convertible, again powered by a 2.0-liter twin-cam four-cylinder engine. Standard equipment was similar to 1981.

X1/9 — FOUR — Except for a price increase, little was new in Fiat's mid-engine, Targa-roofed sports coupe. Standard equipment was similar to 1981.

I.D. DATA: Fiat's 17-symbol Vehicle Identification Number is on the upper left of the dashboard, visible through the windshield. The first four symbols indicate manufacturer, make and vehicle type; symbol five indicates body type; symbol six denotes model; symbol seven is the restraint system; symbol eight identifies the engine, followed by a check digit; symbol ten indicates model year; symbol eleven identifies the assembly plant. The final six digits make up the sequential serial number.

Model	Body Type & Seating	Engine Type/CID	P.O.E. Price	Weight (lbs.)	Prod. Total
STRADA					
DD	2-dr Hatch-4/5P	I4/91	6350	2025	Note 1
DD Custom	2-dr Hatch-4/5P	I4/91	6695	2025	Note 1
DE Custom	4-dr Hatch-4/5P	I4/91	6995	2060	Note 1
SPIDER 2000					
AS	2-dr Conv-2P	I4/122	12290	2310	Note 1
	2-dr Turbo Conv-2P	I4/122	14995	N/A	Note 1
X1/9					
BS	2-dr Targa Cpe-2P	I4/91	10990	2120	Note 1

Note 1: A total of at least 927,370 Fiats (all models) were produced during 1982.

ENGINE DATA: BASE FOUR (Strada, X1/9): Inline, overhead-cam four-cylinder. Cast iron block and aluminum head. **Displacement:** 91.4 cu. in. (1498 cc). **Bore & Stroke:** 3.40 x 2.52 In. (86.4 x 63.9 mm). **Compression Ratio:** 8.5:1. **Brake Horsepower:** 75 (SAE) at 5500 rpm. **Torque:** 79 lbs.-ft. (SAE) at 3000 rpm. Five main bearings. Solid valve lifters. Electronic fuel injection.

BASE FOUR (Spider 2000): Inline, dual-overhead-cam four-cylinder. Cast iron block and aluminum head. **Displacement:** 121.7 cu. in. (1995 cc). **Bore & Stroke:** 3.31 x 3.54 in. (84 x 90 mm). **Compression Ratio:** 8.1:1. **Brake Horsepower:** 102 (SAE) at 5500 rpm. **Torque:** 110 lbs.-ft. (SAE) at 3000 rpm. Five main bearings. Solid valve lifters. Electronic fuel injection.

BASE FOUR (Spider 2000 Turbo): Same as 1995-cc four above, except with turbocharger — **Brake Horsepower:** 120 at 6000 rpm. **Torque:** 130 lbs. ft. at 3600 rpm.

CHASSIS DATA: Wheelbase: (Strada) 96.4 in.; (2000) 89.7 in.; (X1/9) 86.7 in. **Overall Length:** (Strada) 161.0 in.; (2000) 163.0 in.; (X1/9) 156.2 in. **Height:** (Strada) 55.1 in.; (2000) 48.2 in.; (X1/9) 46.4 in. **Width:** (Strada) 64.9 in.; (2000) 63.5 in.; (X1/9) 61.8 in. **Front Tread:** (Strada) 55.1 in.; (2000) 53.2 in.; (X1/9) 53.3 in. **Rear Tread:** (Strada) 55.5 in.; (2000) 52.0 in.; (X1/9) 53.6 in.

TECHNICAL: Layout: (Strada) front-engine, front-drive; (Spider 2000) front-engine, rear-drive; (X1/9) mid-engine, rear-drive. **Transmission:** five-speed manual; three-speed automatic available on Strada and Spider. **Standard Final Drive Ratio:** (Strada) 3.59:1; (Spider 2000) 3.90:1 w/5-speed, 3.58:1 w/automatic; (X1/9) 4.08:1. **Steering:** (Strada, X1/9) rack and pinion; (2000) worm and roller. **Suspension (front):** (Strada) MacPherson struts with coil springs and anti-roll bar; (2000) upper/lower A-arms with coil springs and anti-roll bar; (X1/9) MacPherson struts with lower lateral links, compliance struts and coil springs. **Suspension (rear):** (Strada) Chapman struts with lower A-arms and transverse leaf springs; (2000) rigid axle with trailing arms, Panhard rod and coil springs; (X1/9) Chapman struts with lower A-arms, trailing links and coil springs. **Brakes:** (Strada) front disc, rear drum; (2000, X1/9) front/rear disc. **Body Construction:** steel unibody. **Fuel Tank:** (Strada) 12.1 gal.; (Spider 2000) 11.4 gal.; (X1/9) 12.2 gal.

MAJOR OPTIONS: Automatic transmission: Strada Custom ($426); Spider 2000 ($520). Air conditioning: X1/9 ($695). Leather upholstery: Spider 2000 ($415). Power windows: 2000, X1/9 ($278). Metallic paint: 2000 ($232); X1/9 ($179).

Note: Other Strada options were similar to 1981.

PRODUCTION/SALES: At least 14,113 Fiats were sold in the U.S. during 1982, including 4,824 Spider 2000 and 2,359 X1/9 coupes.

Manufacturer: Fiat S.p.A., Turin, Italy.

Distributor: Fiat Motors of North America Inc., Montvale, New Jersey.

HISTORY: Fiat's 1982 models were introduced in the U.S. in October 1981. This would be the final year of availability for the Strada, as Fiat focused solely on the sports cars for the U.S. market. The Strada had not been selling well anyway. Stradas in Europe could be obtained with a diesel engine, but that did not enter the American market.

1983 FIAT

SPIDER 2000 — FOUR — With the front-drive Strada economy hatchback sedans out of the lineup, Fiat made a last-ditch stab at the American market with its sports car. The long-lived Spider, descended from the 124 Sport Spider of the 1960s, continued with little change. Both naturally-aspirated and turbocharged versions of the 2.0-liter twin-cam four-cylinder engine were available.

X1/9 — FOUR — Fiat's mid-engine, Targa-topped sport coupe continued with little change.

I.D. DATA: Similar to 1982.

Model	Body Type & Seating	Engine Type/CID	P.O.E. Price	Weight (lbs.)	Prod. Total
SPIDER 2000					
AS	2-dr Conv-2P	I4/122	12290	2310	Note 1
	2-dr Turbo Conv-2P	I4/122	14995	N/A	Note 1
X1/9					
BS	2-dr Targa Cpe-2P	I4/91	10990	2120	Note 1

Note 1: A total of 979,390 Fiats (all models) were produced during 1983, plus 2,317 Bertone X1/9 coupes.

ENGINE DATA: BASE FOUR (X1/9): Inline, overhead-cam four-cylinder. Cast iron block and aluminum head. **Displacement:** 91.4 cu. in. (1498 cc). **Bore & Stroke:** 3.40 x 2.52 in. (86.4 x 63.9 mm). **Compression Ratio:** 8.5:1. **Brake Horsepower:** 75 (SAE) at 5500 rpm. **Torque:** 79 lbs.-ft. (SAE) at 3000 rpm. Five main bearings. Solid valve lifters. Electronic fuel injection.

BASE FOUR (Spider 2000): Inline, dual-overhead-cam four-cylinder. Cast iron block and aluminum head. **Displacement:** 121.7 cu. in. (1995 cc). **Bore & Stroke:** 3.31 x 3.54 in. (84 x 90 mm). **Compression Ratio:** 8.1:1. **Brake Horsepower:** 102 (SAE) at 5500 rpm. **Torque:** 110 lbs.-ft. (SAE) at 3000 rpm. Five main bearings. Solid valve lifters. Electronic fuel injection.

BASE FOUR (Spider 2000 Turbo): Same as 1995-cc four above, except with turbocharger — **Brake Horsepower:** 120 at 6000 rpm. **Torque:** 130 lbs.-ft. at 3600 rpm.

CHASSIS DATA: Wheelbase: (2000) 89.7 in.; (X1/9) 86.7 in. **Overall Length:** (2000) 163.0 in.; (X1/9) 156.2 in. **Height:** (2000) 48.2 in.; (X1/9) 46.5 in. **Width:** (2000) 63.5 in.; (X1/9) 61.8 in. **Front Tread:** (2000) 53.2 in.; (X1/9) 53.3 in. **Rear Tread:** (2000) 52.0 in.; (X1/9) 53.6 in.

TECHNICAL: Layout: (Spider 2000) front-engine, rear-drive; (X1/9) mid-engine, rear-drive. **Transmission:** five-speed manual; three-speed automatic available on Spider 2000. **Steering:** (X1/9) rack and pinion; (2000) worm and roller. **Suspension (front):** (2000) upper/lower A-arms with coil springs and anti-roll bar; (X1/9) MacPherson struts with lower lateral links, compliance struts and coil springs. **Suspension (rear):** (2000) rigid axle with trailing arms, Panhard rod and coil springs; (X1/9) Chapman struts with lower A-arms, trailing links and coil springs. **Brakes:** front/rear disc. **Body Construction:** steel unibody.

MAJOR OPTIONS: Similar to 1982.

PERFORMANCE: Acceleration (0-60 mph): (Spider 2000) 9.8 sec. **Fuel Mileage:** (Spider 2000) about 28 mpg average.

PRODUCTION/SALES: Approximately 6,184 Fiats were sold in the U.S. during 1983.

Manufacturer: Fiat S.p.A., Turin, Italy.

Distributor: Fiat Motors of North America Inc., Montvale, New Jersey.

HISTORY: Rather than fade away completely after 1983, production and sale of Spiders continued under the Pininfarina nameplate, while the X1/9 Targa coupe remained available under the Bertone name. See Pininfarina and Bertone listings (below) for details.

1984-85 PININFARINA

AZZURRA — FOUR — Following abandonment of production by Fiat in 1983, the Spider 2000 two-seat convertible enjoyed a short afterlife under the Pininfarina nameplate. Pininfarina had been building the car's bodies anyway, and now turned to full production. Power came from the same 1995-cc four-cylinder engine, rated 102 horsepower (SAE) at 5500 rpm, with 110 pound-feet of torque at 3000 rpm. A GM three-speed automatic transmission could be Installed on models destined for the U.S., which were marketed by the Malcolm Bricklin organization for $17,490 ($495 more than the five-speed manual). Dimensions and other technical data were similar to the former Spider 2000, and this final version was capable of 104 mph. Standard equipment included radio and air conditioning.

Europeans also had a crack at some final two-seaters, marketed as the Spidereuropa with a more potent version of the 1995-cc four. They could even get a "Volumex" variant with a Roots-type supercharger, producing 135 bhp (DIN).

I.D. DATA: Pininfarina's 17-symbol Vehicle Identification Number is on the upper left of the instrument panel, visible through the windshield. Prefix 'ZFRASOOB8' is followed by a number denoting model year ('D' = 1983; 'E' = 1984; 'F' = 1985); number '5' to indicate the Turin assembly plant; and a final six-digit sequential production number.

Model	Body Type & Seating	Engine Type/CID	P.O.E. Price	Weight (lbs.)	Prod. Total
AZZURRA					
	2-dr Conv-2P	I4/122	16995	2360	N/A

Price Note: Azzurra with automatic transmission sold for $17,490.

ENGINE DATA: BASE FOUR: Inline, dual-overhead-cam four-cylinder. Cast iron block and aluminum head. **Displacement:** 121.7 cu. in. (1995 cc). **Bore & Stroke:** 3.31 x 3.54 in. (84 x 90 mm). **Compression Ratio:** 8.1:1. **Brake Horsepower:** 102 (SAE) at 5500 rpm. **Torque:** 110 lbs.-ft. (SAE) at 3000 rpm. Five main bearings. Solid valve lifters. Electronic fuel injection.

CHASSIS DATA: Wheelbase: 89.7 in. **Overall Length:** 163.0 in. **Height:** 48.2 in. **Width:** 63.5 in. **Front Tread:** 53.2 in. **Rear Tread:** 52.0 in.

TECHNICAL: Layout: front-engine, rear-drive. **Transmission:** five-speed manual or three-speed automatic. **Steering:** worm and roller. **Suspension (front):** upper/lower A-arms with coil springs and anti-roll bar. **Suspension (rear):** rigid axle with trailing arms, transverse linkage bar and coil springs. **Brakes:** front/rear disc. **Body Construction:** steel unibody. **Fuel Tank:** 11.4 gallon.

Manufacturer: Pininfarina S.p.A., Turin, Italy.

Distributor: Malcolm Bricklin.

1984-90 BERTONE

X1/9 — FOUR — After 1983, Fiats no longer were imported into the U.S. However, the mid-engined, Targa-topped X1/9 coupe remained available through the 1980s under the Bertone nameplate. Bertone literature referred to the Targa-roofed X1/9 as a "sports car convertible." Standard equipment included an AM/FM stereo radio with cassette player, air conditioning, power windows, tinted glass, electric rear-window defroster, digital clock with stopwatch, and dual luggage compartments. Available body colors included Silver and Red, with red or black interior. Color combinations also included White/Red, White/Black, and Yellow/Black. Malcolm Bricklin took over importation of the Bertone editions.

I.D. DATA: Bertone's 17-symbol Vehicle Identification Number is on the upper instrument panel, visible through the windshield. Symbol one ('Z') indicates Italy. Symbols two and three ('BB') denote the manufacturer, Bertone. Symbol four ('B') indicates model; five ('S') the body type. Symbol 10 identifies the model year ('E' = 1984; 'F' = 1985; 'G' = 1986; 'H' = 1987; 'J' = 1988; 'K' = 1989). Symbol 11 ('7') indicates the assembly plant at Turin, Italy. The final six digits form the sequential production number.

Model	Body Type & Seating	Engine Type/CID	P.O.E. Price	Weight (lbs.)	Prod. Total
X1/9					
	2-dr Targa Cpe-2P	I4/91	13990	2130	Note 1

Note 1: A total of 1,482 Bertone X1/9s were sold in the U.S. during 1986, followed by 845 in 1987, and 325 in 1988.

Price Note: Figure shown was valid in 1984.

ENGINE DATA: BASE FOUR: Inline, overhead-cam four-cylinder. Cast iron block and aluminum head. **Displacement:** 91.4 cu. in. (1498 cc). **Bore & Stroke:** 3.40 x 2.52 in. (86.4 x 63.9 mm). **Compression Ratio:** 8.5:1. **Brake Horsepower:** 75 (SAE) at 5500 rpm. **Torque:** 79.6 lbs.-ft. (SAE) at 3000 rpm. Five main bearings. Solid valve lifters. Electronic fuel injection.

CHASSIS DATA: Wheelbase: 86.7 in. **Overall Length:** 156.3 in. **Height:** 46.4-46.8 in. **Width:** 61.8 in. **Front Tread:** 53.3 in. **Rear Tread:** 53.6 in. **Standard Tires:** 165/70SR13 Pirelli P3.

TECHNICAL: Layout: mid-engine, rear-drive. **Transmission:** five-speed manual (all synchro). **Gear ratios:** (1st) 4.09:1; (2nd) 2.235:1; (3rd) 1.46:1; (4th) 1.033:1; (5th) 0.863:1; (rev) 3.714:1. **Standard Final Drive Ratio:** 4.077:1. **Steering:** rack and pinion. **Suspension (front):** MacPherson struts with coil springs. **Suspension (rear):** MacPherson struts with coil springs, lower wishbones and transverse control bars. **Brakes:** front/rear disc. **Body Construction:** steel unibody. **Fuel Tank:** 12.2 gallon.

PERFORMANCE: Acceleration (0-60 mph): 12.4 sec. (claimed). **Fuel Mileage:** (EPA estimated) 26 mpg city, 37 mpg highway, 30 mpg combined.

Manufacturer: Bertone S.p.A., Turin, Italy.

Distributor: International Automobile Importers Inc., Montvale, New Jersey; (later) Overseas Motors, Livonia, Michigan; and RVD International Distributors, Ramsey, New Jersey.

POSTSCRIPT: As the 1990s began, Fiat remained a major presence in the world vehicle market, but no further Fiats were expected to become available for sale in the U.S. On the other hand, rumors emerged periodically about potential merger between Fiat and a major American automaker.

FORD (British)

Even before the start of World War One, Ford began to set up manufacturing plants outside the U.S., notably in Europe. By 1911, production of the familiar Model A Ford was underway at the Trafford Park facility in Manchester, England. That led to the Model A in 1928, just as it did in America; though the British also issued a variant with a smaller four-cylinder engine, known as the AF. As the V-8 Ford emerged in 1932, production was transferred to another plant, at Dagenham, Essex. There it would remain for the entire period during which British Ford products were exported to the U.S. Both V-8s and four-cylinder Fords were built during the 1930s, concluding before World War Two with the updated Eight and Ten. Both wore new bodies, but were mechanically similar to the former models. Each carried an L-head four-cylinder engine, but the Eight's displaced 939 cc and the Ten measured 1172 cc. Wheelbases of the two models were 90 and 94 inches, respectively.

Production resumed immediately after the war with evolutionary versions of the Eight and Ten, now called Anglia (two-door) and Prefect (four-door). For the home market, the Anglia continued with the smaller (933 cc) engine; but as the pair began to appear on the U.S. market, they both came equipped with the larger (1172 cc) version, producing 30 horsepower. Though never huge sellers in the U.S., the little Fords, which looked rather like miniature versions of prewar American sedans, attracted a certain enthusiastic following, based upon their practical (and economical) virtues as well as the novelty of owning something different. A V-8 Ford reentered production in the early postwar years, but didn't last long, due largely to the fact that the late 1940s were years of austerity in Britain, and a V-8 just didn't fit in.

The postwar look began to fade away by 1951 with the emergence of two modern-styled British Fords: the four-cylinder Consul and six-cylinder Zephyr. Those were joined by a higher-powered Zodiac in 1954. Not only four-door sedans, but two-door drophead coupes were built in each series. The Anglia and Prefect names continued into the mid-1950s, but in sharply different form, similar to that of the larger models. These were the 100E sedans, again powered by L-head engines. Not until the 1960 model year would overhead-valve powerplants enter Anglia and Prefect bonnets, when the nomenclature changed to 105E. The Anglia took on a different look at that time, including a somewhat strange reverse-angled back window, while the Prefect remained in its earlier form. In addition to the sedans, Ford produced a pair of station wagons (Estates)

244

through the late 1950s, based upon the Anglia/Prefect 100E, known as the Escort and Squire. For the home market, Ford continued to produce the prewar-styled Popular through the 1950s.

Another new name appeared by 1963 with the debut of the Cortina. In addition to conventional mid-size (for Britain) models, high-performance Cortinas became available, carrying a twin-cam version of the 1500-cc engine, modified by Lotus. Those Lotus variants came only in two-door form, while other Cortinas came as four-doors and station wagons. Cortina engines grew in size by the 1968 model year, a year after their bodies had adopted a revised form to become the "Model C." By 1970, however, official exports to the U.S. were about to cease. Fords continued to be produced in Britain, of course, but mainly for the family market and seldom sent across the Atlantic.

Note: Some models and updated versions debuted earlier in England than in the U.S.

1945-48 FORD (British)

1946-'47 Ford Anglia two-door.

ANGLIA — E03A — FOUR — Production of a postwar version of the former Eight began soon after World War Two, with a name change to Anglia. Upright and stubby in appearance, the two-door Anglia rode a 90-inch wheelbase and had a distinct prewar look with separate headlamps and a center-hinged hood. Pressed steel, perforated disc wheels held 4.50x17 tires. By 1948, a new 'Anglia' badge was added at the top of the grille. And during that model year, turn signals began to be installed. Anglias sold in Britain carried a 933-cc (57-cid) four-cylinder L-head engine, producing 23 horsepower; but those that came to America generally had the larger 1172-cc version (known as Anglia Ten in Britain), identical to that installed in the four-door Prefect. That one delivered 30 bhp at 4000 rpm.

The early postwar Anglia had worm-and-nut steering, a 16-inch diameter steering wheel with three spokes, and typical Ford transverse leaf springs (nine leaves in the front suspension, and ten at the rear) with double-action hydraulic shock absorbers. A double-drop chassis frame contained three crossmembers. The three-quarter floating rear axle (with 5.5:1 final drive ratio) used a radius rod and torque tube arrangement. The three-speed synchromesh transmission had a floor-mounted gearshift lever, and worked through a single-plate clutch. Brakes were mechanical (not hydraulic), using new 10-inch drums. Moisture-proof, enamelled headlamps were installed. Inside, a single instrument cluster on the dashboard was indirectly lighted and contained a large-diameter speedometer and "zero" ammeter, and a combined ignition and light switch. A full-width parcel shelf went under the belt rail. Front bucket seats were upholstered in leathercloth, and the adjustable driver's seat had a five-inch travel. A pedestal-type rear-view mirror was used. A tool compartment in the trunk contained a tool kit. Standard equipment included dual wipers, full-width front and rear bumpers, combined tail and stop lights, a sunvisor, and a vacuum tank fitted to dashboard (for improved wiper operation).

1946-'47 Ford Prefect four-door.

PREFECT — E93A — FOUR — Both appearance and mechanical details of the four-door Prefect were similar to the Anglia, except that its early grille was made up of horizontal bars, initially with painted radiator slats (later chromed). Export models contained a trunk. 'Ford' lettering was evident on early hubcaps, but plain ones were used by 1948. Smith-type mechanical jacks were added for the 1948 model year. Prefects had under-dash compartments and a rear-window shelf. Space was considered ample for four adults, in "armchair comfort." The sales brochure emphasized the amount of headroom, even in the back seat. Pressed steel wheels with steel hubcaps held 5.00x16 tires. Like the Anglia, the Prefect had mechanical brakes. A center handle on the dashboard opened the one-piece windshield. Starter and choke controls were at the center of the instrument panel, which included a clock. Flush-type (semaphore) turn signals were operated by a self-canceling switch on the steering wheel. A rear-window blind could be operated from the driver's seat. Prefects had running boards, full-width curved-section bumpers, combined tail and stop lights, a vacuum tank behind the grille, sunvisor, interior light, four ashtrays, and a spare wheel in a separate compartment (below the luggage compartment). Leather upholstery was optional at extra cost.

I.D. DATA: Serial number is stamped on left side of cylinder block, near oil filler tube; and on top flange on left-hand chassis side member; and on identification plate with engine number. Motor number plate is under the hood (Anglia) or on tool box lid (Prefect). Starting serial (chassis) number for 1945 models: (Anglia) Y291428. Prefect serial number range: C-323885 to C-386046.

Model	Body Type & Seating	Engine Type/CID	P.O.E. Price	Weight (lbs.)	Prod. Total
ANGLIA					
E-03AF/A	2- dr Sedan-4P	I4/72	1398	1700	Note 1
PREFECT					
E-93AF/A	4-dr Sedan-4P	I4/72	1568	1840	Note 1

Note 1: About 3,223 British Fords were sold in the U.S. in 1948.

Price Note: Price shown is for Prefect with cloth upholstery; price was $1620 with leather upholstery.

ENGINE DATA: BASE FOUR (Anglia, Prefect): Inline, L-head four-cylinder. Cast iron block and head. **Displacement:** 71.55 cu. in. (1172 cc). **Bore & Stroke:** 2.50 x 3.64 in. (63.5 x 92.5 mm). **Compression Ratio:** 6.16:1. **Brake Horsepower:** 30.1 at 4000 rpm. Three main bearings. Solid valve lifters. One Ford/Zenith carburetor. Ford ignition.

Note: Anglias sold in the home market had a smaller (933-cc) engine, rated 23 bhp, with 6.3:1 compression.

CHASSIS DATA: Wheelbase: (Anglia) 90 in.; (Prefect) 94 in. **Overall Length:** (Anglia) 152.25 in.; (Prefect) 156 in. **Height:** 63.5 in. **Width:** 57 in. **Tread:** 45.0 in. **Wheel Type:** pressed steel disc. **Standard Tires:** (Anglia) 4.50x17; (Prefect) 5.00x16.

TECHNICAL: Layout: front-engine, rear-drive. **Transmission:** three-speed manual. **Standard Final Drive Ratio:** 5.5:1. **Steering:** worm and nut. **Suspension (front):** I-beam axle with transverse leaf spring. **Suspension (rear):** rigid axle with transverse leaf spring. **Brakes:** mechanical, front/rear drum. **Body Construction:** welded steel body on open channel frame.

MAJOR OPTIONS: Leather upholstery (Prefect).

PERFORMANCE: Top Speed: 61-62 mph. **Acceleration (0-60 mph):** N/A (0-50 mph in about 27 sec.). **Acceleration (quarter-mile):** (Prefect) under 26 sec.

Manufacturer: Ford Motor Co. Ltd., Dagenham, Essex, England.

Distributor: Ford Motor Co., Dearborn, Michigan.

HISTORY: Introduction of the 1948 models in the U.S. took place in May 1948, several months after their appearance in Britain and elsewhere. Upon its debut just after the war, Ford called the Anglia "Britain's most famous car of its class." The Prefect was billed as the "Tried and tested 10 HP car—the finest value in its class on the road," with all the "feel" of a big horsepower car.

1949 FORD (British)

ANGLIA — FOUR — In addition to appearance modifications, the two-door Ford enjoyed a sharp price cut on the U.S. market. The divided grille was made up of vertical bar, with 'Anglia' script on the side of the hood. Standard equipment included a full-width parcel shelf, leathercloth upholstery, flush-type turn signals, sunvisors, a wiper vacuum tank, combined tail and stop lights, dual windshield wipers, and full-width, curved-section bumpers at front and rear. Passenger space was promoted as "ample" for four people. Steering took just 1-3/4 turns lock to lock, for easy parking. Front bucket seats were "curved for armchair driving comfort."

PREFECT — E493A — FOUR — Prefect four-door sedans also were cheaper in the U.S. for the 1949 model year. Mechanical details were identical to the '48 model. Displaying the same upright profile with flat one-piece windshield and six-window styling, its old-fashioned grille was made up of horizontal bars but an alligator-style hood was used. Built-in headlamps were installed. Prefects were upholstered in either English cloth or leather. Standard equipment included sealed-beam headlamps, full-width curved-section bumpers, a vacuum tank, sunvisors, four ashtrays, flush-type turn signals with a self-cancelling switch on the steering wheel, a rear-window blind operated from the driver's seat, tool kit, pedestal-style rear-view mirror, and dual windshield wipers. Only one door contained a lock. Control knobs were newly-designed. A full-width parcel shelf under the dashboard was cloth-covered, and trimmed with a bakelite molding on the front edge.

I.D. DATA: Serial number is stamped on left side of cylinder block, near oil filler tube; and on top flange on left-hand chassis side member; and on identification plate with engine number. Motor number plate is under the hood (Anglia) or on tool box lid (Prefect). Motor number range: (Anglia) C-386046 to C-412124; (Prefect) C-391372 to C-412351.

Model	Body Type & Seating	Engine Type/CID	P.O.E. Price	Weight (lbs.)	Prod. Total
ANGLIA					
E4930AF/A	2-dr Sedan-4P	I4/72	1004	1700	Note 1
PREFECT					
E493AF/A	4-dr Sedan-4P	I4/72	1122	1800	Note 1

Note 1: Approximately 5,087 British Fords were sold in the U.S. during 1949.

Price Note: Price shown is for Prefect with cloth upholstery; price was $37-$40 higher with leather upholstery. Some U.S. sources quoted prices as low as $947 for the Anglia and $1040 for the Prefect.

ENGINE DATA: BASE FOUR (Anglia, Prefect): Inline, L-head four-cylinder. Cast iron block and head. **Displacement:** 71.55 cu. in. (1172 cc). **Bore & Stroke:** 2.50 x 3.64 in. (63.5 x 92.5 mm). **Compression Ratio:** 6.16:1. **Brake Horsepower:** 30.1 at 4000 rpm. Three main bearings. Solid valve lifters. One Ford/Zenith carburetor. Ford ignition.

Note: Anglias sold in the home market still had a smaller (933-cc) engine, rated 23 bhp, with 6.3:1 compression.

CHASSIS DATA: Wheelbase: (Anglia) 90 in.; (Prefect) 94 in. **Overall Length:** (Anglia) 152.25 in.; (Prefect) 156 in. **Height:** (Anglia) 63 in.; (Prefect) 63.5 in. **Width:** 57 in. **Front Tread:** 45 in. **Rear Tread:** 45 in. **Wheel Type:** pressed steel disc. **Standard Tires:** (Anglia) 4.50x17; (Prefect) 5.00x16.

TECHNICAL: Layout: front-engine, rear-drive. **Transmission:** three-speed manual. Gear ratios: (1st) 3.07:1; (2nd) 1.76:1; (3rd) 1.00:1; (rev) 4.02:1. **Standard Final Drive Ratio:** 5.5:1. **Steering:** worm and nut. **Suspension (front):** I-beam axle with transverse leaf spring (nine leaves). **Suspension (rear):** rigid axle with transverse leaf spring (ten leaves). **Brakes:** mechanical, front/rear drum. **Body Construction:** welded steel body on open channel steel frame. **Fuel Tank:** 8.4 gallons (U.S.).

MAJOR OPTIONS: Leather upholstery.

PERFORMANCE: Top Speed: 61-62 mph. **Acceleration (0-60 mph):** N/A (Prefect, 0-50 mph in under 23 sec.). **Acceleration (quarter-mile):** (Prefect) about 25.4 sec.

Manufacturer: Ford Motor Co. Ltd., Dagenham, Essex, England.

Distributor: Ford Motor Co., Dearborn, Michigan.

HISTORY: Introduction to the U.S. began in December, 1948. "All over America," said Ford's sales brochure, "people have asked for a smaller car with big car reliability and smartness. The Anglia is that car. It's smart — it's fast — it's safe — it's reliable and it saves you money because it uses so much less gasoline and oil....Besides, all maintenance, spare parts and repairs are provided at low prices by selected Ford dealers."

Ford promoted the new Prefect's "smart looks, restrained lines, excellent finish in attractive colors;" plus its "lowest-ever running costs," promising "50 percent more miles per gallon than bigger cars, and smaller costs for maintenance, spares and repairs." It was called "a leader in the smaller car fashion." A Pilot sedan sold in Britain carried a 221-cid V-8 engine, producing 85 horsepower.

1950 FORD (British)

1950 Ford Popular. (William Siuru Jr.)

ANGLIA — FOUR — No significant change was evident in Ford's two-door sedan. Later in the model year, two-tone interior trim became available. Power again came from a 30-bhp L-head four-cylinder engine, except in the home market, where a 23-bhp Anglia remained on sale. Standard equipment included front and rear bumpers, combined tail and stop lamps, twin sunvisors, an adjustable driver's seat, and leathercloth upholstery on bucket-type front seats.

PREFECT — E493A — FOUR — Ford's four-door sedan also had no notable change in either appearance or mechanical details, apart from the later availability of two-tone interior trims. Standard equipment included flush-fitting sealed-beam headlamps, full-width bumpers with overrides, sunvisors, four ashtrays, interior light, and cloth upholstery. Leather upholstery continued as an option.

I.D. DATA: Serial number is stamped on left side of cylinder block, near oil filler tube; and on top flange on left-hand chassis side member; and on identification plate with engine number. Motor number plate is under the hood (Anglia) or on tool box lid (Prefect). Serial/motor number range: (Anglia) C-412125 to C-535703; (Prefect) C-412352 to C-535703.

Model	Body Type & Seating	Engine Type/CID	P.O.E. Price	Weight (lbs.)	Prod. Total
ANGLIA					
	2-dr Sedan-4P	I4/72	1004	1700	Note 1
PREFECT					
E493A	4-dr Sedan-4P	I4/72	1122	1840	Note 1

Note 1: Approximately 1,859 British Fords were sold in the U.S. in 1950.

Price Note: Price shown is for Prefect with cloth upholstery; price was $40 higher with leather upholstery.

ENGINE DATA: BASE FOUR (Anglia, Prefect): Inline, L-head four-cylinder. Cast iron block and head. **Displacement:** 71.55 cu. in. (1172 cc). **Bore & Stroke:** 2.50 x 3.64 in. (63.5 x 92.5 mm). **Compression Ratio:** 6.16:1. **Brake Horsepower:** 30.1 at 4000 rpm. Three main bearings. Solid valve lifters. One Ford/Zenith carburetor. Ford ignition.

245

Note: Anglias sold in the home market still had a smaller (933-cc) engine, rated 23 bhp, with 6.3:1 compression.

CHASSIS DATA: Wheelbase: (Anglia) 90 in.; (Prefect) 94 in. **Overall Length:** (Anglia) 153.5 in.; (Prefect) 156 in. **Height:** (Anglia) 64.3 in.; (Prefect) 63.5 in. **Width:** (Anglia) 56.5 in.; (Prefect) 56.25 in. **Front Tread:** 45 in. **Rear Tread:** 45 in. **Wheel Type:** pressed steel disc. **Standard Tires:** 5.00x16.

TECHNICAL: Layout: front-engine, rear-drive. **Transmission:** three-speed manual. **Standard Final Drive Ratio:** 5.5:1. **Steering:** worm and nut. **Suspension (front):** I-beam axle with transverse leaf spring (nine leaves). **Suspension (rear):** rigid axle with transverse leaf spring (ten leaves). **Brakes:** mechanical, front/rear drum. **Body Construction:** welded steel body on open channel steel frame. **Fuel Tank:** 8.4 gallons (U.S.).

MAJOR OPTIONS: Leather upholstery.

PERFORMANCE: Top Speed: 61-62 mph. **Acceleration (0-60 mph):** N/A (Prefect, 0-50 mph in under 23 sec.). **Acceleration (quarter-mile):** (Prefect) about 25.4 sec.

Manufacturer: Ford Motor Co. Ltd., Dagenham, Essex, England.

Distributor: Ford Motor Co., Dearborn, Michigan.

HISTORY: Introduced to U.S. market in January, 1950. Promotional material for sale in the U.S. made a simple promise: "The Anglia is a pleasure to drive, a pleasure to ride in, a pleasure to own."

1951 FORD
(British)

ANGLIA — FOUR — Production of the small Ford two-door sedan continued with no significant change. See previous listings for details.

PREFECT — E493A — FOUR — Ford's original four-door model also continued with no notable change.

CONSUL — FOUR — Joining the Anglia and Prefect this year was a new, more modern four-door sedan with squarish profile but rounded corners. Styling features included a one-piece curved windshield, rectangular grille made up of narrow vertical bars, and small round parking lights directly below the built-in round headlamps. A bodyside crease ran almost the full length of the car, and curved down ahead of the front wheel opening. Two chrome strips ran down the crown of the front fenders. The four-window design included front vent wings. Wheelbase was 100 inches, and the Consul rode 13-inch tires. Beneath its hood was a new overhead-valve engine, displacing 92 cubic inches (1508 cc) and producing 47 horsepower at 4400 rpm. Inside was Vinylite plastic seat upholstery. A column-mounted gearshift lever operated the three-speed manual transmission. The Consul suspension consisted of coil springs in front and semi-elliptic leaf springs at the rear.

I.D. DATA: Serial number is stamped on left side of cylinder block, near oil filler tube; and on top flange on left-hand chassis side member; and on identification plate with engine number. Motor number plate is under the hood (Anglia), on tool box lid (Prefect), or on right side engine mounting (Consul). Serial/motor number range: (Anglia) C-535704 to C-612990; (Prefect) C-535704 to C-612990; (Consul) EOTA-0001 to EOTA-20414.

Model	Body Type & Seating	Engine Type/CID	P.O.E. Price	Weight (lbs.)	Prod. Total
ANGLIA					
	2-dr Sedan-4P	I4/72	1184	1700	Note 1
PREFECT					
E493A	4-dr Sedan-4P	I4/72	1384	1840	Note 1
CONSUL					
Mk I	4-dr Sedan-4/5P	I4/92	1698	2435	Note 1

Note 1: Approximately 3,508 British Fords were sold in the U.S. during 1951.

ENGINE DATA: BASE FOUR (Anglia, Prefect): Inline, L-head four-cylinder. Cast iron block and head. **Displacement:** 71.55 cu. in. (1172 cc). **Bore & Stroke:** 2.50 x 3.64 in. (63.5 x 92.5 mm). **Compression Ratio:** 6.16:1. **Brake Horsepower:** 30.1 at 4000 rpm. Three main bearings. Solid valve lifters. One Ford/Zenith carburetor. Ford ignition.
BASE FOUR (Consul): Inline, overhead-valve four-cylinder. Cast iron block and head. **Displacement:** 92 cu. in. (1508 cc). **Bore & Stroke:** 3.125 x 3.00 in. (79.4 x 76.2 mm). **Compression Ratio:** 6.8:1. **Brake Horsepower:** 47 at 4400 rpm. Three main bearings. Solid valve lifters. One Zenith carburetor. Lucas ignition.

CHASSIS DATA: Wheelbase: (Anglia) 90 in.; (Prefect) 94 in.; (Consul) 100 in. **Overall Length:** (Anglia) 153.5 in.; (Prefect) 156 in.; (Consul) 164.75 in. **Height:** (Anglia) 64.2 in.; (Prefect) 63.5 in.; (Consul) 60.8 in. **Width:** (Anglia) 56.5 in.; (Prefect) 56.3 in.; (Consul) 64.0 in. **Front Tread:** (Anglia/Prefect) 45 in.; (Consul) 50 in. **Rear Tread:** (Anglia/Prefect) 45 in.; (Consul) 49 in. **Wheel Type:** steel disc. **Standard Tires:** (Anglia/Prefect) 5.00x16; (Consul) 5.90x13.

TECHNICAL: Layout: front-engine, rear-drive. **Transmission:** three-speed manual; (Anglia/Prefect) floor lever; (Consul) column lever. **Standard Final Drive Ratio:** (Anglia/Prefect) 5.5:1; (Consul) 4.625:1. **Steering:** worm and nut. **Suspension (front):** (Anglia/Prefect) transverse leaf spring; (Consul) coil springs. **Suspension (rear):** (Anglia/Prefect) transverse leaf spring; (Consul) rigid axle with semi-elliptic leaf springs. **Brakes:** (Anglia/Prefect) mechanical, front/rear drum; (Consul) Girling hydraulic, front rear drum. **Body Construction:** (Anglia/Prefect) steel body on steel frame; (Consul) steel unibody.

PERFORMANCE: Top Speed: (Consul) 72-74 mph. **Acceleration (0-60 mph):** (Consul) under 26 sec. **Acceleration (quarter-mile):** (Consul) 23.9 sec. **Fuel Mileage:** (Consul) up to 37 mpg.

Manufacturer: Ford Motor Co. Ltd., Dagenham, Essex, England.

Distributor: Ford Motor Co., Dearborn, Michigan.

HISTORY: Introduction of 1951 models to the U.S. market took place in August and November, 1950. Production of the new six-cylinder Zephyr also began for the 1951 model year, but took longer to arrive on the U.S. market. *Motor Trend* called the Consul the "closest thing to a reasonably-priced sports sedan on the market today." The magazine also reported on speculation that the Consul was the car that Ford had been proposing as a smaller American automobile, and that the company would be observing public reaction as it entered the American marketplace, sold by 100 Ford and Lincoln-Mercury dealers.

1952 FORD
(British)

ANGLIA — FOUR — No significant change was evident in the two-door Anglia sedan, which continued its old-fashioned look and L-head four-cylinder engine.

PREFECT — FOUR — Ford's four-door sedan on a 94-inch wheelbase also continued with little change this year.

CONSUL — FOUR — Production of the modern four-cylinder sedan with overhead-valve four-cylinder engine, introduced for the 1951 model year, continued with little change.

ZEPHYR — SIX — The modern-styled, slab-sided Consul was joined by a six-cylinder version on a longer (104-inch) wheelbase. Although the overall profile was similar to that of the Consul, the front end had a considerably different look. The grille was made up of horizontal bars, bulged upward at the center. A bodyside crease ran full length, meeting the top of the grille at the front. Tiny round parking lights sat alongside the grille, below each headlamp. The overhead-valve six-cylinder engine displaced 138 cubic inches (2262 cc) and produced 68 horsepower. Its bore and stroke were identical to the four-cylinder Consul engine. Coil springs were used for the front suspension, with semi-elliptic leaf springs at the rear.

I.D. DATA: Serial number is stamped on left side of cylinder block, near oil filler tube; on top flange on left-hand chassis side member; and on identification plate with engine number. Motor number plate is under the hood (Anglia), on tool box lid (Prefect), or on right-side engine mounting (Consul/Zephyr). Starting serial/motor number: (Anglia/Prefect) C-612991; (Consul) EOTA-20415; (Zephyr) EOTTA-0346.

Model	Body Type & Seating	Engine Type/CID	P.O.E. Price	Weight (lbs.)	Prod. Total
ANGLIA					
	2-dr Sedan-4P	I4/72	1184	1700	Note 1
PREFECT					
E493A	4-dr Sedan-4P	I4/72	1384	1800	Note 1
CONSUL					
Mk I	4-dr Sedan-4/5P	I4/92	1698	2435	Note 1
ZEPHYR					
Mk I	4-dr Sedan-5P	I6/138	1889	2591	Note 1

Note 1: Approximately 3,854 British Fords were sold in the U.S. during 1952.

Price/Weight Note: Some sources quoted higher prices at this time for the Anglia ($1250) and Prefect ($1427). Announced weights also varied, down to 1632 pounds for the Anglia, 2277 for the Consul, and 2464 for the Zephyr.

ENGINE DATA: BASE FOUR (Anglia, Prefect): Inline, L-head four-cylinder. Cast iron block and head. **Displacement:** 71.55 cu. in. (1172 cc). **Bore & Stroke:** 2.50 x 3.64 in. (63.5 x 92.5 mm). **Compression Ratio:** 6.16:1. **Brake Horsepower:** 30.1 at 4000 rpm. Three main bearings. Solid valve lifters. One Ford/Zenith carburetor. Ford ignition.
BASE FOUR (Consul): Inline, overhead-valve four-cylinder. Cast iron block and head. **Displacement:** 92 cu. in. (1508 cc). **Bore & Stroke:** 3.125 x 3.00 in. (79.4 x 76.2 mm). **Compression Ratio:** 6.8:1. **Brake Horsepower:** 47 at 4400 rpm. Three main bearings. Solid valve lifters. One Zenith carburetor. Lucas ignition.
BASE SIX (Zephyr): Inline, overhead-valve six-cylinder. Cast iron block and head. **Displacement:** 138 cu. in. (2262 cc). **Bore & Stroke:** 3.125 x 3.00 in. (79.4 x 76.2 mm). **Compression Ratio:** 6.8:1. **Brake Horsepower:** 68 at 4000 rpm. **Torque:** 112 lbs.-ft. at 2000 rpm. Four main bearings. Solid valve lifters. One Zenith carburetor. Lucas ignition.

CHASSIS DATA: Wheelbase: (Anglia) 90 in.; (Prefect) 94 in.; (Consul) 100 in.; (Zephyr) 104 in. **Overall Length:** (Anglia) 153.5 in.; (Prefect) 156 in.; (Consul) 164.75 in.; (Zephyr) 171.75 in. **Height:** (Anglia) 64.2 in.; (Prefect) 63.5 in.; (Consul) 60.8 in. **Width:** (Anglia) 56.5 in.; (Prefect) 56.3 in.; (Consul) 64.0 in.; (Zephyr) 63.9 in. **Front Tread:** (Anglia/Prefect) 45 in.; (Consul) 50 in. **Rear Tread:** (Anglia/Prefect) 45 in.; (Consul) 49 in. **Wheel Type:** steel disc. **Standard Tires:** (Anglia/Prefect) 5.00x16; (Consul) 5.90x13; (Zephyr) 6.40x13.

TECHNICAL: Layout: front-engine, rear-drive. **Transmission:** three-speed manual; (Anglia/Prefect) floor lever; (Consul/Zephyr) column lever. **Standard Final Drive Ratio:** (Anglia/Prefect) 5.5:1; (Consul) 4.625;1; (Zephyr) 4.375:1. **Steering:** worm and nut. **Suspension (front):** (Anglia/Prefect) transverse leaf spring; (Consul/Zephyr) coil springs. **Suspension (rear):** (Anglia/Prefect) transverse leaf spring; (Consul/Zephyr) rigid axle with semi-elliptic leaf springs. **Brakes:** (Anglia/Prefect) mechanical; (Consul/Zephyr) hydraulic. **Body Construction:** (Anglia/Prefect) steel body on steel frame; (Consul/Zephyr) steel unibody.

PERFORMANCE: Top Speed: (Zephyr) 81 mph. **Acceleration (0-60 mph):** (Zephyr) 18.3 sec. (0-50 mph in 14 sec.). **Acceleration (quarter-mile):** (Zephyr) 20.2-21.8 sec. **Fuel Mileage:** (Zephyr) near 20 mpg.

Manufacturer: Ford Motor Co. Ltd., Dagenham, Essex, England.

Distributor: Ford Motor Co., Dearborn, Michigan.

1953 FORD
(British)

ANGLIA — FOUR — For its final season in the British Ford lineup, the Anglia two-door sedan continued with little change.

PREFECT — FOUR — Ford's smallest four-door sedan continued with little change, in preparation for a restyled model in 1954.

CONSUL — FOUR — The four-cylinder version of Ford's larger series added a a full-length parcel shelf below the dashboard, and instruments were clustered around the steering column. The Consul's one-piece curved windshield was claimed to deliver "full-circle visibility." Pendant-style pedals were new. Independent front suspension consisted of coil springs with two-way shock absorbers and an anti-sway bar. A two-door convertible joined the original sedan, and was similar in appearance. A power-operated top was optional.

ZEPHYR — SIX — Except for interior changes similar to the Consul, the six-cylinder model continued with little revision. A convertible version of the Zephyr also debuted this year, with a power top standard. The plastic top could be positioned in "de ville" position, or folded completely.

I.D. DATA: Anglia/Prefect chassis number is stamped on upper flange of frame, near front shock-absorber bracket. Consul/Zephyr chassis number is stamped around the right front-suspension mounting. Engine number is on the right side of the cylinder block, at motor mount pad except (Consul/Zephyr) stamped on top face of right-side engine mount pad. Starting serial number: (Anglia) C-612652; (Prefect) C-613658; (Consul) EOTA-60960; (Zephyr) EOTTA-16143.

Model	Body Type & Seating	Engine Type/CID	P.O.E. Price	Weight (lbs.)	Prod. Total
ANGLIA					
	2-dr Sedan-4P	I4/72	1184	1700	N/A
PREFECT					
E493A	4-dr Sedan-4P	I4/72	1384	1800	N/A
CONSUL					
Mk1	4-dr Sedan-4/5P	I4/92	1695	2435	N/A
Mk1	2-dr Conv-4P	I4/92	2075	N/A	N/A
ZEPHYR					
Mk I	4-dr Sedan-5P	I6/138	1889	2591	N/A
Mk I	2-dr Conv-4P	I6/138	2425	N/A	N/A

Price Note: Consul convertible with power top cost $2225.

ENGINE DATA: BASE FOUR (Anglia, Prefect): Inline, L-head four-cylinder. Cast iron block and head. **Displacement:** 71.5 cu. in. (1172 cc). **Bore & Stroke:** 2.50 x 3.64 in. (63.5 x 92.5 mm). **Compression Ratio:** 6.16:1. **Brake Horsepower:** 30.1 at 4000 rpm. Three main bearings. Solid valve lifters. One Ford/Zenith carburetor.

BASE FOUR (Consul): Inline, overhead-valve four-cylinder. Cast iron block and head. **Displacement:** 92 cu. in. (1508 cc). **Bore & Stroke:** 3.125 x 3.00 in. (79.4 x 76.2 mm). **Compression Ratio:** 6.8:1. **Brake Horsepower:** 47 at 4400 rpm. **Torque:** 74 lbs.-ft. at 2400 rpm. Three main bearings. Solid valve lifters. One Zenith carburetor.

BASE SIX (Zephyr): Inline, overhead-valve six-cylinder. Cast iron block and head. **Displacement:** 138 cu. in. (2262 cc). **Bore & Stroke:** 3.125 x 3.00 in. (79.4 x 76.2 mm). **Compression Ratio:** 6.8:1. **Brake Horsepower:** 68 at 4000 rpm. **Torque:** 112 lbs.-ft. at 2000 rpm. Four main bearings. Solid valve lifters. One Zenith carburetor.

CHASSIS DATA: Wheelbase: (Anglia) 90 in.; (Prefect) 94 in.; (Consul) 100 in.; (Zephyr) 104 in. **Overall Length:** (Anglia) 153.5 in.; (Prefect) 156 in.; (Consul) 164.75 in.; (Zephyr) 171.75 in. **Height:** (Anglia) 64.2 in.; (Prefect) 63.5 in.; (Consul/Zephyr) 60.8 in. **Width:** (Anglia) 56.5 in.; (Prefect) 56.3 in.; (Consul) 64.0 in.; (Zephyr) 63.9 in. **Front Tread:** (Anglia/Prefect) 45 in.; (Consul/Zephyr) 50 in. **Rear Tread:** (Anglia/Prefect) 45 in.; (Consul/Zephyr) 49 in. **Wheel Type:** steel disc. **Standard Tires:** (Anglia/Prefect) 5.00x16; (Consul) 5.90x13; (Zephyr) 6.40x13.

TECHNICAL: Layout: front-engine, rear-drive. **Transmission:** three-speed manual; (Anglia/Prefect) floor lever; (Consul/Zephyr) column lever. **Standard Final Drive Ratio:** (Anglia/Prefect) 5.5:1; (Consul) 4.625:1; (Zephyr) 4.375:1. **Steering:** worm and sector. **Suspension (front):** (Anglia/Prefect) transverse leaf spring; (Consul/Zephyr) coil springs. **Suspension (rear):** (Anglia/Prefect) transverse leaf spring; (Consul/Zephyr) rigid axle with semi-elliptic leaf springs. **Brakes:** (Anglia/Prefect) mechanical; (Consul/Zephyr) hydraulic front/rear drum. **Body Construction:** (Anglia/Prefect) steel body on steel frame; (Consul/Zephyr) steel unibody.

MAJOR OPTIONS: Radio. Heater/defroster.

PERFORMANCE: Top Speed: (Consul) 74 mph; (Zephyr) 79-81 mph. **Acceleration (0-60 mph):** (Consul) 19 sec.; (Zephyr) 19.2-20.1 sec. **Acceleration (quarter-mile):** (Consul) 24.7 sec. (77 mph); (Zephyr) 21.2 sec. (78 mph). **Fuel Mileage:** (Consul) about 29 mpg; (Zephyr) 21-24 mpg.

Note: Zephyr road-test figures varied considerably, reporting 0-60 mph acceleration times as quick as 14.8 seconds and quarter-mile times down to 19.9 seconds, reaching 92 mph.

Manufacturer: Ford Motor Co. Ltd., Dagenham, Essex, England.

Distributor: Ford Motor Co., Dearborn, Michigan.

1954 FORD (British)

1954 Ford Zephyr four-door sedan.

ANGLIA — 100E — FOUR — A completely different Anglia two-door sedan replaced the former, old-fashioned model. This one displayed the square styling typical of the mid-1950s, with a full-width (slab-sided) body and one-piece curved windshield. Ford promoted its flowing lines and roomier interior. A horizontal trim crease ran the full length of the bodyside. The rectangular Anglia grille was made up of three thick horizontal bars. Parking lights stood just below the built-in round headlamps. Inside were adjustable bucket front seats and a full-width parcel shelf. The new Anglia rode a shorter (87-inch) wheelbase than its predecessor, but still carried an L-head four-cylinder engine. Horsepower got a boost, however, up to 36 at 4400 rpm. Unibody construction replaced the former separate body and frame. The new Anglia also had independent front suspension using coil springs, lower wishbones and sliding kingpins, similar to the setup in the Consul and Zephyr. Semi-elliptic leaf springs brought up the rear. Pendant-style pedals operated the clutch and hydraulic drum brakes. The hood raised forward, and could be locked in the vertical position.

PREFECT — 100E — FOUR — Ford's small four-door sedan also adopted a new, more modern look for 1954, similar to the larger Consul. A rectangular grille opening held concave vertical bars, with a round ornament in the center. The Prefect powertrain was identical to that of the Anglia: the familiar 1172-cc L-head four-cylinder engine, but with six more horsepower than before. Mechanical details also were similar to Anglia, including coil-spring front suspension and semi-elliptic rear leaf springs.

CONSUL — FOUR — Both the four-door sedan and convertible were available, again powered by a 1508-cc four-cylinder engine. Bumpers were restyled, and a wing-style hood ornament was installed. Windshields and back windows added chrome surrounds. At the rear were small oblong taillamps.

ZEPHYR — SIX — A few appearance changes debuted this year on the six-cylinder sedan and convertible, including wing-type hood ornaments, full chrome body trim strips, and a flat center segment on the front bumper bar.

I.D. DATA: Chassis number is stamped around the right front-suspension mounting. Engine number is on the right side of the cylinder block, at motor mount pad except (Consul/Zephyr) stamped on top face of right-side engine mount pad. Serial number ranges: (Anglia) C734998-up and 100E 0001 to 10101; (Prefect) C735087-up and 100E 0001 to 16324; (Consul) EOTA-102232 to -128800; (Zephyr) EOTTA-54168 to -81249.

Model	Body Type & Seating	Engine Type/CID	P.O.E. Price	Weight (lbs.)	Prod. Total
ANGLIA					
100E	2-dr Sedan-4P	I4/72	1398	1618	Note 1
PREFECT					
100E	4-dr Sedan-4P	I4/72	1495	1670	Note 1
CONSUL					
Mk I	4-dr Sedan-4/5P	I4/92	1695	2350	Note 1
Mk I	2-dr Conv-4P	I4/92	N/A	N/A	Note 1
ZEPHYR					
Mk I	4-dr Sedan-5P	I6/138	1889	2542	Note 1
Mk I	2-dr Conv-4P	I6/138	N/A	N/A	Note 2

Note 1: Approximately 1,622 British Fords were sold in the U.S. during 1954, out of total production of 210,000 units.

ENGINE DATA: BASE FOUR (Anglia, Prefect): Inline, L-head four-cylinder. Cast iron block and head. **Displacement:** 71.55 cu. in. (1172 cc). **Bore & Stroke:** 2.50 x 3.64 in. (63.5 x 92.5 mm). **Compression Ratio:** 7.0:1. **Brake Horsepower:** 36 at 4400 rpm. **Torque:** 54 lbs.-ft. at 2150 rpm. Three main bearings. Solid valve lifters. One Solex carburetor.

BASE FOUR (Consul): Inline, overhead-valve four-cylinder. Cast iron block and head. **Displacement:** 92 cu. in. (1508 cc). **Bore & Stroke:** 3.125 x 3.00 in. (79.4 x 76.2 mm). **Compression Ratio:** 6.8:1 (or 7.5:1). **Brake Horsepower:** 47 at 4400 rpm. Three main bearings. Solid valve lifters. One Zenith carburetor.

BASE SIX (Zephyr): Inline, overhead-valve six-cylinder. Cast iron block and head. **Displacement:** 138 cu. in. (2262 cc). **Bore & Stroke:** 3.125 x 3.00 in. (79.4 x 76.2 mm). **Compression Ratio:** 6.8:1 (or 7.5:1). **Brake Horsepower:** 68 at 4000 rpm. Four main bearings. Solid valve lifters. One Zenith carburetor.

CHASSIS DATA: Wheelbase: (Anglia/Prefect) 87 in.; (Consul) 100 in.; (Zephyr) 104 in. **Overall Length:** (Anglia/Prefect) 151.25 in.; (Consul) 164.75 in.; (Zephyr) 171.75 in. **Height:** (Anglia/Prefect) 59.25 in.; (Consul/Zephyr) 60.8 in. **Width:** (Anglia/Prefect) 60.5 in.; (Consul/Zephyr) 64.0 in. **Front Tread:** (Anglia/Prefect) 48 in.; (Consul/Zephyr) 50 in. **Rear Tread:** (Anglia/Prefect) 47.5 in.; (Consul/Zephyr) 49 in. **Wheel Type:** pressed steel disc. **Standard Tires:** (Anglia/Prefect) 5.20x13; (Consul) 5.90x13; (Zephyr) 6.40x13.

TECHNICAL: Layout: front-engine, rear-drive. **Transmission:** three-speed manual; (Anglia/Prefect) floor lever; (Consul/Zephyr) column lever. **Standard Final Drive Ratio:** (Anglia/Prefect) 4.429:1; (Consul) 4.625:1; (Zephyr) 4.375:1. **Steering:** worm and sector. **Suspension (front):** independent, coil springs. **Suspension (rear):** rigid axle with semi-elliptic leaf springs. **Brakes:** hydraulic front/rear drum. **Body Construction:** steel unibody.

PERFORMANCE: Top Speed: (Anglia/Prefect) about 70 mph; (Consul) 74 mph; (Zephyr) 81 mph. **Acceleration (0-60 mph):** N/A (Anglia, 0-50 mph in about 18.5 sec. **Acceleration (quarter-mile):** (Anglia) 23.8 sec.; (Consul) about 24 sec.; (Zephyr) 21.8 sec.

Manufacturer: Ford Motor Co. Ltd., Dagenham, Essex, England.

Distributor: Ford Motor Co., Dearborn, Michigan.

HISTORY: Introduced to U.S. market in January 1954. The new Prefect was described by Ford as a five-star car in every way, giving the customer "power, room and style at less per mile." A more luxurious version of the Zephyr, called Zodiac, entered production for the 1954 model year but took longer to arrive at U.S. dealerships; see next listing for details.

1955 FORD (British)

ANGLIA — 100E — FOUR — Chrome surrounds were added to the windshield and back window of Ford's two-door sedan, introduced in modern form a year earlier. Power again came from the familiar L-head four-cylinder engine, delivering 36 bhp.

PREFECT — 100E — FOUR — Wind-up rear-door windows now were installed on all Prefects. Otherwise, change was minimal.

CONSUL — FOUR — Rectangular taillamps now incorporated reflectors, but little changed otherwise on the larger four-door sedan and convertible.

ZEPHYR/ZODIAC — SIX — Both the standard (Zephyr) and more posh (Zodiac) models were now available, in four-door sedan and drophead coupe (convertible) form. Rectangular taillamps incorporated reflectors. Under each hood was the same 2262-cc overhead-valve six-cylinder engine, but Zodiac's delivered three extra horsepower as a result of increased compression.

I.D. DATA: Chassis number is stamped around the right front-suspension mounting. Engine number is on the right side of cylinder block, at motor mount pad except (Consul/Zephyr/Zodiac) stamped on top face of right-side engine mount pad. Starting serial number: (Anglia) 100E10102; (Prefect) 100E16325; (Consul sedan) EOTA 128801; (Consul conv.) EOTA-137205; (Zephyr/Zodiac sedan) EOTTA-81250; (Zodiac conv.) EOTTA-66101.

Model	Body Type & Seating	Engine Type/CID	P.O.E. Price	Weight (lbs.)	Prod. Total
ANGLIA					
100E	2-dr Sedan-4P	I4/72	1398	1623	Note 1
PREFECT					
100E	4-dr Sedan-4P	I4/72	1495	1721	Note 1

247

Model	Body Type & Seating	Engine Type/CID	P.O.E. Price	Weight (lbs.)	Prod. Total
CONSUL					
Mk I	4-dr Sedan-4/5P	I4/92	1695	2295	Note 1
Mk I	2-dr Conv-4P	I4/92	1917	2495	Note 1
ZEPHYR					
Mk I	4-dr Sedan-5P	I6/138	1889	2475	Note 1
ZODIAC					
Mk I	4-dr Sedan-5P	I6/138	2100	2543	Note 1
Mk I	2-dr Conv-4P	I6/138	2265	2755	Note 1

Note 1: A total of 239,000 British Fords were produced in 1955.

ENGINE DATA: BASE FOUR (Anglia, Prefect): Inline, L-head four-cylinder. Cast iron block and head. **Displacement:** 71.55 cu. in. (1172 cc). **Bore & Stroke:** 2.50 x 3.64 in. (63.5 x 92.5 mm). **Compression Ratio:** 7.0:1. **Brake Horsepower:** 36 at 4400 rpm. Three main bearings. Solid valve lifters. One Solex carburetor.

BASE FOUR (Consul): Inline, overhead-valve four-cylinder. Cast iron block and head. **Displacement:** 92 cu. in. (1508 cc). **Bore & Stroke:** 3.125 x 3.00 in. (79.4 x 76.2 mm). **Compression Ratio:** 6.8:1 (or 7.5:1). **Brake Horsepower:** 47 at 4400 rpm. Three main bearings. Solid valve lifters. One Zenith carburetor.

BASE SIX (Zephyr/Zodiac): Inline, overhead-valve six-cylinder. Cast iron block and head. **Displacement:** 138 cu. in. (2262 cc). **Bore & Stroke:** 3.125 x 3.00 in. (79.4 x 76.2 mm). **Compression Ratio:** 6.8:1 (Zodiac, 7.5:1). **Brake Horsepower:** 68 at 4000 rpm (Zodiac, 71 at 4200). Four main bearings. Solid valve lifters. One Zenith carburetor.

CHASSIS DATA: Wheelbase: (Anglia/Prefect) 87 in.; (Consul) 100 in.; (Zephyr) 104 in. **Overall Length** (Anglia/Prefect) 151.25 in.; (Consul 164.75 in.; (Zephyr/Zodiac) 171.75 in. **Height:** (Anglia/Prefect) 59.25 in.; (Consul/Zephyr) 60.8 in. **Width:** (Anglia/Prefect) 60.5 in.; (Consul/Zephyr) 64.0 in. **Front Tread:** (Anglia/Prefect) 48 in.; (Consul/Zephyr) 50 in. **Rear Tread:** (Anglia/Prefect) 47.5 in.; (Consul/Zephyr) 49 in. **Wheel Type:** pressed steel disc. **Standard Tires:** (Anglia/Prefect) 5.20x13; (Consul) 5.90x13; (Zephyr/Zodiac) 6.40x13.

TECHNICAL: Layout: front-engine, rear-drive. **Transmission:** three-speed manual; (Anglia/Prefect) floor lever; (Consul/Zephyr) column lever. **Standard Final Drive Ratio:** (Anglia/Prefect) 4.429:1; (Consul) 4.625:1; (Zephyr) 4.375:1. **Steering:** worm and sector. **Suspension (front):** coil springs. **Suspension (rear):** rigid axle with semi-elliptic leaf springs. **Brakes:** hydraulic front/rear drum. **Body Construction:** steel unibody.

PERFORMANCE: Top Speed: (Anglia/Prefect) about 70 mph; (Consul) 74 mph; (Zephyr) 81 mph. **Acceleration (0-60 mph):** N/A (Anglia, 0-50 mph in about 18.5 sec. **Acceleration (quarter-mile):** (Anglia) 23.8 sec.; (Consul) about 24 sec.; (Zephyr) 21.8 sec.

Manufacturer: Ford Motor Co. Ltd., Dagenham, Essex, England.

Distributor: Ford Motor Co., Dearborn, Michigan.

HISTORY: Introduced to U.S. market in September 1954. *Motor Trend* applauded the Anglia's and Prefect's "uncanny ability to make time thru traffic...quick and easy steering ...and a fairly soft (but somewhat choppy) ride."

1956 FORD (British)

1956 Ford Zodiac convertible. (William Siuru Jr.)

ANGLIA — 100E — FOUR — No major changes were evident on Ford's small two-door sedan, but the DeLuxe model displayed horizontal chrome strips on its bodysides, as well as chrome headlamp housings. As before, the Anglia grille consisted of three thick horizontal bars, with small rectangular parking lights just below the headlamps. The instrument panel was restyled this year. Standard equipment included fender mirrors. Power again came from an L-head four-cylinder engine, producing 36 horsepower.

PREFECT — 100E — FOUR — The DeLuxe Prefect four-door sedan had chrome headlamp surrounds and bodyside trim strips. Otherwise, little change occurred this year. A close-spaced vertical-bar grille was used again. Powertrain was identical to that of the two-door Anglia.

ESCORT/SQUIRE — 100E — FOUR — Two Estate Cars (station wagons) debuted this year, based on the Anglia and Prefect chassis. Both had a squarish, trucklike profile. The Escort front end and grille was identical to that of the Anglia, while the Squire looked like a Prefect from the front. The Squire also had hardwood bodyside trim and more chrome. Powertrains were identical to the Anglia/Prefect.

CONSUL — Mk I — FOUR — Little change was evident on the mid-size four-door sedan and two-door convertible, except for amber turn-signal lenses.

CONSUL (Second Series) — Mk II — FOUR — A restyled edition of the Consul emerged during the 1956 model year, in both four-door sedan and convertible form. 'CONSUL' letters went above the larger mesh grille. Small round parking lights stood below shrouded headlamps. The four-cylinder engine grew from 1508 to 1703 cc (104 cubic inches) via an increase in both bore and stroke dimensions, and produced 59 horsepower. Compression ratio also was increased, to 7.8:1. Inside was a dished-spoke steering wheel and hydraulically-actuated clutch. A radio and overdrive transmission were available.

ZEPHYR/ZODIAC — Mk I — SIX — Appearance and mechanical details of the standard Zephyr and more luxurious Zodiac changed little, except for amber turn-signal lenses.

ZEPHYR/ZODIAC (Second Series) — Mk II — SIX — Like the smaller Consul, the Zephyr and Zodiac four-door sedans and convertibles went into a second edition at mid-year: longer, wider, and more powerful. Styling was considered closer to U.S. Ford models. The Zephyr wore a wide, open-mesh grille. Taillamps were mounted on fender tips and the gas filler went behind a hinged rear license plate. Overdrive was optional. Zodiac models had a grille made up of horizontal bars, with a fluted chrome band below the trunk and taillamps. Parking lights were built into both grilles. Dimensions of the second series were claimed to have been derived from U.S. army analysis of the "average" man.

I.D. DATA: Chassis number is stamped around the right front-suspension mounting. Engine number is on the right side of the cylinder block, at motor mount pad except (Consul/Zephyr/Zodiac) stamped on top face of right-side engine mount pad. Serial number prefix: (Anglia/Prefect) 100E; (Consul Mk II) 204E; (Zephyr/Zodiac Mk II) 206E.

Model	Body Type & Seating	Engine Type/CID	P.O.E. Price	Weight (lbs.)	Prod. Total
ANGLIA					
100E	2-dr Sedan-4P	I4/72	1398	1623	Note 1
100E	2-dr DeL Sedan-4P	I4/72	1495	1623	Note 1
PREFECT					
100E	4-dr Sedan-4P	I4/72	1495	1721	Note 1
100E	4-dr DeL Sedan-4P	I4/72	1595	1721	Note 1
ESCORT/SQUIRE STATION WAGONS					
100E	2-dr Escort-4/5P	I4/72	1585	1791	Note 1
100E	2-dr Squire-4/5P	I4/72	1695	1800	Note 1
CONSUL					
Mk I	4-dr Sedan-4/5P	I4/92	1695	2295	Note 1
Mk I	2-dr Cond-4P	I4/92	1917	2495	Note 1
CONSUL Mk II (Second Series)					
204E	4-dr Sedan-6P	I4/104	1968	2395	Note 1
204E	2-dr Conv-4P	I4/104	2309	2472	Note 1
ZEPHYR					
Mk I	4-dr Sedan-6P	I6/138	1889	2475	Note 1
Mk I	2-dr Conv-4P	I6/138	2080	2755	Note 1
ZEPHYR Mk II (Second Series)					
206E	4-dr Sedan-6P	I6/156	2149	2582	Note 1
206E	2-dr Conv-4P	I6/156	2508	2611	Note 1
ZODIAC					
Mk I	4-dr Sedan-5P	I6/138	2100	2543	Note 1
ZODIAC Mk II (Second Series)					
206E	4-dr Sedan-6P	I6/156	2321	2627	Note 1

Note 1: A total of 225,121 British Fords were produced in 1956, of which about 4,230 were sold in the U.S.

ENGINE DATA: BASE FOUR (Anglia, Prefect, Escort, Squire): Inline, L-head four-cylinder. Cast iron block and head. **Displacement:** 71.55 cu. in. (1172 cc). **Bore & Stroke:** 2.50 x 3.64 in. (63.5 x 92.5 mm). **Compression Ratio:** 7.0:1. **Brake Horsepower:** 36 at 4400 rpm. **Torque:** 52 lbs.-ft. at 2500 rpm. Three main bearings. Solid valve lifters. One Solex carburetor.

BASE FOUR (Consul Mk I): Inline, overhead-valve four-cylinder. Cast iron block and head. **Displacement:** 92 cu. in. (1508 cc). **Bore & Stroke:** 3.125 x 3.00 in. (79.4 x 76.2 mm). **Compression Ratio:** 6.8:1 (or 7.5:1). **Brake Horsepower:** 47 at 4400 rpm. Three main bearings. Solid valve lifters. One Zenith carburetor.

BASE FOUR (Consul Mk II): Inline, overhead-valve four-cylinder. Cast iron block and head. **Displacement:** 103.9 cu. in. (1703 cc). **Bore & Stroke:** 3.25 x 3.13 in. (82.5 x 79.5 mm). **Compression Ratio:** 7.8:1 (6.9:1 available). **Brake Horsepower:** 59 at 4200 rpm. **Torque:** 92 lbs.-ft. at 2000 rpm. Three main bearings. Solid valve lifters. One Zenith carburetor.

BASE SIX (Zephyr/Zodiac Mk I): Inline, overhead-valve six-cylinder. Cast iron block and head. **Displacement:** 138 cu. in. (2262 cc). **Bore & Stroke:** 3.125 x 3.00 in. (79.4 x 76.2 mm). **Compression Ratio:** 6.8:1 (or 7.5:1). **Brake Horsepower:** 68 at 4000 rpm. Four main bearings. Solid valve lifters. One Zenith carburetor.

BASE SIX (Zephyr/Zodiac Mk II): Inline, overhead-valve six-cylinder. Cast iron block and head. **Displacement:** 155.8 cu. in. (2553 cc). **Bore & Stroke:** 3.25 x 3.13 in. (82.5 x 79.5 mm). **Compression Ratio:** 7.8:1. **Brake Horsepower:** 86 at 4200 rpm. **Torque:** 136 lbs.-ft. at 2000 rpm. Four main bearings. Solid valve lifters. One Zenith carburetor.

CHASSIS DATA: Wheelbase: (Anglia/Prefect/Escort/Squire) 87 in.; (Consul) 100 in.; (Consul Mk II) 104.5 in.; (Zephyr/Zodiac) 104 in.; (Zephyr/Zodiac Mk II) 107 in. **Overall Length:** (Anglia/Prefect) 151.25 in.; (Escort) 141.5 in.; (Squire) 141.8 in.; (Consul) 164.75 in.; (Consul Mk II) 172 in.; (Zephyr/Zodiac) 171.75 in.; (Zephyr Mk II) 178.5 in. (Zodiac Mk II) 180.5 in. **Width:** (Anglia/Prefect) 60.5 in.; (Escort) 60.6 in.; (Consul) 64 in.; (Consul Mk II) 68.6 in.; (Zephyr) 64.0 in.; (Zephyr Mk II) 60.75 in. **Wheel Type:** steel disc. **Standard Tires:** (Anglia/Prefect) 5.20x13; (Escort/Squire) 5.60x13; (Consul) 5.90x13; (Zephyr/Zodiac) 6.40x13.

TECHNICAL: Layout: front-engine, rear-drive. **Transmission:** three-speed manual. **Standard Final Drive Ratio:** (Anglia/Prefect) 4.429:1; (Consul) 4.625:1; (Consul Mk II) 4.11:1; (Zephyr/Zodiac) 4.375:1; (Zephyr/Zodiac Mk II) 3.90:1. **Steering:** worm and sector. **Suspension (front):** coil springs. **Suspension (rear):** rigid axle with semi-elliptic leaf springs. **Brakes:** hydraulic front/rear drum. **Body Construction:** steel unibody.

MAJOR OPTIONS: Overdrive ($150). Fresh-air heater/defroster ($50).

PERFORMANCE: Top Speed: (Anglia) about 70 mph; (Escort/Squire) 65-70 mph; (Consul) about 76 mph; (Zephyr Mk II) 89 mph. **Acceleration (0-60 mph):** (Consul Mk II) 21.6 sec.; (Zephyr Mk II) 15.1 sec. **Acceleration (quarter-mile):** (Consul Mk II) 23 sec.; (Zephyr Mk II) 19.9 sec. **Fuel Mileage:** (Anglia) 25-35 mpg; (Consul) 20-27 mpg.

Manufacturer: Ford Motor Co. Ltd., Dagenham, Essex, England.

Distributor: Ford Motor Co., Dearborn, Michigan.

HISTORY: Introduced to U.S. market on October 15, 1955 (second series models, February 1956). Describing the second-series Consul/Zephyr, *Motor Trend* noted that they "blend old-style economy and new-found liveliness." Ford continued to sell its prewar-styled Popular sedan in Britain, considered to be the world's lowest-priced four-wheel passenger car.

1957 FORD (British)

ANGLIA — 100E — FOUR — Ford's small sedan was unchanged for 1957. The unibodied two-door rode an 87-inch wheelbase and had an independent front suspension with coil springs. The L-head four-cylinder engine produced 36 horsepower and 52 pound-feet of torque. Anglias could deliver fuel economy of 35 miles per gallon. Standard equipment included adjustable front seats, an under-dash parcel tray, and three-speed manual gearbox. Options included a heater and radio.

PREFECT — 100E — FOUR — Like the closely-related Anglia, the small four-door Ford changed little this year. Powertrain was identical to the Anglia's.

ESCORT/SQUIRE — 100E — FOUR — The twin station wagons (known as Estate Cars in the home market) continued with little change, based upon the Anglia/Prefect chassis and drivetrain.

1957 Ford Consul four-door.

CONSUL Mk II — 204E — FOUR — After a restyling for 1956, the mid-range four-door sedan and convertible were back without major change. Styling features included shrouded headlamps, a mesh-type grille, slightly finned rear fenders, mildly wraparound windshield and back window, and large taillamps. A Farnham Estate Car (station wagon) version joined the lineup but took longer to arrive at U.S. dealers; see 1959 listing for details. The overhead-valve four-cylinder engine produced 59 horsepower and 92 pound-feet of torque. Depending on the desire for comfort, Consul interiors could hold four to six passengers. The unibodied model rode a 104.5-inch wheelbase.

1957 Ford Zephyr four-door.

ZEPHYR/ZODIAC Mk II — 206E — SIX — Styling of the larger British Fords, unchanged for 1957, was considered reminiscent of U.S. Ford models. The 156-cid six-cylinder engine produced 86 horsepower (or 80 bhp with the optional low-compression engine). An automatic overdrive unit was available at extra cost, cutting in automatically above 32 mph. Rear seats held side armrests and a center armrest. The more plush Zodiac had a different grille and additional trim, but was otherwise identical to the Zephyr.

I.D. DATA: Chassis number is stamped around the right front-suspension mounting, on firewall. Engine number is on the right side of the cylinder block, at motor mount pad except (Consul/Zephyr/Zodiac) stamped on top face of right-side engine mount pad. Starting serial number. Vehicles first registered on or after September 15, 1956 were considered 1957 models.

Model	Body Type & Seating	Engine Type/CID	P.O.E. Price	Weight (lbs.)	Prod. Total
ANGLIA					
100E	2-dr DeL Sedan-4P	I4/72	1495	1623	Note 1
PREFECT					
100E	4-dr DeL Sedan-4P	I4/72	1595	1721	Note 1
ESCORT/SQUIRE STATION WAGONS					
100E	2-dr Escort Wag-4P	I4/72	1585	1791	Note 1
100E	2-dr Squire Wag-4P	I4/72	1695	1800	Note 1
CONSUL Mk II					
204E	4-dr Sedan-5/6P	I4/104	1995	2295	Note 1
204E	2-dr Conv-4P	I4/104	2307	2495	Note 1
ZEPHYR Mk II					
206E	4-dr Sedan-6P	I6/156	2195	2478	Note 1
206E	2-dr Conv-4P	I6/156	2508	2755	Note 1

Model	Body Type & Seating	Engine Type/CID	P.O.E. Price	Weight (lbs.)	Prod. Total
ZODIAC Mk II					
206E	4-dr Sedan-6P	I6/156	2350	2543	Note 1
206E	2-dr Conv-4P	I6/156	2910	N/A	Note 1

Note 1: Approximately 17,062 of the 239,562 British Fords produced were sold in the U.S.

ENGINE DATA: BASE FOUR (Anglia, Prefect, Escort, Squire): Inline, L-head four-cylinder. Cast iron block and head. **Displacement:** 71.55 cu. in. (1172 cc). **Bore & Stroke:** 2.50 x 3.64 in. (63.5 x 92.5 mm). **Compression Ratio:** 7.0:1. **Brake Horsepower:** 36 at 4500 rpm. **Torque:** 52 lbs.-ft. at 2500 rpm. Three main bearings. Solid valve lifters. One Solex carburetor.

BASE FOUR (Consul Mk II): Inline, overhead-valve four-cylinder. Cast iron block and head. **Displacement:** 103.9 cu. in. (1703 cc). **Bore & Stroke:** 3.25 x 3.13 in. (82.55 x 79.5 mm). **Compression Ratio:** 7.8:1 (6.9:1 optional). **Brake Horsepower:** 59 at 4200 rpm. **Torque:** 92 lbs.-ft. at 2300 rpm. Three main bearings. Solid valve lifters. One Zenith carburetor.

BASE SIX (Zephyr/Zodiac Mk II): Inline, overhead-valve six-cylinder. Cast iron block and head. **Displacement:** 155.8 cu. in. (2553 cc). **Bore & Stroke:** 3.25 x 3.13 in. (82.55 x 79.5 mm). **Compression Ratio:** 7.8:1 (6.9:1 optional). **Brake Horsepower:** 86 at 4200 rpm. **Torque:** 136 lbs.-ft. at 2000 rpm. Four main bearings. Solid valve lifters. One Zenith carburetor.

CHASSIS DATA: Wheelbase: (Anglia/Prefect/Escort/Squire) 87 in.; (Consul) 104.5 in.; (Zephyr/Zodiac) 107 in. **Overall Length:** (Anglia) 149.75 in.; (Prefect) 151 in.; (Escort) 146 in.; (Squire) 141.75 in.; (Consul) 172 in.; (Zephyr) 178.4 in.; (Zodiac) 180.6 in. **Height:** (Anglia/Prefect/Squire) 59 in.; (Escort) 63 in.; (Consul) 61.5 in.; (Zephyr/Zodiac) 62 in. **Width:** (Anglia/Prefect) 60.5 in.; (Consul) 68.6 in.; (Zephyr/Zodiac) 68.9 in. **Wheel Type:** steel disc. **Standard Tires:** (Anglia/Prefect) 5.20x13; (Escort/Squire) 5.60x13; (Consul) 5.90x13; (Zephyr/Zodiac) 6.40x13.

TECHNICAL: Layout: front-engine, rear-drive. **Transmission:** three-speed manual; (Anglia/Prefect) floor lever; (others) column lever. **Standard Final Drive Ratio:** (Anglia/Prefect) 4.429:1; (Consul) 4.11:1; (Zephyr/Zodiac) 3.90:1. **Steering:** worm and sector. **Suspension (front):** coil springs. **Suspension (rear):** rigid axle with semi-elliptic leaf springs. **Brakes:** hydraulic front/rear drum. **Body Construction:** steel unibody.

MAJOR OPTIONS: Automatic transmission (Zephyr/Zodiac).

PERFORMANCE: Similar to 1956.

Manufacturer: Ford Motor Co. Ltd., Dagenham, Essex, England.

Distributor: Ford Motor Co., Dearborn, Michigan.

HISTORY: Introduced to U.S. market as early as September 15, 1956.

1958 FORD (British)

1958 Ford Consul convertible.

ANGLIA — FOUR — A revised mesh-type grille was evident on the Anglia two-door sedan, along with a larger back window and taillamp assembly. Standard models had no belt molding.

PREFECT — FOUR — The four-door's grille was again made up of vertical bars, with a round ornament in the center. Bodies had a larger back window and taillamp assembly, and a triangular badge went on the fender fronts. Standard models had no belt molding. Prefects had a floor gearshift and manual choke.

ESCORT/SQUIRE — FOUR — Little change was evident on the Anglia/Prefect-based station wagons, except that the Squire added chrome bodyside strips. A semi-automatic clutch was available.

CONSUL Mk II — FOUR — Parking lights were restyled this year, and the gearshift was enclosed in the steering column. The steering mechanism switched from the former worm type to recirculating ball. Sedans had a chrome trim piece on each side of the back window.

ZEPHYR/ZODIAC Mk II — SIX — A restyled grille was made up of more horizontal bars, closer together than before. Styling features included thin windshield pillars. Headliners were now made of washable plastic. Options included an automatic clutch. The higher-priced Zodiac came with more trim and could have two-tone paint. Both were powered by a 156-cid six-cylinder, overhead-valve engine. A Borg-Warner automatic transmission was available for six-cylinder models.

I.D. DATA: Chassis numbers are stamped around the right front suspension upper mount, and on a plate attached to the front of the firewall. Engine numbers are stamped on the top face of the engine-mount pad (right side), or the right side of the block.

Model	Body Type & Seating	Engine Type/CID	P.O.E. Price	Weight (lbs.)	Prod. Total
ANGLIA					
100E	2-dr Sedan-4P	I4/72	1441	1648	**Note 1**
100E	2-dr DeL Sed-4P	I4/72	1539	1648	**Note 1**
PREFECT					
100E	4-dr Sedan-4P	I4/72	1490	1697	Note 1
100E	4-dr DeL Sed-4P	I4/72	1639	1697	Note 1

249

Model	Body Type & Seating	Engine Type/CID	P.O.E. Price	Weight (lbs.)	Prod. Total
ESCORT/SQUIRE STATION WAGONS					
100E	2-dr Escort Wag-4P	I4/72	1629	1791	Note 1
100E	2-dr Squire Wag-4P	I4/72	1739	1800	Note 1
CONSUL Mk II					
204E	4-dr Sedan-5/6P	I4/104	2012	2395	Note 1
204E	2-dr Conv-4P	I4/104	2351	2472	Note 1
ZEPHYR Mk II					
206E	4-dr Sedan-6P	I6/156	2193	2582	Note 1
206E	2-dr Conv-4P	I6/156	2552	2611	Note 1
ZODIAC Mk II					
206E	4-dr Sedan-6P	I6/156	2365	2543	Note 1
206E	2-dr Conv-4P	I6/156	2910	N/A	Note 1

Note 1: Of the 287,000 British Fords produced in 1958, about 33,472 were imported and sold in the U.S.

1958 Ford Popular. (William Siuru Jr.)

ENGINE DATA: BASE FOUR (Anglia, Prefect, Escort, Squire): Inline, L-head four-cylinder. Cast iron block and head. **Displacement:** 71.55 cu. in. (1172 cc). **Bore & Stroke:** 2.50 x 3.64 in. (63.5 x 92.5 mm). **Compression Ratio:** 7.0:1. **Brake Horsepower:** 36 at 4500 rpm. **Torque:** 52 lbs.-ft. at 2500 rpm. Three main bearings. Solid valve lifters. One Solex carburetor.

BASE FOUR (Consul): Inline, overhead-valve four-cylinder. Cast iron block and head. **Displacement:** 103.9 cu. in. (1703 cc). **Bore & Stroke:** 3.25 x 3.13 in. (82.55 x 79.5 mm). **Compression Ratio:** 7.8:1 (6.9:1 optional). **Brake Horsepower:** 59 at 4400 rpm. **Torque:** 93 lbs.-ft. at 2300 rpm. Three main bearings. Solid valve lifters. One Zenith carburetor.

BASE SIX (Zephyr/Zodiac): Inline, overhead-valve six-cylinder. Cast iron block and head. **Displacement:** 155.8 cu. in. (2553 cc). **Bore & Stroke:** 3.25 x 3.13 in. (82.55 x 79.5 mm). **Compression Ratio:** 7.8:1 (6.9:1 optional). **Brake Horsepower:** 90 at 4400 rpm. **Torque:** 137 lbs.-ft. at 2000 rpm. Four main bearings. Solid valve lifters. One Zenith carburetor.

CHASSIS DATA: Wheelbase: (Anglia/Prefect/Escort/Squire) 87 in.; (Consul) 104.5 in.; (Zephyr/Zodiac) 107 in. **Overall Length:** (Anglia) 149.75 in.; (Prefect) 151.25 in.; (Consul) 172.2 in.; (Zephyr) 178.5 in.; (Zodiac) 180.6 in. **Height:** (Anglia/Prefect/Escort/Squire) 59 in.; (Escort) 63 in.; (Consul) 61.5 in.; (Zephyr/Zodiac) 62 in. **Width:** (Anglia/Prefect/Escort/Squire) 60.5 in.; (Consul) 68.6 in.; (Zephyr/Zodiac) 68.9 in. **Wheel Type:** steel disc. **Standard Tires:** (Anglia/Prefect) 5.20x13; (Escort/Squire) 5.60x13; (Consul) 5.90x13; (Zephyr/Zodiac) 6.40x13.

TECHNICAL: Layout: front-engine, rear-drive. **Transmission:** three-speed manual; (Anglia/Prefect) floor lever; (others) column lever. **Standard Final Drive Ratio:** (Anglia/Prefect/Escort/Squire) 4.43:1; (Consul) 4.11:1; (Zephyr/Zodiac) 3.90:1. **Steering:** worm and sector. **Suspension (front):** coil springs. **Suspension (rear):** rigid axle with semi-elliptic leaf springs. **Brakes:** hydraulic front/rear drum. **Body Construction:** steel unibody.

MAJOR OPTIONS: Borg-Warner automatic transmission (Zephyr/Zodiac). Overdrive transmission (Consul/Zephyr/Zodiac). Semi-automatic clutch (Squire). Heater/defroster: Anglia/Prefect ($39); others ($49). Radio ($69).

ADDITIONAL MODELS: For the home market, Ford continued to offer its prewar-styled Popular sedan.

PERFORMANCE: Top Speed: (Anglia/Prefect) 70 mph; (Consul) 80 mph; (Zephyr) 85 mph. **Acceleration (0-60 mph):** (Prefect) 32.5 sec.; (Consul) 25.5 sec.; (Zephyr) 18 sec. **Fuel Mileage:** (Prefect) 25-32 mpg; (Consul) 22-30 mpg; (Zephyr) 18-25 mpg.

Manufacturer: Ford Motor Co. Ltd., Dagenham, Essex, England.

Distributor: Ford Motor Co., Dearborn, Michigan.

HISTORY: Introduced to U.S. market on September 15, 1957. Aftermarket conversion kits were available to boost Anglia power. One of them, developed by Willment Speed Shop Ltd., turned the L-head engine into an F-head configuration, raising output to 63 bhp.

1959 FORD (British)

ANGLIA — 100E — FOUR — For its final year in the Ford lineup (in this form), the small two-door sedan continued with little change, powered by the L-head four-cylinder engine that developed 36 horsepower. The standard models had no belt molding.

PREFECT — FOUR — Ford's smallest four-door model continued with little change. The Prefect grille was again made up of vertical bars, with a round ornament in the center. The standard model had no belt molding. Powertrain identical to that of the two-door Anglia.

1959 Ford Squire. (William Siuru Jr.)

ESCORT/SQUIRE — FOUR — No significant change was evident on either the Anglia-based (Escort) or Prefect-based (Squire) station wagon. The Squire version had chrome bodyside trim strips.

CONSUL Mk II — 204E — FOUR — Except for a modification to the front-door lock, little change was evident in the Consul series: sedan, convertible, and Estate Car (station wagon). All were powered by a 104-cid overhead-valve engine, producing 59 or 61 horsepower (depending on compression ratio). During the model year, Consuls adopted a lower roofline and added a stainless steel surround molding to the windshield and rear window, as well as chromed headlamp bezels. The Estate Car became available with two-tone paint.

ZEPHYR/ZODIAC Mk II — 206E — SIX — The front door locking device was modified, but little change was evident otherwise in Ford's largest models, offered in four-door sedan, convertible, and Estate Car (station wagon) form. Seating was provided for up to six passengers, though four or five would be more comfortable. Zodiac, the more luxurious of the pair, was the model most commonly imported into the U.S. It came with a slightly different grille, more chrome trim, and two-tone color combinations.

I.D. DATA: Chassis numbers are stamped around the right front suspension upper mount, and on a plate attached to the front of the firewall. Engine numbers are stamped on the top face of the engine-mount pad (right side), or the right side of the block.

Model	Body Type & Seating	Engine Type/CID	P.O.E. Price	Weight (lbs.)	Prod. Note
ANGLIA					
100E	2-dr Std Sed-4P	I4/72	1464	1623	Note 1
100E	2-dr DeL Sed-4P	I4/72	1561	1623	Note 1
PREFECT					
100E	4-dr Std Sed-4P	I4/72	1517	1721	Note 1
100E	4-dr DeL Sed-4P	I4/72	1661	1721	Note 1
ESCORT/SQUIRE STATION WAGONS					
100E	2-dr Escort Wag-4P	I4/72	1651	1791	Note 1
100E	2-dr Squire Wag-4P	I4/72	1761	1800	Note 1
CONSUL Mk II					
204E	4-dr Sedan-5/6P	I4/104	2034	2395	Note 1
204E	2-dr Conv-4P	I4/104	2373	2472	Note 1
204E	4-dr Sta Wag-5P	I4/104	2772	2624	Note 1
ZEPHYR Mk II					
206E	4-dr Sedan-5/6P	I6/156	2215	2582	Note 1
206E	2-dr Conv-4P	I6/156	2574	2611	Note 1
206E	4-dr Sta Wag-6P	I6/156	2945	2774	Note 1
ZODIAC Mk II					
206E	4-dr Sedan-5/6P	I6/156	2387	2627	Note 1
206E	2-dr Conv-4P	I6/156	2865	2698	Note 1
206E	4-dr Sta Wag-6P	I6/156	3149	2834	Note 1

Note 1: Out of a total of 319,600 British Fords produced, about 42,413 were imported and sold in the U.S. during 1959.

ENGINE DATA: BASE FOUR (Anglia, Prefect, Escort, Squire): Inline, L-head four-cylinder. Cast iron block and head. **Displacement:** 71.55 cu. in. (1172 cc). **Bore & Stroke:** 2.50 x 3.64 in. (63.5 x 92.5 mm). **Compression Ratio:** 7.0:1. **Brake Horsepower:** 36 at 4500 rpm. **Torque:** 52 lbs.-ft. at 2500 rpm. Three main bearings. Solid valve lifters. One Solex carburetor.

BASE FOUR (Consul): Inline, overhead-valve four-cylinder. Cast iron block and head. **Displacement:** 103.9 cu. in. (1703 cc). **Bore & Stroke:** 3.25 x 3.13 in. (82.6 x 79.5 mm). **Compression Ratio:** 7.8:1 (6.9:1 optional). **Brake Horsepower:** 61 at 4200 rpm (59 bhp with lower compression). **Torque:** 93/89 lbs.-ft. at 2300 rpm. Three main bearings. Solid valve lifters. One Zenith carburetor.

BASE SIX (Zephyr/Zodiac): Inline, overhead-valve six-cylinder. Cast iron block and head. **Displacement:** 155.8 cu. in. (2553 cc). **Bore & Stroke:** 3.25 x 3.13 in. (82.6 x 79.5 mm). **Compression Ratio:** 7.8:1 (6.9:1 optional). **Brake Horsepower:** 85/90 at 4400 rpm. **Torque:** 137 lbs.-ft. at 2000 rpm. Four main bearings. Solid valve lifters. One Zenith carburetor.

CHASSIS DATA: Wheelbase: (Anglia/Prefect/Escort/Squire) 87 in.; (Consul) 104.5 in.; (Zephyr/Zodiac) 107 in. **Overall Length:** (Anglia) 149.75 in.; (Prefect) 151.25 in.; (Escort/Squire) 142 in.; (Consul) 172.2 in.; (Zephyr) 178.5 in.; (Zodiac) 180.6 in. **Height:** (Anglia/Prefect/Squire) 59 in.; (Escort) 63 in.; (Consul) 59.6 in.; (Zephyr/Zodiac) 60.3 in. **Width:** (Anglia/Prefect/Escort/Squire) 60.5 in.; (Consul) 68.6 in.; (Zephyr/Zodiac) 69 in. **Front Tread:** (Anglia/Prefect/Escort/Squire) 48 in.; (Consul) 53 in.; (Zephyr/Zodiac) 53 in. **Rear Tread:** (Anglia/Prefect/Escort/Squire) 47.5 in.; (Consul) 52 in.; (Zephyr/Zodiac) 53 in. **Wheel Type:** steel disc. **Standard Tires:** (Anglia/Prefect) 5.20x13; (Escort/Squire) 5.60x13; (Consul) 5.90x13; (Zephyr/Zodiac) 6.40x13.

TECHNICAL: Layout: front-engine, rear-drive. **Transmission:** three-speed manual, synchronized 2nd/3rd; (Anglia/Prefect) floor lever; (others) column lever. **Standard Final Drive Ratio:** (Anglia/Prefect/Escort/Squire) 4.43:1; (Consul) 4.11:1; (Zephyr/Zodiac) 3.90:1. **Steering:** (Anglia/Prefect) worm; (others) recirculating ball. **Suspension (front):** coil springs. **Suspension (rear):** rigid axle with semi-elliptic leaf springs. **Brakes:** hydraulic front/rear drum. **Body Construction:** steel unibody. **Fuel Tank:** (Anglia) 8.3 gal.; (Consul/Zephyr) 13.1 gal.

MAJOR OPTIONS: Automatic transmission (Zephyr/Zodiac). Overdrive transmission (Zephyr/Zodiac).

PERFORMANCE: Top Speed: (Anglia/Prefect) about 70 mph, for cruising at 65 mph; (Consul) 78 mph. **Fuel Mileage:** (Anglia/Prefect) up to 40 mpg.

Manufacturer: Ford Motor Co. Ltd., Dagenham, Essex, England.
Distributor: Ford Motor Co., Dearborn, Michigan.
HISTORY: Introduced to U.S. market in October, 1958.

1960 FORD (British)

1960 Ford Zodiac four-door. (William Siuru Jr.)

ANGLIA — 105E — FOUR — Ford's small two-door sedan gained a new updated body and powertrain this year, including a smaller engine with overhead-valve configuration. The most striking feature of the new sharp-edged body profile was its "Z-line" (reverse-angled) back window. Up front was an angled-forward grille and front-hinged hood, which could be opened to nearly a vertical position, while small fins brought up the rear. The new model rode a longer (90.5-inch) wheelbase than its predecessor and displayed a flatter, narrower roofline. Hooked to the new 61-cid (997-cc) four-cylinder engine was a new four-speed manual gearbox, replacing the former three-speed. This was Ford's first use of a four-speed in its British line. Even though engine displacement diminished, output rose from 36 to 41 horsepower. Bore dimension was ordinary at 3.19 inches, but the new engine had an unusually short stroke: just 1.91 inches. The new body design offered increased interior space, especially in the back seat. External trunk hinges were installed, and bucket front seats had tubular frames. Wedge-shaped parking lights stood at the far ends of the grille, and the windshield had a sharper inclination this year. Chrome bodyside moldings rose at the front to form visors for the headlamps.

PREFECT — 107E — FOUR — Body styling of the four-door Prefect was basically unchanged this year, but under its hood went the new overhead-valve four-cylinder engine and four-speed gearbox, as used in the Anglia. A new standard model came with the same fittings as the former Deluxe version. The familiar Prefect name would last only one more season, not progressing into another form for the mid-1960s like the Anglia.

ESCORT/SQUIRE — 100E — FOUR — Unlike the Anglia and Prefect sedans, which switched to overhead-valve engines and four-speed gearboxes, the twin Estate Cars (station wagons) continued in their prior form. Power still came from an L-head four-cylinder engine, with three-speed transmission.

CONSUL Mk II — 204E — FOUR — No significant change was evident in the mid-range four-door sedan and convertible. Two versions of the 104-cid engine were produced, but only the higher-compression edition, which delivered 61 horsepower, was ordinarily imported into the U.S. Though still produced, the Estate Car version was no longer offered by U.S. dealers.

ZEPHYR/ZODIAC Mk II — 206E — SIX — Little change was evident in Ford's largest, most powerful models. As usual, the more luxurious Zodiac was the one most commonly imported into the U.S. marketplace. The Estate Car (station wagon) was no longer listed in U.S. directories.

I.D. DATA: Chassis numbers are stamped around the right front suspension upper mount, or on a plate attached to the front of the firewall. Engine numbers are stamped on the top face of the engine-mount pad (right side), or the right side of the block. Starting serial number: (Anglia/Prefect) 105E000001; (Escort/Squire) 100E587780; (Consul) 204E170644; (Zephyr/Zodiac) 206E154227.

Model	Body Type & Seating	Engine Type/CID	P.O.E. Price	Weight (lbs.)	Prod. Total
ANGLIA					
105E	2-dr Sedan-4/P	I4/61	1583	1625	Note 1
PREFECT					
107E	4-dr Sedan-4P	I4/61	1661	1765	Note 1
ESCORT/SQUIRE STATION WAGONS					
100E	2-dr Escort Wag-4P	I4/72	1651	1773	Note 1
100E	2-dr Squire Wag-4P	I4/72	1761	1816	Note 1
CONSUL Mk II					
204E	4-dr Sedan-5/6P	I4/104	2034	2395	Note 1
204E	2-dr Conv-5P	I4/104	2373	2473	Note 1
ZEPHYR Mk II					
206E	4-dr Sedan-5/6P	I6/156	2215	2582	Note 1
206E	2-dr Conv-5P	I6/156	2574	2605	Note 1
ZODIAC Mk II					
206E	4-dr Sedan-5/6P	I6/156	2387	2616	Note 1
206E	2-dr Conv-5P	I6/156	2865	2661	Note 1

Note 1: Approximately 23,602 British Fords were imported and sold in the U.S. in 1960.
Model Number Note: Some sources list the Prefect as 105E rather than 107E.

ENGINE DATA: BASE FOUR (Anglia, Prefect): Inline, overhead-valve four-cylinder. Cast iron block and head. Displacement: 61 cu. in. (997 cc). Bore & Stroke: 3.19 x 1.91 in. (81 x 48.4 mm). Compression Ratio: 8.9:1. Brake Horsepower: 41 at 5000 rpm. Torque: 55 lbs.-ft. at 2000 rpm. Three main bearings. Solid valve lifters. One Solex carburetor.

BASE FOUR (Escort, Squire): Inline, L-head four-cylinder. Cast iron block and head. Displacement: 71.55 cu. in. (1172 cc). Bore & Stroke: 2.50 x 3.64 in. (63.5 x 92.5 mm). Compression Ratio: 7.0:1. Brake Horsepower: 36 at 4500 rpm. Torque: 52 lbs.-ft. at 2500 rpm. Three main bearings. Solid valve lifters. One Solex carburetor.

BASE FOUR (Consul): Inline, overhead-valve four-cylinder. Cast iron block and head. Displacement: 103.9 cu. in. (1703 cc). Bore & Stroke: 3.25 x 3.13 in. (82.6 x 79.4 mm). Compression Ratio: 7.8:1 (6.9:1 optional). Brake Horsepower: 61/59 at 4400 rpm. Torque: 93/89 lbs.-ft. at 2300 rpm. Three main bearings. Solid valve lifters. One Zenith carburetor.

BASE SIX (Zephyr/Zodiac): Inline, overhead-valve six-cylinder. Cast iron block and head. Displacement: 155.8 cu. in. (2553 cc). Bore & Stroke: 3.25 x 3.13 in. (82.6 x 79.4 mm). Compression Ratio: 7.8:1 (6.9:1 optional). Brake Horsepower: 85 at 4400 rpm. Torque: 137 lbs.-ft. at 2000 rpm. Four main bearings. Solid valve lifters. One Zenith carburetor.

CHASSIS DATA: Wheelbase: (Anglia) 90.5 in.; (Prefect/Escort/Squire) 87 in.; (Consul) 104.5 in.; (Zephyr/Zodiac) 107 in. Overall Length: (Anglia) 153.5 in.; (Prefect) 150 in.; (Consul) 172.2 in.; (Zephyr) 178.5 in.; (Zodiac) 180.6 in. Height: (Anglia) 54.9 in.; (Prefect) 60 in.; (Escort) 63 in.; (Consul) 58.8 in.; (Zephyr/Zodiac) 59.3 in. Width: (Anglia) 57.5 in.; (Prefect) 60 in.; (Escort/Squire) 60.5 in.; (Consul) 68.6 in.; (Zephyr/Zodiac) 69 in. Front Tread: (Anglia) 46.0 in.; (Prefect/Escort/Squire) 48 in.; (Consul) 53 in.; (Zephyr/Zodiac) 53 in. Rear Tread: (Anglia) 45.8 in.; (Prefect/Escort/Squire) 47.5 in.; (Consul) 52 in.; (Zephyr/Zodiac) 52 in. Wheel Type: steel disc. Standard Tires: (Anglia/Prefect) 5.20x13; (Escort/Squire) 5.60x13; (Consul) 5.90x13; (Zephyr/Zodiac) 6.40x13.

TECHNICAL: Layout: front-engine, rear-drive. Transmission: three-speed manual except (Anglia/Prefect) four-speed manual. Standard Final Drive Ratio: (Anglia/Prefect) 4.125:1; (Escort/Squire) 4.43:1; (Consul) 4.11:1; (Zephyr/Zodiac) 3.90:1. Suspension (front): coil springs. Suspension (rear): rigid axle with semi-elliptic leaf springs. Brakes: hydraulic front/rear drum. Body Construction: steel unibody. Fuel Tank: (Anglia) 8.4 gal.; (Consul/Zephyr) 12.6 gal.

MAJOR OPTIONS: Automatic transmission (Zephyr/Zodiac). Overdrive transmission (Zephyr/Zodiac).

PERFORMANCE: Top Speed: (Anglia) 74-77 mph; (Consul) 78 mph. Acceleration (0-60 mph): N/A (Anglia, 0-50 mph in 16.7 sec. Acceleration (quarter-mile): (Anglia) 22.9 sec.

Manufacturer: Ford Motor Co. Ltd., Dagenham, Essex, England.
Distributor: Ford Motor Co., Dearborn, Michigan.
HISTORY: Introduced to U.S. market on October 1, 1959 except (Anglia) November 20, 1959. Anglia advertisements at this time featured a man in a lion costume, advising readers to "Get the LION's share of driving fun!"

1961 FORD (British)

1961 Ford Prefect four-door. (William Siuru Jr.)

ANGLIA — 105E — FOUR — No major change was evident on the two-door sedan, after its extensive restyling a year earlier. Power again came from an overhead-valve, 997-cc engine, hooked to a four-speed manual gearbox.

PREFECT — 107E — FOUR — For its final year in the Ford lineup, the Prefect four-door sedan continued with no notable change.

ESCORT — 100E — FOUR — The Prefect-based Squire Estate Car (station wagon) dropped out of the lineup first, but the Escort, based upon the older Anglia design, continued for another season without significant change. An L-head four-cylinder engine still provided the power, to a three-speed manual transmission.

CONSUL Mk II — 204E — FOUR — Front disc brakes became available on the mid-range Ford series this year, but no other major change was evident.

ZEPHYR/ZODIAC Mk II — 206E — SIX — No significant change took place in the largest models, except for the availability of front disc brakes.

I.D. DATA: Chassis numbers are stamped around the right front suspension upper mount, or on a plate attached to the front of the firewall. Engine numbers are stamped on the top face of the engine-mount pad (right side), or the right side of the block.

Model	Body Type & Seating	Engine Type/CID	P.O.E. Price	Weight (lbs.)	Prod. Total
ANGLIA					
105E	2-dr Sedan-4P	I4/61	1608	1625	Note 1
PREFECT					
107E	4-dr sedan-4P	I4/61	1686	1721	Note 1
ESCORT STATION WAGON					
100E	2-dr Sta Wag-4P	I4/72	1714	1791	Note 1

Model	Body Type & Seating	Engine Type/CID	P.O.E. Price	Weight (lbs.)	Prod. Total
CONSUL Mk II					
204E	4-dr Sedan-5/6P	I4/104	2059	2395	Note 1
204E	2-dr Conv-5P	I4/104	2398	2473	Note 1
ZEPHYR Mk II					
206E	4-dr Sedan-5/6P	I6/156	2240	2582	Note 1
206E	2-dr Conv-5P	I6/156	2599	2605	Note 1
ZODIAC Mk II					
206E	4-dr Sedan-5/6P	I6/156	2412	2616	Note 1
206E	2-dr Conv-5P	I6/156	2890	2661	Note 1

Note 1: Approximately 8,660 British Fords were imported and sold in the U.S. during 1961.

ENGINE DATA: BASE FOUR (Anglia, Prefect): Inline, overhead-valve four-cylinder. Cast iron block and head. **Displacement:** 61 cu. in. (997 cc). **Bore & Stroke:** 3.19 x 1.91 in. (81 x 48.4 mm). **Compression Ratio:** 8.9:1. **Brake Horsepower:** 41 at 5000 rpm. **Torque:** 55 lbs.-ft. at 2700 rpm. Three main bearings. Solid valve lifters. One Solex carburetor.

BASE FOUR (Escort): Inline, L-head four-cylinder. Cast iron block and head. **Displacement:** 71.55 cu. in. (1172 cc). **Bore & Stroke:** 2.50 x 3.64 in. (63.5 x 92.5 mm). **Compression Ratio:** 7.0:1. **Brake Horsepower:** 36 at 4500 rpm. **Torque:** 52 lbs.-ft. at 2500 rpm. Three main bearings. Solid valve lifters. One Zenith carburetor.

BASE FOUR (Consul): Inline, overhead-valve four-cylinder. Cast iron block and head. **Displacement:** 103.9 cu. in. (1703 cc). **Bore & Stroke:** 3.25 x 3.13 in. (82.6 x 79.4 mm). **Compression Ratio:** 7.8:1 (6.9:1 optional). **Brake Horsepower:** 61/59 at 4400 rpm. **Torque:** 93/89 lbs.-ft. at 2300 rpm. Three main bearings. Solid valve lifters. One Zenith carburetor.

BASE SIX (Zephyr/Zodiac Mk II): Inline, overhead-valve six-cylinder. Cast iron block and head. **Displacement:** 155.8 cu. in. (2553 cc). **Bore & Stroke:** 3.25 x 3.13 in. (82.6 x 79.4 mm). **Compression Ratio:** 7.8:1. **Brake Horsepower:** 85 at 4400 rpm. **Torque:** 137 lbs.-ft. at 2000 rpm. Four main bearings. Solid valve lifters. One Zenith carburetor.

CHASSIS DATA: Wheelbase: (Anglia) 90.5 in.; (Prefect/Escort) 87 in.; (Consul) 104.5 in.; (Zephyr/Zodiac) 107 in. **Overall Length:** (Anglia) 155.6 in.; (Prefect) 150 in.; (Escort) 142 in.; (Consul) 172.2 in.; (Zephyr) 178.5 in.; (Zodiac) 180.6 in. **Height:** (Anglia) 54.8 in.; (Prefect) 60 in.; (Escort) 63 in. **Width:** (Anglia) 57.5 in.; (Prefect) 60 in.; (Escort) 60.5 in.; (Consul) 68.6 in.; (Zephyr/Zodiac) 69 in. **Front Tread:** (Anglia) 46.3 in.; (Prefect/Escort/Squire) 48 in.; (Consul) 53 in.; (Zephyr/Zodiac) 53 in. **Rear Tread:** (Anglia) 46.1 in.; (Prefect/Escort/Squire) 47.5 in.; (Consul) 52 in.; (Zephyr/Zodiac) 52 in. **Wheel Type:** steel disc. **Standard Tires:** (Anglia/Prefect) 5.20x13; (Escort/Squire) 5.60x13; (Consul) 5.90x13; (Zephyr/Zodiac) 6.40x13.

TECHNICAL: Layout: front-engine, rear-drive. **Transmission:** three-speed manual except (Anglia/Prefect) four-speed. **Standard Final Drive Ratio:** (Anglia/Prefect) 4.125:1; (Consul) 4.11:1; (Zephyr/Zodiac) 3.90:1. **Suspension (front):** coil springs. **Suspension (rear):** rigid axle with semi-elliptic leaf springs. **Brakes:** hydraulic front/rear drum; front discs available on Consul/Zephyr/Zodiac. **Body Construction:** steel unibody. **Fuel Tank:** (Anglia) 8.4 gal.

MAJOR OPTIONS: Automatic transmission or overdrive (Zephyr/Zodiac). Overdrive (Consul).

PERFORMANCE: Top Speed: (Anglia) 77 mph; (Consul) 78 mph. **Fuel Mileage:** (Anglia) 44 mpg; (Consul) 23-28 mpg; (Zephyr) 23-25 mpg.

Manufacturer: Ford Motor Co. Ltd., Dagenham, Essex, England.
Distributor: Ford Motor Co., Dearborn, Michigan.

---

headlamps were used, with parking lights outboard of the headlamps. The sedan displayed a back-angled rear window, similar to that introduced earlier in the Anglia. A round 'Consul 315' emblem stood at the hood front, just above the grille; and 'Consul 315' script went below the right taillamp. Power was supplied by an 82-cid (1340-cc) overhead-valve, four-cylinder engine, producing 56.5 horsepower. Either a column-mounted or floor-mounted gearshift lever operated the four-speed transmission. Inside, a long parcel shelf went below the dashboard. In addition to the two- and four-door sedan, a Consul Capri hardtop coupe was introduced.

Note: Some Consul models in the former style were produced, using the 1703-cc engine, and called "Consul 375."

I.D. DATA: Chassis numbers are stamped around the right front suspension upper mount, or on a plate attached to the front of the firewall. Engine numbers are stamped on the top face of the engine-mount pad (right side), or the right side of the block.

Model	Body Type & Seating	Engine Type/CID	P.O.E. Price	Weight (lbs.)	Prod. Total
ANGLIA					
105E	2-dr Sedan-4P	I4/61	1524	1625	N/A
105E	2-dr DeL Sed-4P	I4/61	1573	1625	N/A
105E	2-dr Sta Wag-4P	I4/61	1754	1640	N/A
CONSUL 315					
109E	2-dr Sedan-4/5P	I4/82	1970	2025	N/A
109E	4-dr DeL Sed-4/5P	I4/82	2120	2080	N/A
CONSUL CAPRI					
109E	2-dr HT Cpe-2 + 2P	I4/82	2331	2025	N/A

ENGINE DATA: BASE FOUR (Anglia): Inline, overhead-valve four-cylinder. Cast iron block and head. **Displacement:** 61 cu. in. (997 cc). **Bore & Stroke:** 3.19 x 1.91 in. (81 x 48.4 mm). **Compression Ratio:** 8.9:1 (7.5:1 optional). **Brake Horsepower:** 41 at 5000 rpm. **Torque:** 55 lbs.-ft. at 2700 rpm. Three main bearings. Solid valve lifters. One Solex carburetor.

BASE FOUR (Consul/Capri): Inline, overhead-valve four-cylinder. Cast iron block and head. **Displacement:** 81.8 cu. in. (1340 cc). **Bore & Stroke:** 3.19 x 2.56 in. (81 x 65.1 mm). **Compression Ratio:** 8.5:1 (7.2:1 optional). **Brake Horsepower:** 56.5 at 5000 rpm. **Torque:** 76 lbs.-ft. at 2500 rpm. Three main bearings. Solid valve lifters. One Zenith carburetor.

CHASSIS DATA: Wheelbase: (Anglia) 90.5 in.; (Consul) 99 in. **Overall Length:** (Anglia) 153.5 in.; (Consul) 170.75 in. **Height:** (Anglia) 55 in.; (Consul) 56.3 in.; (Capri) 52.5 in. **Width:** (Anglia) 57.3 in.; (Consul) 65.25 in. **Front Tread:** (Anglia) 46.3 in.; (Consul) 49.5 in. **Rear Tread:** (Anglia) 46.1 in.; (Consul) 48.8 in. **Standard Tires:** (Anglia) 5.20x13; (Consul) 5.60x13.

TECHNICAL: Layout: front-engine, rear-drive. **Transmission:** four-speed manual. **Standard Final Drive Ratio:** (Anglia) 4.125:1; (Consul) 4.125:1. **Steering:** recirculating ball. **Suspension (front):** coil springs with anti-roll bar. **Suspension (rear):** rigid axle with semi-elliptic leaf springs. **Brakes:** hdraulic front/rear drum; front discs available on Consul. **Body Construction:** steel unibody. **Fuel Tank:** (Anglia) 8.4 gal.; (Consul) 10.8 gal.

PERFORMANCE: Top Speed: (Anglia) 75 mph; (Consul) 78 mph. **Fuel Milage:** (Anglia) 30-42 mpg; (Consul) 25-33 mpg.

Manufacturer: Ford Motor Co. Ltd., Dagenham, Essex, England.
Distributor: Ford Motor Co., Dearborn, Michigan.

HISTORY: Consul 315 was introduced to U.S. market in summer 1961.

1962 FORD (British)

1962 Ford Consul 315 two-door sedan.

ANGLIA — 105E — FOUR — The Prefect four-door disappeared, but the Anglia two-door, restyled for 1960 to a sharp-edged look, continued. The grille was restyled this year to a narrower form; its tight-mesh insert ended just inside of the bumper dividers. An emblem with 'ANGLIA' lettering went above the grille. Parking lights again were all the way at the edges of the front panel, at the ends of a chromed full-width bar that served as the upper limit of the grille. Styling features again included a back-angled rear window, "eyebrow" headlamps, and swing-out rear quarter windows. Power came again from an overhead-valve four-cylinder engine, producing 41 horsepower, hooked to a four-speed manual gearbox. Joining the usual two-door sedan, in standard or deluxe trim, was a station wagon version.

Note: Not only the Prefect, but the Escort station wagon, faded away this year.

CONSUL 315 — 109E — FOUR — A new model appeared for 1962, with sculptured bodysides, outward-rolled rear fenders with two round taillamps on each side, and an unusual grille that consisted of five chrome crosses (stars) spaced across the width of its rectangular opening. That grille layout allowed the use of a higher bumper. Quad round

---

1963 FORD (British)

1963 Ford Mark I Lotus two-door. (William Siuru Jr.)

ANGLIA — 105E — FOUR — No significant change was evident in Ford's two-door or station wagon. A small rectangular plate with Ford script was added to the lower rear edge of the right front fender.

CONSUL 315 — 109E — FOUR — Production of the Consul 315 two- and four-door sedan, and the Capri two-door hardtop coupe, continued with little change. Capri's bucket seats had crushed English leather facings over deep foam padding, with space in back for an occasional passenger. A small rectangular plate with Ford script was added to the lower rear edge of the right front fender.

CORTINA — 113E/116E — FOUR — A new name and a new model emerged this year, riding a 98-inch wheelbase and carrying a 1198-cc overhead-valve four-cylinder engine that developed 53.5 horsepower. The Cortina came in two- and four-door sedan form, and as a station wagon, with five-passenger seating capacity. Bodies wore stainless steel trim, while chassis made use of American-size fasteners. Seats, armrests and visors were foam-padded. The four-speed manual transmission was synchronized in each gear. Bucket seats went in front, with a sofa-style rear seat, all padded with foam rubber. Cortina's two-section grille displayed a tight mesh pattern, with a horizontal divider bar. Oval parking lights stood below each round headlamp. A low, simulated scoop sat at the front of the hood.

ZEPHYR/ZODIAC — Mk III — SIX — After a brief absence, the larger British Ford sedans were back again in a new form, but not necessarily imported on a regular basis. Under the hood was the same six-cylinder engine that powered the Mark II edition: 2553-cc displacement, now producing 98 horsepower in the Zephyr and 114 bhp in the Zodiac. Wheelbase was 107 inches, unchanged from the prior version.

I.D. DATA: Chassis numbers are stamped around the right front suspension upper mount, or on a plate attached to the front of the firewall. Engine numbers are stamped on the top face of the engine-mount pad (right side), or the right side of the block.

Model	Body Type & Seating	Engine Type/CID	P.O.E. Price	Weight (lbs.)	Prod. Total
ANGLIA					
105E	2-dr Sedan-4P	I4/61	1532	1625	N/A
105E	2-dr DeL Sed-4P	I4/61	1596	1625	N/A
105E	2-dr Sta Wag-4P	I4/61	1787	1640	N/A
CONSUL 315					
109E	2-dr Sedan-4/5P	I4/82	1980	2025	N/A
109E	4-dr DeL Sed-4/5P	I4/82	2130	2080	N/A
CAPRI					
109E	2-dr HT Cpt-2+2P	I4/82	2210	2025	N/A
CORTINA					
113E	2-dr DeL Sed-5P	I4/73	1820	1775	N/A
113E	4-dr DeL Sed-5P	I4/73	1872	1775	N/A
116E	4-dr Sta Wag-5P	I4/91	N/A	1832	N/A
ZEPHYR/ZODIAC Mk III					
Zephyr	4-dr Sed-6P	I6/156	2656	2740	N/A
Zodiac	4-dr Sed-6P	I6/156	3046	2800	N/A

Availability Note: Consul 315, Zephyr and Zodiac were available in the U.S. on special order only.

ENGINE DATA: BASE FOUR (Anglia): Inline, overhead-valve four-cylinder. Cast iron block and head. **Displacement:** 60.8 cu. in. (997 cc). **Bore & Stroke:** 3.19 x 1.91 in. (81 x 48.4 mm). **Compression Ratio:** 8.9:1. **Brake Horsepower:** 41 at 5000 rpm. **Torque:** 55 lbs.-ft. at 2700 rpm. Three main bearings. Solid valve lifters. One Solex carburetor.

BASE FOUR (Cortina): Inline, overhead-valve four-cylinder. Cast iron block and head. **Displacement:** 73.1 cu. in. (1198 cc). **Bore & Stroke:** 3.19 x 2.29 in. (81 x 58 mm). **Compression Ratio:** 8.7:1. **Brake Horsepower:** 53.5 at 5000 rpm. **Torque:** 68.5 lbs.-ft. at 2700 rpm. Three main bearings. Solid valve lifters. One Zenith carburetor.

BASE FOUR (Consul/Capri): Inline, overhead-valve four-cylinder. Cast iron block and head. **Displacement:** 81.8 cu. in. (1340 cc). **Bore & Stroke:** 3.19 x 2.56 in. (81 x 65.1 mm). **Compression Ratio:** 8.5:1 (7.2:1 optional). **Brake Horsepower:** 56.5 at 5000 rpm. **Torque:** 76 lbs.-ft. at 2500 rpm. Three main bearings. Solid valve lifters. One Zenith carburetor.

BASE FOUR (Cortina wagon); OPTIONAL (Cortina): Inline, overhead-valve four-cylinder. Cast iron block. **Displacement:** 91.5 cu. in. (1498 cc). **Bore & Stroke:** 3.19 x 2.86 in. (81 x 72.7 mm). **Compression Ratio:** 9.0:1. **Brake Horsepower:** 64 at 4600 rpm. Five main bearings. Solid valve lifters. One Weber carburetor.

BASE SIX (Zephyr/Zodiac): Inline, overhead-valve six-cylinder. Cast iron block and head. **Displacement:** 156 cu. in. (2553 cc). **Bore & Stroke:** 3.25 x 3.13 in. (82.5 x 79.5 mm). **Compression Ratio:** 8.3:1. **Brake Horsepower:** (Zephyr) 98 at 4750 rpm; (Zodiac) 114 at 4800. **Torque:** up to 141 lbs.-ft. at 2400 rpm. Four main bearings. Solid valve lifters. One Zenith carburetor.

CHASSIS DATA: Wheelbase: (Anglia) 90.5 in.; (Consul) 99 in.; (Cortina) 98 in.; (Zephyr/Zodiac) 107 in. **Overall Length:** (Anglia) 154.25 in.; (Consul/Capri) 170.8 in.; (Cortina) 168.3 in.; (Zephyr/Zodiac) 182 in. **Height:** (Anglia) 55.5 in.; (Consul Capri) 52.5 in.; (Cortina) 54.6 in.; (Zephyr/Zodiac) 55.5 in. **Width:** (Anglia) 57.3 in.; (Consul/Capri) 65.2 in.; (Cortina) 62.5 in.; (Zephyr/Zodiac) 69 in. **Front Tread:** (Anglia) 46.3 in.; (Consul/Capri) 49.5 in.; (Cortina) 49.5 in. **Rear Tread:** (Anglia) 46.1 in.; (Consul/Capri) 48.8 in.; (Cortina) 49.5 in. **Wheel Type:** steel disc. **Standard Tires:** (Anglia) 5.20x13; (Anglia wag) 5.60x13; (Consul) 5.60x13; (Cortina) 5.60x13; (Cortina wag) 6.00 x 13; (Zephyr/Zodiac) 6.40x13.

TECHNICAL: Layout: front-engine, rear-drive. **Transmission:** four-speed manual (all synchromesh on Cortina). Overall Capri gear ratios: (1st) 16.99:1; (2nd) 9.88:1; (3rd) 5.83:1; (4th) 4.125:1. Overall Cortina gear ratios: (1st) 14.62:1; (2nd) 9.883:1; (3rd) 5.824:1; (4th) 4.125:1. **Standard Final Drive Ratio:** (Anglia) 4.125:1; (Consul) 4.125:1; (Cortina) 4.125:1; (Zephyr/Zodiac) 3.55:1. **Steering:** recirculating ball. **Suspension (front):** coil springs with anti-roll bar. **Suspension (rear):** rigid axle with semi-elliptic leaf springs. **Brakes:** front/rear drum except (Capri/Zodiac) front disc, rear drum. **Body Construction:** steel unibody. **Fuel Tank:** (Anglia) 8.4 gal.; (Capri) 9 gal.; (Cortina) 9.6 gal.; (Zephyr) 10.4 gal.

MAJOR OPTIONS: Automatic transmission: Zephyr/Zodiac ($257). 1498-cc engine (Cortina). Fresh-air heater/defroster. Whitewall tires. Oversize 5.60x13 tires (Cortina). Wheel trims.

PERFORMANCE: Similar to 1962.

Manufacturer: Ford Motor Co. Ltd., Dagenham, Essex, England.

Distributor: Ford Motor Co., Dearborn, Michigan.

HISTORY: Introduced to U.S. market on September 1, 1962. The Mark III Zephyr/Zodiac debuted in spring 1962. "Rakish, debonair with a sports car flair" was Ford's description of the Capri coupe, billed as "a special kind of car for a special kind of people."

1964 FORD (British)

ANGLIA — 105E — FOUR — No change was evident on the basic Anglia two-door sedan, but a new Super model was added. That one carried a 53.5-horsepower Cortina engine instead of the usual 41-bhp powerplant, and came with two-tone body paint as well as bodyside flashes.

CAPRI — 109E/118E — FOUR — A new GT version of the Capri hardtop coupe had a large badge on the right rear panel, below the taillamps. A short gearshift lever went between the bucket seats. Otherwise, the coupe continued with little change. Power came from a 1498-cc (91-cid) engine, as in the Cortina GT.

CORTINA — FOUR — Each Cortina had a restyled dashboad this year, featuring large round instruments. A new GT model displayed dual chrome bodyside strips in a narrow "V" arrangement, coming to a point just behind the headlamps. A shield-shaped medallion went on the GT's rear fenders, just ahead of the downward jut of the lower chrome bodyside strip. Inside was a short gearshift lever and center console, between the bucket seats. Instead of the customary Cortina 73-cid engine, the GT carried a 91-cid version that produced 78 horsepower. Standard GT equipment included a tachometer.

ZODIAC — SIX — Production of the revived six-cylinder Ford continued with little change.

I.D. DATA: Chassis numbers are stamped around the right front suspension upper mount, or on a plate attached to the front of the firewall. Engine numbers are stamped on the top face of the engine-mount pad (right side), or the right side of the block.

Model	Body Type & Seating	Engine Type/CID	P.O.E. Price	Weight (lbs.)	Prod. Total
ANGLIA					
105E	2-dr Std Sed-4P	I4/61	1522	1580	Note 1
105E	2-dr DeL Sed-4P	I4/61	1586	1580	Note 1
105E	2-dr Super Sed-4P	I4/73	1715	1607	Note 1
105E	2-dr Sta Wag-5P	I4/61	1777	1730	Note 1
CAPRI					
109E	2-dr Coupe-2+2P	I4/82	2210	1935	Note 1
118E	2-dr GT Cpe-2+2P	I4/91	2800	2020	Note 1
CORTINA					
113E	2-dr DeL Sed-5P	I4/73	1809	1650	Note 1
113E	4-dr DeL Sed-5P	I4/73	1872	1731	Note 1
116E	2-dr Sta Wag-5P	I4/91	2096	1878	Note 1
118E	2-dr GT Sed-4/5P	I4/91	2225	1739	Note 1
118E	4-dr GT Sed-4/5P	I4/91	2289	1739	Note 1
ZODIAC Mk III					
	4-dr Sed-6P	I6/156	3036	2800	Note 1

Note 1: Approximately 4,100 British Fords were sold in the U.S. during 1964.

Model Availability Note: Some sources also list the Consul 315 two- and four-door sedans as being available again this year, priced at $1980 and $2130 (respectively); see previous listing for details.

ENGINE DATA: BASE FOUR (Anglia): Inline, overhead-valve four-cylinder. Cast iron block and head. **Displacement:** 60.8 cu. in. (997 cc). **Bore & Stroke:** 3.19 x 1.91 in. (81 x 48.4 mm). **Compression Ratio:** 8.9:1. **Brake Horsepower:** 41 at 5000 rpm. **Torque:** 55 lbs.-ft. at 2700 rpm. Three main bearings. Solid valve lifters. One Solex carburetor.

BASE FOUR (Anglia Super, Cortina sedan): Inline, overhead-valve four-cylinder. Cast iron block and head. **Displacement:** 73.1 cu. in. (1198 cc). **Bore & Stroke:** 3.19 x 2.29 in. (81 x 58 mm). **Compression Ratio:** 8.7:1. **Brake Horsepower:** 53.5 at 5000 rpm. **Torque:** 68.5 lbs.-ft. at 2700 rpm. Three main bearings. Solid valve lifters. One Zenith carburetor.

BASE FOUR (Capri): Inline, overhead-valve four-cylinder. Cast iron block and head. **Displacement:** 81.8 cu. in. (1340 cc). **Bore & Stroke:** 3.19 x 2.56 in. (81 x 65.1 mm). **Compression Ratio:** 8.5:1 (7.2:1 optional). **Brake Horsepower:** 56.5 at 5000 rpm. **Torque:** 76 lbs.-ft. at 2500 rpm. Three main bearings. Solid valve lifters. One Zenith carburetor.

BASE FOUR (Capri GT, Cortina GT): Inline, overhead-valve four-cylinder. **Displacement:** 91.5 cu. in. (1498 cc). **Bore & Stroke:** 3.19 x 2.86 in. (81 x 72.7 mm). **Compression Ratio:** 9.0:1. **Brake Horsepower:** 78 (SAE) at 5200 rpm. **Torque:** 91 lbs.-ft. at 3600 rpm. Five main bearings. Solid valve lifters. One Weber carburetor.

BASE FOUR (Cortina wagon): Same as 91.5-cid engine above, but 64 bhp.

Note: Some sources claim the GT engine produced 84 bhp.

BASE SIX (Zodiac): Inline, overhead-valve six-cylinder. Cast iron block and head. **Displacement:** 156 cu. in. (2553 cc). **Bore & Stroke:** 3.25 x 3.13 in. (82.5 x 79.5 mm). **Compression Ratio:** 8.3:1. **Brake Horsepower:** 114 at 4800. **Torque:** up to 141 lbs.-ft. at 2400 rpm. Four main bearings. Solid valve lifters. One Zenith carburetor.

CHASSIS DATA: Wheelbase: (Zodiac) 107 in. **Overall Length:** (Anglia) 155.6 in.; (Anglia wag) 154.1 in.; (Capri) 170.8 in.; (Cortina) 168.3 in.; (Cortina GT) 170 in.; (Zodiac) 182. in. **Height:** (Anglia) 54.8 in.; (Capri) 52.5 in.; (Cortina) 56.6 in.; (Cortina GT) 56.8 in.; (Zodiac) 55.5 in. **Width:** (Anglia) 57.3 in.; (Capri) 65.2 in.; (Cortina) 62.5 in.; (Zodiac) 69 in. **Front Tread:** (Anglia) 46.3 in.; (Capri) 49.5 in.; (Capri GT) 49 in.; (Cortina) 49.5 in. **Rear Tread:** (Anglia) 46.1 in.; (Capri) 48.8 in.; (Capri GT) 49 in.; (Cortina) 49.5 in. **Wheel Type:** steel disc. **Standard Tires:** (Anglia) 5.20x13; (Anglia wag) 5.60 x 13; (Capri) 5.60x13; (Cortina) 5.60x13; (Cortina wag) 6.00x13; (Cortina GT) 5.60x13 or 165x13; (Zodiac) 6.40x13.

TECHNICAL: Layout: front-engine, rear-drive. **Transmission:** four-speed manual (all synchromesh on Anglia Super, Capri GT, Cortina and Zodiac). **Standard Final Drive Ratio:** (Anglia) 4.125:1; (Capri) 4.125:1; (Cortina) 4.125:1; (Cortina GT) 3.90:1. **Steering:** recirculating ball. **Suspension (front):** coil springs. **Suspension (rear):** rigid axle with semi-elliptic leaf springs. **Brakes:** hydraulic front/rear drum except (Cortina GT, Capri GT and Zodiac) front disc, rear drum. **Body Construction:** steel unibody. **Fuel Tank:** (Anglia) 8.4 gal.; (Cortina) 9.6 gal.; (Cortina GT) 10 gal.; (Capri) 9 gal.; (Capri GT) 10.8 gal.; (Zodiac) 10.4 gal,

MAJOR OPTIONS: Automatic transmission: Cortina (except GT) and Zodiac.

PERFORMANCE: Top Speed: (Anglia) 70 mph cruising; (Cortina) 80 mph cruising; (Cortina GT) 90 mph cruising, about 100 mph maximum. **Acceleration (0-60 mph):** (Cortina GT) 12.3 sec. **Acceleration (quarter-mile):** (Cortina GT) 18.7 sed. **Fuel Mileage:** (Anglia) 35-40 mpg; (Cortina) 32 mpg; (Cortina GT) 27 mpg.

Manufacturer: Ford Motor Co. Ltd., Dagenham, Essex, England.

Distributor: Ford Motor Co., Dearborn, Michigan.

HISTORY: Introduced to U.S. market on September 1, 1963. A Lotus-Cortina was already available in England, with the same 105-bhp twin-cam Ford engine used in the Lotus Elan sports car; see 1966 listing for details.

1965 FORD (British)

ANGLIA 1200 — 123E — FOUR — No major visible change was evident in the Anglia two-door sedan, but examples that crossed the Atlantic now carried the larger (1198-cc) four-cylinder engine that had powered the Super in 1964, and become available in England during 1962.

Note: Although the Capri hardtop coupe continued to be listed in some U.S. directories, it was no longer officially available.

CORTINA 1500 — FOUR — A new grille consisted of one heavy horizontal bar that formed a unit with the lower bar, with thinner horizontal bars spaced between them. Round tri-section taillamps were used. New "aeroflow" vent outlets went into rear quarter panels. Cortinas now stopped with front disc brakes. Otherwise, little was new. Both standard and GT sedans were available.

I.D. DATA: Serial numbers are on the firewall or the right side of the engine compartment, under the hood.

Model	Body Type & Seating	Engine Type/CID	P.O.E. Price	Weight (lbs.)	Prod. Total
ANGLIA 1200					
123E	2-dr DeL Sed-4P	I4/73	1598	1625	Note 1

Model	Body Type & Seating	Engine Type/CID	P.O.E. Price	Weight (lbs.)	Prod. Total
CORTINA 1500					
113E	2-dr Sedan-4/5P	I4/91	1796	1744	Note 1
113E	4-dr Sedan-4/5P	I4/91	1920	1803	Note 1
116E	4-dr Sta Wag-4/5P	I4/91	2142	1878	Note 1
118E	2-dr GT Sed-4/5P	I4/91	2162	1870	Note 1

Note 1: Approximately 4,810 British Fords were sold in the U.S. during 1965.

ENGINE DATA: BASE FOUR (Anglia): Inline, overhead-valve four-cylinder. Cast iron block and head. **Displacement:** 73.1 cu. in. (1198 cc). **Bore & Stroke:** 3.19 x 2.29 in. (81 x 58 mm). **Compression Ratio:** 8.7:1. **Brake Horsepower:** 53.5 at 5000 rpm. **Torque:** 66.5 lbs.-ft. at 2700 rpm. Five main bearings. Solid valve lifters. One Solex carburetor.
BASE FOUR (Cortina): Inline, overhead-valve four-cylinder. Cast iron block and head. **Displacement:** 91.4 cu. in. (1498 cc). **Bore & Stroke:** 3.19 x 2.86 in. (81 x 72.7 mm). **Compression Ratio:** 8.3:1 except (GT) 9.0:1. **Brake Horsepower:** 64 at 4500 rpm except (GT) 84 at 5200. **Torque:** 85.5 lbs.-ft. at 2300 rpm except (GT) 97 at 3600. Five main bearings. Solid valve lifters. One carburetor.
CHASSIS DATA: Wheelbase: (Anglia) 90.5 in.; (Cortina) 98 in. **Overall Length:** (Anglia) 153.5 in.; (Cortina) 168.5 in. **Height:** (Anglia) 56.5 in.; (Cortina) 54.3 in. **Width:** (Anglia) 57.3 in.; (Cortina) 62.5 in. **Front Tread:** (Anglia) 46.0 in.; (Cortina) 49.5 in. **Rear Tread:** (Anglia) 48.3 in.; (Cortina) 49.5 in. **Wheel Type:** steel disc. **Standard Tires:** (Anglia) 5.20x13; (Cortina) 5.60x13; (Cortina wag) 6.00x13.
TECHNICAL: Layout: front-engine, rear-drive. **Transmission:** four-speed manual. **Standard Final Drive Ratio:** (Anglia) 4.125:1; (others) 3.90:1. **Steering:** recirculating ball. **Suspension (front):** MacPherson struts with coil springs and anti-roll bar. **Suspension (rear):** rigid axle with semi-elliptic leaf springs. **Brakes:** front/rear drum except (Cortina) front disc, rear drum. **Body Construction:** steel unibody. **Fuel Tank:** (Anglia) 8.4 gal.; (Cortina) 9.6 gal.
Manufacturer: Ford Motor Co. Ltd., Dagenham, Essex, England.
Distributor: Ford Motor Co., Dearborn, Michigan.
HISTORY: Introduced to U.S. market on September 1, 1964. In England, a new Corsair series for the home market, wearing a front end similar to that of the 1961 Thunderbird, introduced a V-4 engine.

1966 FORD
(British)

1966 Ford Mark III Zephyr Estate Wagon. (William Siuru Jr.)

ANGLIA 1200 — FOUR — No major change was visible on the two-door sedan, which carried the 53.5-horsepower engine that had formerly powered Super models.

CORTINA 1500 — FOUR — No significant change was evident on the basic Cortina sedans and station wagon. As before, the GT sedan carried a more powerful version of the 91.5-cid four-cylinder engine, rated 84 horsepower.

LOTUS CORTINA — FOUR — Performance enthusiasts finally had the option of a Lotus-powered Ford, as introduced in England during 1963. The dual-overhead-cam four-cylinder engine was essentially a slightly enlarged version of the basic Ford powerplant, but carried a Lotus-developed cylinder head and twin two-barrel Weber carburetors. Lotus versions were easy to spot, because all were painted white with distinctive tapered olive-green bodyside paint striping that reached around the rear panel, and a blackout grille. Lotus badges replaced the customary GT badges on the trunk and rear side panels. Special Lotus features included a brushed-aluminum instrument panel and Smiths instruments, including a tachometer. The upholstery got extra padding and black vinyl covering, and a simulated wood steering wheel was installed. Lotus editions were lower than stock Cortinas and rode wider wheels/tires.

I.D. DATA: Serial number is on the right fender, under the hood.

Model	Body Type & Seating	Engine Type/CID	P.O.E. Price	Weight (lbs.)	Prod. Total
ANGLIA 1200					
123E	2-dr DeL Sed-4P	I4/73	1569	1685	Note 1
CORTINA 1500					
113E	2-dr Sedan-4/5P	I4/91	1765	1744	Note 1
113E	4-dr Sedan-4/5P	I4/91	1885	1803	Note 1
116E	4-dr Sta Wag-4/5P	I4/91	2102	1878	Note 1
118E	2-dr GT Sed-4/5P	I4/91	2122	1870	Note 1
LOTUS CORTINA					
125E	2-dr Sedan-4/5P	I4/95	3420	2038	Note 2

Note 1: Approximately 7,932 British Fords were imported into the U.S. during 1966.
Note 2: A total of 2,927 Lotus Cortinas (Mark I series) were produced from 1963-66.

1966 Ford Mark III Zodiac four-door. (William Siuru Jr.)

ENGINE DATA: BASE FOUR (Anglia): Inline, overhead-valve four-cylinder. Cast iron block and head. **Displacement:** 73.1 cu. in. (1198 cc). **Bore & Stroke:** 3.19 x 2.29 in. (81 x 58.2 mm). **Compression Ratio:** 9.0:1. **Brake Horsepower:** 53.5 at 5000 rpm. **Torque:** 66.5 lbs.-ft. at 2700 rpm. Five main bearings. Solid valve lifters. One Solex carburetor.
BASE FOUR (Cortina): Inline, overhead-valve four-cylinder. Cast iron block and head. **Displacement:** 91.4 cu. in. (1498 cc). **Bore & Stroke:** 3.19 x 2.86 in. (81 x 72.7 mm). **Compression Ratio:** 8.3:1 except (GT) 9.0:1. **Brake Horsepower:** 65 at 4500 rpm except (GT) 84 at 5200. **Torque:** 85.5 lbs.-ft. at 2300 rpm except (GT) 97 at 3600. Five main bearings. Solid valve lifters. One carburetor.
BASE FOUR (Lotus Cortina): Inline, dual-overhead-cam four-cylinder. Cast iron block and light alloy head. **Displacement:** 95.1 cu. in. (1588 cc). **Bore & Stroke:** 3.25 x 2.86 in. (82.7 x 72.7 mm). **Compression Ratio:** 9.5:1. **Brake Horsepower:** 115 at 5700 rpm. **Torque:** 108 lbs.-ft. at 4000 rpm. Five main bearings. Solid valve lifters. Two Weber two-barrel carburetors.
CHASSIS DATA: Wheelbase: (Anglia) 90.5 in.; (Cortina) 98 in. **Overall Length:** (Anglia) 153.5 in.; (Cortina) 168.5 in.; (Lotus) 168.3 in. **Height:** (Anglia) 56.5 in.; (Cortina) 54.3 in.; (Lotus) 53.4 in. **Width:** (Anglia) 57.3 in.; (Cortina) 62.5 in.; (Lotus) 51.5 in. **Front Tread:** (Anglia) 46.0 in.; (Cortina) 49.5 in.; (Lotus) 51.5 in. **Rear Tread:** (Anglia) 48.3 in.; (Cortina) 49.5 in.; (Lotus) 50.5 in. **Wheel Type:** steel disc. **Standard Tires:** (Anglia) 5.20x13; (Cortina) 5.60x13; (Cortina wag/Lotus) 6.00x13.
TECHNICAL: Layout: front-engine, rear-drive. **Transmission:** four-speed manual. **Standard Final Drive Ratio:** (Anglia) 4.125:1; (Cortina) 3.90:1; (Lotus) 4.125:1. **Steering:** recirculating ball. **Suspension (front):** MacPherson struts with coil springs and anti-sway bar. **Suspension (rear):** rigid axle with semi-elliptic leaf springs (torque arms on GT and Lotus). **Brakes:** (Anglia) front/rear drum; (Cortina) front disc, rear drum. **Body Construction:** steel unibody.
MAJOR OPTIONS: Automatic transmission (except GT).
PERFORMANCE: Top Speed: (Anglia) 84 mph; (Cortina) 84-85 mph; (Cortina GT) 91 mph; (Lotus) 110 mph. **Acceleration (0-60 mph):** (Cortina) 19.0 sec.; (Cortina GT) 12.1 sec.; (Lotus) 9.6 sec. **Acceleration (quarter-mile):** (Lotus) 16.5 sec. (81 mph). **Fuel Mileage:** (Anglia) 31 mpg; (Cortina) 27 mpg; (Cortina GT) 25 mpg; (Lotus) 17 mpg.
Manufacturer: Ford Motor Co. Ltd., Dagenham, Essex, England.
Distributor: Ford Motor Co., Dearborn, Michigan.
HISTORY: Introduced to U.S. market on September 1, 1965. The Lotus Cortina was the joint work of Colin Chapman, designer of Lotus racing cars, and Ford of Britain. Production of the Mark I Lotus Cortina began in 1963. In addition to the special engine, they used lightweight body panels. Assembly was done at Lotus, using parts supplied by Ford. Another Lotus version was produced after 1966, based upon the restyled Cortina, but was not imported to the U.S. Those later examples were built at the Ford plant rather than at Lotus.

1967 FORD
(British)

ANGLIA 1200 — FOUR — No significant change was evident on the two-door Anglia sedan. Powertrain was again the 73.1-cid four-cylinder engine, hooked to a four-speed manual gearbox. The Anglia's most noted styling feature continued to be its reverse-angled back window.

CORTINA 1500 — FOUR — The Cortina series started off identical to the 1966 models, until mid-February when the Model C debuted. The new body style was said to have a "distinctly American flair." Just a fraction of an inch shorter, and riding the same 98-inch wheelbase as before, the new body was some two inches wider, with curved doors and window glass. A wide new grille ran between the round headlamps, and consisted of four sections, each with a pattern of horizontal strips. Width grew by two inches, and both front and rear tread dimensions increased substantially. The GT model no longer had the distinctive chrome side flashes, but wore small badges on each rear quarter panel, as well as on the trunk lid. Both two-door and four-door GTs were available, with lower bodyside striping and 'GT' identification on the lower front fender. Inside was a restyled interior with instruments and controls positioned ahead of the driver, plus a console and sports shifter. Standard bucket seats had color-keyed vinyl leatherette upholstery. Standard safety features included a padded dashboard and sunvisors, four-way flashers, dual braking system, backup lights, and an outside mirror. See next listing for details on the Model C's 1600 engine.

I.D. DATA: Serial number is on the right fender, under the hood.

Model	Body Type & Seating	Engine Type/CID	P.O.E. Price	Weight (lbs.)	Prod. Total
ANGLIA 1200					
22	2-dr DeL Sed-4P	I4/73	1569	1607	Note 1
CORTINA 1500					
74	2-dr Sedan-4/5P	I4/91	1815	1710	Note 1
76	4-dr Sedan-4/5P	I4/91	1935	1731	Note 1
87	4-dr Sta Wag-4/5P	I4/91	2152	1878	Note 1
77	2-dr GT Sed-4/5P	I4/91	2172	1739	Note 1
75	4-dr GT Sed-4/5P	I4/91	2291	1739	Note 1

Note 1: Approximately 16,193 British Fords were imported into the U.S. during 1967.
Model Availability Note: Some sources listed the Cortina Lotus as available for 1967, while others omitted it after 1966 (though production continued as late as 1970); see previous listing for details.

ENGINE DATA: BASE FOUR (Anglia): Inline, overhead-valve four-cylinder. Cast iron block and head. **Displacement:** 73.1 cu. in. (1198 cc). **Bore & Stroke:** 3.19 x 2.29 in. (81 x 58.2 mm). **Compression Ratio:** 9.0:1. **Brake Horsepower:** 53.5 at 5000 rpm. **Torque:** 66.5 lbs.-ft. at 2700 rpm. Five main bearings. Solid valve lifters. One Solex carburetor.
BASE FOUR (Cortina 1500): Inline, overhead-valve four-cylinder. Cast iron block and head. **Displacement:** 91.4 cu. in. (1499 cc). **Bore & Stroke:** 3.19 x 2.87 in. (81 x 72.8 mm). **Compression Ratio:** 8.3:1 except (GT) 9.0:1. **Brake Horsepower:** 64 at 4500 rpm except (GT) 84 at 5200. **Torque:** 89 lbs.-ft. at 2500 rpm except (GT) 98 at 3600. Five main bearings. Solid valve lifters. One Solex carburetor except (GT) twin-choke Weber.
Note: See 1968 listing for details on the Cortina 1600 engine.

CHASSIS DATA: Wheelbase: (Anglia) 90.5 in.; (Cortina) 98 in. **Overall Length:** (Anglia) 153.5 in.; (Cortina) 168 in. **Height:** (Anglia) 56.6 in.; (Cortina) 54.3-54.5 in. **Width:** (Anglia) 57 in.; (Cortina) 62.5 in. **Front Tread:** (Anglia) 46.0 in.; (Cortina) 49.5 in. **Rear Tread:** (Anglia) 48.3 in.; (Cortina) 49.5 in. **Wheel Type:** steel disc. **Standard Tires:** (Anglia) 5.20x13; (Cortina) 5.60x13; (Cortina wag) 6.00x13; (Cortina GT) 165x13 optional.
Note: Model C Cortina was 64.9 inches wide, with 52.5-inch front track and 51-inch rear track.

TECHNICAL: Layout: front-engine, rear-drive. **Transmission:** four-speed manual (fully synchronized). **Standard Final Drive Ratio:** (Anglia) 4.125:1; (Cortina) 3.90:1. **Steering:** recirculating ball. **Suspension (front):** MacPherson struts with coil springs and anti-sway bar. **Suspension (rear):** rigid axle with semi-elliptic leaf springs (torque arms on GT). **Brakes:** (Anglia) front/rear drum; (Cortina) front disc, rear drum. **Body Construction:** steel unibody.

MAJOR OPTIONS: Automatic transmission (except GT).

PERFORMANCE: Top Speed: (Anglia) up to 84 mph; (Cortina) 84-85 mph; (Cortina GT) 91 mph. **Acceleration (0-60 mph):** (Cortina) 19.0-19.5 sec.; (Cortina GT) 12.1 sec. **Fuel Mileage:** (Anglia) 31 mpg; (Cortina) 27 mpg; (Cortina GT) 25 mpg.
Manufacturer: Ford Motor Co. Ltd., Dagenham, Essex, England.
Distributor: Ford Motor Co., Dearborn, Michigan.
HISTORY: Introduced to U.S. market on September 1, 1966.

1968 FORD
(British)

CORTINA 1600 — FOUR — As the 1968 model year began, Ford's Cortina series adopted a larger (1599-cc) four-cylinder engine, and became known popularly as the Model "C" Ford. The new "1600" crossflow engine had the carburetor and exhaust system on opposite sides, and the combustion chamber formed into the piston top. The cylinder-head portion was now flat. As part of the change, the car's battery moved from the right to the left side of the engine compartment. Later in the model year, a number of safety changes were made, in accordance with Federal (U.S.) regulations. Two separate amber turn signal lamps were mounted on the grille, inside each headlamp. Side markers went on each front fender, and at the rear of the station wagon. Dashboards held more padding, and all knobs and gauges were recessed. Finally, the GT's instrument cluster moved to the main part of the dashboard. Cortina's GT package included a tachometer, stiffer springs and shocks, radial tires, higher-powered engine (with modified carburetion and camshaft), and a close-ratio four-speed gearbox.
Note: The Anglia was no longer offered to U.S. customers, though it remained available in Britain in 1968.

I.D. DATA: Serial number is on the right fender, under the hood.

Model	Body Type & Seating	Engine Type/CID	P.O.E. Price	Weight (lbs.)	Prod. Total
CORTINA 1600					
92	2-dr Sedan-4/5P	I4/97	1873	1974	Note 1
93	4-dr Sedan-4/5P	I4/97	1993	2013	Note 1
98	4-dr Sta Wag-4/5P	I4/97	2208	2154	Note 1
96	2-dr GT Sed-4/5P	I4/97	2243	2028	Note 1
97	4-dr GT Sed-4/5P	I4/97	2363	2066	Note 1

Note 1: Of the 553,791 British Fords produced in 1968, approximately 22,983 were imported into the U.S.

ENGINE DATA: BASE FOUR: Inline, overhead-valve four-cylinder. Cast iron block and head. **Displacement:** 97.5 cu. in. (1599 cc). **Bore & Stroke:** 3.19 x 3.06 in. (81 x 77.6 mm). **Compression Ratio:** up to 9.0:1. **Brake Horsepower:** 71 at 5000 rpm except (GT) 88 at 5400. **Torque:** 91.5 lbs.-ft. at 2500 rpm except (GT) 96.6 at 3600. Five main bearings. Solid valve lifters. One Ford-Autolite carburetor except (GT) two-barrel Weber.

CHASSIS DATA: Wheelbase: 98 in. **Overall Length:** (sed) 168.5 in.; (wag) 169.5 in. **Height:** 54.7 in. **Width:** 64.9 in. **Front Tread:** 52.5 in. **Rear Tread:** 51 in. **Standard Tires:** 5.60x13 except (GT) 165x13.

TECHNICAL: Layout: front-engine, rear-drive. **Transmission:** four-speed manual (fully synchronized). GT gear ratios: (1st) 2.972:1; (2nd) 2.01:1; (3rd) 1.397:1; (4th) 1.00:1. **Standard Final Drive Ratio:** 3.90:1. **Steering:** recirculating ball. **Suspension (front):** MacPherson struts with coil springs and anti-sway bar. **Suspension (rear):** rigid axle with semi-elliptic leaf springs. **Brakes:** front disc, rear drum. **Body Construction:** steel unibody. **Fuel Tank:** (GT) 12.0 gal.

MAJOR OPTIONS: Automatic transmission (except GT).

PERFORMANCE: Top Speed: (Cortina) 87 mph; (GT) 95-102 mph. **Acceleration (0-60 mph):** (GT) 14.9 sec. **Acceleration (quarter-mile):** (GT) 18.8 sec. (72.5 mph). **Fuel Mileage:** (Cortina) about 26 mpg; (GT) 24-28 mpg.
Manufacturer: Ford Motor Co. Ltd., Dagenham, Essex, England.
Distributor: Ford Motor Co., Dearborn, Michigan.

1969 FORD
(British)

1969 Ford Mark II Cortina. (William Siuru Jr.)

CORTINA — FOUR — Two new base models were added this year. The GT had a new racing stripe and wood dashboard. Park/signal lamps moved below the front fender, and a new short-throw gearshift lever was installed. Mechanical changes included an automatic choke, high-output generator, aluminized exhaust system, and heavy-duty heater. Otherwise, the Cortina continued as before with the 1599-cc engine introduced a year earlier. In standard trim, that engine delivered up to 71 horsepower; in GT form, with two-barrel Weber carburetion, output rose to about 89 bhp at 5500 rpm.

I.D. DATA: Serial number is on the right fender, under the hood. A 'J' in the serial number indicates an early 1969 model.

Model	Body Type & Seating	Engine Type/CID	P.O.E. Price	Weight (lbs.)	Prod. Total
CORTINA					
92	2-dr Sedan-4/5P	I4/97	1849	1926	Note 1
93	4-dr Sedan-4/5P	I4/97	1964	1970	Note 1
92	2-dr DeL Sed-4/5P	I4/97	1932	1934	Note 1
93	4-dr DeL Sed-4/5P	I4/97	2047	1978	Note 1
98	4-dr Sta Wag-4/5P	I4/97	2270	2143	Note 1
96	2-dr GT Sed-4/5P	I4/97	2313	1962	Note 1
97	4-dr GT Sed-4/5P	I4/97	2430	2000	Note 1

Note 1: Of the 531,623 British Fords produced in 1969, approximately 21,496 were sold in the U.S.

1969 Ford Mark II Cortina Estate Wagon. (William Siuru Jr.)

ENGINE DATA: BASE FOUR: Inline, overhead-valve four-cylinder. Cast iron block and head. **Displacement:** 97.5 cu. in. (1599 cc). **Bore & Stroke:** 3.19 x 3.06 in. (81 x 77.6 mm). **Compression Ratio:** 9.0:1 except (GT) 9.6:1. **Brake Horsepower:** 71 at 5000 rpm except (GT) 89 at 5500. **Torque:** 91.5 lbs.-ft. at 2500 rpm except (GT) 96.6 at 3600. Five main bearings. Solid valve lifters. One Ford-Autolite carburetor except (GT) two-barrel Weber.
Note: Some sources listed base-engine horsepower as only 66.5 bhp. GT-engine torque was variously announced as either 96.6 or 102.5 lbs.-ft.
CHASSIS DATA: Wheelbase: 98 in. **Overall Length:** (sed) 168.5 in.; (wag) 169.5 in. **Height:** 54.7 in. **Width:** 64.9 in. **Front Tread:** 52.5 in. **Rear Tread:** 51 in. **Standard Tires:** 6.00x13 except (GT) 165x13.
TECHNICAL: Layout: front-engine, rear-drive. **Transmission:** four-speed manual (fully synchronized). GT gear ratios: (1st) 2.972:1; (2nd) 2.01:1; (3rd) 1.397:1; (4th) 1.00:1. **Standard Final Drive Ratio:** 3.90:1. **Steering:** recirculating ball. **Suspension (front):** MacPherson struts with coil springs and anti-sway bar. **Suspension (rear):** rigid axle with semi-elliptic leaf springs (power assist on GT/wagon). **Brakes:** front disc, rear drum. **Body Construction:** steel unibody. **Fuel Tank:** 12.0 gal. except (wagon) 9.6 gal.
MAJOR OPTIONS: Automatic transmission ($216).
PERFORMANCE: Top Speed: (Cortina) 85 mph; (GT) 96 mph. **Acceleration (quarter-mile):** (Cortina) 20.8 sec. (64 mph). **Fuel Mileage:** (Cortina) about 26 mpg; (GT) 24-28 mpg.
Manufacturer: Ford Motor Co. Ltd., Dagenham, Essex, England.
Distributor: Ford Motor Co., Dearborn, Michigan.
HISTORY: Introduced to U.S. market on January 1, 1969.

1970 FORD (British)

CORTINA — FOUR — Larger side marker lenses were the major visible change in this final year of official importation into the U.S. An alternator replaced the generator, and new emission-control components were installed. The Cortina GT included a walnut instrument panel, electric clock, tachometer, racing stripes, power brakes, high-lift-cam engine, and stiffer suspension.

I.D. DATA: Serial number is on the right fender, under the hood. Serial number prefix: (2-dr) BA92JK; (2-dr GT) BA96JK; (4-dr) BA93JK; (4-dr GT) BA97JK; (wagon) BA98JK. Starting serial number: 100001.

Model	Body Type & Seating	Engine Type/CID	P.O.E. Price	Weight (lbs.)	Prod. Total
CORTINA					
92	2-dr Sedan-4/5P	I4/97	1889	1938	Note 1
93	4-dr Sedan-4/5P	I4/97	2004	1982	Note 1
92	2-dr DeL Sed-4/5P	I4/97	1977	1941	Note 1
93	4-dr DeL Sed-4/5P	I4/97	2092	1985	Note 1
98	4-dr Sta Wag-4/5P	I4/97	2304	2143	Note 1
96	2-dr GT Sed-4/5P	I4/97	2358	1962	Note 1
97	4-dr GT Sed-4/5P	I4/97	2475	2000	Note 1

Note 1: Approximately 10,216 British Fords were sold in the U.S. in 1970.

ENGINE DATA: BASE FOUR: Inline, overhead-valve four-cylinder. Cast iron block and head. **Displacement:** 97.5 cu. in. (1599 cc). **Bore & Stroke:** 3.19 x 3.06 in. (81 x 77.6 mm). **Compression Ratio:** 9.0:1 except (GT) 9.6:1. **Brake Horsepower:** 71 at 5000 rpm except (GT) 89 at 5500. **Torque:** 91.5 lbs.-ft. at 2500 rpm except (GT) 96.6 at 3600. Five main bearings. Solid valve lifters. One Ford-Autolite carburetor except (GT) Weber two-barrel.

Note: Some sources listed base-engine horsepower as 66.5 bhp. GT-engine torque was variously announced as either 96.6 or 102.5 lbs.-ft.

CHASSIS DATA: Wheelbase: 98 in. **Overall Length:** (sed) 168.5 in.; (wag) 171 in. **Height:** 54.7 in. **Width:** 64.9 in. **Front Tread:** 52.5 in. **Rear Tread:** 51 in. **Standard Tires:** 6.00x13 except (GT) 165x13.

TECHNICAL: Layout: front-engine, rear-drive. **Transmission:** four-speed manual (fully synchronized). **Standard Final Drive Ratio:** 3.90:1. **Steering:** recirculating ball. **Suspension (front):** MacPherson struts with coil springs and anti-sway bar. **Suspension (rear):** rigid axle with semi-elliptic leaf springs. **Brakes:** front disc, rear drum (power assist on GT/wagon). **Body Construction:** steel unibody. **Fuel Tank:** 10.1 gal. except (wagon) 8.6 gal.

MAJOR OPTIONS: Three-speed automatic transmission ($216); N/A on GT. Radial tires: GT ($10)l. Whitewall tires ($33).

PERFORMANCE: Top Speed: (Cortina) 87 mph; (GT) about 96 mph. **Acceleration (0-60 mph):** (Cortina) about 16 sec.; (GT) 12 sec.; (wagon) 17 sec. **Fuel Mileage:** up to 30 mpg except (GT) 25 mpg.

Manufacturer: Ford Motor Co. Ltd., Dagenham, Essex, England.

Distributor: Ford Motor Co., Dearborn, Michigan.

HISTORY: Introduced to U.S. market on October 6, 1969. Importation to the U.S. ceased before the 1971 model year began, but production continued in Britain. In the 1970s, the list of models produced for sale elsewhere in the world included a series of new Escorts and Capris, and a new Granada line with V-6 engines.

1974 Ford Escort GT. (William Siuru Jr.)

FORD GT40

Origins of this short-lived but significant British/American racing car began in the summer of 1962, when Henry Ford II announced a "Total Performance" project that would span a wide range of racing milieus: from Indianapolis to Le Mans. Interest was intensified after Ford failed in an attempt to take over the Ferrari operation. By the mid-1960s, the resulting GT40 would become one of the first small mid-engined race cars and compile an impressive (though less than perfect) string of successes. An early rear-engined Mustang prototype was nixed by Lee Iacocca because of its high cost. Yet that project evolved into a GT race car with 4.2-liter V-8 power, intended to compete at Indy. Before the year ended, the original open car turned into a closed coupe, and Ford elected to focus on Le Mans. Because top speeds in the 185-mph neighborhood were anticipated, wind-tunnel testing helped hone the final shape. Design work was performed by Eric Broadley (who'd styled the Lola GT) and John Wyer (formerly with Aston Martin). Gullwing doors were considered, then rejected. Production began at a plant in Slough, just outside London, using bodies and V-8 engines supplied by Ford in the U.S. Ford needed to build 100 or more examples for racing homologation purposes. The GT40 first appeared at the New York Auto Show in March 1964. Nearly all carried a Ford 289-cid V-8, but a handful were produced with 427-cid power. Though incredibly fast on the straightaways, GT40s lagged in handling on the turns, and made a weak showing at their first Le Mans attempt. In 1965, Shelby American (in California) took over a major portion of further development work, as did Kar Kraft in Detroit. After another Le Mans failure in 1965, Mark II GT40s came in first and second in '66. Roadgoing GT40s had detuned engines (down to 306 bhp) and softer suspensions. The low-production Mk III wore four round headlamps instead of the twin rectangular units. An evolutionary version developed by Kar Kraft, with aluminum chassis, turned into the Mark IV that emerged victorious at the 1967 Le Mans race. Production continued through 1969 under the auspices of JW Automotive (in England), bringing two more Le Mans victories; but by that time, Ford had abandoned the entire race project.

1964-69 FORD GT40

1965 Ford GT40. (Coys of Kensington)

GT40 — Mk I/II/III/IV — V-8 — The GT40's fiberglass body rode a semi-monocoque platform chassis. Early models carried a smaller (256-cid) engine rated 350 bhp, but the majority came with a Ford 289-cid V-8. The '40' in the car's title stood for its height: nominally 40.5 inches, down to only 38.5 inches for the 427-cid models. Six different versions were produced, according to the *Shelby American Guide*. The Mark I and III had the smaller engine; Mark II, Mark IV and Type J the larger. The initial Mark I used a triple dry-plate clutch and unsynchronized four-speed manual gearbox. Subsequent models turned to fully-synchronized transmissions and twin-plate clutches. Suspension was independent all around, with coil springs. Rack-and-pinion steering was employed. Even with the initial all-alloy 4.2-liter V-8, a GT40 was capable of 165 mph and could accelerate from zero to 60 mph in about five seconds.

I.D. DATA: Not available.

Model	Body Type & Seating	Engine Type/CID	P.O.E. Price	Weight (lbs.)	Prod. Total
Mk I	2-dr Coupe-2P	V8/289	N/A	1835	Note 1
Mk IV	2-dr Coupe-2P	V8/427	N/A	2205	Note 2

1965 Ford GT40. (Coys of Kensington)

Note 1: Approximately 111 GT40s with 289-cid V-8 engine were produced, according to the *Shelby American Guide,* including eight prototypes, four closed coupes that were later converted to roadsters, and seven Mk III editions.

Note 2: Approximately 12 GT40s with the 427-cid V-8 were produced (four Type J and eight Mark IV), plus about six Mk II prototypes that were converted from earlier 289-cid models and two converted roadsters.

Weight Note: Figures shown are "dry" weight.

1966 Ford GT40 mid-engined sports two-seater. (Christie's)

ENGINE DATA: BASE V-8 (initial 1964 version): Overhead-valve "vee" type eight-cylinder. Light alloy block and heads. **Displacement:** 256 cu. in. (4195 cc). **Bore & Stroke:** 3.76 x 2.87 in. (95.5 x 72.9 mm). **Brake Horsepower:** 350 at 7200 rpm. Four Weber carburetors.
BASE V-8 (Mk I): 90-degree, overhead-valve "vee" type eight-cylinder (Ford). Cast iron block and head. **Displacement:** 289 cu. in. (4736 cc). **Bore & Stroke:** 4.00 x 2.87 in. (101.6 x 72.9 mm). **Compression Ratio:** 12.5:1 (reduced to 10.6:1 in 1968-69). **Brake Horsepower:** 390 at 7000 rpm. **Torque:** 325 lbs.-ft. at 5000 rpm. Five main bearings. Four Weber two-barrel carburetors (or single Holley four-barrel).
BASE V-8 (Road GT40): Same as 289-cid V-8 above, except — **Compression Ratio:** 9.0:1. **Brake Horsepower:** 335 at 6250 rpm. **Torque:** 330 lbs.-ft. at 5500 rpm.
BASE V-8 (Mk III): Same as 289-cid V-8 above, except — **Compression Ratio:** 10.5:1. **Brake Horsepower:** 306 at 6000 rpm. **Torque:** 329 lbs.-ft. at 4200 rpm. One Holley four-barrel carburetor.
BASE V-8 (Mk II, J): 90-degree, overhead-valve "vee" type eight-cylinder. Cast iron block and head. **Displacement:** 427 cu. in. (6997 cc). **Bore & Stroke:** 4.24 x 3.78 in. (108 x 96 mm). **Compression Ratio:** 10.5:1. **Brake Horsepower:** 485 at 6200 rpm. **Torque:** 475 lbs.-ft. at 5000 rpm. Five main bearings. One Holley four-barrel carburetor.
BASE V-8 (Mk IV): Same as 427-cid V-8 above, except — **Brake Horsepower:** 500 at 5000 rpm. **Torque:** 470 lbs.-ft. at 5000 rpm. Two Holley four-barrel carburetors.

1966 Ford GT40 4.7 liter road/competition coupe. (Christie's)

CHASSIS DATA: Wheelbase: 95 in. except (Mk IV) 95.5 in. **Overall Length:** (prototype) 158.5 in.; (Mk I) 165 in.; (road, Mk IV) 168 in.; (Mk III) 169 in.; (Mk II) 163 in.; (Type J) 164 in. **Height:** 40.5 in. except (Mk III) 41 in.; (Mk IV, J) 38.5 in. **Width:** 70 in. except (J) 69 in. **Front Tread:** (Mk I) 54 in.; (road, J, Mk IV) 55 in.; (J) 55.5 in.; (Mk III) 53.25 in.; (Mk II) 57 in. **Rear Tread:** (Mk I) 54 in.; (road, J, Mk IV) 55 in.; (Mk III) 53.25 in.; (Mk II) 56 in.

TECHNICAL: Layout: mid-engine, rear-drive. **Transmission:** four-speed manual except (road version, Mk III) five-speed. Gearboxes were all-synchro except (Mk I) unsynchronized. **Steering:** rack and pinion. **Suspension (front):** dual control arms with coil springs and anti-roll bar. **Suspension (rear):** independent with dual trailing arms, transverse upper links, lower control arms, coil springs and anti-roll bar. **Brakes:** front/rear disc. **Body Construction:** fiberglass body panels on steel semi-monocoque chassis except (427 V-8) aluminum honeycomb panels.

PERFORMANCE: Top Speed: (4.2-liter prototype) 140-165 mph. **Acceleration (0-60 mph):** (4.2-liter prototype) 5.0 sec. **Acceleration (quarter-mile):** (prototype) 13.8 sec.
Manufacturer: Ford Advanced Vehicles, Slough, England.

FORD (EUROPE) CAPRI

Though commonly considered a German import, the Capri sport coupe, which was sold in the U.S. by Lincoln-Mercury dealers, was actually assembled at Ford plants in Great Britain and Belgium as well as in West Germany. Thus, it qualifies as a European rather than strictly German vehicle. Introduced in England in 1969, as the "car you've always promised yourself," the two-door ponycar began to arrive at U.S. ports the following year as a Mercury model (though it never displayed the Mercury name on its body).

Even more than Mustangers of the 1970s, Capri fans took quite a fancy to their machines. No surprise, perhaps, since Mustangs were quickly losing the panache of their Sixties styling and performance, while the European-built Capris arrived with a sparkle. Capris mixed an attractive body with sprightly performance and capable handling, plus easy servicing at Lincoln-Mercury dealers. In Europe, where Capris came with an awesome selection of trim options and powertrains, they were just about as popular as the Mustang was in the U.S. A total of 1,169,088 Capris were produced in their early form (through 1974), followed by 404,169 Capri II models from 1975-77. In recent years, Capri popularity has reached even beyond its favor when new, and it's become a strong contender for low-budget collectibility.

First Capris off the boat in America came with a 1600-cc "Kent" four-cylinder engine (as used in the British Ford Cortina), offered in a single trim level. That made sense because the engine happened to be emissions-legal, based on earlier applications. Before long, a larger (2.0-liter) four was added, followed by a V-6. The final year of the first version brought a modest restyle and new dashboard.

Late in the 1975 model year came the Capri II (intended as a '76 model), with revised panels on a new hatchback body. Base, luxury Ghia and sporty 'S' models were available. Production (and sales) in Europe continuued until 1987, though imports to the U.S. stopped after 1977, as Mercury awaited its Mustang clone for '79.

Note: Factory literature did not necessarily use the cubic centimeter (1600, 2300, etc.) designations, but those figures were commonly employed in describing Capri models.

1969-70 CAPRI

1600 — FOUR — Produced mainly, but not exclusively, by Ford of (West) Germany, the semi-fastback Capri coupe was powered by a 97.6 cubic-inch (1599-cc) British Ford "Kent" four-cylinder engine. That pushrod overhead-valve design came out of the Ford Cortina, initially rated at 71 horsepower (slightly detuned from the European version) under Capri hoods. A bold bodyside crease tapered down behind the rear wheel, while twin "grilles" stood just ahead of each wheel. The front end held round quad headlamps and a long hood bulge, with separate 'CAPRI' letters at the hood front. Capri's grille was made up of horizontal strips only. The gas filler cap stood high on the right side, to the rear of the quarter window. Seating was provided for four (though closer to a 2+2 configuration). The standard rear seat had vertical pleats and a center armrest, with full-width seat optional. A vinyl top also was optional. Just one trim level was offered at first. Standard equipment included power front disc brakes, radial tires on styled steel wheels, vinyl front bucket seats, a bench-style back seat, full carpeting, and a four-speed manual gearbox (with floor-mounted gearshift lever). Automatic shift was not available in early Capris. Rack-and-pinion steering was used. Two round dials were mounted in the instrument panel, finished in simulated walnut grain.

1969 Ford Capri.

I.D. DATA: An 11-symbol Vehicle Identification Number (VIN) is attached to left windshield pillar post, visible through windshield; and to plate in right fender, to rear of radiator. Engine number is stamped on a horizontal boss on the right side. Symbol one indicates country ('G' = Germany). Symbol two is assembly plant ('A' = Cologne; 'B' = Belgium). Symbols three and four indicate Series ('EC'). Symbol five is the year code ('K' = 1970). Next is a month code, followed by the sequential serial number. Starting serial number: 00001.

Model	Body Type & Seating	Engine Type/CID	P.O.E. Price	Weight (lbs.)	Prod. Total
1600	2-dr Spt Cpe-4P	I4/98	2295	2135	Note 1

Note 1: A total of 17,258 Capris were sold in the U.S. in 1970.

ENGINE DATA: BASE FOUR: Inline, overhead-valve four-cylinder. Cast iron block and head. **Displacement:** 97.6 cu. in. (1599 cc). **Bore & Stroke:** 3.19 x 3.08 in. (81 x 78 mm). **Compression Ratio:** 8.0:1. **Brake Horsepower:** 71 at 5000 rpm. **Torque:** 91 lbs.-ft. at 2800 rpm. Five main bearings. Solid valve lifters. One downdraft carburetor. 12-volt electrical.

CHASSIS DATA: Wheelbase: 100.8 in. **Overall Length:** 167.8 in. **Height:** 52 in. **Width:** 64.8 in. **Front Tread:** 53 in. **Rear Tread:** 52 in. **Wheel Type:** styled steel disc (13x5J). **Standard Tires:** 165x13.

TECHNICAL: Layout: front-engine, rear-drive. **Transmission:** four-speed manual; floor lever. Overall gear ratios: (1st) 13.77:1; (2nd) 9.33:1; (3rd) 5.48:1; (4th) 3.89:1. **Standard Final Drive Ratio:** 3.89:1. **Steering:** rack and pinion. **Suspension (front):** MacPherson struts with coil springs and anti-roll bar. **Suspension (rear):** rigid axle with multi-leaf springs, radius rods and staggered shock absorbers. **Brakes:** front disc, rear drum. **Body Construction:** steel unibody. **Fuel Tank:** 12 gallons.

MAJOR OPTIONS: Air conditioning. Vinyl top. Decor package ($93). 185x13 tires ($25).

PERFORMANCE: Top Speed: 90 mph. **Acceleration (0-60 mph):** 17.3 seconds. **Acceleration (quarter-mile):** 20.4 seconds (65 mph). **Fuel Mileage:** near 25 mpg (average).

PRODUCTION/SALES: A total of 1,169,088 Capri I models were produced through 1974.

Manufacturer: Ford Werke A.G., West Germany; also built in Great Britain.

Distributor: Sold through Lincoln-Mercury dealers, beginning in April 1970.

HISTORY: First shown in London, December 1968; sold in Europe beginning in early 1969. Introduced in U.S. on April 17, 1970. Sales for the first month amounted to 2,011 units, emptying the showrooms.

1971 CAPRI

1600 — FOUR — Production of the 1.6-liter Capri continued as in 1970, with a slight horsepower boost but no significant appearance change in the sport-coupe body. Standard equipment included a heater/defroster, power front disc brakes (in a dual braking system), radial tires on styled steel wheels, two-speed wiper/washer, front/rear bumper guards, and an aluminized exhaust system. Front bucket seats had armrests and adjustable backs. Bucket rear seats came with the deluxe trim package. The interior had simulated woodgrain accents, a sports steering wheel, full carpeting, front and rear ashtrays, and a lighter.

2000 — FOUR — By 1971, a larger 2.0-liter (122 cubic inch) overhead-cam four-cylinder engine was available, rated 100 horsepower. The larger engine could also be ordered with an automatic transmission (floor lever) instead of the standard four-speed manual gearbox.

I.D. DATA: Vehicle Identification Number is in same location as 1969-70. Breakdown is the same as in that listing, except for a change in the year code ('L' = 1971).

Model	Body Type & Seating	Engine Type/CID	P.O.E. Price	Weight (lbs.)	Prod. Total
1600	2-dr Spt Cpe-4P	I4/98	2395	2135	Note 1
2000	2-dr Spt Cpe-4P	I4/122	2445	2210	Note 1

Note 1: A total of 56,120 Capris were sold in the U.S. in 1971.

Price Note: Some sources list the 2000 engine as a $50 option rather than a separate model.

ENGINE DATA: BASE FOUR (1600): Inline, overhead-valve four-cylinder. Cast iron block and head. **Displacement:** 97.6 cu. in. (1599 cc). **Bore & Stroke:** 3.19 x 3.08 in. (81 x 78 mm). **Compression Ratio:** 8.4:1. **Brake Horsepower:** 75 at 5000 rpm. **Torque:** 96 lbs.-ft. at 3000 rpm. Five main bearings. Solid valve lifters. One downdraft carburetor. 12-volt electrical.

BASE FOUR (2000): Inline, single overhead-cam four-cylinder. Cast iron block and head. **Displacement:** 122 cu. in. (1993 cc). **Bore & Stroke:** 3.575 x 3.029 in. (91 x 77 mm). **Compression Ratio:** 8.6:1. **Brake Horsepower:** 100 at 5600 rpm. **Torque:** 120 lbs.-ft. at 3600 rpm. Five main bearings. Solid valve lifters. One downdraft carburetor. 12-volt electrical.

CHASSIS DATA: Wheelbase: 100.8 in. **Overall Length:** 167.8 in. **Height:** 52 in. **Width:** 64.8 in. **Front Tread:** 53 in. **Rear Tread:** 52 in. **Wheel Type:** styled steel disc. **Standard Tires:** 165x13.

TECHNICAL: Layout: front-engine, rear-drive. **Transmission:** four-speed manual (synchro); floor lever. **Standard Final Drive Ratio:** (1600) 3.89:1; (2000) 3.44:1. **Steering:** rack and pinion. **Suspension (front):** MacPherson struts with coil springs. **Suspension (rear):** rigid axle with multi-leaf springs and staggered shock absorbers. **Brakes:** front disc, rear drum. **Body Construction:** steel unibody. **Fuel Tank:** 12 gallons.

MAJOR OPTIONS: 2.0-liter engine ($50). Automatic transmission: 2000 only ($185). Manual sunroof ($120). Black vinyl top ($63). Decor group (blacked-out grille, reclining front bucket seats, rear bucket seats, folding rear armrest, parking-brake light, leather-covered steering wheel and gearshift knob, dual horns, console with clock, and map light) ($119). Air conditioning.

PERFORMANCE: Top Speed: (1600) 90 mph; (2000) 108 mph. **Acceleration (0-60 mph):** (1600) 16-17 seconds; (2000) 11.5 seconds. **Acceleration (quarter-mile):** (2000) 18.5 seconds (75 mph). **Fuel Mileage:** about 25 mpg.

PRODUCTION/SALES: By 1971, about 100,000 Capris had been built in Great Britain and over 200,000 in Germany. A total of 1,169,088 Capri I models were produced through 1974.

Manufacturer: Ford Motor Co., West Germany and Great Britain.

Distributor: Sold through Lincoln-Mercury dealers.

HISTORY: *Road Test* magazine named Capri its "Import Car of the Year" for 1971. "If any modern automotive product ever reaches the universality of the Model T," declared Petersen's *Import Buyer's Guide '71*, "it will be the Capri." Ford of Germany turned out six different models, with engines from 1.3 to 2.1 liters. Great Britain produced seven models of its own, from 1.3 to 3.0 liters. German Capris came with V-4 or V-6 power; British versions with an inline four, V-4 or V6. Capris sold in the U.S. were considerably more limited in scope. The European 2300 (2.3-liter) version got some attention in the American press, but would not arrive until the Capri II emerged for the U.S. market. Petersen's guide declared a modified version of the 2300 to be virtually equivalent to a "Boss 351 Mini-Mustang."

1972 CAPRI

1600 — FOUR — Production of the smaller-engine Capri continued with little change for another season.

2000 — FOUR — Production of the 2.0-liter version continued with little change.

2600 — V-6 — A V-6 engine, offered in Europe since 1969, became available under U.S. Capri hoods for 1972, identifiable by dual exhaust pipes at the back end that delivered a subtle but alluring tone. Horsepower was reduced for the U.S. market, however, from 125 in Europe to 107 on imported Capris. Nevertheless, the German-built V-6 provided a strong performance boost and impetus to sales. Larger tires were installed on V-6 models: 185/70HR13 radials rather than the usual 165 size. Spring rates were revised slightly, and brake drums were a bit wider. Standard equipment included a 140-mph speedometer, 7000-rpm tachometer, trip odometer, clock, and gauges for oil pressure, temperature, voltage and fuel.

I.D. DATA: Vehicle Identication Number is in the same location as 1969-71; see 1969-70 listing for breakdown. Model year code changed to 'M' for 1972. Starting serial number: 00001.

Model	Body Type & Seating	Engine Type/CID	P.O.E. Price	Weight (lbs.)	Prod. Total
1600	2-dr Spt Cpe-4P	I4/98	2477	2135	Note 1
2000	2-dr Spt Cpe-4P	I4/122	2528	2210	Note 1
2600	2-dr Spt Cpe-4P	V6/155	2821	2330	Note 1

Note 1: A total of 91,995 Capris were sold in the U.S. in 1972.

Price Note: Some sources listed the V-6 engine as a $293 option rather than a separate model.

ENGINE DATA: BASE FOUR (1600): Inline, overhead-valve four-cylinder. Cast iron block and head. **Displacement:** 97.6 cu. in. (1599 cc). **Bore & Stroke:** 3.188 x 3.056 in. (81 x 78 mm). **Compression Ratio:** 8.0:1. **Brake Horsepower:** 54 at 4600 rpm. **Torque:** 80 lbs.-ft. at 2400 rpm. Five main bearings. Solid valve lifters. One downdraft carburetor. 12-volt electrical.

BASE FOUR (2000): Inline, overhead-cam four-cylinder. Cast iron block and head. **Displacement:** 122 cu. in. (1993 cc). **Bore & Stroke:** 3.575 x 3.029 in. (91 x 77 mm). **Compression Ratio:** 8.2:1. **Brake Horsepower:** 86 at 5400 rpm. Five main bearings. Solid valve lifters. One downdraft two-barrel carburetor. 12-volt electrical.

BASE V-6 (2600): Overhead-valve, 60-degree vee-type six-cylinder. Cast iron block and head. **Displacement:** 155.5 cu. in. (2548 cc). **Bore & Stroke:** 3.545 x 2.63 in. (90 x 66.8 mm). **Compression Ratio:** 8.2:1. **Brake Horsepower:** 107 at 5000 rpm. **Torque:** 130 lbs.-ft. at 3400 rpm. Four main bearings. Solid valve lifters. One Holley-Weber two-barrel carburetor. 12-volt electrical.

Horsepower Note: Published horsepower and torque figures changed from the former gross measure to net measurements in 1972.

CHASSIS DATA: Wheelbase: 100.8 in. **Overall Length:** 167.8 in. **Height:** 52 in. **Width:** 64.8 in. **Front Tread:** 53 in. **Rear Tread:** 52 in. **Wheel Type:** styled steel disc (13x5J). **Standard Tires:** 165x13 except (2600) 185/70HRx13.

TECHNICAL: Layout: front-engine, rear-drive. **Transmission:** four-speed manual (synchro); floor lever. Gear ratios: (1st) 3.65:1; (2nd) 1.97:1; (3rd) 1.37:1; (4th) 1.00:1. **Standard Final Drive Ratio:** (1600) 3.89:1; (2000) 3.44:1; (2600) 3.22:1. **Steering:** rack and pinion. **Suspension (front):** MacPherson struts with coil springs and anti-roll bar. **Suspension (rear):** rigid axle with trailing arms and semi-elliptic leaf springs. **Brakes:** power front disc, rear drum. **Body Construction:** steel unibody. **Fuel Tank:** 12 gallons.

MAJOR OPTIONS: V-6 engine ($293). Automatic transmission ($182). Manual sunroof ($119). Vinyl top ($63). Decor group (padded steering wheel rim, clock, rear center armrest, etc.) ($117). Air conditioning.

PERFORMANCE: Top Speed: (2600) 110 mph. **Acceleration (0-60 mph):** (1600) 17.3 sec.; (2000) 11.5 sec.; (2600) 10.4 sec. **Acceleration (quarter-mile):** (1600) 20.4 sec.; (2000) 18.5 sec.; (2600) 17.7 sec. **Fuel Mileage:** (1600) about 24.5 mpg; (2000) about 25.5 mpg; (2600) about 24 mpg.

PRODUCTION/SALES: A total of 1,169,088 Capri I models were produced through 1974.

Manufacturer: Ford Werke A.G., West Germany; also built in Great Britain.

Distributor: Sold at Lincoln-Mercury dealers.

1973 CAPRI

1973 Ford Capri.

2000 — FOUR — The 1600 model dropped out after 1972, leaving only one four-cylinder engine. Capri changes for 1973 included a new energy-absorbing bumper to meet U.S. requirements, a new steering wheel and dashboard gauge layout, and new horizontally-pleated upholstery. The grillework ahead of each back wheel also got a restyle for a smaller appearance. Bodies displayed side marker lights and backup lights, bright moldings, a blackout grille, and simulated dual air scoops on the power bulge hood. Power front disc brakes, rack-and-pinion steering, and an all-synchro four-speed manual gearbox remained standard (with automatic transmission available). Interior featurees included a simulated woodgrain dashboard, padded sun visors, looped pile carpet, assist bars, and vinyl upholstery on the adjustable front bucket seats and rear bench seat. Standard equipment also included a two-speed wiper/washer, two-speed heater/defogger, and locking glovebox.

2600 — V-6 — As before, the V-6 Capri rode larger tires than the four-cylinder (185/70HR13 instead of 165x13). The V-6 edition also had heavy-duty springs and shock absorbers, dual exhausts with bright extensions, and blackout rockers and lower back panel. The instrument group consisted of a tachometer, trip odometer, ammeter, and oil pressure gauge.

I.D. DATA: Vehicle Identification Number is in the same location as 1970-72; see 1969-70 listing for breakdown of the 11-symbol VIN. Starting serial number: 42151.

Model	Body Type & Seating	Engine Type/CID	P.O.E. Price	Weight (lbs.)	Prod. Total
2000	2-dr Spt Cpe-4P	I4/122	2983	2231	Note 1
2600	2-dr Spt Cpe-4P	V6/155	3261	2341	Note 1

Note 1: Approximately 113,069 Capris were sold in the U.S. during 1973.

Price Note: Some sources listed specific prices for automatic-transmission models, $216 higher than shown above ($3199 and $3477). Some sources listed the V-6 as an option rather than a separate model.

ENGINE DATA: BASE FOUR (2000): Inline, overhead-cam four-cylinder. Cast iron block and head. **Displacement:** 122 cu. in. (1993 cc). **Bore & Stroke:** 3.575 x 3.029 in. (91 x 77 mm). **Compression Ratio:** 8.2:1. **Brake Horsepower:** 85 at 5600 rpm. Five main bearings. Solid valve lifters. One two-barrel carburetor. 12-volt electrical.

BASE V-6 (2600): Overhead-valve, vee-type six-cylinder. Cast iron block and head. **Displacement:** 155.5 cu. in. (2548 cc). **Bore & Stroke:** 3.545 x 2.63 in. (90 x 67 mm). **Compression Ratio:** 8.2:1. **Brake Horsepower:** 107 at 5000 rpm. **Torque:** 130 lbs.-ft. at 3400 rpm. Four main bearings. Solid valve lifters. One two-barrel carburetor. 12-volt electrical.

CHASSIS DATA: Wheelbase: 100.8 in. **Overall Length:** 173.8 in. **Height:** 52 in. **Width:** 64.8 in. **Front Tread:** 53 in. **Rear Tread:** 52 in. **Wheel Type:** steel disc. **Standard Tires:** 165x13 except (2600) 185/70HRx13.

TECHNICAL: Layout: front-engine, rear-drive. **Transmission:** four-speed manual (all-synchro); floor lever. **Standard Final Drive Ratio:** (2000) 3.44:1; (2600) 3.22:1. **Steering:** rack and pinion. **Suspension (front):** MacPherson struts with coil springs and anti-roll bar. **Suspension (rear):** rigid axle with semi-elliptic leaf springs with staggered shock absorbers. **Brakes:** power front disc, rear drum. **Body Construction:** steel unibody. **Fuel Tank:** 12 gallons.

MAJOR OPTIONS: V-6 engine ($278). Automatic transmission ($216). Metal sunroof ($132). Vinyl top ($79). Decor group (simulated leather-trim steering wheel and gearshift knob, reclining front seats, contour rear bucket seats, console with clock, adjustable map light, electric rear defroster, dual horns) ($169). Instrument group, including tachometer ($76). AM radio ($65). AM/FM radio (dealer-installed). Air conditioning (dealer-installed).

PERFORMANCE: Top Speed: (2000) 100 mph; (2600) 105 mph. **Acceleration (0-60 mph):** (2000) 13.5 sec.; (2600) 10 sec. **Fuel Mileage:** (2000) 20-25 mpg; (2600) 17-23 mpg.

PRODUCTION/SALES: A total of 1,169,088 Capri I models were produced through 1974.
Manufacturer: Ford Werke A.G., West Germany; also built in Great Britain.
Distributor: Sold by Lincoln-Mercury dealers.

HISTORY: Capri's 1973 model year in the U.S. began July 1972.

1974 CAPRI

1974 Ford Cologne Capri RS3100.

2000 — FOUR — Production of the four-cylinder Capri continued with minimal change, except for heavier painted bumpers.

2800 — V-6 — A 2.8-liter V-6 replaced the former 2600 version, but otherwise production continued as before in this final season of the first-generation Capri.

I.D. DATA: Vehicle Identification Number is in the same location as 1970-73; see 1969-70 listing for breakdown of the 11-symbol VIN. Model year code was 'P' for 1974.

Model	Body Type & Seating	Engine Type/CID	P.O.E. Price	Weight (lbs.)	Prod. Total
2000	2-dr Spt Cpe-4P	I4/122	3566	2231	Note 1
2800	2-dr Spt Cpe-4P	V6/171	3807	2341	Note 1

Note 1: Approximately 75,260 Capris were sold in the U.S. during 1974.

ENGINE DATA: BASE FOUR (2000): Inline, overhead-cam four-cylinder. Cast iron block and head. **Displacement:** 122 cu. in. (1993 cc). **Bore & Stroke:** 3.575 x 3.029 in. (91 x 77 mm). **Compression Ratio:** 8.2:1. **Brake Horsepower:** 80 at 5400 rpm. **Torque:** 98 lbs.-ft. at 3000 rpm. Five main bearings. Solid valve lifters. One two-barrel carburetor. 12-volt electrical.

BASE V-6 (2800): Overhead-valve, vee-type six-cylinder. Cast iron block and head. **Displacement:** 170.8 cu. in. (2792 cc). **Bore & Stroke:** 3.66 x 2.70 in. (93 x 69 mm). **Compression Ratio:** 8.2:1. **Brake Horsepower:** 105 at 4600 rpm. **Torque:** 140 lbs.-ft. at 3200 rpm. Four main bearings. Solid valve lifters. One two-barrel carburetor. 12-volt electrical.

CHASSIS DATA: Wheelbase: 100.8 in. **Overall Length:** 174.8 in. **Height:** 50.5-52 in. **Width:** 64.8 in. **Front Tread:** 53.25 in. **Rear Tread:** 52.25 in. **Wheel Type:** steel disc. **Standard Tires:** 165x13 except (V-6) 185/70x13.

TECHNICAL: Layout: front-engine, rear-drive. **Transmission:** four-speed manual (synchro); floor lever. **Standard Final Drive Ratio:** (2000) 3.44:1; (2800) 3.22:1. **Steering:** rack and pinion. **Suspension (front):** MacPherson struts with coil springs and anti-roll bar. **Suspension (rear):** rigid axle with semi-elliptic leaf springs and staggered shock absorbers. **Brakes:** power front disc, rear drum. **Body Construction:** steel unibody. **Fuel Tank:** 12.7 gallons.

MAJOR OPTIONS: V-6 engine ($241). Automatic transmission ($256). Air conditioning ($364). Metal sunroof ($141). Vinyl top ($83). Decor group ($153). AM radio ($53). AM/FM radio ($101).

PERFORMANCE: Top Speed: (2800) 105 mph. **Acceleration (0-60 mph):** (2800) 10 sec. **Fuel Mileage:** (2800) near 19 mpg.

PRODUCTION/SALES: A total of 1,169,088 Capri I models were produced through 1974.
Manufacturer: Ford Werke A.G., West Germany; also built in Great Britain.
Distributor: Sold by Lincoln-Mercury dealers.
HISTORY: The 1974 Capri model year in the U.S. began July 1973.

1975-76 CAPRI II

Note: No Capris were imported for the 1975 model year, but late in that season came the Capri II (intended as a '76 model).
2300 — FOUR — Revised sheetmetal panels with a smoother bodyside look went on a new hatchback sport coupe body in the second-generation Capri, which otherwise looked similar to the first version. Lincoln-Mercury billed it as the "sexy European road car." Quad headlamps were used again, flanking a neat rectangular blackout grille with 'CAPRI' block letters in its center and amber park/signal lights at its outer ends. A horizontal protective molding stretched the full length of the bodyside. Base and luxury Ghia models were offered, as well as a sporty 'S' edition. Under the hood, which had a much shorter bulge than before, a 2.3-liter overhead-cam four-cylinder engine replaced the earlier 2.0-liter. Hood creases reached to the edges of the grille. Inside, seat upholstery returned to vertical pleating. Once again, a vinyl top was among the options.

Standard equipment included full instrumentation, fully reclining bucket seats, fold-down rear seat, 165SRx13 steel-belted radial tires on styled steel wheels, protective bodyside moldings, rack-and-pinion steering, power front disc brakes, front and rear stabilizer bars, and a four-speed manual gearbox. A high-output heater and Flow-Thru power ventilation were standard. The dual hydraulic braking system included a warning light; turn signals included a lane-change feature; and two-speed windshield wiper/washers were installed. Interior features included padded sun visors, coat hooks, self-locking front seatbacks with head restraints, integral lap/shoulder front seat belts, and a safety glovebox latch. Standard body colors were: white, black, dark red, yuellow, orange, and dark brown; plus metallic silver, blue, or green. Interiors came in dark brown, black, light tan, red/black, and dark brown/parchment. The optional vinyl roof came in black, dark brown or white (depending on body/interior colors selected).

The Capri II 'S' came in dramatic black with flashes of gold striping, and virtually no brightwork. The gold-color theme also extended to the wheels, whether standard or optional cast aluminum. A plain white 'S' with gold striping could be ordered instead. Seating surfaces were gold-color cloth with black vinyl trim, accented by black carpeting and a black instrument panel. Standard 'S' equipment included dual racing mirrors, heavy-duty suspension, contoured rear seats, and upgraded sound package.

Capri Ghia added high-back bucket seats (cloth or knit vinyl), cast aluminum wheels, color-keyed wide bodyside moldings, a full console, seatback map pockets, contoured rear seats, clock, woodtone instrument panel, leather-wrapped steering wheel, grab and assist handles, color-keyed racing mirrors (driver's remote), opening quarter windows, and bright exhaust extension. A Capri Decor Group option included embossed vinyl seating surfaces and trim panels, contoured rear seats, a console, map light, woodtone instrument panel, opening quarter windows, glovebox light and lock, assist handles, dual-note horn, lower-door carpeting, and bright exhaust extensions.

2800 — V-6 — The 2.8-liter V-6, introduced in the latter part of the Capri I run, returned to power the second generation. Extras with the V-6 included a heavy-duty four-speed manual gearbox, larger clutch and brakes, 185/70HR13 steel-belted radial tires, dual exhaust system, and larger-capacity cooling system.

I.D. DATA: An 11-symbol Vehicle Identification Number (VIN) is attached to left windshield pillar post, visible through windshield; and included in the identification plate inside the right fender, to rear of radiator. That fender plate also shows codes for paint, rear axle, trim, engine, and transmission type. Engine number is stamped on a horizontal boss on the right side. Symbol one indicates country ('G' = Germany). Symbol two is assembly plant ('A' = Cologne). Symbols three and four indicate Series ('EC'). Symbol five is the year code ('S' = 1976). Next is a month code, followed by the sequential serial number. Starting serial number: 00001.

Model	Body Type & Seating	Engine Type/CID	P.O.E. Price	Weight (lbs.)	Prod. Total
2300	2-dr Hatch Cpe-4P	I4/140	4117	2513	Note 1
2300	2-dr Ghia Cpe-4P	I4/140	4740	2562	Note 1
2300	2-dr 'S' Cpe-4P	I4/140	N/A	N/A	Note 1
2800	2-dr Hatch Cpe-4P	V6/171	4389	2685	Note 1

Note 1: Approximately 54,586 Capris were sold in the U.S. during 1975, followed by 29,904 during 1976.

ENGINE DATA: BASE FOUR (2300): Inline, overhead-cam four-cylinder. Cast iron block and head. **Displacement:** 140 cu. in. (2300 cc). **Bore & Stroke:** 3.78 x 3.13 in. (96 x 79.5 mm). **Compression Ratio:** 9.0:1. **Brake Horsepower:** 88 at 5000 rpm. **Torque:** 116 lbs.-ft. at 2600 rpm. Five main bearings. Solid valve lifters. One Holley-Weber two-barrel carburetor. 12-volt electrical.

BASE V-6 (2800): Overhead-valve, 60-degree vee-type six-cylinder. Cast iron block and head. **Displacement:** 170.8 cu. in. (2795 cc). **Bore & Stroke:** 3.66 x 2.70 in. (93 x 68.6 mm). **Compression Ratio:** 8.2:1. **Brake Horsepower:** 109 at 4800 rpm. **Torque:** 146 lbs.-ft. at 3000 rpm. Four main bearings. Solid valve lifters. One Motorcraft 2150 two-barrel carburetor. 12-volt electrical.

CHASSIS DATA: Wheelbase: 100.9 in. **Overall Length:** 174.8 in. **Height:** 51.0 in. **Width:** 66.9 in. **Front Tread:** 53.3 in. **Rear Tread:** 54.5 in. **Wheel Type:** steel disc. **Standard Tires:** 165SRx13 except (V-6) 185/70HRx13.

TECHNICAL: Layout: front-engine, rear-drive. **Transmission:** four-speed manual; automatic optional. Manual four-cylinder gear ratios: (1st) 3.65:1; (2nd) 1.97:1; (3rd) 1.37:1; (4th) 1.00:1; (rev) 3.66:1. Manual V-6 gear ratios: (1st) 3.36:1; (2nd) 1.81:1; (3rd) 1.36:1; (4th) 1.00:1; (rev) 3.37:1. **Standard Final Drive Ratio:** (2300) 3.44:1; (2800) 3.09:1 exc. 3.22:1 in California. **Steering:** rack and pinion. **Suspension (front):** MacPherson struts with coil springs and stabilizer bar. **Suspension (rear):** rigid axle with four-leaf semi-elliptic springs, staggered shock absorbers and stabilizer bar. **Brakes:** power front disc, rear drum. **Body Construction:** steel unibody. **Fuel Tank:** 12.7 gallons.

MAJOR OPTIONS: V-6 engine ($272). Select-Shift automatic transmission ($276). Air conditioning ($429). Power steering ($129). Decor group ($217). Full tinted glass (required with air conditioning) ($47). Driver's remote racing mirror ($12). Vinyl top ($95). Manual sunroof ($181). Cast aluminum wheels ($113). AM radio ($71). AM/FM radio ($136). Tonneau-style vinyl luggage cover ($29). Electric rear-window defroster ($69). Rear wiper/washer ($48).

PERFORMANCE: Top Speed: (2800) 108 mph. **Acceleration (0-60 mph):** (2800) 10.6 seconds. **Acceleration (quarter-mile):** (2800) 18 seconds (77 mph). **Fuel Mileage:** (2300 manual) EPA 24/34 mpg; (2800 manual) EPA 18/28 mpg.

PRODUCTION/SALES: A total of 404,169 Capri II models were produced from 1975-77.

Manufacturer: Ford Werke A.G., West Germany; also built in Great Britain.

Distributor: Sold by Lincoln-Mercury dealers.

HISTORY: Capri II was introduced in the U.S. in March 1975. Capri sales had been slipping by the mid-1970s, and the downhill slide continued after the Capri II arrived, partly because of its rather hefty price.

1977-78 CAPRI II

2300 — FOUR — Production of the four-cylinder Capri continued with little change in 1977. Standard Capri equipment included a four-speed manual gearbox, power front disc brakes, 165SRx13 radial tires, two-speed wiper/washers, tachometer, trip odometer, color-keyed bumpers, blackout grille with bright molding, blackout rocker and lower back panels, driver's remote mirror, and bright window frames. Interiors held reclining front bucket seats, a fold-down bench rear seat, two-spoke steering wheel, day/night inside mirror, and cut pile carpeting. Capri Ghia added such extras as cast aluminum wheels, color-keyed wide bodyside moldings, bright exhaust extension, flipper-style quarter windows, a clock, color-keyed racing mirrors (driver's remote), dual-note horns, woodtone instrument panel, high-back seats, and contoured bucket back seats. The Le Cat Black 'S' option group consisted of blackout chrome moldings, gold paint/tape accents, gold-finished styled steel wheels, dual racing mirrors, black/gold interior, sports steering wheel, and heavy-duty suspension. The 'S' came with a black or white body, with gold striping. Capri's Decor Group contained contoured rear seats, mini sports console, flipper-type rear quarter windows, black vinyl steering wheel, dual-note horn, adjustable map light, and bright exhaust extension. Standard colors for 1977 were white, red, orange, and yellow; plus metallic clear coat enamels in silver, green, gold, or blue.

2800 — V-6 — Little change was evident in the six-cylinder Capri, which came in the same model selection as the four-cylinder. As before, V-6 Capris had a larger clutch and brake components, bigger 185/70SR13 tires, and dual exhausts.

I.D. DATA: Location and breakdown of the 11-symbol Vehicle Identification Number (VIN) were the same as 1976; see that listing. Model year code changed to 'T' for 1977. Starting serial number: 00001.

Model	Body Type & Seating	Engine Type/CID	P.O.E. Price	Weight lbs.)	Prod. Total
2300	2-dr Hatch Cpe-4P	I4/140	4361	2513	Note 1
2300	2-dr Ghia Cpe-4P	I4/140	4984	2562	Note 1
2800	2-dr Hatch Cpe-4P	V6/71	Note 2	N/A	Note 1

Note 1: A total of 22,458 Capris were sold in the U.S. in 1977, followed by 4,079 in 1978 (its final year).

Note 2: Some sources listed the V-6 engine as an option ($272) rather than a separate model.

ENGINE DATA: BASE FOUR (2300): Inline, overhead-cam four-cylinder. Cast iron block and head. **Displacement:** 140 cu. in. (2300 cc). **Bore & Stroke:** 3.78 x 3.13 in. (96 x 79.5 mm). **Compression Ratio:** 9.0:1. **Brake Horsepower:** 91.5 at 5000 rpm. **Torque:** 117 lbs.-ft. at 2400 rpm. Five main bearings. Solid valve lifters. One Holley-Weber two-barrel carburetor. 12-volt electrical.

BASE V-6 (2800): Overhead-valve, 60-degree vee-type six-cylinder. Cast iron block and head. **Displacement:** 170.8 cu. in. (2795 cc). **Bore & Stroke:** 3.66 x 2.70 in. (93 x 68.6 mm). **Compression Ratio:** 8.7:1. **Brake Horsepower:** 110 at 4800 rpm. **Torque:** 148 lbs.-ft. at 3000 rpm. Four main bearings. Solid valve lifters. One Motorcraft 2150 two-barrel carburetor. 12-volt electrical.

CHASSIS DATA: Wheelbase: 100.9 in. **Overall Length:** 174.8 in. **Height:** 51.0 in. **Width:** 66.9 in. **Front Tread:** 53.3 in. **Rear Tread:** 54.5 in. **Wheel Type:** steel disc. **Standard Tires:** 165SRx13 except (V-6) 185/70SRx13.

TECHNICAL: Layout: front-engine, rear-drive. **Transmission:** four-speed manual; automatic optional. Manual four-cylinder gear ratios: (1st) 3.65:1; (2nd) 1.97:1; (3rd) 1.37:1; (4th) 1.00:1; (rev) 3.66:1. Manual V-6 gear ratios: (1st) 3.36:1; (2nd) 1.81:1; (3rd) 1.36:1; (4th) 1.00:1; (rev) 3.37:1. **Standard Final Drive Ratio:** (2300) 3.22:1; (2800) 3.09:1 exc. 3.22:1 in California. **Steering:** rack and pinion. **Suspension (front):** MacPherson struts with coil springs and stabilizer bar. **Suspension (rear):** rigid axle with four-leaf semi-elliptic springs, staggered shock absorbers and stabilizer bar. **Brakes:** power front disc, rear drum. **Body Construction:** steel unibody. **Fuel Tank:** 12.7 gallons.

MAJOR OPTIONS: V-6 engine ($272). Select-Shift automatic transmission ($276). Air conditioning ($429). Power steering ($129). Le Cat Black 'S' option group ($241). Decor group ($217). Manual sunroof ($181). Vinyl top ($95). Full tinted glass (required with air conditioning) ($47). Electric rear-window defroster ($69). Driver's remote racing mirror ($12). Wide bodyside moldings ($42). Tonneau-style vinyl luggage cover ($29). AM radio ($71). AM/FM radio ($136). AM/FM stereo radio ($216). Cast aluminum wheels ($113). Rear wiper/washer ($48).

Note: Also available was a dealer-installed Rally Cat option that included a twin-striped hood and tail with spoiler, plus larger 'CAPRI' decal striping on the lower door.

PERFORMANCE: Acceleration (0-60 mph): (2300) 13 seconds; (2800) 11 seconds. **Fuel Mileage:** (2300 manual) EPA 24/34 mpg; (2800 manual) EPA 18/28 mpg.

PRODUCTION/SALES: A total of 404,169 Capri II models were produced from 1975-77.

Manufacturer: Ford Werke A.G., West Germany; also built in Great Britain.

Distributor: Sold by Lincoln-Mercury dealers.

HISTORY: The final Capri II model year began in May 1977. Capris were not imported after 1977, though leftovers were sold in that year.

FORD (GERMAN)

Ford's presence in Germany dates back to 1925, when versions of the Model T went into production at Berlin. The Model A followed in 1928, and the Model B in 1931. Then, in the early 1930s, came the Koln, a smaller-engine sedan suitable for the Depression era, built at a new Ford plant in Cologne. In 1935, a variant of the flathead Ford V-8 also debuted. The Taunus name emerged by 1939, but war put a halt to its appearance.

Ford of Germany reintroduced the Taunus after the war, and continued the name into the 1960s and '70s. U.S. imports of the Taunus didn't begin officially until 1958, but a fair number of prior examples were brought home earlier in the Fifties by returning servicemen. Imports ceased after 1960, and through the next decade few German-built Ford products found their way to America. Then came the German/English Capri (listed separately under Ford-Europe), followed for a brief time by the subcompact Fiesta of 1977-80.

1948-51 TAUNUS

1949-'50 Ford Taunus.

TYPE 48 — FOUR — Prewar styling was evident on the first postwar Taunuses, which, except for the rear-hinged ("suicide") doors, looked rather like scaled-down American Fords of 1939 vintage. A low, divided grille was made up of horizontal bars. Headlamps were built into the fenders. A Standard two-door was the first to enter production, followed in 1949 by a two-door cabriolet. A little later in 1949, the Special two-door sedan added round parking lights below the headlamps and switched to a wide grille with two thick horizontal bars and a rounded upper bar. The car's profile now resembled that of a 1947 American Ford. Rectangular parking lights went on the DeLuxe two-door sedan for 1951. Power was provided by an L-head four-cylinder engine of 71.5-cid displacement, delivering 34 horsepower.

I.D. DATA: Chassis serial number is stamped on right frame member, above the first crossmember. Engine number is stamped on the right side of the block.

Model	Body Type & Seating	Engine Type/CID	P.O.E. Price	Weight (lbs.)	Prod. Total
TYPE 48					
Standard	2-dr Sedan	I4/71	N/A	N/A	182
Standard	2-dr Cabriolet	I4/71	N/A	N/A	11,109
Special	2-dr Sedan	I4/71	N/A	N/A	24,443
DeLuxe	2-dr Sedan	I4/71	N/A	N/A	27,059

Production Note: Figure shown for Standard sedan is for 1948 only; cabriolet, 1949-59; Special sedan, 1950-51; DeLuxe, 1951 only.

ENGINE DATA: BASE FOUR: Inline, L-head four-cylinder. **Displacement:** 71.5 cu. in. (1172 cc). **Bore & Stroke:** 2.50 x 3.64 in. (63.5 x 92.5 mm). **Compression Ratio:** 6.6:1. **Brake Horsepower:** 34 at 4200 rpm. Three main bearings. Solid valve lifters. One downdraft carburetor.

CHASSIS DATA: Wheelbase: 94 in. **Overall Length:** 161.5 in. **Width:** 57 in. **Front Tread:** 46.7 in. **Rear Tread:** 48 in. **Wheel Type:** disc. **Standard Tires:** 5.25x16.

TECHNICAL: Layout: front-engine, rear-drive. **Transmission:** three-speed manual. **Standard Final Drive Ratio:** 4.87:1. **Brakes:** front/rear drum.

Manufacturer: Ford-Werke Aktiengesellschaft (A.G.), Koln (Cologne), West Germany.

HISTORY: Introduced: (Standard sed) May 1948; (Standard cabr) April 1949; (Special sed) June 1949; (DeLuxe sed) January 1951. Last examples of the DeLuxe sedan were produced in December 1951.

1952-54 TAUNUS

1954 Ford Taunus 12M DeLuxe convertible.

12M — FOUR — If the first postwar Taunus models looked like scaled-down 1938-48 American Fords, the next generation resembled vaguely the 1949-51 models. An even closer resemblance could be seen to the British Zephyr and Consul Fords, which came to the U.S. earlier (officially) than the Taunus. Models included a two-door sedan, two-door cabriolet (convertible), and a Combi station wagon. Considered a well-built vehicle, the Taunus also was lauded for its attractive (if conventional) lines. Each of the split grille sections contained horizontal bars. Round parking lights stood below the fender-tip headlamps. What appeared to be a large round emblem (actually a foglight) went between the hood and the grille's center bar. Doors were now hinged at the front. Bodyside trim strips ran horizontally along the rear quarter panel and door, but kicked upward above the front wheel openings. Performance was not a strong point, at least to American prospects. Wool fabric was used for upholstery. The cabriolet had a neatly-folding top, though one that bulged a bit in the manner of most German ragtops. In addition to the 12M series, a more basic 12 series was produced with less chrome trim and fewer accessories. Under the hood was the same 1172-cc, L-head four-cylinder engine as the earlier models, with a bit more power (38 bhp).

I.D. DATA: Chassis serial number is stamped on inside of right wheel housing. Engine number is stamped on right side of block.

Model	Body Type & Seating	Engine Type/CID	P.O.E. Price	Weight (lbs.)	Prod. Total
12M	2-dr Sedan-4/5P	I4/71	N/A	1820	Note 1
12M	2-dr Cabr-4/5P	I4/71	N/A	1874	Note 1
12M	2-dr Combi Wag	I4/71	N/A	1950	Note 1

Note 1: A total of 30,685 units of the 12M were produced in 1952, 34,011 in 1953, and 37,858 in 1954.

Model Note: Series 12 sedan and Combi wagon also were available, with less trim.

Price Note: Base price at factory in Germany was about $1,399 for the lowest-cost sedan, up to about $1,649 for the Combi wagon. Estimated price in U.S. for the cabriolet was $2,500.

ENGINE DATA: BASE FOUR: Inline, L-head four-cylinder. **Displacement:** 71.5 cu. in. (1172 cc). **Bore & Stroke:** 2.50 x 3.64 in. (63.5 x 92.5 mm). **Compression Ratio:** 6.8:1. **Brake Horsepower:** 38 at 4250 rpm. **Torque:** 55 lbs.-ft. at 2200 rpm. Three main bearings. Solid valve lifters. One downdraft carburetor. 6-volt electrical.

CHASSIS DATA: Wheelbase: 98 in. **Overall Length:** 159-160 in. **Height:** 61 in. exc. (wag) 63.6 in. **Width:** 62 in. **Front Tread:** 48 in. **Rear Tread:** 48 in. **Wheel Type:** disc. **Standard Tires:** 5.60x13 (5.90x13 optional).

TECHNICAL: Layout: front-engine, rear-drive. **Transmission:** three-speed manual (later, four-speed). **Standard Final Drive Ratio:** 4.37:1. **Suspension (front):** independent; coil springs and stabilizer bar. **Suspension (rear):** rigid axle with semi-elliptic leaf springs. **Brakes:** hydraulic, front/rear drum. **Body Construction:** steel body on steel frame.

PERFORMANCE: Top Speed: 68 mph; (Combi) 65 mph. **Acceleration (0-60 mph):** 20 seconds. **Fuel Mileage:** 28-29 mpg.

Manufacturer: Ford-Werke A.G., Cologne, West Germany.

HISTORY: Taunus was just part of the Ford operation at Cologne. The company also produced trucks, buses, and other commercial vehicles.

1955-57 TAUNUS

1956 Ford Taunus 12M.

12M — FOUR — Production of the 12M series continued, with a switch from horizontal to vertical bars in the split grille, though joined by the 15M with its larger engine. A wide mesh grille replaced the split grille in 1957, when teardrop-shaped (later round) parking lights were added. The four-cylinder engine also gained some power that year, going from 38 to 43 bhp.

15M — FOUR — Appearance of the 15M was similar to the 12M, except for a wide single-unit grille that contained a single horizontal bar and curved upper bar. For 1956, though, the DeLuxe model changed to a grille with seven heavy vertical "teeth" across a horizontal bar. As in prior models, the bodyside trim strip jutted upward in a square above the front wheelwell, and headlamps were slightly hooded. 'Taunus' script was at the cowl, above the bodyside trim strip. A central foglight between the grille and hood looked more like a round emblem. A bigger four-cylinder engine with overhead valves, displacing 91.37 cubic inches, provided output of 55 horsepower, without (or so it was claimed) any loss of fuel economy. Interiors had plastic-covered, foam rubber seats. In addition to the two-door sedan and station wagon, a Combiwagen (minibus) was available.

I.D. DATA: Chassis serial number is stamped on inside of right wheel housing. Engine number is stamped on right side of block.

Model	Body Type & Seating	Engine Type/CID	P.O.E. Price	Weight (lbs.)	Prod. Total
12M					
12M	2-dr Sedan-4/5P	I4/71	N/A	1810	Note 1
12M	2-dr Cabr-4/5P	I4/71	N/A	1874	Note 1
12M	2-dr Station Wag	I4/71	N/A	1950	Note 1

1956 Ford Taunus 15M DeLuxe.

Model	Body Type & Seating	Engine Type/CID	P.O.E. Price	Weight (lbs.)	Prod. Total
15M	2-dr Sedan-4/5P	I4/91	N/A	1904	Note 2
15M	2-dr Cabr-4/5P	I4/91	N/A	N/A	Note 2
15M	2-dr Combi Wag	I4/91	N/A	2055	Note 2

Note 1: A total of 15,787 units of the 12M were produced in 1955, 18,287 in 1956, and 17,094 in 1957.

Note 2: A total of 35,877 units of the 15M were produced in 1955, 38,872 in 1956, and 25,877 in 1957.

Price Note: Base price at factory in Germany for 1957 was about $1,355 for the lowest-cost 12-series sedan, $1,473 for the 15M sedan, and $1,560 for the Combi wagon.

ENGINE DATA: BASE FOUR (12M): Inline, L-head four-cylinder. **Displacement:** 71.5 cu. in. (1172 cc). **Bore & Stroke:** 2.50 x 3.64 in. (63.5 x 92.5 mm). **Compression Ratio:** 6.8:1. **Brake Horsepower:** 38 at 4250 rpm (43 bhp in 1957). **Torque:** 55 lbs.-ft. at 2200 rpm. Three main bearings. Solid valve lifters. One downdraft carburetor. 6-volt electrical.
BASE FOUR (15M): Inline, overhead-valve four-cylinder. **Displacement:** 91.37 cu. in. (1498 cc). **Bore & Stroke:** 3.22 x 2.79 in. (82 x 70.9 mm). **Compression Ratio:** 7.0:1. **Brake Horsepower:** 55 at 4250 rpm. One Solex downdraft carburetor.

CHASSIS DATA: Wheelbase: 98 in. **Overall Length:** 160 in. **Height:** 61 in. exc. (wagon) 63.6 in. **Width:** 62 in. **Front Tread:** 48 in. **Rear Tread:** 48 in. **Wheel Type:** disc. **Standard Tires:** 5.60x13.

TECHNICAL: Layout: front-engine, rear-drive. **Transmission:** three- or four-speed manual. **Suspension (front):** independent; coil springs and stabilizer bar. **Suspension (rear):** rigid axle with semi-elliptic leaf springs. **Brakes:** hydraulic, front/rear drum. **Body Construction:** steel unibody.

MAJOR OPTIONS: Four-speed manual transmission.

PERFORMANCE: Top Speed: (12M) 69 mph; (15M) 78 mph. **Fuel Mileage:** about 29 mpg.

Manufacturer: Ford-Werke A.G., Cologne, West Germany.

HISTORY: A 17M sedan with larger engine yet was added in mid-1957; see next listing. Official Taunus importation to the U.S. began by 1958.

1958 TAUNUS

17M — FOUR — Not only was there a bigger engine under the hood of the next-generation Taunus, but it rode a longer wheelbase: grown from 98 to 102.5 inches. Styling features included a Z-shaped bodyside trim strip, and front fenders that angled sharply forward (not unlike the 1955-58 Plymouth). 'TAUNUS' block letters stood above the grille, which was made up of horizontal strips in the full-width lower section and four side-by-side oval segments above. In addition to the two- and four-door sedans, Taunus came in station wagon form. Rear windows of the sedan pivoted outward for ventilation. Seats were foam rubber, while plastic was used for trim. Instead of the customary knobs, Taunus used a set of "piano-key" controls on the dashboard for headlamps, fan and wipers. A three-speed gearbox with column gearshift lever was standard. Available extras included overdrive and an automatic clutch. Lights on the center roof supports served as auxiliary turn signals or parking lights. Four-doors came with a sunroof. Deluxe models showed a different grille, concave in shape and dipping below the headlamps, in one piece with both horizontal and vertical strips.

12M — FOUR — Production of the smaller-engined Taunus continued for the European market with little change, wearing a mesh grille and round parking lights. A 43-horsepower L-head four-cylinder engine provided the power.

15M — FOUR — The 1498-cc version switched to a mesh grille and teardrop-shaped parking lights for 1958, but was dropped before the model year ended; see prior listing for details.

I.D. DATA: Chassis serial number of the 12M is stamped on inside of right wheel housing; of the 17M, on right body brace. Serial/motor number is stamped on the right side of the engine block. Starting serial number: 1001001.

Model	Body Type & Seating	Engine Type/CID	P.O.E. Price	Weight (lbs.)	Prod. Total
17M	2-dr Sedan-5P	I4/104	2017	2205	Note 1
17M	4-dr Sedan-5P	I4/104	2109	2205	Note 1
17M	2-dr Sta Wag-5P	I4/104	2225	2381	Note 1
17M	2-dr DeL Sed-5P	I4/104	2117	2260	Note 1
17M	2-dr DeL Sed-5P	I4/104	2255	2260	Note 1
17M	2-dr DeL Wag-5P	I4/104	2711	2403	Note 1
12M					
12M	2-dr Sedan-4/5P	I4/71	N/A	1810	Note 2
12M	2-dr Station Wag	I4/71	N/A	N/A	Note 2

Note 1: A total of 67,772 units of the 17M series were produced in 1958; approximately 1,627 were sold in the U.S. during that year.

Note 2: A total of 24,323 units of the 12M series were produced in 1958, but not for the U.S. market.

Price Note: With Taunus imports now official, actual retail prices for the American market were announced.

ENGINE DATA: BASE FOUR (12M): Inline, L-head four-cylinder. **Displacement:** 71.5 cu. in. (1172 cc). **Bore & Stroke:** 2.50 x 3.64 in. (63.5 x 92.5 mm). **Compression Ratio:** 6.8:1. **Brake Horsepower:** 43 at 4250 rpm. **Torque:** 55 lbs.-ft. at 2200 rpm. Three main bearings. Solid valve lifters. One downdraft carburetor. 6-volt electrical.
BASE FOUR (17M): Inline, overhead-valve four-cylinder. **Displacement:** 103.62 cu. in. (1698 cc). **Bore & Stroke:** 3.31 x 3.02 in. (84 x 76.6 mm). **Compression Ratio:** 7.1:1. **Brake Horsepower:** 67 at 4400 rpm. **Torque:** 97.6 lbs.-ft. at 2220 rpm. Three main bearings. Solid valve lifters. One carburetor. 6-volt electrical.

CHASSIS DATA: Wheelbase: (12M) 98 in.; (17M) 102.5 in. **Overall Length:** (12M) 160 in; (17M) 172 in. **Height:** (12M) 61 in.; (17M) 59 in. **Width:** (12M) 62 in.; (17M) 64 in. **Front Tread:** (17M) 50 in. **Rear Tread:** (17M) 50 in. **Wheel Type:** disc. **Standard Tires:** (12M) 5.60x13; (17M) 5.90x13 except (wagon) 6.40x13.

TECHNICAL: Layout: front-engine, rear-drive. **Transmission:** three-speed or four-speed manual (overdrive available). **Standard Final Drive Ratio:** 3.9:1. **Steering:** worm and roller. **Suspension (front):** coil springs and stabilizer bar. **Suspension (rear):** rigid axle with semi-elliptic leaf springs. **Brakes:** hydraulic, front/rear drum. **Body Construction:** steel unibody. **Fuel Tank:** (17M) 11.9 gallons.

MAJOR OPTIONS: Overdrive. Saxomat automatic clutch.

PERFORMANCE: Top Speed: (12M) about 69 mph; (17M) 78-80 mph. **Acceleration (0-60 mph):** (17M) 17.5 seconds. **Fuel Mileage:** (12M) 30 mpg; (17M) 20-28 mpg.

Manufacturer: Ford Werke A.G., Cologne, West Germany.

Distributor: Columbia Motor Co., New York City.

HISTORY: Introduced in U.S. June 1958.

1959 TAUNUS

17M — FOUR — Except for slight price hikes, little changed in the large-engine Taunus, which was the only model commonly sold in the U.S. in the late 1950s. Six body styles included two- and four-door sedans and a two-door Combi station wagon, in both standard and deluxe trim. Interior features included a padded dashboard, adjustable front seatbacks, and folding armrests in back. The standard three-speed gearbox was fully synchronized.

12M — FOUR — Production of the Taunus with L-head engine continued without significant change, but it was augmented by a 12M Super during 1959, with larger 1498-cc engine. The 12M was not listed as available in the U.S. during 1959, but did appear on such lists later. See 1958 and 1960 listings for details.

I.D. DATA: Chassis serial number is stamped on right body brace. Engine number is stamped on right side of block.

Model	Body Type & Seating	Engine Type/CID	P.O.E. Price	Weight (lbs.)	Prod. Total
17M	2-dr Sedan-5P	I4/104	2029	2205	Note 1
17M	4-dr Sedan-5P	I4/104	2121	2205	Note 1
17M	2-dr Combi Wag-5P	I4/104	2237	2381	Note 1
17M	2-dr DeL Sed-5P	I4/104	2175	2260	Note 1
17M	4-dr DeL Sed-5P	I4/104	2267	2260	Note 1
17M	2-dr DeL Wag-5P	I4/104	2383	2403	Note 1

Note 1: Approximately 6,570 Taunuses were sold in the U.S. during 1959.

ENGINE DATA: BASE FOUR (17M): Inline, overhead-valve four-cylinder. **Displacement:** 103.62 cu. in. (1698 cc). **Bore & Stroke:** 3.31 x 3.02 in. (84 x 76.6 mm). **Compression Ratio:** 7.1:1. **Brake Horsepower:** 67 at 4400 rpm. **Torque:** 97.6 lbs.-ft. at 2220 rpm. Three main bearings. Solid valve lifters. One carburetor. 6-volt electrical.

CHASSIS DATA: Wheelbase: 102.5 in. **Overall Length:** 172.2 in. **Height:** 59.1 in. **Width:** 64 in. **Front Tread:** 50 in. **Rear Tread:** 50 in. **Wheel Type:** disc. **Standard Tires:** 5.90x13 except (wagon) 6.40x13.

TECHNICAL: Same as 1958.

MAJOR OPTIONS: Overdrive. Saxomat automatic clutch.

PERFORMANCE: Top Speed: near 78-80 mph. **Acceleration (0-60 mph):** about 20 seconds. **Fuel Mileage:** 22-25 mpg.

Manufacturer: Ford Werke A.G., Cologne, West Germany.

Distributor: Various Ford dealers in U.S.

HISTORY: Introduced: October 8, 1958.

1960 TAUNUS

17M — FOUR — Except for new upholstery patterns, not much was new in the larger Taunus, which was sold by Ford dealers in the U.S. Options included a four-speed manual transmission and Saxomat automatic clutch.

12M — FOUR — Production of the smaller-engined 12M continued with a facelift, including a change to a wide crosshatch grille topped by 'TAUNUS' block letters, and revised taillamps. The version imported to the U.S. was generally the Super, with optional 91 cubic-inch four-cylinder engine rather than the earlier 71.5-cid.

I.D. DATA: Serial/motor number is stamped on the right side of the engine block. Starting serial number: (17M) 1060658.

1960 Ford Taunus 17M four-door.

Model	Body Type & Seating	Engine Type/CID	P.O.E. Price	Weight (lbs.)	Prod. Total
17M	2-dr Sedan-5P	I4/104	2029	2157	Note 1
17M	4-dr Sedan-5P	I4/104	2121	2195	Note 1
17M	2-dr Sta Wag-5P	I4/104	2237	2301	Note 1
17M	2-dr DeL Sed-5P	I4/104	2175	2179	Note 1
17M	2-dr DeL Sed-5P	I4/104	2267	2217	Note 1
17M	2-dr DeL Wag-5P	I4/104	2383	2323	Note 1
12M SUPER					
12M	2-dr Sedan-4/5P	I4/91	1701	1920	Note 1
12M	2-dr Combi Wag	I4/91	1875	N/A	Note 1

Note 1: Total Ford-Werke (German) passenger car production for 1960 was 163,482 units.

ENGINE DATA: BASE FOUR (17M): Inline, overhead-valve four-cylinder. **Displacement:** 103.62 cu. in. (1698 cc). **Bore & Stroke:** 3.31 x 3.02 in. (84 x 76.6 mm). **Compression Ratio:** 7.1:1. **Brake Horsepower:** 67 at 4400 rpm. **Torque:** 97.6 lbs.-ft. at 2220 rpm. Three main bearings. Solid valve lifters. One Solex carburetor. 6-volt electrical.
BASE FOUR (12M Super): Inline, overhead-valve four-cylinder. **Displacement:** 91.4 cu. in. (1498 cc). **Bore & Stroke:** 3.23 x 2.79 in. (82 x 70.9 mm). **Compression Ratio:** 6.8:1. **Brake Horsepower:** 60 at 4250 rpm. **Torque:** 81.7 lbs.-ft. at 2000 rpm. Three main bearings. Solid valve lifters. One carburetor. 6-volt electrical.
Note: 12M models with the older L-head (71.5-cid) engine also were produced, but not normally exported to the U.S.

CHASSIS DATA: Wheelbase: (12M) 98 in.; (17M) 102.5 in. **Overall Length:** (12M) 160 in.; (17M) 172.2 in. **Height:** (12M) 59.5 in.; (17M) 57.7 in. **Width:** (12M) 61.8 in.; (17M) 65.7 in. **Front Tread:** (12M) 48 in.; (17M) 50 in. **Rear Tread:** (12M) 48 in.; (17M) 50 in. **Wheel Type:** disc. **Standard Tires:** (12M) 5.60x13; (17M) 5.90x13 except (wagon) 6.40x13.

TECHNICAL: Layout: front-engine, rear-drive. **Transmission:** three-speed or four-speed manual. **Standard Final Drive Ratio:** 3.27:1. **Steering:** worm and roller. **Suspension (front):** coil springs and stabilizer bar. **Suspension (rear):** rigid axle with semi-elliptic leaf springs. **Brakes:** hydraulic, front/rear drum. **Body Construction:** steel unibody. **Fuel Tank:** (12M) 9 gallons; (17M) 11.9 gallons.

MAJOR OPTIONS: Four-speed transmission. Saxomat automatic clutch.

PERFORMANCE: Top Speed: (12M) 69 mph; (12M Super) 78 mph; (17M) near 78-80 mph. **Acceleration (0-60 mph):** (17M) about 20 seconds. **Fuel Mileage:** (12M) 30 mpg; (12M Super) 27 mpg; (17M) 26-30 mpg.
Manufacturer: Ford Werke A.G., Cologne, West Germany.
Distributor: Various Ford dealers in U.S.
HISTORY: Introduced in U.S. October 1, 1959.

INTERIM NOTE: A restyled Taunus 17M appeared in Germany for 1961, with new oblong headlamps slightly inboard, ahead of the hood front. Park/signal lights were set low in the tips of the sharp-edged front fenders. By this time, however, exports to the U.S. had diminished and Taunus was no longer listed as an official import. Taunus production continued into the 1960s, as did that of other German Ford products. A new version of the 12M, introduced in 1962 (designed in the U.S.) had a V-4 engine and front-wheel drive. A V-4 also went into the rear-drive 17M in 1964, while a V-6 powered a new 20M. Not until the Capri of the 1970s (listed separately under Ford-Europe), and then the subcompact Fiesta (described below), did substantial numbers of Fords again arrive in America from Germany.

1962 Ford Taunus 12M two-door.

1977-80 FIESTA

1979 Ford Fiesta two-door sedan.

60S — FOUR — Actually designed at Ford in Dearborn, Michigan, Fiesta went into production in Germany in 1976 and came to the U.S. in August 1977, sold through more than 5,000 Ford dealers. Billed as the "Wundercar," Ford's front-wheel drive subcompact two-door hatchback sedan rode a 90-inch wheelbase and was powered by a 97.6 cubic-inch transverse-mounted four-cylinder engine. A flag decal strip on the wide back hatch suggested the car's international sales. Up front were single round headlamps and a horizontal-bar grille with 'FORD' on the lower driver's side. The deluxe dashboard held a tachometer on the right-hand side, while seats had separate headrests. Seats had Recaro mechanisms for welcome comfort. Folding back the rear seat brought 29 cubic feet of cargo space, accessible via the rear hatch. Optional Ghia and Sport packages were available. For 1979, the front seatbacks grew taller, adding integrated headrests; and three revised body colors were added (orange, green, and light beige). The Sport package included wider wheels, a rear anti-roll bar, and heavy-duty shock absorbers. The next year brought a new bumper rub strip and a few additional body colors.

I.D. DATA: A 12-symbol Vehicle Identification Number (VIN) plate is attached to left windshield post, visible through the windshield. Symbol one ('G') indicates German manufacture. Symbol two is the plant code. The next two symbols indicate body type ('FB' = hatchback). Symbol five is model year ('T' = 1978; 'U' or 'W' = 1979; 'W' or 'A' = 1980). Next is a symbol for production month, followed by the sequential serial number.

Model	Body Type & Seating	Engine Type/CID	P.O.E. Price	Weight (lbs.)	Prod. Total
60S	2-dr Hatch Sed-4P	I4/98	3680	1760	Note 1

Note 1: A total of 40,549 Fiestas were sold in the U.S. in 1977, 76,145 in 1978, 78,109 in 1979, and 68,595 in 1980.
Price Note: 1978 price shown; rose to $4,198 for 1979 and $4,493 in 1980.

ENGINE DATA: BASE FOUR: Inline, overhead-valve four-cylinder (transverse mounted). Cast iron block and head. **Displacement:** 97.6 cu. in. (1599 cc). **Bore & Stroke:** 3.19 x 3.07 in. (81 x 78 mm). **Compression Ratio:** 8.5:1. **Brake Horsepower:** 66 at 5000 rpm. **Torque:** 88 lbs.-ft. at 3200 rpm. Five main bearings. Solid valve lifters. Weber Two-barrel carburetor.

CHASSIS DATA: Wheelbase: 90 in. **Overall Length:** 147.1 in. **Height:** 52.3 in. **Width:** 61.2 in. **Front Tread:** 52.5 in. **Rear Tread:** 52.0 in. **Standard Tires:** Michelin 145SR12 (155SR12 available).

TECHNICAL: Layout: front-engine, front-drive. **Transmission:** four-speed manual. **Standard Final Drive Ratio:** 3.58:1. **Steering:** rack and pinion. **Suspension (front):** MacPherson struts with coil springs. **Suspension (rear):** rigid axle with four trailing links, Panhard rod, coil springs, and anti-sway bar. **Brakes:** power front disc, rear drum. **Body Construction:** steel unibody. Fuel Tank: 10 gallons.

MAJOR OPTIONS: (1979) Decor trim package ($390). Sport package ($556). Ghia trim package ($722). Flip-up sunroof ($199). Power brakes ($70). Air conditioning ($430). AM radio ($72). AM/FM stereo radio ($161). AM/FM monaural radio ($120). Cast aluminum wheels ($180).

PERFORMANCE: Acceleration (0-60 mph): N/A (Ford claimed 0-50 mph in 8.8 seconds). **Fuel Mileage:** (EPA) 34/46 mpg.
Manufacturer: Ford Werke A.G., West Germany.
Distributor: Ford Motor Company, Dearborn, Michigan (over 5,000 dealers in the U.S.).

HISTORY: Production began for European customers in 1976, and the first Fiestas arrived in the U.S. in August 1977, as 1978 models.

POSTSCRIPT: Like the Taunus two decades earlier, the Fiesta continued in production in Europe, but ceased export to the U.S. This time, the reason was the emergence of the new domestically-built Ford Escort with its own version of front-wheel drive.

263

FRAZER-NASH

"Chain gang" was the term given by Frazer-Nash fans to the early examples of the marque. During the decade prior to World War II, Frazer-Nash became known for one bit of already-antiquated technology: chain drive. That was no surprise, since the company's founder, Archibald (Archie) Frazer-Nash, had worked on the chain-drive GN cyclecar before starting his own firm in 1922. His first order of business, in fact, was to buy surplus parts from the GN company and turn out a handful of Frazer-Nash editions of the cyclecar. A shaft-drive Frazer-Nash also appeared early, but little more than the body came from the new company. In 1924 the first true Frazer-Nash arrived, initially offered with a Plus-Power 1.5-liter engine, then with an Anzani powerplant; and later yet, carrying engines by Meadows and Gough, among others. They performed handily in hillclimbs and other race events. One special supercharged race car was capable of 135 mph. A name change to A.F.N. Ltd. came in 1927, after which control left the hands of Archie Frazer-Nash. H.J. Aldington, who'd been part of the company all along, took over and remained in charge through the postwar decade of production. Throughout its subsequent existence, too, the Frazer-Nash was tied to the HRG (also listed in this Catalog).

A total of 350 Frazer-Nashes were produced by 1939, with 39 built in 1934 alone. Even so, it was always a limited-production automobile and attracted a staunch following among stalwarts who fancied the down-to-basics, cycle-fendered bodywork and its primitive drivetrain/suspension. Comforts were few, but traction was great with the chain drive, which used no differential. Besides that, top speeds reached as high as 90 mph. Both four- and six-cylinder engines were used. Aldington acquired rights to the German BMW in 1934 and began to import Frazer-Nash-BMWs, including the appealing model 328.

H.J. Aldington became a director of the Bristol Aeroplane Co. after World War II, and helped that firm adopt BMW's engine design for the new Bristol automobile. Bristol focused largely on luxury with a series of two-door saloons, while sporty roadster and coupe versions became the province of Frazer-Nash. Designed by Fritz Fiedler, who'd worked on the BMW 328 powerplant, the postwar Frazer-Nashes abandoned the prewar chain drive, but used Bristol engines and transmissions in a new tubular steel chassis. A variety of essentially handmade models came out of the Isleworth plant, headed by the cycle-fendered Le Mans Replica, which fared well in competition (as befitting its name). Other models had modern and curvaceous "envelope" style bodies, including the Milla Miglia, Sebring, Targa Florio, and the Fast Roadster. Careful craftsmanship made the cars expensive and rare, and few ever left Britain. A total of 34 Le Mans Replicas were built by 1953, and no more than 95 postwar Frazer-Nashes in all before the company ceased production in 1957. Final offering was the V-8 Continental, of which even fewer were built.

1948-57 FRAZER-NASH

Postwar Frazer-Nashes came in more than a dozen different varieties, from the first Competition edition of 1948 to the final Continental of 1956-57. With the exception of the

264

Continental (which carried a BMW V-8) and a four-cylinder prototype built in 1952, each was powered by the Bristol six-cylinder engine that evolved from the prewar BMW design. Horsepower ratings ranged from 85 to 150. Body styles were no less numerous, including open roadsters, closed and drophead coupes, and single-seat racing cars. Because each Frazer-Nash was built to order, there was no standard type with strict specifications. Except for the Continental, postwar Frazer-Nashes had an independent front suspension with transverse leaf spring and a rigid rear axle with torsion bars. The Continental switched to coil springs up front. Aluminum bodies rode a tubular ladder-type chassis, with a 96-inch wheelbase.

1950 Frazer-Nash LeMans replica roadster. (William Siuru Jr.)

LE MANS REPLICA — SIX — Best known of the postwar Frazer-Nashes, the Le Mans edition had a stark prewar race-car look with cycle-style fenders. According to the U.S. sales brochure, the hand-built competition two-seater was "guaranteed a replica in specification, performance and construction of the Frazer Nash which was so successful at Le Mans." Separate headlamps were mounted high up, alongside the narrow grille which was made up of vertical bars with a wide center vertical bar, and an insignia in the top of the bright surround molding. Headlamps and "mudguards" (fenders) detached easily. The cowl and hood were loaded with grillework, and a belt held the hood in position. Straight exhaust pipes stuck out the side of the cowl. Bucket-type seats were upholstered in leather. Tubular main body hoops and subsidiary framework for the aluminum body were welded to the chassis, "resulting in exceptional strength and rigidity." Standard equipment included a tonneau cover and twin aero windshields. Body colors were offered to the customer's choice. "One-shot" chassis lubrication was available by pressing a foot pump.
    Early examples offered two versions of the Bristol six-cylinder engine, rated either 110 or 120 bhp (8.5:1 or 9.5:1 compression). A later Mk II was also available with up to 132 bhp.

MILLE MIGLIA — SIX — Specifications were similar to the Le Mans, except that box-section extensions in the main tubular chassis members passed under the rear axle instead of being upswept in form. This permitted an even lower body profile. The Mille Miglia had an envelope-style body with built-in headlamps, and tiny round parking lights below. Its protruding grille had a wide vertical center bar, along with a pattern of horizontal bars, in a surround molding that was rounded at the top. Two tiny aero windshields were installed. The body had full wheel openings, front and rear, plus an air scoop in the hood.

FAST ROADSTER — SIX — This example had a fully faired full-width body, with a 16-gallon petrol tank mounted on upward extensions of the frame immediately behind the seats. That allowed the whole rear of the body to be used as a big trunk. The spare wheel was fully enclosed in a front fender. Large running lights stood inboard of the built-in headlamps, with tiny parking lights down below the small separate bumpers. The hood was more like a lid, not covering the entire top of the front end. The sloping windshield was made of curved glass. A traditional Frazer-Nash radiator design was made up of vertical bars. Color schemes were to the customer's choice. Seats and cockpit trim were upholstered in leather. On the dash was a 5-inch tachometer and 5-inch (100-mph) speedometer. A 90-bhp version of the Bristol six-cylinder engine provided the power, to a four-speed manual gearbox. A later version carried a 105-bhp engine. The roadster body also was available on a competition chassis, with unstressed light alloy panels on a rigid framework of steel tubes, welded to the chassis.

FOURSOME CABRIOLET — SIX — Riding a longer (108-inch) wheelbase than its mates, this model carried an 85-bhp version of the Bristol engine. Autocar described it as "undoubtedly one of the most attractive convertibles yet seen." All wheels were partially enclosed, giving a very sleek look. Built-in bumpers were installed. Front appearance was unique, with a grille made up of horizontal bars and a single vertical bar at the center.

TARGA FLORIO — SIX — Introduced in 1952, the Targa Florio came in two forms: Gran Sport and Turismo. A year earlier, a Frazer-Nash had been the first British car to win the 35th Targa Florio race event, beating a Ferrari and Maserati. This model had full-width, low-drag roadster coachwork but with all-weather protection that included a raked and curved windshield, three-point top, and Perspex side windows. Autocar noted that it was "as easy and comfortable as a convertible, and remarkably warm even when the outside temperature is below freezing." Appearance was similar to the Mille Miglia, but with a narrower and taller vertical-bar grille. The Gran Sport version was identical in technical specifications to the Le Mans Competition model, with three tubular steel body hoops welded to the main chassis members. It used thinner metal for the body than the Turismo, which accounted for its lighter weight. Inside the Targo Florio, Dunopillo seats were upholstered in leather. Seats, steering column rake/height and pedal positions could be adjusted to suit the customer. Plastic three-quarter panels in the soft top were standard (upon request). Under the Turismo hood was a 100-bhp version of the Bristol six-cylinder engine, while the Gran Sport's six delivered 132 bhp.

SEBRING — SIX — Unlike most Frazer-Nashes, which had a vertical-bar type grille, the Sebring had a wide opening with large recessed horizontal bars in a low nose. Headlamps were built into the fender tips, also rather low, with round parking lights inboard, alongside the grille opening. The hood (actually a lid) held an airscoop. The Sebring was introduced in 1954, with a 140-bhp version of the Bristol six-cylinder engine.

LE MANS COUPE — SIX — The Le Mans name emerged again on a far different sort of car than the earlier Replica. This one was a sleek fixed-head coupe, similar in appearance to the Sebring roadster, with a pentagonal grille opening that contained recessed horizontal bars.

CONTINENTAL — V-8 — Rarest of the lot may be the final Frazer-Nash, powered by a BMW V-8 engine in a choice of three displacements. Appearance was similar to the Sebring and Le Mans coupe.

Model Note: Other Frazer-Nashes also were offered with similar appearance and specifications, including Competition models and a High Speed.

1954 Frazer-Nash LeMans fixed-head coupe.

1956 Frazer-Nash Sebring model (left) and fixed head coupe.

I.D. DATA: Not available.

Model	Body Type & Seating	Engine Type/CID	P.O.E. Price	Weight (lbs.)	Prod. Total
LE MANS REPLICA					
	2-dr Rds-2P	I6/120	6850	1484	34
MILLE MIGLIA					
	2-dr Rds-2P	I6/120	7850	1792	Note 1
FAST ROADSTER					
	2-dr Rds-2P	I6/120	N/A	1881	Note 1
FOURSOME CABRIOLET					
	2-dr Conv-2P	I6/120	N/A	2212	Note 1
TARGA FLORIO (1952)					
Gran Spt	2-dr Rds-2P	I6/120	N/A	1710	Note 1
Turismo	2-dr Rds-2P	I6/120	N/A	1824	Note 1
SEBRING (1954)					
	2-dr Coupe-2P	I6/120	N/A	1767	Note 1
LE MANS COUPE (1954)					
	2-dr Coupe-2P	I6/120	7500	1820	Note 1
CONTINENTAL (1956-57)					
	2-dr Coupe-2P	V8	N/A	2052	Note 1

Note 1: A total of only about 84 Frazer-Nash cars were built during the 1948-57 period.
Price Note: Price for the Le Mans Replica in England was 2250 pounds (Sterling).

ENGINE DATA: BASE SIX (Le Mans Replica, Mille Miglia): Inline, overhead-valve six-cylinder. Cast iron block and alloy head. **Displacement:** 120.2 cu. in. (1971 cc). **Bore & Stroke:** 2.60 x 3.78 in. (66 x 96 mm). **Compression Ratio:** 8.5:1 (9.5:1 optional). **Brake Horsepower:** 110 at 5250 rpm (120 at 5500 optional). **Torque:** 121 lbs.-ft. at 3750 rpm (125.5 at 4500 optional). Four main bearings. Solid valve lifters. Three Solex downdraft carburetors. 12-volt electrical.

BASE SIX (Fast Roadster): Same as above, except — **Compression Ratio:** 8.0:1. **Brake Horsepower:** 90 at 4500 rpm.

BASE SIX (Foursome Cabriolet): Same as above, except — **Compression Ratio:** 7.5:1. **Brake Horsepower:** 85 at 4500 rpm.

BASE SIX (Targa Florio): Same as above, except — **Compression Ratio:** (Turismo) 7.5:1; (Gran Spt) 8.5:1. **Brake Horsepower:** (Turismo) 100 at 5000 rpm; (Gran Spt) 140 at 5750 rpm.

BASE SIX (Sebring/Le Mans coupe): Same as above, except — **Compression Ratio:** 8.8:1. **Brake Horsepower:** 140 at 5750 rpm.

BASE V-8 (Continental): Overhead-valve V-8 (BMW). **Displacement:** 2430 cc, 2580 cc, or 3168 cc. **Bore & Stroke:** 72 x 75, 74 x 75, or 82 x 75 mm. **Compression Ratio:** 7.5:1 to 8.2:1. **Brake Horsepower:** 120 to 173.

Engine Note: Because so few Frazer-Nashes were produced, and those were built to order, specifications were not always identical to figures above.

CHASSIS DATA: Wheelbase: 96.0 in. **Overall Length:** (Le Mans Replica) 141 in.; (Mille Miglia/Targa) 150 in.; (Le Mans cpe/Sebring) 156 in.; (Foursome) 164 in. **Height:** (Le Mans Replica) 37 in.; (Mille) 35.5 in.; (Targa) 51 in. to windshield top; (Le Mans cpe/Sebring) 51 in.; (Foursome) 50 in. **Width:** (Le Mans) 59 in.; (Mille/Targa) 58 in.; (Le Mans cpe) 61.5 in.; (Sebring) 61 in.; (Foursome) 64 in. **Front Tread:** 48 in.; (Le Mans cpe) 50 in. **Rear Tread:** 48 in.; (Targa) 49.5 in.; (Sebring) 50 in.; (Le Mans cpe) 52 in. (Foursome) 54 in. **Wheel Type:** disc. **Standard Tires:** 5.25x16 (most models); some 5x50x16 or larger.

TECHNICAL: Layout: front-engine, rear-drive. **Transmission:** four-speed manual; floor lever. Overall Le Mans Replica/Mille Miglia (close-ratio) gearing: (1st) 10.33:1; (2nd) 6.46:1; (3rd) 4.57:1; (4th) 3.54:1; (rev) 10.23:1. Overal Fast Roadster gear ratios: (free-wheeling 1st) 15.26:1; (2nd) 7.72:1; (3rd) 4.51:1; (4th) 3.55:1; (rev) 12.22:1. Targa Florio Gran Sport ratios: (1st) 10.7:1; (2nd) 6.9:1; (3rd) 4.7:1; (4th) 3.6:1; (rev) 10.6:1. Targa Florio Turismo ratios: (1st) 15.5:1; (2nd) 7.8:1; (3rd) 4.7:1; (4th) 3.6:1. Foursome gear ratios: (1st) 16.77:1; (2nd) 8.48:1; (3rd) 5.51:1; (4th) 3.9:1; (rev) 13.43:1. **Standard Final Drive Ratio:** 3.54:1 or 3.55:1 (most models). **Steering:** rack and pinion. **Suspension (front):** independent; top transverse leaf spring and wishbones. **Suspension (rear):** rigid axle with torsion bars. **Brakes:** hydraulic, front/rear drum. **Body Construction:** aluminum body on tubular steel frame. **Fuel Tank:** 20-gallon (plus 2-gallon reserve).

MAJOR OPTIONS: (for Targa Florio and certain other models) Engine with up to 150 bhp and 10:1 compression. Alternate final drive ratios. Alternate gearbox ratios. Center-lock disc wheels. Center-lock wire wheels. Detachable bumpers. Adjustable steering wheel. Large-capacity fuel tank. Auxiliary fuel tank. Racing windshield.

PERFORMANCE: Top Speed: (Le Mans Replica) 118 mph; (Foursome) 89 mph; (Le Mans cpe) 130 mph. **Acceleration (0-60 mph):** (Le Mans cpe) 9.5 seconds (Le Mans Replica, 0-50 in 7 seconds). **Acceleration (quarter-mile):** (Targa Turismo) 17.8 seconds.

Manufacturer: A.F.N. Ltd., London Road, Isleworth, Middlesex, England.
Distributor: Bristol Motors, Inc., New York City.

HISTORY: Introduced: (Le Mans) 1949; (Mille Miglia) 1949; (Fast Roadster) 1949; (Foursome Cabriolet) 1949; (Targa Florio) 1952; (Sebring) 1954; (Continental) 1956. *Autocar* declared the Frazer-Nash showing at Le Mans "a significant performance." The sole Frazer-Nash entered was a standard production 1949 two-liter competition model, privately owned and driven. It wound up with three successes, including third place in the Gran Prix d'Endurance (on actual distance covered in 24 hours at average speed of 78.53 mph) and second in the Rudge-Whitworth Biennial Cup. This continued the prewar Frazer-Nash tradition of success in international competition. A Le Mans Replica also won the first Sebring 12-hour race in the U.S., in 1952. Promotional material referred to Frazer-Nash as "The Competition Car for the Owner-Driver," adding that it could be "Raced As Sold."

GEO (CHEVROLET IMPORTS)

Chevrolet's importation of Japanese-built subcompacts began in 1984 with the Suzuki-built Sprint, followed the next year by the Isuzu-built Spectrum. When a new Geo nameplate was introduced for all Chevrolet imported models for the 1989 model year, the Sprint got a name change to Geo Metro, while the Spectrum continued under the Geo badge for one year. New in 1989 was a Prizm four-door, built in California as a joint venture with Toyota, taking over from the Nova that had been produced by the NUMMI plant there since 1986. A sporty Geo Storm hatchback coupe was added in 1990, built in Japan by Isuzu. Meanwhile, the Geo name also went on a Tracker sport-utility vehicle produced in Japan and Canada.

1984-88 CHEVROLET (IMPORTS)

1985 Chevrolet Spectrum.

SPRINT — FOUR — Chevrolet's smallest offering was the Suzuki-built two-door hatchback sedan, with front-wheel-drive, which went on sale in western states in spring 1984. As sale spread across the country, it was promoted as the lightest, and most economical, production model sold in America. The initial three-cylinder engine produced 48 horsepower, offered only with a five-speed manual gearbox. With an 88.4-inch wheelbase, it measured some 20 inches shorter overall than a domestically-built Chevette and weighed nearly 540 pounds less. A larger four-door hatchback was added for 1986, along with a super-economical E/R model that earned an EPA mileage rating of 55 mpg.

SPECTRUM — FOUR — This front-wheel-drive, five-seat subcompact sedan was introduced first on the East Coast during the 1985 model year. Built by Isuzu in Japan, it came in four-door sedan and two-door hatchback body styles. Both manual and automatic transmissions were available with the 1.5-liter four-cylinder engine.

I.D. DATA: A 17-symbol Vehicle Identification Number is on the upper left of the dashboard, visible through the windshield.

Model	Body Type & Seating	Engine Type/CID	P.O.E. Price	Weight (lbs.)	Prod. Total
SPRINT (1984-88)					
	2-dr Hatch-4P	I3/61	5380	1488	Note 1
E/R	2-dr Hatch-4P	I3/61	5765	N/A	Note 1
Plus	4-dr Hatch-4P	I3/61	5580	1565	Note 1
SPECTRUM (1985-88)					
	2-dr Sedan-5P	I4/91	6928	1874	Note 1
	2-dr Hatch-5P	I4/91	6658	1909	Note 1

Note 1: A total of 13,004 Chevrolet imports were sold in the U.S. during 1984, followed by 84,860 in 1985, 160,363 in 1986, 137,211 in 1987, and 116,435 in 1988.
Price Note: Figures and models shown were valid in 1986.
ENGINE DATA: BASE THREE (Sprint): Inline, overhead-cam three-cylinder. **Displacement:** 61 cu. in. (999 cc). **Bore & Stroke:** 2.91 x 3.03 in. (74 x 77 mm). **Compression Ratio:** 9.5:1. **Brake Horsepower:** 48 at 5100 rpm. **Torque:** 57 lbs.-ft. at 3200 rpm. Two-barrel carburetor.

BASE FOUR (Spectrum): Inline, overhead-cam four-cylinder. **Displacement:** 91 cu. in. (1491 cc). **Bore & Stroke:** 3.03 x 3.11 in. (77 x 79 mm). **Compression Ratio:** 9.6:1. **Brake Horsepower:** 70 at 5400 rpm. **Torque:** 87 lbs.-ft. at 3400 rpm. Two-barrel carburetor.
CHASSIS DATA: Wheelbase: (Sprint 2-dr) 88.4 in.; (Sprint 4-dr) 92.3 in.; (Spectrum) 94.5 in. **Overall Length:** (Sprint 2-dr) 141.1 in.; (Sprint 4-dr) 145.1 in.; (Spectrum 2-dr) 156 in.; (Spectrum 4-dr) 159 in. **Height:** (Sprint) 53.1 in.; (Spectrum) 52 in. **Width:** (Sprint) 60.3 in.; (Spectrum) 63.6 in.
TECHNICAL: Layout: front-engine, front-drive. **Transmission:** five-speed manual or (Spectrum) three-speed automatic. **Steering:** rack and pinion. **Suspension (front):** MacPherson struts with coil springs. **Suspension (rear):** (Sprint) beam axle w/monoleaf springs; (Spectrum) transverse beam with trailing arms and coil springs. **Brakes:** front disc, rear drum. **Body Construction:** steel unibody.
ADDITIONAL MODELS: Chevrolet also produced the Nova in California, as part of a joint venture with Toyota.

1989-90 GEO

1989 Geo Spectrum four-door.

METRO — THREE — Production of the Suzuki-built Sprint continued under the Geo Metro badge. For 1990, three versions were available: ultra-economical XFi two-door hatchback, base two-door or four-door hatchback, and upscale (to a point) twin LSi hatchbacks. Each carried the same three-cylinder engine used on the former Sprint, but now with fuel injection. A two-seat convertible was added during summer 1990 (as a late '90 model).

1989 Geo Tracker.

STORM — FOUR — The sporty new subcompact front-drive 2+2 coupe, produced in Japan by Isuzu, went on sale in the U.S. for the 1990 model year. Intended to rival Honda's CRX as well as the new Mitsubishi Eclipse, it came in two forms. The base model had a single-cam 1.6-liter four-cylinder (12-valve) engine that produced 95 horsepower. Performance fans could get a potent GSi, with a high-revving dual-overhead-cam (16-valve) version of the 1.6-liter engine that delivered 130 bhp. Styling features on the GSi included aero body add-on elements, notable rocker panel extensions and a unique rear end with spoiler, plus integrated halogen foglamps and alloy wheels. Underneath was a road-tuned suspension and quicker steering ratio. Both models came with a driver's-side airbag. Either a five-speed manual gearbox or optional automatic was available. The GSi came only in Flash Yellow; base Storms were offered in six body colors.

Note: The Spectrum also sold under the Geo name in 1989.

I.D. DATA: A 17-symbol Vehicle Identification Number is on the upper left of the dashboard, visible through the windshield.

1990 Geo Prizm hatchback.

1990 Geo Metro convertible.

Model	Body Type & Seating	Engine Type/CID	P.O.E. Price	Weight (lbs.)	Prod. Total
METRO (1989-90)					
XFi	2-dr Hatch-4P	I3/61	5995	N/A	Note 1
	2-dr Hatch-4P	I3/61	6695	1585	Note 1
	4-dr Hatch-4P	I3/61	6995	1693	Note 1
LSi	2-dr Hatch-4P	I3/61	7495	1591	Note 1
LSi	4-dr Hatch-4P	I3/61	7795	1640	Note 1
LSi	2-dr Conv-2P	I3/61	9740	1753	Note 1
STORM (1990)					
	2-dr Hatch-2+2P	I4/97	10390	2282	Note 1
GSi	2-dr Hatch-2+2P	I4/97	11650	2392	Note 1

Note 1: A total of 115,504 Chevrolet imports were sold in the U.S. during 1989, and 128,745 in 1990.

Price Note: Figures and models shown were valid in 1990.

ENGINE DATA: BASE THREE (Metro): Inline, overhead-cam three-cylinder. **Displacement:** 61 cu. in. (999 cc). **Bore & Stroke:** 2.91 x 3.03 in. (74 x 77 mm). **Compression Ratio:** 9.5:1. **Brake Horsepower:** 55 at 5700 rpm. **Torque:** 58 lbs.-ft. at 3300 rpm. Throttle-body fuel injection.
Note: The economy-leader Metro XFi was rated 49 bhp at 4700 rpm.
BASE FOUR (Metro): Inline, overhead-cam four-cylinder. **Displacement:** 97 cu. in. (1588 cc). **Bore & Stroke:** 3.15 x 3.11 in. (80 x 79 mm). **Compression Ratio:** 9.1:1. **Brake Horsepower:** 95 at 5800 rpm. **Torque:** 97 lbs.-ft. at 4800 rpm. Port fuel injection.
BASE FOUR (Storm GSi): Same as 1.6-liter four above, but with dual overhead cams (16-valve). **Compression Ratio:** 9.8:1. **Brake Horsepower:** 130 at 7000 rpm. **Torque:** 102 lbs.-ft. at 5800 rpm.

CHASSIS DATA: Wheelbase: (Metro 2-dr) 89.2 in.; (Metro 4-dr) 93.2 in.; (Storm) 96.5 in. **Overall Length:** (Metro 2-dr) 146.3 in.; (Metro 4-dr) 150.4 in.; (Storm) 163.4 in. **Height:** (Metro) 53.4 in.; (Storm) 51.1 in. **Width:** (Metro 2-dr) 62.0 in.; (Metro 4-dr) 62.7 in.; (Storm) 66.7 in.

TECHNICAL: Layout: front-engine, front-drive. **Transmission:** five-speed manual or (Storm) three-speed automatic, (Storm GSi) four-speed automatic. **Steering:** rack and pinion. **Suspension (front):** MacPherson struts with coil springs. **Suspension (rear):** (Metro) beam axle w/monoleaf springs; (Storm) MacPherson struts with coil springs. **Brakes:** front disc, rear drum. **Body Construction:** steel unibody.

1990 Geo Storm GSi.

ADDITIONAL MODELS: Chevrolet also marketed the domestic-built Prizm sedan, manufactured in California as a joint venture with Toyota (and similar to its Corolla) under the Geo name. Introduced in February 1989 as early '90 models, Prizms were powered by a dual-overhead-cam 1.6-liter four-cylinder engine, producing 102 horsepower (130 bhp in the GSi sport model). Four-door notchback and hatchback bodies were offered, on a 95.7-inch wheelbase.
Also available was the Suzuki-built Tracker sport-utility four-wheel-drive vehicle. Some Trackers were produced in Canada, others in Japan. A squareback Storm 2+2 hatchback joined the original model for 1991, adding considerable space in the back seat.

GLAS

One of the nearly-forgotten German makes, Glas (pronounced GLAHS) actually dates back to 1883, when the Hans Glas GmbH firm was founded in Pilsting an der Isar (later known as Dingolfing). The company became known for the manufacture of agricultural equipment. In 1951, the company built a Goggo motorscooter. By 1955, that evolved into the Goggomobil (listed separately in this Catalog), which became a rival to the BMW Isetta minicar. Two years later came the debut of the larger Isar T600, shown first as a front-drive car, but produced with rear-wheel drive and a 584-cc two-cylinder, two-stroke engine. A subsequent Isar T700 had a larger (688-cc) engine, also of two-stroke configuration. Both Isars featured wraparound windshields.

A sporty 1004 model 2+2 coupe debuted in spring 1962, with a front engine and rear-wheel drive, powered by a 993-cc four-cylinder engine rated 42 horsepower. This was the first production automobile to use a toothed-belt cam drive for the engine, eliminating the customary chain. A convertible and two-door sedan were added in 1963, as well as a 64-bhp TS model. The 1204 was similar in appearance but powered by an 1189-cc engine, rated 53 horsepower (70 bhp in TS form). Engine size grew again (to 1289 cc) for the model 1304, introduced in 1965.

A four-door sedan, styled by Frua, appeared at the Frankfurt Show in 1963, and went into production a year later as the Glas 1700. This one carried a 1682-cc engine, rated 85 horsepower, and was meant to be a rival to the BMW 1600 and 1800. The 1700 TS edition added 15 more horsepower, with dual carburetors. Also at the Frankfurt Show that year was a Frua-styled 1300 GT fastback 2+2 coupe, with the 1289-cc engine from the 1304 TS (rated 75 horsepower). Production of that model began in March 1964, followed a year later by a convertible version. A 1700 GT coupe also debuted, with a 100-bhp engine. That one sold briefly in the U.S. but received a bad review from *Road & Track,* because of its handling, though the magazine called it "one of the most attractive small GT cars we've ever driven."

The 1965 Frankfurt Show brought a Glas V-8 2+2 coupe, with a 2576-cc engine designed and built by Glas. Bore/stroke were identical to the 1289-cc four, so displacement was precisely double. This one used two toothed camshaft belts, as well as a trio of Solex carburetors, and produced up to 150 bhp at 5600 rpm. Prior Glas models had a rigid (live) rear axle, but the V-8 turned to a De Dion setup. The V-8 could accelerate from zero to 62 mph in 11 seconds, and reach 121 mph. Body styling came from Frua.

In 1966, BMW bought up the Glas company, which had been in financial trouble due to a move into larger cars. In fact, none of its products had been earning a profit except for the little Goggomobil. Production continued at the BMW plant in Dingolfing, including the Goggomobil, 1004, 1304 and 1700 models. The 1700 TS was dropped early in

1967, other 1700s later that year; and the 1004 and 1304 lasted through 1967 before biting the dust. The 1304 TS lingered longer.

The 1300 GT and 1700 GT coupes remained, marketed under the BMW badge. In September 1967, they enjoyed a name change to BMW 1600 GT. In this form, the fastback coupe was powered by a BMW 1600ti engine and transmission, rated at 105 bhp (with twin carburetors). BMW's usual semi-trailing arm rear suspension was used, instead of the Glas "live" axle. Otherwise, the 1600 GT had the same look as before, apart from its BMW emblems and center "kidney" grille. A total of 1,255 1600 GT coupes were built, through August 1968. By that time, prices had dropped sharply, and the Glas name faded away.

Also continued under BMW management, however, was the 2.6-liter 2+2 V-8 model, which had been nicknamed "Glasferati" (because of its resemblance to Maseratis, also designed by Frua). Addition of 5 mm to the stroke length in 1967 turned it into a 3.0-liter engine, rated 160 horsepower and capable of 200 kph top speeds. A BMW emblem went on the hood, rear body panel and wheel covers. The Glas name no longer was on the grille, but block letters with that name went below the BMW badge on rear. Only 400 of the late V-8s were sold, called BMW-Glas 3000, before production halted in June 1968.

1963-66 GLAS

1966 Glas 1600 V-8.

1204 — FOUR — One of the basic Glas models was the 1204, powered by an 1189-cc engine. Glas engines used a Solex recirculating carburetor that permitted excess fuel to spill over into a return pipe and be reused, via a special fuel pump. Each engine also had a dry-running, notched plastic timing belt.

1300/1304 — FOUR — A 1289-cc single-overhead-cam four-cylinder engine powered the 1304 sedan and the subsequent 1300 GT coupe. Styled by Frua (in Italy), the German-built Glas 1300 GT fastback 2+2 coupe debuted in spring 1964. Styling features included a wide grille in a slightly rounded nose, with single round headlamps mounted like projectiles at the fender tips. The 1300 GT engine produced 85 horsepower (DIN). A two-seat cabriolet (convertible) also was produced.

1700 — FOUR — A larger (1682-cc) engine rated 85 bhp powered the Glas 1700 four-door sedan, introduced in September 1964. A 1700 TS version produced 100 horsepower, using twin carburetors. The five-seat sedan had front vent wings, wide front/rear bumpers, fold-down front bucket seats, glovebox, parcel shelf behind the rear seats, and four armrests.

1700 GT — FOUR — A more potent version of the 1700 engine went into the 1700 GT coupe, which featured single round headlamps, a long hood scoop, tight crosshatch grille pattern, and Glas emblem at the grille's center. Standard 1700 GT equipment included cushioned sunvisors, windshield washers, backup light, door armrests, heater/defroster, passenger courtesy grip, bumper guards with rubber inserts, full carpeting, door map pockets, vinyl upholstery, courtesy light, tachometer, reclining front seats, and a cushioned anti-glare dashboard.

2600 — V-8 — Styled by Pietro Frua, this rather angular semi-fastback four-seat coupe carried a Glas-built 2576-cc V-8 engine, rated 140 bhp (DIN). The dual-overhead-camshaft engine was essentially a pair of fours (from the 1300 GT) atop a single crank-

case, with twin toothed camshaft drive belts. Three Solex carburetors helped boost horsepower to 150 at 5600 rpm. At the rear was a De Dion axle. Body styling featured rectangular headlamps recessed into curvy housings and thin roof pillars. The grille was made up of horizontal strips with vertical dividers, full-width at the bottom (reaching around the fenders into parking lights), with a large and high center insignia.

I.D. DATA: Not available.

Model	Body Type & Seating	Engine Type/CID	P.O.E. Price	Weight (lbs.)	Prod. Total
1204	2-dr Sedan-4P	I4/72	N/A	N/A	Note 1
1204 TS	2-dr Sedan-4P	I4/72	N/A	N/A	Note 1
1304	2-dr Sedan-4P	I4/79	N/A	1632	Note 1
1304	2-dr Conv-2P	I4/79	N/A	N/A	Note 1
1300 GT	2-dr Coupe-2+2P	I4/79	N/A	1830	Note 1
1700	4-dr Sedan-5P	I4/103	N/A	2249	Note 1
1700 TS	4-dr Sedan-5P	I4/103	N/A	2249	Note 1
1700 GT	2-dr Coupe-2+2P	I4/103	3695	1852	Note 1
2600	2-dr Coupe-4P	V8/157	N/A	2485	Note 1

Note 1: A total of 27,525 Glas cars were produced during 1963, 27,070 in 1964, 29,760 in 1965, and 26,844 in 1966. Approximately 800 model 1300/1700 GT coupes were produced in all.

ENGINE DATA: BASE FOUR (1204): Inline, overhead-cam four-cylinder. **Displacement:** 72.5 cu. in. (1189 cc). **Bore & Stroke:** 2.83 x 2.87 in. (72 x 73 mm). **Compression Ratio:** 8.3:1. **Brake Horsepower:** 53 (SAE) at 5100 rpm. **Torque:** 86 lbs.-ft. (SAE) at 2000 rpm. Solid valve lifters. Solex 32PICB carburetor.
BASE FOUR (1300 GT, 1304): Inline, overhead-cam four-cylinder. Cast iron block and light alloy head. **Displacement:** 78.6 cu. in. (1289 cc). **Bore & Stroke:** 2.95 x 2.87 in. (75 x 73 mm). **Compression Ratio:** 9.3:1. **Brake Horsepower:** 85 (DIN) at 5800 rpm. **Torque:** 79.6 lbs.-ft. at 3000 rpm. Five main bearings. Solid valve lifters. Two Solex 35RH carburetors.
BASE FOUR (1700): Inline, overhead-cam four-cylinder. Cast iron block and light alloy head. **Displacement:** 102.6 cu. in. (1682 cc). **Bore & Stroke:** 3.07 x 3.46 in. (78 x 88 mm). **Compression Ratio:** 8.5:1. **Brake Horsepower:** 85 (DIN) at 4900 rpm. **Torque:** 105 lbs.-ft. at 2700 rpm. Five main bearings. Solid valve lifters. One Solex carburetor.
BASE FOUR (1700 TS, 1700 GT): Same as 1682-cc four above, except — **Compression Ratio:** 9.5:1. **Brake Horsepower:** 100 DIN (112 SAE) at 5500 rpm. **Torque:** 109 lbs.-ft. DIN (127 SAE) at 3000 rpm. Two Solex carburetors.
BASE V-8 (2600): 60-degree, overhead-cam "vee" type eight-cylinder. Cast iron block and light alloy head. **Displacement:** 157.1 cu. in. (2576 cc). **Bore & Stroke:** 2.95 x 2.87 in. (75 x 73 mm). **Compression Ratio:** 9.0:1. **Brake Horsepower:** 140 (DIN) at 5600 rpm. **Torque:** 152 lbs.-ft. at 3000 rpm. Five main bearings. Two Solex carburetors.
Note: With three Solex carburetors, the 2600 engine could produce 150 bhp.

CHASSIS DATA: Wheelbase: (1700/2600) 98.5 in.; (1300/1700 GT) 91.4 in. **Overall Length:** (1700) 173.3 in.; (1300/1700 GT) 159.5 in.; (2600) 182.0 in. **Height:** (1700) 54.3 in.; (1300/1700 GT) 50.5 in.; (2600) 55.1 in. **Width:** (1700) 63.1 in.; (1300/1700 GT) 61 in.; (2600) 68.9 in. **Front Tread:** (1700) 49.5 in.; (1300/1700 GT) 49.5 in.; (2600) 55.9 in. **Rear Tread:** (1700) 49.5 in.; (1300/1700 GT) 47.3 in.; (2600) 55.9 in. **Standard Tires:** (1304) 155x13; (1300 GT) 155x14; (1700) 6.00Sx14; (1700 GT) 6.55x14; (2600) 175x14.

TECHNICAL: Layout: front-engine, rear-drive. **Transmission:** four-speed manual. 1700/1700 GT gear ratios: (1st) 3.82:1; (2nd) 2.07:1; (3rd) 1.33:1; (4th) 1.00:1; (rev) 4.153:1. **Steering:** Gemmer or ZF worm and roller. **Suspension (front):** dual control arms, with coil springs. **Suspension (rear):** rigid axle with semi-elliptic leaf springs. **Brakes:** (1204) front/rear drum; (others) front disc, rear drum. **Body Construction:** steel unibody. **Fuel Tank:** (1204/1304) 10.6 gal.; (1300/1700 GT) 13.2 gal.; (1700) 15.8 gallon.

PERFORMANCE: Top Speed: (1300 GT) near 100 mph; (1700) 100 mph; (1700 TS) 106 mph; (1700 GT) 115 mph; (2600 V-8) 121-125 mph. **Acceleration (0-60 mph):** (1300 GT) about 10.5 sec.; (1700) 13.5 sec.; (1700 TS) 11.5 sec.; (1700 GT) 9.8 sec.; (2600) under 11 sec. **Fuel Mileage:** (1700 GT) 25 mpg average.

ADDITIONAL MODELS: Glas also produced a 1004 series with 993-cid engine, in sedan and cabrioelet form on an 82.7-inch wheelbase. The same company produced the Goggomobil, listed separately in this Catalog.

Manufacturer: Glas-Automobilwerke, Dingolfing, West Germany.

Distributor: Glas Automobile Corp., Beverly Hills, California.

HISTORY: *Road & Track* called the 1700 GT "one of the most attractive small GT cars we've ever driven," displaying "abundant evidence of careful workmanship." *Sports Car Graphic* predicted that the 1700 GT was "(d)estined to carve its own reputation." Promotional literature issued at the London Show in October 1966 claimed the 1700 TS sedan was "not only a powerful and strong mountain climber but also an elegant and comfortable travelling saloon." The company also noted that many extras were available, including an automatic gearbox, pushbutton steel sliding roof, safety 165SR14 tires, and metallic paint.

1967-68 (BMW) GLAS

1600 GT — FOUR — The former 1300/1700 GT coupe became a BMW model under a new number, following the takeover of the Glas company. The 1600 GT was introduced in September 1967. BMW's 1600ti engine with dual carburetors now provided the power, rated at 105 bhp; and BMW's semi-trailing arm rear suspension replaced the former setup. Appearance was similar to former models, but with BMW emblems and the familiar "kidney" grille. Other styling features included a long hood, and quarter windows. A total of 1,255 1600 GT coupes were built, through August 1968.

3000 GT — V-8 — Adoption of a larger (2982-cc) BMW engine gave the V-8 coupe a new designation. Output was now 160 horsepower (DIN). Round blue/white BMW emblems on the hood, trunk and hubcaps differentiated it from the former model. 'Glas' block lettering went below the BMW badge at the rear end. Only 400 were produced.

I.D. DATA: Not available.

Model	Body Type & Seating	Engine Type/CID	P.O.E. Price	Weight (lbs.)	Prod. Total
1600 GT	2-dr Coupe-2+2P	I4/96	N/A	2115	1255
3000 GT	2-dr Coupe-4P	V8/182	N/A	N/A	400

Production Note: A total of 17,861 Glas cars (all models) were produced during 1967, and 7,768 in 1968.

ENGINE DATA: BASE FOUR (1600 GT): Inline, overhead-cam four-cylinder. Cast iron block and light alloy head. **Displacement:** 96 cu. in. (1573 cc). **Bore & Stroke:** 3.31 x 2.80 in. (84 x 71 mm). **Compression Ratio:** 9.5:1. **Brake Horsepower:** 105 DIN (118 SAE at 6200 rpm). **Torque:** 97 lbs.-ft. (DIN) at 4500 rpm. Five main bearings. Solid valve lifters. Two Solex carburetors.
BASE V-8 (3000 GT): 90-degree, overhead-cam "vee" type eight-cylinder. Cast iron block

and light alloy head. **Displacement:** 182 cu. in. (2982 cc). **Bore & Stroke:** 3.07 x 3.07 in. (78 x 78 mm). **Compression Ratio:** 9.2:1. **Brake Horsepower:** 160 (DIN) at 5100 rpm. **Torque:** 174 lbs.-ft. at 3400-4400 rpm. Five main bearings. Three Solex carburetors.
CHASSIS DATA: Wheelbase: (1600 GT) 91.4 in.; (3000 GT) 98.4 in. **Overall Length:** (1600 GT) 161.4 in.; (3000 GT) 182.0 in. **Height:** (1600 GT) 50.4 in.; (3000 GT) 54.3 in. **Width:** (1600 GT) 61 in.; (3000 GT) 68.9 in. **Front Tread:** (1600 GT) 49.2 in.; (3000 GT) 56.4 in. **Rear Tread:** (1600 GT) 49.6 in.; (3000 GT) 55.6 in. **Standard Tires:** (1600 GT) 155x14; (3000 GT) 6.00Sx14.
TECHNICAL: Layout: front-engine, rear-drive. **Transmission:** four-speed manual. **Standard Final Drive Ratio:** (1600 GT) 3.64:1. **Steering:** worm and roller. **Suspension (front):** dual control arms, with coil springs and anti-roll bar. **Suspension (rear):** (1600 GT) semi-trailing arms with coil springs; (3000 GT) De Dion axle. **Brakes:** front disc, rear drum. **Body Construction:** (1600 GT) steel unibody; (3000 GT) steel unibody on platform frame.
PERFORMANCE: Top Speed: (1600 GT) 118 mph; (3000 GT) about 124 mph. **Acceleration (0-60 mph):** N/A (1600 GT, 0-50 mph in 7.5 sec.).
Manufacturer: Bayerische Motoren Werke AG (BMW), Munich, West Germany (built at Dingolfing).

GOGGOMOBIL

The Germans seemed to have a propensity for curious car names in the 1950s, as witness the Goliath and the Goggomobil. In spring 1955, the first Goggomobil left the factory at Dingolfing. Over the next four years, more than 100,000 were built, and the tiny coupes and sedans began to trickle into the U.S., gaining an impressive following. The company's history went back considerably farther, but for other industrial pursuits. Goggomobils were imported into the U.S. through 1961, and remained in production into 1969. More than 280,000 were built in all. The Glas firm also produced a Glas automobile (listed in this Catalog) during the 1960s, both before and after acquisition of the company by BMW.

1955-57 GOGGOMOBIL

T300/TS300 — TWO — Two versions of the tiny Goggomobil arrived on American shores in the mid 1950s: a two-door sedan with plain (solid) front end, and a coupe with vee-shaped grille. Though tiny in dimensions, the pair were rather stylish (especially the attractive coupe, which reminded some observers of the Alfa Romeo coupes). Both lacked the usual econobox look. The sedan had a somewhat stubby front end with very little metal ahead of or behind each front wheel, sizable rear quarter windows, and a similarly short deck. The coupe's profile was more graceful, with a raked windshield angle, longer fenders and hood, and fairly large vertical taillamps tacked onto the tips of the back fenders. Both models held four passengers, but the coupe's back bench seat was far more appropriate for small children. Each was powered by an air-cooled two-cylinder, two-stroke engine mounted in the rear, in a unit with the rear axle. Luggage went into a front compartment. Doors were hinged at the rear, opening from the front. The sedan's interior was more austere than the coupe's, with a less-finished appearance. "A well-built, interesting little car," said Tom McCahill of *Mechanix Illustrated*, whose colleague was pictured easily lifting the front end of a Goggomobil sedan off the ground.

I.D. DATA: Serial number is on the side of the car, above the nameplate or flooring. Engine number is stamped on the right side of the block, alongside the carburetor.

Model	Body Type & Seating	Engine Type/CID	P.O.E. Price	Weight (lbs.)	Prod. Total
T300	2-dr Sedan-4P	I2/18	995	851	N/A
TS300	2-dr Coupe-4P	I2/18	1395	925	N/A

ENGINE DATA: BASE TWO: Parallel two-stroke, two-cylinder (air cooled Glas 02). **Displacement:** 18.06 cu. in. (296 cc). **Bore & Stroke:** 2.28 x 2.21 in. (58 x 56 mm). **Compression Ratio:** 6.0:1. **Brake Horsepower:** 17 at 5000 rpm. 12-volt electrical.

CHASSIS DATA: Wheelbase: 70.8 in. **Overall Length:** (sedan) 114.2 in.; (coupe) 120.1 in. **Width:** (sed) 50.4 in.; (cpe) 53.9 in. **Front Tread:** 43 in. **Rear Tread:** 43 in. **Standard Tires:** (sed) 4.40x10; (cpe) 4.80x10.

TECHNICAL: Layout: rear-engine, rear-drive. **Transmission:** four-speed manual. Overall gear ratios: (1st) 20.62:1; (2nd) 11.0:1; (3rd) 7.18:1; (4th) 5.07:1. **Steering:** rack and pinion. **Suspension (front):** independent; coil springs and swing axle. **Suspension (rear):** independent; coil springs and swing axle. **Brakes:** hydraulic drum. **Body Construction:** steel unibody with pressed steel platform, central tube and diagonal ribs. **Fuel Tank:** (cpe) 6.6 gallons.

MAJOR OPTIONS: Preselector gearbox ($65). Sliding sunroof.

PERFORMANCE: Top Speed: 53-60 mph. **Acceleration (0-60 mph):** (cpe) 29.8 seconds. **Fuel Mileage:** 40-48 mpg (as high as 60-80 mpg reported).
Manufacturer: Hans Glas Isaria-Vertriebe KG, Dingolfing, Bavaria, West Germany.
Distributor: Continental Car Combine, New York City.

1958 Goggomobil T-400 coupe.

1958 Goggomobil T-400 sedan.

T300/TS300 — TWO — Production of the smaller-engined models continued as the more powerful version debuted.

T400/TS400 — TWO — Appearance of the twin Goggomobils was unchanged, but the two-stroke engine grew to 392 cc (nearly 24 cubic inches) and added five horsepower. A two-inch lever sticking out of the dashboard operated the available preselector gearbox. Neutral was in the center of the square shift pattern, with each of the four forward speeds at one corner. Engaging reverse was accomplished via a separate button. After a gear was selected, the driver simply pressed down the clutch to make the shift. An oil pump handled the mixing of oil and gasoline for the two-stroke engine, eliminating the need for addition of lubricant with each fillup.

I.D. DATA: Same as 1955-57.

Model	Body Type & Seating	Engine Type/CID	P.O.E. Price	Weight (lbs.)	Prod. Total
T400	2-dr Sedan-4P	I2/24	1095	1014	Note 1
TS400	2-dr Coupe-4P	I2/24	1495	N/A	Note 1

Note 1: Approximately 539 Goggomobils were sold in the U.S. during 1958.

ENGINE DATA: BASE TWO: Parallel, two-stroke, two-cylinder (Glas 03). **Displacement:** 23.99 cu. in. (392 cc). **Bore & Stroke:** 2.64 x 2.20 in. (67 x 56 mm). **Compression Ratio:** 6.0:1. **Brake Horsepower:** 20 at 5000 rpm. 12-volt electrical.

CHASSIS DATA: Wheelbase: 70.8 in. **Overall Length:** (sedan) 114.2 in.; (coupe) 119.5 in. **Height:** (sed) 51.5 in.; (cpe) 48.6 in. **Width:** (sed) 50.4 in.; (cpe) 53.9 in. **Standard Tires:** (sed) 4.40x10; (cpe) 4.80x10.

TECHNICAL: Layout: rear-engine, rear-drive. **Transmission:** four-speed manual (preselector available). **Standard Final Drive Ratio:** 4.8:1. **Steering:** rack and pinion. **Suspension (front):** independent; coil springs and swing axle. **Suspension (rear):** independent; coil springs and swing axle. **Body Construction:** steel unibody with pressed steel platform, central tube and diagonal ribs.

MAJOR OPTIONS: Preselector gearbox ($65).

PERFORMANCE: Top Speed: 60-62 mph. **Acceleration (0-60 mph):** N/A (0-50 mph in 28 seconds). **Fuel Mileage:** 45-60 mpg.

Manufacturer & Distributor: Same as 1955-57.

HISTORY: Studebaker was rumored to be planning to assemble Goggomobils in the U.S. around this time.

1959 GOGGOMOBIL

T400/TS400 — TWO — Two-stroke Goggomobils remained on the U.S. market for 1959, in both sedan and deVille coupe form, but were joined by a four-stroke T700 series. See previous listing for details on the two-stroke models.

T700 ROYAL — TWO — "Everyday's a HOLIDAY with the new Goggomobil T700!" That's what 1959 ads claimed for the newest edition of the German compact, this one larger and more conventional in appearance, and powered by a Glas 70 four-cycle, two-cylinder engine. Air cooled like the two-stroke engine before it, the new version delivered 30 horsepower, offered a top speed up to 80 mph, and claimed to carry five people 10 miles on just seven cents worth of gasoline. "It go-go-goes through traffic and away like quick-silver, parks in half the space and puts the fun back in driving!"

This Goggomobil had a wide mesh-style grille with round parking lamps alongside, enclosed in the same surround molding. Above were single round headlamps, with a round emblem at the front of the hood. The spare tire was mounted under the hood, and the windshield was wraparound style. At the rear fender tips were round taillamps, with smaller round lenses below. Seats adjusted to reclining position. The brochure from the London show in October 1958 touted the enlarged Goggomobil's "big car" look, and its modern all-steel body with wide wraparound panoramic windshield.

I.D. DATA: Same as 1955-57.

Model	Body Type & Seating	Engine Type/CID	P.O.E. Price	Weight (lbs.)	Prod. Total
T400	2-dr Sedan-4P	I2/24	1095	915	Note 1
TS400	2-dr deV Cpe-4P	I2/24	1450	N/A	Note 1
T700	2-dr Sedan-4/5P	H2/42	N/A	N/A	Note 1

Note 1: Approximately 579 Goggomobils were sold in the U.S. during 1959.
Price Note: A Florida sunroof version of the T400 sedan cost $1135.

ENGINE DATA: BASE TWO (T400): Parallel two-stroke, two-cylinder (air cooled Glas 03). **Displacement:** 23.99 cu. in. (392 cc). **Bore & Stroke:** 2.64 x 2.20 in. (67 x 56 mm). **Compression Ratio:** 6.0:1. **Brake Horsepower:** 20 at 5000 rpm. 12-volt electrical.

BASE TWO (T700): Horizontally opposed, overhead-valve, four-stroke two-cylinder (air cooled). **Displacement:** 41.6 cu. in. (682 cc). **Bore & Stroke:** 3.07 x 2.83 in. (78 x 72 mm). **Brake Horsepower:** 30 at 4900 rpm. 12-volt electrical.

CHASSIS DATA: Wheelbase: (T400) 70.8 in.; (T700) 78.7 in. **Overall Length:** (T400) 114.2 in.; (TS400) 119.5 in.; (T700) 134.8 in. **Height:** (T400) 51.5 in.; (TS400 coupe) 48.6 in.; (T700) 54.3 in. **Width:** (T400) 50.4 in.; (TS400) 53.9 in.; (T700) 57.9 in. **Front Tread:** (TS400) 42.0 in. **Rear Tread:** (TS400) 42.0 in. **Standard Tires:** (T400) 4.40x10; (TS400) 4.80x10; (T700) 4.80x12.

TECHNICAL: Layout: (T400) rear-engine, rear-drive; (T700) front-engine, rear-drive. **Transmission:** four-speed manual (preselector available). **Standard Final Drive Ratio:** 4.8:1. **Steering:** rack and pinion. **Suspension (front):** (T400) coil springs and swing axle; (T700) independent coil springs. **Suspension (rear):** (T400) coil springs and swing axle; (T700) laminated springs. **Brakes:** hydraulic drum. **Body Construction:** steel unibody with pressed steel platform, central tube and diagonal ribs.

PERFORMANCE: Top Speed: (T400) 62 mph; (TS400) 62+ mph; (T700) 65-70 mph. **Fuel Mileage:** 45-60 mpg.

Manufacturer & Distributor: Same as 1955-57.

HISTORY: Goggomobil also continued to produce a less-powerful two-stroke model, as the Regent T300 and Mayfair TS300. Its engine was rated only 15 horsepower. Glas also built a Goggomobil van during this period.

1960-61 GOGGOMOBIL

T400 — TWO — Two-stroke Goggomobils remained on the U.S. market for 1960-61, powered by a 20-horsepower, 392-cc engine. In addition to the former sedan and deVille coupe, a convertible model was available.

T700 ROYAL — TWO — Little change was evident on the larger Goggomobil, which was available not only as a two-door sedan with four-cycle, two-cylinder engine, but also with a sport roadster or Sprint coupe body.

I.D. DATA: Same as 1955-57.

Model	Body Type & Seating	Engine Type/CID	P.O.E. Price	Weight (lbs.)	Prod. Total
T400	2-dr Sedan-4P	I2/24	995	915	N/A
T400	2-dr deV Coupe-4P	I2/24	1395	N/A	N/A
T400	2-dr Conv Cpe	I2/24	1445	N/A	N/A
T700	2-dr Sedan-4P	H2/42	1395	1372	N/A
T700	2-dr Spt Rds	H2/42	1445	N/A	N/A
T700	2-dr Sprint Cpe	H2/42	1695	N/A	N/A

Note: A Florida sunroof version of the T400 sedan cost $1035.

ENGINE DATA: BASE TWO (T400): Parallel two-stroke, two-cylinder (air cooled). **Displacement:** 23.99 cu. in. (392 cc). **Bore & Stroke:** 2.64 x 2.20 in. (67 x 56 mm). **Compression Ratio:** 6.0:1. **Brake Horsepower:** 20 at 5000 rpm. One carburetor. 12-volt electrical.

BASE TWO (T700): Horizontally opposed, overhead-valve, four-stroke two-cylinder (air cooled). **Displacement:** 41.6 cu. in. (682 cc). **Bore & Stroke:** 3.07 x 2.83 in. (78 x 72 mm). **Compression Ratio:** 7.0:1. **Brake Horsepower:** 30 at 4500 rpm. **Torque:** 36.2 lbs.-ft. at 3000 rpm. Two carburetors. 12-volt electrical.

CHASSIS DATA: Wheelbase: (T400) 70.8 in.; (T700) 78.7 in. **Overall Length:** (T400) 114.3 in.; (TS400) 119.5 in.; (T700) 133.8 in. **Height:** (T400) 51.5 in.; (T400 coupe) 48.6 in.; (T700) 54.3 in. **Width:** (T400) 50.4 in.; (T400 cpe) 53.9 in.; (T700) 57.9 in. **Front Tread:** (T400) 42.0 in. **Rear Tread:** (T400) 42.0 in. **Standard Tires:** (T400) 4.40x10; (T400 cpe) 4.80x10; (T700) 4.80x12.

TECHNICAL: Layout: (T400) rear-engine, rear-drive; (T700) front-engine, rear-drive. **Transmission:** four-speed manual (preselector available). **Standard Final Drive Ratio:** 4.8:1. **Steering:** rack and pinion. **Suspension (front):** (T700) coil springs and swing axle; (T700) independent coil springs. **Suspension (rear):** (T400) coil springs and swing axle; (T700) laminated springs. **Brakes:** hydraulic drum. **Body Construction:** steel unibody with pressed steel platform, central tube and diagonal ribs.

MAJOR OPTIONS: Preselector gearbox.
PERFORMANCE: Top Speed: (T400) 62 mph; (T700) 68 mph. **Acceleration (0-60 mph):** N/A (T400 went 0-45 mph in 17 seconds). **Fuel Mileage:** 45-60 mpg.
Manufacturer & Distributor: Same as 1955-57.
HISTORY: Goggomobil also produced a step-in van that was imported to the U.S., selling for $1350.

1962 Goggomobil T-400.

GOLIATH

Production of a Goliath automobile — surely one of the least accurately named vehicles of all time — began in 1924 and resumed in 1948 for building three-wheeled commercial vehicles. By 1950, the first four-wheel passenger car was ready for viewing. Goliath's streamlined Sport Coupe of 1951-52 was one of the first cars to use fuel injection. Production of passenger cars continued until 1961. A few leftovers were sold as late as 1963. Though not a minicar by any means, the German-built compact stood considerably closer to "David" stature than that of a true "Goliath." The Goliath company was an offshoot of Borgward/Hansa, and the final models were called Hansas.

1950-56 GOLIATH

1954 Goliath GP 700 sports.

GP700 — TWO — Postwar Goliath production began with a five-passenger sedan powered by a two-cylinder, 688 cc, two-stroke engine with Bosch fuel injection (though early models were carbureted). First offered in Europe (as was customary), examples of the two-cylinder edition were slipping into the U.S. market as well by the mid-1950s. As *Motor Trend* reported in January 1956, the car may not have been a giant, but it "packs a

mighty wallop." On the minus side, they subsequently criticized the placement of the gas tank above the engine, and the many unidentified knobs on the dashboard. The shift lever for the four-speed transmission stuck out of the dashboard, just below the steering wheel.

The two-stroke engine, mounted crosswise ahead of the front axle (with transmission alongside), actually delivered better gas mileage in the city than on the highway. As in other two-strokes of that day, oil had to be mixed with gasoline during each fillup. It used a thermosyphon cooling system, with auxiliary fan behind the radiator. A whole replacement engine cost only $65.

Goliath's vee-shaped grille was made up of horizontal bars with a center divider. Round headlamps stood above vertical rectangular parking lamps on early models; later ones put parking lamps atop the fenders, and the grille had a more rounded look. Inside, a column lever operated the four-speed gearbox, while instruments and controls were in the center of the dashboard.

1956 Goliath two-door sedan.

GP700 SPORT COUPE — TWO —Far different from the economy sedans, the limited-production Goliath Sport Coupe wore a body handmade by the Rometsch firm of Berlin. In profile, it looked rather like an early Porsche coupe, but with Goliath's horizontal-bar grille up front.

GP900 — TWO — A larger engine powered the Goliaths built in 1955-56, until it was replaced by the new 1100 series. The 886-cc powerplant developed 40 horsepower, good enough for a top speed of 72 mph in U.S. tests. Noting that Goliath was the only car in the world with a two-cylinder, two-stroke, fuel-injected engine, *Road & Track* described it as "solidly built, comfortable, thrifty, and not particularly notable for beauty or grace."

I.D. DATA: Not available.

Model	Body Type & Seating	Engine Type/CID	P.O.E. Price	Weight (lbs.)	Prod. Total
GP700	2-dr Sedan-5P	I2/42	1898	1918	N/A
GP700	2-dr Spt Cpe-2/3P	I2/42	N/A	1750	25
GP900	2-dr Sedan-5P	I2/54	1898	2060	N/A

Production Note: A total of 5,000 Goliaths were built in 1953 alone, and 8,125 were sold in 1956.

ENGINE DATA: BASE TWO (GP700): Inline two-cylinder, two-cycle. **Displacement:** 42 cu. in. (688 cc). **Bore & Stroke:** 2.91 x 3.15 in. (74 x 80 mm). **Compression Ratio:** 6.4:1. **Brake Horsepower:** 24-26 at 4000 rpm. Bosch fuel injection (some carbureted). **Note:** GP700 engine, with fuel injection and 7.7:1 compression, developed 29 horsepower.

BASE TWO (GP900): Inline two-cylinder, two-cycle. **Displacement:** 54 cu. in. (886 cc). **Bore & Stroke:** 3.31 x 3.15 in. (84 x 80 mm). **Compression Ratio:** 7.4:1. **Brake Horsepower:** 40 at 4000 rpm. **Torque:** 54 lbs.-ft. at 2750 rpm. Bosch fuel injection.

CHASSIS DATA: Wheelbase: 90.6 in. **Overall Length:** 163.4 in. exc. (Spt Cpe) 156.8 in. **Height:** 57.1 in. exc. (Spt Cpe) 50 in. **Width:** 63 in. exc. (Spt Cpe) 60 in. **Front Tread:** 49.2 in. **Rear Tread:** 49.2 in. **Standard Tires:** (700) 5.60x15; (900) 5.90x13.

TECHNICAL: Layout: front-engine, front-drive. **Transmission:** four-speed manual (dashboard lever); early models were non-synchronized. Overall gear ratios (GP900): (1st) 18.9:1; (2nd) 11.0:1; (3rd) 6.71:1; (4th) 4.14:1. **Steering:** rack and pinion. **Suspension (front):** two transverse semi-elliptic leaf springs. **Suspension (rear):** longitudinal semi-elliptic leaf springs. **Brakes:** drum. **Body Construction:** steel body on central tube frame; separate unit holds engine/transmission/differential and suspension.

MAJOR OPTIONS: Sunroof ($107). Separate front seats ($15). Reclining seats ($51).

PERFORMANCE: Top Speed: (GP700) 62 mph; (GP900) 72 mph. **Acceleration (0-60 mph):** 31.6 seconds. **Acceleration (quarter-mile):** 23.6 sec. (57 mph). **Fuel Mileage:** 40+ mpg (factory). Road tests achieved 29+ mpg city, 26 mpg highway; some as high as 35 mpg.

Manufacturer: Goliath-Werk GmbH, Bremen, West Germany (part of the Borgward Group).

Distributor: Goliath Distributors, Inc., San Francisco, California.

1957 GOLIATH

1100 — FOUR — "See why you should go Goliath" was the appeal to late 1950s prospects for this offshoot of the Borgward and Hansa, which switched from a two-stroke to four-stroke engine. Promoted as "The Quality Compact" that was "Built to sell for much more," the Goliath was a front-drive compact automobile available in four two-door body styles for the 1957 model year: two sedans, a convertible, and a station wagon.

Goliath's grille curved outward and was made up of horizontal bars with a center vertical bar. 'GOLIATH' block letters stood above the grille. Teardrop-shaped parking lamps sat atop each front fender, above single round headlamps. Rear quarter windows were fixed in position (with opening windows available). Standard equipment included a heater/defroster. Powerplant was a water-cooled flat four, rated 46 horsepower, driving a four-speed manual gearbox. Road testers faulted the car's column shift lever, for difficulty in finding each gear (not an uncommon problem during this period).

I.D. DATA: Serial number is on a riveted plate on left upper corner of firewall, and on the left side of the front spring frame. Starting serial number: 32-01-00001 (prefix '04' for wagon or '02' for convertible). Engine number is on top right of motor, under the generator. Starting engine number: 32-51-00001.

Model	Body Type & Seating	Engine Type/CID	P.O.E. Price	Weight (lbs.)	Total Prod.
1109	2-dr Std Sed-5P	H4/67	1995	1945	Note 1
1110	2-dr Sedan-5P	H4/67	2089	1945	Note 1
1111	2-dr Conv-5P	H4/67	2395	1945	Note 1
1112	2-dr Sta Wag-5P	H4/67	2288	2000	Note 1

Note 1: A total of 12,870 Goliaths were produced in 1957.

ENGINE DATA: BASE FOUR: Horizontally opposed, overhead-valve four-cylinder (water-cooled). Light alloy block with wet cylinder liners. **Displacement:** 66.73 cu. in. (1094 cc). **Bore & Stroke:** 2.91 x 2.52 in. (74 x 64 mm). **Compression Ratio:** 7.3:1. **Brake Horsepower:** 46 at 4250 rpm. **Torque:** 59.3 lbs.-ft. at 2750 rpm. Solex carburetor.

CHASSIS DATA: Wheelbase: 89.4 in. **Overall Length:** 159.8 in. **Height:** 57.1 in. **Width:** 64.2 in. **Front Tread:** 50.8 in. **Rear Tread:** 49.2 in. **Standard Tires:** 5.60x13.

TECHNICAL: Layout: front-engine, front-drive. **Transmission:** four-speed manual (all synchronized; dashboard lever). Overall gear ratios: (1st) 18.86:1; (2nd) 10.84:1; (3rd) 6.60:1; (4th) 4.10:1. **Standard Final Drive Ratio:** 4.714:1. **Steering:** rack and pinion. **Suspension (front):** coil springs. **Suspension (rear):** beam axle with longitudinal semi-elliptic leaf springs. **Brakes:** drum. **Body Construction:** steel unibody on central tube frame; engine/transmission/differential unit and steering on subframe. **Fuel Tank:** 11.9 gallons.

MAJOR OPTIONS: Hinged rear quarter windows. Reclining seats. Sliding sunroof (fabric). Separate front seats.

PERFORMANCE: Top Speed: 77.6 mph (factory). **Acceleration (0-60 mph):** 26.2 sec. **Acceleration (quarter-mile):** 24.2 sec. (54.8 mph). **Fuel Mileage:** 30 mpg (average). **Manufacturer:** Goliath-Werk GmbH, Bremen, West Germany (part of the Borgward Group).

1958 GOLIATH

1100 — FOUR — A two-passenger Tiger sport coupe joined the original sedans, station wagon and convertible this year. So did an Empress Deluxe sedan.

I.D. DATA: Serial number is on a riveted plate on left upper corner of firewall, and on the left side of the front spring frame. Engine number is on top right of motor, under the generator. Numbering is similar to 1957.

Model	Body Type & Seating	Engine Type/CID	P.O.E. Price	Weight (lbs.)	Prod. Total
1109	2-dr Std Sed-5P	H4/67	1995	1945	Note 1
1110	2-dr Sedan-5P	H4/67	2089	1945	Note 1
1111	2-dr Conv-5P	H4/67	2395	1945	Note 1
1112	2-dr Sta Wag-5P	H4/67	2288	2000	Note 1
1107	2-dr Tiger Cpe-2P	H4/67	2835	1975	Note 1
1108	2-dr Empress Sed-5P	H4/67	2481	1945	Note 1

Note 1: Approximately 2,267 Goliaths were sold in the U.S. during 1958.

ENGINE DATA: BASE FOUR: Horizontally opposed, overhead-valve four-cylinder (water-cooled). Light alloy block with wet cylinder liners. **Displacement:** 66.73 cu. in. (1094 cc). **Bore & Stroke:** 2.91 x 2.52 in. (74 x 64 mm). **Compression Ratio:** 7.3:1 (Tiger/Empress, 7.9:1). **Brake Horsepower:** 46 at 4250 rpm (Tiger/Empress, 63 at 5000). **Torque:** 59.3 lbs.-ft. at 2750 rpm; (Tiger/Empress, 60.9 at 4000). Solex carburetor (one or two).

CHASSIS DATA: Wheelbase: 89.4 in. **Overall Length:** 159.8 in. **Height:** 57.1 in. **Width:** 64.2 in. **Front Tread:** 50.8 in. **Rear Tread:** 49.2 in. **Standard Tires:** 5.60x13.

TECHNICAL: Layout: front-engine, front-drive. **Transmission:** four-speed manual (all synchronized; dashboard lever). **Standard Final Drive Ratio:** 4.714:1. **Steering:** rack and pinion. **Suspension (front):** coil springs. **Suspension (rear):** beam axle with longitudinal semi-elliptic leaf springs. **Brakes:** drum. **Body Construction:** steel unibody on central tube frame; engine/transmission/differential unit and steering on subframe. **Fuel Tank:** 11.9 gallons.

MAJOR OPTIONS: Similar to 1957.

PERFORMANCE: Top Speed: 75 mph. **Acceleration (0-60 mph):** 25 seconds. **Manufacturer:** Goliath-Werk GmbH, Bremen, West Germany.

1959 GOLIATH

1100 — FOUR — Prices fell somewhat for the 1959 model year but the model lineup remained the same.

I.D. DATA: Similar to 1957-58.

Model	Body Type & Seating	Engine Type/CID	P.O.E. Price	Weight (lbs.)	Prod. Total
1109	2-dr Std Sed-5P	H4/67	1899	1896	Note 1
1110	2-dr Sedan-5P	H4/67	1949	N/A	Note 1
1111	2-dr Conv-5P	H4/67	2126	N/A	Note 1
1112	2-dr Sta Wag-5P	H4/67	2095	N/A	Note 1
1107	2-dr Tiger Cpe-2P	H4/67	2568	2090	Note 1
1108	2-dr Empress Sed-5P	H4/67	2275	N/A	Note 1

Note 1: Approximately 3,478 Goliaths were sold in the U.S. during 1959.

ENGINE DATA: BASE FOUR: Same as 1958.

CHASSIS DATA: Same as 1958.

TECHNICAL: Same as 1958.

MAJOR OPTIONS: Similar to 1957-58.

PERFORMANCE: Similar to 1957-58.

HISTORY: Introduced in October, 1958.

1960 GOLIATH

1960 Goliath two-door sedan.

1100 — FOUR — The lowest-priced Standard sedan left the lineup this year. Goliath's grille was revised, now made up of nothing other than horizontal strips, though curving outward as before. Both the windshield and back window were almost two inches taller. A new dashboard included upholstered framing beyond the instrument panel. Perhaps more important for drivers was the new gearshift lever: an ordinary column lever to replace the former dashboard unit. As before, two engine horsepowers were available. The attractive Tiger coupe had a tiny bench seat in the back, suitable for children or luggage.

I.D. DATA: Similar to 1957-59.

Model	Body Type & Seating	Engine Type/CID	P.O.E Price	Weight (lbs.)	Prod. Total
1110	2-dr Sedan-5P	H4/67	1949	1896	Note 1
1111	2-dr Conv-5P	H4/67	2126	N/A	Note 1
1112	2-dr Sta Wag-5P	H4/67	2095	N/A	Note 1
1107	2-dr Tiger Cpe-2P	H4/67	2568	1892	Note 1
1108	2-dr Empress Sed-5P	H4/67	2275	N/A	Note 1

Note 1: A total of 7,112 Goliath 1100s were produced in 1960 (plus 1,548 wagons).

ENGINE DATA: BASE FOUR: Same as 1958-59.

CHASSIS DATA: Same as 1958-59.

TECHNICAL: Same as 1958-59.

MAJOR OPTIONS: Similar to 1957-59.

PERFORMANCE: Similar to 1957-59.

Manufacturer: Goliath Werk GmbH, Bremen, West Germany.

Distributor: Goliath Importers, Inc. Burlingame, California.

HISTORY: Introduced on October 1, 1959.

1961 HANSA (GOLIATH)

1100 — FOUR — For its final official outing in the U.S. market, the German compact changed its name to Borgward-Hansa this year.

I.D. DATA: Not available.

Model	Body Type & Seating	Engine Type/CID	P.O.E. Price	Weight (lbs.)	Prod. Total
1110	2-dr Sedan-5P	H4/67	1785	2090	N/A
1112	2-dr Sta Wag-5P	H4/67	1785	N/A	N/A
1107	2-dr Sport Cpe-2P	H4/67	1995	N/A	N/A
1108	2-dr DeLuxe Sed-5P	H4/67	1895	N/A	N/A

Note: The DeLuxe sedan was available with 63-bhp engine for $2100; the Sport Coupe with 63-bhp engine cost $2375.

ENGINE DATA: BASE FOUR: Horizontally opposed, overhead-valve four-cylinder (water-cooled). Light alloy block with wet cylinder liners. **Displacement:** 66.5 cu. in. (1094 cc). **Bore & Stroke:** 2.91 x 2.52 in. (74 x 64 mm). **Compression Ratio:** 7.3:1 (optional, 7.9:1). **Brake Horsepower:** 46 at 4250 rpm (optional, 63 at 5000). **Torque:** 59.3 lbs.-ft. at 2750 rpm (optional, 61 at 4000).

CHASSIS DATA: Wheelbase: 89.3 in. **Overall Length:** 161.4 in. **Height:** 53.5 in. **Width:** 64 in. **Front Tread:** 50.8 in. **Rear Tread:** 49.2 in. **Standard Tires:** 5.60x13.

TECHNICAL: Layout: front-engine, front-drive. **Transmission:** four-speed manual (all synchronized; column lever). **Standard Final Drive Ratio:** 4.71:1. **Steering:** rack and pinion. **Suspension (front):** transverse semi-elliptic leaf spring with A-arms. **Suspension (rear):** beam axle with longitudinal semi-elliptic leaf springs. **Brakes:** drum. **Body Construction:** steel unibody on central tube frame; engine/transmission/differential unit and steering on subframe. **Fuel Tank:** 11.9 gallons.

MAJOR OPTIONS: Similar to 1957-60.

PERFORMANCE: Top Speed: (46-hp) 77 mph; (63-hp) 84 mph. **Fuel Mileage:** (46-hp) 30 mpg; (63-hp) 28 mpg.

PRODUCTION/SALES: During its final official season, approximately 147 U.S. dealers sold Borgward/Hansa/Goliath models.

Manufacturer: Goliath Werk GmbH, Bremen, West Germany.

Distributor: Fenchurch Corp., New York City; and Hansa Corp., Burlingame, California.

POSTSCRIPT: A few Goliaths continued in production into 1963, essentially using left-over components.

GORDON-KEEBLE

For a time in the 1950s and '60s, popping a big American V-8 into a European chassis seemed the fitting course to lure American customers. Adding an Italian-styled body to a British chassis, with a Corvette V-8 under the hood, just might prove irresistible. Do it right, and you might even have a rival to the Ferrari. A good idea, perhaps; but the target buyers for the Gordon-Keeble managed to resist, just as they had the Peerless GT (described elsewhere in this Catalog) a couple of years earlier.

Immediately after the collapse of a Peerless 2+2 coupe project, intended to be powered by a Triumph TR4 engine, John Gordon pondered this blend of British chassis, Bertone body, and Corvette engine. A four-door steel-bodied prototype was designed with a space frame, De Dion rear axle, all-disc brakes, and small-block (4.6-liter) Chevrolet V-8. Journalists praised the prototypes, but the project couldn't quite get moving. Designed by Jim Keeble, a garage owner who'd attracted Gordon's attention by displaying a Peerless coupe into which he'd stuffed a Corvette V-8 engine, the production Gordon-Keeble of 1964 took one route from the earlier Peerless. Over in Italy, the Iso Rivolta took another (but similar) path. Both used not only the 327-cid Corvette V-8, but a De Dion rear axle configuration. Wearing a handsome Bertone-styled body, the Gordon-Keeble close-coupled four-seat coupe offered quick locomotion and good handling. Though handsome, the body design dated back to 1960. That and an unrealistically low selling price led to failure. Few (if any) reached the U.S. at the time, though an active owner's club emerged in Britain.

1964-67 GORDON-KEEBLE

1965 Gordon-Keeble GT sports saloon. (Sotheby's)

GK1/IT — V-8 — Built on an essentially handmade chassis, the Gordon-Keeble GT coupe wore a fiberglass body from Williams & Pritchard, with hardtop styling and large rear quarter windows. Quad round headlamps were installed, with each pair on a slight angle. Round parking lights sat below the headlamp pairs. A fine crosshatch pattern on the wide grille was dominated by horizontal strips, with only six vertical dividers, and the hood contained a small air scoop. Vertical-style taillamps stood in slightly finned back fenders, alongside a sloping deck. The gas filler cap was just to the rear of the back window. Gordon Keebles also displayed a tortoise mascot. The chassis was welded together from many one-inch square-section steel tubes. To maintain silence, the spaces between the tubes were filled with foamed plastic for insulation. Under the hood was a 300-bhp, 327-cid Chevrolet V8 engine and either a Warner four-speed manual gearbox or Powerglide automatic transmission. Dunlop disc brakes on all four wheels used separate front and rear master cylinders, plus two separate vacuum servo units. The De Dion rear axle tube passed behind a Salisbury differential, with two trailing links on each side of the chassis and a transverse Watt linkage. Coil springs handled suspension chores, front and rear. Two versions were built: the IT (International Touring) and GK1. Standard equipment included a radio, fire extinguisher, reclining seats, two-speed wipers/washers, and electric windows.

I.D. DATA: Not available.

Model	Body Type & Seating	Engine Type/CID	P.O.E. Price	Weight (lbs.)	Prod. Total
IT	2-dr Coupe-2+2P	V8/327	Note 1	3150	Note 2
GK1	2-dr Coupe-2+2P	V8/327	Note 1	3150	Note 2

Note 1: Price in England was 2798 pounds (Sterling) for the initial production version in 1964; up to 4058 pounds (Sterling) for the later GK1 edition.

Note 2: About 93 cars were produced at Gordon-Keeble Ltd., up to March 1965; followed by about nine more at the next (Southampton) production site.

ENGINE DATA: BASE V-8: Overhead-valve V-8 (Chevrolet). Cast iron block. **Displacement:** 327 cu. in. (5355 cc). **Bore & Stroke:** 4.00 x 3.29 in. (101.6 x 83.5 mm). **Compression Ratio:** 10.5:1. **Brake Horsepower:** 300 at 5000 rpm. Five main bearings. Hydraulic valve lifters. Carter carburetor.

CHASSIS DATA: Wheelbase: 102 in. **Overall Length:** 189.5 in. **Width:** 68 in. **Front Tread:** 55 in. **Rear Tread:** 55 in. **Wheel Type:** center-lock. **Standard Tires:** 6.70x15.

TECHNICAL: Layout: front-engine, rear-drive. **Transmission:** Warner four-speed manual; Powerglide automatic available. **Standard Final Drive Ratio:** 3.07:1. **Steering:** Marles. **Suspension (front):** coil springs. **Suspension (rear):** De Dion axle with coil springs, two trailing links and transverse Watt linkage. **Brakes:** Dunlop disc, front/rear. **Body Construction:** fiberglass body on separate multi-tubular chassis.

PERFORMANCE: Top Speed: 130-140 mph. **Acceleration (0-60 mph):** near 6 seconds (0-50 mph in 5.5 seconds). **Acceleration (quarter-mile):** 15.6 seconds.

Manufacturer: Gordon-Keeble Ltd., Eastleigh, Hampshire, England; and (1965-67) Keeble Cars Ltd., Southampton, England.

HISTORY: An early version of the Gordon-Keeble was announced at the Geneva auto show in 1960, to be powered by a 283-cid V-8 engine. Production did not begin until 1964, with the larger (327-cid) Corvette V-8. In Italy, the original Peerless/Warwick project evolved into the Iso Rivolta (also described in this Catalog). In March 1965, the company failed; but new financial backing from Harold Smith allowed production to resume on a limited basis, for a GK1 model, at the Southampton location. During 1968, after another corporate failure, resumption of production was announced for a similar model to be called the De Bruyne, aimed at the U.S. market. De Bruyne Motor Car Co. Ltd. was formed at Newmarket, Suffolk by an American, John de Bruyne, and the car appeared at the 1968 New York Auto Show. Only two GT sedans were built this time, before the Peerless/Gordon-Keeble concept faded away completely.

HEALEY

Although best known in America for the popular Austin-Healey sports car and the Nash-Healey (both described elsewhere in this Catalog), Donald Healey had been working on sports cars for two decades before hooking up with the British Motor Corporation (BMC). In the 1920s, he'd been a top European rally driver. Then, in the following decade, Healey became technical director of the Triumph firm, working on (among other projects) rally racers under the Riley and Invicta badges.

Immediately after World II, Healey started his own manufacturing business, at Warwick (near Coventry) in England. Due to minimal operating funds, he elected to make extensive use of components from other manufacturers. Quite a variety of Healey models appeared in the next few years, with bodies built by such British coachbuilders as Tickford, Abbott, Westland, and Elliot. The lineup included four-passenger coupes, as well as convertibles and saloons. Each could hit a hundred miles an hour. Most noted in the U.S. was the lower-priced Silverstone, produced mainly for competition use. The later Healey Hundred, shown in prototype form at the 1952 Earl's Court Motor Show, quickly evolved into the Austin-Healey 100 as a result of strong interest by Sir Leonard Lord of BMC (and by the showgoing public). Other Healey models were built as late as 1954.

1946-54 HEALEY

1946 Healey prototype sports tourer.

HEALEY — FOUR/SIX — Early Healey models rode a box-section platform with 96-inch wheelbase. Trailing arms and coil springs made up the front suspension, which included an anti-roll bar. At the rear was a "live" axle with torque tube, radius arms and coil springs. Powerplant was an overhead-valve, 2.4-liter four-cylinder engine, as used in the Riley RM series. About two dozen of the final Healeys were powered by a 3.0-liter six, borrowed from the Alvis model TA21. Models included the Westland roadster, Duncan sports, Abbott & Tickford saloon, Elliott saloon, and Sportsmobile drophead coupe. Typical standard equipment included leather upholstery, polished walnut interior woodwork, provision for radio and heater, spare tire and tools in compartment below the luggage area, 120-mph speedometer and tachometer.

Fergus Motors of New York City advertised the 1949 Healey drophead sports model as a "symphony in comfort, speed and roadability. Comfort never before associated with a top performance sports car. Through traffic at 15 mph or over the pike at 115 mph....the HEALEY is again first in sports car circles." The model shown had a diamond-shaped vertical-bar grille, with headlamps right alongside, low on the nose, and running lamps mounted at fender tips.

SILVERSTONE — FOUR — While most Healeys were touring machines, the Silverstone, produced from 1949-51, was a true sports car. Its name stemmed from that of the new Grand Prix race course in Britain, where Healeys had taken the Royal Automobile Club team prize in 1949. Few vehicles looked more like racing cars. Instead of the smooth, "semi-envelope" body shape used on other Healeys, with its highly noticeable fender demarcations and overall prewar look, the Silverstone switched to a projectile shape.

1947 Healey 2.4-liter saloon.

1949 Healey Silverstone D-Type.

The body held separate "clamshell" cycle-type fenders (with tiny parking lights on the front fenders), an old-fashioned rectangular windshield, and cutaway doors. Headlamps were set close together, behind a narrow vertical-bar grille in the car's smooth nose. A scoop stood near the front of the small horizontal hood. A fully rounded rear end held the spare tire in a horizontal position, tucked into a slot, where it served as a back bumper of sorts. Not a bad idea, since the Silverstone had no regular bumpers at either end. A gas filler was on top of the deck. One curiosity was the appearance of Buick-style rectangular "portholes" along the Silverstone's cowl. The body, built by Abbey Panel & Sheet Metal Company, included a folding top and removable windshield.

Intended as a lightweight, wholly functional race car that could also go touring, the Silverstone offered only minimal weather protection and weighed close to 500 pounds less than other Healey models. Mostly built by hand, it was somewhat costly. Bodies were not always the most durable, though the tough chassis and drivetrain held up well.

I.D. DATA: Not available.

Model	Body Type & Seating	Engine Type/CID	P.O.E. Price	Weight (lbs.)	Prod. Total
HEALEY (various bodies)					
S'mobile	2-dr Conv Cpe-5P	I4/149	N/A	Note 1	Note 2
	2-dr Coupe-4P	I4/149	N/A	Note 1	Note 2
	2-dr Roadster-2P	I4/149	N/A	Note 1	Note 2
Tickford	2-dr Spt Saloon-4P	I4/149	N/A	Note 1	Note 2
Abbott	2-dr Dhd Cpe-4P	I4/149	N/A	Note 1	Note 2
SILVERSTONE					
	2-dr Roadster-2P	I4/149	3995	2075	105

Note 1: Weights ranged from 2,408 to 2,912 pounds.

Note 2: A total of 676 Healeys were built, in addition to the Silverstone (and the Nash-Healey). Listed above are typical examples, all of which had bodies by British coachbuilders.

Price Note: A supercharged Silverstone carried a price of $4650.

Production Note: Slightly more than half of the Silverstones were "E" types (rather than "D"), with improved interior appointments.

1950 Healey Silverstone roadster. (Coys of Kensington)

1952 Healey fixed-head coupes.

ENGINE DATA: BASE FOUR: Inline, overhead-valve four-cylinder (Riley). **Displacement:** 149 cu. in. (2443 cc). **Bore & Stroke:** 3.17 x 4.72 in. (80.5 x 120 mm). **Compression Ratio:** 6.9:1. **Brake Horsepower:** 104 at 4500 rpm. **Torque:** 132 lbs.-ft. at 3000 rpm. Three main bearings. Solid valve lifters. Two SU carburetors. 12-volt electrics.

BASE SIX (late models): Inline, overhead-valve six-cylinder (Alvis). **Displacement:** 182.6 cu. in. (2993 cc). **Bore & Stroke:** 3.31 x 3.54 in. (84 x 90 mm). **Compression Ratio:** 7.0:1. **Brake Horsepower:** 106 at 4200 rpm. **Torque:** 150 lbs.-ft. at 2500 rpm. Solid valve lifters. Two SU carburetors.

CHASSIS DATA: Wheelbase: 102 in. **Overall Length:** (Silverstone) 168 in.; (others) 168-180 in. **Height:** 55 in. **Width:** (Silverstone) 63 in.; (others) 65 in. **Front Tread:** 54 in. **Rear Tread:** 53 in. **Wheel type:** (Silverstone) perforated steel disc. **Standard Tires:** 5.50x15 and 5.75x15 (larger sizes available).

TECHNICAL: Layout: front-engine, rear-drive. **Transmission:** four-speed manual (floor shift). Silverstone overall gear ratios: (1st) 12.76:1; (2nd) 7.542:1; (3rd) 4.963:1; (4th) 3.5:1. **Standard Final Drive Ratio:** (4-cyl.) 3.50:1; (6-cyl.) 3.77:1. **Steering:** (Silverstone) cam-type. **Suspension (front):** (Silverstone) independent; dual trailing arms, coil springs and anti-roll bar. **Suspension (rear):** (Silverstone) live axle with torque tube, radius arms and coil springs. **Brakes:** front/rear drum. **Body Construction:** aluminum body panels on ash framing; (Silverstone) stressed aluminum alloy skin on channel framework with tubular bracing.

PERFORMANCE: Top Speed: about 100 mph (Silverstone, up to 110 mph). **Acceleration (0-60 mph):** (Silverstone) 11-13 sec. **Acceleration (quarter-mile):** (six-cylinder) 18.7 sec.

PRODUCTION/SALES: Possibly no more than a half-dozen Silverstones were imported into the U.S. when new. Approximately four Healeys of any type were sold in the U.S. in 1948; seven in 1949; seven more in 1950; and two in 1951.

Manufacturer: Donald Healey Motor Co. Ltd., Warwick, England.

1954 Healey Tickford four-seat fixed-head coupe. (Christie's)

HISTORY: The first Healey appeared in January 1946. The Silverstone was introduced in summer 1949, but gained scant attention in the U.S. motoring press. In 1949, Bill Frick and Briggs Cunningham dropped a Cadillac V-8 into a Silverstone, adding a De Dion rear axle in the process. It finished second in the 200-mile Palm Beach road race in January 1950. Another Silverstone finished fourth in the 1950 Le Mans (powered by a Nash Ambassador six-cylinder engine). Other roadsters and saloons did well in the Alpine Trial, Targa Florio, Mille Miglia, and the Belgian 24-Hour race. A Healey sport sedan averaged 100+ mph for one hour at Montlhery, France, streaking through a "flying mile" at 110.8 mph.

Donald Healey's connection with Nash, leading to the Nash-Healey, stemmed from a meeting with Nash president George Mason while both men sailed aboard the Queen Elizabeth transatlantic ship. In later years, Healey became a director of the Jensen company, contributing to the Jensen of the 1970s (described elsewhere in this Catalog).

HEALEY "HUNDRED" POSTSCRIPT: After the Silverstone ended its production run, in 1952, the company developed the Healey Hundred, on a 90-inch wheelbase, using Austin A90 components. About 50 examples were built, carrying a different engine: a 2660-cc (162.2 cubic-inch) four. That engine developed 90 horsepower at 4000 rpm, with 7.5:1 compression and twin carburetors, feeding either a conventional gearbox or one with Laycock de Normanville overdrive. Tires were 5.90x15, and the Hundred was capable of 106 mph. *Automobile Topics* magazine called it "a very fast everyday road car, of superior refinement and with exceptionally fine handling qualities." They reported acceleration to 60 mph in 10.5 seconds, and a run through the quarter-mile in 18 seconds. Price in Britain was 850 pounds (Sterling), and estimated at $3000 in the U.S. Those first examples soon evolved into the Austin-Healey 100, similar in both appearance and specifications, as a result of Healey's hookup with BMC. See that listing for further details.

HILLMAN

Introduced in 1931, the popular compact Minx was by no means the first motorcar from Hillman. Founded in 1907 by William Hillman, the company actually indulged in some surprisingly large vehicles in the early days, starting with a 9654-cc six-cylinder Model 40. Displacements diminished to more reasonable levels by the end of that decade, and most Hillman autos through the teens and 1920s carried engines in the 2-liter class or smaller. The Rootes organization acquired Hillman in 1928, along with Sunbeam-Talbot and Humber. Four years later, the first Minx came off the line, with an L-head, 1185-cc four-cylinder engine beneath its bonnet, good for a top speed in the high 50s.

In Hillman's final complete model year before the outbreak of World War II, more than 55,000 Minxes were built (more than one-third of the total prewar production). They even continued in production, in limited number, for wartime applications. Larger Hillmans also were built right up to 1940, including a 2.6-liter Sixteen, a 3.2-liter Hawk, and a four-cylinder model Fourteen that resembled an outsized Minx. (That latter model evolved into the postwar Humber Hawk, also listed in this Catalog.)

Hillman re-emerged right after the war with a 1946 Minx, but it differed little from the 1939-40 version. Its gearshift moved from the floor to the steering column for 1948, but then an all-new Minx arrived for 1949, with coil springs up front. A bigger four-cylinder engine came for the 1950 model year, followed by a succession of improvements (and frequent model-number changes) through the 1950s: larger overhead-valve engine in 1955, new body the next year, and an available automatic transmission in 1958. Perhaps even more important to the American market was the arrival of the little Husky station wagon in 1955, riding a shorter wheelbase. More potent Super Minxes came in the early 1960s, along with front disc brakes for 1964. Hillman also introduced a rival to the front-drive Austin Mini with its rear-engined Imp, which debuted in 1963. That one also was sold under the Sunbeam name in the U.S. (listed in this Catalog).

Chrysler acquired a substantial share of the Rootes Group (Hillman's parent company) in 1964, gaining full control three years later. By 1970, Rootes was known as Chrysler UK Ltd. Export of Hillmans to the U.S. had already ceased, but a Hunter model was produced for European consumption. A cheaper edition was called Minx, and served as the last of its line. Final model to carry the Hillman name was the Avenger, which debuted in 1970 and lasted until 1981 (though the Hillman name switched to Talbot by 1979).

1946-48 HILLMAN

MINX — Mk I — FOUR — Prior to Hillman's surprisingly successful invasion of the American marketplace, the company re-entered the British market with a Minx nearly identical to the prewar saloon (sedan). Its canted-back, upright vee-shape grille contained horizontal bars, with three vertical bars in the fender aprons alongside. Parking lights rode atop the front fenders. Headlamps were mounted separately. Minxes had unibody construction and carried a 72.3 cid (1185 cc) four-cylinder engine. A drophead coupe joined the sedan in spring 1946. Because the Mk I was limited to the home market, data is not included below.

MINX — Mk II — FOUR — Introduced at the end of 1947, the Mark II Minx looked similar

at a glance to the Mark I, with the same sort of upright grille made up of horizontal bars. Its "distinguished new frontal appearance," however, included a new chromium grille plus "streamlined fenders with quadruple motif" (four horizontal bars in each side grille, low in the fender apron) and built-in headlamps. Parking lights were built into the headlamps. A Hillman insignia stood above the grille, at the hood front. A one-piece flat windshield continued, with Lucas wide-arc twin-blade wipers. Disc wheels replaced the former spoke-style wheels. At the rear was a built-in tail/stop lamp. On the mechanical side, Minx switched from the former floor-mounted gearshift lever to a new Synchromatic column-mounted gearshift for the four-speed transmission. A steering-column switch controlled the self-canceling "trafficators" (turn-signal flags). The three-spoke spring steering wheel was 16.5 inches in diameter.

This modified Minx was described as having a "Cushioned Power" engine and "Vari-Load" springing. Lockheed hydraulic brakes used two leading shoes. Wool cloth and leather were used for the new "duo-tone" interior design, while the fascia panel and interior moldings were finished in jewelescent gray. The driver's seat adjusted to three positions. A wide parcel shelf went behind the rear seat, front doors had large pockets, the back seat had side armrests, and the dashboard contained a large cubbyhole. Front windows had vent louvers. A new easi-lift safety hood could be released from inside the car. For emergencies, Minxes came with a self-locating starter handle. Mud flaps were included. The dashboard had provision for fitting the new "His Master's Voice" six-tube superhet medium and long wave radio. The six-window, all-steel unibody came with a sunshine roof. In addition to the four-door saloon (sedan) body, Minx came as an Estate Car (station wagon) or as a drophead (convertible) coupe with three-position top, which served the purpose of a closed saloon, a coupe de ville, or an open tourer.

Note: Specifications and data below apply to Mark II Minx.

I.D. DATA: A seven-digit serial number is stamped on a plate on the right side of the firewall. Starting serial number: 1800001. Engine number (which may be identical to the chassis number) is stamped on the crankcase, above the starter.

1947 Hillman Minx.

1948 Hillman convertible.

Model	Body Type & Seating	Engine Type/CID	P.O.E. Price	Weight (lbs.)	Prod. Total
MINX					
Mk II	4-dr Sedan-4/5P	I4/72	1778	2016	Note 1
Mk II	2-dr Conv Cpe-4/5P	I4/72	2083	2002	Note 1
Mk II	4-dr Est Wag-4/5P	I4/72	2022	2356	Note 1

Note 1: Approximately 789 Hillmans were sold in the U.S. during 1948.

ENGINE DATA: BASE FOUR: Inline, L-head four-cylinder (monobloc). Cast iron block. **Displacement:** 72.26 cu. in. (1184.5 cc). **Bore & Stroke:** 2.48 x 3.74 in. (63 x 95 mm). **Compression Ratio:** 6.3:1. **Brake Horsepower:** 35 at 4100 rpm (factory). Three main bearings. Solid valve lifters. One Solex downdraft carburetor. Lucas ignition. 12-volt.

CHASSIS DATA: Wheelbase: 92 in. **Overall Length:** 156 in. **Height:** 62.5 in. **Width:** 60.5 in. **Front Tread:** 47.6 in. **Rear Tread:** 48.5 in. **Wheel Type:** "easi-clean" disc. **Standard Tires:** Dunlop 5.00x16.

TECHNICAL: Layout: front-engine, rear-drive. **Transmission:** four-speed manual; Synchromatic column lever; synchronized on 2nd/3rd/4th. Overall gear ratios: (1st) 18.63:1; (2nd) 12.90:1; (3rd) 7.79:1; (4th) 5.22:1; (rev) 24.84:1. **Standard Final Drive Ratio:** 5.22:1. **Steering:** Burman Douglas worm and nut. **Suspension (front):** semi-elliptic leaf springs. **Suspension (rear):** rigid axle, semi-elliptic leaf springs. **Brakes:** Lockheed hydraulic front/rear drum. **Body Construction:** steel unibody with stressed platform frame.

MAJOR OPTIONS: "His Master's Voice" six-tube long/medium wave radio.

PERFORMANCE: Top Speed: (Mk II) 66 mph. **Acceleration (0-60 mph):** N/A (Mk II, 0-50 mph in 25.7 seconds). **Acceleration (quarter-mile):** (Mk II) 25.6 seconds.
Manufacturer: Hillman Motor Car Co. Ltd., Warwickshire, England.

HISTORY: Introduced: (Mk I saloon) August 1945 in England; (Mk II) December 1947.

276

1949 HILLMAN

MINX — Mk III — FOUR — After its period of carrying on the prewar profile, then switching to built-in headlamps, Hillman brought out an all-new "envelope" style body for the next Minx, on a one-inch longer wheelbase with 15-inch tires. A new rectangular grille contained six horizontal bars. 'HILLMAN' block letters went above the grille, with a wing-style insignia at the hood front. A cowl ventilator provided ventilation. Full-width chrome bumpers held bumper guards. A new one-piece Opticurve windshield was installed, along with a similarly-curved back window. At the rear were twin tail/stop lamps. All doors were front-hinged, with concealed hinges. Finished in walnut veneer, the instrument panel used ivory color for the large dial-type speedometer and other instruments and controls, as well as for the spring-spoke steering wheel.

Beneath the Minx bonnet was the same 72-cid (1185 cc) four-cylinder engine, rated 38 horsepower, hooked to a four-speed gearbox with Synchromatic steering-column gearshift lever. Down below came a switch to independent front suspension, with coil springs. Long underslung semi-elliptic rear springs had a torsion bar sway eliminator.

As before, three models were produced: a four-door saloon (sedan), two-door drophead (convertible coupe), and an Estate Car. Unibody construction used boxed side and cross members, welded to the body. An adjustable rear license-plate bracket allowed installation of various size plates. Full-width front seats were capable of carrying two adults and a child. A tool kit fit into a felt-lined trough in the floor of the spare-tire compartment, which was separate from the trunk storage area. Available accessories included a radio, heater, and electric clock. Standard colors included Black or Pastel Green (with brown upholstery), Imperial Blue (blue upholstery), and Dove Grey (red upholstery).

1949 Hillman Minx four-door sedan.

I.D. DATA: A seven-digit serial number is stamped on a plate on the right side of the firewall or inside of the left fender. Starting serial number: 1900001. A three-symbol suffix may be used. Symbol one denotes destination ('L' = export, left-hand drive). Symbol two is body type ('S' = sedan; 'C' = coupe; 'U' = Estate). Symbol three indicates deviations from standard type ('O' = standard; 'X' = deviation). Engine number (which may be identical to the chassis number) is stamped on the crankcase, above the starter.

Model	Body Type & Seating	Engine Type/CID	P.O.E. Price	Weight (lbs.)	Prod. Total
MINX					
Mk III	4-dr Sedan-4/5P	I4/72	1495	1981	Note 1
Mk III	2-dr Conv Cpe-4/5P	I4/72	1745	2016	Note 1
Mk III	4-dr Est Wag-4/5P	I4/72	1825	2184	Note 1

Note 1: Approximately 575 Hillmans were sold in the U.S. during 1949.

ENGINE DATA: BASE FOUR: Inline, L-head four-cylinder (monobloc). Cast iron block. **Displacement:** 72.3 cu. in. (1185 cc). **Bore & Stroke:** 2.48 x 3.74 in. (63 x 95 mm). **Compression Ratio:** 6.6:1. **Brake Horsepower:** 38 at 4100 rpm (factory). Three main bearings. Solid valve lifters. One Solex downdraft carburetor. Lucas ignition. 12-volt.

CHASSIS DATA: Wheelbase: 93 in. **Overall Length:** 159.5 in. **Height:** 60 in. **Width:** 62 in. **Front Tread:** 48.6 in. **Rear Tread:** 48.5 in. **Wheel Type:** "easi-clean" disc. **Standard Tires:** Dunlop 5.50x15.

TECHNICAL: Layout: front-engine, rear-drive. **Transmission:** four-speed manual; column lever. Overall gear ratios: (1st) 18.63:1; (2nd) 12.90:1; (3rd) 7.79:1; (4th) 5.22:1; (rev) 24.84:1. **Standard Final Drive Ratio:** 5.22:1. **Steering:** Burman worm and nut. **Suspension (front):** independent; silico manganese coil springs. **Suspension (rear):** rigid axle with semi-elliptic leaf springs and torsion bar sway eliminator. **Brakes:** Lockheed hydraulic front/rear drum. **Body Construction:** pressed steel unibody.

MAJOR OPTIONS: Radio. Heating and air circulating equipment. Electric clock.

PERFORMANCE: Top Speed: 70 mph. **Acceleration (0-60 mph):** N/A (0-50 mph in 24.1 seconds). **Acceleration (quarter-mile):** 25.3 sec.

Manufacturer: Hillman Motor Car Co. Ltd., Ryton-on-Dunsmore, near Coventry, England; part of Rootes Ltd., London, England.

Distributor: Rootes Motors Inc., Long Island City, New York.

HISTORY: "An original conception in modern automobile design," said the 1949 sales brochure from Fergus Motors in New York City, "the HILLMAN MINX has taken another step in its long and distinguished career." Still promoting the earlier model with upright grille, the brochure noted that it offered "Big car roominess with a proven power unit of 72.6 cubic inches," as well as an "exclusive draughtless ventilation system." In sum, even the prewar-style Hillman was immodestly dubbed "an engineering achievement designed for this modern age."

1950 HILLMAN

MINX — Mk IV — FOUR — A bigger powerplant was the foremost change for the 1950 model, billed as "Hillman Minx Magnificent." The new Plus Power L-head engine, larger in bore dimension but with the same stroke as before, displaced 77.2 cubic inches (1265 cc) and delivered 42 horsepower at 4200 rpm. Appearance was similar to 1949, with the horizontal-bar rectangular grille. Instead of the former parking lights built into the head-lamps, however, the Mark IV had separate round parking lights below. "Unitary construction," said the factory sales brochure, "integrates body and chassis into one assembly of immense strength and power." Independent coil spring suspension continued in front, with semi-elliptic leaf springs at the rear. Dunlop 5.50x15 tires were standard, on "Easi-Clean" disc wheels. Standard colors were: Black with brown upholstery; Black with red; Pastel Green with red; and Pastel Blue with blue; and Pastel Green with dove gray upholstery. Optional accessories include a radio, heating and air circulating equipment, electric clock and thermometer.

Hillman's Estate Car (station wagon) retined the earlier 72.3-cid engine. Wagons had a wider rear track than the sedan and convertible. With an Opticurve windshield and set-back pillars, and large back window, they were claimed to have "observation car" vision. Accessories at extra cost included the "His Master's Voice" radio; heating and air circulation equipment; electric clock; and front or rear bumper overiders (guards).

I.D. DATA: Serial number is located on a plate on the inside of the left fender. The first figure ('1') following the 'A' prefix indicates model (Mink). The second figure indicates model year ('0' = 1950). The next five digits are the sequential serial number. A three-symbol suffix breaks down as follows: symbol one denotes destination ('L' = export, left-hand drive); symbol two is body type ('S' = sedan; 'C' = coupe; 'U' = Estate); symbol three indicates deviations ('O' = standard; 'X' = deviation). Serial number range: A1000001 to A1020611. Engine number is on left side of crankcase, near the rear.

1950 Hillman Minx convertible coupe.

MINX

Model	Body Type & Seating	Engine Type/CID	P.O.E. Price	Weight (lbs.)	Prod. Total
Mk IV	4-dr Sedan-4/5P	I4/77	1495	2002	Note 1
Mk IV	2-dr Conv Cpe-4/5P	I4/77	1745	2016	Note 1
Mk IV	4-dr Estate Car-4/5P	I4/72	1825	2184	Note 1

Note 1: Approximately 3,279 Hillmans were sold in the U.S. during 1950.

ENGINE DATA: BASE FOUR (sedan/conv): Inline, L-head four-cylinder (monobloc). Cast iron block. **Displacement:** 77.2 cu. in. (1265 cc). **Bore & Stroke:** 2.56 x 3.74 in. (65 x 95 mm). **Compression Ratio:** 6.6:1. **Brake Horsepower:** 42 at 4200 rpm. Three main bearings. Solid valve lifters. One Solex downdraft carburetor. Lucas ignition. 12-volt.
BASE FOUR (Estate): Same as above, except — **Displacement:** 72.3 cu. in. (1185 cc). **Bore & Stroke:** 2.48 x 3.74 in. (63 x 95 mm). **Compression Ratio:** 6.6:1. **Brake Horsepower:** 35 at 4100 rpm.

CHASSIS DATA: Wheelbase: 93 in. **Overall Length:** 160 in. **Height:** 60 in. exc. (conv) 58.5 in. **Width:** 62 in. **Front Tread:** 48.6 in. **Rear Tread:** 48.5 in. exc. (Estate) 50.5 in. **Wheel Type:** "easi-clean" disc. **Standard Tires:** Dunlop 5.50x15.

TECHNICAL: Layout: front-engine, rear-drive. **Transmission:** four-speed manual; column lever. Overall gear ratios: (1st) 18.60:1; (2nd) 12.89:1; (3rd) 7.78:1; (4th) 5.22:1; (rev) 24.85:1. **Standard Final Drive Ratio:** 5.22:1. **Steering:** Burman worm and nut. **Suspension (front):** independent; silico manganese coil springs. **Suspension (rear):** rigid axle with semi-elliptic leaf springs and torsion bar sway eliminator. **Brakes:** Lockheed hydraulic front/rear drum. **Body Construction:** pressed steel unibody.

MAJOR OPTIONS: "His Master's Voice" radio. Heating and air circulating equipment. Electric clock and thermometer. Front and rear bumper guards (wagon).

PERFORMANCE: Top Speed: 68 mph. **Acceleration (0-60 mph):** N/A (0-50 mph in 21.4 seconds). **Acceleration (quarter-mile):** 24.6 sec.
Manufacturer: Hillman Motor Car Co. Ltd., Ryton-on-Dunsmore, near Coventry, England; part of Rootes Ltd., London, England.
Distributor: Rootes Motors Inc., Long Island City, New York.
HISTORY: Introduced: (Mark IV) September 1949.

1951 HILLMAN

MINX — Mk IV — FOUR — Appearance and mechanical details were similar to 1950, except that headlamps were almost flush with the front fenders.
I.D. DATA: Serial number is located on a plate on the inside of the left fender. Breakdown is similar to 1950. Starting serial number: A1020612. Engine number is on left side of crankcase, near the rear.

Model	Body Type & Seating	Engine Type/CID	P.O.E. Price	Weight (lbs.)	Prod. Total
MINX					
Mk IV	4-dr Sedan-4/5P	I4/77	1533	1995	Note 1
Mk IV	2-dr Conv Cpe-4/5P	I4/77	1890	2016	Note 1
Mk IV	4-dr Est Car-4/5P	I4/72	1938	2142	Note 1

Note 1: Approximately 3,787 Hillmans were sold in the U.S. during 1951.
ENGINE DATA: Same as 1950.
CHASSIS DATA: Same as 1950.
TECHNICAL: Same as 1950.
PERFORMANCE: Same as 1950.
HISTORY: 1951 models introduced in the U.S. in November, 1950.

1952 HILLMAN

MINX — Mk IV — FOUR — Production of the Mark IV version of the Minx continued, while the DeLuxe (but similar) Mark V was introduced.

MINX — Mk V — FOUR — Appearance of the new DeLuxe Minx was similar to the Mk IV, except that a new chrome 'Hillman' nameplate went above the grille, on a heavy horizontal chromed bar. Alongside the grille were two vertical chromed elements. A horizontal body trim strip on the front fender extended throught part of the front door, and bright guards went on the back doors, just ahead of the wheel wells. As before, the drophead (convertible) coupe had a three-position top.

I.D. DATA: Serial number is on a plate on the inside of the left fender. Starting serial number: (Mark IV) A1050000; (Mark V) A1100001. Engine number is on left side of crankcase, near the rear.

Model	Body Type & Seating	Engine Type/CID	P.O.E. Price	Weight (lbs.)	Prod. Total
MINX					
Mk IV	4-dr Sedan-4/5P	I4/77	1533	1995	Note 1
Mk IV	2-dr Conv-4/5P	I4/77	1845	2016	Note 1
Mk IV	4-dr Est Car-4/5P	I4/77	1938	2142	Note 1
MINX					
Mk V	4-dr Sedan-4/5P	I4/77	1645	1995	Note 1
Mk V	2-dr Conv-4/5P	I4/77	1890	2016	Note 1
Mk V	4-dr Est Car-4/5P	I4/77	1938	2142	Note 1

Note 1: Approximately 4,782 Hillmans were sold in the U.S. during 1952.
ENGINE DATA: BASE FOUR: Inline, L-head four-cylinder (monobloc). Cast iron block. **Displacement:** 77.2 cu. in. (1265 cc). **Bore & Stroke:** 2.56 x 3.74 in. (65 x 95 mm). **Compression Ratio:** 6.6:1. **Brake Horsepower:** 42 at 4200 rpm. Three main bearings. Solid valve lifters. One Solex downdraft carburetor. Lucas ignition. 12-volt.
CHASSIS DATA: Wheelbase: 93 in. **Overall Length:** 160 in. **Height:** 60 in. exc. (conv) 58.5 in. **Width:** 62 in. **Front Tread:** 48.6 in. **Rear Tread:** 48.5 in. exc. (Estate) 50.5 in. **Wheel Type:** "easi-clean" disc. **Standard Tires:** Dunlop 5.50x15.
TECHNICAL: Layout: front-engine, rear-drive. **Transmission:** four-speed manual; column lever. Overall gear ratios: (1st) 18.60:1; (2nd) 12.89:1; (3rd) 7.78:1; (4th) 5.22:1. **Standard Final Drive Ratio:** 5.22:1. **Steering:** Burman worm and nut. **Suspension (front):** independent; silico manganese coil springs. **Suspension (rear):** rigid axle with semi-elliptic leaf springs and torsion bar sway eliminator. **Brakes:** Lockheed hydraulic front/rear drum. **Body Construction:** pressed steel unibody.
PERFORMANCE: Top Speed: (Mk V) 73.2 mph. **Acceleration (0-60 mph):** N/A; (Mk V) 0-50 mph in 17.7 sec. **Acceleration (quarter-mile):** (Mk V) 23.9 seconds.
Manufacturer: Hillman Motor Car Co. Ltd., Ryton-on-Dunsmore, near Coventry, England; part of Rootes Ltd., London, England.
Distributor: Rootes Motors Inc., Long Island City, New York.
HISTORY: Mark V introduced in U.S., February 1952. In a test sponsored by Esso Mile-O-Meter and *Auto Sports Review* magazine, a Minx "scored" 34.6 miles per gallon in New York City traffic.

1953 HILLMAN MINX

MINX — Mk VI — FOUR — While similar to prior Minxes in overall upright profile and basic mechanical details, the Mark VI enjoyed a facelift and what *Automobile Topics* magazine described as "32 improvements" to help the Hillman company's 25th anniversary in the car business. The new wide die-cast grille of the "Continental" style front end was a rectangular oval in shape, with a pattern of slim horizontal bars and 'Hillman'

lettering at the top center of its heavy chromed surround molding. Tiny round parking lights stood below the built-in headlamps, similar to former models. A winged insignia was evident above the grille. Round taillamps now were faired into the rear fenders, some six inches higher than before (partly to meet American requirements). Bumpers were restyled, wrapping about two inches farther around the rear fenders; and pushbutton door handles installed. As in the previous version, a horizontal trim strip ran along the front fender, continuing part of the way along the front door. Hillman broadened its range of body colors and trim this year, up to eight color choices. All models had a standard heater and fresh-air conditioning system, with twin intakes behind the grille. That meant the disappearance of the old-fashioned cowl vent. Turn-signal flashers were used, with indicators on the instrument panel. Inside was a contour front seat and two-spoke steering wheel, and a restyled instrument panel. Less visible were the new shock absorbers and the revised carburetor, heat-controlled manifold and cylinder head. Most notable of the changes, though, was the addition of a Californian hardtop coupe to the lineup. Appearance was virtually identical to the customary convertible, with no 'B' pillar, but with the addition of a solid roof and large wraparound back window. While its name had obvious American inspiration, the Californian hardtop was also sold in England.

I.D. DATA: Serial number is on a plate on the inside of the left fender. Starting serial number: 1300001. Engine number is on left side of crankcase, near the rear.

Model	Body Type & Seating	Engine Type/CID	P.O.E. Price	Weight (lbs.)	Prod. Total
MINX					
Mk VI	4-dr Sedan-4/5P	I4/77	1699	2039	Note 1
Mk VI	2-dr HT Cpe-4/5P	I4/77	1899	2172	Note 1
Mk VI	2-dr Conv-4/5P	I4/77	1899	2074	Note 1
Mk VI	4-dr Est Car-4/5P	I4/77	1949	2207	Note 1

Note 1: Approximately 4,506 Hillmans were sold in the U.S. during 1953.

ENGINE DATA: BASE FOUR: Inline, L-head four-cylinder. Cast iron (monobloc) block. **Displacement:** 77.2 cu. in. (1265 cc). **Bore & Stroke:** 2.56 x 3.74 in. (65 x 95 mm). **Compression Ratio:** 6.6:1. **Brake Horsepower:** 42 at 4200 rpm. Three main bearings. Solid valve lifters. One carburetor. 12-volt.

CHASSIS DATA: Wheelbase: 93 in. **Overall Length:** 160 in. **Height:** 60 in. exc. (conv) 58.5 in. **Width:** 62 in. **Front Tread:** 48.6 in. **Rear Tread:** 48.5 in. **Wheel Type:** disc. **Standard Tires:** 5.50x15.

TECHNICAL: Layout: front-engine, rear-drive. **Transmission:** four-speed manual; column lever. **Standard Final Drive Ratio:** 5.22:1. **Steering:** Burman worm and nut. **Suspension (front):** independent; coil springs. **Suspension (rear):** rigid axle with semi-elliptic leaf springs. **Brakes:** hydraulic front/rear drum. **Body Construction:** pressed steel unibody.

PERFORMANCE: Top Speed: 68 mph. **Fuel Mileage:** 26 mpg.

Manufacturer: Hillman Motor Car Co. Ltd., Ryton-on-Dunsmore, near Coventry, England; part of Rootes Ltd., London, England.

Distributor: Rootes Motors Inc., Long Island City, New York.

HISTORY: Introduced (Mk VI): February 1953.

1954 HILLMAN MINX

MINX — Mk VII — FOUR — This year's Minx had longer rear fenders, vertical taillamps, wraparound rear bumper and a longer decklid with a handle above the license plate, but otherwise looked similar to the prior model. Sedans had a bigger back window. A pushbutton starter now was installed on the dashboard. As before, the Minx had a wide, rectangular oval grille with thin horizontal bars and a bright surround molding, round parking lights below the headlamps, an insignia on the hood front, and rounded (but square-shaped) wheel openings. Vent windows were on front and rear doors. One buyer's guide of the time called attention to Minx for its roominess, comfort, finish and economy, as well as its "rugged hauling power." Coachwork for the convertible and the Californian coupe was done by Thrupp and Maberly, a British company with a history dating back over 200 years.

1954 Hillman Minx Mark VII.

I.D. DATA: Serial number is on a plate on the inside of the left fender. Starting serial number: 1400001. Engine number is on left side of crankcase, near the rear.

Model	Body Type & Seating	Engine Type/CID	P.O.E. Price	Weight (lbs.)	Prod. Total
MINX					
Mk VII	4-dr Sedan-4/5P	I4/77	1699	2053	Note 1
Mk VII	2-dr Hardtop-4/5P	I4/77	1899	2144	Note 1
Mk VII	2-dr Conv-4/5P	I4/77	1899	2060	Note 1
Mk VII	4-dr Est Car-4/5P	I4/77	1949	2207	Note 1

Note 1: Approximately 2,340 Hillmans were sold in the U.S. during 1954.

ENGINE DATA: BASE FOUR: Inline, L-head four-cylinder. Cast iron (monobloc) block. **Displacement:** 77.2 cu. in. (1265 cc). **Bore & Stroke:** 2.56 x 3.74 in. (65 x 95 mm). **Compression Ratio:** 6.6:1. **Brake Horsepower:** 42 at 4200 rpm. Three main bearings. Solid valve lifters. One downdraft carburetor. 12-volt.

CHASSIS DATA: Wheelbase: 93 in. **Overall Length:** 162 in. **Height:** 60 in. exc. (conv) 58.5 in. **Width:** 62 in. **Front Tread:** 48.6 in. **Rear Tread:** 48.5 in. exc. (Estate) 50.5 in. **Wheel Type:** disc. **Standard Tires:** 5.50x15.

TECHNICAL: Layout: front-engine, rear-drive. **Transmission:** four-speed manual; column lever. Overall gear ratios: (1st) 18.60:1; (2nd) 12.89:1; (3rd) 7.78:1; (4th) 5.22:1. **Standard Final Drive Ratio:** 5.22:1. **Steering:** Burman worm and nut. **Suspension (front):** independent; coil springs. **Suspension (rear):** rigid axle with semi-elliptic leaf springs. **Brakes:** Lockheed hydraulic front/rear drum. **Body Construction:** pressed steel unibody.

PERFORMANCE: Top Speed: 68-69 mph. **Acceleration (0-60 mph):** 31 seconds. **Acceleration (quarter-mile):** 25.3 seconds. **Fuel Mileage:** about 28 mpg.

PRODUCTION/SALES: By this time, Minx was probably the most popular of the Rootes Group cars among American buyers. Almost 17,000 had been sold in the U.S. since its 1948 debut.

Manufacturer: Hillman Motor Car Co. Ltd., Ryton-on-Dunsmore, near Coventry, England; part of Rootes Ltd., London, England.

Distributor: Rootes Motors Inc., Long Island City, New York.

1955 HILLMAN MINX

HUSKY — Mk I — FOUR — Hillman's brochure billed the new lower-priced, shorter-wheelbase "Double Duty" Husky Estate Car (station wagon) as "two cars in one. A smart comfortable saloon for personal use...a sturdy load carrier for business transport." Designed to carry four adults plus 250 pounds of baggage, Husky had foam-cushion bucket seats in front and a fold-forward rear seat. Gauges, including a round speedometer, were in the center of the dashboard. Front-end appearance was similar to the current Minx. The side-opening rear door had no tailgate. Husky's price began at $1445. Available extras included two-tone paint schemes, a roof luggage carrier, and whitewall tires. Standard colors were: Golden Sand, Quartz Blue, Mountain Grey, Surf Green. While the newest Minx models moved to an overhead-valve engine, Husky stuck with the familiar L-head four, and the four-speed gearbox was operated by a floor lever.

MINX — Mk VIII — FOUR — A modified front-end greeted buyers of the newest Minx, which had a wide oval rectangular grille with heavy surround molding as before, but added a single horizontal bar across the long row of thin vertical bars. Small round parking lights went below the headlamps. The car's profile was still rather upright, with squared-off wheel openings, front-hinged doors, vent panes on front and rear doors, and exposed trunk hinges. Under the bonnet of the three new models (four-door Deluxe sedan, Californian hardtop coupe, and convertible coupe) was a new overhead-valve engine. Like former Minx models, the new one used chassisless (unibody) steel construction. The Californian had a large wraparound back window, while the convertible's top folded away neatly, virtually out of sight.

Standard colors for the Deluxe saloon and convertible were: Black, Mountain Grey or Golden Sand with bright red leather upholstery; Black with dark fawn upholstery; Black, Claret or Mid Green with light fawn upholstery; Claret with mid grey upholstery; and Severn Blue with light fawn or bright red upholstery. Convertibles could also get a Cream body with bright red upholstery. The Californian came in Cream with black top and bright red upholstery; Balmoral Grey with quartz blue top and blue grey/dark blue upholstery; Pastel Green body with bottle green top and light green/dark green upholstery; Cream body with pippin red top and light fawn/bright red upholstery; Black body with pippin red top and bright red upholstery; or Oxford Blue body with cream top and French grey upholstery. A special sedan powered by the Econimaster engine also was announced, with its own selection of colors.

I.D. DATA: Serial number plate is on bulkhead, under hood. Starting serial number: (Husky) 2400001; (Minx) 1500001. Engine number is on left side of crankcase, near the rear.

Model	Body Type & Seating	Engine Type/CID	P.O.E. Price	Weight (lbs.)	Prod. Total
HUSKY					
Mk I	2-dr Sta Wagon-4P	I4/77	1445	1858	Note 1
MINX					
Mk VIII	4-dr Sedan-4/5P	I4/85	1699	2100	Note 1
MI VIII	2-dr HT Cpe-4/5P	I4/85	1915	2198	Note 1
Mk VIII	2-dr Conv-4/5P	I4/85	1915	2128	Note 1
Mk VIII	4-dr Est Wag-4/5P	I4/77	1965	2172	Note 1

Note 1: A total of 76,700 Hillmans were built in 1955.

ENGINE DATA: BASE FOUR (Husky/Estate): Inline, L-head four-cylinder. Cast iron (monobloc) block. **Displacement:** 77.2 cu. in. (1265 cc). **Bore & Stroke:** 2.56 x 3.74 in. (65 x 95 mm). **Compression Ratio:** 6.6:1. **Brake Horsepower:** 37 at 4100 rpm. Three main bearings. Solid valve lifters. One Zenith carburetor. 12-volt.

BASE FOUR (Minx): Inline, overhead-valve four-cylinder. Cast iron block. **Displacement:** 84.8 cu. in. (1390 cc). **Bore & Stroke:** 3.00 x 3.00 in. (76.2 x 76.2 mm). **Compression Ratio:** 7.0:1. **Brake Horsepower:** 47 at 4400 rpm. Three main bearings. Solid valve lifters. One Zenith carburetor.

CHASSIS DATA: Wheelbase: (Husky) 84 in.; (Minx) 93 in. **Overall Length:** (Husky) 145.5 in.; (Minx) 159.5 in. **Height:** (Husky) 61 in.; (Minx) 61 in. **Width:** (Husky) 62 in.; (Minx) 63.5 in. **Front Tread:** (Minx) 48.6 in. **Rear Tread:** (Minx) 48.5 in. **Wheel Type:** disc. **Standard Tires:** (Husky) 5.00x15; (Minx) 5.60x15.

TECHNICAL: Layout: front-engine, rear-drive. **Transmission:** four-speed manual; (Husky) floor lever; (Minx) column lever. **Standard Final Drive Ratio:** (Husky) 5.22:1 (Minx) 4.77:1. **Steering:** Burman worm and nut. **Suspension (front):** independent; coil springs. **Suspension (rear):** rigid axle with semi-elliptic leaf springs. **Brakes:** Lockheed hydraulic front/rear drum. **Body Construction:** pressed steel unibody. **Fuel Tank:** (Minx) 8.7 gallons.

MAJOR OPTIONS: (Husky) Two-tone paint. Roof luggage carrier. Whitewall tires.

PERFORMANCE: Top Speed: (Husky) about 65 mph; (Minx) 70-75 mph. **Acceleration (0-60 mph):** N/A; (Husky) 0-50 mph in 24.3 seconds; (Minx) 0-50 mph in 17.3 seconds. **Acceleration (quarter-mile):** (Husky) 25.6 sec.; (Minx) 23.4 sec. **Fuel Mileage:** (Minx) about 28 mpg at cruising speed.

Manufacturer: Hillman Motor Car Co. Ltd., Ryton-on-Dunsmore, near Coventry, England; part of Rootes Ltd., London, England.

Distributor: Rootes Motors Inc., Long Island City, New York.

1956 HILLMAN MINX

1957 Hillman Minx DeLuxe four-door sedan.

HUSKY — Mk I — FOUR — Production of the smaller station wagon continued with little change, after its 1955 debut. With only two people aboard, the Husky was capable of carrying 560 pounds of cargo.

MINX — Mk VIIIA — FOUR — Only modest appearance changes differentiated the Mk VIIIA from the former Mk VIII Minx. As before, a wide vertical-bar grille had a single horizontal bar across its front, and round parking lights stood below the headlamps. The Minx Estate Car (station wagon) now used the same overhead-valve engine as the other models. It had front bucket seats, a folding rear bench seat, and washable fabric headlining. Double rear doors had snap-back retaining arms. All models now had tubeless tires.

I.D. DATA: Serial number plate is on bulkhead, under hood. Starting serial number: (Husky) 2400001; (Minx) 1500001. Engine number is on left side of crankcase, near the rear.

Model	Body Type & Seating	Engine Type/CID	P.O.E. Price	Weight (lbs.)	Prod. Total
HUSKY					
Mk I	2-dr Sta Wagon-4P	I4/77	1497	1858	Note 1
MINX					
Mk VIIIA	4-dr Sedan-4/5P	I4/85	1699	2100	Note 1
Mk VIIIA	2-dr HT Cpe-4/5P	I4/85	1915	2198	Note 1
Mk VIIIA	2-dr Conv-4/5P	I4/85	1915	2120	Note 1
Mk VIIIA	4-dr Estate Wag-4/5P	I4/85	1965	2172	Note 1

Note 1: A total of about 60,000 Hillmans were built during 1956.

ENGINE DATA: BASE FOUR (Husky): Inline, L-head four-cylinder. Cast iron (monobloc) block. **Displacement:** 77.2 cu. in. (1265 cc). **Bore & Stroke:** 2.56 x 3.74 in. (65 x 95 mm). **Compression Ratio:** 6.65:1. **Brake Horsepower:** 37.5 at 4100 rpm. Three main bearings. Solid valve lifters. One Zenith carburetor. 12-volt.

BASE FOUR (Mark VIIIA): Inline, overhead-valve four-cylinder. Cast iron (monobloc) block. **Displacement:** 84.8 cu. in. (1390 cc). **Bore & Stroke:** 3.00 x 3.00 in. (76.2 x 76.2 mm). **Compression Ratio:** 7.0:1. **Brake Horsepower:** 47 at 4400 rpm. Three main bearings. Solid valve lifters. One Zenith carburetor. 12-volt.

CHASSIS DATA: Wheelbase: (Husky) 84 in.; (Mark VIIIA) 93 in. **Overall Length:** (Husky) 145.5 in.; (Mark VIIIA) 159.5 in. **Height:** (Husky) 61 in.; (Minx) 61 in.; (Estate) 67.5 in. **Width:** (Husky) 62 in.; (Minx) 63.5 in. **Front Tread:** (Minx) 48.6 in. **Rear Tread:** (Minx) 48.5 in.; (Estate) 50.5 in. **Wheel Type:** disc. **Standard Tires:** (Husky) 5.00x15; (Minx) 5.60x15.

TECHNICAL: Layout: front-engine, rear-drive. **Transmission:** four-speed manual; (Husky) floor lever; (Minx) column lever. **Standard Final Drive Ratio:** (Husky) 5.22:1 (Minx) 4.77:1. **Steering:** Burman worm and nut. **Suspension (front):** independent; coil springs. **Suspension (rear):** rigid axle with semi-elliptic leaf springs. **Brakes:** Lockheed hydraulic front/rear drum. **Body Construction:** pressed steel unibody.

PERFORMANCE: Top Speed: (Husky) 65-70 mph; (Minx) about 75 mph. **Fuel Mileage:** (Husky) up to 40 mpg; (Minx) 35pg.

Manufacturer: Hillman Motor Car Co. Ltd., Ryton-on-Dunsmore, near Coventry, England; part of Rootes Ltd., London, England.

Distributor: Rootes Motors Inc., Long Island City, New York.

HISTORY: Introduced in U.S. on September 15, 1955.

Compression Ratio: 6.63:1. **Brake Horsepower:** 42 at 4100 rpm. Three main bearings. Solid valve lifters. One Zenith carburetor. 12-volt.

BASE FOUR (New Minx): Inline, overhead-valve four-cylinder. Cast iron (monobloc) block. **Displacement:** 84.8 cu. in. (1390 cc). **Bore & Stroke:** 3.00 x 3.00 in. (76.2 x 76.2 mm). **Compression Ratio:** 8.0:1. **Brake Horsepower:** 51 at 4600 rpm. **Torque:** 69.75 lbs.-ft. at 2400 rpm. Three main bearings. Solid valve lifters. One carburetor. 12-volt.

CHASSIS DATA: Wheelbase: (Husky) 84 in.; (New Minx) 96 in. **Overall Length:** (Husky) 145.5 in.; (Minx) 160.5 in. **Height:** (Husky) 61 in.; (Minx) 60.75 in. **Width:** (Husky) 62 in.; (Minx) 60.75 in. **Front Tread:** (Minx) 49 in. **Rear Tread:** (Minx) 48.5 in. **Wheel Type:** disc. **Standard Tires:** (Husky) 5.00x15; (New Minx) 9889x15.

TECHNICAL: Layout: front-engine, rear-drive. **Transmission:** four-speed manual; (Husky) floor lever; (Minx) column lever. Second/third/fourth gears synchronized. **Standard Final Drive Ratio:** (Minx) 4.778:1. **Steering:** Burman worm and nut. **Suspension (front):** independent; transverse control arms with coil springs. **Suspension (rear):** rigid axle with semi-elliptic leaf springs. **Brakes:** Lockheed hydraulic front/rear drum. **Body Construction:** pressed steel unibody.

MAJOR OPTIONS: Heater ($57). Whitewall tires ($25).

PERFORMANCE: Top Speed: (Husky) about 68 mph; (Minx) 75-80 mph. **Acceleration (0-60 mph):** (Minx) 22 sec. **Acceleration (quarter-mile):** (Husky) 25.6 sec.; (Minx) 23.4 sec. **Fuel Mileage:** (Husky) about 38 mpg; (Minx) 24.6-35 mpg.

Manufacturer: Hillman Motor Car Co. Ltd., Ryton-on-Dunsmore, near Coventry, England; part of Rootes Ltd., London, England.

Distributor: Rootes Motors, Inc., New York and Los Angeles (and other locations).

HISTORY: Husky introduced in U.S. October 8, 1956, for the 1957 model year. Hillman claimed to have put in eight years of development work on the new Minx design, including detailed study of American tastes and preferences. "Designed for Americans at home and abroad," read the ads in autumn 1956 for "the dynamic new '57 Hillman Minx." They touted the rugged double-duty Husky; the glamorous three-way convertible; and the roomier, more powerful four-door sedan. "These three exciting new cars," the copy continued, "were designed for the turnpikes here as well as the byways of Europe." Ads further mentioned the overseas delivery plans that enabled visitors to Britain to pick up a Hillman as part of the journey.

1957 HILLMAN

HUSKY — Mk I — FOUR — Production of the smallest Hillman, the short-wheelbase Husky, continued with little change.

NEW MINX — FOUR — Rather than a modest facelift, the New Minx actually looked new, with a more modern profile replacing the old-fashioned upright look. *Motor Trend* called it the "smartest looking Hillman Minx ever to hit these shores." The wide vertical-bar was similar to earlier versions, but in a less-rounded frame with a horizontal bar across the front and parking lights at the outside (contained within the grille). Back doors of the sedan had no vent panes, but their windows were now back-angled for a fresh appearance, especially with the sharply-wraparound rear window. A bodyside trim strip, slightly curved, ran all the way from front to rear. Vertical-style taillamps stood at the tips of rear fenders. The license plate mounted on the trunk lid, which still had exposed hinges. The hood was counterbalanced for easy lifting. Inside were bench seats front and rear, with space for four (five with squeezing) and instruments in the center of the dashboard. Glove compartments lacked doors. Some observers complained about the unconventional shift pattern of the column lever, which required the driver to push the lever forward to reach first and second gears.

Convertible coupe and deluxe sedan bodies arrived first, riding a 96-inch wheelbase (three inches longer than before). Even so, the sedan grew by only half an inch overall. Still, the increased size allowed roomier (and lower) interior dimensions. As in past forms, the convertible's plastic roof could go part way up to the "de ville" position. The overhead-valve engine, with its equal bore/stroke dimensions, got a compression boost to 8:1 (a high value for a British vehicle), for a rating of 51 horsepower. Arriving late in the model year was an Estate Car version of the new Minx design, with protruding rear fenders.

I.D. DATA: Serial number plate is on bulkhead, under hood. Starting serial number: (Minx) A1600001. Engine number is on left side of block.

Model	Body Type & Seating	Engine Type/CID	P.O.E. Price	Weight (lbs.)	Prod. Total
HUSKY					
Mk I	2-dr Sta Wagon-4P	I4/77	1535	1858	Note 1
NEW MINX					
Series I	4-dr Sedan-4/5P	I4/85	1799	2100	Note 1
Series I	2-dr Conv-4/5P	I4/85	1999	2118	Note 1
Series I	4-dr Estate Car-4/5P	I4/85	2172	2172	Note 1

Note 1: A total of about 75,000 Hillmans were built during 1957; approximately 13,036 were sold in the U.S.

ENGINE DATA: BASE FOUR (Husky): Inline, L-head four-cylinder. Cast iron (monobloc) block. **Displacement:** 77.2 cu. in. (1265 cc). **Bore & Stroke:** 2.56 x 3.74 in. (65 x 95 mm).

1958 HILLMAN

HUSKY — SERIES I — FOUR — For the 1958 model year, the littlest Hillman adopted a variant of the bigger (1390 cc) overhead-valve four-cylinder engine of its Minx mate, forsaking the former L-head four. Longer and lower in profile, the restyled Husky two-door station wagon delivered higher performance than its predecessor, along with more passenger and luggage space. The luggage platform was 7.5 inches longer than previous, for 41.5 cubic feet of cargo space and a new maximum load rating of almost 700 pounds. Seating for four was still available, with increased leg and headroom for passengers. The new design allowed space for 300 pounds of luggage. The new 85-cid engine with 8:1 compression delivered 46 horsepower at 4400 rpm, allowing a top speed over 75 mph with fuel mileage in the 30-35 mpg neighborhood. During the model year, Husky adopted the revised Minx grille.

1958 Hillman Minx.

MINX — SERIES II — FOUR — Known this year as the Jubilee Minx, in honor of the 25th birthday of the model (and the 50th anniversary of Hillman cars), the larger Hillman received a moderate front-end restyling, highlighted by a new grille. Parking lights were incorporated within the mesh-patterned grille, which consisted of a chromed surround

molding within the overall surround. 'Hillman' script decorated the grille mesh on the passenger side. Overall appearance was similar to the contemporary Sunbeam Rapier and Singer Gazelle, with full wheel openings that were slightly flared. Two sedans were offered: a Minx Deluxe and lower-priced Hillman Special. Purchasers of a DeLuxe model now had the option of Hillman's Manumatic transmission instead of the usual four-speed manual gearbox.

The Special sedan had the same body and engine as Minx DeLuxe, but less exterior and interior trim and only one available color scheme. Headlamps were unvisored, and the windshield and windows lacked the DeLuxe's chrome moldings. Inside, it had two bucket seats instead of a bench-type front seat, large Husky-derived center-mounted instruments, and the gearshift lever was on the floor rather than the steering column. The fully weatherproofed Minx Sports Convertible had wind-up windows all around and a three-position top that could be put in the "coupe de ville" position, with only the roof over the front seat open. Hillman's Minx four-door station wagon held four passengers plus 400 pounds of luggage. With the rear seat folded down, it could carry half a ton; or two adults and 700 pounds of cargo. A drop-down tailgate was installed at the rear, with a lifting full-width window. Like other DeLuxe Minxes, the wagon came in a wide selection of single or two-tone color schemes. Under each Minx hood was the same 85-cid four-cylinder engine, with a new camshaft this year.

I.D. DATA: Serial number plate is on bulkhead, under hood. Starting serial number: (Husky) 2800001; (Minx) 1800001; (Minx Special) 1865001. Engine number is on left side of block.

Model	Body Type & Seating	Engine Type/CID	P.O.E. Price	Weight (lbs.)	Prod. Total
HUSKY					
I	2-dr Sta Wagon-4P	I4/85	1639	2020	Note 1
MINX (SERIES II)					
Special	4-dr Sedan-4/5P	I4/85	1699	2116	Note 1
DeLuxe	4-dr Sedan-4-5P	I4/85	1849	2135	Note 1
DeLuxe	2-dr Conv-4/5P	I4/85	2099	2148	Note 1
DeLuxe	4-dr Est Wag-4/5P	I4/85	2299	2270	Note1

Note 1: A total of about 100,000 Hillmans were built during 1958; approximately 18,970 were sold in the U.S.

Husky Note: Some 1st Series Husky models were sold early in the model year, with the former smaller engine.

ENGINE DATA: BASE FOUR (Husky): Inline, overhead-valve four-cylinder. Cast iron (monobloc) block. **Displacement:** 84.8 cu. in. (1390 cc). **Bore & Stroke:** 3.00 x 3.00 in. (76.2 x 76.2 mm). **Compression Ratio:** 8.0:1. **Brake Horsepower:** 46 at 4400 rpm. Torque: 71 lbs.-ft. at 2000 rpm. Three main bearings. Solid valve lifters. One Zenith carburetor. 12-volt.

BASE FOUR (Minx): Inline, overhead-valve four-cylinder. Cast iron (monobloc) block. **Displacement:** 84.8 cu. in. (1390 cc). **Bore & Stroke:** 3.00 x 3.00 in. (76.2 x 76.2 mm). **Compression Ratio:** 8.0:1. **Brake Horsepower:** 51 at 4400 rpm. **Torque:** 72 lbs.-ft. at 2200 rpm. Three main bearings. Solid valve lifters. One Zenith carburetor. 12-volt.

CHASSIS DATA: Wheelbase: (Husky) 86 in.; (Minx) 96 in. **Overall Length:** (Husky) 149.5 in.; (Minx) 162 in. **Height:** (Husky) 62 in.; (Minx sed) 59.5 in.; (conv) 58 in.; (Estate) 61 in. **Width:** (Husky) 60.5 in.; (Minx) 60.75 in. **Front Tread:** 49 in. **Rear Tread:** 48.5 in. **Wheel Type:** disc. **Standard Tires:** (Husky/Special) 5.00x15 tubeless; (Minx) 5.60x15; (Estate) 5.90x15. **Fuel Tank:** (Husky) 7.5 gallons (U.S.); (Minx) 8.7 gallons.

TECHNICAL: Layout: front-engine, rear-drive. **Transmission:** four-speed manual; (Husky/Special sedan) floor lever; (Minx) column lever. Second/third/fourth gears synchronized. Minx Special overall gear ratios: (1st) 17.05:1; (2nd) 11.81:1; (3rd) 7.13:1; (4th) 4.78:1. **Standard Final Drive Ratio:** 4.78:1. **Steering:** worm and nut. **Suspension (front):** independent; wishbones and coil springs. **Suspension (rear):** rigid axle with semi-elliptic leaf springs. **Brakes:** Lockheed hydraulic front/rear drum. **Body Construction:** pressed steel unibody.

MAJOR OPTIONS: (Minx) Manumatic transmission. Radio ($71). Heater ($57). Whitewall tires ($27).

PERFORMANCE: Top Speed: (Husky) 74+mph; (Minx) 80 mph. **Acceleration (0-60 mph):** (Husky) 23.7-25 sec.; (Minx) 21.8-24 sec.; (Estate) 28 sec. **Acceleration (quarter-mile):** (Husky) 23.9 sec.; (Minx) 22.9 sec. **Fuel Mileage:** (Husky) 30-35 mpg; (Minx) 30 mpg when touring.

Manufacturer: Hillman Motor Car Co. Ltd., Ryton-on-Dunsmore, near Coventry, England; part of Rootes Ltd., London, England.

Distributor: Rootes Motors, Inc., New York and Los Angeles (and other locations).

1959 HILLMAN

HUSKY — SERIES I — FOUR — Appearance and mechanical details of the small station wagon continued with little change. Unlike the Minx models, Husky did not receive a new grille this year.

1959 Hillman Minx four-door sedan.

MINX — SERIES III — FOUR — Engine growth was the biggest news in the Minx lineup for 1959, along with some revisions in body detailing. Though similar to the previous 85-cid powerplant, the new overhead-valve four-cylinder engine displaced 91.2 cubic inches and developed 52.5 horsepower. Torque output also grew. Less evident was a switch to a larger clutch size, and a new recirculating-ball steering gear. The new one-piece grille insert had a tight crosshatch pattern across the bottom, with parking lights at the outer ends, and five wide air openings across the top. Across the upper panel, just below the hood, the Hillman name was spelled out in block letters. A winged insignia decorated the hood front. Straight horizontal bodyside trim strips created a dividing line for two-tone color schemes. 'Minx' script stood on the driver's door, just above the trim strip. Inside, seats were deeper and the instrument panel displayed a revised group of gauges and controls. Though still open-style, the under-dash glove compartment now extended the full car width. As before, four models were available: Special and DeLuxe sedans, convertible, and Estate Wagon. The lower-cost Special now had a bench seat (formerly buckets).

I.D. DATA: Serial number plate is on bulkhead, under hood. Starting serial number: (Husky) 2805408; (Minx) 1900001; (Special sed) A1965001. Engine number is on left side of block.

Model	Body Type & Seating	Engine Type/CID	P.O.E. Price	Weight (lbs.)	Prod. Total
HUSKY					
I	2-dr Sta Wagon-4P	I4/85	1639	2020	Note 1
MINX (SERIES III)					
Special	4-dr Sedan-4/5P	I4/91	1699	2116	Note 1
DeLuxe	4-dr Sedan-4/5P	I4/91	1849	2156	Note 1
DeLuxe	4-dr Conv Cpe-4/5P	I4/91	2099	2174	Note 1
DeLuxe	4-dr Est Wag-4/5P	I4/91	2299	2289	Note 1

Note 1: A total of about 120,000 Hillmans were built during 1959; approximately 27,335 were sold in the U.S.

ENGINE DATA: BASE FOUR (Husky): Inline, overhead-valve four-cylinder. Cast iron (monobloc) block. **Displacement:** 84.8 cu. in. (1390 cc). **Bore & Stroke:** 3.00 x 3.00 in. (76.2 x 76.2 mm). **Compression Ratio:** 8.0:1. **Brake Horsepower:** 46 at 4400 rpm. Torque: 72 lbs.-ft. at 2200 rpm. Three main bearings. Solid valve lifters. One Zenith carburetor. 12-volt.

BASE FOUR (Minx): Inline, overhead-valve four-cylinder. Cast iron (monobloc) block. **Displacement:** 91.2 cu. in. (1494 cc). **Bore & Stroke:** 3.11 x 3.00 in. (79 x 76.2 mm). **Compression Ratio:** 8.5:1. **Brake Horsepower:** 52.5 at 4400 rpm. **Torque:** 78.3 lbs.-ft. at 2100 rpm. Three main bearings. Solid valve lifters. One Zenith carburetor. 12-volt.

CHASSIS DATA: Wheelbase: (Husky) 86 in.; (Minx) 96 in. **Overall Length:** (Husky) 149.5 in.; (Minx) 162 in. **Height:** (Husky) 62 in.; (Minx sed) 59.5 in.; (conv) 58 in.; (Estate) 61 in. **Width:** (Husky) 60.5 in.; (Minx) 61 in. **Front Tread:** (Husky) 49 in.; (Minx) 49 in. **Rear Tread:** (Husky) 48.5 in.; (Minx) 48.5 in. **Wheel Type:** disc. **Standard Tires:** (Husky/Special) 5.00x15 tubeless; (Minx) 5.60x15; (Estate) 5.90x15. **Fuel Tank:** (Husky) 7.5 gallons (U.S.); (Minx) 8.7 gallons.

TECHNICAL: Layout: front-engine, rear-drive. **Transmission:** four-speed manual; (Husky/Special sedan) floor lever; (Minx) column lever. Second/third/fourth gears synchronized. **Steering:** worm and nut. **Suspension (front):** independent; wishbones and coil springs. **Suspension (rear):** rigid axle with semi-elliptic leaf springs. **Brakes:** Lockheed hydraulic front/rear drum. **Body Construction:** pressed steel unibody.

PERFORMANCE: Top Speed: (Husky) 75+mph; (Minx) 80 mph. **Acceleration (0-60 mph):** (Husky) 23.7 sec.; (Minx) 21.8-24 sec.; (Estate) 28 sec. **Acceleration (quarter-mile):** (Minx) 22.9 sec. **Fuel Mileage:** (Husky) 35-40 mpg; (Minx) 30-35 mpg.

Manufacturer: Hillman Motor Car Co. Ltd., Ryton-on-Dunsmore, near Coventry, England; part of Rootes Motors Ltd., London, England.

Distributor: Rootes Motors, Inc., New York and Los Angeles (and other locations).

1960 HILLMAN

HUSKY — FOUR — A Series II Husky joined the original after the start of the model year, wearing a revised grille with vertical bars decorating the insert and parking lights at the outer ends. Both the windshield and back window grew larger, while the roofline lowered and added an overhang. Headlamps had plated rims and hoods. Mechanical changes included a close-ratio gearbox. Husky continued to use an 85-cid overhead-valve four-cylinder engine, rated 51 bhp, with four-speed manual gearbox.

MINX — SERIES IIIA — FOUR — Hillman prices rose just slightly this year, and Minx bodies wore a new grille. But the major change was the availability of an automatic transmission, making Hillman the first British production automobile with an engine under 1.5 liters to be sold with a fully automatic gearbox. Developed by Smiths Motor Accessories, the "Easidrive" automatic transmission, which worked with twin magnetic-powder clutches and constant-mesh gears, was also available on Singer models this year. That system responded to changes in electrical current to tighten or free the clutches. Hillman claimed it delivered acceleration and economy near that of a manual gearbox, without the customary automatic-transmission "creep." Engine size remained the same as in 1959, but horsepower grew to 57 (gross) at 4600 rpm, a result of switching to a different Zenith carburetor and adopting manifolds from the Singer Gazelle. A floor gearshift lever for the closer-ratio four-speed gearbox was standard for Minxes sold in England, while export models retained the column lever that had drawn complaints from Americans. Minx brakes were bigger this year. The new single-unit grille consisted of two separate horizontal mesh-patterned sections at each end, separated by a center segment with five horizontal slots. Each outer section incorporated rectangular parking lights at the outside ends and wrapped around the front fenders. Just above the grille's center was a winged insignia. 'HILLMAN' block letters stood along the hood front. The central instrument cluster contained a round speedometer, round trio of gauges, separate fuel gauges, and warning lights to supplement the gauge values.

I.D. DATA: Serial number plate is on bulkhead, under hood. Starting serial number: (Husky) A2815001; (Husky II) B2000001; (Special sed) B0000001; (Minx DeL) B1000001. Engine number is on left side of block.

Model	Body Type & Seating	Engine Type/CID	P.O.E. Price	Weight (lbs.)	Prod. Total
HUSKY					
I	2-dr Sta Wagon-4P	I4/85	1639	2020	Note 1
HUSKY (SERIES II)					
ii	2-dr Sta Wagon-4P	I4/85	1679	2032	Note 1

Model	Body Type & Seating	Engine Type/CID	P.O.E. Price	Weight (lbs.)	Prod. Total
MINX (SERIES IIIA)					
Special	4-dr Sedan-4/5P	I4/91	1735	2113	Note 1
DeLuxe	4-dr Sedan-4/5P	I4/91	1875	2163	Note 1
DeLuxe	2-dr Conv Cpe-4/5P	I4/91	2149	2181	Note 1
DeLuxe	4-dr Est Wag-4/5P	I4/91	2299	2286	Note 1

Note 1: A total of about 135,000 Hillmans were built during 1960.

ENGINE DATA: BASE FOUR (Husky): Inline, overhead-valve four-cylinder. Cast iron (monobloc) block. **Displacement:** 84.8 cu. in. (1390 cc). **Bore & Stroke:** 3.00 x 3.00 in. (76.2 x 76.2 mm). **Compression Ratio:** 8.0:1. **Brake Horsepower:** 51 at 4400 rpm. **Torque:** 72 lbs.-ft. at 2200 rpm. Three main bearings. Solid valve lifters. One Zenith carburetor. 12-volt.

BASE FOUR (Minx): Inline, overhead-valve four-cylinder. Cast iron (monobloc) block. **Displacement:** 91.2 cu. in. (1494 cc). **Bore & Stroke:** 3.11 x 3.00 in. (79 x 76.2 mm). **Compression Ratio:** 8.5:1. **Brake Horsepower:** 57 at 4600 rpm. **Torque:** 83 lbs.-ft. at 2000 rpm. Three main bearings. Solid valve lifters. One Zenith carburetor. 12-volt.

CHASSIS DATA: Wheelbase: (Husky) 86 in.; (Minx) 96 in. **Overall Length:** (Husky) 149.5 in.; (Minx) 162 in. **Height:** (Husky) 62 in.; (Minx sed) 59.5 in.; (conv) 58 in.; (Estate) 61 in. **Width:** (Husky) 60.5 in.; (Minx) 61 in. **Front Tread:** (Husky) 49 in.; (Minx) 49 in. **Rear Tread:** (Husky) 48.5 in.; (Minx) 48.5 in. **Wheel Type:** (Minx) ventilated steel disc. **Standard Tires:** (Husky/Special) 5.00x15 or 5.60x15 tubeless; (Minx) 5.60x15 Dunlop tubeless; (Estate) 5.90x15. **Fuel Tank:** (Husky) 7.5 gallons (U.S.); (Minx) 8.7 gallons.

TECHNICAL: Layout: front-engine, rear-drive. **Transmission:** four-speed manual; (Husky/Special sedan) floor lever; (Minx) column lever. Second/third/fourth gears synchronized. Three-speed automatic available on Minx. **Standard Final Drive Ratio:** (Minx) 4.55:1. **Steering:** worm and nut. **Suspension (front):** independent; wishbones, coil springs and anti-roll bar. **Suspension (rear):** rigid axle with semi-elliptic leaf springs. **Brakes:** Lockheed hydraulic front/rear drum. **Body Construction:** pressed steel unibody.

MAJOR OPTIONS: (Minx) Easidrive three-speed automatic transmission ($199).

PERFORMANCE: Top Speed: (Husky) 74-77 mph; (Minx) about 79-82 mph. **Acceleration (0-60 mph):** (Minx automatic) 27.6 sec. **Acceleration (quarter-mile):** (Minx automatic) 23.7 seconds, reaching 58.5 mph. **Fuel Mileage:** (Husky) 37-39 mpg; (Minx) 25-37 mpg.

Manufacturer: Hillman Motor Car Co. Ltd., Ryton-on-Dunsmore, near Coventry, England; part of Rootes Motors Ltd., London, England.

Distributor: Rootes Motors, Inc., Long Island City, New York (and other locations).

HISTORY: Introduced in October 1959 (Husky II, later in model year). In its road test of an Easidrive-equipped Minx, *Motor Life* described the unconventional automatic as a "square peg in a square hole--an automatic transmission custom tailored to a small car."

1961 HILLMAN

HUSKY — SERIES II — FOUR — The revised version of the small station wagon continued with little change. Husky again used an 85-cid overhead-valve four-cylinder engine, rated 51 bhp, with four-speed manual gearbox.

MINX — SERIES IIIB — FOUR — Prices were cut this year, for both the Minx and Husky. Otherwise, little changed. A 57-bhp four-cylinder engine provided the power, via either the standard four-speed manual gearbox or optional "Easidrive" automatic. This year's Standard (formerly Special) sedan received a grille similar to that of the Deluxe sedan. It formerly wore a Husky-style grille. Standard's bodyside moldings and dashboard also adopted the Deluxe style. All Minxes now came with a floor-mounted gearshift lever, but the column-mount gearshift could be requested. Air conditioning ws optional.

I.D. DATA: Serial number plate is on bulkhead, under hood. Starting serial number: (Minx) B1100001; (Special) B0100001. Engine number is on left side of block.

Model	Body Type & Seating	Engine Type/CID	P.O.E. Price	Weight (lbs.)	Prod. Total
HUSKY					
II	2-dr Sta Wagon-4P	I4/85	1579	2080	Note 1
MINX (SERIES IIIB)					
Special	4-dr Sedan-4/5P	I4/91	1599	2122	Note 1
DeLuxe	4-dr Sedan-4/5P	I4/91	1699	2172	Note 1
DeLuxe	2-dr Conv Cpe-4/5P	I4/91	2099	2190	Note 1
DeLuxe	4-dr Est Wag-4/5P	I4/91	2199	2265	Note 1

Note 1: A total of about 72,000 Hillmans were built during 1961.

ENGINE DATA: BASE FOUR (Husky): Inline, overhead-valve four-cylinder. Cast iron (monobloc) block. **Displacement:** 84.8 cu. in. (1390 cc). **Bore & Stroke:** 3.00 x 3.00 in. (76.2 x 76.2 mm). **Compression Ratio:** 8.0:1. **Brake Horsepower:** 51 at 4400 rpm. **Torque:** 72 lbs.-ft. at 2200 rpm. Three main bearings. Solid valve lifters. One Zenith carburetor. 12-volt.

BASE FOUR (Minx): Inline, overhead-valve four-cylinder. Cast iron (monobloc) block. **Displacement:** 91.2 cu. in. (1494 cc). **Bore & Stroke:** 3.11 x 3.00 in. (79 x 76.2 mm). **Compression Ratio:** 8.5:1. **Brake Horsepower:** 57 at 4600 rpm. **Torque:** 83 lbs.-ft. at 2000 rpm. Three main bearings. Solid valve lifters. One Zenith carburetor. 12-volt.

CHASSIS DATA: Wheelbase: (Husky) 86 in.; (Minx) 96 in. **Overall Length:** (Husky) 149.5 in.; (Minx) 162 in. **Height:** (Husky) 62 in.; (Minx) 58 in. **Width:** (Husky) 60.5 in.; (Minx) 60.7 in. **Front Tread:** (Husky) 49 in.; (Minx) 49 in. **Rear Tread:** (Husky) 48.5 in.; (Minx) 48.5 in. **Wheel Type:** (Minx) ventilated steel disc. **Standard Tires:** 5.60x15. **Fuel Tank:** (Husky) 7.5 gallons (U.S.); (Minx) 8.7 gallons.

TECHNICAL: Layout: front-engine, rear-drive. **Transmission:** four-speed manual; (Husky/Special sedan) floor lever; (Minx) column lever. Second/third/fourth gears synchronized. Three-speed automatic optional. **Standard Final Drive Ratio:** 4.55:1. **Steering:** worm and nut. **Suspension (front):** independent; wishbones and coil springs with anti-roll bar. **Suspension (rear):** rigid axle with semi-elliptic leaf springs. **Brakes:** hydraulic front/rear drum. **Body Construction:** pressed steel unibody.

MAJOR OPTIONS: (Minx) Automatic transmission ($199). Air conditioning.

PERFORMANCE: Top Speed: (Husky) 74-77 mph; (Minx) about 79-82 mph. **Acceleration (0-60 mph):** (Minx automatic) 27.6 sec. **Acceleration (quarter-mile):** (Minx automatic) 23.7 sec, reaching 58.5 mph. **Fuel Mileage:** (Husky) 37-39 mpg; (Minx) 25-37 mpg.

Manufacturer: Hillman Motor Car Co. Ltd., Ryton-on-Dunsmore, near Coventry, England; part of Rootes Motors Ltd., London, England.

Distributor: Rootes Motors, Inc., Long Island City, New York (and other locations).

HISTORY: Introduced October 15, 1960. At this time, Hillman also marketed in the U.S. a Commer Caravan (five-passenger station wagon) priced at $2826, and a vehicle in the form of a mobile-home priced at $3655.

1962 HILLMAN

HUSKY — SERIES II — FOUR — Little change was evident at a glance, but the small Hillman station wagon enjoyed some appearance improvements for 1962. The rear section of its roof now was ridged, for one, with a bit of an overhang past the rear door. Overall dimensions also grew slightly larger, and the headlamps added modest hoods. Also up front, the wide grille was concave in shape with a long row of vertical strips, encompassing the parking lights at the outer ends. Powerplant again was an 85-cid overhead-valve four, rated 51 bhp, with four-speed manual gearbox.

MINX — 1600 (SERIES IIIC) — FOUR — A bigger engine was the major change in the next Minx series: 1592 rather than the former 1494 cc, which resulted from increasing the bore dimension. Torque got a substantial boost, but horsepower remained at 57, though peaking at a slower engine speed. Compression dropped slightly, from the former 8.5:1 to 8.3:1. Also modified was the final drive ratio, to 4.22:1. Gearbox ratios also were changed in the manual transmission. Other mechanical improvements included reinforcement of the front suspension crossmember, larger bushings in the rear leaf springs, and the elimination of several lubrication points.

SUPER MINX — FOUR — A much-modified, more potent Minx arrived later in the model year, riding a longer (101-inch) wheelbase and carrying a 66-horsepower version of the "1600" engine. Headlamps were lower than in the other Minx, with hooded parking lights protruding above, at the fender tips. A tall, wide grille dominated by horizontal strips sat between the headlamps, with a small vertical insignia in its center. 'HILLMAN' block letters stood along the hood front, and a bodyside trim strip ran from the front parking lights to the rear end, below the outward-curving tailfins. Tires were 13-inch size, as opposed to the 15-inchers of the regular Minx and Husky.

1962 Hillman Super Minx.

I.D. DATA: Serial number plate is on bulkhead, under hood. Starting serial number: (1600) B0200001; (Super) B1200001. Engine number is on left side of block.

Model	Body Type & Seating	Engine Type/CID	P.O.E. Price	Weight (lbs.)	Prod. Total
HUSKY					
II	2-dr Sta Wagon-4P	I4/85	1599	2032	Note 1
MINX (SERIES IIIC)					
1600	4-dr Sed-4/5P	I4/97	1699	2172	Note 1
1600	2-dr Conv Cpe-4/5P	I4/97	2099	2190	Note 1
1600	4-dr Sta Wag-4/5P	I4/97	2199	2272	Note 1
SUPER MINX					
Super	4-dr Sedan-5P	I4/97	1899	2301	Note 1

Note 1: A total of about 93,000 Hillmans were built during 1962.

ENGINE DATA: BASE FOUR (Husky): Inline, overhead-valve four-cylinder. Cast iron (monobloc) block. **Displacement:** 84.8 cu. in. (1390 cc). **Bore & Stroke:** 3.00 x 3.00 in. (76.2 x 76.2 mm). **Compression Ratio:** 8.0:1. **Brake Horsepower:** 51 at 4400 rpm. **Torque:** 72 lbs.-ft. at 2200 rpm. Three main bearings. Solid valve lifters. One Zenith carburetor. 12-volt.

BASE FOUR (Minx): Inline, overhead-valve four-cylinder. Cast iron (monobloc) block. **Displacement:** 97.1 cu. in. (1592 cc). **Bore & Stroke:** 3.21 x 3.00 in. (81.5 x 76.2 mm). **Compression Ratio:** 8.3:1. **Brake Horsepower:** 57 at 4100 rpm. **Torque:** 87 lbs.-ft. at 2100 rpm. Three main bearings. Solid valve lifters. One Zenith carburetor. 12-volt.

BASE FOUR (Super Minx): Same as Minx engine, except — **Brake Horsepower:** 66 at 4800 rpm. **Torque:** 84 lbs.-ft. at 2800 rpm.

CHASSIS DATA: Wheelbase: (Husky) 86 in.; (Minx) 96 in.; (Super Minx) 101 in. **Overall Length:** (Husky) 152 in.; (Minx) 162 in.; (Super Minx) 165 in. **Height:** (Husky) 60 in.; (Minx) 59.5 in.; (Super Minx) 58.3 in. **Width:** (Husky) 62 in.; (Minx) 60.75 in.; (Super Minx) 62.25 in. **Front Tread:** (Husky) 49 in.; (Minx) 49 in.; (Super Minx) 51.5 in. **Rear Tread:** (Husky) 48.5 in.; (Minx) 48.5 in. **Wheel Type:** (Minx) ventilated steel disc. Standard Tires: (Husky/Minx) 5.60x15; (Super Minx) 5.90x13. **Fuel Tank:** (Husky) 7.5 gallons (U.S.); (Minx) 8.7 gallons; (Super Minx) 13.2 gallons.

TECHNICAL: Layout: front-engine, rear-drive. **Transmission:** four-speed manual; floor lever (column available on Minx); second/third/fourth gears synchronized. Three-speed automatic optional on Minx. **Standard Final Drive Ratio:** (Husky) 4.55:1; (Minx) 4.22:1. Steering: Burman recirculating ball. **Suspension (front):** independent; wishbones and coil springs with anti-roll bar. **Suspension (rear):** rigid axle with semi-elliptic leaf springs. **Brakes:** hydraulic front/rear drum. **Body Construction:** pressed steel unibody.

MAJOR OPTIONS: (Minx) Automatic transmission ($199). Air conditioning.

PERFORMANCE: Top Speed: (Husky) 72 mph; (Minx) 78 mph. Acceleration (0-60 mph): (Husky) 27 sec.; (Minx) 25 sec.; (Super) 19.5 sec. Acceleration (quarter-mile): (Minx automatic) 23.7 sec, reaching 58.5 mph; (Super Minx) 22.8 sec. Fuel Mileage: 25-35 mpg.

Manufacturer: Hillman Motor Car Co. Ltd., Ryton-on-Dunsmore, near Coventry, England; part of Rootes Motors Ltd., London, England.

Distributor: Rootes Motors, Inc., Long Island City, New York (and other locations).

1963 HILLMAN

HUSKY — SERIES II — FOUR — Production of the small Hillman station wagon continued with little change.

MINX — 1600 (SERIES IIIC) — FOUR — Only one model remained in the basic Minx lineup: the four-door sedan, which continued with little change wearing the earlier-style front end. Shorter in wheelbase than the Super Minx, it also differed considerably in front-end appearance.

SUPER MINX — Mk I/II — FOUR — Two versions of the longer-wheelbase Minx entered the 1963 model year: a standard Mark I and Deluxe Mark II. The Mark I wore a grille with only eight horizontal slats, while the Mark II grille contained vertical dividers. Not only did two versions of the Super Minx four-door sedan go on sale this year, but they were joined by a Deluxe convertible coupe and four-door station wagon. Front disc brakes were added to Super Minx models.

1963 Hillman Imp two-door.

I.D. DATA: Serial number plate is on bulkhead, under hood; on hood latch panel; or on body crossmember, ahead of radiator. Starting serial number: (Husky) B2010001; (1600) B1200001; (Super Mk I) B1200001; (Super Mk II) B1300001.

Model	Body Type & Seating	Engine Type/CID	P.O.E. Price	Weight (lbs.)	Prod. Total
HUSKY					
II	2-dr Sta Wagon-4P	I4/85	1599	2017	Note 1
MINX (SERIES IIIC)					
1600	4-dr Sedan-4P	I4/97	1699	2172	Note 1
SUPER MINX					
Mk I	4-dr Sedan-4/5P	I4/97	1899	2301	Note 1
SUPER MINX DELUXE					
Mk II	4-dr Sedan-4/5P	I4/97	1975	2261	Note 1
Mk II	2-dr Conv Cpe-4/5P	I4/97	2449	2332	Note 1
Mk II	4-dr Sta Wag-4/5P	I4/97	2399	2389	Note 1

Note 1: A total of about 115,000 Hillmans were built during 1963.

ENGINE DATA: BASE FOUR (Husky): Inline, overhead-valve four-cylinder. Cast iron (monobloc) block. Displacement: 84.8 cu. in. (1390 cc). Bore & Stroke: 3.00 x 3.00 in. (76.2 x 76.2 mm). Compression Ratio: 8.0:1. Brake Horsepower: 51 at 4400 rpm. Torque: 72 lbs.-ft. at 2200 rpm. Three main bearings. Solid valve lifters. One Zenith carburetor. 12-volt.

BASE FOUR (Minx 1600): Inline, overhead-valve four-cylinder. Cast iron (monobloc) block. Displacement: 97.1 cu. in. (1592 cc). Bore & Stroke: 3.21 x 3.00 in. (81.5 x 76.2 mm). Compression Ratio: 8.3:1. Brake Horsepower: 57 at 4100 rpm. Torque: 87 lbs.-ft. at 2100 rpm. Three main bearings. Solid valve lifters. One Zenith carburetor. 12-volt.

BASE FOUR (Super Minx): Same as Minx engine, except — Brake Horsepower: 66 at 4800 rpm. Torque: 84 lbs.-ft. at 2800 rpm.

CHASSIS DATA: Wheelbase: (Husky) 86 in.; (Minx 1600) 96 in.; (Super Minx) 101 in. Overall Length: (Husky) 152 in.; (Minx 1600) 162 in.; (Super Minx) 165 in. Height: (Husky) 60 in.; (Minx 1600) 59.5 in.; (Super Minx) 58.3 in. Width: (Husky) 62 in.; (Minx 1600) 60.75 in.; (Super Minx) 62.25 in. Front Tread: (Husky) 49 in.; (Minx 1600) 49 in.; (Super Minx) 51.5 in. Rear Tread: (Husky) 48.5 in.; (Minx) 48.5 in. Wheel Type: (Minx) ventilated steel disc. Standard Tires: (Husky/Minx) 5.60x15; (Super Minx) 5.90x13. Fuel Tank: (Husky) 7.5 gallons; (Minx 1600) 8.7 gallons; (Super Minx) 13.2 gallons.

TECHNICAL: Layout: front-engine, rear-drive. Transmission: four-speed manual; floor lever (column available on Minx); second/third/fourth gears synchronized. Three-speed automatic optional on Super Minx. Standard Final Drive Ratio: (Husky) 4.55:1; (Minx) 4.22:1. Steering: Burman recirculating ball. Suspension (front): independent; wishbones and coil springs with anti-roll bar. Suspension (rear): rigid axle with semi-elliptic leaf springs. Brakes: hydraulic front/rear drum except (Super Minx) front disc, rear drum. Body Construction: pressed steel unibody.

MAJOR OPTIONS: (Super Minx) Automatic transmission ($199). Air conditioning.

PERFORMANCE: Top Speed: (Husky) 72 mph; (Minx) 78 mph. Acceleration (0-60 mph): (Husky) 27 sec.; (Minx) 25 sec.; (Super Minx) 19.5 sec. Fuel Mileage: 25-35 mpg.

Manufacturer: Hillman Motor Car Co. Ltd., Ryton-on-Dunsmore, near Coventry, England; part of Rootes Motors Ltd., London, England.

Distributor: Rootes Motors, Inc., Long Island City, New York (and other locations).

HISTORY: Introduced August 15, 1962.

1964 HILLMAN

HUSKY — SERIES III — FOUR — Production continued with minimal change in Husky's final series; see previous listings for details.

MINX — SERIES V — FOUR — Last of the non-Super Minxes, the new Series V was the only car sold in the U.S. for less than $2000 with an American-built automatic transmission. The Type 35 Borg-Warner automatic cost $199 above the car's $1739 base price. The grille was revised this year (similar to Super Minx), and the hood line lowered at the front. Restyling of the rear end allowed the back window to reach higher into the roofline, and eliminated the lip at the top of the back panel. Disc brakes were mounted on front wheels (like the Super Minx). Horsepower got a boost here, up to 62. That was enough to send the basic Minx from zero to 60 mph in about 16 seconds, yet deliver fuel mileage in the 30-mpg neighborhood.

SUPER MINX — Mk II — FOUR — Only one trim level of Super Minx arrived for the 1964 model year, offered in four-door sedan, convertible and station wagon form. Appearance and mechanical details were similar to 1963.

I.D. DATA: Serial number plate is on bulkhead, under hood; or on hood latch panel, above radiator. Starting serial number: (Husky) B2100000; (1600) B0300000; (Super Minx) B1300000.

Model	Body Type & Seating	Engine Type/CID	P.O.E. Price	Weight (lbs.)	Prod. Total
HUSKY					
III	2-dr Sta Wagon-4P	I4/85	1639	2032	Note 1
MINX					
V	4-dr Sedan-5P	I4/97	1739	2165	Note 1
SUPER MINX					
II	4-dr Sedan-5P	I4/97	1975	2261	Note 1
II	2-dr Conv Cpe-5P	I4/97	2449	2332	Note 1
II	4-dr Sta Wagon-5P	I4/97	2399	2402	Note 1

Note 1: A total of about 165,000 Hillmans were built during 1964.

ENGINE DATA: BASE FOUR (Husky): Same as 1963.

BASE FOUR (Minx V): Inline, overhead-valve four-cylinder. Cast iron (monobloc) block. Displacement: 97.1 cu. in. (1592 cc). Bore & Stroke: 3.21 x 3.00 in. (81.5 x 76.2 mm). Compression Ratio: 8.3:1. Brake Horsepower: 62 at 4400 rpm. Torque: 86 lbs.-ft. at 2500 rpm. Three main bearings. Solid valve lifters. One Zenith carburetor. 12-volt.

BASE FOUR (Super Minx): Same as Minx engine, except — Brake Horsepower: 66 at 4800 rpm. Torque: 84 lbs.-ft. at 2800 rpm.

CHASSIS DATA: Wheelbase: (Husky) 86 in.; (Minx V) 96 in.; (Super Minx) 101 in. Overall Length: (Husky) 152 in.; (Minx V) 162 in.; (Super Minx) 165 in. Height: (Husky) 59.5 in.; (Minx V) 58 in.; (Super Minx) 58.3 in. Width: (Husky) 62 in.; (Minx V) 60.75 in.; (Super Minx) 62.25 in. Front Tread: (Husky) 49.0 in.; (Minx V) 51.5 in.; (Super Minx) 51.5 in. Rear Tread: (Husky) 48.5 in.; (Minx) 48.5 in. Standard Tires: (Husky) 5.60x15; (Minx) 5.90/6.00x13. Fuel Tank: (Husky) 7.5 gallons; (Minx V) 12 gallons; (Super Minx) 13.2 gallons.

TECHNICAL: Layout: front-engine, rear-drive. Transmission: four-speed manual; floor lever (column available on Minx); second/third/fourth gears synchronized. Three-speed automatic optional on Minx. Standard Final Drive Ratio: (Husky) 4.22:1; (Minx) 3.89:1. Steering: Burman recirculating ball. Suspension (front): independent; wishbones and coil springs with anti-roll bar. Suspension (rear): rigid axle with semi-elliptic leaf springs. Brakes: (Husky) hydraulic front/rear drum; (Minx) front disc, rear drum. Body Construction: pressed steel unibody.

MAJOR OPTIONS: (Minx) Automatic transmission ($199). Air conditioning.

PERFORMANCE: Top Speed: (Minx) 85 mph. Acceleration (0-60 mph): (Minx) 16 sec. Fuel Mileage: (Minx) about 30 mpg.

Manufacturer: Hillman Motor Car Co. Ltd., Ryton-on-Dunsmore, near Coventry, England; part of Rootes Motors Ltd., London, England.

Distributor: Rootes Motors, Inc., Long Island City, New York (and other locations).

HISTORY: U.S. model year began in September, 1963. Hillman was also producing the new rear-engine Imp by this time, for European consumption, with 53.4 cid (875 cc) displacement and 10:1 compression, rated 42 bhp. Only the Super Minx remained in the Hillman lineup after 1964, as the basic Minx name went on a Sunbeam model; see that listing.

1965 HILLMAN

HUSKY — SERIES III — FOUR — Production of the small Hillman wagon continued, with little change; see prior listings for details.

SUPER MINX — Mk II — FOUR — Only the Super Minx remained on U.S. availability lists, offered in four-door sedan and Estate Wagon form. The convertible was no longer available. Interiors had reclining seats. Models sold later in the season had a fully-synchronized four-speed gearbox (unlike the non-synchro first gear of earlier examples), and a dish-style steering wheel.

I.D. DATA: Serial number plate is on bulkhead, under hood; or on hood latch panel. Starting serial number: (Husky) 21100000; (Super Minx) 14000000.

Model	Body Type & Seating	Engine Type/CID	P.O.E. Price	Weight (lbs.)	Prod. Total
HUSKY					
III	2-dr Sta Wagon-4P	I4/85	1599	2032	Note 1

Model	Body Type & Seating	Engine Type/CID	P.O.E. Price	Weight (lbs.)	Prod. Total
SUPER MINX					
Mk II	4-dr Sedan-5P	I4/97	1999	2261	Note 1
Mk II	4-dr Sta Wagon-5P	I4/97	2349	2261	Note 1

1965 Hillman 1600 Minx four-door sedan.

Note 1: A total of about 120,000 Hillmans were built during 1965.

ENGINE DATA: BASE FOUR (Husky): Same as 1963.

BASE FOUR (Minx): Inline, overhead-valve four-cylinder. Cast iron (monobloc) block. **Displacement:** 97.1 cu. in. (1592 cc). **Bore & Stroke:** 3.21 x 3.00 in. (81.5 x 76.2 mm). **Compression Ratio:** 8.3:1. **Brake Horsepower:** 66 at 4600 rpm. **Torque:** 84 lbs.-ft. at 2800 rpm. Three main bearings. Solid valve lifters. One Zenith carburetor. 12-volt.

CHASSIS DATA: Wheelbase: (Husky) 86 in.; (Super Minx) 101 in. **Overall Length:** (Husky) 152 in.; (Super Minx) 165 in. **Height:** (Husky) 59.5 in.; (Super Minx) 58.3 in. **Width:** (Husky) 62 in.; (Super Minx) 64 in. **Front Tread:** (Husky) 49.0 in.; (Minx) 51.5 in. **Rear Tread:** (Husky) 48.5 in.; (Minx) 48.5 in. **Standard Tires:** (Husky) 5.60x15; (Minx) 5.90/6.00x13. **Fuel Tank:** (Husky) 7.5 gallons; (Minx) 13.2 gallons.

TECHNICAL: Layout: front-engine, rear-drive. **Transmission:** four-speed manual; second/third/fourth gears synchronized. Three-speed automatic optional on Minx. **Standard Final Drive Ratio:** (Husky) 4.22:1; (Minx) 3.89:1. **Steering:** Burman recirculating ball. **Suspension (front):** independent; wishbones and coil springs with anti-roll bar. **Suspension (rear):** rigid axle with semi-elliptic leaf springs. **Brakes:** (Husky) hydraulic front/rear drum; (Minx) front disc, rear drum. **Body Construction:** pressed steel unibody.

MAJOR OPTIONS: (Minx) Automatic transmission ($199). Air conditioning.

PERFORMANCE: Top Speed: (Minx) 85 mph. **Acceleration (0-60 mph):** (Minx) 16 sec. **Fuel Mileage:** (Minx) about 30 mpg.

Manufacturer: Hillman Motor Car Co. Ltd., Ryton-on-Dunsmore, near Coventry, England; part of Rootes Motors Ltd., London, England.

Distributor: Rootes Motors, Inc., Long Island City, New York (and other locations).

HISTORY: Husky introduced August 21, 1964; Minx on October 5, 1964. Although the rear-engine Imp sold under the Hillman name elsewhere in the world, it took a Sunbeam nameplate in the U.S. The former Mk V Minx now was marketed as a Sunbeam Deluxe sedan. See Sunbeam listing for details.

1966 HILLMAN

HUSKY — SERIES III — FOUR — The small Hillman wagon was still offered in the U.S., with little change.

SUPER MINX — Mk III — FOUR — A larger four-cylinder engine went under the Super Minx hood, measuring 105.2 cubic inches and delivering 69.5 horsepower. Appearance was similar to prior models, with a horizontal-bar grille stretching between the headlamps and parking lights in hooded protrusions above the headlamps.

I.D. DATA: Serial number plate is on bulkhead, under hood; or on hood latch panel. Starting serial number: (Husky) 21100000; (Super Minx) 034000000.

Model	Body Type & Seating	Engine Type/CID	P.O.E. Price	Weight (lbs.)	Prod. Total
HUSKY					
III	2-dr Sta Wagon-4P	I4/85	1599	2032	Note 1
SUPER MINX					
III	4-dr Sedan-5P	I4/105	2149	2261	Note 1
III	4-dr Sta Wagon-5P	I4/105	2399	2402	Note 1

Note 1: A total of about 107,400 Hillmans were built during 1966.

ENGINE DATA: BASE FOUR (Husky): Same as 1963-65.

BASE FOUR (Super Minx): Inline, overhead-valve four-cylinder. Cast iron (monobloc) block and head. **Displacement:** 105.2 cu. in. (1725 cc). **Bore & Stroke:** 3.21 x 3.25 in. (81.5 x 82.55 mm). **Compression Ratio:** 8.4:1. **Brake Horsepower:** 69.5 at 4800 rpm. **Torque:** 91.4 lbs.-ft. at 2400 rpm. Three main bearings. Solid valve lifters. One Zenith carburetor. 12-volt.

CHASSIS DATA: Wheelbase: (Husky) 86 in.; (Super Minx) 101 in. **Overall Length:** (Husky) 152 in.; (Super Minx) 165 in. **Height:** (Husky) 59.5 in.; (Super Minx) 58.3 in. **Width:** (Husky) 60.5 in.; (Super Minx) 63.75 in. **Front Tread:** (Husky) 49.0 in.; (Minx) 51.5 in. **Rear Tread:** (Husky) 48.5 in.; (Minx) 48.5 in. **Standard Tires:** (Husky) 5.60x15; (Minx) 6.00x13. **Fuel Tank:** (Husky) 7.5 gallons; (Minx) 13.2 gallons.

TECHNICAL: Layout: front-engine, rear-drive. **Transmission:** four-speed manual; three-speed automatic optional on Minx. **Standard Final Drive Ratio:** (Husky) 4.22:1; (Minx) 3.89:1. **Steering:** Burman recirculating ball. **Suspension (front):** independent; wishbones and coil springs with anti-roll bar. **Suspension (rear):** rigid axle with semi-elliptic leaf springs. **Brakes:** (Husky) hydraulic front/rear drum; (Minx) front disc, rear drum. **Body Construction:** pressed steel unibody.

MAJOR OPTIONS: (Minx) Automatic transmission ($199). Air conditioning.

Manufacturer: Hillman Motor Car Co. Ltd., Ryton-on-Dunsmore, near Coventry, England; part of Rootes Motors Ltd., London, England.

Distributor: Rootes Motors, Inc., Long Island City, New York (and other locations).

HISTORY: Importation of Hillmans to the U.S. ceased after 1966, though they continued in production in England. A "New Minx" was introduced in 1967, with 1496 or 1725 cc engine. Later came a series of Avengers.

HONDA/ACURA

Honda's history in motorcar manufacture dates back only to the early 1960s, but Soichiro Honda was involved with vehicles as early as the 1920s. He honed his skills as an auto mechanic by rebuilding vehicles that had been damaged during Tokyo's massive earthquake of 1923. That experience led to a brief flirtation with racing, and to the manufacture of piston rings shortly before World War II.

Honda's postwar activities included the production of small motorized bicycles and motorcycles, and to the manufacture of his own engines: first two-stroke, then four-stroke. By 1958, his motorcycles began a tiny trickle into the U.S. market, leading to establishment of American Honda Motor Company during 1959.

Already well known worldwide for the manufacture of motorcycles, the Honda Motor Company of Tokyo added automobiles to its lineup in 1962. After producing only 136 cars in 1963, output rose sharply to 87,169 in 1967 and 186,560 in 1968.

Curiously, Honda began with a two-seat sports roadster called the S500, powered by a 531-cc twin-cam four-cylinder engine with four carburetors. Chains sent the power to each rear axle, yet the car could hit speeds of 85 mph. That quickly led to an S600 and, in 1966, an S800 sports convertible and coupe, powered by a 791-cc four-cylinder engine. The S800 two-seater had a wood-rimmed steering wheel, bucket seats, and exposed trunk hinges, and used conventional shaft drive rather than chains. None of the S-series roadsters saw extensive production. In the mid-1960s, Honda also had a brief foray into Formula One competition, running an open-wheeled race car.

Back in ordinary production, by 1966 a mini-style front-drive N360 sedan carried a 354-cc two-cylinder engine. Not until 1969 were the first air-cooled, two-cylinder 600 sedans imported to the U.S., starting on the west coast. It was even available with a three-speed Hondamatic transmission, which included a torque converter. By mid-1972, Honda ranked twelfth in imported-car sales. Honda's Civic, introduced in the U.S. for 1973, soon offered either conventional power or a four-cylinder CVCC (Compound Vortex Controlled Combustion) stratified-charge engine with an auxiliary combustion chamber and extra intake valve for each cylinder. Using this system, a Civic was able to meet U.S. emissions standards that would take effect in 1975. All Civic engines were water-cooled, not air-cooled as the twos had been.

By 1975, the Civic lineup included sedans and a station wagon. A larger Accord hatchback became available in 1976, followed later by a four-door sedan. A sporty Prel-

ude coupe joined for 1979. Both the Accord and Prelude used versions of the CVCC engine. Next came the sporty little CRX two-seater, which debuted in 1984 and hit the U.S. market the following year, riding a Civic platform. Various CRX models emerged, aimed either at miserly fuel economy or snappy performance.

Honda went upscale in 1986 with a new Acura line: the Integra and larger Legend. As the 1990 model year ended, Honda gained considerable attention with its new $60,000 Acura NSX sports car, meant to rival such supercars as "low end" Ferraris, Porsches, and the Corvette ZR-1.

1969-70 HONDA

1970-'72 Honda 600 two-door sedan. (American Honda Motor Co. Inc.)

600 — TWO — Honda's entry into the U.S. market began with the two-door, two-cylinder sedan, which had a four-speed gearbox and front disc brakes. Unlike the Japanese editions, the U.S. models had side clearance lights at the leading edge of front fenders. A Honda emblem stood on the cowl, and the 'H' symbol also appeared at the grille's center. Three sets of cowl vent slots were evident on the hood for 1969, but the total dropped to two for the 1970 model year. The 598-cc overhead-cam engine developed 36 horsepower. A Hondamatic transmission with torque converter became optional. Hondamatic had a seven-position shift quadrant and went through its three forward speeds either automatically or manually. Body colors included red, ivory white, adrian blue, and yellow.

I.D. DATA: Honda's Vehicle Identification Number is on the upper edge of the instrument panel, visible through the windshield. An identification plate is on the hood mounting bracket, under the hood. The engine number is stamped into the clutch casing.

Model	Body Type & Seating	Engine Type/CID	P.O.E. Price	Weight (lbs.)	Prod. Total
600	2-dr Sedan-4P	I2/36	1398	1355	Note 1

Note 1: A total of 232,704 Hondas (all models) were produced in 1969, followed by 276,884 in 1970.

Price Note: Price announced in 1968, prior to actual sale in the U.S., was $1275. Price with Hondamatic transmission was $1522.

ENGINE DATA: BASE TWO: Vertical, overhead-cam two-cylinder (air-cooled). Light alloy block and head. **Displacement:** 36.5 cu. in. (598 cc). **Bore & Stroke:** 2.91 x 2.74 in. (74 x 69.6 mm). **Compression Ratio:** 8.5:1. **Brake Horsepower:** 36 at 6000 rpm. **Torque:** 32 lbs.-ft. at 4000 rpm. Four main bearings. Solid valve lifters. One Keihin-Seiki sidedraft carburetor.

CHASSIS DATA: Wheelbase: 78.75 in. **Overall Length:** 125 in. **Height:** 52.4 in. **Width:** 52.5 in. **Front Tread:** 46.1 in. **Rear Tread:** 44.3 in. **Standard Tires:** 5.20x10.

TECHNICAL: Layout: front-engine, front-drive. **Transmission:** four-speed manual, or optional Hondamatic. **Standard Final Drive Ratio:** 3.04:1. **Steering:** rack and pinion. **Suspension (front):** MacPherson struts with coil springs and lower wishbones. **Suspension (rear):** rigid axle with semi-elliptic leaf springs. **Brakes:** front disc, rear drum. **Body Construction:** steel unibody.

MAJOR OPTIONS: AM radio. Stereo tape player. Tachometer. Roof rack. Ski rack. Folding rear seat. Wood-rim steering wheel. Leather-trimmed steering wheel.

PERFORMANCE: Top Speed: 80 mph (factory claim). **Acceleration (0-60 mph):** as little as 18 seconds reported, with manual gearbox. **Fuel Mileage** 35-40 mpg.

PRODUCTION/SALES: A total of 4,195 Hondas were sold in the U.S. during 1970.

Manufacturer: Honda Motor Co. Ltd., Tokyo, Japan.

Distributor: American Honda Motor Company, Gardena, California.

1971-72 HONDA

600 — TWO — The original two-door sedan was joined by a two-door coupe in 1971, featuring upswept swing-open rear quarter windows. A large round "Coupe" insignia stood to the rear of that quarter window. The coupe, which had a small hatch at the rear, also had a different grille than the sedan, with integral parking lamps. Advertisements lured early coupe customers with the simple claim: "It makes a lot of sense."

I.D. DATA: Honda's Vehicle Identification Number is on the upper edge of the instrument panel, visible through the windshield. An identification plate is on the hood mounting bracket, under the hood. The engine number is stamped into the clutch casing. Starting serial number: 101-0000001.

1971-'72 Honda 600 coupe. (American Honda Motor Co. Inc.)

Model	Body Type & Seating	Engine Type/CID	P.O.E. Price	Weight (lbs.)	Prod. Total
600	2-dr Sedan-4P	I2/36	1395	1356	Note 1
600	2-dr Coupe-4P	I2/36	1543	1312	Note 1

Note 1: A total of 215,256 Hondas (all models) were produced in 1971, followed by 235,248 in 1972.

Price Note: For 1972, the sedan price rose to $1473; the coupe went to $1610.

ENGINE DATA: BASE TWO: Vertical, overhead-cam two-cylinder (air-cooled). Light alloy block and head. **Displacement:** 36.5 cu. in. (598 cc). **Bore & Stroke:** 2.91 x 2.74 in. (74 x 69.6 mm). **Compression Ratio:** 8.5:1. **Brake Horsepower:** 36 at 6000 rpm. **Torque:** 32 lbs.-ft. at 4000 rpm. Four main bearings. Solid valve lifters. One Keihin-Seiki sidedraft carburetor.

CHASSIS DATA: Wheelbase: 78.8 in. **Overall Length:** (sedan) 125.6 in.; (coupe) 123.5 in. **Height:** (sedan) 52.4 in.; (coupe) 50.4 in. **Width:** (sedan) 52.5 in.; (coupe) 51 in. **Front Tread:** (sedan) 46.1 in.; (coupe) 45.9 in. **Rear Tread:** (sedan) 44.6 in.; (coupe) 44.3 in. **Standard Tires:** (sedan) 5.20x10; (coupe) 145SR10.

TECHNICAL: Layout: front-engine, front-drive. **Transmission:** four-speed manual, or optional Hondamatic. Four-speed coupe gear ratios: (1st) 2.47:1; (2nd) 1.50:1; (3rd) 0.97:1; (4th) 0.68:1. **Standard Final Drive Ratio:** 3.03:1. **Steering:** rack and pinion. **Suspension (front):** MacPherson struts with coil springs and lower wishbones. **Suspension (rear):** rigid axle with semi-elliptic leaf springs. **Brakes:** front disc, rear drum. **Body Construction:** steel unibody. **Fuel Tank:** 6.9 gallon.

MAJOR OPTIONS: Hondamatic transmission (with torque converter).

PERFORMANCE: Top Speed: 80 mph (factory claim); (coupe) 78 mph tested. **Acceleration (0-60 mph):** (coupe w/4-spd) 23.6 sec. **Acceleration (quarter-mile):** (coupe w/4-spd) 23.9 sec. (60.4 mph). **Fuel Mileage:** as high as 43 mpg (average) reported.

PRODUCTION/SALES: Approximately 9,509 Hondas were sold in the U.S. during 1971, rising to 20,500 in 1972.

Manufacturer: Honda Motor Co. Ltd., Tokyo, Japan.

Distributor: American Honda Motor Company, Gardena, California.

HISTORY: "Every outing is an adventure" in a Honda 600 coupe, reported *Road & Track* magazine, "figuratively equal to crossing the ocean in a rowboat" but also "fun."

1973-74 HONDA

CIVIC — FOUR — Not everyone realized when Honda's Civic entered U.S. dealerships that it would become a modest phenomenon--not exactly on par with Volkswagen's Beetle, but paving the way for Honda's development as a major player in the world (and American) marketplace. Under the hood of the initial Civic two-door sedan and hatchback was an 1169-cc, water-cooled four-cylinder engine. That engine grew to 1237-cc displacement for 1974, after which the CVCC engine that had been announced earlier became available in American Civics. Either a four-speed manual gearbox or Hondama-

tic two-speed semi-automatic transmission was available. Larger than the former 600, the Civic rode an 86.6-inch wheelbase. The 71.3-cid (1169-cc) engine produced 50 horsepower. Standard equipment included power front disc brakes, reclining front bucket seats, woodgrain dashboard, carpeting, and two-speed wiper/washer. The hatchback added an AM radio, cloth interior, and whitewall tires. Bumper guards were restyled for the 1974 model year, and overall dimensions were increased.

I.D. DATA: Honda's 10-symbol Vehicle Identification Number is on the upper edge of the instrument panel, visible through the windshield. The first two symbols denote the Honda make. Symbol three indicates body style and transmission type. The final seven digits form the sequential serial number. An identification plate is on the hood mounting bracket, under the hood. The engine number is stamped into the clutch casing. Starting serial number: (1973 sedan) SBA-1007001; (1973 sedan w/auto.) SBB-1007001; (1973 hatch) SBC-0000001; (1973 hatch w/auto.) SBD-1007001; (1974 sedan/hatch) SB()-2100001.

Model	Body Type & Seating	Engine Type/CID	P.O.E. Price	Weight (lbs.)	Prod. Total
CIVIC					
SBA	2-dr Sedan-4P	I4/71	2150	1536	Note 1
SBC	2-dr Hatch-4P	I4/71	2250	1552	Note 1

Note 1: A total of 256,962 Hondas (all models) were produced in 1973, followed by 316,012 in 1974.

Price Note: For 1974, a larger engine was installed; the sedan price rose to $2375, the hatchback to $2545.

ENGINE DATA: BASE FOUR (1973): Inline, overhead-cam four-cylinder. Aluminum alloy block and head. **Displacement:** 71.3 cu. in. (1169-cc). **Bore & Stroke:** 2.76 x 2.99 in. (70 x 76 mm). **Compression Ratio:** 8.3:1. **Brake Horsepower:** 50 at 5500 rpm. **Torque:** 59 lbs.-ft. at 3000 rpm. Five main bearings. Solid valve lifters. One Hitachi two-barrel carburetor.

BASE FOUR (1974): Inline, overhead-cam four-cylinder. Aluminum alloy block and head. **Displacement:** 75.5 cu. in. (1237 cc). **Bore & Stroke:** 2.83 x 2.99 in. (72 x 76 mm). **Compression Ratio:** 8.1:1. **Brake Horsepower:** 52 at 5000 rpm. **Torque:** 59 lbs.-ft. at 3000 rpm. Five main bearings. Solid valve lifters. One Hitachi two-barrel carburetor.

CHASSIS DATA: Wheelbase: 86.6 in. **Overall Length:** 139.8 in. **Height:** 53 in. **Width:** 53.3 in. **Front Tread:** 51.2 in. **Rear Tread:** 50.4 in. **Standard Tires:** 600S12.

Note: Sedan dimensions changed for 1974 to 146.9 inches overall, 52.2 inches high, and 59.3 inches wide.

TECHNICAL: Layout: front-engine, front-drive. **Transmission:** four-speed manual, or two-speed Hondamatic. **Standard Final Drive Ratio:** 4.13:1 or 4.93:1. **Steering:** rack and pinion. **Suspension (front):** MacPherson struts with coil springs, lower wishbones and anti-roll bar. **Suspension (rear):** MacPherson struts with coil springs and lower wishbones. **Brakes:** front disc, rear drum. **Body Construction:** steel unibody.

MAJOR OPTIONS: Hondamatic two-speed semi-automatic transmission: sedan ($105); hatch ($150-$162). Air conditioning. Radial tires. Rear defroster. Rear wiper. AM radio.

PERFORMANCE: Top Speed: 85-90 mph. **Acceleration (0-60 mph):** 15.1 sec. **Fuel Mileage:** near 30 mpg.

PRODUCTION/SALES: A total of 38,957 Hondas were sold in the U.S. during 1973, and 43,119 in 1974.

Manufacturer: Honda Motor Co. Ltd., Tokyo, Japan.

Distributor: American Honda Motor Company, Gardena, California.

HISTORY: Honda's early advertising claim for the Civic was certainly modest: "It will get you where you're going." Other ads promised that it would deliver "more miles per gallon than anybody." The CVCC engine was announced in 1972, but did not become available under U.S. Civic hoods until the 1975 model year. The EPA ranked Civic the most economical car of 1974, with a 29.1-mpg rating. Just over one-fourth of Hondas sold in 1973 had automatic shift, and only 8.5 percent were air conditioned.

sions control, and was not available in California. Intake and exhaust valves were on the same side in the CVCC engine, while the conventional four had a crossflow head. The CVCC sedan was more than two inches longer than the ordinary model, that extra space being needed for its engine's exhaust system. New "ram" air intakes went on the hood, but the major difference between the two was a 'CVCC' badge on the right dash panel. A five-speed manual gearbox also became available at this time. The CVCC hatchback with five-speed had a mandatory trim package, which included cloth/vinyl trim, a simulated wood steering wheel, and wood gearshift knob. Only two body colors were offered: yellow and orange.

I.D. DATA: Honda's 10-symbol Vehicle Identification Number is on the upper edge of the instrument panel, visible through the windshield. The first two symbols denote the Honda make. Symbol three indicates body style and transmission type. The final seven digits form the sequential serial number. An identification plate is on the hood mounting bracket, under the hood. The engine number is stamped into the clutch casing. Starting serial number: (CVCC sedan/hatch) SG()-1000001; (CVCC wagon) WBA-1000001; (air-injection sedan/hatch) SB()-3300001. CVCC engines have prefix ED1 (sedan/hatch) or ED2 (wagon); air-injection engines have prefix EB2.

Model	Body Type & Seating	Engine Type/CID	P.O.E. Price	Weight (lbs.)	Prod. Total
CIVIC					
SBA	2-dr Sedan-4P	I4/75	2649	N/A	Note 1
SBC	2-dr Hatch-4P	I4/75	2859	N/A	Note 1
CIVIC CVCC					
SGA	2-dr Sedan-4P	I4/91	2799	1687	Note 1
SGC	2-dr Hatch-4P	I4/91	3009	1720	Note 1
WBA	2-dr Sta Wag-4P	I4/91	3349	1962	Note 1

Note 1: A total of 328,107 Hondas (all models) were produced in 1975.

Model Number Note: Third letter of prefix changed to B or D with Hondamatic transmission; or to E for CVCC hatchback with five-speed transmission. **Price Note:** A CVCC hatchback with five-speed transmission sold for $3369.

ENGINE DATA: BASE FOUR (Civic): Inline, overhead-cam four-cylinder. Aluminum alloy block and head. **Displacement:** 75.5 cu. in. (1237 cc). **Bore & Stroke:** 2.83 x 2.99 in. (72 x 76 mm). **Compression Ratio:** 8.1:1. **Brake Horsepower:** 52 at 5000 rpm. **Torque:** 59 lbs.-ft. at 3500 rpm. Five main bearings. Solid valve lifters. One Hitachi two-barrel carburetor.

BASE FOUR (CVCC): Inline, overhead-cam four-cylinder (stratified-charge). Cast iron block and aluminum alloy head. **Displacement:** 90.8 cu. in. (1488 cc). **Bore & Stroke:** 2.91 x 3.41 in. (74 x 86.5 mm). **Compression Ratio:** 8.1:1. **Brake Horsepower:** 53 at 5000 rpm. **Torque:** 69 lbs.-ft. at 2500 rpm. Five main bearings. Solid valve lifters. One Keihin three-barrel carburetor.

CHASSIS DATA: Wheelbase: (sedan) 86.6 in.; (wagon) 89.9 in. **Overall Length:** (sedan) 147.8 in.; (CVCC sedan) 150 in.; (wagon) 160 in. **Height:** 52.2 in. **Width:** 59.3 in. **Front Tread:** 51.2 in. **Rear Tread:** 50.4 in. **Standard Tires:** (sedan/wagon) 600S12.

TECHNICAL: Layout: front-engine, front-drive. **Transmission:** four-speed manual; five-speed and Hondamatic available. CVCC four-speed gear ratios: (1st) 3.00:1; (2nd) 1.737:1; (3rd) 1.13:1; (4th) 0.778:1. **Standard Final Drive Ratio:** (sedan) 4.93:1; (CVCC sedan) 4.73:1. **Steering:** rack and pinion. **Suspension (front):** MacPherson struts with coil springs, lower wishbones and anti-roll bar. **Suspension (rear):** MacPherson struts with coil springs and lower wishbones. **Brakes:** front disc, rear drum. **Body Construction:** steel unibody.

MAJOR OPTIONS: Hondamatic two-speed transmission ($180). Five-speed manual transmission. 155SR13 radial tires.

PERFORMANCE: Acceleration (0-60 mph): (Civic) 15.1 sec.; (CVCC) 13.8 sec. **Acceleration (quarter-mile):** (CVCC) 19.6 sec. (69.2 mph). **Fuel Mileage:** (CVCC) about 39 mpg average.

PRODUCTION/SALES: A total of 102,389 Hondas were sold in the U.S. during 1975.

Manufacturer: Honda Motor Co. Ltd., Tokyo, Japan.

Distributor: American Honda Motor Company, Gardena, California.

HISTORY: Standard Civic sedans for the 1975 model year were introduced to the U.S. market on March 1, 1975; CVCC models on January 1, 1975; and the station wagon in June 1975. Announced in 1972, the CVCC engine was designed to meet 1975 U.S. emissions standards.

1975 HONDA

1975 Honda Civic hatchback. (American Honda Motor Co. Inc.)

CIVIC — FOUR — An expanded selection of body styles was now available in the Civic line, with either a conventional four-cylinder powerplant or an engine with a difference. The 1488-cc CVCC (Compound Vortex Controlled Combustion) design contained an auxiliary combustion chamber with a spark plug and an extra intake valve for each cylinder. A rich air/fuel mixture was ignited within that chamber, and that combustion in turn ignited the leaner mixture that entered the main combustion chamber. Smaller in displacement than the CVCC, the 1237-cc conventional engine used air injection for emis-

1976-78 HONDA

1977 Honda Civic CVCC five-speed. (American Honda Motor Co. Inc.)

CIVIC — FOUR — Production of the Civic series, with both conventional and CVCC engines, continued with little change except for a modified blackout grille for the 1978 model year. At that time, rear-facing hood louvers were installed, replacing the former side ports. The "1200" model's hood added a raised center section in 1978, while the CVCC's was flat; and turn signals moved to the lower edge of front bumpers. Taillamps also enjoyed a restyling. Standard equipment during this period included a four-speed manual gearbox, power front disc brakes, heater/defroster, two-speed wiper/washer, reclining front bucket seats, and hinged rear side windows. Hatchbacks included an AM radio and fold-down rear seat. The CVCC hatchback with five-speed gearbox in 1977 came with a rear-window defroster, tachometer, sport steering wheel, woodgrain gearshift knob, and houndstooth-pattern upholstery.

1978 Honda Accord. (American Honda Motor Co. Inc.)

ACCORD — FOUR — A larger two-door hatchback joined the Civic for the 1976 model year, powered by a 1600-cc version of the Advanced Stratified Charge CVCC engine. A five-speed manual transmission was standard, with two-speed Hondamatic available. Riding a 93.7-inch wheelbase (seven inches longer than the Civic), the Accord measured close to 163 inches overall. The CVCC engine produced 68 horsepower. Standard equipment on the 1977 model included an AM/FM radio, clock, rear- and side-window defrosters, rear wiper/washer, remote hatch opener, metallic paint, and protective bodyside moldings. Electronic warnings were included for oil change, tire rotation, brake-fluid level, and other maintenance details.

An upscale LX (luxury) model was added for the 1978 model year, offered in silver or burgundy body color with burgundy interior. Standard LX equipment included air conditioning, variable-assist power steering, and a digital clock.

I.D. DATA: Honda's 10-symbol Vehicle Identification Number is on the upper edge of the instrument panel, visible through the windshield. The first three symbols denote the series and body style, and transmission type, followed by a seven-digit sequential serial number. An identification plate is on the hood mounting bracket, under the hood. The engine number is stamped into the clutch casing. Starting serial number (1976 models): (CVCC sedan/hatch) SG()-2000001; (CVCC wagon) WB()-2000001; (air-injection sedan/hatch) SB()-4000001; (Accord) SJE-1000001.

Model	Body Type & Seating	Engine Type/CID	P.O.E. Price	Weight (lbs.)	Prod. Total
CIVIC (1976)					
SBA	2-dr Sedan-4P	I4/75	2729	1610	Note 1
SBC	2-dr Hatch-4P	I4/75	2939	1643	Note 1
CIVIC CVCC (1976)					
SGA	2-dr Sedan-4P	I4/91	2979	1675	Note 1
SGC	2-dr Hatch-4P	I4/91	3189	1708	Note 1
WBA	2-dr Sta Wag-4P	I4/91	3419	1893	Note 1
ACCORD (1976)					
SJE	2-dr Hatch-4P	I4/98	3995	1993	Note 1

Note 1: A total of 473,597 Hondas were produced in 1976, followed by 576,631 in 1977, and 652,920 in 1978.

Model Number Note: Third letter of Civic's prefix changed to B or D with Hondamatic transmission; or to E for CVCC hatchback with five-speed transmission. Third letter of Accord prefix changed to D with Hondamatic instead of five-speed.

Price Note: Civic CVCC hatchback with five-speed transmission sold for $3469 in 1976. Civic prices in 1978 ranged from $3255 for the base two-door sedan to $4325 for a CVCC hatchback with five-speed. Accord prices in 1978 were $5099 for the base model and $5965 for the LX.

ENGINE DATA: BASE FOUR (Civic): Inline, overhead-cam four-cylinder. Aluminum alloy block and head. **Displacement:** 75.5 cu. in. (1237 cc). **Bore & Stroke:** 2.83 x 2.99 in. (72 x 76 mm). **Compression Ratio:** 8.1:1. **Brake Horsepower:** 50 at 5000 rpm. **Torque:** 59 lbs.-ft. at 3500 rpm. Five main bearings. Solid valve lifters. One Hitachi two-barrel carburetor.

BASE FOUR (Civic CVCC): Inline, overhead-cam four-cylinder (stratified-charge). Cast iron block and aluminum alloy head. **Displacement:** 90.8 cu. in. (1488 cc). **Bore & Stroke:** 2.91 x 3.41 in. (74 x 86.5 mm). **Compression Ratio:** 7.9:1. **Brake Horsepower:** 60 at 5000 rpm. **Torque:** 76 lbs.-ft. at 2500 rpm. Five main bearings. Solid valve lifters. One Keihin three-barrel carburetor.

BASE FOUR (Accord): Inline, overhead-cam four-cylinder (CVCC stratified-charge). Cast iron block and aluminum alloy head. **Displacement:** 97.6 cu. in. (1600 cc). **Bore & Stroke:** 2.91 x 3.66 in. (74 x 93 mm). **Compression Ratio:** 8.0:1. **Brake Horsepower:** 68 at 5000 rpm. **Torque:** 85 lbs.-ft. at 3500 rpm. Five main bearings. Solid valve lifters. One Keihin three-barrel carburetor.

CHASSIS DATA: Wheelbase: (Civic sedan) 86.6 in.; (Civic wagon) 89.8 in.; (Accord) 93.7 in. **Overall Length:** (Civic sedan) 147.8 in.; (CVCC sedan) 150 in.; (Civic wagon) 159.5 in.; (Accord) 162.8 in. **Height:** (Civic sedan) 52.2 in.; (CVCC sedan) 52.4 in.; (CVCC 5-spd) 52 in.; (Civic wagon) 54.1 in.; (Accord) 52.4 in. **Width:** (Civic sedan/wagon) 59.3 in.; (Accord) 63.8 in. **Front Tread:** (Civic) 51.2 in.; (Accord) 55.1 in. **Rear Tread:** (Civic sedan/hatch) 50.4 in.; (Civic wagon) 51.2 in. **Standard Tires:** (Civic sedan) 600S12; (Civic five-speed) 155SR12; (Civic CVCC wagon) 6.15x13; (Accord) 155SR13.

TECHNICAL: Layout: front-engine, front-drive. **Transmission:** (Civic) four-speed manual, with five-speed available on hatchback; (Accord) five-speed manual; two-speed Hondamatic available on both models. Accord five-speed gear ratios: (1st) 3.18:1; (2nd) 1.823:1; (3rd) 1.181:1; (4th) 0.846:1; (5th) 0.714:1; (rev) 2.916:1. **Standard Final Drive Ratio:** (Accord) 4.266:1. **Steering:** rack and pinion. **Suspension (front):** MacPherson struts with coil springs, lower wishbones and anti-roll bar. **Suspension (rear):** (Civic) MacPherson struts with coil springs and lower wishbones; (Civic wagon) rigid axle with semi-elliptic leaf springs; (Accord) MacPherson struts with coil springs, lower transverse arms and radius rods. **Brakes:** front disc, rear drum. **Body Construction:** steel unibody. **Fuel Tank:** (Civic) 10 gal.; (CVCC) 10.6 gal.

MAJOR OPTIONS: Hondamatic transmission: Civic hatch/wagon, Accord ($150-$160). Five-speed manual transmission (CVCC hatchback). Air conditioning. AM/FM stereo radio.

PERFORMANCE: Top Speed: (Accord) 90 mph. **Acceleration (0-60 mph):** (Accord) 13.8 sec. **Acceleration (quarter-mile):** (Accord) 19.7-20 sec. (68.1-69.5 mph). **Fuel Mileage:** (Civic CVCC) about 36 mpg average.

PRODUCTION/SALES: A total of 150,929 Hondas were sold in the U.S. during 1976, followed by 223,633 in 1977, and 274,876 in 1978.

Manufacturer: Honda Motor Co. Ltd., Tokyo, Japan.

Distributor: American Honda Motor Company, Gardena, California.

HISTORY: Hondas during this period were introduced to the U.S. market in December for the next model year. The Accord was introduced in summer 1976. Advertising in the late 1970s advised readers that Honda was "what the world is coming to." Other ads promised: "We make it simple." Honda set sales records in 1976, and promoted the Civic CVCC as having the highest EPA mileage rating of any car: 43 mpg highway, 32 mpg city, 36 mpg combined. The Accord was rated 31/44 mpg by the EPA. *Road Test* magazine named Accord "car of the year in the under $5000 category," commenting on its "space-age warning light system." The conventional Civic was promoted as the cheapest car sold in the U.S. By 1976, Honda had close to 600 dealers in the U.S. EPA ratings in 1977 included 41/54 mpg for the Civic CVCC five-speed, and 39/50 mpg for the CVCC four-speed.

1979 HONDA

1978-'79 Honda Civic four-door station wagon. (American Honda Motor Co. Inc.)

CIVIC — FOUR — Two series were offered this year: the Civic 1200 with conventional 1237-cc engine, and the CVCC with the larger CVCC engine. The latter models were identified by 'CVCC' lettering on the side of the grille. The stratified-charge CVCC engine produced 63 horsepower; its smaller mate, 55 bhp. The CVCC hatchback was offered with a five-speed gearbox or the customary four-speed. Optional Hondamatic had a torque converter and two manually-selected forward speeds.

ACCORD — FOUR — A four-door sedan joined the original Accord hatchback this year, measuring close to nine inches longer overall (nearly all of the excess at the rear end). 'CVCC' lettering on the grille displayed the engine type used in Accords, which grew to 107-cid displacement and 72 horsepower. Power steering and an oil cooler were standard. In the rear suspension, springs were now offset on the struts to improve ride quality, while front springs grew stiffer. Larger exhaust-system diameter increased the engine's low-end torque output. A larger radiator was installed at this time, to answer complaints about overheating. A tachometer and electronic warning system were standard.

PRELUDE — FOUR — A sporty coupe joined the Honda lineup for 1979, powered by the same CVCC engine used in the Accord. Clean lines were highlighted by a blackout rectangular grille between single rectangular headlamps, with amber park/signal lights mounted in the front bumper. 'HONDA' lettering went in the corner of the grille. The hood displayed a slight bulge along its center. Standard Prelude equipment included a power moonroof, AM/FM stereo radio, and tachometer.

I.D. DATA: Honda's 10-symbol Vehicle Identification Number is on the upper edge of the instrument panel, visible through the windshield. The first three symbols denote the series and body style, and transmission type, followed by a seven-digit sequential serial number. Starting serial number: (Civic 1200) SB()-7000001; (Civic CVCC 1500) SG()-5000001; (Civic CVCC 1500 wagon) WB()-5000001; (Accord) SM()-1000001; (Prelude) SN()100001.

Model	Body Type & Seating	Engine Type/CID	P.O.E. Price	Weight (lbs.)	Prod. Total
CIVIC 1200					
SBA	2-dr Sedan-4P	I4/75	3649	1610	Note 1
SBC	2-dr Hatch-4P	I4/75	4075	1643	Note 1

Model	Body Type & Seating	Engine Type/CID	P.O.E. Price	Weight (lbs.)	Prod. Total
CIVIC CVCC					
SGA	2-dr Sedan-4P	I4/91	3999	1675	Note 1
SGC	2-dr Hatch-4P	I4/91	4499	1708	Note 1
WBA	2-dr Sta Wag-4P	I4/91	4759	1893	Note 1
ACCORD					
SME	2-dr Hatch-4P	I4/107	5799	2024	Note 1
SMH (LX)	2-dr Hatch-4P	I4/107	6799	2193	Note 1
SMK	4-dr Sedan-4P	I4/107	6365	2203	Note 1
PRELUDE					
SNF	2-dr Coupe-4P	I4/107	6445	2106	Note 1

Note 1: A total of 706,375 Hondas (all models) were produced in 1979.

Model Number Note: Third letter of Civic's prefix changed to B or D with Hondamatic transmission; or to E for CVCC hatchback with five-speed transmission.

ENGINE DATA: BASE FOUR (Civic): Inline, overhead-cam four-cylinder. Aluminum alloy block and head. **Displacement:** 75.5 cu. in. (1237 cc). **Bore & Stroke:** 2.83 x 2.99 in. (72 x 76 mm). **Compression Ratio:** 8.1:1. **Brake Horsepower:** 55 at 5000 rpm. **Torque:** 67 lbs.-ft. at 2500 rpm. Five main bearings. Solid valve lifters. One Hitachi two-barrel carburetor.

BASE FOUR (Civic CVCC): Inline, overhead-cam four-cylinder (stratified-charge). Cast iron block and aluminum alloy head. **Displacement:** 90.8 cu. in. (1488 cc). **Bore & Stroke:** 2.91 x 3.41 in. (74 x 86.5 mm). **Compression Ratio:** 7.9:1. **Brake Horsepower:** 63 at 5000 rpm. **Torque:** 77 lbs.-ft. at 3000 rpm. Five main bearings. Solid valve lifters. One Keihin three-barrel carburetor.

BASE FOUR (Accord, Prelude): Inline, overhead-cam four-cylinder (CVCC stratified-charge). Cast iron block and aluminum alloy head. **Displacement:** 106.8 cu. in. (1751 cc). **Bore & Stroke:** 3.03 x 3.70 in. (77 x 94 mm). **Compression Ratio:** 8.0:1. **Brake Horsepower:** 72 at 4500 rpm. **Torque:** 94 lbs.-ft. at 3000 rpm. Five main bearings. Solid valve lifters. One Keihin three-barrel carburetor.

CHASSIS DATA: Wheelbase: (Civic sedan) 86.6 in.; (Civic wagon) 89.8 in.; (Accord) 93.7 in.; (Prelude) 91.3 in. **Overall Length:** (Civic 1200 sed) 145.5 in.; (CVCC hatch/sedan) 148.6 in.; (Civic wagon) 158.5 in.; (Accord sedan) 163.2 in.; (Accord sedan) 171.9 in.; (Prelude) 161.4 in. **Height:** (Civic sedan) 52.4 in.; (Civic CVCC 5-spd hatch) 52.0 in.; (Civic wagon) 54.3 in.; (Accord hatch) 52.6 in.; (Accord sedan) 53.3 in.; (Prelude) 51.0 in. **Width:** (Civic) 59.3 in.; (Accord) 63.8 in.; (Prelude) 64.4 in. **Front Tread:** (Civic) 51.2 in.; (Accord) 55.5 in.; (Prelude) 55.1 in. **Rear Tread:** (Civic hatch/sedan) 50.4 in.; (Civic wagon) 51.2 in.; (Accord) 55.1 in.; (Prelude) 55.5 in. **Standard Tires:** (Civic hatch/sedan) 600S12; (Civic CVCC 5-spd hatch) 155SR12; (Civic CVCC wagon) 6.15x13; (Accord) 165SR13; (Prelude) 175/70SR13.

TECHNICAL: Layout: front-engine, front-drive. **Transmission:** (Civic) four-speed manual, with five-speed available on hatchback; (Accord/Prelude) five-speed manual; Hondamatic available on all models. **Steering:** rack and pinion. **Suspension (front):** MacPherson struts with coil springs, lower wishbones and anti-roll bar. **Suspension (rear):** (Civic) MacPherson struts with coil springs and lower wishbones; (Civic wagon) rigid axle with semi-elliptic leaf springs; (Accord) MacPherson struts with coil springs, lower transverse arms and radius rods; (Prelude) MacPherson struts with coil springs, trailing and transverse arms, and anti-roll bar. **Brakes:** front disc, rear drum. **Body Construction:** steel unibody. **Fuel Tank:** (Civic) 10.6 gal.; (Civic wagon) 11.1 gal.; (Accord/Prelude) 13.2 gal.

MAJOR OPTIONS: Hondamatic semi-automatic two-speed transmission. Five-speed manual transmission (CVCC hatchback). Air conditioning. AM/FM stereo radio. Aluminum wheels.

PERFORMANCE: Similar to 1976-78.

PRODUCTION/SALES: A total of 353,291 Hondas were sold in the U.S. during 1979.

Manufacturer: Honda Motor Co. Ltd., Tokyo, Japan.

Distributor: American Honda Motor Company, Gardena, California.

HISTORY: Hondas were introduced to the U.S. market in October 1978 for the 1979 model year, except (Prelude) in March 1979. The new Prelude was advertised as "a sports car for grownups."

1980-81 HONDA

CIVIC — FOUR — A restyling for 1980 added a bit of size to Honda's smallest model, as its wheelbase grew by two inches. Two engine displacements were available: 1.3 liters and 1.5 liters, each hooked to either a five-speed manual gearbox (four-speed on base hatchbacks) or optional two-speed Hondamatic semi-automatic. Though retaining the stratified-charge cylinder head, the revised engines no longer promoted the CVCC designation. The conventional engine (two valves per cylinder) was no longer offered. A four-door notchback sedan joined the hatchback and station wagon for 1981, and a three-speed fully automatic transmission replaced the two-speed semi-automatic on the option list.

ACCORD — FOUR — Production of the compact front-drive Honda continued with little change other than minor cosmetics. Both a two-door hatchback and a four-door were available, powered by a 1.8-liter four-cylinder engine that produced 72 horsepower. A three-speed automatic transmission became optional for 1980. The Accord SE, added for 1981, had leather upholstery, power steering, air conditioning, and power windows.

PRELUDE — FOUR — Production of the sporty Honda notchback coupe continued with little change. Preludes rode a Civic platform but were powered by an Accord 1.8-liter four-cylinder engine. A three-speed automatic transmission joined the option list for 1980, and Prelude got a slight facelift for 1981.

I.D. DATA: Honda's Vehicle Identification Number is on the upper left of the instrument panel, visible through the windshield. A 10-symbol number identifies 1980 models. Symbols 1-3 indicate series and body style, followed by the sequential serial number. A 17-symbol number identifies 1981 models. The first three symbols identify manufacturer, make, and vehicle type; symbols four and five denote series and engine, followed by a digit to identify the transmission; symbol seven is the door code, eighth the trim level, followed by a check digit. Symbol ten indicates model year, eleven is the assembly plant. Then comes the six-digit sequential serial number. Serial number prefix (1980 models): (Civic 1300) SLA; (Civic 1300 DX) SLC; (Civic 1500) SRA; (Civic 1500 DX) SRC; (Civic 1500 GL) SRE; (Civic 1500 wag) WDA; (Accord cpe) SME; (Accord sed) SMK; (Accord LX) SMH; (Prelude) SNF. Identification plates may also be on the firewall, and the rear jamb of the driver's door. Engine number is stamped into the clutch casing.

Model	Body Type & Seating	Engine Type/CID	P.O.E. Price	Weight (lbs.)	Prod. Total
CIVIC (1980 Models)					
1300	2-dr Hatch-4P	I4/81	3799	1722	Note 1
1300 DX	2-dr Hatch-4P	I4/81	4275	1736	Note 1
1500	2-dr Hatch-4P	I4/91	4149	1780	Note 1
1500 DX	2-dr Hatch-4P	I4/91	4699	1794	Note 1
1500 GL	2-dr Hatch-4P	I4/91	5049	1822	Note 1
1500	4-dr Sta Wag-4P	I4/91	4999	1951	Note 1
ACCORD (1980 Models)					
	2-dr Hatch Cpe-4P	I4/107	5949	2129	Note 1
LX	2-dr Hatch Cpe-4P	I4/107	6949	2229	Note 1
	4-dr Sedan-4P	I4/107	6515	2239	Note 1
PRELUDE (1980 Model)					
	2-dr Coupe-4P	I4/107	6595	2130	Note 1

Note 1: A total of 845,514 Hondas (all models) were produced in 1980, followed by 852,177 in 1981.

Civic Note: A four-door sedan was added in 1981, selling for $6499. Prices that year ranged from $4599 to $6499.

Accord Note: An SE four-door sedan was added for 1981, selling for $9950. Prices that year started at $6999 for the base hatchback.

ENGINE DATA: BASE FOUR (Civic 1300): Inline, overhead-cam four-cylinder (stratified-charge, three valves per cylinder). **Displacement:** 81.5 cu. in. (1335 cc). **Bore & Stroke:** 2.83 x 3.23 in. (72 x 82 mm). **Compression Ratio:** 7.9:1. **Brake Horsepower:** 55 at 5000 rpm. **Torque:** 64.5 lbs.-ft. at 3500 rpm. Five main bearings. Keihin-Honda three-barrel carburetor.

BASE FOUR (Civic 1500): Inline overhead-cam four-cylinder (stratified-charge, three valves per cylinder). **Displacement:** 90.8 cu. in. (1488 cc). **Bore & Stroke:** 2.91 x 3.41 in. (74 x 86.5 mm). **Compression Ratio:** 8.9:1. **Brake Horsepower:** 67 at 5000 rpm. **Torque:** 79 lbs.-ft. at 3000 rpm. Five main bearings. Keihin-Honda three-barrel carburetor.

BASE FOUR (Accord, Prelude): Inline, overhead-cam four-cylinder (12-valve, stratified-charge). Cast iron block and light alloy head. **Displacement:** 106.8 cu. in. (1751 cc). **Bore & Stroke:** 3.03 x 3.70 in. (77 x 94 mm). **Compression Ratio:** 8.0:1. **Brake Horsepower:** 72 at 4500 rpm. **Torque:** 94 lbs.-ft. at 3000 rpm. Five main bearings. Keihin-Honda three-barrel carburetor.

CHASSIS DATA: Wheelbase: (Civic hatch) 88.6 in.; (Civic sedan/wagon) 91.3 in.; (Accord) 93.7 in.; (Prelude) 91.3 in. **Overall Length:** (Civic hatch) 148 in.; (Civic sedan) 160.8 in.; (Accord cpe) 163.2 in.; (Accord sed) 171.9 in.; (Prelude) 161.4 in. **Height:** (Civic hatch) 53 in.; (Civic wagon) 54.2 in.; (Accord cpe) 52.6 in.; (Accord sed) 53.3 in.; (Prelude) 51.0 in. **Width:** (Civic) 62.2 in.; (Accord) 63.8 in.; (Prelude) 64.4 in. **Front Tread:** (Civic) 53.5 in.; (Accord) 55.5 in.; (Prelude) 55.1 in. **Rear Tread:** (Civic 2-dr) 53.9 in.; (Civic wagon) 54.2 in.; (Accord) 55.1 in.; (Prelude) 55.5 in. **Standard Tires:** (Civic) 600S12; (Accord) 165SR13; (Prelude) 175/70SR13.

TECHNICAL: Layout: front-engine, front-drive. **Transmission:** (Civic) four- or five-speed manual, or optional two-speed semi-automatic (three-speed in 1981); (Accord/Prelude) five-speed manual, with three-speed automatic available. **Steering:** rack and pinion. **Suspension (front):** MacPherson struts with coil springs and anti-roll bar. **Suspension (rear):** MacPherson struts with coil springs (anti-roll bar on Prelude); Civic wagon used parallel leaf springs. **Brakes:** front disc, rear drum. **Body Construction:** steel unibody. **Fuel Tank:** (Civic) 10.8 gal.; (Accord/Prelude) 13.2 gal.

MAJOR OPTIONS: Automatic transmission. Air conditioning. AM/FM stereo. Aluminum wheels.

PRODUCTION/SALES: A total of 375,388 Hondas were sold in the U.S. during 1980, followed by 370,705 in 1981.

Manufacturer: Honda Motor Company Ltd., Tokyo, Japan.

Distributor: American Honda Motor Company, Gardena, California.

HISTORY: Honda's 1980 Civic models were introduced to the U.S. market in October 1979, Accord and Prelude in November 1979. To meet tightening nitrogen oxide emissions standards and new CAFE requirements in the U.S., the Civic CVCC engine needed to be modified to a more conventional design, with a three-way catalytic converter. Civic ads in 1980 promoted the car's 13 percent increase in interior space, and 20 percent growth in window area, as well as the longer wheelbase.

A two-seat sports car from Honda was rumored at this time, and had been seen on the street in Japan. Some observers claimed it appeared to be a cross between a Fiat X1/9 and a Triumph TR7. Honda's CRX two-seater would not arrive in the U.S. until 1985. An aluminum V-6 engine for the larger models also was rumored.

1982 HONDA

1982 Honda Accord. (American Honda Motor Co. Inc.)

CIVIC — FOUR — Production of the restyled Civic continued with little change, except for minor cosmetics. Civics now displayed rectangular headlamps and black bumpers. A new FE (Fuel Economy) model was added, with five-speed gearbox only, rating 41-mpg city and 55-mpg highway on the EPA scale. A three-speed automatic transmission was optional on other models. Standard Civic equipment included power brakes, a locking fuel door, tinted glass, remote hatch or tailgate release, reclining front bucket seats, rear defroster, and intermittent wipers. The 1500 Civic added a rear wiper/washer (except the four-door sedan). The 1500 GL included a digital clock and tachometer.

ACCORD — FOUR — Honda's popular compact was reworked this year into a second-generation hatchback coupe and notchback sedan. This version was longer and lower than its predecessor, but mechanical details changed minimally. Wheelbase grew by 2.8 inches, overall length by less. Styling was new at both front and rear. A revised nose held a full-width grille and quad rectangular headlamps. Below the larger urethane-coated bumpers was a chin-type spoiler. Taillamps were larger, too. Rear ends had a slight spoiler treatment. An electronic warning system was now standard, as was a four-spoke steering wheel. Air conditioning was standard on the LX, which had velour upholstery. All Accords came with a tachometer, clock, electric rear defroster, remote trunk or hatch release, and intermittent wipers.

PRELUDE — FOUR — Production of the sporty Honda coupe continued with little change. An 'H' emblem went on the grille. A new electronic function warning system was added. Standard Prelude equipment included tinted glass, a powered sunroof, remote-control driver's mirror, digital clock, and trip odometer. Variable-assist power steering was included with automatic-shift models.

I.D. DATA: Honda's 17-symbol Vehicle Identification Number is on the upper left of the instrument panel, visible through the windshield. The first three symbols identify manufacturer, make, and vehicle type; symbols four and five denote series and engine, followed by a digit to identify the transmission; symbol seven is the door code, eight the trim level, followed by a check digit. Symbol ten indicates model year, eleven is the assembly plant. Then comes the six-digit sequential serial number.

Model	Body Type & Seating	Engine Type/CID	P.O.E. Price	Weight (lbs.)	Prod. Total
CIVIC					
1300	2-dr Hatch-4P	I4/81	4799	1700	Note 1
1300 FE	2-dr Hatch-4P	I4/81	5899	1733	Note 1
1500 DX	2-dr Hatch-4P	I4/91	5849	1792	Note 1
1500 GL	2-dr Hatch-4P	I4/91	6199	1803	Note 1
1500	4-dr Sedan-4P	I4/91	6749	1896	Note 1
1500	4-dr Sta Wag-4P	I4/91	6249	1940	Note 1
ACCORD					
	2-dr Hatch Cpe-4P	I4/107	7399	1988	Note 1
LX	2- dr Hatch Cpe-4P	I4/107	8449	2076	Note 1
	4-dr Sedan-4P	I4/107	8245	2070	Note 1
PRELUDE					
	2-dr Coupe-4P	I4/107	7995	2056	Note 1

Note 1: A total of 365,865 Hondas were sold in the U.S. during 1982, out of 854,453 produced.

ENGINE DATA: BASE FOUR (Civic 1300): Inline, overhead-cam four-cylinder. **Displacement:** 81.5 cu. in. (1335 cc). **Bore & Stroke:** 2.83 x 3.23 in. (72 x 82 mm). **Compression Ratio:** 8.8:1. **Brake Horsepower:** 62 at 5000 rpm. **Torque:** 69 lbs.-ft. at 3000 rpm. Five main bearings. Keihin-Honda three-barrel carburetor.

BASE FOUR (Civic 1500): Inline overhead-cam four-cylinder. **Displacement:** 90.8 cu. in. (1488 cc). **Bore & Stroke:** 2.91 x 3.41 in. (74 x 86.5 mm). **Compression Ratio:** 8.8:1. **Brake Horsepower:** 69 at 5000 rpm. **Torque:** 78 lbs.-ft. at 3000 rpm. Five main bearings. Keihin-Honda three-barrel carburetor.

BASE FOUR (Accord, Prelude): Inline, overhead-cam four-cylinder. Cast iron block and aluminum alloy head. **Displacement:** 106.8 cu. in. (1751 cc). **Bore & Stroke:** 3.03 x 3.70 in. (77 x 94 mm). **Compression Ratio:** 8.8:1. **Brake Horsepower:** 75 at 4500 rpm. **Torque:** 93 lbs.-ft. at 3500 rpm. Five main bearings. Keihin-Honda three-barrel carburetor.

CHASSIS DATA: Wheelbase: (Civic hatch) 88.6 in.; (Civic 4-dr) 91.3 in.; (Accord) 96.5 in.; (Prelude) 91.3 in. **Overall Length:** (Civic hatch) 148.4 in.; (Civic 4-dr sedan) 161.4 in.; (Civic wagon) 160.8 in.; (Accord cpe) 165.8 in.; (Accord sed) 173.6 in.; (Prelude) 161.4 in. **Height:** (Civic hatch) 53.2 in.; (Civic wagon) 54.1 in.; (Accord cpe) 53.3 in.; (Accord sed) 54.1 in.; (Prelude) 51.0 in. **Width:** (Civic) 61.6 in.; (Accord) 65.0 in.; (Prelude) 64.4 in. **Front Tread:** (Civic) 53.5 in.; (Accord) 56.3 in.; (Prelude) 55.1 in. **Rear Tread:** (Civic) 54.3 in.; (Accord) 55.9 in.; (Prelude) 55.5 in. **Standard Tires:** (Civic 1300) 155SR12; (Civic 1500) 155SR13; (Accord) 185/70SR13; (Prelude) 175/70SR13.

TECHNICAL: Layout: front-engine, front-drive. **Transmission:** (Civic) four- or five-speed manual; (Accord/Prelude) five-speed manual; three-speed automatic available on all models. **Steering:** rack and pinion. **Suspension (front):** MacPherson struts with coil springs and anti-roll bar. **Suspension (rear):** MacPherson struts with coil springs (anti-roll bar on Civic/ Prelude); Civic wagon used parallel leaf springs. **Brakes:** front disc, rear drum. **Body Construction:** steel unibody.

Manufacturer: Honda Motor Company Ltd., Tokyo, Japan.

Distributor: American Honda Motor Company, Gardena, California.

HISTORY: Honda's 1982 models were introduced to the U.S. market in October 1981. Beginning in November 1982, some Accords were built in Marysville, Ohio, making Honda the first Japanese automaker to produce cars in the U.S.

1983 HONDA

CIVIC — FOUR — Production of the restyled Civic continued with little change. A new 'S' model replaced the former 1500 GL, and included an upgraded suspension with rear stabilizer bar and Michelin 165/70SR13 tires. The 1500 S also had red bodyside moldings and bumper accents, tricot sport reclining bucket seats, a tachometer, four-spoke sport steering wheel, and a front spoiler. A 1300 FE (Fuel Economy) model came with a five-speed gearbox that had two overdrive ratios.

ACCORD — FOUR — Production of the second-generation hatchback coupe and notchback sedan continued with little change, except that an optional four-speed (overdrive) automatic transmission replaced the previous three-speed.

PRELUDE — FOUR — A second-generation sporty coupe debuted this year on a longer chassis, with a new 1.8-liter four-cylinder engine and carrying a considerably bigger price tag. A four-speed automatic transmission replaced the three-speed on the option list. Standard equipment included tinted glass, a power moonroof, AM/FM stereo radio with cassette player, side- and rear-window defrosters, rear spoiler, dual remote-control mirrors, tachometer, and knit-pile reclining front bucket seats with lumbar support.

I.D. DATA: Honda's 17-symbol Vehicle Identification Number is on the upper left of the instrument panel, visible through the windshield. The first three symbols identify the manufacturer, make, and vehicle type; symbols four and five denote series and engine, followed by a digit to identify the transmission; symbol seven is the door code, eight the trim level, followed by a check digit. Symbol ten indicates model year, eleven is the assembly plant. Then comes the six-digit sequential serial number.

Model	Body Type & Seating	Engine Type/CID	P.O.E. Price	Weight (lbs.)	Prod. Total
CIVIC					
1300	2-dr Hatch-4P	I4/81	4899	1773	Note 1
1300 FE	2-dr Hatch-4P	I4/81	5999	1803	Note 1
1500 DX	2-dr Hatch-4P	I4/91	5949	1867	Note 1
1500 S	2-dr Hatch-4P	I4/91	6399	1898	Note 1
1500	4-dr Sedan-4P	I4/91	6849	1973	Note 1
1500	4-dr Sta Wag-4P	I4/91	6349	2033	Note 1
ACCORD					
	2-dr Hatch Cpe-4P	I4/107	7499	2102	Note 1
LX	2-dr Hatch Cpe-4P	I4/107	8549	2192	Note 1
	4-dr Sedan-4P	I4/107	8345	2179	Note 1
PRELUDE					
	2-dr Coupe-4P	I4/112	9645	2200	Note 1

Note 1: A total of 356,670 Hondas were sold in the U.S. during 1983 (not including 50,402 domestically-built models).

ENGINE DATA: BASE FOUR (Civic 1300): Inline, overhead-cam four-cylinder. **Displacement:** 81.5 cu. in. (1335 cc). **Bore & Stroke:** 2.83 x 3.23 in. (72 x 82 mm). **Compression Ratio:** 8.8:1. **Brake Horsepower:** 62 at 5000 rpm. **Torque:** 69 lbs.-ft. at 3000 rpm. Five main bearings. Keihin-Honda three-barrel carburetor.

BASE FOUR (Civic 1500): Inline overhead-cam four-cylinder. **Displacement:** 90.8 cu. in. (1488 cc). **Bore & Stroke:** 2.91 x 3.41 in. (74 x 86.5 mm). **Compression Ratio:** 8.8:1. **Brake Horsepower:** 69 at 5000 rpm. **Torque:** 78 lbs.-ft. at 3000 rpm. Five main bearings. Keihin-Honda three-barrel carburetor.

BASE FOUR (Accord): Inline, overhead-cam four-cylinder. Cast iron block and aluminum alloy head. **Displacement:** 106.8 cu. in. (1751 cc). **Bore & Stroke:** 3.03 x 3.70 in. (77 x 94 mm). **Compression Ratio:** 8.8:1. **Brake Horsepower:** 75 at 4500 rpm. **Torque:** 96 lbs.-ft. at 3000 rpm. Five main bearings. Keihin-Honda three-barrel carburetor.

BASE FOUR (Prelude): Inline, overhead-cam four-cylinder. Cast iron block and light alloy head. **Displacement:** 111.6 cu. in. (1829 cc). **Bore & Stroke:** 3.15 x 3.58 in. (80 x 91 mm). **Compression Ratio:** 9.4:1. **Brake Horsepower:** 100 at 5500 rpm. **Torque:** 104 lbs.-ft. at 4000 rpm. Five main bearings. Two horizontal three-barrel carburetors.

CHASSIS DATA: Wheelbase: (Civic hatch) 88.6 in.; (Civic 4-dr) 91.3 in.; (Accord) 96.5 in.; (Prelude) 96.5 in. **Overall Length:** (Civic hatch) 148 in.; (Civic (4-dr) 161 in.; (Civic wagon) 160.8 in.; (Accord cpe) 165.8 in.; (Accord sed) 173.6 in.; (Prelude) 169.1 in. **Height:** (Civic hatch) 53.0 in.; (Civic wagon) 54.1 in.; (Accord cpe) 53.3 in.; (Accord sed) 54.1 in.; (Prelude) 51.0 in. **Width:** (Civic) 61.6 in.; (Accord) 65 in.; (Prelude) 66.5 in. **Front Tread:** (Civic) 53.5 in.; (Accord) 56.3 in.; (Prelude) 57.9 in. **Rear Tread:** (Civic) 54.3 in.; (Accord) 55.9 in.; (Prelude) 57.9 in. **Standard Tires:** (Civic 1300) 155SR12; (Civic 1500) 155SR13; (Civic 1500S) 165/70SR13; (Accord/Prelude) 185/70SR13.

TECHNICAL: Layout: front-engine, front-drive. **Transmission:** (Civic) four- or five-speed manual, or three-speed automatic; (Accord/Prelude) five-speed manual or four-speed automatic. **Steering:** rack and pinion. **Suspension (front):** MacPherson struts with coil springs and anti-roll bar. **Suspension (rear):** MacPherson struts with coil springs (anti-roll bar on Accord/Prelude); parallel leaf springs on Civic wagon. **Brakes:** front disc, rear drum. **Body Construction:** steel unibody.

Manufacturer: Honda Motor Company Ltd., Tokyo, Japan.

Distributor: American Honda Motor Company, Gardena, California.

HISTORY: Honda's 1983 models were introduced to the U.S. market in September 1982, except (Prelude) April 1983. Honda brochures soon boasted of the fact that in 1983 *Road & Track* declared Prelude "a benchmark car, the best car in its class." *Motor Trend* called it "an engineering tour de force," while *Car and Driver* praised Prelude as "a true driver's machine."

1984-85 HONDA

CIVIC — FOUR — Honda's subcompact series got a new platform this year, with an extra five inches of wheelbase, to create the third generation. The station wagon and four-door sedan now rode the same wheelbase as Accord/Prelude. The Civic wagon became known as the "tall boy," because its extra height and modified back-window area gave it a different look than the other body styles. All Civics had the 1.5-liter four-cylinder engine (with new 12-valve cylinder head), except for the base hatchback which came with the 1.3-liter four. The modified suspension included struts and torsion bars in front, with a beam axle and coil springs at the rear.

CIVIC CRX/CRX 1.5 — FOUR — Honda put the Civic drivetrain inside a two-seat sport coupe body to mix snappy performance and sporty handling in an economical package. The new all-aluminum 1.3-liter engine was a mileage champ with EPA ratings of 51 mpg in the city and 67 mph on the highway, while the larger 1.5-liter four (with 12-valve cylinder head) was the choice for performance. Front fenders, wraparound bumpers, lower body panels and the front air dam were made of impact-resistant plastic. Suspension design was the same as the reworked Civic, but on a shorter wheelbase. Primary styling feature was the stubby, cutoff back end. Standard CRX equipment in 1984 included reclining sport bucket seats, a sport steering wheel, tachometer, front air dam, rear spoiler, and tinted glass. Bodies were painted in Greek White, Baltic Blue, or Victoria Red. A CRX HF (High Fuel Economy) model was added in 1985, with lower-powered 1.5-liter engine.

1984 Honda Accord four-door sedan. (American Honda Motor Co. Inc.)

ACCORD — FOUR — A new 1.8-liter four-cylinder engine, as in the Prelude, powered the restyled Accord. A firmer suspension and rear anti-roll bar gave the hatchback coupe sportier handling. Sedans had revised front-end appearance. Coupes displayed a lower hood, blackout body trim, restyled lower grille and bumpers, and a spoiler on the revised hatch lid.

PRELUDE — FOUR — Production of the second-generation sporty coupe, introduced in mid-1983, continued with little change, except that all-disc brakes now were installed. An adjustable steering column was standard, and manual-shift models gained variable-assist power steering. The 1829-cc engine (12-valve) produced 100 horsepower, to either a five-speed manual or four-speed automatic transmission. Standard Prelude equipment in 1984 included a power moonroof, tachometer, four-speaker stereo with cassette player, dual remote mirrors, bodyside moldings, tinted glass, and rear defroster. Bodies came in Arctic Silver, Windsor Blue, or Dominican Red metallic.

1985 Honda Prelude coupe.

I.D. DATA: Honda's 17-symbol Vehicle Identification Number is on the upper left of the instrument panel, visible through the windshield. The first three symbols identify the manufacturer, make, and vehicle type; symbols four and five denote series and engine, followed by a digit to identify the transmission; symbol seven is the door code, eighth the trim level, followed by a check digit. Symbol ten indicates model year, eleven is the assembly plant. Then comes the six-digit sequential serial number.

Model	Body Type & Seating	Engine Type/CID	P.O.E. Price	Weight (lbs.)	Prod. Total
CIVIC					
1300	2-dr Hatch-4P	I4/82	5242	1797	Note 1
1500 DX	2-dr Hatch-4P	I4/91	6292	1863	Note 1
1500 S	2-dr Hatch-4P	I4/91	6842	1907	Note 1
1500	4-dr Sedan-4P	I4/91	7092	1940	Note 1
1500	4-dr Sta Wag-4P	I4/91	6992	2015	Note 1
CIVIC CRX/CRX 1.5					
1300	2-dr Spt Hatch-2P	I4/82	6142	1713	Note 1
1500	2-dr Spt Hatch-2P	I4/91	6592	1803	Note 1
ACCORD					
	2-dr Hatch Cpe-4P	I4/112	7691	2187	Note 1
LX	2-dr Hatch Cpe-4P	I4/112	8841	2235	Note 1
	4-dr Sedan-4P	I4/112	8541	2271	Note 1
LX	4-dr Sedan-4P	I4/112	9941	2341	Note 1
PRELUDE					
	2-dr Coupe-4P	I4/112	9987	2266	Note 1

Note 1: A total of 374,819 Hondas were sold in the U.S. during 1984, followed by 406,413 in 1985 (not including domestically-built models).

ENGINE DATA: BASE FOUR (Civic/CRX 1300): Inline, overhead-cam four-cylinder. Aluminum alloy block and head. **Displacement:** 82 cu. in. (1342 cc). **Bore & Stroke:** 2.91 x 3.07 in. (74 x 78 mm). **Compression Ratio:** 10.0:1. **Brake Horsepower:** 60 at 5500 rpm. **Torque:** 73 lbs.-ft. at 3500 rpm. Five main bearings. One three-barrel carburetor.

BASE FOUR (Civic/CRX 1500): Inline overhead-cam four-cylinder (12-valve). **Displacement:** 90.8 cu. in. (1488 cc). **Bore & Stroke:** 2.91 x 3.41 in. (74 x 86.5 mm). **Compression Ratio:** 9.2:1. **Brake Horsepower:** 76 at 6000 rpm. **Torque:** 84 lbs.-ft. at 3500 rpm. Five main bearings. One three-barrel carburetor.

Note: CRX HF (1985) engine was rated 65 bhp at 5500 rpm, and 81 lbs.-ft. at 3500 rpm.

BASE FOUR (Accord): Inline, overhead-cam four-cylinder (12-valve). Cast iron block and aluminum alloy head. **Displacement:** 111.6 cu. in. (1829 cc). **Bore & Stroke:** 3.15 x 3.58 in. (80 x 91 mm). **Compression Ratio:** 9.0:1. **Brake Horsepower:** 86 at 5800 rpm. **Torque:** 99 lbs.-ft. at 3500 rpm. Five main bearings. One downdraft three-barrel carburetor.

BASE FOUR (Prelude): Same as 1829-cc four above, except with two carburetors. **Compression Ratio:** 9.1:1. **Brake Horsepower:** 100 at 5500 rpm. **Torque:** 104 lbs.-ft. at 4000 rpm.

CHASSIS DATA: Wheelbase: (Civic hatch) 93.7 in.; (Civic 4-dr) 96.5 in.; (CRX) 86.6 in.; (Accord) 96.5 in.; (Prelude) 96.5 in. **Overall Length:** (Civic hatch) 150 in.; (Civic 4-dr) 163.4 in.; (Civic wagon) 157.1 in.; (CRX) 144.6 in.; (Accord cpe) 167.5 in.; (Accord sed) 175.4 in.; (Prelude) 169.1 in. **Height:** (Civic 2-dr) 52.6 in.; (Civic 4-dr) 54.5 in.; (Civic wagon) 58.3 in.; (CRX) 50.8 in.; (Accord cpe) 53.3 in.; (Accord sed) 54.1 in.; (Prelude) 51.0 in. **Width:** (Civic) 64 in.; (CRX) 63.9 in.; (Accord) 65.6 in.; (Prelude) 66.5 in. **Front Tread:** (Civic/CRX) 55.1 in.; (Accord) 56.9 in.; (Prelude) 57.9 in. **Rear Tread:** (Civic/CRX) 55.7 in.; (Accord) 55.9 in.; (Prelude) 57.9 in.

TECHNICAL: Layout: front-engine, front-drive. **Transmission:** (Civic) four- or five-speed manual, or three-speed automatic; (Accord/Prelude) five-speed manual or four-speed automatic. **Steering:** rack and pinion. **Suspension (front):** (Civic/CRX/Accord) MacPherson struts with coil springs and anti-roll bar; (Prelude) upper/lower control arms with coil springs and anti-roll bar. **Suspension (rear):** (Civic/CRX) beam axle with coil springs; (Accord) MacPherson struts with coil springs; (Prelude) MacPherson struts with coil springs and anti-roll bar. **Brakes:** front disc, rear drum except (Prelude) front/rear disc. **Body Construction:** steel unibody.

Manufacturer: Honda Motor Company Ltd., Tokyo, Japan.

Distributor: American Honda Motor Company, Gardena, California.

HISTORY: Honda's 1984 models were introduced to the U.S. market in September 1983; the 1985 models in October 1984. During the 1985 model year, a four-wheel-drive version of the Civic "tall boy" station wagon and a fuel-injected CRX Si debuted; see next listing for details. Through the mid- and late-1980s, *Car and Driver* named Accord one of the best 10 cars sold in America.

1986-87 HONDA

CIVIC — FOUR — Aero-styled flush-mount headlamps were installed at this time, and an optional four-speed automatic transmission replaced the former three-speed. A new Si hatchback included a fuel-injected version of the 1.5-liter four-cylinder engine. The Si included a removable glass sunroof, full wheel covers, full-width taillamp panel, body-colored front air dam, and roof lip rear spoilers. All other engines were carbureted, as before. Introduced during the 1985 model year, the four-wheel drive variant of the "tall boy" wagon came with a six-speed manual gearbox. For 1987, the 4WD system adopted automatic engagement (called Real Time 4WD), replacing the former part-time system.

1986 Honda CRX two-passenger sports car. (American Honda Motor Co. Inc.)

CIVIC CRX — FOUR — A new Si model, introduced during the 1985 model year, carried a fuel-injected, 91-bhp version of the 1.5-liter four-cylinder engine. All CRX engines were 1.5 liters in displacement, but the economy HF (High Fuel Economy) model was rated 58 horsepower, versus 76 bhp for the standard model. The lower-powered engine had an eight-valve head, the base version a 12-valve. Flush-mounted headlamps were new for 1986, as were lower bodyside rub strips. A four-speed automatic transmission replaced the three-speed on the CRX option list. A power glass sunroof was standard on the Si, which wore larger 60-series tires and had body-color front and rear spoilers, and rocker panel extensions. With the Si engine, a CRX could hit 60 mph in less than nine seconds.

ACCORD — FOUR — The all-new, aerodynamically-restyled, next-generation Accord coupe and sedan gained 5.9 inches in wheelbase, and a tad more than 3 inches in overall length. To power the increased weight, the four-cylinder engine grew from 1.8 to 2.0 liters, available either carbureted or (in the upper-rung LXi) with electronic multi-point fuel injection. The fuel-injected four delivered an extra dozen horsepower. The revised suspension used wishbones and coil springs at both ends. Sedans now had a fold-down rear seatback. The LX included an AM/FM stereo radio with cassette player and power antenna, air conditioning, dual remote-control mirrors, power windows and door locks, and passenger-door map pocket. At the upper end, the LXi sedan included a power moonroof and custom alloy wheels.

PRELUDE — FOUR — A fuel-injected Si version of the two-door coupe joined the lineup just before the end of the 1985 model year, and continued into 1986. The Si engine displaced 2.0 liters, versus 1.8 liters for the carbureted base Prelude. Standard Si equipment included air conditioning, power windows and mirrors, driver's lumbar support adjustment, cruise control, custom alloy wheels, body-color spoilers, and a sound system with graphic equalizer. A power moonroof was standard on both models.

289

1987 Honda Accord DX four-door sedan. (American Honda Motor Co. Inc.)

I.D. DATA: Honda's 17-symbol Vehicle Identification Number is on the upper left of the instrument panel, visible through the windshield. The first three symbols identify the manufacturer, make, and vehicle type; symbols four and five denote series and engine, followed by a digit to identify the transmission; symbol seven is the door code, eight the trim level, followed by a check digit. Symbol ten indicates model year, eleven is the assembly plant. Then comes the six-digit sequential serial number.

Model	Body Type & Seating	Engine Type/CID	P.O.E. Price	Weight (lbs.)	Prod. Total
CIVIC (1986 Models)					
	2-dr Hatch-4P	I4/82	5479	1887	Note 1
DX	2-dr Hatch-4P	I4/91	6699	1958	Note 1
Si	2-dr Hatch-4P	I4/91	7999	2033	Note 1
	4-dr Sedan-4P	I4/91	7499	2064	Note 1
	4-dr Sta Wag-4P	I4/91	7395	2084	Note 1
4WD	4-dr Sta Wag-4P	I4/91	8739	2304	Note 1
CIVIC CRX (1986 Models)					
	2-dr Spt Hatch-2P	I4/91	7049	1865	Note 1
HF	2-dr Spt Hatch-2P	I4/91	6729	1713	Note 1
Si	2-dr Spt Hatch-2P	I4/91	8279	1954	Note 1
ACCORD (1986 Models)					
DX	2-dr Hatch Cpe-4P	I4/119	8429	2417	Note 1
LXi	2-dr Hatch Cpe-4P	I4/119	11140	2498	Note 1
DX	4-dr Sedan-4P	I4/119	9299	2421	Note 1
LX	4-dr Sedan-4P	I4/119	10995	2529	Note 1
LXi	4-dr Sedan-4P	I4/119	12675	2569	Note 1
PRELUDE (1986 Models)					
	2-dr Coupe-4P	I4/112	10549	2293	Note 1
Si	2-dr Coupe-4P	I4/119	12995	2426	Note 1

Note 1: A total of 405,399 Hondas were sold in the U.S. during 1986, followed by 312,218 in 1987 (not including domestically-built models).

1987 Honda Prelude Si. (American Honda Motor Co. Inc.)

ENGINE DATA: BASE FOUR (base Civic): Inline, overhead-cam four-cylinder. Aluminum alloy block and head. **Displacement:** 82 cu. in. (1342 cc). **Bore & Stroke:** 2.91 x 3.07 in. (74 x 78 mm). **Compression Ratio:** 10.0:1. **Brake Horsepower:** 60 at 5500 rpm. **Torque:** 73 lbs.-ft. at 3500 rpm. Five main bearings. One three-barrel carburetor.

BASE FOUR (Civic/CRX): Inline overhead-cam four-cylinder (12-valve). **Displacement:** 90.8 cu. in. (1488 cc). **Bore & Stroke:** 2.91 x 3.41 in. (74 x 86.5 mm). **Compression Ratio:** 9.2:1. **Brake Horsepower:** 76 at 6000 rpm. **Torque:** 84 lbs.-ft. at 3500 rpm. Five main bearings. One three-barrel carburetor.

BASE FOUR (Civic/CRX Si): Same as 1488-cc four above, but with fuel injection — **Compression Ratio:** 8.7:1. **Brake Horsepower:** 91 at 5500 rpm. **Torque:** 93 lbs.-ft. at 4500 rpm.

BASE FOUR (CRX HF): Same as 1488-cc four above, but with eight-valve head — **Compression Ratio:** 10.0:1. **Brake Horsepower:** 58 at 4800 rpm. **Torque:** 79 lbs.-ft. at 2500 rpm.

BASE FOUR (Prelude): Inline, overhead-cam four-cylinder. **Displacement:** 111.6 cu. in. (1829 cc). **Bore & Stroke:** 3.15 x 3.58 in. (80 x 91 mm). **Compression Ratio:** 9.1:1. **Brake Horsepower:** 100 at 5500 rpm. **Torque:** 107 lbs.-ft. at 4000 rpm. Five main bearings. Two single-barrel carburetors.

BASE FOUR (Accord): Inline, overhead-cam four-cylinder. **Displacement:** 119 cu. in. (1955 cc). **Bore & Stroke:** 3.26 x 3.58 in. (83 x 91 mm). **Compression Ratio:** 9.2:1. **Brake Horsepower:** 98 at 5500 rpm. **Torque:** 109 lbs.-ft. at 3500 rpm. Five main bearings. One downdraft three-barrel carburetor.

BASE FOUR (Accord LXi, Prelude Si): Same as 1955-cc four above, but with port fuel injection — **Compression Ratio:** 9.4:1. **Brake Horsepower:** 110 at 5500 rpm. **Torque:** 114 lbs.-ft. at 4500 rpm.

1987 Honda Civic hatchback. (American Honda Motor Co. Inc.)

CHASSIS DATA: Wheelbase: (Civic hatch) 93.7 in.; (Civic sedan/wagon) 96.5 in.; (CRX) 86.6 in.; (Accord) 102.4 in.; (Prelude) 96.5 in. **Overall Length:** (Civic hatch) 150 in.; (Civic sedan) 163.4 in.; (Civic wagon) 157.1 in.; (CRX) 144.6 in.; (Accord cpe) 174.8 in.; (Accord sed) 178.5 in.; (Prelude) 169.1 in. **Height:** (Civic hatch) 52.6 in.; (Civic sedan) 54.5 in.; (Civic wagon) 55.7 in.; (CRX) 50.8 in.; (Accord cpe) 52.6 in.; (Accord sed) 53.3 in.; (Prelude) 51.0 in. **Width:** (Civic) 64 in.; (CRX) 63.9 in.; (Accord) 66.7 in.; (Prelude) 66.5 in. **Front Tread:** (Civic/CRX) 55.1 in.; (Accord) 58.3 in.; (Prelude) 57.9 in. **Rear Tread:** (Civic/CRX) 55.7 in.; (Accord) 58.1 in.; (Prelude) 57.9 in.

TECHNICAL: Layout: front-engine, front-drive. **Transmission:** (Civic) four- or five-speed manual, or four-speed automatic; (Civic 4WD) six-speed manual; (others) five-speed manual or four-speed automatic. **Steering:** rack and pinion. **Suspension (front):** (Civic/CRX) MacPherson struts with coil springs and anti-roll bar; (Accord/Prelude) upper/lower control arms with coil springs and anti-roll bar. **Suspension (rear):** (Civic/CRX) beam axle with coil springs; (Accord) upper/lower control arms with coil springs and anti-roll bar; (Prelude) MacPherson struts with coil springs and anti-roll bar. **Brakes:** front disc, rear drum except (Prelude) front/rear disc. **Body Construction:** steel unibody.

Manufacturer: Honda Motor Company Ltd., Tokyo, Japan.

Distributor: American Honda Motor Company, Gardena, California.

HISTORY: Honda's 1986 models were introduced to the U.S. market in September 1985; the 1987 models in September 1986. Production of some Civics began in Canada in 1986.

1986-87 ACURA

INTEGRA — FOUR — Honda went upscale in early spring 1986 with the introduction of two front-drive models under the new Acura badge: an Integra hatchback coupe and sedan, and larger Legend four-door sedan. Focusing more on sportiness than luxury, Integras were powered by a 1.6-liter twin-cam four-cylinder engine that produced 113 horsepower, through a five-speed manual gearbox or available four-speed overdrive automatic.

LEGEND — V-6 — The larger and more plush Legend sedan rode a 108.6-inch wheelbase and measured 189.4 inches overall. Beneath its hood was a 2.5-liter V-6 engine that delivered 151 horsepower. Both a five-speed manual gearbox and four-speed automatic were available. A two-door coupe joined the original four-door sedan during the 1987 model year (with a larger engine), and leather upholstery became optional.

I.D. DATA: See Honda breakdown.

Model	Body Type & Seating	Engine Type/CID	P.O.E. Price	Weight (lbs.)	Prod. Total
INTEGRA (1987 Models)					
RS	2-dr Hatch Cpe-5P	I4/97	9859	2326	Note 1
RS	4-dr Hatch Sed-5P	I4/97	10559	2390	Note 1
LS	2-dr Hatch Cpe-5P	I4/97	11359	2357	Note 1
LS	4-dr Hatch Sed-5P	I4/97	12159	2416	Note 1
LEGEND (1987 Models)					
	2-dr Coupe-5P	V6/163	22458	3089	Note 1
L	2-dr Coupe-5P	V6/163	25718	N/A	Note 1
LS	2-dr Coupe-5P	V6/163	27958	N/A	Note 1
	4-dr Sedan-5P	V6/152	19898	3078	Note 1
Sunroof	4-dr Sedan-5P	V6/152	20523	N/A	Note 1
Luxury	4-dr Sedan-5P	V6/152	22348	N/A	Note 1

Note 1: A total of 52,869 Acuras were sold in the U.S. during 1986, followed by 109,470 in 1987.

ENGINE DATA: BASE FOUR (Integra): Inline, dual-overhead-cam four-cylinder (16-valve). Aluminum alloy block and head. **Displacement:** 97 cu. in. (1590 cc). **Bore & Stroke:** 2.95 x 3.54 in. (75 x 90 mm). **Compression Ratio:** 9.3:1. **Brake Horsepower:** 113 at 6250 rpm. **Torque:** 99 lbs.-ft. at 5500 rpm. Port fuel injection.

BASE V-6 (Legend sedan): Overhead-cam "vee" type six-cylinder (24-valve). **Displacement:** 152 cu. in. (2494 cc). **Bore & Stroke:** 3.30 x 2.95 in. (84 x 75 mm). **Compression Ratio:** 9.0:1. **Brake Horsepower:** 151 at 5800 rpm. **Torque:** 154 lbs.-ft. at 4500 rpm. Port fuel injection.

Note: Legend coupe carried a larger (2.7-liter) V-6 engine; see 1988-89 Acura listing for details.

CHASSIS DATA: Wheelbase: (Integra cpe) 96.5 in.; (Integra sed) 99.2 in.; (Legend cpe) 106.5 in.; (Legend sed) 108.6 in. Overall Length: (Integra cpe) 168.5 in.; (Integra sed) 171.3 in.; (Legend cpe) 188.0 in.; (Legend sed) 189.4 in. Height: (Integra) 53.0 in.; (Legend cpe) 53.9 in.; (Legend sed) 54.7 in. Width: (Integra) 65.6 in.; (Legend cpe) 68.7 in.; (Legend sed) 68.3 in. Front Tread: (Integra) 55.9 in.; (Legend cpe) 59.1 in.; (Legend sed) 59.0 in. Rear Tread: (Integra) 56.5 in.; (Legend cpe) 59.1 in.; (Legend sed) 57.5 in.
TECHNICAL: Layout: front-engine, front-drive. Transmission: five-speed manual or four-speed (overdrive) automatic. Steering: power rack and pinion. Suspension (front): (Integra) MacPherson struts with torsion bars and anti-roll bar; (Legend) upper/lower control arms with coil springs and anti-roll bar. Suspension (rear): (Integra) beam axle with Panhard rods and anti-roll bar; (Legend) MacPherson struts with coil springs and anti-roll bar. Brakes: front/rear disc. Body Construction: steel unibody.
Manufacturer: Honda Motor Company Ltd., Tokyo, Japan.
Distributor: American Honda Motor Company, Gardena, California.
HISTORY: The Legend's platform and V-6 engine also went into the new Sterling sedan, produced in Britain by the Rover Group in a joint venture with Honda.

1988-89 HONDA

CIVIC — FOUR — Honda's long-lived subcompact series got a total redesign for 1988, creating a lineup which replaced the former Si hatchback with a more posh LX sedan. Styling features of the enlarged Civic included flush headlamps, nearly-flush window glass, and a steeper hood angle. Hatchback wheelbase grew by 4.7 inches, but other models gained less. A new 1.5-liter four-cylinder engine with four valves per cylinder had twin throttle-body fuel injection. Honda's 4WD station wagon got an even greater power boost via a new 1.6-liter engine, which produced 105 horsepower; and it could now be ordered with automatic transmission instead of the standard six-speed manual gearbox. Suspensions were now independent at both ends. The Si hatchback was revived for the 1989 model year, powered by the 16-valve engine used in the CRX Si.

CRX — FOUR — Honda's restyled two-seat coupe line grew four inches in wheelbase, and nearly as much overall, and carried a new selection of engines. The economy-oriented HF was powered by an eight-valve version of the new 1.5-liter four, while the base model had a 12-valve variant. Topping the list, the sportier CRX Si gained a 16-valve, 1.6-liter four-cylinder engine that produced 105 horsepower. The Si also came with 14-inch tires on alloy wheels, and included a power sunroof and chin spoiler. Suspension changes were identical to those on the reworked Civic, using twin wishbones at front and rear. A CRX Si could accelerate to 60 mph in about 8.2 seconds.

1989 Honda CRX Si.

1988 Honda Accord DX coupe. (American Honda Motor Co. Inc.)

ACCORD — FOUR — A notchback coupe joined the Accord lineup during the model year, to replace the hatchback body style. Engine modifications boosted horsepower of the LXi engine to 120, as a result of increased compression and intake/exhaust and camshaft revisions. Slight appearance changes included wider taillamps and a deeper front spoiler. An SEi luxury version joined the lineup for 1989, adding leather upholstery and a high-power Bose stereo sound system.

PRELUDE — FOUR — Introduced to the U.S. in July 1987, the third-generation sport coupe came with either a carbureted or fuel-injected version of the new 1958-cc four-cylinder engine, with either a single-cam or twin-cam head. More intriguing than that

was the availability of mechanical four-wheel steering on the Si model. Wheelbase beneath the all-new body grew by 4.5 inches; overall length reached 175.6 inches. The optional four-speed automatic transmission had a driver-selectable "Sport" mode that altered shift points.

I.D. DATA: See 1986-87 Honda listing.

Model	Body Type & Seating	Engine Type/CID	P.O.E. Price	Weight (lbs.)	Prod. Total
CIVIC (1988 Models)					
	2-dr Hatch-4P	I4/91	6095	1933	Note 1
DX	2-dr Hatch-4P	I4/91	7985	1993	Note 1
DX	4-dr Sedan-4P	I4/91	8795	2039	Note 1
LX	4-dr Sedan-4P	I4/91	9675	2161	Note 1
	4-dr Sta Wag-4P	I4/91	9948	2130	Note 1
4WD	4-dr Sta Wag-4P	I4/97	11998	2366	Note 1
CIVIC CRX (1988 Models)					
	2-dr Spt Hatch-2P	I4/91	8635	1922	Note 1
HF	2-dr Spt Hatch-2P	I4/91	8295	1819	Note 1
Si	2-dr Spt Hatch-2P	I4/97	10195	2011	Note 1
ACCORD (1988 Models)					
DX	2-dr Hatch Cpe-4P	I4/119	10535	2513	Note 1
LXi	2-dr Hatch Cpe-4P	I4/119	13695	2641	Note 1
DX	2-dr Coupe-4P	I4/119	11335	2493	Note 1
LXi	2-dr Coupe-4P	I4/119	14295	2646	Note 1
DX	4-dr Sedan-4P	I4/119	11175	2482	Note 1
LX	4-dr Sedan-4P	I4/119	13460	2579	Note 1
LXi	4-dr Sedan-4P	I4/119	15200	2668	Note 1
PRELUDE (1988 Models)					
	2-dr Coupe-4P	I4/119	13495	2522	Note 1
Si	2-dr Coupe-4P	I4/119	16645	2665	Note 1
Si (4WS)	2-dr Coupe-4P	I4/119	17945	2685	Note 1

Note 1: A total of 640,747 Hondas were sold in the U.S. during 1988 (including 375,625 domestically-built models), followed by 251,569 imported models in 1989.

Accord Model Note: An Accord SEi coupe and sedan became available in 1989.

1989 Honda Prelude Si.

ENGINE DATA: BASE FOUR (Civic hatchback): Inline overhead-cam four-cylinder (16-valve). Aluminum alloy block and head. Displacement: 91 cu. in. (1493 cc). Bore & Stroke: 2.95 x 3.32 in. (75 x 84 mm). Compression Ratio: 9.2:1. Brake Horsepower: 70 at 5500 rpm. Torque: 83 lbs.-ft. at 3000 rpm. Twin-injector fuel injection.

BASE FOUR (Civic DX/LX, CRX): Same as 1493-cc four above, but — Brake Horsepower: 92 at 6000 rpm. Torque: 89 lbs.-ft. at 4500 rpm.

BASE FOUR (CRX HF): Same as 1493-cc four above, with eight-valve head configuration — Compression Ratio: 9.6:1. Brake Horsepower: 62 at 4500 rpm. Torque: 90 lbs.-ft. at 2000 rpm.

BASE FOUR (Civic 4WD wagon, CRX Si): Inline overhead-cam four-cylinder (16-valve). Aluminum alloy block and head. Displacement: 97 cu. in. (1590 cc). Bore & Stroke: 2.95 x 3.54 in. (75 x 90 mm). Compression Ratio: 9.1:1. Brake Horsepower: 105 at 6000 rpm. Torque: 98 lbs.-ft. at 5000 rpm. Port (multi-point) fuel injection.

BASE FOUR (Accord DX/LX): Inline, overhead-cam four-cylinder (12-valve). Cast iron block and aluminum alloy head. Displacement: 119.3 cu. in. (1955 cc). Bore & Stroke: 3.26 x 3.58 in. (83 x 91 mm). Compression Ratio: 9.1:1. Brake Horsepower: 98 at 5500 rpm. Torque: 109 lbs.-ft. at 3500 rpm. One two-barrel carburetor.

BASE FOUR (Accord LXi): Same as 1955-cc four above, but with port fuel injection — Brake Horsepower: 120 at 5800 rpm. Torque: 122 lbs.-ft. at 4000 rpm. Sequential fuel injection.

BASE FOUR (Prelude): Inline, overhead-cam four-cylinder (12-valve). Aluminum alloy block and head. Displacement: 119.5 cu. in. (1958 cc). Bore & Stroke: 3.19 x 3.74 in. (81 x 95 mm). Compression Ratio: 9.1:1. Brake Horsepower: 104 at 5800 rpm. Torque: 111 lbs.-ft. at 4000 rpm. Two carburetors.

BASE FOUR (Prelude Si): Inline, dual-overhead-cam four-cylinder (16-valve). Aluminum alloy block and head. Displacement: 119.5 cu. in. (1958 cc). Bore & Stroke: 3.19 x 3.74 in. (81 x 95 mm). Compression Ratio: 9.0:1. Brake Horsepower: 135 at 6200 rpm. Torque: 127 lbs.-ft. at 4500 rpm. Sequential fuel injection.

CHASSIS DATA: Wheelbase: (Civic) 98.4 in.; (CRX) 90.6 in.; (Accord) 102.4 in.; (Prelude) 101.0 in. Overall Length: (Civic hatch) 156.1 in.; (Civic sedan) 166.5 in.; (Civic wagon) 161.6 in.; (CRX) 147.8 in.; (Accord cpe) 174.8 in.; (Accord sed) 179.7 in.; (Prelude) 175.6 in. Height: (Civic hatch) 52.4 in.; (Civic sedan) 53.5 in.; (Civic wagon) 54.0 in.; (CRX) 50.0 in.; (Accord cpe) 52.6 in.; (Accord sed) 53.4 in.; (Prelude) 51.0 in. Width: (Civic hatch) 65.6 in.; (Civic sedan) 65.9 in.; (Civic wagon) 66.1 in.; (CRX) 65.7 in.; (Accord cpe) 66.7 in.; (Accord sed) 67.4 in.; (Prelude) 67.3 in. Front Tread: (Civic/CRX) 57.1 in.; (Accord) 58.3 in.; (Prelude) 58.3 in. Rear Tread: (Civic/CRX) 57.3 in.; (Accord) 58.1 in.; (Prelude) 57.9 in.

TECHNICAL: Layout: front-engine, front-drive. Transmission: (Civic) four- or five-speed manual, or four-speed automatic; (Civic 4WD) six-speed manual; (others) five-speed manual or four-speed automatic. Steering: rack and pinion. Brakes: front disc, rear drum except (Prelude) front/rear disc. Body Construction: steel unibody.
Manufacturer: Honda Motor Company Ltd., Tokyo, Japan.
Distributor: American Honda Motor Company, Gardena, California.

HISTORY: Honda's 1988 models were introduced to the U.S. market in September 1987 except (Civic wagon) January 1988 and (Accord coupe) February 1988. Honda's 1989 models were introduced in September 1988 except (Accord coupe SEi) February 1989. Coupes and hatchbacks were produced only at Honda's plant in Marysville, Ohio; and the coupe was planned for export to Japan. Other Accords were built in Japan. Civics were built in Ohio, Canada, and Japan. By 1988, Accord was the fourth best selling car model in the U.S. market, and Honda the fourth best selling make.

1988-89 ACURA

INTEGRA — FOUR — A new front spoiler adorned the 1988 models, while Integra's 1.6-liter engine gained five horsepower via a compression boost. Otherwise, little change was evident except for the addition of an SE (Special Edition) coupe, introduced in spring 1988 and offered in that year only. Available only in black or white body color, the SE had special aero body elements including a rear spoiler and rocker (sill) extensions, plus a firmer suspension and power windows/mirrors.

LEGEND — V-6 — A larger (2.7-liter) V-6 engine went under Legend sedan hoods for 1988, along with new available safety features: a driver's airbag and anti-lock braking. Each of these additions arrived first on the Legend coupe, when it debuted in spring 1987, and became standard only on upper-level models initially. An electronically-controlled four-speed automatic transmission was available in both models, with normal and sport shift modes. For 1989, the Legend sedan adopted the twin-wishbone rear suspension used in the coupe. Legends were advertised as capable of 125-mph top speed and 0-60 mph acceleration in less than eight seconds.

I.D. DATA: See 1986-87 Honda breakdown.

Model	Body Type & Seating	Engine Type/CID	P.O.E. Price	Weight (lbs.)	Prod. Total
INTEGRA (1988 Models)					
RS	2-dr Hatch Cpe-5P	I4/97	10545	2313	Note 1
RS	4-dr Hatch Sed-5P	I4/97	11300	2390	Note 1
LS	2-dr Hatch Cpe-5P	I4/97	12240	2355	Note 1
LS	4-dr Hatch Sed-5P	I4/97	13030	2396	Note 1
SE	2-dr Hatch Cpe-5P	I4/97	13670	2388	Note 1
LEGEND (1988 Models)					
	2-dr Coupe-5P	V6/163	23096	3089	Note 1
L	2-dr Coupe-5P	V6/163	26578	N/A	Note 1
LS	2-dr Coupe-5P	V6/163	28377	N/A	Note 1
	4-dr Sedan-5P	V6/163	21010	3067	Note 1
Sunroof	4-dr Sedan-5P	V6/163	21848	N/A	Note 1
L	4-dr Sedan-5P	V6/163	24998	N/A	Note 1
LS	4-dr Sedan-5P	V6/163	27541	N/A	Note 1

Note 1: A total of 128,238 Acuras were sold in the U.S. during 1988, followed by 142,061 in 1989.

ENGINE DATA: BASE FOUR (Integra): Inline, dual-overhead-cam four-cylinder (16-valve). Aluminum alloy block and head. **Displacement:** 97 cu. in. (1590 cc). **Bore & Stroke:** 2.95 x 3.54 in. (75 x 90 mm). **Compression Ratio:** 9.5:1. **Brake Horsepower:** 118 at 6500 rpm. **Torque:** 103 lbs.-ft. at 5500 rpm. Port fuel injection.

BASE V-6 (Legend): Overhead-cam "vee" type six-cylinder (24-valve). Aluminum alloy block and head. **Displacement:** 163 cu. in. (2675 cc). **Bore & Stroke:** 3.42 x 2.95 in. (87 x 75 mm). **Compression Ratio:** 9.0:1. **Brake Horsepower:** 161 at 5900 rpm. **Torque:** 162 lbs.-ft. at 4500 rpm. Port fuel injection.

CHASSIS DATA: Wheelbase: (Integra cpe) 96.5 in.; (Integra sed) 99.2 in.; (Legend cpe) 106.5 in.; (Legend sed) 108.6 in. **Overall Length:** (Integra cpe) 168.5 in.; (Integra sed) 171.3 in.; (Legend cpe) 188.0 in.; (Legend sed) 189.4 in. **Height:** (Integra) 53.0 in.; (Legend cpe) 53.9 in.; (Legend sed) 54.7 in. **Width:** (Integra) 65.6 in.; (Legend cpe) 68.7 in.; (Legend sed) 68.3 in. **Front Tread:** (Integra) 55.9 in.; (Legend cpe) 59.1 in.; (Legend sed) 59.0 in. **Rear Tread:** (Integra) 56.5 in.; (Legend cpe) 59.1 in.; (Legend sed) 57.5 in.

TECHNICAL: Layout: front-engine, front-drive. **Transmission:** five-speed manual or four-speed (overdrive) automatic. **Steering:** power rack and pinion. **Suspension (front):** (Integra) MacPherson struts with torsion bars and anti-roll bar; (Legend) upper/lower control arms with coil springs and anti-roll bar. **Suspension (rear):** (Integra) beam axle with Panhard rods and anti-roll bar; (1988 Legend sedan) MacPherson struts with coil springs and anti-roll bar; (Legend cpe/1989 sedan) control arms with coil springs. **Brakes:** front/rear disc. **Body Construction:** steel unibody.

Manufacturer: Honda Motor Company Ltd., Tokyo, Japan.

Distributor: American Honda Motor Company, Gardena, California.

HISTORY: The 1988 Legends were introduced to the U.S. market in September 1987; Integras in January 1988 except (SE) in February 1988. *Car and Driver* named the Legend coupe one of its "10 Best Cars."

1990 HONDA

CIVIC — FOUR — Bumpers and taillamps were restyled this year in the Civic hatchback and sedan. Otherwise, little was new except for a new EX model to replace the former LX. The EX was powered by a 108-bhp 1.6-liter engine (as in the Si and 4WD wagon), versus 92 horsepower for the standard model with its 1.5-liter four and 70 bhp for the hatchback. A four-speed automatic transmission was available on all models except the base hatchback and Si.

CRX — FOUR — Little was new in the Honda two-seater except for new bumpers, front turn signals and taillamps, and a new instrument panel with larger gauges inside. All-disc brakes replaced the usual front-disc/rear-drum layout on the CRX Si, which carried a 108-bhp 1.6-liter engine and five-speed gearbox. The HF engine was rated 62 bhp; the base model, 92 horsepower.

ACCORD — FOUR — The Accord was reworked for the 1990 model year, and powered by a new 16-valve aluminum 2.2-liter engine. Wheelbase of the notchback coupe and four-door sedan grew to 107.1 inches, and flush-mounted headlamps replaced the former concealed units. The two-door hatchback body style was dropped. Dual exhausts

added five extra horsepower to the EX engine. The optional four-speed automatic transmission offered Normal and Sport shift modes.

PRELUDE — FOUR — Modestly restyled for a mid-year 1990 debut, Honda's sporty coupe carried a 1958-cc four-cylinder engine, as before, in single-cam carbureted (2.0 S) or twin-cam fuel-injected (2.0 Si) configuration. New this year in the Si, however, was a larger (2056-cc) 16-valve four, rated 140-horsepower. The new aluminum-alloy engine was cast with aluminum oxide and carbon fiber for strength. Wheelbase was 101 inches, and the Prelude measured 177.6 inches overall. Anti-lock braking and four-wheel steering were optional in the Si. The front air dam was redesigned as part of the front and rear restyling.

1990 Honda Prelude Si. (American Honda Motor Co. Inc.)

I.D. DATA: See 1986-87 Honda listing.

Model	Body Type & Seating	Engine Type/CID	P.O.E. Price	Weight (lbs.)	Prod. Total
CIVIC					
	2-dr Hatch-4P	I4/91	6635	2127	Note 1
DX	2-dr Hatch-4P	I4/91	8695	2165	Note 1
Si	2-dr Hatch-4P	I4/97	10245	2291	Note 1
DX	4-dr Sedan-4P	I4/91	9440	2262	Note 1
LX	4-dr Sedan-4P	I4/91	10450	2322	Note 1
EX	4-dr Sedan-4P	I4/97	11145	2374	Note 1
	4-dr Sta Wag-4P	I4/91	10325	2335	Note 1
4WD	4-dr Sta Wag-4P	I4/97	12410	2628	Note 1
CRX					
	2-dr Spt Hatch-2P	I4/91	9410	2103	Note 1
HF	2-dr Spt Hatch-2P	I4/91	9145	1967	Note 1
Si	2-dr Spt Hatch-2P	I4/97	11130	2174	Note 1
ACCORD					
DX	2-dr Coupe-4P	I4/132	12145	2738	Note 1
LX	2-dr Coupe-4P	I4/132	14695	2822	Note 1
EX	2-dr Coupe-4P	I4/132	16395	2888	Note 1
DX	4-dr Sedan-4P	I4/132	12345	2733	Note 1
LX	4-dr Sedan-4P	I4/132	14895	2857	Note 1
EX	4-dr Sedan-4P	I4/132	16595	2923	Note 1
PRELUDE					
2.0 S	2-dr Coupe-4P	I4/119	13945	2566	Note 1
2.0 Si	2-dr Coupe-4P	I4/119	14945	2639	Note 1
Si	2-dr Coupe-4P	I4/125	16965	2690	Note 1
Si (4WS)	2-dr Coupe-4P	I4/125	18450	2712	Note 1

Note 1: A total of 252,377 imported Hondas were sold in the U.S. during 1990.

ENGINE DATA: BASE FOUR (Civic hatchback): Inline overhead-cam four-cylinder (16-valve). Aluminum alloy block and head. **Displacement:** 91 cu. in. (1493 cc). **Bore & Stroke:** 2.95 x 3.32 in. (75 x 84 mm). **Compression Ratio:** 9.2:1. **Brake Horsepower:** 70 at 5500 rpm. **Torque:** 83 lbs.-ft. at 3000 rpm. Twin-injector fuel injection.

BASE FOUR (Civic DX/LX/2WD wagon, CRX): Same as 1493-cc four above, but — **Brake Horsepower:** 92 at 6000 rpm. **Torque:** 89 lbs.-ft. at 4500 rpm.

BASE FOUR (CRX HF): Same as 1493-cc four above, with eight-valve head configuration — **Compression Ratio:** 9.6:1. **Brake Horsepower:** 62 at 4500 rpm. **Torque:** 90 lbs.-ft. at 2000 rpm.

BASE FOUR (Civic Si/EX/4WD wagon, CRX Si): Inline overhead-cam four-cylinder (16-valve). Aluminum alloy block and head. **Displacement:** 97 cu. in. (1590 cc). **Bore & Stroke:** 2.95 x 3.54 in. (75 x 90 mm). **Compression Ratio:** 9.1:1. **Brake Horsepower:** 108 at 6000 rpm. **Torque:** 100 lbs.-ft. at 5000 rpm. Port (multi-point) fuel injection.

BASE FOUR (Accord DX/LX): Inline, overhead-cam four-cylinder (16-valve). Aluminum alloy block and head. **Displacement:** 132 cu. in. (2156 cc). **Bore & Stroke:** 3.35 x 3.74 in. (85 x 95 mm). **Compression Ratio:** 8.8:1. **Brake Horsepower:** 125 at 5200 rpm. **Torque:** 137 lbs.-ft. at 4000 rpm. Multi-point fuel injection.

BASE FOUR (Accord EX): Same as 2156-cc four above, except with dual exhausts — **Brake Horsepower:** 130 at 5200 rpm. **Torque:** 142 lbs.-ft. at 4200 rpm.

BASE FOUR (Prelude 2.0 S): Inline overhead-cam four-cylinder (12-valve). Aluminum alloy block and head. **Displacement:** 119.5 cu. in. (1958 cc). **Bore & Stroke:** 3.19 x 3.74 in. (81 x 95 mm). **Compression Ratio:** 9.1:1. **Brake Horsepower:** 104-105 at 5800 rpm. **Torque:** 111 lbs.-ft. at 4000 rpm. Multi-point fuel injection.

BASE FOUR (Prelude 2.0 Si): Inline, dual-overhead-cam four-cylinder (16-valve). Aluminum alloy block and head. **Displacement:** 119.5 cu. in. (1958 cc). **Bore & Stroke:** 3.19 x 3.74 in. (81 x 95 mm). **Compression Ratio:** 9.0:1. **Brake Horsepower:** 135 at 6200 rpm. **Torque:** 127 lbs.-ft. at 4000 rpm. Multi-point fuel injection.

BASE FOUR (Prelude Si): Inline, dual-overhead-cam four-cylinder (16-valve). Aluminum alloy block and head. **Displacement:** 125 cu. in. (2056 cc). **Bore & Stroke:** 3.27 x 3.74 in. (83 x 95 mm). **Compression Ratio:** 9.4:1. **Brake Horsepower:** 140 at 5800 rpm. **Torque:** 135 lbs.-ft. at 5000 rpm. Multi-point fuel injection.

CHASSIS DATA: Wheelbase: (Civic) 98.4 in.; (CRX) 90.6 in.; (Accord) 107.1 in.; (Prelude) 101.0 in. **Overall Length:** (Civic hatch) 157.1 in.; (Civic sedan) 168.8 in.; (Civic wagon) 161.7 in.; (CRX) 148.5 in.; (Accord) 184.8 in.; (Prelude) 177.6 in. **Height:** (Civic hatch) 52.5 in.; (Civic sedan) 53.5 in.; (Civic wagon) 56.1 in.; (CRX) 50.1 in.; (Accord cpe) 53.9 in.; (Accord sed) 54.7 in.; (Prelude) 51.0 in. **Width:** (Civic hatch) 66.3 in.; (Civic sedan) 66.7 in.; (Civic wagon) 66.1 in.; (CRX) 65.9 in.; (Accord) 67.9 in.; (Prelude) 67.3 in. **Front Tread:** (Civic/CRX) 57.1 in.; (Civic wagon) 56.8-56.9 in.; (Accord) 58.1 in.; (Prelude) 58.3 in. **Rear Tread:** (Civic/CRX) 57.3 in.; (Civic wagon) 57.2 in.; (Accord) 58.3 in.; (Prelude) 57.9 in.

TECHNICAL: Layout: front-engine, front-drive. **Transmission:** (Civic) four- or five-speed manual, or four-speed automatic; (Civic 4WD) six-speed manual or four-speed automatic; (others) five-speed manual or four-speed automatic. **Steering:** rack and pinion. **Brakes:** front disc, rear drum except (CRX Si and Prelude) front/rear disc. **Body Construction:** steel unibody.
Manufacturer: Honda Motor Company Ltd., Tokyo, Japan.
Distributor: American Honda Motor Company, Gardena, California.
HISTORY: Honda's 1990 models were introduced to the U.S. market in October 1989 except (Accord cpe) December 1989 and (Prelude) March 1990.

1990 ACURA

1990 Acura Legend Coupe LS.

INTEGRA — FOUR — The Integra was reworked for the 1990 model year, made longer, lower, wider, and more powerful. A twin-cam 1.8-liter engine rated 130 bhp provided the power. The suspension was new, as were all major components. Wheelbases grew to 100.4 inches for the coupe, 102.4 for the sedan. A new four-door sedan replaced the former four-door hatchback, offered along with a two-door hatchback coupe. Integra's optional four-speed automatic transmission now had a Sport mode with higher shift points. Anti-lock braking was standard on GS models.

LEGEND — V-6 — Taillamp lenses were modified this year for the Legend, mirrors were painted body-color, and seats were deeper. Coupes got a restyled grille, and the LS coupe added a rear spoiler. All LS models had a burled walnut center console. Otherwise, the Legend was essentially a carryover. Anti-lock braking was standard on L/LS models.

I.D. DATA: See 1986-87 Honda breakdown.

Model	Body Type & Seating	Engine Type/CID	P.O.E. Price	Weight (lbs.)	Prod. Total
INTEGRA					
RS	2-dr Hatch Cpe-5P	I4/112	11950	2549	Note 1
RS	4-dr Sedan-5P	I4/112	12850	2604	Note 1
LS	2-dr Hatch Cpe-5P	I4/112	13725	2608	Note 1
LS	4-dr Sedan-5P	I4/112	14545	2639	Note 1
GS	2-dr Hatch Cpe-5P	I4/112	15825	2639	Note 1
GS	4-dr Sedan-5P	I4/112	15950	6506	Note 1
LEGEND					
	2-dr Coupe-5P	V6/163	24760	3139	Note 1
L	2-dr Coupe-5P	V6/163	27325	3139	Note 1
LS	2-dr Coupe-5P	V6/163	30690	3139	Note 1
	4-dr Sedan-5P	V6/163	22600	3170	Note 1
L	4-dr Sedan-5P	V6/163	25900	3170	Note 1
LS	4-dr Sedan-5P	V6/163	29610	3170	Note 1

Note 1: A total of 138,384 Acuras were sold in the U.S. during 1990.

ENGINE DATA: BASE FOUR (Integra): Inline, dual-overhead-cam four-cylinder. Aluminum alloy block and head (16-valve). **Displacement:** 112 cu. in. (1834 cc). **Bore & Stroke:** 3.19 x 3.50 in. (81 x 88.9 mm). **Compression Ratio:** 9.2:1. **Brake Horsepower:** 130 at 6000 rpm. **Torque:** 121 lbs.-ft. at 5000 rpm. Port fuel injection.
BASE V-6 (Legend): Overhead-cam "vee" type six-cylinder (24-valve). Aluminum alloy block and head. **Displacement:** 163 cu. in. (2675 cc). **Bore & Stroke:** 3.42 x 2.95 in. (87 x 75 mm). **Compression Ratio:** 9.0:1. **Brake Horsepower:** 160 at 5900 rpm. **Torque:** 162 lbs.-ft. at 4500 rpm. Port fuel injection.

CHASSIS DATA: Wheelbase: (Integra cpe) 100.4 in.; (Integra sed) 102.4 in.; (Legend cpe) 106.5 in.; (Legend sed) 108.7 in. **Overall Length:** (Integra cpe) 172.9 in.; (Integra sed) 176.5 in.; (Legend cpe) 188.0 in.; (Legend sed) 190.6 in. **Height:** (Integra cpe) 52.2 in.; (Integra sed) 52.8 in.; (Legend cpe) 53.9 in.; (Legend sed) 54.7 in. **Width:** (Integra) 67.4 in.; (Integra sed) 68.7 in.; (Legend sed) 68.9 in. **Front Tread:** (Integra) 58.1 in.; (Legend cpe) 59.1 in.; (Legend sed) 59.1 in. **Rear Tread:** (Integra) 58.1 in.; (Legend cpe) 59.1 in.; (Legend sed) 57.5 in.

TECHNICAL: Layout: front-engine, front-drive. **Transmission:** five-speed manual or four-speed (overdrive) automatic. **Steering:** power rack and pinion. **Brakes:** front/rear disc; anti-locking on Integra GS and Legend L/LS. **Body Construction:** steel unibody.

Manufacturer: Honda Motor Company Ltd., Tokyo, Japan.
Distributor: American Honda Motor Company, Gardena, California.

HISTORY: The 1988 Integras were introduced to the U.S. market in May 1989; Legends in September 1989.

POSTSCRIPT: Acura's new NSX mid-engine, two-seat sports car was unveiled at the 1989 Chicago Auto Show and introduced in summer 1990 as an early 1991 model. A 2977-cc aluminum V-6 engine with dual overhead cams and four valves per cylinder delivered 270 horsepower at 7100 rpm, and 210 pound-feet of torque at 5300 rpm. The engine featured variable valve timing and lift control, to boost low-end performance. Compression ratio was 10.2:1. Wearing a sleek all-aluminum unibody with 0.32 drag coefficient, atop an all-aluminum fully-independent suspension, the NSX included anti-lock braking and traction control. An NSX was tested by the factory at speeds past 165 mph, could accelerate to 60 mph in less than 6.0 seconds, and could run the quarter-mile in less than 14 seconds. Interior features included a driver's airbag, leather-trimmed power seats, automatic climate control, and an Acura/BOSE music system. Price tag for this near-supercar was $60,000 with a five-speed manual gearbox, and $64,000 with four-speed automatic. With automatic, the engine output dropped to 252 bhp at 6600 rpm. Initial body colors were Formula Red, Berlina Black, and Sebring Silver, with a black or ivory interior. Honda/Acura claimed the NSX as the world's first aluminum production car.

HOTCHKISS

Not many European manufacturers had an American background. Hotchkiss, though a French company, was the exception. Not only was it founded by an American (Benjamin B. Hotchkiss), but the firm's head from 1928 to 1950 was British. Hotchkiss was a munitions maker during the American Civil War before moving to France in 1870, entering armaments production five years later. Orders fell during the years following Hotchkiss' death in 1885, prompting the company to turn to the production of automobile parts. Late in 1903, at the Paris Salon, the first Hotchkiss car appeared, powered by a four-cylinder T-head engine. Its round honeycomb radiator became a virtual trademark for the company. Hotchkiss drive (using an open propeller shaft and "live" axle) was first used in 1905, and would later appear on many other makes as well. Sagging sales led the company to shift to smaller models with L-head four-cylinder engines in the years before World War I. Offerings between the wars included a 4-liter AF, a 2.4-liter 12CV AM and, starting in 1929, a 3-liter, six-cylinder AM80 model. That led to the 3.5-liter Hotchkiss, produced during the 1930s and resumed after World War II. Race victories at the Monte Carlo Rally came to Hotchkiss six times: four times during the 1930s, and again in 1949 and '50. Production of smaller models was enhanced by the acquisition of the Amilcar company in 1937. Nationalization of the French munitions industry hurt the company badly. So did British bombing during the war.

Hotchkiss reentered automobile production after World War II with the same 3.5-liter car that had been sold in the 1930s, marketed as the 686. Sales were sluggish at first, but helped by the resumption of a 2.3-liter four-cylinder model 684. Hotchkiss would remain less than a footnote in American automotive history except for what turned out to be the company's best-known model: the smaller Gregoire, designed by J.A. Gregoire. Only about 180 were built, and few ever reached American shores; but the unorthodox sedan gained a fair amount of publicity in the early 1950s because of its aluminum construction and front-drive layout. (Gregoire was partial to front-wheel drive, having built a Tracta front-drive racer back in 1926; and he got the idea for a lightweight cast-metal chassis in the 1930s.) That modest level of production did nothing to boost the company's profits. Merging with Delahaye in 1954 didn't help either, and passenger cars departed during that year. Until 1970, however, the company continued to produce trucks and Jeeps.

1949-54 HOTCHKISS

1954 Hotchkiss Gregoire convertible.

GREGOIRE — FOUR — Ideas sometimes take time to come to fruition. So it was with the Gregoire, designed and put into prototype form in 1949 but suffering production delays into 1951. While the prototype carried a 2.0-liter four-cylinder engine, the horizontally-opposed powerplant grew to 2.2 liters by the time actual cars came off the line. All four wheels on the front-drive layout had independent suspension. Appearance of the streamlined fastback two-door was reminiscent of some American sedanettes of the immediate postwar period, but with a dramatically curved wraparound rear window and long rear quarter windows. A vee-shaped, squarish grille with rounded upper molding section contained a pattern of horizontal bars with a single center vertical bar and round emblem. Headlamps were mounted somewhat low on the fenders, with auxiliary lights below. Doors held vent panes, and rear fenders could have skirts. A split windshield was used. Most striking of the car's features wasn't its appearance, however, but its construction method, which made use of light alloys for nearly every component. The chassis/body consisted of cast aluminum side members and a one-piece aluminum alloy dashboard. Five separate chassis sections bolted together, along with the crossmembers. Suspension/steering components attached to a cast metal crankcase bracket, while the engine actually hung from the front of the frame. The four-speed transmission included overdrive. With a top speed around 93 mph, the Gregoire was able to deliver fuel mileage of at least 23 mpg on the highway.

I.D. DATA: Not available.

Model	Body Type & Seating	Engine Type/CID	P.O.E. Price	Weight (lbs.)	Prod. Total
GREGOIRE					
	2-dr Sedan-4/5P	H4/133	N/A	2376	180

1954 Hotchkiss Gregoire coupe. (JC)

ENGINE DATA: BASE FOUR: Horizontally-opposed, overhead-valve four-cylinder. **Displacement:** 133 cu. in. (2180 cc). **Bore & Stroke:** 3.54 x 3.38 in. (89.9 x 85.9 mm). **Compression Ratio:** 6.5:1. **Brake Horsepower:** 70 at 4000 rpm. **Torque:** 108 lbs.-ft. at 2000 rpm. Three main bearings.
Note: First announced engine was a 1998-cc (122-cid) four.

CHASSIS DATA: Wheelbase: 98 in. **Overall Length:** 181 in. **Height:** 61 in. **Width:** 68 in. **Front Tread:** 57 in. **Rear Tread:** 52 in. **Standard Tires:** 5.50x16.

TECHNICAL: Layout: front-engine, front-drive. **Transmission:** four-speed manual. **Suspension (front):** independent; coil springs. **Suspension (rear):** independent; coil springs. **Brakes:** front/rear drum. **Body Construction:** aluminum body/chassis.

PERFORMANCE: Top Speed: 93-95 mph. **Fuel Mileage:** 23 + mpg.
Manufacturer: S.A. des Anciens Establissements Hotchkiss, St. Denis-Sur-Seine, France.

ADDITIONAL MODELS: During the late 1940s, Hotchkiss also produced a four-cylinder (2.3-liter) model 684 and a six-cylinder (3.5-liter) model 686 sedan. Those model designations changed to 13.50 Anjou and 20.50 Anjou in the early 1950s. A 20.50 Grand Sport two-door sedan also was offered, with more powerful (130-bhp) six-cylinder engine.

HISTORY: The revised Gregoire appeared at the Geneva (Switzerland) auto show in 1951, with first deliveries planned for that fall. The Hotchkiss-Gregoire chassis also was used for a prototype turbine-powered car, the Socema-Gregoire, which appeared at the 1952 Paris Salon. Its aerodynamic body was claimed to have a drag coefficient of less than 0.20. A four-passenger Hotchkiss-Gregoire convertible was announced in 1953.

POSTSCRIPT: In 1956, after production of the Hotchkiss-Gregoire sedan had eased to a halt, a Gregoire two-passenger sports car was announced. The aluminum convertible's chassis/body consisted of six members bolted together, reinforced with steel cross-members. Its supercharged 2.2-liter (133-cid) engine delivered 130 horsepower at 4500 rpm, with 6.9:1 compression. A variable-rate suspension was used, and the engine was mounted ahead of the front axle (cantilever style) for front-wheel drive. The convertible was expected to sell for about $6000 in the U.S., and debuted at the "Sports Cars in Review" show at the Henry Ford Museum in Michigan, early in 1956.

HRG

While most European automakers could hardly wait to move into the modern era after World War II ended, HRG (sometimes spelled H.R.G.) took a different tack. After producing less than three dozen stark, down-to-business sports cars since the company's founding in 1935, they simply continued with more of the same, carrying on the prewar design. At the same time, they created a modern Aerodynamic model; but when that one failed to attract favorable attention (especially in the U.S.), HRG returned to its roots in the traditional sports car arena.

The company's first car had been a basic two-seater, powered by a 1.5-liter, four-cylinder Meadows overhead-valve engine, rated 58 horsepower and capable of hitting 90 mph. Soon came a switch to a similarly-dimensioned but more powerful overhead-cam Singer engine. Racing successes included a second-place finish (in its class) at the 1937 Le Mans course. A total of 25 cars of the 1.5-liter class were built before the war, plus eight companion 1100 models that carried a smaller, 1074-cc Singer overhead-cam engine. These were rough-looking, rough-riding sports cars, whose superior cornering abilities made up for the lack of amenities.

Production of the same two models continued in 1946, with neither the 1100 nor the 1500 having changed noticeably. An Aerodynamic version of the 1500 also was built, until 1950, on the same prewar-based chassis. Eye-opening, though not the most attractive of modern designs, it failed to find many customers (and those that sold tended to deteriorate later on). A few fared well in competition, however.

Rally and racing successes continued, including two class wins at the 1949 Le Mans event. A year earlier, half a dozen HRGs had entered the French Alpine Rally, taking home several prizes. Sales did not progress as well. Only 40 cars were sold in 1948, slipping to just 11 by 1950.

In 1953, a new Singer-based 1100 WS model appeared, with a shorter-stroke four-cylinder engine. Only about a dozen were produced. Two years later, the company had high hopes for its redesigned, modern Mark II sports car with alloy body and tubular frame, its twin-cam engine delivering more than 100 horsepower. Its curvacously contemporoary race-car styling included oversize wheel openings, and the car was expected to sell for around $4000 in the U.S. Only two or three were built, however. Both the old and the new styles faded away in 1956, as the company turned away from production of automobiles and into the manufacture of components. The HRG firm expired completely in 1965, after producing one more experimental prototype a year earlier.

1946-56 HRG

1946 HRG roadster.

1100/1500 — FOUR — The HRG two-seaters that appeared after the war looked nearly identical to its prewar forerunner: separate fenders, square upright appearance, cutaway doors, and austere interior. Largely assembled by hand, with bodies by various coachbuilders, the HRGs also had prewar-level brakes (mechanical) and suspensions (rigid axles and leaf springs at both ends). The two-door aluminum body had a fold-flat windshield and ground clearance of 6.5 inches. The 1100 rode a shorter wheelbase than the 1500, and carried a smaller engine, but was similar in appearance. As in prewar years, the engine sat well back in the frame. Many variations from basic equipment were possible, with different wheel sizes and fender shapes, an extra spare tire, and interior modifications to suit a specific driver.

Built on the same narrow chassis as the traditional two-seaters, the Aerodynamic 1500 of the late 1940s had a streamlined full-width "envelope" body instead of the customary slim shape. A full set of outriggers attached that body to the car's frame.

1947 HRG roadster.

I.D. DATA: Not available.

Model	Body Type & Seating	Engine Type/CID	P.O.E. Price	Weight (lbs.)	Prod. Total
1946-53					
1100 (S)	2-dr Roadster-2P	I4/65	N/A	1512	49
1500 (W)	2-dr Roadster-2P	I4/91	2450	1568	104
Aero	2-dr Roadster-2P	I4/91	N/A	1792	40

Production Note: Production totals are approximate and include a few models built just before World War II. Some sources indicate a total of 187 cars (138 with the 1500 engine).

Price Note: 1500 price shown is FOB factory in 1952; HRG prices in U.S. ran around $2800.

1953-56 (SM)					
15002	2-dr Roadster-2P	I4/91	2965	1568	12

Note: Price and production are approximate.

ENGINE DATA: BASE FOUR (1100): Inline, overhead-cam four-cylinder. **Displacement:** 65.5 cu. in. (1074 cc). **Bore & Stroke:** 2.36 x 3.74 in. (60 x 95 mm). **Compression Ratio:** 7.75:1. **Brake Horsepower:** 40 at 5100 rpm. Three main bearings. Two SU sidedraft carburetors. 12-volt electrical (coil or magneto ignition).

BASE FOUR (early 1500): Inline, overhead-cam four-cylinder (modified Singer). **Displacement:** 91.3 cu. in. (1496 cc). **Bore & Stroke:** 2.68 x 4.06 in. (68 x 103 mm). **Compression Ratio:** 7.0:1. **Brake Horsepower:** 65 at 4800 rpm. Three main bearings. Two SU sidedraft carburetors. 12-volt electrical.

BASE FOUR (late 1500, 1953-56): Inline, overhead-cam four-cylinder. **Displacement:** 91.4 cu. in. (1496 cc). **Bore & Stroke:** 2.87 x 3.52 in. (73 x 89 mm). **Compression Ratio:** 7.5:1. **Brake Horsepower:** 61-65 at 4800 rpm. **Torque:** 77 lbs.-ft. at 2800 rpm. Two downdraft carburetors. 12-volt electrical.

1954 HRG roadster.

CHASSIS DATA: Wheelbase: (1100) 99.75 in.; (1500) 103 in. **Overall Length:** (1100) 142.5 in.; (1500) 144.0 in.; (Aero) 156 in. **Height:** (1500) 52 in. **Width:** 55 in. exc. (Aero) 58 in. **Front Tread:** 48.0 in. **Rear Tread:** 45.0 in. Wheel type: center-lock wire. **Standard Tires:** 4.75x17 or (later) 5.50x16.

TECHNICAL: Layout: front-engine, rear-drive. **Transmission:** four-speed manual (floor lever). **Standard Final Drive Ratio:** (1100) 4.55:1; (1500) 4.00:1 or 4.55:1. Other ratios available. **Steering:** Marles. **Suspension (front):** rigid tubular axle with quarter-elliptic leaf springs. **Suspension (rear):** rigid axle with semi-elliptic leaf springs. **Brakes:** cable-activated mechanical (Girling hydraulic optional on later models). **Body Construction:** aluminum body on pressed rail chassis. **Fuel Tank:** 10.8 gallons. exc. (Aero) 13.2 gallons.

PERFORMANCE: Top Speed: (1100) 75-80 mph; (1500) 87-90 mph; (Aero) 90-100 mph. **Acceleration (0-60 mph):** (late 1500) 13.5 seconds. Early 1500 did 0-50 mph in 11.2 seconds. **Acceleration (quarter-mile):** (1100) 21.6 seconds; (1500) 19 to 20.4 seconds.

1956 HRG roadster.

PRODUCTION/SALES: Approximately five HRGs were sold in the U.S. in 1949, and one in 1950. About 26 were imported to the U.S. in all.

Manufacturer: HRG Engineering Co. Ltd., Tolworth, Surrey, England.

U.S. Distributor: Jack Wherry, Maquoketa, Iowa.

HISTORY: HRG stood for the initials of the company's three founders in 1935: E.A. Halford, Guy H. Robins and H.R. Godfrey (whose initials alone also happen to be 'HRG'). HRG's primary rival in the postwar era was the MG TC and TD, which were cheaper and available in greater quantities in Britain. Especially when MG switched to front coil springs, the HRG's primitive (and painful) suspension became an ever greater drawback.

HUMBER

Thomas Humber had been building bicycles in Britain for more than 15 years by the time he formed Humber & Co. Ltd. in 1887. While focusing operations on the then-new "safety" bicycle, the new firm also turned to tricycles; and to at least one self-propelled vehicle, powered by compressed air. Thomas had retired a few years before the emergence of a prototype electric automobile in 1895, which did not enter production. By that time, Humber bicycles also were being built in America. At the turn of the

295

century, however, the British firm had turned to motorcycles, and was preparing its first production motorcar. That was followed by a surprisingly broad variety of models, bearing two- or four-cylinder engines (punctuated by a single-cylinder model in 1904, the popular Humberette). T-head engines were the norm at first, switching to side valves around 1911. Production of airplanes also began around that time, followed (just before war broke out) by the Humberette V-twin cyclecar. Motorcycles remained in production as late as 1930, and bicycles a year or two longer. In sum, Humber's early history was a diverse one, and in 1930 the company produced more than 6,000 automobiles.

Two years earlier, Humber had bought the Hillman organization and, by 1932, Rootes Motor Ltd. took over operations. Configurations of the side-valve (L-head) engines were modified in the 1930s, replacing the early versions that had put the intake valves above the exhausts. During the Depression decade, Humber established itself as a strong supplier of motorcars to the upper middle class of Britain. Adoption of such technologies as the automatic clutch, synchromesh transmission, and freewheeling helped enhance its appeal. Both the Snipe and Pullman badges arrived in 1930, on six-cylinder Humbers, which grew from original 3498 cc to 4088 cc displacement in 1936. Snipes saw considerable service during World War II as staff vehicles, and served as the basis for a wartime 4x4.

Offerings after the war came in three forms: the four-cylinder Hawk, which evolved from the prewar Hillman Fourteen; and the six-cylinder Snipe sedan and Pullman limousine. Humbers were restyled for a modern look for 1949, with a steering-column gearshift lever. Overhead-valve engines arrived in 1953, by which time about 800 postwar Humbers had been sold in the U.S. Americans took a particular fancy to the luxurious interiors of the British saloons. The stately, dignified demeanor of the early postwar models faded away somewhat with the appearance of a fully restyled Hawk in 1957, especially when the Super Snipe badge went on the same smaller body. An Imperial limousine re-emerged in the mid-1960s, but by 1967, at the time when Chrysler was taking over the Rootes Group, only the Hawk remained. A year later, that was gone, leaving only the new Humber Sceptre which was little more than a fancy edition of Hillman's Super Minx, rarely seen in the U.S. The grand old name disappeared completely in 1976.

1946-48 HUMBER

1947 Humber Hawk four-door.

HAWK — Mk I/II — FOUR — The name was new but the body was not, having been taken from the final prewar Hillman Fourteen. A four-cylinder, 1944-cc L-head engine provided the power, delivering 56 bhp. Styling of the six-window saloon body was strictly in the prewar model, with a slanted vee-shaped vertical-bar grille, separately-mounted headlamps, rear-hinged ("suicide") front doors, and flat one-piece windshield. A 'Hawk' nameplate stood on hood sides, ahead of the long horizontal air vents. The Mark II version, introduced in 1947, replaced the original floor gearshift with a steering-column lever.

SNIPE — SIX — Appearance of the first postwar Snipe was similar to the new Hawk, since it wore the same basic body. Under the hood was a six-cylinder, L-head engine displacing 2731 cc and putting out 65 horsepower. A 'Snipe' nameplate went on the hood sides.

SUPER SNIPE — Mk I — SIX — Although it looked about the same as the Hawk and Snipe, the Mark I Super Snipe carried a bigger six-cylinder powerplant: 4.1 liters, delivering 100 bhp. A 'Super Snipe' nameplate on the hood was the major identifying feature.

PULLMAN — Mk I — SIX — Humber's limousine was powered by the same 4.1-liter six-cylinder engine as the Super Snipe, and was similar in overall appearance to its mates, but rode a longer (127.5-inch) wheelbase.

I.D. DATA: Hawk chassis serial number is stamped on the chassis frame side member, near the front shock absorber; and on a plate on the firewall, under the hood. Snipe chassis serial number is stamped on a plate on the firewall. Pullman chassis number is at the front of the left chassis member. Starting serial number: (Hawk Mk I) 2710001; (Hawk Mk II) 5800001; (Snipe) 4710001; (Super Snipe Mk I) 8710001; (Pullman Mk I) 6710001. Hawk engine number (which may be identical to the chassis number) is stamped on the chamfered edge of the block.
Breakdown of the seven-digit serial number (beginning with Hawk Mk II) is as follows: First digit is the model ('5' = Hawk; '4' = Snipe; '1' = Super Snipe; '6' = Pullman). Second digit is the year of manufacture ('7' = 1947 or before; '8' = 1948). Digits 3-7 are the sequential serial number. A three-letter suffix is added: letter one indicates destination ('H' = home market; 'L' = export with left-hand drive; 'R' = export with RHD); letter two is body style ('S' = saloon; 'L' = limo; 'E' = Estate Car); letter three indicates a car of standard configuration ('O') or with some deviation ('X'). An additional suffix ('7' or '9') may indicate Snipe axle ratio (3.7:1 or 3.9:1).

Model	Body Type & Seating	Engine Type/CID	P.O.E. Price	Weight (lbs.)	Prod. Total
HAWK					
Mk I	4-dr Saloon	I4/119	N/A	3021	Note 1
Mk II	4-dr Saloon	I4/119	N/A	3021	Note 1
SNIPE					
	4-dr Saloon	I6/167	N/A	3420	Note 1
SUPER SNIPE					
Mk I	4-dr Saloon	I6/249	N/A	3505	Note 1
PULLMAN					
Mk I	4-dr Limo	I6/249	N/A	4190	Note 1

Note 1: Only two Humbers were known to have been sold in the U.S. during 1948.

ENGINE DATA: BASE FOUR (Hawk): Inline, L-head four-cylinder. **Displacement:** 118.6 cu. in. (1944 cc). **Bore & Stroke:** 2.95 x 4.33 in. (75 x 110 mm). **Compression Ratio:** 6.4:1. **Brake Horsepower:** 56 at 3800 rpm. Three main bearings. Solid valve lifters. Stromberg downdraft carburetor.

BASE SIX (Snipe): Inline, L-head six-cylinder. **Displacement:** 166.6 cu. in. (2731 cc). **Bore & Stroke:** 2.74 x 4.72 in. (69.5 x 120 mm). **Compression Ratio:** 6.4:1. **Brake Horsepower:** 65 at 3500 rpm. Four main bearings. Solid valve lifters. Stromberg downdraft carburetor.

BASE SIX (Super Snipe, Pullman): Inline, L-head six-cylinder. **Displacement:** 249.2 cu. in. (4086 cc). **Bore & Stroke:** 3.35 x 4.72 in. (85 x 120 mm). **Compression Ratio:** 6.25:1. **Brake Horsepower:** 100 at 3400 rpm. Four main bearings. Solid valve lifters. Stromberg downdraft carburetor.

CHASSIS DATA: Wheelbase: (Hawk/Snipe) 114 in.; (Pullman) 127.5 in. **Overall Length:** (Hawk/Snipe) 180 in.; (Pullman) 197.5 in. **Width:** (Hawk/Snipe) 69 in.; (Pullman) 73 in. **Rear Tread:** (Hawk/Snipe) 56 in.; (Pullman) 61 in. **Standard Tires:** (Hawk) 5.75x16; (Snipe) 6.00x16; (Pullman) 7.00x16.

TECHNICAL: Layout: front-engine, rear-drive. **Transmission:** four-speed manual; floor lever or (later) column lever. **Standard Final Drive Ratio:** (Hawk) 4.78:1; (Snipe) 4.67:1; (Super Snipe) 4.09:1. **Suspension (front):** transverse leaf spring. **Suspension (rear):** rigid axle, semi-elliptic leaf springs. **Brakes:** front/rear drum. **Body Construction:** steel body on steel frame.

PERFORMANCE: Top Speed: (Hawk) 64 mph; (Snipe) 72 mph. **Acceleration (quarter-mile):** (Hawk) 25.6 sec.; (Snipe) 24.4 sec.

Manufacturer: Humber Ltd., Ryton-on-Dunsmore, Warwickshire, England (part of Rootes Motors Ltd.).

Distributor: Rootes Motors Inc., Long Island City, New York.

HISTORY: First postwar models were introduced in England in August 1945.

1949-50 HUMBER

HAWK — Mk III — FOUR — A new full-width body gave the four-cylinder Humber a totally new and modern look, while a new coil-spring front suspension improved its riding qualities. Headlamps were now built into the fenders, with parking lights incorporated in the same housing. A smaller vertical-bar grille at the center, in a rather flat front-end panel, was flanked by smaller horizontal-bar grilles down in the fender aprons. An Opticurve windshield and rear window improved visibility over the prewar-style bodies. Separate parking lights were added below the headlamps for the 1949 model year. The roomy interior held up to six people, propelled by a 1944-cc four-cylinder engine delivering 56 bhp. A "Synchromatic" (trademark of Humber) steering-column shift lever controlled a four-speed manual transmission. Standard equipment included self-canceling trafficators (turn signals), twin tail/stop lamps, dual wind-tone horns, and a courtesy roof lamp. Standard body colors included Black or Pastel Green with buff upholstery, and jewelescent Satin Bronze with red upholstery.

SUPER SNIPE — Mk II — SIX — Appearance of the restyled six-cylinder Humber was similar to the Hawk up front, but not quite as modern overall. Styling was said to be "modern yet dignified." Running boards were still evident. Its main center grille was made up of vertical bars, protruding forward at the center; flanked by auxiliary grilles on either side, made up of horizontal bars. Round parking lights stood directly below the built-in headlamps. Front doors had adjustable quarter windows.

"Evenkeel" independent transvese-leaf front springs were used, as opposed to the Hawk's new coil springs. At the rear were long semi-elliptic leaf springs and an anti-sway bar. A Synchromatic fingertip gearshift controlled the fully-synchronized four-speed manual transmission. Powerplant was the same as before: a 4.1-liter, L-head, rated at 100 horsepower. Super Snipe was claimed to be a full six-seater, capable of going from 5 to 80 mph in top gear. Wide front doors contained armrests. The fully adjustable, wide front bench seat also had a folding center armrest, while the back seat had one center folding and two side armrests. Standard equipment included twin taillamps with stop lights and backup lights, a cigar lighter, dashboard clock, courtesy roof light, dual wind-tone horns, self-canceling trafficators, and two tool kits in a separate storage compartment. Standard colors included Black with buff or light fawn leather upholstery; Steel Grey with grey leather upholstery; and Almond Green with buff leather upholstery.

Sales brochures referred to the alternate restyled six-cylinder model as "the Humber Super Snipe Touring Limousine." Its vertically-operated glass division window was flanked by side curved panels.

PULLMAN/IMPERIAL — Mk II — SIX — Humber's limousine also gained a new (and longer) body for 1949, but appearance differed considerably from the more modern Hawk/Snipe. Pullmans now had built-in headlamps and an alligator-style hood, but fenders continued the separately-mounted look. A steering-column gearshift lever was now standard. Models without a division window were called Imperials; those intended for a chauffeur were Pullmans.

1949 Humber Super Snipe two-door convertible. (Sotheby's)

I.D. DATA: Hawk chassis serial number is stamped on the chassis frame side member, near the front shock absorber; and on a plate on the firewall, under the hood. Snipe chassis serial number is stamped on a plate on the firewall. Pullman chassis number is at the front of the left chassis member. Starting serial number: (Hawk) 5900001; (Snipe) 8800001; (Pullman) 9800001. Breakdown of the seven-digit serial number and suffixes is similar to 1946-48; see that listing. Hawk engine number (which may be identical to the chassis number) is stamped on the chamfered edge of the block.

Model	Body Type & Seating	Engine Type/CID	P.O.E. Price	Weight (lbs.)	Prod. Total
HAWK					
Mk III	4-dr Saloon-6P	I4/119	N/A	2652	Note 1
SUPER SNIPE					
Mk II	4-dr Saloon-6P	I6/249	N/A	3703	Note 1
PULLMAN/IMPERIAL					
Mk II	4-dr Limo-7/8P	I6/249	N/A	4531	Note 1

Note 1: No more than three Humbers were known to have been sold in the U.S. during 1949, followed by about 89 cars during 1950. Weight Note: Hawk/Snipe figures shown are "dry" weight (no fuel or water).

1950 Humber Super Snipe saloon.

ENGINE DATA: BASE FOUR (Hawk): Inline, L-head four-cylinder. Cast iron block. **Displacement:** 118.6 cu. in. (1944 cc). **Bore & Stroke:** 2.95 x 4.33 in. (75 x 110 mm). **Compression Ratio:** 6.4:1. **Brake Horsepower:** 56 at 3800 rpm. Three main bearings. Solid valve lifters. Stromberg downdraft carburetor.

BASE SIX (Super Snipe, Pullman): Inline, L-head six-cylinder. Cast iron block and alloy head. **Displacement:** 249.2 cu. in. (4086 cc). **Bore & Stroke:** 3.35 x 4.72 in. (85 x 120 mm). **Compression Ratio:** 6.25:1. **Brake Horsepower:** 100 at 3400 rpm. Four main bearings. Solid valve lifters. Stromberg downdraft carburetor.

CHASSIS DATA: Wheelbase: (Hawk) 105 in.; (Snipe) 117.5 in.; (Pullman) 131 in. **Overall Length:** (Hawk) 174 in.; (Snipe) 187.5 in.; (Pullman) 210.25 in. **Width:** (Hawk) 70 in.; (Snipe) 74.5 in.; (Pullman) 74.5 in. **Front Tread:** (Hawk) 56 in.; (Snipe) 57.9 in.; (Pullman) 57.9 in. **Rear Tread:** (Hawk) 57 in.; (Snipe) 61.0 in.; (Pullman) 62.2 in. **Wheel Type:** "easi-clean" disc with chromed center plates. **Standard Tires:** (Hawk) 5.50x15; (Snipe) Dunlop Fort 6.50x16; (Pullman) 7.00x16.

TECHNICAL: Layout: front-engine, rear-drive. **Transmission:** four-speed manual; column shift lever. Hawk overall gear ratios: (1st) 16.14:1; (2nd) 11.24:1; (3rd) 6.78:1; (4th) 4.55:1; (rev) 21.62:1. Snipe overall gear ratios: (1st) 15.95:1; (2nd) 9.59:1; (3rd) 5.89:1; (4th) 4.09:1; (rev) 16.91:1. **Standard Final Drive Ratio:** (Hawk) 4.55:1; (Snipe/Pullman) 4.09:1. **Steering:** Burman worm and nut (recirculating ball); right or left-hand drive. **Suspension (front):** (Hawk) coil springs; (others) transverse leaf springs. **Suspension (rear):** rigid axle with semi-elliptic leaf springs and torsion-bar sway eliminator. **Brakes:** Lockheed hydraulic, front/rear drum. **Body Construction:** steel body on separate welded box-girder steel frame.

MAJOR OPTIONS: "His Master's Voice" radio. Clayton heater.

PERFORMANCE: Top Speed: (Hawk) about 74 mph; (Snipe) about 82 mph. **Acceleration (quarter-mile):** (Hawk) 24.1 sec.; (Snipe) 21.9 sec.

Manufacturer: Humber Ltd., Ryton-on-Dunsmore, Warwickshire, England (part of Rootes Motors Ltd.).

Distributor: Rootes Motors Inc., Long Island City, New York (export agent).

HISTORY: Hawk introduced October 1948; Super Snipe, September 1948.

1951 HUMBER

HAWK — Mk IV — FOUR — Though similar in appearance to the Mark III, with separate parking lights below the built-in headlamps, the revised Hawk carried a larger-displacement engine. The new 138-cid (2267-cc) L-head four delivered 58 horsepower (two more than its predecessor). Tires grew to 6.40x15 size. As before, the Hawk center grille contained many vertical chrome strips, and was flanked by twin side grille openings with horizontal strips. Parking lights stood below the built-in headlamps. Front fenders extended into the body, and running boards were concealed. All doors were hinged at the front.

SUPER SNIPE — Mk III — SIX — Appearance of the six-cylinder four-door sedan and Touring Limousine was similar to the Mark II Snipe, with removable rear fender skirts and rectangular parking lights. Running boards held steel tread plates. Eight-leaf front springs now were installed, with a transverse stabilizer bar added to the rear. Snipe front fenders ended at the front door opening. Wheelbase remained at 117.5 inches, but overall length grew slightly. The same 249-cid engine was used, rated 100 horsepower.

PULLMAN/IMPERIAL — Mk III — SIX — Wraparound bumpers with guards were now standard equipment, but the limousines otherwise continued with little change. Overall length increased slightly, but the wheelbase remained at 131 inches.

I.D. DATA: Hawk serial number is stamped on the chassis frame side member, near the front shock absorber; and/or on a plate on the firewall, under the hood. Snipe chassis serial number is stamped on a plate on the firewall. Pullman chassis number is at the front of the left chassis member. Starting serial number: (Hawk) A5000001; (Snipe) A8000001; (Pullman) A9000001. Engine number is on the right side of the block.

Model	Body Type & Seating	Engine Type/CID	P.O.E. Price	Weight (lbs.)	Prod. Total
HAWK					
Mk IV	4-dr Sedan-5P	I4/138	1997	2748	Note 1
SUPER SNIPE					
Mk III	4-dr Saloon-6P	I6/249	2997	3745	Note 1
PULLMAN/IMPERIAL					
Mk III	4-dr Limo-7/8P	I6/249	N/A	4560	Note 1

Note 1: Approximately 309 Humbers were sold in the U.S. during 1951.

ENGINE DATA: BASE FOUR: Inline, L-head four-cylinder. Cast iron block and aluminum head. **Displacement:** 138.2 cu. in. (2267 cc). **Bore & Stroke:** 3.187 x 4.33 in. (81 x 110 mm). **Compression Ratio:** 6.3:1. **Brake Horsepower:** 58 at 3400 rpm. Three main bearings. Solid valve lifters. One Stromberg downdraft carburetor.

BASE SIX (Super Snipe, Pullman): Inline, L-head six-cylinder. Cast iron block and alloy head. **Displacement:** 249.2 cu. in. (4086 cc). **Bore & Stroke:** 3.35 x 4.72 in. (85 x 120 mm). **Compression Ratio:** 6.25:1. **Brake Horsepower:** 100 at 3400 rpm. Four main bearings. Solid valve lifters. Stromberg downdraft carburetor.

CHASSIS DATA: Wheelbase: (Hawk) 105.5 in.; (Snipe) 117.5 in.; (Pullman) 131.0 in. **Overall Length:** (Hawk) 179.5 in.; (Snipe) 190.8 in.; (Pullman) 211.9 in. **Height:** (Hawk) 64.8 in.; (Snipe) 65.8 in.; (Pullman) 69.0 in. **Width:** (Hawk) 70 in.; (Snipe) 74.8 in.; (Pullman) 74.8 in. **Front Tread:** (Hawk) 56 in.; (Snipe) 57.9 in.; (Pullman) 57.9 in. **Rear Tread:** (Hawk) 57 in.; (Snipe) 61.0 in.; (Pullman) 62.2 in. **Wheel Type:** disc. **Standard Tires:** (Hawk) 6.40x15; (Snipe) 6.50x16; (Pullman) 7.00x16.

TECHNICAL: Layout: front-engine, rear-drive. **Transmission:** four-speed manual; column gearshift lever. **Standard Final Drive Ratio:** (Hawk) 4.55:1; (Snipe/Pullman) 4.09:1. **Steering:** Burman worm and nut. **Suspension (front):** (Hawk) coil springs and anti-sway bar; (Snipe/Pullman) transverse leaf springs. **Suspension (rear):** rigid axle, semi-elliptic leaf springs and anti-sway bar. **Brakes:** hydraulic, front/rear drum. **Body Construction:** steel body on steel frame.

MAJOR OPTIONS: Radio. Heater.

PERFORMANCE: Top Speed: (Hawk) 72-73 mph; (Snipe) about 84 mph; (Pullman) 82 mph. **Acceleration (quarter-mile):** (Hawk) 23.7 sec.; (Snipe) 21.7 sec.; (Pullman) under 23 sec.

Manufacturer: Humber Ltd., Ryton-on-Dunsmore, Warwickshire, England (part of Rootes Motors Ltd.).

Distributor: Rootes Motors Inc., Long Island City, New York (export agent).

HISTORY: Hawk Mk II introduced in Britain by September 1950; Super Snipe Mk III by August 1950; Pullman/Imperial by December 1950. Humbers in U.S. registered prior to December of 1951 were considered 1951 models.

1952 HUMBER

HAWK — Mk IV — FOUR — Production of the four-cylinder Humber continued with no significant change.

SUPER SNIPE — Mk III — SIX — No change was evident in the six-cylinder Humber for the 1952 model year.

PULLMAN/IMPERIAL — Mk III — SIX — Limousines continued production with a division window (Pullman) or without one (Imperial), with little change.

I.D. DATA: Hawk serial (chassis) number is stamped on the frame side member, near the front shock absorber; and/or on a plate on the firewall, under the hood. Snipe chassis serial number is stamped on a plate on the firewall. Pullman chassis number is at the front of the left chassis member. Starting serial number: (Hawk) 5002500; (Super Snipe) A8001990; (Pullman/Imperial) A9000001. Engine number is on the right side of the block.

Model	Body Type & Seating	Engine Type/CID	P.O.E. Price	Weight (lbs.)	Prod. Total
HAWK					
Mk IV	4-dr Sedan-5P	I4/138	2295	2758	Note 1
SUPER SNIPE					
Mk III	4-dr Sedan-5P	I6/249	3369	3745	Note 1
PULLMAN-IMPERIAL					
Mk III	4-dr Imp Sedan-8P	I6/249	5110	4466	Note 1
Mk III	4-dr Pullman Limo-8P	I6/249	5110	4466	Note 1

Note 1: Approximately 226 Humbers were sold in the U.S. during 1952.

ENGINE DATA: BASE FOUR (Hawk): Inline, L-head four-cylinder. Cast iron block and aluminum head. **Displacement:** 138.2 cu. in. (2267 cc). **Bore & Stroke:** 3.187 x 4.33 in. (81 x 110 mm). **Compression Ratio:** 6.3:1. **Brake Horsepower:** 58 at 3400 rpm. Three main bearings. Solid valve lifters. One Stromberg downdraft carburetor.

BASE SIX (Super Snipe, Pullman): Inline, L-head six-cylinder. Cast iron block and aluminum head. **Displacement:** 249.2 cu. in. (4086 cc). **Bore & Stroke:** 3.35 x 4.72 in. (85 x 120 mm). **Compression Ratio:** 6.25:1. **Brake Horsepower:** 100 at 3400 rpm. **Torque:** 198 lbs.-ft. at 1200 rpm. Four main bearings. Solid valve lifters. Stromberg downdraft carburetor.

CHASSIS DATA: Wheelbase: (Hawk) 105.5 in.; (Snipe) 117.5 in.; (Pullman/Imp) 131.0 in. **Overall Length:** (Hawk) 179.5 in.; (Snipe) 190.8 in.; (Pullman/Imp) 211.9 in. **Height:** (Hawk) 64.8 in.; (Snipe) 65.8 in.; (Pullman/Imp) 69.0 in. **Width:** (Hawk) 70 in.; (Snipe) 74.8 in.; (Pullman/Imp) 74.8 in. **Front Tread:** (Hawk) 56 in.; (Snipe) 57.9 in.; (Pullman/Imp) 57.9 in. **Rear Tread:** (Hawk) 57 in.; (Snipe) 61.0 in.; (Pullman/Imp) 62.2 in. **Wheel Type:** disc. **Standard Tires:** (Hawk) 6.40x15; (Snipe) 6.50x16; (Pullman) 7.00x16.

TECHNICAL: Layout: front-engine, rear-drive. **Transmission:** four-speed manual; column gearshift lever. Hawk overall gear ratios: (1st) 14.50:1; (2nd) 11.24:1; (3rd) 6.78:1; (4th) 4.55:1. **Standard Final Drive Ratio:** (Hawk) 4.55:1; (Snipe/Pullman) 4.09:1. **Steering:** Burman worm and nut. **Suspension (front):** (Hawk) coil springs and anti-sway bar; (Snipe/Pullman) transverse leaf springs. **Suspension (rear):** rigid axle, semi-elliptic leaf springs and anti-sway bar. **Brakes:** hydraulic, front/rear drum. **Body Construction:** steel body on steel frame.

MAJOR OPTIONS: Radio. Heater.

PERFORMANCE: Top Speed: (Hawk) 72-73 mph; (Snipe) 81-84 mph; (Pullman) 82 mph. **Acceleration (quarter-mile):** (Hawk) 23.7 sec.; (Snipe) 21.7 sec.; (Pullman) under 23 sec. **Fuel Mileage:** (Hawk) about 19 mpg; (Snipe) average 16.2 mpg; (Pullman) about 12 mpg.

Manufacturer: Humber Ltd., Ryton-on-Dunsmore, Warwickshire, England (part of Rootes Motors Ltd.).

Distributor: Rootes Motors Inc., Long Island City, New York (export agent).

1953 HUMBER

HAWK — Mk V — FOUR — A revised Hawk came in sedan and Touring Limousine form (like the larger Snipe). Restyling included a lowering of the hood line. Air intake grilles were now vertical, enclosed in a chromed surround, and incorporated the parking lights. Wraparound bumpers included standard bumper guards. Rear fenders had chrome moldings and pushbuttons were used for the door locks. Humber described the revised Hawk as "superb from every point of view," in the brochure distributed at the London Motor Show in October 1952. As before, the three-section grille consisted of a center grille with vertical bars and twin side grilles that contained vertical bars, with round parking lights at the outer ends. Powerplant remained the 138-cid L-head four, with an aluminum cylinder head and 58-horsepower output. Seating space was ample for five or six people. Standard colors this year were: Beech Green, Black, or Metallic Quartz Blue with light fawn upholstery; and Black, Gun, or Satin Bronze with red upholstery. Available accessories included a radio, heater and air circulating equipment, and Rootes Group "rim finishers."

SUPER SNIPE — Mk IV — SIX — Appearance differences between the four-cylinder Hawk and six-cylinder Super Snipe diminished with the emergence of a new full-width Hawk-like body, with longer hood and smaller central grille. Round parking lights were mounted within the twin side grilles. A horizontal trim strip ran along the front fender, continuing through part of the front door. Mechanical changes included a switch to an overhead-valve engine (only slightly larger in displacement than the former L-head), and the adoption of coil springs for the front suspension. Inside, the dashboard displayed cowled instruments. Tires were now 15-inch diameter rather than the former 16-inchers.

PULLMAN/IMPERIAL — Mk III — SIX — Production of the large sedan and limousine with L-head six-cylinder engine ceased during the 1953 model year, to be replaced by a new version with overhead-valve engine; see 1954 listing.

I.D. DATA: Hawk serial (chassis) number is stamped on the frame side member, near the front shock absorber; and/or on a plate on the firewall, under the hood. Snipe chassis serial number is stamped on a plate on the firewall, and on the front extension of the car's frame. Pullman chassis number is at the front of the left chassis member. Starting serial number: (Hawk) A5200001; (Snipe) A8200001. Engine number is on right side of block.

Model	Body Type & Seating	Engine Type/CID	P.O.E. Price	Weight (lbs.)	Prod. Total
HAWK					
Mk V	4-dr Sedan-5/6P	I4/138	2399	2821	Note 1
Mk V	4-dr Limo-5/6P	I4/138	2699	2821	Note 1
SUPER SNIPE					
Mk IV	4-dr Sedan-5/6P	I6/253	3295	3873	Note 1
Mk IV	4-dr Limo-5/6P	I6/253	3595	3873	Note 1
PULLMAN/IMPERIAL					
Mk III	4-dr Imp Sedan-8P	I6/249	5110	4466	Note 1
Mk III	4-dr Pullman Limo-8P	I6/249	5110	4466	Note 1

Note 1: Approximately 146 Humbers were sold in the U.S. during 1953.

ENGINE DATA: BASE FOUR (Hawk): Inline, L-head four-cylinder. Cast iron block and aluminum head. **Displacement:** 138.2 cu. in. (2267 cc). **Bore & Stroke:** 3.1875 x 4.33 in. (81 x 110 mm). **Compression Ratio:** 6.32:1. **Brake Horsepower:** 58 at 3400 rpm. **Torque:** 110 lbs.-ft. at 1800 rpm. Three main bearings. Solid valve lifters. Stromberg downdraft carburetor.

BASE SIX (Super Snipe): Inline, overhead-valve six-cylinder. Cast iron block and head. **Displacement:** 252.6 cu. in. (4139 cc). **Bore & Stroke:** 3.50 x 4.375 in. (88.9 x 111.1 mm). **Compression Ratio:** 6.48:1 (7.2:1 optional). **Brake Horsepower:** 113 at 3400 rpm. **Torque:** 206 lbs.-ft. at 1400 rpm. Four main bearings. Solid valve lifters. Zenith or Stromberg carburetor.

BASE SIX (Pullman/Imperial): Same as 1952.

CHASSIS DATA: Wheelbase: (Hawk) 105.5 in.; (Snipe) 115.75 in. **Overall Length:** (Hawk) 180.5 in.; (Snipe) 197 in. **Height:** (Hawk) 64.75 in.; (Snipe) 65 in. **Width:** (Hawk) 70.0 in.; (Snipe) 73.5 in. **Front Tread:** (Hawk) 56.0 in.; (Snipe) 58 in. **Rear Tread:** (Hawk) 57.0 in.; (Snipe) 56 in. **Wheel Type:** disc. **Standard Tires:** (Hawk) 6.40x15; (Snipe) 7.00x15.

Note: See 1952 listing for Pullman/Imperial dimensions.

TECHNICAL: Layout: front-engine, rear-drive. **Transmission:** four-speed manual; steering-column lever. Hawk overall gear ratios: (1st) 14.50:1; (2nd) 11.24:1; (3rd) 6.78:1; (4th) 4.55:1. **Standard Final Drive Ratio:** (Hawk) 4.55:1; (Snipe) 3.7:1; (Pullman/Imp) 4.09:1. **Steering:** Burman worm and nut. **Suspension (front):** (Hawk/Snipe) coil springs and anti-sway bar; (Pullman) transverse leaf springs. **Suspension (rear):** rigid axle, semi-elliptic leaf springs and anti-sway bar. **Brakes:** hydraulic, front/rear drum. **Body Construction:** steel body on steel frame.

MAJOR OPTIONS: Radio. Heater. Wheel covers (Hawk).

PERFORMANCE: Top Speed: (Hawk) 71-73 mph; (Snipe) 90-91 mph; (Pullman) 78-82 mph. **Acceleration (quarter-mile):** (Hawk) 23.7 sec.; (Snipe) 20.9 sec.; (Pullman) under 23 sec. **Fuel Mileage:** (Hawk) about 19 mpg; (Snipe) about 14 mpg; (Pullman) about 12 mpg.

Manufacturer: Humber Ltd., Ryton-on-Dunsmore, Warwickshire, England (part of Rootes Motors Ltd.).

Distributor: Rootes Motors Inc., Long Island City, New York (export agent).

HISTORY: Introduced to U.S. market in January 1953.

1954 HUMBER

1954 Humber Pullman limousine. (Christie's)

HAWK — Mk V — FOUR — Production of the Mark V Hawk continued with no significant change, until it was replaced by the Mark VI during the 1954 model year. See 1955 listing for details on Mark VI.

SUPER SNIPE — Mk IV — SIX — Production of the six-cylinder Humber continued with minimal change, except for the addition of a trim strip that extended all the way across the front door. Powerplant was the overhead-valve engine introduced for the 1953 model year.

PULLMAN/IMPERIAL — Mk IV — SIX — An overhead-valve six-cylinder engine, like that in the Super Snipe, went under the longest Humber's hood for its final stab at the marketplace. The re-powered limos lasted only a single season before leaving the lineup. As before, the Pullman version had a division window; the Imperial did not.

I.D. DATA: Hawk serial number is stamped on the chassis frame side member, near the front shock absorber; and/or on a plate on the firewall, under the hood. Snipe chassis serial number is stamped on a plate on the firewall, and on the front extension of the car's frame. Pullman chassis number is at the front of the left chassis member. Starting serial number: (Hawk) 5200184; (Pullman) 9200001. Engine number is on right side of block.

Model	Body Type & Seating	Engine Type/CID	P.O.E. Price	Weight (lbs.)	Prod. Total
HAWK					
Mk V	4-dr Sedan-5P	I4/138	2399	2821	N/A

Model	Body Type & Seating	Engine Type/CID	P.O.E. Price	Weight (lbs.)	Prod. Total
SUPER SNIPE					
Mk IV	4-dr Sedan-5/6P	I6/253	3295	3941	N/A
Mk IV	4-dr Limo-5/6P	I6/253	3595	4150	N/A
PULLMAN/IMPERIAL					
Mk IV	4-dr Imp Sedan-8P	I6/253	N/A	4760	N/A
Mk IV	4-dr Pullman Limo-8P	I6/253	N/A	4788	N/A

ENGINE DATA: BASE FOUR (Hawk): Inline, L-head four-cylinder. Cast iron block and aluminum head. **Displacement:** 138.2 cu. in. (2267 cc). **Bore & Stroke:** 3.1875 x 4.33 in. (81 x 110 mm). **Compression Ratio:** 6.32:1. **Brake Horsepower:** 58 at 3400 rpm. **Torque:** 110 lbs.-ft. at 1800 rpm. Three main bearings. Solid valve lifters. Stromberg downdraft carburetor.

BASE SIX (Super Snipe): Inline, overhead-valve six-cylinder. Cast iron block and head. **Displacement:** 252.6 cu. in. (4139 cc). **Bore & Stroke:** 3.50 x 4.375 in. (88.9 x 111.1 mm). **Compression Ratio:** 6.48:1 (7.2:1 optional). **Brake Horsepower:** 113 at 3400 rpm. **Torque:** 206 lbs.-ft. at 1400 rpm. Four main bearings. Solid valve lifters. Zenith or Stromberg carburetor.

BASE SIX (Pullman/Imperial): Same as Super Snipe, except — **Compression Ratio:** 6.48:1 (7.1:1 optional). **Brake Horsepower:** 113/116 at 3400 rpm.

CHASSIS DATA: Wheelbase: (Hawk) 105.5 in.; (Snipe) 115.75 in.; (Pullman/Imp) 131 in. **Overall Length:** (Hawk) 180.5 in.; (Snipe) 197 in.; (Pullman/Imp) 212 in. **Height:** (Hawk) 64.75 in.; (Snipe) 65 in. **Width:** (Hawk) 70.0 in.; (Snipe) 73.5 in.; (Pullman/Imp) 74.75 in. **Front Tread:** (Hawk) 56.0 in.; (Snipe) 58 in. **Rear Tread:** (Hawk) 57.0 in.; (Snipe) 56 in. **Wheel Type:** disc. **Standard Tires:** (Hawk) 6.40x15; (Snipe) 7.00x15; (Pullman/Imp) 7.50x16.

TECHNICAL: Layout: front-engine, rear-drive. **Transmission:** four-speed manual; column gearshift lever. **Standard Final Drive Ratio:** (Hawk) 4.55:1; (Snipe) 3.7:1; (Pullman/Imp) 4.09:1. **Steering:** Burman worm and nut. **Suspension (front):** (Hawk/Snipe) coil springs and anti-sway bar; (Pullman/Imp) transverse leaf springs. **Suspension (rear):** rigid axle, semi-elliptic leaf springs and anti-sway bar. **Brakes:** hydraulic, front/rear drum. **Body Construction:** steel body on steel frame.

MAJOR OPTIONS: Similar to 1953.

PERFORMANCE: Top Speed: (Hawk) 71 mph. **Acceleration (0-60 mph):** (Hawk) 25.4 seconds. **Fuel Mileage:** (Hawk) about 18 mpg.

HISTORY: By this time, almost 800 postwar Humbers had been sold in the U.S. (mostly Hawks). Comparing the Super Snipe to domestic rivals, one buying guide for 1954 described the Humber "far superior in craftsmanship and roadability, and pretty much the equal of the Detroit product in performance and economy," with an engine that "has enough flexibility to forgive the lazy operator who forgets to shift." Production of the long-wheelbase Pullman and Imperial ceased during the 1954 model year.

1955 HUMBER

HAWK — Mk VI — FOUR — A new overhead-valve four-cylinder engine went under the Hawk hood for 1955, developing 70 horsepower (12 more than the prior L-head powerplant). Displacement and bore/stroke dimensions were identical to those of the prior L-head engine. Top speed reached 80 miles per hour. Appearance was similar to the Mark V, still with an upright profile and traditional demeanor, but the nameplate that had been mounted on the hood was now at the top of the grille. Bodyside trim strips along the front fenders now extended all the way through the front doors. A taller rear fender line was topped by chromed elements, and the gas cap was concealed. Flashing turn signals were now standard. As before, both front and rear doors were front-hinged, and held vent panes. Laycock de Normanville overdrive was now optional. Both sedan and Touring Limousine models were produced. Available options included a radio, heater, rim finishers, and whitewall tires.

SUPER SNIPE — Mk IV — SIX — Production of the six-cylinder Humber continued with minimal change, powered by the 253-cid overhead-valve engine. Bucket front seats were optional.

I.D. DATA: Serial number is on a plate on the firewall, under the hood. Starting serial number: (Hawk) A5400001; (Snipe) A8204200. Hawk engine number is stamped on the side of the block. Snipe engine number is stamped on the block, above the dipstick.

Model	Body Type & Seating	Engine Type/CID	P.O.E. Price	Weight (lbs.)	Prod. Total
HAWK					
Mk VI	4-dr Sedan-5/6P	I4/138	N/A	2821	Note 1
Mk VI	4-dr Tour Limo-5/6P	I4/138	N/A	N/A	Note 1
SUPER SNIPE					
Mk IV	4-dr Sedan-5/6P	I6/253	N/A	3873	Note 1

Note 1: Approximately 20,000 Humbers were built during 1955.

Price Note: Price at factory in England was $1955 for the Hawk and $2770 for the Super Snipe.

ENGINE DATA: BASE FOUR (Hawk): Inline, overhead-valve four-cylinder. Cast iron block and head. **Displacement:** 138.4 cu. in. (2267 cc). **Bore & Stroke:** 3.1875 x 4.33 in. (81 x 110 mm). **Compression Ratio:** 7.0:1. **Brake Horsepower:** 70 at 3200 rpm. Three main bearings. Solid valve lifters. Stromberg downdraft carburetor.

BASE SIX (Super Snipe): Inline, overhead-valve six-cylinder. Cast iron block and head. **Displacement:** 252.6 cu. in. (4139 cc). **Bore & Stroke:** 3.50 x 4.375 in. (88.9 x 111.1 mm). **Compression Ratio:** 7.13:1. **Brake Horsepower:** 116 at 3400 rpm. Four main bearings. Solid valve lifters. Zenith or Stromberg carburetor.

CHASSIS DATA: Wheelbase: (Hawk) 105.5 in.; (Snipe) 115.75 in. **Overall Length:** (Hawk) 181.5 in.; (Snipe) 197 in. **Height:** (Hawk) 64.75 in.; (Snipe) 65 in. **Width:** (Hawk) 72.0 in.; (Snipe) 73.5 in. **Front Tread:** (Hawk) 56.0 in.; (Snipe) 58 in. **Rear Tread:** (Hawk) 57.0 in.; (Snipe) 56 in. **Wheel Type:** disc. **Standard Tires:** (Hawk) 6.40x15; (Snipe) 7.00x15.

TECHNICAL: Layout: front-engine, rear-drive. **Transmission:** four-speed manual; column gearshift lever. **Standard Final Drive Ratio:** (Hawk) 4.55:1 or 4.22:1; (Snipe) 3.7:1. **Steering:** Burman worm and nut. **Suspension (front):** wishbones, coil springs and anti-sway bar. **Suspension (rear):** rigid axle with semi-elliptic leaf springs and anti-sway bar. **Brakes:** Lockheed hydraulic, front/rear drum. **Body Construction:** steel body on pressed rail steel frame with central crossmembers.

MAJOR OPTIONS: Laycock de Normanville overdrive. Radio. Heater. Rim finishers (wheel covers). Whitewall tires.

PERFORMANCE: Top Speed: (Hawk) 80 mph; (Snipe) 90 mph. **Acceleration (quarter-mile):** (Hawk) 23.3 sec.; (Snipe) 20.9 sec.

1956 HUMBER

HAWK — Mk VI — FOUR — Little of consequence was new on the four-cylinder Humber, except that an Estate Car (station wagon) joined the original four-door sedan. Styling was the same for both models. As before, the center grille consisted of vertical bars, while the twin side grilles used horizontal bars and contained the parking lights. Tubeless tires now were standard, and backup lights were built into the taillamps. Central folding armrests on both front and back seats. Inside, each front door had a large pocket, while both front and back seats had folding center armrests. Six passengers could fit inside the sedan or wagon. Options included separate seats for driver and front passenger, as well as Laycock de Normanville overdrive. Later in the model year, a Mark VIA DeLuxe version added a horizontal trim strip all around the body.

1956 Humber Super Snipe saloon.

SUPER SNIPE — Mk IV — SIX — Changes were minimal for the six-cylinder, six-passenger Humber sedan, apart from a horsepower boost to more than 130 (resulting from a compression increase). Bright trim strips were added to the side windows, and the rear license plate was flush with the trunk lid. Tubeless tires were standard. Snipes had leather upholstery over soft foam rubber. The front seat adjusted both forward and back, and for height and rake. Rear seats had armrests and headrests. Both compartments held deep pile carpeting. Options included Laycock de Normanville electric overdrive, with a switch on control panel. Later in the 1956 model year, an automatic transmission became available; but Super Snipe left the Humber lineup at the end of the season.

I.D. DATA: Serial number is on a plate on the firewall, under the hood. Starting serial number: (Hawk) A5420001; (Snipe) A8410001. Hawk engine number is stamped on the side of the block; Snipe engine number is on the block, above the dipstick.

Model	Body Type & Seating	Engine Type/CID	P.O.E. Price	Weight (lbs.)	Prod. Total
HAWK					
Mk VI	4-dr Sedan-6P	I4/138	N/A	2987	Note 1
Mk VI	4-dr Tour Limo-6P	I4/138	N/A	N/A	Note 1
Mk VI	4-dr Sta Wag-6P	I4/138	N/A	N/A	Note 1
Mk VIA	4-dr DeL Sed-6P	I4/138	N/A	N/A	Note 1
SUPER SNIPE					
Mk IV	4-dr Sedan-6P	I6/253	N/A	3948	Note 1

Note 1: Approximately 15,000 Humbers were built during 1956.

Price Note: Price at factory in England was $2002 for the Hawk and $3066 for the Super Snipe.

1956 Humber four-door Pullman limousine.

ENGINE DATA: BASE FOUR (Hawk): Inline, overhead-valve four-cylinder. Cast iron block and head. **Displacement:** 138.2 cu. in. (2267 cc). **Bore & Stroke:** 3.1875 x 4.33 in. (81 x 110 mm). **Compression Ratio:** 7.0:1. **Brake Horsepower:** 75 at 4000 rpm. Three main bearings. Solid valve lifters. Stromberg downdraft carburetor.

BASE SIX (Super Snipe): Inline, overhead-valve six-cylinder. Cast iron block and head. **Displacement:** 252.6 cu. in. (4139 cc). **Bore & Stroke:** 3.50 x 4.375 in. (88.9 x 111.1 mm). **Compression Ratio:** 7.36:1 (6.48:1 optional). **Brake Horsepower:** 130.5 at 3800 rpm. Four main bearings. Solid valve lifters. Zenith or Stromberg carburetor.

CHASSIS DATA: Wheelbase: (Hawk) 105.5 in.; (Snipe) 115.75 in. **Overall Length:** (Hawk) 181.5 in.; (Snipe) 197 in. **Height:** (Hawk) 65 in.; (Snipe) 66 in. **Width:** (Hawk) 72.0 in.; (Snipe) 73.5 in. **Front Tread:** (Hawk) 56.0 in.; (Snipe) 58 in. **Rear Tread:** (Hawk) 57.0 in.; (Snipe) 56 in. **Wheel Type:** disc. **Standard Tires:** 7.00x15.

TECHNICAL: Layout: front-engine, rear-drive. **Transmission:** four-speed manual; column gearshift lever. **Standard Final Drive Ratio:** (Hawk) 4.55:1 or 4.22:1; (Snipe) 3.7:1. **Steering:** Burman worm and nut. **Suspension (front):** wishbones, coil springs and anti-sway bar. **Suspension (rear):** rigid axle with semi-elliptic leaf springs and anti-sway bar. **Brakes:** Lockheed hydraulic, front/rear drum. **Body Construction:** steel body on pressed rail steel frame with central crossmembers.

MAJOR OPTIONS: Laycock de Normanville overdrive. Radio. Heater. Rim finishers (wheel covers). Whitewall tires.

PERFORMANCE: Top Speed: (Hawk) 80 mph; (Snipe) 97 mph. **Acceleration (quarter-mile):** (Hawk) 23.3 seconds.

Manufacturer: Humber Ltd., Ryton-on-Dunsmore, Warwickshire, England (part of Rootes Motors Ltd.).

Distributor: Rootes Motors Inc., Long Island City, New York.

HISTORY: Super Snipe faded away from the lineup at the end of the 1956 model year, but would return for 1959 in another form.

1957 HUMBER

HAWK — Mk VI/VIA — FOUR — Production of the four-cylinder Hawk continued with little change, but the sedans were dropped at mid-year and the Estate Car (wagon) at the end of the model year.

HAWK — SERIES I — FOUR — A new Hawk, completely different in appearance, went on sale before the end of the 1957 model year; see 1958 listing for details.

I.D. DATA: Serial number is on a plate on the firewall, under the hood. Starting serial number: (Hawk VIA) A5460001. Engine number is on the side of the block.

Model	Body Type & Seating	Engine Type/CID	P.O.E. Price	Weight (lbs.)	Prod. Total
HAWK					
Mk VI	4-dr Sedan-6P	I4/138	N/A	2990	N/A
Mk VI	4-dr Tour Limo-6P	I4/138	N/A	N/A	N/A
Mk VI	4-dr Sta Wag-6P	I4/138	N/A	N/A	N/A
Mk VIA	4-dr Del Sed-6P	I4/138	N/A	N/A	N/A

Note: Prices at factory in England started at $1820.

ENGINE DATA: BASE FOUR (Hawk): Inline, overhead-valve four-cylinder. Cast iron block and head. **Displacement:** 138.2 cu. in. (2267 cc). **Bore & Stroke:** 3.1875 x 4.33 in. (81 x 110 mm). **Compression Ratio:** 7.0:1. **Brake Horsepower:** 75 at 4000 rpm. **Torque:** 119 lbs.-ft. at 2200 rpm. Three main bearings. Solid valve lifters. Stromberg downdraft carburetor.

CHASSIS DATA: Wheelbase: (Hawk) 105.5 in. **Overall Length:** (Hawk) 181.5 in. **Height:** (Hawk) 65 in. **Width:** (Hawk) 72.0 in. **Front Tread:** (Hawk) 56.0 in. **Rear Tread:** (Hawk) 57.0 in. **Wheel Type:** disc. **Standard Tires:** (Hawk) 6.40x15.

TECHNICAL: Layout: front-engine, rear-drive. **Transmission:** four-speed manual; column gearshift lever. **Standard Final Drive Ratio:** 4.55:1 or 4.22:1. **Steering:** Burman worm and nut (recirculating ball). **Suspension (front):** wishbones, coil springs and anti-sway bar. **Suspension (rear):** rigid axle with semi-elliptic leaf springs and anti-sway bar. **Brakes:** Lockheed hydraulic, front/rear drum. **Body Construction:** steel body on pressed rail steel frame with central crossmembers.

MAJOR OPTIONS: Laycock de Normanville overdrive. Radio. Heater. Rim finishers (wheel covers). Whitewall tires.

PERFORMANCE: Top Speed: (Hawk) 80 mph. **Acceleration (quarter-mile):** (Hawk) 23.3 sec.

Manufacturer: Humber Ltd., Ryton-on-Dunsmore, Warwickshire, England (part of Rootes Motors Ltd.).

Distributor: Rootes Motors Inc., Long Island City, New York (export agent).

1958 HUMBER

1958 Humber Hawk station wagon.

HAWK — SERIES I — FOUR — More modern in appearance than its predecessors, the totally restyled Hawk (introduced during the 1957 model year) also lost some of its dignified demeanor, blending into the late 1950s crowd of well-finished motorcars. A wraparound windshield was installed, with vertical 'A' pillars. That and the new wraparound back window improved all-around visibility. The large, nearly full-width, rectangular grille contained a pattern of thin horizontal bars within a bright surround molding (flat at the base but rounded along the top). A wide insignia was above the grille, at the hood front. Small rectangular parking lights were mounted below the slightly hooded headlamps. Bodyside trim strips ran horizontally across the fenders and doors, dipping downward at the far rear, serving as dividing lines for two-tone color schemes. Both front and rear doors held vent panes. Vertical-style taillamps protruded a bit out the back, in the style of very modest tailfins. Hawk's gas filler cap was concealed beneath a reflector. The rather squarish sedan held six passengers. Body and frame were an integral welded assembly. The new sedan was slightly narrower overall, but roomier inside. Both front and back seats were 3.5 inches wider. The front seat adjusted for rake, and included six fore/aft positions. Front and back seats had double-width armrests on each door. A soft "crash pad" framed the dashboard, which contained a deep glove box at the right end. Built-in ventilation included four windshield defroster nozzles.

Both a sedan and a Touring Limousine were produced. A new Hawk Estate Car also replaced the old-style station wagon. Beneath each Hawk hood was the 138.2 cid four-cylinder overhead-valve engine, delivering 78 horsepower at 4400 rpm with 7.5:1 compression. Either a four-speed manual gearbox (with or without overdrive) or Borg-Warner automatic was available. Top speed ran between 85 and 90 mph, with fuel mileage around 25 mpg.

1958 Humber Hawk.

I.D. DATA: Serial number is on a plate on the firewall, under the hood. Starting serial number: A5700001. Engine number is on the side of the block.

Model	Body Type & Seating	Engine Type/CID	P.O.E. Price	Weight (lbs.)	Prod. Total
HAWK					
I	4-dr Sedan-6P	I4/138	N/A	2975	N/A
I	4-dr Tour Limo-5P	I4/138	N/A	N/A	N/A
I	4-dr Sta Wag-6P	I4/138	N/A	3147	N/A

ENGINE DATA: BASE FOUR (Hawk): Inline, overhead-valve four-cylinder. Cast iron block and head. **Displacement:** 138.2 cu. in. (2267 cc). **Bore & Stroke:** 3.1875 x 4.33 in. (81 x 110 mm). **Compression Ratio:** 7.5:1. **Brake Horsepower:** 78 at 4400 rpm. **Torque:** 120 lbs.-ft. at 2300 rpm. Three main bearings. Solid valve lifters. One Zenith downdraft carburetor.

CHASSIS DATA: Wheelbase: (Hawk) 110 in. **Overall Length:** (Hawk) 185 in. **Height:** (Hawk) 61 in. **Width:** (Hawk) 69.5 in. **Front Tread:** (Hawk) 56.0 in. **Rear Tread:** (Hawk) 55.5 in. **Wheel Type:** disc. **Standard Tires:** (Hawk) 6.40x15.

TECHNICAL: Layout: front-engine, rear-drive. **Transmission:** four-speed manual; column gearshift lever. Overdrive and automatic transmission optional. **Standard Final Drive Ratio:** 4.55:1 or 4.22:1. **Steering:** Burman worm and nut. **Suspension (front):** independent; coil springs and swinging links. **Suspension (rear):** rigid axle with semi-elliptic leaf springs and anti-sway bar. **Brakes:** hydraulic, front/rear drum. **Body Construction:** unibody; steel body and frame, welded together.

MAJOR OPTIONS: Automatic transmission. Laycock de Normanville overdrive.

PERFORMANCE: Top Speed: (Hawk) 84-90 mph. **Acceleration (quarter-mile):** (Hawk) 22.2 sec. **Fuel Mileage:** (Hawk) 22-25 mpg.

Manufacturer: Humber Ltd., Ryton-on-Dunsmore, Coventry, England (part of Rootes Motors Ltd.).

Distributor: Rootes Motors Inc., Long Island City, New York.

HISTORY: The new Hawk sedan debuted in May 1957, while the new Estate Car (station wagon) was introduced in October 1957. Super Snipe remained out of the 1958 lineup. Although a handful of Humbers continued to be imported into the U.S. in the mid to late 1950s, and they were included in some consumer-oriented buying guides, they were no longer listed in all of the American price guides for the used car trade.

1959 HUMBER

HAWK — SERIES I — FOUR — Production of the restyled four-cylinder Humber continued with minimal change, in sedan, touring limousine, and station wagon (Estate Car) form. Appearance was similar to 1958, with the new large grille made up of thin horizontal strips, enclosed in a bright surround molding; and rectangular parking lights below the hooded headlamps. A new instrument panel, finished in burr walnut, had a padded safety roll. Door moldings also were finished in burr walnut. Both a Laycock de Normanville overdrive unit and Borg-Warner automatic transmission were optional. Specifications were the same as 1958, with the 138-cid overhead-valve engine producing 78 horsepower.

SUPER SNIPE — SERIES I — SIX — The Snipe was back, in a new form nearly identical to that of the four-cylinder Hawk that had been restyled more than a year earlier. In fact, Snipe took on the same body and chassis as the Hawk's, thus losing a large measure of

its distinctive quality, compared with the earlier, traditional (and dignified) versions. Dimensions were the same as the Hawk and the front-end was similar, except that the grille pattern differed from the Hawk's arrangement of horizontal strips. A separate cross-hatched insert with its own surround molding was mounted within the overall surround opening (which had the same flat base and rounded upper edge as the Hawk's). Parking lights were contained within the grille's chromed surround molding, which extended outward below the hooded headlamps into fluting (decorated by three horizontal trim bars) that wrapped around each front fender, up to the flare of the wheelwell. A new wraparound windshield reached vertical 'A' pillars. On the hood was a special Snipe ornament.

Under the hood was a 162-cid overhead-valve six-cylinder engine with identical bore/stroke dimensions. Unibody construction was used. Sedan, touring limousine, and Estate Car (station wagon) bodies were available, each with standard power brakes. Both an automatic transmission and overdrive were optional in the home market, as was power steering. Super Snipes sold in America typically came with an automatic transmission as standard. Leather seating surfaces held six people, with burr walnut finished woodwork and a glovebox on the passenger side. Each front door held a deep pocket. Behind the back seat was a large storage shelf. Twin folding tables were built into the front seatback. Thick pile carpets had sponge rubber underlay. The built-in ventilation system included a defroster. Backup lights were standard. Over 19.5 cubic feet of luggage space was available. Options included individual reclining front seats and a radio.

I.D. DATA: Serial number is on a plate on the firewall, under the hood. Starting serial number: (Snipe) A8900001. Engine number is on the right side of the block (Snipe) or left side (Hawk).

Model	Body Type & Seating	Engine Type/CID	P.O.E. Price	Weight (lbs.)	Prod. Total
HAWK					
I	4-dr Sedan-6P	I4/138	N/A	2975	Note 1
I	4-dr Tour Limo-6P	I4/138	N/A	N/A	Note 1
I	4-dr Sta Wag-6P	I4/138	N/A	3147	Note 1
SUPER SNIPE					
I	4-dr Sedan-6P	I4/162	3995	3246	Note 1
I	4-dr Tour Limo-6P	I4/162	N/A	N/A	Note 1
I	4-dr Sta Wag-6P	I4/162	4575	N/A	Note 1

Note 1: Approximately 257 Humbers were sold in the U.S. during 1959. Roughly 7,500 Series I/II Super Snipes were produced in 1959-60.

ENGINE DATA: BASE FOUR (Hawk): Inline, overhead-valve four-cylinder. Cast iron block and head. **Displacement:** 138.2 cu. in. (2267 cc). **Bore & Stroke:** 3.1875 x 4.33 in. (81 x 110 mm). **Compression Ratio:** 7.5:1. **Brake Horsepower:** 78 at 4400 rpm. **Torque:** 120 lbs.-ft. at 2300 rpm. Three main bearings. Solid valve lifters. One Zenith downdraft carburetor.

BASE SIX (Super Snipe): Inline, overhead-valve six-cylinder. Cast iron block and head. **Displacement:** 161.8 cu. in. (2651 cc). **Bore & Stroke:** 3.25 x 3.25 in. (82.55 x 82.55 mm). **Compression Ratio:** 7.5:1. **Brake Horsepower:** 112 at 4800 rpm. **Torque:** 139 lbs.-ft. at 2400 rpm. Four main bearings. Solid valve lifters. One Stromberg carburetor.

CHASSIS DATA: Wheelbase: 110 in. **Overall Length:** 185 in. **Height:** 61 in. **Width:** 69.5 in. **Front Tread:** 56.0 in. **Rear Tread:** 55.5 in. **Wheel Type:** disc. **Standard Tires:** (Hawk) 6.00/6.40x15; (Snipe) 6.70x15.

TECHNICAL: Layout: front-engine, rear-drive. **Transmission:** (Hawk) four-speed manual; column gearshift lever; overdrive or automatic available. (Snipe) automatic on export models. **Standard Final Drive Ratio:** (Hawk) 4.55:1 or 4.22:1; (Snipe) 4.55:1. **Steering:** Burman worm and nut. **Suspension (front):** independent; coil springs and swinging links. **Suspension (rear):** rigid axle with semi-elliptic leaf springs and anti-sway bar. **Brakes:** hydraulic, front/rear drum. **Body Construction:** unibody; steel body and frame, welded together.

MAJOR OPTIONS: Borg-Warner automatic transmission. Laycock de Normanville overdrive. Power steering. Individual reclining front seats. Radio. Heater. Whitewall tires.

Note: Super Snipes sold in the U.S. during the late 1950s and 1960s generally had an automatic transmission and heater as standard equipment.

PERFORMANCE: Top Speed: (Hawk) 87-90 mph; (Snipe) 90-96 mph. **Acceleration (quarter-mile):** (Hawk) 22.2 sec.; (Snipe) 21.5 sec. **Fuel Mileage:** (Hawk) 22-25 mpg; (Snipe) about 23 mpg.

Manufacturer: Humber Ltd., Ryton-on-Dunsmore, Coventry, England (part of Rootes Motors Ltd.).

Distributor: Rootes Motors Inc., New York and Los Angeles.

HISTORY: The new Super Snipe was introduced in October 1958.

1960 HUMBER

HAWK — SERIES IA — FOUR — Only minor changes were evident on the four-cylinder Humber as it switched from Series I to IA designation. Bodysides added full-length dual trim strips, tapered toward the front (similar to the Snipe). Door trim panels added a stretch of horizontal pleating. A closer-ratio gearbox was used for manual-transmission models, available with or without overdrive. Both the Hawk and Super Snipe had leather interiors and burr walnut finished woodwork.

SUPER SNIPE — SERIES II — SIX — A larger engine went under Snipe hoods this year, having grown in the bore dimension. Front disc brakes also were new. Twin bodyside trim strips tapered together toward the front of the car, with the space between them serving as the site for an accent color in two-tone schemes. 'HUMBER' block lettering at the hood front, above the grille, replaced the former wide insignia. Though similar in crosshatch pattern, the Snipe grille now contained five horizontal bars (formerly six). Examples imported to the U.S. came with standard Borg-Warner automatic, power brakes and heater (included in the basic price), while a three-speed manual gearbox with optional overdrive continued as standard in the home market. Lower-compression engines also were available in England, with reduced horsepower. Front disc brakes become available this year.

I.D. DATA: Serial number is on a plate on the firewall, under the hood. Starting serial number: (Hawk) B5000001; (Snipe) B8000001. Engine number is on the right side of the block (Snipe) or left side (Hawk).

Model	Body Type & Seating	Engine Type/CID	P.O.E. Price	Weight (lbs.)	Prod. Total
HAWK					
IA	4-dr Sedan-6P	I4/138	N/A	3080	N/A
IA	4-dr Tour Limo-6P	I4/138	N/A	N/A	N/A
IA	4-dr Sta Wag-6P	I4/138	N/A	N/A	N/A

Model	Body Type & Seating	Engine Type/CID	P.O.E. Price	Weight (lbs.)	Prod. Total
SUPER SNIPE					
II	4-dr Sedan-6P	I4/181	3995	3351	Note 1
II	4-dr Tour Limo-6P	I4/181	N/A	N/A	Note 1
II	4-dr Sta Wag-6P	I4/181	4575	N/A	Note 1

Note 1: Roughly 7,500 Series I/II Super Snipes were produced in 1959-60.

ENGINE DATA: BASE FOUR (Hawk): Inline, overhead-valve four-cylinder. Cast iron block and head. **Displacement:** 138.2 cu. in. (2267 cc). **Bore & Stroke:** 3.1875 x 4.33 in. (81 x 110 mm). **Compression Ratio:** 7.5:1. **Brake Horsepower:** 78 at 4400 rpm. **Torque:** 120 lbs.-ft. at 2300 rpm. Three main bearings. Solid valve lifters. One Zenith downdraft carburetor.

BASE SIX (Super Snipe): Inline, overhead-valve six-cylinder. Cast iron block and head. **Displacement:** 180.8 cu. in. (2965 cc). **Bore & Stroke:** 3.44 x 3.25 in. (87.3 x 82.55 mm). **Compression Ratio:** 8.0:1. **Brake Horsepower:** 129 at 4800 rpm. **Torque:** 162 lbs.-ft. at 1800 rpm. Four main bearings. Solid valve lifters. One Zenith carburetor.

CHASSIS DATA: Wheelbase: 110 in. **Overall Length:** 184.75 in. **Height:** 61 in. **Width:** 69.5 in. **Front Tread:** 56.87 in. **Rear Tread:** 55.5 in. **Wheel Type:** disc. **Standard Tires:** (Hawk) 6.00/6.40x15; (Snipe) 6.70x15.

TECHNICAL: Layout: front-engine, rear-drive. **Transmission:** (Hawk) four-speed manual; column gearshift lever; overdrive or automatic available. (Snipe) automatic transmission on export models. **Standard Final Drive Ratio:** (Hawk) 4.55:1 or 4.22:1; (Snipe) 4.55:1. **Steering:** Burman worm and nut. **Suspension (front):** independent; coil springs and swinging links. **Suspension (rear):** rigid axle with semi-elliptic leaf springs and anti-sway bar. **Brakes:** (Hawk) hydraulic, front/rear drum; (Snipe) front disc, rear drum. **Body Construction:** unibody; steel body and frame, welded together.

MAJOR OPTIONS: Borg-Warner automatic transmission. Laycock de Normanville overdrive. Power steering. Individual reclining front seats. Radio. Heater. Whitewall tires.

Note: Super Snipes sold in the U.S. during the 1960s had an automatic transmission and heater as standard equipment.

PERFORMANCE: Top Speed: (Hawk) 87-90 mph; (Snipe) 90-96 mph. **Acceleration (quarter-mile):** (Hawk) 22.2 sec.; (Snipe) 21.5 sec. **Fuel Mileage:** (Hawk) 22-25 mpg; (Snipe) about 22-24 mpg.

Manufacturer: Humber Ltd., Ryton-on-Dunsmore, Coventry, England (part of Rootes Motors Ltd.).

Distributor: Rootes Motors Inc., New York and Los Angeles.

HISTORY: By the 1960s, Super Snipe was considered the most familiar Humber in the U.S. market, rather than the similar-bodied but four-cylinder Hawk.

1961 HUMBER

HAWK — SERIES II — FOUR — Appearance of the four-cylinder Humber was similar to the prior Series IA, but front disc brakes were added. Other equipment made standard included a heater, ammeter, oil pressure gauge, and windshield washers. An automatic transmission was included with export models. Hawk suspensions also were modified this year, though retaining the same coil front/leaf rear spring configuration.

SUPER SNIPE — SERIES III — SIX — Quad (side-by-side) headlamps were the most noticeable change on the facelifted six-cylinder Humber, standing above a revised grille layout. Rectangular parking lights were incorporated into the outer ends of the new full-width grille, which consisted of horizontal strips and wrapped around the front fenders. The grille's upper molding dropped down a bit at the hood edges, to run below the headlamp pairs. Block lettering spelled out the 'HUMBER' name at the hood front, with no ornament or insignia used. A single trim strip decorated the bodyside, changed from the near-parallel twin strips on the prior Super Snipe. The car's front overhang was extended a bit, to accept optional air conditioning. Rich leather/walnut continued to adorn the interior. Polished walnut veneer was evident on the dashboard, sills, and back-seat picnic tables.

Engine output was the same as in 1960, but internal changes included new main bearings, oil pump, and water pump. Dealer-installed power steering was available. Larger front coil springs and rear leaf springs were used. As before, Snipes imported to the U.S. came with standard Borg-Warner automatic, power brakes and heater (included in the basic price).

I.D. DATA: Serial number is on a plate on the firewall, under the hood. Starting serial number: (Hawk) B5100001; (Snipe) B8100001. Engine number is on the left side of the block (Hawk) or right side (Snipe).

Model	Body Type & Seating	Engine Type/CID	P.O.E. Price	Weight (lbs.)	Prod. Total
HAWK					
II	4-dr Sedan-6P	I4/138	N/A	3080	Note 1
II	4-dr Tour Limo-6P	I4/138	N/A	N/A	Note 1
II	4-dr Sta Wag-6P	I4/138	N/A	N/A	Note 1
SUPER SNIPE					
III	4-dr Sedan-6P	I4/181	3995	3351	Note 1
III	4-dr Tour Limo-6P	I4/181	N/A	N/A	Note 1
III	4-dr Sta Wag-6P	I4/181	4575	N/A	Note 1

Note 1: Approximately 8,000 Humbers were produced during 1961. A total of 7,257 Series III Super Snipes were built in 1961-62.

ENGINE DATA: BASE FOUR (Hawk): Inline, overhead-valve four-cylinder. Cast iron block and head. **Displacement:** 138.2 cu. in. (2267 cc). **Bore & Stroke:** 3.1875 x 4.33 in. (81 x 110 mm). **Compression Ratio:** 7.5:1. **Brake Horsepower:** 78 at 4400 rpm. **Torque:** 120 lbs.-ft. at 2300 rpm. Three main bearings. Solid valve lifters. One Zenith downdraft carburetor.

BASE SIX (Super Snipe): Inline, overhead-valve six-cylinder. Cast iron block and head. **Displacement:** 180.8 cu. in. (2965 cc). **Bore & Stroke:** 3.44 x 3.25 in. (87.3 x 82.55 mm). **Compression Ratio:** 8.0:1. **Brake Horsepower:** 129 at 4800 rpm. **Torque:** 162 lbs.-ft. at 1800 rpm. Four main bearings. Solid valve lifters. One Zenith carburetor.

CHASSIS DATA: Wheelbase: 110 in. **Overall Length:** (Hawk) 184.75 in.; (Snipe) 188 in. **Height:** 61 in. **Width:** 69.5 in. **Front Tread:** 56.8 in. **Rear Tread:** 55.5 in. **Wheel Type:** disc. **Standard Tires:** (Hawk) 6.00/6.40x15; (Snipe) 6.70x15.

TECHNICAL: Layout: front-engine, rear-drive. **Transmission:** (Hawk) four-speed manual; column gearshift lever; overdrive or automatic available. (Snipe) automatic transmission available, three-speed manual in home market. **Standard Final Drive Ratio:** (Hawk) 4.22:1; (Snipe) 4.55:1. **Steering:** Burman worm and nut. **Suspension**

(front): independent; coil springs and swinging links. **Suspension (rear):** rigid axle with semi-elliptic leaf springs and anti-sway bar. **Brakes:** front disc, rear drum. **Body Construction:** unibody; steel body and frame, welded together.

MAJOR OPTIONS: Borg-Warner automatic transmission. Laycock de Normanville overdrive. Power steering. Individual reclining front seats. Radio. Whitewall tires.

Note: Super Snipes sold in the U.S. during the 1960s had an automatic transmission and heater as standard equipment.

PERFORMANCE: Top Speed: (Hawk) 87-90 mph; (Snipe) 90-96 mph. **Acceleration (quarter-mile):** (Hawk) 22.2 sec.; (Snipe) 21.5 sec. **Fuel Mileage:** (Hawk) 22-25 mpg; (Snipe) about 22 mpg.

Manufacturer: Humber Ltd., Ryton-on-Dunsmore, Coventry, England (part of Rootes Motors Ltd.).

Distributor: Rootes Motors Inc., New York and Los Angeles.

1962 HUMBER

1962 Humber Super Snipe saloon.

HAWK — SERIES II — FOUR — Production of the Hawk continued with little change.

SUPER SNIPE — SERIES III — SIX — Appearance of the six-cylinder Humber was similar to 1961. One American buyer's guide applauded the modern Series III facelift, noting that the Super Snipe had formerly looked like an overgrown Hillman Minx, though adding that the car's once-dignified stance had diminished.

The Series III Snipe's waistline displayed an abrupt rise (kickup) at the middle of the rear door, sloping downward gradually to the taillamps. The horizontal-ribbed grille encompassed the parking lights and wrapped around the front fenders, almost reaching the wheelwells, its upper molding angled back at the extreme end to match the wheel-well angle. Quad headlamps were hooded. Vertical three-section taillamps stood at fender tips. 'HUMBER' block lettering was on the trunk lid, above the license plate, and on the hood front. As in earlier Super Snipes, burr walnut decorated the dashboard and door cappings, and the dash held a padded safety roll. Borg-Warner automatic was standard in U.S. models. Optional separate reclining front seats had central armrests (recessed into seat edges). Automatic lights for underhood, trunk, and glove compartment were standard. A warning light even showed when the choke was operating. Power front disc brakes were standard; power steering also standard on U.S. models.

I.D. DATA: Serial number is on a plate on the firewall, under the hood. Engine number is on the left side of the block (Hawk) or right side (Snipe).

Model	Body Type & Seating	Engine Type/CID	P.O.E. Price	Weight (lbs.)	Prod. Total
HAWK					
II	4-dr Sedan-6P	I4/138	N/A	3080	Note 1
II	4-dr Tour Limo-6P	I4/138	N/A	N/A	Note 1
II	4-dr Sta Wag-6P	I4/138	N/A	N/A	Note 1
SUPER SNIPE					
III	4-dr Sedan-6P	I4/181	4295	3351	Note 1
III	4-dr Tour Limo-6P	I4/181	N/A	N/A	Note 1
III	4-dr Sta Wag-6P	I4/181	4860	3455	Note 1

Note 1: Approximately 9,000 Humbers were produced during 1962. A total of 7,257 Series III Super Snipes were built in 1961-62.

ENGINE DATA: BASE FOUR (Hawk): Inline, overhead-valve four-cylinder. Cast iron block and head. **Displacement:** 138.2 cu. in. (2267 cc). **Bore & Stroke:** 3.1875 x 4.33 in. (81 x 110 mm). **Compression Ratio:** 7.5:1. **Brake Horsepower:** 78 at 4400 rpm. **Torque:** 120 lbs.-ft. at 2300 rpm. Three main bearings. Solid valve lifters. One Zenith downdraft carburetor.

BASE SIX (Super Snipe): Inline, overhead-valve six-cylinder. Cast iron block and head. **Displacement:** 180.8 cu. in. (2965 cc). **Bore & Stroke:** 3.44 x 3.25 in. (87.3 x 82.55 mm). **Compression Ratio:** 8.0:1. **Brake Horsepower:** 129 at 4800 rpm. **Torque:** 162 lbs.-ft. at 1800 rpm. Four main bearings. Solid valve lifters. One Zenith carburetor.

CHASSIS DATA: Wheelbase: 110 in. **Overall Length:** (Hawk) 184.75 in.; (Snipe) 188 in. **Height:** 61 in. **Width:** 69.5 in. **Front Tread:** 56.8 in. **Rear Tread:** 55.5 in. **Wheel Type:** disc. **Standard Tires:** (Hawk) 6.00/6.40x15; (Snipe) 6.70x15.

TECHNICAL: Layout: front-engine, rear-drive. **Transmission:** (Hawk) four-speed manual; column gearshift lever; overdrive or automatic available. (Snipe) automatic transmission on export models, three-speed manual in home market. **Standard Final Drive Ratio:** (Hawk) 4.22:1; (Snipe) 4.55:1. **Steering:** Burman worm and nut (recirculating ball). **Suspension (front):** independent; coil springs and swinging links. **Suspension (rear):** rigid axle with semi-elliptic leaf springs and anti-sway bar. **Brakes:** front disc, rear drum. **Body Construction:** unibody; steel body and frame, welded together.

MAJOR OPTIONS: Borg-Warner automatic transmission. Laycock de Normanville overdrive. Power steering. Individual reclining front seats. Radio. Whitewall tires.

Note: Super Snipes sold in the U.S. during the 1960s had an automatic transmission and heater as standard equipment.

PERFORMANCE: Top Speed: (Hawk) 87-90 mph; (Snipe) 90-96 mph. **Acceleration (0-60 mph):** (Snipe) 16 seconds. **Acceleration (quarter-mile):** (Hawk) 22.2 sec.; (Snipe) 21.5 sec. **Fuel Mileage:** (Hawk) 22-25 mpg; (Snipe) about 22 mpg.

Manufacturer: Humber Ltd., Ryton-on-Dunsmore, Coventry, England (part of Rootes Motors Ltd.).

Distributor: Rootes Motors Inc., New York and Los Angeles.

HISTORY: Although it remained in production through 1967, in Series III/IV form, the Hawk received diminishing attention in American directories of imported cars. Instead, nearly all of the focus was on the six-cylinder Super Snipe.

1963-64 HUMBER

HAWK — SERIES III — FOUR — Evolution to another Series brought minimal change to the four-cylinder Humber.

SUPER SNIPE — SERIES IV — SIX — Snipe also went to a new series, but with little change evident (other than a price increase in the U.S.). Standard equipment (on U.S. models) included an automatic transmission, heater, power steering, and whitewall tires.

I.D. DATA: Serial number is on the firewall, under the hood.

Model	Body Type & Seating	Engine Type/CID	P.O.E. Price	Weight (lbs.)	Prod. Total
HAWK					
III	4-dr Sedan-6P	I4/138	N/A	3100	Note 1
III	4-dr Sta Wag-6P	I4/138	N/A	N/A	Note 1
SUPER SNIPE					
IV	4-dr Sedan-6P	I4/181	4500	3358	Note 1
IV	4-dr Sta Wag-6P	I4/181	5100	N/A	Note 1

Note 1: Approximately 19,000 Humbers were produced in 1963, and 14,000 in 1964. A total of 6,495 Series IV Super Snipes were built in 1963-64.

ENGINE DATA: BASE FOUR (Hawk): Inline, overhead-valve four-cylinder. Cast iron block and head. **Displacement:** 138.2 cu. in. (2267 cc). **Bore & Stroke:** 3.1875 x 4.33 in. (81 x 110 mm). **Compression Ratio:** 7.5:1. **Brake Horsepower:** 78 at 4400 rpm. **Torque:** 120 lbs.-ft. at 2300 rpm. Three main bearings. Solid valve lifters. One Zenith downdraft carburetor.

BASE SIX (Super Snipe): Inline, overhead-valve six-cylinder. Cast iron block and head. **Displacement:** 180.8 cu. in. (2965 cc). **Bore & Stroke:** 3.44 x 3.25 in. (87.3 x 82.55 mm). **Compression Ratio:** 8.0:1. **Brake Horsepower:** 133 at 5000 rpm. **Torque:** 160 lbs.-ft. at 2600 rpm. Four main bearings. Solid valve lifters. One Zenith carburetor.

CHASSIS DATA: Wheelbase: 110 in. **Overall Length:** (Hawk) 184.75 in.; (Snipe) 188 in. **Height:** 61 in. **Width:** 69.5 in. **Front Tread:** 56.8 in. **Rear Tread:** 55.5 in. **Wheel Type:** disc. **Standard Tires:** (Hawk) 6.40x15; (Snipe) 6.70x15.

TECHNICAL: Layout: front-engine, rear-drive. **Transmission:** (Hawk) four-speed manual; column gearshift lever; overdrive or automatic available. (Snipe) automatic transmission on export models, three-speed manual in home market. **Standard Final Drive Ratio:** (Hawk) 4.22:1; (Snipe) 4.22:1. **Steering:** Burman worm and nut (recirculating ball). **Suspension (front):** independent; coil springs and swinging links. **Suspension (rear):** rigid axle with semi-elliptic leaf springs and anti-sway bar. **Brakes:** front disc, rear drum. **Body Construction:** unibody; steel body and frame, welded together.

MAJOR OPTIONS: Borg-Warner automatic transmission. Laycock de Normanville overdrive. Power steering. Individual reclining front seats. Radio. Whitewall tires.

Note: Super Snipes sold in the U.S. during the 1960s had an automatic transmission, power steering and heater as standard equipment.

PERFORMANCE: Top Speed: (Hawk) 87-90 mph; (Snipe) 90-96 mph. **Acceleration (0-60 mph):** (Snipe) 16 seconds. **Acceleration (quarter-mile):** (Hawk) 22.2 sec.; (Snipe) 21.5 sec. **Fuel Mileage:** (Hawk) 22-25 mpg; (Snipe) about 22 mpg.

Manufacturer: Humber Ltd., Ryton-on-Dunsmore, Coventry, England (part of Rootes Motors Ltd.).

Distributor: Rootes Motors Inc., New York and Los Angeles.

HISTORY: Humber also began to produce a four-cylinder Sceptre model in 1964, with a 97-cid engine, for the European market.

1965-67 HUMBER

HAWK — SERIES IV — FOUR — Evolution into its final series brought minimal change to the Hawk. The familiar four-cylinder engine still developed 78 horsepower, hooking into a four-speed gearbox (overdrive optional).

SUPER SNIPE — SERIES V — SIX — Snipe's ultimate series also continued into its final seasons with little change. Standard equipment in the U.S. included an automatic transmission, power steering, and heater.

IMPERIAL — SIX — Humber revived the Imperial name on a Snipe-based limousine (with no division window), custom-built by Thrupp & Maberly. Specifications and dimensions were similar to the Super Snipe, except for the addition of a broad selection of standard equipment. Imperials had a black vinyl top, fog/driving lights, 'Imperial' script on the front doors, and the Thrupp & Maberly name on door sills. Standard equipment included not only the expected automatic transmission, power brakes and steering, but a

separate heater/defroster system for the front and rear, separate rear radio speakers, reading lamps, and Armstrong Selectaride rear shock absorbers. Interiors were upholstered in Connolly leather and West of England fabric, with Wilton carpeting to cradle the feet.

I.D. DATA: Serial number is on the firewall, under the hood.

Model	Body Type & Seating	Engine Type/CID	P.O.E. Price	Weight (lbs.)	Prod. Total
HAWK					
III	4-dr Sedan-6P	I4/138	N/A	3226	Note 1
III	4-dr Sta Wag-6P	I4/138	N/A	3422	Note 1
SUPER SNIPE					
V	4-dr Sedan-6P	I4/181	4800	3425	Note 2
V	4-dr Sta Wag-6P	I4/181	5400	3491	Note 2
IMPERIAL					
	4-dr Limo	I4/181	5300	3571	Note 3

Note 1: No more than 15,000 Humbers were produced in 1965, about 13,800 in 1966, and 6,500 in 1967.

Note 2: Roughly 3,000 Series V Super Snipes were built in 1965-67.

Note 3: Approximately 2,325 Imperials were built in 1965-67.

Note: Only the Super Snipe and Imperial were commonly listed in U.S. buyers' guides during the final Humber years.

ENGINE DATA: BASE FOUR (Hawk): Inline, overhead-valve four-cylinder. Cast iron block and head. **Displacement:** 138.2 cu. in. (2267 cc). **Bore & Stroke:** 3.1875 x 4.33 in. (81 x 110 mm). **Compression Ratio:** 7.5:1. **Brake Horsepower:** 78 at 4400 rpm. **Torque:** 120 lbs.-ft. at 2300 rpm. Three main bearings. Solid valve lifters. One Zenith downdraft carburetor.

BASE SIX (Super Snipe, Imperial): Inline, overhead-valve six-cylinder. Cast iron block and head. **Displacement:** 180.8 cu. in. (2965 cc). **Bore & Stroke:** 3.44 x 3.25 in. (87.3 x 82.55 mm). **Compression Ratio:** 8.0:1. **Brake Horsepower:** 137 at 5000 rpm. **Torque:** 160 lbs.-ft. at 2600 rpm. Four main bearings. Solid valve lifters. Two Zenith-Stromberg downdraft carburetors.

CHASSIS DATA: Wheelbase: 110 in. **Overall Length:** (Hawk) 184 in.; (Snipe/Imp) 187.5 in. **Height:** (sed) 59.8 in.; (wagon) 62 in. **Width:** 70 in. **Front Tread:** 56.8 in. **Rear Tread:** 55.5 in. **Wheel Type:** steel disc. **Standard Tires:** (Hawk) 6.40x15; (Snipe/Imp) 6.70x15.

TECHNICAL: Layout: front-engine, rear-drive. **Transmission:** (Hawk) four-speed manual; column gearshift lever; overdrive or automatic available. (Snipe) automatic transmission on export models, three-speed manual in home market. **Standard Final Drive Ratio:** 4.22:1. **Steering:** recirculating ball. **Suspension (front):** wishbones, coil springs and anti-sway bar. **Suspension (rear):** rigid axle with semi-elliptic leaf springs and anti-sway bar. **Brakes:** front disc, rear drum (power assisted). **Body Construction:** unibody; steel body and frame, welded together.

MAJOR OPTIONS: Borg-Warner automatic transmission. Laycock de Normanville overdrive. Power steering. Individual reclining front seats. Radio. Whitewall tires.

Note: Super Snipes aand Imperials sold in the U.S. had an automatic transmission, power steering and heater as standard equipment.

PERFORMANCE: Similar to 1964.

Manufacturer: Humber Ltd., Ryton-on-Dunsmore, Coventry, England (part of Rootes Motors Ltd.).

Distributor: Rootes Motors Inc., New York and Los Angeles.

POSTSCRIPT: Production of the Hawk, Super Snipe and Imperial ceased in 1967; but Humber continued to market the four-cylinder, 1725-cc Sceptre in the home market and elsewhere (but not in the U.S.) into the 1970s.

HYUNDAI

South Korea joined the influx of Asian imports to the U.S. for the 1986 model year with its subcompact front-drive Hyundai Excel hatchbacks and four-door sedans. Riding a platform based on the Japanese-built Mitsubishi Mirage, the Excel offered a low price and excellent gas mileage, helping it to become the best-selling first-year imported model in U.S. history.

Hyundai's history dates from 1968, when the company was founded at Ulsan, South Korea to assemble British Fords. British auto executive George Turnbull, in fact, was largely responsible for creating the first true Hyundai, accomplishing that feat in some three years. Famed Italian designer Giorgetto Giugiaro handled the styling, Ital Design the engineering. A prototype of the Hyundai Pony appeared at the Turin (Italy) show in October 1974, and it was in production a year later. Mitsubishi supplied the engine and various mechanical components, while Hyundai assembled the car under license from the Japanese company. More than 100,000 Pony models were produced in 1979 alone. By 1982, a modified Pony carried a larger (1439-cc) engine to replace the original 1238-cc four. Early in 1985, the Pony Excel debuted in Korea, soon to arrive on the U.S. market in similar form.

A larger Sonata sedan joined the Excel for the 1989 model year. Styling of this model, too, was done by

Giugiaro. As the next decade began, Hyundai introduced a sporty new Scoupe to the U.S. market for the 1991 model year.

1986-88 HYUNDAI

EXCEL — FOUR — Introduced to the U.S. market in February 1986, the Excel came in four-door sedan and hatchback form at first, joined a few months later by a two-door hatchback. Built on the same platform as Japan's Mitsubishi Mirage (and closely-related Dodge/Plymouth Colt), the South Korean subcompact was powered by a 1.5-liter four-cylinder engine. Either a five-speed manual gearbox (four-speed on the base model) or three-speed automatic was available. Aerodynamic headlamps were added for the 1987 model year, and the automatic transmission added a lock-up torque converter to minimize slippage. A sporty GS hatchback joined the lineup for 1988. Owners could expect gas mileage in the 34-mpg neighborhood from an Excel with manual shift.

I.D. DATA: A 17-symbol Vehicle Identification Number is atop the instrument panel, visible through the windshield.

EXCEL (1986 Models)

Model	Body Type & Seating	Engine Type/CID	P.O.E. Price	Weight (lbs.)	Prod. Total
	2-dr Hatch-5P	I4/90	4995	2127	Note 1
	4-dr Hatch-5P	I4/90	4996	2127	Note 1
GL	2-dr Hatch-5P	I4/90	5895	2149	Note 1
GL	4-dr Hatch-5P	I4/90	5895	2145	Note 1
GL	4-dr Sedan-5P	I4/90	6045	2145	Note 1
GLS	2-dr Hatch-5P	I4/90	6395	2171	Note 1
GLS	4-dr Hatch-5P	I4/90	6395	2167	Note 1
GLS	4-dr Sedan-5P	I4/90	6545	2167	Note 1

Note 1: A total of 166,882 Hyundais were sold in the U.S. during 1986, followed by 263,610 in 1987, and 264,282 in 1988.

Price Note: An automatic transmission added $370 to prices shown (except base model).

ENGINE DATA: BASE FOUR: Inline, overhead-cam four-cylinder. **Displacement:** 89.6 cu. in. (1468 cc). **Bore & Stroke:** 2.97 x 3.25 in. (75.4 x 82.5 mm). **Compression Ratio:** 9.5:1. **Brake Horsepower:** 68 at 5500 rpm. **Torque:** 82 lbs.-ft. at 3500 rpm. Two-barrel carburetor.

CHASSIS DATA: Wheelbase: 93.7 in. **Overall Length:** (hatchback) 160.9 in.; (sedan) 168 in. **Height:** 54.1 in. **Width:** 63.1 in. **Front Tread:** 54.1 in. **Rear Tread:** 52.8 in. **Standard Tires:** P155/80R13.

TECHNICAL: Layout: front-engine, front-drive. **Transmission:** four- or five-speed manual, or three-speed automatic. **Standard Final Drive Ratio:** 3.47:1 w/manual, 3.60:1 w/automatic. **Steering:** rack and pinion. **Suspension (front):** MacPherson struts with coil springs and anti-roll bar. **Suspension (rear):** independent; trailing arms with coil springs and anti-roll bar. **Brakes:** front disc, rear drum. **Body Construction:** steel unibody. **Fuel Tank:** 10.6 gallon except (GLS w/auto.) 13.2 gallon.

MAJOR OPTIONS (1987): Air conditioning. Power sunroof. AM/FM stereo radio w/cassette player. Right-hand remote mirror, tinted glass and bodyside moldings package. P175/70R13 tires.

Manufacturer: Hyundai Motor Co. Ltd., Seoul, South Korea.

Distributor: Hyundai Motor America.

HISTORY: Even in the short model year, Hyundai sold more Excels than any imported car in the history of the U.S. market for a first-year model. And at the end of the 1986 model year, only 31 states had a Hyundai dealership. The reason for its success was mainly the car's modest price tag: just $4995 for a base model.

Hyundais got an earlier start elsewhere in the world. By 1985, the rear-drive Hyundai Pony was the best-selling imported car in Canada, where a larger Stellar sedan also was marketed.

1989-90 HYUNDAI

1989 Hyundai Excel GS three-door.

EXCEL — FOUR — Production of the subcompact Excel continued with little change into 1989, but enjoyed a major restyling the next year. The engine gained multi-point fuel injection for 1990, adding 13 horsepower. Also in 1990, a four-speed automatic replaced the original three-speed unit, with normal/economy shift-mode selection.

SONATA — FOUR/V-6 — Measuring more than 16 inches longer overall than the Excel sedan, Hyundai's new front-drive sedan rode a 104.3-inch wheelbase and carried a 2351-cc four-cylinder engine. While the Excel was loaded with Mitsubishi components, the Sonata was more of a Hyundai product, borrowing little more than the engine from the Japanese company. An electronically-controlled four-speed automatic transmission was available. For 1990, a 3.0-liter V-6 engine became optional.

I.D. DATA: A 17-symbol Vehicle Identification Number is atop the instrument panel, visible through the windshield.

Model	Body Type & Seating	Engine Type/CID	P.O.E. Price	Weight (lbs.)	Prod. Total
EXCEL (1989 Models)					
	2-dr Hatch-5P	I4/90	5499	2156	Note 1
	4-dr Sedan-5P	I4/90	6199	2156	Note 1
GL	2-dr Hatch-5P	I4/90	6699	2178	Note 1
GL	4-dr Hatch-5P	I4/90	6949	2178	Note 1
GL	4-dr Sedan-5P	I4/90	7149	2178	Note 1
GS	2-dr Hatch-5P	I4/90	7699	2182	Note 1
GLS	4-dr Hatch-5P	I4/90	7599	2178	Note 1
GLS	4-dr Sedan-5P	I4/90	7749	2198	Note 1
SONATA (1989 Models)					
	4-dr Sedan-5P	I4/143	9695	2684	Note 1
GLS	4-dr Sedan-5P	I4/143	11695	2783	Note 1

Note 1: A total of 183,261 Hyundais were sold in the U.S. during 1989, and 137,448 in 1990.

ENGINE DATA: BASE FOUR (1989 Excel): Inline, overhead-cam four-cylinder. Cast iron block and aluminum head. **Displacement:** 89.6 cu. in. (1468 cc). **Bore & Stroke:** 2.97 x 3.25 in. (75.4 x 82.5 mm). **Compression Ratio:** 9.5:1. **Brake Horsepower:** 68 at 5500 rpm. **Torque:** 82 lbs.-ft. at 3500 rpm. Two-barrel carburetor.

BASE FOUR (1990 Excel): Same as 1468-cc four above, except with multi-point fuel injection. **Compression Ratio:** 9.4:1. **Brake Horsepower:** 81 at 5500 rpm. **Torque:** 91 lbs.-ft. at 3000 rpm.

BASE FOUR (Sonata): Inline, overhead-cam four-cylinder. Cast iron block and aluminum head. **Displacement:** 143 cu. in. (2351 cc). **Bore & Stroke:** 3.41 x 3.94 in. (86.5 x 100 mm). **Compression Ratio:** 8.5:1. **Brake Horsepower:** 116 at 4500 rpm. **Torque:** 142 lbs.-ft. at 3500 rpm. Port fuel injection.

OPTIONAL V-6 (1990 Sonata): Overhead-cam "vee" type six-cylinder. Cast iron block and aluminum head. **Displacement:** 181 cu. in. (2972 cc). **Bore & Stroke:** 3.59 x 2.99 in. (91.1 x 76 mm). **Compression Ratio:** 8.9:1. **Brake Horsepower:** 142 at 5000 rpm. **Torque:** 168 lbs.-ft. at 2500 rpm. Port fuel injection.

1990 Hyundai Sonata GLS.

CHASSIS DATA: Wheelbase: (Excel) 93.7 in.; (Sonata) 104.3 in. **Overall Length:** (Excel hatchback) 161 in.; (Excel sedan) 168 in.; (Sonata) 184.3 in. **Height:** (Excel) 54.1 in.; (Sonata) 55.4 in. **Width:** (Excel) 63.1 in.; (Sonata) 68.9 in. **Front Tread:** (Excel) 54.1 in.; (Sonata) 57.3 in. **Rear Tread:** (Excel) 52.8 in.; (Sonata) 56.7 in. **Standard Tires:** (Excel) P155/80R13 except (GS) P175/70R13; (Sonata) P185/70R14 except (V-6) P195/70R14.

TECHNICAL: Layout: front-engine, front-drive. **Transmission:** (Excel) four- or five-speed manual, or three-speed automatic (four-speed in 1990); (Sonata) five-speed manual or four-speed automatic. **Steering:** rack and pinion. **Suspension (front):** MacPherson struts with coil springs and anti-roll bar. **Suspension (rear):** independent; trailing arms with coil springs and anti-roll bar. **Brakes:** front disc, rear drum. **Body Construction:** steel unibody.

MAJOR OPTIONS (1989 Excel): Air conditioning. Power steering. Power sunroof. AM/FM stereo radio w/cassette player. Right-hand remote mirror, tinted glass and bodyside moldings package. P175/70R13 tires. Two-tone paint. Passive restraint system.

Manufacturer: Hyundai Motor Co. Ltd., Seoul, South Korea.

Distributor: Hyundai Motor America, Fountain Valley, California.

POSTSCRIPT: For the 1991 model year, Hyundai introduced a sporty new two-door Scoupe. The 2+2 coupe was powered by an 81-horsepower, 1.5-liter four-cyilnder engine and rode a 93.8-inch wheelbase, measuring 165.9 inches overall.

ISO

Considering that it came out of a company best known in Italy for the manufacture of refrigerators, the Iso sport-touring models produced from 1963 into the 1970s seems quite a sterling achievement. Blending Italian style with American technology, each was powered by a Chevrolet V-8 engine. Iso's steel platform chassis was designed by Giotto Bizzarrini, a former Ferrari engineer, who also produced a handful of cars under his own name (listed separately in this Catalog).

Founded by Renzo Rivolta in 1939, the Isothermos company became Iso Automotoveicoli S.p.A. after the war. Full-size automobiles had to wait a while, however, as they turned first to motor scooters and then, in 1953, to "bubble" cars. This was the company that created and first sold the Isetta, which was later marketed in Europe and the U.S. by BMW (listed in this Catalog). Italian production of the Isetta minicar ceased by 1956, in fact, as BMW and other licensees took over that market. Earnings from the bubble-car venture allowed the firm to turn to GT motorcars, built in a new plant near Milan. The first example, a four-passenger Rivolta, appeared at the Turin (Italy) auto show in late 1962, powered by a 300-bhp Corvette V-8. Sales went well, in both Europe and the U.S. (as well as the Middle East). During the following year, a companion two-seater emerged, the Grifo, which went on sale by 1965. After a time, the original Chevrolet V-8 was replaced by a larger-displacement Ford engine. In 1968, a four-door sedan body appeared in the Fidia, styled by Ghia; but that one found fewer customers. Then came a replacement for the Rivolta, named Lele, which gained less attention than its predecessors. A special edition of the Lele was known as the "Marlboro," named for the cigarette company, which had backed a so-so Iso attempt at Grand Prix racing. Financial difficulties prompted sale of the company to an American refrigerator maker in the early 1970s, which resulted in bankruptcy at mid-decade. A handful of additional Lele and Fidia models were built later, until production finally halted permanently before 1980. "The best of two worlds--Italian body styling and an American V-8.!" That early slogan managed to capture the attention of a fair number of enthusiasts in the mid-1960s, and continues to do so today.

1963-64 ISO

RIVOLTA — V-8 — Bertone penned the first of the Iso models, the four-passenger Rivolta notchback coupe. Aimed at the American market, it carried a 327-cid Chevrolet V-8 and was softer riding than most Italian sports cars of the day. The hardtop (pillarless) coupe body had a pointed nose with crosshatch-patterned grille, full wheel openings, and front vent windows. A horizontal trim strip went along the bodyside. At the cowl, above that trim strip, stood a set of angled horizontal grillework openings. Inside was a full complement of round gauges.

I.D. DATA: Not available.

Model	Body Type & Seating	Engine Type/CID	P.O.E. Price	Weight (lbs.)	Prod. Total
RIVOLTA					
	2-dr Coupe-4P	V8/327	8595	3350	Note 1

Note 1: A total of 799 Rivoltas were produced, through 1970.

ENGINE DATA: BASE V-8: 90-degree, overhead-valve V-8 (Corvette). Cast iron block and head. **Displacement:** 327 cu. in. (5359 cc). **Bore & Stroke:** 4.00 x 3.25 in. (101.6 x 82.55 mm). **Compression Ratio:** 10.5:1 (11.25:1 optional). **Brake Horsepower:** 300 at 5000 rpm (350 at 5800 optional). **Torque:** 360 lbs.-ft. at 2000 rpm. Five main bearings. Hydraulic valve lifters. Carter four-barrel carburetor.

CHASSIS DATA: Wheelbase: 106.3 in. **Overall Length:** 187.4 in. **Height:** 56.1 in. **Width:** 69.0 in. **Front Tread:** 55.5 in. **Rear Tread:** 55.5 in. **Wheel Type:** disc (6Lx15). **Standard Tires:** Pirelli Cinturato HS 185VR15 or 205VR15.

TECHNICAL: Layout: front-engine, rear-drive. **Transmission:** four-speed manual (Borg-Warner), five-speed manual (ZF) or three-speed "Powerglide" automatic (Chevrolet). **Standard Final Drive Ratio:** 2.88:1 or 3.31:1 ("Power Lock" differential available). **Steering:** Burman recirculating ball. **Suspension (front):** coil springs with anti-roll bar. **Suspension (rear):** De Dion axle with coil springs. **Brakes:** Dunlop hydraulic, front/rear discs with servo assist (discs near differential at rear). **Body Construction:** steel body integral with steel platform frame.

MAJOR OPTIONS: Rudge-Whitworth spoked wheels. Elektron wheels. Leather upholstery. Air conditioning.

PERFORMANCE: Top Speed: (300 bhp) 137 mph; (350 bhp) 148 mph. **Acceleration (quarter-mile):** (300 bhp) 16.2 sec.; (350 bhp) 15.8 sec. **Fuel Mileage:** (300 bhp) 15 mpg; (350 bhp) 13.5 mpg.

Manufacturer: Iso Automoveicoli S.p.A., Bresso, Milan, Italy.

Distributor: GT Motorcar Corp, Norwalk, Connecticut.

1965-66 ISO

GRIFO — V-8 — Success of the four-seat Rivolta led to the two-passenger fastback Grifo coupe, also designed by Bertone (with the assistance of Giorgio Giugiaro), which rode a shorter wheelbase and had a more assertive demeanor. The low profile (47-inch height) was highlighted by a large windshield and back window, plus a sliced-off back-end look. Front-end appearance differed from the Rivolta, with quad headlamps at the outer ends of a split grille with dark, tight mesh pattern. Along the cowl, between the wheel well and the door, stretched a set of short engine-cooling grids. According to *Motor Trend,* Bertone unabashedly called the production version of the Iso Grifo coupe his masterpiece. About the only change from the 1963 vintage prototype was movement of the exhaust pipes to the conventional (and cheaper) location. Like the Rivolta, it had a Corvette V-8 engine, synchro four-speed gearbox, and disc brakes. Bertone-designed mag alloy wheels were standard, with the more traditional Borrani wire wheels optional. Limited production began by 1966. Leather upholstery was standard, with PVC headlining.

RIVOLTA — V-8 — Production continued with minimal change through 1970. Rivolta's recessed grille, which protruded ahead of the outboard headlamps, consisted of thin horizontal bars, with a large insignia in the center. Standard equipment included power windows. The sales catalog noted that Rivolta's "excellent visibility and exceptional lightness of steering, the quickness of the engine, obviate tiredness and irritation to driver even on the longest journey." Inside, the wood facia dash had safety padding.

I.D. DATA: Serial number is on a plate at right front, under the hood.

Model	Body Type & Seating	Engine Type/CID	P.O.E. Price	Weight (lbs.)	Prod. Total
GRIFO					
A3/L	2-dr Coupe-2P	V8/327	14986	2826	Note 1
RIVOLTA					
	2-dr Coupe-4P	V8/327	8595	3350	Note 2

Note 1: A total of 412 Grifos were produced during the full model run, through 1974.

Note 2: A total of 799 Rivoltas were produced, through 1970.

ENGINE DATA: BASE V-8: 90-degree, overhead-valve V-8 (Corvette). Cast iron block and head. **Displacement:** 327 cu. in. (5359 cc). **Bore & Stroke:** 4.00 x 3.25 in. (101.6 x 82.55 mm). **Compression Ratio:** 10.5:1. **Brake Horsepower:** 300 (SAE) at 5000 rpm. **Torque:** 360 (SAE) lbs.-ft. at 3200 rpm. Five main bearings. Hydraulic valve lifters. Carter four-barrel carburetor.

OPTIONAL V-8: Same as above, except — **Compression Ratio:** 11.0:1. **Brake Horsepower:** 340 (SAE) at 6200 rpm (Grifo, 365 at 6200). **Torque:** 360-361 lbs.-ft. (SAE) at 4000 rpm. Solid valve lifters. Holley four-barrel carburetor.

Engine Note: Some Isos may have highly-tuned engines whose specifications differ from those above; e.g., with four Weber carburetors.

CHASSIS DATA: Wheelbase: (Grifo) 98.4 in.; (Rivolta) 106.3 in. **Overall Length:** (Grifo) 174.74 in.; (Rivolta) 187.4 in. **Height:** (Grifo) 47 in.; (Rivolta) 56.1 in. **Width:** (Grifo) 69.5 in.; (Rivolta) 69.0 in. **Front Tread:** 55.5 in. **Rear Tread:** 55.5 in. **Wheel Type:** disc (6Lx15). **Standard Tires:** Pirelli Cinturato HS 185VR15 or 205VR15.

TECHNICAL: Layout: front-engine, rear-drive. **Transmission:** four-speed manual (Borg-Warner T-10), five-speed manual (ZF) or three-speed "Powerglide" automatic (Chevrolet). **Standard Final Drive Ratio:** 2.88:1 or 3.07:1 ("Power Lock" differential). **Steering:** Burman recirculating ball. **Suspension (front):** wishbones and coil springs with anti-roll bar. **Suspension (rear):** (Grifo) De Dion axle with longitudinal and transverse links and coil springs; (Rivolta) De Dion with twin parallel upper and lower radial arms and Panhard rod. **Brakes:** Dunlop hydraulic, front/rear discs with servo assist (discs near differential at rear). **Body Construction:** steel body welded to (integral with) steel platform frame.

MAJOR OPTIONS: Borrani triple-laced wire wheels with knock-off hubs. Leather upholstery. Air conditioning. Limited-slip differential. Sunroof. Powerglide automatic transmission.

PERFORMANCE: Top Speed: (Grifo 300-hp) 143 mph; (Grifo 365-hp) 161-165 mph; (Rivolta 300-hp) 137 mph; (Rivolta 340-hp) 148 mph. **Acceleration (0-60 mph):** (Grifo 365-hp) about 7.4 sec. (0-100 mph in 16.6 sec.). **Acceleration (quarter-mile):** (Grifo 300-hp) 15 sec.; (Grifo 365-hp) 14.5-14.9 sec.; (Rivolta 300-hp) 16.2 sec.; (Rivolta 340-hp) 15.8 sec. **Fuel Mileage:** (Grifo 300-hp) 16.5 mpg; (Grifo 365-hp) 15.7 mpg; (Rivolta 300-hp) 15 mpg; (Rivolta 340-hp) 13.5 mpg.

Manufacturer: Iso Automoveicoli S.p.A., Bresso, Milan, Italy.

Distributor: GT Motorcar Corp, Norwalk, Connecticut.

1967-68 ISO

1967 Iso Grifo Lusso coupe.

GRIFO — V-8 — Production of the fastback Grifo coupe continued without significant change, into 1974.

RIVOLTA — V-8 — Production of the four-seater continued through 1970, with minimal change. As before, two engine choices were offered. "Iso," said the sales catalog for 1967, "is a car that can be driven *safely* at high speeds, and possesses the uncanny quality of rewarding the average driver, as well as the expert, with a sense of achievement."

S4 FIDIA — V-8 — A new four-door sedan from Iso borrowed the basic chassis design and powertrain from the Rivolta, but stretched its wheelbase by six inches. This one was styled not by Bertone, but by Ghia, featuring quad rectangular headlamps in a flat nose (with park/signal lights between each headlamp pair) and a comparatively short back end. The grille displayed a single horizontal bar with a center insignia. Both front and rear doors had vent windows. Standard equipment included air conditioning, a center console, full instruments, and bucket seats up front. British writer Douglas Foster-Browne, admiring the Fidia sedan's appearance, suggested that its wheels "explode from each corner of the vast length of this car like a newly opened rose, in a flurry of aluminium sheen and stainless steel shine on each of the petal shaped spokes."

I.D. DATA: Serial number is on a plate on left side, under the hood; or on right side of firewall. Engine number is on right side of block.

Model	Body Type & Seating	Engine Type/CID	P.O.E. Price	Weight (lbs.)	Prod. Total
GRIFO					
GL	2-dr Coupe-2P	V8/327	13750	3043	Note 1
RIVOLTA					
GT	2-dr Coupe-4P	V8/327	8539	3350	Note 2
FIDIA					
S4	4-dr Sedan-4/5P	V8/327	13875	3740	Note 3

Note 1: A total of 412 Grifos were produced during the full model run, through 1974.
Note 2: A total of 799 Rivoltas were produced, through 1970.
Note 3: A total of 192 Fidias were produced, through 1974.
Price Note: Prices shown was effective in 1968.

ENGINE DATA: BASE V-8: 90-degree, overhead-valve V-8 (Corvette Turbofire). Cast iron block and head. **Displacement:** 327 cu. in. (5359 cc). **Bore & Stroke:** 4.00 x 3.25 in. (101.6 x 82.55 mm). **Compression Ratio:** 10.5:1. **Brake Horsepower:** 300 at 5000 rpm. **Torque:** 360 lbs.-ft. at 3200 rpm. Five main bearings. Hydraulic valve lifters. Carter four-barrel carburetor.
OPTIONAL V-8 (Grifo/Rivolta/Fidia): Same as above, except — **Compression Ratio:** 11.0:1. **Brake Horsepower:** 350 (SAE) at 5800 rpm. **Torque:** 360 lbs.-ft. at 3600 rpm.

CHASSIS DATA: Wheelbase: (Grifo) 98.4 in.; (Rivolta) 106.5 in.; (Fidia) 112.2 in. **Overall Length:** (Grifo) 174.4 in.; (Rivolta) 187.4 in.; (Fidia) 195.7 in. **Height:** (Grifo) 47.2 in.; (Rivolta) 52.8 in.; (Fidia) 52.0 in. **Width:** (Grifo) 69.7 in.; (Rivolta) 68.9 in.; (Fidia) 70.1 in. **Front Tread:** 55.5 in. **Rear Tread:** 55.5 in. **Wheel Type:** disc (6Lx15). **Standard Tires:** Pirelli Cinturato HS 185VR15 or 205VR15.

TECHNICAL: Layout: front-engine, rear-drive. **Transmission:** four-speed manual (Borg-Warner T-10), five-speed manual (ZF) or three-speed "Powerglide" automatic (Chevrolet). Four-speed standard gear ratios: (1st) 2.54:1 (2nd) 1.89:1 (3rd) 1.51:1; (4th) 1.00:1. **Standard Final Drive Ratio:** 2.88:1 or 3.07:1 ("Power Lock" differential available). **Steering:** Burman recirculating ball. **Suspension (front):** wishbones and coil springs with anti-roll bar. **Suspension (rear):** (Grifo) De Dion axle with longitudinal and transverse links and coil springs; (Rivolta) De Dion with twin parallel upper and lower radial arms and Panhard rod. **Brakes:** Dunlop hydraulic, front/rear discs with servo assist (discs near differential at rear). **Body Construction:** steel body welded to (integral with) steel platform frame.

MAJOR OPTIONS: Borrani triple-laced wire wheels. Air conditioning. Alloy wheels. Power steering. Detachable roof.

PERFORMANCE: Top Speed: (Grifo 300-hp) 143 mph; (Grifo 350-hp) 165 mph; (Rivolta 300-hp) 137 mph; (Rivolta 350-hp) 148 mph; (Lele) 150 mph. **Acceleration (0-60 mph):** (Grifo 350-hp) about 7.4 sec. **Acceleration (quarter-mile):** (Grifo 300-hp) 15 sec.; (Grifo 350-hp) 14.5 sec.; (Rivolta 300-hp) 16.2 sec.; (Rivolta 350-hp) (15.8 sec. **Fuel Mileage:** (Grifo 300-hp) 16.5 mpg; (Grifo 350-hp) 15.7 mpg; (Rivolta 300-hp) 15 mpg; (350-hp) 13.5 mpg.

Manufacturer: Iso Automoveicoli S.p.A., Bresso, Milan, Italy.
Distributor: Isocars Corp., New York City.

1969-74 ISO

1970 Iso Grifo Targa Series 1, 5.3-liter. (Sportscar Auction Co.)

GRIFO — V-8 — Production of the fastback Grifo coupe continued into 1974. Standard equipment included a heater, air conditioning, power disc brakes, high-speed Pirelli tires, power windows, and heated back window. Grifos also had top-grain leather interiors. Later "7-Litre" models had a Chevrolet big-block (427-cid) V-8 instead of the former 327-cid, with a wide hood bulge to clear the engine's air cleaners. At the very end, a handful had a 351-cid Ford V-8 instead of either Chevrolet powerplant. Second-series models also got a facelift that included partially-concealed headlamps in a lower front end.

RIVOLTA — V-8 — Production of the four-seater continued through 1970, with minimal change. Standard equipment was similar to the Grifo, except that air conditioning was optional.

S4 FIDIA — V-8 — Production of the four-door Iso continued with little change, through 1974. Standard equipment was similar to the Grifo, but without air conditioning. A leather interior and power steering were standard.

LELE — V-8 — This 2+2 fastback was the final addition to the Iso line, arriving in 1969. Like second-series models of its mates, it received semi-concealed headlamps. A 350-cid V-8 was standard, but other engines could be ordered.

I.D. DATA: Serial number is on a plate on left side, under the hood; or on right side of firewall. Engine number is on right side of block.

Model	Body Type & Seating	Engine Type/CID	P.O.E. Price	Weight (lbs.)	Prod. Total
GRIFO					
GL	2-dr Coupe-2P	V8/327	13448	2826	Note 1
RIVOLTA					
GT	2-dr Coupe-4P	V8/327	8539	3350	Note 2
FIDIA					
S4	4-dr Sedan-4/5P	V8/327	13800	3740	Note 3
LELE					
	2-dr Coupe-2+2P	V8/350	24500	3520	317

Note 1: A total of 412 Grifos were produced during the full model run, through 1974.
Note 2: A total of 799 Rivoltas were produced, through 1970.
Note 3: A total of 192 Fidias were produced, through 1974.
Price Note: Lele price shown was effective in 1974; others in 1969. The Grifo 7-Litre price in 1970 was $15,800.

ENGINE DATA: BASE V-8: 90-degree, overhead-valve V-8 (Corvette Turbofire). Cast iron block and head. **Displacement:** 327 cu. in. (5359 cc). **Bore & Stroke:** 4.00 x 3.25 in. (101.6 x 82.55 mm). **Compression Ratio:** 10.5:1. **Brake Horsepower:** 300 at 5000 rpm. **Torque:** 360 lbs.-ft. at 3200 rpm. Five main bearings. Hydraulic valve lifters. Carter four-barrel carburetor.
OPTIONAL V-8: Same as above, except — **Compression Ratio:** 11.0:1. **Brake Horsepower:** 350 (SAE) at 5800 rpm. **Torque:** 360 lbs.-ft. at 3600 rpm.
BASE V-8 (Lele): 90-degree, overhead-valve V-8 (Chevrolet). Cast iron block and head. **Displacement:** 350 cu. in. (5735 cc). **Bore & Stroke:** 4.00 x 3.48 in. (101.6 x 88.4 mm). **Compression Ratio:** 10.2:1. **Brake Horsepower:** 300 (SAE) at 4800 rpm. **Torque:** 380 lbs.-ft. at 3200 rpm. Five main bearings. Hydraulic valve lifters.
OPTIONAL V-8 (7-Litre): 90-degree, overhead-valve V-8 (Chevrolet). Cast iron block and head. **Displacement:** 427 cu. in. (6998 cc). **Bore & Stroke:** 4.25 x 3.76 in. (107.9 x 95.9 mm). **Compression Ratio:** 10.2:1. **Brake Horsepower:** 400 at 5200 rpm. **Torque:** 460 lbs.-ft. at 3600 rpm.

Note: Some Grifos, Fidias and Leles had a 351-cid (5762-cc) Ford V-8.

CHASSIS DATA: Wheelbase: (Grifo) 98.4 in.; (Rivolta) 106.5 in.; (Fidia) 112.2 in.; (Lele) 106.3 in. **Overall Length:** (Grifo) 174.4 in.; (Rivolta) 187.4 in.; (Fidia) 195.7 in.; (Lele) 183.1 in. **Height:** (Grifo) 47.2 in.; (Rivolta) 52.8 in.; (Fidia) 52.0 in.; (Lele) 53.1 in. **Width:** (Grifo) 69.7 in.; (Rivolta) 68.9 in.; (Lele) 68.9 in. **Front Tread:** 55.5 in. **Rear Tread:** 55.5 in. **Wheel Type:** disc (6Lx15). **Standard Tires:** Pirelli Cinturato HS 185VR15 or 205VR15.

TECHNICAL: Layout: front-engine, rear-drive. **Transmission:** four-speed manual (Borg-Warner T-10), five-speed manual (ZF) or three-speed "Powerglide" automatic (Chevrolet). Four-speed standard gear ratios: (1st) 2.54:1; (2nd) 1.89:1; (3rd) 1.51:1; (4th) 1.00:1. **Standard Final Drive Ratio:** 2.88:1 or 3.07:1 ("Power Lock" differential available). **Steering:** Burman recirculating ball. **Suspension (front):** wishbones and coil springs with anti-roll bar. **Suspension (rear):** De Dion axle with twin trailing radius arms, transverse linkage bars and coil springs. **Brakes:** Dunlop hydraulic, front/rear discs with servo assist (discs near differential at rear). **Body Construction:** steel body welded to (integral with) steel platform frame.

MAJOR OPTIONS: Automatic transmission ($150). Air conditioning: Rivolta/Fidia ($495). Power steering. Detachable roof. Leather interior: Rivolta ($375). Alloy wheels. Borrani triple-laced wire wheels.

PERFORMANCE: Top Speed: (Grifo 300-hp) 143 mph; (Grifo 350-hp) 165 mph; (Grifo 7-Litre) 175 mph; (Rivolta 300-hp) 137 mph; (Rivolta 350-hp) 148 mph; (Fidia) 130-143 mph; (Lele) 150-155 mph. **Acceleration (0-60 mph):** (Grifo 350-hp) 6.5-7.4 sec.; (Grifo 7-Litre) 6.0 sec.; (Rivolta) 7.8 sec.; (Fidia) 8.0 sec. **Acceleration (quarter-mile):** (Grifo 300-hp) 15 sec.; (Grifo 350-hp) 14.5 sec.; (Rivolta 300-hp) 16.2 sec.; (Rivolta 350-hp) (15.8 sec. **Fuel Mileage:** (Grifo 300-hp) 16.5 mpg; (Grifo 350-hp) 15.7 mpg; (Rivolta 300-hp) 15 mpg; (350-hp) 13.5 mpg.; (Lele/Fidia) 12.4 mpg.

Manufacturer: Iso Automoveicoli S.p.A., Bresso, Milan, Italy. **Distributor:** Isocars Corp., New York City; or Granturismo Inc., South Norwalk, Connecticut.

ISOTTA FRASCHINI

World-renowned for its prewar luxury automobiles, the Isotta Fraschini carried on briefly into the postwar period before expiring completely. The Italian company was founded in 1899 by Cesare Isotta and Vincenzo Fraschini: first to import cars from France, then (by 1903) to mount French engines in a chassis of their own design. In addition to automobiles, the firm turned to aircraft-engine and truck production during World War I. After the war, in 1919, they announced production of a straight-eight Type 8 model, though it took a while for actual cars to be delivered. A fair number of those big Isotta Fraschinis wound up on the American side of the Atlantic, starting in 1922. With two separate cylinder heads atop a light-alloy block, the early straight eight produced 80 horsepower. Enlargement to 7372-cc displacement in the Type 8A of 1924 boosted output to 120 bhp. A Type 8ASS sporting edition with higher compression was rated 135 bhp, and could hit 100 mph. The final prewar model was the Type 8B, introduced in 1931, which could have a Wilson preselector transmission. Automobile production was abandoned just one year later, but resumed briefly after World War II for one final stab at the world market with the Monterosa.

1947 Isotta-Fraschini covertible coupe.

ENGINE DATA: BASE V-8: Overhead-valve "vee" type eight-cylinder. **Displacement:** 181.8 cu. in. (2980 cc). **Bore & Stroke:** 3.07 x 3.07 in. (78 x 78 mm). **Compression Ratio:** 7.0:1. **Brake Horsepower:** 120 at 4800 rpm. Five main bearings. One downdraft carburetor.

CHASSIS DATA: Wheelbase: 122 in. **Front Tread:** 57.1 in. **Rear Tread:** 57.1 in. **Standard Tires:** 7.00x16.

TECHNICAL: Layout: rear-engine, rear-drive. **Transmission:** five-speed manual. **Standard Final Drive Ratio:** 3.94:1. **Suspension (front):** independent; rubber in compression. **Suspension (rear):** independent; swing axles. **Brakes:** hydraulic, front/rear drum. **Body Construction:** separate body on steel frame. **Manufacturer:** Isotta Fraschini S.A., Milan, Italy.

HISTORY: By the end of 1949, the famed old firm was reported to have been liquidated, its final attempt at success never having gotten off the ground.

1947-49 ISOTTA FRASCHINI

1947 Isotta-Fraschini Tipo 8C Monterosa 3.4-liter saloon. (Autocar)

MONTEROSA — TYPE 8C — V-8 — Designed by Fabio Rapi, the final Isotta Fraschini was powered by a rear-mounted overhead-cam V-8 engine with five-speed (all-synchro) manual transmission. When introduced at the Paris Salon in 1947, the prototypes, with convertible and closed bodies by Touring of Italy, carried 3.4-liter engines. The platform-type chassis used a swing-axle rear suspension. Fewer than 20 were actually produced, according to the *Encyclopedia of Motorcars* (other sources indicate as few as six), with a 2980-cc or 2544-cc engine. Sedan bodies were styled by Touring and Zagato, a convertible by Boneschi.

I.D. DATA: Not available.

Model	Body Type & Seating	Engine Type/CID	P.O.E. Price	Weight (lbs.)	Prod. Total
MONTEROSA					
8C	2-dr Coupe	V8/182	N/A	Note 1	Note 2
8C	4-dr Sedan	V8/182	N/A	Note 1	Note 2
8C	2-dr Conv	V8/182	N/A	Note 1	Note 2

Note 1: Chassis weight was 3197 pounds.
Note 2: Fewer than 20 (possibly as few as six) Monterosas were produced from 1947-49.

ISUZU

Ishikawajima, a predecessor to the Isuzu, was assembling British Wolseleys under license in Japan as early as 1918. That foray led to the manufacture of military vehicles during the 1930s. In 1937, that company joined with another manufacturer and the Tokyo Gas and Electric Company to form a larger organization, which led to the Hino nameplate during World War II. Isuzu Motors was formed in 1949, and the Hino name would wind up as part of Toyota. Production during the 1950s consisted of assembly of Hillman Minxes. Then, in 1959, Isuzu turned out an Elf truck and began to produce a diesel engine. Diesel power wound up in many of the first actual automobiles to come out of Isuzu, named Bellel, as introduced in 1961. Both the Bellel and the subsequent Florian were produced as sedans and as coupes, the latter styled by Ghia and Giugiaro in Italy. General Motors obtained a substantial interest (34.2 percent) in the company in 1971, leading to availability of the LUV pickup truck in Chevrolet showrooms during that decade. An Isuzu model also was marketed by Buick in the late 1970s, as the Opel (in the wake of the demise of the German-built Opel).

Passenger cars under the Isuzu nameplate did not go on general sale in the U.S. until the 1980s, with the debut of the I-Mark. Around the same time, the Trooper 4WD sport-utility vehicle was introduced; and Isuzu sold an extensive line of pickup trucks alongside the 4WDs and passenger cars. By 1983, an Impulse coupe was available at U.S. dealerships, along with the I-Mark. Turbocharged versions of both models gave Isuzu a modest performance image to match its economy-oriented role. In the mid- to late-1980s, Isuzus also were marketed under Chevrolet badges as the Spectrum sedan (see Geo/Chevrolet listing). Yet another 4WD model, the Amigo, joined the Isuzu lineup by 1989.

1961-65 ISUZU

BELLEL — 2000 — FOUR — A diesel four-cylinder engine powered this sedan, which was the first car designed by Isuzu. Though rare in the U.S., it was advertised for sale and listed in some directories of imported models. The four-door sedan had a sharp-edged profile with a large rectangular mesh grille, and large parking lights below the headlamps. 'Bellel Diesel' script went on the cowl, above a full-length bodyside molding. A station wagon also was advertised in 1965. Standard equipment included a four-speed manual transmission, signal-seeking stereo radio, electronic headlamp dimmer, forced-air thermo heater, tinted glass, and nylon whitewall tires. The diesel engine had a Bosch injection system. A top speed up to 80 mph was claimed.

I.D. DATA: Not available.

Model	Body Type & Seating	Engine Type/CID	P.O.E. Price	Weight (lbs.)	Prod. Total
2000	4-dr Sedan-6P	I4/121	2690	3200	Note 1
2000	4-dr Sta Wag-6P	I4/121	2990	N/A	Note 1

Note 1: A total of 36,278 Isuzus (all models) were produced during 1964 alone.

ENGINE DATA: BASE DIESEL FOUR (DL201): Inline, overhead-valve four-cylinder. Cast iron block and head. **Displacement:** 121.5 cu. in. (1991 cc). **Bore & Stroke:** 3.27 x 3.62 in. (83 x 92 mm). **Compression Ratio:** 21.0:1. **Brake Horsepower:** 55 at 3600 rpm. **Torque:** 89 lbs.-ft. at 2000 rpm. Solid valve lifters. Bosch-licensed fuel injection.

OPTIONAL DIESEL FOUR (DL200): Inline, overhead-valve four-cylinder. Cast iron block and head. **Displacement:** 98 cu. in. (1608 cc). **Bore & Stroke:** 3.11 x 3.23 in. (79 x 82 mm). **Compression Ratio:** 21.0:1. **Brake Horsepower:** 52 at 3600 rpm. **Torque:** 87 lbs.-ft. at 2000 rpm. Solid valve lifters. Bosch-licensed fuel injection.

Note: Gasoline-engined Isuzus also were produced during this period, using a 1.5- or 2.0-liter overhead-valve four-cylinder engine.

CHASSIS DATA: Wheelbase: 99.6 in. **Overall Length:** 176 in. **Height:** 59.7 in. **Width:** 66.6 in. **Front Tread:** 52.8 in. **Rear Tread:** 53.6 in. **Standard Tires:** 6.40x14.

Note: Dimensions above were for 2000-series sedan with gasoline engine.

TECHNICAL: Layout: front-engine, rear-drive. **Transmission:** four-speed manual (synchro 2nd/3rd/4th). **Steering:** recirculating ball. **Suspension (front):** wishbones with coil springs. **Suspension (rear):** rigid axle with semi-elliptic leaf springs. **Brakes:** hydraulic, front/rear drum. **Body Construction:** steel unibody. **Fuel Tank:** 10 gallon.

Manufacturer: Isuzu Motors Ltd., Tokyo, Japan.

Distributor: Trans-Alpac Corp., Burbank, California.

HISTORY: Isuzus were not ordinarily imported into the U.S. under their own name until the 1980s, when the I-Mark (and later Impulse) became available. Advertisements for this early example omitted the Isuzu name completely, calling the four-door sedan, simply, the Bellel 2000 Diesel. The U.S. distributor immodestly promoted the Bellel as the "world's greatest getaway car," and as the "lowest priced, highest quality, diesel-powered automobile in the world," offering "classic styling" that didn't change dramatically each year.

1966-80 ISUZU

By 1966, a Bellett model debuted with a 1.5-liter engine, and became available in other displacements as well. At the following year's Tokyo show, a new Florian appeared with an overhead-cam 1.6-liter four, along with a Type 117 sport coupe. By 1971, Florians were in production with 1.8-liter power.

During the 1970s, following the purchase of a sizable share of Isuzu by General Motors, Chevrolet dealers marketed the Isuzu-built LUV pickup. Then a Gemini project, begun in 1974, spawned the release of a version that sold as the Buick Opel (adopting the name formerly used by German-built models). See Opel listing for details on that latter model.

Road Test magazine tested an Isuzu/GM Gemini 1600 for its February 1975 issue, prior to its availability in the U.S. With a 1584-cc overhead-cam engine developing 100 horsepower, the 1600 could accelerate from zero to 60 mph in 13 seconds, and had a claimed top speed of 106 mph.

1981-82 ISUZU

I-MARK — FOUR — After several years of availability in the U.S. under the Opel name, Isuzus finally entered the American marketplace on their own. Both two-door fastback coupes and four-door notchback sedans were available in the early 1980s under the I-Mark name, powered by either gasoline or diesel engines that displaced 1.8 liters. They were closely related to the Buick/Opel sold in the late 1970s, and to GM's Chevette (T-car). Standard Deluxe-model equipment included a five-speed manual gearbox, power brakes, tinted glass, rear defogger, intermittent wipers, clock, console, and reclining front bucket seats. The LS added bodyside stripes and dual sport mirrors. The base coupe lacked some of the Deluxe features. A slight facelift came in 1982.

I.D. DATA: A 17-symbol Vehicle Identification Number is atop the dashboard, visible through the windshield. Symbol one ('J') indicated Japan; symbol two ('A') denotes Isuzu Motors; symbol three ('B') means passenger car; symbol four identifies the restraint system. Symbols six and seven denote the body type ('07' = hatchback cpe; '08'

or '11' = hatchback sedan; '15' = 2-dr sta wag; '19' or '69' = 4-dr sedan; '35' = 4-dr sta wag; '68' = 4-dr hatchback sedan; '77' = 2-dr cpe). Symbol eight is engine type ('B' = gasoline; 'P' = diesel). Symbol ten is model year ('B' = 1981; 'C' = 1982). Final six digits form the sequential production number. Engine number is at upper right corner of block (gasoline) or left rear corner (diesel).

Price/Specification Note: Figures shown below are for 1981 models.

Model	Body Type & Seating	Engine Type/CID	P.O.E. Price	Weight (lbs.)	Prod. Total
I-MARK (GASOLINE)					
AT77B	2-dr DeL Cpe-4P	I4/111	5917	2187	Note 1
AT69B	4-dr DeL Sed-4P	I4/111	6069	2233	Note 1
AT77B	2-dr LS Cpe-4P	I4/111	6535	2202	Note 1
I-MARK (DIESEL)					
AT77P	2-dr Cpe-4P	I4/111	6699	N/A	Note 1
AT77P	2-dr DeL Cpe-4P	I4/111	7044	N/A	Note 1
AT69P	4-dr DeL Sed-4P	I4/111	7194	N/A	Note 1
AT77P	2-dr LS Cpe-4P	I4/111	7660	N/A	Note 1

Note 1: A total of 129,564 passenger cars were produced by Isuzu during 1981, followed by 113,299 in 1982.

ENGINE DATA: BASE FOUR (Gasoline): Inline, overhead-cam four-cylinder (G180Z). Cast iron block and light alloy head. **Displacement:** 111 cu. in. (1817 cc). **Bore & Stroke:** 3.31 x 3.23 in. (84 x 82 mm). **Compression Ratio:** 8.5:1. **Brake Horsepower:** 78-80 at 4800 rpm. **Torque:** 95 lbs.-ft. at 3000 rpm. Five main bearings. Solid valve lifters. Hitachi two-barrel carburetor.

BASE FOUR (Diesel): Inline, overhead-cam four-cylinder (4FB1). Cast iron block and light alloy head. **Displacement:** 111 cu. in. (1817 cc). **Bore & Stroke:** 3.31 x 3.23 in. (84 x 82 mm). **Compression Ratio:** 22.0:1. **Brake Horsepower:** 51 at 5000 rpm. **Torque:** 72 lbs.-ft. at 2000 rpm. Five main bearings. Solid valve lifters. Fuel injection.

CHASSIS DATA: Wheelbase: 94.3 in. **Overall Length:** 171 in. **Height:** (cpe) 52.6 in.; (sed) 53.5 in. **Width:** 61.8 in. **Front Tread:** 51.4 in. **Rear Tread:** 51.4 in. **Standard Tires:** 155SR13 or 175/70R13 except (diesel) 155/70R13.

TECHNICAL: Layout: front-engine, rear-drive. **Transmission:** five-speed manual except (base diesel cpe) four-speed. **Standard Final Drive Ratio:** 3.15:1. **Steering:** rack and pinion. **Suspension (front):** A-arms with coil springs. **Suspension (rear):** rigid axle with coil springs. **Brakes:** front disc, rear drum. **Body Construction:** steel unibody. **Fuel Tank:** 13.7 gallon.

MAJOR OPTIONS: Automatic transmission ($197). Air conditioning. Rally package. AM/FM stereo radio. Power steering.

PRODUCTION/SALES: A total of 17,805 Isuzus were sold in the U.S. during 1981, and 15,462 in 1982.

Manufacturer: Isuzu Motors Ltd., Tokyo, Japan.

Distributor: American Isuzu Motors Inc., Whittier, California.

HISTORY: Isuzu also marketed a series of pickup trucks, including a four-wheel-drive version. On 104.3- or 117.9-inch wheelbases, the pickups carried a 1.8-liter gasoline or 2.0-liter diesel engine. By 1982, Isuzus were sold in about 30 states.

1983-85 ISUZU

1984 Isuzu I-Mark four-door sedan.

I-MARK — FOUR — Production of the I-Mark coupes and sedans continued, though the range of models available in the U.S. shrank each year. In Japan, these were part of the Gemini series.

IMPULSE — FOUR — A sporty new hatchback coupe became available during the 1983 model year in the U.S., powered by a 1949-cc gasoline four-cylinder engine. Introduced two years earlier in Japan, it evolved from an "Ace of Clubs" vehicle designed by Giorgetto Giugiaro, which had appeared at the 1979 Geneva (Switzerland) auto show. Styling features included aerodynamic lines with flush window glass and a steep windshield angle, plus partly hidden headlamps. Impulses lacked exposed body seams and chrome trim. Either a five-speed manual or four-speed automatic transmission was available. Standard equipment included power steering, power windows, cruise control, auto-temp air conditioning, rear- and side-window defoggers, digital clock, stopwatch, power door locks, AM/FM stereo radio, remote hatch release, adjustable control pods, and an adjustable steering column. Four-wheel disc brakes were standard, and the dashboard held a tachometer. Tinted glass included a sunshade band. Aluminum alloy wheels held P195/60R14 raised-black-letter tires. The only Impulse options were a cassette player and premium sound system, and turbine-style wheels.

I.D. DATA: A 17-symbol Vehicle Identification Number is atop the dashboard, visible through the windshield. Breakdown is similar to 1981-82.

Price/Specification Note: Figures shown below are for 1983 models.

Model	Body Type & Seating	Engine Type/CID	P.O.E. Price	Weight (lbs.)	Prod. Total
I-MARK (GASOLINE)					
T77	2-dr DeL Cpe-4P	I4/111	6415	2189	Note 1
T69	4-dr DeL Sed-4P	I4/111	6535	2231	Note 1
T77	2-dr LS Cpe-4P	I4/111	6890	2207	Note 1
T69	4-dr LS Sed-4P	I4/111	7010	2260	Note 1
I-MARK (DIESEL)					
T77	2-dr Cpe-4P	I4/111	6720	2233	Note 1
IMPULSE					
	2-dr Spt Cpe-4P	I4/119	9998	2734	Note 1

1984 Isuzu Impulse GT coupe.

Note 1: A total of 20,731 Isuzus were sold in the U.S. during 1983, followed by 17,233 in 1984, and 26,953 in 1985.

ENGINE DATA: BASE FOUR (I-Mark Gasoline): Inline, overhead-cam four-cylinder (G180Z). Cast iron block and light alloy head. **Displacement:** 111 cu. in. (1817 cc). **Bore & Stroke:** 3.31 x 3.23 in. (84 x 82 mm). **Compression Ratio:** 8.5:1. **Brake Horsepower:** 78 at 4800 rpm. **Torque:** 95 lbs.-ft. at 3000 rpm. Five main bearings. Solid valve lifters. Two-barrel carburetor.
BASE FOUR (I-Mark Diesel): Inline, overhead-cam four-cylinder (4FB1). Cast iron block and light alloy head. **Displacement:** 111 cu. in. (1817 cc). **Bore & Stroke:** 3.31 x 3.23 in. (84 x 82 mm). **Compression Ratio:** 22.0:1. **Brake Horsepower:** 51 at 5000 rpm. **Torque:** 72 lbs.-ft. at 3000 rpm. Five main bearings. Solid valve lifters. Fuel injection.
BASE FOUR (Impulse): Inline, overhead-cam four-cylinder (G200Z). Cast iron block and light alloy head. **Displacement:** 118.9 cu. in. (1949 cc). **Bore & Stroke:** 3.43 x 3.23 in. (87 x 82 mm). **Compression Ratio:** 9.2:1. **Brake Horsepower:** 90 at 5000 rpm. **Torque:** 108 lbs.-ft. at 3000 rpm. Five main bearings. Solid valve lifters. Multi-point fuel injection.

CHASSIS DATA: Wheelbase: (I-Mark) 94.3 in.; (Impulse) 96.0 in. **Overall Length:** (I-Mark) 170.1-170.7 in.; (Impulse) 172.6 in. **Height:** (I-Mark cpe) 52.6 in.; (I-Mark sed) 53.5 in.; (Impulse) 51.4 in. **Width:** (I-Mark) 61.8 in.; (Impulse) 65.2 in. **Front Tread:** (I-Mark) 51.4 in.; (Impulse) 53.4 in. **Rear Tread:** (I-Mark) 51.4 in.; (Impulse) 53.9 in. **Standard Tires:** (I-Mark) 175/70R13 except (diesel) 155/70R13; (Impulse) P195/60R14.

TECHNICAL: Layout: front-engine, rear-drive. **Transmission:** five-speed manual; three-speed automatic (I-Mark) or four-speed automatic (Impulse) available. **Steering:** rack and pinion. **Suspension (front):** A-arms with coil springs and anti-roll bar. **Suspension (rear):** rigid axle with coil springs. **Brakes:** (I-Mark) front disc, rear drum; (Impulse) front/rear disc. **Body Construction:** steel unibody.

MAJOR OPTIONS (1983 I-Mark): Automatic transmission ($332). Air conditioning ($606). AM/FM stereo radio ($235); w/cassette player ($343). Gold aluminum wheels: DeL ($310). Sport package: sedan ($222).

ADDITIONAL MODELS: A series of Isuzu pickup trucks also was sold in the U.S. at this time. The Trooper four-wheel-drive sport-utility vehicle became available in 1984.

Manufacturer: Isuzu Motors Ltd., Tokyo, Japan.
Distributor: American Isuzu Motors Inc., Whittier, California.

HISTORY: A new front-drive I-Mark debuted during the 1985 model year; see next listing for details. The Impulse had debuted in Japan as the Piazza, in 1981.

1986-89 ISUZU

I-MARK — FOUR — A front-wheel-drive version of the I-Mark replaced the original rear-drive model during the 1985 model year, with a smaller (1471-cc) transverse-mounted engine. The diesel engine was no longer available. For 1987, the front end got a restyle that included flush composite headlamps, revised fenders and a no-grille nose, and a turbocharged RS model became available. For 1989, a larger (1588-cc) engine went into the RS series, in a twin-cam (non-turbo) configuration that produced 125 horsepower. That RS could accelerate to 60 mph in 8.1 seconds, and achieve 32 mpg. *Road & Track* advised that the I-Mark RS sounded "like a Cosworth racing engine." Chevrolet marketed a closely-related variant of the I-Mark as the Spectrum (see Geo listing).

IMPULSE — FOUR — Production of the sporty coupe continued with its 1949-cc gasoline four-cylinder engine. Appearance was similar to 1983-85, with partly-concealed headlamps, hidden drip rails, single-arm windshield wiper, and a rounded back end. 'Impulse' lettering went in the center of the smooth rear panel. The aero-shaped hatchback coupe lacked chrome trim and exposed body seams. Rear seats folded down, and front seats had seven-way adjustment with lumbar/thigh support. A turbocharged/intercooled 1994-cc engine also became available during the 1985 model year, delivering 140 horsepower. A limited-production RS turbo also was announced in 1987, with white body and handling suspension. A larger (2254-cc) non-turbo engine became standard in 1988. Suspension modifications from Lotus brought a "Handling by Lotus" insignia to 1988 models. Also in 1988, a "power bulge" went on Impulse hoods, the grille was restyled, and small "doors" no longer covered a portion of the headlamps. Turbo models added a new rear spoiler that year.

I.D. DATA: A 17-symbol Vehicle Identification Number is atop the dashboard, visible through the windshield. Breakdown is similar to 1981-82. I-Mark engine number is on the flange near the transaxle mounting, toward the front of the car.

1986 Isuzu Impulse Turbo hatchback coupe.

Model	Body Type & Seating	Engine Type/CID	P.O.E. Price	Weight (lbs.)	Prod. Total
I-MARK (1986 Models)					
T77	2-dr Hatch-4P	I4/90	7149	1919	Note 1
T69	4-dr Sedan-4P	I4/90	7249	1933	Note 1
I-MARK (1989 Models)					
S	2-dr Hatch-4P	I4/90	7779	1984	Note 1
XS	2-dr Hatch-4P	I4/90	9179	2015	Note 1
RS	2-dr Hatch-4P	I4/97	9359	2167	Note 1
S	4-dr Sedan-4P	I4/90	8179	2011	Note 1
XS	4-dr Sedan-4P	I4/90	9379	2024	Note 1
RS	4-dr Sedan-4P	I4/97	9559	2191	Note 1
LS Turbo	4-dr Sedan-4P	I4/90	11369	2154	Note 1
IMPULSE (1986 Models)					
R07	2-dr Spt Cpe-4P	I4/119	11048	2734	Note 1
R07	2-dr Turbo Cpe-4P	I4/122	13499	2824	Note 1
IMPULSE (1989 Models)					
R07	2-dr Spt Cpe-4P	I4/137	14329	2890	Note 1
R07	2-dr Turbo Cpe-4P	I4/122	16329	2970	Note 1

Note 1: A total of 38,910 Isuzus were sold in the U.S. during 1986, followed by 39,587 in 1987, 24,520 in 1988, and 16,296 in 1989.

1986 Isuzu I-Mark four-door sedan.

ENGINE DATA: BASE FOUR (I-Mark): Inline, overhead-cam four-cylinder. **Displacement:** 89.8 cu. in. (1471 cc). **Bore & Stroke:** 3.03 x 3.11 in. (77 x 79 mm). **Compression Ratio:** 9.6:1. **Brake Horsepower:** 70 at 5400 rpm. **Torque:** 87 lbs.-ft. at 3400 rpm. Solid valve lifters. Two-barrel carburetor.
OPTIONAL TURBO FOUR (1987-89 I-Mark): Same as 1471-cc four above, but with turbocharger and multi-point fuel injection — **Compression Ratio:** 8.0:1. **Brake Horsepower:** 110 at 5400 rpm. **Torque:** 120 lbs.-ft. at 3500 rpm.
BASE FOUR (1989 I-Mark RS): Inline, dual-overhead-cam four-cylinder. **Displacement:** 96.9 cu. in. (1588 cc). **Bore & Stroke:** 3.15 x 3.11 in. (80 x 79 mm). **Compression Ratio:** 9.8:1. **Brake Horsepower:** 125 at 6800 rpm. **Torque:** 102 lbs.-ft. at 5400 rpm. Solid valve lifters. Multi-point fuel injection.
BASE FOUR (1986-87 Impulse): Inline, overhead-cam four-cylinder. **Displacement:** 118.9 cu. in. (1949 cc). **Bore & Stroke:** 3.43 x 3.23 in. (87 x 82 mm). **Brake Horsepower:** 90 at 5000 rpm. **Torque:** 108 lbs.-ft. at 3000 rpm. Solid valve lifters. Multi-point fuel injection.
BASE FOUR (1988-89 Impulse): Inline, overhead-cam four-cylinder. **Displacement:** 137.5 cu. in. (2254 cc). **Bore & Stroke:** 3.52 x 3.54 in. (89.4 x 90 mm). **Compression Ratio:** 8.6:1. **Brake Horsepower:** 110 at 5000 rpm. **Torque:** 127 lbs.-ft. at 3000 rpm. Solid valve lifters. Multi-point fuel injection.
OPTIONAL TURBO FOUR (Impulse): Inline, overhead-cam four-cylinder. Turbocharged with air-to-air intercooler. **Displacement:** 121.7 cu. in. (1994 cc). **Bore & Stroke:** 3.47 x 3.23 in. (88 x 82 mm). **Compression Ratio:** 7.9:1. **Brake Horsepower:** 140 at 5400 rpm. **Torque:** 166 lbs.-ft. at 3000 rpm. I-TEC multi-point fuel injection.

CHASSIS DATA: Wheelbase: (I-Mark) 94.5 in.; (Impulse) 96.1 in. **Overall Length:** (I-Mark hatch) 157.4 in.; (I-Mark sedan) 160.2 in.; (Impulse) 172.6 in. **Height:** (I-Mark) 54.1 in.; (Impulse) 51.4 in. **Width:** (I-Mark) 63.5 in.; (Impulse) 65.2 in. **Front Tread:** (I-Mark) 54.7 in.; (Impulse) 53.3 in. **Rear Tread:** (I-Mark) 54.3 in.; (Impulse) 54.3 in. **Standard Tires:** (I-Mark) 175/70R13 except (RS) 185/60R14; (Impulse) P195/60R14 or P205/60R14.

Note: Dimensions above were for 1988 models.

TECHNICAL: Layout: (I-Mark) front-engine, front-drive; (Impulse) front-engine, rear-drive. **Transmission:** five-speed manual; three-speed automatic (I-Mark) or four-speed automatic (Impulse) available. **Steering:** rack and pinion. **Suspension (front):** (I-Mark)

1988 Isuzu Impulse Turbo.

MacPherson struts with coil springs; (Impulse) twin A-arms with coil springs and anti-roll bar. **Suspension (rear):** (I-Mark) transverse beam axle with trailing arms and coil springs; (Impulse) rigid axle with coil springs and anti-roll bar. **Brakes:** (I-Mark) front disc, rear drum; (Impulse) front/rear disc. **Body Construction:** steel unibody.

MAJOR OPTIONS (1986): Automatic transmission: I-Mark ($380); Impulse ($560). Air conditioning: I-Mark ($630). Power steering: I-Mark ($205). AM/FM stereo radio w/cassette player: I-Mark ($345); w/graphic equalizer ($485). Premium sound system: Impulse ($421). Sunroof: I-Mark ($270). Alloy wheels: Impulse ($100). Cruise control (I-Mark). Leather seat package: Impulse Turbo ($1173).

ADDITIONAL MODELS: A series of Isuzu P'up pickup trucks was sold in the U.S. during this period, as was the Trooper four-wheel-drive sport-utility vehicle. A smaller Isuzu Amigo 4WD vehicle became available in 1989.
Manufacturer: Isuzu Motors Ltd., Tokyo, Japan.
Distributor: American Isuzu Motors Inc., Whittier, California.

1990 Isuzu Impulse XS.

POSTSCRIPT: For 1990, the I-Mark was out of the lineup. All that was left (in addition to the pickup trucks and 4WD vehicles) was a revised front-drive Impulse coupe. The new 2 + 2 XS coupe rode a 96.5-inch wheelbase, measured 166 inches overall, and carried a 1588-cc (96.9-cid) four-cylinder engine that produced 130 horsepower. Tires were 185/60R14 size, and the car weighed 2,411 pounds. It was perhaps better known in the U.S. in its incarnation as the similar Geo Storm, marketed by Chevrolet dealers.

JAGUAR

Origin of the world-renowned Jaguar nameplate began with William Lyons and the SS company in Britain. Founded in the late 1920s, the Swallow Coachbuilding Company changed to SS Cars Ltd. by 1931 as the firm turned from special bodies to complete automobiles.

Partnered with William Walmsley, Lyons had initially worked on Swallow sidecars (as the Swallow Sidecar Co.), then turned to production of bodies for such cars as the Austin Seven, Morris Cowley, and Fiat Tipo. Then, Lyons designed a rakish body for a new Standard chassis, which became known as the SS1, offered in saloon (sedan), coupe, and convertible form. Wearing a long hood and with styling reminiscent of the huge SSK Mercedes, the SS1 captured attention at the 1931 British Motor Show. Among the most famous of the versions that followed was the two-seater SS90, produced in 1935; followed the next year by the even more notable SS100. That SS100 first came with an overhead-valve 2663-cc six (a Standard conversion); then a 125-bhp, 3485-cc engine (mainly SS). With an exposed gas tank, the SS100 was fast and known for good roadholding, though some observers thought the bodies to be excessively flamboyant. Nevertheless, their gracefully curved front fenders, blending beautifully into the running boards and rounded rear fenders, attracted considerable attention on both sides of the Atlantic. Priced reasonably at 445 pounds (Sterling) in Britain, the 3.5-liter SS100 could run from 0-60 mph in about 10.5 seconds, and hit a top speed of about 100 mph. Both before and after World War II, SS100s raced at Brooklands and at British hillclimbs, as well as in rally events. In fall 1935, the Jaguar name was used for the first time. As few as 265 SS100 roadsters were built before the war.

After the war, with the company renamed Jaguar Cars Ltd., the SS100 made no further appearance; but a revival of the prewar saloons gained surprising early popularity in America, powered by a 3.5-liter or 2.5-liter six-cylinder engine. That popularity led to the emergence of a new Mark V saloon for 1949, which also gained a U.S. following. Jaguar also offered a smaller 1.5-liter model, with a four-cylinder engine; but few of those crossed the Atlantic. And when Standard stopped producing the four-cylinder engine that had been used, Jaguar elected to drop the small sedans completely.

Meanwhile, at the Earl's Court Motor Show in fall 1948, a completely different Jaguar, the XK-120 roadster, created nothing short of a sensation. With its name suggesting a 120-mph top speed, the XK soon became the fastest production car in the world, powered by a new 3.4-liter six-cylinder engine that delivered 160 horsepower. That was enough to send an XK-120 to 60 mph in as little as 10 seconds.

Actually, the XK-120 was intended to be a limited-production model, solely to demonstrate the new dual-overhead-camshaft six-cylinder engine (to be used in future saloons). Its immediate success called for complete body tooling to be created in a hurry-up project. Not only was the new roadster practical and reasonably-priced, it was also docile, rode nicely, held the road securely—and beautiful to boot.

Not everyone believed early claims of Jaguar's virtues, so the company held a high-speed demonstration run in Belgium (on the Jabbeke highway). There, an unmodified XK-120 hit 126 mph at first, then 132 mph with its windshield removed. To complete the show, it then ran past journalists at 10 mph in top (fourth) gear. In 1949, three Jaguars entered the British Racing Driver's Club meet at Silverstone, in a one-hour race for production models. They took first and second place, and the third car lost only because of a blown tire.

Many other race victories followed. Stirling Moss won the 1950 Tourist Trophy, while a Jaguar driven by Ian Appleyard won Alpine rallies in 1950/51/52.

Three Jag XK-120s entered the 1950 Le Mans 24-Hour race, not intending to win. And they didn't, as two finished somewhat far back in the pack. This attempt revealed that a special design would be needed for victory, which led to the XK-120C (called C-Type), with its multi-tube frame. One of those won the 1951 Le Mans event, and again in 1953 (with a 220-bhp engine and Dunlop disc brakes).

Joining the roadster at the 1951 Geneva (Switzerland) Motor Show was a new fixed-head coupe, displaying a profile similar to a one-of-a-kind SS100 coupe built in 1938. More civilized in behavior than the roadster, the new solid-top coupe became a better choice for long-distance touring. More pleasing interior detailing included a veneer-trimmed dashboard and wind-up windows. A Special Equipment model, called XK-120M in the U.S. market, had a 180-horsepower engine rather than the usual 160-bhp six.

Two years later, in 1953, a drophead-coupe version was introduced, with a fully-trimmed convertible top. Then, in 1954, the D-Type racer was designed, like the "C" before it, with the intention of winning the Le Mans race. This would become one of the most famous racing sportscars of the 1950s. Wind-tunnel tested, the D-Type used a central monocoque chassis designed around aircraft principles. A modified cylinder head with three Weber carburetors produced 250 horsepower. The rigid rear axle was connected by trailing arms and transverse torsion bars, and Dunlop disc brakes were used on all four wheels. Its first outing at Le Mans produced a second-place finish, partly due to fuel problems. But the D-Type then took both first and second spots in the Rheims 12-Hour race.

Debut of the next generation, the XK-140, came in October 1954. This time, moving the engine forward on the chassis allowed a larger cockpit area. The engine also got a boost to 190 horsepower, and rack-and-pinion steering was added. Drophead and fixed-head coupes offered 2 + 2 seating (though back seats were definitely for kids only).

Aerodynamics were improved on the factory D-Type, which had a longer nose, smooth tail, and more power (at least 250 bhp). That one won Le Mans, setting a 122.39-mph lap record. Factory D-Types had trouble at the next year's Le Mans, but a privately-owned team won the event. In 1957, that private team won again, as the factory dropped out of participation. A limited-production D-Type, with short nose and a bit less power (250 bhp) became available by 1956. Next year, a few of these were marketed, with minimal road gear, known as the XK-SS.

Dunlop disc brakes all around were major features of the XK-150 series, introduced in 1957. Styling changes included a wider hood, larger cockpit, and straight line back from the fenders, which meant the original swoopy profile was gone. Engine access was better, too. A one-piece windshield replaced the former vee-type. Almost all XK-150s had the "special equipment" engine with 210 horsepower, 20 more than the standard version. Only drophead and fixed-head coupes were sold in 1957, but the roadster (which added wind-up windows in this incarnation) became available again in 1958. The "S" engine option was rated 250 horsepower, with a trio of SU carburetors. Engine dimensions grew for 1959, to 3781 cubic centimeters, with 220 horsepower; and the "S" version produced 265 bhp.

Jaguar's racing D-Type evolved into the production E-Type (called XK-E in the U.S.) of 1961, which skyrocketed

in popularity from the start. Pressed-steel monocoque construction used a bolt-on tubular front sub-frame to hold the engine and front suspension. At the rear, another "cage" sub-frame held the final drive and new coil-spring (independent) rear suspension. Under the hood was the "S" variant of the 3.8-liter XK engine. Top speed was now 150 mph, due to improved aerodynamics, and an E-Type could run from 0-60 mph in 6.9 seconds. Two models were offered: an open two-seater or fastback fixed-head coupe, the latter with a back window that opened.

An E-Jag won its first race attempt, driven by Graham Hill. But sports cars were changing, and Jag couldn't really rival the current Ferraris. So its racing career lagged behind the earlier XKs. Even so, a dozen "lightweight" E-Types were built for racing, some with an aluminum monocoque chassis and up to 320 bhp or more using fuel injection. Though driven by some top drivers (Jackie Stewart, Graham Hill), it enjoyed only modest and brief success.

A 4235-cc version of the old XK engine went into the E-Type in 1964, with no horsepower increase but more torque. The gearbox was now fully synchronized. Then, in 1966, a fixed-head 2+2 coupe with nine-inch longer wheelbase was offered, with a more vertical windshield.

Series II of the E-Type, introduced during 1968, dropped its front headlamp covers and added bigger taillamps. Bumpers stood higher up, too, partly as a result of U.S. safety requirements. Then came the Series III with a 5343-cc V-12 engine, producing up to 314 (gross) horsepower, on a longer wheelbase. A two-seat convertible and 2+2 fixed-head coupe were produced. Final editions were built in the winter of 1974-75.

In mid-1975 the XJ-S coupe emerged, also V-12 powered and with full monocoque construction. Its underpan, in fact, evolved from the XJ12 saloon. Not quite a sports car any longer, the XJ was more of a "boulevard" sportster. Before long, all examples had automatic transmissions. An "H.E." version of the engine debuted by 1982, more efficient and economical. In autumn 1983, a cabriolet XJ-S joined the 2+2 coupe, with fixed roll bar above the seats. The cabriolet took several years to arrive in the U.S. market, however. In addition to V-12 power, XJ sedans for 1988 had a new 3.6-liter twin-cam six rated 225 bhp, hooked to a five-speed Getrag manual gearbox. Jaguar continued to do well in production touring car races during the 1980s, and gave official sanction for 1983-84.

Note: For the XK series, factory literature generally used a space between the 'XK' and the following digits: e.g., XK 120. In other printed matter, a hyphen often was used; or in some cases, the letters and digits were run together (e.g., XK120). For clarity in this Catalog, the hyphenated form is used. Like other British models, Jaguar four-doors were called "saloons" at home but were generally referred to as "sedans" in the U.S.

1946-48 JAGUAR

3-1/2 LITRE — SIX — Styling of the first Jaguars to appear after World War II changed little from those offered during the late 1930s. Both the saloon (sedan) and drophead coupe displayed a traditional look with huge separately-mounted, round Lucas bulb-type headlamps, alongside a bright vertical-bar grille. Tiny round parking lights stood atop each separate fender. Bodies also had running boards and "suicide" doors. Atop the grille was a '3-1/2 Litre' badge. Wheelbase was 120 inches, solid axles with leaf springs were used at front and rear, and brakes, though new, were still mechanically actuated. Under the bonnet (hood) was a 3485-cc overhead-valve six-cylinder engine with two SU carburetors and two electric fuel pumps, rated 125 horsepower and hooked to a four-speed manual transmission. Inside was Connolly leather upholstery with plenty of polished walnut wood, but the folding tables offered in prewar models no longer were installed. Standard equipment included a tachometer, twin electric windshield wipers, "trafficator" (semaphore-style) turn signals, wire wheels, a telescopic steering wheel,

twin foglamps, heater/defroster, lighter, and built-in tool kit. The drophead's top adjusted to three positions: up, down, or a midway "DeVille" look. Left-hand-drive Jaguars destined for America had bumper guards. Wire wheels had 'JAGUAR' lettering on their knock-off hubs. During 1947, ignition advance for Jaguar engines was made automatic, no longer controlled by a steering-wheel lever.

2-1/2 LITRE — SIX — Appearance and dimensions of the smaller-engined Jaguar were similar to the larger saloon and drophead coupe, except for a '2-1/2 Litre' badge on the grille. This smaller (2664-cc) version of the overhead-valve six produced 102 horsepower.

1947 Jaguar 1½-liter Mark V saloon. (Coys of Kensington)

1-1/2 LITRE — FOUR — For the home market, Jaguar continued to produce a four-cylinder model on a shorter (113-inch) wheelbase. The engine displaced 1775 cc and produced 65 horsepower.

I.D. DATA: Chassis serial number is stamped on the front of the frame, and on a plate at side of firewall. Engine numbers are stamped on a boss on the rear of the cylinder block, and on the firewall plate. Starting serial number: (3-1/2 Litre RHD saloon) 610001; (3-1/2 Litre LHD saloon) 630001; (3-1/2 Litre RHD coupe) 617001; (3-1/2 Litre LHD coupe) 637001; (2-1/2 Litre RHD saloon) 510001; (2-1/2 Litre LHD saloon) 530001; (2-1/2 Litre RHD coupe) 517001; (2-1/2 Litre LHD coupe) 537001; (1-1/2 Litre RHD) 410001; (1-1/2 Litre LHD) 430001. Starting engine number: (3/1/2 Litre) S26; (2-1/2 Litre) P18; (1-1/2 Litre) KB1001.

Model	Body Type & Seating	Engine Type/CID	P.O.E. Price	Weight (lbs.)	Prod. Total
3-1/2 LITRE					
	4-dr Saloon-5P	I6/213	4633	3500	Note 1
	2-dr Dhd Cpe-5P	I6/213	4745	3750	Note 1
2-1/2 LITRE					
	4-dr Saloon-5P	I6/162	N/A	N/A	Note 1
	2-dr Dhd Cpe-5P	I6/162	N/A	N/A	Note 1
1-1/2 LITRE					
	4-dr Saloon-4/5P	I4/108	N/A	N/A	Note 1
	2-dr Dhd Cpe-4/5P	I4/108	N/A	N/A	Note 1

Note 1: A total of 11,952 Jaguars were produced from 1946 to 1949; of that total, 4,166 were intended for export (including 376 of the 3-1/2 Litre models and 31 of the 2-1/2 Litre).

Price Note: Amounts shown were effective in 1948. Early 1948 ads listed prices of $4488 for the 3-1/2 Litre saloon (sedan) and $4600 for the convertible (drophead) with three-position top.

1948 Jaguar 3½-liter Mark three-position drophead coupe. (Christie's)

ENGINE DATA: BASE SIX (3-1/2 Litre): Inline, overhead-valve six-cylinder. Cast iron block and head. **Displacement:** 212.6 cu. in. (3485 cc). **Bore & Stroke:** 3.23 x 4.33 in. (82 x 110 mm). **Compression Ratio:** 7.2:1 or 6.75:1. **Brake Horsepower:** 125 at 4250 rpm (or 120 at 4500 rpm). **Torque:** 184 lbs.-ft. at 2000 rpm. Seven main bearings. Solid valve lifters. Two SU sidedraft carburetors. 12-volt electrical system.

BASE SIX (2-1/2 Litre): Same as above, except — **Displacement:** 162.4 cu. in. (2664 cc). **Bore & Stroke:** 2.87 x 4.17 in. (73 x 106 mm). **Compression Ratio:** 7.6:1 or 6.9:1. **Brake Horsepower:** 102 at 4600 rpm.

BASE FOUR (1-1/2 Litre): Inline, overhead-valve four-cylinder. Cast iron block and head. **Displacement:** 108 cu. in. (1775 cc). **Bore & Stroke:** 2.87 x 4.17 in. (73 x 106 mm). **Compression Ratio:** 7.5:1 or 6.8:1. **Brake Horsepower:** 65 at 4500 rpm. Three main bearings. Solid valve lifters. One SU carburetor.

Engine Note: Because of the variance in available fuels, each engine was offered with a choice of compression ratios.

CHASSIS DATA: Wheelbase: 120 in. except (1-1/2 Litre) 112.5 in. **Overall Length:** 186 in. except (1-1/2 Litre) 173 in. **Height:** (3-1/2 Litre) 61 in. **Width:** 66 in. **Front Tread:** (2-1/2 and 3-1/2 Litre) 54 in.; (1-1/2 Litre) 52 in. **Rear Tread:** (2-1/2 and 3-1/2 Litre) 56 in.; (1-1/2 Litre) 55 in. **Wheel Type:** Dunlop center-lock wire; wheel discs (covers) available. **Standard Tires:** 5.50x18 except (1-1/2 Litre) 5.25x18.

TECHNICAL: Layout: front-engine, rear-drive. **Transmission:** Moss four-speed manual, floor lever (synchro 2nd/3rd/4th). **Standard Final Drive Ratio:** (3-1/2 Litre) 4.27:1; (2-1/2 Litre) 4.55:1; (1-1/2 Litre) 4.87:1. **Steering:** Burman-Douglas worm and nut. **Suspension (front):** rigid axle with semi-elliptic leaf springs. **Suspension (rear):** rigid axle with semi-elliptic leaf springs. **Brakes:** Girling mechanical, front/rear drum. **Body Construction:** steel body on box-section steel frame. **Fuel Tank:** (3-1/2 Litre) 16.8 gallon.

MAJOR OPTIONS: Radiator ornament. Ace wheel covers. Optional compression ratios.

PERFORMANCE: Top Speed: (3-1/2 Litre) 90+ mph (up to 100 mph claimed); (2-1/2 Litre) 87 mph; (1-1/2 Litre) 71 mph. **Acceleration (0-60 mph):** N/A (0-50 mph, 3-1/2 Litre) 11.9 sec.; (0-50 mph, 2-1/2 Litre) 10.6 sec. **Acceleration (quarter-mile):** (3-1/2 Litre) 21 sec.; (2-1/2 Litre) 20.6 sec. **Fuel Mileage:** (3-1/2 Litre) 18-20 mpg claimed.

PRODUCTION/SALES: Approximately 238 Jaguars were sold in the U.S. during 1948.

Manufacturer: Jaguar Cars Ltd., Coventry, England.

Distributor: Fergus Motors and The Hoffman Motor Car Co., New York City, were the first dealers; Hoffman became eastern distributor early in 1948.

HISTORY: All three models were introduced just after World War II, in September 1945. The first saloons arrived in the U.S. in January 1947; the first drophead coupes at the end of that year, when they gained considerable popularity. Only six-cylinder models were officially imported, and those were mainly 3-1/2 Litre. These 1946-48 models were sometimes referred to as "Mark IV," after the Mark V Jaguar debuted late in 1948, but their only official name was the "Litre" designation. Production of these models ceased in March 1949, after the Mark V had already emerged.

Jaguar wanted to use pressed steel bodies for its early postwar sedans instead of the prewar-style steel-over-ash, but pressed steel was scarce in these years. So they soon mixed a new chassis with the old (3.5-liter) engine, and mounted a traditional-style "interim" body to create the Mark V saloon, until the arrival of the all-new Mark VII.

Early Hoffman ads in the U.S. promoted the 1948 Jaguar 3-1/2 Litre convertible (drop/head coupe) as "The World's Finest Car in its Class," and "the first British-made luxury car to offer conventional American left-hand drive." Customers were further advised that the car's "fleet, low, European lines...attract admiring glances everywhere."

1949 JAGUAR

1949 Jaguar XK120 roadster.

XK-120 — SIX — Jaguar's new two-seat roadster quickly became a favorite with American sports-car fans. Its name was intended to suggest the likely top speed (120 mph). Faired-in sealed-beam headlamps sat alongside the narrow oval, thirteen-vertical-bar grille, which was flanked by twin slim bumpers (without guards). The grille rose as a unit when the narrow, tapered hood was opened. Parking-light nacelles were chrome-plated at first, but changed to body-color about one-third of the way through the production run. After the first 1,772 cars were built, air vents were added to the front fenders, low on the cowl. At the rear, small taillamps stood alongside the long decklid (which contained the license-plate mounting). No horizontal rear bumper was used, but some rear protection was provided by two vertical guards. More than 200 early models were built with aluminum bodies (on a wooden framework), but all Jaguars produced after April 1950 wore steel bodies. Leather upholstery was standard, and leather also was used on the instrument panel and garnish rails. Standard equipment included a twin-blade wiper, cigar lighter, twin blended-note horns, two batteries, 140-mph speedometer, tachometer, and electric clock. The mohair top was concealed behind the seats when folded, while detachable sidescreens stored in a tray in the top's compartment.

The new double-overhead-camshaft six-cylinder engine, producing 160 horsepower (150 bhp with lower compression), had seven main bearings and hemispherical combustion chambers, in a head made of high-strength aluminum alloy. The intake system was designed in collaboration with Harry Weslake. Camshafts were driven by two-stage chain, to inclined overhead valves. Before long, Jaguars could be ordered for U.S. delivery with an optional performance package, including high-lift camshafts, higher compression, racing clutch, dual exhaust system, and wire wheels. A mono windshield was available for racing. Fender skirts also became a popular option, for models equipped with steel disc wheels rather than wires.

MARK V — SIX — Appearance of Jaguar's saloon (sedan) changed dramatically with the arrival of the four-door Mark V. The new 120-inch-wheelbase chassis now featured independent front suspension and hydraulic brakes, whereas the former saloons used leaf springs at both ends and mechanical brakes. Up front, upper/lower wishbones with ball joints worked with longitudinal torsion bars, while the rear end retained its rigid axle and semi-elliptic leaf springs. Sealed-beam headlamps were now semi-faired into the front fenders, no longer separately mounted, alongside a large grille made up of thick vertical bars. Fender lamps also were built-in, while the doors held pushbutton handles and concealed hinges. Front doors displayed a particular elegant curve in their forward edges, to complement the angled-back trailing edge of the hood. Twin bumpers had overriders, vertical vents were evident at the cowl, and the Mark V was highlighted by rakish rear fender skirts. Hubcaps wore 'JAGUAR' lettering. Overall appearance was similar to the new Bentley Mark VI, which had debuted in 1946.

Other new features included the frame, Burman steering, longer rear springs, and the transmission. Under the Mark V hood, however, were the same 2.5- and 3.5-liter six-cylinder engines used in the 1946-48 models. Standard equipment included two foglamps, backup light, two-blade windshield wipers, lighter, self-cancelling trafficators, and built-in "air conditioning" with defroster/demister. Bolt-on pressed-steel disc wheels were now 16-inch size (formerly 18-inch), carrying Dunlop 6.70x16 tires. That helped give the car a lower appearance than its predecessor. On the dashboard were two 5-inch gauges: a 0-120 mph speedometer and a tachometer. The new dashboard design made it easier to produce both left-hand-drive and right-hand-drive versions, but the windshield no longer opened for ventilation. Upholstery was non-pleated Vaumol leather and Dunlopillo. Front bucket seats were installed, with a padded folding rear center armrest, adjustable driver's-seat height, and telescopic steering wheel. Polished walnut decorated the garnish rails, window frames, and instrument panel. Tools were mounted in a specially-shaped, soundproof container in the decklid, with automatic light. The spare tire rested in a separate rear compartment, under the tool locker. A drophead coupe with large landau bars joined the four-door saloon in September 1949.

I.D. DATA: Chassis serial number for XK-120 is stamped atop the chassis side member, opposite the flywheel housing; and on the front crossmember, under the radiator. Chassis number for the Mark V saloon is stamped on front of frame. Starting chassis serial number: (XK-120) 660001 w/RHD, 670001 w/LHD; (Mk V 2.5-Litre RHD saloon) 520001; (Mk V 2.5-Litre RHD cpe) 540001; (Mk V 2.5-Litre LHD saloon) 527001; (Mk V 2.5-Litre RHD cpe) 547001; (Mk V 3.5-Litre RHD saloon) 620001; (Mk V 3.5-Litre RHD cpe) 640001; (Mk V 3.5-Litre LHD saloon) 627001; (Mk V 2.5-Litre RHD cpe) 647001; Engine number for XK-120 is stamped on oil-filter boss on right side of block, and (on later engines) on rear face of camshaft drive housing on the cylinder head; suffix /7 or /8 denotes compression ratio. Engine number for Mark V is stamped on a boss at the rear of the block. Starting engine number: (XK-120) W1001; (Mk V 2.5-Litre) H2001; (Mk V 3.5-Litre) T5001. Engine and chassis numbers for both models also appear on a large firewall plate, which also contains body and gearbox numbers.

Model	Body Type & Seating	Engine Type/CID	P.O.E. Price	Weight (lbs.)	Prod. Total
XK-120	2-dr Roadster-2P	I6/210	3945	2920	Note 1
MARK V					
3.5-Litre	4-dr Saloon-5P	I6/213	3750	3500	Note 2
3.5-Litre	2-dr Dhd Cpe-5P	I6/213	3850	3650	Note 2
2.5-Litre	4-dr Saloon-5P	I6/162	N/A	N/A	Note 2
2.5-Litre	2-dr Dhd Cpe-5P	I6/162	N/A	N/A	Note 2

Note 1: Total XK-120 production (1949-54) came to 12,078 units (7,631 roadsters, 2,678 fixed-head coupes, and 1,769 drophead coupes). Approximately 10,392 were left-hand-drive.

Note 2: Total Mark V production (1949-51) came to 7,814 3.5-Litre saloons (4,690 for export); 1,647 2.5-Litre saloons (533 for export); 977 3.5-Litre drophead coupes (840 for export); and 28 2.5-Litre drophead coupes (all but one for export).

ENGINE DATA: BASE SIX (XK-120): Inline, 70-degree dual-overhead-cam six-cylinder. Cast iron block and aluminum-alloy head. **Displacement:** 210 cu. in. (3442 cc). **Bore & Stroke:** 3.27 x 4.17 in. (83 x 106 mm). **Compression Ratio:** 8.0:1 (or 7.0:1). **Brake Horsepower:** 160 at 5000 rpm (150 at 5000 with 7.0:1 compression). **Torque:** 195 lbs.-ft. at 2500 rpm. Seven main bearings. Solid valve lifters. Two SU H6 sidedraft carburetors. Lucas ignition.

BASE SIX (Mark V 3.5-Litre): Inline, overhead-valve six-cylinder. Cast iron block and head. **Displacement:** 212.6 cu. in. (3485 cc). **Bore & Stroke:** 3.23 x 4.33 in. (82 x 110 mm). **Compression Ratio:** 7.2:1. **Brake Horsepower:** 125 at 4500 rpm. Seven main bearings. Solid valve lifters. Two SU sidedraft carburetors. 12-volt electrical system. Dual exhaust system.

BASE SIX (Mark V 2.5-Litre): Same as above, except — **Displacement:** 162.4 cu. in. (2664 cc). **Bore & Stroke:** 2.87 x 4.17 in. (73 x 106 mm). **Compression Ratio:** 7.3:1. **Brake Horsepower:** 102 at 4600 rpm.

CHASSIS DATA: Wheelbase: (XK-120) 102 in.; (Mark V) 120 in. **Overall Length:** (XK-120) 173 in.; (Mark V) 187 in. **Height:** (XK-120) 52.5 in.; (Mark V) 62.5 in. **Width:** (XK-120) 61.5 in.; (Mark V) 68.5 in. **Front Tread:** (XK-120) 51 in.; (Mark V) 56 in. **Rear Tread:** (XK-120) 50 in.; (Mark V) 57.5 in. **Wheel Type:** pressed steel bolt-on disc. **Standard Tires:** (XK-120) Dunlop 6.00x16; (Mark V) Dunlop 6.70x16.

TECHNICAL: Layout: front-engine, rear-drive. **Transmission:** four-speed manual. Overall XK-120 gear ratios: (1st) 12.29:1; (2nd) 7.22:1; (3rd) 4.98:1; (4th) 3.64:1. Overall Mk V 3.5-Litre gear ratios: (1st) 14.5:1; (2nd) 8.52:1; (3rd) 5.87:1; (4th) 4.3:1. Overall Mk V 2.5-Litre gear ratios: (1st) 15.35:1; (2nd) 9.01:1; (3rd) 6.21:1; (4th) 4.55:1. **Standard Final Drive Ratio:** (XK-120) 3.64:1 (3.27:1, 4.0:1 or 4.3:1 available); (Mk V 3.5-Litre) 4.3:1; (Mk V 2.5-Litre) 4.55:1. **Steering:** Burman recirculating ball. **Suspension (front):** independent; transverse wishbones and long torsion bars (anti-roll bar on XK-120). **Suspension (rear):** rigid axle with semi-elliptic leaf springs. **Brakes:** hydraulic, front/rear drum. **Body Construction:** steel body on box-section steel frame. **Fuel Tank:** (XK-120) 18 gallon (U.S.).

MAJOR OPTIONS: High-capacity 24-gallon fuel tank (XK-120). Two spare wheels (XK-120). Wire wheels (XK-120).

PERFORMANCE: Top Speed: (XK-120) 122-125 mph; (Mk V 3.5) 91 mph. **Acceleration (0-60 mph):** (XK-120) 10.0-11.7 sec.; (Mk V 3.5) N/A (0-50 mph in 9.9 sec.). **Acceleration (quarter-mile):** (XK-120) 17-18.3 sec. (about 74 mph); (Mk V 3.5) 20.2 sec. **Fuel Mileage:** (XK-120) about 18-20 mpg.

PRODUCTION/SALES: Approximately 158 Jaguars were sold in the U.S. during 1949.

Manufacturer: Jaguar Cars Ltd., Coventry, England.

Distributor: The Hoffman Motor Car Co., New York City; and Charles H. Hornburg Jr., Los Angeles.

HISTORY: Production of the XK-120 began in July 1949 and continued until September 1954. Initial deliveries on the east coast of the new XK-120 began in August 1949, when an example with serial number 670005 was received by Hoffman Motors. West-coast shipments began to arrive in September 1949, going to Charles Hornburg.

On May 30, 1949, a standard aluminum-bodied Jaguar XK-120 with 3.5-liter engine, running on ordinary pump fuel, attained 132.6 mph over a flying mile on the Jabbeke-Aeltre road in Belgium. Officially timed by the Royal Automobile Club of Belgium, that was the fastest time ever recorded by a standard production car without a supercharger. Jaguars also finished first and second in the production-car one-hour race at Silverstone, a fact touted in an American ad which advised that orders for the car were being filled "in strict rotation."

"It is typically British that Jaguars never claimed more than 120 mph for this car," said *California Autonews*. The British *Daily Herald* explained that the XK-120 was "the faster ever tourer, yet as docile in heavy traffic as the most expensive and biggest saloon." As for its appearance, *Country Life* noted that the car "reaches a standard of functional beauty never before achieved by a British manufacturer." At the time, the XK's engine was the most powerful production unit available in Europe.

The XK-120 evolved from a "100" experimental coupe done in 1938, which featured a long hood, sloped tail, and rounded cockpit. The XK-120 copied that profile, but added a narrower oval vertical-bar grille and faired-in headlamps. One of the most surprising facts of postwar automotive history is that the XK-120 design arrived almost by accident,

when the company needed a sports roadster body in a hurry to fit atop a cutdown Mark V chassis for display at the fall 1948 Motor Show. The first aluminum-bodied example was produced in a startling six weeks. Though intended as a mere short-term stopgap, then, the new sports car quickly faced huge demand, with most of them ultimately heading toward the U.S. market.

A four-cylinder roadster also was announced, to be called the XK-100. In fact, its two-liter engine allowed Colonel Gardner to break the world speed record in that class, reaching 176 mph in 1948, in an MG Special with higher compression and modified pistons.

The Mark V saloon was introduced in September 1948 as an interim (stopgap) model, after delivery of new bodies in 1947-48 had been delayed and something was needed to ride the awaiting chassis. It was available by March 1949. Bodies were produced by Pressed Steel Ltd. The drophead coupe was added in September 1949. A preliminary announcement called the Mark V a "worthy successor to a car which has fully earned the description of being the finest car of its class in the world."

1950 JAGUAR

1950 Jaguar Mark V saloon. (Jaguar Cars Inc.)

XK-120 — SIX — Appearance and mechanical details of the roadster were the same as 1949. All bodies were now made of steel, and all later models had air vents on trailing ends of the front fenders.

MARK V — SIX — Appearance and mechanical details of the Jaguar saloons were the same as 1949.

I.D. DATA: Serial numbers are in same locations as 1949. Starting serial number: (XK-120) 670001; (Mark V) 627251. Starting engine number: (XK-120) W1016; (Mark V) T5626.

Model	Body Type & Seating	Engine Type/CID	P.O.E. Price	Weight (lbs.)	Prod. Total
XK-120	2-dr Roadster-2P	I6/210	3945	2920	Note 1
MARK V					
3.5-Litre	4-dr Saloon-5P	I6/213	3750	3500	Note 2
3.5-Litre	2-dr Dhd Cpe-5P	I6/213	3850	3650	Note 2
2.5-Litre	4-dr Saloon-5P	I6/162	N/A	N/A	Note 2
2.5-Litre	2-dr Dhd Cpe-5P	I6/162	N/A	N/A	Note 2

Note 1: Total XK-120 production (1949-54) came to 12,078 units (7,631 roadsters, 2,678 fixed-head coupes, and 1,769 drophead coupes).

Note 2: Total Mark V production (1949-51) came to 7,814 3.5-Litre saloons (4,690 for export); 1,647 2.5-Litre saloons (533 for export); 977 3.5-Litre drophead coupes (840 for export); and 28 2.5-Litre drophead coupes (all but one for export).

ENGINE DATA: Same as 1949.

CHASSIS DATA: Same as 1949.

TECHNICAL: Same as 1949.

PERFORMANCE: Same as 1949.

PRODUCTION/SALES: Approximately 912 Jaguars were sold in the U.S. during 1950.

HISTORY: A new Mark VII saloon (sedan) replaced the Mark V in October 1950; see next listing for details. Several privately-owned XK-120s entered the Le Mans race in 1950.

1951 JAGUAR

XK-120 — SIX — A fixed-head (hardtop) coupe joined the original two-seat roadster in August 1951. The coupe had walnut-veneer dashboard trim, versus leather trim on the roadster. With its sharply-sloped fender line, the coupe looked particularly streamlined and handsome when wearing the available rounded rear fender skirts. Footwell vents were added this year, and a heater became standard on the sports roadster by September 1951. Both steel disc and wire wheels were available (no rear skirts with the latter).

XK-120C (C-TYPE) — SIX — Also added to the sports-car lineup in 1951 was a high-performance, competition-oriented "C-Type," with an engine that produced 200 horsepower. The cylinder head contained larger valves and ports than the regular twin-cam six, as well as high-lift camshafts and racing pistons. Unlike the XK-120, the aluminum-bodied C-Type roadster rode a frame made up of welded steel tubes, with a rear suspension that contained a transverse torsion bar and underslung trailing links. Rack-and-pinion steering was installed, and the entire front end hinged forward. The roadster body had only one door. Initial examples had large side louvers at the cowl, but the production version switched to a set of narrow side louvers. Wheelbase of the C-Type was 96 inches (6 inches shorter than the XK-120).

1951 Jaguar Mark VII saloon.

MARK VII — SIX — After a brief period in the lineup, the traditional-styled Mark V saloon was replaced by a completely different Mark VII, which would evolve over the next decade into Mark VIII and Mark IX versions. Up top, some similarity was evident in roof profile between the Mark V and Mark VII; but below the beltline, virtually no resemblance could be noted, as the gracefully-sweeping separate fenders and running boards faded into history. Not only the body, but the powerplant, was completely different, identical to that installed in the XK-120 roadster and coupe, producing 160 horsepower. That was enough to give the four-door sedan a top speed beyond 100 mph. The modern-style, all-steel body now featured faired-in fenders and front-hinged front doors. A small grille contained thin vertical bars, and a split (two-piece) windshield was used. Dual saddle-style gas tanks were installed, as were rear fender skirts. The frame and suspension were identical to that used in the Mark V, but the new XK engine sat five inches farther forward than its predecessor. Brakes had a vacuum booster. Mark VII sedans came with a sunshine roof. The DeLuxe model included a radio and heater.

Model Note: The Mark V remained available into 1951, when it was superceded by the Mark VII; see previous listing for data.

I.D. DATA: Chassis serial number for XK-120 is located on front left chassis member; for Mark VII, on left side of chassis member, above rear engine mounting bracket. Engine number is stamped on right of engine block above oil filter (XK-120); and on front end of cylinder head (Mark VII). Starting chassis serial number: (XK-120 cpe) 669001 w/RHD, 679001 w/LHD; (XK-120C C-Type) XKC001; (Mark VII) 730001. Starting engine number: (Mark VII) A-1001.

Model	Body Type & Seating	Engine Type/CID	P.O.E. Price	Weight (lbs.)	Prod. Total
XK-120	2-dr Roadster-2P	I6/210	4039	2920	Note 1
XK-120	2-dr HT Coupe-2P	I6/210	3850	3050	Note 1
C-TYPE					
XK-120C	2-dr Roadster-2P	I6/210	N/A	2128	Note 2
MARK VII					
Standard	4-dr Sedan-5/6P	I6/210	4170	3700	Note 3
Deluxe	4-dr Sedan-5/6P	I6/210	4290	3700	Note 3

Note 1: Total XK-120 production (1949-54) came to 12,078 units (7,631 roadsters, 2,678 fixed-head coupes, and 1,769 drophead coupes).

Note 2: A total of 53 C-Types were produced from 1951-53 (both racing and "production" versions).

Note 3: A total of 20,908 Mark VII sedans were produced from 1951-55 (12,978 for export).

ENGINE DATA: BASE SIX (XK-120, Mark VII): Inline, dual-overhead-cam six-cylinder. Cast iron block and aluminum-alloy head. **Displacement:** 210 cu. in. (3442 cc). **Bore & Stroke:** 3.27 x 4.17 in. (83 x 106 mm). **Compression Ratio:** 8.0:1 (or 7.0:1). **Brake Horsepower:** 160 at 5000 rpm (150 bhp with 7.0:1 compression). **Torque:** 195 lbs.-ft. at 2500 rpm. Seven main bearings. Solid valve lifters. Two SU sidedraft carburetors. Lucas ignition.

BASE SIX (C-Type): Same as above, except — **Compression Ratio:** 9.0:1 (or 8.0:1). **Brake Horsepower:** 200 at 5800 rpm.

CHASSIS DATA: Wheelbase: (XK-120) 102 in.; (C-Type) 96 in.; (Mk VII) 120 in. **Overall Length:** (XK-120) 173 in.; (C-Type) 157 in.; (Mk VII) 196.5 in. **Height:** (XK-120) 52.5 in.; (Mk VII) 63 in. **Width:** (XK-120) 61.5 in.; (C-Type) 64.5 in.; (Mk VII) 73 in. **Front Tread:** (XK-120) 51 in.; (Mk VII) 56 in. **Rear Tread:** (XK-120) 50 in.; (Mk VII) 57.5 in. **Wheel Type:** steel disc (wire available on XK-120). **Standard Tires:** (XK-120) 6.00x16; (Mk VII) 6.70x16.

TECHNICAL: Layout: front-engine, rear-drive. **Transmission:** four-speed manual. **Standard Final Drive Ratio:** (XK-120) 3.64:1; (Mk VII) 4.27:1. **Steering:** Burman recirculating ball except (C-Type) rack and pinion. **Suspension (front):** independent; transverse wishbones and long torsion bars (anti-roll bar on XK-120). **Suspension (rear):** rigid axle with semi-elliptic leaf springs except (C-Type) transverse torsion bar with underslung trailing links and angled upper link. **Brakes:** hydraulic, front/rear drum. **Body Construction:** steel body on box-section steel frame except (C-Type) aluminum body on tubular steel frame. **Fuel Tank:** (XK-120) 18 gallon (U.S.).

PERFORMANCE: Top Speed: (XK-120 cpe) 120 mph; (C-Type) about 143 mph; (Mk VII) 101 mph. **Acceleration (0-60 mph):** (XK-120 cpe) 9.9 sec.; (C-Type) N/A (0-50 mph in 6.1 sec.); (Mk VII) about 13.4 sec. (0-50 mph in 9.8 sec.). **Acceleration (quarter-mile):** (C-Type) 16.2 sec.; (Mk VII) 19.3 sec.

PRODUCTION/SALES: Approximately 1,702 Jaguars were sold in the U.S. during 1951.

Manufacturer: Jaguar Cars Ltd., Coventry, England.

Distributor: The Hoffman Motor Car Co., New York City; and Charles H. Hornburg Jr., Los Angeles.

HISTORY: The Mark VII sedan debuted at the 35th International Motor Exhibition at Earl's Court in London, in fall 1950; the XK-120 fixed-head coupe debuted at the 1951 Geneva show. One of the new limited-production, high-performance XK-120C roadster won the Le Mans race this year.

1952 JAGUAR

1952 Jaguar XK120 roadster. (Coys of Kensington)

XK-120 — SIX — During 1952, faired-in lights replaced the former chromed sidelight housings atop the front fenders. New this year were XK-120M (modified) versions, with knock-off wire wheels, no fender skirts, and a 180-horsepower version of the twin-cam engine with dual exhausts. That modified engine had high-lift camshafts (from the C-Type racer), stiffer valve springs, and a special crankshaft damper. The 'M' package also included stiffer front torsion bars and rear springs, and added $395 to the car's price. Meanwhile, the basic engine adopted a thicker head gasket this year.

MARK VII — SIX — Production of the four-door sedan, introduced for 1951, continued with little change. Standard Mk VII equipment included a 120-mph speedometer, sliding sunroof, polished walnut instrument panel and interior garnishings, twin locking glove-boxes, five ashtrays, padded armrests, and deep pile carpeting. Seats were upholstered in Vaumol leather over foam rubber. Either five-passenger or six-passenger seating was available.

I.D. DATA: Chassis serial number for XK-120 is located on front left chassis member; for Mark VII, on left side of chassis member, above rear engine mounting bracket. Engine number is stamped on right of engine block above oil filter (XK-120); and on front end of cylinder head (Mark VII). Starting serial number: (XK C-Type) XKC004; (other models) continued in sequence from prior listings. "Special Equipment" models have an 'S' prefix for the chassis number, and 'S' suffix added to the engine number.

Model	Body Type & Seating	Engine Type/CID	P.O.E. Price	Weight (lbs.)	Prod. Total
XK-120	2-dr Roadster-2P	I6/210	4039	2920	Note 1
XK-120	2-dr HT Coupe-2P	I6/210	4065	3050	Note 1
XK-120M (modified)					
XK-120M	2-dr Roadster-2P	I6/210	4434	N/A	Note 1
XK-120M	2-dr HT Coupe-2P	I6/210	4460	N/A	Note 1
C-TYPE					
	2-dr Roadster-2P	I6/210	N/A	2128	Note 2
MARK VII					
Standard	4-dr Sedan-5/6P	I6/210	4120	3700	Note 3
Deluxe	4-dr Sedan-5/6P	I6/210	4290	3775	Note 3

Note 1: Total XK-120 production (1949-54) came to 12,078 units (7,631 roadsters, 2,678 fixed-head coupes, and 1,769 drophead coupes).
Note 2: A total of 53 C-Types were produced from 1951-53 (both racing and "production" versions).
Note 3: A total of 20,908 Mark VII sedans were produced from 1951-55 (12,978 for export).
Equipment Note: Mark VII sedans came with a sunshine roof; DeLuxe model included radio and heater.

ENGINE DATA: BASE SIX (XK-120, Mark VII): Inline, dual overhead-cam six-cylinder. Cast iron block and aluminum-alloy head. **Displacement:** 210 cu. in. (3442 cc). **Bore & Stroke:** 3.27 x 4.17 in. (83 x 106 mm). **Compression Ratio:** 8.0:1 (or 7.0:1). **Brake Horsepower:** 160 at 5000/5200 rpm. **Torque:** 195 lbs.-ft. at 2500 rpm. Seven main bearings. Solid valve lifters. Two SU sidedraft carburetors. Lucas ignition.

BASE SIX (XK-120M): Same as above, except — **Brake Horsepower:** 180 at 5300 rpm.
BASE SIX (C-Type): Same as above, except — **Compression Ratio:** 9.0:1. **Brake Horsepower:** 200 at 5800 rpm.

CHASSIS DATA: Wheelbase: (XK-120) 102 in.; (C-Type) 96 in.; (Mk VII) 120 in. **Overall Length:** (XK-120) 173 in.; (C-Type) 157 in.; (Mk VII) 196.5 in. **Height:** (XK-120) 52.5 in.; (Mk VII) 63 in. **Width:** (XK-120) 61.5 in.; (C-Type) 64.5 in.; (Mk VII) 73 in. **Front Tread:** (XK-120) 51 in.; (C-Type) 50 in.; (Mk VII) 56 in. **Rear Tread:** (XK-120) 50 in.; (Mk VII) 57.5 in. **Wheel Type:** (XK-120) steel disc or wire; (Mk VII) pressed steel bolt-on disc. **Standard Tires:** (XK-120) 6.00x16; (Mk VII) 6.70x16.

TECHNICAL: Layout: front-engine, rear-drive. **Transmission:** four-speed manual. Mark VII overall gear ratios: (1st) 14.4:1; (2nd) 8.56:1; (3rd) 5.84:1; (4th) 4.27:1. **Standard Final Drive Ratio:** (XK-120) 3.64:1; (Mark VII) 4.27:1. **Steering:** Burman recirculating ball except (C-Type) rack and pinion. **Suspension (front):** independent; transverse wishbones and long torsion bars (anti-roll bar on XK-120). **Suspension (rear):** rigid axle with semi-elliptic leaf springs except (C-Type) transverse torsion bar with underslung trailing links and angled upper link. **Brakes:** hydraulic, front/rear drum. **Body Construction:** steel body on box-section steel frame except (C-Type) aluminum body on tubular steel frame. **Fuel Tank:** (XK-120) 18 gallon (U.S.).

PERFORMANCE: Top Speed: (XK-120) 122 mph; (XK-120M) 124 mph; (C-Type) up to 145 mph; (Mk VII) 102 mph. **Acceleration (0-60 mph):** (XK-120) 10.5 sec.; (XK-120M) about 9 sec.; (C-Type) 6.5-8 sec.; (Mk VII) 13.5 sec. **Acceleration (quarter-mile):** (XK-120) 18.5 sec.; (XK-120M) 17.0 sec. (83 mph); (C-Type) 15.2-16.2 sec.; (Mk VII) 19.3 sec. (72 mph).

PRODUCTION/SALES: Approximately 3,349 Jaguars were sold in the U.S. during 1952.
Manufacturer: Jaguar Cars Ltd., Coventry, England.
Distributor: The Hoffman Motor Car Co., New York City; Charles H. Hornburg Jr., Los Angeles; and Peter Satori, California.
HISTORY: By 1951-52, factory information sheets describing performance boosts were available to owners who wished to modify their own cars. Jaguar also offered alternative equipment for sporting events, including a 24-gallon fuel tank and dual spare wheels. Brochures issued at the 1952 Paris Salon called the Mark VII "an entirely new car of unparalleled beauty...powered by the world famous record-breaking XK120 engine." Some U.S. ads omitted the "120" designation of the sports roadster, promoting it as the "XK Super Sports."

1953 JAGUAR

1953 Jaguar XK120 SE roadster. (Coys of Kensington)

XK-120 — SIX — A full-fledged convertible (drophead coupe) joined the roadster and fixed-head coupe for 1953. A "Special Equipment" engine also was available, rated 180 horsepower under the hood of the XK-120M trio. Jaguar also offered a selection of other performance options. Throughout the early 1950s, many XK-120s had the optional center-lock wire wheels instead of the standard steel discs, and wore rear fender skirts.

MARK VII — SIX — An automatic transmission became available for the four-door sedan early in 1953, followed later in the year by a Laycock de Normanville overdrive gearbox. Initially, the Borg-Warner automatic was available only on export models. With overdrive, a 4.55:1 rear axle was installed (versus 4.27:1 with the conventional manual gearbox). Otherwise, production continued with little change.

I.D. DATA: Serial number is located on front left chassis member (XK-120); on left side of chassis member, above rear engine mounting bracket (Mark VII). Engine number is on right of engine block above oil filter, or on front end of cylinder head. Starting serial number: (XK-120 conv) 667001 w/RHD. "Special Equipment" models have an 'S' prefix for the chassis number, and a suffix added to the engine number.

Model	Body Type & Seating	Engine Type/CID	P.O.E. Price	Weight (lbs.)	Prod. Total
XK-120	2-dr Spt Rds-2P	I6/210	4039	2920	Note 1
XK-120	2-dr HT Coupe-2P	I6/210	4065	3050	Note 1
XK-120	2-dr Spt Conv-2P	I6/210	4250	3060	Note 1
XK-120M (modified)					
XK-120M	2-dr Spt Rds-2P	I6/210	4434	N/A	Note 1
XK-120M	2-dr HT Coupe-2P	I6/210	4460	3022	Note 1
XK-120M	2-dr Spt Conv-2P	I6/210	4645	N/A	Note 1
C-TYPE					
	2-dr Roadster-2P	I6/210	5860	2128	Note 2
MARK VII					
Standard	2-dr Sedan-5/6P	I6/210	4170	3700	Note 3

Note 1: Total XK-120 production (1949-54) came to 12,078 units (7,631 roadsters, 2,678 fixed-head coupes, and 1,769 drophead coupes).
Note 2: A total of 53 C-Types were produced from 1951-53 (both racing and "production" versions).
Note 3: A total of 20,908 Mark VII sedans were produced from 1951-55 (12,978 for export). Those were followed by 10,061 Mk VIIM sedans (3,818 for export).
Price Note: Prices of the XK-120 dropped sharply during the year, to the figures shown in 1954 listing ($3345 to $4175).

1953 Jaguar XK120 fixed-head coupe. (Coys of Kensington)

ENGINE DATA: BASE SIX (XK-120, Mark VII): Inline, dual overhead-cam six-cylinder. Cast iron block and aluminum-alloy head. **Displacement:** 210 cu. in. (3442 cc). **Bore & Stroke:** 3.27 x 4.17 in. (83 x 106 mm). **Compression Ratio:** 8.0:1. **Brake Horsepower:** 160 at 5000/5200 rpm. **Torque:** 195 lbs.-ft. at 2500 rpm. Seven main bearings. Solid valve lifters. Two SU sidedraft carburetors. Lucas ignition.

Note: Special Equipment engine for the XK-120M was rated 180 bhp at 5300 rpm, and 203 pound-feet at 4000 rpm.

BASE SIX (C-Type): Same as above, except — **Compression Ratio:** 9.0:1. **Brake Horsepower:** 200 at 5800 rpm.

CHASSIS DATA: Wheelbase: (XK-120) 102 in.; (C-Type) 96 in.; (Mk VII) 120 in. **Overall Length:** (XK-120) 173 in.; (C-Type) 157 in.; (Mk VII) 196.5 in. **Height:** (XK-120) 52.5 in.; (Mk VII) 63 in. **Width:** (XK-120) 61.5 in.; (C-Type) 64.5 in.; (Mk VII) 73 in. **Front Tread:** (XK-120) 51 in.; (Mk VII) 56 in. **Rear Tread:** (XK-120) 50.5 in.; (Mk VII) 57.5 in. **Wheel Type:** (XK-120) steel disc or wire; (Mk VII) pressed steel bolt-on disc. **Standard Tires:** (XK-120) 6.00x16; (Mk VII) 6.70x16.

TECHNICAL: Layout: front-engine, rear-drive. **Transmission:** four-speed manual. Mark VII overall gear ratios: (1st) 14.4:1; (2nd) 8.56:1; (3rd) 5.84:1; (4th) 4.27:1. **Standard Final Drive Ratio:** (XK-120) 3.64:1; (Mark VII) 4.27:1; (Mark VII w/OD) 4.55:1. **Steering:** Burman recirculating ball except (C-Type) rack and pinion. **Suspension (front):** independent; transverse wishbones and long torsion bars (anti-roll bar on XK-120). **Suspension (rear):** rigid axle with semi-elliptic leaf springs except (C-Type) transverse torsion bar with underslung trailing links and angled upper link. **Brakes:** hydraulic, front/rear drum. **Body Construction:** steel body on box-section steel frame except (C-Type) aluminum body on tubular steel frame. **Fuel Tank:** (XK-120) 18 gallon (U.S.).

MAJOR OPTIONS: Automatic transmission: Mark VII ($280).

PERFORMANCE: Top Speed: (XK-120) 122 mph; (XK-120M) 120-124 mph; (C-Type) 139-145 mph; (Mk VII) 102 mph. **Acceleration (0-60 mph):** (XK-120) 8.5-10.5 sec.; (XK-120M) 9-10.4 sec.; (C-Type) 6.5-8 sec.; (Mk VII) 13.5 sec. **Acceleration (quarter-mile):** (XK-120) 18.5 sec.; (XK-120M) 17.0-17.5 sec. (up to 83 mph); (C-Type) 15.2-16.2 sec.; (Mk VII) 19.3 sec. (72 mph).

PRODUCTION/SALES: Approximately 3,914 Jaguars were sold in the U.S. during 1953.

Manufacturer: Jaguar Cars Ltd., Coventry, England.

Distributor: The Hoffman Motor Car Co., New York City; and Charles H. Hornburg Jr., Los Angeles.

HISTORY: A special bubble-topped XK-120 roadster hit 172.412 mph in October 1953, driven for the Belgian Royal Automobile Club by Norman Dewis. Because the engine was essentially stock, that feat helped Jaguar rate as the world's fastest production car. The convertible coupe debuted for the U.S. market at the New York Automobile Show in spring 1953. *Auto Sportsman* magazine reported that the XK-120C was "sold only to drivers or owners who are consistent competitors."

1954 JAGUAR

1954 Jaguar XK120 roadster to rally specifications. (Christie's)

XK-120 — SIX — Production of the three basic sports-car models continued with little change in what would be their final year, before replacement by the XK-140.

D-TYPE — SIX — Another sports-racing evolution of the XK-120 went into (limited) production in 1954, powered by a hopped-up (250-bhp) version of the twin-cam six-cylinder engine, with a new head, three-plate clutch, and fully synchronized four-speed gearbox. Only 87 were produced from 1954-56. Wheelbase was 90 inches (6 inches shorter than the former C-Type), and torsion bars went at both front and rear. The rear suspension was similar to the C-Type, but with upper and lower trailing links at each side. This became the first monocoque (unibodied) Jaguar, with steel tube subframes bolted to an aluminum/magnesium center section, though early models had bodies riveted to a square magnesium tubular frame. Knock-off Dunlop magnesium alloy wheels were standard. Styling features included a short oval nose, small windshield, and large fin behind the headrest. D-Types were offered only to qualified race drivers.

MARK VII — SIX — Production of Jaguar's full-size sedan continued with little change.

I.D. DATA: Serial number is located on front left chassis member (XK-120); or on left side of chassis member, above rear engine mounting bracket (Mark VII). Engine number is on right of engine block above oil filter, or at front end of cylinder head. Serial number range: (D-Type) XKD401-406. "Special Equipment" models have an 'S' prefix for the chassis number, and a suffix added to the engine number.

Model	Body Type & Seating	Engine Type/CID	P.O.E. Price	Weight (lbs.)	Prod. Total
XK-120	2-dr Spt Rds-2P	I6/210	3345	2920	Note 1
XK-120	2-dr HT Coupe-2P	I6/210	3875	3050	Note 1
XK-120	2-dr Spt Conv-2P	I6/210	3975	3060	Note 1

Model	Body Type & Seating	Engine Type/CID	P.O.E. Price	Weight (lbs.)	Prod. Total
XK-120M	2-dr Spt Rds-2P	I6/210	3545	N/A	Note 1
XK-120M	2-dr HT Coup-2P	I6/210	4075	3022	Note 1
XK-120M	2-dr Spt Conv-2P	I6/210	4175	N/A	Note 1
D-TYPE					
	2-dr Rds-2P	I6/210	Note 2	1904	Note 3
MARK VII					
Mk VII	4-dr Sedan-6P	I6/210	4255	3700	Note 4

Note 1: Total XK-120 production (1949-54) came to 12,078 units (7,631 roadsters, 2,678 fixed-head coupes, and 1,769 drophead coupes).

Note 2: D-Type price was 1895 Pounds (Sterling) at the factory, or about $10,000 in the U.S.

Note 3: A total of 87 D-Types were produced from 1954-56 (including 16 that were converted for road operation, starting in 1957).

Note 4: A total of 20,908 Mark VII sedans were produced from 1951-55 (12,978 for export). Those were followed by 10,061 Mk VIIM sedans (3,818 for export).

ENGINE DATA: BASE SIX (XK-120, Mark VII): Inline, dual overhead-cam six-cylinder. Cast iron block and aluminum-alloy head. **Displacement:** 210 cu. in. (3442 cc). **Bore & Stroke:** 3.27 x 4.17 in. (83 x 106 mm). **Compression Ratio:** 8.0:1. **Brake Horsepower:** (XK-120) 160 at 5200 rpm; (Mark VII) 160 at 5000 rpm. **Torque:** 195 lbs.-ft. at 2500 rpm. Seven main bearings. Solid valve lifters. Two SU sidedraft carburetors. Lucas ignition.

Note: Special Equipment engine for the XK-120M was rated 180 bhp at 5300 rpm, and 203 pound-feet at 4000 rpm.

BASE SIX (D-Type): Same as above, except — **Compression Ratio:** 9.0:1. **Brake Horsepower:** 250 at 6000 rpm. Three Weber carburetors.

1954 Jaguar XK120M roadster. (Christie's)

CHASSIS DATA: Wheelbase: (XK-120) 102 in.; (D-Type) 90 in.; (Mk VII) 120 in. **Overall Length:** (XK-120) 173.5 in.; (D-Type) 154 in.; (Mk VII) 196.5 in. **Height:** (XK-120) 52.5 in.; (D-Type) 38 in.; (Mk VII) 63 in. **Width:** (XK-120) 61.5 in.; (D-Type) 65.8 in.; (Mk VII) 73 in. **Front Tread:** (XK-120) 51 in.; (D-Type) 50 in.; (Mk VII) 56 in. **Rear Tread:** (XK-120) 50 in.; (D-Type) 48 in.; (Mk VII) 57.5 in. **Wheel Type:** (XK-120) steel disc or wire; (Mk VII) steel disc. **Standard Tires:** (XK-120) 6.00x16; (D-Type) 6.50x16; (Mk VII) 6.70x16.

TECHNICAL: Layout: front-engine, rear-drive. **Transmission:** four-speed manual. **Standard Final Drive Ratio:** (XK-120) 3.64:1; (Mk VII) 4.27:1. **Steering:** recirculating ball except (D-Type) rack and pinion. **Suspension (front):** independent; transverse wishbones and long torsion bars (anti-roll bar on XK-120). **Suspension (rear):** rigid axle with semi-elliptic leaf springs except (D-Type) torsion bar with upper/lower trailing links. **Brakes:** hydraulic, front/rear drum. **Body Construction:** steel body on box-section steel frame except (D-Type) body riveted to magnesium-tube chassis or, later, aluminum/magnesium monocoque with steel-tube subframes. **Fuel Tank:** (XK-120) 18 gallon (U.S.).

MAJOR OPTIONS: Automatic transmission: Mark VII ($195). Wire wheels (XK-120 rds).

PERFORMANCE: Top Speed: (D-Type) 160 mph. **Acceleration (0-60 mph):** (D-Type) 4.7 sec. **Acceleration (quarter-mile):** (D-Type) 13.7 sec. (107 mph).

PRODUCTION/SALES: Approximately 3,365 Jaguars were sold in the U.S. during 1954.

Manufacturer: Jaguar Cars Ltd., Coventry, England.

Distributor: Hoffman Motor Car Co., New York City; and Charles H. Hornburg Jr., Los Angeles.

HISTORY: Jaguar's replacement for the XK-120, the restyled XK-140, debuted in October 1954; see next listing for details.

1955 JAGUAR

XK-140 — SIX — Although the basic profile was similar to the XK-120, its replacement displayed a number of significant changes, both visible and hidden. Ads in 1955 pointed out the XK-140's redesigned chassis, larger-diameter torsion bars, new rack-and-pinion steering (replacing recirculating ball), new high-lift camshafts, new oil ignition coil, and larger cockpit with increased leg room. Bumpers were bigger, and the cast metal grille was made up of fewer (seven) but heavier vertical bars. More chrome was evident on both the hood and trunk lid. A chrome strip extended the full length of the hood. Tiny park lights remained atop the fenders, which added extra round lights in a low position, just above the bumper. The coupe had a larger backlight and rear quarter windows. Taillamps also increased in size. Tiny back seats in the coupe and convertible, made possible by moving the roof back about seven inches and raising it about 1.5 inches, folded down to carry long parcels.

Underneath was the same box-section chassis and wishbone/torsion-bar front suspension used on the XK-120, offered in the same three body styles: roadster, fixed-head coupe, and drophead coupe (convertible). The roadster kept its side curtains, while its mates carried roll-up windows. The dual-cam 3.4-liter engine was identical in construction, too, but produced 30 more horsepower than its predecessor, turning out 190 bhp at 5500 rpm. The base engine now was comparable to the "Special Equipment" version

offered on later XK-120s, then priced at $800. In this installation, the engine and gearbox sat about three inches farther forward. Weight rose by about 200 pounds heavier, but the XK-140 offered easier handling as well as a roomier interior. That interior featured a blend of walnut and leather in the coupe and convertible, with a plastic steering wheel with flat horn button, and a deep map pocket and fitted tool case in each door. A tool kit and spare tire were recessed beneath the trunk floor. Door handles differed among the three models: inside straps for the roadster, a rotating handle at the door top for the convertible, and pushbuttons lower on the coupe's door. Roadsters still had doors made of aluminum, while the others were steel. Standard equipment included a tachometer, heater, turn signals, electric wipers, electric clock, and automatic backup light. Both a Laycock de Normanville overdrive and Borg-Warner automatic transmission were optional on the coupe and convertible. Top speed rose close to 130 mph with overdrive, while automatic remained a comparative rarity. The XK-140 'M' appearance package included a crankshaft damper, wire wheels (either body-colored or chrome), dual exhaust, twin foglamps, and windshield washers. An 'MC' package included those extras but also added a 'C' type cylinder head that boosted output to 210 horsepower, for $295 above the base price.

D-TYPE — SIX — Small quantities of the competition Jaguar continued to emerge; see 1954 listing for full data.

MARK VIIM — SIX — The basic shape was unchanged, but the next version of Jaguar's full-size sedan had various modifications, starting with a more potent (190-bhp) version of the dual-overhead-cam six-cylinder engine. That same engine went into the new XK-140 sports cars. Appearance modifications included the addition of wraparound bumpers and separately-mounted foglamps (above the bumper), as well as new headlamps. The round holes below the headlamps, formerly occupied by foglamps, now contained horn grilles. Turn-signal flashers were now mounted low on the fenders, and taillamps were larger. Wheel trim rings were new. Acceleration got a boost via the combination of additional power and close-ratio gearing. Stiffer front torsion bars also were installed.

1955 Jaguar XK140 drophead coupe. (William Siuru Jr.)

I.D. DATA: Chassis serial numbers are stamped on the left frame member, above the rear engine mounting bracket, and contained on a brass identification plate at the firewall. Engine number is on right of engine block, above the oil filter; or on front end of cylinder head. Starting chassis serial number: (XK-140 roadster) 810001; (XK-140 coupe) 814001; (XK-140 convertible) 817001; (D-Type) XKD501; (Mk VIIM) 738184. Starting engine number: (XK-140) G1001; (Mk VIIM) D4958. The XK-140M had an 'A' prefix in its serial number. The XK-140MC could be identified by a red plaque on each camshaft cover, and had an 'S' prefix in its serial number when exported to the U.S. Engines with the 'C' head also had that letter cast into the head top.

Model	Body Type & Seating	Engine Type/CID	P.O.E. Price	Weight (lbs.)	Prod. Total
XK-140	2-dr Spt Rds-2P	I6/210	3450	2750	Note 1
XK-140	2-dr HT Cpe-2+2P	I6/210	3795	2860	Note 1
XK-140	2-dr Conv-2+2P	I6/210	3795	2970	Note 1
XK-140M					
XK-140M	2-dr Spt Rds-2P	I6/210	3595	2750	Note 1
XK-140M	2-dr HT Cpe-2+2P	I6/210	3940	2860	Note 1
XK-140M	2-dr Conv-2+2P	I6/210	3940	2970	Note 1
XK-140MC					
XK-140MC	2-dr Spt Rds-2P	I6/210	3745	2750	Note 1
XK-140MC	2-dr HT Cpe-2+2P	I6/210	4090	2860	Note 1
XK-140MC	2-dr Conv-2+2P	I6/210	4090	2970	Note 1
D-TYPE					
	2-dr Rds-2P	I6/210	Note 2	1904	Note 3
MARK VIIM					
Mk VIIM	4-dr Sedan-6P	I6/210	4255	3800	Note 4

Note 1: Total XK-140 production (1954-57) came to 8,884 units (3,347 roadsters, 2,797 fixed-head coupes, and 2,740 drophead coupes). Only 385 of the drophead coupes (convertibles) and 396 of the fixed-head coupes had automatic transmissions.

Note 2: D-Type price was 1895 Pounds (Sterling) at the factory, or about $10,000 in the U.S.

Note 3: A total of 87 D-Types were produced from 1954-56 (including 16 that were converted for road operation, starting in 1957).

Note 4: A total of 10,061 Mark VIIM sedans were produced through the full model run (including 3,818 for export).

ENGINE DATA: BASE SIX (XK-140, Mark VIIM): Inline, dual overhead-cam six-cylinder. Cast iron block and aluminum-alloy head. **Displacement:** 210 cu. in. (3442 cc). **Bore & Stroke:** 3.27 x 4.17 in. (83 x 106 mm). **Compression Ratio:** 8.0:1. **Brake Horsepower:** 190 at 5500 rpm (210 at 5750 rpm with 'C' type head). **Torque:** 210 lbs.-ft. at 2500 rpm (213 lbs.-ft. at 4000 rpm with 'C' head). Seven main bearings. Solid valve lifters. Two SU sidedraft carburetors. Lucas ignition.

BASE SIX (D-Type): Same as above, except — **Compression Ratio:** 9.0:1. **Brake Horsepower:** 250 at 6000 rpm. Three Weber carburetors.

CHASSIS DATA: Wheelbase: (XK-140) 102 in.; (D-Type) 90 in.; (Mk VIIM) 120 in. **Overall Length:** (XK-140) 176 in.; (D-Type) 154 in.; (Mk VIIM) 196.5 in. **Height:** (XK-140) 55 in.; (D-Type) 38 in.; (Mk VIIM) 63 in. **Width:** (XK-140) 64.5 in.; (D-Type) 65.8 in.; (Mk VIIM) 73 in. **Front Tread:** (XK-140) 51.5 in.; (D-Type) 50 in.; (Mk VIIM) 56 in. **Rear Tread:** (XK-140) 50.5 in.; (D-Type) 48 in.; (Mk VIIM) 57.5 in. **Wheel Type:** (XK-140) steel disc or wire; (Mk VIIM) steel disc. **Standard Tires:** (XK-140) 6.00x16; (D-Type) 6.50x16; (Mk VIIM) 6.70x16.

TECHNICAL: Layout: front-engine, rear-drive. **Transmission:** four-speed manual; overdrive and automatic available. **Standard Final Drive Ratio:** (XK-140) 3.54:1; (Mk VIIM) 4.27:1. **Steering:** (XK-140, D-Type) rack and pinion; (Mk VIIM) recirculating ball. **Suspension (front):** independent; transverse wishbones and long torsion bars (anti-roll bar on XK-140). **Suspension (rear):** rigid axle with semi-elliptic leaf springs except (D-Type) torsion bar with upper/lower trailing links. **Brakes:** hydraulic, front/rear drum. **Body Construction:** steel body on box-section steel frame except (D-Type) aluminum/magnesium monocoque with steel-tube subframes.

MAJOR OPTIONS: Automatic transmission: XK-140 cpe/conv ($240); Mk VIIM ($195). Overdrive transmission: XK-140/Mk VIIM ($160).

PERFORMANCE: Top Speed: (XK-140) 120+ mph; (XK-140 w/OD) near 130 mph. **Acceleration (0-60 mph):** (XK-140M) under 8.5 sec. **Acceleration (quarter-mile):** (XK-140) 17.4 sec.

PRODUCTION/SALES: Approximately 3,573 Jaguars were sold in the U.S. during 1955. **Manufacturer:** Jaguar Cars Ltd., Coventry, England.
Distributor: Hoffman Motor Car Co., New York City; and Charles H. Hornburg Jr., Los Angeles.

HISTORY: The Mark VIIM debuted in September 1954.

1956 JAGUAR

XK-140 — SIX — Production of the three body styles continued with little change. As before, both an appearance package ('M') and performance package ('MC') were available.

D-TYPE — SIX — Small numbers of the competition Jaguar continued to emerge; see 1954 listing for full data.

2.4 — SIX — Joining the full-size sedan for 1956 was a new and smaller four-door Jaguar, powered by a 2483-cc (shortened stroke) version of the twin-cam six-cylinder engine and riding a 107.4-inch wheelbase. The engine produced 112 horsepower, allowing a top speed beyond 100 mph and 0-60 mph acceleration in the neighborhood of 14.5 seconds. Styling features of the unibody sedan included inboard headlamps, fender-tip park/signal lights, and a narrow vertical-bar grille. The car's overall profile, however, differed considerably from the Mark VIIM, with a straight-through fenderline rather than the bigger sedan's cutaway into the doors, plus thick roof pillars and window frames. Unibody construction was a "first" for Jaguar, and the 2.4's suspension also was new: coil springs up front, with a rigid axle and cantilever springs at the rear.

MARK VIIM — SIX — Production of the full-size four-door sedan continued with little change, available with either overdrive or automatic transmission.

I.D. DATA: Chassis numbers of the XK-140 and Mark VIIM are located on front left chassis member, above rear engine mounting bracket. Chassis number for the 2.4 sedan is on body channel under the hood on the right side, ahead of the radiator header tank. Engine number is on right of engine block above the oil filter, or at front end of cylinder head. Serial numbers are also found on a brass plate on the firewall. Starting serial number: (XK-140 and Mk VIIM) continued from prior year; (D-Type) XKD601 to XKD606, plus leftovers in the XKD500 series; (2.4-Litre) 940001. Starting engine number: (2.4) BB-1001.

Model	Body Type & Seating	Engine Type/CID	P.O.E. Price	Weight (lbs.)	Prod. Total
XK-140	2-dr Roadster-2P	I6/210	3595	2750	Note 1
XK-140	2-dr HT Cpe-2+2P	I6/210	3995	2860	Note 1
XK-140	2-dr Conv-2+2P	I6/210	3995	2970	Note 1
XK-140M					
XK-140M	2-dr Roadster-2P	I6/210	3755	2750	Note 1
XK-140M	2-dr HT Cpe-2+2P	I6/210	4160	2860	Note 1
XK-140M	2-dr Conv-2+2P	I6/210	4160	2970	Note 1
XK-140MC					
XK-140MC	2-dr Roadster-2P	I6/210	3910	2750	Note 1
XK-140MC	2-dr HT Cpe-2+2P	I6/210	4315	2860	Note 1
XK-140MC	2-dr Conv-2+2P	I6/210	4315	2970	Note 1
D-TYPE					
	2-dr Rds-2P	I6/210	Note 2	1904	Note 3
2.4					
	4-dr Sedan-5/6P	I6/151	3795	2800	Note 4
MARK VIIM					
Mk VIIM	4-dr Sedan-6P	I6/210	4440	3800	Note 5

Note 1: Total XK-140 production (1954-57) came to 8,884 units (3,347 roadsters, 2,797 fixed-head coupes, and 2,740 drophead coupes). Only 385 of the drophead coupes (convertibles) and 396 of the fixed-head coupes had automatic transmissions.

Note 2: D-Type price was 1895 Pounds (Sterling) at the factory, or about $10,000 in the U.S.

Note 3: A total of 87 D-Types were produced from 1954-56 (including 16 that were converted for road operation, starting in 1957).

Note 4: Approximately 19,400 2.4-liter sedans were produced from 1956-59.

Note 5: A total of 10,061 Mark VIIM sedans were produced through the full model run (including 3,818 for export).

ENGINE DATA: BASE SIX (2.4): Inline, dual overhead-cam six-cylinder. Cast iron block and aluminum-alloy head. **Displacement:** 151.5 cu. in. (2483 cc). **Bore & Stroke:** 3.27 x 3.01 in. (83 x 76.5 mm). **Compression Ratio:** 8.0:1. **Brake Horsepower:** 112 at 5750 rpm. **Torque:** 140 lbs.-ft. at 2000 rpm. Seven main bearings. Solid valve lifters. Two Solex carburetors.

BASE SIX (XK-140, Mark VIIM): Inline, dual overhead-cam six-cylinder. Cast iron block and aluminum-alloy head. **Displacement:** 210 cu. in. (3442 cc). **Bore & Stroke:** 3.27 x 4.17 in. (83 x 106 mm). **Compression Ratio:** 8.0:1. **Brake Horsepower:** 190 at 5500 rpm (210 at 5750 rpm with 'C' type head). **Torque:** 210 lbs.-ft. at 2500 rpm (213 lbs.-ft. at 4000 rpm with 'C' head). Seven main bearings. Solid valve lifters. Two SU sidedraft carburetors.

BASE SIX (D-Type): Same as 3442-cc six above, except — **Compression Ratio:** 9.0:1. **Brake Horsepower:** 250 at 6000 rpm. Three Weber carburetors.

CHASSIS DATA: Wheelbase: (XK-140) 102 in.; (D-Type) 90 in.; (2.4) 107.4 in.; (Mark VIIM) 120 in. Overall Length: (XK-140) 176 in.; (D-Type) 154 in.; (2.4) 180.75 in.; (Mark VIIM) 196.5 in. Height: (XK-140) 55 in.; (D-Type) 38 in.; (2.4) 57.5 in.; (Mk VIIM) 63 in. Width: (XK-140) 64.5 in.; (D-Type) 65.8 in.; (2.4) 66.75 in.; (Mk VIIM) 73 in. Front Tread: (XK-140) 51.5 in.; (D-Type) 50 in.; (2.4) 54.6 in.; (Mk VIIM) 56 in. Rear Tread: (XK-140) 50.5 in.; (D-Type) 48 in.; (2.4) 50.1 in.; (Mk VIIM) 57.5 in. Wheel Type: (XK-140) steel disc or wire; (2.4, Mk VIIM) steel disc. Standard Tires: (XK-140) 6.00x16; (D-Type) 6.50x16; (2.4) 6.40x15; (Mk VIIM) 6.70x16.

TECHNICAL: Layout: front-engine, rear-drive. Transmission: four-speed manual; overdrive and automatic available. Standard Final Drive Ratio: (XK-140) 3.54:1; (2.4) 4.55:1 or 4.27:1; (Mk VIIM) 4.27:1. Steering: (XK-140, D-Type) rack and pinion; (2.4) recirculating ball; (Mk VIIM) recirculating ball. Suspension (front): (XK-140) transverse wishbones with torsion bars and anti-roll bar; (2.4) wishbones with coil springs; (Mk VIIM) wishbones with torsion bars. Suspension (rear): XK-140, Mk VIIM rigid axle with semielliptic leaf springs except (D-Type) torsion bar with upper/lower trailing links; (2.4) rigid axle with cantilever springs. Brakes: hydraulic, front/rear drum. Body Construction: steel body on box-section steel frame except (2.4) steel unibody and (D-Type) aluminum/magnesium monocoque with steel-tube subframes.

MAJOR OPTIONS: Automatic transmission: XK-140 ($260); Mk VIIM ($200). Overdrive transmission: XK-140 ($175); Mk VIIM ($160).

PERFORMANCE: Top Speed: (2.4) 100+ mph. Acceleration (0-60 mph): (2.4) 13.4-14.5 sec. Acceleration (quarter-mile): (2.4) 19.2 sec. (71 mph).

PRODUCTION/SALES: Approximately 3,685 Jaguars were sold in the U.S. during 1956.

Manufacturer: Jaguar Cars Ltd., Coventry, England.

Distributor: Jaguar Cars North American Corp., New York City.

HISTORY: Jaguar's 1956 models were introduced to the U.S. market on September 1, 1955. A central parts depot opened in the U.S. in January 1956.

1957 JAGUAR

1957 Jaguar XKSS. (Jaguar Cars Inc.)

XK-140 — SIX — Production of Jaguar's sports car continued with little change. As before, three body styles were offered, with 'M' and 'MC' packages available.

D-TYPE (XK-SS) — SIX — Created as the roadgoing version of the competition D-Type, the XK-SS, made up of leftover D-Type components, qualified as the fastest street Jag ever. With three Weber carburetors, the 3442-cc six produced up to 262 horsepower. Each of the 16 XK-SS models built (until the tooling was destroyed in a 1957 fire) was right-hand-drive, just as the D-Types had been. Bodies displayed a curved windshield, little bumpers, and a rear-deck luggage rack, but lacked the headrest of the D-Type. Seats were upholstered in leather and non-adjustable, with fabric top and side curtains included. As roadgoing vehicles, they came with turn signals and muffler.

2.4 — SIX — Production of the small sedan with 107.4-inch wheelbase and 2483-cc engine continued with little change.

3.4 — SIX — The body was essentially the same as that used on the 2.4 sedan, but this new model carried the bigger (3442-cc) engine. Round parking lights stood outboard of the headlamps. At the center was a rather narrow vertical-bar grille (wider than the one on the 2.4, but with thinner bars). Wheel openings were fully recessed, front and rear, with cutaway rear fender skirts available. Wire wheels were optional. Top speed approached 120 mph with the 210-horsepower twin-cam engine, and a 3.4 sedan could accelerate to 60 mph in close to 9 seconds. It was produced in response to American demand for more power in the smaller sedan. Either an overdrive (manual) transmission or Borg-Warner automatic was available.

MARK VIIM — SIX — Production of the Mark VIIM sedan continued into 1957, as it was replaced by the Mark VIII.

MARK VIII — SIX — Evolution into Mark VIII form brought Jaguar's full-size sedan only a handful of significant changes, including a one-piece windshield and modest revisions to the engine's cylinder head, now in 'B' (green) form. The revised grille had a thicker chrome surround molding and flatter appearance, topped by a "leaping Jaguar" ornament. Cutaway rear fender skirts were installed. Interiors contained walnut picnic tables. Two-tone paint (and interior upholstery) was available, separated by a curvy trim strip on the bodysides. Also available was a Dual-Range Borg-Warner automatic transmission.

I.D. DATA: Chassis serial number for XK-140 and Mark VIIM are located on front left chassis, above the rear engine mounting bracket; for 2.4/3.4 sedans, on body channel under the hood on the right side, ahead of the radiator header tank. Engine number is on right of engine block above oil filter or front end of cylinder head. Serial numbers are also found on a brass plate on the firewall. Starting serial number: (XK-140, 2.4, Mark VIIM) continued from prior listings; (XK-SS) XKSS701; (3.4) 985001; (Mark VIII w/LHD) 780001. Starting engine number: (3.4) KE1001.

Model	Body Type & Seating	Engine Type/CID	P.O.E. Price	Weight (lbs.)	Prod. Total
XK-140	2-dr Roadster-2P	I6/210	3645	2750	Note 1
XK-140	2-dr HT Cpe-2+2P	I6/210	4045	2860	Note 1
XK-140	2-dr Conv-2+2P	I6/210	4045	2970	Note 1
XK-140M					
XK-140M	2-dr Roadster-2P	I6/210	3755	2750	Note 1
XK-140M	2-dr HT Cpe-2+2P	I6/210	4160	2860	Note 1
XK-140M	2-dr Conv-2+2P	I6/210	4160	2970	Note 1
XK-140MC					
XK-140MC	2-dr Roadster-2P	I6/210	3960	2750	Note 1
XK-140MC	2-dr HT Cpe-2+2P	I6/210	4365	2860	Note 1
XK-140MC	2-dr Conv-2+2P	I6/210	4365	2970	Note 1
XK-SS					
	2-dr Rds-2P	I6/210	N/A	1960	16
2.4					
	4-dr Sedan-5/6P	I6/151	3843	2800	Note 2
3.4					
	4-dr Sedan-5/6P	I6/210	4530	3164	Note 3
MARK VIIM					
Mk VIIM	4-dr Sedan-6P	I6/210	4465	3800	Note 4
MARK VIII					
Luxury	4-dr Sedan-6P	I6/210	5770	3752	Note 5

Note 1: Total XK-140 production (1954-57) came to 8,884 units (3,347 roadsters, 2,797 fixed-head coupes, and 2,740 drophead coupes. Only 385 of the drophead coupes (convertibles) and 396 of the fixed-head coupes had automatic transmissions.

Note 2: Approximately 19,400 2.4-liter sedans were produced from 1956-59.

Note 3: Approximately 17,340 3.4-liter sedans were produced from 1956-59.

Note 4: A total of 10,061 Mark VIIM sedans were produced through the full model run (including 3,818 for export).

Note 5: A total of 6,212 Mark VIII sedans were produced from 1957-59 (including 2,448 for export).

ENGINE DATA: BASE SIX (2.4): Inline, dual overhead-cam six-cylinder. Cast iron block and aluminum-alloy head. Displacement: 151.5 cu. in. (2483 cc). Bore & Stroke: 3.27 x 3.01 in. (83 x 76.5 mm). Compression Ratio: 8.0:1. Brake Horsepower: 112 at 5750 rpm. Torque: 140 lbs.-ft. at 2000 rpm. Seven main bearings. Solid valve lifters. Two Solex carburetors.

BASE SIX (XK-140, 3.4, Mark VIIM, Mark VIII): Inline, dual overhead-cam six-cylinder. Cast iron block and aluminum-alloy head. Displacement: 210 cu. in. (3442 cc). Bore & Stroke: 3.27 x 4.17 in. (83 x 106 mm). Compression Ratio: 8.0:1 (9.0:1 optional). Brake Horsepower: (XK-140/Mk VIIM) 190 at 5500 rpm; (XK-140 with 'C' type head) 210 at 5750 rpm; (3.4/Mk VIII) 210 at 5500 rpm. Torque: (XK-140/Mk VIIM) 210 lbs.-ft. at 2500 rpm; (XK-140 with 'C' head) 213 lbs.-ft. at 4000 rpm; (3.4/Mk VIII) 215 lbs.-ft. at 3000 rpm. Seven main bearings. Solid valve lifters. Two SU sidedraft carburetors.

BASE SIX (XK-SS): Same as 3442-cc six above, except — Compression Ratio: 9.0:1. Brake Horsepower: 262 at 6000 rpm. Three Weber DCO3 carburetors.

CHASSIS DATA: Wheelbase: (XK-140) 102 in.; (XK-SS) 90.5 in.; (2.4/3.4) 107.4 in.; (Mark VIIM/VIII) 120 in. Overall Length: (XK-140) 176 in.; (XK-SS) 168 in.; (2.4/3.4) 180.75 in.; (Mk VIIM/VIII) 196.5 in. Height: (XK-140) 55 in.; (2.4) 57.5 in.; (3.4) 57.5 in.; (Mk VIIM/VIII) 63 in. Width: (XK-140) 64.5 in.; (XK-SS) 65.75 in.; (2.4/3.4) 66.75 in.; (Mk VIIM/VIII) 73 in. Front Tread: (XK-140) 51.5 in.; (2.4) 54.6 in.; (3.4) 54.6 in.; (Mk VIIM/VIII) 56 in. Rear Tread: (XK-140) 50.5 in.; (2.4) 50.1 in.; (3.4) 50.1 in.; (Mk VIIM/VIII) 57.5 in. Wheel Type: steel disc; wires available on XK-140. Standard Tires: (XK-140) 6.00x16; (XK-SS) 6.50x16; (2.4) 6.40x15; (3.4) 6.40x15; (Mk VII) 6.70x16; (Mk VIII) 6.70x16.

TECHNICAL: Layout: front-engine, rear-drive. Transmission: four-speed manual; overdrive and Borg-Warner three-speed automatic available. Standard Final Drive Ratio: (XK-140) 3.54:1; (XK-SS) 3.54:1; (2.4) 4.55:1 or 4.27:1; (3.4 w/manual) 3.77:1; (3.4 w/auto.) 3.54:1; (Mk VIIM) 4.27:1; (Mk VIII) 4.27:1. Steering: (XK-140, XK-SS) rack and pinion; (2.4/3.4) recirculating ball; (Mk VIIM/VIII) recirculating ball. Suspension (front): (XK-140) transverse wishbones and long torsion bars with anti-roll bar; (2.4/3.4) wishbones with coil springs; (Mk VIII) wishbones and torsion bars. Suspension (rear): (XK-140, Mk VIII) rigid axle with semi-elliptic leaf springs; (2.4/3.4) rigid axle with cantilever springs. Brakes: hydraulic, front/rear drum. Body Construction: steel body on box-section steel frame except (2.4/3.4) steel unibody.

MAJOR OPTIONS: Automatic transmission: XK-140 ($260); Mark VIIM ($200); Mark VIII ($250); 3.4 sedan. Overdrive transmission: XK-140 ($175); 2.4 ($160); Mark VIIM/VIII ($160).

PERFORMANCE: Top Speed: (XK-140MC) 121 mph; (3.4) near 120 mph; (Mk VIII) 106 mph. Acceleration (0-60 mph): (XK-140MC) 9.1 sec.; (3.4) just over 9 sec. to 10.7 sec. Acceleration (quarter-mile): (3.4) 17.7 sec. (78 mph); (Mk VIII) about 18.4 sec.

PRODUCTION/SALES: Approximately 3,800 Jaguars were sold in the U.S. during 1957.

Manufacturer: Jaguar Cars Ltd., Coventry, England.

Distributor: Jaguar Cars North American Corp., New York City.

HISTORY: Jaguar's 1957 models were introduced to the U.S. market on September 1, 1956. The XK-150 debuted in mid-1957, replacing the XK-140; see next listing for details.

1958 JAGUAR

XK-150 — SIX — Jaguar's third-generation postwar sports car wore new sheetmetal and displayed a revised (higher) beltline, running in a straight line rather than dipping down in the former graceful curve. Thus, front fenders were taller at the cowl. The roofline also was modified, and a curved one-piece windshield replaced the former split "vee" style. The coupe's back window also was curved, wrapping around slightly. Door handles moved upward, too. Up front, a wider grille contained 16 thin vertical bars and had a more oval shape than its predecessor, while the front bumper dipped downward at the center, ahead of the grille. A raised center section on the widened hood (which sloped toward the front of the car) was decorated by a chrome strip. At the rear, the license-plate housing moved from the bumper to the decklid, allowing the bumper to stretch

between vertical guards and wrap around the rear fenders. The coupe and convertible were offered first. Because of a fire, resumption of roadster production was delayed. The roadster debuted nine months later, but now had wind-up windows and lacked the traditional cutaway doors. Rear skirts were still available (except with wire wheels), adding even more to the car's straight-across look. A "leaping Jaguar" hood ornament became optional on the XK-150.

More plush and refined than its predecessors, and roomier inside, the XK-150 also gained weight. Inside, the coupe and convertible lost their burl walnut dashboards, adopting the leather used all along in the roadster. Dunlop four-wheel disc brakes (with servo-assist) were supposedly an option, but installed on virtually all cars. Under the hood was the same 190-bhp engine used in the XK-140, but the 210 horsepower "Special Equipment" option became more popular. The new B-type cylinder head on the "Special Equipment" engine was painted blue, whereas the standard head was unpainted aluminum. Both overdrive and a Borg-Warner automatic transmission were available. In spring 1958, a more potent 'S' engine became available, with straight-port head, three big (two-inch) SU carbs, higher (9.0:1) compression, more radical cam timing, and 250-horsepower rating. Each carburetor supplied only two cylinders, via separate manifolds. All XK-150S models had manual shift with overdrive, and the engine's cylinder head was gold-colored. A small 'S' went on the upper front corner of each door on XK-150S models.

3.4 — SIX — Production of the 3.4 sedan continued with little change, except that disc brakes became optional.

MARK VIII — SIX — Production of the full-size sedan continued with little change, except that disc brakes and wire wheels became optional.

1958 Jaguar XK150 roadster. (Jaguar Cars Inc.)

I.D. DATA: Chassis serial number of XK-150 is stamped on the frame, adjacent to the rear engine mounting; for 3.4 sedan, on body channel under the hood on the right side, ahead of radiator header tank; for Mark VIII, stamped atop frame member above the rear engine mounting bracket. Engine number is on right of engine block, above the oil filter. Starting chassis serial number: (XK-150 cpe) 834001; (XK-150 conv) 83700; (3.4) 985001; (Mark VIII) 780001. Starting engine number: (XK-150) V-1001-8; (3.4) KE-1001-8; (Mark VIII) N-6001-8. Starting engine number: (XK-150) VE1001; (XK-150S) VS1001. Engine and chassis number also appear on a brass plate on the firewall.

Model	Body Type & Seating	Engine Type/CID	P.O.E. Price	Weight (lbs.)	Prod. Total
XK-150	2-dr Roadster-2P	I6/210	4520	3066	Note 1
XK-150	2-dr Coupe-2+2P	I6/210	4475	3108	Note 1
XK-150	2-dr Conv-2+2P	I6/210	4595	3108	Note 1
XK-150S	2-dr Roadster-2P	I6/210	5120	3094	Note 2
3.4					
	4-dr Sedan-5P	I6/210	4460	3164	Note 3
MARK VIII					
Mk VIII	4-dr Sedan-6P	I6/210	5445	3976	Note 4

Note 1: Total XK-150 production (1957-60) came to 7,929 units. Of these, 1,339 were roadsters (42 with 3.8-liter engine), 4,101 were fixed-head coupes (656 with 3.8-liter engine), and 2,489 were drophead coupes (586 with 3.8-liter engine).

Note 2: Total XK-150S production (1958-61) came to 1,466 units. Of these, 924 were roadsters (36 with 3.8-liter engine), 349 were fixed-head coupes (150 with 3.8-liter engine), and 193 were drophead coupes (89 with 3.8-liter engine).

Note 3: Approximately 17,340 3.4-liter sedans were produced from 1957-59.

Note 4: A total of 6,212 Mark VIII sedans were produced from 1957-59 (including 2,448 for export).

Price Note: Figure shown for 3.4 sedan includes overdrive; price was $4560 with automatic.

1958 Jaguar XK150 fixed-head coupe. (Coys of Kensington)

ENGINE DATA: BASE SIX (XK-150, 3.4, Mark VIII): Inline, dual overhead-cam six-cylinder. Cast iron block and aluminum-alloy head. **Displacement:** 210 cu. in. (3442 cc). **Bore & Stroke:** 3.27 x 4.17 in. (83 x 106 mm). **Compression Ratio:** 8.0:1 (9.0:1 optional). **Brake Horsepower:** 210 at 5500 rpm. **Torque:** 216 lbs.-ft. at 3000 rpm. Seven main bearings. Solid valve lifters. Two SU sidedraft carburetors.

XK-150 Engine Note: A lower-powered version of the 3442-cc engine remained available, rated 190 bhp at 5500 rpm and 210 lbs.-ft. at 2500 rpm. The 210-bhp engine described above was actually part of the "Special Equipment" package.

BASE SIX (XK-150S): Same as 3442-cc six above, except — **Compression Ratio:** 9.0:1. **Brake Horsepower:** 250 at 5500 rpm. **Torque:** 240 lbs.-ft. at 4000 rpm. Three SU carburetors.

CHASSIS DATA: Wheelbase: (XK-150) 102 in.; (3.4) 107.4 in.; (Mk VIII) 120 in. **Overall Length:** (XK-150) 177 in.; (3.4) 180.75 in.; (Mk VIII) 196.5 in. **Height:** (XK-150) 55 in.; (XK-150 rds) 52.5 in.; (3.4) 57.5 in.; (Mk VIII) 63 in. **Width:** (XK-150) 64.5 in.; (3.4) 66.75 in.; (Mk VIII) 73 in. **Front Tread:** (XK-150) 51.6 in.; (3.4) 54.6 in.; (Mk VIII) 56 in. **Rear Tread:** (XK-150) 51.6 in.; (3.4) 50.1 in.; (Mk VIII) 57.5 in. **Wheel Type:** steel disc; wire wheels available on XK-150 cpe/conv and 3.4 sedan. **Standard Tires:** (XK-150) 6.00x16; (3.4) 6.40x15; (Mk VIII) 6.70x16.

TECHNICAL: Layout: front-engine, rear-drive. **Transmission:** four-speed manual, with overdrive and three-speed automatic optional; overdrive standard on 3.4 sedan and XK-150S. **Standard Final Drive Ratio:** (XK-150) 3.54:1; (XK-150S) 4.09:1; (3.4) 3.54:1; (Mk VIII) 4.27:1. **Steering:** (XK-150) rack and pinion; (others) recirculating ball. **Suspension:** (XK-150) wishbones and torsion bars with anti-roll bar; (3.4) wishbones with coil springs; (Mk VIII) wishbones and torsion bars. **Suspension (rear):** (XK-150, Mk VIII) rigid axle with semi-elliptic leaf springs; (3.4) rigid axle with cantilever springs. **Brakes:** hydraulic, front/rear drum except (XK-150) front/rear disc; discs optional on 3.4 and Mark VIII sedans. **Body Construction:** steel body on box-section steel frame except (2.4/3.4) steel unibody.

MAJOR OPTIONS: Automatic transmission: XK-150 ($250); 3.4 ($250); Mark VIII ($250). Overdrive transmission: XK-150 ($165); Mark VIII ($165).

PERFORMANCE: Top Speed: (XK-150) 120+ mph; (3.4) 120 mph; (Mk VIII) 106 mph. **Acceleration (0-60 mph):** (XK-150) 8.5 sec. or less; (3.4) 10.4 sec.; (Mk VIII) 11.6 sec. **Acceleration (quarter-mile):** (XK-150) 16.9 sec. (82 mph). **Fuel Mileage:** (XK-150) 18-20 mpg.

PRODUCTION/SALES: A total of 4,607 Jaguars were exported to the U.S. during the year ending July 1958.

ADDITIONAL MODELS: Production of the 2.4-liter sedan (with 2483-cc engine) continued into 1959, when it was replaced by a Mk II version. Only the larger-engined version was commonly exported to the U.S.

Manufacturer: Jaguar Cars Ltd., Coventry, England.
Distributor: Jaguar Cars Inc., New York City.

HISTORY: Jaguar's 1958 models were introduced to the U.S. market on September 1, 1957. Production of the XK-150 began in May 1957 and continued until October 1960, when it was replaced by the E-Type (XK-E).

1959 JAGUAR

1959 Jaguar XK150 2+2 fixed-head coupe. (Christie's)

XK-150 — SIX — Production of the Jaguar sports car, in the usual three body styles, continued with little change. As before, a more potent 'S' version (250 horsepower versus the usual 190/210) was available. By fall 1959, the larger (3.8-liter) engine installed in the new Mark IX sedan also became available for the XK-150. That engine produced 220 horsepower in standard (Special Equipment) form, or 265 bhp for the 'S' version.

3.4 — SIX — Production of the smaller 3.4-liter sedan on 107.4-inch wheelbase continued with little change. An overdrive manual transmission was standard.

MARK IX — SIX — A larger (3.8-liter) engine powered the next generation of Jaguar's full-size sedan. For the U.S. market, it came with standard automatic transmission and power steering, as well as all-disc brakes. The 220-horsepower, 3781-cc six delivered a top speed near 115 mph. A 'Mk IX' emblem was evident on the trunk lid, but otherwise appearance was similar to the Mark VIII. Built-in folding picnic tables continued in the sedan's burl-walnut trimmed interior, adding a clock and lock in this version. The new engine would go into the XK-150 sports car and 3.8 (Mark II) sedan a year later.

I.D. DATA: Chassis serial number of XK-150 is stamped on the frame, adjacent to the rear engine mounting; for 3.4 sedan, on body channel under the hood on the right side, ahead of radiator header tank; for Mark IX, stamped atop frame member above the rear engine mounting bracket. Engine number is on right of engine block, above oil filter. Starting chassis serial number: (XK-150, 3.4) continued from prior listings; (Mark IX w/LHD) 790001. Engine and chassis numbers also appear on a brass firewall plate.

Model	Body Type & Seating	Engine Type/CID	P.O.E. Price	Weight (lbs.)	Prod. Total
XK-150	2-dr Roadster-2P	I6/210	4520	3066	Note 1
XK-150	2-dr Coupe-2+2P	I6/210	4500	3108	Note 1
XK-150	2-dr Conv-2+2P	I6/210	4620	3108	Note 1
XK-150S	2-dr Roadster-2P	I6/210	5120	3094	Note 2
3.4					
	4-dr Sedan-5P	I6/210	4567	3136	Note 3
MARK IX					
Mk IX	4-dr Sedan-5/6P	I6/231	6020	3976	Note 4

Note 1: Total XK-150 production (1957-60) came to 7,929 units. Of these, 1,339 were roadsters (42 with 3.8-liter engine), 4,101 were fixed-head coupes (656 with 3.8-liter engine), and 2,489 were drophead coupes (586 with 3.8-liter engine).

Note 2: Total XK-150S production (1958-61) came to 1,466 units. Of these, 924 were roadsters (36 with 3.8-liter engine), 349 were fixed-head coupes (150 with 3.8-liter engine), and 193 were drophead coupes (89 with 3.8-liter engine).

Note 3: Approximately 17,340 3.4-liter sedans were produced from 1957-59.

Note 4: A total of 10,009 Mark IX sedans were produced from 1959-61 (including 4,647 for export).

Price Note: Figure shown for 3.4 sedan included overdrive transmission; price with automatic was $4667.

ENGINE DATA: BASE SIX (XK-150, 3.4): Inline, dual overhead-cam six-cylinder. Cast iron block and aluminum-alloy head. **Displacement:** 210 cu. in. (3442 cc). **Bore & Stroke:** 3.27 x 4.17 in. (83 x 106 mm). **Compression Ratio:** 8.0:1. **Brake Horsepower:** 210 at 5500 rpm. **Torque:** 216 lbs.-ft. at 3000 rpm. Seven main bearings. Solid valve lifters. Two SU sidedraft carburetors.

XK-150 Engine Note: A lower-powered version of the 3442-cc engine remained available, rated 190 bhp at 5500 rpm and 210 lbs.-ft. at 2500 rpm. The 210-bhp engine described above was actually part of the "Special Equipment" package.

BASE SIX (XK-150S): Same as 3442-cc six above, except — **Compression Ratio:** 9.0:1. **Brake Horsepower:** 250 at 5500 rpm. **Torque:** 240 lbs.-ft. at 4000 rpm. Three SU carburetors.

BASE SIX (Mark IX); OPTIONAL (later XK-150): Inline, dual overhead-cam six-cylinder. Cast iron block and aluminum-alloy head. **Displacement:** 230.6 cu. in. (3781 cc). **Bore & Stroke:** 3.425 x 4.17 in. (87 x 106 mm). **Compression Ratio:** 8.0:1. **Brake Horsepower:** 220 at 5000 rpm. **Torque:** 240 lbs.-ft. at 4000 rpm. Seven main bearings. Solid valve lifters. Two SU sidedraft carburetors.

OPTIONAL SIX (later XK-150S): Same as 3781-cc six above, except — **Compression Ratio:** 9.0:1. **Brake Horsepower:** 265 at 5500 rpm. **Torque:** 260 lbs.-ft. at 4500 rpm. Three SU carburetors.

CHASSIS DATA: Wheelbase: (XK-150) 102 in.; (3.4) 107.4 in.; (Mk IX) 120 in. **Overall Length:** (XK-150) 177 in.; (3.4) 180.75 in.; (Mk IX) 196.5 in. **Height:** (XK-150) 55 in.; (3.4) 57.5 in.; (Mk IX) 63 in. **Width:** (XK-150) 64.5 in.; (3.4) 66.75 in.; (Mk IX) 73 in. **Front Tread:** (XK-150) 51.6 in.; (3.4) 54.6 in.; (Mk IX) 56.5 in. **Rear Tread:** (XK-150) 51.6 in.; (3.4) 50.1 in.; (Mk IX) 58 in. **Standard Tires:** (XK-150) 6.00x16; (3.4) 6.40x15; (Mk IX) 6.70x16.

TECHNICAL: Layout: front-engine, rear-drive. **Transmission:** (XK-150) four-speed manual; overdrive and three-speed automatic optional. Overdrive standard on 3.4 sedan. Automatic transmission standard on Mark IX sedan. **Standard Final Drive Ratio:** (XK-150) 3.54:1; (3.4) 3.77:1; (Mark IX) 4.27:1. **Steering:** (XK-150) rack and pinion; (others) recirculating ball. **Suspension (front):** (XK-150) wishbones and torsion bars with anti-roll bar; (3.4) wishbones with coil springs; (Mk IX) wishbones and torsion bars. **Suspension (rear):** (XK-150, Mk IX) rigid axle with semi-elliptic leaf springs; (3.4) rigid axle with cantilever springs. **Brakes:** (XK-150, Mk IX) front/rear disc; (3.4) discs optional. **Body Construction:** steel body on box-section steel frame except (3.4) steel unibody.

MAJOR OPTIONS: Automatic transmission: XK-150 ($250); 3.4 ($100). Overdrive transmission: XK-150 ($165).

PERFORMANCE: Top Speed: (XK-150) 126 mph; (XK-150S w/3.8 engine) 135+ mph; (3.4) 120 mph; (Mk IX) near 115 mph. **Acceleration (0-60 mph):** (XK-150) 8.5 sec.; (XK-150S w/3.8 engine) about 7 sec.; (3.4) 10.4 sec.; (Mk IX) 11.2 sec. **Acceleration (quarter-mile):** (Mk IX) 18.1 sec. (79 mph).

PRODUCTION/SALES: A total of 5,596 Jaguars were exported to the U.S. during the year ending July 1959. Approximately 5,839 Jaguars were sold in the U.S. during 1959.

ADDITIONAL MODELS: Production of the 2.4-liter sedan (with 2483-cc engine) continued into 1959, when it was replaced by a Mk II version. Only the larger-engined version was commonly exported to the U.S.

Manufacturer: Jaguar Cars Ltd., Coventry, England.

Distributor: Jaguar Cars Inc., New York City.

HISTORY: Jaguar's 1959 models were introduced to the U.S. market on September 1, 1958. The Mark IX debuted at the London show in fall 1958. Mark II versions of the smaller sedan were introduced in fall 1959; see next listing.

1960 JAGUAR

1960 Jaguar XK150 3-liter fixed head coupe. (Christie's)

XK-150 — SIX — For the 1960 model year, the 3.8-liter engine (first used in the Mark IX sedan) was available under XK-150 hoods. The engine produced 220 horsepower in standard form, or 265 bhp in the 'S' version, which came only with manual shift (with overdrive). An 'S' engine was available in each body style. The 3.4-liter engine remained available through the end of XK-150 production.

3.4 — Mk II — SIX — Disc brakes were standard on the revised version of the 3.4-liter sedan, which had a larger rear window, bright trim on window frames, and thinner windshield pillars. Overdrive was standard, with automatic optional. Inside, the speedometer and tachometer now sat ahead of the driver.

3.8 — Mk II — SIX — A bigger-engined version of Jaguar's smaller sedan debuted for 1960, with standard overdrive and available automatic transmission. All-disc brakes were installed. Standard equipment included a tachometer and limited-slip differential. Windshield pillars were thinner than prior models. With the 220-bhp engine, a 3.8 could accelerate to 60 mph in as little as 8.5 seconds and hit 125 mph or more. Except for a '3.8' badge, appearance was nearly identical to the 3.4 sedan.

MARK IX — SIX — Production of the full-size sedan continued with little change. For the U.S. market, an automatic transmission and power steering were standard.

I.D. DATA: Chassis serial number of XK-150 is stamped on the frame, adjacent to the rear engine mounting; for 3.4 sedan, on body channel under the hood on the right side, ahead of radiator header tank; for Mark IX, stamped atop frame member above the rear engine mounting bracket. Engine number is on right of engine block, above oil filter.

Model	Body Type & Seating	Engine Type/CID	P.O.E. Price	Weight (lbs.)	Prod. Total
XK-150	2-dr Roadster-2P	I6/210	4520	3020	Note 1
XK-150	2-dr Coupe-2+2P	I6/210	4643	2912	Note 1
XK-150	2-dr Conv-2+2P	I6/210	4763	3020	Note 1
XK-150S	2-dr Roadster-2P	I6/210	5120	3035	Note 2
XK-150S	2-dr Coupe-2+2P	I6/210	5075	N/A	Note 2
XK-150S	2-dr Conv-2+2P	I6/210	5195	N/A	Note 2
3.4					
Mk II	4-dr Sedan-5P	I6/210	4567	3136	Note 3
3.8					
Mk II	4-dr Sedan-5P	I6/231	4765	3136	Note 4
MARK IX					
Mk IX	4-dr Sedan-5/6P	I6/231	6020	3976	Note 5

Note 1: Total XK-150 production (1957-60) came to 7,929 units. Of these, 1,339 were roadsters (42 with 3.8-liter engine), 4,101 were fixed-head coupes (656 with 3.8-liter engine), and 2,489 were drophead coupes (586 with 3.8-liter engine).

Note 2: Total XK-150S production (1958-61) came to 1,466 units. Of these, 924 were roadsters (36 with 3.8-liter engine), 349 were fixed-head coupes (150 with 3.8-liter engine), and 193 were drophead coupes (89 with 3.8-liter engine).

Note 3: Approximately 28,660 3.4-liter (Mk II) sedans were produced from 1960-67.

Note 4: A total of 30,070 3.8-liter (Mk II) sedans were produced from 1960-67.

Note 5: A total of 10,009 Mark IX sedans were produced from 1959-61 (including 4,647 for export).

XK-150 Engine Note: XK-150s were available with either 3.4- or 3.8-liter engine.

Price Note: Figure shown for 3.4 sedan included overdrive; price was $4667 with automatic. Figure shown for 3.8 sedan included overdrive; price was $4865 with automatic.

ENGINE DATA: BASE SIX (XK-150, 3.4): Inline, dual overhead-cam six-cylinder. Cast iron block and aluminum-alloy head. **Displacement:** 210 cu. in. (3442 cc). **Bore & Stroke:** 3.27 x 4.17 in. (83 x 106 mm). **Compression Ratio:** 8.0:1 (XK-150S, 9.0:1). **Brake Horsepower:** 210 at 5500 rpm except (XK-150S) 250 at 5500 rpm. **Torque:** 216 lbs.-ft. at 3000 rpm except (XK-150S) 240 at 4000 rpm. Seven main bearings. Solid valve lifters. Two SU sidedraft carburetors except (XK-150S) three SU carburetors.

BASE SIX (3.8, Mark IX); OPTIONAL (XK-150): Inline, dual overhead-cam six-cylinder. Cast iron block and aluminum head. **Displacement:** 230.6 cu. in. (3781 cc). **Bore & Stroke:** 3.425 x 4.17 in. (87 x 106 mm). **Compression Ratio:** 8.0:1 (XK-150S, 9.0:1). **Brake Horsepower:** 220 at 5500 rpm except (XK-150S) 265 at 5500 rpm. **Torque:** 240 lbs.-ft. at 4000 rpm except (XK-150S) 260 at 4500 rpm. Seven main bearings. Solid valve lifters. Two SU sidedraft carburetors except (XK-150S) three SU carburetors.

CHASSIS DATA: Wheelbase: (XK-150) 102 in.; (3.4/3.8 sedan) 107.4 in.; (Mark IX) 120 in. **Overall Length:** (XK-150) 177 in.; (3.4/3.8 sedan) 180.75 in.; (Mk IX) 196.5 in. **Height:** (XK-150) 55 in.; (3.4/3.8 sedan) 57.5 in.; (Mk IX) 63 in. **Width:** (XK-150) 64.5 in.; (3.4/3.8 sedan) 66.75 in.; (Mk IX) 73 in. **Front Tread:** (XK-150) 51.6 in.; (3.4/3.8 sedan) 55.7 in.; (Mk IX) 56.5 in. **Rear Tread:** (XK-150) 51.6 in.; (3.4/3.8 sedan) 54.1 in.; (Mk IX) 58 in. **Standard Tires:** (XK-150) 6.00x16; (3.4) 6.40x15; (3.8) 6.40 x 15; (Mk IX) 6.70x16.

TECHNICAL: Layout: front-engine, rear-drive. **Transmission:** (XK-150) four-speed manual; overdrive and three-speed automatic optional. Overdrive standard on 3.4 and 3.8 sedan. Automatic transmission standard on Mark IX. **Standard Final Drive Ratio:** (XK-150) 3.54:1; (3.4) 3.54:1; (3.8) 3.54:1; (Mk IX) 4.27:1. **Steering:** (XK-150) rack and pinion; (others) recirculating ball. **Suspension (front):** (XK-150) wishbones and torsion bars with anti-roll bar; (3.4/3.8) wishbones with coil springs; (Mk IX) wishbones and torsion bars. **Suspension (rear):** (XK-150, Mk IX) rigid axle with semi-elliptic leaf springs; (3.4/3.8) rigid axle with cantilever springs. **Brakes:** front/rear disc. **Body Construction:** steel body on box-section steel frame except (3.4/3.8) steel unibody.

MAJOR OPTIONS: Automatic transmission: XK-150 ($250); 3.4/3.8 ($100). Overdrive transmission: XK-150 ($165).

PERFORMANCE: Top Speed: (XK-150) 126 mph; (XK-150S w/3.8 engine) 135+ mph; (3.4) 120 mph; (3.8) 120-125+ mph; (Mk IX) 115 mph. **Acceleration (0-60 mph):** (XK-150 w/3.8 engine) 8.3 sec.; (XK-150S w/3.8 engine) about 7 sec.; (3.4) 10.4 sec.; (3.8) 8.5-9.2 sec.; (Mk IX) 11.2 sec. **Acceleration (quarter-mile):** (XK-150 w/3.8 engine) 16.7 sec. (82 mph); (XK-150S w/3.8 engine) 15.3 sec. (87 mph).

PRODUCTION/SALES: Approximately 23,000 Jaguars were produced during 1960. A total of 4,934 Jaguars were exported to the U.S. during the year ending July 1960.

ADDITIONAL MODELS: A Mark II version of the 2.4-liter sedan with 120-bhp engine also became available, but was not ordinarily exported to the U.S. A total of 25,070 were produced from 1960-67.

Manufacturer: Jaguar Cars Ltd., Coventry, England.

Distributor: Jaguar Cars Inc., New York City.

HISTORY: Jaguar's 1960 models were introduced to the U.S. market on September 1, 1959. Jaguar acquired the Daimler company in 1960 (see separate listing in this Catalog).

1961 JAGUAR

XK-150 — SIX — This would be the final season for the XK-150 sports cars, as the new and completey different XK-E arrived at mid-year.

XK-E (E-TYPE) — SIX — Completely different in appearance from its XK-120/140/150 predecessors, and more than 400 pounds lighter in weight, the new projectile-shaped E-Type roadster and hatchback coupe debuted in March 1961 at the Geneva Motor Show. Styling was reminiscent of the D-Type racing car of the mid-1950s. Wheelbase was 96 inches (6 inches shorter than the XK-150). What had been the most potent (265-horsepower) 3.8-liter engine option in the the XK-150 became standard in the XK-E, producing top speeds near 150 mph. While the XK-150 had a separate body and frame, the E-Type turned to a monocoque (unibody) bodyshell bolted to a multi-tube front structure. The whole front end tilted forward (as on the D-Type racer). Styling was by Malcolm Sayer, an aerodynamicist, making this the first Jaguar not penned by William Lyons, who'd been knighted by this time. Lyons did provide "much input" toward the design, however, according to the company. The simple oval grille contained a single horizontal bar to match the slim bumper, and a small oval emblem at its center. Headlamps were recessed into nacelles. At the rear was a slim wraparound back bumper and narrow taillamps, plus center dual exhaust pipes. Underneath was a new independent rear suspension, consisting of lower wishbones and coil springs, with a chassis-mounted differential. All-disc brakes were installed. The coupe's rear hatchback opened sideways. Painted wire wheels were standard (chromed versions optional), and would remain so until the Series 3 of 1971. Early (1961-62) models had unpainted center sections of the dashboard.

Model Note: The new sports car was commonly referred to as the XK-E in the U.S., but E-Type in Europe.

1961 Jaguar Mark II 3.8 liter. (Jaguar Cars Inc.)

3.8 — Mk II — SIX — A 220-horsepower XK engine powered the 3.8 sedan, which continued with little change. Automatic transmission and power steering were optional. All-disc brakes were standard.

MARK IX — SIX — For its final full year in the Jaguar lineup before replacement by the Mark X, the full-size sedan continued with little change. As before, U.S. versions came with standard automatic transmission and power steering.

I.D. DATA: Chassis serial number of XK-150 is stamped on the frame, adjacent to the rear engine mounting; for XK-E, on right frame crossmember, above the shock absorber mounting; for 3.8 sedan, on body channel under the hood on the right side, ahead of radiator header tank; for Mark IX, stamped atop frame member above the rear engine mounting bracket. Engine number is on right of engine block, above oil filter. Engine and chassis numbers also appear on a firewall plate.

Model	Body Type & Seating	Engine Type/CID	P.O.E. Price	Weight (lbs.)	Prod. Total
XK-150	2-dr Roadster-2P	I6/210	N/A	3020	Note 1
XK-150	2-dr Coupe-2+2P	I6/210	4642	2912	Note 1
XK-150	2-dr Conv-2+2P	I6/210	4762	3020	Note 1
XK-150S	2-dr Roadster-2P	I6/210	5120	N/A	Note 2
XK-150S	2-dr Coupe-2+2P	I6/210	5142	N/A	Note 2
XK-150S	2-dr Conv-2+2P	I6/210	5162	N/A	Note 2
XK-E (E-Type)					
	2-dr Roadster-2P	I6/231	5595	2464	Note 3
	2-dr Coupe-2P	I6/231	5895	2520	Note 3
3.8					
Mk II	4-dr Sedan-5P	I6/231	4915	3136	Note 4
MARK IX					
Mk IX	4-dr Sedan-5/6P	I6/231	6070	3976	Note 5

Note 1: Total XK-150 production (1957-60) came to 7,929 units. Of these, 1,339 were roadsters (42 with 3.8-liter engine), 4,101 were fixed-head coupes (656 with 3.8-liter engine), and 2,489 were drophead coupes (586 with 3.8-liter engine).
Note 2: Total XK-150S production (1958-61) came to 1,466 units. Of these, 924 were roadsters (36 with 3.8-liter engine), 349 were fixed-head coupes (150 with 3.8-liter engine), and 193 were drophead coupes (89 with 3.8-liter engine).
Note 3: Total XK-E (E-Type) production from 1961-64 (First Series) amounted to about 7,820 roadsters and 7,670 fixed-head coupes.
Note 4: A total of 30,070 3.8-liter (Mk II) sedans were produced from 1960-67.
Note 5: A total of 10,009 Mark IX sedans were produced from 1959-61 (including 4,647 for export).
Price Note: Figure shown for 3.8 sedan included overdrive; price with automatic and power steering was $5195.

ENGINE DATA: BASE SIX (XK-150): Inline, dual overhead-cam six-cylinder. Cast iron block and aluminum-alloy head. **Displacement:** 210 cu. in. (3442 cc). **Bore & Stroke:** 3.27 x 4.17 in. (83 x 106 mm). **Compression Ratio:** 8.0:1 (XK-150S, 9.0:1). **Brake Horsepower:** 210 at 5500 rpm except (XK-150S 250 at 5500 rpm). **Torque:** 216 lbs.-ft. at 3000 rpm except (XK-150S) 240 at 4000 rpm. Seven main bearings. Solid valve lifters. Two SU sidedraft carburetors except (XK-150S) three SU carburetors.

BASE SIX (XK-E, 3.8, Mark IX); OPTIONAL (XK-150): Inline, dual overhead-cam six-cylinder. Cast iron block and aluminum-alloy head. **Displacement:** 230.6 cu. in. (3781 cc). **Bore & Stroke:** 3.425 x 4.17 in. (87 x 106 mm). **Compression Ratio:** (XK-E) 9.0:1; (others) 8.0:1. **Brake Horsepower:** 220 at 5500 rpm except (XK-E, XK-150S) 265 at 5500 rpm. **Torque:** (3.8) 245 lbs.-ft. at 3000 rpm; (Mk IX) 240 lbs.-ft. at 2900 rpm; (XK-E) 260 lbs.-ft. at 4000 rpm. Seven main bearings. Solid valve lifters. Two SU sidedraft carburetors except (XK-E) three SU carburetors.

CHASSIS DATA: Wheelbase: (XK-E) 96 in.; (XK-150) 102 in.; (3.8 sedan) 107.4 in.; (Mk IX) 120 in. **Overall Length:** (XK-E) 175.3 in.; (XK-150) 177 in.; (3.8 sedan) 180.75 in.; (Mk IX) 196.5 in. **Height:** (XK-E) 48 in.; (XK-150) 55 in.; (XK-150 rds) 52.5 in.; (3.8 sedan) 57.5 in.; (Mk IX) 63 in. **Width:** (XK-E) 65.25 in.; (XK-150) 64.5 in.; (3.8 sedan) 66.75 in.; (Mk IX) 73 in. **Front Tread:** (XK-E) 50 in.; (XK-150) 51.6 in.; (3.4/3.8 sedan) 55 in.; (Mk IX) 56.5 in. **Rear Tread:** (XK-E) 50 in.; (XK-150) 51.6 in.; (3.4/3.8 sedan) 53.4 in.; (Mk IX) 58 in. **Standard Tires:** (XK-E) 6.40x15; (XK-150) 6.00x16; (3.8) 6.40x15; (Mk IX) 6.70x16.

TECHNICAL: Layout: front-engine, rear-drive. **Transmission:** (XK-E) four-speed manual; overdrive optional. (XK-150) four-speed manual; overdrive or automatic optional. Overdrive standard on 3.8 sedan. Automatic transmission standard on Mark IX. **Standard Final Drive Ratio:** (XK-E) 3.31:1; (XK-150) 3.54:1; (3.8) 3.54:1 or 3.77:1; (Mark IX) 4.27:1. **Steering:** (XK-E, XK-150) rack and pinion; (others) recirculating ball. **Suspension (front):** (XK-E and XK-150) wishbones and torsion bars with anti-roll bar; (3.8) wishbones and coil springs; (Mark IX) wishbones and torsion bars. **Suspension (rear):** (XK-E) independent with lower wishbones, coil springs and anti-roll bar; (XK-150, Mk IX) rigid axle with semi-elliptic leaf springs; (3.8) rigid axle with cantilever springs. **Brakes:** front/rear disc. **Body Construction:** (XK-E) monocoque (unibody) bodyshell bolted to multi-tube front structure; (XK-150, Mk IX) steel body on box-section steel frame; (3.8) steel unibody.

MAJOR OPTIONS: Automatic transmission: XK-150 ($250); 3.8 sedan ($150). Overdrive transmission: XK-150 ($165). Power steering: 3.8 sedan ($130).

PERFORMANCE: Top Speed: (XK-E) near 150 mph; (XK-150 w/3.8 engine) 126 mph; (3.8) 120 mph; (Mk IX) 115 mph. **Acceleration (0-60 mph):** (XK-E) 6.5-7.0 sec.; (XK-150 w/3.8 engine) 8.3 sec.; (3.8) 10.0-10.8 sec.; (Mk IX) 11.2 sec. **Acceleration (quarter-mile):** (XK-E) 15.3 sec. (93 mph). **Fuel Mileage:** (3.8) 15-19 mpg.

PRODUCTION/SALES: Approximately 25,000 Jaguars were produced during 1961. A total of 3,422 Jaguars were exported to the U.S. during the year ending July 1961. Close to 44,000 XK-E (E-Type) Jaguars would be sold in the U.S. from 1961-75, out of a total of 72,520 produced.

ADDITIONAL MODELS: The 3.4-liter sedan was dropped this year from the U.S. market, but remained available in Britain.
Manufacturer: Jaguar Cars Ltd., Coventry, England.
Distributor: Jaguar Cars Inc., New York City.

HISTORY: Jaguar's 1961 models were introduced to the U.S. market on September 1, 1960. The XK-E appeared at the New York International Auto Show in April 1961, shortly after its debut at the Geneva (Switzerland) show in March. *Autocar* called the E-Type a "breakthrough in design of high-performance vehicles." *Car and Driver* declared its appeal to be "sensual and elemental."

1962 JAGUAR

1962 Jaguar XKE. (Jaguar Cars Inc.)

XK-E (E-TYPE) — SIX — Production of the sleek roadster and hatchback coupe, introduced in 1961, continued with little change. Power again came from a 3.8-liter twin-cam six with three carburetors.

3.8 — Mk II — SIX — Overdrive was standard equipment on the smaller Jaguar sedan, with automatic optional. The 3781-cc engine produced 220 horsepower.

MARK X — SIX — The Mark IX sedan faded away as the 1962 model year began, leaving only the XK-E coupe and roadster and 3.8 (Mark II) sedan in Jaguar's lineup. But at mid-year, a new full-size Mark X sedan arrived, riding the same 120-inch wheelbase as its predecessor but featuring unibody construction. Either an automatic transmission or overdrive gearbox was available on U.S. models. Styling of the new sedan differed considerably from the Mark IX, abandoning the distinctive fenderline that extended through front and rear doors to meet a bulging rear fender, in favor of a straight-through look. The roofline, too, displayed a more modern appearance, while a lower hood met a revised (and lower) vertical-bar grille and quad headlamps. Under the hood was the more powerful (265-bhp) version of the 3.8-liter engine, as in the XK-E sports cars. Up front, the former torsion-bar suspension departed, replaced by coil springs; while independent suspension at the rear used a transverse leaf spring.

I.D. DATA: Serial number for XK-E is stamped on right frame crossmember, above the front shock absorber mounting. For 3.8 sedan, serial number is stamped at the side of the engine compartment, just ahead of the radiator header tank. Serial number of the Mark X sedan is stamped atop the right front wheel's inner panel. Engine number for XK-E is stamped in two places: on the right side of the block above the oil filter, and at the front end of the cylinder head. A suffix (slash plus digit) in the engine number indicates the engine's compression ratio ('/8' = 8.0:1; '/9' = 9.0:1). Engine and chassis numbers also appear on a firewall plate.

Model	Body Type & Seating	Engine Type/CID	P.O.E. Price	Weight (lbs.)	Prod. Total
XK-E					
	2-dr Roadster-2P	I6/231	5595	2460	Note 1
	2-dr Coupe-2P	I6/231	5895	2520	Note 1
3.8					
Mk II	4-dr Sedan-5P	I6/231	5045	3276	Note 2
MARK X					
Mk X	4-dr Sedan-5P	I6/231	7384	3926	Note 3

Note 1: Total XK-E (E-Type) production from 1961-64 (First Series) amounted to about 7,820 roadsters and 7,670 fixed-head coupes.
Note 2: A total of 30,070 3.8-liter (Mk II) sedans were produced from 1960-67.
Note 3: A total of 13,382 Mark X sedans with 3.8-liter engine were produced from 1962-64 (including 5,775 for export).

ENGINE DATA: BASE SIX: Inline, dual overhead-cam six-cylinder. Cast iron block and aluminum-alloy head. Displacement: 230.6 cu. in. (3781 cc). Bore & Stroke: 3.425 x 4.17 in. (87 x 106 mm). Compression Ratio: (3.8) 8.0:1; (XK-E, Mk X) 9.0:1. Brake Horsepower: (3.8) 220 at 5500 rpm; (XK-E, Mk X) 265 at 5500 rpm. Torque: (3.8) 245 lbs.-ft. at 3000 rpm; (XK-E, Mk X) 260 lbs.-ft. at 4000 rpm. Seven main bearings. Solid valve lifters. Two SU sidedraft carburetors (3.8) or three SU carburetors.

CHASSIS DATA: Wheelbase: (XK-E) 96 in.; (3.8) 107.4 in.; (Mark X) 120 in. Overall Length: (XK-E) 175.3 in.; (3.8) 180.75 in.; (Mk X) 202 in. Height: (XK-E) 48 in.; (3.8) 57.5 in.; (Mk X) 54.5 in. Width: (XK-E) 65.25 in.; (3.8) 66.75 in.; (Mk X) 76 in. Front Tread: (XK-E) 50 in.; (3.8) 55 in.; (Mk X) 58 in. Rear Tread: (XK-E) 50 in.; (3.8) 53.4 in.; (Mk X) 58 in. Standard Tires: (XK-E) 6.40x15; (3.8) 6.40x15; (Mk X) 7.50x14.

TECHNICAL: Layout: front-engine, rear-drive. Transmission: (XK-E) four-speed manual; overdrive optional. Overdrive standard on 3.8 and Mark X. Standard Final Drive Ratio: (XK-E) 3.31:1; (3.8) 3.54:1; (Mk X) 3.54:1 w/automatic, 3.77:1 w/overdrive. Steering: (XK-E) rack and pinion; (others) recirculating ball. Suspension (front): (XK-E) wishbones, torsion bars and anti-roll bar; (3.8) wishbones and coil springs; (Mark X) wishbones and coil springs. Suspension (rear): (XK-E) lower wishbones with coil springs and anti-roll bar; (3.8) rigid axle with cantilever springs; (Mark X) independent, with transverse leaf spring. Brakes: front/rear disc. Body Construction: steel unibody.

MAJOR OPTIONS: Automatic transmission and power steering: 3.8 ($280). Removable hardtop: XK-E rds ($252).

PERFORMANCE: Top Speed: (XK-E) up to 150 mph; (Mk X) 115-118 mph. Acceleration (0-60 mph): (XK-E) 6.5-7.0 sec.; (Mk X) 10.6 sec. Acceleration (quarter-mile): (XK-E) 14.8-15.3 sec. (93-97 mph); (Mk X) 17.2 sec. (80 mph).

PRODUCTION/SALES: Approximately 28,000 Jaguars were produced during 1962. A total of 6,716 Jaguars were exported to the U.S. during the year ending July 1962. Approximately 4,442 Jaguars were sold in the U.S. during 1962.

HISTORY: Jaguar's 1962 models were introduced to the U.S. market on September 1, 1961, except for the Mark X, which debuted on February 14, 1962.

1963 JAGUAR

XK-E (E-TYPE) — SIX — Production of the projectile-shaped sports cars continued with little change. As before, a 265-horsepower version of the 3781-cc engine was installed, hooked to a four-speed manual gearbox (with overdrive optional).

3.8 — Mk II — SIX — Little change was evident in the smaller sedan, powered by a 220-bhp version of the twin-cam six-cylinder engine. Overdrive was standard equipment, automatic optional.

MARK X — SIX — Production of the large four-door sedan (saloon), introduced during 1962, continued with little change. The same 3.8-liter engine was used in the XK-E, producing 265 horsepower. An automatic transmission was standard, with overdrive (manual) available.

1963 Jaguar XKE Lightweight. (Coys of Kensington)

I.D. DATA: Serial numbers are in same locations as 1962.

Model	Body Type & Seating	Engine Type/CID	P.O.E. Price	Weight (lbs.)	Prod. Total
XK-E					
	2-dr Roadster-2P	I6/231	5595	2464	Note 1
	2-dr Coupe-2P	I6/231	5895	2520	Note 1
3.8					
Mk II	4-dr Sedan-5P	I6/231	4890	3136	Note 2
MARK X					
Mk X	4-dr Sedan-5P	I6/231	6990	3920	Note 3

Note 1: Total XK-E (E-Type) production from 1961-64 (First Series) amounted to about 7,820 roadsters and 7,670 fixed-head coupes.
Note 2: A total of 30,070 3.8-liter (Mk II) sedans were produced from 1960-67.
Note 3: A total of 13,382 Mark X sedans with 3.8-liter engine were produced from 1962-64 (including 5,775 for export).
Price Note: Figure shown for 3.8-liter sedan included overdrive; price with automatic was $5040. A Mark X sedan with overdrive sold for $6840.
ENGINE DATA: Same as 1962.
CHASSIS DATA: Same as 1962.
TECHNICAL: Layout: front-engine, rear-drive. Transmission: (XK-E) four-speed manual; overdrive optional. Overdrive standard on 3.8; automatic optional. Automatic transmission standard on Mark X (overdrive available). Standard Final Drive Ratio: (XK-E) 3.31:1; (3.8) 3.77:1 w/OD, 3.54:1 w/automatic; (Mark X) 3.77:1 w/OD, 3.54:1 w/automatic. Steering: (XK-E) rack and pinion; (others) recirculating ball. Suspension (front): (XK-E) wishbones, torsion bars and anti-roll bar; (3.8) wishbones and coil springs; (Mark X) wish-

bones and coil springs. Suspension (rear): (XK-E) lower wishbones with coil springs and anti-roll bar; (3.8) rigid axle with cantilever springs; (Mark X) independent, with transverse leaf spring. Brakes: front/rear disc. Body Construction: steel unibody.
MAJOR OPTIONS: Automatic transmission: 3.8 ($150). Power steering: 3.8 ($120).
PERFORMANCE: Similar to 1962.
PRODUCTION/SALES: Approximately 22,500 Jaguars were produced during 1963. A total of 4,113 Jaguars were exported to the U.S. during the year ending July 1963. Approximately 4,421 Jaguars were sold in the U.S. during 1963.
Manufacturer: Jaguar Cars Ltd., Coventry, England.
Distributor: Jaguar Cars Inc., New York City.
HISTORY: Jaguar's 1963 models were introduced to the U.S. market on September 1, 1962.

1964 JAGUAR

1964 Jaguar 3.8-liter XKE Series 1 roadster. (Christie's)

XK-E (E-TYPE) — SIX — Little was new in Jaguar's sports roadster and hatchback coupe, until the larger (4.2-liter) engine arrived late in the year; see next listing for details.

3.8 — Mk II — SIX — Power steering was standard on the smaller Jaguar sedan, which again came with either overdrive or automatic transmission. A longer 'S' version became available this year, with independent rear coil springs replacing the former cantilevered units. The 'S' edition also had a different rear-end look, with flattened (lower) wheel openings, slimmer bumpers, shrouded headlamps, teardrop-shaped turn signals indicators outside the parking lights, and a straight decklid. Inside, the 'S' dashboard had walnut in its center, lacking the bleak leather covering on the standard model.

MARK X — SIX — Automatic transmission and power steering were standard on the full-size sedan, which continued with minimal change. A larger (4.2-liter) engine became available later in the year; see next listing for details.

I.D. DATA: Serial numbers are in same locations as 1962-63.

Model	Body Type & Seating	Engine Type/CID	P.O.E. Price	Weight (lbs.)	Prod. Total
XK-E					
	2-dr Roadster-2P	I6/231	5325	2464	Note 1
	2-dr Coupe-2P	I6/231	5525	2520	Note 1
3.8					
Mk II	4-dr Sedan-5P	I6/231	5220	3248	Note 2
3.8S	4-dr Sedan-5P	I6/231	5850	3440	Note 3
MARK X					
	4-dr Sedan-5P	I6/231	6990	3976	Note 4

Note 1: Total XK-E (E-Type) production from 1961-64 (First Series) amounted to about 7,820 roadsters and 7,670 fixed-head coupes.
Note 2: A total of 30,070 3.8-liter (Mk II) sedans were produced from 1960-67.
Note 3: A total of 15,070 3.8S sedans were produced from 1964-68.
Note 4: A total of 13,382 Mark X sedans with 3.8-liter engine were produced from 1962-64 (including 5,775 for export).
Price Note: Figures shown for 3.8-liter sedan included automatic transmission; price with overdrive was $5070 for the 3.8 Mark II, and $5700 for the 3.8S sedan.
ENGINE DATA: BASE SIX: Inline, dual overhead-cam six-cylinder. Cast iron block and aluminum-alloy head. Displacement: 230.6 cu. in. (3781 cc). Bore & Stroke: 3.425 x 4.17 in. (87 x 106 mm). Compression Ratio: (3.8) 8.0:1; (XK-E, Mk X) 9.0:1. Brake Horsepower: (3.8) 220 at 5500 rpm; (XK-E, Mk X) 265 at 5500 rpm. Torque: (3.8) 240/245 lbs.-ft. at 3000 rpm; (XK-E, Mk X) 260 lbs.-ft. at 4000 rpm. Seven main bearings. Solid valve lifters. Two SU sidedraft carburetors (3.8) or three SU carburetors.
CHASSIS DATA: Wheelbase: (XK-E) 96 in.; (3.8) 107.4 in.; (Mk X) 120 in. Overall Length: (XK-E) 175.3 in.; (3.8) 180.75 in.; (3.8S) 187.75 in.; (Mk X) 202 in. Height: (XK-E) 48 in.; (3.8) 57.5 in.; (Mk X) 54.5 in. Width: (XK-E) 65.25 in.; (3.8) 66.75 in.; (Mk X) 76 in. Front Tread: (XK-E) 50 in.; (3.8) 55 in.; (Mk X) 58 in. Rear Tread: (XK-E) 50 in.; (3.8) 53.4 in.; (Mk X) 58 in. Standard Tires: (XK-E) 6.40x15; (3.8) 6.40x15; (Mk X) 7.50x14.
TECHNICAL: Layout: front-engine, rear-drive. Transmission: (XK-E) four-speed manual, overdrive optional; (3.8) overdrive standard, automatic optional; (Mark X) automatic transmission standard. Standard Final Drive Ratio: (XK-E) 3.31:1; (3.8) 3.54:1; (Mark X) 3.54:1. Steering: (XK-E) rack and pinion; (others) recirculating ball. Suspension (front): (XK-E) wishbones, torsion bars and anti-roll bar; (3.8) wishbones and coil springs; (Mark X) wishbones and coil springs. Suspension (rear): (XK-E) lower wishbones with coil springs and anti-roll bar; (3.8) rigid axle with cantilever springs; (3.8S) coil springs; (Mark X) independent, with transverse leaf spring. Brakes: front/rear disc. Body Construction: steel unibody.

MAJOR OPTIONS: Automatic transmission: 3.8 ($150). Wire wheels (3.8).
PERFORMANCE: Similar to 1962-63.
PRODUCTION/SALES: Approximately 20,000 Jaguars were produced during 1964. A total of 4,037 Jaguars were exported to the U.S. during the year ending July 1964. Approximately 4,018 Jaguars were sold in the U.S. during 1964.

Manufacturer: Jaguar Cars Ltd., Coventry, England.
Distributor: Jaguar Cars Inc., New York City.
HISTORY: Jaguar's 1964 models were introduced to the U.S. market on September 1, 1963.

1965 JAGUAR

1965 Jaguar XKE Lightweight replica. (Coys of Kensington)

XK-E (E-TYPE) — SIX — A bigger (4.2-liter) six-cylinder engine become available this year, with a larger bore than its 3.8-liter predecessor. Torque got a boost to 283 pound-feet, but horsepower remained the same as before (265 bhp). A new all-synchro four-speed gearbox was installed. Seats, clutch, alternator and exhaust system also were new. Lettering on the trunk lid spelled out "E TYPE JAGUAR 4.2."

3.8 — Mk II — SIX — Change was minimal on the smaller sedan, which continued with the 3781-cc twin-cam engine. Power steering was standard. Wire wheels and air conditioning were optional. The 3.8S sedan was 7 inches longer and had a different rear-end appearance, with flattened rear wheel openings and straight decklid (similar to the larger Mark X sedan).

MARK X — 4.2 — SIX — The 4.2-liter engine went into Jaguar's full-size sedan even before it appeared under XK-E (E-Type) hoods. Some sources called the revised model, simply, '4.2,' though 'Mark X' remained part of its name.

I.D. DATA: Chassis serial number for XK-E is stamped on right frame crossmember, above the shock absorber mounting. Mark II (3.8) serial number is stamped in the hood latch channel, ahead of the radiator. Mark X serial number is stamped atop the right front wheel's inner panel. Engine number is stamped on the right side of the block, above the oil filter; and at the front of the cylinder head. Suffix '/8' or '/9' indicates the engine's compression ratio. Starting serial number: (XK-E 4.2 rds) 1E.10001 or 1R.7001; (XK-E 4.2 cpe) 1E.300001 or 1R.25001; (Mark X 4.2) 1D.75001.

Model	Body Type & Seating	Engine Type/CID	P.O.E. Price	Weight (lbs.)	Prod. Total
XK-E					
4.2	2-dr Roadster-2P	I6/258	5384	2464	Note 1
4.2	2-dr Coupe-2P	I6/258	5580	2520	Note 1
3.8					
Mk II	4-dr Sedan-5P	I6/231	5419	3136	Note 2
3.8S	4-dr Sedan-5P	I6/231	5933	3438	Note 3
MARK X					
4.2	4-dr Sedan-6P	I6/258	6990	3920	Note 4

Note 1: Total XK-E (E-Type) production from 1965-68 amounted to about 9,550 roadsters and 7,770 fixed-head coupes (plus 5,600 2+2 coupes).
Note 2: A total of 30,070 3.8-liter (Mk II) sedans were produced from 1960-67.
Note 3: A total of 15,070 3.8S sedans were produced from 1964-68.
Note 4: A total of 5,119 Mark X sedans with 4.2-liter engine were produced in 1965-66 (including 2,291 for export), plus 18 limousines.
Price Note: Figures shown for 3.8-liter sedan included automatic transmission; price with overdrive was $5272 for the 3.8 Mark II, and $5786 for the 3.8S sedan. Figure shown for Mark X included automatic transmission; overdrive was available on special order at $6840.
ENGINE DATA: BASE SIX (3.8 Mk II, 3.8S): Inline, dual overhead-cam six-cylinder. Cast iron block and aluminum-alloy head. **Displacement:** 230.6 cu. in. (3781 cc). **Bore & Stroke:** 3.425 x 4.17 in. (87 x 106 mm). **Compression Ratio:** 8.0:1. **Brake Horsepower:** 220 at 5500 rpm. **Torque:** 240/245 lbs.-ft. at 3000 rpm. Seven main bearings. Solid valve lifters. Two SU sidedraft carburetors.
BASE SIX (XK-E, Mark X): Inline, dual overhead-cam six-cylinder. Cast iron block and aluminum-alloy head. **Displacement:** 258.4 cu. in. (4235 cc). **Bore & Stroke:** 3.625 x 4.17 in. (92.1 x 106 mm). **Compression Ratio:** 9.0:1. **Brake Horsepower:** 265 at 5400 rpm. **Torque:** 283 lbs.-ft. at 4000 rpm. Seven main bearings. Solid valve lifters. Three SU sidedraft carburetors.
CHASSIS DATA: Wheelbase: (XK-E) 96 in.; (3.8 Mk II) 107.4 in.; (Mk X) 120 in. **Overall Length:** (XK-E) 175.3 in.; (3.8 Mk II) 180.75 in.; (3.8S) 187.75 in.; (Mk X) 202 in. **Height:** (XK-E) 48 in.; (3.8 Mk II) 57.5 in.; (3.8S) 54.5 in.; (Mk X) 54.5 in. **Width:** (XK-E) 65.25 in.; (3.8 Mk II) 66.75 in.; (3.8S) 66.75 in.; (Mk X) 76 in. **Front Tread:** (XK-E) 50 in.; (3.8 Mk II) 55 in.; (3.8S) 55 in.; (Mk X) 58 in. **Rear Tread:** (XK-E) 50 in.; (3.8 Mk II) 53.4 in.; (3.8S) 54.25 in.; (Mk X) 58 in. **Standard Tires:** (XK-E) 6.40x15; (3.8 Mk II) 6.40x15; (Mk X) 205x14.
TECHNICAL: Layout: front-engine, rear-drive. **Transmission:** (XK-E) four-speed manual, overdrive optional; (3.8) overdrive standard, automatic optional; (Mark X) automatic transmission standard. **Standard Final Drive Ratio:** (XK-E) 3.54:1; (3.8 Mark II) 3.54:1; (3.8S) 3.77:1; (Mark X 4.2) 3.54:1. **Steering:** (XK-E) rack and pinion; (others) recirculating ball. **Suspension (front):** (XK-E) wishbones and torsion bars with anti-roll bar; (3.8, Mark X) wishbones and coil springs with anti-roll bar. **Suspension (rear):** (XK-E) lower wishbones with coil springs and anti-roll bar; (3.8 Mk II) rigid axle with cantilever leaf springs; (3.8S, Mark X) wishbones with four coil springs and anti-roll bar. **Brakes:** front/rear disc. **Body Construction:** steel unibody.

MAJOR OPTIONS: Air conditioning ($595).
PRODUCTION/SALES: A total of 3,669 Jaguars were exported to the U.S. during the year ending July 1965. Approximately 3,993 Jaguars were sold in the U.S. during 1965.
Manufacturer: Jaguar Cars Ltd., Coventry, England.
Distributor: Jaguar Cars Inc., New York City.
HISTORY: Jaguar's 1965 models were introduced to the U.S. market on October 15, 1964 except (3.8) September 1, 1964.

1966 JAGUAR

1966 Jaguar XKE 2+2 fixed-head coupe. (Christie's)

XK-E 4.2 (E-TYPE) — SIX — In addition to the well-established roadster (convertible) and coupe, Jaguar added a longer 2+2 coupe to the E-Type lineup this year. Both models carried the 4.2-liter engine, rated 265 bhp, and a four-speed manual gearbox. A Borg-Warner automatic transmission became available for the 2+2, which rode a 9-inch longer wheelbase than the original models and displayed a taller roofline. A fiberglass removable hardtop was optional on the roadster. The steering column adjusted for both reach and height.

3.8 Mk II, 3.8S — SIX — Jaguar's 3.8-liter sedan came in two levels: basic Mk II, and the slightly larger and luxurious 'S' model, intended to mix family comfort with sports car character. Power for each model came from a 225-bhp engine with twin carburetors. Overdrive and power steering were standard. Plastic replaced leather in the car's interior in 1966, and new grilles replaced the former foglamps. The 3.8S had slim bumpers, a different rear-wheel opening shape, and different position of the signal/side lights than the Mark II, as well as independent rear suspension with coil springs. The Mark II continued with semi-elliptic leaf springs at the rear.

4.2 (MARK X) — SIX — The largest Jaguar sedan again carried the same engine as the XK-E sports car, displacing 258.4 cubic inches and producing 265 bhp. Standard equipment included variable-ratio power steering, Borg-Warner dual-range automatic transmission, a limited-slip differential, and built-in walnut tables. The 'Mark X' portion of its designation was not always used in these final years.

I.D. DATA: Serial number for XK-E is stamped on right frame crossmember, above the shock absorber mounting; for 3.8 series, on hood latch channel ahead of the radiator; for 4.2 Mark X, atop the right front wheel inner panel. Prefix indicates make and model (and possibly whether car is a U.S. model). Suffix may indicate whether car is equipped with overdrive or automatic transmission, and if left-hand drive (for export). Numerical sequence is the production serial number. Engine number is stamped on the right side of the block, above the oil filter; and at the front of the cylinder head (suffix /8 or /9 indicates compression ratio). Engine and chassis numbers also appear on a brass plate on the firewall. Starting serial number: (XK-E 2+2) 1E.75001 or 1R.40001.

Model	Body Type & Seating	Engine Type/CID	P.O.E. Price	Weight (lbs.)	Prod. Total
XK-E (E-Type)					
4.2	2-dr Roadster-2P	I6/258	5384	2464	Note 1
4.2	2-dr Coupe-2P	I6/258	5580	2520	Note 1
4.2	2-dr Coupe-2+2P	I6/258	6070	N/A	Note 1
3.8					
Mk II	4-dr Sedap-5P	I6/231	5272	3136	Note 2
S	4-dr Sedan-5P	I6/231	5786	3440	Note 3
4.2 (MARK X)					
	4-dr Sedan-6P	I6/258	6990	3920	Note 4

Note 1: A total of approximately 22,922 E-Types were produced from 1965-68 (9,550 roadsters, 7,772 fixed-head coupes, and 5,600 2+2 coupes).
Note 2: A total of 30,070 3.8 Mark II sedans were produced from 1960-67.
Note 3: A total of 15,070 3.8S sedans were produced from 1964-68.
Note 4: A total of 5,119 Mark X sedans with the 4.2-liter engine were produced in 1965-66 (2,291 for exports), plus 18 limousines.
Price Note: XK-E 2+2 coupe with automatic was priced at $6415; 3.8 Mk II with automatic, $5419; 3.8S with automatic was $5933.

ENGINE DATA: BASE SIX (3.8): Inline, dual overhead-cam six-cylinder. Cast iron block and aluminum head. **Displacement:** 230.6 cu. in. (3781 cc). **Bore & Stroke:** 3.425 x 4.17 in. (87 x 106 mm). **Compression Ratio:** 8.0:1. **Brake Horsepower:** 225 at 5500 rpm. **Torque:** 240 lbs.-ft. at 3000 rpm. Seven main bearings. Solid valve lifters. Two SU sidedraft carburetors. Lucas ignition.
BASE SIX (XK-E, 4.2 Mk X): Inline, dual overhead-cam six-cylinder. Cast iron block and aluminum head. **Displacement:** 258.4 cu. in. (4235 cc). **Bore & Stroke:** 3.625 x 4.17 in. (92.1 x 106 mm). **Compression Ratio:** 9.0:1. **Brake Horsepower:** 265 at 5400 rpm. **Torque:** 283 lbs.-ft. at 4000 rpm. Seven main bearings. Solid valve lifters. Three SU sidedraft carburetors. Lucas ignition.

CHASSIS DATA: Wheelbase: (XK-E) 96 in.; (XK-E 2+2) 105 in.; (3.8) 107.4 in.; (4.2) 120 in. **Overall Length:** (XK-E) 175.3 in.; (XK-E 2+2) 184.5 in.; (3.8 Mk II) 180.75 in.; (3.8S) 187.8 in.; (4.2) 202 in. **Height:** (XK-E) 48 in.; (XK-E 2+2) 50 in.; (3.8 Mk II) 57.5 in.; (3.8S) 54.5 in.; (4.2) 54.5 in. **Width:** (XK-E) 65.3 in.; (3.8) 66.8 in.; (4.2) 76.3 in. **Front Tread:** (XK-E) 50 in.; (3.8 Mk II) 55 in.; (3.8S) 55.3 in.; (4.2) 58 in. **Rear Tread:** (XK-E) 50 in.; (3.8 Mk II) 53.4 in.; (3.8S) 54.3 in.; (4.2) 58 in. **Standard Tires:** (XK-E) 6.40x15; (3.8) 205x14; (3.8S) 6.40x15; (4.2) 205x14.

TECHNICAL: Layout: front-engine, rear-drive. **Transmission:** (XK-E, 3.8) four-speed manual; overdrive optional. Borg-Warner automatic transmission standard on 4.2 Mark X sold in U.S., and optional on XK-E 2+2 coupe and 3.8 series. **Standard Final Drive Ratio:** (XK-E) 3.31:1; (3.8 Mk II) 3.54:1; (3.8S) 3.77:1; (4.2) 3.54:1. **Steering:** (XK-E) rack and pinion; (others) recirculating ball. **Suspension (front):** wishbones, torsion bars and anti-roll bar. **Suspension (rear):** (XK-E, 4.2) independent, lower wishbones, trailing lower radius arms, coil springs and anti-roll bar; (3.8 Mk II) rigid axle with trailing radius arms, transverse linkage bar and semi-elliptic leaf springs; (3.8S) independent with coil springs. **Brakes:** front/rear disc. **Body Construction:** (XK-E) integral steel, with front tubular frame; (others) integral steel body and frame.

MAJOR OPTIONS: Automatic transmission: 3.8 sedan, XK-E 2+2 coupe.
PERFORMANCE: Top Speed: (XK-E) up to 150+ mph claimed (but as low as 130 mph reported); (3.8 Mk II) 136-140 mph; (3.8S) 120 mph; (3.8S) 123 mph; (4.2) 120-125 mph. **Acceleration (0-60 mph):** (XK-E) 6.5-7.0 sec.; (XK-E 2+2) 8.9 sec. **Acceleration (quarter-mile):** (XK-E) 15 sec.; (3.8 Mk II) 16.3 sec.; (3.8S) 15 sec. **Fuel Mileage:** (XK-E) 15-16 mpg; (3.8) 15-17 mpg; (4.2) about 14-15 mpg.

PRODUCTION/SALES: Approximately 23,000 Jaguars and Daimlers were produced during 1966. At least 4,635 Jaguars were sold in the U.S. during 1966.
Manufacturer: Jaguar Cars Ltd., Coventry, England.
Distributor: Jaguar Cars Inc., New York City.
HISTORY: Introduced to U.S. market on September 1, 1965. *Car and Driver* called the XK-E 4.2 "a delightful, multi-purpose two-seater which is equally at home in city traffic, on country roads and at racing circuits," though "no faster than the 3.8."

1967 JAGUAR

1967 Jaguar XKE roadster. (Coys of Kensington)

XK-E (E-Type) — SIX — No major change was evident on the roadster (convertible) or coupe, or the enlarged 2+2 coupe introduced for 1966. The 4.2-liter twin-cam six-cylinder engine developed 265 horsepower. A four-speed manual gearbox was standard; dual-range Borg-Warner automatic optional. The 2+2 rode a nine-inch longer wheelbase than the coupe and roadster and had hinged rear quarter windows, and the backs of its rear seats slid forward to enlarge the luggage platform. Wire wheels were available. Instruments included a 160-mph speedometer and tachometer.

340 — SIX — The body was the same, but the name different on Jaguar's compact sedan. Instead of 3.8 Mk II, as before, it was now called the 340 (denoting the 3.4-liter engine size), and carried a considerably smaller price tag. Wheelbase was the same as the Mk II, at 107.4 inches, and the sedan again measured nearly 181 inches long. This model adopted the slim bumpers from the former 3.8S sedan. Separate front seats were upholstered in vinyl leatherette-covered foam. Walnut veneer was used for the window cappings and instrument panel. A tachometer and electric clock were standard, as was the telescopic steering wheel. Standard equipment also included power steering and all-wheel disc brakes, and a four-speed manual gearbox. A Borg-Warner automatic transmission was optional.

420 — SIX — A new version of the Jaguar sedan, on a 107.4-inch wheelbase, mixed the body dimensions of the former 3.8S sedan with the powerplant of the XK-E sports car. However, that engine was reduced in horsepower to 246, using two instead of three carburetors. Front-end appearance of the sports sedan was similar to the larger 420G (which was actually the former Mk X). "Varamatic" power steering was standard on examples for the U.S. market. Four-wheel disc brakes had the usual separate circuits for front and rear. Like the 3.8S before it, this model had an independent rear suspension with coil springs rather than the Mark II's leaf springs. Appearance changes included a new quad-headlamp setup, a larger grille, and a padded dashboard interior. A new impulse-driven tachometer was standard. The new model came with a standard four-speed (overdrive) manual transmission. Options included an automatic transmission, wire wheels, and tinted glass.

420G — SIX — Successor to the Mk X, the new 420G Grand Saloon had the same body dimensions and engine specifications. New features this year included an improved aluminized exhaust system, restyled front seats, new body chrome, and a new padded dashboard. A dual-range Borg-Warner automatic transmission was standard. Polished walnut interior trim included two folding picnic tables. Production lasted into 1970, though the 420G would not remain that long on lists of U.S. imports.

324

I.D. DATA: Serial number for XK-E is stamped on right frame crossmember, above the shock absorber mounting; for 340/420 series, on hood latch channel ahead of the radiator; for 420G, atop the right front wheel inner panel. Prefix indicates make and model (and possibly whether car is a U.S. model). Suffix may indicate whether car is equipped with overdrive or automatic transmission, and if left-hand drive (for export). Numerical sequence is the production serial number. Engine number is stamped on the right side of the block, above the oil filter; and at the front of the cylinder head (suffix /8 or /9 indicates compression ratio). Engine and chassis numbers also appear on a brass plate on the firewall. Starting serial number: (420) 1F.25001; (420G) G1D.77001.

Model	Body Type & Seating	Engine Type/CID	P.O.E. Price	Weight (lbs.)	Prod. Total
XK-E (E-Type)					
	2-dr Roadster-2P	I6/258	5384	2464	Note 1
	2-dr Coupe-2P	I6/258	5580	2520	Note 1
	2-dr Coupe-2+2P	I6/258	5870	2744	Note 1
340					
	4-dr Sedan-4/5P	I6/210	4490	3080	N/A
420 SERIES					
420	4-dr Sedan-5P	I6/258	5786	3440	Note 2
420G	4-dr Sedan-5/6P	I6/258	6990	3920	Note 3

Note 1: A total of approximately 22,922 E-Types were produced from 1965-68 (9,550 roadsters, 7,772 fixed-head coupes, and 5,600 2+2 coupes).
Note 2: A total of 9,600 420 sedans were produced in 1967-68.
Note 3: A total of 5,739 420G sedans were produced from 1967-70 (2,304 for export), plus 24 limousines (10 for export).
Price Note: XK-E 2+2 coupe with automatic transmission was priced at $6120; 340 sedan with automatic, $4723; 420 sedan with automatic was $5933. 420G had automatic as standard equipment.

ENGINE DATA: BASE SIX (340): Inline, dual overhead-cam six-cylinder. Cast iron block and aluminum head. **Displacement:** 210 cu. in. (3442 cc). **Bore & Stroke:** 3.27 x 4.17 in. (83 x 106 mm). **Compression Ratio:** 8.0:1. **Brake Horsepower:** 210 at 5500 rpm. **Torque:** 215 lbs.-ft. at 3000 rpm. Seven main bearings. Solid valve lifters. Two SU sidedraft carburetors.

BASE SIX (XK-E, 420G): Inline, dual overhead-cam six-cylinder. Cast iron block and aluminum head. **Displacement:** 258.4 cu. in. (4235 cc). **Bore & Stroke:** 3.625 x 4.17 in. (92.1 x 106 mm). **Compression Ratio:** 9.0:1. **Brake Horsepower:** 265 at 5400 rpm. **Torque:** 283 lbs.-ft. at 4000 rpm. Seven main bearings. Solid valve lifters. Three SU sidedraft carburetors.

BASE SIX (420): Same as 4.2-liter six above, except — **Compression Ratio:** 8.0:1. **Brake Horsepower:** 246 at 5500 rpm. **Torque:** 282 lbs.-ft. at 3750 rpm. Two SU carburetors.

CHASSIS DATA: Wheelbase: (XK-E) 96 in.; (XK-E 2+2) 105 in.; (340) 107.4 in.; (420) 107.4 in.; (420G) 120 in. **Overall Length:** (XK-E) 175.3 in.; (XK-E 2+2) 184.5 in.; (340) 180.75 in.; (420) 187.8 in.; (420G) 202 in. **Height:** (XK-E) 48 in.; (XK-E 2+2) 50 in.; (340) 57.5 in.; (420) 54.5 in.; (420G) 54.5 in. **Width:** (XK-E) 65.3 in.; (340) 66.8 in.; (420) 66.75 in. (420G) 76.3 in. **Front Tread:** (XK-E) 50 in.; (340) 55 in.; (420) 55.3 in.; (420G) 58 in. **Rear Tread:** (XK-E) 50 in.; (340) 53.4 in.; (420) 54.3 in.; (420G) 58 in. **Wheel Type:** (XK-E) disc or center-lock wire; (others) steel disc. **Standard Tires:** (XK-E) 6.40x15; (340) 6.40x15; (420) 185x15; (420G) 205x14.

TECHNICAL: Layout: front-engine, rear-drive. **Transmission:** (XK-E, 340, 420) four-speed manual; overdrive optional. Borg-Warner automatic transmission standard on 420G, optional on others. **Steering:** (XK-E) rack and pinion; (others) recirculating ball. **Suspension (front):** wishbones, torsion bars and anti-roll bar. **Suspension (rear):** (XK-E, 420G) independent, lower wishbones, trailing lower radius arms, coil springs and anti-roll bar; (340) rigid axle, trailing radius arms, transverse linkage bar and semi-elliptic leaf springs. **Brakes:** front/rear disc. **Body Construction:** (XK-E) integral steel, with front tubular frame; (others) integral steel body and frame.

PERFORMANCE: Top Speed: (XK-E) 140-152 mph; (340) about 110 mph; (420) 120+ mph; (420G) 125 mph. **Acceleration (0-60 mph):** (XK-E) 7.2 to 8 sec.; (340) under 13 sec. **Acceleration (quarter-mile):** (XK-E) about 15 sec. **Fuel Mileage:** (XK-E) 14-20 mpg; (340) 17-25 mpg; (420) about 15 mpg.
PRODUCTION/SALES: At least 5,839 Jaguars were sold in the U.S. during 1967.
Manufacturer: Jaguar Cars Ltd., Coventry, England.
Distributor: Jaguar Cars Inc., New York City.
HISTORY: The Daimler Sovereign was nearly identical to the 420 (and former 3.8S). The 3.8S sedan also remained in production into 1968.

1968 JAGUAR

1968 Jaguar XJ-6 saloon. (Jaguar Cars Inc.)

XK-E (E-Type) — SIX — Only the Jaguar series of sports cars made it to the U.S. for the 1968 model year. The 340/420 sedans faded away. Horsepower was reduced to 246 bhp for the imported edition. Safety bumpers were new this year, and the cockpit was restyled.

Model Availability Note: Importation of Jaguar sedans was prevented in 1968, because of U.S. emissions regulations. A different (XJ) series of sedans would appear for the 1969 model year.

I.D. DATA: Serial number for XK-E is stamped on right frame crossmember, above the shock absorber mounting. Prefix indicates make and model (and possibly whether car is a U.S. model). Suffix may indicate whether car is equipped with overdrive or automatic transmission, and if left-hand drive (for export). Numerical sequence is the production serial number. Engine number is stamped on the right side of the block, above the oil filter; and at the front of the cylinder head (suffix /8 or /9 indicates compression ratio). Engine and chassis numbers also appear on a brass plate on the firewall.

Model	Body Type & Seating	Engine Type/CID	P.O.E. Price	Weight (lbs.)	Prod. Total
XK-E (E-Type)					
	2-dr Roadster-5P	I6/258	5372	2464	Note 1
	2-dr Coupe-2P	I6/258	5559	2520	Note 1
	2-dr Coupe-2 + 2P	I6/258	5739	2744	Note 1

Note 1: A total of approximately 22,922 E-Types were produced from 1965-68 (9,550 roadsters, 7,772 fixed-head coupes, and 5,600 2 + 2 coupes).

Price Note: 2 + 2 coupe with automatic transmission was priced at $5977.

ENGINE DATA: BASE SIX: Inline, dual overhead-cam six-cylinder. Cast iron block and aluminum head. **Displacement:** 258.4 cu. in. (4235 cc). **Bore & Stroke:** 3.625 x 4.17 in. (92.1 x 106 mm). **Compression Ratio:** 9.0:1. **Brake Horsepower:** 246 at 5500 rpm. **Torque:** 263 lbs.-ft. at 3000 rpm. Seven main bearings. Solid valve lifters. Three SU sidedraft carburetors.

Note: Home-market engine was rated 265 bhp (SAE) at 5400 rpm, and 283 lbs.-ft. at 4000 rpm.

CHASSIS DATA: Wheelbase: (XK-E) 96 in.; (XK-E 2 + 2) 105 in. **Overall Length:** (XK-E) 175.3 in.; (XK-E 2 + 2) 184.5 in. **Height:** (XK-E) 48 in.; (XK-E 2 + 2) 50 in. **Width:** 65.3 in. **Front Tread:** 50 in. **Rear Tread:** 50 in. **Wheel Type:** disc or center-lock wire. **Standard Tires:** 6.40x15 or 185x15.

TECHNICAL: Layout: front-engine, rear-drive. **Transmission:** four-speed manual; automatic available on 2 + 2. **Steering:** rack and pinion. **Suspension (front):** wishbones, torsion bars and anti-roll bar. **Suspension (rear):** independent, wishbones, trailing lower radius arms, coil springs and anti-roll bar. **Brakes:** front/rear disc. **Body Construction:** integral steel, with front tubular frame.

PERFORMANCE: Top Speed: (XK-E) 140 + mph. **Acceleration (0-60 mph):** (XK-E) 7.2 to 8 sec. **Acceleration (quarter-mile):** (XK-E) about 15 sec. **Fuel Mileage:** (XK-E) up to 20 mpg.

PRODUCTION/SALES: Approximately 5,179 Jaguars were sold in the U.S. during 1968.

ADDITIONAL MODELS: A total of 2,630 type 340 sedans were produced in 1968, as well as final 3.8S models.

Manufacturer: Jaguar Cars Ltd., Coventry, England.

Distributor: British Motor Holdings (USA) Inc., Ridgefield, New Jersey; or British Leyland Motors, Leonia, New Jersey.

HISTORY: Jaguar's new XJ sedan and the second-series E-Type debuted during 1968; see next listing for details. Also in 1968, British Motor Holdings and Leyland Motors merged to form the British Leyland Motor Company.

I.D. DATA: Serial number for XK-E is stamped on right frame crossmember, above the shock absorber mounting; for XJ, on inner fender panel within engine compartment. Prefix indicates make and model (and possibly whether car is a U.S. model). Suffix may indicate whether car is equipped with overdrive or automatic transmission, and if left-hand drive (for export). Numerical sequence is the production serial number. Engine number is stamped on the right side of the block, above the oil filter; and at the front of the cylinder head (suffix /8 or /9 indicates compression ratio). Engine and chassis numbers also appear on a brass plate on the firewall. Starting serial number: (XK-E rds) 1R7001; (XK-E cpe) 1R25001; (XK-E 2 + 2) 1R40001; (XJ) 1L50001. Starting engine number: (XJ) 7L1001.

Model	Body Type & Seating	Engine Type/CID	P.O.E. Price	Weight (lbs.)	Prod. Total
XK-E (E-Type)					
II	2-dr Roadster-2P	I6/258	5534	2912	Note 1
II	2-dr Coupe-2P	I6/258	5725	2912	Note 1
II	2-dr Coupe-2 + 2P	I6/258	5907	3024	Note 1
XJ					
	4-dr Sedan-5P	I6/258	6270	3556	8085

Note 1: Approximately 18,820 Series II XK-Es were produced from 1968-70 (8,630 roadsters, 4,860 fixed-head coupes, and 5,330 2 + 2 coupes).

Price Note: 2 + 2 coupe with automatic transmission was priced at $6145; XJ with automatic was $6465.

ENGINE DATA: BASE SIX (XK-E, XJ): Inline, dual overhead-cam six-cylinder. Cast iron block and aluminum head. **Displacement:** 258.4 cu. in. (4235 cc). **Bore & Stroke:** 3.625 x 4.17 in. (92.1 x 106 mm). **Compression Ratio:** 9.0:1. **Brake Horsepower:** 246 at 5500 rpm. **Torque:** 263 lbs.-ft. at 3000 rpm. Seven main bearings. Solid valve lifters. Two carburetors.

Engine Note: The home-market E-Type's engine was rated 265 bhp, with 9.0:1 compression and three carburetors. A 2791-cc six-cylinder engine rated 180 horsepower was available in XJ sedans sold in Europe.

CHASSIS DATA: Wheelbase: (XK-E) 96 in.; (XK-E 2 + 2) 105 in.; (XJ) 108.9 in. **Overall Length:** (XK-E) 175.3 in.; (XK-E 2 + 2) 184.4 in.; (XJ) 189.6 in. **Height:** (XK-E) 48 in.; (XK-E 2 + 2) 50.1 in.; (XJ) 52.9 in. **Width:** (XK-E) 65.25 in.; (XJ) 69.75 in. **Front Tread:** (XK-E) 50 in.; (XJ) 58 in. **Rear Tread:** (XK-E) 50 in.; (XJ) 58.6 in. **Standard Tires:** (XK-E) 185x15; (XJ) 195x15.

TECHNICAL: Layout: front-engine, rear-drive. **Transmission:** (XK-E, XJ) four-speed manual; automatic available on 2 + 2 and XJ. **Standard Final Drive Ratio:** 3.54:1. **Steering:** rack and pinion. **Suspension (front):** (XK-E) wishbones, torsion bars and anti-roll bar; (XJ) wishbones and coil springs. **Suspension (rear):** independent with lower wishbones, trailing lower radius arms, coil springs and anti-roll bar. **Brakes:** front/rear disc. **Body Construction:** integral steel, with subframes.

MAJOR OPTIONS: Air conditioning (XJ). Air cond.: XK-E ($482). Wire wheels: XK-E ($132). Power steering: XK-E ($160).

PERFORMANCE: Top Speed: (XK-E) 138 mph (about 120 mph in U.S. form); (XJ) 124 mph. **Acceleration (0-60 mph):** (XK-E) 7.2-8.0 sec.; (XJ) under 9 sec. **Acceleration (quarter-mile):** (XK-E) 15.5-15.7 sec. (88-89 mph); (XJ) 17 sec. (85 mph).

PRODUCTION/SALES: At least 5,700 Jaguars were sold in the U.S. during 1969.

Manufacturer: Jaguar Cars Ltd., Coventry, England.

Distributor: British Leyland Motors, Leonia, New Jersey.

HISTORY: Introduced to U.S. market on August 1, 1968. The new XJ sedan was the last design penned by company co-founder William Lyons, and shared few parts with earlier models. A 2.8-liter version also was produced, but U.S. showrooms normally got only the 4.2-liter engine.

1969 Jaguar XKE Series II roadster. (Coys of Kensington)

XK-E 4.2 (E-Type) — SERIES II — SIX — A second series of Jaguar's sports cars emerged for 1969, displaying safety features that had formerly appeared only on U.S. models. The new model had larger park/signal lights, and headlamps sat farther forward than before. The front air intake also was larger, behind a full-width bumper. Taillamps grew and moved below the back bumper, and side clearance lights were new. The 2 + 2's windshield adopted a revised (steeper) rake angle, accomplished by moving its base forward. The 258-cid twin-cam six-cylinder engine imported to the U.S. was rated 246 horsepower with its emission controls, a result of revised carburetion. Girling all-disc brakes replaced the former Dunlop units. Power steering was optional.

XJ — SIX — A new four-door sedan debuted this year, on a 108.9-inch wheelbase with a different front-end look. The rather large grille was rectangular in shape, made up of horizontal strips. Quad round headlamps were installed, with parking and signal lights immediately below each unit. The XJ carried the same engine as the XK-E sports car. Standard equipment included power steering and four-wheel disc brakes. Options included air conditioning, power windows, automatic transmission, and a heated back window.

1970 Jaguar XKE roadster. (Coys of Kensington)

XK-E 4.2 (E-Type) — SERIES II — SIX — Production of the three sports-car models continued with little change. As before, a roadster (convertible), two-seat coupe, and 2 + 2 coupe were available. Closed models featured a large window in the luggage (hatch) door, and hinged rear quarter windows. Inside were leatherette door panels, leather-upholstered bucket seats that adjusted for reach and rake, padded visors, a grab handle, glove compartment, and map light. The 2 + 2's fully upholstered back seat held two children. Wide-spoke 15-inch wheels had center-lock quick-change hubs and wore Dunlop high-performance tires. Girling four-wheel disc brakes had power assist. Front and rear wraparound bumpers contained overriders (guards). The convertible had a large back window in its folding top.

XJ — SIX — The Jaguar sedan continued with little change after its 1969 debut. Power steering and a Borg-Warner automatic transmission were standard on U.S. models.

325

I.D. DATA: Serial number for XK-E is stamped on right frame crossmember, above the shock absorber mounting; for XJ, on inner fender panel within engine compartment. Prefix indicates make and model (and possibly whether car is a U.S. model). Suffix may indicate whether car is equipped with overdrive or automatic transmission, and if left-hand drive (for export). Numerical sequence is the production serial number. Engine number is stamped on the right side of the block, above the oil filter; and at the front of the cylinder head (suffix /8 or /9 indicates compression ratio). Engine and chassis numbers also appear on a brass plate on the firewall. Starting serial number: (XK-E rds) 1R11052; (XK-E cpe) 1R27051; (XK-E 2+2) 1R42850; (XJ) 1L53203.

Model	Body Type & Seating	Engine Type/CID	P.O.E. Price	Weight (lbs.)	Prod. Total
XK-E (E-Type)					
II	2-dr Roadster-2P	I6/258	5534	2912	Note 1
II	2-dr Coupe-2P	I6/258	5725	2912	Note 1
II	2-dr Coupe-2+2P	I6/258	5907	3136	Note 1
XJ					
	4-dr Sedan-5P	I6/258	6585	3556	17,525

Note 1: Approximately 18,820 Series II XK-Es were produced from 1968-70 (8,630 roadsters, 4,860 fixed-head coupes, and 5,330 2+2 coupes).

XJ Production Note: Figure shown does not include 2,695 equivalent Daimlers built in 1970.

Price Note: 2+2 coupe with automatic transmission was priced at $6145.

ENGINE DATA: BASE SIX (XK-E, XJ): Inline, dual overhead-cam six-cylinder. Cast iron block and aluminum head. **Displacement:** 258.4 cu. in. (4235 cc). **Bore & Stroke:** 3.625 x 4.17 in. (92.1 x 106 mm). **Compression Ratio:** 9.0:1. **Brake Horsepower:** (XK-E) 246 at 5500 rpm; (XJ) 240 at 5500 rpm. **Torque:** 263 lbs.-ft. at 3000 rpm. Seven main bearings. Solid valve lifters. Two Zenith carburetors.

CHASSIS DATA: Wheelbase: (XK-E) 96 in.; (XK-E 2+2) 105 in.; (XJ) 108.9 in. **Overall Length:** (XK-E) 175.3 in.; (XK-E 2+2) 184.4 in.; (XJ) 189.6 in. **Height:** (XK-E) 48 in.; (XK-E 2+2) 50.1 in.; (XJ) 52.9 in. **Width:** (XK-E) 65.25 in.; (XJ) 69.75 in. **Front Tread:** (XK-E) 50 in.; (XJ) 58 in. **Rear Tread:** (XK-E) 50 in.; (XJ) 58.6 in. **Standard Tires:** (XK-E) 185x15; (XJ) 195x15.

TECHNICAL: Layout: front-engine, rear-drive. **Transmission:** (XK-E) four-speed manual; automatic available on 2+2. Automatic standard on XJ in U.S. **Standard Final Drive Ratio:** 3.54:1. **Steering:** rack and pinion. **Suspension (front):** (XK-E) wishbones, torsion bars and anti-roll bar; (XJ) wishbones with coil springs. **Suspension (rear):** independent with lower wishbones, trailing lower radius arms, coil springs and anti-roll bar. **Brakes:** front/rear disc. **Body Construction:** integral steel, with subframes.

MAJOR OPTIONS: Air cond.: XK-E ($482); XJ ($530). Power steering: XK-E ($160). Wire wheels: XK-E ($165). Disc wheels: XK-E 2+2, XJ ($77). Hardtop: XK-E rds ($180). Power windows: XJ ($146). Heated rear window: XJ ($48). Whitewall tires: XK-E ($27); XJ ($36).

PERFORMANCE: Top Speed: (XK-E) about 130 mph; (XJ) 120 mph. **Acceleration (0-60 mph):** (XK-E rds) 7.5 sec.; (XK-E 2+2) 8.7 sec.; (XJ) 8.7 sec. **Fuel Mileage:** (XK-E) 14-16 mpg; (XJ) 14-18 mpg.

PRODUCTION/SALES: As many as 6,732 Jaguars were sold in the U.S. during 1970.

Manufacturer: Jaguar Cars Ltd., Coventry, England.

Distributor: British Leyland Motors, Leonia, New Jersey.

HISTORY: The 1970 models were introduced to U.S. market on December 1, 1969.

1971 JAGUAR

XK-E 4.2 (E-Type) — SERIES II — SIX — The model year began with little change in Jaguar's sports-car trio. Power for the roadster and coupe again came from the familiar 4.2-liter twin-cam six, producing 246 bhp with twin Zenith carburetors. Then at mid-year came the debut of the long-awaited V-12 engine, which would soon became nearly as well-known as the original six.

XK-E (E-Type) — SERIES III — V-12 — Beneath the hood of the next-generation E-Type lay Jaguar's first all-new engine since the debut of the XK-120 (though the long-lived twin-cam six had come in a variety of displacements over the years). The new all-aluminum V-12 was installed in Series III convertible and 2+2 coupe bodies, which displayed an enlarged hood bulge that suggested the power that lurked within. Wheel openings grew taller, highlighted by marked flares, and wider tires produced larger tread dimensions. The formerly plain oval grille now contained a crosshatch insert, while the front end added a chrome molding and revised bumpers. The roadster was dropped, and both remaining bodies now rode the same 105-inch wheelbase, with the same steeper windshield initiated earlier on the 2+2 coupe. Trunk lids displayed 'E Type' lettering. Combustion chambers in the new engine were formed into the piston tops, which worked with flat cylinder heads. Because of emissions changes in the U.S. (and increased weight), the impact of the power boost was somewhat diminished. Wheels were wider now, either in slotted steel or center-lock wire form. Brake rotors, formerly solid, were now vented-type. Models destined for the U.S. wore large black bumper guards. A detachable hardtop was now optional for the convertible.

XJ — SIX — Jaguar's sedan entered its third season with little change. As before, power steering and an automatic transmission were standard on U.S. models. Under the hood once again was the same six-cylinder engine used in the XK-E series, but with compression dropped to 8.0:1.

I.D. DATA: Serial number for XK-E is stamped on right frame crossmember, above the shock absorber mounting; for XJ, on inner fender panel within engine compartment. Prefix indicates make and model (and possibly whether car is a U.S. model). Suffix may indicate whether car is equipped with overdrive or automatic transmission, and if left-hand drive (for export). Numerical sequence is the production serial number. Engine number is stamped on the right side of the block, above the oil filter; and at the front of the cylinder head (suffix /8 or /9 indicates compression ratio). Engine and chassis numbers also appear on a brass plate on the firewall. Starting serial number: (XK-E rds) 2R13716; (XK-E cpe) 2R28084; (XK-E V-12 conv.) 1S20001; (XK-E V-12 cpe) 1S700001; (XJ) 1L55686. Starting engine number: (XK-E V-12) 7S1001.

Model	Body Type & Seating	Engine Type/CID	P.O.E. Price	Weight (lbs.)	Prod. Total
XK-E (E-Type)					
II	2-dr Roadster-2P	I6/258	5734	2966	Note 1
II	2-dr Coupe-2P	I6/258	5925	2966	Note 1
II	2-dr Coupe-2+2P	I6/258	N/A	3136	Note 1
III	2-dr Conv-2P	V12/326	6950	3435	Note 2
III	2-dr Coupe 2+2P	V12/326	7325	3435	Note 2
XJ					
	4-dr Sedan-5P	I6/258	7260	3703	23,546

Note 1: Approximately 18,820 Series II XK-Es were produced from 1968-70 (8,630 roadsters, 4,860 fixed-head coupes, and 5,330 2+2 coupes).

Note 2: A total of 15,290 Series III XK-Es were produced from 1971-75 (7,990 convertibles and 7,300 2+2 coupes).

XJ Production Note: Figure shown does not include 5,158 equivalent Daimlers built in 1971.

Body Style Note: Series III E-Type came with the same open body as the Series II, but was by this time more commonly referred to as a convertible rather than a roadster.

ENGINE DATA: BASE SIX (XK-E Series II, XJ): Inline, dual overhead-cam six-cylinder. Cast iron block and aluminum head. **Displacement:** 258.4 cu. in. (4235 cc). **Bore & Stroke:** 3.625 x 4.17 in. (92.1 x 106 mm). **Compression Ratio:** (XJ) 8.0:1 or 9.0:1; (XK-E) 9.0:1. **Brake Horsepower:** (XK-E) 246 at 5500 rpm; (XJ) 240 at 5500 rpm. **Torque:** 263 lbs.-ft. at 3000 rpm. Seven main bearings. Solid valve lifters. Two Zenith carburetors.

BASE V-12 (XK-E Series III V-12): 60-degree, overhead-cam "vee" type 12-cylinder. Aluminum block and heads. **Displacement:** 326 cu. in. (5343 cc). **Bore & Stroke:** 3.54 x 2.77 in. (90 x 70 mm). **Compression Ratio:** 9.0:1. **Brake Horsepower:** 314 (gross) at 6200 rpm (272 DIN at 5850, or 250 SAE net at 6000 rpm). **Torque:** 349 lbs.-ft. (gross) at 3800 rpm (304 DIN at 3600, or 283 SAE at 3500 rpm). Seven main bearings. Solid valve lifters. Four Zenith carburetors.

CHASSIS DATA: Wheelbase: (XK-E) 96 in.; (XK-E 2+2, XK-E Series III) 105 in.; (XJ) 108.9 in. **Overall Length:** (XK-E) 175.3 in.; (XK-E 2+2) 184.4 in.; (XJ) 189.6 in. **Height:** (XK-E) 48 in.; (XK-E 2+2) 50.1 in.; (XK-E Series III) 51.3 in.; (XJ) 52.9 in. **Width:** (XK-E) 65.25 in.; (XK-E Series III) 66.1 in.; (XJ) 69.75 in. **Front Tread:** (XK-E) 50 in.; (XK-E Series III) 54.3 in.; (XJ) 58 in. **Rear Tread:** (XK-E) 50 in.; (XK-E Series III) 53 in.; (XJ) 58.6 in. **Standard Tires:** (XK-E) 185x15; (XK-E Series III) 6.00x15; (XJ) ER70x15 or 195x15.

TECHNICAL: Layout: front-engine, rear-drive. **Transmission:** (XK-E) four-speed manual; automatic available on 2+2. Three-speed automatic standard on XJ in U.S. **Steering:** rack and pinion. **Suspension (front):** (XK-E) wishbones, torsion bars and anti-roll bar; (XJ) wishbones with coil springs. **Suspension (rear):** independent with lower wishbones, trailing lower radius arms, coil springs and anti-roll bar. **Brakes:** front/rear disc. **Body Construction:** integral steel, with subframes.

MAJOR OPTIONS: Air conditioning: XK-E ($482); XJ ($530). Power steering: XK-E ($160). Wire wheels: XK-E ($165). Chrome disc wheels: XK-E ($77); ($132). Hardtop: XK-E rds ($200). Power windows: XJ ($146). Heated rear window: XK-E cpe ($44); XJ ($48). Whitewall tires ($36).

PERFORMANCE: Top Speed: (XK-E) about 130 mph; (XK-E V-12) 135+ mph; (XJ) 120 mph. **Acceleration (0-60 mph):** (XK-E rds) 7.5 sec.; (XK-E 2+2) 8.7 sec.; (XK-E V-12) 7.5 sec. or less; (XJ) 8.7 sec. **Fuel Mileage:** (XK-E) 14-16 mpg; (XJ) 14-18 mpg.

PRODUCTION/SALES: As many as 5,614 Jaguars were sold in the U.S. during 1971.

Manufacturer: Jaguar Cars Ltd., Coventry, England.

Distributor: British Leyland Motors, Leonia, New Jersey.

HISTORY: The 1971 models were introduced to U.S. market on October 1, 1970 (XK-E V-12 in March 1971). The new V-12 engine had initially been meant for racing, then intended for a new sedan. Instead, it first went into the Jaguar sports car. At the time, only Ferrari and Lamborghini offered a production V-12 powerplant.

1972 JAGUAR

1972 Jaguar XKE V-12 Series III. (Coys of Kensington)

XK-E (E-Type) — SERIES III — V-12 — Six-cylinder E-Types faded out of the U.S. market as the V-12 engine, introduced in March 1971, gained a foothold. Little change was evident this year.

XJ6 — SIX — Changes were minimal on the Jaguar six-cylinder sedan, except that a GM air-conditioner compressor replaced the former York unit. An automatic transmission was standard. Published engine ratings for XJ6 sedans sold in the U.S. dropped sharply during this period, as a result of reduced compression and detuning, and the switch to SAE net (formerly gross) horsepower and torque figures.

I.D. DATA: Serial number for XK-E is stamped on right frame crossmember, above the shock absorber mounting; for XJ, on inner fender panel within engine compartment. Prefix indicates make and model (and possibly whether car is a U.S. model). Suffix may indicate whether car is equipped with overdrive or automatic transmission, and if left-hand drive (for export). Numerical sequence is the production serial number. Engine number is stamped on the right side of the block, above the oil filter; and at the front of the cylinder head (suffix /8 or /9 indicates compression ratio). Engine and chassis numbers also appear on a brass plate on the firewall. Serial number range: (XK-E conv) 1S20103 to 1S20168; (XK-E cpe) 1S72335 to 1S72660; (XJ6) 1L64124 to 1L64774.

Model	Body Type & Seating	Engine Type/CID	P.O.E. Price	Weight (lbs.)	Prod. Total
XK-E (E-Type)					
III	2-dr Conv-2P	V12/326	7338	3435	Note 1
III	2-dr Coupe-2+2P	V12/326	7732	3435	Note 1
XJ6					
	4-dr Sedan-5P	I6/258	7683	3528	14,885

Note 1: A total of 15,290 Series III XK-Es were produced from 1971-75 (7,990 convertibles and 7,300 2 + 2 coupes).

XJ Production Note: Figure shown does not include 3,206 equivalent Daimlers built in 1972 (or 3,703 early V-12 sedans).

ENGINE DATA: BASE SIX (XJ6): Inline, dual overhead-cam six-cylinder. Cast iron block and aluminum head. **Displacement:** 258.4 cu. in. (4235 cc). **Bore & Stroke:** 3.625 x 4.17 in. (92.1 x 106 mm). **Compression Ratio:** 8.0:1. **Brake Horsepower:** 186 (gross), 157 (net) at 4500 rpm in U.S. form. **Torque:** 240 (gross) lbs.-ft. at 3750 rpm. Seven main bearings. Solid valve lifters. Two Zenith-Stromberg 175CD2SE carburetors.

BASE V-12 (XK-E Series III): 60-degree, overhead-cam "vee" type 12-cylinder. Aluminum block and heads. **Displacement:** 326 cu. in. (5343 cc). **Bore & Stroke:** 3.54 x 2.77 in. (90 x 70 mm). **Compression Ratio:** 9.0:1. **Brake Horsepower:** 250 (SAE net) at 6000 rpm. **Torque:** 283 lbs.-ft. at 3500 rpm. Seven main bearings. Solid valve lifters. Four Zenith-Stromberg 175CD2SE carburetors.

CHASSIS DATA: Wheelbase: (XK-E) 105 in.; (XJ) 108.9 in. **Overall Length:** (XK-E) 184.4 in.; (XJ) 189.6 in. **Height:** (XK-E) 51.3 in.; (XJ) 52.9 in. **Width:** (XK-E) 66.1 in.; (XJ) 69.75 in. **Front Tread:** (XK-E) 54.3 in.; (XJ) 58 in. **Rear Tread:** (XK-E) 53 in.; (XJ) 58.6 in. **Standard Tires:** (XK-E) 6.00x15; (XJ) 195x15.

TECHNICAL: Layout: front-engine, rear-drive. **Transmission:** (XK-E) four-speed manual; three-speed automatic available. Automatic standard on XJ6. **Standard Final Drive Ratio:** 3.54:1. **Steering:** rack and pinion. **Suspension (front):** (XK-E) wishbones, torsion bars and anti-roll bar; (XJ) wishbones, lower trailing links, coil springs and anti-roll bar. **Suspension (rear):** independent with lower wishbones, trailing lower radius arms, coil springs and anti-roll bar. **Brakes:** front/rear disc. **Body Construction:** integral steel, with subframes.

MAJOR OPTIONS: Automatic trans.: XK-E ($261). Air conditioning. Power steering (XK-E). Wire wheels (XK-E). Chrome disc wheels. Hardtop (XK-E conv). Power windows (XJ). Heated rear window (XK-E cpe, XJ). Whitewall tires.

PERFORMANCE: Top Speed: (XK-E conv) 135 + mph; (XJ) up to 122 mph. **Acceleration (0-60 mph):** (XK-E conv) 7.4 sec. or less; (XJ) 10.7 sec. **Acceleration (quarter-mile):** (XK-E conv) about 15.4 sec. (93 mph); (XJ) 17.1 sec. **Fuel Mileage:** (XJ) about 15 mpg.

PRODUCTION/SALES: Approximately 5,143 Jaguars were sold in the U.S. during 1972. **Manufacturer:** Jaguar Cars Ltd. (then British Leyland UK Ltd.), Coventry, England. **Distributor:** British Leyland Motors, Leonia, New Jersey.

HISTORY: The 1972 models were introduced to U.S. market on December 13, 1971. By this time, Jaguar had about 301 dealers in the U.S.

XJ Production Note: Figures shown do not include equivalent Daimlers (3,206 six-cylinder and 809 12-cylinder) or early Series II models (1,656 Series II XJ6 and 168 Series II XJ12).

ENGINE DATA: BASE SIX (XJ6): Inline, dual-overhead-cam six-cylinder. Cast iron block and aluminum head. **Displacement:** 258.4 cu. in. (4235 cc). **Bore & Stroke:** 3.625 x 4.17 in. (92.1 x 106 mm). **Compression Ratio:** 7.5:1. **Brake Horsepower:** 150 (net) at 4750 rpm. **Torque:** 213 lbs.-ft. at 3000 rpm. Seven main bearings. Solid valve lifters. Two Zenith-Stromberg 175CD2SE carburetors.

BASE V-12 (XK-E, XJ12): 60-degree, overhead-cam "vee" type 12-cylinder. Aluminum block and heads. **Displacement:** 326 cu. in. (5343 cc). **Bore & Stroke:** 3.54 x 2.77 in. (90 x 70 mm). **Compression Ratio:** 7.8:1. **Brake Horsepower:** 241 (net) at 5750 rpm. **Torque:** 285 lbs.-ft. at 3500 rpm. Seven main bearings. Four Zenith-Stromberg 175CD2SE carburetors.

Note: European V-12 was rated 265 bhp, with 9.0:1 compression.

CHASSIS DATA: Wheelbase: (XK-E) 105 in.; (XJ) 108.8 in. **Overall Length:** (XK-E) 184.4 in.; (XJ) 189.6 in. **Height:** (XK-E) 51 in.; (XJ6/12) 52.9 in. **Width:** (XK-E) 66.1 in.; (XJ) 69.7 in. **Front Tread:** (XK-E) 54.3 in.; (XJ) 58 in. **Rear Tread:** (XK-E) 53 in.; (XJ) 58.6 in. **Standard Tires:** (XK-E) E70VR15; (XJ6) 195x15; (XJ12) 205/70VR15.

TECHNICAL: Layout: front-engine, rear-drive. **Transmission:** (XK-E) four-speed manual; automatic available. Automatic standard on XJ6. **Standard Final Drive Ratio:** (XK-E) 3.54:1; (XJ6) 3.54:1; (XJ12) 3.31:1. **Steering:** rack and pinion. **Suspension (front):** (XK-E) wishbones, torsion bars and anti-roll bar; (XJ) wishbones, lower trailing links, coil springs and anti-roll bar. **Suspension (rear):** independent with lower wishbones, trailing lower radius arms, coil springs and anti-roll bar. **Brakes:** front/rear disc. **Body Construction:** integral steel, with subframes.

MAJOR OPTIONS: Automatic transmission: XK-E ($269). Air conditioning.: XK-E ($521). Chrome wire wheels: XK-E ($275). Chrome turbo disc wheels: XK-E ($133). Removable hardtop: XK-E conv ($363). AM/FM stereo radio ($170). Heated rear window: XK-E cpe ($58). Whitewall tires: XK-E ($45).

PERFORMANCE: Top Speed: (XK-E) about 135 mph; (XJ6) about 115 mph; (XJ12) about 140 mph. **Acceleration (0-60 mph):** (XK-E) about 6.8 to 8 sec.; (XJ6) 10.7 sec.; (XJ12) about 8.5 sec. **Acceleration (quarter-mile):** (XJ6) 17.1 sec. **Fuel Mileage:** (XK-E) 14-18 mpg; (XJ6) about 15 mpg; (XJ12) 10-12 mpg.

PRODUCTION/SALES: Approximately 6,767 Jaguars were sold in the U.S. during 1973. **Manufacturer:** Jaguar (British Leyland UK Ltd.), Coventry, England. **Distributor:** British Leyland Motors, Leonia, New Jersey.

HISTORY: A longer-wheelbase XJ 'L' sedan was available by 1973, but did not reach the U.S. market until the 1974 model year.

1973 JAGUAR

1973 Jaguar XKE V-12 fixed-head coupe. (Coys of Kensington)

XK-E (E-Type) — SERIES III — V-12 — Production of the 12-cylinder coupe and convertible continued with little change. Standard equipment included power rack-and-pinion steering, an adjustable steering column, power disc brakes, wraparound bumpers with overriders, dual exhausts, windshield washers, heater/defroster, reclining bucket seats with adjustable headrests, leather upholstery, and a padded dashboard.

XJ6 — SIX — A switch to larger front-bumper overriders was the major change this year in Jaguar's six-cylinder four-door sedan. Standard equipment included a Borg-Warner three-speed automatic transmission, air conditioning, power windows, tinted glass, rear defroster, and whitewall tires on chrome turbo wheels.

XJ12 — V-12 — A 12-cylinder version of Jaguar's sedan debuted in the U.S. this year. Standard equipment was similar to the XJ6, but with the same engine as the E-Type. Leather reclining seats were standard; an AM/FM stereo radio was the sole option. For the U.S. market, the V-12's compression ratio dwindled from 9.0:1 to 7.8:1 during this period, with a corresponding fall in horsepower and torque.

I.D. DATA: Serial number is on the upper left of the dashboard, visible through the windshield. Prefix indicates make and model (and possibly whether car is a U.S. model). Suffix may indicate whether car is equipped with overdrive or automatic transmission, and if left-hand drive (for export). Numerical sequence is the production serial number. Starting serial number: (XK-E conv) UD1S21029; (XK-E cpe) UD1S73856; (XJ6) US1L69908BW.

Model	Body Type & Seating	Engine Type/CID	P.O.E. Price	Weight (lbs.)	Prod. Total
XK-E (E-Type)					
III	2-dr Conv-2P	V12/326	8475	3462	Note 1
III	2-dr Coupe-2 + 2P	V12/326	8920	3466	Note 1
XJ6/12					
XJ6	4-dr Sedan-5P	I6/258	9500	3769	14,850
XJ12	4-dr Sedan-5P	V12/326	11025	3881	2,894

Note 1: Approximately 15,200 Series III XK-Es were produced from 1971-75 (7,990 convertibles and 7,300 2 + 2 coupes).

1974 JAGUAR

1974 Jaguar XKE V-12 Series III. (Coys of Kensington)

XK-E (E-Type) — SERIES III — V-12 — For its final year in the Jaguar lineup, the convertible's engine continued in detuned form for the U.S. market, with 7.8:1 compression. No coupe was offered this year. Standard equipment included leather-faced, semi-reclining bucket seats with bmala panels on non-wear surfaces; ambla-trimmed interior; tachometer; trip odometer; and Dunlop E70VR15 SP Sport whitewall tires on ventilated chrome disc wheels. Body colors this year were: British Racing Green, Azure Blue, Dark Blue, Fern Grey, Greensand, Old English White, Pale Primrose, Sable, Signal Red, Silver Grey, Regency Red, and Turquoise.

XJ6 — SERIES II — SIX — A longer-wheelbase version of the Jaguar sedan was added during the year, called XJ6L. The body added some four inches, to the rear of the front door. Most examples sold in the U.S. were the long-wheelbase version, so this would be the final year for the shorter-wheelbase sedan. On both models, a shallow front grille held a new rubber bumper. Inside, second-tier instruments were no longer mounted in the center of the dashboard, but sat ahead of the driver. Headlamp/wiper controls moved to stalks attached to the steering column, in the European manner. A different Borg-Warner automatic transmission was installed, along with a new type of padded steering wheel. Automatic climate control air conditioning was installed. Standard equipment included tinted glass, power windows, fully-reclining leather-faced front seats with adjustable head restraints, leather-faced rear seats, deep pile carpeting, a parcel shelf and locking glovebox. Sedan colors were: British Racing Green, Fern Grey, Dark Blue, Greensand, Old English White, Pale Primrose, Sable, Signal Red, Silver Grey, Regency Red, and Turquoise. Whitewall Dunlop E70VR15 Sport tires rode ventilated chrome disc wheels.

XJ12 — SERIES II — V-12 — The 12-cylinder version of Jaguar's sedan adopted the same rubber front bumper as the XJ6; otherwise, change was minimal. Two new models appeared, however: a long-wheelbase XJ12L sedan and, during the year, a pillarless XJ12C two-door coupe. Actuallly, only the XJ12L edition of the long-wheelbase sedan appeared in Jaguar's 1974 U.S. sales brochure; the six-cylinder XJ6L arrived later. Compression ratio for U.S. models dropped to 7.8:1 on the V-12 engine during the previous year, with a corresponding loss of horsepower. European engines retained their earlier potency. Standard equipment was similar to the XJ6, but with larger (205/70VR15) SP Sport tires. An electrically-heated rear window was standard.

327

I.D. DATA: Serial number is on the upper left of the dashboard, visible through the windshield. Prefix indicates make and model. Suffix may indicate whether car is equipped with overdrive or automatic transmission, and if left-hand drive (for export). Numerical sequence is the production serial number.

Model	Body Type & Seating	Engine Type/CID	P.O.E. Price	Weight (lbs.)	Prod. Total
XK-E (E-Type)					
III	2-dr Conv-2P	V12/326	9200	3375	Note 1
XJ6/12					
XJ6	4-dr Sedan-5P	I6/258	10900	4005	Note 2
XJ6L	4-dr Sedan-5P	I6/258	11500	N/A	Note 2
XJ12C	2-dr Coupe-5P	V12/326	N/A	N/A	Note 3
XJ12	4-dr Sedan-5P	V12/326	13000	N/A	Note 3
XJ12L	4-dr Sedan-5P	V12/326	12500	4208	Note 3

Note 1: Approximately 15,200 Series III XK-Es were produced from 1971-75 (7,990 convertibles and 7,300 2 + 2 coupes).

Note 2: Approximately 18,270 XJ6 Jaguars (and 4,282 six-cylinder Daimlers) were produced in 1974.

Note 3: Approximately 4,744 XJ12 Jaguars (and 1,560 V-12 Daimlers) were produced in 1974.

ENGINE DATA: BASE SIX (XJ6): Inline, dual-overhead-cam six-cylinder. Cast iron block and aluminum head. **Displacement:** 258.4 cu. in. (4235 cc). **Bore & Stroke:** 3.625 x 4.17 in. (92.1 x 106 mm). **Compression Ratio:** 7.5:1. **Brake Horsepower:** 150 (net) at 4750 rpm. **Torque:** 213 lbs.-ft. at 3000 rpm. Seven main bearings. Solid valve lifters. Two Zenith-Stromberg 175CD2SE carburetors.

BASE V-12 (XK-E, XJ12): 60-degree, overhead-cam "vee" type 12-cylinder. Aluminum block and heads. **Displacement:** 326 cu. in. (5343 cc). **Bore & Stroke:** 3.54 x 2.77 in. (90 x 70 mm). **Compression Ratio:** 7.8:1. **Brake Horsepower:** 241 (net) at 4750 rpm. **Torque:** 285 lbs.-ft. at 3500 rpm. Seven main bearings. Four Zenith-Stromberg 175CD2SE carburetors. Mark II electronic system.

CHASSIS DATA: Wheelbase: (XK-E) 105 in.; (XJ6/12) 108.8 in.; (XJ6/12L) 112.8 in. **Overall Length:** (XK-E) 189.6 in.; (XJ6L/XJ12) 194.8 in.; (XJ12L) 198.8 in. **Height:** (XK-E) 48.4 in.; (XJ) 54.1 in. **Width:** (XK-E) 66.1 in.; (XJ) 69.75 in. **Front Tread:** (XK-E) 54.4 in.; (XJ) 58 in. **Rear Tread:** (XK-E) 52.75 in.; (XJ) 58.6 in. **Standard Tires:** (XK-E, XJ6) Dunlop E70VR15 SP Sport; (XJ12) Dunlop 205/70VR15 SP Sport.

TECHNICAL: Layout: front-engine, rear-drive. **Transmission:** (XK-E) four-speed manual. Overall XK-E gear ratios: (1st) 10.38:1; (2nd) 6.74:1; (3rd) 4.91:1; (4th) 3.54:1. Automatic available on XK-E. Three-speed automatic standard on XJ sedans. **Standard Final Drive Ratio:** (XK-E w/manual) 3.54:1; (others) 3.31:1. **Steering:** power rack and pinion. **Suspension (front):** (XK-E) wishbones, torsion bars and anti-roll bar; (XJ) wishbones, coil springs and anti-roll bar. **Suspension (rear):** independent with lower wishbones, lower radius arms, coil springs and anti-roll bar. **Brakes:** power front/rear disc. **Body Construction:** integral steel; (XK-E) integral with separate engine subframe.

MAJOR OPTIONS: Automatic trans.: XK-E ($269). Air conditioning: XK-E ($521). Chrome wire wheels: XK-E ($275). Chrome turbo disc wheels: XK-E ($133). Removable hardtop: XK-E conv ($363). AM/FM stereo radio ($170). Heated rear window: XK-E cpe ($58). Whitewall tires: XK-E ($45).

PERFORMANCE: Similar to 1973.

PRODUCTION/SALES: Approximately 5,299 Jaguars were sold in the U.S. during 1974.

Manufacturer: Jaguar (British Leyland UK Ltd.), Coventry, England.

Distributor: British Leyland Motors, Leonia, New Jersey.

HISTORY: Final XK-E (E-Type) coupes were built at the end of the 1973 model year, while the last convertibles came off the line in mid-1974. Reduction to a three-day work week early in 1974 limited shipments of Jaguars to the U.S.

1975 JAGUAR

1975 Jaguar XJ12C two-door hardtop.

XJ6 — SERIES II — SIX — An XJ6C coupe replaced the former short-wheelbase, six-cylinder sedan. Except for a vinyl top and shorter roofline, it was identical to the longer-wheelbase XJ6L. Otherwise, change was minimal, apart from a switch to an automatic choke.

XJ12 — SERIES II — V-12 — Both short- and long-wheelbase versions of the 12-cylinder model were offered this year, with two or four doors (respectively), suffixed 'C' or 'L'. Electronic fuel injection replaced carburetors on the V-12 engine.

Note: No Jaguar sports car was offered in the U.S. this year, as the XK-E (E-Type) had disappeared; but a new XJ-S would arrive for the 1976 model year.

I.D. DATA: Serial number is on the 'A' (windshield) pillar. Prefix indicates make and model (and possibly whether car is a U.S. model). Suffix may indicate whether car is equipped with overdrive or automatic transmission, and if left-hand drive (for export). Numerical sequence is the production serial number. Starting serial number: (XJ6C) UF2J50045BW; (XJ6L) UF2T54779; (XJ12C) UF2G50060BW; (XJ12L) UF2R53930BW.

Model	Body Type & Seating	Engine Type/CID	P.O.E. Price	Weight (lbs.)	Prod. Total
XJ6/12					
XJ6C	2-dr Coupe-5P	I6/258	13750	4022	1,968
XJ6L	4-dr Sedan-5P	I6/258	13100	4053	14,229
XJ12C	2-dr Coupe-5P	V12/326	15650	4005	493
XJ12L	4-dr Sedan-5P	V12/326	14900	4277	2,239

Production Note: Figures shown are approximate and do not include Daimler totals.

Body Style Note: Jaguar literature initially referred to two-door models as sedans rather than coupes.

ENGINE DATA: BASE SIX (XJ6): Inline, dual-overhead-cam six-cylinder. Cast iron block and aluminum head. **Displacement:** 258.4 cu. in. (4235 cc). **Bore & Stroke:** 3.625 x 4.17 in. (92.1 x 106 mm). **Compression Ratio:** 7.5:1. **Brake Horsepower:** 162 at 4750 rpm. **Torque:** 225 lbs.-ft. at 2500 rpm. Seven main bearings. Solid valve lifters. Two Zenith-Stromberg 175CD2SE carburetors.

BASE V-12 (XJ12): 60-degree, overhead-cam, vee-type 12-cylinder. Aluminum block and head. **Displacement:** 326 cu. in. (5343 cc). **Bore & Stroke:** 3.54 x 2.77 in. (90 x 70 mm). **Compression Ratio:** 7.8:1. **Brake Horsepower:** 244 at 5250 rpm. Seven main bearings. Solid valve lifters. Electronic fuel injection.

CHASSIS DATA: Wheelbase: (XJ6/12C) 108.8 in.; (XJ6/12L) 112.8 in. **Overall Length:** (XJ6C) 190.7 in.; (XJ6L) 194.8 in.; (XJ12C) 194.8 in.; (XJ12L) 198.8 in. **Height:** 54.1 in. **Width:** 69.75 in. **Front Tread:** 58 in. **Rear Tread:** 58.6 in. **Standard Tires:** (XJ6) Dunlop E70VR15 SP Sport; (XJ12) Dunlop 205/70VR15 SP Sport.

TECHNICAL: Layout: front-engine, rear-drive. **Transmission:** three-speed automatic. **Steering:** power rack and pinion. **Suspension (front):** wishbones, coil springs and anti-roll bar. **Suspension (rear):** independent with lower wishbones, lower radius arms, coil springs and anti-roll bar. **Brakes:** power front/rear disc. **Body Construction:** integral steel.

PRODUCTION/SALES: Approximately 6,799 Jaguars were sold in the U.S. during 1975.

Manufacturer: Jaguar (British Leyland UK Ltd.), Coventry, England.

Distributor: British Leyland Motors, Leonia, New Jersey.

1976 JAGUAR

1976 Jaguar XJ-S. (Jaguar Cars Inc.)

XJ-S (S-type) — V-12 — An all-new version of Jaguar's sports car debuted for 1976, powered by the now-familiar V-12 engine. This was a 2 + 2 coupe, promoted as "a new breed of cat," with appearance completely different from the former XK-E (E-Type). Styling features included a low-sweeping hood, smooth sides, and rounded corners. Quad round headlamps sat in oval housings at the ends of a squat, wide rectangular grille. A black rubber front bumper contained amber park/signal lights, with side marker lights just ahead of the front wheels. A "flying buttress" profile appeared at the rear, with extensions on each side that reached all the way to the car's tail. The gas filler lid was located on the left-hand panel. Large black moldings sat to the rear of each rear quarter window. Both front and rear spoilers were installed. A bodyside crease line ran the full length of the car, just across the top of the modestly flared rear wheelwell. The 326-cid V-12 engine used Bosch-Lucas electronic fuel injection. Only a Borg-Warner Model 12 three-speed automatic transmission was installed. Standard equipment included air conditioning with automatic temperature control, an AM/FM stereo radio with eight-track tape player, power windows, tinted glass, fully-reclining leather-faced front seats (with adjustable head restraints, electric tachometer, two-speed wipers with washer, heated rear window, and remote-control mirror. All instruments sat in a nacelle ahead of the driver. Standard colors were: British Racing Green, Regency Red, Silver Grey, Greensand, Signal Red, Dark Blue, Fern Grey, Old English White, Squadron Blue, Carriage Brown, and Yellow Gold.

Note: Just as the former coupe and convertible had been called either "XK-E" or "E-Type," the new edition was variously named "XJ-S" or "XJS" or, on occasion (infrequently in the U.S.), "S-type."

XJ6 — SERIES II — SIX — Little change was evident in the six-cylinder model, offered with either short (coupe) or long (sedan) wheelbase.

XJ12 — SERIES II — V-12 — Like the six-cylinder XJ6, the XJ12 came in two-door and four-door form again this year.

I.D. DATA: Serial number is on the 'A' (windshield) pillar. Prefix indicates make and model. Suffix may indicate whether car is equipped with overdrive or automatic transmission, and if left-hand drive (for export). Numerical sequence is the production serial number. Starting serial number: (XJ-S) UF2W500002BW or UG2W50168BW; (XJ6C) UG2J51369BW; (XJ6L) UG2T56746BW; (XJ12C) UG2G50426BW; (XJ12L) UG2R54264BW.

Model	Body Type & Seating	Engine Type/CID	P.O.E. Price	Weight (lbs.)	Prod. Total
XJ-S					
GT	2-dr Coupe-2 + 2P	V12/326	19000	3935	4,020
XJ6/12					
XJ6C	2-dr Coupe-5P	I6/258	14850	4024	2,659
XJ6L	4-dr Sedan-5P	I6/258	14100	4068	15,440
XJ12C	2-dr Coupe-5P	V12/326	16850	4220	979
XJ12L	4-dr Sedan-5P	V12/326	16100	4334	3,283

Production Note: Figures shown are approximate and do not include equivalent Daimlers. In addition, 1976 was an unusually long model year for Jaguar, stretching to 15 months.

ENGINE DATA: BASE SIX (XJ6): Inline, dual-overhead-cam six-cylinder. Cast iron block and aluminum head. **Displacement:** 258.4 cu. in. (4235 cc). **Bore & Stroke:** 3.625 x 4.17 in. (92.1 x 106 mm). **Compression Ratio:** 7.5:1. **Brake Horsepower:** 162 at 4750 rpm. **Torque:** 225 lbs.-ft. at 2500 rpm. Seven main bearings. Solid valve lifters. Two Zenith-Stromberg 175CD2SE carburetors.
BASE V-12 (XJ12, XJ-S): 60-degree, overhead-cam "vee" type 12-cylinder. Aluminum block and head. **Displacement:** 326 cu. in. (5343 cc). **Bore & Stroke:** 3.54 x 2.77 in. (90 x 70 mm). **Compression Ratio:** 8.0:1. **Brake Horsepower:** 244 at 4500/5250 rpm. **Torque:** 269 lbs.-ft. at 4500 rpm. Seven main bearings. Electronic fuel injection.

CHASSIS DATA: Wheelbase: (XJ-S) 102 in.; (XJ6/12C) 108.8 in.; (XJ6/12L) 112.8 in. **Overall Length:** (XJ-S) 192.25 in.; (XJ6/12C) 194.8 in.; (XJ6/12L) 200.5 in. **Height:** (XJ-S) 47.8 in.; (XJ) 54.1 in. **Width:** (XJ-S) 70.6 in.; (XJ) 69.75 in. **Front Tread:** (XJ-S) 58.6 in.; (XJ) 58 in. **Rear Tread:** (XJ-S) 58.65 in.; (XJ) 58.6 in. **Wheel type:** (XJ-S) cast aluminum alloy. **Standard Tires:** (XJ-S) Dunlop 205/70VR15 Sports Super SBR WSW; (XJ6) Dunlop E70VR15 SP Sport; (XJ12) Dunlop 205/70VR15 SP Sport.

TECHNICAL: Layout: front-engine, rear-drive. **Transmission:** three-speed automatic. **Steering:** power rack and pinion. **Suspension (front):** (XJ-S) semi-trailing wishbones with coil springs and anti-roll bar; (XJ) wishbones, coil springs and anti-roll bar. **Suspension (rear):** independent with lower wishbones, lower radius arms, coil springs and anti-roll bar. **Brakes:** power front/rear disc. **Body Construction:** integral steel.

PERFORMANCE: Top Speed: (XJ-S) about 150 mph. **Acceleration (0-60 mph):** (XJ-S) 8.9 sec.; (XJ6C) 11.9 sec. **Acceleration (quarter-mile):** (XJ-S) 15.9 sec. (91.3 mph); (XJ6C) 18.2 sec. (77 mph).

PRODUCTION/SALES: Approximately 7,382 Jaguars were sold in the U.S. during 1976. **Manufacturer:** Jaguar (British Leyland UK Ltd.), Coventry, England. **Distributor:** British Leyland Motors Inc., Leonia, New Jersey.

HISTORY: The XJ-S was the first Jaguar styled solely by an outsider, according to Roger Hicks in his *Jaguar Illustrated History,* without the scrutiny of Sir William Lyons.

1977 JAGUAR

1977 Jaguar XJ6C sports coupe. (William Siuru Jr.)

XJ-S — V-12 — Production of the new 2 + 2 coupe, introduced for 1976, continued with little change, powered by Jaguar's 326-cid V-12 engine and three-speed automatic. A four-speed manual gearbox became available, but not on U.S. models. Standard colors were: British Racing Green, Regency Red, Silver Grey, Greensand, Signal Red, Dark Blue, Fern Grey, Old English White, Squadron Blue, Carriage Brown, and Yellow Gold.

XJ6 — SERIES II — SIX — Little change was evident in the six-cylinder coupe and sedan, which again carried the familiar twin-cam six-cylinder engine. A stereo radio with eight-track tape player and automatic-temperature-control air conditioning were standard.

XJ12 — SERIES II — V-12 — No significant change was evident in the 12-cylinder version of Jaguar's sedan, but the coupe faded out of the picture. For the U.S. market, the fuel-injected engine produced 244 horsepower.

I.D. DATA: An 11-symbol serial number is on the 'A' (windshield) pillar. Symbol one indicates manufacture to U.S. specs. Symbol two denotes model year; three and four, the body style. The remaining symbols make up the sequential serial number. Starting serial number: (XJ-S) UH2W52737BW; (XJ6C) UH2J52842BW; (XJ6L) UH2T63599BW; (XJ12L) UH2R56786BW.

Model	Body Type & Seating	Engine Type/CID	P.O.E. Price	Weight (lbs.)	Prod. Total
XJ-S					
GT	2-dr Coupe-2 + 2P	V12/326	20250	3935	3,861
XJ6/12					
XJ6C	2-dr Coupe-5P	I6/258	15750	4024	1,835
XJ6L	4-dr Sedan-5P	I6/258	15000	4068	10,956
XJ12C	2-dr Coupe-5P	V12/326	N/A	N/A	339
XJ12L	4-dr Sedan-5P	V12/326	17250	4334	1,913

Production Note: Figures shown are approximate and do not include equivalent Daimler sedans.

ENGINE DATA: BASE SIX (XJ6): Inline, dual-overhead-cam six-cylinder. Cast iron block and aluminum head. **Displacement:** 258.4 cu. in. (4235 cc). **Bore & Stroke:** 3.625 x 4.17 in. (92.1 x 106 mm). **Compression Ratio:** 7.5:1. **Brake Horsepower:** 162 at 4750 rpm. **Torque:** 225 lbs.-ft. at 2500 rpm. Seven main bearings. Solid valve lifters. Two Zenith-Stromberg 175CD2SE carburetors.
BASE V-12 (XJ12, XJ-S): 60-degree, overhead-cam "vee" type 12-cylinder. Aluminum block and head. **Displacement:** 326 cu. in. (5343 cc). **Bore & Stroke:** 3.54 x 2.77 in. (90 x 70 mm). **Compression Ratio:** 8.0:1 (XJ12, 7.8:1). **Brake Horsepower:** 244 at 5250 rpm. **Torque:** 269 lbs.-ft. at 2500 rpm. Seven main bearings. Electronic fuel injection.

CHASSIS DATA: Wheelbase: (XJ-S) 102 in.; (XJ cpe) 108.8 in.; (XJ sed) 112.8 in. **Overall Length:** (XJ-S) 192.25 in.; (XJ cpe) 196.5 in.; (XJ sed) 200.5 in. **Height:** (XJ-S) 47.8 in.; (XJ) 54.1 in. **Width:** (XJ-S) 70.6 in.; (XJ) 69.8 in. **Front Tread:** (XJ-S) 58.6 in.; (XJ) 58.2 in. **Rear Tread:** (XJ-S) 58.65 in.; (XJ) 58.9 in. **Wheel type:** (XJ-S) cast aluminum alloy; (XJ) ventilated chrome disc. **Standard Tires:** (XJ-S) Dunlop 205/70VR15 Sports Super SBR WSW; (XJ6) Dunlop ER70VR15; (XJ12) Dunlop 205/70VR15 SBR WSW.

TECHNICAL: Layout: front-engine, rear-drive. **Transmission:** Borg-Warner three-speed automatic. **Standard Final Drive Ratio:** 3.31:1. **Steering:** power rack and pinion. **Suspension (front):** (XJ-S) semi-trailing wishbones with coil springs and anti-roll bar; (XJ) wishbones, coil springs and anti-roll bar. **Suspension (rear):** independent with lower wishbones, lower radius arms, coil springs and anti-roll bar. **Brakes:** power front/rear disc. **Body Construction:** integral steel.

MAJOR OPTIONS: No factory options offered.
PERFORMANCE: Top Speed: (XJ-S) about 140-150 mph; (XJ6) about 115 mph; (XJ12) about 140 mph. **Acceleration (0-60 mph):** (XJ-S) about 8 sec. **Fuel Mileage:** (XJ-S) 9-14 mpg; (XJ) 10-13 mpg city, 14-18 highway (EPA ratings).

PRODUCTION/SALES: Approximately 4,349 Jaguars were sold in the U.S. during 1977. **Manufacturer:** Jaguar (British Leyland UK Ltd.), Coventry, England. **Distributor:** British Leyland Motors Inc., Leonia, New Jersey.

1978 JAGUAR

1978 Jaguar XJ12 V-12 four-door sedan.

XJ-S — V-12 — Production of Jaguar's 2 + 2 coupe continued with little change, again powered by Jaguar's 326-cid V-12 engine and three-speed automatic.

XJ6 — SERIES II — SIX — Jaguar's sedan continued with minimal change, until Lucas/Bosch L-Jetronic fuel injection replaced the twin carburetors in the six-cylinder engine, adding 14 horsepower. Only the four-door sedan was listed for sale in the U.S.

XJ12 — SERIES II — V-12 — No significant change was evident in the 12-cylinder version of Jaguar's sedan.

I.D. DATA: An 11-symbol serial number is on the 'A' (windshield) pillar. Symbol one indicates manufacture to U.S. specs. Symbol two denotes model year; three and four, the body style. The remaining symbols make up the sequential serial number. Starting serial number: (XJ-S) UJ2W54673BW; (XJ6L) UJ2T69451BW; (XJ12L) UJ2R58421BW.
Note: Serial numbering system changed at mid-year (effective in May 1978) to a 14-symbol number. Starting serial number: (XJ-S) JNVEV48C100001; (XJ6) JAVLN48C100001; (XJ12) JBVLV48C100001.

Model	Body Type & Seating	Engine Type/CID	P.O.E. Price	Weight (lbs.)	Prod. Total
XJ-S					
GT	2-dr Coupe-2 + 2P	V12/326	23900	3936	3,217
XJ6/12					
XJ6L	4-dr Sedan-5P	I6/258	19000	4068	15,422
XJ12L	4-dr Sedan-5P	V12/326	23900	4334	3,284

Production Note: Figures shown are approximate and do not include equivalent Daimler sedans.

ENGINE DATA: BASE SIX (early XJ6): Inline, dual-overhead-cam six-cylinder. Cast iron block and aluminum head. **Displacement:** 258.4 cu. in. (4235 cc). **Bore & Stroke:** 3.625 x 4.17 in. (92.1 x 106 mm). **Compression Ratio:** 7.5:1. **Brake Horsepower:** 162 at 4750 rpm. **Torque:** 225 lbs.-ft. at 2500 rpm. Seven main bearings. Solid valve lifters. Two Zenith-Stromberg 175CD2SE carburetors.

BASE SIX (late XJ6): Same as above, but with Lucas/Bosch L-Jetronic fuel injection — **Compression Ratio:** 7.5:1. **Brake Horsepower:** 176 at 4750 rpm. **Torque:** 219 lbs.-ft. at 4500 rpm.

BASE V-12 (XJ12, XJ-S): 60-degree, overhead-cam "vee" type 12-cylinder. Aluminum block and head. **Displacement:** 326 cu. in. (5343 cc). **Bore & Stroke:** 3.54 x 2.77 in. (90 x 70 mm). **Compression Ratio:** 7.8:1 or 8.0:1. **Brake Horsepower:** 244 at 5250 rpm. **Torque:** 269 lbs.-ft. at 4500 rpm. Seven main bearings. Electronic fuel injection.

CHASSIS DATA: Wheelbase: (XJ-S) 102 in.; (XJ sed) 112.8 in. **Overall Length:** (XJ-S) 192.25 in.; (XJ sed) 200.5 in. **Height:** (XJ-S) 47.8 in.; (XJ) 54.1 in. **Width:** (XJ-S) 70.6 in.; (XJ) 69.8 in. **Front Tread:** (XJ-S) 58.6 in.; (XJ) 58.2 in. **Rear Tread:** (XJ-S) 58.65 in.; (XJ) 58.9 in. **Wheel type:** (XJ-S) cast aluminum alloy; (XJ) ventilated chrome disc. **Standard Tires:** (XJ-S) Dunlop 205/70VR15 Sports Super SBR WSW; (XJ6) Dunlop ER70VR15; (XJ12) Dunlop 205/70VR15 SBR WSW.

TECHNICAL: Layout: front-engine, rear-drive. **Transmission:** three-speed automatic. **Standard Final Drive Ratio:** 3.31:1. **Steering:** power rack and pinion. **Suspension (front):** (XJ-S) semi-trailing wishbones with coil springs and anti-roll bar; (XJ) wishbones, coil springs and anti-roll bar. **Suspension (rear):** independent with lower wishbones, lower radius arms, coil springs and anti-roll bar. **Brakes:** power front/rear disc. **Body Construction:** integral steel.

MAJOR OPTIONS: No factory options offered.

PERFORMANCE: Top Speed: (XJ-S) 140-150 mph; (XJ6) about 115 mph; (XJ12) about 140 mph. **Acceleration (0-60 mph):** (XJ-S) about 8 sec.; (XJ12) about 9 sec. **Fuel Mileage:** (XJ-S) 9-14 mpg; (XJ6) 13-18 mpg.

PRODUCTION/SALES: Approximately 4,754 Jaguars were sold in the U.S. during 1978 (1,050 XJ-S, 2,766 XJ6, and 938 XJ12).

Manufacturer: British Leyland UK Ltd. (then Jaguar Rover Triumph Ltd.), Coventry, England.

Distributor: British Leyland Motors Inc., Leonia, New Jersey.

1979 JAGUAR

1979 Jaguar XJ12 V-12 four-door sedan.

XJ-S — V-12 — Jaguar's sport coupe continued with no significant change.

XJ6 — SERIES II — SIX — Jaguar's four-door, six-cylinder sedan continued with no major change, but was now powered by a fuel-injected version of the familiar twin-cam engine. Sole transmission was again the Borg-Warner three-speed automatic. A Series III sedan debuted during the model year.

XJ12 — SERIES II — V-12 — No major change was evident in the 12-cylinder version of Jaguar's four-door sedan. GM's Turbo Hydra-matic three-speed automatic transmission was standard. A Series III version debuted during the model year.

I.D. DATA: A 14-symbol serial number is on the 'A' (windshield) pillar. Symbol one indicates manufacturer. Symbol two denotes model. Symbol three indicates a car made to U.S. specifications. Symbol four identifies the body style. Symbol five indicates engine type; six, the transmission and steering; seven, the model year; eight, the assembly plant. The remaining symbols make up the sequential serial number. Starting serial number: (XJ-S) JNVEV49C100234; (XJ6) JAVLN49C100749; (XJ12) JBVLV49C100770.

Model	Body Type & Seating	Engine Type/CID	P.O.E. Price	Weight (lbs.)	Prod. Total
XJ-S					
GT	2-dr Coupe-2 + 2P	V12/326	25000	3936	2,414
XJ6/12					
XJ6L	4-dr Sedan-5P	I6/258	20000	4068	Note 1
XJ12L	4-dr Sedan-5P	V12/326	22000	4334	Note 2

Note 1: About 1,528 Series II and 6,146 Series III XJ6 sedans were produced in 1979 (not including Daimlers).

Note 2: About 429 Series II and 155 Series III XJ12 sedans were produced in 1979 (not including Daimlers).

ENGINE DATA: BASE SIX (XJ6): Inline, dual-overhead-cam six-cylinder. Cast iron block and aluminum head. **Displacement:** 258.4 cu. in. (4235 cc). **Bore & Stroke:** 3.625 x 4.17 in. (92.1 x 106 mm). **Compression Ratio:** 7.8:1. **Brake Horsepower:** 176 at 4750 rpm. **Torque:** 219 lbs.-ft. at 2500 rpm. Seven main bearings. Solid valve lifters. Electronic fuel injection.

BASE V-12 (XJ12, XJ-S): 60-degree, overhead-cam "vee" type 12-cylinder. Aluminum block and head. **Displacement:** 326 cu.in. (5343 cc). **Bore & Stroke:** 3.54 x 2.77 in. (90 x 70 mm). **Compression Ratio:** 7.8:1. **Brake Horsepower:** 244 at 5250 rpm. **Torque:** 269 lbs.-ft. at 4500 rpm. Seven main bearings. Electronic fuel injection.

CHASSIS DATA: Wheelbase: (XJ-S) 102 in.; (XJ sed) 112.8 in. **Overall Length:** (XJ-S) 192.25 in.; (XJ sed) 200.5 in. **Height:** (XJ-S) 47.8 in.; (XJ) 54.1 in. **Width:** (XJ-S) 70.6 in.; (XJ) 69.8 in. **Front Tread:** (XJ-S) 58.6 in.; (XJ) 58.2 in. **Rear Tread:** (XJ-S) 58.65 in.; (XJ) 58.9 in. **Wheel type:** (XJ-S) cast aluminum alloy; (XJ) ventilated chrome disc. **Standard Tires:** (XJ-S) Dunlop 205/70VR15 Sports Super SBR WSW; (XJ6) Dunlop ER 70VR15; (XJ12) Dunlop 205/70VR15 SBR WSW.

TECHNICAL: Layout: front-engine, rear-drive. **Transmission:** three-speed automatic. **Standard Final Drive Ratio:** 3.31:1. **Steering:** power rack and pinion. **Suspension (front):** (XJ-S) semi-trailing wishbones with coil springs and anti-roll bar; (XJ) wishbones, coil springs and anti-roll bar. **Suspension (rear):** independent with lower wishbones, lower radius arms, coil springs and anti-roll bar. **Brakes:** power front/rear disc. **Body Construction:** integral steel.

MAJOR OPTIONS: No factory options offered.

PERFORMANCE: Top Speed: (XJ-S) 140-150 mph; (XJ6) about 116 mph; (XJ12) about 140 mph. **Acceleration (0-60 mph):** (XJ-S) about 8 sec.; (XJ6) 9.6 sec. **Acceleration (quarter-mile):** (XJ6) 17.7 sec. **Fuel Mileage:** (XJ-S) 10 mpg EPA; (XJ6) 14 mpg EPA, about 17 mpg average.

PRODUCTION/SALES: Approximately 3,551 Jaguars were sold in the U.S. during 1979 (695 XJ-S, 2,313 XJ6, and 543 XJ12).

Manufacturer: Jaguar Rover Triumph Ltd., Coventry, England.

Distributor: Jaguar Rover Triumph Inc., Leonia, New Jersey.

HISTORY: Introduced to U.S. market in June 1978. Series III sedans debuted in mid-1979, as '80 models; see next listing for details.

1980 JAGUAR

XJ-S — V-12 — Once again, Jaguar's 2+2 sports coupe continued with no significant change except for new body colors. Standard colors this year were: Atlantis Blue metallic; Brazilia Brown metallic; Cotswold Yellow; Damson Red; Racing Green metallic; Sebring Red; and Tudor White.

XJ6 — SERIES III — SIX — A revised version of Jaguar's four-door, six-cylinder sedan debuted during the 1979 model year, as an early '80 model. Changes included a taller roofline and slightly larger back window. Rear pillars were slightly narrower, while the windshield grew larger. Wraparound bumpers were added at both front and rear, while restyled taillamps incorporated both backup and stop lights. Mechanical changes were minimal. As before, the sedan was powered by a fuel-injected version of the familiar twin-cam engine, hooked to the Borg-Warner three-speed automatic. However, a five-speed manual gearbox became available (identical to that used in the Rover 3500). Cruise control became available. The V-12 edition was dropped from the U.S. market this year, though it remained in production (and some were sold during the model year). Body colors were the same as XJ-S, except for Sebring Red. Standard equipment included an AM/FM stereo with cassette player, automatic-temperature air conditioning, power windows, tinted glass, heated rear window, and power mirrors.

I.D. DATA: A 14-symbol serial number is on the 'A' (windshield) pillar. Symbol one indicates manufacturer. Symbol two denotes model. Symbol three indicates a car made to U.S. specifications. Symbol four identifies the body style. Symbol five indicates engine type; six, the transmission and steering; seven, the model year; eight, the assembly plant. The remaining symbols make up the sequential serial number. Starting serial number: (XJ6) JAVLN4AC310676. Serial number prefix: (XJ-S) JNVEV.

Model	Body Type & Seating	Engine Type/CID	P.O.E. Price	Weight (lbs.)	Prod. Total
XJ-S					
GT	2-dr Coupe-2 + 2P	V12/326	30000	3936	1,131
XJ6					
XJ6	4-dr Sedan-5P	I6/258	25000	4075	9,836

Production Note: Figures shown are approximate and do not include equivalent Daimler sedans. A total of 814 XJ12 Jaguars also were produced this year (plus 604 12-cylinder Daimlers).

ENGINE DATA: BASE SIX (XJ6): Inline, dual-overhead-cam six-cylinder. Cast iron block and aluminum head. **Displacement:** 258.4 cu. in. (4235 cc). **Bore & Stroke:** 3.625 x 4.17 in. (92.1 x 106 mm). **Compression Ratio:** 7.8:1. **Brake Horsepower:** 176 at 4750 rpm. **Torque:** 219 lbs.-ft. at 2500 rpm. Seven main bearings. Solid valve lifters. Electronic fuel injection.

BASE V-12 (XJ-S): 60-degree, overhead-cam, vee-type 12-cylinder. Aluminum block and head. **Displacement:** 326 cu. in. (5343 cc). **Bore & Stroke:** 3.54 x 2.77 in. (90 x 70 mm). **Compression Ratio:** 7.8:1. **Brake Horsepower:** 244 at 5250 rpm. **Torque:** 269 lbs.-ft. at 4500 rpm. Seven main bearings. Electronic fuel injection.

CHASSIS DATA: Wheelbase: (XJ-S) 102 in.; (XJ6) 112.8 in. **Overall Length:** (XJ-S) 192.25 in.; (XJ6) 199.5 in. **Height:** (XJ-S) 47.8 in.; (XJ6) 54 in. **Width:** (XJ-S) 70.6 in.; (XJ6) 69.7 in. **Front Tread:** (XJ-S) 58.6 in.; (XJ6) 58.3 in. **Rear Tread:** (XJ-S) 58.65 in.; (XJ6) 58.9 in. **Wheel type:** (XJ-S) cast aluminum alloy; (XJ6) ventilated chrome disc. **Standard Tires:** (XJ-S) Dunlop 205/70VR15 Sports Super SBR WSW; (XJ6) Dunlop ER70VR15.

TECHNICAL: Layout: front-engine, rear-drive. **Transmission:** three-speed automatic. Turbo Hydra-matic 400 in XJ-S; Borg-Warner in XJ6. Five-speed manual available in XJ6. **Standard Final Drive Ratio:** 3.31:1 or 3.07:1. **Steering:** power rack and pinion. **Suspension (front):** "anti-dive" with coil springs and anti-roll bar. **Suspension (rear):** independent with lower wishbones, lower radius arms, coil springs and (XJ-S) anti-roll bar. **Brakes:** power front/rear disc. **Body Construction:** integral steel.

MAJOR OPTIONS: No factory options offered.

PERFORMANCE: Top Speed: (XJ-S) 140-150 mph; (XJ6) about 115 mph. **Acceleration (0-60 mph):** (XJ-S) about 8 sec. **Acceleration (quarter-mile):** (XJ6) 17.9 sec. **Fuel Mileage:** (XJ-S) 10 mpg EPA; (XJ6) 14 mpg EPA.

PRODUCTION/SALES: Approximately 2,951 Jaguars were sold in the U.S. during 1980 (420 XJ-S, 2,275 XJ6, and 256 XJ12).

Manufacturer: Jaguar Rover Triumph Ltd. (then Jaguar Cars Ltd.), Coventry, England.

Distributor: Jaguar Rover Triumph Inc., Leonia, New Jersey.

1981 JAGUAR

XJ-S — V-12 — Jaguar's 2+2 sports coupe was not officially listed for sale in the U.S. this year, though a small number were sold.

XJ6 — SERIES III — SIX — Production of the restyled six-cylinder sedan, introduced for the 1980 model year, continued with little change.

I.D. DATA: A 17-symbol Vehicle Identification Number is on the upper left of the instrument panel, visible through the windshield. Symbols 1-3 identify the manufacturer, make, and vehicle type. Symbol four indicates model; five, vehicle class; six, body style; seven, engine. Symbol eight denotes transmission type, followed by a check digit. Symbol 10 indicates model year ('B' = 1981); symbol 11, the assembly plant. The final six digit form the sequential serial number. Starting serial number: (XJ6) SAJAV134()BC320092.

Model	Body Type & Seating	Engine Type/CID	P.O.E. Price	Weight (lbs.)	Prod. Total
XJ-S					
GT	2-dr Coupe-2+2P	V12/326	N/A	N/A	1,252
XJ6					
XJ6	4-dr Sedan-5P	I6/258	27500	4060	10,216

Production Note: Figures shown are approximate and do not include equivalent Daimler sedans. A total of 457 XJ12 Jaguars also were produced (plus 415 12-cylinder Daimlers).

ENGINE DATA: BASE SIX (XJ6): Inline, dual-overhead-cam six-cylinder. Cast iron block and aluminum head. **Displacement:** 258.4 cu. in. (4235 cc). **Bore & Stroke:** 3.625 x 4.17 in. (92.1 x 106 mm). **Compression Ratio:** 7.8:1. **Brake Horsepower:** 176 at 4750 rpm. **Torque:** 219 lbs.-ft. at 2500 rpm. Seven main bearings. Solid valve lifters. Electronic fuel injection.

BASE V-12 (XJ-S): Same as 1980.

CHASSIS DATA: Wheelbase: (XJ-S) 102 in.; (XJ6) 112.8 in. **Overall Length:** (XJ-S) 192.25 in.; (XJ6) 199.5 in. **Height:** (XJ-S) 47.8 in.; (XJ6) 54 in. **Width:** (XJ-S) 70.6 in.; (XJ6) 69.7 in. **Front Tread:** (XJ-S) 58.6 in.; (XJ6) 58.3 in. **Rear Tread:** (XJ-S) 58.65 in.; (XJ6) 58.9 in. **Wheel type:** (XJ-S) cast aluminum alloy; (XJ6) ventilated chrome disc. **Standard Tires:** (XJ-S) Dunlop 205/70VR15 Sports Super SBR WSW; (XJ6) Dunlop ER70VR15.

TECHNICAL: Layout: front-engine, rear-drive. **Transmission:** three-speed automatic or five-speed manual. **Standard Final Drive Ratio:** (XJ6) 3.07:1. **Steering:** power rack and pinion. **Suspension (front):** "anti-dive" with coil springs and anti-roll bar. **Suspension (rear):** independent with lower wishbones, lower radius arms and coil springs. **Brakes:** power front/rear disc. **Body Construction:** integral steel.

MAJOR OPTIONS: No factory options offered.

PERFORMANCE: Similar to 1980.

PRODUCTION/SALES: Approximately 4,688 Jaguars were sold in the U.S. during 1981 (including 232 XJ-S models).

Manufacturer: Jaguar Cars Ltd., Coventry, England.

Distributor: Jaguar Rover Triumph Inc., Leonia, New Jersey.

1982 JAGUAR

XJ-S — V-12 — Jaguar's 12-cylinder coupe continued with little change, except for the adoption of a high-swirl, high-compression cylinder head. That gave it the name H.E. (for "High Efficiency"). The 326-cid (5.3-liter) engine came only with three-speed automatic.

XJ6 — SERIES III — SIX — Production of Jaguar's basic sedan continued with little change. Drivetrain was again the familiar twin-cam 4.2-liter six-cylinder engine with electronic fuel injection, hooked to three-speed automatic. Standard equipment included four-wheel power disc brakes, power steering, power sunroof, power windows and door mirrors, tinted glass, cruise control, automatic-temperature air conditioning, a 25-watt AM/FM digital stereo radio with scan tuning and cassette player, power antenna, central locking, electric rear-window defroster, power driver's seat, and adjustable steering column. Seats wore leather facing.

XJ6 VANDEN PLAS — SIX — A new luxury edition of the six-cylinder four-door sedan added such extra equipment as full leather upholstery, woven throw rugs, wood-veneer dash applique, rear-compartment reading lamps, rear center armrest with built-in storage compartment, and special body emblems.

I.D. DATA: A 17-symbol Vehicle Identification Number is on the top left of the instrument panel, visible through the windshield. Symbols 1-3 indicate origin and make. Symbol four denotes model; symbol five, the restraint system; symbol six, the body style ('1' = four-door sedan; '5' = two-door coupe). Symbol seven is the engine code; symbol eight, the steering and transmission code. Next is a check digit, followed by a letter indicating model year (C = 1982). Symbol 11 (letter C) identifies the assembly plant, followed by a six-digit sequential production number. Starting serial number: (XJ-S) SAJNV5()()()CC105233. (XJ6) SAJAV1()()()CC105233; (Vanden Plas) SAJAY1()()()CC105233.

Model	Body Type & Seating	Engine Type/CID	P.O.E. Price	Weight (lbs.)	Prod. Total
XJ-S					
H.E.	2-dr Coupe-2+2P	V12/326	32100	3980	3,348
XJ6					
III	4-dr Sedan-5P	I6/258	29500	4075	Note 1
Vand Plas	4-dr Sedan-5P	I6/258	32000	4075	Note 1

Note 1: Approximately 14,422 XJ6 sedans were produced in 1982 (plus 2,654 Daimlers). A total of 518 XJ12 (12-cylinder) sedans also were produced, plus 835 12-cylinder Daimlers.

ENGINE DATA: BASE SIX (XJ6): Inline, dual overhead-cam six-cylinder. Cast iron block and aluminum head. **Displacement:** 258 cu. in. (4235 cc). **Bore & Stroke:** 3.63 x 4.17 in. (92 x 106 mm). **Compression Ratio:** 8.1:1. **Brake Horsepower:** 176 at 4750 rpm. **Torque:** 219 lbs.-ft. at 2500 rpm. Seven main bearings. Thimble tappets. Electronic fuel injection.

BASE V-12 (XJ-S): 60-degree, "vee" type overhead-cam twelve-cylinder. Aluminum block and heads. **Displacement:** 326 cu. in. (5343 cc). **Bore & Stroke:** 3.54 x 2.76 in. (90 x 70 mm). **Compression Ratio:** 11.5:1. **Brake Horsepower:** 262 at 5000 rpm. **Torque:** 290 lbs.-ft. at 3000 rpm. Seven main bearings. Thimble tappets. Electronic fuel injection.

CHASSIS DATA: Wheelbase: (XJ-S) 102 in.; (XJ6) 113 in. **Overall Length:** (XJ-S) 192.2 in.; (XJ6) 199.6 in. **Height:** (XJ-S) 49.6 in.; (XJ6) 54.0 in. **Width:** (XJ-S) 70.6 in.; (XJ6) 69.7 in. **Front Tread:** (XJ-S) 58.6 in.; (XJ6) 58.3 in. **Rear Tread:** (XJ-S) 59.2 in.; (XJ6) 58.9 in. **Standard Tires:** (XJ-S) 215/70VR15; (XJ6) 205/70VR15.

TECHNICAL: Layout: front-engine, rear-drive. **Transmission:** three-speed automatic. **Standard Final Drive Ratio:** 2.88:1. **Steering:** rack and pinion, power-assisted. **Suspension (front):** upper/lower control arms, coil springs and anti-roll bar. **Suspension (rear):** independent; lower control arms, longitudinal links, coil springs and anti-roll bar. **Brakes:** front/rear disc. **Body Construction:** steel unibody. **Fuel Tank:** (XJ-S) 24 gal.; (XJ6) 23.6 gallon.

PRODUCTION/SALES: A total of 10,349 Jaguars were sold in the U.S. during 1982 (8,940 XJ6 sedans and 1,409 XJ-S).

Manufacturer: Jaguar Cars Ltd., Coventry, England.

HISTORY: Introduced in U.S. market in October, 1981.

1983 JAGUAR

XJ-S — V-12 — A revised version of the 12-cylinder coupe was anticipated during the 1983 model year, but did not arrive. Instead, this was a carryover model with details little changed from 1982. The V-12 engine continued with its high-swirl cylinder head. Standard equipment was similar to 1982.

XJ6 — SERIES III — SIX — Little change was evident on Jaguar's six-cylinder, four-door sedan, again available in basic or luxury Vanden Plas edition. Standard equipment was similar to 1982.

I.D. DATA: A 17-symbol Vehicle Identification Number is on the top left of the instrument panel, visible through the windshield. Symbols 1-3 indicate origin and make. Symbol four denotes model; symbol five, the restraint system; symbol six, the body style ('1' = four-door sedan; '5' = two-door coupe). Symbol seven is the engine code; symbol eight, the steering and transmission code. Next is a check digit, followed by a letter indicating model year (D = 1983). Symbol 11 (letter C) identifies the assembly plant, followed by a six-digit sequential production number. Starting serial number: (XJ-S) SAJNV5()4()DC000001; (XJ6) SAJAV1()4()DC000001; (Vanden Plas) SAJAY1()4()DC000001.

Model	Body Type & Seating	Engine Type/CID	P.O.E. Price	Weight (lbs.)	Prod. Total
XJ-S					
H.E.	2-dr Coupe-2+2P	V12/326	34000	3950	4,457
XJ6					
III	4-dr Sedan-5P	I6/258	30500	4066	Note 1
Vand Plas	4-dr Sedan-5P	I6/258	33500	4066	Note 1

Note 1: Approximately 17,412 six-cylinder sedans were produced in 1983 (plus 3,206 equivalent Daimlers, 341 XJ12 Jaguars, and 1,668 12-cylinder Daimlers).

ENGINE DATA: BASE SIX (XJ6): Inline, dual overhead-cam six-cylinder. Cast iron block and aluminum head. **Displacement:** 258 cu. in. (4235 cc). **Bore & Stroke:** 3.63 x 4.17 in. (92 x 106 mm). **Compression Ratio:** 8.1:1. **Brake Horsepower:** 176 at 4750 rpm. **Torque:** 219 lbs.-ft. at 2500 rpm. Seven main bearings. Thimble tappets. Electronic fuel injection.

BASE V-12 (XJ-S): 60-degree, "vee" type overhead-cam twelve-cylinder. Aluminum block and heads. **Displacement:** 326 cu. in. (5343 cc). **Bore & Stroke:** 3.54 x 2.76 in. (90 x 70 mm). **Compression Ratio:** 11.5:1. **Brake Horsepower:** 262 at 5000 rpm. **Torque:** 290 lbs.-ft. at 3000 rpm. Seven main bearings. Thimble tappets. Electronic fuel injection.

CHASSIS DATA: Wheelbase: (XJ-S) 102 in.; (XJ6) 113 in. **Overall Length:** (XJ-S) 192.2 in.; (XJ6) 199.6 in. **Height:** (XJ-S) 49.6 in.; (XJ6) 54.0 in. **Width:** (XJ-S) 70.6 in.; (XJ6) 69.7 in. **Front Tread:** (XJ-S) 58.6 in.; (XJ6) 58.3 in. **Rear Tread:** (XJ-S) 59.2 in.; (XJ6) 58.9 in. **Standard Tires:** (XJ-S) 215/70VR15; (XJ6) 205/70VR15.

TECHNICAL: Layout: front-engine, rear-drive. **Transmission:** three-speed automatic. **Standard Final Drive Ratio:** 2.88:1. **Steering:** rack and pinion, power-assisted. **Suspension (front):** upper/lower control arms, coil springs and anti-roll bar. **Suspension (rear):** independent; lower control arms, longitudinal links, coil springs and anti-roll bar. **Brakes:** front/rear disc. **Body Construction:** steel unibody. **Fuel Tank:** (XJ-S) 24 gal.; (XJ6) 23.6 gallon.

PRODUCTION/SALES: A total of 15,815 Jaguars were sold in the U.S. during 1983.

Manufacturer: Jaguar Cars Ltd., Coventry, England.

Distributor: Jaguar Cars Inc., Leonia, New Jersey.

HISTORY: Introduced in U.S. market in November, 1982. A cabriolet version of the XJ-S became available in Europe late in 1983, but would not arrive in the U.S. market until the 1987 model year.

1984 JAGUAR

XJ-S — V-12 — Except for the addition of halogen headlamps and new body color choices, the Jaguar coupe was a carryover from 1983. A total of 10 colors now were offered. As before, the 326-cid (5.3-liter) V-12 engine drove a General Motor THM-400 80 three-speed automatic transmission. Standard equipment included power four-wheel disc brakes, power steering and all the features listed with the XJ6 sedan, plus full leather interior trim, leather-bound steering wheel, and burl-elm instrument panel applique and door inserts.

XJ6 — SERIES III — SIX — Halogen headlamps went on the six-cylinder four-door sedan, again offered in base and Vanden Plas editions. Otherwise, change was minimal. Both models wore 205/70VR15 Pirelli P5 tires. Bodies of the base model came in 10 colors, while the Vanden Plas had a choice of five (versus just two in the prior year). Drivetrain was the same as in 1983: a 4.2-liter inline six, hooked to GM's THM-400 80 three-speed automatic transmission. As before, interiors featured wood dashboard trim

and leather-faced seats. Standard equipment also included power four-wheel disc brakes, power steering, power sunroof, cruise control, automatic air conditioning, AM/FM stereo radio with cassette player and power antenna, tinted glass, central door locking, intermittent wipers, power windows and mirrors, electric rear-window defroster, power driver's seat, and an adjustable steering column. The posher Vanden Plas added rear-compartment reading lamps, woven throw rugs, a wood-veneer dash applique, rear center armrest with storage compartment, full leather upholstery, and special body emblems.

1984 Jaguar XJ-S coupe. (William Siuru Jr.)

I.D. DATA: A 17-symbol Vehicle Identification Number is on the top left of the instrument panel, visible through the windshield. Symbols 1-3 indicate origin and make. Symbol four denotes model; symbol five, the restraint system; symbol six, the body style ('1' = four-door sedan; '5' = two-door coupe). Symbol seven is the engine code; symbol eight, the steering and transmission code. Next is a check digit, followed by a letter indicating model year (E = 1984). Symbol 11 (letter C) identifies the assembly plant, followed by a six-digit sequential production number. Starting serial number: (XJ-S) SAJNV5()4()EC000001; (XJ6) SAJAV1()4()EC000001; (Vanden Plas) SAJAY1()4()EC000001.

Model	Body Type & Seating	Engine Type/CID	P.O.E. Price	Weight (lbs.)	Prod. Total
XJ-S					
H.E.	2-dr Coupe-2 + 2P	V12/326	34700	3950	5,813
XJ6					
III	4-dr Sedan-5P	I6/258	31100	4066	Note 1
Vand Plas	4-dr Sedan-5P	I6/258	34200	4066	Note 1

Note 1: About 19,578 Jaguar sedans were produced during 1984 (plus 3,206 equivalent Daimlers, 1,509 XJ12 sedans, and 1,005 12-cylinder Daimler sedans).

ENGINE DATA: BASE SIX (XJ6): Inline, dual overhead-cam six-cylinder. Cast iron block and aluminum head. **Displacement:** 258 cu. in. (4235 cc). **Bore & Stroke:** 3.63 x 4.17 in. (92 x 106 mm). **Compression Ratio:** 8.1:1. **Brake Horsepower:** 176 at 4750 rpm. **Torque:** 219 lbs.-ft. at 2500 rpm. Seven main bearings. Thimble tappets. Electronic fuel injection.
BASE V-12 (XJ-S): 60-degree, "vee" type overhead-cam twelve-cylinder. Aluminum block and heads. **Displacement:** 326 cu. in. (5343 cc). **Bore & Stroke:** 3.54 x 2.76 in. (90 x 70 mm). **Compression Ratio:** 11.5:1. **Brake Horsepower:** 262 at 5000 rpm. **Torque:** 290 lbs.-ft. at 3000 rpm. Seven main bearings. Thimble tappets. Electronic fuel injection.

CHASSIS DATA: Wheelbase: (XJ-S) 102 in.; (XJ6) 113 in. **Overall Length:** (XJ-S) 191.3 in.; (XJ6) 199.6 in. **Height:** (XJ-S) 49.6 in.; (XJ6) 52.8 in. **Width:** (XJ-S) 70.6 in.; (XJ6) 69.6 in. **Front Tread:** (XJ-S) 58.6 in.; (XJ6) 58.3 in. **Rear Tread:** (XJ-S) 59.2 in.; (XJ6) 58.9 in. **Standard Tires:** (XJ-S) 215/70VR15; (XJ6) 205/70VR15.

TECHNICAL: Layout: front-engine, rear-drive. **Transmission:** three-speed automatic. **Standard Final Drive Ratio:** 2.88:1. **Steering:** rack and pinion, power-assisted. **Suspension (front):** upper/lower control arms, coil springs and anti-roll bar. **Suspension (rear):** independent; lower control arms, longitudinal links, coil springs and anti-roll bar. **Brakes:** front/rear disc. **Body Construction:** steel unibody. Fuel Tank: (XJ-S) 24 gal.; (XJ6) 23.6 gallon.

PRODUCTION/SALES: A total of 18,044 Jaguars were sold in the U.S. during 1984.
Manufacturer: Jaguar Cars Ltd., Coventry, England.
Distributor: Jaguar Cars Inc., Leonia, New Jersey.
HISTORY: Introduced to U.S. market in October, 1983.

XJ-S — V-12 — Appearance and standard equipment for the H.E. (High Efficiency) 12-cylinder coupe were similar to 1984.

XJ6 — SERIES III — SIX — Production of the Jaguar four-door sedan continued with little change. Standard equipment was similar to 1984, with a more powerful (40-watt) stereo radio and cassette player and a trip computer.

I.D. DATA: A 17-symbol Vehicle Identification Number is on the top left of the instrument panel, visible through the windshield. Symbols 1-3 indicate origin and make. Symbol four denotes model; symbol five, the restraint system; symbol six, the body style ('1' = four-door sedan; '5' = two-door coupe). Symbol seven is the engine code; symbol eight, the steering and transmission code. Next is a check digit, followed by a letter indicating model year (F = 1985). Symbol 11 (letter C) identifies the assembly plant, followed by a six-digit sequential production number. Starting serial number: (XJ-S) SAJNV5()4()FC000001; (XJ6) SAJAV1()4()FC000001; (Vanden Plas) SAJAY1()4()FC000001.

Model	Body Type & Seating	Engine Type/CID	P.O.E. Price	Weight (lbs.)	Prod. Total
XJ-S					
H.E.	2-dr Coupe-2 + 2P	V12/326	36000	3980	Note 1
XJ6					
III	4-dr Sedan-5P	I6/258	32250	4075	Note 1
Vand Plas	4-dr Sedan-5P	I6/258	35550	4081	Note 1

Note 1: A total of 20,528 Jaguars were sold in the U.S. during 1985.
ENGINE DATA: BASE SIX (XJ6): Inline, dual overhead-cam six-cylinder. Cast iron block and aluminum head. **Displacement:** 258 cu. in. (4235 cc). **Bore & Stroke:** 3.63 x 4.17 in. (92 x 106 mm). **Compression Ratio:** 8.1:1. **Brake Horsepower:** 176 at 4750 rpm. **Torque:** 219 lbs.-ft. at 2500 rpm. Seven main bearings. Thimble tappets. Electronic fuel injection.
BASE V-12 (XJ-S): 60-degree, "vee" type overhead-cam twelve-cylinder. Aluminum block and heads. **Displacement:** 326 cu. in. (5343 cc). **Bore & Stroke:** 3.54 x 2.76 in. (90 x 70 mm). **Compression Ratio:** 11.5:1. **Brake Horsepower:** 262 at 5000 rpm. **Torque:** 290 lbs.-ft. at 3000 rpm. Seven main bearings. Thimble tappets. Electronic fuel injection.
CHASSIS DATA: Wheelbase: (XJ-S) 102 in.; (XJ6) 113 in. **Overall Length:** (XJ-S) 191.3 in.; (XJ6) 199.6 in. **Height:** (XJ-S) 49.6 in.; (XJ6) 52.8 in. **Width:** (XJ-S) 70.6 in.; (XJ6) 69.6 in. **Front Tread:** (XJ-S) 58.6 in.; (XJ6) 58.3 in. **Rear Tread:** (XJ-S) 59.2 in.; (XJ6) 58.9 in. **Standard Tires:** (XJ-S) 215/70VR15 Pirelli P5.

TECHNICAL: Layout: front-engine, rear-drive. **Transmission:** three-speed automatic. **Standard Final Drive Ratio:** 2.88:1. **Steering:** rack and pinion, power-assisted. **Suspension (front):** upper/lower control arms, coil springs and anti-roll bar. **Suspension (rear):** independent; lower control arms, longitudinal links, coil springs and anti-roll bar. **Brakes:** front/rear disc. **Body Construction:** steel unibody. **Fuel Tank:** (XJ-S) 24 gal.; (XJ6) 23.6 gallon.
Manufacturer: Jaguar Cars Ltd., Coventry, England.
Distributor: Jaguar Cars Inc., Leonia, New Jersey.
HISTORY: Introduced in U.S. in September, 1984. A new all-alloy AJ6 (Advanced Jaguar) six-cylinder engine, as introduced in Europe for the 1984 model year, was expected in U.S. models, along with a new cabriolet (convertible) body style. As offered in Europe, the new 3.6-liter six, which would replace the long-lived XK-derived inline six-cylinder engine, produced 225 bhp and 240 lbs.-ft. of torque, using 9.6:1 compression. The convertible would not arrive until the 1987 model year, the new engine a year later. Jaguar ranked among the top five car models in J.D. Power's Consumer Satisfaction Index for two years in a row, a dramatic change for a company whose products had formerly suffered quality problems.

1986 Jaguar XJ-S cabriolet. (Jaguar Cars Inc.)

XJ-S — V-12 — Appearance and standard equipment for the Jaguar's H.E. 12-cylinder coupe were similar to 1985, except for new body colors (including British Racing Green). Inside were a new burl walnut veneer facia and door inserts. A power sunroof joined the option list, priced at $1300. Though ostensibly a four-seater, even Jaguar described the V-12 coupe's back seat as "occasional seating for two."

XJ6 — SERIES III — SIX — British Racing Green was one of the new color choices for the Jaguar six-cylinder sedan. A new 40-watt Alpine sound system was standard in both the base and posh Vanden Plas models. A walnut finish was added to the center console of the base sedan, while the Vanden Plas added rear-seat headrests. Otherwise, appearance and equipment were similar to 1985, including a trip computer.

I.D. DATA: A 17-symbol Vehicle Identification Number is on the top left of the instrument panel, visible through the windshield. Symbols 1-3 indicate origin and make. Symbol four denotes model; symbol five, the restraint system; symbol six, the body style ('1' = four-door sedan; '5' = two-door coupe). Symbol seven is the engine code; symbol eight, the steering and transmission code. Next is a check digit, followed by a letter indicating model year (G = 1986). Symbol 11 (letter C) identifies the assembly plant, followed by a six-digit sequential production number. Starting serial number: (XJ-S) SAJNV5()4()GC000001; (XJ6) SAJAV1()4()GC000001; (Vanden Plas) SAJAY1()4()GC000001.

Model	Body Type & Seating	Engine Type/CID	P.O.E. Price	Weight (lbs.)	Prod. Total
XJ-S					
H.E.	2-dr Coupe-2 + 2P	V12/326	36000	3980	Note 1
XJ6					
III	4-dr Sedan-5P	I6/258	32250	4064	Note 1
Vand Plas	4-dr Sedan-5P	I6/258	35550	4074	Note 1

Note 1: A total of 24,464 Jaguars were sold in the U.S. during 1986 (19,579 XJ6 sedans and 4,885 XJ-S).

ENGINE DATA: BASE SIX (XJ6): Inline, dual overhead-cam six-cylinder. Cast iron block and aluminum head. **Displacement:** 258 cu. in. (4235 cc). **Bore & Stroke:** 3.63 x 4.17 in. (92 x 106 mm). **Compression Ratio:** 8.1:1. **Brake Horsepower:** 176 at 4750 rpm. **Torque:** 219 lbs.-ft. at 2500 rpm. Seven main bearings. Thimble tappets. Electronic fuel injection.
BASE V-12 (XJ-S): 60-degree, "vee" type overhead-cam twelve-cylinder. Aluminum block and heads. **Displacement:** 326 cu. in. (5343 cc). **Bore & Stroke:** 3.54 x 2.76 in. (90 x 70 mm). **Compression Ratio:** 11.5:1. **Brake Horsepower:** 262 at 5000 rpm. **Torque:** 290 lbs.-ft. at 3000 rpm. Seven main bearings. Thimble tappets. Electronic fuel injection.

CHASSIS DATA: Wheelbase: (XJ-S) 102 in.; (XJ6) 113 in. **Overall Length:** (XJ-S) 191.3 in.; (XJ6) 199.6 in. **Height:** (XJ-S) 49.6 in.; (XJ6) 52.8 in. **Width:** (XJ-S) 70.6 in.; (XJ6) 69.6 in. **Front Tread:** (XJ-S) 58.6 in.; (XJ6) 58.3 in. **Rear Tread:** (XJ-S) 59.2 in.; (XJ6) 58.9 in. **Standard Tires:** (XJ-S) 215/70VR15 Pirelli P5.

TECHNICAL: Layout: front-engine, rear-drive. **Transmission:** three-speed automatic. **Standard Final Drive Ratio:** 2.88:1. **Steering:** rack and pinion, power-assisted. **Suspension (front):** upper/lower control arms, coil springs and anti-roll bar. **Suspension (rear):** independent; lower control arms, longitudinal links, coil springs and anti-roll bar. **Brakes:** front/rear disc. **Body Construction:** steel unibody. **Fuel Tank:** (XJ-S) 24 gal.; (XJ6) 23.6 gallon.

MAJOR OPTIONS: Power sunroof: XJ-S ($1300).
Manufacturer: Jaguar Cars Ltd., Coventry, England.
Distributor: Jaguar Cars Inc., Leonia, New Jersey.
HISTORY: Introduced to the U.S. market in October, 1985. An XJ-SC Targa-roofed cabriolet version of the 12-cylinder coupe appeared in the U.S. in spring 1986; see next listing for details.

1987 JAGUAR

1987 Jaguar XJ-S cabriolet. (Jaguar Cars Inc.)

XJ-S/XJ-SC — V-12 — Biggest news was the arrival of a new XJ-SC two-seat cabriolet to join the original V-12 coupe. It debuted in spring 1986, wearing removable Targa roof panels and a manually-operated folding rear-quarter top. Modifications to a standard coupe were performed in England. For the full 1987 model year, the cabriolet added a removable hardtop section with heated rear glass, which could be mounted in place of the standard folding soft top. The cabriolet included full rear luggage-area carpeting and two locking storage bins. Otherwise, standard equipment and appearance changed little, except that a manual override was added to the climate-control system. Drivetrain again was the 326-cid (5.3-liter) V-12 with three-speed automatic transmission.

1987 Jaguar XJ-6 saloon. (Jaguar Cars Inc.)

XJ6 — SIX — Prices jumped sharply on both the base four-door sedan and the plusher Vanden Plas, for what would be their final season in the form that emerged 18 years earlier, in 1969. The six-cylinder engine had a far longer history, dating back to the original XK series. Standard equipment, drivetrain and appearance were similar to 1986. The Vanden Plas edition came with a special wood-veneer dash applique, special exterior emblems, full leather upholstery, rear center armrest, and rear reading lamps.

I.D. DATA: A 17-symbol Vehicle Identification Number is on the top left of the instrument panel, visible through the windshield. Symbols 1-3 indicate origin and make. Symbol four denotes model; symbol five, the restraint system; symbol six, the body style ('1' = four-door sedan; '5' = two-door coupe; '3' = cabriolet). Symbol seven is the engine code; symbol eight, the steering and transmission code. Next is a check digit, followed by a letter indicating model year (H = 1987). Symbol 11 (letter C) identifies the assembly plant, followed by a six-digit sequential production number. Starting serial number: (XJ-S coupe) SAJNV5()4()HC000001; (XJ-S cabriolet) SAJNV3()4()HC000001; (XJ6) SAJAV1()4()HC000001; (Vanden Plas) SAJAY1()4()HC000001.

Model	Body Type & Seating	Engine Type/CID	P.O.E. Price	Weight (lbs.)	Prod. Total
XJ-S	2-dr Coupe-2 + 2P	V12/326	39700	3980	Note 1
XJ-SC	2-dr Cabriolet-2P	V12/326	44850	4040	Note 1
XJ6					
XJ6	4-dr Sedan-5P	I6/258	36300	4064	Note 1
Vand Plas	4-dr Sedan-5P	I6/258	40100	4074	Note 1

Note 1: A total of 22,919 Jaguars were sold in the U.S. during 1987 (17,539 XJ6 sedans and 5,380 XJ-S).

Convertible Note: A true convertible (converted by Hess & Eisenhardt) was announced during the 1987 model year, priced at $47,000.

ENGINE DATA: BASE SIX (XJ6): Inline, dual overhead-cam six-cylinder. Cast iron block and aluminum head. **Displacement:** 258 cu. in. (4235 cc). **Bore & Stroke:** 3.63 x 4.17 in. (92 x 106 mm). **Compression Ratio:** 8.1:1. **Brake Horsepower:** 176 at 4750 rpm. **Torque:** 219 lbs.-ft. at 2500 rpm. Seven main bearings. Thimble tappets. Electronic fuel injection.

BASE V-12 (XJ-S): 60-degree, "vee" type overhead-cam twelve-cylinder. Aluminum block and heads. **Displacement:** 326 cu. in. (5343 cc). **Bore & Stroke:** 3.54 x 2.76 in. (90 x 70 mm). **Compression Ratio:** 11.5:1. **Brake Horsepower:** 262 at 5000 rpm. **Torque:** 290 lbs.-ft. at 3000 rpm. Seven main bearings. Thimble tappets. Electronic fuel injection.

CHASSIS DATA: Wheelbase: (XJ-S) 102 in.; (XJ6) 113 in. **Overall Length:** (XJ-S) 191.3 in.; (XJ6) 199.6 in. **Height:** (XJ-S) 47.8 in.; (XJ6) 52.8 in. **Width:** (XJ-S) 70.6 in.; (XJ6) 69.6 in. **Front Tread:** (XJ-S) 58.6 in.; (XJ6) 58.3 in. **Rear Tread:** (XJ-S) 59.2 in.; (XJ6) 58.9 in.

TECHNICAL: Layout: front-engine, rear-drive. **Transmission:** three-speed automatic. **Standard Final Drive Ratio:** 2.88:1. **Steering:** rack and pinion, power-assisted. **Suspension (front):** upper/lower control arms, coil springs and anti-roll bar. **Suspension (rear):** independent; lower control arms, longitudinal links, coil springs and anti-roll bar. **Brakes:** front/rear disc. **Body Construction:** steel unibody. **Fuel Tank:** (XJ-S) 24 gal.; (XJ6) 23.6 gallon.

Manufacturer: Jaguar Cars Ltd., Coventry, England.
Distributor: Jaguar Cars Inc., Leonia, New Jersey.
HISTORY: Introduced in U.S. in September, 1986. A replacement for the aging XJ6 sedan was expected in spring 1987, but would not arrive until the 1988 model year. Though referred to inside Jaguar as XJ40, the new sedan would be called XJ6 in the U.S., just like its predecessor. In both dimensions and appearance, the new sedan was expected to be similar to the former version, which debuted in 1969.

1988 JAGUAR

XJ-S — V-12 — In addition to the Targa-style cabriolet, Jaguar's 12-cylinder model added a full-fledged convertible this year, after its appearance had been anticipated for some time. The convertible was actually a conversion performed by Hess & Eisenhart, a custom body builder in Cincinnati, Ohio. It had a power top, and was available only on special order. Coupes and Cabriolets had a new center console with wood veneer trim, heated front-seat cushions, and electrically-adjustable lumbar support for the driver's seat. As before, the V-12 engine was hooked to a three-speed automatic transmission.

XJ6 — SIX — The name was the same and appearance didn't change dramatically, but Jaguar's four-door sedans were new this year, for the first time in nearly two decades. Wheelbase was the same 113 inches as before, but overall length dropped 3.2 inches. The new model was also 9.3 inches wider and 1.5 inches taller, yet weight dropped by some 160 pounds. An improvement in drag coefficient also emerged, from the prior 0.44 down to a more slippery 0.37. Beneath the bonnet, replacing the ancient twin-cam inline six, was a new 3.6-liter aluminum version of the six-cylinder engine with four valves per cylinder and multi-point fuel injection. Replacing the former three-speed automatic transmission was a new ZF four-speed unit with overdrive fourth gear. The same unit was used in BMW and Peugeot models. Fully independent suspension was similar to that of the prior XJ6, but modified. Anti-lock braking was added to the four-wheel disc brake system. Standard equipment now included eight-way power front seats, a 13-function "Vehicle Condition Monitor," heated door locks and mirrors, and heated windshield-washer nozzles. As before, both a base and Vanden Plas edition were offered, the latter adding fold-down burl walnut picnic tables on the front seatbacks, headlamp washers, heated front seats, and a limited-slip differential. No options were offered (as had also been the case with the prior model), but the XJ6 list price rose sharply. Standard equipment included power all-disc brakes, power steering, power sunroof, cruise control, electronic AM/FM stereo radio with cassette player and power antenna, automatic-temperature-control air conditioning, center locking, power windows and mirrors, rear defogger, tinted glass, intermittent wipers, telescoping steering column, trip computer, halogen headlamps, and leather-faced seats. Tires were 205/70VR15 Pirelli P5 radials. The Vanden Plas edition added full leather upholstery, woven throw rubs, special wood-veneer dash applique, special body emblems, rear center armrest built storage compartment, and rear reading lamps.

I.D. DATA: A 17-symbol Vehicle Identification Number is on the top left of the instrument panel, visible through the windshield. Symbols 1-3 indicate origin and make. Symbol four denotes model; symbol five, the restraint system; symbol six, the body style ('1' = four-door sedan; '5' = two-door coupe; '3' = cabriolet). Symbol seven is the engine code; symbol eight, the steering and transmission code. Next is a check digit, followed by a letter indicating model year (J = 1988). Symbol 11 (letter C) identifies the assembly plant, followed by a six-digit sequential production number. Starting serial number: (XJ-S coupe/convertible) SAJNV5()4()JC000001; (XJ-S cabriolet) SAJNA3()4()JC000001; (XJ6) SAJHV1()4()JC000001; (Vanden Plas) SA.JKV1()4()JC000001.

Model	Body Type & Seating	Engine Type/CID	P.O.E. Price	Weight (lbs.)	Prod. Total
XJ-S (V-12)					
XJ-S	2-dr Coupe-2 + 2P	V12/326	41500	4040	Note 1
XJ-S	2-dr Conv-2 + 2P	V12/326	49000	4250	Note 1
XJ-SC	2-dr Cabriolet-2P	V12/326	47450	4040	Note 1
XJ6					
XJ6	4-dr Sedan-5P	I6/219	40500	3903	Note 1
Vand Plas	4-dr Sedan-5P	I6/219	44500	3960	Note 1

Note 1: A total of 20,727 Jaguars were sold in the U.S. during 1988 (15,944 XJ6 sedans and 4,783 XJ-S).

ENGINE DATA: BASE SIX (XJ6): Inline, dual overhead-cam six-cylinder. Aluminum block and head. **Displacement:** 219 cu. in. (3590 cc). **Bore & Stroke:** 3.58 x 3.62 in. (91 x 92 mm). **Compression Ratio:** 8.2:1. **Brake Horsepower:** 181 at 4750 rpm. **Torque:** 221 lbs.-ft. at 3750 rpm. Port fuel injection.

BASE V-12 (XJ-S): 60-degree, "vee" type overhead-cam twelve-cylinder. Aluminum block and heads. **Displacement:** 326 cu. in. (5343 cc). **Bore & Stroke:** 3.54 x 2.76 in. (90 x 70 mm). **Compression Ratio:** 11.5:1. **Brake Horsepower:** 262 at 5000 rpm. **Torque:** 290 lbs.-ft. at 3000 rpm. Seven main bearings. Thimble tappets. Port fuel injection.

CHASSIS DATA: Wheelbase: (XJ-S) 102 in.; (XJ6) 113 in. **Overall Length:** (XJ-S) 191.7 in.; (XJ6) 196.4 in. **Height:** (XJ-S) 47.8 in.; (XJ6) 54.3 in. **Width:** (XJ-S) 70.6 in.; (XJ6) 78.9 in. **Front Tread:** (XJ-S) 58.6 in.; (XJ6) 59.1 in. **Rear Tread:** (XJ-S) 59.2 in.; (XJ6) 59.0 in. **Standard Tires:** (XJ6) 205/70VR15 Pirelli P5.

TECHNICAL: Layout: front-engine, rear-drive. **Transmission:** (XJ-S) three-speed automatic; (XJ6) four-speed automatic. **Standard Final Drive Ratio:** 2.88:1. **Steering:** rack and pinion, power-assisted. **Suspension (front):** upper/lower control arms with coil springs and anti-roll bar. **Suspension (rear):** (XJ6) independent with lower control arms, ride-leveling struts and coil springs; (XJ-S) independent with coil springs. **Brakes:** front/rear disc. **Body Construction:** steel unibody. **Fuel Tank:** (XJ-S) 24 gal.; (XJ6) 23.2 gallon.

Manufacturer: Jaguar Cars Ltd., Coventry, England.
Distributor: Jaguar Cars Inc., Leonia, New Jersey.
HISTORY: Introduced to U.S. market in May 1987 except convertible, July 1987.

1989 JAGUAR

1989 Jaguar XJ-S convertible.

XJ-S — V-12 — A sizable price hike was the major change for Jaguar's 12-cylinder models, along with the adoption of ABS. Rather than the former limited-production conversion model, Jaguar offered a two-seat convertible built in its own plant this year. The former Targa-style cabriolet model was dropped. Both coupe and convertible added anti-lock braking, developed jointly by Jaguar and the Alfred Teves Company. The new convertible had a power top and heated glass back window, plus a locking luggage compartment behind the seats. Other new items included electrically-heated seats with power lumbar adjustment, a new steering wheel, and 235/60VR15 Pirelli P600 tires on new alloy wheels. Powertrain remained the familiar 326-cid (5.3-liter) V-12 engine, driving a three-speed automatic transmission. Standard equipment included a tachometer, power windows and door locks, heated power mirrors, cruise control, trip computer, tinted glass, intermittent wipers, AM/FM stereo with cassette player and power antenna, rear defogger, foglamps, and leather-wrapped steering wheel.

XJ6 — SIX — A shorter final-drive ratio (3.58:1 rather than the former 2.88:1) and more powerful engine were the major changes for the Jaguar six-cylinder sedan, introduced in new form for the 1988 model year. The revised engine got a compression boost to 9.6:1, for output of 195 horsepower (versus 181 bhp in its initial form). That change reduced 0-60 mph acceleration time from 10.4 seconds to 9.6 seconds. Jaguar claimed that the modification did not harm fuel mileage significantly, but it did require the use of premium gasoline. Bosch anti-lock braking and a self-leveling suspension were standard. Other standard equipment included power front bucket seats (with leather facings), power windows, power door locks (with infrared remote control), heated power mirrors, intermittent wipers, trip computer, rear defogger and foglamps, tinted glass, folding rear armrest, seatback pockets, console with cassette storage, and a map light. On the dash was an analog tachometer and speedometer, plus LED gauges, and an electronically-tuned AM/FM stereo with channel-19 CB monitor. Pirelli P5 205/70R15 tires rode alloy wheels. A 3.6-liter six-cylinder drive again was hooked to a four-speed automatic transmission. The posh Vanden Plas model added headlamp washers, a limited-slip differential, heated front seats, walnut picnic tables (on seatbacks), full leather seat trim, rear reading lamps, and a rear storage armrest.

1989 Jaguar Vanden Plas. (Jaguar Cars Inc.)

I.D. DATA: A 17-symbol Vehicle Identification Number is on the top left of the instrument panel, visible through the windshield. Symbols 1-3 indicate origin and make. Symbol four denotes model; symbol five, the restraint system; symbol six, the body style ('1' = four-door sedan; '5' = two-door coupe; '4' = convertible). Symbol seven is the engine code; symbol eight, the steering and transmission code. Next is a check digit, followed by a letter indicating model year (K = 1989). Symbol 11 (letter C) identifies the assembly plant, followed by a six-digit sequential production number. Starting serial number: (XJ-

S coupe) SAJNA5()4()JC000001; (XJ-S convertible) SAJNV4()4()JC000001; (XJ6) SAJHY1()4()KC000001; (Vanden Plas) SAJKY1()4()KC000001.

Model	Body Type & Seating	Engine Type/CID	P.O.E. Price	Weight (lbs.)	Prod. Total
XJ-S (V-12)					
XJ-S	2-dr Coupe-2+2P	V12/326	47000	4015	Note 1
XJ-S	2-dr Conv-2P	V12/326	56000	4190	Note 1
XJ6					
XJ6	4-dr Sedan-5P	I6/219	43500	3903	Note 1
Vand Plas	4-dr Sedan-5P	I6/219	47500	3960	Note 1

Note 1: A total of 18,967 Jaguars were sold in the U.S. during 1989 (14,509 XJ6 sedans and 4,458 XJ-S).

ENGINE DATA: BASE SIX (XJ6): Inline, dual overhead-cam six-cylinder (24-valve). Aluminum block and head. **Displacement:** 219 cu. in. (3590 cc). **Bore & Stroke:** 3.58 x 3.62 in. (91 x 92 mm). **Compression Ratio:** 9.6:1. **Brake Horsepower:** 195 at 5000 rpm. **Torque:** 232 lbs.-ft. at 4000 rpm. Port fuel injection.

BASE V-12 (XJ-S): 60-degree, "vee" type overhead-cam twelve-cylinder. Aluminum block and heads. **Displacement:** 326 cu. in. (5343 cc). **Bore & Stroke:** 3.54 x 2.76 in. (90 x 70 mm). **Compression Ratio:** 11.5:1. **Brake Horsepower:** 262 at 5000 rpm. **Torque:** 290 lbs.-ft. at 3000 rpm. Seven main bearings. Thimble tappets. Port fuel injection.

CHASSIS DATA: Wheelbase: (XJ-S) 102 in.; (XJ6) 113 in. **Overall Length:** (XJ-S) 191.7 in.; (XJ6) 196.4 in. **Height:** (XJ-S) 47.8 in.; (XJ6) 54.3 in. **Width:** (XJ-S) 70.6 in.; (XJ6) 78.9 in. **Front Tread:** (XJ-S) 58.6 in.; (XJ6) 59.1 in. **Rear Tread:** (XJ-S) 59.2 in.; (XJ6) 59.0 in. **Standard Tires:** (XJ-S) Pirelli P600 235/60VR15; (XJ6) Pirelli P5 205/70R15.

TECHNICAL: Layout: front-engine, rear-drive. **Transmission:** (XJ-S) three-speed automatic; (XJ6) ZF four-speed automatic. **Standard Final Drive Ratio:** (XJ-S) 2.88:1; (XJ6) 3.58:1. **Steering:** rack and pinion, power-assisted. **Brakes:** front/rear disc. **Suspension (front):** upper/lower control arms with coil springs and anti-roll bar. **Suspension (rear):** (XJ6) independent with lower control arms, ride-leveling struts and coil springs; (XJ-S) independent with coil springs. **Body Construction:** steel unibody. **Fuel Tank:** (XJ-S) 24 gal.; (XJ6) 23.2 gallon.

Manufacturer: Jaguar Cars Ltd., Coventry, England.
Distributor: Jaguar Cars Inc., Leonia, New Jersey.
HISTORY: Introduced to the U.S. market in September, 1988.

1990 JAGUAR

1990 Jaguar XJ-S Collection Rouge. (Jaguar Cars Inc.)

XJ-S — V-12 — A driver's-side airbag became standard in the 12-cylinder coupe and convertible for 1990. This change caused the telescoping steering column to disappear, but a tilt feature was added to replace it. Drivetrain was again the 262-bhp V-12, with three-speed automatic transmission. Standard equipment and appearance were similar to 1989. A limited-production "Collection Rouge" coupe, offered only in Signal Red color, cost $3000 more than the standard four-seat coupe. It included a Magnolia leather interior, elm burl veneer, and diamond-polished alloy wheels.

XJ6 — SIX — The base sedan dropped in price this year, but Jaguar added two additional upgrade models: the Sovereign and Vanden Plas Majestic, for a total of four sedan models. A larger (4.0-liter), more powerful "AJ6" engine became standard, boosting horsepower from 195 to 223. That increase was claimed to cut 0-60 mph acceleration by a full second, down to 8.6 seconds. A new four-speed automatic transmission included two shift modes: sport and normal. To help improve shift quality, new electronic engine controls would momentarily retard the ignition while the car was accelerating. A Teves anti-lock braking system replaced the former Girling/Bosch version, using a booster operated by an electric pump. Gauges were now all analog in style, with warning lights replacing the former Vehicle Condition Monitor system. The base model kept its former quad round headlamps, but all the upgrade models wore new rectangular headlamps. Two formerly-standard features were gone this year: self-levelling suspension and the power sunroof. Standard equipment on the base model included power front bucket seats, leather seat facings, automatic climate control, power windows and door locks, heated power mirrors, heated door locks and windshield washer nozzles, adjustable steering wheel, remote fuel door and decklid releases, rear defogger, AM/FM stereo with cassette player and channel-19 CB monitor, lighted visor mirrors, map light, console with storage, and a folding rear armrest. The Vanden Plas added a limited-slip differential, headlight washers with heated nozzles, footwell rugs, heated front seats, folding burl walnut picnic tables (on front seatbacks), leather-covered seatbacks, rear-armrest storage, foglamps, and rear reading lights. The Sovereign model added hydraulic ride control, a power sunroof, burl walnut inlays, and rear head restraints. The Majestic, which came only in Regency Red body color, included a magnolia leather interior, diamond-polished alloy wheels, and an alarm system.

1990 Jaguar Sovereign sedan.

I.D. DATA: A 17-symbol Vehicle Identification Number is on the top left of the instrument panel, visible through the windshield. Symbols 1-3 indicate origin and make. Symbol four denotes model; symbol five, the restraint system; symbol six, the body style ('1' = four-door sedan; '5' = two-door coupe). Symbol seven is the engine code; symbol eight, the steering and transmission code. Next is a check digit, followed by a letter indicating model year (L = 1990). Symbol 11 (letter C) identifies the assembly plant, followed by a six-digit sequential production number. Starting serial number: (XJ-S coupe) SAJNW5()4()JC000001; (XJ-S convertible) SAJNW4()4()JC000001; (XJ6) SAJFY1()4()LC000001; (Sovereign) SAJHY1()4()LC000001; (Vanden Plas) SAJKY1()4()LC000001; (Majestic) SAJMY1()4()LC000001.

Model	Body Type & Seating	Engine Type/CID	P.O.E. Price	Weight (lbs.)	Prod. Total
XJ-S	2-dr Coupe-4P	V12/326	48000	4015	Note 1
XJ-S	2-dr Conv-2P	V12/326	57000	4190	Note 1
XJ-S COLLECTION ROUGE					
XJ-S	2-dr Coupe-4P	V12/326	51000	4015	Note 1
XJ6					
XJ-6	4-dr Sedan-5P	I6/243	39700	3903	Note 1
SOVEREIGN					
	4-dr Sedan-5P	I6/243	43000	3980	Note 1
VANDEN PLAS					
	4-dr Sedan-5P	I6/243	48000	3975	Note 1
VANDEN PLAS MAJESTIC					
	4-dr Sedan-5P	I6/243	53000	3980	Note 1

Note 1: A total of 18,728 Jaguars were sold in the U.S. during 1990 (14,013 sedans and 4,715 XJ-S models).

ENGINE DATA: BASE SIX (sedans): Inline, dual overhead-cam six-cylinder (AJ6 24-valve). Aluminum block and head. **Displacement:** 243 cu. in. (3980 cc). **Bore & Stroke:** 3.58 x 4.015 in. (91 x 102 mm). **Compression Ratio:** 9.6:1. **Brake Horsepower:** 223 at 4750 rpm. **Torque:** 278 lbs.-ft. at 3650 rpm. Port fuel injection.
BASE V-12 (XJ-S): 60-degree, "vee" type overhead-cam twelve-cylinder. Aluminum block and heads. **Displacement:** 326 cu. in. (5343 cc). **Bore & Stroke:** 3.54 x 2.76 in. (90 x 70 mm). **Compression Ratio:** 11.5:1. **Brake Horsepower:** 262 at 5000 rpm. **Torque:** 290 lbs.-ft. at 3000 rpm. Seven main bearings. Thimble tappets. Port fuel injection.

CHASSIS DATA: Wheelbase: (XJ-S) 102 in.; (sedans) 113 in. **Overall Length:** (XJ-S) 191.7 in.; (sedans) 196.4 in. **Height:** (XJ-S) 47.8 in.; (sedans) 54.3 in. **Width:** (XJ-S) 70.6 in.; (sedans) 78.9 in. **Front Tread:** (XJ-S) 58.6 in.; (sedans) 59.1 in. **Rear Tread:** (XJ-S) 59.2 in.; (sedans) 59.0 in. **Standard Tires:** (XJ-S) Pirelli P600 235/60VR15; (sedans) 205/70VR15.

TECHNICAL: Layout: front-engine, rear-drive. **Transmission:** (XJ-S) three-speed automatic; (sedans) four-speed automatic. **Standard Final Drive Ratio:** (XJ-S) 2.88:1; (sedans) 3.58:1. **Steering:** rack and pinion, power-assisted. **Suspension (front):** upper/lower control arms with coil springs and anti-roll bar. **Suspension (rear):** independent with lower control arms, ride-leveling struts and coil springs; (XJ-S) independent with coil springs. **Brakes:** front/rear disc. **Body Construction:** steel unibody. **Fuel Tank:** (XJ-S cpe) 24 gal.; (XJ-S conv) 21.6 gal.; (sedans) 23.2 gallon.

Manufacturer: Jaguar Cars Ltd. (Jaguar plc), Coventry, England.

Distributor: Jaguar Cars Inc., Mahwah, New Jersey.

HISTORY: Introduced to U.S. market in October 1989 except (sedans) in November 1989.

POSTSCRIPT: Gaining the most attention as the 1990s began was Jaguar's XJ220 super-car, which first appeared at the Birmingham (England) auto show in fall 1989. With a monocoque body of aluminum and magnesium alloy, bonded to a unitized aluminum "tub" frame, the two-seat coupe was estimated to cost $400,000 or more when it entered limited production. Under the hood would be a 6.2-liter V-12 engine, producing at least 500 horsepower, producing a top speed beyond 200 mph and 0-60 mph acceleration around 3.5 seconds. Rumors of production for the U.S. market surfaced periodically, but were quashed in a hurry. Jaguar made it clear that the tiny handful that might be built in the early 1990s were long since spoken for in the European market, and would not be certified for U.S. sale. Estimates of the ultra-sleek supercar's final price tag continued to rise well beyond the half-million-dollar mark.

JENSEN

Like several other American and European makes, the Jensen series of British motorcars resulted from a collaboration of two brothers, Allan and Richard Jensen. Both be-

gan their automotive careers in the 1920s, Richard as an apprentice for the Wolseley firm, and Allan for a radiator company. In 1923, they tore apart a new Austin Chummy to turn it into a sporty two-seater, entering the modified roadster in a hillclimb. One of the onlookers, an impressed chief engineer from the Standard Motor Company, then asked the brothers to produce a similarly-appealing body on a Standard chassis. The finished product led to a production version, the Avon Standard, late in the decade.

Seeking an opportunity to start their own concern rather than continue to work for others, the brothers first embarked upon expanded careers as directors of a small coachbuilder, W.J. Smith & Sons, and in 1934 took over that company, adopting the name Jensen Motors Ltd. In addition to creating bodies for other manufacturers (including Morris and Wolseley), they yearned to turn out a car under their own name. American actor Clark Gable assisted in that evolution when he shipped a Ford chassis overseas to be fitted with one of Jensen's low-slung bodies. Popularity of replicas of the Gable car led to the introduction of an all-out Jensen, based on a modified Ford V-8 engine and chassis, in 1935. Both 2.5- and 3.5-liter versions were produced, with a standard two-speed Columbia rear axle and hydraulic clutch. Edsel Ford himself authorized the supply of Ford components to the Jensens. An S-type four-door saloon soon joined the original tourer, along with a drophead coupe.

Just before the war came the announcement of a Type H, powered by a Nash straight eight or Lincoln V-12. Production switched instead to military-related vehicles for the duration, but civilian work resumed quickly in 1946, with the announcement of a Meadows-engined PW saloon. That aluminum-block straight-eight powerplant developed problems, but subsequent 4-liter six-cylinder engines came from Austin's big Sheerline series. Those found their way into both the Jensen saloon and the new Interceptor cabriolet (a name that would last through the 1950s and be revived again in the 1960s). The Jensen firm also produced bodies for Austin's A40 sports models in the early '50s. Jensens began to gain modest recognition in the U.S. with the advent of the Interceptor, but imports never reached significant numbers until the 1970s, shortly before the firm's demise.

What was then a startling innovation appeared at the 1953 London Motor Show: the stylish, fiberglass-bodied 541 GT saloon (really a two-door coupe) capable of 115 mph. Corvettes had only recently appeared, and fiberglass was even less commonly seen on European car bodies. Yet another important innovation emerged by 1957: disc brakes on all four wheels. Also in that year came a move to new quarters in West Bromwich. In addition to its own 541 and Interceptor models, Jensen continued to produce bodies for various manufacturers, including Austin-Healeys and the Volvo P1800 and, later, the Sunbeam Tiger. Automatic shift became available in 1960. Then, in 1963, a new Chrysler-powered C-V8 replaced the 541. Two years later came two further innovations, a bit ahead of their time: four-wheel drive and anti-skid braking. The Interceptor name was revived in 1966, this time carrying a 6.2-liter Chrysler V-8 and capable of speeds near 140 mph. Four-wheel drive was available, too.

By 1967, both brothers had retired, but Jensen remained in the car manufacturing business for nearly a decade longer. Financial difficulties led to a takeover by a Norwegian-born American car dealer, Kjell Qvale and the installation of Donald Healey (and his son Geoffrey) on the board. The result of the Healey connection came at the 1972 Geneva Show in the form of a Jensen-Healey that, in production form, ran with a 16-valve slant four-cylinder engine developed by Lotus. Unfortunately, that powerplant had reliability problems that contributed to lack of interest in the car, and consequent weak sales. The addition of a

GT Estate version didn't help. By spring 1976, receivers had taken over and the assets went under the auctioneer's hammer. A different company was formed to handle parts and service, and, later, import cars into Britain. Actually, the Jensen Parts & Services company hung on well into the 1980s, prepared to custom-build all-new Interceptors based on the 1970s design.

Body Type Note: factory brochures referred to the closed two-door Jensens as saloons (sedans), the term used in this Catalog, though American publications often described them as coupes.

1946-48 JENSEN

1947 Jensen "Straight Eight" saloon.

Soon after the end of World War II, Jensen began to produce a PW straight-eight saloon model, to replace the final prewar HC with its 120-horsepower, 257-cid Nash straight eight engine. The PW was intended to carry a 236-cid Meadows straight eight with aluminum block and rating of 130 bhp. Problems with the new engine led to its quick demise, after only about three were built. A handful more were powered by leftover HC (Nash) engines, as in the 1939 design. Not until the arrival of Austin Princess six-cylinder engines for 1949 did production of the PW saloon reach significant numbers. Both saloons were of conventional design with a vee-shaped grille. The prewar HC version had a three-speed transmission plus two-speed rear axle, with a transverse leaf spring for the front suspension and coil springs at the rear. Its box-section steel chassis held aluminum body paneling over a wooden framework. Mechanical brakes were used. Wheelbase was 131 inches and the car measured 198 inches overall. The postwar PW had a four-speed gearbox with overdrive. Wishbones and coil springs were used up front, while the rear held coil springs, radius arms and a Panhard rod. Girling hydraulic drum brakes provided the stopping power. Wheelbase was 126 inches, and the PW measured 197 inches overall.

1949-51 JENSEN

1950 Jensen Interceptor drophead coupe.

336

INTERCEPTOR — SIX — Rakishly handsome, the new open Jensen rode a 112.5-inch wheelbase, and measured 188 inches overall. Beneath the bonnet of the new two-door cabriolet (drophead coupe) was an Austin six-cylinder engine of 3993-cc displacement, rated 130 horsepower. Although the factory claimed top speeds approaching 105 mph, road tests produced velocities closer to 95 mph. Low piston speed, on the other hand, allowed quick cruising with minimal engine wear. The four-speed gearbox was synchronized on the upper three gears, and came with overdrive. Suspension was independent up front, with coil springs and wishbones. Semi-elliptic leaf springs brought up the rear. Aluminum panels were mounted on a wooden framework, atop a box-section steel chassis with tubular center portion. Girling hydraulic drum brakes were used. Appearance was similar to the yet-unannounced Austin A40 Sports model, including the grille shape, which wasn't wholly surprising since the Jensen firm also built that body. The pontoon-profile Interceptor body had full wheel openings, a one-piece windshield, inboard built-in headlamps, and front vent windows. Thick horizontal bars sat in the recessed grille opening, which was flat on the bottom but curved across the top and sides. A wide insignia at the hood front looked almost like an airscoop. Bench-type seating was advertised as being suitable for four. The convertible top's back and quarter windows were made of Perspex, which slipped into body recesses as the roof lowered. Air intake vents for the brakes were added late in 1950, alongside the grille.

PW — SIX — A second-generation PW saloon debuted in 1949 and remained in production into early 1952, powered by the same 3993-cc Austin six-cylinder engine as the new Interceptor.

I.D. DATA: Chassis serial number is stamped on a plate on the bulkhead, under the hood. Starting serial number: (PW) PWA/46799; (Interceptor) INT/12502. Engine number is on the block, below Number 2 spark plug.

Model	Body Type & Seating	Engine Type/CID	P.O.E. Price	Weight (lbs.)	Prod. Total
INTERCEPTOR					
PW	2-dr Cabr-4P	I6/244	Note 2	2800	Note 1
PW	4-dr Saloon	I6/244	N/A	3584	Note 1

Note 1: Only two Jensens were thought to have been sold in the U.S. during 1950, and one in 1951. Auto Age magazine in 1953 claimed there was only one Jensen in the country.

Note 2: Interceptor price was about $3600 at the factory in England.

Weight Note: Interceptor weight shown is "dry" measure.

ENGINE DATA: BASE SIX: Inline, overhead-valve six-cylinder. Cast iron block. **Displacement:** 243.6 cu. in. (3993 cc). **Bore & Stroke:** 3.43 x 4.37 in. (87 x 111 mm). **Compression Ratio:** 6.8:1. **Brake Horsepower:** 130 at 3700/4000 rpm. Four main bearings. Solid valve lifters. Stromberg downdraft carburetor. 12-volt electrical.

CHASSIS DATA: Wheelbase: (Inter) 112.5 in.; (PW) 126 in. **Overall Length:** (Inter) 188 in.; (PW) 197 in. **Height:** (Inter) 58 in. **Width:** (Inter) 66 in.; (PW) 70 in. **Front Tread:** (Inter) 54 in.; (PW) 58 in. **Rear Tread:** (Inter) 57 in.; (PW) 59 in. **Wheel Type:** steel disc. **Standard Tires:** (Inter) 5.50x16; (PW) 6.50x16.

TECHNICAL: Layout: front-engine, rear-drive. **Transmission:** four-speed manual; floor lever. Interceptor overall gear ratios: (1st) 11.05:1; (2nd) 6.06:1; (3rd) 4.11:1; (4th) 3.22:1. **Standard Final Drive Ratio:** (Inter) 3.22:1; (PW) 3.70:1. **Steering:** cam and roller. **Suspension (front):** wishbones and coil springs. **Suspension (rear):** (Inter) rigid axle with semi-elliptic leaf springs; (PW) coil springs with radius arms and Panhard rod. **Brakes:** Girling hydraulic, front/rear drum. **Body Construction:** aluminum body over wooden framework; box-section steel chassis with tubular center section. **Fuel Tank:** (Inter) 15.6 U.S. gallons.

PERFORMANCE: Top Speed: (Inter) about 102 mph. **Acceleration (0-60 mph):** (Inter) 12.5 seconds (0-70 mph in 17.8 seconds). **Acceleration (quarter-mile):** (Inter) about 19 seconds.

Manufacturer: Jensen Motors Ltd., West Bromwich, Staffordshire, England.

HISTORY: Interceptor cabriolet and PW saloon introduced in September 1949. Production of the PW ended by early 1952.

1952 JENSEN

INTERCEPTOR — SIX — A hardtop coupe (called a saloon) version joined the original cabriolet for the 1952 model year, with opening rear quarter windows. Standard equipment included a Smith's heater.

I.D. DATA: Chassis serial number is stamped on a plate on the bulkhead, under the hood. Starting serial number: (Interceptor cabr) INT/62720; (Interceptor saloon) INT/82801. Engine number is on the block, below Number 2 spark plug.

Model	Body Type & Seating	Engine Type/CID	P.O.E. Price	Weight (lbs.)	Prod. Total
INTERCEPTOR					
	2-dr Cabr-4P	I6/244	N/A	3135	N/A
	2-dr Saloon-4P	I6/244	N/A	3135	N/A

ENGINE DATA: BASE SIX: Inline, overhead-valve six-cylinder. Cast iron block. **Displacement:** 243.6 cu. in. (3993 cc). **Bore & Stroke:** 3.43 x 4.37 in. (87 x 111 mm). **Compression Ratio:** 6.8:1. **Brake Horsepower:** 130 at 4000 rpm. Four main bearings. Solid valve lifters. Stromberg/Zenith downdraft carburetor. 12-volt electrical.

CHASSIS DATA: Wheelbase: 112.5 in. **Overall Length:** 188 in. **Height:** 58 in. **Width:** 66 in. **Front Tread:** 54.5 in. **Rear Tread:** 57 in. **Wheel Type:** vented steel disc. **Standard Tires:** Dunlop 6.00x16.

TECHNICAL: Layout: front-engine, rear-drive. **Transmission:** four-speed manual; floor lever. **Standard Final Drive Ratio:** 3.22:1. **Steering:** cam and roller. **Suspension (front):** wishbones and coil springs. **Suspension (rear):** rigid axle with semi-elliptic leaf springs. **Brakes:** hydraulic, front/rear drum. **Body Construction:** aluminum body over wooden framework; box-section steel chassis with tubular center section. **Fuel Tank:** 15.6 U.S. gallons.

PERFORMANCE: Top Speed: 102-105 mph; road tests managed 95-97 mph. **Acceleration (0-60 mph):** 12.5 sec. (0-70 mph in 17 sec.). **Acceleration (quarter-mile):** about 19 seconds.

Manufacturer: Jensen Motors Ltd., West Bromwich, Staffordshire, England.

HISTORY: Interceptor saloon introduced in October 1951.

1953 JENSEN

INTERCEPTOR — SIX — For the 1953 model year, parking lights were moved to the fender tops and bodysides added a bright rub strip. Laycock de Normanville overdrive also became available. Both models were now advertised as being suitable for five passengers. Standard equipment also included a tachometer, ammeter, oil pressure gauge, temperature gauge, fuel gauge, electric clock, trafficators (turn signals), leather-covered instrument panel, and twin-tone horns.

I.D. DATA: Chassis serial number is stamped on a plate on the bulkhead, under the hood. Starting serial number: (Interceptor) INT/233452. Engine number is on the block, below Number 2 spark plug.

Model	Body Type & Seating	Engine Type/CID	P.O.E. Price	Weight (lbs.)	Prod. Total
INTERCEPTOR					
	2-dr Cabr-5P	I6/244	Note 1	3135	N/A
	2-dr Saloon-5P	I6/244	N/A	3135	N/A

Note 1: Cabriolet price in England was 1700 pounds (Sterling), plus purchase tax.

ENGINE DATA: BASE SIX: Inline, overhead-valve six-cylinder. Cast iron block. **Displacement:** 243.6 cu. in. (3993 cc). **Bore & Stroke:** 3.43 x 4.37 in. (87 x 111 mm). **Compression Ratio:** 6.8:1. **Brake Horsepower:** 130 at 4000 rpm. Four main bearings. Solid valve lifters. Stromberg/Zenith downdraft carburetor. 12-volt electrical.

CHASSIS DATA: Wheelbase: 112.5 in. **Overall Length:** 188 in. **Height:** 58 in. **Width:** 66 in. **Front Tread:** 54.5 in. **Rear Tread:** 57 in. **Wheel Type:** vented steel disc. **Standard Tires:** Dunlop 6.00x16.

TECHNICAL: Layout: front-engine, rear-drive. **Transmission:** four-speed manual (plus overdrive); floor lever. Overdrive (overall) gear ratios: (1st) 12.75:1; (2nd) 8.78:1; (3rd) 5.40:1; (4th) 3.77:1; (OD) 2.85:1; (rev) 15.4:1. **Standard Final Drive Ratio:** 3.77:1. **Steering:** cam and roller. **Suspension (front):** wishbones and coil springs. **Suspension (rear):** rigid axle with semi-elliptic leaf springs. **Brakes:** hydraulic, front/rear drum. **Body Construction:** aluminum body over wooden framework; box-section steel chassis with tubular center section. **Fuel Tank:** 13 (Imperial) gallons.

MAJOR OPTIONS: Laycock de Normanville overdrive. H.M.V. radio.

PERFORMANCE: Top Speed: 105 mph (factory); road tests managed 95-97 mph. **Acceleration (0-60 mph):** 13 seconds (factory). **Acceleration (quarter-mile):** 19 seconds (factory). **Fuel Mileage:** 20-24 mpg (British measure); about 15 mpg (U.S.).

Manufacturer: Jensen Motors Ltd., West Bromwich, Staffordshire, England.

HISTORY: 1953 models introduced in September 1952. Exercising the penchant for British understatement, *The Motor* magazine noted that the Interceptor's "good handling and effortless cruising are commendable features."

1954-55 JENSEN

1954 Jensen 541.

INTERCEPTOR — SIX — For the 1954 model year, the Interceptor's hood line was lowered. Front ends also dispensed with the former chromed grille surround molding and badge. The open Interceptor was now called a convertible rather than a cabriolet. For 1955, Interceptors came in standard and Deluxe trim. Deluxe models came with a radio, windshield washer, higher-powered headlamps, pass and driving lamps, and two-speed wiper.

541 — SIX — A shorter-wheelbase Jensen saloon (actually a two-door coupe) joined the Interceptor for the 1954 model year. Although smoother in profile, with a touch of the Italian in its lines, basic appearance was similar to the original model. Body construction, on the other hand, was something far different. The 541 wore a body made of resin-bonded fiberglass — the first four-seater production car to turn to 'glass. Three distinct moldings were used: one for the whole front end, a second for the roof, and a third for the rear end. Doors were made of light alloy. Credit for the design goes to Richard Jensen, with the assistance of Eric Neale. The low, curvy fastback body with rear quarter windows rode a new chassis with coil springs in front and semi-elliptic leaf springs at the rear, similar to the Interceptor. Powerplants also were similar, with the 541 using the same 3993-cc six-cylinder engine, as installed in the Austin Princess, with three carburetors. Top speeds around 112 mph were claimed. A curved one-piece windshield was used. Small round parking lights sat below the built-in headlamps, which flanked an oval grille opening. A front-fender crease tapered to a point at the front and rear. A wraparound back window went into the fastback rear end, and wheel openings were fully rounded.

I.D. DATA: Chassis serial number is stamped on a plate on the bulkhead, under the hood. Starting serial number: (Interceptor) INT/273456; (541) 541/24563. Engine number is on the block, below Number 2 spark plug.

Model	Body Type & Seating	Engine Type/CID	P.O.E. Price	Weight (lbs.)	Prod. Total
INTERCEPTOR					
	2-dr Conv-5P	I6/244	Note 1	3300	N/A
	2-dr Saloon-5P	I6/244	Note 1	3150	N/A
541					
541	2-dr Saloon-4P	I6/244	Note 2	2688	N/A

Note 1: Interceptor price at the factory was about $4777 in 1955.

Note 2: Price for the 541 in England was 2146 pounds (Sterling), or $3610; price in U.S. was estimated at about $4500.

Model Note: Standard and Deluxe versions of the Interceptor saloon and convertible became available for the 1955 model year.

ENGINE DATA: BASE SIX (Interceptor): Inline, overhead-valve six-cylinder. Cast iron block. **Displacement:** 243.6 cu. in. (3993 cc). **Bore & Stroke:** 3.43 x 4.37 in. (87 x 111 mm). **Compression Ratio:** 6.8:1. **Brake Horsepower:** 130 at 4000 rpm. Four main bearings. Solid valve lifters. Stromberg/Zenith downdraft carburetor. 12-volt electrical.

BASE SIX (541): Same as above, except — Three SU carburetors.

CHASSIS DATA: Wheelbase: (Inter) 112.5 in.; (541) 105 in. **Overall Length:** (Inter) 188 in.; (541) 178 in. **Height:** (Inter) 58 in.; (541) 53 in. **Width:** (Inter) 66 in.; (541) 63 in. **Front Tread:** (Inter) 54.5 in.; (541) 52 in. **Rear Tread:** (Inter) 57 in.; (541) 52 in. **Wheel Type:** vented steel disc. **Standard Tires:** (Inter) Dunlop 6.00x16; (541) 5.50x16.

TECHNICAL: Layout: front-engine, rear-drive. **Transmission:** four-speed manual; overdrive available; floor lever. Interceptor w/overdrive (overall) gear ratios: (1st) 12.75:1; (2nd) 8.78:1; (3rd) 5.40:1; (4th) 3.77:1; (OD) 2.85:1; (rev) 15.4:1. **Standard Final Drive Ratio:** (Interceptor) 3.77:1 (changed to 4.09:1 during 1954); (541) 3.31:1 or 3.54:1. **Steering:** cam and roller. **Suspension (front):** wishbones and coil springs. **Suspension (rear):** rigid axle with semi-elliptic leaf springs. **Brakes:** hydraulic, front/rear drum. **Body Construction:** (Inter) aluminum body over wooden framework, on box-section steel chassis with tubular center section; (541) fiberglass body on box-section tubular steel chassis.

MAJOR OPTIONS: (541) Laycock de Normanville overdrive. Special cylinder and intake system. Tachometer. Windshield washer. Heater/demister. Al-fin brake drums. Wire wheels and 6.40x15 Dunlop "road speed" tires. (Interceptor) H.M.V. radio.

PERFORMANCE: Top Speed: (Interceptor) 105 mph (factory) but road tests managed 95-97 mph; (541) 108 mph (factory) w/3.3:1 axle, 115-120 mph w/3.54:1 axle. **Acceleration (0-60 mph):** (Interceptor) 13 seconds (factory); (541) 11.7 seconds (factory w/3.3:1 axle). **Acceleration (quarter-mile):** (Interceptor) 19 seconds (factory); (541) 18 seconds. **Fuel Mileage:** (Interceptor) 20-24 mpg (British measure).

Manufacturer: Jensen Motors Ltd., West Bromwich, Staffordshire, England.

HISTORY: 541 introduced at London Motor Show in October 1953.

1956 JENSEN

1956 Jensen 541.

INTERCEPTOR — SIX — Rectangular air vents were added to the sides of front fenders this year, and Deluxe models added twin horizontal trim strips. Otherwise, both the saloon and convertible continued with little change.

541 — SIX — Little changed this year except for the addition of rectangular air vents and a trim strip on the sides of the front fenders.

I.D. DATA: Chassis serial number is stamped on a plate on the bulkhead, under the hood. Starting serial number: (Interceptor) INT/624993. Engine number is on the block, below Number 2 spark plug.

Model	Body Type & Seating	Engine Type/CID	P.O.E. Price	Weight (lbs.)	Prod. Total
INTERCEPTOR					
	2-dr Conv-5P	I6/244	Note 1	3300	N/A
	2-dr Saloon-5P	I6/244	Note 1	3150	N/A
541					
541	2-dr Saloon-4P	I6/244	Note 2	2688	N/A

Note 1: Interceptor price at the factory was about $4760.

Note 2: Price for the 541 in England was about $3416.

ENGINE DATA: BASE SIX (Interceptor): Inline, overhead-valve six-cylinder. Cast iron block. **Displacement:** 243.6 cu. in. (3993 cc). **Bore & Stroke:** 3.43 x 4.37 in. (87 x 111 mm). **Compression Ratio:** 6.8:1. **Brake Horsepower:** 130 at 4000 rpm. Four main bearings. Solid valve lifters. Stromberg/Zenith downdraft carburetor. 12-volt electrical.

BASE SIX (541): Same as above, except -- Three SU carburetors.

CHASSIS DATA: Wheelbase: (Inter) 112.5 in.; (541) 105 in. **Overall Length:** (Inter) 188 in.; (541) 178 in. **Height:** (Inter) 58 in.; (541) 53 in. **Width:** (Inter) 66 in.; (541); 63 in. **Front Tread:** (Inter) 54.5 in.; (541) 52 in. **Rear Tread:** (Inter) 57 in.; (541) 52 in. **Wheel Type:** vented steel disc. **Standard Tires:** (Inter) Dunlop 6.00x16; (541) 5.50x16.

TECHNICAL: Layout: front-engine, rear-drive. **Transmission:** four-speed manual; overdrive available; floor lever. **Standard Final Drive Ratio:** (541) 3.31:1 or 3.54:1. **Steering:** cam and roller. **Suspension (front):** wishbones and coil springs. **Suspension (rear):** rigid axle with semi-elliptic leaf springs. **Brakes:** hydraulic, front/rear drum. **Body Construction:** (Inter) aluminum body over wooden framework, on box-section steel chassis with tubular center section; (541) fiberglass body on box-section tubular steel chassis.

MAJOR OPTIONS: Similar to 1954-55.

PERFORMANCE: Top Speed: (Interceptor) 105 mph (factory) but road tests managed 95-97 mph; (541) 108 mph (factory) w/3.3:1 axle, 115-120 mph w/3.54:1 axle. **Acceleration (0-60 mph):** (Interceptor) 13 seconds (factory); (541) 11.7 seconds (factory w/3.3:1 axle). **Acceleration (quarter-mile):** (Interceptor) 19 seconds (factory); (541) 18 seconds. **Fuel Mileage:** (Interceptor) 20-24 mpg (British measure).

Manufacturer: Jensen Motors Ltd., West Bromwich, Staffordshire, England.

1957 JENSEN

INTERCEPTOR — SIX — The convertible and saloon continued with minimal change, into the 1957 model year. The five-passenger saloon contained 27 cubic feet of luggage space. The spare tire went below the trunk floor, accessible without disturbing luggage. As before, Interceptors wore an aluminum body on a pressed steel frame.

541 — SIX — A DeLuxe 541 this year brought a major innovation: four-wheel disc brakes. Thus, Jensen became the first production vehicle with discs at all wheels. The DeLuxe also included dual exhausts, overdrive, a higher-compression cylinder head, and 15-inch wheels. An adjustable steering column and power brakes were standard on 541 models.

I.D. DATA: Chassis serial number is stamped on a plate on the bulkhead, under the hood. Starting serial number: (Interceptor conv) INT/795388; (Interceptor saloon) INT/775126; (541 DeL) 541/1265803. Engine number is on the block, below Number 2 spark plug.

Model	Body Type & Seating	Engine Type/CID	P.O.E. Price	Weight (lbs.)	Prod. Total
INTERCEPTOR					
	2-dr Conv-5P	I6/244	N/A	3300	N/A
	2-dr Saloon-5P	I6/244	N/A	3150	N/A
541					
541	2-dr Saloon-4P	I6/244	Note 1	3024	N/A
541 DeL	2-dr Saloon-4P	I6/244	Note 1	30024	N/A

Note 1: Price for the 541 in England was about $4018.

ENGINE DATA: BASE SIX (Interceptor): Inline, overhead-valve six-cylinder. Cast iron block. **Displacement:** 243.6 cu. in. (3993 cc). **Bore & Stroke:** 3.43 x 4.37 in. (87 x 111 mm). **Compression Ratio:** 6.8:1 (7.4:1 optional). **Brake Horsepower:** 130 at 4000 rpm. Four main bearings. Solid valve lifters. Stromberg/Zenith downdraft carburetor. 12-volt electrical.

BASE SIX (541): Same as above, except — Three SU carburetors.

CHASSIS DATA: Wheelbase: (Inter) 112.5 in.; (541) 105 in. **Overall Length:** (Inter) 188 in.; (541) 178 in. **Height:** (Inter) 58 in.; (541) 53 in. **Width:** (Inter) 66 in.; (541); 63 in. **Front Tread:** (Inter) 54.5 in.; (541) 52 in. **Rear Tread:** (Inter) 57 in.; (541) 52 in. **Wheel Type:** vented steel disc. **Standard Tires:** (Inter) Dunlop 6.00x16; (541) 5.50x16 or 6.40x15.

TECHNICAL: Layout: front-engine, rear-drive. **Transmission:** four-speed manual; overdrive available; floor lever. **Standard Final Drive Ratio:** (541) 3.31:1 or 3.54:1. **Steering:** cam and roller. **Suspension (front):** wishbones and coil springs. **Suspension (rear):** rigid axle with semi-elliptic leaf springs. **Brakes:** hydraulic, front/rear drum except (541 DeL) four-wheel disc. **Body Construction:** (Inter) aluminum body over wooden framework, on box-section steel chassis with tubular center section; (541) fiberglass body on box-section tubular steel chassis. **Fuel Tank:** (541) 15 Imperial gallons.

MAJOR OPTIONS: Laycock de Normanville overdrive. Special cylinder head. Dual exhaust system. Tachometer. Windshield washers. Heater. Special leather upholstery.

PERFORMANCE: Top Speed: (Interceptor) about 105 mph; (541) 115+ mph. **Acceleration (0-60 mph):** (Interceptor) about 13 seconds; (541) 11.7 seconds (factory w/3.3:1 axle). **Acceleration (quarter-mile):** (Interceptor) about 19 seconds; (541) 18 seconds. **Fuel Mileage:** (Interceptor) 20-24 mpg; (541) 20-24 mpg.

Manufacturer: Jensen Motors Ltd., West Bromwich, Staffordshire, England.

1958 JENSEN

INTERCEPTOR — SIX — Only the saloon (sedan) version remained for the 1958 model year; the Interceptor convertible was dropped during 1957.

541 — SIX — While the standard and DeLuxe 541 two-door saloons continued with little change, the big news was the appearance of a new 541R model with torpedo-shaped horizontal (protruding) moldings along the front and rear fenders, above the wheel openings. A horizontal trim bar with large round center emblem sat at the front of the tightly mesh-patterned oval grille. The engine was essentially the same Austin-evolved six-cylinder unit as before, but the 541R had a redesigned cylinder head with two SU carburetors on the right side (instead of three on the left) and higher compression, for 10 more horsepower. Rack and pinion steering replaced the usual cam and roller arrangement. Laycock de Normanville overdrive was standard. A swiveling air-intake shutter was

driver-controlled. Leather bucket front seats and a bench rear seat were standard in all 541 models. The whole front end hinged forward. Standard 541 colors included Black, Ivory, Reno Red, Princess Grey, Botticelli Blue, and Deep Carriage Green.

1958 Jensen 541R.

I.D. DATA: Chassis serial number is stamped on a plate on the bulkhead, under the hood. Starting serial number: (541) 541/1973197; (541R) 541R/3013607. Engine number is on the block, below Number 2 spark plug.

Model	Body Type & Seating	Engine Type/CID	P.O.E. Price	Weight (lbs.)	Prod. Total
INTERCEPTOR					
	2-dr Saloon-5P	I6/244	N/A	3584	N/A
541					
541	2-dr Saloon-4P	I6/244	Note 1	2964	N/A
541 DeL	2-dr Saloon-4P	I6/244	Note 1	3078	N/A
541R	2-dr Saloon-4P	I6/244	Note 1	3078	N/A

Note 1: Price for the 541 in England was about $4018; price in U.S. was about $6000 (on special order).

ENGINE DATA: BASE SIX (Interceptor): Inline, overhead-valve six-cylinder. Cast iron block. **Displacement:** 243.6 cu. in. (3993 cc). **Bore & Stroke:** 3.43 x 4.37 in. (87 x 111 mm). **Compression Ratio:** 6.8:1. **Brake Horsepower:** 130 at 4000 rpm. Four main bearings. Solid valve lifters. Stromberg/Zenith downdraft carburetor. 12-volt electrical.

BASE SIX (541): Same as above, except — **Compression Ratio:** (DeL) 7.4:1. Three SU horizontal carburetors.

BASE SIX (541R): Same as above, except — **Compression Ratio:** 7.6:1. **Brake Horsepower:** 140 at 4000 rpm. Two SU carburetors (later, three).

Note: Some American sources reported horsepower ratings as high as 152 for the 541R.

CHASSIS DATA: Wheelbase: (Inter) 112.5 in.; (541) 105 in. **Overall Length:** (Inter) 188 in.; (541) 178 in. **Height:** (Inter) 58 in.; (541) 53 in. **Width:** (Inter) 66 in.; (541); 63 in. **Front Tread:** (Inter) 54.5 in.; (541) 52 in. **Rear Tread:** (Inter) 57 in.; (541) 51.4 in. **Wheel Type:** vented steel disc except (541 DeL) wire. **Standard Tires:** (Inter) 6.00x16; (541) Dunlop 5.50x16; (541 DeL) Dunlop 6.40x15 "Road Speed;" (541R) 5.50x16 or 6.40x15.

TECHNICAL: Layout: front-engine, rear-drive. **Transmission:** four-speed manual; overdrive available; floor lever. **Standard Final Drive Ratio:** (541) 2.93:1 or 3.54:1. **Steering:** cam and roller except (541R) rack and pinion. **Suspension (front):** wishbones and coil springs. **Suspension (rear):** rigid axle with semi-elliptic leaf springs. **Brakes:** hydraulic, front/rear drum except (541R and DeL) four-wheel disc. **Body Construction:** (Inter) aluminum body over wooden framework, on box-section steel chassis with tubular center section; (541) fiberglass body on box-section tubular steel chassis. **Fuel Tank:** (541) 15 Imperial gallons.

MAJOR OPTIONS: (541) Overdrive. Special head and dual exhausts. Tachometer. Heater/demister. 15-inch wire wheels with 6.40x15 tires. Windshield washer.

Note: Options listed above were included in the DeLuxe and 541R models.

PERFORMANCE: Top Speed: (Interceptor) about 105 mph; (541 DeL) 115-120 mph w/3.54:1 axle and OD (factory); (541R) 125 mph (factory). **Acceleration (0-60 mph):** (Interceptor) about 13 seconds; (541) 10.7 seconds (factory); (541R) 9.3 seconds (factory). **Acceleration (quarter-mile):** (Interceptor) about 19 seconds; (541) 18-18.4 seconds (factory); (541R) 17.5 seconds (factory). **Fuel Mileage:** 20-24 mpg (British measurements).

Manufacturer: Jensen Motors Ltd., West Bromwich, Staffordshire, England.

HISTORY: This was the final season for the Interceptor, though the name would return a few years later. The 541R was introduced in October 1957 at the London Motor Show.

1959-60 JENSEN

541R — SIX — The standard and DeLuxe 541s were dropped after 1958 (though a few may have been produced early in the '59 model year; see previous listing for details). All the focus was on the higher-performance 541R, introduced for 1958, which continued with little change. The 541R was capable of a 125-mph top speed, according to the factory, with disc brakes all around to provide stopping power. It could accelerate from a standing start to 100 mph in 27 seconds. Leather upholstery was standard for the seats as well as on protective pads and rail. Either 16-inch Dunlop tires were offered, or 6.40x15 tires on wire wheels. An adjustable steering column was used, with rack-and-pinion steering. In addition to a redesigned head, the 541R had a longer-dwell camshaft and stiffer crankshaft than the ordinary 541. The forward part of the chassis was all new, with a stiffer wall structure. Armstrong piston-type shocks replaced the usual telescopic units. Ahead of the three-spoke steering wheel stood a tachometer and speedometer. The luggage compartment lid was hinged at top, with the spare tire in separate compartment below.

I.D. DATA: Chassis serial number is stamped on a plate on the bulkhead, under the hood. Engine number is on the block, below Number 2 spark plug.

Model	Body Type & Seating	Engine Type/CID	P.O.E. Price	Weight (lbs.)	Prod. Total
541R	2-dr Saloon-4P	I6/244	Note 1	3078	N/A

Note 1: Price for the 541R in England was about $5348.

ENGINE DATA: BASE SIX (541R): Inline, overhead-valve six-cylinder. Cast iron block. **Displacement:** 243.6 cu. in. (3993 cc). **Bore & Stroke:** 3.43 x 4.37 in. (87 x 111 mm). **Compression Ratio:** 7.6:1. **Brake Horsepower:** 140 at 4000 rpm. Four main bearings. Solid valve lifters. Two or three SU horizontal carburetors. 12-volt electrical.

Note: Some American sources reported horsepower ratings as high as 152 for the 541R.

CHASSIS DATA: Wheelbase: 105 in. **Overall Length:** 178 in. **Height:** 53 in. **Width:** 63 in. **Front Tread:** 52 in. **Rear Tread:** 51.4 in. **Wheel Type:** disc or wire. **Standard Tires:** 5.50x16 or Dunlop 6.40x15 "Road Speed."

TECHNICAL: Layout: front-engine, rear-drive. **Transmission:** four-speed manual with overdrive; floor lever. **Standard Final Drive Ratio:** 3.31:1. **Steering:** rack and pinion. **Suspension (front):** wishbones and coil springs. **Suspension (rear):** rigid axle with semi-elliptic leaf springs. **Brakes:** power front/rear disc. **Body Construction:** fiberglass body on box-section tubular steel chassis. **Fuel Tank:** 15 (Imperial) gallons.

PERFORMANCE: Top Speed: 125 mph (factory). **Acceleration (0-60 mph):** 9.3 seconds (factory). **Acceleration (quarter-mile):** 17.5 seconds (factory). **Fuel Mileage:** 20-24 mpg (British measurements).

Manufacturer: Jensen Motors Ltd., West Bromwich, Staffordshire, England.

HISTORY: Production of the 541R continued until the introduction of the 541S in October 1960. Jensen signed an agreement in 1960 to produce bodies for the stylish Volvo P1800 sports car.

1961-62 JENSEN

1961 Jensen four-liter 541S two-door sports saloon. (Christie's)

541S — SIX — One final variant of the six-cylinder 541 appeared for a late 1960 debut, before Jensen turned to V-8 power for its two-door saloons (actually, coupes). Among other changes, an automatic transmission and limited-slip differential became standard, with four-speed manual gearbox optional (and dropped completely during the 1962 model year). The restyled front end of the 541S had a horizontal oval mesh-patterned, slightly recessed grille, with twin round parking and signal lights below each round headlamp. An aggressive-looking air scoop stood at the front of the hood, with its edges curving outward all the way to the grille top. Bodysides displayed the same protruding moldings on front and rear fenders as the earlier 541R, plus a small air-intake opening low on the cowl. Less visible alterations included the movement of chassis side tubes outward, to provide additional passenger space. For cooling purposes, an adjustable internal radiator blind replaced the former swiveling panel. Beneath the 541S bonnet was the same 3993-cc Austin Princess engine as before, with three carburetors. Standard equipment included a radio, spotlights, first-aid kit, and fire extinguisher. This was also the first British car to come with standard seatbelts. By this time, Jensen had a distributor in America.

I.D. DATA: Chassis serial number is stamped on a plate on the firewall, under the hood. Engine number is on the block, below Number 2 spark plug.

Model	Body Type & Seating	Engine Type/CID	P.O.E. Price	Weight (lbs.)	Prod. Total
541S	2-dr Saloon-4P	I6/244	N/A	3306	N/A

1962 Jensen 541S.

ENGINE DATA: BASE SIX: Inline, overhead-valve six-cylinder. Cast iron block. **Displacement:** 243.6 cu. in. (3993 cc). **Bore & Stroke:** 3.43 x 4.37 in. (87 x 111 mm). **Compression Ratio:** 7.4:1. **Brake Horsepower:** 135 at 3700 rpm. Four main bearings. Solid valve lifters. Three SU horizontal carburetors. 12-volt electrical.

Note: American sources reported horsepower ratings of 152-154 at 4100 rpm.

CHASSIS DATA: Wheelbase: 105 in. **Overall Length:** 178 in. **Width:** 67 in. **Front Tread:** 55.2 in. **Wheel Type:** disc. **Standard Tires:** 6.40x15.

TECHNICAL: Layout: front-engine, rear-drive. **Transmission:** four-speed automatic; manual shift optional. **Standard Final Drive Ratio:** 2.93:1. **Steering:** rack and pinion. **Suspension (front):** wishbones and coil springs. **Suspension (rear):** rigid axle with semi-elliptic leaf springs. **Brakes:** power front/rear disc. **Body Construction:** fiberglass body on box-section tubular steel chassis.

PERFORMANCE: Top Speed: about 110 mph. **Acceleration (0-60 mph):** N/A (0-50 in 9.2 seconds). **Acceleration (quarter-mile):** 18.8 seconds.

Manufacturer: Jensen Motors Ltd., West Bromwich, Staffordshire, England.

Distributor: Midland Continental Corp, New York City.

HISTORY: 541S introduced in October 1960. The new C-V8 model debuted in October 1962; see next listing.

1963 JENSEN

C-V8 — Mk I — V-8 — The clean, comparatively attractive styling that characterized earlier Jensens took a rather bizarre turn as a V-8 engine went under the hood of the new model. Quad headlamps replaced the former single units, but because of the diagonal mounting position of each pair within angled nacelles, the front end took on a startling look that few viewed as handsome and some considered downright ugly. The split grille was much lower than before, with a crosshatch pattern, and the hood held a small air scoop. A small winged insignia went above the grille. Protruding bodyside moldings continued from the 541 series, the rear ones leading into a side-by-side trio of round taillamps on each side of the back panel, in a sculpted opening that also contained the license plate. Exposed hinges stood at the top of the trunk lid. The new body was a mix of metals and fiberglass: sheet metal floor, aluminum door panels, and fiberglass roof and rear end. A revised tubular chassis consisted of central parallel tubes rather than the former peripheral-tube design. As in the 541 series, front seats held open-ended panels that permitted the insertion of extra padding. Performance was brisk with the Chrysler V-8, initially displacing 361 cubic inches and hooked to TorqueFlite three-speed automatic. A Powr-Lok limited-slip differential was standard; three-speed manual gearbox (with overdrive) optional. Top speed was claimed to be 132 mph. A "first" for British cars was the C-V8's use of an alternator rather than the former DC generator.

I.D. DATA: Not available.

Model	Body Type & Seating	Engine Type/CID	P.O.E. Price	Weight (lbs.)	Prod. Total
C-V8					
Mk I	2-dr Saloon-4P	V8/361	N/A	3300	Note 1

Note 1: Approximately 314 Mk I and Mk II Jensen C-V8s were produced from late 1962 through 1965.

Body Note: A small number of C-V8 convertibles also were produced.

ENGINE DATA: BASE V-8: Overhead-valve, 90-degree V-8 (Chrysler). Cast iron block. **Displacement:** 361 cu. in. (5916 cc). **Bore & Stroke:** 4.13 x 3.38 in. (105 x 86 mm). **Compression Ratio:** 9.0:1. **Brake Horsepower:** 305 at 4800 rpm. **Torque:** 395 lbs.-ft. at 3000 rpm. Five main bearings. Hydraulic valve lifters. Carter four-barrel carburetor. 12-volt electrical.

CHASSIS DATA: Wheelbase: 105 in. **Overall Length:** 184.5 in. **Height:** 55 in. **Width:** 67 in. **Front Tread:** 55.8 in. **Rear Tread:** 56.1 in. **Wheel Type:** disc. **Standard Tires:** 6.70x15.

TECHNICAL: Layout: front-engine, rear-drive. **Transmission:** TorqueFlite three-speed automatic; manual shift optional. **Standard Final Drive Ratio:** 3.54:1 (Powr-Lok). **Steering:** rack and pinion. **Suspension (front):** wishbones and coil springs. **Suspension (rear):** rigid axle with semi-elliptic leaf springs. **Brakes:** power front/rear disc. **Body Construction:** fiberglass/metal body on box-section tubular steel chassis.

PERFORMANCE: Top Speed: 132 mph. **Acceleration (0-60 mph):** N/A (0-50 in 6.3 seconds). **Acceleration (quarter-mile):** 16 seconds.

Manufacturer: Jensen Motors Ltd., West Bromwich, Staffordshire, England.

Distributor: Midland Continental Corp., New York City.

HISTORY: Introduced at Earl's Court (London) Motor Show in October 1962.

1964 JENSEN

C-V8 — Mk II — V-8 — For its appearance at the October 1963 London show, the C-V8 changed little in appearance but had new Armstrong Selectaride shock absorbers. By the first of the year, the original 361-cid V-8 was replaced by a Chrysler 383, delivering 330 horsepower. Jensen described the C-V8 as "among the fastest full four-seater cars in production and is certainly the most individual." The slanted-headlamp front end made that latter promise come true, though not everyone appreciated the sight. As before, Dunlop disc brakes were installed on all four wheels. Chrysler's three-speed TorqueFlite automatic was standard, feeding a Powr-Lok limited-slip differential. Bucket seats had adjustable reclining backs and provision for the insertion of extra padding, while back seats were described as "virtually armchairs." Standard equipment included a transistorized twin-speaker radio, heating/ventilating system, leather upholstery, front-door map pockets, diagonal front seat belts, rear armrest pockets, map light, two-speed self-parking wipers, and lighted electric clock.

1964 Jensen 541S Grand Touring four-seater. (Christie's)

I.D. DATA: Not available.

Model C-V8	Body Type & Seating	Engine Type/CID	P.O.E. Price	Weight (lbs.)	Prod. Total
Mk II	2-dr Saloon-4P	V8/383	N/A	3333	159

Body Note: A small number of C-V8 convertibles also were produced.

ENGINE DATA: BASE V-8: Overhead-valve, 90-degree V-8 (Chrysler). Cast iron block. **Displacement:** 383 cu. in. (6276 cc). **Bore & Stroke:** 4.25 x 3.38 in. (108 x 86 mm). **Compression Ratio:** 10.0:1. **Brake Horsepower:** 330 at 4600 rpm. Five main bearings. Hydraulic valve lifters. Carter four-barrel carburetor. 12-volt electrical.

Note: Early Mk II models retained the 361-cid Chrysler V-8; see previous listing.

CHASSIS DATA: Wheelbase: 105 in. **Overall Length:** 184.5 in. **Height:** 55 in. **Width:** 67.5 in. **Front Tread:** 55.8 in. **Rear Tread:** 56.1 in. **Wheel Type:** disc. **Standard Tires:** 6.70x15.

TECHNICAL: Layout: front-engine, rear-drive. **Transmission:** TorqueFlite three-speed automatic. **Standard Final Drive Ratio:** 3.07:1 (Powr-Lok). **Steering:** rack and pinion. **Suspension (front):** wishbones and coil springs. **Suspension (rear):** rigid axle with semi-elliptic leaf springs and Armstrong adjustable shock absorbers. **Brakes:** power front/rear Dunlop disc. **Body Construction:** fiberglass/metal body on tubular steel chassis.

PERFORMANCE: Top Speed: 130 + mph (factory). **Acceleration (0-60 mph):** N/A (0-50 in 5 seconds). **Acceleration (quarter-mile):** 14.6-15.5 seconds.

Manufacturer: Jensen Motors Ltd., West Bromwich, Staffordshire, England.

Distributor: Midland Continental Corp., New York City.

HISTORY: Mk II introduced in October 1963. "Driver and passengers can chat or listen to the radio comfortably at well over 100 mph," said *Autocar* magazine, adding that the C-V8 "is a car that more than fulfills great expectations."

1965-66 JENSEN

C-V8 — Mk II — V-8 — Production of the Mark II continued with little change until it was replaced by the Mark III in July 1965.

C-V8 — Mk III/FF — V-8 — Subtle body changes for the Mk III edition included lowering of the cowl and deepening of the windshield, as well as the deletion of brightwork around each diagonal headlamp cluster. A heated back window also became standard, as did a dual braking system. An "FF" version also was introduced, with Ferguson four-wheel drive (like that available in the new Interceptor, introduced late in 1966; see next listing). The C-V8 FF was four inches longer in wheelbase than the standard model. Otherwise, the two were similar.

I.D. DATA: Not available.

Model C-V8	Body Type & Seating	Engine Type/CID	P.O.E. Price	Weight (lbs.)	Prod. Total
Mk II	2-dr Saloon-4P	V8/383	N/A	3333	Note 1
Mk III	2-dr Saloon-4P	V8/383	N/A	3333	Note 1
FF	2-dr Saloon-4P	V8/383	N/A	N/A	Note 1

Note 1: A total of 159 C-V8 models had been produced in 1964, followed by 153 in 1965, and 79 in 1966.

Body Note: A small number of C-V8 convertibles also were produced.

ENGINE DATA: BASE V-8: Overhead-valve, 90-degree V-8 (Chrysler). Cast iron block. **Displacement:** 383 cu. in. (6276 cc). **Bore & Stroke:** 4.25 x 3.38 in. (108 x 86 mm). **Compression Ratio:** 10.0:1. **Brake Horsepower:** 330 at 4600 rpm. **Torque:** 425 lbs.-ft. at 2800 rpm. Five main bearings. Hydraulic valve lifters. Carter four-barrel carburetor. 12-volt electrical.

CHASSIS DATA: Wheelbase: 105 in.; (FF) 109 in. **Overall Length:** 184.5 in.; (FF) 187.5 in. **Height:** 55 in. **Width:** 67.5 in. **Front Tread:** 55.8 in. **Rear Tread:** 56.1 in. **Wheel Type:** disc. **Standard Tires:** 6.70x15.

TECHNICAL: Layout: front-engine, rear-drive. **Transmission:** TorqueFlite three-speed automatic. **Standard Final Drive Ratio:** 3.07:1 (Powr-Lok). **Steering:** rack and pinion. **Suspension (front):** wishbones and coil springs. **Suspension (rear):** rigid axle with semi-elliptic leaf springs; Armstrong adjustable shock absorbers. **Brakes:** power front/rear Dunlop disc. **Body Construction:** fiberglass/metal body on tubular steel chassis.

PERFORMANCE: Top Speed: 130+ mph (factory). **Acceleration (0-60 mph):** N/A (0-50 in 5 seconds). **Acceleration (quarter-mile):** 14.6 seconds.

Manufacturer: Jensen Motors Ltd., West Bromwich, Staffordshire, England.

HISTORY: Mk III introduced in July 1965. The revived Interceptor debuted in late 1966; see next listing. It was preceded by an appearance at the 1965 London Motor Show of a P66 prototype, with aluminum convertible body on a perimeter-type chassis.

1967-69 JENSEN

1967 Jensen.

INTERCEPTOR — Mk I — V-8 — One of the most significant elements of the revival of the Interceptor nameplate was that it brought an end to Jensen's fiberglass bodywork. The steel fastback body had cleaner lines than the C-V8, longer and lower, accented by stainless steel trim. Largely squarish in profile, with a rectangular grille, it was designed by Touring (in Italy) and initially built by the Vignale firm. A huge lift-up rear window was the dominant styling feature, along with back-angled rear quarter windows. Quad headlamps sat side-by-side, above rectangular park/signal lamps. Standard Interceptor equipment included power windows, heated back window, front-door map pockets, reclining front seats, twin-speaker transistorized radio, heat/vent system, tachometer, underhood lighting, map light, lighted clock, and red warning lights in trailing edges of each door. Power disc brakes were standard. The wood-rimmed steering wheel was mounted on an adjustable column. Power was supplied by a Chrysler 383-cid V-8, as in the prior C-V8 series.

INTERCEPTOR — FF — V-8 — In addition to the basic two-wheel-drive model, Jensen produced more than 300 (total) with Ferguson four-wheel drive. FF models were four inches longer in wheelbase, all up front to accommodate the full-time 4WD system. While the two-wheel-drive version had a single near-vertical vent ahead of the cowl, the FF had two. FF models also had a brushed stainless top and deep hood fluting. Power rack-and-pinion steering was standard, as was Maxaret anti-skid braking. Otherwise, the two were similar in both appearance and mechanical details.

I.D. DATA: Not available.

Model INTERCEPTOR	Body Type & Seating	Engine Type/CID	P.O.E. Price	Weight (lbs.)	Prod. Total
I	2-dr Saloon-4P	V8/383	Note 1	3562	Note 3
FF	2-dr Saloon-4P	V8/383	Note 2	3876	Note 4

Note 1: Interceptor price in England was 3742 pounds (Sterling), or $8520.

Note 2: FF price in England was 5340 pounds (Sterling), or $12,160.

Note 3: A total of 17 Interceptors were produced in 1966, 148 in 1967, 444 in 1968, and 529 in 1969.

Note 4: A total of two four-wheel-drive (FF) models were produced in 1966, 24 in 1967, 62 in 1968, and 115 in 1969.

1968 Jensen Interceptor FF Series 1 coupe. (Sotheby's)

ENGINE DATA: BASE V-8: Overhead-valve, 90-degree V-8 (Chrysler). Cast iron block. **Displacement:** 383 cu. in. (6276 cc). **Bore & Stroke:** 4.25 x 3.38 in. (108 x 86 mm). **Compression Ratio:** 10.0:1. **Brake Horsepower:** 325/330 at 4600 rpm. **Torque:** 425 lbs.-ft. at 2800 rpm. Five main bearings. Hydraulic valve lifters. Carter four-barrel carburetor. 12-volt electrical.

CHASSIS DATA: Wheelbase: 105 in.; (FF) 109 in. **Overall Length:** 188 in.; (FF) 191 in. **Height:** 53 in. **Width:** 69 in. **Front Tread:** 55.8 in.; (FF) 56.9 in. **Rear Tread:** 56.5 in.; (FF) 56.9 in. **Wheel Type:** disc. **Standard Tires:** Dunlop R.S. 6.70x15.

TECHNICAL: Layout: front-engine, rear-drive. **Transmission:** TorqueFlite three-speed automatic; four-speed (all-synchro) manual available. FF came with TorqueFlite and Ferguson Formula 4WD unit. Standard TorqueFlite gear ratios: (1st) 7.50:1; (2nd) 4.44:1; (3rd) 3.07:1; (rev) 6.74:1. Manual gear ratios: (1st) 8.16:1; (2nd) 5.86:1; (3rd) 4.26:1; (4th) 3.07:1; (rev) 7.92:1. **Standard Final Drive Ratio:** 3.07:1 (Powr-Lok). **Steering:** rack and pinion; (FF) power-assisted. **Suspension (front):** wishbones and coil springs with stabilizer bar. **Suspension (rear):** rigid axle with semi-elliptic leaf springs and Armstrong adjustable shock absorbers. **Brakes:** power front/rear Dunlop disc; (FF) Dunlop Maxaret anti-skid device. **Body Construction:** steel body on tubular steel chassis.

PRODUCTION/SALES: Total two-wheel-drive Interceptor production from 1966-76 was 6,387. Few were imported to the U.S. until the 1970s. Total FF production from 1966-71 was 318. Even fewer (if any) were imported to the U.S. when new.

PERFORMANCE: Top Speed: 133 mph; (FF) 130 mph. **Acceleration (0-60 mph):** 7.3 seconds. **Acceleration (quarter-mile):** less than 16 seconds.

Manufacturer: Jensen Motors Ltd., West Bromwich, Staffordshire, England.

HISTORY: Interceptor introduced in October 1966. The FF version received the "Car of the Year" award from *Car* magazine in England. An Interceptor Mark II appeared in late 1969; see next listing.

1970-71 JENSEN

1971-'72 Jensen Interceptor III.

INTERCEPTOR — Mk II — V-8 — Modifications were modest for the second generation of the revived Interceptor, again powered by a 383-cid Chrysler V-8. A fully restyled interior was intended to meet all current legal requirements, and included the addition of a second locking glovebox. In addition to thermostatically-controlled heating/ventilation and a rear-window demister, the Interceptor could now be ordered with optional air conditioning. Reclining seats were redesigned, the gas tank enlarged, low-profile radial tires on wider wheels installed, and non-adjustable rear shock absorbers installed. Appearance changes were subtle and limited to the front end. Side-by-side quad headlamps again flanked a horizontal-bar rectangular grille, while parking lights were mounted below the bumper. A divided air-intake slot also stood just below front-bumper level. Interceptor's massive rear hatch provided ample loading space for luggage. Standard equipment included power brakes, steering and windows. Offered in Britain was a special "Director" interior, which turned the grand touring motorcar into a traveling office.

Note: Model name was sometimes given as Mk 2 or, simply, Interceptor II.

INTERCEPTOR — FF — V-8 — The four-wheel-drive version received changes similar to those of the second-generation 2WD Interceptor.

I.D. DATA: Vehicle Identification Number (VIN) is visible through the windshield and also found on right fender skirt, in engine compartment, and on left door pillar post. It consists of a production year code followed by a five-digit serial number. Engine number is on a plate attached to top left cylinder bank and/or stamped on right of block, adjacent to distributor.

Model	Body Type & Seating	Engine Type/CID	P.O.E. Price	Weight (lbs.)	Total Prod.
INTERCEPTOR					
II	2-dr Saloon-4P	V8/383	13500	3500	Note 1
FF	2-dr Saloon-4P	V8/383	N/A	4030	Note 2

Note 1: A total of 526 Interceptors were produced in 1970 and 742 in 1971.

Note 2: A total of 68 four-wheel-drive (FF) models were produced in 1970 and 47 in 1971 (its final year).

ENGINE DATA: BASE V-8: Overhead-valve, 90-degree V-8 (Chrysler). Cast iron block. **Displacement:** 383 cu. in. (6276 cc). **Bore & Stroke:** 4.25 x 3.38 in. (108 x 86 mm). **Compression Ratio:** 9.5:1. **Brake Horsepower:** 330 at 5000 rpm. **Torque:** 425 lbs.-ft. at 3200 rpm. Five main bearings. Hydraulic valve lifters. Four-barrel carburetor. 12-volt electrical.

CHASSIS DATA: Wheelbase: 105 in.; (FF) 109 in. **Overall Length:** 186 in.; (FF) 191 in. **Height:** 53 in. **Width:** 69 in. **Front Tread:** 56.1 in. **Rear Tread:** 56.8 in. **Wheel Type:** disc. **Standard Tires:** ER70x15 or Pirelli GR70VR15

TECHNICAL: Layout: front-engine, rear-drive. **Transmission:** TorqueFlite three-speed automatic; FF came with Ferguson Formula 4WD unit. Gear ratios: (1st) 2.45:1; (2nd) 1.44:1; (3rd) 1.00:1. **Standard Final Drive Ratio:** 2.88:1 (Powr-Lok). **Steering:** power rack and pinion. **Suspension (front):** wishbones and coil springs with stabilizer bar. **Suspension (rear):** rigid axle with semi-elliptic leaf springs and Panhard rod. **Brakes:** power front/rear Dunlop disc; (FF) Dunlop Maxaret anti-skid device. **Body Construction:** steel body on tubular steel chassis. **Fuel Tank:** 24 gallons.

PRODUCTION/SALES: Total two-wheel-drive Interceptor production from 1966-76 was 6,387. Total FF production from 1966-71 was 318. About 50 Jensens were sold in the U.S. in 1970.

PERFORMANCE: Top Speed: up to 142 mph (est). **Acceleration (0-60 mph):** 7.5 seconds (0-100 mph in 18.2 seconds). **Acceleration (quarter-mile):** 15.2 seconds (92 mph).

Manufacturer: Jensen Motors Ltd., West Bromwich, Staffordshire, England.

Distributor: Jensen Motors Inc., San Francisco, California.

HISTORY: Interceptor II introduced in October 1969. To anticipate official importation into the U.S., a federalized version appeared at the New York Auto Show in April 1970. Active merchandising began in the following year. The Mark III and SP Interceptor versions debuted in October 1971; see next listing. As the 1970s began, the Jensen company was in financial trouble. A group led by a Norwegian-born San Francisco distributor for Jensen, Kjell Qvale, gained control and initiated a plan for a different type of car, kin to the departed big Austin-Healey. Since Donald Healey himself wound up as chairman of Jensen's board, the possibilities were especially tempting. With the technical assistance of Kevin Beattie, their efforts resulted in the Jensen-Healey, which debuted at the Geneva (Switzerland) Motor Show in spring 1972.

1972 JENSEN

1972 Jensen Interceptor S.P. (Sotheby's)

JENSEN-HEALEY — FOUR — An all-new, smaller two-seat roadster joined the Interceptor saloon (closed coupe) during 1972, powered by a Lotus-built twin-cam (16-valve) four-cylinder engine. The all-steel unibody had a grille-less front end with recessed headlamps, large amber parking lights below the bumper, and horizontal rectangular taillamps. Its overall profile was angular, with full wheel openings front and rear. Underneath was a mix of British components. Coil-spring front suspension, rack-and-pinion steering and the front disc brakes were borrowed from the Vauxhall Viva. The four-speed manual gearbox came from Sunbeam.

INTERCEPTOR — Mk III — V-8 — Only two-wheel drive remained in the third generation of the revived Interceptor. Appearance changes included restyled headlamp surrounds and, after a time, new five-spoke cast aluminum wheels (introduced first on the SP edition, below). Standard equipment now included many items that had formerly been optional. American imports had air conditioning, radio, power brakes and steering. A plate on the grille identified the series. As the U.S. market opened wider, the standard 383 cubic-inch Chrysler V-8 gave way to a big 440-cid version.

Note: Model name was sometimes given as Mk 3 or, simply, Interceptor III.

INTERCEPTOR — SP — V-8 — Performance fans in Britain could now order an Interceptor with a bigger Chrysler V-8 engine: the 440-cid version, producing 385 horsepower. Because the 'SP' designation stood for "six-pack," it was no surprise to see a trio of two-barrel carburetors sending in the fuel mixture. Just about everything that had formerly been optional was standard on this high-performance edition, including a Lear Jet AM/FM stereo radio with station seeking and eight-track tape player, air conditioning, and power door locks.

I.D. DATA: Interceptor Vehicle Identification Number (VIN) is visible through the windshield and also found on right fender skirt, in engine compartment, and on left door pillar post. It consists of a production year code followed by a five-digit serial number. Engine number is on a plate attached to top left cylinder bank and/or stamped on right of block, adjacent to distributor. Jensen-Healey's five-digit serial number is atop the dashboard, visible through the windshield; and on a plate attached to left door. Engine number is on the rear, near top center.

Model	Body Type & Seating	Engine Type/CID	P.O.E. Price	Weight (lbs.)	Prod. Total
JENSEN-HEALEY					
	2-dr Rds-2P	I4/120	4795	2116	705
INTERCEPTOR					
III	2-dr Saloon-4P	V8/383	13570	3695	922
SP	2-dr Saloon-4P	V8/440	N/A	N/A	121

Production Note: Figures shown are for 1972 only. A total of 19 SP models were produced during 1971, and 88 in 1973 (for a total of 228).

ENGINE DATA: BASE FOUR (Jensen-Healey): Inline, dual overhead cam four-cylinder (inclined 45 degrees). **Displacement:** 120.5 cu. in. (1973 cc). **Bore & Stroke:** 3.75 x 2.73 in. (95.2 x 69.3 mm). **Compression Ratio:** 8.4:1. **Brake Horsepower:** 140 (SAE net) at 6500 rpm. **Torque:** 130 lbs.-ft. at 5000 rpm. Five main bearings. Solid valve lifters. Two carburetors. 12-volt electrical.

BASE V-8 (Interceptor III): Overhead-valve, 90-degree V-8 (Chrysler). Cast iron block. **Displacement:** 383 cu. in. (6276 cc). **Bore & Stroke:** 4.25 x 3.38 in. (108 x 86 mm). **Compression Ratio:** 8.5:1. **Brake Horsepower:** 330 (gross) at 5000 rpm; 250 (net) at 4800 rpm. **Torque:** 425 lbs.-ft. (gross) at 2800 rpm; 325 (net) at 3400 rpm. Five main bearings. Hydraulic valve lifters. Carter four-barrel carburetor. 12-volt electrical.

BASE V-8 (Interceptor SP and later Interceptor III): Same as V-8 above, except — **Displacement:** 440 cu. in. (7212 cc). **Bore & Stroke:** 4.32 x 3.75 in. (109.7 x 95.3 mm). **Compression Ratio:** 8.2:1. **Brake Horsepower:** 385 (330 DIN) at 4700 rpm. Three Holley carburetors.

Note: Horsepower/torque measurements in the U.S. switched from "gross" to "net" figures in 1972.

CHASSIS DATA: Wheelbase: (Healey) 92 in.; (Inter) 105 in. Overall Length: (Healey) 162 in.; (Inter) 188 in. Height: (Healey) 47.75 in.; (Inter) 53 in. Width: (Healey) 63.25 in.; (Inter) 70 in. Front Tread: (Healey) 53.25 in.; (Inter) 56.3 in. Rear Tread: (Healey) 52.5 in.; (Inter) 57.5 in. Wheel Type: cast aluminum. Standard Tires: (Healey) 185/70SR13; (Inter) GR70VR15.

TECHNICAL: Layout: front-engine, rear-drive. Transmission: (Healey) four-speed manual. Overall ratios: (1st) 11.63:1; (2nd) 7.42:1; (3rd) 4.83:1; (4th) 3.73:1; (rev) 12.37:1. (Interceptor) TorqueFlite three-speed automatic. Standard Final Drive Ratio: (Healey) 3.73:1; (Inter) 2.83:1 or 3.07:1 (Powr-Lok). Steering: rack and pinion (Interceptor, power-assisted). Suspension (front): (Healey) double wishbones and coil springs; (Inter) wishbones and coil springs with stabilizer bar. Suspension (rear): (Healey) rigid axle with four links and coil springs; (Inter) rigid axle with semi-elliptic leaf springs and Panhard rod. Brakes: (Healey) power front disc, rear drum; (Inter) power front/rear Dunlop disc. Body Construction: (Healey) undersealed steel unibody; (Inter) steel body on tubular steel chassis. Fuel Tank: (Healey) 13 gallons; (Inter) 24 gallons.

PRODUCTION/SALES: Total two-wheel-drive Interceptor production from 1966-76 was 6,387.

PERFORMANCE: Top Speed: (Healey) 120-125 mph; (Inter) up to 142 mph (est). Acceleration (0-60 mph): (Healey) about 8.1 seconds; (Inter) 7.5 seconds. Acceleration (quarter-mile): (Healey) 16.2 seconds (87 mph); (Inter) 15.2 seconds (92 mph).

Manufacturer: Jensen Motors Ltd., West Bromwich, Staffordshire, England.

Distributor: Jensen Motors Inc., Compton, California and Baltimore, Maryland.

HISTORY: Mark III and SP Interceptors introduced in October 1971. Jensen-Healey introduced at the Geneva show in spring 1972. Kjell Qvale and Donald Healey originally wanted a Vauxhall engine to power the Jensen-Healey roadster, but it wasn't strong enough to do the job so they turned to a Lotus-built twin-cam derivative (which was later used in Lotus vehicles as well). Jensen-Healey's rather nondescript appearance may be attributable to the fact that too many people were involved in its creation.

1973 JENSEN

1973 Jensen Interceptor III sports saloon. (Christie's)

JENSEN-HEALEY — FOUR — The new roadster continued into its first full model year with minor cosmetic changes. Standard equipment included a four-speed manual gearbox, power front disc brakes, map light, twin Hi-Lo horns, two-speed wipers/washers, locking glovebox, console, tonneau cover, tachometer, heater, and diagonal seat belts. Ventilated vinyl seats adjusted for rake angle and had adjustable head restraints. A radio cost $135 extra.

INTERCEPTOR — Mk III — V-8 — Little change was evident on the Interceptor saloon (coupe) for the 1973 model year. Standard equipment included a Lear Jet AM/FM station-seeking radio with eight-track player and four speakers, air conditioning, power windows, power antenna, first aid kit, fire extinguisher, adjustable steering column, lighted clock, and Pirelli GR70VR15 tires. By this time, America-bound Interceptors came with a 440-cid engine, as in the SP version.

INTERCEPTOR — SP — V-8 — The high-performance Interceptor with 440-cid engine continued in production for the home market until July 1973 with little change.

I.D. DATA: Interceptor Vehicle Identification Number (VIN) is visible through the windshield and also found on right fender skirt, in engine compartment, and on left door pillar post. It consists of a production year code followed by a five-digit serial number. Engine number is on a plate attached to top left cylinder bank and/or stamped on right of block, adjacent to distributor. Jensen-Healey's five-digit serial number is atop the dashboard, visible through the windshield; and on a plate attached to left door. Engine number is on the rear, near top center.

Model	Body Type & Seating	Engine Type/CID	P.O.E. Price	Weight (lbs.)	Prod. Total
JENSEN-HEALEY					
	2-dr Rds-2P	I4/120	5195	2116	3,846
INTERCEPTOR					
III	2-dr Saloon-4P	V8/440	15500	3695	1,165
SP	2-dr Saloon-4P	V8/440	N/A	N/A	88

Production Note: Figures shown are for 1973 only.

ENGINE DATA: BASE FOUR (Jensen-Healey): Same as 1972.

BASE V-8 (Interceptor III): Overhead-valve, 90-degree V-8 (Chrysler). Cast iron block. Displacement: 440 cu. in. (7212 cc). Bore & Stroke: 4.32 x 3.75 in. (109.7 x 95.3 mm). Compression Ratio: 8.2:1. Brake Horsepower: 385 (330 DIN) at 4700 rpm (230 net at 3600 rpm). Torque: 350 lbs.-ft. at 2000/2400 rpm. Five main bearings. Hydraulic valve lifters. Four-barrel carburetor. 12-volt electrical.

CHASSIS DATA: Same as 1972.

TECHNICAL: Same as 1972.

PRODUCTION/SALES: Total two-wheel-drive Interceptor production from 1966-76 was 6,387. Total Jensen-Healey production from 1972-76 was 10,453.

PERFORMANCE: Top Speed: (Healey) 120-125 mph; (Inter) 135-142 mph. Acceleration (0-60 mph): (Healey) about 8.1 seconds; (Inter) 7.5 seconds. Acceleration (quarter-mile): (Healey) 16.2 seconds (87 mph); (Inter) 15.2 seconds (92 mph).

Manufacturer: Jensen Motors Ltd., West Bromwich, Staffordshire, England.

Distributor: Jensen Motors Inc., Compton, California and Baltimore, Maryland.

1974 JENSEN

1974 Jensen-Healey.

JENSEN-HEALEY — FOUR — Modest restyling of Jensen's two-seat roadster included the addition of a full-length horizontal bodyside style line, curved headlamp cowl, and some bright trim around the front bumper (including a flash chrome panel). Bright finishers also were added to the rear edge of the hood and to the door tops. A matte black finish was now used on lower sills, and taillamp clusters added chrome surrounds. Two body colors were added: Buttercup Yellow and Malaga Blue. A removable fiberglass roof (with heated back window) became available.

INTERCEPTOR — Mk III — V-8 — Only a few minor interior changes appeared in the larger Jensen model, which carried Chrysler's 440-cid V-8 engine and TorqueFlite automatic. The steering wheel was restyled, and a rheostat now controlled the instrument lighting. The power antenna now worked in conjunction with the radio's on/off switch. Fully reclining seats were upholstered in Connolly leather. Two metallic body colors were added: Brienz Blue and Copper. U.S. (export) models now had fixed rear quarter windows and a louvered hood. Far more notable was the announcement of a convertible coupe, to join the basic closed Interceptor.

I.D. DATA: Interceptor Vehicle Identification Number (VIN) is visible through the windshield and also found on right fender skirt, in engine compartment, and on left door pillar post. It consists of a production year code followed by a five-digit serial number. Saloon code is '2210' except in California, '2211;' convertible's code is '2310' or 2311.' Engine number is on a plate attached to top left cylinder bank and/or stamped on right of block, adjacent to distributor. Jensen-Healey's five-digit serial number is atop the dashboard, visible through the windshield; and on a plate attached to left door. Engine number is on the rear, near top center.

Model	Body Type & Seating	Engine Type/CID	P.O.E. Price	Weight (lbs.)	Prod. Total
JENSEN-HEALEY					
	2-dr Rds-2P	I4/120	5545	2116	4.550
INTERCEPTOR					
III	2-dr Saloon-4P	V8/440	16200	3695	Note 1
III	2-dr Conv-4P	V8/440	N/A	N/A	Note 1

Note 1: Total two-wheel-drive Interceptor production from 1966-76 was 6,387.

Price Note: Jensen-Healey price rose after announcement to $5990.

ENGINE DATA: BASE FOUR (Jensen-Healey): Inline, dual overhead cam four-cylinder (inclined 45 degrees). Displacement: 120.5 cu. in. (1973 cc). Bore & Stroke: 3.75 x 2.73 in. (95.2 x 69.3 mm). Compression Ratio: 8.4:1. Brake Horsepower: 140 (SAE net) at 6500 rpm. Torque: 130 lbs.-ft. at 5000 rpm. Five main bearings. Solid valve lifters. Two carburetors. 12-volt electrical.

BASE V-8 (Interceptor III): Same as 1973.

CHASSIS DATA: Wheelbase: (Healey) 92 in.; (Inter) 105 in. Overall Length: (Healey) 162 in.; (Inter) 188 in. Height: (Healey) 47.75 in.; (Inter) 53 in. exc. (conv) 54.4 in. Width: (Healey) 63.25 in.; (Inter) 69 in. Front Tread: (Healey) 53.25 in.; (Inter) 56.3 in. Rear Tread: (Healey) 52.5 in.; (Inter) 57.6 in. exc. (conv) 56.9 in. Wheel Type: cast aluminum. Standard Tires: (Healey) 185/70SR13; (Inter) ER70VR15 or GR70VR15.

TECHNICAL: Layout: front-engine, rear-drive. Transmission: (Healey) four-speed manual. Overall ratios: (1st) 11.63:1; (2nd) 7.42:1; (3rd) 4.83:1; (4th) 3.73:1; (rev) 12.37:1. (Interceptor) TorqueFlite three-speed automatic. Standard Final Drive Ratio: (Healey) 3.73:1; (Inter) 3.07:1 (Powr-Lok). Steering: rack and pinion (Interceptor, power-assisted). Suspension (front): (Healey) double wishbones and coil springs; (Inter) wishbones and coil springs with stabilizer bar. Suspension (rear): (Healey) rigid axle with four links and coil springs; (Inter) rigid axle with semi-elliptic leaf springs and Panhard rod. Brakes:

(Healey) power front disc, rear drum; (Inter) power front/rear Dunlop disc. **Body Construction:** (Healey) undersealed steel unibody; (Inter) steel body on tubular steel chassis. **Fuel Tank:** (Healey) 13 gallons; (Inter) 24 gallons.

PRODUCTION/SALES: Total Jensen-Healey production from 1972-76 was 10,453.

PERFORMANCE: Top Speed: (Healey) 120-125 mph; (Inter) 135-142 mph. **Acceleration (0-60 mph):** (Healey) about 8.1 seconds; (Inter) 7.5 seconds. **Acceleration (quarter-mile):** (Healey) 16.2 seconds; (Inter) 15.2 seconds (92 mph).

Manufacturer: Jensen Motors Ltd., West Bromwich, Staffordshire, England.

Distributor: Jensen Motors Inc., Compton, California and Baltimore, Maryland.

HISTORY: By 1974, three out of five Jensen-Healeys were being exported to the U.S. and Canada, though sales never reached anticipated levels. Donald Healey dropped out of the project during this period, and his name would not appear on the subsequent GT sportwagon.

1975 JENSEN

JENSEN-HEALEY — FOUR — A five-speed Getrag manual gearbox replaced the former four-speed, but other changes were minimal in the two-seater. Acceleration to 60 mph was actually slower than before, a result of revised rear-axle ratio. Jensen-Healey's price had jumped considerably since the car's introduction in 1972. At mid-year, the roadster dropped out, replaced by a new GT sportwagon; see next listing.

INTERCEPTOR — Mk III — V-8 — Production of the closed and open Interceptors continued without major change. Saloons destined for America had matching lambswool seat panels (one example of an attempt to modify Jensen equipment to target the U.S. market). Standard equipment included air conditioning, tachometer, power windows, rear demister, four-speaker radio with automatic antenna, remote-control gas-filler flap, power rack-and-pinion steering, power four-wheel disc brakes, and Dunlop ER70VR15 tires on cast aluminum wheels.

I.D. DATA: Serial numbers are in same locations as 1974; see that listing.

Model	Body Type & Seating	Engine Type/CID	P.O.E. Price	Weight (lbs.)	Prod. Total
JENSEN-HEALEY					
	2-dr Rds-2P	I4/120	8195	N/A	1,301
INTERCEPTOR					
III	2-dr Saloon-4P	V8/440	N/A	4040	Note 1
III	2-dr Conv-4P	V8/440	N/A	N/A	Note 1

Note 1: Total two-wheel-drive Interceptor production from 1966-76 was 6,387.

Healey Production Note: A final 51 examples were produced during 1976.

Weight Note: Interceptor weight shown is "unladen" measure.

ENGINE DATA: BASE FOUR (Jensen-Healey): Inline, dual overhead cam four-cylinder (inclined 45 degrees). **Displacement:** 120.5 cu. in. (1973 cc). **Bore & Stroke:** 3.75 x 2.73 in. (95.2 x 69.3 mm). **Compression Ratio:** 8.4:1. **Brake Horsepower:** 140 (SAE net) at 6500 rpm. **Torque:** 130 lbs.-ft. at 5000 rpm. Five main bearings. Solid valve lifters. Two Stromberg carburetors. 12-volt electrical.

BASE V-8 (Interceptor III): Overhead-valve, 90-degree V-8 (Chrysler). Cast iron block. **Displacement:** 440 cu. in. (7212 cc). **Bore & Stroke:** 4.32 x 3.38 in. (109.7 x 95.3 mm). **Compression Ratio:** 8.2:1. **Brake Horsepower:** 385 (gross) or 230 (net) at 4700 rpm. Five main bearings. Hydraulic valve lifters. Four-barrel carburetor. 12-volt electrical.

CHASSIS DATA: Wheelbase: (Healey) 92 in.; (Inter) 105 in. **Overall Length:** (Healey) 162 in.; (Inter) 188 in. **Height:** (Healey) 47.75 in.; (Inter) 53 in. exc. (conv) 54.4 in. **Width:** (Healey) 63.25 in.; (Inter) 69 in. **Front Tread:** (Healey) 53.25 in.; (Inter) 56.3 in. **Rear Tread:** (Healey) 52.5 in.; (Inter) 57.6 in. exc. (conv) 56.9 in. **Wheel Type:** cast aluminum. **Standard Tires:** (Healey) 185/70SR13; (Inter) ER70VR15.

TECHNICAL: Layout: front-engine, rear-drive. **Transmission:** (Healey) five-speed manual; (Interceptor) TorqueFlite three-speed automatic. Overall TorqueFlite gear ratios: (1st) 7.50:1; (2nd) 4.44:1; (3rd) 3.07:1; (rev) 6.74:1. **Standard Final Drive Ratio:** (Healey) 3.45:1; (Inter) 3.07:1 (Powr-Lok). **Steering:** rack and pinion (Interceptor, power-assisted). **Suspension (front):** (Healey) double wishbones and coil springs; (Inter) wishbones and coil springs with stabilizer bar. **Suspension (rear):** (Healey) rigid axle with four links and coil springs; (Inter) rigid axle with semi-elliptic leaf springs and Panhard rod. **Brakes:** (Healey) power front disc, rear drum; (Inter) power front/rear Dunlop disc. **Body Construction:** (Healey) undersealed steel unibody; (Inter) steel body on tubular steel chassis. **Fuel Tank:** (Healey) 13 gallons; (Inter) 24 gallons.

PRODUCTION/SALES: Total Jensen-Healey production from 1972-76 was 10,453.

PERFORMANCE: Top Speed: (Healey) 120-125 mph; (Inter) 135-142 mph. **Acceleration (0-60 mph):** (Healey) 9.6 seconds; (Inter) 7.5 seconds. **Acceleration (quarter-mile):** (Healey) 17.9 seconds; (Inter) 15.2 seconds (92 mph).

Manufacturer: Jensen Motors Ltd., West Bromwich, Staffordshire, England.

Distributor: Jensen Motors Inc., Compton, California and Baltimore, Maryland.

HISTORY: A GT sportwagon, replacing the Jensen-Healey roadster, debuted in mid-year 1975.

1976 JENSEN

GT — FOUR — A handful of final Jensen-Healeys were produced during the 1976 model year, but production switched to a wagon-like GT coupe version of the former roadster. Billed as "The Good Thinking Car," it was similar in construction and dimensions to the Jensen-Healey but deleted the Healey badge.

INTERCEPTOR — Mk III — V-8 — Production of the saloon and convertible Interceptors continued (and concluded) without major change.

I.D. DATA: Serial numbers are in same locations as 1974; see that listing.

Model	Body Type & Seating	Engine Type/CID	P.O.E. Price	Weight (lbs.)	Prod. Total
GT	2-dr Coupe-4P	I4/120	9975	2400	N/A
INTERCEPTOR					
III	2-dr Saloon-4P	V8/440	24750	4040	Note 1
III	2-dr Conv-4P	V8/440	N/A	N/A	Note 1

Note 1: Total two-wheel-drive Interceptor production from 1966-76 was 6,387.

Weight Note: GT weight shown is "curb" weight; Interceptor is "unladen" measure.

ENGINE DATA: BASE FOUR (GT): Inline, dual overhead cam four-cylinder (inclined 45 degrees). **Displacement:** 120.5 cu. in. (1973 cc). **Bore & Stroke:** 3.75 x 2.73 in. (95.2 x 69.3 mm). **Compression Ratio:** 8.4:1. **Brake Horsepower:** 140 (SAE net) at 6500 rpm. **Torque:** 130 lbs.-ft. at 5000 rpm. Five main bearings. Solid valve lifters. Two Stromberg carburetors. 12-volt electrical.

BASE V-8 (Interceptor III): Same as 1975.

CHASSIS DATA: Wheelbase: (GT) 92 in.; (Inter) 105 in. **Overall Length:** (GT) 165.8 in.; (Inter) 184.5 in. **Height:** (GT) 48.5 in.; (Inter) 53 in. exc. (conv) 54.4 in. **Width:** (GT) 63.25 in.; (Inter) 69 in. **Front Tread:** (GT) 53.25 in.; (Inter) 56.3 in. **Rear Tread:** (GT) 52.5 in.; (Inter) 57.6 in. exc. (conv) 56.9 in. **Wheel Type:** cast aluminum. **Standard Tires:** (GT) 185/70HR13; (Inter) ER70VR15.

TECHNICAL: Layout: front-engine, rear-drive. **Transmission:** (GT) five-speed manual; (Interceptor) TorqueFlite three-speed automatic. Overall GT gear ratios: (1st) 11.62:1; (2nd) 7.45:1; (3rd) 5.45:1; (4th) 4.28:1; (5th) 3.45:1; (rev) 13.80:1. Overall TorqueFlite gear ratios: (1st) 7.50:1; (2nd) 4.44:1; (3rd) 3.07:1; (rev) 6.74:1. **Standard Final Drive Ratio:** (GT) 3.45:1; (Inter) 3.07:1 (Powr-Lok). **Steering:** rack and pinion (Interceptor, power-assisted). **Suspension (front):** (GT) double wishbones and coil springs; (Inter) wishbones and coil springs with stabilizer bar. **Suspension (rear):** (GT) rigid axle with four links and coil springs; (Inter) rigid axle with semi-elliptic leaf springs and Panhard rod. **Brakes:** (GT) power front disc, rear drum; (Inter) power front/rear Dunlop disc. **Body Construction:** (GT) undersealed steel unibody; (Inter) steel body on tubular steel chassis. **Fuel Tank:** (GT) 14.4 gallons; (Inter) 24 gallons.

PERFORMANCE: Top Speed: (Inter) 135-142 mph. **Acceleration (0-60 mph):** (Inter) 7.5 seconds. **Acceleration (quarter-mile):** (Inter) 15.2 seconds (92 mph).

Manufacturer: Jensen Motors Ltd., West Bromwich, Staffordshire, England.

Distributor: Jensen Motors Inc., Compton, California.

HISTORY: In August 1976, the Jensen plant was closed and production ceased.

JOWETT

Like that of most British automakers of the postwar era, the Jowett history reaches back to the early years of the century: to 1906, in fact, when brothers Ben and Willy Jowett produced a two-cylinder, six-horsepower motorcar. Various light, low-budget autos were built during the prewar period, but the company became known to American enthusiasts only after World War II. As the war ended, the Jowett brothers sold out to a wealthy businessman. Then came the introduction of the stylish fastback Javelin saloon and, for 1950, the Jupiter sports convertible. All postwar models used a 1485-cc horizontally-opposed four-cylinder engine with hydraulic valve lifters.

Goal for the Javelin was to produce a 1.5-liter saloon that blended top British, European and American techniques, adding high-speed performance to comforts for the family. Jupiter would be the company's entry into the sports-car realm, a reasonable route in view of racing successes with the Javelin. "British engineering brains have built a record breaker," declared U.S. ads in 1952. By that time, Jupiter had achieved class victories in nine major trials and races. Other ads even challenged the skills of American drivers, asking: "Can you really handle a race-bred European car?" Jupiter, they added, "can take all the *good* driving you can give it," yet it's "docile in traffic" and offers "big car comfort rare in high-speed sports cars." People tended either to love Jupiter's look or to hate it. Early engine problems also impaired the car's popularity. Competition success and the announcement of a new and totally different "plastic" Jowett didn't help the company survive past 1954.

343

1947-49 JOWETT

1949 Jowett Jupiter.

JAVELIN — FOUR — The four-door saloon was powered by a 1.5-liter, horizontally-opposed four-cylinder engine rated at 50 horsepower, mounted ahead of the radiator. All five passengers (occasionally six) sat between the axles, "insuring a restful ride." Space was provided for five or six suitcases, as well as small gear. The car had independently sprung wheels to "make fast cornering safe and comfortable." The four-cylinder engine was said to give a "smooth high top speed and very lively acceleration," and had oil and air filters as well as "zero lash" hydraulic lifters. The four-speed gearbox was operated by a column shift lever, through a Borg & Beck dry clutch. Torsion bars were used at front and rear, with the front suspension independent.

Jowett was one of the early users of integrated body construction; the integral body and frame was an all-steel welded structure, with sharply sloping (fastback) back end. Bodies were built by Briggs, at Dagenham. The Javelin had fender-mounted headlamps, a deeply-sloped curved windshield, generous-sized windows and alligator-style hood that carried the horizontal-bar grille along with it when raised. A handbrake lever went under the dashboard.

A 1946 brochure announcing the coming-soon Javelin noted that this was "a car the like of which has not been built in England before ... to give you all the verve and smooth riding that drivers of American and Continental cars know so well, coupled with the sturdiness and economy that are a tradition of English engineering." This new model had "successfully come through the most rigorous tests" and it was "hoped to have it ready early in 1947, in quantities that will make it available to critical motorists the world over, and at a price no less interesting than the car itself" (under 500 Pounds Sterling in England).

A 1949 sales brochures pointed out that a Javelin combined "the roominess of a family car, the comfort of a high-priced limousine, the road manners of a sports model, the acceleration of a big American car and a top speed of over 75 mph," while delivering an average of 29 to 33 mpg. For the 1949-50 season, both a standard and DeLuxe Saloon were offered, along with a broader selection of colors and equipment (and a reduced price).

I.D. DATA: Not available.

Model	Body Type & Seating	Engine Type/CID	P.O.E. Price	Weight (lbs.)	Prod. Total
Javelin	4-dr Saloon-5/6P	I4/91	N/A	2184	Note 1

Note 1: Approximately 30,000 Javelins were built from 1947-53.

ENGINE DATA: BASE FOUR: Horizontally-opposed, overhead-valve four-cylinder. Aluminum block (with wet cast iron cylinder liners) and cast iron head. **Displacement:** 90.6 cu. in. (1485 cc). **Bore & Stroke:** 2.85 x 3.54 in. (72.5 x 90 mm). **Compression Ratio:** 7.1:1. **Brake Horsepower:** 50 at 4100 rpm. Three main bearings. Hydraulic valve lifters. Two Zenith carburetors. 12-volt electrical system.

CHASSIS DATA: Wheelbase: 102 in. **Overall Length:** 168 in. (first announced as 164 in.). **Height:** 60.5 in. (ground clearance, 8.5 in.). **Width:** 61 in. **Front Tread:** 51 in. **Rear Tread:** 49 in. **Wheel Type:** pressed steel disc. **Standard Tires:** 5.25x16.

TECHNICAL: Layout: front-engine, rear-drive. **Transmission:** four-speed manual (synchromesh 2nd/3rd/4th); column shift. **Standard Final Drive Ratio:** 4.86:1. **Steering:** internal gear and pinion. **Suspension (front):** torsion bars (independent) with Woodhead Monroe shock absorbers. **Suspension (rear):** transverse torsion bars and Woodhead Monroe shock absorbers. **Brakes:** hydraulic, front/rear drum. **Body Construction:** integral steel body and subframe.

MAJOR OPTIONS: Radio. Heater/ventilator.

PERFORMANCE: Top Speed: 75-80 mph.

PRODUCTION/SALES: Only one Jowett was known to have been sold in the United States in 1948, and none in 1949.
Manufacturer: Jowett Cars Ltd., London W1, England (plant at Idle Bradford, Yorkshire).

HISTORY: Introduced in 1947. Javelins earned several competition victories in the late 1940s, including a 1.5-liter class win at the 1949 Monte Carlo Rally and 2-liter touring class honors at the Belgian 24-hour Grand Prix at Spa (traveling 1,570 miles at 65.5 mph).

344

1950-52 JOWETT

1950 Jowett Javelin four-door sedan.

JAVELIN — FOUR — The four-door saloon contined as before, in standard and Saloon DeLuxe form. Standard equipment included plastic and cloth upholstery, a side jacking system, twin wipers, interior mirror, ashtrays, interior light, two taillamps, driver's sunvisor, bumpers with overriders, and rubber-covered steering wheel with center button horn. The Deluxe model added such extras as armrests and folding elbow rests for driver and passenger, a walnut-grained full instrument panel, and hide upholstery with deeply fluted trim. The DeLuxe also included twin sunvisors (mirror on the passenger side), spotlight, rubber heel mat for the driver, windshield demister and heater, and a radio in walnut grain to match the dashboard. Rope pulls were installed in the rear compartment, with a picnic tray at the back of the front seat and a map drawer under the glovebox. Twin wind-tone horns were used.

Both Javelins had three-abreast seating in front and rear, for a total of up to six passengers. In the DeLuxe model, the folding center armrest could be pulled down when only two people were riding in front. See previous listing for further details.

JUPITER — FOUR — Joining the original saloon was a sports convertible, which soon drew interest in the United States. Announced as "the race bred, high speed 3 seater," it was promoted as primarily a family car, but one with fine performance. Impetus for the arrival of a performance model was the fact that Javelins had made such a strong showing at two major 1949 events: the Monte Carlo Rally and Belgian 24-hour Gran Prix Spa. Although engine displacement was identical to the Javelin (1485 cc), horsepower got a boost from 50 to 60. Special twin carburetors were used, along with special rack-and-pinion steering. Jupiter wore an aluminum body and rode a rigid tubular steel chassis, and had larger Girling hydromechanical brakes and stronger shock absorbers than the family-oriented Javelin. A higher axle ratio (and different transmission ratios) also helped the Jupiter accelerate to 60 mph in about 15 seconds and reach a top speed of more than 90 mph, cruising at 80 mph.

Jupiter's frame was all tubular welded construction with side members of 3-inch diameter chrome molybdenum steel, and 2-inch diameter tubes for struts and torsional stiffness members. Wheelbase was nine inches shorter than the Javelin saloon. Both left- and right-hand drive versions were available. Ground clearance was 7.15 inches, versus 8.5 inches for the Javelin. Standard colors were metallic copper, turquoise blue, British racing green, and scarlet. The walnut dashboard held a 5-inch speedometer and 5-inch tachometer, as well as an oil pressure gauge. Upholstery was fine hide, in either red or beige color. The beige folding convertible top was fabric-lined, and the car had a removable windshield and wind-up windows. Standard equipment included a Stevenson midship jacking system.

Jupiter's recessed center grille was made up of vertical bars, with round headlamps alongside, inboard in nacelles not unlike those of the XK120 Jaguar. Below each headlamp stood a side grille consisting of horizontal bars. Tiny round parking lights sat on the fender tips themselves, with trim strips leading downward to the bumper and back across the top of each fender. The front-fender curve extended into the door to meet the bulging back fender. The entire front end (fenders and hood) hinged upward for access to the engine. With its top raised, the long hood and deck gave the Jupiter a rather stubby cockpit appearance.

I.D. DATA: Not available.

Model	Body Type & Seating	Engine Type/CID	P.O.E. Price	Weight (lbs.)	Prod. Total
Javelin	4-dr Saloon-5/6P	I4/91	1988	2075	Note 1
Jupiter	2-dr Spt Conv-2/3P	I4/91	2548	1792	Note 2

Note 1: Approximately 30,000 Javelins were built from 1947-53.

Note 2: Jupiter was built in limited number.

ENGINE DATA: BASE FOUR: Horizontally-opposed, overhead-valve four-cylinder. Aluminum block (with wet cast iron cylinder liners) and cast iron head. **Displacement:** 90.6 cu. in. (1485 cc). **Bore & Stroke:** 2.85 x 3.54 in. (72.5 x 90 mm). **Compression Ratio:** (Jupiter) 7.2:1 to 8.0:1 (depending on fuel available). **Brake Horsepower:** (Javelin) 50 at 4100 rpm; (Jupiter) 60.5 at 4500 rpm, with 8:1 compression. Three main bearings. Hydraulic valve lifters. Two Zenith downdraft carburetors. 12-volt electrical system.

CHASSIS DATA: Wheelbase: (Jupiter) 93 in.; (Javelin) 102 in. **Overall Length:** (Jup) 163 in.; (Jav) 168 in. **Height:** (Jup) 56 in.; (Jav) 60.5 in. **Width:** (Jup) 62 in.; (Jav) 61 in. **Front Tread:** 51 in. **Rear Tread:** 49 in. **Wheel Type:** pressed steel disc. **Standard Tires:** (Jupiter) 5.50x16; (Javelin) 5.25x16.

TECHNICAL: Layout: front-engine, rear-drive. **Transmission:** four-speed manual (synchromesh 2nd/3rd/4th); column or floor shift. Initial Jupiter overall gear ratios: (1st) 14.62:1; (2nd) 8.91:1; (3rd) 5.63:1; (4th) 4.1:1; (rev) 14.62:1. Later Jupiter overall gear ratios: (1st) 16.25:1; (2nd) 9.9:1; (3rd) 6.25:1; (4th) 4.56:1. **Standard Final Drive Ratio:** (Jupiter) 4.1:1 or, later, 4.56;1; (Javelin) 4.86:1. **Steering:** (Jup) special rack and pinion, either left- or right-hand drive; (Jav) internal gear and pinion. **Suspension (front):** torsion bars (independent) with Woodhead Monroe shock absorbers. **Suspension (rear):** transverse torsion bars and Woodhead Monroe shock absorbers (anti-roll bar on Jupiter). **Brakes:** (Jup) Girling hydromechanical with 10-inch drums; (Jav) front/rear drum. **Body Construction:** (Jup) aluminum body on welded tubular frame; (Jav) integral steel body and subframe. **Fuel Tank:** (Jupiter) 12 gallon.

1951 Jowett Jupiter 2-3 seater.

MAJOR OPTIONS: Floor-mounted gearshift lever. Built-in radio. Smith's fresh air conditioning and heating system. Special body colors.

PERFORMANCE: Top Speed: (Jupiter) 90 + mph; (Javelin) 75 + mph. **Acceleration (0-60 mph):** (Jup) about 15 seconds; (Jav) 22.2-24.3 seconds. **Acceleration (quarter-mile):** (Jupiter) 20.5 seconds. **Fuel Mileage:** 24-28 mpg.

PRODUCTION/SALES: About five Jowetts were sold in the U.S. in 1950, but the total jumped to approximately 46 for 1951 and 110 for 1952.

Manufacturer: Jowett Cars Ltd., Idle, Bradford, Yorkshire, England.

Distributor: The Hoffman Motor Car Co. (New York City); Angell Motors (Pasadena, Calif.); and Sanders Motor Sales (Houston, Texas).

HISTORY: Introduced: (Javelin) 1947; (Jupiter) 1950. Jupiter was first seen at the British Motor Show in New York in April 1950. Credit for its creation goes to Professor Eberan von Eberhorst, who had formerly designed Grand Prix race cars. In its first racing outing, a lone Jupiter won its class at the Grand Prix d'Endurance at Le Mans, France in June 1950, averaging 75.8 mph for 24 hours. Jupiter also took class honors at the 1951 Monte Carlo Rally, while a Javelin saloon finished fourth in the same event. Jowett cars also shared the Stuart trophy for best British performance. Advertisements promised that "your dealer can have your Javelin or Jupiter waiting for you in England for your 1951 vacation."

1953-54 JOWETT

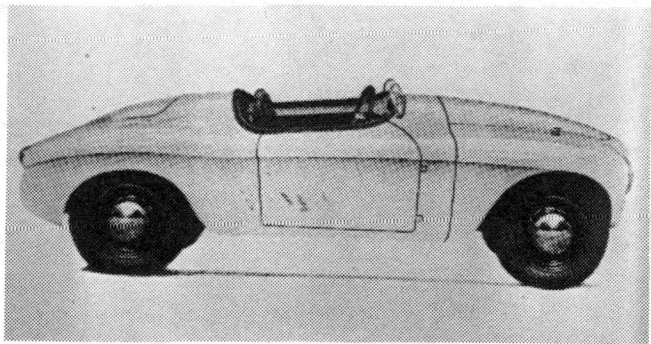

1954 Jowett Jupiter R-4 two-door competition roadster.

JAVELIN — FOUR — A new Series III engine went beneath the bonnet of the Javelin saloon for 1953 (its final year), identical in displacement to the previous flat four but producing 52.5 horsepower. Heavier-gauge bumpers were used now, and interior held fine leather. Headlining material was changed to union cloth. Five grownups could ride a Javelin in comfort, and both driver and front passenger now had a standard sunvisor.

JUPITER — FOUR — Two sports models were available in 1953 (Mark I and Mark IA), both powered by the new Series III engine. That new powerplant had a sturdier crankshaft, new bearings, and improved oil flow, among other technical advances. Along with a longer top, the Mark IA had newly designed luggage accommodation, consisting of a tail locker opening from outside. Its tonneau extended behind the driver's seat, allowing space for small luggage. In the Mark I, luggage was reached from behind the driver's seat only. Jupiters had bench seating and a detachable windshield (which could be replaced by aero screens for competition). The Mark I instrument panel fascia was walnut grain, while Mark IA was painted metal. Standard colors were: metallichrome turquoise with red or beige leather upholstery and beige top; Connaught green with beige leather and top; ivory with red leather and black top; or scarlet with beige leather and top.

I.D. DATA: Serial number is on a metal plate on left side of firewall. Engine number is on left of block, at the front.

Model	Body Type & Seating	Engine Type/CID	P.O.E. Price	Weight (lbs.)	Prod. Total
JAVELIN					
Javelin	4-dr Saloon-5/6P	I4/91	2895	2240	Note 1
JUPITER					
Mark I	2-dr Conv-2/3P	I4/91	3295	1895	Note 2
Mark IA	2-dr Spt Conv-2/3P	I4/91	2795	1895	Note 2

Note 1: Approximately 30,000 Javelins were built from 1947-53.

Note 2: Jupiter was built in limited number.

ENGINE DATA: BASE FOUR: Horizontally-opposed, overhead-valve four-cylinder. Aluminum block (with wet cast iron cylinder liners) and cast iron head. **Displacement:** 90.6 cu. in. (1485 cc). **Bore & Stroke:** 2.85 x 3.54 in. (72.5 x 90 mm). **Compression Ratio:** (Javelin) 7.2:1; (Jupiter) 8.0:1. **Brake Horsepower:** (Javelin) 52.5 at 4500 rpm; (Jupiter) 62.5 at 4500 rpm, with 8:1 compression. **Torque:** (Javelin) 77 lbs.-ft. at 1900 rpm; (Jupiter) 94 at 3000. Three main bearings. Hydraulic valve lifters. Two Zenith carburetors. 12-volt electrical system.

CHASSIS DATA: Wheelbase: (Jup) 93 in.; (Javelin) 102 in. **Overall Length:** (Jup) 168 in.; (Jav) 168 in. **Height:** (Jup) 56 in.; (Jav) 60.5 in. **Width:** (Jup) 62 in.; (Jav) 61 in. **Front Tread:** (Jup) 52 in.; (Jav) 51 in. **Rear Tread:** (Jup) 50.5 in.; (Jav) 49 in. **Wheel Type:** pressed steel disc. **Standard Tires:** (Jupiter) 5.50x16; (Javelin) 5.25x16.

TECHNICAL: Layout: front-engine, rear-drive. **Transmission:** four-speed manual (synchromesh 2nd/3rd/4th); column shift. Jupiter overall gear ratios: (1st) 16.3:1; (2nd) 9.9:1; (3rd) 6.3:1; (4th) 4.56:1. **Standard Final Drive Ratio:** (Jupiter) 4.56:1; (Javelin) 4.88:1. **Steering:** (Jup) special rack and pinion, either left- or right-hand drive; (Jav) internal gear and pinion. **Suspension (front):** torsion bars (independent) with Woodhead Monroe shock absorbers. **Suspension (rear):** transverse torsion bars and Woodhead Monroe shock absorbers (anti-roll bar on Jupiter). **Brakes:** (Jup) Girling hydromechanical with 10-inch drums; (Jav) front/rear drum. **Body Construction:** (Jupiter) aluminum body on tubular frame; (Javelin) integral steel body and subframe.

MAJOR OPTIONS: Similar to 1950-52.

PERFORMANCE: Top Speed: (Jupiter) 90-95 mph; (Javelin) 75 + mph. **Acceleration (0-60 mph):** (Jupiter) 15-16.5 seconds. **Fuel Mileage:** (Jupiter) about 25 mpg.

PRODUCTION/SALES: About 66 Jowetts were sold in the U.S. in 1953.

Manufacturer & Distributor: Same as 1950-52.

HISTORY: Introduced: (Javelin) 1947; (Javelin PE) 1952; (Jupiter) 1950; (Jupiter IA) 1952. The Mark I/IA Jupiter appeared at the London Motor Show in fall 1952. A competition version of the Jupiter also was built, called the R1. With the demise of the conventional Javelin and Jupiter after 1953, Jowett made one more stab at the marketplace with an R4 competition Jupiter. Wearing a streamlined, laminated plastic body, that one rode a shorter (84-inch) wheelbase and had semi-elliptic leaf springs at the rear. Its engine was rated 64 horsepower, rumored to deliver a top speed as high as 120 mph. But that wasn't enough to save the faltering Jowett company.

JUSTICIALISTA

Hardly one of the better-known cars of the world, the Justicialista enjoyed a brief spurt into the marketplace during the mid-1950s. One of the few examples of South American production, it was built in Argentina. Not only a sedan and station wagon, but also a gaudy Gran Sport convertible, were introduced, making an appearance at the International Motor Sports show in New York in February 1954. By 1956, however, the name was gone, never having made a dent in the world market. Thus, it serves more as a curiosity than as an example of production models.

1954-55 JUSTICIALISTA

1954 Justicialista five-passenger sedan.

800 — FOUR — Similar in style and layout to the German DKW, the front-drive 800 sedan carried a two-stroke four-cylinder engine. The two-door sedan looked rather like a truncated 1951 Chevrolet, in miniature, with a split windshield. An Institec station wagon also was produced, with a smaller two-cylinder engine.

SPORT — FOUR/V-8 — This baroque-styled convertible, sometimes referred to as "Gran Sport" or "Super Sports," wore a fiberglass body atop a tubular frame, and carried either a Porsche four-cylinder engine or an air-cooled 3.0-liter V-8. Torsion bars made up the suspension at both ends. Styling features included recessed headlamps, a curved windshield, and a tall, protruding bulged hood that gave the car a heavy appearance. The low grille had a curved upper bar and full-width (wraparound horizontal center bar. A long bodyside trim strip ran just above the front wheel arch, while rear wheels were partly enclosed.

1954 Justicialista Sports prototype.

I.D. DATA: Not available.

Model	Body Type & Seating	Engine Type/CID	P.O.E. Price	Weight (lbs.)	Prod. Total
800	2-dr Sedan-5P	I4/49	N/A	1874	Note 1
800	2-dr Sta Wag-6P	I2	N/A	N/A	Note 1
Sport	2-dr Conv-2/3P	H4/91	N/A	1500	Note 1

Note 1: "Several hundred" Justicialistas were produced in all, according to the *Encyclopedia of Motorcars*, most of them the small sedan.

ENGINE DATA: BASE FOUR (800 sedan): Two-stroke four-cylinder. **Displacement:** 48.8 cu. in. (800 cc). **Bore & Stroke:** 2.28 x 2.99 in. (58 x 76 mm). **Compression Ratio:** 6.5:1. **Brake Horsepower:** 36 at 4400 rpm.

Note: Station wagons were powered by a two-cylinder engine.

BASE FOUR (Sport convertible): Horizontally-opposed, overhead-valve four-cylinder (air cooled). **Displacement:** 90.8 cu. in. (1489 cc). **Bore & Stroke:** 3.15 x 2.91 in. (80 x 74 mm). **Compression Ratio:** 7.0:1. **Brake Horsepower:** 55 at 4400 rpm.

OPTIONAL V-8 (Gran Sport): Air-cooled "vee" type eight-cylinder. **Displacement:** 183 cu. in. (3000 cid). **Bore & Stroke:** 3.14 x 2.95 in. (80 x 75 mm). **Compression Ratio:** 7.0:1. **Brake Horsepower:** 116 at 4300 rpm.

CHASSIS DATA: Wheelbase: (sed) 94 in.; (conv) 94.5 in. **Overall Length:** (sed) 168 in.; (conv) 163.3 in. **Height:** (sed) 57 in.; (conv) 53.2 in. **Width:** (sed) 60 in.; (conv) 61.8 in. **Front Tread:** (conv) 49.2 in. **Rear Tread:** (conv) 49.2 in.

TECHNICAL: Layout: front-engine, front-drive. **Transmission:** (sedan) three-speed manual; (conv) five-speed synchromesh manual. **Suspension (front):** (sed) independent with transverse leaf spring; (conv) independent with longitudinal torsion bars. **Suspension (rear):** (sed) rigid axle with torsion bar; (conv) independent with single transverse torsion bar. **Brakes:** hydraulic, front/rear drum. **Body Construction:** (sedan) on pressed rail chassis; (conv) reinforced plastic monocoque body on tubular frame. **Fuel Tank:** (conv) 15 gallon.

PERFORMANCE: Top Speed: (sedan) 74 mph; (4-cyl conv) 100 mph claimed. **Fuel Mileage:** (sed) 27 mpg; (4-cyl conv) 23.5 mpg claimed; (V-8 conv) 12-15 mpg.

Manufacturer: Industrias Aeronauticas y Mecanicas Estado (I.A.M.E.), Cordoba Province, Argentina.

HISTORY: "Wherever the 'Justicialista Sport' appears," claimed a company sales brochure issued at the New York Motor Sports Show in 1954, "it arouses the astonishment and admiration of all friends of the automobile." Justicialistas were the first vehicles produced by the infant auto industry in Argentina, after I.A.M.E. was established by Argentine President Juan Peron late in 1951. In August 1954, *Motor Trend* reported that only one Sport convertible had been built, and that one was presented to Peron. Also produced during this period was a Rastrojero truck with Willys engine. The sedan design did not expire completely, but was modified by 1960 for production as the Graciela, using a Wartburg (East German) engine.

LAGONDA

Not many British auto companies can trace their origins to an American. Lagonda is the exception, having been founded by Wilbur Gunn, who named the company after the Indian name for a river near his birthplace in Ohio, after moving to Britain as an opera singer. Before the turn of the century, Gunn was building motorcycles in his Staines shop, called Lagonda Engineering Co. By 1905, he switched from two- to three-wheelers, adding a steering wheel the following year. Before long, Gunn turned to four-wheel transport, starting with a shaft-drive model powered by a V-twin engine. Early examples used a primitive form of unit construction. A 16/18 hp version raced at the Brooklands course in 1909. Lagonda soon began selling the bulk of its output to Russia, as a result of victory in the 1910 Reliability Trial that ran from Moscow to St. Petersburg. In 1913, after starting to manufacture their own engines, a new Lagonda Ltd. firm was formed. A smaller 1099-cc four-cylinder model, again with integral construction, was the first offering before the new company turned to armaments manufacture during the Great War.

Gunn himself died in 1920, but the company kept expanding through the 1920s. Between 1913 and 1926, at least 6,000 of the smaller cars were produced. The next model was larger and more expensive, with a twin-cam 1954-cc four-cylinder engine and, once again, integral construction. Even with heavy coachwork, the bigger saloons and tourers managed 60 mph. Sales fell somewhat, but increased profits from the costlier cars kept the company in the black regardless. A "Speed" model and a six-cylinder example arrived by 1927, the latter enlarged to 2931 cc in 1928. Those were followed by a supercharged 2-liter Lagonda. A Lagonda team finished eleventh at Le Mans in 1928, finishing most of the race with a cracked frame and without front brakes. On the technical front, Lagonda incorporated a Maybach eight-speed preselector gearbox into one version of the 3-litre; but it attracted few customers.

Early in the 1930s, a new six-cylinder Lagonda emerged, based on a 1991-cc engine produced by Crossley (but modified at Lagonda). Increased attention to the upper end of the market led to a switch from Lagonda-built bodies to coachwork from outside suppliers. The twin-cam four-cylinder Rapier, introduced in 1933, wore bodies from several coachbuilders. Stepping into larger powerplants, Lagonda put out a 4.5-liter M45 with a Meadows six-cylinder engine (formerly used in the Invicta). Saloons and touring models could be purchased with either Lagonda-built or outside bodies, while all the drophead coupe bodies came from elsewhere. Lagonda M45R Rapides were capable of 100 mph, and one of the 4.5-liter models won the Le Mans race, giving Britain its only victory between 1930 and the 1950s.

Financial troubles resulted from the slack sales in the early Depression years, and in 1935 the company went into receivership. Alan Good bought the assets, forming LG Motors (Staines) Ltd. One of Good's greatest contributions was the fact that he'd secured the designing services of W.O. Bentley. Rapier production was abandoned (though some were built from leftover parts by another company). W.O. Bentley's influence was evident in the final prewar models: the LG45 and LG6, both with Meadows engines. He also designed a new single-cam V-12 version in the late 1930s. Viewed as his masterpiece, the V-12 Lagonda had torsion-bar front suspension and 105-110 mph

speed potential, even when pushing some 5,000 pounds of motorcar. Two special-bodied two-seaters V-12s entered the 1939 Le Mans event, finishing in third and fourth position.

A Lagonda for the postwar era was announced in September 1945, initially named Lagonda-Bentley and powered by a 2580-cc twin-cam six. Rolls-Royce nixed the name, and Alan Good had lost interest in proceeding with its production anyway. Not until 1947 did David Brown, a tractor manufacturer, buy the Lagonda facility for the purpose of installing its engine in the Aston Martin sports cars, which he'd taken over shortly before. Aston Martin Lagonda Ltd. was formed as a subsidiary of the David Brown & Sons company, with production of both makes to take place at Feltham. Finally, in 1948, the new Lagonda emerged in ready-to-sell form, with a cruciform chassis and, unlike other British production cars, all-independent suspension. Grand Touring saloons and drophead coupes were produced. A subsequent 3-liter version was built from 1954-58. Then, after a hiatus, came the Rapide of the early 1960s. Late in the 1970s came the vast Lagonda saloon, which remained in production into the 1990s (see Aston Martin listing for details).

1947 Lagonda 2½-liter drophead coupe.

1948-52 LAGONDA

2-1/2 LITRE — Mk I — SIX — Designed by W.O. Bentley, the 2580-cc Lagonda was built by the David Brown company in the Aston Martin plant (which Brown had purchased). The same six-cylinder, twin-overhead-cam engine (with 60-degree inclined overhead valves) was used in the Aston Martin DB2 and DB2/4 sports cars. With 6.5:1 compression and twin SU carburetors, the engine delivered 105 bhp at 5000 rpm. Some early examples had the Cotal electromagnetic gearbox with preselector, but most used the David Brown manual four-speed transmission with column shift lever, and a Borg & Beck clutch. Suspension chores were handled by coil springs at the front and torsion bars at the rear, with Armstrong double-acting hydraulic shock absorbers. The hypoid bevel final drive was mounted on the frame, which consisted of two 6.5-inch deep beams arranged as a cruciform. Lockheed hydraulic brakes had 12-inch front drums, 11-inch at the rear. Rack- and-pinion steering was used. Disc wheels held 6.00x16 tires.

Both a four-door saloon and two-door drophead coupe were produced, with streamlined bodies essentially handmade by Tickford. A curving-downward, fairly narrow grille was made up of vertical bars with a predominant center bar. Headlamps stood inboard, alongside the grille. Tiny round parking lights stood below and outboard of the headlamps. "Suicide" (rear-hinged) doors held vent windows, and the flat windshield was in one piece. Saloons had a vent window in the rear door, as well as up front. The spare wheel was stowed beneath the floor of the trunk, quickly removable and entirely independent of the luggage compartment. Inside was a 17-inch spring-spoke steering wheel. Colors available were: Black body with beige upholstery; Gray with medium blue; Maroon with beige; Green with gray; polychromatic Blue with gray; or Light Navy with medium blue upholstery.

I.D. DATA: Chassis serial number is stamped on a plate at the front of the bulkhead. Starting serial number (1948 model): LAG/48/4. Engine number is stamped on top of timing cover, and on a plate at the front of the bulkhead. Engine code was LB6A/B.

Model 2-1/2 LITRE	Body Type & Seating	Engine Type/CID	P.O.E. Price	Weight (lbs.)	Prod. Total
Mk I	4-dr Saloon-5/6P	I6/157	6950	3345	359
Mk I	2-dr Dhd Cpe-5P	I6/157	7500	3410	118

Weight Note: Factory reported "dry" weight to be approximately 31 cwt (3,534 pounds).

Production Note: A total of 510 2.5-Litre Lagondas were produced through July 1953 (including 23 unbodied chassis). Figures shown are for the period from October 1948 to July 1952. Of the Mk I saloons, 302 had Hanworth bodies while 57 were built at Tickford. A total of 12 cars were built in 1948, and 61 in 1949.

ENGINE DATA: BASE SIX: Inline, dual-overhead-cam six-cylinder (LB6A/B). Cast iron block and aluminum head. **Displacement:** 157.4 cu. in. (2580 cc). **Bore & Stroke:** 3.07 x 3.54 in. (78 x 90 mm). **Compression Ratio:** 6.5:1. **Brake Horsepower:** 105 at 5000 rpm. Four main bearings. Solid valve lifters. Two SU horizontal carburetors. 12-volt electrical (two 6-volt batteries).

1949 Lagonda fixed-head coupe.

1950 Lagonda 2½-liter four-door saloon. (Sotheby's)

CHASSIS DATA: Wheelbase: 113.5 in. **Overall Length:** 188 in. **Height:** 64 in. **Width:** 68 in. **Front Tread:** 56.4 in. **Rear Tread:** 56.8 in. **Wheel Type:** steel disc. **Standard Tires:** 6.00x16.

TECHNICAL: Layout: front-engine, rear-drive. **Transmission:** four-speed manual; column shift. Overall gear ratios: (1st) 13.60:1; (2nd) 9.15:1; (3rd) 6.20:1; (4th) 4.56:1; (rev) 13.60:1. Some early models had a Cotal electromagnetic (preselector) transmission. **Standard Final Drive Ratio:** 4.56:1. **Steering:** rack and pinion. **Suspension (front):** independent; coil springs. **Suspension (rear):** independent; torsion bar with Armstrong double-acting hydraulic shock absorbers. **Brakes:** hydraulic, front/rear drum. **Body Construction:** separate body on cruciform steel frame. **Fuel Tank:** 22.8 gallons.

PERFORMANCE: Top Speed: 90-91 mph. **Acceleration (0-60 mph):** (saloon) 18.2 seconds; (drophead) 17.6 seconds. **Acceleration (quarter-mile):** (drophead) 21.7 seconds. **Fuel Mileage:** 20-22 mpg (factory; Imperial gallons). Tests produced 18-20 mpg for the saloon and 17 mpg for the drophead coupe.

Manufacturer: Lagonda Ltd., Feltham, Middlesex, England (subsidiary of David Brown & Sons Ltd).

HISTORY: Lagonda promoted its first postwar models as being "for the connoisseur."

1953 LAGONDA

2-1/2 LITRE — Mk II — SIX — Billed as "the thoroughbred 2.6-litre. A David Brown product," the revised Lagonda saloon was described as "Impeccable in performance, smooth as silk." Its engine, the sales brochure went on, had been made famous in the Aston DB2 sports car. Both appearance and mechanical details were similar to the Mk I, including four-wheel independent suspension, hand-built coachwork, inboard headlamps, and separately-mounted auxiliary lights atop the bumper. Small parking lights sat on each fender. Rounded front wheel openings in fenders tapered into vestigial running boards, leading to rounded rear fenders with cutaway wheel openings. Essentially, this was still the prewar upright look with flat windshield and rear-hinged front doors. Gear ratios for the David Brown four-speed synchromesh gearbox changed slightly. The six-cylinder, twin-cam engine again displaced 2580 cc but produced 116 bhp, as a result of a compression increase in the hemispherical combustion chambers. Two variable-jet SU carbs were fed by twin electric fuel pumps. Interiors seated five (possibly six) and had a

distinctive walnut fascia, garnish rails, door lights, thick pile carpets, and leather upholstery. Windshield washers were included with the two-speed wipers. A "Radiomobile" was optional.

I.D. DATA: Chassis serial number is stamped on a plate at the front of the bulkhead. Starting serial number: (Mk II) LAG/50/502. Engine number is stamped on top of timing cover, and on a plate at the front of the bulkhead.

1953 Lagonda three-liter drophead coupe. (Sotheby's)

Model	Body Type & Seating	Engine Type/CID	P.O.E. Price	Weight (lbs.)	Prod. Total
2-1/2 LITRE					
Mk II	4-dr Saloon-5/6P	I6/157	N/A	3306	10

Weight Note: Amount shown is approximate "dry" weight.

Production Note: Figure shown is for September 1952 through July 1953. No drophead coupes were built during this period, but 16 additional chassis were manufactured. A total of 510 2.5-Litre Lagondas (Mk I and Mk II), including unbodied chassis, were produced through July 1953.

ENGINE DATA: BASE SIX: Inline, dual-overhead-cam six-cylinder (LB6E). Cast iron block and aluminum head. **Displacement:** 157.4 cu. in. (2580 cc). **Bore & Stroke:** 3.07 x 3.54 in. (78 x 90 mm). **Compression Ratio:** 7.5:1. **Brake Horsepower:** 116 at 5000 rpm. Solid valve lifters. Two SU horizontal carburetors. 12-volt electrical (two 6-volt batteries).

CHASSIS DATA: Wheelbase: 113.5 in. **Overall Length:** 188 in. **Height:** 64 in. **Width:** 68 in. **Front Tread:** 56.4 in. **Rear Tread:** 56.8 in. **Wheel Type:** steel disc. **Standard Tires:** 6.00x16.

TECHNICAL: Layout: front-engine, rear-drive. **Transmission:** David Brown four-speed manual; column shift. Overall gear ratios: (1st) 13.30:1; (2nd) 9.02:1; (3rd) 6.06:1; (4th) 4.56:1; (rev) 13.30:1. **Standard Final Drive Ratio:** 4.56:1. **Steering:** rack and pinion. **Suspension (front):** independent; coil springs. **Suspension (rear):** independent; torsion bar with Armstrong double-acting hydraulic shock absorbers. **Brakes:** hydraulic, front/rear drum. **Body Construction:** separate body on cruciform steel frame.

PERFORMANCE: Similar to Mk I (1948-52).

Manufacturer: Lagonda Division, The David Brown Corp. Ltd., Feltham, Middlesex, England.

HISTORY: Mark II introduced in October 1952; dropped during 1953 and replaced by 3-liter model late in that year. Lagonda's slogan for the Mk II was: "At any speed...a beautifully mannered car."

1954-56 LAGONDA

1954 Lagonda three-liter two-door Tickford sedan.

3-LITRE — SERIES I — SIX — Larger in both overall dimensions and engine displacement, the restyled Lagonda looked similar at a glance to its predecessor up front, except for headlamps with bright rims mounted in the conventional outboard position on fenders and small round parking lights below. The narrow vertical-bar grille was more steeply angled, and the windshield was curved. In profile, however, the new model looked markedly different, more modern and graceful, with a long tapered deck instead of the former upright shape. Continuous (slab-sided) body panels replaced the earlier separate-fender look. Rear quarter windows opened for ventilation. A horizontal bodyside trim strip began halfway back on the front fender and continued to the rear of the rear door. Standard equipment included leather upholstery and hardwood veneer interior trim, an H.M.V. "Radiomobile" radio, an "air conditioning and demisting unit," twin fog lights at the bumper, four interior door lights, single backup light, a trunk light, and a built-in Smiths hydraulic jacking system at each wheel. On the dashboard was a speedometer with trip and mileage recorder, clock, ammeter, water temperature gauge, combined gas

and oil capacity gauge, oil pressure gauge, tachometer, and lighter. A reserve fuel tank was controlled by a switch. A two-door Sports Saloon and a drophead coupe (bodies by Tickford) were introduced first, followed later by the four-door saloon. Engine construction was similar to the 2580-cc version, but the bore was increased by 5 mm to gain displacement. The same engine went into the Aston Martin DB3S. For 1955, power brakes were installed; and for 1956, a floor gearshift lever became standard (with column lever optional).

I.D. DATA: Chassis serial number is stamped on a plate at the front of the bulkhead. Starting serial number: LB290/24. Engine number is stamped on top of timing cover, and on a plate at the front of the bulkhead. Engine code was VB6J.

Note: Early models had chassis numbers that continued in the 2.6-Litre Mk II sequence.

Model 3-LITRE	Body Type & Seating	Engine Type/CID	P.O.E. Price	Weight (lbs.)	Prod. Total
I	2-dr Saloon-5P	I6/178	Note 1	3556	70
I	4-dr Saloon-5/6P	I6/178	N/A	3615	68
I	2-dr Dhd Cpe-5P	I6/178	N/A	3685	50

Note 1: Estimated at $7160 in U.S.

Production Note: A total of 270 Three-Liter Lagondas (Series I and II), including one Series I chassis, were produced through 1958.

ENGINE DATA: BASE SIX: Inline, dual-overhead-cam six-cylinder (VB6J). Cast iron block with detachable liners; hemispherical combustion chambers in aluminum head. **Displacement:** 178.3 cu. in. (2922 cc). **Bore & Stroke:** 3.267 x 3.543 in. (83 x 90 mm). **Compression Ratio:** 8.2:1. **Brake Horsepower:** 140 at 5000 rpm. **Torque:** 178 lbs.-ft. at 3000 rpm. Solid valve lifters (no tappet adjustment). Two SU variable-jet carburetors. 12-volt.

CHASSIS DATA: Wheelbase: 113.5 in. **Overall Length:** 196 in. **Height:** 62 in. **Width:** 69.5 in. **Front Tread:** 56.8 in. **Rear Tread:** 56.8 in. **Wheel Type:** steel disc with rim embellishers. **Standard Tires:** 6.00x16.

TECHNICAL: Layout: front-engine, rear-drive. **Transmission:** David Brown four-speed manual; column shift (floor shift for 1956). Overall gear ratios: (1st) 13.30:1; (2nd) 9.02:1; (3rd) 6.06:1; (4th) 4.56:1; (rev) 13.30:1. **Standard Final Drive Ratio:** 4.56:1. **Steering:** rack and pinion. **Suspension (front):** independent; coil springs with double-acting hydraulic shock absorbers. **Suspension (rear):** independent; torsion bars with swing axles and double-acting hydraulic shock absorbers. **Brakes:** hydraulic, front/rear drum. **Body Construction:** aluminum body panels on cruciform steel frame. **Fuel Tank:** 19 (Imperial) gallons.

PERFORMANCE: Top Speed: 95-100 mph. **Acceleration (0-60 mph):** 13.5 seconds (0-50 mph in 11.4 seconds). **Acceleration (quarter-mile):** 20.5 seconds. **Fuel Mileage:** about 17.5 mpg (Imperial gallons); estimated 24-26 mpg (U.S.).

Note: Later testing of the Series II, with the same engine output, produced faster speeds; see next listing.

Manufacturer: Lagonda Division, The David Brown Corp. Ltd., Feltham, Middlesex, England.

HISTORY: Two-door saloon and drophead coupe (by Tickford) introduced in October 1953; four-door sedan in October 1954. Production of the two-door saloon ceased in 1955, while the four-door and drophead continued into 1956. Production moved from its original site to a new location at Newport Pagnell during the run of the 3-Litre. Sales literature promoted the new 3-Litre as the "challenging" Lagonda. A saloon built for David Brown himself had a V-12 engine and a grille similar to the V-12 Le Mans Lagonda, suggesting the possibility of a new 12-cylinder model.

1957-58 LAGONDA

3-LITRE — SERIES II — SIX — Modifications were modest for the final Lagonda saloon and drophead coupe, which switched to a floor-mounted gearshift lever. The speedometer was now at the dashboard's center, tachometer at the side; but little other change was evident. Standard equipment was similar to Series I, including leather upholstery, two-speed wiper/washer, a make-up mirror and cigarette case, electric clock, map light, and oil level indicator. Bodies for the four-door saloon and two-door drophead coupe again were built by Tickford.

I.D. DATA: Chassis serial number is stamped on a plate at the front of the bulkhead. Starting serial number: LB290/1/142. Engine number is stamped on top of timing cover, and on a plate at the front of the bulkhead.

Note: Serial numbers overlapped with those of the Series I models.

Model 3-LITRE	Body Type & Seating	Engine Type/CID	P.O.E. Price	Weight (lbs.)	Prod. Total
II	4-dr Saloon-5/6P	I6/178	Note 1	3615	76
II	2-dr Dhd Cpe-5P	I6/178	Note 1	3685	5

Note 1: Price at factory in England estimated at $5586 in 1957.

Production Note: A total of 270 Three-Liter Lagondas (Series I and II) were produced through 1958.

ENGINE DATA: BASE SIX: Same as Series I (1954-56).

CHASSIS DATA: Same as Series I (1954-56).

TECHNICAL: Layout: front-engine, rear-drive. **Transmission:** David Brown four-speed manual; floor shift (column shift optional). Overall gear ratios: (1st) 13.30:1; (2nd) 9.02:1; (3rd) 6.06:1; (4th) 4.56:1; (rev) 13.30:1. **Standard Final Drive Ratio:** 4.56:1. **Steering:** rack and pinion. **Suspension (front):** independent; coil springs with double-acting hydraulic shock absorbers and anti-roll bar. **Suspension (rear):** independent; torsion bars with swing axles and double-acting hydraulic shock absorbers. **Brakes:** Lockheed Phase II hydraulic, front/rear drum; servo assist. **Body Construction:** aluminum body panels on cruciform steel frame. **Fuel Tank:** 19 (Imperial) gallons.

PERFORMANCE: Top Speed: up to 104 mph. **Acceleration (0-60 mph):** 12.9 sec. (0-50 mph in 9.1 seconds). **Acceleration (quarter-mile):** 19.5 seconds. **Fuel Mileage:** about 14.5 mpg.

Manufacturer: The David Brown Corp. Ltd., Lagonda Motors Ltd., Newport Pagnell, Buckinghamshire, England.

HISTORY: Series II introduced in October 1956; production of the drophead coupe ceased in 1957, the saloon early in 1958. Sales literature billed this version as the "illustrious" Lagonda. "Today," the brochure quoted chairman David Brown, "in a world of narrowing scope for personal skills and enthusiasms, the Lagonda commends itself as a rare example of individual endeavor in automobile practice." *Top Gear* magazine said: "It

is interesting to note that performance...is higher than that of the immediately prewar V-12 model, which had an engine capacity of 4-1/2 liters." They added that the drophead coupe "combines saloon comfort with the greatest ease of convertibility. The hood moves smoothly to its three positions according to need."

INTERIM NOTE: After production of the 3-Litre saloon halted early in 1958, Lagonda endured a hiatus until 1961, when the new Rapide appeared.

1961-64 LAGONDA

1962 Lagonda Rapide saloon.

RAPIDE — SIX — After building close to a thousand rather posh saloons and drophead coupes in the 1950s, Lagonda took a different turn when production resumed in the 1960s, turning instead to a high-performance GT four-door saloon. *Superleggera* bodywork came from the Italian firm of Touring (at Milan). Riding an Aston Martin DB4 platform, with longer wheelbase, the Rapide had a De Dion rear suspension and was powered by a slightly detuned version of the DB4's 3995 cc (244 cid) six-cylinder engine. Rapide's sleek profile was marred by its front end, which put four headlamps (two large, two small) high up on the fenders. The narrow vertical rectangular grille had a center divider bar, while twin side grilles with single horizontal bars reached below each headlamp pair, to round parking lights at the fender tips. Bodysides displayed an oval opening at the cowl, with a horizontal trim strip and full wheel openings. Performance got a considerable boost over prior models, however, with top speeds approaching 130 mph. Though offered in the U.S., few Rapides were sold outside Britain.

1963 Lagonda Rapide four-liter four-door sports saloon.

1963 Lagonda Rapide four-door sport sedan. (Christie's)

I.D. DATA: Not available.

Model	Body Type & Seating	Engine Type/CID	P.O.E. Price	Weight (lbs.)	Prod. Total
Rapide	4-dr Saloon-5P	I6/244	13750	3780	55

ENGINE DATA: BASE SIX: Inline, dual-overhead-cam six-cylinder. Cast iron block with aluminum head. **Displacement:** 244 cu. in. (3995 cc). **Bore & Stroke:** 3.78 x 3.62 in. (96 x 92 mm). **Compression Ratio:** 8.25:1. **Brake Horsepower:** 236 at 5000 rpm. **Torque:** 265 lbs.-ft. at 4000 rpm. Solid valve lifters. Two Solex 44PHH carburetors. 12-volt electrical.

CHASSIS DATA: Wheelbase: 114 in. **Overall Length:** 195.5 in. **Height:** 56 in. **Width:** 69.5 in. **Front Tread:** 54 in. **Rear Tread:** 55.5 in. **Standard Tires:** 7.10x15.

TECHNICAL: Layout: front-engine, rear-drive. **Transmission:** four-speed manual or Borg-Warner three-speed automatic. Manual gear ratios: (1st) 2.92:1; (2nd) 1.85:1; (3rd) 1.25:1; (4th) 1.00:1. **Standard Final Drive Ratio:** 3.77:1. **Steering:** rack and pinion. **Suspension (front):** independent; coil springs with double-acting hydraulic shock absorbers and anti-roll bar. **Suspension (rear):** De Dion independent; torsion bars with swing axles and double-acting hydraulic shock absorbers. **Body Construction:** aluminum body panels on platform steel frame.

PERFORMANCE: Top Speed: 125-130 mph.

Manufacturer: Aston Martin Lagonda Ltd., Newport Pagnell, Buckinghamshire, England.

Distributor: J.S. Inskip, Inc., New York City.

POSTSCRIPT: After production of the Rapide ceased in 1964, the Lagonda name essentially disappeared for more than a decade. A V-8 prototype was built for Sir David Brown in 1971, followed by seven early production versions; but serious production of the Aston Martin Lagonda four-door saloon would not resume until October 1976. See Aston Martin listing for details.

LAMBORGHINI

Ferruccio Lamborghini, an Italian manufacturer who'd earned his fortune in tractors and heating appliances, began work on a car of his own car in 1962. Having owned Ferraris, he was certain that he could produce a better high-performance model. Lamborghini bought a new factory at Sant'Agata, Italy (near Bologna and Modena), and hired engineer Giotto Bizzarrini--formerly an engineer at Ferrari and Iso--for design duties. Early in 1963, Giampaolo Dallara (late of Ferrari and Maserati) joined the staff to supervise development of the prototype and head the company, known as Automobili Ferruccio Lamborghini S.p.A. He'd been at Ferrari and Maserati.

Lamborghini wasn't content to develop a dramatic body, with superior handling. He also wanted the car that bore his name to carry its own brand of powerplant, and assigned Bizzarrini to create a four-cam, 60-degree V-12 for that purpose. By the summer of 1963, the first Lambo engine was running, ready to send its power to a five-speed ZF gearbox. With that drivetrain installed, the 350 GTV prototype appeared at the Turin (Italy) show in November 1963. Styling was the work of Franco Scaglione, formerly at Bertone, while the actual body was built by Carrozzeria Sargiotto, in Turin. Design features included retractable headlamps, and the prototype was said by some to bear a certain similarity to the Aston Martin DB4GT Zagato, and the E-Type Jaguar.

Production was rolling in March 1964, with a modified body design by Carrozzeria Touring (of Milan). This production version had a more rounded appearance in the lower portion and a simpler tail design. The retracting headlamps seen on the prototype were abandoned, replaced by exposed oval units. The prototype's gaping air intake was now covered by a conventional grille.

With a slight name change, the 350 GT debuted at the Geneva (Switzerland) show in March 1964. That was followed by the 400 GT, with a larger (3929-cc) version of the four-cam V-12 engine. Then came the suprisingly sexy mid-engined Miura, which set the pace for the supercar league, both among other sports-car manufacturers and for future Lambos.

Lamborghini turned to a true four-seat model (as opposed to a tight 2+2 coupe) with the Espada, which debuted in 1968. Islero, a rebodied replacement for the 400

GT, arrived at the same time but wouldn't last long before it, too, was overtaken--this time by the Jarama of 1970. Also introduced in that year was another mid-engine model, the Urraco, on a slightly shorter wheelbase than the Miura and with V-8 rather than V-12 power.

A Targa roof was only one of the startling styling features of the Silhouette, which appeared at the Geneva show in 1976. That one wouldn't last long, or become available in large numbers. The model that would hang on for a long while had arrived on the market two years earlier, and helped to make the Lamborghini name familiar around the world. Packed with ducts and air intakes and sharp angles, the futuristic and unforgettable Countach lasted into the late 1980s before it was replaced by a slightly less startling, if faster, Diablo. Along the way, the Countach's engine first shrunk in displacement from that installed in the LP500 prototype, which appeared at the Geneva show in 1971. Later, the initial 3929-cc V-12 installed in the first LP400 production Countach grew to 4754 cc in the early 1980s; then expanded to 5167 cc in 1985, adopting a 48-valve configuration in its final Quattrovalvole form. Lamborghini's other sports car for the 1980s, the Jalpa, carried a mid-mounted 3.5-liter V-8. Less known, but no less dramatic, was Lamborghini's version of the sport-utility vehicle, the monstrous, tank-like LM002, which carried the same V-12 powerplant as the Countach.

Specifications Note: Like many high-performance, limited-production sports cars, Lamborghinis were in a constant state of refinement and retuning. Therefore, announced engine horsepower and torque ratings for a given model tended to fluctuate over the years of its existence. Figures shown in this Catalog were valid at some point in each model's lifespan, but a specific engine might have produced different ratings.

1964-65 LAMBORGHINI

350 GT — V-12 — Though Lamborghini eventually would become best known for its mid-engine models, the first Lambo had its V-12 powerplant mounted up front. The 3464-cc four-cam engine produced 280 horsepower at 6500 rpm, using half a dozen Weber carburetors, which was enough to send a 350 GT to 60 mph in about 7.5 seconds. Top speed passed 150 mph. Giotto Bizzarrini was the major force in designing both the engine and the tubular-steel chassis, which featured fully independent suspension: unequal-length A-arms, coil springs and anti-roll bar at both front and rear. Wheelbase was 100.4 inches. Girling discs brakes all around included servo assist. Steering was ZF worm-and-roller type. Oval recessed headlamps sat at the front of fender bulges, outboard of a conventional low grille with two horizontal bars. Parking lights were mounted above slim wraparound bumperettes, which covered a portion of the grille and extended a short distance into the fender sides. Fairly large triangular rear quarter windows were installed, along with a big, tall back window. Rear wheel openings were squared-off, whereas fronts were rounded. A bodyside crease extended from a curve just ahead of the front wheel, along the front fender, and into the door. Most bodies were semi-fastback coupes, though a few convertibles were done by Touring, and Zagato created one special model. Deep leather bucket seats and a leather-covered dashboard were standard. Only 13 examples were produced in 1964, and 120 in all, plus 23 with 3.9-liter power that appeared during 1965-66.

I.D. DATA: Not available.

Model	Body Type & Seating	Engine Type/CID	P.O.E. Price	Weight (lbs.)	Prod. Total
350 GT	2-dr Coupe-2P	V12/211	N/A	2650	Note 1
Spider	2-dr Conv-2P	V12/211	N/A	2734	Note 1

Note 1: Only 13 Lamborghinis were produced during 1964. A total of 120 Type 350 GT coupes were produced, through 1967 (plus 23 with the larger 3.9-liter engine).

ENGINE DATA: BASE V-12: 60-degree, dual-overhead-cam "vee" type twelve-cylinder. Light alloy block and head. **Displacement:** 211.3 cu. in. (3464 cc). **Bore & Stroke:** 3.03 x 2.44 in. (77 x 62 mm). **Compression Ratio:** 9.0:1. **Brake Horsepower:** 280 (DIN) at 6500 rpm. **Torque:** 227 lbs.-ft. at 4800 rpm. Seven main bearings. Solid valve lifters. Six Weber two-barrel carburetors.

Note: In late 1965 and '66, some 350 GT coupes had the 3929-cc engine used on the 400 GT; see next listing for details.

CHASSIS DATA: Wheelbase: 100.4 in. **Overall Length:** 182.7 in. **Height:** 50.4 in. **Width:** 67.9 in. **Front Tread:** 54.3 in. **Rear Tread:** 54.3 in. **Standard Tires:** 205x15.

TECHNICAL: Layout: front-engine, rear-drive. **Transmission:** ZF five-speed manual. Gear ratios: (1st) 2.56:1; (2nd) 1.74:1; (3rd) 1.22:1; (4th) 1.00:1; (5th) 0.81:1. **Standard Final Drive Ratio:** 3.769:1. **Steering:** ZF worm and roller. **Suspension (front):** unequal-length A-arms, coil springs and anti-roll bar. **Suspension (rear):** unequal-length A-arms, coil springs and anti-roll bar. **Brakes:** Girling hydraulic, front/rear disc. **Body Construction:** separate body on tubular steel chassis.

PERFORMANCE: Top Speed: 152-161 mph (but speeds as low as 137 mph were reported). **Acceleration (0-60 mph):** 7.5 sec. **Acceleration (quarter-mile):** 14.9 sec.

Manufacturer: Automobili Ferruccio Lamborghini S.p.A., Sant'Agata Bolognese, Italy.
Distributor: Jake Kaplan's Foreign Cars Ltd., Providence, Rhode Island.
HISTORY: Lamborghini exhibited two 350 GTs at the New York Auto Show in 1965, along with a display version of the forthcoming 3.9-liter engine. The 350 GT was manufactured at Cento, Italy, with bodies done by Carrozzerria Touring of Milan. *Road & Track* magazine issued a simple warning: "Watch out, Ferrari!"

1966-67 LAMBORGHINI

1967 Lamborghini 400 GT 2+2 coupe.

350 GT — V-12 — Production of the initial Lamborghini, with 3464-cc engine, continued through 1967. About 23 examples were produced with the larger (3929-cc) engine, as in the 400 GT.

400 GT — V-12 — Purchasers of the next Lamborghini model could carry along a couple of (small) passengers, as tiny back bucket seats gave it 2+2 capacity. Though similar in basic appearance to the 350 GT, the two models shared no body panels. Quad round headlamps were installed, and the car had a slightly higher roofline. Whereas the 350 GT carried two fuel tanks, the 400 GT used one larger unit. A new gearbox and final-drive unit was designed by Dallara. The four-cam 3929-cc V-12 engine produced 320 horsepower, and eventually would power the early production Countachs in the mid-1970s. Production continued into 1968, with as many as 250 built before the 400 GT was superseded by the Islero.

MIURA — P400 — V-12 — A more potent version of the 3929-cc engine created for the 400 GT went into the new Miura, which served as Lamborghini's first transverse mid-engine model. In this form, the V-12 produced 350 horsepower and 279 pound-feet of torque, for a top speed around 160 mph. The Miura chassis debuted at the 1965 Turin (Italy) show, while the complete car appeared the following spring at the Geneva (Switzerland) event, intended as a show car rather than a pre-production version. Styling came from the pen of Marcello Gandini (of the Bertone firm). *Road & Track* called Miura "one of those beautiful experiences every enthusiast owes himself." Public reaction was so favorable that a production version was deemed essential. Both the front and rear ends tilted upward for access. A pointed snout and sharp-edged rear end helped give the car an extremely low look. Exposed pop-up headlamps were installed in front-fender niches, with parking lights in a low front air intake opening. An air-intake grid served as part of the door, to the rear of the side window. Rear-window louvers were part of the package. 'Lamborghini' and 'Miura' script went on the coupe's back panel, alongside the taillamps. Wheelbase was shorter than the 350/400 GT, at 98.4 inches, and the Miura's integral steel structure was covered with unstressed aluminum body panels.

I.D. DATA: Not available.

Model	Body Type & Seating	Engine Type/CID	P.O.E. Price	Weight (lbs.)	Prod. Total
350 GT/400 GT					
350 GT	2-dr Coupe-2P	V12/211	N/A	2650	Note 1
350 GT	2-dr Conv-2P	V12/211	N/A	2734	Note 1
400 GT	2-dr Coupe-2+2P	V12/240	14250	2646	Note 2
MIURA					
P400	2-dr Coupe-2P	V12/240	N/A	2850	Note 3

Note 1: A total of 120 Type 350 GT coupes were produced from 1964-67 (plus 23 with the 3.9-liter engine).
Note 2: Approximately 247 Type 400 GT coupes were produced from 1966-68.
Note 3: A total of 475 P400 Miura coupes were produced from 1966-70.
Price Note: Figure shown was valid in 1966.
Production Note: Approximately 254 Lamborghinis were produced in 1966 alone.
ENGINE DATA: BASE V-12 (350 GT): 60-degree, dual-overhead-cam "vee" type twelve-cylinder. Light alloy block and head. **Displacement:** 211.3 cu. In. (3464 cc). **Bore & Stroke:** 3.03 x 2.44 in. (77 x 62 mm). **Compression Ratio:** 9.0:1. **Brake Horsepower:** 280 (DIN) at 6500 rpm. **Torque:** 227 lbs.-ft. at 4800 rpm. Seven main bearings. Solid valve lifters. Six Weber two-barrel carburetors.
Note: A November 1965 press release claimed 336 horsepower at 6500 rpm for the 350 GT engine.
BASE V-12 (400 GT): 60-degree, dual-overhead-cam "vee" type twelve-cylinder. Light alloy block and head. **Displacement:** 239.8 cu. in. (3929 cc). **Bore & Stroke:** 3.23 x 2.44 in. (82 x 62 mm). **Compression Ratio:** 9.2:1. **Brake Horsepower:** 320 (DIN) at 6500 rpm. **Torque:** 275 lbs.-ft. at 4500 rpm. Seven main bearings. Solid valve lifters. Six Weber two-barrel carburetors.
BASE V-12 (Miura): Same as 3929-cc V-12 above, except — **Compression Ratio:** 9.8:1. **Brake Horsepower:** 350 at 7000 rpm. **Torque:** 279 lbs.-ft. at 5000 rpm. Four Weber three-barrel carburetors (or six Weber two-barrel carburetors).
CHASSIS DATA: Wheelbase: (350/400 GT) 100.4 in.; (Miura) 98.4 in. **Overall Length:** (350 GT) 182.7 in.; (400 GT) 182.7 in.; (Miura) 171.6 in. **Height:** (350 GT) 50.4 in.; (400 GT) 50.4 in.; (Miura) 41.5 in. **Width:** (350 GT) 67.9 in.; (400 GT) 68.1 in.; (Miura) 69.3 in. **Front Tread:** (350 GT) 54.3 in.; (400 GT) 54.3 in.; (Miura) 55.6 in. **Rear Tread:** (350 GT) 54.3 in.;

(400 GT) 54.3 in.; (Miura) 55.6 in. **Standard Tires:** (350 GT) 205x15; (400 GT) 205x15; (Miura) 210x15.
TECHNICAL: Layout: (350/400 GT) front-engine, rear-drive; (Miura) mid-engine, rear-drive. **Transmission:** five-speed manual. **Standard Final Drive Ratio:** (400 GT) 4.09:1; (Miura) 4.09:1. **Steering:** (350/400 GT) ZF worm and roller; (Miura) rack and pinion. **Suspension (front):** unequal-length A-arms, coil springs and anti-roll bar. **Suspension (rear):** unequal-length A-arms, coil springs and anti-roll bar. **Brakes:** front/rear disc. **Body Construction:** (350/400 GT) separate body on tubular steel chassis; (Miura) integral platform chassis.
PERFORMANCE: Top Speed: (350 GT cpe) 152-161 mph; (400 GT) 156-161 mph; (Miura) 160-170 mph (some sources claim as high as 185 mph). **Acceleration (0-60 mph):** (350 GT) 7.5 sec.; (400 GT) 6.8 sec.; (Miura) 6.0-6.7 sec. **Acceleration (quarter-mile):** (400 GT) 14.9 sec.

Manufacturer: Automobili Ferruccio Lamborghini S.p.A., Sant'Agata, Bolognese, Italy.
Distributor: Jake Kaplan's Foreign Cars Ltd., Providence, Rhode Island.

1968-69 LAMBORGHINI

1968 Lamborghini Miura P400. (Coys of Kensington)

400 GT — V-12 — Production of the 400 GT 2+2 coupe continued into 1968; see previous listing for further details. The basic layout continued in the new Islero (below).

MIURA — P400 — V-12 — Production of the initial Miura continued into 1970 before replacement by the P400 S; see previous listing for further details. Standard equipment included a 200-mph speedometer and 10,000-rpm tachometer.

ESPADA — 400 GT, SERIES I — V-12 — Once again, Marcello Gandini was responsible for the newest Lamborghini model, this one having been inspired by Bertone's rear-engined Marzal show car. Long and low (hardly a surprise from Lambo), the front-engine Espada rode a pressed-steel platform chassis with 104.3-inch wheelbase and carried its powerplant nearly eight inches farther forward than in the 400 GT. Track dimensions grew considerably wider. Under the hood was the same 3929-cc engine offered in the 400 GT coupe, using six Weber carburetors. Espada's low and wide front end, with quad round headlamps at the ends of a blacked-out grille, was taller than that of the Miura, and the wide hood displayed dual NACA ducts. Long, curved-base rear quarter windows were installed in the fastback coupe, along with a huge windshield. An extra glass panel below the back window aided rearward visibility past the chopped-off tail. In profile, the car displayed a nearly-horizontal roofline-into-backlight line, with a rear kickup past its low beltline. Hood and upper fenders tilted forward for engine access. Inside were bucket seats for four, with enough space in the rear for the car to be considered (more or less) a four-seater rather than a tight 2+2. A five-speed gearbox was standard, as usual (though Chrysler's TorqueFlite would become available in later versions of the Espada).

ISLERO — 400 GT — V-12 — A new body went on the tubular chassis that had carried the 400 GT, offering the next-generation Lambo a more contemporary (if less dramatic) look. Wheelbase measured 100.4 inches. The angular notchback coupe had hidden headlamps, ample glass, a long hood, and short deck. Styling was performed by Mario Marazzi, in a roomier interior. 'Lamborghini Islero' script went on the trunk lid. The 3929-cc V-12 engine produced 320 horsepower, as in the final 400 GTs; but rose to 340 bhp in the Islero 'S' version, introduced during 1969. That was enough to deliver a top speed as high as 155 mph and 0-60 acceleration time around 7.5 seconds. Slotted air exhaust vents went behind each 'S' front wheel, the wheel arches added slight flares, and triangular (non-opening) panes were installed ahead of each door window.

I.D. DATA: Not available.

Model	Body Type & Seating	Engine Type/CID	P.O.E. Price	Weight (lbs.)	Prod. Total
400 GT	2-dr Coupe-2+2P	V12/240	N/A	2646	Note 1
MIURA					
P400	2-dr Coupe-2P	V12/240	19260	2850	Note 2
ESPADA (400 GT)					
I	2-dr Coupe-4P	V12/240	21000	3307	Note 3
ISLERO					
400 GT	2-dr Coupe-2+2P	V12/240	18000	2795	Note 4
S	2-dr Coupe-2+2P	V12/240	N/A	2795	Note 4

Note 1: Approximately 247 Type 400 GT coupes were produced from 1966-68.
Note 2: A total of 475 P400 Miura coupes were produced from 1966-70.
Note 3: As many as 1,224 Espadas (Series I through III) were produced from 1968-78; but only 37 in 1968, and a total of 186 Series I coupes.
Note 4: A total of 125 Islero coupes and 100 Islero S coupes were produced from 1968-70.
Price Note: Figures shown were valid in 1969; Islero figure shown is approximate. Miura list price in 1968 was $21,000.
Model Note: The 400 GT designation was sometimes (now always) included with the Espada and Islero names.
ENGINE DATA: BASE V-12 (400 GT): 60-degree, dual-overhead-cam "vee" type twelve-

1969 Lamborghini Miura P400S. (Coys of Kensington)

cylinder. Light alloy block and head. **Displacement:** 239.8 cu. in. (3929 cc). **Bore & Stroke:** 3.23 x 2.44 in. (82 x 62 mm). **Compression Ratio:** 9.2:1. **Brake Horsepower:** 320 (about 360 SAE) at 6500 rpm . **Torque:** 275 lbs.-ft. at 4500 rpm. Seven main bearings. Solid valve lifters. Six Weber two-barrel carburetors.
BASE V-12 (Miura): Same as 3929-cc V-12 above, except — **Compression Ratio:** 9.5:1. **Brake Horsepower:** 350 (about 400 SAE) at 7000 rpm. **Torque:** 279 lbs.-ft. (about 300 SAE) at 5000 rpm.
BASE V-12 (Espada): Same as 3929-cc V-12 above, except — **Compression Ratio:** 9.5:1. **Brake Horsepower:** 325 at 6500 rpm. **Torque:** 276 lbs.-ft. at 4500 rpm.
BASE V-12 (Islero): Same as 3929-cc V-12 above, except — **Compression Ratio:** 9.5:1. **Brake Horsepower:** 320 at 6500 rpm. **Torque:** 278 lbs.-ft. at 5000 rpm.
BASE V-12 (Islero S): Same as 3929-cc V-12 above, except -- **Brake Horsepower:** 340 at 6500 rpm. **Torque:** 289 lbs.-ft. at 5000 rpm.

CHASSIS DATA: Wheelbase: (400 GT) 100.4 in.; (Miura) 98.4 in.; (Espada) 104.3 in.; (Islero) 100.4 in. **Overall Length:** (400 GT) 182.7 in.; (Miura) 171.6 in.; (Espada) 186.5 in.; (Islero) 178.2 in. **Height:** (400 GT) 50.4 in.; (Miura) 41.5 in.; (Espada) 46.6 in.; (Islero) 51.2 in. **Width:** (400 GT) 68.1 in.; (Miura) 69.3 in.; (Espada) 71.4 in.; (Islero) 61.1 in. **Front Tread:** (400 GT) 54.3 in.; (Miura) 55.6 in.; (Espada) 58.7 in.; (Islero) 54.3 in. **Rear Tread:** (400 GT) 54.3 in.; (Miura) 55.6 in.; (Espada) 58.7 in.; (Islero) 54.3 in. **Standard Tires:** (400 GT) 205x15; (Miura) 205x15; (Espada) 205x15; (Islero) 205x15.

TECHNICAL: Layout: (400 GT, Espada, Islero) front-engine, rear-drive; (Miura) mid-engine, rear-drive. **Transmission:** five-speed manual. Miura gear ratios: (1st) 2.52:1; (2nd) 1.735:1; (3rd) 1.225:1; (4th) 1.00:1; (5th) 0.815:1. **Standard Final Drive Ratio:** (400 GT) 4.09:1; (Miura) 4.09:1; (Espada) 4.50:1; (Islero) 4.09:1. **Steering:** (400 GT, Espada, Islero) worm and wheel; (Miura) rack and pinion. **Suspension (front):** unequal-length A-arms, coil springs and anti-roll bar. **Suspension (rear):** unequal-length A-arms, coil springs and anti-roll bar. **Brakes:** front/rear disc. **Body Construction:** (400 GT, Islero) separate body on tubular steel chassis; (Miura) integral chassis; (Espada) integral body on pressed-steel platform.

PERFORMANCE: Top Speed: (400 GT) 156-161 mph; (Miura) 160-163 mph (some sources claimed as high as 185 mph); (Espada) about 140 mph; (Islero) 140+ mph; (Islero S) about 155 mph. **Acceleration (0-60 mph):** (400 GT) 6.8 sec.; (Miura) 6.3-6.7 sec.; (Espada) 7.8 sec.; (Islero S) 7.5 sec. **Acceleration (quarter-mile):** (400 GT) 14.9 sec.; (Miura) 14.5 sec. (101 mph).
Manufacturer: Automobili Ferruccio Lamborghini S.p.A., Sant'Agata, Bolognese, Italy.

HISTORY: In its early 1968 road test, *Road & Track* called the Miura "the most glamorous, exciting and prestigious sports car in the world," adding that "every enthusiast should have at least one." At that time, about a dozen Miuras were in the U.S., though the car did not yet meet federal regulations as a '68 model. One unique open Miura was produced in 1969 with a largely zinc body; a few others may have been converted to Spiders by their owners. Another one-off special was the Jota, lighter in weight and with its engine tuned to 440 bhp, built by Bob Wallace, a Lamborghini engineer.

1970-73 LAMBORGHINI

1970 Lamborghini Espada coupe.

352

MIURA — P400 S/P400 SV — V-12 — The P400 S replaced the original P400 version of the Miura for 1970-71, adding 20 horsepower to the V-12 engine, via higher-lift cams and larger carburetors. Another 15 horsepower arrived in 1972, with the P400 SV edition. The 400 S included Koni shock absorbers and power windows, and a leather-trimmed steering wheel. A fully reworked suspension went into the 400 SV, along with upgraded tires that demanded rear-fender bulges.
ESPADA — 400 GT, SERIES II/III — V-12 — Production of the Series II version of the Espada began in 1970 and continued into 1972 before replacement by the Series III. Horsepower from the 3929-cc engine got a boost to 350. The Series II contained a more attractive steering wheel than the Series I's three-spoke design, as well as an improved dashboard, restyled grille, and vented brakes. The Series III, which first appeared at the Turin show in late 1972, enjoyed a minor grille revision and restyled instrument panel. By the time the Espada III neared the end of its model run (in 1978), horsepower would rise to 365. Air conditioning was standard on Espadas sold in the U.S. Standard Series III equipment also included leather upholstery, a heated rear window, power windows, and tinted glass. Power steering was optional.
ISLERO — S (GTS) — V-12 — Production of the Islero S continued into 1970; see previous listing for further details.

1973 Lamborghini Jarama 400GTS. (Coys of Kensington)

JARAMA — 400 GT/GTS — V-12 — Marcello Gandini, who'd become a familiar name at Lamborghini, was responsible for styling the next 2+2 coupe, which wore its new body atop a shortened version of the Espada chassis. At 93.6 inches between axles, the Jarama wheelbase measured more than 10 inches shorter than the Espada's. The new coupe debuted at the Geneva show in March 1970, and angular-styled production bodies, featuring unit construction, were built by Marazzi. Styling features included prominent wheelwell flares, dual NACA ducts on hood sides (at upper cowl), and partly hidden quad round headlamps with half-lids that rose. Wheels also were restyled. The 3929-cc four-cam V-12 engine produced 350 horsepower. A five-speed manual gearbox was standard, along with a 180-mph speedometer and 9000-rpm tachometer. Lamborghini claimed a top speed of 162 mph (about the same as the Islero), and a Jarama could accelerate to 60 mph in close to 7 seconds. The 400 GTS, which replaced the original model in 1973, added 15 horsepower as well as a wide hood scoop and air-exhaust vents at the upper cowl. Wheels also were restyled. Most Jaramas that reached the U.S. market were 1972-spec models, which were sold through the 1974 model year. Standard GTS equipment included air conditioning, tinted glass, power windows, leather upholstery, and a heated back window.
URRACO — P250 — V-8 — This 2+2 coupe, which was announced in 1970 but didn't go on sale until two years later, served as Lamborghini's response to the debut of the Ferrari Dino and Porsche 911. Power came from a transversely mid-mounted, all-aluminum 2463-cc, 90-degree V-8 that produced 220 horsepower and 166 pound-feet of torque, hooked to a five-speed manual rear transaxle. Marcello Gandini (of Bertone) was responsible for the graceful styling, which included a short hood, sharply raked windshield, hidden headlamps in a pointed nose, and rear-window louvers. Wheelbase was 96.5 inches, and the body was welded to a pressed-steel chassis. The Urraco name came from a breed of fighting bull.

Model Number Note: Company literature sometimes described the second version of the Jarama as S 400 GT rather than 400 GTS. A 400 GT designation was sometimes used for the Espada.

1973 Lamborghini Espada Series III. (Coys of Kensington)

I.D. DATA: Lamborghini used a five-digit sequential serial number. Vehicle Identification Number is on a plate atop the dashboard, visible through the windshield. Miura 400 SV serial number is on a plate in the front trunk compartment. Jarama/Espada serial number is on the left inner fender panel, in the engine compartment; and on a plate attached to left door post. Engine numbers are stamped at top front of block, between the banks.

Model	Body Type & Seating	Engine Type/CID	P.O.E. Price	Weight (lbs)	Prod. Total
MIURA					
P400 S	2-dr Coupe-2P	V12/240	19750	2481	Note 1
P400 SV	2-dr Coupe-2P	V12/240	21000	2745	Note 1
ESPADA (400 GT)					
II	2-dr Coupe-4P	V12/240	19500	3583	Note 2
III	2-dr Coupe-4P	V12/240	N/A	3605	Note 2
ISLERO					
S (GTS)	2-dr Coupe-2+2P	V12/240	13950	2795	Note 3
JARAMA					
400 GT	2-dr Coupe-2+2P	V12/240	23500	3219	Note 4
400 GTS	2-dr Coupe-2+2P	V12/240	N/A	3400	Note 4
URRACO					
P250	2-dr Coupe-2+2P	V8/150	N/A	2426	Note 5

Note 1: A total of 140 P400 S Miura coupes were produced during the full model run, plus 150 P400 SV models.
Note 2: As many as 1,224 Espadas were produced from 1968-78 (including 575 Series II and 483 Series III).

Note 3: A total of 100 Islero S coupes were produced in 1969-70.

Note 4: A total of 177 Jarama 400 GT coupes were produced from 1970-73, followed by 150 Jarama 400 GTS coupes (through 1978).

Note 5: A total of 520 Urraco P250 coupes were produced from 1970-76.

Price Note: Jarama figure shown was valid in 1972.

ENGINE DATA: BASE V-12 (Miura P400 S): 60-degree, dual-overhead-cam "vee" type twelve-cylinder. Light alloy block and heads. **Displacement:** 239.8 cu. in. (3929 cc). **Bore & Stroke:** 3.23 x 2.44 in. (82 x 62 mm). **Compression Ratio:** 10.7:1. **Brake Horsepower:** 370 (DIN) at 7700 rpm. **Torque:** 286 lbs.-ft. at 5750 rpm. Seven main bearings. Solid valve lifters. Four Weber three-barrel carburetors.

BASE V-12 (Miura P400 SV): Same as 3929-cc V-12 above, except — **Compression Ratio:** 10.7:1. **Brake Horsepower:** 385 at 7850 rpm. **Torque:** 294 lbs.-ft. at 5750 rpm.

BASE V-12 (Espada Series II/III): Same as 3929-cc V-12 above, except — **Compression Ratio:** 10.7:1. **Brake Horsepower:** 350 at 7500 rpm. **Torque:** 290 lbs.-ft. at 5500 rpm. Six Weber two-barrel carburetors.

BASE V-12 (Islero S): Same as 3929-cc V-12 above, except — **Brake Horsepower:** 340 at 6500 rpm. **Torque:** 289 lbs.-ft. at 5000 rpm.

BASE V-12 (Jarama 400 GT): Same as 3929-cc V-12 above, except — **Compression Ratio:** 10.7:1. **Brake Horsepower:** 350 at 7500 rpm. **Torque:** 289 lbs.-ft. at 5500 rpm.

BASE V-12 (Jarama 400 GTS): Same as 3929-cc V-12 above, except — **Compression Ratio:** 10.7:1. **Brake Horsepower:** 365 at 7500 rpm. **Torque:** 300 lbs.-ft. at 5500 rpm. Six horizontal Weber 40 DCOE 20-21 two-barrel carburetors.

BASE V-8 (Urraco P250): 90-degree, overhead-cam "vee" type eight-cylinder. Light alloy block and head. **Displacement:** 150.3 cu. in. (2463 cc). **Bore & Stroke:** 3.39 x 2.09 in. (86 x 53 mm). **Compression Ratio:** 10.5:1. **Brake Horsepower:** 220 (DIN) at 7800 rpm. **Torque:** 166 lbs.-ft. at 3500 rpm. Five main bearings. Solid valve lifters. Four Weber two-barrel carburetors.

CHASSIS DATA: Wheelbase: (Miura P400 S/SV) 98.6 in.; (Espada) 104.3 in.; (Islero) 100.4 in.; (Jarama) 93.6 in.; (Urraco) 96.5 in. **Overall Length:** (Miura P400 S/SV) 172.8 in.; (Espada) 186.5 in.; (Islero) 178.2 in.; (Jarama) 176.5 in.; (Urraco) 166.5-167.3 in. **Height:** (Miura P400 S/SV) 43.3 in.; (Espada) 46.6 in.; (Islero) 51.2 in.; (Jarama) 46.8 in.; (Urraco) 43.9 in. **Width:** (Miura P400 S/SV) 70.1 in.; (Espada) 73.2 in.; (Islero) 61.1 in.; (Jarama) 71.6 in.; (Urraco) 69.3 in. **Front Tread:** (Miura P400 SV) 55.6 in.; (Espada) 58.7 in.; (Islero) 54.3 in.; (Jarama) 58.7 in.; (Urraco) 57.5 in. **Rear Tread:** (Miura P400 SV) 60.7 in.; (Espada) 58.7 in.; (Islero) 54.3 in.; (Jarama) 58.7 in.; (Urraco) 57.5 in. **Standard Tires:** (Miura P400 S) GR70VR15; (Miura P400 SV) FR70VR15 front, HR/70VR15 rear; (Espada) 205VR15; (Islero) 205x15; (Jarama) 205VR15 or 215/70VR15; (Urraco) 205VR14.

TECHNICAL: Layout: (Espada/Islero/Jarama) front-engine, rear-drive; (Miura/Urraco) mid-engine, rear-drive. **Transmission:** five-speed manual. **Steering:** (Espada/Islero/Jarama) ZF screw and sector; (Miura/Urraco) rack and pinion. **Suspension (front):** (Miura/Espada/Islero/Jarama) unequal-length A-arms, coil springs and anti-roll bar; (Urraco) MacPherson struts, lower A-arms, coil springs and anti-roll bar. **Suspension (rear):** (Miura/Espada/Islero/Jarama) unequal-length A-arms, coil springs and anti-roll bar; (Urraco) struts with lower A-arms, coil springs and anti-roll bar. **Brakes:** front/rear disc. **Body Construction:** (Islero) separate body on tubular steel chassis; (Jarama) integral steel; (Miura) integral body on box-type platform; (Espada) integral body on pressed-steel platform; (Urraco) body welded to pressed-steel platform, with separate rear auxiliary frame.

MAJOR OPTIONS: Air conditioning: Islero, Miura S ($950). Blaupunkt "New Yorker" stereo ($275) except Miura. Stereo with 8-track tape player ($175). Koni shock absorbers ($100). Power steering.

PERFORMANCE: Top Speed: (Miura P400 S) 174+ mph; (Espada II) 155 mph; (Islero S) about 155 mph; (Jarama) 152 mph; (Jarama S) 162 mph claimed; (Urraco) 150 mph. **Acceleration (0-60 mph):** (Islero) 7.5 sec.; (Jarama) 7.2 sec. (0-100 mph in 18 sec.). **Acceleration (quarter-mile):** (Jarama) 15.6 sec. (97 mph).

PRODUCTION/SALES: A total of 422 Lamborghinis were produced in 1971 (96 Miura, 130 Jarama, and 196 Espada); 318 in 1972 (59 Miura, 63 Jarama, 161 Espada, and 35 Urraco); and 550 in 1973 (78 Jarama, 187 Espada, and 285 Urraco).

Manufacturer: Automobili Ferruccio Lamborghini S.p.A., Sant'Agata, Bolognese, Italy.

Distributor: Jake Kaplan's Lamborghini East, Providence, Rhode Island.

HISTORY: In 1972, *Road & Track* declared Jarama "a capable and fast car and an exciting one to look at," but faulted its ergonomics, noise, ride quality, and low-speed driveability. By that year, a Swiss firm held over half of the Lamborghini company's stock. Lamborghini literature issued in Britain described the Jarama as its "front engined car with the handling of a mid-engine." Much later, Lamborghini described that model as "sensible and deliberately unspectacular...more bold than beautiful." A VIP version of the Espada, created by Bertone, appeared at the Paris show in 1973, containing a TV set, cassette recorder and small bar. That VIP edition was said to be "made on request."

1974-75 LAMBORGHINI

ESPADA — 400 GT SERIES III — V-12 — Production of the third-generation Espada, introduced in 1972, continued into 1978. Chrysler's three-speed TorqueFlite automatic transmission became optional in 1974. See previous listing for additional details.

JARAMA — 400 GTS — V-12 — Production of the second version of the Jarama, introduced in 1973, continued into 1978. Standard Jarama equipment in later years included four-wheel disc brakes, leather seats, heater/defroster, air conditioning, power windows, carpeting, adjustable reclining bucket seats, wood steering wheel, AM/FM stereo radio with cassette player and power antenna, two-speed wiper/washers, electric rear defroster, tinted glass, a sunroof, and magnesium wheels. A TorqueFlite three-speed automatic transmission became optional in 1974.

URRACO — P250/P200/P300 — V-8 — Production of the initial P250 coupe continued into 1976, but P200 and P300 editions were added in 1974, first seen at the Turin show. Intended for the Italian market, the P200 carried a twin-overhead-cam, 121.7-cid (1994-cc) V-8 that produced 182 horsepower (SAE). Under the P300 hood went a 182.8-cid (2996-cc) V-8 with twin-cam heads, rated 265 horsepower (but as little as 180 bhp in U.S. form) for a top speed past 160 mph. Urraco equipment in final years included four-wheel disc brakes, leather seats, air conditioning, heater/defroster, power windows, carpeting, adjustable reclining bucket seats, leather steering wheel, AM/FM stereo radio with cassette player and power antenna, two-speed wiper/washers, electric rear defroster, tinted glass, and magnesium wheels.

COUNTACH — LP400 — V-12 — The translation of the Countach (pronounced COON-tahsh) name says it all. In polite terms, this bit of exclamatory Italian slang means, roughly, "Good Lord!" Or simply, "Wow!" (The precise translation happens to be a tad risque.) Introduced to the European market in 1974 (nearly three years after its March '71 debut at the Geneva Auto Salon as a show car), and sent to America for 1976, the Countach was indeed unlike anything seen before. The bizarre, wildly futuristic shape--chock full of angles, pyramids and geometric patterns--was the work of Marcello Gandini, at Carrozzeria Nuccio Bertone. While stunning, Gandini's earlier efforts were rather sedate in comparision to the Countach. As time went on, the basic sharp-edged shape grew even more extreme, adding a selection of scoops and spoilers and related doodads to enhance the car's sinister, forbidding, virtually evil demeanor. Bodies were supplied by Bertone, but final assembly was done at the Lamborghini facility. Luggage space was nearly nil.

Rather than riding a pressed-steel chassis, the Countach adopted a complex multi-tube space-frame platform (though the show car had used monocoque construction). Articulated front-hinged doors had the "gullwing" look, but swung upward and outward. Under the hood of the prototype lurked a 5.0-liter V-12. By the time the LP400 production version emerged, however, displacement dropped to 3.9 liters. That same 3929-cc V-12 engine had been used in the Miura and other Lamborghinis, with output rated 375 horsepower (DIN) inside the Countach. Rear-wheel-drive came via a power takeoff through the engine pump, to a five-speed gearbox and ZF limited-slip differential. A longitudinal powertrain mounting put the gearbox ahead of the engine (actually between the seats), allowing a direct shift linkage. Inside the wide (if snug) cockpit, the driver faced an aircraft-type dashboard. Dual coil springs were installed at the rear.

I.D. DATA: Lamborghini used a five-digit sequential serial number. Vehicle Identification Number is on a plate atop the dashboard, visible through the windshield. Espada and Jarama serial numbers are on the left inner fender panel, in the engine compartment; and on a plate attached to left door post. Engine numbers are stamped at top front of block, between the banks.

Model	Body Type & Seating	Engine Type C.I.D.	P.O.E. Price	Weight (lbs.)	Prod. Total
ESPADA 400 GT					
III	2-dr Coupe-4P	V12/240	33900	3605	Note 1
JARAMA					
400 GTS	2-dr Coupe-2+2P	V12/240	29900	3219	Note 2
URRACO					
P250	2-dr Coupe-2+2P	V8/150	22500	2426	Note 3
P200	2-dr Coupe-2+2P	V8/122	N/A	N/A	Note 3
P300	2-dr Coupe-2+2P	V8/183	24150	2866	Note 3
COUNTACH					
LP400	2-dr Coupe-2P	V12/240	N/A	3020	Note 4

Note 1: As many as 1,224 Espadas were produced from 1968-78 (including 483 Series III).

Note 2: A total of 150 Jarama 400 GTS coupes were produced from 1973-78.

Note 3: As many as 522 Urraco P250 coupes were produced through 1976, plus 68 P200 and 205 P300 models.

Note 4: A total of 150 LP400 Countach models were produced from 1974-78.

Price Note: Figures shown were valid in 1975.

ENGINE DATA: BASE V-12 (Espada, Jarama 400 GTS): 60-degree, dual-overhead-cam "vee" type twelve-cylinder. Light alloy block and heads. **Displacement:** 239.8 cu. in. (3929 cc). **Bore & Stroke:** 3.23 x 2.44 in. (82 x 62 mm). **Compression Ratio:** 10.7:1. **Brake Horsepower:** 350/365 at 7500 rpm. **Torque:** 290/300 lbs.-ft. at 5500 rpm. Seven main bearings. Solid valve lifters. Six Weber 40 DCOE 20-21 two-barrel carburetors.

BASE V-12 (Countach): Same as 3929-cc V-12 above, except — **Compression Ratio:** 10.5:1. **Brake Horsepower:** 375 (DIN) at 8000 rpm. **Torque:** 268 lbs.-ft. at 5000 rpm. Six Weber two-barrel carburetors.

BASE V-8 (Urraco P250): 90-degree, overhead-cam "vee" type eight-cylinder. Light alloy block and heads. **Displacement:** 150.3 cu. in. (2463 cc). **Bore & Stroke:** 3.39 x 2.09 in. (86 x 53 mm). **Compression Ratio:** 10.5:1. **Brake Horsepower:** 220 at 7500 rpm. **Torque:** 166 lbs.-ft. at 3500 rpm. Five main bearings. Solid valve lifters. Four Weber two barrel carburetors.

BASE V-8 (Urraco P200): 90-degree, overhead-cam "vee" type eight-cylinder. Light alloy block and heads. **Displacement:** 121.7 cu. in. (1994 cc). **Bore & Stroke:** 3.05 x 2.09 in. (77.4 x 53 mm). **Compression Ratio:** 9.8:1. **Brake Horsepower:** 182 (SAE) at 7500 rpm. **Torque:** 130 lbs.-ft. at 3500 rpm. Five main bearings. Solid valve lifters. Four Weber two-barrel carburetors.

BASE V-8 (Urraco P300): 90-degree, dual-overhead-cam "vee" type eight-cylinder. Light alloy block and heads. **Displacement:** 182.8 cu. in. (2996 cc). **Bore & Stroke:** 3.39 x 2.54 in. (86 x 64.5 mm). **Compression Ratio:** 10.0:1. **Brake Horsepower:** 265 (SAE) at 7500 rpm. **Torque:** 202 lbs.-ft. at 3500 rpm. Five main bearings. Solid valve lifters. Four Weber two-barrel carburetors.

Note: Urraco P300 horsepower was reduced considerably in U.S. models.

CHASSIS DATA: Wheelbase: (Espada) 104.3 in.; (Jarama) 93.6 in.; (Urraco P250) 96.5 in.; (Countach) 96.5 in. **Overall Length:** (Espada) 186.5 in.; (Jarama) 176.6 in.; (Urraco P250) 167.3 in.; (Countach) 163.0 in. **Height:** (Espada) 46.6 in.; (Jarama) 46.8 in.; (Urraco P250) 43.9 in.; (Countach) 42 in. **Width:** (Espada) 73.4 in.; (Jarama) 71.6 in.; (Urraco P250) 69.3 in.; (Countach) 74.4 in. **Front Tread:** (Espada) 58.7 in.; (Jarama) 58.7 in.; (Urraco) 57.5 in.; (Countach) 58 in. **Rear Tread:** (Espada) 58.7 in.; (Jarama) 58.7 in.; (Urraco) 57.5 in.; (Countach) 62 in. **Standard Tires:** (Espada) 205VR15; (Jarama) 215/70VR15; (Urraco) 205VR14; (Countach) 205/70VR14 front, 215/70VR14 rear.

TECHNICAL: Layout: (Espada/Jarama) front-engine, rear-drive; (Urraco/Countach) mid-engine, rear-drive. **Transmission:** five-speed manual; Chrysler TorqueFlite three-speed automatic available on Espada/Jarama. **Steering:** (Espada/Jarama) ZF screw and sector; (Urraco/Countach) rack and pinion. **Suspension (front):** (Espada/Jarama/Countach) unequal-length A-arms, coil springs and anti-roll bar; (Urraco) MacPherson struts, lower A-arms, coil springs and anti-roll bar. **Suspension (rear):** (Espada/Jarama) unequal-length A-arms, coil springs and anti-roll bar; (Urraco) MacPherson struts with lower A-arms, coil springs and anti-roll bar; (Countach) upper lateral links, lower A-arms, upper/lower trailing arms, dual coil springs and anti-roll bar. **Brakes:** front/rear disc. **Body Construction:** (Espada/Jarama) integral steel body on steel chassis; (Urraco) monocoque body welded to pressed-steel platform, with separate rear auxiliary frame; (Countach) on multi-tube platform.

MAJOR OPTIONS: Automatic transmission ($500). Power steering ($350).

PERFORMANCE: Top Speed: (Espada) about 155 mph; (Jarama) about 162 mph; (Urraco P250) 140-149 mph; (Urraco P300) 162+ mph; (Countach) 175 mph. **Acceleration (0-60 mph):** (Espada) about 5.5 sec.; (Jarama) about 6.2 sec.; (Countach) under 7 sec. **Fuel Mileage:** (Espada/Jarama) near 7 mpg; (Urraco P250) about 12 mpg.

PRODUCTION/SALES: A total of 355 Lamborghinis were produced in 1974 (27 Jarama, 140 Espada, 162 Urraco, and 26 Countach); and 276 in 1975 (12 Jarama, 48 Espada, 156 Urraco, and 60 Countach).

Manufacturer: Automobili Ferruccio Lamborghini S.p.A., Sant'Agata, Bolognese, Italy.

Distributor: Grossman Motor Car Corp., West Nyack, New York.

HISTORY: "Not just a one-off design exercise by Bertone," claimed early British literature describing the Countach prototype. Instead, it would "be the first practical futuristic car to be put into production by any manufacturer." The show car's 4971-cc engine produced a claimed 440 horsepower at 7400 rpm, on 10.5:1 compression, and the initial Countach was said to be capable of 200+ mph. Except for a reduction in engine displacement, the production version retained many technical features and appearance details of the prototype. Countach sales actually began in 1974, some time after the first production version appeared at the '73 Geneva (Switzerland) show. After certification for official U.S. sale for a brief period, the Countach entered the "grey market" netherworld, but would later wind up being imported through the services of an American company--and later yet, become part of the Chrysler empire.

1976-80 LAMBORGHINI

1977 Lamborghini Silhouette. (William Siuru Jr.)

ESPADA — 400 GT SERIES III — V-12 — Production of the third-generation Espada, introduced in 1972, continued into 1978. Either a five-speed manual or three-speed TorqueFlite automatic transmission was available. See previous listings for additional details.

JARAMA — 400 GTS — V-12 — Production of the second version of the Jarama, introduced in 1973, continued into 1978.

URRACO — P250/P200/P300 — V-8 — Production of the initial P250 coupe continued into 1976, while the P200 and P300 editions had been added in 1974 and would remain into 1979.

COUNTACH — LP400/LP400S — V-12 — Production of the initial Countach continued until 1978, when it was replaced by the LP400S. Changes at that time included a modified suspension and wider Pirelli P7 tires (on five-hole wheels like those installed on the new Silhouette). The Countach body added fiberglass fender flares and a front spoiler. A new optional (huge) adjustable rear wing that stood on two struts above the tail was installed on most examples of the late 1970s and '80s. Different Weber carburetors were used, but engine output remained the same as before. A Series II version of the 'S' appeared by 1980, with a restyled instrument panel that contained larger gauges, plus simpler-looking wheels.

SILHOUETTE — V-8 — This evolution of the Urraco, which appeared at the 1976 Geneva show, was intended to boost Lamborghini sales. By the time production halted early in 1979, no more than 54 had been built. Wearing a new Targa top that slipped behind the seats for storage, the two-seat Silhouette became Lamborghini's first open production model. "Tunnelback" rather than fastback in profile, the Silhouette's roof incorporated a roll cage. Twin straight arches ran between the targa roof section and the rear of the engine compartment, meeting the angled line that extended to the rear panel. Styling came from Bertone, and also featured hidden headlamps, a low, full-length bodyside crease, and squared-off nose. To the rear of the cockpit was an extremely thick 'B' pillar. Wheelarches were flat along the top. A deeper front spoiler held front-brake air scoops and an oil-cooler duct. New 15-inch magnesium wheels, as seen on the 1974 Bravo show car, had five large holes around the hub and held Pirelli P7 high-performance tires. Unibody construction was used, suitably strengthened for the Targa roof. The dual-overhead-cam, 2996-cc V-8 engine produced 265 horsepower (SAE) at 7500 rpm, working through a five-speed manual gearbox.

I.D. DATA: Lamborghini used a five-digit sequential serial number. Vehicle Identification Number is on a plate atop the dashboard, visible through the windshield. Espada and Jarama serial numbers are on the left inner fender panel, in the engine compartment; and on a plate attached to left door post. Engine numbers are stamped at top front of block, between the banks.

Model	Body Type & Seating	Engine Type/CID	P.O.E. Price	Weight (lbs.)	Prod. Total
ESPADA 400 GT					
III	2-dr Coupe-4P	V12/240	N/A	3605	Note 1
JARAMA					
400 GTS	2-dr Coupe-2P	V12/240	N/A	3219	Note 2
URRACO					
P250	2-dr Coupe-2 + 2P	V8/150	N/A	3021	Note 3
P200	2-dr Coupe-2 + 2P	V8/122	N/A	2756	Note 3
P300	2-dr Coupe-2 + 2P	V8/183	N/A	2867	Note 3
COUNTACH					
LP400	2-dr Coupe-2P	V12/240	52000	3020	Note 4
LP400S	2-dr Coupe-2P	V12/240	41000	2915	Note 5
SILHOUETTE (1976-77)					
	2-dr Coupe-2P	V8/183	N/A	2750	Note 6

Note 1: As many as 1,224 Espadas were produced from 1968-78 (including 483 Series III).

Note 2: A total of 150 Jarama 400 GTS coupes were produced from 1973-78.

Note 3: As many as 522 Urraco P250 coupes were produced through 1976, plus 68 P200 and 205 P300 models.

Note 4: Approximately 150 LP400 Countach models were produced from 1974-78.

Note 5: As many as 385 LP400S Countach models were produced from 1978-82.

Note 6: No more than 54 Silhouettes were produced in 1976-79.

Price Note: Countach LP400 price shown was valid in 1976; LP400S, in 1978.

ENGINE DATA: BASE V-12 (Jarama 400 GTS, late Espada III): 60-degree, dual-overhead-cam "vee" type twelve-cylinder. Light alloy block and heads. **Displacement:** 239.8 cu. in. (3929 cc). **Bore & Stroke:** 3.23 x 2.44 in. (82 x 62 mm). **Compression Ratio:** 10.7:1. **Brake Horsepower:** 365 at 7500 rpm. **Torque:** 300 lbs.-ft. at 5500 rpm. Seven main bearings. Solid valve lifters. Six Weber two-barrel horizontal carburetors.

BASE V-12 (early Espada III): Same as 3929-cc V-12 above, except — **Compression Ratio:** 9.55:1. **Brake Horsepower:** 350 at 7500 rpm. **Torque:** 290 lbs.-ft.

BASE V-12 (Countach): Same as 3929-cc V-12 above, except — **Compression Ratio:** 10.5:1. **Brake Horsepower:** 375 (DIN) at 8000 rpm. **Torque:** 268 lbs.-ft. at 5000-5500 rpm. Six Weber horizontal two-barrel carburetors.

BASE V-8 (Urraco P250): 90-degree, overhead-cam "vee" type eight-cylinder. Light alloy block and heads. **Displacement:** 150.3 cu. in. (2463 cc). **Bore & Stroke:** 3.39 x 2.09 in. (86 x 53 mm). **Compression Ratio:** 10.5:1. **Brake Horsepower:** 220 at 7500 rpm. **Torque:** 166 lbs.-ft. at 3500 rpm. Five main bearings. Solid valve lifters. Four Weber two-barrel carburetors.

Note: Output of the Urraco P250 engine was reduced during the late 1970s, to 175 bhp at 7500 rpm and 139 pound-feet at 5750 rpm.

BASE V-8 (Urraco P200): 90-degree, overhead-cam "vee" type eight-cylinder. Light alloy block and heads. **Displacement:** 121.7 cu. in. (1994 cc). **Bore & Stroke:** 3.05 x 2.09 in. (77.4 x 53 mm). **Compression Ratio:** 9.8:1. **Brake Horsepower:** 182 (DIN) at 7500 rpm. **Torque:** 130 lbs.-ft. at 3500 rpm. Five main bearings. Solid valve lifters. Four Weber two-barrel carburetors.

BASE V-8 (Urraco P300, Silhouette): 90-degree, dual-overhead-cam "vee" type eight-cylinder. Light alloy block and heads. **Displacement:** 182.8 cu. in. (2996 cc). **Bore & Stroke:** 3.39 x 2.54 in. (86 x 64.5 mm). **Compression Ratio:** 10.1:1. **Brake Horsepower:** 265 (DIN) at 7500 rpm. **Torque:** 202 lbs.-ft. at 3500 rpm. Five main bearings. Solid valve lifters. Four Weber two-barrel carburetors.

CHASSIS DATA: Wheelbase: (Espada) 104.3 in.; (Jarama) 93.7 in.; (Urraco/Silhouette) 96.5 in.; (Countach) 96.5 in. **Overall Length:** (Espada) 186.5 in.; (Jarama) 176.6 in.; (Urraco) 168.5 in.; (Countach) 163 in.; (Silhouette) 170.1 in. **Height:** (Espada) 46.6 in.; (Jarama) 46.8 in.; (Urraco) 44.9 in.; (Countach LP400S) 42.1 in.; (Silhouette) 44.1 in. **Width:** (Espada) 73.2 in.; (Jarama) 71.6 in.; (Urraco) 68.5 in.; (Countach LP400S) 78.7 in.; (Silhouette) 74 in. **Front Tread:** (Espada) 58.7 in.; (Jarama) 58.7 in.; (Urraco) 57.5 in.; (Countach LP400S) 58.7 in.; (Silhouette) 58.7 in. **Rear Tread:** (Espada) 58.7 in.; (Jarama) 58.7 in.; (Urraco) 57.5 in.; (Countach LP400S) 63.4 in.; (Silhouette) 61 in. **Standard Tires:** (Espada) 205VR15; (Jarama) 215/70VR15; (Urraco) 205/70VR14; (Countach LP400) 205/70VR14 front, 215/70VR14 rear; (Countach LP400S) 205/50VR15 front, 345/35VR15 rear; (Silhouette) 195/50VR15 front, 285/40VR15 rear.

TECHNICAL: Layout: (Espada/Jarama) front-engine, rear-drive; (Urraco/Countach/Silhouette) mid-engine, rear-drive. **Transmission:** five-speed manual; Chrysler TorqueFlite three-speed automatic available on Espada/Jarama. **Steering:** (Espada/Jarama) ZF screw and sector; (Urraco/Countach) rack and pinion. **Suspension (front):** (Espada/Jarama/Countach) unequal-length A-arms, coil springs and anti-roll bar; (Urraco/Silhouette) MacPherson struts, lower A-arms, coil springs and anti-roll bar. **Suspension (rear):** (Espada/Jarama) unequal-length A-arms, coil springs and anti-roll bar; (Urraco/Silhouette) struts with lower A-arms, coil springs and anti-roll bar; (Countach) upper lateral links, lower A-arms, upper/lower trailing arms, dual coil springs and anti-roll bar. **Brakes:** front/rear disc. **Body Construction:** (Espada/Jarama) integral steel chassis; (Urraco) body welded to pressed-steel platform, with separate rear auxiliary frame; (Silhouette) unibody; (Countach) aluminum body panels on multi-tube platform.

PERFORMANCE: Top Speed: (Espada) 155 mph; (Jarama) 162 mph; (Urraco P250) 149 + mph; (Countach LP400S) 174 mph; (Silhouette) 155-158 mph. **Acceleration (0-60 mph):** (Silhouette) 7.6 sec. **Acceleration (quarter-mile):** (Espada) 15.5 sec.; (Jarama) 15 sec.

PRODUCTION/SALES: A total of 201 Lamborghinis were produced in 1976 (8 Jarama, 33 Espada, 110 Urraco, 40 Countach, and 10 Silhouette); 105 in 1977 (24 Espada, 29 Urraco, 30 Countach, and 22 Silhouette); 68 in 1978 (one Jarama, 21 Espada, 9 Urraco, 16 Countach, and 21 Silhouette); 55 in 1979 (7 Urraco, 47 Countach, and one Silhouette); and 64 in 1980 (all Countach).

ADDITIONAL MODELS: In 1977, Lamborghini produced a Cheetah off-road vehicle for military use, which led to the LM series of four-wheel-drives; see next listing for further details.

Manufacturer: Automobili Ferruccio Lamborghini S.p.A., Sant'Agata, Bolognese, Italy.

Distributor: Grossman Motor Car Corp., West Nyack, New York.

HISTORY: Countach coupes were not officially imported into the U.S. from about 1977 to 1982, except via the unofficial "grey market." Other models couldn't be certified during the late 1970s either, which contributed to the firm's inability to remain afloat financially. No Silhouettes were known to have reached American shores. By 1979, both Urraco and Silhouette were gone; only the Countach was left. By that time, too, the Lamborghini company had entered receivership, and would be sold in 1981. Meanwhile, race driver/journalist Paul Frère called Countach "a he-man's car because the steering, gearshift and clutch are quite heavy."

1981-89 LAMBORGHINI

1981 Lamborghini Countach LP 400S. (Coys of Kensington)

COUNTACH — LP400S — V-12 — Production of the LP400S version with 3929-cc engine halted in 1982, replaced by the LP500S; see prior listing for details.

COUNTACH — LP500S — V-12 — A larger (4754-cc) engine went into the next Countach version, introduced in spring 1982. By that time, emissions regulations (worldwide) had reduced the original engine output to 350 bhp. This larger powerplant produced 375 horsepower (DIN), but only 325 bhp (SAE) for U.S. customers.

COUNTACH — 5000 QUATTROVALVOLE — V-12 — The next (and final) version of the flamboyant Countach adopted a larger, 48-valve (four per cylinder) version of the V-12 engine. Displacement reached 5167 cc (315.3 cid), with output of 455 horsepower (DIN); or 420 bhp (SAE) in U.S. form. Introduced in March 1985, the Countach Quattrovalvole would remain available through 1989.

Inside each tight Countach cockpit was a traditional instrument panel with white-numbered black-dial gauges, and a huge center console. Power windows rolled down only a few inches. A Targa top was available. Countach bodies were formed by hand, of thin aluminum.

To mark the 25th birthday of the company (and what would be the final season for this model), a $145,000 Anniversary Countach appeared for 1989. It wore a restyled front air dam, front and side skirting, reshaped hood air intake grilles, large flared wheel wells, and revised one-piece rear bumper. Airscoops were removed to improve air drag, while quarter-panel vents were enlarged. Radiators were repositioned, and a single large fan replace the twin smaller ones formerly used. Immense Pirelli "P-Zero" tires in 345/35ZR15 profile were installed at the rear (even larger than the usual ample Countach rubber). Power windows and seats became standard, and seats grew wider. In all, Lamborghini claimed that more than 500 component changes were made, after the prior model. Only about 400 of the special-editions were to be built. Customers also had a choice of two Alpine 130-watt sound systems (tape cassette or compact disc), with six matched speakers. European versions retained their six Weber carburetors, but fuel injection went into the later Countachs for the U.S. market.

JALPA — P350 GTS (3500) — V-8 — Joining the Countach in March 1981 was a Targa-topped coupe that has been described as Lamborghini's practical exoticar, displaying some of the aggressive characteristics as its V-12 companion but with a more cultivated tone. Though not without appearance kinship to Countach, the Jalpa came across as less intimidating, lacking some of the better-known supercar's doodads--and also some of its startling performance. Evolved from the Silhouette (which in turn descended from the Urraco), the Jalpa carried a 3.5-liter twin-cam V-8 with four Weber two-barrel carburetors, rated 250 horsepower at 7000 rpm in European trim. Torque of close to that figure was produced at a modest 3250 rpm. American editions, when federally-certified, earned similar ratings. Lamborghini claimed a 0-60 mph acceleration time in the mid-six second neighborhood, but independent testers couldn't manage that pace at first. Later evaluations, however, showed even quicker acceleration figures. A Jalpa could whiz through the quarter-mile in about 14.5 seconds, and reach roughly 150 mph.

Named for a region of Spain where fighting bulls were raised, the Jalpa was styled by Marcello Gandini of Bertone, who'd penned most of the prior Lambos. A new "flying buttress" roofline extension, along either side of the engine bay, created a sharp fastback profile; but the large 'B' pillars impaired rearward visibility. Up front, the air dam displayed a cutout segment in the center. Styling features also included a slim back window and solid, sloping rear quarter sections. Inside the leather-trimmed cockpit was a three-spoke steering wheel. Luggage space behind seats was needed to hold the Targa roof panel when removed, but additional storage area was available in the tail. Round gauges were set into square blocks. At chassis level, MacPherson struts and anti-roll bars were installed at both front and rear. Hefty 16-inch Pirelli P7 tires rode alloy wheels: 205/55 cross-section up front, with a 225/50 profile at the rear. The strengthened steel unibody included a separate auxiliary frame to support the mid-mounted V-8 engine.

I.D. DATA: Lamborghini's Vehicle Identification Number is on a plate atop the dashboard, visible through the windshield. Engine numbers are stamped at top front of block, between the banks.

1989 Lamborghini Countach coupe.

Model	Body Type & Seating	Engine Type/CID	P.O.E. Price	Weight (lbs.)	Prod. Total
COUNTACH (1981)					
LP400S	2-dr Coupe-2P	V12/240	102500	2915	Note 1
COUNTACH (1982-85)					
LP500S	2-dr Coupe-2P	V12/290	N/A	2915	Note 2
COUNTACH 5000 QUATTROVALVOLE (1985-89)					
5000	2-dr Coupe-2P	V12/315	100000	3188	N/A
JALPA					
P350 GTS	2-dr Coupe-2P	V8/213	58000	3300	Note 3

Note 1: As many as 385 Countach LP400S coupes were produced from 1978-82.
Note 2: A total of 325 Countach LP5000S coupes were produced from 1982-85.
Note 3: A total of 410 Jalpas were produced from 1981-89.

Price Note: Figures shown were valid in 1985. Countach price rose to $145,000 by 1989, but actual examples were selling for far more as its era drew to a close. Jalpa price rose to $65,000 in 1988, its final year of availability in the U.S. The 25th Anniversary Countach produced in 1989 carried an initial price tag of $145,000, but it soon was selling for as much as $215,000—and, according to *AutoWeek* magazine, up to $513,000 in England.

Model Note: Although generally referred to as LP500S, actual examples of the 1982-85 Countach carried an 'LP5000S' designation on the tail. The subsequent Quattrovalvole edition was sometimes called "LP500S QV" rather than "5000" or "LP5000."

ENGINE DATA: BASE V-12 (Countach LP400S): 60-degree, dual-overhead-cam "vee" type twelve-cylinder. Light alloy block and heads. **Displacement:** 239.8 cu. in. (3929 cc). **Bore & Stroke:** 3.23 x 2.44 in. (82 x 62 mm). **Compression Ratio:** 10.0:1. **Brake Horsepower:** 350/365 at 7500 rpm. **Torque:** 300 lbs.-ft. at 5500 rpm. Seven main bearings. Solid valve lifters. Six Weber two-barrel carburetors.

BASE V-12 (1982-85 Countach LP500S): 60-degree, dual-overhead-cam "vee" type twelve-cylinder. Light alloy block and heads. **Displacement:** 290.3 cu. in. (4754 cc). **Bore & Stroke:** 3.37 x 2.72 in. (85.5 x 69 mm). **Compression Ratio:** 9.2:1. **Brake Horsepower:** 375 (DIN) at 7000 rpm (325 bhp SAE at 7500 rpm in U.S.). **Torque:** 302 lbs.-ft. at 4500 rpm (260 at 5500 in U.S.). Seven main bearings. Solid valve lifters. Six Weber two-barrel carburetors.

BASE V-12 (1985-89 Countach 5000 Quattrovalvole): 60-degree, dual-overhead-cam "vee" type twelve-cylinder (four valves per cylinder). Light alloy block and heads. **Displacement:** 315.3 cu. in. (5167 cc). **Bore & Stroke:** 3.37 x 2.95 in. (85.5 x 75 mm). **Compression Ratio:** 9.5:1. **Brake Horsepower:** 455 DIN at 7000 rpm (420 SAE at 7000 in U.S.). **Torque:** 369 lbs.-ft. at 5200 rpm (341 at 5000 in U.S.). Seven main bearings. Solid valve lifters. Six Weber two-barrel carburetors (or later, Bosch K-Jetronic fuel injection).

BASE V-8 (Jalpa): Single-overhead-cam "vee" type eight-cylinder. Light alloy block and heads. **Displacement:** 212.7 cu. in. (3485 cc). **Bore & Stroke:** 3.39 x 2.95 in. (86 x 75 mm). **Compression Ratio:** 9.2:1. **Brake Horsepower:** 250/255 at 7000 rpm. **Torque:** 229-235 lbs.-ft. at 3250/3500 rpm. Five main bearings. Solid valve lifters. Four Weber two-barrel downdraft carburetors.

Note: Some Jalpa engines had turbochargers and fuel injection, thus different specifications.

1989 Lamborghini Countach Silver Anniversary model.

CHASSIS DATA: Wheelbase: (Countach) 98.4 in.; (Jalpa) 100.0 in. **Overall Length:** (Countach) 163.0-165.4 in.; (Jalpa) 170.6 in. **Height:** (Countach) 42.1 in.; (Jalpa) 44.9 in. **Width:** (Countach) 78.7 in.; (Jalpa) 74.0 in. **Front Tread:** (Countach) 60.5 in.; (Jalpa) 61.2 in. **Rear Tread:** (Countach) 63.2 in.; (Jalpa) 63.4 in. **Standard Tires:** (Countach) 205/50VR15 front, 345/45VR15 rear; (25th Anniversary Countach) 225/50ZR15 front, 345/35ZR15 rear; (Jalpa) 205/55VR16 front, 225/50VR16 rear.

Note: Jalpa dimensions shown are for final models.

TECHNICAL: Layout: mid-engine, rear-drive. **Transmission:** five-speed manual. **Steering:** rack and pinion. **Suspension (front):** (Countach) unequal-length A-arms, coil springs and anti-roll bar; (Jalpa) struts with lower A-arms, coil springs and anti-roll bar. **Suspension (rear):** (Countach) upper lateral links, lower A-arms, upper/lower trailing arms, dual coil springs and anti-roll bar; (Jalpa) struts with lower A-arms, coil springs and anti-roll bar. **Brakes:** front/rear disc. **Body Construction:** (Countach) aluminum body panels on multi-tube platform; (Jalpa) integral with rear auxiliary frame.

PERFORMANCE: Top Speed: (U.S. Countach LP500S) 150 mph; (U.S. Countach 5000) 173 mph; (25th Anniversary Countach) 183.3 mph claimed, 186 mph reported; (Jalpa) 148-155 mph (154 mph claimed). **Acceleration (0-60 mph):** (Countach LP500S) 5.7 sec.; (Countach 5000) 5.2 sec.; (25th Anniversary Countach) 4.7 sec. claimed; (Jalpa) 5.8 to 7.3 sec. **Acceleration (quarter-mile):** (late Countach) 12.9 sec. (110 mph); (Jalpa) 14.5 to 15.4 sec. (92-93 mph).

PRODUCTION/SALES: A total of 89 Lamborghinis were produced in 1981, followed by 110 in 1982 (98 Countach and 12 Jalpa); 184 in 1983 (115 Countach and 69 Jalpa); and 231 in 1984 (132 Countach and 99 Jalpa). A total of 1,997 Countachs were produced over the full model run (all series).

ADDITIONAL MODELS: No discussion of Lamborghini is quite complete without mention of the monstrous LM-series luxury-sport-utility vehicles of the 1980s. The concept originated in 1977, when Lamborghini obtained a contract from Mobility Technology International (MTI, a U.S. firm) to design and produce an all-terrain military vehicle, intended to replace the long-lived Jeep. MTI did not get the hoped-for contract, and Lamborghini's Cheetah prototype, powered by a rear-mounted 360-cid Chrysler V-8, crashed and was destroyed during tests in the California desert. The idea wasn't forgotten, however, and at the 1981 Geneva show Lamborghini displayed a new LM001 model, which could be powered either by a rear-mounted Lamborghini V-12 engine or an American V-8. As actual production turned to reality, the LM002 switched to a front-engine layout, with the 4754-cc Lamborghini V-12 underhood. An even mightier (and rarer) LM004 edition debuted in 1983, with a 7.3-liter V-12 that produced 420 horsepower and 435 pound-feet of torque.

As the Countach adopted a Quattrovalvole (four valves per cylinder) powerplant in 1985, the LM002 also gained that larger engine, with a rating of up to 455 bhp and 368 pound-feet of torque. The four-wheel-drive LM002 wore an aluminum-and-fiberglass body, atop a steel-tube space frame with 118-inch wheelbase. Standing just over six feet tall, it had a full foot of ground clearance. Late 1980s models rode on 325/65VR17 tires, and could hit 118 to 125 mph. An LM002 could accelerate from 0-60 mph in as little as 7.7 seconds, and blast through the quarter-mile in some 16 seconds, reaching 86 mph. That was no small achievement for a vehicle that weighed close to three tons. A 73-gallon gas tank was a virtual necessity, since an LM002 wasn't likely to average more than about 8 miles per gallon.

Manufacturer: Nuova Automobili Ferruccio Lamborghini S.p.A., Sant'Agata, Bolognese, Italy.

Distributor: Lamborghini East, North Bergren, New Jersey.

HISTORY: *Road & Track* applauded the Jalpa's "rumbling exhaust note" and "swoopy, low" silhouette. The Jalpa show-car prototype wore a metallic copper body, with beige/orange striped leather seats inside. Of the 410 built altogether, only a few dozen Jalpas (at most) reached the U.S. during each year of the car's life. Jalpa production ceased by July 1988.

The company name changed to Nuova Automobili Ferruccio Lamborghini when it was sold to the French-Swiss Mimran brothers in 1981, thus averting imminent financial disaster. Chrysler bought the Lamborghini company in 1987, and called the final Countach a "landmark in automotive design."

"Countach is the king of cars," explained Lamborghini technical director Luigi Marmiroli to *Car and Driver* in 1988. "Ferrari is a woman but a Lamborghini is male!" *Road & Track* described the late Countach Quattrovalvole as "perhaps the most otherwordly shape of all, bristling with decks and planes and scoops like a deathship from outer space." *AutoWeek* named the 25th Anniversary Countach "the most powerful production car money can buy," noting that "you immediately feel the car sticking to the ground. It dominates the road and transmits an incredible sensation of safety." Low-speed acceleration was deemed uninspiring, but "from 3000 to 7000 rpm, the car explodes into extraordinary speed."

1990 LAMBORGHINI

DIABLO — V-12 — After a decade and a half in production, the startling Countach finally was replaced by a slightly less dramatic Diablo. Displaying more rounded lines than its predecessor, with a "cab forward" profile and beltline that dipped aft of the A-pillar, the Diablo was no less a supercar, capable of 202-mph top speed. When unveiled at the Chicago Auto Show in February 1990, the Diablo show car carried a mid-mounted 5707-cc (348-cid) V-12 considerably larger in displacement than the V-12 installed in the final Countach. Fitted luggage was to be included for the $211,000 price, when the car went on sale late in 1990. About one-third of the total production was expected to be earmarked for the U.S. market. Styling was by Marcello Gandini (again), with refinements offered by Chrysler. The American company also handled the interior design. The production V-12 engine developed 485 horsepower with sequential fuel injection, working into a hydraulically-controlled clutch and five-speed manual gearbox.

I.D. DATA: Lamborghini's 17-symbol Vehicle Identification Number is on the upper left of the dashboard, visible through the windshield.

Model	Body Type & Seating	Engine Type/CID	P.O.E. Price	Weight (lbs.)	Prod. Total
DIABLO					
	2-dr Coupe-2P	V12/348	211000	3640	N/A

ENGINE DATA: BASE V-12: 60-degree, dual-overhead-cam "vee" type twelve-cylinder. Aluminum block and heads. **Displacement:** 348 cu. in. (5707 cc). **Bore & Stroke:** 3.43 x 3.15 in. (87 x 80 mm). **Compression Ratio:** 10.1:1. **Brake Horsepower:** 485 at 7000 rpm. **Torque:** 428 lbs.-ft. at 5200 rpm. Seven main bearings. Solid valve lifters. Sequential multipoint fuel injection.

CHASSIS DATA: Wheelbase: 104.3 in. **Overall Length:** 175.6 in. **Height:** 43.5 in. **Width:** 80.3 in. **Front Tread:** 59.4 in. **Rear Tread:** 64.6 in. **Standard Tires:** 245/40ZR17 front, 335/35ZR17 rear.

TECHNICAL: Layout: mid-engine, rear-wheel-drive. **Transmission:** five-speed manual. **Steering:** rack and pinion. **Suspension (front):** unequal-length wishbones, coil springs and anti-roll bar. **Suspension (rear):** independent, with unequal-length wishbones, coil springs and anti-roll bar. **Brakes:** power front/rear vented disc. **Body Construction:** aluminum alloy and composite panels, on structure of high-resistance steel alloys and carbon fiber.

MAJOR OPTIONS: Rear wing ($5000). Designer clock.

PERFORMANCE: Top Speed: 202 mph. **Acceleration (0-60 mph):** N/A (0-62 mph in 4.1 sec.). **Fuel Mileage:** about 11 mpg average.

PRODUCTION/SALES: Approximately 156 Lamborghinis were sold in the U.S. during 1990.

Manufacturer: Automobili Lamborghini S.p.A., Sant'Agata, Bolognese, Italy.
Distributor: Lamborghini U.S.A. Inc., Bloomfield Hills, Michigan.

POSTSCRIPT: A Targa-topped replacement for the Jalpa was expected to appear as early as 1992 (possibly with a V-10 engine), along with a possible four-wheel-drive option for the Diablo.

LANCHESTER

Unlike most British automakers who entered the business before the turn of the century, Frederick Lanchester relied upon his own ideas rather than borrowing from Continental creations. After tinkering with the notion, then producing a motorized boat in 1894, he and his younger brother George developed a motorcar in the following year. Some considered it to be the first gasoline-powered automobile built in England. Technical features included an epicyclic gearbox and crankshafts that turned in opposite directions, delivering surprising smoothness. A two-cylinder version followed in 1897.

Joined by a third brother, the Lanchester Gas Engine Company was established late in 1899. Lanchesters stuck with steering tillers as late as 1911, far longer than rival firms; but switched from bodies by outside suppliers to their own coachwork by 1906. Meanwhile, in the wake of financial difficulties, the original company was dissolved and replaced by the new Lanchester Motor Company Ltd. A four-cylinder model emerged during 1904, then a six-cylinder edition. In addition to his work directly for Lanchester, Frederick secured patents for several notable technical devices that were sold to other manufacturers, including a torsional vibration damper and harmonic balancer. He then became a technical adviser to Daimler.

After the First World War, Lanchester focused on a six-cylinder model Forty, evolved from an earlier short-lived 5.5-liter L-head "Sporting" model, now carrying an overhead-cam engine. A 6.2-liter version was followed by a companion of half that displacement. Quite a few were shipped to the U.S., while others enjoyed Royal patronage. A straight-eight Lanchester came in 1928, but production was hampered by the looming Depression. Further financial woes led to merger with the Daimler Company in 1931, and a shift of Lanchester production facilities to Coventry. A pushrod-type overhead-valve six became the standard powerplant in the early 1930s, coupled to a Wilson preselector gearbox with fluid flywheel. Some smaller Lanchesters of the late 1930s came in comparable form under the BSA nameplate (BSA being the owner of Daimler). In fact, quite a few Lanchester components were shared with both Daimler and BSA vehicles, serving to weaken Lanchester's image as a superlative motorcar. Lanchesters even came to be viewed in some circles as "baby Daimlers." The few straight-eight Lanchesters of the late 1930s, in particular, were "all Daimler" except for the radiator design.

By the outbreak of World War II, none of the Lanchester brothers remained with the company. As that war ended, the firm ignored the possibility of a large model and announced instead an overhead-valve four-cylinder Lanchester Ten, again with the fluid flywheel, wearing six-light coachwork by Briggs. A Barker-bodied four-light Ten saloon emerged after 1949. Sales were relatively brisk, even as prices rose. Still, Lanchester was beginnning to fade away. The new model Fourteen of 1951-54 was essentially a Daimler Conquest saloon with four-cylinder power rather than six. In export form (including U.S. models), it wore an all-steel body and was called the Leda. Prior to the company's demise, two very different models were created: a razor-edge Dauphin saloon with Hooper body, and a unibodied Sprite with four-cylinder power and a Hobbs automatic transmission. Though promoted with some vigor, neither went into production. No more than two Dauphins were built, followed by as many as 13 Sprites, the latter in Mark I and Mark II form. By the end of 1955, the distinguished Lanchester name was gone.

1946-50 LANCHESTER

1947 Lanchester Ten saloon.

TEN (BRIGGS) — FOUR — Like most British (and other) marques that re-emerged just after World War II, the first postwar Lanchester carried on prewar styling. In fact, production had been planned for the 1940 model year before hostilities intervened. The Briggs-built six-light (six-window) saloon body had a vee-shaped grille made up of vertical ribs, wider at the top than the bottom, with curved side moldings. Separate headlamps were mounted alongside the grille. Both the front and rear doors were hinged at the rear, "suicide" style, and the flat windshield could be opened for ventilation. The 1.3-liter overhead-valve four-cylinder engine, rated 40 horsepower, was hooked to a fluid flywheel.

TEN (BARKER) — FOUR — A four-light body emerged in 1949, produced by the Barker company. Front-end appearance was similar, but the four-window design has a longer deck and rear doors were hinged at the front. The windshield no longer opened.

I.D. DATA: Chassis serial number is stamped on a plate on a chassis member, alongside the engine. Starting serial number: L-60025. Engine number is stamped on the block, atop the fuel pump boss.

Model	Body Type & Seating	Engine Type/CID	P.O.E. Price	Weight (lbs.)	Prod. Total
LD10	4-dr Saloon-4/5P	I4/78	N/A	2484	Note 1

Note 1: About 3,050 Lanchester Tens (both Barker and Briggs body) were produced from 1946 to 1951.

ENGINE DATA: BASE FOUR: Inline, overhead-valve four-cylinder. Cast iron block. **Displacement:** 78.5 cu. in. (1287 cc). **Bore & Stroke:** 2.50 x 4.00 in. (63.5 x 101.6 mm). **Compression Ratio:** 7.0:1. **Brake Horsepower:** 40 at 4200 rpm. Three main bearings. Solid valve lifters. One Zenith carburetor.

CHASSIS DATA: **Wheelbase:** 99.0 in. **Overall Length:** 158.0 in. **Height:** 63.0 in. **Width:** 58.0 in. **Front Tread:** 48.0 in. **Rear Tread:** 48.0 in. **Wheel Type:** disc. **Standard Tires:** 5.25x16.

TECHNICAL: **Layout:** front-engine, rear-drive. **Transmission:** four-speed preselector; fluid flywheel. **Standard Final Drive Ratio:** 5.00:1. **Suspension (front):** independent; coil springs. **Suspension (rear):** rigid axle with semi-elliptic leaf springs. **Brakes:** front/rear drum. **Body Construction:** steel body on steel frame.

PERFORMANCE: **Top Speed:** 66-69 mph. **Acceleration (0-60 mph):** N/A (0-50 mph in 26 seconds). **Acceleration (quarter-mile):** 27.5 seconds. **Fuel Mileage:** 31 mpg (Imperial).

Manufacturer: Lanchester Motor Co. Ltd. (Daimler Co. Ltd.), Coventry, England.

HISTORY: Production of the Barker-bodied Ten ceased during 1951, after the debut of the new Fourteen (Leda). Around 1948, one or two special Lanchester drophead coupes were built, with 4.1-liter six-cylinder engines rated 110 bhp.

1951-54 LANCHESTER

1954 Lanchester Fourteen four-door sedan.

FOURTEEN/LEDA — FOUR — Available with either right- or left-hand drive, the dramatically redesigned new Fourteen came in one version for the home market and another (Leda) for export. The Leda had an all-steel body, and Lanchester was hoping for increased international sales. All Fourteens featured Daimler's four-speed epicyclic preselector gearbox with fluid transmission. Displaying traditional graceful lines, the Fourteen rode a much different chassis, five inches longer in wheelbase (104 inches) than its predecessor. The vee-shaped grille again wore a pattern of vertical bars, but with a rectangular shape. Headlamps were now built into the fender tips, with small round parking lights below. Front fenders flowed smoothly into the front doors, rather than stopping at the cowl as in prior models. Both front and rear doors were hinged at their front ends, and the six-window profile included vent wings on the front doors.

Moving away from coil springs for the front end, Lanchester adopted square-section laminated or "leaf" torsion bars. A cruciform box-section frame was used. An automatic chassis lubrication system delivered lubricant to selected points as the engine warmed up. The overhead-valve four-cylinder engine grew from 1287 to 1968 cubic centimeters (120 cid), and added 20 horsepower. It had a full-flow oil filter and Zenith carburetor, with both manual and automatic distributor advance adjustment. Standard equipment included a built-in heater/demister, turn signals, "Bevelift" mechanical jacking system, leather upholstery, and gold line treatment. Standard colors included Black with brown, red or green leather; Blue with blue leather; Grey with blue or red leather; Dark Green with green leather; Light Green with beige leather and green piping; Maroon with red leather; or Fawn with green leather and beige piping. Two-tone color schemes were available, following the extended line of the front fender. Each half of the split bench-type front seat was separately adjustable. The rear seat had a fold-down center armrest and fixed side armrests. Provision was made for a radio, with speaker in the roof. Though wearing a personality of its own, the new Lanchester used a large number of components from the six-cylinder Daimler Conquest series, and their chassis were identical in many ways.

Late in 1951, a De Ville convertible coupe appeared, with a power-operated top and power windows. *Motor Trend* noted its kinship with some American custom cars, including what appeared to be a "shaved" nose, dechromed appearance, clean rear deck, and fadeaway front fenders. For the 1953 model year, Ledas added a mascot at the hood's center.

I.D. DATA: Chassis serial number is stamped on a plate atop a chassis member, alongside the starter. Serial number prefix: (Fourteen, RHD) LJ200; (Leda, LHD) LJ201. Starting serial number: (LHD) 66000; (RHD) 65000; (RHD in 1953-54) 67150. Engine number is stamped on the fuel pump boss.

Model	Body Type & Seating	Engine Type/CID	P.O.E. Price	Weight (lbs.)	Prod. Total
Fourteen	4-dr Saloon-4/5P	I4/120	N/A	3136	Note 1
Leda	4-dr Saloon-4/5P	I4/120	2850	3136	Note 1
DeVille	2-dr Conv Cpe	I4/120	N/A	N/A	Note 1

Note 1: About 2,150 Lanchester Fourteens (and Ledas) were produced from late 1950 to 1954.

ENGINE DATA: BASE FOUR: Inline, overhead-valve four-cylinder. Cast iron block. **Displacement:** 120.0 cu. in. (1968 cc). **Bore & Stroke:** 3.00 x 4.25 in. (76.2 x 107.95 mm). **Compression Ratio:** 6.7:1. **Brake Horsepower:** 60 at 4200 rpm. **Torque:** 95 lbs.-ft. at 2000 rpm. Three main bearings. Solid valve lifters. One Zenith downdraft carburetor. Lucas 12-volt ignition.

CHASSIS DATA: **Wheelbase:** 104.0 in. **Overall Length:** 175.6 in. **Height:** 62.0 in. **Width:** 65.9 in. **Front Tread:** 52.0 in. **Rear Tread:** 48.0 in. **Wheel Type:** bolt-on disc. **Standard Tires:** 6.70x15.

TECHNICAL: **Layout:** front-engine, rear-drive. **Transmission:** four-speed preselector; fluid flywheel. Overall gear ratios: (1st) 17.47:1; (2nd) 10.55:1; (3rd) 6.71:1; (4th) 4.55:1; (rev) 23.7:1. **Standard Final Drive Ratio:** 4.55:1. **Steering:** cam gear. **Suspension (front):** independent; laminated torsion bars with wishbone links, torsional stabilizing bar and Girling telescopic shocks. **Suspension (rear):** rigid axle with semi-elliptic leaf springs and Girling telescopic shocks. **Brakes:** Girling hydromechanical, front/rear drum. **Body Construction:** (Leda) all-steel body on box-section, cruciform-braced steel frame. **Fuel Tank:** 18 gallons (U.S.); 2-gallon reserve.

PERFORMANCE: **Top Speed:** about 73 mph. **Acceleration (0-60 mph):** 29.7 seconds.
Manufacturer: The Lanchester Motor Co. Ltd. (Daimler Co. Ltd.), Coventry, England.

HISTORY: "From bumper to bumper," said the *Lanchester News*, "the 'Leda' is a completely new car. It brings together all that is best in up-to-the-minute automobile design, whilst embodying all the fine attributes associated with the name Lanchester. "This "new car at once suggests swiftness and elegance without ostentation....a skil(l)fully proportioned blend of performance, comfort and grace, equally at home in city or rugged country." Acknowledging its "baby Daimler" character, *Auto Age* magazine applauded the Leda's maneuverability during a road test and added that its "coach work is in the finest British tradition." Ledas enjoyed a modest (and brief) spurt of sales success in the U.S., following introduction of the export model during 1952. Leda production came to a halt during 1953, the home-market Fourteen saloon by mid-1954.

The distinctively streamlined, razor-edged Dauphin two-door saloon, with body by Hooper, would have been a marked departure for Lanchester into specialized luxury transport. Extras were to include such items as tip-up armchair-type rear seats. Designed around a wheelbase of the same dimensions as the Fourteen/Leda, the heavier Dauphin show car carried a 92-bhp six-cylinder engine. Sprite, on the other hand, would have been the first British car in the medium-price range (estimated to be $2135 at the factory) with a standard automatic transmission. Wheelbase was 99 inches, with a 60-bhp, 1622-cc four-cylinder engine beneath the bonnet. The Mark II version was slightly larger than the Mark I, but both had unibody construction. As for the epicyclic automatic transmission, one tester slammed it into reverse at 50 mph (at the suggestion of the manufacturer), whereby the experimental Sprite came to a smooth, quick stop. Lanchester's demise in 1955 prevented production of either the posh Dauphin or the middle-range Sprite.

LANCIA

Starting out in life as a bookkeeper might not seem the most auspicious beginning for Vincenzo Lancia, whose name eventually would grace a series of memorable Italian motorcars. In 1899, however, Lancia became head inspector at FIAT (after its takeover of the company for which he'd worked) and, a year later, started an eight-year racing career with the company. Late in 1906, he founded Lancia & Cie, Fabbrica Automobili. Conditions must have looked less than promising when the new company's first automobile was destroyed by fire, just a year later.

Lancia persisted, starting production of the Alfa, with a 2543-cc four-cylinder engine, in 1908. That led in 1909 to the monobloc-engined Beta, with a powerplant grown to 3120 cc. A succession of Greek-letter model names followed: a six-cylinder Dialfa, 3460-cc Gamma, and 4080-cc Delta. By 1911, the Lancia company operated in an expanded headquarters on the outskirts of Turin, Italy. Its products were sold not only in Europe and Russia, but as far away as Argentina. During the Great War, Lancia produced a Theta model with 4940-cc engine and electric starter. Peacetime brought a Kappa, and the debut of a V-12 engine with narrow (22-degree) angle between its cylinders. That powerplant never reached production as announced, but evolved into a model powered by a 4594-cc, 22-degree V-8 (called Trikappa), which was built from 1922-25. Another engine debuted in 1922 to power a new Lambda: a 13-degree V-4 with single-overhead-cam configuration and an alloy block. The Lambda series produced through the 1920s also featured unit construction of its lower body and chassis, and independent coil-spring front suspension. A hardtop was available for the torpedo-style body.

In 1927, plans were made to produce Lancias in the U.S., at the instigation of an American entrepreneur. Lancia Motors of America was formed, and displayed prototypes at

the New York Importers Car Show. The program collapsed, however, proving to be more of a stock-manipulation scheme than an honest stab at American production. Those prototypes didn't exactly fade away, evolving instead into the Dilambda series of 1929-35, powered by a 3960-cc overhead-cam V-8 (with 22 degrees between cylinders). Pinin Farina did some Dilambda bodies, which rode separate chassis and included centralized lubrication; others came from such coachbuilders as James Young in Britain, and Murphy in the U.S. About 20 Dilambdas had left-hand drive, but the vast majority of Lancias retained right-hand drive until the mid-1950s. Meanwhile, three Lancias entered the 1928 Mille Miglia race, one of which finished third.

Other models of the 1930s included the Artena and Astura, which shared bodies but carried different engines: a 1924-cc V-4 and 2604-cc V-8, respectively. By the late 1930s, Asturas grew to 2972-cc and had hydraulic brakes, and wore avant-garde Pinin Farina bodies. Debuting at the 1932 Paris Salon was a smaller-engined, unibodied Augusta sedan, powered by an 1194-cc, single-overhead-cam V-4 engine.

Production of the Aprilia fastback four-door began in 1937 and lasted into the postwar period. Beneath its hood sat an all-new 1352-cc overhead-cam V-4 with hemispherical combustion chambers, rated 47 horsepower. Streamlined Aprilia sedans used unibody construction and a fully independent suspension (torsion-bar rear), with an unsynchronized four-speed gearbox sending power to the back wheels. Vincenzo Lancia died in 1937, before the production version appeared, succeeded by his son Gianni, who would remain in charge until 1955.

In 1939, shortly before war halted Lancia production, a larger (1486-cc) engine went into the Aprilia, and a shrunken Ardea model with 903-cc engine joined the lineup. Aprilias remained in production into 1949; Ardeas as late as 1953.

The company's first all-new postwar model, the Aurelia, came in 1950, designed by Gianni Lancia and Vittorio Jano (who'd formerly worked at Alfa Romeo). Under its hood was a 56-horsepower, 1754-cc overhead-valve (pushrod) V-6, while its four-speed gearbox was integral with the rear axle. A B20 GT coupe with larger (1991-cc) engine that produced 75 bhp joined the original Aurelia four-door sedan in 1951. A GT coupe edition had 80 horsepower available. Its engine then grew to 2266 cc, then again to 2451 cc, producing up to 118 horsepower in GT trim. A De Dion axle became standard in 1954, as left-hand drive became standard. All coupes through 1959 (when production ceased) had a steering-column gearshift lever, while open Spider roadsters had a floor lever. A smaller version of the Aurelia, named Appia, appeared in 1953 with a 1090-cc V-4 engine that produced 38 horsepower.

Gianni Lancia and his mother elected to sell their interest in the company in 1955, and it was taken over by Carlo Pesenti, who constructed a new headquarters at Turin. Vittorio Jano was replaced by Antonio Fessia (who'd been responsible for the popular little Fiat Topolino before the war). Pinin Farina did the styling for the next new model: the four-door Flaminia of 1957, powered by a 98-horsepower, 2458-cc V-6 and carrying a De Dion transaxle. Lancia's traditional sliding-pillar front suspension finally was dropped, replaced by conventional wishbones and coil springs. Shorter GT versions were available by 1958, with 125 horsepower at hand; and disc brakes were installed. By 1963, the original engine grew to 2775 cc. Coupes and convertibles, as built by Pininfarina, Touring and Zagato, sold stronger than the Flaminia sedans. The 3C sport coupe carried a potent 152-bhp version of the 2.8-liter engine. Flaminia expired in 1970.

Next up (in 1961) was the Flavia, with a horizontally-opposed 1500-cc four-cylinder engine, disc brakes, and front-wheel drive. Flavia development was the work of Dr. Fessia. Both four-door sedans and Pininfarina-styled coupes were produced, the GT coupe having 92 horsepower at hand. A 1.8-liter engine became available in 1963. Flavia production contined as late as 1975, with 2-liter engine made standard in 1972.

In 1964, a new Fulvia replaced the Appia, powered by a 1091-cc V-4 engine. The GT edition rated 71 horsepower, sufficient for a top speed of 106 mph. In 1967, Kugelfischer fuel injection became available on the Flavia engine.

Lancia sales sank badly in the late 1960s. Ford was considered as a prospective buyer, but instead the Fiat organization took over in October 1969. For the early 1970s, the Flavia engine grew to 1990 cc and it was renamed, simply, Lancia 2000.

Greek names made another appearance in the Lancia catalog (for the first time since 1929) as a new front-drive Beta fastback sedan debuted at the 1972 Turin show, but took several years to reach the temporarily-abandoned U.S. market. Fiat twin-cam engines provided the power, in 1438-, 1596- and 1756-cc sizes. A five-speed gearbox was standard, and a two-liter engine became available in 1976. Before long, Spyder, coupe and HPE (High Performance Estate) versions joined the original sedan. The rear-drive Monte Carlo coupe of 1975 carried a mid-mounted 1995-cc engine and Pininfarina-styled body. In the U.S. market, that coupe was called Scorpion and carried a smaller (1756-cc) engine, like its Beta mates. On another level, marketed elsewhere in the world, a large Gamma replaced the Fiat 130, powered by a 2.5-liter horizontally-opposed four (or optional 2.0-liter). Even more noteworthy in the 1970s was the dramatic Lancia Stratos two-seater, powered by a Fiat Dino engine, which by 1978 won 14 World Championship Rallies and 68 other international events.

Lancia faded out of the U.S. marketplace after 1982, but continued to build both everyday and sporty cars for sale elsewhere in the world, as part of the Fiat empire. The Beta replacement, called Trevi, could even be purchased with a Roots-type supercharger. Lancia's final model offered in the U.S. was the Zagato targa-topped coupe/convertible.

1946-49 LANCIA

APRILIA — TIPO (TYPE) 438/439/539 (SERIES II) — V-4 — Introduced in 1937, the unibodied Aprilia sedan resumed production soon after World War II was over. A narrow-angle, 1352-cc overhead-cam V-4 engine had provided the power at the beginning, enlarged to 1486 cc in 1939. Only the larger engine was installed in postwar models. Styled with aerodynamics that were quite good for its day, an Aprilia could top 80 mph (according to some sources). All-independent suspension included traditional Lancia sliding pillars up front. Most Aprilias were pillarless four-window, four-door sedans, but a few small number of sporty longer-wheelbase models also were produced. Styling features included separate headlamps and rear-hinged rear doors. Standard Type 438 (series II) sedans, produced from 1939-49, rode a 108.3-inch wheelbase. Aprilia chassis also were produced in 112.2- and 116.1-inch wheelbases.

I.D. DATA: Chassis serial number is stamped on upper edge of right-hand engine louvers, under the hood; and on some cars, also on a bulkhead plate. Prefix '99' is used. Engine number is stamped on right rear of mounting. Production serial number range (Type 438, Series II): 10355-20082. Chassis number range (Type 438, Series II)

Model	Body Type & Seating	Engine Type/CID	P.O.E. Price	Weight (lbs.)	Prod. Total
APRILIA					
438	4-dr Sedan	V4/91	N/A	2094	Note 1
439	4-dr Sedan	V4/91	N/A	N/A	Note 1
539	4-dr Sedan	V4/91	N/A	N/A	Note 1

Note 1: A total of 14,704 Aprilias were produced (including prewar models) from 1937-49.

Weight Note: Figure shown is curb weight of standard Type 438 sedan. Types 439 and 539 were produced as separate chassis and could carry various bodies.

ENGINE DATA: BASE V-4: 17-degree, overhead-cam "vee" type four-cylinder (type 99). **Displacement:** 90.6 cu. in. (1486 cc). **Bore & Stroke:** 2.94 x 3.35 in. (74.6 x 85 mm). **Compression Ratio:** 5.75:1. **Brake Horsepower:** 48 at 4300 rpm. Three main bearings. Solid valve lifters. Zenith 32VIML3 carburetor.

CHASSIS DATA: Wheelbase: (438) 108.3 in.; (439) 112.2 in.; (539) 116.1 in. **Overall Length:** (438) 154.7-157.0 in.; (539) 177.2 in. **Height:** (438) 57.3 in. **Width:** (438) 59 in.; (539) 60.2 in. **Front Tread:** 49.7 in. **Rear Tread:** 51.9 in. **Standard Tires:** 165x400.

TECHNICAL: Layout: front-engine, rear-drive. **Transmission:** four-speed manual. **Standard Final Drive Ratio:** 4.10:1. **Steering:** worm and sector. **Suspension (front):** sliding pillar. **Suspension (rear):** independent; semi-elliptic transverse leaf spring with torsion

bars and trailing arms. **Brakes:** hydraulic, front/rear drum. **Body Construction:** steel unibody.

PERFORMANCE: Top Speed: 72-80 mph.

ADDITIONAL MODELS: Lancia introduced an Ardea four-door sedan (Series III) on a 96-inch wheelbase in 1948. Vaguely resembling a shrunken 1937 Ford, it had front-hinged front doors and rear-hinged rear doors and a one-piece windshield. Power came from a 903-cc four-cylinder engine with 6:1 compression that produced close to 28.8 horsepower at 4600 rpm (30 bhp in the Series IV, produced from 1949-52). Overall length was 143.5 inches, and top speed was 67 mph.

Manufacturer: Fabbrica Automobili Lancia e Cia, Turin, Italy.

1950-52 LANCIA

1951 Lancia Aurelia four-door sedan.

AURELIA — B10/B15/B20/B21/B22 (SERIES 1) — V-6 — A four-door Berlina (sedan) was the first offering under the new Aurelia nameplate, introduced in 1950. A year later, that sedan was joined by a fastback GT coupe (B20), with the same chassis and drivetrain but designed by Pinin Farina. Styling features of both bodies included a vaguely heart-shaped (curved at the base) vertical-bar grille with wider center divider bar. Oval headlamps were built into the fenders, with tiny round parking lamps below. Each model used a sliding-pillar front suspension, like all other Lancias of the time. Through the 1950s, a total of six Aurelia series would appear, through differences weren't great. Under the hood of the first (B10) sedan was a 1754-cc V-6 engine, rated 56 horsepower at 4000 rpm. GT coupes and later sedans carried a 1991-cc (121-cid) V-6, rated from 65 to 90 horsepower. The longer-wheelbase B15 sedan joined the lineup in 1952. Standard GT equipment included a natural wood riveted steering wheel rim, with spring spokes.

I.D. DATA: Aurelia chassis serial number is stamped on a firewall plate, either below the hood hinge mounting bracket or on the right side of the junction box. Engine number is stamped on right side of block, near the fuel pump. Prefix 'B' is followed by a two-digit model designation. Letter 'S' denotes left-hand drive. Chassis serial number range: (B10) 1001-5938; (B10S) 1001-1513; (B15) 1001-1067; (B15S) 1001-1014; (B21) 1001-4250; (B21S) 1001-1530; (B22) 1001-1877; (B22S) 1001-1197; (B20 GT cpe) 1001-1500; (B20S GT cpe) 1001-1255.

Model	Body Type & Seating	Engine Type/CID	P.O.E. Price	Weight (lbs.)	Prod. Total
AURELIA					
B10	4-dr Sedan-5/6P	V6/107	N/A	2435	Note 1
B15	4-dr Sedan-5/6P	V6/121	N/A	2557	Note 1
B21	4-dr Sedan-5/6P	V6/121	N/A	2435	Note 1
B22	4-dr Sedan-5/6P	V6/121	N/A	2435	Note 1
B20	2-dr GT Cpe-2 + 2P	V6/121	N/A	2325	Note 1

Note 1: A total of 12,786 Aurelias were built, through 1955. A total of 3,871 coupes (and 761 later Spider roadsters) were produced during the full model run.

ENGINE DATA: BASE V-6 (B10 sedan): 60-degree, overhead-valve "vee" type six-cylinder. Aluminum block and heads. **Displacement:** 107 cu. in. (1754 cc). **Bore & Stroke:** 2.76 x 2.99 in. (70 x 76 mm). **Compression Ratio:** 6.85:1. **Brake Horsepower:** 56 at 4000 rpm. Solid valve lifters. Solex twin-choke downdraft carburetor.
BASE V-6 (B20 coupe, B15/B21/B22 sedan): 60-degree, overhead-valve "vee" type six-cylinder. Aluminum block and heads. **Displacement:** 121 cu. in. (1991 cc). **Bore & Stroke:** 2.83 x 3.21 in. (72 x 81.5 mm). **Compression Ratio:** (B21/B22) 7.8:1; (B20) 8.4:1. **Brake Horsepower:** (B15) 65 at 4000 rpm; (B20) 75 at 4500 rpm; (B21) 70 at 4800 rpm; (B22) 90 at 5000 rpm. Solid valve lifters. Solex carburetor (B21); Weber twin-choke carburetor (B22); dual Weber carburetors (B20).

CHASSIS DATA: Wheelbase: (GT cpe) 104.7 in.; (sed) 112.6 in.; (B15 sed) 128 in. **Overall Length:** (GT cpe) 168.5 in.; (sed) 174 in.; (B15 sed) 189 in. **Height:** (GT cpe) 53.5 in.; (sed) 59 in.; (B15 sed) 61.3 in. **Width:** (GT cpe) 60.6 in.; (sed) 61.5 in.; (B15 sed) 62.8 in. **Front Tread:** 50.4 in. except (B15) 51 in. **Rear Tread:** 51.2 in. except (B15) 52.2 in. **Wheel Type:** 5.50x16. **Standard Tires:** 165x400 except (B15) 185x400.

TECHNICAL: Layout: front-engine, rear-drive. **Transmission:** four-speed manual. **Steering:** worm and sector. **Suspension (front):** sliding pillar. **Suspension (rear):** independent; coil springs with semi-trailing link. **Brakes:** hydraulic, front/rear drum. **Body Construction:** steel unibody.

PERFORMANCE: Top Speed: (B10 sedan) 84 mph; (B21 sedan) 90 mph; (B22 sedan) 94 mph; (B20 GT coupe) 101 mph.

Manufacturer: Fabbrica Automobili Lancia e Cia S.p.A., Turin (Torino), Italy.

HISTORY: "Everything about this machine is quick, compact, positive, practical and ingenious," reported John Bentley on the Aurelia GT coupe in *Auto Speed and Sport* magazine. That road test involved the only GT then in the U.S., owned by Briggs Cunningham. A Lancia easily won its class at the 1951 Le Mans race, averaging 82.14 mph.

1953-56 LANCIA

1954 Lancia 2½-liter Gran Turismo sports sedan.

AURELIA — B10/B15/B21/B22 (SERIES 1) — V-6 — Production of the four Berlinas (sedans) continued into 1953, and they remained available in the U.S. market into the mid-1950s; see previous listing for full details. Later sedans were identified in the U.S. market as Series 2a (code B12), and carried a larger (2266-cc) engine than the original models. Like the GT coupe, the sedans switched to a De Dion rear axle in 1954. Sedans had pushbutton door handles and a movable center front armrest.

AURELIA GT 2500 — B20 (SERIES 2/3) GT — V-6 — The second series of Lancia's GT fastback coupe got higher (8.8:1) compression for an extra five horsepower (80 bhp). Series three and four, sometimes known as the GT 2500, gained a bigger V-6 engine: 2451 cc (149.5 cid), producing 110 horsepower. Series five, with the same 2451-cc V-6, grew to to 118 bhp. In 1954, Aurelias switched from the former semi-trailing link (independent) rear suspension to a De Dion configuration. The clutch, transmission and differential formed a single unit, suspended from the car's frame at the rear. Styling features of the unibodied Aurelia included a heart-shaped grille with thick surround molding and thin vertical bars, small parking lights below the headlamps, and large inboard rectangular auxiliary lights. Small rectangular air intake grilles sat on each side of the main center grille. The fastback body contained thin 'B' pillars with rear quarter windows and rounded wheel openings. Two or three people could squeeze in front, while the rear seat provided two occasional places. Blue tinted catathermic windows were standard.

1956 B24 Spider GT.

AURELIA — B24 SPIDER (SERIES 4/5) — V-6 — Joining the GT coupe in 1954 was a new two-seat roadster, styled by Pinin Farina on a shorter (96.5-inch) wheelbase. Under its hood was the same 2451-cc V-6 engine that powered the GT coupes, with dual exhaust. The first 240 Spiders wore wraparound windshields, but lacked door windows. Subsequent examples had an ordinary windshield and roll-up windows. At the rear was a De Dion axle. Front-end appearance was similar to the coupe, with the customary Aurelia heart-shaped grille and inboard headlamps. Spiders were marketed exclusively in the U.S. Top speed was reported as high as 115 mph. Standard equipment included a heater/defroster, adjustable steering wheel, racing tires, and carpeted luggage compartment. The spare tire went under the car's floor. Appearance was similar to the GT 2500 coupe but with a more rectangular grille shape, slightly cutdown doors with adjustable side windows, no extra inboard lights or auxiliary lights (as on the coupe), wraparound rear half-bumpers, and a wraparound windshield. The narrow hood held a long airscoop. No outside doors handles were installed, so drivers had to reach through the wind wing to gain entry. External trunk hinges were used. Left-hand drive Spiders could have a floor-mounted gearshift lever, whereas other Lancias up to this time retained column shift. Small taillamps sat at the fender tips.

APPIA — C10 — V-4 — Lancia introduced an Appia four-door sedan in 1953, on a 97.6-inch wheelbase (later increased to 98.8-inch). Appearance was similar to the Aurelia, while power came from a 1090-cc four-cylinder engine that produced 38 horsepower, using 7.4:1 compression. The unusual "vee" type engine had only a 10-degree angle between cylinders. Output would later grow to 43.5 bhp as the Appia remained in production into the 1960s, eventually adding a GT coupe and Giardinetta station wagon to the original sedan. Appias had a four-speed gearbox with column shift, and a vane-type

radiator. Doors, hood, trunk, and rear fenders were made of aluminum. Front-hinged front and rear-hinged rear doors were used for pillarless entry/exit, as in the Aurelia. The heart-shaped grille was made up of thin vertical bars, with center divider bar and thick surround molding. Parking lights stood below the headlamps. Top speed was about 75 mph. A column-mounted gearshift lever operated the four-speed transmission. Appia served as replacement for the Ardea, which had a 900-cc engine.

I.D. DATA: Aurelia chassis serial number is stamped on a firewall plate, either below the hood hinge mounting bracket or on the right side of the junction box. Engine number is stamped on right side of block, near the fuel pump. Prefix 'B' is followed by a two-digit model designation. Letter 'S' denotes left-hand drive. Aurelia serial number range: (B20 Series 2) 1501-2231; (B20 Series 3) 2232-2951; (B20 Series 4) 2952-3696; (B20 Series 5) 3697-3816; (Spider Series 4) 1001-1181; (Spider Series 5) 1182-1331. Appia serial number range: (Series 1) 1001-11257.

Model	Body Type & Seating	Engine Type/CID	P.O.E. Price	Weight (lbs.)	Prod. Total
AURELIA (SERIES 1)					
B10	4-dr Sedan-5/6P	V6/107	N/A	2435	Note 1
B15	4-dr Sedan-5/6P	V6/121	N/A	2557	Note 1
B21	4-dr Sedan-5/6P	V6/121	N/A	2435	Note 1
B22	4-dr Sedan-5/6P	V6/121	N/A	2435	Note 1
AURELIA (SERIES 2/3/4/5)					
B12	4-dr Sedan-5/6P	V6/138	N/A	2576	Note 1
B20 (S2)	2-dr GT Cpe-2+2P	V6/121	N/A	2315	Note 1
B20 (S3)	2-dr GT Cpe-2+2P	V6/150	5800	2425	Note 1
B24 Spider	2-dr Rds-2P	V6/150	5500	2464	Note 1
APPIA					
C10	4-dr Sedan-4/5P	V4/66	N/A	1806	N/A

Note 1: A total of 12,786 Aurelias were built, through 1955. A total of 3,871 Aurelia coupes and 761 Spiders were produced during the full model run. A total of 5,746 Lancias (all models) were produced in 1956 alone.

Price Note: Figures shown are approximate, and were valid in 1958 (GT coupe) and 1956 (Spider). Prices at factory in 1955 were $3699 for Aurelia Series 2 (B12), $4552 for Aurelia GT 2500 (B20, S3), and $2143 for Appia.

Model Note: Models shown are those of greatest historical interest. Other Aurelia body styles were produced, including a four-door station wagon and special custom bodies.

Model Designation Note: Aurelia coupes and Spiders (roadsters) with the 2.5-liter engine were commonly known as GT 2500 models.

ENGINE DATA: BASE V-6 (Aurelia B10 sedan): 60-degree, overhead-valve "vee" type six-cylinder. Aluminum block and heads. **Displacement:** 107 cu. in. (1754 cc). **Bore & Stroke:** 2.76 x 2.99 in. (70 x 76 mm). **Compression Ratio:** 6.85:1. **Brake Horsepower:** 56 at 4000 rpm. Solid valve lifters. Solex twin-choke downdraft carburetor.

BASE V-6 (Aurelia B12 sedan): 60-degree, overhead-valve "vee" type six-cylinder. Aluminum block and heads. **Displacement:** 138.2 cu. in. (2266 cc). **Bore & Stroke:** 2.95 x 3.36 in. (75 x 85.5 mm). **Compression Ratio:** 7.4:1. **Brake Horsepower:** 87 at 4300 rpm. Solid valve lifters. Solex twin-choke downdraft carburetor.

BASE V-6 (Aurelia B15/B21/B22 Series 1 sedans, B20 Series 2 GT coupe): 60-degree, overhead-valve "vee" type six-cylinder. Aluminum block and heads. **Displacement:** 121 cu. in. (1991 cc). **Bore & Stroke:** 2.83 x 3.21 in. (72 x 81.5 mm). **Compression Ratio:** (B21/B22) 7.8:1; (B20) 8.8:1. **Brake Horsepower:** (B15) 65 at 4000 rpm; (B20) 80 at 4700 rpm; (B21) 70 at 4800 rpm; (B22) 90 at 5000 rpm. Solid valve lifters. Solex carburetor (B21); Weber twin-choke carburetor (B22); dual Weber carburetors (B20).

BASE V-6 (Aurelia Series 2-6, 1953-58): 60-degree, overhead-valve "vee" type six-cylinder. Aluminum block and heads. **Displacement:** 149.5 cu. in. (2451 cc). **Bore & Stroke:** 3.07 x 3.37 in. (78 x 85.5 mm). **Compression Ratio:** 8.0:1. **Brake Horsepower:** 110 at 5100 rpm (later, 118 bhp). **Torque:** 133.5 lbs.-ft. at 3000 rpm. Solid valve lifters. Weber twin-choke carburetor.

BASE V-4 (Appia): 10-degree, overhead-valve "vee" type four-cylinder. Cast iron block and light alloy head. **Displacement:** 66.5 cu. in. (1090 cc). **Bore & Stroke:** 2.68 x 2.95 in. (68 x 75 mm). **Compression Ratio:** 7.4:1. **Brake Horsepower:** 38 at 4800 rpm. Hydraulic valve lifters. One Solex carburetor.

CHASSIS DATA: Wheelbase: (Aurelia GT cpe) 104.7 in.; (Aurelia rds) 96.5 in.; (Aurelia sed) 112.6 in.; (Aurelia B15 sed) 128 in.; (Appia) 97.6 in. **Overall Length:** (Aurelia GT cpe) 172 in.; (Aurelia sed) 174 in.; (Aurelia B15 sed) 189 in.; (Appia) 152.2 in. **Height:** (Aurelia GT cpe) 53.5 in.; (Aurelia sed) 59 in.; (Aurelia B15 sed) 61.3 in.; (Appia) 56 in. **Width:** (Aurelia GT cpe) 61 in.; (Aurelia sed) 61.5 in.; (Aurelia B15 sed) 62.8 in.; (Appia) 55.9 in. **Front Tread:** (Aurelia) 50.4 in. except (B15) 51 in.; (Appia) 46.4 in. **Rear Tread:** (Aurelia) 51.2 in. except (B15) 52.2 in.; (Appia) 46.5 in. **Wheel Standard Tires:** (Aurelia) 165x400 except (B15) 185x400; (Appia) 155x15 or 5.60x15.

TECHNICAL: Layout: front-engine, rear-drive. **Transmission:** four-speed manual; column shift except (Spider) floor shift. **Steering:** worm and sector. **Suspension (front):** sliding pillar with solid axle and coil springs. **Suspension (rear):** (Aurelia to 1953) independent; semi-trailing link with coil springs; (Aurelia, 1953-up) De Dion axle with leaf springs; (Appia) rigid axle with semi-elliptic leaf springs. **Brakes:** hydraulic, front/rear drum. **Body Construction:** steel/aluminum unibody.

PERFORMANCE: Top Speed: (Aurelia B12 sedan) 93 mph; (Aurelia GT 2500 cpe) 112-115 mph; (Aurelia Spider) 108-115 mph; (Appia) 74-75 mph. **Acceleration (0-60 mph):** (Aurelia GT 2500 cpe) as little as 10 sec. reported; (Aurelia GT 2500 rds) 14.3 sec. **Acceleration (quarter-mile):** (Aurelia GT 2500 cpe) 18 sec.; (Aurelia GT 2500 rds) 17-19.3 sec.

Manufacturer: Fabbrica Automobili Lancia e Cia S.p.A., Turin (Torino), Italy.

HISTORY: Lancia emerged victorious in the 1953 Mexican road race (*Carrera Panamericana*). Fangio, Taruffi and Castelloti took the top three spots, driving Lancias with a new 3-liter V-6 engine. The winner's average speed was 105.73 mph. A 2.5-liter Sports Sedan won its class at Le Mans, and also captured the 1953 Liege-Rome-Liege Rally. Lancia also was victorious at the 1954 Mille Miglia event.

"Beauty without ostentation, speed without strain." That was Lancia's description of the Gran Turismo 2500 coupe. Was it possible, the Lancia literature reported observers asking, for a sports car to be so beautiful? A striking "Florida" four-door hardtop takeoff on the Aurelia appeared at the Turin show in spring 1955, styled by Pinin Farina and priced at $9500 in Italy. Two headlamp pairs were installed (two in fenders for long distance, and two in the grille for low beam). That "Florida" show car led to the production Flaminia; see next listing for details.

1957-61 LANCIA

AURELIA — V-6 — Production of the Aurelia coupe and Spider roadster continued into 1958, as the Flaminia was phased in as its replacement. Four-door sedans were dropped, in favor of the Flaminia version. Standard Aurelia equipment included a heater/defroster, tachometer, dashboard ashtrays, clock, twin visors, windshield washers, and adjustable front armrest. Pushbutton door handles were used. The low-slung GT 2500 Spider, as styled by Pinin Farina, had a sharply wraparound windshield, forward-angled door windows and vent wings in small doors, and a tapered deck. Inside was a tachometer. Leather seatbacks were individually contoured. The Spider's spare tire fit under the luggage-compartment floor, and it lacked the coupe's occasional rear seat. Horsepower of Aurelia coupes and convertibles imported in the U.S. rose from 110 to 118 in the model's final period.

FLAMINIA — V-6 — A different form of V-6 engine powered the new Flaminia sedan, which was introduced late in 1956, for the 1957 model year. The 2458-cc (150-cid) engine produced 98 horsepower, using 8.0:1 compression. The four-door sedan displayed a modern box-shape design, quite different from its curvy Aurelia predecessor. Pinin Farina penned the body design. Styling features of the pillarless body included a mesh-type rectangular grille, hood scoop, wraparound windshield, and ample glass area. Chrome window frames allowed the continuation of the no-pillar profile. A Farina-styled notchback coupe and Spider convertible followed in 1959. Instead of the customary sliding-pillar front suspension, the Flaminia turned to regular coil springs, set up via quadrilateral crossmembers with swinging steel triangles that pivoted on adjustable bearings. Rear-axle layout was similar to the Aurelia, with semi-elliptic leaf springs. Stabilizer bars went at each end. All-disc brakes were installed. The Flaminia instrument panel contained a tachometer and odometer. The sedan's front seatback folded to horizontal position, and rear-quarter vent windows could be controlled by the driver. Later on, the original models were joined by a selection of special-bodied coupes and Spider roadsters, on shorter chassis, with bodies created by Touring, Zagato, and Ghia. The aluminum-bodied Zagato fastback was generally considered the most stylish of the lot, with its deeply recessed headlamps behind clear lenses and different grille appearance.

1959 Lancia Appia coupe.

APPIA — SERIES 2 — V-4 — Introduced in 1953, the smaller, lower-priced Appia was commonly found on lists of Lancia models available in the U.S. in the late 1950s. Offered initially in four-door sedan form only, the Appia was powered by a 1090-cc (66.5-cid) V-4 engine. In its second-series configuration, the engine produced 43.5 horsepower and 56 pound-feet of torque. Apperance of the pillarless sedan with its rear-hinged back doors was similar to the Aurelia, but on a smaller scale. Additional body styles became available in the late 1950s, included a coupe and convertible with 53-bhp engine. The Vignale-styled two-seat convertible featured roll-up windows, individually-adjustable leather-upholstered seats, a tachometer, and canvas top. A hardtop was available at extra cost. The Farina hardtop coupe had cloth upholstery, with two occasional seats in the back. Horsepower of the basic sedan engine grew to 48 in its Series 3 form.

I.D. DATA: Appia chassis serial number is stamped on center of bulkhead, at left side of coil. Aurelia chassis serial number is stamped on a firewall plate, either below the hood hinge mounting bracket or on the right side of the junction box. Flaminia chassis number is stamped on a plate on the right side of the firewall. Engine number is stamped on right side of block, near the fuel pump except (Appia) behind fuel pump. Appia has a 'C10' prefix. Aurelia prefix 'B' is followed by a two-digit model designation. Flaminia serial numbers have a '813.00' prefix.

Model	Body Type & Seating	Engine Type/CID	P.O.E. Price	Weight (lbs.)	Prod. Total
AURELIA					
GT 2500	2-dr Coupe-2+2P	V6/150	6195	2630	Note 1
GT 2500	2-dr Rds-2+	V6/150	5195	2500	Note 1
GT 2500	2-dr Conv	V6/150	5595	N/A	Note 1
FLAMINIA					
Farina	2-dr Coupe-4/5P	V6/150	6355	3265	Note 2
Zagato	2-dr Fbk Cpe-2+2P	V6/150	6485	2670	Note 2
Spider	2-dr Rds-2P	V6/150	N/A	N/A	Note 2
Farina	4-dr Sedan-5/6P	V6/150	5998	N/A	Note 2
Touring	2-dr GT Cpe-2P	V6/150	6485	N/A	Note 2
APPIA (SERIES 2)					
Farina	2-dr Coupe-2+2P	V4/66	4673	N/A	N/A
Zagato	2-dr Coupe-2P	V4/66	4873	N/A	N/A
Vignale	2-dr Conv-2+2P	V4/66	4565	N/A	N/A
	4-dr Sedan-4/5P	V4/66	2850	1904	N/A
APPIA (SERIES 3)					
Farina	2-dr Coupe-2+2P	V4/66	4438	N/A	N/A
Zagato	2-dr Coupe-2P	V4/66	4558	N/A	N/A
Vignale	2-dr Conv-2+2P	V4/66	4490	N/A	N/A
	4-dr Sedan-4/5P	V4/66	2892	2016	N/A

Note 1: A total of 3,871 Aurelia coupes and 761 Spiders were produced during the full model run.

Note 2: A total of 4,151 Flaminia 2.5-liter coupes and 1,133 2.8-liter coupes were produced during the full model run, plus 2,593 special bodies with 2.5-liter engine and 868 with 2.8-liter engine.

Aurelia Price Note: Figures shown were valid in 1957.

Flaminia Price Note: Figures shown were valid in 1960.

Appia Price Note: Figure shown for Series 2 sedan was valid in 1957; coupes and convertibles in 1959. Figures shown for Series 3 were valid in 1961. A Series 3 sedan sold for $2892 in 1960, when other Lancia models went for as high as $6485.

Model Note: Other Aurelia and Flaminia body styles were produced.

Flaminia Production Note: Flaminia coupes and convertibles, as built by Pininfarina, Touring and Zagato, sold stronger than the sedans (8,663 built, 1959-67).

ENGINE DATA: BASE V-6 (Aurelia): 60-degree, overhead-valve "vee" type six-cylinder. Aluminum block and heads. **Displacement:** 149.5 cu. in. (2451 cc). **Bore & Stroke:** 3.07 x 3.37 in. (78 x 85.5 mm). **Compression Ratio:** 8.0:1/8.4:1. **Brake Horsepower:** 110/112 at 5000/5100 rpm (or 118 at 5000 rpm). **Torque:** 127/133.5 lbs.-ft. at 3000 rpm. Solid valve lifters. Weber carburetor.

BASE V-6 (Flaminia sedan): 60-degree, overhead-valve "vee" type six-cylinder. Aluminum block and heads. **Displacement:** 150 cu. in. (2458 cc). **Bore & Stroke:** 3.15 x 3.23 in. (80 x 81.5 mm). **Compression Ratio:** 8.0:1/8.4:1. **Brake Horsepower:** (initial) 98 at 4800 rpm; (later) 110 at 5200 rpm. **Torque:** (initial) 137.4 lbs.-ft. at 3000 rpm. Four main bearings. Solid valve lifters.

BASE V-6 (Flaminia coupe); OPTIONAL (Flaminia sedan): Same as 2458-cc V-6 above, except — **Compression Ratio:** 9.0:1. **Brake Horsepower:** (coupe) 119 at 5100 rpm; (GT cpe, special sedan) 140 at 5600 rpm.

BASE V-4 (Appia Series 2): 10-degree, overhead-valve "vee" type four-cylinder. Cast iron block and light alloy head. **Displacement:** 66.5 cu. in. (1090 cc). **Bore & Stroke:** 2.68 x

2.95 in. (68 x 75 mm). **Compression Ratio:** 7.8:1. **Brake Horsepower:** 43.5 at 4800 rpm. **Torque:** 56 lbs.-ft. at 3000 rpm. Solid valve lifters. Solex carburetor.

BASE V-4 (Appia coupe/conv): Same as 1090-cc V-4 above, except — **Compression Ratio:** 8.0:1. **Brake Horsepower:** 53 at 5200 rpm. **Torque:** 63.6 lbs.-ft. at 3500 rpm.

BASE V-4 (Appia Series 3): Same as 1090-cc V-4 above, except — **Compression Ratio:** 7.8:1. **Brake Horsepower:** 48 at 5000 rpm. **Torque:** 63 lbs.-ft. at 3000 rpm.

1959 Lancia Appia convertible.

CHASSIS DATA: Wheelbase: (Appia) 98.8 in.; (Aurelia cpe) 104.7 in.; (Aurelia rds) 96.5 in.; (Flaminia sed) 113 in.; (Flaminia cpe) 108.3 in.; (Flaminia Zagato) 99.2 in. **Overall Length:** (Appia) 158 in.; (Aurelia cpe) 172.0 in.; (Aurelia rds) 165.4 in.; (Flaminia sed) 191 in.; (Flaminia cpe) 184.5 in.; (Flaminia Zagato) 177.0 in. **Height:** (Appia) 57 in.; (Aurelia cpe) 53.5 in.; (Flaminia sed) 57.5 in. **Width:** (Appia) 58 in.; (Aurelia cpe) 61 in.; (Aurelia rds) 61.2 in.; (Flaminia sed) 68.9 in. **Front Tread:** (Appia) 46.5 in.; (Aurelia) 50.4 in.; (Flaminia) 53.9 in. **Rear Tread:** (Appia) 46.5 in.; (Aurelia) 51.2 in.; (Flaminia) 53.9 in. **Standard Tires:** (Appia) 155x15 or 5.90x15; (Aurelia) 165x400; (Flaminia) 165x400.

TECHNICAL: Layout: front-engine, rear-drive. **Transmission:** four-speed manual. **Steering:** (Aurelia) worm and sector; (Flaminia) screw and roller. **Suspension (front):** (Aurelia) sliding pillar with coil springs; (Flaminia) transverse trapezoid with external coil springs; (Appia) coil springs. **Suspension (rear):** (Aurelia/Flaminia) De Dion axle with semi-elliptic leaf springs; (Appia) rigid axle with semi-elliptic leaf springs. **Brakes:** (Aurelia, Appia, early Flaminia) front/rear drum; (later Flaminia) front/rear disc. **Body Construction:** (Aurelia/Appia) unibody; (Flaminia) unibody with rear auxiliary frame.

PERFORMANCE: Top Speed: (Aurelia GT 2500 conv) 110 mph; (Aurelia GT 2500 cpe) 112-115 mph; (Flaminia sed) 100 mph; (Flaminia Zagato cpe) 118 mph; (Appia Series 2) about 80 mph; (Appia Series 3) about 90 mph. **Acceleration (0-60 mph):** (Appia Series 2 conv) 10 sec. (estimated).

PRODUCTION/SALES: A total of 10,629 Lancias (all models) were produced during 1957, followed by 10,911 in 1958, 12,130 in 1959, 21,022 in 1960, and 27,119 in 1961. Approximately 853 Lancias were sold in the U.S. during 1959, followed by 675 in 1960.

Manufacturer: Fabbrica Automobili Lancia e Cia S.p.A., Turin (Torino), Italy.

Distributor: Hoffman Motors Corp., New York City and Beverly Hills, California; J.S. Inskip, New York City; British Motor Car Distributors Ltd., Los Angeles and San Francisco.

HISTORY: Aurelia production halted in 1958. Lancia's Flaminia appeared at the Earl's Court show (in England) in October 1956. "Everything about this Lancia Appia is smile and surprise," trumpeted ads in 1960, "machined and articulated like a fine watch." A competition-oriented Flaminia Zagato Special coupe tested by *Sports Car Graphic* in 1961, with 154-bhp version of the 2458-cc V-6 engine, accelerated to 60 mph in 8.4 seconds and achieved a top speed near 132 mph.

A new Flavia entered production in 1961, and appeared at the New York International Automobile Show in April of that year. See next listing for details.

1962-64 LANCIA

1962 Lancia Flaminia GT.

APPIA — SERIES 3 — V-4 — Production of the Appia pillarless sedan and coupe/convertible offshoots continued into 1963; see previous listings for additional details. Wheelbase of these final Appias was 98.8 inches, and the 1090-cc engine was rated 48 horsepower (nearly five bhp more than earlier models, as a result of manifold modifications). As before, the sedan had no central door pillars, but shut using door checks on the floor and roof. Adjustable front shock absorbers had two settings, and the brake system had separate front/rear hydraulics. Stainless steel bumpers, window trim and bodyside moldings were installed. Thermostatic shutters on the radiator controlled the temperature.

FLAMINIA — V-6 — Production of the Flaminia coupe and Spider with 2458-cc V-6 continued into 1963, when it was replaced by a larger (2775-cc) engine that developed 150 horsepower. Flaminia production continued as late as 1970.

1962 Lancia Flavia GT.

FLAVIA — 1500/1800 — FLAT-4 — After years of V-6 and V-4 powerplants, Lancia turned to a horizontally-opposed four-cylinder engine for its next model, which first appeared in 1961. Flavia was the first Italian car with front-wheel-drive. The sedan was introduced first, followed by a sporty Pininfarina-styled four-seat notchback coupe (with quad headlamps), a convertible, and a lightweight-bodied fastback coupe by Zagato. In 1963, the Flavia engine grew from its original 1.5-liter displacement (rated 78 horsepower) to 1.8 liters. Flavias remained in production through 1975, using both carbureted and fuel-injected engines. The four-speed, all-synchro manual transmission had a column-mounted gearshift lever. A transverse leaf spring with anti-roll bar made up the front suspension, while the rear used a rigid axle with semi-elliptic leaf springs and anti-roll bar. Wheelbase was 97.6 inches.

The slim-pillar sedan had front-hinged doors (abandoning the traditional pillarless design), a slightly curved windshield, side windows that curved outward, and a sloping hood. Quad round headlamps were installed. A large insignia went in the relatively small grille, which had angled sides and a wide eggcrate pattern. Large park/signal lights stood immediately below each headlamp pair. The Flavia's engine/gearbox was mounted on three rubber supports, and the fan was behind the fanbelt pulley. All-disc brakes were installed. Inside, the bench-type front seat had seatbacks adjustable for rake. The dashboard was foam-rubber padded, covered in leatherette. Each door contained a map pocket. The car's defrosting system acted on the front side windows as well as the windshield. Warning lights indicated that the manual choke was operating, or the handbrake on.

I.D. DATA: Appia serial number is stamped at center of firewall, under the hood. Flavia/Flaminia serial number is stamped on right edge of hood opening, and on firewall plate. Appia/Flaminia engine number is stamped on right side of crankcase. Flavia engine number is stamped on tappet chamber cover, next to distributor.

Model	Body Type & Seating	Engine Type/CID	P.O.E. Price	Weight (lbs.)	Prod. Total
APPIA SERIES (1962-63)					
	4-dr Sedan-4/5P	V4/66	2938	2016	N/A
Vignale	2-dr Conv-2+2P	V4/66	3998	N/A	N/A
Vignale	2-dr Coupe	V4/66	3952	N/A	N/A
Zagato	2-dr Coupe-2P	V4/66	4055	N/A	N/A
FLAMINIA					
Farina	4-dr Sedan-5/6P	V6/150	5998	N/A	Note 1
Farina	2-dr Coupe-4/5P	V6/150	6355	3265	Note 1
Zagato	2-dr Fbk Cpe-2+2P	V6/150	6485	2670	Note 1
Spider	2-dr Rds-2P	V6/150	6485	N/A	Note 1
FLAVIA 1500 (1962-63)					
Farina	2-dr Coupe-4P	H4/92	4715	N/A	Note 2
Zagato Spt	2-dr Coupe-2+2P	H4/92	5030	2340	Note 2
Vignale	2-dr Conv Cpe-2+2P	H4/92	4830	2530	Note 2
	4-dr Sedan-5P	H4/92	3685	2689	Note 2
FLAVIA 1800 (1963-69)					
	2-dr Coupe-4P	H4/110	N/A	N/A	Note 3
Zagato Spt	2-dr Coupe-2+2P	H4/110	N/A	N/A	Note 3
	2-dr Conv Cpe-2+2P	H4/110	N/A	N/A	Note 3
	4-dr Sedan-5P	H4/110	N/A	N/A	Note 3

Note 1: A total of 4,151 Flaminia 2.5-liter coupes and 1,133 2.8-liter coupes were produced during the full model run, plus 2,593 special bodies with 2.5-liter engine and 868 with 2.8-liter engine.

Note 2: A total of 4,449 Flavia 1500 coupes and convertibles, plus 98 Zagato 1500 Sport models, were produced during the full model run.

Note 3: A total of 64,739 Flavia four-door sedans were built from 1961-70, plus 19,293 Pininfarina coupes. A total of 16,445 Flavia 1800 coupes and convertibles, plus 628 Zagato 1800 Sport models, were produced during the full model run. An additional 15,025 sedans and 6,791 coupes were produced from 1970-74, with 1991-cc engine.

Price Note: Appia and Flaminia figures shown were valid in 1962. Flaminia GT Touring 3C coupes and convertible sold for $6938 in 1963. Flaminia prices in 1964 were $7500 for the Pininfarina coupe, $7088 for the Zagato sport coupe, and $7200 for GT Touring coupe or convertible.

Flaminia Engine Note: A 2.8-liter V-6 succeeded the original 2.5-liter unit in 1963.

ENGINE DATA: BASE V-4 (Appia): 10-degree, overhead-valve "vee" type four-cylinder. Cast iron block and light alloy head. **Displacement:** 66.5 cu. in. (1090 cc). **Bore & Stroke:** 2.68 x 2.95 in. (68 x 75 mm). **Compression Ratio:** 7.8:1. **Brake Horsepower:** 48 at 5000 rpm (cpe/conv, 60 at 5400 rpm). **Torque:** 63 lbs.-ft. at 3000 rpm. Two main bearings. Solid valve lifters.

BASE V-6 (1962-63 Flaminia): 60-degree, overhead-valve "vee" type six-cylinder. Aluminum block and heads. **Displacement:** 150 cu. in. (2458 cc). **Bore & Stroke:** 3.15 x 3.23 in. (80 x 81.5 mm). **Compression Ratio:** 9.0:1. **Brake Horsepower:** 140 at 5600 rpm. **Torque:** 150 lbs.-ft. at 3600 rpm. Four main bearings. Solid valve lifters.

BASE V-6 (1963-up Flaminia): 60-degree, overhead-valve "vee" type six-cylinder. Aluminum block and heads. **Displacement:** 169 cu. in. (2775 cc). **Bore & Stroke:** 3.35 x 3.23 in. (85 x 81.5 mm). **Compression Ratio:** 9.0:1. **Brake Horsepower:** 150 at 5400 rpm. Four main bearings. Solid valve lifters.

BASE FOUR (Flavia 1500): Horizontally-opposed, overhead-valve four-cylinder. Aluminum block and heads. **Displacement:** 91.5 cu. in. (1500 cc). **Bore & Stroke:** 3.23 x 2.79 in. (82 x 71 mm). **Compression Ratio:** 8.3:1 (Sport, 9.3:1). **Brake Horsepower:** 78 at 5200 rpm (Sport, 90 at 5800 rpm). **Torque:** 81.5 lbs.-ft. at 3500 rpm (Sport, 85 at 4500 rpm). Three main bearings. Solid valve lifters. Solex twin-choke carburetor.

Note: SAE ratings for Flavia 1500 engine were listed in the U.S. as 90 bhp at 5200 rpm, and 94 lbs.-ft. at 3500 rpm.

BASE FOUR (Flavia 1800): Horizontally-opposed, overhead-valve four-cylinder. Aluminum block and heads. **Displacement:** 110 cu. in. (1800 cc). **Bore & Stroke:** 3.46 x 2.91 in. (88 x 74 mm). **Compression Ratio:** 9.0:1. **Brake Horsepower:** 92 at 5200 rpm (Sport, 100 at 5800 rpm). Three main bearings. Solid valve lifters. One Solex carburetor.

CHASSIS DATA: Wheelbase: (Appia) 98.8 in.; (Flaminia cpe) 108.3 in.; (Flaminia Zagato) 99.2 in.; (Flavia cpe/conv) 97.6 in.; (Flavia sed) 104.3 in. **Overall Length:** (Appia) 158.25 in.; (Flaminia cpe) 184.5 in.; (Flaminia Zagato) 177.0 in.; (Flavia cpe) 176.5 in.; (Flavia Zagato) 175.6 in.; (Flavia sed) 180.25 in. **Height:** (Appia) 56.8 in.; (Flaminia cpe) 56 in.; (Flavia sed) 59.1 in. **Width:** (Appia) 58.25 in.; (Flaminia cpe) 68.5 in.; (Flavia sed) 63.25 in. **Front Tread:** (Appia) 46.8 in.; (Flaminia) 54 in.; (Flavia) 51.2 in. **Rear Tread:** (Appia) 46.2 in.; (Flaminia) 54 in.; (Flavia) 50.4 in. **Standard Tires:** (Appia) 6.10x16 or 155x14; (Flaminia) 165x400; (Flavia) 6.50x15 or 165x15.

TECHNICAL: Layout: (Appia/Flaminia) front-engine, rear-drive; (Flavia) front-engine, front-drive. **Transmission:** four-speed manual (column gearshift on Appia). **Standard Final Drive Ratio:** (Appia) 4.18:1; (Flaminia) 3.61:1. **Steering:** (Appia) worm and sector; (Flaminia) screw and roller; (Flavia) worm and roller. **Suspension (front):** (Appia) coil springs; (Flaminia) coil springs; (Flavia) transverse leaf spring with wishbones and anti-roll bar. **Suspension (rear):** (Appia/Flaminia) semi-elliptic leaf springs; (Flavia) rigid axle with semi-elliptic leaf springs and anti-roll bar. **Brakes:** (Appia) front/rear drum; (Flaminia/Flavia) front/rear disc. **Body Construction:** steel unibody.

MAJOR OPTIONS: Leather upholstery: Flavia ($175).

PERFORMANCE: Top Speed: (Appia) 80 mph; (Flavia) 92 mph claimed; (early Flavia cpe) 104 mph. **Acceleration (0-60 mph):** (Appia) 24 sec.; (Flavia) 20.5 sec. or less.; (early Flavia cpe) 14.3 sec. **Acceleration (quarter-mile):** (Flavia) about 21 sec. (about 63 mph); (early Flavia cpe) 18.4 sec. (69 mph).

PRODUCTION/SALES: A total of 26,615 Lancias (all models) were produced during 1962, followed by 40,921 in 1963, and 28,988 in 1964.

ADDITIONAL MODELS: A new Fulvia first appeared in 1963, but took longer to reach the U.S. market. See next listing for details.

Manufacturer: Fabbrica Automobili Lancia e Cia S.p.A., Turin (Torino), Italy.

Distributor: Hoffman Motors Corp., New York City and Beverly Hills, California.

1965-68 LANCIA

1967 Lancia Flaminia 2.8 3C GT. (Coys of Kensington)

FLAMINIA — V-6 — Production of the Flaminia sedan, coupe and convertible continued into 1967 (sedans as late as 1970). Directories of cars available in the U.S. continued to list the 2.5-liter engine as late as 1965, though it had been replaced by the 2.8-liter in 1963.

FLAVIA 1800 — FLAT-4 — Production of the 1800 series Flavia, introduced in 1963, continued into 1969. American directories continued to include the 1500 series as well; see previous listing for full details on both models.

FULVIA — V-4 — This would be the final Lancia designed in full by that company, prior to takeover by Fiat in 1969. Introduced in 1963, but taking longer to arrive in the U.S. market, the front-drive Fulvia came in a selection of coupe bodies, as well as sedan form. Power came initially from a 1091-cc engine (for the sedan) and a larger 1216-cc version for the coupes. Each of those overhead-cam V-4 powerplants used a narrow angle between cylinders, and was mounted at a 45-degree angle. Larger engines came later in the car's life (which lasted until 1976), starting with the 1298-cc version of 1967. All-disc brakes were installed. Zagato and HF (high-performance) editions used many aluminum body panels. The two-seat Zagato Sports coupe was longer than the regular 2 + 2 notchback coupe. Sedans rode a 98-inch wheelbase; coupes, a shorter 91.7 inches.

I.D. DATA: Flavia serial number is stamped on right edge of hood opening, and on firewall plate. Flavia engine number is stamped on tappet chamber cover, next to distributor.

Model	Body Type & Seating	Engine Type/CID	P.O.E. Price	Weight (lbs.)	Prod. Total
FLAMINIA 2.5-LITER					
	4-dr Sedan-5P	V6/150	5998	N/A	Note 1
Farina	2-dr Coupe-4P	V6/150	7600	N/A	Note 1
Zagato	2-dr Fbk Cpe-2 + 2P	V6/150	7088	N/A	Note 1
GT Touring	2-dr Conv Cpe	V6/150	7200	N/A	Note 1
FLAMINIA 2.8-LITER					
	4-dr Sedan-5P	V6/169	6158	N/A	Note 1
Farina	2-dr Coupe-4P	V6/169	6586	N/A	Note 1
Zagato	2-dr Fbk Cpe	V6/169	6898	N/A	Note 1
GT Touring	2-dr Conv Cpe	V6/169	6754	N/A	Note 1
GT Touring	2-dr Coupe	V6/169	6754	N/A	Note 1
GT Touring	2-dr Coupe-2 + 2P	V6/169	6959	N/A	Note 1

Model	Body Type & Seating	Engine Type/CID	P.O.E. Price	Weight (lbs.)	Prod. Total
FLAVIA 1800 (1963-69)					
Farina	2-dr Coupe-4P	H4/110	4715	N/A	Note 2
Zagato Spt	2-dr Coupe-2 + 2P	H4/110	5030	N/A	Note 2
Vignale	2-dr Conv Cpe-4P	H4/110	4830	N/A	Note 2
	4-dr Sedan-5/6P	H4/110	3685	2600	Note 2
FULVIA (1.1-Liter, 1963-69)					
	4-dr Sedan-5P	V4/67	N/A	2194	Note 3
FULVIA (1.2-Liter, 1965-67)					
	2-dr Coupe-2 + 2P	V4/74	3450	N/A	Note 3
HF	2-dr Coupe-2 + 2P	V4/74	N/A	N/A	Note 3
	4-dr Sedan-5P	V4/74	2725	N/A	Note 3
FULVIA (1.3-Liter, 1967-76)					
Rally	2-dr Coupe-2 + 2P	V4/79	3385	2039	Note 3
HF	2-dr Coupe-2 + 2P	V4/79	3940	1815	Note 3
Zagato	2-dr Coupe-2 + 2P	V4/79	4150	1990	Note 3
GT	4-dr Sedan-5P	V4/79	2745	2170	Note 3
Cloche	4-dr Sedan-5P	V4/79	2795	N/A	Note 3

Note 1: A total of 4,151 Flaminia 2.5-liter coupes and 1,133 2.8-liter coupes were produced during the full model run, plus 2,593 special bodies with 2.5-liter engine and 868 with 2.8-liter engine.

Note 2: A total of 16,445 Flavia 1800 coupes and convertibles, plus 628 Zagato 1800 Sport models, were produced during the full model run.

Note 3: A total of 20,436 Fulvia 1.2-liter coupes, 490 1.2-liter HF coupes, 202 113,599 1.3-liter coupes, 2,239 1.3-liter HF coupes, and 6,100 1.3-liter Zagatos were produced during the full model run. More than 359,000 Fulvias in all were built, from 1963-76.

Price Note: Flavia figures shown were valid in 1965; Fulvia 1.2-liter, in 1966; Fulvia 1.3-liter, in 1968. Flavias with fuel-injected engine were listed in 1968 at $4139 for the four-door sedan, $6754 for the coupe, $6754 for convertible, $6898 for Supersport coupe, and $6969 for a GT 2 + 2 cpe.

ENGINE DATA: BASE V-6 (Flaminia 2.5-liter): 60-degree, overhead-valve "vee" type six-cylinder. Aluminum block and heads. **Displacement:** 150 cu. in. (2458 cc). **Bore & Stroke:** 3.15 x 3.23 in. (80 x 81.5 mm). **Compression Ratio:** 9.0:1. **Brake Horsepower:** 140 at 5600 rpm. **Torque:** 150 lbs.-ft. at 3600 rpm. Four main bearings. Solid valve lifters.

BASE V-6 (Flaminia 2.8-liter): 60-degree, overhead-valve "vee" type six-cylinder. Aluminum block and heads. **Displacement:** 169 cu. in. (2775 cc). **Bore & Stroke:** 3.35 x 3.23 in. (85 x 81.5 mm). **Compression Ratio:** 9.0:1. **Brake Horsepower:** 150 at 5400 rpm. Four main bearings. Solid valve lifters.

BASE FOUR (Flavia 1800): Horizontally-opposed, overhead-valve four-cylinder. Light alloy block and heads. **Displacement:** 110 cu. in. (1800 cc). **Bore & Stroke:** 3.46 x 2.91 in. (88 x 74 mm). **Compression Ratio:** 9.0:1. **Brake Horsepower:** 115 at 5200 rpm. **Torque:** 115 lbs.-ft. at 3500 rpm. Three main bearings. Solid valve lifters.

BASE V-4 (1963-69 1.1-liter Fulvia sedan): 12-degree, dual-overhead-cam "vee" type four-cylinder. Cast iron block and light alloy head. **Displacement:** 66.6 cu. in. (1091 cc). **Bore & Stroke:** 2.83 x 2.64 in. (72 x 67 mm). **Compression Ratio:** (early) 7.8:1; (1964-69) 9.0:1. **Brake Horsepower:** (early) 58 at 5800 rpm; (1964-69) 71 at 6000 rpm. Three main bearings. Solid valve lifters.

BASE V-4 (1965-67 1.2-liter Fulvia): 12-degree, dual-overhead-cam "vee" type four-cylinder. Cast iron block and light alloy head. **Displacement:** 74 cu. in. (1216 cc). **Bore & Stroke:** 2.99 x 2.64 in. (76 x 67 mm). **Compression Ratio:** 9.0:1. **Brake Horsepower:** 92 at 6000 rpm (80 bhp DIN). **Torque:** 78 lbs.-ft. at 4000 rpm. Three main bearings. Solid valve lifters.

BASE V-4 (1967-76 1.3-liter Fulvia): 12-degree, dual-overhead-cam "vee" type four-cylinder. Cast iron block and light alloy head. **Displacement:** 79 cu. in. (1298 cc). **Bore & Stroke:** 3.03 x 2.74 in. (77 x 69.7 mm). **Compression Ratio:** 9.0:1. **Brake Horsepower:** 101 at 6000 rpm (90 bhp DIN). **Torque:** 84 lbs.-ft. at 4500 rpm. Three main bearings. Solid valve lifters.

BASE V-4 (Fulvia HF coupe): Same as 1.3-liter V-4 above, except — **Compression Ratio:** 10.5:1. **Brake Horsepower:** 115 at 6400 rpm. **Torque:** 97 lbs.-ft. at 4700 rpm.

CHASSIS DATA: Wheelbase: (Flaminia cpe) 99.2 in.; (Flavia cpe) 97.6 in.; (Flavia sed) 105 in.; (Fulvia cpe) 91.7 in.; (Fulvia sed) 98 in. **Overall Length:** (Flaminia cpe) 177.4 in.; (Flavia cpe) 176.5 in.; (Flavia Zagato) 175.6 in.; (Flavia sed) 183 in.; (Fulvia cpe) 156.0 in.; (Fulvia Zagato) 161.0 in.; (Fulvia sed) 162 in. **Height:** (Flaminia cpe) 50.4 in.; (Flavia sed) 60 in.; (Fulvia sed) 52 in.; (Fulvia cpe) 51 in.; (Fulvia Zagato) 47 in. **Width:** (Flaminia cpe) 65.5 in.; (Flavia sed) 64 in.; (Fulvia sed) 62 in.; (Fulvia cpe) 61 in. **Front Tread:** (Flaminia) 54 in.; (Flavia) 51.5 in.; (Fulvia) 52 in. **Rear Tread:** (Flaminia) 54 in.; (Flavia) 50.5 in.; (Fulvia) 50 in. **Standard Tires:** (Flavia) 165x16; (Fulvia) 5.95x14.

TECHNICAL: Layout: (Flaminia) front-engine, rear-drive; (Flavia/Fulvia) front-engine, front-drive. **Transmission:** four-speed manual. **Steering:** (Flaminia) screw and roller; (Flavia/Fulvia) worm and roller. **Suspension (front):** (Flaminia) coil springs; (Flavia/Fulvia) A-arms with transverse leaf spring and anti-roll bar. **Suspension (rear):** (Flaminia) semi-elliptic leaf springs; (Flavia/Fulvia) rigid axle with semi-elliptic leaf springs and anti-roll bar. **Brakes:** front/rear disc. **Body Construction:** steel unibody.

MAJOR OPTIONS: Floor gearshift lever: Fulvia ($50); Flavia ($72). Fuel-injected engine: Flavia ($400). Power steering: Flavia ($228).

Note: Option prices above were valid in 1968.

PRODUCTION/SALES: A total of 25,949 Lancias (all models) were produced during 1965, followed by 36,988 in 1966, 43,172 in 1967, and 36,668 in 1968.

Manufacturer: Fabbrica Automobili Lancia e Cia, Turin, Italy.

HISTORY: Official importation of Fulvias diminished for a time after 1967, though both the Fulvia and Flavia remained listed in directories of imported models.

1969-75 LANCIA

FLAVIA 1800 — FLAT-4 — The second-generation Flavia was replaced by the 2000 in 1969; see prior listings for details on earlier models.

2000 — FLAT-4 — Flavia became the 2000 in 1969, dropping the original name as it adopted a 2.0-liter engine. All body styles except the notchback coupe were dropped, and that got a restyled nose. A Flavia sedan with 2.0-liter remained in directories into 1970, however. Production continued into 1975.

FULVIA — V-4 — A 1584-cc V-4 engine became available under Fulvia hoods in 1969, called the 1.6-liter series. Production of both the 1.3-liter and 1.6-liter versions lasted as late as 1976, though the final Zagatos emerged in 1971. With the 1.6-liter engine, a Fulvia was capable of 110-mph speeds. A Fiat-based Beta model (see next listing) replaced the Fulvia in the mid-1970s.

STRATOS — V-6 — Built for rallies, the strikingly-styled Stratos two-seat coupe was

developed for racing homologation purposes, but was also usable on ordinary roads. Because the front-drive Fulvia coupe had done well in 1960s rallying, the Stratos was meant as its successor, though little about the two cars was shared. The mid-engine Stratos drivetrain was borrowed from the Ferrari Dino 246 GT (also used in a Fiat Dino), which made sense since Fiat took over Lancia in 1969. Bertone was responsible for both styling and construction, which evolved from a Fulvia-engined concept car (also called Stratos) that appeared at the Turin (Italy) show in 1970. A total of 500 needed to be built for homologation. So, in November 1971, a prototype Stratos HF coupe was displayed at the Turin show. Over the following year, prototypes went rallying, taking their first major win at the Spanish Rally in April 1973. Finally, in 1974, the production model was ready.

Styling features of the short, rather wide body included slim, semi-concealed A-pillars, a dramatically upswept door beltline, sharply wraparound windshield, hidden headlamps, and tunnelback roofline. At the rear was a tall spoiler, plus another spoiler at the back window that looked like a carrying handle. On the front hood, an expansive set of air-intake slots was evident. The Stratos unibody itself was made of steel, but fiberglass was used for the tilt-up nose and tail. Inside, bins molded into door panels could hold racing helmets. Door windows swiveled downward. The transversely-mounted 2418-cc twin-cam V-6 engine produced 190 horsepower (SAE) and 166 pound-feet of torque. A five-speed manual gearbox went into the rear transaxle. Rack-and-pinion steering was installed, along with all-disc brakes and fully independent suspension.

I.D. DATA: Not available.

Model	Body Type & Seating	Engine Type/CID	P.O.E. Price	Weight (lbs.)	Prod. Total
FLAVIA 1800 (1963-69)					
	2-dr Coupe-4P	H4/110	N/A	2470	Note 1
Zagato Spt	2-dr Coupe-2+2P	H4/110	N/A	N/A	Note 1
	2-dr Conv Cpe-4P	H4/110	N/A	2447	Note 1
	4-dr Sedan-5/6P	H4/110	N/A	2536	Note 1
2000 (FLAVIA)					
	2-dr Coupe-4P	H4/121	5380	2600	Note 2
LX	4-dr Sedan-5P	H4/121	4305	2645	Note 2
FULVIA (1.3-Liter, 1967-76)					
Rally	2-dr Coupe-2+2P	V4/79	3440	N/A	Note 3
HPE Rally	2-dr Coupe-2+2P	V4/79	4735	1753	Note 3
Zagato	2-dr Coupe-2+2P	V4/79	4150	N/A	Note 3
	4-dr Sedan-5P	V4/79	2950	2205	Note 3
FULVIA (1.6-Liter, 1967-76)					
	2-dr Coupe-2+2P	V4/97	N/A	N/A	Note 4
HF	2-dr Coupe-2+2P	V4/97	N/A	1870	Note 4
Zagato	2-dr Coupe-2+2P	V4/97	N/A	N/A	Note 4
	4-dr Sedan-5P	V4/97	N/A	N/A	Note 4
STRATOS (1974-75)					
	2-dr Coupe-2P	V6/148	N/A	2160	Note 5

Note 1: A total of 16,445 Flavia 1800 coupes and convertibles, plus 628 Zagato 1800 Sport models, were produced during the full model run.

Note 2: A total of 6,791 model 2000 coupes were produced during the full model run.

Note 3: A total of 113,599 Fulvia 1.3-liter coupes, 2,239 1.3-liter HF coupes, and 6,100 1.3-liter Zagatos were produced during the full model run.

Note 4: A total of 3,690 Fulvia 1.6-liter HF coupes and 800 Zagatos were produced during the full model run.

Note 5: A total of 500 Stratos coupes were built in 1974-75, for racing homologation purposes.

Price Note: Figures shown were listed in 1970.

ENGINE DATA: BASE FOUR (Flavia 1800): Horizontally-opposed, overhead-valve four-cylinder. Light alloy block and heads. **Displacement:** 110 cu. in. (1800 cc). **Bore & Stroke:** 3.46 x 2.91 in. (88 x 74 mm). **Compression Ratio:** 9.0:1. **Brake Horsepower:** 96 (SAE) at 5200 rpm. **Torque:** 120 lbs.-ft. at 3000 rpm. Three main bearings. Solid valve lifters. Solex two-barrel carburetor.

BASE FOUR (2000): Horizontally-opposed, overhead-valve four-cylinder. Light alloy block and heads. **Displacement:** 121.5 cu. in. (1990 cc). **Bore & Stroke:** 3.50 x 3.15 in. (89 x 80 mm). **Compression Ratio:** 9.0:1. **Brake Horsepower:** 131 at 5400 rpm. **Torque:** 132 lbs.-ft. at 4200 rpm. Three main bearings. Solid valve lifters.

BASE V-4 (1967-76 1.3-liter Fulvia): 12-degree, dual-overhead-cam "vee" type four-cylinder. Cast iron block and light alloy heads. **Displacement:** 79 cu. in. (1298 cc). **Bore & Stroke:** 3.03 x 2.74 in. (77 x 69.7 mm). **Compression Ratio:** (sedan) 9.0:1; (cpe) 9.5:1. **Brake Horsepower:** (sedan) 95 SAE at 6000 rpm; (cpe) 103 SAE at 6200 rpm. **Torque:** (sedan) 93 lbs.-ft. at 4600; (cpe) 96 lbs.-ft. at 4500 rpm. Three main bearings. Solid valve lifters.

BASE V-4 (1969-76 1.6-liter Fulvia): 12-degree, dual-overhead-cam "vee" type four-cylinder. Cast iron block and light alloy heads. **Displacement:** 97 cu. in. (1584 cc). **Bore & Stroke:** 3.23 x 2.95 in. (82 x 75 mm). **Compression Ratio:** 10.5:1. **Brake Horsepower:** 130 at 6200 rpm. **Torque:** 123 lbs.-ft. at 4500 rpm. Three main bearings. Solid valve lifters.

BASE V-6 (1974-75 Stratos): 65-degree, dual-overhead-cam "vee" type six-cylinder (Fiat Dino). Light alloy block and heads. **Displacement:** 147.6 cu. in. (2418 cc). **Bore & Stroke:** 3.64 x 2.36 in. (92.5 x 60 mm). **Compression Ratio:** 9.0:1. **Brake Horsepower:** 190 (DIN) at 7000 rpm. **Torque:** up to 166 lbs.-ft. at 4000 rpm. Four main bearings. Solid valve lifters.

Note: Early Stratos coupes appeared with a 1584-cc four-cylinder engine, rated 114 bhp (DIN) at 6000 rpm.

CHASSIS DATA: Wheelbase: (Flavia cpe/conv) 97.6 in.; (Flavia sed) 105 in.; (2000 cpe) 97.6 in.; (Fulvia cpe) 91.7 in.; (Fulvia sed) 98.5 in.; (Stratos) 85.8 in. **Overall Length:** (Flavia cpe) 176.5-179 in.; (Flavia Zagato) 175.6 in.; (Flavia conv) 170.9 in.; (Flavia sed) 180.3 in.; (Fulvia cpe) 156.5 in.; (Fulvia Zagato) 161.0 in.; (Fulvia sed) 161.8-163 in.; (Stratos) 144.5 in. **Height:** (Flavia cpe) 52 in.; (Flavia sed) 59 in.; (Fulvia sed) 55.1 in.; (Fulvia cpe) 51.2 in.; (Stratos) 42.5 in. **Width:** (Flavia sed) 64 in.; (Flavia cpe) 63 in.; (Fulvia sed) 61.2 in.; (Fulvia cpe) 61.2; (Fulvia 1.6 HF cpe) 63 in.; (Stratos) 66.9 in. **Front Tread:** (Flavia sed) 52.0 in.; (Flavia cpe) 51.2 in.; (Fulvia) 51.2 in.; (Stratos) 55.1 in. **Rear Tread:** (Flavia) 50.4 in.; (Fulvia) 50.5 in.; (Stratos) 55.1 in. **Standard Tires:** (Flavia) 165x15; (Fulvia 1.3 sedan) 155x14; (Fulvia Rally cpe) 145x14; (Fulvia 1.6 HF cpe) 175x13.

TECHNICAL: Layout: front-engine, front-drive except (Stratos) mid-engine, rear-drive. **Transmission:** four-speed manual; (Stratos) five-speed manual in rear transaxle. **Steering:** (Flavia/Fulvia) worm and roller; (Stratos) rack and pinion. **Suspension (front):** (Flavia/2000/Fulvia) A-arms with transverse leaf spring and anti-roll bar; (Stratos) upper/lower A-arms with coil springs and anti-roll bar. **Suspension (rear):** (Flavia/2000/Fulvia) rigid axle with semi-elliptic leaf springs and anti-roll bar; (Stratos) upper/lower A-arms with Chapman struts, coil springs and anti-roll bar. **Brakes:** front/rear disc. **Body Construction:** steel unibody; (Stratos) monocoque with extensions.

PERFORMANCE: Top Speed: (Flavia cpe) 107 mph; (Fulvia spt cpe) 112 mph; (Fulvia 1.3 Rally cpe) 107 mph; (Stratos) 142-143 mph. **Acceleration (0-60 mph):** (Stratos) 6.6-6.8 sec.

PRODUCTION/SALES: A total of 31,556 Lancias (all models) were produced during 1969, followed by 44,542 in 1970, 52,789 in 1971, 41,778 in 1972, 52,631 in 1973, 44,920 in 1974, and 45,745 in 1975. Approximately 1,011 Lancias were sold in the U.S. during 1975.

Manufacturer: Fabbrica Automobili Lancia e Cia, Turin, Italy.

Distributor: Fiat Distributors Inc. (Lancia of America, a Fiat Division), Montvale, New Jersey.

HISTORY: A Lancia Stratos won the World Rally Championship in 1974-76, and the Monte Carlo Rally in 1979. Official importation of Lancias ceased in the early 1970s. Lancia prepared to reenter the U.S. marketplace in 1975 with a new series: the front-drive Beta, introduced earlier in Europe. See next listing for details.

1976-78 LANCIA

BETA — FOUR — By 1976, Lancia was back on the lists of makes officially available in the U.S., with a new set of models. The front wheel-drive Beta came in three body styles, starting with a two-door coupe and four-door sedan. Those were joined in 1976 by an HPE (High Performance Estate) "wagonback" model. The sedan had six-window fastback styling and quad round headlamps. Beneath each hood was a Fiat twin-cam 1756-cc four-cylinder engine, hooked to a five-speed manual gearbox. Standard equipment included power disc brakes, adjustable steering wheel, two-speed heater/defroster, rear defogger, tinted glass, electric tachometer, trip odometer, and 175/70SR14 tires on alloy wheels. Sedans had styled steel wheels and a fold-down rear center armrest.

SCORPION — FOUR — Complementing the front-engined Beta series was a mid-engined, rear-drive Scorpion coupe with dramatic wedge-profile styling. Though larger, the Scorpion (known in Europe as the Monte Carlo) was related to Fiat's X1/9 two-seat coupe. Power came from a slightly detuned version of the Beta's twin-cam engine, working with a five-speed gearbox. The engine was transversely mounted, ahead of the rear wheels. Standard equipment was similar to the Beta, but added a fabric sunroof and 185/70HR13 tires (rather than the Beta's 14-inchers). A Lancia badge went in the center of the blackout grille. The sunroof was made of soft plastic. New glass panels were added in 1978 to the car's "flying buttress" roofline.

I.D. DATA: Lancia's 12-symbol (Beta) or 11-symbol (Scorpion) serial number is on the upper left corner of the dashboard. The first five or six symbols indicate model and chassis type, followed by a six-digit sequential production number. Starting serial number (1976): (Beta 2-dr) 828AC1-603001; (Beta 4-dr) 828AB6-503001; (Beta HPE) 828AF1-700001; (Scorpion) 137AS-100001. Starting serial number (1977): (Beta 2-dr) 828AC1-607201; (Beta 4-dr) 828CB6-503102; (Beta HPE) 828AF1-700102; (Scorpion) 137AS-101369. Starting serial number (1978): (Beta 2-dr) 828AC1-608001; (Beta 4-dr) 828CB6-505001; (Beta HPE) 828AF1-702001.

Model	Body Type & Seating	Engine Type/CID	P.O.E. Price	Weight (lbs.)	Prod. Total
BETA					
	2-dr Coupe-5P	I4/107	7750	2395	Note 1
HPE	2-dr Estate-5P	I4/107	8860	2514	Note 1
	4-dr Sedan-5P	I4/107	6800	2620	Note 1
SCORPION (1976-77)					
	2-dr Spt Cpe-2P	I4/107	9943	2278	Note 1

Note 1: A total of 63,348 Lancias (all models) were produced during 1976, followed by 68,944 in 1977 and 52,462 in 1978.

Price Note: Prices in 1977 ranged from $6995 for the four-door sedan to $9995 for the Scorpion. Beta prices rose sharply for 1978, to $8803 for the coupe and $8217 for the sedan, though the HPE dropped to $9868.

ENGINE DATA: BASE FOUR: Inline, dual-overhead-cam four-cylinder. Cast iron block and light alloy head. **Displacement:** 107.1 cu. in. (1756 cc). **Bore & Stroke:** 3.31 x 3.12 in. (84 x 79.2 mm). **Compression Ratio:** 8.0:1. **Brake Horsepower:** (Beta) 86 at 6200 rpm; (Scorpion) 81 at 5900 rpm. **Torque:** (Beta) 90 lbs.-ft. at 2800 rpm; (Scorpion) 89 lbs.-ft. at 3200 rpm. Five main bearings. Solid valve lifters. Two-barrel carburetor.

Note: The coupe called Scorpion in the U.S. was sold elsewhere in the world as the Monte Carlo, with a larger (1995-cc) engine that produced 120 bhp (DIN) at 6000 rpm.

CHASSIS DATA: Wheelbase: (Beta cpe) 92.6 in.; (Beta sed) 100 in.; (Scorpion) 90.5 in. **Overall Length:** (Beta cpe) 167 in.; (Beta sed) 178 in.; (Scorpion) 156.1 in. **Height:** (Beta cpe) 50.6 in.; (Beta sed) 55.1 in.; (HPE) 50.6 in.; (Scorpion) 46.8 in. **Width:** (Beta cpe) 65 in.; (Beta sed) 66.5 in.; (HPE) 65 in.; (Scorpion) 66.8 in. **Front Tread:** (Beta) 55.4 in.; (Scorpion) 55.6 in. **Rear Tread:** (Beta) 54.8 in.; (Scorpion) 57.3 in. **Standard Tires:** (Beta) 175/70SR14; (Scorpion) 165HR13 or 185/70HR13.

TECHNICAL: Layout: (Beta) front-engine, front-drive; (Scorpion) mid-engine, rear-drive. **Transmission:** five-speed manual. Scorpion gear ratios: (1st) 3.75:1; (2nd) 2.24:1; (3rd) 1.52:1; (4th) 1.15:1; (5th) 0.92:1. **Standard Final Drive Ratio:** (Scorpion) 3.93:1. **Steering:** rack and pinion. **Suspension (front):** (Scorpion) MacPherson struts with anti-roll bar. **Suspension (rear):** (Scorpion) MacPherson struts with anti-roll bar. **Brakes:** front/rear disc. **Body Construction:** steel unibody.

MAJOR OPTIONS: Power steering: Beta ($333). Air conditioning ($589). Sunroof: Beta ($290). Power windows: sedan ($270); others ($218). Leather upholstery: Scorpion ($299). Metallic paint ($250). Radio: Scorpion ($225).

Note: Option prices shown were valid in 1977 (except radio, 1976).

PERFORMANCE: Top Speed: (Beta) about 103 mph; (Scorpion) 110 mph. **Acceleration (0-60 mph):** 11.5-12 sec.; (Scorpion) 11.8 sec. **Acceleration (quarter-mile):** (Scorpion) 19.2 sec. (78.6 mph).

PRODUCTION/SALES: Approximately 3,710 Lancias were sold in the U.S. during 1976, followed by 5,500 in 1977 and 2,811 in 1978.

Manufacturer: Fabbrica Automobili Lancia e Cia S.p.A., Turin (Torino), Italy.

Distributor: Fiat Distributors Inc. (Lancia of America, a Fiat Division), Montvale, New Jersey.

HISTORY: "Chances are, you've never heard of a Lancia," admitted American ads in late 1975 as the company undertook its comeback into the U.S. market. "But in Europe, our name is a household word." *Motor Trend* called the wedge-shaped Scorpion coupe "one of the wildest-looking cars to hit our shores in some time."

1979-82 LANCIA

BETA — FOUR — Lancia's front-drive coupe, sedan and HPE "wagonback" continued in production into the 1980s, though 1979 literature omitted the Beta name. The coupe rode a shorter wheelbase than the six-window fastback-style sedan, which had long tri-

angular rear quarter windows. The HPE (High-Performance Estate) had long rear side windows and front vent wings; the coupe wore smaller rear side windows that were curved slightly along the top. Power came from a 1995-cc (122-cid) four-cylinder twin-cam engine that produced 87 horsepower in standard form, and 108 bhp in high-performance trim. A five-speed manual gearbox was standard, with three-speed automatic available in all models. New body colors and minor interior modifications were the only changes for 1980. Only the coupe remained for the 1981 model year in the U.S. market; the sedan and HPE remained in production, but not for export to America. Standard coupe equipment included reclining front bucket seats, carpeting, tachometer, digital clock, height-adjustable steering column, intermittent wipers, electric rear defroster, and alloy wheels.

ZAGATO — FOUR — The Scorpion model was gone, but Lancia offered a 2+2 Targa-topped coupe (often called a convertible) that also displayed a certain kinship in appearance to the Fiat X1/9. Zagato coupes used the same engine and drivetrain as the Beta models, however: front-engine rather than mid-engine. Styling was performed by Pininfarina. By 1982, the Zagato edition was the only Lancia remaining in the U.S. market, with a lift-off roof section made of fiberglass. A folding fabric section went behind the central hoop, which served as a rudimentary roll bar. Zagato equipment included variable-assist power rack-and-pinion steering and tinted glass.

Note: Lancias were not officially imported during 1980, but resumed again for 1981 before fading away permanently after 1982.

I.D. DATA: Lancia's 12-symbol serial number for 1979 is on the upper left corner of the dashboard. The first six symbols indicate model and chassis type, followed by a six-digit sequential production number. Starting serial number (1979): (Beta 2-dr) 828BC1-610001; (Beta 4-dr) 828CB1-506001; (Beta wag) 828BF1-703001; (Zagato) 828BS1-200001.

For 1981, Lancia adopted a 17-symbol Vehicle Identification Number, again on the upper left corner of the dashboard. Starting serial number: (Beta) ZLAECHOC()B0612070 or 828BS4-00202011; (Zagato) ZLAFS4OC()B0202070 or 828BS4-00202011.

Model	Body Type & Seating	Engine Type/CID	P.O.E. Price	Weight (lbs.)	Prod. Total
BETA					
	2-dr Coupe-4P	I4/122	9500	2510	Note 1
HPE	2-dr Wagon-4P	I4/122	9985	2460	Note 1
	4-dr Sedan-5P	I4/122	8551	2715	Note 1
ZAGATO					
Spider	2-dr Targa Cpe-2+2P	I4/122	10811	2655	Note 1

Note 1: A total of 60,459 Lancias (all models) were produced during 1979, 110,756 in 1980, 78,257 in 1981, 68,122 in 1982, 104,896 in 1983, and 102,658 in 1984.

Price Note: Figures shown were valid in 1979. Beta coupe price in 1981 was $9975; Zagato, $11,880. Zagato price was $13,852 in 1982.

ENGINE DATA: BASE FOUR: Inline, dual-overhead-cam four-cylinder (Fiat). Cast iron block and light alloy head. **Displacement:** 121.7 cu. in. (1995 cc). **Bore & Stroke:** 3.31 x 3.54 in. (84 x 90 mm). **Compression Ratio:** 8.1:1. **Brake Horsepower:** 87 at 5400 rpm (108 bhp at 5500 rpm available). **Torque:** 105 lbs.-ft. at 2900 rpm (114 lbs.-ft. at 2500 rpm available). Five main bearings. Solid valve lifters. Weber two-barrel carburetor.

Note: Basic engine specifications in California were 83 bhp at 5400 rpm, and 101 lbs.-ft. at 2900 rpm.

CHASSIS DATA: Wheelbase: (Beta cpe) 92.5 in.; (Beta sed/HPE wag) 100.0 in.; (Zagato) 92.5 in. **Overall Length:** (Beta cpe) 162.4 in.; (Beta sed) 178 in.; (Beta HPE wag) 173.8 in.; (Zagato) 164.6 in. **Height:** (Beta cpe) 50.6 in.; (Beta sed) 55.2 in.; (HPE) 51.6 in.; (Zagato) 49.7 in. **Width:** (Beta cpe) 64.6 in.; (Beta sed) 66.2 in.; (HPE) 64.6 in.; (Zagato) 64.6 in. **Front Tread:** 55.35 in. **Rear Tread:** 54.8 in. **Standard Tires:** 175/70SR14.

TECHNICAL: Layout: front-engine, front-drive. **Transmission:** five-speed manual or optional three-speed automatic. Manual gear ratios: (1st) 3.50:1; (2nd) 2.24:1; (3rd) 1.52:1; (4th) 1.15:1; (5th) 0.86:1; (rev) 3.071:1. **Standard Final Drive Ratio:** 4.214:1 w/manual, 4.846:1 w/automatic. **Steering:** rack and pinion. **Suspension (front):** wishbones with MacPherson struts/coil springs and stabilizer bar. **Suspension (rear):** independent; Macpherson struts with coil springs and stabilizer/reaction bar. **Brakes:** front/rear disc. **Body Construction:** steel unibody.

MAJOR OPTIONS: Three-speed automatic transmission ($583). Sunroof: cpe ($315). Power windows ($300). Leather seats ($421). Zagato Special Edition package ($435). AM/FM stereo radio ($328). Air conditioning ($645).

Note: Option prices shown were valid in 1979 except air conditioning, in 1981.

PERFORMANCE: Top Speed: (Zagato) 103 mph. **Acceleration (quarter-mile):** (Zagato) 18.7 sec.

PRODUCTION/SALES: Approximately 1,602 Lancias were sold in the U.S. during 1979, 2,100 in 1980, 1,068 in 1981, and 1,174 in 1982.

Manufacturer: Fabbrica Automobili Lancia e Cia S.p.A., Turin (Torino), Italy.

Distributor: Fiat Distributors Inc. (Lancia of America, a Fiat Division), Montvale, New Jersey.

HISTORY: "Driving Redefined" was the headline of ads promoting the "Limited Edition" Zagato model. Lancia's 1979 models were introduced to the U.S. market in January 1979; 1980 models were not officially imported; and 1981 models were introduced in November 1980. Only the Zagato Targa-top (convertible) remained on the import list for 1982, the final year of Lancia's presence in the U.S. market.

LAND ROVER

Although trucks and related vehicles are beyond the scope of this Catalog, one model deserves inclusion as the British granddaddy of the modern four-wheel-drive sport-utility vehicle, which grew so popular in the 1980s. Just a few years after the war, the Rover firm introduced its answer to the American Jeep, which had won well-deserved fame during World War II for its hard-working exploits. Starting in 1948 with 1595-cc four-cylinder power, the Land Rover's engine grew to 1996 cc in 1952, and 2286 cc in 1958 (a displacement that would remain available for the next three decades). Six-cylinder engines became available in 1967. Meanwhile, Land Rovers starred in dozens of movies, especially those involving safaris into the deep jungle and treks across the barren Sahara desert. The Land Rover's stark, down-to-business appearance endeared it to many, including quite a few who never would venture past the urban jungle or beyond a suitably-tamed desert. Just the sight of that spare tire mounted on the hood of early models, and headlamps peering out from behind a mesh screen, was enough to inspire longing in sports-minded folks, giving the impression that here was a vehicle that could go anywhere. They could also expect a mighty rough ride, of course. In addition to the basic short- and long-wheelbase utility models, shoppers could eventually choose either a gasoline or diesel engine, a pickup truck or van configuration, a station wagon, or various special bodies. Land Rovers through the years have been used by the British Army and local fire departments, as well as for jungle and tundra safaris.

To tempt potential customers who were less enamored of the workhorse Land Rover's practical characteristics and unadorned appearance, a posher Range Rover stablemate debuted in 1970. Though similarly capable of off-road journeys, the Range Rover was intended as a passenger car rather than a truck that happened to haul people into the bush on occasion. Its V-8 engine, which also saw use in Rover sedans, was adapted from the 215-cid aluminum V-8 that had powered General Motors compacts in the early 1960s. Starting in 1980, the V-8 also became available in the utilitarian Land Rover. Exports of that model to the U.S. had faded away by that time; but by 1987, a Range Rover built to U.S. specifications was available in the American market, establishing a modest but growing presence.

1948-51 LAND ROVER

LAND ROVER 4WD — SERIES I — FOUR — Angular lines dominated the design of the upright Land Rover, which initially had fully enclosed front wheels. Early models had their inboard headlamps behind a mesh grille guard. Later on, headlamps would be exposed (eventually moving onto front fenders). The four-speed manual gearbox had high and low ranges for four-wheel drive, with lockup of the front and rear differentials. Light alloy bodies were installed on box-section steel frames. Under the hood of the first Land Rover was a 1595-cc overhead-valve Rover 60 engine, producing 50 horsepower.

I.D. DATA: Serial number plate is on the bulkhead. Engine number is on the left side of the block.

Model	Body Type & Seating	Engine Type/CID	P.O.E. Price	Weight (lbs.)	Prod. Total
	2-dr Utility	I4/97	N/A	2604	Note 1

Note 1: A total of 8,048 Land Rovers were produced and sold during the 1947-49 fiscal period.

ENGINE DATA: BASE FOUR: Inline, overhead-valve four-cylinder. **Displacement:** 97 cu. in. (1595 cc). **Bore & Stroke:** 2.74 x 4.13 in. (69.5 x 105 mm). **Compression Ratio:** 6.8:1. **Brake Horsepower:** 50-55 at 4000 rpm. **Torque:** 88 lbs.-ft. at 2000 rpm. Three main bearings. Solid valve lifters. Solex downdraft carburetor.

CHASSIS DATA: Wheelbase: 80 in. **Overall Length:** 132 in. **Width:** 62.5 in. **Max. Tread:** 50 in. **Wheel Type:** disc. **Standard Tires:** 6.00x16.

TECHNICAL: Layout: front-engine, four-wheel-drive. **Transmission:** four-speed manual (high/low transfer box). Gear ratios: (1st) 3.00:1; (2nd) 2.04:1; (3rd) 1.38:1; (4th) 1.00:1; (rev) 2.54:1. **Standard Final Drive Ratio:** 4.7:1. **Steering:** recirculating ball. **Suspension (front):** rigid axle with semi-elliptic leaf springs. **Suspension (rear):** rigid axle with semi-elliptic leaf springs. **Brakes:** front/rear drum. **Body Construction:** light alloy body on box-section steel frame.

MAJOR OPTIONS: Rear power takeoff. Center power takeoff.

Manufacturer: The Rover Co. Ltd., Solihull, Birmingham, Warwickshire, England.

HISTORY: The first Land Rover appeared at the Amsterdam auto show in April 1948. Only a pickup body was offered initially, followed a few months later by a station wagon. A larger (2-liter) engine was installed during 1951; see next listing for details.

1952-57 LAND ROVER

LAND ROVER 4WD — FOUR — Factory brochures issued in 1951 promised "More power for the Land Rover" with its new 2.0-liter engine, which had the same design as the former 1.6-liter four. The new 1996-cc powerplant produced 58 horsepower at 4000 rpm, and 101 pound-feet of torque at a mere 1500 rpm, using 6.7:1 compression. Standard equipment for export model Land Rovers included two aluminum doors with perspex side screens; a full top with rear panel; cushions and backrests for two front seat passengers; 6.00x16 spare tire; starting handle; towing plate for rear drawbar; pintle hook; socket for trailer light; hand rail; and a windshield ventilator. A variety of options was available as well. Rover described its creation as "the world's most versatile vehicle."

I.D. DATA: Serial number plate is on the bulkhead. Engine number is on the left side of the block. Starting serial number: 2613001. Starting serial numbers for 1957 models: (88-inch) 114700001; (109-inch) 124700001.

Model	Body Type & Seating	Engine Type/CID	P.O.E. Price	Weight (lbs.)	Prod. Total
LAND ROVER (1952)					
	2-dr Utility	I4/122	2244	2594	Note 1
LAND ROVER (1957)					
88	2-dr Sta Wagon	I4/122	2884	3117	Note 1
109	2-dr Sta Wagon	I4/122	3428	3454	Note 1

Note 1: A total of 174,763 Land Rovers were produced and sold in the period from 1949-50 to 1956-57.

Price Note: Figure shown was valid in 1952.

ENGINE DATA: BASE FOUR: Inline, overhead-valve four-cylinder. Cast iron block and head. **Displacement:** 122 cu. in. (1996 cc). **Bore & Stroke:** 3.06 x 4.13 in. (77.8 x 105 mm). **Compression Ratio:** 6.7:1. **Brake Horsepower:** 58 at 4000 rpm. **Torque:** 101 lbs.-ft. at 1500 rpm. Three main bearings. Solid valve lifters. Solex carburetor.

Diesel Engine Note: A diesel power option (2286-cc) became available in 1957, unrelated to the gasoline engine.

CHASSIS DATA: Wheelbase: 80/86/88 in. **Overall Length:** 132/141 in. **Width:** 60/62.6 in. **Tread:** 50 in. **Standard Tires:** Dunlop 6.00x16.

Dimension Note: Wheelbase of the basic model grew from 80 to 86 inches in 1954, adding 9 inches to overall length; and then to 88 inches in 1956. A longer version on 107-inch wheelbase became available in 1955, with 7.00x16 tires; and that one soon grew to 109 inches.

TECHNICAL: Layout: front-engine, four-wheel-drive. **Transmission:** four-speed manual (two-speed transfer box). **Steering:** recirculating ball. **Suspension (front):** rigid axle with semi-elliptic leaf springs. **Suspension (rear):** rigid axle with semi-elliptic leaf springs. **Brakes:** front/rear drum. **Body Construction:** light alloy body on box-section steel frame.

MAJOR OPTIONS: Metal detachable top (covering the driver's and rear compartment). Tropical roof (for metal detachable top). Rear or center power takeoff. Engine governor. Five detachable-rim wheels. 7.00x16 tractor-tread tires. Rear winch. Combined water thermometer and oil pressure gauge. Heater. Accelerator footrest (for right-hand drive only). Hood carrier for spare tire. Front capstan winch. Motorola radio. Trafficators. Brockhouse trailer. Heavy-duty pintle hook. Oil cooler. Rear seats.

Manufacturer: The Rover Co. Ltd., Solihull, Birmingham, Warwickshire, England.

1958-69 LAND ROVER

LAND ROVER 4WD — SERIES II — FOUR/SIX — From the late 1950s to the end of the '60s, both 88 and 109-inch wheelbases were available. Land Rovers came with a soft top, hard top, or in station wagon form. A new 2286-cc four-cylinder gasoline engine was used. Late in 1961, a diesel version of the 2286-cc powerplant replaced the former 2052-cc unit. Six-cylinder power became available in 1967.

I.D. DATA: Serial number plate is on the firewall. Engine number is on the left side of the block. Starting serial number for 1960 models: (88-inch) 144000001; (109-inch) 154000001.

Model	Body Type & Seating	Engine Type/CID	P.O.E. Price	Weight (lbs.)	Prod. Total
88	2-dr Utility-7/8P	I4/140	2595	3228	Note 1
88	2-dr Sta Wagon-10P	I4/140	3325	N/A	Note 1
109	2-dr Utility-7/8P	I4/140	3085	3745	Note 1
109	2-dr Sta Wagon-10P	I4/140	3925	N/A	Note 1

Note 1: Annual sales during this period ranged from 28,371 to 50,561 units, according to Graham Robson in *The Land Rover—Workhorse of the World.*

Model Note: A variety of body styles was available, in addition to the basic utility form.

88 Price Note: Figures shown were valid in 1963. A diesel engine cost $475 extra in 1963. The basic model sold for $3220 in 1961. By 1966, prices were $2748 for the basic model and $3464 for the station wagon. A Deluxe hardtop in 1969 sold for $3295.

109 Price Note: Figures shown were valid in 1963. Price in 1966 was $3202 for the basic model and $4026 for a station wagon.

Weight Note: Figure shown was valid in 1963 for the model 88.

ENGINE DATA: BASE FOUR: Inline, overhead-valve four-cylinder. Cast iron block and head. **Displacement:** 139.5 cu. in. (2286 cc). **Bore & Stroke:** 3.56 x 3.50 in. (90.4 x 88.9 mm). **Compression Ratio:** 7.0:1. **Brake Horsepower:** 77 at 4250/4500 rpm. **Torque:** 124 lbs.-ft. at 2500 rpm. Three main bearings. Solid valve lifters. Solex one-barrel carburetor.

OPTIONAL SIX (1967-up): Inline, overhead-valve six-cylinder. Cast iron block and head. **Displacement:** 160 cu. in. (2625 cc). **Bore & Stroke:** 3.06 x 3.62 in. (77.8 x 92 mm). **Compression Ratio:** 7.8:1. **Brake Horsepower:** 85 (DIN) at 4500 rpm. **Torque:** 132 lbs.-ft. (DIN) at 1500 rpm. Solid valve lifters. Zenith carburetor.

OPTIONAL DIESEL FOUR (1958-61 only): Inline, overhead-valve four-cylinder. Cast iron block and head. **Displacement:** 125 cu. in. (2052 cc). **Bore & Stroke:** 3.375 x 3.50 in. (86 x 88.9 mm). **Brake Horsepower:** 51/55 at 3500 rpm.

OPTIONAL DIESEL FOUR (1961-up): Inline, overhead-valve four-cylinder. Cast iron block

---

and head. **Displacement:** 139.5 cu. in. (2286 cc). **Bore & Stroke:** 3.58 x 3.50 in. (91 x 89 mm). **Compression Ratio:** 23.0:1. **Brake Horsepower:** 62 (SAE) at 4000 rpm. **Torque:** 103 lbs.-ft. at 1800 rpm. Solid valve lifters.

CHASSIS DATA: Wheelbase: (88) 88 in.; (109) 109 in. **Overall Length:** (88) 142.5 in.; (109) 175 in. **Height:** (88) 77.5-77.9 in.; (109) 81.4 in. **Width:** (88) 64.1-66 in.; (109) 66 in. **Front Tread:** 51.5 in. **Rear Tread:** 51.5 in. **Standard Tires:** (88 four) 6.00x16 (later models, 7.10/7.50x15); (six-cylinder) 7.50x16; (109) 7.50x16.

TECHNICAL: Layout: front-engine, four-wheel-drive. **Transmission:** four-speed manual (two-speed transfer box). **Steering:** recirculating ball. **Suspension (front):** rigid axle with semi-elliptic leaf springs. **Suspension (rear):** rigid axle with semi-elliptic leaf springs. **Brakes:** front/rear drum. **Body Construction:** light alloy body on steel box-type ladder frame.

Manufacturer: The Rover Co. Ltd., Solihull, Birmingham, Warwickshire, England.

Distributor: The Rover Motor Company of North America, New York City.

1970-90 LAND ROVER

1979 Land Rover.

LAND ROVER 4WD — SERIES II/III — FOUR/SIX/V-8 — Following the introduction of the luxury Range Rover (listed below), the utilitarian Land Rover remained available as before, powered by a four- or six-cylinder engine (or optional diesel). Series III replaced Series II late in 1971, wearing a new grille and full-width profile, and carrying a new all-synchro gearbox. By 1980, a V-8 engine also was available, but the long-standing four remained as the base powerplant. Long before the Range Rover gained popularity in the late 1980s, however, the Land Rover had faded out of the U.S. marketplace, though it retained a legion of fans and customers elsewhere in the world.

I.D. DATA: Serial number plate is on right side of dashboard, visible through the windshield. Starting serial number (1971): 24440000.

Model	Body Type & Seating	Engine Type/CID	P.O.E. Price	Weight (lbs.)	Prod. Total
LAND ROVER (1970)					
88 Deluxe	2-dr Utility-7P	I4/140	3295	2947	Note 1
109	2-dr Utility-10P	I4/140	N/A	N/A	Note 1
LAND ROVER (1980)					
88	2-dr Utility-7P	I4/140	N/A	N/A	Note 1
109	2-dr Utility-10P	I4/140	N/A	N/A	Note 1
LAND ROVER (1990)					
88	2-dr Utility-7P	I4/140	N/A	N/A	Note 1
109	2-dr Utility-10P	I4/140	N/A	N/A	Note 1

Note 1: A total of 11,028 Land Rovers were produced in 1973, and 12,929 in 1974, shrinking to 2,120 in 1980. The one-millionth Land Rover was built in mid-1976.

Price Note: By 1974, a Series III hardtop Land Rover sold for $4599 in the U.S.

Model Note: A variety of body styles was available, in addition to the basic utility form.

ENGINE DATA: BASE FOUR: Inline, overhead-valve four-cylinder. Cast iron block and head. **Displacement:** 139.5 cu. in. (2286 cc). **Bore & Stroke:** 3.58 x 3.50 in. (91 x 89 mm). **Compression Ratio:** 7.0:1. **Brake Horsepower:** 77 at 4250 rpm. **Torque:** 124 lbs.-ft. at 2500 rpm. Solid valve lifters.

OPTIONAL SIX: Inline, overhead-valve six-cylinder. Cast iron block and head. **Displacement:** 160 cu. in. (2625 cc). **Bore & Stroke:** 3.06 x 3.62 in. (77.8 x 92 mm). **Compression Ratio:** 7.8:1. **Brake Horsepower:** 85 (DIN) at 4500 rpm. **Torque:** 132 lbs.-ft. (DIN) at 1500 rpm. Solid valve lifters. Zenith carburetor.

OPTIONAL V-8 (1980-up): 90-degree, overhead-valve "vee" type eight-cylinder (derived from Buick). Aluminum block and heads. **Displacement:** 215 cu. in. (3528 cc). **Bore & Stroke:** 3.50 x 2.80 in. (89 x 71 mm). **Brake Horsepower:** approx. 100 (91 DIN at 3500 rpm). **Torque:** 167 lbs.-ft. (DIN) at 2000 rpm. Five main bearings. Hydraulic valve lifters. Two Zenith-Stromberg carburetors.

OPTIONAL DIESEL FOUR: Inline, overhead-valve four-cylinder. Cast iron block and head. **Displacement:** 139.5 cu. in. (2286 cc). **Bore & Stroke:** 3.56 x 3.50 in. (90.5 x 88.9 mm). **Compression Ratio:** 23.0:1. **Brake Horsepower:** 62 at 4000 rpm. **Torque:** 103 lbs.-ft. at 1800 rpm. Solid valve lifters.

CHASSIS DATA: Wheelbase: (88) 88 in.; (109) 109 in. **Overall Length:** (88) 142.5 in.; (109) 175 in. **Height:** (88) 77.5-77.9 in.; (109) 81.4 in. **Width:** (88) 64.1-66 in.; (109) 66 in. **Front Tread:** 51.5 in. **Rear Tread:** 51.5 in.

TECHNICAL: Layout: front-engine, four-wheel-drive. **Transmission:** four-speed manual (two-speed transfer box). **Steering:** recirculating ball. **Suspension (front):** rigid axle with semi-elliptic leaf springs. **Suspension (rear):** rigid axle with semi-elliptic leaf springs.

Brakes: front/rear drum. **Body Construction:** light alloy body on box-section steel frame.
Manufacturer: The Rover Co. Ltd. (until 1973); Rover division of British Leyland U.K. Ltd. (1973-75); then Land Rover Ltd., Solihull, Birmingham, Warwickshire, England.
HISTORY: Land Rovers ceased to be exported to the U.S. during 1974, due to tightening safety/emissions regulations. In the prior year (1973), a total of 1,246 were shipped to the U.S.

1970-90 RANGE ROVER

1988 Range Rover.

RANGE ROVER 4WD — V-8 — The Range Rover nameplate began in 1970 with a two-door wagon: a more luxurious, passenger-oriented companion to the familiar Land Rover, riding a 100-inch wheelbase. This one had permanent (full-time) four-wheel-drive beneath its station wagon body. The Range Rover's all-alloy 3528-cc (215-cid) V-8 engine originated in the Buick design from the early 1960s. A four-door model arrived for the 1980s, along with a high-compression edition of the V-8 engine. An automatic transmission became optional in 1982; an improved five-speed manual gearbox the following year. Electronic fuel injection and a new four-speed ZF automatic transmission arrived in 1985, as the engine got a boost to 165 horsepower (in European trim). The first Range Rovers built to U.S. specifications went on sale in March 1987. The most potent engine of all debuted in the U.S. version late in 1988, producing 178 horsepower.

I.D. DATA: Vehicle Identification Number is on the upper dashboard, visible through the windshield.

Model	Body Type & Seating	Engine Type/CID	P.O.E. Price	Weight (lbs.)	Prod. Total
RANGE ROVER (1970)					
	2-dr Sta Wag-5P	V8/215	N/A	3737	Note 1
RANGE ROVER (1980)					
	2-dr Sta Wag-5P	V8/215	N/A	N/A	Note 1
RANGE ROVER (1990)					
	4-dr Sta Wag-5P	V8/241	38025	4389	Note 1
Standard	4-dr Sta Wag-5P	V8/241	40125	4389	Note 1

Note 1: A total of 7,107 Range Rovers were produced in 1973, followed by 8,899 in 1974, 13,600 in 1975, shrinking to 9,700 in 1980.

1990 Range Rover County.

ENGINE DATA: BASE V-8 (1970s): 90-degree, overhead-valve "vee" type eight-cylinder (derived from Buick). Aluminum block and heads. **Displacement:** 215 cu. in. (3528 cc). **Bore & Stroke:** 3.50 x 2.80 in. (88.9 x 71.1 mm). **Compression Ratio:** 8.5:1. **Brake Horse-**

power: 132 (DIN) at 5000 rpm. **Torque:** 186 lbs.-ft. at 2500 rpm. Five main bearings. Hydraulic valve lifters. Two Zenith-Stromberg carburetors.
Note: Horsepower of European engine rose to 165 in mid-1980s, as fuel injection replaced carburetors.
BASE V-8 (1990): Overhead-valve "vee" type eight-cylinder. Aluminum alloy block and heads. **Displacement:** 241 cu. in. (3947 cc). **Bore & Stroke:** 3.70 x 2.80 in. (94 x 71.1 mm). **Compression Ratio:** 8.13:1. **Brake Horsepower:** 178 at 4750 rpm. **Torque:** 220 lbs.-ft. at 3000 rpm. Lucas L-Jetronic fuel injection.
CHASSIS DATA: Wheelbase: 100.0 in. **Overall Length:** 175-176 in. **Height:** 70-70.8 in. **Width:** 70-71.4 in. **Front Tread:** 58.5 in. **Rear Tread:** 58.5 in. **Standard Tires:** 205R16.
TECHNICAL: Layout: front-engine, four-wheel-drive. **Transmission:** ZF four-speed automatic with two-speed reduction. **Steering:** worm and roller. **Suspension (front):** radius arms, Panhard rod and coil springs. **Suspension (rear):** dual-rate coil springs with Boge "Hydromat" self-energizing leveling device. **Brakes:** front/rear disc. **Body Construction:** aluminum (except steel hood, tailgate and rear lower quarter panels) on boxed steel ladder-type frame.
Manufacturer: The Rover Co. Ltd. (until 1973); Rover division of British Leyland U.K. Ltd. (1973-75); then Land Rover Ltd., Solihull, Birmingham, Warwickshire, England.
Distributor: Range Rover of North America Inc., Lanham, Maryland.
HISTORY: The new Range Rover debuted in June 1970, winning a gold medal for its coachwork at the Earl's Court Motor Show in England. In 1971, it won the RAC Dewar Trophy for outstanding technical merit. *CAR* magazine noted in 1976 that they "have still not found a vehicle to challenge the Range Rover." *Playboy* named it "Best 4x4" in 1988, soon after the first U.S.-spec versions arrived. In 1989, Range Rover was named "Four Wheeler of the Year" by *Four Wheeler* magazine, best multi-purpose vehicle by *Motor-Week*, and one of the "World's Ten Best Cars" by *Automobile* magazine.

LEA-FRANCIS

If known at all to American enthusiasts, the Lea-Francis company is remembered for its small two-seater sports car of the late 1940s. While never a major producer, the firm's Coventry-built chassis went beneath a number of different body styles, including four-door saloons and Estate Cars. Before expiring in the early 1950s, Lea-Francis turned out more than 3,400 "Leafs" in the early postwar period.

Bicycles seem to have led many a long-lived British firm into the motorcar trade in its early days. Lea-Francis was no exception. Before the turn of the century, in 1895, Richard Lea and Graham Francis joined forces to build bikes, soon forming Lea & Francis Ltd. in Coventry, England. While continuing with two-wheelers, and turning to motorcycles a few years before the First World War, the partners expanded to the automobile as early as 1903, creating a separate company for the purpose. Designed by Alexander Craig, the 3.5-liter three-cylinder tourer was both expensive and unusual in form, sporting gigantic connecting rods and flywheels of a size more likely in a steam engine. After selling only two, the rights were sold to the Singer organization. Not until after the war was over did Lea and Francis turn once again to four-wheeled transport, this time with a four-cylinder model of much smaller displacement (in the two-liter neighborhood). Less than two dozen of these found buyers, but the partners foraged ahead regardless. Another design, with an engine much smaller yet, entered production in 1923 and brought much greater success. By the mid-1920s, the company was earning a profit on sales of 750 or more cars annually.

In 1924, they made an initial stab at the sport arena, with a 10-hp four-cylinder tourer that performed very well at the Royal Automobile Club's Six-Day Trial. During the next few years came several sport-touring models with overhead-valve engines. Then in 1927, a Lea-Francis appeared with a low-pressure Cozette supercharger (Rootes-type), gear-driven from the crankshaft, mounted on a 1496-cc Meadows engine. Soon after that came a Hyper-Sports supercharged Lea-Francis with rakish radiator design, fabric body, 28-inch wire wheels, and four-speed "crash box." A similar car won the Ulster (Ireland) Tourist Trophy race.

Unfortunately, the success of the Meadows-engined vehicles, coupled with some significant victories in competition during the 1920s, was followed by introduction of the

model LFS 14/40. Its 1.7-liter twin-cam Vulcan-built engine suffered severe reliability problems, harming the Lea-Francis reputation and sales figures. By 1931, the company that never quite got rolling was in receivership. Mr. Francis had dropped out years earlier, and now Richard Lea did likewise. Production continued in small numbers, however, including a new two-liter model and a 2.2-liter six. Annual sales of 29 were nothing to get excited about in 1932; but the figure dropped farther yet over the next few year, with none at all built in 1936, when the company assets were sold. Riding to the rescue of the Lea-Francis nameplate were George Leek and Hugh Rose, who had a car to build and formed Lea-Francis Engineering Ltd. in 1937 to do the job. About a hundred Lea-Francis Twelve and Fourteen models were built by the time World War II broke out, powered by 1496 and 1629 cc twin-cam engines and wearing bodies by New Avon and Charlesworth.

Wartime profits allowed the company to resume Fourteen passenger-car production early in 1946, this time with bodies produced by A.P. Aircraft Ltd. A streamlined Eighteen sedan and a two-seat sports car debuted in 1948. Estate cars (station wagons) also were built, until the company abandoned auto manufacture by 1954, turning instead to other products. At the London Motor Show in autumn 1960, a modernized Ford Zephyr-powered Lea-Francis (known as the Lynx) with a bizarre round grille made an appearance, but drew little attention and disappeared. By 1962, the company assets were sold to a separate organization that later offered parts and service. Another prototype, for a V-8 model known as the Francesca, emerged in 1963; but that also came to nought. Years later, in 1980, yet another prototype for a sports car entered the scene to revamp the old badge, but serious production never happened.

Model	Body Type & Seating	Engine Type/CID	P.O.E. Price	Weight (lbs.)	Prod. Total
TWELVE					
Westland	2-dr Coupe	I4/91	N/A	N/A	Note 1
	4-dr Saloon-5/6P	I4/91	N/A	2850	Note 1

Note 1: A total of 326 Lea-Francis models were sold in 1946, and 565 in 1947.

1947 Lea-Francis four-door four-light saloon.

ENGINE DATA: BASE FOUR (Fourteen): Inline, overhead-valve four-cylinder. **Displacement:** 107.8 cu. in. (1767 cc). **Bore & Stroke:** 2.95 x 3.94 in. (75 x 100 mm). **Compression Ratio:** 7.25:1. **Brake Horsepower:** 65 at 4700 rpm. Three main bearings. Solid valve lifters. One SU horizontal carburetor.
BASE FOUR (Twelve): Same as above, except — **Displacement:** 91.3 cu. in. (1496 cc). **Bore & Stroke:** 2.72 x 3.94 in. (69 x 100 mm). **Brake Horsepower:** 50 at 4800 rpm.
CHASSIS DATA: Wheelbase: 111 in. **Overall Length:** 179 in. **Width:** 64.5 in. **Rear Tread:** 52.3 in. **Wheel Type:** disc. **Standard Tires:** 5.50x17.
TECHNICAL: Layout: front-engine, rear-drive. **Transmission:** four-speed manual. **Standard Final Drive Ratio:** (Fourteen) 4.87:1; (Twelve) 5.12:1. **Steering:** Burman worm and nut. **Suspension (front):** (Fourteen) semi-elliptic leaf springs, or torsion bars; (Twelve) semi-elliptic leaf springs. **Suspension (rear):** rigid axle, semi-elliptic leaf springs. **Brakes:** front/rear drum. **Body Construction:** aluminum body on steel frame.
PERFORMANCE: Top Speed: (Twelve) 70 mph.
Manufacturer: Lea-Francis Cars Ltd., Coventry, England.
HISTORY: Mark I introduced in March 1946; Mark II in January 1947; coupe in April 1947. All Lea-Francis models used a twin semi-overhead cam engine with hemispherical combustion chambers and patented valve gear. Its lightweight reciprocating mechanism ensured minimal wear.

1946-47 LEA-FRANCIS

1946 Lea-Francis roadster.

FOURTEEN — Mk I/II — FOUR — Postwar production began with a series of four-door saloons that carried on postwar styling. Each had an upright vertical-bar grille, separately-mounted headlamps, rear-hinged ("suicide") doors with no vent panes, and solid (windowless) rear quarter panels. Mark II, which debuted early in 1947, was identical to the earlier Mk I except for the switch to a single beltline for the bodyside. A fixed-head coupe, with body by Westland, joined the saloon in the spring of 1947. It had rear quarter windows and a separate central running light ahead of the grille. The 108 cubic-inch four-cylinder engine produced 65 horsepower. Some Lea-Francis chassis used front leaf springs; others had torsion bars.

TWELVE — FOUR — Lea-Francis models with a smaller-displacement (91-cid) four-cylinder engine also were produced.

I.D. DATA: Chassis serial number is stamped on the right side of the firewall, under the hood; and also on a short stiffening member between the front crossmember and the left-hand frame member. Engine number is stamped on the generator boss of the timing cover. Starting serial number: (Mk I) 200; (Mk II) 494.

Model	Body Type & Seating	Engine Type/CID	P.O.E. Price	Weight (lbs.)	Prod. Total
FOURTEEN					
Mk I	4-dr Saloon-5/6P	I4/108	N/A	N/A	Note 1
Mk II	4-dr Saloon-5/6P	I4/108	N/A	N/A	Note 1

1948 LEA-FRANCIS

1948 Lea-Francis 14 hp sports open 2/4 seater. (Christie's)

FOURTEEN — Mk III/IV — FOUR — The next series of saloons (sedans) was similar in appearance to the Mk II. The Deluxe Mk IV version came with standard radio, heater and "air conditioning."

SPORTS TOURER — FOUR — Joining the saloons was a new two-seat Sports Tourer. Its jaunty look was accented by cutdown doors with a graceful curved front edge, notched rear fender skirts, built-in headlamps, and a shorter (99-inch) wheelbase. The roadster came with either the 1.5-liter (Twelve) or 1.8-liter (Fourteen) engine, but higher in horsepower than the saloon version.

TWELVE — FOUR — Production continued of Lea-Francis models with a smaller-displacement (91-cid) four-cylinder engine.

I.D. DATA: Chassis serial number is stamped on the right side of the firewall, under the hood; and also on a short stiffening member between the front crossmember and the left-hand frame member. Engine number is stamped on the generator boss of the timing cover. Starting serial number: (Mk III/IV) 2450; (Spts Tourer) 1300.

Model	Body Type & Seating	Engine Type/CID	P.O.E. Price	Weight (lbs.)	Prod. Total
FOURTEEN					
Mk III	4-dr Saloon-5/6P	I4/108	N/A	2964	Note 1
Mk IV	4-dr DeL Saloon-5/6P	I4/108	N/A	2964	Note 1
Sports	2-dr Spt Tourer-2P	I4/108	N/A	2280	Note 1
TWELVE					
	4-dr Saloon-5/6P	I4/91	N/A	2850	Note 1
1.5-liter	2-dr Spt Tourer-2P	I4/91	N/A	2166	Note 1

Note 1: A total of 551 Lea-Francis models were sold in 1948. Only two were known to have been sold in the U.S. that year.

ENGINE DATA: BASE FOUR (Fourteen): Inline, overhead-valve four-cylinder. **Displacement:** 107.8 cu. in. (1767 cc). **Bore & Stroke:** 2.95 x 3.94 in. (75 x 100 mm). **Compression Ratio:** 7.25:1; (Sports) 8.0:1. **Brake Horsepower:** 65 at 4700 rpm except (Sports Tourer) 87 at 5200. Three main bearings. Solid valve lifters. One SU horizontal carburetor (Sports, two carburetors).

BASE FOUR (Twelve): Same as above, except — **Displacement:** 91.3 cu. in. (1496 cc). **Bore & Stroke:** 2.72 x 3.94 in. (69 x 100 mm). **Brake Horsepower:** 55 at 4700 rpm except (Sports) 64 at 5300.

CHASSIS DATA: Wheelbase: (saloon) 111 in.; (Spts Tourer) 99 in. **Overall Length:** (saloon) 179 in.; (Spts) 165 in. **Width:** (saloon) 64.5 in.; (Spts) 63 in. **Rear Tread:** 52.3 in. **Wheel Type:** disc. **Standard Tires:** (saloon) 5.50x17; (Spts) 5.25x17.

TECHNICAL: Layout: front-engine, rear-drive. **Transmission:** four-speed manual. **Standard Final Drive Ratio:** (14 saloon) 4.87:1; (12 saloon) 5.12:1; (14 Spts) 4.55:1; (12 Spts) 4.87:1. **Steering:** Burman worm and nut. **Suspension (front):** (Fourteen) semi-elliptic leaf springs, or torsion bars; (Twelve) semi-elliptic leaf springs; (Sports) semi-elliptic leaf springs. Suspension (rear): rigid axle, semi-elliptic leaf springs. **Brakes:** front/rear drum. **Body Construction:** aluminum body on steel frame.

PERFORMANCE: Top Speed: (Twelve) 70 mph; (14 Spts) 85 mph.

Manufacturer: Lea-Francis Cars Ltd., Coventry, England.

HISTORY Mark III/IV saloons and Sports Tourer introduced in October 1947.

1949 LEA-FRANCIS

FOURTEEN — Mk V/VI — FOUR — As before, the four-door saloon came in standard (Mk V) and Deluxe (Mk VI) form, the latter with standard sunroof, radio and heater. Appearance was similar to prior models, with separately-mounted headlamps and upright grille; but a wood-panelled four-door Estate Car (station wagon) joined th original saloon. "Twelve" models with the smaller-displacement engine no longer were produced. Sixteen-inch tires became available on saloons.

SPORTS TOURER — FOUR — Production of the 1767-cc roadster continued with little change.

I.D. DATA: Chassis serial number is stamped on the right side of the firewall, under the hood; and also on a short stiffening member between the front crossmember and the left-hand frame member. Engine number is stamped on the generator boss of the timing cover.

Model	Body Type & Seating	Engine Type/CID	P.O.E. Price	Weight (lbs.)	Prod. Total
FOURTEEN					
MK V	4-dr Saloon-5/6P	I4/108	N/A	2964	Note 1
Mk VI	4-dr DeL Saloon-5/6P	I4/108	N/A	2964	Note 1
	4-dr Sta Wagon-5/6P	I4/108	N/A	N/A	Note 1
Sports	2-dr Spt Tourer-2P	I4/108	N/A	2280	Note 1

Note 1: About 500 Lea-Francis models were produced during 1949. Only two were known to have been sold in the U.S. that year.

ENGINE DATA: BASE FOUR: Inline, overhead-valve four-cylinder. **Displacement:** 107.8 cu. in. (1767 cc). **Bore & Stroke:** 2.95 x 3.94 in. (75 x 100 mm). **Compression Ratio:** 7.25:1; (Sports) 8.0:1. **Brake Horsepower:** 65 at 4700 rpm except (Sports Tourer) 87 at 5200. Three main bearings. Solid valve lifters. One SU horizontal carburetor (Sports, two carburetors).

CHASSIS DATA: Wheelbase: (saloon) 111 in.; (Spts Tourer) 99 in. Overall Length: (saloon) 179 in.; (Spt) 165 in. Width: (saloon) 64.5 in.; (Spt) 63 in. Front Tread: 51.5 in. Rear Tread: 52.4 in. Wheel Type: disc. Standard Tires: (saloon) 5.50x17 or 6.00x16; (Spt) 5.25x17.

TECHNICAL: Layout: front-engine, rear-drive. **Transmission:** four-speed manual. **Standard Final Drive Ratio:** (saloon/wagon) 4.87:1; (Spts) 4.55:1. **Steering:** Burman worm and nut. **Supension (front):** (saloon) torsion bars; (Sports) semi-elliptic leaf springs. **Suspension (rear):** rigid axle, semi-elliptic leaf springs. **Brakes:** front/rear drum. **Body Construction:** aluminum body on steel frame.

PERFORMANCE: Top Speed: (Spts) 85 mph.

Manufacturer: Lea-Francis Cars Ltd., Coventry, England.

HISTORY: Mark V/VI saloons and Estate Car introduced in October 1948.

1950 LEA-FRANCIS

FOURTEEN — Mk V/VI — FOUR — Production of the Mk V (standard) and Mk VI (deluxe) saloons continued with little change, except for the addition of Girling hydromechanical brakes. Appearance was similar to earlier models. During the model year, the Estate Car (station wagon) added vertical-opening rear doors.

EIGHTEEN (2.5 LITRE) — Mk VII/SPORTS — FOUR — Joining the 1.8-liter saloons was new series with larger four-cylinder engine, offered in both four-door saloon and Sports Roadster form. Appearance of the long, stately saloon differed from the earlier models, with a front fender line that reached all the way back through the rear fender skirts. A narrow vertical-bar grille stood ahead of a tapered hood, with inboard built-in headlamps alongside. Rear quarter windows now were used, rather than the blank panels of the Fourteen saloon. All doors now were hinged at the front. Roadster appearance was similar to the earlier Sports Tourer, with separate fenders and cutdown doors, but adopted the grille shape of the new saloon. Built-in headlamps were mounted low on front fenders. A slanted windshield met triangular vent panes.

I.D. DATA: Chassis serial number of the Fourteen is stamped on the right side of the firewall, under the hood; and also on a short stiffening member between the front crossmember and the left-hand frame member. Chassis number of the 2.5-Litre models is stamped on the chassis diagonal member, ahead of the engine mount. Engine number is stamped on the generator boss of the timing cover. Starting serial number: (Mk V/VI) 4366.

Model	Body Type & Seating	Engine Type/CID	P.O.E. Price	Weight (lbs.)	Prod. Total
FOURTEEN					
Mk V	4-dr Saloon-5/6P	I4/108	N/A	2828	Note 1
Mk VI	4-dr DeL Saloon-5/6P	I4/108	N/A	2828	Note 1
	4-dr Sta Wag-5/6P	I4/108	N/A	N/A	Note 1
EIGHTEEN (2.5-LITRE)					
Mk VII	4-dr Saloon-5/6P	I4/152	N/A	3000	Note 1
Sports	2-dr Sports Rds-2P	I4/152	N/A	2400	Note 1

Note 1: Almost 700 Lea-Francis models were produced during 1950. Only three were known to have been sold in the U.S. that year.

Weight Note: Figures shown are shipping weights.

ENGINE DATA: BASE FOUR (Fourteen): Inline, overhead-valve four-cylinder. **Displacement:** 107.8 cu. in. (1767 cc). **Bore & Stroke:** 2.95 x 3.94 in. (75 x 100 mm). **Compression Ratio:** 7.25:1. **Brake Horsepower:** 65 at 4700 rpm. Three main bearings. Solid valve lifters. One SU horizontal carburetor.

BASE FOUR (2.5-Litre Eighteen): Inline, overhead-valve four-cylinder. **Displacement:** 152.3 cu. in. (2496 cc). **Bore & Stroke:** 3.35 x 4.33 in. (85 x 110 mm). **Compression Ratio:** 6.0:1; (Sports) 7.0:1. **Brake Horsepower:** 95 at 4000 rpm except (Sports) 100 at 4000. Three main bearings. Solid valve lifters. One SU horizontal carburetor (Sports, two carburetors).

CHASSIS DATA: Wheelbase: (saloon) 111 in.; (Spts) 99 in. **Overall Length:** (saloon) 181 in.; (Spt) 165 in. **Width:** (saloon) 64.5 in.; (Spt) 63 in. **Front Tread:** 51.5 in. **Rear Tread:** 52.4 in. **Wheel Type:** disc. **Standard Tires:** (Fourteen) 5.50x17 or 6.00x16; (2.5-Litre) 6.00x16.

TECHNICAL: Layout: front-engine, rear-drive. **Transmission:** four-speed manual. **Standard Final Drive Ratio:** (Fourteen) 4.87:1; (Eighteen) 3.90:1; (Spts) 3.50:1. **Steering:** Burman worm and nut. **Suspension (front):** torsion bars. **Suspension (rear):** rigid axle, semi-elliptic leaf springs. **Brakes:** Girling hydromechanical, front/rear drum. **Body Construction:** aluminum body on steel form.

PERFORMANCE: Top Speed: (Eighteen) 90 mph; (Spts) 95-100 mph.

Manufacturer: Lea-Francis Cars Ltd., Coventry, England.

HISTORY: Introduced: September 1949. A 102-hp Connaught sports car (based on 1767-cc Lea-Francis parts) did very well in high-speed racing.

1951 LEA-FRANCIS

FOURTEEN (FOUR-LIGHT) — FOUR — A restyled four-door saloon with "Fourteen" 1767-cc four-cylinder engine debuted with built-in headlamps on front fenders. Otherwise, appearance was similar to the earlier Fourteen series.

Note: Both the "Four-Light" and "Fourteen Horsepower" (or "Six-Light" and "Eighteen Horsepower") names were used by Lea-Francis to designate models.

EIGHTEEN (2.5 LITRE) — Mk VII/SPORTS — FOUR — The four-door saloon (sedan) and two-door Sports Roadster continued with little change, powered by a 2496-cc four-cylinder engine. The roadster had a fold-flat windshield and all-weather equipment, with a rakishly curved front edge on its doors. As before, rear fender skirts had a cutout (curved) lower edge. Bucket seats held two up front, while two youngsters could squeeze into the tiny rear compartment. Built-in headlamps stood at front fender tips.

I.D. DATA: Chassis serial number of the Fourteen is stamped on the right side of the firewall, under the hood; and also on a short stiffening member between the front crossmember and the left-hand frame member. Chassis number of the 2.5-Litre models is stamped on the chassis diagonal member, ahead of the engine mount. Engine number is stamped on the generator boss of the timing cover. Starting serial number: (Four-Light) 8190; (2.5-Litre) 5248.

Model	Body Type & Seating	Engine Type/CID	P.O.E. Price	Weight (lbs.)	Prod. Total
FOURTEEN (FOUR-LIGHT)					
	4-dr Saloon-5/6P	I4/108	N/A	2828	Note 1
	4-dr Sta Wag-5/6P	I4/108	N/A	N/A	Note 1
EIGHTEEN (2.5-LITRE)					
Mk VII	4-dr Saloon-5/6P	I4/152	N/A	3024	Note 1
Sports	2-dr Spot Rds-2P	I4/152	3895	2576	Note 1

Note 1: Almost 600 Lea-Francis models were produced during 1951.

Price Note: Price of roadster was about $2795 at the factory in England.

Weight Note: Figures shown are shipping weights; dry weight of roadster was 2446 lbs.

ENGINE DATA: BASE FOUR (Four-Light Fourteen): Inline, overhead-valve four-cylinder. **Displacement:** 107.8 cu. in. (1767 cc). **Bore & Stroke:** 2.95 x 3.94 in. (75 x 100 mm). **Compression Ratio:** 7.25:1. **Brake Horsepower:** 65 at 4700 rpm. Three main bearings. Solid valve lifters. One SU horizontal carburetor.

BASE FOUR (2.5-Litre Eighteen): Inline, overhead-valve four-cylinder (semi-overhead camshafts). **Displacement:** 152.3 cu. in. (2496 cc). **Bore & Stroke:** 3.35 x 4.33 in. (85 x 110 mm). **Compression Ratio:** 6.0:1; (Sports) 7.0:1. **Brake Horsepower:** 95 at 4000 rpm except (Sports) 100 at 4000. Three main bearings. Solid valve lifters. One SU horizontal carburetor (Sports, two carburetors).

CHASSIS DATA: Wheelbase: (saloon) 111 in.; (Spts) 99 in. **Overall Length:** (saloon) 181 in.; (Spt) 165 in. **Height:** (saloon) 60.5 in.; (Spt) 52 in. **Width:** (saloon) 64.5 in.; (Spt) 63 in. **Front Tread:** 51.5 in. **Rear Tread:** 52.4 in. **Wheel Type:** steel disc. **Standard Tires:** (Fourteen) 5.50x17 or 6.00x16; (2.5-Litre) 6.00x16.

TECHNICAL: Layout: front-engine, rear-drive. **Transmission:** four-speed manual. Sports (close-ratio) overall gear ratios: (1st) 12.75:1; (2nd) 7.68:1; (3rd) 5.00:1; (4th) 3.60:1. **Standard Final Drive Ratio:** (Fourteen) 4.87:1; (Eighteen) 3.90:1; (Spts) 3.60:1.

Steering: Burman worm and nut. **Suspension (front):** wishbones and torsion bars. **Suspension (rear):** rigid axle, semi-elliptic leaf springs. **Brakes:** Girling hydromechanical, front/rear drum. **Body Construction:** (Sport) aluminum body panels on steel frame. **Fuel Tank:** (Sports) 18 U.S. gallons.

PERFORMANCE: Top Speed: (Eighteen) 90 mph; (Spts) 95-100 mph. **Acceleration (0-60 mph):** N/A (roadster did 0-50 mph in 8.5 seconds). **Fuel Mileage:** (Sports) 24-28 mpg.

Manufacturer: Lea-Francis Cars Ltd., Coventry, England.

Distributor: Vaughan-Singer Motors, Hollywood, California.

HISTORY: Introduced: (Four-Light) October 1950; (2.5-Litre) January 1951.

1952 LEA-FRANCIS

FOURTEEN (FOUR-LIGHT) — FOUR — Production continued of the four-door saloon with 1767-cc four-cylinder engine, with little change. Late in the model year, full hydraulic brakes became standard, replacing the former hydromechanical system.

EIGHTEEN — 2.5 LITRE — FOUR — Both the four-door saloon (sedan) and two-door Sports Roadster continued with little change, powered by a 2496-cc four-cylinder engine. Late in the model year, full hydraulic brakes replaced the former hydromechanical system.

I.D. DATA: Chassis serial number of the Fourteen is stamped on the right side of the firewall, under the hood; and also on a short stiffening member between the front cross-member and the left-hand frame member. Chassis number of the 2.5-Litre models is stamped on the chassis diagonal member, ahead of the engine mount. Engine number is stamped on the generator boss of the timing cover. Starting serial number: (Four-Light) 8286; (2.5-Litre) 5306.

Model	Body Type & Seating	Engine Type/CID	P.O.E. Price	Weight (lbs.)	Prod. Total
FOURTEEN (FOUR-LIGHT)					
	4-dr Saloon-5/6P	I4/108	N/A	2828	Note 1
	4-dr Sta Wag-5/6P	I4/108	N/A	N/A	Note 1
EIGHTEEN (2.5-LITRE)					
Mk VII	4-dr Saloon-5/6P	I4/152	N/A	3024	Note 1
Sports	2-dr Spt Rds 2P	I4/152	3895	2576	Note 1

Note 1: About 170 Lea-Francis models were produced during 1952.

Weight Note: Figures shown are shipping weights.

ENGINE DATA: BASE FOUR (Four-Light Fourteen): Inline, overhead-valve four-cylinder. **Displacement:** 107.8 cu. in. (1767 cc). **Bore & Stroke:** 2.95 x 3.94 in. (75 x 100 mm). **Compression Ratio:** 7.25:1. **Brake Horsepower:** 65 at 4700 rpm. Three main bearings. Solid valve lifters. One SU horizontal carburetor.
BASE FOUR (2.5-Litre Eighteen): Inline, overhead-valve four-cylinder (semi-overhead camshafts). **Displacement:** 152.3 cu. in. (2496 cc). **Bore & Stroke:** 3.35 x 4.33 in. (85 x 110 mm). **Compression Ratio:** 6.0:1. (Sports) 7.0:1. **Brake Horsepower:** 95 at 4000 rpm except (Sports) 100 at 4000. Three main bearings. Solid valve lifters. One SU horizontal carburetor (Sports, two carburetors).

CHASSIS DATA: Wheelbase: (saloon) 111 in.; (Spts) 99 in. **Overall Length:** (saloon) 181 in.; (Spt) 168 in. **Height:** (saloon) 60.5 in.; (wagon) 64 in.; (Spt) 52 in. **Width:** (saloon) 64.5 in.; (Spt) 63 in. **Rear Tread:** 51.5 in. **Wheel Type:** steel disc. **Standard Tires:** (Four-Light) 5.50x17 or 6.00x16; (2.5-Litre) 6.00x16.

TECHNICAL: Layout: front-engine, rear-drive. **Transmission:** four-speed manual. Sports (close-ratio) overall gear ratios: (1st) 12.75:1; (2nd) 7.68:1; (3rd) 5.00:1; (4th) 3.60:1. **Standard Final Drive Ratio:** (Four-Light) 4.87:1; (2.5-Litre) 3.91:1; (Spts) 3.60:1. **Steering:** Burman worm and nut. **Suspension (front):** wishbones and torsion bars. **Suspension (rear):** rigid axle, semi-elliptic leaf springs. **Brakes:** Girling hydromechanical, front/rear drum. **Body Construction:** (Sport) aluminum body panels on steel frame. **Fuel Tank:** (Sports) 18 U.S. gallons.

PERFORMANCE: Top Speed: (Eighteen) 90 mph; (Spts) 95-100 mph. **Acceleration (0-60 mph):** N/A (roadster did 0-50 mph in 8.5 seconds). **Fuel Mileage:** (Sports) 24-28 mpg.

Manufacturer: Lea-Francis Cars Ltd., Coventry, England.

Distributor: Vaughan-Singer Motors, Hollywood, California.

HISTORY: Lea-Francis exhibited its wares at the London Show for the last time in October 1952.

1953-54 LEA-FRANCIS

FOURTEEN (FOUR-LIGHT) — FOUR — Production of the four-door saloon with 1767-cc four-cylinder engine continued with little change in its final two seasons. The Estate Car (station wagon) had dark mahogany paneling in a light oak framework.

EIGHTEEN (SIX-LIGHT) — 2.5 LITRE — FOUR — Little change was evident in the four-door saloon and two-door Sports Roadster during its final two model years. Sport Roadster body colors were: black, maroon, green, cream, metallic light blue, and metallic grey. Saloons came in black, maroon, and green. These were sometimes referred to as "Six-Light" models.

I.D. DATA: Chassis serial number of the Fourteen is stamped on the right side of the firewall, under the hood; and also on a short stiffening member between the front cross-member and the left-hand frame member. Chassis number of the 2.5-Litre models is stamped on the chassis diagonal member, ahead of the engine mount. Engine number is stamped on the generator boss of the timing cover. Serial number range: (Four-Light) 9520 to 10066; (2.5-Litre) 5334 to 5342.

Model	Body Type & Seating	Engine Type/CID	P.O.E. Price	Weight (lbs.)	Prod. Total
FOURTEEN (FOUR-LIGHT)					
	4-dr Saloon-5/6P	I4/108	N/A	2990	Note 1
	4-dr Sta Wagon-5/6P	I4/108	N/A	3240	Note 1
EIGHTEEN (SIX-LIGHT)					
	4-dr Saloon-5/6P	I4/152	N/A	2900	Note 1
Sports	2-dr Spt Rds-2P	I4/152	3985	2630	Note 1

Note 1: More than 3,400 Lea-Francis models were produced during the postwar period, beginning in 1946.

1954 Lea-Francis Eighteen four-door sedan.

ENGINE DATA: BASE FOUR (Fourteen): Inline, overhead-valve four-cylinder. **Displacement:** 107.8 cu. in. (1767 cc). **Bore & Stroke:** 2.95 x 3.94 in. (75 x 100 mm). **Compression Ratio:** 7.25:1. **Brake Horsepower:** 65 at 4700 rpm. **Torque:** 94 lbs.-ft. at 2250 rpm. Three main bearings. Solid valve lifters. One SU horizontal carburetor.
BASE FOUR (Eighteen): Inline, overhead-valve four-cylinder (semi-overhead camshafts). **Displacement:** 152.3 cu. in. (2496 cc). **Bore & Stroke:** 3.35 x 4.33 in. (85 x 110 mm). **Compression Ratio:** 6.0:1; (Sports) 7.0:1. **Brake Horsepower:** 95 at 4000 rpm except (Sports) 100 at 4000. **Torque:** 140 lbs.-ft. at 2500 rpm except (Sports) 142 at 2800. Three main bearings. Solid valve lifters. One SU horizontal carburetor (Sports, two carburetors).

CHASSIS DATA: Wheelbase: (saloon) 111 in.; (Spt) 99 in. **Overall Length:** (saloon) 181 in.; (Spt) 168 in. **Height:** (saloon) 60.5 in.; (wagon) 64 in.; (Spt) 54 in. **Width:** (saloon) 64.5 in.; (Spt) 63 in. **Front Tread:** 52.2 in. **Rear Tread:** 52.4 in. **Wheel Type:** steel disc. **Standard Tires:** 6.00x16.

TECHNICAL: Layout: front-engine, rear-drive. **Transmission:** four-speed manual. Sports (close-ratio) overall gear ratios: (1st) 12.89:1; (2nd) 7.77:1; (3rd) 5.16:1; (4th) 3.64:1. **Standard Final Drive Ratio:** (Four-Light) 4.87:1; (Six-Light) 3.91:1; (Spts) 3.91:1. **Steering:** Burman worm and nut. **Suspension (front):** wishbones and torsion bars. **Suspension (rear):** rigid axle with semi-elliptic leaf springs. **Brakes:** Girling hydromechanical, front/rear drum. **Body Construction:** aluminum body panels on steel frame. **Fuel Tank:** (Sports) 18 U.S. gallons.

PERFORMANCE: Top Speed: (Four-Light) 75 mph; (Six-Light) 90-95 mph; (Spts) 95-100 mph. **Acceleration (0-60 mph):** N/A (roadster did 0-50 mph in 8.5 seconds). **Fuel Mileage:** (Four-Light) about 21 mpg; (Six-Light) 20-23 mpg; (Sports) 20-28 mpg.

Manufacturer: Lea-Francis Cars Ltd., Coventry, England.

Distributor: Vaughan-Singer Motors, Hollywood, California.

POSTSCRIPT: While Lea-Francis still officially existed as an auto manufacturer after 1952, the company didn't exhibit at either the 1953 or 1954 Earl's Court (London) Motor Show. Car production was discontinued after 1954, presumably because of continuance of the British Purchase Tax (a sales tax of up to 50 percent of the wholesale price). A company official issued a statement to that effect, noting they would return when the tax was reduced or abolished. So the Lea-Francis firm focused instead on aircraft and other work.

LLOYD

One of many minicars that emerged during the 1950s, the Lloyd had a history dating back to 1906, with the formation of Norddeutsche Automobilund Motoren AG. Eventually, after the Second World War, that company wound up as part of the group that included Hansa and Goliath, under the name Lloyd Motoren Werke (part of the Borgward group). Organized by Dr. Carl Borgward, the Lloyd operation revived early in 1949 with the LP300, a 300-cc two-stroke minicar with front-wheel drive, which entered production in May 1950. By 1951, 1,700 Lloyds had been built. Two years later, with 20,000 Lloyds on the road, a 400-cc version debuted, in a line that included a coupe and station wagon as well as the original sedan. Home-market Lloyds had bodies of leatherette, but export models wore steel. Expansion progressed to the point where the Lloyd was on

sale in 72 nations. By 1958, Lloyd was the third largest selling automobile in Germany. The two-stroke engine used on early postwar Lloyds was abandoned in favor of a larger four-cycle powerplant around the time the car began to trickle into America. By that time, after a number of speed records (for its class) had been set by Lloyds with special streamlined bodies, the 600-cc four-stroke had arrived.

1954 Lloyd Model LP 400 two-door sedan.

1956-57 LLOYD

1957 Lloyd two-door.

L/600 SERIES — TWO — Only a handful of Lloyd minicars were imported to the U.S. in its early form, with three-speed gearbox, no trunk, and a flat rear window.

ALEXANDER — TWO — This more powerful Lloyd debuted in 1957; see next listing for details.

I.D. DATA: Serial number is on the right side of the firewall. Engine number is on the left side of the block.

Model	Body Type & Seating	Engine Type/CID	P.O.E. Price	Weight (lbs.)	Prod. Total
LP600	2-dr Sedan-4P	I2/36	1295	1188	Note 1
LC600	2-dr Conv-4P	I2/36	1375	1188	Note 1
LS600	2-dr Sta Wag-4P	I2/36	1345	1210	Note 1

Note 1: A total of about 170,000 LP600 Lloyds were produced. About 29,000 had been built in 1954 alone. A total of 7,687 Series 600 Lloyds were built in 1955, 35,329 in 1956, and 45,907 in 1957.

ENGINE DATA: BASE TWO: Parallel, overhead-valve two-cylinder. **Displacement:** 36.4 cu. in. (597 cc). **Bore & Stroke:** 3.03 x 2.52 in. (77 x 64 mm). **Compression Ratio:** 6.6:1. **Brake Horsepower:** 19 at 4500 rpm. One carburetor. 6-volt electrical system.

CHASSIS DATA: Wheelbase: 78.7 in. **Overall Length:** 137 in. **Height:** 55.1 in. **Width:** 56.4 in. **Front Tread:** 41.5 in. **Rear Tread:** 43.3 in. **Wheel Type:** disc. **Standard Tires:** 4.25x15.

TECHNICAL: Layout: front-engine, front-drive. **Transmission:** three-speed manual; column shift. **Steering:** rack and pinion. **Suspension (front):** (independent) lower transverse semi-elliptic leaf spring, plus auxiliary upper leaf spring. **Suspension (rear):** swing axle with longitudinal semi-elliptic leaf springs. **Brakes:** hydraulic, front/rear drum. **Body Construction:** steel; central backbone with box-section sills.

MAJOR OPTIONS: Sunroof.
Manufacturer: Lloyd Motoren Werke GmbH, Bremen, West Germany.
Distributor: Light Car Motors, Los Angeles, Calif.; and Gallagher Motors, Seattle, Washington.

1958 LLOYD

1958 Lloyd Alexander Kombi.

ALEXANDER — TWO — Adopting the "Alexander" designation, the revised Lloyd added a four-speed manual gearbox, wraparound back window, and a trunk lid for access to luggage from outside. While short in length, the Lloyd was tall enough for easy entry and a roomy interior. Twin front bucket seats adjusted for legs, while their backrest angles could be changed via thumbscrews. Two grownups could fit on the rear bench seat, for a total of four passengers. Slim windshield and back-window pillars permitted easy visibility. Parking/signal lights stood atop the front fenders, above the single round headlamps. The grille consisted of rather thick horizontal bars, with a triangular center divider. The car's overall profile was rounded, and doors hinged at the rear in "suicide" style. Taillamps sat atop the rear quarter panels. A two-door sedan, convertible and station wagon were offered (as well as a larger, rather truck-like wagon with LT600 model designation).

Lloyd's air-cooled parallel twin, overhead-valve engine was of four-cycle design (unlike early models, which used two-strokes) and displaced just under 600 cubic centimeters. Mounted ahead of the front wheels, the engine was hooked to a four-speed manual gearbox with column gearshift lever. Advertisements maintained that "the sturdy, steel muscled Lloyd" was "Europe's leading light car," promoting its 50-mpg fuel economy.

I.D. DATA: Serial number is on the right side of the firewall. Engine number is on the left side of the block.

Model	Body Type & Seating	Engine Type/CID	P.O.E. Price	Weight (lbs.)	Prod. Total
600	2-dr Sedan-4P	I2/36	1295	1188	Note 1
600	2-dr Conv-4P	I2/36	1410	1188	Note 1
600	2-dr Sta Wag-4P	I2/36	1345	1210	Note 1

Note 1: Total Alexander production for 1958 was 46,780 (a record amount).

ENGINE DATA: BASE TWO: Parallel, overhead-valve two-cylinder (four-cycle). **Displacement:** 36.4 cu. in. (597 cc). **Bore & Stroke:** 3.03 x 2.52 in. (77 x 64 mm). **Compression Ratio:** 6.6:1. **Brake Horsepower:** 24 at 4500 rpm. **Torque:** 28.2 lbs.-ft. at 2500 rpm. One carburetor. 6-volt electrical system.

CHASSIS DATA: Wheelbase: 78.3 in. **Overall Length:** 132.0 in. **Height:** 55.8 in. **Width:** 56.4 in. **Front Tread:** 41.5 in. **Rear Tread:** 43.3 in. **Wheel Type:** disc. **Standard Tires:** 4.25x15.

TECHNICAL: Layout: front-engine, front-drive. **Transmission:** four-speed manual (all synchromesh); column shift. **Standard Final Drive Ratio:** 4.87:1. **Steering:** rack and pinion. **Suspension (front):** (independent) lower transverse semi-elliptic leaf spring, plus auxiliary upper leaf spring. **Suspension (rear):** swing axle with longitudinal semi-elliptic leaf springs. **Brakes:** hydraulic, front/rear drum. **Body Construction:** steel; central backbone with box-section sills.

MAJOR OPTIONS: Sunroof.

PERFORMANCE: Top Speed: 63 mph (factory). **Acceleration (0-60 mph):** N/A (0-50 in 27-28.8 seconds). **Acceleration (quarter-mile):** 27 seconds. **Fuel Mileage:** 35-40 mpg city; up to 50 mpg highway (factory).

Manufacturer & Distributor: same as 1956-57.

1959 LLOYD

ALEXANDER TS — TWO — A new TS (Touring Sport) model came with a more powerful (29-horsepower) engine and a revised rear suspension: trailing arms and coil springs, with an anti-roll bar. It was capable of 70 mph, while delivering up to 40 mpg.

I.D. DATA: Serial number is on the right side of the firewall. Engine number is on the left side of the block.

Model	Body Type & Seating	Engine Type/CID	P.O.E. Price	Weight (lbs.)	Prod. Total
TS	2-dr Sedan-4P	I2/36	1395	1188	N/A
TS	2-dr Conv-4P	I2/36	1510	1188	N/A
TS	2-dr Sta Wag-4P	I2/36	1445	1210	N/A

ENGINE DATA: BASE TWO (Alexander TS): Parallel, overhead-valve two-cylinder (four-cycle). **Displacement:** 36.4 cu. in. (597 cc). **Bore & Stroke:** 3.03 x 2.52 in. (77 x 64 mm). **Compression Ratio:** 7.2:1. **Brake Horsepower:** 29 at 5000 rpm. **Torque:** 28.2 lbs.-ft. at 2500 rpm.

CHASSIS DATA: Same as 1958.

TECHNICAL: Same as 1958, except rear suspension: trailing arms, coil springs and anti-roll bar.

MAJOR OPTIONS: Sunroof.

PERFORMANCE: Top Speed: 70 mph. Fuel Mileage: about 40 mpg.

HISTORY: Introduced September 1, 1958.

1960-61 LLOYD

ALEXANDER TS — TWO — Little changed in the basic Lloyd, except for new bumpers and taillamps.

ARABELLA — FOUR — Joining the original two-cylinder series was a new four-cylinder model, with a squarish, more modern profile rather than the familiar rounded look. Headlamps were slightly shrouded, and stood above a wide mesh-patterned grille that led into wraparound park/signal lamps. A bodyside trim strip dipped downward along the door, reaching a low point just to its rear before rising again to continue to the end of the panel. Canted taillamps brought up the rear. Block lettering spelled out the Lloyd name above the grille. Three different horsepower ratings were offered from the four-cylinder engine.

I.D. DATA: Serial number is on the right side of the firewall. Engine number is on the left side of the block.

Model	Body Type & Seating	Engine Type/CID	P.O.E. Price	Weight (lbs.)	Prod. Total
TS	2-dr Sedan-4P	I2/36	1395	1188	N/A
TS	2-dr Conv-4P	I2/36	1510	1188	N/A
TS	2-dr Sta Wag-4P	I2/36	1445	1210	N/A
Arabella	2-dr Sedan-4P	H4/55	1695	1529	N/A

ENGINE DATA: BASE TWO (Alexander TS): Same as 1959.

BASE FOUR (Arabella): Horizontally-opposed, overhead-valve four-cylinder. Displacement: 54.7 cu. in. (897 cc). Bore & Stroke: 2.72 x 2.36 in. (69 x 60 mm). Compression Ratio: 7.5:1. Brake Horsepower: 44 at 4800 rpm (34/38 bhp also available). Torque: 45 lbs.-ft. at 2500 rpm.

CHASSIS DATA: Wheelbase: (TS) 78.8 in.; (Arabella) 86.6 in. Overall Length: (TS) 132.0 in.; (Arabella) 149.5 in. Height: (TS) 55.8 in.; (Arabella) 54.6 in. Width: (TS) 56.4 in.; (Arabella) 59.5 in. Front Tread: (TS) 41.5 in.; (Arabella) 47.2 in. Rear Tread: (TS) 43.3 in.; (Arabella) 47.2 in. Standard Tires: (TS) 4.25x15; (Arabella) 5.20x13.

TECHNICAL: Layout: front-engine, front-drive. Transmission: four-speed manual (all synchromesh); column shift. Standard Final Drive Ratio: (Arabella) 3.88:1. Steering: (TS) rack and pinion. Suspension (front): (TS) lower transverse semi-elliptic leaf spring, plus auxiliary upper leaf spring; (Arabella) wishbones and coil springs. Suspension (rear): (TS) trailing arms, coil springs and anti-roll bar; (Arabella) trailing wishbones, coil springs and anti-roll bar. Brakes: hydraulic, front/rear drum. Body Construction: steel; central backbone with box-section sills.

MAJOR OPTIONS: Sunroof.

PERFORMANCE: Top Speed: (TS) 70 mph; (Arabella) 75 mph. Fuel Mileage: (TS) about 40 mpg; (Arabella) 35 mpg.

Manufacturer: Lloyd Motoren Werke GmbH, Bremen, West Germany.

Distributor: W.A. Simonds Associates, Long Beach, California; Amsko Distributors Inc., New York City.

HISTORY: Introduced September 15, 1959.

LOTUS

Years before the first Lotus went on sale, Colin Chapman developed his first racing vehicles, using highly-tuned Ford and Austin Seven engines. His first Austin Special was finished in Chapman's garage, early in 1948. By 1949, his Mark 2 racer, powered by a Ford Ten engine, was performing well in hillclimbs and speed trials. At the time, Chapman was serving in the Royal Air Force, but continued to develop racing vehicles. That dual role would continue after his discharge from the Air Force, as he became an engineer for the British Aluminum Company. Not until the start of 1955 would Chapman assume a full-time role in the Lotus firm.

An Austin Seven powerplant went into the Mark 3 of 1951, which had independent front suspension and wore a lightweight aluminum body. Two Mark 3 vehicles were offered for sale. Those were followed by the Mark 4, which was the first to use a space-frame chassis. In 1952, Chapman formed a company, Lotus Engineering Company, with partner Michael Allen. Their first production vehicle was the Mark 6, which went to its customers not fully assembled but in kit form. Riding a multi-tube frame with stressed aluminum panels, it carried Ford running gear including a destroked Consul engine.

Frank Costin joined the company in 1953. By 1954, Lotus had evolved into the Mark 8, which used space-frame construction and a choice of engines: either a 1497-cc MG four, or the 1098-cc FWA Coventry-Climax engine. Chassis features included a De Dion rear end and inboard brakes. As the Mark 8 turned into the Mark 9, the De Dion version took the Le Mans nameplate, while a lower-priced Club model included a Ford gearbox and drum brakes (others had disc brakes installed). This numerical progression of vehicle names would continue over the next decade, reaching the Mark 45 level in 1966. Those double-digit numbers were not always used in describing Lotus vehicles, however.

Lotus displayed its wares at the London Motor Show for the first time in 1955. A Mark 11 (Eleven) replaced the Mark 9 in 1956, a year that was also notable for the debut of the first single-seat Lotus race car. In the next year, the Mark 11 adopted a wishbone-type front suspension. The Mark 12 displayed a new type of suspension, which became known as the Chapman strut—similar to the MacPherson strut that would grow almost standard for small cars many years later. Even more significant was the emergence of the Mark 7 (Seven), which appeared in basic form with a British Ford 100E four-cylinder engine. Some form of the cycle-fendered Seven would be included in the Lotus lineup for the next decade and a half, even after the company had become better known for road cars than racers. Over 3,000 Sevens were produced from 1957 to 1973, nearly all of them in kit form.

As it happened, the prototype for the first roadgoing Lotus, the Elite coupe, appeared at the London Motor Show in 1957. Production began in May 1958, though more time passed before actual examples went on sale. Among other distinctive features, the Elite had unibody construction-- but in fiberglass rather than steel. Beneath its bonnet lurked a 1216-cc Coventry Climax engine and a BMC gearbox. Close to a thousand Elites were produced before the name faded away (temporarily, as it turned out).

Back on the racing scene, Stirling Moss won the 1960 Monaco Grand Prix in a privately-entered Lotus 18. The first Lotus official "factory" victory came a year later, at the U.S. Grand Prix. A Super Seven became available in 1961, with a 1340-cc Coventry Climax engine and disc brakes. Then, in 1962, came the next Lotus for the road: the Elan two-seat roadster. Powered by a twin-cam conversion of the 1588-cc Ford Classic 116E engine, the Elan (which ranked as Mark 26 in the Lotus sequence of events) had disc brakes and retracting headlamps. Its box-section steel backbone chassis branched out at each end to hold the engine and the rear Chapman struts. A fixed-head coupe version debuted in 1965, followed by a Series Two and a +2 version. A mid-engined Europa debuted at the end of 1966, initially powered by a Renault R16 engine; then by a series of twin-cam Lotus fours. In 1971, the Elan +2S 130 took on a 126-horsepower engine.

Those traditional Sevens weren't forgotten as the 1970s began, but by 1973 were manufactured by a different company: Caterham Car Sales of Surrey, England, which acquired the rights from Lotus. During 1974, the Elite name was back on a fiberglass-bodied four-seat model with twin-cam Lotus engine and five-speed gearbox. Options included air conditioning, and even an automatic transmission. Two related models followed: the Eclat 2+2 fastback, and the Esprit. By decade's end, the Elite and Eclat were preparing to fade away, at least in the U.S. market; but the Esprit remained in the Lotus export lineup through the 1980s, with a larger (2.2-liter) powerplant. It even gained a turbocharged engine in 1981, not long before Lo-

tus founder Colin Chapman died. By 1986, Lotus was acquired by General Motors. Then, as the 1990s began, Lotus took a cue from its roots, issuing a modern version of the old Elan, with front-wheel-drive drive this time around.

Lotus Model/Series Number Note: Through the early Lotus years, each model had a specific number, starting with Mark 1 and progressing one digit upward at a time. With a few exceptions, however, those numbers were not always used in descriptions or discussions of Lotus cars produced after the Mark 11 (more commonly referred to as the "Eleven"). Even when those numbers were used, the "Mark" prefix often was omitted.

Series numbers were sometimes given with Roman numerals (I, II, etc.) but more often as ordinary digits (S1, S2, etc.). The latter form is used in this Catalog.

1956 Lotus sports racer.

1957 LOTUS

SEVEN — S1 — FOUR — Comforts and conveniences weren't among the extras offered by the first serious production Lotus sports car, which debuted in kit form rather than fully assembled (partly to sidestep the purchase tax in Britain). Later examples came either way. Many considered the spartan Seven a supreme example of the "pure," no-frills sports car--utterly precise in handling and cornering, thus perfect for low-budget racing as well as occasional sport motoring on the road. Colin Chapman was responsible for the design of the lightweight body, with its cycle fenders, free-standing headlamps, tiny cockpit, and upright fold-flat windshield. Most bodies were fashioned of light alloy, atop a multi-tubular space frame. The basic powertrain was an 1172-cc Ford 100E L-head four, hooked to a three-speed manual gearbox. A modified Aquaplane cylinder head was optional, as were dual SU carburetors. Burman worm-and-nut steering was used on the first few dozen examples, after which rack-and-pinion steering became standard. A wide selection of engines (mostly British Ford) eventually became available: old-fashioned L-head, overhead-valve, even twin-cam. Displacements ranged from about 1000 to 1588 cc, horsepowers from 40 to 125 bhp. Austerity also extended to the standard equipment list, as even side curtains and a soft top were optional. Series 1 debuted in 1957 and remained in production until August 1960. See next listing for details on the Super Seven, with Coventry Climax engine; and the Seven America (for export).

ELEVEN — FOUR — Going even farther along the competition scale was the Lotus Eleven (XI), an evolution of the prior Mark 1 through Mark 9 racing cars. Four distinct versions of the open two-seater were available in 1957: the Le Mans 75 and Club, with a twin-cam 66.9-cid engine rated 75 or 83 horsepower; the Le Mans 100, with a 100-bhp, 89.2-cid engine; and the Sports, carrying an 1172-cc L-head four rated as low as 36 bhp. The Le Mans 100 included a wraparound windshield and head fairing; the Club and Sports had a fixed windshield.

I.D. DATA: Chassis serial number for Seven is on a plate on the foot box. Engine number is on the side of the upper block. Serial number range (Seven): 400-499 and 750-892.

Model	Body Type & Seating	Engine Type/CID	P.O.E. Price	Weight (lbs.)	Prod. Total
SEVEN					
S1	2-dr Rds-2P	I4/72	N/A	1655	Note 1
ELEVEN (Competition)					
Sports	2-dr Rds-2P	I4/72	2880	868	N/A
Club	2-dr Rds-2P	I4/67	3665	812	N/A
Le Mans 75	2-dr Rds-2P	I4/67	N/A	854	N/A
Le Mans 100	2-dr Rds-2P	I4/89	4550	854	N/A

Note 1: Approximately 242 S1 Sevens were produced from 1957-60.
Weight Note: Figure shown is average.

ENGINE DATA: BASE FOUR (Seven S1, Eleven Sports): Inline, L-head (side-valve) four-cylinder (British Ford 100E). Cast iron block. **Displacement:** 71.55 cu. in. (1172 cc). **Bore & Stroke:** 2.50 x 3.64 in. (63.5 x 92.5 mm). **Compression Ratio:** 8.5:1. **Brake Horsepower:** 36/40 at 4500 rpm. Three main bearings. Solid valve lifters. Zenith or Solex carburetor.

Note: Some sources give engine ratings as low as 28 bhp at 4500 rpm, with 53 lbs.-ft. of torque at 2500 rpm, for the first Sevens with 100E engine. Sevens soon became available with a wide variety of engine sizes and horsepower ratings; see later listings.
BASE FOUR (Eleven Le Mans 75, Club): Inline, overhead-cam four-cylinder. **Displacement:** 66.9 cu. in. (1097 cc). **Bore & Stroke:** 2.85 x 2.63 in. (72 x 67 mm). **Compression Ratio:** 9.8:1. **Brake Horsepower:** 75 at 6350 rpm (Stage II, 83 at 6800). **Torque:** 68 lbs.-ft. at 5000 rpm. Solid valve lifters.
BASE FOUR (Eleven Le Mans 100): Inline, overhead-cam four-cylinder. **Displacement:** 89.2 cu. in. (1462 cc). **Bore & Stroke:** 3.00 x 3.15 in. (76 x 80 mm). **Compression Ratio:** 8.6:1. **Brake Horsepower:** 100 at 6200 rpm. **Torque:** 92 lbs.-ft. at 4400 rpm. Solid valve lifters.
CHASSIS DATA: Wheelbase: (Seven) 88.0 in.; (Eleven) 85 in. **Overall Length:** 123.0 in. **Height:** (Seven) 28 in.; (Eleven Club) 47 in.; (Eleven Le Mans) 37 in. **Width:** (Seven) 53 in. Max. Tread: (Seven) 47 in.; (Eleven) 47 in. **Standard Tires:** (Seven) 4.50/5.20x15.
TECHNICAL: Layout: front-engine, rear-drive. **Transmission:** (Seven, Sports) three-speed manual; (Eleven Club/Le Mans) four-speed manual. **Steering:** (early Seven) Burman worm and nut; (later Seven) rack and pinion. **Suspension (front):** lower wishbones with coil spring/shock and anti-roll bar. **Suspension (rear):** rigid axle with coil springs, Panhard rod and trailing arms. **Brakes:** front/rear drum except (Club) disc. **Body Construction:** light alloy body panels on tubular space frame.
MAJOR OPTIONS: (Seven) Soft top. Side curtains. Tonneau cover. Twin carburetors. Aquaplane cylinder head. Windshield wiper. Hubcaps. Spare wheel.
PERFORMANCE: Top Speed: (Seven) 81-90 mph; (Eleven Club) 120 mph; (Eleven Sports) 105 mph; (Eleven Le Mans) 145 mph; (Eleven Le Mans 100) 165 mph. **Acceleration (0-60 mph):** (Seven) about 17.8 sec. **Acceleration (quarter-mile):** (Seven) about 20.8 sec.
Manufacturer: Lotus Engineering Co. Ltd., Hornsey, London, England.
Distributor: Jay Chamberlain Lotus Cars, Burbank, California.
HISTORY: Production of the new roadgoing Elite coupe began in April 1958; see next listing for details. Information on the prototype Elite was issued at the Earls Court (London) Motor Show in October 1957.

1958-61 LOTUS

1958 Lotus Type 17. (Coys of Kensington)

SEVEN — S1 — FOUR — Production of the original cycle-fendered Seven continued with minimal change, joined by a Super Seven and Seven America. The basic 1172-cc (71.55-cc) L-head (side-valve) four produced 36/40 horsepower in home-market form, or as much as 45 horsepower at 4500 rpm for export, to a three-speed manual gearbox. The Super Seven carried an 1098-cc Coventry Climax FWA engine and four-speed gearbox, and included a tachometer and knock-on wire wheels. Sevens had a multi-tube space frame and the same front suspension as the Eleven racer. The "America" (export) model Seven had long sweeping front fenders rather than the original "cycle" units, a design that would later become standard on all models. It also came with a 948-cc BMC A-type engine and gearbox. Export versions also included various equipment that was optional on home-market models, including a spare wheel, hubcaps, windshield wiper, tachometer, side curtains, and top. See 1957 listing for additional details on early Sevens.

SEVEN — S2 — FOUR — The second-series Seven debuted in October 1960 and would remain in production into mid-1968. Powerplants included the initial 1172-cc L-head Ford four, as well as BMC 948- and 1098-cc engines. The revised chassis weighed less than its predecessor and used a smaller number of tubes. Body panels and fenders were now made of fiberglass, and the Seven displayed a modified nose. Full-length front fenders were now available, and commonly installed, to replace the initial "cycle" units. Standard equipment now included windshield wipers and a spare wheel, but side curtains remained optional. For roadgoing comfort, a heater also was optional. Both left- and right-hand drive was available in this series, whereas early models were all RHD. Wire wheels no longer were offered.

Two additional engines became available by 1961: a 997-cc Ford Anglia 105E, and Ford Classic 109E (in Super Seven Cosworth). The "America" designation was dropped after 1960, replaced by a Seven A. An all-synchro four-speed gearbox was standard with the 105E engine, which came with SU or Weber carburetors. The 109E version was much larger in displacement (1340 cc) than its British-Ford counterpart and used a Cosworth-modified cylinder head, camshaft and exhaust manifold. With twin Webers carburetors, the engine produced 80 horsepower on 9.5:1 compression. For U.S. racing, even higher compression was available.

ELITE — FOUR — The prototype of the first real "road" Lotus debuted at the Earls Court Motor Show in October 1957. Approximately 988 Elites were produced from 1959-63. While fiberglass body construction was hardly unheard of, the Elite's all-fiberglass integral (monocoque) body/chassis was unique in the industry. The two-seat coupe used virtually no steel body reinforcement, relying wholly on glass-reinforced epoxide and polyester resin. Lotus literature claimed the 'glass would give "exceptional strength, very good impact resistance, first class sound damping and good thermal insulation." It was also remarkably light in weight. The center tunnel and body sills were used as box-section structural members. Tubular steel reinforcement built into cowl extended up-

ward to form the windshield posts. Two light steel reinforcements connected the engine and suspension mounting points, and a transverse tube connected top front strut mountings.

Elite styling features included a hood that sloped downward between the headlamps, low oval air intake, mild wraparound windshield (and curved back window), front vent wings, hinged quarter windows, separate luggage compartment, and cut-off tail. Door glass was fixed (non-movable), an impractical feature that would later be changed. Prior to that time, the windows either had to be removed completely or remain firmly in place. Doors lacked outside handles. The Elite was offered in "several attractive standard colour schemes," typically sold in kit form. Standard equipment included a four-inch, 8000-rpm tachometer and matching 140-mph speedometer. The chassis contained an all-independent suspension and all-disc brakes (inboard at the rear). Coil springs were used in front, with an anti-roll bar. The Series 1 Elite had a MacPherson-style rear suspension (which Lotus called a Chapman strut, named for the company's founder), with "double articulated driveshaft giving also lateral location." Beneath the sloped bonnet lay an all-aluminum 1216-cc overhead-cam, Coventry Climax four, offered in various states of tune starting at 71 horsepower and progressing as high as 105 bhp. A BMC (B-type) four-speed manual gearbox was installed, with a short gearshift lever directly above the selector forks (no remote linkage). A built-in ventilation system used vents above the rear window. Top speeds approached 120 mph. Wheelbase was 88 inches, and an Elite measured 148 inches overall.

Starting at mid-year 1959, the interior protrusion of rear coil springs was capped rather than faired. Series 2 (introduced in 1960) turned to modified lower wishbones at the rear, and substituted a ZF four-speed gearbox for the original BMC unit. Late in 1960, a Special Equipment model became available. This handful of late "Super 95" and "Super 105" versions had more power than the original Elites.

1961 Lotus Elite. (Coys of Kensington)

I.D. DATA: Chassis serial number for Seven is on a plate on the foot box. Elite chassis number is on a plate on the bulkhead. Engine number for the Seven is on the side of the upper block. Starting chassis number: (1958 Elite) 1020. Serial number range: (Seven S2) 1004-2101.

Model	Body Type & Seating	Engine Type/CID	P.O.E. Price	Weight (lbs.)	Prod. Total
SEVEN (S1)					
	2-dr Rds-2P	I4/72	N/A	725	Note 1
America	2-dr Rds-2P	I4/58	N/A	832	Note 1
Super	2-dr Rds-2P	I4/67	N/A	N/A	Note 1
SEVEN (S2)					
	2-dr Rds-2P	I4/72	N/A	N/A	Note 2
America	2-dr Rds-2P	I4/61	N/A	N/A	Note 2
Super	2-dr Rds-2P	I4/67	N/A	N/A	Note 2
ELITE					
S1	2-dr Coupe-2P	I4/74	4108	1204	Note 3

Note 1: Approximately 242 S1 Sevens were produced from 1957-60.

Note 2: As many as 1,370 S2 Sevens were produced from 1960-68. After that, 350 S3 and 1,000 S4 Sevens were produced through 1973, as well as more than 850 S3 versions with Caterham engine.

Note 3: Approximately 988 Elites were produced from 1958-63.

Elite Price Note: Figure shown was valid in 1960-61. Early U.S. price was about $4780; price at factory was about $3640.

Elite Weight Note: Figure shown was announced for early models. Later Elites weighed as much as 1460 pounds.

ENGINE DATA: BASE FOUR (Seven): Inline, overhead-valve four-cylinder (British Ford 100E). Cast iron block and head. **Displacement:** 71.55 cu. in. (1172 cc). **Bore & Stroke:** 2.50 x 3.63 in. (63.5 x 92.5 mm). **Compression Ratio:** 7.0:1 (8.5:1 for export). **Brake Horsepower:** 36/40 at 4500 rpm (45 at 4500 rpm for export). **Torque:** 52 lbs.-ft. at 2500 rpm. Three main bearings. Solid valve lifters. One Solex or Zenith carburetor (export, two SU carburetors).

BASE FOUR (Super Seven): Inline, overhead-cam four-cylinder (Coventry Climax). **Displacement:** 66.9 cu. in. (1098 cc). **Bore & Stroke:** 2.85 x 2.63 in. (72 x 67 mm). **Compression Ratio:** 9.8:1. **Brake Horsepower:** 75 at 6250 rpm. **Torque:** 65 lbs.-ft. at 4000 rpm. Solid valve lifters. Two SU carburetors.

BASE FOUR (Seven America): Inline, overhead-valve four-cylinder (BMC A-type). **Displacement:** 57.8 cu. in. (948 cc). **Bore & Stroke:** 2.48 x 3.00 in. (62.9 x 76.2 mm). **Compression Ratio:** 8.9:1. **Brake Horsepower:** 37 at 4800 rpm. **Torque:** 50 lbs.-ft. at 2500 rpm. Solid valve lifters. SU carburetor.

BASE FOUR (1961 Seven A): Inline, overhead-valve four-cylinder (British Ford Anglia 105E). Cast iron block and head. **Displacement:** 60.8 cu. in. (997 cc). **Bore & Stroke:** 3.19 x 1.91 in. (81 x 48.4 mm). **Compression Ratio:** 8.9:1. **Brake Horsepower:** 39 at 5000 rpm. **Torque:** 52 lbs.-ft. at 2700 rpm. Three main bearings. Solid valve lifters. Two SU carburetors.

BASE FOUR (1961 Super Seven Cosworth 109E): Inline, overhead-valve four-cylinder (Cosworth-modified British Ford 109E). **Displacement:** 81.7 cu. in. (1340 cc). **Bore & Stroke:** 3.19 x 2.56 in. (81 x 65 mm). **Compression Ratio:** 9.5:1. **Brake Horsepower:** 80 at 5800 rpm. **Torque:** 80 lbs.-ft. at 4000 rpm. Solid valve lifters. Two Weber 40DCOE carburetors.

BASE FOUR (Elite): Inline, overhead-cam four-cylinder (Coventry Climax FWE). Aluminum block and head. **Displacement:** 74.2 cu. in. (1216 cc). **Bore & Stroke:** 3.00 x 2.62 in. (76.2 x 66.6 mm). **Compression Ratio:** 8.5:1. **Brake Horsepower:** 71 DIN (75 SAE) at 6100 rpm. **Torque:** 77 lbs.-ft. at 3750 rpm (82 lbs.-ft. SAE at 4900 rpm). Three main bearings. Solid valve lifters. Two SU carburetors.

BASE FOUR (Elite Series 2): Same as 1216-cc four above, except — **Compression Ratio:** 10.0:1. **Brake Horsepower:** 83 (DIN) at 6250 rpm. **Torque:** 75 lbs.-ft. at 4750 rpm. Two SU carburetors.

Elite Engine Note: Higher horsepower ratings also were available in final years (95 or 105 bhp). Horsepower of later standard Elites was announced as 80 at 6100 rpm.

CHASSIS DATA: Wheelbase: (Seven) 88.0 in.; (Elite) 88.2 in. **Overall Length:** (Seven) 123 in.; (Elite) 148 in. **Height:** (Seven) 28 in.; (Elite) 46 in. **Width:** (Seven) 53 in.; (Elite) 58 in. **Front Tread:** (Seven) 47 in.; (Elite) 47 in. **Rear Tread:** (Seven) 47 in.; (Elite) 47 in. **Wheel Type:** (Elite I) knock-on wire. **Standard Tires:** (Seven) 4.50/5.20x15; (Super Seven) 4.50/5.00x15; (Elite) 4.80/4.90x15.

TECHNICAL: Layout: front-engine, rear-drive. **Transmission:** (Seven) three-speed manual; (Super Seven, Elite) four-speed manual. Standard Elite S1 gear ratios: (1st) 3.67:1; (2nd) 2.20:1; (3rd) 1.32:1; (4th) 1.00:1. **Standard Final Drive Ratio:** (Elite S1) 4.55:1 (3.73:1, 3.89:1, 4.22:1, 4.89:1 and 5.125:1 available). **Steering:** rack and pinion. **Suspension (front):** (Seven) lower wishbones, coil spring/shocks and anti-roll bar; (Elite) upper/lower A-arms with coil springs and anti-roll bar. **Suspension (rear):** (Seven) rigid axle with coil springs and trailing arms; (Elite S1) Chapman struts with trailing arms and coil springs; (Elite S2) Chapman struts with double articulated driveshafts and trailing links. **Brakes:** (Seven) front/rear drum; (Elite) front/rear disc (inboard rear). **Body Construction:** (Seven) light alloy/fiberglass body on multi-tube steel frame; (Elite) fiberglass monocoque.

MAJOR OPTIONS: Soft top (Seven). Side curtains (Seven). Tonneau cover (Seven S1). Windshield wiper (Seven S1). Spare wheel (Seven S1). Hubcaps (Seven S1). Heater/demister (Elite). Seatbelts. Quick-release fuel filler cap (Elite). Full race specifications (Elite).

PERFORMANCE: Top Speed: (Seven) up to 90 mph; (Super Seven) near 105 mph; (Elite) 115 mph claimed; (Elite w/83-bhp) 118+ mph. **Acceleration (0-60 mph):** (Seven w/948-cc) about 14.2 sec.; (Super Seven) about 8.3 sec.; (Super Seven Cosworth) about 7.6 sec.; (Elite) 11.8 sec. or less w/83-hp engine (11.1 sec. claimed). **Acceleration (quarter-mile):** (Seven w/948-cc) about 19.1 sec.; (Super Seven) about 16.1 sec.; (Super Seven Cosworth) about 15.8 sec.; **Fuel Mileage:** (Seven) 40-50 mpg; (Seven export) 40 mpg.

ADDITIONAL MODELS: Racing Lotus Elevens also continued in production, in series 75 and 85, as well as Le Mans, Sports and Club editions. Their 66.9-cid (1097-cc) overhead-cam engines produced 85 horsepower at 6800 rpm, for top speeds of 130-135 mph. See previous listing for additional details on the Eleven. Lotus also produced a Fifteen series for competition, with twin-cam 90-cid engine producing 150 bhp at 7200 rpm and 110-lbs.-ft. of torque at 6500 rpm, using 10:1 compression. Top speeds as high as 180 mph were reported. A less-expensive Series 2 version for export used a four-speed gearbox in unit with the engine, and a ZF limited-slip differential.

Manufacturer: Lotus Engineering Co. Ltd., Hornsey, London, England; then Lotus Cars Ltd., Cheshunt, Herts., England.

Distributor: Jay Chamberlain Lotus Cars, Burbank or North Hollywood, California.

HISTORY: The Elite coupe was advertised as the "Brilliant new offspring of the mighty Lotus racers." Literature advised that an Elite kit "is assembled in just twenty-four hours with normal hand tools--simply bolt it together!"

1962-66 LOTUS

1962 Lotus Elite coupe.

SEVEN — S2 — FOUR — Production of the original Seven, now with full-length fenders, continued with minimal change; see prior listings for full details. The Super Seven, as promoted in the U.S., carried a Cosworth-modified 1340-cc (81.8-cid) engine with 9.5:1 compression that produced 85 horsepower at 6000 rpm. In addition to the engines offered earlier, a 1498-cc British Ford 116E Cortina four became available in the Super Seven 1500, as did a Cosworth-modified version of that larger-displacement powerplant.

ELITE — S1/S2 — FOUR — Production of the Elite two-seat coupe, in two series, continued into 1963; see previous listing for full details.

ELAN — S1/S2/S3 (Lotus Type 26/36/45) — FOUR — The next roadgoing Lotus was also the first to use a folded-steel "backbone" chassis below its fiberglass body. Both a two-seat roadster (convertible) and coupe were produced, in four series, from 1962 to 1973. The convertible came first, followed by a fixed-head coupe in September 1965. A hardtop was optional for the convertible soon after its debut. Output of the initial twin-cam 1558-cc (95-cid) Lotus-Ford engine was 105 horsepower at 5500 rpm, with 108 pound-feet of torque developed, using twin-choke Weber carburetors. That engine was employed into 1967, consisting of a British Ford block with Lotus-designed twin-cam aluminum head (also used in the Lotus Cortina). A four-speed manual gearbox was standard. At chassis level was fully independent suspension: unequal-length A-arms with coil springs and anti-roll bar up front, and Chapman struts with lower A-arms and coil springs bringing up the rear. Wheelbase was 84 inches, and an Elan measured 145 inches overall. Rack-and-pinion steering was installed, along with all-disc brakes. Styling features included pop-up (hidden) headlamps, a curved windshield and coupe back window, roll-up side windows, and slim bumpers. Early convertibles were fully open, but fixed window frames were added in 1966. Like other Lotuses, the Elan came in both kit and fully-assembled form. For a short time in the Elan's lifespan, special black/gold paint was available.

Elan's Series 2 (Lotus number 26) came in late 1964; the series 3 fixed-head coupe (Lotus 36), late in 1965. A Series 3 convertible (Lotus 45) arrived later, in mid-1966. Series 2 Elans added chrome gauge bezels, a full-width dashboard with locking glovebox, quick-release gas cap, 3.07:1 final-drive ratio, and new oval taillamps. The battery moved to the trunk, and center-lock wheels became optional. Series 3 Elans came with standard power windows (and window frames) and a new trunk lid. They could also get an optional 3.55:1 axle ratio. Early in 1966, a Special Equipment Elan also became available.

1965 Lotus Elan convertible. (Coys of Kensington)

I.D. DATA: Starting chassis serial number: (Elan) 26/0001; (Elan Series 2) 26/3901; (Elan Series 3 coupe) 36/4510; (Elan Series 3 conv) 45/5702.

Model	Body Type & Seating	Engine Type/CID	P.O.E. Price	Weight (lbs.)	Prod. Total
SEVEN (S2)					
A	2-dr Rds-2P	I4/61	2995	N/A	Note 1
Super	2-dr Rds-2P	I4/82	3445	950	Note 1
Super 1500	2-dr Rds-2P	I4/91	N/A	N/A	Note 1
ELITE					
S1	2-dr Coupe-2P	I4/74	N/A	1204	Note 2
S2	2-dr Coupe-2P	I4/74	4995	1260	Note 2
ELAN					
S1	2-dr Coupe-2P	I4/95	N/A	1515	Note 3
S1	2-dr Conv-2P	I4/95	4194	1515	Note 3
S2	2-dr Coupe-2P	I4/95	4206	N/A	Note 3
S2	2-dr Conv-2P	I4/95	N/A	N/A	Note 3
S3	2-dr Coupe-2P	I4/95	N/A	N/A	Note 3
S3	2-dr Conv-2P	I4/95	N/A	N/A	Note 3

Note 1: A total of 1,350 S2 Sevens were produced from 1960-68. After that came 350 S3 and 1,000 S4 Sevens; plus more than 850 S3 versions with Caterham engine.

Note 2: Approximately 988 Elites were produced from 1959-63.

Note 3: As many as 12,224 Elans were produced from 1962-73 (some sources report totals as low as 9,659 units).

Price Note: Seven, Elite and Elan S1 roadster prices shown were valid in 1964; Elan S2 price shown was valid in 1966. The Elite S2 sold for $4780 in 1963.

Weight Note: Some U.S. sources give Elite weights as 1460 pounds, and Elan weights as low as 1290 pounds. An American road test listed Elan weights as 1420 pounds dry, 1485 pounds curb.

ENGINE DATA: BASE FOUR (Seven A): Inline, overhead-valve four-cylinder (British Ford Anglia 105E). Cast iron block and head. **Displacement:** 60.8 cu. in. (997 cc). **Bore & Stroke:** 3.19 x 1.91 in. (81 x 48.4 mm). **Compression Ratio:** 8.9:1. **Brake Horsepower:** 39 at 5000 rpm. **Torque:** 52 lbs.-ft. at 2700 rpm. Three main bearings. Solid valve lifters. Two SU carburetors.

BASE FOUR (Super Seven): Inline, overhead-valve four-cylinder (Cosworth Ford 109E). **Displacement:** 81.8 cu. in. (1340 cc). **Bore & Stroke:** 3.19 x 2.56 in. (81 x 65 mm). **Compression Ratio:** 9.5:1. **Brake Horsepower:** 85 at 6000 rpm. **Torque:** 80 lbs.-ft. at 4800 rpm. Solid valve lifters. Two Weber carburetors.

BASE FOUR (Super Seven 1500): Inline, overhead-valve four-cylinder (British Ford Cortina 116E). **Displacement:** 91.4 cu. in. (1498 cc). **Bore & Stroke:** 3.19 x 2.86 in. (81 x 72.7 mm). **Compression Ratio:** 8.3:1. **Brake Horsepower:** 66 at 4600 rpm. **Torque:** 78 lbs.-ft. at 2300 rpm. Five main bearings. Solid valve lifters. Weber carburetor.

Note: A Cosworth-modified version of the Cortina 116E engine, with two Weber carburetors, produced 95 bhp at 6000 rpm and 95 lbs.-ft. at 4500 rpm, on 9.5:1 compression.

BASE FOUR (Elite): Inline, overhead-cam four-cylinder (Coventry Climax). Aluminum block and head. **Displacement:** 74.2 cu. in. (1216 cc). **Bore & Stroke:** 3.00 x 2.62 in. (76.2 x 66.6 mm). **Compression Ratio:** 10.0:1. **Brake Horsepower:** 75/80 at 6100 rpm. **Torque:** 72/75 lbs.-ft. at 3400/4750 rpm. Three main bearings. Solid valve lifters. Two SU carburetors.

Elite Engine Note: Higher horsepower ratings were available (83, 95 or 105 bhp).

BASE FOUR (Elan): Inline, dual-overhead-cam four-cylinder (Lotus-Ford). Cast iron block and aluminum alloy head. **Displacement:** 95.1 cu. in. (1558 cc). **Bore & Stroke:** 3.25 x 2.86 in. (82.55 x 72.75 mm). **Compression Ratio:** 9.5:1. **Brake Horsepower:** 105 at 5500 rpm. **Torque:** 108 lbs.-ft. at 4000 rpm. Five main bearings. Solid valve lifters. Two twin-choke Weber 40DCOE sidedraft carburetors.

Elan Engine Note: A small number of early Elans (about 22) came with a 1498-cc engine rated 100 bhp, before Lotus switched to the 1558-cc powerplant. The Elan Special Equipment engine produced 115 bhp at 6000 rpm.

CHASSIS DATA: Wheelbase: (Seven) 88.0 in.; (Elite) 88.0 in.; (Elan) 84.0 in. **Overall Length:** (Seven) 132.0 in.; (Super Seven) 144 in.; (Elite) 148.0 in.; (Elan) 145.25 in. **Height:** (Seven) 44.7 in.; (Super Seven) 43.7 in.; (Elite) 46 in.; (Elan) 45 in. **Width:** (Seven) 55 in.; (Super Seven) 56 in.; (Elite) 58 in.; (Elan) 56 in. **Front Tread:** (Seven) 47 in.; (Elite) 47 in.; (Elan) 47 in. **Rear Tread:** (Seven) 47/48 in.; (Elite) 47 in.; (Elan) 47/48 in. **Wheel Type:** (Elan) bolt-on steel (knock-on optional on S2/S3). **Standard Tires:** (Seven) 5.20x13; (Elite) 4.80x15; (Elan) 5.20x13 or 145x13.

TECHNICAL: Layout: front-engine, rear-drive. **Transmission:** four-speed manual. Elan gear ratios: (1st) 2.971:1; (2nd) 2.009:1; (3rd) 1.395:1; (4th) 1.00:1. Elan close-ratio gears: (1st) 2.51:1; (2nd) 1.635:1; (3rd) 1.23:1; (4th) 1.00:1. **Standard Final Drive Ratio:** (Super Seven) 4.11:1; (Elite) 4.55:1; (Elan) 3.99:1. **Steering:** rack and pinion. **Suspension (front):** (Seven) lower wishbones with coil springs/shocks and anti-roll bar; (Elite) coil springs/shocks with transverse wishbones incorporating anti-roll bar; (Elan) unequal-length A-arms with coil springs and anti-roll bar. **Suspension (rear):** (Seven) rigid axle with coil springs; (Elite S1) Chapman struts with coil springs; (Elite S2) Chapman struts with double articulated driveshafts and trailing links. (Elan) Chapman struts with coil springs and tubular lower A-arms. **Brakes:** (Seven) front/rear drum; (Elite) front/rear disc (inboard rear); (Elan) Girling front/rear disc. **Body Construction:** (Seven) light alloy/fiberglass body on tubular steel frame; (Elite) fiberglass monocoque; (Elan) fiberglass body on box-section "backbone" chassis with extensions at each end.

MAJOR OPTIONS: Soft top (Seven). Side curtains (Seven). ZF four-speed synchro gearbox (Elite).

PERFORMANCE: Top Speed: (Super Seven 1500) near 103 mph; (Elite) 120 mph claimed; (Elan) 112-120 mph. **Acceleration (0-60 mph):** (Super Seven 1500) about 7.7 sec.; (Elan) 7.1 to 9.0 sec.; (Elan S2) 7.5 sec. **Acceleration (quarter-mile):** (Super Seven 1500) about 15.9 sec.; (Elan) 15.7 sec. (87 mph); (Elan S2) 15.9 sec. (87.5 mph).

Manufacturer: Lotus Cars Ltd., Cheshunt, Herts., England.
Distributor: Cox & Pulver Inc., New York City; or Dutchess Auto Co., New York City.

HISTORY: The Elan first appeared in October 1962 and was available in 1963. "Lotus cars are built for drivers who work at it," declared a 1963 U.S. ad for the Elite, described as "a car meant to be driven and driven well." *Car and Driver* advised readers that the "Elan's well-bred manners come from an ultra-soft, all-independent suspension with lots of wheel travel," adding that it qualified as "a boulevardier's car." They ranked it far different from the Elite, which was considered as "noisy as the boiler room of a tramp steamer." Lotus gained a certain measure of publicity when actress Diana Rigg drove an Elan in her role as Mrs. Peel on The Avengers TV series.

1967-68 LOTUS

SEVEN — S2 — FOUR — Production of the Series 2 Seven and Super Seven continued with minimal change into 1968; see 1957-66 listings for full details. Series 3 debuted in 1968, with some technical modifications and new engine selections; see next (1969-70) listing for details.

ELAN — S3/S4 — FOUR — Production of the Elan convertible and coupe continued into 1971, in S3 and S4 series, before giving way to the "Big-Valve" Sprint edition. Series 4 Elans debuted in early spring 1968, wearing slightly flared wheel openings and larger (155x13) tires. They also had new taillamps and a power bulge atop the hood. European Elans eventually switched from twin-choke Weber carburetors to Dell'orto units. "Federalized" U.S. versions, starting in the late 1960s, came with twin Zenith-Stromberg carburetors.

ELAN +2 — FOUR — A longer-wheelbase Elan +2 (also known as Plus Two, or Plus 2) emerged in 1967, with standard 115/118-hp "Special Equipment" engine. As the name suggested, this was ostensibly a 2+2 coupe rather than a two-seater, riding a 96-inch wheelbase (versus 84 inches for the two-seat Elan). Space for those extra two passengers was minimal, but the +2 carried better trim and more equipment than its two-seat counterpart. Unlike the two-seat Elan, the +2 never was sold in kit form.

EUROPA — SERIES 1 (Type 46) — FOUR — Lotus turned to a mid-engine layout with the Europa, which was introduced late in 1966 and went on sale early in the following year. All Series 1 versions, in fact, were sold outside England, Lotus having agreed to limit sales to continental Europe for the first two years of the car's life. Europas appeared officially in the U.S. market, late in 1969. The Europa drivetrain came from the front-drive Renault 16, with its aluminum-alloy engine rotated 180 degrees in this installation, to mount behind the two-seat cockpit. Wheelbase of the rectangular steel "backbone" chassis was 92 inches, and an Europa measured about 157 inches long overall. The fiberglass body was permanently bonded to the frame, and displayed tall, wide sail panels (like vertical fins) to the rear of the doors, giving the early models a rather bizarre rear-quarter profile. Its front end was similar to the Elite, with low nose, small oval air intake, and exposed headlamps in recessed scoops. Those tall rear quarters made the coupe look almost like a small van; hence the nickname, "breadvan." The strange appearance was accented by the squat rear window, which appeared to be little more than a horizontal slit. Later examples would wear lower sail panels, but an Europa still vaguely resembled a tiny pickup truck (though visibility was much improved). Door windows were fixed (non-movable), and seats were non-adjustable. A removable flat cover sat above the engine. The overhead-valve 1470-cc Renault four produced 78 horsepower. The Renault four-speed gearbox was positioned in the rear transaxle. American versions, with a larger 1565-cc engine, were rated 87.5 bhp (SAE). Front disc (rear drum) brakes were installed, along with rack-and-pinion steering that included a telescopic column. At the rear suspension, the driveshafts formed upper and lower links. Europas came either fully assembled or in kit form, like most early Lotus models.

I.D. DATA: Serial number range: (Elan Series 4 coupe) 36/7896 up; (Elan Series 4 conv) 45/7895 up; (Plus 2 coupe) 50/0001 to 50/2407; (U.S. Plus 2 coupe) 50/0857; (Seven) continued from previous listing.

Model	Body Type & Seating	Engine Type/CID	P.O.E. Price	Weight (lbs.)	Prod. Total
SEVEN (S2)					
A	2-dr Rds-2P	I4/61	N/A	N/A	Note 1
Super	2-dr Rds-2P	I4/82	N/A	N/A	Note 1
ELAN					
S3	2-dr Coupe-2P	I4/95	4605	1515	Note 2
S3	2-dr Rds-2P	I4/95	4545	1515	Note 2
S4	2-dr Coupe-2P	I4/95	N/A	1515	Note 2
S4	2-dr Rds-2P	I4/95	N/A	1515	Note 2
ELAN PLUS 2					
+2	2-dr Coupe-2+2P	I4/95	N/A	2085	Note 3
EUROPA					
S1	2-dr Coupe-2P	I4/90	3795	1350	Note 4

Note 1: A total of 1,350 S2 Sevens were produced from 1960-68. After that came 350 S3 and 1,000 S4 Sevens; plus more than 850 S3 versions with Caterham engine.

Note 2: As many as 12,224 Elans were produced from 1962-73 (some sources report totals as low as 9,659 units).

Note 3: Approximately 4,798 Elan +2s were produced from 1967-74 (some sources report totals as low as 3,330 units, or as high as 5,200).

Note 4: A total of 9,230 Europas were produced from 1967-72.

Price Note: Figures shown were valid in 1968.

Weight Note: Elans were listed as weighing as little as 1340 pounds in U.S. directories.

ENGINE DATA: BASE FOUR (Seven S2): Same as 1962-66.

BASE FOUR (Elan S3/S4): Inline, dual-overhead-cam four-cylinder (Lotus). Cast iron block and aluminum alloy head. **Displacement:** 95.1 cu. in. (1558 cc). **Bore & Stroke:** 3.25 x 2.86 in. (82.55 x 72.75 mm). **Compression Ratio:** 9.5:1. **Brake Horsepower:** 105 at 5500/6000 rpm. **Torque:** 108 lbs.-ft. at 4000 rpm. Five main bearings. Solid valve lifters. Two Weber DCOE two-barrel sidedraft carburetors.

Elan Engine Note: U.S. versions used two Zenith-Stromberg carburetors.

BASE FOUR (Elan +2); OPTIONAL (Elan): "Special Equipment" engine was same as 1558-cc four above, except — **Brake Horsepower:** 115/118 at 5500 rpm (125 SAE at 6250 rpm). **Torque:** 112 lbs.-ft. at 4600 rpm.

BASE FOUR (Europa): Inline, overhead-valve four-cylinder (Renault 16). Light alloy block and head. **Displacement:** 89.7 cu. in. (1470 cc). **Bore & Stroke:** 2.99 x 3.19 in. (76 x 81 mm). **Compression Ratio:** 10.25:1. **Brake Horsepower:** 78/82 at 6000 rpm. **Torque:** 76 lbs.-ft. at 4000 rpm. Five main bearings. Solid valve lifters. Solex two-barrel carburetor.

CHASSIS DATA: Wheelbase: (Seven) 88.0 in.; (Elan) 84.0 in.; (Elan +2) 96.0 in.; (Europa) 91.0 in. **Overall Length:** (Seven) 123/132 in.; (Elan) 145.2 in.; (Elan +2) 168.0 in.; (Europa) 157.5 in. **Height:** (Seven) 44.7 in.; (Elan) 45 in.; (Elan +2) 47 in.; (Europa) 42.5 in. **Width:** (Seven) 55 in.; (Elan) 56 in.; (Elan +2) 63.5 in.; (Europa) 64.5 in. **Front Tread:** (Seven) 47 in.; (Elan) 47/48 in.; (Elan +2) 53 in.; (Europa) 53.5 in. **Rear Tread:** (Seven) 47/48 in.; (Elan) 48 in.; (Elan +2) 53 in.; (Europa) 53 in. **Standard Tires:** (Seven) 5.20x13; (Elan) 5.20x13 or 145x13; (Elan +2) 165x13; (Europa) 155x13.

TECHNICAL: Layout: front-engine, rear-drive except (Europa) mid-engine. **Transmission:** four-speed manual. Standard Europa gear ratios: (1st) 3.61:1; (2nd) 2.25:1; (3rd) 1.48:1; (4th) 1.03:1. **Standard Final Drive Ratio:** (U.S. Elan) 3.70:1; (Europa) 3.56:1. **Steering:** rack and pinion. **Suspension (front):** (Seven) lower wishbones with coil spring/shocks and anti-roll bar; (Elan/Europa) unequal-length A-arms with coil springs and anti-roll bar. **Suspension (rear):** (Seven) rigid axle with coil springs; (Elan) Chapman struts with lower A-arms and coil springs; (Europa) lower A-arms with upper lateral links, upper/lower trailing arms, coil springs and anti-roll bar. **Brakes:** (Seven) front/rear drum; (Elan) front/rear disc; (Europa) front disc, rear drum. **Body Construction:** (Seven) light alloy/fiberglass body on steel frame; (Elan) fiberglass body on backbone chassis; (Europa) fiberglass body on steel backbone chassis.

PERFORMANCE: Top Speed: (Elan S2) 112 mph. **Acceleration (0-60 mph):** (Elan S2) 7.5 sec. **Acceleration (quarter-mile):** (Elan S2) 15.9 sec. (87.5 mph).

Performance Note: An Elan S2 was road-tested in the U.S. during this period, even though the S3 already was in production.

Manufacturer: Lotus Cars Ltd., Hethel, Norwich, England.

Distributor: Lotus/East, Salisbury, Connecticut.

HISTORY: "Sophistication is the word for this car," declared the *Car and Driver '67 Yearbook* of the Elan S2, branding it "a purist's dream." While praising the Europa's technical details, *Car Life* noted that "homeliest car in the world" would be a fitting title for the car, which wore "just about as ugly an ill-finished body as could possibly be imagined." At this time, Colin Chapman acquired a larger factory at Hethel (near Norwich).

1969-70 LOTUS

1970 Lotus Elan convertible. (Coys of Kensington)

SEVEN — S3 — FOUR — Series 3 of the Seven sports-racer debuted in 1968 and continued in production into 1970. Exhaust-system mountings were modified, and the systems now extended the full car length. Rear-track width grew, requiring wider rear fenders. Either air-intake louvers or a scoop was installed on S3 hoods. Rocker switches were installed on the instrument panel. An external filler cap now was used for filling the gas tank. Most important, however, was the new crop of engines: Ford Escort 1300-cc, Ford 1600, and the Lotus-Ford 1558-cc Twin-Cam four. The most potent Sevens of this generation (dubbed S or SS) were Holbay-tuned versions of the 1558-cc engine, producing 125 horsepower or more. Series 4 debuted in 1970; see next listing for details.

ELAN — S4 — FOUR — Production of the original Elan continued into 1971, in S4 series. Then, from 1971-73, it would evolve into the Elan Sprint.

ELAN +2/+2S — FOUR — A +2S Elan coupe debuted in March 1969, with an alternator replacing the former DC generator. Otherwise, production continued with minimal change; see previous listing for full details. The 1558-cc four-cylinder engine produced 115 horsepower in the "Special Equipment" form used in the 2+2 model, versus 105 bhp for the regular two-seat Elan.

EUROPA — SERIES 2 — FOUR — Series 2 was announced in 1968 and available by July 1969. (The first version, described in the previous listing, wasn't referred to as Series 1 until later.) Now, the fiberglass body was bolted into position rather than bonded, and electrically-operated windows replaced the former fixed units. The engine cover added a hinge, and luggage space was expanded. The larger 1565-cc Renault engine, as installed in Europas destined for the American market, produced 87 horsepower (SAE). Europas were certified for official sale in the U.S. in late 1969.

I.D. DATA: Starting serial number: (Seven S3) 2102; (Elan Plus 2S) 50/1554. Seven prefix 'SB' or 'SC' indicated Twin Cam engine. Other serial numbers continued from previous listing. A new numbering system went into use in 1970, with numbers starting at 7001-010001. Suffix 'A' indicated the Elan S4 coupe; suffix 'C' was used for the Elan S4 convertible; suffix 'E' identified the Elan S4 Special Equipment (S/E) coupe; suffix 'G' denoted the Elan S4 S/E convertible; and suffix 'L' identified the Elan Plus 2S coupe.

Model	Body Type & Seating	Engine Type/CID	P.O.E. Price	Weight (lbs.)	Prod. Total
SEVEN (S3)					
1300	2-dr Rds-2P	I4/79	N/A	N/A	Note 1
1600	2-dr Rds-2P	I4/97	N/A	N/A	Note 1
Twin Cam	2-dr Rds-2P	I4/95	N/A	N/A	Note 1
ELAN					
S4	2-dr Coupe-2P	I4/95	N/A	1515	Note 2
S4	2-dr Rds-2P	I4/95	4795	1515	Note 2
ELAN PLUS 2					
+2	2-dr Coupe-2+2P	I4/95	5995	2085	Note 3
+2S	2-dr Coupe-2+2P	I4/95	N/A	N/A	Note 3
EUROPA					
S1	2-dr Coupe-2P	I4/90	N/A	1350	Note 4
S2	2-dr Coupe-2P	I4/96	4295	1350	Note 4

Note 1: A total of 350 S3 and 1,000 S4 Sevens were produced from 1968 through 1973, plus more than 850 S3 versions with Caterham engine.

Note 2: As many as 12,224 Elans were produced from 1962-73 (some sources report totals as low as 9,659 units).

Note 3: Approximately 4,798 Elan +2s were produced from 1967-74 (some sources report totals as low as 3,330 units, or as high as 5,200).

Note 4: A total of 9,230 Europas were produced from 1967-72.

Price Note: Figures shown were valid in 1970. A Lotus Seven sports-racer sold in the U.S. for approximately $5500 at this time.

Weight Note: Weight of Elan sold in the U.S. was listed at 1340 pounds; of Europa S2 sold in the U.S., at 1250 pounds.

ENGINE DATA: BASE FOUR (Seven 1300): Inline, overhead-valve four-cylinder (British Ford Escort). Cast iron block and head. **Displacement:** 79.2 cu. in. (1298 cc). **Bore & Stroke:** 3.19 x 2.48 in. (81 x 63 mm). Five main bearings. Solid valve lifters.

BASE FOUR (Seven 1600): Inline, overhead-valve four-cylinder (British Ford 225E). Cast iron block and head. **Displacement:** 97.5 cu. in. (1599 cc). **Bore & Stroke:** 3.19 x 3.05 in. (81 x 77.6 mm). **Compression Ratio:** 9.0:1. **Brake Horsepower:** 84 at 5500 rpm. Five main bearings. Solid valve lifters. Weber downdraft carburetor.

BASE FOUR (Seven Twin Cam): Same as Elan +2 "Special Equipment" engine below, rated 115 hp.

BASE FOUR (Elan S4, Elan +2): Inline, dual-overhead-cam four-cylinder (Lotus). Cast iron block and aluminum-alloy head. **Displacement:** 95 cu. in. (1558 cc). **Bore & Stroke:** 3.27 x 2.87 in. (83 x 73 mm). **Compression Ratio:** 9.5:1. **Brake Horsepower:** 105 at 5500 rpm. **Torque:** 108 lbs.-ft. at 4000 rpm. Five main bearings. Solid valve lifters. Two twin-choke Webers or Dell'orto carburetors (some 1968-69 European versions used Zenith-Stromberg carburetors).

BASE FOUR (Elan +2); **OPTIONAL** (Elan): "Special Equipment" engine was same as 1558-cc four above, except — **Brake Horsepower:** 115/118 at 5500 rpm (125/130 SAE at 6250 rpm). **Torque:** 112 at 4600 rpm.

Note: Elan engines sent to the U.S. used twin Zenith-Stromberg carburetors.

BASE FOUR (Europa): Inline, overhead-valve four-cylinder (Renault). Light alloy block and head. **Displacement:** 90 cu. in. (1470 cc). **Bore & Stroke:** 2.99 x 3.19 in. (76 x 81 mm). **Compression Ratio:** 10.25:1. **Brake Horsepower:** 78/82 at 6000 rpm. **Torque:** 76 lbs.-ft. at 4000 rpm. Five main bearings. Solid valve lifters. Solex two-barrel carburetor.

BASE FOUR (U.S. Europa Series 2): Inline, overhead-valve four-cylinder (Renault 16S). Light alloy iron block and head. **Displacement:** 95.5 cu. in. (1565 cc). **Bore & Stroke:** 3.03 x 3.31 in. (77 x 84 mm). **Compression Ratio:** 10.0:1. **Brake Horsepower:** 87 (SAE) at 6000 rpm. **Torque:** 75 lbs.-ft. at 5500 rpm. Five main bearings. Solid valve lifters.

Note: Some early U.S. Europas were rated 88 bhp (SAE gross) at 5750 rpm, and 87 lbs.-ft. at 3500 rpm.

CHASSIS DATA: Wheelbase: (Seven) 90.0 in.; (Elan) 84.0 in.; (Elan +2) 96.0 in.; (Europa) 91.0 in. **Overall Length:** (Seven) 144.5 in.; (Elan) 145.2 in.; (Elan +2) 168.0 in.; (Europa) 156.5-158 in. **Height:** (Elan) 45 in.; (Elan +2) 47 in.; (Europa) 43 in. **Width:** (Seven) 60.3 in.; (Elan) 56 in.; (Elan +2) 63.5 in.; (Europa) 64.5 in. **Front Tread:** (Elan) 47 in.; (Elan +2) 54 in.; (Europa) 53 in. **Rear Tread:** (Seven) 52.5 in.; (Elan) 48 in.; (Elan +2) 55 in.; (Europa) 53 in. **Standard Tires:** (Seven) 165x13; (Elan) 5.20x13; (Elan +2) 165x13; (Europa) 155x13.

TECHNICAL: Layout: front-engine, rear-drive except (Europa) mid-engine. **Transmission:** four-speed manual. Standard Europa gear ratios: (1st) 3.61:1; (2nd) 2.25:1; (3rd) 1.48:1; (4th) 1.03:1. **Standard Final Drive Ratio:** (U.S. Elan) 3.70:1; (Europa) 3.56:1. Steering: rack and pinion. **Suspension (front):** (Seven) lower wishbones with coil spring/shocks and anti-roll bar; (Elan/Europa) unequal-length A-arms with coil springs and anti-roll bar. **Suspension (rear):** (Seven) rigid axle with coil springs; (Elan) Chapman struts with lower A-arms and coil springs; (Europa) lower A-arms with upper lateral links, upper/lower trailing arms, coil springs and anti-roll bar. **Brakes:** (Elan) front/rear disc; (Seven, Europa) front disc, rear drum. **Body Construction:** (Seven) light alloy/fiberglass body on tubular steel frame; (Elan) fiberglass body on backbone chassis; (Europa) fiberglass body on steel backbone chassis.

Manufacturer: Lotus Cars Ltd., Hethel, Norwich, England.

Distributor: Lotus/East, Salisbury, Connecticut.

1971-75 LOTUS

1972 Lotus Elan Sprint drophead coupe.

SEVEN — S4 — FOUR — Series 4, the final generation of the Lotus Seven (before production was taken over by the Caterham organization) debuted in 1970 and continued into 1973. Bodies were made of fiberglass, atop a tube/ladder chassis with integral steel panels. The hood was hinged at the front, and fixed side windows contained sliding panels. Front suspension was similar to that used in the Europa, with a twin-wishbone anti-roll bar. At the rear was an Escort-type axle with leading and trailing arms. Front disc, rear drum brakes were installed. Powertrains were the same as Series 3, except that no Twin Cam engines were installed in this final series.

ELAN — S4 — FOUR — Production of the original Elan continued into 1971, in S4 series. Then, from 1971-73, it evolved into the Elan Sprint.

ELAN SPRINT — FOUR — A more potent "Big Valve" version of the 1558-cc twin-cam engine, producing 126 horsepower, powered the renamed Elan coupe and convertible.

ELAN +2S 130 — FOUR — Under the hood of this final 2+2 Elan coupe was the same higher-powered engine used in the new Elan Sprint, rated 126 bhp at 6500 rpm. Starting in fall 1972, a five-speed manual gearbox became available. The handful of Elans with this transmission were given the designation '+2S 130/5.'

EUROPA — SERIES 2/3 — FOUR — Production of the Series 2, with 1565-cc four-cylinder engine, continued as late as 1972; see previous listing for full details. The next generation, Series 3 (more often called the Europa Twin Cam) debuted in 1971, carrying the same 105-bhp twin-cam Lotus engine installed in the Elan. Sail panels were lowered a bit, lessening the car's bizarre profile. Top speed also got a boost, reaching about 120 mph. Renault's four-speed transaxle remained standard. New cast alloy wheels were installed. Twin-Cam Europas had a new front spoiler. The tailpipe now exited separately, rather than protruding out the car's back panel.

EUROPA SPECIAL — FOUR — A more powerful version of the Europa emerged late in 1972, carrying a 126-bhp version of the Lotus twin-cam 1558-cc engine (as in the Elan Sprint). A five-speed gearbox was optional (standard in final examples). Top speed on this version went past 125 mph.

1972 Lotus Plus 2S 130 coupe.

I.D. DATA: Serial number plate is atop the instrument panel, visible through the windshield; and on inner edge of left door, or vertical door sill. The six-digit number begins with two digits to identify model year, followed by a four-digit sequential serial number and a suffix to identify model ('J' or 'K' = Elan; 'N' = Plus 2; 'R' = Europa). See 1969-70 listing for additional details.

Model	Body Type & Seating	Engine Type/CID	P.O.E. Price	Weight (lbs.)	Prod. Total
SEVEN (S4)					
1300	2-dr Rds-2P	I4/79	N/A	1310	Note 1
1600	2-dr Rds-2P	I4/97	N/A	N/A	Note 1
ELAN					
S4	2-dr Coupe-2P	I4/95	4895	1515	Note 2
S4	2-dr Rds-2P	I4/95	N/A	1515	Note 2
Sprint	2-dr Coupe-2P	I4/95	N/A	1515	Note 2
Sprint	2-dr Rds-2P	I4/95	N/A	1515	Note 2
ELAN PLUS 2					
+2S	2-dr Coupe-2+2P	I4/95	5495	2085	Note 3
+2S 130	2-dr Coupe-2+2P	I4/95	6800	2085	Note 3
EUROPA					
S2	2-dr Coupe-2P	I4/96	4520	1350	Note 4
Twin-Cam	2-dr Coupe-2P	I4/95	N/A	N/A	Note 4
Special	2-dr Coupe-2P	I4/95	7292	1570	Note 4

Note 1: At least 1,000 S4 Sevens were produced from 1970 through early 1973, plus more than 850 S3 versions with Caterham engine.

Note 2: As many as 12,224 Elans were produced from 1962-73 (some sources report totals as low as 9,659 units).

Note 3: Approximately 4,798 Elan +2s were produced from 1967-74 (some sources report totals as low as 3,330 units).

Note 4: A total of 9,230 Europas were produced during the full model run, from 1967-74.

Price Note: Elan +2S 130 price shown is approximate. Other figures were valid in 1971 except (Europa Special) 1974.

Weight Note: Figures listed for U.S. versions of the Elan were as low as 1340 pounds.

ENGINE DATA: BASE FOUR (Seven 1300): Inline, overhead-valve four-cylinder (British Ford). Cast iron block and head. **Displacement:** 79.2 cu. in. (1298 cc). **Bore & Stroke:** 3.19 x 2.48 in. (81 x 63 mm). **Compression Ratio:** 9.0:1. **Brake Horsepower:** 70 (DIN) at 5700 rpm. **Torque:** 68 lbs.-ft. at 5700 rpm. Five main bearings. Solid valve lifters. Weber carburetor.

BASE FOUR (Seven 1600): Inline, overhead-valve four-cylinder (British Ford). Cast iron block and head. **Displacement:** 97.5 cu. in. (1599 cc). **Bore & Stroke:** 3.19 x 3.05 in. (81 x 77.6 mm). **Compression Ratio:** 9.0:1. **Brake Horsepower:** 84 at 5500 rpm. Five main bearings. Solid valve lifters. Weber carburetor.

BASE FOUR (Elan S4, Elan +2S, Europa Twin Cam): Inline, dual-overhead-cam four-cylinder (Lotus). Cast iron block and light alloy head. **Displacement:** 95.1 cu. in. (1558 cc). **Bore & Stroke:** 3.25 x 2.86 in. (82.55 x 72.75 mm). **Compression Ratio:** 9.5:1. **Brake Horsepower:** 105 at 5500 rpm. **Torque:** 112 lbs.-ft. at 4600 rpm. Five main bearings. Solid valve lifters.

BASE FOUR (Elan Sprint, Elan +2S 130, Europa Special): Same as 1558-cc four above, except — **Compression Ratio:** 10.3:1. **Brake Horsepower:** 126 at 6500 rpm. **Torque:** 113 lbs.-ft. at 5500 rpm.

Note: Horsepower rating of the Sprint/Special Twin Cam engine was as low as 113 in the U.S. market, but a road test in 1972 reported output of 121 bhp at 6000 rpm and 112 lbs.-ft. at 4000 rpm.

BASE FOUR (Europa Series 2): Inline, overhead-valve four-cylinder. Cast iron block and head. **Displacement:** 95.5 cu. in. (1565 cc). **Bore & Stroke:** 3.03 x 3.31 in. (77 x 84 mm). **Compression Ratio:** 10.0:1. **Brake Horsepower:** 83 at 6000 rpm (U.S. version). **Torque:** 75 lbs.-ft. at 5500 rpm. Solid valve lifters.

CHASSIS DATA: Wheelbase: (Seven) 90 in.; (Elan) 84 in.; (Elan +2) 96 in.; (Europa) 91.0 in.; (Europa Special) 92.0 in. **Overall Length:** (Seven) 146 in.; (Elan) 145.25 in.; (Elan +2) 168 in.; (Europa) 158 in. **Height:** (Seven) 42.8 in.; (Elan) 45 in.; (Elan +2) 47 in.; (Europa) 43 in. **Width:** (Seven) 60.5 in.; (Elan) 56 in.; (Elan +2) 63.5 in.; (Europa) 64.5 in. **Front Tread:** (Seven) 48.8 in.; (Elan) 47 in.; (Elan +2) 54 in.; (Europa) 53 in. **Rear Tread:** (Seven) 51.5 in.; (Elan) 48 in.; (Elan +2) 55 in.; (Europa) 53 in. **Standard Tires:** (Seven) 165x13; (Elan) 5.20x13; (Elan Sprint) 155x13; (Elan +2) 165x13; (Europa) 155x13; (later Europa) 175/70VR13 front, 185/70VR13 (rear).

TECHNICAL: Layout: front-engine, rear-drive except (Europa) mid-engine. **Transmission:** four-speed manual; five-speed manual available in Elan +2S 130S and Europa Special. Five-speed gear ratios: (1st) 3.61:1; (2nd) 2.33:1; (3rd) 1.61:1; (4th) 1.21:1; (5th) 0.87:1. **Standard Final Drive Ratio:** (Elan S4) 3.70:1; (Europa S2) 3.66:1; (Europa w/5-spd) 3.78:1. **Steering:** rack and pinion. **Suspension (front):** (Seven) lower wishbones with coil spring/shocks and anti-roll bar; (Elan/Europa) unequal-length A-arms with coil springs and anti-roll bar. **Suspension (rear):** (Seven) rigid axle with coil springs; (Elan) Chapman struts with lower A-arms and coil springs. (Europa) lower A-arms, upper lateral links, upper/lower trailing arms, and coil springs with anti-roll bar. **Brakes:** (Elan) front/rear disc. (Seven/Europa) front disc, rear drum. **Body Construction:** (Seven) fiberglass body on steel frame; (Elan/Europa) fiberglass body on steel backbone chassis.

PERFORMANCE: Top Speed: (Elan +2S 130) 116 mph; (Europa S2) about 109 mph; (Europa Twin Cam S3) 120 mph; (Europa Special) 125+ mph. **Acceleration (0-60 mph):** (Elan +2S 130) 8.8 sec.; (Europa S2) as little as 9.5 sec.; (Europa Twin Cam) 7.0-8.2 sec.; (Europa Special) 6.7-7.7 sec. **Acceleration (quarter-mile):** (Europa Special) 14.9 sec.

PRODUCTION/SALES: A total of 2,830 Lotus cars were produced in 1973, followed by 1,466 in 1974, and as many as 655 in 1975.

Manufacturer: Lotus Cars Ltd., Hethel, Norwich, England.

HISTORY: Beginning in spring 1973, Caterham Car Sales (at Caterham, Surrey) took over production of the Lotus Seven sports-racer, continuing the Super Seven S3 version through the 1970s and into the '80s. These later examples carried 'Caterham 7' (not Lotus) identification. Twin Cam, 1600 GT and Holbay Sprint 1700 engines were installed.

1976-79 LOTUS

ELITE — 501/502/503/504 — FOUR — With the Elan and Europa out of the lineup, and Lotus Seven production assigned to the Caterham organization, Lotus brought out a completely new series of models by 1976. First of the trio was the front-engined Elite, identified by its square tail and carrying the same name as the first roadgoing Lotus, back in the late 1950s. An all-alloy Lotus Type 907 1973-cc twin-cam four provided the power for all three new models. The Elite 501 was the base model; 502 added halogen headlamps, tinted glass and air conditioning; 503 included power steering; and 504 came with a three-speed automatic transmission.

ECLAT — SPRINT 520/521/522/523/524 — FOUR — Joining the new Elite was a front-engined slopeback Eclat (which would later evolve into an Excel). Power came from the same engine as in the Elite, with slightly more horsepower. The base model 520 came with a four-speed gearbox; others, a five-speed or (524) three-speed automatic. Type 522 included halogen headlamps, air conditioning and tinted glass; 523 added power steering.

1976 Lotus Esprit S1.

ESPRIT — S1/S2 — FOUR — Best known and longest-lived of the new Lotus trio was the low and angular mid-engined Esprit. Having first appeared in prototype form at the 1972 Turin (Italy) auto show, mounted on a Europa platform, the Esprit began as a styling exercise by Ital Design, under the direction of Giorgetto Giugiaro (who also named the car). Few changes were evident when the Esprit finally went into production, some time after the production version was displayed at the autumn 1974 motor show. The first examples didn't reach customers until mid-1976. The futuristic design not only looked good, but produced good aerodynamics. Color was impregnated directly into the fiberglass body, rather than painted on. Much more angular and sharp-edged than prior models, the Esprit displayed a distinct wedge profile with low, slim, squared-off nose and a short, sloped tail end. The driver faced a large, steeply-raked windshield, while the back window resided in a lift-up hatch. Mounted in the middle, behind the cockpit, was a 1973-cc (120-cid) Lotus-designed twin-cam four-cylinder engine that produced as much as 160 horsepower (DIN). That same engine was used in the Maserati Merak and Citroen SM, as well as the other two Lotus models. All-disc brakes were installed, along with rack-and-pinion steering and a five-speed manual gearbox. Wheelbase of the Esprit's steel backbone chassis was 96 inches, and the two-seater measured almost 168 inches long overall (considerably longer than the Europa). Tread dimension was six inches wider than the Europa. In European trim, an early Esprit could hit 135 mph, though 120 mph was about the limit of U.S. versions, which carried a lower-powered (140-bhp SAE) engine when they became available in 1977. The long-time Lotus concept of offering its car in both kit and assembled form was now a memory, as the Esprit came only ready-to-roll.

Series 2 became available in 1979, with wider wheels and a front lip spoiler.

I.D. DATA: Serial number plate is on upper edge of instrument panel, visible through the windshield; and on a plate on left or right fender panel, under the hood. The serial number consists of eight digits (the first four denoting year and month built), followed by a suffix that indicates destination. Suffix 'B' = North America.

Model	Body Type & Seating	Engine Type/CID	P.O.E. Price	Weight (lbs.)	Prod. Total
ELITE					
501	2-dr Coupe-2+2P	I4/120	15548	2413	N/A
502	2-dr Coupe-2+2P	I4/120	16417	N/A	N/A
503	2-dr Coupe-2+2P	I4/120	19090	N/A	N/A
504	2-dr Coupe-2+2P	I4/120	19615	N/A	N/A
ECLAT (SPRINT)					
520	2-dr Coupe-2+2P	I4/120	15350	2390	N/A
521	2-dr Coupe-2+2P	I4/120	16698	N/A	N/A
522	2-dr Coupe-2+2P	I4/120	17688	N/A	N/A
523	2-dr Coupe-2+2P	I4/120	18250	N/A	N/A
524	2-dr Coupe-2+2P	I4/120	18755	N/A	N/A
ESPRIT					
S1	2-dr Coupe-2P	I4/120	15990	1980	Note 1
S2	2-dr Coupe-2P	I4/120	27000	1980	Note 1

Note 1: A total of 1,060 Series S1 Esprits were produced from 1976-79, followed by 88 S2.
Price Note: Esprit S1 figure shown was valid in 1976; Esprit S2 in 1979; others in 1978.
Weight Note: Figures shown are curb weights.

1977 Lotus Elite Series 1.

ENGINE DATA: BASE FOUR: Inline, dual-overhead-cam four-cylinder (16-valve, Lotus 907). Aluminum block and head. **Displacement:** 120.4 cu. in. (1973 cc). **Bore & Stroke:** 3.74 x 2.72 in. (95.2 x 69 mm). **Compression Ratio:** 9.5:1. **Brake Horsepower:** (Eclat/Esprit) up to 160 (DIN) at 6200 rpm; (Elite) 155 (DIN) at 6500 rpm. **Torque:** (Eclat/Esprit) 140 lbs.-ft. at 4900 rpm; (Elite) 135 lbs.-ft. at 5000 rpm. Five main bearings. Solid valve lifters. Two Zenith CD2SE (or Dell'orto) carburetors.
Note: Esprit engine output dropped to 140 hp at 6500 rpm in 1977-78, then rose to 156 at 7000 rpm in 1979. U.S. version with 8.4:1 compression was rated about 140 bhp (SAE) at 6500 rpm, using two Zenith-Stromberg carburetors.

CHASSIS DATA: Wheelbase: (Eclat) 97.8 in.; (Elite) 97.6 in.; (Esprit) 96.0 in. **Overall Length:** (Eclat) 175.5 in.; (Elite) 175.5 in.; (Esprit) 165-167.7 in. **Height:** (Eclat) 47.25 in.; (Elite) 47.6 in.; (Esprit) 43.75 in. **Width:** (Eclat) 71.5 in.; (Elite) 71.5 in.; (Esprit) 73.25 in. **Front Tread:** (Eclat) 58.5 in.; (Elite) 58.5 in.; (Esprit) 59.5 in. **Rear Tread:** (Eclat) 59 in.; (Elite) 58.5 in.; (Esprit) 59.5 in. **Standard Tires:** (Eclat) 185/70HR13; (Eclat 521) 205/60VR14; (Elite) 205/60VR14; (Esprit) 195/70HR14 front, 205/70HR14 rear.

TECHNICAL: Layout: (Eclat/Elite) front-engine, front-drive; (Esprit) mid-engine, rear-drive. **Transmission:** (Eclat/Elite) five-speed manual except Eclat 520, four-speed; (Esprit) five-speed manual in rear transaxle. Automatic available in Eclat/Elite. **Steering:** rack and pinion. **Suspension (front):** upper A-arms, lower lateral links, coil springs, and lower longitudinal links serving as anti-roll bar. **Suspension (rear):** upper/lower lateral links, angled trailing arms and coil springs. **Brakes:** front/rear disc. **Body Construction:** fiberglass body on steel backbone frame.

PERFORMANCE: Top Speed: (Euro Esprit) 135 mph; (U.S. Esprit) 120 mph. **Acceleration (0-60 mph):** (Esprit) as low as 6.8 sec. reported; (Elite) 8.5 sec.; (Euro Esprit) about 9 sec.

PRODUCTION/SALES: A total of 931 Lotus cars were produced in 1977, followed by 1,074 in 1977, 1,200 in 1978, and 1,031 in 1979.
Manufacturer: Lotus Cars Ltd., Hethel, Norwich, England.
Distributor: Lotus East Inc., Millerton, New York.
HISTORY: Through the late 1970s and into the '80s, Lotus was only a sporadic entrant into the U.S. market. Not until the advent of the Series 3, in 1983, would the Esprit become a regular player in the American sports-car arena.

1980-89 LOTUS

1989 Lotus Esprit Turbo.

ESPRIT/ESPRIT TURBO — SERIES 2.2/3 — FOUR — A larger (2174-cc) twin-cam engine went into the next Esprit, Series 2.2, though horsepower did not increase. For extra potency, on the other hand, customers could choose a turbocharged version of the new powerplant, producing 210 horsepower (DIN). The Esprit Turbo rode a more rigid chassis and carried a modified rear suspension with 15-inch wheels. Styling modifications included a deep front air dam and aero rocker-panel extensions. That was enough to boost top speed close to the 150-mph mark. By 1983, the normally-aspirated S3 edition adopted all the changes that had formerly gone into the Turbo, along with wider optional wheels/tires. In 1986, the turbocharged engine switched from carburetors to Bosch fuel injection.

I.D. DATA: A 17-symbol Vehicle Identification Number is atop the instrument panel, visible through the windshield; and on a plate attached to left or right fender panel, under the hood. Symbol one ('S') denotes England. Symbols 2-3 ('CC') indicates Lotus company. Symbol four is model ('C' = Esprit; 'F' = Turbo). Symbol five identifies the series ('A' = Series 1; 'B' — Series 2; 'C' — Series 3). Symbol seven is the final digit of the engine type number (type 907, 908, 909, 910, 911 or 912). Symbol 10 indicates model year ('H' = 1987). The final four digits form the sequential serial number.

Model	Body Type & Seating	Engine Type/CID	P.O.E. Price	Weight (lbs.)	Prod. Total
ESPRIT					
S2.2	2-dr Coupe-2P	I4/133	N/A	N/A	Note 1
S3	2-dr Coupe-2P	I4/133	N/A	2249	Note 1
Turbo	2-dr Coupe-2P	I4/133	N/A	2690	Note 1

Note 1: A total of 384 Lotus cars were produced in 1980, followed by 345 in 1981, 572 in 1982, 642 in 1983, 837 in 1984, and 813 in 1985.

ENGINE DATA: BASE FOUR (1980-86 Esprit): Inline, dual-overhead-cam four-cylinder. Light alloy block and head. **Displacement:** 132.7 cu. in. (2174 cc). **Bore & Stroke:** 3.75 x 3.00 in. (95.3 x 76.2 mm). **Compression Ratio:** 9.5:1. **Brake Horsepower:** 160 (DIN) at 6500 rpm. **Torque:** 160 lbs.-ft. at 5000 rpm. Five main bearings. Solid valve lifters. Two Dell'orto carburetors (European).
Note: U.S. version of Esprit engine had 8.4:1 compression and was rated 140 bhp at 5800 rpm, and 160 lbs.-ft. at 5000 rpm.

BASE FOUR (1987-89 Esprit): Same as 2174-cc four above, except — **Brake Horsepower:** 160 (DIN) at 5600 rpm.

BASE FOUR (Esprit Turbo): Same as 2174-cc four above, but with Garrett AiResearch T3 turbocharger — **Compression Ratio:** 7.5:1. **Brake Horsepower:** 210 (DIN) at 6000 rpm. **Torque:** 200 lbs.-ft. at 4000 rpm.
Note: U.S. version of Turbo engine in late 1980s had 8.0:1 compression and was rated 215 bhp at 6250 rpm, and 192 lbs.-ft. at 5000 rpm.

CHASSIS DATA: Wheelbase: 96.0 in. **Overall Length:** 165-167.7 in. **Height:** 44 in. **Width:** 73.9 in. **Front Tread:** 59.5 in. (Turbo, 60.5 in.). **Rear Tread:** 59.5 in. (Turbo, 61.2 in.). **Standard Tires:** 205/60VR14 front, 205/70VR14 rear except (Turbo) 195/60VR15 front, 235/60VR15 rear.
Note: Specifications above were valid in mid-1980s.

TECHNICAL: Layout: mid-engine, rear-drive. **Transmission:** five-speed manual in rear transaxle. **Steering:** rack and pinion. **Suspension (front):** upper A-arms, lower lateral links, coil springs, and lower longitudinal links serving as anti roll bar. **Suspension (rear):** upper/lower lateral links, angled trailing arms and coil springs. **Brakes:** front/rear disc. **Body Construction:** fiberglass body on steel backbone frame.
Manufacturer: Lotus Cars Ltd., Hethel, Norwich, England.
Distributor: Lotus Cars USA Inc., Lawrenceville, Georgia.

HISTORY: General Motors bought Lotus in 1986, with a promise not to interfere in its workings. Producing its own cars has been only a part of the Lotus business in recent years, however, as they turned more to consultancy duties for other manufacturers in such areas as engine design, suspension systems, and techniques for molding fiberglass. The big-screen "James Bond" did Lotus no harm by driving a Turbo Esprit in *The Spy Who Loved Me*. In December 1988, Group Lotus plc established Lotus Cars USA Inc. as its American distributor.

1990 LOTUS

ESPRIT TURBO SE — FOUR — As the 1990s began, the Esprit remained in the Lotus lineup and the American marketplace. This SE (Special Equipment) version had an inflatable restraint system (airbag) and was powered by an evolution of the 2.2-liter aluminum-alloy engine used through the 1980s. In this incarnation, the four-cylinder powerplant produced 264 horsepower, enough to send an Esprit from a standing start to 60 mph in 4.7 seconds--and to 100 mph in 11.9 seconds. Top speed ran close to 165 mph. SE equipment included a leather interior, polished burr elm instrument panel, air conditioning, power windows, power door locks, power fuel flap, heated power mirrors, three-phase ice warning system, removable roof panel (with deflector), tinted glass, and 100-watt Sony XR7100 AM/FM radio with cassette player.

ELAN — FOUR — Lotus introduced its first all-new model since 1975 with the new Elan roadster, available late in 1990. Unlike the car that first bore the Elan name, this one was front-wheel-drive and carried an Isuzu-Lotus 1.6-liter twin-cam turbocharged engine with air-to-air intercooler. A five-speed gearbox was standard, along with power rack-and-pinion steering and front/rear disc brakes. The Elan first appeared at the Detroit and Los Angeles auto shows in January 1990. The body was formed of composite (GRP and steel) panels on a steel backbone chassis. Standard Elan equipment included a leather-rim steering wheel, central door locking, power windows, heated power mirrors, leather upholstery, bronze-tinted glass, an airbag, air conditioning, and alloy wheels.

I.D. DATA: Similar to 1980-89.

Model	Body Type & Seating	Engine Type/CID	P.O.E. Price	Weight (lbs.)	Prod. Total
ESPRIT					
Turbo SE	2-dr Coupe-2P	I4/133	81950	2820	Note 1
ELAN					
	2-dr Rds-2P	I4/97	33900	2249	Note 1

377

Note 1: Approximately 324 Lotus cars were sold in the U.S. during 1990.

Price Note: Elan figure is approximate.

ENGINE DATA: BASE FOUR (Esprit Turbo SE): Inline, dual-overhead-cam four-cylinder (16-valve). Aluminum-alloy block and head. **Displacement:** 132.7 cu. in. (2174 cc). **Bore & Stroke:** 3.74 x 2.72 in. (95.3 x 69 mm). **Compression Ratio:** 9.5:1. **Brake Horsepower:** 264 (DIN) at 6500 rpm. **Torque:** 261 lbs.-ft. at 3900 rpm. Five main bearings. Multi-point fuel injection.

BASE FOUR (Elan): Inline, dual-overhead-cam four-cylinder (16-valve Isuzu-Lotus). Turbocharger with air-to-air intercooler. **Displacement:** 96.9 cu. in. (1588 cc). **Bore & Stroke:** 3.15 x 3.11 in. (80 x 79 mm). **Compression Ratio:** 8.2:1. **Brake Horsepower:** 165 at 6600 rpm. **Torque:** 148 lbs.-ft. at 4200 rpm. Multi-point fuel injection.

CHASSIS DATA: Wheelbase: (Esprit) 96.0 in.; (Elan) 88.6 in. **Overall Length:** (Esprit) 170.5 in.; (Elan) 152.2 in. **Height:** (Esprit) 45.3 in.; (Elan) 48.4 in. **Width:** (Esprit) 73.2 in. **Front Tread:** (Elan) 58.5 in. **Rear Tread:** (Elan) 58.5 in. **Standard Tires:** (Elan) 205/50ZR15.

TECHNICAL: Layout: (Esprit) mid-engine, rear-drive; (Elan) front-engine, front-drive. **Transmission:** five-speed manual. **Steering:** rack and pinion. **Suspension (front):** (Esprit) upper/lower wishbones with coil springs and anti-roll bar; (Elan) "interactive" unequal-length wishbones with coil springs and anti-roll bar. **Suspension (rear):** (Esprit) upper/lower transverse links with radius arms and coil springs. **Brakes:** front/rear disc. **Body Construction:** composite body on steel backbone frame.

PERFORMANCE: Top Speed: (Esprit) 163-165+ mph; (Elan) 137 mph. **Acceleration (0-60 mph):** (Esprit) 4.7 sec.; (Elan) 6.7 sec.

Manufacturer: Lotus Cars Ltd., Hethel, Norwich, England.

Distributor: Lotus Cars USA Inc., Lawrenceville, Georgia.

HISTORY: In 1990, a Lotus Esprit Turbo SE played a role in two American movies: *Pretty Woman* with Julia Roberts and Richard Gere; and *Taking Care of Business,* which starred Charles Grodin and Jim Belushi. By that time, Lotus was selling about 300 Esprit Turbo SE models per year in the U.S. market.

MAICO

"You'll point with pride to your MAICO 500," said the sales brochure distributed at New York's International Auto Show in April 1958. With "its striking Continental look," the Maico was claimed to be "Germany's greatest sports car achievement in its class." Powered by a rear-mounted 452-cc two-cylinder engine, the mini Sport coupe was supposed to "whiz you along at 70 m.p.h. in true sport car fashion," with unbelievable gas mileage. Following the lead of some of the better-known econocars of the late 1950s, Maico-Werke introduced a tiny Volkswagen-like four-seater sedan with top speed above 50 mph to attract the economy-minded, but coupled it with a sleek and swift little coupe. For both models, however, price was the main attraction.

Maico evolved from an earlier German attempt at a minicar, the Champion, which failed to attract buyers in any number. Another firm also tried to turn it into a paying proposition. Then, late in 1955, that company wound up in the hands of the Maisch brothers, known in America for the production of "scrambler" motorcycles at their Maico plant. Featured at the 1957 Frankfurt auto show were both the sedan, with an unmistakable resemblance in profile to the VW Beetle, and the 500 Sport. By late 1957, when *Motor Trend* road-tested the sedan, some 213 examples had been sold in the Michigan-Ohio area alone by the car's Michigan-based importer. Like many of its rivals, the Maico soon faded into obscurity, its virtues not quite strong enough to prevail over the competition in the emerging minicar marketplace. Rumors of a three-cylinder version emerged, but after 1958 the company refocused its attention on motorcycle production. Still, Maicos were sold in the U.S. into 1960.

700 SPORT — TWO — This final version of the Maico sports model was listed in U.S. directories into 1960.

Note: Most specifications below are for the 500 sedan.

I.D. DATA: Not available.

Model	Body Type & Seating	Engine Type/CID	P.O.E. Price	Weight (lbs.)	Prod. Total
	2-dr Sedan-4P	I2/28	1295	1290	Note 1
	2-dr Coupe-2P	I2/28	1845	N/A	Note 1
	2-dr Coupe-2P	I2/28	1845	N/A	Note 1

Note 1: About 102 Maicos were sold in the U.S. during 1958, 82 more in 1959, and 25 in 1960.

Price Note: Deluxe sedan with heater, electric windshield wipers and turn signals sold for $1325 in the U.S.

ENGINE DATA: BASE TWO: Inline two-cylinder (two-stroke). Displacement: 27.67 cu. in. (452 cc). Bore & Stroke: 2.60 x 2.60 in. (66 x 66 mm). Compression Ratio: 7.2:1. Brake Horsepower: 18 at 4000 rpm. One Bing carburetor.

Note: Some early sedans had a smaller (398 cc) engine.

CHASSIS DATA: Wheelbase: 79.5 in. Overall Length: 134.5 in. Height: 55.0 in. Width: 58.5 in. Front Tread: 47.0 in. Rear Tread: 45.5 in. Wheel Type: disc. Standard Tires: 5.20x12.

TECHNICAL: Layout: rear-engine, rear-drive. Transmission: four-speed manual (synchro 2nd/3rd/4th); floor lever. Steering: rack and pinion. Suspension (front): (sedan) individual swinging links with rubber torsion units; (coupe) coil springs. Suspension (rear): swinging half axles with coil springs. Brakes: hydraulic, front/rear drum. Body Construction: aluminum body on central-tube chassis.

PERFORMANCE: Top Speed: (sedan) 56-60 mph; (Sport coupe) 70 mph. Fuel Mileage: (sedan) 45-50 mpg.

Manufacturer: Maico-Werke GmbH, Pfaeffingen-Tuebingen, West Germany.

Distributor: Whizzer International, Pontiac, Michigan.

MARATHON

Introduced at the Paris Salon in 1953, the French-built Marathon Corsaire wore a body shaped similar to Porsche's, but made largely of ultra-light plastic. Prior to this time, the company had specialized in small engines. Powered by a rear-mounted Dyna-Panhard two-cylinder engine, riding a Volkswagen-style chassis, the coupe had aerodynamic, fastback-style lines. Dyna-Panhard engines had been doing well in racing and rally events, before finding their way into a handful of Marathons and other specialty cars (including the Deutsch-Bonnet).

1955-60 MAICO

1959 Maico 700 Sport Coupe.

500 — TWO — Viewed from the front corner, in particular, the two-door sedan looked surprisingly similar to VW's Beetle, though Maico's recessed headlamps were lower and the sloping front lid wider (squared-off at the base). Rather than a fastback profile, though, the 500 had a slight notchback to the rear of its relatively long roofline, with sizable rear quarter windows. Doors were hinged at the rear, handles mounted at the front ("suicide" style), with exposed hinges. Power came from a two-stroke, two-cylinder engine at the rear, delivering 18 horsepower to a four-speed gearbox with floor lever. The water-cooled engine used twin-coil ignition and a combination starter/generator. Upholstery was plaid plastic, with an adjustable bench-style front seat. Rear windows were fixed, while half of each front window slid open for ventilation. A small amount of luggage could be carried in the front compartment, which also held the gas tank and spare tire. A heater was standard.

500 SPORT — TWO — Appearance of the sporty coupe differed considerably from the two-door sedan (just as VW's Karmann Ghia differed from the Beetle). Headlamps were higher, at the forward tips of the taller front fenders. Within the coupe's front panel was a wide oval grille-like design with horizontal trim bar and center insignia, and round parking lights at its outer ends. Long rear quarter panels ended in tiny tailfins, which held the round taillamps.

1953-56 MARATHON

1954 Marathon Corsaire two-door coupe.

CORSAIRE — TWO — Promoted to American prospects as "your car of tomorrow," the aero-styled Marathon coupe, powered by a rear engine, had no grille but displayed a rounded lid for a hood and a one-piece curved windshield. "Suicide" (rear-hinged) doors were dramatically curved at the front edge, and contained vent wings. Both the gas tank and spare tire were up front. Headlamps were built into fender tips, jutting forward a bit and upward (with fenders higher than the hood). Large round foglights were mounted below and inboard, with small round parking lights below the basic headlamps. The

largely plastic body also had rear quarter windows and partly enclosed front and rear wheels, plus wraparound bumpers at both ends. The Volkswagen-type chassis had a tubular backbone with welded steel floor. The 850-cc Dyna-Panhard OHV horizontally-opposed two-cylinder engine, with twin carburetors and dual exhausts, produced 42 horsepower and was mounted at the rear, along with the four-speed manual gearbox. Cooling ducts were integrated with the body, behind the long quarter windows. Luggage space was available under the front hood, in an upholstered compartment, as well as behind the rear seat. The factory claimed that three people could fit in the front seat, and the car also included a small back seat. Simulated leather upholstery came in a choice of six colors. Standard equipment included a heater and defroster, with provision for a radio. Instruments included a tachometer and oil temperature gauge. Factory claims of a 92-mph top speed were doubted by some American observers, who believed 80 mph was more likely.

PIRATE — TWO — The special sports-competition version had a lighter weight body and chassis, highly-tuned engine, two bucket seats, tachometer, floor gearshift lever, deeply finned brake drums, plus a case between the seats to hold cards, a chronometer and other racing items. It was aimed at competition in hill climbs, rallies and road events.

I.D. DATA: Not available.

Model	Body Type & Seating	Engine Type/CID	P.O.E. Price	Weight (lbs.)	Prod. Total
Corsaire	2-dr Coupe-3P	H2/52	2760	1525	N/A
Pirate	2-dr Rds-2P	H2/52	N/A	N/A	N/A

Price/Weight Note: P.O.E. price is estimated; weight is approximate curb weight.

ENGINE DATA: BASE TWO: Horizontally-opposed, overhead-valve two-cylinder (air cooled Dyna-Panhard). **Displacement:** 51.87 cu. in. (850 cc). **Bore & Stroke:** 3.34 x 2.95 in. (84.8 x 74.9 mm). **Compression Ratio:** 7.2:1. **Brake Horsepower:** 42 at 5000 rpm. Two main bearings. Solid valve lifters. Twin downdraft carburetors. 12-volt electrical.

CHASSIS DATA: Wheelbase: 82.25 in. **Overall Length:** 142 in. **Height:** 45 in. **Width:** 59 in. **Front Tread:** 45 in. **Rear Tread:** 44 in. **Standard Tires:** 5.00x15.

TECHNICAL: Layout: rear-engine, rear-drive. **Transmission:** four-speed manual (synchro 2nd/3rd/4th). **Steering:** rack-type. **Suspension (front):** independent; torsion bar. **Suspension (rear):** independent; torsion bar. **Brakes:** Bendix-Lockheed hydraulic, front/rear drum. **Body Construction:** steel/plastic body on steel platform chassis. **Fuel Tank:** 11.1 gallon.

PERFORMANCE: Top Speed: 92 mph (factory claim). **Acceleration (0-60 mph):** 20 seconds. **Fuel Mileage:** 28-36 mpg (factory claimed 48 mpg at 45 mph).

Manufacturer: Automobiles Marathon, Paris, France; Ateliers Roger Loyer (concessionaire), Clichy (Seine) Paris.

Distributor: F. Hardivilliers Inc., New York City.

HISTORY: In an attempt to spark interest in the U.S., the Corsaire appeared at the New York World Motorsport Show in January 1954. Sales literature promised that it would deliver "Big car comfort...Small car economy...Sports car performance."

MARAUDER

What *Motor Trend* described in 1950 as a "fast touring car" was based on a Rover 75 chassis, built by a team that had formerly worked with that company on the production of a single-seat race car. The Marauder had a shorter, lighter version of that box-section frame and a modification of the Rover 75 engine with inclined overhead valves and 7.6:1 compression, rated 80 horsepower. Some of the sports roadster's body panels also came from Rover, but the body was constructed by Richard Mead, who also produced bodies for Alvis and Bentley models. Only a few examples were built, mostly roadsters, but a fixed-head coupe also was offered in England. Marauders were intended for both competition and road use. Though not officially exported to the U.S. at the time (unlike Rovers), the Marauder has a distinctive look that could still attract latter-day enthusiasts.

1950-52 MARAUDER

MODEL A — SIX — Both the engine and chassis of the Marauder originated with the Rover 75, but a compression boost and stiffer valve springs helped to eke out five extra horsepower from the six-cylinder powerplant. Wheelbase was shorter than the Rover's, at 102 inches, and the roadster could reach speeds of 90 mph. A small grille was made up of four thick horizontal bars, with a vertical divider bar in the center. Small round parking lights stood below the headlamps. Doors were rear-hinged ("suicide" style), and the body displayed full wheel openings with flares at the front. The hood reached only part of the length of the car's long nose. A bright rocker panel extended between the wheel openings on each side. Front fenders held flush-fitting trafficators (turn signals). Provision was made for fresh-air heating/ventilation, and for radio installation. Standard features included a combination fuel/oil-level indicator, reserve fuel switch, map light,

cigar lighter, and choke warning light. Sliding "Perspex" side curtains in metal frames attached to the doors via threaded dowels. Woodhead-Monroe telescopic rear shock absorbers were mounted at an inclined angle. Fixed-head coupe bodies differed somewhat from the roadster, with a narrow vertical-style grille and smaller windshield.

MODEL 100 — SIX — A Marauder with a larger, more powerful engine, displacing 2392 cubic centimeters and rated at 105 horsepower, was also produced starting in 1951. Built on special order only, it was capable of reaching at least 100 mph.

1950 Marauder.

I.D. DATA: Not available.

Model	Body Type & Seating	Engine Type/CID	P.O.E. Price	Weight (lbs.)	Prod. Total
A	2-dr Rds-2/3P	I6/128	Note 1	2622	N/A
100	2-dr Rds-2/3P	I6/146	N/A	2622	N/A

Note 1: Price in Britain was about $2600.

Weight Note 1: Figure shown is approximate "dry" weight.

ENGINE DATA: BASE SIX (Model A): Inline six-cylinder (Rover; overhead intake, side exhaust valves). Cast iron block and aluminum head. **Displacement:** 128 cu. in. (2103 cc). **Bore & Stroke:** 2.57 x 4.13 in. (65.2 x 105 mm). **Compression Ratio:** 7.6:1. **Brake Horsepower:** 80 at 4200 rpm. Four main bearings. Solid valve lifters. Two SU horizontal carburetors.

BASE SIX (Model 100): Same as above, except — **Displacement:** 145.9 cu. in. (2392 cc). **Bore & Stroke:** 2.72 x 4.13 in. (69.2 x 105 mm). **Compression Ratio:** 7.5:1. **Brake Horsepower:** 105 at 5000 rpm. Three SU carburetors.

CHASSIS DATA: Wheelbase: 102 in. **Overall Length:** 166 in. **Height:** 52 in. **Width:** 66 in. **Front Tread:** 51.6 in. **Rear Tread:** 50.8 in. **Wheel Type:** ventilated disc. **Standard Tires:** 6.00x15.

1950 Marauder open sport.

TECHNICAL: Layout: front-engine, rear-drive. **Transmission:** four-speed manual. Overall gear ratios: (1st) 14.5:1; (2nd) 8.77:1; (3rd) 5.92:1; (4th) 4.3:1; (rev) 13.17:1. Gear ratios with overdrive: (1st) 10.07:1; (2nd) 6.09:1; (3rd) 4.11:1; (4th) 3.0:1. **Standard Final Drive Ratio:** 4.3:1. **Steering:** Burman recirculating ball. **Suspension (front):** independent; coil springs. **Suspension (rear):** rigid axle with variable-rate semi-elliptic leaf springs. **Brakes:** Girling hydro-mechanical, front/rear drum. **Body Construction:** steel body (with aluminum hood, cowl, doors and trunk lid) on steel frame.

Note: Early literature indicated slightly different gear ratios without overdrive: (2nd) 8.24:1; (3rd) 5.82:1.

MAJOR OPTIONS: Overdrive (0.694:1).

PERFORMANCE: Top Speed: (Model A) 90 mph. **Acceleration (0-60 mph):** N/A (0-50 mph in as little as 13 seconds).

Manufacturer: Wilks, Mackie & Co. Ltd., Dorridge, Warwickshire, England; (later) Marauder Car Co. Ltd., Kenilworth, Warwickshire, England.

MARCOS

Hardly the best known of British sport minicars, the Marcos was the brainchild of Jem Marsh and Frank Costin, its nameplate an amalgamation of the two surnames. Prior to turning to their own automobile, Marsh had worked in the

technical department at Firestone, while Costin was an aircraft designer/engineer who'd contributed ideas to the Lotus company. In 1959, Marsh founded Speedex Casting & Accessories Ltd. for the purpose of supplying parts and fiberglass body shells to other firms. Design of their first vehicle was penned by Costin: a two-seater with a different sort of unibody construction, crafted not in metal but of marine plywood and fiberglass, atop a composite chassis. The first version had gullwing doors and cycle fenders, Triumph Herald steering and front suspension, and Nash Metropolitan (or Standard) rear end, and was powered by a 1.0-liter British Ford engine. That was enough for a top speed around 120 mph. After a period of racing, they turned to a production version with full fenders, forming Marcos Cars Ltd. in 1962. Kit cars rather than fully-assembled vehicles were their major product.

The Marcos GT, introduced in 1964, carried a Volvo 1800 engine and was again plywood-based. That was followed by the 1600GT, with a 1.6-liter Ford four beneath its bonnet. Subsequent examples took their power from V-4 and V-6 Ford engines, or the Volvo inline six.

By 1970, Marcos coupes were available in the U.S., but that wouldn't last long as they couldn't meet the tightening federal vehicle regulations. Their next model was the four-seat Mantis, a Triumph-powered coupe capable of 140 mph. Financial troubles hit the company hard by 1972. Production came to a halt, except for the low-cost fiberglass-bodied Mini-Marcos, which had been introduced in 1965. That one had the distinction of accepting a selection of BMC Mini components. A new company name and ownership came in 1975, allowing production of the Mini-Marcos to continue as late as 1981. That model was joined by a Midas 2+2 coupe. Another name change (to Midas Cars) came in 1981, furthering production of the Midas in kit and assembled form. Meanwhile, co-founder Jem Marsh started yet another company to reintroduce the old GT. By the 1980s, however, awareness of the Marcos had long since evaporated among most American enthusiasts.

1962-72 MARCOS

GT — FOUR/SIX/V-4/V-6 — Long and low in appearance, the Marcos coupe had a steeply raked windshield and door windows, a pointed nose, and full wheel openings. A straight fastback roofline led past a severely curved rear window and trunk lid, to a chopped-off tail. Headlamps were recessed in long nacelles and (in European form) sat behind clear curved windows. The entire nose section hinged forward, and was held in place by side latches. Standard equipment by 1971 included a leather-rimmed steering wheel, front disc brakes, carpeting, tachometer, lighter, two-speed wiper/washer, bucket seats (non-adjustable), adjustable pedals, console, sunroof, power windows, and dual airhorns. The option list included air conditioning and leather seats.

Note: Dimensions and other technical details shown below were valid for early 1970s models.

I.D. DATA: Not available.

Model	Body Type & Seating	Engine Type/CID	P.O.E. Price	Weight (lbs.)	Prod. Total
MARCOS GT					
1600	2-dr Coupe-2P	I4/98	N/A	1892	N/A
1800	2-dr Coupe-2P	I4/109	N/A	N/A	N/A
3-Litre	2-dr Coupe-2P	I6/182	5495	2010	N/A
3-Litre	2-dr Coupe-2P	V6/183	N/A	1949	N/A

Price Note: Figure shown was valid in 1971.
Model Note: Other engines also were available at various times in Marcos history.

ENGINE DATA: BASE FOUR (1967-69 1600): Inline, overhead-valve four-cylinder. Cast iron block and head. **Displacement:** 97.6 cu. in. (1599 cc). **Bore & Stroke:** 3.19 x 3.06 in. (81 x 77.6 mm). **Compression Ratio:** 9.0:1. **Brake Horsepower:** 88 at 5400 rpm. rpm. Five main bearings. Solid valve lifters. Weber two-barrel carburetor.
Note: A higher-performance 1600 also was available, with 10.5:1 compression and up to 120 bhp.
BASE FOUR (1964-68 1800): Inline, overhead-valve four-cylinder (Volvo). Cast iron block and head. **Displacement:** 108.6 cu. in. (1780 cc). **Bore & Stroke:** 3.31 x 3.15 in. (84.1 x 80 mm). **Compression Ratio:** 10.0:1. **Brake Horsepower:** 114 at 5800 rpm. Five main bearings. Solid valve lifters. Two Stromberg carburetors.
BASE SIX (1970-72, 3-Litre U.S. version): Inline, overhead-valve six-cylinder (Volvo). Cast iron block and head. **Displacement:** 181.7 cu. in. (2978 cc). **Bore & Stroke:** 3.50 x 3.15 in. (88.9 x 80 mm). **Compression Ratio:** 9.2:1. **Brake Horsepower:** 145 at 5500 rpm. Solid valve lifters. Two Stromberg carburetors.

BASE V-6 (1971-72, 3-Litre): 60-degree, overhead-valve "vee" type six-cylinder (Ford). Cast iron block and head. **Displacement:** 182.7 cu. in. (2994 cc). **Bore & Stroke:** 3.69 x 2.85 in. (93.7 x 72.4 mm). **Compression Ratio:** 8.9:1. **Brake Horsepower:** 140 at 4750 rpm. Five main bearings. Solid valve lifters. Weber carburetor.
CHASSIS DATA: Wheelbase: 89.5 in. **Overall Length:** 164.5 in. **Height:** 43.3 in. **Width:** 62.5 in. **Front Tread:** 48.75 in. **Rear Tread:** 51 in.
TECHNICAL: Layout: front-engine, rear-drive. **Transmission:** four-speed manual. **Steering:** rack and pinion. **Suspension (front):** wishbones with coil springs. **Suspension (rear):** rigid axle with radius arms, transverse linkage bar and coil springs. **Brakes:** front disc, rear drum. **Body Construction:** fiberglass, on tubular space frame.
PERFORMANCE: Top Speed: (3-Litre) 115 mph. **Acceleration (0-60 mph):** (3-Litre) 6.8 sec. **Fuel Mileage:** (3-Litre) 15-20 mpg.
ADDITIONAL MODELS: Also produced under the Marcos name were the Mini-Marcos, the Mantis, and (later in the 1970s) the Midas.
Manufacturer: Marcos Cars Ltd., Westbury, Wilts., England.
Distributor: Marcos International Inc., New York City.
Manufacturer Note: In 1959, the first company name was Speedex Castings & Accessories Ltd. That changed to Monocoque Chassis & Body Co. Ltd. in 1961; and to Marcos Cars Ltd. in 1962. The company was taken over by D & H Fibreglass Techniques Ltd. in 1975. Starting in 1981, yet another company, Jem Marsh Performance Cars, continued with production.

MASERATI

Although the Maserati brothers didn't form their own manufacturing company in Italy until 1926, they'd been involved with automobiles since the early days of the century. Competition automobiles, that is. Racing, not production, brought Carlo, Bindo, Alfieri, Ettore and Ernesto their early recognition. Bindo and Alfieri worked at Isotta-Fraschini, the latter as a test driver and auto racer. Carlo raced motorcycles (then cars) as early as 1899, on a bike he'd designed and built himself; but he died in 1911, before the company got underway.

Three of the brothers—Alfieri, Bindo and Ettore—started a firm in 1914 at Bologna, for the purpose of tuning Isotta racing cars. They also produced spark plugs during World War I, and worked on Isotta aircraft engines. After the war, by 1919, Alfieri opened a garage and the Maseratis built a four-cylinder racer. They also tried their collective hands at turning out a straight-eight race car, for another company.

When they formed the company that bore their surname in 1926, they chose Neptune's trident (symbol of their town, Bologna) as its insignia. Through the years prior to World War II (and for a few years beyond), the Maseratis turned out only racing models, some with twin-cam engines and superchargers. At best, a handful of them ranked as sport-racers that could conceivably take to the road.

Early in the 1920s, the Maseratis had worked at racing Diatto motorcars; then, at mid-decade, designed a supercharged Grand Prix car with twin-cam engine for that company. When Diatto went bankrupt, that race car wound up in the Maseratis' hands—a fortuitous turn of events that led to the first real Maserati vehicles.

Maserati's 1.5-liter Tipo (Type) 26 led to a class victory by brother Alfieri at the Targa Florio; and in 1927, to the Italian racing championship. In 1929, the company produced a V4 16-cylinder (Sedici Cilindri) engine that consisted of two 2-liter straight eights in a "vee" arrangement, atop a single crankcase. That car could hit the then-astounding speed of 155 mph. Precisely one roadgoing example was built, with a Zagato body. Semi-roadable models included the 4CS-1100 and 4CS-1500 of the early 1930s, along with several straight eights. Then, in 1938, the Maserati family sold their interest to a group headed by industrialist Adolfo Orsi, prompting a move from Bologna, Italy to Modena. For the next decade, the Maseratis remained under contractual obligation to the Orsi organization; but since World War II occupied most of that period, the agreement proved somewhat moot.

Following the war, as the Orsi agreement expired, the remaining Maserati brothers elected to form their own company once again. Thus, the postwar automobiles that bore their name had no input from the Maserati family. The Orsi-controlled company elected to mix racing and road cars. Nevertheless, through the next decade, prior to the debut of the 3500GT, no more than about 130 roadgoing Maseratis were produced.

At the Geneva auto show in March 1947, the Maseratis displayed a Farina-bodied version of the A6/1500 racer. That was actually the final design performed by the Maseratis for Orsi, as they left to form O.S.C.A. Maserati (see OSCA listing in this Catalog). A production version appeared in the following year, with the 1.5-liter single-cam six-cylinder engine, and remained on the market until 1957, evolving to the A6G/1500 and then the A6GC/2000 and A6GCS/2000 racer, the latter pair with 2.0-liter engines. Bodies came from Pinin Farina, Frua, Zagato, and other coachbuilders.

In 1957, a Maserati won the World Championship with Juan Manuel Fangio at the wheel. But at the Venezuelan Grand Prix, a series of accidents destroyed all four entrants. That tragedy brought official Maserati competition to a halt, abetted by the fact that Grand Prix racing had become prohibitively expensive. Production soon shifted into sports-racers and, especially GT (Grand Touring) machines.

The 3500GT series was built as late as 1966, with a 3485-cc engine and (in its second generation) Lucas fuel injection. Maserati also produced a small number of 5000GT models with 5.0-liter V-8 power. By 1964, a Quattroporte (four-door) sedan was in production, with a twin-cam 4136-cc V-8 under its hood, breathing through four Weber carburetors. Other models introduced during the 1960s included the Sebring and Mistral, as well as the Mexico and Ghibli. Another model was called the Indy, marking the two Maserati victories at the Indianapolis 500. That racing car, named the Boyle Special, had been driven by Wilbur Shaw in 1939 and '40. By 1970, the traditional inline sixes and Quattroporte sedan were dropped. A year later, Adolfo Orsi sold his interest in the company.

In 1968, Maserati had joined forces with Citroen, building a V-6 engine. Early in the 1970s, that pairing resulted in the Citroen SM (see Citroen listing).

A mid-engine Bora debuted in 1971, powered by 4.7-liter and 4.9-liter V-8s. Two years later, it was the Khamsin 2+2 coupe, with a 4.9-liter four-cam V-8. By May 1975, Citroen was under the control of Peugeot, and the plan was to liquidate Maserati. Stepping in to save the grand old name was Alejandro de Topmaso, who wound up with a 30 percent interest for himself. De Tomaso added the Frua-bodied Kyalami coupe.

A successor to the Quattroporte sedan was displayed in 1974, but the production version did not emerge until 1979. In 1982, Maserati debuted a Biturbo model which, as the name suggests, had twin turbochargers under its hood, shoving fuel and air into a 2.0-liter V-8 engine. A four-door Biturbo 425 joined later. Later in the decade, Chrysler and Maserati entered into a joint venture to produce Chrysler's TC by Maserati. Under the Maserati nameplate, a Spyder convertible became available, joining the line of sedans.

1946-50 MASERATI

A6/1500 — SIX — Maserati's first real roadgoing machine came in two-seat coupe and cabriolet form, with sleek styling by Pinin Farina. Tiny back seats technically gave some coupes 2+2 capacity. Appearance differed from the prototype, which had cycle fenders as well as disappearing headlamps and a sunroof. Its radiator was similar to that used on racing Maseratis, with a squarish split grille made up of horizontal bars, highlighted by a vertical center bar and twin curved upper bars. Small horizontal-bar intake units went alongside the grille, inboard of the headlamps. A split windshield was installed, along with vent wings and long rear quarter windows. The A6 rode a large-diameter tubular chassis, using coil springs up front and a rigid axle with coil springs at the rear. Under the hood was a 1488-cc (91-cid) single-overhead-cam six-cylinder engine, developing 65 horsepower. A four-speed manual transmission was standard. Wheelbase was 100.4 inches. A handful of Farina spiders (cabriolets) were built, as well as a single coupe with Zagato body.

I.D. DATA: Serial number range (1946-1950): 051 to 0110.

Model	Body Type & Seating	Engine Type/CID	P.O.E. Price	Weight (lbs.)	Prod. Total
A6/1500	2-dr Coupe-2+2P	I6/91	N/A	1765	Note 1
A6/1500	2-dr Cabr-2P	I6/91	N/A	1765	Note 1

Note 1: No more than 61 Maserati A6/1500 coupes and cabriolets were produced during the full model run (1946-50). Approximately three were built in 1947, nine in 1948, 25 in 1949, and 22 in 1950.

ENGINE DATA: BASE SIX: Inline, overhead-cam six-cylinder. **Displacement:** 90.8 cu. in. (1488 cc). **Bore & Stroke:** 2.60 x 2.85 in. (66 x 72.5 mm). **Compression Ratio:** 7.8:1. **Brake Horsepower:** 65 at 4700 rpm. Solid valve lifters. One Weber 36 DCR two-barrel carburetor.

CHASSIS DATA: Wheelbase: 100.4 in. **Overall Length:** 160.0 in. **Height:** 47.2 in. **Front Tread:** 50.2 in. **Rear Tread:** 49.3 in. **Standard Tires:** 5.50x16.

TECHNICAL: Layout: front-engine, rear-drive. **Transmission:** four-speed manual. Gear ratios: (1st) 3.68:1; (2nd) 1.78:1; (3rd) 1.35:1; (4th) 1.00:1. **Suspension (front):** upper/lower wishbones with coil springs. **Suspension (rear):** rigid axle with trailing radius arms and coil springs. **Brakes:** hydraulic, front/rear drum. **Body Construction:** separate body on tubular chassis.

PERFORMANCE: Top Speed: 95 mph (factory claim). **Manufacturer:** Officine Alfieri Maserati S.p.A., Modena, Italy.

HISTORY: Even though the A6/1500 wasn't formally announced until 1947, and shown to the public at the Geneva Salon in that year, two were built in 1946. Its powerplant evolved from the supercharged twin-cam 6CM racing engine used in 1936, and was conceived by Ernesto Maserati. Design work began in 1943.

1951-53 MASERATI

A6G — SIX — The next Maserati was similar in configuration and appearance to the original A6/1500, but had a larger (1954-cc) six-cylinder engine that developed 100 horsepower. Compression ratio was 7.8:1, and the engine breathed through three Weber carburetors. As before, a four-speed was the sole transmission, and the car rode a tubular chassis. Leaf springs now were used at the rear, with coil springs up front. The grille was similar to that used in the A6/1500, but other details differed. Coupe bodies came from Frua, Pinin Farina, and Vignale, plus a handful created by Ghia and Bertone. Cabriolets were done by Frua. Maserati literature described this model as being for grand touring (Grande Tourisme), and promoted its aerodynamic lines.

I.D. DATA: Serial number range: 2013 to 2030.

Model	Body Type & Seating	Engine Type/CID	P.O.E. Price	Weight (lbs.)	Prod. Total
A6G	2-dr Coupe-2+2P	I6/119	N/A	1900	Note 1
A6G	2-dr Cabr-2+2P	I6/119	N/A	1900	Note 1

Note 1: A total of 16 Maserati A6G models with single-cam engine were produced from 1951-54.

Seating Note: Maserati literature claimed 2+2 passenger capacity, but most rear seats were for occasional use only.

Weight Note: Figure shown was average; actual weights varied with custom body.

ENGINE DATA: BASE SIX: Inline, overhead-cam six-cylinder. **Displacement:** 119.2 cu. in. (1954 cc). **Bore & Stroke:** 2.83 x 3.15 in. (72 x 80 mm). **Compression Ratio:** 7.8:1. **Brake Horsepower:** 100 at 5550 rpm. Solid valve lifters. Three Weber carburetors.

CHASSIS DATA: Wheelbase: 100.4 in. **Front Tread:** 50.2 in. **Rear Tread:** 49.3 in. **Wheel Type:** pressed steel (or Borrani wire). **Standard Tires:** 5.50x16.

TECHNICAL: Layout: front-engine, rear-drive. **Transmission:** four-speed manual. **Steering:** recirculating ball. **Suspension (front):** upper/lower wishbones with coil springs. **Suspension (rear):** rigid axle with radius arms and leaf springs. **Brakes:** hydraulic, front/rear drum. **Body Construction:** separate body on tubular chassis.

PERFORMANCE: Top Speed: about 100 mph. **Acceleration (0-60 mph):** 12.5 sec. **Manufacturer:** Officine Alfieri Maserati S.p.A., Modena, Italy.

HISTORY: Production of the A6G began in 1951 and continued into 1957.

1954-56 MASERATI

1954 Maserati Model A6GCS two-door roadster.

A6G — SIX — Production of the A6G with 1954-cc engine continued into 1954; see previous listing for additional details.

A6G/2000 — SIX — Not only was the six-cylinder engine slightly larger in displacement this time, it was a dual-overhead-cam design rather than the single-cam used in the former A6G. The bigger engine was a detuned version of Maserati's Formula 2 powerplant, differing in bore and stroke dimensions from the single-cam A6G engine. Custom-built coupe and spider (convertible) bodies were styled by Vignale, Zagato, Frua, and Allemano. (Pinin Farina had only worked on the earlier A6G models.) Grilles were similar among the bodies, but appearance otherwise differed. The oval-shaped grille dipped at the upper center to form two sections, each containing three horizontal bars and two vertical bars. The Frua spider, to take one example, had a wraparound windshield and a wide grille made up of thin vertical bars with large round trident insignia in the center. Small round parking lights sat below the headlamps, with large auxiliary lights mounted slightly inboard. At the rear were vertical taillamps. A bodyside trim strip ran just below the door handle, between the wheel housings, with identifying script just above (at the cowl). See next listing for additional details.

Note: The model designation A6G54/2000 (to indicate the 1954 debut year) sometimes was used.

I.D. DATA: Serial number range: 2101 to 2198 (not all consecutive numbers were used).

Model	Body Type & Seating	Engine Type/CID	P.O.E. Price	Weight (lbs.)	Prod. Total
A6G	2-dr Coupe-2+2P	I6/119	N/A	1900	Note 1
A6G	2-dr Cabr-2+2P	I6/119	N/A	1900	Note 1
A6G/2000	2-dr Coupe-2+2P	I6/121	Note 2	1900	Note 3
A6G/2000	2-dr Cabr-2+2P	I6/121	N/A	1900	Note 3

Note 1: A total of 16 Maserati A6G models with single-cam engine were produced from 1951-54.
Note 2: Price at the factory was approximately $6330.
Note 3: No more than 61 Maserati A6G/2000 models with twin-cam engine were produced from 1954-57.
Seating Note: Maserati literature claimed 2+2 passenger capacity, but most rear seats were for occasional use only.
Weight Note: Figure shown was average; actual weights varied with custom body.

1956 Maserati A6G/2000. (Coys of Kensington)

ENGINE DATA: BASE SIX (A6G): Inline, overhead-cam six-cylinder. **Displacement:** 119.2 cu. in. (1954 cc). **Bore & Stroke:** 2.83 x 3.15 in. (72 x 80 mm). **Compression Ratio:** 7.8:1. **Brake Horsepower:** 100 at 5500 rpm. Solid valve lifters. Three Weber carburetors.

BASE SIX (A6G/2000): Inline, dual-overhead-cam six-cylinder. **Displacement:** 121.1 cu. in. (1985 cc). **Bore & Stroke:** 3.01 x 2.83 in. (76.5 x 72 mm). **Compression Ratio:** 8.0:1. **Brake Horsepower:** 150 at 6000 rpm. **Torque:** 123 lbs.-ft. at 5000 rpm. Solid valve lifters. Three Weber carburetors.

Note: Engines with higher horsepower ratings also were available.

CHASSIS DATA: Wheelbase: 100.4 in. **Overall Length:** up to 179 in. **Height:** up to 55 in. **Width:** 63.8 in. **Front Tread:** 53.5 in. **Rear Tread:** 48.0 in. **Wheel Type:** center-lock Borrani wire. **Standard Tires:** 6.00x16.

TECHNICAL: Layout: front-engine, rear-drive. **Transmission:** four-speed manual. **Steering:** recirculating ball. **Suspension (front):** upper/lower wishbones with coil springs. **Suspension (rear):** rigid axle with radius arms and leaf springs. **Brakes:** hydraulic, front/rear drum. **Body Construction:** separate body on tubular chassis.

PERFORMANCE: Top Speed: (A6G/2000) 118 mph (some reports claimed as much as 140 mph). **Acceleration (0-60 mph):** (A6G/2000) 10.0 sec.

ADDITIONAL MODELS: Maserati's A6GCS aluminum-bodied sports racing car rode a 90.1-inch wheelbase and measured 144 inches overall. Power came from a twin-cam 121.3-cid six-cylinder engine with three Weber carburetors and 8.75:1 compression, developing at least 160 horsepower at 7000 rpm. The engine evolved from an all-out Formula II racer. The A6GCS was reported to accelerate to 60 mph in about 8 seconds, and be capable of 142 to 150 mph. Aimed at American sports-car racing, it sold for about $8500 in the U.S. and was a top contender in Class E competition. By 1954, the A6GCS used integral fenders, whereas earlier examples had zeus-fastened separate fenders. The oval grille contained vertical bars. One publication in 1954 claimed that only two had been imported into the U.S., though Maserati was building 60 sports cars and a dozen racing cars annually.

Maserati produced other racing models as well, including the 150/S with a 90.5-cid four-cylinder engine; the open-wheel 250F with a 2494-cc (152-cid) six; and the 300/S, powered by a 185.5-cid six. The 250F engine developed 245 horsepower at 7200 rpm, and was said to be capable of 164 mph. It was the last front-engined Maserati racing car, and the one used by Juan Manuel Fangio to win five Grand Prix races in 1957.

Manufacturer: Officine Alfieri Maserati S.p.A., Modena, Italy.

HISTORY: The A6G/2000 debuted at the 1954 Paris Salon and was on sale by spring 1955.

1957-61 MASERATI

1958 Maserati 3500 GT. (Coys of Kensington)

A6G/2000/C — SIX — Production of the successor to the A6/1500 and A6G continued into 1957. With three twin-barrel Weber carburetors, the 2.0-liter twin-cam engine developed 165 horsepower at 6000 rpm. A single-carb version produced 150 bhp. The engine had twin ignition and exhaust headers. Houdaille shocks went on all wheels, and brake drums were finned. A huge trident sat in a round enclosure at the center of the recessed oval grille. Four models were advertised as available in the U.S. in 1957: a Zagato lightweight competition coupe, an Allemano touring coupe, and a Frua-built coupe and convertible. Standard equipment on final examples included an 8500-rpm tachometer and 160-mph speedometer, and a laminated mahogany steering wheel. Allemano coupes included leather upholstery, Borrani knock-off wire wheels, racing brakes, a tool kit, radio and heater. Seats were bolster-style (not buckets). See prior listing for additional details.

3500GT — SIX — The 3500GT was Maserati's first model built in significant quantity. The front end was similar to the A6G/2000, but contained a recessed eggcrate-patterned grille with round trident insignia in the center. Round parking lights and large round auxiliary lights again were installed, with vertical taillamps and a mild wraparound rear window, along with rounded tailfins. Grilled air intakes were installed on the lower cowl, and an airscoop in the hood. Design was the work of Giulio Alfieri (Maserati's chief engineer). Most coupes were built by Touring, while the Spider roadster was done by Vignale, atop a large-diameter tubular chassis similar to that used in the A6 series. Because they were custom-bodied, no two were quite alike. The Touring coupe had a straight fenderline, with air vents behind front wheel wells. The rigid rear axle was connected to the frame by rods above and cantilever leaf springs below. Under each hood was an enlarged twin-cam engine, displacing 3485 cc (213 cid) and developing 220 horsepower. Essentially a detuned version of the 350S racing engine, the six used two spark plugs per cylinder. A ZF four-speed gearbox (all-synchro) was the only transmission at first, with a long angled gearshift lever; but a five-speed became optional in 1960, then standard the next year. Front disc brakes joined the option list in 1959, and were standard in 1960. In 1959, the Touring body added front vent wings, and center-lock wire wheels were optional. So was a limited-slip differential.

I.D. DATA: Not available.

Model	Body Type & Seating	Engine Type/CID	P.O.E. Price	Weight (lbs.)	Prod. Total
A6G/2000/C					
Allemano	2-dr Coupe-2+2P	I6/121	9500	1850	Note 1
Frua	2-dr Cabr-2+2P	I6/121	10450	1900	Note 1
Frua	2-dr Coupe	I6/121	9900	N/A	Note 1
Zagato	2-dr Coupe-2+2P	I6/121	8900	2200	Note 1
3500GT					
	2-dr Coupe-2+2P	I6/213	11400	2800	Note 2
Spider	2-dr Rds-2P	I6/213	12300	2800	Note 2

Note 1: A total of 59 Maserati A6G/2000 models with twin-cam engine were produced from 1953-57.
Note 2: A total of 2,223 Maserati 3500GT (and later GTI) were produced from 1957-64.
Price Note: Figures shown for A6G/2000 were valid in 1957. Figures shown for 3500GT were valid in 1961.
Weight Note: Figures shown were average; actual weights varied with custom bodies.

383

1960 Maserati Tipo 61 "Birdcage." (Coys of Kensington)

ENGINE DATA: BASE SIX (A6G/2000): Inline, dual-overhead-cam six-cylinder. **Displacement:** 121.1 cu. in. (1985 cc). **Bore & Stroke:** 3.03 x 2.83 in. (77 x 72 mm). **Compression Ratio:** 8.0:1. **Brake Horsepower:** 150 at 6000 rpm (165 bhp with three twin-barrel carburetors). **Torque:** 123 lbs.-ft. at 5000 rpm. Solid valve lifters. Three Weber one- or two-barrel carburetors.
BASE SIX (3500GT): Inline, dual-overhead-cam six-cylinder. Aluminum alloy block and head. **Displacement:** 212.7 cu. in. (3485 cc). **Bore & Stroke:** 3.39 x 3.94 in. (86 x 100 mm). **Compression Ratio:** 8.5:1. **Brake Horsepower:** 220 at 5500 rpm. **Torque:** 253 lbs.-ft. at 3500 rpm. Solid valve lifters. Three twin-barrel carburetors.

Note: Other Maserati literature announced 3500GT engine output as 240 bhp at 5500 rpm, with 8.2:1 compression. For 1961, the rating was 220/230 bhp at 5500 rpm with 8.5:1 compression.

CHASSIS DATA: Wheelbase: (A6G/2000) 100.4 in.; (3500GT cpe) 102.3 in.; (3500GT rds) 98.4 in. **Overall Length:** (A6G/2000) up to 179 in.; (3500GT cpe) 184 in.; (3500GT rds) 175 in. **Height:** (A6G/2000) up to 55 in.; (3500GT cpe) 51 in.; (3500GT rds) 51.5 in. **Width:** (A6G/2000) 63.8 in.; (3500GT cpe) 69 in.; (rds) 64.5 in. **Front Tread:** (A6G/2000) 53.5 in.; (3500GT) 54.7 in. **Rear Tread:** (A6G/2000) 48.0 in.; (3500GT) 53.5 in. **Standard Tires:** (A6G/2000) 6.00x16; (3500GT) 6.50x16 (later, 185x16).

TECHNICAL: Layout: front-engine, rear-drive. **Transmission:** four-speed manual; five-speed optional on 3500GT in 1960, standard in 1961. **Steering:** recirculating ball. **Suspension (front):** (A6G/2000) upper/lower A-arms with coil springs; (3500GT) upper/lower A-arms with coil springs and anti-roll bar. **Suspension (rear):** (3500GT) rigid axle with radius arms, elliptical leaf springs and torsion stabilizer bar. **Brakes:** hydraulic, front/rear drum; front discs optional on 3500GT in 1959, standard in 1960. **Body Construction:** separate body on tubular chassis.

PERFORMANCE: Top Speed: (A6G/2000) 117-130 mph (though some reports claimed as much as 140 mph); (3500GT) 140 mph (Maserati claimed 137-145 mph). **Acceleration (0-60 mph):** (A6G/2000) 8.2-10.0 sec.; (Allemano A6G/2000) 12.6 sec.; (3500GT) 8.1 sec. **Acceleration (quarter-mile):** (Allemano A6G/2000) 19.0 sec. (76 mph).

1961 Maserati 3500 GT Spider.

ADDITIONAL MODELS: A total of 31 5000GT road cars were produced from 1959-64, with 5.0-liter V-8 engine. This 2 + 2 coupe rode a 102.3-inch wheelbase and measured 189 inches long, standing 52 inches tall. The four-cam 301.5-inch V-8 (3.70 x 3.50 inch bore/stroke) had 8.5:1 compression and produced 325 horsepower at 5500 rpm. The rear axle used dual cantilever springs and radius rods. Disc brakes had a servo assist. Top speed was claimed to be 168 mph. The 5000GT was listed in directories of imports to the U.S.
Through 1957, Maserati continued to produce a series of racing cars, including a 200S with 2.0-liter engine, the 150/S roadster with 140-bhp four, and the 3.0-liter 300/S. A competition 150/S sold in the U.S. for approximately $8175 in 1957; the 300/S for $11,880. A 200SI had a price tag of $11,475 and could accelerate to 60 mph in 4.4 seconds, according to *Sports Cars Illustrated*. Maserati claimed that its 450/S model with 4.5-liter V-8 engine was the fastest sports car in the world. Early in the 1960s, Maserati "birdcage" racing cars were said to be available on order, to qualified buyers.

Manufacturer: Officine Alfieri Maserati S.p.A., Modena, Italy.
Distributor: Maserati Corp. of America, Westbury, Long Island, New York; Maserati Southwest Distributors, North Hollywood, California; Mille Miglia Motors, San Francisco; Charles Rezzaghi, San Francisco (and others).

HISTORY: The 3500GT appeared at the Geneva Salon early in 1957, and was on sale later that year. Its tubular-steel chassis and drivetrain would continue in the subsequent Sebring and Mistral. *Motor Trend* in 1957 reported Stirling Moss' appraisal in its review of the A6G2000/C, that "there is no better handling sports car in the world" than a Maserati, "with the possible exception of a Ferrari 3.5." While praising the 2000-series handling and beauty in 1957, *Motor Trend* noted that its "noise level is extremely high" and its "ride is choppy."

1962 MASERATI

3500GTI — SIX — Mechanical fuel injection was added to the 3500GT engine, turning it into the 3500GTI and boosting horsepower from 220 to 235. In 1962, this model also added small triangular vent panes at the rear of windows.

SEBRING — SERIES I — SIX — Maserati's successor to the 3500GT series wore a more modern body atop the former tubular-steel chassis and basic drivetrain. All had bodies built by Vignale: two-seat notchback coupes (with occasional rear seats) displaying a straight-through fenderline from front to rear. A recessed blackout mesh-patterned grille contained a trident emblem. Quad round headlamps sat above rounded rectangular park/signal lights. Working air vents went at the rear of front wheel openings. Other styling features included angled 'B' pillars, front vent wings, and triangular rear quarter windows. Vertical-style taillamp housings held two round lenses separated by a small rectangular lens. 'Sebring' script went on the left side of a squared-off rear panel. Wheelbase was 98.4 inches. Initial models were powered by the same 3485-cc six-cylinder engine as the 3500GTI, with Lucas fuel injection. Later, displacement would grow to 3694-cc and then to 4014-cc. A five-speed ZF manual gearbox was standard, with three-speed automatic optional. All-disc brakes were installed. Options included air conditioning, special paint, radio, and wire wheels.

I.D. DATA: Not available.

Model	Body Type & Seating	Engine Type/CID	P.O.E. Price	Weight (lbs.)	Prod. Total
3500GTI					
	2-dr Coupe-2 + 2P	I6/213	11400	2800	Note 1
Spider	2-dr Rds-2P	I6/213	12300	2800	Note 1
SEBRING					
	2-dr Coupe-2 + 2P	I6/213	N/A	3330	Note 2

Note 1: A total of 2,223 Maserati 3500GT (and later GTI) were produced from 1957-64.
Note 2: At least 444 Maserati Sebrings were produced (346 Series I and 98 Series II) from 1962-66.
Weight Note: Figures shown are averages; actual weights varied with custom bodies.
ENGINE DATA: BASE SIX (3500GTI): Inline, dual-overhead-cam six-cylinder Aluminum alloy block and head. **Displacement:** 212.7 cu. in. (3485 cc). **Bore & Stroke:** 3.39 x 3.94 in. (86 x 100 mm). **Compression Ratio:** 8.8:1. **Brake Horsepower:** 235 at 5800 rpm. **Torque:** 261 lbs.-ft. at 4000 rpm. Solid valve lifters. Lucas mechanical fuel injection.

BASE SIX (Sebring): Same as 3485-cc six above, except — **Brake Horsepower:** 235 at 5500 rpm. **Torque:** 232 lbs.-ft. at 4000 rpm.

Note: Later Sebrings had a 3694-cc six-cylinder engine that developed 245 bhp; and later yet, a 4014-cc six rated 155 bhp; see subsequent listings for full data.

CHASSIS DATA: Wheelbase: (3500GTI cpe) 102.3 in.; (3500GTI rds) 98.4 in. (Sebring) 98.4 in. **Overall Length:** (3500GTI cpe) 184 in.; (3500GTI rds) 175 in.; (Sebring) 176.0 in. **Height:** (3500GTI) 51 in.; (Sebring) 51 in. **Width:** (3500GTI cpe) 69 in.; (3500GTI rds) 64.5 in.; (Sebring) 65.4 in. **Front Tread:** (3500GTI) 54.7 in.; (Sebring) 54.7 in. **Rear Tread:** (3500GTI) 53.5 in.; (Sebring) 53.5 in. **Standard Tires:** 6.50x16 or 185x16.

TECHNICAL: Transmission: five-speed manual; three-speed optional on Sebring. **Steering:** recirculating ball. **Suspension (front):** upper/lower A-arms with coil springs and anti-roll bar. **Suspension (rear):** rigid axle with radius arms, semi-elliptic leaf springs and anti-roll bar. **Brakes:** (Sebring) front/rear disc. **Body Construction:** separate body on tubular chassis.

PERFORMANCE: Top Speed: (3500GTI) 146 mph claimed; (Sebring) 135+ mph. **Acceleration (0-60 mph):** (Sebring) 8.4 sec.

ADDITIONAL MODELS: A total of 31 Type 5000GT road cars were produced from 1959-64, with 5.0-liter V-8 engine.

Manufacturer: Officine Alfieri Maserati S.p.A., Modena, Italy.

Distributor: Maserati Representatives of California, Los Angeles; and Rallye Motors Inc., Glen Cove, Long Island, New York.

HISTORY: Maserati's Sebring coupe debuted at the Geneva (Switzerland) auto show in 1962. Maserati had only four dealers in the U.S. in 1962.

1963-64 MASERATI

3500GTI — SIX — Production of the fuel-injected version of the 3500GT continued into 1964; see previous listings for full details.

SEBRING — SIX — Production of the 3500GTI's successor continued into 1966; see previous listing for full detail.

MISTRAL — SIX — Styling changed considerably for the next Maserati model, designed by Pietro Frua as a sporty followup to the Sebring. For one, the occasional rear seats in back were gone, reducing the new fastback coupe to a strict two-seater. This was also a hatchback body, with lift-up back window and no outside trunklid. A Spider roadster (convertible) joined the coupe a bit later. Shorter in wheelbase at 94.5 inches, the Mistral was similar in overall length to the Sebring. Both bodies displayed rounded profiles with a lower beltline and curved glass; a long, sloping hood with small airscoop; and a slim wraparound front bumper above the grille. A low, split air intake went below that bumper. Slim front vent wings were installed. The tall greenhouse contained ample glass area, while a tall (rather stubby) tail with horizontal taillamps brought up the rear. Maserati script and the trident insignia were evident on the back panel, alongside the license plate. The coupe also had a modest kickup at the base of the quarter window.

Aluminum was used for doors, hood and hatch, while the remainder of the body was made of steel. Early examples used the same 3.5-liter six-cylinder engines that powered the 3500GT series and the Sebring; but that would be replaced after 1964 by 3964-cc and 4014-cc versions, as in the Sebring. Named for a hot Mediterranean desert wind, the Mistral proved comparably hot when hitting the gas pedal hard. Either a five-speed manual or three-speed automatic transmission was available.

QUATTROPORTE — V-8 — Having progressed from all-out race cars to sports-racers to road machines, Maserati now turned to a four-door sedan. No ordinary sedan, that is, but a four-seat GT near-supercar, styled by Pietro Frua with an intriguing collection of curves and angles. A split grille held the usual Maserati trident in its center, in a protruding front end. The tall greenhouse had sizable glass area. European models initially had rectangular headlamps; while later versions (and all sent to the U.S.) wore quad round headlamps. Down below was a tubular and box-section chassis, with all-disc brakes. A De Dion rear axle was installed at first, but later examples switched to a conventional rigid axle with semi-elliptic leaf springs. Under the hood was a 4.1-liter, four-cam V-8, evolved from the 450S racing engine. That engine was destined to remain under Maserati hoods through the 1970s, though growing from its initial 4136-cc displacement to 4719-cc in the late 1960s.

I.D. DATA: Serial number is on metal plate attached to inside of right inner fender panel.

Model	Body Type & Seating	Engine Type/CID	P.O.E. Price	Weight (lbs.)	Prod. Total
3500GTI					
	2-dr Coupe-2+2P	I6/213	12000	2800	Note 1
Spider	2-dr Conv-2P	I6/213	13000	2800	Note 1
SEBRING					
	2-dr Coupe-2+2P	I6/225	N/A	3330	Note 2
MISTRAL					
	2-dr Coupe-2P	I6/213	N/A	2800	Note 3
Spider	2-dr Conv-2P	I6/213	N/A	2800	Note 3
QUATTROPORTE					
	4-dr Sedan-4P	V8/252	15000	3638	Note 4

Note 1: A total of 2,223 Maserati 3500GT (and later GTI) were produced from 1957-64.
Note 2: A total of 446 Maserati Sebrings were produced (348 Series I and 98 Series II) from 1962-66.
Note 3: A total of 948 Mistrals (828 coupes and 120 Spiders) were produced from 1963-70.
Note 4: A total of 759 Quattroportes were produced from 1963-69.
3500GTI Price Note: Although the fuel-injected 3500GTI had been available for some time, U.S. directories listed the carbureted version for $500 less than figures shown above.
Weight Note: Figures shown are averages; actual weights varied depending on body.

1963 Maserati 3500 GT. (Coys of Kensington)

ENGINE DATA: BASE SIX (3500GTI, early Mistral): Inline, dual-overhead-cam six-cylinder. Aluminum alloy block and head. **Displacement:** 212.7 cu. in. (3485 cc). **Bore & Stroke:** 3.39 x 3.94 in. (86 x 100 mm). **Compression Ratio:** 8.5:1. **Brake Horsepower:** 235 at 5800 rpm. **Torque:** 261 lbs.-ft. at 4000 rpm. Seven main bearings. Solid valve lifters. Lucas mechanical fuel injection.
Note: A carbureted 3485-cc (3500GT) engine still was listed, rated 220 bhp at 5500 rpm.
BASE SIX (later Sebring): Inline, dual-overhead-cam six-cylinder. Aluminum alloy block and head. **Displacement:** 225 cu. in. (3694 cc). **Bore & Stroke:** 3.39 x 4.17 in. (86 x 106 mm). **Compression Ratio:** 8.8:1. **Brake Horsepower:** 245 at 5200 rpm. **Torque:** 253 lbs.-ft. at 4000 rpm. Seven main bearings. Solid valve lifters. Lucas mechanical fuel injection.
Note: Early Sebrings were powered by the same 3485-cc engine used in the 3500GT series (and early Mistral).
BASE SIX (later Mistral): Same as 3694-cc six above, except — **Brake Horsepower:** 255 at 5500 rpm. **Torque:** 253 lbs.-ft. at 4000 rpm.
BASE V-8 (Quattroporte): 90-degree, dual-overhead-cam "vee" type eight-cylinder. Aluminum alloy block and head. **Displacement:** 252.4 cu. in. (4136 cc). **Bore & Stroke:** 3.46 x 3.35 in. (88 x 85 mm). **Compression Ratio:** 8.5:1. **Brake Horsepower:** 260 at 5000 rpm. Five main bearings. Solid valve lifters. Four Weber carburetors.

CHASSIS DATA: Wheelbase: (3500GTI) 102.3 in.; (Sebring) 102.3 in.; (Mistral) 94.5 in.; (Quattro) 108.3 in. **Overall Length:** (3500GTI) 184 in.; (Sebring) 176.0 in.; (Mistral) 177.0 in.; (Quattro) 196 in. **Height:** (3500GTI) 51 in.; (Sebring) 51 in.; (Mistral) 51 in.; (Quattro) 53.5 in. **Width:** (3500GTI) 69 in.; (Sebring) 65 in.; (Mistral) 65 in.; (Quattro) 68 in. **Front Tread:** (3500GTI/Sebring/Mistral) 54.7 in.; (Quattro) 54.7 in. **Rear Tread:** (3500GTI/Sebring/Mistral) 53.5 in.; (Quattro) 55.1 in. **Standard Tires:** (3500GTI) 5.50x16; (Sebring) 185x16; (Mistral) 205x15; (Quattro) 205x14.

TECHNICAL: Layout: front-engine, rear-drive. **Transmission:** five-speed manual; three-speed automatic optional on Sebring/Mistral. **Steering:** recirculating ball. **Suspension (front):** upper/lower A-arms with coil springs and anti-roll bar. **Suspension (rear):** (3500GTI/Sebring/Mistral) rigid axle with radius arms and semi-elliptic leaf springs; (early 3500GTI/Sebring/Mistral) De Dion axle with leaf springs. **Brakes:** front/rear disc. **Body Construction:** separate body on tubular chassis.

PERFORMANCE: Top Speed: (Mistral) 145+ mph; (Quattroporte) 130 mph. **Acceleration (0-60 mph):** (Mistral) 9.0 sec. or less.

ADDITIONAL MODELS: Directories of imported cars also listed the 5000GT with its fuel-injected 5.0-liter engine, priced at $16,300. A total of 31 Type 5000GT road cars were produced from 1959-64.

Manufacturer: Officine Alfieri Maserati S.p.A., Modena, Italy.
Distributor: Auto Distributors of New York, Woodside, New York; Hoffman Motors Corp., Los Angeles, California.
HISTORY: Mistral would be the last Maserati with a front-mounted inline six-cylinder engine. The Quattroporte sedan appeared at the Turin (Italy) auto show in 1963.

1965-66 MASERATI

1965 Maserati Mistral Spider. (Coys of Kensington)

SEBRING — SERIES II — SIX — Production of the 3500GTI's successor continued into 1966. The second series had a lower hood scoop and hooded headlamps, as well as the larger 3694-cc engine. Some examples had an even larger 4014-cc engine. See previous listing for additional details.

MISTRAL — SIX — Production of the sporty Mistral coupe and Spider continued into 1970, with two engine sizes available; see previous listing for full details.

MEXICO — V-8 — The next new Maserati model, destined to become one of the best-known (even though only 250 were built), was the Mexico notchback coupe. Styled and built by Vignale, the four-seater rode a short-wheelbase variant of the Quattroporte sedan's platform. Styling features included a low beltline with wide hood and grille, squarish rear wheel openings, thin roof pillars, front vent wings, and large pentagonal rear quarter windows. Quad round headlamps stood alongside the rectangular grille with crosshatch pattern and center insignia, and above rectangular park/signal lights. A bodyside trim strip ran from the front wheel opening to the rear panel. A louvered section was evident at the cowl, below the trim strip. 'Maserati' script decorated the back panel, which contained protruding horizontal taillamps. Leaf springs were used for the rear suspension (as on later Quattroportes). Wire wheels were standard. Rather than a 2+2 coupe with minimal back seat, the Mexico ranked as a four-passenger rival to the sedan, allowing those in the rear to enjoy a bit of comfort. Initial Mexico coupes carried the 4719-cc V-8 engine that also was used in later Quattroportes, developing 290 horsepower and hooked to a ZF five-speed manual gearbox. A three-speed automatic transmission also was available. Later on, a 4.1-liter V-8 would be offered. Wheelbase was 103.9 inches, and the tubular chassis included boxed steel sections.

QUATTROPORTE — 4200 — V-8 — Production of Maserati's sedan supercar continued into 1968 with the initial 4136-cc engine, then switched to a 4719-cc version for 1968-69; see previous listing for full details.

I.D. DATA: Not available.

Model	Body Type & Seating	Engine Type/CID	P.O.E. Price	Weight (lbs.)	Prod. Total
SEBRING					
II	2-dr Coupe-2+2P	I6/225	12800	3330	Note 1
MISTRAL					
	2-dr Coupe-2P	I6/225	12925	2866	Note 2
Spider	2-dr Conv-2P	I6/225	N/A	2800	Note 2
MEXICO					
	2-dr Coupe-4P	V8/288	N/A	3640	Note 3
QUATTROPORTE					
4200	4-dr Sedan-4P	V8/252	13350	3638	Note 4

Note 1: A total of 446 Maserati Sebrings were produced (348 Series I and 98 Series II) from 1962-66.
Note 2: A total of 948 Mistrals (828 coupes and 120 Spiders) were produced from 1963-70.
Note 3: A total of 250 Mexico coupes were produced from 1965-68.
Note 4: A total of 759 Quattroporte sedans were produced from 1963-69.
Model Note: Some American directories continued to list the 3500GT coupe, priced at $11,500; the 3500GTI convertible at $13,086; and the 3700GTI coupe at $12,000.
Weight Note: Figures shown are approximate.

ENGINE DATA: BASE SIX (Sebring, Mistral): Inline, dual-overhead-cam six-cylinder. Aluminum alloy block and head. **Displacement:** 225 cu. in. (3694 cc). **Bore & Stroke:** 3.39 x 4.17 in. (86 x 106 mm). **Compression Ratio:** 8.8:1. **Brake Horsepower:** (Sebring) 245 at 5200 rpm; (Mistral) 255 at 5500 rpm. **Torque:** 253 lbs.-ft. at 4000 rpm. Seven main bearings. Solid valve lifters. Lucas mechanical fuel injection.
OPTIONAL SIX (Sebring, Mistral): Inline, dual-overhead-cam six-cylinder. Aluminum alloy block and head. **Displacement:** 245 cu. in. (4014 cc). **Bore & Stroke:** 3.46 x 4.33 in. (88 x 110 mm). **Compression Ratio:** 8.8:1. **Brake Horsepower:** 255 at 5200 rpm. **Torque:** 267 lbs.-ft. at 4000 rpm. Seven main bearings. Solid valve lifters. Lucas mechanical fuel injection.
BASE V-8 (Quattroporte, later Mexico): 90-degree, dual-overhead-cam "vee" type eight-cylinder. Aluminum alloy block and head. **Displacement:** 252.4 cu. in. (4136 cc). **Bore & Stroke:** 3.46 x 3.35 in. (88 x 85 mm). **Compression Ratio:** 8.5:1. **Brake Horsepower:** 260 at 5000 rpm. **Torque:** 268 lbs.-ft. at 4000 rpm. Five main bearings. Solid valve lifters. Four Weber carburetors.

BASE V-8 (Mexico): 90-degree, dual-overhead-cam "vee" type eight-cylinder. Aluminum alloy block and head. **Displacement:** 288 cu. in. (4719 cc). **Bore & Stroke:** 3.70 x 3.35 in. (94 x 85 mm). **Compression Ratio:** 8.5:1. **Brake Horsepower:** 290 at 5500 rpm. **Torque:** 290 lbs.-ft. at 4000 rpm. Five main bearings. Solid valve lifters. Four Weber carburetors.
CHASSIS DATA: Wheelbase: (Sebring) 102.3 in.; (Mistral) 94.5 in.; (Mexico) 103.9 in.; (Quattro) 108.3 in. **Overall Length:** (Sebring) 176.0 in.; (Mistral) 177.0 in.; (Mexico) 187.4 in.; (Quattro) 197 in. **Height:** (Sebring) 51 in.; (Mistral) 51 in.; (Mexico) 53.2 in.; (Quattro) 53.5 in. **Width:** (Sebring) 65 in.; (Mistral) 65 in.; (Mexico) 68.1 in.; (Quattro) 67-68 in. **Front Tread:** (Sebring/Mistral) 54.7 in.; (Quattro/Mexico) 54.7 in. **Rear Tread:** (Sebring/Mistral) 53.5 in.; (Mexico) 53.5 in.; (Quattro) 55.1 in. **Standard Tires:** (Sebring) 185x16; (Mistral/Mexico) 205x15; (Quattro) 6.00x15.
TECHNICAL: Layout: front-engine, rear-drive. **Transmission:** (Sebring) five-speed manual; (Mistral/Quattroporte/Mexico) ZF five-speed manual or three-speed automatic. **Steering:** recirculating ball. **Suspension (front):** upper/lower A-arms with coil springs and anti-roll bar. **Suspension (rear):** rigid axle with radius arms and semi-elliptic leaf springs. **Brakes:** front/rear disc. **Body Construction:** separate body on tubular chassis.
PERFORMANCE: Top Speed: (Mexico) 155+ mph. **Acceleration (0-60 mph):** (Mexico) about 7.5 sec.
Manufacturer: Officine Alfieri Maserati S.p.A., Modena, Italy.
Distributor: Jaguar-Daimler Distributors, Woodside, New York; Hoffman Motors Corp., Los Angeles, California.
HISTORY: Maserati's Ghibli debuted late in 1966; see next listing for details.

1968 4.7-liter Maserati Ghibli Berlinetta. (Christie's)

ENGINE DATA: BASE SIX (Mistral): Inline, dual-overhead-cam six-cylinder. Aluminum alloy block and head. **Displacement:** 225 cu. in. (3694 cc). **Bore & Stroke:** 3.39 x 4.17 in. (86 x 106 mm). **Compression Ratio:** 8.8:1. **Brake Horsepower:** 255 at 5500 rpm. **Torque:** 253 lbs.-ft. at 4000 rpm. Seven main bearings. Solid valve lifters. Lucas mechanical fuel injection.
OPTIONAL SIX (Mistral): Inline, dual-overhead-cam six-cylinder. Aluminum alloy block and head. **Displacement:** 245 cu. in. (4014 cc). **Bore & Stroke:** 3.46 x 4.33 in. (88 x 110 mm). **Compression Ratio:** 8.8:1. **Brake Horsepower:** 255 at 5200 rpm. **Torque:** 267 lbs.-ft. at 4000 rpm. Seven main bearings. Solid valve lifters. Lucas mechanical fuel injection.
BASE V-8 (early Quattroporte, Mexico): 90-degree, dual-overhead-cam "vee" type eight-cylinder. Aluminum alloy block and head. **Displacement:** 252.4 cu. in. (4136 cc). **Bore & Stroke:** 3.46 x 3.35 in. (88 x 85 mm). **Compression Ratio:** 8.5:1. **Brake Horsepower:** 260 at 5000 rpm. **Torque:** 268 lbs.-ft. at 4000 rpm. Five main bearings. Solid valve lifters. Four Weber two-barrel carburetors.
BASE V-8 (late Quattroporte, early Mexico): 90-degree, dual-overhead-cam "vee" type eight-cylinder. Aluminum alloy block and head. **Displacement:** 288 cu. in. (4719 cc). **Bore & Stroke:** 3.70 x 3.35 in. (94 x 85 mm). **Compression Ratio:** 8.5:1. **Brake Horsepower:** 290 at 5500 rpm. **Torque:** 290 lbs.-ft. at 4000 rpm. Five main bearings. Solid valve lifters. Four Weber carburetors.
BASE V-8 (Ghibli); OPTIONAL (Mexico): Same as 4719-cc V-8 above, except — **Compression Ratio:** 8.5:1. **Brake Horsepower:** 330 at 5500 rpm. **Torque:** 290 lbs.-ft. at 4000 rpm.

1967-68 MASERATI

Keith McCormick with a 1967 Maserati Mistral Spider.

MISTRAL — SIX — Production of the sporty Mistral coupe and Spider continued into 1970, with two engine sizes available; see previous listings for full details.
GHIBLI — V-8 — Replacing the Mistral, the two-seat Ghibli displayed low, curvaceous styling from the pen of Giorgetto Giugiaro (then at the Ghia studio), with a long fastback profile reaching back to the angle-chopped tail. Pop-up headlamps and a wide grille sat in the long nose. Small, angular rear quarter windows were installed. Most Ghiblis were fastback coupes, but a handful of Spider convertibles also were built. Some considered the Ghibli one of the loveliest sport/GT automobile designs of all time; or at least, the prettiest Maserati. As was the practice at this time, the car was named for another regional wind. Power came from a 4719-cc four-cam V-8 that developed 330 horsepower. Tubular chassis construction was similar to the Quattroporte and Mexico, with leaf-spring rear suspension. Wheelbase was a bit shorter, at 100.4 inches. A ZF five-speed gearbox was joined later by an optional three-speed Borg-Warner automatic.
MEXICO — V-8 — Production of the four-seat coupe with 4136- or 4719-cc V-8 power continued into 1968; see previous listing for complete details.
Note: Mexico production continued as late as 1973 with the smaller (4136-cc) engine, but in tiny numbers after 1968.
QUATTROPORTE — V-8 — Production of Maserati's sedan supercar continued into 1968 with the initial 4136-cc engine, then switched to a 4719-cc version for 1968-69; see previous listings for full details.
I.D. DATA: Not available.

Model	Body Type & Seating	Engine Type/CID	P.O.E. Price	Weight (lbs.)	Prod. Total
MISTRAL					
	2-dr Coupe-2P	I6/225	13600	2866	Note 1
Spider	2-dr Conv-2P	I6/225	13600	2800	Note 1
GHIBLI					
4700	2-dr Coupe-2P	V8/288	16900	3500	Note 2
MEXICO					
4200	2-dr Coupe-4P	V8/252	15300	3640	Note 3
4700	2-dr Coupe-4P	V8/288	16300	3640	Note 3
QUATTROPORTE					
4200	4-dr Sedan-4P	V8/252	14300	3638	Note 4
4700	4-dr Sedan-4P	V8/288	N/A	3638	Note 4

Note 1: A total of 948 Mistrals (828 coupes and 120 Spiders) were produced from 1963-70.
Note 2: A total of 1,274 Ghiblis (1,149 coupes and 125 Spiders) were produced from 1966-73.
Note 3: A total of 250 Mexico coupes were produced from 1965-68.
Note 4: A total of 759 Quattroporte sedans were produced from 1963-69.
Price Note: Figures shown were valid in 1968. Mistrals with the larger (4014-cc) engine sold for $500 more ($14,100).
Weight Note: Figures shown are approximate.

1968 Maserati Mistral Spider. (Coys of Kensington)

CHASSIS DATA: Wheelbase: (Mistral) 94.5 in.; (Ghibli) 100.4 in.; (Mexico) 103.9 in.; (Quattro) 108.3 in. **Overall Length:** (Mistral) 177.0 in.; (Ghibli) 180.7 in.; (Mexico) 187.4 in.; (Quattro) 196 in. **Height:** (Mistral) 51.2 in.; (Ghibli) 45.6 in.; (Mexico) 53.2 in.; (Quattro) 53.5 in. **Width:** (Mistral) 65 in.; (Ghibli) 70.8 in.; (Mexico) 68.1 in.; (Quattro) 68 in. **Front Tread:** (Mistral/Mexico/Quattro) 54.7 in.; (Ghibli) 56.6 in. **Rear Tread:** (Mistral/Mexico) 53.5 in.; (Ghibli) 55.4 in.; (Quattro) 55.6 in. **Standard Tires:** (Mistral/Mexico/Quattro) 205x15; (Ghibli) 205x15 or 215x15.

TECHNICAL: Layout: front-engine, rear-drive. **Transmission:** five-speed manual; three-speed automatic available on Mistral/Mexico/Quattroporte. **Steering:** recirculating ball. **Suspension (front):** upper/lower A-arms with coil springs and anti-roll bar. **Suspension (rear):** rigid axle with radius arms and semi-elliptic leaf springs. **Brakes:** front/rear disc. **Body Construction:** separate body on tubular chassis.

PERFORMANCE: Top Speed: (Ghibli) 154-160 mph. **Acceleration (0-60 mph):** (Ghibli) 7.5-8.0 sec. **Acceleration (quarter-mile):** (Ghibli) 17.2 sec.
Manufacturer: Officine Alfieri Maserati S.p.A., Modena, Italy.
Distributor: Foreign Car City Inc., West Nyack, New York; Trident Imported Motors Inc., Rosemont, Pennsylvania; and ABC Motors Inc., Tacoma, Washington.

1969-70 MASERATI

MISTRAL — SIX — Production of the sporty Mistral coupe and Spider continued into 1970, with two engine sizes available; see previous listings for full details.

1969 Maserati Ghibli coupe. (Coys of Kensington)

GHIBLI — V-8 — Production of the Mistral's replacement coupe and Spider convertible continued into 1973. Both became available with a larger (4930-cc) engine in 1970, dropping the initial 4719-cc version after that year. The Spider's top fit below a hinged cover. A removable hardtop was optional. Spiders with the bigger engine were called 'SS.' Ghiblis sold in the U.S. had less horsepower than European-spec models. See previous listing for complete details.

INDY — V-8 — Serving as replacement for the Mexico and Sebring, the Indy was styled by Vignale with an extremely long, pointed nose and concealed headlamps, as well as long rear quarter windows. At the rear was a tall tail with a lift-up hatch. Unlike other front-engine V-8 models, the 2+2 fastback coupe had a steel unibody (body/chassis welded together). The long greenhouse had a thick B-pillar, with long rear quarter windows. Wheelbase was longer, too, measuring 102.5 inches. Either a ZF five-speed manual gearbox or optional automatic was available. Power came initially from a 4136-cc twin-cam V-8, developing 260 horsepower. Larger engines came later. The U.S. version was known as the Indy America.

QUATTROPORTE — V-8 — Production of Maserati's super sedan continued into 1969 with the larger 4719-cc engine; see previous listings for full details.

Note: A small number of Mexico coupes were produced from 1969-73, with the smaller (4.1-liter) engine; see previous listings for details.

I.D. DATA: Maserati serial numbers are on a rectangular metal plate attached to inside of right inner fender panel. Vehicle Identification Number is on a plate on the left side of the instrument panel, ahead of the driver.

Model	Body Type & Seating	Engine Type/CID	P.O.E. Price	Weight (lbs.)	Prod. Total
MISTRAL					
	2-dr Coupe-2P	I6/225	13600	2866	Note 1
Spider	2-dr Conv-2P	I6/225	13600	2800	Note 1
GHIBLI					
	2-dr Coupe-2P	V8/288	18900	3500	Note 2
Spider	2-dr Conv-2P	V8/288	19400	3500	Note 2
INDY					
	2-dr Coupe-2+2P	V8/252	17500	3465	Note 3
QUATTROPORTE					
	4-dr Sedan-4P	V8/288	14300	3638	Note 4

Note 1: A total of 948 Mistrals (828 coupes and 120 Spiders) were produced from 1963-70.
Note 2: A total of 1,274 Ghiblis (1,149 coupes and 125 Spiders) were produced from 1967-73.
Note 3: A total of 1,136 Indys were produced from 1969-74.
Note 4: A total of 759 Quattroporte sedans were produced from 1963-69.
Price Note: Mistrals with the larger (4014-cc) engine sold for $500 more ($14,100). A Mexico 4200 coupe with 4.1-liter engine listed for $15,300; the Mexico 4700 with 4.7-liter engine for $16,300.
Weight Note: Figures shown are approximate.

ENGINE DATA: BASE SIX (Mistral): Inline, dual-overhead-cam six-cylinder. Aluminum alloy block and head. **Displacement:** 225 cu. in. (3694 cc). **Bore & Stroke:** 3.39 x 4.17 in. (86 x 106 mm). **Compression Ratio:** 8.8:1. **Brake Horsepower:** 255 at 5500 rpm. **Torque:** 253 lbs.-ft. at 4000 rpm. Seven main bearings. Solid valve lifters. Lucas mechanical fuel injection.
OPTIONAL SIX (Mistral): Inline, dual-overhead-cam six-cylinder. Aluminum alloy block and head. **Displacement:** 245 cu. in. (4014 cc). **Bore & Stroke:** 3.46 x 4.33 in. (88 x 110 mm). **Compression Ratio:** 8.8:1. **Brake Horsepower:** 255 at 5200 rpm. **Torque:** 267 lbs.-ft. at 4000 rpm. Seven main bearings. Solid valve lifters. Lucas mechanical fuel injection.
BASE V-8 (Quattroporte): 90-degree, dual-overhead-cam "vee" type eight-cylinder. Aluminum alloy block and head. **Displacement:** 288 cu. in. (4719 cc). **Bore & Stroke:** 3.70 x 3.35 in. (94 x 85 mm). **Compression Ratio:** 8.5:1. **Brake Horsepower:** 290 at 5000 rpm. **Torque:** 290 lbs.-ft. at 4000 rpm. Five main bearings. Solid valve lifters. Four Weber carburetors.
Note: Some Quattroportes were still available with the original 4136-cc engine, which developed 260 bhp.
BASE V-8 (Ghibli): Same as 4719-cc V-8 above, except — **Compression Ratio:** 8.5:1. **Brake Horsepower:** 330 at 5500 rpm. **Torque:** 290 lbs.-ft. at 4000 rpm.
OPTIONAL V-8 (Ghibli SS): 90-degree, dual-overhead-cam "vee" type eight-cylinder. Aluminum alloy block and head. **Displacement:** 301 cu. in. (4930 cc). **Bore & Stroke:** 3.70 x 3.50 in. (94 x 89 mm). **Brake Horsepower:** 335 at 5500 rpm (reduced rating in U.S.). **Torque:** 354 lbs.-ft. at 4000 rpm (reduced rating in U.S.). Five main bearings. Solid valve lifters.
BASE V-8 (Indy): 90-degree, dual-overhead-cam "vee" type eight-cylinder. Aluminum alloy block and head. **Displacement:** 252.4 cu. in. (4136 cc). **Bore & Stroke:** 3.46 x 3.35 in. (88 x 85 mm). **Compression Ratio:** 8.5:1. **Brake Horsepower:** 260 at 5500 rpm. **Torque:** 268 lbs.-ft. at 4000 rpm. Five main bearings. Solid valve lifters. Four Weber carburetors.

CHASSIS DATA: Wheelbase: (Mistral) 94.5 in.; (Ghibli) 100.4 in.; (Indy) 102.5 in.; (Quattro) 108.3 in. **Overall Length:** (Mistral) 177.0 in.; (Ghibli) 180.7 in.; (Indy) 186.6 in.; (Quattro) 196 in. **Height:** (Mistral) 51.2 in.; (Ghibli) 45.6 in.; (Indy) 48 in.; (Quattro) 53.5 in. **Width:** (Mistral) 65 in.; (Ghibli) 70.8 in.; (Indy) 69.2 in.; (Quattro) 68 in. **Front Tread:** (Mistral) 54.7 in.; (Ghibli) 56.6 in.; (Indy) 58.2 in.; (Quattro) 54.7 in. **Rear Tread:** (Mistral) 53.5 in.; (Ghibli) 55.4 in.; (Indy) 56.5 in.; (Quattro) 55.6 in. **Standard Tires:** (Mistral/Quattro) 205x15; (Ghibli) 205x15/215x15; (Indy) 205VR14.

TECHNICAL: Layout: front-engine, rear-drive. **Transmission:** five-speed manual; three-speed Borg-Warner automatic available. **Steering:** recirculating ball. **Suspension (front):** upper/lower A-arms with coil springs and anti-roll bar. **Suspension (rear):** rigid axle with radius arms and semi-elliptic leaf springs. **Brakes:** front/rear disc. **Body Construction:** separate body on tubular chassis except (Indy) steel unibody.
MAJOR OPTIONS: Automatic transmission. Seats belts and head restraints ($95). Removable hardtop (Ghibli convertible).
PERFORMANCE: Top Speed: (Indy) 136-156 mph. **Acceleration (0-60 mph):** (Indy) 7.5 sec.

Manufacturer: Officine Alfieri Maserati S.p.A., Modena, Italy.
Distributor: Foreign Car City Inc., West Nyack, New York.
HISTORY: Introduced at the 1969 Turin auto show as a Vignale prototype, the Indy soon went on sale. It lasted in the lineup until 1975, when Maserati was taken over (for a time) by Citroen. The connection between those two companies began in the late 1960s.

1971-73 MASERATI

1972 Maserati 4.7-liter Ghibli SS Spider. (Christie's)

MERAK — V-6 — Maserati used the chassis and mid-engine layout from the new Bora (described below) to create the V-6 Merak. This was the same Maserati-designed V-6 engine and five-speed gearbox that went into the Citroen SM (see Citroen listing in this Catalog). In effect, it was the same drivetrain as that of the SM, but rotated halfway around. Even the dashboards (with oval gauges) and steering wheel were identical between the Merak and SM, at least until the separation between the two companies. Unlike the Bora coupe, the Merak had a flat deckline with "flying buttress" panels. Formed from twin beams that extended from the roof to the tail, they added no rigidity to the body, but were installed strictly for appearance. U.S. versions had a bulged decklid that gave clearance for the air cleaner. Wheelbase was identical to the V-8 Bora, at 102.3 inches. Citroen's hydraulic braking system was installed, but was not used to power the seats. Though a 2+2 design, the rear seats were tiny, virtually useless for adults.
BORA — V-8 — Instead of the usual front-engine design, Maserati turned to a mid-engine V-8 configuration with the Bora, which debuted at the 1971 Geneva Salon. Styling came from Giorgetto Giugiaro (now working at Ital Design), who'd also penned the Ghibli. Boras had a short, flat pointed nose with hidden headlamps and a stylized trident emblem. Noticeable bodyside bulges and very thick B-pillars were part of the fastback profile that ended in a sharply cut-off tail. Door windows were upswept at lower rear corners. The fastback roofline looked almost horizontal, with extra-long (and squat) rear quarter windows. Wheelbase was 102.3 inches, identical to the V-6 Merak. This was actually the first automobile to result from the tie between Citroen and Maserati, and exhibited some of the innovative Citroen technology. Brakes and seats, for instance, were powered by high-pressure hydraulics. Boras had a conventional brake pedal, however, rather than the little button installed in Citroens. Europeans got a 4.7-liter V-8 engine through 1974, but a bigger (4930-cc) V-8 soon went into Boras destined for American shores. Engines were mounted longitudinally on a subframe attached to the steel unibody, and hooked to a ZF five-speed manual gearbox in a rear transaxle. Even in U.S. trim, the two-seat coupe could accelerate to 60 mph in 7.5 seconds, and reach at least 160 mph.

GHIBLI — V-8 — Production continued into 1972 with the larger (4930-cc) engine, as introduced in 1970; see previous listings for full details.

INDY — V-8 — Production of the Mexico's replacement continued into 1974, and a larger (4719-cc) engine became available in 1972; see previous listing for full details.

Note: A modest number of Mexico coupes were produced from 1969-73, with the smaller (4.1-liter) engine; see previous listings for details.

I.D. DATA: Maserati serial numbers are on a rectangular metal plate attached to inside of right inner fender panel. Vehicle Identification Number is on a plate on the left side of the instrument panel, ahead of the driver. The VIN consists of a prefix with five, six or seven characters, followed by a sequential production number. Prefix (1973 models): (Ghibli) AM115; (Indy) AM116.49.

Model	Body Type & Seating	Engine Type/CID	P.O.E. Price	Weight (lbs.)	Prod. Total
MERAK					
	2-dr Coupe-2+2P	V6/181	N/A	3200	Note 1
BORA					
	2-dr Coupe-2P	V8/301	26900	3570	Note 2
GHIBLI					
	2-dr Coupe-2P	V8/301	19275	3500	Note 3
Spider	2-dr Conv-2P	V8/301	19900	3500	Note 3
INDY					
	2-dr Coupe-2+2P	V8/252	18865	3465	Note 4

Note 1: A total of 1,666 Meraks were produced from 1972-80, and the Merak SS remained in production into the 1980s.
Note 2: A total of 571 Boras were produced from 1971-80.

Note 3: A total of 1,274 Ghiblis (1,149 coupes and 125 Spiders) were produced from 1967-73.

Note 4: A total of 1,135 Indys were produced from 1969-74.

Price Note: Figures shown for Ghibli and Indy were valid in 1971; figure shown for Bora was valid in 1973.

Weight Note: Figures shown are approximate.

ENGINE DATA: BASE V-6 (Merak): 90-degree, dual-overhead-cam "vee" type six-cylinder. Aluminum alloy block and head. **Displacement:** 181 cu. in. (2965 cc). **Bore & Stroke:** 3.62 x 2.95 in. (92 x 75 mm). **Compression Ratio:** 8.75:1. **Brake Horsepower:** 190 at 6000 rpm (180 SAE at 6000 rpm in U.S.). **Torque:** 188 lbs.-ft. at 4000 rpm (185 SAE at 3000 rpm in U.S.). Four main bearings. Solid valve lifters. Three Weber carburetors.

BASE V-8 (Indy): 90-degree, dual-overhead-cam "vee" type eight-cylinder. Aluminum alloy block and head. **Displacement:** 252.4 cu. in. (4136 cc). **Bore & Stroke:** 3.46 x 3.35 in. (88 x 85 mm). **Compression Ratio:** 8.5:1. **Brake Horsepower:** 260 at 5500 rpm. **Torque:** 268 lbs.-ft. at 4000 rpm. Five main bearings. Solid valve lifters. Four Weber carburetors.

BASE V-8 (Bora): 90-degree, dual-overhead-cam "vee" type eight-cylinder. Aluminum alloy block and head. **Displacement:** 288 cu. in. (4719 cc). **Bore & Stroke:** 3.70 x 3.35 in. (94 x 85 mm). **Compression Ratio:** 8.5:1. **Brake Horsepower:** 310 at 6000 rpm. **Torque:** 325 lbs.-ft. at 4200 rpm. Five main bearings. Solid valve lifters. Four Weber carburetors.

OPTIONAL V-8 (1972-73 Indy): Same as 4719-cc V-8 above, except — **Brake Horsepower:** 290 at 5500 rpm. **Torque:** 289 lbs.-ft. at 4000 rpm.

BASE V-8 (Ghibli); OPTIONAL (1973-74 Indy): 90-degree, dual-overhead-cam "vee" type eight-cylinder. Aluminum alloy block and head. **Displacement:** 301 cu. in. (4930 cc). **Bore & Stroke:** 3.70 x 3.50 in. (94 x 89 mm). **Compression Ratio:** 8.5:1. **Brake Horsepower:** 335 at 5500 rpm. **Torque:** 354 lbs.-ft. at 4000 rpm. Five main bearings. Solid valve lifters.

BASE V-8 (U.S. Bora, 1972-up): Same as 4930-cc V-8 above, except — **Brake Horsepower:** 325 at 4200 rpm. **Torque:** 335 lbs.-ft. at 4200 rpm.

CHASSIS DATA: Wheelbase: (Merak) 102.3 in.; (Bora) 102.3 in.; (Ghibli) 100.4 in.; (Indy) 102.5 in. **Overall Length:** (Merak) 170.7 in.; (Bora) 170.7 in.; (Ghibli) 184.6 in.; (Indy) 186.6 in. **Height:** (Merak) 44.6 in.; (Bora) 44.8 in.; (Ghibli) 45.7 in.; (Indy) 48 in. **Width:** (Merak) 69.6 in.; (Bora) 69.6 in.; (Ghibli) 70.5 in.; (Indy) 69.2 in. **Front Tread:** (Merak) 58.0 in.; (Bora) 58.0 in.; (Ghibli) 56.7 in.; (Indy) 58.2 in. **Rear Tread:** (Merak) 57.0 in.; (Bora) 53.0 in.; (Ghibli) 55.9 in.; (Indy) 56.5 in. **Standard Tires:** (Merak) 185VR15 front, 205VR15 rear; (Bora) 215/70VR15; (Ghibli) 205x15/235x15; (Indy) 205VR14.

Dimension Note: Later Bora and Merak with U.S.-spec bumpers were longer overall; see next listing.

TECHNICAL: Layout: (Bora/Merak) mid-engine, rear-drive; (Ghibli/Indy) front-engine, rear-drive. **Transmission:** (Bora/Merak) five-speed manual in rear transaxle; (Ghibli/Indy) five-speed manual or optional three-speed automatic. **Steering:** (Bora/Merak) rack and pinion; (Ghibli/Indy) recirculating ball. **Suspension (front):** upper/lower A-arms with coil springs and anti-roll bar. **Suspension (rear):** (Bora/Merak) unequal-length A-arms with coil springs and anti-roll bar; (Ghibli/Indy) rigid axle with radius arms and semi-elliptic leaf springs. **Brakes:** front/rear disc. **Body Construction:** (Bora/Merak/Indy) steel unibody; (Ghibli) steel body on tubular chassis.

PERFORMANCE: Top Speed: (Bora) 157-160+ mph; (Merak) 135+ mph. **Acceleration (0-60 mph):** (Bora) 6.2-7.5 sec.; (Merak) 8.2-9.5 sec.

PRODUCTION/SALES: A total of 550 Maseratis were produced in 1971 (including 57 Mexico, 210 Ghibli, 273 Indy, and 10 Bora); 557 in 1972 (including 99 Ghibli, 221 Indy, 220 Bora, and 17 Merak); and 738 in 1973 (including 146 Indy, 157 Bora, 430 Merak, and five early Khamsin).

Manufacturer: Officine Alfieri Maserati S.p.A., Modena, Italy.

Distributor: Grossman Motor Car Corp., West Nyack, New York.

HISTORY: The idea for a mid-engined Maserati came from the company's new administrator, Guy Malleret. Design work on the Bora began in 1968. Introduced in 1971, it remained in production into 1980. The V-6 Merak debuted a year later, and lasted even longer in the Maserati lineup.

1974-76 MASERATI

1974 Maserati Merak Sports Coupe. (Christie's)

MERAK — V-6 — Production of Maserati's mid-engine V-6 model continued into 1983, though exports to the U.S. came to a halt after 1979. Standard Merak equipment included a five-speed ZF manual gearbox, all-disc brakes, power windows, tinted glass, electric clock, adjustable steering wheel, leather upholstery, air conditioning, tachometer, and power antenna. Michelin tires were installed: 185VR15 on the front, and 205VR15 on the rear. A Merak SS model became available in 1976, after the company takeover by Alejandro de Tomaso. That one borrowed its brakes and ZF transaxle from Bora, and had wider tires and a small chin spoiler.

BORA — V-8 — Production of the mid-engined Bora continued into 1980, with a larger (4.9-liter) V-8 installed from 1975 onward. Standard Bora equipment included a ZF five-speed gearbox, 215/70VR15 VWX Michelin tires on 7.5-inch Campagnolo light alloy wheels, heater/defroster, rear defroster, leather upholstery, air conditioning, AM/FM stereo radio, electric clock, power windows, tinted glass, adjustable steering wheel, power seat, and retractable pedals. Stainless steel was used for the roof. Boras were not readily available in the U.S. until 1974.

INDY — V-8 — Production of the Indy continued into 1974, with a 4930-cc engine; see previous listings for full details.

KHAMSIN — V-8 — Maserati's front-engine replacement for the Ghibli was styled by Marcello Gandini (at Bertone), and debuted at the Turin auto show in 1972; but it did not go on sale until 1974. Styling features included a low greenhouse, long tapered rear quarter windows with a curvy kickup at the rear, an extremely long hood that contained asymmetric air-intake louvers for cooling, and concealed headlamps. The windshield was sharply slanted, and front vent wings were installed. A Kamm-style (chopped-off) tail contained a glass panel between the taillamps (between the bumper and hatch) to add rearward visibility. Inside was a small rear bench seat, more suitable for one extra passenger than for two. The fully independent rear suspension consisted of A-arms with coil springs and an anti-roll bar, like that used in front. Thus, the Khamsin was the first front-engine Maserati with independent rear suspension. Citroen's hydraulics were used for power steering, brakes and clutch. Steering required only two turns lock-to-lock, and the wheel would center itself even while the car was at a halt. The leather-covered, padded steering wheel contained three aluminum spokes and adjusted both up/down and in/out. Either a ZF five-speed gearbox or three-speed Borg-Warner automatic transmission was available. All Khamsins were powered by Maserati's 4930-cc V-8 engine. Standard Khamsin equipment included power rack-and-pinion steering, power ventilated disc brakes, 215/70VR15 tires on light alloy wheels, adjustable steering wheel, power windows, tinted glass, leather upholstery, air conditioning, foglamps, reclining seats, clock, and rear defroster.

I.D. DATA: Vehicle Identification Number is on a plate attached to left side of dashboard, and on a plate attached to right fender panel, in the engine compartment. The number consists of a 5-, 6- or 7-symbol prefix, followed by a sequential production number. Engine number is on the left side of the block, near the front. Serial number range: (1974 Bora) AM117-49-628 to AM117-49-844; (1974 Merak) AM122-920 to AM122-1464; (1975 Bora) AM117-49-856 up; (1975 Merak) AM122-2000 up; (1975 Khamsin) AM120-1000 up.

Model	Body Type & Seating	Engine Type/CID	P.O.E. Price	Weight (lbs.)	Prod. Total
MERAK					
	2-dr Coupe-2+2P	V6/181	21700	3200	Note 1
BORA					
	2-dr Coupe-2P	V8/301	30900	3570	Note 2
INDY					
	2-dr Coupe-4P	V8/301	N/A	3465	Note 3
KHAMSIN					
	2-dr Coupe-2+2P	V8/301	32975	3800	Note 4

Note 1: A total of 1,699 Meraks with 3.0-liter engine were produced from 1972-83, plus 133 with 2.0-liter engine.

Note 2: A total of 571 Boras were produced from 1971-80.

Note 3: A total of 1,135 Indys were produced from 1969-74.

Note 4: A total of 421 Khamsins were produced from 1974-82.

Price Note: Figures shown were valid in 1975. A Bora sold for $28,900 in 1974, and a Merak for $19,975.

Weight Note: Figures shown are curb weights.

ENGINE DATA: BASE V-6 (Merak): 90-degree, dual-overhead-cam "vee" type six-cylinder. Aluminum alloy block and head. **Displacement:** 181 cu. in. (2965 cc). **Bore & Stroke:** 3.62 x 2.95 in. (92 x 75 mm). **Compression Ratio:** 8.75:1. **Brake Horsepower:** 190 at 6000 rpm; (SS) 220 at 6500 rpm. **Torque:** 188 lbs.-ft. at 4000 rpm; (SS) 199 at 4500 rpm. Four main bearings. Solid valve lifters. Three Weber two-barrel carburetors.

Note: U.S. version of the basic Merak engine produced 180 bhp at 6000 rpm, and 185 lbs.-ft. at 3000 rpm. For the home market only, 1976-79 Meraks were offered with a 1999-cc V-6 that produced 170 bhp.

BASE V-8 (Indy): 90-degree, dual-overhead-cam "vee" type eight-cylinder. Aluminum alloy block and head. **Displacement:** 301 cu. in. (4930 cc). **Bore & Stroke:** 3.70 x 3.50 in. (94 x 89 mm). **Compression Ratio:** 8.5:1. **Brake Horsepower:** 335 at 5500 rpm. **Torque:** 354 lbs.-ft. at 4000 rpm. Five main bearings. Solid valve lifters. Four Weber two-barrel carburetors.

BASE V-8 (Bora, Khamsin): Same as 4930-cc V-8 listed above, except — **Brake Horsepower:** 320 at 5500 rpm (315 at 5000 rpm in U.S.). **Torque:** (Bora) 308 lbs.-ft. at 3500 rpm (in U.S.).

Bora Engine Note: Boras sold in Europe through 1974 had a 4719-cc V-8; see previous listing.

CHASSIS DATA: Wheelbase: (Bora) 102.3 in.; (Merak) 102.3 in.; (Indy) 102.5 in.; (Khamsin) 100.3 in. **Overall Length:** (Bora) 177 in.; (Merak) 180 in.; (Indy) 186.6 in.; (Khamsin) 180.0 in. **Height:** (Bora) 44.6 in.; (Merak) 44.6 in.; (Indy) 48.0 in.; (Khamsin) 47 in. **Width:** (Bora) 69.6 in.; (Merak) 69.6 in.; (Indy) 69.3 in.; (Khamsin) 71 in. **Front Tread:** (Bora) 58.0 in.; (Merak) 58.0 in.; (Indy) 58.3 in.; (Khamsin) 56.6 in. **Rear Tread:** (Bora) 56.9 in.; (Merak) 56.9 in.; (Indy) 56.5 in.; (Khamsin) 57.7 in. **Standard Tires:** (Bora) 215/70VR15; (Merak) 185VR15 front, 205VR15 rear; (Indy) 205VR15; (Khamsin) 215/70VR15.

TECHNICAL: Layout: (Bora/Merak) mid-engine, rear-drive; (Indy/Khamsin) front-engine, rear-drive. **Transmission:** (Bora/Merak) five-speed manual in rear transaxle; (Khamsin/Indy) ZF five-speed manual or optional automatic. **Steering:** (Bora/Merak/Khamsin) rack and pinion; (Indy) recirculating ball. **Suspension (front):** unequal-length A-arms with coil springs and anti-roll bar. **Suspension (rear):** (Bora/Merak/Khamsin) independent, A-arms with coil springs and anti-roll bar; (Indy) rigid axle with semi-elliptic leaf springs. **Brakes:** front/rear disc. **Body Construction:** (Bora/Merak/Indy) steel unibody; (Khamsin) separate body on tubular chassis.

MAJOR OPTIONS: Automatic transmission: Khamsin ($600). Blaupunkt Berlin AM/FM radio: Khamsin ($1200).

PERFORMANCE: Top Speed: (Merak) about 149 mph (as little as 115 mph in U.S. trim); (Bora) near 170 mph; (Khamsin) 140-174 mph. **Acceleration (0-60 mph):** (Merak) about 7.5 sec.; (Bora) about 6 sec.; (Khamsin) 7.0-8.1 sec. (as little as 6 sec. claimed). **Acceleration (quarter-mile):** (Khamsin) 15.8 sec. (94.2 mph). **Fuel Mileage:** (Khamsin) near 15 mpg in test (EPA rating, 11 mpg).

ADDITIONAL MODELS: A Quattroporte II sedan debuted at the Turin auto show in November 1974, with a four-door body styled by Bertone and a 3-liter V-6 under its hood. Scheduled for production, only five actually were built. Because it resulted from the Citroen connection, the Quattroporte II had a hydro-pneumatic suspension. Wheelbase was 121 inches.

PRODUCTION/SALES: A total of 571 Maseratis were produced in 1974 (including 55 Indy, 85 Bora, 334 Merak, and 97 Khamsin); 201 in 1975 (including 102 Merak and 98 Bora/Khamsin); and 195 in 1976 (including four 3200 sedans, 139 Merak, and 52 Bora/Khamsin/Kyalami).

Manufacturer: Officine Alfieri Maserati S.p.A., Modena, Italy.

Distributor: Grossman Motor Car Corp., West Nyack, New York; or Maserati Automobiles Inc., Los Angeles.

HISTORY: On sale in 1974, the Khamsin was produced through 1981, but dropped from the U.S. market after 1979. It was named for an Egyptian Sahara-desert wind, following the Maserati practice of model names associated with strong breezes. In 1975, Citroen was ready to liquidate the Maserati company, but Alejandro de Tomaso came to its rescue. "If you are a person of means and perceptions," declared Maserati ads, "you will take considerable pleasure in meeting the Maserati challenge" and in driving the "primal yet distinguished Bora." Those ads described the Bora or Merak as a "hand-crafted driving machine of passion and power."

1977-83 MASERATI

1977 Maserati Khamsin. (Coys of Kensington)

MERAK SS — V-6 — Production of Maserati's mid-engine V-6 model continued into 1983, though exports to the U.S. came to a halt after 1979. The SS version, introduced in 1976, had a small chin spoiler and an engine rated up to 220 bhp (182 bhp in U.S. trim). The SS also abandoned Citroen SM dashboard that had formerly been used, as well as the bulging deck. Standard equipment by 1979 included air conditioning, Blaupunkt AM/FM stereo with cassette tape player, and power windows.

Merak Note: A slash sometimes was used ahead of the 'SS' designation (Merak/SS).

BORA — V-8 — Production of the mid-engined Bora continued into 1980, with a 4.9-liter V-8. Standard equipment included air conditioning, tinted glass, power windows, and leather upholstery. See previous listings for full details.

KHAMSIN — V-8 — Production of the Khamsin coupe continued into 1982, though it wasn't shipped to the U.S. after 1979. Standard Khamsin equipment included air conditioning, light alloy wheels, and leather upholstery. A Borg-Warner three-speed automatic transmission was optional. See previous listing for complete details.

KYALAMI — V-8 — Next on the new-model list was a 2 + 2 coupe that evolved from De Tomaso's Longchamp notchback coupe of the early 1970s—which in turn stemmed from the De Tomaso Deauville sedan. This happened becauase Alejandro de Tomaso took over Maserati in 1975, then popped a Maserati engine into his two earlier models. Rather than being named for a wind, this model took its moniker from a Grand Prix race course in South America. Squarish styling was done by Frua, using a steel unibody on a 102.4-inch wheelbase. Quad round headlamps were installed, alongside a rectangular grille with center Maserati trident insignia. The result appeared to be considerably taller than the typical Maserati. The first hundred examples were powered by a 4136-cc V8, rated 255 horsepower (SAE). A larger (4930-cc) V-8 became optional in 1978, rated 280 bhp. Either a ZF five-speed gearbox or three-speed TorqueFlite automatic was available. The rear suspension consisted of half-shafts as upper links, lower lateral links, radius arms and coil springs.

I.D. DATA: Vehicle Identification Number is on a plate attached to left side of dashboard, and on a plate attached to right fender panel, in the engine compartment. The number consists of a 5-, 6- or 7-symbol prefix, followed by a sequential production number. Engine number is on the left side of the block, near the front. Starting serial number: (1978 Bora) AM117US-0000; (1978 Merak) AM122US-0000; (1978 Khamsin) AM120US-0000.

Model	Body Type & Seating	Engine Type/CID	P.O.E. Price	Weight (lbs.)	Prod. Total
MERAK					
SS	2-dr Coupe-2 + 2P	V6/181	29800	3185	Note 1
BORA					
	2-dr Coupe-2P	V8/301	38790	3540	Note 2
KHAMSIN					
	2-dr Coupe-2 + 2P	V8/301	41450	3800	Note 3
KYALAMI					
	2-dr Coupe-2 + 2P	V8/252	N/A	3835	Note 4

Note 1: A total of 1,699 Meraks with 3.0-liter engine were produced from 1972-83, plus 133 with 2.0-liter engine.

Note 2: A total of 571 Boras were produced from 1971-80.

Note 3: A total of 421 Khamsins were produced from 1974-82.

Note 4: A total of 150 Kyalamis were produced from 1977-83.

Price Note: Figures shown were effective in or around 1979.

Weight Note: Figures shown are curb weights.

ENGINE DATA: BASE V-6 (Merak SS): 90-degree, dual-overhead-cam "vee" type six-cylinder. Aluminum alloy block and head. **Displacement:** 181 cu. in. (2965 cc). **Bore & Stroke:** 3.62 x 2.95 in. (92 x 75 mm). **Brake Horsepower:** (SS) 220 DIN at 6500 rpm. **Torque:** (SS) 199 at 4500 rpm. Four main bearings. Solid valve lifters. Three Weber carburetors.

Note: U.S. version of the basic Merak engine produced 182 bhp at 6000 rpm, and 180 lbs.-ft. at 4000 rpm. For the home market only, 1976-79 Meraks were offered with a 1999-cc V-6 that produced 170 bhp.

BASE V-8 (Kyalami): 90-degree, dual-overhead-cam "vee" type eight-cylinder. Aluminum alloy block and head. **Displacement:** 252.4 cu. in. (4136 cc). **Bore & Stroke:** 3.46 x 3.35 in. (88 x 85 mm). **Compression Ratio:** 8.5:1. **Brake Horsepower:** 255 (SAE) at 6000 rpm. **Torque:** 289 lbs.-ft. at 4000 rpm. Five main bearings. Solid valve lifters. Four Weber carburetors.

BASE V-8 (Bora, Khamsin): 90-degree, dual-overhead-cam "vee" type eight-cylinder. Aluminum alloy block and head. **Displacement:** 301 cu. in. (4930 cc). **Bore & Stroke:** 3.70 x 3.50 in. (94 x 89 mm). **Compression Ratio:** 8.5:1. **Brake Horsepower:** 320 at 5500 rpm (315 at 5000 rpm in U.S.). **Torque:** 308 lbs.-ft. at 3500 rpm (in U.S.). Five main bearings. Solid valve lifters. Four Weber carburetors.

OPTIONAL V-8 (Kyalami): Same as 4930-cc V-8 above, except — **Brake Horsepower:** 280 (SAE) at 5600 rpm. **Torque:** 289 lbs.-ft. at 3000 rpm.

CHASSIS DATA: Wheelbase: (Bora) 102.3 in.; (Merak) 102.3 in.; (Khamsin) 100.3 in.; (Kyalami) 102.4 in. **Overall Length:** (Bora) 181.0 in.; (Merak) 181.0 in.; (Khamsin) 180.0 in.; (Kyalami) 180 in. **Height:** (Bora) 44.6 in.; (Merak) 44.6 in.; (Khamsin) 47.0 in.; (Kyalami) 50 in. **Width:** (Bora) 69.6 in.; (Merak) 69.6 in.; (Khamsin) 71.0 in.; (Kyalami) 72.8 in. **Front Tread:** (Bora) 58.0 in.; (Merak) 58.0 in.; (Khamsin) 56.6 in.; (Kyalami) 60.2 in. **Rear Tread:** (Bora) 56.9 in.; (Merak) 56.9 in.; (Khamsin) 57.7 in.; (Kyalami) 60.2 in. **Standard Tires:** (Bora) 215/70VR15; (Merak) 185/70VR15 front, 205/70VR15 rear; (Khamsin) 215/70VR15; (Kyalami) 205/70VR15.

TECHNICAL: Layout: (Bora/Merak) mid-engine, rear-drive; (Khamsin/Kyalami) front-engine, rear-drive. **Transmission:** (Bora/Merak) five-speed manual in rear transaxle; (Khamsin) ZF five-speed manual or optional Borg-Warner three-speed automatic; (Kyalami) ZF five-speed manual or optional three-speed TorqueFlite automatic. **Steering:** rack and pinion. **Suspension (front):** unequal-length A-arms with coil springs and anti-roll bar. **Suspension (rear):** (Bora/Merak/Khamsin) independent, A-arms with coil springs and anti-roll bar; (Kyalami) half-shafts as upper links, lower lateral links, radius arms and coil springs. **Brakes:** front/rear disc. **Body Construction:** steel unibody.

PERFORMANCE: Top Speed: (U.S. Bora) 150 + mph; (European Bora) 174 mph; (U.S. Khamsin) 141 mph.; (Kyalami) 147 mph. **Acceleration (0-60 mph):** (U.S. Khamsin) 9.1 sec.; (Kyalami) 7.6 sec. **Acceleration (quarter-mile):** (European Bora) 14.4 sec.; (U.S. Khamsin) 17.0 sec. (84.5 mph).

PRODUCTION/SALES: As many as 292 Maseratis were produced in 1977 (including 145 Merak 2000/3000, 84 Bora/Khamsin, and 50 Kyalami); 339 in 1978 (including 154 Merak 2000/3000, 111 Bora/Khamsin, and 74 Kyalami); 371 in 1979 (including 194 Merak 2000/3000, 42 Khamsin, and 135 Kyalami); 555 in 1980 (including 150 Merak 2000/3000, 12 Khamsin, and 393 Kyalami); 528 in 1981; 2,265 in 1982 (including 1,888 Biturbo 2000/2500); and 5,333 in 1983 (including 5,053 Biturbo).

ADDITIONAL MODELS: A new Quattroporte four-door sedan was introduced in 1979. Riding a 110.2-inch wheelbase and measuring 199.6 inches overall, the sedan was powered by either of two engines. The 4136-cc V-8 developed 255 horsepower at 6000 rpm. A 4930-cc (301-cid) V-8 that produced 288 horsepower at 5200 rpm and 308 pound-feet of torque at 3000 rpm, using four two-barrel carburetors and 8.6:1 compression.

Manufacturer: Officine Alfieri Maserati S.p.A., Modena, Italy.

Distributor: Maserati Automobiles Inc., Los Angeles.

HISTORY: Maserati's new Biturbo was first shown in December 1981, but did not arrive in the U.S. market until early 1984; see next listing for details.

1984-88 MASERATI

BITURBO — V-6 — Twin turbochargers (one per bank) helped force air and fuel into the 2.0-liter V-6 engine of the next Maserati. This was Maserati's first model intended for high-volume production, far different from the traditional sports cars. A two-door coupe was available first with carbureted engine developing 180 horsepower. A five-speed manual gearbox was standard, with automatic optional (standard on some models sold in the U.S.). Later Biturbos were marketed with the larger (2491-cc) V-6 engine that debuted in the sedan (below).

BITURBO 425/SPYDER — V-6 — A Biturbo sedan also was produced, with 2491-cc V-6 engine that developed 185 horsepower. That engine also went into the handsome Spyder convertible, available in the U.S. in 1986. Initial Spyders came with three-speed automatic transmission. Those sold in the U.S. were upholstered in Connolly leather.

QUATTROPORTE — V-8 — Production of the V-8 sedan, revived in 1979, continued with little change, powered by the larger (4930-cc) engine that developed 288 horsepower in U.S. trim. Standard equipment included an automatic transmission, power steering, radio, and air conditioning. The Quattroporte was renamed Royale in 1987, with top speed claimed at 150 mph.

I.D. DATA: Maserati's 17-symbol Vehicle Identification Number is on the upper left of the dashboard, visible through the windshield.

Model	Body Type & Seating	Engine Type/CID	P.O.E. Price	Weight (lbs.)	Prod. Total
BITURBO (1986 models)					
	2-dr Coupe-5P	V6/122	26874	2394	Note 1
E	2-dr Coupe-5P	V6/122	29112	2394	Note 1
Spyder	2-dr Conv-4P	V6/152	31895	2390	Note 1
425	4-dr Sedan-5P	V6/152	29900	2625	Note 1
QUATTROPORTE (1986 model)					
	4-dr Sedan-5P	V8/301	66710	4650	Note 1

Note 1: A total of 6,180 Maseratis were produced in 1984 (including 5,865 Biturbos), followed by 5,668 in 1985, 4,133 in 1986, 3,658 in 1987, and 3,001 in 1988.

Price Note: Figures shown were valid in 1986. By 1985, both Maserati models were subject to the Federal gas guzzler tax.

ENGINE DATA: BASE V-6 (early Biturbo): 90-degree, overhead-cam "vee" type six-cylinder. Twin IHI turbochargers. Aluminum alloy block and head. **Displacement:** 121.8 cu. in. (1996 cc). **Bore & Stroke:** 3.23 x 2.50 in. (82 x 63.5 mm). **Compression Ratio:** 7.8:1. **Brake Horsepower:** 180 at 6000 rpm. **Torque:** 188 lbs.-ft. at 3500 rpm. Four main bearings. Solid valve lifters. Weber two-barrel carburetor.

BASE V-6 (Biturbo 425, Spyder): 90-degree, overhead-cam "vee" type six-cylinder (three valves per cylinder). Twin turbochargers. Aluminum alloy block and head. **Displacement:** 152 cu. in. (2491 cc). **Bore & Stroke:** 3.61 x 2.48 in. (91.6 x 63 mm). **Compression Ratio:** 7.8:1. **Brake Horsepower:** 185 at 5500 rpm. **Torque:** 208 lbs.-ft. at 3200 rpm. Four main bearings. Solid valve lifters. Weber two-barrel carburetor.

BASE V-8 (Quattroporte): 90-degree, dual-overhead-cam "vee" type eight-cylinder. Aluminum alloy block and head. **Displacement:** 301 cu. in. (4930 cc). **Bore & Stroke:** 3.70 x 3.50 in. (93.9 x 89 mm). **Compression Ratio:** 8.6:1. **Brake Horsepower:** 288 at 5200 rpm. **Torque:** 308 lbs.-ft. at 3000 rpm. Five main bearings. Solid valve lifters. Four Weber two-barrel carburetors.

CHASSIS DATA: Wheelbase: (Biturbo cpe) 99 in.; (Biturbo conv) 94.5 in.; (Quattro) 110.2 in. **Overall Length:** (Biturbo cpe) 163.5 in.; (Biturbo conv) 159.2 in.; (Quattro) 199.6 in. **Height:** (Biturbo cpe) 51.4 in.; (Biturbo conv) 51.6 in.; (Quattro) 53.1 in. **Width:** (Biturbo) 67.5 in.; (Quattro) 70.5 in. **Front Tread:** (Biturbo cpe) 55.9 in.; (Biturbo conv) 56.8 in.; (Quattro) 60 in. **Rear Tread:** (Biturbo cpe) 56.3 in.; (Biturbo conv) 57.2 in.; (Quattro) 60 in.

TECHNICAL: Layout: front-engine, rear-drive. **Transmission:** (Biturbo) five-speed manual or three-speed automatic; (Quattroporte) three-speed automatic. **Steering:** rack and pinion. **Suspension (front):** MacPherson struts with coil springs, A-arms and anti-roll bar. **Suspension (rear):** (Biturbo) MacPherson/Chapman struts with coil springs and A-arms; (Quattroporte) independent with four coil springs, A-arms and anti-roll bar. **Brakes:** front/rear disc. **Body Construction:** steel unibody.

PERFORMANCE: Top Speed: (Biturbo) 125-130 mph. **Acceleration (0-60 mph):** (Biturbo conv) under 7.5 sec. **Acceleration (quarter-mile):** (Biturbo conv) under 16 sec. (about 90 mph).

PRODUCTION/SALES: A total of 2,023 Maseratis were sold in the U.S. during 1984, followed by 1,190 in 1985, and 1,298 in 1986.

ADDITIONAL MODELS: For the home market, Maserati also produced a 228 coupe and 430 sedan; see next listing for details on U.S. versions.

Manufacturer: Officine Alfieri Maserati S.p.A., Modena, Italy.

Distributor: Maserati Automobiles Inc., Baltimore, Maryland.

1989-90 MASERATI

1989 Maserati Spyder.

SPYDER — V-6 — Styled by Zagato, the late 1980s Spyder convertible had softer lines on its hood, fenders and grille, with the goal of improving airflow. Quad rectangular headlamps were installed. Maserati's traditional trident emblem appeared on the front and rear of the car, as well as on the hubs of its alloy wheels. A twin-turbo 2790-cc V-6 produced 225 horsepower, using electronic fuel injection; but the former Biturbo designation no longer was used for the model name. Inside, burled Carpathian elm wood was used as facings for the doors, dashboard and console, and for the gearshift and handbrake handle. Upholstery was available in smooth or suede leather.

228 — V-6 — Maserati also offered a sport coupe, intended to compete with such luxury models as the Cadillac Allanté, BMW 635CSi, and Jaguar XJ-S. The new coupe body was created by Zagato, on a longer wheelbase than prior models, with rounded lines. The front end included a distinctive grille with traditional Maserati trident emblem. Under the hood was the same 2.8-liter V-6 used in the Spyder and 430 sedan.

1989 Maserati 430 sedan.

430 — V-6 — Maserati's sedan adopted a more rounded and aerodynamic look for 1989. Power mirrors were integrated into the design, and the Maserati trident on the fuel filler flap was recessed. A 2.8-liter V-6 with twin turbochargers provided the power: 225 bhp at 5600 rpm. A five-speed manual gearbox was standard, with a four-speed automatic becoming available later. Hand-sewn leather was used on the interior, with briarwood on the door panels, dashboard, console, gearshift knob, and handbrake handle. Six body colors were offered: Silver, Stormy Sky, Rifle Grey, Dark Blue, Old Modena (gold), and Black.

I.D. DATA: Maserati's 17-symbol Vehicle Identification Number is on the upper left of the dashboard, visible through the windshield.

Model	Body Type & Seating	Engine Type/CID	P.O.E. Price	Weight (lbs.)	Prod. Total
SPYDER					
	2-dr Conv-2 + 2P	V6/170	44995	2780	Note 1
228					
	2-dr Coupe-4P	V6/170	52975	3019	Note 1
430					
	4-dr Sedan-5P	V6/170	41500	2915	Note 1

Note 1: Approximately 240 Maseratis were sold in the U.S. during 1990.

Price Note: Figures shown were valid in 1989.

ENGINE DATA: BASE V-6: 90-degree, single-overhead-cam "vee" type six-cylinder (18-valve). Twin IHI turbochargers with air-to-air intercoolers. Aluminum alloy block and heads. **Displacement:** 170 cu. in. (2790 cc). **Bore & Stroke:** 3.70 x 2.64 in. (94 x 67 mm). **Compression Ratio:** 7.4:1. **Brake Horsepower:** 225 at 5600 rpm. Torque: 246 lbs.-ft. at 3500 rpm. Electronic fuel injection.

CHASSIS DATA: Wheelbase: (Spyder) 94.5 in.; (228) 102.4 in.; (430) 102.4 in. **Overall Length:** (Spyder) 159.2 in.; (228) 175.6 in.; (430) 173.2 in. **Height:** (Spyder) 51.6 in.; (228) 52.4 in.; (430) 53.5 in. **Width:** (Spyder) 67.5 in.; (228) 73.4 in.; (430) 68.1 in. **Front Tread:** (Spyder) 59.1 in.; (228) 60.6 in.; (430) 56.8 in. **Rear Tread:** (Spyder) 58.1 in.; (228) 61.0 in.; (430) 57.2 in. **Standard Tires:** (Spyder) Michelin 205/50VR15 front, 225/50VR15 rear; (228) Michelin 225/50VR15 MXV; (430) Michelin 205/55R15 MXV.

TECHNICAL: Layout: front-engine, rear-drive. **Transmission:** ZF five-speed manual; four-speed automatic available on later sedans. **Steering:** power rack and pinion. **Suspension (front):** MacPherson struts with coil springs and anti-roll bar. **Suspension (rear):** (Spyder/430) semi-trailing arms with coil springs and Bilstein gas shock absorbers; (228) struts on semi-trailing arms with coil springs and anti-roll bar. **Brakes:** front/rear disc. **Body Construction:** steel unibody.

PERFORMANCE: Top Speed: (Spyder) 140-150 mph (146 mph claimed); (228) 146 mph; (430) 145-150 mph. **Acceleration (0-60 mph):** (Spyder) near 6 sec.; (228/430) 6.3 sec. est.

Manufacturer: Officine Alfieri Maserati S.p.A., Modena, Italy.

Distributor: Maserati Automobiles Inc., Baltimore, Maryland.

HISTORY: As the 1989 model year began, only the Spyder was officially available for sale because it was exempt from NHTSA passive-restraint standards. Sedans did not yet comply with the current regulations, so their introduction to the U.S. market was delayed.

1989 Chrysler TC by Maserati.

POSTSCRIPT: Maserati cannot be dismissed without mention of one final model: the Chrysler TC by Maserati. This stylish convertible, similar in appearance to the Maserati Spyder, toured the U.S. auto show circuit in 1987 and 1988, amid promises that it would be in the showrooms shortly. Some three years passed before it actually went on sale, which may be part of the reason for its short life in the marketplace. The TC rode a 93.0-inch wheelbase and carried a 2.2-liter four-cylinder engine, which produced 200 horsepower. In 1990, it sold for $35,500; but importation came to a halt in the spring of that year.

MATRA

Two very different French firms happened to come together in the mid-1960s, resulting in development of the Matra sports car. One was the company operated by Rene Bonnet, who, with Andre Deutsch, had created the Deutsch-Bonnet (DB) coupe in the 1950s (listed separately in this Catalog). The other was Mecanique Aviation Traction (MATRA), a major aerospace and armaments firm that had been founded before World War II and was instrumental in developing such items as guided missiles and satellite launchers in the 1950s. That organization was known as Engins Matra. Because Matra's founder, Marcel Chassagny, was a friend of Bonnet, he took over the latter's expiring company in 1964, creating a new division called Matra Sports.

The first Matra to go into production was actually a Bonnet design, the Djet, with a Renault engine. That would remain available into 1968, with a larger engine; but was joined in 1967 by the mid-engined Matra M530 coupe, with Ford V-4 power. In addition to road cars, Matra focused on racing: Formula 1, 2 and 3, then retaining an interest in Grand Prix events well into the 1970s. By that time, the M530 and subsequent M630 sports cars were virtually forgotten as Matra turned to other automotive activities.

1965-69 MATRA

DJET — 5/6 LUXE — FOUR — Evolved from the Rene Bonnet design, the initial Matra Djet 5 two-seat coupe wore a plastic body with a sharply sloping hood and deeply recessed headlamps. Doors extended partly into the cowl, their upper edges curved backward to the level of the window, Small rear quarter windows were installed, along with a steeply-raked wraparound windshield. The chopped-off tail had a pointy look at the top, curving upward at its base from the rounded rear wheel opening. At the rear was an 1108-cc four, rated 70 horsepower (SAE) and hooked to a four-speed manual gearbox. The coupe rode a tubular backbone chassis with 94.5-inch wheelbase, and had a top speed near 109 mph. That was followed by a Djet 6 Luxe version with a 1255-cc overhead-valve four, rated 103 horsepower (SAE).

530 LX — V-4 — Subsequent Matras in the 530 series were similar in overall appearance to the Djet, but wore concealed headlamps and rode a longer wheelbase. The typical 1970s 2+2 coupe had a small oval grille with pointed ends, wraparound half-bumpers on each side of the front end, and a bodyside crease that ran from the front fenderline through the door. Power came from a 1699-cc V-4, rated 75 horsepower (DIN). A 530 SX with quad headlamps also was produced.

I.D. DATA: Not available.

Model	Body Type & Seating	Engine Type/CID	P.O.E. Price	Weight (lbs.)	Prod. Total
DJET SERIES					
Djet 5	2-dr Coupe-2P	I4/68	N/A	1356	Note 1
Djet 6	2-dr Coupe-2P	I4/77	N/A	1565	Note 1
530 SERIES					
530 LX	2-dr Coupe-2 + 2P	V4/104	N/A	2062	Note 1
530 SX	2-dr Coupe-2 + 2P	V4/104	N/A	2062	Note 1

Note 1: Approximately 810 Matra Sports coupes were produced in 1966.

ENGINE DATA: BASE FOUR (Djet 5): Inline, overhead-valve four-cylinder. Cast iron block and light alloy head. **Displacement:** 67.6 cu. in. (1108 cc). **Bore & Stroke:** 2.75 x 2.83 in. (70 x 72 mm). **Compression Ratio:** 10.2:1. **Brake Horsepower:** 70 (SAE) at 6000 rpm. **Torque:** 62 lbs.-ft. at 4500 rpm. Five main bearings. Solid valve lifters. One Zenith two-barrel carburetor.

BASE FOUR (Djet 6 Luxe): Inline, overhead-valve four-cylinder. Cast iron block and light alloy head. **Displacement:** 76.6 cu. in. (1255 cc). **Bore & Stroke:** 2.93 x 2.83 in. (74.5 x 72 mm). **Compression Ratio:** 10.5:1. **Brake Horsepower:** 103 (SAE) at 6750 rpm. **Torque:** 92 lbs.-ft. at 5000 rpm. Five main bearings. Solid valve lifters. Two Weber two-barrel carburetors.

BASE V-4 (530): 60-degree, overhead-valve "vee" type four-cylinder. Cast iron block and heads. **Displacement:** 103.7 cu. in. (1699 cc). **Bore & Stroke:** 3.54 x 2.63 in. (90 x 66.8 mm). **Compression Ratio:** 9.0:1. **Brake Horsepower:** 75 (DIN) at 5000 rpm. **Torque:** 104 lbs.-ft. at 3000 rpm. Three main bearings. Solid valve lifters. One Solex two-barrel carburetor.

CHASSIS DATA: Wheelbase: (Djet 5/6) 94.5 in.; (530 LX) 100.8 in. **Overall Length:** (Djet 5/6) 166.1 in.; (530 LX) 165.2 in. **Height:** (Djet 5/6) 47.2 in.; (530 LX) 47.2 in. **Width:** (Djet 5) 59.1 in.; (Djet 6) 59 in.; (530 LX) 63.8 in. **Front Tread:** (Djet 5/6) 49.6 in.; (530 LX) 52.8 in. **Rear Tread:** (Djet 5/6) 49.2 in.; (530 LX) 53.2 in. **Standard Tires:** (Djet 5/6) 145x380 front, 155x380 rear; (530 LX) 145x14 front, 165x14 rear.

TECHNICAL: Layout: rear-engine, rear-drive. **Transmission:** four-speed manual. **Standard Final Drive Ratio:** (Djet 5) 4.15:1; (Djet 6) 4.125:1; (530 LX) 3.50:1. **Steering:** rack and pinion. **Suspension (front):** (Djet 5/6) wishbones with coil springs; (530 LX) wishbones with coil springs and anti-roll bar. **Suspension (rear):** (Djet 5/6) wishbones with dual coil springs; (530 LX) trailing arms with coil springs and anti-roll bar. **Brakes:** front/rear disc. **Body Construction:** (Djet 5/6) plastic body on tubular backbone chassis; (530 LX) plastic body on platform chassis.

PERFORMANCE: Top Speed: (Djet 5) 109 mph; (Djet 6) about 127 mph; (530 LX) about 109 mph.
Manufacturer: Matra Sports S.A., Lotr-et-Cher, Paris, France.

POSTSCRIPT: By 1969, Matra formed an alliance with Simca, which in turn was part of Chrysler's international empire. Four years later, a mid-engined Baghera coupe with Simca power became available. That was followed by a four-wheel-drive vehicle, called the Rancho--far removed from the little coupes that had worn the Matra name in the '60s. By 1983, Matra was part of the Renault organization.

MAZDA

When Toyo Cork Kogyo Co. was formed at Hiroshima, Japan in 1920, its founders had no inkling of producing motorcars. They began by building machinery, then expanded into small motorcycles after the Tokyo earthquake of 1923. In 1927, the firm was renamed Toyo Kogyo Co. Ltd. (a name it would keep until the 1980s). Four years later, in 1931, came the debut of a three-wheeled truck, with motorcycle origins and 500-cc engine, named the Mazda DA. That Mazda name stemmed from the concept of harmony between good and bad, with Mazda representing the "good" side. A prototype sedan was built in 1940, shortly before the outbreak of war turned the company's activity toward armaments.

Nearly half of the plant was destroyed by the atomic bomb dropped in summer 1945, yet production of three-wheeled trucks resumed by the end of that year, reaching substantial numbers by 1948. Starting in 1950, four-wheel trucks joined the line. Not until 1960, however, did a passenger car enter production. That was the R360 coupe, with an air-cooled 356-cc two-cylinder engine mounted in the rear. In its first year, more than 23,000 were built. A year later, a model 700 two-seater was seen at the Tokyo auto show, but never went into production. The next car offered for sale was the four-seat Carol sedan, with a water-cooled 358-cc four-cylinder engine, which debuted in 1962. That was followed in 1963 by the model 800, and the Familia four, which featured front engines and rear-wheel-drive. Bertone designed the 1500 Luce that appeared in 1966, which accounted for its European appearance. A 1490-cc overhead-cam engine supplied the power, and a Borg-Warner automatic transmission was optional.

Meanwhile, an agreement had been reached in 1961 with the NSU company of Germany, for Toyo Kogyo to produce Wankel (rotary) engines under license—an agreement that would later have major ramifications for the Japanese firm. A rotary-engine prototype was tested in 1963, and displayed at the Tokyo show in that year. Rotor sealing problems began to surface, just as they did on NSU's version of the Wankel engine; but that flaw eventually would be remedied. Starting in 1964, Toyo Kogyo focused on the twin-rotor Wankel design, and took a rotary-engined prototype of the Cosmo sports coupe to the Tokyo show. By 1967, the first twin-rotary-powered production car ever built, the Cosmo 110S coupe, went on sale. In addition to the lack of pistons and other moving parts, the Wankel promised to perform like a conventional engine of twice its displacement. An R100 Familia coupe with rotary power arrived in 1968, followed by an R100 sedan. By spring 1970, the first Mazdas were on their way to America, and a dealer network known as Mazda Motors of America (North West) was created, reflecting the fact that initial sales were confined to the northwestern states. Three years later, Mazda Motors of America Inc. was formed.

The better-known RX-2 sedan debuted in 1970; and two years later it took first, second and third place in the Japanese Grand Prix for sports cars. With a 1587-cc four-cylinder engine under its hood in place of the rotary, the sedan was called model 616—a pattern that would be followed well into the 1970s, with both Wankel and gas engines available in the same cars. Also offered during the make's first years in the U.S. was a larger, Bertone-styled model 1800. Wankel engines grew popular in the U.S. early on, and by 1973 were able to meet the tighter emis-

sions standards expected for 1975. One problem: they tended to guzzle gas, which became a major reason for their precipitous slide in popularity after the 1973-74 fuel crisis, not only in America but worldwide. What saved the company in the mid-1970s was a move toward another conventional-engined sedan, the 323, putting the rotary on the back burner for the time being. Wankels remained available, having evolved into RX-3 and RX-4 form, but the focus shifted to piston engines. The 323, named GLC ("Great Little Car") in the U.S. and "Familiar" in Japan, was a subcompact hatchback with an ordinary 1272-cc four-cylinder engine and rear-wheel-drive. During the 1979 model year, a larger 626 sedan also arrived on the U.S. market, with a bigger piston engine.

Rotaries had another, far more significant, burst of life after 1978, when the RX-7 sports car debuted with a Wankel under its hood. The hatchback coupe with its low hood grabbed considerable attention in the U.S. and elsewhere for its excellent handling and performance, and won the Japanese Car of the Year award. Soon after the RX-7's emergence into the U.S. market, Ford—which had been connected to Toyo Kogyo for some time—increased its ownership to a 25-percent share.

A new front-drive GLC (323) debuted in 1981, followed by a front-drive version of the 626 during 1983. Then, in 1984, Toyo Kogyo finally changed its name to Mazda Motor Corporation. A turbocharged rotary engine became available in the RX-7 by the time of its restyling for 1986, as did a 2 + 2 model; and a ragtop version hit the dealerships two years later. A new 323 subcompact replaced the GLC for 1986, while Mazda entered the luxury arena for 1988 with its new 929 sedan, which carried a V-6 engine. Joining its Japanese-built mates for 1988 was a new MX-6 coupe, based on the 626 sedan; but that was built at Flat Rock, Michigan as part of a joint venture with Ford. If any car was to exceed the RX-7's appeal to sports-car fans, however, it was the cute little Miata two-seater that debuted for 1990, loosely based on the old Lotus Elan of the 1960s. Enthusiasts were clamoring to pay thousands of dollars above the sticker price for the new roadster before the furor began to subside.

Seating Note: Passenger capacities in the 1970s, as was the case with many early subcompact models, were largely a matter of opinion—and the degree to which riders were inclined to squeeze snugly into the back seat. International sources tended to describe even the smallest sedans as five-passenger, whereas American sources leaned toward calling them four-passenger models. Mazda literature in 1974 explained a bit ambiguously that an RX-4 sedan, to take one example, "seats four adults in luxurious comfort."

1967-69 MAZDA

COSMO — SPORT 110S — ROTARY — Following its debut at the October 1963 Tokyo Motor Show, to demonstrate the new Wankel rotary engine, the Cosmo sports coupe went into production and was on sale in Japan in May 1967. It remained available in limited numbers into 1972, serving as the first mass-production car with a Wankel engine. Styling was akin to the Ferrari Super America, with a wide "mouth" grille opening (no mesh) below the slim bumper, along with wide parking lights just below that bumper. Deeply recessed, covered headlamps were used, with mirrors mounted on the fenders. Diagonal air-intake openings stood at the cowl, just above the bodyside crease line, and the hood had a rounded front edge. Squared-off rear wheel openings led to a rather long rear overhang. Little chrome was evident on the body, except for '110S' script at the front of the car, on the driver's side, with an emblem in the center. Large red taillamps were mounted half above and half below the bumper, while wide-spaced 'MAZDA' block letters ran across the rear deck. Inside, full gauges included a tachometer. All Cosmos had right-hand drive. Although the prototype of the twin-rotor Wankel produced just 70 horsepower, the 982-cc (2 x 491) L10A production version was rated 110 bhp at 7000 rpm. In 1968, its L10B successor rose to 128 horsepower.

1970-71 MAZDA

1200 — FOUR — As Mazdas began to drift into the American market, Mazda (Toyo Kogyo) made a point of offering both rotary-powered and conventional-engine models. Thus, the subcompact 1200 with its 64-horsepower, 1169-cc (71.3-cid) piston engine was equivalent to the R100 rotary. A coupe, sedan and station wagon were offered, on an 88.9-inch wheelbase. Neither this model nor the larger 1800 was destined to last long in the Mazda lineup for the U.S. market.

616 — FOUR — Just as the 1200 series was equivalent to the R100 rotary, the 616 coupe and sedan were essentially RX-2 models with 88-horsepower, 1587-cc (96.8-cid) piston engines. Like the RX-2, they rode a 97-inch wheelbase.

1800 — FOUR — Mazda's largest sedan and station wagon did not have a rotary-engined equivalent, but were powered only by a 1796-cc (109.6-cid) four-cylinder piston engine. Wheelbase was 98.4 inches, and the engine produced 98 horsepower. Standard equipment included power front disc brakes, variable-ratio steering, whitewall tires, carpeting, tinted glass, simulated wood dashboard, and stainless steel moldings. Wraparound bumpers were installed on the steel unibody, which displayed quad headlamps.

R100 — ROTARY — A twin-rotor Wankel engine went into the R100 sport coupe, which rode the same 88.9-inch wheelbase as the 1200 coupe. Single headlamps were used. The rotary engine produced 100 horsepower.

RX-2 — ROTARY — Mazda's RX-2 soon would evolve into the RX-3 and RX-4, each helping to make the Mazda name familiar to U.S. customers. By that time, however, the engine's notoriously poor gas mileage would call a quick halt to its early popularity. The RX-2 version of the twin-rotor Wankel engine produced 120 horsepower. Both a coupe and sedan were offered, equivalent (except for engine) to the 616 series, on the same 97-inch wheelbase. Quad round headlamps were installed, and louvers were evident at the rear of the hood. The grille consisted of thin horizontal bars with a center insignia. Four round taillamps brought up the rear, whereas piston-engined models had rectangular taillamps. Standard equipment included fully reclining bucket seats and tinted glass. Even the sedan had full instrumentation including a tachometer, plus a woodgrained steering wheel. Air conditioning was available, either factory- or dealer-installed.

Note: Specifications and prices below were effective in 1971.

I.D. DATA: Mazda's 10- or 11-symbol serial number is on driver's side of dashboard, and on the firewall under the hood. The first three to five symbols indicate the car series, followed by the sequential production number. Starting serial number (1971): (1200) STA144649; (616) SNA33647; (R100) MIOA66862; (RX-2) S122A61649. Engine number for piston engines is on a plate at the upper right front of the block; for rotary engines, the number is stamped on the intermediate housing.

Model	Body Type & Seating	Engine Type/CID	P.O.E. Price	Weight (lbs.)	Prod. Total
CONVENTIONAL ENGINE					
1200	2-dr Sedan-4/5P	I4/71	1798	1575	Note 1
1200	2-dr Coupe-4P	I4/71	1945	1630	Note 1
1200	2-dr Sta Wag-4/5P	I4/71	1938	1650	Note 1
616	2-dr Coupe-4P	I4/97	2350	2130	Note 1
616	4-dr Sedan-4/5P	I4/97	2195	2150	Note 1
1800	4-dr Sedan-4/5P	I4/110	2310	2315	Note 1
1800	4-dr Sta Wag-4/5P	I4/110	2530	2540	Note 1
ROTARY ENGINE					
R100	2-dr Spt Cpe-2 + 2P	Ro/70	2495	2065	Note 1
RX-2	2-dr Coupe-4P	Ro/70	2799	N/A	Note 1
RX-2	4-dr Sedan-4/5P	Ro/70	2750	2270	Note 1

Note 1: A total of 300,980 Mazda passenger cars were produced during 1971.

ENGINE DATA: BASE FOUR (1200): Inline, overhead-cam four-cylinder. Cast iron block and light alloy head. **Displacement:** 71.3 cu. in. (1169 cc). **Bore & Stroke:** 2.80 x 3.00 in. (71 x 76 mm). **Compression Ratio:** 8.6:1. **Brake Horsepower:** 64 at 6000 rpm. **Torque:** 67 lbs.-ft. at 3500 rpm. Five main bearings. Solid valve lifters.
BASE FOUR (616): Inline, overhead-cam four-cylinder. Cast iron block and light alloy head. **Displacement:** 96.8 cu. in. (1587 cc). **Bore & Stroke:** 3.07 x 3.27 in. (78 x 83 mm). **Compression Ratio:** 8.6:1. **Brake Horsepower:** 88 at 6000 rpm. **Torque:** 95 lbs.-ft. at 3500 rpm. Five main bearings. Solid valve lifters.
BASE FOUR (1800): Inline, overhead-cam four-cylinder. Cast iron block and light alloy head. **Displacement:** 109.6 cu. in. (1796 cc). **Bore & Stroke:** 3.07 x 3.70 in. (78 x 94 mm). **Compression Ratio:** 8.6:1. **Brake Horsepower:** 98 at 5500 rpm. **Torque:** 108 lbs.-ft. at 3000 rpm. Five main bearings. Solid valve lifters.
BASE ROTARY (R100, RX-2): Wankel with two coaxial three-lobe rotors. Light alloy block and cast iron rotors. **Displacement:** 70 cu. in. (1146 cc). **Compression Ratio:** 9.4:1. **Brake Horsepower:** (R100) 100 at 7000 rpm; (RX-2) 120 bhp. **Torque:** (R100) 92 lbs.-ft. at 4000 rpm. Two main bearings.

CHASSIS DATA: Wheelbase: (1200) 88.9 in.; (616) 97 in.; (1800) 98.4 in.; (R100) 88.9 in.; (RX-2) 97 in. **Overall Length:** (1200) 149.4 in.; (1200 wag) 145.6 in.; (616) 163 in.; (1800) 172 in.; (R100) 150.8 in.; (RX-2) 163-173 in. **Height:** (1200 cpe) 52.9 in.; (1200 sed) 54.9 in.; (1200 wag) 55.3 in.; (616 cpe) 56 in.; (616 sed) 55 in.; (1800) 56.3 in.; (R100) 52.9 in.; (RX-2) 56 in. **Width:** (1200) 58.3 in.; (616) 62 in.; (1800) 64.2 in.; (R100) 58.3 in.; (RX-2) 62 in. **Front Tread:** (1200) 47.6 in.; (616) 51 in.; (1800) 52.4 in.; (R100) 47.2 in.; (RX-2) 51 in. **Rear Tread:** (1200) 46.8 in.; (616) 51 in.; (1800) 52 in.; (R100) 46.8 in.; (RX-2) 51 in. **Standard Tires:** (1200) 6.15x13; (616) 6.15S13; (1800) 6.45x14; (R100) 145SR14; (RX-2) 165x13.

TECHNICAL: Layout: front-engine, rear-drive. **Transmission:** four-speed manual. **Steering:** recirculating ball. **Suspension (front):** MacPherson struts with coil springs. **Suspension (rear):** (1200, 1800, R100) rigid axle with parallel links and coil springs; (RX-2, 616) rigid axle with semi-elliptic leaf springs. **Brakes:** (RX-2) front disc, rear drum. **Body Construction:** steel unibody.
MAJOR OPTIONS: Automatic transmission: 1800/616 ($180).

PRODUCTION/SALES: A total of 2,098 Mazdas were sold in the U.S. during 1970, followed by 19,629 in 1971 (plus 843 trucks).
Manufacturer: Toyo Kogyo Co. Ltd., Hiroshima, Japan.
Distributor: Mazda Motors of America, Compton, California.

HISTORY: Importation of Mazdas to the U.S. began during 1970, with sales initially limited to Washington and Oregon. More than half of the Mazdas sold in the U.S. in 1971 had Wankel rotary engines. *Motor Trend* called the rotary engine "the biggest innovation in power plants since the turbine." The *Wall Street Journal* noted that the Wankel "has 40% fewer parts and weighs one third to one half less than today's engines."

1972 MAZDA

808 — FOUR — A new designation went on Mazda's smallest piston-engined model, which replaced the 1200 and carried the powerplant from the former 616 series. This one rode a 91-inch wheelbase (two inches longer than the 1200), and its 97-cid four-cylinder engine produced 70 horsepower. A coupe, sedan, and station wagon were offered.

618 — FOUR — Mazda's replacement for the 616 came in coupe and sedan form, with a 1796-cc (109.6-cid) four-cylinder engine under its hood. Dimensions were nearly identical to the former 616 series.

R100 — ROTARY — Production of the Wankel-engined coupe continued with little change. Ratings for the engine dropped to 77 horsepower and 80 pound-feet of torque, but that was due to the change to SAE new (formerly SAE gross) measuring system at this time.

RX-2 — ROTARY — Production of the more powerful rotary-engined coupe and sedan also contined with little change.

RX-3 — ROTARY — Considerably smaller in size than the RX-2 series, its new Wankel-engined companion rode a 91-inch wheelbase and was equivalent to the 808 series. The all-new design shared no sheetmetal with other models. A distinctive rectangular grille protuded forward slightly and carried a triangular center emblem. Quad round recessed headlamps were used. Styling features of the coupe also included a rear-quarter kickup into the triangular windows. The station wagon became the world's first production wagon with a Wankel powerplant. Output from the twin-rotor Wankel engine was lower than the RX-2 version. Standard equipment included a 130-mph speedometer and 8000-rpm tachometer.

I.D. DATA: Mazda's 10- or 11-symbol serial number is on driver's side of dashboard, and on the firewall under the hood. The first three to five symbols indicate the car series, followed by the sequential production number. Starting serial number (1972): (808) SN3A100001; (808 wag) SN3AV100006; (618) SV2A100001; (R100) MIOA103334; (RX-2) S122A96267; (RX-3) S124A100008; (RX-3 wag) S124W100006. Engine number for piston engines is on a plate at the upper right front of the block; for rotary engines, the number is stamped on the intermediate housing or (later models) on front housing.

Model	Body Type & Seating	Engine Type/CID	P.O.E. Price	Weight (lbs.)	Prod. Total
CONVENTIONAL ENGINE					
808	2-dr Coupe-4P	I4/97	2395	1940	Note 1
808	4-dr Sedan-4/5P	I4/97	2295	1960	Note 1
808	4-dr Sta Wag-4/5P	I4/97	2445	2040	Note 1
618	2-dr Coupe-4P	I4/110	2680	2185	Note 1
618	4-dr Sedan-4/5P	I4/110	2530	2205	Note 1
ROTARY ENGINE					
R100	2-dr Coupe-2 + 2P	Ro/70	2795	2065	Note 1
RX-2	2-dr Coupe-4P	Ro/70	3215	2290	Note 1
RX-2	4-dr Sedan-4/5P	Ro/70	3165	2310	Note 1
RX-3	2-dr Coupe-4P	Ro/70	2945	2080	Note 1
RX-3	4-dr Sedan-4/5P	Ro/70	2895	2090	Note 1
RX-3	4-dr Sta Wag-4/5P	Ro/70	2995	2170	Note 1

Note 1: A total of 379,703 Mazda passenger cars were produced during 1972.

ENGINE DATA: BASE FOUR (808): Inline, overhead-cam four-cylinder. Cast iron block and light alloy head. **Displacement:** 96.8 cu. in. (1587 cc). **Bore & Stroke:** 3.07 x 3.27 in. (78 x 83 mm). **Compression Ratio:** 8.6:1. **Brake Horsepower:** 70 at 5000 rpm. **Torque:** 82 lbs.-ft. at 3500 rpm. Five main bearings. Solid valve lifters.

BASE FOUR (618): Inline, overhead-cam four-cylinder. Cast iron block and light alloy head. **Displacement:** 109.6 cu. in. (1796 cc). **Bore & Stroke:** 3.07 x 3.70 in. (78 x 94 mm). **Compression Ratio:** 8.6:1. **Brake Horsepower:** 74 at 5000 rpm. **Torque:** 92 lbs.-ft. at 3000 rpm. Five main bearings. Solid valve lifters.

BASE ROTARY (R100, RX-2): Wankel with two coaxial three-lobe rotors. Light alloy block and cast iron rotors. **Displacement:** 70 cu. in. (1146 cc). **Compression Ratio:** 9.4:1. **Brake Horsepower:** (R100) 77 at 6000 rpm; (RX-2) 102 at 6800 rpm. **Torque:** (R100) 80 lbs.-ft. at 4000 rpm; (RX-2) 98 at 4000 rpm. Two main bearings. One Hitachi-Stromberg carburetor.

BASE ROTARY (RX-3): Wankel with two coaxial three-lobe rotors. Light alloy block and cast iron rotors. **Displacement:** 70 cu. in. (1146 cc). **Compression Ratio:** 9.4:1. **Brake Horsepower:** 90 at 6000 rpm. **Torque:** 96 lbs.-ft. at 4000 rpm. Two main bearings. One Hitachi-Stromberg four-barrel carburetor.

CHASSIS DATA: Wheelbase: (808) 91 in.; (618) 97 in.; (R100) 88.9 in.; (RX-2) 97 in.; (RX-3) 91 in. **Overall Length:** (808 cpe/sed) 160 in.; (808 wag) 161 in.; (618) 163 in.; (R100) 150.8 in.; (RX-2) 163 in.; (RX-3 cpe/sed) 160 in.; (RX-3 wag) 161 in. **Height:** (808 cpe/sed) 53 in.; (808 wag) 55 in.; (618 cpe) 56 in.; (618 sed) 55 in.; (R100) 52.9 in.; (RX-2) 56 in.; (RX-3 cpe/sed) 54 in.; (RX-3 wag) 55 in. **Width:** (808) 63 in.; (618) 62 in.; (R100) 58.3 in.; (RX-2) 62 in.; (RX-3) 63 in. **Front Tread:** (808) 51 in.; (618) 51 in.; (R100) 47.2 in.; (RX-2/RX-3) 51 in. **Rear Tread:** (808) 51 in.; (618) 51 in.; (R100) 46.8 in.; (RX-2/RX-3) 51 in. **Standard Tires:** (808) 6.15x13; (618) 6.15S13; (R100) 145SR14; (RX-2) 165SR13; (RX-3) 155SR13.

TECHNICAL: Layout: front-engine, rear-drive. **Transmission:** four-speed manual. RX-3 gear ratios: (1st) 3.74:1; (2nd) 2.20:1; (3rd) 1.44:1; (4th) 1.00:1. **Standard Final Drive Ratio:** (RX-2, RX-3) 3.70:1. **Steering:** recirculating ball. **Suspension (front):** MacPherson struts with coil springs. **Suspension (rear):** (RX-3, R100, 808) rigid axle with semi-elliptic leaf springs; (RX-2, 618) rigid axle with parallel links and coil springs. **Brakes:** (RX-2, RX-3) front disc, rear drum. **Body Construction:** steel unibody.

MAJOR OPTIONS: Automatic transmission: 808/618 ($235). AM radio: RX-3 ($52).

PERFORMANCE: Top Speed: (RX-2) 120 mph; (RX-3) 112 mph. **Acceleration (0-60 mph):** (RX-2) 10.4 sec.; (RX-3) 10.9 sec. **Acceleration (quarter-mile):** (RX-2) 17.5 sec. (79 mph); (RX-3) 17.8 sec. (79 mph). **Fuel Mileage:** (RX-2) 15 mpg; (RX-3) 18 mpg.

PRODUCTION/SALES: A total of 53,039 Mazda passenger cars were sold in the U.S. during 1972.

ADDITIONAL MODELS: Mazda also sold a B1600 pickup truck in the U.S. market, priced at $2195 in 1972.

Manufacturer: Toyo Kogyo Co. Ltd., Hiroshima, Japan.

Distributor: Mazda Motors of America, Compton, California.

HISTORY: *Road Test* magazine voted RX-2 its "import car of the year."

1973 MAZDA

808 — FOUR — The 618 series left the U.S. market for 1973, but the 808 coupe, sedan, and station wagon remained. Little change was evident. As before, power came from a 1587-cc four-cylinder engine that produced 70 horsepower. Except for the engine, the 808 series was similar to the RX-3.

RX-2 — ROTARY — Production of the Wankel-powered coupe and sedan continued with little change. A vinyl top was optional.

RX-3 — ROTARY — Production of the smaller rotary-engined series, on a 91-inch wheelbase, continued with little change. The station wagon seated five passengers.

I.D. DATA: Mazda's 10- or 11-symbol serial number is on driver's side of dashboard, and on the firewall under the hood. The first three to five symbols indicate the car series, followed by the sequential production number. Starting serial number (1973): (808 cpe) SN3A114948; (808 sed) SN3A114958; (808 wag) SN3AV103366; (RX-2 cpe) S122A-SCA-139686; (RX-2 sed) S122A-S139686; (RX-3 cpe/sed) S124A108467; (RX-3 wag) S124W100006. Engine number for piston engines is on a plate at the upper right front of the block; for rotary engines, the number is stamped on the front housing.

Model	Body Type & Seating	Engine Type/CID	P.O.E. Price	Weight (lbs.)	Prod. Total
CONVENTIONAL ENGINE					
808	2-dr Coupe-4P	I4/97	2695	2000	Note 1
808	4-dr Sedan-4/5P	I4/97	2595	2025	Note 1
808	4-dr Sta Wag-5P	I4/97	2750	2130	Note 1
ROTARY ENGINE					
RX-2	2-dr Coupe-4P	Ro/70	3495	2325	Note 1
RX-2	4-dr Sedan-4/5P	Ro/70	3450	2355	Note 1
RX-3	2-dr Coupe-4P	Ro/70	3295	2150	Note 1
RX-3	4-dr Sedan-4/5P	Ro/70	3195	2180	Note 1
RX-3	4-dr Sta Wag-5P	Ro/70	3395	2265	Note 1

Note 1: A total of 465,734 Mazda passenger cars were produced during 1973.

ENGINE DATA: BASE FOUR (808): Inline, overhead-cam four-cylinder. Cast iron block and light alloy head. **Displacement:** 96.8 cu. in. (1587 cc). **Bore & Stroke:** 3.07 x 3.27 in. (78 x 83 mm). **Compression Ratio:** 8.6:1. **Brake Horsepower:** 70 at 5000 rpm. **Torque:** 82 lbs.-ft. at 3500 rpm. Five main bearings. Solid valve lifters.

BASE ROTARY (RX-2): Wankel with two coaxial three-lobe rotors. Light alloy block and cast iron rotors. **Displacement:** 70 cu. in. (1146 cc). **Compression Ratio:** 9.4:1. **Brake Horsepower:** 97 at 6500 rpm. **Torque:** 96 at 4000 rpm. Two main bearings.

BASE ROTARY (RX-3): Wankel with two coaxial three-lobe rotors. Light alloy block and cast iron rotors. **Displacement:** 70 cu. in. (1146 cc). **Compression Ratio:** 9.4:1. **Brake Horsepower:** 90 at 6000 rpm. **Torque:** 96 lbs.-ft. at 4000 rpm. Two main bearings.

CHASSIS DATA: Wheelbase: (808) 91 in.; (RX-2) 97 in.; (RX-3) 91 in. **Overall Length:** (808) 162 in.; (RX-2) 167 in.; (RX-3 cpe/sed) 162 in.; (RX-3 wag) 163 in. **Height:** (808 cpe/sed) 53 in.; (808 wag) 55 in.; (RX-2 cpe) 55 in.; (RX-2 sed) 56 in.; (RX-3 cpe) 53 in.; (RX-3 sed/wag) 54 in. **Width:** (808) 63 in.; (RX-2) 62 in.; (RX-3) 63 in. **Front Tread:** (808) 51 in.; (RX-2/RX-3) 51 in. **Rear Tread:** (808) 51 in.; (RX-2/RX-3) 51 in. **Standard Tires:** (808) 6.15x13; (RX-2) 165SR13; (RX-3) 155SR13.

TECHNICAL: Layout: front-engine, rear-drive. **Transmission:** four-speed manual. **Steering:** recirculating ball. **Suspension (front):** MacPherson struts with coil springs. **Suspension (rear):** (RX-3, 808) rigid axle with semi-elliptic leaf springs; (RX-2) rigid axle with parallel links and coil springs. **Brakes:** front disc, rear drum. **Body Construction:** steel unibody.

MAJOR OPTIONS: Automatic transmission.

PERFORMANCE: Similar to 1972.

PRODUCTION/SALES: A total of 104,960 Mazda passenger cars were sold in the U.S. during 1973.

ADDITIONAL MODELS: Mazda also sold a B1600 pickup truck in the U.S. market, priced at $2450 in 1973.

Manufacturer: Toyo Kogyo Co. Ltd., Hiroshima, Japan.

Distributor: Mazda Motors of America, Compton, California.

HISTORY: More than 92 percent of Mazdas sold in the U.S. in 1973 had rotary engines.

1974 MAZDA

808 — FOUR — Production of the only Mazda model offered in the U.S. market with a piston-type engine continued with little change, except that the sedan was dropped.

RX-2 — ROTARY — Production of the familiar RX-2 coupe and sedan continued with little change. Standard equipment included a hydraulic clutch, rear defroster, tinted glass, variable-ratio steering, tachometer, electric clock, vinyl upholstery, and four-speed manual transmission. The coupe had roll-down rear quarter windows, a front-passenger memory seat, and styled wheels. Standard RX-2 body colors were Nova White, Flare Yellow, Harschel Orange, Sunset Red, Mercury Blue, Earth Green, Neptune Green, Jewel Green metallic, Concorde Silver metallic, and Alexandria Gold metallic.

RX-3 — ROTARY — Little change was evident in the RX-3 coupe and station wagon, which carried a lower-powered version of the Wankel engine; but the sedan was dropped. Standard colors were the same as RX-2 (except for Neptune Green), and also included Phoenix Blue and Iris Blue metallic. Standard equipment was similar to the RX-2. The coupe had a woodgrain steering wheel and gearshift knob.

RX-4 — ROTARY — A more powerful (110-horsepower) and larger version of the Wankel engine went into this new hardtop coupe, sedan, and station wagon. Engine displacement was 1308 cc (80 cid), versus 1146 cc for the RX-2 and RX-3 engines. The RX-4 was also the largest of the lot, on a 99-inch wheelbase. Standard equipment included power front disc brakes, electric clock, hydraulic clutch, tinted glass, tachometer, urethane-wrapped gearshift knob, three-speed interval wipers, and a four-speed manual gearbox. The hardtop coupe had front bumper overriders, an overhead console, and front-passenger memory seat. Both the coupe and sedan had crushed nylon upholstery, with vinyl optional in the hardtop and wagon. A 130-mph speedometer was included.

I.D. DATA: Mazda's 11- or 12-symbol serial number is on the windshield pillar (driver's side) or on the firewall under the hood. The first three to five symbols indicate the car series, followed by the sequential production number. Starting serial number (1974): (808 cpe) SN3A126448; (RX-2 cpe/sed) S122A211808; (RX-3 cpe) S124A156007; (RX-3 wag) S124W150108; (RX-4 HT/sed) LA235100038; (RX-4 wag) LA23W100011. Engine number for piston engines is on a plate at the upper right front of the block; for rotary engines, the number is stamped on the front housing.

Model	Body Type & Seating	Engine Type/CID	P.O.E. Price	Weight (lbs.)	Prod. Total
CONVENTIONAL ENGINE					
808	2-dr Coupe-4P	I4/97	2995	2100	Note 1
808	4-dr Sta Wag-4/5P	I4/97	3195	2235	Note 1
ROTARY ENGINE					
RX-2	2-dr Coupe-4P	Ro/70	3750	2510	Note 1
RX-2	4-dr Sedan-4/5P	Ro/70	3695	2540	Note 1
RX-3	2-dr Coupe-4P	Ro/70	3495	2335	Note 1
RX-3	4-dr Sta Wag-4/5P	Ro/70	3595	2450	Note 1
RX-4	2-dr HT Cpe-4P	Ro/80	4150	2610	Note 1
RX-4	4-dr Sedan-4/5P	Ro/80	4095	2680	Note 1
RX-4	4-dr Sta Wag-4/5P	Ro/80	4295	2875	Note 1

Note 1: A total of 378,928 Mazda passenger cars were produced during 1974.

ENGINE DATA: BASE FOUR (808): Inline, overhead-cam four-cylinder. Cast iron block and light alloy head. **Displacement:** 96.8 cu. in. (1587 cc). **Bore & Stroke:** 3.07 x 3.27 in. (78 x 83 mm). **Compression Ratio:** 8.6:1. **Brake Horsepower:** 70 at 5000 rpm. **Torque:** 82 lbs.-ft. at 3500 rpm. Five main bearings. Solid valve lifters.

BASE ROTARY (RX-2): Wankel with two coaxial three-lobe rotors. Light alloy block and cast iron rotors. **Displacement:** 70 cu. in. (1146 cc). **Compression Ratio:** 9.4:1. **Brake Horsepower:** 97 at 6500 rpm. **Torque:** 98 at 4000 rpm. Two main bearings.

BASE ROTARY (RX-3): Wankel with two coaxial three-lobe rotors. Light alloy block and cast iron rotors. **Displacement:** 70 cu. in. (1146 cc). **Compression Ratio:** 9.4:1. **Brake Horsepower:** 90 at 6000 rpm. **Torque:** 96 lbs.-ft. at 4000 rpm. Two main bearings.

BASE ROTARY (RX-4): Wankel with two coaxial three-lobe rotors. Light alloy block and cast iron rotors. **Displacement:** 80 cu. in. (1308 cc). **Compression Ratio:** 9.2:1. **Brake Horsepower:** 110 at 6000 rpm. **Torque:** 117 lbs.-ft. at 3500 rpm. Two main bearings.

CHASSIS DATA: Wheelbase: (808) 91 in.; (RX-2) 97 in.; (RX-3) 91 in.; (RX-4) 99 in. **Overall Length:** (808 cpe) 168 in.; (RX-2) 173 in.; (RX-3 cpe) 168 in.; (RX-3 wag) 170 in.; (RX-4 HT) 177 in.; (RX-4 sed) 179 in.; (RX-4 wag) 184 in. **Height:** (808 cpe) 53 in.; (RX-2 cpe) 55 in.; (RX-2 sed) 56 in.; (RX-3 cpe) 53 in.; (RX-3 wag) 55 in.; (RX-4 HT) 54 in.; (RX-4 sed/wag) 56 in. **Width:** (808) 63 in.; (RX-2) 62 in.; (RX-3) 63 in.; (RX-4 HT) 66 in.; (RX-4 sed/wag) 65 in. **Front Tread:** (808) 51 in.; (RX-2/RX-3) 51 in.; (RX-4) 54 in. **Rear Tread:** (808) 51 in.; (RX-2/RX-3) 51 in.; (RX-4) 54 in. **Standard Tires:** (808) 6.15x13; (RX-2) 165SR13; (RX-3) 155SR13; (RX-4) BR70x13.

TECHNICAL: Layout: front-engine, rear-drive. **Transmission:** four-speed manual. **Steering:** recirculating ball. **Suspension (front):** MacPherson struts with coil springs. **Suspension (rear):** (RX-3, RX-4, 808) rigid axle with semi-elliptic leaf springs; (RX-2) rigid axle with parallel links and coil springs. **Brakes:** front disc, rear drum. **Body Construction:** steel unibody.

MAJOR OPTIONS: Automatic transmission ($250) except RX-4 ($270). Air conditioning. Power steering (RX-4). AM radio.

PRODUCTION/SALES: A total of 61,192 Mazda passenger cars were sold in the U.S. during 1974.

ADDITIONAL MODELS: Both piston-engine and rotary-engine pickup trucks were available in the U.S. in 1974. The piston-engined B1600 sold for $2988; the rotary RE for $3495.

Manufacturer: Toyo Kogyo Co. Ltd., Hiroshima, Japan.

Distributor: Mazda Motors of America, Compton, California.

HISTORY: Mazda promoted the RX-4 sedan as the "roomy rotary," one that "seats four adults in luxurious comfort." The RX-4 hardtop was called the "regal rotary."

1975 MAZDA

808 — FOUR — Little change was evident in the piston-engined 808 coupe and station wagon. The narrow grille was similar to that used in the equivalent RX-3, except for the lack of a Wankel badge.

RX-3 — ROTARY — The RX-2 left the lineup, but the RX-3 coupe and station wagon remained with little change.

RX-4 — ROTARY — Production of the RX-4 trio, introduced for 1974, continued with minimal change.

I.D. DATA: Mazda's 11- or 12-symbol serial number is at the lower left corner of the windshield. The first three to five symbols indicate the car series, followed by the sequential production number. Starting serial number (1975): (808 cpe) SN3A137323; (808 wag) SN3AV111247; (RX-3 cpe) S124A166910; (RX-3 wag) S124W160674; (RX-4 HT) LA23S128544; (RX-4 sed) LA23S127229; (RX-4 wag) LA23W115564. Engine number for piston engines is on a plate at the upper right front of the block; for rotary engines, the number is stamped on the front housing.

Model	Body Type & Seating	Engine Type/CID	P.O.E. Price	Weight (lbs.)	Prod. Total
CONVENTIONAL ENGINE					
808	2-dr Coupe-4P	I4/97	2997	2155	Note 1
808	4-dr Sta Wag-4/5P	I4/97	3177	2285	Note 1
ROTARY ENGINE					
RX-3	2-dr Coupe-4P	Ro/70	3697	2365	Note 1
RX-3	4-dr Sta Wag-4/5P	Ro/70	3877	2455	Note 1
RX-4	2-dr HT Cpe-4P	Ro/80	4597	2705	Note 1
RX-4	4-dr Sedan-4/5P	Ro/80	4497	2765	Note 1
RX-4	4-dr Sta Wag-4/5P	Ro/80	4697	2920	Note 1

Note 1: A total of 387,411 Mazda passenger cars were produced during 1975.

ENGINE DATA: BASE FOUR (808): Inline, overhead-cam four-cylinder. Cast iron block and light alloy head. **Displacement:** 96.8 cu. in. (1587 cc). **Bore & Stroke:** 3.07 x 3.27 in. (78 x 83 mm). **Compression Ratio:** 8.6:1. **Brake Horsepower:** 64 at 5000 rpm. **Torque:** 78 lbs.-ft. at 3000 rpm. Five main bearings. Solid valve lifters.

BASE ROTARY (RX-3): Wankel with two coaxial three-lobe rotors. Light alloy block and cast iron rotors. **Displacement:** 70 cu. in. (1146 cc). **Compression Ratio:** 9.4:1. **Brake Horsepower:** 90 at 6000 rpm. **Torque:** 96 lbs.-ft. at 4000 rpm. Two main bearings.

BASE ROTARY (RX-4): Wankel with two coaxial three-lobe rotors. Light alloy block and cast iron rotors. **Displacement:** 80 cu. in. (1308 cc). **Compression Ratio:** 9.2:1. **Brake Horsepower:** 110 at 6000 rpm. **Torque:** 117 lbs.-ft. at 3500 rpm. Two main bearings.

CHASSIS DATA: Wheelbase: (808) 91 in.; (RX-3) 91 in.; (RX-4) 99 in. **Overall Length:** (808 cpe) 168 in.; (808 wag) 169 in.; (RX-3 cpe) 168 in.; (RX-3 wag) 169 in.; (RX-4 HT/sed) 179 in.; (RX-4 wag) 183 in. **Height:** (808 cpe) 53 in.; (RX-3 cpe) 53 in.; (RX-3 wag) 55 in.; (RX-4 HT) 54 in.; (RX-4 sed/wag) 56 in. **Width:** (808) 63 in.; (RX-3) 63 in.; (RX-4 HT) 66 in.; (RX-4 sed/wag) 65 in. **Front Tread:** (808) 51 in.; (RX-3) 51 in.; (RX-4) 54 in. **Rear Tread:** (808) 51 in.; (RX-3) 51 in.; (RX-4) 54 in. **Standard Tires:** (808) 6.15x13; (RX-3) 115Rx13B; (RX-4) BR70x13.

TECHNICAL: Layout: front-engine, rear-drive. **Transmission:** four-speed manual. **Steering:** recirculating ball. **Suspension (front):** MacPherson struts with coil springs. **Suspension (rear):** (RX-3, 808) rigid axle with semi-elliptic leaf springs; (RX-2) rigid axle with parallel links and coil springs. **Brakes:** front disc, rear drum. **Body Construction:** steel unibody.

MAJOR OPTIONS: Automatic transmission: 808 ($260); RX3/RX-4 ($290). Air conditioning. Power steering: RX-4 ($190).

PRODUCTION/SALES: A total of 65,351 Mazda passenger cars were sold in the U.S. during 1975.

ADDITIONAL MODELS: Both piston-engine and rotary-engine pickup trucks were available in the U.S. in 1975. The piston-engined B1600 sold for $3377; the rotary for $3797.

Manufacturer: Toyo Kogyo Co. Ltd., Hiroshima, Japan.

Distributor: Mazda Motors of America, Compton, California.

HISTORY: During 1975, Mazda was offering $500 rebates to push the rotary engine. The Wankel engine in the RX-2 and RX-3 was less successful than anticipated because consumers saw them as economy models, but they guzzled considerably more fuel than expected.

1976 MAZDA

MIZER 808-1300 — FOUR — A smaller four-cylinder piston engine went into the new Mizer series, offered as a two-door coupe, four-door sedan, or four-door station wagon. The 1272-cc (77.6-cid) engine produced 49 horsepower. The Mizer would last only two years in Mazda's U.S. lineup, despite its EPA mileage rating of 42-mpg highway and 32-mpg city. A four-speed gearbox remained standard.

808-1600 — FOUR — Production of the piston-engined Mazda with 96.8-cid displacement continued without major change. Standard equipment included a four-speed manual gearbox, tinted glass, two-speed wiper/washer, carpeting, rear defroster, reclining front bucket seats, and wheel covers.

RX-3 — ROTARY — A modest power boost was the only significant change this year for the smaller Wankel-engined series.

RX-4 — ROTARY — A revised grille went on the larger Wankel-engined series for 1976. Standard equipment included a five-speed manual gearbox, three-speed wiper, tachometer, electric clock, and white-letter tires.

COSMO — ROTARY — Long and low, the new rotary-engined coupe borrowed its name from the very first Wankel-engine model produced in Japan, in the 1960s. This latter Cosmo displayed a curious profile, with triangular rear quarter windows plus small center windows that rolled up/down. 'Cosmo' script went on the front fender, to the rear of the wheel opening. The twin-rotor Wankel engine produced 110 horsepower (same as the RX-4), and the Cosmo also rode a 99-inch wheelbase. All-disc brakes were standard, as was a five-speed manual transmission. Standard equipment included a front spoiler, front and rear stabilizer bars, dual sport mirrors (driver's side remote-controlled), front/rear bumper overriders, 185/70SR14 whitewall tires on Rally wheels with chrome inserts and hubs, and simulated woodgrain instrument panel. Wood was used on the steering wheel, gearshift knob and handbrake handle, and to trim the velour interior. This was Mazda's top-of-the-line model, and the most expensive.

I.D. DATA: Mazda's 9- to 12-symbol serial number is at the lower left corner of the windshield. The first three to five symbols indicate the car series, followed by the sequential production number. Starting serial number (1976): (Mizer cpe) STC-353391; (Mizer sed) STC-353576; (Mizer wag) STCV-203186; (808-1600 cpe) SN3A-151003; (808-1600 sed) SN3A-151099; (808-1600 wag) SN3A-124623; (RX-3 cpe) 3124A-180050; (RX-3 wag) S124W-170026; (RX-4 HT) LA23S-140457; (RX-4 sed) LA23S-140470; (RX-4 wag) LA23W-130170; (Cosmo) CD23C-700001. Engine number for piston engines is on a plate at the upper right front of the block; for rotary engines, the number is stamped on the front housing.

Model	Body Type & Seating	Engine Type/CID	P.O.E. Price	Weight (lbs.)	Prod. Total
CONVENTIONAL ENGINE (MIZER)					
808-1300	2-dr Coupe-4P	I4/78	2995	2090	Note 1
808-1300	4-dr Sedan-4/5P	I4/78	2895	2055	Note 1
808-1300	4-dr Sta Wag-4/5P	I4/78	3275	2205	Note 1
CONVENTIONAL ENGINE (808)					
808-1600	2-dr Coupe-4P	I4/97	3295	2160	Note 1
808-1600	4-dr Sedan-4/5P	I4/97	3195	2190	Note 1
808-1600	4-dr Sta Wag-4/5P	I4/97	3475	2399	Note 1
ROTARY ENGINE					
RX-3	2-dr Coupe-4P	Ro/70	4095	2400	Note 1
RX-3	4-dr Sta Wag-4/5P	Ro/70	4295	2535	Note 1
RX-4	2-dr HT Cpe-4P	Ro/80	4995	2770	Note 1
RX-4	4-dr Sedan-4/5P	Ro/80	4895	2770	Note 1
RX-4	4-dr Sta Wag-4/5P	Ro/80	5095	2920	Note 1
Cosmo	2-dr HT Cpe-4P	Ro/80	5945	2845	Note 1

Note 1: A total of 446,618 Mazda passenger cars were produced during 1976.

ENGINE DATA: BASE FOUR (808-1300 Mizer): Inline, overhead-cam four-cylinder. Cast iron block and light alloy head. **Displacement:** 77.6 cu. in. (1272 cc). **Bore & Stroke:** 2.87 x 2.99 in. (73 x 76 mm). **Compression Ratio:** 9.2:1. **Brake Horsepower:** 49 at 5000 rpm. **Torque:** 64 lbs.-ft. at 3000 rpm. Five main bearings. Solid valve lifters. Two-barrel carburetor.

BASE FOUR (808-1600): Inline, overhead-cam four-cylinder. Cast iron block and light alloy head. **Displacement:** 96.8 cu. in. (1587 cc). **Bore & Stroke:** 3.07 x 3.27 in. (78 x 83 mm). **Compression Ratio:** 8.6:1. **Brake Horsepower:** 64 at 5000 rpm. **Torque:** 78 lbs.-ft. at 3000 rpm. Five main bearings. Two-barrel carburetor. Solid valve lifters.

BASE ROTARY (RX-3): Wankel with two coaxial three-lobe rotors. Light alloy block and cast iron rotors. **Displacement:** 70 cu. in. (1146 cc). **Compression Ratio:** 9.4:1. **Brake Horsepower:** 95 at 6000 rpm. **Torque:** 102 lbs.-ft. at 4000 rpm. Two main bearings.

BASE ROTARY (RX-4, Cosmo): Wankel with two coaxial three-lobe rotors. Light alloy block and cast iron rotors. **Displacement:** 80 cu. in. (1308 cc). **Compression Ratio:** 9.2:1. **Brake Horsepower:** 110 at 6000 rpm. **Torque:** 120 lbs.-ft. at 4000 rpm. Two main bearings.

CHASSIS DATA: Wheelbase: (808) 91 in.; (RX-3) 91 in.; (RX-4) 99 in.; (Cosmo) 99 in. Overall Length: (808 cpe) 166 in.; (808 wag) 168 in.; (RX-3 cpe) 168 in.; (RX-3 wag) 169 in.; (RX-4 HT/sed) 179 in.; (RX-4 wag) 183 in.; (Cosmo) 182 in. Height: (808 cpe) 53 in.; (808 sed) 54 in.; (808 wag) 55 in.; (RX-3 cpe) 53 in.; (RX-3 wag) 55 in.; (RX-4 HT) 54 in.; (RX-4 sed/wag) 56 in.; (Cosmo) 52 in. Width: (808) 63 in.; (RX-3) 63 in.; (RX-4 HT) 66 in.; (RX-4 sed/wag) 65 in.; (Cosmo) 66 in. Front Tread: (808) 51 in.; (RX-3) 51 in.; (RX-4) 54 in.; (Cosmo) 54 in. Rear Tread: (808) 51 in.; (RX-3) 51 in.; (RX-4) 54 in.; (Cosmo) 54 in. Standard Tires: (808) 6.15x13; (RX-3) 115SR13; (RX-4) BR70x13; (Cosmo) 185/70SR14.

TECHNICAL: Layout: front-engine, rear-drive. Transmission: four-speed manual except (RX-4, Cosmo) five-speed manual. Steering: recirculating ball. Suspension (front): MacPherson struts with coil springs. Suspension (rear): (RX-3, RX-4, 808) rigid axle with semi-elliptic leaf springs; (Cosmo) rigid axle with Panhard rod and coil springs. Brakes: front disc, rear drum except (Cosmo) front/rear disc. Body Construction: steel unibody.

MAJOR OPTIONS: Automatic transmission: 808-1600 ($270); others ($300). Air conditioning: 808-1600, RX-3 ($395), RX-4/Cosmo ($450). Power steering ($190). AM radio: RX-3 ($69). AM/FM radio: RX-4/Cosmo ($150). Power windows: Cosmo ($85).

PRODUCTION/SALES: A total of 35,383 Mazda passenger cars were sold in the U.S. during 1976.

ADDITIONAL MODELS: Both piston-engine and rotary-engine pickup trucks were available in the U.S. The piston-engined B1600 sold for $3425; the rotary for $3895.

Manufacturer: Toyo Kogyo Co. Ltd., Hiroshima, Japan.

Distributor: Mazda Motors of America, Compton, California.

1977 MAZDA

MIZER — FOUR — Little was new in the low-budget Mizer coupe, sedan, and station wagon, with their 1272-cc four-cylinder engine. This series ranked fourth in EPA economy rating, at 38-mpg overall.

808 — FOUR — This was the final outing for the 808 series, which was replaced by the new GLC. The sedan came with a standard four-speed manual gearbox; the coupe and wagon could have a five-speed. As before, the 808's four-cylinder engine was larger than that used in the Mizer. A new grey instrument panel went with certain body colors.

GLC — FOUR — The name of this new hatchback model, according to Mazda, "immodestly" stood for "Great Little Car." Mazda pinned great hopes on this piston-engined model, in the wake of fuel-economy and other problems with the Wankel-engined models. Riding a 91.1-inch wheelbase, it replaced the 808 series during the '77 model year. The 1272-cc (77.6-cid) four-cylinder engine produced 52 horsepower. A four-speed gearbox was standard on the basic model. The Deluxe hatchback came with either a four- or five-speed manual gearbox, with automatic optional. Standard equipment included reclining bucket seats, styled disc wheels, and trip odometer. The Deluxe model added a power-operated hatch, rear-window wiper/washer/defroster, and split rear seatbacks that folded down.

RX-3SP — ROTARY — Only one model was left of the RX-3 series: a coupe with sport trim, blackout grille, spoiler, 155SR13 tires, and five-speed manual gearbox. The RX-3's Wankel engine produced 95 horsepower. 'RX-3SP' lettering went on the body and air dam.

RX-4 — ROTARY — Little was new in the larger Wankel-engined RX-4 series, which came with a standard five-speed gearbox. The former hardtop coupe faded away (its role made redundant by the new RX-3SP and the Cosmo), leaving the sedan and station wagon. Those two had restyled taillamps this year. This version of the rotary engine delivered 110 horsepower.

COSMO — ROTARY — Mazda's top model continued with little change apart from restyled taillamps, powered by the same larger Wankel engine as the RX-4. A red reflector strip across the tail replaced the former grey plastic panel. Power remote mirrors were standard, as were an 8000-rpm tachometer and 130-mph speedometer. Wood was used on the gearshift knob, brake handle, and steering wheel.

I.D. DATA: Mazda's 9- or 11-symbol serial number is at the lower left corner of the windshield. The first three to five symbols indicate the car series, followed by the sequential production number. Starting serial number (1977): (GLC hatch) FA4TS-505592; (Mizer cpe/sed) STC413196; (Mizer wag) STCV-220233; (808 cpe/sed) SN3A162253; (808 wag) SN3AV132527; (RX-3 cpe) S124A-181905; (RX-4 sed) LA23S-151372; (RX-4 wag) LA23W-135327; (Cosmo) CD23C-708652. Engine number for piston engines is on a plate at the upper right front of the block, except for the GLC, with its plate at the front of the cylinder lead. For rotary engines, the number is stamped on the front housing.

Model	Body Type & Seating	Engine Type/CID	P.O.E. Price	Weight (lbs.)	Prod. Total
MIZER					
	2-dr Coupe-4P	I4/78	3250	2015	Note 1
	4-dr Sedan-4/5P	I4/78	3150	2050	Note 1
	4-dr Sta Wag-4/5P	I4/78	3450	2155	Note 1
GLC					
Standard	2-dr Hatch-4/5P	I4/78	2945	1965	Note 1
Deluxe	2-dr Hatch-4/5P	I4/78	3245	1965	Note 1
808					
	2-dr Coupe-4P	I4/97	3645	2165	Note 1
	4-dr Sedan-4/5P	I4/97	3695	2170	Note 1
	4-dr Sta Wag-4/5P	I4/97	3765	2295	Note 1
ROTARY ENGINE					
RX-3SP	2-dr Coupe-4P	Ro/70	3945	2360	Note 1
RX-4	4-dr Sedan-4/5P	Ro/80	5470	2765	Note 1
RX-4	4-dr Sta Wag-4/5P	Ro/80	5545	2910	Note 1
Cosmo	2-dr HT Cpe-4P	Ro/80	5945	2820	Note 1

Note 1: A total of 498,691 Mazda passenger cars were produced during 1977.

ENGINE DATA: BASE FOUR (GLC, Mizer): Inline, overhead-cam four-cylinder. Cast iron block and light alloy head. Displacement: 77.6 cu. in. (1272 cc). Bore & Stroke: 2.87 x 2.99 in. (73 x 76 mm). Compression Ratio: 9.2:1. Brake Horsepower: 52 at 5000 rpm. Torque: 64 lbs.-ft. at 3000 rpm. Five main bearings. Solid valve lifters. Two-barrel carburetor.

BASE FOUR (808): Inline, overhead-cam four-cylinder. Cast iron block and light alloy head. Displacement: 96.8 cu. in. (1587 cc). Bore & Stroke: 3.07 x 3.27 in. (78 x 83 mm). Compression Ratio: 8.6:1. Brake Horsepower: 64 at 5000 rpm. Torque: 78 lbs.-ft. at 3000 rpm. Five main bearings. Two-barrel carburetor. Solid valve lifters.

BASE ROTARY (RX-3SP): Wankel with two coaxial three-lobe rotors. Light alloy block and cast iron rotors. Displacement: 70 cu. in. (1146 cc). Compression Ratio: 9.4:1. Brake Horsepower: 95 at 6000 rpm. Torque: 102 lbs.-ft. at 4000 rpm. Two main bearings.

BASE ROTARY (RX-4, Cosmo): Wankel with two coaxial three-lobe rotors. Light alloy block and cast iron rotors. Displacement: 80 cu. in. (1308 cc). Compression Ratio: 9.2:1. Brake Horsepower: 110 at 6000 rpm. Torque: 120 lbs.-ft. at 4000 rpm. Two main bearings.

CHASSIS DATA: Wheelbase: (808) 91 in.; (GLC) 91.1 in.; (RX-3SP) 91 in.; (RX-4) 99 in.; (Cosmo) 99 in. Overall Length: (808 cpe/sed) 166 in.; (808 wag) 168 in.; (GLC) 154.3 in.; (RX-3SP) 168 in.; (RX-4 sed) 179 in.; (RX-4 wag) 183 in.; (Cosmo) 182 in. Height: (808 cpe) 53 in.; (808 sed) 54 in.; (808 wag) 55 in.; (GLC) 53.9 in.; (RX-3SP) 53 in.; (RX-4) 56 in.; (Cosmo) 52 in. Width: (808) 63 in.; (GLC) 63.2 in.; (RX-3SP) 63 in.; (RX-4) 65 in.; (Cosmo) 66 in. Front Tread: (808) 51 in.; (GLC) 51 in.; (RX-3SP) 51 in.; (RX-4) 54 in.; (Cosmo) 54 in. Rear Tread: (808) 51 in.; (GLC) 51.6 in.; (RX-3SP) 51 in.; (RX-4) 54 in.; (Cosmo) 54 in. Standard Tires: (808) 6.15x13; (GLC) 6.15x13; (RX-3SP) 155SR13; (RX-4) BR70x13; (Cosmo) 185/70SR14.

TECHNICAL: Layout: front-engine, rear-drive. Transmission: four- or five-speed manual. Steering: recirculating ball. Suspension (front): MacPherson struts with coil springs. Suspension (rear): (RX-3SP, RX-4, 808) rigid axle with semi-elliptic leaf springs; (GLC, Cosmo) rigid axle with coil springs. Brakes: front disc, rear drum except (Cosmo) front/rear disc. Body Construction: steel unibody.

MAJOR OPTIONS: Automatic transmission: GLC DeL 4-spd ($270); others ($290). Air conditioning ($420). Power steering ($190). AM/FM stereo radio. Aluminum alloy wheels: Cosmo ($190).

PERFORMANCE: Acceleration (0-60 mph): (Cosmo) 11.0 sec. Acceleration (quarter-mile): (Cosmo) 17.8 sec. (78.1 mph). Fuel Mileage: (Cosmo) near 26 mpg average; (GLC w/5-spd) 35/45 mpg EPA rating.

PRODUCTION/SALES: A total of 50,608 Mazda passenger cars were sold in the U.S. during 1977.

ADDITIONAL MODELS: Both piston-engine and rotary-engine pickup trucks were available in the U.S. The piston-engined B1800 sold for $3965; the rotary for $4445.

Manufacturer: Toyo Kogyo Co. Ltd., Hiroshima, Japan.

Distributor: Mazda Motors of America, Compton, California.

HISTORY: "Rest assured," said Mazda's ad for the new RX-3SP, "SP does not stand for slowpoke."

1978 MAZDA

1978-'79 Mazda RX-7.

GLC — FOUR — Only the GLC remained in the piston-engine Mazda lineup for 1978, as the 808/Mizer models faded away. A four-door hatchback joined the original two-door hatchback, the latter marketed in three trim levels. Under the hood was a 1272-cc (77.6-cid) four, delivering 52 bhp. The GLC was shaped somewhat like the Chevrolet Chevette. Added this year was a Sport version with full instruments, a five-speed manual transmission, oversize steel-belted radial tires on sport wheels, and body striping. Other models had a standard four- or five-speed gearbox, with automatic optional.

RX-3SP — ROTARY — As in 1977, only a two-door coupe was offered in the RX-3 series, with a five-speed gearbox. An automatic transmission was available only in certain states.

RX-4 — ROTARY — This would be the final year for the RX-4 series. Only two models were available: the four-door sedan and station wagon. Both were powered by the twin-rotor Wankel engine, rated 110 horsepower.

COSMO — ROTARY — Production of the top Mazda coupe continued with little change, with the same Wankel engine and five-speed gearbox as the RX-4. An automatic transmission was optional.

I.D. DATA: Mazda's 9- or 11-symbol serial number is at the lower left corner of the windshield. The first three to five symbols indicate the car series, followed by the sequential production number. Starting serial number (1978): (GLC) FA4TS-574145; (RX-3) S124A-183776; (RX-4 sed) LA23S-151885; (RX-4 wag) LA23W-136443; (Cosmo) CD23C-709490. Engine number for piston engines is on a plate at the upper right front of the block, except (GLC) at the front of the cylinder head. For rotary engines, the number is stamped on the front housing.

Model	Body Type & Seating	Engine Type/CID	P.O.E. Price	Weight (lbs.)	Prod. Total
GLC					
	2-dr Hatch-4P	I4/78	3145	1930	Note 1
Deluxe	2-dr Hatch-4P	I4/78	3445	1930	Note 1
Sport	2-dr Hatch-4P	I4/78	3830	1930	Note 1
Deluxe	4-dr Hatch-4P	I4/78	3595	1965	Note 1
ROTARY ENGINE					
RX-3SP	2-dr Coupe-4P	Ro/70	4145	2210	Note 1
RX-4	4-dr Sedan-4P	Ro/80	5720	2675	Note 1
RX-4	4-dr Sta Wag-4P	Ro/80	5795	2820	Note 1
Cosmo	2-dr Coupe-4P	Ro/80	6195	2730	Note 1

Note 1: A total of 493,111 Mazda passenger cars were produced during 1978.

395

ENGINE DATA: BASE FOUR (GLC): Inline, overhead-cam four-cylinder. Cast iron block and light alloy head. **Displacement:** 77.6 cu. in. (1272 cc). **Bore & Stroke:** 2.87 x 2.99 in. (73 x 76 mm). **Compression Ratio:** 9.2:1. **Brake Horsepower:** 52 at 5000 rpm. **Torque:** 64 lbs.-ft. at 3000 rpm. Five main bearings. Solid valve lifters. Two-barrel carburetor.

BASE ROTARY (RX-3SP): Wankel with two coaxial three-lobe rotors. Light alloy block and cast iron rotors. **Displacement:** 70 cu. in. (1146 cc). **Compression Ratio:** 9.4:1. **Brake Horsepower:** 95 at 6000 rpm. **Torque:** 102 lbs.-ft. at 4000 rpm. Two main bearings. One four-barrel carburetor.

BASE ROTARY (RX-4, Cosmo): Wankel with two coaxial three-lobe rotors. Light alloy block and cast iron rotors. **Displacement:** 80 cu. in. (1308 cc). **Compression Ratio:** 9.2:1. **Brake Horsepower:** 110 at 6000 rpm. **Torque:** 120 lbs.-ft. at 4000 rpm. Two main bearings. One four-barrel carburetor.

CHASSIS DATA: Wheelbase: (GLC) 91.1 in.; (RX-3SP) 91 in.; (RX-4) 99 in.; (Cosmo) 99 in. **Overall Length:** (GLC) 154.3 in.; (RX-3SP) 166 in.; (RX-4 sed) 179 in.; (RX-4 wag) 183 in.; (Cosmo) 182 in. **Height:** (GLC) 53.9 in.; (RX-3SP) 53 in.; (RX-4) 56 in.; (Cosmo) 52 in. **Width:** (GLC) 63.2 in.; (RX-3SP) 63 in.; (RX-4) 65 in.; (Cosmo) 66 in. **Front Tread:** (GLC) 51 in.; (RX-3SP) 52 in.; (RX-4) 54 in.; (Cosmo) 54 in. **Rear Tread:** (GLC) 51.6 in.; (RX-3SP) 51 in.; (RX-4) 54 in.; (Cosmo) 54 in. **Standard Tires:** (GLC) 6.15x13; (RX-3SP) 155SR13; (RX-4) BR70x13; (Cosmo) 185/70SR14.

TECHNICAL: Layout: front-engine, rear-drive. **Transmission:** four- or five-speed manual. **Steering:** recirculating ball. **Suspension (front):** MacPherson struts with coil springs and anti-roll bar. **Suspension (rear):** (GLC, Cosmo) rigid axle with Panhard rod and coil springs; (RX-3, RX-4) rigid axle with semi-elliptic leaf springs. **Brakes:** front disc, rear drum except (Cosmo) front/rear disc. **Body Construction:** steel unibody.

MAJOR OPTIONS: Automatic transmission. Air conditioning. Power steering. Overdrive (five-speed) gearbox. AM/FM stereo radio.

PRODUCTION/SALES: A total of 75,309 Mazda passenger cars were sold in the U.S. during 1978.

ADDITIONAL MODELS: Only the B1800 piston-engine pickup truck was available in the U.S. for 1978, selling for $3925 in short-bed version.

Manufacturer: Toyo Kogyo Co. Ltd., Hiroshima, Japan.

Distributor: Mazda Motors of America, Compton, California.

HISTORY: Mazda's RX-7 sports car was introduced during 1978, but as a 1979 model; see next listing for details.

1979 MAZDA

GLC — FOUR — A larger 1415-cc (86.4-cid) engine with more power went into the "Great Little Car" for 1979. The four-cylinder unit delivered 65 bhp at 5000 rpm. An automatic choke and split rear seat also were installed, and a station wagon joined the original hatchbacks. The wagon measured 163 inches long overall (9 inches more than the hatchbacks) and carried five passengers. Standard models had brightwork around the headlamps (but not the grille). The Deluxe GLC had a blackout section around the headlamps. Standard equipment on the GLC Sport included a five-speed manual gearbox, clock, wood steering wheel, tachometer, and body stripes. Other models had a standard four-speed transmission. The Deluxe GLC came with a wood-insert dashboard, tinted glass, power hatch release, bodyside moldings, and rear wiper/washer.

626 — FOUR — Mazda's new luxury sport coupe and sedan debuted during the 1979 model year, powered by an 80-bhp, 1970-cc (120-cid) four-cylinder engine. A five-speed manual gearbox was standrad; automatic available. Styling features included a wrap-around back window and recessed single headlamps. Wheelbase was 98.8 inches.

RX-7 — ROTARY — While fortunes of the Wankel engine had declined sharply during the 1970s, the appearance of Mazda's new sports car with rotary power sent its stock soaring once again. This was an improved Wankel engine, ready to give the new coupe dramatic performance and impressive fuel economy. With 100 horsepower on tap from the 1146-cc (70-cid) rotary engine, 0-60 acceleration times around 9 seconds were possible, with top speed beyond 120 mph and average economy of 20 mpg or so (as much as 30 mpg on the highway). The rear-wheel-drive coupe rode a 95.3-inch wheelbase and had an all-glass hatch. Styling features included a sloping hood and concealed (retractable) headlamps. Blackout rub strips extended the full bodyside length. Integrated bumpers contained rubber impact strips, and the front end held an air dam. Two trim levels were offered: the standard 'S' model and a better-equipped GS. Both included an AM/FM stereo radio with power antenna, bucket seats, steel-belted radial tires, front anti-roll bar, quartz clock, full instruments (including tachometer), door-window demisters, rear defroster, locking fuel filler door, tinted glass, reclining bucket seats, leather-covered two-spoke steering wheel, and full carpeting. The RX-7S had a four-speed manual transmission, while the GS came with a five-speed (automatic optional). The GS also had larger (185/70HR13) tires on alloy wheels, versus styled steel wheels for the standard model; plus a rear anti-roll bar, remote hatch release, four-spoke steering wheel, and intermittent wipers. European and Japanese models had tiny back seats, but the American RX-7 was strictly a two-seater. Transistorized ignition and a larger brake booster were added in 1979.

I.D. DATA: Mazda's 11-symbol serial number is at the lower left corner of the windshield. The first two symbols indicate model; the fourth identifies the engine; the fifth denotes body type; and the final six digits make up the sequential production number. Starting serial number (1979): (GLC 2-dr hatch) FA4US-500665; (GLC 4-dr hatch) FA4US-506056; (GLC wagon) FA4UV-501911; (626) CB2MS-500049; (RX-7) SA22C-500025. Engine number for piston engines is on a plate at the upper right front of the block. For rotary engines, the number is stamped on the front housing.

Model	Body Type & Seating	Engine Type/CID	P.O.E. Price	Weight (lbs.)	Prod. Total
GLC					
	2-dr Hatch-4/5P	I4/86	3995	1955	Note 1
Deluxe	2-dr Hatch-4/5P	I4/86	4295	1970	Note 1
Sport	2-dr Hatch-4/5P	I4/86	4695	1970	Note 1
Deluxe	4-dr Hatch-4/5P	I4/86	4395	2030	Note 1
	4-dr Sta Wag-5P	I4/86	4395	2145	Note 1
Deluxe	4-dr Sta Wag-5P	I4/86	4695	2145	Note 1
626					
	2-dr Spt Cpe-5P	I4/120	5795	2585	Note 1
	4-dr Spt Sed-5P	I4/120	5495	2570	Note 1
RX-7					
S	2-dr Coupe-2P	Ro/70	7195	2350	Note 2
GS	2-dr Coupe-2P	Ro/70	7995	2420	Note 2

Note 1: A total of 647,001 Mazda passenger cars (all models) were produced during 1979.

Note 2: A total of 72,692 RX-7s were produced in 1978, followed by 71,617 in 1979.

ENGINE DATA: BASE FOUR (GLC): Inline, overhead-cam four-cylinder. Cast iron block and light alloy head. **Displacement:** 86.4 cu. in. (1415 cc). **Bore & Stroke:** 3.03 x 2.99 in. (77 x 76 mm). **Compression Ratio:** 9.0:1. **Brake Horsepower:** 65 at 5000 rpm. **Torque:** 76 lbs.-ft. at 3000 rpm. Five main bearings. Solid valve lifters. Two-barrel carburetor.

BASE FOUR (626): Inline, overhead-cam four-cylinder. Cast iron block and light alloy head. **Displacement:** 120.2 cu. in. (1970 cc). **Bore & Stroke:** 3.15 x 3.86 in. (80 x 98 mm). **Compression Ratio:** 8.6:1. **Brake Horsepower:** 80 at 4500 rpm. **Torque:** 105 lbs.-ft. at 2500 rpm. Five main bearings. Solid valve lifters. Two-barrel carburetor.

BASE ROTARY (RX-7): Wankel with two coaxial three-lobe rotors. Cast iron side housing, light alloy trochoid housings and cast iron rotors. **Displacement:** 70 cu. in. (1146 cc). **Compression Ratio:** 9.4:1. **Brake Horsepower:** 100 at 6000 rpm. **Torque:** 105 lbs.-ft. at 4000 rpm. Two main bearings.

CHASSIS DATA: Wheelbase: (GLC) 91 in.; (626) 98.8 in.; (RX-7) 95.3 in. **Overall Length:** (GLC) 154.3 in.; (GLC wag) 163.2 in.; (626) 173.8 in.; (RX-7) 169 in. **Height:** (GLC) 53.9 in.; (GLC wag) 56.1 in.; (626) 54.3 in.; (RX-7) 50 in. **Width:** (GLC) 63.2 in.; (626) 65.4 in.; (RX-7) 65 in. **Front Tread:** (GLC) 51 in.; (626) 53.9 in.; (RX-7) 56 in. **Rear Tread:** (GLC) 51.6 in.; (626) 54.3 in.; (RX-7) 55 in. **Standard Tires:** (GLC) 6.15x13; (626) 165SR13; (RX-7) 165SR13; (RX-7GS) 185/70HR13.

TECHNICAL: Layout: front-engine, rear-drive. **Transmission:** four- or five-speed manual. **Steering:** recirculating ball. **Suspension (front):** (GLC/626) MacPherson struts with coil springs and anti-roll bar; (RX-7) MacPherson struts with lower lateral links, compliance struts, coil springs and anti-roll bar. **Suspension (rear):** (GLC) rigid axle with lower trailing arms, upper torque rods and coil springs; (GLC wagon) rigid axle with semi-elliptic leaf springs; (RX-7) rigid axle with lower trailing links, upper angled links (torque rods), Watt linkage and coil springs; (626) rigid axle with lower trailing arms, upper torque rods, Panhard rod and coil springs. **Brakes:** front disc, rear drum. **Body Construction:** steel unibody.

MAJOR OPTIONS: Automatic transmission: GLC ($335); 626 ($295); RX-7GS ($355). Air conditioning: GLC ($460); RX-7 ($525). Five-speed manual transmission: GLC DeL ($145). AM radio: GLC ($88). AM/FM radio: GLC ($125). AM/FM stereo radio: GLC ($170). Woodgrain exterior: GLC wagon ($329). Console: GLC ($39). Aluminum wheels: RX-7GS ($275); w/removable top ($550).

PERFORMANCE: Top Speed: (RX-7) 122 mph. **Acceleration (0-60 mph):** (RX-7) 9.2 sec. **Acceleration (quarter-mile):** (RX-7) 17.0 sec. (83 mph). **Fuel Mileage:** (RX-7) about 22 mpg.

PRODUCTION/SALES: A total of 156,535 Mazda passenger cars were sold in the U.S. during 1979.

ADDITIONAL MODELS: A new B2000 piston-engine pickup truck was available in the U.S. for 1979, selling for $4695 (short-bed) or $4995 (long-bed).

Manufacturer: Toyo Kogyo Co. Ltd., Hiroshima, Japan.

Distributor: Mazda Motors of America, Compton, California.

HISTORY: The RX-7 was introduced to the U.S. market in February 1978, as a '79 model. The revised GLC was introduced in June 1978, the 626 not until March 1979.

Following its debut as an early '79 model, the RX-7 drew hordes of avid customers who waited weeks for delivery of the rotary-engine sports car. Some were willing to pay prices well above the $7000 sticker figure. This was considered to be the first "affordable" sports car on the U.S. market since Datsun's 240Z. Development had begun in 1974, as Project X605, and the RX-7 went on sale in Japan during 1978 (called the Savanna). In 1979, an RX-7 took first and second place at the 24 Hours of Daytona race. Ford held a 25-percent share of Mazda in 1979, and sold Mazda-built Ford Courier pickup trucks into the 1980s.

1980 MAZDA

GLC — FOUR — Apart from restyled seats, carpets and headliners, not much was new for the subcompact GLC hatchbacks and wagon. Modifications to front fenders, grille, headlamps and parking lights gave a more angular front-end look. Power again came from a 1415-cc (86-cid) four, which produced 65 horsepower. Five models were available.

626 — FOUR — Production of the luxury Mazda coupe and sedan, introduced during 1979, continued with minimal change. Under its hood was a 1970-cc (120-cid) overhead-cam four, which produced 75 bhp, hooked to a standard five-speed manual gearbox. Wheelbase was 98.8 inches, and the 626 measured 173.8 inches long, considered a mid-size. Average fuel economy in the 24-mpg neighborhood was considered feasible. Standard equipment included an AM/FM radio, tachometer, color-keyed carpets and interior trim, and radial tires. Only two major options were offered: air conditioning and a three-speed automatic transmission.

RX-7 — ROTARY — Apart from new colors and fabrics, little was new in Mazda's sports car. Some dealers were charging from $1000 to as much as $3500 above sticker price for the popular RX-7 coupes at this time.

I.D. DATA: Mazda's 11-symbol serial number is at the lower left corner of the windshield. The first two symbols indicate model; the fourth identifies the engine; the fifth denotes body type; and the final six digits make up the sequential production number. Starting serial number (1980): (GLC hatch) FA4US-577104; (GLC wagon) FA4UV-530248; (626) CB2MS-549358; (RX-7) SA22C-558503. Engine number for piston engines is on a plate at the upper right front of the block. For rotary engines, the number is stamped on the front housing.

Model	Body Type & Seating	Engine Type/CID	P.O.E. Price	Weight (lbs.)	Prod. Total
GLC					
	2-dr Hatch-4/5P	I4/86	3795	1965	Note 1
Custom	2-dr Hatch-4/5P	I4/86	4195	1965	Note 1
Sport	2-dr Hatch-4/5P	I4/86	4895	1965	Note 1
Custom	4-dr Hatch-4/5P	I4/86	4345	1965	Note 1
Custom	4-dr Sta Wag-4/5P	I4/86	4645	2115	Note 1
626					
	2-dr Spt Cpe-5P	I4/120	6195	2595	Note 1
	4-dr Spt Sed-5P	I4/120	5895	2595	Note 1
RX-7					
S	2-dr Coupe-2P	Ro/70	7645	2395	Note 2
GS	2-dr Coupe-2P	Ro/70	8395	2340	Note 2

Note 1: A total of 736,544 Mazda passenger cars were produced during 1980.

Note 2: A total of 56,317 RX-7s were produced during 1980.

Price Note: Figures shown were valid in spring 1980.

ENGINE DATA: BASE FOUR (GLC): Inline, overhead-cam four-cylinder. Cast iron block and light alloy head. **Displacement:** 86.4 cu. in. (1415 cc). **Bore & Stroke:** 3.03 x 2.99 in. (77 x 76 mm). **Compression Ratio:** 9.0:1. **Brake Horsepower:** 65 at 5000 rpm. **Torque:** 76 lbs.-ft. at 3000 rpm. Five main bearings. Solid valve lifters. Two-barrel carburetor.

BASE FOUR (626): Inline, overhead-cam four-cylinder. Cast iron block and light alloy head. **Displacement:** 120.2 cu. in. (1970 cc). **Bore & Stroke:** 3.15 x 3.86 in. (80 x 98 mm). **Compression Ratio:** 8.6:1. **Brake Horsepower:** 75 at 4500 rpm. **Torque:** 105 lbs.-ft. at 2500 rpm. Five main bearings. Solid valve lifters. Two-barrel carburetor.

BASE ROTARY (RX-7): Wankel with two coaxial three-lobe rotors. Cast iron side housing, light alloy trochoid housings and cast iron rotors. **Displacement:** 70 cu. in. (1146 cc). **Compression Ratio:** 9.4:1. **Brake Horsepower:** 100 at 6000 rpm. **Torque:** 105 lbs.-ft. at 4000 rpm. Two main bearings. Four-barrel carburetor.

CHASSIS DATA: Wheelbase: (GLC) 91 in.; (626) 98.8 in.; (RX-7) 95.3 in. **Overall Length:** (GLC) 156.5 in.; (GLC wag) 165.6 in.; (626) 173.8 in.; (RX-7) 168.7 in. **Height:** (GLC) 53.9 in.; (GLC wag) 56.1 in.; (626) 54.3 in.; (RX-7) 49.6 in. **Width:** (GLC) 63.2 in.; (626) 65.4 in.; (RX-7) 65 in. **Front Tread:** (GLC) 51 in.; (626) 53.9 in.; (RX-7) 55.9 in. **Rear Tread:** (GLC) 51.6 in.; (626) 54.3 in.; (RX-7) 55.1 in. **Standard Tires:** (GLC) 6.15x13 WSW; (626) 165SR13; (RX-7) 165HR13; (RX-7GS) 185/70HR13.

TECHNICAL: Layout: front-engine, rear-drive. **Transmission:** (GLC) four- or five-speed manual; (626/RX-7) five-speed manual. Automatic optional. **Steering:** recirculating ball. **Suspension (front):** MacPherson struts with coil springs and anti-roll bar. **Suspension (rear):** (GLC) rigid axle with lower trailing arms, upper torque rods and coil springs; (GLC wagon) rigid axle with semi-elliptic leaf springs; (RX-7) rigid axle with lower trailing links, upper torque rods, Watt linkage and coil springs; (626) four-link rigid axle with coil springs and latger rod. **Brakes:** front disc, rear drum. **Body Construction:** steel unibody.

MAJOR OPTIONS: Automatic transmission: GLC ($325); 626, RX-7 GS ($360); RX-7S ($390). Air conditioning. Five-speed manual transmission. Sunroof. AM/FM stereo radio. Aluminum wheels.

PRODUCTION/SALES: A total of 161,623 Mazda passenger cars were sold in the U.S. during 1980.

ADDITIONAL MODELS: A B2000 piston-engine pickup truck was available in the U.S. for 1980, selling for $5095 in standard form; $5345 in Sundowner trim; or $5615 for the Sundowner long-bed.

Manufacturer: Toyo Kogyo Co. Ltd., Hiroshima, Japan.

Distributor: Mazda Motors of America, Compton, California.

1981 MAZDA

GLC — FOUR — A larger 1490 cc (90.9-cid) engine went into the new front-wheel-drive version of the "Great Little Car." Dimensions of the new hatchback and four-door sedan were larger than their rear-drive predecessor. The GLC station wagon, however, carried on in rear-wheel-drive form.

626 — FOUR — Production of Mazda's luxury sport coupe and sedan, with 75-horsepower 2.0-liter engine, continued with little change. Both standard and Luxury versions were available this year.

RX-7 — ROTARY — A luxury GSL version of the RX-7 sports car was added for 1981, with leather seats, power windows, cruise control, all-disc brakes, alloy wheels, and limited-slip differential. Other models got a revised dashboard, slight modification at the nose and tail, and a larger fuel tank.

I.D. DATA: Mazda's 17-symbol Vehicle Identification Number is on the upper left of the dashboard, visible through the windshield. The first three symbols ('JM1') indicate manufacturer, make and model; the next five symbols identify the model; the tenth symbol denotes model year ('B' = 1981); the eleventh ('C') identifies the car's assembly plant. The final six digits make up the sequential production number, starting with 500000. Starting serial number (1981): (GLC) JM1BD()()1()BC500000; (626) JM1GB()()1()BC500000; (RX-7) JM1FB331()BC500000. Engine number for piston engines is on a plate at the upper right front of the block. For rotary engines, the number is stamped on the front housing.

Model	Body Type & Seating	Engine Type/CID	P.O.E. Price	Weight (lbs.)	Prod. Total
GLC					
	2-dr Hatch-5P	I4/91	5095	1870	Note 1
Custom	2-dr Hatch-5P	I4/91	5495	1870	Note 1
Custom	4-dr Hatch-5P	I4/91	5795	1915	Note 1
Custom	4-dr Sedan-5P	I4/91	5995	1915	Note 1
Custom	4-dr Sta Wag-5P	I4/91	5745	2130	Note 1
Custom L	2-dr Hatch-5P	I4/91	5895	1880	Note 1
Custom L	4-dr Sedan-5P	I4/91	6495	1925	Note 1
Sport	2-dr Hatch-5P	I4/91	6295	1880	Note 1
626					
	2-dr Spt Cpe-5P	I4/120	7295	2530	Note 1
	4-dr Spt Sed-5P	I4/120	6995	2530	Note 1
Luxury	2-dr Spt Cpe-5P	I4/120	8495	2530	Note 1
Luxury	4-dr Spt Sed-5P	I4/120	8195	2530	Note 1
RX-7					
S	2-dr Coupe-2P	Ro/70	9395	2345	Note 1
GS	2-dr Coupe-2P	Ro/70	9895	2345	Note 1
GSL	2-dr Coupe-2P	Ro/70	11395	2345	Note 1

Note 1: A total of 840,630 Mazda passenger cars (all models) were produced during 1981.

ENGINE DATA: BASE FOUR (GLC): Inline, overhead-cam four-cylinder. Cast iron block and light alloy head. **Displacement:** 90.9 cu. in. (1490 cc). **Bore & Stroke:** 3.03 x 3.15 in. (77 x 80 mm). **Compression Ratio:** 9.0:1. **Brake Horsepower:** 68 at 5000 rpm. **Torque:** 82 lbs.-ft. at 3000 rpm. Five main bearings. Solid valve lifters. Two-barrel carburetor.

BASE FOUR (626): Inline, overhead-cam four-cylinder. Cast iron block and light alloy head. **Displacement:** 120.2 cu. in. (1970 cc). **Bore & Stroke:** 3.15 x 3.86 in. (80 x 98 mm). **Compression Ratio:** 8.6:1. **Brake Horsepower:** 75 at 4500 rpm. **Torque:** 105 lbs.-ft. at 2500 rpm. Five main bearings. Solid valve lifters. Two-barrel carburetor.

BASE ROTARY (RX-7): Wankel with two coaxial three-lobe rotors. Cast iron side housing, light alloy trochoid housings and cast iron rotors. **Displacement:** 70 cu. in. (1146 cc). **Compression Ratio:** 9.4:1. **Brake Horsepower:** 100 at 6000 rpm. **Torque:** 105 lbs.-ft. at 4000 rpm. Two main bearings. Four-barrel carburetor.

CHASSIS DATA: Wheelbase: (GLC) 93.1 in.; (GLC wag) 91 in.; (626) 98.8 in.; (RX-7) 95.3 in. **Overall Length:** (GLC hatch) 159.1 in.; (GLC sed) 166.8 in.; (GLC wag) 165.6 in.; (626) 173.8 in.; (RX-7) 170.1 in. **Height:** (GLC hatch/sed) 54.1 in.; (GLC wag) 56.1 in.; (626) 54.5 in.; (RX-7) 49.6 in. **Width:** (GLC hatch/sed) 64.2 in.; (GLC wag) 63.2 in.; (626) 65.4 in.; (RX-7) 65.7 in. **Front Tread:** (GLC hatch/sed) 54.7 in.; (GLC wag) 51 in.; (626) 53.9 in.; (RX-7) 55.9 in. **Rear Tread:** (GLC hatch/sed) 54.9 in.; (GLC wag) 51.6 in.; (626) 54.3 in.; (RX-7) 55.1 in. **Standard Tires:** (GLC hatch) 6.15x13; (GLC sed/wag) 155SR13; (626) 165SR13; (RX-7) 165HR13; (RX-7GS) 185/70HR13.

TECHNICAL: Layout: front-engine, rear-drive except (GLC hatch/sedan) front-engine, front-drive. **Transmission:** (GLC) four- or five-speed manual; (626, RX-7) five-speed manual. **Steering:** (GLC hatch/sedan) rack and pinion; (GLC wagon, RX-7, 626) recirculating ball. **Suspension (front):** (GLC hatch/sed) MacPherson struts with coil springs; (GLC wagon) MacPherson struts with coil springs and anti-roll bar; (RX-7) MacPherson struts with lower lateral links, compliance struts, coil springs and anti-roll bar; (626) MacPherson struts with transverse arms, trailing rods, coil springs and anti-roll bar. **Suspension (rear):** (GLC hatch/sed) MacPherson struts with coil springs and anti-roll bar; (GLC wagon) rigid axle with semi-elliptic leaf springs; (RX-7) rigid axle with lower trailing links, upper angled links, Watt linkage and coil springs; (626) rigid axle with lower trailing arms, upper torque rods, Panhard rod and coil springs. **Brakes:** (GLC/RX-7/626) front disc, rear drum; (RX-7GSL) front/rear disc. **Body Construction:** steel unibody.

MAJOR OPTIONS: Automatic transmission: GLC ($275-$420); 626 ($325); RX-7 GS/GSL ($355); RX-7S ($390). Air conditioning. Five-speed manual transmission. Sunroof. Aluminum wheels.

PRODUCTION/SALES: A total of 166,088 Mazda passenger cars were sold in the U.S. during 1981.

ADDITIONAL MODELS: A B2000 piston-engine pickup truck was available in the U.S. for 1981, selling for $5895 in standard form; $6195 in Sundowner trim; or $6445 for the Sundowner long-bed.

Manufacturer: Toyo Kogyo Co. Ltd., Hiroshima, Japan.

Distributor: Mazda Motors of America, Compton, California.

1982 MAZDA

GLC — FOUR — Production of the front-drive hatchback and sedan (and rear-drive wagon) continued without major change. Under each hood was a 1490-cc (90.9-cid) four-cylinder engine, rated 68 horsepower. Either a four- or five-speed manual gearbox was standard.

626 — FOUR — No major change was evident on Mazda's luxury series, which was powered by a 74-horsepower, 1970-cc (120.2-cid) four-cylinder engine. A five-speed gearbox was standard; automatic optional.

RX-7 — ROTARY — Little was new in Mazda's sports car with its twin-rotor Wankel engine, again rated 100 horsepower. As before, three models were offered: S, GS, and luxury GSL.

I.D. DATA: Mazda's 17-symbol Vehicle Identification Number is on the upper left of the dashboard, visible through the windshield. Breakdown is similar to 1981; see that listing.

Model	Body Type & Seating	Engine Type/CID	P.O.E. Price	Weight (lbs.)	Prod. Total
GLC					
	2-dr Hatch-5P	I4/91	5295	1870	Note 1
Custom	2-dr Hatch-5P	I4/91	5695	1870	Note 1
Custom	4-dr Sedan-5P	I4/91	6245	1915	Note 1
Custom	4-dr Sta Wag-5P	I4/91	5995	2130	Note 1
Custom L	2-dr Hatch-5P	I4/91	6095	1900	Note 1
Custom L	4-dr Sedan-5P	I4/91	6745	1915	Note 1
Sport	2-dr Hatch-5P	I4/91	6545	1890	Note 1
626					
	2-dr Spt Cpe-5P	I4/120	7545	2530	Note 1
	4-dr Spt Sed-5P	I4/120	7245	2530	Note 1
Luxury	2-dr Spt Cpe-5P	I4/120	9345	2530	Note 1
Luxury	4-dr Spt Sed-5P	I4/120	8845	2530	Note 1
RX-7					
S	2-dr Coupe-2P	Ro/70	9695	2345	Note 1
GS	2-dr Coupe-2P	Ro/70	10295	2345	Note 1
GSL	2-dr Coupe-2P	Ro/70	11895	2345	Note 1

Note 1: A total of 824,247 Mazda passenger cars (all models) were produced during 1982.

ENGINE DATA: BASE FOUR (GLC): Inline, overhead-cam four-cylinder. Cast iron block and light alloy head. **Displacement:** 90.9 cu. in. (1490 cc). **Bore & Stroke:** 3.03 x 3.15 in. (77 x 80 mm). **Compression Ratio:** 9.0:1. **Brake Horsepower:** 68 at 5000 rpm. **Torque:** 82 lbs.-ft. at 3000 rpm. Five main bearings. Solid valve lifters. Two-barrel carburetor.

BASE FOUR (626): Inline, overhead-cam four-cylinder. Cast iron block and light alloy head. **Displacement:** 120.2 cu. in. (1970 cc). **Bore & Stroke:** 3.15 x 3.86 in. (80 x 98 mm). **Compression Ratio:** 8.6:1. **Brake Horsepower:** 74 at 4500 rpm. **Torque:** 105 lbs.-ft. at 2500 rpm. Five main bearings. Solid valve lifters. Two-barrel carburetor.

BASE ROTARY (RX-7): Wankel with two coaxial three-lobe rotors. Cast iron side housing, light alloy trochoid housings and cast iron rotors. **Displacement:** 70 cu. in. (1146 cc). **Compression Ratio:** 9.4:1. **Brake Horsepower:** 100 at 6000 rpm. **Torque:** 105 lbs.-ft. at 4000 rpm. Two main bearings. Four-barrel carburetor.

CHASSIS DATA: Wheelbase: (GLC) 93.1 in.; (GLC wag) 91 in.; (626) 98.8 in.; (RX-7) 95.3 in. **Overall Length:** (GLC hatch) 159.1 in.; (GLC sed) 166.8 in.; (GLC wag) 165.4 in.; (626) 173.8 in.; (RX-7) 170.1 in. **Height:** (GLC hatch/sed) 54.1 in.; (GLC wag) 56.3 in.; (626) 54.5 in.; (RX-7) 49.6 in. **Width:** (GLC hatch/sed) 64.2 in.; (GLC wag) 62.8 in.; (626) 65.4 in.; (RX-7) 65.7 in. **Front Tread:** (GLC hatch/sed) 54.7 in.; (GLC wag) 51 in.; (626) 53.9 in.; (RX-7) 55.9 in. **Rear Tread:** (GLC hatch/sed) 54.9 in.; (GLC wag) 51.6 in.; (626) 54.3 in.; (RX-7) 55.1 in.

TECHNICAL: Layout: front-engine, rear-drive except (GLC hatch/sedan) front-engine, front-drive. **Transmission:** four- or five-speed manual. **Steering:** (GLC hatch/sedan) rack and pinion; (GLC wagon, 626, RX-7) recirculating ball. **Suspension (front):** (GLC hatch/sed) MacPherson struts with coil springs; (GLC wagon) MacPherson struts with coil springs and anti-roll bar; (RX-7) MacPherson struts with lower lateral links, compliance struts, coil springs and anti-roll bar; (626) MacPherson struts with transverse arms, trailing rods, coil springs and anti-roll bar. **Suspension (rear):** (GLC hatch/sed) MacPherson struts with coil springs and anti-roll bar; (GLC wagon) rigid axle with semi-elliptic leaf springs; (RX-7) rigid axle with lower trailing links, upper angled links, Watt linkage and coil springs; (626) rigid axle with lower trailing arms, upper torque rods, Panhard rod and coil springs. **Brakes:** (GLC/626/RX-7) front disc, rear drum; (RX-7GSL) front/rear disc. **Body Construction:** steel unibody.

MAJOR OPTIONS: Automatic transmission ($250-$420). Air conditioning. Aluminum wheels. Removable top: RX-7GS ($325).

PRODUCTION/SALES: A total of 163,638 Mazda passenger cars were sold in the U.S. during 1982.

ADDITIONAL MODELS: A B2000 piston-engine pickup truck was available in the U.S. for 1982, selling for $5895 to $7095.

Manufacturer: Toyo Kogyo Co. Ltd., Hiroshima, Japan.
Distributor: Mazda Motors of America, Compton, California.

1983 MAZDA

GLC — FOUR — A new Sport four-door notchback sedan joined the GLC lineup this year, to complement the Sport two-door. Both Sport models had front and rear anti-roll bars, plus specially-calibrated shock absorbers. Seats in Sport models and Custom L sedans added lumbar support adjustment. A new feedback carburetor linked to an oxygen sensor in the exhaust manifold delivered more precise mixture control. Joining the GLC option list this year were power steering, power door locks, and a power sunroof, the latter two offered only for the Sport models. The rear-drive station wagon continued without change.

626 — FOUR — Mazda's luxury series switched to front-wheel-drive during the 1983 model year. Models included a coupe and four-door sedan, plus a four-door Touring hatchback. Standard equipment included a front air dam, bumper rub strips, digital clock, rear defroster, side-window demisters, remote-control fuel filler door and hatch release, tinted glass, halogen headlamps, dual remote-control mirrors, front/rear anti-roll bars, tachometer, a padded steering wheel with tilt column, and intermittent wipers. Styled steel wheels held 165SR14 tires. The coupe came with new electronically-variable shock absorbers. Luxury models added power door locks, dual remote mirrors, an AM/FM stereo radio with cassette player, 10-way driver's seat with memory, power brakes/steering, full console, bodyside pinstripings, and 185/70HR14 tires. Touring hatchbacks also included electronically-variable shock absorbers. The 1998-cc (121.9-cid) engine produced 84 horsepower, sent to a standard five-speed manual transmission. The coupe body included molded rear-quarter trim, black window-frame moldings, and protective bodyside moldings.

RX-7 — ROTARY — Modifications were minor this year for Mazda's sports car, which added little more than a standard maintenance-free battery. A removable roof panel was now standard in GS and GSL coupes. Seats in all models offered improved cushion support, with lumbar adjustment. Standard equipment on the 'S' model included tinted glass, side-window demisters, rear defroster, electronic check panel, bodyside moldings, front/rear stabilizer bars, tachometer, two-speed intermittent wipers, analog clock, remote-control fuel filler door, and vinyl/velour reclining bucket seats. Styled steel wheels held 165HR13 tires. The RX-7GS added a digital clock, halogen headlamps, dual power remote-control mirrors, AM/FM stereo radio with cassette player, velour bucket seats, four-spoke sport steering wheel, luggage hold-down straps, a driver's footrest, and 185/70HR13 tires. The GSL version came with all-disc brakes, an electronically-tuned AM/FM stereo radio with cassette and graphic equalizer, striped tweed bucket seats, limited-slip differential, cruise control, removable sunroof, power windows, and 185/70HR13 tires on aluminum wheels. A Limited Edition RX-7 also was announced, with Chateau Silver body paint and red pinstripes, red velour interior trim, air conditioning, Bridgestone 195/60HR14 tires on special forged aluminum wheels, sunroof, and cruise control.

I.D. DATA: Mazda's 17-symbol Vehicle Identification Number is on the upper left of the dashboard, visible through the windshield. Breakdown is similar to 1981; see that listing.

Model	Body Type & Seating	Engine Type/CID	P.O.E. Price	Weight (lbs.)	Prod. Total
GLC					
	2-dr Hatch-5P	I4/91	5295	1870	Note 1
Custom	2-dr Hatch-5P	I4/91	5695	1870	Note 1
Custom	4-dr Sedan-5P	I4/91	6245	1915	Note 1
Custom	4-dr Sta Wag-5P	I4/91	6245	2132	Note 1
Custom L	2-dr Hatch-5P	I4/91	6095	1900	Note 1
Custom L	4-dr Sedan-5P	I4/91	6745	1915	Note 1
Sport	2-dr Hatch-5P	I4/91	6545	1890	Note 1
Sport	4-dr Sedan-5P	I4/91	7145	N/A	Note 1
626					
	2-dr Spt Cpe-5P	I4/122	7895	N/A	Note 1
	4-dr Spt Sed-5P	I4/122	7595	N/A	Note 1
Luxury	2-dr Spt Cpe-5P	I4/122	9295	N/A	Note 1
Luxury	4-dr Spt Sed-5P	I4/122	8895	N/A	Note 1
Luxury	4-dr Hatch-5P	I4/122	9895	N/A	Note 1
RX-7					
S	2-dr Coupe-2P	Ro/70	9695	2345	Note 1
GS	2-dr Coupe-2P	Ro/70	10595	2345	Note 1
GSL	2-dr Coupe-2P	Ro/70	12195	2345	Note 1
Limited	2-dr Coupe-2P	Ro/70	12320	2345	Note 1

Note 1: A total of 861,580 Mazda passenger cars were produced during 1983, including 57,864 RX-7s.

ENGINE DATA: BASE FOUR (GLC): Inline, overhead-cam four-cylinder. Cast iron block and light alloy head. **Displacement:** 90.9 cu. in. (1490 cc). **Bore & Stroke:** 3.03 x 3.15 in. (77 x 80 mm). **Compression Ratio:** 9.0:1. **Brake Horsepower:** 68 at 5000 rpm. **Torque:** 82 lbs.-ft. at 3000 rpm. Five main bearings. Solid valve lifters. Two-barrel carburetor.

BASE FOUR (626): Inline, overhead-cam four-cylinder. Cast iron block and light alloy head. **Displacement:** 121.9 cu. in. (1998 cc). **Bore & Stroke:** 3.39 x 3.39 in. (86 x 86 mm). **Compression Ratio:** 8.6:1. **Brake Horsepower:** 84 at 4800 rpm. **Torque:** 112 lbs.-ft. at 2500 rpm. Five main bearings. Solid valve lifters. Two-barrel carburetor.

BASE ROTARY (RX-7): Wankel with two coaxial three-lobe rotors. Cast iron side housing, light alloy trochoid housings and cast iron rotors. **Displacement:** 70 cu. in. (1146 cc). **Compression Ratio:** 9.4:1. **Brake Horsepower:** 100 at 6000 rpm. **Torque:** 105 lbs.-ft. at 4000 rpm. Two main bearings. Four-barrel carburetor.

CHASSIS DATA: Wheelbase: (GLC) 93.1 in.; (GLC wag) 91 in.; (626) 98.8 in.; (RX-7) 95.3 in. **Overall Length:** (GLC hatch) 159.1 in.; (GLC sed) 166.8 in.; (GLC wag) 165.4 in.; (626) 177.8 in.; (RX-7) 170.1 in. **Height:** (GLC hatch/sed) 54.1 in.; (GLC wag) 56.3 in.; (626 cpe/hatch) 53.7 in.; (626 sed) 55.5 in.; (RX-7) 49.6 in. **Width:** (GLC hatch/sed) 64.2 in.; (GLC wag) 62.8 in.; (626) 66.5 in.; (RX-7) 65.7 in. **Front Tread:** (GLC hatch/sed) 54.7 in.; (GLC wag) 51 in.; (626) 56.3 in.; (RX-7) 55.9 in. **Rear Tread:** (GLC hatch/sed) 54.9 in.; (GLC wag) 51.6 in.; (626) 56.1 in.; (RX-7) 55.1 in.

TECHNICAL: Layout: front-engine, rear-drive except (GLC hatch/sedan, late 626) front-engine, front-drive. **Transmission:** four- or five-speed manual; automatic available. **Steering:** (GLC hatch/sedan) rack and pinion; (GLC wagon, RX-7) recirculating ball; (626) rack and pinion. **Suspension (front):** (GLC hatch/sed) MacPherson struts with coil springs; (GLC wagon) MacPherson struts with coil springs and anti-roll bar; (RX-7) MacPherson struts with lower lateral links, compliance struts, coil springs and anti-roll bar; (626) MacPherson struts with coil springs, plus electronically-adjustable shocks on coupe/hatchback. **Suspension (rear):** (GLC hatch/sed) MacPherson struts with coil springs and anti-roll bar; (GLC wagon) rigid axle with semi-elliptic leaf springs; (RX-7) rigid axle with lower trailing links, upper angled links, Watt linkage and coil springs; (626) MacPherson struts with trailing arms, trapezoidal links and anti-roll bar, plus

electronically-adjustable shocks on coupe/hatchback. **Brakes:** front disc, rear drum except (RX-7GSL) front/rear disc. **Body Construction:** steel unibody.

MAJOR OPTIONS: Automatic transmission: GLC ($290); 626 ($325); RX-7 GS/GSL ($355). Air conditioning: GLC ($590); GLC wagon ($540); 626 ($650); RX-7 ($630). Digital instrument panel: 626 Touring sedan ($630); w/sunroof ($1060). Aluminum wheels: GLC Sport ($245); 626 ($300-$635); RX-7 ($340-$650). Removable top: RX-7GS ($310). Leather package: RX-7 GSL ($650). Sunroof: GLC Cust L/Spt ($265). Moonroof: GLC Sport ($500). Electric sunroof: 626 Luxury ($430). Power steering: GLC Cust L/Sport sedan ($180); base 626 ($195).

PRODUCTION/SALES: A total of 173,388 Mazda passenger cars were sold in the U.S. during 1983.

ADDITIONAL MODELS: Mazda pickup trucks remained available in the U.S.
Manufacturer: Toyo Kogyo Co. Ltd., Hiroshima, Japan.
Distributor: Mazda Motors of America, Compton, California.

1984-85 MAZDA

GLC — FOUR — Mazda's rear-drive wagon was dropped this year, leaving only a front-drive two-door hatchback and four-door sedan. Offered in three price levels, they continued without change. Nothing changed for 1985 except for new body colors.

626 — FOUR — Reworked to front-drive for 1983, the 626 continued with little change. Three body styles were offered: two-door coupe, four-door sedan, and four-door hatchback touring sedan. The coupe and touring sedan came with Electronic Variable Shock Absorbers that adjusted to Normal/Sport/Auto via a dashboard button. They could also be equipped with optional digital instruments and low-profile 15-inch tires.

RX-7 — ROTARY — A four-speed (overdrive) automatic transmission with lockup torque converter became optional on Mazda's rotary-engined sports car for 1984, as did variable-assist power steering. Automatic was available only on the GS and GSL models; power steering only on the GSL. A new instrument panel contained round dial controls. Outside, the front air dam added a slit for brake cooling. Down below, rear control arms were relocated. A new larger high-performance, fuel-injected engine (code 13B) rated 135 horsepower appeared in the GSL-SE model, introduced in 1984. The GSL-SE included low-profile Pirelli P6 tires (205/60VR14 size) on alloy wheels, firmer suspension, and larger disc brakes. Also standard on the GSL-SE were a sunroof, AM/FM stereo radio with cassette player and graphic equalizer, cruise control, air conditioning, and power windows. No RX-7 changes came for 1985, except for revised final-drive ratios.

I.D. DATA: Mazda's 17-symbol Vehicle Identification Number is on the upper left of the dashboard, visible through the windshield. Breakdown is similar to 1981; see that listing.

Model	Body Type & Seating	Engine Type/CID	P.O.E. Price	Weight (lbs.)	Prod. Total
GLC					
	2-dr Hatch-5P	I4/91	4995	1870	Note 1
Deluxe	2-dr Hatch-5P	I4/91	5895	1870	Note 1
Deluxe	4-dr Sedan-5P	I4/91	6445	1915	Note 1
Luxury	2-dr Hatch-5P	I4/91	6495	1890	Note 1
Luxury	4-dr Sedan-5P	I4/91	7095	1915	Note 1
626					
Deluxe	2-dr Coupe-5P	I4/122	8295	2530	Note 1
Deluxe	4-dr Sedan-5P	I4/122	7895	2530	Note 1
Luxury	2-dr Coupe-5P	I4/122	9845	2530	Note 1
Luxury	4-dr Sedan-5P	I4/122	9445	2530	Note 1
Touring	4-dr Hatch-5P	I4/122	10395	N/A	Note 1
RX-7					
S	2-dr Coupe-2P	Ro/70	10195	2345	Note 1
GS	2-dr Coupe-2P	Ro/70	11295	2345	Note 1
GSL	2-dr Coupe-2P	Ro/70	13095	N/A	Note 1
GSL-SE	2-dr Coupe-2P	Ro/80	15095	N/A	Note 1

Note 1: A total of 764,309 Mazda passenger cars were produced during 1984, including 63,959 RX-7s; followed by 815,074 in 1985, including 63,105 RX-7s.

Price Note: Figures shown were valid in 1984.

ENGINE DATA: BASE FOUR (GLC): Inline, overhead-cam four-cylinder. Cast iron block and light alloy head. **Displacement:** 90.9 cu. in. (1490 cc). **Bore & Stroke:** 3.03 x 3.15 in. (77 x 80 mm). **Compression Ratio:** 9.0:1. **Brake Horsepower:** 68 at 5000 rpm. **Torque:** 82 lbs.-ft. at 3000 rpm. Five main bearings. Solid valve lifters. Two-barrel carburetor.

BASE FOUR (626): Inline, overhead-cam four-cylinder. Cast iron block and light alloy head. **Displacement:** 121.9 cu. in. (1998 cc). **Bore & Stroke:** 3.39 x 3.39 in. (86 x 86 mm). **Compression Ratio:** 8.6:1. **Brake Horsepower:** 84 at 4800 rpm. **Torque:** 112 lbs.-ft. at 2500 rpm. Five main bearings. Solid valve lifters. Two-barrel carburetor.

BASE ROTARY (RX-7): Wankel with two coaxial three-lobe rotors. Cast iron side housing, light alloy trochoid housings and cast iron rotors. **Displacement:** 70 cu. in. (1146 cc). **Compression Ratio:** 9.4:1. **Brake Horsepower:** 101 at 6000 rpm. **Torque:** 107 lbs.-ft. at 4000 rpm. Two main bearings. Four-barrel carburetor.

BASE ROTARY (RX-7 GSL-SE): Wankel with two coaxial three-lobe rotors. **Displacement:** 80 cu. in. (1308 cc). **Compression Ratio:** 9.4:1. **Brake Horsepower:** 135 at 6000 rpm. **Torque:** 133 lbs.-ft. at 2750 rpm. Two main bearings. Port fuel injection.

CHASSIS DATA: Wheelbase: (GLC) 93.1 in.; (626) 98.8 in.; (RX-7) 95.3 in. **Overall Length:** (GLC hatch) 159.1 in.; (GLC sed) 166.8 in.; (626) 177.8 in.; (RX-7) 170.1 in. **Height:** (GLC) 54.1 in.; (626 cpe/hatch) 53.7 in.; (626 sedan) 55.5 in.; (RX-7) 49.6 in. **Width:** (GLC) 64.2 in.; (626) 66.5 in.; (RX-7) 65.7 in. **Front Tread:** (GLC) 54.7 in.; (626) 56.3 in.; (RX-7) 55.9 in. **Rear Tread:** (GLC) 54.9 in.; (626) 56.1 in.; (RX-7) 55.1 in.

TECHNICAL: Layout: front-engine, front-drive except (RX-7) front-engine, rear-drive. **Transmission:** (GLC) four- or five-speed manual; (626/RX-7) five-speed manual. Three-speed automatic available on GLC and 626; four-speed automatic on RX-7. **Steering:** (GLC/626) rack and pinion; (RX-7) recirculating ball. **Suspension (front):** (GLC) MacPherson struts with coil springs; (RX-7) MacPherson struts with coil springs and anti-roll bar; (626) MacPherson struts with coil springs, plus electronically-adjustable shocks on coupe/hatchback. **Suspension (rear):** (GLC) MacPherson struts with coil springs and anti-roll bar; (RX-7) rigid axle with four links, Watt linkage, coil springs and anti-roll bar; (626) MacPherson struts with trailing arms, trapezoidal links and anti-roll bar, plus electronically-adjustable shocks on coupe/hatchback. **Brakes:** front disc, rear drum except (RX-7 GSL/GSL-SE) front/rear disc. **Body Construction:** steel unibody.

MAJOR OPTIONS: Similar to 1983.

PERFORMANCE: Top Speed: (RX-7 GSL-SE) 126 mph. **Acceleration (0-60 mph):** (RX-7 GSL-SE) 8.2-8.5 sec. **Acceleration (quarter-mile):** (RX-7 GSL-SE) 16.4 sec. (84-86.5 mph). **Fuel Mileage:** (RX-7 GSL-SE) about 15 mpg city, 24 mpg highway (EPA city/highway ratings: 18/29 mpg).

PRODUCTION/SALES: A total of 169,666 Mazda passenger cars were sold in the U.S. during 1984, rising to 211,093 in 1985.

ADDITIONAL MODELS: Mazda pickup trucks remained available in the U.S.

Manufacturer: Mazda Motor Corp., Hiroshima, Japan.

Distributor: Mazda Motors of America, Compton, California.

HISTORY: Toyo Kogyo changed its name to Mazda in 1984.

1986 MAZDA

323 — FOUR — Mazda's replacement for the GLC was slightly longer in wheelbase and overall length, and also heavier. Some of that increase translated to a more spacious interior, now ranking as a compact (formerly subcompact) as defined by the EPA's volume index. The 323 came in two-door hatchback and four-door sedan form, powered by a new fuel-injected 1.6-liter four-cylinder engine that produced 82 horsepower. A five-speed manual gearbox was standard, except for the base two-door which came with a four-speed. A new three-speed automatic with lockup torque converter was optional. Styling features included a low, wedge-shaped front end, integrated bumpers, and flush-mounted headlamps.

626 — FOUR — Mazda's larger compact got a restyling for 1986, while port fuel injection added some power to its 2.0-liter engine. A sporty GT model came complete with turbocharger, its engine rated 120 horsepower (versus 93 for the base powerplant). Flush aero-style headlamps were installed this year, and the front air dam added brake cooling slots. Taillamps also got a more integrated look. Modifications in the adjustable shock absorber system gave it a new name: Auto Adjusting Suspension. That system was now optional on certain models, rather than standard equipment.

RX-7 — ROTARY — Not only did Mazda's two-seat get a restyling for 1986, it added a 2+2 model. Dimensions didn't change dramatically, but the car added some 240 pounds. Exterior dimensions were the same for both body styles. All models carried the larger (1.3-liter) rotary engine introduced in 1984 on the GSL-SE, hooked to either a five-speed manual or four-speed automatic transmission. The old rigid rear axle was gone, replaced by fully independent suspension (called the Dynamic Tracking Suspension System. Rack-and-pinion replaced the former recirculating-ball unit, with electrically variable power assist. Four-wheel disc brakes now became standard. The hidden headlamps contained little windows that allowed use of flash-to-pass even with the lights turned off. The upgraded GXL models had 15-inch wheels/tires, versus 14-inchers on the base models. Also standard on the GXL was Auto Adjusting Suspension, as on the 626 series, offering a choice of Normal or Sport ride.

Though not a dramatic departure from the original, the new shape had an impressive drag coefficient of 0.31. An optional Sports Package, consisting of a front air dam, rocker-panel skirts and loop-style spoiler, knocked the figure down to 0.29. Not only did the 13B rotary engine have more power than when it first appeared under the GSL-SE hood; an intercooled Turbo II edition added 36 more bhp. Turbo models, which joined during the 1986 model year, carried vented disc brakes. The 2+2 version had been available in Europe and Japan earlier, but could now be enjoyed by Americans as well. Turbos, however, came only in two-seat form. The Turbo edition had a wide hood scoop, front air dam, side skirts, rear spoiler, and 16-inch alloy wheels. Standard Turbo equipment include a sport-tuned suspension, limited-slip differential, air conditioning, electric sunroof, tilt wheel, 100-watt stereo, power windows, and power door locks.

I.D. DATA: Mazda's 17-symbol Vehicle Identification Number is on the upper left of the dashboard, visible through the windshield. Breakdown is similar to 1981; see that listing.

Model	Body Type & Seating	Engine Type/CID	P.O.E. Price	Weight (lbs.)	Prod. Total
323					
	2-dr Hatch-5P	I4/97	5645	2060	Note 1
Deluxe	2-dr Hatch-5P	I4/97	6995	2075	Note 1
Deluxe	4-dr Sedan-5P	I4/97	7495	2115	Note 1
Luxury	2-dr Hatch-5P	I4/97	7695	2115	Note 1
Luxury	4-dr Sedan-5P	I4/97	8095	2170	Note 1
626					
Deluxe	2-dr Coupe-5P	I4/122	9245	2450	Note 1
Deluxe	4-dr Sedan-5P	I4/122	8995	2450	Note 1
Luxury	2-dr Coupe-5P	I4/122	10945	2480	Note 1
Luxury	4-dr Sedan-5P	I4/122	10645	2485	Note 1
Luxury	4-dr Hatch-5P	I4/122	11545	2555	Note 1
GT	2-dr Coupe-5P	I4/122	12595	2565	Note 1
GT	4-dr Sedan-5P	I4/122	12295	2570	Note 1
GT	4-dr Hatch-5P	I4/122	13195	2640	Note 1
RX-7					
	2-dr Coupe-2P	Ro/80	12895	2625	Note 1
GXL	2-dr Coupe-2P	Ro/80	17495	2625	Note 1
2+2	2-dr Coupe-2+2P	Ro/80	13395	N/A	Note 1
GXL 2+2	2-dr Coupe-2+2P	Ro/80	17995	N/A	Note 1

Note 1: A total of 811,371 Mazdas were produced during 1986, including 72,760 RX-7s.

ENGINE DATA: BASE FOUR (323): Inline, overhead-cam four-cylinder. **Displacement:** 97 cu. in. (1597 cc). **Bore & Stroke:** 3.07 x 3.29 in. (78 x 84 mm). **Compression Ratio:** 9.3:1. **Brake Horsepower:** 82 at 5000 rpm. **Torque:** 92 lbs.-ft. at 2500 rpm. Solid valve lifters. Multi-point fuel injection.

BASE FOUR (626): Inline, overhead-cam four-cylinder. Cast iron block and light alloy head. **Displacement:** 121.9 cu. (1998 cc). **Bore & Stroke:** 3.39 x 3.39 in. (86 x 86 mm). **Compression Ratio:** 8.6:1. **Brake Horsepower:** 93 at 5000 rpm. **Torque:** 115 lbs.-ft. at 2500 rpm. Five main bearings. Solid valve lifters. Multi-point fuel injection.

BASE TURBO FOUR (626 GT): Same as 1998-cc four above, except with turbocharger. **Compression Ratio:** 7.8:1. **Brake Horsepower:** 120 at 5000 rpm. **Torque:** 150 lbs.-ft. at 3000 rpm.

BASE ROTARY (RX-7): Wankel with two coaxial three-lobe rotors. **Displacement:** 80 cu. in. (1308 cc). **Compression Ratio:** 9.4:1. **Brake Horsepower:** 146 at 6500 rpm. **Torque:** 138 lbs.-ft. at 3500 rpm. Two main bearings. Multi-point fuel injection.

OPTIONAL TURBO ROTARY (RX-7): Same as above, except with turbocharger — **Compression Ratio:** 8.5:1. **Brake Horsepower:** 182 at 6500 rpm. **Torque:** 183 lbs.-ft. at 3500 rpm.

CHASSIS DATA: Wheelbase: (323) 94.5 in.; (626) 98.8 in.; (RX-7) 95.7 in. **Overall Length:** (323 hatch) 161.8 in.; (323 sedan) 169.7 in.; (626) 177.8 in.; (RX-7) 168.9 in. **Height:** (323) 54.7 in.; (626 cpe/hatch) 53.7 in.; (626 sedan) 55.5 in.; (RX-7) 49.8 in. **Width:** (323) 64.8 in.; (626) 66.5 in.; (RX-7) 66.5 in. **Front Tread:** (323) 54.7 in.; (626) 56.3 in.; (RX-7) 57.1 in. **Rear Tread:** (323) 54.7 in.; (626) 56.1 in.; (RX-7) 56.7 in.

TECHNICAL: Layout: front-engine, front-drive except (RX-7) front-engine, rear-drive. **Transmission:** (323) four- or five-speed manual; (626/RX-7) five-speed manual. Three-speed automatic available on 323 and 626; four-speed automatic on RX-7. **Steering:** rack and pinion. **Suspension (front):** (323/RX-7) MacPherson struts with coil springs and anti-roll bar; (626) MacPherson struts with coil springs, plus electronically-adjustable shocks on coupe/hatchback. **Suspension (rear):** (323) independent with struts, trailing arms, trapezoidal links, coil springs and anti-roll bar; (RX-7) independent with trailing arms, camber-control links, semi-trailing links, coil springs and anti-roll bar; (626) MacPherson struts with trailing arms, trapezoidal links and anti-roll bar, plus electronically-adjustable shocks on coupe/hatchback. **Brakes:** front disc, rear drum except (RX-7) front/rear disc. **Body Construction:** steel unibody.

MAJOR OPTIONS: Automatic transmission. Air conditioning. Aluminum wheels. Sunroof.

PERFORMANCE: Top Speed: (RX-7) 125-135+ mph. **Acceleration (0-60 mph):** (RX-7) as low as 8.5 sec.; (RX-7 Turbo) 6.7 sec.

PRODUCTION/SALES: A total of 222,716 Mazda passenger cars were sold in the U.S. during 1986.

ADDITIONAL MODELS: Mazda pickup trucks remained available in the U.S.

Manufacturer: Mazda Motor Corp., Hiroshima, Japan.

Distributor: Mazda Motors of America, Compton, California.

HISTORY: Improvements to the RX-7 sports car came in part from meetings with consumers, as advice from Mazda's American design center, based in California.

1987 MAZDA

323 — FOUR — A four-door station wagon joined the former two-door hatchback and four-door sedan as the first Mazda wagon since the '83 GLC. The wagon had 60/40 split rear seatbacks that folded flat, and came only in Deluxe trim.

626 — FOUR — A four-speed (overdrive) automatic transmission replaced the former three-speed unit as an option for Mazda's large compact. The new unit had a lockup torque converter, as well as "economy"and "power" shift modes.

RX-7 — ROTARY — Anti-lock braking became optional for 1987 on Turbo and GXL versions of Mazda's sports car. All models had four-wheel disc brakes. Those with five-speed manual gearboxes now had a starter interlock, which required pushing the clutch pedal all the way down before the engine could be started.

I.D. DATA: Mazda's 17-symbol Vehicle Identification Number is on the upper left of the dashboard, visible through the windshield. Breakdown is similar to 1981; see that listing.

Model	Body Type & Seating	Engine Type/CID	P.O.E. Price	Weight (lbs.)	Prod. Total
323					
	2-dr Hatch-5P	I4/97	5999	2060	Note 1
Deluxe	2-dr Hatch-5P	I4/97	7649	2075	Note 1
Deluxe	4-dr Sedan-5P	I4/97	8199	2115	Note 1
Deluxe	4-dr Sta Wag-5P	I4/97	8799	2170	Note 1
Luxury	4-dr Sedan-5P	I4/97	8799	2170	Note 1
626					
Deluxe	2-dr Coupe-5P	I4/122	9899	2450	Note 1
Deluxe	4-dr Sedan-5P	I4/122	9849	2450	Note 1
Luxury	2-dr Coupe-5P	I4/122	11799	2480	Note 1
Luxury	4-dr Sedan-5P	I4/122	11599	2485	Note 1
Luxury	4-dr Hatch-5P	I4/122	12299	2555	Note 1
GT	2-dr Coupe-5P	I4/122	13349	2565	Note 1
GT	4-dr Sedan-5P	I4/122	13049	2570	Note 1
GT	4-dr Hatch-5P	I4/122	13949	2640	Note 1
RX-7					
	2-dr Coupe-2P	Ro/80	14199	2625	Note 1
Sport	2-dr Coupe-2P	Ro/80	15749	2625	Note 1
LX	2-dr Coupe-2P	Ro/80	15799	2625	Note 1
GXL	2-dr Coupe-2P	Ro/80	18449	2625	Note 1
Turbo	2-dr Coupe-2P	Ro/80	20399	2850	Note 1
RX-7 2+2					
	2-dr Coupe-2+2P	Ro/80	14699	2645	Note 1
LX	2-dr Coupe-2+2P	Ro/80	16299	2645	Note 1
GXL	2-dr Coupe-2+2P	Ro/80	18949	2645	Note 1

Note 1: A total of 853,309 Mazdas (all models) were produced during 1987.

ENGINE DATA: BASE FOUR (323): Inline, overhead-cam four-cylinder. **Displacement:** 97 cu. in. (1597 cc). **Bore & Stroke:** 3.07 x 3.29 in. (78 x 84 mm). **Compression Ratio:** 9.3:1. **Brake Horsepower:** 82 at 5000 rpm. **Torque:** 92 lbs.-ft. at 2500 rpm. Solid valve lifters. Multi-point fuel injection.

BASE FOUR (626): Inline, overhead-cam four-cylinder. Cast iron block and light alloy head. **Displacement:** 121.9 cu. in. (1998 cc). **Bore & Stroke:** 3.39 x 3.39 in. (86 x 86 mm). **Compression Ratio:** 8.6:1. **Brake Horsepower:** 93 at 5000 rpm. **Torque:** 115 lbs.-ft. at 2500 rpm. Five main bearings. Solid valve lifters. Multi-point fuel injection.

BASE TURBO FOUR (626 GT): Same as 1998-cc four above, except with turbocharger. **Compression Ratio:** 7.8:1. **Brake Horsepower:** 120 at 5000 rpm. **Torque:** 150 lbs.-ft. at 3000 rpm.

BASE ROTARY (RX-7): Wankel with two coaxial three-lobe rotors. **Displacement:** 80 cu. in. (1308 cc). **Compression Ratio:** 9.4:1. **Brake Horsepower:** 146 at 6500 rpm. **Torque:** 138 lbs.-ft. at 3500 rpm. Two main bearings. Multi-point fuel injection.

OPTIONAL TURBO ROTARY (RX-7): Same as above, except with turbocharger -- **Compression Ratio:** 8.5:1. **Brake Horsepower:** 182 at 6500 rpm. **Torque:** 183 lbs.-ft. at 3500 rpm.

CHASSIS DATA: Wheelbase: (323) 94.5 in.; (626) 98.8 in.; (RX-7) 95.7 in. **Overall Length:** (323 hatch) 161.8 in.; (323 sedan/wagon) 169.7 in.; (626) 177.8 in.; (RX-7) 168.9 in. **Height:** (323 hatch/sed) 54.7 in.; (323 wagon) 55.5 in.; (626 cpe/hatch) 53.7 in.; (626 sedan) 55.5 in.; (RX-7) 49.8 in. **Width:** (323) 64.8 in.; (626) 66.5 in.; (RX-7) 66.5 in. **Front Tread:** (323) 54.7 in.; (626) 56.3 in.; (RX-7) 57.1 in. **Rear Tread:** (323) 55.7 in.; (626) 56.1 in.; (RX-7) 56.7 in.

TECHNICAL: Layout: front-engine, front-drive except (RX-7) front-engine, rear-drive. **Transmission:** (323) four- or five-speed manual; (626/RX-7) five-speed manual. Three-speed automatic available on 323; four-speed automatic on 626 and RX-7. **Steering:** rack and pinion. **Suspension (front):** (323/RX-7) MacPherson struts with coil springs and anti-roll bar; (626) MacPherson struts with coil springs, plus electronically-adjustable shocks on GT. **Suspension (rear):** (323) independent with struts, trailing arms, trapezoidal links, coil springs and anti-roll bar; (RX-7) independent with trailing arms, camber control links, coil springs and anti-roll bar; (626) MacPherson struts with trailing arms, trapezoidal links and anti-roll bar, plus electronically-adjustable shocks on GT. **Brakes:** front disc, rear drum except (RX-7) front/rear disc. **Body Construction:** steel unibody.

PERFORMANCE: Top Speed: (RX-7 Turbo) 140 mph (est.). **Acceleration (0-60 mph):** (RX-7 Turbo) 6.7 sec. **Acceleration (quarter-mile):** 15.2 sec. (est.).
PRODUCTION/SALES: A total of 208,025 Mazda passenger cars were sold in the U.S. during 1987.
Manufacturer: Mazda Motor Corp., Hiroshima, Japan.
Distributor: Mazda Motors of America, Compton, California.
HISTORY: Mazda began to build cars in the U.S. in 1987, at a plant in Flat Rock, Michigan (where Ford Probes also would be produced).

1988-89 MAZDA

323 — FOUR — A new four-wheel-drive GTX hatchback and a turbocharged sport sedan joined the lineup for 1988. The GTX was the first 4WD model marketed by Mazda in the U.S., and used a full-time system. Both the GTX and the GT sport sedan were powered by a twin-cam, turbocharged 1.6-liter engine with four valves per cylinder, which produced 132 horsepower. Both models came only with the five-speed manual gearbox. A new four-speed automatic transmission was now optional on all models except the GT and wagons.

626/MX-6 — FOUR — For its third-generation restyling, Mazda's compact series split into two models: 626 notchback sedans and hatchback touring sedans, and a new MX-6 coupe series that actually was built in the U.S. as well as in Japan. The revised sedans rode a longer (101.4-inch) wheelbase, and carried a larger (2.2-liter) four-cylinder engine. With a 12-valve cylinder head (two intake valves per cylinder), the new engine produced 110 horsepower. A turbocharged edition squeezed out 145 horsepower. Even more intriguing was the emergence of four-wheel steering on one version of the Turbo four-door notchback sedan. Mazda's system was hydraulically-operated (whereas Honda's Prelude offered mechanical 4WS at this time), reacting to both car speed and steering-wheel angle. Below 22 mph, the rear wheels steered opposite to the fronts; above that speed, each wheel turned in the same direction. While Honda's system was limited to a 1.5-degree difference in parallel-turn mode, Mazda's went as far as 5 degrees. Turbo models now had four-wheel disc brakes, with anti-locking optional.

As a result of weak sales, four-wheel steering went on the MX-6 coupe for the 1989 model year, instead of the 626 sedan.

1988 Mazda 929 sedan.

929 — V-6 — Mazda introduced a new luxury sedan for 1988, rivaling the Acura Legend. The rear-wheel-drive four-door carried a 3.0-liter V-6 engine and had fully independent suspension, power rack-and-pinion steering, and four-wheel disc brakes. Anti-locking and Auto Adjusting Suspension were optonal. The V-6 produced 158 horsepower, and was available with either five-speed manual or a new four-speed electronically-controlled automatic transmission. For 1989, only automatic was available, and a power moonroof and power driver's seat became standard (formerly optional).

1988 Mazda 10th anniversary RX-7.

RX-7 — ROTARY — A convertible joined the original hatchback coupe (and 2 + 2 hatchback) for 1988, aimed at enhancing comfort in cooler temperatures. The soft top not only offered a half-open mode, but three positions: open, closed, or Targa-style. It also included a Windblocker device that prevented air from entering the cockpit from the rear. This unit, which consisted of a hinged panel, was also claimed to reduce wind noise and

air turbulence. Complemented by a high-output heater, convertible riders could expect to maintain some degree of warmth with the top down when the weather turned chilly. The convertible came only with the 146-bhp non-turbo engine and five-speed manual gearbox. A theft-deterrent system was now standard on all models.

I.D. DATA: Mazda's 17-symbol Vehicle Identification Number is on the upper left of the dashboard, visible through the windshield. Breakdown is similar to 1981; see that listing.

Model	Body Type & Seating	Engine Type/CID	P.O.E. Price	Weight (lbs.)	Prod. Total
323					
	2-dr Hatch-5P	I4/97	5999	2060	Note 1
	4-dr Sedan-5P	I4/97	6949	2115	Note 1
	4-dr Sta Wag-5P	I4/97	7849	2170	Note 1
SE	2-dr Hatch-5P	I4/97	6799	2065	Note 1
SE	4-dr Sedan-5P	I4/97	7649	2075	Note 1
LX	4-dr Sedan-5P	I4/97	8999	2115	Note 1
DX	4-dr Sta Wag-5P	I4/97	9149	2170	Note 1
GT	4-dr Spt Sedan-5P	I4/97	11499	2290	Note 1
GTX (4WD)	2-dr Hatch-5P	I4/97	11055	2290	Note 1
626					
DX	4-dr Sedan-5P	I4/133	10499	2450	Note 1
LX	4-dr Sedan-5P	I4/133	12399	2450	Note 1
Turbo	4-dr Sedan-5P	I4/133	13999	2570	Note 1
Turbo 4WS	4-dr Sedan-5P	I4/133	17149	N/A	Note 1
Touring	4-dr Hatch-5P	I4/133	12599	N/A	Note 1
Turbo	4-dr Hatch-5P	I4/133	14199	2640	Note 1
MX-6					
DX	2-dr Coupe-4P	I4/133	10599	2530	Note 1
LX	2-dr Coupe-4P	I4/133	12499	2585	Note 1
GT Turbo	2-dr Coupe-4P	I4/133	14499	2675	Note 1
929					
	4-dr Sedan-5P	V6/180	18950	3211	Note 1
RX-7					
SE	2-dr Coupe-2P	Ro/80	15480	2625	Note 1
GTU	2-dr Coupe-2P	Ro/80	17350	2625	Note 1
GXL	2-dr Coupe-2P	Ro/80	19160	2625	Note 1
Turbo	2-dr Coupe-2P	Ro/80	21800	2850	Note 1
	2-dr Conv-2P	Ro/80	20500	2880	Note 1
RX-7 2 + 2					
SE	2-dr Coupe-2 + 2P	Ro/80	15980	2645	Note 1
GXL	2-dr Coupe-2 + 2P	Ro/80	19660	2645	Note 1

Note 1: A total of 880,181 Mazdas (all models) were produced during 1988.
Price Note: Figures shown were valid in 1988. An RX-7 convertible with an option package consisting of leather trim and a compact-disc player sold for $22,900.

1989 Mazda RX-7 convertible.

ENGINE DATA: BASE FOUR (323): Inline, overhead-cam four-cylinder. **Displacement:** 97 cu. in. (1597 cc). **Bore & Stroke:** 3.07 x 3.29 in. (78 x 84 mm). **Compression Ratio:** 9.3:1. **Brake Horsepower:** 82 at 5000 rpm. **Torque:** 92 lbs.-ft. at 2500 rpm. Multi-point fuel injection.
BASE TURBO FOUR (323 GT/GTX): Inline, dual-overhead-cam four-cylinder with turbocharger. **Displacement:** 97 cu. in. (1597 cc). **Bore & Stroke:** 3.07 x 3.29 in. (78 x 84 mm). **Compression Ratio:** 7.9:1. **Brake Horsepower:** 132 at 6000 rpm. **Torque:** 136 lbs.-ft. at 3000 rpm. Multi-point fuel injection.
BASE FOUR (626, MX-6): Inline, overhead-cam four-cylinder. **Displacement:** 133.2 cu. in. (2184 cc). **Bore & Stroke:** 3.39 x 3.70 in. (86 x 94 mm). **Compression Ratio:** 8.6:1. **Brake Horsepower:** 110 at 4700 rpm. **Torque:** 130 lbs.-ft. at 3000 rpm. Five main bearings. Multi-point fuel injection.
BASE TURBO FOUR (626/MX-6 Turbo models): Same as 2184-cc four above, except with turbocharger. **Compression Ratio:** 7.8:1. **Brake Horsepower:** 145 at 4300 rpm. **Torque:** 190 lbs.-ft. at 4300 rpm.
BASE V-6 (929): Overhead-cam "vee" type six-cylinder. **Displacement:** 180.3 cu. in. (2954 cc). **Bore & Stroke:** 3.50 x 3.00 in. (88.9 x 76 mm). **Compression Ratio:** 8.5:1. **Brake Horsepower:** 158 at 5500 rpm. **Torque:** 170 lbs.-ft. at 4000 rpm. Multi-point fuel injection.
BASE ROTARY (RX-7): Wankel with two coaxial three-lobe rotors. **Displacement:** 80 cu. in. (1308 cc). **Compression Ratio:** 9.4:1. **Brake Horsepower:** 146 at 6500 rpm. **Torque:** 138 lbs.-ft. at 3500 rpm. Two main bearings. Multi-point fuel injection.
OPTIONAL TURBO ROTARY (RX-7): Same as above, except with turbocharger — **Compression Ratio:** 8.5:1. **Brake Horsepower:** 182 at 6500 rpm. **Torque:** 183 lbs.-ft. at 3500 rpm.

CHASSIS DATA: Wheelbase: (323) 94.5 in.; (MX-6) 99.0 in.; (626) 101.4 in.; (929) 106.7 in.; (RX-7) 95.7 in. **Overall Length:** (323 hatch) 161.8 in.; (323 sedan/wagon) 169.7 in.; (MX-6) 177.0 in.; (626) 179.3 in.; (929) 193.1 in.; (RX-7) 168.9 in. **Height:** (323 hatch/sed) 54.7 in.; (323 wagon) 55.5 in.; (MX-6) 53.5 in.; (626 sedan) 55.5 in.; (626 hatch) 54.1 in.; (929) 54.5 in.; (RX-7) 49.8 in. **Width:** (323) 64.8 in.; (626/MX-6) 66.5 in.; (929) 66.9 in.; (RX-7) 66.5 in. **Front Tread:** (323) 54.7 in.; (626/MX-6) 57.3 in.; (929) 56.9 in.; (RX-7) 57.1 in. **Rear Tread:** (323) 55.7 in.; (626/MX-6) 57.7 in.; (929) 57.5 in.; (RX-7) 56.7 in.

TECHNICAL: Layout: front-engine, front-drive except (929, RX-7) front-engine, rear-drive; (323 GTX) four-wheel-drive. **Transmission:** (323) four- or five-speed manual; (626/MX-6/RX-7) five-speed manual; (1988 929) five-speed manual. Three- or four-speed automatic available on 323; four-speed automatic on 626/929/MX-6 and RX-7. Automatic standard on 929 in 1989. **Steering:** rack and pinion. **Suspension (front):** (323/RX-7) MacPherson struts with coil springs and anti-roll bar; (626) MacPherson struts with coil

springs, plus electronically-adjustable shocks on Turbo. **Suspension (rear):** (323) independent with struts, trailing arms, trapezoidal links, coil springs and anti-roll bar; (RX-7) independent with trailing arms, camber control links, coil springs and anti-roll bar; (626) MacPherson struts with trailing arms, trapezoidal links and anti-roll bar, plus electronically-adjustable shocks on Turbo. **Brakes:** front disc, rear drum except (RX-7 and 626/MX-6 Turbo) front/rear disc. **Body Construction:** steel unibody.

1989 Mazda 626 Turbo touring sedan.

PRODUCTION/SALES: A total of 256,050 Mazda passenger cars were sold in the U.S. during 1988, followed by 263,378 in 1989.
Manufacturer: Mazda Motor Corp., Hiroshima, Japan.
Distributor: Mazda Motor of America Inc., Irvine, California.

HISTORY: Mercury's subcompact Tracer, built in Mexico, followed the same design as the Mazda 323 and used Mazda engines and transmissions. The new MX-6 coupes were built in Flat Rock, Michigan, and also in Japan. Ford soon would introduce its new Probe coupe, closely related to the MX-6. Mazda's eastern and central operations in the U.S. were consolidated in 1988, to form Mazda Motor of America. A facelifted RX-7 with more power arrived during the 1989 model year, as a late '89 model; see next listing for details.

1990 MAZDA

1990 Mazda MX-5 Miata roadster.

MIATA — MX-5 — FOUR — Not many cars have earned such frenzied attention and consumer demand as Mazda's retro two-seat sports car. Patterned after the 1960s Lotus Elan, the Miata was conceived in the U.S., at Mazda's design headquarters in California, though developed and built in Japan. The curvaceous little rear-drive roadster drew plenty of admiring glances during its appearance at the Chicago Auto Show in February 1989. By the time of its debut that summer, as an early '90 model, eager customers were clamoring to pay thousands of dollars above the car's $13,800 sticker price to be one of the first to own one. Comparatively small supply was part of the reason, as only 20,000 were expected to go on sale during 1989, and another 40,000 in 1990. More than that, the little two-seater managed to finish the job of rekindling the American fancy for open-air motoring, after the way had been paved by a handful of domestic and imported ragtops during the 1980s. A 1.6-liter twin-cam engine provided the power, hooked to a five-speed manual gearbox. That was enough to produce 0-60 mph acceleration around 8.6 seconds, yet permit impressive fuel economy. An optional automatic would come later. The engine had hydraulic valve-lash adjusters and a stainless tuned exhaust header. Fully independent suspension used dual wishbones, coil springs, and an anti-roll bar at both front and rear. Standard equipment included four-wheel disc brakes, a

driver's-side airbag, and an easy-folding manual top. A removable hardtop cost $1100 extra. Two option packages were available, plus separate air conditioning, limited-slip differential, and a compact-disc player. In short, Miata offered much of the fun of the old British roadsters, but was packed with modern high-tech to eliminate most of the reliability problems of the past. Mazda promoted its roadster as "the return of the affordable sports car."

323/PROTEGE — FOUR — Restyling of Mazda's subcompact produced two model designations: 323 for the two-door hatchback, and 323 Protege for the four-door sedan. Though similar in appearance up front, the two models shared no sheetmetal and rode different wheelbases. The 323 kept its 1.6-liter engine, rated 82 horsepower. Protege was powered by a 1.8-liter four, which produced 103 horsepower. The top-of-the-line Protege LX used a twin-cam version of the 1.8-liter engine, rated 125 bhp. A four-wheel-drive sedan arrived later in the model year. The prior turbocharged engine was no longer available.

626/MX-6 — FOUR — Anti-lock braking became optional on LX models for 1990 (formerly only on the GT). Restyling features for the 626 sedan and hatchback included a modified grille and taillamps. The MX-6 coupe wore new bumpers, a body-colored grille, restyled taillamps, and wider bodyside moldings.

929 — V-6 — A new 929 S sedan debuted this year, with a 190-bhp, twin-cam version of the 3.0-liter V-6 and dual exhausts. The base sedan kept its single-cam, 158-bhp engine. A mild facelift included a new grille and bumpers, contrasting-color lower-body paint, and lower body cladding. The Automatic Adjusting Suspension was no longer offered, a result of lack of buyer interest.

RX-7 — ROTARY — Mazda's long-lived, larger sports car earned a facelift and mechanical modifications during 1989, arriving as a late '89 model. The standard twin-rotor engine gained 14 horsepower, and the turbo got an 18-bhp boost. The available four-speed automatic transmission added electronic shift controls, and became optional on the convertible. For 1990, a driver's airbag became standard on the convertible.

I.D. DATA: Mazda's 17-symbol Vehicle Identification Number is on the upper left of the dashboard, visible through the windshield. Breakdown is similar to 1981; see that listing.

Model	Body Type & Seating	Engine Type/CID	P.O.E. Price	Weight (lbs.)	Prod. Total
MIATA					
MX-5	2-dr Conv-2P	I4/97	13800	2093	Note 1
323					
	2-dr Hatch-5P	I4/97	6599	2060	Note 1
SE	2-dr Hatch-5P	I4/97	8329	N/A	Note 1
PROTEGE					
SE	4-dr Sedan-5P	I4/112	9339	2267	Note 1
LX	4-dr Sedan-5P	I4/112	10349	2269	Note 1
4WD	4-dr Sedan-5P	I4/112	N/A	2545	Note 1
626					
DX	4-dr Sedan-5P	I4/133	12459	2521	Note 1
LX	4-dr Sedan-5P	I4/133	13929	2521	Note 1
LX Touring	4-dr Hatch-5P	I4/133	14129	2621	Note 1
GT Touring	4-dr Hatch-5P	I4/133	15699	2621	Note 1
MX-6					
DX	2-dr Coupe-4P	I4/133	12279	2530	Note 1
LX	2-dr Coupe-4P	I4/133	13769	2585	Note 1
GT	2-dr Coupe-4P	I4/133	16029	2675	Note 1
GT 4WS	2-dr Coupe-4P	I4/133	17229	2680	Note 1
929					
	4-dr Sedan-5P	V6/180	23300	3241	Note 1
S	4-dr Sedan-5P	V6/180	24800	N/A	Note 1
RX-7					
GTU	2-dr Coupe-2P	Ro/80	17880	2625	Note 1
GTU S	2-dr Coupe-2P	Ro/80	20180	N/A	Note 1
GXL	2-dr Coupe-2P	Ro/80	22330	2625	Note 1
Turbo	2-dr Coupe-2P	Ro/80	26530	2850	Note 1
	2-dr Conv-2P	Ro/80	26530	2880	Note 1
RX-7 2+2					
GXL	2-dr Coupe-2+2P	Ro/80	22830	2625	Note 1

Note 1: A total of 153,055 Mazdas were sold in the U.S. during 1990, including 35,944 Miatas, 9,743 RX-7s, 16,535 929 sedans, and 224 imported MX-6 coupes.

1990 Mazda Protege 4WD sedan.

ENGINE DATA: BASE FOUR (Miata): Inline, dual-overhead-cam four-cylinder (16-valve). **Displacement:** 97.45 cu. in. (1597 cc). **Bore & Stroke:** 3.07 x 3.29 in. (78 x 83.6 mm). **Compression Ratio:** 9.4:1. **Brake Horsepower:** 116 at 6500 rpm. **Torque:** 100 lbs.-ft. at 5500 rpm. Hydraulic valve lifters. Multi-point fuel injection.

BASE FOUR (323): Inline, overhead-cam four-cylinder. **Displacement:** 97 cu. in. (1597 cc). **Bore & Stroke:** 3.07 x 3.29 in. (78 x 84 mm). **Compression Ratio:** 9.3:1. **Brake Horsepower:** 82 at 5000 rpm. **Torque:** 92 lbs.-ft. at 2500 rpm. Hydraulic valve lifters. Multi-point fuel injection.

BASE FOUR (Protege SE, 4WD): Inline, overhead-cam four-cylinder. **Displacement:** 112 cu. in. (1839 cc). **Bore & Stroke:** 3.27 x 3.35 in. (83 x 85 mm). **Compression Ratio:** 8.9:1. **Brake Horsepower:** 103 at 5500 rpm. **Torque:** 111 lbs.-ft. at 4000 rpm. Hydraulic valve lifters. Multi-point fuel injection.

BASE FOUR (Protege LX): Inline, dual-overhead-cam four-cylinder. **Displacement:** 112 cu. in. (1839 cc). **Bore & Stroke:** 3.27 x 3.35 in. (83 x 85 mm). **Compression Ratio:** 9.0:1. **Brake Horsepower:** 125 at 6500 rpm. **Torque:** 114 lbs.-ft. at 4500 rpm. Hydraulic lifters. Multi-point fuel injection.

BASE FOUR (626, MX-6): Inline, overhead-cam four-cylinder. **Displacement:** 133.2 cu. in. (2184 cc). **Bore & Stroke:** 3.39 x 3.70 in. (86 x 94 mm). **Compression Ratio:** 8.6:1. **Brake Horsepower:** 110 at 4700 rpm. **Torque:** 130 lbs.-ft. at 3000 rpm. Five main bearings. Hydraulic valve lifters. Multi-point fuel injection.

BASE TURBO FOUR (626/MX-6 Turbo models): Same as 2184-cc four above, except with turbocharger. **Compression Ratio:** 7.8:1. **Brake Horsepower:** 145 at 4300 rpm. **Torque:** 190 lbs.-ft. at 4300 rpm.

BASE V-6 (929): Overhead-cam "vee" type six-cylinder. **Displacement:** 180.3 cu. in. (2954 cc). **Bore & Stroke:** 3.50 x 3.00 in. (88.9 x 76 mm). **Compression Ratio:** 8.5:1. **Brake Horsepower:** 158 at 5500 rpm. **Torque:** 170 lbs.-ft. at 4000 rpm. Hydraulic valve lifters. Multi-point fuel injection.

BASE V-6 (929 S): Dual-overhead-cam "vee" type six-cylinder (24-valve). **Displacement:** 180.3 cu. in. (2954 cc). **Bore & Stroke:** 3.50 x 3.00 in. (88.9 x 76 mm). **Compression Ratio:** 8.5:1. **Brake Horsepower:** 190 at 5600 rpm. **Torque:** 191 lbs.-ft. at 4500 rpm. Hydraulic valve lifters. Multi-point fuel injection.

BASE ROTARY (RX-7): Wankel with two coaxial three-lobe rotors. **Displacement:** 80 cu. in. (1308 cc). **Compression Ratio:** 9.7:1. **Brake Horsepower:** 160 at 7000 rpm. **Torque:** 140 lbs.-ft. at 4000 rpm. Two main bearings. Multi-point fuel injection.

OPTIONAL TURBO ROTARY (RX-7): Same as above, except with turbocharger — **Compression Ratio:** 9.0:1. **Brake Horsepower:** 200 at 6500 rpm. **Torque:** 196 lbs.-ft. at 3500 rpm.

CHASSIS DATA: Wheelbase: (Miata) 89.2 in.; (323) 96.5 in.; (Protege) 98.4 in.; (MX-6) 99.0 in.; (626) 101.4 in.; (929) 106.7 in.; (RX-7) 95.7 in. **Overall Length:** (Miata) 155.4 in.; (323) 163.6 in.; (Protege) 171.5 in.; (MX-6) 177.0 in.; (626) 179.3 in.; (929) 193.9 in.; (RX-7) 169.9 in. **Height:** (Miata) 48.2 in.; (323) 54.3 in.; (Protege) 54.1 in.; (MX-6) 53.5 in.; (626 sedan) 55.5 in.; (626 hatch) 54.1 in.; (929) 54.5 in.; (RX-7) 49.8 in. **Width:** (Miata) 65.9 in.; (323) 65.7 in.; (Protege) 65.9 in.; (626/MX-6) 66.5 in.; (929) 67.9 in.; (RX-7) 66.5 in.

TECHNICAL: Layout: front-engine, front-drive except (929, RX-7) front-engine, rear-drive; (Protege 4WD) four-wheel-drive. **Transmission:** five-speed manual; four-speed automatic available. **Steering:** rack and pinion. **Body Construction:** steel unibody.

ADDITIONAL MODELS: Mazda also marketed a multi-purpose vehicle in the U.S. (introduced late in 1988), as well as the line of pickup trucks.
Manufacturer: Mazda Motor Corp., Hiroshima, Japan.
Distributor: Mazda Motor of America Inc., Irvine, California.

POSTSCRIPT: Although demand for Mazda's Miata two-seater retreated somewhat from its initial frenzy, the roadster remained highly popular into the 1991 model year. At least customers no longer had to pay dealers many thousands of dollars above list price to obtain one. In 1991, the roadster became available painted in British Racing Green.

MERCEDES-BENZ

Not until 1926 did two early auto manufacturers—both of which laid claim to creating the first automobile—merge into the German marque that would later produce some of the most dramatic four-wheelers of them all. In that year, the Daimler and Benz firms joined to form Daimler-Benz AG. By that time, however, both companies had 40 years of experience with motorcar production.

Thus, Mercedes-Benz had good cause to celebrate in 1986, a year that marked the hundredth anniversary of the German automaker's origin. Precisely a century earlier, in 1886, Karl Benz obtained a patent for a three-wheeled vehicle with a 984-cc single-cylinder engine. In that same year, Benz invented the spark plug, while Gottlieb Daimler built a four-wheeled carriage with a 469-cc, single-cylinder gas engine that he'd patented three years earlier. Amazingly, considering that the two men would turn out their motorcars in the same region of Germany, they were never destined to meet.

Daimler, who'd apprenticed as a gunsmith before turning to engineering, became technical director of the Deutz Gas Engine Works in 1872, working under Gustav Otto, who would gain fame for his own engine creation. Head designer at Deutz was Wilhelm Maybach (yet another famous person in early automotive and aviation history, whose name would be attached to the Zeppelin created at the turn of the century). By 1881, Daimler and Maybach departed from Deutz and moved into their own shop. The Daimler gasoline engine provided power for a motorcycle and motorboat, even before it went into the four-wheeled vehicle of late 1886. That one was essentially a horseless carriage with an engine rather than a purpose-built motorized vehicle. Three years later, however, Daimler and Maybach turned out a full-fledged automobile, powered by a

vee-type two-cylinder engine. Displayed at the 1889 World's Fair in Paris, their creation was called the *Stahlradwagen* (steel-wheeled car). The engine soon went into Panhard et Levassor motorcars, built in France; and even entered production in America, courtesy of William Steinway (of piano-manufacturing fame). In 1894, a Peugeot with a Daimler engine won the Paris-Rouen race. Late in the 1890s, Daimler and Maybach developed a Phonix automobile with front engine and chain drive, along with a four-cylinder model.

Over at the Benz camp, what some consider to be the world's first "production" automobile, the Benz Velo, arrived in 1894. Nine years later, in 1903, Karl Benz built a four-cylinder engine that remained in production up to the 1914 outbreak of World War I. In that year came the first six-cylinder (6.5-liter) Benz.

Meanwhile, the Mercedes name came into existence on the Daimler side of the equation. Mercedes happened to be the name of the daughter of Emil Jellinek, the Austro-Hungarian Consul at Nice, France, around the turn of the century. In the final years of the 1890s, Jellinek had become an agent for Daimler, selling a small number of cars in southern France. Jellinek used the Mercedes name for a car he entered in the Nice Speed Week competition. By 1900, he suggested that Daimler develop a more modern motorcar, one that was lower in profile, faster, and more powerful. He even agreed to accept the first three dozen, provided that he be granted full rights to sell them in France, Austro-Hungary, Belgium, and even the U.S.; and also that the new car be named after his daughter.

Thus appeared the 1901 Mercedes, designed by Wilhelm Maybach and Paul Daimler, whose father Gottlieb died in 1900. That first Mercedes sported a honeycomb radiator and angled steering column, with a 5913-cc T-head four-cylinder engine and gated four-speed transmission driving the rear wheels. By 1902, Daimler registered the Mercedes name as a trademark and it went onto all passenger cars (but not on trucks, which kept the Daimler designation). Expansion of the models available helped to strengthen the Mercedes reputation, to the point that many other companies began to replicate its vehicles. According to the *World Guide to Automobile Manufacturers*, companies as diverse as Fiat (Italy), Ariel (England) and Locomobile (U.S.) "based their 1904-5 models on Mercedes' patterns." Mercedes car also were turned out by Steinway, in Connecticut, from 1904 to 1907. Offerings from the Daimler/Mercedes firm itself ranged from modest 1.6-liter models all the way up to a trio of chain-driven behemoths, with engines displacing as much as 9.6 liters.

As for competition, a 120-bhp Mercedes won the Grand Prix at Dieppe, France in 1908. In 1912, Ralph de Palma drove a Grand Prix Mercedes at the Indianapolis 500. Though he led the pack for a time, de Palma suffered engine trouble near the end. Three years later, however, he won at Indy.

Another form of trademark, the three-pointed star, also came from Daimler, said to represent the triple-threat perceived value of his engine on land, sea and air. First registered in 1909, it appeared on Daimler's motorcars by about 1911.

In 1911, Daimler had a new model powered by an overhead-valve four-cylinder engine, with three valves per cylinder and a vee-shaped radiator. Production resumed quickly after World War I, carrying on 4-liter and 7.2-liter models. Early in the 1920s, Daimler (Mercedes) became the first manufacturer to install a supercharger on a production model. Supercharging was first used on the 6/25/40 1.6-liter four, and also on the 10/40/65 2614-cc engine. Following the retirement of Paul Daimler, his role as head engineer was taken by Ferdinand Porsche, who designed a line of six-cylinder overhead-cam engines. Porsche remained with Mercedes until 1928.

Negotiations for the Daimler-Benz merger began as early as 1923, and were completed in 1926. The modern insignia was created by placing Daimler's tripointed star inside the laurel wreath that had been seen on Benz vehicles. The first supercharged model produced after the merger was the 24/100/Type K: essentially an old model with a new name. Then came the 1926 Stuttgart (2-liter) and Mannheim (3-liter) L-head engines, followed by the Nurburg straight eight.

In 1928, Mercedes debuted the Type S (called the 26 120/180 in Germany), rated 120 horsepower unblown and 180 with a supercharger in action. Displacement of the six-cylinder engine was 6789 cc, riding in a lower chassis than the more ordinary Type K. The famed 7.1-liter SS and SSK were characterized by long hoods, with three exhaust pipes passing out the side. Only about 173 of the Type SS and a mere 45 Type SSK (on a shorter chassis) were produced from 1928 to 1934.

Two very different Mercedes-Benz models emerged as the 1930s began. At the 1930 Paris Motor Show, Mercedes displayed a 7.7-liter straight-eight "Grosser." At the other extreme was the Type 170 with a 1.7-liter engine and four-wheel independent suspension, introduced in 1931. Then came the rear-engined 130H and 170H, on a backbone chassis. Mercedes introduced the 260D, the world's first diesel-engine production car, in 1935, powered by a 2545-cc four. In 1936, a new front-engined 170V on a tubular backbone frame replaced the original 170. At the upper end of the scale, later in the 1930s, was the dramatic 540K, with a supercharged 5401-cc straight eight under its massive hood. Developing 115 horsepower under ordinary conditions, the 540K's blower went into action by stomping the gas pedal to the floor. Mercedes also produced similar models with 3.8- and 5-liter engines.

By early 1945, Stuttgart stood in ruins as a result of Allied bombing during World War II. Most of the Daimler-Benz factory was destroyed. Nevertheless, by February of 1946, a handmade prototype of the upcoming 170V sedan was created, ready for production in June of that year. Not surprisingly, Max Hoffman of New York became the first importer of postwar Mercedes-Benz models into the U.S., a service he would perform for a number of other European makes. In 1949, a diesel-engined counterpart of the 170 went into production, followed by a more luxurious 170S edition with a larger gasoline engine.

Each of those 170-series sedans displayed prewar styling, but the 220 and 300 introduced in 1951 had a more modern look, with overhead-cam six-cylinder engines under their hoods. Also in 1951, Daimler-Benz patented front/rear crush zones in a rigid passenger compartment.

During 1953, a monocoque-bodied 180 replaced the 170 series, offered with both gasoline and (later) diesel engines. More important to Mercedes history were the 300SL racing cars created in 1952, with an alloy body on a multitubular space frame. Finishing in the top three spots at the Le Mans race, they attracted so much attention (especially in the U.S.) that Daimler-Benz turned to a production version that became one of the most famous and distinctive sports cars of all time. A 240-bhp (SAE) version of the 300 sedan's 2996-cc overhead-cam engine provided the power, becoming the first production car with fuel injection (a Bosch mechanical system). With at least a 130-mph top speed (some reports claimed much swifter velocities), the gullwing-door 300SL quickly became the fastest car in the world. A straight-eight engine powered the 300SLR racing car of 1955.

Gullwing production lasted only a few years, ceasing in 1957. Its 300SL roadster successor had conventional doors. A smaller 190SL edition, with an 1897-cc four-cylinder engine, sold in far greater numbers through 1963.

By the late 1950s, Daimler-Benz established a connection with Studebaker-Packard in the U.S., whereby the latter company undertook distribution of Mercedes-Benz products. That tie lasted until the demise of Studebaker's operation at South Bend, Indiana in early 1964.

Daimler-Benz attempted to diversify in the late 1950s and early '60s, taking control of the Auto Union company in 1958 and contributing to the design of the DKW models and new Audis of the mid-1960s. By 1964, Daimler-Benz was losing interest in the DKW/Audi connection. Thus, Volkswagen became joint owner of the Audi operation and, by 1968, took over completely.

By 1959, fuel injection was available on the 220SE sedan (E = injection). A year later, the 220 series was wearing a new body. A 230SL roadster replaced the original 190SL/300SL duo in 1963, and could be ordered with an automatic transmission and removable hardtop. Also new was the massive and luxurious Type 600 sedan, on a 126-inch wheelbase and powered by a 6329-cc V-8, yet capable of top speeds beyond 125 mph. A Pullman limousine version (later available with six doors) rode a vast 153.5-inch wheelbase, stretching 246 inches overall. This "Grosser" Mercedes ranked as the world's longest car. A lesser-known Landaulette variant also became available, used primarily by heads of state. Little more than a handful of the 600 sedans reached the U.S. between 1963 and 1980, out of the total of 2,190 sedans and 487 Pullmans built.

In the mid-1960s, the 230 and 250 series sedans replaced the former 220. Then, the 230SL roadster turned into the 250SL; and after only a year, transformed again into the 280SL. New bodies and revised suspensions were installed on smaller Mercedes-Benz models in 1968, known as the "New Generation." In addition, a new 280 series (with 2778-cc engine) replaced the 250SE and 300SE. By the end of the decade, a 3499-cc V-8 engine went into the 300SE, which displayed quad vertical headlamps, and also was used for the 280-series coupe and convertible. The big 6.3-liter V-8, as in the "Grosser," also became available in some 300-series sedans. By this time, the Mercedes-Benz lineup was growing quite complex, and most of the models produced were finding their way into the U.S. market.

A 350SL two-seat roadster replaced the 280SL in 1971, with a 3499-cc V-8 under its hood. (U.S. versions turned to a bigger 4520-cc V-8.) New S-Class sedans began to arrive in 1972, with '280' and '350' prefixes. Also new was the S-Class 450 series, with the longer-stroke V-8 that displaced 4520 cc, on a 112.8-inch wheelbase. The 450SEL was longer yet.

Mercedes-Benz introduced its first five-cylinder diesel in 1974, under the hood of the 300D. A turbocharger became available by 1978, ranking as the world's first production car with turbodiesel power. Topping the engine scale was the 450SEL 6.9, with a 6834-cc enlargement of the earlier 6.3-liter V-8.

In 1976, the smaller models got a reworking into a new W123 series, on a 110-inch wheelbase, with lower and wider bodies. Station wagons were added later.

A new aluminum-alloy 4973-cc V-8 went into the European 450SL roadster in 1978; then into all-new S-class models. A 3818-cc version also was produced. These S-Class bodies were lighter and more aerodynamic, on a 115.6-inch (or longer) wheelbase. In European trim, at least, a 500SE could do 140 mph, while a 280SE or 380SE might top 130 mph. As the 1980s began, an S-Class body went on the 300SD Turbodiesel, targeting the U.S. market.

Late in 1982 came a smaller 190 series, with a 1997-cc four-cylinder engine. That was followed by a 16-valve, 2.3-liter version of the 190 engine, developed by Cosworth, which went into U.S. versions. A new 124-series body re-

placed the W123 versions at mid-decade, using the 190's rear suspension and a 110.2-inch wheelbase. Late in 1985, Mercedes introduced a set of revised S-class engines, up to the 5549-cc V-8. Daimler-Benz also developed 4-Matic four-wheel-drive, which engaged as soon as wheel slip was detected, introduced on the 300E/TE. By the end of the decade, the eagerly-awaited replacement for the long-lived SL-series sports cars finally arrived, in both six-cylinder and V-8 form as the 300SL and 500SL.

Through all the postwar years, Mercedes-Benz exported most of its significant models to the U.S., though not always in precisely the same form, or with the same engine ratings, as examples marketed elsewhere in the world.

Model Number Note: As a rule, the initial digits of each model indicate the number of liters (multiplied by 100); but there were numerous exceptions. Suffix E denotes fuel injection (*einspritzung;* S indicates a senior (generally bigger, more costly) model. The 'SL' suffix initially stood for super light (*sehr leicht,* or very light), though later SL convertibles added quite a few pounds and no longer literally qualified for that designation.

1946-50 MERCEDES-BENZ

170V/170S — FOUR — Prewar-style in appearance, the first postwar 170V four-door sedan had separate headlamps, rear-hinged front doors ("suicide" style), and front-hinged rear doors. A flat one-piece windshield was installed. Under the hood went a 1697-cc L-head engine that developed 38 horsepower (DIN). Wheelbase was 112 inches, and a 170V could hit about 65 mph.

A heavier 170S sedan was added in 1949, with 15-inch wheels and a larger (1767-cc) engine that developed 52 horsepower (DIN). Styling was similar to the prewar Type 230, and the 170S became available in cabriolet as well as sedan form. In 1950, that bigger engine also went into the 170Va (170V successor), but detuned to 45 bhp. Even so, it could travel about 10 mph faster than the original 170V (about 75 mph), and switched to tubular shock absorbers. Both the 170V and 170S rode a tubular oval-section cruciform chassis with tubular outriggers. Rear suspensions used coil springs and swing axles. Up front, the 170V had a transverse leaf spring, while the 170S switched to a wishbone/coil-spring setup with anti-sway bar.

170D — DIESEL FOUR — Allied forces initially prohibited production of a Mercedes with a diesel engine, but one became available during 1949. Styling was virtually identical to the gasoline-engine 170V sedan. The 1697-cc overhead-valve four produced 38 bhp. As in prewar diesels, fuel was injected into a pre-combustion chamber, with an electric glow plug to aid starting. Mercedes-Benz claimed a top speed of 62 mph.

I.D. DATA: Chassis serial number for 170 series is on a firewall plate. Engine number is on lower left of block.

Model	Body Type & Seating	Engine Type/CID	P.O.E. Price	Weight (lbs.)	Prod. Total
170V	4-dr Sedan-5P	I4/103	Note 1	2550	Note 2
170Va	4-dr Sedan-5P	I4/108	N/A	2575	Note 2
170S	4-dr Sedan-5P	I4/108	Note 1	2685	Note 2
170D (Dsl)	4-dr Sedan-5P	I4/103	N/A	2750	Note 2

Note 1: Approximate price of the 170V sedan was $1860; the 170S sedan, $2400.

Note 2: A total of 214 Mercedes-Benz cars were produced during 1946, followed by 1,045 in 1947, 5,116 in 1948, 17,417 in 1949, and 33,906 in 1950.

Model Note: The 170S, produced until 1952, also came in cabriolet form (either two- or five-seat).

ENGINE DATA: BASE FOUR (170V): Inline, L-head four-cylinder. Cast iron block. **Displacement:** 103.5 cu. in. (1697 cc). **Bore & Stroke:** 2.89 x 3.94 in. (73.5 x 100 mm). **Compression Ratio:** 6.0:1. **Brake Horsepower:** 38 (DIN) at 3700 rpm. Three main bearings. Solid valve lifters. One downdraft carburetor.

DIESEL FOUR (1949-up 170D): Inline, overhead-valve four-cylinder. **Displacement:** 103.5 cu. in. (1697 cc). **Bore & Stroke:** 2.89 x 3.94 in. (73.5 x 100 mm). **Compression Ratio:** 19.0:1. **Brake Horsepower:** 38 (DIN) at 3200 rpm. Three main bearings. Solid valve lifters.

BASE FOUR (later 170Va, 170S): Inline, L-head four-cylinder. Cast iron block. **Displacement:** 107.8 cu. in. (1767 cc). **Bore & Stroke:** 2.95 x 3.94 in. (75 x 100 mm). **Compression Ratio:** 6.5:1. **Brake Horsepower:** (170Va) 45 at 3650 rpm; (170S) 52 at 4000 rpm. Three main bearings. Solid valve lifters. One downdraft carburetor.

CHASSIS DATA: Wheelbase: 112 in. **Overall Length:** 169 in. **Width:** 64 in. **Front Tread:** (170V) 51.6 in.; (170D) 51.8 in. **Rear Tread:** (170V) 51.0 in.; (170D) 52.8 in. **Standard Tires:** (1946-48 170V) 5.50x16; (1949-up 170V) 5.50x15; (170S) 6.40x15.

TECHNICAL: Layout: front-engine, rear-drive. **Transmission:** four-speed manual. **Suspension (front):** (170V) transverse leaf spring; (170S) wishbones and coil springs, with anti-sway bar. **Suspension (rear):** swing axles with coil springs. **Brakes:** hydraulic, front/rear drum. **Body Construction:** steel body on tubular cruciform frame.

PERFORMANCE: Top Speed: (170V) 65 mph; (170S) 75 mph. **Acceleration (0-60 mph):** N/A (factory claimed 0-60 mph acceleration in 36 sec. for 170V, and 32 sec. for 170S).

Manufacturer: Daimler-Benz AG, Stuttgart, West Germany.
Distributor: Hoffman Motors Corp., New York City.

HISTORY: The 170V sedan debuted in 1946. Its successor, the 170Va sedan debuted in May 1950 and was produced until May 1952. Production of the 170S sedan began in May 1949 and continued until March 1952. Original production of the 170V dated back to 1936. By 1950, Mercedes-Benz cars were using tubular shock absorbers.

1951-53 MERCEDES-BENZ

1952 Mercedes-Benz 300S cabriolet. (Coys of Kensington)

170 SERIES — FOUR — Production of the 170Va and 170S sedans continued into the early 1950s, with various technical changes. Early in 1952, the 170S got a column-mounted gearshift. During that year, the 170V added transverse vent slots in its hood. By 1952, Mercedes-Benz issued an improved 170Sb version of the 170S with hypoid rear axle, dashboard-mounted starter button, wider track, and improved heater. A similarly-modified 170Vb also was introduced. Then, in mid-1953, a 170S-V sedan replaced both models, with a redesigned front transverse leaf spring and the earlier detuned 45-bhp engine (as in the 170V), intended to keep the selling price low.

170D SERIES — DIESEL FOUR — Diesel changes paralleled those on the gasoline-powered version of the 170 series, starting during the 1950 model year with a jump to 1767-cc displacement (and 40-bhp rating) with the 170Da. Then, in 1952-53, came the 170Db with a bigger windshield and revised hood. The 170DS (1952-53) and 170S-D (1953-55) were diesel versions of the gasoline-engined 170S sedan, with a redesigned front transverse leaf spring. The 170DS had cloth and artificial leather door panels and seats. Diesels in this series were built as late as September 1955, in 170S-D form. The earlier versions were dropped by the end of 1953 .

180 — FOUR — A Type 180 sedan joined the Mercedes-Benz lineup in mid-1953, powered by a 52 bhp version of the 1767-cc engine used in the 170S-V. Wheelbase was 104.3 inches, compared to 112 inches for the 170 series. New and modern styling was evident, atop a chassis coded W120. The conservative, boxy shape was similar to that which would appear on small Mercedes sedans for years to come. The traditional upright grille was angled back a bit, with the Mercedes tristar emblem on top. High sectional steel side members were welded to the floor platform, with subframes for suspension and drive-train.

220 SERIES — SIX — Debut of the midrange 220 series took place in mid-1951, ahead of the 300 series. Both a sedan and cabriolet were introduced, with large grilles and "suicide" front doors, but carrying on basic prewar styling (though with a rounded appearance). Sedans had built-in headlamps, while the cabriolet retained separate headlamps and included landau bars. An overhead-cam six-cylinder engine displaced 2195 cc (134 cid) and developed 80 horsepower (DIN). Wheelbase was 112 inches, on what was essentially a 170 chassis. Both the 170 and 220 still had semaphore-type turn signals.

300 SERIES — SIX — Introduced at the Frankfurt Auto Show in late 1951, the stately Type 300 was the first Mercedes-Benz model intended for export, and aimed squarely at Americans. It was destined to last 11 years in the Mercedes lineup.

An overhead-cam six-cylinder engine with aluminum cylinder head displaced 2996 cc (183 cid), and developed 115 horsepower (DIN) using twin Solex downdraft carburetors with a triple-jet system. The engine block had open sides covered by plates, allowing inspection of water jackets. Valve positions were staggered. The four-speed transmission was synchronized in all forward gears, controlled by a column gearshift lever.

Independent swing-axle rear suspension with coil springs also included auxiliary springs that cushioned the rear-axle movements, to improve riding qualities over rough roads. That auxiliary springing could be brought into or out of operation from the driver's seat, according to the load of the car, and the Type 300 was the first car to be fitted with such a device. Its hypoid bevel gear axle was the first such installation on a German automobile. Front suspension consisted of frictionless soft coil springs, telescopic shocks and forged A-arms. A new hydraulic steering damper consisted of a telescopic shock between the frame and a section of the three-piece steering linkage, to absorb road shocks. Wheelbase was 120 inches, and the top speed of 96 mph was claimed to be easily attainable. Type 300 models also had a switch for one-shot chassis lubrication.

Styling features of the 300 series included a curved windshield and built-in headlamps for its "envelope" style body, which had a more modern appearance than the smaller models. The large grille was in traditional upright Mercedes style, with tight mesh pattern. Sweeping fenders faded into the front doors (which hinged at the front), passing alongside an expansive hood. In addition to a plain slim-pillar sedan with quarter windows, Mercedes-Benz offered a four-door Convertible D, with landau bars, along with a two-door convertible coupe. Three people fit in the rear seat of the 300. A column-mounted gearshift controlled the four-speed transmission. The two-spoke steering wheel held the familiar Mercedes horn ring. Both front and rear seats had fixed side armrests. Rear seats had, in addition, a center armrest which folded away. The dashboard contained a large locking glovebox. A pushbutton-tuned radio was optional.

Standard 300 equipment included dual foglamps, backup lights, a triple horn, electric clock, lighter, locking glovebox, and octane-rating compensator switch. Interior features included door armrests, retracting center rear armrest, dual sunvisors, and front door pockets. Sedans had two long hand rails with sliding coat hooks. Cabriolets had two short hand rails for the front seats, plus two holding straps for the rear compartment.

300S — SIX — The 'S' stood for Super, when the 300S was introduced in mid-1952 after an earlier appearance at the Paris Salon (in autumn 1951). Available initially with a convertible body or as a five-passenger sedan, the 300S blended features of both the upcoming SL sports car and the recently-introduced long-wheelbase 300 series. Its existence occurred virtually by accident, in fact, after the SL program was delayed. As on the basic 300 series, handsome styling focused on long, flowing lines, with front fenders reached ahead of the upright radiator, with its three-pointed star. At the rear was a beautifully curved deck. Concealed running boards sat between the front and rear fenders.

A 150-bhp (DIN) hop-up of the Type 300's 2996-cc engine breathed through two (later three) Solex carburetors, using 7.8:1 compression. Both floor and column-mounted gearshifts were available. The cruciform chassis consisted of oval tubes and tubular outriggers.

Functional landau bars decorated the cabriolet body, whose convertible top rode in a big rear bustle. A roadster (sans landau bars) also became available, with a top that disappeared completely. Each open style offered 2+2 seating with fold-down rear seats, and rolled/pleated leather upholstery. Customers had a choice of wood veneers: either straight-grain or burled walnut. Fitted luggage was available, too. Two spare-tire wells sat in the trunk. On the dashboard was a control for ignition timing. Standard equipment included a signal-seeking radio, no-glare mirrors, vacuum-assisted brakes, backup lights, reclining seats, and windshield washers.

Top speed of the 300S was about 110 mph, and it could accelerate to 60 mph in about 14 seconds. Both the 300 and 300S had a turn signal combined with the horn ring, operated by rotating the ring. Each model also had turn-signal lights instead of the semaphore units stlll used on the 170/220 series. Rear signal lights stood tall, at the top of back fenders (just below the beltline).

The 300S roadster appeared at the Paris Salon in late 1952, powered by the 150-bhp engine and with a claimed top speed of 110 mph. Heavy chrome moldings went around the headlamps, with separately-mounted auxiliary lights above the bumper. A one-piece curved windshield was installed. Fender bulges extended a short distance into the doors. At the front was the usual upright grille topped by the Mercedes tristar emblem, with long parking lights atop the fenders. According to *Motor Trend*, this model was called the "sister car to the 300SL model, which made such a terrific showing in the Mexican Road Race."

1953 Mercedes-Benz 300 four-door cabriolet. (Christie's)

I.D. DATA: Chassis serial number is under the hood, on the right side of the firewall. Engine number is on lower left or right front of block.

Model	Body Type & Seating	Engine Type/CID	P.O.E. Price	Weight (lbs.)	Prod. Total
170 SERIES (Gasoline)					
170Va	4-dr Sedan-5P	I4/108	N/A	2575	Note 1
170Vb	4-dr Sedan-5P	I4/108	N/A	2607	Note 1
170S	4-dr Sedan-5P	I4/108	N/A	2685	Note 1
1/0Sb	4-dr Sedan-5P	I4/108	N/A	2750	Note 1
170S-V	4-dr Sedan-5P	I4/108	N/A	2685	Note 1
170D SERIES (Diesel					
170Da	4-dr Sedan-5P	I4/108	N/A	2750	Note 1
170Db	4-dr Sedan-5P	I4/108	N/A	2750	Note 1
170DS	4-dr Sedan-5P	I4/108	3590	2805	Note 1
170S-D	4-dr Sedan-5P	I4/108	N/A	2860	Note 1
180 SERIES					
180	4-dr Sedan-5P	I4/108	N/A	2596	Note 1
220 SERIES					
220	4-dr Sedan-5P	I6/134	N/A	2970	Note 2
220	2-dr Conv Sed-4P	I6/134	N/A	N/A	Note 2
220	2-dr Cabr-2/3P	I6/134	N/A	N/A	Note 2
220	2-dr Coupe	I6/134	N/A	N/A	Note 2
300 SERIES					
300	4-dr Sedan-5/6P	I6/183	N/A	3916	Note 3
300	4-dr Cabr-5/6P	I6/183	N/A	N/A	Note 3
300	2-dr Coupe	I6/183	N/A	N/A	Note 3
300S	4-dr Sedan-5/6P	I6/183	12500	3880	Note 4
300S	2-dr Cabr-2+2P	I6/183	12680	3616	Note 4
300S	2-dr Coupe-2+2P	I6/183	N/A	2845	Note 4
300S	2-dr Rds-2+2P	I6/183	N/A	N/A	Note 4

Note 1: A total of 42,222 Mercedes-Benz passenger cars (all models) were produced during 1951, followed by 36,824 in 1952, and 34,975 in 1953. Production in 1952 included 3,034 cars in the 300 series, 10,343 Type 220, and more than 23,000 Type 170.
Note 2: Approximately 16,154 first-series 220 sedan and 2,360 open models were produced through mid-1955.
Note 3: A total of 6,214 Type 300 and subsequent 300b sedans (and 591 convertibles) were produced between late 1951 and summer 1955.
Note 4: Approximately 560 Type 300S models (216 sedans and 344 other bodies) were produced through August 1955.

ENGINE DATA: BASE FOUR (170/180 gasoline series): Inline, L-head four-cylinder. Cast iron block. **Displacement:** 107.8 cu. in. (1767 cc). **Bore & Stroke:** 2.95 x 3.94 in. (75 x 100 mm). **Compression Ratio:** 6.5:1. **Brake Horsepower:** (170Va/b, 170S-V) 45 at 3650 rpm; (170S/Sb, 180) 52 at 4000 rpm. Three main bearings. Solid valve lifters.

BASE DIESEL FOUR (170D series): Inline, overhead-valve four-cylinder. Cast iron block. **Displacement:** 107.8 cu. in. (1767 cc). **Bore & Stroke:** 2.95 x 3.94 in. (75 x 100 mm). **Compression Ratio:** 19.0:1. **Brake Horsepower:** 40 at 3200 rpm.

BASE SIX (220): Inline, overhead-cam six-cylinder. Cast iron block. **Displacement:** 133.9 cu. in. (2195 cc). **Bore & Stroke:** 3.15 x 2.87 in. (80 x 72.8 mm). **Compression Ratio:** 6.5:1. **Brake Horsepower:** 80 (DIN) at 3600 rpm. Solid valve lifters. One carburetor.

BASE SIX (300): Inline, overhead-cam six-cylinder. Cast iron block and aluminum head. **Displacement:** 182.8 cu. in. (2996 cc). **Bore & Stroke:** 3.35 x 3.46 in. (85 x 88 mm). **Compression Ratio:** 6.4:1. **Brake Horsepower:** 115 (DIN) at 4600 rpm. **Torque:** 144 lbs. ft. at 2500 rpm. Seven main bearings. Solid valve lifters. Two Solex 32 PAJAT carburetors.

BASE SIX (300S): Same as 2996-cc six above, with two or three Solex carburetors — **Compression Ratio:** 7.5:1/7.8:1. **Brake Horsepower:** 150 (DIN) at 4850-5100 rpm. Three Solex 40 PBJC carburetors.

CHASSIS DATA: Wheelbase: (170) 112 in.; (180) 104.3 in.; (220 sed) 112 in.; (300) 120 in.; (300S) 114 in. **Overall Length:** (170) 169 in.; (170DS) 175.3 in.; (180) 176 in.; (220 sed) 178 in.; (300) 195 in.; (300S) 181.1 in. **Height:** (170) 62.8-63.4 in.; (170DS) 63.3 in.; (180) 61 in.; (220 sed) 63.4 in.; (300) 64.5 in.; (300S) 59.5 in. **Width:** (170) 63.5 in.; (170DS) 66.3 in.; (180) 69 in.; (220) 66.4 in.; (300) 72.5 in. **Front Tread:** (170) 51.0 in.; (170DS) 51.8 in.; (180) 55.9 in.; (220) 51.8 in.; (300) 56.7 in.; (300S) 58.3 in. **Rear Tread:** (170) 53.0 in.; (170DS) 56.5 in.; (180) 57.1 in.; (220) 56.5 in.; (300) 60.0 in.; (300S) 60.0 in. **Standard Tires:** (170) 5.50x16; (180) 6.40x13; (220) 6.40x15; (300) 7.10x15; (300S) 6.70x15.

TECHNICAL: Layout: front-engine, rear-drive. **Transmission:** four-speed manual. **Suspension (front):** (170V, 170S-V) transverse leaf spring; (180/220) wishbones with coil springs; (300S) wishbones with coil springs and anti-roll bar. **Suspension (rear):** swing axles with coil springs. **Brakes:** hydraulic, front/rear drum. **Body Construction:** steel body on steel frame except (180) steel unibody.

PERFORMANCE: Top Speed: (170S-V) 70 mph; (170DS) 62 mph; (180) 78 mph; (220) 90 mph; (300) 96-98 mph; (300S) 110 mph. **Acceleration (0-60 mph):** (300) 16.1 sec.; (300S) 14 sec. **Acceleration (quarter-mile):** (300) 20 sec. **Fuel Mileage:** (300) about 17 mpg (U.S.).

PRODUCTION/SALES: Approximately 288 Mercedes-Benz passenger cars were sold in the U.S. in 1953, including about 100 with diesel engines.

ADDITIONAL MODELS: In its first outing, at the Mille Miglia in May 1952, a 300SL racing car finished second (not far behind the winner). Late in 1952, both the 300SL Le Mans racing coupe and the 300S roadster appeared at the Paris Salon. The 300SL had a lightweight tubular frame, and was powered by a 183-cid six-cylinder engine that developed 175 horsepower at 5200 rpm, on 8:1 compression with three Solex carburetors. Racers were developed by Rudolf Uhlenhaut. Wearing a Mercedes tristar emblem ahead of its oval grille, the 300SL had turned in a powerful one-two finish at the *Carrera Panamericana* race in Mexico, as well as at Le Mans, and led to the production version of 1954-57; see next listings for details.

Manufacturer: Daimler-Benz AG, Stuttgart, West Germany.
Distributor: Hoffman Motors Corp., New York City.

HISTORY: Type 300 models were built at the coachworks in Sindelfingen. The 300's engine was the first overhead-cam design used on a Mercedes-Benz since 1932. The first-series 300 sedan became available in late 1951 and lasted through March 1954. Production of the four-door convertible began in April 1952. Production of the 300S began in July 1952. Production of the 220 convertible and coupe continued through 1955. Both the 220 and 330 had engines designed by Josef Muller. The 220 was considered to be a replacement for the prewar 230 series, while the 300 evolved from the prewar 320 and 500K sedans.

Road & Track noted that the 300S "has caused a quiet riot of enthusiasm with its low, sleek lines and its attitude of 'going' even when standing still." The magazine called it "one of the finest road vehicles in the world today." Motor Trend wasn't wholeheartedly impressed by the 170DS diesel, first pointing out that the body looked to be "about 1936 vintage, and not a very flashy '36 at that." When the engine fired up, they added, it "breaks into a harsh clatter that sounds exactly as though you had just thrown three rods." On the other hand, they liked the car's luxury touches and ride quality, said to be "equal to virtually any Detroit car."

1954 Mercedes-Benz 220a cabriolet. (Coys of Kensington)

170S-V — FOUR — Production of the 170S-V sedan continued into early 1955 with little change. All of the other 170-series models with gasoline engines faded away during 1953.

170S-D — DIESEL FOUR — Production of the diesel-engine version of the 170 sedan also continued into 1955, with little change.

180/180D — GAS/DIESEL FOUR — The original 180 sedan remalned in the Mercedes lineup halfway through 1957, joined this year by a diesel-powered edition. With the same 1767-cc displacement as the gasoline engine, the diesel developed 40 horsepower.

220a SERIES — SIX — A new, more modern 220a sedan debuted in March 1954, edging aside the older-style 220 series. This one had a more boxy profile, a much different fender line and smaller grille, with parking lights atop the fenders. Wheelbase was 111 inches (106 inches on some models).

300 SERIES — SIX — A 300b series replaced the original 300 during the 1954 model year, with its 3.0-liter engine producing an additional 10 horsepower (now 125). Brakes also were larger. No change was evident in the 300S series.

300SL — SIX — As of August 1954, the production version of the 300SL racing car was ready to become available to regular customers—and soon afterward, shipped to sports-car fans in the United States. Max Hoffman, importer of Mercedes-Benz cars into America, is generally credited with instigating the existence of the famed gullwing coupe, by ordering a thousand of the roadgoing editions ahead of time. The production 300SL first appeared at the New York Auto Show in February 1954.

Drivetrain and suspension were essentially the same as those used on the 300-series sedans and coupes, on a chassis with 94.5-inch wheelbase. The "high-pivot" swing-axle rear suspension allowed extreme oversteering, a flaw that would later be corrected on

the roadster followup of 1957. The front suspension consisted of upper and lower A-arms with coil springs and anti-roll bar. The 300SL used a multi-tube space-frame chassis, and was best known for the coupe's half-height gullwing doors, which opened upward. In fact, the complex tubular space framework virtually demanded gullwing doors. Though creating a dramatic appearance, those doors with their tall, wide sills also made it difficult to enter and exit from one of the coupes, and also tended to leak during rainy periods. The car's steering wheel was hinged at the base of the hub, tilting almost upside down, to ease entry/exit somewhat.

Although the 300SL prototype had inset door windows (a window within the window), the production version did not. The Mercedes-Benz tristar emblem sat at the center of a horizontal bar across the wide grille. This was the only model lacking the traditional upright, tight-mesh grille. Of course, no one was likely to mistake a gullwing 300SL for any other Mercedes, past or present. Other styling touches included long bulges over the wheel openings, longitudinal hood bulges, and anodized aluminum beltline trim moldings. Large angled eggcrate-patterned grillework in the front fenders (at the cowl) was almost as noticeable a feature as the gullwing doors, and would appear on many other cars in later years. A small round insignia stood at the front of the hood. Round park lamps went below the headlamps. Horizontal wraparound taillamps sat just above the back bumper. Wind-up windows were standard.

The 300SL's single-overhead-cam, 2996-cc (182.8-cid) six-cylinder engine developed 215 horsepower DIN (240 SAE at 6100 rpm). Torque output was 210 pound-feet (SAE). The engine was inclined 50 degrees, contained a forged-steel crankshaft, and used dry-sump lubrication. Bosch mechanical fuel injection replaced the usual carburetors. A remote oil tank sat in the left fender, with an oil cooler next to the regular radiator. A four-speed, all-synchro manual transmission and drum brakes (Alfin drums at first) were installed, along with a single dry-plate clutch. Early models had a long, bent gearshift lever that extended from the transmission tunnel. In 1955, that would change to a remote-control linkage. A ZF self-locking differential contained a standard 3.64:1 axle ratio on U.S. models (but other ratios were available, from 3.25:1 to 4.11:1). With 3.25:1 gearing, the speedometer read up to 180 mph; others had a 160-mph speedometer installed. The gas tank held 34.5 gallons (45 gallons on racing models). Tires were 6.50x16 size.

Aluminum was used for the doors, forward-opening hood, trunklid, rocker panels, belly pan, and interior sheetmetal, but the balance of the body was made of steel. All-aluminum competition bodies were available on special order. A total of 29 aluminum-bodied 300SLs were built. Those aluminum-bodied cars used Plexiglas windows (but a glass windshield) and had Rudge center-lock wheels. Steel bodies could be ordered with competition springs, which were standard on aluminum-bodied cars.

I.D. DATA: Chassis serial number is under the hood, on the right side of the firewall. Engine number is on lower left or right front of block.

Model	Body Type & Seating	Engine Type/CID	P.O.E. Price	Weight (lbs.)	Prod. Total
170 SERIES					
170S-V	4-dr Sedan-5P	I4/108	N/A	2685	Note 1
170S-D (Dsl)	4-dr Sedan-5P	I4/108	N/A	2860	Note 1
180 SERIES					
180	4-dr Sedan-5P	I4/108	3350	2535	Note 1
180D (Dsl)	4-dr Sedan-5P	I4/108	3575	2535	Note 1
220a SERIES					
220a	4-dr Sedan-5P	I6/134	4175	2860	Note 1
220a	2-dr Conv Sed-4P	I6/134	5600	2860	Note 1
220a	2-dr Cabr-2/3P	I6/134	6150	2860	Note 1
220a	2-dr Coupe	I6/134	N/A	2860	Note 1
300 SERIES					
300	4-dr Sedan-5/6P	I6/183	6780	3916	Note 2
300	4-dr Cabr-5/6P	I6/183	8111	3902	Note 2
300	2-dr Coupe-4/5P	I6/183	N/A	N/A	Note 2
300b	4-dr Sedan-5/6P	I6/183	N/A	3916	Note 2
300b	4-dr Cabr-5/6P	I6/183	N/A	N/A	Note 2
300b	2-dr Coupe-4/5P	I6/183	N/A	N/A	Note 2
300S	4-dr Sedan-5/6P	I6/183	N/A	3800	Note 3
300S	2-dr Cabr-2+2P	I6/183	12500	3800	Note 3
300S	2-dr Coupe-2+2P	I6/183	12500	3800	Note 3
300S	2-dr Rds-2+2P	I6/183	12500	3800	Note 3
300SL					
300SL	2-dr Coupe-2P	I6/183	11000	2750	Note 4

Note 1: A total of 48,816 Mercedes-Benz cars (all models) were produced during 1954. That production included 1,455 Type 300 models.

Note 2: A total of 6,214 Type 300 and 300b sedans (and 591 convertibles) were produced between late 1951 and summer 1955.

Note 3: Approximately 560 Type 300S models (216 sedans and 344 other bodies) were produced through August 1955).

Note 4: A total of 1,400 Type 300SL gullwing coupes were produced from 1954-57 (146 in 1954, 867 in 1955, 311 in 1956, and 76 in 1957).

Price Note: 300SL figure is early price; sales in U.S. did not begin until 1955, when the price dropped to $7463.

ENGINE DATA: BASE FOUR (170S-V): Inline, L-head four-cylinder. Cast iron block. **Displacement:** 107.8 cu. in. (1767 cc). **Bore & Stroke:** 2.95 x 3.94 in. (75 x 100 mm). **Compression Ratio:** 6.5:1. **Brake Horsepower:** 45 at 3600 rpm. Three main bearings. Solid valve lifters.

BASE FOUR (180): Same as 1767-cc four above, except — **Compression Ratio:** 6.7:1. **Brake Horsepower:** 52 at 4000 rpm.

BASE DIESEL FOUR (170S-D series): Inline, overhead-valve four-cylinder. Cast iron block. **Displacement:** 107.8 cu. in. (1767 cc). **Bore & Stroke:** 2.95 x 3.94 in. (75 x 100 mm). **Compression Ratio:** 19.0:1. **Brake Horsepower:** 40 at 3200 rpm.

BASE DIESEL FOUR (180D): Same as 1767-cc diesel four above, except — **Brake Horsepower:** 40.

BASE SIX (220a): Inline, overhead-cam six-cylinder. Cast iron block. **Displacement:** 133.9 cu. in. (2195 cc). **Bore & Stroke:** 3.15 x 2.87 in. (80 x 72.8 mm). **Compression Ratio:** 7.6:1. **Brake Horsepower:** 85 (DIN) at 4800 rpm. Solid valve lifters. One carburetor.

BASE SIX (300): Inline, overhead-cam six-cylinder. Cast iron block and aluminum head. **Displacement:** 182.8 cu. in. (2996 cc). **Bore & Stroke:** 3.35 x 3.46 in. (85 x 88 mm). **Compression Ratio:** 6.4:1. **Brake Horsepower:** 115 (DIN) at 4600 rpm. **Torque:** 144 lbs.-ft. at 2500 rpm. Seven main bearings. Solid valve lifters. Two Solex 32 PAJAT carburetors.

BASE SIX (300b): Same as 2996-cc six above, except — **Compression Ratio:** 7.4:1. **Brake Horsepower:** 125 (DIN). Two dual-barrel carburetors.

BASE SIX (300S): Same as 2996-cc six above, with three Solex 40 PBJC carburetors — **Compression Ratio:** 7.8:1. **Brake Horsepower:** 150 (DIN) at 5100 rpm.

BASE SIX (300SL): Same as 2996-cc six, above, with Bosch mechanical fuel injection (code M198) — **Compression Ratio:** 8.5:1. **Brake Horsepower:** 215 (DIN) at 5800 rpm (240 SAE at 6100 rpm). **Torque:** 206 lbs.-ft. (DIN) at 4600 rpm (217 lbs.-ft. SAE at 4800 rpm).

CHASSIS DATA: Wheelbase: (170S-V) 112 in.; (180) 104.3 in.; (220a sed) 111 in.; (300) 120 in.; (300S) 114 in.; (300SL) 94.5 in. **Overall Length:** (170S-V) 175 in.; (180) 176 in.; (220a sed) 185 in.; (300) 195 in.; (300S) 181 in.; (300SL) 180 in. **Height:** (170S-V) 65.5 in.; (180) 61.5 in.; (220a sed) 62 in.; (300) 64 in.; (300S) 59.5 in.; (300SL) 49.8 in. **Width:** (170S-V) 64 in.; (180) 68.5 in.; (220a sed) 69 in.; (300/S) 71.7 in.; (300SL) 70.5 in. **Front Tread:** (170S-V) 51.8 in.; (180) 55.9 in.; (300) 52.8 in.; (300S) 58.3 in.; (300SL) 54.5. **Rear Tread:** (170S-V) 56.5 in.; (180) 57.1 in.; (300) 60.0 in.; (300S) 60.0 in.; (300SL) 56.5. **Standard Tires:** (170S-V) 5.50x16; (180) 6.40x13; (220a) 6.70x15; (300) 7.10x15; (300S) 6.70x15; (300SL) 6.50x15.

TECHNICAL: Layout: front-engine, rear-drive. **Transmission:** four-speed manual. Gear ratios for the first 300SL coupes: (1st) 3.14:1; (2nd) 1.85:1; (3rd) 1.31:1; (4th) 1.00:1. Gear ratios for subsequent 300SL coupes: (1st) 3.34:1; (2nd) 1.97:1; (3rd) 1.39:1; (4th) 1.00:1. **Standard Final Drive Ratio:** (300SL) 3.64:1 on U.S. models (optional 3.25:1, 3.42:1, 3.89:1 and 4.11:1). **Suspension (front):** upper/lower A-arms with coil springs; (300S/SL) upper/lower A-arms with coil springs and anti-roll bar. **Suspension (rear):** swing axles with coil springs; (300SL) high-pivot swing axles with radius arms and coil springs. **Brakes:** hydraulic, front/rear drum. **Body Construction:** steel body on steel frame except (180/220) steel unibody; (300SL) steel/aluminum body on tubular space frame. **Fuel Tank:** (300SL) 34.5 gallon (45 gallons on racer).

Note: About 29 early 300SLs had an aluminum body.

PERFORMANCE: Top Speed: (300) 96 mph; (300S) 110 mph; (300SL cpe) 120-146 mph (as much as 165 mph claimed). **Acceleration (0-60 mph):** (300S) 14 sec.; (300SL) 7.6-8.8 sec. **Acceleration (quarter-mile):** (300SL) 16.1 sec. (84 mph).

PRODUCTION/SALES: Approximately 437 Mercedes-Benz passenger cars were sold in the U.S. in 1954.

ADDITIONAL MODELS: A total of nine 300SLR racing versions were built (two with coupe body). The 300SLR racer differed from an ordinary 300SL in various ways, though the tubular-truss chassis and 3.0-liter engine displacement were the same. The SLR powerplant, however, was a straight eight, canted in the engine bay, with power takeoff at the center to a ZF five-speed gearbox/differential. Inboard brakes were used, along with 16-inch wire wheels. A lightweight Elektron (magnesium alloy) body weighed only 1830 pounds. The 300SLR was not sold to the general public.

Manufacturer: Daimler-Benz AG, Stuttgart, West Germany.

Distributor: Hoffman Motors Corp., New York City.

HISTORY: "The effect is electrifying," declared the British magazine *Autocar* in describing second-gear acceleration of 300SL. Passengers "feel they are being rocketed through space." Their test car managed to accelerate to 60 mph in 8.8 seconds, and to 100 in 21 seconds, with a top speed beyond 120 mph. *Motor Trend* found 300SL acceleration "a trifle disappointing," with a 0-60 time of 8.5 seconds; but expressed greater appreciation for the 16.1-second quarter-mile time. Their test car neared 135 mph. Mercedes-Benz announced the 190SL roadster in 1954, along with the 300SL gullwing coupe, and it was featured in magazines early that year; but production did not begin until 1955.

1955 MERCEDES-BENZ

1955 Mercedes-Benz 300SL Gullwing coupe. (Christie's)

170S-V, 170S-D — FOUR — Production of the gasoline- and diesel-engine 170 series sedans ended during 1955. Little change was evident in this final season.

180/180D — FOUR — Production of the modern, boxy-styled Mercedes with gasoline or diesel engine continued with little change.

190SL — FOUR — By spring of 1955, Mercedes-Benz was ready with its second member of the "SL" generation: the 190SL two-seat touring sports roadster. Actually, the 190SL had been featured in magazine articles a year earlier, alongside the new 300SL coupe; but production did not commence until the beginning of 1955.

Power came from a single-overhead-cam four-cylinder engine with 1897-cc (116-cid) displacement, developing 105 horsepower DIN (120 SAE) at 5700 rpm. The same engine would go into 180-series sedans in 1957. A four-speed manual gearbox was standard. Prototypes had a column gearshift, but production models turned to a floor shift. Prototypes also had a hood scoop, but that too disappeared in production.

Wheelbase was 94.5 inches, and the 190SL was styled to resemble the 300SL; but intended as a sporty tourer rather than all-out sports car. The front end, in particular was similar to the 300SL, but it had no cowl grillework. The 190SL had a rounded overall look with a low nose, wide grille with large tristar in center, and long horizontal bulges above the wheel wells. A short horizontal trim strip decorated the front and rear fenders. The roadster had a rather long deck and ample trunk space, on a shortened version of the 180 (W120-series) sedan platform, which debuted in 1953. This design (code W121 for the 190SL) was known as "Pontoon" style, because of its steel unibody structure. The roadster's body was welded to its frame. The engine, transmission and front axle were mounted in a removable front subframe. The all-independent suspension was similar to that used in the 180 sedan, with single-pivot swing axles at the rear (different from the setup used on the 300SL).

The roadster came with a heater, roll-up windows, easy-to-operate convertible top, windshield washers, and backup lights. The gearbox was synchronized in all forward gears, and a round tachometer and speedometer sat just ahead of the driver. *Road & Track* magazine said performance of the 190SL was "a function of intelligent use of the gearbox." A detachable steel hardtop soon became optional. Later yet, a fixed-roof hard-top would become available.

220a SERIES — SIX — Production of the 220a with 2195-cc overhead-cam engine, in four body styles, continued with little change.

300 SERIES — SIX — Production of the 300b, introduced during 1954, continued with little change until it was replaced by the 300c late in 1955 (see next listing for details). The 300S, with a more powerful version of the 3.0-liter engine, also continued with little change.

300SL — SIX — Introduced in 1954, the gullwing coupe was officially on sale in the U.S. in 1955.

I.D. DATA: Chassis serial number is under the hood, on the right side of the firewall. Engine number is on lower left or right front of the block.

Model	Body Type & Seating	Engine Type/CID	P.O.E. Price	Weight (lbs.)	Prod. Total
170 SERIES					
170S-V	4-dr Sedan-5P	I4/108	N/A	2685	Note 1
170S-D (Dsl)	4-dr Sedan-5P	I4/108	N/A	2860	Note 1
180 SERIES					
180	4-dr Sedan-5P	I4/108	3395	2596	Note 1
180D (Dsl)	4-dr Sedan-5P	I4/108	3595	2684	Note 1
190SL					
190SL	2-dr Rds-2P	I4/116	3998	2550	Note 2
220a SERIES					
220a	4-dr Sedan-5P	I6/134	4588	2860	Note 1
220a	2-dr Conv-4/5P	I6/134	N/A	N/A	Note 1
220a	2-dr Cabr-4/5P	I6/134	6290	N/A	Note 1
220a	2-dr Coupe-4/5P	I6/134	6450	N/A	Note 1
300 SERIES					
300b	4-dr Sedan-5/6P	I6/183	6988	3916	Note 1
300b	4-dr Cabr-5/6P	I6/183	8328	N/A	Note 1
300b	2-dr Coupe	I6/183	N/A	N/A	Note 1
300S	4-dr Sedan-5/6P	I6/183	N/A	3880	Note 3
300S	2-dr Cabr-2+2P	I6/183	12457	N/A	Note 3
300S	2-dr Coupe-2+2P	I6/183	12457	N/A	Note 3
300S	2-dr Rds-2+2P	I6/183	12457	N/A	Note 3
300SL					
300SL	2-dr Coupe-2P	I6/183	7463	2885	Note 4

Note 1: A total of 63,683 Mercedes-Benz cars (all models) were produced during 1955.
Note 2: A total of 25,881 190SL models were produced during the full model run, 1955-63 (1,727 built in 1955 alone).
Note 3: A total of 560 Type 300S models were produced during the full model run, from 1952-55 (216 coupes, 203 cabriolets and 141 roadsters).
Note 4: A total of 1,400 gullwing 300SL coupes were produced during the full model run, 1954-57 (867 in 1955 alone).

ENGINE DATA: BASE FOUR (170S-V, 180): Inline, L-head four-cylinder. Cast iron block. **Displacement:** 107.8 cu. in. (1767 cc). **Bore & Stroke:** 2.95 x 3.94 in. (75 x 100 mm). **Compression Ratio:** 6.7:1. **Brake Horsepower:** (170S-V) 50 at 3600 rpm; (180) 58 at 4000 rpm. **Torque:** (180) 82 lbs.-ft. at 1800 rpm. Three main bearings. Solid valve lifters. One carburetor.

BASE DIESEL FOUR (170S D, 180D): Inline, overhead-valve four-cylinder. **Displacement:** 107.8 cu. in. (1767 cc). **Bore & Stroke:** 2.95 x 3.94 in. (75 x 100 mm). **Compression Ratio:** 19.0:1. **Brake Horsepower:** 40/43 at 3200 rpm.

BASE FOUR (190SL): Inline, overhead-cam four-cylinder (code M121). Cast iron block. **Displacement:** 116 cu. in. (1897 cc). **Bore & Stroke:** 3.35 x 3.29 in. (85 x 83.6 mm). **Compression Ratio:** 8.5:1. **Brake Horsepower:** 105 (DIN) at 5700 rpm (120 bhp SAE). **Torque:** 105 lbs.-ft. (DIN) at 3200 rpm. Two Solex carburetors.

BASE SIX (220a): Inline, overhead-cam six-cylinder. Cast iron block. **Displacement:** 133.9 cu. in. (2195 cc). **Bore & Stroke:** 3.15 x 2.87 in. (80 x 72.8 mm). **Compression Ratio:** 7.5:1. **Brake Horsepower:** 92 at 4800 rpm. **Torque:** 116 lbs.-ft. at 2400 rpm. Solid valve lifters. One carburetor.

BASE SIX (300b): Inline, overhead-cam six-cylinder. Cast iron block and aluminum head. **Displacement:** 183 cu. in. (2996 cc). **Bore & Stroke:** 3.35 x 3.46 in. (85 x 88 mm). **Compression Ratio:** 7.5:1. **Brake Horsepower:** 136 at 4500 rpm. **Torque:** 162 lbs.-ft. at 2600 rpm. Seven main bearings. Solid valve lifters. Two Solex carburetors.

BASE SIX (300S): Same as 2996-cc six above, but with three Solex carburetors — **Compression Ratio:** 7.8:1. **Brake Horsepower:** 163 at 5000 rpm. **Torque:** 170 lbs.-ft. at 3800 rpm.

BASE SIX (300SL): Same as 2996-cc six, above, with Bosch mechanical fuel injection — **Compression Ratio:** 8.55:1. **Brake Horsepower:** 215 (DIN) at 5800 rpm (240 SAE at 6100 rpm). **Torque:** 206 lbs.-ft. (DIN) at 4600 rpm (217 lbs.-ft. SAE at 4800 rpm).

CHASSIS DATA: Wheelbase: (170S-V) 112 in.; (180) 104.3 in.; (190SL) 94.5 in.; (220a sed) 111 in.; (300b) 120 in.; (300S) 114.2 in.; (300SL) 94.5 in. **Overall Length:** (170S-V) 175.3 in.; (180) 175.5 in.; (190SL) 166 in.; (220a sed) 186 in.; (300b) 199 in.; (300S) 186 in.; (300SL) 178 in. **Height:** (170S-V) 62.7 in.; (180) 61.3 in.; (190SL) 52 in.; (220a sed) 61.5 in.; (300b) 63 in.; (300S) 60 in.; (300SL) 51.3 in. **Width:** (170S-V) 66.3 in.; (180) 68.6 in.; (190SL) 68.5 in.; (220a sed) 68.6 in.; (300b) 72.4 in.; (300S) 75.3 in.; (300SL) 71 in. **Front Tread:** (170S-V) 51.8 in.; (180) 51.8 in.; (190SL) 56.3 in.; (220a) 56.3 in.; (300b) 58.3 in.; (300S) 58.3 in.; (300SL) 54.5. **Rear Tread:** (170S-V) 56.7 in.; (180) 57.2 in.; (190SL) 57.9 in.; (220a) 57.9 in.; (300b) 60.0 in.; (300S) 60.0 in.; (300SL) 56.5. **Standard Tires:** (170S-V) 5.50x16; (180) 6.40x13; (190SL) 6.40x13; (220a) 6.70x13; (300b) 7.10x15; (300S) 6.70x15; (300SL) 6.50x15.

TECHNICAL: Layout: front-engine, rear-drive. **Transmission:** four-speed manual. **Suspension (front):** upper/lower A-arms with coil springs; (190SL/300SL) upper/lower A-arms with coil springs and anti-roll bar. **Suspension (rear):** swing axles with coil springs; (190SL) single-joint swing axles as upper lateral arms, with radius arms and coil springs; (300SL) high-pivot swing axles with radius arms and coil springs. **Brakes:** hydraulic, front/rear drum. **Body Construction:** steel body on steel frame except (180/220) steel unibody; (300SL) steel/aluminum body on tubular space frame.

MAJOR OPTIONS: Detachable hardtop (190SL). Automatic antenna (190SL). Sliding sunroof (180). Reclining seats (180).

PERFORMANCE: Top Speed: (190SL) 105-112 mph (factory claimed 111.8 mph); (300b) 100 mph; (300S) 110 mph; (300SL) 120-146 mph (as much as 165 mph claimed). **Acceleration (0-60 mph):** (190SL) 11.6-14.5 sec.; (300S) 14 sec.; (300SL) 7.4-8.8 sec. **Acceleration (quarter-mile):** (190SL) 18.7-18.9 sec. (76 mph). **Fuel Mileage:** (190SL) 16-20 mpg.

ADDITIONAL MODELS: The 300SLR racing coupe evolved from the single-seat Grand Prix car, with a longer (93.3-inch) wheelbase and two seats. During 1955, the 300SLR was victorious at the Mille Miglia, Targa Florio and Tourist Trophy events. As tested by *Motor Trend,* it was capable of traveling 176 mph and could accelerate to 60 mph in 6.8 seconds, using first and second gears. Accelerating to 100 mph took 13.6 seconds. The 2976-cc inline eight-cylinder engine developed 296 horsepower at 7450 rpm, and 228 pound-feet of torque at 5950 rpm.
Manufacturer: Daimler-Benz AG, Stuttgart, West Germany.
Distributor: Hoffman Motors Corp., New York City.

HISTORY: At the 1955 Le Mans race, a 300SLR driven by Pierre Levegh flew into the grandstand. This tragedy prompted Mercedes-Benz's abandonment of motor racing.

1956-57 MERCEDES-BENZ

1956 Mercedes-Benz 190SL two-seat roadster. (Christie's)

180 SERIES — FOUR — Production of the original 180 sedan continued with little change into mid-1957, when it was replaced by the 180a, with a larger (1897-cc) engine. The earlier engine was a 1767-cc L-head design. Diesel (180D) production continued into 1959 with the original smaller engine.

190 SERIES — FOUR — A 190 gasoline engine sedan was added, with the same styling as the 180 but new single-pivot swing-axle rear suspension (on the W121 chassis). Power came from an overhead-cam, 1897-cc four as in the 190SL roadster, but developing 75 horsepower (84 bhp SAE). Wheelbase was 104 inches.

190SL — FOUR — Production of the two-seat roadster continued with little change. A removable hardtop was optional (sometimes described as a coupe model). The coupe was available in a choice of colors, from classic black down to pale two-tone finishes. Second gear was claimed to be usable at 47 mph; third, to 75 mph; fourth, from 105-113 mph.

219/220 SERIES — SIX — A new series of sedans, coupes and cabriolets (convertibles) joined the lineup during 1956. The Type 220S served as successor to the prior 220a, offered as a four-door sedan, two-door coupe, and two-door cabriolet. The 219 came only as a sedan, with single rear window. Wheelbase was 108.3 inches (chassis code W105) for the 219, and 111 inches (chassis W180) for the 220S sedan. Two-door 220S models rode a W128 chassis with 106.3-inch wheelbase. Both models carried a 2195-cc (134-cid) six-cylinder overhead-cam engine, but with different ratings. The engine initially developed 85 horsepower on 7.6:1 compression under Type 219 hoods; but that grew to 90 hp during 1957, as a result of a compression boost to 8.7:1. In the Type 220, the engine used twin two-barrel carburetors for a rating of 100 or 106 horsepower.

300 SERIES — SIX — A 300c sedan with automatic transmission became available late in 1955, soon followed by a 300Sc series with fuel-injected engine (replacing the abandoned 300S). The 300Sc series came in sedan, cabriolet and roadster form. Using Bosch direct fuel injection and 8.55:1 compression, its 2996-cc engine developed 175 horsepower (DIN). The 300Sc introduced Hydrovac power brakes to the Mercedes-Benz line. Although the 300c engine used dual compound carburetion, it offered no increase in horsepower. Appearance of the 300Sc was similar to the former 300S, except for two extra horizontal trim strips along the former's hood.

1957 Mercedes-Benz 300SL two-seat roadster. (Christie's)

300SL — SIX — Production of the gullwing coupe continued through spring 1957. A new roadster entered production in August of that year, and became available for the 1958 model year; see next listing for details.

I.D. DATA: Chassis serial number is on the right side of the firewall. Engine number is on top, or on right side of block.

Model	Body Type & Seating	Engine Type/CID	P.O.E. Price	Weight (lbs.)	Prod. Total
180 SERIES					
180	4-dr Sedan-5P	I4/108	3150	2535	Note 1
180D (Dsl)	4-dr Sedan-5P	I4/108	3438	2645	Note 1
190 SERIES					
190	4-dr Sedan-5P	I4/116	3298	2645	Note 1
190SL	2-dr Rds-2P	I4/116	3998	2510	Note 2
190SL	2-dr HT Cpe-2P	I4/116	4295	2510	Note 2
219 SERIES					
219	4-dr Sedan-6P	I6/134	3680	2780	Note 4
220 SERIES					
220a	4-dr Sedan-5/6P	I6/134	N/A	N/A	Note 1
220S	4-dr Sedan-5/6P	I6/134	4494	2955	Note 3
220S	2-dr Conv Cpe	I6/134	7138	3142	Note 3
220S	2-dr Coupe	I6/134	N/A	N/A	Note 3
300 SERIES					
300c	4-dr Sedan-6P	I6/183	7078	4210	Note 5
300c	4-dr Limo-6P	I6/183	7368	4210	Note 5
300c	4-dr Cabr-6P	I6/183	N/A	N/A	Note 5
300c	2-dr Coupe	I6/183	N/A	N/A	Note 5
300S	4-dr Sedan-6P	I6/183	N/A	3880	Note 1
300S	2-dr Cabr-3P	I6/183	12898	3925	Note 1
300S	2-dr Coupe-3P	I6/183	12898	3925	Note 1
300S	2-dr Rds-3P	I6/183	12898	3925	Note 1
300Sc	4-dr Sedan-6P	I6/183	N/A	N/A	Note 6
300Sc	2-dr Cabr-3P	I6/183	N/A	N/A	Note 6
300Sc	2-dr Rds-3P	I6/183	N/A	N/A	Note 6
300SL					
300SL	2-dr Coupe-2P	I6/183	7295	3000	Note 7

Note 1: A total of 69,601 Mercedes-Benz cars (all models) were produced during 1956, and 80,899 in 1957.

Note 2: A total of 25,881 190SL models were produced during the full model run, 1955-63.

Note 3: Total 220S production over the full model run (1956-59) included 55,279 four-door sedans and 3,429 coupes/convertibles.

Note 4: A total of 27,845 Type 219 sedans were produced from 1956-59.

Note 5: A total of 1,432 Type 300c sedans and 51 other bodies were produced from late 1955 into mid-1956.

Note 6: A total of 200 Type 300Sc models were produced over the full model run, from late 1955 to early 1958 (98 sedans, 49 cabriolets and 53 roadsters).

Note 7: A total of 1,400 gullwing 300SL coupes were produced during the full model run, 1954-57.

Model Note: Official production of the 300S series halted late in 1955, but they remained on lists of models sold in the U.S. for the following year.

Price Note: Figures shown were valid in 1956. In 1957, the 190SL sold for $4652 ($4949 with hardtop), and the 300SL for $7967. Other models rose in price by smaller amounts.

1957 Mercedes-Benz 300SL sport roadster. (Christie's)

ENGINE DATA: BASE FOUR (180): Inline, L-head four-cylinder. Cast iron block. **Displacement:** 107.8 cu. in. (1767 cc). **Bore & Stroke:** 2.95 x 3.94 in. (75 x 100 mm). **Compression Ratio:** 6.7:1. **Brake Horsepower:** 58 at 4000 rpm. **Torque:** 82 lbs.-ft. at 1800 rpm. Three main bearings. Solid valve lifters. One carburetor.

Diesel Note: The overhead-valve diesel version of the 1767-cc engine produced 46 horsepower (SAE) at 3500 rpm, on 19:1 compression.

BASE FOUR (180a): Inline, overhead-cam four-cylinder. Cast iron block. **Displacement:** 116 cu. in. (1897 cc). **Bore & Stroke:** 3.35 x 3.29 in. (85 x 83.6 mm). **Compression Ratio:** 6.8:1. **Brake Horsepower:** 74 at 4700 rpm. **Torque:** 104 lbs.-ft. at 2800 rpm. Solid valve lifters.

BASE FOUR (190SL): Same as 1897-cc four above, except — **Compression Ratio:** 8.5:1. **Brake Horsepower:** 105 (DIN) at 5700 rpm (120 SAE at 5800 rpm). **Torque:** 105 lbs.-ft. (DIN) at 3200 rpm. Two Solex horizontal compound carburetors.

BASE FOUR (190 sedan): Same as 1897-cc four above, except — **Compression Ratio:** 7.5:1. **Brake Horsepower:** 84 (SAE) at 4800 rpm.

BASE SIX (219, 220S): Inline, overhead-cam six-cylinder. Cast iron block. **Displacement:** 133.9 cu. in. (2195 cc). **Bore & Stroke:** 3.15 x 2.87 in. (80 x 72.8 mm). **Compression Ratio:** (early) 7.6:1; (late) 8.7:1. **Brake Horsepower:** (219) 85/90 (up to 100 SAE at 5000 rpm); (220S) 100/106 (112/120 SAE at 5000/5200 rpm); **Torque:** (late 220S) 128.8 lbs.-ft. at 3800 rpm. Solid valve lifters. One carburetor except (220S) dual two-barrel carburetors.

BASE SIX (300c): Inline, overhead-cam six-cylinder. Cast iron block and aluminum head. **Displacement:** 183 cu. in. (2996 cc). **Bore & Stroke:** 3.35 x 3.46 in. (85 x 88 mm). **Compression Ratio:** 7.5:1. **Brake Horsepower:** 115 DIN (136 SAE) at 4500 rpm. Seven main bearings. Solid valve lifters. Two carburetors.

BASE SIX (300Sc): Same as 2996-cc six above, but with Bosch fuel injection — **Compression Ratio:** 8.55:1. **Brake Horsepower:** 175 (DIN) at 5400 rpm. **Torque:** 188/191 lbs.-ft. at 4300 rpm.

BASE SIX (300SL): Same as 2996-cc six, above, with Bosch fuel injection — **Compression Ratio:** 8.55:1. **Brake Horsepower:** 215 (DIN) at 5800 rpm (240 SAE at 6100 rpm). **Torque:** 206 lbs.-ft. (DIN) at 4600 rpm (217 lbs.-ft. SAE at 4800 rpm).

CHASSIS DATA: Wheelbase: (180) 104.3 in.; (190 sed.) 104.3 in.; (190SL) 94.5 in.; (220S sed.) 111 in.; (220S conv.) 106.3 in.; (219) 108.25 in.; (300c sed.) 120 in.; (300S) 114.25 in.; (300SL) 94.5 in. **Overall Length:** (180) 175.6 in.; (190 sed.) 176.6 in.; (190SL) 165.3 in.; (220S sed.) 185.5 in.; (220S conv.) 185 in.; (219) 182.7 in.; (300c sed.) 199 in.; (300S) 185 in.; (300SL) 178 in. **Height:** (180) 61.4 in.; (190 sed.) 61.4 in.; (190SL) 52 in.; (219) 61.4 in.; (220S sed.) 61.6 in.; (220S conv.) 60.3 in.; (300c sed.) 63 in.; (300S) 59.5 in.; (300SL) 51.4 in. **Width:** (180/190/190SL/219/220S sed.) 68.5 in.; (220S conv.) 70 in.; (300c sed.) 72.4 in.; (300S sed.) 75.4 in.; (300SL) 70.5 in. **Front Tread:** (180) 56.1 in.; (190/190SL/219/220S sed.) 56.3 in.; (300c sed.) 58.3 in.; (300S) 54.5 in. **Rear Tread:** (180) 57.5 in.; (190/190SL/219/220S sed.) 57.9 in.; (300c sed.) 60.0 in.; (300S) 60.0 in.; (300SL) 56.5 in. **Standard Tires:** (180/190/190SL/219) 6.40x13; (220S sed.) 6.70x13; (300/S) 7.60x15; (300SL) 6.50x15/6.70x15.

TECHNICAL: Layout: front-engine, rear-drive. **Transmission:** four-speed manual (automatic on 300c series). **Suspension (front):** upper/lower A-arms with coil springs. **Suspension (rear):** swing axles with coil springs. **Brakes:** hydraulic, front/rear drum. **Body Construction:** (180/220) steel unibody; (300SL) steel/aluminum body on tubular space frame.

MAJOR OPTIONS: Automatic transmission: 300 ($350). Sliding sunroof (180/190/219/220S sedans).

PERFORMANCE: Top Speed: (190SL) 105-113 mph; (220S) 100 mph; (219) 92 mph; (300c) 100 mph; (300Sc) 112+ mph; (300SL cpe) 145-165 mph. **Acceleration (0-60 mph):** (300Sc) 12-13 sec.; (300SL cpe) 7.6-8.8 sec.

PRODUCTION/SALES: Approximately 3,000 Mercedes-Benz passenger cars were sold in the U.S. in 1957.

Manufacturer: Daimler-Benz AG, Stuttgart, West Germany.

Distributor: Mercedes-Benz Sales, Inc. (Studebaker-Packard Corp.), South Bend, Indiana.

HISTORY: "Whoever sees the Mercedes-Benz Type 190SL for the first time gets the urge to step in and speed away—such is the stunning beauty of this car." That was its beauty in the eyes of Mercedes-Benz copywriters, at any rate. By 1957, Studebaker-Packard was handling distribution of Mercedes-Benz automobiles in the U.S. The roadster version of the 300SL appeared at the London show in October 1957, and was available in the U.S. for the 1958 model year. Dealers complained when the 300 series was about to be cancelled, so a 300d version arrived late in 1957. See next listing for details on both models.

1958-59 MERCEDES-BENZ

1958 Mercedes-Benz 190SL roadster. (Coys of Kensington)

180 SERIES — FOUR — Production of the 180a sedan, introduced during 1957, continued with little change. The 1897-cc engine developed 74 horsepower. Upholstery was new for 1958, including duo-tone door trim and padded sunvisors. A 180b edition with extra horsepower debuted during the 1959 model year. Also introduced during the 1959 model year was a 180Db version of the diesel.

190 SERIES — FOUR — Little was new in the 190 sedan, except that a 190b edition with more power arrived late in the 1959 model year. A diesel version debuted during the 1958 model year, with a 55-bhp engine. In 1959, the 190SL engine was upgraded to 8.8:1 compression and the hardtop got a larger back window.

219/220 SERIES — SIX — Production of the 220S and 219 continued into 1958-59 with little change, powered by the more potent engines introduced during 1957. For the 1959 model year, they were joined by a 220SE series (sedan, cabriolet and coupe) with fuel-injected engine. Rear license plate lighting was now in the bumper guards. A Hydrak automatic clutch with fluid flywheel was optional, allowing two-pedal operation.

300 SERIES — SIX — After an absence of more than a year, a 300d version of the 300 series debuted for 1958. Restyling gave it a more modern look, without sacrificing the "classic" design. New taillamps went into rear fenders. The 300d had a fuel-injected engine and slightly revised body, with longer (124-inch) wheelbase. The roofline was flatter and more square; rear fenders longer; grille a tad wider. The sedan was now actually a four-door hardtop (without pillars). The fuel-injected engine developed 160 horsepower DIN (180 SAE). Either leather or fabric upholstery was available. A Borg-Warner three-speed automatic transmission was now standard (manual shift on special order). American versions got a 5.11:1 axle ratio for better acceleration. A total of 3,077 sedans were built through early 1962, but only 65 convertible sedans (all to special order). The 300Sc series faded away early in 1958 (see previous listing for details).

300SL — SIX — By the 1958 model year, a 300SL roadster replaced the gullwing coupe. With its tubular frame lowered, the roadster used conventional front-hinged doors. Engine displacement remained the same, but the overhead-cam six got a 10-bhp boost via an increase in compression ratio (to 9.5:1). The roadster used a low-pivot swing axle with transverse compensating spring, as in the Mercedes W196 Grand Prix racing car,

which improved handling. Parking lamps no longer were separate and round, but now sat in bright housings below the headlamps. European-spec cars had big "bubble" headlamp housings. The roadster's windshield was more rounded than that used in the gullwing coupe. A removable steel hardtop became optional, with a deep sloping wraparound window. The standard 300SL roadster had a rear-axle ratio of 3.64:1. Four other ratios were available: 3.25:1, 3.42:1, 3.89:1, or 4.11:1.

I.D. DATA: Chassis serial number is on the right side of the firewall. Engine number is on top, or on right side of block.

Model	Body Type & Seating	Engine Type/CID	P.O.E. Price	Weight (lbs.)	Prod. Total
180 SERIES					
180a	4-dr Sedan-5/6P	I4/116	3240	2570	Note 1
180D (Dsl)	4-dr Sedan-5/6P	I4/108	3517	2645	Note 1
190 SERIES					
190	4-dr Sedan-5/6P	I4/116	3431	2645	Note 1
190D (Dsl)	4-dr Sedan-5/6P	I4/116	3708	N/A	Note 1
190SL	2-dr Rds-2P	I4/116	5020	2515	Note 2
190SL	2-dr HT Cpe-2P	I4/116	5232	2515	Note 2
219 SERIES					
219	4-dr Sedan-5/6P	I6/134	3823	2780	Note 1
220 SERIES					
220S	4-dr Sedan-5/6P	I6/134	4283	2955	Note 1
220S	2-dr Conv-2/3P	I6/134	7641	3065	Note 1
220S	2-dr Conv-4/5P	I6/134	N/A	3065	Note 1
220SE	4-dr Sedan-5/6P	I6/134	N/A	3014	Note 3
220SE	2-dr Conv-2/3P	I6/134	N/A	N/A	Note 3
220SE	2-dr Conv-4/5P	I6/134	N/A	N/A	Note 3
300 SERIES					
300d	4-dr HT Sed-6P	I6/183	10418	4400	Note 1
300d	4-dr Conv-6P	I6/183	13655	N/A	Note 1
300SL					
300SL	2-dr Rds-2P	I6/183	10928	3000	Note 4

Note 1: A total of 99,209 Mercedes-Benz cars (all models) were produced during 1958, and 108,440 in 1959.

Note 2: A total of 25,881 190SL models were produced during the full model run, 1955-63.

Note 3: A total of 1,974 220SE four-door sedans were produced over the full model run (through 1960), plus 1,942 two-door models.

Note 4: A total of 1,858 300SL roadsters were produced during the full model run, from late 1957 into 1963.

Price Note: Figures shown were valid in 1958 and 1959, except 190D was not listed for sale in U.S. until 1959. A "convertible coupe" version of the 300SL roadster (with hardtop) sold for $11,106.

Production Note: See previous listing for additional breakdowns.

1959 Mercedes-Benz 220SE coupe.

ENGINE DATA: BASE FOUR (190SL): Inline, overhead-cam four-cylinder. Cast iron block. **Displacement:** 116 cu. in. (1897 cc). **Bore & Stroke:** 3.35 x 3.29 in. (85 x 83.6 mm). **Compression Ratio:** 8.5:1 (8.8:1 in 1959). **Brake Horsepower:** 105 (DIN) at 5700 rpm (120 SAE at 5800 rpm). **Torque:** 105 lbs.-ft. (DIN) at 3200 rpm. Solid valve lifters. Two Solex carburetors.

BASE FOUR (180a): Same as 1897-cc four above, except — **Compression Ratio:** 6.8:1. **Brake Horsepower:** 74 (SAE) at 4700 rpm. **Torque:** 104 lbs.-ft. at 2800 rpm. Solex carburetor.

BASE FOUR (190 sedan): Same as 1897-cc four above, except — **Compression Ratio:** 7.5:1. **Brake Horsepower:** 84 (SAE) at 4800 rpm. **Torque:** 107 lbs.-ft. at 2500 rpm.

Note: A 190b sedan debuted during 1959 with a 90-bhp engine.

Diesel Note: The diesel version of the 1897-cc four produced 55 horsepower (SAE) at 4000 rpm in the 190D on 21:1 compression. The 180D series continued to use a 1767-cc diesel rated 46 horsepower (SAE) with 19:1 compression.

BASE SIX (219, 220S): Inline, overhead-cam six-cylinder. Cast iron block. **Displacement:** 133.9 cu. in. (2195 cc). **Bore & Stroke:** 3.15 x 2.87 in. (80 x 72.8 mm). **Compression Ratio:** 8.7:1. **Brake Horsepower:** (219) 100 (SAE) at 5000 rpm; (220S) 120 (SAE) at 5000 rpm. **Torque:** (219) 130 lbs.-ft. at 2700 rpm; (220S) 137 lbs.-ft. at 3600 rpm. Solid valve lifters. One carburetor except (220S) two Solex 32 PAJAT carburetors.

BASE SIX (220SE): Same as 2195-cc six above, but with Bosch mechanical fuel injection — **Brake Horsepower:** 115 DIN (130 SAE at 5000 rpm). **Torque:** 146 lbs. ft. (SAE) at 3800 rpm.

BASE SIX (300d): Inline, overhead-cam six-cylinder. Cast iron block and aluminum head. **Displacement:** 182.8 cu. in. (2996 cc). **Bore & Stroke:** 3.35 x 3.46 in. (85 x 88 mm). **Compression Ratio:** 8.5:1. **Brake Horsepower:** 160 DIN (180 SAE at 5500 rpm). **Torque:** 191.7 lbs.-ft. (SAE) at 4500 rpm. Seven main bearings. Solid valve lifters.

BASE SIX (300SL): Same as 2996-cc six, above, with Bosch fuel injection — **Compression Ratio:** 9.5:1. **Brake Horsepower:** 225 (DIN) at 5900 rpm (250 SAE at 6200 rpm). **Torque:** 228 lbs.-ft. (SAE) at 5000 rpm.

CHASSIS DATA: Wheelbase: (180a) 104.3 in.; (190 sed) 104.3 in.; (190SL) 94.5 in.; (220S sed) 111 in.; (220S conv) 106.3 in.; (219) 108.25 in.; (300d) 124 in.; (300SL) 94.5 in. **Overall Length:** (180a) 175.6 in.; (190 sed) 176.6 in.; (190SL) 165 in.; (220S sed) 185.5 in.; (220S conv) 185 in.; (219) 182.7 in.; (300d) 204.3 in.; (300SL) 178 in. **Height:** (180a) 61.4 in.; (190 sed) 61.4 in.; (190SL) 52 in.; (220S sed) 61.6 in.; (220S conv) 60.3 in.; (300d) 63.5 in.; (300SL) 51.3 in. **Width:** (180a/190/190SL/219/220S sed) 68.5 in.; (220S conv) 70.5 in.; (300d) 73.25 in.; (300SL) 70.5 in. **Front Tread:** (180a) 55.9 in.; (190 sed) 54.1 in.; (190SL) 56 in.; (220S conv) 56.3 in.; (300d) 59.2 in.; (300SL) 53.5 in. **Rear Tread:** (180a) 57.5 in.; (190 sed) 57.9 in.; (190SL) 55 in.; (220S conv) 57.9 in.; (300d) 60.4 in.; (300SL) 57 in. **Standard Tires:** (180/190/190SL/219) 6.40x13; (220S sed) 6.70x13; (219) 6.40x13; (300D) 7.60x15; (300SL) 6.50/6.70x15.

TECHNICAL: Similar to 1956-57.

MAJOR OPTIONS: Hydrak automatic clutch: 220S/219 ($165).

PERFORMANCE: Top Speed: (180D) 69 mph claimed; (190 sed) 87 mph claimed; (190D) 75 mph; (190SL) 105-113 mph; (220S) 100 mph claimed; (300d) 105 mph; (300SL rds) 129-155 mph claimed. **Acceleration (0-60 mph):** (190D) 31 sec.; (190SL) 11.0 sec.; (220S) about 15 sec.; (300SL) about 7 sec. **Acceleration (quarter-mile):** (190D) 28.9 sec. (57 mph).

PRODUCTION/SALES: Approximately 13,739 Mercedes-Benz passenger cars were sold in the U.S. in 1959.

Manufacturer: Daimler-Benz AG, Stuttgart, West Germany.

Distributor: Mercedes-Benz Sales, Inc. (Studebaker-Packard Corp.), South Bend, Indiana.

HISTORY: At the London Motor Show in October 1957, Mercedes-Benz literature explained that "the dynamic flow lines of its sprawling body are the outward promise of the pent-up power which the Type 300SL roadster can release within the second, in response to your command." *Sports Cars Illustrated* tested a 300SL roadster with 3.89:1 axle, achieving 0-60 mph acceleration in 7.8 seconds and hitting 100 mph in 19.2 seconds, with a 124-mph top speed. *Road & Track* managed to accelerate to 60 mph in 7.6 seconds, but took 20.5 seconds to reach 100 mph.

1960-62 MERCEDES-BENZ

1960 Mercedes-Benz 190SL sport roadster. (Christie's)

180 SERIES — FOUR — The new 180b sedan had a slightly more powerful version of the 1897-cc engine, as well as a lower hood, wider radiator, and larger taillamp cluster than the 180a. The 180Db diesel differed little from its predecessor, but the 180Dc edition that arrived during 1961 added extra horsepower.

190 SERIES — FOUR — During 1959, a 190b sedan replaced the original 190, and a 190Db replaced the 190D diesel. Except for a horsepower increase in the gasoline engine, little was new for 1960. By this time, the 190SL's optional lift-off hardtop had a wraparound rear window. Restyling prior to the 1962 model year produced a 190c (and 190Dc) sedan with the same engines, but a more boxy body on a 106.3-inch wheelbase.

219/220 SERIES — SIX — By 1960, a 220b replaced the 219 sedan, a 220SB sedan replaced the 220S, and a 220SEb series replaced the 220SE. The overhead-cam 2195-cc engine added a few horsepower in each version. All models had wraparound front and rear windows, with a vertically-styled headlamp/parking-light unit, and horizontal taillamps below subtle but sharp-edged tailfins.

300 SERIES — SIX — Production of the 300d sedan continued with little change, until early 1962. A 300SE series was added during 1961, powered by a 160-bhp (185 bhp SAE) version of the 2996-cc overhead-cam engine. Wheelbase was only 108.3 inches, comparable to the 220 series.

300SL — SIX — Production of the two-seat roadster continued with little change, into 1963.

I.D. DATA: Chassis serial number is on the right side of the firewall. Engine number is on top, or on right front of block.

Model	Body Type & Seating	Engine Type/CID	P.O.E. Price	Weight (lbs.)	Prod. Total
180 SERIES					
180b	4-dr Sedan-5/6P	I4/116	3250	2570	Note 1
180Db (Dsl)	4-dr Sedan-5/6P	I4/108	3527	2670	Note 1
190 SERIES					
190b	4-dr Sedan-5/6P	I4/116	3441	2645	Note 1
190Db (Dsl)	4-dr Sedan-5/6P	I4/116	3718	2670	Note 1
190SL	2-dr Rds-2P	I4/116	5032	2500	Note 2
190SL	2-dr HT Cpe-2P	I4/116	5244	2500	Note 2
220 SERIES					
220b	4-dr Sedan-5/6P	I6/134	4283	2890	Note 1
220Sb	4-dr Sedan-5/6P	I6/134	4583	2940	Note 1
220SEb	4-dr Sedan-5/6P	I6/134	5018	2980	Note 1
220SEb	2-dr Coupe-4P	I6/134	8091	3020	Note 1
220SEb	2-dr Conv	I6/134	8091	3095	Note 1

Model	Body Type & Seating	Engine Type/CID	P.O.E. Price	Weight (lbs.)	Prod. Total
300 SERIES					
300d	4-dr HT Sed-6P	I6/183	10070	4400	Note 1
300d	4-dr Conv Sed-6P	I6/183	12644	4585	Note 1
300SE	4-dr Sedan-6P	I6/183	N/A	3650	Note 1
300SE	2-dr Cabr-5/6P	I6/183	N/A	N/A	Note 1
300SE	2-dr Coupe-5/6P	I6/183	N/A	N/A	Note 1
300SL					
300SL	2-dr Rds-2P	I6/183	10950	3000	Note 3
300SL	2-dr HT Cpe-2P	I6/183	11128	3000	Note 3

Note 1: A total of 122,684 Mercedes-Benz cars (all models) were produced during 1960, followed by 137,431 in 1961, and 146,393 in 1962.

Note 2: A total of 25,881 190SL models were produced during the full model run, 1955-63.

Note 3: A total of 1,858 300SL roadsters were produced during the full model run, 1957-63.

Price Note: Figures shown were valid in 1960 and 1961.

1961 Mercedes-Benz 300SL roadster. (Coys of Kensington)

ENGINE DATA: BASE FOUR (190SL): Inline, overhead-cam four-cylinder. Cast iron block. **Displacement:** 116 cu. in. (1897 cc). **Bore & Stroke:** 3.35 x 3.29 in. (85 x 83.6 mm). **Compression Ratio:** 8.5:1 (8.8:1 in 1959). **Brake Horsepower:** 105 (DIN) at 5700 rpm (120 SAE at 5800 rpm). **Torque:** 114 lbs.-ft. (SAE) at 3800 rpm. Solid valve lifters. Two Solex carburetors.

BASE FOUR (180b/180c): Same as 1897-cc four above, except — **Compression Ratio:** 7.0:1. **Brake Horsepower:** 78 (SAE) at 4500 rpm. **Torque:** 107 lbs.-ft. at 2500 rpm.

BASE FOUR (190b sedan): Same as 1897-cc four above, except — **Compression Ratio:** 8.5:1. **Brake Horsepower:** 90 (SAE) at 4500 rpm. **Torque:** 111 lbs.-ft. at 3000 rpm.

Diesel Note: The diesel version of the 1897-cc engine produced 55 horsepower (SAE) at 4000 rpm in the 190D series, on 21:1 compression. A 1767-cc diesel was installed in the 180D series until mid-1961, rated 43 horsepower DIN (46 SAE) with 19:1 compression. After that came 180Dc and 190Dc versions with 1987-cc engines, rated 48/55 bhp DIN (52/60 bhp SAE).

BASE SIX (220 series): Inline, overhead-cam six-cylinder. Cast iron block. **Displacement:** 133.9 cu. in. (2195 cc). **Bore & Stroke:** 3.15 x 2.87 in. (80 x 72.8 mm). **Compression Ratio:** 8.7:1. **Brake Horsepower:** (220b) 105 (SAE) at 5000 rpm; (220Sb) 124 at 5200 rpm; (220SEb) 134 at 5000 rpm. **Torque:** (220b) 133 lbs.-ft. at 3000 rpm; (220Sb) 139 lbs.-ft. at 3700 rpm; (220SEb) 152 lbs.-ft. at 4100 rpm. Solid valve lifters. Two Solex carburetors except (220SE) Bosch fuel injection.

BASE SIX (300d): Inline, overhead-cam six-cylinder. Cast iron block and aluminum head. **Displacement:** 182.8 cu. in. (2996 cc). **Bore & Stroke:** 3.35 x 3.46 in. (85 x 88 mm). **Compression Ratio:** 8.5:1. **Brake Horsepower:** 180 (SAE) at 5500 rpm. **Torque:** 192 lbs.-ft. at 4500 rpm. Seven main bearings. Solid valve lifters. Bosch fuel injection.

BASE SIX (300SE): Same as 2996-cc six above, except — **Compression Ratio:** 9.0:1. **Brake Horsepower:** 185 (SAE) at 5200 rpm. **Torque:** 205 lbs.-ft. at 4000 rpm.

BASE SIX (300SL): Same as 2996-cc six above, with Bosch fuel injection — **Compression Ratio:** 9.5:1. **Brake Horsepower:** 225 (DIN) at 5900 rpm (250 SAE at 6200 rpm). **Torque:** 228 lbs.-ft. (SAE) at 5000 rpm.

1962 Mercedes-Benz 190SL roadster with hardtop.

410

CHASSIS DATA: Wheelbase: (180b) 104.3 in.; (190b sed) 104.3 in.; (190c sed) 106.3 in.; (190SL) 94.5 in.; (220b/220Sb) 108.3 in.; (220SEb sed) 108.3 in.; (220SEb cpe/conv) 106.3 in.; (300d) 124 in.; (300SE) 108.3 in.; (300SL) 94.5 in. **Overall Length:** (180b) 177.2 in.; (190b sed) 177.2 in.; (190SL) 166 in.; (220b/220Sb) 192.2 in.; (220SEb cpe/conv) 185 in.; (220SEb sed) 192.2 in.; (300d) 204.3 in.; (300SE) 192 in.; (300SL) 179.9 in. **Height:** (180b/190b sed) 61.4 in.; (190SL) 52 in.; (220Sb) 59.5 in.; (300d) 64 in.; (300SE) 57.5 in.; (300SL) 51.3 in. **Width:** (180b/190b/190SL) 68.5 in.; (220b) 70.7 in.; (300d) 73.25 in.; (300SL) 70.5 in. **Front Tread:** (180b/190b) 56.3 in.; (190SL) 56.3 in.; (220Sb) 57.9 in.; (300d) 58.3 in.; (300SL) 55.5 in. **Rear Tread:** (180b/190b) 58.1 in.; (190SL) 57.9 in.; (220Sb) 58.5 in.; (300d) 60.0 in.; (300SE) 58.6 in.; (300SL) 57 in. **Standard Tires:** (180b/190b/190SL) 6.40x13; (220Sb) 7.25x13; (300d) 7.60x15; (300SE) 7.50x13; (300SL) 6.50/6.70x15.

TECHNICAL: Layout: front-engine, rear-drive. **Transmission:** four-speed manual or (300 series) three-speed automatic. **Suspension (front):** upper/lower A-arms with coil springs. **Suspension (rear):** swing axles with coil springs. **Brakes:** front/rear drum except (late 220S/SE) front disc, rear drum.

MAJOR OPTIONS: Automatic transmission: 300 series ($985). Bench-type rear seat: 220SE ($93).

PERFORMANCE: Similar to 1958-59.

PRODUCTION/SALES: Approximately 14,435 Mercedes-Benz passenger cars were sold in the U.S. in 1960, 12,903 in 1961, and 11,075 in 1962.

Manufacturer: Daimler-Benz AG, Stuttgart, West Germany.

Distributor: Mercedes-Benz Sales, Inc. (Studebaker-Packard Corp.), South Bend, Indiana.

HISTORY: "The engineering and construction of Mercedes-Benz is aimed at perfection," claimed advertisements in 1961. "This 300SL, for example, starts its life as an entirely hand-built space frame. Its tubes are cut, balanced and welded by devoted craftsmen. Its brakes and wheels are added carefully. Then its hand-welded body slips firmly over the geometric symmetry of its skeleton. Finally, its fuel-injection powerplant, fresh from its test bench, is lowered into place. Then the 300SL is road tested and checked with a thoroughness that leaves no secrets." Daimler-Benz celebrated its Diamond Jubilee in 1961, electing a new chairman: Walter Hitzinger.

A 300 Automatic, declared *Motor Trend* in 1961, "combines maximum dignity and impressiveness with minimum ostentation." Its "interior is a symphony in tasteful luxury." As for the 220S coupe, its "woodwork and leather are works of art."

1963 MERCEDES-BENZ

1963 Mercedes-Benz 220SEb four-seat cabriolet. (Christie's)

180 SERIES — FOUR — Production of the 180c sedan ceased in 1963, and the diesel version even earlier, though both continued to be listed in some directories of imported vehicles this year.

190 SERIES — FOUR — This would be the final year for the 190SL roadster. Production of the 190-series sedans continued with little change.

220 SERIES — SIX — Production of the 'b' series models continued with little change, each powered by a variant of the 2195-cc overhead-cam engine.

230SL — SIX — In 1963, Mercedes-Benz introduced its replacement (more or less) for the 190/300SL. The "pagoda-roof" 230SL roadster (code W113) debuted at the Geneva (Switzerland) auto show. Rather than a sports car per se, the 230SL ranked as a sports tourer: comparable to the 190SL in size and performance, but more posh. The engine and monocoque body/chassis came from the sedans that debuted in 1959. The overhead-cam six had been used in the 220SE, but bored to 2308-cc displacement in this installation. Multi-point Bosch fuel injection was used instead of the former single-point system, boosting horsepower by 30 (DIN). The low-pivot swing-axle rear suspension included a transverse camber-compensating spring. Girling front disc brakes were installed, with Al-Fin rear drums (vacuum assisted). Though not much longer than the 190SL, this new version was considerably heavier. It was also available with a four-speed Daimler-Benz semi-automatic transmission, which included a fluid coupling but no torque converter. The all-synchro four-speed manual gearbox remained standard. Styling was much more angular than on the 190/300SL, kin to the sedans, but the grille with its large center tristar was similar to prior installations. The optional hardtop's "pagoda" roofline curved upward a bit at the side. Leather upholstery was included.

300 SERIES — SIX — The big 300d series was gone, but the short 300SE continued, joined this year by a longer 300SEL on a 112.2-inch wheelbase.

300SL — SIX — This was the final year for the 300SL roadster.

I.D. DATA: Chassis serial number is on the right side of the firewall (230SL), or on right front fender skirt or hood lock panel. The complete serial number includes a six-digit chassis number, a model year suffix letter, and the model designation. Engine number is on right front of block.

Model	Body Type & Seating	Engine Type/CID	P.O.E. Price	Weight (lbs.)	Prod. Total
180 SERIES					
180c	4-dr Sedan-5/6P	I4/116	3484	2429	Note 1
180Dc (Dsl)	4-dr Sedan-5/6P	I4/121	3704	2550	Note 1
190 SERIES					
190c	4-dr Sedan-6P	I4/116	3844	2629	Note 1
190Dc (Dsl)	4-dr Sedan-6P	I4/121	4047	2739	Note 1
190SL	2-dr Rds-2P	I4/116	5215	2458	Note 2
190SL	2-dr HT Cpe-2P	I4/116	5443	2505	Note 2
220 SERIES					
220b	4-dr Sedan-5/6P	I6/134	4349	2739	Note 1
220Sb	4-dr Sedan-5/6P	I6/134	4818	2833	Note 1
220SEb	4-dr Sedan-5/6P	I6/134	5187	2877	Note 1
220SEb	2-dr Coupe	I6/134	8761	2901	Note 1
220SEb	2-dr Conv	I6/134	9562	3190	Note 1
230SL					
230SL	2-dr Rds-2P	I6/141	N/A	2900	Note 3
230SL	2-dr Coupe-2P	I6/141	N/A	N/A	Note 3
300 SERIES					
300SE	4-dr Sedan-6P	I6/183	8662	3531	Note 1
300SE	2-dr Cabr-5P	I6/183	N/A	N/A	Note 1
300SE	2-dr Coupe-5P	I6/183	N/A	3452	Note 1
300SEL	4-dr Sedan-6P	I6/183	N/A	3600	Note 1
300SL					
300SL	2-dr Rds-2P	I6/183	11099	2811	Note 4
300SL	2-dr HT Cpe-2P	I6/183	11573	2895	Note 4

Note 1: A total of 153,182 Mercedes-Benz cars (all models) were produced during 1963.
Note 2: A total of 25,881 190SL models were produced during the full model run, 1955-63.
Note 3: A total of 19,831 230SL models were produced during the full model run, 1963-66.
Note 4: A total of 1,858 300SL roadsters were produced during the full model run, 1957-63.

ENGINE DATA: BASE FOUR (190SL): Inline, overhead-cam four-cylinder. Cast iron block. **Displacement:** 116 cu. in. (1897 cc). **Bore & Stroke:** 3.35 x 3.29 in. (85 x 83.6 mm). **Compression Ratio:** 8.8:1. **Brake Horsepower:** 105 (DIN) at 5700 rpm (120 SAE at 5800 rpm). **Torque:** 105 lbs.-ft. (DIN) at 3200 rpm.

BASE FOUR (180c): Same as 1897-cc four above, except — **Compression Ratio:** 7.0:1. **Brake Horsepower:** 78 (SAE) at 4500 rpm. **Torque:** 107 lbs.-ft. at 2500 rpm.

BASE FOUR (190c sedan): Same as 1897-cc four above, except — **Compression Ratio:** 8.7:1. **Brake Horsepower:** 90 (SAE) at 5000 rpm. **Torque:** 111 lbs.-ft. at 3000 rpm.

DIESEL FOUR (180Dc, 190Dc): **Displacement:** 121.2 cu. in. (1987 cc). **Bore & Stroke:** 3.42 x 3.29 in. (87 x 83.6 mm). **Compression Ratio:** 21:1. **Brake Horsepower:** (180Dc) 52 at 3800 rpm; (190Dc) 60 at 4200 rpm.

BASE SIX (220 Series): Inline, overhead-cam six-cylinder. Cast iron block. **Displacement:** 133.9 cu. in. (2195 cc). **Bore & Stroke:** 3.15 x 2.87 in. (80 x 72.8 mm). **Compression Ratio:** 8.7:1. **Brake Horsepower:** (220b) 105 (SAE) at 5000 rpm; (220Sb) 124 at 5200 rpm; (220SEb) 134 at 5000 rpm. **Torque:** (220b) 133 lbs.-ft. at 3000 rpm; (220Sb) 139 lbs.-ft. at 3700 rpm; (220SEb) 152 lbs.-ft. at 4100 rpm. Four main bearings. Solid valve lifters. Two carburetors except (220SE) fuel injection.

BASE SIX (230SL): Inline, overhead-cam six-cylinder. Cast iron block and aluminum head. **Displacement:** 140.8 cu. in. (2308 cc). **Bore & Stroke:** 3.23 x 2.87 in. (82 x 73 mm). **Compression Ratio:** 9.3:1. **Brake Horsepower:** 170 (SAE) at 5500 rpm. **Torque:** 159 lbs.-ft. at 4500 rpm. Four main bearings. Solid valve lifters. Bosch multi-point fuel injection.

BASE SIX (300SE): Inline, overhead-cam six-cylinder. Cast iron block and aluminum head. **Displacement:** 183 cu. in. (2996 cc). **Bore & Stroke:** 3.35 x 3.46 in. (85 x 88 mm). **Compression Ratio:** 9.0:1. **Brake Horsepower:** 185 (SAE) at 5200 rpm. **Torque:** 205 lbs.-ft. at 4000 rpm. Seven main bearings. Solid valve lifters.

BASE SIX (300SEL): Same as 2996-cc six above, except — **Compression Ratio:** 195 at 5500 rpm. **Torque:** 203 lbs.-ft. at 4100 rpm.

BASE SIX (300SL): Same as 2996-cc six above, with Bosch fuel injection — **Compression Ratio:** 9.5:1. **Brake Horsepower:** 225 (DIN) at 5900 rpm (250 SAE at 6200 rpm). **Torque:** 228 lbs.-ft. (SAE) at 5000 rpm.

CHASSIS DATA: Wheelbase: (180) 104.5 in.; (190 sed.) 106.3 in.; (190SL) 94.5 in.; (220/220S) 108.3 in.; (230SL) 94.5 in.; (300SE) 108.3 in.; (300SEL) 112.2 in.; (300SL) 94.5 in. **Overall Length:** (180) 177.2 in.; (190 sed) 186.5 in.; (190SL) 166 in.; (220 sedan) 192.2 in.; (230SL) 169 in.; (300SE) 192.2 in.; (300SL) 179.9 in. **Height:** (190 sed) 58.8 in.; (190SL) 52 in.; (220 sedan) 59.5 in.; (300SE) 56.0 in.; (300SE cpe) 55.7 in. **Width:** (180) 68.5 in.; (190 sed) 68.5 in.; (190SL) 68.5 in.; (220) 70.7 in.; (230SL) 69.3 in.; (300SE) 73.25 in.; (300SL) 70.5 in. **Standard Tires:** (180) 6.40x13; (190 sed) 7.00x13; (190SL) 6.40x13; (220) 7.25x13; (230SL) 185x14; (300SL) 7.60x15; (300SE) 6.50x15.

TECHNICAL: Layout: front-engine, rear-drive. **Transmission:** four-speed manual (automatic standard on 300, optional on other models). **Suspension (front):** upper/lower A-arms with coil springs. **Suspension (rear):** swing axles with coil springs. **Brakes:** front/rear drum except (230SL) front disc, rear drum.

MAJOR OPTIONS: Automatic transmission.

PERFORMANCE: Top Speed: (230SL) 114-124 mph. **Acceleration (0-60 mph):** (230SL) 9.9-10.7 sec. **Acceleration (quarter-mile):** (230SL) 17-18 sec.

PRODUCTION/SALES: Approximately 11,234 Mercedes-Benz passenger cars were sold in the U.S. in 1963.

Manufacturer: Daimler-Benz AG, Stuttgart, West Germany.
Distributor: Mercedes-Benz Sales, Inc. (Studebaker-Packard Corp.), South Bend, Indiana.
HISTORY: A 230SL won the Spa-Sofia-Liege rally in its first year. This would be the final year for distribution by the Studebaker-Packard dealer organization.

1964-65 MERCEDES-BENZ

190 SERIES — FOUR — The 180 series sedan was gone, but the 190 remained, in both gasoline- and diesel-powered form. The 190SL sports car was replaced by the new 230SL (below). This would be the final year for the 190 sedans.

220 SERIES — SIX — Three models (220b, 220Sb and 220SEb) were identical in wheelbase and interior dimension, differing in equipment and performance. An automatic transmission was optional; front disc brakes were standard on 220S/SE. The 2195-cc engine became available with fuel injection.

1964 Mercedes-Benz 230SL convertible sports two-seater. (Christie's)

230SL — SIX — Production of the Mercedes two-seat sports car, introduced in 1963, continued with little change. As usual, the 'SL' suffix stood for Super Light, meaning that doors, trunk and hood were made of aluminum. Under the hood was a 2308-cc six-cylinder engine with fuel injection, hooked to a four-speed manual gearbox. A four-speed automatic transmission was optional, using a fluid coupling rather than a torque converter. The front end, with its large tristar emblem in the center of the single horizontal grille bar, was similar to prior 190/300SL models, even though the angular body differed considerably from predecessors.

300SE — SIX — The full-size Mercedes came in four-door sedan, long four-door sedan, coupe and convertible form. Standard equipment included an air suspension, automatic transmission, and power steering.

600/PULLMAN — GRAND MERCEDES — V-8 — Mercedes' most monstrous model, the 600 Pullman seven-passenger limousine, rode a 153.5-inch wheelbase and measured 246 inches overall. Power came from a 6.3-liter V-8 engine that developed 300 horsepower. A shorter-wheelbase 600 also became available. Both were offered on special order in the U.S. market. Styling was similar to the 300SE, with a sharper-edged roofline and back window. The 600 series lacked chrome bodyside trim strips, but front/rear wheel openings, rocker panels and pillar posts all had chrome trim. A four-speed automatic transmission with column lever was standard.

1964 Mercedes-Benz 220SEbC fixed-head pillarless coupe. (Christie's)

I.D. DATA: Chassis serial number is on the right fender skirt or hood lock panel; or on the right side of the firewall (230SL). Engine number is on right side of block.

Model	Body Type & Seating	Engine Type/CID	P.O.E. Price	Weight (lbs.)	Prod. Total
190 SERIES					
190c	4-dr Sedan-5/6P	I4/116	3844	2629	Note 1
190Dc (Dsl)	4-dr Sedan-5/6P	I4/121	4047	2739	Note 1
220 SERIES					
220b	4-dr Sedan-5/6P	I6/134	4349	2833	Note 1
220Sb	4-dr Sedan-5/6P	I6/134	4818	2833	Note 1
220SEb	4-dr Sedan-5/6P	I6/134	5187	2877	Note 1
220SEb	2-dr Coupe-5P	I6/134	8761	2901	Note 1
220SEb	2-dr Conv-5P	I6/134	9562	3190	Note 1
230SL					
230SL	2-dr Rds-2P	I6/141	7506	2749	Note 2
230SL	2-dr Coupe-2P	I6/141	7625	2793	Note 2
230SL	2-dr Cpe/Rds-2P	I6/141	7907	N/A	Note 2
300SE SERIES					
300SE	4-dr Sedan-5/6P	I6/183	8662	3366	Note 1
300SE	2-dr Coupe-5P	I6/183	11770	N/A	Note 1
300SE	2-dr Conv-5P	I6/183	12573	N/A	Note 1
300SEL	4-dr Ext Sedan	I6/183	9910	N/A	Note 1
600/PULLMAN (GRAND MERCEDES)					
600	4-dr Sedan-5/6P	V8/386	22000	N/A	Note 1
Pullman	4-dr Sedan-7P	V8/386	24000	5799	Note 1

Note 1: A total of 165,532 Mercedes-Benz passenger cars (all models) were produced during 1964, followed by 174,007 in 1965.

Note 2: A total of 19,831 230SL models were produced during the full model run, 1963-66.

Price Note: Model 600 figures shown are approximate.

ENGINE DATA: BASE FOUR (190): Inline, overhead-cam four-cylinder. Cast iron block and aluminum head. **Displacement:** 116 cu. in. (1897 cc). **Bore & Stroke:** 3.35 x 3.29 in. (85 x 83.6 mm). **Compression Ratio:** 8.7:1. **Brake Horsepower:** 90 (SAE) at 5200 rpm. **Torque:** 113 lbs.-ft. at 2700 rpm. Three main bearings. Solid valve lifters.

DIESEL FOUR (190D): Inline, overhead-cam four-cylinder. **Displacement:** 121.3 cu. in. (1988 cc). **Bore & Stroke:** 3.43 x 3.29 in. (87 x 83.6 mm). **Compression Ratio:** 21.0:1. **Brake Horsepower:** 60 at 4200 rpm. **Torque:** 87 lbs.-ft. at 2400 rpm. Fuel injection.

BASE SIX (220, 220S, 220SE): Inline, overhead-cam six-cylinder. Cast iron block and aluminum head. **Displacement:** 133.9 cu. in. (2195 cc). **Bore & Stroke:** 3.15 x 2.87 in. (80 x 72.8 mm). **Compression Ratio:** 8.7:1. **Brake Horsepower:** (220S) 124 at 5200 rpm; (220SE) 134 at 5000 rpm. **Torque:** (220S) 139 lbs.-ft. at 3700 rpm; (220SE) 152 lbs.-ft. at 4100 rpm. Four main bearings. Solid valve lifters.

BASE SIX (230SL): Inline, overhead-cam six-cylinder. Cast iron block and aluminum head. **Displacement:** 140.8 cu. in. (2308 cc). **Bore & Stroke:** 3.23 x 2.87 in. (82 x 73 mm). **Compression Ratio:** 9.3:1. **Brake Horsepower:** 170 (SAE) at 5600 rpm. **Torque:** 159 lbs.-ft. at 4500 rpm. Four main bearings. Solid valve lifters. Bosch multi-point fuel injection.

BASE SIX (300SE): Inline, overhead-cam six-cylinder. Aluminum alloy block and head. **Displacement:** 183 cu. in. (2996 cc). **Bore & Stroke:** 3.35 x 3.46 in. (85 x 88 mm). **Compression Ratio:** 9.0:1. **Brake Horsepower:** 185 (SAE) at 5200 rpm. **Torque:** 205 lbs.-ft. at 4000 rpm. Seven main bearings. Solid valve lifters.

BASE V-8 (600 Pullman): 90-degree, overhead-valve, "vee" type eight-cylinder. Cast iron block and aluminum heads. **Displacement:** 386.2 cu. in. (6329 cc). **Bore & Stroke:** 4.05 x 3.74 in. (103 x 95 mm). **Compression Ratio:** 9.0:1. **Brake Horsepower:** 300 at 4100 rpm. **Torque:** 369 lbs.-ft. at 2800 rpm. Five main bearings. Solid valve lifters. Bosch fuel injection.

CHASSIS DATA: Wheelbase: (190 sed) 106.3 in.; (220S/SE) 108.3 in.; (230SL) 94.5 in.; (300SE) 108.3 in.; (300SEL) 112.2 in.; (600) 126 in.; (600 Pullman) 153.5 in. **Overall Length:** (190 sed) 186.5 in.; (220S/220SE) 192.2 in.; (230SL) 169 in.; (300SE) 192.2 in.; (600) 218 in.; (600 Pullman) 246 in. **Height:** (190 sed) 58.8 in.; (220S) 59.5 in.; (220SE) 56.0 in.; (230SL) 51.7 in.; (300SE sed) 57.5 in.; (300SE cpe) 55.7 in.; (600) 58.9 in.; (600 Pullman) 59.4 in. **Width:** (190 sed) 68.5 in.; (220) 70.7 in.; (230SL) 69.3 in.; (300SE) 73.25 in.; (600) 76.8 in. **Front Tread:** (190 sed) 57.8 in.; (220S) 57.8 in.; (220SE) 58.4 in.; (230SL) 58.5 in.; (300SE) 58.4 in.; (600 Pullman) 62.4 in. **Rear Tread:** (190 sed) 58.5 in.; (220) 58.5 in.; (230SL) 58.5 in.; (300SE) 58.7 in.; (600 Pullman) 62 in. **Standard Tires:** (190 sed) 7.00x13; (220) 7.25x13; (230SL) 185x14 or 7.25x14; (300SE) 7.50x13; (600/Pullman) 9.00x15.

TECHNICAL: Layout: front-engine, rear-drive. **Transmission:** four-speed manual except (300SE, 600) automatic standard; automatic optional on 220/230SL. Manual 230SL gear ratios: (1st) 4.42:1; (2nd) 2.28:1; (3rd) 1.53:1; (4th) 1.00:1; (rev) 3.92:1. **Standard Final Drive Ratio:** (230SL) 3.75:1. **Steering:** recirculating ball. **Suspension (front):** (220 series, 230SL) unequal-length A-arms, coil springs and anti-roll bar; (300SE) wishbones with air springs, automatic leveling and anti-roll bar; (600) wishbones with air springs, automatic leveling and anti-roll bar. **Suspension (rear):** (220 series, 230SL) single low-pivot swing axles with trailing arms and coil springs; (300SE, 600) swinging semi-axles with trailing lower radius arms, air springs, automatic leveling and anti-roll bar. **Brakes:** (190) front/rear drum; (220S/SE, 230SL) front disc, rear drum; (300SE, 600) front/rear disc. **Body Construction:** steel unibody with auxiliary front frame.

MAJOR OPTIONS: Automatic transmission. Power steering ($175). Air conditioning ($359-$400). Sunroof ($200).

PERFORMANCE: Top Speed: (190) about 90 mph; (220) about 96 mph; (220S) about 102 mph; (220SE) about 106 mph; (230SL) about 125 mph; (300SE) about 109 mph; (600) about 128 mph. **Acceleration (0-60 mph):** (230SL) 9.9 sec. **Acceleration (quarter-mile):** (230SL) 17.0 sec. (83 mph). **Fuel Mileage:** (190) about 22 mpg; (190D) about 35 mpg; (220) about 21 mpg; (230SL) near 19 mpg; (300SE) about 16-17 mpg.

PRODUCTION/SALES: A total of 2,190 Model 600 sedans and 487 long-wheelbase (Pullman) versions were produced between 1963 and 1982. Approximately 11,234 Mercedes-Benz passenger cars were sold in the U.S. in 1964, followed by 12,117 vehicles in 1965 (including tourist deliveries).

Manufacturer: Daimler-Benz AG, Stuttgart, West Germany.

Distributor: Mercedes-Benz Sales Inc., South Bend, Indiana; then Mercedes-Benz of North America Inc., Fort Lee, New Jersey.

HISTORY: By 1965, approximately 400 dealers in the U.S. sold Mercedes-Benz automobiles.

1966 MERCEDES-BENZ

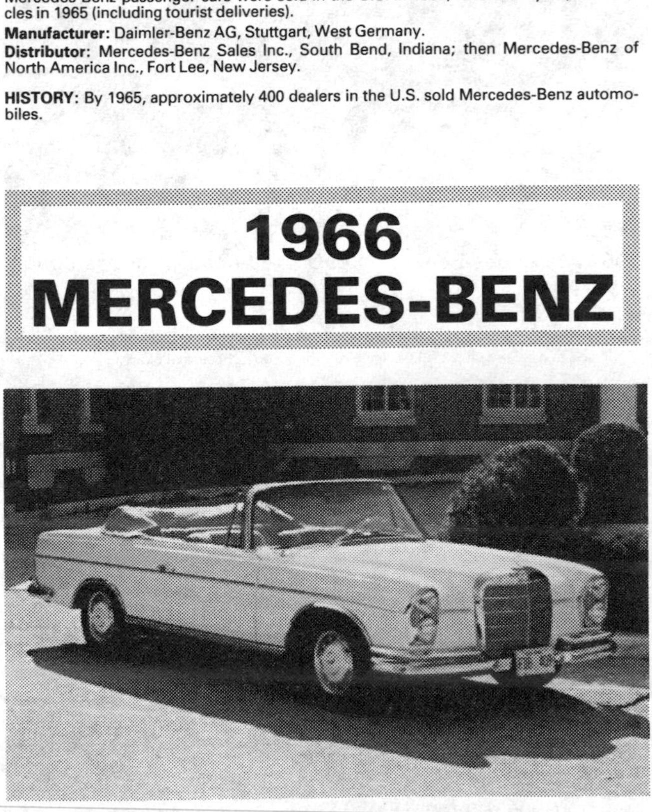

1966 Mercedes-Benz 300SE convertible.

200 SERIES — FOUR — A new 200 four-door sedan replaced the former 190 series, again powered by either a gasoline or diesel engine. The gasoline-powered 1988-cc (121-cid) four developed 105 horsepower using two single-barrel carburetors. The diesel four produced 60 bhp.

220SE — SIX — Only one model in the 220 series remained for 1966, available in coupe and convertible form. The 2195-cc (134-cid) six-cylinder engine developed 134 horsepower, using Bosch fuel injection.

230 SERIES — SIX — This new four-door sedan was similar in appearance to the 200, powered by a new 2308-cc (141-cid), 118-bhp engine. The 230S version, which replaced the 220S, had the same rear fender design (with modified semi-tailfin) as the 200/230, but wore a front end like the 250 with single headlamps and an upper bumper guard bar. The 230S engine used twin two-barrel carburetors and produced 135 bhp.

230SL — SIX — Production of the replacement for the original 190/300SL sports cars continued until late 1966, when it was superseded by the 250SL.

250S/SE — SIX — Another new model was the 250SE, which was built as a coupe, convertible or four-door sedan. Power came from a 2496-cc (152.3-cid) engine, rated 170 bhp with Bosch fuel injection. A lower-priced 250S sedan used a carbureted version of the engine, rated 146 bhp. These were the first examples of the "New Generation" body/chassis, which would be used on the full range of 220-280 series sedans in 1968.

300SE — SIX — Production of the 300SE sedan continued, with a 2996-cc (183-cid) engine under its hood.

600/PULLMAN — GRAND MERCEDES — V-8 — The monstrous Mercedes continued in limited production, and would remain so for another decade and a half.

I.D. DATA: Chassis serial number is on a plate under the hood, on the right side of the firewall. Starting serial number: (200) 160963; (200D) 225648; (230) 000001; (230S) 069693; (220SE cpe) 008909. Engine number is on right side of block.

Model	Body Type & Seating	Engine Type/CID	P.O.E. Price	Weight (lbs.)	Prod. Total
200 SERIES					
200	4-dr Sedan-5/6P	I4/121	3955	2684	Note 1
200D (Dsl)	4-dr Sedan-5/6P	I4/121	4170	2794	Note 1
220SE					
220SE	2-dr Coupe-5P	I6/134	8632	2901	Note 1
220SE	2-dr Conv-5P	I6/134	9420	3190	Note 1
230 SERIES					
230	4-dr Sedan-5/6P	I6/141	4140	2750	Note 1
230S	4-dr Sedan-5/6P	I6/141	4785	2816	Note 1
230SL					
230SL	2-dr Rds-2P	I6/141	6185	2855	Note 2
230SL	2-dr Coupe-2P	I6/141	6343	2855	Note 2
230SL	2-dr Cpe/Rds-2P	I6/141	6587	N/A	Note 2
250 SERIES					
250S	4-dr Sedan-5/6P	I6/152	5747	N/A	Note 1
250SE	2-dr Coupe-5P	I6/152	8959	3063	Note 1
250SE	2-dr Conv-5P	I6/152	9748	3352	Note 1
250SE	4-dr Sedan-5/6P	I6/152	6385	N/A	Note 1
300SE					
300SE	4-dr Sedan-5/6P	I6/183	8048	N/A	Note 1
600/PULLMAN (GRAND MERCEDES)					
600	4-dr Sedan-5P	V8/386	22299	N/A	Note 1
Pullman	4-dr Limo-7P	V8/386	25582	5799	Note 1

Note 1: A total of 191,625 Mercedes-Benz passenger cars (all models) were produced during 1966.

Note 2: A total of 19,831 230SL models were produced during the full model run, 1963-66.

Model Note: Some directories also listed a 300SEL series, priced at $9946 for the sedan, $11,590 for the coupe, and $12,370 for the convertible.

ENGINE DATA: BASE FOUR (200): Inline, overhead-cam four-cylinder. Cast iron block and aluminum head. **Displacement:** 121.3 cu. in. (1988 cc). **Bore & Stroke:** 3.43 x 3.29 in. (87 x 83.6 mm). **Compression Ratio:** 9.0:1. **Brake Horsepower:** 105 (SAE) at 5400 rpm. **Torque:** 123 lbs.-ft. at 3800 rpm. Three main bearings. Solid valve lifters. Two Solex carburetors.

DIESEL FOUR (200D): Inline, overhead-cam four-cylinder. **Displacement:** 121.3 cu. in. (1988 cc). **Bore & Stroke:** 3.43 x 3.29 in. (87 x 83.6 mm). **Compression Ratio:** 21.0:1. **Brake Horsepower:** 60 at 4200 rpm. **Torque:** 87 lbs.-ft. at 2400 rpm. Fuel injection.

BASE SIX (220SE): Inline, overhead-cam six-cylinder. Cast iron block and aluminum head. **Displacement:** 133.9 cu. in. (2195 cc). **Bore & Stroke:** 3.15 x 2.87 in. (80 x 72.8 mm). **Compression Ratio:** 8.7:1. **Brake Horsepower:** 134 (SAE) at 5000 rpm. **Torque:** 152 lbs.-ft. at 4100 rpm. Four main bearings. Solid valve lifters. Bosch fuel injection.

BASE SIX (230, 230S, 230SL): Inline, overhead-cam six-cylinder. Cast iron block and aluminum head. **Displacement:** 140.8 cu. in. (2308 cc). **Bore & Stroke:** 3.23 x 2.87 in. (82 x 72.8 mm). **Compression Ratio:** (230/S) 9.0:1; (230SL) 9.3:1. **Brake Horsepower:** (230) 118 at 5400 rpm; (230S) 135 at 5600 rpm; (230SL) 170 at 5600 rpm. **Torque:** (230) 137 lbs.-ft. at 3800 rpm; (230S) 145 lbs.-ft. at 4200 rpm; (230SL) 159 lbs.-ft. at 4500 rpm. Four main bearings. Solid valve lifters. Two Solex single-barrel carburetors (230); two twin-barrel carburetors (230S); or Bosch multi-point fuel injection (230SL).

BASE SIX (250S, 250SE): Inline, overhead-cam six-cylinder. Cast iron block and aluminum head. **Displacement:** 152.3 cu. in. (2496 cc). **Bore & Stroke:** 3.23 x 3.10 in. (82 x 78.8 mm). **Compression Ratio:** 9.3:1. **Brake Horsepower:** (250) 146 at 5600 rpm; (250SE) 170 (SAE) at 5600 rpm. **Torque:** 174 lbs.-ft. at 4500 rpm. Four main bearings. Solid valve lifters. Two two-barrel carburetors (250S) or Bosch fuel injection (250SE).

BASE SIX (300SE): Inline, overhead-cam six-cylinder. Aluminum alloy block and head. **Displacement:** 183 cu. in. (2996 cc). **Bore & Stroke:** 3.35 x 3.46 in. (85 x 88 mm). **Compression Ratio:** 9.0:1. **Brake Horsepower:** 185 (SAE) at 5200 rpm. **Torque:** 205 lbs.-ft. at 4000 rpm. Seven main bearings. Solid valve lifters. Fuel injection.

BASE V-8 (600/Pullman): 90-degree, overhead-valve, "vee" type eight-cylinder. Cast iron block and aluminum heads. **Displacement:** 386.2 cu. in. (6329 cc). **Bore & Stroke:** 4.05 x 3.74 in. (103 x 95 mm). **Compression Ratio:** 9.0:1. **Brake Horsepower:** 300 at 4100 rpm. **Torque:** 435 lbs.-ft. at 3000 rpm. Five main bearings. Solid valve lifters. Bosch fuel injection.

CHASSIS DATA: Wheelbase: (200) 106.3 in.; (220SE) 108.3 in.; (230) 106.3 in.; (230S) 108.3 in.; (230SL) 94.5 in.; (250SE/300SE) 108.3 in.; (600) 126 in.; (600 Pullman) 153.5 in. **Overall Length:** (200) 186.2 in.; (220SE) 192.1 in.; (230) 186.2 in.; (230S) 191.9 in.; (230SL) 169 in.; (250SE/300SE) 192 in.; (600) 218 in.; (600 Pullman) 245.7 in. **Height:** (200) 58.9 in.; (220SE) 55.9 in.; (230) 58.9 in.; (230S) 59.1 in.; (230SL) 51.3 in.; (250SE sed) 56.7 in.; (600 Pullman) 59.4 in. **Width:** (200) 70.7 in.; (220SE) 72.7 in.; (230/S) 70.7 in.; (230SL) 69.2 in.; (250SE/300SE) 72.7 in.; (600 Pullman) 76.8 in. **Front Tread:** (200) 58.4 in.; (220SE) 58.4 in.; (230/S) 58.4 in.; (230SL) 58.5 in.; (250SE/300SE) 58.4 in.; (600 Pullman) 62.4 in. **Rear Tread:** (200) 58.5 in.; (220SE) 58.5 in.; (230SL) 58.5 in.; (230/S) 58.5 in.; (250SE) 58.5 in.; (300SE) 58.7 in.; (600 Pullman) 62 in. **Standard Tires:** (200) 7.00x13; (220SE) 7.25x13; (230) 7.00x13; (230S) 7.25x13; (230SL) 7.25x14; (250SE) 7.25x13; (600 Pullman) 9.00x15.

TECHNICAL: Layout: front-engine, rear-drive. **Transmission:** four-speed manual except (300SE, 600) automatic standard; automatic optional on other models. **Steering:** recirculating ball. **Suspension (front):** (200/220/230 series) unequal-length A-arms, coil springs and anti-roll bar; (300SE, 600) wishbones with air springs, automatic leveling and anti-roll bar. **Suspension (rear):** (200, 220SE, 230SL) single low-pivot swing axles with trailing arms and coil springs; (230/250 series) single low-pivot swing axles with trailing arms, coil springs and automatic leveling; (300SE, 600) swinging semi-axles with trailing lower radius arms, air springs, automatic leveling and anti-roll bar. **Brakes:** (200/220/230/250 series) front disc, rear drum; (300SE, 600) front/rear disc. **Body Construction:** steel unibody with auxiliary front frame.

MAJOR OPTIONS: Automatic transmission ($342). Power steering.

PERFORMANCE: Top Speed: (200) about 99 mph; (200D) about 85 mph; (220SE) about 106 mph; (230) about 109 mph; (230SL) 125 mph; (300SE) about 118 mph. **Acceleration (0-60 mph):** (230SL) 9.9 sec. **Acceleration (quarter-mile):** (230SL) 17.0 sec. (83 mph). **Fuel Mileage:** (200) about 21 mpg; (200D) about 35 mpg; (220SE) about 22 mpg; (230) about 21 mpg; (230SL) about 17 mpg; (300SE) about 19 mpg.

PRODUCTION/SALES: Approximately 16,465 Mercedes-Benz vehicles were sold in the U.S. in 1966.

Manufacturer: Daimler-Benz AG, Stuttgart, West Germany.

Distributor: Mercedes-Benz of North America Inc., Fort Lee, New Jersey.

HISTORY: Production of the next generation of the Mercedes two-seater (250SL) began in 1966; see next listing for details. By this time, the 220 and 300 series were fading out of the lineup.

1967 MERCEDES-BENZ

200 SERIES — FOUR — Production of the smallest-engined Mercedes models continued with little change.

230 SERIES — SIX — Production of the sedan with 2308-cc (141-cid) engine continued with little change.

250 SERIES — SIX — Only the four-door sedans were listed as available in the U.S. this year, in either 250S form (146 bhp) or as a 250SE (170 bhp). The former engine used two carburetors; the latter was fuel injected.

250SL — SIX — A larger engine went into the next edition of the Mercedes two-seat sports car, which would remain in production for only one year. The 2496-cc overhead-cam six had a 6-mm longer stroke than its predecessor powerplant, and produced the same horsepower (170). Torque output got a boost by 15, however, to 174 pound-feet. The new engine had seven main (crankshaft) bearings, versus four for the former version. Disc brakes were now used at both front and rear, and the 250SL had an axle ratio of 3.69:1. New standard equipment included a collapsible steering wheel.

600/PULLMAN — V-8 — The giant Mercedes "Grosser" sedan remained available on special order in the U.S., with little change evident.

I.D. DATA: Chassis serial number is on the right side of the firewall, or on the radiator cowl. Engine number is on right side of block.

Model	Body Type & Seating	Engine Type/CID	P.O.E. Price	Weight (lbs.)	Prod. Total
200 SERIES					
200	4-dr Sedan-5/6P	I4/121	4084	2684	Note 1
200D (Dsl)	4-dr Sedan-5/6P	I4/121	4305	2794	Note 1
230 SERIES					
230	4-dr Sedan-5/6P	I6/141	4280	2750	Note 1
230S	4-dr Sedan-5/6P	I6/141	4910	2816	Note 1
250 SERIES					
250S	4-dr Sedan-5/6P	I6/152	5747	3014	Note 1
250SE	4-dr Sedan-5/6P	I6/152	6385	3080	Note 1
250SL					
250SL	2-dr Rds-2P	I6/152	6485	2749	Note 2
250SL	2-dr Coupe-2P	I6/152	6647	2793	Note 2
250SL	2-dr Cpe/Rds-2P	I6/152	6897	2848	Note 2
600/PULLMAN (GRAND MERCEDES)					
600	4-dr Sedan-5P	V8/386	22299	N/A	Note 1
Pullman	4-dr Limo-7P	V8/386	25582	5799	Note 1

Note 1: A total of 200,470 Mercedes-Benz passenger cars (all models) were produced during 1967.

Note 2: A total of 5,196 250SL models were produced during the full (short) model run, 1966-67.

Model Note: Leftover 230SL sports cars were listed in U.S. directories in 1967, priced as in 1966 (their final production year).

ENGINE DATA: BASE FOUR (200): Inline, overhead-cam four-cylinder. Cast iron block and aluminum head. **Displacement:** 121.3 cu. in. (1988 cc). **Bore & Stroke:** 3.43 x 3.29 in. (87 x 83.6 mm). **Compression Ratio:** 9.0:1. **Brake Horsepower:** 105 (SAE) at 5400 rpm. **Torque:** 123 lbs.-ft. at 3800 rpm. Three main bearings. Solid valve lifters. Two Solex carburetors.

DIESEL FOUR (200D): Inline, overhead-cam four-cylinder. **Displacement:** 121.3 cu. in. (1988 cc). **Bore & Stroke:** 3.43 x 3.29 in. (87 x 83.6 mm). **Compression Ratio:** 21.0:1. **Brake Horsepower:** 60 at 4200 rpm. **Torque:** 87 lbs.-ft. at 2400 rpm. Fuel injection.

BASE SIX (230, 230S): Inline, overhead-cam six-cylinder. Cast iron block and aluminum head. **Displacement:** 140.8 cu. in. (2308 cc). **Bore & Stroke:** 3.23 x 2.87 in. (82 x 72.8 mm). **Compression Ratio:** 9.0:1. **Brake Horsepower:** (230) 118 at 5400 rpm; (230S) 135 at 5600 rpm. **Torque:** (230) 137 lbs.-ft. at 3800 rpm; (230S) 145 lbs.-ft. at 4200 rpm. Four main bearings. Solid valve lifters. Two single-barrel carburetors (230) or two two-barrel carburetors (230S).

BASE SIX (250S, 250SE): Inline, overhead-cam six-cylinder. Cast iron block and aluminum head. **Displacement:** 152.3 cu. in. (2496 cc). **Bore & Stroke:** 3.23 x 3.10 in. (82 x 78.8 mm). **Compression Ratio:** 9.3:1. **Brake Horsepower:** (250) 146 at 5600 rpm; (250SE) 170 (SAE) at 5600 rpm. **Torque:** 174 lbs.-ft. at 4500 rpm. Four main bearings. Solid valve lifters. Two two-barrel carburetors (250S) or Bosch fuel injection (250SE).

BASE SIX (250SL): Inline, overhead-cam six-cylinder. Cast iron block and aluminum head. **Displacement:** 152.3 cu. in. (2496 cc). **Bore & Stroke:** 3.23 x 3.10 in. (82 x 78.8 mm). **Compression Ratio:** 9.3:1. **Brake Horsepower:** 170 (SAE) at 5600 rpm. **Torque:** 174 lbs.-ft. at 4500 rpm. Seven main bearings. Solid valve lifters. Bosch fuel injection.

BASE V-8 (600/Pullman): 90-degree, overhead-valve, "vee" type eight-cylinder. Cast iron block and aluminum heads. **Displacement:** 386.2 cu. in. (6329 cc). **Bore & Stroke:** 4.05 x 3.74 in. (103 x 95 mm). **Compression Ratio:** 9.0:1. **Brake Horsepower:** 300 at 4100 rpm. **Torque:** 435 lbs.-ft. at 3000 rpm. Five main bearings. Solid valve lifters. Bosch fuel injection.

CHASSIS DATA: Wheelbase: (200) 106.3 in.; (230) 106.3 in.; (230S) 108.3 in.; (250SL) 94.5 in.; (250SE) 108.3 in.; (600 Pullman) 153.5 in. **Overall Length:** (200) 186.2 in.; (230) 186.2 in.; (230S) 191.9 in.; (250SL) 168.7 in.; (250SE) 192 in.; (600 Pullman) 245.7 in. **Height:** (200) 58.9 in.; (230) 58.9 in.; (230S) 59.1 in.; (250SL) 52 in.; (250SE) 56.7 in.; (600 Pullman) 59.4 in. **Width:** (200) 70.7 in.; (230/S) 70.7 in.; (250SL) 69.2 in.; (250SE) 72.7 in.; (600 Pullman) 76.8 in. **Front Tread:** (200) 58.4 in.; (230/S) 58.4 in.; (250SL) 58.4 in.; (600 Pullman) 62.4 in. **Rear Tread:** (200) 58.5 in.; (230/S) 58.5 in.; (250SL) 58.5 in.; (250S/SE) 58.5 in.; (600 Pullman) 62 in. **Standard Tires:** (200) 7.00x13; (230) 7.00x13; (230S) 7.25x13; (250SL) 7.25x14 or 185x14; (250SE) 7.25x13; (600 Pullman) 9.00x15.

TECHNICAL: Layout: front-engine, rear-drive. **Transmission:** four-speed manual except (600) automatic standard; automatic optional on other models. **Steering:** recirculating ball. **Suspension (front):** (200/230/250 series) unequal-length A-arms, coil springs and anti-roll bar; (600) wishbones with air springs, automatic leveling and anti-roll bar. **Suspension (rear):** (200, 250SL) single low-pivot swing axles with trailing arms and coil springs; (230/250 series) single low-pivot swing axles with trailing arms, coil springs and automatic leveling; (600) swinging semi-axles with trailing lower radius arms, air springs, automatic leveling and anti-roll bar. **Brakes:** (200/230/250 series) front disc, rear drum; (250SL, 600) front/rear disc. **Body Construction:** steel unibody with auxiliary front frame.

MAJOR OPTIONS: Automatic transmission ($342). Power steering.

PERFORMANCE: Similar to 1966.

PRODUCTION/SALES: Approximately 20,691 Mercedes-Benz vehicles were sold in the U.S. in 1967.

Manufacturer: Daimler-Benz AG, Stuttgart, West Germany.

Distributor: Mercedes-Benz of North America Inc., Fort Lee, New Jersey.

1968-69 MERCEDES-BENZ

200/220 SERIES — FOUR — Production of the 200 sedans (gas and diesel) continued into early 1968, when they were replaced by the "New Generation" 220 and 220D. A total restyling of the Mercedes sedan lineup followed the design introduced in 1966 with the 250 series. The new grille kept the traditional look, but was considerably lower and wider. No evidence of vestigial tailfins remained. The new sedans had a lower hood, deeper beltline, and flatter rear deck. This new chassis rode a 108.3-inch wheelbase. For these "junior" Mercedes models, the new chassis was designated W114/115 and had thinner C-pillars than on the senior models. Each Mercedes sedan had huge amber parking lights below each headlamp.

230 SERIES — SIX — The six-cylinder version of the "junior" Mercedes also benefited from "New Generation" styling, powered by a 2308-cc (141-cid) engine.

250 SERIES — SIX — Since this was the first series to adopt the new styling, it continued with less change than the other Mercedes sedans.

280 SERIES — SIX — Known as the S-Class, the upper-level Mercedes' version of the "New Generation" got the designation W108. Under the hood was a 2778-cc engine that developed 157 horsepower in 'S' form, or 180 bhp with Bosch fuel injection in the 280SE.

280SL — SIX — After only one year with a 2496-cc engine, the Mercedes two-seat sports car moved up to a 2778-cc six, as the result of an increase in bore dimension. That boosted output by 10 bhp, to 180 horsepower (SAE); and torque rose by 19 pound-feet, to 193. Also new was an optional ZF five-speed manual gearbox, with a $500 price tag. The U.S. version of the 280SL had a 4.08:1 final-drive ratio, with 3.69:1 and 3.92:1 available on request. Side-marker lights also were installed.

300SEL — 2.8 — SIX — A longer-wheelbase (W109) chassis was used for the largest standard Mercedes, measuring 112.2 inches between the wheels. Power came from the same 2.8-liter engine used in the 280SL sports car.

600/PULLMAN — V-8 — The giant Mercedes seven-passenger sedan remained available in the U.S., with little change evident. An automatic transmission was standard.

I.D. DATA: Chassis serial number is on the right side of the firewall, or on the radiator cowl. Engine number is on right side of block. Starting serial number (1968): 000001. Beginning in 1969, the serial number consists of 14 symbols. The first six symbols (all digits) indicate the model; the next two indicate standard (10) or automatic (12) transmission. The final six digits form the sequental production number.

Model	Body Type & Seating	Engine Type/CID	P.O.E. Price	Weight (lbs.)	Prod. Total
220 SERIES					
220	4-dr Sedan-5P	I4/134	4360	2948	Note 1
220D (Dsl)	4-dr Sedan-5P	I4/134	4494	3036	Note 1
230 SERIES					
230	4-dr Sedan-5P	I6/141	4544	3036	Note 1
250 SERIES					
250	4-dr Sedan-5P	I6/152	5060	3080	Note 1
280 SERIES					
280S	4-dr Sedan-5P	I6/169	5897	3278	Note 1
280SE	4-dr Sedan-5P	I6/169	6222	3344	Note 1
280SE	2-dr Coupe-5P	I6/169	9174	3454	Note 1
280SE	2-dr Conv-5P	I6/169	9967	3630	Note 1
280SEL	4-dr Sedan-5P	I6/169	6622	N/A	Note 1
280SL					
280SL	2-dr Rds-2P	I6/169	6485	3102	Note 2
280SL	2-dr Coupe-2P	I6/169	6647	3102	Note 2
280SL	2-dr Cpe/Rds-2P	I6/169	6897	3102	Note 2
300 SERIES					
300SEL 2.8	4-dr Sedan-5/6P	I6/169	9400	N/A	Note 1
600/PULLMAN (GRAND MERCEDES)					
600	4-dr Sedan-5P	V8/386	22299	N/A	Note 1
Pullman	4-dr Limo-7P	V8/386	25582	5799	Note 1

Note 1: A total of 216,284 Mercedes-Benz passenger cars (all models) were produced during 1968, followed by 256,713 in 1969.

Note 2: A total of 23,885 280SL models were produced during the full model run, 1967-71.

Price Note: Figures shown were valid in 1968. Prices rose for 1969, ranging from $4560 for the 220 sedan to $6802 for the 280SL roadster (convertible) and $10,472 for the 280SE convertible.

ENGINE DATA: BASE FOUR (220): Inline, overhead-cam four-cylinder. Cast iron block and aluminum head. **Displacement:** 134 cu. in. (2195 cc). **Bore & Stroke:** 3.15 x 2.87 in. (80 x 72.8 mm). **Compression Ratio:** 9.0:1. **Brake Horsepower:** 116 at 5200 rpm. **Torque:** 142 lbs.-ft. at 3000 rpm. Five main bearings. Solid valve lifters. Two carburetors.

DIESEL FOUR (220D): Inline, overhead-cam four-cylinder. **Displacement:** 134 cu. in. (2195 cc). **Bore & Stroke:** 3.15 x 2.87 in. (80 x 72.8 mm). **Compression Ratio:** 21.0:1. **Brake Horsepower:** 65 at 4200 rpm. **Torque:** 96 lbs.-ft. at 2400 rpm. Fuel injection.

BASE SIX (230): Inline, overhead-cam six-cylinder. Cast iron block and aluminum head. **Displacement:** 140.7 cu. in. (2308 cc). **Bore & Stroke:** 3.23 x 2.87 in. (82 x 72.8 mm). **Compression Ratio:** 9.0:1. **Brake Horsepower:** 135 at 5600 rpm. **Torque:** 145 lbs.-ft. at 3800 rpm. Four main bearings. Solid valve lifters. Two carburetors.

BASE SIX (250): Inline, overhead-cam six-cylinder. Cast iron block and aluminum head. **Displacement:** 152.3 cu. in. (2496 cc). **Bore & Stroke:** 3.23 x 3.10 in. (82 x 78.8 mm). **Compression Ratio:** 9.0:1. **Brake Horsepower:** 146 at 5600 rpm. **Torque:** 161 lbs.-ft. at 3800 rpm. Solid valve lifters. Two carburetors.

BASE SIX (280S): Inline, overhead-cam six-cylinder. Cast iron block and aluminum head. **Displacement:** 169.5 cu. in. (2778 cc). **Bore & Stroke:** 3.41 x 3.10 in. (86.6 x 78.8 mm). **Compression Ratio:** 9.0:1. **Brake Horsepower:** 157 at 5400 rpm. **Torque:** 181 lbs.-ft. at 3800 rpm. Seven main bearings. Solid valve lifters. Two carburetors.

BASE SIX (280SE/SEL, 280SL, 300SEL): Same as 2778-cc six above, except — **Compression Ratio:** 9.5:1. **Brake Horsepower:** 180 at 5750 rpm. **Torque:** 193 lbs.-ft. at 4500 rpm. Bosch fuel injection.

BASE V-8 (600/Pullman): 90-degree, overhead-valve, "vee" type eight-cylinder. Cast iron block and aluminum heads. **Displacement:** 386.2 cu. in. (6329 cc). **Bore & Stroke:** 4.05 x 3.74 in. (103 x 95 mm). **Compression Ratio:** 9.0:1. **Brake Horsepower:** 300 at 4100 rpm. **Torque:** 434 lbs.-ft. at 3000 rpm. Five main bearings. Solid valve lifters. Bosch fuel injection.

CHASSIS DATA: Wheelbase: (220/230/250/280) 108.3 in.; (280SL) 94.5 in.; (300SEL) 112.2 in.; (600) 126 in.; (600 Pullman) 153.5 in. **Overall Length:** (220/230/250) 184.5 in.; (280) 192.9 in.; (280SL) 168.7 in.; (300SEL) 197 in.; (600) 218 in.; (600 Pullman) 245.7 in. **Height:** (220/230/250/280) 56.7 in.; (280SL) 52.0 in.; (300SEL) 55.7 in.; (600) 58.5 in.; (600 Pullman) 59.1 in. **Width:** (220/230/250) 69.7 in.; (280) 71.3 in.; (280SL) 69.3 in.; (300SEL) 71.3 in.; (600) 76.8 in. **Front Tread:** (220/230/250) 56.8 in.; (280) 58.4 in.; (280SL) 58.4 in.; (300SEL) 58.4 in.; (600) 62.5 in. **Rear Tread:** (220/230/250) 56.7 in.; (280) 58.5 in.; (280SL) 58.5 in.; (300SEL) 58.7 in.; (600) 62.2 in. **Standard Tires:** (220/230/250) 6.95x14; (280) 7.35x14; (280SL) 185x14; (300SEL) 7.35x13; (600 Pullman) 9.00x15.

TECHNICAL: Layout: front-engine, rear-drive. **Transmission:** four-speed manual except (600) automatic standard; automatic optional on other models; ZF five-speed optional on 280SL. **Steering:** recirculating ball. **Suspension (front):** (220/230/250/280 series) unequal-length A-arms, coil springs and anti-roll bar; (600) wishbones with air springs, automatic leveling and anti-roll bar. **Suspension (rear):** (220, 280SL) single low-pivot swing axles with trailing arms and coil springs; (230/250 series) single low-pivot swing axles with trailing arms, coil springs and automatic leveling; (600) swinging semi-axles with trailing lower radius arms, air springs, automatic leveling and anti-roll bar. **Brakes:** (200/230/250/280 series) front disc, rear drum (later, four-wheel disc); (280SL, 600) front/rear disc. **Body Construction:** steel unibody with auxiliary front frame.

MAJOR OPTIONS: Four-speed automatic transmission ($342). Power steering ($171-$200). Air conditioning ($417-$562). Sliding steel sunroof. Leather upholstery. Power windows. AM/FM radio. Whitewall tires. Tinted glass. Rear jump seat (280SL). Roof ski brackets (280SL). Removable steel hardtop (280SL).

PRODUCTION/SALES: Approximately 24,553 Mercedes-Benz vehicles were sold in the U.S. in 1968, followed by 26,193 in 1969.

Manufacturer: Daimler-Benz AG, Stuttgart, West Germany.

Distributor: Mercedes-Benz of North America Inc., Fort Lee, New Jersey.

HISTORY: Mercedes-Benz promoted the 280SL as "the sum total of everything the Mercedes-Benz engineers have learned about high-performance sporting machinery."

1970 MERCEDES-BENZ

1970 Mercedes-Benz 280SE 3.5 cabriolet. (Christie's)

220 SERIES — FOUR — Production of the gas- and diesel-engine "junior" Mercedes continued with little change.

250 SERIES — SIX — A new 250C hardtop coupe with all-disc brakes joined the 250 sedan this year. Under the coupe's hood was the 2778-cc (169.5-cid) six-cylinder engine, whereas the sedan kept the smaller 2496-cc six. Otherwise, little change was evident.

280 SERIES — SIX — Production of the six-cylinder 280 series continued with minimal change. The 280S carried a carbureted 169.5-cid engine that developed 157 horsepower; the 280SE/SEL had a 180-bhp version, as in the 280SL sports car.

280SE — 3.5 — V-8 — A new 213.5-cid V-8 engine with Bosch fuel injection that developed 230 horsepower went into the 280SE coupe and converible. Power steering, air conditioning and a radio were standard.

280SL — SIX — Production of the Mercedes two-seat sports car continued with little change.

300SEL — 3.5/6.3 — V-8 — Automatic transmission, power steering, air conditioning and radio were standard in the upper-ranked Mercedes sedan, which could have either the 213.5-cid V-8 or the big 386-cid V-8 (as in the 600 Pullman).

600/PULLMAN — V-8 — The giant Mercedes seven-passenger sedan remained available in the U.S., with little change evident. The shorter-wheelbase version also was available. An automatic transmission, power steering, air conditioning and radio were standard.

I.D. DATA: Chassis serial number is under the hood on the right side of the firewall, or at the left front near the A-pillar. The chassis serial number consists of 14 symbols. The first six symbols (all digits) indicate the model; the next two indicate standard (10) or automatic (12) transmission. The final six digits form the sequental production number. Starting serial number: (220) 037069; (220D) 084964; (250) 033533; (250C) 000001; (280S) 035214; (280SE/SEL sedan) 036081; (280SL) 011948; (280SE cpe/conv) 003549; (300SEL 3.5 sedan) 002221; (300SEL 6.3 sedan) 002839; (600 sedan) 001435.

Model	Body Type & Seating	Engine Type/CID	P.O.E. Price	Weight (lbs.)	Prod. Total
220 SERIES					
220	4-dr Sedan-5P	I4/134	4680	2948	Note 1
220D (Dsl)	4-dr Sedan-5P	I4/134	4782	3036	Note 1
250 SERIES					
250	4-dr Sedan-5P	I6/152	5208	3080	Note 1
250C	2-dr Coupe-5P	I6/169	6260	3100	Note 1
280 SERIES					
280S	4-dr Sedan-5P	I6/169	6273	3278	Note 1
280SE	4-dr Sedan-5P	I6/169	6561	3344	Note 1
280SEL	4-dr Sedan-5P	I6/169	N/A	N/A	Note 1
280SE 3.5	2-dr Coupe-5P	V8/213	11111	3454	Note 1
280SE 3.5	2-dr Conv-5P	V8/213	11924	3630	Note 1
280SL					
280SL	2-dr Rds-2P	I6/169	6952	3102	Note 2
280SL	2-dr Coupe-2P	I6/169	7118	3102	Note 2
280SL	2-dr Cpe/Rds-2P	I6/169	7374	3102	Note 2
300SEL					
3.5	4-dr Sedan-5/6P	V8/213	11327	N/A	Note 1
6.3	4-dr Sedan-5/6P	V8/386	15122	N/A	Note 1
600/PULLMAN (GRAND MERCEDES)					
600	4-dr Sedan-5P	V8/386	24600	N/A	Note 1
Pullman	4-dr Limo-7P	V8/386	28120	5820	Note 1

Note 1: A total of 280,419 Mercedes-Benz passenger cars (all models) were produced during 1970.

Note 2: A total of 23,885 280SL models were produced during the full model run, 1967-71.

Price Note: Figures shown for 300SEL and 600 include dealer preparation charges.

ENGINE DATA: BASE FOUR (220): Inline, overhead-cam four-cylinder. Cast iron block and aluminum head. **Displacement:** 134 cu. in. (2195 cc). **Bore & Stroke:** 3.15 x 2.87 in. (80 x 72.8 mm). **Compression Ratio:** 9.0:1. **Brake Horsepower:** 116 at 5200 rpm. **Torque:** 142 lbs.-ft. at 3000 rpm. Five main bearings. Solid valve lifters.

DIESEL FOUR (220D): Inline, overhead-cam four-cylinder. **Displacement:** 134 cu. in. (2195 cc). **Bore & Stroke:** 3.15 x 2.87 in. (80 x 72.8 mm). **Compression Ratio:** 21.0:1. **Brake Horsepower:** 65 at 4200 rpm. **Torque:** 96 lbs.-ft. at 2400 rpm. Fuel injection.

BASE SIX (250): Inline, overhead-cam six-cylinder. Cast iron block and aluminum head. **Displacement:** 152.3 cu. in. (2496 cc). **Bore & Stroke:** 3.23 x 3.10 in. (82 x 78.8 mm). **Compression Ratio:** 9.0:1. **Brake Horsepower:** 146 at 5600 rpm. **Torque:** 161 lbs.-ft. at 3800 rpm. Four main bearings. Solid valve lifters.

BASE SIX (250C, 280S): Inline, overhead-cam six-cylinder. Cast iron block and aluminum head. **Displacement:** 169.5 cu. in. (2778 cc). **Bore & Stroke:** 3.41 x 3.10 in. (86.6 x 78.8 mm). **Compression Ratio:** 9.0:1. **Brake Horsepower:** 157 at 5400 rpm. **Torque:** 181 lbs.-ft. at 3800 rpm. Seven main bearings. Solid valve lifters.

BASE SIX (280SE/SEL, 280SL): Same as 2778-cc six above, except — **Compression Ratio:** 9.5:1. **Brake Horsepower:** 180 at 5750 rpm. **Torque:** 193 lbs.-ft. at 4500 rpm.

BASE V-8 (280SE 3.5 cpe/conv, 300SEL 3.5): 90-degree, overhead-cam, "vee" type eight-cylinder. Cast iron block and aluminum heads. **Displacement:** 213.5 cu. in. (3499 cc). **Bore & Stroke:** 3.62 x 2.59 in. (92 x 65.8 mm). **Compression Ratio:** 9.5:1. **Brake Horsepower:** 230 at 6050 rpm. **Torque:** 231 lbs.-ft. at 4200 rpm. Five main bearings. Solid valve lifters. Bosch fuel injection.

BASE V-8 (300SEL 6.3, 600/Pullman): 90-degree, overhead-valve, "vee" type eight-cylinder. Cast iron block and aluminum heads. **Displacement:** 386.2 cu. in. (6329 cc). **Bore & Stroke:** 4.05 x 3.74 in. (103 x 95 mm). **Compression Ratio:** 8.1:1. **Brake Horsepower:** 300 at 4100 rpm. **Torque:** 434 lbs.-ft. at 3000 rpm. Five main bearings. Solid valve lifters. Bosch fuel injection.

CHASSIS DATA: Wheelbase: (220/250/280) 108.3 in.; (280SL) 94.5 in.; (280SEL, 300SEL) 112.2 in.; (600) 126 in.; (600 Pullman) 153.5 in. **Overall Length:** (220/250) 184.5 in.; (280) 192.9 in.; (280SL) 168.7 in.; (280SEL, 300SEL) 197 in.; (600) 218 in.; (600 Pullman) 245.7 in. **Height:** (220/250/280 sed) 56.7 in.; (250C) 54.9 in.; (280SL) 52 in.; (280SE 3.5 cpe/conv) 55.9 in.; (300SEL) 55.5-55.9 in.; (600) 58.5 in.; (600 Pullman) 59 in. **Width:** (220/250) 69.7 in.; (250C) 70.5 in.; (280) 71.3 in.; (280SL) 69.3 in.; (280SE 3.5 cpe/conv) 72.6 in.; (300SEL) 71.3 in.; (600) 76.8 in. **Front Tread:** (220/250) 56.8 in.; (280) 58.4 in.; (280SL) 58.4 in.; (280SE 3.5 cpe/conv) 58.3 in.; (300SEL 3.5) 58.3 in.; (300SEL 6.3) 58.7 in.; (600) 62.5 in. **Rear Tread:** (220/250) 56.7 in.; (280) 58.5 in.; (280SL) 58.5 in.; (280SE 3.5 cpe/conv) 58.7 in.; (300SEL 3.5) 58.7 in.; (300SEL 6.3) 58.5 in.; (600) 62.2 in. **Standard Tires:** (220/230/250) 6.95x14; (280) 7.35x14; (280SL) 185x14; (280SE 3.5 cpe/conv) 7.35x14; (300SEL 3.5) 7.35x14; (300SEL 6.3) 195x14; (600 Pullman) 9.00x15.

TECHNICAL: Layout: front-engine, rear-drive. **Transmission:** four-speed manual except (300SEL, 600) automatic standard; automatic optional on other models; ZF five-speed optional on 280SL. **Steering:** recirculating ball. **Suspension (front):** unequal-length A-arms, coil springs and anti-roll bar; (600) wishbones with air springs, automatic leveling and anti-roll bar. **Suspension (rear):** single low-pivot swing axles with coil springs and anti-roll bar; (600) swinging semi-axles with trailing lower radius arms, air springs, automatic leveling and anti-roll bar. **Brakes:** front/rear disc. **Body Construction:** steel unibody with auxiliary front frame.

MAJOR OPTIONS: Automatic transmission. Power steering. Air conditioning.

PRODUCTION/SALES: Approximately 29,108 Mercedes-Benz vehicles were sold in the U.S. in 1970.

Manufacturer: Daimler-Benz AG, Stuttgart, West Germany.

Distributor: Mercedes-Benz of North America Inc., Fort Lee, New Jersey.

1971 MERCEDES-BENZ

1971 Mercedes-Benz 300SEL 6.3-liter saloon. (Christie's)

220 SERIES — FOUR — Production of the only four-cylinder Mercedes-Benz sedans continued with little change, except for a substantial price hike this year. Both engines were 134-cid displacement, developing 116 horsepower (gasoline) or 65 bhp (diesel). Even these least-expensive models had fully independent suspension and all-disc brakes. An automatic transmission was optional; four-speed manual gearbox standard.

250 SERIES — SIX — A substantial price hike was the major change for the 250 coupe and sedan, both now powered by a 2778-cc (169.5-cid) six-cylinder engine that developed 157 horsepower. Dimensions were virtually identical to the four-cylinder 220 series.

280 SERIES — SIX — Production of the 280S, SE and SEL sedans continued with little change. Each was powered by a 169.5-cid six-cylinder engine, but the latter two had 180 horsepower available and the 280S had only 157 bhp.

280SE 3.5 — V-8 — A fuel-injected 213.5-cid V-8 engine powered the coupe and convertible of the 280 series, which were similar in size to their six-cylinder sedan mates. Not all U.S. directories of imported models listed the coupe and convertible this year.

280SL — SIX — This would be the final season in America for the 280SL sports car. Late in 1971, a new R107 generation emerged, to be named 350SL, taking advantage of technical advances from Daimler-Benz.

300SEL — 3.5/6.3 — V-8 — Two very different V-8 engines were available under the hood of the 112.2-inch wheelbase 300SEL. The 300SEL 3.5 used a 213.5-cid V-8 that developed 230 horsepower, while the 300SEL 6.3 adopted the big 386-cid V-8 as installed in the mighty 600 series.

600/PULLMAN — V-8 — The giant Mercedes seven-passenger sedan and its five-passenger counterpart remained minimally available in the U.S., with little change evident.

I.D. DATA: Depending on the model, the Mercedes-Benz chassis serial number is under the hood on the right side of the firewall, on right front frame rail, on the radiator cowl, at the B-pillar, or atop the instrument panel. The chassis serial number consists of 14 symbols. The first six symbols (all digits) indicate the model; the next two indicate standard (10) or automatic (12) transmission. The final six digits form the sequential production number. Starting serial number: (220) 057330; (220D) 142680; 250) 000001; (250C) 002362; (280S) 054244; (280SE) 059236; (280SL) 018506. Engine number is on right side of block.

Model	Body Type & Seating	Engine Type/CID	P.O.E. Price	Weight (lbs.)	Prod. Total
220 SERIES					
220	4-dr Sedan-5P	I4/134	5312	2880	Note 1
220D (Dsl)	4-dr Sedan-5P	I4/134	5419	2961	Note 1
250 SERIES					
250	4-dr Sedan-5P	I6/169	6378	2989	Note 1
250C	2-dr Coupe-5P	I6/169	7373	2993	Note 1
280 SERIES					
280S	4-dr Sedan-5P	I6/169	7370	3148	Note 1
280SE	4-dr Sedan-5P	I6/169	7661	3206	Note 1
280SEL	4-dr Sedan-5P	I6/169	8492	3298	Note 1
280SE 3.5	2-dr Cpe-5P	V8/213	13766	3687	Note 1
280SE 3.5	2-dr Conv-5P	V8/213	14509	3687	Note 1
280SL					
280SL	2-dr Rds-2P	I6/169	7469	2891	Note 2
280SL	2-dr Coupe-2P	I6/169	7642	2891	Note 2
280SL	2-dr Cpe/Rds-2P	I6/169	7909	2891	Note 2
300SEL					
3.5	4-dr Sedan-5P	V8/213	12886	3838	Note 1
6.3	4-dr Sedan-5P	V8/386	16275	4070	Note 1
600/PULLMAN (GRAND MERCEDES)					
600	4-dr Sedan-5P	V8/386	26530	5469	Note 1
Pullman	4-dr Limo-7P	V8/386	30120	6031	Note 1

Note 1: A total of 284,230 Mercedes-Benz cars (all models) were produced during 1971.

Note 2: A total of 23,885 280SL models were produced during the full model run, 1967-71.

Model Number Note: Some directories included a /8 suffix with each model number (e.g., 220/8).

Weight Note: Figures shown for 280SE 3.5 and 300SEL are "unladen" amounts; others are shipping weights.

ENGINE DATA: BASE FOUR (220): Inline, overhead-cam four-cylinder. Cast iron block and aluminum head. **Displacement:** 134 cu. in. (2195 cc). **Bore & Stroke:** 3.15 x 2.87 in. (80 x 72.8 mm). **Compression Ratio:** 9.0:1. **Brake Horsepower:** 116 at 5200 rpm. **Torque:** 142 lbs.-ft. at 3000 rpm. Five main bearings. Solid valve lifters.

DIESEL FOUR (220D): Inline, overhead-cam four-cylinder. **Displacement:** 134 cu. in. (2195 cc). **Bore & Stroke:** 3.15 x 2.87 in. (80 x 72.8 mm). **Compression Ratio:** 21.0:1. **Brake Horsepower:** 65 at 4200 rpm. **Torque:** 96 lbs.-ft. at 2400 rpm. Solid valve lifters. Fuel injection.

BASE SIX (250, 250C, 280S): Inline, overhead-cam six-cylinder. Cast iron block and aluminum head. **Displacement:** 169.5 cu. in. (2778 cc). **Bore & Stroke:** 3.41 x 3.10 in. (86.6 x 78.8 mm). **Compression Ratio:** 9.0:1. **Brake Horsepower:** 157 at 5400 rpm. **Torque:** 181 lbs.-ft. at 3800 rpm. Seven main bearings. Solid valve lifters.

BASE SIX (280SE, 280SEL, 280SL): Same as 2778-cc six above, except — **Compression Ratio:** 9.5:1. **Brake Horsepower:** 180 at 5750 rpm. **Torque:** 193 lbs.-ft. at 4500 rpm.

BASE V-8 (280SE 3.5 cpe/conv, 300SEL 3.5): 90-degree, overhead-valve, "vee" type eight-cylinder. Cast iron block and aluminum heads. **Displacement:** 213.5 cu. in. (3499 cc). **Bore & Stroke:** 3.62 x 2.59 in. (92 x 65.8 mm). **Compression Ratio:** 9.5:1. **Brake Horsepower:** 230 at 6050 rpm. **Torque:** 231 lbs.-ft. at 4200 rpm. Five main bearings. Solid valve lifters. Bosch fuel injection.

BASE V-8 (300SEL 6.3, 600): 90-degree, overhead-valve, "vee" type eight-cylinder. Cast iron block and aluminum heads. **Displacement:** 386.2 cu. in. (6329 cc). **Bore & Stroke:** 4.05 x 3.74 in. (103 x 95 mm). **Compression Ratio:** 8.1:1. **Brake Horsepower:** 300 at 4100 rpm. **Torque:** 434 lbs.-ft. at 3000 rpm. Five main bearings. Solid valve lifters. Bosch fuel injection.

1971 Mercedes-Benz 280SL convertible sports two-seater. (Christie's)

CHASSIS DATA: Wheelbase: (220/250/280) 108.3 in.; (280SL) 94.5 in.; (280SEL, 300SEL) 112.2 in.; (600) 126 in.; (600 Pullman) 153.5 in. **Overall Length:** (220/250) 184.5 in.; (280) 192.9 in.; (280SL) 168.7 in.; (280SEL, 300SEL) 197 in.; (600) 218 in.; (600 Pullman) 245.7 in. **Height:** (220/250/280 sed) 56.7 in.; (250C) 54.9 in.; (280SL) 52 in.; (280SE 3.5 cpe/conv) 55.9 in.; (300SEL 3.5) 55.5 in. (300SEL 6.3) 55.9 in.; (600) 58.5 in.; (600 Pullman) 59 in. **Width:** (220/250) 69.7 in.; (250C) 70.5 in.; (280) 71.3 in.; (280SL) 69.3 in.; (280SE 3.5 cpe/conv) 72.6 in.; (300SEL 3.5) 71.3 in.; (600) 76.8 in. **Front Tread:** (220/250) 56.8 in.; (280) 58.4 in.; (280SL) 58.4 in.; (280SE 3.5 cpe/conv) 58.3 in.; (300SEL 3.5) 58.3 in.; (300SEL 6.3) 58.7 in.; (600) 62.5 in. **Rear Tread:** (220/250) 56.7 in.; (280) 58.5 in.; (280SL) 58.5 in.; (280SE 3.5 cpe/conv) 58.7 in.; (300SEL 3.5) 58.7 in.; (300SEL 6.3) 58.5 in.; (600) 62.2 in. **Standard Tires:** (220/250) 6.95x14; (280) 7.35x14; (280SL) 185x14; (280SE 3.5 cpe/conv) 7.35x14; (300SEL 3.5) 7.35x14; (300SEL 6.3) 195x14; (600 Pullman) 9.00x15.

TECHNICAL: Layout: front-engine, rear-drive. **Transmission:** (220, 280SL) four-speed manual, automatic optional; (others) automatic standard. **Steering:** recirculating ball. **Suspension (front):** unequal length A-arms, coil springs and anti-roll bar; (600) wishbones with air springs, automatic leveling and anti-roll bar. **Suspension (rear):** single low-pivot swing axles with coil springs and anti-sway bar; (600) swinging semi-axles with trailing lower radius arms, air springs, automatic leveling and anti-roll bar. **Brakes:** front/rear disc. **Body Construction:** steel unibody with auxiliary front frame.

MAJOR OPTIONS: Automatic transmission ($392). Power steering ($198). Air conditioning ($597). Sunroof.

PRODUCTION/SALES: Approximately 35,192 Mercedes-Benz passenger cars were sold in the U.S. in 1971.

Manufacturer: Daimler-Benz AG, Stuttgart, West Germany.

Distributor: Mercedes-Benz of North America Inc., Fort Lee, New Jersey.

HISTORY: The 1971 models were introduced to the U.S. market on October 1, 1970. The 350SL replacement for the 280SL was in production in Europe, and would arrive in the U.S. for the 1972 model year.

1972 MERCEDES-BENZ

220 SERIES — FOUR — Except for a slight reduction in horsepower/torque ratings from the gasoline engine, little was new on the four-cylinder Mercedes-Benz models.

250 SERIES — SIX — Little change was evident on the 250 sedan and 250C coupe, powered by a 2778-cc (169.5-cid) engine that devleoped 150 horsepower.

280SE — SIX — Only one version of the six-cylinder sedan in the 280 series remained for 1972, with its engine producing 175 horsepower.

280SE/280SEL 4.5 — V-8 — Two V-8 versions of the 280 sedan got a displacement boost to 276 cid this year. The enlarged V-8 was rated 230 horsepower and 278 pound-feet of torque.

300SEL 4.5 — V-8 — Like other models in the Mercedes lineup for 1972, the 300SEL gained displacement for its basic V-8 engine, now measuring 4.5 liters (276 cid). On the other hand, the former 6.3 version (386-cid) no longer was offered.

1972 Mercedes-Benz rotary coupe. (Indianapolis Motor Speedway)

350SL — V-8 — A 4.5-liter (276-cid) V-8 engine went under the hood of the next Mercedes-Benz two-seat roadster, coded R107. It was longer, plusher, more expensive, and squarely aimed at American customers. This version used steel body panels instead of the former aluminum panels, adding several hundred pounds to the car's weight. Quad round headlamps and black rubber bumpers went on U.S. versions. Some observers criticized the restyling as being overly "Americanized," but it became a strong seller and would remain in the lineup through the late 1980s, evolving into the 450SL, 380SL, 500SL and 560SL editions. European versions of the 350SL had the more logical 3.5-liter V-8 engine, also rated at 230 bhp; but only the bigger 4.5 V-8 came to America.

600/PULLMAN — V-8 — Although the 600 "Grosser" Mercedes remained in production through 1980, it seldom appeared in listings of American imports after 1972.

I.D. DATA: Depending on the model, the Mercedes-Benz chassis serial number is atop the instrument panel (visible through the windshield), on the radiator cowl, or at the driver's door B-pillar. The chassis serial number consists of 14 symbols. The first six symbols (all digits) indicate the model; the next two indicate standard (10) or automatic (12) transmission. The final six digits form the sequential production number. Starting serial number: (220) 115.010-12-081308; (220D) 115.110-10-208608; (250) 114.011-12-007030; (250C) 114.023-12-005231; (280SE) 108.018-12-087244; (350SL) 107.044-12-000001. Engine number is on left front or right rear of block.

Model	Body Type & Seating	Engine Type/CID	P.O.E. Price	Weight (lbs.)	Prod. Total
220 SERIES					
220	4-dr Sedan-5P	I4/134	6267	2983	Note 1
220D (Dsl)	4-dr Sedan-5P	I4/134	6020	3055	Note 1
250 SERIES					
250	4-dr Sedan-5P	I6/169	7218	3159	Note 1
250C	2-dr Coupe-5P	I6/169	8069	3159	Note 1
280SE					
280SE	4-dr Sedan-5P	I6/169	9503	3386	Note 1
280SE 4.5	4-dr Sedan-5P	V8/276	10076	3549	Note 1
280SEL 4.5	4-dr Sedan-5P	V8/276	10634	3766	Note 1
300SEL					
4.5	4-dr Sedan-5P	V8/276	13768	3877	Note 1
350SL					
350SL	2-dr Cpe/Rds-2P	V8/276	10540	3597	Note 2
600/PULLMAN (GRAND MERCEDES)					
600	4-dr Sedan-5P	V8/386	32695	5469	Note 1
Pullman	4-dr Limo-7P	V8/386	37928	6031	Note 1

Note 1: A total of 323,878 Mercedes-Benz cars (all models) were produced during 1972.

Note 2: A total of 15,304 350SL models were produced during the full model run, 1970-80 (sold as late as 1980 in the international market).

Model Number Note: Some directories included a /8 suffix with each model number (e.g., 220/8).

Price Note: Figure shown for 220D included manual transmission; automatic cost $393 more.

Weight Note: Figures shown for 280SEL 4.5 and 300SEL 4.5 are "unladen" amounts; others are shipping weights.

ENGINE DATA: BASE FOUR (220): Inline, overhead-cam four-cylinder. Cast iron block and aluminum head. **Displacement:** 134 cu. in. (2195 cc). **Bore & Stroke:** 3.15 x 2.87 in. (80 x 72.8 mm). **Compression Ratio:** 8.0:1. **Brake Horsepower:** 110 at 5300 rpm. **Torque:** 127 lbs.-ft. at 3300 rpm. Five main bearings. Solid valve lifters.

DIESEL FOUR (220D): Inline, overhead-cam four-cylinder. **Displacement:** 134 cu. in. (2195 cc). **Bore & Stroke:** 3.15 x 2.87 in. (80 x 72.8 mm). **Compression Ratio:** 21.0:1. **Brake Horsepower:** 65 at 4200 rpm. **Torque:** 96 lbs.-ft. at 2400 rpm. Solid valve lifters. Fuel injection.

BASE SIX (250, 250C): Inline, overhead-cam six-cylinder. Cast iron block and aluminum head. **Displacement:** 169.5 cu. in. (2778 cc). **Bore & Stroke:** 3.41 x 3.10 in. (86.6 x 78.8 mm). **Compression Ratio:** 9.0:1. **Brake Horsepower:** 150 at 5300 rpm. **Torque:** 166 lbs.-ft. at 3800 rpm. Seven main bearings. Solid valve lifters.

BASE SIX (280SE): Same as 2778-cc six above, except — **Brake Horsepower:** 175 at 5700 rpm. **Torque:** 174 lbs.-ft. at 4500 rpm.

BASE V-8 (280SE 4.5, 280SEL 4.5, 300SEL 4.5, 350SL): 90-degree, overhead-cam, "vee" type eight-cylinder. Cast iron block and aluminum heads. **Displacement:** 275.8 cu. in. (4520 cc). **Bore & Stroke:** 3.62 x 3.35 in. (92 x 85 mm). **Compression Ratio:** 8.0:1. **Brake Horsepower:** 230 at 5000 rpm. **Torque:** 278 lbs.-ft. at 3200 rpm. Five main bearings. Solid valve lifters. Bosch fuel injection.

BASE V-8 (600): 90-degree, overhead-valve, "vee" type eight-cylinder. Cast iron block and aluminum heads. **Displacement:** 386.2 cu. in. (6329 cc). **Bore & Stroke:** 4.05 x 3.74 in. (103 x 95 mm). **Compression Ratio:** 8.0:1. **Brake Horsepower:** 270 at 4200 rpm. **Torque:** 370 lbs.-ft. at 2900 rpm. Five main bearings. Solid valve lifters. Bosch fuel injection.

CHASSIS DATA: Wheelbase: (220/250/280) 108.3 in.; (280SE 4.5) 108.3 in.; (280SEL 4.5, 300SEL 4.5) 112.2 in.; (350SL) 96.9 in.; (600) 126 in.; (600 Pullman) 153.5 in. **Overall Length:** (220/250) 184.5 in.; (280SE) 192.9 in.; (280SE/SEL 4.5) 196.8 in.; (300SEL 4.5) 196.9 in.; (350SL) 172.1 in.; (600) 218 in.; (600 Pullman) 245.7 in. **Height:** (220/250/280 sed) 56.7 in.; (250C) 54.9 in.; (300SEL/SEL 4.5) 56.7 in.; (350SL) 51.2 in.; (600) 58.5 in.; (600 Pullman) 59 in. **Width:** (220/250) 69.7 in.; (250C) 70.5 in.; (280 series) 71.3 in.; (300SEL) 70.5 in.; (350SL) 71.3 in.; (600) 76.8 in. **Front Tread:** (220/250) 56.8 in.; (280 series) 58.4 in.; (300SEL 4.5) 58.3 in.; (350SL) 57.2 in.; (600) 62.5 in. **Rear Tread:** (220/250) 56.7 in.; (280) 58.5 in.; (300SEL 4.5) 58.5 in.; (350SL) 56.7 in.; (600) 62.2 in. **Standard Tires:** (220/250) 6.95x14; (280 series) 7.35x14; (350SL) 205VR14; (600) 9.00x15.

TECHNICAL: Layout: front-engine, rear-drive. **Transmission:** (220D) four-speed manual, automatic optional; (others) automatic standard. **Steering:** recirculating ball. **Suspension (front):** unequal-length A-arms, coil springs and anti-roll bar; (600) wishbones with air springs, automatic leveling and anti-roll bar. **Suspension (rear):** single low-pivot swing axles with coil springs and anti-sway bar; (600) swinging semi-axles with trailing lower radius arms, air springs, automatic leveling and anti-roll bar. **Brakes:** front/rear disc. **Body Construction:** steel unibody with auxiliary front frame.

MAJOR OPTIONS: Automatic transmission (220D). Power steering (220). Air conditioning. Sunroof. Leather seats.

PRODUCTION/SALES: Approximately 41,998 Mercedes-Benz passenger cars were sold in the U.S. in 1972.

Manufacturer: Daimler-Benz AG, Stuttgart, West Germany.

Distributor: Mercedes-Benz of North America Inc., Fort Lee, New Jersey.

HISTORY: The 1972 models were introduced to the U.S. market on August 2, 1971. The 350SL two-seater was not destined for long life in the Mercedes lineup, replaced by the 450SL (part of the new 450 series) for the 1973 model year.

1973 MERCEDES-BENZ

220 SERIES — FOUR — Advertised horsepower/torque figures were lower by 1973, as a result of the switch from SAE gross to SAE net standards. Otherwise, little change was evident in the four-cylinder Mercedes-Benz sedans, which again came with either a gasoline or diesel engine. Only the diesel four had a standard four-speed manual gearbox (automatic optional). All other Mercedes-Benz models had an automatic as standard equipment.

280 SERIES — SIX — Both a coupe and sedan were offered in the new 280 series (which replaced the 250 series, wearing the same body), with a new 167.6-cid dual-overhead-cam six-cylinder engine producing 130 horsepower. An automatic transmission was standard. A radio and air conditioning were standard. The V-8 versions of the 280 series were dropped, as was the 300SEL.

450SL — V-8 — After a brief stay in the Mercedes-Benz lineup, the 350SL two-seater was replaced by a 450SL. As it happened, this one was powered by the same 4.5-liter (276-cid) V-8 engine that went under the 350SL's hood in American trim. (The 3.5-liter edition had been marketed in Europe.) So in effect, little had changed. The 4.5-liter V-8 was rated 190 horsepower (SAE net) at 4750 rpm, producing 240 pound-feet of torque. Appearance was similar to the 350SL, with the customary Mercedes-Benz tristar emblem at the center of a horizontal grille bar, flanked by quad round headlamps. Wheelbase was 96.9 inches. The two-seater measured 172.5 inches long overall and stood 51.2 inches tall, riding 205x14 tires.

450SE/SEL/SLC — V-8 — Mercedes-Benz now marketed a selection of body styles with the same 4.5-liter V-8 engine used in the 450SL two-seater: a 450SE four-door sedan, 450SEL sedan, and 450SLC coupe. Styling of these models was similar to the other Mercedes models, but wheelbases varied: 112.8 inches for the 450SE, 116.5 inches for the 450SEL, and 111 inches for the 450SLC.

Note: Although the 600 "Grosser" Mercedes remained in production through 1980, it seldom appeared in listings of American imports after 1972.

I.D. DATA: The Mercedes-Benz chassis serial number is atop the instrument panel (visible through the windshield), on the radiator cowl, or at the driver's door B-pillar; or for 450SE/SEL models, it may be at the center of the firewall, in the engine compartment. The chassis serial number consists of 14 symbols. The first six symbols (all digits) indicate the model; the next two indicate standard (10) or automatic (12) transmission. The final six digits form the sequential production number. Starting serial number: (220) 115.010-12-105672; (220D) 115.110-10-277011; (280) 114.060-12-000001; (280C) 114.073-12-000001; (280SE) 108.018-12-014245; (450SL) 107.044-12-005794; (450SLC) 107.024-12-000001. Engine number is on left front or right rear of block.

Model	Body Type & Seating	Engine Type/CID	P.O.E. Price	Weight (lbs.)	Prod. Total
220 SERIES					
220	4-dr Sedan-5P	I4/134	6889	2960	Note 1
220D (Dsl)	4-dr Sedan-5P	I4/134	6662	3000	Note 1
280 SERIES					
280	4-dr Sedan-5P	I6/168	9319	3285	Note 1
280C	2-dr Coupe-5P	I6/168	9994	3285	Note 1
450SL					
450SL	2-dr Cpe/Rds-2P	V8/276	12773	3555	Note 2
450 SERIES					
450SE	4-dr Sedan-5P	V8/276	13396	3843	Note 1
450SEL	4-dr Sedan-5P	V8/276	14605	N/A	Note 1
450SLC	2-dr Coupe-4P	V8/276	16498	3625	Note 1

Note 1: A total of 331,682 Mercedes-Benz cars (all models) were produced during 1973.

Note 2: A total of 66,298 450SL models were produced during the full model run, 1971-80.

Price Note: Figure shown for 220D included manual transmission; automatic cost $438 more.

ENGINE DATA: BASE FOUR (220): Inline, overhead-cam four-cylinder. Cast iron block and aluminum head. **Displacement:** 134 cu. in. (2195 cc). **Bore & Stroke:** 3.15 x 2.87 in. (80 x 72.8 mm). **Compression Ratio:** 8.0:1. **Brake Horsepower:** 85 at 4500 rpm. **Torque:** 124 lbs.-ft. at 2500 rpm. Five main bearings. Solid valve lifters.

DIESEL FOUR (220D): Inline, overhead-cam four-cylinder. **Displacement:** 134 cu. in. (2195 cc). **Bore & Stroke:** 3.15 x 2.87 in. (80 x 72.8 mm). **Compression Ratio:** 21.0:1. **Brake Horsepower:** 57 at 4200 rpm. **Torque:** 88 lbs.-ft. at 2400 rpm. Solid valve lifters. Fuel injection.

BASE SIX (280): Inline, dual-overhead-cam six-cylinder. Cast iron block and aluminum head. **Displacement:** 167.6 cu. in. (2746 cc). **Bore & Stroke:** 3.39 x 3.10 in. (86 x 78.8 mm). **Compression Ratio:** 8.0:1. **Brake Horsepower:** 130 at 5000 rpm. **Torque:** 150 lbs.-ft. at 3500 rpm. Seven main bearings. Solid valve lifters.

BASE V-8 (450 series): 90-degree, overhead-cam, "vee" type eight-cylinder. Cast iron block and aluminum heads. **Displacement:** 275.8 cu. in. (4520 cc). **Bore & Stroke:** 3.62 x 3.35 in. (92 x 85 mm). **Compression Ratio:** 8.0:1. **Brake Horsepower:** 190 at 4750 rpm. **Torque:** 240 lbs.-ft. at 3000 rpm. Five main bearings. Solid valve lifters. Bosch fuel injection.

CHASSIS DATA: Wheelbase: (220/280) 108.3 in.; (450SL) 96.9 in.; (450SE) 112.8 in.; (450SEL) 116.5 in.; (450SLC) 111 in. **Overall Length:** (220/280) 184.5 in.; (450SL) 172.5 in.; (450SE) 195.3 in.; (450SEL) 199.2 in.; (450SLC) 186.6 in. **Height:** (220/280 sed) 56.7 in.; (280C) 54.9 in.; (450SL) 51.2 in.; (450SE) 56.1 in.; (450SEL) 56.3 in.; (450SLC) 52.4 in. **Width:** (220/280 sed) 69.7 in.; (280C) 70.5 in.; (450SL/SLC) 70.5 in.; (450SE) 73.4 in.; (450SEL) 73.4 in. **Front Tread:** (220/280) 57 in.; (450SL/SLC) 57.2 in.; (450SE/SEL) 60 in. **Rear Tread:** (220/280) 56.7 in.; (450SL) 56.7 in.; (450SE/SEL) 59.3 in.; (450SLC) 56.7 in. **Standard Tires:** (220/280) 175x14; (450SL/SLC) 205x14; (450SE/SEL) 205x14.

TECHNICAL: Layout: front-engine, rear-drive. **Transmission:** (220D) four-speed manual, automatic optional; (others) automatic standard. **Steering:** recirculating ball. **Suspension (front):** unequal-length A-arms, coil springs and stabilizer bar. **Suspension (rear):** diagonal swing axles with coil springs and stabilizer bar. **Brakes:** front/rear disc. **Body Construction:** steel unibody with auxiliary front frame.

MAJOR OPTIONS: Automatic transmission (220D). Power steering (220/D). Air conditioning (220/D). Sunroof. Leather seats.

PRODUCTION/SALES: Approximately 41,865 Mercedes-Benz passenger cars (plus 540 trucks) were sold in the U.S. during 1973. The year's total included 10 Model 600 sedans (described in prior listings).

Manufacturer: Daimler-Benz AG, Stuttgart, West Germany.

Distributor: Mercedes-Benz of North America Inc., Montvale, New Jersey.

HISTORY: The 1973 models were introduced to the U.S. market on September 11, 1972 except (280/C) November 1, 1972.

1974 MERCEDES-BENZ

230 — FOUR — A new sedan with 141-cid four-cylinder engine became available for the 1974 model year. The engine produced 95 horsepower at 4800 rpm, using a cross-draft carburetor. A four-speed automatic transmission with torque converter was standard. As in all the 2-series models, roof pillars were redesigned to divert rain from side windows, and doors had a new "safety cone" lock. A lever to the left of the steering column controlled the turn signals, high/low beams, and wipers. Standard equipment included power steering, tinted glass, vinyl upholstery, and an electrically-heated rear window.

240D — FOUR — The 220 series was gone, replaced by a 240D sedan (diesel engine only). The new 146.7-cid engine developed 62 horsepower. Standard equipment was similar to the gas-engine 230 sedan.

280 SERIES — SIX — As before, both a coupe and sedan were offered in the 280 series, powered by a 167.6-cid dual-overhead-cam six-cylinder engine that developed 130 horsepower. A four-barrel carburetor handled the "breathing" duties, and a four-speed automatic transmission was standard. Standard equipment included air conditioning, front armrest, power steering, tinted glass, central locking, vinyl upholstery, AM/FM radio, halogen foglamps, and an electrically-heated rear window.

450SL — V-8 — Production of the Mercedes-Benz two-seat coupe/roadster continued with little change, with the 4.5-liter (276-cid) V-8 engine under its hood. A three-speed automatic transmission was standard. The 450SL could be driven as an open roadster, a convertible with the soft top erected, or with the steel hardtop fitted in position.

450SE/SEL/SLC — V-8 — Little change was evident in the trio of other Mercedes-Benz models with the 4.5-liter V-8 engine, rated at 190 horsepower and 240 pound-feet of torque. Leather upholstery was standard on the 450SEL sedan and 450SLC coupe. All 450-series models included a tachometer and quartz clock ahead of the driver. The 450SEL offered extra legroom and wider doors than its shorter 450SE companion. Each model had air conditioning, a three-speed automatic transmission, cruise control, central locking, halogen foglamps, power windows, AM/FM stereo radio with automatic antenna, height-adjustable front seats, and radial tires. Upholstery was vinyl on the 450SE, leather on the 450SEL sedan and 450SLC coupe.

Note: Although the 600 "Grosser" Mercedes remained in production through 1980, and a handful were exported to the U.S.,it seldom appeared in listings of American imports through the 1970s; see earlier listings for details.

I.D. DATA: The Mercedes-Benz chassis serial number is atop the instrument panel (visible through the windshield), on the radiator cowl, or at the driver's door B-pillar; or for 450SE/SEL models, it may be at the center of the firewall, in the engine compartment. The chassis serial number consists of 14 symbols. The first six symbols (all digits) indicate the model; the next two indicate standard (10) or automatic (12) transmission. The final six digits form the sequential production number. Starting serial number: (230) 115.017-12-000001; (240D) 115.117-10-000001; (280) 114.060-12-100666; (280C) 114.073-12-100168; (450SE) 116.032-12-013479; (450SEL) 116.033-12-013446; (450SL) 107.044-12-015082; (450SLC) 107.024-12-004128. Engine number is on left front or right rear of block.

Note: Various serial numbers that didn't follow the sequences listed above also were considered 1974 models.

Model	Body Type & Seating	Engine Type/CID	P.O.E. Price	Weight (lbs.)	Prod. Total
230	4-dr Sedan-5P	I4/141	8420	3040	Note 1
240D (Diesel)					
240D	4-dr Sedan-5P	I4/147	8715	3080	Note 1
280 SERIES					
280	4-dr Sedan-5P	I6/168	10950	3330	Note 1
280C	2-dr Coupe-5P	I6/168	11630	3330	Note 1
450SL					
450SL	2-dr Cpe/Rds-2P	V8/276	15450	3580	Note 2
450 SERIES					
450SE	4-dr Sedan-5P	V8/276	15820	3910	Note 1
450SEL	4-dr Sedan-5P	V8/276	17400	3940	Note 1
450SLC	2-dr Coupe-4P	V8/276	19450	3630	Note 1

Note 1: A total of 340,006 Mercedes-Benz cars (all models) were produced during 1974.

Note 2: A total of 66,298 450SL models were produced during the full model run, 1971-80.

Price Note: Figure shown for 240D included manual transmission; automatic cost $575 more.

ENGINE DATA: BASE FOUR (230): Inline, overhead-cam four-cylinder. Cast iron block and aluminum head. **Displacement:** 140.8 cu. in. (2308 cc). Bore & Stroke: 3.69 x 3.29 in. (94 x 83.6 mm). **Compression Ratio:** 8.0:1. **Brake Horsepower:** 95 at 4800 rpm. **Torque:** 128 lbs.-ft. at 2500 rpm. Five main bearings. Solid valve lifters. Cross-draft carburetor.

DIESEL FOUR (240D): Inline, overhead-cam four-cylinder. Cast iron block and head. **Displacement:** 146.7 cu. in. (2404 cc). **Bore & Stroke:** 3.58 x 3.64 in. (91 x 92.5 mm). **Compression Ratio:** 21.0:1. **Brake Horsepower:** 62 at 4000 rpm. **Torque:** 97 lbs.-ft. at 2400 rpm. Five main bearings. Solid valve lifters. Fuel injection.

BASE SIX (280): Inline, dual-overhead-cam six-cylinder. Cast iron block and aluminum head. **Displacement:** 167.6 cu. in. (2746 cc). **Bore & Stroke:** 3.39 x 3.10 in. (86 x 78.8 mm). **Compression Ratio:** 8.0:1. **Brake Horsepower:** 130 at 5000 rpm. **Torque:** 150 lbs.-ft. at 3500 rpm. Seven main bearings. Solid valve lifters. Four-barrel carburetor.

Note: California 280-series engine was rated 123 bhp and 143 pound-feet.

BASE V-8 (450 series): 90-degree, overhead-cam, "vee" type eight-cylinder. Cast iron block and aluminum heads. **Displacement:** 275.8 cu. in. (4520 cc). **Bore & Stroke:** 3.62 x 3.35 in. (92 x 85 mm). **Compression Ratio:** 8.0:1. **Brake Horsepower:** 190 at 4750 rpm. **Torque:** 240 lbs.-ft. at 3000 rpm. Five main bearings. Solid valve lifters. Bosch fuel injection.

Note: California 450-series engine was rated 180 bhp and 232 pound-feet.

CHASSIS DATA: Wheelbase: (230/240D/280) 108.3 in.; (450SL) 96.9 in.; (450SLC) 111.0 in.; (450SE) 112.8 in.; (450SEL) 116.7 in. **Overall Length:** (230/240D/280) 195.5 in.; (450SL) 182.3 in.; (450SLC) 196.4 in.; (450SE) 205.5 in.; (450SEL) 209.4 in. **Height:** (230/240D/280 sed) 56.7 in.; (280C) 54.9 in.; (450SL) 50.8 in.; (450SLC) 52.4 in.; (450SE) 56.1 in.; (450SEL) 56.3 in. **Width:** (230/240D/280) 69.7 in.; (450SL/SLC) 70.5 in.; (450SE/SEL) 73.6 in. **Front Tread:** (230/240D/280) 57.0 in.; (450SL/SLC) 57.2 in.; (450SE/SEL) 60.0 in. **Rear Tread:** (230/240D/280) 56.7 in.; (450SL/SLC) 56.7 in.; (450SE/SEL) 59.3 in. **Standard Tires:** (230/240D/280) 175x14; (450 SL/SLC) 205/70x14; (450SE/SEL) 205/70x14.

TECHNICAL: Layout: front-engine, rear-drive. **Transmission:** (240D) four-speed manual, four-speed automatic optional; (230/280) four-speed automatic standard; (450 series) three-speed automatic standard. **Steering:** recirculating ball. **Suspension (front):** unequal-length A-arms, coil springs and stabilizer bar. **Suspension (rear):** diagonal swing axles with coil springs and stabilizer bar. **Brakes:** front/rear disc. **Body Construction:** steel unibody.

MAJOR OPTIONS: Automatic transmission (240D). Air conditioning (230/240D). Sliding metal sunroof. Leather seats. Velour upholstery (280/280C). Automatic antenna. Power windows. Fitted luggage. Parcel nets (on front seatbacks). Front seats with orthopedic backrests. Central locking. Halogen foglamps. Signal-seeking Grand Prix radio (450SL). Light alloy wheels (450-series).

PRODUCTION/SALES: Approximately 37,230 Mercedes-Benz passenger cars (plus 656 trucks) were sold in the U.S. during 1974, plus about 2,876 delivered to tourists in Europe.

Manufacturer: Daimler-Benz AG, Stuttgart, West Germany.

Distributor: Mercedes-Benz of North America Inc., Montvale, New Jersey.

HISTORY: The 1974 models were introduced to the U.S. market on September 30, 1973. This year's Mercedes-Benz catalog focused on safety features, pointing out that the company had "been concerned with automobile safety long before the public discussion began on the subject."

1975-76 MERCEDES-BENZ

230 — FOUR — Production of the four-cylinder Mercedes with 141-cid engine continued with little change.

240D — FOUR — Mercedes' four-cylinder diesel remained in production with minimal change. The 146.7-cid engine developed 62 horsepower.

300D — FIVE — Mercedes turned to a five-cylinder powerplant for its next diesel sedan. The 183.4-cid engine developed 77 horsepower and 115 pound-feet of torque.

280 SERIES — SIX — Once again, a coupe and sedan were offered in the 280 series, powered by a 167.6-cid dual-overhead-cam six-cylinder engine with four-barrel carburetor that developed 120 horsepower. This year, a 280S four-door sedan also was available, on a longer (112.2-inch) wheelbase. A four-speed automatic transmission was standard. Standard equipment was similar to 1974.

450SL — V-8 — Production of the two-seat coupe/roadster with removable hardtop continued with little change, powered by a 4.5-liter (276-cid) V-8 engine that developed 180 bhp. An automatic transmission was standard.

450SE/SEL/SLC — V-8 — Each of the larger 450-series models continued with little change, powered by the same engine used in the 450SL. Standard equipment was similar to 1974. By 1976, the 4.5-liter engine's fuel-injection system changed to Bosch K-Jetronic.

I.D. DATA: The Mercedes-Benz chassis serial number is atop the instrument panel (visible through the windshield), on the radiator cowl, or at the driver's door B-pillar; or for 450SE/SEL models, it may be at the center of the firewall, in the engine compartment. The chassis serial number consists of 14 symbols. The first six symbols (all digits) indicate the model; the next two indicate standard (10) or automatic (12) transmission. The final six digits form the sequential production number. Starting serial number (1975 models): (230) 115.017-12-025972; (240D) 115.117-10-056706; (300D) 115.114-12-000001; (280) 114.060-12-112062; (280C) 114.073-12-103729; (280S) 116.020-12-029633; (450SE) 116.032-12-029673; (450SEL) 116.033-12-029418; (450SL) 107.044-12-021762; (450SLC) 107.024-12-008203. Engine number is on left front or right rear of block.

Note: Various serial numbers that didn't follow the sequences listed above also were considered 1975 models.

Model	Body Type & Seating	Engine Type/CID	P.O.E. Price	Weight (lbs.)	Prod. Total
230	4-dr Sedan-5P	I4/141	9172	3110	Note 1
240D/300D (Diesel)					
240D	4-dr Sedan-5P	I4/147	9811	3100	Note 1
300D	4-dr Sedan-5P	I5/183	12194	3340	Note 1
280 SERIES					
280	4-dr Sedan-5P	I6/168	12756	3440	Note 1
280S	4-dr Sedan-5P	I6/168	15057	3770	Note 1
280C	2-dr Coupe-5P	I6/168	13520	3450	Note 1

Model	Body Type & Seating	Engine Type/CID	P.O.E. Price	Weight (lbs.)	Prod. Total
450SL	2-dr Cpe/Rds-2P	V8/276	17653	3640	Note 2
450 SERIES					
450SE	4-dr Sedan-5P	V8/276	18333	3945	Note 1
450SEL	4-dr Sedan-5P	V8/276	19775	3990	Note 1
450SLC	2-dr Coupe-4P	V8/276	22053	3680	Note 1

Note 1: A total of 356,477 Mercedes-Benz cars (all models) were produced during 1975, followed by 370,348 in 1976.

Note 2: A total of 66,298 450SL models were produced during the full model run, 1971-80.

Price Note: Figure shown for 240D included manual transmission; automatic cost $639 more. Prices shown were valid during the 1975 model year; for 1976, they ranged from $9930 for the 240D (manual shift) to $23,976 for the 450SLC coupe.

ENGINE DATA: BASE FOUR (230): Inline, overhead-cam four-cylinder. Cast iron block and aluminum head. **Displacement:** 140.8 cu. in. (2308 cc). **Bore & Stroke:** 3.69 x 3.29 in. (94 x 83.6 mm). **Compression Ratio:** 8.0:1. **Brake Horsepower:** 93 at 4800 rpm. **Torque:** 125 lbs.-ft. at 2500 rpm. Five main bearings. Solid valve lifters. Single-barrel carburetor.

DIESEL FOUR (240D): Inline, overhead-cam four-cylinder. Cast iron block and head. **Displacement:** 146.7 cu. in. (2404 cc). Bore & Stroke: 3.58 x 3.64 in. (91 x 92.4 mm). **Compression Ratio:** 21.0:1. **Brake Horsepower:** 62 at 4000 rpm. **Torque:** 97 lbs.-ft. at 2400 rpm. Five main bearings. Solid valve lifters. Fuel injection.

DIESEL FIVE (300D): Inline, overhead-cam five-cylinder. Cast iron block and head. **Displacement:** 183.4 cu. in. (3005 cc). **Bore & Stroke:** 3.58 x 3.64 in. (91 x 92.4 mm). **Compression Ratio:** 21.0:1. **Brake Horsepower:** 77 at 4400 rpm. **Torque:** 115 lbs.-ft. at 2400 rpm. Six main bearings. Solid valve lifters. Fuel injection.

BASE SIX (280): Inline, dual-overhead-cam six-cylinder. Cast iron block and aluminum head. **Displacement:** 167.6 cu. in. (2746 cc). **Bore & Stroke:** 3.39 x 3.10 in. (86 x 78.8 mm). **Compression Ratio:** 8.0:1. **Brake Horsepower:** 120 at 4800 rpm. **Torque:** 143 lbs.-ft. at 2800 rpm. Seven main bearings. Solid valve lifters. Four-barrel carburetor.

BASE V-8 (450 series): 90-degree, overhead-cam, "vee" type eight-cylinder. Cast iron block and aluminum heads. **Displacement:** 275.8 cu. in. (4520 cc). **Bore & Stroke:** 3.62 x 3.35 in. (92 x 85 mm). **Compression Ratio:** 8.0:1. **Brake Horsepower:** 180 at 4750 rpm. **Torque:** 220 lbs.-ft. at 3000 rpm. Five main bearings. Solid valve lifters. Bosch fuel injection.

CHASSIS DATA: Wheelbase: (230/240D/280/300D) 108.3 in.; (280S) 112.2 in.; (450SL) 96.9 in.; (450SLC) 111.0 in.; (450SE) 112.8 in.; (450SEL) 116.7 in. **Overall Length:** (230/240D/280/300D) 195.5 in.; (450SL) 182.3 in.; (450SLC) 196.4 in.; (450SE) 205.5 in.; (450SEL) 209.4 in. **Height:** (230/240D/280/300D sed) 56.7 in.; (280C) 54.9 in.; (280S) 56.1 in.; (450SL) 50.8 in.; (450SLC) 52.4 in.; (450SE) 56.1 in.; (450SEL) 56.3 in. **Width:** (230/240D/280/300D) 69.7 in.; (450SL/SLC) 70.5 in.; (450SE/SEL) 73.6 in. **Front Tread:** (230/240D/280/300D) 57.0 in.; (450SL/SLC) 57.2 in.; (450SE/SEL) 60.0 in. **Rear Tread:** (230/240D/280/300D) 56.7 in.; (450SL/SLC) 56.7 in.; (450SE/SEL) 59.3 in. **Standard Tires:** (230/240D/300D) 175x14; (280 series) 185x14; (450 series) 205/70x14.

TECHNICAL: Layout: front-engine, rear-drive. **Transmission:** (240D) four-speed manual, four-speed automatic optional; (230/280/300D) four-speed automatic standard; (450 series) three-speed automatic standard. **Steering:** recirculating ball. **Suspension (front):** unequal-length A-arms, coil springs and stabilizer bar. **Suspension (rear):** diagonal swing axles with coil springs and stabilizer bar. **Brakes:** front/rear disc. **Body Construction:** steel unibody.

MAJOR OPTIONS: Similar to 1974.

PRODUCTION/SALES: Approximately 42,232 Mercedes-Benz passenger cars (plus 1,218 trucks) were sold in the U.S. during 1975, plus about 3,027 cars delivered to tourists in Europe, for a total of 45,259. Approximately 39,075 Mercedes-Benz cars were sold in the U.S. during 1976, plus 4,130 tourist deliveries, for a total of 43,205.

Manufacturer: Daimler-Benz AG, Stuttgart, West Germany.

Distributor: Mercedes-Benz of North America Inc., Montvale, New Jersey.

HISTORY: The 1975 models were introduced to the U.S. market in September 1974; the 1976 models, in November 1975.

1977-78 MERCEDES-BENZ

230 — FOUR — Wheelbase grew from 108.3 to 110 inches but overall length actually became shorter on the 230/240/280/300 sedans with their new W123 body/chassis. This was the first redesign of the basic Mercedes body since 1968, featuring a wider shape and wider radiator grille. Mechanically, production of the four-cylinder Mercedes with its 141-cid engine continued with little change, though horsepower dropped to 86. Cruise control became standard in 1978, on models with automatic transmissions.

240D — DIESEL FOUR — Only a modest change in dimensions was evident in Mercedes' four-cylinder diesel with its new body, again powered by a 146.7-cid engine that developed 62 horsepower.

300D SERIES — DIESEL FIVE — The most powerful Mercedes diesel sedan (until the turbocharged version arrived) used a five-cylinder engine, producing 77 horsepower. For the 1978 model year, a 300CD diesel coupe became available. Just a few months before the start of the 1979 model year, Mercedes introduced a 300SD turbodiesel sedan on a 112.8-inch wheelbase. The 300SD was powered by a more potent version of the five-cylinder engine, initially rated at 110 horsepower. Acceleration to 60 mph took less than 14 seconds.

280 SERIES — SIX — Only a pair of sedans remained of the 280 series, on two different wheelbases: 110 inches for the 280E and 112.8 inches for the 280SE. The 168-cid six now developed 142 horsepower, using fuel injection instead of carburetion. For 1978, a headlamp-on buzzer was added. A 280CE coupe joined in 1978, with a roofline 1.5 inches lower than the sedan, plus a sharper-angled windshield and back window.

Body Note: W123 was the Mercedes-Benz internal code for the shorter-wheelbase 230/240/280/300 body group. Some 280/300 models rode a longer wheelbase and were actually part of the larger S-Class category.

450SL — V-8 — Production of the two-seat coupe/roadster with removable hardtop continued with little change. As before, the 4.5-liter (276-cid) V-8 engine developed 180 bhp and an automatic transmission was standard.

450SEL/SLC — V-8 — The 450SE sedan was dropped for 1977, but the other two variants remained. Power came again from the same 4.5-liter engine used in the 450SL coupe/roadster.

(450SEL) 6.9 — V-8 — A new and plush (and more expensive) sedan joined the Mercedes lineup, carrying a 417-cid V-8 engine that developed 250 horsepower. Wheelbase was 116.5 inches, and the 6.9 cost $15,000 more than the regular 450SEL sedan. The "450SEL" prefix was not always included in its model designation.

I.D. DATA: The Mercedes-Benz chassis serial number is atop the instrument panel (visible through the windshield), on the radiator cowl, or at the driver's door B-pillar; or for 450SE/SEL models, it may be at the center of the firewall, in the engine compartment. The chassis serial number consists of 14 symbols. The first six symbols (all digits) indicate the model; the next two indicate and standard (10) or automatic (12) transmission. The final six digits form the sequential production number. Starting serial number (1977 models): (230) 123.023-12-016749; (240D) 123.123-10-008892; (300D) 123.130-12-013872; (280E) 123.033-12-013707; (280SE) 116.024-12-072034; (450SEL) 116.033-12-059127; (450SL) 107.044-12-035387; (450SLC) 107.024-12-015075. Engine number is on left front or right rear of block.

Model	Body Type & Seating	Engine Type/CID	P.O.E. Price	Weight (lbs.)	Prod. Total
230	4-dr Sedan-5P	I4/141	12509	3070	Note 1
240D/300D (Diesel)					
240D	4-dr Sedan-5P	I4/147	11573	3080	Note 1
300D	4-dr Sedan-5P	I5/183	16107	3385	Note 1
280 SERIES					
280E	4-dr Sedan-5P	I6/168	16616	3405	Note 1
280SE	4-dr Sedan-5P	I6/168	19411	3750	Note 1
450SL					
450SL	2-dr Cpe/Rds-2P	V8/276	21943	3670	Note 2
450 SERIES					
450SEL	4-dr Sedan-5P	V8/276	24506	3925	Note 1
450SLC	2-dr Coupe-4P	V8/276	27090	3715	Note 1
6.9	4-dr Sedan-5P	V8/417	39377	4235	Note 1

Note 1: A total of 401,250 Mercedes-Benz cars (all models) were produced during 1977, followed by 382,622 in 1978.

Note 2: A total of 66,298 450SL coupe/roadsters were produced during the full model run, 1971-80.

Price Note: Figures shown above were valid during 1977. Figure shown for 240D included manual transmission; automatic cost $12,379. Prices in 1978 ranged from $14,872 for the 240D sedan to $44,923 for the 6.9 sedan.

1978 Model Note: Three models were added during the 1978 model year. The 300CD coupe sold for $21,472; the 300SD turbodiesel sedan for $23,878; and the 280CE coupe sold for $22,141.

ENGINE DATA: BASE FOUR (230): Inline, overhead-cam four-cylinder. Cast iron block and aluminum head. **Displacement:** 140.8 cu. in. (2308 cc). **Bore & Stroke:** 3.69 x 3.29 in. (94 x 83.6 mm). **Compression Ratio:** 8.0:1. **Brake Horsepower:** 86 at 4800 rpm. **Torque:** 125 lbs.-ft. at 2500 rpm. Five main bearings. Solid valve lifters. Single-barrel carburetor.

DIESEL FOUR (240D): Inline, overhead-cam four-cylinder. Cast iron block and head. **Displacement:** 146.7 cu. in. (2404 cc). **Bore & Stroke:** 3.58 x 3.64 in. (91 x 92.4 mm). **Compression Ratio:** 21.0:1. **Brake Horsepower:** 62 at 4000 rpm. **Torque:** 97 lbs.-ft. at 2400 rpm. Five main bearings. Solid valve lifters. Fuel injection.

DIESEL FIVE (300D): Inline, overhead-cam five-cylinder. Cast iron block and head. **Displacement:** 183.4 cu. in. (3005 cc). **Bore & Stroke:** 3.58 x 3.64 in. (91 x 92.4 mm). **Compression Ratio:** 21.0:1. **Brake Horsepower:** 77 at 4000 rpm. **Torque:** 115 lbs.-ft. at 2400 rpm. Six main bearings. Solid valve lifters. Fuel injection.

BASE SIX (280): Inline, dual-overhead-cam six-cylinder. Cast iron block and aluminum head. **Displacement:** 167.6 cu. in. (2746 cc). **Bore & Stroke:** 3.39 x 3.10 in. (86 x 78.8 mm). **Compression Ratio:** 8.0:1. **Brake Horsepower:** 142 at 5750 rpm. **Torque:** 149 lbs.-ft. at 4600 rpm. Seven main bearings. Solid valve lifters. Fuel injection.

BASE V-8 (450 series): 90-degree, overhead-cam, "vee" type eight-cylinder. Cast iron block and aluminum heads. **Displacement:** 275.8 cu. in. (4520 cc). **Bore & Stroke:** 3.62 x 3.35 in. (92 x 85 mm). **Compression Ratio:** 8.0:1. **Brake Horsepower:** 180 at 4750 rpm. **Torque:** 220 lbs.-ft. at 3000 rpm. Five main bearings. Hydraulic valve lifters. Bosch fuel injection.

BASE V-8 (6.9 sedan): 90-degree, overhead-cam, "vee" type eight-cylinder. Cast iron block and aluminum heads. **Displacement:** 417 cu. in. (6834 cc). **Bore & Stroke:** 4.21 x 3.74 in. (107 x 95 mm). **Compression Ratio:** 8.0:1. **Brake Horsepower:** 250 at 4000 rpm. **Torque:** 360 lbs.-ft. at 2500 rpm. Five main bearings. Hydraulic valve lifters. Bosch K-Jetronic fuel injection.

CHASSIS DATA: Wheelbase: (230/240D/280/300D) 110 in.; (280SE) 112.8 in.; (450SL) 96.9 in.; (450SLC) 111.0 in.; (450SEL) 116.7 in.; (6.9) 116.5 in. **Overall Length:** (230/240D/280/300D) 190.9 in.; (280SE) 205.5 in.; (450SL) 182.3 in.; (450SLC) 196.4 in.; (450SE) 205.5 in.; (450SEL) 209.4 in.; (6.9) 210 in. **Height:** (230/240D/280/300D) 56.6 in.; (280SE) 56.1 in.; (450SL) 50.8 in.; (450SLC) 52.4 in.; (450SEL) 56.3 in.; (6.9) 55.5 in. **Width:** (230/240D/280/300D) 70.3 in.; (280SE) 73.6 in.; (450SL/SLC) 70.5 in.; (450SEL) 73.6 in.; (6.9) 73.6 in. **Front Tread:** (230/240D/280/300D) 58.6 in.; (280SE) 59.9 in.; (450SL/SLC) 57.2 in.; (450SE/SEL) 60.0 in.; (6.9) 59.5 in. **Rear Tread:** (230/240D/280/300D) 56.9 in.; (280SE) 59.3 in.; (450SL/SLC) 56.7 in.; (450SEL) 59.3 in.; (6.9) 59.3 in. **Standard Tires:** (230/240D) 175SR14; (300D) 195/70HR14; (280E) 195/70HR14; (280SE) 185HR14; (450 series) 205/70HR14; (6.9) 215/70HR14.

TECHNICAL: Layout: front-engine, rear-drive. **Transmission:** (240D) four-speed manual, four-speed automatic optional; (230/280/300D) four-speed automatic standard; (450 series) three-speed automatic standard. **Steering:** recirculating ball. **Suspension (front):** unequal-length A-arms, coil springs and stabilizer bar. **Suspension (rear):** diagonal swing axles with coil springs and stabilizer bar. **Brakes:** front/rear disc. **Body Construction:** steel unibody.

MAJOR OPTIONS: Air conditioning (230/240D). Automatic transmission (240D). AM/FM stereo. Alloy wheels. Sunroof. Leather seats.

PRODUCTION/SALES: A total of 48,872 Mercedes-Benz passenger cars were sold in the U.S. during 1977, plus about 4,946 cars delivered to tourists in Europe. A total of 46,695 passenger cars were sold in the U.S. during 1978, plus 3,569 cars delivered to tourists in Europe.

Manufacturer: Daimler-Benz AG, Stuttgart, West Germany.

Distributor: Mercedes-Benz of North America Inc., Montvale, New Jersey.

HISTORY: The 1977 models were introduced to the U.S. market in December 1976; the 1978 models, in November 1977. Consumer Guide's *Auto '78* ranked the 300D as top Mercedes, for its mix of "prestige, quality and excellent fuel economy." Only its high price kept the 300D from being named one of the top cars in any class.

1979-80 MERCEDES-BENZ

1980 Mercedes-Benz 350SLC coupe.

240D — DIESEL FOUR — Production of the four-cylinder diesel sedan continued with little change, powered by a 146.7-cid engine that developed 62 horsepower. The 230 sedan with four-cylinder gasoline engine was dropped.

300D/CD/TD — DIESEL FIVE — A five-cylinder diesel engine again powered the 300D sedan and 300CD coupe. During 1979, a 300TD station wagon was added, with the same 77-bhp engine and 110-inch wheelbase. An automatic rear load leveler on the wagon operated from a hydraulic pump at the engine. An optional rear-facing seat could be ordered (suitable for two children). Roof rails were standard, a roof rack optional. A manual sliding roof was standard on the wagon.

300SD — TURBODIESEL FIVE — Production of the turbodiesel sedan, introduced late in the 1978 model year, continued with little change.

280 SERIES — SIX — The 280CE coupe and 280E sedan continued with little change, on the same 110-inch wheelbase as in 1978. The 280SE sedan rode a longer (112.8-inch) wheelbase. Under the hood of each model was the 168-cid six, producing 142 horsepower.

Body Note: W123 was the Mercedes-Benz internal code for the shorter-wheelbase 240/280/300 body group. Some 280/300 models rode a longer wheelbase and were actually part of the larger S-Class category.

450SL — V-8 — Little change was evident in the two-seat coupe/roadster, which included a removable hardtop. As before, the 4.5-liter (276-cid) V-8 engine developed 180 bhp and an automatic transmission was standard.

450SEL/SLC — V-8 — Two additional 450-series models remained, a coupe and sedan, again carrying the same 4.5-liter engine used in the 450SL coupe/roadster.

(450SEL) 6.9 — V-8 — The most powerful and expensive sedan, introduced in 1978 with its 417-cid V-8 engine, lasted through 1979 before departing from the lineup of Mercedes models sold in the U.S.

Engine Note: Engine horsepower/torque ratings changed for the 1980 model year; see data below.

I.D. DATA: The Mercedes-Benz chassis serial number is atop the instrument panel (visible through the windshield). firewall, in the engine compartment. The chassis serial number consists of 14 symbols. The first six symbols (all digits) indicate the model; the next two indicate and standard (10) or automatic (12) transmission. The final six digits form the sequential production number. Starting serial number (1979 models): (240D) 123.123-10-085343; (300D) 123.130-12-107713; (300CD) 123.150-12-002879; (300SD) 116.120-12-001944; (300TD) 123.190-12-000001; (280E) 123.033-12-044014; (280CE) 123.053-12-010847; (450SEL) 116.033-12-083626; (450SL) 107.044-12-049156; (450SLC) 107.024-12-022921; (6.9) 116.036-12-004609.

Model	Body Type & Seating	Engine Type/CID	P.O.E. Price	Weight (lbs.)	Prod. Total
240D/300D (Diesel)					
240D	4-dr Sedan-5P	I4/147	15068	3010	Note 1
300D	4-dr Sedan-5P	I5/183	20911	3385	Note 1
300CD	2-dr Coupe-4/5P	I5/183	23619	N/A	Note 1
300TD	4-dr Sta Wag-5P	I5/183	23619	3635	Note 1
300SD (Turbodiesel)					
300SD	4-dr Sedan-5P	I5/183	26265	3705	Note 1
280 SERIES					
280E	4-dr Sedan-5P	I6/168	22318	3415	Note 1
280CE	2-dr Coupe-5P	I6/168	24951	3365	Note 1
280SE	4-dr Sedan-5P	I6/168	26177	3670	Note 1
450SL					
450SL	2-dr Cpe/Rds-2P	V8/276	30729	3595	Note 2
450 SERIES					
450SEL	4-dr Sedan-5P	V8/276	32858	3860	Note 1
450SLC	2-dr Coupe-4P	V8/276	36519	3650	Note 1
6.9	4-dr Sedan-5P	V8/417	50190	4285	Note 1

Note 1: A total of 393,754 Mercedes-Benz cars (all models) were produced during 1979, followed by 401,848 in 1980.

Note 2: A total of 66,298 450SL coupe/roadsters were produced during the full model run, 1971-80.

Price Note: Figures shown above were valid during 1979. Figure shown for 240D included manual transmission; automatic cost $16,313. Prices in 1980 ranged from $17,533 for the 240D sedan to $42,592 for the 450SLC coupe.

ENGINE DATA: BASE DIESEL FOUR (240D): Inline, overhead-cam four-cylinder. Cast iron block and head. **Displacement:** 146.7 cu. in. (2404 cc). **Bore & Stroke:** 3.58 x 3.64 in. (91 x 92.4 mm). **Compression Ratio:** 21.0:1. **Brake Horsepower:** 62 at 4000 rpm (67 bhp in 1980). **Torque:** 97 lbs.-ft. at 2400 rpm. Five main bearings. Solid valve lifters. Fuel injection.

BASE DIESEL FIVE (300D): Inline, overhead-cam five-cylinder. Cast iron block and head. **Displacement:** 183.4 cu. in. (3005 cc). **Bore & Stroke:** 3.58 x 3.64 in. (91 x 92.4 mm). **Compression Ratio:** 21.0:1. **Brake Horsepower:** 77 at 4000 rpm (83 bhp at 4200 rpm in 1980). **Torque:** 115 lbs.-ft. at 2400 rpm (120 lbs.-ft. in 1980). Six main bearings. Solid valve lifters. Fuel injection.

BASE TURBODIESEL FIVE (300SD): Same as 300S-cc five above, but with turbocharger — **Compression Ratio:** 21.5:1. **Brake Horsepower:** 110 at 4200 rpm (120 bhp at 4350 rpm in 1980). **Torque:** 168 lbs.-ft. at 2400 rpm (170 at 2400 rpm in 1980).

BASE SIX (280): Inline, dual-overhead-cam six-cylinder. Cast iron block and aluminum head. **Displacement:** 167.6 cu. in. (2746 cc). **Bore & Stroke:** 3.39 x 3.10 in. (86 x 78.8 mm). **Compression Ratio:** 8.0:1. **Brake Horsepower:** 142 at 5750 rpm (140 at 5500 rpm in 1980). **Torque:** 149 lbs.-ft. at 4600 rpm (145 at 4500 rpm in 1980). Seven main bearings. Solid valve lifters. Fuel injection.

BASE V-8 (450 series): 90-degree, overhead-cam, "vee" type eight-cylinder. Cast iron block and aluminum heads. **Displacement:** 275.8 cu. in. (4520 cc). **Bore & Stroke:** 3.62 x 3.35 in. (92 x 85 mm). **Compression Ratio:** 8.0:1. **Brake Horsepower:** 180 at 4750 rpm (160 at 4200 rpm in 1980). **Torque:** 220 lbs.-ft. at 3000 rpm (230 at 2500 rpm in 1980). Five main bearings. Hydraulic valve lifters. Bosch fuel injection.

BASE V-8 (6.9 sedan): 90-degree, overhead-cam, "vee" type eight-cylinder. Cast iron block and aluminum heads. **Displacement:** 417 cu. in. (6834 cc). **Bore & Stroke:** 4.21 x 3.74 in. (107 x 95 mm). **Compression Ratio:** 8.0:1. **Brake Horsepower:** 250 at 4000 rpm. **Torque:** 360 lbs.-ft. at 2500 rpm. Five main bearings. Hydraulic valve lifters. Bosch K-Jetronic fuel injection.

CHASSIS DATA: Wheelbase: (240D/280/300D) 110 in.; (280SE) 112.8 in.; (300CD) 106.7 in.; (300SD) 112.8 in.; (300TD) 110 in.; (450SL) 96.9 in.; (450SLC) 111.0 in.; (450SEL) 116.7 in.; (6.9) 116.5 in. **Overall Length:** (240D/280/300D) 190.9 in.; (280SE) 205.5 in. (300CD) 187.5 in.; (300SD) 205.5 in.; (300TD) 190.9 in.; (450SL) 182.3 in.; (450SLC) 196.4 in.; (450SE) 205.5 in.; (450SEL) 209.4 in.; (6.9) 210 in. **Height:** (240D/280/300D) 56.6 in.; (280SE) 56.1 in.; (300CD) 54.9 in.; (300SD) 56.1 in.; (300TD) 57.9 in.; (450SL) 50.8 in.; (450SLC) 52.4 in.; (450SEL) 56.3 in.; (6.9) 55.5 in. **Width:** (240D/280/300D) 70.3 in.; (280SE) 73.6 in.; (300CD/TD) 70.3 in.; (300SD) 73.6 in.; (450SL/SLC) 70.5 in.; (450SEL) 73.6 in.; (6.9) 73.6 in. **Front Tread:** (240D/280/300D) 58.6 in.; (280SE) 59.9 in.; (450SL/SLC) 57.2 in.; (450SE/SEL) 60.0 in.; (6.9) 59.5 in. **Rear Tread:** (240D/280/300D) 56.9 in.; (280SE) 59.3 in.; (450SL/SLC) 56.7 in.; (450SEL) 59.3 in.; (6.9) 59.3 in. **Standard Tires:** (240D) 175SR14; (300D) 195/70HR14; (300CD/TD) 195/70SR14 or 195/70SR14; (280E) 195/70HR14; (280SE) 185HR14; (450 series) 205/70HR14; (6.9) 215/70HR14.

TECHNICAL: Layout: front-engine, rear-drive. **Transmission:** (240D) four-speed manual, or optional automatic; (others) automatic standard. **Steering:** recirculating ball. **Suspension (front):** unequal-length A-arms, coil springs and stabilizer bar. **Suspension (rear):** diagonal swing axles with coil springs and stabilizer bar. **Brakes:** front/rear disc. **Body Construction:** steel unibody.

MAJOR OPTIONS: Air conditioning (240D). Automatic transmission (240D). AM/FM stereo. AM/FM stereo with tape player. Alloy wheels. Sunroof. Leather or velour seats.

PRODUCTION/SALES: A total of 52,820 Mercedes-Benz passenger cars were sold in the U.S. during 1979, followed by 53,790 in 1980.

Manufacturer: Daimler-Benz AG, Stuttgart, West Germany.

Distributor: Mercedes-Benz of North America Inc., Montvale, New Jersey.

HISTORY: The 1979 models were introduced to the U.S. market in September 1978 (except station wagon, March 1979). Sales in the U.S. broke a record in 1979. Of the total sold, more than 70 percent had a diesel engine.

1981-82 MERCEDES-BENZ

240D — DIESEL FOUR — Production of the four-cylinder diesel sedan continued with little change. As before, a four-speed manual gearbox was standard; automatic transmission optional.

300 SERIES — DIESEL/TURBODIESEL FIVE — A quartet of models made up the five-cylinder diesel series. Each sedan rode a 110-inch wheelbase except the 300SD sedan, which measured 115.6 inches (and was actually part of the larger S-Class series). The 300CD coupe had a 106.7-inch wheelbase. The five-cylinder engine developed 120 horsepower under the 300SD/TD hoods, or 83 bhp for other models. For the 1982 model year, all diesel models were turbocharged, including the 300D and 300CD.

280E/CE — SIX — The 280-series coupe and sedan lasted through the 1981 model year, powered by a 168-cid six-cylinder engine that developed 140 horsepower.

Note: W123 was the Mercedes-Benz internal code for the shorter-wheelbase 240/280/300 body group.

380SL/SEL/SLC — S-CLASS — V-8 — An all-aluminum 3.8-liter V-8 engine went under the hood of the series of replacements for the 450 series. Leading the list was the 380SL two-seater coupe/roadster (again coded R107), joined by a 380SEL sedan and 380SLC coupe. The 380SL rode a carryover W116 platform, whereas the other 380-series platforms were now coded W126.

I.D. DATA: The 17-symbol Vehicle Identification Number is on the upper left of the instrument panel, visible through the windshield. Symbols 1-3 indicate country, make and vehicle type. Symbols 4-7 indicate model. The next symbol identifies the restraint system. Symbol 10 indicates model year ('B' – 1981; 'C' = 1982). Symbol 11 identifies the assembly plant. The final six digits form the sequential production number. Starting serial number (1981 models): (240D) WDBAB23A4BB213229; (300D) WDBAB30A6BB214778; (300CD) WDBAB50A6BB006797;(300TD-T) WDBAB93A6BN000094; (280E) WDBAA33A4BB081307; (380SEL) WDBCA33AXBB006202; (380SL) WDBBA45A6BB000654; (380SLC) WDBBA25A250BB000735.

Model	Body Type & Seating	Engine Type/CID	P.O.E. Price	Weight (lbs.)	Prod. Total
240D (Diesel)					
240D	4-dr Sedan-5P	I4/147	19312	3020	Note 1
300 SERIES (Diesel/Turbodiesel)					
300D	4-dr Sedan-5P	I5/183	25640	3295	Note 1
300CD	2-dr Coupe-4/5P	I5/183	29231	3285	Note 1
300SD	4-dr Sedan-5P	I5/183	34185	3625	Note 1
300TD	4-dr Sta Wag-5P	I5/183	31373	3615	Note 1
280 SERIES (1981 models)					
280E	4-dr Sedan-5P	I6/168	26848	3330	Note 1
280CE	2-dr Coupe-4/5P	I6/168	30314	3320	Note 1

Model	Body Type & Seating	Engine Type/CID	P.O.E. Price	Weight (lbs.)	Prod. Total
380 SERIES					
380SL	2-dr Rds-2P	V8/234	38993	3460	Note 1
380SEL	4-dr Sedan-5P	V8/234	44298	3570	Note 1
380SLC	2-dr Coupe-4/5P	V8/234	46638	3440	Note 1

Note 1: A total of 414,527 Mercedes-Benz passenger cars (all models) were produced during 1981, followed by 428,725 in 1982.

Model Note: A 380SEC coupe was added in 1982.

Price Note: Figures shown were valid in 1981. Figure shown for 240D included manual gearbox; a 240D with automatic cost $20,558 in 1981.

ENGINE DATA: BASE DIESEL FOUR (240D): Inline, overhead-cam four-cylinder. Cast iron block and head. **Displacement:** 146.7 cu. in. (2404 cc). **Bore & Stroke:** 3.58 x 3.64 in. (91 x 92.4 mm). **Compression Ratio:** 21.0:1. **Brake Horsepower:** 67 at 4000 rpm. **Torque:** 97 lbs.-ft. at 2400 rpm. Five main bearings. Solid valve lifters. Fuel injection.
BASE DIESEL FIVE (1981 300D/CD): Inline, overhead-cam five-cylinder. Cast iron block and head. **Displacement:** 183.4 cu. in. (3005 cc). **Bore & Stroke:** 3.58 x 3.64 in. (91 x 92.4 mm). **Compression Ratio:** 21.0:1. **Brake Horsepower:** 83 at 4200 rpm. **Torque:** 120 lbs.-ft. at 2400 rpm. Six main bearings. Solid valve lifters. Fuel injection.
BASE TURBODIESEL FIVE (300SD/TD): Same as 3005-cc five above, but with turbocharger — **Compression Ratio:** 21.5:1. **Brake Horsepower:** 120 at 4350 rpm. **Torque:** 170 lbs.-ft. at 2400 rpm.
BASE SIX (280 Series): Inline, dual-overhead-cam six-cylinder. Cast iron block and aluminum head. **Displacement:** 167.6 cu. in. (2746 cc). **Bore & Stroke:** 3.39 x 3.10 in. (86 x 78.8 mm). **Compression Ratio:** 8.0:1. **Brake Horsepower:** 140 at 5500 rpm. **Torque:** 145 lbs.-ft. at 4500 rpm. Seven main bearings. Fuel injection.
BASE V-8 (380 Series): Overhead-valve "vee" type eight-cylinder. Aluminum block and heads. **Displacement:** 234 cu. in. (3839 cc). **Bore & Stroke:** 3.46 x 3.11 in. (88 x 79 mm). **Compression Ratio:** 8.3:1. **Brake Horsepower:** 155 at 4750 rpm. **Torque:** 196 lbs.-ft. at 2750 rpm. Five main bearings. Hydraulic valve lifters. Fuel injection.

CHASSIS DATA: Wheelbase: (240D/300D/300TD) 110.0 in.; (300CD cpe) 106.7 in.; (300SD) 115.6 in.; (280E) 110.0 in.; (280CE cpe) 106.7 in.; (380SL) 96.9 in.; (380SEC) 112.2 in.; (380SLC) 111 in.; (380SEL) 121.1 in. **Overall Length:** (240D/300D/300TD) 190.9 in.; (300CD cpe) 187.5 in.; (280E) 190.9 in.; (280CE cpe) 187.5 in.; (380SL) 182.3 in.; (380SEC) 199.2 in.; (300SD) 202.6 in.; (380SLC) 196.4 in.; (380SEL) 208.1 in. **Height:** (240D/300D) 56.6 in.; (300CD cpe) 54.9 in.; (300TD wag) 57.9 in.; (300SD) 56.3 in.; (280E) 56.6 in.; (280CE cpe) 54.9 in.; (380SL) 50.8 in.; (380SEC) 55.4 in.; (380SLC) 52.4 in.; (380SEL) 56.7 in. **Width:** (240D/300D/300CD/300TD) 70.3 in.; (300SD) 71.7 in.; (280) 70.3 in.; (280CE) 70.3 in.; (380SL/SLC) 70.5 in.; (380SEC) 72.0 in.; (380SEL) 71.7 in. **Front Tread:** (240D/300D/300CD/300TD) 58.6 in.; (300SD) 60.8 in.; (380SL/SLC) 57.2 in.; (380SEL) 60.8 in. **Rear Tread:** (240D/300D) 56.9 in.; (300SD) 59.7 in.; (300TD wag) 57.2 in.; (380SL/SLC) 56.7 in.; (380SEL) 59.7 in.

TECHNICAL: Layout: front-engine, rear-drive. **Transmission:** (240D) four-speed manual, or optional four-speed automatic; (others) automatic standard. **Steering:** power recirculating ball. **Suspension (front):** upper/lower A-arms with coil springs and anti-roll bar. **Suspension (rear):** independent, semi-trailing arms with coil springs and anti-roll bar. **Brakes:** front/rear disc. **Body Construction:** steel unibody.

PRODUCTION/SALES: A total of 63,059 Mercedes-Benz passenger cars were sold in the U.S. during 1981, and 65,963 in 1982.

Manufacturer: Daimler-Benz AG, Stuttgart, West Germany.
Distributor: Mercedes-Benz of North America Inc., Montvale, New Jersey.

HISTORY: European versions of the 380SL carried a 5.0-liter version of the V-8 engine, consequently offering swifter performance. That difference created a demand for the bigger engines in the U.S., which was satisfied in some cases by "grey market" importation.

Note: W123 was the Mercedes-Benz internal code for the shorter-wheelbase 240/300 body group. The 300SD sedan rode a longer wheelbase and was part of the larger S-Class category.

300/380 SERIES — S-CLASS — V-8 — The Mercedes senior S-class lineup changed little for 1983. Models included the 300SD sedan with five-cylinder turbodiesel engine, and three 380-series models with V-8 power: the four-passenger 380SEC coupe, two-seat 380SL roadster, and 380SEL sedan on a long (121-inch) wheelbase. The all-aluminum 3.8-liter V-8, introduced in 1981, produced 155 horsepower. The 380SL roadster rode the old W116 platform, but the others used the W126 platform that debuted in 1981. This year, the V-8 engine got some modest modifications in the ignition system and electronic idle-speed control, and the dashboard displayed a different speedometer (unlike the 85-mph unit installed formerly). A power remote passenger mirror was now standard. The only transmission choice was a four-speed automatic.

I.D. DATA: The 17-symbol Vehicle Identification Number is on the upper left of the instrument panel, visible through the windshield. Symbols 1-3 indicate country, make and vehicle type. Symbols 4-7 indicate model. The next symbol identifies the restraint system. Symbol 10 indicates model year ('D' = 1983). Symbol 11 identifies the assembly plant. The final six digits form the sequential production number.

Model	Body Type & Seating	Engine Type/CID	P.O.E. Price	Weight (lbs.)	Prod. Total
240D (Diesel)					
240D	4-dr Sedan-5P	I4/147	22470	3155	Note 1
300 SERIES (Turbodiesel)					
300D	4-dr Sedan-5P	I5/183	30530	3450	Note 1
300CD	2-dr Coupe-5P	I5/183	33750	3450	Note 1
300SD	4-dr Sedan-5P	I5/183	37970	3650	Note 1
300TD	4-dr Sta Wag-5P	I5/183	33850	3660	Note 1
380 SERIES					
380SL	2-dr Rds-2P	V8/234	43030	3505	Note 1
380SEL	4-dr Sedan-5P	V8/234	47870	3640	Note 1
380SEC	2-dr Coupe-4/5P	V8/234	53570	3615	Note 1

Note 1: A total of 483,359 Mercedes-Benz passenger cars (all models) were produced during 1983.

ENGINE DATA: BASE DIESEL FOUR (240D): Inline, overhead-cam four-cylinder. Cast iron block and head. **Displacement:** 146.7 cu. in. (2404 cc). **Bore & Stroke:** 3.58 x 3.64 in. (91 x 92.4 mm). **Compression Ratio:** 21.0:1. **Brake Horsepower:** 67 at 4000 rpm. **Torque:** 97 lbs.-ft. at 2400 rpm. Five main bearings. Solid valve lifters. Fuel injection.
BASE TURBODIESEL FIVE (300 Series): Inline, overhead-cam five-cylinder, with turbocharger. Cast iron block and head. **Displacement:** 183 cu. in. (2998 cc). **Bore & Stroke:** 3.58 x 3.64 in. (91 x 92.4 mm). **Compression Ratio:** 21.5:1. **Brake Horsepower:** 120 at 4350 rpm. **Torque:** 170 lbs.-ft. at 2400 rpm. Six main bearings. Solid valve lifters. Fuel injection.
BASE V-8 (380 Series): Overhead-cam "vee" type eight-cylinder. Light alloy block and heads. **Displacement:** 234 cu. in. (3839 cc). **Bore & Stroke:** 3.46 x 3.11 in. (88 x 79 mm). **Compression Ratio:** 8.3:1. **Brake Horsepower:** 155 at 4750 rpm. **Torque:** 196 lbs.-ft. at 2750 rpm. Five main bearings. Fuel injection.

CHASSIS DATA: Wheelbase: (240D) 110.0 in.; (300 cpe) 106.7 in.; (300 sed/wag) 110.0 in.; (380SL) 96.9 in.; (380SEC) 112.2 in.; (300SD) 115.6 in.; (380SEL) 121.1 in. **Overall Length:** (240D) 190.9 in.; (300 cpe) 187.5 in.; (300 sed/wag) 190.9 in.; (380SL) 182.3 in.; (380SEC) 199.2 in.; (300SD) 202.6 in.; (380SEL) 208.1 in. **Height:** (240D) 56.6 in.; (300 cpe) 54.9 in.; (300 sed) 56.6 in.; (300 wag) 58.7 in.; (380SL) 50.8 in.; (380SEC) 55.4 in.; (300SD) 56.3 in.; (380SEL) 56.7 in. **Width:** (240D) 70.3 in.; (300) 70.3 in.; (380SL) 70.5 in.; (380SEC) 72.0 in.; (300SD) 71.7 in.; (380SEL) 71.7 in. **Front Tread:** (240D) 58.6 in.; (300 cpe/sed) 56.9 in.; (300 wag) 57.2 in.; (380SL) 57.2 in.; (380SEC) 60.8 in.; (300SD) 60.8 in. **Rear Tread:** (240D) 56.9 in.; (300 cpe/sed) 56.9 in.; (300 wag) 57.2 in.; (380SL) 56.7 in.; (380SEC) 59.7 in.; (300SD) 59.7 in.; (380SEL) 59.7 in.

TECHNICAL: Layout: front-engine, rear-drive. **Transmission:** (240D) four-speed manual, or optional four-speed automatic; (others) four-speed automatic. **Steering:** power recirculating ball. **Suspension (front):** upper/lower A-arms with coil springs and anti-roll bar. **Suspension (rear):** independent, semi-trailing arms with coil springs and anti-roll bar. **Brakes:** front/rear disc. **Body Construction:** steel unibody.

PRODUCTION/SALES: A total of 73,692 Mercedes-Benz cars were sold in the U.S. during 1983.

Manufacturer: Daimler-Benz AG, Stuttgart, West Germany.
Distributor: Mercedes-Benz of North America Inc., Montvale, New Jersey.

1983 MERCEDES-BENZ

1983 Mercedes-Benz 300D.

240D — DIESEL FOUR — Powered by a diesel four-cylinder (non-turbo) engine, the 240D four-door sedan changed little this year. A remote-control passenger door mirror was now standard, the speedometer now displayed readings above 85 mph, and windshield post moldings were restyled. Either a four-speed manual or four-speed automatic transmission was available.

300 SERIES — TURBODIESEL FIVE — Changes to the 300D turbodiesel sedan were similar to the 240D, and all three of these models got the revised speedometer and remote mirror. The 3.0-liter (183-cid) five-cylinder inline engine produced 120 horsepower, and came only with four-speed automatic.

1984-85 MERCEDES-BENZ

1985 Mercedes-Benz 380SE sedan.

190 SERIES — GAS/DIESEL FOUR — Both gasoline and diesel four-cylinder engines were available in the new Mercedes compact luxury sedan series, driving either a five-speed manual or four-speed automatic transmission. The former 240 sedan was dropped, making the 190 the least costly model. The 190 four-door had fully independent suspension and front/rear disc brakes. Basic appearance and details were typical Mercedes, led by the familiar grille shape. A driver's airbag became optional during the 1984 model year. A revised camshaft and intake manifold gave the 2.3-liter gasoline engine a horsepower boost for 1985 (from 113 to 120).

300 SERIES — TURBODIESEL FIVE — Little was new on the turbodiesel series, except for a slight change in engine horsepower (due not to mechanical modifications but to a revised method of measurement). A revised four-speed automatic became standard for 1985, with a different torque converter that was intended to help overcome turbo lag and boost low-speed acceleration.

300/380 SERIES — S-CLASS — V-8 — Only two models made up the 380 series for 1984: the two-seat 380SL roadster and 380SE four-door sedan. A larger V-8 engine went into the SEL sedan and SEC coupe, to create a new 500 series. The 380SE was essentially a gasoline-powered version of the 300SD diesel sedan (also a member of the S-Class), with larger tires. All S-series models now included an anti-theft alarm and outside-temperature sensor. Power seats included a two-position memory. A driver's airbag was now optional. For 1985, anti-lock braking became standard.

1985 Mercedes-Benz 500SEC.

500 SERIES — S-CLASS — V-8 — A new all-aluminum 5.0-liter overhead-cam V-8 powered the 500SEC coupe and long-wheelbase 500SEL sedan, which formerly carried the smaller (3.8-liter) engine. An anti-theft alarm and outside-temperature sensor were standard, and an airbag became optional. Front seats were electrically heated in the 500SEC coupe, while all passengers in the 500SEL sedan enjoyed that extra comfort. Anti-lock braking became standard on the 1985 models, along with the driver's airbag, electrically-adjustable headrests, and heated outside mirrors.

I.D. DATA: The 17-symbol Vehicle Identification Number is on the upper left of the instrument panel, visible through the windshield. Symbols 1-3 indicate country, make and vehicle type. Symbols 4-7 indicate model. The next symbol identifies the restraint system. Symbol 10 indicates model year ('E' = 1984; 'F' = 1985). Symbol 11 identifies the assembly plant. The final six digits form the sequential production number.

Model	Body Type & Seating	Engine Type/CID	P.O.E. Price	Weight (lbs.)	Prod. Total
190 SERIES					
190E	4-dr Sedan-5P	I4/140	22850	2575	Note 1
190D (Dsl)	4-dr Sedan-5P	I4/134	22930	2555	Note 1
300 SERIES (Turbodiesel)					
300D	4-dr Sedan-5P	I5/183	31490	3360	Note 1
300CD	2-dr Coupe-5P	I5/183	35220	3360	Note 1
300SD	4-dr Sedan-5P	I5/183	39500	3605	Note 1
300TD	4-dr Sta Wag-5P	I5/183	35310	3630	Note 1
380 SERIES					
380SL	2-dr Rds-2P	V8/234	43820	3505	Note 1
380SE	4-dr Sedan-5P	V8/234	42730	3540	Note 1
500 SERIES					
500SEL	4-dr Sedan-5P	V8/303	51200	3730	Note 1
500SEC	2-dr Coupe-5P	V8/303	56800	3605	Note 1

Note 1: A total of 469,385 Mercedes-Benz passenger cars (all models) were produced during 1984, and 537,909 in 1985.

Price Note: Figures shown were valid in 1984 and 1985.

ENGINE DATA: BASE FOUR (190E): Inline, overhead-cam four-cylinder. Cast iron block and light alloy head. **Displacement:** 140.3 cu. in. (2300 cc). **Bore & Stroke:** 3.76 x 3.16 in. (95.5 x 80.2 mm). **Compression Ratio:** 8.0:1. **Brake Horsepower:** (1984) 113 at 5000 rpm; (1985) 120 at 5000 rpm. **Torque:** (1984) 133 lbs.-ft. at 3500 rpm; (1985) 136 lbs.-ft. at 3500 rpm. Five main bearings. Multi-point fuel injection.

BASE DIESEL FOUR (190D): Inline, overhead-cam four-cylinder. **Displacement:** 134 cu. in. (2197 cc). **Bore & Stroke:** 3.43 x 3.64 in. (87 x 92.4 mm). **Compression Ratio:** 22.0:1. **Brake Horsepower:** 72 at 4200 rpm. **Torque:** 96 lbs.-ft. at 2800 rpm. Five main bearings. Fuel injection.

BASE TURBODIESEL FIVE (300 Series): Inline, overhead-cam five-cylinder, with turbocharger. Cast iron block and head. **Displacement:** 183 cu. in. (2998 cc). **Bore & Stroke:** 3.58 x 3.64 in. (91 x 92.4 mm). **Compression Ratio:** 21.5:1. **Brake Horsepower:** 123 at 4350 rpm. **Torque:** 184 lbs.-ft. at 2400 rpm. Six main bearings. Solid valve lifters. Fuel injection.

BASE V-8 (380 Series): Overhead-cam "vee" type eight-cylinder. Light alloy block and heads. **Displacement:** 234 cu. in. (3839 cc). **Bore & Stroke:** 3.46 x 3.11 in. (88 x 79 mm). **Compression Ratio:** 8.3:1. **Brake Horsepower:** 155 at 4750 rpm. **Torque:** 196 lbs.-ft. at 2750 rpm. Five main bearings. Multi-point fuel injection.

BASE V-8 (500 Series): Overhead-cam "vee" type eight-cylinder. Light alloy block and heads. **Displacement:** 303 cu. in. (4973 cc). **Bore & Stroke:** 3.80 x 3.35 in. (96.5 x 85 mm). **Compression Ratio:** 8.0:1. **Brake Horsepower:** 184 at 4500 rpm. **Torque:** 247 lbs.-ft. at 2000 rpm. Five main bearings. Multi-point fuel injection.

CHASSIS DATA: Wheelbase: (190) 104.9 in.; (300 cpe) 106.7 in.; (300 sed/wag) 110.0 in.; (380SL) 96.9 in.; (500SEC) 112.0 in.; (300SD/380SE) 115.6 in.; (500SEL) 120.9 in. **Overall Length:** (190) 175.0 in.; (300 cpe) 187.5 in.; (300 sed/wag) 190.9 in.; (380SL) 180.3 in.; (500SEC) 199.2 in.; (300SD/380SE) 202.6 in.; (500SEL) 208.1 in. **Height:** (190) 54.4 in.; (300 cpe) 54.9 in.; (300 sed) 56.6 in.; (300 wag) 58.7 in.; (380SL) 50.8 in.; (500SEC) 55.4 in.; (300SD) 56.3 in.; (380SE) 56.5 in.; (500SEL) 55.5 in. **Width:** (190) 66.1 in.; (300) 70.3 in.; (380SL) 70.5 in.; (500SEC) 72.0 in.; (380SE) 71.7 in.; (500SEL) 71.7 in. **Front Tread:** (190) 56.2 in.; (300) 58.6 in.; (380SL) 57.2 in.; (500SEC) 60.8 in.; (300SD, 380SE) 60.8 in.; (500SEL) 60.8 in. **Rear Tread:** (190) 55.7 in.; (300 cpe/sed) 56.9 in.; (300 wag) 57.2 in.; (380SL) 56.7 in.; (500SEC) 59.7 in.; (300SD, 380SE) 59.7 in.; (500SEL) 59.7 in.

TECHNICAL: Layout: front-engine, rear-drive. **Transmission:** (190) five-speed manual, or optional four-speed automatic; (others) four-speed automatic. **Steering:** power recirculating ball. **Suspension (front):** upper/lower A-arms with coil springs and anti-roll bar except (190) modified MacPherson struts with coil springs and anti-roll bar. **Suspension (rear):** independent, semi-trailing arms with coil springs and anti-roll bar except (190) five-link independent with coil springs and anti-roll bar. **Brakes:** front/rear disc. **Body Construction:** steel unibody.

PRODUCTION/SALES: A total of 79,222 Mercedes-Benz cars were sold in the U.S. during 1984, and 86,903 in 1985.

Manufacturer: Daimler-Benz AG, Stuttgart, West Germany.

Distributor: Mercedes-Benz of North America Inc., Montvale, New Jersey.

1986 MERCEDES-BENZ

1986 Mercedes-Benz 300E.

190 SERIES — GAS FOUR/DIESEL FIVE — A new 2.5-liter five-cylinder engine now was installed in diesel versions of the 190 sedan. Besides that, a more potent 16-valve variant of the 2.3-liter four went into a new sports model, known as the 190E 2.3-16 (or 16V). Exhausting through tubular headers, the dual-overhead-cam sport engine developed 167 horsepower, versus 121 bhp for the regular four. Standard equipment on the sport versions include anti-lock braking, a limited-slip differential, 205/55VR15 tires (on wider wheels), thicker stabilizer bars, and a hydraulic rear-leveling system. Aero add-on components on the outside, including a front air dam, made the sport edition easier to spot. Passenger capacity was diminished by one, however, as the sport model's back seat was shaped to hold only two people.

300E/300D — GAS/TURBODIESEL SIX — Mercedes introduced a new mid-size sedan for 1986, powered by an inline gasoline six-cylinder engine that developed 177 horsepower. The gasoline-powered sedan was joined by a turbodiesel version, with slightly larger engine displacement and rated 148 bhp. These two replaced the W123 series. Only slightly taller than its predecessor, and a tad longer in wheelbase, the new sedan was shorter and narrower overall, and lost some 200 pounds. Styling followed the wedge profile introduced with the 190 series. The windshield had a steeper angle than before, with a lower nose and taller trunk lid. Standard equipment included a driver's airbag, anti-lock braking, headlamp wiper/washers, central locking, and an anti-theft alarm system.

300SDL/420SEL — S-CLASS — TURBODIESEL SIX/GAS V-8 — A new 420-series sedan joined the Mercedes lineup in 1986, powered by an enlarged (4.2-liter) V-8 engine that developed 201 horsepower. Its turbodiesel counterpart was the 300SDL, with a 3.0-liter six under its hood. Wheelbases were longer than predecessors, measuring 121.1 inches.

560 SERIES — S-CLASS — V-8 — A 5.6-liter V-8 engine went into the new 560 series, which included the two-seat 560SL coupe/roadster, as well as a 560SEL sedan and 560SEC coupe. A four-speed automatic transmission was standard. Appearance and dimensions were similar to the prior 380 series. The new 560SL had larger brakes, wheels and tires, as well as a recalibrated suspension.

I.D. DATA: The 17-symbol Vehicle Identification Number is on the upper left of the instrument panel, visible through the windshield. Symbols 1-3 indicate country, make and vehicle type. Symbols 4-7 indicate model. The next symbol identifies the restraint system. Symbol 10 indicates model year ('G' = 1986). Symbol 11 identifies the assembly plant. The final six digits form the sequential production number.

Model	Body Type & Seating	Engine Type/CID	P.O.E. Price	Weight (lbs.)	Prod. Total
190 SERIES					
190E	4-dr Sedan-5P	I4/140	23700	2660	Note 1
190E 2.3-16	4-dr Sedan-4P	I4/140	34800	2930	Note 1
190D (Dsl)	4-dr Sedan-5P	I5/152	23700	2765	Note 1
300 SERIES (Gasoline)					
300E	4-dr Sedan-5P	I6/181	33900	3190	Note 1
300 SERIES (Diesel)					
300D	4-dr Sedan-5P	I6/183	N/A	3255	Note 1
300SDL	4-dr Sedan-5P	I6/183	43800	3680	Note 1
420 SERIES					
420SEL	4-dr Sedan-5P	V8/256	45100	3705	Note 1
560 SERIES					
560SEL	4-dr Sedan-5P	V8/338	58300	3980	Note 1
560SEC	2-dr Coupe-4P	V8/338	58700	3815	Note 1
560SL	2-dr Rds-2P	V8/338	48200	3650	Note 1

Note 1: A total of 591,916 Mercedes-Benz passenger cars (all models) were produced during 1986.

ENGINE DATA: BASE FOUR (190E): Inline, overhead-cam four-cylinder. Cast iron block and light alloy head. **Displacement:** 140.3 cu. in. (2300 cc). **Bore & Stroke:** 3.76 x 3.16 in. (95.5 x 80.2 mm). **Compression Ratio:** 8.0:1. **Brake Horsepower:** 121 at 5000 rpm. **Torque:** 136 lbs.-ft. at 3500 rpm. Five main bearings. Hydraulic valve lifters. Multi-point fuel injection.

BASE FOUR (190E 2.3-16): Same as above, except dual-overhead-cam (16-valve). **Brake Horsepower:** 167 at 5800 rpm. **Torque:** 162 lbs.-ft. at 4750 rpm.

BASE DIESEL FIVE (190D): Inline, overhead-cam five-cylinder. **Displacement:** 152 cu. in. (2492 cc). **Bore & Stroke:** 3.43 x 3.31 in. (87 x 84 mm). **Compression Ratio:** 22.0:1. **Brake Horsepower:** 93 at 4600 rpm. **Torque:** 122 lbs.-ft. at 2800 rpm. Five main bearings. Fuel injection.

BASE SIX (300E): Inline, overhead-cam six-cylinder. **Displacement:** 180.8 cu. in. (2964 cc). **Bore & Stroke:** 3.48 x 3.16 in. (88 x 80 mm). **Compression Ratio:** 9.2:1. **Brake Horsepower:** 177 at 5700 rpm. **Torque:** 188 lbs.-ft. at 4400 rpm. Hydraulic valve lifters. Multi-point fuel injection.

BASE TURBODIESEL SIX (300D, 300SDL): Inline, overhead-cam six-cylinder, with turbocharger. Cast iron block and head. **Displacement:** 183 cu. in. (2998 cc). **Bore & Stroke:** 3.43 x 3.31 in. (87 x 84 mm). **Compression Ratio:** 22.0:1. **Brake Horsepower:** 148 at 4600 rpm. **Torque:** 201 lbs.-ft. at 2400 rpm. Fuel injection.

BASE V-8 (420SEL): Overhead-cam "vee" type eight-cylinder. Light alloy block and heads. **Displacement:** 256 cu. in. (4197 cc). **Bore & Stroke:** 3.62 x 3.11 in. (92 x 79 mm). **Compression Ratio:** 9.0:1. **Brake Horsepower:** 201 at 5200 rpm. **Torque:** 228 lbs.-ft. at 3600 rpm. Five main bearings. Hydraulic valve lifters. Multi-point fuel injection.

BASE V-8 (560 Series): Overhead-cam "vee" type eight-cylinder. Light alloy block and heads. **Displacement:** 338.5 cu. in. (5549 cc). **Bore & Stroke:** 3.80 x 3.73 in. (96.5 x 94.7 mm). **Compression Ratio:** 9.0:1. **Brake Horsepower:** 238 at 5200 rpm. **Torque:** 287 lbs.-ft. at 3500 rpm. Five main bearings. Hydraulic valve lifters. Multi-point fuel injection.

CHASSIS DATA: Wheelbase: (190) 104.9 in.; (300D/E) 110.2 in.; (300SDL/420SEL) 121.1 in.; (560SL) 96.7 in.; (560SEC) 112.0 in.; (560SEL) 120.9 in. **Overall Length:** (190) 175.0 in.; (300D/E) 187.2 in.; (300SDL/420SEL) 208.1 in.; (560SL) 180.3 in.; (560SEC) 199.2 in.; (560SEL) 208.1 in. **Height:** (190) 54.4 in.; (300D/E) 56.9 in.; (300SDL/420SEL) 56.7 in.; (560SL) 50.8 in.; (560SEC) 55.6 in.; (560SEL) 55.7 in. **Width:** (190) 66.1 in.; (300D/E) 68.5 in.; (300SDL/420SEL) 71.7 in.; (560SL) 70.5 in.; (560SEC) 72.0 in.; (560SEL) 71.7 in. **Front Tread:** (190) 56.2 in.; (190E 2.3-16) 56.9 in.; (300D/E) 58.9 in.; (300SDL/420SEL) 61.2 in.; (560SL) 57.6 in.; (560SEC/SEL) 61.2 in. **Rear Tread:** (190) 55.7 in.; (190E 2.3-16) 56.3 in.; (300D/E) 58.6 in.; (300SDL/420SEL) 60.1 in.; (560SL) 57.7 in.; (560SEC/SEL) 60.1 in.

TECHNICAL: Layout: front-engine, rear-drive. **Transmission:** (190) five-speed manual, or optional four-speed automatic; (others) four-speed automatic standard. **Steering:** power recirculating ball. **Suspension (front):** upper/lower A-arms with coil springs and anti-roll bar except (190) modified MacPherson struts with coil springs and anti-roll bar; (300) gas-pressurized struts with coil springs and anti-roll bar. **Suspension (rear):** independent, semi-trailing arms with coil springs and anti-roll bar except (190/300) five-link independent with coil springs and anti-roll bar. **Brakes:** front/rear disc. **Body Construction:** steel unibody.

PRODUCTION/SALES: A total of 99,314 Mercedes-Benz cars were sold in the U.S. during 1986.

Manufacturer: Daimler-Benz AG, Stuttgart, West Germany.

Distributor: Mercedes-Benz of North America Inc., Montvale, New Jersey.

1987 MERCEDES-BENZ

190 SERIES — GAS FOUR/SIX, DIESEL FIVE — The 190 series grew considerably more complex for 1987, with five different engines and two new models added later in the season. A new 190E 2.6 adopted the 2.6-liter six-cylinder engine installed in the larger 260E sedan. A turbocharged version of the five-cylinder diesel engine went into a new 190D 2.5 Turbo sedan. Each of the new models included a special front air dam, intended to boost engine cooling. All 190-series sedans gained new aero halogen headlamps. The 190E's gasoline four-cylinder engine got a boost in compression and horsepower this year. Headlamp washers became standard on the high-performance 190E 2.3-16, which continued with its dual-overhead-cam version of the four-cylinder engine.

260E/300 SERIES — GAS/TURBODIESEL SIX — The mid-size Mercedes lineup expanded its model offerings for 1987 with a new 260E sedan, powered by a new 2.6-liter six-cylinder engine. In addition to that, a 300D Turbo sedan and 300TD Turbo station wagon were available. The wagon included a hydropneumatic self-leveling rear suspension.

300SDL/420SEL — S-CLASS — TURBODIESEL SIX/GAS V-8 — Little was new in the two long-wheelbase sedans, powered by a six-cylinder turbodiesel or a 4.2-liter gasoline V-8 engine.

560 SERIES — S-CLASS — V-8 — Each of the three 560-series models was carried over with little change.

I.D. DATA: The 17-symbol Vehicle Identification Number is on the upper left of the instrument panel, visible through the windshield. Symbols 1-3 indicate country, make and vehicle type. Symbols 4-7 indicate model. The next symbol identifies the restraint system. Symbol 10 indicates model year ('H' = 1987). Symbol 11 identifies the assembly plant. The final six digits form the sequential production number.

Model	Body Type & Seating	Engine Type/CID	P.O.E. Price	Weight (lbs.)	Prod. Total
190 SERIES (Gasoline)					
190E 2.3	4-dr Sedan-5P	I4/140	26400	2780	Note 1
190E 2.3-16	4-dr Sedan-4P	I4/140	39600	2900	Note 1
190E 2.6	4-dr Sedan-5P	I6/159	30300	2750	Note 1
190 SERIES (Diesel)					
190D 2.5	4-dr Sedan-5P	I5/152	26400	2750	Note 1
190TD Turbo	4-dr Sedan-4P	I5/152	29800	2920	Note 1
260 SERIES					
260E	4-dr Sedan-5P	I6/159	33700	3100	Note 1
300 SERIES (Gasoline)					
300E	4-dr Sedan-5P	I6/181	38600	3110	Note 1
300 SERIES (Turbodiesel)					
300D	4-dr Sedan-5P	I6/183	39500	3255	Note 1
300TD	4-dr Sta Wag-5P	I6/183	42500	3550	Note 1
300SDL	4-dr Sedan-5P	I6/183	47000	3680	Note 1
420 SERIES					
420SEL	4-dr Sedan-5P	V8/256	52000	3695	Note 1
560 SERIES					
560SEL	4-dr Sedan-5P	V8/338	61500	3925	Note 1
560SEC	2-dr Coupe-4P	V8/338	68000	3750	Note 1
560SL	2-dr Rds-2P	V8/338	55300	3570	Note 1

Note 1: A total of 595,765 Mercedes-Benz passenger cars (all models) were produced during 1987.

ENGINE DATA: BASE FOUR (190E): Inline, overhead-cam four-cylinder. Cast iron block and light alloy head. **Displacement:** 140.3 cu. in. (2300 cc). **Bore & Stroke:** 3.76 x 3.16 in. (95.5 x 80.2 mm). **Compression Ratio:** 9.0:1. **Brake Horsepower:** 130 at 5100 rpm. **Torque:** 146 lbs.-ft. at 3500 rpm. Five main bearings. Hydraulic valve lifters. Multi-point fuel injection.

BASE FOUR (190E 2.3-16): Same as above, except dual-overhead-cam (16-valve). **Brake Horsepower:** 167 at 5800 rpm. **Torque:** 162 lbs.-ft. at 4750 rpm.

BASE DIESEL FIVE (190D): Inline, overhead-cam five-cylinder. **Displacement:** 152 cu. in. (2492 cc). **Bore & Stroke:** 3.43 x 3.31 in. (87 x 84 mm). **Compression Ratio:** 22.0:1. **Brake Horsepower:** 93 at 4600 rpm. **Torque:** 122 lbs.-ft. at 2800 rpm. Five main bearings. Fuel injection.

BASE TURBODIESEL FIVE (190TD): Same as diesel five above, but with turbocharger — **Brake Horsepower:** 123 at 4600 rpm. **Torque:** 168 lbs.-ft. at 2400 rpm.

BASE SIX (190E 2.6, 260E): Inline, overhead-cam six-cylinder. **Displacement:** 158.6 cu. in. (2600 cc). **Bore & Stroke:** 3.26 x 3.16 in. (83 x 80 mm). **Compression Ratio:** 9.2:1. **Brake Horsepower:** 158 at 5800 rpm. **Torque:** 162 lbs.-ft. at 4600 rpm. Multi-point fuel injection.

BASE SIX (300E): Inline, overhead-cam six-cylinder. **Displacement:** 180.8 cu. in. (2964 cc). **Bore & Stroke:** 3.48 x 3.16 in. (88 x 80 mm). **Compression Ratio:** 9.2:1. **Brake Horsepower:** 177 at 5700 rpm. **Torque:** 188 lbs.-ft. at 4400 rpm. Hydraulic valve lifters. Multi-point fuel injection.

BASE TURBODIESEL SIX (300D Series): Inline, overhead-cam six-cylinder, with turbocharger. Cast iron block and head. **Displacement:** 183 cu. in. (2998 cc). **Bore & Stroke:** 3.43 x 3.31 in. (87 x 84 mm). **Compression Ratio:** 22.0:1. **Brake Horsepower:** 143 at 4600 rpm. **Torque:** 195 lbs.-ft. at 2400 rpm. Fuel injection.

BASE V-8 (420SEL): Overhead-cam "vee" type eight-cylinder. Light alloy block and heads. **Displacement:** 256 cu. in. (4197 cc). **Bore & Stroke:** 3.62 x 3.11 in. (92 x 79 mm). **Compression Ratio:** 9.0:1. **Brake Horsepower:** 201 at 5200 rpm. **Torque:** 228 lbs.-ft. at 3600 rpm. Five main bearings. Hydraulic valve lifters. Multi-point fuel injection.

BASE V-8 (560 Series): Overhead-cam "vee" type eight-cylinder. Light alloy block and heads. **Displacement:** 338.5 cu. in. (5549 cc). **Bore & Stroke:** 3.80 x 3.73 in. (96.5 x 94.7 mm). **Compression Ratio:** 9.0:1. **Brake Horsepower:** 238 at 4800 rpm (227 at 4750 rpm in 560SL). **Torque:** 287 lbs.-ft. at 3500 rpm (279 at 3250 rpm in 560SL). Five main bearings. Hydraulic valve lifters. Multi-point fuel injection.

CHASSIS DATA: Wheelbase: (190) 104.9 in.; (260E, 300D/E) 110.2 in.; (300SDL/420SEL) 121.1 in.; (560SL) 96.7 in.; (560SEC) 112.0 in.; (560SEL) 120.9 in. **Overall Length:** (190E) 175.1 in.; (190E 2.3-16) 174.4 in.; (190D) 175.0 in.; (260E, (300D/E) 187.2 in.; (300SDL/420SEL) 208.1 in.; (560SL) 180.3 in.; (560SEC) 199.2 in.; (560SEL) 208.1 in. **Height:** (190D/E) 54.7 in.; (190E 2.3-16) 53.6 in.; (260E, 300D/E) 56.9 in.; (300SDL/420SEL) 56.7 in.; (560SL) 51.5 in.; (560SEC) 55.0 in.; (560SEL) 56.3 in. **Width:** (190D/E) 66.1 in.; (190E 2.3-16) 67.2 in.; (260E, 300D/E) 68.5 in.; (300SDL/420SEL) 71.7 in.; (560SL) 70.5 in.; (560SEC) 72.0 in.; (560SEL) 71.7 in. **Front Tread:** (190D/E) 56.6 in.; (190E 2.3-16) 56.9 in.; (260E, 300D/E) 58.9 in.; (300SDL/420SEL) 61.2 in.; (560SL) 57.7 in.; (560SEC/SEL) 61.2 in. **Rear Tread:** (190D/E) 55.8 in.; (190E 2.3-16) 56.3 in.; (260E, 300D/E) 58.6 in.; (300SDL/420SEL) 60.1 in.; (560SL) 57.7 in.; (560SEC/SEL) 60.1 in.

TECHNICAL: Layout: front-engine, rear-drive. **Transmission:** (190E 2.3) five-speed manual, or optional four-speed automatic; (others) four-speed automatic standard. **Steering:** power recirculating ball. **Suspension (front):** upper/lower A-arms with coil springs and anti-roll bar except (190) modified MacPherson struts with coil springs and anti-roll bar; (260/300) gas-pressurized struts with coil springs and anti-roll bar. **Suspension (rear):** independent, semi-trailing arms with coil springs and anti-roll bar except (190/260/300) five-link independent with coil springs and anti-roll bar. **Brakes:** front/rear disc. **Body Construction:** steel unibody.

PRODUCTION/SALES: A total of 89,918 Mercedes-Benz cars were sold in the U.S. during 1987.

Manufacturer: Daimler-Benz AG, Stuttgart, West Germany.

Distributor: Mercedes-Benz of North America Inc., Montvale, New Jersey.

1988 MERCEDES-BENZ

1988 Mercedes-Benz 300E sedan (rear); 1988 Mercedes-Benz 300CE (front).

190 SERIES — GAS FOUR/SIX, DIESEL FIVE — The sporty, high-performance 190E 2.3-16 model dropped out this year, as did the turbodiesel five. Thus, only one diesel model was offered. A five-speed manual gearbox was standard on all gasoline models, including the 2.6-liter engine (formerly offered only with the four-speed automatic).

260/300 SERIES — SIX — A four-seat 300CE coupe joined the former sedan and station wagon this year, but the turbodiesel six-cylinder engine faded away so all models had gasoline engines. Wheelbase of the new coupe was shorter than the sedan, and it displayed a steeper windshield as well as frameless window glass. Leather upholstery was standard on the coupe, with velour optional. A five-speed manual gearbox was now standard in the 260E and 300E, with four-speed automatic optional (standard in other models).

300SE/300SEL/420SEL — S-CLASS — SIX/V-8 — Because the six-cylinder turbodiesel engine was dropped this year, the 300SDL sedan faded away; but it was replaced by a 300SEL with gasoline six. Otherwise, change was minimal in the long-wheelbase sedans. A 300SE on 115.6-inch wheelbase was added later in the model year.

560 SERIES — S-CLASS — V-8 — Little change was evident in the 5.6-liter versions of the upper Mercedes lineup.

I.D. DATA: The 17-symbol Vehicle Identification Number is on the upper left of the instrument panel, visible through the windshield. Symbols 1-3 indicate country, make and vehicle type. Symbols 4-7 indicate model. The next symbol identifies the restraint system. Symbol 10 indicates model year ('J' = 1988). Symbol 11 identifies the assembly plant. The final six digits form the sequential production number.

Model	Body Type & Seating	Engine Type/CID	P.O.E. Price	Weight (lbs.)	Prod. Total
190 SERIES					
190E 2.3	4-dr Sedan-5P	I4/140	29190	2705	Note 1
190E 2.6	4-dr Sedan-5P	I6/159	33500	2795	Note 1
190D (Dsl)	4-dr Sedan-5P	I5/152	29960	2795	Note 1
260 SERIES					
260E	4-dr Sedan-5P	I6/159	37250	3065	Note 1
300 SERIES					
300E	4-dr Sedan-5P	I6/181	42680	3090	Note 1
300TE	4-dr Sta Wag-5P	I6/181	46980	3360	Note 1
300CE	2-dr Coupe-4P	I6/181	52500	3200	Note 1
300SE	4-dr Sedan-5P	I6/181	49900	N/A	Note 1
300SEL	4-dr Sedan-5P	I6/181	52650	3630	Note 1
420 SERIES					
420SEL	4-dr Sedan-5P	V8/256	58150	3740	Note 1
560 SERIES					
560SEL	4-dr Sedan-5P	V8/338	68660	3940	Note 1
560SEC	2-dr Coupe-4P	V8/338	75850	3775	Note 1
560SL	2-dr Rds-2P	V8/338	61130	3570	Note 1

Note 1: A total of 553,772 Mercedes-Benz passenger cars (all models) were produced during 1988.

ENGINE DATA: BASE FOUR (190E): Inline, overhead-cam four-cylinder. Cast iron block and light alloy head. **Displacement:** 140.3 cu. in. (2300 cc). **Bore & Stroke:** 3.76 x 3.16 in. (95.5 x 80.2 mm). **Compression Ratio:** 9.0:1. **Brake Horsepower:** 130 at 5100 rpm. **Torque:** 146 lbs.-ft. at 3500 rpm. Five main bearings. Hydraulic valve lifters. Multi-point fuel injection.

BASE DIESEL FIVE (190D): Inline, overhead-cam five-cylinder. **Displacement:** 152 cu. in. (2492 cc). **Bore & Stroke:** 3.43 x 3.31 in. (87 x 84 mm). **Compression Ratio:** 22.0:1. **Brake Horsepower:** 93 at 4600 rpm. **Torque:** 122 lbs.-ft. at 2800 rpm. Five main bearings. Fuel Injection.

BASE SIX (190E 2.6, 260E): Inline, overhead-cam six-cylinder. **Displacement:** 158.6 cu. in. (2600 cc). **Bore & Stroke:** 3.26 x 3.16 in. (83 x 80 mm). **Compression Ratio:** 9.2:1. **Brake Horsepower:** 158 at 5800 rpm. **Torque:** 162 lbs.-ft. at 4600 rpm. Multi-point fuel injection.

BASE SIX (300): Inline, overhead-cam six-cylinder. **Displacement:** 180.8 cu. in. (2964 cc). **Bore & Stroke:** 3.48 x 3.16 in. (88 x 80 mm). **Compression Ratio:** 9.2:1. **Brake Horsepower:** 177 at 5700 rpm. **Torque:** 188 lbs.-ft. at 4400 rpm. Hydraulic valve lifters. Multi-point fuel injection.

BASE V-8 (420SEL): Overhead-cam "vee" type eight-cylinder. Light alloy block and heads. **Displacement:** 256 cu. in. (4197 cc). **Bore & Stroke:** 3.62 x 3.11 in. (92 x 79 mm). **Compression Ratio:** 9.0:1. **Brake Horsepower:** 201 at 5200 rpm. **Torque:** 228 lbs.-ft. at 3600 rpm. Five main bearings. Hydraulic valve lifters. Multi-point fuel injection.

BASE V-8 (560 Series): Overhead-cam "vee" type eight-cylinder. Light alloy block and heads. **Displacement:** 338.5 cu. in. (5549 cc). **Bore & Stroke:** 3.80 x 3.73 in. (96.5 x 94.7 mm). **Compression Ratio:** 9.0:1. **Brake Horsepower:** 238 at 4800 rpm (227 at 4750 rpm in 560SL). **Torque:** 287 lbs.-ft. at 3500 rpm (279 at 3250 rpm in 560SL). Five main bearings. Hydraulic valve lifters. Multi-point fuel injection.

CHASSIS DATA: Wheelbase: (190) 104.9 in.; (260E, 300E/TE) 110.2 in.; (300CE) 106.9 in.; (300SE) 115.6 in.; (300SEL/420SEL/560SEL) 121 in.; (560SL) 96.7 in.; (560SEC) 112.0 in. **Overall Length:** (190E) 175.1 in.; (190D) 175.0 in.; (260E/300E) 187.2 in.; (300E) 183.9 in.; (300TE) 188.2 in.; (300SE) 202.6 in.; (300SEL/420SEL) 208.1 in.; (560SL) 180.3 in.; (560SEC) 199.2 in.; (560SEL) 208.1 in. **Height:** (190) 54.7 in.; (260E, 300E/TE) 56.9 in.; (300CE) 55.5 in.; (300SE/300SEL/420SEL) 56.7 in.; (560SL) 51.1 in.; (560SEC) 55.0 in.; (560SEL) 56.3 in. **Width:** (190D/E) 66.1 in.; (260E/300) 68.5 in.; (300SE/300SEL/420SEL) 71.7 in.; (560SL) 70.5 in.; (560SEC) 72.0 in.; (560SL) 71.7 in. **Front Tread:** (190D/E) 56.6 in.; (260E/300) 58.9 in.; (300SE/300SEL/420SEL) 61.2 in.; (560SL) 57.7 in.; (560SEC/SEL) 61.2 in. **Rear Tread:** (190D/E) 55.8 in.; (260E/300) 58.6 in.; (300SE/300SEL/420SEL) 60.1 in.; (560SL) 57.7 in.; (560SEC/SEL) 60.1 in.

TECHNICAL: Layout: front-engine, rear-drive. **Transmission:** (190/260E/300E) five-speed manual, or optional four-speed automatic; (others) four-speed automatic standard. **Steering:** power recirculating ball. **Suspension (front):** upper/lower A-arms with coil springs and anti-roll bar except (190) modified MacPherson struts with coil springs and anti-roll bar; (260/300) gas-pressurized struts with coil springs and anti-roll bar. **Suspension (rear):** independent, semi-trailing arms with coil springs and anti-roll bar except (190/260/300) five-link independent with coil springs and anti-roll bar. **Brakes:** front/rear disc. **Body Construction:** steel unibody.

PRODUCTION/SALES: A total of 83,727 Mercedes-Benz cars were sold in the U.S. during 1988.
Manufacturer: Daimler-Benz AG, Stuttgart, West Germany.
Distributor: Mercedes-Benz of North America Inc., Montvale, New Jersey.

HISTORY: Although the prospect of a replacement for the aging 560SL coupe/roadster was rumored through the late 1980s, it would not arrive until the 1990 model year (as the 300SL/500SL).

1989 MERCEDES-BENZ

1989 Mercedes-Benz 300SE.

190 SERIES — GAS SIX, DIESEL FIVE — Only the six-cylinder gasoline engine and five-cylinder diesel remained for 1989, as four-cylinder power faded away. Diesel popularity had waned sharply in the late 1980s and no other Mercedes model offered a diesel engine (which was unavailable in California). Anti-lock brakes were now standard on all models. Otherwise, apart from a modest facelift that included the addition of wide bodyside moldings, restyled bumpers and a deeper front air dam, little was changed for 1989.

260/300 SERIES — SIX — The Mercedes mid-size lineup was carried over with little change, except for the addition of a passenger airbag to the option list. Power again came from one of two six-cylinder engines, offered only with an automatic transmission; the five-speed manual gearbox was dropped.

300SE/300SEL/420SEL — S-CLASS — SIX/V-8 — Except for the addition of a passenger's airbag as an option, and new soft leather upholstery as standard equipment, little was new among the long-wheelbase models, available with a 3.0-liter six or 4.2-liter V-8 engine.

560 SERIES — S-CLASS — V-8 — Little change was evident in the biggest-engined series, except for an optional passenger's airbag on the 560SEL sedan and 560SEC coupe.

I.D. DATA: The 17-symbol Vehicle Identification Number is on the upper left of the instrument panel, visible through the windshield. Symbols 1-3 indicate country, make and vehicle type. Symbols 4-7 indicate model. The next symbol identifies the restraint system. Symbol 10 indicates model year ('K' = 1989). Symbol 11 identifies the assembly plant. The final six digits form the sequential production number.

Model	Body Type & Seating	Engine Type/CID	P.O.E. Price	Weight (lbs.)	Prod. Total
190 SERIES					
190E 2.6	4-dr Sedan-5P	I6/159	31590	2870	Note 1
190D (Dsl)	4-dr Sedan-5P	I5/152	30980	2860	Note 1
260 SERIES					
260E	4-dr Sedan-5P	I6/159	39200	N/A	Note 1
300 SERIES					
300E	4-dr Sedan-5P	I6/181	44850	3155	Note 1
300TE	4-dr Sta Wag-5P	I6/181	48210	3415	Note 1
300SE	4-dr Sedan-5P	I6/181	51400	3585	Note 1
300CE	2-dr Coupe-4P	I6/181	53800	3200	Note 1
300SEL	4-dr Sedan-5P	I6/181	55100	3630	Note 1
420 SERIES					
420SEL	4-dr Sedan-5P	V8/256	61210	3740	Note 1
560 SERIES					
560SEL	4-dr Sedan-5P	V8/338	72280	3940	Note 1
560SEC	2-dr Coupe-4P	V8/338	79840	3775	Note 1
560SL	2-dr Rds-2P	V8/338	64230	3570	Note 1

Note 1: A total of 75,714 Mercedes-Benz cars were sold in the U.S. during 1989.

1989 Mercedes-Benz 560SL coupe/roadster.

ENGINE DATA: BASE DIESEL FIVE (190D): Inline, overhead-cam five-cylinder. **Displacement:** 152 cu. in. (2492 cc). **Bore & Stroke:** 3.43 x 3.31 in. (87 x 84 mm). **Compression Ratio:** 22.0:1. **Brake Horsepower:** 90 at 4600 rpm. **Torque:** 117 lbs.-ft. at 2800 rpm. Five main bearings. Fuel injection.

BASE SIX (190E 2.6, 260E): Inline, overhead-cam six-cylinder. **Displacement:** 158.6 cu. in. (2600 cc). **Bore & Stroke:** 3.26 x 3.16 in. (83 x 80 mm). **Compression Ratio:** 9.2:1. **Brake Horsepower:** 158 at 5800 rpm. **Torque:** 162 lbs.-ft. at 4600 rpm. Multi-point fuel injection.

BASE SIX (300): Inline, overhead-cam six-cylinder. **Displacement:** 180.8 cu. in. (2964 cc). **Bore & Stroke:** 3.48 x 3.16 in. (88 x 80 mm). **Compression Ratio:** 9.2:1. **Brake Horsepower:** 177 at 5700 rpm. **Torque:** 188 lbs.-ft. at 4400 rpm. Hydraulic valve lifters. Multi-point fuel injection.

BASE V-8 (420SEL): Overhead-cam "vee" type eight-cylinder. Light alloy block and heads. **Displacement:** 256 cu. in. (4197 cc). **Bore & Stroke:** 3.62 x 3.11 in. (92 x 79 mm). **Compression Ratio:** 9.0:1. **Brake Horsepower:** 201 at 5200 rpm. **Torque:** 228 lbs.-ft. at 3600 rpm. Five main bearings. Hydraulic valve lifters. Multi-point fuel injection.

BASE V-8 (560 Series): Overhead-cam "vee" type eight-cylinder. Light alloy block and heads. **Displacement:** 338.5 cu. in. (5549 cc). **Bore & Stroke:** 3.80 x 3.73 in. (96.5 x 94.7 mm). **Compression Ratio:** 9.0:1. **Brake Horsepower:** 238 at 4800 rpm (227 at 4750 rpm in 560SL). **Torque:** 287 lbs.-ft. at 3500 rpm (279 at 3250 rpm in 560SL). Five main bearings. Hydraulic valve lifters. Multi-point fuel injection.

1989 Mercedes-Benz 300SEL.

CHASSIS DATA: Wheelbase: (190) 104.9 in.; (260E, 300E/TE) 110.2 in.; (300CE) 106.9 in.; (300SE) 115.6 in.; (300SEL/420SEL/560SEL) 121.1 in.; (560SL) 96.7 in.; (560SEC) 112.2 in. **Overall Length:** (190) 175.1 in.; (260E/300E) 187.2 in.; (300CE) 183.9 in.; (300TE) 188.2 in.; (300SE) 202.6 in.; (300SEL/420SEL) 208.1 in.; (560SL) 180.3 in.; (560SEC) 199.2 in.; (560SEL) 208.1 in. **Height:** (190) 54.7 in.; (260E/300) 56.9 in.; (300CE) 55.5 in.; (300TE) 59.8 in.; (300SE) 56.6 in.; (300SEL/420SEL) 56.7 in.; (560SL) 51.1 in.; (560SEC) 55.0 in.; (560SEL) 56.3 in. **Width:** (190D/E) 66.5 in.; (260E/300) 68.5 in.; (300SE) 56.6 in.; (560SEL) 51.1 in.; (300SE/300SEL/420SEL) 71.7 in.; (560SL) 70.5 in.; (560SEC) 72.0 in.; (560SEL) 71.7 in. **Front Tread:** (190D/E) 56.6 in.; (260E/300) 58.9 in.; (300SE/300SEL/420SEL) 61.5 in.; (560SL) 57.7 in.; (560SEC/SEL) 61.5 in. **Rear Tread:** (190D/E) 55.8 in.; (260E/300) 58.6 in.; (300SE/300SEL/420SEL) 60.4 in.; (560SL) 57.7 in.; (560SEC/SEL) 60.4 in.

TECHNICAL: Layout: front-engine, rear-drive. **Transmission:** (190E 2.6) five-speed manual, or optional four-speed automatic; (others) four-speed automatic standard. **Steering:** power recirculating ball. **Suspension (front):** upper/lower A-arms with coil springs and anti-roll bar except (190) modified MacPherson struts with coil springs and anti-roll bar; (260/300) gas-pressurized struts with coil springs and anti-roll bar. **Suspension (rear):** independent, semi-trailing arms with coil springs and anti-roll bar except (190/260/300) five-link independent with coil springs and anti-roll bar. **Brakes:** front/rear disc. **Body Construction:** steel unibody.

Manufacturer: Daimler-Benz AG, Stuttgart, West Germany.

Distributor: Mercedes-Benz of North America Inc., Montvale, New Jersey.

1990 MERCEDES-BENZ

1990 Mercedes-Benz 300SL convertible.

190E 2.6 — SIX — Only a single version of the 190 series remained this year, powered by the 2.6-liter gasoline engine. Diesel power departed from the entry-level Mercedes line. Either a five-speed manual gearbox or four-speed automatic was available.

260/300 SERIES — SIX — Automatic 4Matic four-wheel-drive became available this year on both the 300E sedan and 300TE station wagon, again powered by a 3.0-liter six-cylinder engine. The 300CE coupe added 40 extra horsepower by virtue of a new dual-overhead-cam version of the 3.0-liter six (a detuned version of the engine used in the new 300SL roadster). The 260E with its smaller 2.6-liter engine adopted the designation 300E 2.6. Later in the season, a 300D 2.5 turbodiesel sedan joined the series, with a 2.5-liter five-cylinder engine.

300SE/300SEL/420SEL — S-CLASS — SIX/V-8 — Except for a new fuel-injection system, little was new in the smaller-engined members of the S-Class. A passenger airbag was optional.

350SDL — TURBODIESEL SIX — Late in the model year, a 350SDL sedan was added, powered by a 3.5-liter turbodiesel six (the first Mercedes turbodiesel since 1987).

560 SERIES — S-CLASS — V-8 — A new fuel-injection system was the only significant change for the S-Class coupe and sedan, again powered by a 5.6-liter V-8 engine.

1990 Mercedes-Benz 500SL.

300SL/500SL — V-8 — At last, the long-awaited replacement for the aged 560SL coupe/roadster was ready for the marketplace, on an all-new platform. The former design had been around for some 18 years, so a new version was much needed—and appreciated, once observers got a chance to gaze upon one. Again rear-drive, the two-seaters rode a 99-inch wheelbase with a far rounder, smoother and more aerodynamic appearance than their predecessors. The customary Mercedes-Benz tristar emblem again sat in the center of the grille, which had a new angled profile rather than the former upright look. Aero-shaped, flush-style headlamps stood alongside wraparound parking lights. Small air-extractor vents ahead of the doors served as reminders of the original 300SL gullwing coupe. Among the new technical features was a rollbar that normally sat flush with the tonneau cover, but was designed to rise in three-tenths of a second if sensors detected an imminent rollover accident. The bar could also be raised into place at any time, by pushing a button. Each roadster came with both a folding top and removable aluminum hardtop. Two dual-overhead-cam engines were available: a 3.0-liter (24-valve) six in the 300SL, and a 5.0-liter (32-valve) V-8 in the 500SL, the latter rated 322 horsepower. An electro-hydraulic mechanism automatically adjusted the engine's valve timing, for higher torque at midrange and more power at higher engine speeds. A five-speed manual gearbox was standard in the 300SL, with five-speed automatic (overdrive fifth gear) optional. The 500SL came only with a four-speed automatic. Airbags were installed for both the driver and passenger.

1990 Mercedes-Benz 300TE station wagon.

I.D. DATA: The 17-symbol Vehicle Identification Number is on the upper left of the instrument panel, visible through the windshield. Symbols 1-3 indicate country, make and vehicle type. Symbols 4-7 indicate model. The next symbol identifies the restraint system. Symbol 10 indicates model year ('L' = 1990). Symbol 11 identifies the assembly plant. The final six digits form the sequential production number.

Model	Body Type & Seating	Engine Type/CID	P.O.E. Price	Weight (lbs.)	Prod. Total
190E	4-dr Sedan-5P	I6/159	31600	2870	Note 1
300 SERIES					
300E 2.6	4-dr Sedan-5P	I6/159	39950	3155	Note 1
300E	4-dr Sedan-5P	I6/181	45950	3210	Note 1
300E 4WD	4-dr Sedan-5P	I6/181	52550	3505	Note 1
300TE	4-dr Sta Wag-5P	I6/181	49650	3450	Note 1
300TE 4WD	4-dr Sta Wag-5P	I6/181	56250	3725	Note 1
300CE	2-dr Coupe-4P	I6/181	55700	3395	Note 1
300SE	4-dr Sedan-5P	I6/181	52950	3595	Note 1
300SEL	4-dr Sedan-5P	I6/181	56800	3640	Note 1
300/350 SERIES (Turbodiesel)					
300D 2.5	4-dr Sedan-5P	I5/152	39700	N/A	Note 1
350SDL	4-dr Sedan-5P	I6/208	56800	N/A	Note 1
420SEL					
420SEL	4-dr Sedan-5P	V8/256	62500	3770	Note 1
300/500SL					
300SL	2-dr Cpe/Rds-2P	I6/181	72500	3850	Note 1
500SL	2-dr Cpe/Rds-2P	V8/304	83500	4025	Note 1
560 SERIES					
560SEL	4-dr Sedan-5P	V8/338	73800	3960	Note 1
560SEC	2-dr Coupe-4P	V8/338	81500	3770	Note 1

Note 1: A total of 78,375 Mercedes-Benz cars were sold in the U.S. during 1990.

ENGINE DATA: BASE SIX (190E 2.6, 300E 2.6): Inline, overhead-cam six-cylinder. **Displacement:** 158.6 cu. in. (2600 cc). **Bore & Stroke:** 3.26 x 3.16 in. (83 x 80 mm). **Compression Ratio:** 9.2:1. **Brake Horsepower:** 158 at 5800 rpm. **Torque:** 162 lbs.-ft. at 4600 rpm. Multi-point fuel injection.

BASE SIX (300): Inline, overhead-cam six-cylinder. **Displacement:** 180.8 cu. in. (2964 cc). **Bore & Stroke:** 3.48 x 3.16 in. (88.5 x 80.2 mm). **Compression Ratio:** 9.2:1. **Brake Horsepower:** 177 at 5700 rpm. **Torque:** 188 lbs.-ft. at 4400 rpm. Hydraulic valve lifters. Multi-point fuel injection.

BASE SIX (300CE): Inline, dual-overhead-cam six-cylinder. **Displacement:** 180.8 cu. in. (2964 cc). **Bore & Stroke:** 3.48 x 3.16 in. (88.5 x 80.2 mm). **Compression Ratio:** 10.0:1. **Brake Horsepower:** 217 at 6400 rpm. **Torque:** 195 lbs.-ft. at 4600 rpm.

BASE SIX (300SL): Inline, dual-overhead-cam six-cylinder (24-valve). Aluminum cross-flow head. **Displacement:** 180.8 cu. in. (2964 cc). **Bore & Stroke:** 3.48 x 3.16 in. (88.5 x 80.2 mm). **Compression Ratio:** 10.0:1. **Brake Horsepower:** 228 at 6300 rpm. **Torque:** 201 lbs.-ft. at 4600 rpm.

300SL Engine Note: Outside North America, a variant of the 300SL with a 12-valve six-cylinder engine was marketed.

BASE TURBODIESEL FIVE (300D 2.5): Inline, overhead-cam five-cylinder, with turbocharger. **Displacement:** 152 cu. in. (2492 cc). **Bore & Stroke:** 3.43 x 3.31 in. (87 x 84 mm). **Compression Ratio:** 22.0:1. **Brake Horsepower:** 121 at 4600 rpm. **Torque:** 165 lbs.-ft. at 2400 rpm. Fuel injection.

BASE TURBODIESEL SIX (350SDL): Inline, overhead-cam six-cylinder, with turbocharger. **Displacement:** 208 cu. in. (3407 cc). **Bore & Stroke:** 3.50 x 3.60 in. (89 x 91 mm). **Compression Ratio:** 22.0:1. **Brake Horsepower:** 121 at 4600 rpm. **Torque:** 165 lbs.-ft. at 2400 rpm. Fuel injection.

BASE V-8 (420SEL): Overhead-cam "vee" type eight-cylinder. Light alloy block and heads. **Displacement:** 256 cu. in. (4197 cc). **Bore & Stroke:** 3.62 x 3.11 in. (92 x 79 mm). **Compression Ratio:** 9.0:1. **Brake Horsepower:** 201 at 5200 rpm. **Torque:** 228 lbs.-ft. at 3600 rpm. Five main bearings. Hydraulic valve lifters. Multi-point fuel injection.

BASE V-8 (500SL): Dual-overhead-cam "vee" type eight-cylinder (32-valve). Aluminum alloy block. **Displacement:** 304 cu. in. (4983 cc). **Bore & Stroke:** 3.80 x 3.35 in. (96.5 x 85 mm). **Compression Ratio:** 10.0:1. **Brake Horsepower:** 322 at 5500 rpm. **Torque:** 332 lbs.-ft. at 4000 rpm. Bosch KE 5 CIS multi-point fuel injection.

BASE V-8 (560 Series): Overhead-cam "vee" type eight-cylinder. Light alloy block and heads. **Displacement:** 338.5 cu. in. (5549 cc). **Bore & Stroke:** 3.80 x 3.73 in. (96.5 x 94.7 mm). **Compression Ratio:** 9.0:1. **Brake Horsepower:** 238 at 4800 rpm. **Torque:** 287 lbs.-ft. at 3500 rpm. Five main bearings. Hydraulic valve lifters. Multi-point fuel injection.

CHASSIS DATA: Wheelbase: (190) 104.9 in.; (300E/TE) 110.2 in.; (300CE) 106.9 in.; (300SE) 115.6 in.; (300SEL/420SEL/560SEL) 121.1 in.; (300/500SL) 99.0 in.; (560SEC) 112.2 in. **Overall Length:** (190) 175.1 in.; (300E) 187.2 in.; (300CE) 183.9 in.; (300TE) 188.2 in.; (300SE) 202.6 in.; (300SEL/420SEL) 208.1 in.; (300/500SL) 176.0 in.; (560SEC) 199.2 in.; (560SEL) 208.1 in. **Height:** (190) 54.1 in.; (300) 56.3 in.; (300E 4WD) 57.1 in.; (300CE) 54.9 in.; (300TE) 59.8 in.; (300SE) 56.6 in.; (300SEL/420SEL) 56.7 in.; (300/500SL) 50.7 in.; (560SEC) 55.0 in.; (560SEL) 56.3 in. **Width:** (190) 66.5 in.; (300) 68.5 in.; (300SE/300SEL/420SEL) 71.7 in.; (300/500SL) 71.3 in.; (560SEC) 72.0 in.; (560SEL) 71.7 in. **Front Tread:** (190) 56.7 in.; (300) 59.1 in.; (300TE, 300E 4WD) 58.9 in.; (300SE/300SEL/420SEL) 61.5 in.; (300/500SL) 60.4 in.; (560SEC/SEL) 61.5 in. **Rear Tread:** (190) 55.9 in.; (300) 58.7 in.; (300TE, 300E 4WD) 58.5 in.; (300SE/300SEL/420SEL) 60.4 in.; (300/500SL) 60.0 in.; (560SEC/SEL) 60.4 in.

TECHNICAL: Layout: front-engine, rear-drive. **Transmission:** (190E 2.6) five-speed manual, or optional four-speed automatic; (300SL) five-speed manual or five-speed automatic; (others) four-speed automatic standard. **Steering:** power recirculating ball. **Suspension (front):** upper/lower A-arms with coil springs and anti-roll bar except (190) modified MacPherson struts with coil springs and anti-roll bar; (300) gas-pressurized struts with coil springs and anti-roll bar; (300/500SL) struts with coil springs on A-arms and torsion-bar stabilizer. **Suspension (rear):** independent, semi-trailing arms with coil springs and anti-roll bar except (190/300) five-link independent with coil springs and anti-roll bar; (300/500SL) multi-link independent with coil springs, torsion-bar stabilizer and level control. **Brakes:** front/rear disc. **Body Construction:** steel unibody.

PERFORMANCE: Top Speed: (300SL) 143 mph claimed; (500SL) 155 mph claimed. **Acceleration (0-60 mph):** (300SL) about 8.3 sec. claimed; (500SL) about 6.3 sec. claimed.

Manufacturer: Daimler-Benz AG, Stuttgart, West Germany.

Distributor: Mercedes-Benz of North America Inc., Montvale, New Jersey.

MERKUR

Certain Lincoln-Mercury dealers added an import model to their showroom floor, starting with the 1985 model year. By the time the cars began to arrive from Germany, some 800 dealers had purchased the separate franchise that was required. The Merkur XR4Ti was a variation of the German-built Ford Sierra XR4i hatchback, which had been marketed in Europe since early 1983. Among its features was a turbocharged four-cylinder engine. For the 1988 model year, a Scorpio four-door hatchback with V-6 power joined the two-door XR4Ti. Though the Merkur found a certain following in the U.S., sales started slow and never hit startling levels. Except for a few leftovers, only the Scorpio four-door remained after 1989, and the Merkur name finally faded away during the 1990 model year.

1985-87 MERKUR

XR4Ti — FOUR — Power for the two-door hatchback came from Ford's 2.3-liter turbocharged overhead-cam four-cylinder engine, which produced 175 horsepower. That engine was similar to the one used in the Mustang SVO, but without an intercooler. A five-speed manual gearbox was standard; three-speed automatic optional. Standard equipment included air conditioning, power windows, power (heated) outside mirrors,

AM/FM stereo radio with cassette player, variable-ratio power steering, and Pirelli P6 tires. Analog instruments included a turbo boost gauge. Styling features of the rear-drive coupe included a bi-plane rear spoiler, claimed to "provide superior stability and performance at highway speeds." Slim triangular rear quarter windows went behind the larger rear side windows, separated by a rather wide pillar. Only a handful of options were offered, including heated front seats and a moonroof. Larger wheels and Pirelli tires (195/60HR15) became standard for the 1987 model year.

I.D. DATA: Merkur's 17-symbol Vehicle Identification Number is on the upper left of the instrument panel, visible through the windshield.

Model	Body Type & Seating	Engine Type/CID	P.O.E. Price	Weight (lbs.)	Prod. Total
MERKUR					
XR4Ti	2-dr Hatch Cpe-5P	I4/140	16361	2910	Note 1

Note 1: A total of 8,974 Merkurs were sold in the U.S. during 1985, followed by 14,315 in 1986 and 14,301 in 1987.

Price Note: Figure shown was valid in 1985-86. Price rose to $17,832 in 1987.

1985 Merkur XR4Ti.

ENGINE DATA: BASE TURBO FOUR: Inline, overhead-cam four-cylinder with turbocharger. Cast iron block and head. **Displacement:** 140 cu. in. (2294 cc). **Bore & Stroke:** 3.78 x 3.12 in. (96 x 79.5 mm). **Compression Ratio:** 8.0:1. **Brake Horsepower:** 175 at 5000 rpm. **Torque:** 200 lbs.-ft. at 3000 rpm. Five main bearings. Hydraulic valve lifters. Multi-point fuel injection.

Note: XR4Ti engines with automatic transmission were rated 145 bhp at 4400 rpm, and 180 lbs.-ft. at 3600 rpm.

CHASSIS DATA: Wheelbase: 102.7 in. **Overall Length:** 178.4 in. **Height:** 54.8 in. **Width:** 68.0 in. **Front Tread:** 57.2 in. **Rear Tread:** 57.8 in. **Standard Tires:** P195/60HR14 (P195/60HR15 for 1987).

TECHNICAL: Layout: front-engine, rear-drive. **Transmission:** five-speed manual or optional three-speed automatic. **Standard Final Drive Ratio:** 3.64:1 w/manual, 3.38:1 w/automatic. **Steering:** power rack and pinion. **Suspension (front):** modified MacPherson struts with anti-roll bar. **Suspension (rear):** independent with semi-trailing arms and coil springs. **Brakes:** front disc, rear drum. **Body Construction:** steel unibody. **Fuel Tank:** 15 gallon.

MAJOR OPTIONS: Three-speed automatic transmission. Convenience group (incl. power windows and central locking). Heated front seats. Tilt/slide moonroof. Grey leather interior.

PERFORMANCE: Acceleration (0-60 mph): 7.8 sec. **Fuel Mileage:** 19 mpg city, 24 mpg highway (EPA ratings).

Manufacturer: Ford of Germany (Ford Werke AG), Koln-Deutz, West Germany.

Distributor: Lincoln-Mercury Division, Ford Motor Company, Dearborn, Michigan.

HISTORY: The XR4Ti was essentially the same as the Ford Sierra sold in Europe. Both evolved from the Probe III show car that had appeared at the Frankfurt Auto Show in 1981. Sales techniques in the U.S. market included a "Disk Drive Test Drive," which allowed potential customers to view the car's features and details on the screen of a personal computer. A five-stage series of high-performance conversion kits for the XR4Ti was offered by the Rapido Group in Brea, California.

1988-90 MERKUR

XR4Ti — FOUR — A revised rear spoiler (single-plane instead of the former bi-plane style), bodyside cladding, and color-coordinated bumpers were the major changes for the two-door hatchback Merkur for 1988. Power still came from Ford's turbocharged 2.3-liter four, which produced 175 horsepower with five-speed manual shift or 145 bhp with three-speed automatic. Dual accent tape stripes were added to the body for 1989, and black inserts replaced brightwork on the bodysides and bumpers. The XR4Ti was dropped after 1989.

SCORPIO — V-6 — Sales of the V-6 Merkur began in May 1987. Appearance and construction were similar to the XR4Ti, but the Scorpio was a four-door hatchback touring sedan rather than a two-door coupe. The 2.9-liter V-6 was rated 144 horsepower. Standard equipment included a five-speed manual gearbox, anti-locking disc brakes, four-way power front seats, fold-down 60/40 split rear seatbacks with separate recliners, power steering, power windows, central locking, automatic-temperature air conditioning, heated power mirrors, and P205/60HR15 Pirelli P6 tires on cast aluminum wheels. A power front-seat recliner was added after the 1988 model year began. A four-speed automatic transmission, Touring Package (including power moonroof, leather seats and trip computer), and the power moonroof alone were the only options. For 1990, the V-6 engine got a compression boost (to 9.5:1), adding one horsepower and eight pound-feet of torque. Also in 1990, the optional four-speed automatic transmission added electronic lockup in upper gears; a different standard five-speed manual gearbox was installed; driver/passenger airbags were installed; and bumpers, grille and bodyside cladding became color-keyed.

I.D. DATA: Merkur's 17-symbol Vehicle Identification Number is on the upper left of the instrument panel, visible through the windshield.

Model	Body Type & Seating	Engine Type/CID	P.O.E. Price	Weight (lbs.)	Prod. Total
MERKUR					
XR4Ti	2-dr Hatch Cpe-5P	I4/140	19065	2853	Note 1
Scorpio	4-dr Hatch Sed-5P	V6/178	24048	3137	Note 1

Note 1: A total of 15,261 Merkurs were sold in the U.S. during 1988, followed by 8,765 in 1989 and 2,622 in 1990.

Price Note: Figures shown were valid in 1988.

ENGINE DATA: BASE TURBO FOUR (XR4Ti): Inline, overhead-cam four-cylinder with turbocharger. Cast iron block and head. **Displacement:** 140 cu. in. (2294 cc). **Bore & Stroke:** 3.78 x 3.12 in. (96 x 79.5 mm). **Compression Ratio:** 8.0:1. **Brake Horsepower:** 175 at 5000 rpm. **Torque:** 200 lbs.-ft. at 3000 rpm. Five main bearings. Hydraulic valve lifters. Multi-point fuel injection.

Note: Merkur XR4Ti engines with automatic transmission were rated 145 bhp at 4400 rpm, and 180 lbs.-ft. at 3600 rpm.

BASE V-6 (Scorpio): Overhead-valve, "vee" type six-cylinder. **Displacement:** 178 cu. in. (2933 cc). **Bore & Stroke:** 3.66 x 2.83 in. (93 x 72 mm). **Compression Ratio:** 9.0:1 (9.5:1 in 1990). **Brake Horsepower:** 144 at 5500 rpm (145 bhp in 1990). **Torque:** 162 lbs.-ft. at 3000 rpm (170 lbs.-ft. in 1990). Hydraulic valve lifters. Multi-point fuel injection.

CHASSIS DATA: Wheelbase: (XR4Ti) 102.7 in.; (Scorpio) 108.7 in. **Overall Length:** (XR4Ti) 178.4 in.; (Scorpio) 186.4 in. **Height:** (XR4Ti) 54.8 in.; (Scorpio) 54.6 in. **Width:** (XR4Ti) 68.0 in.; (Scorpio) 69.5 in. **Front Tread:** (XR4Ti) 57.2 in.; (Scorpio) 58.1 in. **Rear Tread:** (XR4Ti) 57.8 in.; (Scorpio) 58.1 in. **Standard Tires:** (XR4Ti) P195/60HR15; (Scorpio) P205/60HR15.

TECHNICAL: Layout: front-engine, rear-drive. **Transmission:** five-speed manual; optional three-speed automatic (XR4Ti) or four-speed automatic (Scorpio). **Steering:** power rack and pinion. **Suspension (front):** modified MacPherson struts with anti-roll bar. **Suspension (rear):** independent with semi-trailing arms and coil springs. **Brakes:** (XR4Ti) front disc, rear drum; (Scorpio) front/rear disc with anti-locking. **Body Construction:** steel unibody. **Fuel Tank:** (XR4Ti) 15 gallon; (Scorpio) 16.9 gallon.

OPTIONS: Three-speed automatic transmission (XR4Ti). Four-speed automatic (Scorpio). Heated front seats (XR4Ti). Grey leather interior (XR4Ti). Tilt/slide moonroof (XR4Ti). Power moonroof (Scorpio). Touring Package (Scorpio).

Manufacturer: Ford of Germany (Ford Werke AG), Koln-Deutz, West Germany.

Distributor: Lincoln-Mercury Division, Ford Motor Company, Dearborn, Michigan.

HISTORY: "Engineered to put a grin on your face" was Merkur's 1988 slogan for the XR4Ti, while the newly-arrived Scorpio was claimed to stand apart from some other German sedans by offering "a reward for past sacrifices, not reason for yet another." Both cars, according to the sales literature, "don't conform to traditional standards. They challenge them." Prior to its arrival in the U.S. market, Scorpio had been voted "Car of the Year" in Europe, in 1986. American promotional methods for the Scorpio included a "Guaranteed Resale Value Program." Meanwhile, the XR4Ti was performing well in SCCA Trans-Am racing. That wasn't enough to keep the duo on the market, however, and both faded away early in 1990.

MESSERSCHMITT

Not every car enthusiast is aware that the company best known for the manufacture of German fighter planes during World War II also turned out a passenger automobile during the 1950s. In addition to the famed ME109 fighter, the company that had been founded by Professor Willy Messerschmitt in 1923 even developed an early jet plane during the war. With peacetime came a switch to auto parts and such products as sewing machines. Meanwhile, Fritz Fend had been producing a series of small three-wheeled vehicles. Wishing to expand production, Fend inquired about the Messerschmitt facility. In 1953, his design had evolved into the KR175 Messerschmitt Kabinenroller (cabin scooter). Closer to a motor scooter in operation than to an automobile, right down to handlebar-type steering, that model even lacked a reverse gear and required a pull rope for starting the engine. Two people sat in tandem (one behind the other), again like a motor scooter. About 10,000 were sold in all.

That original design was modified for 1955 into the KR200, which added a reverse gear and was powered by a larger (191 cubic centimeter) two-stroke engine. Popular as low-budget transportation for a time in their home country, Messerschmitts were more of a novelty item in the U.S. Their popularity waned before long, however, amid competition from such minicars as BMW's Isetta, which let its passengers sit side by side. By 1956, too, Messerschmitt had returned to aircraft production, turning the three-wheeled car operation over to Fend. Messerschmitts remained in production until 1964.

1955-64 MESSERSCHMITT

1956 Messerschmitt KR-200. (William Siuru Jr.)

KR175 — ONE — The original Messerschmitt, with a 175-cc, 9.5-horsepower engine, moved forward only and was mainly for the home market. U.S. customers took to the slightly more powerful KR200 model.

KR200 — ONE — Looking more like a motor scooter with a body than an automobile, the Messerschmitt had seating for two (in tandem) and full weather protection beneath the tilt-over, cockpit-style bubble canopy top, which was made of plexiglas. Headlamps were mounted close together, just below the windshield. Bubble-style covers surrounded the twin front wheels. The Fichtel and Sachs 191-cc two-stroke engine developed only a tad more power than the original (smaller) powerplant, working through a four-speed motorcycle-style gearbox. That meant drivers had to go through all four gears to gain speed, and back down through all four when coming to a stop. A handlebar of sorts did the steering, and controls resembled those of a motorcycle (including a rotary hand-grip throttle). The KR200 had a reverse gear, though, and a self-starter. The driver's seat had a dozen fore-and-aft adjustment positions. Standard equipment included an electrical windshield wiper. Price in Germany was the equivalent of $560.

1959 Messerschmitt two-passenger roadster.

I.D. DATA: Not available.

Model	Body Type & Seating	Engine Type/CID	P.O.E. Price	Weight (lbs.)	Prod. Total
KR175	2-dr Coupe-2P	I1/11	N/A	385	Note 1
KR200	2-dr Coupe-2P	I1/12	1073	N/A	Note 1

Note 1: About 10,000 original KR175s and 40,000 KR200s were built, including at least 12,000 in 1955 alone.

Price Note: Price shown is for 1956 model (on West Coast).

1961 Messerschmitt.

ENGINE DATA: BASE ONE (KR175): One-cylinder (two-stroke). **Displacement:** 10.65 cu. In. (175 cc). **Bore & Stroke:** 2.44 x 2.28 in. (62 x 58 mm). **Compression Ratio:** 6.6:1. **Brake Horsepower:** 9.5 at 5250 rpm.

BASE ONE (KR200): One-cylinder (two-stroke). — **Displacement:** 11.65 cu. in. (191 cc). **Bore & Stroke:** 2.56 x 2.28 in. (65 x 58 mm). **Compression Ratio:** 6.6:1. **Brake Horsepower:** 10.

CHASSIS DATA: **Wheelbase** 80 in. **Height:** 47 in. **Front Tread:** 36.3 in. **Rear Tread:** none (single wheel).

TECHNICAL: **Layout:** rear-engine, rear-drive. **Transmission:** four-speed manual (motorcycle-type). **Steering:** dual-track. **Suspension (front):** rubber torsilastic. **Suspension (rear):** rubber torsilastic. **Brakes:** mechanical, front/rear drum.

MAJOR OPTIONS: Bumpers ($50).

PERFORMANCE: **Top Speed:** 62 mph (factory). **Fuel Mileage:** 60-100 mpg.

Manufacturer: Messerschmittwerke, Stuttgart, West Germany.

Distributor: Frank Sennes Motor Corp., Glendale, Calif.

HISTORY: Messerschmitts received a belated compliment of sorts in the 1980s, as an American company marketed a build-it-yourself model of the nearly-forgotten three-wheeler.

METROPOLITAN

Hardly the fastest car of its day, and not the most agile either, the Nash Metropolitan surely qualifies as one of the cutest. Its curious appeal continues today. In addition to the Metro's aesthetic attributes, it served as one of the early examples of postwar joint ventures, whereby a car would mix mechanical components and styling from two countries--then be marketed in a third nation, which had supplied the original concept. In that respect, at least, it served as a forerunner to the Cadillac Allanté of the late 1980s and '90s, but with a low-budget price tag even for the mid-1950s. The Metropolitan might also be considered the first U.S. subcompact, made available just after the formation of American Motors (merging Nash and Hudson) in May 1954.

In the Metropolitan's case, the drivetrain came from England, in the form of the Austin A40 overhead-valve four. In fact, the entire car was assembled by Austin in Britain, from a design penned by Pinin Farina. Development cost about $2 million (considered an amazingly modest sum at that time). The ultimate Metropolitan evolved from an NXI (Nash Experimental International) prototype, which in turn became the NKI (Nash-Kelvinator International). The idea reached back to the period just after World War II, when Nash president George W. Mason ordered research to begin on an economy car. Soon, he looked over a design submitted by Bill Flajole, an independent stylist, based on the chassis and running gear of a tiny Fiat 500. In fact, early rumors suggested that the resulting car would use a Fiat engine.

George Romney, later to become head of American Motors, displayed the prototype NXI to dealers and the press at a series of private functions starting in January 1950, to gauge public reaction. Among other features, the hood and fenders of the NXI lifted as a unit, to give easy engine access, while the grille and nose stayed in place. *Motor Trend* reported in 1950 that the car was expected to sell for $1000. Late in 1953, arrangements were made with Austin to begin volume production. Bodies would be built in Britain by Fisher & Ludlow, in Birmingham, then shipped to the Austin plant at Longbridge. Metropolitans went on sale early in 1954. A second series, the 1500, debuted in April 1956, with a bigger engine (Austin A50) and more power, as well as bright two-tone color schemes.

Metropolitans were marketed under both the Nash and Hudson badges, until the latter's demise after 1957 as the AMC (American Motors) name took over. Then, Metropolitan became a separate make, adding such extras as a trunklid and vent wings in 1959. Metropolitans remained in full production into 1960, with a few leftovers available in the U.S. for two more years. A total of 94,986 were produced in all.

1954-55 METROPOLITAN

1954 Metropolitan convertible.

SERIES A (1954) & B (1955) — FOUR — The two-seat Metropolitan came in hardtop coupe and convertible body styles, the former with two-tone paint. One distinctive feature was the cutout at the top of each door. A low, one-piece rear-hinged hood held a decorative air scoop. The grille consisted of a single die-cast horizontal bar, with central medallion. Fenders stood taller than the hood. Above the hood, at the cowl, was a fresh-air intake for the optional Weather Eye system. Round park/signal lights stood directly below the headlamps. Both front and rear wheels were partly enclosed (a Nash "trademark" at this time). Wraparound front and rear bumpers included standard guards. A "Continental" (external) spare-tire mounting was standard equipment, and came with a vinyl cover. The rear license-plate bracket and light was mounted on the spare wheel's hubcap. Square-cut doors had pushbutton handles. Chrome window frames could be lowered completely. Inside, upholstery was done in leather and nylon cord. A single cluster ahead of the driver held the speedometer, fuel gauge, and warning lights. A manual choke was standard, and the glove-compartment area was open. The tubular-steel seat frame adjusted four inches, the rear cushion could be removed, and the seatback swung forward to give access to the luggage area (which offered more than six cubic feet of storage space). The 12-volt battery rested beneath a mat covering the barely-existent back seat, described by Motor Trend as "actually little more than a padded shelf." Standard equipment included dual Lucas horns, twin sunvisors, ashtray, lighter, 17-inch steering wheel, glovebox, map light, and rear-view mirror.

The 1200-cc (73-cid) Austin A40 engine produced 42 horsepower. The sole transmission was a three-speed manual unit with column-mounted gearshift lever (which actually emerged from the instrument panel). A single-plate Borg & Beck clutch was used. Front suspension was Nash's "Airflex" setup, with a coil spring between the wheel housing and upper control arm; and Metropolitans also adopted the Nash "Airflyte" unit body construction. Standard body colors for 1954 included Spruce Green, Canyon Red, Caribbean Blue, and Croton Green. The hardtop came only in Mist Gray on the upper body. The vinyl convertible top came in tan or black, depending on body color. Upholstery was Old Ivory leather with beige nylon-faced Bedford cord (black/yellow striped). Options included a Weather Eye Conditioned Air System, radio with manual antenna, and white-wall tires. A flat one-piece windshield and three-piece curved rear window were standard with both body styles.

1955 Metropolitan.

I.D. DATA: Chassis serial number is located on the right side of the cowl, under the hood. Engine number is on right center of block. Starting chassis number: (Series A) E-1001; (Series B) E-11001. Starting engine number: (Series A) 1G-881459; (Series B) GS-5-10003.

Model	Body Type & Seating	Engine Type/CID	P.O.E. Price	Weight (lbs.)	Prod. Total
METROPLITAN (NASH & HUDSON)					
541	2-dr Conv-2/3P	I4/73	1469	1785	Note 1
542	2-dr HT Cpe-2/3P	I4/73	1445	1825	Note 1

Note 1: A total of 13,095 Metropolitans were produced during 1954 (including 743 early examples built in 1953), followed by 6,096 in 1955.

Seating Note: American Motors claimed three-passenger capacity for the Metroplitan's front seat, which is a tight squeeze; the miniature utility seat in back was barely suitable for a child.

Price Note: Figures shown were valid during 1954 and 1955.

Weight Note: Figures shown are shipping weights for initial models.

ENGINE DATA: BASE FOUR: Inline, overhead-valve four-cylinder (Austin A40). Cast iron block and head. **Displacement:** 73.2 cu. in. (1200 cc). **Bore & Stroke:** 2.58 x 3.50 in. (65.5 x 88.9 mm). **Compression Ratio:** 7.2:1. **Brake Horsepower:** 42 at 4500 rpm. **Torque:** 62 lbs.-ft. at 2400 rpm. Three main bearings. Solid valve lifters. One Zenith downdraft carburetor.

CHASSIS DATA: Wheelbase: 85 in. Overall Length: 149.5 in. Height: 54.5 in. Width: 61.5 in. Front Tread: 45.3 in. Rear Tread: 44.8 in. Wheel Type: pressed steel disc. Standard Tires: 5.20x13.

TECHNICAL: Layout: front-engine, rear-drive. Transmission: three-speed manual (column shift). Gear ratios: (1st) 2.436:1; (2nd) 1.535:1; (3rd) 1.00:1; (rev) 3.489:1. Standard Final Drive Ratio: 4.625:1. Steering: cam and lever. Suspension (front): Airflex with direct-acting, extra-long coil springs. Suspension (rear): rigid axle with semi-elliptic leaf springs. Brakes: Girling hydraulic, front/rear drum. Body Construction: steel unibody (Airflyte). Fuel Tank: 10.5 gallon.

MAJOR OPTIONS: Radio ($60). Weather Eye heater ($69). Whitewall tires.

PERFORMANCE: Top Speed: 70+ mph claimed; about 77 mph in early test. Acceleration (0-60 mph): as much as 23-27.5 sec. and as little as 19.2 sec. reported. Fuel Mileage: about 30-32 mpg city, 37-40 mpg highway.

PRODUCTION/SALES: Approximately 6,617 Metropolitans (401 Hudson versions) were sold in the U.S. during 1954.

Manufacturer: The Austin Motor Co. Ltd., Longbridge, Birmingham, England (bodies from Fisher & Ludlow Ltd., Birmingham, England).

Distributor: American Motors Corp., Detroit, Michigan.

HISTORY: In a fuel-economy test prior to the car's debut, a Metropolitan achieved 41.57 mpg at an average speed of 34.83 mph, going 24 hours nonstop. In an endurance test at the same time, the Metropolitan averaged 61.24 mph, covering 1469.7 miles in 24 hours. Observed by NASCAR, these tests were held at the one-mile asphalt track in Raleigh, North Carolina. *Motor Trend* called the new Metropolitan "a scaled-down version of everything good in a Nash, which is saying plenty." Initial dealer stocks, according to the company, were sold out the day after its introduction.

1956-62 METROPOLITAN

SERIES B — FOUR — Availability of the original Metropolitan with 42-bhp engine continued into 1957, but it was eclipsed by the higher-powered 1500. See previous listing for engine data.

SERIES 1500 — FOUR — A larger and more powerful Austin A50 engine went into the second-generation Metropolitan, which otherwise remained largely unchanged. The 1489-cc (91-cid) overhead-valve four produced 52 horsepower (24 percent more than the initial A40 engine). That gave top speed a boost to about 78 mph. A larger clutch was installed (8-inch rather than the former 7.25-inch). Metropolitans displayed a new cellular-style oval grille with heavy chrome surround molding and a round Nash or Hudson medallion in the center. Hoods no longer contained an airscoop. Bodyside trim was modified to give the car a fresh look. The bodyside molding began at the headlamps, dipped to the lower portion of the car (just behind the door), and continued hori-

zontally to the rear. That molding served as a separation line for two-tone paint. Standard upper-body colors were Caribbean Green, Sunburst Yellow, and Coral Red (above the molding and on the hood, deck and windshield posts). The second color (Snowberry White) went below the molding. The standard "Continental" spare tire was covered in black vinyl, trimmed in white vinyl. Inside, gray/black upholstery had off-white vinyl trim. Window vent wings and a trunk lid (for outside access) were added during 1959, along with tubless tires. An Austin A55 engine went into final Metropolitans, rated 55 bhp.

1956 Metropolitan hardtop.

I.D. DATA: Chassis serial number is located on the right side of the cowl, under the hood. Engine number is on right center of block. Starting serial number (series 1500): E-21008. Starting engine number: 1H-14004.

Model	Body Type & Seating	Engine Type/CID	P.O.E. Price	Weight (lbs.)	Prod. Total
METROPOLITAN 1500 (NASH/HUDSON/AMERICAN MOTORS)					
561	2-dr Conv-2/3P	I4/91	1551	1803	Note 1
562	2-dr HT Cpe-2/3P	I4/91	1527	1843	Note 1

Note 1: A total of 9,068 Metropolitans were produced during 1956, followed by 15,317 in 1957, 13,128 in 1958, 22,309 in 1959, and 13,103 in 1960. A final 853 examples became available in 1962, and 412 in 1962.

Seating Note: As before, American Motors claimed three-passenger capacity for the Metropolitan's front seat.

Price Note: Figures shown were valid in 1956. Prices rose to $1673 for the hardtop and $1697 for the convertible by 1960. Later examples without a trunklid sold for $47 less.

1957 Metropolitan hardtop.

1958 Metropolitan hardtop.

1959 Metropolitan hardtop.

1960 Metropolitan convertible.

ENGINE DATA: BASE FOUR: Inline, overhead-valve four-cylinder (Austin A50). Cast iron block and head. **Displacement:** 90.9 cu. in. (1489 cc). **Bore & Stroke:** 2.875 x 3.50 in. (73 x 88.9 mm). **Compression Ratio:** 7.2:1. **Brake Horsepower:** 52 at 4500 rpm. **Torque:** 77 lbs.-ft. at 2500 rpm. Three main bearings. Solid valve lifters. One Zenith downdraft carburetor.

CHASSIS DATA: Wheelbase: 85 in. **Overall Length:** 149.5 in. **Height:** 54.5 in. **Width:** 61.5 in. **Front Tread:** 45.3 in. **Rear Tread:** 44.8 in. **Wheel Type:** pressed steel disc. **Standard Tires:** 5.20x13 (later, 5.60x13).

1961 Metropolitan convertible and hardtop.

1962 Metropolitan hardtop.

TECHNICAL: Layout: front-engine, rear-drive. **Transmission:** three-speed manual (column shift). **Standard Final Drive Ratio:** 4.3:1. **Steering:** cam and lever. **Suspension (front):** A-arms with coil springs. **Suspension (rear):** rigid axle with semi-elliptic leaf springs. **Brakes:** Girling hydraulic, front/rear drum. **Body Construction:** steel unibody (Airflyte). **Fuel Tank:** 10.5 gallon.

MAJOR OPTIONS: Weather Eye heater. Radio. Whitewall tires.

PERFORMANCE: Top Speed: (1500) 78 mph claimed. **Acceleration (0-60 mph):** (1500) 19.5-22.0 sec. (0-50 mph in 16.1 sec.). **Fuel Mileage:** 40 mpg claimed; 32-39 mpg reported.

PRODUCTION/SALES: Approximately 7,145 Metropolitans were sold in the U.S. during 1956, followed by 11,791 in 1957, and 8,657 in 1961.

Manufacturer: The Austin Motor Co. Ltd., Longbridge, Birmingham, England (bodies from Fisher & Ludlow Ltd., Birmingham, England).

Distributor: American Motors Corp., Detroit, Michigan.

HISTORY: The Metropolitan 1500 went on display April 9, 1956 at Nash and Hudson dealers. After the Nash and Hudson names faded away in 1957, Metropolitans were marketed as American Motors models, sold by Rambler dealers.

MG

Few cars have enjoyed the popularity of the MG two-seater roadster. Few have had such a strong influence on sports car ownership in America, or on amateur racing. More than any other single make, MG was responsible for introducing the joys (and quirks) of traditional-styled sports cars to American enthusiasts in the early Fifties. Although various derivations of the name have been bandied about, the two letters simply stand for "Morris Garages." Through its long life, the marque has been identified by an octagonal symbol contained those two letters. MG itself became known for the motto, "Safety Fast."

Long known in Britain for its light, open cars, sold at reasonable prices, MG actually descended from a line of surprisingly large vehicles, beginning with the Bullnose Morris of 1923. The first MG 14/40 of the 1920s carried a 1.8-liter engine, while the later Mk I/II/III series were powered by 2.5-liter Morris overhead-cam sixes. In 1928 the sporty M-type Midget appeared, based upon the Morris Minor of that day and powered by engines of only 746-cc and 847-cc displacement. That first Midget was followed by a series of similar models, dubbed C, D, J, PA and PB. Also in the 1930s came the Magna and Magnette sedans, powered by 1.1- and 1.3-liter engines. In 1930, the company turned to five memorable years of British racing, bringing home victories in the Brooklands 500, Double-Twelve, and Grand Prix events. Tazio Nuvolari drove a supercharged K3 Magnette to win the 1933 Ulster Tourist Trophy. Over a five-year period, in fact, MGs won 37 major international events. MG also created the first 750-cc car to reach 120 mph; and later on, the first car of any kind to top 200 mph.

J-Types, produced over a brief period from 1932 to 1934, were rough riders with 847-cc engines, capable of nearly 80 mph, and served as the first Midget series with a four-speed gearbox in every model. A handful of supercharged J3/J4 roadsters also were built. Longer than the J-Type, the PA, built for only a few months in 1935, was the First Midget with a running board. Its successor, the PB, came in roadster and tourer form, along with a few Airline coupes. P-series MGs were the last to carry overhead-cam engines.

The true predecessors to MGs most familiar to American audiences arrived in the mid-1930s: VA and SA saloons with 1.5-, 2.25- and 2.5-liter powerplants and, most important, the TA and TB Midget sports roadsters that were powered by 1292-cc (then 1250-cc) fours. By 1936, the earlier overhead-cam engines had given way to a pushrod (ohv) design that was destined to continue into postwar MG models.

Cecil Kimber of the Morris Garages firm is credited with production of the first MG sports car, and then with the T-series of the late 1930s, using components from other Nuffield Group models. Production of the TA started in 1936, one year after Lord Nuffield sold his Morris Garages firm to the Nuffield Organization (which in turn had evolved from the original Morris Motors). Therefore, T-series development was the responsibility of the Morris firm. The TA used a long-stroke four-cylinder engine. Unlike the prototype, the production models had a slab-shaped gas tank at the rear, which would soon become familiar to MG devotees around the world. Longer in wheelbase (94 inches) than the former P-series, the TA also had a wider tread, but wore the same 19-inch wire wheels. Lockheed hydraulic brakes provided the stopping power. Initial TAs had a "crash box," but before long the transmission was altered so that only first gear was non-synchronized. With the windshield folded down, a TA could come close to 80 mph, and reach 60 mph in a tad over 23 seconds.

For 1939, the TB Midget turned to a shorter-stroke (but still nearly an inch longer than the bore) overhead-valve engine, known as the XPAG. While bore/stroke dimensions of the TA had been 63.5 x 102 mm, the TB had a 66.5-mm bore and 90-mm stroke, and developed 54.4 horsepower at 5200 rpm. Only 3,003 TA and 379 TB models were built; but total MG production by the time World War Two broke out was about 22,454.

The TC, announced in late 1945 at the London Motor Show, was only slightly modified from the final prewar (1939) TB design, though the body was four inches wider and the running board narrower. Only a comparatively modest number of prewar MGs had ever reached America (though more than some people suspect); but the TC changed all that and helped to ignite a near-fanatical fondness for sports cars in the 1950s. American servicemen returning from England, in particular, took a powerful fancy to the traditional-styled roadster and brought back quite a few when they returned home. By 1947, MG had an expanding distribution network in the U.S.; but even before the war, Motor Sport Inc. (in New York City) had served as official importer.

Traditionalists pounced upon the news that the revised roadster for 1950, called the TD, would have independent front suspension and actual bumpers. Later on, however, that model grew even more popular than its predecessor, a virtual icon of sports car history. The TF, produced from fall 1953 to spring '55, was the last traditional model before the arrival of the more modern MGA for 1956. Performance fans welcomed the arrival of the Twin-Cam version in 1958, but their excitement turned to dismay as the potent powerplant experienced durability problems. Late in 1961 came the MG Midget, followed by the MGB, a unibodied successor to the A model. Through the 1960s, extensive modifications occurred on both models, including a veritable maze of engine size and horsepower/torque changes and the emergence of a GT coupe companion to the MGB roadster. A six-cylinder MGC appeared late in the 1960s; and even a V-8 in the 1970s (for the home market). More important, in the 1970s came a pattern of diminished power and unappreciated design changes for both roadsters, which resulted from more stringent U.S. emissions and safety regulations. By the mid-1970s, the roadsters wore big black polyurethane bumper/grilles instead of their former handsome bright grillework, clearly created as "quickie" reactions to the shifting standards.

MG sedans have been overshadowed by the popular roadsters, but have their own modest legions of fans, starting with the Y-Type that emerged along with the TC roadster. Before the T-series turned into the more modern

MGA, a rounded Magnette sedan appeared. Early in the 1960s, however, the original Magnette design disappeared, replaced by a clone of other British models as a result of MG's absorption into the British Motor Corporation (BMC) earlier in the 1950s. A smaller front-drive 1100 sedan joined the revised Magnette, but neither achieved the popularity of earlier sedans, largely because they had little identity of their own. A total of 512,880 vehicles were built before MG production finally came to a halt in 1980.

Company Note: Early factory literature called these automobiles "M.G." as produced by "The M.G. Car Company Ltd." In America, a simple "MG" (without the periods) became common. That latter usage is followed in this catalog, except when naming the actual company.

1945-49 MG

1946 MG Midget Series TC.

TC — FOUR — The first TC models began to trickle into America not too long after production in England commenced in late 1945 (shortly after the war ended). Returning GIs had taken an interest in the "classic" British sports car, and quite a few looked forward to bringing one home. Imports reached sizable numbers by 1948.

The traditional design was little changed from its TA and TB predecessors of the late 1930s, before World War II had halted British motorcar production. Nothing remotely like the TC was offered by Detroit, and newfound fans were able to overlook the little roadster's drawbacks: namely a harsh ride, cramped cockpit, and performance far more sluggish than its rakish lines suggested. All TCs had right-hand drive, too, which presented obvious problems in American traffic. Neither a radio nor a heater was included. Still, nothing else on the market offered such a pure look, so much automotive character--and for a fairly modest price, too. On top of that, the TC was economical to drive and easy to maintain. And because these early British roadsters tended to demand plenty of regular maintenance and repair, that latter trait proved particularly valuable. All told, the TC's flaws and idi- osyncracies were easily offset by its many charms.

A ladder-type chassis with channel-section side members differed little from prewar designs. Neither did the rigid front and rear axles with short semi-elliptic springs and lever-type shock absorbers. Wood framing held the car's steel body panels, in a construction style closer to that of American cars of the 1920s than the late 1940s. Sweeping, separate fenders with freestanding headlamps led into short running boards, narrower than the prewar model and with two step strips. The body was itself four inches wider than the prewar TB, but overall width remained the same. Adding to the rakish lines were rear-hinged cutaway-style doors. Ahead of the long hood stood a traditional vertical-bar grille. The low windshield could be folded down for true "wind-in-the-face" motoring, at a time when American cars no longer even had crank-open windshields. For inclement weather, a soft top fit over a rather complex metal frame, assisted by snap-inside curtains. Putting up the top and curtains was a daunting and tedious task, and hardy drivers tended not to bother. Bumpers were not included, though a badge bar was available.

The TC's 1250-cc engine hooked to a four-speed gearbox (nonsynchronized in first gear), which emitted a lovely sound out the exhaust that served as part of the car's charm. The XPAG engine differed little from the 1939 version used in the TB, producing the same 54.4 horsepower. Because of the hard springs, ride was bouncy over even modest bumps. The car might turn shaky around quick corners, too, though expert drivers could easily control its tendency to scamper sideways. Inside, the speedometer sat ahead of the passenger. All TCs had right-hand drive. Brakes were Lockheed hydraulic, front and rear drums. Performance fans could install such extras as a Shorrock supercharger, which cut the 0-60 mph acceleration time in a 1949 U.S. test from more than 20 seconds to a mere 14.2 seconds.

Y (YA/YT) — FOUR — Nearly forgotten in the excitement over the TC roadster was the MG saloon (sedan), introduced as the "One and a Quarter Liter" model, which rode a shorter (99-inch) wheelbase. Designed just before World War II, the saloon had rack-and-pinion steering with an adjustable Bluemel steering wheel, and independent front suspension. Like the TC, it had a vertical-bar grille split into two sections, and separate headlamps. Both front and rear doors were hinged at the center post. A Smiths Jackall hydraulic jacking system was standard. Also standard: a sliding steel sunroof, single foglights, and rear-window shade. A top-hinged windshield was used. Separate front

bucket seats and a back bench seat were upholstered in leather, and half of the polished veneer instrument panel held twin gauges with octagonal rims. Beneath the bonnet was MG's 1.25-liter four with single carburetor, rated at 45 horsepower. Bumpers were included. Not many sedans arrived in the U.S. until the emergence of the subsequent Magnette in the 1950s. To lure American buyers, however, MG also produced a two-door Tourer edition in the late 1940s, with cutdown doors similar to those on the TC roadster and a twin-carburetor engine.

Note: The first postwar saloons were referred to as either a "Y" or "YA" model. **I.D. DATA:** Serial number plate is located on front of cowl (left side), under the hood. Motor number is alongside the serial number, and on the side of the engine block. Starting serial number: (1945 TC) TC0251; (1948 TC) TC5200. Starting engine number: (1948 TC) 5800.

1949 MG TC roadster.

1947 MG TC roadster.

Model	Body Type & Seating	Engine Type/CID	P.O.E. Price	Weight (lbs.)	Prod. Total
TC	2-dr Roadster-2P	I4/76	2238	1735	Note 1
Y SERIES					
YA	4-dr Saloon-4P	I4/76	2658	2280	Note 2
YT	2-dr Tourer-4P	I4/76	2875	2137	Note 3

Note 1: A total of 10,000 TCs were produced (3,085 in 1948 alone).
Note 2: Approximately 6,158 YA saloons were produced.
Note 3: About 877 YT Tourers were produced, into 1950.

Price Note: Initial TC price in 1946 was $1995 (East coast). TC price rose to $2395 by 1949; YA saloon to $2875.

PRODUCTION/SALES: Out of the total TC production 10,000 units, 3,408 were sold in Britain and only 2,001 were officially exported to the U.S. Additional examples were brought to the U.S. by individuals. An estimated 682 MGs were sold in the U.S. during 1948, and 857 in 1949.
Manufacturer: The M.G. Car Company Ltd. (part of Nuffield Exports Ltd.), Cowley, Oxford, England; plant at Abingdon-on-Thames, Berkshire.
Distributor: Motor Sport Inc., New York City; British Motor Car Distributors Ltd., San Francisco, California; then Hambro Trading Co. of America, New York City.
HISTORY: TC production began in late 1945. Production of the Y-series saloon began in 1947; the Y Tourer in late 1948, continuing into early 1950. The MG company later called the TC "the sports car America loved first." A TC could cruise at 60 mph or so, and hit about 75. But acceleration to 60 mph was considerably slower than typical American cars. MG engines were capable of tight tuning for race purposes, but the car's poor aerodynamics cut back on racing performance. On the other hand, its short wheelbase and quick steering soon made it a popular choice for the rallies and gymkhanas that began to flourish in the 1950s. In October 1948, a group of TCs entered the first Watkins Glen Grand Prix race in New York state, the quickest of which took third place.

1948 MG TC roadster.

1950 MG

1950 MG TD. (Christie's)

TD — FOUR — Many purists were horrified when the upright-looking TC faded away, replaced by the lowered, upstart TD. Smoother, more modern lines replaced the TC's vertical look. Company sales literature promised that its "very lines suggest action," adding that "Hollywood stars acclaim the Midget as the greatest little sports car in the world." A dramatically lower stance resulted from the use of 15-inch tires rather than the original 19-inchers. The replacement also switched to independent front suspension, with twin control arms and coil springs.

The TD platform was a revised version of the box-section chassis used on the Y-series saloon (sedan), hurriedly developed for a late 1949 debut in the new roadster. A "kickup" above the rear wheels allowed the use of softer springs and increased wheel travel, to complement the softer ride of the new front suspension. Wire wheels were gone, replaced by steel discs. Wearing fresh body panels, the TD was notably wider than its predecessor and looked less angular. Because straight-across bumpers were now included, overall length was greater. The upright grille again consisted to vertical bars, with an emblem in the upper center. Headlamps remained separate from the body, while fenders were lower than on the TC. Under the cowl was a frame-mounted roll bar. Twin horns and an oil-bath air cleaner were standard. The leather-upholstered bench seat was similar to that in the TC, while the dual cowl was covered in leatherette. Side curtains could be used even with the top not erected. Ahead of the driver were both the five-inch speedometer and tachometer, as well as the familiar 'MG' octagon within the spring-spoke steering wheel's hub, which stood on an adjustable steering column. The flat windshield could still be folded down.

ENGINE DATA: BASE FOUR (TC, YT Tourer): Inline, overhead-valve four-cylinder (XPAG). Cast iron block and head. **Displacement:** 76.3 cu. in. (1250 cc). **Bore & Stroke:** 2.62 x 3.54 in. (66.1 x 90 mm). **Compression Ratio:** 7.25:1. **Brake Horsepower:** 54.4 at 5200 rpm. **Torque:** 64 lbs.-ft. at 2600 rpm. Three main bearings. Solid valve lifters. Two SU semi-downdraft carburetors. 12-volt electrical system.

BASE FOUR (YA saloon): Same as above, except — **Compression Ratio:** 7.1:1. **Brake Horsepower:** 45 at 4800 rpm. One SU carburetor.

CHASSIS DATA: Wheelbase: (TC) 94 in.; (Y) 99 in. **Overall Length:** (TC) 139.5 in.; (YA) 161.2 in.; (YT) 164 in. **Height:** (TC) 53 in.; (YA) 57 in. **Width:** (TC) 56 in.; (Y) 59 in. **Front Tread:** (TC) 45 in.; (Y) 47.4 in. **Rear Tread:** (TC) 45 in.; (Y) 50 in. **Wheel Type:** (TC) knock-off wire; (YA) disc. **Standard Tires:** (TC) 4.50x19; (Y) 5.25x16.

TECHNICAL: Layout: front-engine, rear-drive. **Transmission:** four-speed manual (floor lever). Overall TC gear ratios: (1st) 17.32:1; (2nd) 10.0:1; (3rd) 6.93:1; (4th) 5.125:1. **Standard Final Drive Ratio:** (TC) 5.125:1; (YA/YT) 5.143:1. **Steering:** (TC) cam and lever; (Y) rack and pinion. **Suspension (front):** (TC) rigid axle with semi-elliptic leaf springs; (Y) unequal-length wishbones and coil springs. **Suspension (rear):** rigid axle with semi-elliptic leaf springs. **Brakes:** Lockheed hydraulic, front/rear drum. **Body Construction:** steel body with wood framing, on box-section steel frame.

PERFORMANCE: Top Speed: (TC) 80-82 mph (74-78 mph in Britain); (YA saloon) 70-72 mph; (YT Tourer) 73-75 mph. **Acceleration (0-60 mph):** (TC) 19.5-22.7 sec.; (TC w/blower) 14.2 sec.; (YA) 29 seconds. **Acceleration (quarter-mile):** (TC) 21.8 sec.; (YA) 23.2 seconds. **Fuel Mileage:** (TC) 25-32 mpg.

431

Drivetrain changes were slight. Beneath the long, louvered hood sat the same engine as in the TC, still rated 54.4 horsepower. Top speed rose a bit to 80 mph, but acceleration suffered because of a weight increase. The major change from an American viewpoint was the availability of left-hand drive.

Y (YA/YT) -- FOUR -- Production of the "One and a Quarter Liter" saloon and Tourer continued with minimal change. MG claimed that "it looks...it rides...it drives like a sports car."

I.D. DATA: Serial number plate is located on on front of cowl (left side), under the hood. Motor number is alongside the serial number, and on the side of the engine block. Starting serial number: (TD) TD0251.

Model	Body Type & Seating	Engine Type/CID	P.O.E. Price	Weight (lbs.)	Prod. Total
TD	2-dr Rds-2P	I4/76	1850	2016	Note 1
Y SERIES					
YA	4-dr Saloon-4P	I4/76	2250	2280	Note 2
YT	2-dr Tourer-4P	I4/76	N/A	2137	Note 3

Note 1: A total of 29,664 TDs were produced from 1949-53.
Note 2: Approximately 6,158 YA saloons were produced.
Note 3: About 877 YT Tourers were produced, into 1950.
Price Note: P.O.E. price was as low as $1850 in 1950.

ENGINE DATA: BASE FOUR (TD, YT Tourer): Inline, overhead-valve four-cylinder. Cast iron block and head. **Displacement:** 76.3 cu. in. (1250 cc). **Bore & Stroke:** 2.62 x 3.54 in. (66.5 x 90 mm). **Compression Ratio:** 7.25:1. **Brake Horsepower:** 54.4 at 5200 rpm. **Torque:** 64 lbs.-ft. at 2600 rpm. Three main bearings. Solid valve lifters. Two SU semi-downdraft carburetors. 12-volt electrical system.

BASE FOUR (YA saloon): Same as above, except — **Compression Ratio:** 7.1:1. **Brake Horsepower:** 45 at 4800 rpm.

CHASSIS DATA: Wheelbase: (TD) 94 in.; (YA) 99 in. **Overall Length:** (TD) 145 in.; (YA) 161.2 in. **Height:** (TD) 53 in.; (YA) 57 in. **Width:** (TD) 58.6 in.; (YA) 59 in. **Front Tread:** (TD) 47.4 in.; (YA) 47.4 in. **Rear Tread:** (TD) 50 in.; (YA) 50 in. **Wheel Type:** (TD) 4.00x15 well-base, five-stud steel disc; (YA) five-stud steel disc. **Standard Tires:** (TD) Dunlop 5.50x15; (YA) 5.25x16.

TECHNICAL: Layout: front-engine, rear-drive. **Transmission:** four-speed manual (2nd/3rd/4th synchro). Overall TD gear ratios: (1st) 17.938:1; (2nd) 10.609:1; (3rd) 7.098:1; (4th) 5.125:1. **Standard Final Drive Ratio:** (TD) 5.125:1 (4.875:1 or 4.555:1 available); (YA) 5.143:1. **Steering:** rack and pinion. **Suspension (front):** independent; control arms and coil springs. **Suspension (rear):** rigid axle and semi-elliptic leaf springs. **Brakes:** hydraulic, front/rear drum. **Body Construction:** steel body with wood framework, on box-section steel frame.

MAJOR OPTIONS: "His Master's Voice" radio.

PERFORMANCE: Top Speed: (TD) 80-83 mph. **Acceleration (0-60 mph):** (TD) 23.5 sec. **Fuel Mileage:** (TD) 39 mpg at 30 mph (claimed in Britain).

PRODUCTION/SALES: A total of 29,664 TDs were produced from 1949-53, of which 23,488 were sold in the United States. An estimated 1,576 MGs were sold in the U.S. during 1950.

Manufacturer: The M.G. Car Company Ltd. (part of Nuffield Exports Ltd.), Cowley, Oxford, England; plant at Abingdon-on-Thames, Berkshire.

Distributor: Hambro Trading Co. of America, New York City.

HISTORY: Created by Cecil Cousins, who'd been with MG since the 1920s, the TD entered production in October 1949. The Nuffield Organization wanted a cheap and simple successor to the increasingly-popular TC, and wanted it fast. The traditional look had to continue, but with independent front suspension rather than the old-fashioned rigid axle. Though improved and even more appealing to American customers, especially with left-hand drive, the TD was still a crude vehicle with cumbersome top and side curtains, so-so performance, and tight cockpit. "They have made many new friends, especially in America," declared The Autocar in 1950, referring to the recent invasion of MG TCs into the export market. "And from these new friends have gradually come various suggestions, mostly requesting modernization."

1951-53 MG

1951 MG TD roadster.

TD — FOUR — MG's basic roadster was little changed from its 1950 debut. Series II, starting in mid-1951, added a few technical changes, such as a bigger clutch, but no appearance revisions. (The "II" designation was seldom seen in referring to ordinary 1951-53 models.) Standard body colors for 1953 were: Black or Ivory with red or green leather upholstery; M.G. Red with red upholstery; Silver Streak Grey with red upholstery; and Woodland Green with green upholstery. Standard equipment included leather upholstery, side curtains, fold-flat windshield, spring-spoke steering wheel on adjustable column, full-width bumpers with overriders, twin stop and taillamps, twin wind-tone horns, 5.50x15 tires on disc wheels, and a glovebox.

TDC (Mk II) — FOUR — Starting in mid-1951, a limited-production Mark II competition version became available with increased compression and horsepower. With 8.0:1 compression in the new cylinder head and larger 1.5-inch SU carburetors, plus twin fuel pumps, horsepower first rose to 57 (versus the standard 54); then up to 60 bhp. Andrex friction-type shock American dealers began to sell conversion kits as early as 1951, and the performance edition became known in the U.S. as the TDC (TD Competition). Both punched-hole disc wheels and wire wheels were available. Owners of ordinary TDs could also obtain instructions for the upgrade. An official Mark II edition had a small metal identifying marker, just to the rear of the headlamp.

YB — FOUR — The next version of MG's saloon was similar in appearance to the initial YA, but switched to smaller (15-inch) tires and hypoid final drive. A compression boost increased horsepower to 48, and the front suspension contained an anti-roll bar. Bumpers contained overriders.

1951-'54 MG YB sedan.

1952 MG TD roadster.

I.D. DATA: Serial number plate is located on on front of cowl (left side), under the hood. Motor number is alongside the serial number, and on the side of the engine block. Starting serial number: (TD) continued from 1950.

Model	Body Type & Seating	Engine Type/CID	P.O.E. Price	Weight (lbs.)	Prod. Total
TD II	2-dr Rds-2P	I4/76	1945	2065	Note 1
TD Mk II					
TDC	2-dr Rds-2P	I4/76	2145	2115	1,022
Y SERIES					
YB	4-dr Saloon-4P	I4/76	N/A	2337	1,301

Note 1: A total of 29,664 TDs were produced from 1949-53 (10,838 in 1952 alone).
Price Note: Prices rose in 1952-53 to $2115 for the basic roadster and $2360 for the TDC.

ENGINE DATA: BASE FOUR (TD): Inline, overhead-valve four-cylinder. Cast iron block and head. **Displacement:** 76.3 cu. in. (1250 cc). **Bore & Stroke:** 2.62 x 3.54 in. (66.5 x 90 mm). **Compression Ratio:** 7.25:1 **Brake Horsepower:** 54.4 at 5200 rpm. **Torque:** 64 lbs.-ft. at 2600 rpm. Three main bearings. Solid valve lifters. Two SU carburetors.

BASE FOUR (TDC Mark II): Same as above, except — **Compression Ratio:** 8.0:1/8.6:1. **Brake Horsepower:** 57/60 at 5500 rpm.

BASE FOUR (YB): Same as above, except — **Compression Ratio:** 7.4:1. **Brake Horsepower:** 48 at 4800 rpm. One SU carburetor.

CHASSIS DATA: Wheelbase: (TD) 94 in.; (YB) 99 in. **Overall Length:** (TD) 145 in.; (YB) 164 in. **Height:** (TD) 53 in. **Width:** (TD) 58.6 in.; (YB) 59 in. **Front Tread:** (TD) 47.4 in.; (YB) 47.4 in. **Rear Tread:** (TD) 50 in.; (YB) 50 in. **Wheel Type:** (TD) 4.00x15 well-base, five-stud steel disc; (YB) five-stud steel disc. **Standard Tires:** (TD) Dunlop 5.50x15; (YB) 5.50x15.

1953 MG TD roadster.

TECHNICAL: Layout: front-engine, rear-drive. **Transmission:** four-speed manual (2nd/3rd/4th synchro). Overall TD gear ratios: (1st) 17.938:1; (2nd) 10.609:1; (3rd) 7.098:1; (4th) 5.125:1. **Standard Final Drive Ratio:** (TD) 5.125:1 (4.875:1 or 4.555:1 available); (YB) 5.143:1. **Steering:** rack and pinion. **Suspension (front):** (TD) independent; control arms and coil springs; (YB) control arms, coil springs and anti-roll bar. **Suspension (rear):** rigid axle and semi-elliptic leaf springs. **Brakes:** hydraulic, front/rear drum. **Body Construction:** steel body with wood framework, on box-section steel frame.

MAJOR OPTIONS: TD OPTIONS: Chrome-plated external luggage rack. Chromium badge bar and two mounting brackets. Spotlight. Radio (fits in glovebox). Twin spare-wheel carrier with six-inch rear tires and wheels (for competition).

PERFORMANCE: Same as 1950.

PRODUCTION/SALES: A total of 29,664 TDs were produced from 1949-53, 23,488 of which were sold in the United States. Of the total, 1,022 were Mark II (TDC) versions. An estimated 3,790 MGs were sold in the U.S. during 1951, 7,449 during 1952, and 6,606 in 1953. YB saloon was produced from early 1952 to late 1953.

Manufacturer: The M.G. Car Company Ltd. (part of Nuffield Exports Ltd.), Cowley, Oxford, England; plant at Abingdon-on-Thames, Berkshire.

Distributor: Hambro Trading Co. of America, New York City.

HISTORY: At the Earl's Court Motor Show in London, in October 1952, MGs were advertised for sale to Americans at $1460. Sales brochures called MG "the one you've always wanted to drive," claiming that the roadster "Goes like a flash...grips the road like a limpet." A 1953 American advertisement promised a new MG for $2157, or less than $65 per month after minimum down payment. "No other sports car can boast such bloodlines," it continued, "such a history of continuous successes. It brings the *fun* back to driving."

The competition-oriented Mark II was advertised as "for the enthusiast--the fellow who wants just that little bit extra." That rare Mark II (TDC) edition could also get suspension and other modifications out of MG's competition catalog. In fact, the catalog listed a variety of engine tuning kits (Stage II, Stage III, etc.) that could be used with any TD model. In August 1951, a stock Mark II version set 23 Class F records at the Bonneville (Utah) Salt Flats, with a 12-hour run averaging 75.34 mph. MG faced serious competition in the marketplace from the Triumph TR2, which had a much more powerful engine and 105-mph top speed, as well as more modern amenities. By 1953, the Nuffield Organisation had become part of the British Motor Corporation.

American distributors turned out several modified MG models that appeared at the 1953 International Motor Show in New York. S.H. Arnolt in Chicago produced about 90 Mark II specials in 1952, with aluminum four-seat coupe or drophead bodywork by Bertone. Barely recognizable as MGs, the fastback specials wore a tight crosshatch-patterned grille and contained bult-in headlamps. Inskip Motors in New York also created a four-seater, but built no more than four examples.

1954 MG

TF — FOUR — Introduced for 1954, the revised roadster did not change radically in appearance or mechanically from the prior TD. A lower, more sharply sloped hood line stood behind a smaller modified, curved radiator grille that displayed fewer vertical bars and a revised rake, with a non-functional radiator cap up top. Headlamps and the smaller grille were now faired into the fenders. Center-lock wire wheels became optional (frequently found on U.S. models), with disc wheels standard; some later disc examples had a punched-hole design. Both the gas tank and outside spare tire also showed a more rakish angle. The dashboard was restyled, using three octagonal gauges (following the MG insignia) in the center, rather than the former round ones. Open gloveboxes stood at each end of the dash. Bucket seats were independently adjustable, and the cowl line was taller than before.

Construction was the same as before: steel body panels over a wooden skeleton frame. Body changes were limited to the front and rear of the car. The XPAG engine developed 3 more horsepower than its predecessor, incorporating modifications made for the earlier Mark II version (larger valves and a higher axle ratio). Performance also got a boost, but engine access became tighter. Louvers on the hood sides were shorter than before. Hood sides were fixed in place, with the center-hinged top section opened by pushbuttons on either side.

1954 MG TF roadster.

ZA MAGNETTE — FOUR — Following the success of the MG roadster, the company introduced the sporty ZA Magnette sedan for 1954, with a larger (91 cu. in.) engine. "Safety fast in airsmoothed style," said the Magnette's sales brochure. Unlike the traditional look of the roadster, the saloon (sedan) four-door body displayed modern, curvaceous lines with overtones of the MGA roadster that would arrive for 1956. Although it attracted little interest in America at first, and never became a major collector's item, the Magnette eventually drew a modest following.

The Y-type saloon of 1947-53, carrying some body panels that originated in prewar Morris Twelves, had never sold in large numbers, though it had been an official American import. However, the Magnette, which entered production during 1953, began to arrive on U.S. shores in significant, if limited, numbers during the Fifties. The Magnette used a Wolseley 4/44 body and was powered by a B-series Austin engine. The Magnette name had been used on prewar MG models. A trim strip extended along the front fender, just over the rounded wheel opening and partly across the front door. Tiny parking lights sat below the built-in headlamps, which flanked a vertical-bar grille. Separate fog lights were available. Perforated disc wheels held 5.50x15 tires. Standard body colors were: Grey with grey upholstery; Green with green or biscuit upholstery; Maroon with maroon or biscuit upholstery; and Black with maroon, biscuit or green upholstery.

I.D. DATA: Serial number plate is located on on front of cowl (left side), under hood on dashboard panel. Motor number is alongside the serial number, and on a plate on the right side of the engine block. Starting serial number: (TF) TF501; (ZA) 501.

Model	Body Type & Seating	Engine Type/CID	P.O.E. Price	Weight (lbs.)	Prod. Total
TF	2-dr Rds-2P	I4/76	2195	1936	6,200
MAGNETTE					
ZA	4-dr Sedan-4/5P	I4/91	2595	2464	Note 1

Note 1: A total of 12,754 Magnettes were built during the 1953-56 period.

Price Note: TF with wire wheels was priced at $2330.

ENGINE DATA: BASE FOUR (TF): Inline, overhead-valve four-cylinder. Cast iron block and head. **Displacement:** 76.3 cu. in. (1250 cc). **Bore & Stroke:** 2.62 x 3.54 in. (66.5 x 76.28 mm). **Compression Ratio:** 8.0:1. **Brake Horsepower:** 57.5 at 5500 rpm. **Torque:** 65 lbs.-ft. at 3000 rpm. Three main bearings. Solid valve lifters. Two SU carburetors.

BASE FOUR (Magnette): Inline, overhead-valve four-cylinder. Cast iron block and head. **Displacement:** 91 cu. in. (1489 cc). **Bore & Stroke:** 2.87 x 3.50 in. (73 x 88.9 mm). **Compression Ratio:** 7.15:1. **Brake Horsepower:** 60 at 4600 rpm. **Torque:** 78.3 lbs.-ft. at 3000 rpm. Three main bearings. Solid valve lifters. Two SU carburetors.

CHASSIS DATA: Wheelbase: (TF) 94 in.; (Magnette) 102 in. **Overall Length:** (TF) 147 in.; (Magnette) 169 in. **Height:** (TF) 52.5 in.; (Magnette) 58 in. **Width:** (TF) 59 in.; (Magnette) 63 in. **Front Tread:** (TF) 47.4 in.; (TF w/wire wheels) 48.2 in.; (Magnette) 51 in. **Rear Tread:** (TF) 50 in.; (TF w/wire wheels) 50.8 in.; (Magnette) 51 in. **Wheel Type:** (TF) 4.00x15 well-base, five-stud steel disc; (Magnette) ventilated four-stud disc. **Standard Tires:** Dunlop 5.50x15.

TECHNICAL: Layout: front-engine, rear-drive. Transmission: four-speed manual (floor lever); 2nd/3rd/4th synchro. Overall TF gear ratios: (1st) 17.06:1; (2nd) 10.09:1; (3rd) 6.725:1; (4th) 4.875:1. **Standard Final Drive Ratio:** (TF) 4.875:1 (5.125:1 or 4.55:1 available); (Magnette) 4.875:1. **Steering:** rack and pinion. **Suspension (front):** independent; control arms and coil springs. **Suspension (rear):** rigid axle and semi-elliptic leaf springs. **Brakes:** hydraulic, front/rear drum. **Body Construction:** steel body panels over wood framework, on box-section steel frame with tubular crossmembers.

MAJOR OPTIONS: TF OPTIONS: Wire wheels. Badge bar. Luggage carrier. Outside rearview mirror. Foglight. "H.M.V." radio.

MAGNETTE OPTIONS: Radio ($70). Heater ($64). Foglights ($29). Turn signals ($29). Windshield washers ($11).

PERFORMANCE: Top Speed: (TF) 80-82 mph; (Magnette) 81-83 mph. **Acceleration (0-60 mph):** (TF) 18.9-22.2 sec.; (Magnette) 22.5-22.8 sec. **Acceleration (quarter-mile):** (TF) 22.6 sec. (61 mph); (Magnette) 22.6 sec. (60.6 mph). **Fuel Mileage:** (TF) about 23 mpg; (Magnette) about 22 mpg.

PRODUCTION/SALES: Production of both models began in October 1953. A total of 6,200 TF models were produced in 1953 and '54. A total of 12,754 Magnettes were built during the 1953-56 period. Approximately 3,454 MGs were sold in the U.S. during 1954. By 1954, about 20,000 MG roadsters had been sold in America.

Manufacturer: The M.G. Car Company Ltd. (part of Nuffield Exports Ltd.), Cowley, Oxford, England; plant at Abingdon-on-Thames, Berkshire.

Distributor: Hambro Automotive Corp., New York City.

HISTORY: The new TF design, introduced in autumn 1953, received considerable criticism at the time for not being a step in the right direction, though many later deemed it the most graceful of the T-series MGs--possibly even the most desirable. Many disagree, however, preferring the more stark lines of the TC and TD. Though improved, the TF was mainly a facelift that couldn't compete with the Triumph TR2 in performance and power. The automotive press was not kind to the final traditional MG, probably because of its lackluster performance--and the fact that the company wasn't eager to issue loaner models to the enthusiast magazines. A bigger engine appeared in mid-1954 for a TF 1500 series (see 1955 listing).

1955 MG

1955 MG TF roadster.

TF 1500 — FOUR — Little change was evident from the 1954 version, except for a switch to the bigger (1.5-liter) engine. A small metal 'TF 1500' marker on each side of the hood (near the front) provided the only visual evidence of the bigger engine. The 1466-cc XPEG engine, derived from the powerplant that ran 120 mph at the Bonneville Salt Flats, produced 63 horsepower and 76 pound-feet of torque. Identification plates on the dashboard and engine indicated the 'XPEG' powerplant.

ZA MAGNETTE — FOUR — Little change from 1954.

I.D. DATA: Continuation of 1954.

Model	Body Type & Seating	Engine Type/CID	P.O.E. Price	Weight (lbs.)	Prod. Total
TF 1500	2-dr Rds-2P	I4/91	1995	1904	3,400
MAGNETTE					
ZA	4-dr Sedan-4/5P	I4/91	2475	2464	Note 1

Note 1: A total of 12,754 Magnettes were built during the 1953-56 period.
Price Note: TF with wire wheels cost $2130.

ENGINE DATA: BASE FOUR (TF 1500): Inline, overhead-valve four-cylinder (XPEG). Cast iron block and head. **Displacement:** 90.9 cu. in. (1466 cc). **Bore & Stroke:** 2.875 x 3.54 in. (72 x 90 mm). **Compression Ratio:** 8.3:1. **Brake Horsepower:** 63 at 5500 rpm. **Torque:** 76 lbs.-ft. at 3000 rpm. Three main bearings. Solid valve lifters. Two SU carburetors.

BASE FOUR (Magnette): Inline, overhead-valve four-cylinder. Cast iron block and head. **Displacement:** 91 cu. in. (1489 cc). **Bore & Stroke:** 2.87 x 3.50 in. (73 x 88.9 mm). **Compression Ratio:** 7.15:1. **Brake Horsepower:** 60 at 4600 rpm. **Torque:** 78.3 lbs.-ft. at 3000 rpm. Three main bearings. Solid valve lifters. Two SU carburetors.

CHASSIS DATA: Wheelbase: (TF) 94 in.; (Magnette) 102 in. **Overall Length:** (TF) 147 in.; (Magnette) 169 in. **Height:** (TF) 52.5 in.; (Magnette) 58 in. **Width:** (TF) 59.75 in.; (Magnette) 63 in. **Front Tread:** (TF) 47.4 in.; (TF w/wire wheels) 48.2 in.; (Magnette) 51 in. **Rear Tread:** (TF) 50 in.; (TF w/wire wheels) 50.8 in.; (Magnette) 51 in. **Wheel Type:** steel disc. **Standard Tires:** (TF) 5.50x15; (Magnette) 5.50x15.

TECHNICAL: Same as 1954.

MAJOR OPTIONS: Similar to 1954.

PERFORMANCE: Top Speed: (TF 1500) 85-89 mph; (Magnette) 80-84 mph. **Acceleration (0-60 mph):** (TF 1500) 15.3-17.3 sec. **Acceleration (quarter-mile):** (TF 1500) 20.7 sec.; (Magnette) 22.2-22.9 sec. **Fuel Mileage:** (TF 1500) about 25 mpg; (Magnette) about 22 mpg.

PRODUCTION/SALES: TF 1500 production began in July 1954, and a total of 3,400 were produced in 1954 and early '55. A total of 9,600 TF roadsters had been built when production halted in March 1955, while the Magnette continued until October 1956. Approximately 3,001 MGs were sold in the U.S. during 1955.

Manufacturer: The M.G. Car Company Ltd. (part of Nuffield Exports Ltd.), Cowley, Oxford, England; plant at Abingdon-on-Thames, Berkshire.
Distributor: Hambro Automotive Corp., New York City.

HISTORY: A prototype for an MG with non-traditional, modern styling had appeared in 1952, but was sent to the back burner. An experimental EX-182 sports car with B-series engine in an advanced state of tune appeared at Le Mans in 1955. Both soon led to the MGA roadster and coupe.

1956 MG

1955-'60 Arnolt MG.

A SERIES — 1500 — FOUR — "At long last" (in the words of *Motor Trend,* at least), MG "abandoned its old-but-handsome lines for new and handsomer ones...considerably slicker than its Le Mans prototype suggested." Not everyone was pleased by the change, but MG's roadster was indeed totally restyled, with a modern rounded look to replace the traditional squarish profile. Except for the front suspension and emblem, in fact, just about everything was new: body, chassis, gearbox, brakes, differential.

Change was less drastic beneath the MG bonnet, which now held a modified BMC B-series 90.88-cid (1489-cc) overhead-valve four-cylinder engine, rated at 68 horsepower (five more than the final TF 1500). While the new four-speed transmission stemmed from that used in the Magnette sedan, reverse gear was now positioned to the left (alongside second). The familiar 'MG' octagonal emblem continued, mounted at the upper center of the new rectangular grille, which contained side-by-side blocks of vertical ribs. The one-piece "alligator-style" hood was hinged at the rear, in the conventional style. In this revised MG's chassis, the deep box-section steel side members were swept outward, to place the roadster's two occupants between the frame rails (not above them). Six tubular crossmembers added rigidity to the structure. The front suspension used twin A-arms with coil springs, while the rear held semi-elliptic leaf springs.

Doors were now hinged at the front, but still held no outside handles. The streamlined body included an enclosed trunk and slightly curved windshield. Instruments were now round rather than octagonal, and turn signals were standard. Two Lucas 6-volt batteries were mounted behind the seats, and the four-inch white-on-black tachometer and speedometer were positioned on either side of the steering column. Adjustable bucket-type seats had leather-covered cushions and backs. Each door contained a storage pocket. Standard equipment included tools, a center-mounted mirror, quick-release gas cap, and a spring-spoke steering wheel. Detachable sidescreens contained a spring-loaded flap that could be opened when needed, at toll booths and the like. Standard colors were Black with red or green upholstery (Ice Blue or black top); Orient Red or Old English White with red or black upholstery (black top); and Tyrolite Green or Glacier Blue with grey or black upholstery (Ice Blue top).

Motor Trend praised the new MG's handling qualities, noting that "there just don't seem to be many ways you can get into trouble" in this car that "certainly puts the fun back into driving." The magazine's tester managed to achieve acceleration times quicker than those of the final TF roadster.

ZA MAGNETTE — FOUR — This year, both the roadster and the Magnette sedan carried the same basic engine, but the BMC B-series produced a bit less power beneath the four-door's bonnet, rated at 60 horsepower. Magnette's body and chassis consisted of a single rigid unit, measuring 169 inches overall. Inside was an instrument panel of polished wood. Standard equipment included a heater, foglights, windshield washer, and whitewall tires.

Model Note: The new roadster series was variously identified in print as the M.G.A., MG-A, MG A, and MGA; but the latter version became the common form in the U.S., just as MGB did in the 1960s. The "1500" designation was not used initially but became common later, especially when engine size grew to 1600 cc.

I.D. DATA: Serial number is on a plate on the left front of the firewall, under the hood. Engine number is on the right side of the block, and also on the firewall plate.

Model	Body Type & Seating	Engine Type/CID	P.O.E. Price	Weight (lbs.)	Prod. Total
MGA					
1500	2-dr Rds-2P	I4/91	2195	1900	Note 1
MAGNETTE					
ZA	4-dr Sedan-4/5P	I4/91	2475	2464	Note 2

Note 1: A total of 58,750 MGAs were built from 1955 through May 1959, and more than 13,000 in 1956 alone.

Note 2: A total of 12,754 ZA Magnettes were built during the 1953-56 period.

Price Note: Roadster with wire wheels cost $2330.

ENGINE DATA: BASE FOUR (MGA): Inline, overhead-valve four-cylinder. Cast iron block and head. **Displacement:** 90.88 cu. in. (1489 cc). **Bore & Stroke:** 2.875 x 3.50 in. (73.025 x 88.9 mm). **Compression Ratio:** 8.3:1. **Brake Horsepower:** 68 at 5500 rpm. **Torque:** 77 lbs.-ft. at 3500 rpm. Three main bearings. Solid valve lifters. Two SU semi-downdraft carburetors.

BASE FOUR (Magnette): Same as above, except — **Compression Ratio:** 7.15:1. **Brake Horsepower:** 60 at 4600 rpm. **Torque:** 78.3 lbs.-ft. at 3000 rpm.

CHASSIS DATA: Wheelbase: (MGA) 94 in.; (Magnette) 102 in. **Overall Length:** (MGA) 156 in.; (Magnette) 169 in. **Height:** (MGA) 50 in.; (Magnette) 58 in. **Width:** (MGA) 57.3 in.; (Magnette) 63 in. **Front Tread:** (MGA) 47.5 in.; (Magnette) 51 in. **Rear Tread:** (MGA) 48.75 in.; (Magnette) 51 in. **Wheel Type:** (MGA) 4.00Jx15 well-base, four-stud steel disc. **Standard Tires:** (MGA) Dunlop 5.60x15; (Magnette) 5.50x15.

TECHNICAL: Layout: front-engine, rear-drive. **Transmission:** four-speed manual (floor lever) with hydraulically-operated clutch. MGA overall gear ratios: (1st) 15.652:1; (2nd) 9.52:1; (3rd) 5.908:1; (4th) 4.3:1; (rev) 20.468:1. **Standard Final Drive Ratio:** (MGA) 4.3:1; (Magnette) 4.875:1. **Steering:** rack and pinion. **Suspension (front):** independent; twin wishbones and coil springs. **Suspension (rear):** rigid axle and semi-elliptic leaf springs. **Brakes:** hydraulic, front/rear drum. **Body Construction:** (MGA) steel body on box-section steel frame; (Magnette) steel unibody. **Fuel Tank:** (MGA) 12 gallons.

MAJOR OPTIONS: MGA OPTIONS: "H.M.V." radio. Fresh-air heater/demister. Adjustable telescopic steering column. Fresh-air cockpit ventilator. 4.55:1 axle ratio. Twin horns. Fender-mounted mirror. External luggage carrier. Foglamp. Overall tonneau cover. Chrome-plated rim embellishers (wheel covers). Radiator blind. Windshield washer. Whitewall tires. Center-lock wire wheels. 5.90x15 Road Speed tires.

PERFORMANCE: Top Speed: (MGA) 90-98 mph; (Magnette) 81-83 mph. **Acceleration (0-60 mph):** (MGA) 14.5-15.9 sec.; (Magnette) 24.7 sec. **Acceleration (quarter-mile):** (MGA) 19.6-20.4 sec. (about 68 mph); (Magnette) 23.1 sec. (58 mph). **Fuel Mileage:** (MGA) about 30 mpg; (Magnette) average 26 mpg.

PRODUCTION/SALES: MGA production began in September 1955. Approximately 6,044 MGs were sold in the U.S. during 1956. Production of the ZA Magnette continued until October 1956.

Manufacturer: The M.G. Car Co. Ltd., Cowley, Oxford, England (plant at Abingdon-on-Thames, Berkshire).

Distributor: Hambro Automotive Corp., New York City; Gough Industries Inc., Los Angeles, California.

HISTORY: Two aluminum-bodied EX.182 prototypes of the restyled MG finished fifth and sixth in their class at the 24-hour race in Le Mans, France in 1955. Like the production MGA, the prototypes had swept-out frame side members that permitted lower seating. The BMC B-series engine, identical in displacement to that in the Magnette sedan (and production A series), produced 82 horsepower. An earlier (1952) prototype had used TD running gear, but because BMC had since taken over the MG operation, the new one adopted one of BMC's engines. The production version of the MGA appeared at the London Motor Show in October, 1955. Proving tests included high-speed runs at the MIRA track in Montlhery, and on the Nurburgring; plus extensive testing in the Alps. A factory-sponsored trio won the team award at the 1956 Sebring (Florida) 12-hour race.

1957-58 MG

1957 MGA coupe.

A SERIES — 1500 — FOUR — A hardtop coupe with roll-up glass windows and small vent wings joined the original MGA roadster this year, while the engine added four horsepower and stronger bearings. The coupe had a wraparound windshield and back window, vertical inside door handles, and outside door handles. The trunk opened from inside, via a handle behind the driver's seat. Better streamlining gave the coupe a considerably higher top speed (over 100 mph) than the roadster. A removable hardtop also became available for the soft-top roadster.

ZB MAGNETTE — FOUR — A ZB series replaced the original ZA Magnette for 1957, and the four-cylinder engine gained horsepower via a rise to 8.3:1 compression and the use of 1.5-inch SU carburetors. In fact, it was identical in output (68 bhp) to the engine used in the prior year's MGA. Appearance was similar to the ZA series. Inside was a restyled dashboard and safety steering wheel. Two versions were offered: standard, which had trafficators; and Duotone, which came with standard turn-signal flashers. Varitone (also called Duotone) models used the high horizontal bodyside trim strip that stretched from the grille along the hood and doors, following the upper curve of the back fenders, as a dividing line for the two body colors used on most examples. Pedals were hinged at the firewall. Bucket front seats and a bench rear seat were upholstered in pleated leather. Deluxe Magnettes had a wraparound back window, and all could be ordered with a Manumatic clutch, for semi-automatic clutch-free driving.

I.D. DATA: Serial number is on a plate on the left front of the firewall, under the hood. Engine number is on the right side of the block, and also on the firewall plate.

Model	Body Type & Seating	Engine Type/CID	P.O.E. Price	Weight (lbs.)	Prod. Total
MGA					
1500	2-dr Rds-2P	I4/91	2269	1997	Note 1
1500	2-dr Cpe-2P	I4/91	2620	1990	Note 1
MAGNETTE					
ZB	4-dr Sedan-4/5P	I4/91	2535	2464	Note 2

Note 1: A total of 58,750 MGA 1500s were built during the 1955-59 period.
Note 2: A total of 23,846 ZB Magnettes were built during the 1956-58 period.
Price Note: Roadster price shown is for disc wheels.
1958 Price Note: Prices rose to $2462 for the MGA roadster, $2695 for the coupe, and $2740 for the Magnette ($2819 for a Deluxe version of the Magnette sedan).

1958 MGA Twin Cam coupe.

ENGINE DATA: BASE FOUR (MGA): Inline, overhead-valve four-cylinder. Cast iron block and head. **Displacement:** 90.88 cu. in. (1489 cc). **Bore & Stroke:** 2.875 x 3.50 in. (73.025 x 88.9 mm). **Compression Ratio:** 8.3:1. **Brake Horsepower:** 72 at 5500 rpm. **Torque:** 77.4 lbs.-ft. at 3500 rpm. Three main bearings. Solid valve lifters. Two SU semi-downdraft carburetors.
BASE FOUR (ZB Magnette): Same as above, except -- **Compression Ratio:** 8.3:1. **Brake Horsepower:** 68 at 5500 rpm. **Torque:** 83 lbs.-ft. at 3500 rpm.

CHASSIS DATA: Same as 1956.

TECHNICAL: Layout: front-engine, rear-drive. **Transmission:** four-speed manual (floor lever) with hydraulically-operated clutch. MGA overall gear ratios: (1st) 15.652:1; (2nd) 9.52:1; (3rd) 5.908:1; (4th) 4.3:1; (rev) 20.468:1. **Standard Final Drive Ratio:** (MGA) 4.3:1; (Magnette) 4.55:1. **Steering:** rack and pinion. **Suspension (front):** independent; twin (unequal-length) wishbones and coil springs. **Suspension (rear):** rigid axle and semi-elliptic leaf springs. **Brakes:** hydraulic, front/rear drum. **Body Construction:** (MGA) steel body on box-section steel frame; (Magnette) steel unibody. **Fuel Tank:** (MGA) 12 gal.; (Magnette) 9.25 gallons.

MAJOR OPTIONS: MGA OPTIONS: Removable hardtop. H.M.V. radio ($65). Fresh-air heater/demister ($65). Adjustable telescopic steering column ($17.50). Fresh-air cockpit ventilator. 4.55:1 axle ratio. Twin horns. Fender-mounted mirror. External luggage carrier ($49.95). Foglamp. Overall tonneau cover. Chrome-plated rim embellishers (wheel covers). Radiator blind. Windshield washer ($17.50). Whitewall tires ($45). Center-lock wire wheels ($135). 5.90x15 Road Speed tires.
MAGNETTE OPTION: Manumatic clutch.

PERFORMANCE: Top Speed: (MGA rds) about 93 mph; (MGA cpe) 102 mph; (Magnette) 81-85 mph. **Acceleration (0-60 mph):** (MGA cpe) 12.3-14.2 sec.; (Magnette) 20.5-24.7 sec. **Acceleration (quarter-mile):** (MGA cpe) 19 sec. (73.6 mph); (Magnette) 23.1 sec. (58 mph). **Fuel Mileage:** (MGA rds) 25+ mpg; (MGA cpe) average 24 mpg; (Magnette) average 26 mpg.

PRODUCTION/SALES: Approximately 13,496 MGs were sold in the U.S. during 1957 and 16,250 in 1958. Production of the ZB Magnette began in October 1956 and continued into late 1958.

Manufacturer: The M.G. Car Co. Ltd., Cowley, Oxford, England (plant at Abingdon-on-Thames, Berkshire).

Distributor: Hambro Automotive Corp., New York City; Gough Industries Inc., Los Angeles, California.

HISTORY: MGA coupe was introduced at the October 1956 London Motor Show. The Twin-Cam MGA was announced in April 1958; see next listing for details.

1959 MG

1959 MGA Twin Cam. (Coys of Kensington)

MGA — 1500 — FOUR — Production of the standard roadster and coupe continued for most of the 1959 model year, with the same 1489-cc engine and little change otherwise. Late in the season, a 1600 series with larger engine was introduced; see 1960 listing for details.

MGA — TWIN-CAM — FOUR — In the spring of 1958, enthusiasts took careful note of the announcement of the new Twin-Cam MGA, which promised a sharp gain in performance. Not only was the new dual-overhead-cam four-cylinder engine larger in displacement than the standard four, at 1588 cc (97 cid), but it delivered a whopping 108 bhp: 50 percent more than the regular powerplant. The potent mill used larger (1.75-inch) SU carburetors, 80-degree inclined valves, hemispherical combustion chambers, and inverted bucket-style tappets. It also demanded high-octane fuel. At announcement time, the hopped-up MG with its cross-flow aluminum-alloy cylinder head sounded tempting to many fans. Later on, the engine would also develop reliability problems, notably detonation (and possible burnt pistons) especially when run at high rpm; and also became known as an oil burner. By the time modifications were made, including a drop in compression from the initial 9.9:1, the damage had been done and the Twin-Cam was doomed to extinction.

Twin-Cams came with standard four-wheel Dunlop disc brakes, and were capable of 115-to 120-mph top speed. Acceleration from a standing start to 100 mph was claimed to take about 30 seconds. The factory advised that engineering changes for the Twin-Cam were so extensive that conversion of existing models would be impractical. MGA steering mechanisms had to be altered, for instance, to allow clearance for the engine. Center-lock vented disc wheels were standard (no wire wheels available). Except for an oval air vent on each side of the hood, appearance was virtually identical to the other MGA models. Twin-Cam roadsters came in Black with red or green upholstery (blue or black top); Orient Red or Old English White with red or black upholstery (black top); and Ash Green or Glacier Blue with grey or black upholstery (blue top). Coupe colors were: Black with red or green upholstery; Orient Red or Old English White with red or black upholstery; and Ash Green or Mineral Blue with grey or black upholstery.

MAGNETTE — Mk III — FOUR — A completely different sedan took on the Magnette name for 1959, no longer designed or built at MG's own Abingdon facility. Pininfarina styling wasn't enough to suit MG fans, who tended to shun the new model with its wider vertical-bar grille, squarish profile, and full vertical taillamps at the ends of finned back fenders. Measuring nine inches longer than the ZA/ZB series, the new Magnette was nearly identical to the Morris Oxford, and differed from the Austin and Wolseley sedans mainly in grille and trim details. Semi-bucket front seats were upholstered in leather, with walnut interior trim. Under the hood was the same 1489-cc BMC B-series engine. New wheels held 14-inch tires, but performance was more sluggish than the former Z-series.

I.D. DATA: Serial number is on a plate on the left front of the firewall, under the hood. Engine number is on the right side of the block, and also on the firewall plate. The Twin-Cam had its own serial number sequence, starting at 501.

Model	Body Type & Seating	Engine Type/CID	P.O.E. Price	Weight (lbs.)	Prod. Total
MGA					
1500	2-dr Rds-2P	I4/91	2462	1904	Note 1
1500	2-dr Cpe-2P	I4/91	2695	2004	Note 1
TWIN-CAM MGA					
A	2-dr Rds-2P	I4/97	3320	2185	Note 2
A	2-dr Cpe-2P	I4/97	3640	2245	Note 2
MAGNETTE					
III	4-dr Sedan-4/5P	I4/91	2695	2492	Note 3

Note 1: A total of 58,750 MGA 1500s were built during the 1955-59 period.

Note 2: Approximately 2,210 Twin-Cam MGAs were built from 1958 to 1961.

Note 3: A total of 15,676 Magnette Mark III sedans were built during the 1959-61 period.

Price Note: Basic roadster with wire wheels cost $2546; coupe, $2785.

ENGINE DATA: BASE FOUR (MGA): Inline, overhead-valve four-cylinder. Cast iron block and head. **Displacement:** 90.88 cu. in. (1489 cc). **Bore & Stroke:** 2.875 x 3.50 in. (73.025 x 88.9 mm). **Compression Ratio:** 8.3:1. **Brake Horsepower:** 72 at 5500 rpm. **Torque:** 77.4 lbs.-ft. at 3500 rpm. Three main bearings. Solid valve lifters. Two SU semi-downdraft carburetors.

BASE FOUR (Magnette): Same as above, except — **Compression Ratio:** 8.3:1. **Brake Horsepower:** 66.5 at 5200 rpm.

BASE FOUR (Twin-Cam MGA): Inline, dual-overhead-cam four-cylinder (chain drive). Cast iron block and aluminum-alloy head. **Displacement:** 96.91 cu. in. (1588 cc). **Bore & Stroke:** 2.969 x 3.50 in. (75.4 x 88.9 mm). **Compression Ratio:** 9.9:1. **Brake Horsepower:** 108 at 6700 rpm. **Torque:** 104 lbs.-ft. at 4500 rpm. Three main bearings. Solid valve lifters. Two SU H6 semi-downdraft carburetors.

Note: Factory initially announced Twin-Cam rating of 107 bhp at 6500 rpm. A lower-powered version (100 bhp) emerged later.

CHASSIS DATA: Wheelbase: (MGA) 94 in.; (Magnette) 99.2 in. **Overall Length:** (MGA) 156 in.; (Magnette) 178 in. **Height:** (MGA) 50 in.; (Magnette) 59.8 in. **Width:** (MGA) 57.3 in.; (Magnette) 63.5 in. **Front Tread:** (MGA) 47.5 in.; (Magnette) 48.6 in.; (Twin-Cam) 47.9 in. **Rear Tread:** (MGA) 48.8 in.; (Magnette) 49.9 in. **Wheel Type:** (MGA) 4Jx15 well-base, four-stud steel disc; (Twin-Cam) center-lock disc. **Standard Tires:** (MGA) Dunlop 5.60x15; (Magnette) 5.60x14; (Twin-Cam) Dunlop 5.90x15 Road Speed.

TECHNICAL: Layout: front-engine, rear-drive. **Transmission:** four-speed manual (floor lever) with hydraulically-operated clutch. MGA overall gear ratios: (1st) 15.652:1; (2nd) 9.52:1; (3rd) 5.908:1; (4th) 4.3:1; (rev) 20.468:1. **Standard Final Drive Ratio:** (MGA) 4.3:1; (Magnette) 4.3:1. **Steering:** rack and pinion except (Magnette) cam and lever. **Suspension (front):** independent; twin (unequal-length) wishbones and coil springs. **Suspension (rear):** rigid axle and semi-elliptic leaf springs. **Brakes:** hydraulic, front/rear drum except (Twin-Cam) four-wheel Dunlop disc. **Body Construction:** (MGA) steel body on box-section steel frame; (Magnette) steel unibody. **Fuel Tank:** 12 gallons.

MAJOR OPTIONS: MGA OPTIONS: "H.M.V." radio. Heater. Cold-air ventilator. Competition windshield. Oil cooler. Windshield washer. Overall tonneau cover. Sliding windows. Deluxe seats. Various other items were available through suppliers, including twin horns, fender mirror, external luggage carrier, foglamps, cigar lighter, radiator blind, ashtray, badge bar, detachable hardtop, and a sunvisor (coupe only).

PERFORMANCE: Top Speed: (MGA rds) about 93 mph; (MGA cpe) 102 mph; (Twin-Cam) 115-120 mph. **Acceleration (0-60 mph):** (MGA cpe) 12.3-14.2 sec.; (Twin-Cam) 9.0-9.9 sec. **Acceleration (quarter-mile):** (MGA cpe) 19 sec. (73.6 mph); (Twin-Cam) 18.1 sec. **Fuel Mileage:** (MGA rds) 25+ mpg; (MGA cpe) average 24 mpg; (Twin-Cam) about 19.5 mpg.

Performance Note: Some Twin-Cam road tests produced much slower acceleration times (for example, 0-60 in 13.1 seconds).

PRODUCTION/SALES: Approximately 17,693 MGs were sold in the U.S. during 1959.

Manufacturer: The M.G. Car Co. Ltd., Cowley, Oxford, England (plant at Abingdon-on-Thames, Berkshire).

Distributor: Hambro Automotive Corp., New York City.

HISTORY: The Twin-Cam MGA was announced in April 1958 and continued in production into spring 1960. Two twin-cam prototype engines had been assembled and tested earlier in the decade, one of which powered the car entered in the 1955 Tourist Trophy race. As it happened, the other version went into production. The MGA 1600 (Mark I) debuted in May 1959; see next listing.

1960-61 MG

1960 MGA 1600.

MGA — 1600 Mk I — FOUR — A bigger engine was the major change for MG's roadster and coupe, as suggested by the model designation. The enlarged four-cylinder engine displaced 1588 cc (96.9 cid) and produced close to 80 horsepower. In essence, it was a pushrod overhead-valve version of the Twin-Cam's powerplant, with much lower compression. Appearance was similar to the prior models, but with amber front turn-signal lenses. Lockheed front disc brakes were used. Standard roadster colors for 1960 were: Black with red or beige upholstery and grey top; Chariot Red with red or beige upholstery and beige top, or black upholstery and grey top; Iris Blue with black upholstery and blue top; Alamo Beige with red upholstery and beige top; Dove Grey with red upholstery and grey top; and Old English White with red or black upholstery and grey top. Coupe colors were: Black with red or beige upholstery; Chariot Red with red, beige or black upholstery; Iris Blue with black upholstery; Alarm Beige or Dove Grey with red upholstery; and Old English White with red or black upholstery.

MGA — TWIN-CAM — FOUR — Production of the Twin-Cam roadster and coupe continued with little change, into early 1960.

DeLuxe MGA Note: Starting late in 1960, after production of the Twin-Cam ceased, a small number of DeLuxe MGA 1600 roadsters and coupes were built, but not listed in the usual charts and directories. They had the Twin-Cam's chassis with four-wheel disc brakes, along with the 1622-cc engine that would soon arrive for the Mark II version.

MAGNETTE — Mk III — FOUR — Little change was evident in the revised Magnette until the Mark IV version arrived in late 1961; see next listing. Duotone color schemes were available and a heater was standard. So were full-width bumpers with overriders.

1960 MGA Twin Cam coupe. (Sotheby's)

I.D. DATA: Serial number is on a plate on the left front of the firewall, under the hood. Engine number is on the right side of the block, and also on the firewall plate. Starting chassis number: (MGA 1600) 70222. Engine number: (MGA 1600): 16GA-U-H101 to -31660.

Model	Body Type & Seating	Engine Type/CID	P.O.E. Price	Weight (lbs.)	Prod. Total
MGA 1600					
Mk I	2-dr Rds-2P	I4/97	2444	1904	Note 1
Mk I	2-dr Cpe-2P	I4/97	2667	2004	Note 1
TWIN-CAM MGA					
A	2-dr Rds-2P	I4/97	3069	2185	Note 2
A	2-dr Cpe-2P	I4/97	3263	2245	Note 2
MAGNETTE					
Mk III	4-dr Sedan-4/5P	I4/91	2695	2476	Note 3

Note 1: A total of 31,501 MGA 1600 Mk I models were built during the 1959-61 period (plus about 82 DeLuxe models; also see next listing).

Note 2: Approximately 2,210 Twin-Cam MGAs were built from 1958 to 1961.

Note 3: A total of 15,676 Magnette Mark III sedans were built during the 1959-61 period.

Price Note: MGA with wire wheels cost $100 extra.

ENGINE DATA: BASE FOUR (MGA 1600): Inline, overhead-valve four-cylinder. Cast iron block and head. **Displacement:** 96.9 cu. in. (1588 cc). **Bore & Stroke:** 2.968 x 3.50 in. (75.4 x 88.9 mm). **Compression Ratio:** 8.3:1. **Brake Horsepower:** 79.5 at 5600 rpm. **Torque:** 87 lbs.-ft. at 3800 rpm. Three main bearings. Solid valve lifters. Two SU semi-downdraft carburetors.

BASE FOUR (Twin-Cam MGA): Inline, dual-overhead-cam four-cylinder (chain drive). Cast iron block and aluminum-alloy head. **Displacement:** 96.91 cu. in. (1588 cc). **Bore & Stroke:** 2.97 x 3.50 in. (75.4 x 88.9 mm). **Compression Ratio:** 9.9:1. **Brake Horsepower:** 108 at 6700 rpm. **Torque:** 104 lbs.-ft. at 4500 rpm. Three main bearings. Solid valve lifters. Two SU H6 semi-downdraft carburetors.

Note: A lower-powered Twin-Cam engine (100 bhp) was introduced in response to problems with the high-compression original.

BASE FOUR (Magnette): Inline, overhead-valve four-cylinder. Cast iron block and head. **Displacement:** 90.88 cu. in. (1489 cc). **Bore & Stroke:** 2.875 x 3.50 in. (73.025 x 88.9 mm). **Compression Ratio:** 8.3:1. **Brake Horsepower:** 66.5 at 5200 rpm. **Torque:** 85 lbs.-ft. at 5200 rpm. Three main bearings. Solid valve lifters. Two SU semi-downdraft carburetors.

CHASSIS DATA: Wheelbase: (MGA) 94 in.; (Magnette) 99.2 in. **Overall Length:** (MGA) 156 in.; (Magnette) 178 in. **Height:** (MGA) 50 in.; (Magnette) 59.8 in. **Width:** (MGA) 57.3 in.; (Magnette) 63.5 in. **Front Tread:** (MGA) 47.5 in.; (Magnette) 48.9 in. **Rear Tread:** (MGA) 48.8 in.; (Magnette) 49.9 in. **Wheel Type:** (MGA) 4Jx15 well-base, four-stud steel disc; (Twin-Cam) center-lock disc. **Standard Tires:** (MGA) Dunlop 5.60x15; (Magnette) 5.90x14; (Twin-Cam) 5.90x15.

TECHNICAL: Layout: front-engine, rear-drive. **Transmission:** four-speed manual (floor lever) with hydraulically-operated clutch. MGA overall gear ratios: (1st) 15.652:1; (2nd) 9.52:1; (3rd) 5.908:1; (4th) 4.3:1; (rev) 20.468:1. **Standard Final Drive Ratio:** (MGA) 4.3:1; (Magnette) 4.3:1. **Steering:** rack and pinion except (Magnette) cam and lever. **Suspension (front):** independent; wishbones and coil springs. **Suspension (rear):** rigid axle and semi-elliptic leaf springs. **Brakes:** (MGA 1600) front disc, rear drum; (Twin-Cam) four-wheel Dunlop disc; (Magnette) front/rear drum. **Body Construction:** (MGA) steel body on box-section steel frame; (Magnette) steel unibody. **Fuel Tank:** 12 gallons.

MAJOR OPTIONS: MGA OPTIONS: Removable hardtop ($275). Heater. Cold-air ventilation. Radio. Adjustable telescopic steering column. Twin horns. Fender mirror. External luggage carrier (with fender mirror). Foglamp. Battery covers. Tonneau cover. Competition windshield. Competition deluxe seats. Badge bar. Headlamps flasher switch. 4.55:1 axle ratio. Anti-roll bar. Radiator blind. Windshield washer. Ashtray. Lighter. Whitewall tires. Wire wheels. 5.90x15 tires.

PERFORMANCE: Top Speed: (MGA rds) 100 mph; (Twin-Cam) 115-120 mph. **Acceleration (0-60 mph):** (MGA) 13.3 sec.; (Twin-Cam) 9.0-9.9 sec. **Acceleration (quarter-mile):** (MGA) 19.0 sec.; (Twin-Cam) 18.1 sec. **Fuel Mileage:** (MGA 1600) about 28 mpg; (Twin-Cam) about 19.5 mpg.

PRODUCTION/SALES: Approximately 13,069 MGs were sold in the U.S. during 1960 and 8,806 in 1961.

Manufacturer: The M.G. Car Co. Ltd., Cowley, Oxford, England (plant at Abingdon-on-Thames, Berkshire).

Distributor: Hambro Automotive Corp., New York City.

HISTORY: Production of the Twin-Cam MGA continued until April 1960, but slowed to a trickle in the final months. Production of the 1600 Mark I halted in April 1961.

1962 MG

1962 MGA roadster.

MIDGET — Mk I (GAN1) — FOUR — Just as Austin-Healey had added its smaller Sprite, the MGA was joined by a new Midget for 1962. Cynics called it simply a "badge-engineered" version of the recently-restyled Sprite II, which lost its original "bugeye" look. True enough, but the new roadster, though differing from the Sprite in little more than grille and trim details, helped MG sales for nearly two decades. Introduced in June 1961, the Midget had a 948-cc four-cylinder engine (like that in the Morris Minor) producing 46 horsepower, with close-ratio four-speed gearbox. Within a few months of the roadster's debut, a high-compression head became available, raising the output to 50 bhp. Midgets had a wide vertical-bar grille, rectangular parking lights below the built-in round headlamps, squared-off wheel arches, small vent windows, a conventional trunk, and a long horizontal bodyside trim strip just above the front wheel opening. Wheelbase of the unibody design was 80 inches. Though truly a two-seater, a tiny carpeted area behind the bucket seats could (barely) hold small children. A tachometer was standard, along with a windshield washer, bumper overriders, and stowage bags for the top and sliding side curtains. Standard colors included Tartan Red with red or black interior and red top; Clipper Blue with dark blue interior and top; Farina Grey, Old English White or Black with red interior and grey top; and Old English White with black interior and grey top.

MGA — 1600 Mk II — FOUR — A revised edition of the 1600 series carried a larger engine yet, now grown to 1622 cubic centimeters and producing 90 horsepower. A compression boost to 8.9:1 meant premium fuel was required, but top speed reached the 105-mph mark. This version was produced for only one year, before it was replaced by the all-new MGB. For the first time since the A series debuted, the final drive ratio was changed, to 4.10:1. Mark II MGs destined for the U.S. had oil coolers on their engines. Center-lock (knock-off) wire wheels remained available, though the factory recommended the usual bolt-on steel disc wheels. Appearance was similar to the earlier 1600, except that the vertical grille bars were now recessed at the base (with the center divider bar jutting forward), and a single horizontal lens served for taillamps.

MAGNETTE — Mk IV — FOUR — MG's four-door sedan got a larger (1622 cc) engine for the Mark IV edition, wheelbase grew an inch, and a Borg-Warner automatic transmission became optional. Though identical in displacment to the four-cylinder engine in the MGA, the Magnette version had less horsepower. Even so, it was quicker than the former Mark III, able to run from zero to 60 mph in about 17 seconds. This version lasted until 1967. Appearance was identical to the Mark III, except for a new bodyside trim strip.

I.D. DATA: Serial number for MGA is on a plate on the left front of the firewall, under the hood. MGA engine number is on the right side of the block, and also on the firewall plate. Serial number for Midget is stamped on a plate on the left inner wheel arch valance, under the hood. Midget engine number is on a plate attached to right side of block, above the generator. Midget body number is stamped on a plate attached to left door pillar. Serial number range: (Midget) GAN1/101 to /16183; (MGA 1600 Mk II) 100352 to 109070. Engine number range: (Midget) 9CG/Da/H101 to -36711; (MGA 1600 Mk II) 16GC-U-H101 to -1851.

Model	Body Type & Seating	Engine Type/CID	P.O.E. Price	Weight (lbs.)	Prod. Total
MIDGET Mk I					
GAN1	2-dr Rds-2P	I4/58	1939	1566	Note 1
MGA 1600					
Mk II	2-dr Rds-2P	I4/99	2449	1960	Note 2
Mk II	2-dr Cpe-2P	I4/99	2685	2060	Note 2
MAGNETTE					
Mk IV	4-dr Sedan-4/5P	I4/99	2695	2476	Note 3

Note 1: A total of 16,080 MG Midget Mk I (GAN1) roadsters were built from June 1961 to October 1962.

Note 2: A total of 8,719 MGA 1600 Mk II models were built from June 1961 to June 1962 (plus 313 DeLuxe models).

Note 3: A total of 13,738 Magnette Mark IV sedans were built during the 1961-68 period.

Weight Note: Midget "dry" weight was about 1,342 pounds.

ENGINE DATA: BASE FOUR (Midget): Inline, overhead-valve four-cylinder. Cast iron block and head. **Displacement:** 57.87 cu. in. (948 cc). **Bore & Stroke:** 2.478 x 3.00 in. (62.9 x 76.2 mm). **Compression Ratio:** 8.3:1. **Brake Horsepower:** 46.4 at 5500 rpm. Three main bearings. Solid valve lifters. Two SU HS2 semi-downdraft carburetors.

BASE FOUR (later Midget): Same as above, except — **Compression Ratio:** 9.0:1. **Brake Horsepower:** 50 at 5500 rpm. **Torque:** 52.5 lbs.-ft. at 4000 rpm.

BASE FOUR (MGA 1600): Inline, overhead-valve four-cylinder. Cast iron block and head. **Displacement:** 99 cu. in. (1622 cc). **Bore & Stroke:** 3.00 x 3.50 in. (76.2 x 88.9 mm). **Compression Ratio:** 8.9:1. **Brake Horsepower:** 90 at 5500 rpm. **Torque:** 97 lbs.-ft. at 4000 rpm. Three main bearings. Solid valve lifters. Two SU semi-downdraft carburetors.

BASE FOUR (Magnette): Same as 1622-cc four above, except — **Compression Ratio:** 8.3:1. **Brake Horsepower:** 68 at 5000 rpm. **Torque:** 83 lbs.-ft. at 3000 rpm.

CHASSIS DATA: Wheelbase: (Midget) 80 in.; (MGA) 94 in.; (Magnette) 100.25 in. **Overall Length:** (Midget) 136 in.; (MGA) 156 in.; (Magnette) 178 in. **Height:** (Midget) 49.75 in.; (MGA) 50 in.; (Magnette) 59.8 in. **Width:** (Midget) 53 in.; (MGA) 57.3 in.; (Magnette) 63.5 in. **Front Tread:** (Midget) 45.75 in.; (MGA) 47.5 in.; (Magnette) 50.6 in. **Rear Tread:** (Midget) 44.75 in.; (MGA) 48.8 in.; (Magnette) 51.4 in. **Wheel Type:** (Midget) four-stud ventilated disc; (MGA) 4Jx15 well-base, four-stud steel disc. **Standard Tires:** (Midget) Dunlop 5.20x13; (MGA) Dunlop 5.60x15; (Magnette) 5.60x14.

TECHNICAL: Layout: front-engine, rear-drive. **Transmission:** four-speed manual (floor lever). MGA gear ratios: (1st) 3.64:1; (2nd) 2.214:1; (3rd) 1.374:1; (4th) 1.00:1; (rev) 4.76:1. MGA could have a close-ratio gearbox, as follows: (1st) 2.44:1; (2nd) 1.62:1; (3rd) 1.27:1; (4th) 1.00:1; (rev) 3.20:1. Midget gear ratios: (1st) 3.20:1; (2nd) 1.916:1; (3rd) 1.357:1; (4th) 1.00:1; (rev) 4.114:1. Midget could have other first-gear ratios (3.63:1 or 2.93:1). **Standard Final Drive Ratio:** (Midget) 4.22:1; (MGA) 4.10:1; (Magnette) 4.30:1. Midget and MGA could have a variety of alternate axle ratios. **Steering:** rack and pinion except (Magnette) cam and lever. **Suspension (front):** independent; wishbones and coil springs with lever shock absorbers (anti-roll bar standard on Midget). **Suspension (rear):** (Midget) trailing arms and quarter-elliptic leaf springs with lever shock absorbers; (MGA) rigid axle and semi-elliptic leaf springs with lever shock absorbers. **Brakes:** (Midget) front/rear drum; (MGA 1600) front disc, rear drum; (Magnette) front/rear drum. **Body Construction:** (MGA) steel body on box-section steel frame; (Midget/Magnette) steel unibody. **Fuel Tank:** (Midget) 7.2 gal.; (MGA) 12 gal.; (Magnette) 12 gallons.

MAJOR OPTIONS: MIDGET OPTIONS: Radio. Heater. Ace Mercury wheel discs. Removable hardtop. Whitewall tires. Heavy-duty tires. Twin horns. Luggage carrier. Rear compartment cushion. Lighter. Fender mirror. Tonneau cover, rail and stowage bag. Locking gas cap.

MGA OPTIONS: Wire wheels ($100). Tonneau cover ($35). Heater/defroster ($65). Windshield washer ($15). Whitewall tires ($35). Detachable hardtop ($275). Dunlop Roadspeed 5.90x15 tires ($45). Four-wheel disc brakes with knock-off disc wheels and Road Speed tires ($250). 4.55:1 axle ratio ($50). Many other options were dealer-installed.

PERFORMANCE: Top Speed: (Midget) 85-89 mph; (MGA) 103-105 mph; (Magnette) 90 mph. **Acceleration (0-60 mph):** (Midget) 20.3 sec.; (MGA) 12.8-14.2 sec.; (Magnette) 17-19 sec. **Acceleration (quarter-mile):** (Midget) 21.9 sec.; (MGA) 18.7-19+ sec. (about 73 mph). **Fuel Mileage:** (MGA) 21-30 mpg; (Magnette) 23-29 mpg.

PRODUCTION/SALES: Approximately 9,319 MGs were sold in the U.S. during 1962.

Manufacturer: The M.G. Car Co. Ltd., Cowley, Oxford, England (plant at Abingdon-on-Thames, Berkshire).

Distributor: Hambro Automotive Corp., New York City.

HISTORY: Production of the MGA ceased in June 1962, after just one year of the Mk II 1600 version. Production of the MGB began in October 1962. "More power to your safety" was the theme of the more potent MGA: "Power to overtake with safety. Power to surmount difficulties." As for the Midget, its sales brochures promoted "sporting appeal from a sporting heritage," adding that the Midget "starts ahead with love at first sight." Both the Austin-Healey Sprite and MG Midget were built at the Abingdon plant.

1963 MG

MIDGET — Mk I (GAN2) — FOUR — Disc brakes were added to the front of the Midget in its second version (still called Mark I, however), along with a larger (1098-cc) four-cylinder engine. Clutch diameter also was enlarged, to handle the increased power of the higher-compression motor. Midgets still had a separate key and starter (using a pull cable), and lacked outside door handles and a glovebox.

MGB — Mk I — FOUR — Slightly smaller than its predecessor MGA, the new slab-sided roadster rode a 91-inch wheelbase and measured 153 inches in length. Overall profile was much more square than the MGA, with a horizontal upper line, full-length bodyside trim molding, and flattened rear wheel openings. Its low, wide horizontal-style grille contained a pattern of tightly-spaced vertical ribs, not unlike those of the Midget. Headlamps sat back a bit from the grille, above rectangular parking lights. The windshield had a greater warparound curve. At the rear were vertical-style taillamps. Adjustable bucket seats were upholstered in leather. Though commonly referred to as a roadster, the MGB had roll-up windows, outside door handles and vent wings, unlike the open MGA. Behind the seats was an open luggage area, where the top could be stored. The traditional "fly-off" handbrake was gone, replaced by an ordinary version, and the glovebox was on the passenger side of the instrument panel. Beneath the hood was a 1798-cc version of the BMC B-series four, with a larger bore than the final MGA's engine. Horsepower was only modestly boosted, but torque got a sizable increase. Structurally, there was a big change, as the MGB used unibody construction (with double-box-section sills below the doors) rather than the former separate body and frame. Suspension was similar to the MGA, with control arms and coil springs up front and semi-elliptic leaf springs at the rear (but with one less leaf than before). Lever-type shock absorbers remained standard.

1100 — FOUR — Two sports sedans went under the MG banner starting in 1963 model year. Like the carryover Magnette, the new, smaller one stemmed not from an MG design but from the BMC group. Designed by Alec Issigonis, the sedan was close kin to the Austin, Morris and Vandan Plas 1100 models. Measuring 147 inches overall in its initial four-door form (a two-door was added later), the unibodied four-seater carried a trnasverse-mounted BMC A-series engine, identical in displacement to that in the revised Midget. This was also the first MG with front-wheel drive. "Hydrolastic" four-wheel independent suspension used wishbone-type control arms in front and trailing arms at the rear, but no conventional springs or shock absorbers at all. Instead, hermetically-sealed rubber cones contained special liquid, and the units at front and rear were connected together to produce a common supply of fluid. Styling touches included slim windshield and door pillars, and curved-glass side windows. All windows cranked down in the four-door, while two-door models had front-hinged rear (side) windows. The grille was similar to that on the Magnette, with multiple vertical bars split into two side-by-side sections by a center bar. Front bucket seats and front disc brakes were standard. Though a strong seller in the home market, not so many 1100 mini sedans found customers in the U.S.

MAGNETTE — Mk IV — FOUR — Production of the Mk IV sedan continued through 1967 with little change.

I.D. DATA: Serial number for MGB is on a plate on the left fender valance, ahead of the radiator; MGB engine number is on the right side of the block. Serial number for Midget is stamped on a plate on the left inner wheel arch valance, under the hood; Midget engine number is on a plate attached to right side of block, above the generator. Midget body number is stamped on a plate attached to left door pillar. 1100 chassis number is stamped on plate attached to hood locking platform; 1100 engine number is on right side of block, above oil filter. Serial number range: (Midget) GAN2/16184 to /25787; (MGB) GHN3L/101 up; (1100) GG2S1L/101 up (or GA2S3L/101 up). Engine number range: (Midget) 10 CG/Da/H101 to /21048.

Model	Body Type & Seating	Engine Type/CID	P.O.E. Price	Weight (lbs.)	Prod. Total
MIDGET Mk I					
GAN2	2-dr Rds-2P	I4/67	1939	1456	Note 1
MGB					
Mk I	2-dr Rds-2P	I4/110	2658	1920	Note 2
1100					
	2-dr Sedan-4P	I4/67	1898	1806	Note 3
	4-dr Sedan-4P	I4/67	2169	1806	Note 3
MAGNETTE					
Mk IV	4-dr Sedan-4/5P	I4/99	2779	2520	Note 4

Note 1: A total of 9,601 MG Midget Mk I (GAN2) roadsters were built.

Note 2: More than half a million MGBs (387,675 roadsters and 125,597 GT models) were built from 1962 to 1980. Over 23,000 were built during 1963 alone. A total of 300,274 raodsters were exported to the U.S.

Note 3: In all, 116,827 type 1100 sedans were produced from 1961 to 1967.

Note 4: A total of 13,738 Magnette Mark IV sedans were built during the 1961-68 period.

Price Note: MGB with wire wheels cost $2758. Price of the 1100 four-door sedan was later reduced to $1998, after the two-door emerged.

ENGINE DATA: BASE FOUR (Midget): Inline, overhead-valve four-cylinder. Cast iron block and head. **Displacement:** 67 cu. in. (1098 cc). **Bore & Stroke:** 2.54 x 3.29 in. (64.58 x 83.72 mm). **Compression Ratio:** 8.9:1. **Brake Horsepower:** 55 at 5500 rpm. **Torque:** 61 lbs.-ft. at 2500 rpm. Three main bearings. Solid valve lifters. Two SU semi-downdraft carburetors.

BASE FOUR (1100): Same as Midget engine above, but transversely mounted.

BASE FOUR (MGB): Inline, overhead-valve four-cylinder. Cast iron block and head. **Displacement:** 109.7 cu. in. (1798 cc). **Bore & Stroke:** 3.16 x 3.50 in. (80.26 x 88.9 mm). **Compression Ratio:** 8.75:1. **Brake Horsepower:** 94 at 5500 rpm. **Torque:** 107 lbs.-ft. at 3500 rpm. Three main bearings. Solid valve lifters. Two SU semi-downdraft carburetors.

BASE FOUR (Magnette): Inline, overhead-valve four-cylinder. Cast iron block and head. **Displacement:** 99 cu. in. (1622 cc). **Bore & Stroke:** 3.00 x 3.50 in. (76.2 x 88.9 mm). **Compression Ratio:** 8.3:1. **Brake Horsepower:** 68 at 5000 rpm. **Torque:** 83 lbs.-ft. at 3000 rpm. Three main bearings. Solid valve lifters. Two SU semi-downdraft carburetors.

CHASSIS DATA: Wheelbase: (Midget) 80 in.; (MGB) 91 in.; (1100) 93.5 in.; (Magnette) 100.25 in. **Overall Length:** (Midget) 137.8 in.; (MGB) 153.25 in.; (1100) 146.75 in.; (Magnette) 178 in. **Height:** (Midget) 49.75 in.; (MGB) 49.4 in.; (1100) 52.75 in.; (Magnette) 59.8 in. **Width:** 53 in.; (MGB) 60 in.; (1100) 60 in.; (Magnette) 63.5 in. **Front Tread:** (Midget) 45.75 in.; (MGB) 49.0 in.; (1100) 51.5 in.; (Magnette) 50.6 in. **Rear Tread:** (Midget) 44.75 in.; (MGB) 49.25 in.; (1100) 50.9 in.; (Magnette) 51.4 in. **Wheel Type:** (Midget) four-stud ventilated disc; (MGB) steel disc (wire available). **Standard Tires:** (Midget) Dunlop 5.20x13; (MGB) 5.60x14; (1100) 5.50x12; (Magnette) 5.60x14.

TECHNICAL: Layout: front-engine, rear-drive except (1100) front-drive. **Transmission:** four-speed manual (floor lever). MGB gear ratios: (1st) 3.63:1; (2nd) 2.21:1; (3rd) 1.37:1; (4th) 1.00:1. Midget gear ratios: (1st) 3.20:1; (2nd) 1.916:1; (3rd) 1.357:1; (4th) 1.00:1; (rev) 4.114:1. Midget could have other first-gear ratios (3.63:1 or 2.93:1). **Standard Final Drive Ratio:** (Midget) 4.22:1; (MGB) 3.91:1; (1100) 4.13:1; (Magnette) 4.30:1. Midget could have a variety of alternate axle ratios. **Steering:** rack and pinion except (Magnette) cam and lever. **Suspension (front):** (Midget/MGB) wishbones and coil springs with lever shock absorbers; (1100) Hydrolastic with wishbones; (Magnette) wishbones with coil springs and anti-roll bar. **Suspension (rear):** (Midget) trailing arms and quarter-elliptic leaf springs with lever shock absorbers; (MGB) rigid axle and semi-elliptic leaf springs with lever shock absorbers; (1100) Hydrolastic with trailing arms and anti-roll bar; (Magnette) rigid axle with semi-elliptic leaf springs and anti-roll bar. **Brakes:** (Midget/MGB/1100) front disc, rear drum; (Magnette) front/rear drum. **Body Construction:** steel unibody. **Fuel Tank:** (Midget) 7.2 gal.; (MGB) 12 gal.; (1100) 10 gal.; (Magnette) 12 gallons.

MAJOR OPTIONS: MIDGET OPTIONS: Radio. Heater. Ace Mercury wheel discs. Removable hardtop. Whitewall tires. Heavy-duty tires. Twin horns. Luggage carrier. Rear compartment cushion. Lighter. Fender mirror. Tonneau cover, rail and stowage bag. Locking gas cap.

PERFORMANCE: Top Speed: (Midget) near 92 mph; (MGB) 103-105 mph; (1100) 80-82 mph; (Magnette) 90 mph. **Acceleration (0-60 mph):** (MGB) 11-12.5 sec.; (1100) 18-22.2 sec.; (Magnette) 17-19 sec. **Acceleration (quarter-mile):** (Midget) 20.1 sec.; (MGB) 18.1-18.5 sec. (about 75 mph); (1100) 22.4 sec. (61 mph). **Fuel Mileage:** (MGB) 22-30 mpg; (1100) 28-36 mpg; (Magnette) 23-29 mpg.

PRODUCTION/SALES: Approximately 21,270 MGs were sold in the U.S. during 1963.

Manufacturer: The M.G. Car Co. Ltd., Cowley, Oxford, England (plant at Abingdon-on-Thames, Berkshire).

Distributor: Hambro Automotive Corp., New York City.

HISTORY: MGB was introduced at the London Motor Show in October 1962, four months after the final MGA had been produced. The new roadster had been under development for four years. A prototype by Frua (of Italy) had been rejected, so the final design was done by MG itself, directed by Syd Enever. Both a roadster and GT coupe were planned, but only the roadster was available in the first three years of production.

1964 MG

MIDGET — Mk I (GAN2) — FOUR — For the early part of the model year, the Mark I version of the Midget continued without change; then, it was replaced by the Mark II.

MIDGET — Mk II (GAN3) — FOUR — Roll-up windows and vent wings were the major change for the Mark II which appeared during the 1964 model year. The A-series engine added a few horsepower, the windshield was taller and more curved, and locking outside door handles were installed. A combined ignition/starter switch replaced the former cable-operated starter, and self-canceling turn signals became standard. Center-lock Dunlop wire wheels were now available as an option, and were found on most U.S. examples. At chassis level, semi-elliptic rear springs replaced the former quarter-elliptic units, but lever-type shock absorbers remaind.

MGB — Mk I — FOUR — Little change was evident in the larger roadster, introduced for 1963. A Laycock de Normanville overdrive unit became available, operating on third and fourth gears via a toggle switch; but took longer to arrive on examples destined for the U.S.

1100 — FOUR — During the model year, a more luxurious Princess four-door sedan joined the standard 1100 two- and four-door models. The Princess had coachbuilt bodywork and a posh interior that included a polished walnut dashboard and folding picnic tables. No MG emblem stood atop the grille, which was flanked by rectangular parking lights.

MAGNETTE — Mk IV — FOUR — Production of the Mk IV sedan continued through 1967 with little change, but Magnettes were available in the U.S. only on special order, and not listed in all imported-car directories.

I.D. DATA: Serial number for MGB is on a plate on the left fender valance, ahead of the radiator; MGB engine number is on the right side of the block. Serial number for Midget is stamped on a plate on the left inner wheel arch valance, under the hood; Midget engine number is on a plate attached to right side of block, above the generator. Midget body number is stamped on a plate attached to left door pillar. 1100 chassis number is stamped on plate attached to hood locking platform; 1100 engine number is on right side of block, above oil filter. Serial number range: (Midget Mk I) GAN2/16184 to /25787; (Midget Mk II) GAN3/25788 up; (MGB) continuation of 1963. Starting engine number: (Midget Mk II) 10CC/Da/H101.

Model	Body Type & Seating	Engine Type/CID	P.O.E. Price	Weight (lbs.)	Prod. Total
MIDGET Mk I					
GAN2	2-dr Rds-2P	I4/67	1945	1456	Note 1
MIDGET Mk II					
GAN3	2-dr Rds-2P	I4/67	1945	1566	Note 2
MGB					
Mk I	2-dr Rds-2P	I4/110	2658	1920	Note 3
1100					
	2-dr Sedan-4P	I4/67	1898	1806	Note 4
	4-dr Sedan-4P	I4/67	1998	1806	Note 4
Princess	4-dr Sedan-4P	I4/67	3016	N/A	Note 4
MAGNETTE					
Mk IV	4-dr Sedan-4/5P	I4/99	2779	2520	Note 5

Note 1: A total of 9,601 MG Midget Mk I (GAN2) roadsters were built, from October 1962 into 1964.

Note 2: A total of 26,601 Midget Mk II roadsters were built, through October 1966.

Note 3: More than a half a million MGBs (approximately 387,675 roadsters and 125,597 GT models) were built from 1962 to 1980. A total of 300,274 roadsters were exported to the U.S.

Note 4: A total of 116,827 model 1100 sedans were produced from 1961 to 1967.

Note 5: A total of 13,738 Magnette Mark IV sedans were built during the 1961-68 period.

Price Note: MGB with wire wheels cost $2758; Midget Mk II, $2045.

ENGINE DATA: BASE FOUR (Midget Mk I, 1100): Inline, overhead-valve four-cylinder. Cast iron block and head. **Displacement:** 67 cu. in. (1098 cc). Bore & Stroke: 2.54 x 3.29 in. (64.58 x 83.72 mm). **Compression Ratio:** 8.9:1. **Brake Horsepower:** 55 at 5500 rpm. **Torque:** 61 lbs.-ft. at 2500/2750 rpm. Three main bearings. Solid valve lifters. Two SU semi-downdraft carburetors.

BASE FOUR (Midget Mk II): Same as above, except — **Compression Ratio:** 9.0:1. **Brake Horsepower:** 59 at 5750 rpm. **Torque:** 61 lbs.-ft. at 3250 rpm.

BASE FOUR (MGB): Inline, overhead-valve four-cylinder. Cast iron block and head. **Displacement:** 109.7 cu. in. (1798 cc). **Bore & Stroke:** 3.16 x 3.50 in. (80.26 x 88.9 mm). **Compression Ratio:** 8.75:1. **Brake Horsepower:** 94 at 5500 rpm. **Torque:** 107 lbs.-ft. at 3500 rpm. Three main bearings. Solid valve lifters. Two SU semi-downdraft carburetors.

BASE FOUR (Magnette): Same as 1963.

CHASSIS DATA: Wheelbase: (Midget) 80 in.; (MGB) 91 in.; (Magnette) 100.25 in. **Overall Length:** (Midget) 137.8 in.; (MGB) 153.25 in.; (1100) 146.75 in.; (Magnette) 178 in. **Height:** (Midget) 49.75 in.; (MGB) 49.4 in.; (1100) 52.75 in.; (Magnette) 59.8 in. **Width:** (Midget) 53 in.; (MGB) 60 in.; (1100) 60 in.; (Magnette) 63.5 in. **Front Tread:** (Midget) 45.75 in.; (MGB) 49.0 in.; (1100) 51.5 in.; (Magnette) 50.6 in. **Rear Tread:** (Midget) 44.75 in.; (MGB) 49.25 in.; (1100) 50.9 in.; (Magnette) 51.4 in. **Wheel Type:** (Midget) four-stud ventilated disc; (MGB) steel disc. Wire wheels available for Midget/MGB. **Standard Tires** (Midget) Dunlop 5.20x13; (MGB) 5.60x14; (1100) 5.50x12; (Magnette) 5.60x14.

TECHNICAL: Layout: front-engine, rear-drive except (1100) front-drive. **Transmission:** four-speed manual (floor lever). MGB gear ratios: (1st) 3.64:1; (2nd) 2.22:1; (3rd) 1.41:1; (4th) 1.00:1. Midget gear ratios: (1st) 3.20:1; (2nd) 1.916:1; (3rd) 1.357:1; (4th) 1.00:1; (rev) 4.114:1. Midget could have other first-gear ratios (3.63:1 or 2.93:1). **Standard Final Drive Ratio:** (Midget) 4.22:1; (MGB) 3.91:1; (1100) 4.13:1; (Magnette) 4.30:1. Midget could have a variety of alternate axle ratios. **Steering:** rack and pinion except (Magnette) cam and lever. **Suspension (front):** (Midget/MGB) wishbones and coil springs with lever shock absorbers; (1100) Hydrolastic with wishbones; (Magnette) wishbones with coil springs and anti-roll bar. **Suspension (rear):** (Midget Mk I) trailing arms and quarter-elliptic leaf springs with lever shock absorbers; (Midget Mk II) rigid axle with semi-elliptic leaf springs and lever shock absorbers; (MGB) rigid axle and semi-elliptic leaf springs with lever shock absorbers; (1100) Hydrolastic with trailing arms and anti-roll bar; (Magnette) rigid axle with semi-elliptic leaf springs and anti-roll bar. **Brakes:** (Midget/MGB) front disc, rear drum; (Magnette) front/rear drum. **Body Construction:** steel unibody. **Fuel Tank:** (Midget) 7.2 gal.; (MGB) 12 gal.; (1100) 10 gal.; (Magnette) 12 gallons.

MAJOR OPTIONS: MIDGET OPTIONS: Similar to 1963. MGB OPTIONS: Removable hardtop ($225). Wire wheels ($100).

PERFORMANCE: Top Speed: (Midget Mk II) 93 mph; (MGB) 103-150 mph; (1100) 80-82 mph; (Magnette) 90 mph. **Acceleration (0-60 mph):** (MGB) 11.12.5 sec.; (1100) 18-22.2 sec.; (Magnette) 17-19 seconds. **Acceleration (quarter-mile):** (MGB) 18.1-18.5 sec. (about 75 mph); (1100) 22.4 sec. (61 mph). **Fuel Mileage:** (MGB) 22-30 mpg; (1100) 28-36 mpg; (Magnette) 23-29 mpg.

PRODUCTION/SALES: Approximately 24,128 MGs were sold in the U.S. during 1964.

Manufacturer: The M.G. Car Co. Ltd., Cowley, Oxford, England (plant at Abington-on-Thames, Berkshire).

Distributor: Hambro Automotive Corp., New York City.

HISTORY: Both the Mk II Midget and 1100 Princess were introduced at mid-year, in spring 1964.

1965 MG

1965 MGT GT.

MIDGET — Mk II (GAN3) — FOUR — Midget production continued with little change, after introduction of the Mark II version during the 1964 model year.

MGB — Mk I — FOUR — Inside the MGB's four-cylinder engine was a new five-bearing crankshaft, replacing the former three-main configuration; plus a new oil cooler and revised rear oil seal. For competition purposes, at least, the three-main crank had suffered too much "whipping." On the MGB dashboard was a new electric tachometer. The Laycock de Normanville overdrive unit was optional.

1100 — FOUR — Little change was evident in the small sports sedan, again offered in both standard and posh Princess editions.

MAGNETTE — Mk IV — FOUR — Production of the Mk IV sedan continued through 1967 with little change, available in the U.S. only on special order.

I.D. DATA: Serial number for MGB is on a plate on the left fender valance, ahead of the radiator; MGB engine number is on the right side of the block. Serial number for Midget is stamped on a plate on the left inner wheel arch valance, under the hood; Midget engine number is on a plate attached to right side of block, above the generator. Midget body number is stamped on plate attached to hood locking platform; 1100 chassis number is stamped on plate attached to hood locking platform; 1100 engine number is on right side of block, above oil filter. Serial number range: (Midget Mk II) continuation from 1963; (MGB) continuation from 1963. Starting engine number: (MGB w/5 mains) 18GB-H101.

Model	Body Type & Seating	Engine Type/CID	P.O.E. Price	Weight (lbs.)	Prod. Total
MIDGET Mk II					
GAN3	2-dr Rds-2P	I4/67	2055	1566	Note 1
MGB					
Mk I	2-dr Rds-2P	I4/110	2607	1920	Note 2
1100					
	2-dr Sedan-4P	I4/67	1861	1806	Note 3
	4-dr Sedan-4P	I4/67	1959	1806	Note 3
Princess	4-dr Sedan-4P	I4/67	2646	1884	Note 3
MAGNETTE					
Mk IV	4-dr Sedan-4/5P	I4/99	N/A	2520	Note 4

Note 1: A total of 26,601 Midget Mk II roadsters were built, through October 1966.

Note 2: More than half a million MGBs (approximately 387,675 roadsters and 125,597 GT models) were built from 1962 to 1980. A total of 300,274 roadsters were exported to the U.S.

Note 3: A total of 116,827 model 1100 sedans were produced from 1961 to 1967.

Note 4: A total of 13,738 Magnette Mark IV sedans were built during the 1961-68 period.

ENGINE DATA: BASE FOUR (1100): Inline, overhead-valve four-cylinder. Cast iron block and head. **Displacement:** 67 cu. in. (1098 cc). **Bore & Stroke:** 2.54 x 3.29 in. (64.58 x 83.72 mm). **Compression Ratio:** 8.9:1. **Brake Horsepower:** 55 at 5500 rpm. **Torque:** 61 lbs.-ft. at 2500 rpm. Three main bearings. Solid valve lifters. Two SU HS2 semi-downdraft carburetors.

BASE FOUR (Midget Mk II): Inline, overhead-valve four-cylinder. Cast iron block and head. **Displacement:** 67 cu. in. (1098 cc). **Bore & Stroke:** 2.54 x 3.29 in. (64.58 x 83.72 mm). **Compression Ratio:** 8.9:1. **Brake Horsepower:** 59 at 5750 rpm. **Torque:** 62 lbs.-ft. at 3250 rpm. Three main bearings. Solid valve lifters. Two SU semi-downdraft carburetors.

BASE FOUR (MGB): Inline, overhead-valve four-cylinder. Cast iron block and head. **Displacement:** 109.7 cu. in. (1798 cc). **Bore & Stroke:** 8.8:1. **Brake Horsepower:** 98 at 54 rpm. **Torque:** 110 lbs.-ft. at 3000 rpm. Five main bearings. Solid valve lifters. Two SU semi-downdraft carburetors.

BASE FOUR (Magnette): Same as 1963-64.

CHASSIS DATA: Wheelbase: (Midget) 80 in.; (MGB) 91 in.; (1100) 93.5 in.; (Magnette) 100.25 in. **Overall Length:** (Midget) 136.5 in.; (MGB) 153.2 in.; (1100) 146.75 in.; (Magnette) 178 in. **Height:** (Midget) 49.75 in.; (MGB) 49.4 in.; (1100) 53 in.; (Magnette) 59.8 in. **Width:** (Midget) 53 in.; (MGB) 60 in.; (1100) 60.5 in.; (Magnette) 63.5 in. **Front Tread:** (Midget) 45.75 in.; (MGB) 49.0 in.; (1100) 51.5 in.; (Magnette) 50.6 in. **Rear Tread:** (Midget) 44.75 in.; (MGB) 49.25 in.; (1100) 50.9 in.; (Magnette) 51.4 in. **Wheel Type:** (Midget) four-stud ventilated disc; (MGB) steel disc. Wire wheels available for Midget/MGB. **Standard Tires:** (Midget) Dunlop 5.20x13; (MGB) 5.60x14; (1100) 5.50x12; (Magnette) 5.60x14.

TECHNICAL: Layout: front-engine, rear-drive except (1100) front-drive. **Transmission:** four-speed manual (floor lever). MGB gear ratios: (1st) 3.64:1; (2nd) 2.22:1; (3rd) 1.41:1; (4th) 1.00:1; (overdrive) 0.85:1. Midget gear ratios: (1st) 3.20:1; (2nd) 1.916:1; (3rd) 1.357:1; (4th) 1.00:1; (rev) 4.114:1. Midget could have other first-gear ratios (3.63:1 or 2.93:1). **Standard Final Drive Ratio:** (Midget) 4.22:1; (MGB) 3.91:1; (1100) 4.13:1; (Magnette) 4.30:1. Midget could have a variety of alternate axle ratios. **Steering:** rack and pinion except (Magnette) cam and lever. **Suspension (front):** (Midget/MGB) wishbones and coil springs with lever shock absorbers; (1100) Hydrolastic with wishbones; (Magnette) wishbones with coil springs and anti-roll bar. **Suspension (rear):** (Midget/MGB) rigid axle with semi-elliptic leaf springs and lever shock absorbers; (1100) Hydrolastic with trailing arms and anti-roll bar; (Magnette) rigid axle with semi-elliptic leaf springs and anti-roll bar. **Brakes:** (Midget/MGB/1100) front disc, rear drum; (Magnette) front/rear drum. **Body Construction:** steel unibody. **Fuel Tank:** (Midget) 7.2 gal.; (MGB) 12 gal.; (1100) 10 gal.; (Magnette) 12 gallons.

MAJOR OPTIONS: MIDGET OPTIONS: Similar to 1963-64, plus wire wheels. MGB OPTIONS: Removable hardtop ($225). Wire wheels ($100). Laycock de Normanville overdrive.

PERFORMANCE: Top Speed: (Midget Mk II) 93 mph; (MGB) 105-110 mph; (1100) about 90 mph. **Acceleration (0-60 mph):** (Midget Mk II) about 18.3 sec.; (MGB) about 11.0 sec.; (1100) 19.6 seconds. **Acceleration (quarter-mile):** (MGB) 18.0 sec. (77 mph); (1100) 21.8 sec. (68 mph). **Fuel Mileage:** (MGB) 22-28 mpg; (1100) 28-36 mpg.

PRODUCTION/SALES: Approximately 22,326 MGs were sold in the U.S. during 1965.

Manufacturer: The M.G. Car Co. Ltd., Cowley, Oxford, England (plant at Abingdon-on-Thames, Berkshire).

Distributor: BMC/Hambro Automotive Corp. Ridgefield, New Jersey.

1966 MG

1966 MGB-1800 sports coupe. (Christie's)

MIDGET — Mk II (GAN3) — FOUR — Midget production continued for one more season with little change, until the introduction of the Mark III for 1967.

MGB/GT — Mk I — FOUR — Joining the original roadster (with roll-up windows) was a new hatchback GT coupe, designed in part by Pininfarina and aimed at the American market, with long rear quarter windows. Mechanically identical to the open MGB, the coupe was capable of 107-mph top speeds and had a cramped bench seat in the back that could hold small children.

1100 — FOUR — Both standard and Princess versions of the small sports sedan remained available this year, though some directories listed only the Princess. Features on the Princess included leather upholstery, deep-pile carpeting, polished walnut dashboard and door sills, folding picnic tables, and independently-adjustable backrests on the front bucket seats.

MAGNETTE NOTE: The Magnette remained available on special order into 1967, but was no longer listed in directories; see previous listings for details.

I.D. DATA: Serial number for MGB is on a plate on the left fender valance, ahead of the radiator; MGB engine number is on the right side of the block. Serial number for Midget is stamped on a plate on the left inner wheel arch valance, under the hood; Midget engine number is on a plate attached to right side of block, above the generator. Midget body number is stamped on a plate attached to left door pillar. 1100 chassis number is stamped on plate attached to hood locking platform; 1100 engine number is on right side of block, above oil filter. Serial number range: (Midget Mk II) continuation of 1963; (MGB) continuation of 1963; (GT) G-HD3-71933 up.

Model	Body Type & Seating	Engine Type/CID	P.O.E. Price	Weight (lbs.)	Prod. Total
MIDGET Mk II					
GAN3	2-dr Rds-2P	I4/67	2055	1566	Note 1
MGB					
Mk I	2-dr Rds-2P	I4/110	2607	1920	Note 2
Mk I	2-dr GT Cpe-2+2P	I4/110	3095	N/A	Note 2
1100					
	2-dr Sedan-4P	I4/67	1861	1806	Note 3
	4-dr Sedan-4P	I4/67	1959	1806	Note 3
Princess	4-dr Sedan-4P	I4/67	2646	1884	Note 3

Note 1: A total of 26,601 Midget Mk II roadsters were built, through October 1966.

Note 2: More than half a million MGBs (approximately 387,675 roadsters and 125,597 GT models) were built from 1962 to 1980. A total of 300,274 roadsters were exported to the U.S.

Note 3: A total of 116,827 model 1100 sedans were produced from 1961 to 1967.

Price Note: Midget price shown included wire wheels. MGB roadster was $2705 with wire wheels.

ENGINE DATA: BASE FOUR (1100): Inline, overhead-valve four-cylinder. Cast iron block and head. **Displacement:** 67 cu. in. (1098 cc). **Bore & Stroke:** 2.54 x 3.29 in. (64.58 x 83.72 mm). **Compression Ratio:** 8.9:1. **Brake Horsepower:** 55 at 5500 rpm. **Torque:** 61 lbs.-ft. at 2500 rpm. Three main bearings. Solid valve lifters. Two SU HS2 semi-downdraft carburetors.

BASE FOUR (Midget Mk II): Inline, overhead-valve four-cylinder. Cast iron block and head. **Displacement:** 67 cu. in. (1098 cc). **Bore & Stroke:** 2.54 x 3.29 in. (64.58 x 83.72 mm). **Compression Ratio:** 8.9:1. **Brake Horsepower:** 59 at 5750 rpm. **Torque:** 62 lbs.-ft. at 3250 rpm. Three main bearings. Solid valve lifters. Two SU semi-downdraft carburetors.

BASE FOUR (MGB): Inline, overhead-valve four-cylinder. Cast iron block and head. **Displacement:** 109.7 cu. in. (1798 cc). **Bore & Stroke:** 3.16 x 3.50 in. (80.26 x 88.9 mm). **Compression Ratio:** 8.8:1. **Brake Horsepower:** 98 at 5400 rpm. **Torque:** 110 lbs.-ft. at 3000 rpm. Five main bearings. Solid valve lifters. Two SU semi-downdraft carburetors.

CHASSIS DATA: Wheelbase: (Midget) 80 in.; (MGB) 91 in.; (1100) 93.5 in. **Overall Length:** (Midget) 136.5 in.; (MGB) 153.2 in.; (1100) 146.75 in. **Height:** (Midget) 49.75 in.; (MGB) 49.4 in.; (1100) 53 in. **Width:** (Midget) 53 in.; (MGB) 59.9 in.; (1100) 60.5 in. **Front Tread:** (Midget) 45.75 in.; (MGB) 49.0 in.; (1100) 51.5 in. **Rear Tread:** (Midget) 44.75 in.; (MGB) 49.25 in.; (1100) 50.9 in. **Wheel Type:** (Midget) four-stud ventilated disc, but most U.S. examples had wire wheels; (MGB) steel disc or wire. **Standard Tires:** (Midget) Dunlop 5.20x13; (MGB) 5.60x14; (1100) 5.50x12.

TECHNICAL: Layout: front-engine, rear-drive except (1100) front-drive. **Transmission:** four-speed manual (floor lever). MGB gear ratios: (1st) 3.64:1; (2nd) 2.22:1; (3rd) 1.41:1; (4th) 1.00:1; (overdrive) 0.85:1. Midget gear ratios: (1st) 3.20:1; (2nd) 1.916:1; (3rd) 1.357:1; (4th) 1.00:1; (rev) 4.114:1. **Standard Final Drive Ratio:** (Midget) 4.22:1; (MGB) 3.91:1; (1100) 4.13:1. Midget could have a variety of alternate axle ratios. **Steering:** rack and pinion. **Suspension (front):** (Midget/MGB) wishbones and coil springs with lever shock absorbers; (1100) Hydrolastic with wishbones. **Suspension (rear):** (Midget/MGB) rigid axle with semi-elliptic leaf springs and lever shock absorbers; (1100) Hydrolastic with trailing arms and anti-roll bar. **Brakes:** front disc, rear drum. **Body Construction:** steel unibody. **Fuel Tank:** (Midget) 7.2 gal.; (MGB) 12 gal.; (1100) 10 gal.

MAJOR OPTIONS: MGB OPTIONS: Removable hardtop. Wire wheels. Heater. Anti-roll bar. Overdrive.

PERFORMANCE: Top Speed: (Midget Mk II) 93 mph; (MGB) 105-110 mph; (1100) about 90 mph. **Acceleration (0-60 mph):** (Midget Mk II) about 18.3 sec.; (MGB) about 11.0 sec.; (GT) 13.6 sec.; (1100) 19.6 sec. **Acceleration (quarter-mile):** (MGB) 18.0 sec. (77 mph); (GT) 19.6 sec.; (1100) 21.8 sec. (68 mph). **Fuel Mileage:** (MGB) 22-28 mpg; (1100) 28-36 mpg.

PRODUCTION/SALES: Approximately 21,709 MGs were sold in the U.S. during 1966.

Manufacturer: The M.G. Car Co. Ltd., Cowley, Oxford, England (plant at Abingdon-on-Thames, Berkshire).

Distributor: BMC/Hambro Automotive Corp., Ridgefield, New Jersey.

1967 MG

1967-1969 MG C roadster and GT coupe. (William Siuru Jr.)

MIDGET — Mk III — FOUR — A larger version of the BMC A-series engine went into the Midget roadster for 1967, measuring 1275 cubic centimeters in displacement and producing 65 horsepower. Compression was reduced slightly, to 8.8:1, and the engine added an air injection system for emissions control. An oil cooler was optional. This was the same engine used in the Mini Cooper 'S' but in detuned form, and cut the Midget's 0-60 mph time considerably. A modified folding top no longer required manual installation of bows and top ribs.

MGB/GT — Mk I/II — FOUR — Late in the 1967 model year, a Mark II version of the MGB roadster and GT hatchback coupe became available. Engine size remained the same, and the new all-synchromesh gearbox kept the same ratios as its predecessor.

1100 — FOUR — Production of the 1100 sports sedan series continued with little change, but the Princess faded away. During the 1967 model year, a new 1300 sedan superseded the 1100; see next listing for details.

MAGNETTE NOTE: The Magnette remained available on special order into 1967, but was no longer mentioned in most American directories; see previous listings for details.

I.D. DATA: Serial number for MGB is on a plate on the left fender valance, ahead of the radiator; MGB engine number is on the right side of the block. Serial number for Midget is stamped on a plate on the left inner wheel arch valance, under the hood; Midget engine number is on a plate attached to right side of block, above the generator. Midget body number is stamped on a plate attached to left door pillar. 1100 chassis number is stamped on plate attached to hood locking platform; 1100 engine number is on right side of block, above oil filter. Serial number range: (Midget Mk III) GAN4/52390 up; (MGB/GT) continuation of 1966. Engine number range: (Midget) 12CC-Da-H101 up; (MGB/GT) continuation of 1966.

Model	Body Type & Seating	Engine Type/CID	P.O.E. Price	Weight (lbs.)	Prod. Total
MIDGET Mk III					
GAN4	2-dr Rds-2P	I4/78	2174	1512	Note 1
MGB					
Mk II	2-dr Rds-2P	I4/110	2615	1920	Note 2
Mk II	2-dr GT Cpe-2+2P	I4/110	3095	2190	Note 2
1100					
	2-dr Sedan-4P	I4/67	1861	1806	Note 3
	4-dr Sedan-4P	I4/67	1959	1806	Note 3

Note 1: As many as 99,896 Midget Mk III roadsters were built, through 1974.

Note 2: More than half a million MGBs (approximately 387,675 roadsters and 125,597 GT models) were built from 1962 to 1980. A total of 300,274 roadsters were exported to the U.S.

Note 3: A total of 116,827 model 1100 sedans were produced from 1961 to 1967.

Price Note: Midget price in U.S. included wire wheels.

1967 MG Sebring Works car. (Coys of Kensington)

ENGINE DATA: BASE FOUR (1100): **Displacement:** 67 cu. in. (1098 cc). **Bore & Stroke:** 2.54 x 3.29 in. (64.58 x 83.72 mm). **Compression Ratio:** 8.9:1. **Brake Horsepower:** 55 at 5500 rpm. **Torque:** 61 lbs.-ft. at 2500 rpm. Three main bearings. Solid valve lifters. Two SU HS2 semi-downdraft carburetors.

BASE FOUR (Midget Mk III): Inline, overhead-valve four-cylinder. Cast iron block and head. **Displacement:** 77.8 cu. in. (1275 cc). **Bore & Stroke:** 2.78 x 3.20 in. (70.6 x 81.3 mm). **Compression Ratio:** 8.8:1. **Brake Horsepower:** 65 at 6000 rpm. **Torque:** 72 lbs.-ft. at 3000 rpm. Three main bearings. Solid valve lifters. Two SU semi-downdraft carburetors.

BASE FOUR (MGB): Inline, overhead-valve four-cylinder. Cast iron block and head. **Displacement:** 109.7 cu. in. (1798 cc). **Bore & Stroke:** 3.16 x 3.50 in. (80.26 x 88.9 mm). **Compression Ratio:** 8.8:1. **Brake Horsepower:** 98 at 5400 rpm. **Torque:** 110 lbs.-ft. at 3000 rpm. Five main bearings. Solid valve lifters. Two SU semi-downdraft carburetors.

CHASSIS DATA: Wheelbase: (Midget) 80 in.; (MGB) 91 in.; (1100) 93.5 in. **Overall Length:** (Midget) 137.6 in.; (MGB) 153.2 in.; (1100) 146.75 in. **Height:** (Midget) 48.6 in.; (MGB) 49.75 in.; (1100) 53 in. **Width:** (Midget) 54.9 in.; (MGB) 59.9 in.; (1100) 60.5 in. **Front Tread:** (Midget) 46.3 in.; (MGB) 49.0 in.; (1100) 51.5 in. **Rear Tread:** (Midget) 44.8 in.; (MGB) 49.25 in.; (1100) 50.9 in. **Wheel Type:** (Midget) four-stud ventilated disc, but most U.S. examples had wire wheels; (MGB) steel disc or wire. **Standard Tires:** (Midget) Dunlop 5.20x13; (MGB) 5.60x14; (1100) 5.50x12.

TECHNICAL: Layout: front-engine, rear-drive except (1100) front-drive. **Transmission:** four-speed manual (floor lever). MGB gear ratios: (1st) 3.64:1; (2nd) 2.22:1; (3rd) 1.41:1; (4th) 1.00:1; (overdrive) 0.85:1. Midget gear ratios: (1st) 3.20:1; (2nd) 1.916:1; (3rd) 1.357:1; (4th) 1.00:1; (rev) 4.114:1. **Standard Final Drive Ratio:** (Midget) 4.22:1; (MGB) 3.91:1; (1100) 4.13:1. Midget could have a variety of alternate axle ratios. **Steering:** rack and pinion. **Suspension (front):** (Midget/MGB) wishbones and coil springs with lever shock absorbers; (1100) Hydrolastic with wishbones. **Suspension (rear):** (Midget/MGB) rigid axle with semi-elliptic leaf springs and lever shock absorbers; (1100) Hydrolastic with trailing arms and anti-roll bar. **Brakes:** front disc, rear drum. **Body Construction:** steel unibody. **Fuel Tank:** (Midget) 7.5 gal.; (MGB) 12 gal.; (1100) 10 gal.

MAJOR OPTIONS: MGB OPTIONS: Removable hardtop. Wire wheels. Heater. Anti-roll bar. Overdrive.

PERFORMANCE: Top Speed: (Midget Mk III) 94-96 mph; (MGB) 105-110 mph. **Acceleration (0-60 mph):** (Midget Mk III) about 14.7 sec.; (MGB) about 11.0 sec.; (1100) 19.6 sec. **Acceleration (quarter-mile):** (Midget Mk III) 19.9 sec.; (MGB) 18.0 sec. (77 mph); (1100) 21.8 sec. (68 mph). **Fuel Mileage:** (Midget Mk III) about 24-32 mpg; (MGB) 22-28 mpg; (1100) 28-36 mpg.

PRODUCTION/SALES: Approximately 22,387 MGs were sold in the U.S. during 1967.

Manufacturer: The M.G. Car Co. Ltd., Cowley, Oxford, England (plant at Abingdon-on-Thames, Berkshire). Changed to MG Division of British Leyland by 1968.

Distributor: BMC/Hambro Automotive Corp., Ridgefield, New Jersey.

HISTORY: Mark III Midget was introduced at the London motor show in October 1966.

1968-69 MG

MIDGET — Mk III — FOUR — Little change was evident in the Mark III version of the Midget, which continued with a 1275-cc four-cylinder engine.

MGB/GT — Mk II — FOUR — Production continued of the Mark II version of the MGB roadster and GT hatchback coupe, introduced late in the 1967 model year, with little change except for a drop in horsepower due to a new emission control system. An automatic transmission was available, but only about 5,000 would be installed before that option was abandoned in 1973.

MGC — SIX — Success of the four-cylinder roadsters over so many years led this year to an experiment with six-cylinder power, using an engine originally intended for the Austin-Healey (now departed). Torsion bars and wishbones replaced the usual front coil springs, to allow space for the larger powerplant. The seven-main six displaced 2912 cc and was actually an evolution of the MG four, with identical stroke but a larger bore dimension. Incorporating an oil cooler, the sump held eight quarts. Identifying an MG six wasn't difficult, even though no special badge was installed, as the MGC's hood held a sizable pair of humps (one inside the other). At the ground were 15-inch tires. Both overdrive and three-speed automatic transmissions were available (the latter priced at $90 extra in the U.S.), and the six was offered in both roadster and coupe form. Top speed reached about 122 mph, but acceleration didn't improve as much as might be expected. Not many MGC editions reached the U.S. marketplace, though they were listed in pricing directories by 1969, with standard wire wheels.

1300 — FOUR — The new sports sedan, sometimes referred to a "1275," carried the same size engine as the upgraded Midget: 1275 cc, but with a single SU carburetor. Early in 1968, that engine added twin carburetors for horsepower to match the Midget. A four-speed automatic transmission was optional.

I.D. DATA: Serial number for MGB is on a plate on the left fender valance, ahead of the radiator; MGB engine number is on the right side of the block. Serial number for Midget is stamped on a plate on the left inner wheel arch valance, under the hood; Midget engine number is on a plate attached to right side of block, above the generator. Midget body number is stamped on a plate attached to left door pillar. Serial number range: (Midget Mk III) continuation of 1967; (later Midget) GAN5UA74886 up; (MGB) GHN4U148401; (GT) GHD4U139472; (MGC) G-CD1-101 up. Engine number range: (MGC) 29GA-H101 up.

Model	Body Type & Seating	Engine Type/CID	P.O.E. Price	Weight (lbs.)	Prod. Total
MIDGET Mk III					
GAN4/5	2-dr Rds-2P	I4/78	2215	1512	Note 1
MGB					
Mk II	2-dr Rds-2P	I4/110	2670	1920	Note 2
Mk II	2-dr GT Cpe-2+2P	I4/110	3160	2190	Note 2
MGC					
	2-dr Rds-2P	I6/178	3350	2445	Note 3
	2-dr GT Cpe-2+2P	I6/178	3715	2595	Note 3
1300					
	4-dr Sedan-4P	I4/78	N/A	N/A	Note 4

Note 1: As many as 99,896 Midget Mk III roadsters were built, through 1974.

Note 2: More than half a million MGBs (approximately 387,675 roadsters and 125,597 GT models) were built from 1962 to 1980. A total of 300,274 roadsters were exported to the U.S.

Note 3: A total of 8,999 MGC models were produced through September 1969 (4,550 roadsters and 4,449 GT coupes).

Note 4: A total of 26,240 series 1300 sedans were built, through 1971.

Price Note: Midget and GT prices in U.S. included wire wheels. The MGB roadster cost $2770 with wire wheels.

1969 Price Note: Midget price rose to $2252; MGB roadster to $2817; MGB GT coupe to $3202. MGC prices shown above are for 1969 (with overdrive).

ENGINE DATA: BASE FOUR (Midget Mk III): Inline, overhead-valve four-cylinder. Cast iron block and head. **Displacement:** 77.8 cu. in. (1275 cc). **Bore & Stroke:** 2.78 x 3.20 in. (70.6 x 81.3 mm). **Compression Ratio:** 8.8:1. **Brake Horsepower:** 62 at 6000 rpm. **Torque:** 72 lbs.-ft. at 3000 rpm. Three main bearings. Solid valve lifters. Two SU semi-downdraft carburetors.

BASE FOUR (1300): Same as 1275-cc Midget above, except — **Brake Horsepower:** 65 at 6000 rpm. One SU carburetor (later, two carburetors).

BASE FOUR (MGB): Inline, overhead-valve four-cylinder. Cast iron block and head. **Displacement:** 109.7 cu. in. (1798 cc). **Bore & Stroke:** 3.16 x 3.50 in. (80.26 x 88.9 mm). **Compression Ratio:** 8.8:1. **Brake Horsepower:** 92 at 5400 rpm. **Torque:** 110 lbs.-ft. at 3000 rpm. Five main bearings. Solid valve lifters. Two SU semi-downdraft carburetors.

Note: MGB output dropped to 92 bhp by 1969.

BASE SIX (MGC): Inline, overhead-valve six-cylinder. Cast iron block and head. **Displacement:** 177.7 cu. in. (2912 cc). **Bore & Stroke:** 3.28 x 3.50 in. (83.34 x 88.9 mm). **Compression Ratio:** 9.0:1. **Brake Horsepower:** 145 at 5250 rpm. **Torque:** 174 lbs.-ft. at 3500 rpm. Seven main bearings. Solid valve lifters. Two SU horizontal carburetors.

CHASSIS DATA: Wheelbase: (Midget) 80 in.; (MGB) 91 in.; (MGC) 91 in.; (1300) 93.5 in. **Overall Length:** (Midget) 137.6 in.; (MGB) 153.2 in.; (1300) 146.75 in. **Height:** (Midget) 48.6 in.; (MGB) 49.75 in.; (1300) 52 in. **Width:** (Midget) 54.9 in.; (MGB) 59.9 in.; (1300) 60.5 in. **Front Tread:** (Midget) 46.3 in.; (MGB) 49.0 in.; (MGC) 50 in.; (1300) 51.5 in. **Rear Tread:** (Midget) 44.8 in.; (MGB) 49.25 in.; (MGC) 49.25 in.; (1300) 50.9 in. **Wheel Type:** (Midget) four-stud ventilated disc, but most U.S. examples had wire wheels; (MGB) steel disc or wire; (MGC) 5Jx15. **Standard Tires:** (Midget) Dunlop 5.20x13; (MGB) 5.60x14; (MGC) 165.15; (1300) 5.50x12.

TECHNICAL: Layout: front-engine, rear-drive except (1300) front-drive. **Transmission:** four-speed manual (floor lever). MGB gear ratios: (1st) 3.64:1; (2nd) 2.22:1; (3rd) 1.41:1; (4th) 1.00:1; (overdrive) 0.85:1. Midget gear ratios: (1st) 3.20:1; (2nd) 1.916:1; (3rd) 1.357:1; (4th) 1.00:1; (rev) 4.114:1. MGC gear ratios: (1st) 3.44:1; (2nd) 2.17:1; (3rd) 1.38:1; (4th) 1.00:1; (overdrive) 0.82:1. (Final MGC models had revised gear ratios.) **Standard Final Drive Ratio:** (Midget) 4.22:1; (MGB) 3.91:1; (MGC) 3.307:1 w/overdrive. **Steering:** rack and pinion. **Suspension (front):** (Midget/MGB) wishbones and coil springs with lever shock absorbers; (MGC) longitudinal torsion bars and anti-roll bar; (1300) Hydrolastic with wishbones. **Suspension (rear):** (Midget/MGB) rigid axle with semi-elliptic leaf springs and lever shock absorbers; (1300) Hydrolastic with trailing arms and anti-roll bar. **Brakes:** front disc, rear drum. **Body Construction:** steel unibody. **Fuel Tank:** (Midget) 7.5 gal.; (MGB) 14 gallons.

MAJOR OPTIONS: MGB OPTIONS: Removable hardtop. Wire wheels. Heater. Anti-roll bar. Overdrive.

PERFORMANCE: Top Speed: (Midget Mk III) 94-96 mph; (MGB) 105-110 mph; (MGC) about 122 mph; (1300) about 82 mph. **Acceleration (0-60 mph):** (Midget Mk III) about 14.7 sec.; (MGB) about 11.0 sec.; (MGC) 10.0 sec.; (1300) 18.4 sec. **Acceleration (quarter-mile):** (Midget Mk III) 19.9 sec.; (MGB) 18.0 sec. (77 mph). **Fuel Mileage:** (Midget Mk III) about 24-32 mpg; (MGB) 22-28 mpg.

PRODUCTION/SALES: Approximately 17,834 MGs were sold in the U.S. in 1968, and 22,114 in 1969.

Manufacturer: MG Division of British Leyland Corp. Ltd., Longbridge, Birmingham, England.

Distributor: British Leyland Motors Inc., Leonia, New Jersey.

HISTORY: Limited production of MGC began in October 1967 and continued until September 1969.

1970-71 MG

1971 MG Midget.

MIDGET — Mk III — FOUR — Little significant change was evident for the 1970 model year. As before, the Mark III, billed as the "lowest-priced true sports car made," carried a 1275-cc engine and the four-speed gearbox was synchronized on the upper three gears. Standard Midget equipment included twin windtone horns, two-speed wipers/washers, backup lights, heater/defroster, reclining washable ambia bucket seats with adjustable head restraints, three-point seatbelts, lighter, gearshift gaiter, fitted carpeting, rubber floor mats, padded sunvisors, and front/rear lighted side markers. Roll-up windows and hinged vent wings were standard. Midgets were available in the same body colors as the MGB (listed below). For the 1971 model year, Midgets had standard mag-style wheels and radial tires, with a new heater and ashtray.

MGB/GT — Mk II — FOUR — More than 20 styling changes were announced for the 1970 model year, but most were less noticeable than the switch to a recessed blacked-out grille (inside a thin, bright surround molding) with center emblem. Amber rectangular parking lights again stood below the recessed headlamps. Models destined for the U.S. had side marker lights ahead of the front fenders and, by 1971, added rubber-tipped bumper guards. Mag-style (Rostyle) wheels were standard, with 155x14 radial tires (165x14 for the MGB/GT coupe). Inside, vinyl replaced leather on the adjustable bucket seats, and a leather-covered steering wheel was standard on both models. Standard equipment included reclining ambia bucket seats with adjustable head restraints, padded sunvisors, three-point seatbelts, heater/defroster, front-rear lighted side markers, lighter and ashtray, map pocket, fitted carpeting, rubber floor mats, and sill kick plates. As before, the GT coupe had space for occasional rear seating, which folded flat for extra luggage storage. Both models had roll-up windows and hinged vent wings. Standard colors were: Flame Red, Bronze Yellow, British Racing Green, Blue Royale, Pale Primrose, and Glacier White. For the 1971 model year, the MGB and MGB/GT grille received yet another restyling, again in blacked-out form. Steering-column locks also became standard.

1300 NOTE: Although the MG sedans remained in production into 1971, they no longer appeared in U.S. import-car directories. See previous listing for details.

I.D. DATA: Serial number on a plate on the fender well or firewall, on the left side of the dashboard (visible through the windshield), and/or on the left door post. Engine number plates are attached to left of block, near the front. Starting serial number: (1970 Midget Mk III) GAN5UA74886; (1971 Midget) GAN5UB89515; (1970 MGB) GHN5UA187218; (1971 MGB) GHN5UB219021; (1970 GT) GHD5UA187841; (1971 GT) GHD5UB219355.

Model	Body Type & Seating	Engine Type/CID	P.O.E. Price	Weight (lbs.)	Prod. Total
MIDGET Mk III					
GAN5	2-dr Rds-2P	I4/78	2279	1512	Note 1
MGB					
Mk II	2-dr Rds-2P	I4/110	2875	1920	Note 2
Mk II	2-dr GT Cpe-2+2P	I4/110	3260	2190	Note 2

Note 1: As many as 99,896 Midget Mk III roadsters were built, through 1974.

Note 2: More than half a million MGBs (approximately 387,675 roadsters and 125,597 GT models) were built from 1962 to 1980. A total of 300,274 roadsters were exported to the U.S.

1971 Price Note: Midget price rose to $2395 in 1971; MGB to $3140; and MGB/GT to $3495.

ENGINE DATA: BASE FOUR (Midget Mk III): Inline, overhead-valve four-cylinder. Cast iron block and head. **Displacement:** 77.9 cu. in. (1275 cc). **Bore & Stroke:** 2.78 x 3.20 in. (70.6 x 81.3 mm). **Compression Ratio:** 8.8:1. **Brake Horsepower:** 62 at 6000 rpm. Torque: 72 lbs.-ft. at 3000 rpm. Three main bearings. Solid valve lifters. Two SU semi-downdraft carburetors.

BASE FOUR (MGB): Inline, overhead-valve four-cylinder. Cast iron block and head. **Displacement:** 109.8 cu. in. (1798 cc). **Bore & Stroke:** 3.16 x 3.50 in. (80.26 x 88.9 mm). **Compression Ratio:** 8.8:1. **Brake Horsepower:** 92 at 5400 rpm. **Torque:** 110 lbs.-ft. at 3000 rpm. Five main bearings. Solid valve lifters. Two SU semi-downdraft carburetors.

CHASSIS DATA: Wheelbase: (Midget) 80 in.; (MGB) 91 in. **Overall Length:** (Midget) 137.6 in.; (MGB) 153.2 in. **Height:** (Midget) 48.6 in.; (MGB) 49.5 in. **Width:** (Midget) 54.9 in.; (MGB) 59.9 in. **Front Tread:** (Midget) 46.3 in.; (MGB) 49.0 in. **Rear Tread:** (Midget) 44.8 in.; (MGB) 49.25 in. **Wheel Type:** (Midget) wire; (MGB) Rostyle, or optional center-lock wire. **Standard Tires:** (Midget) 145x13 radial; (MGB) 155x14 radial; (MGB/GT) 165x14 radial.

TECHNICAL: Layout: front-engine, rear-drive. **Transmission:** four-speed manual (floor lever); all-synchro on MGB. Overall Midget gear ratios: (1st) 12.5:1; (2nd) 7.5:1; (3rd) 5.3:1; (4th) 3.9:1. Overall MGB gear ratios: (1st) 13.45:1; (2nd) 8.47:1; (3rd) 5.40:1; (3rd o/d) 4.43:1; (4th) 3.91:1; (4th o/d) 3.20:1. **Standard Final Drive Ratio:** (Midget) 3.90:1; (MGB) 3.91:1. Steering: rack and pinion. **Suspension (front):** (Midget) wishbones and coil springs with anti-roll bar optional; lever shock absorbers. **Suspension (rear):** (Midget) rigid axle with semi-elliptic leaf springs and lever shock absorbers; (MGB) rigid axle with semi-elliptic leaf springs and hydraulic shock absorbers. **Brakes:** front disc, rear drum. **Body Construction:** steel unibody. **Fuel Tank:** (Midget) 7.25 gal.; (MGB) 14 gallons.

MAJOR OPTIONS: MIDGET OPTIONS: Removable hardtop. Tonneau cover. Anti-roll bar. Oil cooler. Solid-state AM radio. Electric clock. Wood-rim steering wheel. Wood gearshift knobs. Whitewall tires. Selection of SCCA-approved competition parts.
MGB OPTIONS: Removable hardtop. Dunlop 60-spoke center-lock wire wheels (painted or chrome). Heater. Electrically-heated rear window (GT). Overdrive. Solid-state AM radio. Solid-state AM/FM radio. Center console with electric clock. Center armrest. Wood-rim steering wheel. Wood gearshift knob. Rubber floor mats. Whitewall tires. Selection of SCCA-approved competition parts.

PERFORMANCE: Top Speed: (Midget Mk III) 92 mph; (MGB) 105+ mph. **Acceleration (0-60 mph):** (Midget Mk III) 15.3 sec.; (MGB) 11.8 sec. **Acceleration (quarter-mile):** (Midget Mk III) 19.9 sec.; (MGB) 18.45 sec. (77 mph).

PRODUCTION/SALES: Approximately 32,020 MGs were sold in the U.S. in 1970, and 31,848 in 1971.

Manufacturer: MG Division of British Leyland Corp. Ltd., Longbridge, Birmingham, England.

Distributor: British Leyland Motors Inc., Leonia, New Jersey.

HISTORY: "The Midget's got a price tag to match its name," said the 1970 sales brochure, "and the kind of track performance that puts some so called 'sports cars' to shame." A Midget, they claimed, was the "choice of the guy who makes the young way his way." MGB was promoted as "America's largest-selling imported sports car....the obvious choice for the man who wants to be different." As for the MGB/GT coupe, it was an "authentic GT with continental flair and American spirit....for men wanting power and comfort in equal measure." While women were pictured with the cars, no suggestion was made of the fact, obvious by the 1970s, that a female person might actually want to buy one. Austin-Healey's Sprite, which differed little from the MG Midget except for trim and emblem, was dropped in 1971; so only the MG version remained through the rest of the company's existence.

1972-73 MG

1972 MGB-GT.

MIDGET — Mk III — FOUR — Production of the smaller two-seaters continued with little evident change, other than rounded rear wheel openings. Engine compression was modified in response to emissions regulations. Mag-style wheels held radial tires, and the restyled dashboard contained a new locking glovebox.

MGB/GT — Mk III — FOUR — A new version of the MGB emerged for the 1972 model year, but changes were modest except for a new center console and armrests. A restyled instrument panel held a locking glovebox. Under the hood, the 1798-cc four-cylinder engine was modified for use with low-lead or regular fuel. Seats in the GT coupe had leather inserts. Three new body colors were added: gold, aqua, and dark green. For 1973, the grille was revised again, with its emblem returned to the upper grille molding.

I.D. DATA: Serial number is on a plate on the left front fender valance or firewall; or on the upper dash panel. Engine number plates are attached to left of block, near the front. Starting serial number: (1973 Midget) GAN5UD123731; (1973 MGB) GHN5UD294261; (1973 GT) GHD5UD296001.

Model	Body Type & Seating	Engine Type/CID	P.O.E. Price	Weight (lbs.)	Prod. Total
MIDGET Mk III					
GAN5	2-dr Rds-2P	I4/78	2520	1512	Note 1

442

Model	Body Type & Seating	Engine Type/CID	P.O.E. Price	Weight (lbs.)	Prod. Total
MGB					
Mk III	2-dr Rds-2P	I4/110	3320	1920	Note 2
Mk III	2-dr GT Cpe-2+2P	I4/110	3615	2190	Note 2

Note 1: As many as 99,896 Midget Mk III roadsters were built, through 1974.

Note 2: More than half a million MGBs (approximately 387,675 roadsters and 125,597 GT models) were built from 1962 to 1980. A total of 300,274 roadsters were exported to the U.S.

1973 Price Note: Midget price rose to $2795 in 1973; MGB to $3695; and MGB/GT to $4070.

1973 MG B/GT and roadster. (William Siuru Jr.)

ENGINE DATA: BASE FOUR (Midget Mk III): Inline, overhead-valve four-cylinder. Cast iron block and head. **Displacement:** 77.9 cu. in. (1275 cc). **Bore & Stroke:** 2.78 x 3.20 in. (70.6 x 81.3 mm). **Compression Ratio:** 8.0:1. **Brake Horsepower:** 54.5 at 5500 rpm. **Torque:** 67 lbs.-ft. at 3250 rpm. Three main bearings. Solid valve lifters. Two SU semi-downdraft carburetors.

BASE FOUR (MGB): Inline, overhead-valve four-cylinder. Cast iron block and head. **Displacement:** 109.8 cu. in. (1798 cc). **Bore & Stroke:** 3.16 x 3.50 in. (80.26 x 88.9 mm). **Compression Ratio:** 8.0:1. **Brake Horsepower:** 78.5 at 5500 rpm. **Torque:** 94 lbs.-ft. at 3000 rpm. Five main bearings. Solid valve lifters. Two SU semi-downdraft carburetors.

CHASSIS DATA: Wheelbase: (Midget) 80 in.; (MGB) 91 in. **Overall Length:** (Midget) 137.6 in.; (MGB) 153.2 in. **Height:** (Midget) 48.6 in.; (MGB) 49.5 in. **Width:** (Midget) 54.9 in.; (MGB) 59.9 in. **Front Tread:** (Midget) 46.3 in.; (MGB) 49.25 in. **Rear Tread:** (Midget) 44.8 in.; (MGB) 49.25 in. **Wheel Type:** (Midget) Mag-style; (MGB) Rostyle, or optional center-lock wire. **Standard Tires:** (Midget) 145x13 radial; (MGB) 155x14 radial; (MGB/GT) 165x14 radial.

TECHNICAL: Same as 1970-71.

MAJOR OPTIONS: Similar to 1970-71.

PERFORMANCE: Top Speed: (Midget Mk III) 92 mph. **Acceleration (0-60 mph):** (Midget Mk III) 15.3 sec. **Acceleration (quarter-mile):** (Midget Mk III) 19.9 sec.

PRODUCTION/SALES: Approximately 31,584 MGs were sold in the U.S. in 1972, and 31,991 in 1973.

Manufacturer: MG Division of British Leyland Corp. Ltd. (plant at Abingdon-on-Thames, Berkshire, England).

Distributor: British Leyland Motors Inc., Leonia, New Jersey.

HISTORY: Mark III version of MGB was introduced in October 1971. In the summer of 1973, a V-8 version of the MGB debuted in England; see next listing.

1974 MG

1974 MG Midget roadster.

MIDGET — Mk III — FOUR — Little change was evident in the smallest MG for its final season in Mark III form, except for huge, soft black padded bumper guards. Midgets also had a collapsible steering column.

MGB/GT — Mk III — FOUR — This was also the final model year for the Mark III version of the MGB and MGB/GT, which continued with little change except for the new thick bumper guards, which added to the car's overall length. Prices took a sharp jump this year.

MGB V-8 — V-8 — Production of an MG with V-8 power lasted longer than the earlier six-cylinder MGC, but amounted to considerably less in total numbers built. This seldom-seen model was identified by V-8 badges in the grille, and ahead of the doors. The concept began with Ken Costello, the British proprietor of an engine tuning shop who'd begun to install aluminum-block Rover 3.5-liter V-8 engines (evolved from a Buick design of the 1960s) into MG bodies. These production engine installations were performed at MG's Abingdon plant, and resulted in an MGB with 137 horsepower and 193 pound-feet of torque. That was enough to send a V-8 model to 60 miles an hour in close to seven seconds.

I.D. DATA: Serial number is on a plate on the left front fender valance or firewall; or on the upper dash panel. Engine number plates are attached to left of block, near the front. Starting serial number: (1974 Midget Mk III) GAN5UE138801; (1974 MGB) GHN5UE328101; (1974 GT) GHD5UE328801.

Model	Body Type & Seating	Engine Type/CID	P.O.E. Price	Weight (lbs.)	Prod. Total
MIDGET Mk III					
GAN5	2-dr Rds-2P	I4/78	2995	1698	Note 1
MGB					
Mk III	2-dr Rds-2P	I4/110	3925	2314	Note 2
Mk III	2-dr GT Cpe-2+2P	I4/110	4325	2346	Note 2
V-8	2-dr Rds-2P	V8/215	N/A	2427	Note 3

Note 1: As many as 99,896 Midget Mk III roadsters were built, through 1974.

Note 2: More than half a million MGBs (approximately 387,675 roadsters and 125,597 GT models) were built from 1962 to 1980. A total of 300,274 roadsters were exported to the U.S.

Note 3: Fewer than 2,600 V-8 MGBs were produced through 1976.

ENGINE DATA: BASE FOUR (Midget Mk III): Inline, overhead-valve four-cylinder. Cast iron block and head. **Displacement:** 77.9 cu. in. (1275 cc). **Bore & Stroke:** 2.78 x 3.20 in. (70.6 x 81.3 mm). **Compression Ratio:** 8.0:1. **Brake Horsepower:** 54.5 at 5500 rpm. **Torque:** 67 lbs.-ft. at 3250 rpm. Three main bearings. Solid valve lifters. Two SU semi-downdraft carburetors.

BASE FOUR (MGB): Inline, overhead-valve four-cylinder. Cast iron block and head. **Displacement:** 109.8 cu. in. (1798 cc). **Bore & Stroke:** 3.16 x 3.50 in. (80.26 x 88.9 mm). **Compression Ratio:** 8.0:1. **Brake Horsepower:** 78.5 at 5500 rpm. **Torque:** 94 lbs.-ft. at 3000 rpm. Five main bearings. Solid valve lifters. Two SU semi-downdraft carburetors.

BASE V-8 (MGB V-8): Overhead-valve V-8. Aluminum block. **Displacement:** 215.2 cu. in. (3528 cc). **Bore & Stroke:** 3.50 x 2.80 in. (88.9 x 71.1 mm). **Compression Ratio:** 8.25:1. **Brake Horsepower:** 137 at 5000 rpm. **Torque:** 193 lbs.-ft. at 2900 rpm. Two SU horizontal carburetors.

CHASSIS DATA: Wheelbase: (Midget) 80 in.; (MGB) 91 in. **Overall Length:** (Midget) 144.6 in.; (MGB) 159.2 in. **Height:** (Midget) 48.6 in.; (MGB) 49.5 in. **Width:** (Midget) 54.9 in.; (MGB) 59.9 in. **Front Tread:** (Midget) 46.3 in.; (MGB) 49.25 in. **Rear Tread:** (Midget) 44.8 in.; (MGB) 49.25 in. **Wheel Type:** (Midget) mag-style; (MGB) Rostyle, or optional center-lock wire. **Standard Tires:** (Midget) 145x13 radial; (MGB) 155SR14 radial; (MGB/GT) 165SR14 radial; (V-8) 175HR14.

TECHNICAL: Layout: front-engine, rear-drive. **Transmission:** four-speed manual (floor lever); all-synchro on MGB. Overall Midget gear ratios: (1st) 12.5:1; (2nd) 7.5:1; (3rd) 5.3:1; (4th) 3.9:1.Overall MGB gear ratios: (1st) 13.45:1; (2nd) 8.47:1; (3rd) 5.40:1; (3rd o/d) 4.43:1; (4th) 3.91:1; (4th o/d) 3.20:1. MGB V-8 gear ratios: (1st) 3.138:1; (2nd) 1.974:1; (3rd) 1.259:1; (4th) 1.00:1; (o/d) 0.82:1. **Standard Final Drive Ratio:** (Midget) 3.90:1; (MGB) 3.91:1; (MGB V-8) 3.07:1; (MGB V-8 w/overdrive) 3.307:1. **Steering:** rack and pinion. **Suspension (front):** (Midget) wishbones and coil springs with lever shock absorbers, anti-roll bar optional; (MGB) wishbones and coil springs with anti-roll bar and hydraulic shock absorbers. **Suspension (rear):** (Midget) rigid axle with semi-elliptic leaf springs and lever shock absorbers; (MGB) rigid axle with semi-elliptic leaf springs and hydraulic shock absorbers. **Brakes:** front disc, rear drum. **Body Construction:** steel unibody.

MAJOR OPTIONS: Similar to 1970-71.

PERFORMANCE: Top Speed: (MGB V-8) 121.8 (claimed). **Acceleration (0-60 mph):** (MGB V-8) 7.7 seconds or less. **Fuel Mileage:** (Midget) 22.4 mpg EPA; (MGB) 18.7 mpg EPA; (MGB/GT) 16.3 mpg EPA.

PRODUCTION/SALES: Approximately 25,015 MGs were sold in the U.S. in 1974.

Manufacturer: MG Division of British Leyland Corp. Ltd., Longbridge, Birmingham, England.

Distributor: British Leyland Motors Inc., Leonia, New Jersey.

HISTORY: MGB V-8 was introduced in August 1973 and continued in production into 1976. Initial plans to ship V-8 models to the U.S. on a regular basis never came to fruition.

1975-77 MG

MIDGET — Mk IV — FOUR — With a massive rubber nose made of soft black polyurethane to replace the former chromed grille, the Mark IV (1500) Midget was easy enough to spot. No grille was evident at all; just a low, wide opening with tiny center 'MG' octagon emblem. A similarly deformable black bumper went at the rear this year, MG's far-from-elegant response to stricter U.S. regulations. Under the hood was a bigger Triumph Spitfire engine, of 1493-cc displacement, which came as a result of MG's merger into British Leyland in the late 1960s. With a single carburetor (rather than the traditional twin SU units), the four-cylinder engine produced 55 horsepower in U.S. tune. The four-speed gearbox was now fully synchronized, while a taller suspension raised the headlamp level. On the appearance side, the Midget's rear wheel openings, which had been rounded for a few years, reverted again to a flat top. In home-market form, a Midget could squeeze past 100 mph and hit sixty in about 12.5 seconds. Detuned American versions were slower. In 1976, a third wiper was added to meet visibility standards. Standard body colors in 1977 were: Brooklands Green, Chartreuse, Damask Red, Flamenco, Glacier White, Sandglow, and Tahiti Blue; with interiors in Autumn Leaf or Black.

MGB — Mk IV — FOUR — Like the smaller Midget, MG's larger sports car slipped into the Mark IV version, with the most noticeable change being the large matte black polyurethane nose and tail sections. For the remainder of the car's production, no chrome bumpers or grille would be seen. The GT coupe version was dropped. Beneath the bonnet, the four-cylinder engine switched from twin carburetors to a single Zenith-Stromberg unit, losing plenty of horsepower in the process. Transmission gear ratios changed for better gas mileage. MG fans were saddened by the loss in both appearance and performance for this final series. In 1977, the roadster added a zip-in rear window. Standard 1977 colors were the same as the Midget.

MGB V-8 — V-8 — Production of the V-8 MG continued into 1976; see previous listing for details.

1977 MG midget roadster.

I.D. DATA: Serial number is on a plate on the left front fender valance or firewall; or on the upper dash panel. Engine number plates are attached to left of block, near the front. Starting serial number: (1976 Midget) GAN6UG166301G; (1977 Midget) GAN6UH188001. (1976 MGB) GHN5UG386601G; (1977 MGB) GHN5UH410001.

Model	Body Type & Seating	Engine Type/CID	P.O.E. Price	Weight (lbs.)	Prod. Total
MIDGET Mk IV					
1500	2-dr Rds-2P	I4/91	3549	1854	Note 1
MGB					
Mk IV	2-dr Rds-2P	I4/110	4350	2287	Note 2
V-8	2-dr Rds-2P	V8/215	N/A	2427	Note 3

Note 1: About 72,185 Midget Mk IV roadsters were built, through 1979.

Note 2: More than half a million MGBs (approximately 387,675 roadsters and 125,597 GT models) were built from 1962 to 1980. A total of 300,274 roadsters were exported to the U.S.

Note 3: Fewer than 2,600 V-8 MGBs were produced from 1973 through 1976.

1976 Price Note: For 1976, the Midget price rose to $3949; MGB to $4795.

1977 Price Note: In 1977, the Midget price rose to $4150; MGB to $5150.

ENGINE DATA: BASE FOUR (Midget Mk IV): Inline, overhead-valve four-cylinder. Cast iron block and head. **Displacement:** 91.0 cu. in. (1493 cc). **Bore & Stroke:** 2.90 x 3.44 in. (73.7 x 87.5 mm). **Compression Ratio:** 9.1:1. **Brake Horsepower:** 55.5 at 5000 rpm. **Torque:** 67.1 lbs.-ft. at 2500 rpm. Three main bearings. Solid valve lifters. One Zenith CD4 carburetor.

BASE FOUR (MGB): Inline, overhead-valve four-cylinder. Cast iron block and head. **Displacement:** 109.8 cu. in. (1798 cc). **Bore & Stroke:** 3.16 x 3.50 in. (80.26 x 88.9 mm). **Compression Ratio:** 8.0:1. **Brake Horsepower:** 62.5 at 5500 rpm. Torque: 86 lbs.-ft. at 2500 rpm. Five main bearings. Solid valve lifters. One Zenith 175CD5T carburetor.

BASE V-8 (MGB V-8): Same as 1974.

CHASSIS DATA: Wheelbase: (Midget) 80 in.; (MGB) 91.1 in. **Overall Length:** (Midget) 141 in.; (MGB) 158.3 in. **Height:** (Midget) 48.3 in.; (MGB) 51 in. **Width:** (Midget) 54 in.; (MGB) 59.9 in. **Front Tread:** (Midget) 46.3 in.; (MGB) 49.5 in. **Rear Tread:** (Midget) 44.8 in.; (MGB) 49.75 in. **Wheel Type:** (Midget) 4.5Jx13; (MGB) 4.5Jx14 Rostyle. **Standard Tires:** (Midget) 145x13 radial; (MGB) 165SR14 radial; (V-8) 175HR14.

TECHNICAL: Layout: front-engine, rear-drive. **Transmission:** four-speed manual (floor lever); all-synchro. Midget gear ratios: (1st) 3.412:1; (2nd) 2.112:1; (3rd) 1.433:1; (4th) 1.00:1. MGB gear ratios: (1st) 3.3:1; (2nd) 2.21:1; (3rd) 1.40:1; (4th) 1.00:1. MGB V-8 gear ratios: (1st) 3.138:1; (2nd) 1.974:1; (3rd) 1.259:1; (4th) 1.00:1; (o/d) 0.82:1. **Standard Final Drive Ratio:** (Midget) 3.90:1; (MGB) 3.909:1; (MGB V-8) 3.07:1; (MGB V-8 w/overdrive) 3.307:1. **Steering:** rack and pinion. **Suspension (front):** (Midget) wishbones and coil springs with lever shock absorbers, anti-roll bar optional; (MGB) wishbones and coil springs with anti-roll bar and lever shock absorbers. **Suspension (rear):** (Midget) rigid axle with semi-elliptic leaf springs and lever shock absorbers; (MGB) rigid axle with semi-elliptic leaf springs, anti-roll bar and lever shock absorbers. **Brakes:** front disc, rear drum. **Body Construction:** steel unibody.

MAJOR OPTIONS: Overdrive transmission: MGB ($240). Tonneau cover: Midget ($50); MGB ($55). AM/FM radio: MGB ($150). AM/FM stereo radio, with or without tape player (MGB). Anti-roll bar: Midget ($15). Painted center-lock wire wheels: Midget ($135); MGB ($145). Whitewall tires ($45-$50).

Note: Option prices shown were effective in 1977.

PRODUCTION/SALES: Approximately 27,946 MGs were sold in the U.S. in 1975, 28,436 in 1976, and 34,794 in 1977.

Manufacturer: MG Division of British Leyland Corp. Ltd., Longbridge, Birmingham, England.

Distributor: British Leyland Motors Inc., Leonia, New Jersey.

HISTORY: Production of the MGB V-8 continued into 1976. The final Mk IV version of the Midget was introduced in October 1974 and production continued into summer 1979. The Mark IV MGB appeared at the London Motor Show in October 1974 but arrived in the U.S. market late in the 1975 model year, and remained in production until 1980. During 1975, an MGB GT Jubilee edition was produced, in British Racing Green with gold V-8 wheels.

1978-80 MG

1978 MG Midget convertible.

1980 MGB convertible.

MIDGET — Mk IV — FOUR — Production of the final Midget version continued into summer 1979 with little change, except for substantial price hikes. Standard equipment included an anti-roll bar, bucket seats with knit-back expanded vinyl, locking glovebox, three-spoke steering wheel with padded rim, tachometer, tripmeter, 145SR13 radial tires on mag-style 13-inch wheels, opening vent wings, two-speed wiper/washer, lighter, and trunk light.

MGB — Mk IV — FOUR — Production of the larger open MG continued into 1980 with minimal change. Engine cooling was handled by twin electric fans, but horsepower remained low compared to earlier models. Prices jumped sharply for each of the MGB's final model years. Standard equipment included a tonneau cover, power front disc brakes, four-spoke steering wheel with padded rim, 165SR14 tires, and a zip-out rear window.

I.D. DATA: Serial number is on a plate on the left front fender valance or firewall; or on the upper dash panel. Engine number plates are attached to left of block, near the front. Starting serial number: (1978 Midget) GAN6UJ200001J; (1979 Midget) 212001G. (1978 MGB) GHN5UJ447001; (1979 MGB) 4710016; (1980 MGB) GVVDJ2AG501001.

Model	Body Type & Seating	Engine Type/CID	P.O.E. Price	Weight (lbs.)	Prod. Total
MIDGET Mk IV					
1500	2-dr Rds-2P	I4/91	4495	1826	Note 1
MGB					
Mk IV	2-dr Rds-2P	I4/110	5649	2338	Note 2

Note 1: About 72,185 Midget Mk IV roadsters were built, through 1979.

Note 2: More than half a million MGBs (approximately 387,675 roadsters and 125,597 GT models) were built from 1962 to 1980. A total of 300,274 roadsters were exported to the U.S.

1979 Price Note: For 1979, the Midget price rose to $5200; MGB to $6550.

1980 Price Note: In 1980, the MGB price rose to $7950.

1979 MGB convertible.

ENGINE DATA: BASE FOUR (Midget Mk IV): Inline, overhead-valve four-cylinder. Cast iron block and head. **Displacement:** 91.0 cu. in. (1493 cc). **Bore & Stroke:** 2.90 x 3.44 in. (73.7 x 87.5 mm). **Compression Ratio:** 9.1:1. **Brake Horsepower:** 50 at 5000 rpm. **Torque:** 67 lbs.-ft. at 2500 rpm. Three main bearings. Solid valve lifters. One Zenith CD4 carburetor.

BASE FOUR (MGB): Inline, overhead-valve four-cylinder. Cast iron block and head. **Displacement:** 109.8 cu. in. (1798 cc). **Bore & Stroke:** 3.16 x 3.50 in. (80.26 x 88.9 mm). **Compression Ratio:** 8.0:1. **Brake Horsepower:** 62.5 at 5500 rpm. **Torque:** 88 lbs.-ft. at 2500 rpm. Five main bearings. Solid valve lifters. One Zenith 175CD5T carburetor.

CHASSIS DATA: Wheelbase: (Midget) 80 in.; (MGB) 91.1 in. **Overall Length:** (Midget) 141-143 in.; (MGB) 158.3 in. **Height:** (Midget) 48.3 in.; (MGB) 51 in. **Width:** (Midget) 54 in.; (MGB) 59.9 in. **Front Tread:** (Midget) 46.3 in.; (MGB) 49.5 in. **Rear Tread:** (Midget) 44.8 in.; (MGB) 49.8 in. **Wheel Type:** (Midget) 4.5Jx13 Rostyle; (MGB) 4.5Jx14 Rostyle. **Standard Tires:** (Midget) 145SR13 radial; (MGB) 165SR14 radial.

TECHNICAL: Layout: front-engine, rear-drive. **Transmission:** four-speed manual (floor lever); all-synchro. Midget gear ratios: (1st) 3.412:1; (2nd) 2.112:1; (3rd) 1.433:1; (4th) 1.00:1. MGB gear ratios: (1st) 3.3:1; (2nd) 2.21:1; (3rd) 1.40:1; (4th) 1.00:1. **Standard Final Drive Ratio:** (Midget) 3.90:1; (MGB) 3.909:1. **Steering:** rack and pinion. **Suspension (front):** wishbones and coil springs with lever shock absorbers and anti-roll bar. **Suspension (rear):** (Midget) rigid axle with semi-elliptic leaf springs and lever shock absorbers; (MGB) rigid axle with semi-elliptic leaf springs, anti-roll bar and lever shock absorbers. **Brakes:** front disc, rear drum. **Body Construction:** steel unibody.

MAJOR OPTIONS: Overdrive transmission: MGB ($250). Tonneau cover: Midget ($65). AM/FM radio ($150). Anti-roll bar: Midget ($15). Painted wire wheels ($155). Whitewall tires ($60).

Note: Option prices shown were effective in 1978.

PRODUCTION/SALES: A total of 26,656 MGs (9,385 Midgets and 17,271 MGBs) were sold in the U.S. during 1978; a total of 26,025 (9,165 Midgets and 16,860 MGBs) were sold in the U.S. during 1979.

Manufacturer: MG Division of British Leyland Corp. Ltd., Longbridge, Birmingham, England.

Distributor: British Leyland Motors Inc., Leonia, New Jersey.

HISTORY: Midget production halted in summer 1979, MGB in October 1980. Final MGBs to enter the U.S. were 1980 "Limited Edition," all black with gunmetal-gray stripes along the bodyside bottom, with a front spoiler below the polyurethane nose. For the home market, a final thousand "Limited" models were produced: 420 bronze-colored roadsters and 580 pewter-colored GT coupes.

POSTSCRIPT: Just as many observers in the 1970s kept expecting that MG would finally boost its horsepower up toward earlier levels and otherwise return the roadsters to their former glory, rumors of a revived MG have persisted. The appearance of an EX-E experimental prototype in the mid-1980s sparked such talk. And as the 1990s began, further speculation of a modern MG continued to appear in the trade and consumer automotive press.

On a more tangible note, British Motor Heritage Ltd. (a subsidiary of the Rover Group), began to produce complete bodyshells for the 1962-80 MGB, to replace those unibodied structures that have deteriorated beyond repair. The first such reproduction bodyshell was assembled in February 1988, intended to become available to restorers in both Britain and the U.S. Late in 1989, company representatives toured the U.S. in a rebodied MGB, appearing at automotive shows and trade events to publicize the availability of the all-metal bodies, created using some of the original tooling.

MITSUBISHI

For more than a decade prior to Mitsubishi's appearance in the U.S. market under its own name, the Japanese company sold thousands of cars with Dodge and Plymouth badges. Few were aware, then, that Mitsubishi had actually built the first series-production car in Japan, with its Model A of 1917. Only about 20 were built, as it happened, before the company turned to building planes and trucks instead, as an adjunct to its earlier shipbuilding function.

Corporate history reaches back even further, to 1870, when the Tsukomo Shokai shipping company was founded by Yataro Iwasaki. By the turn of the century, that

firm expanded into part of a holding company called Mitsubishi Goshi Kaisha Ltd.

Not until 1960 did Mitsubishi turn out its next passenger car, though scooters and three-wheelers had been produced during the 1950s. Mitsubishi had also built Henry J two-doors and Jeeps, under license from Kaiser (U.S.). The Mitsubishi 500, introduced in 1960, was powered by a two-cylinder, 20-bhp engine at the rear. Two years later, it evolved into the Colt 600, taking on the name that would, in the following decade, bring Mitsubishi products into the U.S. market. A Colt 1000 and a new Debonair series were available in 1963, followed the next year by a fastback Colt 800. In 1969, the Colt Galant was introduced, heralding the eventual appearance of yet another name for U.S. models.

Through the 1970s, Mitsubishi subcompacts sold in the U.S. under the Dodge and Plymouth banners (see Dodge listing), though not everyone was aware of their precise origin. Finally, for the 1983 model year, Mitsubishi introduced a trio of models under its own name (which translates to "three diamonds"), mechanically related to the existing Colts, Challengers and Sapporos. One difference: the new Starion coupe carried a turbocharged version of Mitsubishi's 2.6-liter engine with twin balance shafts. Turbo power became available on the Cordia and Tredia for 1984. Two new models joined the lineup for 1985: Mirage and Galant. By the end of the 1980s, Mitsubishi became particularly noteworthy for two new models ready for the '90s: the high-performance 3000GT sports car, built in Japan; and the Eclipse sport coupe, produced in Normal, Illinois at a new Diamond-Star plant, as part of a joint venture with Chrysler.

1982-83 MITSUBISHI

CORDIA — FOUR — Mitsubishi's sporty coupe used various components from the Dodge/Plymouth Colt, built by the same company. Power came from a "Silent Shaft" 1.8-liter, four-cylinder engine that produced 82 horsepower. The base model had a conventional five-speed manual gearbox, whereas the L and LS editions carried a "4+4" transmission, similar to the Twin-Stick unit used in the Colts. A three-speed automatic was optional, with electronically-controlled damper clutch. The Cordia LS included LCD digital and graphic instruments.

TREDIA — FOUR — Mechanical details of the four-door notchback sedan were similar to the Cordia coupe, including the engine and transmissions, and fully independent suspension. The base model came with a five-speed gearbox; L and LS with the "4+4" dual-range four-speed unit. Standard equipment on the LS included power steering, "one-touch" electric windows, and an AM/FM stereo radio with cassette player.

STARION — FOUR — Turbocharging was a star attraction of Mitsubishi's rear-drive sport/luxury hatchback coupe, which was otherwise mechanically similar to the Dodge Challenger and Plymouth Sapporo. The turbocharged edition of the 2.6-liter, four-cylinder balance-shaft engine used throttle-body fuel injection and produced 145 horsepower. All-disc brakes and power steering were standard, along with power windows and alloy wheels. The LS model included air conditioning, six-way front seats, digital instruments, and an eight-speaker stereo system. Only a five-speed manual gearbox was available. An optional Technical Performance Package included electronic anti-skid control for the rear brakes.

I.D. DATA: Mitsubishi's 17-symbol Vehicle Identification Number is on the upper left of the dashboard, visible through the windshield. Symbols 1-3 denote country of origin, manufacturer, and vehicle type. The next symbol four indicates restraint sytem. Symbols 5-7 identify the model; symbol 8, the engine. Symbol 10 indicates model year; symbol 11, the assembly plant; followed by a six-digit sequential production number.

Model	Body Type & Seating	Engine Type/CID	P.O.E. Price	Weight (lbs.)	Prod. Total
CORDIA					
	2-dr Hatch-4P	I4/110	7089	2101	Note 1
L	2-dr Hatch-4P	I4/110	7849	2156	Note 1
LS	2-dr Hatch-4P	I4/110	9449	2189	Note 1
TREDIA					
	4-dr Sedan-5P	I4/110	6539	2123	Note 1
L	4-dr Sedan-5P	I4/110	7259	2145	Note 1
LS	4-dr Sedan-5P	I4/110	8349	2200	Note 1
STARION					
	2-dr Coupe-2+2P	I4/156	12079	2679	Note 1
LS	2-dr Coupe-2+2P	I4/156	13919	2758	Note 1

Note 1: A total of 5,260 Mitsubishis were sold in the U.S. during 1982, followed by 41,994 in 1983 (including 7,691 Mighty Max pickup trucks and 1,612 Montero sport-utility vehicles).

ENGINE DATA: BASE FOUR (Cordia, Tredia): Inline, overhead-cam four-cylinder. Cast iron block and light alloy head. **Displacement:** 109.5 cu. in. (1795 cc). **Bore & Stroke:** 3.17 x 3.46 in. (81 x 88 mm). **Compression Ratio:** 8.5:1. **Brake Horsepower:** 82 at 5000 rpm. **Torque:** 93 lbs.-ft. at 3000 rpm. Five main bearings. Solid valve lifters. Two-barrel carburetor.

BASE FOUR (Starion): Inline, overhead-cam four-cylinder with turbocharger. Cast iron block and light alloy head. **Displacement:** 156 cu. in. (2555 cc). **Bore & Stroke:** 3.59 x 3.86 in. (91.1 x 98 mm). **Compression Ratio:** 7.0:1. **Brake Horsepower:** 145 at 5000 rpm. **Torque:** 185 lbs.-ft. at 2500 rpm. Five main bearings. Solid valve lifters. Fuel injection (twin injectors).

CHASSIS DATA: Wheelbase: (Cordia/Tredia) 96.3 in.; (Starion) 95.9 in. **Overall Length:** (Cordia) 173.0 in.; (Tredia) 172.4 in.; (Starion) 173.2 in. **Height:** (Cordia) 51.6 in.; (Tredia) 53.7 in.; (Starion) 51.8 in. **Width:** (Cordia) 65.4 in.; (Tredia) 65.4 in.; (Starion) 66.3 in. **Front Tread:** (Cordia/Tredia) 55.5 in.; (Starion) 54.9 in. **Rear Tread:** (Cordia/Tredia) 54.1 in.; (Starion) 55.1 in. **Standard Tires:** (Cordia/Tredia) 165/80R13; (Starion) 195/70R14.

TECHNICAL: Layout: (Cordia/Tredia) front-engine, front-drive; (Starion) front-engine, rear-drive. **Transmission:** (Cordia/Tredia) five-speed manual or "4+4" dual-range four-speed, with three-speed automatic optional; (Starion) five-speed manual. **Steering:** (Cordia/Tredia) rack and pinion; (Starion) recirculating ball. **Suspension (front):** MacPherson struts with coil springs and anti-roll bar. **Suspension (rear):** (Cordia/Tredia) independent with trailing arms and coil springs; (Starion) independent with semi-trailing arms, coil spring struts and anti-roll bar. **Brakes:** (Cordia/Tredia) front disc, rear drum; (Starion) front/rear disc. **Body Construction:** steel unibody.

MAJOR OPTIONS: Automatic transmission (Cordia/Tredia L/LS). Power steering (Tredia L). Power windows (Cordia/Tredia L). Power door locks (Tredia L/LS). AM/FM stereo radio (base Cordia/Tredia). Electronic-tuning stereo with cassette player (Cordia/Tredia L). P185/70R13 tires on alloy wheels (Cordia L). Alloy wheels (Tredia L/LS). Technical Performance Pkg. (Starion). Sunroof (Starion). Cruise control (Tredia L/LS, Starion). Leather seat facings (Starion LS). Two-tone paint (Starion LS). Road Wheel Pkg. including P215/60R15 tires on alloy wheels (Starion).

ADDITIONAL MODELS: Mitsubishi also marketed 2WD and 4WD versions of its Mighty Max pickup truck in the U.S., along with a Montero two-door sport-utility vehicle.
Manufacturer: Mitsubishi Motors Corp., Tokyo, Japan.
Distributor: Mitsubishi Motor Sales of America Inc., Fountain Valley, California.
HISTORY: Initially limited to sales in the coastal regions of the U.S., the Mitsubishi trio soon spread across the country. Sales began during 1982, as '83 models.

1984 MITSUBISHI

CORDIA — FOUR — A larger (2.0-liter) engine powered the hatchback coupe for 1984, while a new Turbo model kept the same 1.8-liter displacement used in the initial Cordia. The new Turbo engine had throttle-body fuel injection and produced 116 horsepower, and came with a firmer suspension and high-performance tires. A five-speed manual gearbox was standard on all Cordias this year, with three-speed automatic optional (except on the Turbo).

TREDIA — FOUR — Mitsubishi's sedan also gained a Turbo model this year, as in the Cordia coupe, and the base engine grew to 2.0 liters. Only the L/LS models came with the Dual Range manual gearbox this year; others carried a conventional five-speed. Three-speed automatic was optional, except for the Turbo.

STARION — FOUR — A few styling modifications came this year on Mitsubishi's turbocharged sport coupe, including the deletion of the simulated hood scoop. The front air dam now slanted rearward, while twin foglamps were installed in the front bumpers. Taillamps added smoked lenses. Three models were available this time: LS, LE (Luxury Edition), and ES (EuroSport). The latter came with anti-lock rear brakes, 15-inch cast alloy wheels, and a limited-slip differential.

I.D. DATA: Mitsubishi's 17-symbol Vehicle Identification Number is on the upper left of the dashboard, visible through the windshield. Symbols 1-3 denote country of origin, manufacturer, and vehicle type. The next symbol four indicates restraint sytem. Symbols 5-7 identify the model; symbol 8, the engine. Symbol 10 indicates model year; symbol 11, the assembly plant; followed by a six-digit sequential production number.

Model	Body Type & Seating	Engine Type/CID	P.O.E. Price	Weight (lbs.)	Prod. Total
CORDIA					
	2-dr Hatch-4P	I4/122	6989	2101	Note 1
L	2-dr Hatch-4P	I4/122	7889	2156	Note 1
LS	2-dr Hatch-4P	I4/122	9059	2189	Note 1
Turbo	2-dr Hatch-4P	I4/110	9459	N/A	Note 1
TREDIA					
	4-dr Sedan-4P	I4/122	6599	2123	Note 1
L	4-dr Sedan-4P	I4/122	7579	2145	Note 1
LS	4-dr Sedan-4P	I4/122	8649	2200	Note 1
Turbo	4-dr Sedan-4P	I4/110	8989	N/A	Note 1
STARION					
LS	2-dr Coupe-2+2P	I4/156	12509	2679	Note 1
LE	2-dr Coupe-2+2P	I4/156	14279	2758	Note 1
ES	2-dr Coupe-2+2P	I4/156	14559	2758	Note 1

Note 1: A total of 56,741 Mitsubishis were sold in the U.S. during 1984 (including 14,945 Mighty Max pickup trucks and 2,673 Montero sport-utility vehicles).

ENGINE DATA: BASE FOUR (Cordia, Tredia): Inline, overhead-cam four-cylinder. Cast iron block and light alloy head. **Displacement:** 122 cu. in. (1997 cc). **Bore & Stroke:** 3.35 x 3.46 in. (85 x 88 mm). **Compression Ratio:** 8.5:1. **Brake Horsepower:** 88 at 5000 rpm. **Torque:** 108 lbs.-ft. at 3500 rpm. Five main bearings. Solid valve lifters. Two-barrel carburetor.

BASE TURBO FOUR (Cordia/Tredia Turbo): Inline, overhead-cam four-cylinder with turbocharger. Cast iron block and light alloy head. **Displacement:** 109.5 cu. in. (1795 cc). **Bore & Stroke:** 3.17 x 3.46 in. (81 x 88 mm). **Compression Ratio:** 7.5:1. **Brake Horsepower:** 116 at 5500 rpm. **Torque:** 129 lbs.-ft. at 3000 rpm. Five main bearings. Solid valve lifters. Throttle-body fuel injection.

BASE FOUR (Starion): Inline, overhead-cam four-cylinder with turbocharger. Cast iron block and light alloy head. **Displacement:** 156 cu. in. (2555 cc). **Bore & Stroke:** 3.59 x 3.86 in. (91.1 x 98 mm). **Compression Ratio:** 7.0:1. **Brake Horsepower:** 145 at 5000 rpm. **Torque:** 185 lbs.-ft. at 2500 rpm. Five main bearings. Solid valve lifters. Fuel injection (twin injectors).

CHASSIS DATA: Wheelbase: (Cordia/Tredia) 96.3 in.; (Starion) 95.9 in. **Overall Length:** (Cordia) 173.0 in.; (Tredia) 172.4 in.; (Starion) 173.2 in. **Height:** (Cordia) 49.4 in.; (Tredia) 51.6 in.; (Starion) 50.2 in. **Width:** (Cordia) 65.4 in.; (Tredia) 65.4 in.; (Starion) 66.3 in. **Front Tread:** (Cordia/Tredia) 55.5 in.; (Starion) 54.9 in. **Rear Tread:** (Cordia/Tredia) 54.1 in.; (Starion) 55.1 in. **Standard Tires:** (Cordia/Tredia) 165/80R13; (Starion) 195/70R14.

445

TECHNICAL: Layout: (Cordia/Tredia) front-engine, front-drive; (Starion) front-engine, rear-drive. **Transmission:** (Cordia) five-speed manual or (Tredia) five-speed manual or "4 + 4" dual-range four-speed, with three-speed automatic optional; (Starion) five-speed manual. **Steering:** (Cordia/Tredia) rack and pinion; (Starion) recirculating ball. **Suspension (front):** MacPherson struts with coil springs and anti-roll bar. **Suspension (rear):** (Cordia/Tredia) independent with trailing arms and coil springs; (Starion) independent with MacPherson struts, coil springs and anti-roll bar. **Brakes:** (Cordia/Tredia) front disc, rear drum; (Starion) front/rear disc. **Body Construction:** steel unibody.

MAJOR OPTIONS: Similar to 1983.

ADDITIONAL MODELS: Mitsubishi continued to market 2WD and 4WD versions of its Mighty Max pickup truck in the U.S., along with a Montero two-door sport-utility vehicle.

Manufacturer: Mitsubishi Motors Corp., Tokyo, Japan.

Distributor: Mitsubishi Motor Sales of America Inc., Fountain Valley, California.

HISTORY: Chrysler marketed a version of the Starion as the Conquest.

1985-86 MITSUBISHI

1985 Mitsubishi Mirage turbo.

MIRAGE — FOUR — This two-door hatchback was nearly identical to the Dodge/Plymouth Colt, as restyled for 1985. Four versions were available, three with a 1.5-liter engine and one with a 1.6-liter turbo four. The Mirage Turbo included high-performance 14-inch tires, a firmer suspension, roof spoiler, bigger front air dam, and sport seats. Base Mirages had a standard four-speed manual gearbox, while a five-speed went into other models (with three-speed automatic optional).

CORDIA/TREDIA — FOUR — Apart from a reshuffling of models available, Mitsubishi's subcompact coupe and sedan continued with minor changes, again available with a 2.0-liter four or 1.8-liter turbo four. The Dual Range four-speed gearbox was dropped, so all models came with a standard five-speed. Tredias wore new grilles and full-width taillamps. Engines added automatic valve lash adjustment. All models got new grilles and aero-style headlamps for 1986, while the Cordia Turbo added color-keyed air dam extensions, rocker sill extensions, and a rear spoiler.

GALANT — FOUR — Mitsubishi's new mid-size sedan had front-wheel drive and a 2.4-liter engine, with dual stabilizers to reduce vibration. The engine produced 101 horsepower, and was available only with a four-speed automatic transmission. A lockout button was provided for the overdrive fourth gear. Variable-assist power steering was electronically-controlled, adjusting boost to car speed. Options included an electronically-controlled suspension that adjusted both firmness and ride height. For 1986, the engine added 9 horsepower and alloy wheels became standard. An ECS package for the Galant included four-wheel disc brakes, 195/60HR15 tires on alloy wheels, and the electronically-controlled suspension.

STARION — FOUR — Several mechanical changes appeared for 1985 on the turbocharged coupe. Turbo bearings were now water-cooled (formerly oil-cooled). Steering-wheel switches for the stereo system were standard on the LE, optional on the ES. Standard LE (Luxury Edition) equipment included bronze tinted glass, leather upholstery, a lighted vanity mirror, and LCD digital instrument cluster. High-performance Yokohama P215/60VR15 tires on alloy wheels went on the ES model. A new 'Turbo' logo went on the rear-window shade of all Starions. During the 1985 model year, an ESI model was added, with an intercooled turbocharger and 25 extra horsepower. During 1986, that sportiest version got a name change to ESI-R, adding rocker sill extensions, integrated fender flares and 16-inch wheels/tires. The ESI-R came only with a five-speed manual gearbox, and its intercooled turbo was rated 176 bhp at 5000 rpm.

I.D. DATA: Mitsubishi's 17-symbol Vehicle Identification Number is on the upper left of the dashboard, visible through the windshield. Symbols 1-3 denote country of origin, manufacturer, and vehicle type. The next symbol four indicates restraint sytem. Symbols 5-7 identify the model; symbol 8, the engine. Symbol 10 indicates model year; symbol 11, the assembly plant; followed by a six-digit sequential production number.

Model	Body Type & Seating	Engine Type/CID	P.O.E. Price	Weight (lbs.)	Prod. Total
MIRAGE					
	2-dr Hatch-4P	I4/90	5389	1904	Note 1
L	2-dr Hatch-4P	I4/90	6189	1949	Note 1
LS	2-dr Hatch-4P	I4/90	6669	1982	Note 1
Turbo	2-dr Hatch-4P	I4/97	7689	2145	Note 1
CORDIA					
L	2-dr Hatch-4P	I4/122	8449	2306	Note 1
Turbo	2-dr Hatch-4P	I4/110	9959	2374	Note 1
TREDIA					
	4-dr Sedan-4P	I4/122	6989	2310	Note 1
L	4-dr Sedan-4P	I4/122	8189	2310	Note 1
Turbo	4-dr Sedan-4P	I4/110	9279	2394	Note 1
GALANT					
	4-dr Sedan-5P	I4/143	11989	2778	Note 1

Model	Body Type & Seating	Engine Type/CID	P.O.E. Price	Weight (lbs.)	Prod. Total
STARION					
LS	2-dr Coupe-2 + 2P	I4/156	12629	2828	Note 1
LE	2-dr Coupe-2 + 2P	I4/156	14869	2915	Note 1
ES	2-dr Coupe-2 + 2P	I4/156	14489	2926	Note 1
ESI	2-dr Coupe-2 + 2P	I4/156	N/A	N/A	Note 1
ESI-R	2-dr Coupe-2 + 2P	I4/156	17569	N/A	Note 1

Note 1: A total of 76,453 Mitsubishis were sold in the U.S. during 1985 (including 24,032 Mighty Max pickup trucks and 2,707 Montero sport-utility vehicles), followed by 84,418 in 1986 (including 28,307 Mighty Max and 6,672 Montero).

Price Note: Figures above were valid in 1985, except for the Starion ESI-R, which became available during the 1986 model year.

1985½ Mitsubishi Starion ESI.

ENGINE DATA: BASE FOUR (Mirage): Inline, overhead-cam four-cylinder. Cast iron block and light alloy head. **Displacement:** 89.6 cu. in. (1468 cc). **Bore & Stroke:** 2.97 x 3.23 in. (75.4 x 82 mm). **Compression Ratio:** 9.4:1. **Brake Horsepower:** 68 at 5500 rpm. **Torque:** 82 lbs.-ft. at 3500 rpm. Five main bearings. Two-barrel carburetor.

BASE FOUR (Mirage Turbo): Inline, overhead-cam four-cylinder. Cast iron block and light alloy head. **Displacement:** 97.4 cu. in. (1597 cc). **Bore & Stroke:** 3.03 x 3.39 in. (77 x 86 mm). **Compression Ratio:** 7.6:1. **Brake Horsepower:** 102 at 5500 rpm. **Torque:** 122 lbs.-ft. at 3000 rpm. Five main bearings. Throttle-body fuel injection (twin injectors).

BASE FOUR (Cordia, Tredia): Inline, overhead-cam four-cylinder. Cast iron block and light alloy head. **Displacement:** 122 cu. in. (1997 cc). **Bore & Stroke:** 3.35 x 3.46 in. (85 x 88 mm). **Compression Ratio:** 8.5:1. **Brake Horsepower:** 88 at 5000 pm. **Torque:** 108 lbs.-ft. at 3500 rpm. Five main bearings. Two-barrel carburetor.

BASE TURBO FOUR (Cordia/Tredia Turbo): Inline, overhead-cam four-cylinder with turbocharger. Cast iron block and light alloy head. **Displacement:** 109.5 cu. in. (1795 cc). **Bore & Stroke:** 3.17 x 3.46 in. (81 x 88 mm). **Compression Ratio:** 7.5:1. **Brake Horsepower:** 116 at 5500 pm. **Torque:** 129 lbs.-ft. at 3000 rpm. Five main bearings. Throttle-body fuel injection.

BASE FOUR (Galant): Inline, overhead-cam four-cylinder. Cast iron block and light alloy head. **Displacement:** 143 cu. in. (2350 cc). **Bore & Stroke:** 3.41 x 3.94 in. (86.6 x 100 mm). **Compression Ratio:** 8.5:1. **Brake Horsepower:** 101 at 5000 rpm. **Torque:** 131 lbs.-ft. at 2500 rpm. Five main bearings. Throttle-body fuel injection.
Note: Galant engine output rose to 110 bhp at 4500 rpm and 138 lbs.-ft. at 3500 rpm for 1986, using multi-point fuel injection.

BASE FOUR (Starion): Inline, overhead-cam four-cylinder with turbocharger. Cast iron block and light alloy head. **Displacement:** 156 cu. in. (2555 cc). **Bore & Stroke:** 3.59 x 3.86 in. (91.1 x 98 mm). **Compression Ratio:** 7.0:1. **Brake Horsepower:** 145 at 5000 rpm. **Torque:** 185 lbs.-ft. at 2500 rpm. Five main bearings. Fuel injection (twin injectors).

BASE FOUR (Starion ESI, ESI-R): Same as 2555-cc turbo four above, but with intercooler. **Brake Horsepower:** (ESI) 170; (ESI-R) 176 at 5000 rpm. **Torque:** (ESI) 220 lbs.-ft.; (ESI-R) 223 lbs.-ft. at 2500 rpm.

CHASSIS DATA: Wheelbase: (Mirage) 93.7 in.; (Cordia/Tredia) 96.3 in.; (Galant) 102.4 in.; (Starion) 95.9 in. **Overall Length:** (Mirage) 157.3 in.; (Cordia) 173.0 in.; (Tredia) 172.4 in.; (Galant) 183.1 in.; (Starion) 173.2 in. **Height:** (Mirage) 50.8 in.; (Cordia) 49.4 in.; (Tredia) 51.6 in.; (Galant) 51.6 in.; (Starion) 50.2 in. **Width:** (Mirage) 64.4 in.; (Cordia) 65.4 in.; (Tredia) 65.4 in.; (Galant) 66.7 in.; (Starion) 66.3 in. **Front Tread:** (Mirage) 54.7 in.; (Cordia/Tredia) 55.5 in.; (Galant) 56.9 in.; (Starion) 54.9 in.; (Starion ESI-R) 57.7 in. **Rear Tread:** (Mirage) 52.8 in.; (Cordia) 54.1 in.; (Galant) 55.3 in.; (Starion) 55.1 in.; (Starion ESI-R) 57.3 in.

TECHNICAL: Layout: (Mirage/Cordia/Tredia/Galant) front-engine, front-drive; (Starion) front-engine, rear-drive. **Transmission:** (Mirage) four- or five-speed manual; (Cordia/Tredia/Starion) five-speed manual; (Galant) four-speed automatic. Three-speed automatic optional on Mirage/Cordia/Tredia, four-speed automatic on Starion (except ESI/ESI-R). **Steering:** rack and pinion except (Starion) recirculating ball. **Suspension (front):** MacPherson struts with coil springs and anti-roll bar. **Suspension (rear):** (Mirage/Cordia/Tredia) independent with trailing arms and coil springs; (Galant) beam axle with trailing arms, coil springs and anti-roll bar; (Starion) independent with MacPherson struts, coil springs and anti-roll bar. **Brakes:** front disc, rear drum except (Starion) front/rear disc. **Body Construction:** steel unibody.

MAJOR OPTIONS: Automatic transmission: Mirage ($370); Mirage Turbo ($570); Cordia/Tredia L ($380); Starion ($550). Power steering: base Tredia ($203). ECS package: Galant ($631). Air conditioning: Mirage ($630); Cordia/Tredia ($656). Sunroof: Cordia ($265); Galant ($429); Mirage Turbo ($265); Starion ($265). Leather/digital package: Starion LE ($604). Cast alloy wheels: Mirage Turbo ($294).
Note: Option prices shown were valid in 1986.

PERFORMANCE: Top Speed: (Starion ESI-R) about 125 mph. **Acceleration (0-60 mph):** (Starion ESI-R) about 7.5 sec. **Acceleration (quarter-mile):** (Starion ESI-R) about 16 sec.

ADDITIONAL MODELS: Mitsubishi continued to market 2WD and 4WD versions of its Mighty Max pickup truck in the U.S., along with a Montero two-door sport-utility vehicle.

Manufacturer: Mitsubishi Motors Corp., Tokyo, Japan.

Distributor: Mitsubishi Motor Sales of America Inc., Fountain Valley, California.

1987-88 MITSUBISHI

1988 Mitsubishi Galant Sigma.

MIRAGE — FOUR — A four-door sedan, closely related to the sedan offered under the Dodge/Plymouth Colt name since 1985, joined the original Mirage for 1987. The sedan came only with the non-turbocharged engine. Like the Colt models, Mirage got a front-end restyling for 1987 with new sheetmetal and aero halogen headlamps.

PRECIS — FOUR — Though similar in mechanical details to the Mirage, the Precis was produced in Korea rather than Japan, built for Mitsubishi by Hyundai. For that reason, its appearance was similar to Hyundai's Excel. Precis joined the Mitsubishi lineup during the 1987 model year, as a complement to the Mirage. Power came from the same 1.5-liter four as the Mirage. The base model came with a four-speed manual gearbox; others, a five-speed. Base and LS models were offered in 1987, with an RS edition added for 1988.

CORDIA/TREDIA — FOUR — Except for the addition of an electronically-tuned stereo radio with cassette player as standard equipment, little was new In the Cordia hatchback coupe or Tredia four-door sedan for 1987. The base Tredia was dropped. For 1988, the Cordia Turbo got the same body appearance (and tires) as the Turbo edition.

GALANT — FOUR — Mitsubishi's mid-size, front-drive luxury sedan was now available with a five-speed manual gearbox instead of the usual four-speed automatic. An electronIc theft deterrent system became standard, along with heated ouside mirrors. This Galant was joined during the model year by a Sigma (below) with V-6 power.

GALANT SIGMA — V-6 — Introduced for the 1988 model year, the next Galant turned in Its six-cylinder engine for a 3.0-liter V-6, which produced 142 horsepower. Styling changes included flush headlamps, integrated bumpers, and a front air dam. Galants with the five-speed gearbox added a rear spoiler. The sedan's rear nameplate displayed the Greek letter "sigma" rather than the spelled-out name. Anti-lock brakes were now optional, four-wheel discs now standard.

STARION — FOUR — Apart from a new theft-deterrent system and heated outside mirrors, little was new for Mitsubishi's turbo coupe in 1987. Only two models were offered: the LE and ESI-R, the latter with intercooled turbo engine. For 1988, the base (LE) model was dropped, replaced by an ESI edition. Both carried a more powerful intercooled engine, rated 188 horsepower. A new Sport Handling package for the ESI-R (which included anti-lock rear brakes) added larger tires on wider wheels, as well as adjustable shock absorbers. All Starions got a modified front alr dam and stainless steel exhaust system for 1988.

I.D. DATA: Mitsubishi's 17-symbol Vehicle Identification Number is on the upper left of the dashboard, visible through the windshield. Symbols 1-3 denote country of origin, manufacturer, and vehicle type. The next symbol four indicates restraint sytem. Symbols 5-7 identify the model; symbol 8, the engine. Symbol 10 indicates model year; symbol 11, the assembly plant; followed by a six-digit sequential production number.

Model	Body Type & Seating	Engine Type/CID	P.O.E. Price	Weight (lbs.)	Prod. Total
MIRAGE					
	2-dr Hatch-4P	I4/90	6059	1984	Note 1
L	2-dr Hatch-4P	I4/90	7319	2018	Note 1
	4-dr Sedan-4P	I4/90	7859	2095	Note 1
Turbo	2-dr Hatch-4P	I4/97	8479	2172	Note 1
PRECIS					
	2-dr Hatch-4P	I4/90	5195	2130	Note 1
LS	2-dr Hatch-4P	I4/90	6499	2141	Note 1
LS	4-dr Hatch-4P	I4/90	6799	2153	Note 1
CORDIA					
L	2-dr Hatch-4P	I4/122	9759	2337	Note 1
Turbo	2-dr Hatch-4P	I4/110	11329	2458	Note 1
TREDIA					
L	4-dr Sedan-4P	I4/122	9369	2370	Note 1
LS	4-dr Sedan-4P	I4/122	10379	2469	Note 1
Turbo	4-dr Sedan-4P	I4/110	10429	2469	Note 1
GALANT (1987)					
Luxury	4-dr Sedan-5P	I4/143	13999	2811	Note 1
Sigma	4-dr Sedna-5P	V6/181	16199	2811	Note 1
GALANT SIGMA (1988)					
	4-dr Sedan-5P	V6/181	16549	2811	Note 1
STARION					
LE	2-dr Coupe-2+2P	I4/156	15469	2988	Note 1
ESI-R	2-dr Coupe-2+2P	I4/156	17989	3087	Note 1

Note 1: A total of 119,816 Mitsubishis were sold in the U.S. during 1987, followed by 113,492 in 1988 (including Mighty Max pickup trucks, Montero sport-utility vehicles, vans, and wagons).

Price Note: Figures above were valid in 1987. Starion ESI, which replaced the LE in 1988, sold for $17,129, while the ESI-R rose in that year to $19,789.

ENGINE DATA: BASE FOUR (Mirage, Precis): Inline, overhead-cam four-cylinder. Cast iron block and light alloy head. **Displacement:** 89.6 cu. in. (1468 cc). **Bore & Stroke:** 2.97 x 3.23 in. (75.4 x 82 mm). **Compression Ratio:** 9.4:1. **Brake Horsepower:** 68 at 5500 rpm. **Torque:** 85 lbs.-ft. at 3500 rpm. Five main bearings. Two-barrel carburetor.

BASE FOUR (Mirage Turbo): Inline, overhead-cam four-cylinder. Cast iron block and light alloy head. **Displacement:** 97.4 cu. in. (1597 cc). **Bore & Stroke:** 3.03 x 3.39 in. (77 x 86 mm). **Compression Ratio:** 7.6:1. **Brake Horsepower:** 105 at 5500 rpm. **Torque:** 122 lbs.-ft. at 3500 rpm. Five main bearings. Throttle-body fuel injection.

BASE FOUR (Cordia, Tredia): Inline, overhead-cam four-cylinder. Cast iron block and light alloy head. **Displacement:** 122 cu. in. (1997 cc). **Bore & Stroke:** 3.35 x 3.46 in. (85 x 88 mm). **Compression Ratio:** 8.5:1. **Brake Horsepower:** 88 at 5000 pm. **Torque:** 108 lbs.-ft. at 3500 rpm. Five main bearings. Two-barrel carburetor.

BASE TURBO FOUR (Cordia/Tredia Turbo): Inline, overhead-cam four-cylinder with turbocharger. Cast iron block and light alloy head. **Displacement:** 109.5 cu. in. (1795 cc). **Bore & Stroke:** 3.17 x 3.46 in. (81 x 88 mm). **Compression Ratio:** 7.5:1. **Brake Horsepower:** 116 at 5500 pm. **Torque:** 129 lbs.-ft. at 3000 rpm. Five main bearings. Throttle-body fuel injection.

BASE FOUR (Galant): Inline, overhead-cam four-cylinder. Cast iron block and light alloy head. **Displacement:** 143 cu. in. (2350 cc). **Bore & Stroke:** 3.41 x 3.94 in. (86.6 x 100 mm). **Compression Ratio:** 8.5:1. **Brake Horsepower:** 110 at 4500 rpm. **Torque:** 138 lbs.-ft. at 3500 rpm. Five main bearings. Multi-point fuel injection.

BASE V-6 (Galant Sigma): Overhead-cam, "vee" type six-cylinder. **Displacement:** 181 cu. in. (2972 cc). **Bore & Stroke:** 3.59 x 2.99 in. (91 x 76 mm). **Compression Ratio:** 8.9:1. **Brake Horsepower:** 142 at 5000 rpm. **Torque:** 168 lbs.-ft. at 2500 rpm. Five main bearIngs. Multi-point fuel injection.

BASE FOUR (1987 Starion): Inline, overhead-cam four-cylinder with turbocharger. Cast iron block and light alloy head. **Displacement:** 156 cu. in. (2555 cc). **Bore & Stroke:** 3.59 x 3.86 in. (91.1 x 98 mm). **Compression Ratio:** 7.0:1. **Brake Horsepower:** 145 at 5000 rpm. **Torque:** 185 lbs.-ft. at 2500 rpm. Five main bearings. Fuel injection (twin injectors).

BASE FOUR (1987 Starion ESI-R): Same as 2555-cc turbo four, but with intercooler. **Brake Horsepower:** 176 at 5000 rpm. **Torque:** 223 lbs.-ft. at 2500 rpm.

BASE FOUR (1988 Starion ESI, ESI-R): Same as intercooled turbo above, except -- **Brake Horsepower:** 188 at 5000 rpm. **Torque:** 234 lbs.-ft. at 2500 rpm.

CHASSIS DATA: Wheelbase: (Mirage/Precis) 93.7 in.; (Cordia/Tredia) 96.3 in.; (Galant) 102.4 in.; (Starion) 95.9 in. **Overall Length:** (Mirage hatch) 157.3 in.; (Mirage sed) 169.1 in.; (Precis) 160.9 in.; (Cordia) 173.0 in.; (Tredia) 172.4 in.; (Galant) 183.1 in.; (Starion) 173.2 in. **Height:** (Mirage) 53.5 in.; (Precis) 54.1 in.; (Cordia) 49.4 in.; (Tredia) 51.6 in.; (Galant) 51.6 in.; (Starion) 50.2 in. **Width:** (Mirage hatch) 63.8 in.; (Mirage sed) 64.4 in.; (Precis) 63.1 in.; (Cordia) 65.4 in.; (Tredia) 65.4 in.; (Galant) 66.7 in.; (Starion) 66.8 in. **Front Tread:** (Mirage) 55.5 in.; (Precis) 54.1 in.; (Cordia/Tredia) 55.5 in.; (Galant) 56.9 in.; (Starion) 55.5 in.; (Starion ESI-R) 57.7 in. **Rear Tread:** (Mirage/Precis) 52.8 in.; (Cordia/Tredia) 54.1 in.; (Galant) 55.3 in.; (Starion) 55.1 in.; (Starion ESI-R) 57.3 in.

TECHNICAL: Layout: front-engine, front-drive except (Starion) front-engine, rear-drive. **Transmission:** (Precis, 1987 Mirage) four- or five-speed manual; (Cordia/Tredia/Starion, 1988 Mirage) five-speed manual; (Galant) five-speed manual or four-speed automatic. Three-speed automatic optional, except four-speed automatic on Starion. **Steering:** rack and pinion except (Starion) recirculating ball. **Suspension (front):** MacPherson struts with coil springs and anti-roll bar. **Suspension (rear):** (Mirage/Cordia/Tredia) independent with trailing arms and coil springs; (Galant) beam axle with trailing arms, coil springs and anti-roll bar; (Starion) independent with MacPherson struts, coil springs and anti-roll bar. **Brakes:** front disc, rear drum except (Starion, Galant Sigma) front/rear disc. **Body Construction:** steel unibody.

MAJOR OPTIONS: Automatic transmission: Cordia L ($430); Tredia L ($420); Mirage ($410); Mirage Turbo ($630); Starion LE ($570). ECS package: Galant ($663). Air conditioning: Cordia/Tredia ($698); Mirage ($677). Sunroof: Cordia/Starlon ($278). Power sunroof: Galant ($530); Mirage Turbo ($461). Leather seats: Galant ($609); Starion ($389). Power windows: Cordia ($142). Cast alloy wheels: Mirage Turbo ($265).

Note: Option prices shown were valid in 1987.

ADDITIONAL MODELS: Mitsubishi continued to market 2WD and 4WD versions of its Mighty Max pickup truck in the U.S., along with a Montero two-door sport-utility vehicle and a minivan.
Manufacturer: Mitsubishi Motors Corp., Tokyo, Japan.
Distributor: Mitsubishi Motor Sales of America Inc., Fountain Valley, California.

1989-90 MITSUBISHI

1989 Mitsubishi Mirage hatchback.

MIRAGE — FOUR — Restyling wasn't the only change to the Mirage for 1989. The new version no longer was closely tied mechanically to the Korean-built Precis. The base two-door hatchback carried a fuel-injected 1.5-liter four that produced 81 horsepower, and a standard three-speed automatic transmission. The notchback four-door sedan had a standard five-speed manual gearbox, with automatic optional. A larger twin-cam Turbo engine only came under hatchback hoods, churning out 135 horsepower—considerably more than the prior Turbo, though displacement was identical. Wheelbase was 96.7 inches for the sedan, versus 93.9 inches for the hatchback. The same hatchback was sold as a Dodge/Plymouth Colt, while the sedan could be purchased under Chrysler's Eagle nameplate, as a Summit. For 1990, the Turbo edition was dropped and a "Value Leader" model added, along with "exe Special Edition" variants and a sporty RS version.

447

PRECIS — FOUR — Essentially a carryover from 1988, the Korean-built hatchbacks added an audible brake-wear indicator and got a few interior changes for 1989. The 1.5-liter engine still used a carburetor that year, but switched to fuel injection for 1990, adding 13 horsepower. That engine was the same as the one used in the Mirage.

1989 Mitsubishi Galant GS four-door sedan.

GALANT — FOUR — The name was old but the car was new. Replacing the former Tredia was a larger Galant compact four-door sedan, powered by a 2.0-liter four that produced 102 horsepower. A five-speed manual gearbox was standard on the base model; four-speed automatic on the LS. A sporty GS edition carried a twin-cam (16-valve) version of the 2.0-liter engine, rated 135 horsepower. Early examples of the GS came only with manual shift, and it had four-wheel disc brakes and Active-Electronically Controlled Suspension. Anti-lock braking was optional on the GS. All Galants had power steering, a tilt steering column, reclining front bucket seats, and tachometer. The LS and GS added power door locks, windows and mirrors. An all-wheel-drive Galant GSX was added for 1990, powered by the GS engine with five-speed gearbox.

SIGMA — V-6 — What had formerly been called the Galant, then the Galant Sigma, was now just plain Sigma. Wheelbase was the same as the new version of the Galant (above), but it carried a 3.0-liter V-6 engine and more luxury equipment. Anti-lock brakes were available either alone, or as part of a Eurotech Package that also included an Electronically Controlled Suspension. The driver's power windows added an automatic-down feature for 1990. A driver's airbag was added for 1990.

STARION — FOUR — Only the ESI-R remained for the rear-drive Starion's final (1989) season in the Mitsubishi lineup. This time, it came only with a five-speed manual gearbox and the 188-bhp turbocharged/intercooled engine.

1990 Mitsubishi Sigma four-door sedan.

I.D. DATA: Mitsubishi's 17-symbol Vehicle Identification Number is on the upper left of the dashboard, visible through the windshield. Symbols 1-3 denote country of origin, manufacturer, and vehicle type. The next symbol four indicates restraint sytem. Symbols 5-7 identify the model; symbol 8, the engine. Symbol 10 indicates model year; symbol 11, the assembly plant; followed by a six-digit sequential production number.

Model	Body Type & Seating	Engine Type/CID	P.O.E. Price	Weight (lbs.)	Prod. Total
MIRAGE					
	2-dr Hatch-5P	I4/90	9159	N/A	Note 1
	4-dr Sedan-5P	I4/90	8859	2095	Note 1
LS	4-dr Sedan-5P	I4/90	10209	2095	Note 1
Turbo	2-dr Hatch-5P	I4/97	11969	2172	Note 1
PRECIS					
	2-dr Hatch-4/5P	I4/90	5499	2130	Note 1
RS	2-dr Hatch-4/5P	I4/90	6699	2135	Note 1
LS	2-dr Hatch-4/5P	I4/90	7349	2141	Note 1
LS	4-dr Hatch-4/5P	I4/90	7599	2153	Note 1
GALANT					
	4-dr Sedan-5P	I4/122	10971	2512	Note 1
LS	4-dr Sedan-5P	I4/122	13579	2512	Note 1
GS	4-dr Sedan-5P	I4/122	15269	2710	Note 1
SIGMA					
	4-dr Sedan-5P	V6/181	17069	2811	Note 1
STARION (1989)					
ESI-R	2-dr Coupe-2 + 2P	I4/156	19859	2988	Note 1

Note 1: A total of 150,476 Mitsubishis were sold in the U.S. during 1989 (including Mighty Max pickup trucks, Montero sport-utility vehicles, vans, and 32,018 early Eclipse models). A total of 99,630 Mitsubishi imports were sold in the U.S. during 1990 (including 1,542 early 3000GT sports cars).

Price Note: Figures above were valid in 1989.

448

1990 Mitsubishi Galant GS four-door sedan.

ENGINE DATA: BASE FOUR (Mirage, 1990 Precis): Inline, overhead-cam four-cylinder. Cast iron block and light alloy head. **Displacement:** 89.6 cu. in. (1468 cc). **Bore & Stroke:** 2.97 x 3.23 in. (75.4 x 82 mm). **Compression Ratio:** 9.4:1. **Brake Horsepower:** 81 at 5500 rpm. **Torque:** 91 lbs.-ft. at 3000 rpm. Five main bearings. Multi-point fuel injection.

BASE FOUR (1989 Mirage Turbo): Inline, overhead-cam four-cylinder. Cast iron block and light alloy head. **Displacement:** 97.4 cu. in. (1597 cc). **Bore & Stroke:** 3.03 x 3.39 in. (77 x 86 mm). **Compression Ratio:** 7.6:1. **Brake Horsepower:** 135 at 6000 rpm. **Torque:** 141 lbs.-ft. at 3000 rpm. Five main bearings. Multi-point fuel injection.

BASE FOUR (1989 Precis): Inline, overhead-cam four-cylinder. Cast iron block and light alloy head. **Displacement:** 89.6 cu. in. (1468 cc). **Bore & Stroke:** 2.97 x 3.23 in. (75.4 x 82 mm). **Compression Ratio:** 9.4:1. **Brake Horsepower:** 68 at 5500 rpm. **Torque:** 85 lbs.-ft. at 3500 rpm. Five main bearings. Two-barrel carburetor.

BASE FOUR (Galant): Inline, overhead-cam four-cylinder. Cast iron block and light alloy head. **Displacement:** 122 cu. in. (1997 cc). **Bore & Stroke:** 3.35 x 3.46 in. (85 x 88 mm). **Compression Ratio:** 8.5:1. **Brake Horsepower:** 102 at 5000 pm. **Torque:** 116 lbs.-ft. at 4500 rpm. Five main bearings. Multi-point fuel injection.

BASE FOUR (Galant GS): Inline, dual-overhead-cam four-cylinder. Cast iron block and light alloy head. **Displacement:** 122 cu. in. (1997 cc). **Bore & Stroke:** 3.35 x 3.46 in. (85 x 88 mm). **Compression Ratio:** 9.0:1. **Brake Horsepower:** 135 at 6000 pm. **Torque:** 125 lbs.-ft. at 5000 rpm. Five main bearings. Multi-point fuel injection.

BASE V-6 (Sigma): Overhead-cam, "vee" type six-cylinder. **Displacement:** 181 cu. in. (2972 cc). **Bore & Stroke:** 3.59 x 2.99 in. (91 x 76 mm). **Compression Ratio:** 8.9:1. **Brake Horsepower:** 142 at 5000 rpm. **Torque:** 168 lbs.-ft. at 2500 rpm. Five main bearings. Multi-point fuel injection.

BASE FOUR (1989 Starion): Inline, overhead-cam four-cylinder with turbocharger. Cast iron block and light alloy head. **Displacement:** 156 cu. in. (2555 cc). **Bore & Stroke:** 3.59 x 3.86 in. (91.1 x 98 mm). **Compression Ratio:** 7.0:1. **Brake Horsepower:** 188 at 5000 rpm. **Torque:** 234 lbs.-ft. at 2500 rpm. Five main bearings. Fuel injection (twin injectors).

1990 Mitsubishi Mirage four-door sedan.

1990 Mitsubishi Eclipse GSX coupe.

CHASSIS DATA: Wheelbase: (Mirage hatch) 93.9 in.; (Mirage sed) 96.7 in.; (Precis) 93.7 in.; (Galant) 102.4 in.; (Sigma) 102.4 in.; (Starion) 95.9 in. Overall Length: (Mirage hatch) 158.7 in.; (Mirage sed) 170.1 in.; (Precis) 160.9 in.; (Galant) 183.9 in.; (Sigma) 185.8 in.; (Starion) 173.2 in. Height: (Mirage hatch) 52.0 in.; (Mirage sed) 52.8 in.; (Precis) 54.1 in.; (Galant) 53.5 in.; (Sigma) 51.6 in.; (Starion) 50.2 in. Width: (Mirage) 65.7 in.; (Precis) 63.1 in.; (Galant) 66.7 in.; (Sigma) 66.7 in.; (Starion) 68.3 in. Front Tread: (Mirage) 56.3 in.; (Precis) 54.1 in.; (Galant) 57.5 in.; (Sigma) 56.9 in.; (Starion) 57.7 in. Rear Tread: (Mirage) 56.3 in.; (Precis) 52.8 in.; (Galant) 57.5 in.; (Sigma) 55.7 in.; (Starion) 57.3 in.

TECHNICAL: Layout: front-engine, front-drive except (Starion) front-engine, rear-drive. Transmission: (Precis) four- or five-speed manual; (Sigma) four-speed automatic; (others) five-speed manual. Three-speed automatic available (standard on base Mirage hatchback), except four-speed automatic on Galant/Starion. Steering: rack and pinion except (Starion) recirculating ball. Brakes: front disc, rear drum except (Sigma/Starion) front/rear disc. Body Construction: steel unibody.

ADDITIONAL MODELS: Mitsubishi continued to market 2WD and 4WD versions of its Mighty Max pickup truck in the U.S., along with a Montero two-door sport-utility vehicle and a minivan.

Manufacturer: Mitsubishi Motors Corp., Tokyo, Japan.
Distributor: Mitsubishi Motor Sales of America Inc., Cypress, California.

POSTSCRIPT: Highlight of the 1990 Mitsubishi was not a Japanese model, but the new Eclipse, built at a new Diamond-Star plant in Normal, Illinois, as part of a joint venture with Chrysler (which had owned a substantial share of Mitsubishi for some years). The front-drive Eclipse hatchback sport coupe actually debuted in January 1989, as a very early '90 model. An all-wheel-drive version was added shortly before the start of the regular 1990 model year. Styling came from Chrysler designers, but the mechanical components were Mitsubishi-based. Base and GS models were powered by a 1.8-liter four-cylinder engine, rated 92 horsepower. A 2.0-liter twin-cam four went into the GS DOHC, rated 135 horsepower. That 2.0-liter four got a turbocharger and intercooler to power the GS DOHC Turbo and the AWD GSX, producing 190-195 bhp. Eclipses attracted considerable attention (and plenty of customers) in their first year, as did the closely-related versions marketed by Chrysler as the Plymouth Laser and Eagle Talon.

If an Eclipse Turbo wasn't exciting enough, Mitsubishi had even greater thrills in store back in Japan, in the form of the 3000GT sports car. Introduced as a 1991 model, along with the similar (but by no means identical) Dodge Stealth, the sleek, low 3000GT sent Mitsubishi toward the near-supercar league, at least with the 300-horsepower twin-turbo VR-4 version that sold for $30,800 as the 1991 season began.

MONTEVERDI

Peter Monteverdi, a BMW automobile importer and manufacturer of M.B.M. racing cars, put Switzerland on the motoring map in 1967 by announcing development of a new high-performance sports car. Like many another supercar of that day, the new semi-fastback GT coupe displayed at the 1967 Frankfurt show blended Italian styling with American V-8 power, but stood atop a tubular-steel chassis designed by Monteverdi himself. Body styling was performed by Pietro Frua, working from ideas issued by Monteverdi. Actual bodies were produced by Fissore (also in Italy), and most components came from outside suppliers. Final assembly took place in the Monteverdi shop at Basle-Binningen. A four-passenger (actually 2+2) coupe soon joined the original two-seater, as did a two-seat 375C cabriolet that debuted in 1969. Monteverdi didn't stop there, but lengthened the chassis to slip under a big sedan body, which qualified as a virtual limousine. A 400-bhp version, called 400SS, also had been announced early on.

By 1971, a mid-engined 450SS Hai debuted, with Chrysler Hemi power and a five-speed ZF manual gearbox, capable of 160-180 mph speeds. Then, early in 1975, a shortened cabriolet called the Palm Beach Spider was introduced. Monteverdis were mainly sold in Europe, with little effort made to tempt U.S. customers. Tightening Federal regulations at this time created a major hurdle for such specialty manufacturers anyway, so few Monteverdis ever managed to cross the Atlantic.

1967-77 MONTEVERDI

1971 Monteverdi two-door.

375 SERIES — V-8 — The two-seat 375S carried coil springs up front and a De Dion axle out back, with a 440-cid (7210-cc) Chrysler V-8 under its sloping hood. That standard V-8 churned out 375 horsepower (SAE gross), which accounted for the car's nomenclature. Also available, however, was a "High Speed Hemi" edition carrying the famed 426-cid Chrysler hemi V-8. Either a four-speed manual or the standard three-speed automatic transmission was available. Most examples had the TorqueFlite unit installed, though a five-speed manual also became available in the 1970s.

The 375S two-seater debuted first, followed by the 375L 2+2, and then the cabriolet. Wheelbase of each model was 105 inches, except for the 375 4 sedan/limo (which measured 125 inches), and the later Palm Beach Spider, which rode a 98-inch wheelbase. Styling features included slim pillars and wide, eggcrate-patterned (large "hole") grilles. The initial 375S coupe had single recessed headlamps and a low grille, while later entries wore quad headlamps.

I.D. DATA: Not available.

Model	Body Type & Seating	Engine Type/CID	P.O.E. Price	Weight (lbs.)	Prod. Total
375 SERIES					
375S	2-dr Coupe-2P	V8/440	N/A	3528	N/A
375L	2-dr Coupe-2+2P	V8/440	N/A	N/A	N/A
375C	2-dr Conv-2P	V8/440	N/A	N/A	N/A
375 4	4-dr Sedan-4/5P	V8/440	N/A	3638	N/A
Palm Beach	2-dr Conv-2P	V8/440	N/A	N/A	N/A
450SS HAI					
450SS	2-dr Coupe-2P	V8/426	N/A	N/A	N/A

Price Note: The basic 375S sold in Britain for 7283 Pounds (Sterling) in 1972.

ENGINE DATA: BASE V-8: 90-degree, overhead-valve "vee" type eight-cylinder (Chrysler). Cast iron block and heads. Displacement: 440 cu. in. (7210 cc). Bore & Stroke: 4.32 x 3.75 in. (109.7 x 95.2 mm). Compression Ratio: 10.1:1. Brake Horsepower: 375 (SAE gross) at 4600 rpm. Torque: 481 lbs.-ft. at 3200 rpm. Five main bearings. Hydraulic valve lifters. Carter four-barrel carburetor.

OPTIONAL HEMI V-8: 90-degree, overhead-valve "vee" type eight-cylinder (Chrysler). Cast iron block and head. Displacement: 426 cu. in. (6974 cc). Bore & Stroke: 4.25 x 3.75 in. (107.9 x 95.2 mm). Compression Ratio: 10.2:1. Brake Horsepower: 450 (SAE gross) at 5000 rpm. Torque: 490 lbs.-ft. at 4000 rpm. Five main bearings. Hydraulic valve lifters. Two Carter four-barrel carburetors.

CHASSIS DATA: Wheelbase: 104.7 in. except (sedan) 125.2 in.; (Palm Beach) 98 in. Overall Length: (375S) 181.1 in.; (375L) 189 in. (375 4) 209 in. Height: (375S) 50 in.; (375 4) 52.4 in. Width: 70.7 in. Front Tread: 59.1 in. Rear Tread: 57.5 in. Standard Tires: GR70x15.

TECHNICAL: Layout: front-engine, rear-drive. Transmission: four-speed manual or three-speed TorqueFlite automatic. Steering: ZF worm and roller (power assisted). Suspension (front): upper/lower A-arms, coil springs and anti-roll bar. Suspension (rear): De Dion axle with Watt linkage, trailing radius arms and coil springs. Brakes: front/rear disc. Body Construction: steel body on box-section space frame.

PERFORMANCE: Top Speed: (375 series) 152-162 mph. Acceleration (0-60 mph): about 6.3 sec.

Manufacturer: Automobile Monteverdi, Basle-Binningen, Switzerland.

HISTORY: Production came to a virtual halt in the mid-1970s. By 1977, Peter Monteverdi gave up on the car that bore his name and instead took up the production of Fissore-styled Sierras (modified Dodge Aspen sedans) and Safari four-wheel-drive vehicles (similar to the Range Rover). A subsequent Sahara 4WD vehicle used International Scout running gear. Palm Beach Spiders remained available on special order for a time, but by 1981, only the Sierra and Safari were listed for sale.

MORETTI

Organized for automobile production just after World War II, in 1945, by Giovanni Moretti, this small Italian sports-car firm turned out small numbers of hand-built roadsters and coupes. Moretti himself had been involved with motorcy-

cle design and specialty auto work for two decades before turning to sports cars. His first postwar effort was a 250-cc two-cylinder model, followed by a 350-cc engine, then four-cylinder powerplants in two sizes. In addition to the 600, which used a single-overhead-cam engine, the company produced a considerably more powerful 750 Gran Sport with dual-overhead-cam powerplant and twin carbs; and later, a 1200 GT series. Numerous victories in Class H (under 750 cc) came the company's way during the 1950s. That list of wins included both first and second place in the 10,000-mile Transafrican Rallye. The company also built a rear-engined Monoposto single-seat race car that weighed only 1,000 pounds and was capable of 108 mph; plus a broad variety of small trucks and vans. When Moretti coupes began to arrive in the U.S. around 1954, they created "an immediate sensation," according to *Sports Cars Illustrated,* because of their "small size, amazing performance, and beautiful Ghia body."

1950-58 MORETTI

1954 Moretti Model 600 convertible.

600 — FOUR — Powered by a single-overhead-cam four-cylinder engine, the handbuilt compact came in coupe and convertible form, along with a station wagon. Riding a short (82-inch) wheelbase, Morettis looked short overall but had space for four passengers. Up front was an oval grille made up of horizontal bars, with a horizontal hood lid. Small round parking lamps stood below the single headlamps. Front and rear fenders held short horizontal trim strips.

750 GRAN SPORT — FOUR — A pair of two-door body styles were available with the larger twin-cam engine: a Berlinetta coupe and open Barchetta. Coupes had a fastback roofline, front vent windows, rear quarter windows, and a wraparound back window. The 750-cc Morettis became popular for racing in the U.S.

1200 — FOUR — A large-engine Moretti joined its smaller mates later, offered only in hardtop coupe form.

I.D. DATA: Serial number is on left side of firewall. Engine number is on right side of block.

Model	Body Type & Seating	Engine Type/CID	P.O.E. Price	Weight (lbs.)	Prod. Total
600	2-dr Conv-2P	I4/36	2700	1225	Note 1
600	2-dr Berlina-4P	I4/36	N/A	1200	Note 1
600	2-dr Sta Wag-4P	I4/36	N/A	1300	Note 1
750	2-dr Rds-2P	I4/46	4195	1210	Note 1
750	2-dr Coupe-2P	I4/46	4195	1240	Note 1
1200	2-dr Rds-2P	I4/74	N/A	N/A	Note 1
1200	2-dr HT Cpe-5/6P	I4/74	4495	2156	Note 1

Note 1: A total of 116 Morettis were produced in 1958 alone.

Price Note: 600 price is estimated; 750/1200 prices are for 1957 models.

ENGINE DATA: BASE FOUR (600): Inline, overhead-cam four-cylinder. **Displacement:** 36.11 cu. in. (592 cc). **Bore & Stroke:** 2.26 x 2.22 in. (57 x 56 mm). **Compression Ratio:** 7.0:1. **Brake Horsepower:** 27 at 4250 rpm.

BASE FOUR (750): Inline, overhead-cam four-cylinder. **Displacement:** 45.57 cu. in. (747 cc). **Bore & Stroke:** 2.36 x 2.60 in. (60 x 66 mm). **Compression Ratio:** 7:1 or 7.5:1. **Brake Horsepower:** 51-52 at 6000 rpm (58 at 7000 with twin carbs). One or two carburetors.

BASE FOUR (1200): Inline, overhead-cam four-cylinder. **Displacement:** 73.69 cu. in. (1208 cc). **Bore & Stroke:** 2.83 x 2.91 in. (72 x 74 mm). **Compression Ratio:** 7.5:1. **Brake Horsepower:** 62 at 5500 rpm.

CHASSIS DATA: Wheelbase: (600) 81.9 in.; (750) 83.8 in.; (1200) 95.6 in. **Overall Length:** (600) 132.6 in.; (750) 136 in. **Height:** (600) 54.2 in.; (1200) 55.3 in. **Width:** (600) 51.5 in. **Front Tread:** (600) 42.9 in. **Rear Tread:** (600) 42.9 in. **Standard Tires:** (600) 4.25x15.

TECHNICAL: Layout: front-engine, rear-drive. **Transmission:** four-speed manual. **Suspension (front):** transverse leaf spring (independent). **Suspension (rear):** rigid axle with semi-elliptic leaf springs. **Brakes:** hydraulic, front/rear drum. **Body Construction:** aluminum body on steel frame.

PERFORMANCE: Top Speed: (600) 65 mph; (750 Spt) 100 mph; (1200) 112 mph. **Fuel Mileage:** (600) about 40 mpg.

Manufacturer: Fabbrica Automobili Moretti, Turin, Italy.

Distributor: Italia Motors, Los Angeles, California.

HISTORY: Purchasing a Moretti in the mid-1950s wasn't so easy. U.S. customers had to pay at least half the purchase price up front, before the car was built. Custom-built bodies were fitted to the Moretti-built chassis at various companies in the Turin region.

1959-60 MORETTI

750 — FOUR — Tiny round parking lamps remained below the headlamps on later Morettis, but their grilles also contained running lights in their outer segments. The 750 sedan had five vertical bars in its grille, while the coupe had four (and lacked an air intake on its hood). Four different body types were offered: a convertible (Spider), a Turismo GT coupe, a four-door sedan, and a station wagon.

1200 — FOUR — Morettis with the larger four-cylinder engine also continued in production.

I.D. DATA: Serial number is one left side of firewall. Engine number is on right side of block.

Model	Body Type & Seating	Engine Type/CID	P.O.E. Price	Weight (lbs.)	Prod. Total
750	2-dr Conv	I4/46	2745	1612	N/A
750GT	20dr Coupe-2P	I4/46	2495	1640	N/A
750	4-dr Sedan-4P	I4/46	2495	1840	N/A
750	4-dr Sta Wag-4/5P	I4/46	2580	1868	N/A
750	4-dr Sta Wag-6/7P	I4/46	2664	1868	N/A
1200GT	2-dr Spt Conv	I4/73	4345	N/A	N/A

Note: In 1960 a Super Coupe Turismo also was offered, for $2995.

ENGINE DATA: BASE FOUR (750): Inline, overhead-cam four-cylinder. **Displacement:** 45.89 cu. in. (748 cc). **Bore & Stroke:** 2.36 x 2.60 in. (60 x 66 mm). **Compression Ratio:** 7.5:1. **Brake Horsepower:** 35 at 4800 rpm (Spider convertible and Super Coupe, 43 bhp at 4800). One Solex or two-barrel Weber carburetor.

BASE FOUR (750GT): Same as above, but -- **Brake Horsepower:** 55 at 6500 rpm. **Torque:** 70 lbs.-ft. at 3200 rpm.

OPTIONAL FOUR: Same as above, but -- **Brake Horsepower:** 75 at 8000 rpm. Two Weber two-barrel carburetors.

BASE FOUR (1200GT): Inline, overhead-cam four-cylinder. **Displacement:** 73.4 cu. in. (1204 cc). **Bore & Stroke:** 2.83 x 2.91 in. (72 x 74 mm). **Brake Horsepower:** 80 at 7000 rpm.

CHASSIS DATA: Wheelbase: 84.5 in. **Overall Length:** 141.75-145 in. **Height:** 57 in. **Width:** 59 in. **Tread:** 46.5 in. **Standard Tires:** 5.20x12; (750GT) 4.25x15; (1200GT) 5.20x14.

TECHNICAL: Layout: front-engine, rear-drive. **Transmission:** four-speed manual. **Steering:** worm and sector shaft. **Suspension (front):** independent; transverse leaf spring with upper/lower control arms. **Suspension (rear):** two transverse leaf springs. **Brakes:** hydraulic, front/rear drum. **Body Construction:** unibody.

PERFORMANCE: Top Speed: (750) 76 mph; (Turismo) 88-92 mph; (1200) 110 mph. **Acceleration (0-60 mph):** N/A (Turismo, 0-45 mph in 12.4 seconds). **Fuel Mileage:** (750) 40; (1200) 24 mpg.

Manufacturer: Fabbrica Automobili Moretti SpA, Turin, Italy.

Distributor: J.F.R. Company, North Attleboro, Massachusetts.

POSTSCRIPT: Although production of Morettis faded after 1960, they continued to be listed in U.S. directories through the early '60s. In later years, the Moretti company built conversions of Fiat models, including off-road cars and open variants of Fiat sedans.

MORGAN

H.F.S. Morgan was a son and grandson of clergymen, but he turned instead to engineering. After graduating from engineering college, he apprenticed at the Great Western Railway as a mechanical engineer. Rather than choose the railroad as a career, he opened a garage in 1906 at Malvern Link in Worcestershire, England--a site that would remain the home of Morgan for decades to come. After a short flurry as a sales agent and rental-car provider, Morgan turned to experiments with his own designs, starting with a motorcycle in 1908. By 1909, he'd built a three-wheeled, single-seat motorcar with vee-twin Peugeot engine, with

an eye toward the tax benefits of lightweight vehicles. Power approached the single rear wheel through a driveshaft within a tube, which also formed the chassis of the car. Dog clutches and chain drives made up the two-speed transmission, which operated in forward only. A sliding-pillar setup with coil springs, at the end of a solid axle, was his choice for a front suspension. Not only was this one of the first forms of independent front suspension, its basic design would continue onto modern-day Morgans.

H.F.S. set up Morgan Motor Co. Ltd. in 1910, displaying two cars at the Olympia motorcycle show late that year. Those didn't create a stir, but the two-seater he developed the following year attracted greater interest. Harrods, the famed London department store, became the first agent for Morgan motorcars.

By the time World War I erupted, Morgan was turning out nearly a thousand cars annually, aided by victories in trials and races. In 1912, H.F.S. Morgan himself had gained the One-hour Record at Brooklands by traveling 59.8 miles in 60 minutes. A prototype four-wheeler was built during the war, but when peace returned, Morgan stuck strictly with three-wheelers into the mid-1930s. He did create a four-seat model, however, first offered in 1919. A French version also was produced, under license, called the Darmont. Through the 1920s, Morgan added electric starting, front-wheel brakes and other improvements, as well as more power from their vee-twin, motorcycle-based engines. In addition to their other appealing points, Morgans were inexpensive, the price falling to only 75 Pounds (Sterling) in the early Depression years.

Morgan's first four-wheeler, the 4/4, was announced at the end of 1935--a fortuituous choice, since three-wheelers no longer were selling so strongly. An 1122-cc Coventry-Climax four-cylinder engine powered the first four-wheelers, replaced shortly before World War II broke out by a 1267-cc Standard four. A drophead coupe was introduced in November 1938, according to Ken Hill in *The Morgan: 75 Years on the Road,* and 61 of those were built (including the prototype) before the war began.

Production resumed late in 1945, with most Morgans going to the U.S. and other export markets rather than remaining at home. Neither as quick nor as agile as the MG TC/TD of that day, the Morgan was similar in character and generally appealed to the same sort of driver--those willing to exchange a comfortable ride and luxuries for superior handling and outright enjoyment. Among other idiosyncracies, Morgan retained its wooden framework under the steel body panels, at a time when virtually all other manufacturers had eliminated wood from their vehicles. A new Plus Four model, which didn't look much different from the 4/4 but carried a bigger and more powerful Standard Vanguard engine, emerged in 1950. Less than two years later, too, three-wheeler production came to a halt.

A Ford engine powered the replacement for the original 4/4, which returned in Series II form in 1955 as the lower-cost Morgan, complementing the Plus Four. The latter model switched to an engine from the Triumph TR2, and would later borrow the evolving powerplants from the TR3 and TR4.

Production of the decidedly different Plus Four Plus, with a modern-style coupe body, began by 1964 but only a handful were built. Tightening Federal regulations in the U.S. sent Morgan away from that market after 1966. Two years later, a V-8 engine debuted in the Plus 8. Based on a Buick powerplant (and also installed in Rovers), that version was acceptable for the U.S. market in the 1970s. Fuel injection was added to the V-8 in 1984, and mid-1980s models came with a choice of Ford or Fiat engines. Meanwhile, U.S. regulations evicted Morgan from the import market once again, except for propane conversions that were created by an American firm. On the whole, Morgans produced in recent years have remained surprisingly simi-lar in shape and construction--and traditional "feel"--to that first 4/4 of the mid-1930s. That slowness to change is undoubtedly a major reason why this throwback to the era of "real" sports cars has had such a hard time meeting modern-day safety/emissions standards.

1945-50 MORGAN

1948 Morgan 4/4 drophead coupe.

4/4 — SERIES I — FOUR — Morgan's initial postwar model had actually been introduced a decade earlier, at the height of the Depression, in 1936. A total of 824 examples of the first four-wheel Morgan sports roadster had been built before the war. Like the three-wheelers that had first brought Morgan fame, the four-wheeled 4/4 adopted the traditional design and engineering and would keep many of those details for years--indeed decades--to come. That included Morgan's sliding-pillar front suspension and Z-section frame side members. Upright in profile, traditionally-styled in the manner of 1930s sports cars, the 4/4 came as an open roadster or drophead coupe (convertible), the latter with a full top. Separately-mounted headlamps and fenders were used. The wood-framed body was produced at the Morgan facility. Although prewar examples had carried Coventry-Climax engines, the first postwar versions used four-cylinder powerplants from the Standard Motor Company (known as the "Standard Special"). The 1267-cc (77-cid) overhead-valve engine produced 40 horsepower at 4300 rpm, which was enough for a top speed around 70 mph. Wheelbase was 92 inches, and each two-passenger model measured less than 140 inches overall. A three-spoke steering wheel was added during 1947.

I.D. DATA: Chassis serial number is stamped on the crossmember beneath front seats. Engine number is stamped on the left of the block. Serial number begins with prefix 'Q.' Serial number range (1945-50): 1000-2090.

Model	Body Type & Seating	Engine Type/CID	P.O.E. Price	Weight (lbs.)	Prod. Total
4/4					
I	2-dr Rds-2P	I4/77	N/A	1568	Note 1
I	2-dr Rds-2 + 2P	I4/77	N/A	1568	Note 1
I	2-dr Dhd Cpe-2P	I4/77	N/A	1568	Note 1

Note 1: Approximately 578 Morgan 4/4s were produced from 1946-50, in addition to the 824 built before World War II.

Weight Note: Figure shown is average for all body styles.

ENGINE DATA: BASE FOUR: Inline, overhead-valve four-cylinder (Standard Special). Cast iron block with replaceable cylinder liners. **Displacement:** 77 cu. in. (1267 cc). **Bore & Stroke:** 2.50 x 3.94 in. (63.5 x 100 mm). **Compression Ratio:** 7.1:1. **Brake Horsepower:** 40 at 4300 rpm. Three main bearings. Solid valve lifters. Solex carburetor.

CHASSIS DATA: Wheelbase: 92 in. **Overall Length:** (rds) 136 in.; (conv) 139.5 in. **Width:** 55 in. **Front Tread:** 45 in. **Rear Tread:** 45 in. **Standard Tires:** 4.50x17 (or 5.00x16).

TECHNICAL: Layout: front-engine, rear-drive. **Transmission:** four-speed manual. **Standard Final Drive Ratio:** 4.72:1. **Suspension (front):** sliding pillars with coil springs. **Suspension (rear):** rigid axle with semi-elliptic leaf springs. **Brakes:** hydraulic, front/rear drum. **Body Construction:** steel body with wood framing, on steel chassis.

PERFORMANCE: Top Speed: about 70 mph.

PRODUCTION/SALES: Less than half a dozen Morgans were known to have been sold in the U.S. during 1948-49.

ADDITIONAL MODELS: A small number of three-wheeled Morgans were built after World War II, in three versions. One series used a Matchless engine, produced mainly for export; the others carried Ford engines. Ken Gross explained in *Special Interest Autos* (1978) that a final shipment of 10 MX4 Super Sports was sent to Australia, made up from leftover parts. The FJ-type three-wheelers remained officially available until 1952. The heyday of the fabulous Morgan three-wheelers, however, was back in the 1930s.

Manufacturer: The Morgan Motor Co. Ltd., Malvern Link, Worcestershire, England.

HISTORY: Production was slow to resume after the war, partly due to steel restrictions in Britain. Ken Hill, author of *The Morgan: 75 Years on the Road,* explains that a "Worth Waiting For" ad appeared early in 1948, indicating that Morgan would be ready with cars for the Motor Show in October of that year. The new Plus Four, intended to replace the 4/4, debuted at the Earls Court Show in October 1950; see next listing for details.

1951-54 MORGAN

1954 Morgan Plus Four two-door roadster.

1952 Morgan roadster.

PLUS FOUR — FOUR — A little bigger and a lot more powerful than its 4/4 predecessor, the Plus Four carried on the familiar Morgan construction technique of steel body panels over a wooden framework, all atop a ladder-type steel chassis with "Z-section" side members. As before, the bodies themselves were crafted at the Morgan facility, but almost all other components came from outside suppliers. The new roadster rode a 96-inch wheelbase and carried a 2088-cc Standard-Triumph overhead-valve four-cylinder engine (as in the Standard Vanguard sedan, though modified), rated 68 horsepower. Taking up that power was a Moss four-speed manual gearbox, similar to that used in the Jaguar XK120. Evolutionary versions of the Standard-Triumph engine would remain under Morgan hoods through the 1950s and '60s, starting with the 1991-cc unit that became available in 1954. Later in the 1950s and into the '60s, the Plus Four would adopt each Triumph engine as it emerged: TR2, then TR3, then TR4.

Appearance was similar to the 4/4, including separate fenders and headlamps, a two-piece center-hinged hood, rear-hinged doors, hidden gas tank, and minimal (but definitely existent) running boards. Removable side curtains gave only rudimentary weather protection. Some examples included a leather hood strap. Twin spare tires were externally-mounted on the early roadsters, though that would change later.

The Morgan front end went through a three-step evolutionary process. Early models retained the flat vertical-bar grille used on the prior 4/4. Then, only a few were built with an intermediate semi-cowled grille, introduced at the 1953 London show. Neither upright like the 4/4's nor curved like its successor would be, it was rather a flat angled-back unit, with a large, bright upper section faired into the nose. In addition, headlamps were semi-faired-in (rather than separately mounted, as before), installed inboard on the fenders. The center foglight that had been standard on initial models was dropped. Next, in 1954, that interim unit was replaced by the curved "cowled" design that would become familiar for decades to come, also with vertical bars (but no surround molding). The center foglight also enjoyed a rebirth. Later models also had a smoother tail and more sloping nose, as well as the semi-faired-in headlamps. All body styles would also switch in the mid-1950s to a single spare tire, abandoning the traditional dual spares at the rear that appeared on 1950-54 models. Each version displayed louvers on its hood. Inside, the later models added a 6000-rpm tachometer, but lacked a glove compartment. Turn signals were optional. Plus Four bodies were normally steel, but aluminum bodies were available on special order.

Morgan's model lineup consisted of a two-seat roadster, a 2+2 roadster, two-seat drophead coupe (convertible) and, for a brief period starting in 1951, a 2+2 convertible. The extra seats were possible because of the car's added length, but were suitable for no more than "occasional" occupancy. Those convertible tops could be positioned half-open. The suspension was unchanged: sliding pillars with coil springs up front, and a rigid rear axle with underslung semi-elliptic leaf springs.

Standard body colors available in 1952, as described in the brochure issued at that year's London Show, included Black, British Racing Green, Nile Blue, and Carnation Red. Upholstery was black. Other body and upholstery colors were available at a modest extra charge (5 Pounds Sterling in 1952). The instrument panel with polished walnut surround contained a speedometer and electric clock on the driver's side, and other gauges on the passenger side. The drophead coupe (convertible) came with detachable side curtains. Open models could run with the windshield folded flat. The Two-Seater Sports model still had twin spare wheels/tires mounted on the back, and a quick-action gas filler neck in the luggage area behind the seats. The four-seater's gas filler was below the rear seats, and it had only one spare tire. The "Drop Head Coupe" (as it was spelled in Morgan literature) included sliding glass windows in its side curtains. The window framework could be removed completely when desired.

1953 Morgan roadster.

452

I.D. DATA: Chassis serial number is stamped on top of crossmember beneath front seat (two-seat) or behind front seat (2+2). Engine number is stamped on a boss on the block, behind the ignition coil. Serial number begins with prefix 'V' and ends with suffix 'ME.' Starting serial number (1950): 2100.

Model	Body Type & Seating	Engine Type/ICD	P.O.E. Price	Weight (lbs.)	Prod. Total
PLUS FOUR					
I	2-dr Rds-2P	I4/127	2450	1680	Note 1
I	2-dr Rds-2 + 2P	I4/127	2500	1736	Note 1
I	2-dr Dhd Cpe-2P	I4/127	2650	1792	Note 1
I	2-dr Dhd Cpe-2 + 2P	I4/127	N/A	N/A	Note 1

Note 1: As many as 4,754 Plus Fours were produced from 1950-68, including approximately 893 with the 2088-cc Vanguard engine (at least 245 of those in this early period).

Price Note: Figures shown were valid in 1954. Prices in Britain in late 1952 were 565 Pounds (Sterling) for the two-seat roadster, 580 for the four-seat roadster, and 620 for the drophead coupe (convertible), not including purchase tax.

ENGINE DATA: BASE FOUR (1950-54): Inline, overhead-valve four-cylinder (Standard Vanguard). Cast iron block and head. **Displacement:** 127.4 cu. in. (2088 cc). **Bore & Stroke:** 3.35 x 3.62 in. (85 x 92 mm). **Compression Ratio:** 6.7:1. **Brake Horsepower:** 68 at 4300 rpm. **Torque:** 108 lbs.-ft. at 2000 rpm. Three main bearings. Solid valve lifters. Solex carburetor.

BASE FOUR (1954-62): Inline, overhead-valve four-cylinder (Triumph TR2). Cast iron block and head. **Displacement:** 121.5 cu. in. (1991 cc). **Bore & Stroke:** 3.27 x 3.62 in. (83 x 92 mm). **Compression Ratio:** 8.5:1. **Brake Horsepower:** 90 at 4800 rpm. **Torque:** 117 lbs.-ft. at 3000 rpm. Three main bearings. Solid valve lifters. Two SU carburetors.

Note: Triumph engine was not offered on the 2+2 drophead coupe.

CHASSIS DATA: Wheelbase: 96 in. **Overall Length:** 140-144 in. **Height:** (early) 47.5 in; (later 2P rds) 52.5 in.; (later 2+2P) 50.5 in. **Width:** 56 in. **Front Tread:** 47 in. **Rear Tread:** 47 in. **Wheel Type:** four-stud pressed steel disc with chromed cap. **Standard Tires:** Dunlop 5.25x16.

TECHNICAL: Layout: front-engine, rear-drive. **Transmission:** Moss four-speed manual. Overall gear ratios: (1st) 13.5:1; (2nd) 8.0:1; (3rd) 5.4:1; (4th) 4.1:1. **Standard Final Drive Ratio:** 4.1:1. **Steering:** Burman Douglas. **Suspension (front):** sliding pillars with coil springs. **Suspension (rear):** rigid axle with semi-elliptic leaf springs. **Brakes:** Girling hydraulic, front/rear drum. **Body Construction:** steel or aluminum body with wood framing, on steel chassis with Z-shaped side members.

PERFORMANCE: Top Speed: 84-86 mph. **Acceleration (0-60 mph):** 14.1-17.9 sec. **Acceleration (quarter-mile):** 19.5 sec.

PRODUCTION/SALES: Approximately 46 Morgans were sold in the U.S. during 1952, and 59 in 1954.

Manufacturer: The Morgan Motor Co. Ltd., Malvern Link, Worcestershire, England.

Distributor: Fergus Motors, New York City; and Angell Motors, Pasadena, California.

HISTORY: The Plus Four debuted at the Earl's Court (London) Motor Show in October 1950, billed as "a small car with a larger engine & a wonderful all round performance." *The Motor* (Britain) praised the Plus Four's "vivid performance" for a "moderately-priced sports car."

By 1951, Morgan had a new distributor on the West Coast: Angell Motors, in Pasadena. Literature at the 1952 London Show described the Morgan as a "comfortable long distance touring car and one that will give a long life of economical and trouble free motoring." The larger Vanguard engine, according to the company, was installed especially to please overseas markets. The Plus Four's chassis frame was claimed to be more rigid, with larger tires on wide-base rims, with greater width and legroom inside, as well as improved weather protection in open models.

An advertisement for the 1954 Plus Four two-seater read: "Going Places—the sporty Morgan Plus 4 gets you there quicker!" Its "sloping radiator shell, faired headlamps, restyled wings (fenders) and streamlined tail/petrol tank unit, give a new look to the 1954 Morgan 2-seater." Delivering "lively performance and delightful handling qualities," driving a Morgan was claimed to offer "sports motoring at its best!"

1955-62 MORGAN

PLUS FOUR — FOUR — Production of the basic Morgan, introduced in 1950, continued with periodic mechanical improvements. The 1991-cc Triumph TR2 engine was standard, as introduced during 1954, producing 90 horsepower. That would evolve into the TR3 and TR4 powerplants as those became available. Morgan literature, however, continued to offer the original Vanguard engine as well. Most Morgans of this period wore light alloy bodies.

As described in the 1955 Morgan catalog, each seat in the Two Seater Tourer (with TR2 engine) had its own pneumatic cushion with a single back squab, while its dashboard held a speedometer and tachometer. Only that two-seat model kept dual spare tires mounted at the rear, and not for long. The Four Seater Tourer had a smaller gas tank

beneath the rear seats, and came with either the Vanguard or TR2 engine. That was also true of the Two Seater Coupe, which had sliding windows that could be removed in a few minutes for fully open motoring. Standard Plus Four equipment included a "Brooklands" race-type steering wheel, badge bar, tachometer, foglamp, bumpers with overriders, and leather (or leatherette) upholstery. Standard 1955 colors were Larch Green, Kingfisher Blue, Ivory, Carnation Red, Ming Blue, and Black. Advertising in the U.S. during 1955 noted the use of larger (16-inch) "Indianapolis" type wheels and higher gear ratios, with upholstery offered in three colors (black, red and beige).

Morgan's 1956 sales catalog listed a tempting selection of options: tonneau cover (for either two- or four-seater); pass lamp; foglamp; badge bar; Smith's heater; Horvell wheel trims; leather upholstery; front bumper overriders; Brooklands steering wheel; and flashing indicators (turn signals). Special color paint or upholstery also was available. Models offered for 1956 were the two-seater tourer, two-seater coupe, and four-seater tourer. Both the two-seater coupe and the four-seater tourer were available with either the Vanguard 2088-cc engine, or the TR2 powerplant.

Standard body colors for 1956 were Larch Green, Wembley Blue, and Carnation Red. Upholstery was black. Special body or upholstery colors cost 10 Pounds (Sterling) extra in Britain. Three bodies were offered that year: the two-seat drophead, open two-seater, and open four-seater. The drophead (convertible) featured detachable sliding side windows, with a top that folded neatly into the back of the body. Open models had a fold-flat windshield. Body widths of two-seat models grew by four inches in 1957, and four-passenger models followed suit the next year.

For 1958, the model selection was again a two-seater tourer, four-seater tourer, and two-seater coupe. Width of the two-seater (then the four-seater) grew by four inches by this time, and the two-seater's fuel tank moved farther down in the chassis, which deleted the curve of the car's back panel. Options were similar to 1956, but added a windshield washer and knock-on wire wheels. Those center-lock wire wheels could replace the standard steel discs, and were optional in the 1959 model year. Morgan's 1959 catalog listed the TR (Triumph) engine only, finally omitting the old Vanguard powerplant. Front disc brakes replaced the original front/rear drum setup by 1960. By 1962, Morgan introduced a 2138-cc (130.5-cid) TR4 engine, rated 100-105 horsepower. Many racing options became available, including an aluminum body that sold for an extra $175 in 1961.

PLUS FOUR SUPER SPORTS — FOUR — A Super Sports model debuted in 1961, with hopped-up engines specially tuned by the Chris Lawrence organization. The forthcoming 2138-cc engine was tuned to 115 bhp at 5500 rpm, with 9.0:1 compression and two Weber carburetors. Super Sports wore light alloy bodies and 5.60x15 tires. Engines were sent to Westerham Motors, in Acton, for modification. Chores there included an increase in compression, polishing of the cylinder head, installation of a high-life camshaft, component balancing, mounting of a square-section four-branch exhaust manifold, and installation of Weber 42 or 45 DCOE carburetors. An oil cooler went behind the Super Sports grille.

4/4 — SERIES II/III/IV — FOUR — Though completely different from the earlier 4/4 (introduced in the 1930s), this one was meant to replace it, after a five-year absence from the lineup. The Plus Four had become more powerful by the mid-1950s, and Morgan wanted to complement it with a lower-powered model. Engines were the major difference. While the Plus Four relied on Standard-Triumph power, the 4/4 engines came from Ford (Britain). The gearbox formed a unit with the engine, whereas it was separate in the Plus Four layout. Otherwise, appearance was nearly identical to the Plus Four, with the same cowled (rounded) vertical-bar radiator grille, sloped tail, and semi-faired-in headlamps. Those features have remained Morgan "trademarks" ever since.

Only a two-passenger roadster (called "Two Seater Tourer" in Britain) was offered initially. A three-speed manual gearbox was standard until 1960, when it was replaced by a four-speed. Chassis construction was nearly identical to the Plus Four, with a front suspension that consisted of sliding pillars with coil springs, and a rigid axle with semi-elliptic leaf springs at the rear. Front/rear drum brakes were used until 1960, when front discs were installed: first optionally, then (by '61) as standard equipment. Wheelbase was identical to the Plus Four, at 96 inches.

Initial power for the 4/4 Series II came from an 1172-cc L-head (side-valve) Ford 100E engine (sometimes called the Ford Ten), which produced 36 horsepower. Starting in 1960, with the Series III, an oversquare overhead-valve "Kent" 997-cc four was installed, as in the 105E Anglia, rated at 39 horsepower. A four-speed gearbox replaced the former three-speed unit. At the same time, side-curtain fasteners moved to the outside of the doors, and taillamps were restyled. The Series III also featured toggle switches on a new dashboard. Since it remained in production for only one year, the Series III qualifies as the rarest 4/4, according to Gregory Houston Bowden's pictorial history, *More Morgan.*

Then, in 1961, came a 1340-cc (81.7-cid) engine that produced 54 horsepower, for the Series IV. That was a Ford "Consul Classic" engine, also offered for only a short period. It reduced 0-60 mph acceleration time from about 26 to as little as 10.5 seconds, while boosting top speed from about 80 to 92 mph. Yet another Series (V) would come in 1963, as the engine grew to 1498 cc. Later yet, a 1.6-liter four would take over as the car's name changed to 4/4 1600; and descendants of the 4/4 would remain available from Morgan into the 1980s.

Morgan's sales catalog of 1958 listed a 4/4 Series II competition model with specially-tuned engine, which had debuted prior to the 1957 Motor Show. Specifications were similar to other 4/4s, but this one sported a carefully-assembled engine with aquaplane aluminum head, improved intake and exhaust manifolds, twin SU carburetors, and compression raised to 8:1. Horsepower got a boost to 40 at 5100 rpm. Several aftermarket firms also offered tuning kits for the 4/4.

I.D. DATA: Plus Four chassis serial number is stamped on top of crossmember beneath front seat (two-seat) or behind front seat (2+2). Plus Four engine number is stamped on a boss on the block, behind the ignition coil. Plus Four serial number begins with prefix 'V' and ends with suffix 'ME.'

Chassis serial number for 4/4 (prefix 'A') is stamped on crossmember beneath the front seats. Engine number (prefix '100E') is on right side of block. Chassis serial number range: (Series II) A200-A586; (Series III) A589-A648; (Series IV) B650-B855.

Model	Body Type & Seating	Engine Type/CID	P.O.E. Price	Weight (lbs.)	Prod. Total
PLUS FOUR					
I	2-dr Rds-2P	I4/122	2595	1848	Note 1
I	2-dr Rds-2+2P	I4/122	2645	1904	Note 1
I	2-dr Dhd Cpe-2P	I4/122	2695	1960	Note 1
Super Spts	2-dr Rds-2P	I4/131	N/A	N/A	Note 1
4/4 (1955-59)					
II	2-dr Rds-2P	I4/72	1995	1430	Note 2
4/4 (1960-61)					
III	2-dr Rds-2P	I4/61	2240	1430	Note 2
4/4 (1961-63)					
IV	2-dr Rds-2P	I4/82	N/A	1430	Note 2

Note 1: As many as 4,754 Plus Fours were produced from 1950-68.

Note 2: A total of 387 model 4/4 Series II Morgans were produced, followed by 59 Series III, and 106 Series IV.

Price Note: Figures shown were advertised for 1955 models (except 4/4 Series II, in 1956; and 4/4 Series III, in 1961). In 1961-62, the Plus Four two-seat roadster sold for $2810, the four-seat roadster for $2850, and the drophead coupe for $2970.

British Price Note: Prices in Britain in late 1955 were 595 Pounds (Sterling) for the Plus Four two-seat Tourer (roadster), 610 for the four-seat roadster, and 640 for the drophead coupe (convertible), not including purchase tax. The four-seater and drophead were still listed with the early Vanguard 2088-cc engine for 30 Pounds less than those amounts (580 and 610 Pounds, respectively). Price of the 4/4 was 450 Pounds (Sterling).

Production Note: By the late 1980s, some 6,500 Morgan 4/4s had been produced.

ENGINE DATA: BASE FOUR (1954-62 Plus Four): Inline, overhead-valve four-cylinder (Triumph TR2). Cast iron block and head. **Displacement:** 121.5 cu. in. (1991 cc). **Bore & Stroke:** 3.27 x 3.62 in. (83 x 92 mm). **Compression Ratio:** 8.5:1. **Brake Horsepower:** 90 at 4800 rpm (rated 100 bhp at 5000 rpm in U.S. in late 1950s). **Torque:** 117-118 lbs.-ft. at 3000 rpm. Three main bearings. Solid valve lifters. Two SU carburetors.

BASE FOUR (Plus Four Super Sports): Inline, overhead-valve four-cylinder (Triumph). Cast iron block and head. **Displacement:** 130.5 cu. in. (2138 cc). **Bore & Stroke:** 3.39 x 3.62 in. (86 x 92 mm). **Compression Ratio:** 9.0:1. **Brake Horsepower:** 115 at 5500 rpm. **Torque:** 128 lbs.-ft. at 3400 rpm. Three main bearings. Solid valve lifters. Two Weber carburetors.

Plus Four Engine Note: Morgan catalog for 1955-56 continued to list the original 2088-cc Vanguard engine (with 7.1:1 compression and 68 horsepower), as well as the TR2 powerplant described above. By 1960, the TR3 engine was available, rated 100 bhp at 5000 rpm. For 1962, Plus Four engine size grew to 2138-cc (130.5-cid), as in the Super Sport (above), but rated 105 bhp at 4750 rpm.

BASE FOUR (1955-59 4/4 Series II): Inline, L-head four-cylinder (Ford 100E). Cast iron block and head. **Displacement:** 71.55 cu. in. (1172 cc). **Bore & Stroke:** 2.50 x 3.64 in. (63.5 x 92.5 mm). **Compression Ratio:** 7.0:1. **Brake Horsepower:** 36-39 at 4400 rpm. **Torque:** 52 lbs.-ft. at 2500 rpm. Three main bearings. Solid valve lifters. One Solex downdraft carburetor.

Note: The 4/4 competition engine had an aluminum head, twin carburetors, and modified camshaft, and was rated 40 bhp at 5100 rpm using 8.0:1 compression.

BASE FOUR (1960-61 4/4 Series III): Inline, overhead-valve four-cylinder (Ford 105E). Cast iron block and head. **Displacement:** 60.8 cu. in. (997 cc). **Bore & Stroke:** 3.19 x 1.90 in. (81 x 48.4 mm). **Compression Ratio:** 8.9:1. **Brake Horsepower:** 39 at 5000 rpm. Three main bearings. Solid valve lifters. One Solex downdraft carburetor.

BASE FOUR (1961-63 4/4 Series IV): Inline, overhead-valve four-cylinder (Ford). Cast iron block and head. **Displacement:** 81.7 cu. in. (1340 cc). **Bore & Stroke:** 3.19 x 2.56 in. (81 x 65.1 mm). **Compression Ratio:** 8.5:1. **Brake Horsepower:** 54 at 5000 rpm. Three main bearings. Solid valve lifters. One Solex downdraft carburetor.

CHASSIS DATA: Wheelbase: (Plus Four) 96 in.; (4/4) 96 in. **Overall Length:** (Plus Four) 144 in.; (4/4) 144 in. **Height:** (Plus Four 2P rds) 52 in.; (Plus Four 2+2P rds) 53 in.; (Plus Four dhd) 51 in.; (4/4) 50 in. **Width:** (Plus Four) 56 in.; (4/4) 56 in. **Front Tread:** (Plus Four) 47 in.; (4/4) 47 in. **Rear Tread:** (Plus Four) 47 in.; (4/4) 47 in. **Wheel Type:** (Plus Four) four-stud pressed steel disc with chromed cap; (4/4) steel disc. Wire wheels optional by 1959. **Standard Tires:** (Plus Four) Dunlop 5.25x16 (5.00x16 or 5.50x16 available); (4/4 Series II) 5.00x16; (4/4 Series III/IV) 5.20x15.

TECHNICAL: Layout: front-engine, rear-drive. **Transmission:** (Plus Four) Moss four-speed manual. Overall Plus Four gear ratios: (1st) 12.85:1; (2nd) 7.38:1; (3rd) 5.24:1; (4th) 3.73:1; (rev) 12.85:1. (4/4) three-speed manual. Overall 4/4 gear ratios: (1st) 15.07:1; (2nd) 8.25:1; (3rd) 4.4:1; (rev) 19.71:1. **Standard Final Drive Ratio:** (Plus Four) 3.73:1; (4/4) 4.4:1. **Steering:** cam gear. **Suspension (front):** sliding pillars with coil springs. **Suspension (rear):** rigid axle with semi-elliptic leaf springs. **Brakes:** Girling hydraulic, front/rear drum (front disc, rear drum by 1960). **Body Construction:** steel or aluminum body with wood framing, on steel chassis with Z-shaped side members.

PERFORMANCE: Top Speed: (Plus Four) 96-103 mph; (later Plus Four) 105 mph; (Plus Four Super Sports) 115 mph; (4/4 Series II) 75-78 mph; (4/4 Series IV) 92 mph. **Acceleration (0-60 mph):** (Plus Four) 11.2-11.4 sec. (just over 10 sec. claimed); (Plus Four Super Sports) 7.8 sec.; (4/4 Series II) 26.9-29 sec.; (4/4 Series IV) 16.5 sec. (as little as 10.5 sec. reported). **Acceleration (quarter-mile):** (Plus Four) 17.1-18.5 sec. (about 76 mph); (4/4) 21.4 sec.; (4/4 competition Series II) 20.2-21.4 sec. **Fuel Mileage:** (Plus Four) up to 35 mpg claimed; (4/4 Series II) 20-22 mpg reported.

ADDITIONAL MODELS: A Plus Four four-seater coupe had been announced at the 1954 London Motor Show, according to *The Morgan: 75 Years on the Road,* and produced sporadically over the next 2-1/2 years. Only 51 were built, each carrying the Standard Vanguard engine.

Manufacturer: The Morgan Motor Co. Ltd., Malvern Link, Worcestershire, England.

Distributor: Fergus Imported Cars Inc., New York City; and Worldwide Import Inc., West Los Angeles, California.

HISTORY: "Four Magnificent Models to chosse from," promised the Morgan catalog issued at the London show in October 1955, including the new 4/4 Series II. A 1955 ad for the Plus Four four-seat sports drophead coupe, "the latest addition" to the Morgan line, promised that it was "ideally suited for the 'family man." The TR2-engined version was advertised as the "New Super Morgan." *Motor Trend* in 1957 called the 4/4 Series II the "lowest priced sports car in America," with a price tag of $1995. The Plus Four was advertised in the U.S. as "last of the real classics," a car "designed and engineered for those who demand the finest." American ads also touted the Morgan's race victories, including a win in the 2-liter class at the Thompson Speedway in October 1954, and 1st and 2nd in its class (2-liter series production cars under $3000) at the Sebring Grand Prix of Endurance in March 1955.

Peter Morgan became managing director of the company following the death of H.F.S. Morgan in 1959. The 4/4 Series III became known as Morgan's "Anniversary Model," since it appeared half a century after the company's founding; but that was not its official designation. On the competition scene, Chris Lawrence and Richard Shepherd-Baron won their class at the 1962 Le Mans race, traveling 2,565 miles at an average of 94 mph.

1963-67 MORGAN

PLUS FOUR — FOUR — Production of the Plus Four continued as described in prior listings, but since 1962 powered by the latest version of the Triumph engine: the 2138-cc (130.5-cid) TR4 edition. This one produced 100-105 horsepower, using two Stromberg carburetors. As before, a more potent version of the engine was tuned by the Chris Lawrence organization, installed in the Super Sports roadster. In 1966, a lower body was adopted for two-seat models.

PLUS FOUR PLUS — FOUR — In its long history, Morgan made only one swing away from the traditional (prewar) look, turning out a small number of modern-styled Plus Four Plus coupes. Introduced in 1963, the slim "bubbletop" two-seater coupe body rode a standard (unaltered) Plus Four chassis. That skinny-looking top gave the coupe a weird, if distinctive, upper profile that some called "bell-shaped," and was not universally loved. Otherwise, it was basically a slab-sided (though rounded) body, with straight fenderlines, a vertical look at front and rear ends, and full rounded wheel openings. Instead of the usual steel-over-wood construction, the coupe wore a fiberglass body, but with the familiar small Morgan vertical-bar grille shape and bumper up front. Headlamps were fully built into the fenders, with rounded rectangular parking lights below. Air intake openings stood low, alongside the grille, adorned by horizontal bars. The coupe's curved windshield was yet another "first" for Morgan, as were the wind-down semicircular glass windows (which didn't wind down quite all the way). Styling features also included two round taillamps on each side, in a vertical panel, a separate trunk with external hinges, and a gas filler just ahead of the trunk lid. Overall, there was little to remind the observer of anything reminiscent of the usual Morgans, with their cutdown doors and old-fashioned look.

Under the hood was Morgan's then-current version of the Triumph "TR" engine: the 2138-cc four, as in the regular Plus Four roadster (above), producing 105 bhp. Most coupes had center-lock wire wheels, and delivered the same sort of rough ride that roadster drivers had learned to love (or hate). Morgan planned to build only 50 coupes, but barely reached half that total, producing only 26 through 1966. The Plus Four Plus could hit about 110 mph, and reach 60 mph in about 12.5 seconds. Standard colors were Westminster Green, Kingfisher Blue, Crimson, and White.

4/4 — SERIES IV/V — FOUR — Production of the Series IV version of the 4/4 roadster, with 1340-cc engine, came to a halt in 1963. That was replaced by the Series V, with a 1498-cc (91.4-cid) edition of the Ford powerplant. In basic trim, the engine produced 65 horsepower, but more potent editions for competition also were marketed. A four-speed manual gearbox was the only transmission choice, and front disc (rear drum) brakes remained standard.

"Small car, Big performance" was the claim for the competition version of the Series V 4/4. Compression was increased from 8.3:1 to 9.0:1, and the engine switched from a Zenith 33N to Weber DCD22 carburetor. A closer-ratio gearbox also was installed, cutting 0-60 mph acceleration time down to 11.9 seconds, and raising top speed to 95-100 mph. Wire wheels were available at extra cost.

1966 Morgan Plus 4 roadster.

I.D. DATA: Plus Four chassis serial number is stamped on top of crossmember beneath front seat (two-seat) or behind front seat (2+2). Plus Four engine number is stamped on a boss on the left side of the block, behind the ignition coil. Chassis serial number for 4/4 is stamped on crossmember beneath the front seats. Serial number range: (4/4 Series IV) B650-B855; (4/4 Series V) B856-B1495.

Model	Body Type & Seating	Engine Type/CID	P.O.E. Price	Weight (lbs.)	Prod. Total
PLUS FOUR					
	2-dr Rds-2P	I4/131	2962	1764	Note 1
	2-dr Rds-2+2P	I4/131	3048	N/A	Note 1
	2-dr Dhd Cpe-2P	I4/131	3352	N/A	Note 1
PLUS FOUR SUPER SPORTS					
	2-dr Rds-2P	I4/131	3893	N/A	Note 2
PLUS FOUR PLUS					
	2-dr Coupe-2P	I4/131	Note 3	1820	26
4/4					
IV	2-dr Rds-2P	I4/82	2394	1456	Note 4
V	2-dr Rds-2P	I4/91	2664	1456	Note 4

Note 1: As many as 4,754 Morgan Plus Fours were produced from 1950-68, including up to 1,523 with the 2138-cc engine.

Note 2: A total of 101 Super Sports roadsters with the high-performance Lawrence-tuned engine were produced.

Note 3: Price of the Plus Four Plus coupe in England was 1250 Pounds (Sterling), including tax.

Note 4: A total of 206 model 4/4 Series IV Morgans were produced, followed by 639 Series V.

Price Note: Figures shown were valid in 1963, except (4/4 Series V) in 1964. In 1966, the Plus Four roadster sold for $3123; the four-seat roadster for $3238; the drophead (convertible) for $3527; the Le Mans Super Sport for $3961; a GT competition roadster for $3475; and GT hardtop coupe for $4030. Price of the 4/4 (Series V) in 1966 was $2752 ($2857 for a competition GT version).

ENGINE DATA: BASE FOUR (1962-68 Plus Four, 1963-66 Plus Four Plus): Inline, overhead-valve four-cylinder (Triumph). Cast iron block and head. **Displacement:** 130.5 cu. in. (2138 cc). **Bore & Stroke:** 3.39 x 3.62 in. (86 x 92 mm). **Compression Ratio:** 9.0:1. **Brake Horsepower:** 100/105 at 4750/5000 rpm. **Torque:** 117/128 lbs.-ft. at 3000/3350 rpm. Three main bearings. Solid valve lifters. Two SU carburetors.

BASE FOUR (Plus Four Super Sports): Same as above, except rated 115/120 bhp at 5000/5500 rpm, and 128 lbs.-ft. at 3400 rpm.

BASE FOUR (1962-63 4/4 Series IV): Inline, overhead-valve four-cylinder (Ford). Cast iron block and head. **Displacement:** 81.7 cu. in. (1340 cc). **Bore & Stroke:** 3.19 x 2.56 in. (81 x 65.1 mm). **Compression Ratio:** 8.5:1. **Brake Horsepower:** 54 at 5000 rpm. Five main bearings. Solid valve lifters. One Solex downdraft carburetor.

BASE FOUR (1963-68 4/4 Series V): Inline, overhead-valve four-cylinder (Ford "Kent"). Cast iron block and head. **Displacement:** 91.4 cu. in. (1498 cc). **Bore & Stroke:** 3.19 x 2.86 in. (81 x 73 mm). **Compression Ratio:** 8.3:1. **Brake Horsepower:** 65 at 4600 rpm. **Torque:** 89 lbs.-ft. at 2500 rpm. Five main bearings. Solid valve lifters. One Zenith single-barrel carburetor.

OPTIONAL FOUR (Competition 4/4 Series V): Same as 1498-cc four above, except — **Compression Ratio:** 9.0:1. **Brake Horsepower:** 78/83.5 at 5200 rpm. **Torque:** 91/97 lbs.-ft. at 3600 rpm. Weber two-barrel carburetor.

CHASSIS DATA: Wheelbase: (Plus Four) 96 in.; (4/4) 96 in. **Overall Length:** (Plus Four) 144 in.; (Plus Four Plus) 152 in.; (4/4) 144 in. **Height:** (Plus Four 2P rds) 52 in.; (Plus Four 2+2P rds) 53 in.; (Plus Four dhd) 51 in.; (Plus Four Plus) 51 in.; (4/4) 52 in. **Width:** (Plus Four) 56 in.; (Plus Four Plus) 61 in.; (4/4) 56 in. **Front Tread:** (Plus Four) 47 in.; (Plus Four Plus) 49 in.; (4/4) 47 in. **Rear Tread:** (Plus Four) 47/49 in.; (Plus Four Plus) 49 in.; (4/4) 47/48 in. **Wheel Type:** steel disc (wire wheels optional). **Standard Tires:** (Plus Four) 5.60x15; (Plus Four Plus) 5.60x15; (4/4) 5.20x15 or 5.60x15.

TECHNICAL: Layout: front-engine, rear-drive. **Transmission:** four-speed manual. **Standard Final Drive Ratio:** (Plus Four) 3.73:1; (Plus Four Plus) 3.78:1; (4/4 Series V) 4.56:1. **Steering:** cam gear. **Suspension (front):** sliding pillars with coil springs. **Suspension (rear):** rigid axle with semi-elliptic leaf springs. **Brakes:** front disc, rear drum. **Body Construction:** steel or aluminum body with wood framing, on steel chassis with Z-shaped side members except (Plus Four Plus) fiberglass body.

PERFORMANCE: Top Speed: (Plus Four) 107 mph; (Plus Four Super Sports) 120 mph; (Plus Four Plus) about 110 mph; (4/4 Series V) 85 mph; (competition 4/4 Series V) 95-100 mph. **Acceleration (0-60 mph):** (Plus Four Plus) about 12.5 sec.; (competition 4/4 Series V) 11.9 sec. **Acceleration (quarter-mile):** (Plus Four) 16.8 sec.; (Plus Four Super Sports) 15.4 sec.; (4/4) 20.9 sec.

Manufacturer: Morgan Motor Co. Ltd., Malvern Link, Worcestershire, England.

Distributor: Fergus Motors Inc., New York City.

HISTORY: The Plus Four Plus coupe was announced at the 1963 British Motor Show, and later performed well in a few rallies. "The enthusiast," Morgan claimed, "will find this the ideal sports car for tireless long-distance travelling." Handling was as good as other Morgans, but the public wasn't enamored of the stying, even though ads promised "new smooth sweeping lines." Other ads encouraged customers to "Make friends with a Morgan Plus Four Plus;" and to "Drive well and influence people with your new Morgan Plus Four Plus." Most of the 26 examples produced over its four-year official life were exported. John H. Sheally stated in *Morgan--Pride of the British* that 10 of them were sold in the U.S.

"There's something about a Morgan," said one British ad for the 4/4 Series V. "Each car is assembled by craftsmen; each is road tested before collection; each carries the unmistakable stamp of the individualist." Another ad advised: "You're a driver to reckon with in a Morgan."

1968-69 MORGAN

PLUS FOUR — FOUR — Production of the Plus Four series with 2138-cc engine ceased by early 1969; see prior listings for full data.

PLUS 8 — V-8 — With the demise of the Plus Four in 1968, Morgan made a major move into V-8 power for its traditional-style roadster. Part of the impetus for the change arose from the fact that Triumph had dropped its latest (TR4A) engine. As fortune would have it, Rover was just beginning to install a V-8 engine in its sedans, and made it available to Morgan. The all-aluminum 3528-cc (215-cid) V-8 was a Buick design, used early in the 1960s in the Buick Special, Oldsmobile F-85 and Pontiac Tempest. Now, it was built under license by Rover, in Britain. Except for the installation of SU carburetors, it differed little from the original GM powerplant, and, surprisingly, weighed no more than the Triumph four that it replaced.

To make space for the new powerplant, the Plus Four's chassis side-members had to be moved farther apart, and fenders widened to accept bigger wheels and tires. Wheelbase grew by two inches, to 98 inches. Cast alloy wheels replaced the former center-lock wire wheels. Only a two-seat roadster was produced. Most examples wore a steel body over the customary wooden framework, but some were made of aluminum. Inside, rocker switches replaced the traditional toggles and matte-black instrument panels replaced the prior chrome units. A steel floor replaced the former wood section, according to *The Morgan: 75 Years on the Road,* from the pedal board to the seat mounting area; and bucket seats replaced the traditional bench seat. A triple-wiper setup also was added. External appearance, however, differed little from prior Morgans, with the same cutaway doors and separate-fender look.

Performance, to no one's great surprise, was considerably swifter than that provided by the Triumph four-cylinder engines, with a top speed approaching 125 mph. Except for some engine changes later on, and widening of fenders and tread dimensions, the Plus 8 remained quite similar to the original concept over the next two decades.

4/4 — SERIES V — FOUR — Production of the Series V came to a halt in 1968, replaced by the 4/4 1600; see prior listing for full data.

4/4 1600 — FOUR — Yet another engine went into the 4/4 at this time, prompting a name change to "1600." That identified the 1599-cc (97.6-cid) Ford four, which gave the revised 4/4 a top speed in the 100-mph neighborhood, and 0-60 acceleration just under 10 seconds. This same engine went into Ford Capris and Cortinas (and even early Pintos), and would remain available into the early 1980s. By this time, too, a four-seater was available. The 4/4 body was widened somewhat in 1969, to match the Plus 8 at the windshield level.

I.D. DATA: Plus Four chassis serial number is stamped on top of crossmember beneath front seat (two-seat) or behind front seat (2+2). Plus Four engine number is stamped on a boss on the block, behind the ignition coil. Chassis serial number for 4/4 is stamped on crossmember beneath the front seats. Starting serial number (4/4 1600): B1600.

Model	Body Type & Seating	Engine Type/CID	P.O.E. Price	Weight (lbs.)	Prod. Total
PLUS FOUR (through 1968)					
	2-dr Rds-2P	I4/131	N/A	1764	Note 1
	2-dr Rds-2+2P	I4/131	N/A	N/A	Note 1
	2-dr Dhd Cpe-2P	I4/131	N/A	N/A	Note 1
Super Spts	2-dr Rds-2P	I4/131	N/A	1792	Note 2
PLUS 8					
	2-dr Rds-2P	V8/215	N/A	1988	Note 3
4/4 (through 1968)					
V	2-dr Rds-2P	I4/91	N/A	1456	Note 4
4/4 1600					
	2-dr Rds-2P	I4/98	N/A	1455	N/A
	2-dr Rds-2+2P	I4/98	N/A	N/A	N/A

Note 1: Approximately 1,523 Plus Fours with the 2138-cc engine were produced, through 1968.

Note 2: A total of 101 Super Sports with the high-performance engine were produced.

Note 3: By the late 1980s, more than 2,600 Plus 8 Morgans had been produced.

Note 4: A total of 639 model 4/4 Series V Morgans were produced, through 1968.

ENGINE DATA: BASE FOUR (1962-68 Plus Four): Inline, overhead-valve four-cylinder (Triumph). Cast iron block and head. **Displacement:** 130.5 cu. in. (2138 cc). **Bore & Stroke:** 3.39 x 3.62 in. (86 x 92 mm). **Compression Ratio:** 9.0:1. **Brake Horsepower:** 100/105 at 4750/5000 rpm. **Torque:** 117/128 lbs.-ft. at 3000/3350 rpm. Three main bearings. Solid valve lifters. Two SU carburetors.

BASE FOUR (Plus Four Super Sports): Same as above, except rated 115 bhp.

BASE V-8 (Plus 8): 90-degree, overhead-valve "vee" type eight-cylinder (Rover). Aluminum-alloy block and heads. **Displacement:** 215 cu. in. (3528 cc). **Bore & Stroke:** 3.50 x 2.80 in. (88.9 x 71.1 mm). **Compression Ratio:** 10.5:1. **Brake Horsepower:** 184 at 5200 rpm. **Torque:** 226 lbs.-ft. at 3600 rpm. Five main bearings. Hydraulic valve lifters. Two SU carburetors.

Plus 8 Engine Note: Some U.S. sources listed V-8 output as low as 143 bhp (DIN) at 5000 rpm, and 202 lbs.-ft. at 2700 rpm.

BASE FOUR (1963-68 4/4 Series V): Inline, overhead-valve four-cylinder (Ford "Kent"). Cast iron block and head. **Displacement:** 91.4 cu. in. (1498 cc). **Bore & Stroke:** 3.19 x 2.86 in. (81 x 73 mm). **Compression Ratio:** 8.3:1. **Brake Horsepower:** 65 at 4600 rpm. **Torque:** 89 lbs.-ft. at 2500 rpm. Five main bearings. Solid valve lifters. One Zenith single-barrel carburetor.

OPTIONAL FOUR (Competition 4/4 Series V): Same as 1498-cc four above, except — **Compression Ratio:** 9.0:1. **Brake Horsepower:** 78/83.5 at 5200 rpm. **Torque:** 91/97 lbs.-ft. at 3600 rpm. Weber two-barrel carburetor.

BASE FOUR (4/4 1600): Inline, overhead-valve four-cylinder (Ford). Cast iron block and head. **Displacement:** 97.6 cu. in. (1599 cc). **Bore & Stroke:** 3.19 x 3.06 in. (81 x 77.6 mm). **Compression Ratio:** 9.0:1. **Brake Horsepower:** 74 at 4750 rpm. **Torque:** 98 lbs.-ft. at 2500 rpm. Five main bearings. Solid valve lifters. One Weber carburetor.

4/4 1600 Engine Note: More potent competition versions were available, rated 88-96 bhp at 4750-5500 rpm.

CHASSIS DATA: Wheelbase: (Plus Four) 96 in.; (Plus 8) 98 in.; (4/4) 96 in. **Overall Length:** (Plus Four) 144 in.; (Plus 8) 152 in.; (4/4) 144 in. **Height:** (Plus Four 2P rds) 52 in.; (Plus Four 2+2P rds) 53 in.; (Plus Four dhd) 51 in.; (Plus 8) 49 in.; (4/4) 51 in. **Width:** (Plus Four) 56 in.; (Plus 8) 57 in.; (4/4) 56 in. **Max. Tread:** (Plus Four) 47 in.; (Plus 8) 51 in.; (4/4) 47 in. **Wheel Type:** (Plus Four, 4/4) steel disc (wire wheels optional); (Plus 8) cast alloy. **Standard Tires:** (Plus Four) 5.60x15; (Plus 8) 185x15; (4/4) 5.60x15; (4/4 1600) 165x15.

TECHNICAL: Layout: front-engine, rear-drive. **Transmission:** four-speed manual. **Standard Final Drive Ratio:** (Plus Four) 3.73:1; (Plus 8) 3.58:1; (4/4 Series V) 4.56:1. **Steering:** cam gear. **Suspension (front):** sliding pillars with coil springs. **Suspension (rear):** rigid axle with semi-elliptic leaf springs. **Brakes:** front disc, rear drum. **Body Construction:** steel or aluminum body with wood framing, on steel chassis with Z-shaped side members.

PERFORMANCE: Top Speed: (Plus Four) 107 mph; (Plus 8) 123-125 mph; (4/4 1600) about 100 mph. **Acceleration (0-60 mph):** (Plus 8) about 9.8 sec.; (Plus 8) as little as 6.5 sec. **Acceleration (quarter-mile):** (Plus Four) 16.8 sec.; (Plus 8) about 15 sec.

Manufacturer: The Morgan Motor Co. Ltd., Malvern Link, Worcestershire, England.

HISTORY: "For 1968 a brand new Morgan, the +8," promised British ads. "Leap to the legal limit in a staggering 7.5 seconds," they added, "when acceleration is needed." By the late 1960s, Morgans were disappearing from the lists of cars imported into the U.S., victims of the tightening Federal regulations. That status would persist into the 1970s and '80s, with certification remaining elusive.

1970-90 MORGAN

1975 Morgan Plus 8 roadster.

PLUS 8 — V-8 — Production of the eight-cylinder Morgan continued into the 1970s and beyond, though Americans weren't entitled to an officially-certified version. Over the course of its long life, Plus 8 fenders and tread dimensions were widened several times to accommodate bigger tires. In May 1972, an all-synchro Rover four-speed manual transmission replaced the former Moss gearbox and engine horsepower was modified. Early in 1977, that was replaced by a five-speed unit, as the V-8 engine was revised again. In the mid-1980s, Morgans adopted a fuel-injected version of the Rover V-8, as well as rack-and-pinion steering. Beginning in the late 1970s, a handful of Plus 8s trickled into the U.S. via a California company, with their engines converted to propane, waiting for the time when the Rover engine (as used in the Range Rover luxury sport-utility vehicle) earned emissions-certification.

4/4 1600 — FOUR — Production of the 1.6-liter version of the 4/4 continued as introduced in 1968, with the Ford Capri/Cortina engine. In 1982, a five-speed replaced the four-speed unit. Starting at that time, too, buyers could get either a British Ford "CVH" engine (related to that used in the American Ford Escort), or a twin-cam Fiat powerplant.

I.D. DATA: Similar to 1968-69.

Model PLUS 8	Body Type & Seating	Engine Type/CID	P.O.E. Price	Weight (lbs.)	Prod. Total
	2-dr Rds-2P	V8/215	N/A	1876	Note 1

Model 4/4 1600	Body Type & Seating	Engine Type/CID	P.O.E. Price	Weight (lbs.)	Prod. Total
	2-dr Rds-2P	I4/98	N/A	1460	N/A
	2-dr Rds-2 + 2P	I4/98	N/A	1568	N/A

Note 1: A total of 484 Plus 8 models were built with the early Moss gearbox, before a Rover unit was installed in 1972. By the late 1980s, more than 2,600 Plus 8 Morgans had been produced.

Weight Note: Figures shown are "dry" weights, valid in the early 1970s.

ENGINE DATA: BASE V-8 (Plus 8 to 1972): 90-degree, overhead-valve "vee" type eight-cylinder (Rover). Aluminum-alloy block and heads. **Displacement:** 215 cu. in. (3528 cc). **Bore & Stroke:** 3.50 x 2.80 in. (89 x 71 mm). **Compression Ratio:** 10.5:1. **Brake Horsepower:** up to 184 (DIN) at 5200 rpm. **Torque:** up to 226 lbs.-ft. at 3000 rpm. Five main bearings. Hydraulic valve lifters. Two SU carburetors.

BASE V-8 (1972-77 Plus 8): Same as 3528-cc V-8 above, except — **Brake Horsepower:** 151 (DIN) at 5000 rpm. **Torque:** 210 lbs.-ft. at 2700 rpm.

BASE V-8 (1977-85 Plus 8): Same as 3528-cc V-8 above, except — **Compression Ratio:** 9.3:1. **Brake Horsepower:** 155 at 5250 rpm. **Torque:** 199 lbs.-ft. at 2500 rpm.

BASE V-8 (1985-90 Plus 8): Same as 3528-cc V-8 above, except — **Brake Horsepower:** 190 (DIN) at 5200 rpm. **Torque:** 220 lbs.-ft. at 4000 rpm.

Plus 8 Engine Note: To meet U.S. emissions requirements in the 1970s and '80s, a number of Morgans were converted to run on propane.

BASE FOUR (1970-81 4/4 1600): Inline, overhead-valve four-cylinder (Ford). Cast iron block and head. **Displacement:** 97.6 cu. in. (1599 cc). **Bore & Stroke:** 3.19 x 3.06 in. (81 x 77.6 mm). **Compression Ratio:** 9.0:1. **Brake Horsepower:** 88 at 5400 rpm. **Torque:** 96 lbs.-ft. at 3600 rpm. Five main bearings. Solid valve lifters.

BASE FOUR (1982-87 4/4 1600): Inline, overhead-cam four-cylinder (Ford XR3 "CVH"). Cast iron block and light alloy head. **Displacement:** 97.4 cu. in. (1596 cc). **Bore & Stroke:** 3.14 x 3.12 in. (80 x 79.5 mm). **Compression Ratio:** 9.5:1. **Brake Horsepower:** 96 (DIN) at 6000 rpm. **Torque:** 98 lbs.-ft. at 4000 rpm. Five main bearings. Solid valve lifters. One Weber two-barrel carburetor.

OPTIONAL FOUR (1982-90 4/4 1600): Inline, dual-overhead-cam four-cylinder (Fiat). Cast iron block and light alloy head. **Displacement:** 96.7 cu. in. (1585 cc). **Bore & Stroke:** 3.31 x 2.81 in. (84 x 71.5 mm). **Compression Ratio:** 9.5:1. **Brake Horsepower:** 97/98 (DIN) at 6000 rpm. **Torque:** 94 lbs.-ft. at 3800-4000 rpm. Five main bearings. Solid valve lifters. Weber or Solex two-barrel carburetor.

Note: A 2.0-liter Fiat engine, as in the 124 sports car, went into the Plus Four that was revived in the late 1980s.

CHASSIS DATA: Wheelbase: (Plus 8) 98 in.; (4/4 1600) 96 in. **Overall Length:** (Plus 8) 146-147 in.; (4/4 1600) 144 in. **Height:** (Plus 8) 49 in.; (4/4 1600) 51 in. **Width:** (Plus 8) 57 in.; (4/4 1600) 56 in. **Front Tread:** (Plus 8) 48-49 in.; (4/4 1600) 47 in.; (competition 4/4) 48 in. **Rear Tread:** (Plus 8) 50-51 in.; (4/4 1600) 49 in.; (competition 4/4) 50 in. **Wheel Type:** (4/4 1600) steel disc; (Plus 8) cast alloy. **Standard Tires:** (Plus 8) 185x15; (4/4) 165x15.

Dimension Note: By the 1980s, Plus 8 tread dimensions grew to 52 inches (front) and 53 inches (rear), and width to 62 inches, with 205x15 tires.

TECHNICAL: Layout: front-engine, rear-drive. **Transmission:** four-speed manual (five-speed on Plus 8 by 1977, and on 4/4 by 1982). **Steering:** cam gear except (late Plus 8) rack and pinion. **Suspension (front):** sliding pillars with coil springs. **Suspension (rear):** rigid axle with semi-elliptic leaf springs. **Brakes:** front disc, rear drum. **Body Construction:** steel or aluminum body with wood framing, on steel chassis with Z-shaped side members.

PERFORMANCE: Top Speed: (Plus 8) up to 130 mph; (4/4 1600) as much as 115 mph in early 1980s. **Acceleration (0-60 mph):** (Plus 8) 5.6-6.5 sec.; (4/4 1600) about 9.8 sec. **Acceleration (quarter-mile):** (Plus 8) about 14.5 sec. in early 1980s.

Manufacturer: Morgan Motor Co. Ltd., Malvern Link, Worcestershire, England.

HISTORY: Ads for the 1970 4/4 1600 called it "The Birthday Car," noting the 60th anniversary of Morgan's founding. "Disc brakes, vivid acceleration, positive control, a little comfort and a lot of fun," was the promise for purchasers, who could get a standard, mildly tuned, or four-seater edition of the 4/4. More than 600 Morgans (including 100 three-wheelers) showed up for a 60th anniversary celebration at Prescott, organized by Morgan clubs in Britain.

No Morgans were officially exported to the U.S. in the 1972-75 period; and in fact, they'd disappeared from lists of available models earlier than that. Starting in 1976, Morgans became available through Isis Imports in San Francisco. To meet U.S. regulations, they had to have roll bars, door bracing and safety bumpers installed. Other safety revisions were made at the same time, including the addition of sunvisors, backup lights and side marker lights, and the repositioning of taillamps. When the Rover V-8 engine finally achieved emissions certification for sale in the U.S., it was thought that Morgans, too, might have a clear field ahead. Emissions were only part of the problem, but the only Morgans officially available for sale in the U.S. during the 1980s were those converted to propane power. Not only emissions, but bumpers and side-impact regulations had to be met—no small matter for a small company with such limited production. Meanwhile, British ads in 1982 promoted Morgan as "first of the real sports cars."

MORRIS

Like many another pioneering British automaker, William Morris (later to become Lord Nuffield) was in the bicycle business in the 1890s. Around the turn of the century, he began to build motorcycles as well; but slipped out of the manufacturing end by 1905. For the next seven years, Morris sold bicycles and automobiles, but was waiting for an opportunity to produce a light car of his own design. In 1919, he formed WRM Motors Ltd. with a factory at Cowley, in Oxford; then created a prototype Morris Oxford. Available for sale by spring of the following year, the Oxford was powered by a 1018-cc T-head four-cylinder engine. The rounded radiator shape of its two-seater body brought the nickname "Bulletnose" and, later, the better-

known "Bullnose." Before long, drophead coupe and sports models were available, as well as a delivery van, and Morris was on its way to success. A larger-engined (1548 cc) Cowley joined the Oxford in 1915, after the First World War had broken out in Europe, with powerplants supplied by the Continental company of Detroit. Production expanded after the war, under the name Morris Motors Ltd. Postwar models carried engines based upon the Continental design, but built by the British branch of the French Hotchkiss firm. Both the basic Cowley and a more deluxe Oxford were offered. Sales zoomed upward, from barely more than 3,000 in 1921 to more than 54,000 in 1925, making Morris Number One in Britain. A six-cylinder Oxford produced in the early 1920s had less success than the fours, but subsequent sixes would fare better. Morris also bought several suppliers during the 1920s, including the SU carburetor company and the Hotchkiss engine manufacturer.

By 1927, the new Morris models displayed a flat-front radiator, causing a nickname change from "Bullnose" to "Flatnose." Takeover of the Wolseley company at that time brought Morris a new overhead-cam engine, first seen under the hoods of the new 847-cc Minor series of 1928-34. Rival to the Austin Seven, the Minor also came with a side-valve (L-head) engine that sold somewhat better than the overhead-cam version. A variant of the Minor turned into the M-type MG Midget, with a thrilling history of its own, as the 'MG' badge was adopted from the name Morris Garages. Morris models available in the 1930s ranged from the little Minor to the six-cylinder Oxford, Isis and Major; topped in dimensions by the Oxford 25 with its 3486-cc engine and 120-inch wheelbase. In 1935 came a fresh small-size model, the "Eight," with a new L-head engine displacing 918 cubic centimeters. Then, just as England was becoming embroiled in another war, the Eight earned a streamlined new body, with faired-in headlamps and without running boards.

Two Morrises, the Eight and the 1140-cc Ten, resumed production right after World War II, in September 1945, but only as a stopgap until the emergence of the all-new Minor (and Oxford) late in 1948. Designed by Alec Issigonis, the Minor carried the same 918-cc L-head engine as the prior Eight, but wore a rounded all-steel unibody. Rack-and-pinion steering was installed, and the front suspension used torsion bars, delivering handling well beyond what was ordinarily expected in a light family automobile. Few of those involved thought the Minor would last more than a few years, but its basic design hung on until 1971, with over 1.5 million produced in all.

Both the Minor and the bigger-engined Oxford sold in the U.S. in the 1950s, though Minors became far more popular. Late in 1951, the two-millionth Morris was produced. And early the next year, the Nuffield Organization (including Morris) joined with Austin to form the British Motor Corp. (BMC). That merger put Austin's 803-cc overhead-valve four-cylinder engine under Morris Minor hoods in 1953. Installation of the larger (948-cc) Austin A35 version into the Minor 1000 added some welcome power and performance by 1957. Through the 1960s, Minors remained in production with 1098-cc engines, but were less-frequently found in America. Other Morrises, which became virtual clones of various BMC models, were rarer yet in the U.S. market. One notable exception was the front-rive Mini, another design by Alec Issigonis, which sold under both the Austin and Morris names (and even as a Riley). One last Morris model, the Marina, emerged in 1971 and lasted through that decade. Facelifted in form by the Ital Design company (of Italy), it became known as the Morris Ital before disappearing at the end of 1983. Actually, Ital dies were then sent to Pakistan to give the car another lease on life, but the Morris name no longer existed.

By that time, in any case, Morris had long since faded away from the memories of most American car purchasers, except for those who retained a fond recollection of those cute little Minors of the 1950s.

1946-48 MORRIS

1947 Morris Eight Series "E" two-door saloon.

Starting by October 1945, just after peace returned to Europe, Morris reentered the marketplace with two carryover models: the Eight and Ten sedans. Riding an 89-inch wheelbase, the little Eight had a sloping grille made up of vertical bars, semi-faired-in headlamps, and an optional sunroof. Both two- and four-door sedans were built, along with a two-seat roadster and four-seat touring model. Under the hood was the same 918-cc L-head four-cylinder engine used in final prewar examples, and which would soon appear in the new Minor. The Ten initially had a more upright grille made up of horizontal bars, separate headlamps, and an 1140-cc overhead-valve four-cylinder engine producing 37 horsepower. Only a four-door sedan was available, with sunroof optional. For the 1947 model year, the Ten's grille became more rounded. Both models were discontinued as the new Minor and Oxford arrived in late 1948.

1949 MORRIS

1949 Morris Minor two-door sedan.

MINOR — MM — FOUR — Dubbed "the world's supreme small car" by its maker, the rounded-look Minor, designed by Alec Issigonis, attracted considerable attention in America from the start. Both a two-door sedan and a similarly-styled convertible were introduced and, as early ads noted, there was "No price penalty on convertibles." Special features included unibody construction with turret-top (sedan) roof and a one-piece floor pressing, rack-and-pinion steering, a semi-floating hypoid rear axle, and vernier-trimmed torsion bars for the front suspension to deliver a "Lull-abye" ride. Headlamps stood low, alongside the grille and beneath its curved upper surround molding. The grille insert displayed a chrome mesh pattern dominated by three vertical bars and two horizontal bars. Single round taillamps in initial models were replaced by separate (twin) stop and tail units, early in the model year. Doors contained vent panels, and a vee-type split windshield was used. Chrome-plated window frames formed the upper half of each "safety" door, which was hinged at the front. The driver's door had a lock; the passenger's, a safety catch. Horizontal pull-out door handles followed the line of the horizontal bodyside trim strip, and sat over recessed oval hand openings. Rear side windows were large and fixed in position, while wheel openings were fully rounded.

Under the "alligator" hood, with internal lock release, the "Bulldog" 918.6-cc four-cylinder side-valve (L-head) engine was hooked to a four-speed manual gearbox. Instruments were grouped in the dashboard, which included a hinged glovebox lid and deep full-width tray. Vynide-covered front bucket seats hinged at the front to tip forward for access to the rear seats. The driver's seat adjusted fore and aft, altering height at the same time. Rear seatbacks folded forward for access to the seven-cubic-foot luggage compartment, or to form a flat space for storage. A hand switch operated the trafficators, which included a warning light. Twin wind-tone horns were installed. Standard colors were: Maroon, Romain Green, Platinum Grey, and Black. Interiors came in "tastefully neutral shades." Convertibles had an easy-to-erect, fully weatherproofed top with wind-up windows in the doors. U.S. export models gained a modified front end early in 1949, with headlamps mounted on front fenders. European Minors kept the original low-headlamp design until the 1951 model year.

OXFORD — FOUR — Shaped similar to the Minor, the Oxford came only as a four-door sedan, with fender-mounted headlamps separate from the large grille, which had a crosshatch pattern of small holes between its thick bars. Parking lights were built into the headlamps. Both front and rear doors held vent panes. Late in the model year, twin oblong stop/taillamps replaced the original round units and tires grew from 5.25x15 to 5.50x15 size. Powerplant was a 1476-cc L-head four, producing 41 horsepower, driving a four-speed manual gearbox.

I.D. DATA: Serial number plate is on the right front of the firewall, under the hood. Engine number is on flywheel or right side of crankcase, and on the firewall plate. Starting serial number: (Minor) SMM-100; (Oxford) SMO-100. Engine number prefix: (Minor) USHM-2; (Oxford) VS15M. A suffix in the serial number indicated body paint type: 'C' = cellulose (used on early models); 'S' = Synobel; 'SYN' = synthetic.

Model	Body Type & Seating	Engine Type/CID	P.O.E Price	Weight (lbs.)	Prod. Total
MINOR					
MM	2-dr Sedan-4P	I4/56	1570	1732	Note 1
MM	2-dr Conv-4P	I4/56	1570	1680	Note 1
OXFORD					
MO	4-dr Sedan-4P	I4/90	2150	2324	Note 1

Note 1: Approximately 298 Morris cars were sold in the U.S. in 1949. During 1948, its first partial year of existence, about 1,172 Minors were produced. A total of 171,021 MM series Minors were produced through July 1952, including about 82,000 with the early low-headlamp front end.

ENGINE DATA: BASE FOUR (Minor): Inline, L-head four-cylinder. Cast iron block and head. **Displacement:** 56 cu. in. (918.6 cc). **Bore & Stroke:** 2.244 x 3.543 in. (57 x 90 mm). **Compression Ratio:** 6.5:1 (6.7:1 optional). **Brake Horsepower:** 27.5 at 4400 rpm. **Torque:** 39 lbs.-ft. at 2400 rpm. Three main bearings. Solid valve lifters. One SU automatic piston-type carburetor. 12-volt electrical system.

BASE FOUR (Oxford): Inline, L-head four-cylinder. Cast iron block and head. **Displacement:** 90 cu. in. (1476 cc). **Bore & Stroke:** 2.894 x 3.425 in. (73.5 x 87 mm). **Compression Ratio:** 6.6:1. **Brake Horsepower:** 41 at 4200 rpm. Three main bearings. Solid valve lifters. One SU piston-type carburetor. 12-volt electrical system.

CHASSIS DATA: Wheelbase: (Minor) 86 in.; (Oxford) 97 in. **Overall Length:** (Minor) 148 in.; (Oxford) 167 in. **Height:** (Minor) 60 in.; (Oxford) 63 in. **Width:** (Minor) 61 in.; (Oxford) 65 in. **Front Tread:** (Minor) 50.6 in.; (Oxford) 53.5 in. **Rear Tread:** (Minor) 50.3 in.; (Oxford) 53.0 in. **Wheel Type:** (Minor) four-bolt disc with plated hub embellishers; (Oxford) five-bolt disc. **Standard Tires:** (Minor) Dunlop 5.00x14; (Oxford) 5.25x15 (later 5.50x15).

TECHNICAL: Layout: front-engine, rear-drive. **Transmission:** four-speed manual; synchro 2nd/3rd/4th. Minor gear ratios: (1st) 3.95:1; (2nd) 2.3:1; (3rd) 1.54:1; (4th) 1.00:1; (rev) 3.95:1. **Standard Final Drive Ratio:** (Minor) 4.55:1; (Oxford) 4.55:1. **Steering:** (Minor) rack and pinion. **Suspension (front):** wishbones and torsion bars. **Suspension (rear):** long semi-elliptic leaf springs. **Brakes:** Lockheed front/rear drum. **Body Construction:** steel unibody.

PERFORMANCE: Top Speed: (Minor) 62 mph; (Oxford) 72 mph. **Acceleration (0-60 mph):** (Minor) N/A (0-50 mph in 24.2 sec.); (Oxford) N/A (0-50 mph in 19.5 seconds). **Acceleration (quarter-mile):** (Minor) 26.3 sec.; (Oxford) 24.5 seconds. **Fuel Mileage:** (Minor) 35-40 mpg advertised.

Manufacturer: Morris Motors Ltd. (Nuffield Exports Ltd.), Cowley, Oxford, England.

ADDITIONAL MODELS: Morris also produced a six-cylinder MS series with 135-cid (2215 cc) overhead-cam engine, rated at 65 horsepower, on a 110-inch wheelbase. Overall profile of the four-door six was similar to the Oxford, but with an upright vertical grille.

HISTORY: Both the Minor and Oxford were introduced in October 1948. Attempting to interest parties who might favor a larger model, Morris called the Minor "the small car interpretation of a Big Car specification." Still, the sales brochure stressed economy in its various forms, adding that owners reported gas mileage of 35-40 mpg. They further claimed that a 200-mile trip could be undertaken for as little as $1.30 in fuel cost. Minors, said the brochures, were "thoroughly tested, new from radiator badge to rear bumper (to bring) motoring perfection within reach by satisfying your ideals and pocket." While bemoaning the lack of power from the original L-head four, *Auto Sport Review* later called the Minor "one of the most delightful small cars in the world to drive." Because designer Alec Issogonis wanted the Minor to be four inches wider than the prototype, a band of that width was added to the center of the hood. Early models also had a three-piece bumper, with a black segment in the center, as evidence of that growth in width. While most Minors imported to the U.S. through the 1950s and '60s had flashing turn signals, a blank metal section, the same size as the standard semaphore-style trafficators, remained evident on the bodysides.

1950 MORRIS

MINOR — MM — FOUR — Painted door window frames replaced the original chromed frames early in the 1950 model year. Later on, control knobs added identifying letters. Otherwise, appearance and mechanical details were the same as 1949. As more examples arrived in the U.S., the Minor's Port-of-Entry price fell, reaching as low as $1295.

OXFORD — FOUR — Although not listed in U.S. directories for 1950, production of the larger-engined Morris continued with little change (as did the six-cylinder model); and the Oxford appeared again in listings for 1951 and beyond. Rear doors added armrests, and control knobs added letters.

I.D. DATA: Serial numbers are in same locations as 1949, continuing in the same sequence.

Model	Body Type & Seating	Engine Type/CID	P.O.E Price	Weight (lbs.)	Prod. Total
MINOR					
MM	2-dr Sedan-4P	I4/56	1295	1732	Note 1
MM	2-dr Conv-4P	I4/56	1295	1680	Note 1
OXFORD					
MO	4-dr Sedan-4P	I4/90	N/A	2324	Note 1

Note 1: Approximately 695 Morris cars were sold in the U.S. in 1950. Total MM series Minor production from 1948-52 was 171,021.

ENGINE DATA: Same as 1949.

CHASSIS DATA: Same as 1949.

TECHNICAL: Same as 1949.

PERFORMANCE: Same as 1949.

1951 MORRIS

1951 Morris Minor MM convertible. (Christie's)

MINOR — MM — FOUR — A four-door Minor joined the original open and closed two-doors. Headlamps on European Minors moved upward from their original position alongside the grille, to mounting on the fenders. (U.S. versions had those higher headlamps starting in early 1949.) During the model year, painted grilles replaced the chrome-plated originals. Grille patterns consisted of a series of thin vertical bars, three thicker vertical bars, and two horizontal bars. Small round parking lights stood alongside the grille, beneath the curved upper molding that reached down to bumper level. Above that molding was a small Morris badge.

OXFORD — FOUR — The bigger four-cylinder Morris added separate round parking lights below its headlamps, as well as telescopic rear shock absorbers. A six-bladed fan replaced the former four-blade unit. Otherwise, little change was evident, but later in the model year, the chrome-plated grilles gave way to painted units.

I.D. DATA: Serial numbers are in same locations as 1949-50, continuing in the same sequence.

Model	Body Type & Seating	Engine Type/CID	P.O.E Price	Weight (lbs.)	Prod. Total
MINOR					
MM	2-dr Sedan-4P	I4/56	1420	1670	Note 1
MM	2-dr Conv-4P	I4/56	1399	1609	Note 1
MM	4-dr Sedan-4P	I4/56	1570	1778	Note 1
OXFORD					
MO	4-dr Sedan-4P	I4/90	1950	2218	Note 1

Note 1: Approximately 1,583 Morris cars were sold in the U.S. in 1951. A total of 171,021 MM series Minors were built from 1948-52, nearly half of which had the early low-headlamp front end.

ENGINE DATA: BASE FOUR (Minor): Inline, L-head four-cylinder. Cast iron block and head. **Displacement:** 56 cu. in. (918.6 cc). **Bore & Stroke:** 2.244 x 3.543 in. (57 x 90 mm). **Compression Ratio:** 6.6:1. **Brake Horsepower:** 27.5 at 4400 rpm. **Torque:** 39 lbs.-ft. at 2400 rpm. Three main bearings. Solid valve lifters. One SU automatic piston-type carburetor. 12-volt electrical system.

BASE FOUR (Oxford): Inline, L-head four-cylinder. Cast iron block and head. **Displacement:** 90 cu. in. (1476 cc). **Bore & Stroke:** 2.894 x 3.425 in. (73.5 x 87 mm). **Compression Ratio:** 6.6:1. **Brake Horsepower:** 41 at 4200 rpm. Three main bearings. Solid valve lifters. One SU piston-type carburetor. 12-volt electrical system.

CHASSIS DATA: Wheelbase: (Minor) 86 in.; (Oxford) 97 in. **Overall Length:** (Minor) 148 in.; (Oxford) 167 in. **Height:** (Minor) 60 in.; (Oxford) 63 in. **Width:** (Minor) 61 in.; (Oxford) 65 in. **Front Tread:** (Minor) 50.6 in.; (Oxford) 53.5 in. **Rear Tread:** (Minor) 50.3 in.; (Oxford) 53.0 in. **Wheel Type:** (Minor) four-bolt disc with plated hub embellishers; (Oxford) five-bolt disc. **Standard Tires:** (Minor) Dunlop 5.00x14; (Oxford) 5.50x15.

TECHNICAL: Layout: front-engine, rear-drive. **Transmission:** four-speed manual; synchro 2nd/3rd/4th. **Standard Final Drive Ratio:** (Minor) 4.55:1. **Steering:** (Minor) rack and pinion. **Suspension (front):** wishbones and torsion bars. **Suspension (rear):** long semi-elliptic leaf springs. **Brakes:** Lockheed front/rear drum. **Body Construction:** steel unibody.

PERFORMANCE: Top Speed: (Minor) 62-69 mph; (Oxford) 72 mph. **Acceleration (0-60 mph):** (Minor) 31-39.2 sec.; (Oxford) N/A (0-50 mph in 19.5 seconds). **Acceleration (quarter-mile):** (Minor) 26.3 sec.; (Oxford) 24.5 seconds. **Fuel Mileage:** (Minor) up to 41 mpg (U.S.) claimed.

Manufacturer: Morris Motors Ltd. (Nuffield Exports Ltd.), Cowley, Oxford, England.

Distributor: The Hambro Trading Co. of America, Chicago, Illinois (and others).

ADDITIONAL MODELS: Morris continued to produce the six-cylinder Morris Six sedan, with overhead-cam 2215-cc engine and 110-inch wheelbase.

HISTORY: Four Minors entered the Sebring (Florida) International Grand Prix of Endurance in 1951, finishing the full 12 hours for what U.S. dealer J.S. Inskip described as "one of the most impressive team performances of the day."

1952 MORRIS

MINOR — MM — FOUR — Little change was evident in the Minor except for an ashtray added to the upper center of the facia. Headlamp warning lights were added during the model year. Most models that reached the U.S. by this time lacked the earlier chrome grille and hubcaps.

OXFORD — FOUR — Changes were minimal on the larger four-cylinder Morris, except for the deletion of the rear blind and moving the battery's location.

I.D. DATA: Serial numbers are in same locations as 1949-51, continuing in the same sequence.

Model	Body Type & Seating	Engine Type/CID	P.O.E. Price	Weight (lbs.)	Prod. Total
MINOR					
MM	2-dr Sedan-4P	I4/56	1450	1670	Note 1
MM	4-dr Sedan-4P	I4/56	1575	1778	Note 1
MM	2-dr Conv-4P	I4/56	1475	1609	Note1
OXFORD					
MO	4-dr Sedan-4P	I4/90	2200	2218	Note 1

Note 1: Approximately 1,945 Morris cars were sold in the U.S. in 1952. A total of 171,021 MM Minors were produced from 1948-52.

ENGINE DATA: Same as 1951.

CHASSIS DATA: Same as 1951.

TECHNICAL: Same as 1951.

PERFORMANCE: Same as 1951.

HISTORY: Just one solitary Minor ran in the 1952 Sebring (Florida) endurance race, winning its class. It was one of only 17 cars to finish at all. J.S. Inskip Inc. in New York City described the Minor as "the economy car with the racing performance....a real little thoroughbred--designed and manufactured by those responsible for the famous MG racing car and built in the same tradition to give fast, rugged performance." Production of the MM series Minor ended in July 1952.

1953 MORRIS

1953 Morris Minor Series II convertible. (Sotheby's)

MINOR — SERIES II — FOUR — An overhead-valve engine from the Austin A30, displacing 803 cc, went under the Morris hood this year. That significant drop brought little boost in the basic performance figures, even though horsepower was higher. No matter, claimed the sales catalog, Morris "establishes a new class in economy motoring." In fact, *Auto Sport Review* praised the new engine's acceleration in high gear, noting that "hills you used to have to churn up in third gear now can be negotiated in fourth." They further praised the Minor as "one of the easiest-handling, best-cornering, most convenient small cars on the market." Early sales literature for the 1953 model year still described the side-valve (L-head) engine, and the overhead-valve unit arrived first on the four-door sedan, for export only; then later on the two-door models. Standard body colors announced at that time for the four-door sedan were: Thames Blue with green upholstery; Gascoyne Grey with brown upholstery; Mist Green with green upholstery; and Black with red upholstery. Two-door models could have Thames Blue, Mist Green or Gascoyne Grey, each with beige upholstery; or Black with red upholstery.

OXFORD — FOUR — A Traveller Estate Car (station wagon) joined the original four-door sedan this year. Early in the model year, Oxford grilles also switched to two heavy horizontal bars instead of four. Standard body colors announced for 1953 were: Black with red upholstery; Gascoyne Grey with brown upholstery; and Mist Green or Thames Blue with green upholstery. Front seats upholstered in leather.

I.D. DATA: Serial number plate is on the right front of the firewall, under the hood. Engine number is on a ledge below the front spark plug or the right side of the crankcase, and on the firewall plate. Serial number prefix: (Minor) SMM; (Oxford) SMO. Sequential numbering continued from 1949-52. Engine number prefix: (Oxford) VS15M.

Model	Body Type & Seating	Engine Type/CID	P.O.E. Price	Weight (lbs.)	Prod. Price
MINOR					
II	2-dr Sedan-4P	I4/49	1450	1670	Note 1
II	4-dr Sedan-4P	I4/49	1575	1778	Note 1
II	2-dr Conv-4P	I4/49	1475	1609	Note 1
OXFORD					
MO	4-dr Sedan-4P	I4/90	2200	2218	Note 1
MO	4-dr Sta Wag-5P	I4/90	N/A	N/A	Note 1

Note 1: A total of 322,400 Series II Minors were produced through 1956. By the end of 1953, nearly 7,000 had been sold in America.

ENGINE DATA: BASE FOUR (Minor): Inline, overhead-valve four-cylinder (Austin A30). Cast iron block and head. **Displacement:** 49 cu. in. (803 cc). **Bore & Stroke:** 2.28 x 3.00 in. (58 x 76 mm). **Compression Ratio:** 7.2:1. **Brake Horsepower:** 30 at 4800 rpm. **Torque:** 40 lbs.-ft. at 2400 rpm. Three main bearings. Solid valve lifters. One SU H1 carburetor. 12-volt electrical system.

Note: Some early 1953 Minors retained the former L-head engine; see previous listings.

BASE FOUR (Oxford): Inline, L-head four-cylinder. Cast iron block and head. **Displacement:** 90 cu. in. (1476 cc). **Bore & Stroke:** 2.894 x 3.425 in. (73.5 x 87 mm). **Compression Ratio:** 6.6:1. **Brake Horsepower:** 41 at 4000 rpm. Three main bearings. Solid valve lifters. One SU piston-type carburetor. 12-volt electrical system.

CHASSIS DATA: **Wheelbase:** (Minor) 86 in.; (Oxford) 97 in. **Overall Length:** (Minor) 148 in.; (Oxford) 167 in. **Height:** (Minor) 60 in.; (Oxford) 63 in. **Width:** (Minor) 61 in.; (Oxford) 65 in. **Front Tread:** (Minor) 50.6 in.; (Oxford) 53.5 in. **Rear Tread:** (Minor) 50.3 in.; (Oxford) 53.0 in. **Wheel Type:** (Minor) four-bolt disc; (Oxford) five-bolt disc. **Standard Tires:** (Minor) Dunlop 5.00x14; (Oxford) Dunlop 5.50x15.

TECHNICAL: **Layout:** front-engine, rear-drive. **Transmission:** four-speed manual; synchro 2nd/3rd/4th. **Standard Final Drive Ratio:** (Minor) 5.375:1; (Oxford) 4.875:1. **Steering:** rack and pinion. **Suspension (front):** wishbones and torsion bars. **Suspension (rear):** long semi-elliptic leaf springs. **Brakes:** Lockheed hydraulic, front/rear drum. **Body Construction:** steel unibody.

PERFORMANCE: **Top Speed:** (Minor) 62-66 mph; (Oxford) 72 mph. **Acceleration (0-60 mph):** (Minor) 39.9 sec.; (Oxford) N/A (0-50 mph in 19.5 seconds). **Acceleration (quarter-mile):** (Minor) 26.2-26.9 sec.; (Oxford) 24.5 seconds. **Fuel Mileage:** (Minor) 32-42 mpg.

Manufacturer: Morris Motors Ltd. (Nuffield Exports Ltd.), Cowley, Oxford, England (part of British Motor Corp.).

ADDITIONAL MODELS: Morris produced the Morris Six sedan, with overhead-cam 2215-cc six-cylinder engine rated 70 bhp and riding a 110-inch wheelbase, into 1954. Though similar in profile to the Oxford, its vertical-style grille gave the Six a much different appearance. All Morris models had unibody construction and split windshields.

HISTORY: Advertisements placed by British Motor Car Distributors Ltd. in San Francisco, late in 1953, called the more potent Minor four-door the "biggest small car buy on earth." Promoting both compact size and economy, the ads further noted that "There's always room for a 'Morris' no matter how small the parking space or how small the budget."

1954 MORRIS

1954 Morris Minor Series II four-door tourer.

MINOR — SERIES II — FOUR — A Traveller Estate Car (station wagon) joined the Minor sedan and convertible this year, though it took a little longer to arrive on the U.S. market. Otherwise, changes were minimal. *Auto Age*, testing a new wagon, claimed that Morrises "will actually outhandle MGs, Jags and practically any other sports car you can name," because of their superb suspension and quick rack-and-pinion steering.

OXFORD — FOUR — A DeLuxe sedan with additional chrome trim and other extras became available in England, but early in 1954 the first Oxford series was discontinued. Series II had a one-piece windshield, and a grille that consisted of one heavy center bar. Replacing the L-head four was a new 1489-cc overhead-valve four-cylinder engine.

I.D. DATA: Serial numbers are in same locations as 1953.

Model	Body Type & Seating	Engine Type/CID	P.O.E. Price	Weight (lbs.)	Prod. Price
MINOR					
II	2-dr Sedan-4P	I4/49	1430	1685	Note 1
II	4-dr Sedan-4P	I4/49	1550	1775	Note 1
II	2-dr Tour Conv-4P	I4/49	1455	1606	Note 1
II	2-dr Sta Wag-4P	I4/49	N/A	1848	Note 1
OXFORD					
MO	4-dr Sedan-4P	I4/90	2108	2296	Note 1
MO	4-dr Sta Wag-5P	I4/90	2355	2440	Note 1

Note 1: Approximately 955 Morris cars were sold in the U.S. in 1954. A total of 322,400 Series II Minors were built, from 1952 through 1956.

Price Note: Deluxe models of the Minor cost about $41-45 more than the base models.

ENGINE DATA: BASE FOUR (Minor): Inline, overhead-valve four-cylinder (Austin A30). Cast iron block and head. **Displacement:** 49 cu. in. (803 cc). **Bore & Stroke:** 2.28 x 3.00 in. (58 x 76 mm). **Compression Ratio:** 7.2:1. **Brake Horsepower:** 30 at 4800 rpm. **Torque:** 40 lbs.-ft. at 2400 rpm. Three main bearings. Solid valve lifters. One SU H1 carburetor. 12-volt electrical system.

BASE FOUR (Oxford): Inline, L-head four-cylinder. Cast iron block and head. **Displacement:** 90 cu. in. (1476 cc). **Bore & Stroke:** 2.894 x 3.425 in. (73.5 x 87 mm). **Compression Ratio:** 6.6:1. **Brake Horsepower:** 41 at 4000 rpm. Three main bearings. Solid valve lifters. One SU piston-type carburetor. 12-volt electrical system.

BASE FOUR (Oxford Series II): Inline, overhead-valve four-cylinder. Cast iron block and head. **Displacement:** 90.8 cu. in. (1489 cc). **Bore & Stroke:** 2.875 x 3.50 in. (73 x 88.9 mm). **Compression Ratio:** 7.4:1. **Brake Horsepower:** 50 at 4800 rpm. Three main bearings. Solid valve lifters. One SU carburetor. 12-volt electrical system.

CHASSIS DATA: Wheelbase: (Minor) 86 in.; (Oxford) 97 in. **Overall Length:** (Minor) 148 in.; (Oxford) 167 in. **Height:** (Minor) 60 in.; (Oxford) 63 in. **Width:** (Minor) 61 in.; (Oxford) 65 in. **Front Tread:** (Minor) 50.6 in.; (Oxford) 53.5 in. **Rear Tread:** (Minor) 50.3 in.; (Oxford) 53.0 in. **Wheel Type:** (Minor) four-bolt disc; (Oxford) five-bolt disc. **Standard Tires:** (Minor) Dunlop 5.00x14; (Oxford) Dunlop 5.50x15.

TECHNICAL: Layout: front-engine, rear-drive. **Transmission:** four-speed manual; synchro 2nd/3rd/4th. **Standard Final Drive Ratio:** (Minor) 5.375:1; (Oxford) 4.875:1. **Steering:** rack and pinion. **Suspension (front):** wishbones and torsion bars. **Suspension (rear):** long semi-elliptic leaf springs. **Brakes:** Lockheed hydraulic, front/rear drum. **Body Construction:** steel unibody.

PERFORMANCE: Top Speed: (Minor) 62-66 mph; (Minor wag) 67-69 mph; (Oxford) 72 mph. **Acceleration (0-60 mph):** (Minor) 29-39.9 sec.; (Minor wag) N/A (0-50 mph in 24.2 seconds); (Oxford) N/A (0-50 mph in 19.5 seconds). **Acceleration (quarter-mile):** (Minor) 26.2-26.9 sec.; (Oxford) 24.5 seconds. **Fuel Mileage:** (Minor) 32-42 mpg.

Manufacturer: Morris Motors Ltd. (Nuffield Exports Ltd.), Cowley, Oxford, England (part of British Motor Corp.).

ADDITIONAL MODELS: During 1954, production of the Morris Six sedan ceased. Later, in 1955, it would be replaced by a new Isis six with larger engine. By this time, too, the Oxford was fast disappearing from American directories of imported cars, leaving the Morris Minor as the only official contender for U.S. sales.

1955-56 MORRIS

1955 Morris Minor convertible.

MINOR — SERIES II — FOUR — A new rectangular grille made up of five horizontal bars was the major change this year. It sat within a larger bright surround molding. Small round parking lights stood below the headlamps. Inside, the Minor's dashboard held a round instrument/control panel in its center, with open gloveboxes at each end and a wide parcel shelf below. An optional radio could be positioned in the center of that shelf. Minors still had a split windshield, and a pull-button starter with manual choke. Only the driver's seat was adjustable, but both two-door front seats hinged forward. Neither the convertible nor the two-door sedan's rear side windows rolled down. Each of the four body styles was available with either basic or deluxe trim.

I.D. DATA: Serial numbers are in same locations as 1953.

Model	Body Type & Seating	Engine Type/CID	P.O.E. Price	Weight (lbs.)	Prod. Price
MINOR					
II	2-dr Sedan-4P	I4/49	1430	1685	Note 1
II	4-dr Sedan-4P	I4/49	1550	1775	Note 1
II	2-dr Conv-4P	I4/49	1455	1606	Note 1
II	2-dr Sta Wag-4P	I4/49	N/A	1848	Note 1

Note 1: Approximately 145,000 Morris cars were produced in 1955, and 115,000 in 1956. A total of 322,400 Series II Minors were built, 1952-56.

Price Note: Deluxe models of the Minor cost about $30-45 more than the base models.

1956 Price Note: During 1956, the Minor two-door sedan sold for $1465; the four-door for $1545; convertible, $1463; and station wagon, $1645.

1956 Morris Minor station wagon.

ENGINE DATA: BASE FOUR (Minor): Inline, overhead-valve four-cylinder (Austin A30, BMC A-series). Cast iron block and head. **Displacement:** 49 cu. in. (803 cc). **Bore & Stroke:** 2.28 x 3.00 in. (58 x 76 mm). **Compression Ratio:** 7.2:1. **Brake Horsepower:** 30 at 4800 rpm. **Torque:** 40 lbs.-ft. at 2400 rpm. Three main bearings. Solid valve lifters. One SU H1 carburetor. 12-volt electrical system.

CHASSIS DATA: Wheelbase: 86 in. **Overall Length:** 148 in.; (wag) 149 in. **Height:** 60 in. **Width:** 61 in. **Front Tread:** 50.6 in. **Rear Tread:** 50.3 in. **Wheel Type:** four-bolt disc. **Standard Tires:** Dunlop 5.00x14.

TECHNICAL: Layout: front-engine, rear-drive. **Transmission:** four-speed manual; synchro 2nd/3rd/4th. **Standard Final Drive Ratio:** 5.375:1. **Steering:** rack and pinion. **Suspension (front):** wishbones and torsion bars. **Suspension (rear):** long semi-elliptic leaf springs. **Brakes:** Lockheed hydraulic, front/rear drum. **Body Construction:** steel unibody. **Fuel Tank:** 6.0 gallons (U.S.).

PERFORMANCE: Top Speed: 62-66 mph. **Acceleration (0-60 mph):** 29-39.9 seconds. **Acceleration (quarter-mile):** 26.2-26.9 seconds. **Fuel Mileage:** 32-44 mpg (35+ mpg at cruising speed).

Manufacturer: Morris Motors Ltd. (Nuffield Exports Ltd.), Cowley, Oxford, England (part of British Motor Corp.).

Distributor: Hambro Trading Company of America, Inc., New York City and Los Angeles.

ADDITIONAL MODELS: Oxford sedan and station wagon production continued in its Series II form, with a 1489-cc overhead-valve engine rated 50 bhp. A new Isis six emerged in 1955, with a 2639-cc engine and 107.5-inch wheelbase, in four-door sedan and station wagon bodies. Output of the Isis engine was 86 horsepower, and a Borg-Warner overdrive transmission was optional. Neither of these larger models was officially imported into the U.S. Morris also introduced a new upright-look Cowley sedan before the 1955 model year began, with a 1200-cc, 42-bhp four-cylinder engine and 97-inch wheelbase (same as the Oxford), measuring 168 inches long. Cowley's grille consisted of a single thick horizontal bar and curved upper bar, over a pattern of thin horizontal slits. That model, too, was not aimed at the U.S. market.

HISTORY: Production of the Series II Minor began in July 1952 and continued until September 1956.

1957-59 MORRIS

MINOR 1000 — FOUR — A larger engine entered the Minor's hood for 1957, displacing 948 cubic centimeters and producing 37 horsepower. *Motor Trend* welcomed the more powerful motor, describing it as a "happy sounding little buzz bomb." Appearance was similar to the final Series II, with a grille that consisted of five horizontal slats and a larger molding surrounding it. Round parking lights stood just outside that outer molding, below the headlamps. A one-piece curved windshield replaced the former split glass, and a large back window was installed. A new rack-and-pinion gearbox was introduced, and the new remote-control gearshift made it unnecessary to lift the lever to reach reverse. Final-drive ratio was lowered this year. Replacing the former dashboard-mounted turn-signal switch was a new trafficator switch (with built-in horn control) on the steering column. A central side-jacking system was intended to simplify tire-changing. As before, the Minor came in four body styles: two- and four-door sedan, convertible, and Traveller Estate Car (station wagon). Both standard and deluxe models were offered. Standard equipment included a heater and sunvisor. One round center gauge contained the speedometer and warning lights, with covered gloveboxes at each end of the dashboard. Morris now advertised the Minor as capable of carrying five passengers, with seven cubic feet of luggage space. For the 1958 model year, convertible tops switched from canvas to plastic material. For the 1959 model year, courtesy light switches were added to front doors.

1957 Morris Minor 1000 four-door sedan.

I.D. DATA: An identification plate on the right front of the firewall, under the hood, contains the Car Number and Engine Number. The engine number is also on a pad below the No. 1 (front) spark plug. Serial number breakdown: first prefix letter is make ('M'); second prefix indicates is engine size ('A' = 800-999 cc); third prefix is body type ('J' = convertible; '2S' = two-door sedan; 'S' = four-door sedan); fourth prefix indicates series; fifth prefix is steering ('L' = left-hand drive).

Model	Body Type & Seating	Engine Type/CID	P.O.E. Price	Weight (lbs.)	Prod. Total
MINOR					
1000	2-dr Sedan-5P	I4/58	1549	1652	Note 1
1000	4-dr Sedan-5P	I4/58	1649	1708	Note 1
1000	2-dr Conv-5P	I4/58	1549	1624	Note 1
1000	2-dr Sta Wag-5P	I4/58	1769	1764	Note 1

Note 1: Approximately 125,000 Morris cars were produced in 1957, 140,000 in 1958, and 147,000 in 1959. About 5,375 were sold in the U.S. during 1957. A total of 544,048 Series 1000 Minors were produced from September 1956 to September 1962.

Price Note: Deluxe models of the Minor cost about $30-45 more than the base models. 1958 Price Note: The two-door sedan rose to $1705, the four-door to $1794, the convertible (Tourer) to $1689, and the station wagon to $1912. Deluxe models cost $1751, $1860, $1745 and $1967, respectively.

1959 Price Note: See 1960 listing for Morris Minor prices.

1958 Morris Minor 1000.

ENGINE DATA: BASE FOUR (Minor): Inline, overhead-valve four-cylinder (BMC A-series). Cast iron block and head. **Displacement:** 57.8 cu. in. (948 cc). **Bore & Stroke:** 2.48 x 3.00 in. (62.9 x 76.2 mm). **Compression Ratio:** 8.3:1. **Brake Horsepower:** 37 at 4800 rpm. **Torque:** 48 lbs.-ft. at 3000 rpm. Three main bearings. Solid valve lifters. One SU H2 carburetor. 12-volt electrical system.

Note: Minors with lower compression (7.2:1) and 34-bhp output were sold in Europe.

CHASSIS DATA: Wheelbase: 86 in. **Overall Length:** 148 in.; (wag) 149 in. **Height:** 60 in. **Width:** 61 in. **Front Tread:** 50.6 in. **Rear Tread:** 50.3 in. **Wheel Type:** four-bolt disc. **Standard Tires:** Dunlop 5.00x14.

TECHNICAL: Layout: front-engine, rear-drive. **Transmission:** four-speed manual; synchro 2nd/3rd/4th. **Standard Final Drive Ratio:** 4.55:1. **Steering:** rack and pinion. **Suspension (front):** wishbones and torsion bars. **Suspension (rear):** long semi-elliptic leaf springs. **Brakes:** Lockheed hydraulic, front/rear drum. **Body Construction:** steel unibody. **Fuel Tank:** 7.8 gallons (U.S.).

PERFORMANCE: Top Speed: 73-75 mph. **Acceleration (0-60 mph):** 28 sec. (0-50 mph in 18.7 seconds). **Acceleration (quarter-mile):** 24.1 seconds (57.2 mph). **Fuel Mileage:** about 32 mpg average (40 mpg claimed).

Manufacturer: Morris Motors Ltd. (Nuffield Exports Ltd.), Cowley, Oxford, England (part of British Motor Corp.).

Distributor: Hambro Automotive Corp., New York City.

ADDITIONAL MODELS: Both the Cowley sedan and the more deluxe Oxford (Series III) sedan and station wagon were now powered by a BMC 1489-cc overhead-valve four-cylinder engine, rated 55 bhp. Each had front torsion bars and rack-and-pinion steering, and could be obtained with a Manumatic clutch. The Series II version of the Isis six retained the 2639-cc engine and 107.5-inch wheelbase, but engine output was up to 90 horsepower. Both a Borg-Warner overdrive and fully automatic transmission were optional on the Isis. At this time, only the Minor was officially imported into the U.S. It was also the only model to keep the rounded profile; all of the others had an upright appearance. Production of the Isis halted in 1958, and all Morris models through the 1960s would have four cylinders. Production of the Cowley sedan ceased early in 1959 as the Oxford sedan and station wagon evolved to Series V designation (see next listing).

1959 Morris Minor 1000.

HISTORY: *Motor Trend* ranked the pepped-up Minor as "one of the best buys in the growing small car field....as easy and delightful to drive as it is economical to operate and maintain." In 1958, Morris announced a new Major model, "big brother of the Morris Minor," derived from the Wolseley 1500.

1960-62 MORRIS

1961 Morris Minor 1000 convertible. (Sotheby's)

MINOR 1000 — FOUR — Changes were minimal on the Minor, which again was powered by BMC's 948-cc four-cylinder engine, producing 37 horsepower. Deluxe models included bumper overriders, leather-covered seat cushions and backs, and a passenger sunvisor on sedans. Standard 1960 sedan/convertible colors were: Black, Off-White or Dark Grey with red upholstery, and Blue Grey with blue grey upholstery. Convertibles could have an off-white top with Black or Blue-Grey body, or a maroon top with the Dark Grey or Off-White body. Wagons came in Black or Dark Grey with red upholstery.

MINI-MINOR — 850 — FOUR — An all-new model adopted the Morris nameplate for the 1960 model, virtually identical to the tiny front-drive Mini sedan that took the Austin name except for the grille pattern and hood badge. A transversely-mounted, 848-cc (51.7-cid) four-cylinder engine produced 34 horsepower, sufficient to give the minicar plenty of performance. Weighing just 1,331 pounds (unladen) and measuring only 10 feet in length, the Mini-Minor could be parked in a space only a foot and a half longer than its own maximum dimension. Cone-shaped rubber springs were installed at all four corners. Mini's grille consisted of a pattern of small horizontal slots, arranged in four rows, below a curved upper surround molding. Parking lights stood alongside that grille molding, below the round headlamps. Sliding door windows were used. Rear windows were fixed on standard models, but hinged on deluxe versions. Standard Mini-Minor colors were White, Red or Blue, with grey and black fleck upholstery. Road wheels were white on all models. Deluxe versions (for export) added an accessory group that included two-color leathercloth upholstery and foam rubber seat cushions, windshield washer, adjustable front passenger's seat, wheel hub embellishers, bumper overriders, bright plastic sill finishers and windshield/back-window surrounds, and a passenger's sunvisor. A little station wagon joined the original sedan for 1961. For additional details of this and subsequent Mini-Minors (including the performance-oriented Cooper and Cooper 'S' versions), see the Austin Mini listing.

OXFORD — SERIES V/VI — FOUR — After an absence of several years, the larger Oxford sedan began to appear in American directories of imported cars available. The new "Farina" design, introduced during the 1959 model year, had a much more upright, squared-off profile than the Minor, with a nearly-vertical front panel, and rode a longer (99.25-inch) wheelbase. A wide rectangular grille was made up of horizontal bars. Wider (full-width) surround moldings below the grille contained parking lamps at their ends. Under the hood was the same 1489-cc four-cylinder engine as in prior Oxford models, developing 55 horsepower. By the 1962 model year, a modified Series VI emerged on a slightly longer wheelbase yet (100.25 inches), with a 1622-cc engine delivering 61 bhp.

1962 Morris Mini-Cooper.

I.D. DATA: An identification plate on the right front of the firewall, under the hood, contains the Car Number and Engine Number. Minor engine number is also on a pad below the No. 1 (front) spark plug. Mini-Minor engine number is on the right upper front of the block. Serial number breakdown: first prefix letter is make ('M'); second prefix indicates is engine size ('A' = 800-999 cc); third prefix is body type ('J' = convertible; '2S' = two-door sedan; 'S' = four-door sedan); fourth prefix indicates series; fifth prefix is steering ('L' = left-hand drive).

Model	Body Type & Seating	Engine Type/CID	P.O.E. Price	Weight (lbs.)	Prod. Total
MINOR					
1000	2-dr Sedan-5P	I4/58	1495	1652	Note 1
1000	4-dr Sedan-5P	I4/58	1678	1708	Note 1
1000	2-dr Conv-5P	I4/58	1574	1624	Note 1
1000	2-dr Sta Wag-5P	I4/58	1798	1764	Note 1
MINOR DELUXE					
1000	2-dr Sedan-5P	I4/58	1599	1652	Note 1
1000	4-dr Sedan-5P	I4/58	1718	1708	Note 1
1000	2-dr Conv-5P	I4/58	1636	1624	Note 1
1000	2-dr Sta Wag-5P	I4/58	1825	1764	Note 1
MINI-MINOR					
850	2-dr Sedan-2P	I4/52	1295	1331	Note 1
850	2-dr Sta Wag-4P	I4/52	1669	N/A	Note 1
OXFORD					
V	4-dr Sedan-5P	I4/91	2259	2464	Note 1

Note 1: Approximately 155,000 Morris cars were produced in 1960, 145,000 in 1961, and 185,000 in 1962. About 7,725 Minors were sold in the U.S. in 1961. A total of 544,048 Minor 1000s were built from 1956 to September 1962.

1962 Morris Minor 1000.

ENGINE DATA: BASE FOUR (Minor): Inline, overhead-valve four-cylinder (BMC A-series). Cast iron block and head. **Displacement:** 57.8 cu. in. (948 cc). **Bore & Stroke:** 2.48 x 3.00 in. (62.9 x 76.2 mm). **Compression Ratio:** 8.3:1. **Brake Horsepower:** 37 at 4800 rpm (later, 40 at 5000). **Torque:** 50 lbs.-ft. at 2500 rpm. Three main bearings. Solid valve lifters. One SU H2 carburetor. 12-volt electrical system.

BASE FOUR (Mini-Minor): Inline, overhead-valve four-cylinder. Cast iron block and head. **Displacement:** 51.7 cu. in. (848 cc). **Bore & Stroke:** 2.48 x 2.69 in. (63 x 68.3 mm). **Compression Ratio:** 8.3:1. **Brake Horsepower:** 34/37 at 5500 rpm. **Torque:** 44 lbs.-ft. at 2900 rpm. Three main bearings. Solid valve lifters. One SU HS2 carburetor. 12-volt electrical system.

BASE FOUR (Mini-Minor Cooper): Inline, overhead-valve four-cylinder. Cast iron block and head. **Displacement:** 60.8 cu. in. (997 cc). **Bore & Stroke:** 2.46 x 3.20 in. (62.4 x 81.3 mm). **Compression Ratio:** 9.0:1. **Brake Horsepower:** 55 at 6000 rpm. **Torque:** 54 lbs.-ft. at 3600 rpm. Three main bearings. Solid valve lifters. Two SU HS2 carburetors. 12-volt electrical system.

Cooper Note: The first Cooper edition was introduced during 1961.

BASE FOUR (Oxford): Inline, overhead-valve four-cylinder. Cast iron block and head. **Displacement:** 90.9 cu. in. (1489 cc). **Bore & Stroke:** 2.875 x 3.50 in. (73 x 88.9 mm). **Compression Ratio:** 8.3:1. **Brake Horsepower:** 55 at 4350 rpm. **Torque:** 83 lbs.-ft. at 2100 rpm. Three main bearings. Solid valve lifters. One SU HS2 carburetor. 12-volt electrical system.

Note: Engines with lower compression (7.2:1) and reduced horsepower were available in Europe.

CHASSIS DATA: Wheelbase: (Minor) 86 in.; (Mini) 80 in.; (Oxford) 99.2 in. **Overall Length:** (Minor) 148 in.; (Mini) 120 in.; (Oxford) 175.4 in. **Height:** (Minor) 60 in.; (Mini) 53 in.; (Oxford) 59.75 in. **Width:** (Minor) 61 in.; (Oxford) 63.5 in. **Front Tread:** (Minor) 50.6 in.; (Mini) 47.75 in.; (Oxford) 48.9 in. **Rear Tread:** (Minor) 50.3 in.; (Mini) 45.9 in.; (Oxford) 49.9 in. **Wheel Type:** disc. **Standard Tires:** (Minor) Dunlop 5.00x14; (Mini) 5.20x10; (Oxford) 5.90x14.

TECHNICAL: Layout: front-engine, rear-drive except (Mini) front-drive. **Transmission:** four-speed manual; synchro 2nd/3rd/4th. **Standard Final Drive Ratio:** (Minor/Oxford) 4.55:1; (Mini) 3.765:1. **Steering:** rack and pinion. **Suspension (front):** (Minor) wishbones and torsion bars; (Mini) rubber springs; (Oxford) coil springs. **Suspension (rear):** semi-elliptic leaf springs except (Mini) rubber springs. **Brakes:** hydraulic, front/rear drum. **Body Construction:** steel unibody. **Fuel Tank:** (Minor) 7.8 gal.; (Mini) 6.6 gal.; (Oxford) 12 gallons.

MAJOR OPTIONS: MINI OPTIONS: Heater. Whitewall tires. PVC seating and adjustable passenger seat.

OXFORD OPTIONS: Heater/demister. Whitewall tires. Two-tone paint. Six-ply tires.

PERFORMANCE: Top Speed: (Minor) 73-75 mph; (Mini) 72-74 mph; (Oxford) about 78 mph. **Acceleration (0-60 mph):** (Minor) 28 sec. (0-50 mph in 18.7 seconds); (Mini) 26.5 sec.; (Oxford) N/A (0-50 mph in 16.6 seconds). **Acceleration (quarter-mile):** (Minor) 24.1 sec. (57.2 mph); (Mini) 23.3-23.7 sec.; (Oxford) 22.8 seconds. **Fuel Mileage:** (Minor) 35-45 mpg; (Mini) 40-50 mpg.

Manufacturer: Morris Motors Ltd. (Nuffield Exports Ltd.), Cowley, Oxford, England (part of British Motor Corp.)

Distributor: Hambro Automotive Corp., New York City.

HISTORY: 1960 models were introduced in the U.S. on October 1, 1959. Production of the Oxford Series V sedan ceased in 1961, but the Series VI continued through the decade for the home market, on a 100.25-inch wheelbase with 1622-cc four-cylinder engine.

1963-71 MORRIS

1964 Morris Oxford Series VI saloon. (Sotheby's)

MINOR 1000 — FOUR — By 1963, the four-door version of the Minor disappeared from American directories of imported cars, while the two-door sedan, convertible and Traveller station wagon remained available. Then, for 1963, the long-lived Minor made its last major mechanical change, adopting a larger (1098-cc) four-cylinder engine rated at 48 horsepower. That bigger engine powered the Minor through its final season, in 1971, though the model continued under the name '1000.' By the mid-1960s, however, Morris disappeared from most lists of cars available on the U.S. market; and after 1967, no Morris models were officially imported. Scattered examples may have arrived later, however, with specifications similar to those listed below. Minors of the mid-1960s had 'MINOR 1000' lettering on the decklid, and on the hood at the cowl (both sides). The hood emblem consisted of a circle within a circle, with straight elements going upward and to the sides; 'MORRIS' lettering; and a red bull in the center. A handle-style hood ornament was decorated by a styling 'M' letter. The Minor's grille consisted of five horizontal slats. Red/amber taillamps were installed at the rear, and amber/clear round parking lights at the front. Hubcaps displayed an 'M' letter. An open glovebox stood at the left end of the dashboard, with an enclosed box at the right, with a large round center dial that contained the speedometer and fuel gauge.

MINI-MINOR — 850 — FOUR — The tiny front-drive Mini went through a series of model changes and high-performance variants before expiring in 1969. The basic 848-cc model continued in production into 1967, while the basic 997-cc Mini Cooper disappeared in 1964, replaced by a 998-cc version. During 1963, the Cooper 'S' became available, with a 1071-cc engine rated 67.5 horsepower. In the following year, both a smaller-engine (970-cc) and larger-engine (1275-cc) Mini Cooper 'S' became available. Then, during 1967, the Mk II versions of the Mini were introduced, with 848- or 998-cc engines. See Austin Mini listing in this Catalog for additional details, since the two models were virtually identical except for grille design and similar details.

I.D. DATA: Serial number plates are on the firewall, under the hood. Starting serial numbers in 1963: (Minor 2-dr sed) MA2S3L/934674; (Minor 1098-cc 2-dr sed) MA2S5L/990290; (Minor conv) MAT3L/934674; (Minor 1098-cc conv) MAT5L/990290; (Mini Cooper) KA2S4L/138311. A separate plate at the firewall carried a number with prefix BMC/63, BMC/64, etc. to indicate the model year. An engine number plate was mounted horizontally on the right of the engine, on a ledge below the No. One spark plug.

Model	Body Type & Seating	Engine Type/CID	P.O.E. Price	Weight (lbs.)	Prod. Total
MINOR					
1000	2-dr Sedan-4P	I4/67	1682	1652	Note 1
1000	2-dr Conv-4P	I4/67	1669	1624	Note 1
1000	2-dr Sta Wag-4P	I4/67	1885	1764	Note 1
1000	2-dr DeL Wag-4P	I4/67	1916	1764	Note 1
MINI-MINOR					
850	2-dr Sedan-4P	I4/52	1295	1330	Note 1
850	2-dr Sta Wag-4P	I4/52	1669	N/A	Note 1

Note 1: Approximately 273,000 Morris cars were produced in 1963, 285,000 in 1964, 224,600 in 1965, 255,300 in 1966, and 233,000 in 1967. A total of 303,443 Minor 1000s were produced from September 1962 to April 1971.

1967 Morris Minor 1000 convertible. (Christie's)

1971 Morris Mini-Cooper S Mark III. (Sotheby's)

ENGINE DATA: BASE FOUR (Minor): Inline, overhead-valve four-cylinder. Cast iron block and head. **Displacement:** 67 cu. in. (1098 cc). **Bore & Stroke:** 2.54 x 3.30 in. (64.6 x 83.7 mm). **Compression Ratio:** 8.5:1. **Brake Horsepower:** 48 at 5100 rpm. Three main bearings. Solid valve lifters. One SU carburetor. 12-volt electrical system.

BASE FOUR (Mini-Minor): Inline, overhead-valve four-cylinder. Cast iron block and head. **Displacement:** 51.7 cu. in. (848 cc). **Bore & Stroke:** 2.48 x 2.69 in. (63 x 68.3 mm). **Compression Ratio:** 8.3:1. **Brake Horsepower:** 34/37 at 5500 rpm. **Torque:** 44 lbs.-ft. at 2900 rpm. Three main bearings. Solid valve lifters. One SU carburetor.

BASE FOUR (Mini-Minor Mk II 1000, 1967-69): Same as above, except — **Displacement:** 60.9 cu. in. (998 cc). **Bore & Stroke:** 2.54 x 3.00 in. (64.6 x 76.2 mm). **Compression Ratio:** 8.3:1. **Brake Horsepower:** 38 at 5200 rpm.

BASE FOUR (Mini-Minor Cooper to 1964): Inline, overhead-valve four-cylinder. Cast iron block and head. **Displacement:** 60.8 cu. in. (997 cc). **Bore & Stroke:** 2.46 x 3.20 in. (62.4 x 81.3 mm). **Compression Ratio:** 9.0:1. **Brake Horsepower:** 55 at 6000 rpm. **Torque:** 54 lbs.-ft. at 3600 rpm. Three main bearings. Solid valve lifters. Two SU HS2 carburetors.

BASE FOUR (Mini-Minor Cooper, 1964-65): Same as above, except — **Displacement:** 60.9 cu. in. (998 cc). **Bore & Stroke:** 2.54 x 3.00 in. (64.6 x 76.2 mm). **Compression Ratio:** 9.0:1. **Brake Horsepower:** 55 at 5800 rpm. **Torque:** 57 lbs.-ft. at 3000 rpm.

BASE FOUR (Mini-Minor Cooper 1071 'S'): Same as above, except — **Displacement:** 65.3 cu. in. (1071 cc). **Bore & Stroke:** 2.78 x 2.69 in. (70.6 x 68.3 mm). **Compression Ratio:** 9.0:1. **Brake Horsepower:** 70 at 6000 rpm. **Torque:** 62 lbs.-ft. at 4500 rpm.

BASE FOUR (Mini-Minor Cooper 970 'S'): Same as above, except — **Displacement:** 59.2 cu. in. (970 cc). **Bore & Stroke:** 2.78 x 2.44 in. (70.6 x 61.9 mm). **Compression Ratio:** 9.75:1. **Brake Horsepower:** 65 at 6500 rpm.

BASE FOUR (Mini-Minor Cooper 1275 'S'): Same as above, except — **Displacement:** 77.8 cu. in. (1275 cc). **Bore & Stroke:** 2.78 x 3.20 in. (70.6 x 81.3 mm). **Compression Ratio:** 9.5:1. **Brake Horsepower:** 76 at 5800 rpm. **Torque:** 79 lbs.-ft. at 3000 rpm.

CHASSIS DATA: Similar to 1960-62.

TECHNICAL: Similar to 1960-62.

PERFORMANCE: Top Speed: (Minor) 73-74 mph; (Mini) 72-74 mph; (Cooper) 84 mph; (Cooper 'S') 90+ mph. **Acceleration (0-60 mph):** (Minor) N/A (0-50 mph in 16.1 seconds); (Mini) 26.5 seconds. **Acceleration (quarter-mile):** (Minor) 22.8 sec.; (Mini) 23.3-23.7 sec.; (Cooper) 21.1 sec.; (Cooper 'S') 18.4-19.2 seconds.

Manufacturer: Morris Motors Ltd., Cowley, Oxford, England (part of British Motor Corp.).

Distributor: British Motor Corp./Hambro Inc., Ridgefield, New Jersey.

ADDITIONAL MODELS: In addition to the Minor and Mini-Minor, Morris turned out for the home market an 1100 series sedan and station wagon from 1962-71, a 1300 version from 1967-71 (including a GT sedan), and an 1800 series sedan. The final Morris line, a Marina coupe and sedan, was introduced in 1971 and hung on through the end of the 1970s. Nearly all of these last examples were virtual clones of MG, Wolseley, and other other BMC models.

HISTORY: Production of the Minor convertible ended in 1969; the sedan at the end of 1970; and the Traveller station wagon lasted until April 1971.

MINI-MINOR PRODUCTION NOTE: A total of 1,884 Morris Cooper 1071S models were built, and 487 of the 970S series. See Austin for additional details and production totals.

MOSKVICH

When automobiles of the Soviet Union were spoken of in the years after World War II, the big ZIM and ZIS limousines got most of the attention in the western press. Russians who drove cars, on the other hand, were far more likely to covet the Moskvich models, which entered production in 1947. Not until the small Fiat-based models of the late 1970s arrived would the early Opel-based Moskvich and its all-new descendants of the 1950s and '60s be eclipsed as the prototype family car for Soviet citizens.

Shortly before the war broke out, the Soviet government formed a company to create a small automobile, which resulted in the KIM-10, with an 1172-cc L-head engine. Prototypes of both two- and four-door models were developed. A few hundred two-doors were produced before the war, while the four-door evolved after the war into the first Moskvich. That initial model 400 bore close resemblance to the prewar Opel Kadett, which was no surprise since it borrowed that car's body as well as its engine. That happened because the tooling for the Opel wound up in Russian hands as war reparations. The Moskvich 400 had a distinctly prewar look (as did most cars of that period), with semi-built-in headlamps alongside the upright "vee" grille, which consisted of thick and thin curved horizontal ribs with a center vertical divider. A flat one-piece windshield was used. The 400 weighed 1,856 pounds, and its 1074-cc (65.5-cid) engine developed 23 horsepower. Wheelbase was 92 inches, and the 400 could reach 56-61 mph. By 1949, those early Moskviches were being exported to Europe. Details and finish, according to *Motor Trend*, were better than in the original German Opel. By 1954, when it appeared at the Brussels show, the Moskvich (spelled "Moskvitch" in early brochures) engine was rated 27 bhp at 3600 rpm, on 6.3:1 compression.

A totally different Moskvich 402 emerged in 1956, wearing a modern sedan body and powered by a larger (1220-cc) overhead-valve engine. That was followed by the Model 407, with a bigger engine yet. Displacement grew over the next decade, reaching 1478 cubic centimeters by

1968 for the Model 412. Meanwhile, by 1960, the Moskvich had been making a modest (and little-noticed) stab at the American marketplace, especially with its station wagon body style. Moskviches remained in production into the 1980s, and were the only cars offered in the Soviet Union without the need to sign up for a waiting list. Their brief foray into the U.S. market, however, never was repeated.

1956-64 MOSKVICH

Moskvich 2140 DeLuxe. (Novosti)

1956 Moskvich four-door sedan.

402 — FOUR — No Opel origins were evident in the completely different Moskvich series that debuted in the mid-1950s, all steel in construction and styled like many another four-door econocar of its day. The initial Model 402 engine displaced 1220 cc (74 cid) and produced 36-40 horsepower. Coil springs were used up front, semi-elliptic leafs at the rear. Its rear seat was larger than that of the prior model, the trunk larger, and turn-signal flashers were installed. A sedan debuted first, followed a year later by a station wagon.

407 — FOUR — Introduced two years after the 402, the 407 carried a larger engine. The Moskvich station wagon that appeared on the U.S. market by 1960 rode a 93-inch wheelbase and came as either a two-seat or four-seat model, with three-speed transmission. The 1360-cc, 45-horsepower engine in the Model 407 had removable cylinder liners. A radio and heater were standard. The conventional body design had a wide grille that consisted of a single horizontal bar with center insignia, matching curved upper bar, and parking lights contained at its ends. A horizontal bodyside trim molding dipped downward at the front wheel, providing a separation line for two-tone paint. Standard equipment included a mechanical windshield wiper, twin sunvisors, glovebox, ashtray, two clothing hooks, rubber floor mats, adjustable front seat with reclining backrests, and tool/accessory kit.

I.D. DATA: Not available.

Model	Body Type & Seating	Engine Type/CID	P.O.E. Price	Weight (lbs.)	Prod. Total
402 SERIES (1956-58)					
	4-dr Sedan-4P	I4/74	Note 1	2170	N/A
	4-dr Sta Wag-4P	I4/74	N/A	N/A	N/A
407 SERIES (1958-64)					
	4-dr Sedan-4P	I4/83	N/A	1984	N/A
	4-dr Sta Wag-4P	I4/83	N/A	2006	N/A

Note 1: Price at the factory was about $540.

ENGINE DATA: BASE FOUR (402): Inline, overhead-valve four-cylinder. **Displacement:** 74.4 cu. in. (1220 cc). **Bore & Stroke:** 2.83 x 2.95 in. (72 x 75 mm). **Compression Ratio:** 7.0:1. **Brake Horsepower:** 36 at 4200 rpm. **Torque:** 51 lbs.-ft. at 2400 rpm. Solid valve lifters. One carburetor.

BASE FOUR (407): Inline, overhead-valve four-cylinder. **Displacement:** 83 cu. in. (1360 cc). **Bore & Stroke:** 2.99 x 2.95 in. (76 x 75 mm). **Compression Ratio:** 7.0:1. **Brake Horsepower:** 45 at 4500 rpm. **Torque:** 65 lbs.-ft. at 2600 rpm. Solid valve lifters. One downdraft carburetor.

Note: Chassis and technical specifications below, for the Model 407, were valid in 1960, and differed little from the earlier 402.

CHASSIS DATA: Wheelbase: 93.3 in. **Overall Length:** 159.6 in. **Height:** 61.4 in. **Width:** 60.8 in. **Front Tread:** 48 in. **Rear Tread:** 48 in. **Wheel Type:** pressed disc. **Standard Tires:** 5.60x15.

TECHNICAL: Layout: front-engine, rear-drive. **Transmission:** three-speed manual (column shift). Model 407 gear ratios: (1st) 3.53:1; (2nd) 1.74:1; (3rd) 1.0:1; (rev) 4.61:1. **Standard Final Drive Ratio:** 4.71:1. **Steering:** worm with double roller. **Suspension (front):** coil springs with cross arms and anti-roll bar. **Suspension (rear):** rigid axle with semi-elliptic leaf springs. **Brakes:** hydraulic, front/rear drum. **Body Construction:** all steel.

PERFORMANCE: Top Speed: (407) 71.5 mph claimed.

ADDITIONAL MODELS: Along with the Moskvich 407, the Soviet Union produced a larger Volga M-21 in the late 1950s and early 1960s. The Volga rode a 106-inch wheelbase, measured 190 inches overall, and was powered by a 2445-cc four-cylinder engine that produced 80 bhp at 4000 rpm. Claimed top speed was 84 mph. According to promotional literature, the Volga received the Grand Prix award at the Universal and International Exhibition at Brussels (Belgium) in 1958. Volgas were produced at the Molotov Automobile Plant in Gorky.

Earlier in the 1950s, the Molotov plant had produced the more costly Pobeda (which translates to "Victory"), with a 129-cid L-head engine and 106-inch wheelbase. The Pobeda selection included a four-wheel-drive version as well as a convertible sedan and panel delivery. Appearance of the fastback sedan was reminiscent of various 1946-48 American cars, including Ford and Plymouth.

Manufacturer: Moskowskii Zavod Malolitrajnikh Avtomobilei (MZMA), Moscow, Soviet Union.

HISTORY: Model 402 was introduced in 1956; Model 407 in 1958. By the mid-1960s, interest in further importation into the U.S. had ceased. The Moskvich name remained on subsequent models, however, starting with the 408 of 1964, which carried an 83-cid engine rated 60.5 horsepower. That led to the 412, with its 1478-cc overhead-cam engine. In 1975, the 1500 series debuted, with an 83-bhp engine. Moskviches of the 1980s carried a 2141 or 21412 designation, with 1.5- and 1.6-liter engines rated 73/78 horsepower (DIN) and top speeds in the 95-mph neighborhood.

NARDI

Enrico Nardi's impressive prewar credentials in Italy included stints as a race driver, engineer and mechanic for Enzo Ferrari and for the Lancia firm, as well as construction of a front-drive race car of his own. After World War II, he and his new partner, Renato Danese, focused on rear-drive racing models with tubular chassis and motorcycle-type engines. Powerplants ranged from a 750-cc BMW two-cylinder and a Dyna-Panhard twin to Crosley and Fiat fours, and even derivatives of the early Ferrari straight eight. In 1949, a Nardi with 1100-cc engine entered four Swiss races, winning three and beating some 1500-cc supercharged cars in the process. By 1950, Nardi had a distributor in the U.S. A name change to Nardi & Co. came in 1951. In addition to relatively conventional race cars, led by the four-cylinder ND 750 (which came as close to a "standard" model as anything out of the Nardi plant), Nardi produced a few curiosities. One was the 118-mph Bisiluro, styled like a catamaran with the twin-cam engine in one "pontoon," and the driver in the other. A special coupe built for Chrysler used the regular Nardi ND chassis, but a Plymouth V-8 for the power. General production remained small, however, and only a few examples made it to America, mainly for racing. By 1957, Nardi was turning away from manufacturing to the tuning and accessories end of the competition business; but his Fiat-based Nardi-Vignale coupe appeared at international shows in 1958 and received favorable comment in America.

1947-54 NARDI

1952 Nardi.

Early postwar Nardi competition models came with a variety of two-cylinder engines, including the 750-cc BMW (for the 750ND model) and a Dyna-Panhard version. Mechanical details are similar to later models (below).

A 33.6-cid (550 cc) American Crosley engine also was used, with horsepower boosted from the customary 27.5 at 5200 rpm to 42 bhp at 5500. Compression was raised to 9.2:1, using the original Crosley pistons. Two Solex carburetors rode a special intake manifold. Nardi's tubular chassis was made up of welded straight tubes, small in diameter. An independent front suspension was used, while the rear had a floating axle with quarter-elliptic leaf springs. All gears except first were synchronized in the four-speed transmission, which sat horizontally between the bucket seats.

1955-57 NARDI

ND 750 — FOUR — Because Nardi built his cars primarily for racing, they came with a variety of powertrains and body details. A typical Nardi competition model would have a cutdown windshield and a wide oval grille with thick surround molding, a large round insignia in the center, and large-hole eggcrate pattern (13 vertical bars and one horizontal bar), and tiny tailfins. Carrozzeria Frua, the Italian custom coachbuilder, designed the streamlined barchetta body typical of Nardis in the early and mid-1950s.

ND 850 — FOUR — Production continued of a model with a BMW two-cylinder engine. With 8.8:1 compression, it delivered 46 horsepower.

Note: In addition to the examples listed here, Nardi offered to supply competition models with engines ranging from 500 cc to 4.5 liters.

I.D. DATA: Not available.

Model	Body Type & Seating	Engine Type/CID	P.O.E. Price	Weight (lbs.)	Prod. Total
ND 750	2-dr Rds-2P	I4/45	N/A	880	N/A
ND 750	2-dr Cpe-2P	I4/45	N/A	880	N/A
ND 850	2-dr Rds-2P	H2/45	N/A	1103	N/A
ND 850	2-dr Cpe-2P	H2/45	N/A	1103	N/A

ENGINE DATA: BASE FOUR (ND 750): Inline, overhead-valve four-cylinder. Cast iron block. **Displacement:** 45.3 cu. in. (743 cc). **Bore & Stroke:** 2.49 x 2.32 in. (63.2 x 58.9 mm). **Brake Horsepower:** 43 at 5500 rpm. Solid valve lifters. Two downdraft carburetors.

BASE TWO (ND 850): Horizontally-opposed two-cylinder (BMW). **Displacement:** 45.45 cu. in. (745 cc). **Bore & Stroke:** 3.07 x 3.07 in. (78 x 78 mm). **Compression Ratio:** 8.8:1. **Brake Horsepower:** 46 at 5700 rpm. Two downdraft carburetors.

CHASSIS DATA: Wheelbase: 74.8 in. **Height:** 45.7 in. **Max. Tread:** 46 in. **Standard Tires:** 4.00x15.

TECHNICAL: Layout: front-engine, rear-drive. **Transmission:** four-speed manual. **Suspension (front):** independent; transverse leaf springs. **Suspension (rear):** rigid (floating) axle and quarter-elliptic leaf springs. **Brakes:** front/rear drum. **Body Construction:** separate body on tubular (aircraft-style) steel chassis.

PERFORMANCE: Top Speed: 87-88 mph (competition version, 100 mph). **Fuel Mileage:** about 30 mpg.

Manufacturer: Nardi & Co., Torino (Turin), Italy.

Distributor: John Edgar, Los Angeles, California (circa 1950); S.H. Arnolt, Chicago, Illinois (circa 1954).

1958-59 NARDI

ND 750 — FOUR — Competition models using the 750-cc four-cylinder engine as well as Crosley and other powerplants continued to be produced on a limited basis; see previous listing for details.

NARDI-VIGNALE — FOUR — Based on the little Fiat 600, the new Nardi-Vignale coupe combined cuteness and sprightly performance in an attempt to gain American attention. Nardi gave the powertrain considerable attention first, even though this car wasn't intended for all-out competition. The original 600-cc engine was stroked to 2.56 inches, a high-compression cylinder head added (with bigger valves and double valve springs), ports enlarged in the intake manifold, high-compression pistons and hotter cam installed, and each component properly balanced. That resulted in a doubling of horsepower, from the original 22 to 45.5 bhp, reached at a high-winding 6500 rpm. Bodywork was performed in steel by the Vignale organization, also in Italy, following a design by Michelotti.

Seats, headlining and door panels were upholstered in a light tan synthetic material. On the dual-purpose gauge ahead of the driver, the outer dial served as a tachometer while the inner needle acted as the speedometer. Extra touches included a steering wheel of aluminum and laminated wood. The clean body design featured a sharply wraparound windshield and matching back window, rounded full wheel openings, and non-opening wind wings at the rear portion of each door. Headlamps were recessed into nacelles, with tiny round parking lights below and inboard. A front lid with exposed hinges and center trim strip provided access to the front luggage compartment, spare tire and tools. A round taillamp stood at each end of the rear air-intake grille. Twin portholes on the rear fenders also supplied air to the engine. A horizontal bodyside trim strip reached nearly the full length of the car, just above the portholes. Production models had an extra rear-deck airscoop and larger bumpers than the prototype (which arrived for U.S. appearances with thin tubular bumpers).

I.D. DATA: Not available.

Model	Body Type & Seating	Engine Type/CID	P.O.E. Price	Weight (lbs.)	Prod. Total
NARDI-VIGNALE					
	2-dr Coupe-2P	I4/45	3195	1300	N/A

ENGINE DATA: BASE FOUR: Inline, overhead-valve four-cylinder (derived from Fiat 600). Cast iron block. **Displacement:** 45.45 cu. in. (750 cc). **Bore & Stroke:** 2.38 x 2.56 in. (60.5 x 65 mm). **Compression Ratio:** 9.0:1. **Brake Horsepower:** 45.5 at 6500 rpm. **Torque:** 42.83 lbs.-ft. at 4500 rpm. Solid valve lifters. Weber or Solex carburetor.

Note: A high-performance Nardi coupe also was produced, using a Lancia engine with twin Weber carburetors, rated 138 bhp at 5400 rpm.

CHASSIS DATA: Wheelbase: 78.7 in. **Overall Length:** 154.5 in. **Height:** 45.7 in. **Width:** 55.1 in. **Front Tread:** 45.3 in. **Rear Tread:** 45.4 in. **Wheel Type:** 3.5x12. **Standard Tires:** 5.20x12.

TECHNICAL: Layout: rear-engine, rear-drive. **Transmission:** four-speed manual (2nd/3rd/4th synchro). **Steering:** worm and sector. **Suspension (front):** independent; transverse leaf spring and upper swinging arms. **Suspension (rear):** coil springs and swinging arms. **Brakes:** hydraulic, front/rear drum. **Body Construction:** steel body on steel frame. **Fuel Tank:** 7.4 gallon.

PERFORMANCE: Top Speed: 90-95 mph. **Fuel Mileage:** 37.5 mpg (factory).

Manufacturer: Nardi & Co., Torino (Turin), Italy.

Distributor: Auto Bernardini Inc., North Hollywood, California.

NASH-HEALEY

While most new car models are developed after lengthy deliberations, the impetus for the Nash-Healey stemmed from a chance encounter. Late in 1949, George Mason, the president of Nash-Kelvinator, was sailing home from Europe on the liner Queen Elizabeth. Also on board was Donald Healey, of British sports-car fame. (See Healey and Austin-Healey, also listed in this Catalog.) At the time, Mason was seeking an image boost for his Nashes, which were considered a bit stodgy. Healey was in the market for a source of engines for his sports car, preferring the new Cadillac V-8. No V-8s could come from the Nash organization, of course; but the two men nevertheless agreed on the value of a British-American hybrid sports car that would use Nash mechanical components.

A prototype two-seater roadster appeared at 1950 auto shows, in both London and Paris. Panelcraft produced the car's aluminum body, which sat atop an ordinary Healey chassis with trailing-link front suspension. Under the hood was a modified Nash Ambassador six-cylinder engine, with a hotter camshaft, aluminum cylinder head, higher (8.1:1) compression, and fed by dual SU carburetors. Nash torque-tube drive fed the power to the back wheels. The slab-sided body wore a grille, headlamps and other body items that originated in the Ambassador Airflyte sedan. Production began before the end of 1950. Early examples were sold in Britain, continental Europe and Canada; but before long, the U.S. became the sole outlet. In February 1951, the new sports car debuted at the Chicago Auto Show, wearing a price tag of $4063.

Nash-Healeys quickly took up racing, powered by the Le Mans Dual Jetfire Ambassador Six engine that would later go into domestically-built sedans. The very first Nash-Healey, wearing a special monoposto body, took 9th place in the 1950 Mille Miglia, and a 4th at the Le Mans 24 Hours event. That experimental model averaged 87.6 mph in the 2100-mile race. The same car, with a new coupe body, wound up 3rd in its class (6th overall) at Le Mans the next year. At the 1952 Le Mans, an open version ranked 3rd overall, taking 2nd in the Index of Performance. Nash-Healey was also 4th in its class (7th overall) at the '52 Mille Miglia. Then, in 1953, a Nash-Healey convertible finished 11th overall at Le Mans.

For its second (1952) season, Pinin Farina did a restyle of the roadster, as he was also creating the design for the '52 Nash sedans. This one had a lower, one-piece windshield and rear-fender bulges, minimizing the slab-sided appearance. By this time, a steel body replaced aluminum. A larger engine with Carter carburetors (and 15 more horsepower) came during the year. Nash sent drivetrains and other parts to Healey, whose company did the rolling chassis; then, in Italy, Pinin Farina installed the body and finished assembly.

In 1953, a Le Mans coupe on a longer wheelbase (with rear quarter windows) joined the open model, which was now called a convertible. For its final year, only the Le Mans version remained, wearing a three-piece wrap-around rear window and with its price cut sharply. All told, over its four-year life, 506 Nash-Healeys had been produced.

Note: Because the Nash-Healey was sold by Nash dealers along with domestic models, it is also described briefly in the Standard Catalog of American Cars 1946-75.

1951 Nash-Healey roadster.

SERIES 25 — SIX — Debuting in the U.S. on February 16, 1951, the Nash-Healey roadster wore a two-seat body with body panels and other structural parts made of aluminum. At the center of the broad, low hood was a small airscoop with vertical chromed grille. Front-end appearance was similar to the familiar Nash Airflyte. Its grille consisted of outward-curved vertical chrome bars, within a heavy chrome molding. Model designations were evident on the front fenders, to the rear of the wheel opening. The roadster measured only 38 inches to the top of its hood. Inside was a leather-finished instrument panel. The adjustable single seat was upholstered in English leather over latex foam cushions, while the folding fabric top contained a soft plastic rear window. Side windows made of hard plastic lowered into the door panels. The spare tire and luggage compartment were reached through a nearly horizontal deck. Standard equipment included an adjustable steering wheel, turn signals, and chrome wheel covers.

Under the hood rested a 125-bhp version of the 234.8-cid (3847-cc) Nash Dual Jetfire Ambassador six-cylinder engine, with 8.1:1 compression, an aluminum racing head (with sealed-in intake manifold), and twin SU horizontal carburetors. Premium fuel was required. Coil springs were installed at all four wheels, with the Healey trailing link suspension up front. Each front wheel was mounted on a swinging arm pivoted ahead of the wheel center line. At the rear, coil springs worked with direct-acting shock absorbers, similar to those in the Nash Ambassador. Duo servo brakes were installed, along with a 3.54:1 axle and 6.40x15 whitewall tires. The three-speed transmission came with standard overdrive.

I.D. DATA: Serial number is located on right fender panel, under the hood. Engine number is located on right front of block. Serial number range (1951 models): N-2001 to N-2109. Starting engine number: NHA-1001.

Model	Body Type & Seating	Engine Type/CID	P.O.E. Price	Weight (lbs.)	Prod. Total
25162	2-dr Spt Rds-2P	I6/235	4063	2600	104

Weight Note: Figure shown was announced as "curb weight" by the manufacturer. Other sources gave a figure of 2690 pounds.

ENGINE DATA: BASE SIX: Inline, overhead-valve six-cylinder (Nash Dual Jet Fire). Cast iron block and aluminum head. **Displacement:** 234.8 cu. in. (3847 cc). **Bore & Stroke:** 3.375 x 4.375 in. (86 x 111 mm). **Compression Ratio:** 8.1:1. **Brake Horsepower:** 125 at 4000 rpm. **Torque:** 210 lbs.-ft. at 1600 rpm. Seven main bearings. Solid valve lifters. Two SU horizontal carburetors.

CHASSIS DATA: Wheelbase: 102 in. **Overall Length:** 170 in. **Height:** 55.5 in. **Width:** 66 in. **Front Tread:** 53 in. **Rear Tread:** 53 in. **Standard Tires:** 6.40x15 whitewall.

TECHNICAL: Layout: front-engine, rear-drive. **Transmission:** three-speed manual (with overdrive). **Standard Final Drive Ratio:** 3.54:1 (overall net, 2.48:1). **Suspension (front):** Healey trailing link with coil springs and anti-roll bar. **Suspension (rear):** rigid axle with coil springs and track bar. **Brakes:** hydraulic, front/rear drum (Bendix duo servo). **Body Construction:** aluminum body on steel frame. **Fuel Tank:** 16 gallon.

PERFORMANCE: Top Speed: 102-104 mph (factory initially claimed an estimated 125 mph). **Acceleration (0-60 mph):** about 12 sec.
Manufacturer: Nash Motors; and Donald Healey Motor Co. Ltd., Warwick, England.
Distributor: Nash Motors (Division, Nash-Kelvinator Corp.), Detroit, Michigan.

HISTORY: An early press release called the Nash-Healey the "first American sports car introduced by an established automobile manufacturer since the mid-20's," adding that prices would be "substantially higher" than other Nash models. Nash estimated top speed rather optimistically, at 125 mph. The car was scheduled to undergo "exhaustive" engineering tests at Daytona, Salt Lake Flats, and Indianapolis Speedway. Production/sales were to be "limited" in 1951, until after the American market was "thoroughly explored."

Nash-Healeys were assembled by Healey at Warwick, England, and sold by Nash dealers in the U.S. Tom McCahill of *Mechanix Illustrated* wrote that he'd never "driven a sports car that handled better or gave the driver so much control." *Motor Trend* advised that "the Nash-Healey rides far better than the average sports car without any apparent ill effect upon handling qualities."

1952 NASH-HEALEY

1953 Nash-Healey roadster.

1952 Nash-Healey roadster with George Mason and Pinin Farina.

SERIES 25 — SIX — Since Pinin Farina was performing a restyle in Italy for the 1952 Nash sedan line, penning a revision of the roadster seemed a reasonable extra task. This second version looked less boxlike than the first, with its lower windshield and bulged back fenders with minimal fins. Inboard headlamps sat within a thick oval (rounded rectangular) front opening that held a grille made up of nothing more than two horizontal bars, with a round insignia in the center. Small round parking lights stood at the fender tips. Atop the hood was a tiny center scoop. This time, a steel body was used rather than aluminum. Power initially came from the same 234.8-cid (3847-cc) engine as the original, but a larger (252.6-cid) engine with Carter carburetors became available during the year. As before, the engine and mechanical components were supplied to Healey by Nash. After completing the chassis, Healey sent the result to Farina in Italy for body installation.

I.D. DATA: Serial number is located on right fender panel, under the hood. Engine number is located on right front of block. Serial number range (1952 models): N-2200 up (but a few with lower numbers were produced: N-2086, 2103, 2104 and 2106). Starting serial number w/253-cid engine: N-2250. Starting engine number: NHA-1088 (but numbers did not necessarily follow in sequence).

Model	Body Type & Seating	Engine Type/CID	P.O.E. Price	Weight (lbs.)	Prod. Total
25262	2-dr Spt Rds-2P	I6/253	5868	2750	150

ENGINE DATA: BASE SIX (early 1952): Inline, overhead-valve six-cylinder (Nash Dual Jetfire). Cast iron block and aluminum head. **Displacement:** 234.8 cu. in. (3847 cc). **Bore & Stroke:** 3.375 x 4.375 in. (86 x 111 mm). **Compression Ratio:** 8.1:1. **Brake Horsepower:** 125 at 4000 rpm. **Torque:** 210 lbs.-ft. at 1600 rpm. Seven main bearings. Solid valve lifters. Two SU horizontal carburetors.

BASE SIX (late 1952): Inline, overhead-valve six-cylinder (LeMans Dual Jetfire). Cast iron block and aluminum head. **Displacement:** 252.6 cu. in. (4140 cc). **Bore & Stroke:** 3.50 x 4.375 in. (88.9 x 111 mm). **Compression Ratio:** 8.0:1. **Brake Horsepower:** 140 at 4000 rpm. **Torque:** 230 lbs.-ft. at 2000 rpm. Seven main bearings. Solid valve lifters. Two Carter carburetors.

CHASSIS DATA: Wheelbase: 102 in. **Overall Length:** 170.75 in. **Height:** 48.65 in. **Width:** 64 in. **Front Tread:** 53 in. **Rear Tread:** 54.9 in. **Standard Tires:** 6.40x15 whitewall.

TECHNICAL: Layout: front-engine, rear-drive. **Transmission:** three-speed manual (with overdrive). **Steering:** walking beam type. **Suspension (front):** Healey trailing link with coil springs and anti-roll bar. **Suspension (rear):** rigid axle with coil springs and track bar. **Brakes:** hydraulic, front/rear drum. **Body Construction:** steel body on steel frame.

PERFORMANCE: Top Speed: about 104 mph. **Acceleration (0-60 mph):** 11.5-14.5 sec.

Manufacturer: Nash Motors; Donald Healey Motor Co. Ltd., Warwick, England; and Pinin Farina, Turin, Italy.

Distributor: Nash Motors (Division, Nash-Kelvinator Corp.), Detroit, Michigan.

1953 Nash-Healey hardtop coupe.

I.D. DATA: Serial number is located on right fender panel, under the hood. Engine number is located on right front of block. Starting serial number: (1953 conv): N-2290; (1953 HT) N-3000. Serial numbers for 1954 models included N-3027, 3036, 3037, 3039-3041, 3043, 3046, 3067-3069, and 3071 up. Starting engine number: (1953 conv) NHA-1203; (1953 HT) NHA-1223.

Model	Body Type & Seating	Engine Type/CID	P.O.E. Price	Weight (lbs.)	Prod. Total
25362	2-dr Spt Conv-2P	I6/253	5909	2750	Note 1
LE MANS					
25367	2-dr HT Cpe-2P	I6/253	6399	2970	Note 1

Note 1: A total of 162 Nash-Healeys were produced in 1953, followed by 90 in 1954.

Price Note: List price of convertible dropped to $5555 in 1954, while the Le Mans coupe sold for only $5128. Prices as low as $4721 were published in U.S. directories for final models.

ENGINE DATA: BASE SIX: Inline, overhead-valve six-cylinder (LeMans Dual Jetfire). Cast iron block and aluminum head. **Displacement:** 252.6 cu. in. (4140 cc). **Bore & Stroke:** 3.50 x 4.375 in. (88.9 x 111 mm). **Compression Ratio:** 8.0:1. **Brake Horsepower:** 140 at 4000 rpm. **Torque:** 230 lbs.-ft. at 2000 rpm. Seven main bearings. Solid valve lifters. Two Carter carburetors.

1953-54 NASH-HEALEY

SERIES 25 — SIX — Production of the two-seat convertible continued with its Pinin Farina body and 252.6-cid (4140-cc) engine, which produced 140 horsepower. That was joined in 1953 by a Le Mans hardtop coupe with a steel top and rear quarter windows, which rode a longer (108-inch) wheelbase. That coupe, too, had been styled by Pinin Farina and was shown for the first time at the Chicago Auto Show in March 1953. Its low hood and high fender contour extended beyond the cowl, through the windshield and out the rear window, onto the rear deck, without interruption. Trailing rear-fender fins accented the flowing front-to-rear lines. Rear fenders rose slightly above the rear deck, forming a "molded" part of the body. Headlamps were mounted within a "racing air scoop" grille. Smoothly rounded front fenders extended forward of the grille line. Standard equipment included leather upholstery, whitewall tires, tachometer, wheel covers, lighter, and ashtray. For 1954, only the Le Mans edition remained, with a three-piece wraparound rear window added.

1954 Nash-Healey roadster.

466

1954 Nash-Healey coupe.

CHASSIS DATA: Wheelbase: (conv) 102 in.; (HT) 108 in. **Overall Length:** (conv) 170.75 in.; (HT) 180.5 in. **Height:** (conv) 48.65 in.; (HT) 55 in. **Width:** (conv) 64 in.; (HT) 65.9 in. **Front Tread:** 53 in. **Rear Tread:** 54.9 in. **Standard Tires:** 6.40x15 whitewall.
TECHNICAL: Layout: front-engine, rear-drive. **Transmission:** three-speed manual (with overdrive). **Standard Final Drive Ratio:** 4.1:1. **Steering:** walking beam type. **Suspension (front):** Healey trailing link with coil springs and anti-roll bar. **Suspension (rear):** rigid axle with coil springs and track bar. **Brakes:** hydraulic, front/rear drum. **Body Construction:** aluminum body on steel frame. **Fuel Tank:** 20 gallon.
MAJOR OPTIONS: Weather Eye heater.
PERFORMANCE: Similar to 1952.
Manufacturer: Nash Motors; Donald Healey Motor Co. Ltd., Warwick, England; and Pinin Farina, Turin, Italy.
Distributor: Nash Motors (Division, Nash-Kelvinator Corp.), Detroit, Michigan.
HISTORY: The last Nash-Healey was produced in August 1954.

NSU

Known primarily for motorcycle manufacture, the NSU Werke in Germany turned to production of a minicar in the mid-1950s. That wasn't their first foray into automobile-related production. Founded in 1873 by Christian Schmidt and Heinrich Stoll to manufacture knitting machines, the original company moved to Neckarsulm in Lower Swabia in 1880, then expanded into bicycle production. As early as 1888, that predecessor to NSU was building the first chassis frames for German Daimler (Benz) vehicles. The NSU name arrived in 1892, using three letters taken from the plant site (Neckarsulm); and by 1901 the company turned to motorcycles, continuing in that field until the 1960s.

NSU's first automobile, a luxury model produced under license from the Belgian Pipe company, was assembled in 1905. Within a year, the company turned to its own smaller models, mainly with T-head four-cylinder engines. Just as war broke out, NSU introduced the Type 5/15, which continued into the mid-1920s. Even in the midst of World War I, NSU continued to turn out cars and trucks as well as motorcycles. Larger models were abandoned in the 1920s, but NSU achieved some success in racing, taking the top three positions in the 1923 Avus event at Berlin. Four supercharged sixes grabbed first through fourth in the 1.5-liter class of the 1926 Avus race.

NSUs of the 1920s featured narrow pointed radiators and four-wheel brakes. By decade's end, six-cylinder models were available for non-racing customers, some with superchagers. Financial troubles precipitated by the Depression in Germany called a halt to car production by 1929, though motorcycles continued to leave the assembly lines.

After selling part of its automobile operation to Fiat in 1929, a new company (NSU Automobil AG) began to assemble NSU-Fiats.

Five years later, in 1934, Dr. Ferdinand Porsche developed three prototypes for the "people's car," having been commissioned for that project by NSU. Before production could begin, however, NSU backed away and returned to motorcycles, leaving the path clear for the emergence of Volkswagen as the builder of the "people's car."

By 1949, motorcycle production had resumed at the Neckarsulm facility, which had been renamed NSU-Werke AG shortly before the war. Not only full-fledged motorcycles but also Lambretta motorscooters, produced under license, were built up to 1957, when the plant turned to a new two-cylinder Prinz econocar. Two-wheeler production then began to slack off, ceasing completely by 1967.

Arriving on the market at the height of interest in European minicars, the Prinz sold rather well in the U.S. and elsewhere. A sports coupe joined the original two-door sedan for the 1959 model year. Then, in the mid-1960s, NSU began to produce models carrying the Wankel rotary engine, starting with the Wankel Spider. An Ro 80 twin-rotor version with front-wheel drive followed, but suffered a disastrous series of warranty claims because of the engine's propensity to wear out in a hurry (if it didn't seize completely by that time). For a small car, the Ro 80 was also a guzzler, which didn't fare well during the oil crisis of the 1970s. In 1969, NSU had merged with Auto Union, with both makes controlled by Volkswagen. As the Ro 80 faded away, so too did the NSU nameplate. By 1977, it was merely a memory.

1958 NSU

1958 NSU Sport Prinz.

PRINZ — TWO — After achieving international popularity with two-stroke motorcycle engines, NSU switched to the four-cycle mode for its automobile offerings, but retained certain motorcycle ideas including the gearbox operation. According to the company history, the Prinz (Prince) was "deliberately kept small and functional, while cutting a pert, lively figure among its contemporaries." Promotional material issued at New York's Auto Show in 1958 called the new econocar the "culmination of automotive accomplishment by NSU Werke." Those same promotional sheets issued by NSU's U.S. distributor promised five-passenger capacity, but most testers at the time cut that figure down to a more realistic four-seat ranking. 'Prinz' script was evident at the cowl, with a wide "vee" trim strip across the front panel, which was flanked by hooded headlamps. Dual horizontal trim lines, the upper one full-length and the lower one shorter, gave the bodyside a "gouged out" look. Sliding panels were used for the front and rear windows, and vent openings were visible in the rear engine lid. The 35.6-cid vertical twin-cylinder engine, mounted transversely at the back, produced 26 horsepower. That engine had twin ignition coils and a Dynastart starter/generator unit, while the chassis rode on four-wheel independent suspension. The chassis had only two lubrication points (none at the rack-and-pinion steering or the suspension). A motorcycle-style four-speed gearbox used constant-mesh gears for "easy and silent gear change," operating with a single-plate clutch. Curved rear glass permitted broad visibility. Luggage and the spare tire fit into the front storage compartment. Standard equipment included a fresh-air heating/ventilating system.

I.D. DATA: Serial number plate is under the luggage compartment lid. Engine number is on the housing, on left side of engine compartment, behind the air duct.

Model	Body Type & Seating	Engine Type/CID	P.O.E. Price	Weight (lbs.)	Prod. Total
PRINZ					
	2-dr Sedan-4/5P	I2/36	1398	1080	Note 1

Note 1: Approximately 29 NSU Prinz models were sold in the U.S. during 1958. A total of 35,934 NSU passenger cars were produced in 1958 (versus 6,403 in 1956 and 16,651 in 1957).

ENGINE DATA: BASE TWO: Inline (vertical), overhead-cam two-cylinder (air cooled, four-stroke). Cast iron block and light alloy head. **Displacement:** 35.6 cu. in. (583 cc). **Bore & Stroke:** 2.95 x 2.60 in. (75 x 66 mm). **Compression Ratio:** 7.2:1. **Brake Horsepower:** 26 at 4600 rpm. **Torque:** 30 lbs.-ft. at 2300 rpm. Two main bearings. One downdraft carburetor. 12-volt electrical system.

CHASSIS DATA: Wheelbase: 78.75 in. **Overall Length:** 123.75 in. **Height:** 53.75 in. **Width:** 55.75 in. **Front Tread:** 47 in. **Rear Tread:** 47 in. **Standard Tires:** 4.40x12.

TECHNICAL: Layout: rear-engine, rear-drive. **Transmission:** four-speed manual (floor lever). Gear ratios: (1st) 4.14:1; (2nd) 2.21:1; (3rd) 1.41:1; (4th) 1.00:1; (rev) 5.38:1. **Standard Final Drive Ratio:** 4.41:1. **Steering:** rack and pinion with divided track rod. **Suspension (front):** independent; swing arms and coil springs. **Suspension (rear):** independent; swing axles and coil springs. **Brakes:** hydraulic, front/rear drum. **Body Construction:** steel unibody. **Fuel Tank:** 6.75 gallons.

PERFORMANCE: Top Speed: 65 mph (factory). **Acceleration (0-60 mph):** N/A (factory claimed 0-37 mph in 11 seconds). **Fuel Mileage:** average 45-50 mpg; factory claimed 51 mpg at constant 50 mph speed.

Manufacturer: NSU Werke AG, Neckarsulm, West Germany.

Distributor: Fadex Commercial Corp., New York City and Long Beach, California.

HISTORY: Introduced in September 1957, the Prinz appeared at New York's International Auto Show in April, 1958. At the rugged Nurburgring race in October 1958, NSU models won the first four places in the 750-cc class, averaging as much as 58.5 mph. By this time, a rotating-piston engine had been run on a test stand and Curtiss-Wright (the American aircraft engine manufacturer) was assisting in its development.

1959 NSU

PRINZ — I/II — TWO — "Great genius is behind the Prinz." So read the immodest ads in 1959, at any rate, which touted speeds up to 70 mph and economy in the 50-mpg neighborhood. The economy sedan came in two forms for its second season in the U.S.: Prinz I was the standard version, Prinz II the deluxe, which had different trim and interior fittings. Appearance and specifications were similar to 1958. A sliding sunroof was available for each model.

SPORT PRINZ — TWO — After a taste of success with the mini sedan, NSU introduced a sport edition with a more powerful (36-bhp) two-cylinder engine, identical in displacement to that in the sedan. Top speed got a jump to 85 mph, with claimed average fuel mileage of 47 mpg. Styling by Nuccio Bertone veered sharply away from the sedan, featuring a fastback profile with tailfins, a raked wraparound windshield and back window, triangular rear quarter windows, and wind-down door windows. Small round parking lights stood below the single round headlamps. 'SPORT Prinz' script was displayed at the cowl, directly above the bodyside trim strip that began to the rear of the headlamp and extended only part way into the front door. That strip also held flashing turn signal lights. *Motor Trend* described the Sport Prinz as similar in design to the Alfa Romeo Giulietta Sprint coupe. Standard equipment included a heater/defroster, locking glove compartment and ashtrays, with provision for popular makes of radios. While the Sport Prinz could hold two children in the back seats, the factory claimed that it could accommodate grownups only "on short distance journeys," and otherwise became "gigantic luggage space." The engine, four-speed gearbox and differential made up a single unit, with a backward-hinged engine cover at the rear.

I.D. DATA: Prinz serial number plate is under the luggage compartment lid; Sport Print serial number is on right side of luggage compartment. Prinz engine number is on the housing on the left side of engine, behind the air duct; Sport Prinz engine number is on top of crankcase housing.

Model	Body Type & Seating	Engine Type/CID	P.O.E. Price	Weight (lbs.)	Prod. Total
PRINZ (SEDAN)					
I	2-dr Sedan-4/5P	I2/36	1398	1080	Note 1
II	2-dr DeL Sed-4/5P	I2/36	1458	1080	Note 1
SPORT PRINZ					
Sport	2-dr Coupe-2 + 2P	I2/36	2245	1188	Note 1

Note 1: Approximately 3,247 NSU Prinz models were sold in the U.S. during 1959. A total of 33,376 NSU cars were produced that year.

Price Note: A sunroof Prinz I sedan cost $1487; Prinz II, $1547.

ENGINE DATA: BASE TWO (Prinz I/II): Inline (vertical), overhead-cam two-cylinder (air cooled, four-stroke). Cast iron block and light alloy head. **Displacement:** 35.6 cu. in. (583 cc). **Bore & Stroke:** 2.95 x 2.60 in. (75 x 66 mm). **Compression Ratio:** 7.2:1. **Brake Horsepower:** 26 at 4600 rpm. **Torque:** 30 lbs.-ft. at 2300 rpm. Two main bearings. One downdraft carburetor. 12-volt electrical system.

BASE TWO (Sport Prinz): Same as above, except 36 bhp.

CHASSIS DATA: Wheelbase: (sed) 78.75 in. (Sport) 78.25 in. **Overall Length:** (sed) 123.75 in.; (Sport) 141 in. **Height:** (sed) 53.75 in.; (Sport) 49 in. **Width:** (sed) 55.75 in.; (Sport) 57 in. **Front Tread:** (sed) 47 in. **Rear Tread:** (sed) 47 in.; (Sport) 47.25 in. **Wheel Type:** pressed steel. **Standard Tires:** 4.40x12.

TECHNICAL: Layout: rear-engine, rear-drive. **Transmission:** four-speed manual (floor lever). Sport Prinz overall gear ratios: (1st) 18.74:1; (2nd) 10.00:1; (3rd) 6.39:1; (4th) 4.52:1; (rev) 24.35:1. **Standard Final Drive Ratio:** (sed) 4.41:1; (Sport) 4.52:1. **Steering:** rack and pinion with divided track rod. **Suspension (front):** independent; wishbones and coil springs. **Suspension (rear):** independent; swing axles and coil springs. **Brakes:** hydraulic, front/rear drum. **Body Construction:** steel unibody. **Fuel Tank:** (sed) 5.5 gal.; (Sport) 6.5 gallons.

MAJOR OPTIONS: Sliding sunroof. Automatic clutch.

PERFORMANCE: Top Speed: (sedan) 65 mph; (Sport) 85 mph (factory figures). **Acceleration (0-60 mph):** N/A (factory claimed 0-37 mph in 11 seconds for sedan; 0-50 mph in 16.4 seconds for the Sport). **Fuel Mileage:** (sedan) average 45-50 mpg; (Sport) factory claimed approximately 47 mpg.

Manufacturer: NSU Werke AG (Aktiengesellschaft), Neckarsulm, West Germany.

Distributor: Fadex Commercial Corp., New York City and California.

HISTORY: Introduced in autumn 1958, the new Sport Prinz appeared at the International Auto Show in New York, in April 1959. In autumn 1959, a Prinz won its class in the "Little Le Mans" eight-hour endurance race at Lime Rock, Connecticut. "With the Sport Prinz," said the sales brochure, "you can conquer any traffic conditions....and "you will always be a step ahead." In 1959, a NSU/Wankel rotary piston engine was shown to the automotive press.

1960 NSU

1960 NSU Prinz.

PRINZ/PRINZ 30 — TWO — Both the original 26-bhp Prinz and a more potent Prinz 30 (with the 36-bhp Sport engine) were offered by 1960.

SPORT PRINZ — TWO — Production of the Sport model continued with little change.

I.D. DATA: Serial numbers are in same locations as 1959.

Model	Body Type & Seating	Engine Type/CID	P.O.E. Price	Weight (lbs.)	Prod. Total
PRINZ (SEDAN)					
	2-dr Sedan-4/5P	I2/36	1398	1106	Note 1
30	2-dr Sedan-4/5P	I2/36	1498	1106	Note 1
SPORT PRINZ					
Sport	2-dr Coupe-2 + 2P	I2/36	2198	1188	Note 1

Note 1: Approximately 2,493 NSU Prinz models were sold in the U.S. during 1960. A total of 30,031 NSU cars were produced that year.

Price Note: A basic Prinz sedan with sunroof cost $1487.

ENGINE DATA: BASE TWO (Prinz sedan): Inline (vertical), overhead-cam two-cylinder (air cooled, four-stroke). Cast iron block and light alloy head. **Displacement:** 35.6 cu. in. (583 cc). **Bore & Stroke:** 2.95 x 2.60 in. (75 x 66 mm). **Compression Ratio:** 6.8:1. **Brake Horsepower:** 26 at 4800 rpm. **Torque:** 30 lbs.-ft. at 2250 rpm. Two main bearings. One downdraft carburetor with starting device. 12-volt electrical system.

BASE TWO (Prinz 30, Sport Prinz): Same as above, except — **Brake Horsepower:** 36 at 5500 rpm. **Torque:** 31 lbs.-ft. at 3000 rpm.

CHASSIS DATA: Wheelbase: (sed) 78.75 in.; (Sport) 78.25 in. **Overall Length:** (sed) 122.75 in.; (Sport) 141 in. **Height:** (sed) 54 in.; (Sport) 49 in. **Width:** (sed) 57 in.; (Sport) 56 in. **Front Tread:** 47.25 in. **Rear Tread:** 47.25 in. **Wheel Type:** steel disc with chromed hubcaps. **Standard Tires:** 4.40x12.

TECHNICAL: Layout: rear-engine, rear-drive. **Transmission:** four-speed manual (floor lever). Sedan overall gear ratios: (1st) 19.8:1; (2nd) 10.57:1; (3rd) 6.74:1; (4th) 4.78:1; Sport Prinz overall gear ratios: (1st) 18.74:1; (2nd) 10.00:1; (3rd) 6.39:1; (4th) 4.52:1; (rev) 24.35:1. **Steering:** rack and pinion with symmetrical divided track rods. **Suspension (front):** independent; wishbones and coil springs. **Suspension (rear):** independent; swing axles and coil springs. **Brakes:** hydraulic, front/rear drum. **Body Construction:** steel unibody. **Fuel Tank:** (sed) 5.5 gal.; (Sport) 6.5 gallons.

MAJOR OPTIONS: Sliding sunroof. Automatic clutch.

PERFORMANCE: Top Speed: (sedan) about 70 mph; (Sport) 85 mph (factory figures). **Acceleration (0-60 mph):** N/A (factory claimed 0-37 mph in 11 seconds for sedan; 0-50 mph in 16.4 seconds for the Sport). **Fuel Mileage:** (sedan) about 50 mpg; (Sport) 47 mpg (factory figures).

Manufacturer: NSU Werke AG (Aktiengesellschaft), Neckarsulm, West Germany.

Distributor: Fadex Commercial Corp., New York City and California.

HISTORY: The corporate name was changed to NSU Motorenwerke Aktiengesellschaft (AG) at this time.

1961 NSU

PRINZ II/PRINZ 30 — TWO — NSU's economy sedan continued with little change, powered by a vertical twin cylinder with either 26 or 36 horsepower.

SPORT PRINZ — TWO — Little change was evident in the Sport model, except for a $200 price cut.

I.D. DATA: Serial numbers are in same locations as 1959.

Model	Body Type & Seating	Engine Type/CID	P.O.E. Price	Weight (lbs.)	Prod. Total
PRINZ (SEDAN)					
II	2-dr Sedan-4/5P	l2/36	1398	1106	Note 1
30	2-dr Sedan-4/5P	l2/36	1498	1106	Note 1
SPORT PRINZ					
Sport	2-dr Coupe-2 + 2P	l2/36	1998	1188	Note 1

Note 1: A total of 35,914 NSU passenger cars were produced during 1961.

Price Note: A sunroofed basic Prinz sedan cost $1487.

ENGINE DATA: BASE TWO (Prinz II): Inline (vertical), overhead-cam two-cylinder (air cooled, four-stroke). Cast iron block and light alloy head. **Displacement:** 35.6 cu. in. (583 cc). **Bore & Stroke:** 2.95 x 2.60 in. (75 x 66 mm). **Compression Ratio:** 6.8:1. **Brake Horsepower:** 26 at 4800 rpm. **Torque:** 30 lbs.-ft. at 2200 rpm. Two main bearings. One downdraft carburetor with starting device. 12-volt electrical system.

BASE TWO (Prinz 30, Sport Prinz): Same as above, except — **Compression Ratio:** 7.6:1. **Brake Horsepower:** 36 at 5500 rpm.

CHASSIS DATA: Wheelbase: (sed) 78.75 in.; (Sport) 78.25 in. **Overall Length:** (sed) 122.75 in.; (Sport) 142.5 in. **Height:** (sed) 54 in.; (Sport) 49 in. **Width:** (sed) 56 in.; (Sport) 57 in. **Front Tread:** 47.25 in. **Rear Tread:** 47.25 in. **Wheel Type:** steel disc with chromed hubcaps. **Standard Tires:** 4.40x12.

TECHNICAL: Layout: rear-engine, rear-drive. **Transmission:** four-speed manual (floor lever). Sedan overall gear ratios: (1st) 19.8:1; (2nd) 10.57:1; (3rd) 6.74:1; (4th) 4.78:1; Sport Prinz overall gear ratios: (1st) 18.74:1; (2nd) 10.00:1; (3rd) 6.39:1; (4th) 4.52:1; (rev) 24.35:1. **Steering:** rack and pinion with symmetrical divided track rods. **Suspension (front):** independent; wishbones and coil springs. **Suspension (rear):** independent; swing axles and coil springs. **Brakes:** hydraulic, front/rear drum. **Body Construction:** steel unibody.

MAJOR OPTIONS: Sliding sunroof. Automatic clutch.

PERFORMANCE: Top Speed: (sedan) about 70 mph; (Prinz 30) 80 mph; (Sport) 85 mph. **Acceleration (0-60 mph):** N/A (factory claimed 0-37 mph in 11 seconds for sedan; 0-50 mph in 16.4 seconds for the Sport). **Fuel Mileage:** (sedan) about 50 mpg; (Sport) 47 mpg (factory figures).

Manufacturer: NSU Motorenwerke AG (Aktiengesellschaft), Neckarsulm, West Germany.

Distributor: Transcontinental Motors Inc., New York City.

HISTORY: An NSU Prinz won the third Mobilgas Import Economy Run with the highest average of all competitors: 62.29 mpg. The Prinz 4 debuted in 1961, replacing the smaller I and II, with a larger interior and luggage compartment. By the end of 1964, 145,000 were built and the model lasted for over a decade. By 1973, 582,000 were sold.

1962-63 NSU

PRINZ III/PRINZ 30 — TWO — Little was new in the basic NSU sedans, which were joined by the larger-engine Prinz 4.

PRINZ 4 — TWO — A revised edition of the NSU economy sedan arrived for 1962, with slightly more displacement (from 583 to 598 cc) and 36 horsepower. The factory claimed a 0-50 mph acceleration time of 14 seconds, with economy in the area of 50 miles per gallon.

SPORT PRINZ — TWO — No major changes took place in the NSU two-seater sport coupe (with its back seat for two youngsters or one cramped grownup). As before, the fastback coupe displayed wide doors, wraparound bumpers, and rounded, squared-off tailfins that held the taillamps. Triangular rear quarter windows followed the fastback roofline. One bodyside trim strip, between the wheel openings, was a bit lower than bumper level; a thinner one stood just below the level of the door handle, stretching only along the front fender and part way into the door. Pointed round parking lights stood below the headlamps, which were contained in bright hooded housings. Ventilating covers were on the rear deck's engine cover. Separate front seats adjusted forward and back, and had adjustable backrest angles. The dashboard contained no gas gauge, but a reserve switch released enough for 25-30 miles.

I.D. DATA: Prinz serial number plate is under the luggage compartment lid. Sport Prinz serial number is on right side of luggage compartment.

Model	Body Type & Seating	Engine Type/CID	P.O.E. Price	Weight (lbs.)	Prod. Total
PRINZ (SEDAN)					
III	2-dr Sedan-4/5P	l2/36	1398	1106	Note 1
30	2-dr Sedan-4/5P	l2/36	1498	1106	Note 1
4	2-dr Sedan-4/5P	l2/36	1598	1245	Note 1
SPORT PRINZ					
Sport	2-dr Coupe-2 + 2P	l2/36	1998	1188	Note 1

Note 1: A total of 55,598 NSU cars were produced during 1962, and 76,045 in 1963.

Price Note: A sunroofed basic Prinz sedan cost $1487. A deluxe Prinz 4 was added later, priced at $1666.

ENGINE DATA: BASE TWO (Prinz III): Inline (vertical), overhead-cam two-cylinder (air cooled, four-stroke). Cast iron block and light alloy head. **Displacement:** 35.6 cu. in. (583 cc). **Bore & Stroke:** 2.95 x 2.60 in. (75 x 66 mm). **Compression Ratio:** 6.8:1. **Brake Horsepower:** 27 at 4600 rpm. **Torque:** 30 lbs.-ft. at 2250 rpm. Two main bearings. One downdraft carburetor with starting device. 12-volt electrical system.

BASE TWO (Prinz 30, Sport Prinz): Same as above, except — **Compression Ratio:** 7.6:1. **Brake Horsepower:** 36 at 5500 rpm.

BASE TWO (Prinz 4): Same as above, except — **Displacement:** 36.4 cu. in. (598 cc). **Bore & Stroke:** 2.99 x 2.60 in. (76 x 66 mm). **Compression Ratio:** 7.5:1. **Brake Horsepower:** 36 at 5500 rpm. **Torque:** 33 lbs.-ft. at 3250 rpm.

CHASSIS DATA: Wheelbase: (sed) 78.75 in.; (Sport) 78.7 in.; (Prinz 4) 80.3 in. **Overall Length:** (sed) 123.8 in.; (Sport) 142.5 in.; (Prinz 4) 135.5 in. **Height:** (sed) 54 in.; (Sport) 49 in.; (Prinz 4) 53.5 in. **Width:** (sed) 56 in.; (Sport) 57.1 in. **Front Tread:** 47.25 in.; (Prinz 4) 48.4 in. **Rear Tread:** 47.25 in.; (Prinz 4) 47.2 in. **Wheel Type:** steel disc. **Standard Tires:** (sed) 4.40x12; (Prinz 4) 4.80x12.

TECHNICAL: Layout: rear-engine, rear-drive. **Transmission:** four-speed manual (floor lever). **Steering:** rack and pinion with symmetrical divided track rods. **Suspension (front):** independent; wishbones and coil springs. **Suspension (rear):** independent; swing axles and coil springs. **Brakes:** hydraulic, front/rear drum. **Body Construction:** steel unibody.

PERFORMANCE: Top Speed: (sedan) about 70 mph; (Prinz 30) 80 mph; (Sport) 75-85 mph. **Acceleration (0-60 mph):** (Prinz 4) N/A (0-50 mph in 14 sec.); (Sport) 28 seconds. **Fuel Mileage:** (sedan) about 50 mpg; (Sport) 47 mpg (factory figures).

Manufacturer: NSU Motorenwerke AG (Aktiengesellschaft), Neckarsulm, West Germany.

Distributor: Transcontinental Motors Inc., New York City.

1964-65 NSU

1964 NSU Prinz 1000 two-door.

Two new models joined the NSU lineup this year: a 1000 sedan with four-cylinder engine and, far more significant historically, the Wankel (rotary-engine) Spider convertible. Carried over from before were the Sport Prinz and Prinz 4, both with two-cylinder engines.

PRINZ 4 — TWO — Continued from its 1962 debut with little change, the Prinz 4 again carried a 598-cc two-cylinder engine rated at 36 horsepower. Both standard and Deluxe models were available.

SPORT PRINZ — TWO — Little was new in the basic Sport Prinz two-seat coupe, which was powered by the same two-cylinder engine as the Prinz 4 sedan.

1000 — FOUR — After several years of experience with two-cylinder power, NSU moved up to four cylinders. The 996-cc engine was air cooled, like the two. Unlike prior models, the 1000 displayed quad headlamps in oval housings. Large block letters spelled out 'NSU PRINZ 1000' across a trip strip in the front panel.

WANKEL SPIDER — ROTARY — Built in relatively modest numbers, partly to test public reaction to the revolutionary engine designed by Felix Wankel, the Spider wore a cute two-seat convertible body. It was the first production automobile with rotary power. Styling of the body, which evolved from the Sport Prinz, was by Bertone; and the unibodied construction was similar to that of the Prinz sedans. The water-cooled, 500-cc single-rotor engine was mounted in the tail end, behind the rear axle, for rear-wheel drive. At the front of the car was its radiator, with filler cap in the rear trunk. From outside, it wasn't easy to determine where the engine was located, much less what it was. The four-speed all-synchro gearbox sat ahead of the rear axle, with a hydraulically-operated clutch. Reliability problems surfaced soon, but not so severely as in the subsequent Ro 80 twin-rotor model. Wankel Spiders had a split grille with vee center that contained an insignia, and a thin horizontal bar in each grille section. Pointed round parking lights stood directly below the headlamps. 'SPIDER' lettering went on the cowl, above the upper bodyside trim strip. Slight tailfins contained the vertical taillamps. Wankels were guaranteed to go 94.5 mph (and test cars managed more than that). Standard equipment included a tachometer, heater and turn signals.

I.D. DATA: Serial numbers are in same locations as 1962-63.

Model	Body Type & Seating	Engine Type/CID	P.O.E. Price	Weight (lbs.)	Prod. Total
PRINZ					
4	2-dr Sedan-4/5P	l2/36	1598	1245	Note 1
4	2-dr DeL Sed-4/5P	l2/36	1666	1245	Note 1
Sport	2-dr Coupe-2 + 2P	l2/36	1998	1106	Note 1
1000	2-dr Sedan-4/5P	l4/61	1798	1367	Note 1
WANKEL					
Spider	2-dr Conv-2P	Rotary	2998	1510	Note 2

Note 1: A total of 86,752 NSU cars were produced during 1964, and 91,873 in 1965.

Note 2: Approximately 5,000 Wankel Spiders were produced, through 1966.

1965 Price Note: A 1000L Prinz was added for 1965, priced at $1998.

ENGINE DATA: BASE TWO (Prinz 4, Sport Prinz): Inline (vertical), overhead-cam two-cylinder (air cooled, four-stroke). Cast iron block and light alloy head. **Displacement:** 36.4 cu. in. (598 cc). **Bore & Stroke:** 2.99 x 2.60 in. (76 x 66 mm). **Compression Ratio:** 7.5:1. **Brake Horsepower:** 36 at 5500 rpm. **Torque:** 33 lbs.-ft. at 3250 rpm.

BASE FOUR (Prinz 1000): Inline, overhead-cam four-cylinder (air cooled). **Displacement:** 60.8 cu. in. (996 cc). **Bore & Stroke:** 2.72 x 2.62 in. (69 x 66.6 mm). **Compression Ratio:** 8.0:1. **Brake Horsepower:** 51 at 5000 rpm. **Torque:** 52 lbs.-ft. at 2000 rpm.

BASE ROTARY (Wankel): Single-rotor (water cooled). **Displacement:** 30.5 cu. in. (500 cc). **Compression Ratio:** 8.6:1. **Brake Horsepower:** 50 (DIN) at 6000 rpm (64 SAE at 5000). **Torque:** 52 lbs.-ft. at 2500 rpm (54 SAE at 3000). Solex sidedraft carburetor.

CHASSIS DATA: Wheelbase: (Sport) 78.7 in.; (Prinz 4) 80.3 in.; (1000) 88 in.; (Wankel) 79.5 in. **Overall Length:** (Sport) 140 in.; (Prinz 4) 135.5 in.; (1000) 150 in.; (Wankel) 141 in. **Height:** (Sport) 49 in.; (Prinz 4) 53.5 in.; (1000) 53.5 in.; (Wankel) 49.5 in. **Width:** (Sport) 57.1 in.; (Wankel) 60 in. **Front Tread:** (Sport) 47.25 in.; (Prinz 4) 48.4 in.; (1000) 50 in.; (Wankel) 49 in. **Rear Tread:** (Sport) 47.25 in.; (Prinz 4) 47.2 in.; (1000) 49 in.; (Wankel) 48.3 in. **Wheel Type:** steel disc. **Standard Tires:** (Sport/Prinz 4) 4.80x12; (1000) 5.50x12; (Wankel) 5.00x12.

TECHNICAL: Layout: rear-engine, rear-drive. **Transmission:** four-speed manual (floor lever). Wankel Spider gear ratios: (1st) 3.08:1; (2nd) 1.77:1; (3rd) 1.17:1; (4th) 0.85:1; (rev) 3.43:1. **Standard Final Drive Ratio:** (Wankel) 4.43:1. **Steering:** rack and pinion. **Suspension (front):** independent; wishbones and coil springs; anti-roll bar in Wankel Spider. **Suspension (rear):** independent; swing axles and coil springs. **Brakes:** hydraulic, front/rear drum except (Wankel) front disc, rear drum. **Body Construction:** steel unibody. **Fuel Tank:** (Sport) 6.75 gal.; (Prinz 4) 9.9 gal.; (Wankel) 8.2 gallons.

PERFORMANCE: Top Speed: (Prinz) up to 85 mph claimed; (Wankel) 92-98 mph. **Acceleration (0-60 mph):** (Wankel) 14.2-15.0 seconds. **Acceleration (quarter-mile):** (Wankel) 20.5-21.8 seconds (69-73 mph). **Fuel Mileage:** (Prinz) up to 50 mpg claimed.

Manufacturer: NSU Motorenwerke AG (Aktiengesellschaft), Neckarsulm, West Germany. Distributor: Transcontinental Motors Inc., New York City.

HISTORY: The Wankel Spider (Spyder) was announced at the Frankfurt International Automobile Exhibition in 1964, and sold at the factory in Germany for 8500 Deutsche Marks (about $2125). A twin-rotor engine rated 110 bhp was at the Frankfurt show in 1965. The first Wankel Spiders arrived in the U.S. during 1965.

1966-67 NSU

PRINZ 4 — TWO — No significant change was evident in the two-cylinder sedan.

SPORT PRINZ — TWO — Little change occurred in the Sport Prinz two-seat coupe, which again was powered by the same two-cylinder engine as the Prinz 4 sedan.

1000 — FOUR — NSU's four-cylinder model added a 1000S (Super) edition and 1000TT, but changed little otherwise. The 1000S had special equipment and 'S' identification at the rear. The 1000TT (Tourist Trophy) model had a larger (1085-cc) engine as in the 110 series, with higher horsepower.

110 — FOUR — Another four-cylinder NSU series became available for 1966, considerably larger in dimensions than the 1000 sedan. The 66-cid engine developed 66 bhp in basic trim. Features included a low beltline and narrow roof pillars, with more instruments than the 1000 and a wood-trimmed dashboard.

WANKEL SPIDER — ROTARY — For its third season in the NSU lineup, the revolutionary rotary Wankel continued with minimal change.

I.D. DATA: Serial numbers are in same locations as 1962-63.

Model	Body Type & Seating	Engine Type/CID	P.O.E. Price	Weight (lbs.)	Prod. Price
PRINZ					
4	2-dr Sedan-4/5P	I2/36	1510	1245	Note 1
4	2-dr DeL Sed-4/5P	I2/36	1598	1245	Note 1
Sport	2-dr Coupe-2 + 2P	I2/36	1998	1106	Note 1
1000	2-dr Sedan-4/5P	I4/61	1708	1367	Note 1
1000L	2-dr Sedan-4/5P	I4/61	1846	1367	Note 1
1000S	2-dr Sedan-4/5P	I4/61	1898	1367	Note 1
1000TT	2-dr Sedan-4/5P	I4/66	1998	N/A	Note 1
110	2-dr Sedan-4/5P	I4/66	1939	1565	Note 1
WANKEL					
Spider	2-dr Conv-2P	Rotary	2497	1510	Note 2

Note 1: A total of 103,680 NSU passenger cars were produced in 1966, and 102,770 in 1967.

Note 2: Approximately 5,000 Wankel Spiders were produced, through 1966.

Price Note: Sunroof versions of the 1000 series sold for $1802 to $2091.

ENGINE DATA: BASE TWO (Prinz 4, Sport Prinz): Inline (vertical), overhead-cam two-cylinder (air cooled, four-stroke). Cast iron block and light alloy head. **Displacement:** 36.4 cu. in. (598 cc). **Bore & Stroke:** 2.99 x 2.60 in. (76 x 66 mm). **Compression Ratio:** 7.5:1. **Brake Horsepower:** 36 at 5500 rpm. **Torque:** 33 lbs.-ft. at 3250 rpm.

BASE FOUR (Prinz 1000): Inline, overhead-cam four-cylinder (air cooled). **Displacement:** 60.8 cu. in. (996 cc). **Bore & Stroke:** 2.72 x 2.62 in. (69 x 66.6 mm). **Compression Ratio:** 8.0:1. **Brake Horsepower:** 51 at 5000 rpm. **Torque:** 52 lbs.-ft. at 2000 rpm.

BASE FOUR (110, 1000TT): Inline, overhead-cam four-cylinder. **Displacement:** 66.2 cu. in. (1085 cc). **Bore & Stroke:** 2.84 x 2.62 in. (72 x 66.6 mm). **Compression Ratio:** 8.0:1 (1000TT, 9.0:1). **Brake Horsepower:** 66 at 5800 rpm (1000TT, 69 bhp). **Torque:** 58 lbs.-ft. at 2500 rpm. Solex one-barrel carburetor.

BASE ROTARY (Wankel): Single-rotor (water cooled). **Displacement:** 30.5 cu. in. (500 cc). **Compression Ratio:** 8.6:1. **Brake Horsepower:** 50 (DIN) at 6000 rpm (64 SAE at 5000). **Torque:** 52 lbs.-ft. at 2500 rpm (54 SAE at 3000). Solex sidedraft carburetor.

CHASSIS DATA: Wheelbase: (Sport) 78.7 in.; (Prinz 4) 80.3 in.; (1000) 88 in.; (Wankel) 79.5 in.; (110) 96.1 in. **Overall Length:** (Sport) 140 in.; (Prinz 4) 135.5 in.; (1000) 150 in.; (Wankel) 141 in.; (110) 157.5 in. **Height:** (Sport) 49 in.; (Prinz 4) 53.5 in.; (1000) 53.5 in.; (Wankel) 49.5 in.; (110) 55 in. **Width:** (Sport) 57.1 in.; (Wankel) 60 in.; (110) 59 in. **Front Tread:** (Sport) 47.25 in.; (Prinz 4) 48.4 in.; (1000) 50 in.; (Wankel) 49 in.; (110) 50.4 in. **Rear Tread:** (Sport) 47.25 in.; (Prinz 4) 47.2 in.; (1000) 49 in.; (Wankel) 48.3 in.; (110) 49.2 in. **Wheel Type:** steel disc. **Standard Tires:** (Sport/Prinz 4) 4.80/5.00x12; (1000) 5.50x12; (Wankel) 5.00x12.

TECHNICAL: Layout: rear-engine, rear-drive. **Transmission:** four-speed manual (floor lever). Wankel Spider gear ratios: (1st) 3.08:1; (2nd) 1.77:1; (3rd) 1.17:1; (4th) 0.85:1; (rev) 3.43:1. **Steering:** rack and pinion. **Standard Final Drive Ratio:** (Wankel) 4.43:1. **Suspension (front):** independent; wishbones and coil springs; anti-roll bar in Wankel Spider. **Suspension (rear):** independent; swing axles and coil springs. **Brakes:** hydraulic, front/rear drum except (Wankel and 1000TT) front disc, rear drum. **Body Construction:** steel unibody. **Fuel Tank:** (Sport) 6.75 gal.; (Prinz 4) 9.9 gal.; (Wankel) 8.2 gallons.

PERFORMANCE: Top Speed: (110) 87 mph; (Wankel) 92-98 mph. **Acceleration (0-60 mph):** (110) about 18 sec.; (Wankel) 14.2-15.0 seconds. **Acceleration (quarter-mile):** (Wankel) 20.5-21.8 seconds (69-73 mph).

Manufacturer: NSU Motorenwerke AG, Neckarsulm, West Germany.

Distributor: Transcontinental Motors Inc., New York City.

HISTORY: A twin-rotor engine, soon to become available in the Ro 80, was made available for automotive journalists to test-drive during 1966. An NSU Wankel Spider won the German GT Rally championship this year, and the 500,000th NSU car was produced. NSU also introduced a new 1200 series with 1.2-liter engine.

1968-77 NSU

1970 NSU Rotary RO-80 four-door sedan.

NSU's twin-rotor engine, installed in the new Ro 80, debuted in Europe in autumn 1967, but did not arrive on the American market until 1969. Production of the rear-engined NSU models continued (except for the Sport Coupe) into the 1970s.

Ro 80 — ROTARY — Acceptance of the Wankel rotary-engine concept in the Spider led NSU to create a twin-rotor version of the engine, mounted in an aero-styled four-door sedan. With a price tag in the $5000 neighborhood in the U.S., it was intended to capture the luxury compact end of the European and American market spectrum. Built with displacement equivalent to that of a 1000-cc engine of conventional design, the 129-bhp rotary delivered its power to the front wheels, via a semi-automatic torque-converter transmission. Applauded at first, the new engine soon proved unreliable, especially because its rotor seals tended to leak and didn't last long. Designed in NSU's own studio, the six-window sedan had a low nose, short but tall deck, and large, steeply-raked curved windshield. Its low rectangular grille, stretched between side-by-side round quad headlamps in recessed housings, was made up of horizontal strips with five vertical dividers. A bodyside crease ran the full length of the car, at the level of the door handles. A drag coefficient of 0.36 made the Ro 80 one of the most aerodynamic vehicles produced up to that time and, as *Motor Trend* reported, it was "almost totally insensitive to crosswinds." Upholstery came in either cloth vinyl or natural leather. European models had large rectangular headlamps and foglights beneath the bumper.

WANKEL SPIDER — ROTARY — Still offered for sale in the U.S., even after production in Germany came to a halt, the Spider convertible had a single-rotary Wankel engine developing 64 horsepower.

SPORT (BERTONE) — TWO — The two-cylinder sport coupe on 78.75-inch wheelbase continued on sale, after production came to a halt, with little change.

1000 — FOUR — No longer listed under the Prinz name, the 1000 two-door sedan rode an 88-inch wheelbase and carried a rear-mounted 60.8-cid four-cylinder engine.

110/TT — FOUR — NSU's 110 and TT two-door sedans had a 66-cid four-cylinder engine developing 66 or 69 horsepower. The TTS carried a smaller (60.8-cid) engine. Wheelbase of the 110 series was 96 inches; the others, 88 inches.

1200C — FOUR — Riding a 96-inch wheelbase, this new two-door sedan, with dimensions similar to the 110, had a 1.2-liter four-cylinder engine developing up to 73 horsepower.

I.D. DATA: Serial number (1971 models) is on a metal plate attached to upper left of dashboard, and on the firewall in front luggage compartment.

Model	Body Type & Seating	Engine Type/CID	P.O.E. Price	Weight (lbs.)	Prod. Total
WANKEL					
Spider	2-dr Conv-2P	Rotary	2998	1510	Note 1
Ro 80	4-dr Sedan-5P	Rotary	4995	2668	Note 2
SPORT (BERTONE)					
Sport	2-dr Coupe-2 + 2P	I2/36	1998	1106	Note 3
1000/110/TT/1200					
1000	2-dr Sedan-4/5P	I4/61	1708	1367	Note 3
110	2-dr Sedan-4/5P	I4/66	2158	1587	Note 3
TT	2-dr Sedan-4/5P	I4/66	2258	1411	Note 3
TTS	2-dr Sedan-4/5P	I4/61	2808	1435	Note 3
1200C	2-dr Sedan-4/5P	I4/74	2198	1587	Note 3

Note 1: Approximately 5,000 Wankel Spider convertibles were built.

Note 2: A total of 47,400 Ro 80s were built, through 1977.

Note 3: A total of 127,530 NSU passenger cars were produced in 1968.

Price Note: A sunroofed version of the 1000 sedan sold for $1798 in 1968; the 110 sedan, $2278; the 1200 sedan, $2318; and the TT sedan, $2348. A Wankel Spider with hardtop cost $3196.

Ro 80 Price Note: Figure shown was announced for 1968, but actual models did not arrive for sale in the U.S. until late 1969.

ENGINE DATA: BASE TWO (Sport): Inline (vertical), overhead-cam two-cylinder (air cooled, four-stroke). Cast iron block and light alloy head. **Displacement:** 36.4 cu. in. (598 cc). **Bore & Stroke:** 2.99 x 2.60 in. (76 x 66 mm). **Compression Ratio:** 7.5:1. **Brake Horsepower:** 36 at 5500 rpm. **Torque:** 33 lbs.-ft. at 3250 rpm.

BASE FOUR (1000): Inline, overhead-cam four-cylinder (air cooled). **Displacement:** 60.8 cu. in. (996 cc). **Bore & Stroke:** 2.72 x 2.62 in. (69 x 66.6 mm). **Compression Ratio:** 8.0:1. **Brake Horsepower:** 51 at 5000 rpm. **Torque:** 52 lbs.-ft. at 2000 rpm.

BASE FOUR (TTS): Same as above, except — **Compression Ratio:** 10.5:1. **Brake Horsepower:** 85 at 6150 rpm. **Torque:** 60 lbs.-ft. at 5500 rpm.

BASE FOUR (110, TT): Inline, overhead-cam four-cylinder. **Displacement:** 66.2 cu. in. (1085 cc). **Bore & Stroke:** 2.84 x 2.62 in. (72 x 66.6 mm). **Compression Ratio:** 8.0:1 (TT, 9.0:1). **Brake Horsepower:** 66 at 5500 rpm (TT, 69 at 5800). **Torque:** 58 lbs.-ft. at 2500 rpm. Solex one-barrel carburetor.

BASE FOUR (1200C): Inline, overhead-cam four-cylinder. **Displacement:** 71.8 cu. in. (1177 cc). **Bore & Stroke:** 2.95 x 2.62 in. (75 x 66.6 mm). **Compression Ratio:** 8.0:1. **Brake Horsepower:** 69 at 5600 rpm (later, 73 at 5500). **Torque:** up to 58 lbs.-ft. at 2500 rpm.

BASE ROTARY (Wankel): Single-rotor (water cooled) NSU/Wankel. **Displacement:** 30.5 cu. in. (500 cc). **Compression Ratio:** 8.6:1. **Brake Horsepower:** 64 (SAE) at 5000 rpm. **Torque:** 54 lbs.-ft. at 3000 rpm. Solex sidedraft carburetor.

BASE ROTARY (Ro 80): Twin-rotor (water cooled) NSU/Wankel. **Displacement:** 61.3 cu. in. (1000 cc). **Compression Ratio:** 9.0:1. **Brake Horsepower:** 129 at 5500 rpm. **Torque:** 112 lbs.-ft. at 4500 rpm.

CHASSIS DATA: Wheelbase: (Sport) 78.75 in.; (1000/TT/TTS) 88 in.; (Wankel) 79.5 in.; (110/1200C) 96 in.; (Ro 80) 112.5 in. **Overall Length:** (Sport) 123.8 in.; (1000/TT/TTS) 150 in.; (Wankel) 141 in.; (110/1200C) 157.5 in.; (Ro 80) 188 in. **Height:** (Sport) 53.75 in.; (1000/TT) 53.5 in.; (TTS) 54.5 in.; (Wankel) 49 in.; (110/1200C) 54.7 in.; (Ro 80) 55.5 in. **Width:** (Sport) 59.8 in.; (1000/TT/TTS) 58.5 in.; (Wankel) 59.75 in.; (110/1200C) 58.5 in.; (Ro 80) 69 in. **Front Tread:** (Sport) 47.25 in.; (1000) 50 in.; (TT) 49 in.; (TTS) 50.6 in.; (110/1200C) 50.4 in.; (Wankel) 50 in.; (Ro 80) 58.5 in. **Rear Tread:** (Sport) 47.25 in.; (1000) 49 in.; (TT) 48.5 in.; (TTS) 49.1 in.; (110/1200C) 49.1 in.; (Wankel) 48 in.; (Ro 80) 56.5 in. **Wheel Type:** steel disc. **Standard Tires:** (Sport) 4.80x12; (1000) 5.50x12; (TT/TTS/1200C) 135x13; (110) 155x13; (Wankel) 4.80x12; (Ro 80) 175SR14.

TECHNICAL: Layout: rear-engine, rear-drive except (Ro 80) front-engine, front-drive. Transmission: four-speed manual (floor lever) except (Ro 80) semi-automatic. **Standard Final Drive Ratio:** (Wankel) 4.43:1; (Ro 80) 4.86:1. **Steering:** rack and pinion. **Suspension (front):** independent, wishbones and coil springs; anti-roll bar in Wankel Spider except (Ro 80) MacPherston struts with wishbones. **Suspension (rear):** independent; swing axles and coil springs except (Ro 80) inclined trailing arms with struts and coil springs. **Brakes:** hydraulic, front/rear drum except (Wankel) front disc, rear drum; (Ro 80) four-wheel disc, front inboard. **Body Construction:** steel unibody. **Fuel Tank:** (Sport) 6.75 gal.; (1000/TT) 9.6 gal.; (110) 11.6 gal.; (TTS/1200C) 9.8 gal.; (Wankel) 8.2 gal.; (Ro 80) 18 gallons.

PERFORMANCE: Top Speed: (Wankel) 92-98 mph; (Ro 80) 112 mph claimed. **Acceleration (0-60 mph):** (Wankel) 14.2-15.0 seconds; (Ro 80) 12.2 seconds. **Acceleration (quarter-mile):** (Wankel) 20.5-21.8 seconds (69-73 mph); (Ro 80) 20.35 seconds (71.55 mph).

Manufacturer: NSU Motorenwerke AG (Aktiengesellschaft), Neckarsulm, West Germany; later, Audi NSU Auto Union AG.

Distributor: Transcontinental Motors Inc., New York City.

HISTORY: At the Frankfurt (Germany) auto show in 1967, the Ro 80 was voted "car of the year." *Road Test* magazine called it "one of the most exciting cars to appear in the last 20 years," adding that "the superb suspension invites exuberant handling." In 1969, NSU established a connection with Volkswagen by merging with Auto Union GmbH, to become Audi NSU Auto Union AG (wholly owned by Volkswagenwerk). Production of the Ro 80 continued into spring 1977, as did some of the smaller and more conventional rear-engined cars. By the early 1970s, if not before, NSU began to disappear from lists of American imported models. Other experimental rotaries were constructed and tested by NSU, and a Wankel engine was considered for the Audi 100 series, but abandoned. So, after the demise of the Ro 80, Toyo Kogyo (Mazda) in Japan became the sole producer of rotary-engined vehicles.

OPEL

Adam Opel, for whom the famed German automotive firm eventually was named, was born at Russelsheim in 1837. After training as a mechanic, he entered the sewing machine business in 1862. By the 1870s, Opel's company dominated that industry. Largely because of his sons' fascination with bicycles, Opel turned to that product in 1886, quickly advancing from the typical high-wheeler model to a new "safety" bicycle.

By the time of Adam Opel's death in 1895, his sons were looking for another product to manufacture and found it in the automobile. They began in 1897 by purchasing rights to produce the Lutzmann. A year later, the first Opel-Lutzmann was ready, powered by a rear-mounted single-cylinder engine. Unlike their earlier products, automobile manufacture did not develop so quickly. Two dozen cars rolling out of the plant in 1900 couldn't keep the company afloat, so they soon arranged to produce Opel-Darracqs under license, installing locally-produced bodies on the French chassis.

Opel's first car under its name alone came in 1902: the 10/12PS, with a two-cylinder engine. Through the early years of the new century, Opel's two-cylinder models became known as the "doctor's car," according to the *World Guide to Automobile Manufacturers*. Racing victories came early, with over 100 first-place finishes recorded by 1905. Along with motorcars, the Opel firm produced a modest number of motorcycles through the years, remaining in the two-wheeler business as late as 1925.

A serious fire nearly destroyed the Opel factory in 1911, prompting the abandonment of sewing-machine manufacture. When production resumed, Opel was clearly in the vehicle business. By 1913, the company ranked sixth in Europe.

Following World War I, Opel resumed production of prewar models. Not until 1924 did a change occur. At that time, Opel rebuilt its plant with a focus on moving conveyor-style assembly lines for mass production (a "first" in Europe). They also introduced a new smaller model for working people, to rival Citroen's 5CV: the 4PS. As the decade ended, not only were Opel's automotive fortunes rising, but the company ranked as Number One bicycle manufacturer in the world.

Opel's interest in tying a knot with the U.S. market was no secret. Shortly after the company was reorganized as Adam Opel AG in 1929, General Motors bought 80 percent of the new firm's stock. Two years later, GM purchased the balance, becoming sole owner of Opel. In 1935, honoring the Olympic Games to be held in Berlin, the unibodied Olympia debuted with a 1279-cc engine. Next year, it was the Kadett with a smaller (1074-cc) powerplant. Finally, Opel gave up two-wheelers, selling its bicycle operation to NSU. Late in 1940, as the war grew more serious in Europe, GM released its interest in Opel and production came to a halt for the duration. By that time, Opel was the second-ranked auto producer in Europe.

Despite extensive bombing, production was underway again in mid-1946. Only trucks began to roll off the line, however, as the Russians had carted away the tooling for the Kadett passenger car as part of its reparations. That design soon would reappear as the Soviet-built Moskvich. Back at Russelsheim, the first car to go into postwar production was the Olympia. Then came the larger Kapitan, with a 2473-cc engine. By November 1948, General Motors was back in the saddle in West Germany.

A new design arrived in 1953, evolved from the Olympia and named Rekord. In fact, the Olympia name continued as a commonly-used prefix. Starting with a 1488-cc four-cylinder engine, it grew late in the decade to 1680-cc displacement. Then in the mid-1960s came an overhead-cam four of 1897-cc size. By 1958, Rekords were being exported to the U.S. on a regular basis, along with Caravan station wagons, marketed and serviced by Buick Motor Division. Kapitan engines also grew in size, but that model was seldom seen in the U.S. market. Neither were the Admiral and Diplomat V-8 models introduced in 1964.

The model that made Opel's name in the U.S. market was the revived Kadett, an econocar introduced in 1962 with a 1.0-liter engine. By 1964, half a million cars annually were coming off the line and Kadetts were available in the U.S. market. For the 1966 model year, a second-generation Kadett emerged with more rounded lines. Then, in mid-1967, came the Opel Rallye coupe, which would make a surprisingly strong showing in U.S. competition as well as a popular choice for ordinary driving.

What clinched Opel's position in the ranks of memorable motor vehicles was the GT sports car, introduced in the U.S. during the 1969 model year. Styled like a mini Corvette with pop-up headlamps, the GT coupe mixed brash looks and peppy performance—at least with the available overhead-cam engine. By 1973, the Kadett name was gone, leaving the GT, the Manta series (including Rallye coupe) and the larger series 1900, offered in four-door sedan and coupe form.

As of 1976, German-built Opels no longer were exported to the U.S., but the Opel name continued—this name on a series built in Japan by Isuzu. Like their German predecessors, these Opel Isuzus were sold and serviced by Buick dealers, and remained available through 1979. Even though no further German Opels entered the U.S. market, that company remained a strong force in the European and international arenas.

1947-52 OPEL

1951 Opel Kapitan four-door.

OLYMPIA — FOUR — The prewar-styled Olympia sedan, which resumed production at the end of 1947, wore a grille made up of horizontal bars. Power came from a 91-cid four-cylinder engine that produced 43 horsepower at 4000 rpm.

KAPITAN — SIX — Opel's larger sedan also retained prewar styling, with grille bars that extended along the hood sides and 16-inch wheels. A 151-cid overhead-valve engine provided 60 horsepower. The front end was restyled in 1951, as the Kapitan switched to 15-inch wheels.

I.D. DATA: Chassis serial number is on the right front wheelhouse, and on right side of the cowl face. Engine number is on right front of crankcase.

Model	Body Type & Seating	Engine Type/CID	P.O.E. Price	Weight (lbs.)	Prod. Total
OLYMPIA					
	2-dr Sedan	I4/91	N/A	1955	Note 1
KAPITAN					
	4-dr Sedan	I6/151	N/A	2557	Note 1

Note 1: A total of 20 Opels (all models) were produced during 1947, followed by 6,028 in 1948, 27,990 in 1949, 59,990 in 1950, 61,900 in 1951, and 66,744 in 1952.

ENGINE DATA: BASE FOUR (Olympia): Inline, overhead-valve four-cylinder. **Displacement:** 90.8 cu. in. (1488 cc). **Bore & Stroke:** 3.15 x 2.91 in. (80 x 74 mm). **Compression Ratio:** 6.0:1. **Brake Horsepower:** 43 at 4000 rpm. Four main bearings. Solid valve lifters. One carburetor.

BASE SIX (Kapitan): Inline, overhead-valve six-cylinder. **Displacement:** 150.9 cu. in. (2473 cc). **Bore & Stroke:** 3.15 x 3.23 in. (80 x 82 mm). **Compression Ratio:** 6.1:1. **Brake Horsepower:** 60 at 3500 rpm. Solid valve lifters. One carburetor.

CHASSIS DATA: Wheelbase: (Olympia) 94.3 in.; (Kapitan) 106.1 in. **Overall Length:** (Olympia) 159.4 in.; (Kapitan) 181.9 in. **Height:** (Olympia) 62.2 in.; (Kapitan) 64.6 in. **Width:** (Olympia) 61.6 in.; (Kapitan) 65.4 in. **Front Tread:** (Olympia) 46.9 in.; (Kapitan) 53.1 in. **Rear Tread:** (Olympia) 49.2 in.; (Kapitan) 52.2 in. **Standard Tires:** (Olympia) 5.00x16; (early Kapitan) 5.50x16; (later Kapitan) 15-inch.

TECHNICAL: Layout: front-engine, rear-drive. **Transmission:** three-speed manual. **Standard Final Drive Ratio:** (Olympia) 4.57:1; (Kapitan) 4.30:1. **Brakes:** hydraulic, front/rear drum. **Body Construction:** steel unibody.

Manufacturer: Adam Opel AG, Russelshelm, West Germany.

HISTORY: Production of the Olympia resumed late in 1947; of the Kapitan, in 1948.

1953-57 OPEL

1956 Opel Kapitan four-door.

OLYMPIA REKORD — FOUR — A curved windshield and rear window highlighted the changes for the modernized Olympia, which had a full-width body, wraparound bumpers, and rectangular parking lights. Two bright three-section lamps at the rear contained the taillight, stoplight and direction light. 'Rekord' script went on the front of the car, half surrounding the round emblem at the front of the hood. 'Opel' was spelled out in block letters just above the mouth-like grille, which consisted merely of a large opening with several vertical elements above the bumper. Under the hood was a 90.8-cid overhead-valve four-cylinder engine, developing 50 horsepower and hooked to a three-speed manual gearbox with column-mounted gearshift lever. Drop-center 4Jx13 wheels held 5.60x13 tires. Helical coil springs were installed in front. The all-steel body had space for four passengers. Divided folding backs for the front seats had tilt-in action. Opel described the Rekord as "soundly styled, trimly streamlined, thoroughly modern without being freakish." Overall, the modern Opel resembled a smaller-scale 1953 or '54 Chevrolet, with overtones of Plymouth.

A new grille with single horizontal bar and protruding rectangular parking lights came on the 1955 models. 'Rekord' script went on front fenders, above the bodyside crease line. Then, for 1956, a mesh-patterned oval-shaped grille was installed.

A wholly redesigned body arrived for the 1957 models: lower, broader, with a more dashing look (according to Opel, at any rate). Hooded headlamps were the dominant feature, with large horizontal parking lights just above the bumper and a lowered hood. The new rounded rectangular grille was made up of vertical bars, complemented by a single horizontal bar. Under the reworked hood was an improved 1.5-liter engine, hooked to a fully synchronized transmission.

CARAVAN — FOUR — In addition to the Rekord two-door sedan, a Caravan two-door station wagon became available with similar specifications.

KAPITAN — SIX — A 150.9-cid six-cylinder engine again went under Kapitan hoods, even after they received a new full-width body (similar to the Rekord) in 1954. By the 1956 model year, Kapitans switched from a single-bar grille to a pattern of thin vertical bars in an elliptical opening. For 1957, the transmission was fully synchronized.

1957 Opel Kapitan four-door.

I.D. DATA: Chassis serial number is on a plate on the right front wheelhouse, and on the right side of the cowl face. Engine number is on right front of crankcase. Starting serial number: (1953 Rekord) 53-LZ-000001; (1954 Kapitan) 54-LV-000001.

Model	Body Type & Seating	Engine Type/CID	P.O.E. Price	Weight (lbs.)	Prod. Total
OLYMPIA REKORD					
	2-dr Sedan-4P	I4/91	1995	1909	Note 1
CARAVAN					
	2-dr Sta Wag-4/5P	I4/91	2300	2083	Note 1
KAPITAN					
	4-dr Sedan	I6/151	N/A	2667	Note 1

Note 1: A total of 83,624 Opel passenger cars (all models) were produced during 1953, followed by 130,342 in 1954, 142,795 in 1955, 163,143 in 1956, and 186,292 in 1957.

Price Note: Figures shown were valid in 1956 (Caravan is approximate).

1957 Opel Olympia Caravan station wagon.

ENGINE DATA: BASE FOUR (1953 Rekord): Inline, overhead-valve four-cylinder. **Displacement:** 90.8 cu. in. (1488 cc). **Bore & Stroke:** 3.15 x 2.91 in. (80 x 74 mm). **Compression Ratio:** 6.7:1. **Brake Horsepower:** 50 (SAE) at 4400 rpm. **Torque:** 77.3 lbs.-ft. (SAE) at 2000 rpm. Four main bearings. Solid valve lifters. One carburetor. 6-volt electrical system.

BASE FOUR (1956-57 Rekord): Same as above, except — **Compression Ratio:** 6.9:1. **Brake Horsepower:** 51.3 at 4200 rpm. **Torque:** 78.8 lbs.-ft. at 2000 rpm.

BASE SIX (Kapitan): Inline, overhead-valve six-cylinder. **Displacement:** 150.9 cu. in. (2473 cc). **Bore & Stroke:** 3.15 x 3.23 in. (80 x 82 mm). **Compression Ratio:** 7.0:1. **Brake Horsepower:** 78 at 3900 rpm. Solid valve lifters. One carburetor.

Kapitan Note: The initial announcement in 1953 for the restyled Kapitan claimed only 68 bhp at 3700 rpm.

CHASSIS DATA: Wheelbase: (Rekord) 97.9 in.; (Kapitan) 108.3 in. **Overall Length:** (Rekord) 166.9 in.; (Kapitan) 185.4 in. **Height:** (Rekord) 59.0 in.; (Kapitan) 62.2 in. **Width:** (Rekord) 64.0 in.; (Kapitan) 69.3 in. **Front Tread:** (Rekord) 47.2 in.; (Kapitan) 52.8 in. **Rear Tread:** (Rekord) 49.9 in.; (Kapitan) 54.0 in. **Standard Tires:** (Rekord) 5.60x13; (Caravan) 6.40x13.

TECHNICAL: Layout: front-engine, rear-drive. **Transmission:** (1953 Rekord) three-speed manual (synchro 2nd/3rd); column lever. Gear ratios: (1st) 3.57:1; (2nd) 1.66:1; (3rd) 1.00:1; (Rev) 3.57:1. (1957 Rekord had all-synchro transmission.) **Standard Final Drive Ratio:** (Rekord) 3.9:1. **Suspension (front):** (Rekord) coil springs. **Suspension (rear):** rigid axle with semi-elliptic leaf springs. **Brakes:** hydraulic, front/rear drum. **Body Construction:** steel unibody.

PERFORMANCE: Top Speed: (Rekord) about 76 mph. **Acceleration (0-60 mph):** (Rekord) N/A (0-50 mph in 20.1 sec.); (Caravan) 26.9 sec. **Acceleration (quarter-mile):** (Caravan) 25.6 sec. (55 mph). **Fuel Mileage:** (Caravan) 25-35 mpg.

PRODUCTION/SALES: Approximately 1,000 Opels were sold in the U.S. during 1957.

Manufacturer: Adam Opel AG, Russelsheim, West Germany.

Distributor: Vaughan Imported Cars, New York City.

HISTORY: Opels were not yet officially available in the U.S., but by 1956 dealers were importing a few on special order. In addition, quite a few were brought back from Europe by returning military personnel.

1958-59 OPEL

1958 Opel Olympia Caravan station wagon.

OLYMPIA REKORD — SERIES II — FOUR — "German made, American style." That's how the Rekord was described as official importation began, for sale through Buick dealers. "Germany's popular precision-built car, Opel offers refinements unique in a car priced as low as this one." Opel promoted the Rekord for its practical family size, as an economical import with "American big-car ideas." Offering seating for four or five, the Rekord was similar to the form taken in its late-1959 revamping, but wore a recessed oval rectangular grille made up of slim vertical bars, and a wraparound windshield and rear window. Parking lights wrapped around the front fenders. 'Rekord' lettering went at the front of front fenders, above the bodyside molding that swept down to the rear wheel opening before continuing horizontally to the rear of the car. 'Opel' block letters went above the grille, below a round insignia. Power came from a 56-bhp version of the famil-

iar 1488-cc (90.8-cid) overhead-valve, four-cylinder engine. Standard Rekord equipment included a heater, defroster, red-line speedometer, dual sunvisors, and turn indicators. Whitewall tires cost extra. Opel also produced a less-deluxe Olympia into 1959, but that was not normally exported to the U.S.

CARAVAN — FOUR — Opel also marketed a two-door station wagon in the U.S., with specifications similar to the Rekord. 'Olympia' script went on the front of the front fenders. Opel advertised a load-carrying capacity of 34 cubic feet, with space for four or five passengers.

1959 Opel Rekord two-door.

I.D. DATA: Serial number is on a plate on the right front wheelhouse. First two digits identify the model. Starting serial number: (1958 sedan) 110607112; (1958 Caravan): 140607112. Engine number is stamped on the right front of the block, below the pushrod cover. Starting engine number for 1958: 1.5-0000001.

Model	Body Type & Seating	Engine Type/CID	P.O.E. Price	Weight (lbs.)	Prod. Total
REKORD					
28	2-dr Sedan-4/5P	I4/91	1988	1911	Note 1
CARAVAN					
29	2-dr Sta Wag-4/5P	I4/91	2400	2077	Note 1

Note 1: A total of 231,406 Opel passenger cars were produced during 1958, followed by 239,286 in 1959. A total of 64,938 (Kombi) wagons were produced in 1958, followed by 72,603 in 1959.

ENGINE DATA: BASE FOUR: Inline, overhead-valve four-cylinder. Cast iron block. **Displacement:** 90.8 cu. in. (1488 cc). **Bore & Stroke:** 3.15 x 2.91 in. (80 x 74 mm). **Compression Ratio:** 7.5:1. **Brake Horsepower:** 56 at 4400 rpm. Four main bearings. Solid valve lifters. One downdraft carburetor. 6-volt electrical system.

Note: Earlier engines of the same 1488-cc displacement were rated 51.3 bhp at 4200 rpm on 6.9:1 compression.

CHASSIS DATA: Wheelbase: 100.4 in. **Overall Length:** 174 in. **Height:** (Rekord) 59 in.; (Caravan) 63 in. **Width:** 63.6 in. **Front Tread:** 49.6 in. **Rear Tread:** 50.0 in. **Standard Tires:** (sed) 5.60x13; (Caravan) 6.40x13.

TECHNICAL: Layout: front-engine, rear-drive. **Transmission:** three-speed manual. Gear ratios: (1st) 3.235:1; (2nd) 1.681:1; (3rd) 1.000:1; (rev) 3.466:1. **Standard Final Drive Ratio:** (sed) 3.9:1; (Caravan) 4.22:1. **Steering:** recirculating ball. **Suspension (front):** A-arms with coil springs. **Suspension (rear):** rigid axle with semi-elliptic leaf springs. **Brakes:** hydraulic, front/rear drum. **Body Construction:** steel unibody (box-section frame).

PERFORMANCE: Top Speed: (Rekord) near 78 mph claimed. **Acceleration (0-60 mph):** (Rekord) 21.4 sec. **Acceleration (quarter-mile):** (Rekord) 26.1 sec. **Fuel Mileage:** (Rekord) about 24 mpg.

PRODUCTION/SALES: Approximately 15,686 Opels were sold in the U.S. during 1958, followed by 39,320 in 1959.
Manufacturer: Adam Opel AG, Russelsheim, West Germany.
Distributor: Buick Motor Division, Flint, Michigan.
HISTORY: Opels were introduced officially to the U.S. market in October 1957 (for the 1958 model year), and on January 1, 1959 (for the 1959 model year). A brief mention of Opel in the November 1957 issue of *Motor Trend* asked: "Buick's newest small car?" Six-cylinder Kapitans (described in previous listing) remained in production into the 1960s, but rarely entered the U.S. market.

1960 OPEL

OLYMPIA REKORD — FOUR — Appearance of the revamped Rekord was similar to the late 1950s version, except that the bodyside trim strip followed a straight path from headlamps to rear end, tapering downward more sharply to the rear of the door. Tires grew to 5.90x13 size.
CARAVAN — FOUR — Production of Opel's station wagon continued with minimal change.

I.D. DATA: Serial number is on a plate on the right front wheelhouse. Starting serial number: (sedan) 28-11-1190533; (Caravan) 29-14-1190548. Engine number is stamped on the right front of the block, below the pushrod cover.

Model	Body Type & Seating	Engine Type/CID	P.O.E. Price	Weight (lbs.)	Prod. Total
REKORD					
28	2-dr Sedan-4/5P	I4/91	1988	1911	Note 1
CARAVAN					
29	2-dr Sta Wag-4/5P	I4/91	2292	2077	Note 1

Note 1: A total of 290,627 Opel passenger cars were produced during 1960, along with 60,324 (Kombi) wagons.

ENGINE DATA: BASE FOUR: Inline, overhead-valve four-cylinder. Cast iron block. **Displacement:** 90.8 cu. in. (1488 cc). **Bore & Stroke:** 3.15 x 2.91 in. (80 x 74 mm). **Compression Ratio:** 7.5:1. **Brake Horsepower:** 56 at 4400 rpm. **Torque:** 84 lbs.-ft. at 2600 rpm. Four main bearings. Solid valve lifters. One downdraft carburetor.

CHASSIS DATA: Wheelbase: 100.4 in. **Overall Length:** 174 in. **Height:** 58.6 in. **Width:** 63.6 in. **Front Tread:** 49.6 in. **Rear Tread:** 50.0 in. **Standard Tires:** (sed) 5.90x13; (Caravan) 6.40x13.

TECHNICAL: Layout: front-engine, rear-drive. **Transmission:** three-speed manual. **Standard Final Drive Ratio:** (sed) 3.9:1; (Caravan) 4.22:1. **Steering:** recirculating ball. **Suspension (front):** A-arms with coil springs. **Suspension (rear):** rigid axle with semi-elliptic leaf springs. **Brakes:** hydraulic, front/rear drum. **Body Construction:** steel unibody.

PERFORMANCE: Similar to 1958-59.

PRODUCTION/SALES: Approximately 25,533 Opels were sold in the U.S. during 1960.
Manufacturer: Adam Opel AG, Russelsheim, West Germany.
Distributor: Buick Motor Division, Flint, Michigan.

HISTORY: Opel's 1960 models were introduced to the U.S. market on September 1, 1959. A larger (1.7-liter) engine was available under Rekord hoods in 1960, but not installed in U.S. models until the 1961 model year.

1961-62 OPEL

1962 Opel Kadett two-door.

OLYMPIA REKORD — FOUR — Opel's two-door sedan grew a few inches by 1961, stretching to 177.8 inches overall, as restyling altered a number of details. Neither front nor rear fenders displayed the modest downward curve that had been evident in earlier models. Rear ('C') pillars now angled backward, since the back window had a reduced curve and no longer wrapped around. A redesigned, taller grille consisted of horizontal bars rather than the curved vertical bars used previously, and wrapped around to enclose the park/signal lights. Under the hood was a larger overhead-valve four-cylinder engine, displacing 1680 cc (102.5 cubic inches) and developing 64 horsepower. Electric windshield wipers were standard.

CARAVAN — FOUR — Production of Opel's station wagon continued with the larger engine under its hood.

I.D. DATA: Serial number is on a plate on the right front wheelhouse. Starting serial number: (1961 sedan) 11-1547092; (1961 Caravan wagon) 14-1593171. Engine number is stamped on the right front of the block, below the pushrod cover.

Model	Body Type & Seating	Engine Type/CID	P.O.E. Price	Weight (lbs.)	Prod. Total
REKORD					
11	2-dr Sedan-4/5P	I4/102	1988	1966	Note 1
CARAVAN					
14	2-dr Sta Wag-4/5P	I4/102	2293	2109	Note 1

Note 1: A total of 289,486 Opel passenger cars were produced during 1961, followed by 294,885 during 1962. A total of 68,806 Gorky wagons were produced in 1961, followed by 64,620 in 1962.
Price Note: Figures shown were valid in 1962.

ENGINE DATA: BASE FOUR: Inline, overhead-valve four-cylinder. Cast iron block. **Displacement:** 102.5 cu. in. (1680 cc). **Bore & Stroke:** 3.35 x 2.91 in. (85 x 74 mm). **Compression Ratio:** 7.8:1. **Brake Horsepower:** 64 at 4200 rpm. **Torque:** up to 98 lbs.-ft. at 2500 rpm. Four main bearings. Solid valve lifters. One downdraft Carter carburetor.

CHASSIS DATA: Wheelbase: 100.0 in. **Overall Length:** 177.8 in. **Height:** 55.9 in. **Width:** 64.3 in. **Front Tread:** 49.8 in. **Rear Tread:** 50.4 in. **Standard Tires:** (sed) 5.90x13; (Caravan) 6.40x13.

TECHNICAL: Layout: front-engine, rear-drive. **Transmission:** three-speed manual. **Standard Final Drive Ratio:** (sed) 3.9:1. **Steering:** recirculating ball. **Suspension (front):** A-arms with coil springs. **Suspension (rear):** rigid axle with semi-elliptic leaf springs. **Brakes:** hydraulic, front/rear drum. **Body Construction:** steel unibody.

PERFORMANCE: Top Speed: (Rekord) about 80 mph. **Fuel Mileage:** (Rekord) 22-25 mpg.

Manufacturer: Adam Opel AG, Russelsheim, West Germany.
Distributor: Buick Motor Division, Flint, Michigan.
HISTORY: Opel's 1961 models were introduced to the U.S. market on December 13, 1960.

1963 OPEL

1963 Opel Rekord two-door.

Partly because of the debut of Buick's domestically-built compact Special, interest in the Opel Rekord began to decline after 1961. Although they were listed in U.S. directories without comment (Rekord sedans carrying a higher $2106 price tag), no Opels were imported officially into the United States for the 1963 model year. The new Kadett debuted in the U.S. market for the 1964 model year.

1964-65 OPEL

1964 Opel Kapitan four-door.

KADETT — FOUR — Opel's Rekord sedan was gone, replaced by a smaller Kadett that came in two-door sedan, sport coupe, and station wagon form. Beneath the hood was a much smaller engine, displacing 987 cc (60.2 cubic inches) and developing 46 horsepower. A four-speed manual transmission was standard. Kadetts had rack-and-pinion steering, front bucket seats, and a narrow upright, squarish profile atop 6.00x12 tires. Single headlamps flanked a horizontal-bar grille, and sedan bodysides displayed a long horizontal trim strip. A sculpted center line decorated the hood. 'Kadett' script went on the front fenders of the sedan; on the lower deck of the coupe. A horizontal 90-mph speedometer went inside. A sliding sunroof was available. The sport coupe had a more powerful engine with 8.8:1 compression and 54 horsepower. Coupes lacked bodyside moldings and had a less-upright roofline, as well as headlamps mounted in square housings.

I.D. DATA: Serial number is on a plate on the right front wheelhouse. Starting serial number: (1964 sedan) 310128612; (1964 coupe) 320137821; (1964 wagon) 340128634; (1965 sedan) 310399251; (1965 coupe) 320299268; (1965 wagon) 340399253. Engine number is stamped on the right front of the block, below the pushrod cover.

Model	Body Type & Seating	Engine Type/CID	P.O.E. Price	Weight (lbs.)	Prod. Total
KADETT					
31	2-dr Sedan-4/5P	I4/60	1655	1408	Note 1
32	2-dr Spt Cpe-4P	I4/60	1818	1411	Note 1
34	2-dr Sta Wag-4/5P	I4/60	1793	1518	Note 1

Note 1: A total of 555,772 Opel passenger cars (not including Kombis) were produced during 1964, followed by 512,997 during 1965.
Price Note: Figures shown were valid during 1964. Prices dropped slightly in 1965 ($1618 to $1753).

ENGINE DATA: BASE FOUR: Inline, overhead-valve four-cylinder. Cast iron block and head. **Displacement:** 60.2 cu. in. (987 cc). **Bore & Stroke:** 2.84 x 2.40 in. (72 x 61 mm). **Compression Ratio:** 7.8:1 except (spt cpe) 8.8:1. **Brake Horsepower:** 46 at 5200 rpm except (spt cpe) 54 at 5500 rpm. **Torque:** 54 lbs.-ft. at 2600-3200 rpm except (spt cpe) 56 lbs.-ft. at 3800 rpm. Three main bearings. Solid valve lifters. One Carter carburetor.

CHASSIS DATA: Wheelbase: 91.5 in. **Overall Length:** 154.4 in. except (spt cpe) 157.1 in. **Height:** (sed) 55.5 in. **Width:** 57.9 in. except (sta wag) 58.4 in. **Front Tread:** 47.2 in. **Rear Tread:** 47.4 in. **Standard Tires:** 6.00x12.

1965 Opel Kadett sports coupe.

TECHNICAL: Layout: front-engine, rear-drive. **Transmission:** four-speed manual (floor lever). Sedan gear ratios: (1st) 3.764:1; (2nd) 2.156:1; (3rd) 1.406:1; (4th) 1.00:1. **Standard Final Drive Ratio:** 3.89:1. **Steering:** rack and pinion. **Suspension (front):** A-arms with lower transverse semi-elliptic leaf spring. **Suspension (rear):** rigid axle with semi-elliptic leaf springs. **Brakes:** hydraulic, front/rear drum. **Body Construction:** steel unibody.

MAJOR OPTIONS: Sliding sunroof ($86).

PERFORMANCE: Top Speed: (Kadett sed) 75-76 mph. **Acceleration (0-60 mph):** (Kadett sed) 21.2-23.0 sec. **Acceleration (quarter-mile):** (Kadett sed) 21.7-22.0 sec. (59-60.6 mph). **Fuel Mileage:** (Kadett sed) 30-35 mpg.

PRODUCTION/SALES: Approximately 14,788 Opels were sold in the U.S. during 1964, followed by 17,378 in 1965. The U.S. Department of Commerce reported that 14,077 Opels were imported in 1964, and 16,216 during 1965.

1965 Opel Kadett two-door sedan.

ADDITIONAL MODELS: Following introduction of the Kadett, the prior Rekord sedan no longer was imported into the U.S. Elsewhere in the world, Opel offered not only the Rekord but a trio of new models, up to the top-of-the-line Diplomat with its V-8 engine. Diplomats had rectangular headlamps and a rectangular mesh grille. Even though its styling displayed an obvious American influence, the Diplomat rarely was seen in the U.S. market. Its 283-cid V-8 engine was borrowed from Chevrolet, producing the same 220-bhp as the Chevelle. Opel's Kapitan and Admiral were similar in design but used a 159-cid inline six-cylinder engine, rated 115 horsepower. Opel claimed a top speed of 124 mph for the Diplomat and 96 mph for six-cylinder models. Each of the three new Opel sedans rode a 112-inch wheelbase and measured 194.8 inches overall.
Manufacturer: Adam Opel AG, Russelsheim, West Germany.
Distributor: Buick Motor Division, Flint, Michigan.

HISTORY: Opel's 1964 models were introduced to the U.S. market on January 17, 1964; the 1965 models arrived on November 16, 1964. By 1965, approximately 500 Buick dealers were selling Opels. Kadetts and the other Opel models of the mid-1960s were created by a fresh design team, headed by Hans Mersheimer on the engineering front and Clare MacKichan, an American who was responsible for styling. Kadett development had begun as early as 1957, intended to rival the Volkswagen Beetle and comparable European imports.

1966-67 OPEL

KADETT — FOUR — Restyling to more rounded contours brought a different look to Opel's Kadett, which was now available in both two- and four-door sedan form, along with a sport coupe and station wagon. Dimensions were larger (on a 95.1-inch wheelbase), and tires grew to 13-inch diameter. A bodyside crease line ran the full length of the car, starting at the single headlamps. Grilles displayed a pattern of horizontal strips and wide-spaced vertical dividers, with a thicker center horizontal bar. Sport coupes had a semi-fastback roofline and upswept rear quarter windows with three trim creases. 'Kadett' script went on the lower cowl, just to the rear of the front wheel opening. Engine displacement grew to 1077 cc (65.8 cid), available in standard form developing 54 horsepower, or in "Super" trim at 60 bhp. Front disc brakes were available with the Super option. The four-door sedan lasted only one season, no longer available for the 1967 model year. All 1967 Kadetts gained thicker sheetmetal in hood, doors and decklid.

475

1967 Opel Kadett L two-door fastback.

RALLYE — FOUR — Introduced during the 1967 model year, Opel's Rallye coupe was created with performance in mind, and wore twin auxiliary lights at the center of the front end, just above the bumper. Based on the regular Kadett sport coupe, the Rallye edition carried a more potent engine with higher (9.2:1) compression and twin Solex carburetors, rated 67 horsepower. Standard equipment included power front disc brakes, radial tires on larger wheels, a dual-exhaust system, rally stripes, three-spoke simulated wood steering wheel, and sport-shift console with gauges.

I.D. DATA: Serial number is on a plate on the right front wheelhouse or on the upper left corner of the instrument panel. Starting serial number: (1966 2-dr sedan) 310655705; (1966 Deluxe 2-dr sedan) 380656131; (1966 4-dr sedan) 370659912; (1966 coupe) 320655651; (1966 wagon) 390655633; (1967 2-dr sedan) 310957604; (1967 coupe) 320957603; (1967 wagon) 390957662; (mid-1967 Rallye coupe) 321041613. Engine number is stamped on the the block, just above the dipstick. An 'S' prefix identifies the Super (60-bhp) engine.

Model	Body Type & Seating	Engine Type/CID	P.O.E. Price	Weight (lbs.)	Prod. Total
KADETT					
31	2-dr Sedan-4/5P	I4/66	1657	1544	Note 1
32	2-dr Spt Cpe-4P	I4/66	1816	1588	Note 1
38 (Deluxe)	2-dr Sedan-4/5P	I4/66	1780	1566	Note 1
37 (Deluxe)	4-dr Sedan-4/5P	I4/66	1868	1620	Note 1
39 (Deluxe)	2-dr Sta Wag-4/5P	I4/66	1898	1654	Note 1
RALLYE (mid-1967)					
32	2-dr Spt Cpe-4P	I4/66	2192	1719	Note 1

Note 1: A total of 552,427 Opel passenger cars (all models except Kombi) were produced during 1966, followed by 448,531 during 1967.

Price Note: Figures shown were valid in 1966. Prices in 1967 were $1695 for the two-door sedan, $1905 for the sport coupe, and $1980 for the Deluxe station wagon.

1967 Opel Kadett two-door.

ENGINE DATA: BASE FOUR: Inline, overhead-valve four-cylinder (model 11). Cast iron block and head. **Displacement:** 65.8 cu. in. (1077 cc). **Bore & Stroke:** 2.95 x 2.40 in. (75 x 61 mm). **Compression Ratio:** 7.8:1. **Brake Horsepower:** 54 at 5600 rpm. **Torque:** 59 lbs.-ft. at 2800-3000 rpm. Three main bearings. Solid valve lifters. One Solex carburetor.

OPTIONAL FOUR (Super): Same as above, except — **Compression Ratio:** 8.8:1. **Brake Horsepower:** 60 at 5600 rpm. **Torque:** 63 lbs.-ft. at 2800-3200 rpm.

BASE FOUR (1967.5 Rallye coupe): Same as above, except — **Compression Ratio:** 9.2:1. **Brake Horsepower:** 67 at 6000 rpm. **Torque:** 62 lbs.-ft. at 5000 rpm. Two Solex carburetors.

1967 Opel Kadett L station wagon.

CHASSIS DATA: Wheelbase: 95.1 in. **Overall Length:** (sed) 161.6 in.; (cpe) 164 in. **Height:** (sed) 53.2 in.; (cpe) 53.9 in. **Width:** 61.9 in. **Front Tread:** 49.2 in. **Rear Tread:** 50.4 in. **Standard Tires:** 6.00x13.

TECHNICAL: Layout: front-engine, rear-drive. **Transmission:** four-speed manual (floor lever). **Standard Final Drive Ratio:** 3.89:1. **Steering:** rack and pinion. **Suspension (front):** A-arms with lower transverse semi-elliptic leaf spring. **Suspension (rear):** rigid axle with semi-elliptic leaf springs. **Brakes:** hydraulic, front/rear drum except (Super option) front disc, rear drum. **Body Construction:** steel unibody.

MAJOR OPTIONS: Sliding sunroof.

PERFORMANCE: Top Speed: (Kadett sed) 75 mph. **Acceleration (0-60 mph):** (Kadett sed) 21.2 sec.

PRODUCTION/SALES: Approximately 32,033 Opels were sold in the U.S. during 1966, followed by 51,693 in 1967. The U.S. Department of Commerce reported that 31,555 Opels were imported in 1966, and 50,866 in 1967.

Manufacturer: Adam Opel AG, Russelsheim, West Germany.

Distributor: Buick Motor Division, Flint, Michigan.

HISTORY: Opel's 1966 models were introduced to the U.S. market on November 15, 1965; the 1967 models arrived on November 17, 1966.

1968 OPEL

KADETT — FOUR — Opel's Kadett series gained another rounded-look restyling, though one that lacked dramatic change except for a revised front end. A revamped grille contained two horizontal bars between the single headlamps. Park/signal lights were now incorporated within the front-end assembly, and airscoops went into the bumper panel. Two new optional overhead-cam engines were introduced this year, joining the basic 1077-cc overhead-valve four. The 1491-cc (91-cid) four developed 80 horsepower; an even larger 1897-cc (115.8-cid) engine produced 102 bhp. Both used two-barrel carburetion.

KADETT RALLYE/SPORT — FOUR — After a half-year with Opel's smaller engine, the Rallye coupe switched to the new 91-cid engine with its 80 horsepower and adopted a "92" model designation. The bigger 115.8-cid engine was optional. Other new models were added this year: the 95 sport coupe, 99 LS sport coupe, and 91 sport sedan. Appearance was similar to the basic 31/39 series Kadett sedan and station wagon (above), except that the Rallye Coupe could have wide bodyside striping and contrasting-color hood.

I.D. DATA: Serial number is on a plate on the right front wheelhouse or on the upper left corner of the instrument panel. Starting serial number: (2-dr sedan) 311243154; (2-dr wagon) 391242823; (2-dr spt sedan) 911260133; (Rallye coupe) 921280093; (LS spt cpe) 991286203. Engine number is stamped on the the block, just above the dipstick.

Model	Body Type & Seating	Engine Type/CID	P.O.E. Price	Weight (lbs.)	Prod. Total
KADETT					
31	2-dr Sedan-4/5P	I4/66	1785	1693	Note 1
39	2-dr Sta Wag-4/5P	I4/66	2070	1781	Note 1
RALLYE/SPORT SERIES					
92 Rallye	2-dr Spt Cpe-4P	I4/91	2314	1925	Note 1
91	2-dr Spt Sed-4/5P	I4/66	1944	1715	Note 1
99	2-dr LS Cpe-4P	I4/66	2163	1735	Note 1
95 (Deluxe)	2-dr Spt Cpe-4P	I4/66	2041	1715	Note 1

Note 1: A total of 539,099 Opel passenger cars (all models except Kombi) were produced during 1968.

ENGINE DATA: BASE FOUR: Inline, overhead-valve four-cylinder. Cast iron block and head. **Displacement:** 65.8 cu. in. (1077 cc). **Bore & Stroke:** 2.95 x 2.40 in. (75 x 61 mm). **Compression Ratio:** 8.2:1. **Brake Horsepower:** 55 at 5600 rpm. **Torque:** 57-59 lbs.-ft. at 2850-3400 rpm. Three main bearings. Solid valve lifters. One Solex carburetor.

BASE FOUR (Rallye coupe); OPTIONAL (other models): Inline, overhead-cam four-cylinder. **Displacement:** 91.0 cu. in. (1491 cc). **Bore & Stroke:** 3.25 x 2.75 in. (83 x 69.8 mm). **Compression Ratio:** 9.0:1. **Brake Horsepower:** 80 at 5100 rpm. **Torque:** 87-89 lbs.-ft. at 3400-4400 rpm. Solid valve lifters. Solex two-barrel carburetor.

OPTIONAL FOUR: Inline, overhead-cam four-cylinder. Cast iron block and light alloy head. **Displacement:** 115.8 cu. in. (1897 cc). **Bore & Stroke:** 3.66 x 2.75 in. (93 x 69.8 mm). **Compression Ratio:** 9.0:1. **Brake Horsepower:** 102 at 5200 rpm. **Torque:** 115 lbs.-ft. at 3100 rpm. Five main bearings. Solid valve lifters. Solex two-barrel carburetor.

CHASSIS DATA: Wheelbase: 95.1 in. **Overall Length:** (sed) 161.6 in.; (cpe) 164.6 in.; (wag) 164.4 in. **Height:** (sed) 53 in.; (cpe) 52.8-53.3 in. **Width:** 61.9 in. **Front Tread:** 49.2 in. **Rear Tread:** 50.2 in. **Standard Tires:** 155x13 except (Rallye cpe) 155SR13.

TECHNICAL: Layout: front-engine, rear-drive. **Transmission:** four-speed manual (floor lever). **Standard Final Drive Ratio:** 3.89:1 except (Rallye cpe) 3.67:1. **Steering:** rack and pinion. **Suspension (front):** A-arms with lower transverse semi-elliptic leaf spring. **Suspension (rear):** rigid axle with coil springs. **Brakes:** hydraulic, front/rear drum; front discs optional (standard on Rallye). **Body Construction:** steel unibody.

PERFORMANCE: Similar to 1966-67.

PRODUCTION/SALES: Approximately 84,680 Opels were sold in the U.S. during 1968. The U.S. Department of Commerce reported that 80,366 Opels were imported in 1968.

Manufacturer: Adam Opel AG, Russelsheim, West Germany.

Distributor: Buick Motor Division, Flint, Michigan.

HISTORY: Opel's 1968 models were introduced to the U.S. market in October 1967. Opel advertising in the late 1960s dubbed these cars "Mini-Brute."

1969 OPEL

KADETT — FOUR — Production of the basic Opel two-door sedan and station wagon continued with little change. The short-lived 1491-cc engine faded away, leaving only the original 1077-cc (65.8-cid) four.

KADETT RALLYE/SPORT — FOUR — The sporty variants of Opel's Kadett returned with minimal change. The Rallye coupe came with a 67-bhp version of the 1077-cc engine. A three-speed automatic transmission was available this year, with the larger (1.9-liter) engine. Options included a vinyl top.

GT — 93 — FOUR — After more than a decade on the U.S. market with sedans and conventional (if sporty) coupes, Opel introduced a two-seat sports car during the 1969 model year. Styling of the GT coupe was unmistakably similar to that of the latest Corvette, down to the pop-up headlamps in a sharp, low nose and the slim bumper. Headlamp rotation was manually-actuated, via a lever in the cockpit. At the rear was a sliced-off tail with a quartet of round lenses and lacking an external trunklid; again, not far removed from the Corvette design. Base engine was the 67-bhp version of the 1077-cc Opel four, with an overhead-cam 1.9-liter four optional. Although differing dramatically in appearance from the Opel Kadett sedan, the GT rode the same chassis. As part of the conversion, the engine was moved about a foot rearward, along with the passenger compartment. Wheelbase was 95.7 inches (only slightly longer than a Kadett). Front disc brakes were standard.

476

1969 Opel GT coupe.

I.D. DATA: Serial number is on a plate on the right front wheelhouse or at the upper left corner of the instrument panel. Starting serial number: (2-dr sedan) 31-1555227 or 9090017; (2-dr wagon) 39-1555181 or 9089057; (2-dr spt sedan) 91-1535504 or 908821; (Rallye/sport coupe) 92-1555131 or 90895608. Engine number is stamped on the block, just above the dipstick.

Model	Body Type & Seating	Engine Type/CID	P.O.E. Price	Weight (lbs.)	Prod. Total
KADETT					
31	2-dr Sedan-4/5P	I4/66	1862	1625	Note 1
39	2-dr Sta Wag-4/5P	I4/66	2153	1742	Note 1
RALLYE/SPORT SERIES					
92 Rallye	2-dr Spt Cpe-4P	I4/66	2365	1717	Note 1
91	2-dr Spt Sed-4/5P	I4/66	2033	1664	Note 1
95 (Deluxe)	2-dr Spt Cpe-4P	I4/66	2132	1664	Note 1
GT					
93	2-dr Coupe-2P	I4/66	3395	1815	Note 2

Note 1: A total of 665,754 Opel passenger cars (all models except Kombi) were produced during 1969.

Note 2: Approximately 103,373 Opel GT coupes with the 1.9-liter engine were produced during the full model run (1969-73).

ENGINE DATA: BASE FOUR: Inline, overhead-valve four-cylinder. Cast iron block and head. **Displacement:** 65.8 cu. in. (1077 cc). **Bore & Stroke:** 2.95 x 2.40 in. (75 x 61 mm). **Compression Ratio:** 8.2:1. **Brake Horsepower:** 60 at 6000 rpm. **Torque:** 58 lbs.-ft. at 4000 rpm. Three main bearings. Solid valve lifters. One Solex carburetor.
BASE FOUR (Rallye coupe, GT coupe): Same as above, except — **Compression Ratio:** 9.2:1. **Brake Horsepower:** 67 at 6000 rpm. **Torque:** 62 lbs.-ft. at 5000 rpm. Solid valve lifters. Two Solex single-barrel carburetors.
OPTIONAL FOUR: Inline, overhead-cam four-cylinder. Cast iron block and light alloy head. **Displacement:** 115.8 cu. in. (1897 cc). **Bore & Stroke:** 3.66 x 2.75 in. (93 x 69.8 mm). **Compression Ratio:** 9.0:1. **Brake Horsepower:** 102 at 5200-5400 rpm. **Torque:** 115 lbs.-ft. at 3100 rpm. Five main bearings. Solid valve lifters. Solex two-barrel carburetor.

CHASSIS DATA: Wheelbase: (Kadett) 95.1 in.; (GT) 95.7 in. **Overall Length:** (sed) 161.6 in.; (cpe) 164.6 in.; (wag) 164.4 in.; (GT cpe) 161.9 in. **Height:** (sed) 53 in.; (cpe) 52.8-53.3 in.; (wag) 53.9 in.; (GT cpe) 47.7 in. **Width:** (Kadett) 61.9 in.; (GT cpe) 62.2 in. **Front Tread:** (Kadett) 49.2 in.; (GT cpe) 49.6 in. **Rear Tread:** (Kadett) 50.2 in.; (GT cpe) 50.6 in. **Standard Tires:** (Kadett) 155x13 except (Rallye cpe) 155SR13; (GT cpe) 165HR13.
TECHNICAL: Layout: front-engine, rear-drive. **Transmission:** four-speed manual (floor lever); three-speed automatic optional. GT gear ratios: (1st) 3.43:1; (2nd) 2.16:1; (3rd) 1.37:1; (4th) 1.00:1. **Standard Final Drive Ratio:** (Kadett) 4.11:1 or 3.67:1; (GT cpe) 3.44:1. **Steering:** rack and pinion. **Suspension (front):** A-arms with lower transverse semi-elliptic leaf spring. **Suspension (rear):** rigid axle with coil springs. **Brakes:** hydraulic, front/rear drum; front discs optional (standard on Rallye and GT). **Body Construction:** steel unibody.
MAJOR OPTIONS: Automatic transmission ($190). Air conditioning. 1.9-liter engine: GT ($99). Rear defroster: GT ($19). Vinyl top.
PERFORMANCE: Top Speed: (Kadett sed) about 101 mph; (1.9-liter GT cpe) 111 mph. **Acceleration (0-60 mph):** (1.9-liter GT cpe) 10.2 sec. **Acceleration (quarter-mile):** (1.9-liter GT cpe) 17.4 sec. (79 mph). **Fuel Mileage:** (1.9-liter GT cpe) 22-26 mpg.
PRODUCTION/SALES: Approximately 93,520 Opels were sold in the U.S. during 1969 (including 11,880 GTs).
Manufacturer: Adam Opel AG, Russelsheim, West Germany.
Distributor: Buick Motor Division, Flint, Michigan.
HISTORY: In its initial evaluation of the smaller-engined model (in European trim), *Car and Driver* described Opel's new GT as a "teeny-bopper Corvette with a mini-powerplant." *Car Life* noted that "it looks like a Mini-Vette, and handles more like a 'Vette than an Opel." The GT evolved from an experimental sports car that had been displayed at the Frankfurt Auto Show in 1964. Bodies were produced in France, by Brissonneau and Lotz, from a design created largely by Clare MacKichan of GM, then working at Opel.

1970 OPEL

KADETT/RALLYE — FOUR — All Kadett models (except the Rallye coupe) got a modest boost in horsepower this year, to 63 bhp, via twin single-barrel carburetors. Otherwise, the "Mini-Brute" (as Opel described the entire Kadett line) continued with minimal change. As before, the Rallye coupe carried a 67-bhp version of the 1077-cid (65.8-cid) four-cylinder engine, with higher compression. Either a floor-mounted four-speed or console-mounted three-speed automatic was available. As before, the 1.9-liter engine was optional, known as the 1900 Super Kadett. Available on all models except the two-

door sedan, that engine package included front disc brakes and heavy-duty powertrain components. The Super Deluxe sport coupe included a three-spoke steering wheel and simulated walnut instrument panel. Body colors this year were: Rallye Orange (on Rallye coupe only), Aztec Gold, Brilliant White, Flame Red, Spring Green, Copper Bronze, Chrome Yellow, and Strato Blue. Interiors came in black, buckskin or red vinyl (depending on body color). Rallye Kadett interiors were black or buckskin.

1970 Opel 1800 GT.

GT — 93 — FOUR — Production of the Opel two-seat sports car continued with little change, available with either a 67-bhp overhead-valve four or 102-bhp overhead-cam four-cylinder engine. A tachometer was standard, along with sculptured bucket seats, a transistorized radio, electric clock, and dual chrome-plated tailpipe outlets. A three-speed automatic transmission was optional, only with the 1.9-liter engine. Body colors this year were Strato Blue, Brilliant White, Flame Red, GT Chartreuse, Sunburst Yellow, and Rallye Orange. Interiors were black vinyl, except red with White body color and buckskin with Strato Blue body color.

I.D. DATA: Serial number is on a plate on the right front wheelhouse or at the upper left corner of the instrument panel. Starting serial number: (2-dr sedan) 311892279 or 319226095; (2-dr wagon) 391891974 or 399226972; (2-dr FB sedan) 911898801 or 9192266160; (Rallye FB coupe) 921892066 or 929226061; (GT cpe) 931892645 or 941888818. Engine number is stamped on the block, just above the dipstick.

Model	Body Type & Seating	Engine Type/CID	P.O.E. Price	Weight (lbs.)	Prod. Total
KADETT					
31	2-dr Sedan-4/5P	I4/66	1877	1640	Note 1
39	2-dr Sta Wag-4/5P	I4/66	2159	1762	Note 1
RALLYE/SPORT (FB) SERIES					
92 Rallye	2-dr Spt Cpe-4P	I4/66	2378	1729	Note 1
91	2-dr Spt Sed-4/5P	I4/66	2043	1671	Note 1
95 (DeL)	2-dr Spt Cpe-4P	I4/66	2139	1673	Note 1
GT					
93	2-dr Coupe-2P	I4/66	3328	1780	Note 2

Note 1: A total of 698,622 Opel passenger cars (all models except Kombi) were produced during 1970.

Note 2: Approximately 103,373 Opel GT coupes with the 1.9-liter engine were produced during the full model run (1969-73).

1970 Opel Kadett wagon.

ENGINE DATA: BASE FOUR: Inline, overhead-valve four-cylinder. Cast iron block and head. **Displacement:** 65.8 cu. in. (1077 cc). **Bore & Stroke:** 2.95 x 2.40 in. (75 x 61 mm). **Compression Ratio:** 8.2:1. **Brake Horsepower:** 63 at 6000 rpm. **Torque:** 59 lbs.-ft. at 4200 rpm. Three main bearings. Solid valve lifters. Two single-barrel carburetors.
BASE FOUR (Rallye coupe, GT coupe): Same as above, except — **Compression Ratio:** 9.2:1. **Brake Horsepower:** 67 at 6000 rpm. **Torque:** 62 lbs.-ft. at 4600-5400 rpm. Two single-barrel Solex carburetors.
OPTIONAL FOUR: Inline, overhead-cam four-cylinder. Cast iron block and light alloy head. **Displacement:** 115.8 cu. in. (1897 cc). **Bore & Stroke:** 3.66 x 2.75 in. (93 x 69.8 mm). **Compression Ratio:** 9.0:1. **Brake Horsepower:** 102 at 5400 rpm. **Torque:** 115 lbs.-ft. at 3000 rpm. Five main bearings. Solid valve lifters. Single Solex two-barrel carburetor.

CHASSIS DATA: Wheelbase: (Kadett) 95.1 in.; (GT) 95.7 in. **Overall Length:** (sed) 161.6 in.; (cpe) 164.6 in.; (wag) 164.4 in.; (GT cpe) 161.9 in. **Height:** (sed) 53 in.; (cpe) 52.8-53.3 in.; (wag) 53.9 in.; (GT cpe) 48.2 in. **Width:** (Kadett) 61.9 in.; (GT cpe) 62.2 in. **Front Tread:** (Kadett) 49.2 in.; (GT cpe) 49.4 in. **Rear Tread:** (Kadett) 50.2 in.; (GT cpe) 50.3 in. **Standard Tires:** (Kadett) 155x13 except (Rallye cpe) 155SR13; (GT cpe) 165HR13.

1970 Opel Manta 1.6S.

TECHNICAL: Layout: front-engine, rear-drive. **Transmission:** four-speed manual (floor lever); three-speed automatic optional. Kadett four-speed gear ratios: (1st) 3.867:1; (2nd) 2.215:1; (3rd) 1.432:1; (4th) 1.00:1; (rev) 3.90:1. Kadett four-speed gear ratios with 1.9-liter engine: (1st) 3.428:1; (2nd) 2.156:1; (3rd) 1.366:1; (4th) 1.00:1. GT gear ratios: (1st) 3.43:1; (2nd) 2.16:1; (3rd) 1.37:1; (4th) 1.00:1. **Standard Final Drive Ratio:** (Kadett w/4-spd) 4.11:1; (1.9-liter Kadett w/4-spd) 3.18:1 or 3.67:1; (GT cpe) 4.11:1; (GT cpe w/1.9-liter engine) 3.44:1. **Steering:** rack and pinion., **Suspension (front):** A-arms with lower transverse semi-elliptic leaf spring. **Suspension (rear):** rigid axle with coil springs. **Brakes:** hydraulic, front/rear drum; front discs optional (standard on Rallye and GT). **Body Construction:** steel unibody. **Fuel Tank:** (Kadett) 10.6 gallon; (GT) 13.2 gallon.

MAJOR OPTIONS: Automatic transmission ($190). Air conditioning. 1.9-liter engine: GT ($99). Vinyl top. Chrome wheels (Rallye).

PERFORMANCE: Top Speed: (1.9-liter GT cpe) about 110 mph. **Acceleration (0-60 mph):** (1.9-liter GT cpe) 10.1 sec. **Acceleration (quarter-mile):** (1.9-liter GT cpe) 17.4 sec. (79.7 mph). **Fuel Mileage:** (1.9-liter GT cpe) 21-24 mpg.

PRODUCTION/SALES: Approximately 86,630 Opels were sold in the U.S. during 1970 (including 21,240 GTs).

Manufacturer: Adam Opel AG, Russelsheim, West Germany.

Distributor: Buick Motor Division, Flint, Michigan.

HISTORY: Opel's 1970 models were introduced to the U.S. market in August 1969.

1971-72 OPEL

1971 Opel GT coupe.

KADETT — FOUR — A four-door sedan was offered in the Kadett series for 1971, along with the two-door sedan and station wagon. Both sedans came in either base or Deluxe trim. This year's 1077-cc (65.8-cid) engine produced 56 horsepower, as a result of reduced compression.

1900 SERIES — 51/53/54/57 — FOUR — A new and slightly larger model joined the Opel lineup, powered by the same 1897-cc (115.8-cid) engine installed in the GT sports car. This Opel had coil-spring front suspension and front disc brakes. In addition to the four-door sedan, body styles included a two-door sedan, two-door station wagon, and standard or Rallye coupe. Styling was credited to Chuck Jordan, then working on German-built General Motors products but who later (in the 1980s) became head of GM styling. Coupes sold in Europe were known as Mantas, but that name was not used until later for models imported into the U.S. market. Sedans and station wagons took the Ascona name outside of the U.S. market. The Rallye coupe included such extras as foglamps, striping, and a stiffer suspension.

GT — 77 — FOUR — Opel's two-seat sports car continued with little change, except for a revision of its model number. The initial 1077-cc engine no longer was commonly available in U.S. models, which turned to the formerly-optional 1897-cc four, now rated at 90 horsepower on reduced compression.

1972 Opel Commodore four-door sedan.

I.D. DATA: Serial number is on the right side of the cowl, under the hood; and at the upper left corner of the instrument panel. The two-digit prefix identifies the model number, followed by a seven-digit sequential production number. Engine number is on the block, above the mount. Engine number consists of a three-symbol prefix, followed by the sequential production number. Starting in 1972, a 13-digit Vehicle Identification Number was used; see next listing for details.

Model	Body Type & Seating	Engine Type/CID	P.O.E. Price	Weight (lbs.)	Prod. Total
KADETT					
31	2-dr Sedan-4/5P	I4/66	1878	1635	Note 1
31D (DeL)	2-dr Sedan-4/5P	I4/66	1994	1640	Note 1
36	4-dr Sedan-4/5P	I4/66	1903	1679	Note 1
36D (DeL)	4-dr Sedan-4/5P	I4/66	2069	1684	Note 1
39 (DeL)	2-dr Sta Wag-4/5P	I4/66	2294	1762	Note 1
1900 SERIES					
51	2-dr Sedan-5P	I4/116	2226	2037	Note 1
53	4-dr Sedan-5P	I4/116	2306	N/A	Note 1
54	2-dr Sta Wag-5P	I4/116	2331	2128	Note 1
57	2-dr Spt Cpe-5P	I4/116	2331	2066	Note 1
57R	2-dr Rallye Cpe-5P	I4/116	2490	2088	Note 1
GT					
77	2-dr Coupe-2P	I4/116	3339	2009	Note 2

Note 1: A total of 730,118 Opel passenger cars (plus 101,754 Kombis) were produced during 1971, followed by 777,292 (and 94,072 Kombis) in 1972.

Note 2: A total of 14,715 Opel GT coupes were produced during 1971, followed by 17,398 in 1972.

Price Note: Figures shown were valid in 1971. Kadett rose for 1972, starting at $2049 for the two-door sedan; 1900 prices rose only slightly; and the GT for $3333.

ENGINE DATA: BASE FOUR (Kadett): Inline, overhead-valve four-cylinder. Cast iron block and head. **Displacement:** 65.8 cu. in. (1077 cc). **Bore & Stroke:** 2.95 x 2.40 in. (75 x 61 mm). **Compression Ratio:** 7.6:1. **Brake Horsepower:** 56 at 5800 rpm. **Torque:** 55 lbs.-ft. at 4400 rpm. Three main bearings. Solid valve lifters.
BASE FOUR (1900, GT): Inline, overhead-cam four-cylinder. Cast iron block and light alloy head. **Displacement:** 115.8 cu. in. (1897 cc). **Bore & Stroke:** 3.66 x 2.75 in. (93 x 69.8 mm). **Compression Ratio:** 7.6:1. **Brake Horsepower:** 90 at 5200 rpm. **Torque:** 111 lbs.-ft. at 3400 rpm. Five main bearings. Solid valve lifters.

CHASSIS DATA: Wheelbase: (Kadett) 95.1 in.; (1900/GT) 95.7 in. **Overall Length:** (Kadett) 161.6 in.; (Kadett wag) 164.4 in.; (1900 sed) 164.6 in.; (1900 cpe) 171 in.; (GT cpe) 161.9 in. **Height:** (Kadett sed) 53 in.; (Kadett wag) 53.9 in.; (1900 2-dr sed) 52.6 in.; (1900 4-dr sed) 54.5 in.; (1900 wag) 53.3 in.; (1900 cpe) 50.9-51.2 in.; (GT cpe) 47.4 in. **Width:** (Kadett) 61.9 in.; (1900) 64.3 in.; (GT cpe) 62.2 in. **Front Tread:** (Kadett) 49.2 in.; (1900) 52.4 in.; (GT cpe) 49.4 in. **Rear Tread:** (Kadett) 50.2 in.; (1900) 52 in.; (GT cpe) 50.6 in. **Standard Tires:** (Kadett) 155x13; (1900) 165AR13; (GT cpe) 165HR13.

TECHNICAL: Layout: front-engine, rear-drive. **Transmission:** four-speed manual (floor lever); three-speed automatic optional. **Standard Final Drive Ratio:** (Kadett) 4.11:1; (1900) 3.44:1; (1900 Rallye cpe) 3.69:1; (GT) 3.44:1. **Steering:** rack and pinion. **Suspension (front):** (Kadett/GT) A-arms with lower transverse semi-elliptic leaf spring; (1900) A-arms with coil springs. **Suspension (rear):** rigid axle with coil springs. **Brakes:** (1900/GT) front disc, rear drum. **Body Construction:** steel unibody.

MAJOR OPTIONS: Automatic transmission ($196). Air conditioning.

PRODUCTION/SALES: As many as 88,535 Opels were sold in the U.S. during 1971, including 13,696 Opel GTs and 8,378 series 1900 models. Approximately 69,407 Opels were sold in the U.S. during 1972, including 12,055 GTs and 10,647 series 1900.

Manufacturer: Adam Opel AG, Russelsheim, West Germany.

Distributor: Buick Motor Division, Flint, Michigan.

HISTORY: Opel's 1971 models were introduced to the U.S. market on October 26, 1970; the 1972 models on September 21, 1971. By 1972, more than 90 percent of Opels sold in the U.S. had the larger (115.8-cid) engine. A total of 2,128 Buick dealers had Opels available. This would be the final season for the Kadett series.

1973 OPEL

1900 SERIES — 51/53/54 — FOUR — Three models entered the 1973 model year in the 1900 series: two- and four-door sedans, and a deluxe station wagon. Each carried a 115.8-cid four-cylinder engine, now rated 75 horsepower (SAE net).

MANTA — 57 — FOUR — Sport coupe versions of the 1900 series adopted the Manta name that had been used earlier in Europe. The coupe came in base, Luxus or Rallye form. Luxus coupes had cord cloth upholstery and four-spoke wheels; base models contained vinyl upholstery.

GT — 77 — FOUR — For its final season in the U.S. marketplace, Opel's sports car got a price hike. Four-spoke wheels were new this year.

I.D. DATA: Opel's 13-symbol Vehicle Identification Number is on lower left windshield pillar, visible through the windshield. Symbol one ('O') indicates manufacturer (Opel). The next three symbols indicate series and body type ('L11' = 2-dr sedan; 'L69' = 4-dr sedan; 'L15' = station wagon; 'L77' = Manta coupe; 'Y07' = GT). Symbol five denotes engine ('N' = 1.9-liter). Symbol six indicates model year ('C' = 1973). Symbol seven is assembly plant ('2' = Bochum; '5' = Russelsheim; '9' = Antwerp). The final six digits form the sequential serial number.

Model	Body Type & Seating	Engine Type/CID	P.O.E. Price	Weight (lbs.)	Prod. Total
1900 SERIES					
51	2-dr Sedan-5P	I4/116	2520	2063	Note 1
53	4-dr Sedan-5P	I4/116	2611	2108	Note 1
54	2-dr Sta Wag-5P	I4/116	2997	2152	Note 1
MANTA					
57	2-dr Spt Cpe-5P	I4/116	2850	2108	Note 1
57L (Luxus)	2-dr Spt Cpe-5P	I4/116	3059	2108	Note 1
57R	2-dr Rallye Cpe-5P	I4/116	3047	2108	Note 1
GT					
77	2-dr Coupe-2P	I4/116	3713	2030	Note 2

Note 1: A total of 788,662 Opel passenger cars (plus 79,520 Kombis) were produced during 1973.
Note 2: A total of 11,380 Opel GT coupes were produced during 1973.

1973 Opel Manta Luxus two-door sport coupe.

ENGINE DATA: BASE FOUR: Inline, overhead-cam four-cylinder. Cast iron block and light alloy head. **Displacement:** 115.8 cu. in. (1897 cc). **Bore & Stroke:** 3.66 x 2.75 in. (93 x 69.8 mm). **Compression Ratio:** 7.6:1. **Brake Horsepower:** 75 (SAE net) at 4800 rpm. **Torque:** 92 lbs.-ft. at 3400 rpm. Five main bearings. Solid valve lifters.

CHASSIS DATA: Wheelbase: 95.7 in. **Overall Length:** (1900) 164.6 in; (Manta cpe) 171 in.; (GT cpe) 161.0 in. **Height:** (1900) 53.3 in.; (Manta cpe) 51.3 in.; (GT cpe) 47.4 in. **Width:** (1900/Manta) 64.3 in.; (GT cpe) 62.2 in. **Front Tread:** (1900/Manta) 52.4 in.; (GT cpe) 49.4 in. **Rear Tread:** (1900/Manta) 52 in.; (GT cpe) 50.6 in. **Standard Tires:** 165x13.

TECHNICAL: Layout: front-engine, rear-drive. **Transmission:** four-speed manual (floor lever); three-speed automatic optional. **Standard Final Drive Ratio:** 3.44:1 or 3.67:1. **Steering:** rack and pinion. **Suspension (front):** (GT) A-arms with lower transverse semi-elliptic leaf spring; (1900/Manta) A-arms with coil springs. **Suspension (rear):** rigid axle with coil springs. **Brakes:** front disc, rear drum. **Body Construction:** steel unibody.

MAJOR OPTIONS: Automatic transmission ($233). Air conditioning.
PRODUCTION/SALES: A total of 68,400 Opels were sold in the U.S. during 1973, including 11,693 Opel GTs, 8,360 Manta Rallye coupes, and 17,536 Manta Luxus coupes.
Manufacturer: Adam Opel AG, Russelsheim, West Germany.
Distributor: Buick Motor Division, Flint, Michigan.
HISTORY: Opel's 1973 models were introduced to the U.S. market on September 15, 1972. This was the final year for the Opel GT in the U.S. market.

1974-75 OPEL

1900/MANTA — FOUR — Only the station wagon (Sportwagon) remained of the 1900 sedan/wagon series as the 1974 model year began, though the two-door sedan returned again later. Manta coupes again came in three trim levels: base, Luxus and Rallye. Under each hood was Opel's 1897-cc (115.8-cid) four-cylinder engine, rated 75 bhp. The engine added fuel injection for 1975, adding a few horsepower.

I.D. DATA: Opel's 13-symbol Vehicle Identification Number is on lower left windshield pillar, visible through the windshield. Symbol one ('O') indicates manufacturer (Opel). The next three symbols indicate series and body type ('L11' = 2-dr sedan; 'L15' = station wagon; 'L77' = Manta coupe). Symbol five denotes engine ('N' = 1.9-liter). Symbol six indicates model year ('D' = 1974; 'E' = 1975). Symbol seven is assembly plant ('2' = Bochum; '5' = Russelsheim; '9' = Antwerp). The final six digits form the sequential serial number.

Model	Body Type & Seating	Engine Type/CID	P.O.E. Price	Weight (lbs.)	Prod. Total
1900					
51	2-dr Sedan-5P	I4/116	3175	2151	Note 1
54	2-dr Sta Wag-5P	I4/116	3442	2172	Note 1
MANTA					
57	2-dr Spt Cpe-5P	I4/116	3275	2128	Note 1
57L (Luxus)	2-dr Spt Cpe-5P	I4/116	3512	2139	Note 1
57R	2-dr Rallye Cpe-5P	I4/116	3500	2139	Note 1

Note 1: A total of 507,204 Opel passenger cars (plus 71,060 Kombis) were produced during 1974, followed by 593,270 (and 62,607 Kombis) in 1975.

Price Note: Figures shown were valid in 1974. During 1975, final prices rose to $3645 for the 1900 two-door sedan, $3962 for the 1900 wagon, and $3745 for the base Manta coupe.
ENGINE DATA: BASE FOUR (1974): Inline, overhead-cam four-cylinder. Cast iron block and light alloy head. **Displacement:** 115.8 cu. in. (1897 cc). **Bore & Stroke:** 3.66 x 2.75 in. (93 x 69.8 mm). **Compression Ratio:** 7.6:1. **Brake Horsepower:** 75 at 4800 rpm. **Torque:** 92 lbs.-ft. at 3400 rpm. Five main bearings. Solid valve lifters.
BASE FOUR (1975): Same as above, except with Bosch fuel injection. **Brake Horsepower:** 81 at 5000 rpm. **Torque:** 96 lbs.-ft. at 2200 rpm.
CHASSIS DATA: Wheelbase: 95.7 in. **Overall Length:** (1900) 170.2 in.; (Manta cpe) 176.1 in. **Height:** (1900) 53.7 in.; (Manta cpe) 51.3-51.8 in. **Width:** 64.3 in. **Front Tread:** 52.4 in. **Rear Tread:** 52 in. **Standard Tires:** 165x13.
TECHNICAL: Layout: front-engine, rear-drive. **Transmission:** four-speed manual (floor lever); three-speed automatic optional. **Standard Final Drive Ratio:** 3.44:1 or 3.67:1. **Steering:** rack and pinion. **Suspension (front):** A-arms with coil springs. **Suspension (rear):** rigid axle with coil springs. **Brakes:** front disc, rear drum. **Body Construction:** steel unibody.
MAJOR OPTIONS: Automatic transmission ($254). Air conditioning.
PRODUCTION/SALES: A total of 68,400 Opels were sold in the U.S. during 1974, including 7,959 Rallye coupes and 14,026 Luxus coupes. A total of 15,118 Opels were sold in the U.S. during 1975.
Manufacturer: Adam Opel AG, Russelsheim, West Germany.
Distributor: Buick Motor Division, Flint, Michigan.

HISTORY: Partly because of a weakening ratio between U.S. and German currency, and rising prices in general, the German Opel left the U.S. market after the 1975 model year.

1976-79 OPEL

OPEL ISUZU — 77 AND 69 SERIES — FOUR — Not only was the 1976 edition sold in America a completely different Opel, it came from a different country: Japan instead of Germany. A two-door coupe was the only body style offered for 1976, in base or Deluxe trim. Under the hood was a 1817-cc (111-cid) four-cylinder engine that produced 80 horsepower, hooked to a four-speed manual gearbox. Both a five-speed manual and three-speed automatic transmission were optional.

The Isuzu-built coupe rode a 94.3-inch wheelbase. Air conditioning was optional. For the 1977 model year, a four-door sedan joined the coupe, featuring a center console, clock, simulated woodgrain trim on the instrument panel, and front/rear bumper guards. Deluxe models added a tachometer, ammeter, oil pressure gauge, clock, window and rocker-panel moldings, and bumper guards. Then, for 1978, came a W77 Sport Coupe, which had body-colored bumpers, a front air dam, blacked-out grille and trim, sport mirrors, rally-style wheels, and wide black lower bodyside striping. A sport suspension with specially-tuned springs and thicker front stabilizer bar also was included with the sport coupe. All coupes had swing-out rear-quarter windows. Each model switched to rectangular headlamps for 1979.

This Isuzu series was called the Gemini in Japan, and used the same engine as the "Luv" compact pickup truck sold by Chevrolet dealers. Six body colors were available in 1977: blue, white, yellow, tan, red, and green. For 1979, the colors were blue, cream, brown, red, silver, and white.

I.D. DATA: Opel's 13-symbol Vehicle Identification Number is on lower left windshield pillar, visible through the windshield. Symbol one ('4') indicates manufacturer. The next symbol indicates series ('T' = standard 2-dr; 'Y' = deluxe 2-dr and 4-dr; 'W' = sport coupe). Symbols three and four denote body type ('69' = 4-dr; '77' = 2-dr). Symbol five ('B') is the engine code. Symbol six is model year ('7' = 1977; '8' = 1978; '9' = 1979). The final six digits form the sequential serial number, starting with 400001 for four-door sedans and 700001 for two-doors.

Model	Body Type & Seating	Engine Type/CID	P.O.E. Price	Weight (lbs.)	Prod. Total
OPEL ISUZU (1976 models)					
77	2-dr Coupe-4/5P	I4/111	3282	2061	Note 1
77 DeL	2-dr Coupe-4/5P	I4/111	3595	2081	Note 1
OPEL ISUZU (1979 models)					
T77	2-dr Coupe-4/5P	I4/111	4335	2083	Note 1
Y77 (DeL)	2-dr Coupe-4/5P	I4/111	4645	2101	Note 1
Y69 (DeL)	4-dr Sedan-4/5P	I4/111	4726	2152	Note 1
W77 (Spt)	2-dr Coupe-4/5P	I4/111	4779	2097	Note 1

Note 1: A total of 10,483 Opel Isuzus were sold in the U.S. during 1976, followed by 29,067 in 1977, and 19,222 in 1978.

ENGINE DATA: BASE FOUR: Inline, overhead-cam four-cylinder. Cast iron block and aluminum head. **Displacement:** 110.8 cu. in. (1817 cc). **Bore & Stroke:** 3.31 x 3.23 in. (84 x 82 mm). **Compression Ratio:** 8.5:1. **Brake Horsepower:** 80 at 4800 rpm. **Torque:** 95 lbs.-ft. at 3000 rpm. Five main bearings. Solid valve lifters. Two-barrel carburetor.

CHASSIS DATA: Wheelbase: 94.3 in. **Overall Length:** (cpe) 168; (sed) 170.5 in. **Height:** (cpe) 52.6 in.; (sed) 53.5 in. **Width:** 61.8 in. **Front Tread:** 51.4 in. **Rear Tread:** 51.4 in. **Standard Tires:** 6.15x13.

TECHNICAL: Layout: front-engine, rear-drive. **Transmission:** four-speed (floor lever); five-speed manual or three-speed Turbo Hydra-Matic optional. **Standard Final Drive Ratio:** 3.55:1. **Steering:** rack and pinion. **Suspension (front):** unequal-length A-arms with coil springs. **Suspension (rear):** three-link rigid axle with coil springs. **Brakes:** power front disc, rear drum. **Body Construction:** steel unibody.

MAJOR OPTIONS: Automatic transmission. Five-speed manual transmission. AM/FM radio. Air conditioning. Instrument package (including tachometer). Electric rear defogger.
Manufacturer: Isuzu Motors Ltd., Tokyo, Japan.
Distributor: Buick Motor Division, Flint, Michigan.

HISTORY: Opel Isuzus were introduced to the U.S. market on April 29, 1976, again sold and serviced by Buick dealers. The new model was first called "Opel by Isuzu," but after sluggish early sales, the name was changed to "Buick Opel," identified as such by large block lettering on bodyside striping. EPA gas mileage estimates reached as high as 38 mpg highway (25 mpg city) in 1977, with a five-speed transmission.

After 1979, the Opel name disappeared from the U.S. market, though Isuzu models soon appeared under their own name. Opels remained in production in Germany through the late 1970s, 1980s and beyond, but never resumed export to America.

OSCA

The Maserati name turns up in connection with several Italian sports/racing makes of the postwar period, including OSCA. Not long before the outbreak of World War II, the Maserati brothers had sold their interest in the original Maserati company to Adolfo Orsi (though they remained under contract until 1947). Soon after the war, their contract having expired, the remaining three brothers wished to reenter the racing car business on their own. So they founded *Officina Specializzata Costruzione Automobili Fratelli Maserati* at Bologna, Italy. The first four elements of that sizable name formed the acronym, OSCA.

Their initial race car carried a 1096-cc four-cylinder engine, mounted on a ladder-type tubular chassis. This basic design remained in production for some years, with engine sizes as large as 1452 cc (and as small as 749 cc). Meanwhile, the brothers got an order to create a 4.5-liter V-12 engine for Grand Prix competition, to be raced by Prince Bira (of Siam), a well-known racing driver in the early 1950s. That engine was installed in a Maserati 4CLT chassis. The OSCA company also was developing a tubular chassis of its own design. OSCA's cigar-shaped 1500 Sport helped Stirling Moss and Bill Lloyd to take the class victory at the Sebring race in 1954—a win that drew the attention of American enthusiasts. Other racing OSCAs fared well in U.S. competition, driven by Briggs Cunningham and Jim Kimberly.

In a 1955 test by *Road & Track,* the OSCA 1490-cc Spyder delivered a 0-60 time of 7.0 seconds, traveling through the quarter-mile acceleration run in 15.7 seconds. By 1956, the company was producing an ample selection of two-seat racing cars, with engines up to two liters in displacement. As many as 30 cars annually were leaving the OSCA facility, wearing bodies that came from outside suppliers. Alejandro de Tomaso, whose name would later be connected with the modern-day Maserati as well as the De Tomaso line of sports cars, served as a factory driver for OSCA in the late 1950s, bringing home the Index of Performance from the Le Mans event of 1958.

As the result of an agreement with Fiat in 1959, a larger version of OSCA's twin-cam four-cylinder engine went into the Fiat 1500S sports car. Not long afterward, when OSCA decided to enter the everyday sports-car end of the business with a roadgoing GT model, it carried that Fiat engine.

OSCA's entry into sports cars for ordinary driving didn't last long, however. In 1963, the Maserati brothers sold out to Count Domenico Agusta, a manufacturer of racing motorcycles. The final OSCAs of 1966-67, powered by V-4 engines from Ford of Germany, were nothing special and the OSCA name soon evaporated with little notice.

1947-55 OSCA

1490-cc SPYDER — MT4/1400 — FOUR — By the mid-1950s, OSCAs were trickling into the U.S. for competition purposes. In 1955, Road & Track had an opportunity to test a car that had recently raced in California. Their test car had the longest (4.37:1) final-drive ratio available. Except for an oval (nearly round) grille made up of vertical bars, in a moderately protruding nose, the car was relatively ordinary in appearance—for a racing model, at any rate—and would not have looked too far out of place on an ordinary road. Not that it would have been suitable for such a purpose. Because of "its aluminum body that tends to rattle a bit, no top or windshield, and a rather 'fierce' clutch," the OSCA was "not a machine suitable for tooling around town."

1954 Osca MT-4 Mille Miglia racing roadster.

Note: Specifications below are valid only for the single model tested in 1955. Details for other examples varied, since each OSCA racing car was virtually handbuilt.

I.D. DATA: Not available.

Model	Body Type & Seating	Engine Type/CID	P.O.E. Price	Weight (lbs.)	Prod. Total
MT4/1400	2-dr Rds-2P	I4/91	10000	1280	N/A

ENGINE DATA: BASE FOUR: Inline, dual-overhead-cam four-cylinder. **Displacement:** 90.9 cu. in. (1490 cc). **Bore & Stroke:** 3.07 x 3.07 in. (78 x 78 mm). **Compression Ratio:** 8.8:1. **Brake Horsepower:** 110 at 6200 rpm.

Note: The initial OSCA four-cylinder engine had a displacement of 1096 cc (67 cid) and developed 94 bhp at 6800 rpm, via 9:1 compression. Engine size grew to 1452 cc (88.5 cid) by 1955.

CHASSIS DATA: Wheelbase: 86.6 in. **Front Tread:** 47.2 in. **Rear Tread:** 45.3 in. **Standard Tires:** 5.00x15/5.50x15.

TECHNICAL: Layout: front-engine, rear-drive. **Transmission:** four-speed manual. Overall gear ratios: (1st) 14.8:1; (2nd) 8.85:1; (3rd) 5.81:1; (4th) 4.37:1. **Standard Final Drive Ratio:** 4.37:1. **Suspension (front):** coil springs. **Suspension (rear):** rigid axle with leaf springs. **Body Construction:** on tubular chassis.

PERFORMANCE: Top Speed: 124 mph (factory claim). **Acceleration (0-60 mph):** 7.0 sec. **Acceleration (quarter-mile):** 15.7 sec.
Manufacturer: Officina Specializzata Costruzione Automobili Fratelli Maserati, Bologna, Italy.
Distributor: Harry Allen Chapman, Tucson, Arizona (western U.S.).

1956-60 OSCA

S187/S273/1500 SERIES — FOUR — In the late 1950s, OSCA produced engines in three displacements: roughly 750, 1100, and 1500 cc. A 2000-cc engine also was produced. The competition-oriented two-seaters rode a tubular chassis with front coil springs. Chassis consisted of two large-diameter tubes, joined by crossmembers. By the late 1950s, bodies (built by the Morelli brothers) were more streamlined than before. The 1500 model ranked as a Formula Two car with its passenger compartment covered, lack of lighting, and magneto ignition.

I.D. DATA: Not available.
Note: Models shown and data below were valid in 1959.

Model	Body Type & Seating	Engine Type/CID	P.O.E. Price	Weight (lbs.)	Prod. Total
S187	2-dr Rds-2P	I4/45	N/A	950	N/A
S273	2-dr Rds-2P	I4/67	N/A	1050	N/A
1500	2-dr Rds-2P	I4/91	9500	1150	N/A

ENGINE DATA: BASE FOUR (S187): Inline, overhead-cam four-cylinder. **Displacement:** 45.2 cu. in. (749 cc). **Bore & Stroke:** 2.43 x 2.43 in. (62 x 62 mm). **Compression Ratio:** 9.0:1. **Brake Horsepower:** 70 at 7500 rpm. Two Weber carburetors.
BASE FOUR (S273): Inline, dual-overhead-cam four-cylinder. **Displacement:** 66.6 cu. in. (1092 cc). **Bore & Stroke:** 2.76 x 2.80 in. (70 x 71 mm). **Compression Ratio:** 9.5:1. **Brake Horsepower:** 95 at 7000 rpm. Two Weber carburetors.
BASE FOUR (1500): Inline, dual-overhead-cam four-cylinder. **Displacement:** 90.9 cu. in. (1490 cc). **Bore & Stroke:** 3.07 x 3.07 in. (78 x 78 mm). **Compression Ratio:** 9.5:1. **Brake Horsepower:** 135 at 6600 rpm. Two Weber carburetors.

CHASSIS DATA: Wheelbase: 86.6 in. **Tread:** 47.2 in. **Standard Tires:** (S187) 5.15x15; (S273) 5.20x14; (1500) 5.25x15/5.90x15.

TECHNICAL: Layout: front-engine, rear-drive. **Transmission:** four-speed manual. S187 overall gear ratios: (1st) 16.1:1; (2nd) 9.6:1; (3rd) 6.5:1; (4th) 4.8:1. S273 overall gear ratios: (1st) 15.9:1; (2nd) 9.0:1; (3rd) 5.7:1; (4th) 4.4:1. 1500 overall gear ratios: (1st) 12.8:1; (2nd) 7.7:1; (3rd) 5.2:1; (4th) 3.8:1. **Suspension (front):** unequal-length A-arms with coil springs. **Suspension (rear):** rigid axle with trailing arms and coil springs. **Body Construction:** on tubular chassis.
Manufacturer: Officina Specializzata Costruzione Automobili Fratelli Maserati, Bologna, Italy.
Distributor: Almar Motors, Tucson, Arizona; E. Fronteras, Jackson Heights, New York.

1961-65 OSCA

1964 Osca-Maserati 1600 GTS Zagato. (Coys of Kensington)

1600 GT/GTS — FOUR — By 1961, OSCA had a roadgoing two-seat coupe ready for the market, displayed at the Turin Auto Show in autumn of that year. The coupe had relatively large quarter windows, a curved windshield, and a low oval grille with mesh pattern that contained the small park/signal lights. Power came from a 1570-cc four-cylinder engine that produced 95 horsepower (140 bhp in competition form). Four-wheel independent suspension consisted of wishbones and coil springs at each corner.

I.D. DATA: Not available.

Model	Body Type & Seating	Engine Type/CID	P.O.E. Price	Weight (lbs.)	Prod. Total
1600 GT	2-dr Cpe-2P	I4/96	N/A	1731	N/A
1600 GTS	2-dr Cpe-2P	I4/96	N/A	1653	N/A

ENGINE DATA: BASE FOUR (1600 GT): Inline, dual-overhead-cam four-cylinder. **Displacement:** 95.7 cu. in. (1570 cc). **Bore & Stroke:** 3.15 x 3.07 in. (80 x 78 mm). **Compression Ratio:** 9.0:1. **Brake Horsepower:** 95 (DIN) at 6000 rpm. **Torque:** 97 lbs.-ft. at 4800 rpm. Two Weber two-barrel carburetors.
Note: Competition 1600 GTS engine developed 140 bhp at 7200 rpm.

CHASSIS DATA: Wheelbase: 88.6 in. **Length:** 153 in. **Height:** 48 in. **Width:** 59.5 in. **Front Tread:** 50 in. **Rear Tread:** 48.2 in. **Standard Tires:** 155x15.

TECHNICAL: Layout: front-engine, rear-drive. **Transmission:** four-speed manual (overdrive optional). 1600 GT gear ratios: (1st) 3.08:1; (2nd) 1.98:1; (3rd) 1.38:1; (4th) 1.00:1. **Standard Final Drive Ratio:** 3.90:1 (3.70:1, 4.10:1 and 4.30:1 optional). **Suspension (front):** wishbones with coil springs and anti-roll bar. **Suspension (rear):** independent; wishbones with coil springs and anti-roll bar. **Brakes:** four-wheel disc.

ADDITIONAL MODELS: By 1965, a fiberglass-bodied 1050S coupe and Spider (roadster) were available, with a 64.5-cid engine that produced 63 horsepower.
Manufacturer: Officina Specializzata Costruzione Automobili (O.S.C.A.) Fratelli Maserati S.p.A., Bologna, Italy.

1965 Osca 1600 Zagato, chassis 004. (Sportscar Auction Co.)

1966-67 OSCA

1600 GT/GTS — FOUR — Production of the 1570-cc models continued; see previous listing for data.
1700 — V-4 — OSCA's final new model came in 2+2 coupe and two-seat Spider (roadster) form, powered by an overhead-valve 1699-cc four-cylinder engine. Rounded rectangular headlamps were recessed into nacelles above the park/signal lights mounted in the ends of a tight mesh-patterned grille, with round center insignia.

I.D. DATA: Not available.

Model	Body Type & Seating	Engine Type/CID	P.O.E. Price	Weight (lbs.)	Prod. Total
1700	2-dr Cpe-2 + 2P	V4/104	N/A	1565	N/A
1700	2-dr Rds-2P	V4/104	N/A	1410	N/A

ENGINE DATA: BASE V-4: 60-degree, overhead-valve "vee" type four-cylinder. **Displacement:** 103.7 cu. in. (1699 cc). **Bore & Stroke:** 3.54 x 2.63 in. (90 x 66.8 mm). **Compression Ratio:** 9.0:1. **Brake Horsepower:** 95 (SAE) at 5800 rpm. **Torque:** 112 lbs.-ft. at 2800 rpm. Three main bearings. Two Solex single-barrel carburetors.
CHASSIS DATA: Wheelbase: (cpe) 92.5 in.; (rds) 86.6 in. **Length:** (cpe) 159.5 in.; (rds) 151.6 in. **Height:** (cpe) 48 in.; (rds) 47.2 in. **Width:** 61 in. **Front Tread:** 51.2 in. **Rear Tread:** 49 in. **Standard Tires:** 5.90x13.

TECHNICAL: Layout: front-engine, rear-drive. **Transmission:** four-speed manual. Gear ratios: (1st) 4.03:1; (2nd) 2.33:1; (3rd) 1.48:1; (4th) 1.00:1. **Standard Final Drive Ratio:** 3.56:1. **Steering:** recirculating ball. **Suspension (front):** wishbones with coil springs. **Suspension (rear):** independent; wishbones with transverse leaf spring and anti-roll bar. **Brakes:** four-wheel disc.

PERFORMANCE: Top Speed: (cpe) near 112 mph; (rds) near 109 mph.
Manufacturer: Officina Specializzata Costruzione Automobili (O.S.C.A.) Fratelli Maserati S.p.A., Bologna, Italy.

PANHARD

Not many automakers can match the illustrious history of the Panhard et Levassor firm of Paris, France, which dates back to 1891 and before. Like Daimler-Benz, it's one of the grand old names of motoring. Corporate history actually began in 1867, when Rene Panhard became a partner in a woodworking shop, joined several years later by a friend, Emile Levassor. By 1875, the firm was manufacturing Deutz gas engines, designed by a company that employed Gottlieb Daimler as head engineer. Later, in the 1880s, when Daimler needed a production facility for his own engines, he turned to Panhard and Levassor. Their company also began to manufacture Benz engines and, in 1890, supplied powerplants for Peugeot.

By 1891, the partners had begun to experiment with cars of their own creation, and in fact sold two of them. A full-scale sales catalog was issued in the following year, at a time when Duryea and other American inventors had yet to display their initial products. By 1894, about 55 Panhard et Levassor automobiles were in customers' hands, each with a steering wheel, front-mounted engine, and chain drive to rear wheels. Emile Levassor died in 1897, a year after being injured in the Paris-Marseilles race. Retaining the memory of both founders, the company adopted the name Societe Anonyme des Anciens Etablissements Panhard et Levassor. By 1902, they were producing more than 1,000 vehicles per year. Panhard died in 1908, but his descendants remained active in the firm until its demise in the 1960s. Among the company's innovations was four-wheel steering, installed on military vehicles before World War II. Knight sleeve-valve engines powered most Panhards, initially known as "SS" models for their *sans soupapes* (without valves) construction, right through the 1920s and '30s. In addition to four-cylinder engines, some straight eights were built, also with sleeve valves. A straight-eight with racing body broke the one-hour world record in 1926 at the Montlhery track, averaging 120.5 mph. In 1937, a futuristic-looking unibodied "Dynamic" series appeared, with faired-in headlamps, enclosed front wheels, a central steering wheel, and independent torsion bar suspension at all four wheels.

After planning to introduce some large automobiles after World War II, evolving from the prewar Dynamic, Panhard et Levassor instead released a smaller Dyna Panhard. Based upon a front-drive design created in the war years, it was powered by a horizontally-opposed two-cylinder engine and wore a light alloy body. Production rose quickly, reaching 10,000 in 1950. No less important, Panhard's air-cooled flat-twin engine was finding its way into many low-production sports cars and other automobiles, including the DB (Deutsch-Bonnet), and was responsible for hundreds of wins at Le Mans and other racing events, both in their class and for index of performance. A modified Dyna appeared in 1954, with the same engine configuration and another light alloy body, with a distinctive front end. A year later, Citroen bought a one-fourth interest in the company. Starting in 1958, bodies were built of steel rather than alloys. Panhard production continued until 1967, but exports to America had already slacked off early in that decade.

482

1946-53 PANHARD

1950 Panhard Dyna four-door.

Though considerably different in appearance from the Panhards that would arrive in the U.S. later in the 1950s, the first postwar Dyna sedan had a kindred grille shape, with a round element in its center. Three slim horizontal bars reached outward from each side of that center piece, which was partly enclosed by long horizontal upper and lower moldings. Headlamps were only partly faired-in, mounted inboard of the separate rounded front fenders. A flat windshield was used, and front doors of the aluminum four-door sedan body were hinged at the rear, "suicide" style. The Dyna Luxe Type 110's two-cylinder engine displaced 37.2 cubic inches (610 cc) and delivered 24 horsepower. Wheelbase was 83 inches, and the gearbox had four forward speeds.

Panhard also introduced the "Junior" roadster in 1951, with a 745-cc two-cylinder engine. By 1952, the Dyna engine came in three displacements: 610, 745 or 850 cc, obtained by altering the bore dimension. Six Dyna Panhards completed the 1950 French Alpine Trial over 2,000 miles of mountain roads, without any points lost.

1951 Panhard "Luxe."

1954-55 PANHARD

DYNA 54 — TWO — Viewed from the front, in particular, no one was likely to mistake the new Dyna Panhard for any other car. A low, wide, vaguely oval-shaped grille opening used the front bumper as its lower molding, while the upper molding extended outward to wrap around the front fenders. Within that opening, taking up most of the available space, was a wide horizontal decorative insignia. Headlamps were built into the fenders, but somewhat inboard. Round protruding parking lights went below the headlamps (but were not evident on the early examples). Dyna's well-rounded body and chassis were made of light alloy (mainly aluminum) panels, welded together. The complete structure, including doors, weighed only 202 pounds. Front and rear tube assemblies were bolted to that structure. The front assembly held the engine, gearbox and front-wheel-drive differential, as well as the rack-and-pinion steering mechanism and transverse-leaf suspension. That 850-cc air-cooled, flat-twin engine delivered 42 horsepower to a four-speed gearbox (top gear overdrive). Panhard claimed six-passenger capacity for the four-door sedan, though some observers considered five to be more realistic.

DYNA JUNIOR — TWO — Panhard also offered a smaller roadster with different appearance. Only 145 inches long, on an 83.75-inch wheelbase, the Junior had a vertical front panel with a thick horizontal bar across its oval grille opening, and round parking lights below the headlamps. Doors were rear-hinged. Under the Junior's hood was the same 850-cc engine as the Dyna 54 sedan, but a 750-cc version was optional for class racing. Both standard and special bodies were available.

1954 Panhard Dyna 54 four-door sedan.

I.D. DATA: Serial number is on the right side of the firewall, under the hood.

Model DYNA	Body Type & Seating	Engine Type/CID	P.O.E. Price	Weight (lbs.)	Prod. Total
54	4-dr Sedan-6P	H2/52	2600	1386	Note 1
Junior	2-dr Rds-2P	H2/52	2200	1350	Note 1

Note 1: Approximately 20 Panhards were sold in the U.S. in 1954, before full distribution became available.

Weight Note: A Dyna 54 weighed prior to a road test came to 1,570 pounds, ready to roll.

ENGINE DATA: BASE TWO: Horizontally-opposed, overhead-valve two-cylinder (air-cooled, four-cycle). Light alloy cylinders with cast iron liners. **Displacement:** 51.9 cu. in. (850 cc). **Bore & Stroke:** 3.35 x 2.95 in. (85 x 75 mm). **Compression Ratio:** 7.25:1. **Brake Horsepower:** 42 at 5000 rpm. Two main bearings. Solid valve lifters. Twin-choke Solex carburetor. 12-volt electrical system.

CHASSIS DATA: Wheelbase: (Dyna 54) 101 in.; (Junior) 83.75 in. **Overall Length:** (Dyna 54) 183 in.; (Junior) 145 in. **Height:** (Dyna 54) 56 in.; (Junior) 50.5 in. **Width:** (Dyna 54) 63 in. **Front Tread:** (Dyna 54) 51 in.; (Junior) 44.7 in. **Rear Tread:** (Dyna 54) 51 in.; (Junior) 44.7 in. **Standard Tires:** (Dyna 54) 145x400; (Junior) 135x400.

TECHNICAL: Layout: front-engine, front-drive. **Transmission:** four-speed manual; column lever. **Steering:** rack and pinion. **Suspension (front):** independent; two transverse leaf springs. **Suspension (rear):** (Dyna 54) rigid axle with torsion bars; (Junior) V-shaped axle with flexible center mounting and six transverse torsion bars. **Brakes:** hydraulic, front/rear drum. **Body Construction:** (Dyna 54) aluminum/magnesium body and platform chassis, welded together; (Junior) pressed rail chassis.

PERFORMANCE: Top Speed: (Dyna 54) 70-80 mph; (Junior) 73-77 mph. **Acceleration (0-60 mph):** (Dyna 54) N/A (0-50 mph in 10.2 seconds claimed, but 17 seconds in test); (Junior) about 25 seconds. **Acceleration (quarter-mile):** (Dyna 54) 23.4 seconds. **Fuel Mileage:** (Dyna 54) 34-45 mpg; (Junior) about 44 mpg.

ADDITIONAL MODELS: Panhard later began to produce a convertible version of the Dyna 54. Other Panhard models included a Dyna series 110 sedan and convertible; 120 Berline two- and four-door sedans; and 130 Berline four-door sedan.

Manufacturer: Panhard et Levassor, Paris, France.

Distributor: Robert Perreau, Los Angeles, California.

1956-57 PANHARD

1956 Panhard Dyna.

DYNA 54 — TWO — Several technical improvements appeared on Panhard's four-door sedan, including hydraulic tappets and stronger connecting rods. The engine was now mounted on a flexible, vibration-damped cradle. A new synchromesh gearbox offered direct drive in third gear, with overdrive fourth. Headlamps added visor rims, and new sweep-around bumpers were installed. Otherwise, appearance and construction were the same as 1954-55. Dyna Panhard sedans were now readily available in the U.S., through a West Coast distributor. A convertible was also produced, but rarely seen outside Europe.

DYNA JUNIOR — TWO — Still available in Europe were the smaller roadster and convertible; see previous listing for details.

I.D. DATA: Serial number is on the right side of the firewall, under the hood. Engine number is on the left front of the block.

1956 Panhard Dyna.

Model DYNA	Body Type & Seating	Engine Type/CID	P.O.E. Price	Weight (lbs.)	Prod. Total
54	4-dr Sedan-6P	H2/52	2195	1546	Note 1
54	2-dr Conv-5/6P	H2/52	N/A	N/A	Note 1

Note 1: A total of 25,703 Panhard passenger cars were produced in 1956, and 37,991 in 1957.

Weight Note: Figure shown is "dry" weight.

ENGINE DATA: BASE TWO: Horizontally-opposed, overhead-valve two-cylinder (air-cooled, four-cycle). Light alloy cylinders with cast iron liners. **Displacement:** 51.9 cu. in. (850 cc). **Bore & Stroke:** 3.35 x 2.95 in. (85 x 75 mm). **Compression Ratio:** 7.25:1. **Brake Horsepower:** 42 at 5000 rpm. Two main bearings. Twin-choke Solex carburetor. 12-volt electrical system.

CHASSIS DATA: Wheelbase: 101.25 in. **Overall Length:** 180 in. **Height:** 57 in. **Width:** 62 in. **Front Tread:** 51.25 in. **Rear Tread:** 51.25 in. **Standard Tires:** Michelin 145x400.

TECHNICAL: Layout: front-engine, front-drive. **Transmission:** four-speed manual (fourth gear overdrive); column lever. Overall gear ratios: (1st) 16.3:1; (2nd) 9.2:1; (3rd) 6.15:1; (4th) 4.7:1 overdrive. **Steering:** rack and pinion. **Suspension (front):** independent; two transverse leaf springs. **Suspension (rear):** rigid trailing axle with transverse torsion bars. **Brakes:** hydraulic, front/rear drum. **Body Construction:** aluminum/magnesium body and platform chassis, welded together.

PERFORMANCE: Top Speed: up to 85 mph claimed. **Acceleration (quarter-mile):** 23.4 seconds. **Fuel Mileage:** 40-45 mpg.

Manufacturer: Panhard et Levassor, Paris, France.

Distributor: French Motors Inc., Los Angeles, California.

HISTORY: 1957 model was introduced in the U.S. on October 1, 1956. Sales literature promoted the fact that a Panhard-powered sports model broke a world's record, covering 126.18 miles in one hour. Up to this time, racing cars were driven almost exclusively by private owners, yet Panhards and Panhard-powered cars had won more than 600 victories in international competition. Citroen now owned a one-fourth interest in the Panhard company, and soon began to distribute the cars in the U.S.

1958 PANHARD

DYNA 58 — TWO — While appearance was similar to prior models, the Dyna four-door sedan by 1958 abandoned its light-alloy body and switched to steel paneling. The "Isodyne" suspension also was revised, and brakes were more powerful. Standard equipment included two-color leatherette upholstery for the two bench seats, a heater/defroster, windshield washer, trip odometer, and whitewall tires. The entire nose section tilted backward for engine access. Under the hood, ahead of the axle, was the same 850-cc two-cylinder engine, with roller-bearing crankshaft and torsion-bar valve springs.

I.D. DATA: Serial number is on the right side of the firewall, under the hood. Engine number is on the left front of the block.

Model DYNA	Body Type & Seating	Engine Type/CID	P.O.E. Price	Weight (lbs.)	Prod. Total
58	4-dr Sedan-6P	H2/52	1995	1764	Note 1

Note 1: A total of 34,784 Panhard passenger cars were produced in 1958.

Weight Note: Figure shown is "curb" weight.

ENGINE DATA: Horizontally-opposed, overhead-valve two-cylinder (air-cooled, four-cycle). Light alloy cylinders with cast iron liners. **Displacement:** 51.9 cu. in. (850 cc). **Bore & Stroke:** 3.35 x 2.95 in. (85 x 75 mm). **Compression Ratio:** 7.25:1. **Brake Horsepower:** 50 at 5200 rpm. **Torque:** 50.6 lbs.-ft. at 2250 rpm. Two main bearings. Solex 30 PAAI, Zenith-Stromberg 32 NDIX, or Zenith-Stromberg 36Wi carburetor. 12-volt electrical system.

Note: 42-bhp version also remained available.

CHASSIS DATA: Wheelbase: 101 in. **Overall Length:** 180 in. **Height:** 57.5 in. **Width:** 63 in. **Front Tread:** 51.25 in. **Rear Tread:** 51.25 in. **Standard Tires:** Michelin 145x400.

TECHNICAL: Layout: front-engine, front-drive. **Transmission:** four-speed manual (fourth gear overdrive); column lever. Overall gear ratios: (1st) 16.2:1; (2nd) 9.2:1; (3rd) 6.14:1; (4th) 4.71:1 overdrive. **Standard Final Drive Ratio:** 6.14:1. **Steering:** rack and pinion. **Suspension (front):** independent; two transverse leaf springs. **Suspension (rear):** semi-independent; rigid trailing axle with transverse torsion bars. **Brakes:** hydraulic, front/rear drum. **Body Construction:** steel body/chassis.

PERFORMANCE: Top Speed: 85 mph (claimed). **Acceleration (0-60 mph):** 24-30 seconds. **Fuel Mileage:** 35-42 mpg (claimed); 33-40 mpg in test.

Manufacturer: Panhard et Levassor, Paris, France.

Distributor: Citroen Cars Corp., New York City.

HISTORY: 1958 model was introduced in the U.S. on October 1, 1957. Panhard ads in 1958 promoted the 800 sports-car victories achieved by the two-cylinder engine, in such events as the 24-hour Le Mans race (with six wins). "Stop pouring money down the gas tank!" warned some of the ads in a push for economy as well as performance, and "go farther for less." Others ads also stressed economy, but led off with "On the ROAD...or at the RALLYE." Panhards, they continued, offer "the penny-wise thrift of a small car, the 'living' room comforts of the larger car, and the precision performance of a sports car." *Car Life* magazine criticized the gadgety control console that straddled the car's steering column, especially the fact that a single lever operated the lights, horn and turn signals.

1959 PANHARD

DYNA 58 — TWO — A Deluxe Super sedan was added this year, with two-tone body paint. Solid disc wheels also were introduced this year, and bodyside trim was modified. Otherwise, appearance and mechanical details were the same as 1958.

I.D. DATA: Serial number is on the right side of the firewall, under the hood. Engine number is on the left front of the block.

Model DYNA 58	Body Type & Seating	Engine Type/CID	P.O.E. Price	Weight (lbs.)	Prod. Total
DeL	4-dr Sedan-6P	H2/52	1995	1764	Note 1
DeL Super	4-dr Sedan-6P	H2/52	2065	N/A	Note 1

Note 1: A total of 24,427 Panhard passenger cars were produced in 1959.

ENGINE DATA: Same as 1958.
CHASSIS DATA: Same as 1958.
TECHNICAL: Same as 1958.
PERFORMANCE: Same as 1958.

1960 PANHARD

1960 Panhard Dyna convertible.

PL-17 — TWO — Prices dropped sharply this year, for the basic DeLuxe sedan and the step-up Grand Standing model. Appearance changed considerably too, highlighted by sculptured areas around the hood, headlamps, taillamps, and rear deck. Protruding creases ran backward from the headlamps, along the front fenders. The grille opening now consisted of a thin horizontal slit above the front bumper. Two ratings of the two-cylinder engine were available: standard 42-bhp version, and a 50-bhp Tiger edition that produced a top speed around 90 mph. Panhards still had rear-hinged front doors. According to *Foreign Cars Illustrated* and *Auto Sport* magazine, "only the French would have the courage to market an automobile in some of the color combinations found on the Panhard."

I.D. DATA: Serial number is on the right side of the firewall, under the hood. Engine number is on the left front of the block.

Model	Body Type & Seating	Engine Type/CID	P.O.E. Price	Weight (lbs.)	Prod. Total
PL-17	4-dr Sedan-5/6P	H2/52	1697	1764	Note 1
Grand St.	4-dr Sedan-5/6P	H2/52	1725	1764	Note 1

Note 1: A total of 34,050 Panhard passenger cars were produced in 1960.
Model Note: A convertible also was offered for sale.

ENGINE DATA: BASE TWO: Horizontally-opposed, overhead-valve two-cylinder (air-cooled, four-cycle). Light alloy cylinders with cast iron liners. **Displacement:** 51.9 cu. in. (850 cc). **Bore & Stroke:** 3.35 x 2.95 in. (85 x 75 mm). **Compression Ratio:** 7.25:1. **Brake Horsepower:** 42 at 5000 rpm. **Torque:** 51 lbs.-ft. at 2500 rpm. Two main bearings. 12-volt electrical system.

OPTIONAL (TIGER) TWO: Same as above, except — **Brake Horsepower:** 50 at 5300 rpm. Zenith downdraft carburetor.

CHASSIS DATA: Wheelbase: 101 in. **Overall Length:** 180 in. **Height:** 57.5 in. **Width:** 63 in. **Front Tread:** 51.25 in. **Rear Tread:** 51.25 in. **Standard Tires:** Michelin 145x380.

TECHNICAL: Layout: front-engine, front-drive. **Transmission:** four-speed manual (fourth gear overdrive); column lever. **Steering:** rack and pinion. **Suspension (front):** independent; two transverse leaf springs. **Suspension (rear):** semi-independent; rigid trailing axle with transverse torsion bars. **Brakes:** hydraulic, front/rear drum. **Body Construction:** steel body/chassis with large transverse tubes in frame pan.

PERFORMANCE: Top Speed: 81 mph claimed (90 mph with 50-bhp engine); 84 mph achieved in test of 50-hp version. **Acceleration (0-60 mph):** 22.3 seconds. **Acceleration (quarter-mile):** 25.8 sec. (63 mph). **Fuel Mileage:** 40 mpg claimed; average 34 mpg.

Manufacturer: Panhard et Levassor, Paris, France.
Distributor: Citroen Cars Corp., Los Angeles, California.
HISTORY: 1960 models were introduced on August 12, 1959.

1961-62 PANHARD

1962 Panhard PL-17.

NICE/MONTE CARLO — TWO — A modified model lineup was the only significant change for 1961. Both the standard (42-bhp) and Tiger (50-bhp) engines again were available. Both the sedans and a Tiger convertible appeared on American lists of imported cars for these final years.

I.D. DATA: Serial number is on the right side of the firewall, under the hood. Engine number is on the left front of the block.

Model	Body Type & Seating	Engine Type/CID	P.O.E. Price	Weight (lbs.)	Prod. Total
Nice	4-dr Sedan-6P	H2/52	1795	1764	Note 1
Monte Carlo	4-dr Sedan-6P	H2/52	1998	1764	Note 1
Tiger	2-dr Conv-5/6P	H2/52	2695	N/A	Note 1

Note 1: A total of 29,746 Panhard passenger cars were produced in 1961, and 33,698 in 1962.

Price Note: Nice and Monte Carlo models were available with Tiger engine, priced at $1895 and $2095 in 1961.

ENGINE DATA: BASE TWO: Horizontally-opposed, overhead-valve two-cylinder (air-cooled, four-cycle). Light alloy cylinders with cast iron liners. **Displacement:** 51.9 cu. in. (850 cc). **Bore & Stroke:** 3.35 x 2.95 in. (85 x 75 mm). **Compression Ratio:** 7.25:1. **Brake Horsepower:** 42 at 5000 rpm. **Torque:** 51 lbs.-ft. at 2500 rpm. Two main bearings. 12-volt electrical system.

OPTIONAL (TIGER) TWO: Same as above, except — **Brake Horsepower:** 50 at 5300 rpm. Zenith downdraft carburetor.

CHASSIS DATA: Wheelbase: 101 in. **Overall Length:** 180 in. **Height:** 57.5 in. **Width:** 63 in. **Front Tread:** 51.25 in. **Rear Tread:** 51.25 in. **Standard Tires:** Michelin 145x380 (5.20x15).

TECHNICAL: Layout: front-engine, front-drive. **Transmission:** four-speed manual (fourth gear overdrive); column lever. **Steering:** rack and pinion. **Suspension (front):** independent; two transverse leaf springs. **Suspension (rear):** semi-independent; rigid trailing axle with transverse torsion bars. **Brakes:** hydraulic, front/rear drum. **Body Construction:** steel body/chassis with large transverse tubes in frame pan.

PERFORMANCE: Top Speed: 81 mph claimed (90 mph with 50-bhp engine). **Acceleration (0-60 mph):** 22.3 seconds. **Acceleration (quarter-mile):** 25.8 sec. (63 mph). **Fuel Mileage:** 40 mpg claimed; average 34 mpg.

Manufacturer: Panhard et Levassor, Paris, France.
Distributor: Citroen Cars Corp., Los Angeles, California.

HISTORY: Panhard remained in production into the mid-1960s, but disappeared from most lists of available imported cars in the U.S. well before the end. A total of 31,195 were produced during 1963, 27,910 in 1964, and 11,613 in 1965.

PANTHER

Although replicars are not a part of this Catalog, one example of that lot is worthy of mention: the neoclassic Panther series of the 1970s and '80s. Starting in the 1960s, motor-racing fan Robert Jankel was producing about one specialty car per year in Britain—a far cry from his regular occupation in the fashion industry. In 1971, Jankel abandoned fashion and founded Panther Westwinds Ltd. at Surrey, England. His first official product was styled like an early Rolls-Royce. His second car, the J-72 roadster, bore a closer resemblance to the (Jaguar) SS100, and indeed was Jaguar-powered. That one remained in production through the decade.

Panthers became known for their use of high quality components and carefully-finished coachwork. In fact, prior to commencing production of complete automobiles, the Panther firm supplied custom interiors for Rolls-Royce motorcars. Additional models were created through the 1970s, though most were produced in extremely limited number, and some never entered production at all. Late in 1980, the Panther firm was acquired by a South Korean businessman named Young Chull Kim. By 1981, each of the existing models was abandoned, and the company focused on conversions of other makes. A successor to the J-72, built in Korea, was announced in 1982. Other models, including the comparatively popular Lima, were assembled in England using Korean-manufactured aluminum bodies. By the mid-1980s, the Kallista (which evolved from the Lima by 1982) was offered in the U.S. market.

1972-80 PANTHER

1972 Panther J72 3.4 liter sports car. (Panther Westwinds Ltd.)

J-72 — SIX — Styled with a kinship to the SS100 roadster of the late 1930s, the aluminum-bodied J-72 carried a 4.2-liter Jaguar six-cylinder engine, producing 190 horsepower. This was hooked to a Jaguar four-speed manual transmission (with overdrive). Scoops on each side of the louvered hood allowed space for the XK-evolved engine, which was wider than the powerplant originally used in the SS100. The ladder-type frame, with 111-inch wheelbase, was welded from square steel tubing. Jaguar components formed the front suspension, while coil springs and a limited-slip differential brought up the rear. Knock-off wire wheels held 225/70VR15 tires, which required wider fenders than the SS100. Sealed-beam headlamps were used instead of the old Lucas P-100 units, though the housings were similar in size to the original design. Sliding side windows were made of acrylic. Inside were leather seats and a gauge-filled dashboard. For a brief period in the early 1970s, V-12 engines were available for the roadster.

DEVILLE — V-12 — Whereas the J-72 used Jaguar's SS100 as its inspiration, the larger DeVille roughly followed the lines of the massive Bugatti Royale—though on a smaller scale. As in its smaller roadster companion, Jaguar mechanical components were installed, including suspension elements modified from those used in the XJ sedan. Wheelbase was 142 inches; overall length a surprisingly short 204 inches, a result of the car's minimal overhang at each end. Beneath the bonnet sat a Jaguar 326-cid V-12 engine, hooked to GM's Turbo Hydra-Matic 400 transmission. The interior held four leather bucket seats, complemented by burled walnut veneer on the dashboard and door sills. While the J-72 did indeed bear a reasonable resemblance to the SS100, the DeVille veered considerably farther away from its Bugatti Royale spark, largely because of its reduced size and inevitable distortion of proportions. In addition, the DeVille was a four-door sedan, although that body style was not used on Royales. An open-topped two-door variant of the DeVille was offered starting in 1976.

LIMA — FOUR/V-6 — Starting in 1976, a smaller Panther roadster became available, with a fiberglass body atop a Vauxhall chassis. The initial engine was a 2279-cc Vauxhall four, but later models could have a V-6 engine.

I.D. DATA: Not available.

Model	Body Type & Seating	Engine Type/CID	P.O.E. Price	Weight (lbs.)	Prod. Total
J-72	2-dr Rds-2P	I6/258	35000	2576	Note 1
DeVille	4-dr Sedan-4P	V12/326	92000	4360	Note 1
DeVille	2-dr Conv-4P	V12/326	N/A	N/A	Note 1
Lima	2-dr Rds-2P	I4/139	9300	N/A	Note 1

Note 1: A total of 550 Panthers (all models) were produced during 1978 alone.
Price Note: Figures shown were valid in late 1970s.
Model Note: J-72 was available starting in 1972; DeVille in 1974; Lima by 1977.

1977 Panther DeVille convertible. (Panther Westwinds Ltd.)

ENGINE DATA: BASE SIX (J-72): Inline, dual-overhead-cam six-cylinder (Jaguar). Cast iron block and aluminum alloy head. **Displacement:** 258 cu. in. (4235 cc). **Bore & Stroke:** 3.63 x 4.17 in. (92 x 106 mm). **Compression Ratio:** 8.0:1. **Brake Horsepower:** 190 (DIN) at 5000 rpm. **Torque:** 200 lbs.-ft. at 2000 rpm. Seven main bearings. Solid valve lifters. Two SU carburetors.
BASE V-12 (DeVille): 60-degree, overhead-cam "vee" type 12-cylinder (Jaguar). **Displacement:** 326 cu. in. (5343 cc). **Bore & Stroke:** 3.54 x 2.76 in. (90 x 70 mm). **Compression Ratio:** 9.0:1. **Brake Horsepower:** 244 at 5250 rpm. Seven main bearings. Solid valve lifters. Lucas-Bosch fuel injection.
BASE FOUR (Lima): Inline, overhead-valve four-cylinder (Vauxhall). Cast iron block and head. **Displacement:** 139.2 cu. in. (2279 cc). **Bore & Stroke:** 3.84 x 3.00 in. (97.5 x 76.2 mm). **Compression Ratio:** 8.5:1. **Brake Horsepower:** 108 (DIN) at 5000 rpm. **Torque:** 138 lbs.-ft. at 3000 rpm. Solid valve lifters. Zenith-Stromberg one-barrel carburetor.
Note: Limas were available with Holley-Weber carburetor and AiResearch turbocharger. Later Limas could have a 200-cid V-6 engine, rated 110 bhp at 3000 rpm.

CHASSIS DATA: Wheelbase: (J-72) 111 in.; (DeVille) 142 in.; (Lima) 97 in. **Overall Length:** (J-72) 165 in.; (DeVille) 204 in.; (Lima) 142.1 in. **Height:** (J-72) 49 in.; (DeVille) 61 in.; (Lima) 48 in. **Width:** (J-72) 68.5 in.; (DeVille) 71 in.; (Lima) 63.4 in. **Front Tread:** (J-72) 58.5 in.; (DeVille) 58 in.; (Lima) 52.3 in. **Rear Tread:** (J-72) 58.5 in.; (DeVille) 58 in.; (Lima) 52 in.

TECHNICAL: Layout: front-engine, rear-drive. **Transmission:** (J-72) four-speed manual or Borg-Warner 65 automatic; (DeVille) three-speed Turbo Hydra-Matic 400 or four-speed manual; (Lima) four-speed manual or three-speed automatic. **Steering:** (J-72) recirculating ball; (DeVille/Lima) rack and pinion. **Suspension (front):** A-arms, coil springs and anti-roll bar. **Suspension (rear):** (J-72) rigid axle with trailing arms, Panhard rod and coil springs; (DeVille) independent with trailing links and dual coil springs on each side; (Lima) rigid axle with coil springs and anti-roll bar. **Brakes:** (J-72) front disc, rear drum; (DeVille/Lima) front/rear disc. **Body Construction:** aluminum body on ladder-type steel-tube frame except (Lima) fiberglass body.

PERFORMANCE: Top Speed: (J-72) 128 mph; (DeVille) 115 mph. **Acceleration (0-60 mph):** (J-72) under 10 sec. **Acceleration (quarter-mile):** (J-72) 17 sec. (about 90 mph); (DeVille) 17 sec. (90 mph). **Fuel Mileage:** (J-72) about 15 mpg; (DeVille) about 10 mpg.

ADDITIONAL MODELS: Panther displayed a Ferrari-based replica, following the pattern of the early 125S, at the Geneva auto show in 1974. Around the same time, Panther also produced an aluminum-bodied version of the Triumph Dolomite, named the Rio. With a 2.0-liter four that developed 127 horsepower, a Rio was claimed to accelerate to 60 mph in 8.7 seconds and hit 115 mph. Doubtless the most startling Panther of the lot was a six-wheeled Super Six convertible displayed at the London Motor Show in 1977, powered by a mid-mounted Cadillac V-8 with turbocharger.
Manufacturer: Panther Westwinds Ltd., Byfleet, Surrey, England.
Distributor: Buckingham Motor Imports Inc., Los Angeles, California.

HISTORY: The J-72 was introduced in 1972; the DeVille in late 1974. Late in 1982, after the company had been acquired by Young Chull Kim, the Vauxhall-based Lima evolved into the Kallista (see next listing).

485

1981-85 PANTHER

KALLISTA — FOUR/V-6 — Successor to the Lima of the 1970s, the Kallista roadster was introduced in 1982 with either four-cylinder or V-6 power (both engines from Ford). The chassis and aluminum body came from South Korea, but the car was assembled in Britain.

I.D. DATA: Not available.

Model	Body Type & Seating	Engine Type/CID	P.O.E. Price	Weight (lbs.)	Prod. Total
KALLISTA					
1.6	2-dr Rds-2P	I4/97	Note 1	1918	Note 3
2.8	2-dr Rds-2P	V6/170	Note 2	2073	Note 3

Note 1: Price in Britain was 6945 Pounds (Sterling) in 1982.
Note 2: Price in Britain was 7485 Pounds (Sterling) in 1982 (8985 Pounds with fuel-injected engine).
Note 3: A total of 350 Panthers (all models) were produced during 1982 alone.

ENGINE DATA: BASE FOUR (1.6): Inline, overhead-cam four-cylinder. Cast iron block and light alloy head. **Displacement:** 97.4 cu. in. (1597 cc). **Bore & Stroke:** 3.15 x 3.13 in. (80 x 79.5 mm). **Compression Ratio:** 9.5:1. **Brake Horsepower:** 96 (DIN) at 6000 rpm. **Torque:** 98 lbs.-ft. at 4000 rpm. Five main bearings. Hydraulic valve lifters. Weber-Venturi carburetor.
BASE V-6 (2.8): 60-degree, overhead-valve "vee" type six-cylinder. Cast iron block and head. **Displacement:** 170.4 cu. in. (2792 cc). **Bore & Stroke:** 3.66 x 2.70 in. (93 x 68.5 mm). **Compression Ratio:** 9.2:1. **Brake Horsepower:** 135 (DIN) at 5200 rpm. **Torque:** 162 lbs.-ft. at 3000 rpm. Four main bearings. Solex-Venturi carburetor.
Note: Bosch K-Jetronic fuel-injected 2.8-liter V-6 was rated 150 bhp at 5700 rpm and 159 lbs.-ft. at 4000 rpm.

CHASSIS DATA: Wheelbase: 100.4 in. **Overall Length:** 153.7 in. **Height:** 49 in. **Width:** 67.3 in. **Front Tread:** 57.5 in. **Rear Tread:** 54.3 in.
TECHNICAL: Layout: front-engine, rear-drive. **Transmission:** five-speed manual or three-speed automatic. **Steering:** rack and pinion. **Suspension (front):** A-arms with coil springs. **Suspension (rear):** rigid axle with trailing arms, Panhard rod and coil springs. **Brakes:** front disc, rear drum. **Body Construction:** aluminum body on ladder-type box frame.
PERFORMANCE: Top Speed: (2.8) 110 mph; (fuel-injected 2.8) 123 mph.
Manufacturer: Panther Car Company Ltd., Byfleet, Surrey, England.
POSTSCRIPT: By 1985 the Kallista was offered in the U.S. market, powered by a Mustang 2.3-liter four-cylinder engine. In 1989, a Kallista listed for $24,000 and could be ordered with a four-speed manual or three-speed automatic transmission.

PEERLESS

Even when a specialty motorcar doesn't quite succeed, it often leads to something better; or at least to something else. So went the short-lived Peerless, a British-built four-seat sports coupe of the late 1950s. Produced by a new company that had been formed by Bernard Rodger, the prototype coupe (first called Warwick) was announced in August 1957 and appeared at the Paris Salon that fall. Its grille, in fact, displayed a 'W' letter in the center. The name stemmed from the fact that production took place in a garage which, long before (in the years following the First World War), had served as a site for the sale of reconditioned (American) Peerless trucks.

Wearing a 16-gauge aluminum body (with fiberglass moldings for the floor, bulkhead, trunk area, etc.), the prototype Gran Turismo coupe rode a tubular space frame. Performance wasn't its only "plus" factor. "The Peerless G.T.," said the sales brochure at the Paris show, "is, for the first time in a small car, a real 4-seater for full-sized adults," with "over 7 cubic feet of usable space" for luggage. The brochure further promised European motorists economy in the 30-mpg neighborhood. To keep servicing problems to a minimum, the Peerless was mostly Triumph mechanically, including a TR3 engine and gearbox. Sending the power to the wheels was a De Dion axle. As posh as it was sporty, the Peerless contained fine leather upholstery and plenty of amenities. Options included Dunlop center-lock wire wheels and a Laycock de Normanville overdrive (on the upper three gears of the four-speed box).

By mid-1958, bodies were built in fiberglass rather than aluminum, manufactured by James Whitson and Co. Ltd. In Britain, the standard model sold for 998 pounds (Sterling); in the U.S., just under $4000. American observers praised the Peerless as being more civilized than a TR3. *Road & Track* proclaimed the coupe to be worth its asking price in the U.S. and, during testing, reached 110 mph (with fuel economy in the 32-mpg neighborhood). "There is a certain pleasure in driving a 'fooler,'" they added, "but it is a great deal more satisfying to have a car which invites comments from fellow enthusiasts. The Peerless assures both fun and comments." Compared to the Triumph TR3, *Road & Track* noted that Peerless "has the same engine noises and exhaust notes, but...is a distinctive and quite different automobile" with its own "feel." During testing, they found the Peerless to be "nearly as good to 70 mph, slightly better over the standing quarter-mile and definitely faster to 90," adding that "once the Peerless gets over 70 mph its streamlining is enough to offset the disadvantage of its 3.7 axle and it will equal the performance of the TR3 with the 4.10 axle ratio."

That kind of performance wasn't enough to capture a sufficient number of American customers. Neither was the car's attractive profile. Predictions of production at levels of 25 cars per week never materialized, and the cars built were criticized for being poorly assembled and finished, as well as too noisy for a car of their caliber. Bankruptcy was filed early in 1960; but that wasn't the end of the story. Bernard Rodger went on to produce a successor called the Warwick; and the basic concept later evolved into the Gordon-Keeble.

1958-60 PEERLESS

G.T. — FOUR — Initial Peerless models had an aluminum body; but by mid-1958, fiberglass became standard. The aero-styled profile was made of polyester resin reinforced with fiberglass. Beneath the hood was a conventional Triumph TR3 engine and other mechanical components, to ensure easy servicing and maintenance. The interior held genuine foam-padded leather seats, carpeting, an adjustable wood-rim steering wheel, a fresh air heater/defroster, electric wipers, and a recessed instrument panel. In back was a center dividing armrest, and the luggage compartment held eight cubic feet of cargo. The space-frame chassis was formed of rectangular steel tubing, electrically welded. Twin wishbones and coil springs were used for the independent front suspension; a De Dion tube on semi-elliptic leaf springs went at the rear, with Salisbury differential and Layrub propeller shaft. Sankey 15-inch 4J steel disc wheels held 5.50x15 Avon Turbo-Speed tires. Dunlop center-lock wire wheels with 4J rims were optional. Two side-mounted gas tanks held seven gallons each. Either left or right hand steering was available. Air slats provided ventilation.

The four-seat coupe's clean, rather upright profile featured long rear quarter windows and rounded wheel openings. A simple oval front opening held crossbar-style grille bars and a round insignia with the letter 'P' in its center. Tiny round parking lights stood below the headlamps. Slim wraparound bumpers were installed. Standard body colors were red, white, blue, grey, and British Racing Green.

"Phase 2" for 1959 brought a few improvements, notably in body finish, recessed headlamp moldings, a mesh grille pattern, and the addition of tiny sharp-edged tailfins at the rear; but no chassis modifications. Seats, floor tray, wheel arches, etc. were made of the same fiberglass-reinforced polyester resin material as the body. The black padded Vynide facia board had a typewriter finish on the recessed instrument panel. A carpet-lined glovebox was used. Wraparound rear bumpers went within a few inches of the back wheels but stopped just inside the vertical taillamps, and the battery was moved to the engine compartment, inside the left front fender. A quick-release gas cap stood on the left side, just below the swing-out rear quarter window. The fiberglass/polyester resin body was produced by James Whitson and Co. Ltd. (coachbuilders).

I.D. DATA: Serial number is inside the fender, on the left side, under the hood. Engine number is stamped on the left side of the block.

Model	Body Type & Seating	Engine Type/CID	P.O.E. Price	Weight (lbs.)	Prod. Total
G.T.	2-dr Spts Cpe-4P	I4/121	3985	2072	Note 1

Note 1: About 325 Peerless coupes were built from 1958-60 (about 250 in a one-year period).

Price Note: Later sources give U.S. price as $3995.

Weight Note: Figure shown is approximate "dry" weight; "curb" weight was 2,400 pounds.

ENGINE DATA: BASE FOUR: Inline, overhead-valve four-cylinder (Triumph TR3). Cast iron block. **Displacement:** 121.45 cu. in. (1991 cc). **Bore & Stroke:** 3.27 x 3.62 in. (83 x 92 mm). **Compression Ratio:** 8.5:1. **Brake Horsepower:** 100 at 5000 rpm. **Torque:** 117.5 lbs.-ft. at 3000 rpm. Three main bearings. Solid valve lifters. Two SU H.6 sidedraft carburetors. Lucas 12-volt electrical system.

CHASSIS DATA: Wheelbase: 94.5 in. **Overall Length:** 163 in. **Height:** 50 in. **Width:** 63 in. **Front Tread:** 51 in. **Rear Tread:** 51 in. **Wheel Type:** Sankey 15x4J steel disc. **Standard Tires:** 5.50x15 Avon Turbo-Speed.

TECHNICAL: Layout: front-engine, rear-drive. **Transmission:** four-speed manual (synchromesh 2nd/3rd/4th). Overall gear ratios: (1st) 12.5:1; (2nd) 7.4:1; (top) 3.7:1. Ratios with overdrive: (2nd) 6.07:1; (3rd) 4.02:1; (top) 3.03:1. **Standard Final Drive Ratio:** 3.7:1. **Steering:** worm and peg with three-piece track rod and slave arm. **Suspension (front):** independent; double unequal-length wishbones with coil springs. **Suspension (rear):** De Dion axle with semi-elliptic leaf springs. **Brakes:** Girling front disc, rear drum. **Body Construction:** fiberglass body on space-frame chassis of rectangular steel tubing (early models had aluminum body). **Fuel Tank:** 14 gallons.

MAJOR OPTIONS: Laycock de Normanville overdrive. Dunlop center-lock wire wheels.

PERFORMANCE: Top Speed: 117+ mph (factory). **Acceleration (0-60 mph):** 10.5-12.4 seconds (factory claimed 0-50 mph in 6.8 seconds; 0-80 in 17.5 sec.) **Acceleration (quarter-mile):** 18.1 seconds (75 mph). **Fuel Mileage:** 26-32 mpg.

Manufacturer: Peerless Cars Ltd., Farnham Road, Slough, Buckinghamshire, England.

Distributor: European Motors, Inc., Detroit, Michigan.

HISTORY: The first "Warwick" prototype was announced in August 1957, but not offered for sale in England as a Peerless until after the Earl's Court (London) Auto Show of October 1958. Production continued until January 1960, when the company went into bankruptcy. Ads for the Peerless G.T. Two-Litre announced a "fine English Gran Tourismo four-seater coupe with competition performance and a moderate price." In addition to abundant luggage space, they continued, the Peerless "combines exhilirating performance, extraordinary roadholding characteristics, and four-seat passenger comfort to make it a highly desirable car for all-around driving."

1961 Peerless.

POSTSCRIPT: After the bankruptcy, Bernard Rodger participated in the setup of a new Warwick firm, serving as technical director, to build a presumably improved Peerless. Manufactured from 1960 to 1962, the Warwick GT (Warwick had actually been the name of the first Peerless prototype) used a 100-bhp Triumph TR3 engine and transmission. Bodies again came from the James Whitson firm. Similar in appearance to the Peerless, the Warwick GT had a recessed oval grille with crosshatch pattern and vertical center divider, tiny round parking lights below the headlamps, and a sloping hood (with fenders at a higher level). Large rear quarter windows were used. Price in Britain was 1620 pounds (Sterling) with standard overdrive. Dunlop wire wheels were the only option. Expectations of building five cars per week never materialized, as the company ran out of cash quickly. No more than 59 Warwicks were produced (some sources suggest half that number). Bernard Rodger bought the company in December 1960, but it didn't last much longer. Rodger and Rowland Ham (managing director, later chairman) then began experiments with a Warwick powered by a 3.5-liter Buick aluminum V-8, aimed at America. That one came into existence in summer 1961, remaining in production until 1964, two years longer than the Triumph-engined version. However, the concept evolved into the Gordon-Keeble (also described in this Catalog).

PEGASO

Surprise was in the air when the striking Spanish-built Pegaso sports car emerged at the Paris Salon in 1951, powered by a four-cam V-8 engine. Named for the mythical winged horse, Pegasus, the dramatically-styled two-seat coupe suggested real-life performance to match that of its imagined namesake. Empresa Nacional de Automocamiones S.A. (ENASA), the company that built Pegasos for half a dozen years in the 1950s, was created by the Spanish government right after World War II, becoming known mainly for truck production (and those only in limited numbers). Still, the fact that in 1946 it absorbed the remnants of a famous old Spanish motorcar firm, Hispano-Suiza Fabrica de Automoviles S.A., suggests that something more than commercial vehicles may have been intended. For one thing, Wilfredo Ricart, technical director of the company, had formerly worked on high-performance automobiles at Alfa Romeo. In 1922, at the tender age of 24, Ricart had designed and built a four-cylinder twin-

cam engine with 16 valves and hemispherical combustion chambers, producing 62 bhp. He'd also designed a Type 162 Alfa Romeo 3-litre model with a two-stage supercharged V-16, rated at 600 bhp but never raced.

Starting with a 2.5-liter engine, the Pegaso's powerplants grew as large as 4.7 liters. For a time, it qualified as the fastest production car in the world, capable of 140 to 150 mph—faster even than Ferraris of that day. Pegaso's power/weight ratio was no less startling than its shape: in the neighborhood of 10 pounds per horsepower, at least with the larger engines. Prices of $15,000 to $35,000 were quoted by the mid-1950s, making Pegaso one of the costliest cars in the world. Production came to a halt after Ricart retired in 1958, with the company turning back to commercial vehicles. No more than about 125 cars were built, more for the purposes of prestige and publicity than as a serious attempt to create an ongoing sports-car industry in Spain. Because motorcars were a sideline to ENASA, few sales and service agents existed, anywhere in the world. Still, few cars produced in such limited numbers attracted as much attention and admiration as the Pegaso, in the United States and elsewhere in the world.

1951-55 PEGASO

1951 Pegaso Z102.

Z-102/2.5 — V-8 — Essentially handmade, in a former Hispano-Suiza plant at Barcelona, Pegasos had a semi-monocoque steel underbody topped by either factory-designed or custom bodies. No two were quite alike. Created mainly for high-speed grand touring, Pegasos had an extremely distinctive look. Early models typically displayed full wheel openings, a large rectangular grille opening with horizontal bars, and recessed headlamps above huge round parking lights. Italian influences were evident in the styling, prompting speculation that an Italian designer may have been responsible. In fact, bodies came from such renowned coachbuilders as Saoutchik and Carrozzeria Touring, the latter producing a lightweight Superleggera version. Pegasos had De Dion rear axles with integral five-speed manual gearboxes. The torsion-bar rear suspension had finned inboard brake drums fitted close to the differential. Aircraft-style instruments were installed inside the cockpit.

Some examples looked considerably different. The factory's own "Barcelona" coupe, for instance, had an unusually smooth and curvy front end with enclosed front fenders, minuscule parking lights below the built-in headlamps, a lid-style hood with bulge, and wide rectangular grille opening with crossbar pattern. Rear fenders held airscoops for the tires and brakes. Mufflers were installed below the doors, and a transparent tail section allowed full rear visibility. Pegasos could have power windows and built-in traveling accessories. Most models had thigh-high crash belts plus shoulder safety harnesses.

The basic model came with a 2472-cc (151-cid) V-8 delivering 140 horsepower. Crankcase and block formed a single light-alloy casting, with steel cylinder liners that used rubber seals for watertightness. Cylinder heads were made of light alloy. Cam drive was via roller chain on sports models, but race engine used a gear tower. An oil radiator was built into the lower section of the regular cooling radiator. Smooth operation was said to be possible with fuel as low as 72 octane. Optional compression ratios were offered for higher-octane fuel; and up to 13:1 with special racing fuels (and pistons). Among other attributes, Pegaso engines were claimed to display a straight horsepower curve.

Z-102B/2.8 — V-8 — A larger V-8 displacing 2816 cc (172 cid) also was available, with an output of 180 horsepower. Some of the four-cam V-8 engines contained a supercharger, boosting output to 250 horsepower.

Z-102B/3.2 — V-8 — Largest engine of the lot was the 3178-cc (194-cid) V-8, producing 210 horsepower in basic tune, which arrived by 1955. A 275-hp version also became available.

Note: Because Pegasos were essentially one-of-a-kind, specifications varied considerably. So, to an even greater extent than usual for limited-production models, the data given below is typical rather than absolute.

Early '50s Pegaso convertible.

1954 Pegaso Z102 2.8 two-passenger "Thrill Berlinetta." (Christie's)

I.D. DATA: Not available.

Model	Body Type & Seating	Engine Type/CID	P.O.E. Price	Weight (lbs.)	Prod. Total
Z-102/2.5	2-dr Coupe-2/3P	V8/151	N/A	2160	Note 1
Z-102/2.5	2-dr Luxe-2/3P	V8/151	N/A	2820	Note 1
Z-102B/2.8	2-dr Coupe-2/3P	V8/172	18000	2480	Note 1
Z-102BS/2.8	2-dr Coupe-2/3P	V8/172	19300	2480	Note 1
Z-102B/3.2	2-dr Coupe-2/3P	V8/172	N/A	N/A	Note 1
Z-102BSS/3.2	2-dr Coupe-2/3P	V8/172	29500	N/A	Note 1

Note 1: A total of between 100 and 125 Pegasos were produced from 1951 to 1958. About 20 were built in 1956 alone.

Price Note: A basic Pegaso cost about $8400 in Spain (about $5600 for the chassis alone, sans body). The U.S. price for a 280-bhp Pegaso was reported by *Motor Trend* in 1953 as $29,500.

HISTORY: Among the cars scheduled for display at the Sports Cars Unlimited show at the Henry Ford Museum in 1954 was the Pegaso. It had also been seen at the World Motor Sports Show in New York's Madison Square Garden, early in 1953; and at the International Motor Show in Hartford, Connecticut. The Pegaso at the New York event was owned by Generalissimo Rafael Trujillo, former ruler of the Dominican Republic, and wore a price tag of $29,200. Figures of that magnitude seemed to turn away quite a few prospects for the car.

While observers lauded the Pegaso's appearance and roadability, its racing performance was less than startling (seldom raced at all, in fact). Racing success just wasn't in the cards for the Spanish sports car. Only one of three coupes entering the 1952 Monaco race even managed to qualify. Following a fatality in the 1953 Spanish Grand Prix, a trio of supercharged models ran in the next year's event but couldn't come close to Ferrari and C-type Jaguars. Greater success appeared imminent in the Mexican Carrera Panamericana race, but after a strong showing in one segment the car suffered two collisions and failed to finish.

"Pegaso gives an immediate impression of ruggedness," said *Motor Trend* testers of the example driven in the Mexican road race, "fully capable of mastering the open highway in the hands of a driver who wants a man's car." By 1955, only four Pegasos had been imported into the U.S.

1953 Pegaso coupe.

ENGINE DATA: BASE V-8 (Z-102/2.5): 90-degree, four-overhead-cam V-8. Cast iron block and light alloy heads. **Displacement:** 150.5 cu. in. (2472 cc). **Bore & Stroke:** 2.95 x 2.76 in. (75 x 70 mm). **Compression Ratio:** 8.0:1. **Brake Horsepower:** 140. **Torque:** 136 lbs.-ft. at 3900 rpm. Five main bearings. One carburetor.

Note: 2.5-liter V-8 also was available with 8.5:1 compression and four carburetors, producing about 165 bhp at 6200 rpm.

BASE V-8 (Z-102B/2.8): Same as above, except — **Displacement:** 171.5 cu. in. (2816 cc). **Bore & Stroke:** 3.14 x 2.76 in. (80 x 70 mm). **Compression Ratio:** 7.8:1, 8.0:1 or 8.8:1. **Brake Horsepower:** 170/180 at 6300 rpm. **Torque:** 160-167 lbs.-ft. at 3600 rpm. One or four Weber carburetors.

BASE V-8 (Z-102BS/2.8): Supercharged version of 2816-cc engine with 6:1 compression, rated 250 hp at 6500 rpm, and 238 lbs.-ft. at 4000 rpm.

BASE V-8 (Z-102BS/3.2): Same as 2816-cc V-8 above, except — **Displacement:** 194 cu. in. (3178 cc). **Bore & Stroke:** 3.35 x 2.76 in. (85 x 70 mm). **Compression Ratio:** 8.0:1. **Brake Horsepower:** 200/210.

BASE V-8 (Z-102BSS/3.2): Supercharged version of the Z-102B/3.2 V-8 produced 275-280 horsepower at 6700 rpm, and 289 lbs.-ft. at 3800 rpm.

CHASSIS DATA: Wheelbase: 92 in. **Overall Length:** 160.8 in. (typical). **Height:** 50.1 in. **Width:** 63 in. **Front Tread:** 52 in. **Rear Tread:** 50.8 in. **Standard Tires:** 5.50x16, 6.00x16 or 6.50x16 (6.00x17 and 6.50x17 available for special purposes).

TECHNICAL: Layout: front-engine, rear-drive. **Transmission:** five-speed manual. **Standard Final Drive Ratio:** 4.18:1 (3.75:1, 4.36:1, 4.72:1, 5.20:1 and other ratios were available). **Steering:** worm. **Suspension (front):** independent; unequal-length control arms and torsion bars. **Suspension (rear):** De Dion axle with torsion bars. **Brakes:** Lockheed hydraulic, front/rear drum. **Body Construction:** semi-integral with platform chassis.

MAJOR OPTIONS: Bosch magneto. Four carburetors. Radio. Air conditioning. Extra-large fuel tank. Fitted luggage. 17-inch tires.

PERFORMANCE: Top Speed: 115-127 mph (up to 144-160 mph for model with supercharged 2.8-liter V-8). **Acceleration (0-60 mph):** (blown 2.8-liter) 6 seconds. **Fuel Mileage:** 21 mpg; (blown 2.8-liter) about 15 mpg.

Manufacturer: Empresa Nacional de Autocamiones S.A. (ENASA), Madrid and Barcelona, Spain.

Distributor: Brewster Automobile Corp., Long Island, New York.

1956-58 PEGASO

1956 Pegaso Superlegera body by Touring. (JC)

Z-102B — V-8 — Production of the earlier Pegaso series with smaller V-8 engine continued, but displacement was now 3.2 liters. Inside were bucket seats, a race-type steering wheel, and tachometer. Rectangular park/signal lights stood below the crossbar-style grille in a typical example. As before, custom bodies were installed that differed considerably from the norm. Late bodies were created by Jose Serra, at Barcelona. An open-top Spyder version was available, with supercharged engine rated 290 horsepower and competition-based construction. Airscoops stood in the hood and at the cowl. A wraparound windshield was installed, and the hood wore a bulge.

Z-103 — V-8 — The new Pegaso series was offered with two larger V-8 engine displacements: 3.9-liter and 4.5-liter. The 3.9-liter's Berlinetta body was produced by Touring, and its supercharged engine was rated 350 bhp. Pegaso called this model "the fastest and highest quality car built to date," while *Motor Trend* added that it was also the most expensive. The simple recessed grille pattern used a crossbar formed of a single vertical bar and the wraparound bumper. Air-intake grillework stood at the cowl. Both a supercharger and Bosch magneto could be installed, along with multiple Weber carburetors.

I.D. DATA: Not available.

Model	Body Type & Seating	Engine Type/CID	P.O.E. Price	Weight (lbs.)	Prod. Total
Z-102B/3.2	2-dr Coupe-2/3P	V8/195	N/A	2200	Note 2
Z-102B/3.2	2-dr Spyder-2/3P	V8/195	N/A	2359	Note 2
Z-103/3.9	2-dr Coupe-2/3P	V8/238	Note 1	2160	Note 2
Z-103/4.5	2-dr Coupe-2/3P	V8/274	Note 1	2820	Note 2

Note 1: Basic price at factory in Spain was about $8000.

Note 2: A total of between 100 and 125 Pegasos were produced from 1951 to 1958.

ENGINE DATA: BASE V-8 (Z-102B/3.2): 90-degree, four-overhead-cam V-8. Cast iron block and light alloy heads. **Displacement:** 195.0 cu. in. (3197 cc). **Bore & Stroke:** 3.35 x 2.76 in. (85 x 70 mm). **Compression Ratio:** 6.0:1. **Brake Horsepower:** N/A (290 at 5800 rpm in supercharged form). Five main bearings.

1956 Pegaso two-seater convertible with body by Saoutchik of France.

BASE V-8 (Z-103/3.9): 90-degree, four-overhead-cam V-8. Cast iron block and light alloy heads. **Displacement:** 237.9 cu. in. (3900 cc). **Bore & Stroke:** 3.46 x 3.23 in. (88 x 82 mm). **Compression Ratio:** 8.0:1 (9.0:1 optional). **Brake Horsepower:** 270 at 5800 rpm (350 bhp when supercharged). Five main bearings.

BASE V-8 (Z-103/4.5): 90-degree, four-overhead-cam V-8. Cast iron block and light alloy heads. **Displacement:** 274.5 cu. in. (4500 cc). **Bore & Stroke:** 3.66 x 3.23 in. (93 x 82 mm). **Compression Ratio:** 8.0:1 (9.0:1 optional). **Brake Horsepower:** 300 at 5800 rpm. Five main bearings.

1956 Pegaso with Superleggera body designed by Touring of Italy.

CHASSIS DATA: Wheelbase: 92 in. **Overall Length:** 160.8 in. (typical). **Height:** 53 in. **Width:** about 63 in. **Front Tread:** 52 in. **Rear Tread:** 50.8 in.

TECHNICAL: Layout: front-engine, rear-drive. **Transmission:** five-speed manual. **Steering:** worm. **Suspension (front):** independent; unequal-length control arms and torsion bars. **Suspension (rear):** De Dion axle with torsion bars. **Brakes:** hydraulic, front/rear drum. **Body Construction:** semi-integral with platform chassis.

MAJOR OPTIONS: Bosch magneto. Multiple carburetors. Supercharger. Radio. Air conditioning. Extra-large fuel tank. Fitted luggage. 17-inch tires.

PERFORMANCE: Top Speed: (Z-103/3.9) 143 mph; (Z-103/4.5) 158 mph.

Manufacturer: Empresa Nacional de Autocamiones S.A. (ENASA), Madrid and Barcelona, Spain.

PEUGEOT

Only a handful of existing automobile manufacturers trace their roots back to the 19th century. Peugeot's history of automobile production reaches back as far as anyone's: to 1889, when the French company turned out a total of four vehicles, and became the first automaker to sell a car to a private owner.

Prior to that time, according to the *World Guide to Automobile Manufacturers,* the Peugeot (pronounced Pooj-Oh) family had been involved in manufacturing for at least four generations. The company's history dated back to Jean-Jacques Peugeot, who'd operated a cotton mill; his son Jean-Pierre Peugeot, who'd constructed hand tools in the 18th century; and to the foundry set up in 1810 by Jean-Pierre's two sons, where the cold rolling mill was invented. By 1819, Peugeot's "lion" was "widely recognized" (ac-

cording to the company) as a "symbol of manufacturing quality." *Societe Peugeot Freres Aines* was formed in 1832, to produce a variety of tools and home products, ultimately ranging from clock springs and coffee mills to hoop-skirt frames and corset stays.

By 1880, the firm had changed its name to *Les Fils de Peugeot Freres,* headed by Jules and Emile Peugeot. Starting in 1885, bicycles joined the list of items produced by the Peugeot plants, instigated by Armand Peugeot (Emile's son), who'd become a cycling fan while studying in England. Three years later, work began on the rear-engined, three-wheeled steam automobile, exhibited by Armand Peugeot at the 1889 Paris Exposition, as the Eiffel Tower was dedicated. Rather than moving forward with steam, however, the Peugeots turned instead to the internal combustion engine. Armand had seen a Panhard et Levassor engine at that Paris Exposition, and bought one to install in a Peugeot chassis. Peugeot entered into an agreement to produce cars with gasoline engines designed by Gottlieb Daimler's firm and manufactured by Panhard et Levassor.

Peugeot's entry of one of its first automobiles into the 1500-mile Paris-Brest-Paris bicycle race of 1891 didn't exactly bring home a victory. The two-cylinder Peugeot with handlebar steering was last across the line, beaten by the bicyclists. Even so, the publicity from finishing at all proved valuable. No other car had ever completed such a grueling distance. Later in the 1890s, Peugeots participated in a number of competitions that featured vehicles with engines. Peugeots ranked first (tied with Panhard), third and fifth in the 1894 Paris-Rouen Trials, for example. A year later, the Michelins put pneumatic tires on a Peugeot for the Paris-Bordeaux-Paris race, but it finished in last place after suffering almost 50 flats.

In 1894, Peugeot introduced the boxy Type 10, which some considered to be the world's first station wagon. Peugeot claimed that their late-1890s vehicles cost only about a penny a mile to operate, and could maintain 15-mph road speeds.

Armand Peugeot formed *Societe Anonyme des Automobiles Peugeot* in 1897, headquartered at Audincourt, France. By the turn of the century, electric ignition was used and up to 500 cars a year were being produced. Less than a decade later, the total rose to some 2,300 annually. By that time, nearly all Peugeots used shaft drive, powered by two- or four-cylinder engines, with the exception of a chain-driven monstrosity with a massive 11,150-cc six-cylinder engine. At the other extreme was the lightweight Bebe, with a single-cylinder engine and tubular chassis.

A separate series of smaller-engined cars, known as Lion-Peugeots, were built by a relative, Robert Peugeot, who'd begun as a motorcycle manufacturer. The first "lion" insignia appeared on a Peugeot automobile by 1907, and remains in use to the present day.

In 1910, a new company was founded to reunite the two branches of the family, called *Societe Anonyme des Automobiles et des Cycles Peugeot,* and a new facility at Sochaux, France went into operation. Among the many different Peugeot models in the early years of the 20th century was the 856-cc Bebe of 1912, designed by Ettore Bugatti. Jules Goux won the Indianapolis 500 in 1913, driving a Peugeot with 7-liter engine. Peugeots also won the 1916 and 1919 Indy races. After World War II, Peugeot put two models on the market: the 153 and 163, with 2.8- and 1.4-liter four-cylinder engines. A few years later came a small-size update of the Bebe, called the Quadrilette, with a 667-cc engine and narrow body that demanded the passenger to sit behind the driver. Also during the 1920s, Peugeot turned out costly models with sleeve-valved engines. Peugeot had created the world's first diesel car in 1922, and it went into production by 1928.

By 1930, annual production passed 43,300. Now the company was ready with a new low-priced car, the Type 201. With a 1.1-liter four-cylinder engine under its hood, the 201 was the first Peugeot to adopt the three-digit numbering system that continues to the present day. The first digit indicates chassis size; the third denotes series. By 1932, the 201 C (which stood for comfort) had independent front suspension using a transverse leaf spring; two years later, a synchromesh transmission. By the time it was succeeded by the 202 in 1938, a total of 143,309 had been built.

Farther up the scale in the early 1930s were the Types 401 and 601 (six-cylinder). Cabriolet versions could be obtained with powered lift-off steel convertible tops as early as 1934, qualifying as true hardtop convertibles. The top lowered into the trunk area in about 15 seconds. Peugeot also had a 301, powered by a 1.5-liter engine. Their 202/302/402 successors, led by the 402 sedan in 1935, gained a dramatic restyling that delivered the look of a Chrysler Airflow, with headlamps mounted behind the grille and skirts covering the rear wheels. A Sports version performed well at Le Mans in 1937. Experiments began with an automatic transmission for the larger models, but only the Cotal electromagnetic setup actually was offered to prewar customers. By the time production halted for World War II, Peugeot had become the second strongest auto manufacturer in France, behind Renault.

Production resumed surprisingly soon: before the war officially ended, in fact, early in 1945. Only the Type 202 returned, however, with its 1133-cc engine; bigger Peugeots were abandoned for the next decade or so. In 1948 came the Type 203 sedan, which used unibody construction and had a more modern look with headlamps built into the fenders, powered by a 1290-cc engine. A Type 403 sedan with 1468-cc engine was added in 1955, adopting the boxy profile that was becoming commonplace, with Italian styling by Pinin Farina. Cabriolet and station wagon versions also were introduced, as well as a diesel edition. An automatic transmission became available in 1958. Peugeot production rose from 44,250 (including trucks) in 1949 to 166,521 (also including trucks) in 1957, of which one-fourth were exported. Official importation into the U.S. began in 1958.

Pininfarina (now spelled as one word) also designed the even boxier and angular 404, with 1618-cc engine, which emerged in 1960 and soon became noteworthy for its silent running. This was also the first Peugeot available with a fuel-injected engine. By 1960, production of the 203 had halted, but a replacement 204 didn't arrive until 1965, also penned by Pininfarina. The 204 had front-wheel drive, with a transversely-mounted, overhead-cam aluminum-alloy 1130-cc engine, plus fully independent suspension and front disc brakes. This model was not ordinarily exported to the U.S. When Roland Peugeot took over as president in 1964, he became the eighth generation of the family to head a Peugeot organization.

Three years later, in 1968, came the rear-drive Type 504, with a 1796-cc engine, either carbureted or fuel injected. A Type 304 joined in 1969, riding the same 102-inch wheelbase as the 204 but with a larger (1288-cc) engine and bigger trunk, as well as trapezoidal headlamps. As usual, new models took a little longer to reach American shores. Peugeot turned to a smaller model for the first time in decades with the front-drive Type 104 of 1972, which carried a transverse 954-cc overhead-cam engine. Peugeot claimed that it was "the smallest four-door car in the world," though it, too, bypassed American showrooms.

A new PRV V-6 engine, developed jointly by Peugeot, Renault and Volvo by 1974-75, first went into the 504 models; then, for the American market, into the posh 604 sedan. By 1976, Peugeot held full control of the Citroen firm,

forming the PSA Peugeot-Citroen group, and turned out a Citroen-engined version of the Type 104 as the Citroen LN. Late in the following year, a 305 sedan replaced the former 304, powered by either a 1290- or 1472-cc overhead-cam four. Then, in 1979, a Type 505 emerged; but was produced alongside the existing 504 for the next several years.

By 1978, Peugeot had acquired all of Chrysler's operations in Europe, giving the new organization the Talbot name. The entire group took the name Peugeot S.A. in 1980.

A Type 205 replacement for the 204 entered the market in 1983, on the same wheelbase as the 104. Sporty, more potent GT and GTI editions of the 205 followed, as did a much-modified 200-bhp Turbo 16 version developed for homologation in rally events. By 1985, Peugeots also were produced in Britain and the 505 got a restyling, soon to replace the 604 as top Peugeot. A new aerodynamic 405 sedan emerged during 1987, aimed at the U.S. market for the following year, after first earning Car of the Year status from the European motoring press.

Each year since 1958, at least one or two Peugeot models have entered the U.S. market—a fairly consistent seller, if not exactly an overpoweringly popular European import. More recently, 505 Turbo sedans were claimed to be "dominating their class in...Sports Car Club of America competition." Nevertheless, sagging sales totals caused Peugeot to halt export of cars to the U.S., as of August 1991.

1945-48 PEUGEOT

202 — FOUR — Peugeot reintroduced its prewar-styled sedan early in 1945, several months before the end of World War II. Headlamps stood behind the grille bars. "Suicide" front doors (rear-hinged) were installed. Under the hood was an 1133-cc (69-cid) overhead-valve four-cylinder engine, developing about 30 horsepower at 4000 rpm. A three-speed gearbox was installed. More than 14,000 Type 202s were produced in 1946 alone. Production of the Type 202 halted early in 1949, by which time the new Type 203 was on the market.

1949-54 PEUGEOT

203 — FOUR — Peugeot's first new postwar model had a wide grille made up of horizontal bars (wider at the base), following the curve of the headlamps that were built into the fenders. Round parking lights stood below and outboard of the headlamps, and wheel openings were rounded. Appearance was completely different from the prewar "Airflow" style, though the 203 resembled various prewar and early postwar American sedans. Both short- and long-wheelbase versions were produced (102 or 110 inches). Front doors of the four-door sedans were rear-hinged ("suicide" style) with exposed hinges, while back doors were front-hinged. A sunroof was included. A four-door convertible also was produced, with pillars above the doors (not unlike the early 1950s Nash Rambler convertible). Peugeot also built a six-passenger family limousine. Under the hood was a 1290-cc (79-cid) four-cylinder engine, developing at least 40 horsepower and hooked to a four-speed gearbox. Fourth gear was an overdrive ratio. The engine featured hemispherical combustion chambers and wet cylinder liners. An underslung worm/wormwheel final drive allowed a low driveshaft position.

Early models had a metal strip atop front fenders, but that was dropped in 1950. Late that year, the trafficator control moved from the top to the side of the steering wheel. By 1952, bright metal bumpers replaced the former painted units, which had only a chrome strip. A larger rear window went into 1954 models, which had a fuel filler concealed in the rear fender.

I.D. DATA: Serial number is on a plate on the right side of the firewall, under the hood. Engine number is on front right side of block. Starting serial number: 1100201.

Model	Body Type & Seating	Engine Type/CID	P.O.E. Price	Weight (lbs.)	Prod. Total
203	4-dr Sedan-4P	I4/79	N/A	1980	Note 1
203	4-dr Family Limo-6P	I4/79	N/A	N/A	Note 1
203	2-dr Cabr-4P	I4/79	N/A	N/A	Note 1
203	4-dr Conv-4P	I4/79	N/A	N/A	Note 1

Note 1: Approximately 150,000 Peugeot 203s were produced between 1949 and 1951.

ENGINE DATA: BASE FOUR (203): Inline, overhead-valve four-cylinder. **Displacement:** 78.7 cu. in. (1290 cc). **Bore & Stroke:** 2.95 x 2.87 in. (75 x 73 mm). **Compression Ratio:** 6.8:1/7.0:1. **Brake Horsepower:** 40-48 at 4500 rpm. **Torque:** up to 59 lbs.-ft. at 2500 rpm. Three main bearings. Solid valve lifters. One carburetor.

CHASSIS DATA: Wheelbase: 102 in. or 110 in. **Overall Length:** 171 in. **Height:** 61.5 in. **Width:** 63.5 in. **Front Tread:** 52.0 in. **Rear Tread:** 52.0 in. **Standard Tires:** 155x400, 5.00x16 or 6.00x16.

TECHNICAL: Layout: front-engine, rear-drive. **Transmission:** four-speed manual. **Steering:** rack and pinion. **Suspension (front):** coil springs. **Suspension (rear):** rigid axle with semi-elliptic leaf springs. **Brakes:** hydraulic, front/rear drum. **Body Construction:** steel unibody.

PERFORMANCE: Top Speed: about 72 mph. **Acceleration (0-60 mph):** about 34 sec. **Fuel Mileage:** about 24-26 mpg.

PRODUCTION/SALES: Approximately 20 Peugeots were imported into the U.S. during 1949-50.

Manufacturer: S.A. des Automobiles Peugeot, Paris, France.

HISTORY: The Type 203 was introduced in 1948, and was the only Peugeot model built for the next seven years. It remained in production into early 1960, with only moderate changes along the way. A Peugeot 203 won the 6500-mile Australian reliability run in 1953.

1955-57 PEUGEOT

1956 Peugeot 203-C four-door sedan.

203 — FOUR — Production of Peugeot's first true postwar model continued with minimal change. Trunk handles added a key lock, and windshield washers were added. First-gear was now synchromesh. Both a sedan and station wagon were produced, but the wagon faded away after 1956. See previous listing for complete data.

403 — FOUR — The next Peugeot took on a far different look with its rounded, boxy full-width slab-sided body, which put the fenders in a continuous line with the doors. Styling of the unibodied four-door sedan was performed by Pinin Farina. An oval grille had a horizontal bar and center insignia. This time, all four doors were front-hinged, opening forward. A bodyside crease line ran the full length of the car, just above the door handles, enhancing the illusion of length. Parking lights were immediately below the headlamps. Vertical taillamps stood at fender tips. A '403' model designation went on the hood front.

Under the hood was a 1468-cc overhead-valve four-cylinder engine, developing 58 horsepower (French rating), with hemispherical combustion chambers and detachable wet cylinder liners. The four-speed synchromesh gearbox had overdrive on the top gear. The gearshift lever, lighting control and trafficator switch went under the steering wheel. Independently sprung front wheels used a transverse leaf spring. At the rear were coil springs and a transverse stabilizer bar, and a worm-driven rear axle. Rack and pinion steering was installed. Tires were 165x380 size (5.90x15). Upholstery was done in Vynide. Front and rear windows rolled all the way down, and optional seats could turn into beds. Body fittings were made of stainless steel, with pushbutton door handles. After the first model year, a pushbutton starter replaced the original pull-type unit. A convertible coupe joined the sedan during 1956, as did a four-door station wagon and a 7/8-passenger Family sedan.

1956 Peugeot 403 four-door sedan.

I.D. DATA: Serial number is on upper right corner of firewall. Engine number is on a boss on the left side of the block. Starting serial number: (sedan) 2000001; (convertible) 1046226.

Model	Body Type & Seating	Engine Type/CID	P.O.E. Price	Weight (lbs.)	Prod. Total
403	4-dr Sedan-5/6P	I4/90	1995	2375	Note 1
403L	4-dr Family Sed-7/8P	I4/90	N/A	N/A	Note 1
403	4-dr Sta Wag-5/6P	I4/90	N/A	N/A	Note 1
403	2-dr Conv Cpe-2/3P	I4/90	N/A	N/A	Note 1

Note 1: A total of 92,086 Peugeot passenger cars (all models) were produced in 1955, followed by 112,223 in 1956, and 126,902 in 1957.

Model Note: Only the four-door sedan was offered initially.

Price Note: Figure shown was valid on the East Coast in 1956, for a stripped model. With a sliding sunroof, overdrive, folding seats, heater/defroster, radiator warm-up blind, full-flow oil filters, front/rear armrests, dual sunvisors and folding rear center armrest, the price was $2595.

ENGINE DATA: BASE FOUR: Inline, overhead-valve four-cylinder. Cast iron block and aluminum head. **Displacement:** 89.6 cu. in. (1468 cc). **Bore & Stroke:** 3.15 x 2.87 in. (80 x 73 mm). **Compression Ratio:** 7.0:1. **Brake Horsepower:** 58 at 4900 rpm. **Torque:** 75 lbs.-ft. at 2500 rpm. Solid valve lifters. One downdraft carburetor.

CHASSIS DATA: Wheelbase: 105 in. except (Family sedan) 114 in. **Overall Length:** 176 in. **Height:** 57.8 in. **Width:** 66 in. **Front Tread:** 53 in. **Rear Tread:** 52 in. **Standard Tires:** 165x380 or 5.90x15.

TECHNICAL: Layout: front-engine, rear-drive. **Transmission:** four-speed manual (overdrive fourth gear available). **Steering:** rack and pinion. **Suspension (front):** control arms and transverse leaf spring. **Suspension (rear):** rigid axle with coil springs and stabilizer bar except (Family sedan) semi-elliptic leaf springs. **Brakes:** hydraulic, front/rear drum. **Body Construction:** steel unibody.

PERFORMANCE: Top Speed: 78-80 mph. **Acceleration (0-60 mph):** 22.6-24.0 sec. **Acceleration (quarter-mile):** 22.2 sec. (60.7 mph). **Fuel Mileage:** 22-27 mpg.

Manufacturer: S.A. des Automobiles Peugeot, Paris, France.

Distributor: Vaughn Imported Cars, New York City; and John L. Green Jr., Los Angeles.

HISTORY: A handful of Peugeots were trickling into the U.S. before official importation began in April 1958.

1958-59 PEUGEOT

1958-'60 Peugeot 403 convertible at the Chateau de Vincennes.

403 — FOUR — Available officially in the U.S. market late in the 1958 model year, the 403 changed little from its previous (1955-57) form. As before, models included a four-door sedan that held five or six passengers; a convertible coupe with space for two or three; and a 403L family sedan with seven or eight seats, four side doors and a rear door, six side windows, and seats that converted to beds. A station wagon also was produced. Coupes had wire-wheel embellishers and inset foglamps. Flashing turn signals were incorporated into rear lights and front foglamps, with repeaters in the side parking lamps.

Only the standard four-door sedan was offered by U.S. dealers, with a 65-horsepower overhead-valve engine that displaced 1468 cc (89.6-cid). A sliding sunroof was standard on Peugeots destined for America, as was a four-speed gearbox (overdrive top gear) with column-mounted gearshift. The gas-filler cap hid beneath the left taillamp, and hubcaps bolted onto the three-lug wheels at the center. Peugeot even included a hand crank.

1958 Peugeot 403 station wagon.

I.D. DATA: Serial number is on a plate at the upper right corner of the firewall. Engine number is on left side of block, above the fuel pump.

Model	Body Type & Seating	Engine Type/CID	P.O.E. Price	Weight (lbs.)	Prod. Total
403	4-dr Sedan-5/6P	I4/90	2175	2322	Note 1
403L	4-dr Family Sed-7/8P	I4/90	N/A	N/A	Note 1
403	4-dr Sta Wag-5/6P	I4/90	N/A	N/A	Note 1
403	2-dr Conv Cpe-2/3P	I4/90	N/A	N/A	Note 1

Note 1: A total of 145,346 Peugeot passenger cars (all models) were produced in 1958, followed by 154,729 in 1959.

Price Note: Sedan price was $2245/$2295 on West Coast and $2215 on Gulf Coast. Price rose to $2250 for the 1959 model year.

1959 Peugeot 403 convertible.

ENGINE DATA: BASE FOUR: Inline, overhead-valve four-cylinder. Cast iron block and aluminum head. **Displacement:** 89.6 cu. in. (1468 cc). **Bore & Stroke:** 3.15 x 2.87 in. (80 x 73 mm). **Compression Ratio:** 7.5:1. **Brake Horsepower:** 65 at 4750 rpm. **Torque:** 75 lbs.-ft. at 2800 rpm. Solid valve lifters. One Solex downdraft carburetor.

CHASSIS DATA: Wheelbase: 105 in. **Overall Length:** 176 in. except (403L) 181.5 in. **Height:** (sedan) 59 in.; (conv) 58 in.; (403L) 61 in. **Width:** 66 in. **Front Tread:** 52.8 in. **Rear Tread:** 52 in. **Standard Tires:** 5.90x15.

TECHNICAL: Layout: front-engine, rear-drive. **Transmission:** four-speed manual (overdrive top gear). **Standard Final Drive Ratio:** 5.75:1. **Steering:** rack and pinion. **Suspension (front):** control arms and transverse leaf spring. **Suspension (rear):** rigid axle with coil springs and stabilizer bar except (Family sedan) semi-elliptic leaf springs. **Brakes:** hydraulic, front/rear drum. **Body Construction:** steel unibody.

PERFORMANCE: Top Speed: 85-87 mph. **Acceleration (0-60 mph):** 16.9-21.6 sec. **Acceleration (quarter-mile):** 22.9 sec. (62.2 mph). **Fuel Mileage:** 30 mpg claimed; 22.8 mpg in road test.

PRODUCTION/SALES: A total of 6,867 Model 403 sedans were sold in the U.S. during 1958, more than doubling to 15,787 in 1959.

ADDITIONAL MODELS: The smaller 203 sedan, as described in the previous listing, remained available elsewhere in the world.

Manufacturer: S.A. des Automobiles Peugeot, Paris, France.

Distributor: Peugeot Inc., New York.

HISTORY: Peugeot's first public showing in the U.S. was at the International Automobile Show in New York, in April 1958. Francois de Peyrecave, president and general manager of Peugeot Inc. (New York) announced that initial plans called for importing 8,000 cars that year, and the first shipment contained 325 cars. Sales and service would be handled by the same distributor/dealer network used for Renaults, but Peugeot and Renault would operate as separate companies. Waiting time in France for delivery of a 403 at this time was two years. A diesel engine became available in 1958, but was not installed in Peugeots destined for America. Peugeot also developed an automatic transmission by 1958, but nothing other than manual shift was installed in U.S. models until the mid-1960s.

With only "one or two exceptions," Tom McCahill of *Mechanix Illustrated* declared the Peugeot "one of the best import buys available in the world." McCahill was especially displeased with the steering, which he found difficult to operate and demonstrating "a definite nose-heavy feel." On the other hand, he noted that other publications had praised the 403's "sports-car-like handling" and "ease of steering and accuracy." A restyled station wagon joined the sedan late in the 1959 model year; see next listing for details.

1960 PEUGEOT

403 — FOUR — A longer station wagon joined the Peugeot lineup for the U.S. market, as of May 1959. Otherwise, little change was evident except for a revision in the style of the '403' model designation on the hood. A cooling fan with electromagnetic coupling was now standard (formerly an option).

I.D. DATA: Serial number is on a plate at the upper right corner of the firewall, and on left side of engine block, above the fuel pump. Serial number range: 2357801 to 2377069.

Model	Body Type & Seating	Engine Type/CID	P.O.E. Price	Weight (lbs.)	Prod. Total
403	4-dr Sedan-5/6P	I4/90	2250	2260	Note 1
403	4-dr Sta Wag-5/6P	I4/90	2490	2600	Note 1

Note 1: A total of 11,373 Model 403s were available for sale in the U.S. during 1960, out of a total of 173,571 Peugeot passenger cars (all models) built that year.

ENGINE DATA: BASE FOUR: Inline, overhead-valve four-cylinder. Cast iron block and aluminum head. **Displacement:** 89.6 cu. in. (1468 cc). **Bore & Stroke:** 3.15 x 2.87 in. (80 x 73 mm). **Compression Ratio:** 7.5:1. **Brake Horsepower:** 65 at 4750 rpm. **Torque:** 85 lbs.-ft. at 3000 rpm. Three main bearings. Solid valve lifters. One Solex downdraft carburetor.

CHASSIS DATA: Wheelbase: (sedan) 105 in.; (wagon) 116 in. **Overall Length:** (sedan) 176 in.; (wagon) 184.4 in. **Height:** 59 in. **Width:** 66 in. **Front Tread:** 52.8 in. **Rear Tread:** 52 in. **Standard Tires:** 5.90x15.

1960 Peugeot 404 four-door sedan.

1960½ Peugeot 403 four-door sedan. (Peugeot Motors of America Inc.)

TECHNICAL: Layout: front-engine, rear-drive. **Transmission:** four-speed manual (overdrive top gear). **Standard Final Drive Ratio:** 5.75:1. **Steering:** rack and pinion. **Suspension (front):** control arms and transverse leaf spring. **Suspension (rear):** rigid axle with coil springs and stabilizer bar. **Brakes:** hydraulic, front/rear drum. **Body Construction:** steel unibody.

PERFORMANCE: Similar to 1958-59.

ADDITIONAL MODELS: The smaller 203 sedan faded away during 1960, but other 403 models (including the larger Family sedan and the convertible coupe) remained available, though not ordinarily exported to the U.S. During the 1960 model year, Peugeot introduced a low-budget 403-7 sedan, with the 403 body and 203 engine, and a different (mesh-patterned) grille.

Manufacturer: S.A. des Automobiles Peugeot, Paris, France.

Distributor: Peugeot Inc., New York City.

HISTORY: The 1960 model was introduced to the U.S. market on October 15, 1959. Peugeots were sold by Renault dealers.

1961-62 PEUGEOT

403 — FOUR — Production of the 403 sedan and station wagon continued with little change, except that the front bumper guards no longer extended below the edge of the bumper itself. Spoke-style full wheel covers were now standard, as were a padded dashboard, clock, and windshield washers. Starting was now performed by the ignition key, replacing the former pushbutton starter. Standard equipment on U.S. models included a sliding metal sunroof, whitewall (or Michelin X) tires, four-speed transmission, heater/defroster, safety padded dashboard, leatherette (or cloth) upholstery, reclining seats, electric clock, windshield washers, trip mileage counter, wheel trim rings, and outside mirror. Peugeot claimed that this equipment list was valued at $365, and no extra-cost options were offered. The 403 remained available in the U.S. into 1966, sold alongside the new 404.

404 — FOUR — Styling for the new 404 sedan again came from the pen of Pininfarina. This one had a more squarish profile, with a flatter roofline than the 403, and crisper lines in general. Little overhang was evident at the rear. The grille consisted of four horizontal bars with a large Peugeot crest in the center. Rectangular parking lights stood beneath the headlamps. Tall vertical taillamps were installed at quarter-panel tips.

The new four-cylinder engine was mounted at a 45-degree angle to lower the hoodline, thus making servicing easier. Displacement was larger than the 403, at 1618 cc (98.7 cid), and the engine developed 72 horsepower. A new four-speed transmission was fully synchronized, with fourth gear direct-drive (not overdrive, as in the 403). The automatic fan clutch was claimed to lower engine drag and increase fuel mileage, allowing the fan to run free when not needed (at temperatures below 167 degrees). Front suspension differed from the 403, consisting of struts with coil springs. Airliner-type reclining seats could be converted into a bed, and came with either cloth or leatherette upholstery. No optional extras were offered. Accessories conservatively valued at $525 (according to Peugeot) were installed at the factory and included in the basic price. That included a sunroof, heater/defroster, whitewall or Michelin X tires, reclining seats, automatic fan clutch, and electric clock. Body colors for 1961 were red, turquoise, ivory, light gray, medium metallic gray, and black.

I.D. DATA: Serial number is on a plate at the upper right corner of the firewall, and on left side of engine block, above the fuel pump. Serial number range: (1961 403) 2377070 to 2488999; (1961 404) 4005100 to 4102899; (1962 403 sedan) 2489000 to 2554223; (1962 403 wagon) 2880700 up; (1962 404) 4102900 to 4223804.

Model	Body Type & Seating	Engine Type/CID	P.O.E. Price	Weight (lbs.)	Prod. Total
403	4-dr Sedan-5/6P	I4/90	2250	2260	Note 1
403	4-dr Sta Wag-5/6P	I4/90	2490	2600	Note 1
404					
404	4-dr Sedan-5/6P	I4/99	2575	2244	Note 1

Note 1: A total of 193,338 Peugeot passenger cars (all models) were produced in 1961, followed by 217,840 in 1962.

ENGINE DATA: BASE FOUR (403): Inline, overhead-valve four-cylinder. Cast iron block and aluminum head. **Displacement:** 89.6 cu. in. (1468 cc). **Bore & Stroke:** 3.15 x 2.87 in. (80 x 73 mm). **Compression Ratio:** 7.5:1. **Brake Horsepower:** 65 at 4750 rpm. **Torque:** 85 lbs.-ft. at 3000 rpm. Three main bearings. Solid valve lifters. One downdraft carburetor.

BASE FOUR (404): Inline, overhead-valve four-cylinder. Cast iron block and aluminum head. **Displacement:** 98.7 cu. in. (1618 cc). **Bore & Stroke:** 3.31 x 2.87 in. (84 x 73 mm). **Compression Ratio:** 7.4:1. **Brake Horsepower:** 72 at 5400 rpm. **Torque:** 94 lbs.-ft. at 2250 rpm. Three main bearings. Solid valve lifters. One downdraft carburetor.

CHASSIS DATA: Wheelbase: (403 sedan) 105 in.; (403 wagon) 116 in.; (404) 104.3 in. **Overall Length:** (403 sedan) 176 in.; (403 wagon) 184.4 in.; (404) 174 in. **Height:** (403) 59 in.; (404) 57.1 in. **Width:** (403) 66 in.; (404) 64.2 in. **Front Tread:** (403) 52.8 in.; (404) 53.2 in. **Rear Tread:** (403) 52 in.; (404) 50.4 in. **Standard Tires:** (403) 5.90x15; (404) 5.90x15 or 165x380 (whitewall or Michelin X).

TECHNICAL: Layout: front-engine, rear-drive. **Transmission:** four-speed manual (overdrive top gear on 403). Overall 404 gear ratios: (1st) 17.14:1; (2nd) 9.29:1; (3rd) 5.97:1; (4th) 4.20:1; (rev) 18.50:1. **Standard Final Drive Ratio:** (403) 5.75:1; (404) 4.20:1. **Steering:** rack and pinion. **Suspension (front):** (403) control arms and transverse leaf spring; (404) single lower wishbones, struts and coil springs. **Suspension (rear):** rigid axle with coil springs and stabilizer bar. **Brakes:** hydraulic, front/rear drum. **Body Construction:** steel unibody.

PERFORMANCE: Top Speed: (404) 90 mph claimed; 88 in test. **Acceleration (0-60 mph):** (404) near 19 sec. **Acceleration (quarter-mile):** (404) about 21 sec. **Fuel Mileage:** (404) 29-30 mpg claimed.

PRODUCTION/SALES: A total of 577 Model 403s became available for sale in the U.S. during 1961, but more than that number (1,502) were shipped back to France; a total of 1,709 were available for sale in 1962. A total of 2,652 Model 404 sedans became available for sale in the U.S. during 1961, and 3,011 in 1962.

Manufacturer: S.A. des Automobiles Peugeot, Paris, France.

Distributor: Peugeot Inc., New York City.

HISTORY: The new 404 sedan was introduced to the U.S. market in February 1961, and appeared at the International Automobile Show in New York that spring. *Sports Cars Illustrated* declared that the 404's styling "will undoubtedly become a classic in years to come." Peugeot literature called it a "pleasing blend of modern and conservative." *Road & Track* called Peugeot "one of the seven best-made cars in the world." By 1962, there were 422 Peugeot dealers in the U.S. At the Paris and Turin shows in 1961, Peugeot displayed a 404 convertible, also created by Pininfarina.

1963-64 PEUGEOT

403 — FOUR — Only the sedan remained in the 403 line, as the station wagon was dropped for 1963. Otherwise, production continued with little change. A restyled grille for 1964 abandoned the long-lived oval shape with a single horizontal bar. Instead, dual horizontal dividers stood ahead of a vertical mesh pattern, with a larger emblem at the center. Later models adopted amber parking lights.

404 — FOUR — No change was evident in the appearance of the squarish Peugeot sedan, with its larger (1618-cc) engine. During the 1963 model year, a new "full reflex" strut-type front suspension was installed. Very late in that 1963 model year, a new XC5 engine with five main bearings and internal modifications went under 404 hoods. The 1964 models added chrome headlamp rims, a chrome strip on rocker panels, and restyled wheel covers with concentric rings. A 404 station wagon was introduced late in 1962 and became available in the U.S. by the 1964 model year.

I.D. DATA: Serial number is on a plate at the upper right corner of the firewall, and on left side of engine block, above the fuel pump. Serial number range: (1963 403 sedan) 2554224 to 2582322; (1963 404 sedan) 4223805 to 4403000; (1964 403 sedan) 2582323 up; (1964 404 sedan) 4403001 up; (1964 404 wagon) 1921039 up.

Model	Body Type & Seating	Engine Type/CID	P.O.E. Price	Weight (lbs.)	Prod. Total
403	4-dr Sedan-5/6P	I4/90	2295	2262	Note 1
404					
404	4-dr Sedan-5/6P	I4/99	2645	2249	Note 1
404	4-dr Sta Wag-5/6P	I4/99	2795	2440	Note 1

Note 1: A total of 273,185 Peugeot passenger cars (all models) were produced in 1963, followed by 265,698 in 1964.

ENGINE DATA: BASE FOUR (403): Inline, overhead-valve four-cylinder. Cast iron block and aluminum head. **Displacement:** 89.6 cu. in. (1468 cc). **Bore & Stroke:** 3.15 x 2.87 in. (80 x 73 mm). **Compression Ratio:** 7.5:1. **Brake Horsepower:** 65 at 4750 rpm. **Torque:** 85 lbs.-ft. at 3000 rpm. Three main bearings. Solid valve lifters. One downdraft carburetor.

BASE FOUR (early 404): Inline, overhead-valve four-cylinder. Cast iron block and aluminum head. **Displacement:** 98.7 cu. in. (1618 cc). **Bore & Stroke:** 3.31 x 2.87 in. (84 x 73 mm). **Compression Ratio:** 7.4:1. **Brake Horsepower:** 72 at 5400 rpm. **Torque:** 94 lbs.-ft. at 2250 rpm. Three main bearings. Solid valve lifters. One downdraft carburetor.

BASE FOUR (late 404): Same as above, except with five main bearings.

CHASSIS DATA: Wheelbase: (403) 105 in.; (404) 104.3 in. **Overall Length:** (403) 176 in.; (404 sedan) 174 in.; (404 wagon) 180 in. **Height:** (403) 59 in.; (404 sedan) 57.1 in.; (404 wagon) 58.3 in. **Width:** (403) 66 in.; (404) 64.2 in. **Front Tread:** (403) 52.8 in.; (404) 53.2 in. **Rear Tread:** (403) 52 in.; (404 sedan) 50.4 in.; (404 wagon) 51.2 in. **Standard Tires:** (403) 5.90x15; (404) 5.90x15 or 165x380.

TECHNICAL: Layout: front-engine, rear-drive. **Transmission:** four-speed manual (overdrive top gear on 403). **Standard Final Drive Ratio:** (404 sedan) 4.20:1; (404 wagon) 4.75:1. **Steering:** rack and pinion. **Suspension (front):** (403) control arms and transverse leaf spring; (404) single lower wishbones, struts and coil springs. **Suspension (rear):** rigid axle with coil springs and stabilizer bar. **Brakes:** hydraulic, front/rear drum. **Body Construction:** steel unibody.

PERFORMANCE: Top Speed: (403) 84 mph; (404) 90 mph. **Fuel Mileage:** 25-28 mpg.

PRODUCTION/SALES: A total of 648 Model 403 Peugeots became available for sale in the U.S. during 1963, followed by 632 in 1964. A total of 1,798 Model 404 Peugeots became available for sale in the U.S. during 1963, and 2,060 in 1964.

Manufacturer: S.A. des Automobiles Peugeot, Paris, France.

Distributor: Peugeot Inc., Rego Park, New York.

HISTORY: Peugeot's 1964 models were introduced to the U.S. market on November 1, 1963.

1965-67 PEUGEOT

1967 Peugeot 404 four-door sedan. (Peugeot Motors of America Inc.)

403 — FOUR — Introduced in Europe a decade earlier, the 403 sedan remained available in the U.S. as late as the 1966 model year. A slightly larger grille emblem was installed in these final models. Sedans with an optional vinyl interior had full-ribbed simulated leather seats and door panels. A sliding sunroof remained standard.

404 — FOUR — Though seldom seen, a convertible version of the 404 joined the sedan and station wagon on the U.S. market for the 1965 model year. The 1618-cc (98.7-cid) engine now developed 76 horsepower. Reclining front seats and a sliding sunroof were standard. Power brakes became standard late in 1965. An automatic transmission became available for the 404 sedan late in 1966, and the engine gained four horsepower for the 1967 model year. Also for 1967, a hypoid rear axle replaced the torque-tube (worm and roller) that had been standard in Peugeots up to this time, and round dials were installed in the instrument panel. Either whitewalls or Michelin X tires were available on 404 models, for the same price.

I.D. DATA: Serial number is on a plate at the upper right corner of the firewall; and on left side of engine block, above the fuel pump. Starting serial number: (1965 403 sedan) 2651489; (1965 404 sedan) 5029151; (1965 404 conv) 4438001; (1965 wagon) 1923370; (1966 403 sedan) 2664234; (1966 404 sedan) 5183338; (1966 404 conv) 4498275; (1966 404 wagon) 1925732; (1967 404 sedan) 5311001; (1967 404 conv) 4498001; (1967 404 wagon) 1928101.

Model	Body Type & Seating	Engine Type/CID	P.O.E. Price	Weight (lbs.)	Prod. Total
403	4-dr Sedan-5/6P	I4/90	2250	2262	Note 1
404					
404	4-dr Sedan-5/6P	I4/99	2595	2249	Note 1
404	4-dr Sta Wag-5/6P	I4/99	2740	2440	Note 1
404	2-dr Conv-5P	I4/99	3899	2270	Note 1

Note 1: A total of 260,141 Peugeot passenger cars (all models) were produced in 1965, followed by 332,184 in 1966, and 374,028 in 1967.

ENGINE DATA: BASE FOUR (403): Inline, overhead-valve four-cylinder. Cast iron block and aluminum head. **Displacement:** 89.6 cu. in. (1468 cc). **Bore & Stroke:** 3.15 x 2.87 in. (80 x 73 mm). **Compression Ratio:** 7.3:1. **Brake Horsepower:** 66 at 4750 rpm. **Torque:** 85 lbs.-ft. at 2500 rpm. Three main bearings. Solid valve lifters. One Solex downdraft carburetor.

BASE FOUR (404): Inline, overhead-valve four-cylinder. Cast iron block and aluminum head. **Displacement:** 98.7 cu. in. (1618 cc). **Bore & Stroke:** 3.31 x 2.87 in. (84 x 73 mm). **Compression Ratio:** 7.6:1. **Brake Horsepower:** 76 at 5500 rpm. **Torque:** 96 lbs.-ft. at 2500 rpm. Five main bearings. Solid valve lifters. One Solex downdraft carburetor.

Note: Model 404 engine for 1967 was rated 80 bhp at 5500 rpm, on 8.3:1 compression.

CHASSIS DATA: Wheelbase: (403) 105 in.; (404 sedan) 104.3 in.; (404 wagon) 111.8 in. **Overall Length:** (403) 176 in.; (404 sedan) 174 in.; (404 wagon) 180 in. **Height:** (403) 59 in.; (404 sedan) 57.1 in.; (404 wagon) 58.3 in. **Width:** (403) 66 in.; (404) 64.2 in. **Front Tread:** (403) 52.8 in.; (404) 53 in. **Rear Tread:** (403) 52 in.; (404 sedan) 50.4 in.; (404 wagon) 51.2 in. **Standard Tires:** 5.90x15.

TECHNICAL: Layout: front-engine, rear-drive. **Transmission:** four-speed manual; automatic available in late 1966. **Standard Final Drive Ratio:** (404 sedan) 4.20:1; (404 wagon) 4.75:1. **Steering:** rack and pinion. **Suspension (front):** (403) control arms and transverse leaf spring; (404) single lower wishbones, struts and coil springs. **Suspension (rear):** rigid axle with coil springs and stabilizer bar. **Brakes:** hydraulic, front/rear drum. **Body Construction:** steel unibody.

PERFORMANCE: Top Speed: (403) about 81 mph; (404) 89-93 mph. **Fuel Mileage:** (403) about 27 mpg; (404) 21-22 mpg.

PRODUCTION/SALES: A total of 635 Model 403s became available for sale in the U.S. during 1965, followed by 665 in 1966. According to Peugeot, only a single leftover went to a U.S. dealer in 1967. A total of 1,916 Model 404s became available for sale in the U.S. during 1965, followed by 2,689 in 1966, and 3,593 in 1967.

ADDITIONAL MODELS: Peugeot also produced a 204 series with 1130-cc engine for sale in Europe and elsewhere in the world.

Manufacturer: S.A. des Automobiles Peugeot, Paris, France.

Distributor: Peugeot Inc., Rego Park, New York.

HISTORY: Peugeot's 1966 models were introduced to the U.S. market on August 23, 1965; the 1967 models on September 12, 1966.

1968-69 PEUGEOT

1969 Peugeot 404 station wagon.

404 — FOUR — Peugeot's four-door sedan and station wagon remained available in the U.S., with few changes. Front disc brakes were now standard, in addition to the usual sliding sunroof and reclining front seats. Both the sedan and station wagon could have an optional automatic transmission. The shift pattern for the four-speed manual gearbox adopted the conventional form. Seatbelts were installed at both front and rear, and the dashboard was fully padded. Backup lights also were installed, along with side reflector lenses. For the 1969 model year, the 404 had smaller bolt-on hubcaps on grey wheels. In addition, during manufacture the bodies were fully immersed in a paint primer, which was said to virtually eliminate the prospect of body rust. Convertibles were available only on special order.

I.D. DATA: Serial number is on a plate at the upper right corner of the firewall; and on left side of engine block, above the fuel pump. Starting serial number: (1968 sedan) 8325001; (1968 wagon) 1932385; (1969 sedan) 8350001; (1969 sedan with automatic) 8352701; (1969 wagon) 1934601; (1969 wagon with automatic) 7101001.

Model	Body Type & Seating	Engine Type/CID	P.O.E. Price	Weight (lbs.)	Prod. Total
404	4-dr Sedan-5/6P	I4/99	2699	2244	Note 1
404	4-dr Sta Wag-5/6P	I4/99	2799	2525	Note 1
404	2-dr Conv-5P	I4/99	N/A	N/A	Note 1

Note 1: A total of 362,207 Peugeot passenger cars (all models) were produced in 1968, followed by 440,717 in 1969.

Price Note: Figures shown were for 1968 models with manual shift. An automatic transmission cost $199 extra. The station wagon cost $100 more in 1969.

ENGINE DATA: BASE FOUR (404): Inline, overhead-valve four-cylinder. Cast iron block and aluminum head. **Displacement:** 98.7 cu. in. (1618 cc). **Bore & Stroke:** 3.31 x 2.87 in. (84 x 73 mm). **Compression Ratio:** 8.3:1. **Brake Horsepower:** 80 at 5500 rpm. **Torque:** 97.5 lbs.-ft. at 2500 rpm. Five main bearings. Solid valve lifters. One Solex downdraft single-barrel carburetor.

CHASSIS DATA: Wheelbase: (sedan) 104.3 in.; (wagon) 111.8 in. **Overall Length:** (sedan) 175 in.; (wagon) 180 in. **Height:** (sedan) 57.1 in.; (wagon) 58.8 in. **Width:** (sedan) 64 in. **Front Tread:** (sedan) 53.2 in.; (wagon) 53 in. **Rear Tread:** (sedan) 49.2 in.; (wagon) 51.1 in. **Standard Tires:** 5.90x15.

TECHNICAL: Layout: front-engine, rear-drive. **Transmission:** four-speed manual; three-speed automatic optional. **Standard Final Drive Ratio:** (sedan) 4.20:1; (wagon) 4.63:1. **Steering:** rack and pinion. **Suspension (front):** single lower wishbones, struts, coil springs and stabilizer bar. **Suspension (rear):** rigid axle with coil springs and stabilizer bar. **Brakes:** front disc, rear drum. **Body Construction:** steel unibody.

PERFORMANCE: Top Speed: about 90-93 mph. **Fuel Mileage:** 21-22 mpg mpg.

PRODUCTION/SALES: A total of 4,684 Model 404 Peugeots became available for sale in the U.S. during 1968, followed by 2,681 in 1969.

Manufacturer: S.A. des Automobiles Peugeot, Paris, France.

Distributor: Peugeot Western Distributors Inc., Long Beach, California (and others).

HISTORY: Peugeot's 1968 models were introduced to the U.S. market on August 25, 1967; the 1969 models on October 1, 1967. Peugeots were promoted in America as "the toughest bargain you can drive."

1970 PEUGEOT

1970 Peugeot four-door sedan.

404 — FOUR — This would be the final year for the 404 series, offered only in station wagon form. Under its hood was the same engine used in the new 504 series.

504 — FOUR — The new Peugeot model was a luxury four-door sedan with a different body and larger engine. As before, Pininfarina was responsible for the styling. A rectangular horizontal-bar grille with center Peugeot insignia sat between quad round headlamps, with '504' designation on the protruding lip just ahead of the hood. Four-wheel power disc brakes and four-wheel independent suspension were standard. So were the expected sliding steel sunroof and reclining seats. Wheelbase was 108 inches, and the 1796-cc (109.8 cid) four-cylinder engine produced 90 horsepower.

I.D. DATA: Serial number is on a plate at the upper right corner of the firewall, or on driver's door post. Starting serial number: (404 wagon) 7160001; (404 wagon w/automatic) 7162001; (504 sedan) 1078611 or 1119001; (504 sedan w/automatic) 1120401.

Model	Body Type & Seating	Engine Type/CID	P.O.E. Price	Weight (lbs.)	Prod. Total
404	4-dr Sta Wag-5/6P	I4/110	2995	2535	Note 1
504					
504	4-dr Sedan-5P	I4/110	3195	2650	Note 1

Note 1: A total of 525,201 Peugeot passenger cars (all models) were produced in 1970.

Price Note: Figures shown were for models with manual shift. A 404 wagon with automatic transmission cost $3194; a 504 with automatic sold for $3395.

ENGINE DATA: BASE FOUR: Inline, overhead-valve four-cylinder. Cast iron block and aluminum head. **Displacement:** 109.8 cu. in. (1796 cc). **Bore & Stroke:** 3.30 x 3.20 in. (84 x 81 mm). **Compression Ratio:** 8.3:1. **Brake Horsepower:** (404) 87 at 5500 rpm; (504) 90 at 5600 rpm. **Torque:** 108 lbs.-ft. at 3000 rpm. Five main bearings. Solid valve lifters.

CHASSIS DATA: Wheelbase: (404 wagon) 111.8 in.; (504 sedan) 108 in. **Overall Length:** (404 wagon) 180 in.; (504 sedan) 177 in. **Height:** (404 wagon) 58.8 in.; (504 sedan) 57.5 in. **Width:** (404 wagon) 64 in.; (504 sedan) 66.5 in. **Front Tread:** (404 wagon) 53 in.; (504 sedan) 56.5 in. **Rear Tread:** (404 wagon) 51.1 in.; (504 sedan) 53.5 in. **Standard Tires:** (404 wagon) 5.90x15 or 165x15; (504 sedan) 175x14.

TECHNICAL: Layout: front-engine, rear-drive. **Transmission:** four-speed manual; three-speed automatic optional. **Standard Final Drive Ratio:** (404 wagon) 4.63:1; (504 sedan) 3.89:1. **Steering:** rack and pinion. **Suspension (front):** (404 wagon) single lower wishbones, struts, coil springs and anti-roll bar; (504 sedan) MacPherson struts with coil springs and anti-roll bar. **Suspension (rear):** (404 wagon) rigid axle with coil springs and anti-roll bar; (504 sedan) independent with semi-trailing arms, coil springs and anti-roll bar. **Brakes:** (404 wagon) front disc, rear drum; (504 sedan) four-wheel disc. **Body Construction:** steel unibody.

PERFORMANCE: Top Speed: 97 mph. **Acceleration (quarter-mile):** (404 w/automatic) 20.8 sec.; (504) 19.8 sec. **Fuel Mileage:** (504) near 25 mpg.

PRODUCTION/SALES: A total of 1,051 Model 404 Peugeots were offered for sale in the U.S. during 1970. A total of 4,738 Peugeot 504s were offered for sale in the U.S. during 1970 (plus 752 early examples in late 1969).

Manufacturer: S.A. des Automobiles Peugeot, Paris, France.

Distributor: Peugeot Inc., Forest Hills, New York.

HISTORY: *Road Test* magazine described the new 504 sedan as "a harmonious blend of Italian lines and proper people packaging," wearing a body with "low nose and chopped tail" that "will look as fresh years from now as it does today."

1971-72 PEUGEOT

304 — FOUR — A new smaller sedan became available for the 1971 model year, serving as Peugeot's first front-wheel-drive model. The transverse-mounted 1288-cc (78.6-cid) engine produced 70 horsepower. Wheelbase was 101.9 inches. Appearance was similar to the 504 sedan, but on a smaller scale. The rectangular grille was made up of horizontal bars with a center Peugeot lion insignia, set between quad round headlamps. A station wagon joined the sedan later. After 1972, the 304 disappeared from the U.S. market.

504 — FOUR — Production of Peugeot's luxury four-door sedan continued with little change, except for a larger engine. A bore increase brought the four-cylinder engine to 1971-cc (120.3-cid) displacement. A four-door station wagon joined the sedan during this period.

I.D. DATA: Serial number is on a plate at the upper right corner of the firewall, or on the driver's door post. Starting serial number: (1971 Model 304) 302001; (1971 Model 504) 1180001; (1972 Model 304 sedan) 3227896; (1972 Model 304 wagon) 3242094; (1972 Model 504 sedan) 1335387; (1972 Model 504 wagon) 1371867.

Model	Body Type & Seating	Engine Type/CID	P.O.E. Price	Weight (lbs.)	Prod. Total
304	4-dr Sedan-4/5P	I4/79	2625	1920	Note 1
304	4-dr Sta Wag-4/5P	I4/79	2895	2000	Note 1
504					
504	4-dr Sedan-5P	I4/120	3735	2525	Note 1
504	4-dr Sta Wag-5P	I4/120	4095	2800	Note 1

Note 1: A total of 559,480 Peugeot passenger cars (all models) were produced in 1971, followed by 603,421 in 1972.

Price Note: Figures shown were valid in 1972, for models with manual shift. Prices in 1971 were $2479 for the 304 sedan, $2799 for the 304 wagon, and $3478 for the 504 sedan.

ENGINE DATA: BASE FOUR (304): Inline, overhead-cam four-cylinder. Aluminum alloy block and head. **Displacement:** 78.6 cu. in. (1288 cc). **Bore & Stroke:** 2.99 x 2.80 in. (76 x 71 mm). **Compression Ratio:** 8.8:1. **Brake Horsepower:** 70 at 6000 rpm (58 bhp net in 1972). **Torque:** 74 lbs.-ft. at 3750 rpm (65 lbs.-ft. net in 1972). Five main bearings. Solid valve lifters. Solex single-barrel carburetor.

BASE FOUR (504): Inline, overhead-valve four-cylinder. Cast iron block and aluminum head. **Displacement:** 120.3 cu. in. (1971 cc). **Bore & Stroke:** 3.46 x 3.20 in. (88 x 81 mm). **Compression Ratio:** 8.4:1. **Brake Horsepower:** 98 at 5500 rpm (92 bhp net in 1972). **Torque:** 124.5 lbs.-ft. at 3000 rpm (119 lbs.-ft. net in 1972). Five main bearings. Solid valve lifters. Solex two-barrel carburetor.

CHASSIS DATA: Wheelbase: (304) 101.9 in.; (504 sedan) 108 in. **Overall Length:** (304 sedan) 162.9 in.; (304 wagon) 158 in.; (504 sedan) 177 in. **Height:** (304 sedan) 55.4 in.; (304 wagon) 56 in.; (504 sedan) 57.5 in. **Width:** (304) 61.8 in.; (504 sedan) 66.5 in. **Front Tread:** (304) 51.9 in.; (504 sedan) 56.5 in. **Rear Tread:** (304) 49.5 in.; (504 sedan) 53.5 in. **Standard Tires:** (304) 145x14; (504 sedan) 175x14.

TECHNICAL: Layout: (304) front-engine, front-drive; (504) front-engine, rear-drive. **Transmission:** four-speed manual; three-speed automatic optional. **Standard Final Drive Ratio:** (304) 4.07:1; (504 sedan) 3.89:1. **Steering:** rack and pinion. **Suspension (front):** MacPherson struts with coil springs and anti-roll bar. **Suspension (rear):** (304) trailing arms with coil springs and anti-roll bar; (504) independent with semi-trailing arms, coil springs and anti-roll bar. **Brakes:** (304) front disc, rear drum; (504) four-wheel disc. **Body Construction:** steel unibody.

PRODUCTION/SALES: A total of 2,153 Peugeot 404s were offered for sale in the U.S. during 1971 (plus 1,407 early examples in late 1970); followed by only 709 in 1972. A total of 3,158 Peugeot 504s were offered for sale in the U.S. during 1971, followed by 3,884 in 1972.

Manufacturer: S.A. des Automobiles Peugeot, Paris, France.

Distributor: Peugeot Inc., Forest Hills, New York.

1973-76 PEUGEOT

504 — FOUR — For the next four years, only the Peugeot 504 sedan and station wagon were available on the U.S. market. A diesel engine with larger displacement (128.8 cid) joined the original gasoline four in 1974.

I.D. DATA: Peugeot's serial number is on the driver's door post (1973) or at the upper left corner of the instrument panel, visible through the windshield; and on a plate attached to right front fender in engine compartment. Starting in 1974, a 10- or 13-symbol Vehicle Identification Number was used. The first symbols identify the body style ('504A' = sedan; '504D' = station wagon). The next two digits denote transmission type ('91' = manual shift; '93' = automatic) or diesel engine ('90' = diesel). The final seven digits form the sequential serial number. Starting serial number: (1973) 504-1528595; (1974 sedan) A91-1669569; (1974 sedan w/automatic) A93-1665582; (1974 wagon) D91-1669609; (1974 wagon w/automatic) D93-1669623; (1975 sedan) A91-1897001; (1975 sedan w/auto.) A93-1897001; (1975 wagon) D91-1897001; (1975 wagon w/auto.) D93-1897001; (1975 diesel sedan) A90-1927538; (1975 diesel wagon) D90-1950577; (1976 sedan) GL- or SL-504A91-2198704; (1976 wagon) 504D91-2191029; (1976 diesel sedan) 504A90-2200193; (1976 diesel wagon) 504D90-2191024.

Model	Body Type & Seating	Engine Type/CID	P.O.E. Price	Weight (lbs.)	Prod. Total
504 (1973 models)					
504	4-dr Sedan-5P	I4/120	4230	2750	Note 1
504	4-dr Sta Wag-5P	I4/120	4670	2932	Note 1
504 (1974 models)					
	4-dr Sedan-5P	I4/120	4830	2800	Note 1
	4-dr Sta Wag-5P	I4/120	5380	3000	Note 1
Diesel	4-dr Sedan-5P	I4/129	5880	2880	Note 1
Diesel	4-dr Sta Wag-5P	I4/129	6350	3090	Note 1
504 (1975 models)					
	4-dr Sedan-5P	I4/120	5610	2860	Note 1
	4-dr Sta Wag-5P	I4/120	6220	3105	Note 1
Diesel	4-dr Sedan-5P	I4/129	6630	3000	Note 1
Diesel	4-dr Sta Wag-5P	I4/129	7240	3230	Note 1
504 (1976 models)					
GL504	4-dr Sedan-5P	I4/120	6470	2879	Note 1
SL504	4-dr Sedan-5P	I4/120	6970	2879	Note 1
504	4-dr Sta Wag-5P	I4/120	7420	3156	Note 1
Diesel	4-dr Sedan-5P	I4/120	8020	3029	Note 1
Diesel	4-dr Sta Wag-5P	I4/120	8470	3260	Note 1

Note 1: A total of 684,538 Peugeot passenger cars (all models) were produced in 1973, followed by 634,479 in 1974, 578,125 in 1975, and 655,760 in 1976.

ENGINE DATA: BASE FOUR (504): Inline, overhead-valve four-cylinder. Cast iron block and aluminum head. **Displacement:** 120.3 cu. in. (1971 cc). **Bore & Stroke:** 3.46 x 3.20 in. (88 x 81 mm). **Compression Ratio:** 7.6:1. **Brake Horsepower:** 82-88 at 5200-5500 rpm. **Torque:** 104.7-110 lbs.-ft. at 2900-3000 rpm. Five main bearings. Solid valve lifters. Two single-barrel carburetors.

BASE DIESEL FOUR (1974-76): Inline, overhead-valve four-cylinder. Cast iron block. **Displacement:** 128.8 cu. in. (2111 cc). **Bore & Stroke:** 3.54 x 3.26 in. (90 x 83 mm). **Compression Ratio:** 22.2:1. **Brake Horsepower:** 65 at 4500 rpm. **Torque:** 87.5 lbs.-ft. at 2500 rpm. Solid valve lifters. Fuel injection.

CHASSIS DATA: Wheelbase: (sedan) 108 in.; (wagon) 114 in. **Overall Length:** (sedan) 177-182.8 in.; (wagon) 189-194.4 in. **Height:** (sedan) 57 in.; (wagon) 61 in. **Width:** 66.7 in. **Front Tread:** 56 in. **Rear Tread:** 53.5 in. **Standard Tires:** (sedan) 175HR14; (wagon) 185SR14.

TECHNICAL: Layout: front-engine, rear-drive. **Transmission:** four-speed manual; three-speed automatic optional. **Standard Final Drive Ratio:** (gas sedan) 3.9:1; (gas wagon) 4.11:1. **Steering:** rack and pinion. **Suspension (front):** MacPherson struts with coil springs and anti-roll bar. **Suspension (rear):** independent with semi-trailing arms, coil springs and anti-roll bar. **Brakes:** (sedan) four-wheel disc; (wagon) front disc, rear drum. **Body Construction:** steel unibody.

MAJOR OPTIONS: Automatic transmission ($255 up). Air conditioning. Power steering.

PRODUCTION/SALES: A total of 2,690 Peugeot model 504s were offered for sale in the U.S. during 1973; total U.S. sales came to 4,010 units. A total of 7,948 Peugeots were sold in the U.S. during 1974, rising to 11,850 in 1975, then slipping to 9,497 in 1976.

ADDITIONAL MODELS: In Europe, Peugeot also offered the new subcompact model 104, as well as the larger 204, 304 and 404 series.

Manufacturer: S.A. des Automobiles Peugeot, Paris, France.

Distributor: Peugeot Inc., Clifton, New Jersey.

HISTORY: The luxurious 604 was introduced late in 1976; see next listing for details.

1977-79 PEUGEOT

504 — FOUR — Production of the 504 sedan and station wagon continued with minimal change. They were marketed alongside the new and larger 604 sedan. The diesel engine grew larger in displacement, to 2304 cc (140.6 cid). Appearance was little changed from prior models, with quad round headlamps alongside a blacked-out grille with two bright horizontal bars and center Peugeot insignia. The '504' model designation was easy to see on the protruding lip ahead of the forward-sloping hood. 'Peugeot' script went on the cowl, above the bodyside trim strip. Four-wheel disc brakes were standard on the sedan.

604/604 SL — V-6 — Peugeot moved from four-cylinder to V-6 power with the new 604 sedan. The 2664-cc (163-cid) engine, a joint project of Peugeot, Renault and Volvo, produced 133 horsepower (less in California). *Car and Driver* described the posh 604's interior as "immense and thoughtfully designed," with "authentically sumptuous" appointments. Quad rectangular headlamps flanked a narrow blacked-out rectangular grille. Parking lights wrapped around the front fenders. Four-wheel power disc brakes, reclining seats and air conditioning were standard. Both a four-speed manual gearbox and three-speed automatic transmission were available. Features that didn't necesssarily earn praise included a turn-signal switch on the right side of the steering column, and the tall steering wheel mounted in a nearly-horizontal position. An 'SL' suffix was commonly added to the model designation.

I.D. DATA: Peugeot's 13-symbol Vehicle Identification is atop the left side of the instrument panel. The first three symbols identify the model. Symbol four indicates body type. Symbol five is the engine code; symbol six identifies the powertrain. The final seven digits form the sequential production number. Starting serial number: (1977 504 gas-engine) 2570001; (1977 504 diesel) 2401001; (1977 604) 6547151; (1977 604 w/automatic) 6536246.

Model	Body Type & Seating	Engine Type/CID	P.O.E. Price	Weight (lbs.)	Prod. Total
504 (1977 models)					
SL504	4-dr Sedan-5P	I4/120	7360	3020	Note 1
504	4-dr Sta Wag-5P	I4/120	7840	3230	Note 1
Diesel	4-dr Sedan-5P	I4/141	8660	3130	Note 1
Diesel	4-dr Sta Wag-5P	I4/141	9140	3375	Note 1
604 (1977 models)					
604	4-dr Sedan-5P	V6/163	10990	3345	Note 1

Note 1: A total of 676,109 Peugeot passenger cars (all models) were produced in 1977, followed by 742,303 in 1978, and 754,448 in 1979.

Price Note: By 1979, prices rose to $8040 for the 504 gasoline-engined sedan and $12,840 for the 604 SL sedan.

ENGINE DATA: BASE FOUR (504): Inline, overhead-valve four-cylinder. Cast iron block and aluminum head. **Displacement:** 120.3 cu. in. (1971 cc). **Bore & Stroke:** 3.46 x 3.20 in. (88 x 81 mm). **Compression Ratio:** 8.0:1. **Brake Horsepower:** 88 at 5000 rpm. **Torque:** 109 lbs.-ft. at 3000 rpm. Five main bearings. Solid valve lifters. Two single-barrel carburetors.

BASE DIESEL FOUR (504): Inline, overhead-valve four-cylinder. Cast iron block. **Displacement:** 140.6 cu. in. (2304 cc). **Bore & Stroke:** 3.70 x 3.26 in. (94 x 83 mm). **Compression Ratio:** 22.2:1. **Brake Horsepower:** 71 at 4500 rpm. **Torque:** 99 lbs.-ft. at 2500 rpm. Solid valve lifters. Fuel injection.

BASE SIX (604): 90-degree, overhead-cam "vee" type six-cylinder. Light alloy block and head. **Displacement:** 162.6 cu. in. (2664 cc). **Bore & Stroke:** 3.46 x 2.87 in. (88 x 73 mm). **Compression Ratio:** 8.2:1. **Brake Horsepower:** 133 at 5750 rpm. **Torque:** 147 lbs.-ft. at 3500 rpm. Four main bearings. Solid valve lifters. One single-barrel and one two-barrel carburetor.

Note: A larger (2.8-liter) V-6 was installed in Peugeot 604 sedans in 1979; see next listing for data.

CHASSIS DATA: Wheelbase: (504 sedan) 108 in.; (504 wagon) 114 in.; (604) 110.2 in. **Overall Length:** (504 sedan) 182.4 in.; (504 wagon) 194.4 in.; (604) 192.3 in. **Height:** (504 sedan) 57 in.; (504 wagon) 61 in.; (604) 56.3 in. **Width:** (504) 66.7 in.; (604) 69.7 in. **Front Tread:** (504) 56 in.; (604) 58.7 in. **Rear Tread:** (504) 53.5 in.; (604) 56.3 in. **Standard Tires:** (504 sedan) 175HR14; (504 wagon) 185SR14; (604) 175HR14.

TECHNICAL: Layout: front-engine, rear-drive. **Transmission:** four-speed manual; three-speed automatic optional. **Standard Final Drive Ratio:** (504 gas sedan) 3.89:1; (504 gas wagon) 4.11:1; (604) 3.7:1. **Steering:** rack and pinion. **Suspension (front):** MacPherson struts with coil springs and anti-roll bar. **Suspension (rear):** independent with semi-trailing arms, coil springs and anti-roll bar. **Brakes:** (504 wagon) front disc, rear drum; (504 sedan, 604) four-wheel disc. **Body Construction:** steel unibody.

MAJOR OPTIONS: Automatic transmission ($430 up). Air conditioning (504). Sunroof (604). Leather interior (604). AM/FM stereo.

PERFORMANCE: Acceleration (0-60 mph): (604 SL) 13.7 sec. **Acceleration (quarter-mile):** (604 SL) 19.7 sec. (72.2 mph). **Fuel Mileage:** (604 SL) about 18 mpg.

PRODUCTION/SALES: A total of 10,295 Peugeots were sold in the U.S. during 1977, followed by 9,061 in 1978.

Manufacturer: S.A. des Automobiles Peugeot, Paris, France.

Distributor: Peugeot Inc., Clifton, New Jersey; then Peugeot Motors of America Inc., Lyndhurst, New Jersey.

HISTORY: The new 604 sedan debuted in mid-summer of 1977. In 1978, a Peugeot won the Eastern African Safari event for the sixth time.

1980-81 PEUGEOT

1981 Peugeot 504 SRD four-door sedan.

505/504 — FOUR — By 1980, Peugeot's 120.3-cid four-cylinder gasoline engine switched from carburetion to fuel injection, gaining some horsepower in the process. The new 505 sedan was several inches longer than the previous 504, as well as a little wider and taller. The 504 station wagon remained in the lineup. An optional 'S' package included an electric sliding steel sunroof, power windows, cruise control, air conditioning, and AM/FM stereo radio. A turbodiesel engine was added for 1981.

604 SL — V-6 — Production of the six-cylinder Peugeot continued into 1980 with little change, powered by the 2849-cc engine that became available in 1979.

I.D. DATA: Peugeot's Vehicle Identification Number is on the upper left of the dashboard, visible through the windshield. For 1980 models, see previous listing. Starting in 1981, a 17-symbol number was used. Symbols 1-3 ('VF3') indicate country and manufacturer. Symbol four identifies the model, five the body style, six the engine, seven the restraint system. Symbol eight identifies the transmission, folowed by a check digit. Symbol 10 denotes the model year ('B' = 1981); symbol 11 ('S'), the assembly plant. The six final digits form the sequential serial number. Starting serial number: VF3BA()1()()BS300001.

Model	Body Type & Seating	Engine Type/CID	P.O.E. Price	Weight (lbs.)	Prod. Total
505/504 (1980 models)					
505	4-dr Sedan-5P	I4/120	10400	3020	Note 1
505 (Dsl)	4-dr Sedan-5P	I4/141	11350	3200	Note 1
504 (Dsl)	4-dr Sta Wag-5P	I4/141	10923	3300	Note 1
505 TURBODIESEL (1981 model)					
505	4-dr Sedan-5P	I4/141	12980	3250	Note 1
604 (1980 model)					
604 SL	4-dr Sedan-5P	V6/174	15496	3418	Note 1

Note 1: A total of 12,930 Peugeots were sold in the U.S. during 1980, followed by 16,725 in 1981.

Price Note: Prices for the 505/504 series rose in 1981 to $10,990, $11,990 and $11,660 (respectively).

ENGINE DATA: BASE FOUR (505): Inline, overhead-valve four-cylinder. Cast iron block and aluminum head. **Displacement:** 120.3 cu. in. (1971 cc). **Bore & Stroke:** 3.46 x 3.19 (88 x 81 mm). **Compression Ratio:** 8.35:1. **Brake Horsepower:** 96 at 4900 rpm. **Torque:** 116 lbs.-ft. at 3300 rpm. Five main bearings. Fuel injection.

BASE DIESEL FOUR (505/504): Inline, overhead-valve four-cylinder. **Displacement:** 140.6 cu. in. (2304 cc). **Bore & Stroke:** 3.70 x 3.27 (94 x 83 mm). **Compression Ratio:** 22.4:1/23.0:1. **Brake Horsepower:** 71 at 4500 rpm. **Torque:** 99 lbs.-ft. at 2500 rpm. Five main bearings. Fuel injection.

BASE TURBODIESEL (1981 505): Same as diesel above, but turbocharged — **Compression Ratio:** 21.0:1. **Brake Horsepower:** 80 at 4150 rpm. **Torque:** 135.6 lbs.-ft. at 2000 rpm.

BASE SIX (604): Overhead-cam "vee" type six-cylinder. **Displacement:** 174 cu. in. (2849 cc). **Bore & Stroke:** 3.58 x 2.87 in. (91 x 73 mm). **Compression Ratio:** 8.2:1. **Brake Horsepower:** 133 at 5250 rpm. **Torque:** 162.5 lbs.-ft. at 3000 rpm. Four main bearings. Solid valve lifters.

1981 Peugeot 305 GR four-door sedan.

CHASSIS DATA: Wheelbase: (505) 107.9 in.; (504 wagon) 114 in.; (604) 110.2 in. **Overall Length:** (505) 186.6 in.; (504 wagon) 194.4 in.; (604) 192.3 in. **Height:** (505) 57.1 in.; (504 wagon) 61 in.; (604) 56.3 in. **Width:** (505) 68.3 in.; (504) 66.7 in.; (604) 69.7 in. **Front Tread:** (505) 57.5 in.; (504) 56 in.; (604) 58.7 in. **Rear Tread:** (505) 56.4 in.; (504) 53.5 in.; (604) 56.3 in. **Standard Tires:** (505) 175x14; (604) 190/65HR390.

TECHNICAL: Layout: front-engine, rear-drive. **Transmission:** five-speed manual except (diesel/turbodiesel) four-speed manual; three-speed automatic available. **Steering:** power rack and pinion. **Suspension (front):** modified MacPherson struts with lower control arms, coil springs and anti-roll bar. **Suspension (rear):** independent, semi-trailing arms with coil springs and anti-roll bar except (504 wagon) rigid axle with coil springs. **Brakes:** front/rear disc. **Body Construction:** steel unibody.

MAJOR OPTIONS: Automatic transmission ($360). 'S' package ($2530). Air conditioning.

Note: Option prices shown above were valid in 1981.

Manufacturer: Peugeot S.A., Paris, France.

Distributor: Peugeot Motors of America Inc., Lyndhurst, New Jersey.

HISTORY: The revised 505 sedan debuted in mid-1980 for the U.S. market. Availability of the gasoline-engine 604 sedan in the U.S. market faded away during this period, but a turbodiesel version would emerge for the 1982 model year.

1982 PEUGEOT

505/504 — FOUR — Production of the 505 sedan and 504 station wagon continued with little change. The station wagon came only with a diesel engine, and its design dated back to 1968. Three trim levels of the 505 sedan were offered. A turbodiesel had been added in 1981, giving three engine possibilities for the sedan. An 'S' package included air conditioning, an electric sunroof, power windows, alloy wheels, central locking, and driver's-seat height adjustment.

604 TD — FOUR — A turbodiesel four powered the modified 604 sedan, instead of the former gasoline V-6. The same engine was used in the 505 Turbodiesel. Except for its engine, the new 604 was similar to the sedan that had faded away in 1980. Standard equipment included a sunroof, air conditioning, power windows, Michelin TRX tires on alloy wheels, and a stereo radio with cassette player. A five-speed gearbox was standard; three-speed automatic optional.

I.D. DATA: Peugeot's 17-digit Vehicle Identification Number is on the upper left of the dashboard, visible through the windshield. Symbols 1-3 ('VF3') indicate country and manufacturer. Symbol four identifies the model, five the body style, six the engine, seven the restraint system. Symbol eight identifies the transmission, folowed by a check digit. Symbol 10 denotes the model year ('C' = 1982); symbol 11 ('S'), the assembly plant. The six final digits form the sequential serial number, starting with 000001.

Model	Body Type & Seating	Engine Type/CID	P.O.E. Price	Weight (lbs.)	Prod. Total
505/504					
505	4-dr Sedan-5P	I4/120	10990	2965	Note 1
505 S	4-dr Sedan-5P	I4/120	13990	3075	Note 1
505 STI	4-dr Sedan-5P	I4/120	14990	3075	Note 1
505 (Dsl)	4-dr Sedan-5P	I4/141	12390	3130	Note 1
504 (Dsl)	4-dr Sta Wag-5P	I4/141	11900	3410	Note 1
505/604 TURBODIESEL					
505	4-dr Sedan-5P	I4/141	13570	3140	Note 1
505 S	4-dr Sedan-5P	I4/141	16175	3250	Note 1
604 TD	4-dr Sedan-5P	I4/141	19595	3500	Note 1

Note 1: A total of 14,323 Peugeots were sold in the U.S. during 1982.

ENGINE DATA: BASE FOUR: Inline, overhead-valve four-cylinder. Cast iron block and light alloy head. **Displacement:** 120.3 cu. in. (1971 cc). **Bore & Stroke:** 3.46 x 3.19 (88 x 81 mm). **Compression Ratio:** 8.35:1. **Brake Horsepower:** 96 at 4900 rpm. **Torque:** 116 lbs.-ft. at 3000 rpm. Five main bearings. Fuel injection.

DIESEL FOUR: Inline, overhead-valve four-cylinder. Cast iron block. **Displacement:** 140.6 cu. in. (2304 cc). **Bore & Stroke:** 3.70 x 3.27 (94 x 83 mm). **Compression Ratio:** 23.0:1. **Brake Horsepower:** 71 at 4500 rpm. **Torque:** 99 lbs.-ft. at 2500 rpm. Five main bearings. Fuel injection.

TURBODIESEL FOUR: Inline, overhead-valve four-cylinder. Cast iron block. **Displacement:** 140.6 cu. in. (2304 cc). **Bore & Stroke:** 3.70 x 3.27 (94 x 83 mm). **Compression Ratio:** 21.0:1. **Brake Horsepower:** 80 at 4150 rpm. **Torque:** 136 lbs.-ft. at 2000 rpm. Five main bearings. Fuel injection.

CHASSIS DATA: Wheelbase: (505) 107.9 in.; (504 wagon) 114 in.; (604) 110.2 in. **Overall Length:** (505) 186.7 in.; (504 wagon) 194.4 in.; (604) 192.3 in. **Height:** (505) 56.4 in.; (504 wagon) 61 in.; (604) 56.3 in. **Width:** (505) 68.4 in.; (504 wagon) 66.7 in.; (604) 69.7 in. **Front Tread:** (505) 57.5 in.; (504 wagon) 56 in.; (604) 58.7 in. **Rear Tread:** (505) 56.5 in.; (504 wagon) 53.5 in.; (604) 56.3 in.

TECHNICAL: Layout: front-engine, rear-drive. **Transmission:** five-speed manual except (diesel/turbodiesel) four-speed manual; three-speed automatic available. **Steering:** power rack and pinion. **Suspension (front):** modified MacPherson struts with lower control arms, coil springs and anti-roll bar. **Suspension (rear):** independent, semi-trailing arms with coil springs and anti-roll bar except (504 wagon) rigid axle with coil springs. **Brakes:** front/rear disc. **Body Construction:** steel unibody.

MAJOR OPTIONS: Leather upholstery: 505 Turbodiesel ($675). Metallic paint: 505/504 ($295); 604 ($375). Taxi-Yellow paint ($195).

Manufacturer: Peugeot S.A., Paris, France.

Distributor: Peugeot Motors of America Inc., Lyndhurst, New Jersey.

HISTORY: Peugeot's 1982 models were introduced to the U.S. market In September 1981.

1983 PEUGEOT

1983 Peugeot 505 S four-door sedan.

505/504 — FOUR — Little change was evident on the four-door sedan series, except for a few equipment and option revisions. Both base and sporty (STI) gas-engine models appeared again, along with the diesel-powered and turbodiesel versions. All models added a maintenance-free battery this year, and were wired for foglamp installation. Door and dashboard trim was darker in color than before. A leather-wrapped steering wheel went into the STI. Diesel-engine models added a water-in-fuel warning. The leather upholstery option now included a heated driver's seat. A 505 station wagon had debuted in Europe early in 1982, but did not enter the U.S. market; only the 504 diesel wagon was offered. Standard 505 equipment included power brakes and steering, tinted glass, electric rear defroster, reclining front bucket seats, velour upholstery, rear center armrest, clock, intermittent wipers, full carpeting, bodyside protection moldings, passenger assist handles, and a trip odometer. Gas-engine models included a tachometer. The 505 S added a power sunroof, power windows, AM/FM stereo with cassette player and power antenna, central locking, alloy wheels, and driver's seat height adjustment. The gas-engine 505 S included cruise control. Extras on the 505 STI included an uprated suspension, leather upholstery, special paint, and Michelin TRX radial tires.

604 — FOUR — The older Peugeot sedan model, on a longer (110.2-inch) wheelbase, came only with the Turbodiesel engine but was otherwise similar to the 505.

I.D. DATA: Peugeot's 17-digit Vehicle Identification Number is on the upper left of the dashboard, visible through the windshield. Symbols 1-3 ('VF3') indicate country and manufacturer. Symbol four identifies the model, five the body style, six the engine, seven the restraint system. Symbol eight identifies the transmission, followed by a check digit. Symbol 10 denotes the model year ('D' = 1983); symbol 11, the assembly plant. The six final digits form the sequential serial number, starting with 000001.

Model	Body Type & Seating	Engine Type/CID	P.O.E. Price	Weight (lbs.)	Prod. Total
505/504					
505	4-dr Sedan-5P	I4/120	11865	3020	Note 1
505 S	4-dr Sedan-5P	I4/120	14175	N/A	Note 1
505 STI	4-dr Sedan-5P	I4/120	15215	N/A	Note 1
505 (Dsl)	4-dr Sedan-5P	I4/141	12575	3190	Note 1
504 (Dsl)	4-dr Sta Wag-5P	I4/141	12085	3300	Note 1
505/604 TURBODIESEL					
505	4-dr Sedan-5P	I4/141	14445	3250	Note 1
505 S	4-dr Sedan-5P	I4/141	16360	N/A	Note 1
604	4-dr Sedan-5P	I4/141	19780	3500	Note 1

Note 1: A total of 15,241 Peugeots were sold in the U.S. in 1983.
Price Note: Automatic transmission added $370 to prices shown. 604 Turbodiesel with leather interior sold for $20,510 with five-speed and $20,910 with automatic.

ENGINE DATA: BASE FOUR: Inline, overhead-valve four-cylinder. Cast iron block and light alloy head. **Displacement:** 120.3 cu. in. (1971 cc). **Bore & Stroke:** 3.46 x 3.19 (88 x 81 mm). **Compression Ratio:** 8.35:1. **Brake Horsepower:** 97 at 5000 rpm. **Torque:** 116 lbs.-ft. at 3500 rpm. Five main bearings. Fuel injection.
DIESEL FOUR: Inline, overhead-valve four-cylinder. Cast iron block and light alloy head. **Displacement:** 140.6 cu. in. (2304 cc). **Bore & Stroke:** 3.70 x 3.27 (94 x 83 mm). **Compression Ratio:** 23.0:1. **Brake Horsepower:** 71 at 4500 rpm. **Torque:** 99 lbs.-ft. at 2500 rpm. Five main bearings. Fuel injection.
TURBODIESEL FOUR: Inline, overhead-valve four-cylinder. Cast iron block and light alloy head. **Displacement:** 140.6 cu. in. (2304 cc). **Bore & Stroke:** 3.70 x 3.27 (94 x 83 mm). **Compression Ratio:** 21.0:1. **Brake Horsepower:** 80 at 4150 rpm. **Torque:** 136 lbs.-ft. at 2000 rpm. Five main bearings. Fuel injection.

CHASSIS DATA: Wheelbase: (505) 107.9 in.; (604) 110.2 in. **Overall Length:** (505) 186.7 in.; (604) 192.3 in. **Height:** (505) 56.4 in.; (604) 56.3 in. **Width:** (505) 68.4 in.; (604) 69.7 in. **Front Tread:** (505) 57.5 in.; (604) 58.7 in. **Rear Tread:** (505) 56.5 in.; (604) 56.3 in.

TECHNICAL: Layout: front-engine, rear-drive. **Transmission:** five-speed manual except (diesel/turbodiesel) four-speed manual; three-speed automatic available. **Standard Final Drive Ratio:** (505 w/manual) 3.58:1; (505 w/auto.) 3.88:1; (diesel w/manual) 3.70:1; (diesel w/auto.) 3.78:1; (turbo w/manual) 3.58:1; (turbo w/auto) 3.08:1. **Steering:** power rack and pinion. **Suspension (front):** modified MacPherson struts with lower control arms, coil springs and anti-roll bar. **Suspension (rear):** independent, semi-trailing arms with coil springs and anti-roll bar. **Brakes:** front/rear disc. **Body Construction:** steel unibody. **Fuel Tank:** 18.0 gallon.

MAJOR OPTIONS: Leather upholstery: 505 Turbodiesel ($675). Metallic paint: 505/504 ($295); 604 ($375). Taxi-Yellow paint ($195).

Manufacturer: Peugeot S.A., Paris, France.

Distributor: Peugeot Motors of America Inc., Lyndhurst, New Jersey.

1984 PEUGEOT

505 — FOUR — A new 505 gas-engined station wagon arrived this year, on a longer (114.2-inch) wheelbase, offering 79.1 cubic feet of cargo space. Two versions were offered: basic GL and upper-rung S, with either the 2.0-liter four-cylinder gas engine or the 2.3-liter turbodiesel. The wagon used a different rear suspension than the sedan, with a live axle and variable-rate coil springs. Sedans came in three price levels this season: GL, S, and the sporty STI. A revised front end displayed dual rectangular halogen headlamps instead of the former quad round units. STI models included leather upholstery and heated seat (also optional on other models).

604 — FOUR — As before, the 604 sedan rode a longer (110.2-inch) wheelbase than the 505 version, but was otherwise similar. It came only with turbodiesel power.

I.D. DATA: Peugeot's 17-digit Vehicle Identification Number is on the upper left of the dashboard, visible through the windshield. Symbols 1-3 ('VF3') indicate country and manufacturer. Symbol four identifies the model, five the body style, six the engine, seven the restraint system. Symbol eight identifies the transmission, followed by a check digit. Symbol 10 denotes the model year ('E' = 1984); symbol 11, the assembly plant. The six final digits form the sequential serial number, starting with 000001.

Model	Body Type & Seating	Engine Type/CID	P.O.E. Price	Weight (lbs.)	Prod. Total
505 GL	4-dr Sedan-5P	I4/120	11300	3020	Note 1
505 S	4-dr Sedan-5P	I4/120	14845	3250	Note 1
505 STI	4-dr Sedan-5P	I4/120	15800	3020	Note 1
505 GL	4-dr Sta Wag-5P	I4/120	11990	3230	Note 1
505 S	4-dr Sta Wag-5P	I4/120	16495	3240	Note 1
505/604 TURBODIESEL					
505 GL	4-dr Sedan-5P	I4/141	12800	3250	Note 1
505 S	4-dr Sedan-5P	I4/141	16345	3250	Note 1
505 STI	4-dr Sedan-5P	I4/141	17300	3250	Note 1
505 GL	4-dr Sta Wag-5P	I4/141	13860	3430	Note 1
505 S	4-dr Sta Wag-5P	I4/141	17965	3430	Note 1
604	4-dr Sedan-5P	I4/141	20885	3500	Note 1

Note 1: A total of 20,007 Peugeots were sold in the U.S. in 1984.

ENGINE DATA: BASE FOUR: Inline, overhead-valve four-cylinder. Cast iron block and light alloy head. **Displacement:** 120.3 cu. in. (1971 cc). **Bore & Stroke:** 3.46 x 3.19 (88 x 81 mm). **Compression Ratio:** 8.35:1. **Brake Horsepower:** 97 at 5000 rpm. **Torque:** 116 lbs.-ft. at 3500 rpm. Five main bearings. Fuel injection.
OPTIONAL DIESEL FOUR: Inline, overhead-valve four-cylinder. Cast iron block and light alloy head. **Displacement:** 140.6 cu. in. (2304 cc). **Bore & Stroke:** 3.70 x 3.27 (94 x 83 mm). **Compression Ratio:** 23.0:1. **Brake Horsepower:** 71 at 4500 rpm. **Torque:** 99 lbs.-ft. at 2500 rpm. Five main bearings. Fuel injection.
Diesel Note: Availability of the non-turbo diesel engine diminished during 1984.
TURBODIESEL FOUR: Inline, overhead-valve four-cylinder. Cast iron block and light alloy head. **Displacement:** 140.6 cu. in. (2304 cc). **Bore & Stroke:** 3.70 x 3.27 (94 x 83 mm). **Compression Ratio:** 21.0:1. **Brake Horsepower:** 80 at 4150 rpm. **Torque:** 136 lbs.-ft. at 2000 rpm. Five main bearings. Fuel injection.

CHASSIS DATA: Wheelbase: (505 sed) 107.9 in.; (505 wag) 114.2 in.; (604) 110.2 In. **Overall Length:** (505 sed) 186.7 in.; (505 wag) 198.9 in.; (604) 192.3 in. **Height:** (505 sed) 56.4 in.; (505 wag) 58.3 in.; (604) 56.3 in. **Width:** (505) 68.4 in.; (604) 69.7 in. **Front Tread:** (505 sed) 57.5 in.; (505 wag) 61.1 in.; (604) 58.7 in. **Rear Tread:** (505 sed) 56.5 in.; (505 wag) 57.1 in.; (604) 56.3 in. **Standard Tires:** (505) 175HR14; (505 diesel) 175SR14; (604) Michelin TRX 190/65HR390.

TECHNICAL: Layout: front-engine, rear-drive. **Transmission:** five-speed manual except (diesel) four-speed manual; three-speed automatic available. **Standard Final Drive Ratio:** (505 w/manual) 3.58:1; (505 w/auto.) 3.88:1; (diesel w/manual) 3.70:1; (diesel w/auto.) 3.78:1; (turbo w/auto) 3.08:1. **Steering:** power rack and pinion. **Suspension (front):** modified MacPherson struts with lower control arms, coil springs and anti-roll bar. **Suspension (rear):** (sedan) independent, semi-trailing arms with coil springs and anti-roll bar; (wagon) live axle with variable-rate coil springs. **Brakes:** front/rear disc. **Body Construction:** steel unibody. **Fuel Tank:** 18.0 gallon.

MAJOR OPTIONS: 'S' package: 505 gas ($2310); 505 Turbodiesel ($1915). STI package: 505 gas ($3350). Automatic transmission: 505 ($370); 604 ($400). Air conditioning: 505 diesel ($690). Leather upholstery: 505 Turbodiesel ($675); 604 ($730). Metallic paint: 505 ($295); 604 ($375). Taxi-Yellow paint ($195).

Manufacturer: Peugeot S.A., Paris, France.

Distributor: Peugeot Motors of America Inc., Lyndhurst, New Jersey.

HISTORY: Peugeot's 1984 models were introduced to the U.S. market in October 1983.

497

1985 PEUGEOT

1985 Peugeot 505 STI sport sedan.

505 — FOUR — A new 505 Turbo sedan joined the non-turbo gas-engined models and turbodiesels, carrying a 2.2-liter overhead-cam four. Displaying a front air dam and rear spoiler, the Turbo wore 15-inch spoke-type alloy wheels and came only with the five-speed manual gearbox. The normally-aspirated diesel engine was dropped, and a new 2.5-liter turbodiesel added (for sedans only), joining the former 2.3-liter turbodiesel that was available in station wagons. Base engine remained the 2.0-liter gas four. A change in the method for measuring cargo volume allowed Peugeot to claim 92.5 cubic feet for the station wagons.

Note: The 604 sedan was dropped after 1984, as a result of poor sales.

I.D. DATA: Peugeot's 17-digit Vehicle Identification Number is on the upper left of the dashboard, visible through the windshield. Symbols 1-3 ('VF3') indicate country and manufacturer. Symbol four ('B') identifies the model, five the body style ('A' = sedan; 'D' = wagon), six the engine, seven the restraint system. Symbol eight identifies the transmission, followed by a check digit. Symbol 10 denotes the model year ('F' = 1985); symbol 11 ('S'), the assembly plant. The six final digits form the sequential serial number, starting with 000001.

Model	Body Type & Seating	Engine Type/CID	P.O.E. Price	Weight (lbs.)	Prod. Total
505 GL	4-dr Sedan-5P	I4/120	11900	3020	Note 1
505 S	4-dr Sedan-5P	I4/120	15580	3075	Note 1
505 STI	4-dr Sedan-5P	I4/120	16630	3075	Note 1
505 Turbo	4-dr Sedan-5P	I4/131	18150	3131	Note 1
505 GL	4-dr Sta Wag-5P	I4/120	12440	3230	Note 1
505 S	4-dr Sta Wag-5P	I4/120	17075	3230	Note 1
505 TURBODIESEL					
505 GL	4-dr Sedan-5P	I4/152	13220	3197	Note 1
505 S	4-dr Sedan-5P	I4/152	16900	3252	Note 1
505 STI	4-dr Sedan-5P	I4/152	17950	3252	Note 1
505 GL	4-dr Sta Wag-5P	I4/141	13860	3417	Note 1
505 S	4-dr Sta Wag-5P	I4/141	17965	3417	Note 1

Note 1: A total of 15,636 Peugeots were sold in the U.S. in 1985.
Price Note: An automatic transmission added $380 to prices shown.

1985 Peugeot 505 station wagon.

ENGINE DATA: BASE FOUR: Inline, overhead-valve four-cylinder. Cast iron block and light alloy head. **Displacement:** 120.3 cu. in. (1971 cc). **Bore & Stroke:** 3.46 x 3.19 (88 x 81 mm). **Compression Ratio:** 8.35:1. **Brake Horsepower:** 97 at 5000 rpm. **Torque:** 116 lbs.-ft. at 3500 rpm. Five main bearings. Fuel injection.

TURBO FOUR (505 Turbo): Inline, overhead-cam four-cylinder. Cast iron block and light alloy head. **Displacement:** 131.5 cu. in. (2155 cc). **Bore & Stroke:** 3.61 x 3.21 (91.7 x 81.6 mm). **Compression Ratio:** 7.0:1. **Brake Horsepower:** 142 at 5600 rpm. **Torque:** 163 lbs.-ft. at 3800 rpm. Five main bearings. Fuel injection.

TURBODIESEL FOUR (505 station wagons): Inline, overhead-valve four-cylinder. Cast iron block and light alloy head. **Displacement:** 140.6 cu. in. (2304 cc). **Bore & Stroke:** 3.70 x 3.26 (94 x 83 mm). **Compression Ratio:** 21.1:1. **Brake Horsepower:** 80 at 4150 rpm. **Torque:** 136 lbs.-ft. at 2000 rpm. Five main bearings. Fuel injection.

TURBODIESEL FOUR (505 sedans): Inline, overhead-valve four-cylinder. Cast iron block and light alloy head. **Displacement:** 152.4 cu. in. (2498 cc). **Bore & Stroke:** 3.70 x 3.52 (94 x 89.4 mm). **Compression Ratio:** 21.0:1. **Brake Horsepower:** 95 at 4150 rpm. **Torque:** 133 lbs.-ft. at 2000 rpm. Five main bearings. Fuel injection.

CHASSIS DATA: Wheelbase: (sed) 107.9 in.; (wag) 114.2 in. **Overall Length:** (sed) 186.7 in.; (wag) 198.9 in. **Height:** (sed) 56.4 in.; (wag) 58.3 in. **Width:** 68.4 in. **Front Tread:** (sed) 57.5 in.; (wag) 61.1 in. **Rear Tread:** (sed) 56.5 in.; (wag) 57.1 in. **Standard Tires:** 175/SR14 Michelin XZX except (STI) Michelin TRX; (Turbo) 195/60HR15 Michelin MXV speed-rated.

TECHNICAL: Layout: front-engine, rear-drive. **Transmission:** five-speed manual; three-speed automatic available. **Standard Final Drive Ratio:** (505 w/manual) 3.58:1 except (STI) 4.11:1; (505 w/auto.) 3.89:1; (Turbo) 3.46:1; (turbodiesel) 3.46:1 except (sedan w/auto.) 2.87:1. **Steering:** power rack and pinion. **Suspension (front):** modified MacPherson struts with lower control arms, coil springs and anti-roll bar. **Suspension (rear):** (sedan) independent, semi-trailing arms with coil springs and anti-roll bar; (wagon) live axle with variable-rate coil springs. **Brakes:** front/rear disc. **Body Construction:** steel unibody. **Fuel Tank:** 18.0 gallon.

MAJOR OPTIONS: Air conditioning: GL ($750). Leather upholstery: Turbo, S wagon ($675). Metallic paint: GL ($350).

Manufacturer: Peugeot S.A., Paris, France.

Distributor: Peugeot Motors of America Inc., Lyndhurst, New Jersey.

HISTORY: Peugeot's 1985 models were introduced to the U.S. market in October 1984.

1986 PEUGEOT

505 — FOUR — A Turbo version of the Peugeot station wagon joined the lineup this year, with body and suspension modifications similar to those of the Turbo sedan. It rode the same 15-inch alloy wheels, too. Turbo horsepower got a boost to 150 bhp, as a result of a smaller turbocharger unit with intercooler and water-cooled bearing. Four-speed automatic also became available in the Turbo models. New interiors on all models included a restyled dashboard, new seats with adjustable lumbar support, four-way adjustable headrests, and new upholstery. An Alpine sound system was installed in all models, but upscale editions got six speakers plus a cassette player and graphic equalizer.

I.D. DATA: Peugeot's 17-digit Vehicle Identification Number is on the upper left of the dashboard, visible through the windshield. Symbols 1-3 ('VF3') indicate country and manufacturer. Symbol four ('B') identifies the model, five the body style ('A' = sedan; 'D' = wagon), six the engine, seven the restraint system. Symbol eight identifies the transmission, followed by a check digit. Symbol 10 denotes the model year ('G' = 1986); symbol 11 ('S'), the assembly plant. The six final digits form the sequential serial number, starting with 000001.

Model	Body Type & Seating	Engine Type/CID	P.O.E. Price	Weight (lbs.)	Prod. Total
505 GL	4-dr Sedan-5P	I4/120	12615	2915	Note 1
505 S	4-dr Sedan-5P	I4/120	15965	3065	Note 1
505 STI	4-dr Sedan-5P	I4/120	17065	3065	Note 1
505 Turbo	4-dr Sedan-5P	I4/131	18740	3155	Note 1
GL Turbo	4-dr Sedan-5P	I4/131	16465	3100	Note 1
505 GL	4-dr Sta Wag-5P	I4/120	13185	3120	Note 1
505 S	4-dr Sta Wag-5P	I4/120	17130	3220	Note 1
505 Turbo	4-dr Sta Wag-5P	I4/131	20435	3280	Note 1
505 TURBODIESEL					
505 S	4-dr Sedan-5P	I4/152	17950	3235	Note 1
505 S	4-dr Sta Wag-5P	I4/141	19600	3420	Note 1

Note 1: A total of 14,296 Peugeots were sold in the U.S. in 1986.
Price Note: An automatic transmission added $550 to prices shown.
Turbodiesel Note: Peugeots with the turbodiesel engine were not listed in all directories of imported cars for the 1986 model year.

ENGINE DATA: BASE FOUR: Inline, overhead-valve four-cylinder. Cast iron block and light alloy head. **Displacement:** 120.3 cu. in. (1971 cc). **Bore & Stroke:** 3.46 x 3.19 (88 x 81 mm). **Compression Ratio:** 8.35:1. **Brake Horsepower:** 97 at 5000 rpm. **Torque:** 116 lbs.-ft. at 3500 rpm. Five main bearings. Multi-point fuel injection.

TURBO FOUR (505 Turbo): Inline, overhead-cam four-cylinder. Cast iron block and light alloy head. **Displacement:** 131.5 cu. in. (2155 cc). **Bore & Stroke:** 3.61 x 3.21 (91.7 x 81.6 mm). **Compression Ratio:** 7.0:1. **Brake Horsepower:** 150 at 5200 rpm. **Torque:** 184 lbs.-ft. at 2500 rpm. Five main bearings. Multi-point fuel injection.

TURBODIESEL FOUR (505 station wagons): Inline, overhead-valve four-cylinder. Cast iron block and light alloy head. **Displacement:** 140.6 cu. in. (2304 cc). **Bore & Stroke:** 3.70 x 3.26 (94 x 83 mm). **Compression Ratio:** 21.1:1. **Brake Horsepower:** 80 at 4150 rpm. **Torque:** 136 lbs.-ft. at 2000 rpm. Five main bearings. Fuel injection.

TURBODIESEL FOUR (505 sedans): Inline, overhead-valve four-cylinder. Cast iron block and light alloy head. **Displacement:** 152.4 cu. in. (2498 cc). **Bore & Stroke:** 3.70 x 3.52 (94 x 89.4 mm). **Compression Ratio:** 21.0:1. **Brake Horsepower:** 95 at 4150 rpm. **Torque:** 133 lbs.-ft. at 2000 rpm. Five main bearings. Fuel injection.

CHASSIS DATA: Wheelbase: (sed) 107.9 in.; (wag) 114.2 in. **Overall Length:** (sed) 186.7 in.; (wag) 198.9 in. **Height:** (sed) 56.4 in.; (wag) 58.3 in. **Width:** 68.4 in. **Front Tread:** (sed) 57.5 in.; (wag) 61.1 in. **Rear Tread:** (sed) 56.5 in.; (wag) 57.1 in. **Standard Tires:** 175/SR14 Michelin XZX except (STI) Michelin TRX; (Turbo) 195/60HR15 Michelin MXV speed-rated.

TECHNICAL: Layout: front-engine, rear-drive. **Transmission:** five-speed manual; three-speed automatic available (four-speed in Turbo). **Standard Final Drive Ratio:** (505 w/manual) 3.58:1; (505 w/auto.) 3.89:1; (Turbo) 3.46:1. **Steering:** power rack and pinion. **Suspension (front):** modified MacPherson struts with lower control arms, coil springs and anti-roll bar. **Suspension (rear):** (sedan) independent, semi-trailing arms with coil springs and anti-roll bar; (wagon) live axle with variable-rate coil springs. **Brakes:** front/rear disc. **Body Construction:** steel unibody. **Fuel Tank:** 18.0 gallon.

MAJOR OPTIONS: Air conditioning: GL ($910). Leather upholstery: Turbo, S wagon ($750-$775). Metallic paint: GL/S/STI ($355).

Manufacturer: Peugeot S.A., Paris, France.

Distributor: Peugeot Motors of America Inc., Lyndhurst, New Jersey.

HISTORY: Peugeot's 1986 models were introduced to the U.S. market in October 1985.

1987 PEUGEOT

505 — FOUR/V-6 — Two new engines became available this year: a 2.2-liter overhead-cam four, rated 120 horsepower, made standard in most GL, GLS and STI models; and a 145-bhp, 2.8-liter V-6 (used in the STI/STX V-6 sedans). Teves anti-lock braking became standard in the STX and Turbo S sedans, and optional in the STI V-6 model. A limited-production Liberte series, intended to commemorate the 100th anniversary of the Statue of Liberty, came with the former 2.0-liter overhead-valve four and automatic transmission. Peugeot's 2.5-liter turbodiesel engine gained electronic (formerly mechanical) fuel injection.

I.D. DATA: Peugeot's 17-digit Vehicle Identification Number is on the upper left of the dashboard, visible through the windshield. Symbols 1-3 ('VF3') indicate country and manufacturer. Symbol four ('B') identifies the model, five the body style ('A' = sedan; 'D' = wagon), six the engine, seven the restraint system. Symbol eight identifies the transmission, followed by a check digit. Symbol 10 denotes the model year ('H' = 1987); symbol 11 ('S'), the assembly plant. The six final digits form the sequential serial number, starting with 000001.

Model	Body Type & Seating	Engine Type/CID	P.O.E. Price	Weight (lbs.)	Prod. Total
505 GL	4-dr Sedan-5P	I4/132	13900	2870	Note 1
505 GLS	4-dr Sedan-5P	I4/132	15950	2920	Note 1
505 Turbo	4-dr Sedan-5P	I4/131	18650	3075	Note 1
Turbo S	4-dr Sedan-5P	I4/131	22600	3140	Note 1
505 STI	4-dr Sedan-5P	I4/132	18400	3030	Note 1
505 STI	4-dr Sedan-5P	V6/174	20700	3120	Note 1
505 STX	4-dr Sedan-5P	V6/174	23250	3135	Note 1
Liberte	4-dr Sedan-5P	I4/120	15600	3090	Note 1
Liberte	4-dr Sta Wag-5P	I4/120	16600	3245	Note 1
505 Turbo	4-dr Sta Wag-5P	I4/131	19980	3360	Note 1
Turbo S	4-dr Sta Wag-5P	I4/131	22250	3405	Note 1
505 TURBODIESEL					
505 GLS	4-dr Sedan-5P	I4/152	18100	3160	Note 1
505 GLS	4-dr Sta Wag-5P	I4/152	18900	3175	Note 1

Note 1: A total of 9,422 Peugeots were sold in the U.S. in 1987.

ENGINE DATA: BASE FOUR (Liberte): Inline, overhead-valve four-cylinder. Cast iron block and light alloy head. **Displacement:** 120.3 cu. in. (1971 cc). **Bore & Stroke:** 3.46 x 3.19 (88 x 81 mm). **Compression Ratio:** 8.3:1. **Brake Horsepower:** 97 at 5000 rpm. **Torque:** 116 lbs.-ft. at 3500 rpm. Five main bearings. Multi-point fuel injection.

BASE FOUR (505 GL/GLS/STI): Inline, overhead-cam four-cylinder. Aluminum alloy block and head. **Displacement:** 132.1 cu. in. (2165 cc). **Bore & Stroke:** 3.46 x 3.50 (88 x 89 mm). **Compression Ratio:** 8.8:1. **Brake Horsepower:** 120 at 5000 rpm. **Torque:** 131 lbs.-ft. at 3500 rpm. Five main bearings. Multi-point fuel injection.

TURBO FOUR (505 Turbo): Inline, overhead-cam four-cylinder. Cast iron block and aluminum alloy head. **Displacement:** 131.5 cu. in. (2155 cc). **Bore & Stroke:** 3.61 x 3.21 (91.7 x 81.6 mm). **Compression Ratio:** 7.5:1. **Brake Horsepower:** 150 at 5200 rpm. **Torque:** 180 lbs.-ft. at 2750 rpm. Five main bearings. Multi-point fuel injection.

TURBODIESEL FOUR: Inline, overhead-valve four-cylinder. Cast iron block and light alloy head. **Displacement:** 152.4 cu. in. (2498 cc). **Bore & Stroke:** 3.70 x 3.52 (94 x 89.4 mm). **Compression Ratio:** 21.0:1. **Brake Horsepower:** 95 at 4150 rpm. **Torque:** 133 lbs.-ft. at 2000 rpm. Five main bearings. Electronic fuel injection.

BASE V-6 (505 V-6): Overhead-cam, vee-type six-cylinder (Peugeot-Ranault-Volvo). Aluminum alloy block and heads. **Displacement:** 174 cu. in. (2849 cc). **Bore & Stroke:** 3.58 x 2.87 (91 x 73 mm). **Compression Ratio:** 9.5:1. **Brake Horsepower:** 145 at 5000 rpm. **Torque:** 173 lbs.-ft. at 3750 rpm. Multi-point fuel injection.

CHASSIS DATA: Wheelbase: (sed) 108.0 in.; (wag) 114.2 in. **Overall Length:** (sed) 186.7 in.; (wag) 198.9 in. **Height:** (sed) 56.7 in.; (wag) 58.3 in. **Width:** (sed) 68.3 in.; (wag) 68.4 in. **Front Tread:** (sed) 58.4 in.; (wag) 58.9 in. **Rear Tread:** (sed) 56.9 in.; (wag) 57.2 in. **Standard Tires:** (sed) 185/70R14 Michelin MXL; (wag) 195/70R14; (STI) Michelin MXV 195/60R15; (Turbo) 205/60R15 Michelin MXV.

TECHNICAL: Layout: front-engine, rear-drive. **Transmission:** five-speed manual or four-speed automatic. **Steering:** power rack and pinion. **Suspension (front):** modified MacPherson struts with lower control arms, coil springs and anti-roll bar. **Suspension (rear):** (sedan) independent, semi-trailing arms with coil springs and anti-roll bar; (wagon) live axle with variable-rate coil springs. **Brakes:** front/rear disc. **Body Construction:** steel unibody. **Fuel Tank:** 18.0 gal.

MAJOR OPTIONS: Automatic transmission: GL ($700); others ($600). Air conditioning: GL ($910). Leather upholstery: Turbo/S sedan ($750); Turbo/S wagon ($775). Metallic paint ($355).

Manufacturer: Peugeot S.A., Paris, France.

Distributor: Peugeot Motors of America Inc., Lyndhurst, New Jersey.

HISTORY: Peugeot's 1987 models were introduced to the U.S. market in October 1986.

1988 PEUGEOT

505 — FOUR/V-6 — A more powerful turbocharged four became available this year, installed in the Turbo S sedan. The new intercooled engine produced 180 horsepower, versus 150 bhp for the former turbo. That version was offered in the Turbo S wagon. A 200-watt Alpine stereo radio with cassette player and 12 speakers became standard in the Turbo S sedan, optional in other models, and included anti-theft circuitry. The turbodiesel models were dropped this year. Base engine was the 2.2-liter four, rated 120 horsepower, offered in the new DL series as well as the higher-priced GLS/STI. Another station wagon, the SW8 (with eight-passenger seating) joined the lineup after the start of the model year. Standard DL equipment included power brakes/steering, limited-slip differential, automatic air conditioning, intermittent wipers, heated front bucket seats, central locking, tinted glass, and 185/70R14 tires. The GLS added power front windows, heated power mirrors, AM/FM stereo with cassette player, power sunroof, and cruise control, as well as velour trim. The STI added infrared remote-control locking, driver's seat height adjustment, adjustable lumbar support, power rear windows, leather steering wheel trim, Alpine stereo, and eight-spoke alloy wheels. The STX included anti-lock braking.

I.D. DATA: Peugeot's 17-digit Vehicle Identification Number is on the upper left of the dashboard, visible through the windshield. Symbols 1-3 ('VF3') indicate country and manufacturer. Symbol four ('B') identifies the model, five the body style, six the engine, seven the restraint system. Symbol eight identifies the transmission, followed by a check digit. Symbol 10 denotes the model year ('J' = 1988); symbol 11 ('S'), the assembly plant. The six final digits form the sequential serial number, starting with 420001.

Model	Body Type & Seating	Engine Type/CID	P.O.E. Price	Weight (lbs.)	Prod. Total
505 DL	4-dr Sedan-5P	I4/132	15495	2870	Note 1
505 GLS	4-dr Sedan-5P	I4/132	17775	2920	Note 1
Turbo S	4-dr Sedan-5P	I4/131	24615	3140	Note 1
505 STI	4-dr Sedan-5P	I4/132	20295	3085	Note 1
505 GLX	4-dr Sedan-5P	V6/174	19850	3040	Note 1
505 STX	4-dr Sedan-5P	V6/174	23995	3135	Note 1
505 DL	4-dr Sta Wag-5P	I4/132	16485	3130	Note 1
505 GLS	4-dr Sta Wag-5P	I4/132	17995	3175	Note 1
SW8	4-dr 3S Wag-8P	I4/132	18545	3260	Note 1
Turbo S	4-dr Sta Wag-5P	I4/131	23645	3405	Note 1

Note 1: A total of 6,713 Peugeots were sold in the U.S. in 1988.

Price Note: An automatic transmission added $625 to prices shown (except the STI sedan and Turbo wagon, which came with standard automatic).

ENGINE DATA: BASE FOUR (505): Inline, overhead-cam four-cylinder. Aluminum alloy block and head. **Displacement:** 132.1 cu. in. (2165 cc). **Bore & Stroke:** 3.46 x 3.50 (88 x 89 mm). **Compression Ratio:** 8.8:1. **Brake Horsepower:** 120 at 5000 rpm. **Torque:** 131 lbs.-ft. at 3500 rpm. Five main bearings. Multi-point fuel injection.

TURBO FOUR (505 Turbo Wagon): Inline, overhead-cam four-cylinder. Cast iron block and aluminum alloy head. **Displacement:** 131.5 cu. in. (2155 cc). **Bore & Stroke:** 3.61 x 3.21 (91.7 x 81.6 mm). **Compression Ratio:** 7.5:1. **Brake Horsepower:** 150 at 5000 rpm. **Torque:** 180 lbs.-ft. at 2750 rpm. Five main bearings. Multi-point fuel injection.

TURBO FOUR (505 Turbo S sedan): Same as turbocharged four above, but with intercooler — **Brake Horsepower:** 180 at 5200 rpm. **Torque:** 205 lbs.-ft. at 2500 rpm.

BASE V-6 (505 V-6): Overhead-cam, vee-type six-cylinder (Peugeot-Ranault-Volvo). Aluminum alloy block and heads. **Displacement:** 174 cu. in. (2849 cc). **Bore & Stroke:** 3.58 x 2.87 (91 x 73 mm). **Compression Ratio:** 9.5:1. **Brake Horsepower:** 145 at 5000 rpm. **Torque:** 173 lbs.-ft. at 3750 rpm. Multi-point fuel injection.

CHASSIS DATA: Wheelbase: (sed) 108.0 in.; (wag) 114.2 in. **Overall Length:** (sed) 186.7 in.; (wag) 198.9 in. **Height:** (sed) 56.7 in.; (wag) 58.3 in. **Width:** (sed) 68.3 in.; (wag) 68.4 in. **Front Tread:** (sed) 58.3 in.; (wag) 58.9 in. **Rear Tread:** (sed) 56.9 in.; (wag) 57.2 in. **Standard Tires:** (DL) 185/70R14 Michelin MXL/T; (GLS) 185/65R15 Michelin MXV/H.

TECHNICAL: Layout: front-engine, rear-drive. **Transmission:** five-speed manual; four-speed automatic. **Steering:** power rack and pinion. **Suspension (front):** modified MacPherson struts with lower control arms, coil springs and anti-roll bar. **Suspension (rear):** (sedan) independent, semi-trailing arms with coil springs and anti-roll bar; (wagon) live axle with variable-rate coil springs. **Brakes:** front/rear disc. **Body Construction:** steel unibody. **Fuel Tank:** 18.0 gal.

MAJOR OPTIONS: Leather upholstery: STI/STX/Turbo ($940). Metallic or special lacquered paint ($395). 200-watt AM/FM stereo system.

Manufacturer: Peugeot S.A., Paris, France.

Distributor: Peugeot Motors of America Inc., Lyndhurst, New Jersey.

HISTORY: Peugeot's 1988 models were introduced to the U.S. market in November 1987.

1989 PEUGEOT

1989 Peugeot 405 station wagon.

405 — FOUR — A new, smaller front-drive sedan joined the rear-drive 505 this year, riding a 105.1-inch wheelbase and measuring 177.7 inches overall. Each of the three models had four-wheel independent suspension, power rack-and-pinion steering, power four wheel disc brakes, central locking, automatic air conditioning, and an adjustable steering column. S and Mi 16 sedans also included a power moonroof, infrared remote locking, heated front seats, heated mirrors, power windows, cruise control, and alloy wheels. Leather upholstery was standard on the Mi 16, along with an Alpine anti-theft AM/FM stereo with cassette player, and larger (195/60R14) tires on alloy wheels. Anti-lock braking was optional on the Mi 16, and included in a Luxury Touring Package for the S model. A single-overhead-cam, 1.9-liter four-cylinder engine rated 110 horsepower powered the DL and S models; a twin-cam version, producing 150 bhp, went under Mi 16 hoods. A four-speed automatic transmission was optional on the DL and S, but the Mi 16 came only with five-speed manual shift.

505 — FOUR/V-6 — Appearance changes for 1989 included a deeper front air dam, integrated front and rear bumpers, wider bodyside moldings, and lowered side skirts and rear valance. A trunk-mounted wing spoiler was installed on the 505 Turbo, which carried a 180-bhp turbocharged four-cylinder engine (160-bhp in the wagon). Base powerplant was again a 2.2-liter four, rated 120 horsepower, while V-6 models carried a 2.8-liter overhead-cam V-6 engine. Turbo wagons came only with four-speed automatic transmission, while other models could have either the standard five-speed manual or optional automatic. SW8 wagons held eight passengers, with a third forward-facing seat. Anti-lock braking was standard in the Turbo sedan and the STX.

1989 Peugeot 405 DL four-door sedan.

I.D. DATA: Peugeot's 17-digit Vehicle Identification Number is on the upper left of the dashboard, visible through the windshield. Symbols 1-3 ('VF3') indicate country and manufacturer. Symbol four identifies the model ('B' = 505; 'D' = 405), five the body style ('A' = sedan; 'D' = wagon; 'F' = 8P wagon), six the engine, seven the restraint system. Symbol eight identifies the transmission, followed by a check digit. Symbol 10 denotes the model year ('K' = 1989); symbol 11 ('S'), the assembly plant. The six final digits form the sequential serial number. Starting serial number: (405) 500001; (505) 426001.

Model	Body Type & Seating	Engine Type/CID	P.O.E. Price	Weight (lbs.)	Prod. Total
405					
DL	4-dr Sedan-5P	I4/116	14500	2460	Note 1
S	4-dr Sedan-5P	I4/116	17700	2580	Note 1
Mi 16	4-dr Sedan-5P	I4/116	20700	2715	Note 1
505					
S	4-dr Sedan-5P	I4/132	19295	2998	Note 1
S	4-dr Sedan-5P	V6/174	21435	3086	Note 1
STX	4-dr Sedan-5P	V6/174	25895	3230	Note 1
Turbo	4-dr Sedan-5P	I4/131	26335	3230	Note 1
DL	4-dr Sta Wag-5P	I4/132	17590	3274	Note 1
Turbo	4-dr Sta Wag-5P	I4/131	25540	3440	Note 1
SW8	4-dr 3S Wag-8P	I4/132	19995	3296	Note 1
SW8 Turbo	4-dr 3S Wag-8P	I4/132	25695	3506	Note 1

Note 1: A total of 6,095 Peugeots were sold in the U.S. in 1989.

1989 Peugeot 505 Turbo station wagon.

ENGINE DATA: BASE FOUR (405): Inline, overhead-cam four-cylinder. Aluminum alloy block and head. **Displacement:** 116 cu. in. (1905 cc). **Bore & Stroke:** 3.27 x 3.46 (83 x 88 mm). **Compression Ratio:** 8.4:1. **Brake Horsepower:** 110 at 5200 rpm. **Torque:** 120 lbs.-ft. at 4250 rpm. Multi-point fuel injection.
BASE FOUR (Mi 16): Inline, dual-overhead-cam four-cylinder (16-valve). Aluminum alloy block and head. **Displacement:** 116 cu. in. (1905 cc). **Bore & Stroke:** 3.27 x 3.46 (83 x 88 mm). **Compression Ratio:** 9.5:1. **Brake Horsepower:** 150 at 6400 rpm. **Torque:** 128 lbs.-ft. at 5000 rpm. Multi-point fuel injection.
BASE FOUR (505): Inline, overhead-cam four-cylinder. Aluminum alloy block and head. **Displacement:** 132.1 cu. in. (2165 cc). **Bore & Stroke:** 3.46 x 3.50 (88 x 89 mm). **Compression Ratio:** 8.8:1. **Brake Horsepower:** 120 at 5000 rpm. **Torque:** 131 lbs.-ft. at 3500 rpm. Five main bearings. Multi-point fuel injection.
TURBO FOUR (505 Turbo Wagon): Inline, overhead-cam four-cylinder. Cast iron block and aluminum alloy head. **Displacement:** 131.5 cu. in. (2155 cc). **Bore & Stroke:** 3.61 x 3.21 (91.7 x 81.6 mm). **Compression Ratio:** 7.5:1. **Brake Horsepower:** 160 at 5000 rpm. **Torque:** 205 lbs.-ft. at 2500 rpm. Five main bearings. Multi-point fuel injection.
TURBO FOUR (505 Turbo sedan): Same as turbocharged four above, but with inter-cooler — **Brake Horsepower:** 180 at 5200 rpm. **Torque:** 205 lbs.-ft. at 2500 rpm.
BASE V-6 (505 V-6): 90-degree, overhead-cam, vee-type six-cylinder (Peugeot-Ranault-Volvo). Aluminum alloy block and heads. **Displacement:** 174 cu. in. (2849 cc). **Bore & Stroke:** 3.58 x 2.87 (91 x 73 mm). **Compression Ratio:** 9.5:1. **Brake Horsepower:** 145 at 5000 rpm. **Torque:** 176 lbs.-ft. at 2800 rpm. Multi-point fuel injection.

CHASSIS DATA: Wheelbase: (405) 105.1 in.; (505 sed) 108.0 in.; (505 wag) 114.2 in. **Overall Length:** (405) 177.7 in.; (505 sed) 181.4 in.; (505 wag) 194.5 in. **Height:** (405) 55.4 in.; (505 sed) 57.0 in.; (505 wag) 60.1 in. **Width:** (405) 67.6 in.; (505) 67.7 in. **Front Tread:** (405) 57.1 in.; (505) 58.7 in. **Rear Tread:** (405) 56.8 in.; (505 sed) 57.3 in.; (505 wag) 57.1 in. **Standard Tires:** (405) 185/65R14 Michelin MXV; (Mi 16) 195/60R14; (505) 185/65R15 Michelin MXV; (505 STX) 205/60HR15 Michelin MXV.

TECHNICAL: Layout: (405) front-engine, front-drive; (505) front-engine, rear-drive. **Transmission:** five-speed manual or four-speed automatic available. **Steering:** power rack and pinion. **Suspension (front):** modified MacPherson struts with lower control arms, coil springs and anti-roll bar. **Suspension (rear):** (405) independent, trailing arms with coil springs and anti-roll bar; (505 sedan) independent, semi-trailing arms with coil springs and anti-roll bar; (505 wagon) live axle with variable-rate coil springs. **Brakes:** front/rear disc. **Body Construction:** steel unibody. **Fuel Tank:** (405) 17.2 gal.; (505) 18.0 gal.

MAJOR OPTIONS: Four-speed automatic trans.: 405 DL/S, 505 ($650). Anti-lock braking: Mi 16. Leather pkg. incl. Alpine stereo: 405 S ($1300). Leather Touring pkg. incl. ABS: 405 S. Leather upholstery: 505 Turbo sed ($960). Metallic or black lacquered paint: 505 ($395). Metallic paint: 405 ($375).
Manufacturer: Peugeot S.A., Paris, France.
Distributor: Peugeot Motors of America Inc., Lyndhurst, New Jersey.
HISTORY: Peugeot's 1989 models were introduced in the U.S. in August 1988. Prior to its appearance in the U.S., the 405 had been voted 1987 "Car of the Year" in Europe, by a wide margin. Peugeot referred to the older 505 as a "contemporary classic."

1990 PEUGEOT

1990 Peugeot 405 S four-door sedan.

405 — FOUR — A Sportwagon designed by Pininfarina joined the original 405 sedan. Both came in DL and S trim, powered by the 110-bhp, 1.9-liter four. As before, the Mi 16 carried a 150-bhp twin-cam version of that engine; but added anti-lock braking this year, plus new 15-inch tires on alloy wheels. DL/S sedans added a reflective red strip at the rear.
505 — FOUR/V-6 — This year, a Turbo engine came only in the station wagon. Base engine remained the 2.2-liter four, rated 120 bhp. Otherwise, little change was evident.

I.D. DATA: Peugeot's 17-digit Vehicle Identification Number is on the upper left of the dashboard, visible through the windshield. As before, symbols 1-3 ('VF3') indicate country and manufacturer. Symbol four identifies the model, five the body style, six the engine, seven the restraint system. Symbol eight identifies the transmission, followed by a check digit. Symbol 10 denotes the model year ('L' = 1990); symbol 11 ('S'), the assembly plant. The six final digits form the sequential serial number. Starting serial number: (405) 515001.

Model	Body Type & Seating	Engine Type/CID	P.O.E. Price	Weight (lbs.)	Prod. Total
405					
DL	4-dr Sedan-5P	I4/116	15390	2460	Note 1
S	4-dr Sedan-5P	I4/116	17700	N/A	Note 1
DL	4-dr Sta Wag-5P	I4/116	15990	2680	Note 1
S	4-dr Sta Wag-5P	I4/116	18495	2753	Note 1
Mi 16	4-dr Sedan-5P	I4/116	21990	N/A	Note 1
505					
S	4-dr Sedan-5P	I4/132	19945	2998	Note 1
S	4-dr Sedan-5P	V6/174	22485	3086	Note 1
DL	4-dr Sta Wag-5P	I4/132	18590	3230	Note 1
SW8	4-dr 3S Wag-8P	I4/132	20400	3296	Note 1
Turbo	4-dr Sta Wag-5P	I4/131	25940	3440	Note 1
SW8 Turbo	4-dr 3S Wag-8P	I4/132	26100	3506	Note 1

Note 1: A total of 4,292 Peugeots were sold in the U.S. in 1990.

1990 Peugeot 505 station wagon.

1990 Peugeot 405 Mi 16 four-door sedan.

ENGINE DATA: BASE FOUR (405): Inline, overhead-cam four-cylinder. Aluminum alloy block and head. **Displacement:** 116 cu. in. (1905 cc). **Bore & Stroke:** 3.27 x 3.46 (83 x 88 mm). **Compression Ratio:** 8.4:1. **Brake Horsepower:** 110 at 5200 rpm. **Torque:** 120 lbs.-ft. at 4250 rpm. Multi-point fuel injection.

BASE FOUR (Mi 16): Inline, dual-overhead-cam four-cylinder (16-valve). Aluminum alloy block and head. **Displacement:** 116 cu. in. (1905 cc). **Bore & Stroke:** 3.27 x 3.46 (83 x 88 mm). **Compression Ratio:** 9.5:1. **Brake Horsepower:** 150 at 6400 rpm. **Torque:** 128 lbs.-ft. at 5000 rpm. Multi-point fuel injection.

BASE FOUR (505): Inline, overhead-cam four-cylinder. Aluminum alloy block and head. **Displacement:** 132.1 cu. in. (2165 cc). **Bore & Stroke:** 3.46 x 3.50 (88 x 89 mm). **Compression Ratio:** 8.8:1. **Brake Horsepower:** 120 at 5200 rpm. **Torque:** 131 lbs.-ft. at 3500 rpm. Five main bearings. Multi-point fuel injection.

TURBO FOUR (505 Turbo Wagon): Inline, overhead-cam four-cylinder. Cast iron block and aluminum alloy head. **Displacement:** 131.5 cu. in. (2155 cc). **Bore & Stroke:** 3.61 x 3.21 (91.7 x 81.6 mm). **Compression Ratio:** 7.5:1. **Brake Horsepower:** 160 at 5000 rpm. **Torque:** 205 lbs.-ft. at 2500 rpm. Five main bearings. Multi-point fuel injection.

BASE V-6 (505 V-6): 90-degree, overhead-cam, vee-type six-cylinder (Peugeot-Renault-Volvo). Aluminum alloy block and heads. **Displacement:** 174 cu. in. (2849 cc). **Bore & Stroke:** 3.58 x 2.87 (91 x 73 mm). **Compression Ratio:** 9.5:1. **Brake Horsepower:** 145 at 5000 rpm. **Torque:** 176 lbs.-ft. at 2800 rpm. Multi-point fuel injection.

CHASSIS DATA: Wheelbase: (405) 105.1 in.; (505 sed) 108.0 in.; (505 wag) 114.2 in. **Overall Length:** (405 sed) 177.7 in.; (405 wag) 175.1 in.; (505 sed) 181.4 in.; (505 wag) 194.5 in. **Height:** (405 sed) 55.4 in.; (405 wag) 56.0 in.; (505 sed) 57.0 in.; (505 wag) 60.1 in. **Width:** (405 sed) 67.6 in.; (405 wag) 67.5 in.; (505) 67.7 in. **Front Tread:** (405) 57.1 in.; (505) 58.7 in.; (505 Turbo) 59.1 in. **Rear Tread:** (405) 56.8 in.; (505) 57.3 in.; (505 wag) 57.1 in. **Standard Tires:** (405) 185/65R14 Michelin MXV; (Mi 16) 195/55x15 Michelin MXV2/V; (505) 185/65HR15 Michelin MXV.

TECHNICAL: Layout: (405) front-engine, front-drive; (505) front-engine, rear-drive. **Transmission:** five-speed manual or four-speed automatic available. **Steering:** power rack and pinion. **Suspension (front):** modified MacPherson struts with lower control arms, coil springs and anti-roll bar. **Suspension (rear):** (405) independent, trailing arms with coil springs and anti-roll bar; (505 sedan) independent, semi-trailing arms with coil springs and anti-roll bar; (505 wagon) live axle with variable-rate coil springs. **Brakes:** front/rear disc. **Body Construction:** steel unibody. **Fuel Tank:** (405) 17.2 gal.; (505) 18.0 gal.

MAJOR OPTIONS: Four-speed automatic trans.: 405, 505 wag ($650). Leather upholstery: 405 S sed ($990). Metallic or black lacquered paint: 405 ($375); 505 ($395).

Manufacturer: Peugeot S.A., Paris, France.

Distributor: Peugeot Motors of America Inc., Lyndhurst, New Jersey.

HISTORY: Peugeot's 1990 models were introduced to the U.S. market in August 1989.

POSTSCRIPT: After peaking at just over 20,000 U.S. sales in 1984 Peugeot slid steadily through the balance of the decade, bottoming close to the 4,200 mark in 1990. Peugeot's diesel engines had earned a fair share of popularity during the era of concern over fuel availability, but diesels quickly fell out of favor as gasoline prices stabilized. Rising competition in Peugeot's market niche didn't help, either. The 1990s showed no prospect for improvement, with only 2,223 cars sold in the first seven months of 1991. Therefore, in August 1991 Peugeot Motors of America announced that no more cars would be produced for the U.S. market. At the time, the company had 151 dealers in America.

PLYMOUTH (imports)

Two distinct series of passenger cars were imported by Chrysler under the Plymouth nameplate during the 1970s, from two different countries. The short-lived Cricket, marketed in the U.S. from 1971 to 1973, came from Britain. Virtually the same car was sold in England as the Hillman Avenger.

In 1976, five years after Chrysler began to import subcompacts from Japan, to be marketed under the Dodge name, the Plymouth nameplate gained its own line of Mitsubishi-built models. Though similar to the Dodge Colt,

with a comparable range of engines, Plymouth's Arrow series was slightly smaller. For 1978, the Arrow sedans were joined by a sporty Sapporo coupe, differing little from Dodge's Challenger. Front-wheel-drive Champ models, introduced for 1979, were equivalent to the reworked Dodge Colts. By 1983, a single Colt series was marketed by both Dodge and Plymouth dealers.

1971-73 PLYMOUTH

1971 Plymouth Cricket four-door sedan.

CRICKET — FOUR — A British-built four-door sedan entered the U.S. market under the Plymouth nameplate for the 1971 model year, priced as $1915 and billed as "the little car that can." The subcompact had curved side windows, quad round headlamps and a divided grille. A 91.4-cid four-cylinder engine produced 70 horsepower, to either a four-speed manual gearbox or automatic transmission. A four-door station wagon joined the sedan during 1972. Power front disc brakes and rack-and-pinion steering were standard.

I.D. DATA: Plymouth's 13-symbol Vehicle Identification Number is located on the upper left of the instrument panel. Symbols 1-4 form the model number (shown below). Symbol five indicates engine; symbol six is model year ('2' = 1972); symbol seven identifies the assembly plant. The final six digits make up the sequential production number, starting with 100001.

Model	Body Type & Seating	Engine Type/CID	P.O.E. Price	Weight (lbs.)	Prod. Total
CRICKET (1971 models)					
4B41	4-dr Sedan-4P	I4/91	1915	1907	Note 1
CRICKET (1972 models)					
4B41	4-dr Sedan-4P	I4/91	2017	1958	Note 1
4C45	4-dr Sta Wag-4P	I4/91	2399	N/A	Note 1

Note 1: A total of 27,682 Crickets were sold in the U.S. during 1971, followed by 13,882 in 1972.

1972 Plymouth Cricket four-door sedan.

ENGINE DATA: BASE FOUR (1971): Inline, overhead-valve four-cylinder. Cast iron block and head. **Displacement:** 91.4 cu. in. (1498 cc). **Bore & Stroke:** 3.39 x 2.53 in. (86 x 64.2 mm). **Compression Ratio:** 8.0:1. **Brake Horsepower:** 70 at 5200 rpm. **Torque:** 83 lbs.-ft. at 3000 rpm. Five main bearings. Solid valve lifters. Single Zenith carburetor.

BASE FOUR (1972-73): Same as above, except — **Compression Ratio:** 8.5:1. **Brake Horsepower:** 55 at 5000 rpm. **Torque:** 70 lbs.-ft. at 3000 rpm.

OPTIONAL FOUR (1972-73): Same as above, except — **Compression Ratio:** 8.5:1. **Brake Horsepower:** 70 at 5400 rpm. **Torque:** 74 lbs.-ft. at 3500 rpm. Two Zenith carburetors.

501

1973 Plymouth Cricket station wagon.

CHASSIS DATA: Wheelbase: 98 in. **Overall Length:** (sed) 162 in.; (wag) 166.9 in. **Height:** 54.6-54.9 in. **Width:** 62.5 in. **Front Tread:** 51 in. **Rear Tread:** 51.3 in. **Standard Tires:** 155x13 (5.60/6.10x13).

TECHNICAL: Layout: front-engine, rear-drive. **Transmission:** four-speed manual, or optional automatic. **Steering:** rack and pinion. **Suspension (front):** MacPherson struts with coil springs. **Suspension (rear):** rigid axle with coil springs. **Brakes:** front disc, rear drum. **Body Construction:** steel unibody.

MAJOR OPTIONS: Automatic transmission ($178). Air conditioning ($338).

Note: Option prices shown above were valid in 1972.

Manufacturer: Chrysler United Kingdom Ltd., Ryton-on-Dunsmore, Warwickshire, England.

Distributor: Chrysler-Plymouth Division, Chrysler Corp., Detroit, Michigan.

HISTORY: Crickets were introduced to the U.S. market in January 1971 and left the market after 1973 (though sold elsewhere in the world). No imports were sold under the Plymouth name in 1974-75.

1976-77 PLYMOUTH

1977 Plymouth Arrow GT two-door coupe.

ARROW — 160/160 GT/160 GS — FOUR — Plymouth's Mitsubishi-built series of rear-drive subcompacts reached the U.S. market a year earlier than the second-generation Dodge Colt. Though slightly smaller than their Dodge cousins in wheelbase and overall length, Arrows were similar in design and construction. Most Arrows came with the basic 1597-cc (98-cid) overhead-cam four-cylinder engine, hooked to a four-speed manual gearbox. A larger (2.0-liter) "Silent Shaft" powerplant also was offered, and available with a five-speed manual gearbox or a three-speed automatic transmission. Only one body style was marketed: a two-door hatchback coupe, with fold-down rear seat. Base and GT models were available in 1976, joined by a midrange GS version in 1977.

I.D. DATA: Plymouth's 13-symbol Vehicle Identification Number is located on the upper left of the instrument panel. Symbols 1-4 form the model number (shown below). Symbol five indicates engine; symbol six is model year ('6' = 1976); symbol seven identifies the assembly plant. The final six digits make up the sequential production number, starting with 100001.

Model	Body Type & Seating	Engine Type/CID	P.O.E. Price	Weight (lbs.)	Prod. Total
ARROW (1976 models)					
7L24	2-dr Hatch-4P	I4/98	3175	2110	Note 1
7P24 (GT)	2-dr Hatch-4P	I4/98	3748	2290	Note 1

Model	Body Type & Seating	Engine Type/CID	P.O.E. Price	Weight (lbs.)	Prod. Total
ARROW (1977 models)					
7L24	2-dr Hatch-4P	I4/98	3379	2110	Note 1
7H24 (GS)	2-dr Hatch-4P	I4/98	3654	2110	Note 1
7P24 (GT)	2-dr Hatch-4P	I4/98	4098	2090	Note 1

Note 1: A total of 30,430 Arrows were sold in the U.S. during 1976, followed by 47,599 in 1977.

ENGINE DATA: BASE FOUR: Inline, overhead-cam four-cylinder. Cast iron block and light alloy head. **Displacement:** 97.5 cu. in. (1597 cc). **Bore & Stroke:** 3.03 x 3.39 in. (76.9 x 86 mm). **Compression Ratio:** 8.5:1. **Brake Horsepower:** 83 at 5500 rpm. **Torque:** 89 lbs.-ft. at 3500 rpm. Five main bearings. Solid valve lifters. Two-barrel carburetor.

OPTIONAL FOUR (GS/GT): Inline, overhead-cam four-cylinder ("Silent Shaft"). Cast iron block and light alloy head. **Displacement:** 121.7 cu. in. (1995 cc). **Bore & Stroke:** 3.31 x 3.54 in. (84.1 x 89.9 mm). **Compression Ratio:** 8.5:1. **Brake Horsepower:** 96 at 5500 rpm. **Torque:** 109 lbs.-ft. at 3500 rpm. Five main bearings. Solid valve lifters. Two-barrel carburetor.

CHASSIS DATA: Wheelbase: 92.1 in. **Overall Length:** 167.3 in. **Height:** 52.2 in. **Width:** 63.4 in. **Front Tread:** 51.2 in. **Rear Tread:** 50.0 in.

TECHNICAL: Layout: front-engine, rear-drive. **Transmission:** four-speed or five-speed manual; or three-speed automatic. **Steering:** recirculating ball. **Suspension (front):** MacPherson struts with coil springs. **Suspension (rear):** rigid axle with semi-elliptic leaf springs. **Brakes:** front disc, rear drum. **Body Construction:** steel unibody.

MAJOR OPTIONS: Air conditioning ($395). Vinyl top ($92). Rear-window defroster ($79).

Note: Option prices shown above were valid in 1977.

Manufacturer: Mitsubishi Motors Corp. (Mitsubishi Heavy Industries), Tokyo, Japan.

Distributor: Chrysler-Plymouth Division, Chrysler Corp., Detroit, Michigan.

HISTORY: Arrows were introduced to the U.S. market in January 1976.

1978 PLYMOUTH

1978 Plymouth Arrow GT two-door coupe.

ARROW — 160 — FOUR — Production of the two-door hatchback series continued with little change. Mitsubishi's MCA-Jet engine system was supposed to deliver improved mileage and emissions. Standard equipment included reclining bucket seats, fold-down rear seats, and power front disc brakes. GT versions included gauges and a tachometer, plus a sport steering wheel and radial tires. An Arrow Jet option package, painted in flat black and orange, included black bumpers, special graphics, and twin racing mirrors.

SAPPORO — FOUR — Plymouth introduced a sporty rear-drive coupe for 1978, nearly identical to the Dodge Challenger and promoted as "the sophisticated new car from Plymouth." Under the hood was either the same 1597-cc MCA-Jet four-cylinder engine as installed in Arrows, with a new lean-combustion system; or an optional 2.6-liter four. Both engines were of "Silent Shaft" design. A gauge cluster around the tilt steering wheel included a tachometer, speedometer, trip odometer and oil/amp indicators, on a woodgrained dashboard. A digital clock was mounted in an overhead console. Reclining bucket seats were standard. Styling features included a horizontal-bar grille with rectangular headlamps, a canopy vinyl roof, and large wraparound taillamps.

I.D. DATA: Plymouth's 13-symbol Vehicle Identification Number is located on the upper left of the instrument panel. Symbols 1-4 form the model number (shown below). Symbol five indicates engine; symbol six is model year ('8' = 1978); symbol seven identifies the assembly plant. The final six digits make up the sequential production number, starting with 100001.

Model	Body Type & Seating	Engine Type/CID	P.O.E. Price	Weight (lbs.)	Prod. Total
ARROW					
7L24	2-dr Hatch-4P	I4/98	4206	2175	Note 1
7H24 (GS)	2-dr Hatch-4P	I4/98	4541	2180	Note 1
7P24 (GT)	2-dr Hatch-4P	I4/98	5199	2175	Note 1
SAPPORO					
3H29	2-dr Coupe-4P	I4/98	6087	2455	Note 2

Note 1: As many as 28,296 Arrows were sold in the U.S. during the 1978 model year.

Note 2: A total of 12,777 Sapporos were sold in the U.S. during the 1978 model year (plus 1,406 early examples in 1977).

ENGINE DATA: BASE FOUR: Inline, overhead-cam four-cylinder. Cast iron block and light alloy head. **Displacement:** 97.5 cu. in. (1597 cc). **Bore & Stroke:** 3.03 x 3.39 in. (76.9 x 86 mm). **Compression Ratio:** 8.5:1. **Brake Horsepower:** 77 at 5200 rpm. **Torque:** 87 lbs.-ft. at 3000 rpm. Five main bearings. Solid valve lifters.

OPTIONAL FOUR (Arrow GS/GT): Inline, overhead-cam four-cylinder ("Silent Shaft"). Cast iron block and light alloy head. **Displacement:** 121.7 cu. in. (1995 cc). **Bore & Stroke:** 3.31 x 3.54 in. (84.1 x 89.9 mm). **Compression Ratio:** 8.5:1. **Brake Horsepower:** 93 at 5200 rpm. **Torque:** 108 lbs.-ft. at 3000 rpm. Five main bearings. Solid valve lifters. Two-barrel carburetor.

OPTIONAL FOUR (Sapporo): Inline, overhead-cam four-cylinder ("Silent Shaft"). Cast iron block and light alloy head. **Displacement:** 155.9 cu. in. (2555 cc). **Bore & Stroke:** 3.59 x 3.86 in. (91.1 x 98 mm). **Compression Ratio:** 8.2:1. **Brake Horsepower:** 105 at 5200 rpm. **Torque:** 139 lbs.-ft. at 3000 rpm. Five main bearings. Solid valve lifters. Two-barrel carburetor.

1978 Plymouth Sapporo two-door coupe.

CHASSIS DATA: Wheelbase: (Arrow) 92.1 in.; (Sapporo) 99.0 in. **Overall Length:** (Arrow) 167.3 in.; (Sapporo) 183.1 in. **Height:** (Arrow) 52.2 in.; (Sapporo) 52.2 in. **Width:** (Arrow) 63.4 in.; (Sapporo) 65.6 in. **Front Tread:** (Arrow) 51.2 in.; (Sapporo) 53.9 in. **Rear Tread:** (Arrow) 50.0 in.; (Sapporo) 53.3 in.

TECHNICAL: Layout: front-engine, rear-drive. **Transmission:** (Arrow) four-speed or five-speed manual, or optional three-speed automatic; (Sapporo) five-speed manual, or optional three-speed automatic. **Steering:** recirculating ball. **Suspension (front):** MacPherson struts with coil springs and anti-sway bar. **Suspension (rear):** (Arrow) rigid axle with semi-elliptic leaf springs; (Sapporo) rigid axle with coil springs. **Brakes:** power front disc, rear drum. **Body Construction:** steel unibody.

MAJOR OPTIONS: Premium package: Sapporo ($486). Arrow Jet package: Arrow ($240). Air conditioning: Arrow ($493); Sapporo ($471). Vinyl or halo roof (Arrow). Rear-window defroster: Arrow ($94).
Manufacturer: Mitsubishi Motors Corp. (Mitsubishi Heavy Industries), Tokyo, Japan.
Distributor: Chrysler-Plymouth Division, Chrysler Corp., Detroit, Michigan.

HISTORY: The 1978 Arrow/Sapporo models were introduced to the U.S. market in October 1977. Sapporo was named for the Japanese city in which the 1976 Olympic games had been held.

1979-83 PLYMOUTH

1979 Plymouth Champ hatchback.

CHAMP — FOUR — A new front-drive subcompact series, also produced by Mitsubishi, joined the rear-drive Arrows for the 1979 model year. These were closely related to the revised Dodge Colt, bearing some resemblance to Chevrolet's Chevette. Beneath this new hood was a transverse-mounted 1.4-liter four-cylinder engine, with a 1.6-liter four optional. Many Champs had the curious Twin-Stick dual-range manual transmission, with eight forward speeds that could be used for performance or economy operation. The base model came with racing mirrors, side-window defrosters, and reclining bucket seats. The Custom added special cloth/vinyl upholstery, tinted glass, a sport steering wheel, rear defogger, and carpeted cargo area. An eggcrate-patterned grille and rectangular headlamps appeared on 1981 models. An LS option package (for the Custom model) included a rally handling package, two-tone paint, whitewall tires on cast aluminum wheels, twin electric remote mirrors, and a rear wiper/washer. A four-door hatchback joined the original two-door hatchback for the 1982 model year.

ARROW — FOUR — Plymouth's Mitsubishi-built rear-drive hatchbacks continued for two more seasons with modest change, marketed alongside the new front-drive Champs. A new horizontal grille and rectangular headlamps were installed for 1979, along with larger bumpers and a bigger back window. The Fire Arrow performance option package for the GT came with a standard 2.6-liter "Silent Shaft" MCA-Jet engine, as well as 185/70HR14 radial tires on cast aluminum wheels and four-wheel disc brakes.

1979 Plymouth Sapporo two-door coupe.

SAPPORO — FOUR — The sporty rear-drive coupe, close kin to Dodge's Challenger, remained on sale in the U.S. market through 1983. Some of its original trim was deleted for the 1979 model year, and the vinyl roof was dropped. The coupe's sail panel had a plainer appearance, and the deck lost its original bright applique. Full-length black vinyl rub moldings were installed. By 1980, the formerly-optional 2.6-liter "Silent Shaft" engine became the standard powerplant, replacing the 1.6-liter four. A five-speed manual gearbox was standard; three-speed automatic optional. Restyling in 1981 caused the Challenger and Sapporo to look more alike. Changes included an eggcrate-patterned grille, taller rear deck, and wraparound back window.

1981 Plymouth Champ hatchback.

I.D. DATA: Plymouth's 13-symbol Vehicle Identification Number is located on the upper left of the instrument panel. Symbols 1-4 form the model number (shown below). Symbol five indicates engine; symbol six is model year ('9' = 1979); symbol seven identifies the assembly plant. The final six digits make up the sequential production number, starting with 100001. Beginning in 1981, a 17-symbol Vehicle Identification Number was used.

Model	Body Type & Seating	Engine Type/CID	P.O.E. Price	Weight (lbs.)	Prod. Total
CHAMP (1979 models)					
1M24	2-dr Hatch-4P	I4/86	4425	1730	Note 1
1H24	2-dr Cust Hatch-4P	I4/86	4743	1775	Note 1
ARROW (1979 models)					
7L24	2-dr Hatch-4P	I4/98	4647	2100	Note 1
7H24 (GS)	2-dr Hatch-4P	I4/98	5005	2105	Note 1
7P24 (GT)	2-dr Hatch-4P	I4/98	5696	2140	Note 1
SAPPORO (1979 model)					
3H29	2-dr Coupe-4P	I4/98	6486	2410	Note 1

Note 1: A total of 27,031 Champs, 21,829 Arrows and 12,322 Sapporos were sold in the U.S. during 1979, followed by 39,756 Champs, 15,718 Arrows and 10,263 Sapporos in 1980.

1982 Plymouth Sapporo two-door coupe.

ENGINE DATA: BASE FOUR (1979 Champ): Inline, overhead-cam four-cylinder. Cast iron block and light alloy head. **Displacement:** 86.0 cu. in. (1410 cc). **Bore & Stroke:** 2.91 x 3.23 in. (74 x 82 mm). **Compression Ratio:** 8.8:1. **Brake Horsepower:** 70 at 5200 rpm. **Torque:** 78 lbs.-ft. at 3000 rpm. Five main bearings. Solid valve lifters. Two-barrel carburetor.
BASE FOUR (1979 Arrow, Sapporo): Inline, overhead-cam four-cylinder ("Silent Shaft"). Cast iron block and light alloy head. **Displacement:** 97.5 cu. in. (1597 cc). **Bore & Stroke:** 3.03 x 3.39 in. (76.9 x 86 mm). **Compression Ratio:** 8.5:1. **Brake Horsepower:** 77 at 5200 rpm. **Torque:** 87 lbs.-ft. at 3000 rpm. Five main bearings. Solid valve lifters. Two-barrel carburetor.

OPTIONAL FOUR (1979 Arrow): Inline, overhead-cam four-cylinder ("Silent Shaft"). Cast iron block and light alloy head. **Displacement:** 121.7 cu. in. (1995 cc). **Bore & Stroke:** 3.31 x 3.54 in. (84.1 x 89.9 mm). **Compression Ratio:** 8.5:1. **Brake Horsepower:** 93 at 5200 rpm. **Torque:** 108 lbs.-ft. at 3000 rpm. Five main bearings. Solid valve lifters. Two-barrel carburetor.

BASE FOUR (1979 Fire Arrow, 1980-up Sapporo); OPTIONAL FOUR (1979 Sapporo): Inline, overhead-cam four-cylinder ("Silent Shaft"). Cast iron block and light alloy head. **Displacement:** 155.9 cu. in. (2555 cc). **Bore & Stroke:** 3.59 x 3.86 in. (91.1 x 98 mm). **Compression Ratio:** 8.2:1. **Brake Horsepower:** 105 at 5200 rpm. **Torque:** 139 lbs.-ft. at 3000 rpm. Five main bearings. Solid valve lifters. Two-barrel carburetor.

CHASSIS DATA: Wheelbase: (Champ) 90.6 in.; (Arrow) 92.1 in.; (Sapporo) 99.0 in. **Overall Length:** (Champ) 156.8 in.; (Arrow) 169.9 in.; (Sapporo) 183.1 in. **Height:** (Champ) 53.1 in.; (Arrow) 50.8 in.; (Sapporo) 51.8 in. **Width:** (Champ) 62.4 in.; (Arrow) 63.4 in.; (Sapporo) 66.7 in. **Front Tread:** (Champ) 53.9 in.; (Arrow) 51.2 in.; (Sapporo) 53.9 in. **Rear Tread:** (Champ) 52.8 in.; (Arrow) 50.0 in.; (Sapporo) 53.3 in.

1983 Plymouth Sapporo two-door coupe.

TECHNICAL: Layout: (Champ) front-engine, front-drive; (Arrow/Sapporo) front-engine, rear-drive. **Transmission:** (Champ) four-speed manual or four/two-speed Twin-Stick; (Arrow) four-speed or five-speed manual, or optional three-speed automatic; (Sapporo) five-speed manual, or optional three-speed automatic. **Steering:** (Champ) rack and pinion; (Arrow/Sapporo) recirculating ball. **Suspension (front):** MacPherson struts with coil springs and anti-sway bar. **Suspension (rear):** (Champ) independent with trailing arms and coil springs; (Arrow) rigid axle with semi-elliptic leaf springs; (Sapporo) rigid axle with coil springs. **Brakes:** power front disc, rear drum except (Fire Arrow and Sapporo w/2.6-liter engine) all-disc. **Body Construction:** steel unibody.

1983 Plymouth Colt four-door hatchback.

MAJOR OPTIONS: Fire Arrow package: Arrow ($719). Arrow Jet package: Arrow ($256). Premium package: Champ ($487); Sapporo ($489). Air conditioning ($517). Halo roof: Arrow ($107). Rear-window defroster: Arrow ($94). Speed control: Sapporo ($107). Flip-up glass sunroof: Champ ($177). Luggage rack: Champ ($79).
Note: Option prices shown above were valid in 1979.
Manufacturer: Mitsubishi Motors Corp. (Mitsubishi Heavy Industries), Tokyo, Japan.
Distributor: Chrysler-Plymouth Division, Chrysler Corp., Detroit, Michigan.
HISTORY: Marketing of the Mitsubishi-built front-drive subcompacts continued through 1982 under separate Dodge (Colt) and Plymouth (Champ) banners. After that time, it became just plain Colt, sold by both Dodge and Plymouth dealers. See Dodge listing for details on 1983-90 models.

POBEDA

One of three major passenger cars produced in the Soviet Union during the early postwar years, the Pobeda didn't last as long as the others. Introduced in 1949, the Pobeda (which translates to "victory" in Russian) came in four-door sedan form, along with a convertible sedan and panel delivery. Pobedas were built in the same plant at Gorky as the Moskvich (also listed in this Catalog).

504

1949-58 POBEDA

1954 Pobeda M-20 four-door.

M-20 — FOUR — The Pobeda's fastback bodies bore some resemblance to various 1946-48 American makes, notably Chevrolet; but owed even more to the German Opel design. One guide to world automobiles of the early 1950s reached even further, claiming that the Pobeda steering wheel was similar to that used in Jeeps, while the dashboard appeared similar to Plymouth's. The grille was made up of horizontal bars, narrower at the upper center where it met the hood. Horizontal parking lights sat below the headlamps. Power came from a 129-cid L-head four-cylinder engine that produced 50 bhp, hooked to a three-speed gearbox. Motor Trend noted the resemblance of the engine to that used in Jeeps that went to the Soviet Union during the early postwar years. Upholstery was done in wool. A new Model 72 sedan was added in 1955, with special low-pressure tires and four-wheel drive for travel through rough country.

I.D. DATA: Not available.

Model	Body Type & Seating	Engine Type/CID	P.O.E. Price	Weight (lbs.)	Prod. Total
M-20	4-dr Sedan-5P	I4/129	Note 1	3000	N/A
M-20	4-dr Cabriolet	I4/129	N/A	N/A	N/A

Note 1: Price at the factory was about $4000.

ENGINE DATA: BASE FOUR: Inline, L-head four-cylinder. Cast iron block and head (cast in one piece); aluminum alloy cylinders. **Displacement:** 129.4 cu. in. (2121 cc). **Bore & Stroke:** 3.23 x 3.94 in. (82 x 100 mm). **Compression Ratio:** 6.2:1/6.5:1. **Brake Horsepower:** 50-52 at 3600 rpm. Solid valve lifters.

CHASSIS DATA: Wheelbase: 106 in. **Overall Length:** 184.25 in. **Height:** 64.5 in. **Width:** 65.5 in. **Front Tread:** 53.5 in. **Rear Tread:** 53.5 in. **Standard Tires:** 6.00x16.

TECHNICAL: Layout: front-engine, rear-drive except (Model 72) four-wheel drive. **Transmission:** three-speed manual. **Suspension (front):** wishbones with coil springs. **Suspension (rear):** rigid axle with semi-elliptic leaf springs. **Brakes:** hydraulic, front/rear drum. **Body Construction:** steel monocoque.

PERFORMANCE: Top Speed: 65-68 mph. **Acceleration (0-60 mph):** 34 sec. **Fuel Mileage:** about 25 mpg.

Manufacturer: Zavod Imeni Molotov (Molotov Works), Gorky, U.S.S.R.

HISTORY: A small number of Pobedas were exported to Sweden, Finland and Belgium. They also were built in Poland as the Warzawa M-20. Motor Trend in late 1952 ran a report on Stanley F. Slotkin, an American businessman and car enthusiast who'd smuggled a Pobeda out of Russia. While in Finland on business, he'd been impressed by the comfortable ride in a Pobeda taxicab and wanted to purchase one. Even in the Soviet Union, few Pobedas were in private hands. Slotkin's tale ended with the arrival of an unassembled Pobeda at dockside in San Pedro, California. He chose not to drive the car in the U.S., but planned to display it at charitable events.

PORSCHE

Considering the ultimate achievements of the Porsche nameplate, it's surprising to note that the first Austrian-built two-seaters of 1948 were considered to be little more than sporty versions of the Volkswagen Beetle—which hadn't yet arrived on American shores. Ferdinand Porsche's sports-car project had its origin long before that time, of course. After a brief trial at the family metalsmith business as a teenager in the 1880s, Porsche took an interest in electricity and, in 1890, built a fully electrical system for the family home. While at college in Vienna, Austria, he

also served an apprenticeship and, by 1898, became manager of the test department at an electrical equipment firm. A year later, however, Porsche joined with Jacob Lohner to develop automobiles with both electric and gasoline/electric engines, notably a front-drive model with a gasoline engine driving a generator. Porsche not only worked on design, but drove some of his own creations in competition.

Porsche moved to Austro-Daimler in 1905, in the post of technical director. His interest expanded into aircraft engines. In fact, the air-cooled flat-four powerplant he designed in 1912 would serve, decades later, as the foundation for the Volkswagen/Porsche rear-mounted engines. Porsche's son Ferry, whose design work would ultimately become as renowned as his father's, was born in 1909.

By the end of World War I, the elder Porsche had moved up to managing director at Austro-Daimler and been granted an honorary doctorate by the University of Vienna. Thus arose the title by which he came to be known: Herr Doktor Ingenieur (engineer) Porsche. The additional title of "Professor" was granted years later, by Adolf Hitler. In 1923, he moved to Daimler-Benz as a designer, working on the mighty SSK and SSKL road racers. Then, in 1929, Porsche jumped over to the Steyr organization as head engineer. All this time, however, he'd been thinking about small cars, not just the large models to which he'd contributed at Austro-Daimler, Daimler-Benz, and Steyr.

An opportunity to follow his personal urges came with the formation of his own design firm, at Stuttgart, Germany, late in 1930. Joining him at the fledgling company was Karl Rabe, also from Austro-Daimler, who would remain in the capacity of Porsche chief engineer as late as 1966. Young Ferry Porsche also became part of the staff, having served his own apprenticeship at both the Steyr and Bosch organizations. So did Joseph Kales, an expert in air-cooled engines with experience at the Czechoslovakian Skoda and Tatra companies, and designer Erwin Komenda.

Project 7 was the first order of business: a small car ordered by the Wanderer company. Zundapp and NSU also ordered designs for small vehicles; but neither of those went into production. One project that did indeed go into production began in 1934: Project 60, which would become the spectacularly successful Volkswagen Beetle: the "people's car," as requested by Adolf Hitler himself. Two years later, the first three VW prototypes were ready. Porsche also spent time on a completely different type of car: the massive mid-engined V-16 Auto Union Grand Prix racing models.

Both Ferdinand Porsche and his son Ferry were arrested by American occupation forces shortly after World War II, and imprisoned by the French. His incarceration also happened to encompass design work, as he was ordered by the French authorities to help with the creation of the Renault 4CV, as well as the Cisitalia racing car. Ferry Porsche was released in 1946, but his father remained in jail for more than a year longer. By that time, both men were ready to begin work on the sporting variant of the Volkswagen, which became project number 356. Actually, the design for the first Porsche had originated before the war, with the mid-engined Type 114 F-Wagen.

Even before Ferdinand Porsche was released from prison, son Ferry had been working with Karl Rabe to develop the new two-seater, largely based on Volkswagen components. That meant a tuned version of the VW air-cooled engine, and Volkswagen suspension. Development began at the company's small headquarters in the village of Gmund (Austria). A chassis was ready by March 1948, and soon was wearing an open body with a low windshield of the sort that would help give Porsches their special identity. Later that summer, a streamlined closed coupe was finished. Actual production began, with each car virtually hand-assembled, late in 1948; and the first examples appeared at the Geneva show the next spring. Those first Porsches carried a 1086-cc engine, even though initial advertisements had promised a larger (1131-cc) unit. Between 1948 and 1950, about 47 cars were produced, each wearing aluminum body panels. These early cars had non-synchromesh VW transmissions, but that soon would change as Porsche developed its own gearbox.

By the time the first few dozen cars were built, permission had been granted to return to the company's original (larger) facility at Zuffenhausen, just outside Stuttgart, West Germany. Thus, the first German-built Porsches emerged in April 1950. Less than a year later, Ferdinand Porsche died of a stroke, but the work was carried on by son Ferry.

Importation of Porsches into the U.S. began early in 1950, carried out by Max Hoffman of New York, a family friend of the Porsches and first importer of many European makes.

At the 1951 Frankfurt show, Porsche displayed two new models with bigger (1300-cc) engines: the 356/1 and 356/3, rated 44 bhp rather than the former 40. By 1951, Porsches came with any of three engine displacements, including the biggest 1488-cc version. One of the hottest and best-remembered Porsches, the racy open-topped Speedster, arrived in 1954, and gained particular popularity in the U.S. By the mid-1950s, in fact, three-fourths of the Porsches built were heading westward to American shores. By 1956, a 1.6-liter engine replaced the earlier 1.5-liter version. Throughout the 1950s and early '60s, the 356 underwent a sizable series of improvements.

Finally, late in 1964, the 356 was replaced by the new 911 series, with a 1991-cc flat-six engine, initially rated 130 bhp. A year later, the 912 series replaced the 356C, keeping the latter's 1582-cc four-cylinder engine. Fuel injection became available in the 911 series in 1970, and its engine grew several times in the early years of that decade. A Carrera RS became available in 1973. Two years later, a turbocharged variant of the 911 took the 930 Carrera designation and, according to the World Guide to Automobile Manufacturers, became one of the quickest-accelerating cars in existence—then or later. Its 3299-cc engine developed 253 bhp.

Late in the 1960s, Porsche was contemplating a full partnership with Volkswagen, and the two companies launched a VW-Porsche model 914. After Volkswagen took over Porsche distribution, the proposed joint venture fell through.

Porsche's financial standing was faltering in the 1970s, before the new (lower-cost) 924 and the more posh 928 helped trigger an impressive recovery. Unlike its predecessors, the 924 carried a front-mounted four-cylinder engine, cooled by water instead of air and driving the back wheels. The 928 kept the same configuration, but ran with V-8 power through a rear-mounted transmission.

A turbocharged 924 came in 1979. Then, in the 1980s, Porsche introduced such disparate models as the moderately-priced 944, a 911 cabriolet, and the ultimate Porsche: the four-wheel-drive 959 supercar with a 450-bhp six-cylinder engine and Kevlar body. Sales in modern times weren't always as strong as Porsche might have liked, but the car's reputation for quality and performance has grown into a legend.

Note: The listings in this Catalog focus on roadgoing Porsches. A broad variety of racing models also were produced through the years.

1948-53 PORSCHE

1948 Porsche "Gmund" coupe owned by Chuck Stoddard. (Dennis Schrimpf)

356 — FLAT FOUR — In prototype form, Porsche's first creation had a tubular space frame but was otherwise based on Volkswagen Type 1 (Beetle) components. Prototypes had the engine mounted ahead of the rear axle, but in production it moved rearward. Production models also rode a platform of sheet steel rather than the tubular type, with a central tunnel and boxed sills. Out back was a 40-bhp version of the Volkswagen flat-four engine, breathing through twin carburetors and sporting higher compression and bigger valves. The rear suspension was Volkswagen's torsion-bar and swing-axle setup, but reversed. Up front: VW torsion bars. Wheelbase was 82.7 inches, and the car measured just under 152 inches overall. The first Austrian-built Porsches had tiny round taillamps, a wraparound back bumper (with no guards, and swing-out trafficators in the front fenders. Inside was a "banjo" type steering wheel, as well as a 160-kph speedometer.

A closed coupe came first, followed in 1951 by an open cabriolet (convertible). Modest restyling accompanied the move from Austria to Germany in 1950, accomplished by Erwin Komenda. A larger split windshield was installed, flat except at the edges where the glass curved to meet the A-pillars. At the rear were two round and two rectangular taillamps. Early examples had wind wings, but those soon were abandoned. An oil temperature gauge was added, but a gas gauge was not. Instead, owners had to use a measuring stick, or rely on the reserve fuel tank (as in Volkswagens of the 1950s). Hydraulic brakes replaced the cable-operated mechanical units installed on Austrian-built Porsches. During 1951, tubular rear shock absorbers replaced the original lever-type shocks. Until the 1952 models, Porsches kept the divided windshield (slightly "vee" shaped), which curved at the outer edges. Then, the two largely flat sections were joined together in the center. Also in 1952, a folding rear seat was added, and the spare tire moved forward (standing almost vertical). Brakes drums also grew in diameter, from 9 to 11 inches.

By 1951, Porsche offered a choice of three engines: 1086, 1286 and 1488 cc, rated 40, 44 and 60 bhp (DIN), respectively. With the 44-bhp engine, a Porsche 356 could top 90 mph. The 1.5-liter engine used a roller-bearing crankshaft, with 10-mm longer stroke than the 1.3-liter version. A tachometer was optional. Although these early Porsches carried the Volkswagen's non-synchromesh transmission, by 1952 Porsche developed its own unit, using synchronizing split rings instead of the customary cones.

A Super series (1500S) engine arrived in 1952, developing 70 horsepower. A year later, it was the 1300S with 60 bhp. Offered only in the U.S., in very limited number, was the "America" version of the 1500S, a roadster with aluminum body by Glaser, which suggested the Speedster that soon would emerge. The Hirth crankshafts used in the first 1.5-liter engines had proven troublesome, and were replaced in 1953 by a forged-steel crankshaft. Both Normal and Super versions of the three engines were available.

Note: Porsches built at Gmund, Austria from late 1948 to early 1950 were designated 356/2, and came only with 1.1-liter engines.

1949 Porsche 356 coupe.

I.D. DATA: Serial number is on driver's door post. Serial number range: (1950 models) 5001 to 5410; (1951 1100) 5411 to 5600; (1951 1300) 10350 to 10432; (late 1951 1500) 10531 to 11125; (1952 1000 conv) 10433 to 10469; (1952 1300 cpe) 11126 to 12084; (1952 1500 conv) 12301 to 12387; (late 1952 1500 cpe) 50001 to 50098; (late 1952 1500S) 15001 to 16116; (1953 cpe) 50099 to 51645; (1953 conv) 60001 to 60394. Engine number is stamped on generator post.

Model	Body Type & Seating	Engine Type/CID	P.O.E. Price	Weight (lbs.)	Prod. Total
356/2 (1948-1950)					
356/2	2-dr Coupe-2+2P	H4/66	N/A	N/A	Note 1
356/2	2-dr Cabr-2P	H4/66	N/A	N/A	Note 1
356 (1950-up)					
356	2-dr Coupe-2+2P	H4/91	4284	1675	Note 1
356	2-dr Cabr-2P	H4/91	4584	1830	Note 1
356 AMERICA (1953 models)					
356	2-dr Coupe-2+2P	H4/91	3395	N/A	Note 1
356	2-dr Rds-2P	H4/91	3645	N/A	Note 2

Note 1: Only four Porsches were produced in 1948, and 25 in 1949. Approximately 410 coupes were produced in 1950; 170 coupes and 999 cabriolets (convertibles) in 1951; 1,057 coupes and 240 convertibles in 1952; plus 1,547 coupes and 394 convertibles in 1953.
Note 2: At least 16 special lightweight "America" roadsters were produced.
Price Note: Figures shown were valid in 1953, for Super (1488-cc) engine and equipment that included a radio and tachometer.
Engine Note: In the early 1950s, any of three engine sizes were available.
ENGINE DATA: BASE FOUR (356/2, 1100): Horizontally opposed, overhead-valve four-cylinder (air cooled). Cast iron cylinder liners. **Displacement:** 66.3 cu. in. (1086 cc) **Bore & Stroke:** 2.89 x 2.52 in. (73.5 x 64 mm). **Compression Ratio:** 7.0:1. **Brake Horsepower:** 40 DIN (46 SAE) at 4000-4200 rpm. **Torque:** 50-52 lbs.-ft. at 2800 rpm. Four main bearings. Solid valve lifters. Two Solex carburetors.
OPTIONAL FOUR, 1951-up (1300): Horizontally opposed, overhead-valve four-cylinder (air cooled). Aluminum cylinder liners. **Displacement:** 78.5 cu. in. (1286 cc) **Bore & Stroke:** 3.15 x 2.52 in. (80 x 64 mm). **Compression Ratio:** 6.5:1. **Brake Horsepower:** 44 DIN (50 SAE) at 4000-4500 rpm. **Torque:** 58-59 lbs.-ft. at 2500-2800 rpm. Four main bearings. Solid valve lifters. Two Solex carburetors.
OPTIONAL FOUR, late 1953-up (1300S): Same as 1286-cc four above, except — **Compression Ratio:** 8.2:1. **Brake Horsepower:** 60 DIN (70 SAE) at 5500-5700 rpm. **Torque:** 63-65 lbs.-ft. at 3600 rpm.
OPTIONAL FOUR, 1951-up (1500): Horizontally opposed, overhead-valve four-cylinder (air cooled). **Displacement:** 90.8 cu. in. (1488 cc) **Bore & Stroke:** 3.15 x 2.91 in. (80 x 74 mm). **Compression Ratio:** 6.5:1. **Brake Horsepower:** (1951-52) 60 DIN (70 SAE) at 4800-5000 rpm; (1952-up) 55 DIN (64 SAE) at 4400 rpm. **Torque:** (1951-52) 73 lbs.-ft. at 2800 rpm; (1952-up) 76 lbs.-ft. at 2800 rpm. Four main bearings. Solid valve lifters. Two Solex carburetors.
OPTIONAL FOUR, 1952-up (Super 1500): Same as 1488-cc four above, except — **Compression Ratio:** 8.2:1. **Brake Horsepower:** 70 DIN (82 SAE) at 5000-5400 rpm. **Torque:** 77 lbs.-ft. at 3600 rpm.
CHASSIS DATA: Wheelbase: 82.7 in. **Overall Length:** 151.6 in. **Height:** 51.2 in. **Width:** 65.4 in. **Front Tread:** 50.8 in. **Rear Tread:** 49.2 in. **Standard Tires:** 5.00x16.
TECHNICAL: Layout: rear-engine, rear-drive. **Transmission:** four-speed manual (initially non-synchromesh) in rear transaxle. Gear ratios: (1st) 3.18:1; (2nd) 1.76:1; (3rd) 1.13:1; (4th) 0.81:1; (rev) 3.56:1. **Standard Final Drive Ratio:** 4.375:1. **Steering:** worm and peg. **Suspension (front):** parallel trailing arms with transverse laminated torsion bars. **Suspension (rear):** swing axles with transverse torsion bars. **Brakes:** hydraulic, front/rear drum (mechanical brakes on early Gmund cars). **Body Construction:** steel unibody with boxed, pressed-steel platform chassis (first Porsches had aluminum body panels).
PERFORMANCE: Top Speed: (1100) 87 mph claimed; (1300) 90 mph claimed; (1500) 96 mph claimed; (1500 Super) near 109 mph claimed. **Acceleration (0-60 mph):** N/A (0-62 mph in 14.6 sec. claimed).
PRODUCTION/SALES: An industry source offered production figures that differed from those noted above, reporting that a total of 335 Porsches were produced during 1950, followed by 1,112 in 1951, 1,303 in 1952, and 1,978 in 1953. Approximately 30 Porsches were sold in the U.S. during 1951, followed by 141 in 1952 and 573 in 1953.
Manufacturer: Dr. Ing. h.c. F. Porsche KG, Zuffenhausen, Stuttgart, West Germany.
Distributor: Hoffman Motors, New York City.
HISTORY: Porsche's 356 first appeared at the Geneva (Switzerland) auto show in March 1949. Importation into the U.S. began early in 1950. Initial models, known as the 356/2, were built from 1948-50 at Gmund, Austria. By April 1950, production had moved to Stuttgart and Porsches took the simple 356 designation. Porsche became a design consultant to the Volkswagen company late in 1948, thus establishing the tight connection between the two makes as they evolved in the 1950s.
A Porsche entered the Le Mans race in June 1950, finishing in twelfth position; but later Porsches would fare far better on the racing circuit. By spring 1951, Porsche Number 500 had been built. Road & Track noted that its 356/4 Porsche "seems to behave perfectly on the road." John von Neumann undertook the high-speed runs, claiming that the Porsche delivered sensations akin "to those felt in a DC-6's pilot seats...the drive feels more as though he were airborne than bound to the highway." Summing up, the magazine called it "The Car of Tomorrow."
Porsche's familiar emblem, featuring a black horse on a yellow shield (the Stuttgart coat of arms) atop the staghorn crest of Baden-Wurttemburg, first appeared on the 1952 models. Porsche expert Dean Batchelor explains that the design was first sketched by Ferry Porsche on a napkin, while he was having lunch with American importer Max Hoffman.

1954-55 PORSCHE

356 — FLAT FOUR — No more 1.1-liter Porsches were sent to the U.S. after 1953, since importer Max Hoffman believed that engine was too small to satisfy Americans; and even the 1.3-liter wasn't quite sufficient. Elsewhere in the world, Porsche buyers could get any of six engines, but the 1.5-liter version became the only powerplant commonly offered to American customers, offered either in base or 1500S form. Super engines had roller-bearing Hirth crankshafts, larger carburetors, higher compression, and sports camshafts. The 1500S (Super) model sold in the U.S. included such extras as aluminum wheel trim rings, radio, and an adjustable passenger-side seatback.
Porsche's Speedster appeared in September 1954. In essence, it was a lightweight roadster version of the earlier cabriolet, but lacking its roll-up windows and padded convertible top. Its most striking feature was the severely chopped one-piece windshield, standing 3.5 inches lower than that of a regular cabriolet. Priced at $2995 (heater and

tachometer extra), the Speedster proved a big hit, sold initially only in the U.S. Another $500 brought the Super engine. A Super Speedster could hit 120 mph and accelerate to 60 mph in about 10 seconds. By the time Speedster production came to a halt in 1959, more than 4,000 had been built.

All models got a front anti-sway bar during 1954. For 1955, the prior 16-inch wheels were gone, replaced by 15-inchers. By that time, engines had a three-piece aluminum crankcase (formerly made of magnesium, in two sections). Overall, the 356 was making use of fewer and fewer Volkswagen components, a trend that would continue as Porsche established its own separate identity. Porsches sold in the U.S. took the "Continental" designation, but that quickly faded away as Lincoln introduced a model of that name.

1954 Porsche Type 356: 1500 Super convertible.

I.D. DATA: Serial number is on driver's door post. Serial number range: (1954 cpe) 51646 to 53008; (1954 conv) 60395 to 60722; (1954 Speedster) 80001 to 80200; (1955 cpe) 53009 to 55390; (1955 conv) 60723 to 61069; (1955 Speedster) 80201 to 81200. Engine number is stamped on generator post or on a plate attached to center of engine, at the rear.

Model	Body Type & Seating	Engine Type/CID	P.O.E. Price	Weight (lbs.)	Prod. Total
356					
1500	2-dr Coupe-2+2P	H4/91	3445	1870	Note 1
1500	2-dr Cabr-2P	H4/91	3695	1870	Note 1
Super	2-dr Coupe-2+2P	H4/91	4284	N/A	Note 1
Super	2-dr Cabr-2P	H4/91	4584	N/A	Note 1
SPEEDSTER					
356	2-dr Rds-2P	H4/91	2995	1675	Note 1
356 Super	2-dr Rds-2P	H4/91	3495	N/A	Note 1

Note 1: Approximately 1,363 coupes, 328 convertibles and 200 Speedsters were produced during 1954; followed by 1,992 coupes, 278 convertibles and 1,700 Speedsters in 1955 (totals include early 356A models).

Price Note: Figures shown were valid in 1955.

1954 Porsche 356 coupe.

ENGINE DATA: BASE FOUR (1100): Horizontally opposed, overhead-valve four-cylinder (air cooled). Cast iron cylinder liners. **Displacement:** 66.3 cu. in. (1086 cc). **Bore & Stroke:** 2.89 x 2.52 in. (73.5 x 64 mm). **Compression Ratio:** 7.0:1. **Brake Horsepower:** 40 DIN (46 SAE) at 4000 rpm. **Torque:** 50-52 lbs.-ft. at 2800 rpm. Four main bearings. Solid valve lifters. Two Solex carburetors.

OPTIONAL FOUR (1300): Horizontally opposed, overhead-valve four-cylinder (air cooled). Aluminum cylinder liners. **Displacement:** 78.5 cu. in. (1286 cc). **Bore & Stroke:** 3.15 x 2.52 in. (80 x 64 mm). **Compression Ratio:** 6.5:1. **Brake Horsepower:** 44 DIN (50 SAE) at 4000 rpm. **Torque:** 58-59 lbs.-ft. at 2500-2800 rpm. Four main bearings. Solid valve lifters. Two Solex carburetors.

OPTIONAL FOUR (1300S): Same as 1286-cc four above, except — **Compression Ratio:** 8.2:1. **Brake Horsepower:** 60 DIN (70 SAE) at 5500 rpm. **Torque:** 63-65 lbs.-ft. at 3600 rpm.

Note: 1086-cc and 1288-cc engines no longer were commonly exported to the U.S.

OPTIONAL FOUR (1500): Horizontally opposed, overhead-valve four-cylinder (air cooled). **Displacement:** 90.8 cu. in. (1488 cc). **Bore & Stroke:** 3.15 x 2.91 in. (80 x 74 mm). **Compression Ratio:** 6.5:1. **Brake Horsepower:** 55 DIN (64 SAE) at 4400 rpm. **Torque:** 76 lbs.-ft. at 2800 rpm. Four main bearings. Solid valve lifters. Two Solex carburetors.

OPTIONAL FOUR (1500 Super): Same as 1488-cc four above, except — **Compression Ratio:** 8.2:1. **Brake Horsepower:** 70 DIN (82 SAE) at 5000 rpm. **Torque:** 79 lbs.-ft. at 3500 rpm.

CHASSIS DATA: Wheelbase: 82.7 in. **Overall Length:** 151.6 in. **Height:** 51.2 in. **Width:** 65.4 in. **Front Tread:** 50.8 in. **Rear Tread:** 49.2 in. **Standard Tires:** 5.00x16 (5.25x16 optional); changed to 15-inch in 1955.

TECHNICAL: Layout: rear-engine, rear-drive. **Transmission:** four-speed manual (initially non-synchromesh) in rear transaxle. Gear ratios: (1st) 3.18:1; (2nd) 1.76:1; (3rd) 1.13:1; (4th) 0.81:1; (rev) 3.56:1. **Standard Final Drive Ratio:** 4.375:1. **Steering:** worm and peg. **Suspension (front):** parallel trailing arms with transverse laminated torsion bars. **Suspension (rear):** swing axles with transverse torsion bars. **Brakes:** hydraulic, front/rear drum. **Body Construction:** steel unibody with boxed, pressed-steel platform chassis.

1955 Porsche 356 Speedster. (Coys of Kensington)

PERFORMANCE: Top Speed: (1100) 87 mph claimed; (1300) 90 mph claimed; (1500) 96 mph claimed; (1500 Super) 106 mph claimed; (Super Speedster) about 120 mph. **Acceleration (0-60 mph):** (1500 Speedster) 14.7 sec.; (Super Speedster) about 10 sec. **Acceleration (quarter-mile):** (1500 Speedster) 19.9 sec. (68.5 mph).

PRODUCTION/SALES: An industry source offered production figures that differed from those noted above, reporting that a total of 1,934 Porsches were produced during 1954, followed by 2,952 in 1955. Approximately 588 Porsches were sold in the U.S. during 1954.

Manufacturer: Dr. Ing. h.c. F. Porsche KG, Zuffenhausen, Stuttgart, West Germany.
Distributor: Hoffman Motors, New York City.

HISTORY: The Model 550 racing Porsche of the mid-1950s had an aluminum body with stabilizing fins, and a 110-bhp four-overhead-cam engine that ran with four carburetors and dual ignition. Top speed was 140 mph. One of its predecessors had finished well ahead of its class in the Mexican road race.

1956-59 PORSCHE

1956 Porsche Carrera 356A cabriolet.

356A/CARRERA — FLAT FOUR — By 1956, when the 356A designation was adopted for a revised Porsche, five different engines were available (but only three in America). A new 1582-cc overhead-valve engine replaced the old 1.5-liter engine, producing either 70 horsepower (SAE) or, in Super form, 88 bhp. Speedsters were available with any engine except the smaller 1300.

A 1500GS engine, available for racing and adapted from the 550 Spyder competition model, had dual-overhead-cam cylinder heads design and a roller-bearing crankshaft, as well as one-piece connecting rods (also using roller bearings). With 8.7:1 compression to develop as much as 128 horsepower (SAE) at 6400 rpm, the 1500GS breathed through twin Solex 40 PJ1 two-barrel carburetors. That model, better known as the Carrera, could accelerate to 60 mph in 8.7 seconds (1.3 seconds faster than a 1600 Super). It could also hit 125 mph or more.

As before, three body styles were offered: coupe, convertible (cabriolet), and Speedster. Bodies were supplied by the Reutter company, in Stuttgart. The 356A had a curved one-piece windshield, horn grilles below the headlamps, and a fuel gauge inside.

Coupes and cabriolets added rub rails along the rocker-panel area. Suspension modifications included a removal of leaves from the front torsion bars, and lengthening of the rear torsion bars, which delivered a softer ride. Tires were 15-inch size. A new flat-faced instrument panel had a padded top, with a tachometer mounted between the speedometer and fuel/oil gauge. Legroom was increased due to a lowering of the car's floor. Fitted luggage became available for Porsche models.

In 1957, horizontal teardrop-shaped taillamps replaced the earlier quartet of round units, and the license-plate light moved downward, below the plate itself. For 1957, vent wings were back (unseen since the very first Porsches), at least on the cabriolet. Coupes got a different version, outside the window frames. Exhaust-pipe tips, which had formerly protruded separately, close to the ground, now exited through the bumper guards. Up front, a twin-bow overrider went on the bumper, replacing the former single-bow unit. Both open-topped Porsches gained larger back windows. By 1958, too, Speedsters could be ordered with a lift-off fiberglass top, manufactured either in Germany or America. By this time, the 1300 (1286-cc) engine was gone, and the 1600 reverted to plain bearings, abandoning the roller units. In Normal form, the 1600 engine also reverted to cast iron cylinders. Carrera editions switched to the 1587-cc engine. Each engine now breathed through Zenith 32 NDIX carburetors. Finally, a different steering gear was installed: a ZF worm and lever arrangement, rather than the former worm and peg setup as in VWs. Porsches had now evolved a considerable distance beyond their Volkswagen origins.

In summer 1958, a Convertible D (for Drauz, the body supplier) with a taller windshield and folding top replaced the original racy Speedster.

1957 Porsche 356A coupe. (Coys of Kensington)

I.D. DATA: Serial number is on driver's door post. Serial number range: (1956 cpe) 55391 to 58311; (1956 conv) 61070 to 61499; (1956 Speedster) 81201 to 82189; (1957 1300/S cpe) 58312 to 59090; (1957 1300/S conv) 61500 to 61700; (1957 1300/S Speedster) 82190 to 83691; (1957 1600/S cpe) 100001 to 102504; (1957 1600/S conv) 61701 to 61892, then 150001 to 150149; (1957 1600/S Speedster) 83792 to 84366; (1958 1600/S cpe) 102505 to 106174; (1958 1600/S conv) 150150 to 151531; (1958 1600/S Speedster) 84367 to 85886; (1959 1600/S cpe) 106175 to 108917; (1959 1600/S conv) 151532 to 152475; (1959 1600/S Speedster/Convertible D) 83887 to 86830. Engine number is on a plate attached to center of engine, at the rear.

Model	Body Type & Seating	Engine Type/CID	P.O.E. Price	Weight (lbs.)	Prod. Total
356A (1956 Standard models)					
356A	2-dr Coupe-2+2P	H4/96	3665	1870	Note 1
356A	2-dr Cabr-2P	H4/96	3915	1870	Note 1
Speedster	2-dr Rds-2P	H4/96	3215	1675	Note 1
356A (1956 1500GS/Carrera models)					
356A	2-dr Coupe-2+2P	H4/91	5665	1945	Note 1
356A	2-dr Cabr-2P	H4/91	5915	1945	Note 1
Speedster	2-dr Rds-2P	H4/91	5215	1745	Note 1
356A (1959 Standard models)					
356A	2-dr Coupep2+2P	H4/96	3665	1874	Note 1
356A	2-dr HT Cpe-2+2P	H4/96	3830	1874	Note 1
356A	2-dr Cabr-2P	H4/96	3915	1874	Note 1
Conv D	2-dr Rds-2P	H4/96	3581	N/A	Note 1
356A (1959 1600GS/Carrera models)					
356A	2-dr Coupe-2+2P	H4/97	5665	2046	Note 1
356A	2-dr HT Cpe-2+2P	H4/97	5830	2046	Note 1
356A	2-dr Cabr-2P	H4/97	5915	2046	Note 1

Note 1: Approximately 390 coupes, 69 convertibles and 100 Speedsters were produced late in 1955, as early examples of the 356A series. Then, 2,921 coupes, 430 convertibles and 850 Speedsters were produced during 1956; 3,283 coupes, 542 convertibles and 1,416 Speedsters in 1957; 3,670 coupes, 1,382 convertibles, 556 Speedsters and 386 early Convertible D models in 1958; and finally, 2,743 coupes, 944 convertibles and 944 Convertible D models in 1959.

Price Note: Figures shown for 1959 standard models included base 1600 engine; the Super engine added $400 to $450 to amounts shown.

1958 Porsche 356 Speedster. (Coys of Kensington)

ENGINE DATA: OPTIONAL FOUR (1300): Horizontally opposed, overhead-valve four-cylinder (air cooled). **Displacement:** 78.5 cu. in. (1286 cc). **Bore & Stroke:** 3.15 x 2.52 in. (80 x 64 mm). **Compression Ratio:** 6.5:1. **Brake Horsepower:** 44 DIN (50 SAE) at 4200 rpm. **Torque:** 59 lbs.-ft. at 2800 rpm. Four main bearings. Solid valve lifters. Two Solex carburetors.

OPTIONAL FOUR (1300S): Same as 1286-cc four above, except — **Compression Ratio:** 8.2:1. **Brake Horsepower:** 60 DIN (71 SAE) at 5500 rpm. **Torque:** 63-65 lbs.-ft. at 3600 rpm.

Note: Neither 1300 engine was ordinarily exported to the U.S.

BASE FOUR (1600): Horizontally opposed, overhead-valve four-cylinder (air cooled). **Displacement:** 96.5 cu. in. (1582 cc). **Bore & Stroke:** 3.25 x 2.91 in. (82.5 x 74 mm). **Compression Ratio:** 7.5:1. **Brake Horsepower:** 60 DIN (70 SAE) at 4500 rpm. **Torque:** 81 lbs.-ft. at 2800 rpm. Four main bearings. Solid valve lifters. Two Solex or Zenith carburetors.

OPTIONAL FOUR (1600S): Same as 1582-cc four above, except — **Compression Ratio:** 8.5:1. **Brake Horsepower:** 75 DIN (88 SAE) at 5000 rpm. **Torque:** 86 lbs.-ft. at 3700 rpm.

OPTIONAL FOUR (1956-57 1500GS/GT Carrera): Horizontally opposed, dual-overhead-cam four-cylinder (air cooled). **Displacement:** 91.5 cu. in. (1498 cc). **Bore & Stroke:** 3.35 x 2.59 in. (85 x 66 mm). **Compression Ratio:** 8.7:1. **Brake Horsepower:** 100/110 DIN (up to 128 SAE) at 6200 rpm. **Torque:** 85/88 lbs.-ft. at 5200 rpm. Four main bearings. Solid valve lifters. Two Solex 40 PJI two-barrel carburetors.

OPTIONAL FOUR (1958-59 1600GS/GT Carrera): Horizontally opposed, dual-overhead-cam four-cylinder (air cooled). **Displacement:** 96.8 cu. in. (1587 cc). **Compression Ratio:** 9.5:1. **Bore & Stroke:** 3.45 x 2.59 in. (87.5 x 66 mm). **Brake Horsepower:** 105/115 at 6500 rpm. **Torque:** 89/100 lbs.-ft. at 5000 rpm. Four main bearings. Solid valve lifters. Two Weber carburetors.

1959 Porsche 356A cabriolet. (Coys of Kensington)

CHASSIS DATA: **Wheelbase:** 82.7 in. **Overall Length:** 155.5 in. **Height:** 51.6 in. **Width:** 65.7 in. **Front Tread:** 51.4 in. **Rear Tread:** 50 in. **Standard Tires:** 5.60x15 except (GS/GT Carrera) 5.90x15.

TECHNICAL: **Layout:** rear-engine, rear-drive. **Transmission:** four-speed manual in rear transaxle. **Steering:** worm and peg (later, ZF worm and lever). **Suspension (front):** parallel trailing arms with transverse laminated torsion bars and anti-roll bar. **Suspension (rear):** swing axles with transverse torsion bars. **Brakes:** hydraulic, front/rear drum. **Body Construction:** steel unibody with boxed, pressed-steel platform chassis.

MAJOR OPTIONS: Coupe seats ($45). Side curtains ($10). Lift-off hardtop.

PERFORMANCE: **Top Speed:** (1300) 90 mph claimed; (1300S) 100 mph claimed; (1600) 100 mph claimed; (1600S) 110 mph claimed; (1500GS Carrera) 125 mph claimed; (1600S Speedster) 106 mph. **Acceleration (0-60 mph):** (1600S Speedster) 10.1 sec.; (Carrera) 8.7 sec. **Acceleration (quarter-mile):** (1600S Speedster) 18.3 sec. **Fuel Mileage:** (1600S Speedster) about 25 mpg average.

PRODUCTION/SALES: An industry source offered production figures that differed from those noted above, reporting that a total of 4,264 Porsches were produced during 1956, followed by 5,191 in 1957, 5,998 in 1958, and 7,055 in 1959.

Manufacturer: Dr. Ing. h.c. F. Porsche KG, Zuffenhausen, Stuttgart, West Germany. **Distributor:** Porsche of America Corp., Teaneck, New Jersey.

HISTORY: The 356A first appeared at the Frankfurt automobile show in September 1955; then at the New York Automobile Show in April 1956.

1960-62 PORSCHE

356B — FLAT FOUR — The next incarnation of the 356 series appeared at the Frankfurt show in late 1959. Bumpers were heavier and considerably taller than before, wearing large vertical guards, and the hood had a revised slope. Headlamps also rode higher from the ground, now meeting the top of the fenderline. Amber parking lights went below the headlamps, alongside small horn grilles. Below the bumper sat air intakes for the brake system. What had briefly been called the Convertible D (descended from the Speedster) now took the Roadster designation. All models soon had vent wings in the doors. Digits on the rear deck identified the 1600 (1582-cc) engine. New cast aluminum brake drums had a radial-fin design, with cast iron liners. One new engine became available: the 1600 Super 90, rated 90 horsepower (DIN). In fact, all engines now were of 1.6-liter displacement.

Koni shock absorbers became standard in 1961, on both the 1600S and Super 90. A transverse leaf spring was installed at the rear of Super 90 models, and could go in others as well. During 1960-61, lightweight GT coupe bodies (with Carrera-tuned engines) came from the Reutter company. Roadster bodies were done by Druaz or D'leteren Freres, while the Karmann firm produced a new notchback coupe.

For 1962, the front lid had a flatter appearance, while the engine lid out back switched from a single to dual air-intake grilles, and coupes gained larger back windows. A gas-filler neck now hid beneath a flap in the right front fender. By spring 1962, the race/rally Carrera 2 was available, powered by a 2.0-liter engine that developed 130 horsepower (DIN). This was the first Porsche with all-disc brakes, a feature that would also appear on the final 356 version: the 356C, introduced in mid-1963.

Standard equipment on final 356B examples included a variable-speed electric windshield wiper/washer, backup lights, tool kit (with spare fan belt), rear defroster for coupe window, tachometer, reserve fuel tank, and padded dashboard.

1962 Porsche 356B coupe. (Coys of Kensington)

I.D. DATA: Serial number is on driver's door post. Serial number range: (1960 cpe) 108918 to 114650; (1960 conv) 152476 to 154560; (1960 roadster) 86831 to 88920; (1961 cpe) 114651 to 117476; (1961 Karmann) 200001 to 201048; (1961 conv) 154561 to 155569; (1961 roadster) 88921 to 89483; (1962 cpe) 117601 to 121099; (1962 Karmann) 201601 to 202299; (1962 conv) 155601 to 156999; (1962 roadster) 89601 to 89800. Engine number is on a plate attached to center of engine, at the rear.

Model	Body Type & Seating	Engine Type/CID	P.O.E. Price	Weight (lbs.)	Prod. Total
356B	2-dr Coupe-2+2P	H4/96	3700	1874	Note 1
356B	2-dr HT Cpe-2+2P	H4/96	3865	1874	Note 1
356B	2-dr Cabr-2P	H4/96	3950	1874	Note 1
Roadster	2-dr Rds-2P	H4/96	3580	1874	Note 1
Carrera 2	2-dr Coupe-2P	H4/120	7600	2230	Note 2

Note 1: Approximately 1,320 coupes, 468 cabriolets and 100 Roadsters were produced late in 1959, as early examples of the 356B series. Then, 4,413 coupes, 1,617 cabriolets and 1,529 Roadsters were produced during 1960; 4,176 coupes, 3,257 cabriolets and 563 Roadsters in 1961; plus 4,092 coupes and 1,667 cabriolets in 1962.
Note 2: A total of 1,810 Carrera 2 coupes were produced in 1962-63.
Price Note: Figures shown were valid in 1960. By 1962, prices ranged from $3884 for the Roadster to $4523 for the Cabriolet. Carrera 2 price is approximate, for 1962 model.

ENGINE DATA: BASE FOUR (1600): Horizontally opposed, overhead-valve four-cylinder (air cooled). **Displacement:** 96.5 cu. in. (1582 cc). **Bore & Stroke:** 3.25 x 2.91 in. (82.5 x 74 mm). **Compression Ratio:** 7.5:1. **Brake Horsepower:** 60 DIN (70 SAE) at 4500 rpm. **Torque:** 81 lbs.-ft. at 2800 rpm. Four main bearings. Solid valve lifters. Two Zenith carburetors.
OPTIONAL FOUR (1600S): Same as 1582-cc four above, except — **Compression Ratio:** 8.5:1. **Brake Horsepower:** 75 DIN (88 SAE) at 5000 rpm. **Torque:** 86 lbs.-ft. at 3700 rpm.
OPTIONAL FOUR (1600S 90): Same as 1582-cc four above, except — **Compression Ratio:** 9.0:1. **Brake Horsepower:** 90 DIN (102 SAE) at 5500 rpm. **Torque:** 89 lbs.-ft. at 4300 rpm. Two Solex carburetors.
BASE FOUR (Carrera 2): Horizontally opposed, dual-overhead-cam four-cylinder (air cooled). **Displacement:** 120.0 cu. in. (1966 cc). **Bore & Stroke:** 3.62 x 2.91 in. (92 x 74 mm). **Compression Ratio:** 9.5:1. **Brake Horsepower:** 130 DIN (152 SAE) at 6200 rpm. **Torque:** 116 lbs.-ft. (131 SAE) at 4600 rpm. Four main bearings. Solid valve lifters. Two Solex carburetors.

CHASSIS DATA: Wheelbase: 82.7 in. **Overall Length:** 158 in. **Height:** 52.4 in. **Width:** 65.8 in. **Front Tread:** 51.4 in. **Rear Tread:** 50.1 in. **Standard Tires:** 5.60x15 except (Carrera) 5.90x15.

TECHNICAL: Layout: rear-engine, rear-drive. **Transmission:** four-speed manual in rear transaxle. Gear ratios: (1st) 3.09:1; (2nd) 1.765:1; (3rd) 1.13:1; (4th) 0.852:1; (rev) 3.56:1. **Steering:** ZF worm and lever. **Suspension (front):** parallel trailing arms with transverse laminated torsion bars and anti-roll bar. **Suspension (rear):** swing axles with transverse torsion bars. **Brakes:** hydraulic, front/rear drum. **Body Construction:** steel unibody with boxed, pressed-steel platform chassis. **Fuel Tank:** 13.2 gallon (including 1.6-gallon reserve).

MAJOR OPTIONS: Special-design luggage. Ski or luggage rack. Power steel sunroof. Detachable steel hardtop (cabriolet). Leather seats. Foglamps with yellow lens. Removable headlamp grilles. Outside mirror. Safety belts. Luggage straps. Radio (AM or AM/FM). Headrests. Top cover (cabriolet).
PERFORMANCE: Top Speed: (1600) 110 mph claimed; (1600S) 109 mph; (1600S 90) 115 mph.
PRODUCTION/SALES: An industry source offered production figures that differed from those noted above, reporting that a total of 7,598 Porsches were produced during 1960, followed by 7,664 in 1961, and 8,205 in 1962.
Manufacturer: Dr. Ing. h.c. F. Porsche KG, Zuffenhausen, Stuttgart, West Germany.
Distributor: Porsche of America Corp., Teaneck, New Jersey.
HISTORY: The 356B was introduced in September 1959. A Porsche won the 1962 Grand Prix of France, driven by Dan Gurney. Commenting on the Porsche 356B in *Playboy* magazine, Ken Purdy wrote that it "may be the most fun to drive of anything in the world." In a Porsche, he added, "you can, with small effort, believe that the seat of your trousers is part of the automobile."

1963-64 PORSCHE

356B/C — 1600 C/SC — FOUR — Production of the 356B continued until July 1963, when it was replaced by the 356C. Dunlop four-wheel disc brakes became standard, but except for new flat-face hubcaps, little change was evident. Only three engines remained available: the 1600 C (formerly 1600 Super), 1600 SC (former Super 90), and 2.0-liter

four-cam Carrera 2. Engines marketed in America now had positive crankcase ventilation. Only coupe and cabriolet bodies were produced for these final evolutions of the 356 series. A 'Porsche C' designation went below the grille panel on the rear deck of the basic model.

1963 Porsche 911 coupe. (William Siuru Jr.)

I.D. DATA: Serial number is on driver's door post. Starting serial number: (1963 cpe) 121100 up; (1963 Karmann cpe) 210900 up; (1963 cabr) 157000; (1964 cpe) 126001; (1964 Karmann cpe) 215001; (1964 cabr) 159001. Engine number is on a plate attached to center of engine, at the rear.

Model	Body Type & Seating	Engine Type/CID	P.O.E. Price	Weight (lbs.)	Prod. Total
356C					
1600 C	2-dr Coupe-2+2P	H4/96	4195	1980	Note 1
1600 SC	2-dr Coupe-2+2P	H4/96	4753	1980	Note 1
1600 C	2-dr Cabr-2P	H4/96	4564	1980	Note 1
1600 SC	2-dr Cabr-2P	H4/96	5096	1980	Note 1
CARRERA 2					
Carrera 2	2-dr Coupe-2P	H4/120	7585	N/A	Note 2
Carrera 2	2-dr Coupe-2P	H4/120	8051	2230	Note 2

Note 1: Approximately 2,104 Type 356C coupes, 2,229 hardtops and 832 cabriolets were produced during 1963; followed by 3,823 coupes, 1,745 hardtops and 1,745 cabriolets in 1964; plus a final three coupes, 1,097 hardtops and 588 cabriolets in the first half of 1965.
Note 2: A total of 2,134 Type 356C Carrera 2 coupes (included in totals above).
Price Note: Figures shown were valid in 1964.

1964 Porsche 356SC coupe.

ENGINE DATA: BASE FOUR (1600 C): Horizontally opposed, overhead-valve four-cylinder (air cooled). **Displacement:** 96.5 cu. in. (1582 cc). **Bore & Stroke:** 3.25 x 2.91 in. (82.5 x 74 mm). **Compression Ratio:** 8.5:1. **Brake Horsepower:** 75 DIN (88 SAE) at 5200 rpm. **Torque:** 88 lbs.-ft. at 3600 rpm. Four main bearings. Solid valve lifters. Two Zenith carburetors.
OPTIONAL FOUR (1600 SC): Same as 1582-cc four above, except — **Compression Ratio:** 9.5:1. **Brake Horsepower:** 95 DIN (107 SAE) at 5800 rpm. **Torque:** 88 lbs.-ft. at 4200 rpm. Two Solex carburetors.
BASE FOUR (Carrera 2): Horizontally opposed, dual-overhead-cam four-cylinder (air cooled). **Displacement:** 120.0 cu. in. (1966 cc). **Bore & Stroke:** 3.62 x 2.91 in. (92 x 74 mm). **Compression Ratio:** 9.5:1. **Brake Horsepower:** 130 DIN (145 SAE) at 6200 rpm. **Torque:** 116 lbs.-ft. (131 SAE) at 4600 rpm. Four main bearings. Solid valve lifters. Two Solex carburetors.

CHASSIS DATA: Wheelbase: 82.7 in. **Overall Length:** 158 in. **Height:** 52.4 in. **Width:** 65.8 in. **Front Tread:** 51.4 in. **Rear Tread:** 50.1 in. **Standard Tires:** 5.60x15 except (Carrera) 5.90x15.

TECHNICAL: Layout: rear-engine, rear-drive. **Transmission:** four-speed manual in rear transaxle. **Steering:** ZF worm and lever. **Suspension (front):** parallel trailing arms with transverse laminated torsion bars and anti-roll bar. **Suspension (rear):** swing axles with transverse torsion bars. **Brakes:** hydraulic, front/rear disc. **Body Construction:** steel unibody with boxed, pressed-steel platform chassis.

MAJOR OPTIONS: Specially-designed luggage. Ski or luggage rack. Power steel sunroof. Detachable steel hardtop (cabriolet). Leather seats. Foglamps with yellow lens. Removable headlamp grilles. Outside mirror. Safety belts. Luggage straps. Radio (AM or AM/FM). Headrests. Top cover (cabriolet).

PERFORMANCE: Top Speed: (1600 C) about 109 mph; (1600 SC) 125 mph; (Carrera) 125 mph. **Fuel Mileage:** about 30 mpg except (Carrera) about 24 mpg.

PRODUCTION/SALES: An industry source offered production figures that differed from those noted above, reporting that a total of 9,672 Porsches were built in 1963 and 10,808 in 1964.

ADDITIONAL MODELS: During 1963-64, Porsche produced about 100 Type 904 GTS racing cars for GT competition. Power came from a mid-mounted 2.0-liter dual-overhead-cam four, as in the Carrera, developing as much as 180 horsepower (DIN); or 155 bhp in road trim, of which only a handful were built. A five-speed manual gearbox was used, along with coil springs all around. Top speed approached 160 mph, and a 904 could accelerate to 60 mph in as little as 5.3 seconds. The 904's shapely fiberglass body was designed by Ferdinand "Butzi" Porsche, a grandson of the company's founder who also penned the upcoming 901/911.

Manufacturer: Dr. Ing. h.c. F. Porsche KG, Zuffenhausen, Stuttgart, West Germany.

Distributor: Porsche of America Corp., Teaneck, New Jersey.

HISTORY: Production of the 356C continued until September 1965, when it was replaced by the new 911; and soon afterward, the 912 series. A total of 76,303 examples of the 356 series had been produced since the beginning.

As early as the summer of 1963, Porsche announced the Type 901, which soon would transform itself into the long-lived 911 series. The 901 announcement began by denying that Porsche was about to introduce a four-seater, but insisting that its next model would be in keeping with the Porsche motto: "Driving in its purest form." It would also be even more aerodynamically smooth than the 356, on a longer wheelbase, and able to deliver the performance of a Carrera. Changes announced at this time included a switch to MacPherson struts in the front suspension, rack-and-pinion steering and a five-speed transmission. See next listing for details on the actual production version 901/911.

1965-66 PORSCHE

1965 Porsche 356C coupe. (Coys of Kensington)

356 — 1600 C/SC — FLAT FOUR — Final 356C and 356SC models were the only Porsches available in the U.S. at the start of the 1965 model year; see previous listings for additional details. Coupe bodies came from either Reutter or Karmann.

911 — 2000 (A-Series) — FLAT SIX — After a considerable number of rumors, the six-cylinder successor to the original 356 series finally arrived on the U.S. market during the 1965 model year. About six inches longer overall than its predecessor, the 911 rode a wheelbase that measured 4.4 inches longer. Styling was similar on the whole, but the 911 displayed more of a fastback profile, including a "knife-edged" appearance at the front end, with its nose extending downward into the bumper line. It also looked narrower toward the rear, with a low beltline. Air intakes extended into the hood/fender line, while turn-signal indicators wrapped around the front fenders. A long horizontal, one-piece air intake went at the top of the rear deck. Horizontal rectangular taillamps wrapped around the rear fenders, while the back bumper extended to the rear of the wheel openings.

Porsche's horizontally-opposed, air-cooled 2.0-liter six-cylinder engine with single overhead camshafts developed 148 horsepower, working through a five-speed manual gearbox. That was enough to warrant announcement of a zero-to-60 time around eight seconds, with a top speed of 130 mph. Racing-style disc brakes went on all four wheels. Porsche promoted the new model for its aerodynamic design, equal fore/aft weight distribution, low center of gravity, and tight suspension. Instead of being pushed as a conventional sports car, it was described as a "gran turismo" vehicle, in the European sense of that term: "a fast, comfortable, high-performance car to go about your business in." A wood-trimmed instrument panel held five gauges.

912 — 1600 — FLAT FOUR — For the 1966 model year, a new four-cylinder coupe joined the 911, with the same body, brakes and suspension as its six-cylinder mate. Providing the power was the same engine used in the 356SC (Super 90) series, but in detuned form. Referred to as the 616/36 engine, it developed 102 horsepower (SAE) at 5800 rpm, for a top speed of about 115 mph. Two versions were offered: a 912/4 with four-speed gearbox, and a 912/5 with five-speed. Standard equipment included three-speed windshield wipers with quad-jet washers, reclining bucket seats, backup lights, dual horns, 7000-rpm tachometer, a parcel shelf behind rear seats, two padded sunvisors, and a touch-up paint dispenser. As in the 356 series, two occasional back seats were available for small passengers. Only three gauges were installed on the instrument panel, which had no wood trim.

1966 Porsche 912 Targa. (William Siuru Jr.)

I.D. DATA: Serial number is on driver's door-hinge post, or on a plate in front luggage compartment (near gas tank). Starting serial number: (1965 Reutter-bodied 356 cpe) 130512; (1965 Karmann-bodied 356 cpe) 219070; (1965 356 cabr) 160751; (1965 911 cpe) 000001; (1966 911 cpe) 300.001; (1966 912/4 cpe) 350.001; (1966 912/5 cpe) 450.001. Engine number is on a plate attached to center of engine, at the rear.

Model	Body Type & Seating	Engine Type/CID	P.O.E. Price	Weight (lbs.)	Prod. Total
356 (1965 models)					
1600 C	2-dr Coupe-2 + 2P	H4/96	4099	1980	Note 1
1600 SC	2-dr Coupe-2 + 2P	H4/96	4577	1980	Note 1
1600 C	2-dr Cabr-2P	H4/96	4460	1980	Note 1
1600 SC	2-dr Cabr-2P	H4/96	4873	1980	Note 1
911					
2000	2-dr Coupe-2 + 2P	H6/121	6490	2376	Note 2
912 (1966 models)					
912/4	2-dr Coupe-2 + 2P	H4/96	4690	2134	Note 3
912/5	2-dr Coupe-2 + 2P	H4/96	4770	2134	Note 3

Note 1: Approximately three Type 356 coupes, 1,097 hardtops and 588 cabriolets were produced during 1965.

Note 2: Approximately 36,533 Type 911 Porsches (A-Series) were produced over the full model run, from 1965 to 1968.

Note 3: Approximately 6,440 Type 912 Porsches were produced during 1965, followed by 8,700 in 1966.

ENGINE DATA: BASE FOUR (356/1600 C): Horizontally opposed, overhead-valve four-cylinder (air cooled). Light alloy block and heads. **Displacement:** 96.5 cu. in. (1582 cc). **Bore & Stroke:** 3.25 x 2.91 in. (82.5 x 74 mm). **Compression Ratio:** 8.5:1. **Brake Horsepower:** 75 DIN (88 SAE) at 5200 rpm. **Torque:** 88 lbs.-ft. at 3600 rpm. Four main bearings. Solid valve lifters. Two carburetors.

OPTIONAL FOUR (356/1600 SC): Same as 1582-cc four above, except — **Compression Ratio:** 9.5:1. **Brake Horsepower:** 95 DIN (107 SAE) at 5800 rpm. **Torque:** 88 lbs.-ft. at 4200 rpm.

BASE FOUR (912): Same as 1582-cc four above, except — **Compression Ratio:** 9.3:1. **Brake Horsepower:** 90 DIN (102 SAE) at 5800 rpm. **Torque:** 91 lbs.-ft. at 3500 rpm. Two Solex 40P II-4 carburetors.

BASE SIX (911): Horizontally opposed, overhead-cam six-cylinder (air cooled). **Displacement:** 121.5 cu. in. (1991 cc). **Bore & Stroke:** 3.15 x 2.60 in. (80 x 66 mm). **Compression Ratio:** 9.0:1. **Brake Horsepower:** 130 DIN (148 SAE) at 6100 rpm. **Torque:** 129 lbs.-ft. at 4200 rpm (140 SAE at 4300 rpm). Eight main bearings. Two Solex 40 BI carburetors.

CHASSIS DATA: Wheelbase: (356) 82.7 in.; (911/912) 87.1 in. **Overall Length:** (356) 158 in.; (911/912) 164.0 in. **Height:** (356) 52.4 in.; (911/912) 52 in. **Width:** (356) 65.8 in.; (911/912) 63.4 in. **Front Tread:** (356) 51.4 in.; (911) 52.7 in.; (912) 52.6 in. **Rear Tread:** (356) 50.1 in.; (911/912) 51.9 in. **Standard Tires:** (356) 5.60x15; (911) 165HR15; (912) 6.95H15 (165HR15 optional).

TECHNICAL: Layout: rear-engine, rear-drive. **Transmission:** (356, 912/4) four-speed manual in rear transaxle; (911, 912/5) five-speed manual. 911 gear ratios: (1st) 2.835:1; (2nd) 1.778:1; (3rd) 1.218:1; (4th) 0.962:1; (5th) 0.822:1. **Steering:** (356) ZF worm and lever; (911/912) rack and pinion. **Suspension (front):** (356) parallel trailing arms with transverse laminated torsion bars and anti-roll bar; (911/912) MacPherson Struts with single lower transverse A-arms, longitudinal torsion bars and anti-roll bar. **Suspension (rear):** (356) swing axles with transverse torsion bars; (911/912) independent with semi-trailing arms and transverse torsion bars. **Brakes:** front/rear disc. **Body Construction:** steel monocoque (unibody).

PERFORMANCE: Top Speed: (911) 130 mph claimed; (912) 115 mph claimed. **Acceleration (0-60 mph):** (911) 8 sec. claimed (7.0-9.0 sec. in tests); (912) under 12 sec. claimed (11.7 sec. in test). **Acceleration (quarter-mile):** (911) 16.5 sec. (86 mph). **Fuel Mileage:** 24.5 mpg claimed (14-19 mpg average in test).

PRODUCTION/SALES: An industry source reported that 11,243 Porsches (all models) were built in 1965, followed by 13,134 in 1966. Approximately 4,599 Porsches were sold in the U.S. during 1965, followed by 6,195 in 1966.

Manufacturer: Dr. Ing. h.c. F. Porsche KG, Zuffenhausen, Stuttgart, West Germany.

Distributor: Porsche of America Corp., Teaneck, New Jersey.

HISTORY: The first new Porsche in 17 years, the 911 was introduced to the western U.S. market in July 1965, at Albany, California. The four-cylinder 912 was available by the start of the 1966 model year, in September 1965. Meanwhile, production of the old 356 series had extended into 1965, but only for export to the U.S.

1967 PORSCHE

1967 Porsche 911 coupe.

911/911S — 2000 (A-Series) — FLAT SIX — A high-performance 911S coupe joined the original 911 this year. With 9.8:1 compression rather than the usual 9.0:1, and twin three-barrel carburetors, its 2.0-liter engine developed 180 horsepower instead of the 911's 148 bhp. Both engines used Weber carburetors.

912 — 1600 — FLAT FOUR — Production of the four-cylinder coupe continued with little change. The 102-bhp engine came with a standard four-speed manual transmission.

I.D. DATA: Serial number is on a plate in front luggage compartment, near the gas tank. Starting serial number: (911 cpe) 305.001; (911S cpe) 500.000; (912 cpe) 354.001 or 458.101. Engine number is on a plate attached to center of engine, at the rear.

Model	Body Type & Seating	Engine Type/CID	P.O.E. Price	Weight (lbs.)	Prod. Total
911	2-dr Coupe-2+2P	H6/121	5990	2376	Note 1
911S	2-dr Coupe-2+2P	H6/121	6990	2270	Note 1
912					
912	2-dr Coupe-2+2P	H4/96	4790	2134	Note 2

Note 1: Approximately 36,533 Type 911 Porsches (A-Series) were produced over the full model run, from 1965 to 1968.
Note 2: Approximately 3,239 Type 912 Porsches were produced during 1967.

ENGINE DATA: BASE FOUR (912): Horizontally opposed, overhead-valve four-cylinder (air cooled). Light alloy block and heads. **Displacement:** 96.5 cu. in. (1582 cc). **Bore & Stroke:** 3.25 x 2.91 in. (82.5 x 74 mm). **Compression Ratio:** 9.3:1. **Brake Horsepower:** 90 DIN (102 SAE) at 5800 rpm. **Torque:** 91 lbs.-ft. at 3500 rpm. Four main bearings. Two Solex carburetors.

BASE SIX (911): Horizontally opposed, overhead-cam six-cylinder (air cooled). **Displacement:** 121.5 cu. in. (1991 cc). **Bore & Stroke:** 3.15 x 2.60 in. (80 x 66 mm). **Compression Ratio:** 9.0:1. **Brake Horsepower:** 130 DIN (148 SAE) at 6100 rpm. **Torque:** 129 lbs.-ft. at 4200 rpm (140 SAE at 4300 rpm). Eight main bearings. Two Weber carburetors.

BASE SIX (911S): Same as 1991-cc six above, except — **Compression Ratio:** 9.8:1. **Brake Horsepower:** 180 (SAE) at 6600 rpm. **Torque:** 144 lbs.-ft. at 5200 rpm. Two Weber carburetors.

CHASSIS DATA: Wheelbase: 87.1 in. **Overall Length:** 163.9 in. **Height:** 52 in. **Width:** 63.4 in. **Front Tread:** (911S) 53.4 in. **Rear Tread:** (911S) 52.2 in. **Standard Tires:** (911) 165HR15; (912) 6.95x15.

TECHNICAL: Layout: (912) four-speed manual in rear transaxle; (911) five-speed manual. 911S gear ratios: (1st) 3.09:1; (2nd) 1.89:1; (3rd) 1.32:1; (4th) 1.04:1; (5th) 0.79:1. **Steering:** rack and pinion. **Suspension (front):** MacPherson Struts with single lower transverse A-arms, longitudinal torsion bars and anti-roll bar. **Suspension (rear):** independent with semi-trailing arms and transverse torsion bars. **Brakes:** front/rear disc. **Body Construction:** steel monocoque (unibody).

MAJOR OPTIONS: Air conditioning ($500). Sunroof ($395).

PERFORMANCE: Top Speed: (911) 130 mph; (911S) 140 mph; (912) 115 mph. **Acceleration (0-60 mph):** (911S) 6.5 sec. **Acceleration (quarter-mile):** (911S) 15.2 sec. (92 mph).

PRODUCTION/SALES: An industry source reported that 10,941 Porsches were built in 1967. Approximately 6,700 Porsches were sold in the U.S. during 1967.
Manufacturer: Dr. Ing. h.c. F. Porsche KG, Zuffenhausen, Stuttgart, West Germany.
Distributor: Porsche of America Corp., Teaneck, New Jersey.
HISTORY: Porsche's 1967 models were introduced to the U.S. market on October 1, 1966.

1968 PORSCHE

911/911L — 2000 (A-Series) — FLAT SIX — The high-performance 911S coupe dropped out of the lineup temporarily, replaced by a detuned 911L (luxury) model with the same 148-bhp engine as the base Porsche. Extra 911L features included a leather-covered steering wheel and forged aluminum wheels. Each model was available not only in the expected closed coupe form, but with a new Targa "convertible" top, which included a large built-in rollbar. A tinted, heated rear window cost $120 extra. Also new was a Sportomatic semi-automatic transmission option, which amounted to little more than an ordinary four-speed gearbox with a torque converter and automatic clutch added. A four-speed manual gearbox was standard; five-speed optional.

912 — 1600 — FLAT FOUR — Like its 911 companion, the four-cylinder Porsche came in both closed-coupe and Targa "convertible" this year. A four-speed manual gearbox was standard, with five-speed available at extra cost.

I.D. DATA: Serial number is located in front luggage compartment, near the gas tank. Starting serial number: (911 cpe) 118.3.0001; (911 Targa) 118.8.0001; (911L cpe) 118.0.5001; (911L Targa) 118.5.5001; (912 cpe) 128.0.0001 or 128.2.0001; (912 Targa) 128.7.0001. Engine number is on a plate attached to center of engine, at the rear.

Model	Body Type & Seating	Engine Type/CID	P.O.E. Price	Weight (lbs.)	Prod. Total
911/L					
911	2-dr Coupe-2+2P	H6/121	6190	2376	Note 1
911	2-dr Targa-2+2P	H6/121	6590	2376	Note 1
911L	2-dr Coupe-2+2P	H6/121	6790	2376	Note 1
911L	2-dr Targa-2+2P	H6/121	7190	2376	Note 1
912					
912	2-dr Coupe-2+2P	H4/96	4950	2134	Note 2
912	2-dr Targa-2+2P	H4/96	5350	2134	Note 2

Note 1: Approximately 36,533 Type 911 Porsches (A-Series) were produced over the full model run, from 1965 to 1968.
Note 2: Approximately 11,921 Type 912 Porsches were produced during the 1968-69 period.

ENGINE DATA: BASE FOUR (912): Horizontally opposed, overhead-valve four-cylinder (air cooled). Light alloy block and heads. **Displacement:** 96.5 cu. in. (1582 cc). **Bore & Stroke:** 3.25 x 2.91 in. (82.5 x 74 mm). **Compression Ratio:** 9.3:1. **Brake Horsepower:** 102 (SAE) at 5800 rpm. **Torque:** 90 lbs.-ft. at 4200 rpm. Four main bearings. Two Solex carburetors.

BASE SIX (911): Horizontally opposed, overhead-cam six-cylinder (air cooled). **Displacement:** 121.5 cu. in. (1991 cc). **Bore & Stroke:** 3.15 x 2.60 in. (80 x 66 mm). **Compression Ratio:** 9.0:1. **Brake Horsepower:** 148 (SAE) at 6100 rpm. **Torque:** 145 lbs.-ft. at 4200 rpm. Eight main bearings. Two Weber carburetors.

CHASSIS DATA: Wheelbase: 87.1 in. **Overall Length:** 163.9 in. **Height:** 52 in. **Width:** 63.4 in. **Front Tread:** 53.3 in. **Rear Tread:** 52 in. **Standard Tires:** (911) 165x15; (912) 6.95x15.

TECHNICAL: Layout: rear-engine, rear-drive. **Transmission:** four-speed manual in rear transaxle; five-speed manual or Sportomatic optional. **Steering:** rack and pinion. **Suspension (front):** MacPherson Struts with single lower transverse A-arms, longitudinal torsion bars and anti-roll bar. **Suspension (rear):** independent with semi-trailing arms and transverse torsion bars. **Brakes:** front/rear disc. **Body Construction:** steel monocoque (unibody).

MAJOR OPTIONS: Five-speed manual transmission ($80). Semi-automatic transmission: 911 ($280). Tinted/heated rear window: Targa ($120). Air conditioning. Sunroof.

PERFORMANCE: Top Speed: (911) 130 mph; (911 w/Sportomatic) 120 mph; (912) 115 mph. **Acceleration (0-60 mph):** (911 w/Sportomatic) 9.3 sec. **Acceleration (quarter-mile):** (911 w/Sportomatic) 16.8 sec. (82 mph). **Fuel Mileage:** (911 w/Sportomatic) about 15-19 mpg.

PRODUCTION/SALES: An industry source reported that 14,133 Porsches were built in 1968. Approximately 7,458 Porsches were sold in the U.S. during 1968.
Manufacturer: Dr. Ing. h.c. F. Porsche KG, Zuffenhausen, Stuttgart, West Germany.
Distributor: Porsche of America Corp., Teaneck, New Jersey.
HISTORY: Porsche's 1968 models were introduced to the U.S. market in October 1967. Car and Driver was not impressed by the Sportomatic transmission, claiming that it reminded them "of Detroit's bizarre efforts at clutchless shifting that died a merciful death in the middle Fifties."

1969 PORSCHE

1969 Porsche 911S coupe.

911 — B-Series — FLAT SIX — Changes weren't exactly dramatic for the second-generation 911, but were enough to make a difference. For starters, the coupe's wheelbase grew by 2.2 inches, to 89.3 inches. Flared wheel openings went into the body, allowing for wider tires. Different axle half-shafts were installed, and weight distribution improved. Three models were offered this time: base 911T, 911E, and (after a one year's

absence) the high-performance 911S, with a 190-bhp version of the 2.0-liter engine. Instead of the customary MacPherson struts with torsion bars, the 911E version included Boge self-leveling front struts; but that change didn't last long. Targa coupes turned to a fixed wraparound back window (prior versions were zippered plastic as standard, with heated glass optional). Back at the engine bay, the 911T stuck with twin Weber carburetors, but the other two went into Bosch mechanical fuel injection. Only a five-speed manual gearbox was available in the 911S, while the others could have either a four-speed, five-speed, or Sportomatic. Targa "convertibles" now had fluting in the stainless steel roll bar.

912 — 1600 — FLAT FOUR — Production of the four-cylinder Porsche continued with minimal change, on the same extended wheelbase as the 911. As before, the 912 was offered in either coupe or Targa form.

I.D. DATA: Serial number plate is located in front luggage compartment. Starting serial number: (911T cpe) 11.910.0001 or 11.912.0001; (911T Targa) 11.911.0001; (911E cpe) 11.920.0001 or 11.922.0001; (911E Targa) 11.921.0001; (911S cpe) 11.930.0001 or 11.932.0001; (911S Targa) 11.931.0001; (912 cpe) 12.900.0001 or 12.902.0001; (912 Targa) 12.901.0001. Engine number is on a plate attached to center of engine, at the rear.

Model	Body Type & Seating	Engine Type/CID	P.O.E. Price	Weight (lbs.)	Prod. Total
911T	2-dr Coupe-2+2P	H6/121	5795	2249	Note 1
911T	2-dr Targa-2+2P	H6/121	6315	2249	Note 1
911E	2-dr Coupe-2+2P	H6/121	6995	2249	Note 1
911E	2-dr Targa-2+2P	H6/121	7515	2249	Note 1
911S	2-dr Coupe-2+2P	H6/121	7695	2249	Note 1
911S	2-dr Targa-2+2P	H6/121	8215	2249	Note 1
912					
912	2-dr Coupe-2+2P	H4/96	5095	2094	Note 2
912	2-dr Targa-2+2P	H4/96	5615	2094	Note 2

Note 1: Approximately 14,446 Type 911 Porsches (B-Series) were produced during 1969.

Note 2: Approximately 11,921 Type 912 Porsches were produced during the 1968-69 period.

ENGINE DATA: BASE FOUR (912): Horizontally opposed, overhead-valve four-cylinder (air cooled). Light alloy block and heads. **Displacement:** 96.5 cu. in. (1582 cc). **Bore & Stroke:** 3.25 x 2.91 in. (82.5 x 74 mm). **Compression Ratio:** 9.3:1. **Brake Horsepower:** 102 (SAE) at 5800 rpm. **Torque:** 90 lbs.-ft. at 4200 rpm. Four main bearings. Two carburetors.

BASE SIX (911T): Horizontally opposed, overhead-cam six-cylinder (air cooled). **Displacement:** 121.5 cu. in. (1991 cc). **Bore & Stroke:** 3.15 x 2.60 in. (80 x 66 mm). **Compression Ratio:** 8.6:1. **Brake Horsepower:** 125 (SAE) at 5800 rpm. **Torque:** 131 lbs.-ft. at 4200 rpm. Eight main bearings. Two Weber carburetors.

BASE SIX (911E): Same as 1991-cc six above, except — **Compression Ratio:** 9.1:1. **Brake Horsepower:** 158 (SAE) at 6500 rpm. **Torque:** 145 lbs.-ft. at 4500 rpm. Bosch mechanical fuel injection.

BASE SIX (911S): Same as 1991-cc six above, except — **Compression Ratio:** 9.9:1. **Brake Horsepower:** 190 (SAE) at 6800 rpm. **Torque:** 149-152 lbs.-ft. at 5500 rpm. Bosch mechanical fuel injection.

CHASSIS DATA: Wheelbase: 89.3 in. **Overall Length:** 163.9 in. **Height:** 52 in. **Width:** 63.4 in. **Front Tread:** (911T) 53.8 in.; (911E) 54.1 in.; (911S) 54.2 in. **Rear Tread:** (911T) 53.0 in.; (911E) 53.4 in.; (911S) 53.5 in. **Standard Tires:** (911E) 185/70VR15; (911S) 185/70VR15; (912) 165x15.

TECHNICAL: Layout: rear-engine, rear-drive. **Transmission:** four-speed manual in rear transaxle except (911S) five-speed; five-speed manual or Sportomatic optional on all except 911S. **Steering:** rack and pinion. **Suspension (front):** MacPherson Struts with single lower transverse A-arms and longitudinal torsion bars (anti-roll bar on 911T), except (911E) self-leveling struts. **Suspension (rear):** independent with semi-trailing arms and transverse torsion bars (anti-roll bar on 911S). **Brakes:** front/rear disc. **Body Construction:** steel monocoque (unibody).

MAJOR OPTIONS: Five-speed manual transmission. Sportomatic transmission. Air conditioning. Sunroof.

PRODUCTION/SALES: An industry source reported that 15,292 Porsches were built in 1969. Approximately 5,893 Porsches were sold in the U.S. during 1969.

Manufacturer: Dr. Ing. h.c. F. Porsche KG, Zuffenhausen, Stuttgart, West Germany.

Distributor: Porsche of America Corp., Teaneck, New Jersey.

HISTORY: This was the last year for the four-cylinder 912, which faded away to leave room the new mid-engine 914. Later, for the 1976 model year (after the 914 had proved to be a sluggish seller), the 912 designation was destined to return for another short-lived stab at the market.

1970-71 PORSCHE

911 — C-Series/D-Series — FLAT SIX — A larger (2.2-liter) horizontally-opposed engine went into the next 911 generation, boosting horsepower and torque ratings accordingly. Attachment points for the front suspension were moved forward slightly, with the intention of reducing steering effort. Brakes also were improved. A ZF limited-slip differential was now optional. Production of the three 911 models continued with little change, offered again in both closed coupe and Targa coupe (convertible) body styles. As before, the 911T engine was carbureted (now with Zenith rather than Weber units); the others retained Bosch mechanical fuel injection. The self-leveling suspension struts of the 911E (optional on other models) faded away during the model year. The D-Series of 1971 showed little change.

914 — FLAT FOUR/SIX — A completely different Porsche emerged for the 1970 model year, to replace the rather short-lived 912. This one carried either a 1679-cc Volkswagen four-cylinder engine (rated 85 SAE horsepower), or the earlier 2.0-liter Porsche flat six with its 125-bhp rating. The big difference was that the engines were mid-mounted. The 914 was a joint venture between Porsche and Volkswagen, with bodies created by Karmann. The two-seat targa-topped coupe was built to a Porsche design, with suspension components adapted from the 911 (but lacking anti-roll bars). Coil springs went at the rear, instead of the customary torsion bars. Bilstein gas-filled shock absorbers could be ordered to replace the standard Boge units. Four-wheel (non-vented) disc brakes were installed. The four-cylinder VW engine used Bosch electronic fuel injection, and worked through a five-speed manual gearbox. Styling differed considerably from the usual Porsche (or Volkswagen), displaying a somewhat square profile with raised front fender tips and a long deck. Large sail panels held the roof bar and formed the base for the removable fiberglass top, which could be stored in the trunk. The six-cylinder version, called 914/6, arrived later in the 1970 model year with wider tires on light alloy wheels, and vented-type front brakes. It also had more complete instrumentation, as in the 911 series.

I.D. DATA: Serial number is on a plate at front of hood opening, or (1971) on left windshield column post. Starting serial number (1970 models): (911T cpe) 9110100001; (911T Targa) 9110110001; (911E cpe) 9110200001; (911E Targa) 9110210001; (911S) 9110300001; (914/4) 4702000001; (914/6) 9140430001. Engine number is on a plate attached to center of engine, at the rear.

Model	Body Type & Seating	Engine Type/CID	P.O.E. Price	Weight (lbs.)	Prod. Total
911T	2-dr Coupe-2+2P	H6/134	6430	2250	Note 1
911T	2-dr Targa-2+2P	H6/134	7105	2250	Note 1
911E	2-dr Coupe-2+2P	H6/134	7895	2250	Note 1
911E	2-dr Targa-2+2P	H6/134	8570	2250	Note 1
911S	2-dr Coupe-2+2P	H6/134	8675	2250	Note 1
911S	2-dr Targa-2+2P	H6/134	9350	2250	Note 1
914					
914/4	2-dr Targa-2P	H4/102	3595	1982	Note 2
914/6	2-dr Targa-2P	H6/121	5999	2070	Note 2

Note 1: Approximately 10,234 Type 911 Porsches (C-Series) were produced during 1970, followed by at least 10,599 (D-Series) in 1971.

Note 2: Approximately 16,231 Type 914 Porsches were produced during 1970, followed by 21,440 in 1971.

ENGINE DATA: BASE SIX (911T): Horizontally opposed, overhead-cam six-cylinder (air cooled). **Displacement:** 134 cu. in. (2195 cc). **Bore & Stroke:** 3.31 x 2.60 in. (84 x 66 mm). **Compression Ratio:** 8.6:1. **Brake Horsepower:** 142 (SAE) at 5800 rpm (125 bhp DIN). **Torque:** 148 lbs.-ft. at 4200 rpm. Eight main bearings. Two Zenith carburetors.

BASE SIX (911E): Same as 2195-cc six above, except — **Compression Ratio:** 9.0:1. **Brake Horsepower:** 175 (SAE) at 6200 rpm (155 bhp DIN). **Torque:** 160 lbs.-ft. at 4500 rpm. Bosch fuel injection.

BASE SIX (911S): Same as 2195-cc six above, except — **Compression Ratio:** 9.8:1. **Brake Horsepower:** 200 (SAE) at 6500 rpm (180 bhp DIN). **Torque:** 164 lbs.-ft. at 5200 rpm. Bosch fuel injection.

BASE FOUR (914/4): Horizontally opposed, overhead-valve four-cylinder (air-cooled Volkswagen). **Displacement:** 102.5 cu. in. (1679 cc). **Bore & Stroke:** 3.54 x 2.60 in. (90 x 66 mm). **Compression Ratio:** 8.2:1. **Brake Horsepower:** 85 (SAE) at 5000 rpm (80 bhp DIN). **Torque:** 99.6 lbs.-ft. at 3500 rpm. Four main bearings. Bosch electronic fuel injection.

BASE SIX (914/6): Horizontally opposed, overhead-cam six-cylinder (air cooled). **Displacement:** 121.5 cu. in. (1991 cc). **Bore & Stroke:** 3.15 x 2.60 in. (80 x 66 mm). **Compression Ratio:** 8.6:1. **Brake Horsepower:** 125 (SAE) at 5800 rpm (110 bhp DIN). **Torque:** 131 lbs.-ft. at 4200 rpm. Eight main bearings. Two Weber three-barrel carburetors.

CHASSIS DATA: Wheelbase: (911) 89.3 in.; (914) 96.5 in. **Overall Length:** (911) 163.9 in.; (914) 156.8 in.; **Height:** (911) 52 in.; (914) 48.4 in. **Width:** (911) 63.4 in.; (914) 65.0 in. **Front Tread:** (911T) 53.6 in.; (911E) 53.7 in.; (911S) 54.2 in.; (914/4) 52.8 in.; (914/6) 53.6 in. **Rear Tread:** (911T) 52.9 in.; (911E) 53 in.; (911S) 53.5 in.; (914) 54.5 in. **Standard Tires:** (911T) 165HR14; (911E) 185HR14; (911S) 185/70VR15; (914/4) 155SR15; (914/6) 165HR15.

TECHNICAL: Layout: rear-engine, rear-drive. **Transmission:** (911T) four-speed manual in rear transaxle, with five-speed manual or four-speed Sportomatic optional; (911E) five-speed manual, with Sportomatic optional; (911S) five-speed manual; (914) five-speed manual. **Steering:** rack and pinion. **Suspension (front):** MacPherson struts with single lower transverse A-arms and longitudinal torsion bars (anti-roll bar on 911E/S) except (early 911E) self-leveling struts. **Suspension (rear):** (911) independent with semi-trailing arms and transverse torsion bars, plus anti-roll bar on 911S; (914) semi-trailing arms with coil springs. **Brakes:** front/rear disc. **Body Construction:** steel monocoque (unibody).

MAJOR OPTIONS: Five-speed manual transmission (911T). Sportomatic transmission: 911T/E ($315). Air conditioning ($635-$650). Sunroof: 911 ($360). Appearance group (914). Alloy wheels (911). AM/FM stereo radio w/tape player.

PRODUCTION/SALES: An industry source reported that 16,757 Porsches were built in 1970, followed by 10,905 in 1971 (not including VW-Porsche 914s). Approximately 13,898 Porsches were sold in the U.S. during 1970, followed by 17,239 in 1971.

Manufacturer: Dr. Ing. h.c. F. Porsche KG, Zuffenhausen, Stuttgart, West Germany.

Distributor: Volkswagen of America Inc., Englewood Cliffs, New Jersey.

HISTORY: Porsche's 914/4 appeared at the Frankfurt auto show in September 1969 and went on sale in Europe in February 1970, reaching U.S. showrooms a month later. The 914/6 came later in the year. Type 914s were marketed in Europe as "VW-Porsche" models, but carried only the Porsche designation in the U.S. market. Volkswagen and Porsche formed a new company with 'VG' designation to handle sales of both makes. The six-cylinder 914 was destined to last only until the 1972 model year, a victim of weak sales, while the four-cylinder version hung on into 1976.

1972 PORSCHE

1972 Porsche 911 Targa.

911 — E-Series — FLAT SIX — Stroking the flat-six engine brought another increase in displacement to the trio of Porsche 2+2 sports cars. The 2341-cc (143-cid) six now produced 157, 185 or 210 SAE horsepower (for the 911T, 911E and 911S respectively). All three engines were now fuel-injected. Curiously, the 911's engine-lid badges this year carried a '2.4' label, though the actual displacement was closer to 2.3 liters. This year's 911S added a small lip spoiler under its front bumper (optional on the other two models). Because of reduced compression, all 911s sold in the U.S. could now operate on regular gasoline. The five-speed gearbox also was modified this year, to give a more conventional H-pattern for shifting. Wheelbase grew this year, but only by an insignificant 3 millimeters.

914 — FLAT FOUR — Only the four-cylinder 914 was listed in most U.S. directories of imported cars this year, as the six-cylinder version faded out of the lineup.

I.D. DATA: Porsche's 10-digit serial number for 911 is at driver's door-hinge post, visible through the windshield; or on a plate in the luggage compartment, near the hood latch. Serial number for 914 is on driver's windshield pillar post, on a plate at right headlamp casing, and on a plate attached to right front fender panel in luggage compartment. The first three digits indicate model; digit four denotes the model year; digit six identifies the engine; digit seven is body type; followed by the sequential production number. Starting serial number: (911T) 9112100001; (911E) 9112200001; (911S) 9112300001; (914) 4722900001. Engine number for 911 is on right rear of block, below the generator support bracket; for 914, on left upper portion of crankcase, below the breather column.

Model	Body Type & Seating	Engine Type/CID	P.O.E. Price	Weight (lbs.)	Prod. Total
911T	2-dr Coupe-2+2P	H6/143	7250	2230	Note 1
911T	2-dr Targa-2+2P	H6/143	7985	2238	Note 1
911E	2-dr Coupe-2+2P	H6/143	7995	2238	Note 1
911E	2-dr Targa-2+2P	H6/143	8730	2238	Note 1
911S	2-dr Coupe-2+2P	H6/143	9495	2238	Note 1
911S	2-dr Targa-2+2P	H6/143	10230	2238	Note 1
914					
914	2-dr Targa-2P	H4/102	3755	1973	Note 2

Note 1: Approximately 14,266 Type 911 Porsches were produced during 1972, according to industry sources.

Note 2: Approximately 27,660 Type 914 Porsches were produced during 1972.

ENGINE DATA: BASE SIX (911T): Horizontally opposed, overhead-cam six-cylinder (air cooled). **Displacement:** 142.8 cu. in. (2341 cc). **Bore & Stroke:** 3.31 x 2.76 in. (84 x 70 mm). **Compression Ratio:** 7.5:1. **Brake Horsepower:** 157 (SAE) at 5600 rpm (130 bhp DIN). **Torque:** 166 lbs.-ft. at 4000 rpm. Eight main bearings. Bosch fuel injection.

BASE SIX (911E): Same as 2341-cc six above, except — **Compression Ratio:** 8.0:1. **Brake Horsepower:** 185 (SAE) at 6200 rpm (165 bhp DIN). **Torque:** 174 lbs.-ft. at 4800 rpm. Bosch fuel injection.

BASE SIX (911S): Same as 2341-cc six above, except — **Compression Ratio:** 8.5:1. **Brake Horsepower:** 210 (SAE) at 6500 rpm (190 bhp DIN). **Torque:** 181 lbs.-ft. at 5200 rpm. Bosch fuel injection.

BASE FOUR (914): Horizontally opposed, overhead-valve four-cylinder (air-cooled Volkswagen). **Displacement:** 102.5 cu. in. (1679 cc). **Bore & Stroke:** 3.54 x 2.60 in. (90 x 66 mm). **Compression Ratio:** 8.2:1. **Brake Horsepower:** 85 (SAE) at 5000 rpm (80 bhp DIN). **Torque:** 99.5 lbs.-ft. at 3500 rpm. Four main bearings. Bosch fuel injection.

CHASSIS DATA: Wheelbase: (911) 89.4 in.; (914) 96.5 in. **Overall Length:** (911) 168.9 in.; (914) 157 in. **Height:** (911) 52 in.; (914) 48.4 in. **Width:** (911) 63.4 in.; (914) 65.0 in. **Front Tread:** (911T) 53.8 in.; (911E/S) 54.1 in.; (914) 52.7 in. **Rear Tread:** (911T) 52.9 in.; (911E/S) 53.3 in.; (914) 54.3 in. **Standard Tires:** (911T) 165HR14; (911E) 185VR14; (911S) 185/70VR15; (914) 155SR15.

TECHNICAL: Layout: rear-engine, rear-drive. **Transmission:** (911T/E) four-speed manual in rear transaxle, with five-speed manual or four-speed Sportomatic optional; (911S) five-speed manual, with Sportomatic optional; (914) five-speed manual. **Steering:** rack and pinion. **Suspension (front):** MacPherson struts with single lower transverse A-arms and longitudinal torsion bars (anti-roll bar on 911E/S). **Suspension (rear):** (911) independent with semi-trailing arms and transverse torsion bars, plus anti-roll bar on 911S; (914) semi-trailing arms with coil springs. **Brakes:** front/rear disc. **Body Construction:** steel monocoque (unibody).

MAJOR OPTIONS: Five-speed manual transmission (911T/E). Sportomatic transmission (911). Air conditioning. Sunroof (911). Appearance group: 914 ($300). Alloy wheels (911). AM/FM stereo radio w/tape player.

PRODUCTION/SALES: An industry source reported that 14,503 Porsches were built in 1972 (not including VW-Porsche 914s). A total of 20,464 Porsches were sold in the U.S. during 1972 (5,120 Type 911 and 15,344 Type 914).

Manufacturer: Dr. Ing. h.c. F. Porsche KG, Zuffenhausen, Stuttgart, West Germany.

Distributor: Volkswagen of America Inc., Englewood Cliffs, New Jersey.

1973 PORSCHE

1973 Porsche Carrera RS touring. (Coys of Kensington)

911 — F-Series — FLAT SIX — Production of the 911 trio continued with little change, but this would be the final year for the T/E suffixes.

914 — FLAT FOUR — Two four-cylinder 914s were available for 1973: the familiar 1679-cc Volkswagen-engined version, and a new 2.0-liter edition with larger bore/stroke dimensions.

I.D. DATA: Porsche's 10-digit serial number for 911 is on driver's door-hinge post, visible through the windshield; or on a plate in the luggage compartment, near the hood latch. Serial number for 914 is on driver's windshield pillar post, on a plate at right headlamp casing, and on a plate attached to right front fender panel in luggage compartment. The first three digits indicate model; digit four denotes the model year; digit six identifies the engine; digit seven is body type; followed by the sequential production number. Starting serial number: (911T) 3100001; (911T Targa) 3110001; (911E) 3200001; (911E Targa) 32110001; (911S) 3300001; (911S Targa) 3310001; (914) 4732900001. Engine number for 911 is on right rear of block, below the generator support bracket; for 914, on left upper portion of crankcase, below the breather column.

Model	Body Type & Seating	Engine Type/CID	P.O.E. Price	Weight (lbs.)	Prod. Total
911T	2-dr Coupe-2+2P	H6/143	7960	2250	Note 1
911T	2-dr Targa-2+2P	H6/143	8760	2250	Note 1
911E	2-dr Coupe-2+2P	H6/143	8960	2250	Note 1
911E	2-dr Targa-2+2P	H6/143	9760	2250	Note 1
911S	2-dr Coupe-2+2P	H6/143	10060	2250	Note 1
911S	2-dr Targa-2+2P	H6/143	10860	2250	Note 1
914					
914-1.7	2-dr Targa-2P	H4/102	4499	2029	Note 2
914-2.0	2-dr Targa-2P	H4/120	5049	2029	Note 2

Note 1: Approximately 14,074 Type 911 Porsches (all models) were produced during 1973, according to industry sources.

Note 2: Approximately 28,403 Type 914 Porsches were produced during 1973, according to industry sources (identified in statistics as VW-Porsches with 1700-, 1800- or 2000-cc engines).

ENGINE DATA: BASE SIX (911T): Horizontally opposed, overhead-cam six-cylinder (air cooled). **Displacement:** 142.8 cu. in. (2341 cc). **Bore & Stroke:** 3.31 x 2.76 in. (84 x 70 mm). **Compression Ratio:** 7.5:1. **Brake Horsepower:** 134 (SAE net) at 5600 rpm. **Torque:** 140 lbs.-ft. at 4000 rpm. Eight main bearings. Bosch fuel injection.

BASE SIX (911E): Same as 2341-cc six above, except — **Compression Ratio:** 8.0:1. **Brake Horsepower:** 157 (SAE net) at 6200 rpm. **Torque:** 147 lbs.-ft. at 4500 rpm. Bosch fuel injection.

BASE SIX (911S): Same as 2341-cc six above, except — **Compression Ratio:** 8.5:1. **Brake Horsepower:** 181 (SAE net) at 6500 rpm. **Torque:** 154 lbs.-ft. at 5200 rpm. Bosch fuel injection.

BASE FOUR (914-1.7): Horizontally opposed, overhead-valve four-cylinder (air-cooled Volkswagen). **Displacement:** 102.5 cu. in. (1679 cc). **Bore & Stroke:** 3.54 x 2.60 in. (90 x 66 mm). **Compression Ratio:** 8.2:1. **Brake Horsepower:** 76 (SAE net) at 4900 rpm. **Torque:** 76 lbs.-ft. at 4900 rpm. Four main bearings. Bosch fuel injection.

BASE FOUR (914-2.0): Horizontally opposed, overhead-valve four-cylinder (air cooled). **Displacement:** 120.3 cu. in. (1971 cc). **Bore & Stroke:** 3.70 x 2.80 in. (94 x 71 mm). **Compression Ratio:** 7.6:1. **Brake Horsepower:** 91 (SAE net) at 4900 rpm. **Torque:** 108.5 lbs.-ft. at 3500 rpm. Four main bearings. Bosch fuel injection.

CHASSIS DATA: Wheelbase: (911) 89.4 in.; (914) 96.5 in. **Overall Length:** (911) 168.4 in.; (914) 159.4 in. **Height:** (911) 52 in.; (914) 48.4 in. **Width:** (911) 63.4 in.; (914) 65.0 in. **Front Tread:** (911T) 53.6 in.; (911S) 54.1 in.; (914) 52.4 in. **Rear Tread:** (911T) 52.9 in.; (911S) 53.3 in.; (914) 54.0 in. **Standard Tires:** (911T) 165HR15; (911E) 185VR15; (911S) 185/70VR15; (914-1.7) 155SR15; (914-2.0) 165SR15.

TECHNICAL: Layout: rear-engine, rear-drive. **Transmission:** (911T) four-speed manual in rear transaxle, with five-speed manual or four-speed Sportomatic optional; (914) five-speed manual. **Steering:** rack and pinion. **Suspension (front):** MacPherson struts with single lower transverse A-arms and longitudinal torsion bars (anti-roll bar on 911E/S). **Suspension (rear):** (911) independent with semi-trailing arms and transverse torsion bars, plus anti-roll bar on 911S; (914) semi-trailing arms with coil springs. **Brakes:** front/rear disc. **Body Construction:** steel monocoque (unibody).

MAJOR OPTIONS: Five-speed manual transmission: 911 ($165). Sportomatic transmission: 911 ($355). Air conditioning. Sunroof. Appearance group: 914 ($300). Alloy wheels (911). AM/FM stereo w/tape player.

PRODUCTION/SALES: An industry source reported that 15,415 Porsches were built in 1973 (not including VW-Porsche 914s). A total of 23,771 Porsches were sold in the U.S. during 1973 (5,838 Type 911 and 17,933 Type 914).

Manufacturer: Dr. Ing. h.c. F. Porsche KG, Zuffenhausen, Stuttgart, West Germany.

Distributor: Volkswagen of America Inc., Englewood Cliffs, New Jersey.

HISTORY: Porsche's 1973 models were introduced to the U.S. market in August 1972.

1974-75 PORSCHE

911 — FLAT SIX — The next generation of the 911 carried yet another enlarged engine, grown to 2687 cc (164 cid) this time. Two basic models were offered: a base 911 and high-performance 911S, again in either closed coupe or Targa-topped form. Although styling was basically similar to prior 911s, the new models wore body-colored integrated bumpers, designed to meet U.S. bumper-strength requirements. Each model had a front air spoiler, while interiors contained new high-back front seats with integral headrests. Bosch K-Jetronic fuel injection was installed on both versions of the new engine, instead of the earlier mechanical system. In addition to the two basic models, a Carrera edition emerged. Evolved from the more potent European Carrera RS, this one used the same engine as the 911S but had larger wheels/tires (wider at the rear). Carrera extras included a rubber-rimmed "ducktail" rear spoiler on the engine cover, and identifying lettering on the lower bodysides. Standard colors were: Light Yellow, Lime Green, Orange, Chocolate Brown, Grand Prix White, India Red, Peru Red, Desert Beige, Mexico Blue, Aubergine, Copper Brown metallic, Gazelle metallic, Ice Green metallic, and Salmon metallic. Metallic colors were not available on Carrera models. For the 1975 model year, the base 911 dropped out, leaving only the 911S and Carrera, with revised horsepower/torque ratings. The Carrera edition added a "whale tail" rear spoiler, along with a deeper front spoiler. Approximately 750 examples of the 911S were painted in Diamond Silver metallic and marketed as the Silver Anniversary edition.

914 — FLAT FOUR — A slightly larger (1795-cc) base engine went into the 914 Targa coupe for 1974, while the optional powerplant remained the same as in 1973. The optional appearance group included a leatherette-covered steering wheel, center console with clock and gauges, leather boot for gearshift lever, dual-tone horn, and bumper-mounted foglamps. A performance group consisting of cast alloy wheels, a front spoiler and front/rear stabilizer bars also was available. Standard colors were: Light Ivory, Bahia

Red, Olympic Blue, Saturn Yellow, Phoenix Red, Ravenna Green, Zambezi Green, Sunflower Yellow, Signal Orange, Black, Gold metallic, Marathon Blue metallic, Alaska Blue metallic, and Silver metallic.

I.D. DATA: Porsche's 10-digit serial number for the 911 is on driver's door-hinge post, visible through the windshield; or on a plate in the luggage compartment, near the hood latch. Serial number for Type 914 is on driver's windshield pillar post, on a plate at right headlamp casing, and/or on a plate attached to right front fender panel in luggage compartment. The first three digits indicate model; digit four denotes the model year; digit six identifies the engine; digit seven is body type; followed by the sequential production number. Starting serial number (1974 models): (911) 9114100011; (911 Targa) 9114110011; (911S) 9114300011; (911S Targa) 9114310011; (Carrera) 9114400011; (Carrera Targa) 9114410011; (914) 4742900014. Starting serial number (1975 models): (911S) 9115200011 or 9115210011; (Carrera) 9115400011 or 9115410011; (914) 4752900014. Engine number for 911 is on right rear of block, below the generator support bracket; for 914, on left upper portion of crankcase, below the breather column.

Model	Body Type & Seating	Engine Type/CID	P.O.E. Price	Weight (lbs.)	Prod. Total
911/CARRERA					
911	2-dr Coupe-2+2P	H6/164	9950	2315	Note 1
911	2-dr Targa-2+2P	H6/164	10800	2315	Note 1
911S	2-dr Coupe-2+2P	H6/164	11875	2315	Note 1
911S	2-dr Targa-2+2P	H6/164	12725	2315	Note 1
Carrera	2-dr Coupe-2+2P	H6/164	13575	2315	Note 1
Carrera	2-dr Targa-2+2P	H6/164	14425	2315	Note 1
914					
914-1.8	2-dr Targa-2P	H4/109	5400	2029	Note 2
914-2.0	2-dr Targa-2P	H4/120	6050	2029	Note 2

Note 1: Approximately 7,124 Type 911 Porsches were produced during 1974, plus 2,257 Type 911S and 2,243 Carreras. Approximately 2,236 Type 911 Porsches were produced in 1975, plus 651 Type 911S, 3,827 U.S 911S versions, and 715 Carreras.

Note 2: Approximately 17,012 Type 914 Porsches were produced during 1974, according to industry sources (identified in statistics as VW-Porsches with 1800- or 2000-cc engines).

Model Note: The base 911 was not offered in the U.S. for the 1975 model year. An Anniversary Edition of the 911S that year cost $11,775 in closed coupe form, or $12,625 as a Targa coupe.

Price Note: Figures shown were valid in 1974. Prices in 1975 ranged from $6300 for the 914-1.8 Targa coupe to $15,795 for the 911 Carrera Targa coupe.

ENGINE DATA: BASE SIX (911): Horizontally opposed, overhead-cam six-cylinder (air cooled). **Displacement:** 163.9 cu. in. (2687 cc). **Bore & Stroke:** 3.54 x 2.76 in. (90 x 70 mm). **Compression Ratio:** 8.0:1. **Brake Horsepower:** 143 (SAE net) at 5700 rpm. **Torque:** 168 lbs.-ft. at 3800 rpm. Eight main bearings. Bosch K-Jetronic fuel injection.

BASE SIX (911S, Carrera): Same as 2687-cc six above, except — **Compression Ratio:** 8.5:1. **Brake Horsepower:** 167 (SAE net) at 5800 rpm (157 at 5800 in 1975). **Torque:** 168 lbs.-ft. at 4000 rpm (166 lbs.-ft. in 1975). Bosch K-Jetronic fuel injection.

BASE FOUR (914-1.8): Horizontally opposed, overhead-valve four-cylinder (air cooled). **Displacement:** 109.5 cu. in. (1795 cc). **Bore & Stroke:** 3.66 x 2.60 in. (93 x 66 mm). **Compression Ratio:** 7.3:1. **Brake Horsepower:** 72.5 (SAE net) at 4800 rpm. **Torque:** 94 lbs.-ft. at 3400 rpm (89 at 4000 rpm in 1975). Four main bearings. Bosch fuel injection.

BASE FOUR (914-2.0): Horizontally opposed, overhead-valve four-cylinder (air cooled). **Displacement:** 120.3 cu. in. (1971 cc). **Bore & Stroke:** 3.70 x 2.80 in. (94 x 71 mm). **Compression Ratio:** 7.6:1. **Brake Horsepower:** 91 (SAE net) at 4900 rpm (84 bhp in 1975). **Torque:** 105 lbs.-ft. at 3500 rpm (97 at 4000 in 1975). Four main bearings. Bosch fuel injection.

CHASSIS DATA: Wheelbase: (911) 89.4 in.; (914) 96.5 in. **Overall Length:** (911) 168.4 in.; (914) 161.2 in. **Height:** (911) 52 in.; (914) 48.4 in. **Width:** (911) 63.4 in.; (Carrera) 65 in.; (914) 65.0 in. **Front Tread:** (911) 53.5 in.; (911S/Carrera) 54 in.; (914) 52.9 in. **Rear Tread:** (911) 52.9 in.; (911S) 53.3 in.; (Carrera) 54.9 in.; (914) 54.4 in. **Standard Tires:** (911) 165HR15; (911S/Carrera) 185/70VR15; (914-1.8) 165SR15; (914-2.0) 165HR15.

TECHNICAL: Layout: rear-engine, rear-drive. **Transmission:** (911) four-speed manual in rear transaxle, with five-speed manual or four-speed Sportomatic optional; (914) five-speed manual. **Steering:** rack and pinion. **Suspension (front):** MacPherson struts with single lower transverse A-arms and longitudinal torsion bars (anti-roll bar on 911). **Suspension (rear):** (911) independent with semi-trailing arms, transverse torsion bars and anti-roll bar; (914) semi-trailing arms with coil springs. **Brakes:** front/rear disc. **Body Construction:** steel monocoque (unibody).

MAJOR OPTIONS: Five-speed manual transmission: 911 ($250). Sportomatic transmission: 911 ($425). Air conditioning: 911 ($1125); 914 ($650). Electric sunroof: 911 ($615). Appearance group: 914 ($300). Alloy wheels: 911 ($605). AM/FM stereo radio: 914 ($289). AM/FM stereo w/tape player. Chrome bumpers: 914 ($145). Heated rear window: 914 ($50). Tinted glass: 914 ($115). Front/rear stabilizer bars: 914 ($145). Bilstein shock absorbers: 914 ($150). Cast alloy wheels: 914 ($325). Forged alloy wheels: 914 ($380). Front spoiler: 914 ($115). Metallic paint: 914 ($270).

Note: Option prices shown above were valid in 1974.

PERFORMANCE: Top Speed: (914-1.8) 107 mph claimed; (914-2.0) 115 mph claimed. **Acceleration (0-60 mph):** N/A (914-1.8, 0-62 mph in 14 sec.; 914-2.0, 0-62 mph in 11 sec.).

PRODUCTION/SALES: An industry source reported that 9,915 Porsches were built in 1974 (not including VW-Porsche 914s), followed by 9,424 in 1975. A total of 21,029 Porsches were sold in the U.S. during 1974 (4,868 Type 911 and 16,161 Type 914); followed by 16,224 in 1975 (5,024 Type 911 and 11,200 Type 914).

Manufacturer: Dr. Ing. h.c. F. Porsche AG, Zuffenhausen, Stuttgart, West Germany.
Distributor: Volkswagen of America Inc., Englewood Cliffs, New Jersey.

HISTORY: Porsche's 1974 models were introduced to the U.S. market in August 1973 except (914-1.8) November 1973; the 1975 models in August 1974.

1976 PORSCHE

911S/CARRERA — FLAT SIX — Production of the high-performance 911S closed coupe and Targa coupe continued with modest change, except that the 911S now had just about as much standard equipment as the former Carrera, including intermittent wipers and tinted glass. A five-speed gearbox was standard (though a four-speed continued in European models).

TURBO CARRERA — 930 — FLAT SIX — Offered in Europe during the 1975 model year, a turbocharged Porsche hit U.S. shores for 1976, quickly becoming known as the fastest road Porsche ever--and possibly even the swiftest car available in America. Power came from a turbocharged 3.0-liter version of the flat six, with 6.5:1 compression, developing 234 horsepower in U.S. trim. With its four-speed manual transaxle (the only transmission available), a Turbo could accelerate to 60 mph in 4.9 seconds, and reach 156 mph. Styling features included a "whale tail" spoiler out back, as well as aggressively-flared wheelarches atop wide tires on cast aluminum wheels. Bilstein gas/oil shock absorbers were standard, as was an oil cooler. Not that the driver and passenger lacked comfort. Standard equpment included air conditioning, leather upholstery, AM/FM stereo radio, and power windows. A sliding (electrically-powered) sunroof was optional. Only the closed coupe body was used, with no Targa top available.

912E — FLAT FOUR — The 912 designation returned for a short stint on a four-cylinder coupe, meant to give Porsche an extra model to offer American customers while waiting for the new front-engine 924 coupe. Similar in appearance to the 911, the 912E carried a fuel-injected 2.0-liter Volkswagen engine, borrowed from the fading-fast 914. A five-speed gearbox was standard.

914 — FLAT FOUR — For its final year in the Porsche lineup, little change was evident in the two-seat 914 Targa coupe. Only the 2.0-liter engine was offered in the U.S.

I.D. DATA: Porsche's 10-digit serial number for the 911 is on driver's windshield pillar post, visible through the windshield; or on a plate in the luggage compartment, near the hood latch. Serial number for Type 914 is on driver's windshield pillar post, on a plate at right headlamp casing, and/or on a plate attached to right front fender panel in luggage compartment. The first three digits indicate model; digit four denotes the model year; digit six identifies the engine; digit seven is body type; followed by the sequential production number. Starting serial number: (911S) 9116200001; (Turbo Carrera) 9306800001; (912E) 9126000001; (914) 4762900001. Engine number for 911 is on right rear of block, below the generator support bracket; for 914, on left upper portion of crankcase, below the breather column.

Model	Body Type & Seating	Engine Type/CID	P.O.E. Price	Weight (lbs.)	Prod. Total
911S	2-dr Coupe-2+2P	H6/164	13845	2315	Note 1
911S	2-dr Targa-2+2P	H6/164	14795	2315	Note 1
TURBO CARRERA					
Carrera	2-dr Coupe-2+2P	H6/183	25850	2514	Note 2
912E					
912E	2-dr Coupe-2+2P	H4/120	10845	2420	Note 3
914					
914-2.0	2-dr Targa-2P	H4/120	7250	2125	Note 4

Note 1: Approximately 3,444 Type 911 Porsches were produced during 1976, plus 4,254 Type 911S for the U.S. market (one industry source put the total at 8,928 units).

Note 2: Approximately 1,389 Turbo Carrera coupes were produced in 1976.

Note 3: As many as 2,099 Type 912E coupes were produced in 1976 (one industry source claimed the total was only 1,216 units).

Note 4: Approximately 7,924 Type 914 Porsches were produced during 1976 (identified in industry statistics as VW-Porsches with 1800- or 2000-cc engines).

Model Note: A 911S Signature Edition cost $400 extra.

ENGINE DATA: BASE SIX (911S): Horizontally opposed, overhead-cam six-cylinder (air cooled). **Displacement:** 163.9 cu. in. (2687 cc). **Bore & Stroke:** 3.54 x 2.76 in. (90 x 70 mm). **Compression Ratio:** 8.5:1. **Brake Horsepower:** 157 (SAE net) at 5800 rpm. **Torque:** 166 lbs.-ft. at 4000 rpm. Eight main bearings. Bosch K-Jetronic fuel injection.

BASE SIX (Turbo Carrera): Horizontally opposed, overhead-cam six-cylinder (air cooled) with turbocharger. **Displacement:** 182.6 cu. in. (2993 cc). **Bore & Stroke:** 3.74 x 2.76 in. (95 x 70 mm). **Compression Ratio:** 6.5:1. **Brake Horsepower:** 234 (SAE net) at 5500 rpm. **Torque:** 245 lbs.-ft. at 4000 rpm. Bosch K-Jetronic fuel injection.

BASE FOUR (912E): Horizontally opposed, overhead-valve four-cylinder (air cooled). **Displacement:** 120.3 cu. in. (1971 cc). **Bore & Stroke:** 3.70 x 2.80 in. (94 x 71 mm). **Compression Ratio:** 7.6:1. **Brake Horsepower:** 86 (SAE net) at 4900 rpm. **Torque:** 93 lbs.-ft. at 4000 rpm. Four main bearings. Bosch fuel injection.

BASE FOUR (914-2.0): Horizontally opposed, overhead-valve four-cylinder (air cooled). **Displacement:** 120.3 cu. in. (1971 cc). **Bore & Stroke:** 3.70 x 2.80 in. (94 x 71 mm). **Compression Ratio:** 7.6:1. **Brake Horsepower:** 84 (SAE net) at 4900 rpm. **Torque:** 97 lbs.-ft. at 4000 rpm. Four main bearings. Bosch fuel injection.

CHASSIS DATA: Wheelbase: (911S/Turbo) 89.4 in.; (912E) 89.4 in.; (914) 96.5 in. **Overall Length:** (911S/Turbo) 168.9 in.; (912E) 168.9 in.; (914) 161.2 in. **Height:** (911S/Turbo) 52 in.; (912E) 52.8 in.; (914) 48.4 in. **Width:** (911S) 63.4 in.; (Turbo) 69.9 in.; (912E) 63.4 in.; (914) 65.0 in. **Front Tread:** (911S) 54.1 in.; (Turbo) 56.3 in.; (912E) 53.5 in.; (914) 52.9 in. **Rear Tread:** (911S) 53.3 in.; (Turbo) 59.1 in.; (912E) 52.4 in.; (914) 54.4 in. **Standard Tires:** (911S) 185/70VR15; (Turbo) 215/60VR15; (912E) 165HR15; (914) 165HR15.

TECHNICAL: Layout: rear-engine, rear-drive. **Transmission:** (911S) five-speed manual in rear transaxle, Sportomatic optional; (Turbo) wide-ratio four-speed manual; (912E, 914) five-speed manual. **Steering:** rack and pinion. **Suspension (front):** MacPherson struts with single lower transverse A-arms, longitudinal torsion bars and anti-roll bar (except 914). **Suspension (rear):** (911S/Turbo) independent with semi-trailing arms, transverse torsion bars and anti-roll bar; (912E) semi-trailing arms with transverse torsion bars; (914) semi-trailing arms with coil springs. **Brakes:** front/rear disc. **Body Construction:** steel monocoque (unibody).

MAJOR OPTIONS: Sportomatic transmission: 911S ($295). Other options similar to 1974-75.

PERFORMANCE: Top Speed: (Turbo Carrera) up to 156 mph. **Acceleration (0-60 mph):** (Turbo Carrera) 4.9 sec. **Acceleration (quarter-mile):** (Turbo Carrera) 13.5 sec.

PRODUCTION/SALES: Approximately 32,554 Porsches were built in 1976 (not including VW-Porsche 914s). A total of 14,192 Porsches were sold in the U.S. during 1976 (plus 284 tourist deliveries). The sales total included 4,300 Type 911S, 626 Turbo Carreras, and 4,534 early Type 924s.

Manufacturer: Dr. Ing. h.c. F. Porsche AG, Zuffenhausen, Stuttgart, West Germany.
Distributor: Volkswagen of America Inc., Englewood Cliffs, New Jersey.

HISTORY: Availability of Porsche's 914 ceased early in the 1976 model year. The front-engine Type 924 went on sale in Europe for the 1976 model year, but did not arrive in the U.S. until the 1977 model year; see next listing for details.

1977 PORSCHE

911S — FLAT SIX — As in 1976, only one 911-series closed coupe and Targa coupe were available in the U.S., powered by a 157-bhp engine. Little change was evident for its final year in this form, apart from new flush door locks.

TURBO CARRERA — FLAT SIX — Production of the turbocharged coupe, introduced in U.S. form for 1976, continued with little change, powered by a 3.0-liter engine.

924 — FOUR — All the attention went to Porsche's first front-engine model, which also featured water cooling rather than the customary air cooling. Quite a few components (including suspension, steering and brakes) were borrowed from Volkswagen models. In fact, the 924 was initially conceived as a VW product. The Audi 2.0-liter single-overhead-cam inline four-cylinder engine, with Bosch K-Jetronic fuel injection, developed 95

horsepower in its U.S. form (30 bhp less than European versions with their DIN rating). Oddly enough, the same engine saw service under the hood of AMC's Gremlin during this era. Halfway through the 1977 model year, engine output got a boost to 110 horsepower. Even though the engine went up front, the four-speed manual transaxle stuck to the rear of the 924. A three-speed automatic transmission (also from Audi) became available during the 1977 model year. Drum-type rear brakes were installed, instead of the usual four-wheel disc setup. Styling was a dramatic departure from Porsche's traditional profile, highlighted by a large compound-curved hatch-style back window and small rear quarter windows. Though supposedly a replacement for the 914, there appeared to be little similarity between the two. Options included a tilt-type removable sunroof, anti-roll bars, and alloy wheels.

1977 Porsche 935. (Christie's)

I.D. DATA: Porsche's 10-digit serial number is on driver's windshield pillar post, visible through the windshield; or on a plate in the luggage compartment, near the hood latch. The first three digits indicate model; digit four denotes the model year; digit six identifies the engine; digit seven is body type; followed by the sequential production number. Starting serial number: (911S) 9117200001; (911S Targa) 91172100001; (Turbo Carrera) 9307800001; (924) 9247200001. Engine number for 911S is on right rear of block, below the generator support bracket.

Model	Body Type & Seating	Engine Type/CID	P.O.E. Price	Weight (lbs.)	Prod. Total
911S	2-dr Coupe-2+2P	H6/164	14995	2315	Note 1
911S	2-dr Targa-2+2P	H6/164	15945	2315	Note 1
TURBO CARRERA					
Carrera	2-dr Coupe-2+2P	H6/183	28000	2490	Note 2
924					
924	2-dr Coupe-2+2P	I4/121	9395	2344	Note 3

Note 1: Approximately 4,173 Type 911 Porsches were produced during 1977, plus 6,135 Type 911S for the U.S. market.

Note 2: An industry source reported that 839 Turbo Carrera coupes with the 3.0-liter engine were produced in 1977.

Note 3: Approximately 21,956 Type 924 Porsches were produced in 1977.

ENGINE DATA: BASE SIX (911S): Horizontally opposed, overhead-cam six-cylinder (air cooled). **Displacement:** 163.9 cu. in. (2687 cc). **Bore & Stroke:** 3.54 x 2.76 in. (90 x 70 mm). **Compression Ratio:** 8.5:1. **Brake Horsepower:** 157 (SAE net) at 5800 rpm. **Torque:** 166 lbs.-ft. at 4000 rpm. Eight main bearings. Bosch K-Jetronic fuel injection.
BASE SIX (Turbo Carrera): Horizontally opposed, overhead-cam six-cylinder (air cooled) with turbocharger. **Displacement:** 182.6 cu. in. (2993 cc). **Bore & Stroke:** 3.74 x 2.76 in. (95 x 70 mm). **Compression Ratio:** 6.5:1. **Brake Horsepower:** 234 (SAE net) at 5500 rpm. **Torque:** 245 lbs.-ft. at 4000 rpm. Bosch K-Jetronic fuel injection.
BASE FOUR (924): Inline, overhead-cam four-cylinder (water cooled). **Displacement:** 121.1 cu. in. (1985 cc). **Bore & Stroke:** 3.41 x 3.32 in. (86.5 x 84.4 mm). **Compression Ratio:** 8.0:1. **Brake Horsepower:** 95 (SAE net) at 5500 rpm. **Torque:** 109 lbs.-ft. at 3000 rpm. Five main bearings. Bosch K-Jetronic fuel injection.
BASE FOUR (late 924): Same as 1985-cc four above, except — **Compression Ratio:** 8.5:1. **Brake Horsepower:** 110 (SAE net) at 5750 rpm. **Torque:** 111 lbs.-ft. at 3500 rpm.

CHASSIS DATA: Wheelbase: (911S/Turbo) 89.4 in.; (924) 94.5 in. **Overall Length:** (911S/Turbo) 168.9 in.; (924) 170.1 in. **Height:** (911S/Turbo) 52 in.; (924) 50 in. **Width:** (911S) 63.4 in.; (Turbo) 69.9 in.; (924) 66.3 in. **Front Tread:** (911S) 53.6 in.; (Turbo) 56.4 in.; (924) 55.9 in. **Rear Tread:** (911S) 52.8 in.; (Turbo) 59.1 in.; (924) 54 in. **Standard Tires:** (911S) 185/70VR15; (Turbo) 225/50VR16; (924) 165HR14.

TECHNICAL: Layout: (911S/Turbo) rear-engine, rear-drive; (924) front-engine, rear-drive. **Transmission:** (911S) five-speed manual in rear transaxle, Sportomatic optional; (Turbo) wide-ratio four-speed manual; (924) four-speed manual, with three-speed automatic optional. **Steering:** rack and pinion. **Suspension (front):** MacPherson struts with single lower transverse A-arms, longitudinal torsion bars (anti-roll bar on 911S/Turbo). **Suspension (rear):** (911S/Turbo) independent with semi-trailing arms, transverse torsion bars and anti-roll bar; (924) semi-trailing arms with transverse torsion bars. **Brakes:** (911S/Turbo) front/rear disc; (924) front disc, rear drum. **Body Construction:** steel monocoque (unibody).

MAJOR OPTIONS: Sportomatic transmission: 911S ($295). Three-speed automatic (924). Air conditioning ($548-$895). Removable tilt sunroof: 924 ($330). Electric sunroof ($710). Alloy wheels w/oversize tires: 924 ($295). Front/rear anti-roll bars: 924 ($105). Metallic paint: 924 ($295). AM/FM stereo w/tape player.

PERFORMANCE: Top Speed: (924) 110 mph; (Turbo Carrera) up to 156 mph. **Acceleration (0-60 mph):** (924) 12.5 sec. or less; (Turbo Carrera) 4.9 sec. **Acceleration (quarter-mile):** (Turbo Carrera) 13.5 sec.

PRODUCTION/SALES: Approximately 36,130 Porsches were built in 1977. A total of 19,896 Porsches were sold in the U.S. during 1977 (plus 375 tourist deliveries). The sales total included 5,709 Type 911S, 517 Turbo Carreras, and 13,670 Type 924s.
Manufacturer: Dr. Ing. h.c. F. Porsche AG, Zuffenhausen, Stuttgart, West Germany.
Distributor: Volkswagen of America Inc., Englewood Cliffs, New Jersey.
HISTORY: Porsche's 1977 models were introduced to the U.S. market in September 1976.

1978-79 PORSCHE

1978 Porsche 928 coupe.

911SC — FLAT SIX — A bigger (3.0-liter) engine went into the next version of the familiar 911 coupe and Targa coupe, identical in displacement to the flat six initially used in the Turbo. In U.S. form, it developed 172 horsepower. A new crankshaft contained larger bearings, and the new engine used an aluminum crankcase (formerly magnesium). Power brakes and heated mirrors became standard for 1979, by which time 16-inch tires were available and the Sportomatic semi-automatic transmission option faded away. Among the options was a "whale tail" rear spoiler.
TURBO — 930 — FLAT SIX — The Turbo's engine grew to 3.3-liter size for 1978, with an air-to-air intercooler to give some extra muscle to the turbocharger. The Carrera designation no longer was used. Brakes got a performance boost, adopting the ventilated, cross-drilled discs used earlier in the racing 917 Porsche. After 1979, as another energy crisis erupted, the Turbo left the U.S. market and would not reappear until 1986.
924 — FOUR — A Getrag five-speed manual gearbox was available for the front-engine Porsche, starting in 1978; and became standard the following year. Customers could also elect a fully automatic transmission. A jump in compression during the 1977 model year had helped boost output of the U.S.-spec engine to 110 horsepower, around the time the automatic transmission became available.
928 — V-8 — Intended as a replacement for the 911, which itself replaced the original 356 series, the 928 displayed a sleek and well-rounded profile (though some complained that it looked too chubby). Styling features included a long nose and retractable, but exposed, headlamps. Door windows had a curious parallelogram shape, rear quarter windows formed long triangles, and bumpers were body-colored. Aluminum was used for the doors, hood and hatch, while the nose and tail were made of polyurethane. Like the recently-introduced 924, this one had a front-mounted, water-cooled engine rather than the traditional air-cooled rear engine. Unlike any predecessors, it was an all-aluminum alloy 4474-cc (273-cid) V-8 with single overhead camshafts, putting out 219 horsepower in U.S. trim. A twin-disc clutch sent power to either a five-speed manual or three-speed automatic transmission (from Daimler-Benz). Coil springs were installed at each corner, with a "Weissach" axle at the rear. All-disc brakes used ventilated discs.

I.D. DATA: Porsche's 10-digit serial number is on driver's windshield pillar post, visible through the windshield; or on a plate in the luggage compartment, near the hood latch. The first three digits indicate model; digit four denotes the model year; digit six identifies the engine; followed by the five-digit sequential production number. Starting serial number (1978 models): (911SC) 9118200001; (911SC Targa) 91182100001; (Turbo) 9308800001; (924) 9248200001; (928) 9288200001. For 1979, the fourth digit changed from '8' to '9.' Engine number for 911SS is on right rear of block, below the generator support bracket.

Model	Body Type & Seating	Engine Type/CID	P.O.E. Price	Weight (lbs.)	Prod. Total
911SC	2-dr Coupe-2+2P	H6/183	19500	2315	Note 1
911SC	2-dr Targa-2+2P	H6/183	20775	2315	Note 1
TURBO					
930	2-dr Coupe-2+2P	H6/201	36700	2746	Note 2
924					
924	2-dr Coupe-2+2P	I4/121	11995	2344	Note 3
928					
928	2-dr Coupe-2+2P	V8/273	28500	3144	Note 4

Note 1: Approximately 8,283 Type 911 Porsches were produced during 1978 (4,719 coupes and 3,564 Targas), followed by 8,940 in 1979 (5,333 coupes and 3,607 Targas).
Note 2: Approximately 1,515 Turbo coupes were produced in 1978, followed by 1,652 in 1979.
Note 3: Approximately 22,154 Type 924 Porsches were produced in 1978, followed by 20,713 in 1979.
Note 4: Approximately 4,927 Type 928 Porsches were produced in 1978, followed by 4,706 in 1979.
Price Note: Figures shown were valid in 1978. Prices in 1979 ranged from $14,600 for the 924 coupe, to $42,520 for the 930 Turbo.

1979 Porsche 935. (Coys of Kensington)

1980 Porsche 911SC. (William Siuru Jr.)

ENGINE DATA: BASE SIX (911SC): Horizontally opposed, overhead-cam six-cylinder (air cooled). **Displacement:** 182.6 cu. in. (2993 cc). **Bore & Stroke:** 3.74 x 2.77 in. (95 x 70.4 mm). **Compression Ratio:** 8.5:1. **Brake Horsepower:** 172 (SAE net) at 5500 rpm. **Torque:** 189 lbs.-ft. at 4200 rpm. Eight main bearings. Bosch K-Jetronic fuel injection.

BASE SIX (Turbo 930): Horizontally opposed, overhead-cam six-cylinder (air cooled) with turbocharger. **Displacement:** 201.3 cu. in. (3299 cc). **Bore & Stroke:** 3.82 x 2.93 in. (97 x 74.4 mm). **Compression Ratio:** 7.0:1. **Brake Horsepower:** 253 (SAE net) at 5500 rpm. **Torque:** 282 lbs.-ft. at 4200 rpm. Bosch K-Jetronic fuel injection.

BASE FOUR (924): Inline, overhead-cam four-cylinder (water cooled). **Displacement:** 121.1 cu. in. (1985 cc). **Bore & Stroke:** 3.41 x 3.32 in. (86.5 x 84.4 mm). **Compression Ratio:** 8.5:1. **Brake Horsepower:** 110 (SAE net) at 5750 rpm. **Torque:** 111 lbs.-ft. at 3500 rpm. Five main bearings. Bosch K-Jetronic fuel injection.

BASE V-8 (928): 90-degree, overhead-cam "vee" type eight-cylinder. Aluminum alloy block and heads. **Displacement:** 273 cu. in. (4474 cc). **Bore & Stroke:** 3.74 x 3.11 in. (95 x 78.9 mm). **Compression Ratio:** 8.5:1. **Brake Horsepower:** 219 (SAE net) at 5250 rpm. **Torque:** 254 lbs.-ft. at 3600 rpm. Hydraulic valve lifters. Bosch K-Jetronic fuel injection.

CHASSIS DATA: Wheelbase: (911SC/Turbo) 89.4 in.; (924) 94.5 in.; (928) 98.3 in. **Overall Length:** (911SC/Turbo) 168.9 in.; (924) 170.1 in.; (928) 175.7 in. **Height:** (911SC) 52 in.; (Turbo) 51.6 in.; (924) 50 in.; (928) 51.7 in. **Width:** (911SC) 65 in.; (Turbo) 69.9 in.; (924) 66.3 in.; (928) 72.3 in. **Front Tread:** (911SC) 53.5 in.; (Turbo) 56.4 in.; (924) 55.9 in.; (928) 60.8 in. **Rear Tread:** (911SC) 52.8 in.; (Turbo) 59.1 in.; (924) 54 in.; (928) 59.6 in. **Standard Tires:** (911SC) 185/70VR15 front, 215/60VR15 rear; (Turbo) 205/55VR16; (924) 185/70HR14; (928) 225/50VR16.

TECHNICAL: Layout: (911SC/Turbo) rear-engine, rear-drive; (924/928) front-engine, rear-drive. **Transmission:** (911SC) five-speed manual in rear transaxle, Sportomatic optional through 1978; (Turbo) wide-ratio four-speed manual; (924) four-speed manual, with three-speed automatic optional; (928) five-speed manual, with three-speed automatic optional. **Steering:** rack and pinion. **Suspension (front):** (911SC/Turbo/924) MacPherson struts with single lower transverse A-arms, longitudinal torsion bars (anti-roll bar on 911SC/Turbo); (928) upper A-arms with lower trailing arms, coil springs and anti-roll bar. **Suspension (rear):** (911SC/Turbo) independent with semi-trailing arms, transverse torsion bars and anti-roll bar; (924) semi-trailing arms with transverse torsion bars; (928) upper transverse links with lower trailing arms, coil springs and anti-roll bar. **Brakes:** front/rear disc except (924) front disc, rear drum. **Body Construction:** steel monocoque (unibody).

MAJOR OPTIONS: Sportomatic transmission (1978 911SC). Three-speed automatic (924/928). Air conditioning ($695). Removable tilt sunroof: 924 ($395). Electric sunroof ($795). Alloy wheels: 911SC ($1230). Power windows: 911SC ($300). Speed control: 911SC ($270). AM/FM stereo w/tape player: 911SC ($500). Sport seats: 911SC/930 ($330). Leather seats: 911SC ($680). Full leather interior: 911SC ($1450). Front/rear spoilers: 911SC ($650).
Note: Option prices shown above were valid in 1979.

911SC — FLAT SIX — By 1980, Type 911SC coupes sold in the U.S. had plenty of standard equipment, including air conditioning and power windows. Otherwise, apart from the addition of halogen headlamps for 1981, little significant change was evident. The flat six-cylinder engine again developed 172 horsepower in U.S. trim. For 1982, leather front seats and headlamp washers became standard.

1981 Porsche 924 Turbo.

924 — FOUR — Biggest news in the Porsche camp was the arrival of a Turbo edition of the front-drive 924 coupe. Identical in displacement to the conventional engine, the Turbo developed 143 horsepower in U.S. form (33 bhp more than the regular 924). Turbo models had special alloy wheels and front and rear spoilers, the latter integral with the hatchback glass. A quartet of air slots in the nose (just above the bumper) shot air to the radiator and oil cooler, while an operating NACA-style air duct in the hood sent cool air to the turbocharger. The engine had a special cylinder head with modified hemispherical combustion chambers and a 7.5:1 compression ratio. A five-speed manual transaxle now was standard in each 924 (Getrag in the Turbo); three-speed automatic optional at no extra cost. Halogen headlamps went into the 1981 models, as did rear disc brakes.

PERFORMANCE: Top Speed: (911SC) 126-139 mph; (Turbo) 156 mph; (928) 138+ mph; (928 w/automatic) 133 mph. **Acceleration (0-60 mph):** (911SC) 6.3-7.0 sec.; (Turbo) 5.0 sec.; (928) 7.0 sec. or less.; (928 w/automatic) 8.3 sec.

PRODUCTION/SALES: Approximately 36,879 Porsches were built in 1978, followed by 36,011 in 1979. A total of 17,018 Porsches were sold in the U.S. during 1978 (plus 131 tourist deliveries). That sales total included 4,484 Type 911SC, 566 Turbo 930s, 10,433 Type 924, and 1,535 Type 928. A total of 13,818 Porsches were sold in the U.S. in 1979 (3,267 Type 911SC, 652 Turbo 930s, 7,710 Type 924, 635 Type 924 Turbos, and 1,554 Type 928).
Manufacturer: Dr. Ing. h.c. F. Porsche AG, Zuffenhausen, Stuttgart, West Germany.
Distributor: Volkswagen of America Inc., Englewood Cliffs, New Jersey.

HISTORY: Porsche's 1978 models were introduced to the U.S. market in August 1977; the 1979 models in October 1978. *Automotive News* advised its trade readers that attributes of the 911SC included "high road speeds and jackrabbit starts."
The new 928 first appeared at the Geneva show in March 1977. Styling was the work of Anatole "Tony" Lapine. A 924 Turbo became available during 1979; see next listing for details.
"Outrageous" was *Road & Track* magazine's capsule description of the Porsche Turbo, a result of its "unrestrained performance" that included a 0-60 mph acceleration time of 5.0 seconds. The 911SC was summed up as "one of the best GTs in the world, exoticars notwithstanding. Its performance, handling, looks, ride and quality are second to none...."

1982 Porsche 928.

928 — V-8 — Production of the front-engine V-8 Porsche continued without major change. Standard equipment by 1982 included reclining front bucket seats, front/rear headrests, power steering, a remote-control driver's mirror with electric defroster, power door locks, a tilting steering column and instrument cluster, leather-wrapped steering wheel, and either leather or cloth upholstery.

Note: Porsche's 930-series Turbo was dropped from the U.S. market after 1979.

I.D. DATA: For 1980, Porsche's 10-symbol serial number is on driver's windshield pillar post, visible through the windshield; or on a plate in the luggage compartment, near the hood latch. The first two digits indicate model; digit three and four denote the model year; followed by the six-digit sequential production number. Starting serial number (1980 models): (911SC) 91A0140001; (924) 92A0430001; (924 Turbo) 93A0150001; (928) 92A0810001.

For 1981, Porsche switched to a 17-symbol Vehicle Identification Number on the left windshield pillar post, visible through the windshield. Symbol one indicates country; symbols two and three identify the manufacturer; symbol four is the series; symbols seven and eight indicate car line ('91' = 911; '92' = 924/928; '93' = 924 Turbo); symbol 10 indicates model year ('B' = 1981). The final six digits form the sequential production number. Starting serial number (1981 models): (911SC) WPOAA91()BS120001; (911SC Targa) WPOEA091()BS160001; (924) WPOAA092()BN450001; (924 Turbo) WPOAA093()BN150001; (928) WPOJA092()BS820001.

Model	Body Type & Seating	Engine Type/CID	P.O.E. Price	Weight (lbs.)	Prod. Total
911SC	2-dr Coupe-2+2P	H6/183	27700	2315	Note 1
911SC	2-dr Targa-2+2P	H6/183	29150	2315	Note 1
924					
924	2-dr Coupe-2+2P	I4/121	16770	2344	Note 1
Turbo	2-dr Coupe-2+2P	I4/121	20875	2719	Note 1
928					
928	2-dr Coupe-2+2P	V8/273	37930	3144	Note 1

Note 1: Approximately 28,622 Porsches (all models) were produced during 1980, followed by 31,734 in 1981 and 36,329 in 1982.

Price Note: Figures shown were valid in 1980. Prices in 1981 rose to $21,500 for the 924 Turbo, $28,365 for the 911SC coupe, $29,850 for the 911SC Targa coupe, and $38,850 for the 928; the base 924 did not change. Prices rose only slightly for the 1982 model year, ranging from $16,900 for the 924 to $39,500 for the 928.

ENGINE DATA: BASE SIX (911SC): Horizontally opposed, overhead-cam six-cylinder (air cooled). **Displacement:** 182.6 cu. in. (2993 cc). **Bore & Stroke:** 3.74 x 2.77 in. (95 x 70.4 mm). **Compression Ratio:** 8.5:1. **Brake Horsepower:** 172 (SAE net) at 5500 rpm. **Torque:** 189 lbs.-ft. at 4200 rpm. Eight main bearings. Bosch K-Jetronic fuel injection.

BASE FOUR (924): Inline, overhead-cam four-cylinder (water cooled). **Displacement:** 121.1 cu. in. (1985 cc). **Bore & Stroke:** 3.41 x 3.32 in. (86.5 x 84.4 mm). **Compression Ratio:** 8.5:1. **Brake Horsepower:** 110 (SAE net) at 5750 rpm. **Torque:** 111 lbs.-ft. at 3500 rpm. Five main bearings. Bosch K-Jetronic fuel injection.

BASE FOUR (924 Turbo): Same as 1985-cc four above, but with German KKK turbocharger — **Compression Ratio:** 7.5:1. **Brake Horsepower:** 143 (SAE net) at 5500 rpm. **Torque:** 147 lbs.-ft. at 3000 rpm.

BASE V-8 (928): 90-degree, overhead-cam "vee" type eight-cylinder. Aluminum alloy block and heads. **Displacement:** 273 cu. in. (4474 cc). **Bore & Stroke:** 3.74 x 3.11 in. (95 x 78.9 mm). **Compression Ratio:** 8.5:1. **Brake Horsepower:** 220 (SAE net) at 5450 rpm. **Torque:** 265 lbs.-ft. at 3600 rpm. Hydraulic valve lifters. Bosch K-Jetronic fuel injection.

CHASSIS DATA: Wheelbase: (911SC) 89.4 in.; (924) 94.5 in.; (928) 98.3 in. **Overall Length:** (911SC) 168.9 in.; (924) 170.1 in.; (924 Turbo) 168.9 in.; (928) 175.1 in. **Height:** (911SC) 52 in.; (924) 50 in.; (924 Turbo) 50.2 in.; (928) 51.7 in. **Width:** (911SC) 65 in.; (924) 66.3 in.; (928) 72.3 in. **Front Tread:** (911SC) 53.6 in.; (924) 55.9 in.; (928) 61.1 in. **Rear Tread:** (911SC) 52.8 in.; (924) 54 in.; (928) 60.2 in. **Standard Tires:** (911SC) 215/60VR15; (924) 185/70HR14; (924 Turbo) 185/70VR15; (928) 215/60VR15.

TECHNICAL: Layout: (911SC) rear-engine, rear-drive; (924/928) front-engine, rear-drive. **Transmission:** (911SC) five-speed manual in rear transaxle; (924/928) five-speed manual, with three-speed automatic optional. **Steering:** rack and pinion. **Suspension (front):** (911SC/924) MacPherson struts with single lower transverse A-arms, longitudinal torsion bars (anti-roll bar on 911SC); (928) upper A-arms with lower trailing arms, coil springs and anti-roll bar. **Suspension (rear):** (911SC) independent with semi-trailing arms, transverse torsion bars and anti-roll bar; (924) semi-trailing arms with transverse torsion bars; (928) upper transverse links with lower trailing arms, coil springs and anti-roll bar. **Brakes:** front/rear disc except (924 through 1980) front disc, rear drum. **Body Construction:** steel monocoque (unibody).

MAJOR OPTIONS: Three-speed automatic transmission (924/928). Air conditioning: 924 ($750). Removable tilt sunroof: 924 ($485). Electric sunroof. Alloy wheels. Speed control (911SC). AM/FM stereo w/tape player ($665). Sport seats: 911SC ($385). Leather seats ($850). Full leather interior: 911SC ($1820). Sports group: 924 ($1960).

Note: Option prices shown above were valid in 1980.

PERFORMANCE: Acceleration (0-60 mph): (924 Turbo) about 9 sec. claimed.

PRODUCTION/SALES: A total of 10,490 Porsches were sold in the U.S. during 1980 (including 3,459 Type 911, 1,925 Type 924 Turbos, and 197 Type 930 Turbos). A total of 11,241 Porsches were sold in the U.S. in 1981, and 14,407 in 1982.

Manufacturer: Dr. Ing. h.c. F. Porsche AG, Zuffenhausen, Stuttgart, West Germany.

Distributor: Volkswagen of America Inc., Englewood Cliffs, New Jersey.

HISTORY: Porsche's 1980 models were introduced to the U.S. market in October 1979. The European 928 (called 928S) gained a larger engine by 1980, but that did not enter the U.S. market until 1983. A cabriolet version of the 911SC appeared at the Geneva (Switzerland) auto show in March 1982, and soon would join the U.S. lineup.

1983 PORSCHE

911SC — FLAT SIX — For the first time in some 18 years, Porsche offered a true open cabriolet to join the Targa-roofed coupe and closed coupe. Only a limited number of cabriolets (convertibles) were expected to be available. Otherwise, production continued without major change.

944 — FOUR — Evolved from the 924 series, the 944 carried a Porsche engine rather than the Volkswagen/Audi-based four that had been used. The single-overhead-cam, 2479-cc (151-cid) four developed 143 horsepower via 9.5:1 compression. To keep vibration down, the engine contained dual balance shafts, not unlike the system used by Mitsubishi (but following a principle that dated back to 1911). Though similar in overall appearance to the 924, the new model had a different nose and tail, as well as fatter fenders (with wider tires underneath). Four-wheel disc brakes were installed.

928S — V-8 — An 'S' suffix brought a larger V-8 engine under the (front) hood of the 928 coupe. The 4644-cc (283-cid) V-8 produced 234 horsepower and came with a standard four-speed (overdrive) automatic transmission. A five-speed manual gearbox was the option, at no extra cost.

1983 Porsche 928S.

I.D. DATA: Porsche's 17-symbol Vehicle Identification Number is on a plate attached to left windshield pillar, visible through the windshield. Symbol one indicates country; symbols two and three identify the manufacturer; symbol four is the series; symbols seven and eight indicate car line ('91' = 911; '92' = 928; '94' = 944); symbol 10 indicates model year ('D' = 1983). The final six digits form the sequential production number, starting with 000001.

Model	Body Type & Seating	Engine Type/CID	P.O.E. Price	Weight (lbs.)	Prod. Total
911SC	2-dr Coupe-2+2P	H6/183	29950	2615	Note 1
911SC	2-dr Targa-2+2P	H6/183	31450	2615	Note 1
911SC	2-dr Cabr-2+2P	H6/183	34450	2615	Note 1
944					
944	2-dr Coupe-2+2P	I4/151	18980	2675	Note 1
928S					
928S	2-dr Coupe-2+2P	V8/283	43000	3210	Note 1

Note 1: Approximately 48,288 Porsches (all models) were produced during 1983.

Model Note: Some directories of imported cars continued to list the 928 with smaller (273-cid) V-8 engine rather than the newer 928S.

ENGINE DATA: BASE SIX (911SC): Horizontally opposed, overhead-cam six-cylinder (air cooled). **Displacement:** 182.6 cu. in. (2993 cc). **Bore & Stroke:** 3.74 x 2.77 in. (95 x 70.4 mm). **Compression Ratio:** 8.5:1. **Brake Horsepower:** 172 (SAE net) at 5500 rpm. **Torque:** 189 lbs.-ft. at 4200 rpm. Eight main bearings. Bosch K-Jetronic fuel injection.

BASE FOUR (944): Inline, overhead-cam four-cylinder (water cooled). **Displacement:** 151.3 cu. in. (2479 cc). **Bore & Stroke:** 3.94 x 3.11 in. (100 x 78.9 mm). **Compression Ratio:** 9.5:1. **Brake Horsepower:** 143 (SAE net) at 5500 rpm. **Torque:** 137 lbs.-ft. at 3000 rpm. Five main bearings. Bosch LE-Jetronic fuel injection.

BASE V-8 (928S): 90-degree, overhead-cam "vee" type eight-cylinder. Light alloy block and heads. **Displacement:** 283 cu. in. (4644 cc). **Bore & Stroke:** 3.82 x 3.11 in. (97 x 78.9 mm). **Compression Ratio:** 9.3:1. **Brake Horsepower:** 234 (SAE net) at 5500 rpm. **Torque:** 263 lbs.-ft. at 400 rpm. Bosch fuel injection.

CHASSIS DATA: Wheelbase: (911SC) 89.4 in.; (944) 94.5 in.; (928S) 98.4 in. **Overall Length:** (911SC) 168.9 in.; (944) 168.9 in.; (928S) 175.7 in. **Height:** (911SC) 52 in.; (944) 50.2 in.; (928S) 50.5 in. **Width:** (911SC) 65 in.; (944) 68.3 in.; (928S) 72.3 in. **Front Tread:** (911SC) 53.6 in.; (944) 58.2 in.; (928S) 61.1 in. **Rear Tread:** (911SC) 52.8 in.; (944) 57.1 in.; (928S) 60.2 in.

TECHNICAL: Layout: (911SC) rear-engine, rear-drive; (944/928S) front-engine, rear-drive. **Transmission:** (911SC) five-speed manual in rear transaxle; (944) five-speed manual, with three-speed automatic optional; (928) four-speed overdrive automatic, with five-speed manual optional. **Steering:** rack and pinion. **Suspension (front):** (911) MacPherson struts with single lower transverse A-arms, longitudinal torsion bars and anti-roll bar; (944) MacPherson struts with lower A-arms, coil springs and anti-roll bar; (928S) upper A-arms with lower trailing arms, coil springs and anti-roll bar. **Suspension (rear):** (911) semi-trailing arms with transverse torsion bars and anti-roll bar; (944) semi-trailing arms with transverse torsion bars; (928S) "Weissach" system with upper transverse links, lower semi-trailing arms, coil springs and anti-roll bar. **Brakes:** front/rear disc. **Body Construction:** steel monocoque (unibody).

PRODUCTION/SALES: A total of 21,831 Porsches were sold in the U.S. during 1983.

Manufacturer: Dr. Ing. h.c. F. Porsche AG, Zuffenhausen, Stuttgart, West Germany.

Distributor: Porsche/Audi Division, Volkswagen of America Inc., Troy, Michigan.

HISTORY: Porsche's 944 debuted in spring 1982, as an early '83 model. The other 1983 models were introduced to the U.S. market in October 1982.

1984-85 PORSCHE

911 CARRERA — FLAT SIX — The 'SC' designation disappeared after 1983, replaced by the Carrera name, which had been used on various special and racing Porsche models as early as 1953. At the same time, the 911 engine grew to 3.2 liters (and a 200-bhp rating), and a Bosch "Motronic" control system replaced the former K-Jetronic fuel injection. Among other changes, the foglights now were mounted in the front spoiler, and brakes were larger. An optional "Turbo Look" equipment package delivered the appearance of the Turbo 930 model, which had departed from the U.S. lineup late in the 1970s.

That package included a firmer suspension, bigger tires, spoilers and flared fenders. Separate options at this time included 15-inch forged alloy wheels and a rear spoiler.

944 — FOUR — A new DME (Digital Motor Electronics) fuel-injection/ignition control system replaced the original Bosch LE-Jetronic fuel injection on the 944's 2479-cc (151-cid) four-cylinder engine. Power steering and a power hatch release became standard. Joining the option list: cruise and an electric tilting sunroof.

928S — V-8 — Production of the 928S with 4644-cc (283-cid) V-8 engine continued into 1984 without major change. For 1985, however, displacement grew to 5.0 liters and horsepower jumped to 288 bhp. The new engine was a dual-overhead-cam V-8 with Bosch LH-Jetronic fuel injection. A four-speed automatic transmission was now standard, with five-speed manual gearbox optional. Standard 928S equipment now included a powered hatch release and central locking console switch, as well as a locking storage compartment.

I.D. DATA: Porsche's 17-symbol Vehicle Identification Number is on a plate attached to left windshield pillar, visible through the windshield. Symbol one indicates country; symbols two and three identify the manufacturer; symbol four is the series; symbols seven and eight indicate car line ('91' = 911; '92' = 928; '94' = 944); symbol 10 indicates model year ('E' = 1984; 'F' = 1985). The final six digits form the sequential production number, starting with 000001.

Model	Body Type & Seating	Engine Type/CID	P.O.E. Price	Weight (lbs.)	Prod. Total
911 CARRERA					
911	2-dr Coupe-2 + 2P	H6/193	31950	2615	Note 1
911	2-dr Targa-2 + 2P	H6/193	32450	2615	Note 1
911	2-dr Cabr-2 + 2P	H6/193	36450	2615	Note 1
944					
944	2-dr Coupe-2 + 2P	I4/151	21440	2675	Note 1
928S (1984 model)					
928S	2-dr Coupe-2 + 2P	V8/283	44000	3210	Note 1
928S (1985 model)					
928S	2-dr Coupe-2 + 2P	V8/302	50000	3288	Note 1

Note 1: Approximately 44,017 Porsches (all models) were produced during 1984, followed by 54,458 in 1985.
Price Note: Figures shown were valid in 1984-85.

ENGINE DATA: BASE SIX (911 Carrera): Horizontally opposed, overhead-cam six-cylinder (air cooled). **Displacement:** 193.1 cu. in. (3165 cc). **Bore & Stroke:** 3.74 x 2.93 in. (95 x 74.4 mm). **Compression Ratio:** 9.5:1. **Brake Horsepower:** 200 (SAE net) at 5900 rpm. **Torque:** 185 lbs.-ft. at 4800 rpm. Eight main bearings. Bosch Motronic (DME) fuel injection.
BASE FOUR (944): Inline, overhead-cam four-cylinder (water cooled). **Displacement:** 151.3 cu. in. (2479 cc). **Bore & Stroke:** 3.94 x 3.11 in. (100 x 78.9 mm). **Compression Ratio:** 9.5:1. **Brake Horsepower:** 143 (SAE net) at 5500 rpm. **Torque:** 137 lbs.-ft. at 3000 rpm. Five main bearings. Bosch DME fuel injection system.
BASE V-8 (1984 928S): 90-degree, overhead-cam "vee" type eight-cylinder. Light alloy block and heads. **Displacement:** 283 cu. in. (4644 cc). **Bore & Stroke:** 3.82 x 3.11 in. (97 x 78.9 mm). **Compression Ratio:** 9.3:1. **Brake Horsepower:** 234 (SAE net) at 5500 rpm. **Torque:** 263 lbs.-ft. at 4000 rpm. Bosch fuel injection.
BASE V-8 (1985 928S): 90-degree, dual-overhead-cam "vee" type eight-cylinder (32-valve). **Displacement:** 302 cu. in. (4957 cc). **Bore & Stroke:** 3.94 x 3.11 in. (100 x 78.9 mm). **Compression Ratio:** 10.0:1. **Brake Horsepower:** 288 (SAE net) at 5500-5750 rpm. **Torque:** 302 lbs.-ft. at 2700 rpm. Bosch LH-Jetronic fuel injection.

CHASSIS DATA: Wheelbase: (911) 89.5 in.; (944) 94.5 in.; (928S) 98.4 in. **Overall Length:** (911) 168.9 in.; (944) 168.9 in.; (928S) 175.7 in. **Height:** (911) 51.6 in.; (944) 50.2 in.; (928S) 50.5 in. **Width:** (911) 65 in.; (944) 68.3 in.; (928S) 72.3 in. **Front Tread:** (911) 53.9 in.; (944) 58.2 in.; (928S) 61.1 in. **Rear Tread:** (911) 54.3 in.; (944) 57.1 in.; (928S) 61.8 in.

TECHNICAL: Layout: (911) rear-engine, rear-drive; (944/928S) front-engine, rear-drive. **Transmission:** (911) five-speed manual in rear transaxle; (944) five-speed manual, with three-speed automatic optional; (928) four-speed overdrive automatic, with five-speed manual optional. **Steering:** rack and pinion. **Suspension (front):** (911) MacPherson struts with single lower transverse A-arms, longitudinal torsion bars and anti-roll bar; (944) MacPherson struts with lower A-arms, coil springs and anti-roll bar; (928S) upper A-arms with lower trailing arms, coil springs and anti-roll bar. **Suspension (rear):** (911) semi-trailing arms with transverse torsion bars and anti-roll bar; (944) semi-trailing arms with transverse torsion bar; (928S) "Weissach" system with upper transverse links, lower semi-trailing arms, coil springs and anti-roll bar. **Brakes:** front/rear disc. **Body Construction:** steel monocoque (unibody).

PRODUCTION/SALES: A total of 20,024 Porsches were sold in the U.S. during 1984, followed by 25,306 in 1985.
Manufacturer: Dr. Ing. h.c. F. Porsche AG, Zuffenhausen, Stuttgart, West Germany.
Distributor: Porsche/Audi Division, Volkswagen of America Inc., Troy, Michigan; then Porsche Cars North America Inc., Reno, Nevada.
HISTORY: Porsche's 1984 models were introduced to the U.S. in October 1983; the 1985 models in November 1984, except (928S) in December 1984. By 1985, Porsche had its own sales subsidiary: Porsche Cars North America, in Reno, Nevada.

1986 PORSCHE

911 CARRERA — FLAT SIX — The Turbo was back in the 911 line after a lengthy absence (but not called 930 Turbo this time). Powered by a 3299-cc (201-cid), 282-bhp flat six, the Turbo wore flared rear fenders and a "whale tail" spoiler out back. Non-turbo models continued with little change.

944 — FOUR — A turbocharged 944 debuted for 1986, with different front and rear spoilers than the basic model. Integrated headlamps rode in a revised nose, which covered the front bumper. A rear skirt in the Turbo served as an underbody spoiler. Otherwise, no major change was evident.

928S — V-8 — Anti-lock braking became standard this year on the 928S coupe, but little was new otherwise.

I.D. DATA: Porsche's 17-symbol Vehicle Identification Number is on a plate attached to left windshield pillar, visible through the windshield. Symbol one indicates country; symbols two and three identify the manufacturer; symbol four is the series; symbols seven and eight indicate car line ('91' = 911; '92' = 928; '94' = 944); symbol 10 indicates model year ('G' = 1986). The final six digits form the sequential production number, starting with 000001.

Model	Body Type & Seating	Engine Type/CID	P.O.E. Price	Weight (lbs.)	Prod. Total
911 CARRERA					
911	2-dr Coupe-2 + 2P	H6/193	31950	2606	Note 1
911	2-dr Targa-2 + 2P	H6/193	33450	2606	Note 1
911	2-dr Cabr-2 + 2P	H6/193	36450	2606	Note 1
Turbo	2-dr Coupe-2 + 2P	H6/201	48000	N/A	Note 1
944					
944	2-dr Coupe-2 + 2P	I4/151	22950	2637	Note 1
Turbo	2-dr Coupe-2 + 2P	I4/151	29500	2758	Note 1
928S					
928S	2-dr Coupe-2 + 2P	V8/302	50000	3288	Note 1

Note 1: Approximately 52,939 Porsches (all models) were produced during 1986.

ENGINE DATA: BASE SIX (911 Carrera): Horizontally opposed, overhead-cam six-cylinder (air cooled). **Displacement:** 193.1 cu. in. (3165 cc). **Bore & Stroke:** 3.74 x 2.93 in. (95 x 74.4 mm). **Compression Ratio:** 9.5:1. **Brake Horsepower:** 200 (SAE net) at 5900 rpm. **Torque:** 185 lbs.-ft. at 4800 rpm. Eight main bearings. Bosch Motronic (DME) fuel injection.
BASE TURBO SIX (911 Turbo): Horizontally opposed, overhead-cam six-cylinder (air cooled) with turbocharger. **Displacement:** 201.3 cu. in. (3299 cc). **Bore & Stroke:** 3.82 x 2.93 in. (97 x 74.4 mm). **Compression Ratio:** 7.0:1. **Brake Horsepower:** 282 (SAE net) at 5500/5900 rpm. **Torque:** 278 lbs.-ft. at 4000/4800 rpm.
BASE FOUR (944): Inline, overhead-cam four-cylinder (water cooled). **Displacement:** 151.3 cu. in. (2479 cc). **Bore & Stroke:** 3.94 x 3.11 in. (100 x 78.9 mm). **Compression Ratio:** 9.5:1. **Brake Horsepower:** 143 (SAE net) at 5500 rpm. **Torque:** 137 lbs.-ft. at 3000 rpm. Five main bearings. Bosch DME fuel injection system.
BASE TURBO FOUR (944 Turbo): Same as 2479-cc four above, but with turbocharger — **Compression Ratio:** 8.0:1. **Brake Horsepower:** 217 (SAE net) at 5800 rpm. **Torque:** 243 lbs.-ft. at 3500 rpm.
BASE V-8 (928S): 90-degree, dual-overhead-cam "vee" type eight-cylinder (32-valve). **Displacement:** 302 cu. in. (4957 cc). **Bore & Stroke:** 3.94 x 3.11 in. (100 x 78.9 mm). **Compression Ratio:** 10.0:1. **Brake Horsepower:** 288 (SAE net) at 5500/5750 rpm. **Torque:** 302 lbs.-ft. at 2700 rpm. Bosch LH-Jetronic fuel injection.

CHASSIS DATA: Wheelbase: (911) 89.5 in.; (944) 94.5 in.; (928S) 98.4 in. **Overall Length:** (911) 168.9 in.; (944) 168.9 in.; (928S) 175.7 in. **Height:** (911) 52 in.; (911 Turbo) 51.6 in.; (944) 50.2 in.; (928S) 50.5 in. **Width:** (911) 65 in.; (911 Turbo) 69.9 in.; (944) 68.3 in.; (928S) 72.3 in. **Front Tread:** (911) 53.9 in.; (944) 58.2 in.; (928S) 61.1 in. **Rear Tread:** (911) 54.3 in.; (944) 57.1 in.; (928S) 61.8 in.

TECHNICAL: Layout: (911) rear-engine, rear-drive; (944/928S) front-engine, rear-drive. **Transmission:** (911) five-speed manual in rear transaxle; (944) five-speed manual, with three-speed automatic optional; (928) four-speed overdrive automatic, with five-speed manual optional. **Steering:** rack and pinion. **Suspension (front):** (911) MacPherson struts with single lower transverse A-arms, longitudinal torsion bars and anti-roll bar; (944) MacPherson struts with lower A-arms, coil springs and anti-roll bar; (928S) upper A-arms with lower trailing arms, coil springs and anti-roll bar. **Suspension (rear):** (911) semi-trailing arms with transverse torsion bars and anti-roll bar; (944) semi-trailing arms with transverse torsion bar; (928S) independent "Weissach" system with upper transverse links, lower semi-trailing arms, coil springs and anti-roll bar. **Brakes:** front/rear disc. **Body Construction:** steel monocoque (unibody).

PERFORMANCE: Top Speed: (all models) 150 + mph claimed.
PRODUCTION/SALES: A total of 30,471 Porsches were sold in the U.S. during 1986.
Manufacturer: Dr. Ing. h.c. F. Porsche AG, Zuffenhausen, Stuttgart, West Germany.
Distributor: Porsche Cars North America Inc., Reno, Nevada.
HISTORY: Porsche's 1986 models were introduced to the U.S. in October 1985.

1987-88 PORSCHE

1987 Porsche 924S. (William Siuru Jr.)

911 CARRERA — FLAT SIX — The non-turbo engine added 14 horsepower for 1987, reaching 214 bhp. A new "slant-nose" option for the Turbo delivered the look of a Porsche 935 racing car, but was no bargain at $23,244. For 1988, that option package returned, including sloped front fenders, retractable headlamps, and air vents to provide cooling air for the brakes and engine. The Turbo engine was available in all three body styles: coupe, Targa coupe, and cabriolet (convertible).

924S — FOUR — A low-budget (relatively low, that is) Porsche joined the lineup as of June 1986, styled like the old 924 but carrying the 944's engine and suspension. Tires were smaller than those on the 944, however. For 1988, the non-turbo engine in 924/944 models added 11 horsepower, as a result of a freer-flowing exhaust system.

944/944S — FOUR — A new 944S edition powered by a dual-cam, 16-valve variant of the usual 2.5-liter four-cylinder engine appeared for 1987. With its engine developing 188 horsepower, a 944S was capable of 142-mph top speed. Identification was provided by '944S' lettering at the rear and a '16-Valve' label on fenders. Anti-lock braking was now optional. Driver and passenger airbags were standard on the Turbo, optional on others. For 1988, the non-turbo engine added 11 horsepower, due to a freer-flowing exhaust system, and airbags became standard on the 944S.

928S4 — V-8 — A '4' suffix was added to the 928S model number (to denote the fourth series) as it gained a more powerful version of the dual-overhead-cam V-8 engine. Again running with four valves per cylinder, the 4957-cc (302-cid) V-8 produced an extra 28 horsepower, reaching 316 bhp at 5750 rpm. Additions for 1987 included a new spoiler and wraparound taillamps. A minor front-end restyle featured a more rounded nose, and low air intake. No significant change was evident for 1988.

I.D. DATA: Porsche's 17-symbol Vehicle Identification Number is on a plate attached to left windshield pillar, visible through the windshield. Symbol one indicates country; symbols two and three identify the manufacturer; symbol four is the series; symbols seven and eight indicate car line; symbol 10 indicates model year ('H' = 1987; 'J' = 1988). The final six digits form the sequential production number, starting with 000001.

Model	Body Type & Seating	Engine Type/CID	P.O.E. Price	Weight (lbs.)	Prod. Total
911 CARRERA					
911	2-dr Coupe-2+2P	H6/193	38500	2606	Note 1
911	2-dr Targa-2+2P	H6/193	40500	2606	Note 1
911	2-dr Cabr-2+2P	H6/193	44500	2606	Note 1
Turbo	2-dr Coupe-2+2P	H6/201	58750	2826	Note 1
Turbo	2-dr Targa-2+2P	H6/201	69300	2826	Note 1
Turbo	2-dr Cabr-2+2P	H6/201	76500	2826	Note 1
924S					
924S	2-dr Coupe-2+2P	I4/151	19900	2627	Note 1
944					
944	2-dr Coupe-2+2P	I4/151	25500	2637	Note 1
944S	2-dr Coupe-2+2P	I4/151	28250	2637	Note 1
Turbo	2-dr Coupe-2+2P	I4/151	33250	2758	Note 1
928S4					
928S4	2-dr Coupe-2+2P	V8/302	58900	3288	Note 1

Note 1: Approximately 48,520 Porsches (all models) were produced during 1987.

Price Note: Figures shown above were valid in 1987. Prices rose in 1988, ranging from $24,935 for the 924S to $89,180 for the 911 Turbo cabriolet.

ENGINE DATA: BASE SIX (911 Carrera): Horizontally opposed, overhead-cam six-cylinder (air cooled). **Displacement:** 193.1 cu. in. (3165 cc). **Bore & Stroke:** 3.74 x 2.93 in. (95 x 74.4 mm). **Compression Ratio:** 9.5:1. **Brake Horsepower:** 214 (SAE net) at 5900 rpm. **Torque:** 195 lbs.-ft. at 4800 rpm. Eight main bearings. Bosch Motronic (DME) fuel injection.

BASE TURBO SIX (911 Turbo): Horizontally opposed, overhead-cam six-cylinder (air cooled) with turbocharger. **Displacement:** 201.3 cu. in. (3299 cc). **Bore & Stroke:** 3.82 x 2.93 in. (97 x 74.4 mm). **Compression Ratio:** 7.0:1. **Brake Horsepower:** 282 (SAE net) at 5500 rpm. **Torque:** 278 lbs.-ft. at 4000 rpm.

BASE FOUR (924S, 944): Inline, overhead-cam four-cylinder (water cooled). Aluminum alloy block and head. **Displacement:** 151.3 cu. in. (2479 cc). **Bore & Stroke:** 3.94 x 3.11 in. (100 x 78.9 mm). **Compression Ratio:** 9.7:1. **Brake Horsepower:** 147 (SAE net) at 5500 rpm (158 at 5900 rpm in 1988). **Torque:** 140 lbs.-ft. at 3000 rpm (155 at 4500 rpm in 1988). Five main bearings. Bosch DME fuel injection.

BASE FOUR (944S): Inline, dual-overhead-cam four-cylinder (16-valve, water cooled). **Displacement:** 151.3 cu. in. (2479 cc). **Bore & Stroke:** 3.94 x 3.11 in. (100 x 78.9 mm). **Compression Ratio:** 10.9:1. **Brake Horsepower:** 188 (SAE net) at 6000 rpm. **Torque:** 170 lbs.-ft. at 4300 rpm. Five main bearings. Bosch DME fuel injection.

BASE TURBO FOUR (944 Turbo): Same as 2479-cc four above, but with turbocharger — **Compression Ratio:** 8.0:1. **Brake Horsepower:** 217 (SAE net) at 5800 rpm. **Torque:** 243 lbs.-ft. at 3500 rpm.

BASE V-8 (928S4): 90-degree, dual-overhead-cam "vee" type eight-cylinder (32-valve). Aluminum alloy block and heads. **Displacement:** 302 cu. in. (4957 cc). **Bore & Stroke:** 3.94 x 3.11 in. (100 x 78.9 mm). **Compression Ratio:** 10.0:1. **Brake Horsepower:** 316 (SAE net) at 5750 rpm. **Torque:** 317 lbs.-ft. at 2700 rpm. Five main bearings. Bosch LH-Jetronic fuel injection.

CHASSIS DATA: Wheelbase: (911) 89.5 in.; (924/944) 94.5 in.; (928S4) 98.4 in. **Overall Length:** (911) 168.9 in.; (924/944) 168.9 in.; (928S4) 178.1 in. **Height:** (911) 52 in.; (911 Turbo) 51.6 in.; (924/944) 50.2 in.; (928S4) 50.5 in. **Width:** (911) 65 in.; (911 Turbo) 69.9 in.; (924S/944) 66.3 in.; (944S) 68.3 in.; (928S4) 72.3 in. **Front Tread:** (911) 53.9 in.; (911 Turbo) 56.4 in.; (924) 55.8 in.; (944) 58.2 in.; (928S4) 61.1 in. **Rear Tread:** (911) 54.3 in.; (911 Turbo) 58.7 in.; (924) 54.8 in.; (944) 57.1 in.; (928S4) 61 in.

TECHNICAL: Layout: (911) rear-engine, rear-drive; (924S/944/928S4) front-engine, rear-drive. **Transmission:** (911) five-speed manual in rear transaxle; (911 Turbo) four-speed manual; (924S/944) five-speed manual, with three-speed automatic optional; (944S/Turbo) five-speed manual; (928S4) four-speed overdrive automatic, with five-speed manual optional. **Steering:** rack and pinion. **Suspension (front):** (911) MacPherson struts with single lower transverse A-arms, longitudinal torsion bars and anti-roll bar; (924/944 series) MacPherson struts with lower A-arms, coil springs and anti-roll bar; (928S) upper A-arms with lower trailing arms, coil springs and anti-roll bar. **Suspension (rear):** (911) semi-trailing arms with transverse torsion bars and anti-roll bar; (924/944 series) semi-trailing arms with transverse torsion bar; (928S4) "Weissach" system with upper/lower A-arms, coil springs and anti-roll bar. **Brakes:** front/rear disc. **Body Construction:** steel monocoque (unibody).

PRODUCTION/SALES: A total of 23,632 Porsches were sold in the U.S. during 1987, dropping to 15,737 in 1988.

ADDITIONAL MODELS: Porsche's four-wheel-drive supercar, the 959, made its initial appearance in 1987, whetting the appetites of super-performance fans worldwide. Loosely based on the 911 Carrera but basically built from the ground up, the 959's composite body was an amalgamation of curves, ducts, spoilers and intakes. Early prototypes, dating from 1983 and aimed at Group B racing, had proven successful in African rallies. When first announced for production, the twin-cam flat-six engine with two-stage twin turbochargers was claimed to develop 450 horsepower (DIN) and 369 pound-feet of torque. Acceleration times as quick as 3.7 seconds to 60 mph were claimed, with a top speed in the 200-mph neighborhood. The car was said to have zero lift, with a 0.31 drag coefficient. Most of the body was made of fiberglass-reinforced Kevlar, with aluminum doors and front lid, and a polyurethane nose cap. Huge Bridgestone tires (235/45VR17 in front, 255/40VR17 in back) rode alloy wheels with hollow spokes. Sensors in the wheels warned of pressure loss, and the tires could run flat for 50 miles or more—a wise precaution since no spare tire was included. A six-speed manual gearbox was installed. Two versions were announced: one for "Comfort," the other for "Sport." Initially priced around $180,000, the actual selling prices soon shot skyward. A couple of Porsche fans brought 959s into the U.S. during the late 1980s, despite the fact that the car wasn't certified for the U.S. market. They could not be driven on the street, but turned up at dealerships, drawing plenty of gawkers.

Manufacturer: Dr. Ing. h.c. F. Porsche AG, Zuffenhausen, Stuttgart, West Germany.

Distributor: Porsche Cars of North America Inc., Reno, Nevada.

HISTORY: Porsche's 1987 models were introduced to the U.S. market in September 1986, except (924S) in June 1986. The 924S dropped out after two years in the lineup.

1989 PORSCHE

1989 Porsche 911 Carrera 4.

911 CARRERA SERIES — FLAT SIX — A four-wheel-drive Carrera 4 became available later in the 1989 model year, borrowing the basics of its "intelligent" full-time 4WD system from the 959 supercar. Styling was similar to the customary 911, but with some extra aerodynamic touches. A 3.6-liter enlargement of the 911's flat six developed 247 horsepower. Anti-lock braking and power steering were standard on the Carrera 4, which also had a rear spoiler that raised automatically at speeds above 50 mph. As for the regular Carrera models, little was new except for a switch to 16-inch tires from the former 15-inchers. Turbo models turned to a five-speed manual gearbox instead of the four-speed unit they'd used all along.

Also added during the model year was a two-seat 911 Speedster, wearing the basic 911 body but with a cutdown windshield. Carrying on the tradition that began with the early 356 Speedsters, the modern edition had a single-layer convertible top that fit beneath a tonneau cover, lacking the padding and the power operation that were standard in the regular 911 cabriolet. If that wasn't enough, those few customers lucky enough to get a 911 Speedster could order a special Turbo-look body.

944/944S2 — FOUR — The 944's base engine grew slightly in displacement for 1989, to 2.7 liters from the former 2.5-liter size. That change added just four horsepower. A new 944S2 model wore a body similar to the 944 Turbo, complete with spoilers, and carried a 16-valve, 3.0-liter four that developed 208 horsepower. That model replaced the former 944S, with its 188-bhp engine, and included anti-lock braking, an electric sunroof, and passenger-seat height adjustment. This year's 944 Turbo was rated 247 horsepower (30 more than its predecessor), and came with anti-lock braking, a limited-slip differential, transmission oil cooler, a sport suspension, and forged alloy wheels.

A cabriolet (convertible) body style was announced as a new member of the 944S2 lineup, converted from a coupe in Germany by a branch of ASC; but it was delayed for the U.S. market until the 1990 model year.

928S4 — V-8 — Little change was evident on the front-engined V-8 Porsche coupe.

Note: The lower-cost 924S coupe was dropped after a two-year revival.

I.D. DATA: Porsche's 17-symbol Vehicle Identification Number is on a plate attached to left windshield pillar, visible through the windshield. Symbol one indicates country; symbols two and three identify the manufacturer; symbol four is the series; symbols seven and eight indicate car line; symbol 10 indicates model year ('K' = 1989'). The final six digits form the sequential production number, starting with 000001.

Model	Body Type & Seating	Engine Type/CID	P.O.E. Price	Weight (lbs.)	Prod. Total
911 CARRERA					
911	2-dr Coupe-2+2P	H6/193	51205	2606	Note 1
911	2-dr Targa-2+2P	H6/193	52435	2606	Note 1
911	2-dr Cabr-2+2P	H6/193	59200	2606	Note 1
Turbo	2-dr Coupe -2+2P	H6/201	70975	2826	Note 1
Turbo	2-dr Targa-2+2P	H6/201	77065	2826	Note 1
Turbo	2-dr Cabr-2+2P	H6/201	85060	2826	Note 1
911 SPEEDSTER					
	2-dr Cabr-2P	H6/193	65480	N/A	Note 1
911 CARRERA 4					
911	2-dr Coupe-2+2P	H6/220	69500	3197	Note 1
944					
944	2-dr Coupe-2+2P	I4/164	36360	2637	Note 1
944S2	2-dr Coupe-2+2P	I4/182	45285	2637	Note 1
Turbo	2-dr Coupe-2+2P	I4/151	47600	2758	Note 1
928S4					
928S4	2-dr Coupe-2+2P	V8/302	74545	3288	Note 1

Note 1: A total of 9,479 Porsches were sold in the U.S. during 1989.

Note: The 911 Speedster was a limited-production model, offered only in 1989.

ENGINE DATA: BASE SIX (911 Carrera, Speedster): Horizontally opposed, overhead-cam six-cylinder (air cooled). Aluminum alloy block and head. **Displacement:** 193.1 cu. in. (3165 cc). **Bore & Stroke:** 3.74 x 2.93 in. (9.5 x 74.4 mm). **Compression Ratio:** 9.5:1. **Brake Horsepower:** 214 (SAE net) at 5900 rpm. **Torque:** 195 lbs.-ft. at 4800 rpm. Eight main bearings. DME ignition/fuel injection.

BASE TURBO SIX (911 Turbo): Horizontally opposed, overhead-cam six-cylinder (air cooled) with turbocharger. **Displacement:** 201.3 cu. in. (3299 cc). **Bore & Stroke:** 3.82 x 2.93 in. (97 x 74.4 mm). **Compression Ratio:** 7.0:1. **Brake Horsepower:** 282 (SAE net) at 5500 rpm. **Torque:** 288 lbs.-ft. at 4000 rpm.

BASE SIX (911 Carrera 4): Horizontally opposed, overhead-cam six-cylinder (air cooled). Aluminum alloy block and head. **Displacement:** 219.7 cu. in. (3602 cc). **Bore & Stroke:** 3.94 x 3.01 in. (100 x 76.5 mm). **Compression Ratio:** 11.3:1. **Brake Horsepower:** 247 (SAE net) at 6100 rpm. **Torque:** 228 lbs.-ft. at 4800 rpm. Eight main bearings. DME ignition/fuel injection.

BASE FOUR (944): Inline, overhead-cam four-cylinder (water cooled). Aluminum alloy block and head. **Displacement:** 163.6 cu. in. (2682 cc). **Bore & Stroke:** 4.09 x 3.11 in. (104 x 78.9 mm). **Compression Ratio:** 10.9:1. **Brake Horsepower:** 162 (SAE net) at 5800 rpm. **Torque:** 166 lbs.-ft. at 4200 rpm. Five main bearings. Multi-point fuel injection. DME ignition/fuel injection.

BASE FOUR (944S2): Inline, dual-overhead-cam four-cylinder (16-valve, water cooled). **Displacement:** 182.5 cu. in. (2992 cc). **Bore & Stroke:** 4.09 x 3.46 in. (104 x 88 mm). **Compression Ratio:** 10.9:1. **Brake Horsepower:** 208 (SAE net) at 5800 rpm. **Torque:** 207 lbs.-ft. at 4100 rpm. Five main bearings. DME ignition/fuel injection.

BASE TURBO FOUR (944 Turbo): Inline, dual-overhead-cam four-cylinder (16-valve, water cooled) with turbocharger. **Displacement:** 151.3 cu. in. (2479 cc). **Bore & Stroke:** 3.94 x 3.11 in. (100 x 78.9 mm). **Compression Ratio:** 8.0:1. **Brake Horsepower:** 247 (SAE net) at 6000 rpm. **Torque:** 258 lbs.-ft. at 4000 rpm. Five main bearings. Bosch DME fuel injection.

BASE V-8 (928S4): 90-degree, dual-overhead-cam "vee" type eight-cylinder (32-valve). Aluminum alloy block and heads. **Displacement:** 302.5 cu. in. (4957 cc). **Bore & Stroke:** 3.94 x 3.11 in. (100 x 78.9 mm). **Compression Ratio:** 10.0:1. **Brake Horsepower:** 316 (SAE net) at 6000 rpm. **Torque:** 317 lbs.-ft. at 3000 rpm. Five main bearings. Bosch LH-Jetronic fuel injection.

CHASSIS DATA: Wheelbase: (911) 89.5 in.; (944) 94.5 in.; (928S4) 98.4 in. **Overall Length:** (911) 168.9 in.; (911 Carrera 4) 167.3 in.; (944) 170 in.; (944 Turbo) 168.9 in.; (928S4) 178.1 in. **Height:** (911) 52 in.; (911 Turbo) 51.6 in.; (944) 50.2 in.; (928S4) 50.5 in. **Width:** (911) 65 in.; (911 Turbo) 69.9 in.; (944) 68.3 in.; (928S4) 72.3 in. **Front Tread:** (911) 54.0 in.; (911 Carrera 4) 54.3 in.; (911 Turbo) 56.4 in.; (944) 58.2 in.; (944 Turbo) 57.4 in.; (928S4) 61.1 in. **Rear Tread:** (911) 55.3 in.; (911 Carrera 4) 54.1 in.; (911 Turbo) 58.7 in.; (944) 57.1 in.; (944 Turbo) 56.5 in.; (928S4) 60.9 in.

TECHNICAL: Layout: (911) rear-engine, rear-drive; (911 Carrera 4) rear-engine, four-wheel drive; (944/928S4) front-engine, rear-drive. **Transmission:** (911) five-speed manual in rear transaxle; (944) five-speed manual, with three-speed automatic optional; (944S2/Turbo) five-speed manual; (928S4) four-speed overdrive automatic, with five-speed manual optional. **Steering:** rack and pinion. **Suspension (front):** (911) MacPherson struts with single lower transverse A-arms, longitudinal torsion bars and anti-roll bar; (911 Carrera 4) struts with lower A-arms, coil springs and anti-roll bar; (944) MacPherson struts with lower A-arms, coil springs and anti-roll bar; (928S) upper A-arms with lower trailing arms, coil springs and anti-roll bar. **Suspension (rear):** (911) semi-trailing arms with transverse torsion bars and anti-roll bar; (944) semi-trailing arms with transverse torsion bar; (928S4) "Weissach" system with upper/lower A-arms, coil springs and anti-roll bar. **Brakes:** front/rear disc. **Body Construction:** steel monocoque (unibody).

Manufacturer: Dr. Ing. h.c. F. Porsche AG, Zuffenhausen, Stuttgart, West Germany.
Distributor: Porsche Cars of North America Inc., Reno, Nevada.
HISTORY: Porsche's 1989 models were introduced to the U.S. market in September 1988. Sales in the U.S. were declining steadily, down to only 9,479 for the year after peaking at 30,471 in 1986.

1990 PORSCHE

1990 Porsche 944 S2 cabriolet.

911 CARRERA SERIES — FLAT SIX — Porsche's 911 Turbo dropped out of the lineup, at least temporarily. Returning were the base Carrera and the four-wheel-drive Carrera 4, each powered by the 3.6-liter flat six that previously had been used only in the Carrera 4. A four-speed overdrive automatic transmission, called Tiptronic, became available on the two-wheel-drive models. That was the first automatic-shift ever offered on the 911 series. Although initially available only in closed coupe form, the Carrera 4 later came in all three body styles. All models had anti-lock brakes and dual front airbags. This year, both rear-drive and 4WD models had coil springs up front instead of the traditional torsion bars. An automatic-raising rear spoiler also was installed on both models.

944S2 — FOUR — The cabriolet (convertible) that had been anticipated for 1989 became available for the 1990 model year, powered by the same 208-bhp engine as the 944S2 hatchback coupe. Each had anti-lock braking and dual front airbags. The former base model was gone; so was the 944 Turbo. Only a five-speed manual gearbox was available.

928 — V-8 — Only a few changes hit the 928 coupe for 1990, beyond the loss of its 'S' model-number suffix. Improvements included airbags for both driver and front passenger, a new tire-pressure monitoring system, and the addition of a limited-slip differential. The powertrain was unchanged: a 4957-cc (302-cid) V-8 with either four-speed automatic or five-speed manual transmission.

I.D. DATA: Porsche's 17-symbol Vehicle Identification Number is on a plate attached to left windshield pillar, visible through the windshield. Symbol one indicates country; symbols two and three identify the manufacturer; symbol four is the series; symbols seven and eight indicate car line; symbol 10 indicates model year ('L' = 1990'). The final six digits form the sequential production number, starting with 000001.

Model	Body Type & Seating	Engine Type/CID	P.O.E. Price	Weight (lbs.)	Prod. Total
911 CARRERA					
Carrera 2	2-dr Coupe-2+2P	H6/220	58500	2891	Note 1
Carrera 2	2-dr Targa-2+2P	H6/220	59900	2891	Note 1
Carrera 2	2-dr Cabr-2+2P	H6/220	66800	2891	Note 1
Carrera 4	2-dr Coupe-2+2P	H6/220	69500	3252	Note 1
Carrera 4	2-dr Targa-2+2P	H6/220	70900	3252	Note 1
Carrera 4	2-dr Cabr-2+2P	H6/220	77800	3252	Note 1
944S2					
944S2	2-dr Coupe-2+2P	I4/182	41900	2857	Note 1
944S2	2-dr Cabr-2+2P	I4/182	48600	2968	Note 1
928					
928	2-dr Coupe-2+2P	V8/302	74545	3288	Note 1

Note 1: A total of 9,139 Porsches were sold in the U.S. during 1990.

1990 Porsche 928 automatic.

ENGINE DATA: BASE SIX (911 Carrera): Horizontally opposed, overhead-cam six-cylinder (air cooled). Aluminum alloy block and head. **Displacement:** 219.7 cu. in. (3602 cc). **Bore & Stroke:** 3.94 x 3.01 in. (100 x 76.5 mm). **Compression Ratio:** 11.3:1. **Brake Horsepower:** 247 (SAE net) at 6100 rpm. **Torque:** 228 lbs.-ft. at 4800 rpm. Eight main bearings. DME ignition/fuel injection.

BASE FOUR (944S2): Inline, dual-overhead-cam four-cylinder (16-valve, water cooled). **Displacement:** 182.5 cu. in. (2992 cc). **Bore & Stroke:** 4.09 x 3.46 in. (104 x 88 mm). **Compression Ratio:** 10.9:1. **Brake Horsepower:** 208 (SAE net) at 5800 rpm. **Torque:** 207 lbs.-ft. at 4100 rpm. Five main bearings. DME ignition/fuel injection.

BASE V-8 (928): 90-degree, dual-overhead-cam "vee" type eight-cylinder (32-valve). Aluminum alloy block and heads. **Displacement:** 302.5 cu. in. (4957 cc). **Bore & Stroke:** 3.94 x 3.11 in. (100 x 78.9 mm). **Compression Ratio:** 10.0:1. **Brake Horsepower:** 316 (SAE net) at 6000 rpm. **Torque:** 317 lbs.-ft. at 3000 rpm. Five main bearings. Bosch LH-Jetronic fuel injection.

CHASSIS DATA: Wheelbase: (911) 89.5 in.; (944S2) 94.5 in.; (928) 98.4 in. **Overall Length:** (911) 168.3 in.; (944S2) 168.9 in.; (928) 178.1 in. **Height:** (911) 52 in.; (944S2) 50.2 in.; (928) 50.5 in. **Width:** (911) 65 in.; (944S2) 68.3 in.; (928) 72.3 in. **Front Tread:** (911) 54.0 in.; (911 Carrera 4) 54.3 in.; (944S2) 58.2 in.; (928) 61.5 in. **Rear Tread:** (911) 55.3 in.; (911 Carrera 4) 54.1 in.; (944S2) 57.1 in.; (928) 61.6 in.

TECHNICAL: Layout: (911 Carrera 2) rear-engine, rear-drive; (911 Carrera 4) rear-engine, four-wheel drive; (944S2/928) front-engine, rear-drive. **Transmission:** (911) five-speed manual in rear transaxle, or four-speed automatic; (944S2) five-speed manual; (928) four-speed overdrive automatic or five-speed manual. **Steering:** rack and pinion. **Suspension (front):** (911) struts with lower A-arms, coil springs and anti-roll bar; (944) MacPherson struts with lower A-arms, coil springs and anti-roll bar; (928) upper A-arms with lower trailing arms, coil springs and anti-roll bar. **Suspension (rear):** (911) semi-trailing arms with transverse torsion bars and anti-roll bar; (944) semi-trailing arms with transverse torsion bar; (928) "Weissach" system with upper/lower A-arms, coil springs and anti-roll bar. **Brakes:** front/rear disc. **Body Construction:** steel monocoque (unibody).

Manufacturer: Dr. Ing. h.c. F. Porsche AG, Zuffenhausen, Stuttgart, West Germany.
Distributor: Porsche Cars of North America Inc., Reno, Nevada.

HISTORY: Porsche's 1990 models were introduced to the U.S. market in October 1989 except (911 Targa/cabrio) in November 1989. A 911 Turbo returned to the Porsche lineup for 1991.

RELIANT

Early in 1935, designer Tom L. Williams founded the British firm that adopted the Reliant name, creating a three-wheeled prototype with one-cylinder engine and chain drive. Williams was no stranger to powered three-wheelers, having designed the Safety Seven a few years earlier, while he worked for the Raleigh Cycle Company. When Raleigh discontinued its three-wheel van, Williams obtained the rights and began to arrange for production on his own. In mid-1935, the first such van was ready for delivery. A two-cylinder version arrived in the following year, propelled by shaft drive; followed by a four-cylinder model (using an Austin Seven engine) in 1938. Reliant was building its own bodies by 1936. By the time World War II erupted, Reliant was turning out its own engine, similar to the Austin design. Van production resumed early in 1946, months after the war ended.

Passenger-car production began in 1952 with the Regal, an open four-seater with three-wheel layout. The light-weight design could be registered as a motorcycle in Britain. Within a year, examples of the compact three-wheeler began to arrive on the West Coast of the U.S. A switch from the original metal bodies to fiberglass construction came in 1956.

Unlike most automakers of that day, Reliant didn't stick close to home, but helped initiate operations in developing nations. Starting in 1958, a Sussita station wagon based on a Reliant design was being produced in Israel. That was followed by a Sabra sports car (listed separately in this Catalog). In the late 1960s and early 1970s, Reliant-based designs went into production in Turkey, Greece, and India.

For the 1961 model year, Reliant introduced a variant of that Israeli-built sports car for the British market, under the Sabre nameplate. First powered by a four-cylinder Ford engine, it soon became available as a six-cylinder coupe. A four-seat, four-wheeled minisedan called the Rebel arrived in 1964. Also in that year came a model which, though seldom seen on U.S. shores, gained considerably publicity among sports/GT fans: the Scimitar. An Estate (station wagon) version of the Scimitar was added in 1968, with a V-6 engine replacing the original inline six. A convertible Scimitar arrived in 1980.

Three-wheelers remained in production throughout the period. In 1985, a new SS1 sports car replaced the long-lived Scimitar. Except for the smattering of three-wheelers that arrived during the 1950s, Reliants have been rare in the U.S., and all examples are right-hand drive. A lone Scimitar was displayed at the British Auto Festival in Illinois in 1990. The owner of that 1973 GTE purchased and drove the car for several years in Britain before bringing it across the Atlantic.

Regal's engine rested between the two front seats, and drove a four-speed constant-mesh gearbox. Hydraulic brakes were used. The four-seater body was steel over wood, on a chassis with a 74-inch wheelbase, measuring 123 inches overall. Top speed was claimed to be 65 mph, with fuel mileage of 45-50 mpg. The simple rectangular grille had horizontal ribs. Inside was synthetic leather upholstery. Under the hinged hood lid was a spare tire and tool area, with trunk space at the rear. The Mark III version, introduced in 1956, wore a fiberglass body instead of the original steel, and came in closed coupe and well as roadster form.

1954 Reliant Regal DeLuxe roadster.

I.D. DATA: Not available.

Model	Body Type & Seating	Engine Type/CID	P.O.E. Price	Weight (lbs.)	Prod. Total
Regal	2-dr Rds-4P	I4/46	Note 1	896	N/A
Regal	2-dr Coupe-4P	I4/46	Note 1	N/A	N/A

Note 1: Price in the U.S. was about $1200 in 1953. Price at the factory in Britain was approximately $840 in 1955, raised to $902 in 1956 and $924 by 1957.

ENGINE DATA: BASE FOUR: Inline, L-head four-cylinder (Austin Seven). Cast iron block with aluminum crankcase. **Displacement:** 45.59 cu. in. (747.5 cc). **Bore & Stroke:** 2.20 x 3.00 in. (55.9 x 76.2 mm). **Compression Ratio:** 5.7:1. **Brake Horsepower:** 16 at 4000 rpm. **Torque:** 28 lbs.-ft. at 2000 rpm. Solex carburetor.

CHASSIS DATA: Wheelbase: 74 in. **Overall Length:** 123 in. **Height:** 53 in. **Width:** 54 in. (later, 59.25 in.). **Tread:** 45 in. **Standard Tires:** 4.50x14 (5.00x14 for export).

TECHNICAL: Layout: front-engine, rear-drive (three-wheel). **Transmission:** four-speed manual (constant mesh). **Standard Final Drive Ratio:** 5.14:1. **Suspension (front):** torsion bar with double-acting shock absorber. **Suspension (rear):** semi-elliptic leaf springs with double-acting shock absorber. **Brakes:** hydraulic, front/rear drum. **Body Construction:** composite hardwood framing with metal panels, on pressed rail frame.

PERFORMANCE: Top Speed: 65 mph. **Acceleration (0-60 mph):** 30 sec. **Fuel Mileage:** 45-50 mpg.

Manufacturer: The Reliant Engineering Co. Ltd., Tomworth, England.

HISTORY: A Regent Delivery Van also was available, with similar specifications and 1350-pound payload.

1952-60 RELIANT

REGAL — FOUR — Reliant's three-wheeler, powered by an Austin Seven L-head four-cylinder engine, first came in open form with a metal body. Before long, its American debut took place in Los Angeles. In California, according to the October 1953 issue of *CARS* magazine, the three-wheeler "caused quite a stir among the normally blase members of the celluloid set." Hollywood actress Polly Bergen (who also owned an MG) was pictured behind the wheel. Two men were shown lifting the front end of the British light-weight.

1961-63 RELIANT

1962 Reliant Sabre.

SABRE GT — FOUR/SIX — Based on the Sabra sports car that was produced in Israel (from a Reliant design by Leslie Bellamy), the Sabre two-seater first came with a four-cylinder Ford Console engine. Though lacking a front bumper as such, it wore huge vertical overriders (guards). The engine was offered in three states of tune: standard, Stage One (with 8.9:1 compression), and Stage Two (with twin SU carbs instead of the usual single Zenith). For the 1963 model year, a six-cylinder version became available, with Ford Zodiac engine. That one also had a Ford gearbox, unlike the ZF four-speed used in the original Sabre. Appearance also was modified, adopting a more conventional GT/sports coupe look with clean, uncluttered lines and 2+2 seating capacity. Full rounded wheel openings surrounding wire wheels and modestly finned rear fenders helped give the fastback coupe an attractive stance.

521

1967 Reliant Scimitar three-liter.

SCIMITAR GT — V-6 — A 3.0-liter V-6 engine replaced the inline six in 1967, followed by an optional smaller (2.5-liter) V-6 engine for Reliant's sports coupe. Otherwise, specifications remained similar to 1966. Production of the coupe body ceased after 1970, leaving only the GTE (Estate) version.

SCIMITAR GTE — V-6 — Introduced in 1968 was a new Grand Touring Estate (GTE) station wagon body style with long rear side windows. According to the sales brochure, it "combines the features of a grand touring and an estate car." The GTE came with the larger (3.0-liter) V-6 and rode a longer wheelbase than the original coupe. Even with automatic shift (available later), a GTE went from 0-60 in less than 10 seconds. Quad round headlamps stood in slightly recessed housings alongside the small rectangular grille, which consisted of thin horizontal bars. 'SCIMITAR' block letters went above the grille. A sword emblem sat ahead of the hood, and on the cowl. Body colors in the mid-1970s included Nevada Yellow, Wessex Green, Shetland Blue, Highland Purple, Everest White, Beaujolais Red, Capricorn Blue, and Ivory Beige. Interiors came in Black or Tan. Standard features included a 140-mph speedometer, 7000-rpm tachometer, upward-opening rear window, reclining aero-type front seats upholstered in leathercloth, fold-down rear seats, clock, lighter, front and rear wiper/washers, and two-speaker Radiomobile radio. Overdrive was available as an option, followed by a Borg-Warner three-speed automatic transmission. Production continued until 1985, but later models adopted a 2.8-liter V-6 engine.

I.D. DATA: Not available.

Model	Body Type & Seating	Engine Type/CID	P.O.E. Price	Weight (lbs.)	Prod. Total
SCIMITAR					
GT	2-dr Coupe-2 + 2P	V6/183	Note 1	2226	Note 3
GT	2-dr Coupe-2 + 2P	V6/152	N/A	N/A	Note 3
GTE	2-dr Estate-4P	V6/183	Note 2	2226	Note 3

Note 1: Basic price in Britain was 1232 pounds (Sterling) in 1968.

Note 2: Basic price in Britain was 1902 pounds (Sterling) in 1972.

Note 3: A total of about 3,438 Reliants were produced in 1968, and 3,850 in 1969. In 1973, the Reliant Group produced 2,405 cars, rising to 3,247 in 1976, but down to only 820 in 1978.

1973 Reliant Scimitar GTE.

ENGINE DATA: BASE V-6 (Scimitar GT/GTE): Overhead-valve, vee-type six-cylinder (60-degree). Cast iron block and head. **Displacement:** 182.7 cu. in. (2994 cc). **Bore & Stroke:** 3.69 x 2.85 in. (93.7 x 72.4 mm). **Compression Ratio:** 8.9:1. **Brake Horsepower:** 128 DIN (144 SAE) at 4750 rpm except (GTE) 135 (DIN) at 5000. **Torque:** 172 lbs.-ft. DIN (192 SAE) at 3000 rpm. Four main bearings. Weber two-barrel carburetor.

OPTIONAL V-6 (Scimitar GT): Overhead-valve, vee-type six-cylinder. Cast iron block and head. **Displacement:** 152.2 cu. in. (2495 cc). **Bore & Stroke:** 3.69 x 2.38 in. (93.7 x 60.4 mm). **Compression Ratio:** 9.1:1. **Brake Horsepower:** 119 (SAE) at 4750 rpm. **Torque:** 146 lbs.-ft. (SAE) at 3000 rpm. Four main bearings. Zenith two-barrel carburetor.

I.D. DATA: Not available.

Model	Body Type & Seating	Engine Type/CID	P.O.E. Price	Weight (lbs.)	Prod. Total
Sabre 4	2-dr Coupe-2P	I4/104	N/A	N/A	N/A
Sabre 6	2-dr Coupe-2 + 2P	I6/156	N/A	N/A	N/A

ENGINE DATA: BASE FOUR (Sabre 4): Inline, overhead-valve four-cylinder (Ford Consul). Cast iron block and head. **Displacement:** 103.9 cu. in. (1703 cc). **Bore & Stroke:** 3.25 x 3.13 in. (82.6 x 79.5 mm). **Compression Ratio:** 7.8:1. **Brake Horsepower:** 57 at 4400 rpm. Solid valve lifters. Zenith carburetor.

Note: Four-cylinder engine was available with 8.9:1 compression and two SU carburetors, producing up to 73 horsepower.

BASE SIX (Sabre 6): Inline, overhead-valve six-cylinder (Ford Zephyr). Cast iron block and head. **Displacement:** 155.78 cu. in. (2553 cc). **Bore & Stroke:** 3.25 x 3.13 in. (82.6 x 79.5 mm). **Compression Ratio:** 8.3:1. **Brake Horsepower:** 98 at 4750 rpm. Solid valve lifters. Zenith carburetor.

CHASSIS DATA: Wheelbase: 90 in. **Overall Length:** (four) 165 in.; (six) 159.5 in. **Width:** 61 in. **Tread:** (four) 48 in.; (six) 50 in. **Standard Tires:** (four) 155x15; (six) 165x15.

TECHNICAL: Layout: front-engine, rear-drive. **Transmission:** four-speed manual. **Standard Final Drive Ratio:** 3.55:1 or 3.58:1. **Suspension (front):** coil springs. **Suspension (rear):** coil springs. **Brakes:** hydraulic; front disc, rear drum. **Body Construction:** fiberglass.

PERFORMANCE: Top Speed: (four) 90-93 mph; (six) 107 mph. **Acceleration (quartermile):** (four) about 20 sec.; (six) 17.6 seconds.

Manufacturer: The Reliant Engineering Co. Ltd., Tomworth, England; changed to Reliant Motor Co. Ltd. in 1963.

HISTORY: Production of three-wheeled Regals also continued, replaced by a new 3/25 three-wheeler in 1963. Reliant's own engine replaced the former L-head Austin Seven.

1964-66 RELIANT

REBEL — FOUR — With the debut of this two-door mini sedan, Reliant was considered to be the first new British family car manufacturer to appear since World War II. Small but roomy inside, the unitary-bodied four-seat Rebel wore a fiberglass body on a steel chassis. Space was provided for 12 cubic feet of luggage. Under the hood was an aluminum 600-cc, four-cylinder engine with four-speed gearbox (as in the 3/25 three-wheeler).

SCIMITAR GT — SE4 — SIX — Like other Reliants, the new grand touring coupe wore a fiberglass body, this one styled by David Ogle Associates. Replacing the former Sabre, it was powered initially by a specially-tuned version of the Ford Zephyr inline six-cylinder engine, producing 120 horsepower. Center-lock wire wheels held 165x15 tires. Quad headlamps sat in recessed housings, with a protruding crease between them. An insignia stood just ahead of the horizontal hood lid. Doors held vent windows. A bodyside trim crease followed the line of the front wheel opening, extending all the way to the rear of the car. Optional overdrive for the four-speed (all-synchro) transmission provided direct drive in top gear, controlled by a dashboard switch.

I.D. DATA: Not available.

Model	Body Type & Seating	Engine Type/CID	P.O.E. Price	Weight (lbs.)	Prod. Total
REBEL					
Rebel	2-dr Sedan-4P	I4/36	Note 1	1178	Note 3
SCIMITAR					
SE4	2-dr Coupe-2 + 2P	I6/156	Note 2	2200	Note 3

Note 1: Base price in Britain was 433 pounds (Sterling).

Note 2: Base price in Britain was 1068 pounds (Sterling).

Note 3: A total of about 15,000 Reliants were produced in 1964 alone, and 15,000 in 1966.

ENGINE DATA: BASE FOUR (Rebel): Inline, overhead-valve four-cylinder. Aluminum block and head. **Displacement:** 36.49 cu. in. (600 cc). **Bore & Stroke:** 2.20 x 2.40 in. (56 x 61 mm). **Compression Ratio:** 8.45:1. **Brake Horsepower:** 28 at 5250 rpm. **Torque:** 31 lbs.-ft. at 3000 rpm. Solid valve lifters. Solex carburetor.

BASE SIX (Scimitar): Inline, overhead-valve six-cylinder. Cast iron block and head. **Displacement:** 155.78 cu. in. (2553 cc). **Bore & Stroke:** 3.25 x 3.13 in. (82.6 x 79.5 mm). **Compression Ratio:** 8.3:1. **Brake Horsepower:** 120 (DIN) at 5000 rpm. **Torque:** 140 lbs.-ft. (DIN) at 2600 rpm. Four main bearings. Solid valve lifters. Three SU HS4 carburetors.

CHASSIS DATA: Wheelbase: (Rebel) 89 in.; (Scimitar) 92 in. **Overall Length:** (Rebel) 137 in.; (Scimitar) 168 in. **Height:** (Rebel) 56.5 in.; (Scimitar) 50.5 in. **Width:** (Rebel) 58 in.; (Scimitar) 61.5 in. **Front Tread:** (Rebel) 48 in.; (Scimitar) 50 in. **Rear Tread:** (Rebel) 46.5 in.; (Scimitar) 50 in. **Wheel Type:** (Rebel) ventilated steel disc; (Scimitar) center-lock wire. **Standard Tires:** (Rebel) 5.50x12; (Scimitar) 165x15.

TECHNICAL: Layout: front-engine, rear-drive. **Transmission:** four-speed manual (Scimitar, all synchro). **Standard Final Drive Ratio:** (Rebel) 4.38:1; (Scimitar) 3.88:1. **Steering:** (Rebel) cam and peg; (Scimitar) rack and pinion. **Suspension (front):** wishbones with coil springs. **Suspension (rear):** (Rebel) rigid axle with semi-elliptic leaf springs and lever shocks; (Scimitar) rigid axle with coil springs and modified Watt linkage. **Brakes:** hydraulic front disc, rear drum. **Body Construction:** (Rebel) fiberglass unibody on ladder-type steel chassis; (Scimitar) fiberglass. **Fuel Tank:** (Rebel) 7.1 gal.; (Scimitar) 24 gallon.

MAJOR OPTIONS: Overdrive (Scimitar).

PERFORMANCE: Top Speed: (Rebel) 73 mph; (Scimitar) 117-121 mph. **Acceleration (0-60 mph):** (Scimitar) N/A (0-50 in 8.5 seconds). **Acceleration (quarter-mile):** (Scimitar) 18 sec. **Fuel Mileage:** (Rebel) 51 mpg; (Scimitar) about 19 mpg.

Manufacturer: Reliant Motor Car Co. Ltd., Tomworth, England.

HISTORY: In addition to the four-wheeled Rebel and Scimitar, Reliant produced about three-fourths of all British three-wheelers.

OPTIONAL V-6 (later Scimitar): Overhead-valve, vee-type six-cylinder (Ford Granada). **Displacement:** 170.4 cu. in. (2792 cc). **Bore & Stroke:** 3.66 x 2.70 in. (93.0 x 68.5 mm). **Compression Ratio:** 9.2:1. **Brake Horsepower:** 135 (DIN) at 5200 rpm. **Torque:** 152 lbs.-ft. at 3000 rpm. Twin-choke carburetor.

CHASSIS DATA: Wheelbase: (Scimitar GT) 92 in.; (GTE) 99.5 in. **Overall Length:** (Scimitar GT) 168 in.; (GTE) 171 in. **Height:** (Scimitar GT) 51.5 in.; (GTE) 52 in. **Width:** (Scimitar GT) 62.75 in.; (GTE) 64.5 in. **Front Tread:** (Scimitar GT) 51.5 in.; (GTE) 55 in. **Front Tread:** (Scimitar GT) 50.5 in.; (GTE) 53 in. **Wheel Type:** pressed steel disc. **Standard Tires:** (Scimitar GT) 165x15; (GTE) 185x14.

TECHNICAL: Layout: front-engine, rear-drive. **Transmission:** four-speed manual (all synchro). **Standard Final Drive Ratio:** (Scimitar GT) 3.58:1; (GTE) 3.07:1 w/manual, 3.31:1 w/overdrive or automatic. **Steering:** rack and pinion. **Suspension (front):** wishbones with coil springs and anti-roll bar. **Suspension (rear):** rigid axle with coil springs and modified Watts linkage. **Brakes:** hydraulic front disc, rear drum. **Body Construction:** fiberglass body on box-type ladder frame. **Fuel Tank:** (GTE) 20.3 gallon.

MAJOR OPTIONS: Overdrive. Wire wheels (GT). Manual or power sunroof (GT). Borg-Warner 35 automatic transmission (later GTE). 3.07:1 axle ratio (GTE). Light alloy wheels (GTE). Heated rear window (GTE). Radiomobile 8-track stereo tape player/radio. Cast alloy wheels. Fog and spot lamps. Leather upholstery. Power windows. Quartz halogen lamps. Full tinted glass. Auxiliary cooling fan. Non-standard body colors. Note: Not all options were available in every year.

PERFORMANCE: Top Speed: (Scimitar GT) 121-125 mph; (GTE) 117-123 mph. **Acceleration (0-60 mph):** (Scimitar GT) N/A (0-50 in 7.2 seconds); (GTE) 8.6-8.9 seconds, or 9.8 seconds with automatic transmission. **Acceleration (quarter-mile):** (Scimitar GT) 17.1 sec.; (GTE) 16.4-16.8 seconds, or 17.6 with automatic. **Fuel Mileage:** (Scimitar GT) near 21 mpg.

ADDITIONAL MODELS: Production of the Rebel minicar continued into 1974 (see previous listing for details). By 1974, a Robin three-wheeled sedan was available. Next year came a replacement for the four-wheel Rebel minicar, called the Kitten.

Manufacturer: Reliant Motor Co. Ltd., Tomworth, Staffordshire, England.

HISTORY: Reliant bought out the Bond company (another producer of three-wheeled vehicles) in 1969.

1980-85 RELIANT

SCIMITAR GTE — V-6 — Production of the Estate sports car continued into 1985, with a 2.8-liter V-6 engine. Reliant claimed that the GTE was "accepted throughout the motoring world as the original high performance estate." Sales literature described it as "reminiscent of traditional sports cars in its performance and feel, (providing) the modern inter-city executive with effortless motorway travel." Appearance was similar to earlier models, but inner headlamps were smaller than the outer units and their housings had a rectangular shape, which connected with the blackout rectangular grille. Standard equipment included a 140-mph speedometer, 7000-rpm tachometer, heated rear window, two-speed wipers with intermittent facility, tinted windshield, gas-strut rear-window opening, reclining front seats, and two interior lights with delay action. Twelve body colors were available. Interiors came in Black, Dark Blue, Chocolate, or Tan. Factory literature promised "high maximum speed approaching 120 mph, vivid acceleration and economical fuel consumption." Rear seats folded down individually. An overdrive four-speed manual transmission was standard; three-speed automatic optional.

SCIMITAR GTC — V-6 — A convertible version of Reliant's sports car arrived in 1980, joining the GTE Estate. Reliant called it a "stylish and sophisticated high performance 4 seater....destined to become a classic in its own right....a reminder of your earlier sports car days or the realisation of a dream." Rear seats folded down individually, and the GTS was promoted as offering "exhiliration of an open car...for the whole family." Appearance and specifications were similar to the GTE, with a slim targa bar evident when the top was folded.

I.D. DATA: Not available.

Model	Body Type & Seating	Engine Type/CID	P.O.E. Price	Weight (lbs.)	Prod. Total
SCIMITAR					
GTE	2-dr Estate-4P	V6/170	Note 1	2790	Note 3
GTC	2-dr Conv-4P	V6/170	Note 2	2790	Note 3

Note 1: Price in Britain in 1982 was 11,790 pounds (Sterling).

Note 2: Price in Britain in 1982 was 14,490 pounds (Sterling).

Note 3: A total of 135 four-wheeled Reliant cars were produced in 1984 alone. About 7,000 Reliant vehicles were built in 1980.

ENGINE DATA: BASE V-6: Overhead-valve, 60-degree vee-type six-cylinder. Cast iron block and head. **Displacement:** 170.4 cu. in. (2792 cc). **Bore & Stroke:** 3.66 x 2.70 in. (93.0 x 68.5 mm). **Compression Ratio:** 9.2:1. **Brake Horsepower:** 135 (DIN) at 5200 rpm. **Torque:** 152 lbs.-ft. (DIN) at 3000 rpm. Four main bearings. Twin-choke carburetor.

CHASSIS DATA: Wheelbase: 103.8 in. **Overall Length:** 174.5 in. **Height:** 52.0 in. **Width:** 67.75 in. **Front Tread:** 58.1 in. **Front Tread:** 56.1 in. **Wheel Type:** cast alloy 6.00x14. **Standard Tires:** 185HR14.

TECHNICAL: Layout: front-engine, rear-drive. **Transmission:** four-speed manual (overdrive 3rd and 4th). **Standard Final Drive Ratio:** 3.54:1. **Steering:** power rack-and-pinion. **Suspension (front):** wishbones with coil springs and anti-roll bar. **Suspension (rear):** rigid axle with trailing arms, coil springs and Watts linkage. **Brakes:** vacuum-servo hydraulic front disc, rear drum. **Body Construction:** fiberglass on box-section pressed steel chassis.

MAJOR OPTIONS: Automatic transmission. Phillips mono radio with stereo cassette player. Phillips stereo radio/cassette player. Cast alloy wheels. Power steering. Leather upholstery. Front auxiliary lamps. Tinted glass. Power windows. Power mirror. Power antenna. Hollandia sunroof (GTE). Two-tone paint.

PERFORMANCE: Top Speed: 120 mph. **Fuel Mileage:** 29.8 mpg at 56 mph.

Manufacturer: Reliant Motor Car Co. Ltd., Tomworth, Staffordshire, England.

POSTSCRIPT: In 1985, Reliant announced a new and completely different SS1 replacement for the Scimitar, powered by either a 1.3-liter or 1.6-liter Ford engine and designed by Michelotti. Billed as the "affordable small sports car," this open two-seater achieved some notoriety when Britain's Princess Anne was stopped for speeding in one. A 1.8-liter turbocharged engine became optional in 1986. In addition to its other work, the Reliant firm earned the right to build 200 bodies for Ford's RS200 rally car in 1985.

RENAULT

Shortly before the turn of the century—late in 1898 to be exact—youthful Louis Renault turned his De Dion-Bouton three-wheeled quadricycle into a four-wheeled motorcar in his workshop. The shop was actually a shed, on the grounds of the family home at Billancourt, France (a suburb of Paris). With that ambitious step, Louis paved the way for Renault eventually to become one of the major automobile producers in the world. Among other technical details, that initial two-seat vehicle was the first to employ a direct-drive third (top) gear, and fed power through a propeller shaft and differential.

Although that first vehicle was built for pleasure, essentially as a hobby, friends quickly expressed interest in acquiring one for themselves. According to *Road Test* magazine, a dozen Renault friends plunked down deposits on the evening of its very first outing, on Christmas Eve in 1898. Fortunately for Louis, his elder brothers Marcel and Fernand were able to provide essential funds for this new venture, because the family's button/drapery business was doing well at the time. So Renault Freres (brothers) was formed in February, 1899. At the Paris Automobile Salon that year, the brothers obtained orders for some 60 *voiturette* motorcars. Production quickly got underway on the grounds of the family home, turning out cars with single-cylinder engines and closed coupe bodies.

Racing also drew the brother's attention, starting with the Paris-Trouville trek in 1899. A single-cylinder Renault took the top spot in its class at the Paris-to-Berlin race in 1901. A 3.8-liter four-cylinder model took top honors overall in the Paris-to-Vienna event the following year, with Marcel Renault at the helm. Renault's first major production automobile was the Model K, introduced in 1902, with a 2554-cc L-head four-cylinder engine and tubular-type chassis. Its thermo-syphon cooling system was destined to become a standard feature on Renaults, and powerplants were produced by the Renault firm.

Marcel Renault's death in 1903 at the Paris-Madrid race prompted brother Louis to abandon racing and focus instead on production vehicles. A 1060-cc two-cylinder Model AX debuted in 1905, wearing the coal-scuttle-shaped hood (introduced a year earlier) that would become a virtual Renault "trademark." Also standard on Renaults from that time until the late 1920s was a dashboard-mounted radiator. Renault soon returned to competition, winning the first Grand Prix in 1906; but racing never again became a major part of the company's activities.

Fernand Renault died in 1908, and the company underwent a name change to *SA des Usines Renault.* Top-of-the-line by that time was a six-cylinder model, with an immense 9.5-liter engine and vast 156-inch wheelbase. Whereas Renault eventually would become best known for economy models, this one cost more than a Rolls-Royce of that day. Renault had also become a prominent supplier of taxicabs worldwide, based on the AX and related AG series. Aircraft engines were another part of the operation, starting in 1907 with an air-cooled V-8 version. For a short time, the Renault aero engine was produced by Rolls-Royce in England. By the time war broke out in 1914, Renault had become the foremost motor-vehicle manufacturer in France and was selling its automobiles throughout the world, including the U.S. Among other contributions to the war effort, some 600 Renault taxis were removed from Paris streets and used to transport troops to the Battle of the Marne. Renault also produced "Whippet" light tanks and other war material.

Postwar production included a trio of four-cylinder models, plus a huge six-cylinder 40CV introduced in 1921 with a 9.1-liter engine, wood wheels, and 147- or 157-inch wheelbase. A streamlined edition of the 40CV ran 100 mph for a 24-hour period in 1926. Meanwhile, Renault debuted a far smaller car in 1922: the KJ, with a 951-cc four-cylinder engine and disc wheel. *Societe Anonyme des Usines Renault* continued to diversify, becoming strong in trucks and buses as well as taxis and aircraft engines. Starting by 1927, Renaults also were final-assembled in Britain (at Acton, in west London), using British upholstery and lights.

A 7.1-liter straight-eight Reinastella with front-mounted radiator replaced the 40CV in 1928. Two years later came another straight-eight, the 4.2-liter Nervastella; and in 1932, the 4.8-liter Nervasport. In 1935, a variant of the Nervastella won both the Monte Carlo and Liege-Rome-Liege rallies. Four- and six-cylinder models also were produced into the 1930s. Synchromesh gearboxes emerged in 1933, and became standard the next year. The Monaquatre of 1936 had a 2383-cc L-head four-cylinder engine and dashboard-mounted transmission lever. That gearbox style also went into the 8CV Juvaquatre of 1938, which featured unibody construction and a 1003-cc engine. As early as 1935, some Renaults had headlamps set into the fenders and were losing their exposed running boards.

Partly because Louis Renault continued to produce the Juvaquatre automobile after World War II broke out, he was arrested by French authorities soon after the liberation of Paris, accused of collaborating with the Nazis. The company had fallen under German control during the war, after the invasion and fall of France. Louis Renault died in prison in 1944, following a month of incarceration. The Renault firm then came under the jurisdiction of Pierre Lefaucheux, who'd fought in the Resistance. Then, in February 1945, the company was nationalized under the name *Regie Nationale des Usines Renault.*

Postwar production began with an update of the prewar-styled Juvaquatre, but prototypes of a new 4CV had been tested during the war, and it was destined to lead the Renault lineup of the 1950s. The 4CV first appeared at the Paris Salon in 1946, powered by a rear-mounted 760-cc four-cylinder engine and featuring four-wheel independent suspension with coil springs. By spring 1949, Renault was turning out 300 of the tiny four-door sedans each day. By 1952, the 4CV represented one-third of the total production of French automobiles and more than a quarter-million had been produced. Production continued until 1961, with a slightly smaller (747-cc) engine used from 1951 onward. A small number were assembled in Britain, and also in Japan (under license). Renault's Fregate sedan of 1951 had a conventional front-mounted 2-liter engine, but never became a big seller.

Although the 4CV established Renault's presence in America, it was the Dauphine—introduced in 1956—that enhanced its position. More than 200,000 entered the U.S. market by 1960, powered by an 845-cc engine. Within a month after its debut, Dauphines took the first through fourth sports in their class at the Mille Miglia race. In 1958, a Dauphine won the Monte Carlo rally. Specially-tuned examples, done by Amedee Gordini, also grew popular. A Dauphine-derived Floride coupe and convertible joined the lineup in 1959, later marketed in America as the Caravelle.

A replacement for the 4CV arrived in 1961, known as the R4; but that one did not cross the Atlantic like its predecessor. Replacing the Dauphine in 1962, for both European and North American consumption, was a new R8 with four-wheel disc brakes and a rear-mounted 956-cc engine. A larger Renault for the home market debuted in 1963, shaped similar to American Motors' Rambler (and built under license from that company).

Also produced in the late 1960s was a medium-size Model 16 fastback (hatchback), with front-wheel drive and a 1.5-liter engine. The 16 could have an electronically-controlled automatic transmission as early as 1969. Rear-mounted engines were starting to lose appeal. Front-drive seemed to signal the future, and Renault finally abandoned rear engines in 1972.

Renault entered the growing youth-oriented mini-size market in the early 1970s with its Model 5 hatchback. By the time it was replaced in 1984, the "5" had become the top selling French automobile ever. A large Model 30TS arrived in 1975, powered by the new Peugeot-Renault-Volvo (PRV) V-6 engine. Starting in 1977, the company also sold the Alpine GT coupe, having obtained control of Automobiles Alpine (see Alpine-Renault listing in this Catalog).

In 1979, Renault entered into an agreement with American Motors Corporation whereby the American company would sell Renault's Model 5, renamed "Le Car." On the other side of the Atlantic, Renault would distribute AMC Jeeps. Renault also made a substantial investment in AMC, soon holding a share of 46.9 percent.

A new Fuego coupe with curved-glass hatch debuted in Europe in 1980, soon offered also in turbocharged form. It look two years longer to reach America. A "9" sedan arrived in 1981, with a transverse-mounted engine (1108- or 1397-cc) driving the front wheels. By 1983-84, versions of the "9" and hatchback "11" were being produced in Kenosha, Wisconsin, marketed as the Alliance and Encore (respectively). Those died out by the end of the decade, after Chrysler purchased AMC.

Meanwhile, Fuegos left the imported-car list after 1985, and the last Sportwagons sold in the U.S. under the Renault name left dealerships in 1986. Starting a year later, however, the Renault "21" was sold by AMC in the U.S., named Medallion. The Giugiaro-styled Eagle Premier of the late 1980s and early '90s, though built in North America, was a rebodied version of Renault's "25." Though out of the American market, Renault continues as one of the foremost manufacturers of automobiles in the world.

Note: Through the 1960s, 1970s and 1980s, only selected Renault models were ordinarily imported into the U.S. Thus, the total model lineup was much larger than indicated in the listings below.

1946-48 RENAULT

JUVAQUATRE — FOUR — The revived Juvaquatre added hydraulic brakes but otherwise retained its prewar styling and mechanical details. Literature in 1946 described the car as *"Rapide Elegante."*

4CV — FOUR — On sale in 1947, after a debut late in 1946, the 4CV was known in France as *"La Quatre Chevaux"* (4-hp). Initial prototoypes were two-door models, but the production version had four doors. The four-seat sedan had four-wheel independent suspension and a 760-cc four-cylinder engine, mounted in the rear and driving a three-speed gearbox. Top speed was claimed to be 90 kilometers per hour (56 mph), and the initial car weighed 1,146 pounds. Wheelbase was 83 inches, and the first engine developed about 16 horsepower, able to deliver fuel mileage of 47 mpg. Lockheed hydraulic brakes were installed. Early literature responded to the question: *"Pourquois le Moteur Arriere?"* (why the motor in the back?). See next listing for additional details on the 4CV as it arrived in the American market.

1949 RENAULT

4CV — 760 — FOUR — By 1949, Renault's 4CV was on sale in the U.S., sometimes referred to as the "Green Renault" because its sole U.S. distributor was the John L. Green company. Far different in appearance than anything else sold in the U.S., the chubby 4CV had a short front hood and sloping tail. Six wide horizontal bars across its front panel gave the appearance of a grille, even though the engine was mounted in the back, beneath a louvered engine lid. "Suicide" (rear-hinged) front doors were installed, while rear doors were hinged at the front. Front doors bulged to mate with front fenders. Air-intake slots went ahead of the rear fenders. Sliding windows were used. The radiator cap was mounted externally, below the rear window. The fuel filler went under the engine lid. Inside, the starter and handbrake were found between the seats. A three-speed manual gearbox had constant-mesh second and third gears.

I.D. DATA: Serial number is on a diamond-shaped plaque on the rear wall of the front luggage compartment, or on an oval plate in the same location. Engine number is on the right side of the block, below the fuel pump. Starting serial number: 1132067. Starting engine number: 0575.

Model	Body Type & Seating	Engine Type/CID	P.O.E. Price	Weight (lbs.)	Prod. Total
4CV					
Standard	4-dr Sedan-4P	I4/46	1035	1200	Note 1
Grand Luxe	4-dr Sedan-4P	I4/46	1085	1200	Note 1

Note 1: A total of 63,920 Renaults were produced in 1949.

ENGINE DATA: BASE FOUR: Inline, overhead-valve four-cylinder. Cast iron block and aluminum head (removable cylinder sleeves). **Displacement:** 46.3 cu. in. (760 cc). **Bore & Stroke:** 2.16 x 3.15 in. (55 x 80 mm). **Compression Ratio:** 6.7:1. **Brake Horsepower:** 19 at 4000 rpm. **Torque:** 32.6 lbs.-ft. at 1500 rpm. Three main bearings. Solid valve lifters. One inverted carburetor. 6-volt electrical system.

CHASSIS DATA: Wheelbase: 83 in. **Overall Length:** 141.5 in. **Height:** 56 in. **Width:** 56 in. **Front Tread:** 47 in. **Rear Tread:** 47 in. **Standard Tires:** 5.00x15.

TECHNICAL: Layout: rear-engine, rear-drive. **Transmission:** three-speed manual (floor lever). **Standard Final Drive Ratio:** 4.3:1. **Steering:** rack and pinion. **Suspension (front):** independent with coil springs. **Suspension (rear):** independent with swing axles and coil springs. **Brakes:** Lockheed hydraulic, front/rear drum. **Body Construction:** steel unibody.

PERFORMANCE: Fuel Mileage: up to 50 mpg claimed.

PRODUCTION/SALES: Approximately 1,402 Renaults were sold in the U.S. during 1949.

Manufacturer: Regie Nationale des Usines Renault, Billancourt, France.

Distributor: John L. Green Operations Corp., New York City (regional offices in Los Angeles and Atlanta).

HISTORY: Introduced in Europe two years earlier, Renault's 4CV was on sale in the U.S. by 1949. "Europe's largest factory," said literature issued that year, "is NOW producing and delivering large quantities to the United States each month." The car was claimed to be "designed to American standards, combining the ultimate in performance with unbelievable economy" and with "the motor right where it applies the power...in the rear." The 4CV also was described as the "most advanced car on the road."

1950 RENAULT

1950 Renault 4CV four-door sedan.

4CV — 760 — FOUR — Taillamps were restyled for 1950, but otherwise the 4CV continued with little change.

I.D. DATA: Serial number is on a diamond-shaped plaque on the rear wall of the front luggage compartment, or on an oval plate in the same location. Engine number is on the right side of the block, below the fuel pump. Starting serial number: 1283658. Starting engine number: 71229.

Model	Body Type & Seating	Engine Type/CID	P.O.E. Price	Weight (lbs.)	Prod. Total
4CV					
Grand Luxe	4-dr Sedan-4P	I4/46	1035	1200	Note 1

Note 1: A total of 83,107 Renaults were produced in 1950.

ENGINE DATA: BASE FOUR: Same as 1949.

CHASSIS DATA: Same as 1949.

TECHNICAL: Same as 1949.

PRODUCTION/SALES: Approximately 1,551 Renaults were sold in the U.S. during 1950.

Manufacturer: Regie Nationale des Usines Renault, Billancourt, France.

Distributor: John L. Green Operations Corp., New York City (regional offices in Los Angeles and Atlanta).

HISTORY: "It's smart...It's thrifty...It's French." Such ads in 1950 billed the 4CV as the "lowest-priced 4-door, 4-passenger sedan in America," claimed that it could deliver 40-50 mpg economy and had "44 improvements over all previous models." Late in 1950, the 4CV's engine displacement shrunk slightly; see next listing.

1951 RENAULT

1951 Renault Fregate four-door sedan.

4CV — 750 (R-1060/1062) — FOUR — A slightly smaller engine went into the 1951 version of the 4CV sedan, displacing 747 cc rather than the original 760 cc, but developing 4 more horsepower. Air intakes ahead of the rear fenders had chrome wire guards. Deluxe models had leather upholstery. Windows were available in new roll-down style instead of the former sliding panes. The 4CV was available with a small sliding sunroof (above the front seat only), or as a full-fledged convertible with a long sliding roof that exposed all passengers to the sun.

I.D. DATA: Serial number is on a diamond-shaped plaque on the rear wall of the trunk. Engine number is on the right side of the block, below the fuel pump. Starting serial number: (R-1060) 1436114; (R-1062 Luxe) 1439086; (R-1062 w/sliding roof) 1437073.

Model	Body Type & Seating	Engine Type/CID	P.O.E. Price	Weight (lbs.)	Prod. Total
4CV (Sliding Windows)					
R-1060	4-dr Sedan-4P	I4/46	1095	1200	Note 1
4CV LUXE (Rolldown Windows)					
R-1062	4-dr Sedan-4P	I4/46	1195	1200	Note 1
4CV SUPER GRAND LUXE (Rolldown Windows)					
R-1062	4-dr Sedan-4P	I4/46	1335	N/A	Note 1
R-1062	4-dr Conv-4P	I4/46	1495	N/A	Note 1

Note 1: A total of 167,259 Renaults were produced in 1951 (including almost 100,000 4CVs).

Price Note: Luxe with sliding roof cost $1266. Super Grand Luxe sedan with sliding roof cost $1410.

ENGINE DATA: BASE FOUR: Inline, overhead-valve four-cylinder. Cast iron block and aluminum head (removable cylinder sleeves). **Displacement:** 45.6 cu. in. (747 cc). **Bore & Stroke:** 2.15 x 3.15 in. (54.5 x 80 mm). **Compression Ratio:** 7.25:1. **Brake Horsepower:** 23 at 4000 rpm. Three main bearings. Solid valve lifters. One inverted carburetor. 6-volt electrical system.

CHASSIS DATA: Wheelbase: 83 in. **Overall Length:** 142 in. **Height:** 57.8 in. **Width:** 56.3 in. **Front Tread:** 47.6 in. **Rear Tread:** 47.6 in. **Standard Tires:** 5.00x15.

TECHNICAL: Layout: rear-engine, rear-drive. **Transmission:** three-speed manual. **Standard Final Drive Ratio:** 3.9:1. **Steering:** rack and pinion. **Suspension (front):** independent with coil springs. **Suspension (rear):** independent with swing axles and coil springs. **Brakes:** hydraulic, front/rear drum. **Body Construction:** steel unibody.

PRODUCTION/SALES: Approximately 777 Renaults were sold in the U.S. during 1951.

ADDITIONAL MODELS: During the winter of 1950-51, Renault introduced a new Fregate family-size model in the French market, powered by a 2-liter (122-cid) overhead-valve four-cylinder engine. The Fregate briefly entered the U.S. market by 1953.

Manufacturer: Regie Nationale des Usines Renault, Billancourt, France.

HISTORY: Renault's 1951 model was introduced to the U.S. market in October 1950, with the smaller (and more powerful) engine.

1952 RENAULT

4CV — 750 (R-1062) — FOUR — Prices rose slightly, but little change was evident. All 4CVs sold in the U.S. now had roll-up windows.

I.D. DATA: Serial number is on a diamond-shaped plaque on the rear wall of the trunk. Engine number is on the right side of the block, below the fuel pump. Starting serial number: 1510151A. Starting engine number: 40212.

Model	Body Type & Seating	Engine Type/CID	P.O.E. Price	Weight (lbs.)	Prod. Total
4CV LUXE					
R-1062	4-dr Sedan-4P	I4/46	1221	1200	Note 1
4CV SUPER GRAND LUXE					
R-1062	4-dr Sedan-4P	I4/46	1364	1200	Note 1
R-1062	4-dr Conv-4P	I4/46	1528	1200	Note 1

Note 1: A total of 121,026 Renaults were produced in 1952.

Price Note: Luxe sedan with sliding sunroof cost $1294. Super Grand Luxe sedan with sliding sunroof cost $1441.

Weight Note: Figures shown are approximate.

ENGINE DATA: BASE FOUR: Same as 1951.

CHASSIS DATA: Same as 1951.

TECHNICAL: Same as 1951.

PRODUCTION/SALES: Approximately 374 Renaults were sold in the U.S. during 1952.

Manufacturer: Regie Nationale des Usines Renault, Billancourt, France.

1953-54 RENAULT

1954 Renault Fregate two-liter convertible.

4CV — 750 (R-1062) — FOUR — Little change was evident in the small Renault four-door sedan. The Luxe sedan came with or without a sliding roof, while the Grand Luxe series faded away. The Super Grand Luxe ranked as a convertible, with its full-length sliding roof.

FREGATE — R-1100 — FOUR — Renault's larger sedan, with a front-mounted engine and rear-wheel drive, made a brief stab at the American market. Power came from a 2.0-liter four-cylinder engine.

I.D. DATA: Serial number is on a diamond-shaped plaque on the rear wall of the trunk. Engine number is on the right side of the block, below the fuel pump. Starting serial number: (1953) 1648076; (1954 model 4CV) 1960985.

Model	Body Type & Seating	Engine Type/CID	P.O.E. Price	Weight (lbs.)	Prod. Total
4CV LUXE (SPORT LINE)					
R-1062	4-dr Sedan-4P	I4/46	1495	1200	Note 1
4CV SUPER GRAND LUXE (SPORT LINE)					
R-1062	4-dr Conv-4P	I4/46	1695	1200	Note 1
FREGATE					
R-1100	4-dr Sedan	I4/122	2595	2789	Note 1

Note 1: A total of 120,460 Renaults were produced in 1953, followed by 157,701 in 1954.

Price Note: Figures shown were valid in 1953. Luxe sedan with sliding sunroof cost $1595. Price of the 4CV sedan in 1954 dropped to $1295 ($1395 with sunroof); the convertible sold in that year for $1495.

ENGINE DATA: BASE FOUR (4CV): Inline, overhead-valve four-cylinder. Cast iron block and aluminum head (removable cylinder sleeves). **Displacement:** 45.6 cu. in. (747 cc). **Bore & Stroke:** 2.15 x 3.15 in. (54.5 x 80 mm). **Compression Ratio:** 7.25:1. **Brake Horsepower:** 23 at 4000 rpm. Three main bearings. Solid valve lifters. Solex downdraft carburetor. 6-volt electrical system.

BASE FOUR (Fregate): Inline, overhead-valve four-cylinder. **Displacement:** 121.8 cu. in. (1997 cc). **Bore & Stroke:** 3.35 x 3.46 in. (85 x 88 mm). **Compression Ratio:** 6.6:1. **Brake Horsepower:** 56-60 at 4200 rpm. Solid valve lifters.

CHASSIS DATA: Wheelbase: (4CV) 83 in.; (Fregate) 110.25 in. **Overall Length:** (4CV) 142 in.; (Fregate) 185 in. **Height:** (4CV) 57.8 in.; (Fregate) 61 in. **Width:** (4CV) 56.3 in.; (Fregate) 67.8 in. **Front Tread:** (4CV) 47.6 in.; (Fregate) 55.1 in. **Rear Tread:** (4CV) 47.6 in.; (Fregate) 55.1 in. **Standard Tires:** (4CV) 5.00x15; (Fregate) 6.40x15.

1954-'56 Renault 4CV four-door sedan.

TECHNICAL: Layout: (4CV) rear-engine, rear-drive; (Fregate) front-engine, rear-drive. **Transmission:** three-speed manual. **Standard Final Drive Ratio:** 3.9:1. **Steering:** rack and pinion. **Suspension (front):** (4CV) independent with coil springs and torsion bar. **Suspension (rear):** (4CV) independent with swing axles and coil springs. **Brakes:** hydraulic, front/rear drum. **Body Construction:** steel unibody.

PRODUCTION/SALES: Approximately 110 Renaults were sold in the U.S. during 1953.

Manufacturer: Regie Nationale des Usines Renault, Billancourt, France.

Distributor: Renault Selling Branch Inc., New York City.

HISTORY: Renault's 4CV lineup in the U.S. was known as the "Quintette Series." A panel delivery version also was marketed.

1955-56 RENAULT

4CV — FOUR — Production of the four-door sedan continued with little change, offered in sedan, sunroof and convertible (long sunroof) form. The 747-cc engine was now rated 28 horsepower (SAE) in Renaults destined for America. A Ferlec automatic clutch was optional. The dashboard contained an open glovebox on the right, a hooded instrument cluster ahead of the driver, and a decorative panel in the center that could accept a radio. Standard equipment included a heater, defroster, directional signals, and leatherette upholstery.

Features of the 1956 model sold in the U.S. included a new rubber-mounted front wheel suspension and an automatic choke, plus semi-pliable plastic steering wheel, sunvisors and interior door handles. Rubber safety trim cushioned the lower edge of the dashboard and the upper edge of the windshield frame. Both front seats could be adjusted. An oval-shaped rear-view mirror also was new. All seats were now upholstered in smart red leatherette. Nieman locks with weatherproof spring shutters were provided on front doors of American models. Deluxe models also had those locks on the front hood; and on the convertible, in front and rear hoods.

I.D. DATA: Serial number is on a diamond-shaped plaque on the rear wall of the front trunk. Engine number is on the right side of the block, below the fuel pump. Starting serial number: (1955 models) 2169444; (1956 models) 2362858.

Model	Body Type & Seating	Engine Type/CID	P.O.E. Price	Weight (lbs.)	Prod. Total
4CV LUXE (SPORT LINE)					
R-1062	4-dr Sedan-4P	I4/46	1295	1200	Note 1
4CV SUPER GRAND LUXE					
R-1062	4-dr Conv-4P	I4/46	1495	1200	Note 1

Note 1: Approximately 176,260 Renaults (all models) were produced in 1955, followed by 214,921 in 1956.

Price Note: Luxe sedan with sliding sunroof cost $1350.

ENGINE DATA: BASE FOUR: Inline, overhead-valve four-cylinder. Cast iron block and aluminum head (removable cylinder sleeves). **Displacement:** 45.6 cu. in. (747 cc). **Bore & Stroke:** 2.15 x 3.15 in. (54.5 x 80 mm). **Compression Ratio:** 7.25:1. **Brake Horsepower:** 28 (SAE) at 4500 rpm. Three main bearings. Solid valve lifters. Solex downdraft carburetor. 6-volt electrical system.

CHASSIS DATA: Wheelbase: 82.7 in. **Overall Length:** 143 in. **Height:** 57.8 in. **Width:** 56.3 in. **Front Tread:** 48 in. **Rear Tread:** 48 in. **Standard Tires:** 5.00x15.

TECHNICAL: Layout: rear-engine, rear-drive. **Transmission:** three-speed manual. **Standard Final Drive Ratio:** 3.9:1. **Steering:** rack and pinion. **Suspension (front):** independent with coil springs. **Suspension (rear):** independent with swing axles and coil springs. **Brakes:** hydraulic, front/rear drum. **Body Construction:** steel unibody.

MAJOR OPTIONS: Ferlec clutch ($95).

PERFORMANCE: Top Speed: 66 mph (up to 72 mph claimed). **Acceleration (0-60 mph):** N/A (0-50 mph in 21.6 sec.). **Fuel Mileage:** 34-45 mpg (up to 50 mpg claimed).

ADDITIONAL MODELS: In addition to the 4CV and new Dauphine (see next listing), Renault in 1956 offered two larger models in the U.S. market. The 12CV Domaine station wagon had a fold-flat rear seat (serving as either a six-seater or a three-seater with 80 cubic feet of loading space), and was priced at $2695. Power came from a 77-bhp, 2141-cc engine, claimed to deliver 28 mpg economy and a top speed of 85 mph. Appearance in no way resembled either the 4CV or the Dauphine, but was an evolution of the earlier Fregate series. The top-of-the-line 12CV Grand Pavois sedan was a two-tone six-seater with concours d'elegance styling, a new grille design and a Sofica air conditioner, priced at $2795. It also carried the 77-bhp engine and had variable-ratio steering. The new Dauphine was initially listed at $1595.

Manufacturer: Regie Nationale des Usines Renault, Billancourt, France.

Distributor: Renault of France, Direct Factory Branch, New York City.

1957-59 RENAULT

1957 Renault Dauphine four-door sedan.

4CV — FOUR — Production of the original postwar four-door sedan continued with little change; see previous listing for full details.

DAUPHINE — 5CV — FOUR — Renault's next model soon grabbed a far bigger chunk of the American market than the 4CV. The stylish four-door Dauphine also had a rear engine, but enlarged to 845-cc (51.5-cid) displacement and rated 30 horsepower. The Dauphine's body was longer and wider than the 4CV, rounded but more boxy (in the modern mid-1950s mode). Headlamps were mounted on the hood, not the front fenders. Both front and rear doors were hinged at the front. Front doors have roll-down windows and no-draft vent wings, while rear door windows slid forward and back. Weight distribution was modified by moving the spare tire and gas tank. The spare tire sat in a receptable hidden by the swing-down front license plate. Like the 4CV, the Dauphine had four-wheel independent suspension that used coil springs all around. A Ferlec automatic electric clutch was optional with the three-speed manual gearbox, giving some of the advantages of automatic shifting without detracting from performance. According to *Motor Trend,* new synchromesh for 2nd and 3rd gears made that transmission "nearly clash-proof." Wheelbase was longer than the 4CV, at 89 inches, and the sedan was available with or without a sliding sunroof. The 7-cubic-foot front luggage compartment opened forward for safety. Standard equipment included a semi-flexible steering wheel, two glove compartments, provision for radio, large ashtray, two adjustable sunvisors, and day/night rear-view mirror.

I.D. DATA: Serial number is on a diamond-shaped plaque on the rear wall of the front trunk (4CV), or on the right wall (Dauphine). Engine number is on the right side of the block, below the fuel pump (4CV), or at the rear above the timing case (Dauphine). Starting serial number: (1957 model 4CV) 2605867; (1957 Dauphine) 2671625; (1958 model 4CV) 3124105; (1958 Dauphine) 2935703. Starting engine number: (1957 model 4CV) 664957; (1957 Dauphine) 30420.

Model	Body Type & Seating	Engine Type/CID	P.O.E. Price	Weight (lbs.)	Prod. Total
4CV (SPORT LINE)					
R-1062	4-dr Sedan-4P	I4/46	1345	1200	Note 1
DAUPHINE					
R-1090	4-dr Sedan-5P	I4/52	1645	1397	Note 1

Note 1: Approximately 265,522 Renaults (all models) were produced in 1957, followed by 363,924 in 1958 and 457,894 in 1959.

Price Note: 4CV sedan with sliding sunroof cost $1400; Dauphine with sunroof cost $1700.

1958 Renault 4CV four-door sedan.

ENGINE DATA: BASE FOUR (4CV): Inline, overhead-valve four-cylinder. Cast iron block and aluminum head (removable cylinder sleeves). **Displacement:** 45.6 cu. in. (747 cc). **Bore & Stroke:** 2.15 x 3.15 in. (54.5 x 80 mm). **Compression Ratio:** 7.25:1. **Brake Horsepower:** 28 (SAE) at 4500 rpm. Three main bearings. Solid valve lifters. Solex downdraft carburetor. 6-volt electrical system.

BASE FOUR (Dauphine): Inline, overhead-valve four-cylinder ("Ventoux"). Cast iron block and aluminum head (removable cylinder sleeves). **Displacement:** 51.5 cu. in. (845 cc). **Bore & Stroke:** 2.28 x 3.15 in. (58 x 80 mm). **Compression Ratio:** 7.25:1. **Brake Horsepower:** 30 (SAE) at 4250 rpm. **Torque:** 48 lbs.-ft. at 2000 rpm. Three main bearings. Solid valve lifters. Solex downdraft carburetor. 6-volt electrical system.

Note: Later 845-cc Dauphine engines were rated 32 bhp at 4500 rpm and 50 lbs.-ft. at 2000 rpm.

CHASSIS DATA: Wheelbase: (4CV) 82.7 in.; (Dauphine) 89 in. **Overall Length:** (4CV) 143 in.; (Dauphine) 155 in. **Height:** (4CV) 57.8 in.; (Dauphine) 57 in. **Width:** (4CV) 56.3 in.; (Dauphine) 60 in. **Front Tread:** (4CV) 48 in.; (Dauphine) 49 in. **Rear Tread:** (4CV) 48 in.; (Dauphine) 48 in. **Standard Tires:** (4CV) 5.00x15; (Dauphine) 5.00x15 (135x380 mm).

1959 Renault Dauphine four-door.

TECHNICAL: Layout: rear-engine, rear-drive. **Transmission:** three-speed manual. Dauphine gear ratios: (1st) 3.7:1; (2nd) 1.81:1; (3rd) 1.07:1; (rev) 3.7:1. **Standard Final Drive Ratio:** (4CV) 3.9:1; (Dauphine) 4.37:1. **Steering:** rack and pinion. **Suspension (front):** independent with coil springs and torsion stabilizer. **Suspension (rear):** independent with swing axles and coil springs. **Brakes:** hydraulic, front/rear drum. **Body Construction:** steel unibody.

MAJOR OPTIONS: Ferlec automatic clutch ($95). Whitewall tires. Radio.

PERFORMANCE: Top Speed: (4CV) 66 mph; (Dauphine) 71 mph (71-75 mph claimed). **Acceleration (0-60 mph):** (4CV) N/A (0-50 mph in 21.6 sec.); (Dauphine) 31.6 sec. (0-50 mph in 17.7-20 sec.). **Acceleration (quarter-mile):** (Dauphine) 22.6 sec. (57 mph). **Fuel Mileage:** (4CV) 34-45 mpg; (Dauphine) 34-42 mpg.

PRODUCTION/SALES: Approximately 22,586 Renaults were sold in the U.S. during 1957, followed by 48,148 in 1958 and 91,073 in 1959.

ADDITIONAL MODELS: Gordini-tuned versions of the Dauphine were available starting in 1957, with four-speed gearboxes and hopped-up engines that developed 37.5 to 40 horsepower.

Manufacturer: Regie Nationale des Usines Renault, Billancourt, France.

Distributor: Renault of France, Direct Factory Branch, New York City.

HISTORY: Early road-testing of the new Dauphine (which means "princess" in French) took place on the island of Corsica, prior to its 1956 debut. More than 2 million test miles had been driven by prototypes, in the arctic regions of Norway, in the Swiss Alps, through African jungle and desert, and other rough environments. More than the 4CV, the Dauphine was built as a rival to Volkswagen's Beetle. *Motor Trend* testers reached over 80 mph on downhill roads and were "amazed by the lack of wind noise and in fact of any excessive noise." Advertisements promoted the Dauphine as a "50-mile-a-gallon 4-door sedan with a Mille Miglia pedigree...appropriately christened The Princess." On the non-production front, Renault's experimental Shooting Star was clocked at 191.2 mph (faster by 40 mph than any previous turbine-powered car).

By 1958, ads were appearing for such add-ons as a Judson supercharger, claimed to add 50 percent more horsepower to the Dauphine engine. Speed Age magazine noted that "the Dauphine engine takes to souping like an Offy to Alky." Renault's Floride coupe and convertible were introduced during 1959; see next listing for details.

1960-62 RENAULT

1961 Renault R4L four-door.

4CV — FOUR — Production of the original postwar sedan continued with little change until 1961, and it remained available in America in 1960-61. Like earlier models, the 4CV wore an imitation front grille made up of three horizontal bars. Compression had been boosted to 7.75:1 in 1959, but horsepower did not change.

1961 Renault Dauphine four-door.

DAUPHINE — FOUR — Production of the Dauphine continued with minimal change, into 1966. Changes for 1960 included adoption of a higher top-gear ratio, stainless steel trim moldings, rear safety locks, and hold-open catches on the door stays. The 845-cc engine was rated 32 horsepower. Dauphine body colors for the 1960 model year were Imperial Red, Tulip Yellow, Marlin Blue, Pompadour Grey, DuBarry Blue, and White. Dauphines came with a deluxe heater, city-horn/country-horn, and what was described as a "terrific 6-month warranty with no mileage limitations." A sunroof was optional. Rectangular parking lights were installed for the 1962 model year.

GORDINI (SUPER DAUPHINE) — FOUR — A Gordini-tuned variant of the Dauphine also was marketed in 1961-62. Gordinis were known as the "Super Dauphine," with a 40-horsepower version of the 845-cc engine. This was a deluxe Dauphine with all the interior trimmings, plus standard whitewalls, chrome wheels, four-speed gearbox, Aerostable suspension, and the finely-tuned engine, which included a special cam. A Gordini could accelerate to 62 mph (100 kph) in a claimed 21 seconds, and hit 80 mph. The Gordini nameplate was evident on the front fenders and rear decklid.

CARAVELLE (FLORIDE) — FOUR — Named Floride in Europe, but marketed as the Caravelle in America, the sleek Dauphine-derived coupe and convertible debuted in the U.S. in December 1959, in time for the 1960 model year. Details of this semi-sports car were revealed at the Waldorf-Astoria Hotel, simultaneously with similar ceremonies in 17 other major cities. "A dream car come true" was its merchandising slogan. Available in six metal-hue colors, the Caravelle contained "harmonizing" leatherette and/or fabric upholstery.

Caravelles used the same basic rear-engine layout and independent four-wheel suspension as the Dauphine. Three models were offered: a soft-top convertible (whose top was recessed into a hideaway compartment behind the rear seat); a hardtop convertible (including a detachable hardtop); and a hardtop coupe. Each had a rear seat that could hold two. The soft top had a vinyl back window. Styling features included a long, low hood with sheer line at its nose; no conventional grille; deeply-recessed headlamps with a scoop at their base; and round parking lights below the headlamps. A full-length chrome molding went all along the beltline. Caravelles had wraparound chrome-plated bumpers in three pieces, front and rear. Doors contained vent windows with chrome-plated frames. Roll-down framed windows were completely concealed when opened. Final assembly of the all-steel chassis and body (unibody) was done by Brissonneau and Lotz, of Creil, France. Body colors were: Metallic Green, Metallic Tan, White, Red, Light Blue, and Dark Blue.

At the rear was a four-cylinder engine with the same 845-cc displacement as the Dauphine, but rated 40 horsepower (SAE). A three-speed transmission (floor lever) was standard; four speeds optional. Also optional: an automatic Ferlec clutch (with three-speed gearbox only) controlled by an electromagnetic system. Wheelbase was 89 inches, and the car measured 167.8 inches long (more than a foot longer than a Dauphine). Tires were 5.50x15 size, and the gas tank held 8.5 gallons. Heating/defrosting was accomplished by a Sofica hot-water system. The curved dashboard had space at the center for a radio, plus a glove compartment with pushbutton door to the right.

A new suspension, called Aerostable, combined conventional coil springs and shocks with unique rubber pads and pneumatic bags, which varied the flexibility of the springs according to the load (or the impact transmitted from the road). Under minimum load, as with the driver riding alone, the flexible coil springs would give a soft ride. As load increased, the depression of the springs rose, sending the auxiliary suspension into action. That suspension consisted of rubber pads surrounding the rods of the shocks and, at the rear, pneumatic bags filled with air at atmospheric pressure. Pistons compressed those bags in proportion with the load.

1962 Renault Floride S convertible.

I.D. DATA: Serial number is on a diamond-shaped plaque on the rear wall of the front trunk. 4CV and Dauphine have a '60' stamped on the serial number plate. Serial number prefix: (Caravelle) 2401. Engine number is on the right side of the block, below the fuel pump (4CV), or at the rear above the timing case (Dauphine).

Model	Body Type & Seating	Engine Type/CID	P.O.E. Price	Weight (lbs.)	Prod. Total
4CV (1960-61)					
R-1062	4-dr Sedan-4P	I4/46	1345	1200	Note 1
Sunroof	4-dr Sedan-4P	I4/46	1405	1200	Note 1
DAUPHINE					
R-1090	4-dr Sedan-4/5P	I4/52	1645	1397	Note 1
Sunroof	4-dr Sedan-4/5P	I4/52	1700	1397	Note 1
GORDINI (1961-62)					
R-1091A	4-dr Spt Sed-4/5P	I4/52	1596	N/A	Note 1
CARAVELLE					
R-1092	2-dr Conv-4P	I4/52	2445	1645	Note 1
R-1092	2-dr Cpe-4P	I4/52	2395	1675	Note 1
R-1092	2-dr HT Conv-4P	I4/52	2525	N/A	Note 1

Note 1: Approximately 464,122 Renaults (all models) were produced in 1960, followed by 309,744 in 1961 and 471,288 in 1962.

Model Note: A "Ghia" Resort Special 4CV was marketed in 1960.

Price Note: Figures shown were valid in 1960 (except Gordini, in 1962). For 1961, prices dropped to $1095 for the 4CV, $1385 for the Dauphine, and $2295 for the Caravelle coupe. A base Dauphine sold for $1395 in 1962, a deluxe version for $100 more.

ENGINE DATA: BASE FOUR (4CV): Inline, overhead-valve four-cylinder. Cast iron block and aluminum head (removable cylinder sleeves). **Displacement:** 45.6 cu. in. (747 cc). **Bore & Stroke:** 2.15 x 3.15 in. (54.5 x 80 mm). **Compression Ratio:** 7.75:1. **Brake Horsepower:** 28 (SAE) at 4100 rpm. **Torque:** 43 lbs.-ft. at 1800 rpm. Three main bearings. Solid valve lifters. Single downdraft carburetor.

BASE FOUR (Dauphine): Inline, overhead-valve four-cylinder. Cast iron block and aluminum head (removable cylinder sleeves). **Displacement:** 51.5 cu. in. (845 cc). **Bore & Stroke:** 2.28 x 3.15 in. (58 x 80 mm). **Compression Ratio:** 7.25:1. **Brake Horsepower:** 32 (SAE) at 4200 rpm. **Torque:** 50 lbs.-ft. at 2000 rpm. Three main bearings. Solid valve lifters. Single downdraft carburetor.

BASE FOUR (Caravelle, Gordini): Same as 845-cc four above, except — **Compression Ratio:** 8.0:1. **Brake Horsepower:** 40 (SAE) at 5000 rpm. **Torque:** 47.8 lbs.-ft. at 3300 rpm. Reversed type Solex PIBT32 carburetor (Gordini); Solex 32 PICBT (Caravelle).

CHASSIS DATA: Wheelbase: (4CV) 83 in.; (Dauphine/Caravelle) 89 in. **Overall Length:** (4CV) 142 in.; (Dauphine) 155 in.; (Carav.) 167.8 in. **Height:** (4CV) 58 in.; (Dauphine) 57 in.; (Carav.) 51.5 in. **Width:** (4CV) 56.3 in.; (Dauphine) 60 in.; (Carav.) 62 in. **Front Tread:** (4CV) 48 in.; (Dauphine/Carav.) 49 in. **Rear Tread:** (4CV) 48 in.; (Dauphine/Carav.) 48 in. **Standard Tires:** (4CV) 5.00x15; (Dauphine/Carav.) 5.50x15.

1962 Renault R8 four-door.

TECHNICAL: Layout: rear-engine, rear-drive. **Transmission:** three-speed manual; four-speed optional on Caravelle, standard on Gordini. Caravelle three-speed gear ratios: (1st) 3.7:1; (2nd) 1.8:1; (3rd) 1.035:1; (rev) 3.7:1. Caravelle/Gordini four-speed gear ratios: (1st) 3.7:1; (2nd) 2.1:1; (3rd) 1.46:1; (4th) 1.035:1; (rev) 3.7:1. **Standard Final Drive Ratio:** (4CV) 4.71:1; (Dauphine/Carav) 4.37:1. **Steering:** rack and pinion. **Suspension (front):** independent with coil springs. **Suspension (rear):** independent with swing axles and coil springs. **Brakes:** hydraulic, front/rear drum. **Body Construction:** steel unibody.

PRODUCTION/SALES: Approximately 62,772 Renaults were sold in the U.S. during 1960, followed by 44,122 in 1961 and 29,763 in 1962.

ADDITIONAL MODELS: For the home market, Renault introduced a replacement for the 4CV in 1961; but that R4 did not come to America like its predecessor. At the 1960 New York show, Renault also showed its new light truck for the first time, in two models: the Petite Panel and the Hi-Boy.
Manufacturer: Regie Nationale des Usines Renault, Billancourt, France.
Distributor: Renault Inc., New York City.

HISTORY: Renault's Caravelle first appeared at the Paris Salon in October 1958 (as the Floride). More than 12,800 American motorists had placed orders for the Caravelle "even before they knew the price, specifications or approximate delivery date," according to the company. Advertisements referred to the car's "sculptured snoot" and its "lush fittings and interiors."
Promotional literature touted the Dauphine as "the frisky, thrifty family car." American ads in 1961 for the Dauphine-based Gordini called it "a truly high-performance economy car."
Renaults won various classes in the 1960 Mobil Mileage Rally. A 4CV won 1st place in class A with 49.18 mpg; Dauphine got 2nd place in class B with 48.54 mpg; and Caravelle got 3rd place in class E with 50.13 mpg.

1963-66 RENAULT

1965 Renault Caravelle 1100 coupe.

DAUPHINE — FOUR — Production of the Dauphine continued into 1966, and the car remained available in the U.S. through that year. A pushbutton automatic transmission became available for 1964, as did an air conditioner. Tilt-back front seats and an all-synchro gearbox became standard for the 1964 model year. A "40" series became available in that year, with automatic transmission and the 40-bhp engine.

CARAVELLE S — FOUR — Horsepower of the coupe and convertible rose to 51 for the 1963 model year, as the engine grew in displacement (to 58 cid), prompting the addition of an 'S' suffix to the Caravelle name. Horizontal trim bars on the scoop ahead of rear wheels were eliminated, and front disc brakes became standard. For the 1964 model year, an 1108-cc engine was installed in the convertible, bringing horsepower up to 55. Also at that time, 'CARAVELLE' block letters replaced the medallion above the front grille. Only the convertible remained by 1965, with removable hardtop option.

R8 — FOUR — Introduced during 1962 as a replacement for the Dauphine, the new R8 was intended for both European and North American consumption. Powered by a rear-mounted 956-cc engine, it had four-wheel disc brakes. The compact sedan had a squarish profile, a single horizontal trim moldings between the headlamps (with vertical diamond medallion at the left), and round turn-signal lights above front-wheel openings. An 1108-cc engine became standard for the 1964 model year on manual-shift R8 sedans; automatic-equipped sedans kept the smaller engine. Pushbutton automatic shift and air conditioning joined the option list. Tilt-back front seats also became standard. A more potent Gordini edition of the R8 was marketed in 1965-66. Gordini engines had two dual-barrel Solex carburetors and were rated 95 horsepower, on 10.5:1 compression. They also included a heavy-duty suspension and a tachometer. Four-wheel disc brakes were made standard by 1966.

I.D. DATA: Serial number is on a plate in the front luggage compartment. Starting serial number: (1963 Dauphine R-1090/1094) 6825009; (1963 Dauphine "40" series R-1091/1095) 7000001; (1963 Caravelle S) 0073001; (1963 R8) 1507300; (1964 Dauphine R-1094) R-10940600001; (1964 Dauphine R-1095) R-10950050001; (1964 Caravelle conv) R-11330190001; (1964 R8 R-1130) R-1130/2906685; (1964 R8 R-1132) R-1132/3450001. Engine number is at right rear of block.

Model	Body Type & Seating	Engine Type/CID	P.O.E. Price	Weight (lbs.)	Prod. Total
DAUPHINE					
R-1090	4-dr Sedan-4/5P	I4/52	1495	1397	Note 1
CARAVELLE S (1963)					
R-1133	2-dr Conv-4P	I4/58	2561	1770	Note 1
R-1131	2-dr Cpe-4P	I4/58	2475	1695	Note 1
	2-dr HT Cpe-4P	I4/58	2595	N/A	Note 1
CARAVELLE (1964-66)					
R-1133	2-dr Conv-4P	I4/58	2295	1760	Note 1
R-1131	2-dr Cpe-4P	I4/58	2295	1770	Note 1
R8					
R-1130	4-dr Sedan-4/5P	I4/58	1795	1595	Note 1
R8 1100 (1964-66)					
R-1132	4-dr Sedan-4/5P	I4/68	1695	1676	Note 1
R8 GORDINI (1965-66)					
R-1134	4-dr Sedan-4/5P	I4/68	2345	1753	Note 1

Note 1: Approximately 559,408 Renaults (all models) were produced in 1963, followed by 421,808 in 1964, 479,707 in 1965, and 666,224 in 1966.

Price Note: Figures shown were valid in 1963 (or in first year of period stated).

ENGINE DATA: BASE FOUR (Dauphine): Inline, overhead-valve four-cylinder. Cast iron block and aluminum head (removable cylinder sleeves). **Displacement:** 51.5 cu. in. (845 cc). **Bore & Stroke:** 2.28 x 3.15 in. (58 x 80 mm). **Compression Ratio:** 7.25:1. **Brake Horsepower:** 32 (SAE) at 4200 rpm. **Torque:** 50 lbs.-ft. at 2000 rpm. Three main bearings. Solid valve lifters. Single downdraft carburetor.
BASE FOUR (1963 Caravelle S): Inline, overhead-valve four-cylinder. Cast iron block and aluminum head. **Displacement:** 58.3 cu. in. (956 cc). **Bore & Stroke:** 2.56 x 2.83 in. (65 x 72 mm). **Compression Ratio:** 9.5:1. **Brake Horsepower:** 51 at 5500 rpm. **Torque:** 55 lbs.-ft. at 3500 rpm. Three main bearings.
BASE FOUR (R8): Same as 956-cc four above, except — **Compression Ratio:** 8.5:1. **Brake Horsepower:** 48 at 5200 rpm. **Torque:** 55 lbs.-ft. at 2500 rpm.
BASE FOUR (R8 1100, later Caravelle conv): Inline, overhead-valve four-cylinder. Cast iron block and aluminum head. **Displacement:** 67.6 cu. in. (1108 cc). **Bore & Stroke:** 2.76 x 2.83 in. (70 x 72 mm). **Compression Ratio:** 8.5:1. **Brake Horsepower:** 51 at 5100 rpm. **Torque:** 65 lbs.-ft. at 2500 rpm.

CHASSIS DATA: Wheelbase: 89 in. **Overall Length:** (Dauphine) 155 in.; (Carav) 170 in.; (R8) 157 in. **Height:** (Dauphine) 57 in.; (Carav) 53 in.; (R8) 56 in. **Width:** (Dauphine) 60 in.; (Carav) 62 in. **Front Tread:** 49 in. **Rear Tread:** 48 in. **Standard Tires:** 5.50x15.

TECHNICAL: Layout: rear-engine, rear-drive. **Transmission:** four-speed manual; automatic available from 1964. **Steering:** rack and pinion. **Suspension (front):** independent with coil springs. **Suspension (rear):** independent with swing axles and coil springs. **Brakes:** (1963) front/rear drum except (Caravelle) front disc, rear drum; all front/rear disc from 1964. **Body Construction:** steel unibody.

PRODUCTION/SALES: Approximately 22,621 Renaults were sold in the U.S. during 1963, followed by 18,432 in 1964, 12,697 (including tourist deliveries) in 1965, and 12,106 in 1966.
Manufacturer: Regie Nationale des Usines Renault, Billancourt, France.
Distributor: Renault Inc., New York City.

1967-68 RENAULT

10 (R-10) — FOUR — Renault's Dauphine and sporty Caravelle were fading away, and the R8 sedan was replaced by a Renault 10, with 68-cid engine. The model 10 had four-wheel disc brakes, backup lights, side safety marker lights at the front of front fenders, reclining bucket seats, rubber-covered bumper guards, and an optional pushbutton three-speed automatic transmission. Styling and basic layout evolved from the Dauphine and R8, with squared-off lines and single headlamps in a "controlled crush" front end. Horizontal taillamps were larger than the R8's. Overhang was considerably larger than on the R8, allowing some 25 percent more luggage space. The car's front bumper had a curious shape, upswept in the center, while bodysides displayed a thin horizontal trim strip. Claimed top speed was 84 mph. Cloth upholstery was standard, with vinyl a $38 option. Renault called the 10 its "luxury compact model."

Model Number Note: In advertisements through the late 1960s and '70s, Renault generally referred to its models by a single number (e.g., Renault 10). other sources used an 'R' prefix, usually (but not always) followed by a hyphen.

I.D. DATA: Renault's 12-symbol serial number is on a plate on the firewall, in the front luggage compartment. Symbols 1-3 identify the model, followed by a 9-digit sequential production number. Starting serial number: (1967) R-11906488785; (1968) R-11906968202.

Model	Body Type & Seating	Engine Type/CID	P.O.E. Price	Weight (lbs.)	Prod. Total
10 (R-10)					
R-1190	4-dr Sedan-4/5P	I4/68	1647	1775	Note 1

Note 1: Approximately 706,622 Renault passenger cars (all models) were produced in 1967, followed by 734,455 in 1968.

Price Note: Figure shown was valid in 1968; rose to $1745 in 1969.

Model Note: Dauphines and the Caravelle convertible were still marketed in the U.S. during 1967, priced at $1409 ($1550 with automatic) and $2100, respectively. See previous listing for full details.

ENGINE DATA: BASE FOUR: Inline, overhead-valve four-cylinder. Cast iron block and aluminum head. **Displacement:** 67.6 cu. in. (1108 cc). **Bore & Stroke:** 2.76 x 2.83 in. (70 x 72 mm). **Compression Ratio:** 8.5:1. **Brake Horsepower:** 48 at 4600 rpm. **Torque:** 57 lbs.-ft. at 3000 rpm. Five main bearings.

CHASSIS DATA: Wheelbase: 89 in. **Overall Length:** 167.5 in. **Height:** 55.5 in. **Width:** 60 in. **Front Tread:** 49 in. **Rear Tread:** 48 in. **Standard Tires:** 5.50x15.

TECHNICAL: Layout: rear-engine, rear-drive. **Transmission:** four-speed manual; automatic available. **Steering:** rack and pinion. **Suspension (front):** wishbones with coil springs and anti-roll bar. **Suspension (rear):** independent with swing axles and coil springs. **Brakes:** front/rear disc. **Body Construction:** steel unibody.

PRODUCTION/SALES: Approximately 21,219 Renaults were sold in the U.S. during 1967, followed by 21,662 in 1968.
Manufacturer: Regie Nationale des Usines Renault, Billancourt, France.
Distributor: Renault Inc., Englewood Cliffs, New Jersey.

HISTORY: Ads in the U.S. promoted the 10 as "the Renault for people who swore they would never buy another one." Renault admitted that earlier models "were not fully prepared to meet the demands of America, where sustained high speeds are normal, where a heavy foot with the clutch is normal, and where people are not used to fixing their own cars."

1969-70 RENAULT

1969 Renault 16 four-door sedan.

10 (R-10) — FOUR — Production of the rear-drive model 10 sedan continued into 1969 with little change, except for the installation of a nameplate above the left front wheel opening. Park/signal lights sat the outer extremities of front fenders, next to single round headlamps. For 1970, a larger (79-cid) engine was installed, promising an estimated 86-mph top speed. The optional automatic transmission actually was more like an automatic clutch with manual (pushbutton) override.

16 (R-16) — FOUR — Renault turned from rear-drive to front-drive with the model 16 fastback sedan wagon, which had a front-mounted four-cylinder engine. Styling differed considerably from the model 10, including quad round headlamps alongside a three-segment grille made up of horizontal strips. At the rear was a large hatchback lid; triangular rear quarter windows were installed; and the roof had indentations. The 1565-cc (95.5-cid) engine developed 70 horsepower.

I.D. DATA: Renault's 12-symbol serial number is on a plate on the firewall, in the front luggage compartment. Symbols 1-3 identify the model, followed by a 9-digit sequential production number. Starting serial number: (1969 R-10) R11906980201; (1969 R-16) R11529700001.

Model	Body Type & Seating	Engine Type/CID	P.O.E. Price	Weight (lbs.)	Prod. Total
10 (R-10)					
R-1190	4-dr Sedan-4/5P	I4/68	1775	1825	Note 1
16 (R-16)					
R-1152	4-dr Sed Wag-5/6P	I4/95	2445	2249	Note 1

Note 1: Approximately 911,264 Renault passenger cars (all models) were produced in 1969, followed by 1,055,803 in 1970.
Price Note: Figures shown were valid in 1969.

ENGINE DATA: BASE FOUR (1969 R-10): Inline, overhead-valve four-cylinder. Cast iron block and aluminum head. **Displacement:** 67.6 cu. in. (1108 cc). **Bore & Stroke:** 2.76 x 2.83 in. (70 x 72 mm). **Compression Ratio:** 8.5:1. **Brake Horsepower:** 48 at 4600 rpm. **Torque:** 57 lbs.-ft. at 3000 rpm.

BASE FOUR (1970 R-10): Inline, overhead-valve four-cylinder. Cast iron block and aluminum head. **Displacement:** 78.6 cu. in. (1289 cc). **Bore & Stroke:** 2.87 x 3.03 in. (73 x 77 mm). **Compression Ratio:** 8.0:1. **Brake Horsepower:** 56 at 4800 rpm. **Torque:** 70 lbs.-ft. at 2500 rpm. Solex two-barrel carburetor.

BASE FOUR (R-16): Inline, overhead-valve four-cylinder. Light alloy block and head. **Displacement:** 95.5 cu. in. (1565 cc). **Bore & Stroke:** 3.03 x 3.31 in. (77 x 84 mm). **Compression Ratio:** 8.6:1. **Brake Horsepower:** 70 at 5200 rpm. **Torque:** 86 lbs.-ft. at 2500 rpm. Five main bearings. Solex downdraft carburetor.

CHASSIS DATA: Wheelbase: (R-10) 89 in.; (R-16) 105.8 in. **Overall Length:** (R-10) 167.5 in.; (R-16) 170 in. **Height:** (R-10) 55.5 in.; (R-16) 57.3 in. **Width:** (R-10) 60 in.; (R-16) 64.9 in. **Front Tread:** (R-10) 49 in.; (R-16) 52.8 in. **Rear Tread:** (R-10) 48 in.; (R-16) 50.9 in. **Standard Tires:** (R-10) 5.50x15; (R-16) 155x14.

TECHNICAL: Layout: (R-10) rear-engine, rear-drive; (R-16) front-engine, front-drive. **Transmission:** four-speed manual; automatic available. **Steering:** rack and pinion. **Suspension (front):** (R-10) wishbones with coil springs and anti-roll bar; (R-16) wishbones with torsion bars and anti-roll bar. **Suspension (rear):** (R-10) independent with swing axles and coil springs; (R-16) trailing arms with torsion bars and anti-roll bar. **Brakes:** front/rear disc. **Body Construction:** steel unibody.

PRODUCTION/SALES: Approximately 20,419 Renaults were sold in the U.S. during 1969, rising to 23,373 in 1970.
Manufacturer: Regie Nationale des Usines Renault, Billancourt, France.
Distributor: Renault Inc., Englewood Cliffs, New Jersey.

1971-75 RENAULT

10 (R-10) — FOUR — Availability of the rear-drive sedan continued into 1971, after which all Renaults had front-wheel drive.

12 (R-12) — FOUR — Added late in the 1971 model year, the Renault 12 notchback four-door sedan and station wagon had a 95.5-cid engine that developed 69 horsepower. Wheelbase was 96 inches, versus 89 inches for the R-10. A larger (100.5-cid) engine was installed for the 1973 model year.

15 (R-15) — FOUR — After focusing only on four-doors for several years, Renault turned out a fastback coupe. Available starting in mid-1972, the model 15 had a 96-inch wheelbase like the R-12, and a 95.5-cid engine. Displacement grew to 100.5 cid for 1973.

16 (R-16) — FOUR — Availability of the front-drive sedan wagon continued into 1972.

17 (R-17) — FOUR — Introduced for 1972, the R-17 Sports Coupe used a high-performance, 107-bhp version of the 95.5-cid engine, with Bosch electronic fuel injection. Styling features include a series of angled slats along the long rear sail panels, and pushbutton-controlled doors. An early R-17 could hit 103 mph and accelerate to 60 mph in 12.5 seconds. A Gordini edition of the R-17 was available starting in 1974.

I.D. DATA: Renault's 12-symbol serial number is on a plate on the firewall, in the front luggage compartment. Symbols 1-3 identify the model, followed by a 9-digit sequential production number. In 1973, a shorter (7-digit) serial number was used, omitting the prefix.

Model	Body Type & Seating	Engine Type/CID	P.O.E. Price	Weight (lbs.)	Prod. Total
R-10 (1971 only)					
	4-dr Sedan-4/5P	I4/79	1845	1907	Note 1
R-12 (1972-up)					
	4-dr Sedan-4/5P	I4/95	2195	2050	Note 1
	4-dr Sta Wag-4/5P	I4/95	2595	2161	Note 1
R-15 (1972-up)					
	2-dr Coupe-4P	I4/95	2995	2172	Note 1
R-16 (1971-72 only)					
	4-dr Sed Wag-5/6P	I4/95	2565	2271	Note 1
R-17 (1972-up)					
	2-dr Spt Cpe-4P	I4/95	3975	2337	Note 1

Note 1: Approximately 1,069,070 Renault passenger cars (all models) were produced in 1971, followed by 1,202,486 in 1972, 1,292,991 in 1973, 1,355,799 in 1974, and 1,293,551 in 1975.
Price Note: Figures shown were valid in 1971 (R-10 and R-16) or 1972 (R-12, R-15 and R-17).

ENGINE DATA: BASE FOUR (R-10): Inline, overhead-valve four-cylinder. Cast iron block and aluminum head. **Displacement:** 78.6 cu. in. (1289 cc). **Bore & Stroke:** 2.87 x 3.03 in. (73 x 77 mm). **Compression Ratio:** 8.8:1. **Brake Horsepower:** 56 at 4600 rpm. **Torque:** 70 lbs.-ft. at 2300 rpm.
BASE FOUR (R-16): Inline, overhead-valve four-cylinder. Light alloy block and head. **Displacement:** 95.5 cu. in. (1565 cc). **Bore & Stroke:** 3.03 x 3.31 in. (77 x 84 mm). **Compression Ratio:** 8.6:1. **Brake Horsepower:** 70 at 5200 rpm. **Torque:** 86 lbs.-ft. at 2500 rpm. Five main bearings. Solex downdraft carburetor.

BASE FOUR (1972 R-12): Same as 1565-cc four above, except — **Brake Horsepower:** 69 at 5000 rpm. **Torque:** 88 lbs.-ft. at 3000 rpm.
BASE FOUR (early R-17): Same as 1565-cc four above, except with Bosch electronic fuel injection — **Compression Ratio:** 9.0:1. **Brake Horsepower:** 107 at 6000 rpm. **Torque:** 96 lbs.-ft. at 4500 rpm.
BASE FOUR (1973-up R-12, R-15, R-17): Inline, overhead-valve four-cylinder. **Displacement:** 100.5 cu. in. (1647 cc). **Bore & Stroke:** 3.11 x 3.31 in. (79 x 84 mm). **Compression Ratio:** 7.5:1. **Brake Horsepower:** 65 at 5000 rpm. **Torque:** 88 lbs.-ft. at 2500 rpm.
CHASSIS DATA: Wheelbase: (R-10) 89 in.; (R-12/R-15/R-17) 96 in.; (R-16) 105.8 in. **Overall Length:** (R-10) 167.5 in.; (R-12 sed) 172.5 in.; (R-12 wag) 170.5 in.; (R-15/R-17) 170 in.; (R-16) 168.4 in. **Height:** (R-10) 55.5 in.; (R-12 sed) 56.5 in.; (R-12 wag) 57 in.; (R-15/R-17) 51.5 in.; (R-16) 57.3 in. **Width:** (R-10) 60 in.; (R-12) 64.5 in.; (R-15/R-17) 64 in.; (R-16) 64.9 in. **Front Tread:** (R-10) 49 in.; (R-12/R-15) 51.5 in.; (R-16) 52.8 in.; (R-17) 52.7 in. **Rear Tread:** (R-10) 48 in.; (R-12/R-15) 51.5 in.; (R-16) 50.9 in.; (R-17) 52.5 in. **Standard Tires:** (R-12/R-15) 155x13; (R-16) 155x14; (R-17) 165x13.
TECHNICAL: Layout: (R-10) rear-engine, rear-drive; (others) front-engine, front-drive. **Transmission:** four-speed manual (five-speed on later R-17 Gordini); automatic available. **Steering:** rack and pinion. **Suspension (front):** (R-10/R-12/R-15/R-17) wishbones with coil springs and anti-roll bar; (R-16) wishbones with torsion bars and anti-roll bar. **Suspension (rear):** (R-10) independent with swing axles and coil springs; (R-12/R-15/R-17) rigid axle with coil springs and anti-roll bar; (R-16) trailing arms with torsion bars and anti-roll bar. **Brakes:** front/rear disc. **Body Construction:** steel unibody.
PRODUCTION/SALES: Approximately 18,601 Renaults were sold in the U.S. during 1971, followed by 14,465 in 1972, 9,284 in 1973, 8,756 in 1974, and 5,780 in 1975.
Manufacturer: Regie Nationale des Usines Renault, Billancourt, France.
Distributor: Renault Inc., Englewood Cliffs, New Jersey.

1976-80 RENAULT

1978 Renault LeCar two-door sedan.

R-5 (LE CAR) — FOUR — Renault took careful aim at the low-budget subcompact market with its next new model, the two-door hatchback front-drive model 5, billed as "the incredible little car a million Europeans drive." *Automotive News*, on the other hand, described the R-5 as a "box with wheels at the four corners," noting that it was the shortest car in its class sold in the U.S. Renault countered by noting that it had a "longer wheelbase than any other car in its class." A carbureted 1289-cc (78.6-cid) four-cylinder developed 58 horsepower. Wheelbase differed on the left and right sides of the car. Options included striping, mag wheels, and rear wiper/washer. Top speed of 87 mph was claimed. The 5TL came with rubber floor mats and non-reclining front seats. Renault's 5GTL was better equipped, with reclining seats, carpeting, a package shelf behind rear seats, front map pockets, padded steering wheel, and cloth sunroof.

The name changed to Le Car for the 1977 model year, when black bumpers were added. A fabric sunroof and luggage rack were optional.

For the 1980 model year, only the Le Car remained of Renault's selection, with a larger (1397-cc) engine but no horsepower increase. The 1980 version had a slightly different front end, with an air dam incorporated in the new bumper. Rectangular headlamps replaced the former round units, and a new instrument panel went inside. Formerly required only in California, a catalytic converter now was installed in all Le Cars.

R-12TL/GTL — FOUR — Renault's R-12 sedan and station wagon remained available in 1976-77, powered by a 1647-cc (100.5-cid) engine.

R-15TL — FOUR — The 15-series coupe left the U.S. lineup after 1976.

R-17 — FOUR — Although the basic series 17 Sports Coupe (commonly described as a coupe/convertible, with its sunroof) remained available only through 1977, the Gordini edition lasted through 1979. The fuel-injected engine in a Gordini R-17 was rated at 95 horsepower.

I.D. DATA: Renault's 12-symbol serial number is on a plate on the right side of the wheel opening panel, and on the left side of the dashboard. Symbols 1-5 identify the model, followed by a 7-digit sequential production number.

Model	Body Type & Seating	Engine Type/CID	P.O.E. Price	Weight (lbs.)	Prod. Total
R-5 (1976)					
R-5TL	2-dr Hatch-4P	I4/79	3295	1777	Note 1
R-5GTL	2-dr Hatch-4P	I4/79	3627	1777	Note 1
LE CAR (1977-up)					
TL	2-dr Hatch-4P	I4/79	3345	1777	Note 1
GTL	2-dr Hatch-4P	I4/79	3695	1777	Note 1
R-12 (1976-77 only)					
R-12TL	4-dr Sedan-4/5P	I4/100	3899	2101	Note 1
R-12GTL	4-dr Sedan-4/5P	I4/100	4198	2156	Note 1
R-12	4-dr Sta Wag-4/5P	I4/100	4498	2242	Note 1

Model	Body Type & Seating	Engine Type/CID	P.O.E. Price	Weight (lbs.)	Prod. Total
R-15 (1976 only)					
R-15TL	2-dr Coupe-4P	I4/100	4795	2243	Note 1
R-17					
R-17TL	2-dr Cpe/Conv-4P	I4/100	5895	2356	Note 1
Gordini	2-dr Cpe/Conv-4P	I4/100	6665	2434	Note 1

Note 1: Approximately 1,218,358 Renault passenger cars (all models) were produced in 1976, followed by 1,259,038 in 1977, 1,240,941 in 1978, 1,405,330 in 1979, and 1,492,339 in 1980.

Price Note: Figures shown were valid in 1976 except (Le Car) 1977. By 1980, Le Car prices rose to $4587 for the base model and $5193 for a deluxe version.

Note: Specifications below were valid in 1976, except as indicated.

1979 Renault LeCar two-door sedan.

ENGINE DATA: BASE FOUR (R-5, Le Car): Inline, overhead-valve four-cylinder. **Displacement:** 78.6 cu. in. (1289 cc). **Bore & Stroke:** 2.87 x 3.03 in. (73 x 77 mm). **Compression Ratio:** 8.5:1. **Brake Horsepower:** 58 at 6000 rpm. **Torque:** 70 lbs.-ft. at 3500 rpm. Two-barrel carburetor.

BASE FOUR (1980 Le Car): Inline, overhead-valve four-cylinder. **Displacement:** 85.3 cu. in. (1397 cc). **Bore & Stroke:** 2.99 x 3.03 in. (76 x 77 mm). **Compression Ratio:** 8.8:1. **Brake Horsepower:** 51 at 5000 rpm. **Torque:** 70 lbs.-ft. at 3000 rpm.

BASE FOUR (R-12, R-15, R-17): Inline, overhead-valve four-cylinder. **Displacement:** 100.5 cu. in. (1647 cc). **Bore & Stroke:** 3.11 x 3.31 in. (79 x 84 mm). **Compression Ratio:** 8.0:1. **Brake Horsepower:** 72 at 5500 rpm. **Torque:** 84 lbs.-ft. at 3500 rpm. Two-barrel carburetor.

BASE FOUR (R-17 Gordini): Same as 1647-cc four above, but with fuel injection — **Compression Ratio:** 9.3:1. **Brake Horsepower:** 95 at 5250 rpm. **Torque:** 90 lbs.-ft. at 3500 rpm.

CHASSIS DATA: Wheelbase: (R-5) 94.6/95.8 in.; (R-12/R-15/R-17) 96 in. **Overall Length:** (R-5) 141.5 in.; (R-12 sed) 174 in.; (R-12 wag) 176 in.; (R-15/R-17) 172 in. **Height:** (R-5) 55 in.; (R-12 sed) 56.6 in.; (R-12 wag) 57 in.; (R-15/R-17) 51.5 in. **Width:** (R-5) 60 in.; (R-12) 64.5 in.; (R-15/R-17) 64 in. **Front Tread:** (R-5) 50.7 in.; (R-12/R-15/R-17) 51.5 in. **Rear Tread:** (R-5) 49 in.; (R-12/R-15/R-17) 51.5 in. **Standard Tires:** (R-5) 135SR-13; (R-12/R-15/R-17) 155x13; (R-17 Gordini) 165x13.

TECHNICAL: Layout: front-engine, front-drive. **Transmission:** four-speed manual (five-speed on R-17 Gordini); automatic available. **Steering:** rack and pinion. **Suspension (front):** (R-5/Le Car) unequal-length A-arms with torsion bars; (R-12/R-15/R-17) wishbones with coil springs and anti-roll bar. **Suspension (rear):** (R-5/Le Car) trailing arms with torsion bars; (R-12/R-15/R-17) rigid axle with coil springs and anti-roll bar. **Brakes:** (R-5/Le Car) front disc, rear drum; (R-12/R-15/R-17) front/rear disc. **Body Construction:** steel unibody.

PRODUCTION/SALES: Approximately 6,819 Renaults were sold in the U.S. during 1976, followed by 13,198 in 1977, 15,739 in 1978, 18,862 in 1979, and 25,365 in 1980.

Manufacturer: Regie Nationale des Usines Renault, Billancourt, France.

Distributor: Renault Inc., Englewood Cliffs, New Jersey.

HISTORY: Switching to the Le Car name caused Renault sales in the U.S. to rise sharply, soon reaching the 18th spot. Ads for Le Car claimed that sales doubled in 1977, and promised that "the small car of the future is here today." In the first six months of 1977, Le Cars secured a total of 57 first, second and third place finishes, out of 52 SCCA races. Said *Road Test* magazine of Le Car: "...blasting across a railroad track at full speed becomes not only possible, but delightful," while the car "seems built like a tank." By 1979, Renault's plan to build cars in conjunction with American Motors was already publicized, and Renaults were being sold by AMC dealers. In return, Renault sold AMC's Jeeps in Europe.

1981 RENAULT

LE CAR — FOUR — Availability of the subcompact Le Car continued, with the 1397-cc engine that debuted in the 1980 model year. Facelifted modestly in 1980, appearance changed little this year. A "Black Beauty" appearance package was available, as it had been the prior year. Only Deluxe models could have an optional sunroof, air conditioning, and rear wiper/washer. Standard equipment on the Deluxe included reclining bucket seats and a day/night mirror. A four-door hatchback joined the original two-door hatchback body style at mid-year.

1981 Renault 18i station wagon.

18i — FOUR — New this year was a larger sedan and station wagon, powered by a 1.6-liter four-cylinder engine that developed 81.5 horsepower. Two trim levels were offered. Standard equipment included a four-speed gearbox, reclining front bucket seats with vinyl upholstery, and bodyside moldings. The deluxe version added cloth seats, console, electric rear defroster, tachometer, passenger map light, tilt steering, wheel lip moldings, and body striping.

I.D. DATA: Renault's 17-digit Vehicle Identification Number is on the upper left of the dashboard, visible through the windshield. Symbols 1-3 ('VF1') indicate country, make and vehicle type. Symbol four identifies the engine, five the transmission. Symbols 6-7 identify the series and body style ('22' = Le Car 2-dr; '39' = Le Car 4-dr; '34' = 18i sedan; '35' = 18i wagon). The next symbol indicates the restraint system type, followed by a check digit. Symbol 10 denotes the model year ('B' = 1981); symbol 11, the assembly plant. The six final digits form the sequential serial number, starting with 000001.

Model	Body Type & Seating	Engine Type/CID	P.O.E. Price	Weight (lbs.)	Prod. Total
LE CAR					
	2-dr Hatch-4P	I4/85	5200	1820	Note 1
Deluxe	2-dr Hatch-4P	I4/85	5600	1820	Note 1
Deluxe	4-dr Hatch-4P	I4/85	5827	1865	Note 1
18i					
	4-dr Sedan-4/5P	I4/100	7398	2261	Note 1
	4-dr Sta Wag-4/5P	I4/100	7858	2405	Note 1
Deluxe	4-dr Sedan-4/5P	I4/100	7898	2261	Note 1
Deluxe	4-dr Sta Wag-4/5P	I4/100	8358	2405	Note 1

Note 1: A total of 1,295,713 Renault passenger cars (all models) were produced in 1981.

1981 Renault LeCar two-door sedan.

ENGINE DATA: BASE FOUR (Le Car): Inline, overhead-valve four-cylinder. Cast iron block and light alloy head. **Displacement:** 85.2 cu. in. (1397 cc). **Bore & Stroke:** 2.99 x 3.03 in. (76 x 77 mm). **Compression Ratio:** 8.8:1. **Brake Horsepower:** 51 at 5000 rpm. **Torque:** 70 lbs.-ft. at 3000 rpm. Five main bearings. Two-barrel carburetor.

BASE FOUR (18i): Inline, overhead-valve four-cylinder. Light alloy block and head. **Displacement:** 100.5 cu. in. (1647 cc). **Bore & Stroke:** 3.11 x 3.31 in. (79 x 84 mm). **Compression Ratio:** 8.6:1. **Brake Horsepower:** 81.5 at 5500 rpm. **Torque:** 86 lbs.-ft. at 2500 rpm. Five main bearings. Bosch L-Jetronic fuel injection.

CHASSIS DATA: Wheelbase: (Le Car) 95.2 in.; (18i) 96.1 in. **Overall Length:** (Le Car) 142.5 in.; (18i sed) 178.7 in.; (18i wag) 181.5 in. **Height:** (Le Car) 55.0 in.; (18i sed) 55.3 in.; (18i wag) 55.2 in. **Width:** (Le Car) 60.0 in.; (18i) 66.5 in. **Front Tread:** (Le Car) 50.9 in.; (18i) 55.7 in. **Rear Tread:** (Le Car) 49.2 in.; (18i) 53.4 in. **Standard Tires:** (Le Car) 145x13; (18i) 175/70R13.

TECHNICAL: Layout: front-engine, front-drive. **Transmission:** four-speed manual. **Steering:** rack and pinion. **Suspension (front):** (Le Car) upper/lower control arms with longitudinal torsion bars and anti-roll bar; (18i) lower control arms, upper transverse arms and reaction arms, coil springs and anti-roll bar. **Suspension (rear):** (Le Car) independent, trailing arms with transverse torsion bars and anti-roll bar; (18i) beam axle with coil springs and anti-roll bar. **Brakes:** front disc, rear drum. **Body Construction:** steel unibody.

MAJOR OPTIONS: LE CAR OPTIONS: Sunroof (DeL). Air conditioning (DeL). AM/FM stereo (DeL). Black Beauty pkg. (DeL). Tinted glass. Rear wiper/washer (DeL).

18i OPTIONS: Air conditioning ($595). Three-speed automatic ($395). Five-speed manual transmission ($199). Cruise control ($165). Convenience group ($359). Driving group ($339). Touring package incl. leather seats ($598). AM/FM stereo w/cassette.

1981 Renault 18i sedan.

PRODUCTION/SALES: A total of 31,077 Renaults were sold in the U.S. in 1981 (including 208 tourist deliveries).
Manufacturer: Regie Nationale des Usines Renault, Boulogne Billancourt, France.
Distributor: Renault USA Inc., New York City and American Motors Corp., Southfield, Michigan.
HISTORY: Renaults for the 1981 model year were introduced to the U.S. market in September 1980.

1982 RENAULT

1982 Renault LeCar.

LE CAR — FOUR — Except for a redesigned steering-column stalk, little was new in the Le Car. Since mid-1981, two hatchback body styles had been offered. A Sport package was optional on the two-door only.
FUEGO — FOUR — Joining Renault's lineup late in the model year (spring 1982), the new coupe carried a 1.6-liter (100.5-cid) normally aspirated four-cylinder engine or, later, an optional smaller Turbo four.
18i — FOUR — For its second season in the Renault lineup, the larger sedan and wagon continued with the 1.6-liter four-cylinder engine.
I.D. DATA: Renault's 17-digit Vehicle Identification Number is on the upper left of the dashboard, visible through the windshield. Symbols 1-3 ('VF1') indicate country, make and vehicle type. Symbol four identifies the engine, five the transmission. Symbols 6-7 identify the series and body style ('22' = Le Car 2-dr; '39' = Le Car 4-dr; '34' = 18i sedan; '35' = 18i wagon; '36' = Fuego). The next symbol indicates the restraint system type, followed by a check digit. Symbol 10 denotes the model year ('C' = 1982); symbol 11, the assembly plant. The six final digits form the sequential serial number, starting with 000001.

Model	Body Type & Seating	Engine Type/CID	P.O.E. Price	Weight (lbs.)	Prod. Total
LE CAR					
	2-dr Hatch-4P	I4/85	4995	1820	Note 1
Deluxe	2-dr Hatch-4P	I4/85	5295	1820	Note 1
Deluxe	4-dr Hatch-4P	I4/85	5595	1865	Note 1
FUEGO					
	2-dr Coupe-4P	I4/100	8495	2204	Note 1
18i					
	4-dr Sedan-4/5P	I4/100	7398	2263	Note 1
	4-dr Sta Wag-4/5P	I4/100	7858	2426	Note 1
Deluxe	4-dr Sedan-4/5P	I4/100	7898	N/A	Note 1
Deluxe	4-dr Sta Wag-4/5P	I4/100	8358	N/A	Note 1

Note 1: A total of 1,491,853 Renault passenger cars (all models) were produced in 1982.
ENGINE DATA: BASE FOUR (Le Car): Inline, overhead-valve four-cylinder. Cast iron block and light alloy head. **Displacement:** 85.2 cu. in. (1397 cc). **Bore & Stroke:** 2.99 x 3.03 (76 x 77 mm). **Compression Ratio:** 8.8:1. **Brake Horsepower:** 51 at 5100 rpm. **Torque:** 70 lbs.-ft. at 3000 rpm. Five main bearings. Two-barrel carburetor.

532

BASE FOUR (18i, Fuego): Inline, overhead-valve four-cylinder. Light alloy block and head. **Displacement:** 100.5 cu. in. (1647 cc). **Bore & Stroke:** 3.11 x 3.31 (79 x 84 mm). **Compression Ratio:** 8.6:1. **Brake Horsepower:** 81.5 at 5500 rpm. **Torque:** 86 lbs.-ft. at 2500 rpm. Five main bearings. Fuel injection.
Turbo Note: A turbocharged Fuego also became available; see next listing for data.
CHASSIS DATA: Wheelbase: (Le Car) 95.2 in.; (Fuego/18i) 96.1 in. **Overall Length:** (Le Car) 142.5 in.; (Fuego) 176.8 in.; (18i sed) 178.7 in.; (18i wag) 181.5 in. **Height:** (Le Car) 55.0 in.; (Fuego) 50.5 in.; (18i sed) 55.3 in.; (18i wag) 55.2 in. **Width:** (Le Car) 60.0 in.; (Fuego) 66.6 in.; (18i) 66.5 in. **Front Tread:** (Le Car) 50.9 in.; (Fuego) 56.4 in.; (18i) 55.7 in. **Rear Tread:** (Le Car) 49.2 in.; (Fuego) 53.0 in.; (18i) 53.4 in. **Standard Tires:** (Le Car) 145x13; (18i) 175/70R13.
TECHNICAL: Layout: front-engine, front-drive. **Transmission:** (Le Car/18i) four-speed manual; (Fuego) five-speed manual. **Steering:** rack and pinion. **Suspension (front):** (Le Car) upper/lower control arms, longitudinal torsion bars and anti-roll bar; (Fuego/18i) lower control arms, upper transverse arms and reaction arms, coil springs and anti-roll bar. **Suspension (rear):** (Le Car) independent, trailing arms with transverse torsion bars and anti-roll bar; (Fuego) beam axle with A-shape control bracket, lateral trailing arms, coil springs and anti-roll bar; (18i) beam axle with four links, coil springs and anti-roll bar. **Brakes:** front disc, rear drum. **Body Construction:** steel unibody.
PRODUCTION/SALES: A total of 37,702 Renaults were sold in the U.S. in 1982 (including 162 tourist deliveries).
Manufacturer: Regie Nationale des Usines Renault, Boulogne Billancourt, France.
Distributor: American Motors Corp., Southfield, Michigan.
HISTORY: Renaults for the 1982 model year were introduced to the U.S. market in September 1981 except (Fuego) March 1982.

1983 RENAULT

LE CAR — FOUR — Little was changed on Renault's smallest imported model, except for a shift in final drive ratio from 3.63:1 to 3.10:1. The two-barrel carburetor also was revised this year, to improve cold-start and hot-start performance. Base models had leatherette upholstery. Deluxe models included reclining front seats with fabric upholstery, passenger assist handles, carpeting, lighter, soft-feel steering wheel, swing-out (or rolldown) rear side windows, power brakes, electric rear defroster, deluxe lower door panel trim, and body striping.
FUEGO — FOUR — Introduced in spring 1982, the Renault coupe came with either a 1.6-liter (100.5-cid) normally aspirated four-cylinder engine, or a smaller Turbo four. Both models switched from three-stalk to two-stalk steering-column controls for lights and wiper/washer. Two new options were offered: an "infrawave" remote door-lock system, and power remote mirrors. Standard equipment was similar to the 18i, but added a digital clock, split-back rear seat, leather-wrapped steering wheel (on adjustable column), four-speaker stereo, driver's remote mirror, and remote liftgate release. The Fuego Turbo included Michelin TRX tires on aluminum wheels, air conditioning, and special body striping.
18i — FOUR — Except for a switch to two-stalk controls (as on the Fuego), and a change from 3.78:1 to 3.54:1 final drive, Renault's sedan and wagon continued as before. A five-speed gearbox replaced the former standard four-speed, and the base-trim edition was dropped. Power came from the same 1.6-liter (normally aspirated) engine used in the Fuego coupe. Standard equipment included reclining front bucket seats, intermittent wipers, cloth upholstery, full carpeting, analog clock, center console, padded steering wheel, tachometer, passenger vanity mirror, AM/FM stereo radio, electric rear defroster, power brakes/steering, and tinted glass. The wagon included a rear wiper/washer.

1983 Renault Vesta.

I.D. DATA: Renault's 17-digit Vehicle Identification Number is on the upper left of the dashboard, visible through the windshield. Symbols 1-3 ('VF1') indicate country, make and vehicle type. Symbol four identifies the engine, five the transmission. Symbols 6-7 identify the series and body style ('22' = Le Car 2-dr; '34' = Le Car 4-dr; '34' = 18i sedan; '35' = 18i wagon; '36' = Fuego). The next symbol indicates the restraint system type, followed by a check digit. Symbol 10 denotes the model year ('D' = 1983); symbol 11, the assembly plant. The six final digits form the sequential serial number, starting with 000001.

Model	Body Type & Seating	Engine Type/CID	P.O.E. Price	Weight (lbs.)	Prod. Total
LE CAR					
	2-dr Hatch-4P	I4/85	4795	1820	Note 1
Deluxe	2-dr Hatch-4P	I4/85	4995	1820	Note 1
Deluxe	4-dr Hatch-4P	I4/85	5295	1865	Note 1
FUEGO					
	2-dr Coupe-4P	I4/100	8695	2379	Note 1
Turbo	2-dr Coupe-4P	I4/95	11095	N/A	Note 1
18i					
Deluxe	4-dr Sedan-5P	I4/100	8395	2263	Note 1
Deluxe	4-dr Sta Wag-5P	I4/100	8855	2426	Note 1

Note 1: A total of 1,639,405 Renault passenger cars were produced during 1983.
ENGINE DATA: BASE FOUR (Le Car): Inline, overhead-valve four-cylinder. Cast iron block and light alloy head. Displacement: 85.2 cu. in. (1397 cc). Bore & Stroke: 2.99 x 3.03 (76 x 77 mm). Compression Ratio: 8.8:1. Brake Horsepower: 51 at 5100 rpm. Torque: 70 lbs.-ft. at 3000 rpm. Five main bearings. Two-barrel carburetor.
BASE FOUR (18i, Fuego): Inline, overhead-valve four-cylinder. Light alloy block and head. Displacement: 100.5 cu. in. (1647 cc). Bore & Stroke: 3.11 x 3.31 (79 x 84 mm). Compression Ratio: 8.6:1. Brake Horsepower: 81.5 at 5500 rpm. Torque: 86 lbs.-ft. at 2500 rpm. Five main bearings. Fuel injection.
BASE FOUR (Fuego Turbo): Inline, overhead-valve four-cylinder. Light alloy block and head. Displacement: 95.5 cu. in. (1565 cc). Bore & Stroke: 3.03 x 3.30 (77 x 84 mm). Compression Ratio: 8.0:1. Brake Horsepower: 107 at 5500 rpm. Torque: 120 lbs.-ft. at 2500 rpm. Five main bearings. Fuel injection.
CHASSIS DATA: Wheelbase: (Le Car) 95.2 in.; (Fuego/18i) 96.1 in. Overall Length: (Le Car) 142.5 in.; (Fuego) 176.8 in.; (18i sed) 178.7 in.; (18i wag) 181.5 in. Height: (Le Car) 55.0 in.; (Fuego) 50.5 in.; (18i sed) 55.3 in.; (18i wag) 55.2 in. Width: (Le Car) 60.0 in.; (Fuego) 66.6 in.; (18i) 66.5 in. Front Tread: (Le Car) 55.0 in.; (Fuego) 56.4 in.; (18i) 55.7 in. Rear Tread: (Le Car) 50.9 in.; (Fuego) 53.0 in.; (18i) 53.4 in. Standard Tires: (Le Car) 145SR13; (18i) 175/70R13.
TECHNICAL: Layout: front-engine, front-drive. Transmission: (Le Car) four-speed manual; (Fuego/18i) five-speed manual. Standard Final Drive Ratio: (Le Car) 3.10:1; (Fuego/18i) 3.54:1; (Fuego Turbo) 3.78:1. Steering: rack and pinion (power assist on Fuego/18i). Suspension (front): (Le Car) upper/lower control arms, longitudinal torsion bars and anti-roll bar; (Fuego/18i) lower control arms, upper transverse arms and reaction arms, coil springs and anti-roll bar. Suspension (rear): (Le Car) independent, trailing arms with transverse torsion bars and anti-roll bar; (Fuego) beam axle with A-shape control bracket, lateral trailing arms, coil springs and anti-roll bar; (18i) beam axle with four links, coil springs and anti-roll bar. Brakes: front disc, rear drum. Body Construction: steel unibody. Fuel Tank: (Le Car) 10.0 gal.; (Fuego) 14.8 gal.; (18i sed) 14.0 gal.; (18i wag) 15.0 gallon.
MAJOR OPTIONS: LE CAR OPTIONS: Air cond. (DeL). Black Beauty pkg. (DeL). Electric rear defroster (base). Tinted glass. AM/FM stereo (DeL). AM/FM stereo w/cassette (DeL). Sunroof. Rear washer/wiper (DeL). Wheel covers (DeL). Aluminum wheels (DeL). Sport steering wheel (DeL). Fabric upholstery (DeL).
FUEGO/18i OPTIONS: Air cond. ($640). Three-speed automatic ($365); N/A on Turbo. Cruise control ($170). Cast aluminum wheels: 18i ($360). Cast aluminum wheels with Michelin TRX tires: Fuego ($440). Convenience group: Fuego ($525); 18i ($375). Front floormats ($30). AM/FM stereo w/cassette ($149). Roof rack: 18i wag ($115). Metallic paint ($135). Touring interior ($645). Deluxe vinyl seats: 18i wag ($26). Electric vinyl sunroof: Fuego ($425). Visibility group: Fuego ($140).
PRODUCTION/SALES: A total of 33,229 Renaults were sold in the U.S. in 1983.
Manufacturer: Regie Nationale des Usines Renault, Boulogne Billancourt, France.
Distributor: American Motors Corp. (AMC), Southfield, Michigan.
HISTORY: Renault's imported models for the 1983 model year were introduced to the U.S. market in September 1982. New this year was the Renault Alliance, designed in France but built in Kenosha, Wisconsin; see Standard Catalog of American Cars 1976-86 for details. This was the final year for the Le Car subcompact.

1984 RENAULT

FUEGO — FOUR — A larger four-cylinder engine powered the Renault coupe, evolved from the former 1.6-liter four. Bosch L-Jetronic fuel injection was installed. Turbo models continued with the 1.6-liter four. A new Turbo handling package this year included larger-diameter stabilizer bars and revised shock-absorber calibrations. Otherwise, standard tires grew to P185/70R13 size, and a leather-wrapped sports steering wheel became standard. Joining the option list: an electronically-tuned stereo system with six speakers, and garnet leather seats.

SPORTWAGON — FOUR — The former 18i station wagon took a new name this year, as the four-door sedan faded away. Under its hood was the same larger engine as installed in the Fuego. New this year: standard air conditioning, a leather-wrapped steering wheel, black roof rack, and "bio-formed" individual front seats. Automatic-transmission models included cruise control.

I.D. DATA: Renault's 17-digit Vehicle Identification Number is on the upper left of the dashboard, visible through the windshield. Symbols 1-3 ('VF1') indicate country, make and vehicle type. Symbol four identifies the engine, five the transmission. Symbols 6-7 identify the series and body style ('35' = Sportwagon; '36' = Fuego). The next symbol indicates the restraint system type, followed by a check digit. Symbol 10 denotes the model year ('E' = 1984); symbol 11, the assembly plant. The six final digits form the sequential serial number, starting with 000001.

Model	Body Type & Seating	Engine Type/CID	P.O.E. Price	Weight (lbs.)	Prod. Total
FUEGO					
	2-dr Coupe-4P	I4/132	8995	2480	Note 1
Turbo	2-dr Coupe-4P	I4/95	N/A	N/A	Note 1
SPORTWAGON					
	4-dr Sta Wag-5P	I4/132	9595	2579	Note 1

Note 1: A total of 1,429,138 Renault passenger cars were produced during 1984.
ENGINE DATA: BASE FOUR (Fuego, Sportwagon): Inline, overhead-valve four-cylinder. Light alloy block and head. Displacement: 132 cu. in. (2165 cc). Bore & Stroke: 3.47 x 3.50 (88 x 89 mm). Compression Ratio: 8.7:1. Brake Horsepower: N/A. Torque: N/A. Five main bearings. Port fuel injection.
Note: AMC, which marketed the Renault imports in the U.S., did not announce horsepower/torque figures.
BASE FOUR (Fuego Turbo): Inline, overhead-valve four-cylinder. Light alloy block and head. Displacement: 95.5 cu. in. (1565 cc). Bore & Stroke: 3.03 x 3.30 (77 x 84 mm). Compression Ratio: 8.0:1. Brake Horsepower: 107 at 5500 rpm. Torque: 120 lbs.-ft. at 2500 rpm. Five main bearings. Fuel injection.
CHASSIS DATA: Wheelbase: (Fuego) 96.1 in. Overall Length: (Fuego) 176.8 in.; (Sportwagon) 181.5 in. Height: (Fuego) 50.5 in.; (Sportwagon) 55.2 in. Width: (Fuego) 66.6 in.; (Sportwagon) 66.5 in. Front Tread: (Fuego) 56.4 in.; (Sportwagon) 55.7 in. Rear Tread: (Fuego) 53.0 in.; (Sportwagon) 53.4 in. Standard Tires: (Fuego) P185/70R13.

TECHNICAL: Layout: front-engine, front-drive. Transmission: five-speed manual; three-speed automatic available. Standard Final Drive Ratio: 3.10:1 w/manual, 3.56:1 w/automatic except (Fuego Turbo) 3.78:1. Steering: power rack and pinion. Suspension (front): lower control arms, upper transverse arms, coil springs and anti-roll bar. Suspension (rear): (Fuego) beam axle with lateral trailing arms, coil springs and anti-roll bar; (Sportwagon) beam axle with four links, coil springs and anti-roll bar. Brakes: front disc, rear drum. Body Construction: steel unibody. Fuel Tank: (Fuego) 14.8 gal.; (Sportwagon) 15.0 gallon.
MAJOR OPTIONS: Air conditioning. Three-speed automatic transmission (N/A on Turbo). Cruise control. Sunroof (Fuego). Convenience group. AM/FM stereo w/cassette (Sportwagon). Roof rack (Sportwagon). Metallic paint.
PRODUCTION/SALES: A total of 12,243 Renaults were sold in the U.S. in 1984.
Manufacturer: Regie Nationale des Usines Renault, Boulogne Billancourt, France.
Distributor: American Motors Corp. (AMC), Southfield, Michigan.
HISTORY: Imported Renaults for the 1984 model year were introduced to the U.S. market in September 1983; Sportwagon did not appear until February 1984. A new Encore model joined the Alliance, built in Wisconsin; see Standard Catalog of American Cars 1976-86 for details.

1985 RENAULT

1985 Renault Fuego.

FUEGO — FOUR — The turbocharged version of Renault's coupe disappeared this year, leaving only the 2.2-liter aluminum four-cylinder engine. Larger (14-inch) wheels and tires became standard. Added to the option list: aluminum wheels, a seven-function trip computer, and a color-keyed cargo area cover. Cruise control was now available with manual shift, as well as automatic.

SPORTWAGON — FOUR — The biggest change in Renault's station wagon was a switch to 14-inch steel wheels and tires. Aluminum wheels were optional. The Touring Edition included an electronically-tuned AM/FM stereo radio with cassette player, leather interior, dual remote mirrors, power front windows, power door locks, and cast aluminum wheels with Michelin radial tires.

I.D. DATA: Renault's 17-digit Vehicle Identification Number is on the upper left of the dashboard, visible through the windshield. Symbols 1-3 ('VF1') indicate country, make and vehicle type. Symbol four identifies the engine, five the transmission. Symbols 6-7 identify the series and body style ('35' = Sportwagon; '36' = Fuego). The next symbol ('B') indicates the restraint system type, followed by a check digit. Symbol 10 denotes the model year ('F' = 1985); symbol 11, the assembly plant. The six final digits form the sequential serial number, starting with 000001.

Model	Body Type & Seating	Engine Type/CID	P.O.E. Price	Weight (lbs.)	Prod. Total
FUEGO					
	2-dr Coupe-4P	I4/132	9295	2480	Note 1
SPORTWAGON					
	4-dr Sta Wag-5P	I4/132	9895	2579	Note 1

Note 1: A total of 1,322,887 Renault passenger cars were produced during 1985.
ENGINE DATA: BASE FOUR: Inline, overhead-valve four-cylinder. Light alloy block and head. Displacement: 132 cu. in. (2165 cc). Bore & Stroke: 3.47 x 3.50 (88 x 89 mm). Compression Ratio: 8.7:1. Brake Horsepower: N/A. Torque: N/A. Five main bearings. Port fuel injection.

1985 Renault Sportwagon.

Note: AMC, which marketed the Renault imports in the U.S., did not announce horsepower/torque figures.

CHASSIS DATA: Wheelbase: 96.1 in. **Overall Length:** (Fuego) 176.8 in.; (Sportwagon) 181.5 in. **Height:** (Fuego) 50.5 in.; (Sportwagon) 55.2 in. **Width:** (Fuego) 66.6 in.; (Sportwagon) 66.5 in. **Front Tread:** (Fuego) 56.4 in.; (Sportwagon) 55.7 in. **Rear Tread:** (Fuego) 53.0 in.; (Sportwagon) 53.4 in. **Standard Tires:** 185/65R14.

TECHNICAL: Layout: front-engine, front-drive. **Transmission:** five-speed manual; three-speed automatic available. **Standard Final Drive Ratio:** 3.10:1 w/manual, 3.56:1 w/automatic. **Steering:** power rack and pinion. **Suspension (front):** lower control arms, upper transverse arms, coil springs and anti-roll bar. **Suspension (rear):** (Fuego) beam axle with lateral trailing arms, coil springs and anti-roll bar; (Sportwagon) beam axle with four links, coil springs and anti-roll bar. **Brakes:** front disc, rear drum. **Body Construction:** steel unibody. **Fuel Tank:** (Fuego) 14.8 gal.; (Sportwagon) 15.0 gallon.

MAJOR OPTIONS: Air cond.: Fuego ($755). Three-speed automatic ($438). Cruise control ($203). Sunroof: Fuego ($490). Convenience group: Fuego ($568); Sportwagon ($375). AM/FM stereo w/cassette and equalizer: Fuego ($417). Leather touring interior: Fuego ($714). Trip computer: Fuego ($225). Visibility group: Fuego ($242). Aluminum wheels with P195/60R14 Michelin TRX tires: Fuego ($490). Metallic paint ($156).

PRODUCTION/SALES: A total of 7,205 Renaults were sold in the U.S. in 1985.
Manufacturer: Regie Nationale des Usines Renault, Boulogne Billancourt, France.
Distributor: American Motors Corp. (AMC), Southfield, Michigan.

HISTORY: Imported Renaults for the 1985 model year were introduced to the U.S. market in October 1984.

1986 RENAULT

1986 Renault Sportwagon.

SPORTWAGON — FOUR — Only the station wagon in Renault's imported-car lineup for this, its final year in the U.S. market. No change was evident. Like the Alliance/Encore that were built in the U.S., the Sportwagon came with AMC's 5/50 Plus (5-year/50,000-mile) warranty, initiated in March 1985.

I.D. DATA: Renault's 17-digit Vehicle Identification Number is on the upper left of the dashboard, visible through the windshield. Starting serial number: VF1FD35B_G_000001.

Model	Body Type & Seating	Engine Type/CID	P.O.E. Price	Weight (lbs.)	Prod. Total
SPORTWAGON					
	4-dr Sta Wag-5P	I4/132	10199	2579	Note 1

Note 1: A total of 1,305,191 Renault passenger cars were produced during 1986.

ENGINE DATA: BASE FOUR: Inline, overhead-valve four-cylinder. Light alloy block and head. **Displacement:** 132 cu. in. (2165 cc). **Bore & Stroke:** 3.47 x 3.50 (88 x 89 mm). **Compression Ratio:** 8.7:1. **Brake Horsepower:** N/A. **Torque:** N/A. Five main bearings. Port fuel injection.
Note: AMC, which marketed the Renault imports in the U.S., did not announce horsepower/torque figures.

CHASSIS DATA: Wheelbase: 96.1 in. **Overall Length:** 181.5 in. **Height:** 55.2 in. **Width:** 66.5 in. **Front Tread:** 55.7 in. **Rear Tread:** 53.4 in. **Standard Tires:** 185/65R14.

TECHNICAL: Layout: front-engine, front-drive. **Transmission:** five-speed manual; three-speed automatic available. **Standard Final Drive Ratio:** 3.10:1 w/manual, 3.56:1 w/automatic. **Steering:** power rack and pinion. **Suspension (front):** lower control arms, upper transverse arms, coil springs and anti-roll bar. **Suspension (rear):** beam axle with four links, coil springs and anti-roll bar. **Brakes:** front disc, rear drum. **Body Construction:** steel unibody. **Fuel Tank:** 15.0 gallon.

MAJOR OPTIONS: Three-speed automatic ($438). Cruise control ($203). Convenience group ($375). Metallic paint ($156).

PRODUCTION/SALES: A total of 4,152 Renaults were sold in the U.S. in 1986.
Manufacturer: Regie Nationale des Usines Renault, Boulogne Billancourt, France.
Distributor: American Motors Corp. (AMC), Southfield, Michigan.

HISTORY: Sportwagons for the 1986 model year were introduced to U.S. market in October 1985.

RILEY

Like several other British motorcar makers, the Riley company traces its origin to fabrics: specifically, to the manufacture of woven materials and the machines to create them. By 1890, when the weaving business was fading fast, William Riley added a bicycle plant to his operation. Percy Riley, one of William's five sons, created a two-seat motorized vehicle with single-cylinder engine by 1898, especially notable for its use of mechanically-actuated intake valves. Just before the turn of the century, the Riley Cycle Company had both three-wheel and four-wheel powered cycles for sale.

After a few years of relying on engines from outside sources, three of the younger Rileys set up a separate firm to produce their own powerplants, using the valve configuration created by Percy. By 1907, their vehicles sported steering wheels and other automobile-like details, so they turned to a full-fledged car, powered by a 12/18 hp 90-degree V-twin engine and wearing the world's first detachable wire wheels. Oddly, the company became best known for the production of those wire wheels in the years preceding World War I. So, yet another separate firm was founded to concentrate on the production of automobiles, with both two- and four-cylinder engines.

Through the early 1920s, Riley turned out a new open four-seater with 2.5-liter four-cylinder engine and four-speed gearbox. The Redwinger version, in particular, earned a fair number of racing trophies. By 1926, the famed Riley Nine was ready for the marketplace, carrying an engine design that would be used for the next three decades. Pushrods from twin camshafts high on each side of the cylinder block actuated the inclined overhead valves, while pistons reached toward hemispherical combustion chambers. More than 10,000 Nines were built through 1938, including at least 100 low-slung Brooklands editions and about 75 short-wheelbase Imps.

Fluid flywheels and Wilson preselectors became available on Rileys by 1934. A year later came the 1496-cc four-cylinder engine, destined to power 1.5-liter Rileys for two decades. Among the notable bodies to carry the 1.5-liter four were the Kestrel and the limited-production Sprite two-seater, introduced in 1936. A handful of six-cylinder and V-8 Rileys appeared during the 1930s, including the rare MPH two-seater of 1934-35, but four-cylinder engines remained the company's forte. Financial woes led to receivership in 1938, followed by acquisition by Lord Nuffield and subsequent takeover by Morris Motors, under a new company name.

Postwar production began early, with a new 1.5-liter "Twelve" saloon ready in late 1945. That model was joined late in the following year by a "Big Four" model with a 2443-cc engine, but the same basic saloon body. That larger engine had been developed just before the war. Roadster and drophead-coupe bodies soon followed. In 1948, Riley production moved from its long-standing site at Coventry to the MG plant at Abingdon. For 1954, a new, modern-looking Pathfinder replaced the more traditional 2-1/2 Litre series, but powered by the same twin-cam 2443-cc engine; and the smaller Riley enjoyed a modest restyling. By this time, Rileys had already begun to lose much of their distinctive quality, being squeezed into the British Motor Corporation (BMC) mold, following absorption into that group in 1952. The last new full-size Riley, for instance, the Two-Point-Six, differed little except in trim from one of the Wolseley models of that period. As a final

irony (some might say insult), the distinguished diamond-shaped Riley badge found itself on a selection of other BMC clones in the 1960s, including the Mini-based Elf and 1100-level Kestrel. Final Rileys were produced in 1969, but the last "real" examples had entered the market long before that year.

1946-47 RILEY

1947 Riley 1½-liter saloon.

Postwar production began before the end of 1945 with an all-new 1-1/2 Litre "Twelve" four-door saloon, wearing a fresh body but carrying on Riley's traditional look. A successor to the similarly-engined saloon of 1939-40, the postwar version had a redesigned chassis with torsion-bar front suspension. Inboard, semi-built-in headlamps, a vertical-bar grille and a wide front-end appearance differentiated the new Riley from its prewar predecessor. The 1496-cc (91-cid) four-cylinder engine evolved from that used in the old Riley Nine, with twin camshafts in the block acting upon short pushrods for the 90-degree inclined overhead valves. Late in 1946, a similar-looking 2-1/2 Litre model joined the smaller Riley, also offered only in four-door saloon form but on a longer wheelbase. See 1948-50 listing below for details on both models, and on the drophead coupe and roadster that arrived during 1948.

1948-50 RILEY

1949 Riley with custom body by W. Kong.

2-1/2 LITRE — FOUR — Three body styles were available by 1948 with the 2.5-liter four-cylinder engine: four-door saloon, two-door drophead (convertible) coupe, and a three-seater roadster. Up front was a vee-shaped vertical-bar grille, slightly slanted, with inboard faired-in headlamps alongside. Tiny parking lights rode atop the front fenders. Auxiliary lights were mounted separately, on the front bumper. Both the front and rear end held split bumpers. A vee-type fixed (split) windshield was used. Front and rear saloon doors were hinged at the center pillar, and did not contain vent wings. All models wore vestigial running boards, more for decoration than utility. Riley's "torsionic front suspension," said the sales brochure, "keeps you on a level keel—*all* the time." Torsion bars ran parallel to the frame sides. A rigid axle with semi-elliptic leaf springs brought up the rear. A separate compartment held the spare tire. Inside were separately adjustable front seats, a Bluemel three-spoke steering wheel on an adjustable column, English

leather upholstery, and walnut wood trim. Riley's 149-cid (2443 cc) engine had twin camshafts in the block, with short pushrods and rockers, plus valves set at 90 degrees and hemispherical combustion chambers. That engine delivered 100 horsepower, sufficient for a claimed top speed of 100 mph (though actual road tests did not reach that pace).

Aimed largely at the American market, the twin open models introduced in 1948 never quite caught on with the sales success that had been expected, largely because of their high price and low power. The drophead coupe was described as a "smart, sleek, open-to-the-air, high performer for those days when the sun makes you feel it's good to be alive." It had wind-up door windows and adjustable forward vent panels, with directional indicators below the body's center line. Riley's Sports three-seater roadster had a fold-down flat windshield, rakish cutdown rear-hinged doors with the same gracefully curved leading edges as on the saloon and drophead, and specially-designed bumper overriders. Company literature claimed that the roadster's trunk would "carry easily four suitcases, two attache cases and a bag of golf clubs."

For 1949, Riley hoods were released from the dashboard rather than outside. Instruments were grouped on a mahogany center facia panel with a round clock on one side and matching speedometer on the other. Standard saloon/coupe colors in 1950 were: Black with beige, maroon, green or brown upholstery; Autumn Red with beige or maroon upholstery; Almond Green with beige or green upholstery; and Sun Bronze with maroon upholstery. Roadster colors were: Black with beige, red or green upholstery; Clipper Blue with beige upholstery; Almond Green with beige upholstery; Red with beige or red upholstery; and Ivory with red or green upholstery. These larger-engined models had a light blue 'Riley' diamond-shaped badge.

1-1/2 LITRE — FOUR — Only a four-door saloon was offered with the 1496-cc engine, which produced 55 horsepower. Though not considered to be officially marketed in the U.S., the smaller-engine Riley was included in sales brochures issued by some American dealers. Appearance was similar to the 2-1/2 Litre saloon, but on a shorter (112.5-inch) wheelbase and with a dark blue 'Riley' badge. Technical details, including the twin-cam engine construction, were similar to the larger model.

1950 Riley drophead four-passenger coupe.

I.D. DATA: Serial number plate is on the right front of the dashboard, under the hood; and/or on the chassis frame member, alongside the engine. Engine number is stamped on the block, adjacent to the starter; atop left side of bellhousing flange; or on a diamond-shaped plate on the left or right side of the block. Starting serial number: (1-1/2 Litre, beginning in late 1945) 10001; (2-1/2 Litre, starting in late 1946) 2000.

Model	Body Type & Seating	Engine Type/CID	P.O.E. Price	Weight (lbs.)	Prod. Total
2-1/2 LITRE					
	4-dr Saloon-5P	I4/149	3350	3220	Note 1
	2-dr Dhd Cpe-4/5P	I4/149	3600	3220	Note 1
	2-dr Spt Rds-3P	I4/149	3500	N/A	Note 1
1-1/2 LITRE					
	4-dr Saloon-5P	I4/91	Note 2	2716	Note 1

Note 1: Approximately 25 Rileys were sold in the U.S. in 1949, and 117 in 1950. A total of 502 drophead coupes and 507 roadsters were produced, from 1948 through 1951.

Note 2: Price at the factory in England was approximately $1999 for the 1-1/2 Litre saloon, and $2682 for the 2-1/2 Litre Sport Roadster.

ENGINE DATA: BASE FOUR (2-1/2 Litre): Inline, overhead-valve (twin-cam) four-cylinder. Cast iron block. **Displacement:** 149 cu. in. (2443 cc). **Bore & Stroke:** 3.169 x 4.725 in. (80.5 x 120 mm). **Compression Ratio:** 6.8:1. **Brake Horsepower:** 100 at 4500 rpm. **Torque:** 134 lbs.-ft. at 3000 rpm. Three main bearings. Solid valve lifters. Two SU H4 carburetors. 12-volt electrical system.

BASE FOUR (1-1/2 Litre): Inline, overhead-valve (twin-cam) four-cylinder. Cast iron block. **Displacement:** 91 cu. in. (1496 cc). **Bore & Stroke:** 2.72 x 3.94 in. (69 x 100 mm). **Compression Ratio:** 6.8:1. **Brake Horsepower:** 55 at 4500 rpm. **Torque:** 76 lbs.-ft. at 3000 rpm. Three main bearings. Solid valve lifters. One SU carburetor. 12-volt electrical system.

CHASSIS DATA: Wheelbase: (1.5-Litre) 112.5 in.; (2.5-Litre) 119 in. **Overall Length:** (1.5-Litre) 179 in.; (2.5-Litre) 186 in. **Height:** (1.5-Litre) 59 in.; (2.5-Litre) 59.5 in.; (Rds) 55 in.; (Dhd Cpe) 59 in. **Width:** 63.5 in.; (Rds) 66 in. **Front Tread:** 52.25 in. **Rear Tread:** 52.25 in. **Wheel Type:** 4.50x16 steel disc. **Standard Tires:** (1.5-Litre) Dunlop 5.75x16; (2.5-Litre) Dunlop 6.00x16.

TECHNICAL: Layout: front-engine, rear-drive. **Transmission:** four-speed manual; floor lever. Overall 2.5-Litre gear ratios: (1st) 15.0:1; (2nd) 8.86:1; (3rd) 5.83:1; (4th) 4.11:1; (rev) 15.0:1. Overall 1.5-Litre gear ratios: (1st) 19.42:1; (2nd) 11.2:1; (3rd) 7.23:1; (4th) 4.89:1; (rev) 19.42:1. **Standard Final Drive Ratio:** (2.5-Litre) 4.11:1; (1.5-Litre) 4.89:1. **Steering:** rack and pinion. **Suspension (front):** "Torsionic;" wishbones and long torsion bars. **Suspension (rear):** rigid axle with underslung semi-elliptic leaf springs. **Brakes:** Girling hydro-mechanical, front/rear drum. **Body Construction:** steel/aluminum body over hardwood framework, on box-section steel chassis.

MAJOR OPTIONS: "His Master's Voice" radio.

535

HISTORY: Riley's 1-1/2 Litre saloon was introduced late in 1945, the 2-1/2 Litre a year later. The Sports Roadster appeared in spring 1948, and the drophead coupe late in 1948. Production of the drophead coupe ceased during 1950, and the roadster in 1951. The 2-1/2 Litre saloon continued until the end of the 1953 model year, and the smaller saloon through 1954. When the roadster first appeared, no price at all was announced for the home market.

A sales brochure distributed by Falvey Sales & Service in Detroit promoted "The Riley Aces...for Magnificent Motoring." Both the 1-1/2 and 2-1/2 Litre models were featured. Other literature immodestly described the drophead as "another thoroughbred Riley of grace and power...swift and smooth-running. Built by men of creative genius."

PERFORMANCE: Top Speed: (2.5-Litre) 90-95 mph (but up to 100 mph claimed); (2.5-Litre Rds) 98 mph; (1.5-Litre) about 78 mph. **Acceleration (0-60 mph):** (2.5-Litre) 15.2-16.85 seconds; (2.5-Litre Rds) 19 seconds; (1.5-Litre) 25.1-31.8 seconds. **Acceleration (quarter-mile):** (2.5-Litre) 19.2-21.1 seconds (near 95 mph); (1.5-Litre) 23-24.3 seconds.

Manufacturer: Riley Motors Ltd. (Nuffield Exports Ltd.), Cowley, Oxford, England.

1951 Riley roadster.

2-1/2 LITRE — FOUR — No change was evident for the 1951 model year, except for a moderate price rise in the U.S. and an increase in brake size. Full-length front bumpers went on all Riley saloons for 1952, double bumpers at the rear. Hydro-mechanical brakes became full Girling hydraulics late in the 1952 model year. Standard colors for 1953 were: Black with beige, green or brown upholstery; Autumn Red with beige or maroon upholstery; Woodland Green with beige or green upholstery; and Silver Streak Grey with maroon upholstery.

1-1/2 LITRE — FOUR — Except for a few interior modifications, including the addition of a squarish instrument panel and recessed sunvisors in 1951, not much changed in the smaller Riley through 1953. Full-length front bumpers and double rear bumpers were added for 1952, followed by a switch to Girling hydraulic brakes.

I.D. DATA: Serial numbers are in same locations as 1948-50.

Model	Body Type & Seating	Engine Type/CID	P.O.E. Price	Weight (lbs.)	Prod. Total
2-1/2 LITRE					
	4-dr Saloon-5P	I4/149	3450	3214	Note 1
	2-dr Dhd Cpe-4/5P	I4/149	3700	3164	Note 1
	2-dr Spt Rds-3P	I4/149	3340	3164	Note 1
1-1/2 LITRE					
	4dr-Saloon-5P	I4/91	N/A	2716	Note 1

Note 1: Approximately 226 Rileys were sold in the U.S. in 1951, and 49 in 1952.
Model Note: Even though production of the drophead coupe and roadster ceased before 1952, both open models were still listed in U.S. directories, along with the saloon.

ENGINE DATA: Same as 1948-50.
CHASSIS DATA: Same as 1948-50.

TECHNICAL: Layout: front-engine, rear-drive. Transmission: four-speed manual; floor lever. Overall 2.5-Litre gear ratios: (1st) 15.0:1; (2nd) 8.86:1; (3rd) 5.83:1; (4th) 4.11:1; (rev) 15.0:1. Overall 1.5-Litre gear ratios: (1st) 19.42:1; (2nd) 11.2:1; (3rd) 7.23:1; (4th) 4.89:1; (rev) 19.42:1. **Standard Final Drive Ratio:** (2.5-Litre) 4.11:1; (1.5-Litre) 4.89:1; (later 1.5-Litre) 5.125:1. **Steering:** rack and pinion. **Suspension (front):** "Torsionic;" wishbones and long torsion bars. **Suspension (rear):** rigid axle with underslung semi-elliptic leaf springs. **Brakes:** Girling hydro-mechanical, front/rear drum; changed to Girling hydraulic late in 1952. **Body Construction:** steel/aluminum body over hardwood framework, on box-section steel chassis.

Note: Revised gear ratios were announced for 1953. Overall 2.5-Litre ratios: (1st) 14.9:1; (2nd) 8.84:1; (3rd) 5.8:1; (4th) 4.1:1; (rev) 14.9:1. Overall 1.5-Litre ratios: (1st) 20.7:1; (2nd) 11.7:1; (3rd) 7.585:1; (4th) 5.125:1; (rev) 20.4:1.

MAJOR OPTIONS: "His Master's Voice" radio.
PERFORMANCE: Similar to 1948-50.
Manufacturer: Riley Motors Ltd. (Nuffield Exports Ltd.), Cowley, Oxford, England.

HISTORY: Production of the roadster ceased during 1951. Corporate literature for all three models promised 100-mph speed from the 2-1/2 Litre, with the thrill of sports car performance. A Riley, it added, "can be all things to all men. Its proverbial high speed, exceptional roadholding, and safe braking make it a thrill to drive. Its fine styling makes it a thrill to own. " Ads in 1953 by J.S. Inskip Inc. in New York City promised "the touring car with sports car performance," quoting a price of $3700. The 2-1/2 Litre, they went on, was "For the man who wants an automobile that performs like a racer yet has the refinements of a luxury, all-purpose car." Ads further noted Riley's "remarkable successes in the most competitive events all over the world, including Monte Carlo Rallies and Alpine Trials." In 1952, British Motor Corp. (BMC) was formed by the merger of Austin and Morris (including Riley).

1954 Riley 2½-liter Pathfinder four-door sedan.

PATHFINDER — FOUR — Riley's replacement for the 2-1/2 Litre saloon wore a rounded, all-steel, full-width modern body. Headlamps were now mounted in the conventional position on front fenders, but the vertical-bar grille was similar to that on prior models. A wide curved one-piece windshield was installed, matched by a curved back window, and doors were hinged at the front. Grille and hood lifted as a single counterbalanced unit. Under the hood was the same 2443-cc twin-cam four-cylinder engine that powered the former model, developing 102 horsepower at first (then 110 bhp). This would be the last model powered by a Riley engine. Riley's "Torsionic" front suspension also continued, but the rear end now used coil springs and torque arms rather than leafs. Servo-assisted Girling hydraulic brakes used 12-inch drums. Between-the-axles seating was provided for five or six people.

A cam-gear arrangement replaced the former rack-and-pinion steering. The floor-mounted gearshift lever was on the left side of the driver (for left-hand-drive models), to permit unrestricted entry into the car from either side. Choices included fully adjustable individual front seats or a bench seat with wide center armrest, both upholstered in leather. A polished walnut facia contained instruments illuminated by black light. Standard equipment included two flush-fitting foglights, backup lights, two-speed wiper/washers, twin wind-tone horns, tachometer, a map reading light, two sunvisors (one with vanity mirror), and full-width bumpers with overriders. Standard colors were: Black with maroon, green or biscuit upholstery; Maroon with biscuit or maroon upholstery; Green with biscuit or green upholstery; Blue with grey upholstery; and Grey with maroon or grey upholstery. Initial models had 6.70x16 tires, but switched to 6.00x16 size late in 1954. A central jacking system also was added at that time. For the 1956 model year, the clutch was operated hydraulically and overdrive became available. In addition, painted lines replaced the former chrome side strips. A larger glovebox stood above a map pocket.

1-1/2 LITRE — FOUR — Production of the smaller-engined Riley continued through 1954, with a moderate restyling of its traditional-look body. Parking lights were now faired into the front fenders and foglights recessed in the fender valances. Running boards were eliminated. The "greatly improved" body held adjustable front bucket seats and a rear seat with folding center armrest. Seat cushions were leather-covered. New colors were: Black with maroon, green or biscuit upholstery; Maroon with maroon or biscuit upholstery; Green with green or biscuit upholstery; Blue with grey upholstery; Grey with rust, maroon or green upholstery; and Ivory with rust or maroon upholstery. A new 1.5-liter Riley would not arrive until the One-Point-Five, late in 1957.

I.D. DATA: Pathfinder serial/engine number plate is on the firewall, above the battery. Starting serial number: (Pathfinder) RMH/500.

Model	Body Type & Seating	Engine Type/CID	P.O.E. Price	Weight (lbs.)	Prod. Total
PATHFINDER					
	4-dr Saloon-5/6P	I4/149	3970	3280	N/A
1-1/2 LITER					
	4-dr Saloon-4/5P	I4/91	Note 1	2768	N/A

Note 1: Price at factory was about $2390.
Weight Note: Figures shown are "dry" weight. Pathfinder "curb" weight was 3,426 pounds; 1-1/2 Liter was 2,928 pounds.

ENGINE DATA: BASE FOUR (Pathfinder): Inline, overhead-valve (twin-cam) four-cylinder. Cast iron block. **Displacement:** 149 cu. in. (2443 cc). **Bore & Stroke:** 3.169 x 4.725 in. (80.5 x 120 mm). **Compression Ratio:** 6.8:1 (later, 7.25:1). **Brake Horsepower:** 102 at 4400 rpm (later, 110 at 4400). Three main bearings. Solid valve lifters. Two SU carburetors. 12-volt electrical system.

BASE FOUR (1-1/2 Litre): Inline, overhead-valve (twin-cam) four-cylinder. Cast iron block. **Displacement:** 91 cu. in. (1496 cc). **Bore & Stroke:** 2.72 x 3.94 in. (69 x 100 mm). **Compression Ratio:** 6.8:1. **Brake Horsepower:** 55 at 4500 rpm. **Torque:** 76 lbs.-ft. at 3000 rpm. Three main bearings. Solid valve lifters. One SU carburetor. 12-volt electrical system.

1955 Riley RMe 1½-liter sports saloon. (Sotheby's)

CHASSIS DATA: Wheelbase: (Pathfinder) 113.5 in.; (1.5-Litre) 112.5 in. **Overall Length:** (Pathfinder) 183 in.; (1.5-Litre) 179 in. **Height:** (Pathfinder) 60 in.; (1.5-Litre) 61 in. **Width:** (Pathfinder) 67 in.; (1.5-Litre) 63.5 in. **Front Tread:** (Pathfinder) 54.5 in; (1.5-Litre) 52.25 in. **Rear Tread:** (Pathfinder) 54.5 in.; (1.5-Litre) 52.26 in. **Wheel Type:** five-stud disc. **Standard Tires:** (Pathfinder) 6.70x16 (later, 6.00x16); (1.5-Litre) 5.75x16.

TECHNICAL: Layout: front-engine, rear-drive. **Transmission:** four-speed manual; floor lever. Overall Pathfinder gear ratios: (1st) 13.59:1; (2nd) 8.446:1; (3rd) 5.88:1; (4th) 4.1:1; (rev) 18.42:1. Overall 1.5-Litre gear ratios: (1st) 20.372:1; (2nd) 11.736:1; (3rd) 7.585:1; (4th) 5.125:1; (rev) 20.372:1. **Standard Final Drive Ratio:** (Pathfinder) 4.1:1; (1.5-Litre) 5.125:1. **Steering:** (Pathfinder) cam-type; (1.5-Litre) rack-and-pinion. **Suspension (front):** "Torsionic;" wishbones and torsion bars. **Suspension (rear):** (Pathfinder) rigid axle with long coil springs, torque arms and anti-sway bar; (1.5-Litre) semi-elliptic leaf springs. **Brakes:** Girling hydraulic, front/rear drum. **Body Construction:** all-steel body on box-section steel chassis.

MAJOR OPTIONS: "His Master's Voice" radio. Borg-Warner overdrive (1956 Pathfinder)

PERFORMANCE: Top Speed: (Pathfinder) 100 mph. **Acceleration (0-60 mph):** (Pathfinder) about 17 seconds. **Acceleration (quarter-mile):** (Pathfinder) 20.8 seconds. **Fuel Mileage:** (Pathfinder) about 18 mpg.

Manufacturer: Riley Motors Ltd. (Nuffield Exports Ltd.), Cowley, Oxford, England (part of British Motor Corp.).

HISTORY: Production of the original 1-1/2 Litre saloon ceased in 1955, while the Pathfinder began in late 1953 and continued through 1956.

1957 RILEY

PATHFINDER — FOUR — For the final few months of its existence, the Pathfinder switched from rear coil springs to semi-elliptic leaf rear springs. Production continued until January 1957.

TWO-POINT-SIX — SIX — By summer 1957, a six-cylinder Riley was available for sale, similar in appearance to the already-extinct Pathfinder except for small round parking and signal lights below the slightly shrouded headlamps. Large auxiliary lamps were positioned above the bumper overriders. A thick, bright surround molding enclosed the familiar vertical-bar grille, now more upright in profile, and which no longer contained a dummy filler cap. The hood top and grille no longer lifted as a unit. Beneath that hood, the new engine was an ordinary BMC C-series overhead-valve design, far removed from the long-lived twin-cam Riley configuration. The same basic engine was found in the Austin A95/105, Morris Isis, and Wolseley Six-Ninety. Displacement wasn't much larger than the former four, at 2639 cc (161 cubic inches). Rear-axle ratio was 3.9:1 (versus 4.1:1 for the Pathfinder). Both a Borg-Warner overdrive unit (operating in third and fourth gears) and a fully automatic B-W transmission were available as options. Up front were splayed telescopic shock absorbers and converging torsion bars; at the rear, rubber-insulated leaf springs. Standard equipment included leather upholstery (leather-cloth on non-wearing parts), bucket or bench front seats, a three-passenger rear seat with folding center armrest, tachometer, locking glovebox, two sunvisors, windshield washer, foglight, and map reading light. Full-width bumpers came equipped with over-riders. Inside was a polished walnut wood facia with leather-covered sponge-rubber protection rail, plus polished wood door cappings and surrounds. Round instruments had white-on-black dials.

"Created by enthusiasts...for enthusiasts," said the Riley sales brochure for the new model, though latter-day enthusiasts would bemoan the loss of the familiar engine and distinctive qualities as the BMC influence grew. Standard Two-Point-Six body colors were: Black with either two-color green upholstery and green carpet, two-color maroon upholstery and maroon carpet, or biscuit and brown upholstery and maroon carpet; Basilica Blue and Teal Blue with two-color grey upholstery and blue carpet; Shannon Green and Leaf Green with either two-color green upholstery and green carpet or biscuit and brown upholstery and green carpet; Charcoal Grey and Frilford Grey; Maroon and Kashmir Beige; Black and Frilford Grey; and, finally, Black and Chartreuse Yellow. Those final four combinations came with a choice of upholstery colors.

I.D. DATA: Pathfinder serial/engine number plate is on the firewall, above the battery. Two-Point-Six serial number plate is on the right side of the firewall, and its engine number is on the side of the crankcase. Starting serial number: (Two-Point-Six) 501.

Model	Body Type & Seating	Engine Type/CID	P.O.E. Price	Weight (lbs.)	Prod. Total
PATHFINDER					
	4-dr Saloon-5/6P	I4/149	3970	3280	N/A
TWO-POINT-SIX					
	4-dr Saloon-5/6P	I6/161	N/A	3505	N/A

ENGINE DATA: BASE FOUR (Pathfinder): Inline, overhead-valve (twin-cam) four-cylinder. Cast iron block. **Displacement:** 149 cu. in. (2443 cc). **Bore & Stroke:** 3.169 x 4.725 in. (80.5 x 120 mm). **Compression Ratio:** 7.25:1. **Brake Horsepower:** 110 at 4400 rpm. Three main bearings. Solid valve lifters. Two SU carburetors. 12-volt electrical system.

BASE SIX (Two-Point-Six): Inline, overhead-valve six-cylinder (BMC C-series). Cast iron block. **Displacement:** 161 cu. in. (2639 cc). **Bore & Stroke:** 3.125 x 3.50 in. (79.4 x 88.9 mm). **Compression Ratio:** 8.3:1. **Brake Horsepower:** 101 at 4750 rpm. **Torque:** 141.5 lbs.-ft. at 2500 rpm. Four main bearings. Solid valve lifters. Two SU H4 carburetors. 12-volt electrical system.

CHASSIS DATA: Wheelbase: 113.5 in. **Overall Length:** (Pathfinder) 183 in.; (Two-Point-Six) 185.5 in. **Height:** (Pathfinder) 60 in.; (Two-Point-Six) 61 in. **Width:** 67 in. **Front Tread:** 54.5 in. **Rear Tread:** 54.5 in. **Wheel Type:** five-stud disc. **Standard Tires:** (Pathfinder) 6.00x16; (Two-Point-Six) Dunlop 6.70x15.

TECHNICAL: Layout: front-engine, rear-drive. **Transmission:** four-speed manual; floor lever. Overall Two-Point-Six gear ratios: (1st) 12.93:1; (2nd) 8.03:1; (3rd) 5.60:1; (4th) 3.90:1; (rev) 17.52:1. **Standard Final Drive Ratio:** (Two-Point-Six) 3.90:1; (Pathfinder) 4.1:1. **Steering:** cam and lever. **Suspension (front):** (Pathfinder) "Torsionic" wishbones and torsion bars; (Two-Point-Six) wishbones and torsion bars, with vernier adjustment. **Suspension (rear):** rigid axle with semi-elliptic leaf springs. **Brakes:** (Two-Point-Six) Lockheed hydraulic, front/rear drum with vacuum servo assist. **Body Construction:** all-steel body on box-section steel chassis.

MAJOR OPTIONS: Automatic transmission. Overdrive. Radio.

PERFORMANCE: Top Speed: (Pathfinder) 100 mph; (Two-Point-Six) about 100 mph. **Acceleration (0-60 mph):** (Pathfinder) about 17 seconds. **Acceleration (quarter-mile):** (Pathfinder) 20.8 seconds; (Two-Point-Six) 20.6 seconds. **Fuel Mileage:** (Pathfinder) about 18 mpg.

Manufacturer: Riley Motors Ltd. (Nuffield Exports Ltd.), Cowley, Oxford, England (part of British Motor Corp.).

1958 RILEY

1958 Riley 1.5 saloon.

ONE-POINT-FIVE — FOUR — After an absence of several years, a 1.5-liter Riley again became available, this time on a short (86-inch) wheelbase. Sales literature described the new One-Point-Five as a "family four-seater of outstanding comfort and flashing performance." Basic structure and engine were the same as the Wolseley 1500, but Riley's version was more powerful. This was the first Riley to use unibody construction. Its vertical-bar grille was similar to other Riley models, with a thick bright surround molding, but displayed a more curved shape. Unadorned side grille openings extended outward from the lower portion of that center grille, below a bright curved molding. At the base level, just above the bumper, was a full-width grille trim strip with five horizontal bars, which contained round and nearly-rectangular parking and signal lights as it wrapped around the front fenders. Below the partial-length horizontal bodyside trim strip, above the front wheel opening, was 'Riley One-Point-Five' script. Both front and rear doors contained vent wings. Inside "the lively One-Point-Five" was a polished walnut wood dashboard panel that included a tachometer, and upholstery in two shades of leather. Rack and pinion steering was used, as in the earlier 1.5-liter model. The BMC B-series overhead-valve four-cylinder engine with dual carburetors displaced 1489 cc (90.88 cu-

bic inches) and produced 68 horsepower. Standard equipment included a heater, bucket seats, twin sunvisors, windshield washer, and twin wind-tone horns. A radio was optional.

TWO-POINT-SIX — SIX — Introduced late in the 1957 model year, the six-cylinder Riley continued with little change. Both an automatic transmission and overdrive were available. Leather/leathercloth upholstery covered the bucket or bench-type front seats. Standard body colors were: Black, Basilica Blue, Yukon Grey, Maroon, Shannon Green, Basilica Blue with Florentine Blue, Black with Birch Grey, Maroon with Kashmir Beige, Shannon Green with Leaf Green, and Yukon Grey with Birch Grey.

I.D. DATA: Serial/engine number plate is on the firewall, above the battery. One-Point-Five engine number is on the side of the block, below No. 2 and 3 spark plugs; Two-Point Six, on the side of the crankcase. Starting serial number: (One-Point-Five) 501.

Model	Body Type & Seating	Engine Type/CID	P.O.E. Price	Weight (lbs.)	Prod. Total
ONE-POINT-FIVE					
	4-dr Saloon-4P	I4/91	N/A	2060	N/A
TWO-POINT-SIX					
	4-dr Saloon-5/6P	I6/161	N/A	3505	N/A

ENGINE DATA: BASE FOUR (One-Point-Five): Inline, overhead-valve four-cylinder (BMC B-series). Cast iron block. **Displacement:** 90.88 cu. in. (1489 cc). **Bore & Stroke:** 2.875 x 3.50 in. (73 x 88.9 mm). **Compression Ratio:** 8.3:1. **Brake Horsepower:** 68 at 5400 rpm. Solid valve lifters. Two SU carburetors. 12-volt electrical system.

BASE SIX (Two-Point-Six): Inline, overhead-valve six-cylinder (BMC C-series). Cast iron block. **Displacement:** 161 cu. in. (2639 cc). **Bore & Stroke:** 3.125 x 3.50 in. (79.4 x 88.9 mm). **Compression Ratio:** 8.3:1. **Brake Horsepower:** 101 at 4500 rpm. **Torque:** 141.5 lbs.-ft. at 2500 rpm. Four main bearings. Solid valve lifters. Two SU H4 carburetors. 12-volt electrical system.

CHASSIS DATA: Wheelbase: (One-Point-Five) 86 in.; (Two-Point-Six) 113.5 in. **Overall Length:** (One-Point-Five) 153 in.; (Two-Point-Six) 185.5 in. **Height:** (One-Point-Five) 60 in.; (Two-Point-Six) 61 in. **Width:** (One-Point-Five) 61 in.; (Two-Point-Six) 67 in. **Front Tread:** (One-Point-Five) 50.9 in.; (Two-Point-Six) 54.4 in. **Rear Tread:** (One-Point-Five) 50.3 in.; (Two-Point-Six) 54.5 in. **Wheel Type:** disc. **Standard Tires:** (One-Point-Five) Dunlop 5.00x14; (Two-Point-Six) Dunlop 6.70x15.

TECHNICAL: Layout: front-engine, rear-drive. **Transmission:** four-speed manual; floor lever. **Standard Final Drive Ratio:** (One-Point-Five) 3.73:1; (Two-Point-Six) 3.90:1. **Steering:** (One-Point-Five) rack and pinion; (Two-Point-Six) cam and lever. **Suspension (front):** wishbones and torsion bars, with vernier adjustment. **Suspension (rear):** rigid axle with semi-elliptic leaf springs. **Brakes:** (One-Point-Five) Girling hydraulic, front/rear drum; (Two-Point-Six) Lockheed hydraulic, front/rear drum. **Body Construction:** (One-Point-Five) steel unibody; (Two-Point-Six) all-steel body on box-section steel chassis. **Fuel Tank:** (One-Point-Five) 8.4 U.S. gallons; (Two-Point-Six) 15.5 U.S. gallons.

MAJOR OPTIONS: TWO-POINT-SIX OPTIONS: Automatic transmission. Overdrive. Radio (also available in One-Point-Five).

PERFORMANCE: Top Speed: (One-Point-Five) 90 mph; (Two-Point-Six) about 100 mph. **Acceleration (0-60 mph):** (One-Point-Five) about 18 seconds (0-50 mph in 13 seconds); (Two-Point-Six) N/A (0-50 mph in 11.8 seconds). **Acceleration (quarter-mile):** (One-Point-Five) 21.1 seconds; (Two-Point-Six) 20.6 seconds. **Fuel Mileage:** (One-Point-Five) about 27-30 mpg; (Two-Point-Six) about 25 mpg.

Manufacturer: Riley Motors Ltd. (Nuffield Exports Ltd.), Cowley, Oxford, England (part of British Motor Corp.).

HISTORY: Production of the Two-Point-Six halted by spring 1959, for a total life of less than two years. The One-Point-Five, introduced late in 1957, enjoyed a longer existence that stretched into 1965. "In the tradition of the famous Riley Nine," claimed the Riley sales brochure of the new One-Point-Five, "but brilliantly modern from stem to stern."

1959-61 RILEY

ONE-POINT-FIVE — FOUR — Production of the four-cylinder Riley continued with little change, except for a switch from 5.00x14 to 5.60x14 tires during the 1959 model year.

TWO-POINT-SIX — SIX — Production of the six-cylinder model continued only into spring 1959.

4/SIXTY EIGHT — FOUR — A new "Farina" four-cylinder model joined the One-Point-Five during the 1959 model year. Front-end appearance was similar to its four-cylinder mate, except that the vertical-bar grille was closer to square in shape, with a slight "vee" in the upper bar. Directly above that bar stood a diamond-shaped Riley emblem. No air-intake openings were evident above the full-width wraparound "grille" element, made up of horizontal bars that contained the park/signal lights. In profile, the 4/Sixty Eight had a more squarish appearance, with taillfins at the rear and a low hoodline. Instead of the customary torsion bars, this model used coil springs up front. Though powered by a BMC B-series four-cylinder engine, similar to that in the MG Magnette III, the 4/Sixty Eight actually was intended more as a replacement for the larger six-cylinder Riley.

I.D. DATA: Serial/engine number plate is on the firewall, above the battery; or on a plate attached to driver's door post. One-Point-Five and 4/Sixty Eight engine numbers are on the side of the block, below No. 2 and 3 spark plugs; Two-Point Six, on the side of the crankcase. Starting serial number: (4/Sixty Eight) R/HS1.101.

Model	Body Type & Seating	Engine Type/CID	P.O.E. Price	Weight (lbs.)	Prod. Total
ONE-POINT-FIVE					
	4-dr Saloon-4P	I4/91	2316	2060	Note 1
4/SIXTY EIGHT					
	4-dr Saloon-4/5P	I4/91	N/A	2480	Note 1
TWO-POINT-SIX					
	4-dr Saloon-5/6P	I6/161	N/A	3505	Note 1

Note 1: Approximately 7,000 Rileys were produced in 1961.

ENGINE DATA: BASE FOUR (One-Point-Five, 4/Sixty Eight): Inline, overhead-valve four-cylinder (BMC B-series). Cast iron block. **Displacement:** 90.88 cu. in. (1489 cc). **Bore & Stroke:** 2.875 x 3.50 in. (73 x 88.9 mm). **Compression Ratio:** 8.3:1. **Brake Horsepower:** 68 at 5400 rpm (4/Sixty Eight, 66.5 bhp). **Torque:** 83 lbs.-ft. at 3200 rpm. Solid valve lifters. Two SU carburetors. 12-volt electrical system.

BASE SIX (Two-Point-Six): Inline, overhead-valve six-cylinder (BMC C-series). Cast iron block. **Displacement:** 161 cu. in. (2639 cc). **Bore & Stroke:** 3.125 x 3.50 in. (79.4 x 88.9 mm). **Compression Ratio:** 8.3:1. **Brake Horsepower:** 101 at 4500 rpm. **Torque:** 141.5 lbs.-ft. at 2500 rpm. Four main bearings. Solid valve lifters. Two SU H4 carburetors. 12-volt electrical system.

CHASSIS DATA: Wheelbase: (One-Point-Five) 86 in.; (4/Sixty Eight) 99 in.; (Two-Point-Six) 113.5 in. **Overall Length:** (One-Point-Five) 153 in.; (4/Sixty Eight) 178 in.; (Two-Point-Six) 185.5 in. **Height:** (One-Point-Five) 60 in.; (4/Sixty Eight) 59.8 in.; (Two-Point-Six) 61 in. **Width:** (One-Point-Five) 61 in.; (4/Sixty Eight) 63.5 in.; (Two-Point-Six) 67 in. **Front Tread:** (One-Point-Five) 50.9 in.; (Two-Point-Six) 54.4 in. **Rear Tread:** (One-Point-Five) 50.3 in.; (Two-Point-Six) 54.5 in. **Wheel Type:** disc. **Standard Tires:** (One-Point-Five) 5.60x14; (4/Sixty Eight) 5.90x14 in.; (Two-Point-Six) Dunlop 6.70x15.

TECHNICAL: Layout: front-engine, rear-drive. **Transmission:** four-speed manual; floor lever. **Standard Final Drive Ratio:** (One-Point-Five) 3.73:1; (4/Sixty Eight) 4.3:1; (Two-Point-Six) 3.90:1. **Steering:** (One-Point-Five) rack and pinion; (Two-Point-Six) cam and lever. **Suspension (front):** wishbones and torsion bars, with vernier adjustment except (4/Sixty Eight) coil springs. **Suspension (rear):** rigid axle with semi-elliptic leaf springs. **Brakes:** (One-Point-Five) Girling hydraulic, front/rear drum; (Two-Point-Six) Lockheed hydraulic, front/rear drum. **Body Construction:** (One-Point-Five and 4/Sixty Eight) steel unibody; (Two-Point-Six) all-steel body on box-section steel chassis. **Fuel Tank:** (One-Point-Five) 8.4 U.S. gallons; (Two-Point-Six) 15.5 U.S. gallons.

MAJOR OPTIONS: TWO-POINT-SIX OPTIONS: Automatic transmission. Overdrive. Radio.

PERFORMANCE: Top Speed: (One-Point-Five) 85+ mph; (4-Sixty Eight) 88 mph; (Two-Point-Six) 100 mph. **Acceleration (0-60 mph):** (One-Point-Five) about 18 seconds; (4/Sixty Eight) N/A (0-50 mph in 12.9 seconds). **Acceleration (quarter-mile):** (One-Point-Five) 21.1 seconds; (4/Sixty Eight) 21.2 seconds; (Two-Point-Six) 20.6 seconds. **Fuel Mileage:** (One-Point-Five) about 27-30 mpg; (Two-Point-Six) about 25 mpg.

Manufacturer: Riley Motors Ltd. (Nuffield Exports Ltd.), Cowley, Oxford, England (part of British Motor Corp.).

HISTORY: Production of the Two-Point-Six halted in spring 1959, after less than two years on the market. The One-Point-Five remained on the Riley list into 1965.

1962-63 RILEY

1962 Riley 1.5 saloon.

ONE-POINT-FIVE — FOUR — Production continued into 1965, with no major changes. Sales literature for 1962 described this sports saloon as offering "All the luxury of a superbly appointed limousine. All the pep and pace of a thoroughbred sports car."

4/SEVENTY TWO — FOUR — Similar in appearance and structure to the 4/Sixty Eight, its replacement had a larger (1622-cc) four-cylinder engine with twin carburetors and was available with automatic transmission. Longer in both wheelbase and track dimensions, it had anti-roll and stabilizer bars for the front and rear suspensions.

ELF — I — FOUR — Introduced at the same time as the 4/Seventy Two was the first of a series of Rileys based on the new front-drive Austin/Morris Mini. Differing mainly in its notchback body profile and plusher interior, the Elf was described as "The world's first baby car to offer big-car luxury in the true RILEY tradition." Elf I, produced until 1963, had an 848-cc four-cylinder engine and was capable of over 70 mph. Elfs had diamond-shape Riley badges at the top of the grille, which carried on the familiar vertical-bar look, albeit in shrunken form. Alongside the center grille were twin side grilles, with horizontal bars that reached outward to the parking lights.

I.D. DATA: Serial numbers are in same locations as 1959-61.

Model	Body Type & Seating	Engine Type/CID	P.O.E. Price	Weight (lbs.)	Prod. Total
ONE-POINT-FIVE					
	4-dr Saloon-4P	I4/91	N/A	2100	Note 1
4/SEVENTY TWO					
	4-dr Saloon-4/5P	I4/99	N/A	2515	Note 1
ELF					
I	2-dr Saloon-4P	I4/52	N/A	1342	Note 1

Note 1: Approximately 9,000 Rileys were produced in 1962, and 17,000 in 1963.

ENGINE DATA: BASE FOUR (One-Point-Five): Inline, overhead-valve four-cylinder (BMC B-series). Cast iron block. **Displacement:** 90.88 cu. in. (1489 cc). **Bore & Stroke:** 2.875 x 3.50 in. (73 x 88.9 mm). **Compression Ratio:** 8.3:1. **Brake Horsepower:** 63.5 at 5000 rpm. Solid valve lifters. Two SU carburetors. 12-volt electrical system.

BASE FOUR (4/Seventy Two): Same as above, except — **Displacement:** 98.9 cu. in. (1622 cc). **Bore & Stroke:** 3.00 x 3.50 in. (76.2 x 88.9 mm). **Compression Ratio:** 8.3:1. **Brake Horsepower:** 68 at 5000 rpm.

BASE FOUR (Elf): Inline, overhead-valve four-cylinder. Cast iron block. **Displacement:** 51.7 cu. in. (848 cc). **Bore & Stroke:** 2.48 x 2.69 in. (62.9 x 68.3 mm). **Compression Ratio:** 8.3:1. **Brake Horsepower:** 37 at 5500 rpm. Solid valve lifters. SU carburetor. 12-volt electrical system.

CHASSIS DATA: Wheelbase: (One-Point-Five) 86 in.; (4/Seventy Two) 100.25 in.; (Elf) 80 in. **Overall Length:** (One-Point-Five) 153 in.; (4/Seventy Two) 178 in.; (Elf) 128.75 in. **Height:** (One-Point-Five) 59.75 in.; (4/Seventy Two) 59.75 in.; (Elf) 53 in. **Width:** (One-Point-Five) 61 in.; (4/Seventy Two) 63.5 in.; (Elf) 55.5 in. **Front Tread:** (One-Point-Five) 50.9 in.; (4/Seventy Two) 50.6 in.; (Elf) 47.4 in. **Rear Tread:** (One-Point-Five) 50.3 in.; (4/Seventy Two) 51.9 in.; (Elf) 45.9 in. **Wheel Type:** disc.

TECHNICAL: Layout: front-engine, rear-drive except (Elf) front-drive. **Transmission:** four-speed manual; floor lever. **Standard Final Drive Ratio:** (One-Point-Five) 3.73:1; (4/Seventy Two) 4.3:1; (Elf) 3.765:1. **Suspension (front):** (One-Point-Five) wishbones and torsion bars; (4/Seventy Two) wishbones and coil springs; (Elf) independent rubber cone springs. **Suspension (rear):** rigid axle with semi-elliptic leaf springs except (Elf) independent rubber cone springs. **Brakes:** hydraulic, front/rear drum.

MAJOR OPTIONS: Automatic transmission (4/Seventy Two).

Manufacturer: Riley Motors Ltd. (Nuffield Exports Ltd.), Cowley, Oxford, England (part of British Motor Corp.).

HISTORY: Both the 4/Seventy Two and Elf were introduced late in 1961, for the 1962 model year.

POSTSCRIPT: Through the 1960s, Riley identity submerged even farther into the BMC mold, continuing to serve largely as upscale clones of models produced under the MG, Wolseley and Austin badges. During 1963, the Elf II engine grew to 998 cc. Engine size remained the same for the Mk III Elf, built from 1966 to 1969, but that one adopted BMC's Hydrolastic suspension.

Another series that arrived in 1965, named Kestrel (a famous Riley model of the 1930s), was actually a clone of the front-drive MG 1100 sedan. Its original 1098-cc engine grew to 1275 as the name changed to 1300 in 1967. A horsepower increase sent the Kestrel 1300 into a second series for 1968-69, after which the Riley name disappeared forever. All Kestrel models had the Hydrolastic suspension. For additional details on these 1960s Riley models, see the related British Motor Corp. (BMC) listings in this Catalog.

ROLLS-ROYCE

As the name implies, Rolls-Royce came into existence as a result of the efforts of two men: Charles Stewart Rolls and Frederick Henry Royce. While Rolls was a member of the British aristocracy, Royce came from a working-class background.

Royce, the son of an impoverished miller, started work as a newspaper vendor and then, in 1877, became an apprentice at the Great Northern Railway Locomotive Works. In 1880, having gained considerable knowledge of engineering basics (but never finishing the apprenticeship), Royce went to work at a machine tool firm in Leeds; and then to a London electric-light company. Not yet 20 years of age, he then moved to Liverpool and a post as technical advisor to the Lancashire Maxim and Western Electric Company. Within three years, he was in business for himself (with a partner), producing electrical devices.

Not until 1903 did fate turn to automotive endeavors, when he purchased a secondhand Decauville motorcar. Displeased with its unreliability, and tiring of tinkering with its mechanical and electrical components, he quickly announced his intention to produce an automobile himself. Soon afterward, in the spring of 1904, the first Royce automobile came into existence. The 1.8-liter, two-cylinder engine had an F-head (intake-over-exhaust) configuration and was notable for its near-silent running.

Charles Rolls, meanwhile, obtained a degree in Mechanical Engineering and Applied Sciences at Cambridge University. While at the university, he took an interest in the motorcar industry and purchased a Peugeot—the first automobile of any kind to appear on the campus. By graduation time, Rolls had become one of the most skilled drivers in England. He won a 1000-mile reliability trial and, in 1903, set a world land-speed record at the wheel of an 80-horsepower Mors, reaching 93 mph. By that time, Rolls was in the motorcar sales business under the name C.S. Rolls and Company, dealing in expensive foreign-built automobiles.

Rolls wanted his name to be associated with the finest motorcar available, and set out to find such a vehicle in the British marketplace. Informed by a Royce Ltd. stockholder about the recently-debuted Royce automobile, he was at first uncertain of its qualities, but elected to take a closer look. As soon as he took the wheel, Rolls became a convert, later claiming, according to the company history, that Royce "was the man I have been looking for for years." Rolls quickly obtained rights to sell all the Royce motorcars that could be produced.

At the Paris Salon in December 1904, two complete Royce cars were displayed, along with several chassis and engines. Days later, an agreement between the two companies stipulated that the motorcars would henceforth be named "Rolls-Royce." In 1906, Rolls-Royce Ltd. was formed. Late in that year, the first Rolls-Royce arrived in America. From the beginning until the outbreak of World War II in 1939, Rolls-Royce produced only chassis, with coachbuilders creating bodies to suit specific customers.

Early models had two, three, four or six cylinders, but none proved too popular. Only three Royce models and 16 Rolls-Royces were built.

Then came their first major joint creation, introduced at the Olympia Show in London in 1906 and available for the following year: the 40/50 HP, which soon became known as Silver Ghost and was the first Rolls-Royce billed as "best car in the world." The Silver Ghost actually was applied to the thirteenth chassis built, which wore an aluminum-finished 4/5-seat touring body and carried silver-plated lights and fittings. Autocar reported that the 40/50 engine "might be a silent sewing machine [offering] no realisation of driving propulsion; the feeling as the passenger sits either at the front or back of the vehicle is one of being wafted through the landscape." One of the first examples traveled 2,000 miles in the Scottish Reliability Trial, then trekked 14,371 miles to set a new long-distance record.

As destiny would have it, Charles Rolls never lived to see the car that bore his name develop into the "best in the world." He died in 1910, as the result of an aircraft accident. Henry Royce became ill shortly afterward, and was warned by doctors to stay away from the plant; but he remained in touch with operations from home, until his death in 1933.

Over the years, the traditional Rolls-Royce grille would grow larger, but the basic design never changed. The only exception is that when Sir Henry Royce died in 1933, the

monogram changed from red to black. The mascot atop the radiator was created in 1911 by Sir Charles Sykes, and known as The Silver Lady, or The Spirit of Effortless Flight.

During World War I, Rolls-Royce 40/50 HP motorcars served as ambulances and staff cars—even as armored vehicles. Some were used by T.E. Lawrence, who gained fame as "Lawrence of Arabia." The company also became widely known for production of aircraft engines, first of Renault (V-8) design, but then a V-12 that was wholly Rolls-Royce.

Of the 7,870 Silver Ghosts produced from 1907 to 1925, a surprising 1,700 were built in America, at Springfield, Massachusetts. By 1931, however, U.S. production came to a halt as customers expressed a lack of interest in Rolls-Royces that weren't exported from Britain. Both long- and short-wheelbase versions of the Silver Ghost were built.

From 1922 to 1929, the company also produced a "baby Rolls-Royce," the 20 HP. Greeted with some scorn by purists, the "20" (Twenty) achieved considerable popularity, permitting ownership of a Rolls-Royce by people who'd formerly been unable to consider one, or who didn't care for the larger dimensions of the "standard" models. A total of 2,940 were built, and elements of its engine design would remain evident through the 1950s, when the six-cylinder powerplant finally disappeared. Starting with the Twenty, Rolls-Royce took to recommending bodies built by specific firms, rather than strictly supplying the chassis alone. Creating such bodies in modest quantities rather than individually helped keep prices more reasonable. By this time, too, more mechanical and electrical components were purchased from outside suppliers, whereas in the early days Rolls-Royce had generally produced its own.

The next "big" Rolls-Royce was the Phantom I, introduced in 1925 to replace the Silver Ghost. This one used an overhead-valve engine. A total of 3,437 were produced (plus 1,225 in the U.S. plant) before it was replaced by the Phantom II. Most British Phantom I bodies were supplied by Hooper, Barker and Windovers, while the American firm of Brewster did like service for the American editions. A total of 1,672 Phantom IIs were built (all in Britain) from 1929 to 1935. That total included a number of "Continental" models, which rode a shorter chassis.

Evolution also came to the 20 HP, which was replaced in 1929 by the 20/25 HP with a larger-displacement engine. A 20/25 could hit 77 mph or so, and with the increased power could handle heavier bodies. A total of 3,827 were built, into 1936.

In 1931, Rolls-Royce acquired the Bentley company, founded by W.O. Bentley, which had fallen into receivership. Two years later came the first Bentley produced under the new ownership: the 3-1/2 liter "Silent Sports Car," powered by a modification of the Rolls-Royce 20/25 engine. Through most of the subsequent company history, Rolls-Royce and Bentley models used similar, if not identical, powertrains and chassis, and were built at the same facility. See Bentley listing in this Catalog for details on all Bentley models.

A larger 25/30 Rolls-Royce replaced the 20/25 in 1936, with a larger (4257-cc) six-cylinder engine. By the time production came to a halt in 1938, a total of 1,201 were built. Also in 1936, a Phantom III replaced the Phantom II, carrying a big 7340-cc V-12 engine. Only 710 were built through 1939, but the Phantom III could top 100 mph and ranked as the first Rolls-Royce with independent front suspension. Next came the Wraith of 1938-39, a descendant of the Twenty with a modified version of the 4257-cc engine and

independent front suspension. A revised engine-mounting setup made this "probably the quietest of all Rolls-Royce motor cars between the wars," according to a company brochure. Only 491 were built over its two-year life.

Rolls-Royce aircraft engines were installed in several cars in the 1930s, to capture the world land-speed record. "Merlin" aircraft engines also saw extensive service in planes, of course, as World War II erupted.

By 1947, Rolls-Royce was back in production with a Silver Wraith, which carried an F-head (intake-over-exhaust) variant of the 4257-cc six-cylinder engine used in prewar models. Silver Wraiths demanded custom-built bodies, in keeping with tradition, though the postwar Bentley Mark VI could be ordered with a "factory" body, created by the Pressed Steel company but assembled at the Rolls-Royce plant in Crewe. Two years later, a Rolls-Royce version of that "standard" saloon, named Silver Dawn, became available. By the time Silver Dawn production ceased in 1955, engine size grew from its initial 4257-cc displacement to 4566 cc. Only 785 Silver Dawns were built in all, mostly for export. Production of the Silver Wraith continued into 1959, by which time 1,783 were produced, in both short- and long-wheelbase form. Hydra-matic transmissions were installed in Rolls-Royces, starting in 1952. Power steering became available in 1956.

In these postwar years, differences between the Rolls-Royce and lower-priced Bentley grew slighter—typically little more than the grille pattern. Still, according to a company brochure, Bentleys "have a distinctly different heritage" from Rolls-Royce throughout their history "and have attracted a distinctly different type of driver."

Next in line was the Silver Cloud, which served as the last six-cylinder Rolls-Royce and had a more modern-looking, streamlined body. A total of 2,359 were built before the Silver Cloud II arrived in 1959, powered by an aluminum 6230-cc V-8 engine. Also in 1959, a Phantom V took over the role of the Silver Wraith, similar in appearance to the Silver Cloud but on a 22-inch longer chassis, which used a huge tubular member to maintain rigidity. Powertrains were the same as those used on the smaller Silver Cloud, while bodies came from H.J. Mulliner, Park Ward or James Young, and a few other coachbuilders—of the handful still in existence. A total of 2,716 Silver Cloud II and 832 Phantom V models were produced, the latter remaining in the lineup into 1968. The Silver Cloud III, of which 2,376 were built from 1962 to 1966, used a modification of the original V-8 engine but had a lower hoodline and quad headlamps.

Only one Rolls-Royce saloon model was produced from 1965 to 1977: the Silver Shadow, of which 20,604 were built. This was the first unibodied Rolls-Royce, which, among other things, made it virtually impossible for coachbuilders to supply special bodies. Thus, the era of custom-built Rolls-Royces just about came to an end. The Silver Shadow also had four-wheel independent suspension, front/rear disc brakes, and automatic leveling. A two-door edition with coachbuilt saloon body appeared in 1966, followed the next year by a convertible. That evolved into the Corniche convertible of 1971, with body by H.J. Mulliner/Park Ward—a model that would remain in production into the 1990s, having achieved surprising popularity. At one point in the 1970s, potential purchasers of a Rolls-Royce convertible had to face a four-year waiting list.

Partly because Rolls-Royce had difficulty fulfilling a contract with Lockheed for aircraft engines in 1969, having promised them at a low price, the company faced financial

disaster and asked the British government for assistance. Following official bankruptcy, the company was nationalized in 1971, with automobile production under the control of a new organization: Rolls-Royce Motors Ltd. In 1980, that entity became part of Vickers Ltd.

A two-door Camargue arrived in 1975 with coachbuilt body styled by Pininfarina (but built at Crewe). Among other extras, the Camargue had new dual-level automatic air conditioning. Over the period ending in 1986, a total of 534 were built. The Silver Shadow II and longer Silver Wraith II each debuted in 1977, and remained in the lineup for only three years. A total of 8,425 Silver Shadow IIs and 2,135 Silver Wraith IIs were built in this comparatively short lifespan. Rolls-Royce models available in the 1980s included the Silver Spirit (successor to the Shadow), the Silver Spur, an evolution of the Cornice convertible, and the minimal-production Phantom VI, which was built to customer order. In 1985, the 100,000th Rolls-Royce left the factory at Crewe.

Engine Note: Traditionally, horsepower figures never were quoted for Rolls-Royce (or Bentley) engines. Therefore, all figures given in the listings below are estimates.

1946-50 ROLLS-ROYCE

1948 Rolls-Royce Silver Wraith four-door sports saloon. (Coys of Kensington)

SILVER WRAITH — SIX — Introduced soon after World War II, the first postwar Rolls retained the look of its prewar predecessor, with its separately-mounted Lucas headlamps. Engine size was identical to the prewar version (4257-cc), but F-head (overhead intake and side exhaust valves) rather than the former overhead-valve configuration. The postwar Wraith's chassis was new, though similar to the prior model, with front coil springs (no longer oil-cased) and semi-elliptic rear springs. Disc wheels replaced the earlier Wraith's wire wheels, and the four-wheel hydraulic jacking system was abandoned. Only the rear shock absorbers were adjustable, via a hydraulic pump. A pull-type hand brake was installed. Early right-hand-drive models had a floor gearshift, but left-hand-drive editions turned to a column-mounted lever. Bodies, as usual, came from a selection of coachbuilders: Sedanca deVille and Touring Saloon by H.J. Mulliner & Co.; four-door saloon and seven-seat limousine by Park Ward & Co.; Touring Limousine by Hooper & Co. Ltd.; Sports Saloon by James Young. Other bodies were created by Freestone & Webb. Silver Wraith body/upholstery color schemes were: Black with brown, grey, blue or beige furniture hide (leather); Maroon with maroon or beige hide; Dark Blue with brown or blue hide; Pearl Metallic with blue hide; Metallic Grey with grey hide; and Two-tone Grey with blue hide.

SILVER DAWN — SIX — "Hitherto," declared promotional literature for the next postwar model (which debuted in July 1949), "the Rolls-Royce has been regarded as the car of those who prefer to be chauffeur-driven. In the less formal mood of today, however, many who still require all that the Rolls-Royce traditionally bestows prefer to drive themselves. The Rolls-Royce Silver Dawn is intended specifically for these owner-drivers." This new saloon (sedan) wore an all steel body and was, as the sales literature declared, "Produced in its entirety by the makers of 'the best car in the world.'"

Except for the traditional Rolls grille, with inboard semi-integrated headlamps alongside, styling was similar to Bentley's Mark VI. Color schemes were: Black with brown, beige or tan furniture hide (leather); Dark Blue with beige hide; Pearl metallic finish with light blue hide; Metallic Grey with grey hide; Two-tone Grey with light blue hide; and Moss green with beige hide.

Beneath the early Dawn's bonnet lay the same 4257-cc F-head six-cylinder engine used in the Silver Wraith, which developed approximately 126 horsepower, via 6.4:1 compression. Instead of the Bentley's dual SU carburetors, the Silver Dawn used a single Stromberg unit. A column gearshift operated the four-speed manual transmission. Instruments were grouped in the center of the dashboard. Two separate sliding front seats were installed, plus a three-passenger seat in the rear. All seats were upholstered in leather in "pleated and bolster" style. Folding tables were fitted into the backs of each front seat, with footrests below. Most Silver Dawns wore a standardized body like that used for the Bentley Mark VI, but a small number came with coachbuilt bodies (notably drophead coupes done by Park Ward).

1949 Rolls-Royce Silver Wraith Sedanca deVille by H.J. Mulliner & Co. Ltd.

I.D. DATA: Serial number plate is located on the left side of the firewall, under the hood. Engine number is on the left side of the crankcase at lower front, or (later) in upper front corner of left side of crankcase.

Model	Body Type & Seating	Engine Type/CID	P.O.E. Price	Weight (lbs.)	Prod. Total
SILVER WRAITH					
Park Ward	4-dr Saloon-5P	16/260	Note 1	4480	Note 2
Park Ward	4-dr Limo-7P	16/260	Note 1	4480	Note 2
Mulliner	2-dr Sedanca DeV	16/260	Note 1	4480	Note 2
Mulliner	4-dr Touring Limo	16/260	Note 1	4480	Note 2
Hooper	2-dr Dhd Coupe	16/260	Note 1	4480	Note 2
Hooper	4-dr Touring Limo	16/260	Note 1	4480	Note 2
J. Young	4-dr Spt Saloon	16/260	Note 1	4480	Note 2
J. Young	4-dr Limousine	16/260	Note 1	4480	Note 2
Freestone	4-dr Saloon	16/260	Note 1	4480	Note 2
Freestone	4-dr Limousine	16/260	Note 1	4480	Note 2
Freestone	2-dr Coupe	16/260	Note 1	4480	Note 2
Freestone	4-dr Spt Saloon	16/260	Note 1	4480	Note 2
SILVER DAWN (1949-up)					
Standard	4-dr Saloon-5P	16/260	N/A	4030	Note 3
Farina	4-dr Spec Saloon	16/260	N/A	4030	Note 3
Freestone	4-dr Saloon-5P	16/260	N/A	4030	Note 3
Park Ward	2-dr Dhd Coupe	16/260	N/A	4030	Note 3
Park Ward	2-dr Coupe	16/260	N/A	4030	Note 3

Note 1: Chassis price alone was 2035 pounds (Sterling). A Sedanca deVille sold for 3875 pounds (Sterling) plus purchase tax; four-door saloon for 3590 pounds; Hooper Touring Limo for 3900 pounds; Park Ward limousine for 3750 pounds; James Young four-door sports saloon for 3885 pounds; and H.J. Mulliner Touring Saloon for 3900 pounds.

Note 2: A total of 1,783 Silver Wraiths were produced over the full model run from 1946 to 1959 (1,144 short-wheelbase and 639 long-wheelbase).

Note 3: A total of 785 Silver Dawns were produced over the full model run, from 1949 to 1955.

Weight Note: Figures shown are approximate.

1950 Rolls-Royce Silver Wraith drophead coupe.

ENGINE DATA: BASE SIX: Inline, F-head six-cylinder. Cast iron block and aluminum head. **Displacement:** 260 cu. in. (4257 cc). **Bore & Stroke:** 3.50 x 4.50 in. (88.9 x 114.3 mm). **Compression Ratio:** 6.4:1. **Brake Horsepower:** 126 at 3750 rpm (estimated). Seven main bearings. Solid valve lifters. Stromberg carburetor. 12-volt electrical system.

CHASSIS DATA: Wheelbase: (Wraith) 127 in.; (Dawn) 120 in. **Overall Length:** (Wraith) 206 in.; (Dawn) 192 in. **Width:** (Wraith) 73 in.; (Dawn) 69 in. **Front Tread:** (Wraith) 58 in.; (Dawn) 56 in. **Wheel Type:** steel disc. **Standard Tires:** (Wraith) 6.50x17; (Dawn) 6.50x16.
Note: Dimensions of custom bodies vary.

TECHNICAL: Layout: front-engine, rear-drive. **Transmission:** four-speed manual, column or floor lever (synchro 2nd/3rd/4th). Overall Wraith gear ratios: (1st) 11.125:1; (2nd) 7.514:1; (3rd) 5.002:1; (4th) 3.727:1; (rev) 11.757:1. **Standard Final Drive Ratio:** 3.727:1. **Steering:** cam and roller follower. **Suspension (front):** wishbones and coil springs. **Suspension (rear):** rigid axle with semi-elliptic leaf springs. **Brakes:** hydraulic front, mechanical rear (servo-assisted). **Body Construction:** steel body on steel frame (standard model); custom bodies may have aluminum body paneling.

PRODUCTION/SALES: Approximately six Rolls-Royces were sold in the U.S. in 1948, followed by three in 1949, and 18 in 1950.

ADDITIONAL MODELS: Beginning in 1950, Rolls-Royce also produced the Phantom IV, on a 145-inch wheelbase with Park Ward limousine body. A straight-eight F-head engine (code B80) of 5675-cid displacement was used, developing about 164 horsepower. Only 18 Phantom IV limos were built from 1950-56.
Manufacturer: Rolls-Royce Ltd., London and Crewe, England.

HISTORY: The Silver Dawn was intended as an alternate to the Bentley Mark VI, created especially to attract American customers.

1951-54 ROLLS-ROYCE

1951 Rolls-Royce Silver Wraith Limoby Hooper.

SILVER WRAITH — SIX — Starting in 1951, a larger (4566-cc) F-head engine went into the Silver Wraith. A long-wheelbase version (133-inch) became available, and was standard by 1952. Tires changed to 7.50x16 size. A four-speed automatic transmission became optional in 1952, initially on export models. Automatic had three forward speed ranges, marked 2, 3 and 4; plus reverse and neutral.

SILVER DAWN — SIX — The larger (4566-cc) Rolls-Royce engine also went into the smaller model. Body colors were: Black, Midnight Blue, Shell Grey, Tudor Grey, two-tone Grey, Silver, and Velvet Green. Furniture hide upholstery came in brown, tan, beige, light blue, maroon, red, or grey.

1953 Rolls-Royce Silver Wraith two-passenger drophead coupe. (Christie's)

542

1953 Rolls-Royce Silver Dawn Sports saloon. (Coys of Kensington)

I.D. DATA: Serial number plate is located on the left side of the firewall, under the hood. Engine number is in upper front corner of left side of crankcase.

Model	Body Type & Seating	Engine Type/CID	P.O.E. Price	Weight (lbs.)	Prod. Total
SILVER WRAITH					
Park Ward	4-dr Limousine-7P	I6/278	Note 1	5150	Note 2
Park Ward	4-dr Saloon-5P	I6/278	Note 1	5150	Note 2
Mulliner	4-dr Limousine-7P	I6/278	Note 1	5150	Note 2
Mulliner	4-dr Touring Limo	I6/278	Note 1	5150	Note 2
Hooper	4-dr Touring Limo	I6/278	Note 1	5150	Note 2
J. Young	4-dr Spt Saloon	I6/278	Note 1	5150	Note 2
Freestone	2-dr Coupe	I6/278	Note 1	5150	Note 2
Freestone	4-dr Spt Saloon	I6/278	Note 1	5150	Note 2
SILVER DAWN					
Standard	4-dr Saloon-5P	I6/278	N/A	4200	Note 3
Park Ward	2-dr Dhd Coupe	I6/278	N/A	4200	Note 3

Note 1: Prices of export models in late 1952 were 2185 pounds (Sterling) for chassis alone; 4230 pounds for Six Light Saloon by Park Ward; 4275 pounds for Touring Limousine by Hooper; 4560 pounds for Seven-Seat Limousine by H.J. Mulliner (or Park Ward); 4455 pounds for Touring Limousine by H.J. Mulliner; and 4460 pounds for Sport Saloon by James Young.

Note 2: A total of 1,783 Silver Wraiths were produced over the full model run from 1946 to 1959 (1,144 short-wheelbase and 639 long-wheelbase).

Note 3: A total of 785 Silver Dawns were produced over the full model run, from 1949 to 1955.

Weight Note: Figures shown are approximate.

1954 Rolls-Royce Silver Dawn Foursome drophead coupe. (Christie's)

ENGINE DATA: BASE SIX: Inline, F-head six-cylinder. Cast iron block and aluminum head. **Displacement:** 278.5 cu. in. (4566 cc). **Bore & Stroke:** 3.62 x 4.50 in. (92.1 x 114.3 mm). **Compression Ratio:** 6.4:1. **Brake Horsepower:** 150 (estimated). Seven main bearings. Solid valve lifters. Stromberg carburetor. 12-volt electrical system.

CHASSIS DATA: Wheelbase: (1951 Wraith SWB) 127 in.; (Wraith LWB) 133 in.; (Dawn) 120 in. **Overall Length:** (Wraith SWB) 206 in.; (Wraith LWB) 211 in.; (Dawn) 199.5 in. **Height:** (Wraith SWB) 72.5 in.; (Dawn) 66 in. **Width:** (Wraith SWB) 73 in.; (Wraith LWB) 77 in.; (Dawn) 71 in. **Front Tread:** (Wraith SWB) 58 in.; (Dawn) 56.5 in. **Rear Tread:** (Dawn) 58.5 in. **Wheel Type:** steel disc. **Standard Tires:** (Wraith) 7.50x16; (Dawn) 6.50x16.
Note: Dimensions of custom bodies vary.

TECHNICAL: Layout: front-engine, rear-drive. **Transmission:** four-speed manual, column lever (floor shift available); synchro 2nd/3rd/4th. Automatic transmission available from 1952. **Standard Final Drive Ratio:** 3.727:1. **Steering:** cam and roller follower. **Suspension (front):** wishbones and coil springs. **Suspension (rear):** rigid axle with semi-elliptic leaf springs. **Brakes:** hydraulic front, mechanical rear (servo-assisted). **Body Construction:** steel body on steel frame (standard model); custom bodies may have aluminum body paneling.

PRODUCTION/SALES: Approximately 14 Rolls-Royces were sold in the U.S. in 1951, followed by 34 in 1952, 85 in 1953, and 30 in 1954.

1954 Rolls-Royce Silver Dawn four-door sedan.

ADDITIONAL MODELS: Occasional production of the rare Phantom IV continued into 1956; see previous listing for details.

Manufacturer: Rolls-Royce Ltd., London and Crewe, England.

HISTORY: "In common with all Rolls-Royce cars," declared *Autocar* magazine in Britain, "the Silver Wraith has an indefinable something about it. A delicacy of behaviour, which escapes definition in written words. It is a car for the connoisseur in cars."

1955-58 ROLLS-ROYCE

1955 Rolls-Royce Silver Dawn four-door sedan.

SILVER WRAITH — SIX — Another enlargement of the F-head six-cylinder engine's bore brought displacement to 4887 cc, and output to approximately 178 horsepower.

SILVER CLOUD — SIX — Introduced in Britain in the spring of 1955, the Silver Cloud served as replacement for the Silver Dawn and was comparable to Bentley's new 'S' (S1) series. Wheelbase was 3 inches longer than the Silver Dawn, at 123 inches, and overall length reached 212 inches. A new frame allowed a lower stance. Styling differed from previous models, dominated by curvaceous fender lines and a softened knife-edge appearance. The Silver Cloud had a gently sloping hood, curved windshield, and large rear window. Twin foglamps incorporated flashing filaments for turn signals. A switch operated the flap covering the gas filler, and one switch controlled two-speed wiper/washers.

A softer suspension allowed more wheel travel. The Silver Cloud's front suspension consisted of unequal-length wishbones and coil springs. At the rear were semi-elliptic leaf springs with electrically-controlled shocks and a 'Z' type anti-roll bar. A two-position ride control switch varied the action of the rear shocks. The closed box-section frame was made of welded steel, with cruciform center bracing. While the Silver Dawn and Wraith had 16-inch tires, the Cloud turned to 8.20x15 tires on 15-inch, five-stud disc wheels. As before, hydraulic brakes were used in front, but hydromechanical brakes were installed at the rear, with servo assist. Cam and roller box steering included a transverse link to a three-piece track linkage; power steering was optional starting in 1956. An automatic transmission was standard equipment. Features again included a central pressure lube system, operated via a pedal under the instrument panel.

Leather pile upholstery was standard. Front and rear seats held folding center armrests, and the front backrests adjusted independently for rake. Vanity mirrors, cigar lighters, picnic trays and a map reading light were standard. Picnic trays and ashtrays pulled out from under the facia panel. Garnish rails were finished with French walnut veneers. Interior space was sufficient for five or six people. Top speed was well over 100 mph. Air conditioning was optional.

Both single colors and two-tones were available. Single colors included: Black, Black Pearl, Midnight Blue, Velvet Green, Maroon, or Lugano Blue. Two-tones were (upper color listed first): Shell Grey and Tudor Grey; Sage Green and Smoke Green; Sand and Sable; Shell Grey and Black Pearl; or Shell Grey and Velvet Green. Upholstery came in tan, red, blue, brown, beige, grey, or green. In addition to the basic owner-driven Silver Cloud, by 1957 customers could order one with a longer wheelbase and division window. A Silver Cloud Countryman also became available, with special interior fittings by Radford of London.

1956 Rolls-Royce Silver Cloud I, body by Freestone & Webb.

I.D. DATA: Serial number plate is located on the left side of the firewall, under the hood. Engine number is in upper front corner of left side of crankcase.

Model	Body Type & Seating	Engine Type/CID	P.O.E. Price	Weight (lbs.)	Prod. Total
SILVER WRAITH					
Hooper	4-dr Limousine	l6/298	N/A	5150	Note 1
Hooper	4-dr Saloon	l6/298	N/A	5150	Note 1
Mulliner	4-dr Touring Limo	l6/298	N/A	5150	Note 1
Park Ward	4-dr Limousine-7P	l6/298	N/A	5150	Note 1
Park Ward	4-dr Saloon-5P	l6/298	N/A	5150	Note 1
SILVER CLOUD					
Standard	4-dr Saloon-5/6P	l6/298	N/A	4200	Note 2
J. Young	4-dr Saloon-5/6P	l6/298	N/A	4200	Note 2
Park Ward	4-dr LWB Saloon	l6/298	N/A	4200	Note 2
Mulliner	2-dr Dhd Coupe	l6/298	N/A	4200	Note 2

Note 1: A total of 1,783 Silver Wraiths were produced over the full model run from 1946 to 1959 (1,144 short-wheelbase and 639 long-wheelbase).

Note 2: A total of 2,359 Silver Clouds (first series) were produced over the full model run, from 1955 to 1959 (121 with long wheelbase).

Weight Note: Figures shown are approximate.

1957 Rolls-Royce Silver Cloud Hooper sedan.

1958 Rolls-Royce Silver Cloud four-door sedan.

543

ENGINE DATA: BASE SIX: Inline, F-head six-cylinder. Cast iron block and aluminum alloy head. **Displacement:** 298.2 cu. in. (4887 cc). **Bore & Stroke:** 3.75 x 4.50 in. (95 x 114 mm). **Compression Ratio:** 6.6/6.8:1. **Brake Horsepower:** 178 (estimated). Seven main bearings. Solid valve lifters. Two SU carburetors. 12-volt electrical system.

CHASSIS DATA: **Wheelbase:** (Wraith LWB) 133 in.; (Cloud) 123 in.; (Cloud LWB) 127 in. **Overall Length:** (Wraith LWB) 211 in.; (Cloud) 212 in. **Height:** (Cloud) 64.25 in. **Width:** (Wraith LWB) 77 in.; (Cloud) 74.75 in. **Max. Tread:** (Wraith) 64 in.; (Cloud) 60 in. **Wheel Type:** steel disc. **Standard Tires:** (Wraith) 7.50x16; (Cloud) 8.20x15.

Note: Dimensions of custom bodies vary.

TECHNICAL: **Layout:** front-engine, rear-drive. **Transmission:** four-speed automatic. Silver Cloud overall gear ratios: (1st) 13.06:1; (2nd) 9.00:1; (3rd) 4.96:1; (4th) 3.42:1; (rev) 14.72:1, **Steering:** cam and roller follower. **Suspension (front):** unequal-length wishbones and coil springs. **Suspension (rear):** (Wraith) rigid axle with semi-elliptic leaf springs; (Cloud) rigid axle with semi-elliptic leaf springs, Z-type anti-roll bar and electrically-controlled shock absorbers. **Brakes:** hydraulic front, hydromechanical rear (servo-assisted). **Body Construction:** steel body on steel frame (standard model); custom bodies may have aluminum body paneling.

ADDITIONAL MODELS: Occasional production of the rare Phantom IV continued into 1956; see 1947-50 listing for details.

Manufacturer: Rolls-Royce Ltd., London and Crewe, England.

HISTORY: "With the distinguished appearance of the Rolls-Royce design," declared the Silver Cloud sales brochure, "goes a performance which fulfills a motorist's most exacting requirements in every respect."

1959-61 ROLLS-ROYCE

1959 Rolls-Royce Silver Cloud I drophead coupe.

SILVER CLOUD II — V-8 — Rolls-Royce turned to V-8 power for the second-generation Silver Cloud, introduced in fall 1959. Made mainly of aluminum, with steel wet cylinder liners, the 6230-cc (380-cid) V-8 had twin SU carburetors and 8:1 compression. Standard equipment for all Rolls-Royces sold in the U.S. included power-assisted steering, power brakes, automatic transmission, radio, whitewalls, heater, defroster and ventilating units. Standard colors were: Black, Black Pearl, Midnight Blue, Velvet Green, Porcelain White, Tudor Grey, Steel Blue, Smoke Green, Sage Green, Blue Grey, Sable, Pacific Green, Metal Grey, Shell Grey, Sand, and Opal.

In addition to the usual saloons (sedans) and long-wheelbase limousines with division window, a two-door convertible coupe became available, with bucket front seats to replace the normal Silver Cloud bench seat. Bodywork was done by H.J. Mulliner. English hide upholstery was used throughout, with fitted pile carpets to match the leather. A power top and power windows were available, as was an electric radio antenna. Two folding picnic trays went on the back of front seats. Another tray was recessed under the center of the instrument panel.

I.D. DATA: Serial number plate is located on the left side of the firewall, under the hood.

Model	Body Type & Seating	Engine Type/CID	P.O.E. Price	Weight (lbs.)	Prod. Total
SILVER CLOUD II					
Standard	4-dr Saloon-5/6P	V8/380	15655	4424	Note 1
	4-dr LWB Saloon	V8/380	19185	N/A	Note 1
Mulliner	2-dr Conv Coupe	V8/380	22750	N/A	Note 1
J. Young	4-dr Limousine	V8/380	N/A	N/A	Note 1
Radford	4-dr Countryman	V8/380	N/A	N/A	Note 1

Note 1: A total of 2,716 Silver Clouds IIs were produced over the full model run, from late 1959 to 1962 (299 with long wheelbase).

Price Note: Figures shown were valid in 1961.

ENGINE DATA: BASE V-8: 90-degree, overhead-valve "vee" type eight-cylinder. Cast aluminum block and heads. **Displacement:** 380 cu. in. (6230 cc). **Bore & Stroke:** 3.99 x 3.60 in. (101.4 x 91.5 mm). **Compression Ratio:** 8.0:1. **Brake Horsepower:** 185 (estimated). Five main bearings. Hydraulic valve lifters. Two SU diaphragm-type carburetors. 12-volt electrical system.

CHASSIS DATA: **Wheelbase:** (SWB) 123 in.; (LWB) 127 in. **Overall Length:** 211.75 in. **Height:** 64 in. **Width:** 74.75 in. **Front Tread:** 58.5 in. **Rear Tread:** 60 in. **Wheel Type:** steel disc. **Standard Tires:** 8.20x15.

Note: Dimensions of custom bodies vary.

TECHNICAL: **Layout:** front-engine, rear-drive. **Transmission:** four-speed automatic. Silver Cloud overall gear ratios: (1st) 11.75:1; (2nd) 8.10:1; (3rd) 4.46:1; (4th) 3.08:1; (rev) 13.25:1, **Steering:** cam and roller (power assisted). **Suspension (front):** unequal-length wishbones and coil springs with anti-roll torsion bar. **Suspension (rear):** rigid axle with semi-elliptic leaf springs, radius rod and electrically-controlled shock absorbers. **Brakes:** hydraulic front, hydromechanical rear (servo-assisted). **Body Construction:** steel body on steel frame (standard model); custom bodies may have aluminum body paneling.

1960 Rolls-Royce Silver Cloud II drophead coupe. (Christie's)

PRODUCTION/SALES: A total of 618 Rolls-Royces were sold in the U.S. in 1960, which was claimed to be about 35 percent higher than in 1959.

ADDITIONAL MODELS: Rolls-Royce also introduced a Phantom V, using the same new V-8 engine but on a 144-inch wheelbase, measuring 238 inches overall. The seven-passenger limousine bodywork was done by Park Ward or James Young, but H.J. Mulliner produced a 5/6-seat Touring Limousine version. The Phantom V seven-passenger limo was the same series as the Royal limousine used by Queen Elizabeth, designed to be the most spacious car obtainable anywhere. It had an electrically-operated glass partition, and two forward-facing occasional seats which swung outward from the back of that division. The Phantom V had a sliding roof extension over the front seats, operated by a single quick-release handle. Interiors held veneer folding tables and a cocktail cabinet. A total of 832 examples of the Phantom V were produced over the full model run, from late 1959 to 1968. A Phantom V was priced at $27,617 in the U.S., in 1961.

Manufacturer: Rolls-Royce Ltd., London and Crewe, England.

1961 Rolls-Royce Silver Cloud II.

HISTORY: Availability of the Silver Cloud II began in late 1959 and continued into early 1962, when it was replaced by the Silver Cloud III. Rolls-Royce promoted the fact that each engine was run for seven hours at full throttle before installation, and each car test driven for hundreds of miles. A technical editor of *The Motor* was the one who said: "At 60 miles an hour, the loudest noise comes from the electric clock."

1962-65 ROLLS-ROYCE

1962 Rolls-Royce Silver Cloud II drophead convertible by H.J. Mulliner. (Coys of Kensington)

1963 Rolls-Royce Silver Cloud III four-door sedan.

SILVER CLOUD III — V-8 — Inboard quad headlamps and a lower grille with revised hoodline were the major changes for the Silver Cloud's third series, which was introduced in autumn 1962 along with the equivalent Bentley S3. Engine compression rose from 8.0:1 to 9.0:1, and carburetors grew larger. Individually adjustable front seats were added, in a more spacious interior. As usual, custom bodies were installed by coachbuilders; but this would be their last real opportunity, since the next Rolls-Royce would have unibody construction. Power steering delivered more assist than before, for a lighter feel. Standard equipment included a four-speed automatic transmission, power brakes, radio and heater, with air conditioning optional.

1964 Rolls-Royce Silver Cloud III two-door drophead coupe. (Christie's)

I.D. DATA: Serial number plate is located on the left side of the firewall, under the hood.

Model	Body Type & Seating	Engine Type/CID	P.O.E. Price	Weight (lbs.)	Prod. Total
SILVER CLOUD III					
Standard	4-dr Saloon-5/6P	V8/380	16655	4659	Note 1
Mulliner	2-dr Saloon	V8/380	N/A	N/A	Note 1
Mulliner	2-dr Dhd Coupe	V8/380	N/A	N/A	Note 1
Mulliner	4-dr Flying Spur	V8/380	N/A	N/A	Note 1
Park Ward	2-dr Dhd Coupe	V8/380	N/A	N/A	Note 1
Park Ward	4-dr LWB Limo	V8/380	N/A	N/A	Note 1
J. Young	4-dr Spt Saloon	V8/380	N/A	N/A	Note 1
J. Young	2-dr Coupe	V8/380	N/A	N/A	Note 1
J. Young	4-dr SWB Tr Limo	V8/380	N/A	N/A	Note 1
J. Young	4-dr LWB Tr Limo	V8/380	N/A	N/A	Note 1

Note 1: A total of 2,376 Silver Clouds IIIs were produced over the full model run, from late 1962 to 1966 (including 253 with long wheelbase).

Price Note: Figure shown was valid in 1963.

1965 Rolls-Royce Phantom V touring limousine with body by Young, Bromley. (Christie's)

ENGINE DATA: BASE V-8: 90-degree, overhead-valve "vee" type eight-cylinder. Cast aluminum block and heads. **Displacement:** 380 cu. in. (6230 cc). **Bore & Stroke:** 3.99 x 3.60 in. (101.4 x 91.5 mm). **Compression Ratio:** 9.0:1. **Brake Horsepower:** 200 (estimated). Five main bearings. Hydraulic valve lifters. Two SU diaphragm-type carburetors. 12-volt electrical system.

CHASSIS DATA: Wheelbase: (SWB) 123 in.; (LWB) 127 in. **Overall Length:** 211.75 in. **Height:** 64 in. **Width:** 74 in. **Front Tread:** 58.5 in. **Rear Tread:** 60 in. **Wheel Type:** steel disc. **Standard Tires:** 8.20x15.

Note: Dimensions of custom bodies vary.

TECHNICAL: Layout: front-engine, rear-drive. **Transmission:** four-speed automatic. **Steering:** cam and roller (power assisted). **Suspension (front):** unequal-length wishbones and coil springs with anti-roll torsion bar. **Suspension (rear):** rigid axle with semi-elliptic leaf springs, radius rod and electrically-controlled shock absorbers. **Brakes:** hydraulic front, hydromechanical rear (servo-assisted). **Body Construction:** steel body on steel frame (standard model); custom bodies may have aluminum body paneling.

ADDITIONAL MODELS: Production of the Phantom V continued into 1968. Landaulette and limousine bodies were created by H.J. Mulliner-Park Ward, while Park Ward did a limousine version, and James Young turned out both a limousine and a Sedanca de Ville.

Manufacturer: Rolls-Royce Ltd., London and Crewe, England.

Distributor: Rolls-Royce Inc., New York City.

HISTORY: Production of the Silver Cloud III began in late 1962 and continued until October 1965, when the Silver Shadow debuted. "Many people have paid the price of the best car in the world without ever owning it," declared a 1965 Rolls-Royce ad in American publications.

1966-76 ROLLS-ROYCE

1967 Rolls-Royce Silver Shadow I drophead coupe by Mulliner, Park Ward. (Coys of Kensington)

SILVER SHADOW — V-8 — Not everyone applauded the next Rolls-Royce generation when it first appeared. Some criticized the Shadow for its differences from the past, its breaking with tradition. New monocoque (unibody) construction, for one, signaled a virtual end to traditional custom bodies on Rolls-Royces, and the only coachbuilt examples were produced in the early part of the period. James Young created 35 two-door models (the last in early 1967), while Mulliner-Park Ward was responsible for some 571 coupes and 505 convertibles through 1970. Still, each of these was built by simply stretching and modifying the basic saloon, not by creating a truly new body.

Furthermore, the overall appearance of the basic car was different, with nearly vertical bodysides and a less striking stance. On the other hand, the new model delivered improved performance, better handling and a more pleasing ride; and the reshaped body tended to grow on people. The Silver Shadow was comparable to Bentley's new 'T' series.

The Silver Shadow's new suspension incorporated high-pressure leveling to keep the same ride height regardless of load. New cylinder heads were installed on the 6230-cc (380-cid) V-8 engine, which was otherwise similar to that used in the Silver Cloud. Spark plugs now sat above the manifolds. GM's Hydra-matic was used on early examples, but models destined for export got a General Motors 400 three-speed unit instead. By 1968, that transmission was installed in all Shadows. Power windows were standard, as were all-disc brakes.

Starting in 1970, the Rolls-Royce V-8 engine gained displacement, enlarged to 6750 cc (412 cid). For 1971, central door locking was installed, which locked the transmission in "park" as the ignition key was withdrawn. As on most cars destined for the U.S. market in the early 1970s, compression was reduced, dropped to 7.3:1 by 1975. Wheel arches were added during 1974 to accommodate larger tires. Lucas electronic ignition was added for the 1976 model year.

CORNICHE — V-8 — A Rolls-Royce coupe and convertible under a new name debuted in 1971, replacing the earlier Silver Shadow two-doors. A revised camshaft and slightly larger exhaust-pipe increased horsepower a bit over the basic Shadow engine. Later examples also had a tachometer. Ventilated disc brakes and cruise control were standard. Top speed was in the 120-mph neighborhood, and a heavyweight Corniche could accelerate to 60 mph in less than 10 seconds. Bodies were produced by H.J. Mulliner-Park Ward.

CAMARGUE — V-8 — Styling of the next Rolls-Royce two-door model was accomplished by Pininfarina, in Italy. Faired-in headlamps were added, giving a different front-end look that would later emerge on conventional Rolls-Royces. The radiator grille angled forward slightly, whereas other models retained the traditional vertical grille. Intended as a "personal" car, though heavier than a Corniche, the low-production Camargue had several special features, including dual exhaust pipes and split-level air conditioning.

I.D. DATA: Serial number plate is located on the left side of the firewall, under the hood. A new numbering system was adopted for the Silver Shadow. The number consists of three letters, followed by four digits. Letter one indicates model ('S' = standard; 'L' = long wheelbase; 'C' = coachbuilt; 'D' = drophead; 'P' = Phantom VI). Letter two indicates make ('R' = Rolls-Royce). Letter three indicates right-hand or left-hand drive ('H' = RHD; 'X' = LHD). On later North American models, the third letter denotes the year ('A' = 1972; 'B' = 1973; 'C' = 1974; 'D' = 1975; 'E' = 1976). Serial number range (1966-67): 1000-5999; (1968-69) 6000-8999.

1968 Rolls-Royce Silver Shadow four-door sedan.

Model	Body Type & Seating	Engine Type/CID	P.O.E. Price	Weight (lbs.)	Prod. Total
SILVER SHADOW					
Standard	4-dr Saloon-5/6P	V8/380	19700	4636	16,717
LWB	4-dr Saloon	V8/380	N/A	N/A	2,776
Mulliner	2-dr Coupe	V8/380	N/A	N/A	571
Mulliner	2-dr Conv Coupe	V8/380	N/A	N/A	505
J. Young	2-dr Coupe	V8/380	N/A	N/A	35
CORNICHE (1971-76)					
Mull-P.W.	2-dr Coupe-4P	V8/412	33000	4760	780
Mull-P.W.	2-dr Conv Cpe-4P	V8/412	35600	4700	1,233
CAMARGUE (1975-76)					
	2-dr Coupe-5P	V8/412	N/A	5175	Note 1

Note 1: A total of 534 Camargues were produced through 1986.

Production Note: Total production came to 20,604 Silver Shadows, from late 1965 to the end of 1976.

Price Note: Figure shown for Silver Shadow was valid in 1966; for Corniches, in 1972. By then, a Silver Shadow sold for $25,200 ($28,700 for long-wheelbase version).

1970 Rolls-Royce Silver Shadow fixed-head coupe by Mulliner, Park Ward. (Coys of Kensington)

1971 Rolls-Royce Silver Shadow four-door sedan.

ENGINE DATA: BASE V-8 (1965-70): 90-degree, overhead-valve "vee" type eight-cylinder. Cast aluminum block and heads. **Displacement:** 380 cu. in. (6230 cc). **Bore & Stroke:** 3.99 x 3.60 in. (101.4 x 91.5 mm). **Compression Ratio:** 9.0:1. **Brake Horsepower:** 200 (estimated). Five main bearings. Hydraulic valve lifters. Two SU diaphragm-type carburetors. 12-volt electrical system.
BASE V-8 (1970-up): 90-degree, overhead-valve "vee" type eight-cylinder. Cast aluminum block and heads. **Displacement:** 412 cu. in. (6750 cc). **Bore & Stroke:** 4.10 x 3.90 in. (104.1 x 99 mm). **Compression Ratio:** 9.0:1 (8.0:1 later; 7.3:1 in 1975). **Brake Horsepower:** 220 (estimated). Five main bearings. Hydraulic valve lifters. Two SU diaphragm-type carburetors. 12-volt electrical system.

1973 Rolls-Royce Corniche convertible. (Christie's)

CHASSIS DATA: Wheelbase: (Shadow SWB, Corniche) 119.5 in.; (Shadow LWB) 123.5 in.; (Camargue) 120.1 in. **Overall Length:** (Shadow SWB, Corniche) 203.5 in.; (Shadow LWB, Camargue) 207.5 in. **Height:** (Shadow) 59.75 in.; (Corn) 58.75 in.; (Camargue) 58.2 in. **Width:** (Shadow) 71 in.; (Corn) 72 in.; (Camargue) 75.5 in. **Front Tread:** 57.5 in. except (Camargue) 60 in. **Rear Tread:** 57.5 in. except (Camargue) 59.6 in. **Wheel Type:** steel disc. **Standard Tires:** 8.45x15 or 205x15 (later, HR70x15).

TECHNICAL: Layout: front-engine, rear-drive. **Transmission:** GM 400 three-speed automatic (four-speed Hydra-matic on early home-market models). **Steering:** recirculating ball (variable power assisted). **Suspension (front):** wishbones and coil springs, with automatic leveling. **Suspension (rear):** independent, semi-trailing arms with coil springs and automatic leveling. **Brakes:** front/rear disc. **Body Construction:** steel unibody with front and rear auxiliary frames.

1976 Rolls-Royce Silver Shadow four-door saloon. (William Siuru Jr.)

ADDITIONAL MODELS: Production of the Phantom V continued into 1968, when it was supplanted by the Phantom VI. Never officially available in the U.S., the next Phantom retained the 6230-cc V-8 engine until 1978, rather than switching to the enlarged version in 1970 like the Silver Shadow. Drum brakes also were retained. Appearance was similar to the Phantom V, except the rear doors were front-hinged (rear-hinged on the Phantom V). Approximately 300 were produced through 1982.
Manufacturer: Rolls-Royce Ltd., London and Crewe, England.
Distributor: Rolls-Royce Inc., New York City.
HISTORY: Prototypes for the Silver Shadow had been created as early as 1957. The Shadow debuted in October 1965 and remained available, with changes, into 1976. The Rolls-Royce company faced bankruptcy in 1971, followed by a restructuring.

1977-80 ROLLS-ROYCE

SILVER SHADOW II — V-8 — Revisions were relatively modest in the second generation of the Silver Shadow, which changed little in appearance except for the deletion of air-intake grilles alongside the radiator grille. Modifications included a switch to rack-and-pinion steering, bi-level automatic air conditioning, plus new carburetors and a dual exhaust system for the 6750-cc (412-cid) V-8 engine. A smaller, asymmetric seven-blade

plastic fan was limited to 1700 rpm, and an electric booster fan turned on when coolant reached a certain temperature. Rolls-Royce claimed a 10 percent reduction in fuel usage. European models got a front air dam and headlamp wipers, but those destined for U.S. lacked those extras. A reshaped central console was installed, however, and the restyled instrument panel had large round gauges. Ten warning lights sat alongside the switch panel, the cruise-control selector was now on the steering-column stalk, and the steering wheel was smaller in diameter. An electronic odometer registed to a million miles. The Silver Shadow was equivalent to Bentley's T2 series. By 1977, it was claimed that the Silver Shadow had undergone more than 2,000 changes in its 12-year history.

SILVER WRAITH II — V-8 — An old name resurfaced for the long-wheelbase version of the Silver Shadow, which had a smaller rear window. An inside division window was not available on Wraiths exported to the U.S. An Everflex-covered roof was standard.

CORNICHE — V-8 — Production of the Rolls-Royce convertible and coupe continued with little change, except as noted for the Silver Shadow. Bodies were produced by Mulliner-Park Ward, and took approximately five months to build. Bentley convertibles and coupes also were produced under the "Corniche" designation.

CAMARGUE — V-8 — Production of the Pininfarina-styled two-door "personal" coupe continued with little change.

I.D. DATA: Serial number plate is located on the left side of the firewall, under the hood. A new numbering system was adopted for the Silver Shadow. The number consists of three letters, followed by four digits. Letter one indicates model ('S' = standard; 'L' = long wheelbase; 'C' = coachbuilt; 'D' = drophead; 'P' = Phantom VI). Letter two indicates make ('R' = Rolls-Royce). On North American models, the third letter denotes the year ('F' = 1977; 'G' = 1978; 'K' = 1979; 'L' = 1980).

Model	Body Type & Seating	Engine Type/CID	P.O.E. Price	Weight (lbs.)	Prod. Total
SILVER SHADOW II					
	4-dr Saloon-5P	V8/412	65400	4700	8,425
SILVER WRAITH II					
LWB	4-dr Saloon-5P	V8/412	74500	4850	2,135
CORNICHE					
	2-dr Coupe-4P	V8/412	102900	5000	Note 1
	2-dr Conv Cpe-4P	V8/412	109800	5000	Note 1
CAMARGUE					
	2-dr Coupe-5P	V8/412	115000	5175	Note 2

Note 1: A total of 326 Corniche coupes and 1,361 convertibles (including Bentley versions) were produced from 1977 through 1983.

Note 2: A total of 534 Camargues were produced through 1986.

Price Note: Figures shown were valid in 1979.

ENGINE DATA: BASE V-8: 90-degree, overhead-valve "vee" type eight-cylinder. Cast aluminum block and heads. **Displacement:** 412 cu. in. (6750 cc). **Bore & Stroke:** 4.10 x 3.90 in. (104.1 x 99 mm). **Compression Ratio:** 7.3:1. **Brake Horsepower:** 220 (estimated). Five main bearings. Hydraulic valve lifters. Two carburetors.

CHASSIS DATA: Wheelbase: (Shadow/Wraith) 119.5 in.; (Wraith) 123.5 in.; (Camargue) 120.1 in. **Overall Length:** (Shadow) 203.5 in.; (Wraith) 211.5 in.; (Corniche/Camargue) 207.5 in. **Height:** (Shadow/Wraith) 59.75 in.; (Corn.) 58.75 in.; (Camargue) 58.2 in. **Width:** (Shadow/Wraith) 71.8 in.; (Corn.) 72.7 in.; (Camargue) 75.5 in. **Front Tread:** 57.5 in. except (Camargue) 60 in. **Rear Tread:** 57.5 in. except (Camargue) 59.6 in. **Wheel Type:** steel disc. **Standard Tires:** HR70x15.

TECHNICAL: Layout: front-engine, rear-drive. **Transmission:** GM 400 three-speed automatic. **Steering:** rack and pinion. **Suspension (front):** wishbones and coil springs. **Suspension (rear):** independent, semi-trailing arms with coil springs and automatic leveling. **Brakes:** front/rear disc. **Body Construction:** steel unibody with front and rear auxiliary frames.

ADDITIONAL MODELS: Production of the Phantom VI continued with little change, except that it adopted the larger (6750-cc) V-8 engine in 1978. See previous listing for additional details.

Manufacturer: Rolls-Royce Motors Ltd., Crewe, Cheshire, England.

Distributor: Rolls-Royce Motors Inc., Paramus, New Jersey.

HISTORY: In 1980, Rolls-Royce merged with Vickers Ltd.

1981-90 ROLLS-ROYCE

1981 Rolls-Royce Corniche convertible.

SILVER SPIRIT — V-8 — The Rolls-Royce for the 1980s was less angular and upright in appearance, with more rounded bodyside panels and slightly wider, lower dimensions. Front-end appearance was somewhat akin to the limited-production Camargue. Headlamps were faired into the fenders, and a short "kick-up" was evident along the rear of the back window's base. Inside, veneered door cappings no longer were installed. Mechanical details were similar to the final Silver Shadows. The Silver Spirit was comparable to the new Bentley Mulsanne.

By 1985, the Silver Spirit added such features as a headlamp washer and heated door mirrors.

1982 Rolls-Royce Corniche convertible.

1983 Rolls-Royce Silver Spirit four-door sedan.

SILVER SPUR — V-8 — The long-wheelbase version of the Silver Spirit adopted the "Spur" designation. A seven-passenger limousine became available in the U.S. in 1985, priced at $185,000. This was the first limo sent to the U.S. market by Rolls-Royce in 18 years. Limousine options included an electric sunroof over the passenger compartment, power rear seat, lady's vanity case in the rear armrest, curtains in the passenger compartment, and a flag mast.

CORNICHE — V-8 — Production of the Corniche convertible continued through the 1980s, but the coupe was dropped. By 1989, the Corniche II convertible was priced at $205,500.

CAMARGUE — V-8 — Production of the Camargue coupe continued, adopting the rear suspension of the Silver Spirit.

I.D. DATA: A 17-symbol Vehicle Identification Number is on the upper left of the dashboard, visible through the windshield. Symbol one is the letter 'S'. Symbol two ('C') identifies the company. Symbol three denotes make ('R' = Rolls-Royce). Symbol four is the letter 'Z' (except 'P' = Phantom VI). Symbol five gives the body type ('S' = shortwheelbase four-door; 'L' = LWB four-door w/division; 'N' = LWB four-door without division; 'D' = Corniche conv; 'J' = Camargue; 'M' = Phantom VI limo; 'T' = Phantom VI Landaulette). Symbol ten indicates year built ('B' = 1981, 'C' = 1982, etc.). Symbol 11 identifies the assembly plant ('C' = Crewe). Symbol 12 indicates steering-wheel position ('H' = RHD; 'X' = LHD). Symbols 13-17 form the sequential serial number.

Model	Body Type & Seating	Engine Type/CID	P.O.E. Price	Weight (lbs.)	Prod. Total
SILVER SPIRIT					
	4-dr Saloon-5P	V8/412	111000	4700	N/A
SILVER SPUR					
LWB	4-dr Saloon-5P	V8/412	119000	4850	N/A
CORNICHE					
	2-dr Conv Cpe	V8/412	162500	5000	Note 1
CAMARGUE					
	2-dr Coupe	V8/412	158600	5175	Note 2

Note 1: A total of 326 Corniche coupes and 1,361 convertibles (including Bentley versions) were produced from 1977 through 1983.

Note 2: A total of 534 Camargues were produced through 1986.

Model Note: A Silver Spur limousine became available in 1985, priced at $185,000.

Price Note: Figures shown were valid in 1982.

1990 Rolls-Royce Corniche III convertible.

1990 Rolls-Royce Silver Spirit II.

ENGINE DATA: BASE V-8: 90-degree, overhead-valve "vee" type eight-cylinder. Cast aluminum block and heads. **Displacement:** 412 cu. in. (6750 cc). **Bore & Stroke:** 4.10 x 3.90 in. (104.1 x 99 mm). **Compression Ratio:** 8.0:1 (U.S. models). Five main bearings. Hydraulic valve lifters. Bosch K-Jetronic fuel injection (U.S. models).

CHASSIS DATA: Wheelbase: (Spirit) 120.5 in.; (Spur) 124.5 in.; (Corniche) 119.5 in.; (Camargue) 120.1 in. **Overall Length:** (Spirit) 207.8 in.; (Spur) 211.8 in.; (Corniche/Camargue) 207.5 in. **Height:** (Spirit/Spur) 58.5 in.; (Corn) 59.8 in.; (Camargue) 58.2 in. **Width:** (Spirit) 74.3 in.; (Spur) 74 in.; (Corn) 72.7 in.; (Camargue) 75.5 in. **Front Tread:** (Spirit/Spur) 60.5 in.; (Corn) 57.5 in.; (Camargue) 60 in. **Rear Tread:** (Spirit/Spur) 60.5 in. except; (Corn) 57.5 in.; (Camargue) 59.6 in.

TECHNICAL: Layout: front-engine, rear-drive. **Transmission:** three-speed automatic. **Steering:** rack and pinion. **Suspension (front):** lower wishbones with coil springs and anti-roll bar. **Suspension (rear):** independent, semi-trailing arms with coil springs, anti-roll bar and automatic leveling. **Brakes:** front/rear disc. **Body Construction:** steel unibody with front and rear auxiliary frames.

ADDITIONAL MODELS: Production of the Phantom VI continued with little change.

Manufacturer: Rolls-Royce Motors Ltd., Crewe, Cheshire, England.

Distributor: Rolls-Royce Motors Inc., Lyndhurst, New Jersey.

ROVER

Motorcar production in Britain under the Rover name started in 1904, but the company's history as a bicycle manufacturer reaches back into the 19th century, and the founding of the Coventry Sewing Machine Company in 1861. By 1868, partners James Starley and Josiah Turner changed the company name to Coventry Machinists Co. Ltd. and, among other products, began to turn out veloci-pedes. Mr. Starley departed the partnership in 1870, set-ting off on his own to produce "Penny Farthing" bicycles and, later in the decade, tricycles and tandem four-wheelers.

Yet another bicycle firm was founded in 1877 by Star-ley's nephew John. In 1884, that company first used the Rover name on a bicycle. Soon afterward, they came out with the "Safety" cycle, which quickly evolved into the

two-wheeler design that became familiar in the 20th cen-tury.

John Starley's firm became a publicly-held company in 1896, named Rover Cycle Co. Ltd. A year later, he began to import Peugeot motorcycles for research, following up an interest in motorized two-wheel transport that he'd held for a decade. Before anything came out of that venture, Starley died; but the first Rover motorcycles debuted late in 1902.

Because several other manufacturers in the Coventry area had turned to motorcars, Rover head Harry Smith de-cided to follow the trend. Their first product, designed by E.W. Lewis with a tubular steel backbone frame and front-mounted 1327-cc single-cylinder engine, emerged in 1904. A lower-priced model with chassis partly made of wood and a smaller (780-cc) engine also became available.

Four-cylinder and two-cylinder models followed as the company underwent another name change in 1906, to Rover Motor Co. Ltd., even though bicycles were still the primary product. After a brief flirtation with sleeve-valve engines, Rover developed a 2.3-liter L-head four that was used from 1912 to 1924, switching to a detachable cylinder head after World War I. Rover turned to a light car in the early 1920s, with a 998-cc two-cylinder engine. Bicycles re-mained in production as late as 1923, and motorcycles lasted two years longer.

A new light car, the Eight, with an air-cooled, 998-cc flat two-cylinder engine debuted in 1920 and was offered over the next five years. That evolved later in the decade into water-cooled 9/20 and 10/25 models, produced along with larger Rovers (14/45 and 16/50). Designed by Peter Poppe, the big cars had overhead-cam engines with hemispheri-cal combustion chambers. Even a displacement increase to 2413 cc didn't deliver stunning performance, so that en-gine was replaced in 1928 by a 2.0-liter L-head six. The Light Six that debuted in 1930 had a raked windshield and cycle-style fenders, and a top speed of 70 mph. In a race through France, a Rover Light Six beat the famed "Blue Train."

Sunroofs were available by 1929 on the big Ten. By that time, Rover was faltering financially, saved from extinction largely by a management change that put Spencer Wilks (formerly of Hillman) in the driver's seat. A former Hillman engineer named Major B. Thomas then designed a new 1410-cc "Pilot" six-cylinder engine, which evolved into the powerplant used by Rovers through the 1930s.

Starting in 1931, Rovers had vee-shaped radiators and lower chassis. Features added during the Depression years included no-clutch gearshifting with freewheeling in 1933, and four-speed gearboxes by 1934. To help attract middle-class customers, interiors turned to leather and wood trim, while new steel bodies were supplied by the Pressed Steel company. Hydraulic brakes were tried, but in 1936 Rover reverted to mechanically-activated binders. An experimental light Scarab with air-cooled rear two-cylinder engine never entered the marketplace. Production rose considerably, however, from less than 5,000 cars in 1933 to more than 11,000 in 1939. Rovers were restyled in 1937, and that same basic body would reappear after the war. Synchromesh transmissions became available in 1939, and disc wheels replaced the traditional wires a year later.

Wartime production focused on aircraft and tank en-gines. As the war ended, automobile production resumed at the Solihull plant, starting with a series of prewar-styled P2 sedans with a choice of four engines. In 1948, those were replaced by a new P3 series, which served as a half-way measure until Rover could introduce a wholly modern lineup. The P3 cars had 1595-cc four-cylinder or 2103-cc six-cylinder F-head (intake over exhaust valve) engines and front coil springs. Their "60" and "75" model designa-tions were intended to denote approximate horsepower ratings (though actual bhp ratings were lower).

A fully restyled P4 Rover "75" emerged in 1949, evidently influenced—according to the *World Guide to Automobile Manufacturers*—by Raymond Loewy's 1946 Studebaker design. Early examples even had a center "cyclops" headlight. The slab-sided, full-width body had built-in headlamps, and gearboxes used a column-mounted lever. Hydraulic brakes replaced the initial hydro-mechanical units after two years. Not until 1964 would this basic Rover profile change.

Rover also debuted a new four-wheel-drive Land Rover early in 1948, which is listed separately in this Catalog. Experiments also were underway on gas turbine engines and in 1950, Rover demonstrated the world's first turbine-powered automobile. That one was a two-seater, but later turbine prototypes came in sedan and four-wheel-drive coupe form. With a rear-mounted 200-horsepower engine, that first turbine hit 151.965 mph through the flying kilometer in 1952. Like other turbine experiments of the time, Rover's never developed into the production stage.

Two more engines joined the lineup in 1954: a 2.0-liter four and 2.6-liter six, the latter developing 90 horsepower. Overdrive became available on the Rover "90" in 1956, as the old freewheeling faded away. A 105-bhp edition of the "90" was introduced for 1957, called the 105S. Rover debuted its own two-speed automatic transmission, but that soon was replaced by a Borg-Warner version.

A larger P5 series with unibody construction joined the P4 in 1959, powered by a 3.0-liter engine. Front disc brakes became standard by the 1960 model year, while power steering debuted in 1961. Next model of note was the P6 2000, with an overhead-cam 2.0-liter four-cylinder engine, which appeared in 1963 and carried a De Dion rear axle. A TC variant of the 2000 debuted with a twin-carb 114-bhp engine. An automatic transmission also was available.

Corporate adjustments came in the mid-1960s, as Rover purchased the Alvis company (to acquire its military vehicles). In 1967, Leyland took over the Rover operation, soon merging with British Motor Corporation to become British Motor Holdings. That organization in turn evolved into British Leyland.

Rover turned to eight-cylinder power in 1968, using the aluminum 215-cid V-8 that had been developed earlier for Buick compacts. Offered only with automatic shift, the initial 3.5 series (evolved from the former 3.0-liter) with its 160-horsepower engine could hit 108 mph. Within a year, the V-8 went into the 2000 series. With a V-8 under its hood, the Rover was named P6 3500—typically known as, simply, the 3500 (just as its four-cylinder predecessor was generally called the 2000). It could reach speeds in the 114-mph neighborhood. A larger (2.2-liter) four-cylinder engine went into the 2000 in 1974.

A fresh series debuted in 1976, starting with a wedge-profile SD1 hatchback sedan with V-8 power. Features included a self-leveling suspension and central door locking. Two years later, that was joined by 2.3- and 2.6-liter overhead-cam six-cylinder versions.

Importation of Rovers into the U.S. had ceased early in the 1970s, but resumed again (briefly) by the 1980 model year. A 3500 hatchback sedan was the last car to be offered in the U.S. market under the Rover name (apart from the Land Rovers and posh Range Rovers). By 1981, the company was known as Austin Rover Ltd. and soon established a connection with Honda. That tie would result in the Sterling sedan, which was exported to America from 1987 until 1991 (and listed separately in this Catalog).

1945-49 ROVER

1946 Rover Twelve four-door saloon. (Christie's)

1947 Rover Twelve sport tourer. (Christie's)

1948 Rover 12 hp four-seat tourer. (Sotheby's)

TEN — FOUR — Rover's prewar-styled Ten was introduced in its postwar guise late in 1945, powered by an overhead-valve engine that displaced 1389 cc. Wheelbase was 105 inches. Production of the Ten, Twelve, Fourteen and Sixteen continued into 1948.

TWELVE — FOUR — A larger (1496-cc) four-cylinder engine went under the hood of the Twelve sedan, which rode a 112-inch wheelbase and came in four- or six-window form. The Sports sedan had a 105-inch wheelbase.

FOURTEEN — SIX — Rover's largest sedan rode a 115-inch wheelbase and carried a 1901-cc six-cylinder overhead-valve engine. Like its smaller mates, the sedan had "suicide" doors front and rear, and separately-mounted headlamps.

SIXTEEN — SIX — The 115-inch wheelbase sedan also came with a 2147-cc, overhead-valve six-cylinder engine.

SIXTY (60)/SEVENTY-FIVE (75) — P3 — FOUR/SIX — Two versions of the Rover with an interim P3 body debuted in 1948 and lasted into 1949, when they were replaced by the more modern P4 series. Wheelbase was 110.5 inches, and the sedans measured 169.8 inches long overall. A four-cylinder 1595-cc F-head engine was installed in the Sixty sedan, while a 2103-cc six-cylinder version with the same bore and stroke dimensions went into the Seventy-Five.

Note: A modern slab-sided Rover 75 was introduced late in 1949, for the 1950 model year; see next listing.

1950-53 ROVER

SEVENTY-FIVE (SERIES 75) — P4 — SIX — Rover dismissed its prewar body with separate headlamps for the 1950 model year. Styling features of the new, modern sedan (saloon) included recessed inboard headlamps in squarish housings that bulged upward slightly into the fender tops. Rectangular air intake grilles sat directly below the headlamps, while tiny round lights were installed in the outboard position. The horizontal-bar grille had a center crossbar and a foglight in the middle of that crossbar. The front fender line extended through the car's body. Easy-clean wheels held Dunlop 6.00x15 tires and hubcaps with a Rover center symbol.

Leather upholstery was standard, and a Rover could seat five with ease. Three people could fit in the front seat, which could be used with a wide central armrest if only two passengers were present. Side armrests were adjustable in height. A hand-rubbed mahogany dashboard contained two glove compartments, and had provision for a radio. A curved one-piece windshield was installed. Standard colors were: Connaught Green with grey upholstery; Lakeside Green with green or grey upholstery; Pastel Blue with blue upholstery; Ivory with red or green upholstery; and Black with green, red, blue, tan or grey upholstery. The spare tire went into a separate compartment.

Telescopic shock absorbers were now used at front and rear, along with variable-rate rear leaf springs. Well-tried features such as controlled freewheeling and clutchless gear-change were retained, but the gearshift lever was now on the steering column (which also held the trafficator control and headlamp switch). Under the hood was a 2103-cc, F-head six-cylinder engine that developed 75 horsepower.

After 1951, the central foglight and fender air intake grilles were dropped, giving the front end a modified appearance. Instead of a horizontal-bar grille, this one was made up of thin vertical bars surrounded by a chromed rectangular frame. Headlamps now sat farther forward, rather than deep into rectangular recesses. A valance strip filled in the space between the front bumper and the car body. A ventilator was now mounted ahead of the windshield, operated from inside the car (eliminating the need for those earlier air-intake openings). Inside was a smaller, round horn ring.

I.D. DATA: Serial number plate is on the left front door hinge post. Chassis numbers also were stamped along the left chassis member. Engine number is on the left side of the block. Starting serial number (1950) 04300001; (1951) 14330001 or 14360001; (1952) 243301; (1953) 34330001 or 34300000.

Model	Body Type & Seating	Engine Type/CID	P.O.E. Price	Weight (lbs.)	Prod. Total
75					
P4	4-dr Sedan-5P	I6/128	2497	3166	N/A

Price Note: Figure shown was valid in 1951. Price rose to $2697 in 1952, and $2899 in 1953.

ENGINE DATA: BASE SIX: Inline, F-head six-cylinder. Cast iron block and aluminum alloy head. **Displacement:** 128.4 cu. in. (2103 cc). **Bore & Stroke:** 2.57 x 4.13 in. (65.2 x 105 mm). **Compression Ratio:** 7.25:1. **Brake Horsepower:** 75 at 4200 rpm. **Torque:** 111 lbs.-ft. at 2500 rpm. Four main bearings. Solid valve lifters. Two SU horizontal carburetors.

CHASSIS DATA: **Wheelbase:** 111 in. **Overall Length:** 178.25 in. **Height:** 63.3 in. **Width:** 65.5 in. **Front Tread:** 52 in. **Rear Tread:** 51.5 in. **Standard Tires:** Dunlop 6.00x15.

TECHNICAL: **Layout:** front-engine, rear-drive. **Transmission:** four-speed manual (3rd/4th synchro). Overall gear ratios: (1st) 14.49:1; (2nd) 8.77:1; (3rd) 5.92:1; (4th) 4.3:1; (rev) 12.77:1. **Standard Final Drive Ratio:** 4.3:1. **Steering:** recirculating ball (worm and nut). **Suspension (front):** coil springs. **Suspension (rear):** rigid axle with semi-elliptic leaf springs. **Brakes:** Girling front/rear drum. **Body Construction:** separate body on box-section steel frame.

PERFORMANCE: **Top Speed:** 83-85 mph. **Acceleration (0-60 mph):** 18.5 sec. **Acceleration (quarter-mile):** 22 sec.

PRODUCTION/SALES: Approximately 66 Rovers were sold in the U.S. in 1950, followed by 241 in 1951, 371 in 1952, and 422 in 1953.
Manufacturer: The Rover Co. Ltd., Solihull, Birmingham, Warwickshire, England.
Distributor: Rootes Motors Inc., New York City.

HISTORY: Rover devoted considerable attention to experiments with gas turbine automobiles in the early 1950s, and produced the first operative example, a three-seat open car with engine ahead of the rear axle. After display at the British Automobile & Motorcycle Show, its first public trial took place on March 9, 1950. In test runs on Belgium's Jabbeke highway in the summer of 1952, a Rover with gas turbine engine traveled at average speeds of 151.196 mph. The person responsible for turbine development at the Rover company was F.R. Bell, a designer and expert in airplane jet engines who worked under chief engineer Maurice Wilks.

A four-cylinder Rover 60 became available during 1953; see next listing for details.

1954-58 ROVER

1954 Rover Model 90 four-door sedan.

60 — P4 — FOUR — A four-cylinder Rover joined the "75" for 1954, with the same four-door sedan body. As its model number suggested, the 1997-cc F-head four developed 60 horsepower. Appearance was similar to the Rover 75 sedan.

75 — P4 — SIX — Production of the "75" sedan continued into 1956, but a larger (2230-cc) engine was installed by the 1955 model year.

90 — P4 — SIX — The same basic sedan body used for the "60" and "75" formed the basis for a new series, introduced for 1954, with a 2638-cc (161-cid) six-cylinder engine. Horsepower rating was 90 at 4500 rpm, and the new engine produced 128 pound-feet of torque at 2000 rpm.

105 — P4 — SIX — Introduced late in 1956, the "105" sedan was yet another variant of the same basic Rover body. Under the hood was a more potent version of the 2638-cc engine installed in the Rover 90, developing 108 horsepower at 4250 rpm and using twin SU carburetors. The 105R had a Roverdrive automatic transmission (with built-in overdrive), while the 105S had a regular four-speed synchromesh gearbox with automatic overdrive. Standard equipment included power brakes, individually-adjustable leather-upholstered front bucket seats with map pockets, twin foglights, backup lights, lighter, and full instruments (including an oil level gauge) in a genuine walnut dashboard.

1957 Rover 90 four-door sedan.

I.D. DATA: Serial number plate is on the left front door hinge post. Chassis numbers also were stamped atop the left chassis member. Engine number is on the left side of the block. Starting serial number (60) 43300001; (1955 "75" w/2230-cc) 54300001; (90) 45300001; (105R) 615700001; (105S) 620700001.

Model	Body Type & Seating	Engine Type/CID	P.O.E. Price	Weight (lbs.)	Prod. Total
P4 (60/75/90) SERIES					
60	4-dr Sedan-5P	I4/122	N/A	3106	N/A
75 (1954)	4-dr Sedan-5P	I6/128	N/A	3262	N/A
75 (1955)	4-dr Sedan-5P	I6/136	N/A	3262	N/A
90	4-dr Sedan-5P	I6/161	N/A	3267	N/A
P4 105 SERIES (1957-58)					
105R	4-dr Sedan-5P	I6/161	3750	3420	N/A
105R DeL	4-dr Sedan-5P	I6/161	N/A	3473	N/A
105S	4-dr Sedan-5P	I6/161	N/A	3382	N/A

Price Note: Figure shown for 105R was valid in 1958.

ENGINE DATA: BASE FOUR (60): Inline, F-head four-cylinder. Cast iron block and aluminum alloy head. **Displacement:** 122 cu. in. (1997 cc). **Bore & Stroke:** 3.06 x 4.13 in. (77.8 x 105 mm). **Compression Ratio:** 6.9:1. **Brake Horsepower:** 60 at 4000 rpm. Three main bearings. Solid valve lifters. One SU carburetor.
BASE SIX (Rover 75 through 1954): Inline, F-head six-cylinder. Cast iron block and aluminum alloy head. **Displacement:** 128.4 cu. in. (2103 cc). **Bore & Stroke:** 2.57 x 4.13 in. (65.2 x 105 mm). **Compression Ratio:** 7.25:1. **Brake Horsepower:** 75 at 4200 rpm. **Torque:** 111 lbs.-ft. at 2500 rpm. Four main bearings. Solid valve lifters. Two SU horizontal carburetors.
BASE SIX (Rover 75, 1955-up): Inline, F-head six-cylinder. Cast iron block and aluminum alloy head. **Displacement:** 136 cu. in. (2230 cc). **Bore & Stroke:** 2.87 x 3.50 in. (73 x 88.9 mm). **Compression Ratio:** 6.9:1. **Brake Horsepower:** 80 at 4500 rpm. Four main bearings. Solid valve lifters. One SU carburetor.
BASE SIX (90): Inline, F-head six-cylinder. Cast iron block and aluminum alloy head. **Displacement:** 161 cu. in. (2638 cc). **Bore & Stroke:** 2.87 x 4.13 in. (73 x 105 mm). **Compression Ratio:** 6.7/7.5:1. **Brake Horsepower:** 90/93 at 4500 rpm. **Torque:** 128 lbs.-ft. at 2000 rpm. Four main bearings. Solid valve lifters. One SU carburetor.

BASE SIX (105 series): Same as 2638-cc six above, except — **Compression Ratio:** 8.5:1. **Brake Horsepower:** 108 at 4250 rpm. Two SU carburetors.

CHASSIS DATA: Wheelbase: 111 in. **Overall Length:** 178.25 in. **Height:** 63.8 in. **Width:** 65.4 in. **Front Tread:** 52 in. **Rear Tread:** 51.5 in. **Standard Tires:** 6.00x15.

TECHNICAL: Layout: front-engine, rear-drive. **Transmission:** four-speed manual except (105R) Roverdrive automatic; (105S) automatic overdrive. **Steering:** recirculating ball (worm and nut). **Suspension (front):** coil springs with anti-roll bar. **Suspension (rear):** rigid axle with semi-elliptic leaf springs. **Brakes:** Girling front/rear drum. **Body Construction:** separate body on box-section steel frame.

PERFORMANCE: Top Speed: (60) 78 mph; (75) 80 mph; (90) 82 mph; (90 w/overdrive) 90 mph; (105R) 94-98 mph; (105S w/overdrive) 100 mph. **Acceleration (0-60 mph):** (60) 26 sec.; (75) 20 sec.; (90) 18 sec.; (105R) 21-23 sec.; (105S) 15 sec.

Manufacturer: The Rover Co. Ltd., Solihull, Birmingham, Warwickshire, England.
Distributor: Rootes Motors Inc., New York City.

HISTORY: When displayed at the New York auto show in spring 1958, the Rover 105R was described as "one of Britain's fine cars."

1959-63 ROVER

1961 Rover three-liter Mark III four-door saloon. (Sotheby's)

100 — P4 — SIX — A new Rover 100 took over the spot vacated by the fading-away Rover 90 and 105. Said to combine the silent and economical running of the 90 with the fast acceleration of the 105, this model was marketed in the U.S. in the early 1960s, along with the new 3-Litre. A new 2625-cc version of the familiar F-head engine, essentially a short-stroke variant of the powerplant used in the 3-Litre, developed 104 horsepower. The 100 sedan had "prime" leather upholstery, polished solid English wood trim, adjustable front seats, fitted carpets, and an aircraft-type instrument panel. Ten body colors were available. Laycock de Normanville overdrive was optional.

Starting in 1962, the P4 body evolved into the Rover 95 and 110, with the same engine displacement, before dropping out during 1964.

105 — P4 — SIX — Rover's 105 series remained in production (and available in the U.S.) into 1959.

3-LITRE — P5 (SERIES I/II) — SIX — A new and large (by European standards) full-width body debuted late in 1958, powered by a 2995-cc enlargement of Rover's F-head engine. Low and wide in appearance, the conservative styling was claimed to provide slow obsolescence. Standard equipment included a fresh-air heater, windshield washers, reserve gas tank, backup light, prime quality hide upholstery, deep-pile carpets and underlay, dashboard tool tray, cigar lighter, directional signals, "dowager" straps, twin sunvisors, wheel trim rings, and laminated glass windshield. A rubber-fitted drawer of tools sat below the instrument panel. Instruments were grouped in a binnacle ahead of the driver. Individual bucket-type front seats were optional.

Girling front disc brakes (rear drum) were installed. Independent front suspension consisted of upper wishbones and radius links with laminated torsion bars and double-acting shocks. At the rear were progressive-rate semi-elliptic leaf springs with telescopic shocks. Laycock de Normanville overdrive was included with the standard-transmission model. An automatic transmission was optional. Second-gear hold lock control allowed the driver to manually engage and bypass first gear, for safer movement on snow and ice, on hills, and in traffic, from 0 to 65 mph. Standard body colors were: Dover White, Light Grey, Dove Grey, Smoke Grey, Rush Green, Shadow Green, Light Brown, Heather Brown, Black, and Dark Blue. Two-tone combinations also were available.

Engine output grew to 121 horsepower in the Series II, which became available by 1963.

Note: Production of the Rover 75 and 90 continued into mid-1959; see previous listing for details.

I.D. DATA: Serial number plate is on the left front door hinge post. Chassis numbers also were stamped atop the left chassis member. Engine number is on the left side of the block. Starting serial number: (60) 43300001; (1955 "75" w/2230-cc) 54300001; (90) 45300001; (105R) 615700001; (105S) 620700001.

Model	Body Type & Seating	Engine Type/CID	P.O.E. Price	Weight (lbs.)	Prod. Total
P4 SERIES					
100	4-dr Sedan-5P	I6/160	N/A	3305	Note 1
105 DeL	4-dr Sedan-5P	I6/161	3625	N/A	Note 1
3-LITRE (P5)					
	4-dr Sedan-5P	I6/183	4620	3360	Note 1

Note 1: Approximately 18,000 Rovers (all models) were produced in 1960, followed by 11,000 in 1961, 12,000 in 1962, and 12,500 in 1963.

Price Note: Figure shown for 105 was valid in 1959; for 3-Litre in 1960, with bench front seat. A 3-Litre with overdrive and individual front seats sold for $4840; with automatic and bench seat, $4985.

ENGINE DATA: BASE SIX (100): Inline, F-head six-cylinder. Cast iron block and aluminum alloy head. **Displacement:** 160 cu. in. (2625 cc). **Bore & Stroke:** 3.06 x 3.63 in. (77.8 x 92.1 mm). **Compression Ratio:** 7.8:1. **Brake Horsepower:** 104 at 4750 rpm. Solid valve lifters. One SU carburetor.

BASE SIX (105): Inline, F-head six-cylinder. Cast iron block and aluminum alloy head. **Displacement:** 161 cu. in. (2638 cc). **Bore & Stroke:** 2.87 x 4.13 in. (73 x 105 mm). **Compression Ratio:** 8.5:1. **Brake Horsepower:** 108 at 4250 rpm. Four main bearings. Solid valve lifters. Two SU carburetors.

BASE SIX (3-Litre): Inline, F-head six-cylinder. Cast iron block and aluminum alloy head. **Displacement:** 183 cu. in. (2995 cc). **Bore & Stroke:** 3.06 x 4.13 in. (77.8 x 105 mm). **Compression Ratio:** 8.75:1. **Brake Horsepower:** 115 at 4500 rpm (later, 121 at 4800). **Torque:** 164 lbs.-ft. at 1500 rpm. Seven main bearings. Solid valve lifters. One SU carburetor.

CHASSIS DATA: Wheelbase: (100/105) 111 in.; (3-Litre) 110.5 in. **Overall Length:** (100/105) 178.25 in.; (3-Litre) 186.5 in. **Height:** (100/105) 63.8 in.; (3-Litre) 60.3 in. **Width:** (100/105) 65.4 in.; (3-Litre) 70 in. **Front Tread:** (100) 52.5 in.; (105) 52 in.; (3-Litre) 55 in. **Rear Tread:** (100/105) 51.5 in.; (3-Litre) 56.5 in. **Standard Tires:** (100) 6.00/6.40x15; (3-Litre) 6.70x15.

TECHNICAL: Layout: front-engine, rear-drive. **Transmission:** four-speed manual; automatic available. **Steering:** recirculating ball (worm and nut). **Suspension (front):** (100/105) coil springs with anti-roll bar; (3-Litre) upper wishbones and radius links with laminated torsion bars. **Suspension (rear):** rigid axle with semi-elliptic leaf springs. **Brakes:** (3-Litre) front disc, rear drum. **Body Construction:** separate body on box-section steel frame.

ADDITIONAL MODELS: From 1959-62, Rover also produced a model 80 with the P4 body, which used a 2268-cc four-cylinder engine.

Manufacturer: The Rover Company Ltd., Solihull, Birmingham, Warwickshire, England.
Distributor: Rover Motor Company of North America, New York City.

HISTORY: In late 1958, at the Earl's Court Motor Show, Rover introduced its 3-Litre line as the first completely new Rover since 1949. Simultaneouly, Rover begin the establishment of factory branches to serve dealers and owners in the U.S. At the 1959 Earl's Court show, the 3-Litre won a gold medal for best coachwork in its class. At the 1960 New York auto show, Rover displayed its recently-introduced 100 sedan (priced at $3795) and the larger 3-Litre sedan, along with the 4WD Land Rover. Rovers also appeared at the Import Show in New York, in June 1960. Each Rover was road-tested on the company's test track.

1964-68 ROVER

1964 Rover P4 "100" saloon. (William Siuru Jr.)

2000 SERIES — P6 — FOUR — With the debut of the P6 body on a shorter (103.4-inch) wheelbase, Rover abandoned the familiar F-head engine and turned instead to an overhead-cam four. In the original 2000 sedan, the 1978-cc (121-cid) engine developed 90 horsepower. A compression boost for the 2000TC, introduced in 1966, brought engine output to 124 bhp using twin carburetors. Styling of the four-door sport sedan was completely different from prior models, with a wide horizontal-bar grille that contained the quad underslung headlamps and had a triangular insignia at its center. The 2000 used unibody construction, with separate members for doors, roof and outside panels. All-wheel disc brakes were installed (inboard at the rear). Special features on the 2000 included an "Icealert" that detected road ice.

3-LITRE — P5 (SERIES II/III) — SIX — Production of the 3-Litre with its F-head engine continued into 1967. Two four-door models were marketed, the sportier (four-seat) version referred to as a "coupe" rather than a saloon (sedan). Production continued into 1967.

I.D. DATA: Serial number plate is on the left front door hinge post.

Model	Body Type & Seating	Engine Type/CID	P.O.E. Price	Weight (lbs.)	Prod. Total
2000 (P6)					
P6	4-dr Spt Sed-4/5P	I4/121	3998	2767	Note 1
2000TC (1966-up)					
P6	4-dr Spt Sed-4/5P	I4/121	4198	2810	Note 1

Model	Body Type & Seating	Engine Type/CID	P.O.E. Price	Weight (lbs.)	Prod. Total
3-LITRE (P5)					
II	4-dr Sedan-5P	I6/183	5009	3654	Note 1
II	4-dr Coupe-4P	I6/183	5890	3741	Note 1
III	4-dr Sedan-5P	I6/183	6064	3654	Note 1
III	4-dr Coupe-4P	I6/183	6497	3741	Note 1

Note 1: Approximately 25,000 Rovers (all models) were produced in 1964, followed by as many as 36,300 in 1965, 39,600 in 1966, 42,600 in 1967, and 46,775 in 1968 (1966-68 totals are for Rover-Alvis).

Price Note: Figures shown were valid in 1966.

ENGINE DATA: BASE FOUR (2000): Inline, overhead-cam four-cylinder. Cast iron block and aluminum alloy head. **Displacement:** 120.8 cu. in. (1978 cc). **Bore & Stroke:** 3.37 x 3.37 in. (85.7 x 85.7 mm). **Compression Ratio:** 9.0:1. **Brake Horsepower:** 90 at 5000 rpm. Five main bearings. Solid valve lifters. One SU carburetor.

BASE FOUR (2000TC): Same as above, but with twin carburetors — **Compression Ratio:** 10.0:1. **Brake Horsepower:** 124 at 5500 rpm. **Torque:** 132 lbs.-ft. at 4000 rpm.

BASE SIX (3-Litre): Inline, F-head six-cylinder. Cast iron block and aluminum alloy head. **Displacement:** 183 cu. in. (2995 cc). **Bore & Stroke:** 3.06 x 4.13 in. (77.8 x 105 mm). **Compression Ratio:** 8.75:1 (8.0:1 w/automatic). **Brake Horsepower:** 134 at 5000 rpm (129 at 4750 w/automatic). **Torque:** 169 lbs.-ft. at 1750 rpm. Seven main bearings. Solid valve lifters. One SU carburetor.

1966 Rover P3 three-liter saloon. (Sotheby's)

CHASSIS DATA: Wheelbase: (2000) 103.4 in.; (3-Litre) 110.5 in. **Overall Length:** (2000) 178.5 in.; (3-Litre) 186.5 in. **Height:** (2000) 54.75 in.; (3-Litre sed) 59.3; (3-Litre cpe) 57.3 in. **Width:** (2000) 66.5 in.; (3-Litre) 70 in. **Front Tread:** (2000) 53.4 in.; (3-Litre) 55.3 in. **Rear Tread:** (2000) 52.5 in.; (3-Litre) 56 in. **Standard Tires:** (2000) 6.50x14 or 165x14; (2000TC) 165x14; (3-Litre) 6.70x15.

TECHNICAL: Layout: front-engine, rear-drive. **Transmission:** four-speed manual (overdrive on 3-Litre); Borg-Warner automatic available. **Steering:** (2000) worm and roller; (3-Litre) recirculating ball (worm and nut). **Suspension (front):** (2000) upper/lower arms with horizontal coil springs and anti-roll bar; (3-Litre) upper wishbones and radius links with laminated torsion bars. **Suspension (rear):** (2000) De Dion rigid axle with semi-axles, Watt linkage and coil springs; (3-Litre) rigid axle with semi-elliptic leaf springs. **Brakes:** (2000) front/rear disc; (3-Litre) front disc, rear drum. **Body Construction:** (2000) unibody; (3-Litre) separate body and frame.

PERFORMANCE: Top Speed: (2000) 110 mph (estimated); (2000TC) 108-116 mph. **Acceleration (0-60 mph):** (2000) 14.4 sec.; (2000TC) 11.5-12.6 sec. **Acceleration (quarter-mile):** (2000) 19.2 sec. (69 mph); (2000TC) 18.3-18.9 sec. (73.8-76 mph).

Manufacturer: The Rover Company Ltd., Solihull, Birmingham, Warwickshire, England.

Distributor: Rover Motor Company of North America, New York City.

HISTORY: During this period, Rover became a part of British Leyland. Advertisements claimed that Rover's 2000 was "the world's safest car." As noted by *Car and Driver*, a Rover was often described as the "poor man's Rolls Royce."

1969-71 ROVER

2000/2000TC — P6 — FOUR — Production of the four-cylinder 2000 series continued into 1973, after which it evolved into a 2200 series. As before, the 2000TC used a dual-carburetor engine with higher horsepower.

3500/3500S — P6 — V-8 — Starting during 1968, Rover dropped a 3528-cc (215-cid) aluminum V-8 engine into the familiar 2000-series (P6) body. This was the V-8 used in Buick Specials in the early 1960s, later acquired by Rover for use in various British automobiles. The 3500 was available only with automatic transmission at first, then with manual shift as the 3500S. As marketed in the U.S. through 1971, the V-8 developed 184 horsepower at 5200 rpm.

I.D. DATA: Not available.

Model	Body Type & Seating	Engine Type/CID	P.O.E. Price	Weight (lbs.)	Prod. Total
2000 SERIES (1969-72)					
2000	4-dr Spt Sed-4/5P	I4/121	3998	2767	N/A
2000TC	4-dr Spt Sed-4/5P	I4/121	4198	2810	N/A
3500S					
	4-dr Sedan-4/5P	V8/215	5398	3184	N/A

Price Note: Figures shown for 2000 series were valid in 1970; for 3500S in 1971.

1970 Rover 3500 S. (William Siuru Jr.)

ENGINE DATA: BASE FOUR (2000): Inline, overhead-cam four-cylinder. Cast iron block and aluminum alloy head. **Displacement:** 120.8 cu. in. (1978 cc). **Bore & Stroke:** 3.37 x 3.37 in. (85.7 x 85.7 mm). **Compression Ratio:** 9.0:1. **Brake Horsepower:** 99 at 5000 rpm. **Torque:** 121 lbs.-ft. at 3600 rpm. Five main bearings. Solid valve lifters. One SU carburetor.

BASE FOUR (2000TC): Same as above, but with twin carburetors — **Compression Ratio:** 10.0:1. **Brake Horsepower:** 124 at 5500 rpm. **Torque:** 132 lbs.-ft. at 4000 rpm.

BASE V-8 (3500S): 90-degree, overhead-valve, "vee" type eight-cylinder. Aluminum alloy block and aluminum alloy heads. **Displacement:** 215 cu. in. (3528 cc). **Bore & Stroke:** 3.50 x 2.80 in. (88.9 x 71.1 mm). **Compression Ratio:** 10.5:1. **Brake Horsepower:** 184 at 5200 rpm. **Torque:** 226 lbs.-ft. at 3000 rpm. Five main bearings. Hydraulic valve lifters. Two SU semi-downdraft carburetors.

CHASSIS DATA: Wheelbase: (2000) 103.4 in.; (3-Litre) 110.5 in. **Overall Length:** (2000) 178.5 in.; (3-Litre) 186.5 in. **Height:** (2000) 54.75 in.; (3-Litre sed) 59.3; (3-Litre cpe) 57.3 in. **Width:** (2000) 66.5 in.; (3-Litre) 70 in. **Front Tread:** (2000) 53.4 in.; (3-Litre) 55.3 in. **Rear Tread:** (2000) 52.5 in.; (3-Litre) 56 in. **Standard Tires:** (2000) 6.50x14 or 165x14; (2000TC) 165x14; (3-Litre) 6.70x15.

TECHNICAL: Layout: front-engine, rear-drive. **Transmission:** four-speed manual (overdrive on 3-Litre); Borg-Warner automatic available. **Steering:** (2000) worm and roller; (3-Litre) recirculating ball (worm and nut). **Suspension (front):** (2000) upper/lower arms with horizontal coil springs and anti-roll bar; (3-Litre) upper wishbones and radius links with laminated torsion bars. **Suspension (rear):** (2000) De Dion rigid axle with semi-axles, Watt linkage and coil springs; (3-Litre) rigid axle with semi-elliptic leaf springs. **Brakes:** (2000) front/rear disc; (3-Litre) front disc, rear drum. **Body Construction:** (2000) unibody; (3-Litre) separate body and frame.

PERFORMANCE: Top Speed: (3500S) 114 mph. **Acceleration (0-60 mph):** (3500S) 12.5 sec. (another road test claimed 0-60 mph in 8.1 sec.). **Acceleration (quarter-mile):** 18.9 sec. (76 mph).

Manufacturer: The Rover Company Ltd., Solihull, Birmingham, Warwickshire, England.

Distributor: Rover Motor Company of North America, New York City.

HISTORY: A V-8 engine was first used in the older P5 body, during 1967 only, before it went into the P6 (2000-series) body. *Road Test* magazine declared that the Rover 3500 "must rate among the best engineered cars produced in the automotive world today."

1972-80 ROVER

1980 Rover V-8 with ex-Buick engine. (Elliott Kahn)

Rover left the U.S. market after the 1971 model year, except for the 4WD Land Rover, which remained available as late as 1974 (see that listing). The 2000 series evolved into a 2200 series by 1974, and the 3500S remained available elsewhere in the world into 1976. Then came a new wedge-shaped Rover SD1 hatchback sedan, also with V-8 power. Early ratings for the SD1's V-8 were 155 bhp at 5250 rpm and 198 pound-feet of torque at 2500 rpm. Standard features included a self-leveling suspension. Top speed was claimed to be 125 mph, with 0-60 mph acceleration under 9 seconds. Overhead-cam six-cylinder engines went into that model later in the decade.

For the 1980 model year, Rover made one more (brief) stab at the American market with the 3500 hatchback sedan, marketed by Jaguar-Rover-Triumph in Leonia, New Jersey. Ads promoted the 3500 as being "logical as a sedan...practical as a station wagon ...responsive as a sports car." The four-door body had a sloped front hood and swept-back roofline, with a front spoiler. Wheelbase was 110.8 inches, and the sedan measured 191 inches long. Three engines were offered in Britain, but only the 3528-cc (215-cid) V-8 came to America this time. That engine was rated 133 horsepower at 5000 rpm, with 165 pound-feet of torque at 3250 rpm. Either a five-speed manual gearbox or three-speed automatic was available. MacPherson struts made up the front suspension, with coil springs at the rear. Velour upholstery was installed. Power rack-and-pinion steering and air conditioning were standard, as were cruise control, power windows, power door locks, and a signal-seeking stereo radio with cassette player. Tires were 195/70x14 size. A total of 481 of these last-ditch Rovers were sold in the U.S. during 1980, priced at $15,900 (plus $350 for automatic transmission).

SAAB

Airplanes to automobiles isn't the most common switch for a company to make, though certain obvious similarities exist between the two. That's the route taken by the Swedish Saab, a decade after the Svenska Aeroplan Aktiebolaget (AB) had been formed to produce military aircraft. Because of the rising threat of war in Europe, the privately-run company was encouraged by the Swedish government to start up in 1937, to help strengthen the country's air force and thereby assist it to maintain neutrality. Production commenced near the industrial town of Trollhattan, with technical assistance from several American aircraft firms. The Type 21 pusher-prop, in particular, led to the development of Saab's first jet plane after the war.

Well before hostilities ceased, however, Saab was contemplating the prospects for automobile production, anticipating a rising need for private transport that could not be filled by devastated European concerns. Late in 1945, with peace at hand, they decided to proceed with Project 92. Saab's design team was headed by engineer Gunnar Ljungstrom, who'd formerly worked at Rover and Standard in Britain. He and others were most impressed by the prewar front-drive DKW, and many details from that German-built auto wound up on the first Saabs. In addition to front-wheel-drive, the Saab would eschew the customary four-cycle engine and carry a two-stroke powerplant instead. Two-strokes, it was felt, were simpler and cheaper to build (with fewer parts), more reliable, easier to repair, and would start more easily during cold Swedish winters. Because of Ljungstrom's desire for a streamlined, lightweight model, Saab chose to use unibody construction. Body design came from outsider Sixten Sason, who'd penned unibody cars before the war, largely because early in-house attempts looked too much like American autos. His creation was projectile-shaped below the beltline, but up top looked almost exactly like the ultimate production Saab. An early prototype, built partly from junkyard parts, was running in 1946.

In June 1947, a Saab was shown to the press. Not until summer 1949 did the first batch of 25 sedans come off the line; and significant production did not begin until December of that year. Unorthodox it was, but displaying a charm of its own, and with some of Saab's aircraft construction techniques evident. In fact, their distinctive fastback profile made Saabs one of the easiest cars to spot from a distance. For 1953, a modestly-modified 92B replaced the original 92, adding a larger rear window and a trunk lid. Then came a three-cylinder version, logically called the Type 93. Marketing of the 93 in the U.S. began early in 1957, after Saab had established an office in New York. In addition to the basic sedan, a high-performance 750 Granturismo became available. A Type 95 station wagon appeared during 1959, followed by a 96 sedan the following year.

Major additions for 1967 included a German Ford V-4 engine to augment (then replace) the original two-stroke powerplants, and a new Sonett II sports car. The Sonett name had actually appeared on a prototype in the mid-1950s, but never went into production. Although the original fastback two-door sedan design continued through the 1970s, it disappeared from the U.S. market by 1974, having been eclipsed by the new and different series 99, introduced five years earlier. With that restyled sedan, initially powered by a Triumph-built engine, Saab began to alter its image, gradually establishing itself in America as an upscale automobile for the rising number of young professionals. All the more so when the 99 evolved into the longer-wheelbase 900 and, later, the 9000 series. Turbocharged engines, which first appeared in 1977, mixed performance with comfort, helping to keep Saab sales strong in the U.S. marketplace. Convertibles added even more panache to the marque's sport/luxury image in the 1980s.

1950-52 SAAB

92 — TWO — Saab design chief Gunnar Ljungstrom's desire for a streamlined, modern automobile--roomy inside and with adequate ground clearance, yet offering a relatively low center of gravity--was evident in the first production Saab. Unibody construction blended strength with light weight, and space was provided for four (possibly five) passengers.

A two-cylinder, two-stroke engine with light-alloy head and hemispherical combustion chambers went transversely ahead of the front axle, with three-speed gearbox alongside, allowing passenger feet to fit between the front wheels. Though similar to DKW's, the Saab engine had a number of distinct features, including roller main bearings along with ball bearings. Saab's initial intention of using a Dynastart combination starter/generator (like DKW) was abandoned, in favor of separate units. Unlike most generators, though, Saab's was driven by the gearbox. Thermo-syphon cooling and a radiator blind eliminated a water pump, but the need for one would soon become evident. It would not arrive until the model 93, in the mid-1950s. Freewheeling made gear changes easy.

Early Saabs had independent torsion-bar suspension all around, as well as a flat floorpan and rack-and-pinion steering. Low placement of back-seat passengers allowed the fastback shape, with low drag coefficient, that would became a Saab trademark into the 1960s. That continuous roofline stretched from the windshield all the way to the tail end, with large triangular side windows following that profile. A smooth body line also ran from the bottom of the front fender's leading edge to the rear fender's lower trailing edge. Convex bodysides displayed slight fairing above rather small wheel openings. All early Saabs were painted green. A low, shallow grille opening contained four horizontal bars, with a Saab badge above. Along the hood was a small central spine. Small round parking lights sat below and outboard of the vertical-style headlamps. Semaphore-style turn signals were mounted high on center pillars. Quarter-type bumpers reached around onto the fenders and included overriders. Below the split windshield was a small air scoop.

To help cut costs, Saab used a back window smaller than planned, and omitted a trunk lid. Lack of each item was later criticized, but changes would not come for some years. Lack of a trunk lid allowed the gas filler cap to go below the back window, while a vertical back panel held the taillamps and license plate. Doors were hinged at the rear. Cloth upholstery covered the seats. All instruments, including a strip-style speedometer, sat in a long rectangular panel, ahead of the driver, with an open glovebox to the right and a rear-view mirror atop the dashboard. A pull-cable started the engine. DeLuxe models added a clock and temperature gauge, plus a rear center armrest and extra horn.

I.D. DATA: Serial number plate is on left side of firewall, under the hood. Engine number is on a boss on the side of the block. Starting chassis serial number: 5/001.

Model	Body Type & Seating	Engine Type/CID	P.O.E. Price	Weight (lbs.)	Prod. Total
92	2-dr Sedan-4/5P	I2/47	N/A	1680	Note 1

Note 1: A total of 1,246 Saabs were produced during 1950, 2,179 in 1951, and 2,298 in 1952.

ENGINE DATA: BASE TWO: Inline, two-stroke two-cylinder. Cast iron block and light alloy head. **Displacement:** 46.6 cu. in. (764 cc). **Bore & Stroke:** 3.15 x 2.99 in. (80 x 76 mm). **Compression Ratio:** 6.6:1. **Brake Horsepower:** 25 at 3800 rpm. Solex 32 AIC downdraft carburetor. Two-coil ignition (6-volt).

CHASSIS DATA: Wheelbase: 97 in. **Overall Length:** 154 in. **Height:** 56 in. **Width:** 64 in. **Front Tread:** 46 in. **Rear Tread:** 46 in. **Wheel Type:** steel disc. **Standard Tires:** 5.00x15.

TECHNICAL: Layout: front-engine, front-drive. **Transmission:** three-speed manual transaxle (2nd/3rd synchro). Overall gear ratios: (1st) 18.5:1; (2nd) 8.55:1; (3rd) 5.35:1; (rev) 24.65:1. **Standard Final Drive Ratio:** 5.35:1. **Steering:** rack and pinion. **Suspension (front):** independent; transverse torsion bars. **Suspension (rear):** independent; transverse torsion bars. **Brakes:** hydraulic, front/rear drum. **Body Construction:** steel unibody.

PERFORMANCE: Top Speed: about 65 mph (early reports claimed only about 50 mph, but 40 mpg fuel mileage).

Manufacturer: Svenska Aeroplan Aktiebolaget (AB), Trollhattan, Sweden.

HISTORY: Saab's overall appearance, as described by Britain's *Motor* magazine, offered the "low, sleek lines of a super-sports coupe." On the minus side, testers criticized the car's lack of rearward visibility, the need to mix gas and oil for the two-stroke engine, lack of a trunk lid, and tendency to oversteer. They liked the car's flat floor, and the easy gear changing that freewheeling permitted (though many observers complained that it often caused the engine to stall). Many modifications were made during the next years, in response to reported problems. Rolf Mellde, for example, drove a Saab in the 1950 Monte Carlo Rally, complaining of what turned out to be carburetor icing. So in 1951, a removable preheater pipe was fitted. Earlier, within weeks of the emergence of the first production models, Mellde had driven a Saab to victory in the Swedish Winter Rally, the first of many such rally wins to follow in succeeding years.

1953 SAAB

92B — TWO — In response to complaints about lack of visibility and luggage access, the next Saab model had a trunk lid and larger back window. The gas tank moved to the inside of the left rear fender; the battery from inside the trunk to under the hood. Rear

seats could be removed to expand luggage space, and front seats added curved seat-backs plus foam rubber padding. Separate parking lights were installed. While the early 92 came only in green, its replacement had a choice of six: light grey, blue grey, black, light green, tan, and maroon.

I.D. DATA: Serial number plate is on left side of firewall, under the hood. Engine number is on a boss on the side of the block. Starting serial number (92B): 5/3001.

Model	Body Type & Seating	Engine Type/CID	P.O.E. Price	Weight (lbs.)	Prod. Total
92B	2-dr Sedan-4/5P	I2/47	N/A	1680	Note 1

Note 1: A total of 3,424 Saabs were produced during 1953.

ENGINE DATA: BASE TWO: Same as 1950-52.

CHASSIS DATA: Wheelbase: 97 in. **Overall Length:** 154 in. **Height:** 56 in. **Width:** 64 in. **Front Tread:** 46 in. **Rear Tread:** 46 in. **Wheel Type:** steel disc. **Standard Tires:** 5.00x15.

TECHNICAL: Same as 1950-52.

Manufacturer: Svenska Aeroplan AB, Trollhattan, Sweden.

1954-55 SAAB

1954 Saab Model 92 two-door sedan.

92B — TWO — Horsepower of the two-cylinder engine rose from 25 to 28 for the final version of the 92B. Late in 1953, synthetic paint had replaced the former cellulose variety. Road wheels added perforations to improve brake cooling. Bright metal strips were mounted above wheel openings. Small clear "perspex" triangles went across upper rear corner of door windows, to cut drafts into passenger areas. Upholstery now came in either cloth, or plastic with cloth inserts. Later in this period, small separate parking lights were dropped, replaced by lights built into the headlamps. The grille also was modified.

I.D. DATA: Serial number plate is on left side of firewall, under the hood. Engine number is on a boss on the side of the block.

Model	Body Type & Seating	Engine Type/CID	P.O.E. Price	Weight (lbs.)	Prod. Total
92B	2-dr Sedan-4/5P	I2/47	N/A	1680	Note 1

Note 1: A total of 5,138 Saabs were produced during 1954, and 5,620 in 1955. Including a final 680 examples built in 1956, total production of the Type 92 was 20,128 (including 14,800 Type 92B).

ENGINE DATA: BASE TWO: Inline, two-stroke two-cylinder. Cast iron block and light alloy head. **Displacement:** 46.6 cu. in. (764 cc). **Bore & Stroke:** 3.15 x 2.99 in. (80 x 76 mm). **Compression Ratio:** 6.6:1. **Brake Horsepower:** 28 at 4000 rpm. Solex 32 AIC downdraft carburetor. Two-coil ignition.

CHASSIS DATA: Wheelbase: 97 in. **Overall Length:** 154 in. **Height:** 56 in. **Width:** 64 in. **Front Tread:** 46 in. **Rear Tread:** 46 in. **Wheel Type:** steel disc. **Standard Tires:** 5.00x15.

TECHNICAL: Same as 1950-53.

Manufacturer: Svenska Aeroplan AB, Trollhattan, Sweden.

HISTORY: Production of the 92B continued into 1956, after the debut of the new Type 93.

1956-57 SAAB

93 — THREE — As part of the next evolutionary step of the Saab, a three-cylinder engine replaced the former twin-cylinder, but it was also a two-stroke that required mixing of oil and gas. Displacement was actually a bit smaller than the former two-cylinder, and horsepower remained about the same, but it offered smoother operation and more torque output, as well as improved economy. Convex-type pistons were used, again with hemispherical combustion chambers. Layout was altered from transverse to longitudinal, with the engine rotated so it sat ahead of the gearbox instead of alongside. A conventional ignition system was installed, with a distributor and single coil. To improve cooling, a water pump was installed, as a unit with the generator. The radiator grew in

size and was positioned behind the engine, and its blind moved forward to just behind the grille. In an attempt to rid the Saab of its oversteering propensity, the suspension was reworked substantially, switching from torsion bars to coil springs. While the front suspension remained independent, using transverse links and a stabilizer bar along with its coil springs, the rear was not. Instead, the back end used a U-shaped tubular, rigid axle and trailing arms with the coil springs, with two longitudinal links in progressively-acting rubber mounts. Track increased by almost two inches with the new arrangement.

Saab's hood was hinged at the front, and could be removed completely for access to engine space. Engine, clutch, gearbox and differential consisted of a single unit which lifted easily out of the car. As before, the column-shift gearbox gave three forward speeds, and could be shifted between 2nd and 3rd without using the clutch, because of freewheeling. Gear ratios were modified this year. Second gear, according to company literature, was usable to about 45 mph for passing. A two-spoke steering wheel was used, with rack-and-pinion steering. The spare tire rode in a separate section under the luggage compartment.

Overall appearance was similar to the Type 92, with the same split windshield and rear-hinged doors but a modified nose, with a slightly flatter front panel. Front wheel openings were higher than before. A much narrower, taller central grille, with a square-mesh pattern and tapering inward at the top, was accompanied by twin side "grilles," each with two horizontal aluminum slats that stretched outward below the headlamps. Those slightly-recessed headlamps, again mounted inboard of the fenders, had full and dipped beams, with parking lights built into the hood. New flat-fronted bumpers included overriders. At the rear were twin taillamps. Semaphore-style directional indicators again were built into rear-door pillars. Standard equipment included heater/defroster, dual horns, dual wipers, ceiling lights, chrome-plated bumpers, twin sunvisors, and draft shields at the windows. The 93's gauges had gold letters on black backgrounds, and a roller-type gas pedal was still used. Back windows did not open, but Saab interiors could be turned into sleeping space for two. Entry into the U.S. market in 1956 brought only a few changes for those export models, including the addition of scuff guards to back fenders. Whitewall tires also were common on American Saabs.

1956 Saab 93. (William Siuru Jr.)

I.D. DATA: Serial number plate is on left side of firewall, under the hood. Engine number is on a boss on the right side of the block.

Model	Body Type & Seating	Engine Type/CID	P.O.E. Price	Weight (lbs.)	Prod. Total
93	2-dr Sedan-4/5P	I3/46	1895	1734	Note 1

Note 1: A total of 6,320 Saabs were produced during 1956 (including 680 final Type 92 sedans), and 9,847 in 1957.

Weight Note: Figure shown is "empty" weight (no fuel or water).

ENGINE DATA: BASE THREE: Inline, two-stroke three-cylinder. Cast iron block and aluminum alloy head. **Displacement:** 45.6 cu. in. (748 cc). **Bore & Stroke:** 2.59 x 2.87 in. (66 x 72.9 mm). **Compression Ratio:** 7.3:1. **Brake Horsepower:** 37.5 at 5000 rpm. **Torque:** 52.1 lbs.-ft. at 2000 rpm. Four main bearings. Solex 40 AI downdraft carburetor. Distributor-type ignition (12-volt).

CHASSIS DATA: Wheelbase: 98 in. **Overall Length:** 157.1 in. **Height:** 57.1 in. **Width:** 61.5 in. **Front Tread:** 48 in. **Rear Tread:** 48 in. **Wheel Type:** 4-inch disc. **Standard Tires:** 5.00x15.

TECHNICAL: Layout: front-engine, front-drive. **Transmission:** three-speed manual transaxle (2nd/3rd synchro and freewheeling); column lever. Overall gear ratios: (1st) 16.74:1; (2nd) 8.31:1; (3rd) 5.10:1; (rev) 20.46:1. **Standard Final Drive Ratio:** 5.10:1. **Steering:** rack and pinion. **Suspension (front):** independent; coil springs with transverse links and anti-roll bar. **Suspension (rear):** rigid U-shaped tubular axle with trailing arms and coil springs. **Brakes:** hydraulic, front/rear drum. **Body Construction:** steel unibody.

PERFORMANCE: Top Speed: 70-74 mph. **Acceleration (0-60 mph):** 24.9 sec. (0-50 mph in about 16.3 seconds). **Acceleration (0-60 mph):** 22.6 sec. (57 mph). **Fuel Mileage:** about 32-37 mpg.

Manufacturer: Svenska Aeroplan AB, Trollhattan, Sweden. **Distributor:** Saab Motors Inc., New York City.

HISTORY: Appearing at the New York International Automobile Show in April/May 1956, the 93B became the first Swedish automobile offered to the American market. To assist in that export effort, Saab opened an office in New York City. The first boatload of Saabs arrived in December 1956, and in the first full year (1957), about 1,400 were sold in the U.S.

Press releases from that New York show of 1956 also described Saab's new experimental sports car, the Super Sport Sonett, displayed for the first time outside Sweden. Sonett's body was made of laminated fiberglass plastic, on a chassis similar to the 93 sedan. The three-cylinder engine was boosted to 57.7 horsepower at 5000 rpm with twin carburetors, working through a four-speed gearbox. A lightweight Sonett (1,150 pounds) was expected to reach 120 mph with the top up and accelerate from 0-60 mph in 12 seconds or less. Unfortunately, only half a dozen prototypes were built, and the Sonett name would not emerge on a production sports car for another decade (see 1967 listing). Ads in 1957 promoted Saab's victories at rally events, including the Great American Mountain Rallye, which consisted of four grueling days through New England snow and ice. Saab won the team prize as well as 750-cc and touring class victories at that event in late 1956.

1958-59 SAAB

1959 Saab 93B two-door sedan.

93B — THREE — Improvements for 1958 that turned the Type 93 sedan into a 93B included a new wraparound curved windshield (replacing the former split unit), plus new rectangular flashing turn signals in front fenders to replace the former semaphore trafficators. An anti-theft device was built into the ignition switch (actually an armored cable between the switch and coil), and windshield wipers were improved. A self-mixing gas tank also was installed, eliminating the need to premix oil and fuel (except in severe weather). The ratio of oil to gas was reduced. Front seats now had anchorages for safety belts, while the rear seat had a height adjustment that made use of a wooden cam.

For the 1959 model year, only a few modifications were evident in the basic Saab two-door model. Seatbacks added deeper foam-rubber padding and could be adjusted to seven rake angles. Windshield washers and a locking glovebox lid were added, along with padded sunvisors. Brake drums were enlarged from 8-inch to 9-inch diameter.

GT750 — THREE — Introduced in spring 1958, the high-performance Granturismo 750 was aimed at the American market and carried a more potent version of the three-cylinder two-stroke engine (called the Sonett sports). Compression got a hefty boost. A twin-choke Solex 44 PII carburetor was mounted on a special intake manifold, with sports-type air filters and twin SU electric fuel pumps. Appearance was similar to the 93B, but two chrome trim strips ran along the lower body, between the wheel openings, to meet the scuff guards at the rear fenders. Large, well-shaped bucket seats reclined fully and had extra pads on their backrests. They adjusted to 14 positions. Rear seats had little padding, and were intended only for occasional use. Extra features included racing tires, oversize brakes, a shoulder harness, wood-rimmed light-alloy steering wheel, twin chromed driving lights, tachometer, plus a Halda Speed-Pilot (average-speed computer) and grab handle at the right of the dashboard. Special GT wheels had been developed for the first Sonett. An optional factory tuning kit boosted the normal 50-bhp rating to 57.

95 — THREE — During the 1959 model year, a Type 95 station wagon joined the sedan; see next listing for details.

I.D. DATA: Serial number plate is on left side of firewall. Engine number is on the right side of the block.

Model	Body Type & Seating	Engine Type/CID	P.O.E. Price	Weight (lbs.)	Prod. Total
93B	2-dr Sedan-4/5P	I3/46	1895	1735	Note 1
GT750	2-dr Spt Sed-2 + 2P	I3/46	2568	1750	Note 1

Note 1: A total of 13,968 Saabs were produced during 1958, and 17,836 in 1959.

ENGINE DATA: BASE THREE (93B): Inline, two-stroke three-cylinder. Cast nickel alloy steel block and aluminum head. **Displacement:** 45.6 cu. in. (748 cc). **Bore & Stroke:** 2.59 x 2.87 in. (66 x 72.9 mm). **Compression Ratio:** 7.3:1. **Brake Horsepower:** 38 at 5000 rpm. **Torque:** 52 lbs.-ft. at 2000 rpm. Four main bearings. Solex 40 AI downdraft carburetor.

BASE THREE (GT750): Same as above, except — **Compression Ratio:** 9.0:1. **Brake Horsepower:** 50 at 5000 rpm. **Torque:** 61 lbs.-ft. at 3500 rpm. Twin-choke Solex 44 PII carburetor.

Note: Modified GT750 engine with twin carburetors produced 57 bhp.

CHASSIS DATA: Wheelbase: 98 in. **Overall Length:** 158 in. **Height:** 58 in. **Width:** 62 in. **Front Tread:** 48 in. **Rear Tread:** 48 in. **Wheel Type:** disc. **Standard Tires:** 5.00x15.

TECHNICAL: Layout: front-engine, front-drive. **Transmission:** three-speed manual; column lever. **Steering:** rack and pinion. **Suspension (front):** independent; coil springs with transverse links and stabilizer bar. **Suspension (rear):** U-shaped tubular axle with trailing arms and coil springs. **Brakes:** hydraulic, front/rear drum. **Body Construction:** steel unibody. **Fuel Tank:** 9.5 gallon.

MAJOR OPTIONS: Automatic clutch ($100). Sunroof ($155). Factory tuning kit for GT750 (twin carburetors, special manifold and exhaust; 57 bhp).

PERFORMANCE: Top Speed: (93B) 78-85 mph; (GT750) 93 mph; (GT750 w/speed kit) 100 mph. **Acceleration (0-60 mph):** 28.5 seconds. **Fuel Mileage:** (93B) 25-35 mpg.

Manufacturer: Svenska Aeroplan AB, Trollhattan, Sweden.

Distributor: Saab Motors Inc., New York City.

HISTORY: At the New York Auto Show in spring 1958, Saab displayed the 93B, a Saxomat automatic-clutch model, the new Granturismo 750, and a cutaway full working model of the three-cylinder engine. A promotional brochure at that show noted that Saab stood for: Safe and Sturdy; Aerodynamic construction; Acceleration Plus; Better mpg. A Saab had recently won the Great Florida Rally. Corporate literature described the 750 as "an automobile of exceptional performance, suitable for transcontinental touring or rally race competition."

1960 SAAB

93F — THREE — For its final season, the 93B evolved into the 93F, the latter wearing doors hinged at the front instead of the rear.

95 — THREE — Saab's two-door station wagon was introduced in June 1959, with a larger three-cylinder engine (still two-stroke). Bore was increased from 66 to 70 mm, but stroke remained the same. The new engine had a 12-bolt head, versus eight bolts for the smaller three-cylinder version, partly to solve the problem of blown head gaskets. A restyled rear end followed the line of the door window (instead of the sedan's familiar downward curve). Because they reached a tad past that back end, the rear fenders formed a trace of tailfin. Twin round taillamp pairs were mounted one over the other. The rear bumper reached farther around the bodyside than usual, with the license plate between its guards (overriders). Tires grew to 5.60x15 size, and the gas tank had a larger capacity. Both rear and auxiliary rear seats could fold downward to create a long cargo area, or be used as a bed. That cargo floor was plastic-coated sheetmetal. With all seats erect, the 95 wagon could carry as many as seven people. Initial Type 95 wagons retained the rear-hinged doors of the 93B doors, then switched to front-hinged doors as on the 93F.

GT750 — THREE — Production of the GT750 continued with little change, except for a switch to front-hinged doors like the 93F. When the new 96 sedan appeared during the 1960 model year, the GT750 adopted that body but retained the smaller engine so it would remain eligible to compete in the under-750-cc racing class. A four-speed gearbox also replaced the former three-speed. See next listing for details on both models.

I.D. DATA: Serial number plate is on left side of firewall. Engine number is on the right side of the block.

Model	Body Type & Seating	Engine Type/CID	P.O.E. Price	Weight (lbs.)	Prod. Total
93B/F	2-dr Sedan-4/5P	I3/46	1895	1735	Note 1
GT750	2-dr Spt Sed-2 + 2P	I3/46	2568	1750	Note 1
95	2-dr Sta Wagon-6/7P	I3/51	N/A	N/A	Note 1

Note 1: A total of 26,066 Saabs were produced during 1960, including 5,042 final Type 93 models.

ENGINE DATA: BASE THREE (93F): Inline, two-stroke three-cylinder. Cast nickel alloy steel block and aluminum head. **Displacement:** 45.6 cu. in. (748 cc). **Bore & Stroke:** 2.59 x 2.87 in. (66 x 72.9 mm). **Compression Ratio:** 7.3:1. **Brake Horsepower:** 38 at 5000 rpm. **Torque:** 52 lbs.-ft. at 2000 rpm. Four main bearings. Solex 40 AI downdraft carburetor.

BASE THREE (GT750): Same as above, except — **Compression Ratio:** 9.0:1. **Brake Horsepower:** 50 at 5000 rpm. **Torque:** 61 lbs.-ft. at 3500 rpm. Twin-choke Solex 44 PII carburetor.

Note: Modified GT750 engine with twin carburetors produced 57 bhp.

BASE THREE (95): Inline, two-stroke three-cylinder. Cast nickel alloy steel block and aluminum head. **Displacement:** 51.3 cu. in. (841 cc). **Bore & Stroke:** 2.76 x 2.87 in. (70 x 72.9 mm). **Compression Ratio:** 7.3:1. **Brake Horsepower:** 42 at 5000 rpm. **Torque:** 59 lbs.-ft. at 3000 rpm. Four main bearings. Solex 40 AI downdraft carburetor.

CHASSIS DATA: Wheelbase: 98 in. **Overall Length:** (93) 158 in.; (95) 162 in. **Height:** (93) 58 in.; (95) 57.9 in. **Width:** (93) 62 in.; (95) 61.8 in. **Front Tread:** 48 in. **Rear Tread:** 48 in. **Wheel Type:** disc. **Standard Tires:** (93) 5.00x15; (95) 5.60x15.

TECHNICAL: Layout: front-engine, front-drive. **Transmission:** (93F/95) three-speed manual; (GT750) four-speed manual, all synchro. **Standard Final Drive Ratio:** 5.43:1. **Steering:** rack and pinion. **Suspension (front):** independent; coil springs with transverse links and stabilizer bar. **Suspension (rear):** U-shaped tubular axle with trailing arms and coil springs. **Brakes:** hydraulic, front/rear drum. **Body Construction:** steel unibody. **Fuel Tank:** 9.5 gallon.

MAJOR OPTIONS: Automatic clutch ($100). Sunroof ($124). Factory tuning kit for GT750 (twin carburetors, special manifold and exhaust; 57 bhp).

PERFORMANCE: Top Speed: (93B) 78-80 mph. **Fuel Mileage:** (93B) 35-40 mpg.

Manufacturer: Svenska Aeroplan AB, Trollhattan, Sweden.

Distributor: Saab Motors Inc., New York City.

HISTORY: The four-speed version of the GT750, wearing a new Type 96 body, made its world debut at the New York Auto Show in April 1960. See next listing for details on that GT750 and the new 96 sedan, which debuted in February 1960 as a '61 model. Other Saabs at the New York event were the 93F sedan, a sunroof sedan, and the series 95 station wagon. A press release for that show was titled: "Saab - the small car for big men." At the 1960 Monte Carlo Rally, Carl Bremer of the Saab team finished 9th overall (1st in class) while Greta Molander finished 16th.

1961-62 SAAB

96 — THREE — Powered by the larger three-cylinder engine that appeared earlier under the new Type 95 station wagon's hood, the revised two-door replacement for the 93 series debuted in February 1960, but as a 1961 model. Saab called the new series "a sure-footed family car with sports car spirit," which was "built with aircraft quality." The five-passenger body was described as a "happy reconciliation of safety with beauty," featuring a front end that gently curved with no sharp projections and a restyled rear end with larger wraparound back window. The new sedan, they added, was modified to fulfill the requirements of American motorists, including widening the rear seat by some 10 inches to accommodate three adults; increasing trunk space to 13 cubic feet; and enlarging the rear window area by 117 percent. Basic appearance was similar to the former 93, with the same fastback profile. A bigger wraparound windshield was used, while side windows were both larger and reshaped. New extractor vents for the flow-through heat/vent system were added between side and back windows. An enlarged trunk lid now held the license plate, below a chrome handle. Larger taillamps were mounted on the trailing edge of rear fenders. The revised rear end displayed a softer 'S' curve of the rear fender panel, with slimmer corner posts. A round medallion stood on the rear post, between the back and side windows. Both the 96 sedan and 95 wagon had a more powerful version of the famous two-stroke engine, rated 42 bhp (SAE). Early brochures announced a three-speed gearbox, as in former models; but that would switch later to a four-speed.

1962 Saab 96.

Rear sections of both bodies could be made into a double bed. Saab's many safety features included heavily-padded sunvisors and dashboard. Steel replaced plywood as the material for the car's firewall. An all-new fascia was painted to match the body color: red, beige, blue or green. Dark grey safety padding was installed, and the instrument panel consisted of a dark grey aluminum casting. A strip-type speedometer used a fluorescent strip (no needle). Control knobs were cream-colored at first (as in the 93); then switched to dark grey. A few months after the first models became available, both road wheels and fascia switched to light grey color. Standard 96 equipment included twin padded sunvisors, windshield washers, self-canceling turn signals, ashtrays front and rear, locking glovebox, heater/defroster, low-fuel warning light, and seven-position seatbacks. Standard colors for 1962 were: pearl grey, black, light blue, grey, white, and red.

95 — THREE — Production of Saab's two-door station wagon, introduced in June 1959, continued with little change. Wagons now had front-hinged doors, like the 96 sedan. During the 1961 model year, the 95 wagon adopted instruments from the 96 sedan, replacing the original 93-type gauges. Rear pillars abandoned their chromed cappings, while the back end of the wagon's roof added an airfoil. Saab claimed the wagon could carry 925 pounds or seat seven passengers. A four-speed gearbox was listed as optional.

GT750 — THREE — Production of the GT750 continued with little change, wearing the 96-style body but retaining the smaller (748 cc) three-cylinder engine. That permitted the Granturismo to maintain eligibility for racing in the under-750-cc class. A four-speed gearbox was now standard. Saab sometimes referred to the 750 as a "sports coupe" rather than a sedan, even though its basic body was virtually identical to the standard model. This performance Saab lacked the usual chrome moldings that ran along the bodyside bottoms, and had chrome wheel rims, open-up rear side windows, badges on front fenders, and backup lights. Standard equipment also included twin shoulder harness seatbelts, fully reclining seats (with headrest on passenger side), racing tires, front-mounted high-speed driving lights, twin outside mirrors, front/rear carpeting, windshield washers, and wood-rimmed racing steering wheel. Full instrumentation included a tachometer and the Halda Speed Pilot. Custom-fitted compartments were included, under the rear seat and armrests. A "Super" GT750 tuning kit with twin Solex carburetors boosted horsepower to 57 and added $130 to the car's price.

I.D. DATA: Serial number plate is on left side of firewall. Engine number is on the right side of the block. Starting serial number for 1961 models: (96) 112501; (GT750) 100001; (wag) 1701. Starting serial number for 1962 models: (96) 139601; (wag) 3685.

Model	Body Type & Seating	Engine Type/CID	P.O.E. Price	Weight (lbs.)	Prod. Total
96	2-dr Sedan-5P	I3/51	1895	1817	Note 1
95	2-dr Sta Wag-6/7P	I3/51	2265	2050	Note 1
GT750	2-dr Spt Sed-2+2P	I3/46	2790	1900	Note 1

Note 1: A total of 33,040 Saabs were produced during 1961, and 35,890 in 1962.

ENGINE DATA: BASE THREE (95/96): Inline, two-stroke three-cylinder. Cast nickel alloy steel block and aluminum head. **Displacement:** 51.3 cu. in. (841 cc). **Bore & Stroke:** 2.76 x 2.87 in. (70 x 72.9 mm). **Compression Ratio:** 7.3:1. **Brake Horsepower:** 42 (SAE) at 5000 rpm. Torque: 59 lbs.-ft. at 3000 rpm. Four main bearings. Solex 40 AI downdraft carburetor.

BASE THREE (GT750): Inline, two-stroke three-cylinder. Cast nickel alloy steel block and aluminum head. **Displacement:** 45.6 cu. in. (748 cc). **Bore & Stroke:** 2.59 x 2.87 in. (66 x 72.9 mm). **Compression Ratio:** 9.0:1. **Brake Horsepower:** 50 at 5000 rpm. **Torque:** 61 lbs.-ft. at 3500 rpm. Four main bearings. Twin-choke Solex 44 PII carburetor.

CHASSIS DATA: Wheelbase: 98 in. **Overall Length:** (96/GT750) 158 in.; (95) 162 in. Height: (96/GT750) 58 in.; (95) 57.9 in. **Width:** (96/GT750) 62 in.; (95) 61.8 in. **Front Tread:** 48 in. **Rear Tread:** 48 in. **Wheel Type:** (96) 4Jx15 wide-base artillery type. **Standard Tires:** (96) 5.00/5.20x15; (95) 5.60x15; (GT750) 155x15.

TECHNICAL: Layout: front-engine, front-drive. **Transmission:** (96/95) three-speed manual standard, four-speed available on 95 wagon and later on 96 sedan; (GT750) four-speed manual. **Standard Final Drive Ratio:** (96) 5.43:1; (95) 4.61:1. **Steering:** rack and pinion. **Suspension (front):** independent; coil springs with wishbones. **Suspension (rear):** U-shaped tubular (rigid) axle with coil springs. **Brakes:** hydraulic, front/rear drum. **Body Construction:** steel unibody. **Fuel Tank:** (96) 10.5 gal.; (95) 11.4 gallon.

MAJOR OPTIONS: Saxomat automatic clutch ($100). Four-speed transmission: 95 wagon ($130). Sunroof: 96 sedan ($125). Radio. "Super" factory tuning kit for GT750 with twin carburetors, special manifold and exhaust, 57-bhp ($130).

PERFORMANCE: Top Speed: (96/95) 80 mph; (GT750) 85 mph; (GT750 Super) 95 mph. **Fuel Mileage:** (96/95) about 30 mpg; (GT750) about 28 mpg.

Manufacturer: Svenska Aeroplan AB, Trollhattan, Sweden.

Distributor: Saab Motors Inc., New York City.

HISTORY: The four-speed GT made its world premiere at the New York International Automobile Show in April 1960. The new 96 sedan debuted early in 1960, and was introduced in the U.S. on October 1, 1960. Britain's *Autosport* magazine noted of the 96 that the "two best features of the car are its roadholding and the exceptional silence of its cruising at speeds close to the maximum." Erik Carlsson was 4th overall at the 1961 Monte Carlo race, and earned an upset victory in the 1962 event. Saabs continued to make a good showing at many rally events. Late in 1962, a GT850 with the larger Saab engine replaced the GT750; see next listing for details.

1963 SAAB

96/95 — THREE — Little change was evident on the sedan and wagon, except that the 'Saab' name was now cast into the upper center of the grille, whereas it had formerly been separate, above the grille. Inside, both models had a semicircle horn ring. A four-speed manual gearbox became available for the sedan, as well as the station wagon. Body colors for 1963 were: green, dark blue, light blue, grey, white, and red.

GT850 — THREE — Saab's Granturismo sports sedan switched to the larger (841-cc) engine for 1963. In Europe, it was generally called the "Saab Sport;" and would soon adopt the name "Monte Carlo" in the U.S. Under GT hoods, the three-cylinder engine delivered 57 horsepower (52 bhp DIN), using three parallel-linked carburetors. A separate lubrication system, using a tank alongside the engine, eliminated the need to mix oil and gasoline. This was the first production Saab with front disc brakes. Unlike the GT750, this new version abandoned the Halda Speedpilot as standard equipment, but it remained available as an option. A new instrument panel was kin to that used in the 96 sedan. Standard GT850 equipment included white-on-black VDO instruments, a 7000-rpm tachometer, 120-mph speedometer, clock, fresh-air heater, wood-rimmed steering wheel, lighter, windshield washer, and outside rear-view mirrors.

I.D. DATA: Serial number plate is on left side of firewall. Engine number is on the right side of the block. Starting serial number: (96) 168001; (wag) 6624.

Model	Body Type & Seating	Engine Type/CID	P.O.E. Price	Weight (lbs.)	Prod. Total
96	2-dr Sedan-5P	I3/51	1895	1820	Note 1
95	2-dr Sta Wag-6/7P	I3/51	2195	2050	Note 1
GT850	2-dr Spt Sed-4/5P	I3/51	2790	2000	Note 1

Note 1: A total of 40,374 Saabs were produced during 1963. A total of 4,117 were imported and sold in the U.S. that year.

ENGINE DATA: BASE THREE (95/96): Inline, two-stroke three-cylinder. Cast nickel alloy steel block and aluminum head. **Displacement:** 51.3 cu. in. (841 cc). **Bore & Stroke:** 2.76 x 2.87 in. (70 x 72.9 mm). **Compression Ratio:** 7.3:1. **Brake Horsepower:** 42 (SAE) at 5000 rpm. **Torque:** 59 lbs.-ft. at 3000 rpm. Four main bearings. Solex 40 AI downdraft carburetor.

BASE THREE (GT850): Same as above, except — **Compression Ratio:** 9.0:1. **Brake Horsepower:** 57 at 5000 rpm. **Torque:** 68 lbs.-ft. at 3500 rpm. Four main bearings. Three Solex carburetors.

CHASSIS DATA: Wheelbase: 98 in. **Overall Length:** (96/GT850) 158 in.; (95) 162 in. **Height:** 58 in. **Width:** 62 in. **Front Tread:** 48 in. **Rear Tread:** 48 in. **Wheel Type:** (96) 4Jx15 wide-base artillery type. **Standard Tires:** (96) 5.00/5.20x15; (95) 5.60x15; (GT850) 155x15.

TECHNICAL: Layout: front-engine, front-drive. **Transmission:** (96/95) three-speed manual standard, four-speed available; (GT850) four-speed manual. GT850 gear ratios: (1st) 3.56:1; (2nd) 2.12:1; (3rd) 1.28:1; (4th) 0.84:1. **Standard Final Drive Ratio:** (GT850) 5.14:1. **Steering:** rack and pinion. **Suspension (front):** independent; coil springs with wishbones. **Suspension (rear):** U-shaped tubular (rigid) axle with coil springs. **Brakes:** (96/95) hydraulic, front/rear drum; (GT850) front disc, rear drum. **Body Construction:** steel unibody. Fuel Tank: (96) 10.5 gal.; (95) 11.4 gallon.

MAJOR OPTIONS: Saxomat automatic clutch ($100). Four-speed transmission: 95/96 ($100). Sunroof ($125). Radio.

PERFORMANCE: Top Speed: (96/95) 80+ mph; (GT850) 87-90+ mph. **Acceleration (0-60 mph):** (GT850) 21.2 seconds. **Acceleration (quarter-mile):** (GT850) 21.9 sec. (61 mph). **Fuel Mileage:** (96/95) 28-35 mpg; (GT850) about 26 mpg.

Manufacturer: Svenska Aeroplan AB, Trollhattan, Sweden.

Distributor: Saab Motors Inc., New Haven, Connecticut.

HISTORY: Erik Carlsson again won the Monte Carlo rally in a Saab.

1964 SAAB

96/95 — THREE — Except for the addition of a large Saab badge on the trunk lid (and the wagon's tailgate), little change was evident on Saab's basic sedan and wagon. Sedans actually displayed the Saab name in eight places around the body. All Saabs adopted a new diagonally-split braking system. Inside, the handbrake took on a modified position, standing nearly vertical when engaged and about 45 degrees forward when released. A restyled instrument panel contained a large round speedometer to replace the former strip-type unit, while a charge indicator light replaced the ammeter gauge. Four-speed Saabs in some markets added an anti-theft device, which prevented removal of the ignition key unless the gearshift lever was in reverse. Operational problems caused that device to be deleted later. Body colors for 1964 were: Glacier Blue, Dark Blue, Savannah Brown, Grey, White, and Red. Actually, red was a popular color because it had been used for years on rallying Saabs. All Saabs now had three-point seatbelts installed, adding to such familiar safety features as a pop-out windshield and padded dashboard and sunvisors.

MONTE CARLO 850 — THREE — A name change was the only significant alteration to Saab's Granturismo sports sedan, formerly known as the GT850 (successor to the GT750). Under the hood again was a more potent version of Saab's 841-cc three-cylinder engine.

I.D. DATA: Serial number plate is on left side of firewall. Engine number is on the right side of the block. Starting serial number: (96) 201401; (wag) 10801.

Model	Body Type & Seating	Engine Type/CID	P.O.E. Price	Weight (lbs.)	Prod. Total
96	2-dr Sedan-5P	I3/51	1895	1820	Note 1
95	2-dr Sta Wag-6/7P	I3/51	2345	2050	Note 1
MONTE CARLO					
850	2-dr Spt Sed-4/5P	I3/51	2790	1940	Note 1

Note 1: A total of 43,493 Saabs were produced during 1964.

ENGINE DATA: BASE THREE (95/96): Inline, two-stroke three-cylinder. Cast nickel alloy steel block and aluminum head. **Displacement:** 51.3 cu. in. (841 cc). **Bore & Stroke:** 2.76 x 2.87 in. (70 x 72.9 mm). **Compression Ratio:** 7.3:1. **Brake Horsepower:** 42 (SAE) at 5000 rpm. **Torque:** 59 lbs.-ft. at 3000 rpm. Four main bearings. Solex 40 AI downdraft carburetor.

BASE THREE (Monte): Same as above, except — **Compression Ratio:** 9.0:1. **Brake Horsepower:** 57 at 5000 rpm. **Torque:** 68 lbs.-ft. at 3500 rpm. Four main bearings. Three Solex downdraft carburetors.

CHASSIS DATA: Wheelbase: 98 in. **Overall Length:** (96/Monte) 158 in.; (95) 162 in. **Height:** 58 in. **Width:** 62 in. **Front Tread:** 48 in. **Rear Tread:** 48 in. **Wheel Type:** (96) 4Jx15 wide-base artillery type. **Standard Tires:** (96) 5.00/5.20x15; (95) 5.60x15; (Monte) 155x15.

TECHNICAL: Layout: front-engine, front-drive. **Transmission:** (96) three-speed manual standard, four-speed available; (95/Monte) four-speed manual. Monte Carlo 850 gear ratios: (1st) 3.56:1; (2nd) 2.12:1; (3rd) 1.28:1; (4th) 0.84:1. **Standard Final Drive Ratio:** (96/95) 5.23:1; (Monte) 5.14:1. **Steering:** rack and pinion. **Suspension (front):** independent; coil springs with wishbones. **Suspension (rear):** U-shaped tubular (rigid) axle with coil springs. **Brakes:** (96/95) front/rear drum; (Monte) front disc, rear drum. **Body Construction:** steel unibody. **Fuel Tank:** (96/Monte) 10.5 gal.; (95) 11.4 gallon.

MAJOR OPTIONS: Saxomat automatic clutch ($100). Four-speed transmission: 96 ($100). Sunroof: 96 sedan ($125). Radio.

PERFORMANCE: Top Speed: (96/95) 80+ mph; (Monte) 87-90+ mph. **Acceleration (0-60 mph):** (Monte) 21.2 seconds. **Acceleration (quarter-mile):** (Monte) 21.9 sec. (61 mph). **Fuel Mileage:** (96/95) 28-35 mpg; (Monte) 24-30 mpg.

Manufacturer: Svenska Aeroplan AB, Trollhattan, Sweden.

Distributor: Saab Motors Inc., New Haven, Connecticut.

HISTORY: Erik Carlsson again won the Monte Carlo rally in a Saab.

1965 SAAB

1965 Saab Monte Carlo 850.

96/95 — THREE — For the first time in nine years, Saab's front end underwent a dramatic alteration as the car grew by close to six inches (nearly all of it at the overhang past the front wheels, including a four-inch growth in fender length). Front fenders that formerly had been gently curved now reached to a nearly-vertical front panel. Saab's full-width checkered grille now consisted merely of perforations in the panel's metal, with no brightwork insert installed at all. Single round headlamps sat within that pierced panel, at the upper corners. A bright framework was partly on the hood, and partly over the perforated area. Twin bright strips ran from the headlamps to that center frame, which displayed a shield-shaped badge with 'Saab' lettering at its midpoint. Four slits were evident below that center frame. Flattened hood edges highlighted its elevated center section, which tapered to a narrow width at the front, meeting the new grille shield. A raised sculpture line ran along the hood's center, splitting it into two segments. Rectangular parking/signal lights now were mounted in lower corners of the front panel, instead of on the fenders. Single chrome trim strips ran along the tops of each wheel opening. Thinner, shallower bumpers on the sedan had slim vertical faces, lacking the former plates between bumper and body. Wagons retained the earlier back bumper. Hoods no longer were hinged at the bumper overrides, but tilted forward only after sliding ahead on runners. The radiator now sat ahead of the engine, allowing the deletion of air-extractor vents at the wheel openings. Suspended-style pedals were installed, and clutches operated hydraulically. Engine output got a slight boost. Body colors for 1965 were: Glacier Blue, Dark Blue, Savannah Brown, Olive, White, and Red.

MONTE CARLO 850 — THREE — Body and structural changes for the 96/95 also emerged on the sports sedan, and the high-performance engine also got a modest increase in horsepower. Monte Carlos had two chrome strips along each rocker panel. A single three-barrel carburetor replaced the former tri-carb setup.

I.D. DATA: Serial number plate is on left side of firewall. Engine number is on the right side of the block. Starting serial number: (96) 311001; (wag) 23101.

Model	Body Type & Seating	Engine Type/CID	P.O.E. Price	Weight (lbs.)	Prod. Total
96	2-dr Sedan-5P	I3/51	1985	1820	Note 1
95	2-dr Sta Wag-6/7P	I3/51	2375	2050	Note 1
MONTE CARLO					
850	2-dr Spt Sed-4/5P	I3/51	2750	1960	Note 1

Note 1: A total of 48,517 Saabs were produced during 1965. Approximately 5,462 were sold in the U.S. that year.

ENGINE DATA:
BASE THREE (95/96): Inline, two-stroke three-cylinder. Cast nickel alloy steel block and aluminum head. **Displacement:** 51.3 cu. in. (841 cc). **Bore & Stroke:** 2.76 x 2.87 in. (70 x 72.9 mm). **Compression Ratio:** 8.1:1. **Brake Horsepower:** 44 at 5000 rpm. **Torque:** 62 lbs.-ft. at 2800 rpm. Four main bearings. Solex downdraft carburetor.
BASE THREE (Monte): Same as above, except — **Compression Ratio:** 9.0:1. **Brake Horsepower:** 60 at 5000 rpm. **Torque:** 66 lbs.-ft. at 3800 rpm. Three-barrel carburetor.

CHASSIS DATA: Wheelbase: 98 in. **Overall Length:** (96/Monte) 164 in.; (95) 168 in. **Height:** 58 in. **Width:** 62 in. **Front Tread:** 48 in. **Rear Tread:** 48 in. **Standard Tires:** (96) 5.00/5.20x15; (95) 5.60x15; (Monte) 155x15.

TECHNICAL: Layout: front-engine, front-drive. **Transmission:** (96) three-speed manual standard, four-speed available; (95/Monte) four-speed manual. Monte Carlo 850 gear ratios: (1st) 3.56:1; (2nd) 2.12:1; (3rd) 1.28:1; (4th) 0.84:1. **Standard Final Drive Ratio:** (96/95) 5.23:1; (Monte) 5.14:1. **Steering:** rack and pinion. **Suspension (front):** independent; coil springs with wishbones. **Suspension (rear):** U-shaped tubular (rigid) axle with coil springs. **Brakes:** (96/95) front/rear drum; (Monte) front disc, rear drum. **Body Construction:** steel unibody. **Fuel Tank:** (96/Monte) 10.5 gal.; (95) 11.4 gallon.

MAJOR OPTIONS: Four-speed transmission: 96 ($60). Sunroof. Radio.

Manufacturer: Saab AB, Trollhattan, Sweden. **Distributor:** Saab Motors Inc., New Haven, Connecticut.

1966 SAAB

96/95 — THREE — Replacing the single carburetor with three separate units gave a small horsepower boost and helped to transform the two-stroke Saab's "putt-putt" sound into a more pleasing whine. All Saabs now had a four-speed manual gearbox. Except for a slight modification of hubcaps and taillamps, little change was evident externally. In addition to the basic sedan and station wagon, "Special" models were offered this year, with the more powerful Monte Carlo engine, front disc brakes, and a tachometer.

MONTE CARLO 850 — THREE — No change was evident on Saab's sports sedan, but its engine gained an alternator and the differential had a revised final drive ratio. By this time, the Monte Carlo name was adopted worldwide for the performance model, formerly called "Sport" outside the U.S. Monte Carlos could be identified by their twin chrome bodyside trim strips and full wheel covers.

I.D. DATA: Serial number plate is on left side of firewall. Engine number is on the right side of the block. Starting serial number: (96) 370001; (wag) 30001.

Model	Body Type & Seating	Engine Type/CID	P.O.E. Price	Weight (lbs.)	Prod. Total
96	2-dr Sedan-5P	I3/51	1997	1770	Note 1
96 Special	2-dr Sedan-5P	I3/51	2320	1795	Note 1
95	2-dr Sta Wag-6/7P	I3/51	2227	1930	Note 1
95 Special	2-dr Sta Wag-6/7P	I3/51	2550	1955	Note 1
MONTE CARLO					
850	2-dr Spt Sed-4/5P	I3/51	2750	1905	Note 1

Note 1: A total of 37,009 Saabs were produced during 1966. A total of 6,947 were imported into the U.S. that year.

ENGINE DATA: BASE THREE (95/96): Inline, two-stroke three-cylinder. Cast nickel alloy steel block and aluminum head. **Displacement:** 51.3 cu. in. (841 cc). **Bore & Stroke:** 2.76 x 2.87 in. (70 x 72.9 mm). **Compression Ratio:** 8.5:1. **Brake Horsepower:** 46 at 5000 rpm. **Torque:** 60 lbs.-ft. at 3000 rpm. Four main bearings. Three Solex downdraft carburetors.

BASE THREE (Monte Carlo, 96/95 Special): Same as above, except — **Compression Ratio:** 9.0:1. **Brake Horsepower:** 60 at 5000 rpm. **Torque:** 68 lbs.-ft. at 3800 rpm. Four main bearings. Three Solex carburetors.

CHASSIS DATA: Wheelbase: 98 in. **Overall Length:** (96/Monte) 164 in.; (95) 168 in. **Height:** 58 in. **Width:** 62 in. **Front Tread:** 48 in. **Rear Tread:** 48 in. **Standard Tires:** (96) 5.00/5.20x15; (95) 5.60x15; (Monte) 155x15.

TECHNICAL: Layout: front-engine, front-drive. **Transmission:** four-speed manual; column lever. **Standard Final Drive Ratio:** (96/95) 5.43:1; (Monte) 4.88:1. **Steering:** rack and pinion. **Suspension (front):** independent; coil springs with wishbones and anti-roll bar. **Suspension (rear):** U-shaped tubular (rigid) axle with trailing radius rods and coil springs. **Brakes:** (96/95) front/rear drum; (Monte/Special) front disc, rear drum. **Body Construction:** steel unibody. **Fuel Tank:** (96/Monte) 10.5 gal.; (95) 11.4 gallon.

MAJOR OPTIONS: Saxomat automatic clutch: 96 ($125). Sunroof: 96/Monte ($160).

PERFORMANCE: Top Speed: (96/95) 79-81 mph; (Monte) up to 93 mph. **Fuel Mileage:** (96/95) about 27 mpg.

Manufacturer: Saab AB, Trollhattan, Sweden. **Distributor:** Saab Motors Inc., New Haven, Connecticut.

HISTORY: 1966 models were introduced in August 1965, and on sale in America on September 15, 1965. Because Saab had performed well in European rallies for years, a full-fledged sports model seemed logical, especially to please American fans. Back in 1956-57, nothing had come of the first Sonett roadster, which never progressed beyond prototype form. Early in the 1960s, however, what was first called a Saab 97 took a completely different path, starting with two designs. One of those, penned by Bjorn Karlstrom and built by Malmo Aircraft Industry, was a two-seat fastback coupe with squared-off tail, nearly horizontal wraparound back window, and no rear quarter windows. The second was created in-house by Sixten Sason, and built by ASJ. That one used a 96 sedan floorpan/underbody and had a targa top and concave back window, with a tiny grille up front and deeply recessed headlamps with transparent covers. Karlstrom's design was selected, and the first prototype (with steel body) appeared at the Hedenlunda Rally in February 1965. By spring 1966, a total of 24 prototypes had been completed, each differing in some ways, with bodies made of fiberglass. The production version appeared for the 1967 model year; see next listing.

1967 SAAB

96/95 — V-4 — After nearly two decades of two-stroke power, Saab turned to a four-cycle V-4 engine supplied by Ford of Germany. For the 1967 model year, both three-cylinder and V-4 Saabs were produced. As part of the V-4 debut, seat upholstery switched from hessian-type cloth inserts to close-weave nylon, and front compartments

added removable storage bins. American 96 sedans with the V-4 now wore the same body trim as the sporty Monte Carlo, while in Europe they looked like the two-stroke version. All V-4 Saabs had front disc brakes and an alternator. Identification was made by chrome 'V4' emblems on the rear deck and left fender, and chrome strips on lower bodysides. Saab's familiar freewheeling transmission was retained for the four-cylinder model.

96/95 — SHRIKE — THREE — Saab named its carryover two-stroke models "Shrike" when the V-4 edition appeared. They retained drum brakes, a DC generator, one-speed wipers, and all-vinyl upholstery. The "Special" model with Monte Carlo engine no longer was offered. Two-stroke Saabs now came with an "original owner" lifetime guarantee for the engine. 'L' models had an automatic oil-injection system (using a separate oil tank), while the 96M and 95M still required mixing of oil and gasoline.

MONTE CARLO 850 — THREE/V-4 — Like the 96, the Monte Carlo sports sedan adopted the new four-stroke engine early in the 1967 model year, taking the name "Monte Carlo V4." The Monte Carlo's three-cylinder version had oil injection for its high-performance engine.

1967 Saab Sonett II. (William Siuru Jr.)

SONETT II — THREE — Production of Saab's sports car began late in 1966. Similar in appearance to the first prototype (and the 24 prototypes that emerged by 1966), the production version had a fiberglass coupe body with sharply truncated, "sawed-off" back end and a large wraparound back window. Four round taillamps stood in a vertical back panel. Air extractors went behind the door windows, on B-pillars. A low, pointed nose held a grille made up of horizontal slats, down near the ground (below the thin rubber bumper strip at the leading edge). That grille was flanked by small round parking/signal lights, with narrow black rubber bumperettes at the front. Atop the hood, at the cowl, was an air scoop and a modest squarish bulge. That bulge would grow considerably larger when the V-4 engine arrived later. Both the hood and front fenders hinged forward, and the coupe had no trunk lid. Wheel openings were flared. On the wood dashboard, two large round dials were flanked by two smaller ones. Four round taillamps came from the 95 station wagon. Floorpan and drivetrain came from the 96-based Monte Carlo sedan. So did the 60-bhp, 841-cc three-cylinder (two-stroke) engine with special tri-carb setup, and the front disc brakes. A four-speed transaxle was operated with a column gearshift lever.

I.D. DATA: Serial number plate is on left side of firewall. Engine number is on the right side of the block. Starting serial number: (96) 370081; (wag) 30010.

Model	Body Type & Seating	Engine Type/CID	P.O.E. Price	Weight (lbs.)	Prod. Total
96M-S	2-dr Sedan-5P	I3/51	1795	1775	Note 1
96LD	2-dr Sedan-5P	I3/51	2095	1775	Note 1
96V-4	2-dr Sedan-5P	V4/91	2295	1885	Note 1
95M	2-dr Sta Wag-6/7P	I3/51	2145	1930	Note 1
95L	2-dr Sta Wag-6/7P	I3/51	2295	1930	Note 1
95V-4	2-dr Sta Wag-6/7P	V4/91	2575	2040	Note 1
MONTE CARLO					
850	2-dr Spt Sed-4/5P	I3/51	2770	1905	Note 1
V-4	2-dr Spt Sed-4/5P	V4/91	N/A	N/A	Note 1
SONETT					
II	2-dr Coupe-2P	I3/51	3500	1565	Note 2

Note 1: A total of 45,325 Saabs were produced during 1967. A total of 10,529 were imported into the U.S. that year.

Note 2: A total of 60 Sonetts were built in 1966 (the first partial season), and 455 in 1967. Only 258 had the three-cylinder (two-stroke) engine. Sonett production through 1969 came to 1,868 units.

ENGINE DATA: BASE THREE (95/96): Inline, two-stroke three-cylinder. Cast nickel alloy steel block and aluminum head. **Displacement:** 51.3 cu. in. (841 cc). **Bore & Stroke:** 2.76 x 2.87 in. (70 x 72.9 mm). **Compression Ratio:** 8.5:1. **Brake Horsepower:** 46 at 5000 rpm. **Torque:** 60 lbs.-ft. at 3000 rpm. Four main bearings. One Solex one-barrel carburetor.

BASE THREE (Monte Carlo, Sonett): Same as above, except — **Compression Ratio:** 9.0:1. **Brake Horsepower:** 60 at 5300 rpm. **Torque:** 67 lbs.-ft. at 3800 rpm. Four main bearings. Three Solex downdraft carburetors (Sonett, three horizontal carburetors).

BASE V-4 (96/95/Monte Carlo V-4): Overhead-valve, four-stroke 60-degree V-4 (German Ford Taunus M15). Cast iron block. **Displacement:** 91.4 cu. in. (1498 cc). **Bore & Stroke:** 3.54 x 2.32 in. (89 x 58 mm). **Compression Ratio:** 9.0:1. **Brake Horsepower:** 73 at 4700 rpm. **Torque:** 85 lbs.-ft. at 2500 rpm. Three main bearings. Solid valve lifters. Solex one-barrel carburetor.

CHASSIS DATA: Wheelbase: 98 in. except (Sonett) 85 in. **Overall Length:** (96/Monte) 164 in.; (95) 168 in.; (Sonett) 149 in. **Height:** 58 in. except (Sonett) 46 in. **Width:** 62 in. except (Sonett) 57 in. **Front Tread:** 48 in. **Rear Tread:** 48 in. **Standard Tires:** (96) 5.00/5.20x15; (95) 5.60x15; (Monte) 155x15; (Sonett) 155x15.

TECHNICAL: Layout: front-engine, front-drive. **Transmission:** four-speed manual; column lever. V-4 gear ratios: (1st) 3.48:1; (2nd) 2.09:1; (3rd) 1.29:1; (4th) 0.84:1; (rev) 3.18:1. **Standard Final Drive Ratio:** (96/95) 5.43:1; (Monte) 4.88:1; (V-4) 4.88:1. **Steering:** rack and pinion. **Suspension (front):** independent; coil springs with upper/lower wishbones and anti-roll bar. **Suspension (rear):** U-shaped tubular (rigid) axle with trailing radius rods and coil springs. **Brakes:** (96/95 two-stroke) front/rear drum; (others) front disc, rear drum. **Body Construction:** steel unibody. **Fuel Tank:** (96/Monte) 10.5 gal.; (95) 11.4 gallon.

MAJOR OPTIONS: Saxomat automatic clutch: 96 ($125). Sunroof: 96/Monte ($160).

PERFORMANCE: Top Speed: (96/95) 81 mph; (Monte) about 85 mph; (V-4) about 87 mph. **Acceleration (0-60 mph):** (Monte) 18.9 seconds; (V-4) 15.0 seconds. **Acceleration (quarter-mile):** (V-4) 20 seconds (68 mph). **Fuel Mileage:** (V-4) 26-32 mpg.

Manufacturer: Saab AB, Trollhattan, Sweden.

Distributor: Saab Motors Inc., New Haven, Connecticut.

HISTORY: Sonetts were aimed almost exclusively at the U.S. market, and sold rather well. The V-4 engine emerged on the Swedish market in August 1966, but took a bit longer to get to America and elsewhere. Sales brochures for the '67 models made no mention of the new engine's existence, which was described only in supplementary material later. As a reflection of the hurried nature of their introduction, early V-4s had decals rather than the metal badges that appeared later on front fenders. Saab promoted the V-4 in terms of safety, asking "could we add another safety feature to the Saab?" Their answer was simple: "The dynamic acceleration of the new V4 Saab." Rally wins with the V-4 began with victory in the 1967 Finnish Riihimaki event. Saab's was the first V-4 engine to enter the U.S. market.

1968 SAAB

96/95 — V-4 — Slight reworking gave the Saab sedan a larger back window this year, as well as a deeper windshield. Electric windshield washers were added, and wipers enlarged. The instrument panel was now dark grey, and a black steering wheel had a large padded hub. A V-4D (DeLuxe) replaced the Monte Carlo V-4, using the same body trim and instruments as the prior Monte Carlo. It carried a 'DeLuxe V-4' emblem on the lower cowl, as opposed to a plain 'V-4' badge for the standard sedan.

96M/95M — SHRIKE — THREE — Two-stroke versions of the sedan and station wagon remained available, but with the former body (smaller windshield and back window). American versions had a shrunken, detuned engine (795 cc), because displacement had to be below 50 cid to be exempt from new emission rules. Two-strokes kept lighter grey fascia and rubber mats; all were red with grey upholstery.

SONETT II — V-4 — After a year on the market with two-stroke power, Saab's sports car acquired the German Ford V-4 engine available in other models. With a boost of five horsepower and substantial torque increase, it delivered a top speed of 100 mph or more. The original column shift was replaced by a floor lever. Aerodynamic Sonetts had a drag coefficient of only 0.32. The V-4 version had a large hood bulge with 'SONETT V4' lettering, plus front rubber overriders (no actual bumper). 'SAAB' lettering was on the left side of the hood, ahead of the hood bulge. All Sonetts had roll bar behind seats.

I.D. DATA: Serial number plate is on left side of firewall. Engine number is on the right side of the block. Starting serial number: (96 V-4) 470001; (96M) 427488; (95 V-4) 52001; (95M) 49383.

Model	Body Type & Seating	Engine Type/CID	P.O.E. Price	Weight (lbs.)	Prod. Total
96M	2-dr Sedan-5P	I3/48	1995	1800	Note 1
96V-4S	2-dr Sedan-5P	V4/91	2295	1940	Note 1
96V-4D	2-dr Sedan-5P	V4/91	2550	1950	Note 1
95M	2-dr Sta Wag-6/7P	I3/48	2225	1960	Note 1
95V-4	2-dr Sta Wag-6/7P	V4/91	2650	2080	Note 1
SONETT					
II	2-dr Coupe-2P	V4/91	3695	1520	Note 2

Note 1: A total of 52,551 Saabs were produced during 1968. A total of 10,871 were imported into the U.S. that year.

Note 2: A total of 1,868 Sonett IIs were built through 1969 (1,610 with the V-4 engine).

ENGINE DATA: BASE THREE (95M/96M): Inline, two-stroke three-cylinder. Cast nickel alloy steel block and aluminum head. **Displacement:** 48.5 cu. in. (795 cc). **Compression Ratio:** 8.5:1. **Brake Horsepower:** 40 at 5000 rpm. **Torque:** 58.5 lbs.-ft. at 3000 rpm. Four main bearings.

BASE V-4 (96/95 V-4, Sonett): Overhead-valve, four-stroke 60-degree V-4 (German Ford Taunus M15). Cast iron block and heads. **Displacement:** 91.4 cu. in. (1498 cc). **Bore & Stroke:** 3.54 x 2.32 in. (89 x 58 mm). **Compression Ratio:** 9.0:1. **Brake Horsepower:** 73 at 5000 rpm. **Torque:** 87 lbs.-ft. at 2700 rpm. Three main bearings. Solid valve lifters. One Solex carburetor.

CHASSIS DATA: Wheelbase: 98 in. except (Sonett) 85 in. **Overall Length:** (96) 164 in.; (95) 168 in.; (Sonett) 149 in. **Height:** 58 in. except (Sonett) 46 in. **Width:** 62 in. except (Sonett) 57 in. **Front Tread:** 48 in. **Rear Tread:** 48 in. **Standard Tires:** (96/95) 5.60x15; (Sonett and 96V-4D) 155x15.

TECHNICAL: Layout: front-engine, front-drive. **Transmission:** four-speed manual; column lever (Sonett) floor lever. **Standard Final Drive Ratio:** (96M/95M) 5.43:1; (96/95 V-4) 4.88:1; (Sonett) 4.67:1. **Steering:** rack and pinion. **Suspension (front):** independent; coil springs with upper/lower wishbones and anti-roll bar. **Suspension (rear):** U-shaped tubular (rigid) axle with trailing radius rods and coil springs. (Sonett) beam axle with radium arms and coil springs. **Brakes:** (96/95 two-stroke) front/rear drum; (others) front disc, rear drum. **Body Construction:** steel unibody. **Fuel Tank:** (96) 10.5 gal.; (95) 11.3 gal.; (Sonett) 15.8 gallon.

MAJOR OPTIONS: Saxomat automatic clutch. Sunroof.

PERFORMANCE: Top Speed: (96M) 81 mph; (96/95 V-4) about 87 mph; (Sonett V-4) 100 mph. **Acceleration (0-60 mph):** (96 V-4) 15.0 seconds; (Sonett V-4) 12-12.5 seconds. **Acceleration (quarter-mile):** (96 V-4) about 20 seconds (68 mph). **Fuel Mileage:** (96/95 V-4) 26-32 mpg.

Manufacturer: Saab AB, Trollhattan, Sweden.

Distributor: Saab Motors Inc., New Haven, Connecticut.

HISTORY: Advertisements that called the Sonett an "expensive toy," adding that "You can find it in the toy department," probably didn't help sales in the U.S.

1969 SAAB

96/95 — V-4 — The traditional Saab sedan and station wagon enjoyed a restyle this year to give a more modern front-end look, similar to that of the new 99 series. The center grille remained, with an enamelled-disc Saab badge (aircraft style, on a blue background) at its midpoint; but its formerly perforated metal construction was replaced by a dozen chromed horizontal bars. Four slits no longer were present below the grille, but side grilles had a pattern of thin horizontal slots, with a single vertical divider on each side. Air-extractor vents of the station wagon displayed another blue badge, and its taillamp cluster now contained backup lights. European Saabs got rectangular headlamps and pear-shaped mirrors this year, but American versions kept their round headlamps and mirrors. Parking/signal lights moved to the fenders, alongside the recessed headlamps. Hubcaps also were restyled, minimizing the domed look. Bumper overriders added rubber inserts, and a telescopic steering column was installed. Vacuum-assisted brakes became standard. Three-cylinder (two-stroke) Saabs finally faded away from the marketplace.

99 — FOUR — Only a couple of years had elapsed between the arrival of Saab's V-4 four-stroke engine and the emergence of an all-new model, this time with a single-overhead-cam inline four-cylinder powerplant. Appearance of the new two-door was markedly different from the familiar 96 fastback sedan, and served as the first of Saab's upscale models, aimed at affluent customers. Basic profile of the new design evolved into the Saabs of the 1980s and '90s. A vertical front panel contained quad round headlamps, with rectangular parking/signal lights below and outside, near bumper level. Though smaller, the center grille was similar to the 96/95 shape, as was the pattern of thin horizontal slots in its side grilles, which reached out to the headlamps. A concave shape was noticeable in the profile of the large back window and rear deck, above an angled-back rear panel that contained rectangular taillamps flanking the license plate mounting. Small horizontal grilles below the rear pillars, ahead of the gas filler cap, served as the only bodyside adornment. Wheel openings were rounded. The 1709-cc engine was supplied by Standard Triumph, in England, to Saab specifications. It was mounted above the four-speed manual gearbox, which was controlled by a floor lever. Suspension was similar to that of the 96 design, with coil springs. To improve the ride for back-seat passengers, Saab chose a conventional straight rear axle rather than the customary U-shaped axle. For stopping chores, four-wheel disc brakes were installed. Inside were round white-on-black gauges.

SONETT II — V-4 — Production of the Saab sports car continued with little change for its final season. Among other features, Sonetts had a built-in roll bar.

I.D. DATA: Serial number plate is on left side of firewall. Engine number is on the right side of the block. Starting serial number: (96 V-4) 520001; (95 V-4) 65001; (99) 1001; (Sonett) 1000.

Model	Body Type & Seating	Engine Type/CID	P.O.E. Price	Weight (lbs.)	Prod. Total
96V-4	2-dr Sedan-5P	V4/91	2295	1960	Note 1
96V-4D	2-dr DeL Sed-5P	V4/91	2550	1960	Note 1
95V-4	2-dr Sta Wag-6/7P	V4/91	2650	2105	Note 1
99					
99	2-dr Sedan-5P	I4/104	2899	2435	Note 1
SONETT					
II	2-dr Coupe-2P	V4/91	3695	1520	Note 2

Note 1: A total of 61,711 Saabs were produced during 1969. Approximately 10,898 were sold in the U.S. during that year.

Note 2: A total of 1,868 Sonett IIs were built from 1966 through 1969 (1,610 with the V-4 engine).

ENGINE DATA: BASE V-4 (96/95, Sonett): Overhead-valve, four-stroke 60-degree V-4 (German Ford). Cast iron block. **Displacement:** 91.4 cu. in. (1498 cc). **Bore & Stroke:** 3.54 x 2.32 in. (89 x 58 mm). **Compression Ratio:** 9.0:1. **Brake Horsepower:** 73 at 5000 rpm. Torque: 87 lbs.-ft. at 2700 rpm. Three main bearings. Solid valve lifters. One Autolite one-barrel carburetor.

BASE FOUR (99): Inline, overhead-cam slant four-cylinder. Cast iron block and light alloy head. **Displacement:** 104.3 cu. in. (1709 cc). **Bore & Stroke:** 3.29 x 3.07 in. (83.6 x 78 mm). **Compression Ratio:** 9.0:1. **Brake Horsepower:** 87 at 5500 rpm. **Torque:** 97 lbs.-ft. at 3000 rpm. Five main bearings. One Zenith-Stromberg 175CD carburetor.

CHASSIS DATA: Wheelbase: (95/95) 98 in.; (99) 97.3 in.; (Sonett) 85 in. **Overall Length:** (96) 165 in.; (95) 169 in.; (99) 171.2 in.; (Sonett) 149 in. **Height:** (96/95) 58 in.; (99) 57.1 in.; (Sonett) 46 in. **Width:** (96/95) 62 in.; (99) 66.1 in.; (Sonett) 57 in. **Front Tread:** 48 in. except (99) 54.7 in. **Rear Tread:** 48 in. except (99) 55.1 in. **Standard Tires:** (96/95) 5.60x15; (99) 155SR15; (Sonett) 155x15.

TECHNICAL: Layout: front-engine, front-drive. **Transmission:** four-speed manual; column lever except (99) floor lever. 96 sedan gear ratios: (1st) 3.48:1; (2nd) 2.09:1; (3rd) 1.29:1; (4th) 0.84:1. **Standard Final Drive Ratio:** (96/95) 4.88:1; (99) 4.88:1; (Sonett) 4.67:1. **Steering:** rack and pinion. **Suspension (front):** independent; coil springs with upper/lower wishbones and anti-roll bar. **Suspension (rear):** (95/96) U-shaped tubular (rigid) axle with trailing radius rods and coil springs; (99) rigid axle with Panhard rod and coil springs; (Sonett) beam axle with radius arms and coil springs. **Brakes:** front disc, rear drum except (99) four-wheel disc. **Body Construction:** steel unibody. **Fuel Tank:** (96) 10.5 gal.; (95) 11.3 gal.; (99) 12.4 gal.; (Sonett) 15.8 gallon.

MAJOR OPTIONS: Sunroof.

PERFORMANCE: Top Speed: (96/95 V-4) about 87 mph; (99) 97-99 mph; (Sonett V-4) 100-110 mph. **Acceleration (0-60 mph):** (96 V-4) 15.0 sec.; (99) 14.5 sec.; (Sonett V-4) 12-12.5 seconds. **Acceleration (quarter-mile):** (96 V-4) about 20 seconds (68 mph). **Fuel Mileage:** (96/95 V-4) 26-32 mpg.

Manufacturer: Saab AB, Trollhattan, Sweden.

Distributor: Saab Motors Inc., New Haven, Connecticut.

HISTORY: As far back as the early 1950s, Saab designers had been pondering the shape of a future model. By the latter part of that decade, those thoughts were focusing on a profile with a low nose and tall tail end. The finished 99 sedan evolved from a "Gudmond" prototype, and looked quite similar to a prototype completed in 1965. After ruling out the recently-introduced V-4 design, and briefly considering a V-8, Saab engineers turned to an inline four being developed by Standard Triumph, entering an agreement with that company in 1965. Early in 1966, Saab put a drivable prototype of the new 99 through a two-month test on wintry Swedish roads. In autumn 1967, two examples were shown to the press, with test drives given and questionnaires filled out. Then, in 1968, Saab issued 36 cars to motorists for trial, with a lengthy form to be filled out after about 10,000 miles of use. In August of that year, the 99 was available to the public at home; but as usual, it took a bit longer to cross the Atlantic. Neither in Europe nor in America did everyone take to the new design without reservations. *Motor* magazine in Britain, for instance, said the newest Saab "is not exceptional for speed, nor indeed for a strong sporting character." Even so, testers there considered the 99 refined, safe to handle, with fine interior, adding that it "is something of a trendsetter that we much admire." On the racing front, a privately-owned Sonett V-4 entered the 1969 Monte Carlo Rally, finishing 9th overall. In 1969, too, Saab merged with Scania-Vabis (a Swedish truck manufacturer and Porsche/VW importer), to form Saab-Scania. By this year, Saab had about 353 dealers in the U.S. and production was taking place in Finland as well as Sweden.

1970 SAAB

96/95 — V-4 — Production of the traditional-styled sedan and station wagon continued with a number of minor changes. A recessed gas cap was used. The new instrument panel had two large round dials (white-on-black speedometer at the left, temperature and gas gauges at the right). Replacing the center-mounted clock was a black square with chrome surround molding and '95' or '96' designation. Headlamps now switched off along with the ignition. Door and side panels were color-matched to the seat sides. Mechanically, little changed except for the addition of an aluminized exhaust system. The V-4 DeLuxe model was dropped.

99 — FOUR — Saab's newest model entered its second season with virtually no change, other than the addition of a lighter and an extra ashtray in the back. In the spring of 1970, however, a four-door sedan joined the original two-door, and both could be obtained with a Borg-Warner three-speed automatic transmission. Both were "firsts" for Saab. Engines in automatic-shift sedans could have Bosch D-Jetronic fuel injection, for 95 bhp at 5500 rpm (versus 87 horsepower for the carbureted version). Features included a fold-down rear seat and side-window defrosters.

SONETT III — V-4 — A restyled sports car replaced the Sonett II, offering a smoother, sleeker appearance in its fiberglass body. Wheelbase was identical, but the III measured five inches longer overall, at 154 inches, evident in both the extended rear overhang and longer nose. Concealed (pop-up) headlamps rode in that longer sloping nose, which reached to the vertical front panel with its blacked-out grille above a larger bumper that still amounted to no more than than a narrow rubber strip. Those headlamps had to be raised manually. Driving lights were mounted behind the thin horizontal bars of the grille. Raised a bit in its center, they contained small round parking lights at its ends. An airscoop was evident in the hood center, to the rear of a black bulge. Small rear quarter windows were added. Both standard and luxury models were offered. The new version used the same central body structure as the Sonett II, but had a longer tail. Gone was the wraparound back window, replaced by a large, flat frameless hatchback window with exposed hinges at the top. An improved black-crackle dashboard held three round gauges (including tachometer) on a cowled housing ahead of the driver. A grab handle sat below the glovebox, which had a lid. The short gearshift lever rested in a small console. Seats adjusted for lumbar support. Frame and drivetrain again came from the 96 sedan, but a larger (1.7-liter) German Ford V-4 engine delivered more power. Additional car weight offset that increase, however.

I.D. DATA: Serial number plate is on left side of firewall or left door jamb. Engine number is on the right side of the block. Starting serial number: (96) 562732; (95) 80822; (99) 21682; (Sonett) 70500001.

Model	Body Type & Seating	Engine Type/CID	P.O.E. Price	Weight (lbs.)	Prod. Total
96	2-dr Sedan-5P	V4/91	2449	1995	Note 1
95	2-dr Sta Wag-6/7P	V4/91	2769	2150	Note 1
99					
99	2-dr Sedan-5P	I4/104	2990	2360	Note 1
99	4-dr Sedan-5P	I4/104	3190	N/A	Note 1
SONETT III					
97	2-dr Coupe-2P	V4/104	3995	1785	Note 2

Note 1: A total of 73,982 Saabs were produced during 1970. Approximately 11,123 were sold in the U.S. during that year.

Note 2: A total of 8,351 Sonett IIIs were produced from 1970 through 1974.

Price Note: A 99E two-door sedan with automatic transmission and fuel-injected engine sold for $3299.

ENGINE DATA: BASE V-4 (96/95): Overhead-valve, four-stroke 60-degree V-4 (German Ford). Cast iron block. **Displacement:** 91.4 cu. in. (1498 cc). **Bore & Stroke:** 3.54 x 2.32 in. (89 x 58 mm). **Compression Ratio:** 9.0:1. **Brake Horsepower:** 73 at 5000 rpm. **Torque:** 87 lbs.-ft. at 2700 rpm. Three main bearings. Solid valve lifters. One single-barrel carburetor.

BASE V-4 (Sonett): Overhead-valve, four-stroke 60-degree V-4 (German Ford). Cast iron block. **Displacement:** 103.7 cu. in. (1699 cc). **Bore & Stroke:** 3.54 x 2.63 in. (90 x 66.8 mm). **Compression Ratio:** 9.0:1. **Brake Horsepower:** 75 (DIN) at 5000 rpm. **Torque:** 94 (DIN) lbs.-ft. at 2500 rpm. Three main bearings. Solid valve lifters.

BASE FOUR (99): Inline, overhead-cam four-cylinder. Cast iron block and light alloy head. **Displacement:** 104.3 cu. in. (1709 cc). **Bore & Stroke:** 3.29 x 3.07 in. (83.6 x 78 mm). **Compression Ratio:** 9.0:1. **Brake Horsepower:** 87 at 5500 rpm. **Torque:** 98 lbs.-ft. at 3000 rpm. Five main bearings. One Zenith-Stromberg 175CD carburetor.

OPTIONAL FOUR (99E): Same as 1709-cc above, except — **Brake Horsepower:** 95 at 5500 rpm. Bosch D-Jetronic fuel injection.

CHASSIS DATA: Wheelbase: (96/95) 98 in.; (99) 97.4 in.; (Sonett) 84.6 in. **Overall Length:** (96) 165 in.; (95) 169 in.; (99) 171.2 in.; (Sonett) 153.5 in. **Height:** (96/95) 58 in.; (99) 57.1 in.; (Sonett) 46.9 in. **Width:** (96/95) 62 in.; (99) 66.1 in.; (Sonett) 59 in. **Front Tread:** 48 in. except (99) 54.7 in. **Rear Tread:** 48 in. except (99) 55.1 in. **Standard Tires:** (96/95) 5.60x15; (99) 155SR15; (Sonett) 155SR15.

TECHNICAL: Layout: front-engine, front-drive. **Transmission:** four-speed manual; column lever except (99/Sonett) floor lever. **Standard Final Drive Ratio:** (96/95) 4.88:1; (99) 4.22:1; (Sonett) 4.67:1. **Steering:** rack and pinion. **Suspension (front):** independent; coil springs with upper/lower wishbones. **Suspension (rear):** (95/96) U-shaped tubular (rigid) axle with trailing radius rods and coil springs; (99) rigid axle with Watts linkage, Panhard rod and coil springs; (Sonett) beam axle with radius arms and coil springs. **Brakes:** front disc, rear drum except (99) four-wheel disc. **Body Construction:** steel unibody. **Fuel Tank:** (96) 10.5 gal.; (95) 11.3 gal.; (99) 12.4 gal.; (Sonett) 15.8 gallon.

MAJOR OPTIONS: Automatic transmission (series 99). Air conditioning: 95/96 ($276); 99 ($325). AM radio ($75-$76). AM/FM radio ($101-$123).

PERFORMANCE: Top Speed: (96/95) about 87 mph; (99) 99 mph; (Sonett) 100 mph. **Acceleration (0-60 mph):** (96) 15.0 sec.; (Sonett) 14.4 seconds. **Acceleration (quarter-mile):** (96 V-4) about 20 seconds (68 mph); (99) 19.7 sec. (68 mph). **Fuel Mileage:** (96/95 V-4) 26-32 mpg.

Manufacturer: Saab-Scania (Saab Car Division), Nykoping, Sweden.
Distributor: Saab-Scania of America Inc., Orange, Connecticut.

HISTORY: Aimed at American buyers, the Sonett III debuted at the spring 1970 New York Auto Show. Most of the Sonett III design work was by Sergio Coggiola.

1971 SAAB

96/95 — V-4 — For the 1971 model year, U.S. emissions requirements compelled a change in V-4 engine size for the American market. Therefore, it grew to 1.7 liters and compression was lowered to 8:1, so horsepower remained the same as before. Bright trim strips on fenders (used since 1954) were dropped this year, replaced by a low, single rubber-mounted bodyside molding that ran along the bottom of the door and rear quarter panel. Headlamp frames were modified. Ridged black plastic was now used for the cap at bottom leading edge of rear fenders. All Saabs were electrodip primed. European models got headlamp wiper/washers, but U.S. versions with their round headlamps did not.

99 — FOUR — The 99's standard engine also grew in size this year, from the original 1709 cc up to 1854 cc, as a result of growth in bore dimension. That same engine would soon appear in the Triumph Dolomite, but with more power. With automatic shift, the new engine could be carbureted, or equipped with Bosch D-Jetronic fuel injection for additional power. Carbureted versions went into manual-shift models. Freewheeling was abandoned as the bigger powerplants emerged. The former 1.7-liter four remained available for this final year. As for appearance, two small grilles were added below the main grille. Inside, three round, deeply recessed gauges sat on the padded dashboard, ahead of the driver: speedometer in the center, clock on the right. Like all Saab sedans, the 99 had mudflaps. Front bucket seats with "see-thru" head restraints were infinitely-adjustable, and the front passenger had a grab handle.

SONETT III — V-4 — Wheels got a restyle for 1971, and the alloy rims (formerly on luxury model) were dropped. Otherwise, Sonett production continued as before, powered by the 1.7-liter four-cylinder V-4 engine.

I.D. DATA: Serial number plate is on left side of firewall. Engine number is on the right side of the block. Starting serial number: (96) 600001; (95) 095001; (99) 050001; (Sonett) 71500001.

Model	Body Type & Seating	Engine Type/CID	P.O.E. Price	Weight (lbs.)	Prod. Total
96	2-dr Sedan-5P	V4/104	2532	2025	Note 1
95	2-dr Sta Wag-6/7P	V4/104	2732	2195	Note 1
99					
99-2CM	2-dr Sedan-5P	I4/104	3240	2425	Note 1
99-4CM	4-dr Sedan-5P	I4/104	3375	2490	Note 1
SONETT					
III	2-dr Coupe-2P	V4/104	3995	1765	Note 2

Note 1: A total of 72,960 Saabs were produced during 1971. Approximately 12,653 were sold in the U.S. during that year.
Note 2: A total of 8,351 Sonett IIIs were produced from 1970 through 1974.
Price Note: 99 prices shown are for manual-shift models with carbureted engine. A two-door sedan with fuel-injected engine sold for $3360; with automatic transmission, $3540. A four-door with fuel-injection sold for $3495; with automatic, $3675.

ENGINE DATA: BASE V-4 (96/95, Sonett): Overhead-valve, four-stroke 60-degree V-4 (German Ford). Cast iron block and head. **Displacement:** 103.6 cu. in. (1698 cc). **Bore & Stroke:** 3.54 x 2.63 in. (90 x 66.8 mm). **Compression Ratio:** 8.1:1. **Brake Horsepower:** 73 at 5000 rpm. **Torque:** 87 lbs.-ft. at 2700 rpm. Three main bearings. Solid valve lifters. One downdraft carburetor.
BASE FOUR (99): Inline, overhead-cam four-cylinder. Cast iron block and light alloy head. **Displacement:** 104.5 cu. in. (1709 cc). **Bore & Stroke:** 3.29 x 3.07 in. (83.6 x 78 mm). **Compression Ratio:** 9.0:1. **Brake Horsepower:** 95 at 5500 rpm. **Torque:** 97 lbs.-ft. at 3000 rpm. Bosch D-Jetronic fuel injection.
Note: The carbureted version of the 1709-cc engine was rated at 87 bhp.
OPTIONAL FOUR (99): Same as above, except — **Displacement:** 113.1 cu. in. (1854 cc). **Bore & Stroke:** 3.42 x 3.07 in. (87 x 78 mm). **Compression Ratio:** 9.0:1. **Brake Horsepower:** up to 97 at 5200 rpm. **Torque:** up to 106 lbs.-ft. at 3200 rpm. One Stromberg carburetor or Bosch fuel injection.

CHASSIS DATA: Wheelbase: (95/95) 98 in.; (99) 97.3 in.; (Sonett) 84.6 in. **Overall Length:** (96) 165 in.; (95) 169 in.; (99) 171.2 in.; (Sonett) 153.5 in. **Height:** (96/95) 58 in.; (99) 57.1 in.; (Sonett) 46.9 in. **Width:** (96/95) 62 in.; (99) 66.1 in.; (Sonett) 59 in. **Front Tread:** 48 in. except (99) 54.7 in. **Rear Tread:** 48 in. except (99) 55.1 in. **Standard Tires:** (96/95) 5.60x15; (99) 155x15; (Sonett) 155SR15.

TECHNICAL: Layout: front-engine, front-drive. **Transmission:** four-speed manual; column lever except (99/Sonett) floor lever. **Standard Final Drive Ratio:** (96/95) 4.88:1; (99) 4.22:1; (Sonett) 4.67:1. **Steering:** rack and pinion. **Suspension (front):** coil springs with upper/lower wishbones. **Suspension (rear):** (95/96) U-shaped tubular (rigid) axle with trailing radius rods and coil springs; (99) rigid axle with Watts linkage, Panhard rod and coil springs; (Sonett) beam axle with radius arms and coil springs. **Brakes:** power front disc, rear drum except (99) four-wheel disc. **Body Construction:** steel unibody. **Fuel Tank:** (96) 10.5 gal.; (95) 11.3 gal.; (99) 12.4 gal.; (Sonett) 15.8 gallon.

MAJOR OPTIONS: Air conditioning. Automatic transmission (99 series).

PERFORMANCE: Top Speed: (Sonett) 100 mph. **Acceleration (0-60 mph):** (Sonett) 14.4 seconds.
Manufacturer: Saab-Scania (Saab Car Division), Nykoping, Sweden.
Distributor: Saab-Scania of America Inc., Orange, Connecticut.

HISTORY: In 1971, Saab established a Road Accident Investigation Group, to study serious accidents.

1972 Saab 99E four-door sedan.

A heated driver's seat was introduced this year: a "first" for any manufacturer. All Saabs got new wheels with rectangular holes that replaced the former round perforations. All models also got new rear mudflaps with a simpler Saab emblem to replace the old aircraft symbol. Single horns replaced the former twin ones. Inline four-cylinder engines for the 99 series built by Saab rather than Triumph were now available.

96/95 — V-4 — Even as the upscale 99 sedans grew in popularity, Saab continued to produce the familiar-looking 96 sedan and 95 station wagon. This year, both received new bumper guards of molded black rubber (though the wagon's rear kept the old ones). A different sound emanated from the V-4's back end this year, because its two exhaust pipes were now equal in length.

99 — FOUR — New impact-absorbing bumpers this year were designed to meet anticipated U.S. regulations. Slightly curved (U-shaped) steel rails held blocks of cellular plastic that had a honeycomb appearance, covered by black rubber sheathing and a bright metal trim strip. No provision was made for mounting front spotlights. A much larger parking/signal light cluster was installed, on the fenders alongside the headlamps. The 1.7-liter engine was dropped this year, leaving only the 1.85-liter version, available with carburetors or fuel-injection on both manual and automatic-transmission cars. During the model year, a new deluxe sports model arrived, the 99EMS (for Electronic Manual Special). Offered only in two-door form with manual shift, it carried a new Swedish-built 2-liter (1985-cc) engine, derived from the 1.85-liter by enlarging the distance between cylinder axes, thus permitting larger bores (90 instead of 87 mm). Stroke size remained the same. A duplex timing chain replaced the customary single-row chain. Compression was lower than that of the standard engine, at 8.7:1. The enlarged engine easily passed U.S. emissions tests. The 99EMS had metallic paint, alloy wheels, and a blackout grille with a single horizontal chrome strip. The smaller-diameter steering wheel had a padded leather rim, and a tachometer (with small integral clock) replaced the regular clock on the dashboard. Suspension components also got an upgrade.

1972 Saab Sonett III coupe.

SONETT III — V-4 — Saab's sports car received a new black plastic grille, shaped similar to that used on other Saabs. A small round insignia sat in the center of the wide hexagon-shaped grille unit, which resided with a full-width panel that contained parking/signal lights at its outer ends. The rear panel also switched to black, and wider aluminum wheels were installed. Standard equipment included molded fiberglass bucket seats, a leather-trimmed steering wheel, alloy wheels, a 120-mph speedometer and 7000-rpm tachometer. Rollover bars were installed in the windshield pillars, with a roll bar built-in behind the seats.

I.D. DATA: Serial number plate is on left side of firewall. Starting serial number: 722000001; (Sonett) 97725000001. Engine number is on the side of the block.

Model	Body Type & Seating	Engine Type/CID	P.O.E. Price	Weight (lbs.)	Prod. Total
96	2-dr Sedan-5P	V4/104	2595	2030	Note 1
95	2-dr Sta Wag-6/7P	V4/104	2795	2180	Note 1

Model	Body Type & Seating	Engine Type/CID	P.O.E. Price	Weight (lbs.)	Prod. Total
99-CM	2-dr Sedan-5P	I4/113	3395	N/A	Note 1
99-2EM	2-dr Sedan-5P	I4/113	3695	2480	Note 1
99-4EM	4-dr Sedan-5P	I4/113	3795	2550	Note 1
99EMS	2-dr Sedan-5P	I4/121	N/A	N/A	Note 1
SONETT III					
97	2-dr Coupe-2P	V4/104	3795	1805	Note 2

Note 1: A total of 83,997 Saabs were produced during 1972. Approximately 14,410 were sold in the U.S. during that year.

Note 2: A total of 8,351 Sonett IIIs were produced from 1970 through 1974, and 2,080 during 1972.

Price Note: An automatic transmission added $200 to the 99-EM price.

Model Note: 'C' after 99 model number indicates carbureted engine; 'E' indicates fuel injection; 'M' indicates manual shift.

ENGINE DATA: BASE V-4 (96/95, Sonett): Overhead-valve, four-stroke 60-degree V-4 (German Ford). Cast iron block and head. **Displacement:** 103.6 cu. in. (1698 cc). **Bore & Stroke:** 3.54 x 2.63 in. (90 x 66.8 mm). **Compression Ratio:** 8.0:1. **Brake Horsepower:** 65 (SAE) at 4700 rpm. **Torque:** 85 lbs.-ft. (SAE) at 2500 rpm. Three main bearings. Solid valve lifters. One one-barrel carburetor.

BASE FOUR (99): Inline, overhead-cam four-cylinder. Cast iron block and light alloy head. **Displacement:** 113.1 cu. in. (1854 cc). **Bore & Stroke:** 3.42 x 3.07 in. (87 x 78 mm). **Compression Ratio:** 9.0:1. **Brake Horsepower:** 97 at 5200 rpm. **Torque:** 105 lbs.-ft. at 3200 rpm. Five main bearings. Solid valve lifters. Bosch D-Jetronic fuel injection.

Note: Carbureted version of the 1854-cc engine, as in the 99-CM, was rated 86 bhp at 5000 rpm.

BASE 2-LITER FOUR (99EMS): Same as 1854-cc engine above, except — **Displacement:** 121 cu. in. (1985 cc). **Bore & Stroke:** 3.54 x 3.07 in. (90 x 78 mm). **Compression Ratio:** 8.7:1. **Brake Horsepower:** 110 at 5500 rpm. **Torque:** 123 lbs.-ft. at 3500 rpm. Bosch D-Jetronic fuel injection.

CHASSIS DATA: Wheelbase: (96/95) 98 in.; (99) 97.4 in.; (Sonett) 84.6 in. **Overall Length:** (96) 165 in.; (95) 169 in.; (99) 171.2 in.; (Sonett) 153.5 in. **Height:** (96/95) 58 in.; (99) 56.7 in.; (Sonett) 46.9 in. **Width:** (96/95) 62 in.; (99) 66.5 in.; (Sonett) 59 in. **Front Tread:** (96/95) 48 in.; (99) 54.7 in.; (Sonett) 48.5 in. **Rear Tread:** (96/95) 48 in.; (99) 55.1 in.; (Sonett) 48.5 in. **Standard Tires:** (96/95) 5.60x15; (99) 155x15; (Sonett) 155SR15.

TECHNICAL: Layout: front-engine, front-drive. **Transmission:** four-speed manual; column lever except (99/Sonett) floor lever. **Standard Final Drive Ratio:** (96/95) 4.88:1; (99) 4.22:1; (Sonett) 4.67:1. **Steering:** rack and pinion. **Suspension (front):** independent; coil springs with upper/lower wishbones. **Suspension (rear):** (95/96) U-shaped tubular (rigid) axle with trailing radius rods and coil springs; (99) rigid axle with Watts linkage, Panhard rod and coil springs; (Sonett) beam axle with radius arms and coil springs. **Brakes:** power front disc, rear drum except (99) four-wheel disc. **Body Construction:** steel unibody. **Fuel Tank:** (96) 10.5 gal.; (95) 11.3 gal.; (99) 12.4 gal.; (Sonett) 15.8 gallon.

MAJOR OPTIONS: Automatic transmission ($200). Air conditioning. AM radio. AM/FM radio. AM/FM stereo radio. Vinyl top (99 series).

PERFORMANCE: Top Speed: (99E) 98 mph; (Sonett) 95-110 mph. **Acceleration (0-60 mph):** (99E) 12.7 sec.; (Sonett) 12-14.4 seconds. **Acceleration (quarter-mile):** (99E) 18.4 sec. (72 mph); (Sonett) 18.6 seconds (70 mph). **Fuel Mileage:** (99E) about 22 mpg; (Sonett) 26-30 mpg.

Manufacturer: Saab-Scania (Saab Car Division), Nykoping, Sweden.

Distributor: Saab-Scania of America Inc., Orange, Connecticut.

HISTORY: Saab-Scania split into two separate divisions this year: Saab Car Division and a Scania Division. Saab headquarters moved form Sodertalje to Nykoping.

1973 SAAB

1973 Saab 99EMS sedan.

96/95 — V-4 — Production of the traditional sedan and station wagon continued without change.

99 — FOUR — The base 99 sedan was called a 99L this year, with 99LE the mid-range model and 99EMS the sporty top-of-the-line edition, offered only as a two-door sedan with manual shift. A more basic, frill-free 99 version (no suffix) with plain window frames and bumpers was added later. The 2-liter four-cylinder engine became standard, with either carburetion or fuel injection. All 99 grilles were black this year with a single chrome trim strip, while that of the EMS added an extra bright trim strip. A new nameplate on the rear end had chromed edges and black letters. Instruments added amber fluorescent pointers. Doors were strengthened for side impact, using rectangular steel beams welded into place. European 99s got halogen headlamp bulbs, but U.S. Saabs kept their former lighting systems.

1973 Saab Sonett III. (William Siuru Jr.)

SONETT III — V-4 — The sports coupe added front/rear impact-type bumpers, as on the 99 sedan a year before. Large 'SAAB' lettering as part of the striping along the lower bodyside made Sonetts easy to spot. As before, equipment included a leather-covered steering wheel, dual built-in roll bars, and molded bucket seats. Saab literature promoted the fact that only 2,500 Sonetts were built each year.

I.D. DATA: Serial number plate is on left side of firewall. Engine number is on the right side of the block. Starting serial number: (96) 96730000001; (95) 95732000001; (99) 99732000001; (Sonett) 97735000001.

Model	Body Type & Seating	Engine Type/CID	P.O.E. Price	Weight (lbs.)	Prod. Total
96	2-dr Sedan-5P	V4/104	2995	2030	Note 1
95	2-dr Sta Wag-6/7P	V4/104	3095	2180	Note 1
99					
99	2-dr Sedan-5P	I4/121	3545	N/A	Note 1
99L	2-dr Sedan-5P	I4/121	3745	2480	Note 1
99L	4-dr Sedan-5P	I4/121	3845	2540	Note 1
99LE	2-dr Sedan-5P	I4/121	4095	2500	Note 1
99LE	4-dr Sedan-5P	I4/121	4145	2560	Note 1
99EMS	2-dr Sedan-5P	I4/121	4445	2490	Note 1
SONETT III					
97	2-dr Coupe-2P	V4/104	4175	1875	Note 2

Note 1: A total of 89,467 Saabs were produced during 1973.

Note 2: A total of 8,351 Sonett IIIs were produced from 1970 through 1974.

ENGINE DATA: BASE V-4 (96/95, Sonett): Overhead-valve, four-stroke 60-degree V-4 (German Ford). Cast iron block. **Displacement:** 103.6 cu. in. (1698 cc). **Bore & Stroke:** 3.54 x 2.63 in. (90 x 66.8 mm). **Compression Ratio:** 8.0:1. **Brake Horsepower:** 65 (SAE) at 4700 rpm. **Torque:** 85 lbs.-ft. at 2500 rpm. Three main bearings. Solid valve lifters. Autolite downdraft carburetor.

BASE FOUR (99LE/EMS): Inline, overhead-cam four-cylinder. Cast iron block and light alloy head. **Displacement:** 121.1 cu. in. (1985 cc). **Bore & Stroke:** 3.54 x 3.07 in. (90 x 78 mm). **Compression Ratio:** 8.7:1. **Brake Horsepower:** 110 at 5500 rpm. **Torque:** 123 lbs.-ft. at 3700 rpm. Five main bearings. Solid valve lifters. Bosch D-Jetronic fuel injection.

Note: The carbureted version of the 1985-cc engine, used in the 99L, was rated 95 bhp at 5200 rpm and 116 lbs.-ft. at 3500 rpm.

CHASSIS DATA: Wheelbase: (96/95) 98.3 in.; (99) 97.4 in.; (Sonett) 84.6 in. **Overall Length:** (96) 167.3 in.; (95) 171.3 in.; (99) 173.2 in.; (Sonett) 159.8 in. **Height:** (96) 58.7 in.; (95) 57.9 in.; (99) 56.7 in.; (Sonett) 46.9 in. **Width:** (96/95) 62.6 in.; (99) 66.5 in.; (Sonett) 59.1 in. **Front Tread:** (96/95) 48 in.; (99) 54.7 in.; (99EMS) 55.1 in.; (Sonett) 48.5 in. **Rear Tread:** (96/95) 48 in.; (99) 55.1 in.; (99EMS) 55.5 in.; (Sonett) 48.5 in. **Standard Tires:** 155SR15.

TECHNICAL: Layout: front-engine, front-drive. **Transmission:** four-speed manual; column lever except (99/Sonett) floor lever. **Standard Final Drive Ratio:** (96/95) 4.88:1; (99) 4.22:1; (99EMS) 3.89:1; (Sonett) 4.67:1. **Steering:** rack and pinion. **Suspension (front):** independent; coil springs with upper/lower wishbones. **Suspension (rear):** (95/96) U-shaped tubular (rigid) axle with trailing radius rods and coil springs; (99) rigid axle with Watts linkage, Panhard rod and coil springs; (Sonett) beam axle with radius arms and coil springs. **Brakes:** power front disc, rear drum except (99) four-wheel disc. **Body Construction:** steel unibody. **Fuel Tank:** (96) 10 gal.; (95) 11.1 gal.; (99) 11.9 gal.; (Sonett) 15.8 gallon.

MAJOR OPTIONS: Automatic transmission: 99LE sed ($250). Air conditioning.

PERFORMANCE: Top Speed: (Sonett) 100 mph. **Acceleration (0-60 mph):** (Sonett) 14.4 seconds.

Manufacturer: Saab-Scania (Saab Car Division), Nykoping, Sweden.

Distributor: Saab-Scania of America Inc., Orange, Connecticut.

1974 SAAB

99 — FOUR — New seats in LE and EMS models had integral head restraints (with "hole" in the center). The performance-oriented EMS also added new door/side panels, nylon/velour and vinyl seats, and a center rear armrest. Other EMS features included mag-type wheels, tachometer, clock, black racing stripes, and color-coordinated racing mirrors. Windshield wipers were now black. Power steering became optional on the LE with automatic, and 165-series tires replaced 155s on the 2-liter sedans. Waxy oil was now sprayed over the underside of all models, and into box sections, to cut corrosion. Quad round headlamps resided in bright metal housings, flanking the blacked-out grille with bright horizontal bar and a bright-framed center grille with 'SAAB' lettering in its center. Stylized 'ems' lettering went below the Saab name in the EMS center grille.

Large amber signal/marker lights wrapped around front fenders. Standard colors this year were: Sunset Orange, Sienna Brown, Verona Green, Toreador Red, Polar White, Caroline Blue, Sepia metallic, and Sterling Silver metallic. At mid-year, a new 99LE two-door hatchback, dubbed "Wagon Back" (known overseas as the Combi Coupe) appeared. Designed by Bjorn Envall, it had the same roofline as the sedan and a huge tailgate, with new taillamps at the corners. These hatchbacks were promoted as a combination sedan and station wagon.

SONETT III — V-4 — For its final season in the lineup, Saab's sports car added bumpers like those on the 99 sedan, to meet U.S. safety rules. Headlamp wipers were added to European models.

1974 Saab 99. (Saab Cars USA Inc.)

I.D. DATA: Serial number is on the driver's side door post or atop the instrument panel. Starting serial number: (99) 99742000001; (Sonett) 97745000001.

Model	Body Type & Seating	Engine Type/CID	P.O.E. Price	Weight (lbs.)	Prod. Total
99L (C2M)	2-dr Sedan-5P	I4/121	4448	2500	Note 1
99LE	2-dr Sedan-5P	I4/121	4698	2492	Note 1
99LE	4-dr Sedan-5P	I4/121	4848	2558	Note 1
99LE	3-dr Hatch-5P	I4/121	5248	2720	Note 1
99EMS	2-dr Sedan-5P	I4/121	5198	2422	Note 1
SONETT III					
97	2-dr Coupe-2P	V4/104	4898	1875	Note 2

Note 1: A total of 92,554 Saabs were produced during 1974, and 13,590 were sold in the U.S. (including 1,115 EMS models).

Note 2: A total of 8,351 Sonett IIIs were produced from 1970 through 1974 (1,595 in 1974 alone).

ENGINE DATA: BASE V-4 (Sonett): Overhead-valve, four-stroke 60-degree V-4 (German Ford). Cast iron block and heads. **Displacement:** 103.6 cu. in. (1699 cc). **Bore & Stroke:** 3.54 x 2.63 in. (89.9 x 66.8 mm). **Compression Ratio:** 8.0:1. **Brake Horsepower:** 65 at 4700 rpm. **Torque:** 85 lbs.-ft. at 2500 rpm. Three main bearings. Solid valve lifters. One downdraft carburetor.

BASE FOUR (99L): Inline, overhead-cam four-cylinder. Cast iron block and light alloy head. **Displacement:** 121.1 cu. in. (1985 cc). **Bore & Stroke:** 3.54 x 3.07 in. (90 x 78 mm). **Compression Ratio:** 8.7:1. **Brake Horsepower:** 95 at 5200 rpm. **Torque:** 116 lbs.-ft. at 3500 rpm. Five main bearings. Solid valve lifters. One carburetor.

BASE FOUR (99LE/EMS): Same as 1985-cc engine above, except — **Brake Horsepower:** 110 at 5500 rpm. **Torque:** 123 lbs.-ft. at 3700 rpm. Bosch D-Jetronic fuel injection.

CHASSIS DATA: Wheelbase: (99) 97.4 in.; (Sonett) 84.6 in. **Overall Length:** (99) 173.9 in.; (99 hatch) 178.3 in.; (Sonett) 160 in. **Height:** (99) 56.7 in.; (Sonett) 46.9 in. **Width:** (99) 66.5 in.; (Sonett) 59 in. **Front Tread:** (99) 54.7 in.; (99EMS) 55.1 in.; (Sonett) 48.5 in. **Rear Tread:** (99) 55.1 in.; (99EMS) 55.5 in.; (Sonett) 48.5 in. **Standard Tires:** (99) 165SR15; (Sonett) 155SR15.

TECHNICAL: Layout: front-engine, front-drive. **Transmission:** four-speed manual; floor lever. **Standard Final Drive Ratio:** (99) 3.89:1; (Sonett) 4.67:1. **Steering:** rack and pinion. **Suspension (front):** independent; coil springs with upper/lower wishbones. **Suspension (rear):** (99) rigid axle with Watts linkage, Panhard rod and coil springs; (Sonett) beam axle with radius arms and coil springs. **Brakes:** (99) power four-wheel disc; (Sonett) front disc, rear drum. **Body Construction:** steel unibody. **Fuel Tank:** (99) 11.9 gal.; (99 hatch) 14.5 gal.; (Sonett) 15.8 gallon.

MAJOR OPTIONS: Automatic transmission: 99LE ($250). Air conditioning: 99 ($450).

PERFORMANCE: Top Speed: (Sonett) 95-110 mph. **Acceleration (0-60 mph):** (Sonett) 12-14.4 seconds. **Fuel Mileage:** (99LE w/4-spd) 19.4 mpg EPA; (Sonett) 21.7 mpg EPA, 26.8 mpg in test.

Manufacturer: Saab-Scania (Saab Car Division), Nykoping, Sweden.
Distributor: Saab-Scania of America Inc., Orange, Connecticut.

HISTORY: The traditional 96 sedan and 95 station wagon remained available elsewhere in the world, but exports to the U.S. ceased.

1975 Saab 99. (Saab Cars USA Inc.)

99 — FOUR — The restyled, wider grille that went on the hatchback model (introduced at mid-year in 1974) appeared on all 99s this year. The performance-oriented EMS had a somewhat different grille with an inner framework line in addition to the main one. EMS also displayed a new rear badge. All models were powered by Saab's 2-liter engine. Bosch constant-injection mechanical fuel injection replaced the former Jetronic system. Sedan gas tanks grew to 14.5 gallons, to match the hatchback.

I.D. DATA: Serial number is on the top of the instrument panel (driver's side). First two digits are the model number; second two digits indicate model year; fifth digit indicates plant location; followed by sequential serial number. Starting serial number: 9975-000001.

Model	Body Type & Seating	Engine Type/CID	P.O.E. Price	Weight (lbs.)	Prod. Total
99LE	2-dr Sedan-5P	I4/121	5198	2485	Note 1
99LE	4-dr Sedan-5P	I4/121	5398	2535	Note 1
99LE	3-dr Hatch-5P	I4/121	5748	2555	Note 1
99EMS	2-dr Sedan-5P	I4/121	5798	2485	Note 1

Note 1: A total of 90,962 Saabs were produced during 1975, and 13,731 were sold in the U.S. (including 1,965 EMS models).

ENGINE DATA: BASE FOUR (99): Inline, overhead-cam four-cylinder. Cast iron block and light alloy head. **Displacement:** 121.1 cu. in. (1985 cc). **Bore & Stroke:** 3.54 x 3.07 in. (90 x 78 mm). **Compression Ratio:** 8.7:1. **Brake Horsepower:** 115 at 5500 rpm. **Torque:** 123 lbs.-ft. at 3500 rpm. Five main bearings. Solid valve lifters. Bosch mechanical (continuous) fuel injection.

CHASSIS DATA: Wheelbase: 97.4 in. **Overall Length:** (sed) 174 in.; (hatch) 178 in. **Height:** 56.5 in. **Width:** 66.5 in. **Front Tread:** 54.7 in.; (EMS) 55.25 in. **Rear Tread:** 55.2-55.5 in.; (EMS) 56 in. **Standard Tires:** 165SR15.

TECHNICAL: Layout: front-engine, front-drive. **Transmission:** four-speed manual; floor lever. **Standard Final Drive Ratio:** 3.89:1. **Steering:** rack and pinion. **Suspension (front):** independent; coil springs with upper/lower wishbones. **Suspension (rear):** rigid axle with Watts linkage, Panhard rod and coil springs. **Brakes:** power four-wheel disc. **Body Construction:** steel unibody. **Fuel Tank:** 14.5 gallon.

MAJOR OPTIONS: Automatic transmission: 99LE ($280). Air conditioning ($475). Power steering ($200); N/A on EMS or LE two-door. Sunroof: EMS ($300).

PERFORMANCE: Similar to 1974.

Manufacturer: Saab-Scania (Saab Car Division), Nykoping, Sweden.
Distributor: Saab-Scania of America Inc., Orange, Connecticut.

HISTORY: U.S. models were introduced on November 1, 1974. Up to this time, Saab's 2-liter had been able to pass all U.S. (Federal) and California emissions regulations. This year, California required modification so Saabs got an air-injection pump and partial exhaust-gas recirculation, causing power to drop. Saab's ad theme at this time was "It's what a car should be."

99 — FOUR — Saab claimed over 40 engineering refinements for 1976, including new rear brake caliper pistons and a simpler trip odometer. The 99LE Saab of 1975 turned into the 99GL this year. A new front spoiler went onto the performance-oriented 99EMS, which wore wider black bodyside moldings with thin racing accent striping. Saab's hatchback two-door was identified by 'Wagon Back' script on a plate on the rear quarter panel. A luxury GLE, trimmed like the EMS but with four doors, arrived in the U.S. during the 1976 season, with automatic transmission only. Its alloy wheels had gold trim (versus black on the EMS). GLE features included remote-control electric mirrors, stereo speakers in the doors, tinted glass all around, and metallic paint (usually charcoal grey). As the GLE debuted, the 99EMS got stiffer springs, Bilstein shocks, and the large front spoiler. Other 99 sedans got new hubcaps that lacked the former Saab design. Prices rose sharply this year.

1976 Saab 99. (Saab Cars USA Inc.)

I.D. DATA: Saab's 11-digit serial number is on the top of the instrument panel (driver's side). First two digits are the model number; second two digits indicate model year; fifth digit indicates plant location; followed by sequential serial number. Starting serial number: 9976-000001.

Model	Body Type & Seating	Engine Type/CID	P.O.E. Price	Weight (lbs.)	Prod. Total
99GL	2-dr Sedan-5P	I4/121	6298	2480	Note 1
99GL	4-dr Sedan-5P	I4/121	6498	2550	Note 1
99GL	3-dr Hatch-5P	I4/121	6648	2550	Note 1
99EMS	2-dr Sedan-5P	I4/121	6798	2470	Note 1
99GLE	4-dr Sedan-5P	I4/121	N/A	N/A	Note 1

Note 1: A total of 95,927 Saabs were produced during 1976, and 9,866 were sold in the U.S.

ENGINE DATA: BASE FOUR (99): Inline, overhead-cam four-cylinder. Cast iron block and light alloy head. **Displacement:** 121 cu. in. (1985 cc). **Bore & Stroke:** 3.54 x 3.07 in. (90 x 78 mm). **Compression Ratio:** 8.7:1. **Brake Horsepower:** 115 at 5500 rpm. **Torque:** 123 lbs.-ft. at 3500 rpm. Solid valve lifters. Bosch continuous fuel injection.

CHASSIS DATA: Wheelbase: 97.5 in. **Overall Length:** (sed) 175 in.; (hatch) 179 in. **Height:** 56.5 in. **Width:** 66.5 in. **Front Tread:** 54.8 in. **Rear Tread:** 55.2 in. **Standard Tires:** 165SR15.

TECHNICAL: Layout: front-engine, front-drive. **Transmission:** four-speed manual; floor lever. **Standard Final Drive Ratio:** 3.89:1. **Steering:** rack and pinion. **Suspension (front):** independent; coil springs with upper/lower wishbones. **Suspension (rear):** rigid axle with Watts linkage, Panhard rod and coil springs. **Brakes:** power four-wheel disc. **Body Construction:** steel unibody. **Fuel Tank:** 14.5 gallon.

MAJOR OPTIONS: Automatic transmission and power steering: 99GL ($400). Air conditioning ($475). Sunroof: EMS ($300).

PERFORMANCE: Acceleration (quarter-mile): (99EMS) near 80 mph. **Fuel Mileage:** (99EMS) 20+ mpg.

Manufacturer: Saab-Scania (Saab Car Division), Nykoping, Sweden.

Distributor: Saab-Scania of America Inc., Orange, Connecticut.

HISTORY: The one-millionth Saab was built early in 1976. U.S. models were introduced in November 1975. A four-door version of the hatchback debuted in January 1976 at the Brussels Motor Show, but would not appear in the U.S. until the '77 model year. Ads this year began: "We believe a car should help correct the driver's mistakes. Not vice versa."

1977 SAAB

1977 Saab GL. (Saab Cars USA Inc.)

564

99 — FOUR — Front turn signals and parking lights grew deeper this year, extending the full grille depth. Sedan taillamps grew to twice the former size (but not those on the "Wagon Back" model). A five-door "Wagon Back" (hatchback) was available this year, with an opera window on the rear panel. Both were considered part of the GL series. The luxury GLE came with standard automatic transmission and power steering. Standard equipment on the 99EMS included a heated driver's seat, aluminum-alloy wheels, gas-filled Bilstein shock absorbers, and a leather-wrapped steering wheel.

I.D. DATA: Serial number is on the top of the instrument panel (driver's side). First two digits are the model number; second two digits indicate model year; fifth digit indicates plant location; followed by sequential serial number. Starting serial number: 9977-000001.

Model	Body Type & Seating	Engine Type/CID	P.O.E. Price	Weight (lbs.)	Prod. Total
99GL	2-dr Sedan-5P	I4/121	6698	2550	Note 1
99GL	4-dr Sedan-5P	I4/121	6898	2670	Note 1
99GL	3-dr Hatch-5P	I4/121	6948	2600	Note 1
99GL	5-dr Hatch-5P	I4/121	7148	2750	Note 1
99EMS	2-dr Sedan-5P	I4/121	7198	2548	Note 1
99GLE	4-dr Sedan-5P	I4/121	7298	2634	Note 1

Note 1: A total of 76,498 Saabs were produced during 1977, and 13,120 were sold in the U.S.

ENGINE DATA: BASE FOUR (99): Inline, overhead-cam four-cylinder. Cast iron block and light alloy head. **Displacement:** 121.1 cu. in. (1985 cc). **Bore & Stroke:** 3.54 x 3.07 in. (90 x 78 mm). **Compression Ratio:** 9.25:1. **Brake Horsepower:** 115 at 5500 rpm. **Torque:** 123 lbs.-ft. at 3500 rpm. Five main bearings. Solid valve lifters. Bosch continuous fuel injection.

Note: Saabs sold in California had 8.7:1 compression for 110 bhp at 5500 rpm, and 119 lbs.-ft. at 3500 rpm.

CHASSIS DATA: Wheelbase: 97.5 in. **Overall Length:** (sed) 175 in.; (hatch) 179 in. **Height:** 56.5 in. **Width:** 66.5 in. **Front Tread:** 54.8 in.; (EMS) 55.25 in. **Rear Tread:** 55.3-55.5 in.; (EMS) 56 in. **Standard Tires:** 165SR15; (EMS) 175/70HR15.

TECHNICAL: Layout: front-engine, front-drive. **Transmission:** four-speed manual; floor lever. **Overall gear ratios:** (1st) 13.37:1; (2nd) 8.06:1; (3rd) 5.41:1; (4th) 3.89:1; (rev) 14.70:1. **Standard Final Drive Ratio:** 3.89:1. **Steering:** rack and pinion. **Suspension (front):** independent; coil springs with upper/lower wishbones. **Suspension (rear):** rigid axle with Watts linkage, Panhard rod and coil springs. **Brakes:** power four-wheel disc. **Body Construction:** steel unibody. **Fuel Tank:** 14.5 gallon.

MAJOR OPTIONS: Automatic transmission and power steering ($400). Air conditioning ($475). Sunroof: EMS/GLE ($300). Metallic paint ($160). AM/FM stereo.

PERFORMANCE: Acceleration (0-60 mph): (99) 12.5 sec.; (99EMS) 12 sec.; (Calif. 99EMS) 11.3 seconds. **Acceleration (quarter-mile):** (99EMS) 18.1 seconds (75.2 mph); (Calif. 99EMS) 18.5 seconds (71.5 mph). **Fuel Mileage:** (99) 19/28 mpg EPA; (Calif. 99EMS) 28-29 mpg.

Manufacturer: Saab-Scania (Saab Car Division), Nykoping, Sweden.

Distributor: Saab-Scania of America Inc., Orange, Connecticut.

HISTORY: U.S. models were introduced in December 1976. A Lambda sensor for emissions control (developed in concert with Bosch), was announced this year and installed on all Saabs destined for California and the west. A ceramic plug inserted into the manifold monitored the fuel/air mixture and signaled the fuel injection system. With the Lambda system, only a three-way catalyst converter was required except that automatic-transmission models also needed an EGR device. Saabs during this era were billed as "the command performance car." Ads promoted the praise for Saabs published in *Road Test* magazine, which stated that "It is difficult to imagine a better family sedan."

1978 SAAB

1978 Saab 99 Turbo. (Saab Cars USA Inc.)

99 — FOUR — Turbocharging was the big news for 1978, offered in the three-door hatchback (Wagon Back) model. Production turbos used a stock block, crankshaft, bearings and rods, but new pistons. Compression dropped from the usual 9.2:1 to 7.2:1. Exhaust valves got sodium cores for cooling, and a milder camshaft was installed. Turbos also had a larger radiator and an oil cooler, and a thicker exhaust-system bore dimension. A pressure switch would cut off fuel in case of excess pressure, and a distributor switch would isolate the ignition in case the engine was over-revved (beyond 6000 rpm). The turbocharged four developed 135 bhp at 5000 rpm (versus 115 at 5500 for normal engines). A very flat torque curve reached 160 pound-feet, versus 123 for the standard four. Turbocharger effect began around 1000 rpm, and would turn up to 80,000

rpm at top engine speed. Suspension was similar to the EMS, with blacked-out trim close to the GLE. A rear deck spoiler went below the back window. Turbos sported unique alloy wheels and a front air dam. Atop the dashboard was a turbo boost gauge. A 'Turbo' nameplate appeared on the grille, and 'Saab Turbo' on the lower section of the door. Top speed reached beyond 120 mph. Other 1978 models changed little. The EMS was available only as a three-door hatchback, the GLE as a five-door. Thus, five of the seven models sold in the U.S. were now hatchbacks.

I.D. DATA: Serial number is on the top of the instrument panel (driver's side). First two digits are the model number; second two digits indicate model year; fifth digit indicates plant location; followed by sequential serial number. Starting serial number: 99781000001.

Model	Body Type & Seating	Engine Type/CID	P.O.E. Price	Weight (lbs.)	Prod. Total
99L	2-dr Sedan-5P	I4/121	5998	2470	Note 1
99GL	2-dr Sedan-5P	I4/121	6298	2476	Note 1
99Gl	3-dr Hatch-5P	I4/121	6998	2542	Note 1
99GL	5-dr Hatch-5P	I4/121	7398	2608	Note 1
99EMS	3-dr Hatch-5P	I4/121	7858	2539	Note 1
99GLE	5-dr Hatch-5P	I4/121	7798	2649	Note 1
99 Turbo	3-dr Hatch-5P	I4/121	9998	2628	Note 1

Note 1: A total of 72,516 Saabs were produced during 1978, and 15,662 were sold in the U.S.

ENGINE DATA: BASE FOUR (99): Inline, overhead-cam four-cylinder. Cast iron block and light alloy head. **Displacement:** 121 cu. in. (1985 cc). **Bore & Stroke:** 3.54 x 3.07 in. (90 x 78 mm). **Compression Ratio:** 9.2:1. **Brake Horsepower:** 115 at 5500 rpm. **Torque:** 123 lbs.-ft. at 3500 rpm. Five main bearings. Solid valve lifters. Bosch mechanical fuel injection.

BASE FOUR (Turbo): Same as above, except — **Compression Ratio:** 7.2:1. **Brake Horsepower:** 135 at 5000 rpm. **Torque:** 160 lbs.-ft. at 3500 rpm.

CHASSIS DATA: Wheelbase: 97.4 in. **Overall Length:** (sed) 175 in.; (hatch) 179 in. **Height:** 56.7 in. **Width:** 66.5 in. **Front Tread:** 55.1 in. **Rear Tread:** 55.9 in. **Standard Tires:** 165SR15.

TECHNICAL: Layout: front-engine, front-drive. **Transmission:** four-speed manual; floor lever. **Steering:** rack and pinion. **Suspension (front):** independent; coil springs with upper/lower wishbones. **Suspension (rear):** rigid axle with trailing links, Panhard rod and coil springs. **Brakes:** power four-wheel disc. **Body Construction:** steel unibody. **Fuel Tank:** 14.5 gallon.

MAJOR OPTIONS: Automatic transmission and power steering ($400). Air conditioning. Sunroof ($300). AM/FM stereo.

PERFORMANCE: Top Speed: (Turbo) 120+ mph. **Fuel Mileage:** (99) 26-30 mpg highway (EPA).

Manufacturer: Saab-Scania (Saab Car Division), Nykoping, Sweden.

Distributor: Saab-Scania of America Inc., Orange, Connecticut.

HISTORY: U.S. models were introduced in November 1977. The Turbo was introduced in Europe in September 1977, and arrived in the U.S. later in the model year. Saab had taken an interest in the BMW 2002's failed turbocharger a few years earlier, thinking in terms of a turbo version of the 2-liter engine that would peak at fairly low speed. Turbo V-4s had already been used for rallycross events. Turbocharging, it was felt, would enhance Saab's upscale image generally and turn away from the somewhat staid conception of the 99. Around this time, Garrett (in the U.S.) introduced a compact turbo unit, roughly the size of an alternator. Saab chose a design of that sort, but added a wastegate to prevent problems of excess pressure. "The performance car perfected" was Saab's description of the new Turbo in 1978 ads, which added that "Nothing performs like a Saab." A competition version of the turbocharged engine was tuned to develop 240 horsepower.

1979 SAAB

99 — FOUR — Only one 99 model remained in Saab's lineup, as the new 900 series arrived. Added this year were the front springs from the new 900, plus wheels and seats from the 900GL.

900 — FOUR — Introduced at the October 1978 Paris Motor Show, the new 900 series was a trifle larger (and more expensive) than the 99, aimed upward at the executive end of the car market. Styling was based upon the "Wagon Back" (Combi Coupe) version of the 99, with wheelbase lengthened from 97.4 to 99.4 inches to give extra passenger space. Front wheel openings also moved forward. Overall length was nearly a foot greater than the equivalent 99. Front tread grew, too. Quite a few structural members were now made of aluminum rather than steel. Rack-and-pinion steering was still used, with a new Saginaw mechanism, but the safety steering wheel consisted of a deformable metal frame covered by a plastic pressure-distribution box and a soft plastic pad. Standard steel wheels on the basic 900GL had triangular cooling slots and a sculptured look. The luxury 900GLE carried spoke-like hubcaps instead of alloy wheels (as on the former 99GLE). Five-door Turbos wore alloy wheels with a fine-spoke look. Michelin TRX tires went on the five-door Turbo, but the three-door wore Pirelli P6 rubber. Grilles were restyled for the 900 series, with the GL and GLE using a horizontally-divided unit with small grillework in its center. Grilles of both Turbos and the EMS had three vertical slots at each end, and a plain center section. Parking/signal lights were larger than those of the 99, and faired into the body metal. For the first time, U.S. Saabs had recessed rectangular headlamps, though of single sealed-beam design; so both the European and American versions looked essentially similar. The 900EMS included a heavy-duty suspension, aluminum alloy wheels, a front air dam, clock, tachometer, and sport steering wheel.

Under the 900's hood sat the same inline four-cylinder engine as used in the 99, rated 115 or (with turbo) 135 horsepower. Turbocharged models had 'turbo' lettering on the cowl. The all-new dashboard was split into two sections, with the driver's half curved a bit. Deeply-recessed gauges sat under a non-reflective panel, with green lighting and a center-mounted speedometer. Instead of the customary clock on the left and combination gauge on the right, both the EMS and Turbo had a tachometer on the left and small clock at bottom, plus a boost pressure gauge on the right (for the Turbo). Saab's heat/vent system included a pollen-removing filter, and windshield wipers took on an asymmetrical configuration.

I.D. DATA: Serial number is on the top of the instrument panel (driver's side). First two digits are the model number; second two digits indicate model year; fifth digit indicates plant location; followed by sequential serial number. Starting serial number: (99GL) 99792000001; (900) 90791000001.

Model	Body Type & Seating	Engine Type/CID	P.O.E. Price	Weight (lbs.)	Prod. Total
99GL	2-dr Sedan-5P	I4/121	6798	2470	Note 1
900					
900GL	3-dr Hatch-5P	I4/121	8198	2595	Note 1
900GLE	5-dr Hatch-5P	I4/121	9348	2690	Note 1
900EMS	3-dr Hatch-5P	I4/121	9473	2640	Note 1
900 Turbo	3-dr Hatch-5P	I4/121	10923	2690	Note 1
900 Turbo	5-dr Hatch-5P	I4/121	11968	2795	Note 1

Note 1: A total of 83,758 Saabs were produced during 1979, and 15,142 were sold in the U.S.

ENGINE DATA: BASE FOUR: Inline, overhead-cam four-cylinder. Cast iron block and light alloy head. **Displacement:** 121 cu. in. (1985 cc). **Bore & Stroke:** 3.54 x 3.07 in. (90 x 78 mm). **Compression Ratio:** 9.2:1. **Brake Horsepower:** 115 at 5500 rpm. **Torque:** 123 lbs.-ft. at 3500 rpm. Five main bearings. Solid valve lifters. Fuel injection.

BASE FOUR (Turbo): Same as above, except — **Brake Horsepower:** 135 at 5500 rpm. **Torque:** 160 lbs.-ft. at 3500 rpm.

CHASSIS DATA: Wheelbase: (99) 97.4 in.; (900) 99.4 in. **Overall Length:** (99) 175 in.; (900) 186.6 in. **Height:** (99) 56.6 in.; (900) 55.9 in. **Width:** 66.5 in. **Front Tread:** (99) 55.3 in.; (900) 55.9 in.; (Turbo 3-dr) 56.3 in. **Rear Tread:** (99) 56 in.; (900) 56.3 in.; (Turbo 3-dr) 56.7 in. **Standard Tires:** (99/900) 165SR15; (Turbo 3-dr) 195/60HR15; (Turbo 5-dr) 180/65HR15.

TECHNICAL: Layout: front-engine, front-drive. **Transmission:** four-speed manual; floor lever. **Standard Final Drive Ratio:** 3.89:1. **Steering:** rack and pinion. **Suspension (front):** coil springs with upper/lower wishbones. **Suspension (rear):** rigid axle with trailing arms, Panhard rod and coil springs. **Brakes:** power four-wheel disc. **Body Construction:** steel unibody. **Fuel Tank:** 14.5 gallon.

MAJOR OPTIONS: Automatic transmission and power steering: 900GL/EMS ($500). Automatic transmission: 900GLE ($350). Air conditioning. Sunroof: 900GLE ($375). AM/FM stereo.

PERFORMANCE: Top Speed: (Turbo) 111 mph. **Acceleration (quarter-mile):** (Turbo) 17.7 seconds. **Fuel Mileage:** (Turbo) 19 mpg (EPA).

Manufacturer: Saab-Scania (Saab Car Division), Nykoping, Sweden.

Distributor: Saab-Scania of America Inc., Orange, Connecticut.

HISTORY: The 99GL for 1979 was introduced in the U.S. in November 1978, the new 900 series a month later.

1980 SAAB

99 — FOUR — For one more season, the 99GL was available in the U.S., only as a two-door sedan with manual shift. New front seats had lower backs and adjustable head restraints. Taillamps were larger this year. A 99 two-door Turbo became available in Europe, but not in the U.S., as the 99 series began to fade away. Otherwise, the biggest change was a sharp price hike in the U.S.

900 — FOUR — This year, the grille introduced on the Turbo 900 went on all 900 models, and restyled taillamp clusters now contained built-in rear foglights. A space-saver spare tire now was included. A five-speed gearbox (overdrive fifth gear) became optional on the Turbo and EMS, and first gear got a higher ratio. For the first time, the 900GLE was offered with manual shift, partly in response to American preferences. All Saabs had "Lambda Guard" emissions control, as used in California models in 1979, which consisted of a three-way catalyst and sensor to measure oxygen content in the exhaust. A mini-computer then kept the air/fuel mixture close to the optimum (14.5:1) ratio. Headrests adjusted vertically by four inches. Prices rose sharply this year.

I.D. DATA: Serial number is on the top of the instrument panel (driver's side). First two digits are the model number; second two digits indicate model year; fifth digit indicates plant location; followed by sequential serial number. Starting serial number: (99GL) 99806000001; (900GL) 9980-000001; (900) 9080-000001.

Model	Body Type & Seating	Engine Type/CID	P.O.E. Price	Weight (lbs.)	Prod. Total
99GL	2-dr Sedan-5P	I4/121	7995	2500	Note 1
900					
900GL	3-dr Hatch-5P	I4/121	9295	2630	Note 1
900GLE	5-dr Hatch-5P	I4/121	10295	2790	Note 1
900EMS	3-dr Hatch-5P	I4/121	10795	2690	Note 1
900 Turbo	3-dr Hatch-5P	I4/121	12595	2760	Note 1
900 Turbo	5-dr Hatch-5P	I4/121	13695	2880	Note 1

Note 1: A total of 65,754 Saabs were produced during 1980, and 13,558 were sold in the U.S.

ENGINE DATA: BASE FOUR: Inline, overhead-cam four-cylinder. Cast iron block and light alloy head. **Displacement:** 121 cu. in. (1985 cc). **Bore & Stroke:** 3.54 x 3.07 in. (90 x 78 mm). **Compression Ratio:** 9.25:1. **Brake Horsepower:** 110 at 5250 rpm. **Torque:** 119 lbs.-ft. at 3500 rpm. Five main bearings. Solid valve lifters. Fuel injection.

BASE FOUR (Turbo): Same as above, except — **Compression Ratio:** 7.2:1. **Brake Horsepower:** 135 at 4800 rpm. **Torque:** 160 lbs.-ft. at 3500 rpm.

CHASSIS DATA: Wheelbase: (99) 97.4 in.; (900) 99.4 in. **Overall Length:** (99) 176.3 in.; (900) 187.6 in. **Height:** (99) 56.7 in.; (900) 55.9 in. **Width:** 66.5 in. **Front Tread:** (99) 55.5 in.; (900) 55.9 in.; (Turbo 3-dr) 56.3 in. **Rear Tread:** (99) 56 in.; (900) 56.3 in.; (Turbo 3-dr) 56.7 in. **Standard Tires:** (99/900) 165SR15; (Turbo 3-dr) 195/60HR15; (Turbo 5-dr) 180/65HR15.

TECHNICAL: Layout: front-engine, front-drive. **Transmission:** four-speed manual; floor lever. **Standard Final Drive Ratio:** 3.89:1. **Steering:** rack and pinion. **Suspension (front):** coil springs with upper/lower wishbones. **Suspension (rear):** rigid axle with trailing arms, Panhard rod and coil springs. **Brakes:** power four-wheel disc. **Body Construction:** steel unibody. **Fuel Tank:** 14.5 gallon.

MAJOR OPTIONS: Automatic transmission ($395). Power steering (GLi). Air conditioning. Touring package: GLE ($1795). Metallic paint ($325) except GLi. AM/FM stereo.

Manufacturer: Saab-Scania (Saab Car Division), Nykoping, Sweden.

Distributor: Saab-Scania of America Inc., Orange, Connecticut.

HISTORY: 1980 models were introduced in the U.S. in October 1979. The 99GL ceased to be available in the U.S. after 1980.

1981-82 SAAB

1981 Saab 900 four-door notchback sedan. (Saab Cars USA Inc.)

900 — FOUR — A four-door notchback sedan became available for 1981, in both Turbo and regular form. Turbos could be obtained with a reinforced Borg-Warner three-speed automatic transmission this year. Other models had a standard four-speed manual shift, optional five-speed, or automatic. A four-door notchback sedan version of the basic 900 became available for the 1982 model year.

I.D. DATA: A 17-symbol Vehicle Identification Number (VIN) is on the upper left of the instrument panel, visible through the windshield. First three symbols ('900') are the manufacturer's code; fourth letter ('Y') indicates the product line; fifth and sixth characters indicate series and body style; seventh digit denotes the engine; eighth character indicates the type of restraint system; ninth is a check digit; tenth symbol indicates the model year; eleventh is the assembly plant. The final six digits make up the sequential serial number. Starting serial number: 000001.

Model	Body Type & Seating	Engine Type/CID	P.O.E. Price	Weight (lbs.)	Prod. Total
900	3-dr Hatch-5P	I4/121	10400	2580	Note 1
900	4-dr Sedan-5P	I4/121	10700	2630	Note 1
900S	3-dr Hatch-5P	I4/121	12100	2650	Note 1
900S	4-dr Sedan-5P	I4/121	12700	2690	Note 1
900 Turbo	3-dr Hatch-5P	I4/121	14600	2770	Note 1
900 Turbo	4-dr Sedan-5P	I4/121	15100	2810	Note 1

Note 1: A total of 66,392 Saabs were produced during 1981, and 14,613 were sold in the U.S. A total of 83,556 Saabs were built in 1982, with 18,463 sold in the U.S.

1982 Saab 900 Turbo three-door hatchback. (Saab Cars USA Inc.)

ENGINE DATA: BASE FOUR: Inline, overhead-cam four-cylinder. Cast iron block and light alloy head. **Displacement:** 121.1 cu. in. (1985 cc). **Bore & Stroke:** 3.54 x 3.07 in. (90 x 78 mm). **Compression Ratio:** 9.25:1. **Brake Horsepower:** 110 at 5250 rpm. **Torque:** 119 lbs.-ft. at 3500 rpm. Five main bearings. Solid valve lifters. Fuel injection. BASE FOUR (Turbo): Same as above, except -- **Compression Ratio:** 7.2:1. **Brake Horsepower:** 135 at 4800 rpm. **Torque:** 160 lbs.-ft. at 3500 rpm.

CHASSIS DATA: Wheelbase: 99.4 in. **Overall Length:** 187.6 in. **Height:** 55.9 in. **Width:** 66.5 in.; **Front Tread:** 55.9 in.; (Turbo 3-dr) 56.3 in. **Rear Tread:** 56.3 in.; (Turbo 3-dr) 56.7 in. **Standard Tires:** 165SR15; (Turbo 3-dr) 195/60HR15; (Turbo 5-dr) 180/65HR15.

TECHNICAL: Layout: front-engine, front-drive. **Transmission:** four-speed manual; floor lever. **Standard Final Drive Ratio:** 3.89:1. **Steering:** rack and pinion. **Suspension (front):** transverse control arms and coil springs. **Suspension (rear):** rigid axle with trailing arms, Panhard rod and coil springs. **Brakes:** power four-wheel disc. **Body Construction:** steel unibody. **Fuel Tank:** 16.6 gallon.

MAJOR OPTIONS: Automatic transmission ($350). Air conditioning. AM/FM stereo.
Manufacturer: Saab-Scania (Saab Car Division), Nykoping, Sweden.
Distributor: Saab-Scania of America Inc., Orange, Connecticut.
HISTORY: 1982 models were introduced in the U.S. in October 1981.

1983 SAAB

1983 Saab 900 four-door. (Saab Cars USA Inc.)

900 — FOUR — Minor refinements were the only notable change this year, including running lights added to each side of the grille. Parking/marker lights remained at the outer ends of the car's nose. Asbestos-free pads were now used for the disc braking system (semi-metallic in front). Both front and rear seats now had three-point shoulder/lap belts in outboard positions. Non-turbo Saabs no longer needed an exhaust gas recirculation system for emissions control. As before, three-door hatchback and four-door notchback sedans were offered, in base, 'S' or Turbo form. Turbo models had gas-pressurized shock absorbers on both ends. Standard equipment on the base model included the 121-cid (2.0-liter) engine, five-speed (overdrive) manual gearbox, power steering and brakes, tachometer, clock, electric rear-window defroster, intermittent wipers, tinted glass, reclining front bucket seats, driver's seat tilt/height adjustment, and AM/FM stereo radio. The 900S added electrically-heated front seats, manual sunroof, and fold-down rear center armrest. Turbo models included air conditioning, halogen headlamps, power remote mirrors, power front-door windows (four-door model), and upgraded suspension/tires. Three-door Turbos had front and rear spoilers.

I.D. DATA: VIN is in same location, with same breakdown, as prior models; see 1981 listing.

Model	Body Type & Seating	Engine Type/CID	P.O.E. Price	Weight (lbs.)	Prod. Total
900	3-dr Hatch-5P	I4/121	10750	2600	Note 1
900	4-dr Sedan-5P	I4/121	11050	2640	Note 1
900S	3-dr Hatch-5P	I4/121	13550	2710	Note 1
900S	4-dr Sedan-5P	I4/121	13950	2750	Note 1
900 Turbo	3-dr Hatch-5P	I4/121	16510	2790	Note 1
900 Turbo	4-dr Sedan-5P	I4/121	16910	2820	Note 1

Note 1: A total of 26,323 Saabs were sold in the U.S. during 1983.

ENGINE DATA: BASE FOUR: Inline, overhead-cam four-cylinder. Cast iron block and light alloy head. **Displacement:** 121 cu. in. (1985 cc). **Bore & Stroke:** 3.54 x 3.07 in. (90 x 78 mm). **Compression Ratio:** 9.25:1. **Brake Horsepower:** 110 at 5250 rpm. **Torque:** 119 lbs.-ft. at 3500 rpm. Five main bearings. Solid valve lifters. Fuel injection. BASE FOUR (Turbo): Same as above, except — **Compression Ratio:** 8.5:1. **Brake Horsepower:** 135 at 4800 rpm. **Torque:** 160-172 lbs.-ft. at 3500 rpm.

CHASSIS DATA: Wheelbase: 99.1 in. **Overall Length:** 187.6 in. **Height:** 55.9 in. **Width:** 66.5 in. **Front Tread:** 56.3 in. **Rear Tread:** 56.7 in.

TECHNICAL: Layout: front-engine, front-drive. **Transmission:** five-speed manual; automatic available. **Standard Final Drive Ratio:** 3.67:1. **Steering:** power rack and pinion. **Suspension (front):** transverse control arms and coil springs. **Suspension (rear):** rigid axle with trailing arms, Panhard rod and coil springs. **Brakes:** power four-wheel disc. **Body Construction:** steel unibody. **Fuel Tank:** 16.6 gallon.

MAJOR OPTIONS: Automatic transmission ($370). Metallic or special black paint ($350).
Manufacturer: Saab-Scania (Saab Car Division), Nykoping, Sweden.
Distributor: Saab-Scania of America Inc., Orange, Connecticut.
HISTORY: 1983 models were introduced in the U.S. in September 1982.

1984 SAAB

900 — FOUR — A restyled grille was the major change for 1984, to complement the rounded shape of the nose and front bumper extensions. A new twin-belt alternator was installed, and the Lambda emissions control system was modified to improve cold starting. Turbos got a new exhaust with deeper tone, with an oval tailpipe visible at the back end. Turbo sound systems now had electronic tuning and a graphic equalizer. A new time-delay switch held the inside lights on for a time after the car's doors were shut. An optional luxury package for the Turbo included leather upholstery, power sunroof, cruise control, and foglights.

1984 Saab 900 Turbo. (Saab Cars USA Inc.)

I.D. DATA: VIN is in same location, with same breakdown, as prior models; see 1981 listing.

Model	Body Type & Seating	Engine Type/CID	P.O.E. Price	Weight (lbs.)	Prod. Total
900	3-dr Hatch-5P	I4/121	11110	2600	Note 1
900	4-dr Sedan-5P	I4/121	11420	2640	Note 1
900S	3-dr Hatch-5P	I4/121	13850	2710	Note 1
900S	4-dr Sedan-5P	I4/121	14310	2750	Note 1
900 Turbo	3-dr Hatch-5P	I4/121	16940	2790	Note 1
900 Turbo	4-dr Sedan-5P	I4/121	17400	2830	Note 1

Note 1: A total of 33,631 Saabs were sold in the U.S. during 1984.

ENGINE DATA: Same as 1983.

CHASSIS DATA: Wheelbase: 99.1 in. **Overall Length:** 186.6 in. **Height:** 56.1 in. **Width:** 66.5 in. **Front Tread:** 56.3 in. **Rear Tread:** 56.7 in.

TECHNICAL: Same as 1983.

MAJOR OPTIONS: Automatic transmission. Metallic or special black paint.

Manufacturer: Saab-Scania (Saab Car Division), Nykoping, Sweden.

Distributor: Saab-Scania of America Inc., Orange, Connecticut.

HISTORY: 1984 models were introduced in the U.S. in September 1983.

1985 SAAB

900 — FOUR — Turbocharged Saabs had a modified engine this year, the same size as before but operating with twin overhead cams (four valves per cylinder). Horsepower rose by 25, to 160 bhp. Both the three-door and four-door Turbos also wore new spoke-style alloy wheels. An optional Special Performance Group with aero body add-ons became available later in the season for the three-door. Cruise control was now standard in both the 900S and Turbo, while base Saabs rode new 15-inch steel wheels. Hoods all displayed the Saab logo.

I.D. DATA: VIN is in same location, with same breakdown, as prior models; see 1981 listing.

Model	Body Type & Seating	Engine Type/CID	P.O.E. Price	Weight (lbs.)	Prod. Total
900	3-dr Hatch-5P	I4/121	11850	2558	Note 1
900	4-dr Sedan-5P	I4/121	12170	2595	Note 1
900S	3-dr Hatch-5P	I4/121	15040	2607	Note 1
900S	4-dr Sedan-5P	I4/121	15510	2658	Note 1
900 Turbo	3-dr Hatch-5P	I4/121	18150	2739	Note 1
900 Turbo	4-dr Sedan-5P	I4/121	18620	2779	Note 1

Note 1: A total of 39,068 Saabs were sold in the U.S. during 1985.

ENGINE DATA: BASE FOUR: Inline, overhead-cam four-cylinder. Cast iron block and light alloy head. **Displacement:** 121 cu. in. (1985 cc). **Bore & Stroke:** 3.54 x 3.07 in. (90 x 78 mm). **Compression Ratio:** 9.25:1. **Brake Horsepower:** 110 at 5250 rpm. **Torque:** 119 lbs.-ft. at 3500 rpm. Five main bearings. Solid valve lifters. Port fuel injection.

BASE FOUR (Turbo): Inline, dual-overhead-cam four-cylinder (16-valve). **Displacement:** 121 cu. in. (1985 cc). **Bore & Stroke:** 3.54 x 3.07 in. (90 x 78 mm). **Compression Ratio:** 9.0:1. **Brake Horsepower:** 160 at 5500 rpm. **Torque:** 188 lbs.-ft. at 3000 rpm.

CHASSIS DATA: Wheelbase: 99.1 in. **Overall Length:** 186.6 in. **Height:** 56.1 in. **Width:** 66.5 in. **Front Tread:** 56.3 in. **Rear Tread:** 56.7 in.

TECHNICAL: Layout: front-engine, front-drive. **Transmission:** five-speed manual; three-speed automatic available. **Standard Final Drive Ratio:** 3.67:1. **Steering:** power rack and pinion. **Suspension (front):** transverse control arms and coil springs. **Suspension (rear):** rigid axle with trailing arms, Panhard rod and coil springs. **Brakes:** power four-wheel disc. **Body Construction:** steel unibody. **Fuel Tank:** 16.6 gallon.

MAJOR OPTIONS: Automatic transmission ($400). Exclusive Appointment Group: Turbo ($1330). Metallic or special black paint ($385); N/A on base 900.

Manufacturer: Saab-Scania (Saab Car Division), Nykoping, Sweden.

Distributor: Saab-Scania of America Inc., Orange, Connecticut.

HISTORY: 1985 models were introduced in the U.S. in September 1984.

1986 SAAB

900 — FOUR — A two-door notchback sedan joined the 900S hatchback and four-door sedan this year, while the four-door version of the Turbo was dropped (replaced by the new five-door 9000 Turbo). A new twin-cam engine became standard in the 900S, with 15 extra horsepower. The single-cam engine, identical in displacement, remained standard in the base 900. Built-in circuitry for the 900S radio was designed to disable it if stolen. A Turbo convertible (built in Finland) arrived late in the model year, in small numbers at first; see next listing for details.

9000 — FOUR — Available earlier in Europe, the new Saab 9000 finally arrived in the U.S. for 1986, the first all-new model since the debut of the 99 series in 1969. Wheelbase of the five-door hatchback was 105 inches, some six inches longer than the 900. Overall profile and the large rear glass actually belied the fact that it was a hatchback rather than a notchback design. Split rear seatbacks folded down to add cargo space. Manual-shift ignition locks were on the steering column, rather than the usual spot on the floor. The 9000's hood also hinged at the rear rather than the front. Under that hood sat the same engine as in the 900 Turbo, but mounted transversely in this model.

I.D. DATA: VIN is in same location, with same breakdown, as prior models; see 1981 listing.

Model	Body Type & Seating	Engine Type/CID	P.O.E. Price	Weight (lbs.)	Prod. Total
900	3-dr Hatch-5P	I4/121	12285	2643	Note 1
900	4-dr Sedan-5P	I4/121	12685	2629	Note 1
900S	2-dr Sedan-5P	I4/121	15595	2671	Note 1
900S	3-dr Hatch-5P	I4/121	15895	2684	Note 1
900S	4-dr Hatch-5P	I4/121	16295	2737	Note 1
900 Turbo	3-dr Hatch-5P	I4/121	18695	2766	Note 1
900 Turbo	2-dr Conv-5P	I4/121	25390	N/A	Note 1
9000					
Turbo	5-dr Hatch-5P	I4/121	21945	2835	Note 1

Note 1: A total of 48,246 Saabs were sold in the U.S. during 1986.

ENGINE DATA: BASE FOUR (900): Inline, overhead-cam four-cylinder. Cast iron block and light alloy head. **Displacement:** 121 cu. in. (1985 cc). **Bore & Stroke:** 3.54 x 3.07 in. (90 x 78 mm). **Compression Ratio:** 9.25:1. **Brake Horsepower:** 110 at 5250 rpm. **Torque:** 119 lbs.-ft. at 3500 rpm. Five main bearings. Solid valve lifters. Port fuel injection.

BASE FOUR (900S): Inline, dual-overhead-cam four-cylinder (16-valve). **Displacement:** 121 cu. in. (1985 cc). **Bore & Stroke:** 3.54 x 3.07 in. (90 x 78 mm). **Compression Ratio:** 10.0:1. **Brake Horsepower:** 125 at 5500 rpm. **Torque:** 123 lbs.-ft. at 3000 rpm. Solid valve lifters. Port fuel injection.

BASE FOUR (900/9000 Turbo): Inline, dual-overhead-cam four-cylinder (16-valve); turbocharged and intercooled. **Displacement:** 121 cu. in. (1985 cc). **Bore & Stroke:** 3.54 x 3.07 in. (90 x 78 mm). **Compression Ratio:** 9.0:1. **Brake Horsepower:** 160 at 5500 rpm. **Torque:** 188 lbs.-ft. at 3000 rpm.

CHASSIS DATA: Wheelbase: (900) 99.1 in.; (9000) 105.2 in. **Overall Length:** (900) 186.6 in.; (9000) 181.9 in. **Height:** (900) 56.1 in.; (9000) 55.9 in. **Width:** (900) 66.5 in.; (9000) 69.4 in. **Front Tread:** (900) 56.3 in.; (9000) 59.9 in. **Rear Tread:** (900) 56.7 in.; (9000) 58.7 in. **Standard Tires:** 195/60R15.

TECHNICAL: Layout: front-engine, front-drive. **Transmission:** five-speed manual; three-speed automatic available. **Standard Final Drive Ratio:** (900) 3.67:1. **Steering:** power rack and pinion. **Suspension (front):** transverse control arms and coil springs. **Suspension (rear):** rigid axle with trailing arms, Panhard rod and coil springs. **Brakes:** power four-wheel disc. **Body Construction:** steel unibody. **Fuel Tank:** (900) 16.6 gallon.

MAJOR OPTIONS: Automatic transmission: 900 ($400); 9000 ($500). Special Performance Group: 900 Turbo 3-dr ($2870). Exclusive Appointment Group: 900 Turbo 3-dr ($1390). Leather pkg.: 9000 Turbo 5-dr ($1830). Power sunroof.: 9000 Turbo 5-dr ($920). Metallic or special black paint: 900S/9000 Turbo ($395).

Manufacturer: Saab-Scania (Saab Car Division), Nykoping, Sweden.

Distributor: Saab-Scania of America Inc., Orange, Connecticut.

HISTORY: 1986 models were introduced in the U.S. in September 1985.

1987 SAAB

1987 Saab 900 Turbo. (Saab Cars USA Inc.)

900 — FOUR — A convertible arrived during the 1986 model year, while the two-door notchback sedan was dropped for '87. A notchback four-door came in both base and S trim, and three versions of the three-door hatchback were offered. A fresh front-end look similar to that of the 9000 series consisted of a sloped chrome grille, new headlamps, and wraparound integrated bumper. A Special Performance Group option package for the Turbo included aero body fairings and a firmer suspension, as well as Pirelli P6 tires, foglamps, and a power sunroof.

1987 Saab 9000S five-door hatchback. (Saab Cars USA Inc.)

9000 — FOUR — After a year of availability only in Turbo form, the larger 9000 five-door hatchback came with or without a turbocharger this year. Automatic transmissions had been made available during the '86 model year, and became more plentiful in 1987. Both models wore Pirelli P600 tires. Leather upholstery was standard on the Turbo and optional on the non-turbo 9000S. Standard equipment included a five-speed manual gearbox, power windows, central locking, AM/FM stereo with cassette and graphic equalizer, power antenna, automatic climate control, halogen headlamps, front/rear reading lights, adjustable height/tilt sport driver's seat with lumbar and thigh support, 195/60R15 tires, and telescopic steering column. Both engines displaced 2.0 liters, and the Turbo's included an intercooler. A four-speed overdrive automatic transmission was optional.

I.D. DATA: VIN is in same location, with same breakdown, as prior models; see 1981 listing.

Model	Body Type & Seating	Engine Type/CID	P.O.E. Price	Weight (lbs.)	Prod. Total
900	3-dr Hatch-5P	I4/121	14115	2744	Note 1
900	4-dr Sedan-5P	I4/121	14515	2724	Note 1
900S	3-dr Hatch-5P	I4/121	17585	2819	Note 1
900S	4-dr Sedan-5P	I4/121	17985	2852	Note 1
900 Turbo	3-dr Hatch-5P	I4/121	20405	2875	Note 1
900 Turbo	2-dr Conv-5P	I4/121	26580	2920	Note 1
9000					
9000S	5-dr Hatch-5P	I4/121	21805	2967	Note 1
Turbo	5-dr Hatch-5P	I4/121	25515	3048	Note 1

Note 1: A total of 45,106 Saabs were sold in the U.S. during 1987.

ENGINE DATA: BASE FOUR (900): Inline, overhead-cam four-cylinder. Cast iron block and light alloy head. **Displacement:** 121 cu. in. (1985 cc). **Bore & Stroke:** 3.54 x 3.07 in. (90 x 78 mm). **Compression Ratio:** 9.25:1. **Brake Horsepower:** 110 at 5250 rpm. **Torque:** 119 lbs.-ft. at 3500 rpm. Five main bearings. Solid valve lifters. Port fuel injection.

BASE FOUR (900S, 9000S): Inline, dual-overhead-cam four-cylinder (16-valve). **Displacement:** 121 cu. in. (1985 cc). **Bore & Stroke:** 3.54 x 3.07 in. (90 x 78 mm). **Compression Ratio:** 10.0:1. **Brake Horsepower:** 125 at 5500 rpm. **Torque:** 123 lbs.-ft. at 3000 rpm. Port fuel injection.

BASE FOUR (900/9000 Turbo): Inline, dual-overhead-cam four-cylinder (16-valve); turbocharged and intercooled. **Displacement:** 121 cu. in. (1985 cc). **Bore & Stroke:** 3.54 x 3.07 in. (90 x 78 mm). **Compression Ratio:** 9.0:1. **Brake Horsepower:** 160 at 5500 rpm. **Torque:** 188 lbs.-ft. at 3000 rpm. Port fuel injection.

Note: 900 Turbos with the Special Performance Group option produced 165 bhp and 195 lbs.-ft. of torque.

CHASSIS DATA: Wheelbase: (900) 99.1 in.; (9000) 105.2 in. **Overall Length:** (900) 184.3-184.5 in.; (9000) 181.9 in. **Height:** (900) 56.1 in.; (9000) 55.9 in. **Width:** (900) 66.5 in.; (9000) 69.4 in. **Front Tread:** (900) 56.3 in.; (9000) 59.9 in. **Rear Tread:** (900) 56.7 in.; (9000) 58.7 in. **Standard Tires:** 195/60R15.

TECHNICAL: Layout: front-engine, front-drive. **Transmission:** five-speed manual; three-speed automatic available (four-speed on 9000). **Standard Final Drive Ratio:** (900) 3.67:1; (9000S w/5-spd) 4.45:1; (9000 Turbo w/5-spd) 4.21:1; (9000 w/automatic) 4.28:1. **Steering:** power rack and pinion. **Suspension (front):** (900) transverse control arms and coil springs, with stabilizer bar on 900S and Turbo; (9000) MacPherson struts with coil springs and stabilizer bar. **Suspension (rear):** rigid axle with trailing arms, Panhard rod and coil springs; stabilizer bar on 900S, 900 Turbo and 9000. **Brakes:** power four-wheel disc. **Body Construction:** steel unibody. **Fuel Tank:** (900) 16.6 gallon; (9000) 17.9 gallon.

MAJOR OPTIONS: Three-speed automatic transmission: 900 ($430). Four-speed automatic transmission: 9000 ($550). Special Performance Group: 900 Turbo ($2630). Leather package: 9000 ($1010).

Manufacturer: Saab-Scania (Saab Car Division), Nykoping, Sweden.

Distributor: Saab-Scania of America Inc., Orange, Connecticut.

HISTORY: 1987 models were introduced in the U.S. in September 1986.

1988 SAAB

900 — FOUR — A modified braking system with ventilated front discs (formerly solid) went into the smaller Saabs for 1988, while the 900 Turbo added a new water-cooling circuit. Turbos now had a standard Clarion 80-watt stereo system with cassette player and graphic equalizer. Upholstery was new, except on the base model. As before, a five-speed manual gearbox was standard; three-speed automatic optional.

1988 Saab 9000 Turbo five-door hatchback. (Saab Cars USA Inc.)

9000 — FOUR — Teves-developed anti-lock braking became standard on the larger Saab hatchback sedan. Joining the option list was a compact disc player, while the new 80-watt Clarion stereo system with graphic equalizer became standard on the 9000 Turbo. Leather upholstery again was standard on the Turbo, optional on the 9000S. A four-speed automatic transmission also was optional.

I.D. DATA: VIN is in same location, with same breakdown, as prior models; see 1981 listing.

Model	Body Type & Seating	Engine Type/CID	P.O.E. Price	Weight (lbs.)	Prod. Total
900	3-dr Htchk-5P	I4/121	14983	2695	Note 1
900	4-dr Sedan-5P	I4/121	15471	2735	Note 1
900S	3-dr Hatch-5P	I4/121	18718	2826	Note 1
900S	4-dr Sedan-5P	I4/121	19206	2846	Note 1
900 Turbo	3-dr Hatch-5P	I4/121	21995	2895	Note 1
900 Turbo	2-dr Conv-5P	I4/121	29740	2985	Note 1
9000					
9000S	5-dr Hatch-5P	I4/121	23337	3022	Note 1
Turbo	5-dr Hatch-5P	I4/121	28141	3096	Note 1

Note 1: A total of 39,829 Saabs were sold in the U.S. during the 1988 model year.

Price Note: Prices rose during the model year, ranging from $15,432 to $28,985.

1988 Saab Turbo convertible. (Saab Cars USA Inc.)

ENGINE DATA: BASE FOUR (900): Inline, overhead-cam four-cylinder. Cast iron block and light alloy head. **Displacement:** 121 cu. in. (1985 cc). **Bore & Stroke:** 3.54 x 3.07 in. (90 x 78 mm). **Compression Ratio:** 9.25:1. **Brake Horsepower:** 110 at 5250 rpm. **Torque:** 119 lbs.-ft. at 3500 rpm. Five main bearings. Solid valve lifters. Port fuel injection.

BASE FOUR (900S, 9000S): Inline, dual-overhead-cam four-cylinder (16-valve). **Displacement:** 121 cu. in. (1985 cc). **Bore & Stroke:** 3.54 x 3.07 in. (90 x 78 mm). **Compression Ratio:** 10.0:1. **Brake Horsepower:** 125 at 5500 rpm. **Torque:** 125 lbs. ft. at 3000 rpm. Port fuel injection.

BASE FOUR (900/9000 Turbo): Inline, dual-overhead-cam four-cylinder (16-valve); turbocharged and intercooled. **Displacement:** 121 cu. in. (1985 cc). **Bore & Stroke:** 3.54 x 3.07 in. (90 x 78 mm). **Compression Ratio:** 9.0:1. **Brake Horsepower:** 160 at 5500 rpm. **Torque:** 188 lbs.-ft. at 3000 rpm. Port fuel injection.

Note: 900 Turbos with the Special Performance Group option produced 165 bhp and 195 lbs.-ft. of torque.

CHASSIS DATA: Wheelbase: (900) 99.1 in.; (9000) 105.2 in. **Overall Length:** (900) 184.3-184.5 in.; (9000) 181.9 in. **Height:** (900) 56.1 in.; (9000) 55.9 in. **Width:** (900) 66.5 in.; (9000) 69.4 in. **Front Tread:** (900) 56.3-56.4 in.; (9000) 59.9 in. **Rear Tread:** (900) 56.7-56.8 in.; (9000) 58.7 in. **Standard Tires:** 185/65R15; (9000 Turbo) 205/55VR15.

TECHNICAL: Layout: front-engine, front-drive. **Transmission:** five-speed manual; three-speed automatic available (four-speed on 9000). **Steering:** power rack and pinion. **Suspension (front):** (900) transverse control arms and coil springs, with stabilizer bar on 900S and Turbo; (9000) MacPherson struts with coil springs and stabilizer bar. **Suspension (rear):** rigid axle with trailing arms, Panhard rod and coil springs; stabilizer bar on 900S, 900 Turbo and 9000. **Brakes:** power four-wheel disc. **Body Construction:** steel unibody. **Fuel Tank:** (900) 16.6 gallon; (9000) 17.9 gallon.

MAJOR OPTIONS: Three-speed automatic transmission: 900 ($458). Four-speed automatic transmission: 9000 ($591). Special Performance Group: 900 Turbo 3-dr ($2874); 9000S ($1117). Leather package: 900 Turbo 3-dr ($1117); 9000S ($1117).

Manufacturer: Saab-Scania (Saab Car Division), Nykoping, Sweden.

Distributor: Saab-Scania of America Inc., Orange, Connecticut.

HISTORY: 1988 models were introduced in the U.S. in September 1987.

1989 SAAB

1989 Saab 900 Turbo 16 Cabriolet. (William Siuru Jr.)

900 — FOUR — All Saabs were powered by a twin-cam engine for 1989, with a modest horsepower increase, as the single-cam version was dropped. Following a three-year absence, a four-door notchback Turbo sedan joined the lineup. Saab's SPG had a higher-powered version of the four-cylinder engine, sport suspension, aero body components, leather-wrapped steering wheel, and wider tires. Base models now had front and rear stabilizer bars, as well as gas shock absorbers.

9000 — FOUR — A 9000 CD four-door notchback sedan (with regular trunk) joined the five-door hatchbacks this year. More than six inches longer than the hatchback, the sedan offered 19.8 cubic feet of storage area. Extra CD features included extra backup lights, a front spoiler and foglights, in a smoother front end different from the other 9000 models. A smoked accent panel stretched between the 9000 CD taillamps, and it wore wider bodyside moldings. Both the CD and the Turbo were powered by Saab's turbo-charged, intercooled 2.0-liter four-cylinder engine. Power front seats became standard in the five-door Turbo.

I.D. DATA: VIN is in same location, with same breakdown, as prior models; see 1981 listing.

Model	Body Type & Seating	Engine Type/CID	P.O.E Price	Weight (lbs.)	Prod. Total
900	3-dr Hatch-5P	I4/121	16995	2708	Note 1
900	4-dr Sedan-5P	I4/121	17515	2763	Note 1
900S	3-dr Hatch-5P	I4/121	19695	2790	Note 1
900S	4-dr Sedan-5P	I4/121	20245	2821	Note 1
900 Turbo	3-dr Hatch-5P	I4/121	23795	2901	Note 1
SPG Turbo	3-dr Sedan-5P	I4/121	26895	N/A	Note 1
900 Turbo	4-dr Sedan-5P	I4/121	24345	2946	Note 1
900 Turbo	2-dr Conv-4P	I4/121	32095	2967	Note 1
9000					
9000S	5-dr Hatch-5P	I4/121	24445	3004	Note 1
Turbo	5-dr Hatch-5P	I4/121	30795	3147	Note 1
9000 CD	4-dr Sedan-5P	I4/121	30895	3151	Note 1

Note 1: A total of 34,901 Saabs were sold in the U.S. during the 1989 model year.

1989 Saab 9000S five-door hatchback. (Saab Cars USA Inc.)

ENGINE DATA: BASE FOUR (900/S, 9000S): Inline, dual-overhead-cam four-cylinder (16-valve). **Displacement:** 121 cu. in. (1985 cc). **Bore & Stroke:** 3.54 x 3.07 in. (90 x 78 mm). **Compression Ratio:** 10.0:1. **Brake Horsepower:** 128 at 6000 rpm. **Torque:** 128 lbs.-ft. at 3000 rpm. Port fuel injection.

BASE FOUR (900 Turbo, 9000 Turbo/CD): Inline, dual-overhead-cam four-cylinder (16-valve); turbocharged and intercooled. **Displacement:** 121 cu. in. (1985 cc). **Bore & Stroke:** 3.54 x 3.07 in. (90 x 78 mm). **Compression Ratio:** 9.0:1. **Brake Horsepower:** 160 at 5500 rpm. **Torque:** 188 lbs.-ft. at 3000 rpm. Port fuel injection.

Note: 900 SPG Turbos with the Special Performance Group produced 165 bhp and 195 lbs.-ft. of torque.

CHASSIS DATA: Wheelbase: (900) 99.1 in.; (9000) 105.2 in. **Overall Length:** (900) 184.3-184.5 in.; (9000 hatch) 181.9 in.; (9000 sedan) 188.2 in. **Height:** (900) 56.1 in.; (9000) 55.9 in. **Width:** (900) 66.5 in.; (9000) 69.4 in. **Front Tread:** (900) 56.3-56.4 in.; (9000) 59.9 in. **Rear Tread:** (900) 56.7-56.8 in.; (9000) 58.7 in. **Standard Tires:** 185/65R15; (9000 Turbo) 205/55VR15; (9000 CD) 195/65R15.

1989 Saab 900 Turbo four-door sedan. (Saab Cars USA Inc.)

TECHNICAL: Layout: front-engine, front-drive. **Transmission:** five-speed manual; three-speed automatic available (four-speed on 9000). **Steering:** power rack and pinion. **Suspension (front):** (900) transverse control arms and coil springs, with stabilizer bar; (9000) MacPherson struts with coil springs and stabilizer bar. **Suspension (rear):** rigid axle with trailing arms, Panhard rod and coil springs; stabilizer bar on 900S, 900 Turbo and 9000. **Brakes:** power four-wheel disc. **Body Construction:** steel unibody. **Fuel Tank:** (900) 16.6 gallon; (9000) 17.9 gallon.

MAJOR OPTIONS: Three-speed automatic transmission: 900 ($525). Four-speed automatic transmission: 9000 ($695). Leather package: 900 Turbo hatch/sed ($1295); 9000S ($1595). Metallic or special black paint ($485).

Manufacturer: Saab-Scania (Saab Car Division), Nykoping, Sweden.
Distributor: Saab-Scania of America Inc., Orange, Connecticut.

1990 SAAB

1990 Saab 900 three-door hatchback. (Saab Cars USA Inc.)

900 — FOUR — Anti-lock braking was now standard on all Saabs, after introduction on the 9000 series two years earlier. So was an airbag on the driver's side. A larger (18-gallon) gas tank was installed. A new Mitsubishi-built turbocharger went into the SPG model, adding 10 horsepower to the engine's output. The SPG came in Talladega Red or Saab Black, with grey leather interior and a leather-wrapped four-spoke steering wheel.

9000 — FOUR — All models had a driver's airbag this year, and the Turbo added a Saab Direct Ignition (SDI) system. A new T25 turbocharger (made by Garrett in the U.S.) was intended to boost low-speed response, and added five horsepower to the engine's output. Narrower tires were used on the Turbo this year, along with self-leveling rear shock absorbers. The 9000 CD included leather seating surfaces (heated), a tilt-up power sunroof, one-touch power front windows, and heated mirrors.

I.D. DATA: VIN is in same location, with same breakdown, as prior models; see 1981 listing.

Model	Body Type & Seating	Engine Type/CID	P.O.E. Price	Weight (lbs.)	Prod. Total
900	3-dr Hatch-5P	I4/121	16995	2732	N/A
900	4-dr Sedan-5P	I4/121	17515	2787	N/A
900S	3-dr Hatch-5P	I4/121	20995	2790	N/A
900S	4-dr Sedan-5P	I4/121	21545	2821	N/A
900 Turbo	3-dr Hatch-5P	I4/121	25495	2901	N/A
SPG Turbo	3-dr Hatch-5P	I4/121	28995	2945	N/A
900 Turbo	4-dr Sedan-5P	I4/121	26045	2946	N/A
900 Turbo	2-dr Conv-4P	I4/121	32995	2967	N/A
9000					
9000S	5-dr Hatch-5P	I4/121	25495	3004	N/A
Turbo	5-dr Hatch-5P	I4/121	32495	3147	N/A
9000S	4-dr Sedan-5P	I4/121	25995	3022	N/A
9000 CD	4-dr Sedan-5P	I4/121	32995	3151	N/A

1990 Saab 9000 CD Turbo. (Saab Cars USA Inc.)

ENGINE DATA: BASE FOUR (900/S, 9000S): Inline, dual-overhead-cam four-cylinder (16-valve). Cast iron block and light alloy head. **Displacement:** 121 cu. in. (1985 cc). **Bore & Stroke:** 3.54 x 3.07 in. (90 x 78 mm). **Compression Ratio:** 10.0:1. **Brake Horsepower:** 128 at 6000 rpm (9000S, 130 bhp). **Torque:** 128 lbs.-ft. at 3000 rpm (9000S, 128 at 3750). Bosch LH port fuel injection.

BASE FOUR (900 Turbo, 9000 Turbo/CD): Inline, dual-overhead-cam four-cylinder (16-valve); turbocharged and intercooled. **Displacement:** 121 cu. in. (1985 cc). **Bore & Stroke:** 3.54 x 3.07 in. (90 x 78 mm). **Compression Ratio:** 9.0:1. **Brake Horsepower:** 160 at 5500 rpm (9000, 165 bhp). **Torque:** 188 lbs.-ft. at 3000 rpm (9000, 195 at 3000). Bosch LH port fuel injection.

BASE FOUR (900 Turbo SPG): Same as above, except — **Brake Horsepower:** 175 at 5500 rpm. **Torque:** 195 lbs.-ft. at 3000 rpm.

CHASSIS DATA: Wheelbase: (900) 99.1 in.; (9000) 105.2 in. **Overall Length:** (900) 184.3-184.5 in.; (9000 hatch) 181.9 in.; (9000 sedan) 188.2 in. **Height:** (900) 56.1 in.; (900 SPG) 55.3 in.; (900 Turbo conv) 55.1 in.; (9000) 55.9 in. **Width:** (900) 66.5 in.; (900 SPG) 66.7 in.; (9000) 69.4 in. **Front Tread:** (900) 56.3-56.4 in.; (900 SPG) 57.3 in.; (9000) 59.9 in. **Rear Tread:** (900) 56.7-56.8 in.; (900 SPG) 57.7 in.; (9000) 58.7 in. **Standard Tires:** 185/65R15; (900 Turbo) 195/60VR15; (9000 CD/Turbo) 195/65VR15.

TECHNICAL: Layout: front-engine, front-drive. **Transmission:** five-speed manual; three-speed automatic available (four-speed on 9000). **Steering:** power rack and pinion. **Suspension (front):** (900) transverse control arms and coil springs, with stabilizer bar; (9000) MacPherson struts with coil springs and stabilizer bar. **Suspension (rear):** rigid axle with trailing arms, Panhard rod and coil springs; stabilizer bar on 900S, 900 Turbo and 9000. **Brakes:** power four-wheel disc. **Body Construction:** steel unibody. **Fuel Tank:** (900) 18.0 gallon; (9000) 17.4 gallon.

MAJOR OPTIONS: Three-speed automatic transmission: 900 ($580). Four-speed automatic transmission: 9000 ($765). Leather package: 9000S ($1995). Metallic or special black paint ($535).

Manufacturer: Saab-Scania (Saab Car Division), Nykoping,, Sweden.

Distributor: Saab-Scania of America Inc., Orange, Connecticut.

SABRA

During the 1950s and '60s, several developing countries that had never been known for auto manufacture made a stab at vehicle production. Israel was one of them. Reliant, the British firm, made Israel's production attempt possible by supplying its three-wheeled vehicles in kit form. As early as 1954, Autocars Ltd. was formed at Haifa to investigate the problems involved and to test Reliant's fiberglass bodies in the Israeli desert climate. Not until 1959 did serious assembly begin, with an order for 500 unassembled four-wheel estate cars, named Sussita. The new four-wheelers used Ford Anglia four-cylinder powertrains. A thousand more were ordered in 1960, another thousand the next year. To the surprise of some, Israel even began to export a few of its assembled examples to the U.S. Autocars would never be remembered for those mini pickup trucks and station wagons, however. What puts the company into the import-car history rolls is the Sabra, a Ford-engined sports car that was also initiated by Reliant (and built in Britain as the Sabre). Introduced to the U.S. market at the New York Auto Show in spring 1961, the Sabra soon began production. Sabra, which is the name of the cactus that serves as Israel's national symbol, became the marque name for all Israeli-built models in 1963, including a new Carmel sedan. Reliant ceased supplying un-

assembled vehicles in 1966, but production continued with components obtained directly from manufacturers. By that time, interest in the Israeli sports car had long since peaked (and fallen) in the U.S. Production of the Sabra continued, however, even after the name changed to Rom Carmel in 1974. Triumph engines were used, starting in the late 1960s. Not until 1981 did the little-known Israeli line of vehicles evaporate completely.

1959-61 SABRA

SUSSITA — FOUR — For the first few years of production, only a station wagon, pickup truck and delivery van were built, offered for sale in the U.S. starting by 1961. They were the first utility vehicles to be built of fiberglass. Riding an 85-inch wheelbase, they measured 150 inches overall. Each was powered by a 61-cid Ford Anglia four-cylinder engine, rated 39 bhp. The wagon was capable of carrying two people plus 880 pounds of cargo, or four people and their luggage. Wagons included a radio, heater, and whitewall tires. Prices in 1961 were $1999 for the two-door station wagon and $1899 for the delivery van.

1962-64 SABRA

1962 Sabra Sports.

SUSSITA — FOUR — Importation continued of the station wagon and panel truck, along with a sedan version; see previous listing for details.

SABRA SPORTS — FOUR — "Motoring in the Continental Manner" was the promise of sales literature for the Sabra sports car. Introduced at the 1961 New York Auto Show, the two-seat roadster was described by *Motor Trend* as having "sleek, graceful lines and a removable hard top." Power came from a Ford Consul four-cylinder engine of 103.9 cubic-inch (1703 cc) displacement, producing 61 horsepower. Riding a 90-inch wheelbase, the curvaceous fiberglass-bodied roadster had front disc brakes and wind-up windows. The low, protruding nose carried a tilted grille, while the hood held an air scoop and the windshield was curved. Massive twin vertical bumpers were mounted alongside the oval grille opening, which contained two vertical center ribs. Headlamps with bright rims stood far back from the nose, whereas the front fenders bulged above hood level. Round parking lights were farther forward, alongside the bumpers. Front wheel openings were rounded; rear openings squared-off. At the rear was a molded-in wraparound bumper, vertical-style taillamps (with backup lights at the base and round lamps alongside), and a recessed gas filler cap on the left side. The front-hinged nose gave full access to the engine for servicing, while a lid at the rear gave access to a small luggage area. Luggage access was limited, however, as the lid could not open fully. A hydraulically-operated clutch hooked up with the four-speed synchromesh gearbox. Both an open two-seater with folding soft top and, later, a closed Gran Turismo (GT) coupe were available. Bodies were molded in reinforced fiberglass. Inside, the cockpit was said to be spacious enough to permit "straight arm" driving if desired. Hooded instruments in the glare-free, aircraft-type fascia included a speedometer, tachometer, water temperature and oil pressure gauges, and clock. Aero-style seats gave "maximum support for the fast cornering of which the Sabra is capable." Standard equipment included a wood-rimmed steering wheel, carpeting, a heater, and simulated knock-off wheel covers.

I.D. DATA: Not available.

Model	Body Type & Seating	Engine Type/CID	P.O.E. Price	Weight (lbs.)	Prod. Total
Sussita	2-dr Sta Wag-4P	I4/61	1754	N/A	Note 1
Sports	2-dr Rds-2P	I4/104	2995	1756	Note 1
Sports	2-dr GT Cpe-2P	I4/104	3595	1950	Note 1

Note 1: Only one car was imported from Israel in 1959, followed by 75 cars during 1960, and 21 in 1961.

Price Note: The delivery van and pickup truck sold for $1651 each in 1962. A hardtop version of the Sports roadster was listed by 1964, at $3285.

Note: Specifications below are for the Sports models.

ENGINE DATA: BASE FOUR (Sports): Inline, overhead-valve four-cylinder (British Ford Consul). Cast iron block and head. **Displacement:** 103.9 cu. in. (1703 cc). **Bore & Stroke:** 3.25 x 3.13 in. (82.6 x 79.5 mm). **Compression Ratio:** 7.8:1. **Brake Horsepower:** 61 (gross) at 4400 rpm. **Torque:** 91 lbs.-ft. at 2300 rpm. Three main bearings. Solid valve lifters. One Zenith downdraft carburetor.
BASE FOUR (GT): Same as above, except -- **Compression Ratio:** 8.9:1. **Brake Horsepower:** 110 at 5000 rpm. **Torque:** 98 lbs.-ft. at 2600 rpm.

CHASSIS DATA: Wheelbase: 90 in. **Overall Length:** 165 in. **Height:** 50 in. **Width:** 51 in. **Front Tread:** 48 in. **Rear Tread:** 48 in. **Wheel Type:** 4Jx15 pressed steel. **Standard Tires:** 155x15.

TECHNICAL: Layout: front-engine, rear-drive. **Transmission:** four-speed manual (all synchro). Gear ratios: (1st) 2.53:1; (2nd) 1.71:1; (3rd) 1.23:1; (4th) 1.00:1; (rev) 2.59:1. **Standard Final Drive Ratio:** 3.55:1. **Steering:** rack and pinion. **Suspension (front):** independent; coil springs with tubular suspension arms. **Suspension (rear):** live axle with coil springs and modified Watt linkage. **Brakes:** hydraulic, front disc, rear drum. **Body Construction:** fiberglass body on box-section steel frame. **Fuel Tank:** 10 gallons (U.S.).

PERFORMANCE: Top Speed: 99 mph. **Acceleration (0-60 mph):** 16.5 seconds. **Acceleration (quarter-mile):** 22.6 sec. (70 mph). **Fuel Mileage:** 28 mpg average.
Manufacturer: Autocars Company Ltd., Haifa, Israel.
Distributor: Sabra Motors Corp. of America, New York City and Beverly Hills, California.

HISTORY: While deploring the "ugly, protruding nose" of an early British-built Sabra, which "spoils any possibility of balanced lines," *Sports Car Graphic* road-testers were impressed with the car's tight turning circle. They did not care for the car's high-mounted steering wheel, distortion in the windshield, or the vigorous transmission of road bumps "resulting in wrist-breaking snaps of the steering wheel." Rarity might well be the Sabra's strongest feature.

SALMSON

Best known during World War One for the production of nine-cylinder, liquid-cooled aircraft engines, the Salmson company of France developed an air-cooled overhead-valve four for GN cars in 1920. Later came a water-cooled 1097-cc powerplant with twin overhead cams. Designer Emile Petit also created a car under the Salmson name, which raced to a number of victories during the Twenties. Salmson became a popular small car during that decade, but some larger models also emerged, one of which put twin superchargers on a straight eight engine. That combination was quite potent in hill climbs and road races. A 1750-cc road car introduced in 1929 kept quite a few features that had been tested on the racing models, including the twin-overhead-cam engine. Small luxury models took over from the former sports-car lineup in the 1930s, again with twin-cam power. Models included a 1.5-liter pointed tail sports two seater. Later, there was also a British Salmson with larger overhead-cam engine, based on the French S4C design. By 1935, Salmson (in France) was producing an S4D model using the Cotal four-speed electromagnetic gearbox.

Production resumed in 1946, after World War Two, with a handful of competition models as well as road cars, which were similar to the S4 series of the 1930s. More than a thousand Salmsons were sold in 1950 alone. A new Randonee model appeared for 1951, with a 2.2-liter aluminum engine and Cotal transmission. That was followed two years later by the 2300 Sport GT coupe, powered by a 2.3-liter twin-cam engine. Although the 2300 was capable of speeds beyond 100 mph and scored a number of racing victories, sales weren't sufficient to keep the company operating. Following the appearance of a final four-door sedan version of the 2300, the Salmson name disappeared in 1957.

1951-52 SALMSON

1952 Salmson Cabriolet E72.

RANDONEE — FOUR — Wearing a handmade aluminum body by Tolerie Automobile Industrielle atop its Randonee (touring) chassis, the first new postwar Salmson was powered by a 2.2-liter twin-cam four-cylinder engine. Those camshafts were driven by a vertical shaft and worm gear. As in prior models, this aluminum-bodied two-door Berline coupe used a Cotal electromagnetic four-speed transmission, in unit with the engine and operated by a switch on the steering column. That basic engine was redesigned at this time, using aluminum or light alloy for its head, block, crankcase, oil pan, and connecting rods. The rear suspension consisted of a cantilever spring arrangement, with anti-roll bar in a cross tube.

I.D. DATA: Not available.

Model	Body Type & Seating	Engine Type/CID	P.O.E. Price	Weight (lbs.)	Prod. Total
72	2-dr Coupe-4P	I4/137	Note 1	2755	N/A

Note 1: Estimated price in U.S. was $6200 (in 1954).

ENGINE DATA: BASE FOUR: Inline, dual-overhead-cam four-cylinder. Aluminum alloy block and head. **Displacement:** 137 cu. in. (2248 cc). **Bore & Stroke:** 3.23 x 4.13 in. (82 x 105 mm). **Brake Horsepower:** 71 at 4000 rpm.

CHASSIS DATA: Wheelbase: 111 in. **Overall Length:** 179 in. **Height:** 59.3 in. **Width:** 66.6 in. **Front Tread:** 53.8 in. **Rear Tread:** 53.8 in. **Standard Tires:** 6.00x16.

TECHNICAL: Layout: front-engine, rear-drive. **Transmission:** four-speed Cotal-type preselector. **Suspension (front):** independent; transverse leaf springs. **Suspension (rear):** rigid axle with semi-cantilever leaf springs. **Body Construction:** aluminum body on pressed-rail steel frame.

PERFORMANCE: Top Speed: 110 mph. **Acceleration (0-60 mph):** 12 seconds. **Fuel Mileage:** about 18 mpg.

Manufacturer: Societe des Moteurs Salmson, Billancourt (Seine), France.
HISTORY: The Randonee debuted at the 1951 Geneva Motor Show, featuring considerable use of light alloy materials.

1953-57 SALMSON

1954 Salmson Model E-72 two-door Berline.

2300 SPORT — FOUR — Salmson's new low-slung GT coupe with sweeping lines was billed as "the first French sport car," capable of 112 mph yet delivering 22 mpg at 65 mph. Under the hood was a 2.3-liter version of the familiar twin-cam four-cylinder engine, hooked to either a Cotal electromagnetic transmission or ZF four-speed manual gearbox. The curved-top, flat-base grille opening contained just two horizontal bars. Built-in headlamps stood at fender tips, displaying a jutting-forward look, while auxiliary lights were mounted above the bumper at the outer corners of the grille opening. A

horizontal bodyside trim strip reached from the headlamps all the way to the rear of the car, just above the door handles. Long rear quarter windows were used, and doors contained vent wings. Wire wheels were installed.

1956 Salmson 2300 Sport Coupe.

I.D. DATA: Not available.

Model	Body Type & Seating	Engine Type/CID	P.O.E. Price	Weight (lbs.)	Prod. Total
2300	2-dr Coupe-4P	I4/141	Note 1	2888	227

Note 1: Price at the factory in France was about $4500.

Model Note: A small number of open two-seat roadsters and four-door sedans also were produced.

ENGINE DATA: BASE FOUR (2300): Inline, dual-overhead-camshaft four-cylinder. Aluminum alloy block and head. **Displacement:** 141.5 cu. in. (2320 cc). **Bore & Stroke:** 3.31 x 4.13 in. (84 x 105 mm). **Compression Ratio:** 7.5:1. **Brake Horsepower:** 110 at 5000 rpm. Solid valve lifters. Horizontal twin-choke carburetor.

CHASSIS DATA: Wheelbase: 106 in. Overall Length: 173.6 in. Height: 59 in. Width: 65.7 in. Front Tread: 55 in. Rear Tread: 54 in. Wheel Type: bolt-on wire. Standard Tires: 5.50x16.

1957 Salmson convertible.

TECHNICAL: Layout: front-engine, rear-drive. **Transmission:** four-speed; Cotal preselector. **Steering:** rack and pinion with automatic adjustment. **Suspension (front):** transverse control arms and longitudinal torsion bars. **Suspension (rear):** rigid axle with semi-elliptic leaf springs. **Brakes:** hydraulic, front/rear drum. **Body Construction:** aluminum body on pressed-rail box-type steel chassis.

PERFORMANCE: Top Speed: 112 mph. **Fuel Mileage:** 22 mpg at 65 mph. **Manufacturer:** Societe des Moteurs Salmson, Billancourt (Seine), France.

HISTORY: The 2300 Sport appeared at the October 1952 Paris Auto Show. Salmson promoted a series of first-place finishes in European races during 1954 for the 2300 Sport, either in its class or overall. They included in-class victories at the Charbonnieres and "Tulipes" Rallies. Salmson's engine was billed as "the only mass produced one in France with double overhead camshafts."

SIATA

Even though Societa Italiana Applicazione Trasformazione Automobilistiche (SIATA) was founded in 1926 at Turin, Italy, automobile production did not begin until after World War II. The original company was formed by Giorgio Ambrosini, an amateur race-car driver, to provide performance/tuning equipment and engine conversions for a variety of cars—but especially for Fiats, establishing a connection that would last until the firm's eventual demise.

Tuning gear for the Fiat 508 and 508S Balillas of the early 1930s included special gearboxes as well as overhead-valve kits for the engine. Siata tuning could boost a Balilla's engine output from its original 22 horsepower to a more promising 48 bhp. A supercharged version was more potent yet, dishing out 55 horsepower when installed in a single-seat racing car. When Fiat introduced its 500 Topolino in 1936, Siata soon was ready with an overhead-valve conversion for that engine as well. Among other special models, Siata created a cabriolet version of the Topolino with a vee-shaped grille, plus an aero-styled coupe that could hit 75 mph.

A Siata model debuted soon after World War II, in 1948. Named Bersaglieri, it had a rear-mounted aluminum four-cylinder engine with dual overhead cams, as well as tubular chassis and four-wheel independent suspension. Hardly a conventional design, it was set up with three seats, the driver occupying the center position.

The first true production Siata was the Amica, powered by an overhead-valve Fiat 500B/C engine that developed 22 horsepower in standard form. Modified to 750-cc displacement, the engine yielded 25 bhp. The Amica came in two-seat spider (convertible) and coupe form, on a tubular frame with full-width body. A special racing edition of the Amica, with a five-speed gearbox and 42-bhp engine, won the Italian championship in 1948.

Fiat's 1400 became the Daina when modified by Siata starting in 1950, capable of topping 90 mph. Siata's two-seat Rallye touring model, also 1400-based, came with a five-speed gearbox and looked similar to the recently-introduced MG TD. Engine ratings on the 1400 (Daina) initially ranged from 44 to 65 horsepower, but higher-output versions also were announced. This series was produced as late as 1958, with both open and closed bodies.

Surprisingly, in 1952 Siata turned to American powerplants: from the little 720-cc overhead-valve Crosley four all the way up to Chrysler's "hemi" V-8. The V-8 models used torsion bars for the front suspension and a De Dion axle at the rear. Siata became quite well known in the U.S. market during the early 1950s, working with Briggs Cunningham and producing specialty automobiles for celebrities.

Variants of the Fiat 8V with a 2.0-liter V-8 engine (introduced at the 1952 Geneva show) came next, wearing bodies created by Vignale and containing five-speed gearboxes. In fact, the 8V itself had been developed as a joint effort by Fiat and Siata. Produced from 1952 to 1955, the Siata versions were available in the U.S. (priced around $6000) and could hit 110 mph. The 208S America coupe went faster yet, said to be capable of 120 mph or more. Among other features, it had retracting headlamps. A Siata entered the 1953 Carrera Panamericana road race in 1953, driven by Ernie McAfee, the company's U.S. importer.

In 1954, Siata turned from sports cars to minicars with the Mitzi, which carried a tiny 398-cc two-cylinder L-head engine at the rear. The little car had fully independent sus-

pension using torsion bars. Through the late 1950s, however, Fiat-based automobiles continued to be Siata's mainstay—especially those based on the Fiat 600 and 1100 series.

Siata joined with Abarth—another Italian producer of Fiat sports-car derivatives—in 1959, changing the company name to Siata-Abarth. The union didn't last long. By 1961, another name change created the Siata Auto company, which it would remain into the marque's demise in 1970. See Abarth listing in this catalog for further details.

Early in the 1960s, after the Siata-Abarth dissolution, Siata concentrated on conversions of the Fiat 1300 and 1500 series. By 1964, output consisted primarily of dual-carb, 94-horsepower modifications of the Fiat 1500, in GT coupe form. About 1,400 Siatas were built in that year alone. One notable example was the TS 1600 coupe of 1966, which carried a 1578-cc engine.

The final Siata was the Spring, a two-seater that vaguely resembled T-series MGs of the 1930s to early '50s. The open roadster held a rear-mounted Fiat 850 engine, and was produced until 1970. A fair number of Springs came to the U.S. market, especially in the western states, though fewer were seen elsewhere in the country.

Note: Early Siatas often were custom-built to order rather than standardized, so descriptions below did not necessarily apply to all related models.

1949-51 SIATA

AMICA — FOUR — Introduced in 1949, Siata's first actual production model was powered by Fiat's overhead-valve 500B/C engine, developing 22 horsepower. Siata also offered a modification of 750-cc displacement, rated 25 horsepower. Both two-seat spiders and coupes were produced, with full-width bodies mounted on tubular frames.

DAINA — FOUR — Not long after Fiat introduced its 1400 series, Siata was ready with a conversion, which entered production in 1950. Top speed was 90 mph or more. A two-seat Rallye touring edition arrived a year later, with styling overtones kin to the MG TD and a five-speed manual gearbox. Prices for the Grand Sport versions in the U.S., according to a letter issued by Fergus Motors of New York City in 1951, were $5850 for the cabriolet and $5650 for the coupe.

1952-58 SIATA

1953 Siata, Volvo-powered. (William Siuru Jr.)

1400 (DAINA) — FOUR — By 1953, at least three different versions of the Daina were available, having evolved from the Fiat 1400. The Gran Turismo carried a 109.5-cid four-cylinder engine, while the Daina Sport held a 90.2-cid four. The basic 1400 Gran Sport had an 85-cid (1395-cc) overhead-valve four that developed 72 horsepower. A typical Gran Turismo (208C) featured a wide eggcrate grille, wider at the bottom and narrower in the upper center; a tapered hood lid with airscoop; and tiny round parking lights below round headlamps. Horizontal bodyside trim strips were installed. The two-seat Sports Coupe had an aluminum body by Vignale. Borrani-Rudge knock-off wire wheels were available. Siata Spyder roadsters also were produced with 750-cc (American) Crosley four-cylinder engines, and supercharging was available for the 1400 powerplant.

208S — V-8 — Fiat's 2.0-liter V-8, introduced in the limited-production 8V model, was the basis for this series of Siatas. The 122-cid engine developed 125 horsepower, feeding a five-speed manual gearbox. Bodies were created by Vignale. This series was produced from 1952-55. The 208S America coupe with retractable headlamps had a reported top speed of 112 to 120 mph (possibly higher).

200CS — V-8 — Chrysler's "hemi" V-8 went under the hood of Siatas starting in 1952. Cadillac V-8s also were available.

I.D. DATA: Not available.

Model	Body Type & Seating	Engine Type/CID	P.O.E. Price	Weight (lbs.)	Prod. Total
DAINA SERIES					
Gran Sport	2-dr Cabr-2P	I4/85	4000	2000	N/A
Grand Sport	2-dr Cabr-2P	I4/90	4000	1940	N/A
GT 208C	2-dr Cabr-2P	I4/109	6000	2090	N/A
208S					
GT	2-dr Cabr-2P	V8/122	5350	2460	N/A
200CS					
	2-dr Cabr-2P	V8/331	N/A	N/A	N/A

Price/Model Note: Figures shown are approximate. Closed coupes also were available.

1954 Siata Daina Gran Turismo 208C sports coupe.

ENGINE DATA: BASE FOUR (1400 Gran Sport): Inline, overhead-valve four-cylinder. **Displacement:** 85.1 cu. in. (1395 cc). **Bore & Stroke:** 3.22 x 2.51 in. (82 x 66 mm). **Compression Ratio:** 6.7:1. **Brake Horsepower:** 72 at 5800 rpm. Solid valve lifters. Two Weber downdraft carburetors.
Note: Early ads the U.S. offered supercharging for the 1400 engine.
BASE FOUR (Daina Sport): Inline, overhead-valve four-cylinder. **Displacement:** 90.2 cu. in. (1479 cc). **Bore & Stroke:** 3.23 x 2.76 in. (82 x 70 mm). **Compression Ratio:** 8.5:1. **Brake Horsepower:** 91 at 6000 rpm. **Torque:** 83 lbs.-ft. at 4400 rpm. Solid valve lifters.
BASE FOUR (Daina GT): Inline, overhead-valve four-cylinder. **Displacement:** 109.5 cu. in. (1795 cc). **Bore & Stroke:** 3.31 x 3.23 in. (84 x 82 mm). **Compression Ratio:** 7.2:1. **Brake Horsepower:** 79 at 4500 rpm. **Torque:** 108 lbs.-ft. at 3400 rpm. Solid valve lifters.
BASE FOUR (208S GT): Overhead-valve, "vee" type eight-cylinder (Fiat 8V). **Displacement:** 121.8 cu. in. (1997 cc). **Bore & Stroke:** 2.83 x 2.41 in. (72 x 61 mm). **Compression Ratio:** 7.5:1. **Brake Horsepower:** 125 at 6500 rpm. **Torque:** 99 lbs.-ft. at 4000 rpm.
BASE FOUR (200CS): Overhead-valve, "vee" type eight-cylinder (Chrysler). **Displacement:** 331 cu. in. (5426 cc). **Bore & Stroke:** 3.81 x 3.63 in. (97 x 92 mm). **Brake Horsepower:** up to 300.
Note: Siata Spyder roadsters also were sold with 750-cc Crosley four-cylinder engines.

CHASSIS DATA: Wheelbase: (Daina 1400) 94 in.; (208S) 106 in. **Overall Length:** (Daina 1400) 152 in. **Height:** (Daina 1400) 53 in.; (208S) 57 in. **Width:** (Daina 1400) 62 in. **Front Tread:** (Daina 1400) 51.8 in.; (208S) 51 in. **Rear Tread:** (Daina 1400) 51.5 in.; (208S) 51 in. **Standard Tires:** (Daina GT 208C) 5.90x14 (5.50x15 optional); (Daina Sport) 5.50x15; (208S) 6.50x16.

TECHNICAL: Layout: front-engine, rear-drive. **Transmission:** four-speed or five-speed manual. **Standard Final Drive Ratio:** (1400 Gran Sport) 4.44:1. **Steering:** worm and roller. **Suspension (front):** upper/lower wishbones with coil springs and anti-roll bar except (Chrysler V-8) torsion bars. **Suspension (rear):** rigid axle with semi-elliptic leaf springs and anti-roll bar except (Chrysler V-8) De Dion axle. **Brakes:** hydraulic, front/rear drum. **Body Construction:** steel or light alloy unibody with platform chassis.

PERFORMANCE: Top Speed: (1400 Gran Sport) near 86 mph; (Daina 208C) about 105 mph. **Acceleration (0-60 mph):** (1400 Gran Sport) under 20 sec.; (Daina 208C) 16 sec.

ADDITIONAL MODELS: Siata continued to produce the Amica with a 66-cid engine that developed 34 horsepower, as well as a 750 Spider whose 46-cid four-cylinder engine produced 45 horsepower. These were much lighter in weight than the models described above, on an 83-inch wheelbase. Price of the Amica in 1953 was approximately $3000, while a Spider 750 ran around $3100. Amicas were available with either Fiat or Crosley engines.

Siata also introduced a cute little two-seat minicar, the Mitzi, with a 398-cc two-cylinder engine that developed 10 horsepower at 4000 rpm. Tires were 4.00x13 size, and a torsion-bar suspension was installed. Riding a 67-inch wheelbase, the tiny coupe displayed almost the same profile whether headed forward or backward. Features included rounded wheel openings and "suicide" doors with external hinges. This model was not ordinarily exported to the U.S.

Manufacturer: Societa Italiana Applicazione Trasformazione Automobilistiche (SIATA), Turin, Italy,

HISTORY: Ads in 1952 from dealer Tony Pompeo in New York City noted that Siata "has in production new and powerful sports cars which should intrigue the American Automotive Sportsman." Bodies were "built to the customer's specifications." A Siata was shown at the Henry Ford Museum in 1953.

1959-67 SIATA

1300/1500/1600 — FOUR — From 1959 to 1961, Siata operated jointly with Abarth. After that "marriage" broke up, Siata turned back to Fiat-based conversions on its own, focusing on the 1300 and 1500 series. Most notable were its twin-carb modifications of the Fiat 1500, with an engine that developed 94 horsepower. The TS 1600, available in 1966, held a 1578-cc engine. Styling features of that 2 + 2 coupe included a rectangular eggcrate grille, rectangular single headlamps, and large triangular rear quarter windows that were curved along the upper edge.

I.D. DATA: Not available.

Model	Body Type & Seating	Engine Type/CID	P.O.E. Price	Weight (lbs.)	Prod. Total
1300	2-dr Cabr-2P	I4/79	N/A	N/A	Note 1
1300	2-dr Coupe-2P	I4/79	N/A	N/A	Note 1
1500/1600					
1500	2-dr Cabr-2P	I4/90	N/A	N/A	Note 1
1500	2-dr Coupe-2P	I4/90	N/A	N/A	Note 1
TS 1600	2-dr Coupe-2 + 2P	I4/96	N/A	1918	Note 1

Note 1: A total of 1,400 Siatas were produced in 1964 alone.

ENGINE DATA: BASE FOUR (1300): Inline, overhead-valve four-cylinder (Fiat). **Displacement:** 79 cu. in. (1295 cc). **Bore & Stroke:** 2.83 x 3.13 in. (72 x 79.5 mm). Solid valve lifters.
BASE FOUR (1500): Inline, overhead-valve four-cylinder (Fiat). **Displacement:** 90.4 cu. in. (1481 cc). **Bore & Stroke:** 3.03 x 3.13 in. (77 x 79.5 mm). **Brake Horsepower:** 94. Solid valve lifters.
BASE FOUR (TS 1600): Inline, overhead-valve four-cylinder. Cast iron block and light alloy head. **Displacement:** 96.3 cu. in. (1578 cc). **Bore & Stroke:** 3.13 x 3.13 in. (79.5 x 79.5 mm). **Compression Ratio:** 9.8:1. **Brake Horsepower:** 106 (SAE) at 6000 rpm. Torque: 103 lbs.-ft. (SAE) at 4200 rpm. Three main bearings. Solid valve lifters. Solex or Weber two-barrel carburetor.

CHASSIS DATA: Wheelbase: (TS 1600) 98.6 in. **Overall Length:** (TS 1600) 168.5 in. **Height:** (TS 1600) 51.2 in. **Width:** (TS 1600) 61.4 in. **Front Tread:** (TS 1600) 51 in. **Rear Tread:** (TS 1600) 50.1 in. **Standard Tires:** (TS 1600) 155x14.

TECHNICAL: Layout: front-engine, rear-drive. **Transmission:** (TS 1600) four-speed manual. **Steering:** worm and roller. **Suspension (front):** upper/lower wishbones with coil springs and anti-roll bar. **Suspension (rear):** rigid axle with semi-elliptic leaf springs. **Brakes:** front disc, rear drum. **Body Construction:** steel unibody.
Manufacturer: Siata-Abarth (1959-61); Siata Auto (1961-70); Turin, Italy.

1968-70 SIATA

SPRING — FOUR — Styled to be reminiscent of early T-series MGs, the Spring roadster focused on the American market. "Suddenly it's 'Spring,'" declared the U.S. sales literature for "America's newest fun car," billed as "the sportive car for all seasons." A rear-mounted 823-cc Fiat 850/S engine was mounted at the rear, developing 42.4 horsepower. Wheelbase was 79.8 inches. Top speed was claimed to approach 80 mph, with gas mileage of up to 37 mpg. Weight distribution was 35/65 front/rear. Styling features included a long decklid with rear-mounted spare tire, large high-mounted rectangular taillamps, large rectangular vertical-bar grille, separately-mounted headlamps, and external door hinges. The dashboard contained three round gauges.

I.D. DATA: Not available.

Model	Body Type & Seating	Engine Type/CID	P.O.E. Price	Weight (lbs.)	Prod. Total
SPRING					
	2-dr Rds-2P	I4/50	1995	1359	N/A

Price Note: Price in U.S. reached $2395 in 1969.

ENGINE DATA: BASE FOUR: Inline, overhead-valve four-cylinder (Fiat 850/S). **Displacement:** 50.2 cu. in. (823 cc). **Compression Ratio:** 8.5:1. **Brake Horsepower:** 42.4 at 5000 rpm. Solid valve lifters.

CHASSIS DATA: Wheelbase: 79.8 in. **Overall Length:** 139.6 in. **Height:** 47.2 in. **Width:** 54.3 in. **Front Tread:** 45.1 in. **Rear Tread:** 47.7 in. **Wheel Type:** wire or pressed steel. **Standard Tires:** 5.50x12 radial.

TECHNICAL: Layout: rear-engine, rear-drive. **Transmission:** five-speed manual. **Suspension (front):** independent, with anti-roll bar. **Suspension (rear):** independent, with anti-roll bar.

MAJOR OPTIONS: Wire wheels. Deluxe steering wheel. Deluxe windows. Tachometer. Side-view mirror. Hardtop.

Manufacturer: Siata Auto, Turin, Italy.

Distributor: Siata International USA Inc., Newark, New Jersey.

HISTORY: Car and Driver described the Spring as "$1995 worth of campiness," like an "overblown" MG TD. Rather than a serious car, it was considered "a toy, an automotive aberration, a plaything."

SIMCA

Like that of many European auto manufacturers, the Simca name is an acronym, which stands for Societe Industrielle de Mecanique et de Carrosserie Automobile. Founded in France in 1934 by Henri-Theodore Pigozzi, the new organization first built Fiats, under license from that Italian firm. Thus, the prewar Simcas were merely Fiats that happened to be manufactured in France, using a factory that had formerly been used to produce the Donnet.

Production started with their version of the 508 Balilla. The two-seat Simca Cinq (Five), introduced in 1936, was the French edition of the famed Fiat 500 Topolino, powered by a 570-cc engine. After that came the Huit (Eight), which was a close relative of Fiat's 508C Millecento 1100, and carried a 1089-cc overhead-valve four-cylinder engine. Even before World War II, Amedee Gordini was applying his tuning skills to Simcas. In fact, Gordini himself won the Le Mans Index of Performance in 1939, at the wheel of a Simca. Gordini managed to hop up the tiny Topolino engine to eke out 28 horsepower.

A small number of cars emerged from the Simca plant even during the war, though the company fell under German control in 1940. Peacetime production resumed gradually starting in 1946, with continuations of the prewar Cinq and Huit as well as a new Six. A sport-coupe edition of the Huit with 50-horsepower engine debuted in 1949, a year in which total production passed the 26,000 mark. Competition helped gain publicity for the company, including class victories at three major events: the Spa 24-hour race, and Alpine and Monte Carlo rallies. Simcas began to arrive in the U.S. market by 1948. The Huit (Eight) was restyled in 1950, powered by a 1.2-liter engine that developed 40 horsepower and used a column-mounted gearshift lever.

Production of a new Aronde sedan featuring unibody construction began in mid-1951, adopting the engine from the Huit but placed in a brand-new body. The engine was rated at 45 horsepower, and independent front suspension consisted of wishbones and coil springs. One of the longest-lasting models of the period, the Aronde remained in the Simca lineup as late as 1964, though dropped from U.S. lists earlier. A 51-horsepower sports version of the Aronde debuted in 1952. A year later, Simcas adopted Gemmer cam steering.

Also in 1954, Simca acquired the French Ford company, releasing the former Ford Vedette, with its 2.3-liter V-8 engine, under a Simca nameplate. Eventually, the Ford plant at Poissy became the site of all Simca production, and the original facility at Nanterre went to Citroen in 1961, at which time production of the V-8 model ceased in France.

Meanwhile, Arondes got a more potent 1.3-liter engine in 1956, rated 48 horsepower or, in tuned form under sport coupe and convertible hoods, 57 bhp. A family sedan called Ariane, introduced in 1957 (and available in the U.S. by 1959), blended the Vedette body with the Aronde's smaller engine.

Chrysler obtained a 15-percent minority share in Simca in 1958. A year later, Simca took over the Talbot operation and the engine from the Vedette wound up in the Talbot Lago coupe (listed separately in this Catalog). Then, by 1963, Chrysler owned the majority share (close to two-thirds) of the entire Simca company. Simca's founder, H.T. Pigozzi, died a year later.

Simca debuted a completely different model in 1962: the 1000, with a rear-mounted 944-cc engine and radiator alongside, intended to compete with Citroen's Ami. Sales

proved impressive, not only in France but on the export market. Within a year, in fact, the 1000 was France's best-selling exported automobile. The 1000 had fully independent suspension and a four-speed all-synchro gearbox. A coupe edition of the 1000 came in 1963, with body by Bertone and all-disc brakes. More important to enthusiasts at the time was the new connection with Carlo Abarth, which led to a Simca-Abarth with twin-cam 1300-cc engine. (See Abarth listing for additional details.) The 1000 became available with a semi-automatic transmission in 1966, while the larger 1500 series could get a Borg-Warner automatic.

After Chrysler acquired an even larger stake in Simca in 1967, the Chrysler pentastar insignia wound up on all Simca models. Simca turned to front-drive a year later with the 1100-series sedan, which carried a transverse-mounted engine and front disc brakes. Another merger came in 1969, as Simca took over Matra, the sports-car builder (also listed in this Catalog).

By mid-1970, Chrysler held virtually all of Simca's shares, which resulted in a name change to Chrysler France SA. Subsequent models were introduced under the Chrysler name, alongside further Simcas. The latter included a 1.2-liter version of the 1100, introduced in 1971 and destined quickly to become the top-selling automobile in France. Also produced until 1976 were 1301 and 1501 sedans, evolved from models introduced early in the 1960s. Simca's Horizon, which blended features of the Alpine fastback and 1100 sedan, also was manufactured in the U.S. under Dodge and Plymouth names. After 1979, when the 1000 faded out of the picture, all Simcas were front-wheel-drive.

By 1978, however, Chrysler of France was in financial difficulty, not unlike that of its American parent. Thus, the entire operation—Simca included—wound up in the hands of Peugeot-Citroen. The Simca nameplate lasted a little longer on the 1100, and appeared jointly as Talbot-Simca on some other models, before it vanished completely after late 1981.

1946-50 SIMCA

1950 Simca Eight Sport convertible.

CINQ (5) — FOUR — This was a carryover of the prewar design, based upon the Fiat 500 Topolino coupe. A 570-cc L-head four-cylinder engine was installed, rated 12 horsepower via 6:1 compression. Wheelbase was 79 inches, and the "Five" measured 127 inches long. A sunroofed model was available.

SIX (6) — FOUR — A new coupe debuted late in 1948, based on Fiat's 500C and with a front end and grille that resembled a scaled-down 1941-48 Chevrolet, including built-in headlamps. The coupe body style with "suicide" doors was known as a *Berline Decapotable* in France. Wheelbase was 79 inches, and overall length came to 134 inches. Tires were 4.25x15 size. Engine displacement was identical to the Five, at 570 cc, but the overhead-valve unit developed 16 horsepower. A sunroofed model was available.

HUIT (8) — 1100 — FOUR — Simca also continued production of the prewar Eight two-door sedan, which was powered by an overhead-valve 1089-cc four-cylinder engine that developed 32 horsepower on 6:1 compression.

HUIT (8) — 1200 — FOUR — Styling was similar to the prior "Eight," with a vertical-bar grille and separately-mounted inboard headlamps, but engine displacement grew to 1221 cc. A four-door sedan, coupe and cabriolet were produced, each on a 95-inch wheelbase and measuring 158 inches overall. With 6.25:1 compression, the engine developed 40 horsepower at 4400 rpm.

A 50-bhp sports version known as the 8CV or 8 Sport became available by 1950, with bodywork performed by Facel Metallon from a Pinin Farina design. The 8 Sport was an open two-seat roadster (or coupe), capable of a claimed 83.9 mph, with a horizontal-bar grille and split windshield. Tires were 5.25x15 or 5.50x15 size, versus 5.00x15 for standard models. European models included two small jump seats in the rear and a floor shift, but American imports were strictly two-seaters with a column-mounted gearshift lever. Grand Sport and Competition versions also were produced.

I.D. DATA: Chassis serial number is on the right side of the chassis, opposite the generator (Five/Six); or on a plate on the firewall (Eight). Engine number is on the right front of the block. Serial/engine number may also be on the tool box, under the hood.

Model	Body Type & Seating	Engine Type/CID	P.O.E. Price	Weight (lbs.)	Prod. Total
5	2-dr Coupe-2P	I4/35	987	1375	Note 1
6	2-dr Coupe-2P	I4/35	1040	1375	Note 1
8 (1100)	4-dr Sedan-4P	I4/66	1535	2000	Note 1
8 (1100)	2-dr Bus Cpe	I4/66	1535	2000	Note 1
8 (1100)	2-dr Conv Cpe	I4/66	1735	1875	Note 1
8 (1200)	4-dr Sedan-4P	I4/75	N/A	N/A	Note 1
8 (1200)	2-dr Bus Cpe	I4/75	N/A	N/A	Note 1
8 (1200)	2-dr Conv Cpe	I4/75	N/A	N/A	Note 1
8 Sport	2-dr Rds-2P	I4/75	2495	1840	Note 1

Note 1: A total of 5,770 Simca passenger cars were produced in 1946, followed by 7,650 in 1947, 9,271 in 1948, and 21,471 in 1949.

Price Note: Figures shown were valid in 1948, except (8 Sport) in 1950.

ENGINE DATA: BASE FOUR (5): Inline, L-head four-cylinder. **Displacement:** 34.7 cu. in. (570 cc). **Bore & Stroke:** 2.05 x 2.64 in. (52 x 67 mm). **Compression Ratio:** 6.0:1. **Brake Horsepower:** 12 at 3600 rpm. Two main bearings. Solid valve lifters. One carburetor.

BASE FOUR (6): Inline, overhead-valve four-cylinder. **Displacement:** 34.7 cu. in. (570 cc). **Bore & Stroke:** 2.05 x 2.64 in. (52 x 67 mm). **Compression Ratio:** 6.3:1. **Brake Horsepower:** 16 at 4400 rpm. Two main bearings. Solid valve lifters. One carburetor.

BASE FOUR (1946-49 8—1100): Inline, overhead-valve four-cylinder. **Displacement:** 66.4 cu. in. (1089 cc). **Bore & Stroke:** 2.68 x 2.95 in. (68 x 75 mm). **Compression Ratio:** 6.0:1. **Brake Horsepower:** 32 at 4000 rpm. Solid valve lifters. One carburetor.

BASE FOUR (1949 8—1200): Inline, overhead-valve four-cylinder. **Displacement:** 74.5 cu. in. (1221 cc). **Bore & Stroke:** 2.83 x 2.95 in. (72 x 75 mm). **Compression Ratio:** 6.25:1. **Brake Horsepower:** 40 at 4400 rpm. Three main bearings. Solid valve lifters. One carburetor.

BASE FOUR (8 Sport): Same as 1221-cc four above, except —**Compression Ratio:** 7.7:1. **Brake Horsepower:** 50. One Solex carburetor.

CHASSIS DATA: Wheelbase: (5/6) 79 in.; (8) 95 in. **Overall Length:** (5) 127 in.; (6) 134 in.; (8) 158 in. **Width:** (5/6) 50 in.; (8) 58 in. **Standard Tires:** (5) 4.00x15; (6) 4.25x15; (8) 5.00x15; (8 Sport) 5.25/5.50x15.

TECHNICAL: Layout: front-engine, rear-drive. **Transmission:** four-speed manual. **Suspension (front):** coil springs. **Suspension (rear):** rigid axle with semi-elliptic leaf springs. **Brakes:** hydraulic, front/rear drum. **Body Construction:** steel unibody.

PRODUCTION/SALES: Approximately 331 Simcas were sold in the U.S. during 1948, dropping to 45 in 1949.

Manufacturer: Societe Industrielle de Mecanique et de Carrosserie Automobile (SIMCA), Nanterre, Seine, France.

HISTORY: Surprisingly, Simcas entered the U.S. market for the 1948 model year, and were listed in directories of available models. According to those sources, however, none were officially imported during 1949. A reviewer for *Motor Trend* commented on the Sport's "beautiful exhaust note," which "drones like a small Bugatti." Simcas scored two class victories at the 1950 Le Mans race.

1951-55 SIMCA

1951 Simca 8 sport two-door coupe with Facel/Pininfarina coachwork. (Sotheby's)

HUIT (8) SPORT — FOUR — Production of the Simca "Eight" Sport, offered as a roadster (convertible) or coupe, continued into 1952. The 1952 model was said to have "a refined silhouette with new radiator shell, a side molding, longer and fuller rear bumper, and newly designed rear lights." Low-hung seats were upostered with Dunlopillo, and doors contained pockets. See previous listing for additional details.

ARONDE — NINE — FOUR — Simca's first modern postwar sedan wore a full-width body with built-in headlamps and came in two- and four-door form, along with a station wagon. The grille had a narrow air intake with heavy chrome surround molding. Body elements were electrically welded along their total length. All four doors were front-hinged, all windows lowered completely, and the curved windshield had no anchor posts.

The four-door sedan was claimed to "reach 75 mph swiftly." Arondes had worm and roller steering, a coil-spring front suspension with stabilizer, and leaf springs at the rear. A four-speed gearbox was standard, with the upper three ratios synchronized. An anti-theft device was incorporated in the column gearshift lever. The 1221-cc overhead-valve engine developed 45 horsepower at 4500 rpm.

A stylish and low coupe was added for 1952, carrying a 51-horsepower version of the 1221-cc engine. It was billed as a sports car capable of 84 mph when displayed at the New York International Motor Sports Show in February 1954. In 1955, the engine in the Coup de Ville developed 60 horsepower, for a top speed of 90 mph.

I.D. DATA: Chassis serial number is on a plate on the firewall. Engine number is on the right front of the block. Serial/engine number may also be on the tool box, under the hood.

Model	Body Type & Seating	Engine Type/CID	P.O.E. Price	Weight (lbs.)	Prod. Total
HUIT (8)					
8 Sport	2-dr Rds-2P	I4/75	3495	1840	Note 1
8 Sport	2-dr Cpe-2P	I4/75	3495	1840	Note 1
ARONDE					
	2-dr Sedan-4P	I4/75	N/A	N/A	Note 1
	4-dr Sedan-4P	I4/75	1995	1918	Note 1
	2-dr Sta Wag-4P	I4/75	N/A	N/A	Note 1
	2-dr HT Cpe-2P	I4/75	N/A	2086	Note 1

Note 1: A total of 40,991 Simca passenger cars were produced in 1951, followed by 69,030 in 1952, 50,996 in 1953, 74,213 in 1954, and 141,900 in 1955.

Price Note: Figures shown were valid in 1952. In 1955, a four-door sedan sold for $1697; a two-door wagon for $1899; hardtop coupe for $1997; and a Coup de Ville with 60-bhp engine for $2495.

1954 Simca Grand Large pillarless two-door sports sedan.

ENGINE DATA: BASE FOUR: Inline, overhead-valve four-cylinder. **Displacement:** 74.5 cu. in. (1221 cc). **Bore & Stroke:** 2.83 x 2.95 in. (72 x 75 mm). **Compression Ratio:** 6.7:1. **Brake Horsepower:** 45 at 4500 rpm. Three main bearings. Solid valve lifters. One carburetor.

BASE FOUR (8 Sport): Same as 1221-cc four above, except —**Compression Ratio:** 7.7:1. **Brake Horsepower:** 50. One Solex carburetor.

BASE FOUR (Aronde Nine Sport): Same as 1221-cc four above, except —**Compression Ratio:** 7.8:1. **Brake Horsepower:** 51.

CHASSIS DATA: Wheelbase: (8 Sport) 95 In.; (Aronde) 96 in. **Overall Length:** (8 Sport) 161 in.; (Aronde) 160 in.; (Aronde Sport) 167 in. **Height:** (8 Sport) 51.25 in. **Width:** (8 Sport) 61 in.; (Aronde) 61 in. **Standard Tires:** (8 Sport) 5.25/5.50x15; (Aronde) 5.50x15 (later, 14-inch).

TECHNICAL: Layout: front-engine, rear-drive. **Transmission:** four-speed manual (column lever). **Suspension (front):** coil springs. **Suspension (rear):** rigid axle with semi-elliptic leaf springs. **Brakes:** hydraulic, front/rear drum. **Body Construction:** steel unibody.

PERFORMANCE: Top Speed: (Aronde) 75 mph claimed. **Acceleration (0-60 mph):** (Aronde) 27.3 sec. claimed.

PRODUCTION/SALES: Approximately 50 Simcas were sold in the U.S. during 1951, followed by 46 in 1952, and 27 in 1953.

Manufacturer: Societe Industrielle de Mecanique et de Carrosserie Automobile (SIMCA), Nanterre, Seine, France.

Distributor: Hoffman Motors, New York City; International Motor Inc., Los Angeles.

HISTORY: *Motor Trend* in 1951 described the Simca 8 Sport as "one of the most significant cars on the American market today." Simca claimed of the final Sport that "people insist" it "is the finest car known....a first-rate all-around car." Ads in 1952 promoted Simcas "For Sport - Elegance - Economy." Later, a stock Simca sedan went 63,000 miles at 65 mph, without ever being shut off, setting 38 international records. In 1954, Simca acquired Ford of France.

1956-58 SIMCA

1957 Simca Aronde Grand Large two-door.

ARONDE 1300 — FOUR — A larger (1290-cc) engine went into the next Aronde series, which included Deluxe and Elysee four-door sedans, Grand Large two-door hardtop sedan, and Chatelaine two-door station wagon. A Simcamatic automatic clutch was optional.

VEDETTE — V-8 — An L-head, 2351-cc (143.5-cid) V-8 engine provided the power for the Vedette series, which was marketed in the U.S. in the late 1950s. This was a modern version of the earlier French Ford, with squarish styling and an update of the prewar Ford V8-60 engine. A Versailles model was sold in 1956-57; Versailles and Trianon in 1958. Standard equipment included foglights, windshield washer, rear center armrest, two-tone colors (inside and out), a three-way horn, and custom wheel discs.

I.D. DATA: Chassis serial number is on a plate on the firewall (Aronde); or on the left fender apron, front right X-member or upper front of chassis (Vedette). Engine number is on the lower left of the block (Aronde); or at front of cylinder head on right side (Vedette).

Model	Body Type & Seating	Engine Type/CID	P.O.E. Price	Weight (lbs.)	Prod. Total
ARONDE 1300					
Deluxe	4-dr Sedan-5P	I4/79	1595	2053	Note 1
Elysee	4-dr Sedan-5P	I4/79	1745	2053	Note 1
Plein Ciel	2-dr Sedan-5P	I4/79	2688	2072	Note 1
Grand Large	2-dr HT Cpe-5P	I4/79	2095	2053	Note 1
Chatelaine	2-dr Sta Wag-5P	I4/79	1899	2127	Note 1
Oceane	2-dr Conv-2P	I4/79	2888	2072	Note 1
VEDETTE					
Versailles	4-dr Sedan-6P	V8/143	2199	2596	Note 1

Note 1: A total of 160,761 Simca passenger cars were produced in 1956, followed by 151,405 in 1957, and 189,010 in 1958.

Price Note: Figures shown were valid in 1957. The Versailles sold for $2495 in 1956.

ENGINE DATA: BASE FOUR (Aronde): Inline, overhead-valve four-cylinder (Flash). **Displacement:** 78.7 cu. in. (1290 cc). **Bore & Stroke:** 2.91 x 2.95 in. (74 x 75 mm). **Compression Ratio:** 6.8:1. **Brake Horsepower:** 48 at 4800 rpm. Three main bearings. Solid valve lifters. One Solex 32 PBICT carburetor.

BASE FOUR (Aronde Oceane and Plein Ciel): Flash Special engine; same as 1221-cc four above, except with aluminum head — **Compression Ratio:** 7.8:1. **Brake Horsepower:** 57 at 5200 rpm.

BASE V-8 (Vedette): L-head, "vee" type eight-cylinder. **Displacement:** 143.5 cu. in. (2351 cc). **Bore & Stroke:** 2.60 x 3.37 in. (66 x 86 mm). **Compression Ratio:** 7.2:1. **Brake Horsepower:** 85 at 4600 rpm. Solid valve lifters.

CHASSIS DATA: Wheelbase: (Aronde) 96.2 in.; (Vedette) 106 in. **Overall Length:** (Aronde) 162-168 in.; (Vedette) 178 in. **Width:** (Aronde) 61.3 in.; (Vedette) 68.1 in. **Front Tread:** (Aronde) 49.4 in.; (Vedette) 54 in. **Rear Tread:** (Aronde) 49.2 in.; (Vedette) 53 in. **Standard Tires:** (Aronde) 5.60x14; (Vedette) 6.40x13.

TECHNICAL: Layout: front-engine, rear-drive. **Transmission:** (Aronde) four-speed manual; (Vedette) three-speed manual (column lever). **Steering:** worm and roller. **Suspension (front):** control arms with coil springs. **Suspension (rear):** rigid axle with semi-elliptic leaf springs. **Brakes:** hydraulic, front/rear drum. **Body Construction:** steel unibody.

PERFORMANCE: Top Speed: (Aronde) 82 mph; (Vedette) 95 mph claimed, 88.5 mph in test. **Acceleration (0-60 mph):** (Aronde) N/A (0-50 mph in 16.2 sec.); (Vedete) 17.9 sec. **Acceleration (quarter-mile):** (Aronde) 23 sec.; (Vedette) 21.2 sec. (63 mph).

PRODUCTION/SALES: Approximately 5,766 Simcas were sold in the U.S. during 1957.

Manufacturer: Societe Industrielle de Mecanique et de Carrosserie Automobile (SIMCA), Nanterre, Seine, France.

Distributor: Paris Auto Inc., Long Island City, New York; Witkin-Wolf Co. Inc., Los Angeles; then Chrysler Corp., Detroit, Michigan.

HISTORY: Ads for the Vedette Versailles encouraged customers to "drive it...compare it...and begin your love affair with this saucy French bomb." Arondes were advertised as offering "a little more of everything...the roomiest, most luxurious 4-Door Sedan in its price class," a car that was "more fun to drive...for a family of five."

Simca held 14 world records for endurance, having run 62,137 consecutive miles at 70.02 mph. A stock Simca had hauled a 9-ton bus from a dead halt. Simca was also chosen "Best Import Buy" by *Mechanix Illustrated*. By the late 1950s, Chrysler was importing Simcas into the U.S.

1959-61 SIMCA

1961 Simca 1000 four-door sedan.

ARONDE — SERIES I/II — FOUR — Production of the Aronde continued into 1959, with little change. Standard equipment on the Super Deluxe model included reclining seats, trip mileage indicator, heater, defroster, and electric wipers. A second series arrived at mid-year 1959, with four revised bodies: Elysee sedan, Grand Large hardtop, Montlhery sedan, and Monaco hardtop.

The Elysee had an oval-shaped vertically-striped chrome grille, forward-sloping hood, lowered silhouette, large curved windshield, full wraparound rear window with visor, and deeper door windows. Total glass area was enlarged 30 percent. A silver arrow of bright metal extended the full length of the car, from the hooded headlamps to the tip of the slightly finned rear fenders. 'Simca' in chromed block letters was arched over the grille, and also appeared on the rear of the new models. A tubular guard protected the front grille. Oval-shaped rubber-tipped guards were fixed to both front and rear wrap-around bumpers. Special chrome wheel covers were set off by a circle of black dashes. Brocade upholstery came in four colors: blue, green, red or brown, combined with vinyl. They harmonized with eight basic single-tone colors, including Diamond Black, Chinese Ivory, Copenhagen Green, Princess Gray, Burning Coal Red, Venetian Beige, Leman Blue, and Periwinkle Blue. Two-tone combinations were available. Optional at extra cost was an anodized aluminum insert in the arrow-like side molding. A Simcamatic semi-automatic clutch was available on all Arondes. An Aronde Etoile sedan with 50-bhp engine debuted in November 1959.

VEDETTE — V-8 — Production of the V-8 Simca continued with little change, now called the Beaulieu series. Vedettes came in 10 body colors.

ARIANE — FOUR/V-8 — Both four-cylinder and V-8 power were available in the Ariane series, which was promoted as having its own body but actually was a less-trimmed version of the Vedette's, on the same 106-inch wheelbase. A four-speed gearbox was installed, instead of the three-speed on the Vedette. Both the Ariane and Vedette had parking lights incorporated into the grille, visored headlamps, a wraparound windshield, slender roof pillars, and curved rear windows. Taillamps, backup lights and directional signals were grouped in sweptback fins, placed high for visibility and security.

I.D. DATA: Chassis serial number is on a plate on the firewall (Aronde); or on the left fender apron, front right X-member or upper front of chassis (Vedette). Engine number is on the lower left of the block (Aronde); or at front of cylinder head on right side (Vedette).

Model	Body Type & Seating	Engine Type/CID	P.O.E. Price	Weight (lbs.)	Prod. Total
ARONDE					
Deluxe	4-dr Sedan-5P	I4/79	1698	1925	Note 1
Super DeL	4-dr Sedan-5P	I4/79	1798	1920	Note 1
Elysee	4-dr Sedan-5P	I4/79	N/A	1925	Note 1
Montlhery	4-dr Sedan-5P	I4/79	N/A	1975	Note 1
Grand Large	2-dr HT Cpe-5P	I4/79	N/A	2040	Note 1
Plein Ciel	2-dr HT Cpe-5P	I4/79	2947	2045	Note 1
Chatelaine	2-dr Sta Wag-5P	I4/79	1963	2020	Note 1
Oceane	2-dr Conv-2P	I4/79	3167	2115	Note 1
ARONDE (SECOND SERIES 1959)					
Elysee	4-dr Sedan-5P	I4/79	1898	1980	Note 1
Montlhery	4-dr Sedan-5P	I4/79	1971	1975	Note 1
Grand Large	2-dr HT Cpe-5P	I4/79	2071	2040	Note 1
Monaco	2-dr HT Cpe-5P	I4/79	2146	2040	Note 1
Etoile	4-dr Sedan-5P	I4/79	1659	1995	Note 1
VEDETTE					
Beaulieu	4-dr Sedan-6P	V8/143	2298	2520	Note 1
ARIANE					
Four	4-dr Sedan-6P	I4/79	1998	2255	Note 1
V-8	4-dr Sedan-6P	V8/143	2098	2415	Note 1

Note 1: A total of 225,897 Simca passenger cars were produced in 1959, followed by 204,213 in 1960, and 201,621 in 1961.

Price Note: Figures shown were valid in 1959.

ENGINE DATA: BASE FOUR (Aronde): Inline, overhead-valve four-cylinder (Flash). **Displacement:** 78.7 cu. in. (1290 cc). **Bore & Stroke:** 2.91 x 2.95 in. (74 x 75 mm). **Compression Ratio:** 6.8:1. **Brake Horsepower:** 48 at 4800 rpm. **Torque:** 65 lbs.-ft. at 2800 rpm. Three main bearings. Solid valve lifters. One single-barrel downdraft carburetor.

OPTIONAL FOUR (Aronde): Flash Special engine; same as 1221-cc four above, except with aluminum head — **Compression Ratio:** 7.9:1. **Brake Horsepower:** 57 at 5200 rpm.

BASE V-8 (Vedette, Ariane V-8): L-head, "vee" type eight-cylinder. **Displacement:** 143.5 cu. in. (2351 cc). **Bore & Stroke:** 2.60 x 3.37 in. (66 x 86 mm). **Compression Ratio:** 7.5:1. **Brake Horsepower:** 84 at 4800 rpm. **Torque:** 112 lbs.-ft. at 2750 rpm. Solid valve lifters. Dual downdraft Zenith 32NDIX.

CHASSIS DATA: Wheelbase: (Aronde) 96.3 in.; (Vedette) 106 in. **Overall Length:** (Aronde) 158-162 in.; (Vedette) 187 in. **Height:** (Aronde) 59.8 in.; (Vedette) 57 in. **Width:** (Aronde) 61.3 in.; (Vedette) 69.7 in. **Front Tread:** (Aronde) 49.4 in.; (Vedette) 54 in. **Rear Tread:** (Aronde) 49.2 in.; (Vedette) 53 in. **Standard Tires:** (Aronde) 5.60x14; (Aronde wag) 5.75x15; (Vedette) 6.50x15 or 165x380.

TECHNICAL: Layout: front-engine, rear-drive. **Transmission:** (Aronde/Ariane) four-speed manual; (Vedette) three-speed manual (column lever). **Steering:** worm and roller. **Suspension (front):** control arms with coil springs. **Suspension (rear):** rigid axle with semi-elliptic leaf springs. **Brakes:** hydraulic, front/rear drum. **Body Construction:** steel unibody.

Manufacturer: Societe Industrielle de Mecanique et de Carrosserie Automobile (SIMCA), Nanterre, Seine, France.

Distributor: Chrysler Corp., Detroit, Michigan.

HISTORY: After 1961, the Aronde, Ariane and Vedette series faded out of the American market. Their replacements, the new 5 series and, by 1963, the rear-drive 1000, were considerably different in character.

1962-68 SIMCA

1963 Simca 1500 four-door sedan.

5 — FOUR — Simca's next model was more ordinary in appearance than the Aronde, with a more squared-off profile. The less distinctive grille had a curved upper molding, far different from the inverted vee shape of the Aronde's, no longer reaching to the outer extremities of the fenders. The 79-cid engine developed 65 horsepower.

1000 — FOUR — Simca turned to a rear-mounted engine for its next series, available in the U.S. in 1963. The 944-cc engine developed up to 52 horsepower. In addition to an ordinary, if practical, squarish sedan, Simca issued a low, handsome coupe with a body by Bertone. Front-end appearance was similar to the sedan, but the coupe had long rear quarter windows and a rakishly slanted roofline.

I.D. DATA: Serial number is on firewall, on left rear wheelhousing in engine compartment, stamped into upper rear flange of left side of engine compartment, or (Bertone cpe) on a plate in the front luggage compartment.

Model	Body Type & Seating	Engine Type/CID	P.O.E. Price	Weight (lbs.)	Prod. Total
5	4-dr Sedan-5P	I4/79	1650	1890	Note 1
1000					
Bertone	2-dr Coupe-4P	I4/58	N/A	N/A	Note 1
1000	4-dr Sedan-5P	I4/58	1595	1609	Note 1

Note 1: A total of 245,909 Simca passenger cars (all models) were produced in 1962, followed by 272,202 in 1963, 271,154 in 1964, 237,486 in 1965, 327,433 in 1966, 275,785 in 1967, and 350,083 in 1968.

Price Note: Figures shown were valid in 1963. Bertone coupe sold for $1653 in 1965, by which time the 1000 sedan dropped to $1536.

1963 Simca 1300.

ENGINE DATA: BASE FOUR (5): Inline, overhead-valve four-cylinder. **Displacement:** 78.7 cu. in. (1290 cc). **Bore & Stroke:** 2.91 x 2.95 in. (74 x 75 mm). **Compression Ratio:** 8.5:1. **Brake Horsepower:** 65 at 5200 rpm. **Torque:** 73.7 lbs.-ft. at 2600 rpm. Five main bearings. Solid valve lifters.

BASE FOUR (1000): Inline, overhead-valve four-cylinder. **Displacement:** 57.6 cu. in. (944 cc). **Bore & Stroke:** 2.68 x 2.56 in. (68 x 65 mm). **Compression Ratio:** 8.5:1. **Brake Horsepower:** 50 at 5400 rpm (coupe, 52 at 5200 rpm). **Torque:** 55 lbs.-ft. at 3500 rpm. Five main bearings. Solid valve lifters.

CHASSIS DATA: Wheelbase: (5) 96.3 in.; (1000) 87.3 in.; (1000 cpe) 87.7 in. **Overall Length:** (5) 164.9 in.; (1000) 149.2 in.; (1000 cpe) 154.5 in. **Height:** (5) 56.5 in.; (1000) 54.8 in.; (1000 cpe) 49.5 in. **Width:** (5) 58.2 in.; (1000) 60 in. **Front Tread:** (5) 49.4 in.; (1000) 49.2 in. **Rear Tread:** (5) 49.2 in.; (1000) 48 in. **Standard Tires:** (5) 5.60x14; (1000) 6.00x13.

TECHNICAL: Layout: (5) front-engine, rear-drive; (1000) rear-engine, rear-drive. **Transmission:** four-speed manual. **Steering:** (1000) cam and roller. **Suspension (front):** (5) control arms with coil springs; (1000) upper control arms with transverse leaf springs. **Suspension (rear):** (5) rigid axle with semi-elliptic leaf springs; (1000) independent with trailing swinging arms and coil springs. **Brakes:** (1000) front/rear drum; (1000 cpe) front/rear disc. **Body Construction:** steel unibody.

Manufacturer: Societe Industrielle de Mecanique et de Carrosserie Automobile (SIMCA), Nanterre, Seine, France.

Distributor: Chrysler Corp., Detroit, Michigan.

HISTORY: *Motor Sport Illustrated* called the Simca 1000 "one of the most engaging, amiable and drivable cars to come down the pike in a long time." Added *Motor Trend:* "It's cute, fun to drive, well built, and takes five a long way on a gallon of gas."

1969-71 SIMCA

1971 Simca 1100 two-door hatchback.

1118/1204 — FOUR — For its final years in the American marketplace, Simca turned from rear-wheel-drive to front-drive. The 1118 sedan had an 1118-cc engine, the 1204's displaced 1204 cc, but the models also differed in appearance. The 1118 was a notch-back four-door sedan with no vent wings on the back doors, and a low wraparound front grille. The 1204 had a hatchback body and a narrower, but taller grille.

I.D. DATA: Simca's nine-symbol serial number is on left side of engine compartment.

Model	Body Type & Seating	Engine Type/CID	P.O.E. Price	Weight (lbs.)	Prod. Total
1118					
GL	4-dr Sedan-4/5P	I4/68	1622	1725	Note 1
GLS	4-dr Sedan-4/5P	I4/68	1670	1725	Note 1
1204					
LS	2-dr Sedan-4/5P	I4/73	1693	1910	Note 1
GLS	2-dr Sedan-4/5P	I4/73	1788	1945	Note 1
GLS	4-dr Sedan-4/5P	I4/73	1869	2023	Note 1
GLS	2-dr Sta Wag-4/5P	I4/73	1963	1995	Note 1
GLS	4-dr Sta Wag-4/5P	I4/73	2043	2043	Note 1

Note 1: A total of 7,776 Simcas were sold in the U.S. in 1969, followed by 6,035 in 1970, and 2,600 in 1971 (their final year).

Price Note: Figures shown were valid in 1969.

ENGINE DATA: BASE FOUR (1118): Inline, overhead-valve four-cylinder. **Displacement:** 68.2 cu. in. (1118 cc). **Bore & Stroke:** 2.91 x 2.56 in. (74 x 65 mm). **Compression Ratio:** 9.0:1. **Brake Horsepower:** 56 at 5600 rpm. **Torque:** 56.5 lbs.-ft. at 2600 rpm. Solid valve lifters. Solex carburetor.

BASE FOUR (1204): Inline, overhead-valve four-cylinder. **Displacement:** 73.4 cu. in. (1204 cc). **Bore & Stroke:** 2.91 x 2.76 in. (74 x 70 mm). **Compression Ratio:** 8.7:1. **Brake Horsepower:** 62 at 5800 rpm. **Torque:** 65 lbs.-ft. at 3400 rpm. Solid valve lifters. Solex carburetor.

CHASSIS DATA: Wheelbase: (1118) 87.4 in.; (1204) 99.2 in. **Overall Length:** (1118) 149.5 in.; (1204) 155.3 in. **Height:** (1118) 53.4 in.; (1204) 55.7 in. **Width:** (1118) 58.5 in.; (1204) 62.5 in. **Front Tread:** (1118) 49.2 in.; (1204) 53.8 in. **Rear Tread:** (1118) 48.6 in.; (1204) 52.6 in. **Standard Tires:** (1118) 5.70x13; (1204) 6.10x13.

TECHNICAL: Layout: front-engine, front-drive. **Transmission:** four-speed manual. **Steering:** (1000) cam and roller. **Suspension (front):** (1118) transverse leaf springs; (1204) torsion bars. **Suspension (rear):** (1118) coil springs; (1204) torsion bars. **Brakes:** (1118) front/rear drum; (1204) front disc, rear drum. **Body Construction:** steel unibody.
Manufacturer: Societe Industrielle de Mecanique et de Carrosserie Automobile (SIMCA), Nanterre, Seine, France.
Distributor: Chrysler-Plymouth, Detroit, Michigan.

POSTSCRIPT: Production of both rear- and front-drive Simcas continued through the 1970s, after exports to the U.S. stopped; then came to a complete halt after the company went under the control of Peugeot-Citroen. The final use of the Simca name came in 1981.

SINGER

Almost forgotten by all except enthusiasts today, Singer was one of the old-time British motorcar firms, founded by George Singer at Coventry in 1905. Like many other early British manufacturers, Singer had started with bicycles, turning out "Xtraordinary" two-wheelers—as well as tricycles—at his own plant beginning in 1876. In 1901, Singer obtained rights to the Perks and Birch motor wheel, which allowed the company to produce motorized bicycles and tricycles with power applied to the front wheel. Those evolved into a series of three-wheeled vehicles with steering wheels, which remained available until 1907.

Automobiles entered the Singer picture in 1905, with the debut of two models that had their engines beneath the floorboards. None was an original Singer creation, however. Instead, each was manufactured under license from Lea-Francis. Engine cylinders were horizontal, and used connecting rods that measured 30 inches in length. Additional models arrived the following year, powered by two-, three- and four-cylinder engines, the latter of more conventional construction. Not long after that initial infatuation with horizontal engines, each Singer model had its power-plant mounted vertically up front, in the customary manner.

Singer almost disappeared in 1908, when financial woes forced receivership. Singer himself died the next year, but Singer and Co. Ltd. was revived and re-formed. Most engines during the next few years were supplied by White and Poppe, though some were produced by Singer itself. Known for comparatively small-engined cars through its history, the biggest of the lot came early: the 4.1-liter model that was available in the early Teens, prior to the outbreak of World War I. At the other end of the scale, a 1.1-liter Ten debuted in 1912 and remained in the lineup after the Armistice. Motorcycle production came to a halt in 1915.

After the war, Singer introduced a sports edition of the Ten, capable of 60 mph. A Singer powered by a 2.0-liter, L-head six-cylinder engine emerged in 1922. Four-wheel brakes became available two years later. Starting in 1926, the lineup also included a four-seat Junior, with an overhead-cam 848-cc engine. Juniors turned out to be quite popular, selling at least 25,000 copies over a four-year period. The basic design was destined to continue on Singers built all the way up to 1956.

Singer's Ten turned into a Senior by 1927, with a 1.3-liter engine. Cone clutches departed in 1928, as the Junior turned to four-wheel braking. In 1932, a Singer Nine replaced the Junior. By that time, Singers were available with left-hand drive for the export market. A total of eight models were available for sale in 1932.

Singer turned to the sports end of the spectrum with a sporty 972-cc variant of the Nine in 1933. These Nines performed well in reliability trials. Sadly for Singer, its entries into the Tourist Trophy race of 1935 suffered a number of severe steering failures, which didn't help the car's sporty image.

Certain Singers adopted no-clutch gearshifting in 1934, and independent front suspension was installed on the new Eleven, which carried an overhead-cam engine. The Eleven even came in an aerodynamically-styled Airstream version, whose designer was said to have been inspired by the Czechoslovakian Tatra. Customers didn't care too much for that car's unconventional look.

Singer introduced a Bantam model in 1936. Plant closures and financial ills during the Depression years led to a reshuffling and name change in 1937, to Singer Motors Ltd. Over the next decade and a half, Singer engines wound up beneath the bonnets of the limited-production HRG sports car (also listed in this Catalog).

Shortly before World War II erupted, Singer introduced a Nine roadster, which continued in production after the war. Postwar Singers were produced at the plant in Birmingham, rather than at Coventry. Also carried over were the prewar Ten and Twelve. In 1949, Singer introduced the model that would become best known in America: the SM1500, with a full-width slab-sided body and 1.5-liter engine. Only 428 sedans in that series were produced in its first year, but that jumped to a peak of 6,358 by 1952. The SM1500 had a column-mounted gearshift lever and front coil springs. More notable to enthusiasts were the SM1500 roadster, of which 3,450 were built. Engines with twin carburetors became available in 1953. Singer also debuted a Hunter sedan series in 1954, with a body similar to the SM.

Late in 1955, Singer was acquired by Roote Motors, the company controlled by William Rootes. Thus came a Singer Gazelle, which was essentially a Hillman Minx with Singer overhead-cam engine. The Singer name continued to appear on automobiles as late as 1970, but after 1958 they were little more than badge-engineered variants of other models in the Rootes stable. The era of Singer as a separate entity was gone.

1946-47 SINGER

NINE — FOUR — Singer re-entered the market after World War II with carryovers of the Nine roadster, as well as the Ten and Twelve sedans. See next listing for details on the Nine, which was marketed in America.

SUPER TEN — FOUR — Singer's Ten saloon (sedan) had a nearly-vertical rear panel and four "suicide" (rear-hinged) doors. Styling was strictly prewar, including separately-mounted headlamps and disc wheels with holes around the rim. Wheelbase was 95 inches, and the 1193-cc overhead-cam four-cylinder engine developed 38 horsepower, hooked to a four-speed gearbox. Its grille was similar to that used in the Nine saloon, with long vertical slats. Production ceased in mid-1949. A small number of Tens may have been imported, as sales literature was distributed by Fergus Motors in New York City.

TWELVE — FOUR — A 1525-cc engine powered the larger Twelve sedan, which also had "suicide" doors but rode a 103-inch wheelbase. The engine was rated 43 horsepower. Twelves came with a sunroof and protruding trunk. Production halted in mid-1949.

1948-49 SINGER

NINE — FOUR — Singer's four-passenger sport roadster had adjustable front bucket seats with a leather-upholstered interior. Headlamps were mounted between the fenders and radiator, and tiny parking lights sat atop the fenders. The chromed radiator grille, which contained long wide vertical slats, sat ahead of the four-panel hood. The Nine also had a sloping rear deck. Knurled nuts permitted adjustment of the flat one-piece windshield. The 1074-cc four-cylinder engine developed 37 horsepower, hooked to a three-speed gearbox. "Easy Clean" wheels held 5.00x16 tires. Underneath, the frame was underslung at the rear. Wheelbase was 91 inches, and the Nine measured 149.75 inches overall (including bumpers). Cutdown doors were front-hinged. Side curtains with rigid glass and chrome-plated bumpers were included. Improvements over the prewar model, according to sales literature, included moving the engine three inches farther forward to permit additional space between front and rear seats and also improve the car's ride. Standard colors available on early postwar Nine roadsters included Maroon with fawn or burgundy upholstery; Black with brown, fawn or signal red upholstery; and Signal Red with matching red upholstery.

I.D. DATA: Serial number is on the left side of the firewall, under the hood; and atop the frame. Engine number is on the right side of the flywheel housing. Starting serial number: 101 with suffix 'Q' (starting in 1946); 857 with suffix 'R' (starting early in 1948). Prefix 'A' signifies a roadster. Engine number is stamped atop the flywheel housing.

Model	Body Type & Seating	Engine Type/CID	P.O.E. Price	Weight (lbs.)	Prod. Total
NINE					
SM-9	2-dr Spt Rds-4P	I4/66	2195	1736	N/A

ENGINE DATA: BASE FOUR: Inline, overhead-cam four-cylinder. **Displacement:** 65.6 cu. in. (1074 cc). **Bore & Stroke:** 2.36 x 3.74 in. (60 x 95 mm). **Compression Ratio:** 6.9:1. **Brake Horsepower:** 36-37 at 5000 rpm. Three main bearings. Solid valve lifters. SU downdraft carburetor. 12-volt electrical system.

CHASSIS DATA: Wheelbase: 91 in. **Overall Length:** 149.75 in. **Height:** 56 in. **Width:** 55.75 in. **Tread:** 45 in. **Standard Tires:** 5.00x16.

TECHNICAL: Layout: front-engine, rear-drive. **Transmission:** three-speed manual. Overall gear ratios: (1st) 18.08:1; (2nd) 9.9:1; (3rd) 5.43:1. **Standard Final Drive Ratio:** 5.43:1. **Steering:** Burman worm and nut. **Suspension (front):** semi-elliptic leaf springs. **Suspension (rear):** semi-elliptic leaf springs. **Brakes:** Girling front/rear drum. **Body Construction:** aluminum-paneled body on channel-section steel frame, underslung at the rear.

PERFORMANCE: Top Speed: 65 mph (British test). **Acceleration (0-60 mph):** 37.6 sec. (British test). **Acceleration (quarter-mile):** 24.7 sec. (British test).

ADDITIONAL MODELS: Singer also continued production of the prewar-styled Ten and Twelve sedans; see previous listing for details.
Manufacturer: Singer Motors Ltd., Coventry and Birmingham, England.
Distributor: Fergus Motors, New York City.

HISTORY: According to company literature issued soon after World War II, the Nine had "new post-war improvements" that made it "the perfect light roadster of today." A Nine "combines excellent performance with smart lines and ample body-space. Economical to run, simple to handle, it is the ideal car for every driver who desires speed with flexibility and mileage with low petrol-consumption." Singer's SM1500 became available in 1949 and was offered in the U.S. for the 1950 model year; see next listing for details.

1950 SINGER

NINE — SERIES 4A — FOUR — Modifications to the Nine roadster gave it a 4A designation, and cut the price in the U.S. market dramatically. Singer sales literature advised that the revised model had some "really worth-while improvements," including a four-speed gearbox, which would deliver "a new thrill, as well as an entirely fresh conception of light car performance." Greater seating capacity was offered, along with refined trim in the "perfect light Roadster of today." Nines now were upholstered in Vynide imitation leather. Real leather was optional (formerly standard). Glass windows for the sidecurtains also were optional. Standard colors included Maroon with burgundy upholstery, Black or Signal Red with signal red upholstery, Grey with red upholstery, and Green with brown upholstery.

SM1500 — FOUR — Singer's first new postwar saloon (sedan) had an all-new notchback profile for its full-width, slab-sided four-door body, which held five or six passengers. Three people could sit up front because of the column-mounted gearshift lever. Flush-style fenders contained built-in headlamps, and the grille was made up of horizontal bars (longer at the base, forming a curve at left and right). Round, small parking lights sat directly below the headlamps, on a nearly flat front panel. Inside, bench-type seats had either cloth, Vynide or leather upholstery. Wishbones and coil springs were used for the front suspension; long multi-leaf springs at the rear. Goodyear 5.50x16 tires rode pressed steel wheels. Under the hood was a 1506-cc overhead-cam four-cylinder engine that developed 50 horsepower. A four-speed manual gearbox was installed. Standard body colors were Geneva Blue, Cotswold Beige, Warwick Green, and Black, each with beige upholstery. Standard equipment included twin sunvisors, a rear blind, center armrest, front and rear ashtray, and glovebox. The instrument panel contained a speedometer, electric clock and gauges ahead of the driver.

Note: In Singer literature, the new model was generally described as the 'S.M. 1500.'

I.D. DATA: Serial number is on the left side of the bulkhead, under the hood; and also at the front of the frame. Starting serial number: (SM1500) 101. Engine number is on the right side of the flywheel housing.

Model	Body Type & Seating	Engine Type/CID	P.O.E. Price	Weight (lbs.)	Prod. Total
NINE					
4A	2-dr Spt Rds-4P	I4/66	1495	1736	N/A
SM1500					
SM1500	4-dr Sedan-5/6P	I4/92	2195	2520	N/A

ENGINE DATA: BASE FOUR (Nine 4A): Inline, overhead-cam four-cylinder. **Displacement:** 65.6 cu. in. (1074 cc). **Bore & Stroke:** 2.36 x 3.74 in. (60 x 95 mm). **Compression Ratio:** 7.0:1. **Brake Horsepower:** 37 at 5000 rpm. Three main bearings. Solid valve lifters. Solex downdraft carburetor. 12-volt electrical system.

BASE FOUR (SM1500): Inline, overhead-cam four-cylinder. Cast iron block. **Displacement:** 91.9 cu. in. (1506 cc). **Bore & Stroke:** 2.87 x 3.54 in. (73 x 90 mm). **Compression Ratio:** 7.0:1. **Brake Horsepower:** 50 at 4500 rpm. Three main bearings. Solid valve lifters. Solex F.A.I. downdraft carburetor.

CHASSIS DATA: Wheelbase: (Nine rds) 91 in.; (SM1500) 107.5 in. **Overall Length:** (Nine rds) 151.75 in.; (SM1500) 174 in. **Height:** (Nine rds) 56 in.; (SM1500) 64 in. **Width:** (Nine rds) 55.75 in.; (SM1500) 63 in. **Tread:** (Nine rds) 45 in.; (SM1500) 50.5 in. front, 51 in. rear. **Standard Tires:** (Nine rds) 5.00x16; (SM1500) 5.50x16.

TECHNICAL: Layout: front-engine, rear-drive. **Transmission:** four-speed manual. Overall 4A gear ratios: (1st) 19.5:1; (2nd) 12.3:1; (3rd) 7.96:1; (4th) 5.43:1; (rev) 19.5:1. **Standard Final Drive Ratio:** (Nine 4A) 5.43:1; (SM1500) 5.125:1. **Steering:** (Nine 4A) Burman worm and nut; (SM1500) worm and ball. **Suspension (front):** (Nine 4A) semi-elliptic leaf springs; (SM1500) wishbones with coil springs and anti-roll device. **Suspension (rear):** rigid axle with semi-elliptic leaf springs. **Brakes:** (Nine 4A) Girling front/rear drum; (SM1500) Lockheed front/rear drum. **Body Construction:** (Nine 4A) aluminum-paneled body on channel-section steel frame, underslung at the rear; (SM1500) steel body integral with pressed steel frame.

Manufacturer: Singer Motors Ltd., Coventry and Birmingham, England.
Distributor: Vaughan Motors, New York City; and Vaughan-Singer Motors, Hollywood, California.

579

1951-56 SINGER

1952 Singer SM 1500 roadster.

NINE — SERIES 4A/4AB — FOUR — Production of the Nine roadster continued into 1952. Hoods now had fixed sides (formerly a four-panel design), and disc wheels replaced the former spoke-type wheels. Final examples switched to independent front suspension. Two versions were marketed in the U.S. this year: the standard 4A and more expensive 4AB.

SM1500 — FOUR — Production of the modern-styled sedan continued with little change, but the big news was the debut of the new SM roadster. According to the company brochure, the roadster was created exclusively for export and displayed at the Paris show in 1951. This was an open four-seater, on the same 91-inch wheelbase as the Nine but with a 1497-cc overhead-cam engine. Essentially, it was the same 1.5-liter engine introduced a year earlier in the SM1500 sedan, but reduced slightly in stroke length so displacement edged below the 1500-cc mark. Appearance was quite similar to the Nine, except for a facelift that included twin taillamps and a shortening of the grille, so its lower edge ended at the bumper line. Front fenders were lengthened, and the rear fenderline modified to meet what *Motor Trend* described as a "beaver-tailed" back end. Otherwise, the coachbuilt body still displayed low sporting lines that included the traditional separate headlamps. Cutdown doors had external hinges. Standard body colors were Salvador Blue, Black, Signal Red, Grey, and Warwick Green, all with beige upholstery. Both left- and right-hand drive versions were available. Standard equipment in the U.S. included a tonneau cover. Sliding glass sidescreens were available as options. The roadster's spare tire went beneath the sloping rear deck.

Note: The new roadster was sometimes referred to as, simply, 'SM' or 'SM Sports' rather than 'SM1500.'

I.D. DATA: Serial number is on the left side of the bulkhead, under the hood; and also at the front of the frame. Starting serial number: (1951 Nine) 6000; (1952 SM1500 rds) 4AD 220. Engine number is on the right side of the flywheel housing.

Model	Body Type & Seating	Engine Type/CID	P.O.E. Price	Weight (lbs.)	Prod. Total
NINE					
4A	2-dr Spt Rds-4P	I4/66	1570	1736	N/A
4AB	2-dr Spt Rds-4P	I4/66	1695	1758	N/A
SM1500					
SM1500	4-dr Sedan-5/6P	I4/91	2195	2520	Note 1
SM1500	2-dr Spt Rds-4P	I4/91	1995	1848	Note 2

Note 1: A total of 6,358 Singer SM1500 sedans were produced during 1952 alone.
Note 2: A total of 3,450 Singer SM1500 roadsters were produced over the full model run.
Price Note: Price for the SM1500 sedan rose to $2595 in 1952.

1954 Singer SMX roadster.

ENGINE DATA: BASE FOUR (Nine): Inline, overhead-cam four-cylinder. **Displacement:** 65.6 cu. in. (1074 cc). **Bore & Stroke:** 2.36 x 3.74 in. (60 x 95 mm). **Compression Ratio:** 7.0:1. **Brake Horsepower:** 36-37 at 5000 rpm. Three main bearings. Solid valve lifters. Solex downdraft carburetor. 12-volt electrical system.

BASE FOUR (SM1500): Inline, overhead-cam four-cylinder. Cast iron block. **Displacement:** 91.4 cu. in. (1497 cc). **Bore & Stroke:** 2.87 x 3.52 in. (73 x 89.4 mm). **Compression Ratio:** 7.0:1. **Brake Horsepower:** 48/50 at 4500 rpm. Three main bearings. Solid valve lifters. Solex F.A.I. downdraft carburetor.

CHASSIS DATA: Wheelbase: (Nine rds) 91 in.; (SM1500 rds) 91 in.; (SM1500 sed) 107.5 in. **Overall Length:** (Nine rds) 149.75-151.75 in.; (SM1500 rds) 151-152 in.; (SM1500 sed) 174 in. **Height:** (Nine rds) 56 in.; (SM1500 rds) 58.5 in.; (SM1500 sed) 64 in. **Width:** (Nine rds) 55.75 in.; (SM1500 rds) 58 in.; (SM1500 sed) 63 in. **Tread:** (Nine rds) 45 in.; (SM1500 rds) 46.75 in.; (SM1500 sed) 50.5 in. front, 51 in. rear. **Standard Tires:** (Nine rds) 5.00x16; (SM1500) 5.50x16.

TECHNICAL: Layout: front-engine, rear-drive. **Transmission:** four-speed manual. Overall SM1500 roadster gear ratios: (1st) 14.5:1; (2nd) 9.45:1; (3rd) 6.12:1; (4th) 4.87:1. **Standard Final Drive Ratio:** (Nine rds) 5.43:1; (SM1500 rds) 4.87:1; (SM1500 sed) 5.125:1. **Steering:** (Nine rds) Burman worm and nut; (SM1500) worm and ball. **Suspension (front):** (Nine) semi-elliptic leaf springs (later, independent); (SM1500) wishbones with coil springs and anti-roll device. **Suspension (rear):** rigid axle with semi-elliptic leaf springs. **Brakes:** front/rear drum. **Body Construction:** (Nine, SM1500 rds) aluminum-paneled body on channel-section steel frame; (SM1500 sed) steel body integral with pressed steel frame.

PERFORMANCE: Top Speed: (Nine rds) 64 mph; (SM1500 rds) 73-77 mph. **Acceleration (0-60 mph):** (Nine rds) 36.4 sec.; (SM1500 rds) 18.9 to 24.3 sec. (two different road tests) **Acceleration (quarter-mile):** (Nine rds) 22.6 sec.; (SM1500 rds) 20.3-20.9 sec.

ADDITIONAL MODELS: A Singer Hunter sedan, similar in appearance to the SM1500, replaced that model in 1954 and was produced into 1956. The 1497-cc engine developed 48/50 horsepower, but a twin-cam version introduced in 1955 (called the Hunter 75) produced 75 bhp and had twin Solex carburetors.

Manufacturer: Singer Motors Ltd., Coventry and Birmingham, England.
Distributor: Vaughan Motors, New York City; and Vaughan-Singer Motors, Hollywood, California.

HISTORY: Ads in 1951 showed comedienne Lucille Ball sitting in her Singer Nine roadster. "For economy minded America," ads read, "the perfect light roadster of today is the .. four passenger Singer....It's thrifty, it's smart, it's dependable...and it's the easiest handling car you've ever owned."

Other ads in 1952 focused on California, advising that a Singer SM Sports Roadster was "your answer to California's challenge of the open road."

Production of the SM1500 sedan continued with little change into 1953-54, while the roadster lasted into 1956. A twin-carbureted version of the 1497-cc engine became available in 1953. With two Solex carburetors, that engine developed 58 horsepower, helped by a compression boost to 7.4:1. Later roadsters added a new finish for the instrument panel, an improved hood latch, and repositioned controls.

1957-58 SINGER

GAZELLE — FOUR — After 1956, when Singer had become part of the Rootes group, the cars that carried a Singer nameplate were essentially rebadged versions of other Rootes products, but initially with Singer engines. First came the Singer Gazelle, introduced for the 1957 model year with the same overhead-cam 1497-cc engine used in the SM series, now rated 52.5 horsepower at 4500 rpm, on 7.5:1 compression. Top speed of the Gazelle was claimed to be 80 mph. Though structurally similar to the former SM1500, the Gazelle had a different appearance with a narrow vertical-bar grille and auxiliary side grilles that contained the parking/signal lights. At the rear was a wraparound back window. Both a sedan and drophead coupe (convertible) were offered. According to *Motor Trend*, the Gazelle's chassis was similar to that used in the Sunbeam Rapier. Two-tone bodies were available.

I.D. DATA: Chassis serial number is stamped on a plate on the firewall. Starting serial number: A7600001. Engine number is on the right side of the block.

Model	Body Type & Seating	Engine Type/CID	P.O.E. Price	Weight (lbs.)	Prod. Total
GAZELLE					
	4-dr Sedan-5/6P	I4/91	N/A	2240	N/A
	2-dr Conv-4P	I4/91	N/A	N/A	N/A

ENGINE DATA: BASE FOUR: Inline, overhead-cam four-cylinder. Cast iron block. **Displacement:** 91.4 cu. in. (1497 cc). **Bore & Stroke:** 2.87 x 3.52 in. (73 x 89.4 mm). **Compression Ratio:** 7.5:1. **Brake Horsepower:** 52.5 at 4500 rpm. Three main bearings. Solid valve lifters. Solex downdraft carburetor.

CHASSIS DATA: Wheelbase: 96 in. **Overall Length:** 163.5 in. **Height:** (sedan) 59.5 in.; (conv) 58 in. **Width:** 60.75 in. **Tread:** 49 in. **Standard Tires:** Goodyear 5.60x15.

TECHNICAL: Layout: front-engine, rear-drive. **Transmission:** four-speed manual. Overall gear ratios: (1st) 17.045:1; (2nd) 11.81:1; (3rd) 7.13:1; (4th) 4.78:1. **Standard Final Drive Ratio:** 4.78:1. **Steering:** Burman worm and nut. **Suspension (front):** wishbones with coil springs. **Suspension (rear):** rigid axle with semi-elliptic leaf springs. **Brakes:** front/rear drum.

PERFORMANCE: Top Speed: 80 mph claimed. **Acceleration (0-60 mph):** 19.6 sec. (British test). **Acceleration (quarter-mile):** 21.4 sec. (British test).
Manufacturer: Singer Motors Ltd., Ryton-on-Dunsmore, Warwickshire, England.

POSTSCRIPT: After 1958, the Singer engine was dropped in favor of a Hillman overhead-valve 1494-cc four, which developed 60 horsepower. Subsequent Gazelle models and the Vogue series of 1961-70 were rebadged variants of contemporary Hillman Minx and Super Minx models. By 1959, a station wagon was available on the American market. An Easidrive automatic transmission was optional at $189 by 1960. At that time, prices in the U.S. were $2095 for the sedan, $2349 for the convertible, and $2425 for the station wagon. The final Singer was called the Chamois, based on Hillman's Imp and produced from 1964-70. See Hillman listing for additional details on comparable models.

SKODA

Not only did the Czechoslovakian-built Skoda begin to appear in U.S. showrooms during the late 1950s, the small-car line managed to sell in fair numbers to American customers. Quite a feat for an automobile built in a Communist country, at the height of the Cold War. In fact, an occasional earlier postwar Skoda had managed to trickle into North America, headed for Canada if not for U.S. ports.

Determining a date for the first production of an automobile is no easier for Skoda than for many other makes. Company history reaches all the way back to 1869, when Emil Skoda took over a plant in Plzen for the purpose of manufacturing armaments. Automobile production began much later, in 1923, when Skoda obtained a license to build Hispano-Suizas, including some of the bodies for that luxury model. Another licensing agreement involved production of a steam wagon. Meanwhile, in 1925, Skoda had acquired an old car/truck plant at Mlada Boleslav, and three years later had a Type A ready for sale, with 890-cc four-cylinder engine. Both fours and sixes were produced through the 1930s, along with a few dozen straight eights. In 1933, the new model 420 featured a backbone-type frame and independent suspension on all four wheels. Within a few years, all Skodas were riding that backbone chassis.

Skoda was never a big producer, setting a prewar record in 1937 with a mere 4,452 cars coming out of the plant. Not many of those went farther than neighboring nations, either. After the war, production resumed with the 1100 series, changed little mechanically from the final prewar models but with a more modern look. Elements of Chevrolets of that era can be seen easily within the 1100's lines and details (but on a smaller scale). Skoda had operated independently as an automaker for a quarter-century before the firm was nationalized in 1948, at a time when they planned to produce a 1.2-liter car (abandoning the 1101/1102 with its 1089-cc engine). That larger engine emerged in the 1200 series of the early 1950s. An early stab at export sales to the U.S. failed, but the S440 series of the late 1950s did much better. With a name change to Octavia and Felicia, Skodas continued export to the U.S. through much of the 1960s before fading away like many rivals as the import-car marketplace was shaken down (and the Japanese models were gaining strength). Long after Skoda was virtually forgotten by American small-car fans, the Czech-built cars continued to find homes elsewhere in the world.

1946-51 SKODA

1101/1102 — FOUR — Evolved from the prewar "Popular" model, the first postwar Skodas used the same constructional principles, developed for comfortable travel over long stretches of bad roads. At a glance, the new and modern body (especially the two-door cabriolet convertible) resembled a scaled-down 1939-48 Chevrolet coupe, with faired-in headlamps but also with rear-hinged doors and vertical-style ventilators at the cowl. 'Skoda' block lettering stood at the very front of the tapered hood. Tiny parking lights sat in long, bright housings atop each fender. At the center, ahead of a long trim strip, was a hood ornament. Skoda's horizontal-bar grille had a center divider bar and five main bars: narrow at the top, tapering to wide at the bottom. Models available included a two-door sedan, a four-seat cabriolet (with easily-folding roof), and a delivery van. Under each hood was a 1089-cc overhead-valve four-cylinder engine. Transverse leaf springs in front and swing axles at the rear provided four-wheel independent suspension. The four-speed manual transmission had a floor shift lever. Provision was made for a radio, and the new ventilating system was said to be draft-free. Front and rear seats

could be "readily changed to offer the most luring invitation to rest or sleep thereon comfortably." Skodas had a central lubrication system, automatic ignition control, hand-brake lever on the dashboard, clock on the glovebox lid, triple-arm steering wheel, and rear armrests. Luggage was accessible from inside or outside the car.

I.D. DATA: Not available.

Model	Body Type & Seating	Engine Type/CID	P.O.E. Price	Weight (lbs.)	Prod. Total
1101	2-dr Sedan-4/5P	I4/66	N/A	2045	Note 1
1101	2-dr Cabr-4P	I4/66	N/A	2045	Note 1

Note 1: A total of 67,000 series 1101 and 1102 models were produced from 1946 to 1951.

ENGINE DATA: BASE FOUR: Inline, overhead-valve four-cylinder. **Displacement:** 66.43 cu. in. (1089 cc). **Bore & Stroke:** 2.68 x 2.95 in. (68 x 75 mm). **Compression Ratio:** 6.3:1. **Brake Horsepower:** 32. Three main bearings. Solid valve lifters. One horizontal carburetor. 6-volt electrical system.

CHASSIS DATA: Wheelbase: 97.1 in. **Overall Length:** 159.5 in. **Height:** 60 in. **Width:** 59.0 in. **Front Tread:** 47.25 in. **Rear Tread:** 49.25 in. **Wheel Type:** disc. **Standard Tires:** 5.00x16.

TECHNICAL: Layout: front-engine, rear-drive. **Transmission:** four-speed manual (3rd/4th synchro). **Standard Final Drive Ratio:** 4.78:1. **Steering:** screw and nut. **Suspension (front):** independent; transverse leaf springs. **Suspension (rear):** independent; swing axles. **Brakes:** hydraulic, front/rear drum. **Body Construction:** steel body on steel backbone chassis.

PERFORMANCE: Top Speed: 65 mph (factory). **Fuel Mileage:** 35 mpg (factory). **Manufacturer:** Motokov Ltd., Praha (Prague), Czechoslovakia.

HISTORY: Skoda's slogan was "Performance—Elegance—Economy." The first postwar Skoda, according to the company, was "developed to suit the latest requirements of our customers all over the world, and is the result of many years of ingenious work of our technical experts." The promotional material further stated that "Everything is tasteful, solid, to the purpose. Everything has been intended to enhance your comfort when traveling, and to make you enjoy every moment you spend in the car most delightfully." An early sales brochure promoted "30 Principal Novel Achievements" for the 1101, ranging from an enlarged wheelbase and four-speed gearbox to "tasteful combinations of colours of upholstery and varnish."

1952-55 SKODA

1954 Skoda Model 1200 four-door sedan.

1200 — FOUR — A larger (74.5 cid) four-cylinder engine went under the hood of the next Skoda model, developing 36 horsepower. Far different from the 1100 series, the 1200 blended European and American styling. Built-in headlamps sat somewhat low on the fenders. The grille was made up of only two thick horizontal bars, with 'SKODA' lettering above the curved trim strip at the hood front. Central chassis lubrication was installed, as in the 1101/1102. Five body colors were available. Semaphore turn signals continued to be used at first, as did a split windshield. New for 1955 was a set of three separate lights on each rear fender (taillamp, stop light, and an amber bulb that glowed when slowing down).

I.D. DATA: Not available.

Model	Body Type & Seating	Engine Type/CID	P.O.E. Price	Weight (lbs.)	Prod. Total
1200	4-dr Sedan-5P	I4/74	1950	2150	N/A
1200	4-dr Sta Wag-5P	I4/74	N/A	N/A	N/A

Price Note: Figure shown is approximate; price at factory in Czechoslovakia was about $1173.

ENGINE DATA: BASE FOUR: Inline, overhead-valve four-cylinder. **Displacement:** 74.5 cu. in. (1221 cc). **Bore & Stroke:** 2.83 x 2.95 in. (72 x 75 mm). **Compression Ratio:** 6.5:1. **Brake Horsepower:** 36 at 4000 rpm. **Torque:** 54 lbs.-ft. at 2500 rpm. Solid valve lifters.

CHASSIS DATA: Wheelbase: 106 in. **Overall Length:** 176 in. **Height:** 60 in. **Width:** 66 in. **Front Tread:** 49 in. **Rear Tread:** 52 in. **Wheel Type:** disc. **Standard Tires:** 5.50x16.

TECHNICAL: Layout: front-engine, rear-drive. **Transmission:** four-speed manual. **Standard Final Drive Ratio:** 5.25:1. **Steering:** worm and nut. **Suspension (front):** independent; transverse leaf spring. **Suspension (rear):** independent; transverse leaf spring with floating half-axles. **Brakes:** hydraulic, front/rear drum. **Body Construction:** steel body on tubular central beam steel frame.

PERFORMANCE: Top Speed: about 65 mph. **Acceleration (0-60 mph):** about 26 seconds. **Fuel Mileage:** about 28 mpg.

Manufacturer: Motokov Ltd., Praha (Prague), Czechoslovakia.

HISTORY: The Skoda 1200 was built at the same factory that had produced the larger, rear-engined Tatra. Czechoslovakia was said to be developing a Spartak People's Car; but in the mid-1950s, after the demise of Tatra, Skoda was the only automobile produced in that country. A handful of Skoda 1200 models made their way to U.S. dealers on the East Coast in the mid-1950s, but failed to attract customers. The next (440) model would fare better. Skoda also produced a panel truck version of the 1200.

1956-57 SKODA

1956 Skoda Model 440 two-door sedan.

440 — FOUR — Smaller than the 1200, the new Skoda 440 came in two-door sedan and station wagon form, each powered by a 66.4-cid four-cylinder engine with automatic vacuum advanced, rated 40 horsepower. Suspension was independent on all four wheels. The modern slab-sided steel body had a rounded, sculptured look. Skoda's new grille contained a single horizontal bar with center insignia, plus two side-by-side openings above (each containing a pattern of vertical bars). Little "eyebrows" stood over the headlamps. A trim strip ran horizontally along the front fender, back from the headlamps. Windshields and back windows were interchangeable. Two-tone paint and whitewall tires were available. The spare tire sat at an angle in the trunk. In addition to the export model (with column shift), there was a stripped version with floor shift, less chrome trim, and no rear shocks.

1200/1201 — FOUR — Production of the 1200 series continued, as the new 440 became available. For 1956, new turn signal "blinkers" used an electromagnetic contract breaker; the horn and stoplights operated even when the ignition key was not inserted; heating was made more efficient; the hood locked from inside; and the ceiling's foam rubber was replaced with homogeneous rubber. The larger Skoda's grille consisted of two thick horizontal bars, with a center insignia on the lower one. Round parking lights sat below and outboard of the low-mounted, somewhat-inboard, headlamps. Standard equipment included a heater/defroster and column shift. For 1957, the 1201 model had more power (45 bhp) from the same basic engine.

I.D. DATA: Chassis number (440) was stamped on a plate on the right side of the firewall, and on the right side member of the frame. Engine number (identical to chassis number) was stamped on an oil pump boss on the right side of the crankcase. Starting serial number (440): 258601.

Model	Body Type & Seating	Engine Type/CID	P.O.E. Price	Weight (lbs.)	Prod. Total
440	2-dr Sedan-4P	I4/66	1595	2066	N/A
440	2-dr Sta Wag-4P	I4/66	N/A	2066	N/A
1200					
1200	4-dr Sedan-5P	I4/74	Note 1	2249	N/A
1200	4-dr Sta Wag-5P	I4/74	N/A	N/A	N/A

Note 1: Price at the factory was about $774.

Model Note: Export version of the 440 was called "S440 America" in the U.S.

Weight Note: "Dry" weights shown. Curb weight of 440 sedan sold in U.S. was 2,138 pounds.

ENGINE DATA: BASE FOUR (440): Inline, overhead-valve four-cylinder. Aluminum block and head. **Displacement:** 66.4 cu. in. (1089 cc). **Bore & Stroke:** 2.68 x 2.95 in. (68 x 75 mm). **Compression Ratio:** 7.0:1. **Brake Horsepower:** 40 at 4200 rpm. **Torque:** 54 lbs.-ft. at 2300 rpm. Solid valve lifters. One downdraft carburetor.

BASE FOUR (1200): Inline, overhead-valve four-cylinder. **Displacement:** 74.5 cu. in. (1221 cc). **Bore & Stroke:** 2.83 x 2.95 in. (72 x 75 mm). **Compression Ratio:** 6.5:1. **Brake Horsepower:** 36 at 4000 rpm. **Torque:** 54 lbs.-ft. at 2500 rpm. Solid valve lifters.

BASE FOUR (1201): Same as above, except — **Compression Ratio:** 7.0:1. **Brake Horsepower:** 45 at 4200 rpm. **Torque:** 63 lbs.-ft. at 2500 rpm.

CHASSIS DATA: Wheelbase: (440) 94.5 in.; (1200) 105.5 in. **Overall Length:** (440) 160.0 in.; (1200) 177.1 in. **Height:** (440) 56.3 in.; (1200) 59.9 in. **Width:** (440) 63.0 in.; (1200) 66.9 in. **Front Tread:** (440) 47.6 in.; (1200) 49.25 in. **Rear Tread:** (440) 49.2 in.; (1200) 52 in. **Wheel Type:** disc; (440) 3.50Dx15. **Standard Tires:** (440) 5.50x15; (1200) 5.50x16; (1201 wag) 6.00x16.

TECHNICAL: Layout: front-engine, rear-drive. **Transmission:** (440) four-speed manual, 2nd/3rd/4th synchro; (1200) four-speed manual, 3rd/4th synchro. Overall 440 gear ratios: (1st) 20.4:1; (2nd) 11.8:1; (3rd) 7.6:1; (4th) 4.8:1. **Standard Final Drive Ratio:** (440) 4.78:1; (1200) 5.25:1. **Steering:** worm and nut. **Suspension (front):** (440) independent trapezoidal with forked upper arms, transverse semi-elliptic leaf springs and lever-type shock absorbers; (1200) independent with wishbone arm. **Suspension (rear):** swing axles and transverse semi-elliptic leaf spring, with telescopic shock absorbers. **Brakes:** hydraulic, front/rear drum. **Body Construction:** (440) steel body on backbone chassis with two crossmembers. **Fuel Tank:** (440) 7.5 gallons.

PERFORMANCE: Top Speed: (440) 69-72 mph; (1200) 65 mph; (1201) 72-78 mph. **Acceleration (0-60 mph):** (440) 34.3 seconds. **Fuel Mileage:** (440) 27-36 mpg in U.S.; (1201) 22-33 mpg.

Manufacturer: Motokov Ltd., Praha (Prague), Czechoslovakia.

Distributor: Continental Car Combine, New York City.

HISTORY: The 440 was introduced in Europe in October 1955, but took longer to arrive in America. Promotional material for the export model called it "a noble representative of the famous name and tradition" that "blends the requirements of discerning customers, ingenious contrivances of modern automotive engineering and 60 years of experience in building high quality motor vehicles." Skoda's U.S. distributor advertised the export-version "S440 America" as offering a 78-mph and 40-mpg fuel economy, along with "big car comfort of an American car...the small car comfort of a European car." Although the 1200 series continued in production for the home market as late as 1962 (1969 for the station wagon), American attention focused solely on the S440 series, which was exported to many countries.

1958-59 SKODA

S440/S445 — FOUR — Appearance of the Skoda "America" sedan was unchanged for 1958-59, but a full line of models was available in the U.S., including a series of convertibles. Both standard and Deluxe sedan versions were offered, the latter with a larger four-cylinder engine (as in the prior 1200 series).

SS450 — FOUR — The new Sports convertible had a completely different front-end appearance than the sedan, centering on an oval grille with crosshatch (mesh) pattern dominated by the vertical bars. Round parking lights stood outboard of, and below, the hooded headlamps (as on the sedan). Under the hood was the same engine as the standard sedan, measuring 1089 cubic centimeters, but with additional horsepower.

I.D. DATA: Serial number is on left side of firewall. Engine number is on left side of firewall, and right side of crankcase.

Model	Body Type & Seating	Engine Type/CID	P.O.E. Price	Weight (lbs.)	Prod. Total
S440	2-dr Sedan-4P	I4/66	1687	1984	Note 1
S445	2-dr DeL Sed-4P	I4/74	1787	N/A	Note 1
SS450	2-dr Conv-4P	I4/66	2395	2000	Note 1
VSS	2-dr Spts Conv-4P	I4/66	2985	N/A	Note 1
VSS	2-dr Spts Cpe-4P	I4/66	3085	N/A	Note 1

Note 1: Approximately 370 Skodas were sold in the U.S. during 1958, and 721 in 1959.

ENGINE DATA: BASE FOUR (440/450): Inline, overhead-valve four-cylinder. Aluminum block and head. **Displacement:** 66.4 cu. in. (1089 cc). **Bore & Stroke:** 2.68 x 2.95 in. (68 x 75 mm). **Compression Ratio:** (440) 7.0:1; (450) 8.4:1. **Brake Horsepower:** (440) 40 at 4200 rpm; (450) 50 at 5500. Solid valve lifters. Jikov carburetor.

BASE FOUR (445): Inline, overhead-valve four-cylinder. **Displacement:** 74.5 cu. in. (1221 cc). **Bore & Stroke:** 2.83 x 2.95 in. (72 x 75 mm). **Compression Ratio:** 7.0:1. **Brake Horsepower:** 45 at 4200 rpm. Solid valve lifters.

CHASSIS DATA: Wheelbase: 94.5 in. **Overall Length:** 160 in. **Height:** 56.3 in. **Width:** 63 in. **Front Tread:** 47.6 in. **Rear Tread:** 49.2 in. **Wheel Type:** disc. **Standard Tires:** 5.50x15.

TECHNICAL: Layout: front-engine, rear-drive. **Transmission:** (440) four-speed manual, 2nd/3rd/4th synchro. Overall 440 gear ratios: (1st) 20.4:1; (2nd) 11.8:1; (3rd) 7.6:1; (4th) 4.8:1. **Standard Final Drive Ratio:** (440) 4.78:1. **Steering:** worm and nut. **Suspension (front):** independent trapezoidal with forked upper arms, transverse semi-elliptic leaf springs and lever-type shock absorbers. **Suspension (rear):** swing axles and transverse semi-elliptic leaf spring, with telescopic shock absorbers. **Brakes:** hydraulic, front/rear drum. **Body Construction:** (440) steel body on backbone chassis with two crossmembers. **Fuel Tank:** (440) 7.5 gallons.

PERFORMANCE: Top Speed: (440) 69-72 mph. **Acceleration (0-60 mph):** (440) 34.3 seconds. **Fuel Mileage:** (440) 27-36 mpg in U.S.

Manufacturer: Motokov Ltd., Praha (Prague), Czechoslovakia.

Distributor: Continental Car Combine, New York City.

HISTORY: Skoda's limited dealer network was mainly on the East Coast at first, with a few in the west.

1960-62 SKODA

OCTAVIA — FOUR — Promotional material at the New York Auto Show in spring 1960 called the Skoda Octavia "a small car for great service," and "the youngest member of the good old Skoda family." Replacing the former 440 series, the sedan was powered by the same 66.4-cid (1089 cc) four-cylinder overhead-valve engine. In basic form, that engine produced 43 horsepower; in Super trim, 47 bhp. Standard Octavia body colors were: Granada Beige, Lemon Yellow, Dove Grey, Clematis Grey-Blue, Tonus Blue, Chrysopras Green, Turqoise Green, Coffee Brown, Torrero Red, and Jet Black. Octavias switched in 1961 from the original horizontal-bar grille to an oval mesh pattern (like the Felicia convertible). By 1961, a Touring Sport sedan also was available.

FELICIA — FOUR — Skoda's convertible, formerly known as the SS450, had an oval grille with crosshatch (mesh) pattern dominated by the vertical bars. Round parking lights stood outboard of, and below, the hooded headlamps. Convertibles had the same engine as the standard sedan, measuring 1089 cubic centimeters, but with additional horsepower. Underneath was a tubular steel chassis with fully-independent suspension.

I.D. DATA: Serial number is on left side of firewall. Engine number is on left side of firewall, and right side of crankcase.

1960 Skoda convertible.

OCTAVIA

Model	Body Type & Seating	Engine Type/CID	P.O.E. Price	Weight (lbs.)	Prod. Total
Octavia	2-dr Sedan-4P	I4/66	1575	1962	N/A
Super	2-dr DeL Sed-4P	I4/66	1675	1962	N/A
Tour Spt	2-dr DeL Sed-4P	I4/66	1775	N/A	N/A

FELICIA

Model	Body Type & Seating	Engine Type/CID	P.O.E. Price	Weight (lbs.)	Prod. Total
Felicia	2-dr Conv-4P	I4/66	1995	N/A	N/A

Price Note: A Felicia convertible with removable hardtop (and soft top) cost $2150.

ENGINE DATA: BASE FOUR (Octavia): Inline, overhead-valve four-cylinder. Aluminum block and head. **Displacement:** 66.4 cu. in. (1089 cc). **Bore & Stroke:** 2.68 x 2.95 in. (68 x 75 mm). **Compression Ratio:** 8.4:1. **Brake Horsepower:** 43 (SAE) at 4600 rpm (Super, 47 at 4600). Solid valve lifters. One Jikov carburetor.

BASE FOUR (Felicia): Same as above, except — **Brake Horsepower:** 50 at 5500 rpm. **Torque:** 54 lbs.-ft. at 3500 rpm. Two downdraft carburetors.

1962 Skoda Felicia convertible.

CHASSIS DATA: Wheelbase: 94.5 in. **Overall Length:** 159 in. **Height:** (sed) 56.3 in.; (conv) 54 in. **Width:** 63 in. **Front Tread:** 47.6 in. **Rear Tread:** 49.2 in. **Wheel Type:** disc. **Standard Tires:** 5.50x15.

TECHNICAL: Layout: front-engine, rear-drive. **Transmission:** four-speed manual. Gear ratios: (1st) 4.27:1; (2nd) 2.46:1; (3rd) 1.59:1; (4th) 1.0:1; (rev) 5.61:1. **Standard Final Drive Ratio:** 4.78:1. **Steering:** worm and nut. **Suspension (front):** independent trapezoidal with forked upper arms, transverse semi-elliptic leaf springs and lever-type shock absorbers. **Suspension (rear):** swing axles and transverse semi-elliptic leaf spring, with telescopic shock absorbers. **Brakes:** hydraulic, front/rear drum. **Body Construction:** steel body on backbone chassis with two crossmembers. **Fuel Tank:** 6.5 gallons.

PERFORMANCE: Top Speed: (Octavia) 73 mph; (Super) 80 mph; (Felicia) 90-94 mph. **Fuel Mileage:** (Octavia) 40.36 mpg; (Super) 37.7 mpg; (Felicia) 40 mpg.

Manufacturer: Motokov Ltd., Praha (Prague), Czechoslovakia.

Distributor: Amsko Distributors Inc., New York City; Rosben Imports Corp., Brooklyn, New York.

1963-65 SKODA

OCTAVIA — FOUR — Production continued of the Skoda sedan, along with a two-door station wagon, both of which remained available in the U.S. Prices were reduced in 1963, and again in 1964.

FELICIA — FOUR — Skoda's convertible also remained in production, and available in America, into the mid-1960s. Prices were cut like those of the Octavia. After a period with the 1089-cc engine, it became available with a 1221-cc four.

1965 Skoda 1000 MB.

I.D. DATA: Serial number is on left side of firewall. Engine number is on left side of firewall, and right side of crankcase.

Model	Body Type & Seating	Engine Type/CID	P.O.E. Price	Weight (lbs.)	Prod. Total
Octavia	2-dr Sedan-4P	I4/66	1395	2350	N/A
	2-dr Sta Wag-4P	I4/66	1865	N/A	N/A

FELICIA

Model	Body Type & Seating	Engine Type/CID	P.O.E. Price	Weight (lbs.)	Prod. Total
Felicia	2-dr Conv-4P	I4/74	1645	2405	N/A

Price Note: A Felicia convertible with removable hardtop (and soft top) cost $150 more in 1963. Prices dropped in 1964 to $1315 for the sedan, $1695 for the station wagon, and $1545 for the Felicia convertible. An automatic clutch added $100 to the Octavia sedan price.

Weight Note: Figures shown are "curb" weights.

Model Note: A Touring Sport sedan cost $1515 in 1965.

ENGINE DATA: BASE FOUR (Octavia): Inline, overhead-valve four-cylinder. Aluminum block and head. **Displacement:** 66.4 cu. in. (1089 cc). **Bore & Stroke:** 2.68 x 2.95 in. (68 x 75 mm). **Compression Ratio:** 7.0:1. **Brake Horsepower:** 40 at 4200 rpm. **Torque:** 51 lbs.-ft. at 2800 rpm. Solid valve lifters. One Jikov carburetor.

BASE FOUR (Felicia): Inline, overhead-valve four-cylinder. **Displacement:** 74.5 cu. in. (1221 cc). **Bore & Stroke:** 2.83 x 2.95 in. (72 x 75 mm). **Compression Ratio:** 8.4:1. **Brake Horsepower:** 53 at 5100 rpm. **Torque:** 61 lbs.-ft. at 3000 rpm. Two Jikov carburetors.

CHASSIS DATA: Wheelbase: 94.5 in. **Overall Length:** 159 in. **Height:** (sed) 56.3 in.; (conv) 54 in. **Width:** 63 in. **Front Tread:** 47.6 in. **Rear Tread:** 49.2 in. **Wheel Type:** disc. **Standard Tires:** 5.50x15.

TECHNICAL: Layout: front-engine, rear-drive. **Transmission:** four-speed manual. Gear ratios: (1st) 4.27:1; (2nd) 2.46:1; (3rd) 1.59:1; (4th) 1.0:1; (rev) 5.61:1. **Standard Final Drive Ratio:** 4.78:1. **Steering:** worm and nut. **Suspension (front):** wishbones and coil springs. **Suspension (rear):** swing axles and transverse semi-elliptic leaf spring. **Brakes:** hydraulic, front/rear drum. **Body Construction:** steel body on backbone chassis with two crossmembers. **Fuel Tank:** 6.5 gallons.

PERFORMANCE: Similar to 1960-62.

Manufacturer: Motokov Ltd., Praha (Prague), Czechoslovakia.

Distributor: Rosben Imports Corp., Brooklyn, New York.

1966-67 SKODA

1000 MB — FOUR — This final Skoda offered for sale in the U.S. looked considerably different from earlier models, generally more utilitarian, less attractive and distinctive. Headlamps stood far out on the fenders, alongside a wide luggage lid. Gilled air scoops stood in quarter panels, below the wraparound back window. 'SKODA' block letters ran across the grille area. At the rear were slanted vertical taillamps. Skoda's powerplant was now a rear-mounted slant four of 60.3-cid displacement, producing 45 horsepower. The four-speed, all-synchro transmission used a hydraulic clutch. Reclining front seats were available, while each rear seat folded down for luggage storage. Another seating arrangement was available that converted to single or double sleeping space. Safety was a paramount feature in the new design, which displayed a lack of sharp projections in the passenger compartment, and included a padded instrument panel.

OCTAVIA — FOUR — Only a Combi station wagon remained available in the U.S., in the Octavia series. A 1221-cc four-cylinder engine was mounted in front.

I.D. DATA: Not available.

Model	Body Type & Seating	Engine Type/CID	P.O.E. Price	Weight (lbs.)	Prod. Total
1000 MB	4-dr Sedan-4/5P	I4/60	1480	1600	N/A
OCTAVIA					
Octavia	2-dr Combi Wag-4P	I4/74	N/A	2125	N/A

ENGINE DATA: BASE FOUR (1000 MB): Inline, overhead-valve four-cylinder. **Displacement:** 60.3 cu. in. (988 cc). **Bore & Stroke:** 2.68 x 2.68 in. (68 x 68 mm). **Compression Ratio:** 8.3:1. **Brake Horsepower:** 45 at 4650 rpm. **Torque:** 54 lbs.-ft. at 3000 rpm. Solid valve lifters. Jekoz one-barrel downdraft carburetor.

BASE FOUR (Octavia): Inline, overhead-valve four-cylinder. **Displacement:** 74.5 cu. in. (1221 cc). **Bore & Stroke:** 2.83 x 2.95 in. (72 x 75 mm). **Compression Ratio:** 7.5:1. **Brake Horsepower:** 47 at 4500 rpm. One carburetor.

CHASSIS DATA: Wheelbase: 94.5 in. **Overall Length:** (1000) 153.2 in.; (Octavia) 160 in. **Height:** (1000) 54.7 in.; (Octavia) 56.3 in. **Width:** (1000) 52.4 in.; (Octavia) 63 in. **Front Tread:** (1000) 50.4 in.; (Octavia) 47.6 in. **Rear Tread:** (1000) 49.2 in.; (Octavia) 49.2 in. **Wheel Type:** steel disc. **Standard Tires:** (1000) 6.00x14; (Octavia) 5.90x15.

TECHNICAL: Layout: (1000) rear-engine, rear-drive; (Octavia) front-engine, rear-drive. Transmission: four-speed manual (all synchro). Steering: worm and nut. Suspension (front): wishbones, coil springs and anti-roll bar. Suspension (rear): swing axles, radius arms and coil springs. Brakes: hydraulic, front/rear drum.
PERFORMANCE: Top Speed: (1000) about 75 mph.
Manufacturer: Motokov Ltd., Praha (Prague), Czechoslovakia.
Distributor: Felicia Motors Corp., Long Island City, New York.
HISTORY: Production continued into the 1970s and beyond, but official Skoda importation to America ceased in the late 1960s.

STANDARD

Among the small British sedans that briefly entered the gradually-developing American marketplace just after World War II was the Standard (often referred to as Standard Vanguard, for the series that became best known). As is typically the case, origins of the company began nearly half a century earlier, in 1903 to be exact, when R.W. Maudslay released a single-cylinder motorcar with its engine mounted beneath the floorboard. Engine design was the work of Alex Craig, who also created powerplants for such early British makes as Singer and Lea-Francis. Standard also offered two- and four-cylinder vehicles in the early days and, in 1906, an L-head six-cylinder model. Before long, the sixes became the temporary mainstay of the company, lasting until 1912, after which only four-cylinder engines were used.

Next, in 1913, came the compact-size Rhyl 9.5, on a 90-inch wheelbase with a 1087-cc engine. Two years later, the Rhyl 9.5 was available with electric lights. Larger Standards had four-cylinder engines of 2.4- and 3.3-liter displacement.

After World War I, a new SLS evolution of the Rhyl carried a 1.3-liter four-cylinder engine. An SLO with larger (1.6-liter) four with exposed overhead valves arrived in 1921. More popular was the SLO4 (13.9 HP), with an overhead-valve 1944-cc engine, produced until 1928. By 1927, Standard sedans could be ordered with sliding roofs. A year later, in an attempt to head off financial woes, Standard introduced a smaller Nine with an 1155-cc engine and fabric body. Sports two-seaters even had supercharged engines as the 1920s came to a close. Special Avon Standard Specials also appeared at this time, and continued to be built on various Standard chassis through the 1930s.

New six-cylinder engines introduced in 1929, with seven-bearing crankshafts, would remain under Standard bonnets until 1940 and the outbreak of World War II. A Big Nine emerged in 1931, with a 1287-cc L-head four-cylinder engine. Standard also offered Sixteen and Twenty models with six cylinders, but added a Little Nine in 1932 with a 1006-cc four. William Lyons borrowed the Standard chassis to create his S.S. cars in the early 1930s, which later evolved into the Jaguar. In fact, the four-cylinder Jaguars produced just after World War II still had Standard engines.

A few Standard models could have preselector gearboxes in 1933, followed by freewheeling and synchromesh the next year. A new Ten debuted in 1934, with a 1343-cc L-head four-cylinder engine. Fastback Flying Standards arrived in 1936, with spare tires integrated into their tails. A year later, that body style was the "standard" for Standard. A V-8 engine became available in 1937, displacing 2686 cc and mounted in a Standard Twelve chassis. The Standard Eight of 1939 ranked as Britain's first small sedan with independent front suspension.

The models and engines described amount to only a fraction of the total number of Standards available in the prewar years. After World War II, only three models returned: the Eight, Twelve, and Fourteen. By that time, Triumph was part of the Standard "empire," having been acquired in 1945.

Standard was ready for the 1948 model year with an all-new car, the Vanguard, powered by a 2088-cc four-cylinder overhead-valve engine. With little delay, that sedan was available in the U.S. market. Its full-width body could hold six passengers and the Vanguard had a column-shift three-speed transmission. This engine also was used in larger Triumph models, as well as in Morgan sports cars. Overdrive became available in 1950. A body restyle for 1953 produced the Vanguard II. Shortly afterward, Standard introduced a smaller model: the Eight, with an 803-cc engine. Its companion of a year later, the Ten, added a trunk lid. Other smaller models of the late 1950s were the Companion and Pennant, on the same 84-inch wheelbase as the Eight and Ten; and the Ensign, on a 102-inch wheelbase and powered by a 1670-cc engine.

A diesel engine became available in the Vanguard in 1954, but lasted only a short time. Further restylings of the Vanguard came in 1956 and 1959. A luxury-oriented Sportsman edition was produced in 1956-57, with a more potent (90-horsepower) engine. Automatic transmissions became available late in the decade, soon before the Vanguard four was abandoned in 1961.

Standard became part of the Leyland organization in 1961, leading to the debut of a Vanguard six. Along with a revived version of the Ensign, with a larger engine, these were the final automobiles to bear the Standard name. Ironically, according to *The Complete Catalogue of British Cars* and other sources, the car's name was part of the problem. Early in the century, "standard" had positive connotations. Sixty years later, the word meant something other than "deluxe." And that just wouldn't do for car purchasers of the 1960s.

1945-48 STANDARD

EIGHT — FOUR — Introduced in 1939, the Eight was revived after World War II. The two-door sedan had "suicide" doors and separately-mounted headlamps, and a generally stubby profile with flowing vertical grille. The drophead coupe (convertible) had rakish cutdown doors and a long folding top. Wheelbase was 83 inches, and power came from a 1009-cc side-valve (L-head) four-cylinder engine that developed 28 horsepower. Top speed was about 60 mph.

TWELVE — FOUR — Standard introduced a new four-door sedan and drophead coupe (convertible) just after the war, on a 100-inch wheelbase. A 1609-cc four-cylinder engine provided the power: 44 horsepower at 4000 rpm, to be precise. Appearance was similar to the Eight, but on a somewhat larger scale. The convertible had no quarter windows but included landau bars and a deck-mounted spare tire.

FOURTEEN — FOUR — On the same 100-inch wheelbase as the Twelve, the Fourteen carried a larger (1776-cc) engine that developed 49 horsepower. Both a four-door sedan and drophead coupe were offered.

VANGUARD — FOUR — The new Vanguard was introduced in mid-1947, and reached the U.S. market by 1949; see next listing for details.

1949 STANDARD

VANGUARD — PHASE I — FOUR — The first new postwar Standard model wore a slab-sided "six light" body in the modern rounded style, with headlamps built into the fenders and a fastback rear end. The four-door sedan's grille was made up of thin horizontal bars, tapering outward from the top and forming a wider rectangle at the base. A split windshield was installed, along with a spring-balanced hood, front vent wings, and rear quarter windows. Both doors hinged at the front. Up to six passengers could be seated. Power came from a 2088-cc four-cylinder overhead-valve engine that developed

68 horsepower, hooked to a three-speed gearbox with column-mounted lever. Independent front suspension used coil springs, while semi-elliptic leaf springs brought up the rear. Wheelbase was 94 inches, and the car measured 164 inches long overall. Claimed top speed was 80 mph. Instruments, including an electric clock, were grouped ahead of the driver. Front doors contained pockets, and sunvisors were standard. Self-canceling "trafficators" were controlled from the center of the steering wheel. Provision was made for a radio and heater/demister.

I.D. DATA: Serial number is on right side of firewall, under the hood. Starting serial number: V-1-LDL. Engine number is on a boss on left side of block (off center). Starting engine number: V-1-E.

Model	Body Type & Seating	Engine Type/CID	P.O.E. Price	Weight (lbs.)	Prod. Total
I	4-dr Sedan-5/6P	I4/127	1850	2700	Note 1

Note 1: Approximately 34 Standard models were sold in the U.S. during 1949.

ENGINE DATA: BASE FOUR: Inline, overhead-valve four cylinder. **Displacement:** 127 cu. in. (2088 cc). **Bore & Stroke:** 3.35 x 3.62 in. (85 x 92 mm). **Compression Ratio:** 6.7:1. **Brake Horsepower:** 68 at 4200 rpm. Three main bearings. Solid valve lifters. Solex downdraft carburetor.

CHASSIS DATA: Wheelbase: 94 in. **Overall Length:** 164 in. **Height:** 64 in. **Width:** 69 in. **Front Tread:** 51 in. **Rear Tread:** 54 in. **Standard Tires:** 5.50x16.

TECHNICAL: Layout: front-engine, rear-drive. **Transmission:** three-speed manual (column lever). **Standard Final Drive Ratio:** 4.62:1. **Steering:** cam and roller. **Suspension (front):** independent with coil springs. **Suspension (rear):** rigid axle with semi-elliptic leaf springs and anti-sway bar. **Brakes:** Lockheed hydraulic, front/rear drum. **Body Construction:** steel body on steel frame.

MAJOR OPTIONS: Heater/demister. Radio.

PERFORMANCE: Top Speed: 80 mph claimed. **Acceleration (0-60 mph):** N/A (0-50 mph in 16.1 sec., in British test). **Acceleration (quarter-mile):** 22.4 sec. (British test).

Manufacturer: The Standard Motor Company Ltd., Coventry, Warwickshire, England.

Distributor: Fergus Motors Inc., New York City.

HISTORY: The Vanguard was introduced in Britain in July 1947, and became available in the U.S. by the 1949 model year.

1950-52 STANDARD

VANGUARD — PHASE I — FOUR — Both a four-door sedan and an Estate Car (station wagon) were available in the American market by 1950. Mechanical details were similar to the prior model. Appearance also was similar, except that rear wheels on later models were enclosed (with detachable covers) and separate parking lights were installed. Both the sedan and station wagon had a center armrest in the front seat, which folded to allow space for three people. A simple operation was claimed to convert the Estate Car from a comfortable six-seat saloon (sedan) into an all-purpose luggage carrier. Basic sedans came with Vynide upholstery. Options included leather upholstery, a heater/demister, pushbutton Radiomobile, and (starting 1950) Laycock de Normanville overdrive.

The Vanguard grille was modified for 1952, using a thick horizontal bar that reached to the parking lights. Pushbutton door handles were installed.

I.D. DATA: Serial number is on right side of firewall, under the hood. Starting serial number (1952 models): V-150013. Engine number is on a boss on left side of block (off center).

Model	Body Type & Seating	Engine Type/CID	P.O.E. Price	Weight (lbs.)	Prod. Total
I	4-dr Sedan-5/6P	I4/127	2250	2700	Note 1
I	4-dr Sta Wag-5/6P	I4/127	2550	2700	Note 1

Note 1: Approximately 30 Standard models were sold in the U.S. during 1950, followed by 19 in 1951.

ENGINE DATA: BASE FOUR: Inline, overhead-valve four-cylinder. **Displacement:** 127 cu. in. (2088 cc). **Bore & Stroke:** 3.35 x 3.62 in. (85 x 92 mm). **Compression Ratio:** 6.7:1. **Brake Horsepower:** 68 at 4200 rpm. Three main bearings. Solid valve lifters. Solex downdraft carburetor.

CHASSIS DATA: Wheelbase: 94 in. **Overall Length:** (sedan) 164 in.; (wagon) 162.75 in. **Height:** 64 in. **Width:** 69 in. **Front Tread:** 51 in. **Rear Tread:** 54 in. **Standard Tires:** (1950 sed) 5.50x16; (1951-52 sed) 5.75x16; (wagon) 5.75x16.

TECHNICAL: Layout: front-engine, rear-drive. **Transmission:** three-speed manual (column lever). **Standard Final Drive Ratio:** 4.62:1. **Steering:** cam and roller. **Suspension (front):** independent with coil springs. **Suspension (rear):** rigid axle with semi-elliptic leaf springs and anti-sway bar. **Brakes:** Lockheed hydraulic, front/rear drum. **Body Construction:** steel body on steel frame.

MAJOR OPTIONS: Heater/demister. Pushbutton radio. Leather upholstery. Laycock de Normanville overdrive.

PERFORMANCE: Top Speed: 80 mph claimed. **Acceleration (0-60 mph):** N/A (0-50 mph in 16.1 sec., in British test). **Acceleration (quarter-mile):** 22.4 sec. (British test).

Manufacturer: The Standard Motor Company Ltd., Coventry, Warwickshire, England.

Distributor: Fergus Motors Inc., New York City.

1953-55 STANDARD

VANGUARD — PHASE II — FOUR — Vanguard's second series switched to "four light" styling (no separate rear quarter windows), with a protruding trunk. That meant a notchback rather than the original fastback profile. The grille was extended horizontally to encompass the parking lights. All four doors had pivoting vent wings. Detachable rear wheel covers no longer were available. A hydraulic clutch was standard and tires grew to 6.00x16 size, but no major mechanical changes were undertaken. Both two-door and four-door Estate Cars (station wagons) were available, but the two-door didn't last long.

1954 Standard Eight four-door sedan.

I.D. DATA: Serial number is on right side of firewall, under the hood. Starting serial number (1953 sedan): V200001. Engine number is on a boss on left side of block (off center).

Model	Body Type & Seating	Engine Type/CID	P.O.E. Price	Weight (lbs.)	Prod. Total
II	4-dr Sedan-5/6P	I4/127	N/A	2690	N/A
II	2-dr Sta Wag-5/6P	I4/127	N/A	N/A	N/A
II	4-dr Sta Wag-5/6P	I4/127	N/A	N/A	N/A

ENGINE DATA: BASE FOUR: Inline, overhead-valve four-cylinder. **Displacement:** 127 cu. in. (2088 cc). **Bore & Stroke:** 3.35 x 3.62 in. (85 x 92 mm). **Compression Ratio:** 7.0:1. **Brake Horsepower:** 68 at 4200 rpm. Three main bearings. Solid valve lifters. Solex downdraft carburetor.

CHASSIS DATA: Wheelbase: 94 in. **Overall Length:** (sedan) 168 in.; (wagon) 163 in. **Height:** 65 in. **Width:** 69 in. **Front Tread:** 51 in. **Rear Tread:** 54 in. **Standard Tires:** 6.00x16.

TECHNICAL: Layout: front-engine, rear-drive. **Transmission:** three-speed manual (column lever). **Standard Final Drive Ratio:** 4.62:1. **Steering:** cam and roller. **Suspension (front):** independent with coil springs. **Suspension (rear):** rigid axle with semi-elliptic leaf springs and anti-sway bar. **Brakes:** Lockheed hydraulic, front/rear drum. **Body Construction:** steel body on steel frame.

MAJOR OPTIONS: "Air conditioning" (Smith's heater/demister). Pushbutton radio. Leather upholstery. Laycock de Normanville overdrive.

PERFORMANCE: Top Speed: 80 mph claimed. **Acceleration (0-60 mph):** 19.9 sec. (British test). **Acceleration (quarter-mile):** 21.6 sec. (British test).

ADDITIONAL MODELS: A diesel engine became available in 1954, with displacement almost identical to the gasoline four but different bore/stroke dimensions. The diesel developed 40 horsepower. For the home market, Standard also introduced smaller Eight and Ten sedans on an 84-inch wheelbase, with 803- and 948-cc four-cylinder engines.

Manufacturer: The Standard Motor Company Ltd., Coventry, Warwickshire, England.

HISTORY: Though available in the U.S. in the late 1940s and early 1950s, by the time the Phase II arrived, Vanguards no longer were listed in all directories of imported cars. Standard engines, however, were installed in Morgan sports cars and were modified for Triumph's TR series.

1956-58 STANDARD

1956 Standard Vanguard four-door sedan.

VANGUARD — PHASE III — FOUR — The next series carried the same 2088-cc four-cylinder engine, but was revised in appearance with a rectangular oval grille that contained a wide, thick horizontal bar. Wheelbase grew to 102 inches. Bodysides had a sculptured cutout that extended from the forward portion of the front door to near the rear end. This Vanguard employed unit construction. An automatic transmission and four-speed floor shift became available by 1958.

SPORTSMAN — FOUR — Standard also debuted a high-performance variant of the Vanguard, called the Sportsman. With twin SU carburetors, the 2088-cc engine developed 90 horsepower. The Sportsman had a unique large, split grille with a thick curved upper molding. Parking lights sat just above the bumper.

I.D. DATA: Serial number is on right side of firewall, under the hood. Engine number is on a boss on left side of block.

Model	Body Type & Seating	Engine Type/CID	P.O.E. Price	Weight (lbs.)	Prod. Total
VANGUARD					
III	4-dr Sedan-5/6P	I4/127	N/A	2575	N/A
III	4-dr Sta Wag-5/6P	I4/127	N/A	N/A	N/A
SPORTSMAN					
	4-dr Sedan-5/6P	I4/127	N/A	2690	N/A

ENGINE DATA: BASE FOUR (Vanguard III): Inline, overhead-valve four-cylinder. **Displacement:** 127 cu. in. (2088 cc). **Bore & Stroke:** 3.35 x 3.62 in. (85 x 92 mm). **Compression Ratio:** 7.5:1. **Brake Horsepower:** 68 at 4200 rpm. Three main bearings. Solid valve lifters. Solex downdraft carburetor.
BASE FOUR (Sportsman): Same as above, except — **Compression Ratio:** 8.0:1. **Brake Horsepower:** 90 at 4500 rpm. Two SU carburetors.

CHASSIS DATA: Wheelbase: 102 in. **Overall Length:** (Vanguard) 171.5 in.; (Sportsman) 173.5 in. **Width:** 67.5 in. **Max. Tread:** 51.5 in. **Standard Tires:** 5.50x16 or 5.90x15.

TECHNICAL: Layout: front-engine, rear-drive. **Transmission:** three-speed manual (column lever); automatic and four-speed manual optional on later models. **Suspension (front):** independent with coil springs. **Suspension (rear):** rigid axle with semi-elliptic leaf springs. **Brakes:** hydraulic, front/rear drum. **Body Construction:** steel unibody.

ADDITIONAL MODELS: Two smaller models emerged in 1955 for the home market, on the same 84-inch wheelbase as the Eight and Ten. Both the Companion Estate Car and Pennant sedan used a 948-cc engine. Introduced in 1957, the Ensign sedan rode a 102-inch wheelbase and carried a 1670-cc engine.
Manufacturer: The Standard Motor Company Ltd., Coventry, Warwickshire, England.

1959-60 STANDARD

VANGUARD — VIGNALE — FOUR — The final Vanguard version, before the company was taken over by Leyland, wore a Vignale body that was similar in appearance to its predecessors, but had a large eggcrate grille pattern. Parking and signal lights stood alongside the grille.

I.D. DATA: Serial number is on right side of firewall, under the hood. Engine number is on a boss on left side of block.

Model	Body Type & Seating	Engine Type/CID	P.O.E. Price	Weight (lbs.)	Prod. Total
VANGUARD					
Vignale	4-dr Sedan-5/6P	I4/127	N/A	2575	N/A
	4-dr Sta Wag-5/6P	I4/127	N/A	N/A	N/A

ENGINE DATA: BASE FOUR: Inline, overhead-valve four-cylinder. **Displacement:** 127 cu. in. (2088 cc). **Bore & Stroke:** 3.35 x 3.62 in. (85 x 92 mm). **Compression Ratio:** 7.5:1. **Brake Horsepower:** 68 at 4200 rpm. Three main bearings. Solid valve lifters. Solex downdraft carburetor.

CHASSIS DATA: Wheelbase: 102 in. **Overall Length:** 171.5 in. **Width:** 67.5 in. **Max. Tread:** 51.5 in. **Standard Tires:** 5.90x15.

TECHNICAL: Layout: front-engine, rear-drive. **Transmission:** three-speed manual; four-speed and automatic optional. **Suspension (front):** independent with coil springs. **Suspension (rear):** rigid axle with semi-elliptic leaf springs. **Brakes:** hydraulic, front/rear drum. **Body Construction:** steel unibody.
Manufacturer: The Standard Motor Company Ltd., Coventry, Warwickshire, England.

1961-63 STANDARD

VANGUARD — SIX — For its final stab at the marketplace, after the Leyland takeover, Standard abandoned the familiar four-cylinder engine in favor of six-cylinder power. The 1998-cc six (actually smaller in displacement than the former four) developed 80 horsepower, using twin Solex carburetors.

I.D. DATA: Serial number is on right side of firewall, under the hood. Engine number is on a boss on left side of block.

Model	Body Type & Seating	Engine Type/CID	P.O.E. Price	Weight (lbs.)	Prod. Total
VANGUARD					
	4-dr Sedan-5/6P	I6/122	N/A	2550	N/A
	4-dr Sta Wag-5/6P	I6/122	N/A	N/A	N/A

ENGINE DATA: BASE SIX: Inline, overhead-valve six-cylinder. **Displacement:** 122 cu. in. (1998 cc). **Bore & Stroke:** 2.94 x 2.99 in. (74.7 x 76 mm). **Compression Ratio:** 8.0:1. **Brake Horsepower:** 80 at 4500 rpm. Solid valve lifters. Two Solex carburetors.

CHASSIS DATA: Wheelbase: 102 in. **Overall Length:** 173.5 in. **Width:** 67.5 in. **Max. Tread:** 51.5 in. **Standard Tires:** 5.90x15.

TECHNICAL: Layout: front-engine, rear-drive. **Transmission:** three-speed manual; four-speed and automatic optional. **Suspension (front):** independent with coil springs. **Suspension (rear):** rigid axle with semi-elliptic leaf springs. **Body Construction:** steel unibody.

ADDITIONAL MODELS: A second version of the Ensign also was introduced during the final years of the Standard nameplate, with a larger (2138-cc) four-cylinder engine.
Manufacturer: The Standard Motor Company Ltd., Coventry, Warwickshire, England (now part of the Leyland organization).

STERLING

For half a dozen years after the Rover finally gave up on the American passenger-car market with its last-ditch 3500 hatchback, that British company offered no cars in the U.S. Then came the product of a joint British/Japanese effort between Austin Rover and Honda. Under the terms of their agreement, Austin Rover was building Acura Legends for sale in Europe, while Honda produced Rover 800s for sale in Japan.

Introduced to the U.S. during the 1987 model year, this British-built Sterling lasted only a few years before giving up like its Rover predecessor, a victim of sales that never managed to take off. The Sterling sedan was based on Honda's Acura Legend, and came first with a 2.5-liter V-6; later with the larger 2.7-liter V-6 that debuted initially in the Legend. Early in 1990, Sterling achieved the dubious distinction of offering what may have been the largest rebate of all time ($6000), in an effort to perk up sales. Finally, in August 1991, the company announced that no more Sterlings would be coming to the U.S. market.

Note: See Rover listing in this Catalog for details on the 3500 and earlier Rover models; and Land Rover listing for data on the four-wheel-drive models that were marketed in America.

1987-88 STERLING

1988 Sterling 825SL four-door sedan.

825 SERIES — V-6 — Appearance of the Sterling was similar to the Acura Legend, though not identical. Both cars shared mechanical components, but sheetmetal differed. Sterling's narrow grille consisted of two horizontal slots, flanked by large wraparound aero-styled headlamps. Inside, the Sterling had its own dashboard and burled walnut trim. Under the hood was Honda's 2.5-liter overhead-cam V-6 engine, developing 151 horsepower. Sterlings were four-door sedans and had front-wheel drive. A five-speed manual gearbox was standard on the base 825S, while the deluxe 825SL added a four-speed automatic transmission, leather upholstery, and Bosch anti-lock braking. Each of those items also was optional on the 825S. Standard equipment included cruise control, intermittent wipers, tachometer, Philips six-speaker AM/FM stereo with cassette player, tilt steering, power moonroof, and central locking. The 825SL included a power driver's seat with four-position memory, power passenger seat, trip computer, graphic display, and eight-speaker stereo.

I.D. DATA: Sterling's Vehicle Identification Number is on the upper left of the instrument panel, visible through the windshield.

Model	Body Type & Seating	Engine Type/CID	P.O.E. Price	Weight (lbs.)	Prod. Total
825S	4-dr Sedan-5P	V6/152	19000	3164	Note 1
825SL	4-dr Sedan-5P	V6/152	23900	3252	Note 1

Note 1: A total of 14,171 Sterlings were sold in the U.S. during 1987, followed by 8,901 in 1988.

Price Note: Figures shown were valid in 1987. Prices rose to $20,804 and $25,995 in 1988.

ENGINE DATA: BASE V-6: Overhead-cam, "vee" type six-cylinder. Aluminum alloy block and heads. **Displacement:** 152.2 cu. in. (2494 cc). **Bore & Stroke:** 3.31 x 2.95 in. (84 x 75 mm). **Compression Ratio:** 9.0:1. **Brake Horsepower:** 151 at 5800 rpm. **Torque:** 154 lbs.-ft. at 4500 rpm. Multi-point fuel injection.

CHASSIS DATA: Wheelbase: 108.6 in. **Overall Length:** 188.8 in. **Height:** 54.8 in. **Width:** 68.1 in. **Front Tread:** 58.8 in. **Rear Tread:** 57.1 in. **Standard Tires:** 195/65VR15.

TECHNICAL: Layout: front-engine, front-drive. **Transmission:** five-speed manual or four-speed overdrive automatic. **Steering:** power rack and pinion. **Suspension (front):** upper/lower control arms with coil springs and anti-roll bar. **Suspension (rear):** struts with coil springs. **Brakes:** front/rear disc. **Body Construction:** steel unibody.

MAJOR OPTIONS: Five-speed manual transmission (825SL). Four-speed automatic transmission (825S). Connolly leather upholstery (825S). Anti-lock braking (825S). Metallic paint (825S). Power rear seat (825SL).

Manufacturer: Austin Rover Group, London, England.
Distributor: Austin Rover Cars of North America, Miami, Florida.

HISTORY: When introduced to the U.S. market in January 1987, Sterling had approximately 145 dealers. The Acura Legend, which served as the basis for this car, had gone on sale in the U.S. nearly a year earlier, during the 1986 model year. The European version was known as the Rover 800.

1989-90 STERLING

1989 Sterling 827SLi four-door sedan.

827 SERIES — V-6 — Not only did Sterling adopt the 2.7-liter V-6 that had been installed on Acura Legends a year earlier, but a five-door hatchback (known as 827SLi) joined the original four-door sedan. Sedans had a self-leveling rear suspension, but the hatchback did not. The new V-6 developed 161 horsepower, up 10 from the prior engine. A Limited Edition 827SL was available in 1989, with leather and suede upholstery and a power rear recliner, painted only in green metallic. An 827Si was added for 1990, with equipment similar to the 827SL.

I.D. DATA: Sterling's Vehicle Identification Number is on the upper left of the instrument panel, visible through the windshield.

Model	Body Type & Seating	Engine Type/CID	P.O.E. Price	Weight (lbs.)	Prod. Total
827S	4-dr Sedan-5P	V6/163	23300	3097	Note 1
827SL	4-dr Sedan-5P	V6/163	29675	3183	Note 1
827SLi	5-dr Hatch-5P	V6/163	29675	3230	Note 1

Note 1: A total of 5,907 Sterlings were sold in the U.S. during 1989, followed by 4,015 in 1990.

Price Note: Figures shown were valid in 1989. A Limited Edition 827SL was available in 1989, priced at $30,150. Prices in 1990 were $23,550 for the 827S, $26,500 for the 827Si hatchback, $28,500 for the 827SL, and $28,500 for the 827SLi.

1990 Sterling Oxford Edition four-door sedan.

ENGINE DATA: BASE V-6: Overhead-cam, "vee" type six-cylinder. Aluminum alloy block and heads. **Displacement:** 163 cu. in. (2675 cc). **Bore & Stroke:** 3.43 x 2.95 in. (87 x 75 mm). **Compression Ratio:** 9.0:1. **Brake Horsepower:** 161 at 5900 rpm. **Torque:** 162 lbs.-ft. at 4500 rpm. Multi-point fuel injection.

CHASSIS DATA: Wheelbase: 108.6 in. **Overall Length:** 188.8 in. **Height:** 54.8 in. **Width:** 68.1 in. **Front Tread:** 58.8 in. **Rear Tread:** 57.1 in.

TECHNICAL: Layout: front-engine, front-drive. **Transmission:** five-speed manual or four-speed overdrive automatic. **Steering:** power rack and pinion. **Suspension (front):** upper/lower control arms with coil springs and anti-roll bar. **Suspension (rear):** struts with coil springs, lower control arms and anti-roll bar. **Brakes:** front/rear disc. **Body Construction:** steel unibody.

MAJOR OPTIONS: Five-speed manual transmission (827SL). Four-speed automatic transmission (827S). Leather upholstery (827S). Anti-lock braking (827S). Metallic paint (827S). Power rear seat (827SL).

Manufacturer: Rover Group PLC, London, England.

Distributor: Austin Rover Cars of North America, Miami, Florida; then Sterling Motor Cars, New York City.

POSTSCRIPT: Despite minimal sales, Sterling stuck out the 1991 model year. In August 1991, however, the company announced that it would halt sales in the U.S.

SUBARU

Although Fuji Heavy Industries Ltd. (the producer of Subarus) was founded in Japan in 1953, its first vehicle wasn't a car, but a motorscooter: the Rabbit, which debuted in 1956. Fuji actually had evolved from the Nakajima Aircraft Company, which dissolved after World War II. Subaru is the Japanese name for a six-star constellation known as "Pleiades."

The first automobile to carry that Subaru name was the rear-engined 360, which debuted in 1958. The transverse-mounted, air-cooled two-stroke engine, with two cylinders and 356-cc displacement, developed 16 horsepower. A three-speed gearbox was standard initially, but a four-speed became available by 1964. Torsion bars were used for both the front and rear suspension. Malcolm Bricklin began to import 360s into the U.S. in the late 1960s, but the Subaru image was thrown for a loss when *Consumer Reports* branded the 360 "the most unsafe car on the market." Years would pass, and many totally different Subarus would be introduced, before that unpleasant early image began to fade.

A full-size FE Subaru with front-mounted 997-cc engine became available in 1968. This overhead-valve engine was water-cooled and had four horizontally-opposed cylinders—a configuration that would continue into the 1990s. Thus, that engine type would become almost a Subaru trademark—similar to the experience of the Volkswagen Beetle, which also used a flat four. Unlike the Beetle, however, these Subarus were front-wheel-drive. A Sport version with a more powerful engine and front disc brakes also was produced. Fuji became part of the Nissan group in 1968, assembling certain cars for that company in subsequent years.

Larger engines came in the early 1970s: first 1088 cc, then 1267 and 1361 cc. Topping the FF series by 1972 was the Leone GSR coupe, with a 93-bhp engine and 106-mph top speed. Bigger Subarus were available in the U.S. by 1971, under the FF-1 (Star) designation. Through the 1970s, Subaru's flat-four engines grew from 1.1 to 1.8 liters. Before long, some American publications were impressed with the larger Subarus. *Road & Track,* for instance, named the GF "import car of the year" in 1975.

Subaru's minicars were improved and offered for sale elsewhere in the world during the 1970s, but steered clear of the American market. A configuration that did gain favor in the U.S. was four-wheel-drive, introduced much earlier on Subarus than on most other makes. A four-wheel-drive wagon debuted in 1973 and was available in the U.S. within two years. For the Japanese market, Subaru intro-

duced a Rex two-cylinder sedan, which started small but grew to a whopping 544-cc displacement by 1978. Subaru's slogan in the U.S. in the late 1970s was: "Inexpensive. And built to stay that way." Subaru naturally promoted its EPA fuel-economy estimates, which reached as high as 50 mpg (highway) late in the decade.

Two notable Subarus entered the U.S. market in the 1980s, in addition to the conventional (for Subaru) family sedans and wagons. Small in size, the Justy was significant technically with its continuously-variable transmission. The unit actually was produced under license from the the Van Doorne firm in Holland, not unlike the transmission used earlier in the DAF (also listed in this Catalog). A four-wheel-drive sport coupe, the XT, also attracted a modest following in the U.S., despite (or perhaps because of) its curious squarish styling. The XT was succeeded during 1991 by a dramatically-styled SVX coupe, which got into trouble with critics early as a result of advertisements that claimed—allegedly tongue in cheek—that "You can drive it so fast you'll get so many tickets you'll lose your license." TV commercials toned down the message, pointing out that an SVX was intended only to travel at legal speeds.

1958-70 SUBARU

1968-'70 Subaru.

360 — TWO — Production of the 360 coupe began in 1958, though imports to the U.S. did not commence until a decade later, handled by Malcolm Bricklin. The 360 had partly-recessed headlamps alongside a rounded triangular front luggage lid, "suicide" (rear-hinged) doors, and 10-inch tires. By the time the car reached the American market, its air-cooled two-cylinder, two-stroke engine with 356-cc (21.7-cid) displacement developed 25 horsepower. Wheelbase was less than 71 inches. Up until the mid-1960s, these first Subarus had mechanical brakes.

1970 Subaru two-door.

588

I.D. DATA: Serial number is stamped on the end of the floor tunnel, and is on a decal attached to firewall inside the front compartment.

Model	Body Type & Seating	Engine Type/CID	P.O.E. Price	Weight (lbs.)	Prod. Total
360	2-dr Coupe-4P	I2/22	1297	900	Note 1
360 Custom	2-dr Coupe-4P	I2/22	N/A	1000	Note 1

Note 1: A total of 22,319 Subarus (all models) were produced during 1961, followed by 12,442 in 1962, rising to 103,746 in 1968, 124,877 in 1969, and 158,259 in 1970.

ENGINE DATA: BASE TWO: Inline two-stroke, two-cylinder (air cooled). **Displacement:** 21.7 cu. in. (356 cc). **Bore & Stroke:** 2.42 x 2.36 in. (61.5 x 60 mm). **Compression Ratio:** 6.7:1. **Brake Horsepower:** 25 at 5500 rpm. **Torque:** 25 lbs.-ft. at 4500 rpm. One Hitachi carburetor.

CHASSIS DATA: Wheelbase: 70.9 in. **Overall Length:** 118 in. **Height:** 53.1-53.6 in. **Width:** 51.2 in. **Front Tread:** 44.9 in. **Rear Tread:** 41.7-42.1 in. **Standard Tires:** 4.80x10.

TECHNICAL: Layout: rear-engine, rear-drive. **Transmission:** four-speed manual (early models, three-speed). **Steering:** rack and pinion. **Suspension (front):** trailing arms with torsion bars and coil springs. **Suspension (rear):** independent with semi-axles and torsion bars. **Brakes:** front/rear drum (hydraulic by late 1960s). **Body Construction:** steel unibody.

PRODUCTION/SALES: A total of 5,590 Subarus were sold in the U.S. during 1970.
Manufacturer: Fuji Heavy Industries Ltd., Tokyo, Japan.
Distributor: Malcolm Bricklin.

1971 SUBARU

FF-1 STAR — 1100 — FLAT FOUR — Subaru abandoned the tiny 360 after a short and largely unsuccessful foray into the U.S. marketplace, turning instead to the larger models with their horizontally-opposed four-cylinder engines. The 1100 "Star" series had a 1088-cc engine that developed 62 horsepower. Whereas the 360 had been rear-engine, rear-wheel-drive, the 1100 had a front-mounted engine and front-wheel drive. Wheelbase was 95.2 inches. Single round headlamps were slightly recessed, and sat alongside a blackout-patterned rectangular grille with center insignia and bright surround molding. Amber wraparound park/signal lights were installed. Standard equipment included reclining seats, a four-speed manual gearbox, heater/defroster, vinyl upholstery, padded sunvisors, and bumper guards. A top speed of 90 mph was claimed.

I.D. DATA: Subaru's 10-symbol serial number is atop the dashboard on the driver's side and on the driver's door pillar post. The first four symbols identify the model; the fifth indicates body style; and the final five digits are the sequential production number.

Model	Body Type & Seating	Engine Type/CID	P.O.E. Price	Weight (lbs.)	Prod. Total
FF-1 STAR					
1100	2-dr Sedan-5P	H4/66	1699	1520	Note 1
1100	4-dr Sedan-5P	H4/66	1799	1530	Note 1
1100	4-dr Sta Wag-5P	H4/66	1899	1640	Note 1

Note 1: A total of 115,466 Subarus (all models) were produced during 1971.

Price Note: Figures shown were listed in sales brochure; other sources listed prices as $50 higher.

ENGINE DATA: BASE FOUR: Horizontally-opposed four-cylinder (model EA61). **Displacement:** 66.4 cu. in. (1088 cc). **Bore & Stroke:** 2.99 x 2.36 in. (76 x 60 mm). **Compression Ratio:** 9.0:1. **Brake Horsepower:** 62 at 6000 rpm. **Torque:** 62.9 lbs.-ft. at 3200 rpm.

CHASSIS DATA: Wheelbase: 95.2 in. **Overall Length:** (sed) 155 in.; (wag) 152.8 in. **Height:** (sed) 54.7 in.; (wag) 55.7 in. **Width:** 58.3 in. **Front Tread:** 48.2 in. **Rear Tread:** (sed) 47.6 in.; (wag) 48.5 in. **Standard Tires:** 6.15x13.

TECHNICAL: Layout: front-engine, front-drive. **Transmission:** four-speed manual. **Steering:** rack and pinion. **Suspension (front):** wishbones with torsion bars. **Suspension (rear):** independent with trailing arms and torsion bars. **Brakes:** front/rear drum. **Body Construction:** steel unibody.

PRODUCTION/SALES: A total of 14,116 Subarus were sold in the U.S. during 1971.
Manufacturer: Fuji Heavy Industries Ltd., Tokyo, Japan.
Distributor: Subaru of America, Pennsauken, New Jersey and Newport Beach, California.

1972 SUBARU

1300 SERIES — FLAT FOUR — A larger (1267-cc) engine went into the next Subaru series offered in the U.S., developing 80 gross horsepower (61 net). The grille now consisted of two slim horizontal bars, parallel at the center and diverging at the ends. At mid-year, a GL coupe joined the sedans, on a slightly longer (96.6-inch) wheelbase and with a larger grille.

I.D. DATA: Subaru's 10-symbol serial number is atop the dashboard on the driver's side and on the driver's door pillar post. The first four symbols identify the model; the fifth indicates body style; and the final five digits are the sequential production number. Engine number is stamped on the crankcase, behind the distributor.

Model	Body Type & Seating	Engine Type/CID	P.O.E. Price	Weight (lbs.)	Prod Total
1300					
A15L	2-dr Sedan-5P	H4/77	2040	1620	Note 1
A15L	4-dr Sedan-5P	H4/77	2138	1640	Note 1
A44L	4-dr Sta Wag-5P	H4/77	2346	1750	Note 1
GL	2-dr Coupe-4/5P	H4/77	2499	1750	Note 1

Note 1: A total of 130,339 Subarus (all models) were produced during 1972.

ENGINE DATA: BASE FOUR: Horizontally-opposed, overhead-valve four-cylinder. **Displacement:** 77.3 cu. in. (1267 cc). **Bore & Stroke:** 3.23 x 2.36 in. (82 x 60 mm). **Compression Ratio:** 9.0:1. **Brake Horsepower:** 61 (SAE net) at 5600 rpm. **Torque:** 65 lbs.-ft. (SAE net) at 4000 rpm. Two-barrel carburetor.

CHASSIS DATA: **Wheelbase:** 95.3 in. **Overall Length:** (sed) 153.5 in.; (wag) 152.8 in. **Height:** (sed) 54.7 in.; (wag) 55.7 in. **Width:** 58.3 in. **Front Tread:** 48.2 in. **Rear Tread:** (sed) 47.4 in.; (wag) 48.6 in. **Standard Tires:** 6.15x13.

TECHNICAL: **Layout:** front-engine, front-drive. **Transmission:** four-speed manual. **Steering:** rack and pinion. **Suspension (front):** wishbones with torsion bars. **Suspension (rear):** independent with trailing arms and torsion bars. **Brakes:** front/rear drum. **Body Construction:** steel unibody.

PRODUCTION/SALES: A total of 24,056 Subarus were sold in the U.S. during 1972. **Manufacturer:** Fuji Heavy Industries Ltd., Tokyo, Japan. **Distributor:** Subaru of America Inc., Pennsauken, New Jersey.

1973-76 SUBARU

1400 DL/GL — FLAT FOUR — Engine displacement of the horizontally-opposed four grew again by 1973, to 1361 cc (83.2-cid). So did the car's dimensions. Output started at 61 horsepower (SAE net), but dropped to 58 bhp by 1975. A GF two-door hardtop joined the original coupe, sedans and station wagon for 1975. Also added in that year was a four-wheel-drive version of the station wagon. A five-speed manual gearbox and an automatic transmission also became available in 1975.

I.D. DATA: Subaru's 10-symbol serial number is atop the dashboard on the driver's side and on the driver's door pillar post. The first four symbols identify the model; the fifth indicates body style; and the final five digits are the sequential production number. Engine number is stamped on the crankcase, behind the distributor.

Model	Body Type & Seating	Engine Type/CID	P.O.E. Price	Weight (lbs.)	Prod. Total
1400					
DL	2-dr Sedan-5P	H4/83	2040	1620	Note 1
DL	4-dr Sedan-5P	H4/83	2138	1640	Note 1
DL	4-dr Sta Wag-5P	H4/83	2346	1750	Note 1
GL	2-dr Coupe-4/5P	H4/83	2499	1750	Note 1

Note 1: A total of 130,730 Subarus (all models) were produced during 1973, followed by 102,209 in 1974, 108,663 in 1975, and 108,179 in 1976.

Price Note: Figures shown were valid in 1974. The GF hardtop coupe added for 1975 sold for $3589, while the four-wheel-drive station wagon brought $3999.

ENGINE DATA: BASE FOUR: Horizontally-opposed, overhead-valve four-cylinder. **Displacement:** 83.2 cu. in. (1361 cc). **Bore & Stroke:** 3.35 x 2.36 in. (85 x 60 mm). **Compression Ratio:** 9.0:1 (later 8.5:1). **Brake Horsepower:** 61 at 5600 rpm (later 58 at 5200 rpm). **Torque:** 69 lbs.-ft. at 3600 rpm (later 68 at 2400 rpm). Two-barrel carburetor.

CHASSIS DATA: **Wheelbase:** 96.7 in. except (4WD wagon) 96.1 in. **Overall Length:** (cpe/sed) 164.4 in.; (wag) 165.2 in.; (4WD wag) 158.7 in. **Height:** (cpe) 53.0 in.; (sed) 54.5 in.; (wag) 55.9 in.; (4WD wag) 57.5 in. **Width:** 59.2 in. **Front Tread:** 50.2 in. except (4WD wag) 49.4 in. **Rear Tread:** (cpe/sed) 48 in.; (wag) 47.8 in.; (4WD wag) 47.4 in. **Standard Tires:** 6.15x13 or 155SR13.

TECHNICAL: **Layout:** front-engine, front-drive. **Transmission:** four-speed manual (five-speed and automatic available by 1975). **Steering:** rack and pinion. **Suspension (front):** wishbones with torsion bars (or MacPherson struts with coil springs). **Suspension (rear):** independent with trailing arms and torsion bars. **Brakes:** front/rear drum. **Body Construction:** steel unibody.

Manufacturer: Fuji Heavy Industries Ltd., Tokyo, Japan. **Distributor:** Subaru of America Inc., Pennsauken, New Jersey.

PRODUCTION/SALES: A total of 37,793 Subarus were sold in the U.S. during 1973, followed by 22,980 in 1974, 41,587 in 1975, and 48,928 in 1976.

HISTORY: The 1600 series with a 1595-cc engine debuted in 1976, marketed along with the 1400; see next listing for details.

1977-79 SUBARU

1979 Subaru two-door coupe.

1600 SERIES — FLAT FOUR — After its debut as an option for 1976 models, the larger 1595-cc (97-cid) engine became standard on all Subarus sold in the U.S. for 1977. This came as a response to charges that the smaller engine's performance was too sluggish.

Mechanical details remained the same but styling revisions came for the 1978 model year, including flattened bodysides and the deletion of the deep crease that formerly ran from fender to fender. Park/signal lamps now sat on the outer portion of the fenders, to give a wider look to the car. Also cleaned up was the rear panel, and the taillamps. Inside, the instrument panel was new. The top-of-the-line GF hardtop and the four-wheel-drive wagon now had quad headlamps, along with a revised grille shape.

I.D. DATA: Subaru's 10-symbol serial number is atop the dashboard on the driver's side and on the driver's door pillar post. The first four symbols identify the body style, followed by the sequential production number. Engine number is stamped on the crankcase, behind the distributor.

Model	Body Type & Seating	Engine Type/CID	P.O.E. Price	Weight (lbs.)	Prod. Total
1600 SERIES					
STD	2-dr Sedan-5P	H4/97	2974	1975	Note 1
DL	2-dr Sedan-5P	H4/97	3299	1980	Note 1
DL	4-dr Sedan-5P	H4/97	3499	2030	Note 1
DL	2-dr Coupe-4P	H4/97	3499	2000	Note 1
GF	2-dr HT Cpe-4P	H4/97	3949	2045	Note 1
DL	4-dr Sta Wag-5P	H4/97	3749	2145	Note 1
DL 4WD	4-dr Sta Wag-5P	H4/97	4199	2210	Note 1

Note 1: A total of 155,705 Subarus (all models) were produced during 1977, followed by 140,229 in 1978, and 153,841 in 1979.

Price Note: Figures shown were valid in 1977. In 1978, the four-wheel-drive BRAT sold for $4329.

1979 Subaru DL four-door sedan.

ENGINE DATA: BASE FOUR: Horizontally-opposed, overhead-valve four-cylinder. **Displacement:** 97 cu. in. (1595 cc). **Bore & Stroke:** 3.62 x 2.36 in. (92 x 60 mm). **Compression Ratio:** 8.5:1. **Brake Horsepower:** 67 at 5200 rpm. **Torque:** 81 lbs.-ft. at 2400 rpm. Two-barrel carburetor.

CHASSIS DATA: **Wheelbase:** 96.7 in. except (4WD wagon) 96.1 in. **Overall Length:** (cpe/sed) 164 in.; (wag) 165.2 in.; (4WD wag) 158.7 in. **Height:** (cpe) 53 in.; (sed) 54.5 in.; (wag) 55.9 in.; (4WD wag) 57.5 in. **Width:** 59.1-59.3 in. **Front Tread:** 50.2 in. except (4WD wag) 49.4 in. **Rear Tread:** (cpe/sed) 48 in.; (wag) 47.8 in.; (4WD wag) 47.4 in. **Standard Tires:** 155SR13.

TECHNICAL: **Layout:** front-engine, front-drive. **Transmission:** four- or five-speed manual; automatic available. **Steering:** rack and pinion. **Suspension (front):** MacPherson struts with coil springs. **Suspension (rear):** independent with semi-trailing arms and torsion bars. **Brakes:** front disc, rear drum. **Body Construction:** steel unibody.

PRODUCTION/SALES: A total of 80,826 Subarus were sold in the U.S. during 1977, followed by 103,274 in 1978, and 127,871 in 1979.

ADDITIONAL MODELS: Subaru introduced the four-wheel-drive BRAT to the U.S. market for 1978, styled like a miniature pickup truck but with two rear-facing seats in the "bed." The curious choice of a name was actually an acronym for Bi-drive Recreational All-Terrain Transporter.

Manufacturer: Fuji Heavy Industries Ltd., Tokyo, Japan. **Distributor:** Subaru of America Inc., Pennsauken, New Jersey.

HISTORY: Subaru's slogan during this period was: "Inexpensive, and built to stay that way."

1980-84 SUBARU

1600/1800 SERIES — FLAT FOUR — Subarus were fully redesigned for 1980, to give a more European look. Clean, contemporary lines were compared by some to the Honda Accord. In addition to sedans and station wagons, and a hardtop coupe, two-door hatchbacks were available. Only the BRAT multi-purpose four-wheel-drive vehicle kept the old appearance. A larger (1781-cc) engine became available, joining the former 1595-cc horizontally-opposed four. In addition, hatchbacks and wagons were available with either front-drive or four-wheel drive. Options (depending on model) included air conditioning, a five-speed manual gearbox, and an automatic transmission. After 1981, the bigger engine became standard on wagons and GL models. A turbocharged version of the 1.8-liter engine was available in the 4WD wagon for 1983, and in the 4WD sedan the next year. By 1984, all Subarus could have four-wheel drive.

I.D. DATA: Subaru's 17-symbol Vehicle Identification Number is atop the left side of the instrument panel, visible through the windshield.

Model	Body Type & Seating	Engine Type/CID	P.O.E. Price	Weight (lbs.)	Prod. Total
1600/1800 SERIES					
STD	2-dr Hatch-4P	H4/97	3999	2020	Note 1
STD 4WD	2-dr Hatch-4P	H4/97	4799	2155	Note 1
DL	2-dr Hatch-4P	H4/97	4749	2035	Note 1
DL 4WD	2-dr Hatch-4P	H4/97	5399	2170	Note 1
DL	4-dr Sedan-4/5P	H4/97	4899	2070	Note 1
DL	2-dr HT Cpe-4P	H4/97	5099	2060	Note 1
DL	4-dr Sta Wag-4/5P	H4/97	5149	2185	Note 1
DL 4WD	4-dr Sta Wag-4/5P	H4/97	5899	2305	Note 1
GL	4-dr Sedan-4/5P	H4/97	5249	2125	Note 1
GL	4-dr Sta Wag-4/5P	H4/97	5499	2225	Note 1
GL 4WD	4-dr Sta Wag-4/5P	H4/97	6149	2310	Note 1
GLF	2-dr HT Cpe-4P	H4/97	5449	2115	Note 1

Note 1: A total of 202,038 Subarus (all models) were produced during 5449 1980, followed by 190,451 in 1981, and 201,388 in 1982.

Price Note: Figures shown were valid in 1980. In that year, the four-wheel-drive BRAT sold for $5299 in DL trim, or $5599 as a GL.

ENGINE DATA: BASE FOUR: Horizontally-opposed, overhead-valve four-cylinder. **Displacement:** 97 cu. in. (1595 cc). **Bore & Stroke:** 3.62 x 2.36 in. (92 x 60 mm). **Compression Ratio:** 8.5:1. **Brake Horsepower:** 67 at 5200 rpm. **Torque:** 81 lbs.-ft. at 2400 rpm. Two-barrel carburetor.

OPTIONAL FOUR: Horizontally-opposed, overhead-valve four-cylinder. **Displacement:** 109 cu. in. (1781 cc). **Bore & Stroke:** 3.62 x 2.64 in. (92 x 67 mm). **Compression Ratio:** 8.7:1. **Brake Horsepower:** 72 at 4800 rpm. **Torque:** 92 lbs.-ft. at 2400 rpm. Two-barrel carburetor.

Turbo Note: A turbocharged version of the 1781-cc engine, rated 95 bhp, was available in 1983-84.

CHASSIS DATA: Wheelbase: 96.9 in. except (hatch) 93.7 in.; (wagon) 96.7 in. **Overall Length:** (cpe/sed) 168.1 in.; (hatch) 156.9 in.; (wag) 168.3 in. **Height:** (cpe) 53.2 in.; (hatch/sed) 53.7 in.; (wag) 54.7 in. **Width:** 63.4-63.6 in. **Front Tread:** 52.4 in. except (wag) 52.2 in. **Rear Tread:** 53 in.

TECHNICAL: Layout: front-engine, front-drive or four-wheel drive. **Transmission:** four- or five-speed manual; automatic available. **Steering:** rack and pinion. **Suspension (front):** MacPherson struts with coil springs. **Suspension (rear):** independent with semi-trailing arms and torsion bars. **Brakes:** front disc, rear drum. **Body Construction:** steel unibody.

PRODUCTION/SALES: A total of 142,968 Subarus (including 12,003 BRATS) were sold in the U.S. during 1980, followed by 152,062 (including 5,546 BRATS) in 1981, and 150,335 (including 6,909 BRATS) in 1982.

Manufacturer: Fuji Heavy Industries Ltd., Tokyo, Japan.
Distributor: Subaru of America Inc., Pennsauken, New Jersey.

1985-86 SUBARU

STD/DL/GL — FLAT FOUR — Extensive restyling gave the standard Subaru sedans and wagons a longer look for 1985. Wheelbases grew only slightly, but overall lengths added several inches. Interiors also were roomier, and cargo volume in the station wagon grew by 25 percent. Under most sedan and wagon hoods was a new overhead-cam 1.8-liter engine, still horizontally-opposed. The new engine came with a two-barrel carburetor, port fuel injected, or fuel injected with a turbocharger. Standard hatchbacks continued to use the overhead-valve 1.6-liter engine from the prior generation, and certain other models retained the earlier 1.8-liter version. The four-wheel-drive Turbo sedan had a new computer-controlled air-spring suspension.

XT — FLAT FOUR — A sleek, dramatic new sport coupe joined the Subaru lineup during 1985, with either a conventional or turbocharged engine. The angular, wedge-shaped profile attracted considerable attention.

I.D. DATA: Subaru's 17-symbol Vehicle Identification Number is atop the left side of the instrument panel, visible through the windshield.

Model	Body Type & Seating	Engine Type/CID	P.O.E. Price	Weight (lbs.)	Prod. Total
STD/DL/GL					
STD	2-dr Hatch-4P	H4/97	4989	2050	Note 1
DL	4-dr Sedan-5P	H4/109	7096	2145	Note 1
DL	4-dr Sta Wag-5P	H4/109	7334	2420	Note 1
GL	2-dr Hatch-4P	H4/109	6924	2120	Note 1
GL 4WD	2-dr Hatch-4P	H4/109	7474	2240	Note 1
GL	4-dr Sedan-5P	H4/109	7646	2190	Note 1
GL 4WD	4-dr Sedan-5P	H4/109	9104	2385	Note 1
GL	4-dr Sta Wag-5P	H4/109	7884	2330	Note 1
GL 4WD	4-dr Sta Wag-5P	H4/109	8434	2475	Note 1
TURBO RX/GL					
RX 4WD	4-dr Sedan-5P	H4/109	10743	2510	Note 1
GL 4WD	4-dr Sedan-5P	H4/109	11130	2565	Note 1
XT					
DL	2-dr Coupe-4P	H4/109	7889	2270	Note 1
GL	2-dr Coupe-4P	H4/109	9899	2415	Note 1
4WD Turbo	2-dr Coupe-4P	H4/109	13589	2610	Note 1

Note 1: A total of 178,175 Subarus were sold in the U.S. during 1985, followed by 179,100 in 1986.

Price Note: Figures shown were valid in 1985.

ENGINE DATA: BASE FOUR (STD - Standard): Horizontally-opposed, overhead-valve four-cylinder. **Displacement:** 97 cu. in. (1595 cc). **Bore & Stroke:** 3.62 x 2.36 in. (92 x 60 mm). **Compression Ratio:** 9.0:1. **Brake Horsepower:** 69 at 4800 rpm. **Torque:** 86 lbs.-ft. at 2800 rpm. Two-barrel carburetor.

BASE FOUR (DL): Horizontally-opposed, overhead-valve four-cylinder. **Displacement:** 109 cu. in. (1781 cc). **Bore & Stroke:** 3.62 x 2.64 in. (92 x 67 mm). **Compression Ratio:** 8.7:1. **Brake Horsepower:** 73 at 4400 rpm. **Torque:** 94 lbs.-ft. at 2400 rpm. Two-barrel carburetor.

OPTIONAL FOUR: Horizontally-opposed, overhead-cam four-cylinder. **Displacement:** 109 cu. in. (1781 cc). **Bore & Stroke:** 3.62 x 2.64 in. (92 x 67 mm). **Compression Ratio:** 9.0:1. **Brake Horsepower:** 82 at 4800 rpm. **Torque:** 101 lbs.-ft. at 2800 rpm. Two-barrel carburetor.

OPTIONAL FOUR: Same as overhead-cam four above, except with multi-point fuel injection — **Brake Horsepower:** 94 at 5200 rpm. **Torque:** 101 lbs.-ft. at 2800 rpm.

TURBO FOUR: Same as overhead-cam four above, but with turbocharger and multi-point fuel injection — **Brake Horsepower:** 111 at 4800 rpm. **Torque:** 134 lbs.-ft. at 2800 rpm.

CHASSIS DATA: Wheelbase: (hatch) 93.7 in.; (sedan) 97.2 in.; (wagon) 97.0 in.; (XT cpe) 97.1 in. **Overall Length:** (hatch) 157.9 in.; (sedan) 172.0 in.; (wag) 173.6 in.; (XT cpe) 175.2 in. **Height:** (hatch) 53.7 in.; (sed) 52.5 in.; (wag) 53.0 in.; (XT cpe) 49.4 in. **Width:** (hatch) 63.6 in.; (sed/wag) 65.4 in.; (XT cpe) 66.5 in. **Front Tread:** (hatch) 52.8 in.; (sed) 56.1 in.; (wag) 55.9 in.; (XT cpe) 56.5 in. **Rear Tread:** (hatch) 53.0 in.; (sed/wag) 56.1 in.; (XT cpe) 56.1 in.

TECHNICAL: Layout: front-engine, front-drive or four-wheel drive. **Transmission:** four- or five-speed manual; three-speed automatic and Dual Range manual gearboxes available. **Steering:** rack and pinion. **Suspension (front):** MacPherson struts with coil springs (adjustable air springs on Turbo sedan). **Suspension (rear):** independent with trailing arms and coil springs (torsion bars on hatchback); adjustable air springs on Turbo sedan. **Brakes:** front disc, rear drum except (Turbo) all-disc. **Body Construction:** steel unibody.

Manufacturer: Fuji Heavy Industries Ltd., Tokyo, Japan.
Distributor: Subaru of America Inc., Pennsauken, New Jersey.

1987-89 SUBARU

1988 Subaru XT6 two-door coupe.

JUSTY — THREE — A three-cylinder overhead-cam engine powered the new subcompact Subaru, introduced to the U.S. for the 1987 model year. The 1.2-liter engine developed 66 horsepower. A year later, on-demand four-wheel-drive became available. Early Justys came only with a five-speed manual gearbox, but the 1989 model could have a gearless electronic continuously variable transmission. A system of pulleys were used to vary the ratio of engine speed to drive-wheel speed, following the pattern of the Dutch DAF introduced some three decades earlier. Justy also was restyled for 1989, gaining a more rounded appearance and six inches of overall length.

STD/DL/GL SERIES — FLAT FOUR — Full-time four-wheel drive became available in 1987 on the coupe and sedan, and on the wagon in 1988. Otherwise, production continued without major change. One holdover from the prior generation, the lowest-priced "Standard" hatchback, remained on the market with a 1.6-liter engine for 1987, then switched to 1.8 liters and was called, simply, "hatchback." All others were 1.8-liter, with either overhead-valve or overhead-cam configuration.

XT/XT6 — FLAT FOUR/SIX — Production of the sleek coupe with four-cylinder power continued until 1988, when it was replaced by an XT6 coupe with 2.7-liter six-cylinder engine and electronic power steering.

1989 Subaru 4WD station wagon.

I.D. DATA: Subaru's 17-symbol Vehicle Identification Number is atop the left side of the instrument panel, visible through the windshield.

Model	Body Type & Seating	Engine Type/CID	P.O.E. Price	Weight (lbs.)	Prod. Total
JUSTY					
DL	2-dr Hatch-4P	I3/73	5695	1655	Note 1
GL	2-dr Hatch-4P	I3/73	6595	1675	Note 1
GL 4WD	2-dr Hatch-4P	I3/73	7195	1785	Note 1
RS 4WD	2-dr Hatch-4P	I3/73	7666	1785	Note 1
HATCHBACK					
GL	2-dr Hatch-4P	H4/109	7995	2120	Note 1
GL 4WD	2-dr Hatch-4P	H4/109	8795	2240	Note 1
DL/GL					
DL	2-dr Hatch-5P	H4/109	9295	2260	Note 1
DL	4-dr Sedan-5P	H4/109	8995	2220	Note 1
DL	4-dr Sta Wag-5P	H4/109	9595	2350	Note 1
DL 4WD	4-dr Sta Wag-5P	H4/109	9995	2510	Note 1
GL	2-dr Hatch-5P	H4/109	10695	2325	Note 1
GL 4WD	2-dr Hatch-5P	H4/109	11395	2475	Note 1
GL	4-dr Sedan-5P	H4/109	10395	2270	Note 1
GL 4WD	4-dr Sedan-5P	H4/109	11095	2425	Note 1
GL	4-dr Sta Wag-5P	H4/109	10995	2420	Note 1
GL 4WD	4-dr Sta Wag-5P	H4/109	11695	2580	Note 1
TURBO RX					
RX 4WD	2-dr Hatch-5P	H4/109	14995	2615	Note 1
RX 4WD	4-dr Sedan-5P	H4/109	14995	2615	Note 1
XT					
DL	2-dr Coupe-4P	H4/109	10195	2375	Note 1
GL	2-dr Coupe-4P	H4/109	12195	2435	Note 1
GL 4WD	2-dr Coupe-4P	H4/109	12895	2625	Note 1
XT6 (1988-up)					
	2-dr Coupe-4P	H6/163	16995	2795	Note 1
4WD	2-dr Coupe-4P	H6/163	17745	2865	Note 1

Note 1: A total of 175,864 Subarus were sold in the U.S. during 1987, followed by 155,946 in 1988, and 136,111 in 1989.

Price Note: Figures shown were valid in 1988.

ENGINE DATA: BASE THREE (Justy): Inline, overhead-cam three-cylinder. **Displacement:** 73 cu. in. (1189 cc). **Bore & Stroke:** 3.07 x 3.27 in. (78 x 83 mm). **Compression Ratio:** 9.1:1. **Brake Horsepower:** 66 at 5200 rpm. **Torque:** 70 lbs.-ft. at 3600 rpm. Two-barrel carburetor.

BASE FOUR (1987 Standard Hatchback): Horizontally-opposed, overhead-valve four-cylinder. **Displacement:** 97 cu. in. (1595 cc). **Bore & Stroke:** 3.62 x 2.36 in. (92 x 60 mm). **Compression Ratio:** 9.0:1. **Brake Horsepower:** 69 at 4800 rpm. **Torque:** 86 lbs.-ft. at 2800 rpm. Two-barrel carburetor.

BASE FOUR (DL): Horizontally-opposed, overhead-valve four-cylinder. **Displacement:** 109 cu. in. (1781 cc). **Bore & Stroke:** 3.62 x 2.64 in. (92 x 67 mm). **Compression Ratio:** 8.7:1. **Brake Horsepower:** 73 at 4400 rpm. **Torque:** 94 lbs.-ft. at 2400 rpm. Two-barrel carburetor.

OPTIONAL FOUR: Horizontally-opposed, overhead-cam four-cylinder. **Displacement:** 109 cu. in. (1781 cc). **Bore & Stroke:** 3.62 x 2.64 in. (92 x 67 mm). **Compression Ratio:** 9.0:1. **Brake Horsepower:** 84 at 5200 rpm. **Torque:** 101 lbs.-ft. at 3200 rpm. Two-barrel carburetor.

OPTIONAL FOUR: Same as overhead-cam four above, except with multi-point fuel injection — **Brake Horsepower:** 90 at 5200 rpm. **Torque:** 101 lbs.-ft. at 2800 rpm.

TURBO FOUR: Same as overhead-cam four above, but with turbocharger and multi-point fuel injection — **Brake Horsepower:** 115 at 5200 rpm. **Torque:** 134 lbs.-ft. at 2800 rpm.

BASE SIX (XT6): Horizontally-opposed, overhead-cam six-cylinder. **Displacement:** 163 cu. in. (2672 cc). **Bore & Stroke:** 3.62 x 2.64 in. (92 x 67 mm). **Compression Ratio:** 9.5:1. **Brake Horsepower:** 145 at 5200 rpm. **Torque:** 156 lbs.-ft. at 4000 rpm. Multi-point fuel injection.

CHASSIS DATA: Wheelbase: (Justy) 90.0 in.; (std hatch) 93.7 in.; (hatch/sed/wag) 97.2 in.; (XT cpe) 97.1 in. **Overall Length:** (early Justy) 139.1 in.; (1989 Justy) 145.5 in.; (std hatch) 156.9 in.; (hatch/sed) 174.6 in.; (wag) 176.8 in.; (XT cpe) 175.2 in. **Height:** (early Justy) 54.7 in.; (1989 Justy) 55.9 in.; (std hatch) 53.7 in.; (hatch) 51.8 in.; (sed) 52.5 in.; (wag) 53.0 in.; (XT cpe) 49.4 in. **Width:** (Justy) 60.4 in.; (std hatch) 63.4 in.; (hatch/sed/wag) 65.4 in.; (XT cpe) 66.5 in. **Front Tread:** (Justy) 52.4 in.; (std hatch) 52.8 in.; (hatch/sed) 56.1 in.; (wag) 55.9 in.; (XT cpe) 56.5 in. **Rear Tread:** (Justy) 50.8 in.; (std hatch) 53.0 in.; (hatch/sed/wag) 56.1 in.; (XT cpe) 56.1 in.

TECHNICAL: Layout: front-engine, front-drive or four-wheel drive. **Transmission:** four- or five-speed manual; three-speed automatic available except (Justy) five-speed manual or, in 1989, ECVT gearless unit. **Steering:** rack and pinion. **Suspension (front):** MacPherson struts with coil springs. **Suspension (rear):** independent with trailing arms and coil springs (torsion bars on standard hatchback). **Brakes:** front disc, rear drum except (Turbo) all-disc. **Body Construction:** steel unibody.

Manufacturer: Fuji Heavy Industries Ltd., Tokyo, Japan.

Distributor: Subaru of America Inc., Cherry Hill, New Jersey.

1990 Subaru Justy five-door.

Subaru kept two of its existing models, renamed one of them, and introduced a new one for the 1990 model year. A four-door hatchback joined the original two-door in the Justy lineup, and the 1.2-liter three-liter engine acquired fuel injecton (except in the base model, which retained the carbureted version). Fuel-injection added 7 horsepower to the engine's output: 73 bhp versus 66 for the carbureted edition. The optional electronic continuously variable transmission was now available on Justys with front-drive or four-wheel-drive, though a five-speed manual gearbox remained standard. Little was changed in the XT/XT6 coupe, except that the four-cylinder version no longer was available with four-wheel-drive.

The existing subcompact sedan, wagon and three-door hatchback coupe remained in the lineup, but under the Loyale nameplate. The prior DL, GL and GL-10 designations were dropped, leaving only a single trim level. Under the hood was the same overhead-cam flat-four engine, rated 90 horsepower; or a turbocharged version rated 115 bhp. All body styles were available with front-drive, on-demand four-wheel-drive, or permanent 4WD.

A new Legacy series was introduced as an early 1990 model, in four-door sedan and station-wagon form. More luxurious than the Loyale models, they rode a longer wheelbase (101.6 inches versus 97.2 inches) and could be categorized as compacts rather than subcompacts. They also carried a bigger horizontally-opposed engine. The new 2.2-liter overhead-cam flat four developed 130 horsepoer at 5400 rpm, using multi-point fuel injection. Either a five-speed manual or four-speed automatic transmission was available, and four-wheel disc brakes were standard. Some Legacy sedans were manufactured in Lafayette, Indiana rather than in Japan, as part of joint venture between Subaru and Isuzu.

1990 Subaru Loyale station wagon.

POSTSCRIPT: For the 1992 model year, Subaru introduced a dramatically-styled (some called it bizarre) coupe to replace the XT and XT6, known as the SVX. Its most noticed feature was a "window-within-a-window," which allowed the driver to lower a segment of glass while leaving the major portion in place. Wheelbase was .4 inches longer than the XT. All of the coupes came with permanent four-wheel-drive. Power came from a 3.3-liter flat six, rated 230 horsepower. A driver's airbag and anti-lock brakes were standard.

1990 SUBARU

1990 Subaru Legacy L four-door sedan.

SUNBEAM & SUNBEAM-TALBOT

John Marston's business in late 19th-century Great Britain was metal lacquering. His avocation was cycling. Thus, in 1887 he formed the Sunbeamland Cycle Factory, at Wolverhampton. That evolved in 1895 to John Marston Ltd. and, in 1899, the company's first prototype automobile came out of the shop.

A two-cylinder vehicle followed in 1901, soon leading to the first production models. Known as Sunbeam Mabley

Voiturettes, they were of unconventional layout, with the wheels arranged in a diamond-shaped pattern (claimed to be skidproof) and passengers facing the outside. A De Dion engine was used. A more conventional chain-drive 12-hp model also was produced, with four-cylinder engine, marketed under the Sunbeam name starting in 1903. A six-cylinder car was produced in 1904, but didn't last long. Instead, the company turned mainly to T-head four-cylinder powerplants for a time.

A separate company was formed in 1905: Sunbeam Motor Car Co. Ltd. By 1909, Sunbeam offered a selection of L-head four-cylinder models, still with chain drive. Then came a T-head 14/18-hp model available with either chain or shaft drive. Sunbeam had become involved in racing during these early years, which helped the firm's bottom line. So did production of ambulances during World War I, as well as aircraft and marine engines.

Peacetime found Sunbeam turning out two models: a four-cylinder 16/40 (evolved from the prewar 12/16) and a six-cylinder 24-hp, the latter with a 4.5-liter engine. Sunbeam joined with Talbot and Darracq in 1920, to form a group known as STD Motors Ltd. The familiar 16- and 24-hp models were redesigned by 1922 with overhead-valve engines. Some of Sunbeam's sport/touring models of the 1920s carried overhead-cam engines obtained from Talbot. By 1927, too, Sunbeams set the world land speed record on five separate occasions. Sunbeam offered a straight-eight engine in 1926, which grew from 4.8 liters to 5.4 liters by the time it dropped out at the end of the decade. Four-cylinder models were eliminated after 1927, leaving Sunbeam to focus on sixes.

Hydraulic brakes and radiator shutters were added in 1931. At that time, the 16-hp model grew to 2193-cc, while the 20-hp engine displaced 3.3 liters. Synchromesh arrived in 1933, as did a Speed Model 20 with 2.9-liter engine (and non-synchro gearbox). The only four-cylinder model was the Dawn of 1934-35, with a 1627-cc engine that lacked power. Sunbeam ceased to exist as an independent company after 1935, as the STD (Sunbeam-Talbot-Darracq) combine failed and went into receivership. Rootes then purchased what was left of Sunbeam.

By 1938, several upscale and sporting variants of Rootes' Hillman Minx and Humber Super Snipe were on the market, under the Sunbeam-Talbot nameplate, with 1.2-liter (Ten) and 3.2-liter engines, respectively. Thus, little remained of the Sunbeam tradition that had risen in the 1920s and early '30s. A new company was formed for this venture: Sunbeam-Talbot Ltd. A 2-Litre model also debuted under this new name, and reappeared—along with the Ten—after World War II. Those two were produced into 1948, then followed by the Sunbeam-Talbot 80 and 90 saloons and drophead coupes.

With an 1185-cc engine, the type 80 lasted only until 1950, but the 90's engine grew from 1944 to 2267 cc. That car (and engine) formed the basis for the Alpine two-seat sports car, introduced in 1953. Because early postwar cars had been marketed as Sunbeams in France (so Sunbeam-Talbot wouldn't be confused with the Talbot-Lago), the Talbot suffix was dropped for the sports car. So too did the 90 saloons and dropheads become, simply, Sunbeam Mk III. Sunbeam-Talbot Ltd. remained the corporate name until 1970, however, with cars built at Ryton-on-Dunsmore, in Warwickshire.

Another Sunbeam joined for 1956: the Hillman Minx-based Rapier sedan. In fact, a variety of sporty variants of Hillmans wound up with Sunbeam nameplates over the next decade.

The original Alpine lasted only into 1955, but was revived for a completely different sports car introduced during 1959, featuring unibody construction. Beneath that car's handsome surface lurked, surprisingly, a Hillman Husky chassis and Rapier mechanical components, including the 1494- and 1592-cc engines. By the mid-1960s, an all-synchro manual gearbox and an automatic transmission were available on Alpines, and the engine grew to 1725-cc displacement for its final incarnation as the Alpine V.

Meanwhile, the folks at Sunbeam had another idea: pop an American V-8 under the hood of an Alpine, and call it the Tiger. Despite the fact that the Rootes Group was closely allied with Chrysler, this swift two-seat machine carried a 4261-cc (260-cid) Ford V-8 or, later, a 289-cid V-8, along with rack-and-pinion steering. Also marketed in the U.S. was a Sunbeam version of Hillman's Imp.

A new Rapier appeared in 1968, based on the Hillman Hunter with a fastback body said to have been inspired by the Plymouth Barracuda. The Alpine dropped out that year, and Sunbeams quickly disappeared from the American market. Chrysler took over the company by 1970, and the Sunbeam name lingered on for a time on those Rapier fastbacks, built through 1976.

1945-48 SUNBEAM-TALBOT

TEN — FOUR — Produced as a saloon (sedan) and drophead coupe, the Sunbeam-Talbot Ten was based in the Hillman Minx. About 4,000 Tens were built from 1945-48 (plus about 7,000 before World War II). Styling was in the prewar mode, on a 94-inch wheelbase, with fender-mounted headlamps and an upright profile. An L-head 1185-cc engine with Stromberg carburetor developed 41 horsepower, via 6.8:1 compression. Tires were 5.25x16 size. A Sunbeam-Talbot was capable of 68 mph.

2-LITRE — FOUR — Close kin to the Hillman 14, the Sunbeam-Talbot 2-Litre came in saloon and drophead coupe body styles. A total of 1,124 were built from 1945-48. A 1944-cc L-head four-cylinder engine produced 56 horsepower at 3800 rpm, on 6.4:1 compression. Wheelbase was 97.5 inches, and the 2-Litre measured close to 160 inches long. Top speed was 72 mph.

Note: The Sunbeam-Talbot 80 and 90 became available in mid-1948 to replace the Ten and 2-Litre; see next listing for details.

1949-50 SUNBEAM-TALBOT

80 — FOUR — An overhead-valve engine went into the replacement for the Sunbeam-Talbot Ten, which remained in production only into 1950. The L-head engines were abandoned. Displacing 1185 cc (72.3 cid), the four-cylinder engine developed 47 horsepower at 4800 rpm, using 6.88:1 compression. A column-mounted gearshift operated the four-speed transmission. Semi-elliptic springs were used at both front and rear, as on prior models. The all-steel body was all new and far more streamlined, with headlamps built low into fenders, and a curved one-piece windshield and rear window. A painted center grille was made up of vertical chrome strips. Front fender lines swept downward into the front doors. Door pillars sat farther back than before. Both a saloon and drophead (convertible) coupe were available, with rear fender skirts standard.

90 — FOUR — A larger engine went into the 90 series, but the body was the same as the Sunbeam-Talbot 80. Whereas the 80 was not destined to remain for long, the series 90 would evolve into Mk II and Mk IIA editions through 1954; and then into the Sunbeam Mk III. Displacement was 1944 cc (118.6 cid), and the engine yielded 64 horsepower at 4100 rpm, via 6.59:1 compression.

I.D. DATA: Serial number is on a plate on the firewall, under the hood. Engine number is on the left side of the block. Starting serial number: (1949) 3800001; (1950) 3801501.

Model	Body Type & Seating	Engine Type/CID	P.O.E. Price	Weight (lbs.)	Prod. Total
80					
Mk I	4-dr Sedan-4P	I4/72	N/A	2520	Note 1
Mk I	2-dr Conv Cpe-4P	I4/72	N/A	N/A	Note 1
90					
90	4-dr Sedan-4P	I4/119	2995	2723	Note 1
90	2-dr Conv Cpe-4P	I4/119	3345	2660	Note 1

Note 1: Approximately 17 Sunbeam-Talbots were sold in the U.S. during 1949, followed by 120 in 1950. Only the series 90 was ordinarily imported into the U.S.

Price Note: Figures shown were valid in 1949; prices for the Sunbeam-Talbot dropped to $2395 and $2695 in 1950.

ENGINE DATA: BASE FOUR (80): Inline, overhead-valve four-cylinder. **Displacement:** 72.3 cu. in. (1185 cc). **Bore & Stroke:** 2.48 x 3.74 in. (63 x 95 mm). **Compression Ratio:** 6.88:1. **Brake Horsepower:** 47 at 4800 rpm. Solid valve lifters. One Stromberg carburetor.

BASE FOUR (90): Inline, overhead-valve four-cylinder. **Displacement:** 118.6 cu. in. (1944 cc). **Bore & Stroke:** 2.95 x 4.33 in. (75 x 110 mm). **Compression Ratio:** 6.59:1. **Brake Horsepower:** 64 at 4100 rpm. Three main bearings. Solid valve lifters. One Stromberg downdraft carburetor.

CHASSIS DATA: Wheelbase: 97.5 in. Overall Length: 167.5 in. Height: (sed) 60.75 in.; (conv) 59 in. Width: 62.5 in. Front Tread: 47.5 in. Rear Tread: 50.5 in. Standard Tires: 5.50x16.

TECHNICAL: Layout: front-engine, rear-drive. Transmission: four-speed manual. Standard Final Drive Ratio: (80) 5.22:1; (90) 4.3:1. Steering: Suspension (front): rigid axle with semi-elliptic leaf springs. Suspension (rear): rigid axle with semi-elliptic leaf springs. Brakes: front/rear drum. Body Construction: steel body on steel frame.

PERFORMANCE: Top Speed: (80) near 73 mph; (90) near 77 mph. Acceleration (quarter-mile): (80) 24.4 sec.; (90) 23.1 sec.

Manufacturer: Sunbeam-Talbot Ltd., Ryton-on-Dunsmore, Warwickshire, England (part of Rootes Group).

1951-52 SUNBEAM-TALBOT

90 — Mk II — FOUR — An independent front suspension with coil springs was installed in the modification of the Sunbeam-Talbot 90, again offered in saloon (sedan) and drophead coupe (convertible) form. Engine displacement grew to 2267 cc (138 cid), with 6.45:1 compression and a rating of 70 horsepower at 4000 rpm. Auxiliary side grilles contained horizontal strips, with parking lights below the headlamps. Sunbeam-Talbot literature claimed a top speed of 90 mph for the series 90. Synchromatic column shift was used, and both right and left hand steering were available. Standard equipment included two sunvisors (passenger one with a vanity mirror); an electric clock neatly faired into the top screen rail; plus a tray of fitted tools in the luggage compartment lid, in a rattle-proof felt lining. Standard colors were: Sapphire Blue, Beech Green or Black with light fawn upholstery; Gun with grey upholstery; Black, Alpine Mist or Satin Bronze with bright red upholstery. Options included a heater and "His Master's Voice" radio.

I.D. DATA: Serial number is on a plate on the firewall, under the hood. Engine number is on the left side of the block. Starting serial number: (1951) A3000001; (1952) A3000180. Vehicles registered in the U.S. after December 1, 1951 were considered 1952 models.

Model 90	Body Type & Seating	Engine Type/CID	P.O.E. Price	Weight (lbs.)	Prod. Total
Mk II	4-dr Sedan-4P	I4/138	2395	2807	Note 1
Mk II	2-dr Conv Cpe-4P	I4/138	2645	2744	Note 1

Note 1: Approximately 133 Sunbeam-Talbots were sold in the U.S. during 1951, followed by 281 in 1952 and 809 in 1953.

Price Note: Figures shown were valid in 1951. Prices rose to $2685 and $2911 in 1952.

ENGINE DATA: BASE FOUR: Inline, overhead-valve four-cylinder. Displacement: 138.2 cu. in. (2267 cc). Bore & Stroke: 3.19 x 4.33 in. (81 x 110 mm). Compression Ratio: 6.45:1. Brake Horsepower: 70 at 4000 rpm. Three main bearings. Solid valve lifters. One Stromberg downdraft carburetor.

CHASSIS DATA: Wheelbase: 97.5 in. Overall Length: 167.5 in. Height: (sed) 60.75 in.; (conv) 59 in. Width: 62.5 in. Front Tread: 47.5 in. Rear Tread: 50.5 in. Standard Tires: 5.50x16.

TECHNICAL: Layout: front-engine, rear-drive. Transmission: four-speed manual (column lever). Overall gear ratios: (1st) 12.43:1 or 13.905:1; (2nd) 9.633:1; (3rd) 5.811:1; (4th) 3.90:1. Standard Final Drive Ratio: 3.90:1. Steering: Burman variable-ratio. Suspension (front): coil springs with torsion bar. Suspension (rear): rigid axle with semi-elliptic leaf springs and transverse stabilizer. Brakes: hydraulic, front/rear drum. Body Construction: steel body on box-section steel frame.

PERFORMANCE: Top Speed: 90 mph claimed; (conv) 84 mph in test. Acceleration (0-60 mph): (conv) 21.8 sec. Acceleration (quarter-mile): about 22.4 sec.

Manufacturer: Sunbeam-Talbot Ltd., Ryton-on-Dunsmore, Warwickshire, England (part of Rootes Group).

Distributor: Rootes Motors Inc.; New York and Long Island City, New York; Beverly Hills and San Francisco, California.

HISTORY: Sales brochures advised that a Sunbeam had been the first car to exceed 200 mph; and Talbot, the first to cover 100 miles in an hour. Sunbeam-Talbots also had been winners in the international Alpine rallies, in 1948, 1949, 1950 and 1952. Count Kolaczkowski won the Fidelity Prize at the 1952 Alpine rally in a Sunbeam-Talbot, while the race was won by G. Murray-Frame of the factory team. Two other Sunbeam-Talbots took second and third place.

1953-54 SUNBEAM-TALBOT/SUNBEAM

1954 Sunbeam Talbot Alpine roadster.

90 — Mk IIA — FOUR — The next evolution of the 90 series enjoyed some technical advances, including a heavier clutch, improved carburetion, revised transmission ratios, and restyled vented (perforated) wheels to improve brake cooling. Braking area was 27 percent larger. Rear fender skirts were deleted. Top speed was near 90 mph, with average fuel economy of 25 mpg claimed. As before, this Sunbeam-Talbot had a narrow vertical-bar grille. Two small auxiliary grilles contained horizontal bars, and tiny round parking lights sat below the headlamps.

ALPINE — Mk IIA/III — FOUR — A two-seat sport roadster joined the Sunbeam-Talbot sedan and drophead coupe, taking the Alpine designation. Styling features included a louvered hood and a sizable trunk, with exposed hinges on its lid. The Alpine had a vertical-bar grille and auxiliary side grilles, with tiny parking lights at outboard tips of the fenders. The 2267-cc engine had a special cylinder high-compression cylinder head (7.4:1) with enlarged and polished intake ports. Initial output was 77 horsepower, raised to 80 bhp by the Mk III edition. A hand-controlled override for the automatic ignition was installed. Synchromatic fingertip gearchange operated a close-ratio gearbox. Inside were contour-correct individual bucket seats, with the cockpit surround finished in padded leather. Detachable side windows included sliding panes, and doors lacked outside handles. A full range of options included plastic racing windshields and "Plus Performance Kits" for competition, as well as a heater, radio, cockpit cover, tachometer, badge bar, outside mirror, and windshield washer. Standard colors were: Alpine Mist or Ivory with bright red upholstery; Coronation Red or Sapphire Blue with light fawn upholstery. Wheels were finished in body color, except for Ivory body which came with bright red wheels.

Note: The sport roadster was marketed under the Sunbeam name, omitting the -Talbot suffix.

1954 Sunbeam Talbot 90 Mark II A four-door saloon.

I.D. DATA: Serial number is on a plate on the firewall, under the hood. Engine number is on the left side of the block. Starting serial number: (1953 models) A3009809; (1954 90) A3010015; (1954 Alpine) 3012468.

Model	Body Type & Seating	Engine Type/CID	P.O.E. Price	Weight (lbs.)	Prod. Total
SUNBEAM-TALBOT 90					
Mk IIA	4-dr Sedan-4P	I4/138	2699	2856	Note 1
Mk IIA	2-dr Conv Cpe-4P	I4/138	2899	2856	Note 1
SUNBEAM ALPINE					
Mk IIA	2-dr Spt Rds-2P	I4/138	2899	2848	Note 1

Note 1: Approximately 809 Sunbeam-Talbots were sold in the U.S. during 1953, followed by 553 in 1954.

ENGINE DATA: BASE FOUR (90): Inline, overhead-valve four-cylinder. Displacement: 138.2 cu. in. (2267 cc). Bore & Stroke: 3.19 x 4.33 in. (81 x 110 mm). Compression Ratio: 6.45:1. Brake Horsepower: 70 at 4000 rpm. Three main bearings. Solid valve lifters. One Stromberg downdraft carburetor.

BASE FOUR (Alpine); OPTIONAL (90): Same as above, except — Compression Ratio: 7.4:1. Brake Horsepower: 77 at 4200 rpm.

Note: By 1954, output of Alpine engine was given as 80 bhp.

CHASSIS DATA: Wheelbase: 97.5 in. Overall Length: (90) 167.5 in.; (Alpine) 168.25 in. Height: (90 sed) 60.75 in.; (90 conv) 59 in. Width: 62.5 in. Front Tread: 47.5 in. Rear Tread: 50.5 in. Standard Tires: 5.50x16.

TECHNICAL: Layout: front-engine, rear-drive. Transmission: four-speed manual (column lever). Overall Alpine (close-ratio) gear ratios: (1st) 11.04:1; (2nd) 8.54:1; (3rd) 5.19:1; (4th) 3.90:1; (rev) 13.96:1. Standard Final Drive Ratio: 3.90:1 (4.22:1 available on Alpine). Steering: Burman variable-ratio. Suspension (front): coil springs with torsion bar. Suspension (rear): rigid axle with semi-elliptic leaf springs and transverse stabilizer. Brakes: hydraulic, front/rear drum. Body Construction: steel body on box-section steel frame.

PERFORMANCE: Top Speed: (90) about 93 mph; (Alpine) about 95 mph. Acceleration (quarter-mile): (Alpine) 21.1 sec. (British test).

Manufacturer: Sunbeam-Talbot Ltd., Ryton-on-Dunsmore, Warwickshire, England (part of Rootes Group).

Distributor: Rootes Motors Inc.; New York and Long Island City, New York; Beverly Hills and San Francisco, California.

HISTORY: An American ad early in 1953 referred to the Alpine Sports roadster as the "new queen among sports cars," which was "Bred in the Alps." Another advised readers to "Drive a Sunbeam...and leave others in the shade." Motor Trend called the Alpine more of a "touring car" than a sports car. Sheila Von Damm was the first woman to hit 120 mph in a production sports car, driving a Sunbeam on the track at Jabbeke, Belgium.

1955 SUNBEAM

Mk III — FOUR — The Sunbeam-Talbot 90 evolved into the Mk III, dropping the -Talbot suffix in the process. Production of the drophead (convertible) coupe lasted only through 1955, but the sedan hung on into 1956. In this final form, the 2267-cc engine developed 80 horsepower (like the Alpine), with a slight compression increase to 7.5:1; and top speed was claimed at 95 mph. Laycock de Normanville overdrive was a new option. Again available with either right- or left-hand drive, the steering wheel was almost vertical and framed all essential instruments. Restyling of the sport sedan included a chromed air intake grille embracing the side lamps. Three distinctive chrome air vents sat on each side of the hood, to aid engine cooling at high speeds. Two-speed automatic-parking windshield wipers were installed. Standard colors were: Black, Light Gun or Alpine Mist with bright red upholstery; Black or Sapphire Blue with french grey upholstery; Crystal Green with light green upholstery. Options included a radio, tachometer, ignition override and foglamp controls, whitewall tires, and bumper overriders.

ALPINE — Mk III — FOUR — Production of the Alpine roadster continued through 1955, with the same 80-bhp engine used in the Mk III sedan and convertible. See previous listing for additional details.

I.D. DATA: Serial number is on a plate on the firewall, under the hood. Engine number is on the left side of the block. Starting serial number: A3500001.

Model	Body Type & Seating	Engine Type/CID	P.O.E. Price	Weight (lbs.)	Prod. Total
Mk III	4-dr Sedan-4P	I4/138	2675	2924	N/A
Mk III	2-dr Conv Cpe-4P	I4/138	2899	2924	N/A
ALPINE					
Mk III	2-dr Spt Rds-2P	I4/138	2699	2800	N/A

Price Note: Overdrive cost $154 extra on U.S. models.

ENGINE DATA: BASE FOUR: Inline, overhead-valve four-cylinder. **Displacement:** 138.2 cu. in. (2267 cc). **Bore & Stroke:** 3.19 x 4.33 in. (81 x 110 mm). **Compression Ratio:** 7.5:1. **Brake Horsepower:** 80 at 4400 rpm. Three main bearings. Solid valve lifters. One Stromberg downdraft carburetor.

CHASSIS DATA: Wheelbase: 97.5 in. **Overall Length:** (sed/conv) 168 in.; (Alpine) 168.25 in. **Width:** 62.5 in. **Front Tread:** 47.5 in. **Rear Tread:** 50.5 in. **Standard Tires:** 5.50x16.

TECHNICAL: Layout: front-engine, rear-drive. **Transmission:** four-speed manual (column lever). Overall sed/conv gear ratios: (1st) 12.43:1; (2nd) 9.633:1; (3rd) 5.811:1; (4th) 3.90:1; (rev) 15.74:1. Overall Alpine (close-ratio) gear ratios: (1st) 11.04:1; (2nd) 8.54:1; (3rd) 5.19:1; (4th) 3.90:1; (rev) 13.96:1. **Standard Final Drive Ratio:** 3.90:1 (4.22:1 available on Alpine). **Steering:** Burman variable-ratio. **Suspension (front):** coil springs with torsion bar. **Suspension (rear):** rigid axle with semi-elliptic leaf springs and transverse stabilizer. **Brakes:** hydraulic, front/rear drum. **Body Construction:** steel body on box-section steel frame.

PERFORMANCE: Top Speed: (Mk III sed) 95 mph claimed; (Alpine) about 95 mph. **Acceleration (quarter-mile):** (Mk III sed) 21.2 sec. (British test).

Manufacturer: Sunbeam-Talbot Ltd., Ryton-on-Dunsmore, Warwickshire, England (part of Rootes Group).

Distributor: Rootes Motors Inc.; New York and Long Island City, New York; Beverly Hills and San Francisco, California.

HISTORY: Production of the Mk III sedan continued through 1956, but the convertible coupe and Alpine roadster dropped out after 1955. However, both continued to be listed in some directories of imported models.

---

valve engine developed 62 horsepower, which was sufficient for a claimed top speed of 90 mph. An R67 dual-carbureted engine was rated 67 bhp to give "more zip." Standard overdrive operated on top and 3rd gears. Inside the Rapier were pendant-type pedals, a hydraulically-assisted clutch, and ignition key starter. Whitewalls, radio, heater, tachometer, clock, and bumper overriders were optional.

RAPIER — II — FOUR — A larger (1494-cc) Rally-Master engine went into the Rapier III, which debuted during 1958 with a 73-bhp rating. Styling revisions including the use of a European version of tailfins, claimed to be the first such usage on an imported car. Instead of a cramped, boxy look, the revised Rapier allegedly displayed "sports car sweeping lines finishing in discreetly flared tailfins housing the rear lamp clusters." A new grille added an extra element of rakishness, according to the company. The modified Rapier also was claimed to have lighter steering, bigger brakes, and a "race-bred" front suspension, "to appeal to the appreciative and discriminating driver." Seating was adequate for four (possibly five) adults. The convertible's top could be fully closed, completely opened, or placed in the "coupe de ville" halfway position. A two-door hardtop also was available again. Standard equipment included a large speedometer, tachometer, water temperature, oil pressure and fuel gauges. Ammeter and panel lights, ignition and flashing tail indicators, all set in a padded dashboard.

I.D. DATA: Serial number is on a plate on the firewall, under the hood. Engine number is on the left side of the block. Starting serial number: (1956) A3600001; (1957) A3603375; (1958) A3800001; (1959) A3802161.

Model	Body Type & Seating	Engine Type/CID	P.O.E. Price	Weight (lbs.)	Prod. Total
RAPIER I (1956-58)					
I	2-dr HT Cpe-4P	I4/85	2499	2280	Note 1
RAPIER II (1958-59)					
II	2-dr HT Cpe-4P	I4/91	2499	2280	Note 1
II	2-dr Conv Cpe-4P	I4/91	2649	2276	Note 1

Note 1: Approximately 749 Sunbeams were sold in the U.S. during 1957.

ENGINE DATA: BASE FOUR (Rapier I): Inline, overhead-valve four-cylinder. **Displacement:** 85 cu. in. (1390 cc). **Bore & Stroke:** 3.00 x 3.00 in. (76.2 x 76.2 mm). **Compression Ratio:** 8.0:1. **Brake Horsepower:** 62 at 5400 rpm. Three main bearings. Solid valve lifters. One Stromberg carburetor.

BASE FOUR (later Rapier I): Same as above, except with two Zenith carburetors — **Brake Horsepower:** 67 at 5400 rpm.

BASE FOUR (Rapier II): Inline, overhead-valve four-cylinder. **Displacement:** 91.2 cu. in. (1494 cc). **Bore & Stroke:** 3.11 x 3.00 in. (79 x 76.2 mm). **Compression Ratio:** 8.5:1. **Brake Horsepower:** 73 at 5200 rpm. Three main bearings. Solid valve lifters. Two Zenith downdraft carburetors.

CHASSIS DATA: Wheelbase: 96 in. **Overall Length:** (I) 160.5 in.; (II) 162 in. **Height:** 58 in. **Width:** 60.75 in. **Front Tread:** 49 in. **Rear Tread:** 48.5 in. **Standard Tires:** 5.60x15.

TECHNICAL: Layout: front-engine, rear-drive. **Transmission:** four-speed manual with overdrive (column lever). Overall Rapier I gear ratios: (1st) 16.642:1; (2nd) 12.633:1; (3rd) 7.788:1; (4th) 5.22:1; (rev) 21.08:1. Overall Rapier II gear ratios: (1st) 14.518:1; (2nd) 11.258:1; (3rd) 6.794:1; (4th) 4.55:1; (rev) 21.08:1. **Standard Final Drive Ratio:** (Rapier I) 5.22:1; (Rapier II) 4.55:1. **Steering:** Burman worm and nut (reciculating ball). **Suspension (front):** coil springs with swinging links. **Suspension (rear):** rigid axle with semi-elliptic leaf springs. **Brakes:** Lockheed hydraulic, front/rear drum. **Body Construction:** steel unibody.

PERFORMANCE: Top Speed: (67-bhp) 85+ mph; (73-bhp) 90-95 mph claimed. **Acceleration (0-60 mph):** (67-bhp) 20.6 sec.; (73-bhp) 17 sec. claimed, 19.6 sec. in test. **Acceleration (quarter-mile):** (67-bhp) 21.3 sec.

Manufacturer: Sunbeam-Talbot Ltd., Ryton-on-Dunsmore, Warwickshire, England (part of Rootes Group).

Distributor: Rootes Motors Inc.; New York City and Los Angeles.

HISTORY: Early American ads billed the Rapier as "the classic car of the future." Advertisements in late 1957 claimed "surging acceleration from zero to sixty miles per hour in under 20 seconds," with "perfect spacing of six gear ratios." The sports convertible debuted in the U.S. at the New York auto show in April 1958. Promotional literature promised "sports-car performance combined with family-style comfort." By that time, Sunbeam had more than 700 dealers in North America.

1956-59 SUNBEAM

1959 Sunbeam Rapier. (Coys of Kensington)

RAPIER — I — FOUR — Based on the Hillman Minx, the next Sunbeam model differed considerably from its predecessors. Only a two-door (pillarless) hardtop coupe was offered in its initial incarnation. According to early literature, the unibodied coupe displayed "a waistline of color to accentuate its fleet flowing lines." Other styling features included a curved rear window, built-in taillamps, and small round parking lamps formed into the front grille, which was made up of horizontal bars. Round headlamps had bright surround moldings, with little hoods over the top. Standard equipment included a tachometer, ammeter, thermometer, two-speed wipers, and lighter. A 1390-cc overhead-

---

1960-63 SUNBEAM

1961 Sunbeam Alpine.

ALPINE — I/II/III — FOUR — A completely different sport roadster revived the Alpine name for the 1960 model year. Like the early 1950s Sunbeam-Talbot Alpine, this version borrowed a number of elements from the sedan of the time, which in this case was the Hillman Minx-based Rapier. Drivetrains came from the Rapier, atop a chassis from the Hillman Husky station wagon. Engineering and initial assembly work was performed not by Rootes (Sunbeam-Talbot) itself, but by the Armstrong-Siddeley firm. Styling was wholly contemporary in the American mode, including long sharp-pointed (but otherwise rounded) tailfins that contained the taillamps, a curved windshield, and a squat

grille with curved upper bar and slim horizontal bars. Round parking lights sat below the slightly hooded headlamps. Roll-up windows and a tachometer were standard. So were front disc brakes and a close-ratio four-speed gearbox. Options included a clock, ammeter and lighter. A padded center armrest included a lock-up compartment. A hardtop was available to turn the roadster into a closed coupe. Standard colors were: Thistle Grey or Moonstone with scarlet upholstery; Carnival Red, Glen Green, Embassy Black or Moonstone with black upholstery. Both soft and hard tops were black.

Under early hoods went the 1494-cc engine installed in the Rapier III, rated 78 horsepower (83.5 bhp as marketed in the U.S.). The Alpine II, which debuted a year later (October 1960), switched to a 1592-cc four. Series III (introduced in March 1963) had a slightly detuned version of the 1.6-liter engine for a GT model, which came with a removable hardtop but had no folding soft top. Laycock de Normanville overdrive was optional.

A seldom-seen Le Mans edition of the Alpine was available in 1962-63. This fastback coupe, created by Harrington coachbuilders, looped off the tailfins and added a fiberglass roof. Stage 2 and Stage 3 tuning of the engine resulted in ratings of 88, 93 or 100 horsepower. A Le Mans sold for $3995 in the U.S., and only 250 were built.

RAPIER — III/IIIA — FOUR — A more powerful (78-bhp) version of the 1494-cc engine went into the Rapier III, which debuted during 1959. Compression got a boost to 9.2:1. Then, in 1961, a 1592-cc engine was installed, with an aluminum cylinder head, dual carburetors and 9.1:1 compression, developing 80 horsepower at 5100 rpm. The close-ratio four-speed gearbox used a short-stick floor shift, and top speed went past 90 mph. Front disc brakes were installed.

1962 Sunbeam Rapier hardtop.

I.D. DATA: Serial number is on a plate on the firewall, under the hood. Engine number is on the left side of the block. Serial number range: (Alpine Series I) B9000001 to B9011904; (Alpine II) B9100001 to B9119956; (Alpine III) B9200001 to B92505863.

Model	Body Type & Seating	Engine Type/CID	P.O.E. Price	Weight (lbs.)	Prod. Total
ALPINE					
I	2-dr Spt Rds-2P	I4/91	2595	2082	11,904
II	2-dr Spt Rds-2P	I4/97	2595	2082	19,956
III	2-dr Spt Rds-2P	I4/97	2595	2180	5,863
III GT	2-dr Spt Rds-2P	I4/97	2749	2230	Note 1
Le Mans	2-dr Fbk Cpe-2P	I4/97	3995	2112	250
RAPIER					
III	2-dr HT Cpe-4P	I4/91	2499	2250	Note 2
III	2-dr Conv Cpe-4P	I4/91	2649	2244	Note 2
IIIA	2-dr HT Cpe-4P	I4/97	2399	2250	Note 2
IIIA	2-dr Conv Cpe-4P	I4/97	2695	2265	Note 2

Note 1: Production is included in Series III figure.
Note 2: Approximately 12,000 Sunbeams (all models) were produced during 1961, followed by 16,000 in 1962, and 13,000 in 1963.
Price Note: Figures shown for Rapier III were valid in 1960-61; for Rapier IIIA, in 1963.

1963 Sunbeam Alpine.

ENGINE DATA: BASE FOUR (Alpine I, Rapier III): Inline, overhead-valve four-cylinder. **Displacement:** 91.2 cu. in. (1494 cc). **Bore & Stroke:** 3.11 x 3.00 in. (79 x 76.2 mm). **Compression Ratio:** 9.2:1. **Brake Horsepower:** (Alpine) 83.5 at 5300 rpm; (Rapier) 78 at 5400 rpm. **Torque:** (Alpine) 89.5 lbs.-ft. at 3600 rpm; (Rapier) 83 lbs.-ft. at 3500 rpm. Three main bearings. Solid valve lifters. Two Zenith downdraft carburetors.

BASE FOUR (Alpine II/III, Rapier IIIA): Inline, overhead-valve four-cylinder. **Displacement:** 97.2 cu. in. (1592 cc). **Bore & Stroke:** 3.21 x 3.00 in. (81.5 x 76.2 mm). **Compression Ratio:** 9.1:1. **Brake Horsepower:** (Alpine) 80 DIN (86 SAE) at 5000 rpm. (Rapier) 80 at 5100 rpm. **Torque:** (Alpine) 94 lbs.-ft. at 3800 rpm; (Rapier) 88 lbs.-ft. at 3900 rpm. Three main bearings. Solid valve lifters. Two Zenith downdraft carburetors.

CHASSIS DATA: Wheelbase: (Alpine) 86 in.; (Rapier) 96 in. **Overall Length:** (Alpine) 155.2 in.; (Rapier) 162.5 in. **Height:** (Alpine) 51.5 in.; (Rapier) 58.5 in. in. **Width:** (Alpine) 60.5 in.; (Rapier) 60.75 in. **Front Tread:** (Alpine) 51 in.; (Rapier) 49.75 in. **Rear Tread:** 48.5 in. **Standard Tires:** (Alpine) 5.60x13; (Rapier) 5.60x15.

TECHNICAL: Layout: front-engine, rear-drive. **Transmission:** four-speed manual. Overall Alpine I gear ratios: (1st) 13.013:1; (2nd) 8.324:1; (3rd) 5.413:1; (4th) 3.89:1; (rev) 16.483:1. **Standard Final Drive Ratio:** (Alpine I) 3.89:1. 4.55:1. **Steering:** Burman recirculating ball. **Suspension (front):** coil springs with swinging links. **Suspension (rear):** rigid axle with semi-elliptic leaf springs. **Brakes:** (Alpine) Girling front disc, rear drum. **Body Construction:** steel unibody.

MAJOR OPTIONS: (Alpine). Hardtop. Radio. Heater. Wire wheels. Road Speed and whitewall tires.

PERFORMANCE: Top Speed: (Alpine I) up to 100 mph claimed. **Acceleration (0-60 mph):** (Alpine I) 18.8 sec. or less. (as little as 14.4 sec. reported). **Acceleration (quarter-mile):** (Alpine I) 19.5 sec. (/3 mph).

Manufacturer: Sunbeam-Talbot Ltd., Ryton-on-Dunsmore, Warwickshire, England (part of Rootes Group).

Distributor: Rootes Motors Inc.; New York City, Long Island City, San Francisco and Los Angeles.

HISTORY: "Sleek - Swift - Spectacular." That was Sunbeam's description of the new Alpine for 1960 in the U.S. sales literature. The roadster was created as a rival to the MG B and Triumph TR3, named for the mountain passes where prototypes had been tested.

1964-67 SUNBEAM

1965 Sunbeam Tiger sport roadster. (Coys of Kensington)

ALPINE — IV/V — FOUR — Two more evolutions of the Alpine roadster arrived in early 1964 (IV) and late 1965 (V). Series IV retained the former 1592-cc engine, but Series V switched to a 1725-cc version. An all-synchro gearbox debuted during the run of the Series IV, in September 1964.

TIGER — 260/289 — V-8 — Though not the only example of a British roadster stuffed full of V-8 Power, Sunbeam's Tiger ranks as one of the most memorable. The folks at Rootes surely were aware of Carroll Shelby's Cobra, and sought a comparable power boost for their Alpine, which wasn't known for startling performance. Although the Chrysler connection was well established by the time the Tiger arrived, engines were supplied by Ford: first a 260-cid V-8 that developed 164 horsepower; then, for the Mk II edition, a 289-cid V-8. The reason was simple enough: Chrysler's own 273-cid V-8 simply would not fit into the Alpine's engine compartment.

A four-speed gearbox was installed, but one of Ford's design rather than the usual Rootes unit. Rack-and-pinion steering was used, also to help cope with space problems. Although horsepower rose sharply from the usual Alpine, weight also went up. Thus, several chassis modifications were required, including stiffening of springs. No change was made to the front-disc/rear-drum braking system. Tigers differed only slightly in appearance from a basic Alpine, adding a slim full-length bodyside trim strip. Assembly was performed by the Jensen firm. Tiger IIs added an eggcrate-patterned grille inserts and dual rocker-panel stripes, plus 'Sunbeam V-8' badging to replace the earlier ones that said "Powered by Ford 260."

RAPIER — IV/V — FOUR — Like the Alpine, Rapiers continued with the 1592-cc engine, but then switched to a larger 1725-cc four. Unlike earlier Rapiers, however, these came only in sedan form. The Rapier name was not used for final examples marketed in the U.S.

I.D. DATA: Serial number is on a plate on the firewall, under the hood. Engine number is on the left side of the block. Serial number range: (Alpine Series IV) B9400001 to B9407936; (Alpine IV w/all-synchro) B94100001 to B94104470; (Alpine V) B395000001 to B395019122; (1964 Tiger Mk I) B9470001 to B9471649; (1966 Tiger Mk I) B9471650 to B9473756; (1965 Tiger Mk IA) B382000001 to B382000913; (1966 Tiger Mk IA): B382000912 to B382002694; (1966 Tiger Mk II) B382100001 to B382100045; (1967 Tiger Mk II) B382100046 to B382100633.

Model	Body Type & Seating	Engine Type/CID	P.O.E. Price	Weight (lbs.)	Prod. Total
ALPINE					
IV	2-dr Spt Rds-2P	I4/97	2595	2180	12,406
IV GT	2-dr Spt Rds-2P	I4/97	2749	2230	Note 1
V	2-dr Spt Rds-2P	I4/105	2567	2091	19,122

Model	Body Type & Seating	Engine Type/CID	P.O.E. Price	Weight (lbs.)	Prod. Total
TIGER					
I	2-dr Spt Rds-2P	V8/260	3425	2407	3,756
IA	2-dr Spt Rds-2P	V8/260	N/A	N/A	2,694
II	2-dr Spt Rds-2P	V8/289	N/A	N/A	633
RAPIER					
IV	4-dr Sedan-4P	I4/97	N/A	N/A	Note 2
V	4-dr Sedan-4P	I4/105	1799	2095	Note 2

Note 1: Production is included in Series IV figure.

Note 2: Approximately 17,000 Sunbeams (all models) were produced during 1964, followed by 10,800 in 1965, 17,200 in 1966, and 11,400 in 1967.

ENGINE DATA: BASE FOUR (Alpine IV, Rapier IV): Inline, overhead-valve four-cylinder. **Displacement:** 97.2 cu. in. (1592 cc). **Bore & Stroke:** 3.21 x 3.00 in. (81.5 x 76.2 mm). **Compression Ratio:** 9.1:1. **Brake Horsepower:** (Alpine) 90 at 5200 rpm; (Rapier) 80 at 5100 rpm. **Torque:** (Alpine) 93 lbs.-ft. at 3600 rpm. Three main bearings. Solid valve lifters. Solex carburetor.

Note: Harrington (Le Mans) engines had higher horsepower ratings.

BASE FOUR (Alpine V, Rapier V): Inline, overhead-valve four-cylinder. **Displacement:** 105.3 cu. in. (1725 cc). **Bore & Stroke:** 3.21 x 3.25 in. (81.5 x 82.55 mm). **Compression Ratio:** 9.2:1. **Brake Horsepower:** (Alpine) 103 bhp. at 5500 rpm. **Torque:** (Alpine) 103 lbs.-ft. at 3700 rpm. Three main bearings. Solid valve lifters. Two Stromberg carburetors (Alpine).

BASE V-8 (Tiger Mk I/IA): Overhead-valve "vee" type eight-cylinder (Ford). Cast iron block and heads. **Displacement:** 260 cu. in. (4261 cc). **Bore & Stroke:** 3.80 x 2.87 in. (96.5 x 73 mm). **Compression Ratio:** 8.8:1. **Brake Horsepower:** 164 at 4400 rpm. **Torque:** 258 lbs.-ft. at 2200 rpm. Five main bearings. Ford two-barrel carburetor.

BASE V-8 (Tiger Mk II): Overhead-valve "vee" type eight-cylinder (Ford). Cast iron block and heads. **Displacement:** 289 cu. in. (4737 cc). **Bore & Stroke:** 4.00 x 2.87 in. (101.6 x 73 mm). **Compression Ratio:** 9.3:1. **Brake Horsepower:** 200 at 4400 rpm. **Torque:** 282 lbs.-ft. at 2400 rpm. Ford carburetor.

1966 Sunbeam Mark I Tiger. (Coys of Kensington)

CHASSIS DATA: Wheelbase: (Alpine) 86 in.; (Rapier) 96 in. **Overall Length:** (Alpine) 155.2 in.; (Rapier) 161.5 in. **Height:** (Alpine) 51.5 in.; (Rapier) 58.5 in. in. **Width:** (Alpine) 60.5 in.; (Rapier) 61 in. **Front Tread:** (Alpine) 51 in.; (Rapier) 51.5 in. **Rear Tread:** 48.5 in. **Standard Tires:** (Alpine/Rapier) 6.00x13; (Tiger) 5.90x13.

TECHNICAL: Layout: front-engine, rear-drive. **Transmission:** four-speed manual. Overall Tiger 260 gear ratios: (1st) 6.68:1; (2nd) 4.87:1; (3rd) 3.72:1; (4th) 2.88:1 (other ratios were available). **Steering:** reciculating ball except (Tiger) rack and pinion. **Suspension (front):** wishbones with coil springs and anti-roll bar. **Suspension (rear):** rigid axle with semi-elliptic leaf springs. **Brakes:** (Alpine) Girling front disc, rear drum. **Body Construction:** steel unibody.

PERFORMANCE: Top Speed: (Alpine V) 118 mph; (Tiger 260) up to 124 mph. **Acceleration (0-60 mph):** (Alpine V) 11.5 sec.; (Tiger 260) 8.4 sec. (as little as 7.8 sec. reported). **Acceleration (quarter-mile):** (Alpine V) 18.6 sec. (74 mph); (Tiger 260) 16.5 sec. (89 mph).

ADDITIONAL MODELS: Starting in 1964, Sunbeam also marketed its version of the subcompact Imp in the U.S. With a 42-bhp overhead-cam engine and riding an 82-inch wheelbase, the Imp sport sedan sold for $1495 in 1964.

Manufacturer: Sunbeam-Talbot Ltd., Ryton-on-Dunsmore, Warwickshire, England (part of Rootes Group).

Distributor: Rootes Motors Inc.; New York City, Long Island City, San Francisco and Los Angeles.

HISTORY: Sunbeam's Ford-powered Tiger debuted at the New York Auto Show in April 1964. Tiger had been the name of the Sunbeam special V-12 that set the land-speed record way back in 1926. Production of both the Alpine and Tiger halted in 1967.

1968-70 SUNBEAM

The Alpine and Tiger roadsters were gone, but a revised Rapier appeared in 1968, based on the Hillman Hunter. The fastback body was supposedly inspired by Plymouth's Barracuda. This fastback coupe was marketed in the U.S. for a brief period as the Alpine, with a 105-cid engine developing either 73 horsepower or (in GT guise) 94 bhp. Selling price in 1969 was $2299 for the base coupe, and $2475 for the GT coupe. In these final years in the U.S. market, Sunbeam also offered an Arrow four-door sedan on the same 98.5-inch wheelbase. Fastback Rapiers (Alpine) were produced as late as 1976, but the Sunbeam name disappeared from lists of cars imported into America after 1970.

596

SUZUKI

Suzuki, one of the lesser-known Japanese firms, dates back to 1939, but none of its products entered the American market under their own name until nearly half a century later. The company evolved from the Suzuki Loom Manufacturing Company, founded in 1920 by Michio Suzuki, who'd entered the business 11 years earlier. Because the Japanese government was encouraging domestic production of automobiles in the years just before World War II, Suzuki decided to enter that business. A few prototypes were built, but war called a temporary halt to further development. Instead, the Suzuki plants were used for military equipment.

After V-J Day, loom production resumed, and Suzuki also turned out other products—but the prewar interest in automobiles took longer to resurface. Motorized bicycles came first, starting with a "Power Free" model in 1952 that used a tiny 36-cc engine. After studying various automobiles produced by European manufacturers, Suzuki created the front-drive Suzulight in 1955, using a 360-cc air-cooled two-stroke engine. Half a dozen years later, as automobile production expanded, the textile part of the business was severed from the motorcar element.

An evolution of the Suzulight, called the 800 Fronte, emerged in 1967, powered by a three-cylinder two-stroke engine. Water cooling arrived in 1974. The first Suzuki with a four-stroke engine came in 1977. Two years later, Suzuki offered a selection of overhead-cam powerplants for both passenger cars and off-road vehicles. An Alto hatchback debuted in 1981, with a 797-cc three-cylinder engine. By the mid-1980s, another hatchback model, the Cultus, was available with a 1.3-liter engine. That one was exported to the U.S., but not as a Suzuki. Instead, it was named the Chevrolet Sprint (listed separately in this Catalog), as a result of the fact that General Motors owned a share of the Suzuki operation.

Suzuki entered the U.S. market under its own name for the 1986 model year not with a passenger car, but with a four-wheel-drive sport-utility vehicle: the Samurai. Though rather popular, the Samurai became the target of safety experts in 1988, when *Consumer Reports* claimed it was subject to rollover accidents as a result of fast changes in direction. One reason cited was that the Samurai had too short a wheelbase. Suzuki denied the charges, and the National Highway Traffic Safety Administration eventually ruled that they lacked sufficient validity. Still, sales slumped badly.

Meanwhile, Suzuki introduced a larger sport-utility vehicle called the Sidekick, which was built in Canada. That one also was marketed as the Geo Tracker.

For the 1989 model year, Suzuki introduced a version of the minicar that had been marketed as a Chevrolet Sprint, and which later changed its name to the Geo Metro. Suzuki called it the Swift. Instead of promoting the Swift strictly as an econocar, as Chevrolet/Geo (with a three-cylinder engine) was doing, Suzuki also focused on performance and sportiness. In addition to a basic 70-horsepower version of the 1.3-liter four-cylinder engine, installed in the four-door hatchback GLX, Suzuki offered a more potent twin-cam variant. That higher-powered engine used multi-point fuel injection and developed 100 horsepower, and was installed in the Swift GTi two-door hatchback. The GTi even

had sporty body add-ons; namely, a front spoiler (which contained foglamps) and a set of rocker-panel extensions. Suzuki claimed that the GTi could accelerate to 60 mph in a swift 8.2 seconds with the five-speed manual gearbox. An electronically-controlled three-speed automatic also was available. The GTi used all-disc brakes, versus front discs and rear drums for the GLX.

For 1990, a four-door notchback sedan replaced the four-door hatchback, and the model selection broadened. The sporty edition with 100-horsepower twin-cam engine now was called GT, as Volkswagen hadn't been pleased with the use of Suzuki's GTi designation a year earlier.

1990 Suzuki Swift GT two-door.

TALBOT-LAGO

While the history of this French firm reaches back toward the turn of the century, its renown for striking production models solidified after a 1935 takeover by Antonio Lago, its head engineer and plant manager. During the 1920s, the Talbot-Darracq company had earned fame for its Grand Prix cars. After the takeover, the cars adopted the Talbot-Lago name. In Britain and other countries, however, the Darracq name continued in use, to avoid confusion with the Sunbeam-related Talbot. The French cars were sometimes known as Lago-Talbots.

Lago, who'd had a taste of racing experience earlier in the 1930s while working as general manager of the Wilson Self-Changing Gear Company, improved upon the prior Talbot-Darracq line with new 2.7- and 3.0-liter six-cylinder engines. Another new powerplant, displacing 4.0 liters and producing from 115 to 165 horsepower, went into a Speciale model. It was also employed for racing cars (soon enlarged to 4.5 liters). Other sports racers used a 3.5-liter engine. Even the race cars used a Wilson preselector gearbox, which let the driver choose the next gear before a change was needed. The actual shift took place as the clutch was pushed down toward the floor. Both factory and custom bodies were used, including a two-seat coupe by Figoni and Falaschi, which, according to *World's Great Cars,* had a steeply-raked windshield, pontoon rear fenders, oval grille, and "a spiked tail in the manner of the Type 57 Bugatti Atlantic."

Production resumed just after World War Two, with new Record and Grand Sport coupes, each powered by a 4.5-liter six-cylinder engine but riding the prewar-style chassis. Neither was a lightweight, so they needed the 170 or 195 horsepower available. High camshafts in the twin-cam, long-stroke engine actuated short, crossover-type pushrods. Even with balance shafts, vibration was a major problem, causing the company to display a "redline" of only 4200 rpm on the tachometer. Also available was a lower-cost Quinze Luxe model, available with either the big six or a 2.7-liter four-cylinder engine.

In 1950 came the Bebe (Baby) model, powered by the 2.7-liter four, which now delivered 118 horsepower. Two years later, all models were restyled. Although Talbot-Lagos fared well at LeMans races, and attracted considerable attention at the 1953 Paris Automobile Salon, financial troubles loomed and the company neared extinction in the early 1950s. Introduction of a new 2.5-liter GT coupe in 1955, followed by an "America" version for export (with BMW V-8 power) helped the firm last a while longer. A mere dozen "Americas" were built, however. Final models carried a Simca V-8 engine. With the death of Antonio Lago in 1960 came the demise of the company he'd virtually created, and the memory of some strikingly handsome GT machines.

1946-54 TALBOT-LAGO

RECORD — SIX — Debuting shortly after the war, in 1946, the Lago Record carried a 170-horsepower, 273-cid six-cylinder engine. The standard high-beltline sedan wore a curved windshield and wraparound rear window. As with all Talbot-Lago models, however, custom bodies could be ordered that differed sharply from the norm. Like other cars from the company, the Record used a Wilson preselector transmission.

1947 Talbot-Lago Record Type 26. (Coys of Kensington)

GRAND SPORT — TYPE 26 — SIX — Also arriving early was a Grand Sport coupe which, according to *World's Great Cars,* had lines "somewhat reminiscent of an Aston Martin DB2 with a similar suggestion of speed and brute force coupled with elegance." Engine size was the same as that in the Record, but rated at 195 horsepower. That was enough to produce top speeds beyond 110 mph, despite the car's hefty weight. Graber convertible and sports sedan bodies became available. Later models (by 1954) switched from the original transverse leaf springs up front to coil springs, and used both hydraulic and friction shock absorbers. Wheelbase also grew, so both two- and four-seat bodies could be accommodated.

QUINZE-LUXE — FOUR/SIX — Both four- and six-cylinder power was offered for the next Talbot-Lago model, a lower-priced version that wore disc wheels.

BABY (BEBE) — FOUR — Last of the new models introduced in the early postwar period was the Bebe, powered by the same four-cylinder engine as the Quinze-Luxe. Its debut came in 1949-50.

1948 Talbot-Lago coupe.

I.D. DATA: Not available.

Note: Because many Talbot-Lagos had custom bodies, dimensions and other specifications varied considerably.

Model	Body Type & Seating	Engine Type/CID	P.O.E. Price	Weight (lbs.)	Prod. Total
Baby	4-dr Sedan 5P	I4/164	N/A	3306	Note 1
Q-Luxe	2-dr Coupe	I4/164	N/A	N/A	Note 1
Q-Luxe	2-dr Coupe	I6/164	N/A	N/A	Note 1
Record	4-dr Sedan-5P	I6/273	5718	3968	Note 1
Record Spt	4-dr Sedan-5P	I6/273	N/A	3386	Note 1
Record Spt	2-dr Coupe-2P	I6/273	N/A	3950	Note 1
G. Sport	4-dr Sedan-5P	I6/273	9850	3556	Note 1
G. Sport	2-dr Coupe-4P	I6/273	6760	3417	Note 1
G. Sport	2-dr Conv Cpe	I6/273	N/A	N/A	Note 1

Note 1: About 433 Talbot-Lagos were produced during 1950, followed by only 80 in 1951.

1950 Talbot-Lago T 26 Record. (Coys of Kensington)

1951 Talbot-Lago 4½-liter Grand Sport two-seater coupe. (Christie's)

ENGINE DATA: BASE FOUR (Quinze-Luxe): Inline, overhead-valve four-cylinder (twin camshafts). Cast iron block and head. **Displacement:** 164 cu. in. (2690 cc). **Bore & Stroke:** 3.66 x 3.90 in. (93 x 99 mm). **Compression Ratio:** 6.5:1. **Brake Horsepower:** 110 at 4500 rpm. Three main bearings. Two carburetors. 12-volt electrical system.

BASE FOUR (Baby): Same as above, except 118-120 bhp with 7.0:1 compression.

BASE SIX (Quinze-Luxe): Inline, overhead-valve six-cylinder (twin camshafts). Cast iron block and head. **Displacement:** 164 cu. in. (2693 cc). **Bore & Stroke:** 3.46 x 2.91 in. (88 x 73.8 mm). **Compression Ratio:** 6.5:1. **Brake Horsepower:** 110. Seven main bearings. Two carburetors. 12-volt electrical system.

BASE SIX (Record): Inline, overhead-valve six-cylinder. Cast iron block and head. **Displacement:** 273 cu. in. (4482 cc). **Bore & Stroke:** 3.66 x 4.33 in. (93 x 110 mm). **Compression Ratio:** 6.5:1 or 7.0:1. **Brake Horsepower:** 170 at 4200 rpm. **Torque:** 240 lbs.-ft. at 2800 rpm. Seven main bearings. Two carburetors.

BASE SIX (Grand Sport): Same as Record engine above, except — **Compression Ratio:** 7.5:1. **Brake Horsepower:** 190-195 bhp at 4000 rpm. Three Zenith carburetors.

Note: Later versions of the Grand Sport engine (also used in the Record Sport) were rated 210 bhp at 4200 rpm, with 8.0:1 compression.

1954 Talbot-Lago Grand Sport T 26 GSL.

1954 Talbot-Lago Grand Sport Graber sports sedan.

CHASSIS DATA: Wheelbase: (Baby) 115 in.; (Quinze/Record) 123 in.; (Record Sport) 113 in.; (Grand Sport) 103/110 in. **Overall Length:** (Baby) 191 in.; (Quinze/Record) 196 in. **Width:** (Baby/Quinze/Record) 69 in.; (Grand Sport) 67.4 in. **Front Tread:** (Quinze/Record) 55.9 in.; (Grand Sport) 58.3 in. **Rear Tread:** 58.5 in. **Wheel Type:** (Quinze-Luxe) 4.00x16 disc; (Record/Grand Sport) 3.62x18 Rudge wire. **Standard Tires:** (Baby/Quinze-Luxe) 6.00x16; (Record/Grand Sport) 6.00x18.

TECHNICAL: Layout: front-engine, rear-drive. **Transmission:** four-speed manual with optional Wilson preselector gearchange. **Steering:** worm and nut. **Suspension (front):** independent coil springs with stabilizer except (Grand Sport) transverse leaf spring. **Suspension (rear):** rigid axle with semi-elliptic leaf springs (stabilizer, except Grand Sport). **Brakes:** hydraulic, front/rear drum. **Body Construction:** aluminum. **Fuel Tank:** 100 liters.

PERFORMANCE: Top Speed: (Record) 106 mph; (Grand Sport) to 124 mph. **Acceleration (0-60 mph):** (Grand Sport) 10 seconds. **Fuel Mileage:** about 11 mpg.

Manufacturer: Automobiles Talbot, Suresnes, France.

1955-60 TALBOT-LAGO

1956 Talbot-Lago Grand Sport.

2.5-LITRE — GT — FOUR — Similar to the former Bebe, the new 2.5-liter four-cylinder model came in two versions: Tourisme Rapide and Sport Speciale. As before, the inclined-overhead-valve, twin-cam engine operated its valve via pushrods, into hemispherical combustion chambers. Styling features included slim bumpers and wire wheels. Appearance of the stylish coupe was similar to the V-8 "America" model introduced for export.

AMERICA — V-8 — Similar in appearance to the European GT coupe, Talbot-Lago's export model (introduced in 1957) carried a BMW 2.5-liter V-8 engine and ZF four-speed gearbox. *Road & Track* felt that the coupe's "traditional but rather awkward Talbot radiator grille rather spoils the front end, though this is a matter of taste and/or opinion." And in fact, others have a far more favorable view of the car's front end with its grille made up of vertical bars in a bright surround molding, and small round parking lights just above the bumper. Those bumpers were now stronger than before, and roll-up windows were installed. The hood held an airscoop, and a four-hole "grille" stood at the cowl. Fiberglass was used for the roof; plexiglass for the unusually wide wraparound back window. Decklid hinges for the roomy trunk were exposed, and the rear end featured gracefully smooth, rounded "fins" that led to twin tiny round taillamps on each fender. Inside was a leather-covered dashboard (which extended into the engine compartment and a four-spoke steering wheel. A tachometer stood to the right of the steering column; the speedometer to the left. A thumbscrew on the sill locked each vent window on the door. Fully rounded wheel openings highlighted the Borrani wire wheels. The V-8 engine used dual exhaust pipes.

I.D. DATA: Not available.

Model	Body Type & Seating	Engine Type/CID	P.O.E. Price	Weight (lbs.)	Prod. Total
2.5-LITRE GT					
Rapide	2-dr Coupe-2P	I4/152	Note 1	2300	Note 2
Special	2-dr Coupe-2P	I4/152	Note 1	N/A	Note 2
AMERICA					
America	2-dr Coupe-2P	V8/151	6995	2650	12

Note 1: Price at the factory in France was $4995 for the Rapide and $5520 for the Speciale.

Note 2: Approximately 70 GT Talbot-Lagos were produced. "America" production also is approximate.

ENGINE DATA: BASE FOUR (2.5-Litre): Inline, overhead-valve four-cylinder (twin camshafts). **Displacement:** 152 cu. in. (2491 cc). **Bore & Stroke:** 3.52 x 3.90 in. (89.5 x 99 mm). **Compression Ratio:** 7.6:1. **Brake Horsepower:** 120 at 5000 rpm. **Torque:** 144 lbs.-ft. at 2200 rpm. Five main bearings. Solid valve lifters. Two Zenith carburetors. 12-volt electrical system.

Note: Final European GT model contained a 2.3-liter Simca V-8 engine, rated 95 bhp.

BASE V-8 (America): Overhead-valve, vee-type eight-cylinder (BMW). Aluminum block and head. **Displacement:** 151 cu. in. (2476 cc). **Bore & Stroke:** 2.85 x 2.95 in. (72.4 x 74.9 mm). **Compression Ratio:** 7.6:1. **Brake Horsepower:** 138 at 5000 rpm. **Torque:** 156 lbs.-ft. at 2600 rpm. Solid valve lifters. Two two-barrel Zenith carburetors.

CHASSIS DATA: Wheelbase: 98.4 in. **Overall Length:** (2.5-Litre) 165.1 in.; (America) 166 in. **Height:** (2.5-Litre) 51.6 in.; (America) 52.4 in. **Width:** 64.6 in. **Front Tread:** 51.2 in. **Rear Tread:** 51.2 in. **Wheel Type:** (America) Borrani wire. **Standard Tires:** (2.5-Litre) 6.50x15; (America) 6.00x16.

TECHNICAL: Layout: front-engine, rear-drive. **Transmission:** four-speed manual. "America" gear ratios: (1st) 3.39:1; (2nd) 2.07:1; (3rd) 1.36:1; (4th) 1.00:1. **Standard Final Drive Ratio:** (America) 3.92:1. **Suspension (front):** transverse control arms and leaf springs. **Suspension (rear):** rigid axle with semi-elliptic leaf springs. **Brakes:** hydraulic, front/rear drum. **Body Construction:** separate body on tubular frame.

PERFORMANCE: Top Speed: (2.5-Litre) 110-120 mph; (America) 118-124 mph. **Acceleration (0-60 mph):** (America) 10.6 seconds. **Acceleration (quarter-mile):** (America) 17.4 sec. (82 mph).

Manufacturer: Automobiles Talbot, Suresnes, France.

Distributor: Lago America Automobiles, Santa Monica, California; and Milani International Automotive Imports, Chicago, Illinois.

HISTORY: The "America" debuted on the West Coast in August 1958 and attracted ample attention, but few paying customers. Only a dozen or so were built altogether. Each car, according to factory sources reporting to *Sportscar Quarterly*, was "road tested prior to delivery by the 1948 French Grand Prix champion, Y. Giraud-Cabantous." Talbot-Lagos continued to be called Darracqs in Britain, to avoid confusion with the Sunbeam-Talbot. Production ceased officially in 1960, with the death of Antonio Lago; but it was already almost extinct. A year earlier, the company had been taken over by Simca. Two decades later, the Talbot nameplate resurfaced, as Automobiles Talbot S.A. became the name for cars built by Chrysler in Europe. But those elegant French GT coupes were long since gone.

TATRA

One of the first rear-engined cars to enter production, the Czechoslovakian-built Tatra was also one of the world's most progressive vehicles, a pioneer in (among other advances) unibody construction and streamlined design. Evolved from the Schustala wagon factory, which dated back to 1853, the company formed at Nesseldorf entered the automobile business in 1897, when Czechoslovakia was still part of the Austro-Hungarian empire. An experimental "Prasident" vehicle, powered by a two-cylinder engine designed by Hans Ledwinka, led to production of 10 motorcars in 1899. Each had a different name, but by 1901 the Nesseldorf name was adopted. A 3.3-liter model S with overhead-cam engine appeared in 1906, and six-cylinder engines came into use by 1914. By that time, too, the cars had independent suspensions and four-wheel brakes. After World War One, when the Czechoslovakian nation was formed, the town of Nesseldorf adopted a new name. So the car produced there became known as the Tatra, named for the mountain range where they underwent testing.

The Type 11 that arrived in 1923 had such advanced features as air cooling, swing axles and tubular backbone-style chassis, and was powered by a horizontally-opposed two-cylinder engine. By the 1930s, the model lineup had ranged from three-wheelers with one-cylinder power to a limited-production V-12. Meanwhile, the company had become no less renowned for the manufacture of trucks and railway locomotives.

In 1934 came the car that put Tatra's name in the history books: the Type 77 fastback sedan, powered by a rear-mounted V-8 engine, with styling cues similar to the Chrysler Airflow but a potent personality of its own. It was capable of speeds near 100 mph with the 3380-cc, 75-bhp engine. Design features included triple headlights. A similarly-shaped T87 came later, along with a smaller (3-liter) overhead-cam V-8 engine.

Also in the 1930s, a smaller rear-engined prototype was built that later was found to bear a strong resemblance to what would become the Volkswagen. Many years later, in 1967, Tatra's lawsuit against Volkswagen for patent infringement was rewarded with a judgment of 3 million Marks.

Nationalization of the Tatra company under the new Communist government came after World War II. Production of the T600 Tatraplan--similar in teardrop appearance to the advanced prewar sedan but with four-cylinder power--began in 1948, though on a small scale. By 1957, the T603 debuted with a rear V-8 engine instead of the former flat four. Two years later, the body got a facelift from Vignale and a more potent V-8. In 1969, a total of 250 cars were produced by Tatra, but that was a small part of the company's total output, which consisted of some 4,000 vehicles. Trucks remained the mainstay of the firm. Though seldom seen in the U.S., early postwar Tatra sedans are prime examples of advanced technology and design--all the more amazing since the basic structure so closely followed the pattern set down in the 1930s.

1951 Tatra four-door.

TATRAPLAN — T600 — FLAT FOUR — Nobody would be likely to mistake the teardrop-shaped Tatraplan for any other car, with its huge bulge on the back end of the fastback (actually hatchback) four-door sedan body. Air intakes at the sides of that back bulge fed cooling air to the rear-mounted flat-four engine, which formed a single unit with the gearbox and differential. Large rear fender skirts added to the car's impression of vast length and sleekness. The rear hatch lid contained small windows alongside a narrow "fin." Front "suicide" doors (hinged at the rear) were used, with exposed door hinges at the center pillar. Semaphore turn signals were mounted on that 'B' pillar between the doors. A smooth nose contained protruding built-in headlamps, low on the fenders, with a horizontal-bar grille between them. Four tiny round taillamps were mounted on the low rear panel, just above the bumper. Ample space was provided for six passengers, in what the sales brochure described as an interior "created in co-operation with artist-designers so that its comely arrangement and spaciousness satisfy even the most pretentious motorist." A column lever operated the four-speed manual transmission.

1952 Tatra Tatraplan 107.

I.D. DATA: Not available.

Model	Body Type & Seating	Engine Type/CID	P.O.E. Price	Weight (lbs.)	Prod. Total
T600	4-dr Sedan-6P	H4/119	Note 1	2640	Note 2

Note 1: Price at the factory in 1953 was about $2800, but around 1950 a U.S. serviceman could buy one in Germany for $1450.

Note 2: By 1953, some 850 U.S. servicemen stationed in Europe were said to have bought a Tatraplan.

1954 Tatra Tatraplan four-door sedan.

ENGINE DATA: BASE FOUR: Horizontally opposed, overhead-valve four-cylinder (air cooled). **Displacement:** 119.0 cu. in. (1950 cc). **Bore & Stroke:** 3.35 x 3.39 in. (85 x 86 mm). **Compression Ratio:** 6.0:1. **Brake Horsepower:** 52 at 4000 rpm. **Torque:** 87 lbs.-ft. at 2000 rpm. Two carburetors. 12-volt electrical system.

CHASSIS DATA: Wheelbase: 106.2 in. **Overall Length:** 179.0 in. **Height:** 59.8 in. **Width:** 65.8 in. **Front Tread:** 51.2 in. **Rear Tread:** 51.2 in. **Wheel Type:** E 4.00x16. **Standard Tires:** 6.00x16.

TECHNICAL: Layout: rear-engine, rear-drive. **Transmission:** four-speed manual (2nd/3rd/4th synchro). V-8 gear ratios: (1st) 4.7:1; (2nd) 2.95:1; (3rd) 1.56:1; (4th) 1.04:1. **Standard Final Drive Ratio:** 4.09:1. **Steering:** rack and pinion. **Suspension (front):** two transverse leaf springs. **Suspension (rear):** torsion rods with swing axles. **Brakes:** hydraulic, front/rear drum. **Body Construction:** unibody; double steel shell welded to backbone frame. **Fuel Tank:** 12 gallon.

PERFORMANCE: Top Speed: 78-85 mph (about 80 mph claimed). **Acceleration (0-60 mph):** 32 seconds. **Fuel Mileage:** estimates ranged from about 19 mpg (overall) to 32 mpg at 50 mph.

Manufacturer: Tatra National Corp., Koprivnice, Praha (Prague), Czechoslovakia.

HISTORY: "The new streamlined automobile TATRA," said the English-language sales brochure in 1948, "is coming onto the market in the jubilee years of its makers," offering a "new thrill of driving." Tatra also issued an announcement in 1948 of a V-8 version, as in the prewar period, but a modern V-8 would not go into production until the mid-1950s. After introduction at the Prague Motor Show in late 1947, a Tatraplan was featured at the Brussels (Belgium) show in 1950. "Studying the form of a drop of water in free fall," said *Auto Sport Review* in 1953, Tatra "engineers decided on the basic form of the body." Wind-tunnel testing gave the curious motorcar a low drag characteristic. An open Tatra sports model using "mostly stock parts" was clocked at 110 mph, according to *Auto Sport Review*.

1957-64 TATRA

1962 Tatra 603.

TATRAPLAN — T603 — V-8 — Appearance of the next-generation Tatra was similar to the T600 (and to the prewar 77/87). The large, fast six-passenger four-door sedan wore an updated version of the streamlined body with fastback styling. Grilled air intakes between the back window and rear wheels fed air to a rear-mounted V-8 engine. Twin headlamps plus a third light of similar size all fit within a rectangular oval grille opening, far inboard of the fenders. 'TATRA' letters stood at the hood front, ahead of an airscoop.

I.D. DATA: Not available.

Model	Body Type & Seating	Engine Type/CID	P.O.E. Price	Weight (lbs.)	Prod. Total
T603	4-dr Sedan-6P	V8/155	N/A/	3175	N/A

ENGINE DATA: BASE V-8: Overhead-valve V-8 (air cooled). **Displacement:** 155.2 cu. in. (2544 cc). **Bore & Stroke:** 2.95 x 2.83 in. (74.9 x 72 mm). **Compression Ratio:** 6.5:1. **Brake Horsepower:** 100 at 4800 rpm. **Torque:** 115 lbs.-ft. at 3000 rpm.

CHASSIS DATA: Wheelbase: 108 in. **Overall Length:** 201 in. **Height:** 61 in. **Max. Tread:** 55.2 in. **Standard Tires:** 6.50x15S.

TECHNICAL: Layout: rear-engine, rear-drive. **Transmission:** four-speed manual. **Steering:** rack and pinion. **Suspension (front):** independent; coil springs. **Suspension (rear):** independent; coil springs. **Brakes:** hydraulic, front/rear drum. **Body Construction:** steel unibody.

PERFORMANCE: Top Speed: 105.6 mph. **Fuel Mileage:** about 24 mpg.

Manufacturer: Motokov, Praha (Prague), Czechoslovakia.

1965-68 TATRA

TATRAPLAN — 2-603 — V-8 — A smaller V-8 engine powered the next Tatra variant, which took on a considerably different look. Though still unconventional in appearance, the new fastback four-door displayed a less-startling six-window fastback profile, with air intakes in the rear fenders and small fins leading to the vertical taillamps. Four head-lamps were mounted low, at the center of the front panel, in a two-section housing, far inboard of the front fenders. Separate auxiliary lights were mounted above the bumper guards, just outside the headlight panel. 'TATRA' lettering stood just ahead of a front airscoop.

I.D. DATA: Not available.

Model	Body Type & Seating	Engine Type/CID	P.O.E. Price	Weight (lbs.)	Prod. Total
2-603	4-dr Sedan-6P	V8/151	N/A	3241	N/A

ENGINE DATA: BASE V-8: Overhead-cam V-8 (air cooled). Light alloy block and head. **Displacement:** 150.9 cu. in. (2472 cc). **Bore & Stroke:** 2.95 x 2.76 in. (75 x 70 mm). **Compression Ratio:** 8.2:1. **Brake Horsepower:** 125 (SAE) at 4800 rpm. **Torque:** 123 lbs.-ft. (DIN) at 4000 rpm. Two Jikov two-barrel carburetors.

CHASSIS DATA: Wheelbase: 108.3 in. **Overall Length:** 199.4 in. **Height:** 60.2 in. **Width:** 75.2 in. **Front Tread:** 58.5 in. **Rear Tread:** 55.1 in. **Standard Tires:** 6.70x15.

TECHNICAL: Layout: rear-engine, rear-drive. **Transmission:** four-speed manual. **Steering:** rack and pinion. **Suspension (front):** independent; longitudinal trailing arms, coil springs and anti-roll bar. **Suspension (rear):** swing axles, trailing arms and coil springs. **Brakes:** hydraulic, front/rear drum. **Body Construction:** steel unibody.

PERFORMANCE: Top Speed: 100.6 mph. **Fuel Mileage:** near 19 mpg.

Manufacturer: Motokov, Praha (Prague), Czechoslovakia.

POSTSCRIPT: Additional horsepower arrived in the next Tatra model, the T613, introduced in 1969 with a 165-hp engine and styling by Vignale. Tatra passenger cars continued in production into 1975; but output dropped sharply after that time as the company focused on commercial and industrial vehicles.

TOYOTA

Many an automaker began with bicycles or motorcycles, but Toyota evolved instead from a textile firm in Japan. Sakichi Toyoda formed the Toyoda Automatic Loom Works in 1926. Sale of patent rights to a British company allowed Toyoda's son Kiichiro to add an automobile department to the business. Experiments began by 1930 with a two-cylinder engine, followed by an Atsuta prototype. Then, in 1935, came a more successful A-1 prototype, followed by production versions named AA (for the four-door sedan) and AB (for the touring model).

Under AA/AB hoods was a six-cylinder overhead-valve engine patterned after Chevrolet's, developing 65 horse-power. In fact, the chassis and gearbox came directly from Chevrolet, though styling was akin to the streamlined Chrysler Airflow of the mid-1930s. By 1937, a separate company named Toyota Motor Co. Ltd. was in operation. In the years leading to World War II, Toyota turned out not only cars, but also trucks and buses. The original family name (Toyoda) was retained for the company's steel plant—initiated in 1940—and other non-automotive operations.

Truck production resumed quickly after the war, but cars didn't begin to trickle off the line until 1947. Toyopet was the name chosen for the new SA two-door sedan, which used a 27-bhp engine and rode a backbone-style chassis; but only a couple of hundred were built through 1952. By that time, Toyota also was producing a four-wheel-drive Land Cruiser, which would later join the international market.

Part of the reason for minimal sales in Japan was the limited number of people who knew how to drive. Toyota started a separate sales organization in 1950 to help change that picture. Starting in 1955, a four-cylinder Crown was available, with 1453-cc engine and three-speed column shift. That was followed by the Corona, with 1.0-liter engine. Production finally began to rise swiftly, from about 700 cars a month in 1955 to 11,750 in 1958—and as many as 50,000 monthly by 1964. English-language sales catalogs first appeared in 1956, and the first Toyopets (Crowns) began to trickle into the U.S. two years later.

Restyling of Coronas and Crowns in 1964 was carried out with export in mind. A two-cylinder Publica was offered in the home market, and Crowns came with six-cylinder and V-8 engines. In the U.S., however, the Corona began to attract considerable attention with its unique angled-back front end and 1.9-liter four-cylinder engine. So did the 4WD Land Cruiser, entering a market niche that

was occupied only by the American Jeep and British Land Rover. Six-cylinder Crowns also sold in modest numbers during the late 1960s and into 1971. Hino became part of the Toyota empire in 1966, and was the name subsequently used for trucks. Toyota also took over control of Daihatsu, one year later.

Corolla imports began for the 1969 model year, some two years after that subcompact debuted in Japan. A two-door Carina sedan with the Corolla's 1588-cc engine sold briefly in the U.S, in 1972-73. Compact pickup trucks also became available.

Sportiness became part of the Toyota image in the U.S. with the debut of the Celica coupe for the 1971 model year. Sports models had been introduced in the 1960s—the Sports 800 in 1964, and the better-known 2000 GT a year later—but neither had made an impact in the U.S. marketplace. With a five-speed gearbox and front disc brakes, Celicas were capable of competition, ready to rival such European roadsters as the Fiat 124 and MGB.

During 1971, Toyota exported its 10-millionth car. By mid-1976, Toyota turned out its 20-millionth automobile. By 1980, Toyota slipped ahead of Chevrolet as the world's leading producer of private automobiles, with plants in 40 countries.

A larger, top-line Cressida with six-cylinder engine entered the U.S. market for the 1978 model year. Near the other end of the spectrum was the front-drive Tercel, added at the start of the 1980s decade. Tercels had longitudinally-mounted engines, rack-and-pinion steering, and front disc brakes. Smallest of all was the rear-drive Starlet, introduced a year later (though offered through most of the 1970s elsewhere in the world).

A front-drive Camry debuted in the U.S. for 1983. Toyota entered the sports-car arena with the mid-engine MR2, which debuted during 1984 with a 16-valve, 1.6-liter powerplant. Sporting fans also had the choice of a rear-drive Supra. Best known for its full line of family sedans, Toyota also offered a variety of specialty vehicles, from the rough-and-tumble Land Cruiser to utilitarian vans and pickups. For the 1991 model year, the angular-shaped MR2 two-seater enjoyed a curvaceous restyle, and a rounded Previa van replaced its squarish predecessor.

1954 Toyopet four-door sedan.

1956 Toyopet Crown RS four-door sedan.

1958-60 TOYOPET (TOYOTA)

1959 Toyopet four-door sedan.

CROWN — FOUR — Early examples of the Crown series arrived in America not as Toyotas, but under the Toyopet nameplate. Riding a 99.6-inch wheelbase, the Crown sedan carried a 1453-cc (88.7-cid) four-cylinder engine that developed 60 horsepower at 4400 rpm. Twin oval grille sections sat side-by-side, each containing a pattern of vertical bars. Standard colors for the Crown Deluxe were: Velvet Blue metallic, Lyons Green metallic, Gold Bronze metallic, or Black.

Literature issued at the New York Auto Show in April 1960 described the Crown Custom family sedan (on a 172-inch wheelbase) and the Custom station wagon (on 173.7-inch wheelbase). Wagons were available in the 1960 model year.

I.D. DATA: Serial and motor number is on a plate attached to the radiator. Starting serial number: R161009.

Model	Body Type & Seating	Engine Type/CID	P.O.E. Price	Weight (lbs.)	Prod. Total
CROWN					
RSL	4-dr Sedan-6P	I4/89	2187	2650	N/A

Price Note: Figures shown were valid in 1958. A year later, a base Crown sold for $1989, while the Custom (RS22L) cost $2329. Price in 1960 was $1999 for the sedan, $2111 for a two-door station wagon, and $2211 for a four-door wagon.

1960 Toyopet four-door sedan.

ENGINE DATA: BASE FOUR: Inline, overhead-valve four-cylinder. **Displacement:** 88.7 cu. in. (1453 cc). **Bore & Stroke:** 3.03 x 3.07 in. (77 x 78 mm). **Compression Ratio:** 8.0:1. **Brake Horsepower:** 60 at 4400 rpm. **Torque:** 79.5 lbs.-ft. at 2600 rpm (later, 83.6 at 3600 rpm). Three main bearings.

CHASSIS DATA: **Wheelbase:** 99.6 in. **Overall Length:** (sed) 172-175 in.; (wag) 173.7 in. **Height:** 60 in. **Width:** 66 in. **Front Tread:** 52.2 in. **Rear Tread:** 53.9 in. **Standard Tires:** 6.50x15, 7.00x14 or 6.40x13.

TECHNICAL: **Layout:** front-engine, rear-drive. **Transmission:** three-speed manual (column shift). **Standard Final Drive Ratio:** 5.2:1. **Steering:** worm and sector. **Suspension (front):** unequal-length A-arms and coil springs. **Suspension (rear):** rigid axle with semi-elliptic leaf springs. **Brakes:** hydraulic, front/rear drum. **Body Construction:** on box-section steel frame.

MAJOR OPTIONS: Radio ($94). Whitewall tires ($35).

PERFORMANCE: **Top Speed:** 78-80 mph claimed. **Acceleration (0-60 mph):** 25.9 sec. **Acceleration (quarter-mile):** 23.5 sec. (58 mph). **Fuel Mileage:** average 23.5 mpg in test.

ADDITIONAL MODELS: Toyota's 4WD Land Cruiser (initially spelled Landcruiser) debuted in the U.S. by 1960, powered by a six-cylinder engine that developed 135 horsepower. Price was $2930 with a canvas top, or $3365 with a steel top. At the New York Auto Show in 1960, the Land Cruiser was described as the "most powerful sports-utility vehicle in the world."

Manufacturer: Toyota Motor Co. Ltd., Toyota City, Japan.

HISTORY: In a test of 12 hours of city driving, reported in Chicago's *American* newspaper, a Toyopet Crown Custom sedan got 34.59 mpg in city traffic. The car was driven for 12 hours non-stop within corporate limits of Chicago, including a trip through the Loop at the height of the rush hour.

1961-66 TOYOPET (TOYOTA)

1962 Toyopet Tiara.

TIARA — FOUR — This was Toyopet's "economy" sedan, on a shorter (94.5-inch) wheelbase than the current Crown, with the 89-cid engine that had powered prior Crowns. It debuted at the New York Auto Show in April 1960. Tires were 5.60x13 size.

CROWN — FOUR — Production of the six-passenger Crown sedan and station wagon continued, with a larger (116-cid), 95-horsepower engine.

I.D. DATA: Serial number is on a plate attached to the radiator cowl; on the frame near the front bumper; or on the right inner fender panel under the hood (Tiara).

Model TIARA	Body Type & Seating	Engine Type/CID	P.O.E. Price	Weight (lbs.)	Prod. Total
	4-dr Sedan-4/5P	I4/89	1613	2160	Note 1
CROWN					
Custom	4-dr Sedan-6P	I4/116	1795	2700	Note 1
Custom	4-dr Sta Wag-6P	I4/116	2080	N/A	Note 1

Note 1: A total of 73,830 Toyota passenger cars (all models) were produced during 1961, followed by 74,515 in 1962, 128,843 in 1963, 181,738 in 1964, 236,143 in 1965, and 316,189 in 1966.

Price Note: Figures shown were valid in 1961.

1966-'67 Toyota 2000 GT.

ENGINE DATA: BASE FOUR (Tiara): Inline, overhead-valve four-cylinder. **Displacement:** 88.7 cu. in. (1453 cc). **Bore & Stroke:** 3.03 x 3.07 in. (77 x 78 mm). **Compression Ratio:** 8.3:1. **Brake Horsepower:** 75 at 4500/5000 rpm. **Torque:** 84 lbs.-ft. at 3000 rpm.
BASE FOUR (Crown): Inline, overhead-valve four-cylinder. **Displacement:** 115.8 cu. in. (1879 cc). **Bore & Stroke:** 3.46 x 3.07 in. (88 x 78 mm). **Compression Ratio:** 8.4:1. **Brake Horsepower:** 95 at 5000 rpm. **Torque:** 110 lbs.-ft. at 3000 rpm.

CHASSIS DATA: Wheelbase: (Tiara) 94.5 in.; (Crown) 99.6 in. **Overall Length:** (Tiara) 157.2 in.; (Crown sed) 172 in. **Height:** (Tiara) 55.1-56.7 in.; (Crown sed) 60.2 in.; (Crown wag) 62.0 in. **Width:** (Tiara) 58.3 in.; (Crown) 66.0-66.8 in. **Front Tread:** (Tiara) 48.5 in.; (Crown) 52 in. **Rear Tread:** (Tiara) 48.5 in.; (Crown) 54 in. **Standard Tires:** (Tiara) 5.60x13; (Crown) 6.40x13.

TECHNICAL: Layout: front-engine, rear-drive. **Transmission:** three-speed manual (column shift). **Steering:** worm and sector. **Suspension (front):** unequal-length A-arms and coil springs. **Suspension (rear):** rigid axle with semi-elliptic leaf springs. **Brakes:** hydraulic, front/rear drum.

PERFORMANCE: Top Speed: (Tiara) 85 mph claimed; (Crown) 80 mph claimed.

PRODUCTION/SALES: Approximately 1,096 Toyotas (all models) were sold in the U.S. during 1963, followed by 2,029 in 1964, 6,404 in 1965, and 20,908 in 1966.

ADDITIONAL MODELS: Toyota's 4WD Land Cruiser remained available, priced at $2425 up in 1962. By the mid-1960s, Toyota also introduced a Stout pickup truck.
Manufacturer: Toyota Motor Co. Ltd., Toyota City, Japan.
Distributor: Toyota Motor Sales U.S.A. Inc., Torrance, California.
HISTORY: By 1964, the Toyopet name was dropped in the U.S. market and all cars were known as Toyotas.

1967-68 TOYOTA

1967 Toyota 2000 GT.

CORONA — FOUR — While the larger Crown had brought in a modest number of American customers, and the 4WD Land Cruiser earned its own separate following, the Corona was the car that established Toyota's presence in the U.S. With its angled back quad-headlamp front end, the Corona quickly became one of the most distinctive—easy to spot—cars on the road. Coronas came in sedan and hardtop coupe form, powered by a 115.8-cid four-cylinder engine (as in the earlier Crown) that developed 90 horsepower at 4600 rpm. An automatic transmission was optional.

CROWN — SIX — The luxury Crown remained in production through the late 1960s, now powered by an overhead-cam six-cylinder engine and on a longer (105.9-inch) wheelbase.

2000 GT — SIX — No discussion of Toyotas is complete without mention of the company's early but short-lived entrant into the GT sports-car arena. Styling features included concealed headlamps, a dramatic wraparound windshield, and rear quarter windows that came to a point at the rear. Under the hood of the sleek two-seater lurked a dual-overhead-cam inline six-cylinder Yamaha engine of 1988-cc displacement, whipping up 150 horsepower and 130 pounds-feet of torque. Actually built by Yamaha, the fastback coupe could accelerate to 60 mph in a claimed 10.1 seconds, and run the quarter-mile in 15.9 seconds. An all-synchro five-speed gearbox sent the power to the rear wheels, and all-disc brakes were installed. Fully independent suspension consisted of unequal-length A-arms with coil springs and anti-roll bars, at front and rear. Standard equipment included a 160-mph speedometer and 9000-rpm tachometer. A 2000 GT appeared at the New York Auto Show in April 1967. A modified convertible version was seen in the James Bond movie, "You Only Live Twice," which was filmed in Japan. A 2000 GT broke three world records and 13 international records for speed and endurance in October 1966, averaging 128.76 mph over a 72-hour period. A total of 337 2000 GTs were produced, of which about 53 were exported to the U.S. Production ended in 1968. Competition versions were rated 200 horsepower via higher compression and a hotter camshaft, among other modifications.

I.D. DATA: Serial number is on a plate attached to the radiator cowl; on the frame near the front bumper; or on a plate on the right side of the firewall, under the hood.

Model CORONA	Body Type & Seating	Engine Type/CID	P.O.E. Price	Weight (lbs.)	Prod. Total
	4-dr Sedan-4P	I4/116	1790	2100	Note 1
	2-dr HT Cpe-4P	I4/116	1995	2145	Note 1
CROWN					
	4-dr Sedan-5P	I6/137	2765	2765	Note 1
	4-dr Sta Wag-5P	I6/137	3070	2955	Note 1
2000 GT					
	2-dr Fbk Cpe-2P	I6/121	N/A	2470	337

Note 1: A total of 476,807 Toyota passenger cars (all models) were produced during 1967, followed by 659,189 in 1968.

Price Note: Figures shown were valid in 1968.

ENGINE DATA: BASE FOUR (Corona): Inline, overhead-valve four-cylinder. **Displacement:** 115.8 cu. in. (1879 cc). **Bore & Stroke:** 3.46 x 3.07 in. (88 x 78 mm). **Compression Ratio:** 8.0:1. **Brake Horsepower:** 90 at 4600 rpm. **Torque:** 110 lbs.-ft. at 2600 rpm.
BASE SIX (Crown): Inline, overhead-cam six-cylinder. **Displacement:** 137.5 cu. in. (2254 cc). **Bore & Stroke:** 2.95 x 3.35 in. (75 x 85 mm). **Compression Ratio:** 8.8:1. **Brake Horsepower:** 115 at 5200 rpm. **Torque:** 127 lbs.-ft. at 3600 rpm.
BASE SIX (2000 GT): Inline, dual-overhead-cam six-cylinder. **Displacement:** 121.3 cu. in. (1988 cc). **Bore & Stroke:** 2.95 x 2.95 in. (75 x 75 mm). **Compression Ratio:** 8.4:1. **Brake Horsepower:** 150 at 6600 rpm. **Torque:** 130 lbs.-ft. at 5000 rpm. Three Solex sidedraft carburetors.

CHASSIS DATA: Wheelbase: (Corona) 95.3 in.; (Crown) 105.9 in.; (2000 GT) 91.7 in. **Overall Length:** (Corona) 162.4 in.; (Crown sed) 183.7 in.; (Crown wag) 184.6 in.; (2000 GT) 164.4 in. **Height:** (Corona) 55.9 in.; (Crown sed) 56.9 in.; (Crown wag) 57.7 in.; (2000 GT) 45.7 in. **Width:** (Corona) 61.0 in.; (Crown) 66.5 in.; (2000 GT) 63.0 in. **Front Tread:** (Corona) 48.5 in.; (Crown) 53.9 in.; (2000 GT) 51.2 in. **Rear Tread:** (Corona) 48.5 in.; (Crown) 54.3 in.; (2000 GT) 51.2 in. **Standard Tires:** (Corona) 5.60x13; (Crown) 6.95x14; (2000 GT) 165HR15.

TECHNICAL: Layout: front-engine, rear-drive. **Transmission:** three-speed manual (column shift); four-speed and Toyoglide automatic available; except (2000 GT) five-speed manual. 2000 GT gear ratios: (1st) 3.143:1; (2nd) 1.636:1; (3rd) 1.179:1; (4th) 1.00:1; (5th) 0.844:1; (rev) 3.238:1. **Standard Final Drive Ratio:** (2000 GT) 4.375:1 (4.111:1 or 4.625:1 available). **Steering:** worm and sector except (2000 GT) rack and pinion. **Suspension (front):** unequal-length A-arms and coil springs. **Suspension (rear):** rigid axle with semi-elliptic leaf springs except (2000 GT) independent with wishbones, coil springs and torsion-bar stabilizer. **Brakes:** hydraulic, front/rear drum except (2000 GT) front/rear disc. **Body Construction:** (Corona) steel unibody; (2000 GT) on backbone frame.

PERFORMANCE: Top Speed: (Corona HT) 91 mph; (2000 GT) 128 mph in test (137 mph claimed). **Acceleration (0-60 mph):** (Corona HT w/4-spd) 14.0 sec.; (2000 GT) 10.0-11.0 sec. in tests (10.1 sec. claimed). **Acceleration (quarter-mile):** (Corona HT w/4-spd) 19.7 sec. (70.5 mph); (2000 GT) 16.3-16.6 sec. (83-87 mph) in test, but 15.9 sec. claimed.

PRODUCTION/SALES: Approximately 38,073 Toyotas (all models) were sold in the U.S. in 1967, followed by 71,463 in 1968.

ADDITIONAL MODELS: Toyota's 4WD Land Cruiser remained available, priced at $2705 up in 1968.

Manufacturer: Toyota Motor Co. Ltd., Toyota City, Japan.

Distributor: Toyota Motor Sales U.S.A. Inc., Torrance, California.

1969-70 TOYOTA

1970 Toyota Corona 1900 Mk II four-door sedan.

COROLLA — FOUR — Introduced during summer 1968, the subcompact Corolla rode a 90-inch wheelbase and carried a 65.8-cid engine, rated 60 horsepower. Displacement grew to 71 cid for 1970. Corollas came in three body styles: coupe, four-door sedan, and two-door wagon.

CORONA — FOUR — Production of the original Corona continued with little change.

CORONA MARK II — FOUR — A second-generation Corona rode a longer (98.8-inch) wheelbase and carried a smaller (113.4-cid) engine. Three body styles were available.

CROWN — SIX — Toyota continued to offer its large six-cylinder model, described as "a new prestige car for America." Both a four-door sedan and four-door wagon were available, with 137.5-cid overhead-cam six-cylinder engine.

I.D. DATA: Toyota's serial number is on upper left of dashboard, and on the firewall in the engine compartment.

Model	Body Type & Seating	Engine Type/CID	P.O.E. Price	Weight (lbs.)	Prod. Total
COROLLA					
	2-dr Sedan-4P	I4/66	1686	1642	Note 1
	2-dr Fbk Cpe-4P	I4/66	1816	1642	Note 1
	2-dr Sta Wag-4P	I4/66	1836	1730	Note 1
CORONA					
	4-dr Sedan-4/5P	I4/116	1950	2235	Note 1
	2-dr HT Cpe-4/5P	I4/116	2135	2235	Note 1
CORONA Mk II					
Mk II	4-dr Sedan-4/5P	I4/113	2130	2180	Note 1
Mk II	2-dr HT Cpe-4/5P	I4/113	2280	2180	Note 1
Mk II	4-dr Sta Wag-4/5P	I4/113	2360	2300	Note 1
CROWN					
	4-dr Sedan-5P	I6/137	2785	2765	Note 1
	4-dr Sta Wag-5P	I6/137	3089	3065	Note 1

Note 1: A total of 964,088 Toyota passenger cars (all models) were produced during 1969, followed by 1,068,321 in 1970.

Price Note: Figures shown were valid in 1969.

ENGINE DATA: BASE FOUR (1969 Corolla): Inline, overhead-valve four-cylinder. **Displacement:** 65.8 cu. in. (1079 cc). **Bore & Stroke:** 2.95 x 2.40 in. (75 x 61 mm). **Compression Ratio:** 9.0:1. **Brake Horsepower:** 60 at 6000 rpm. **Torque:** 61.5 lbs.-ft. at 3800 rpm.

BASE FOUR (1970 Corolla): Inline, overhead-valve four-cylinder. **Displacement:** 71.1 cu. in. (1166 cc). **Bore & Stroke:** 2.95 x 2.60 in. (75 x 66 mm). **Compression Ratio:** 9.0:1. **Brake Horsepower:** 73 at 6000 rpm. **Torque:** 74 lbs.-ft. at 3800 rpm.

BASE FOUR (Corona): Inline, overhead-valve four-cylinder. **Displacement:** 115.8 cu. in. (1879 cc). **Bore & Stroke:** 3.46 x 3.07 in. (88 x 78 mm). **Compression Ratio:** 8.0:1. **Brake Horsepower:** 90 at 4600 rpm. **Torque:** 110 lbs.-ft. at 2600 rpm.

BASE FOUR (Mk II): Inline, overhead-valve four-cylinder. **Displacement:** 113.4 cu. in. (1859 cc). **Bore & Stroke:** 3.39 x 3.15 in. (86 x 80 mm). **Compression Ratio:** 9.0:1. **Brake Horsepower:** 108 at 5500 rpm. **Torque:** 117 lbs.-ft. at 3600 rpm.

BASE SIX (Crown): Inline, overhead-cam six-cylinder. **Displacement:** 137.5 cu. in. (2254 cc). **Bore & Stroke:** 2.95 x 3.35 in. (75 x 85 mm). **Compression Ratio:** 8.8:1. **Brake Horsepower:** 115 at 5200 rpm. **Torque:** 127 lbs.-ft. at 3600 rpm.

CHASSIS DATA: Wheelbase: (Corolla) 90 in.; (Corona) 95.3 in.; (Mk II) 98.8 in.; (Crown) 105.9 in. **Overall Length:** (Corolla cpe/sed) 151.8 in.; (Corolla wag) 154 in.; (Corona) 162.4 in.; (Mk II) 170.5-171.5 in.; (Crown sed) 183.7 in.; (Crown wag) 184.6 in. **Height:** (Corolla cpe/sed) 54.3 in.; (Corolla wag) 55.1 in.; (Corona sed) 55.9 in.; (Corona cpe) 54.1 in.; (Mk II) 54.9-56.1 in.; (Crown sed) 56.9 in.; (Crown wag) 57.7 in. **Width:** (Corolla) 58.5-58.7 in.; (Corona) 61.0-61.6 in.; (Mk II) 63.2-63.4 in.; (Crown) 66.5 in. **Front Tread:** (Corolla) 49 in.; (Corona) 50 in.; (Mk II) 52.2 in.; (Crown) 53.9 in. **Rear Tread:** (Corolla) 48 in.; (Corona) 50 in.; (Mk II) 52 in.; (Crown) 54.3 in. **Standard Tires:** (Corolla) 6.00x12; (Corona) 6.00x13; (Crown) 6.95x14.

TECHNICAL: Layout: front-engine, rear-drive. **Transmission:** four-speed manual; automatic available. **Steering:** (Corolla/Corona) worm and roller; (Crown) recirculating ball. **Suspension (front):** (Corolla) struts with lower arms and transverse semi-elliptic leaf springs; (Corona/Crown) unequal-length A-arms and coil springs. **Suspension (rear):** rigid axle with semi-elliptic leaf springs. **Brakes:** (Corolla) front/rear drum; (Crown) front disc, rear drum. **Body Construction:** steel unibody.

PERFORMANCE: Top Speed: (Crown) 96 mph. **Acceleration (0-60 mph):** (Crown) 15.3 sec. **Acceleration (quarter-mile):** (Crown) 19.7 sec. (69 mph).

PRODUCTION/SALES: Approximately 130,044 Toyotas (all models) were sold in the U.S. during 1969, followed by 208,315 in 1970.

ADDITIONAL MODELS: Toyota's 4WD Land Cruiser remained available, priced at $2703 with a soft top.

Manufacturer: Toyota Motor Co. Ltd., Toyota City, Japan.

Distributor: Toyota Motor Sales U.S.A. Inc., Torrance, California.

1971-77 TOYOTA

1971 Toyota 2600 Crown four-door sedan.

COROLLA — FOUR — Production of the original Corolla continued, but a 1600 model with larger engine joined the lineup in 1971.

CELICA — FOUR — A sporty coupe was the next new Toyota model, introduced during the 1971 model year. From 1971-74, its engine was a 1967-cc four, rated 97 horsepower. Displacement then grew to 2189 cc (133.6 cid).

CORONA — FOUR — An 1859-cc engine powered the 1971 Corona; but that grew to 1967 cc for 1972-74, then to 2189 cc.

MARK II — FOUR — For the 1971 model year, an 1859-cc four continued. That evolved into a 1967-cc four for 1972, after which the four-cylinder Mark II faded away.

CROWN — SIX — Toyota's original Crown remained available only into 1971.

MX MARK II — SIX — Replacing the Crown, a new MX series started with a 2254-cc engine, then moved up to a 2563-cc version.

I.D. DATA: Toyota's serial number is on upper left of dashboard, and on the firewall in the engine compartment.

Model Year Note: Prices and specifications in this section are for 1971 models only. Engines changed over the 1971-77 period, as noted above.

Model	Body Type & Seating	Engine Type/CID	P.O.E. Price	Weight (lbs.)	Prod. Total
COROLLA					
1200	2-dr Sedan-4P	I4/71	1798	1725	Note 1
1200	2-dr Coupe-4P	I4/71	1918	1715	Note 1
1200	2-dr Sta Wag-4P	I4/71	1958	1805	Note 1
1600	2-dr Sedan-4P	I4/97	1918	N/A	Note 1
1600	4-dr Sedan-4P	I4/97	1993	N/A	Note 1
1600	2-dr Coupe-4P	I4/97	2038	N/A	Note 1
1600	2-dr Sta Wag-4P	I4/97	2078	N/A	Note 1
CELICA					
	2-dr Coupe-4P	I4/120	2598	2270	Note 1

604

Model	Body Type & Seating	Engine Type/CID	P.O.E. Price	Weight (lbs.)	Prod. Total
CORONA					
	4-dr Sedan-4/5P	I4/113	2150	2170	Note 1
	2-dr HT Cpe-4/5P	I4/113	2310	2170	Note 1
CORONA Mk II					
Mk II	4-dr Sedan-4/5P	I4/113	2280	2310	Note 1
Mk II	2-dr HT Cpe-4/5P	I4/113	2430	2310	Note 1
Mk II	4-dr Sta Wag-4/5P	I4/113	2510	2430	Note 1
CROWN (1971 only)					
	4-dr Sedan-5P	I6/137	2849	2965	Note 1
	4-dr Sta Wag-5P	I6/137	3154	3140	Note 1

Note 1: A total of 1,400,186 Toyota passenger cars (all models) were produced during 1971, followed by 1,487,661 in 1972, 1,631,940 in 1973, 1,484,737 in 1974, 1,714,836 in 1975, 1,730,767 in 1976, and 1,884,260 in 1977.

Price Note: Figures shown were valid in 1971.

ENGINE DATA: BASE FOUR (Corolla 1200): Inline, overhead-valve four-cylinder. **Displacement:** 71.1 cu. in. (1166 cc). **Bore & Stroke:** 2.95 x 2.60 in. (75 x 66 mm). **Compression Ratio:** 9.0:1. **Brake Horsepower:** 73 at 6000 rpm. **Torque:** 74 lbs.-ft. at 3800 rpm.

BASE FOUR (Corolla 1600): Inline, overhead-valve four-cylinder. **Displacement:** 96.9 cu. in. (1588 cc). **Bore & Stroke:** 3.35 x 2.76 in. (85 x 70 mm). **Compression Ratio:** 8.5:1. **Brake Horsepower:** 102 at 6000 rpm. **Torque:** 101 lbs.-ft. at 3800 rpm.

BASE FOUR (Celica): Inline, overhead-valve four-cylinder. **Displacement:** 120 cu. in. (1967 cc). **Bore & Stroke:** 3.48 x 3.15 in. (88 x 80 mm). **Compression Ratio:** 8.5:1. **Brake Horsepower:** 97 at 5500 rpm. **Torque:** 106 lbs.-ft. at 3600 rpm.

BASE FOUR (Corona/Mk II): Inline, overhead-valve four-cylinder. **Displacement:** 113.4 cu. in. (1859 cc). **Bore & Stroke:** 3.39 x 3.15 in. (86 x 80 mm). **Compression Ratio:** 9.0:1. **Brake Horsepower:** 108 at 5500 rpm. **Torque:** 117 lbs.-ft. at 3600 rpm.

BASE SIX (Crown): Inline, overhead-cam six-cylinder. **Displacement:** 137.5 cu. in. (2254 cc). **Bore & Stroke:** 2.95 x 3.35 in. (75 x 85 mm). **Compression Ratio:** 8.8:1. **Brake Horsepower:** 115 at 5200 rpm. **Torque:** 127 lbs.-ft. at 3600 rpm.

CHASSIS DATA: Wheelbase: (Corolla) 91.9 in.; (Corona) 95.7 in.; (Mk II) 98.8 in.; (Crown) 105.9 in. **Overall Length:** (Corolla 1200) 161.4-161.8 in.; (Corolla 1600) 157.5 in.; (Corona) 166.7-166.9 in.; (Mk II) 171.5 in.; (Crown sed) 183.7 in.; (Crown wag) 184.6 in. **Height:** (Corolla 1200) 54.1-55.3 in.; (Corolla 1600) 54.1 in.; (Corona sed) 54.5-55.1 in.; (Mk II) 54.9-56.1 in.; (Crown) 56.9 in. **Width:** (Corolla) 59.3 in.; (Corona) 61.8 in.; (Mk II) 63.2 in.; (Crown) 66.5 in. **Front Tread:** (Corolla) 49.3-49.4 in.; (Corona) 51.2 in.; (Mk II) 52.2 in.; (Crown) 53.9 in. **Rear Tread:** (Corolla) 49 in.; (Corona) 50 in.; (Mk II) 52 in.; (Crown) 54.3 in. **Standard Tires:** (Corolla 1200) 6.00x12; (Corolla 1600) 6.15x13; (Corona/Mk II) 6.00x13; (Crown) 6.95x14.

TECHNICAL: Layout: front-engine, rear-drive. **Transmission:** four-speed manual; five-speed and automatic available on some models. **Steering:** recirculating ball. **Suspension (front):** (Corolla/Celica) MacPherson struts with coil springs; (Corona/Crown) unequal-length A-arms and coil springs. **Suspension (rear):** rigid axle with semi-elliptic leaf springs. **Body Construction:** steel unibody.

PRODUCTION/SALES: Approximately 309,363 Toyotas (all models) were sold in the U.S. during 1971, followed by 311,278 in 1972, 326,844 in 1973, 235,874 in 1974, 283,909 in 1975, 346,920 in 1976, and 439,048 in 1977. Figures include Land Cruisers and (in some years) pickup trucks.

ADDITIONAL MODELS: Toyota's 4WD Land Cruiser remained available. Toyota also marketed a Carina sedan in 1972-73.

Manufacturer: Toyota Motor Co. Ltd., Toyota City, Japan.

Distributor: Toyota Motor Sales U.S.A. Inc., Torrance, California.

1978-83 TOYOTA

1979 Toyota Corolla SR-5 liftback.

COROLLA — FOUR — Toyota's top-selling model was reworked for 1980, still on a rear-drive chassis. Wheelbase was 94.5 inches, and the Corolla came in two- and four-door sedan form, along with notchback and hatchback coupes and a station wagon. Four-speed overdrive automatic became available in 1982. The 1.7-liter (108-cid) engine used in 1980-82 developed 73-75 horsepower, while the 1.6-liter overhead-cam version of 1983 was rated 70 bhp.

TERCEL — FOUR — Toyota's first front-drive model arrived for 1980, offered as a two-door sedan and three-door liftback coupe, as well as a four-door notchback sedan. Wheelbase was 98.4 inches. The 1.5-liter (89-cid) engine developed 60-62 horsepower. Fresh sheetmetal went onto a restyled Tercel for 1983, and wheelbase shrunk to 95.7 inches.

STARLET — FOUR — This was Toyota's rear-drive minicar, available only from 1981 to 1984. The three-door liftback used a 1.3-liter (79-cid) engine that developed 58 horsepower.

CELICA — FOUR — The sporty second-generation Celica came as a two-door notchback coupe or three-door liftback, powered by a 2.2-liter (134-cid) four-cylinder engine that developed 90-95 horsepower. Displacement grew to 2.4 liters (144 cid) for the 1981 model year. Wheelbase was 98.4 inches. Major restyling for 1982 gave a different look, but did not change dimensions or drivetrain by much.

CELICA SUPRA — SIX — Introduced in 1979, the Celica Supra was a six-cylinder version of the Celica, on a longer (103.5-inch) wheelbase. A larger 2.6-liter (156-cid) six yielded 116 to 121 horsepower. A larger (2.8-liter) engine with fuel injection became standard in 1981. Restyling for 1982 was accompanied by a switch to a twin-cam 2.8-liter engine, developing 145 horsepower. Independent rear suspension replaced the original solid axle at that time.

SUPRA — SIX — A restyled performance-oriented coupe debuted in mid-year 1986, dropping the former Celica prefix. Added pounds did not help performance, even though the engine grew to 3.0-liter (180-cid) displacement and a 200-horsepower rating. An intercooled turbo edition with 30 extra horsepower arrived the next year. Anti-lock braking became optional in 1987.

1979 Toyota Corona four-door hatchback.

CORONA — FOUR — The familiar Corona got a restyling for 1979, and came as a four-door sedan, five-door hatchback, or station wagon. A larger four-cylinder engine replaced the initial 2.2-liter for 1981, but actually rated slightly lower in horsepower. Availability continued into 1982, after which the Corona was replaced by a new front-drive Camry.

CRESSIDA — SIX — Toyota introduced a luxury model for 1978, and gave it a restyling for the 1981 model year. Wheelbase was 104.1 inches in both instances. In its first incarnation, a 2.6-liter (156.4-cid) six-cylinder engine went under the hood. A 2.8-liter (168-cid) engine went into the second generation, rated 116 horsepower. That engine adopted a twin-cam configuration for 1983, boosting horsepower to 143 and beyond. Also in 1983, Cressida gained independent rear suspension and all-wheel disc brakes, plus a five-speed manual gearbox.

1979 Toyota Celica GT liftback coupe.

I.D. DATA: Toyota's serial number is on upper left of dashboard, and (until 1981) on the firewall in the engine compartment.

Model Year Note: Prices and specifications in this section are for 1981 models only.

Model	Body Type & Seating	Engine Type/CID	P.O.E. Price	Weight (lbs.)	Prod. Total
COROLLA					
	2-dr Sedan-4/5P	I4/108	5178	2140	Note 1
Deluxe	2-dr Sedan-4/5P	I4/108	5688	2210	Note 1
Deluxe	4-dr Sedan-4/5P	I4/108	5808	2240	Note 1
Deluxe	4-dr Sta Wag-5P	I4/108	6178	2280	Note 1
Deluxe	2-dr HT Coupe-4P	I4/108	6258	2185	Note 1
SR5	2-dr HT Coupe-4P	I4/108	6658	2230	Note 1
Deluxe	3-dr Liftbk-4P	I4/108	5998	2265	Note 1
Deluxe	2-dr Spt Cpe-4P	I4/108	6128	N/A	Note 1
SR5	3-dr Liftbk-4P	I4/108	6708	2310	Note 1
SR5	2-dr Spt Cpe-4P	I4/108	6808	2315	Note 1
TERCEL					
	2-dr Sedan-4P	I4/89	4748	1900	Note 1
Deluxe	2-dr Sedan-4P	I4/89	5248	1905	Note 1
	4-dr Sedan-4P	I4/89	5078	1935	Note 1
Deluxe	3-dr Liftbk-4P	I4/89	5408	1915	Note 1
SR5	3-dr Liftbk-4P	I4/89	6038	1955	Note 1

Model	Body Type & Seating	Engine Type/CID	P.O.E. Price	Weight (lbs.)	Prod. Total
STARLET					
	3-dr Liftbk-4P	I4/79	5148	1724	Note 1
CELICA					
ST	2-dr Spt Cpe-4P	I4/144	6699	2597	Note 1
GT	2-dr Spt Cpe-4P	I4/144	7429	2610	Note 1
GT	3-dr Liftbk-4P	I4/144	7659	2641	Note 1
CELICA SUPRA					
GT	2-dr Spt Cpe-4P	I6/168	11298	2866	Note 1
CORONA					
Deluxe	4-dr Sedan-5P	I4/144	6719	2514	Note 1
Deluxe	5-dr Sta Wag-5P	I4/144	7099	2574	Note 1
LE	4-dr Sedan-5P	I4/144	8254	2597	Note 1
LE	5-dr Liftbk-5P	I4/144	8089	2559	Note 1
CRESSIDA					
Luxury	4-dr Sedan-4/5P	I6/168	11599	2851	Note 1
Luxury	4-dr Sta Wag-4/5P	I6/168	12049	2895	Note 1

Note 1: A total of 441,800 Toyotas were sold in the U.S. during 1978, followed by 507,816 in 1979, 582,204 in 1980, 576,491 in 1981, 530,246 in 1982, 555,766 in 1983, and 557,981 in 1984.
Price Note: Figures shown were valid in 1981.

1979 Toyota Cressida Luxury sedan.

ENGINE DATA: BASE FOUR (Corolla): Inline, overhead-cam four-cylinder. **Displacement:** 108 cu. in. (1770 cc). **Bore & Stroke:** 3.35 x 3.07 in. (85 x 78 mm). **Compression Ratio:** 9.0:1. **Brake Horsepower:** 73/75 at 5000 rpm. **Torque:** up to 95 lbs.-ft. at 2600 rpm. Two-barrel carburetor.

BASE FOUR (Starlet): Inline, overhead-valve four-cylinder. **Displacement:** 79 cu. in. (1290 cc). **Bore & Stroke:** 2.95 x 2.90 in. (75 x 74 mm). **Compression Ratio:** 9.0:1. **Brake Horsepower:** 58 at 5200 rpm. **Torque:** 67 lbs.-ft. at 3600 rpm. Two-barrel carburetor.

BASE FOUR (Tercel): Inline, overhead-cam four-cylinder. **Displacement:** 89 cu. in. (1452 cc). **Bore & Stroke:** 3.05 x 3.03 in. (77.5 x 77 mm). **Compression Ratio:** 9.0:1. **Brake Horsepower:** 62 at 4800 rpm. **Torque:** 75 lbs.-ft. at 2800 rpm. Two-barrel carburetor.

BASE FOUR (Celica, Corona): Inline, overhead-cam four-cylinder. **Displacement:** 144 cu. in. (2366 cc). **Bore & Stroke:** 3.62 x 3.50 in. (92 x 89 mm). **Compression Ratio:** 9.0:1. **Brake Horsepower:** 96 at 4800 rpm. **Torque:** 129 lbs.-ft. at 2800 rpm. Two-barrel carburetor.

BASE SIX (Celica Supra, Cressida): Inline, overhead-cam six-cylinder. **Displacement:** 168 cu. in. (2759 cc). **Bore & Stroke:** 3.27 x 3.35 in. (83 x 85 mm). **Compression Ratio:** 8.0:1. **Brake Horsepower:** 116 at 4800 rpm. **Torque:** 145 lbs.-ft. at 3600 rpm. Fuel injection.

1980 Toyota Viper coupe.

CHASSIS DATA: Wheelbase: (Corolla) 94.5 in.; (Tercel) 98.4 in.; (Starlet) 90.6 in.; (Celica) 98.4 in.; (Supra) 103.5 in.; (Corona) 99.4 in.; (Cressida) 104.1 in. **Overall Length:** (Corolla) 166.3-168.9 in.; (Tercel) 161.4 in.; (Starlet) 152.2 in.; (Celica) 175.5 in.; (Supra) 181.7 in.; (Corona) 175.0-178.7 in.; (Cressida) 184.8-185.2 in. **Height:** (Corolla) 50.8-53.0 in.; (Tercel) 52.8 in.; (Starlet) 54.3 in.; (Celica) 50.8-51.2 in.; (Supra) 51.8 in.; (Corona) 53.0-54.3 in.; (Cressida) 55.7-57.1 in. **Width:** (Corolla) 63.4-64.0 in.; (Tercel) 61.2 in.; (Starlet) 60.0 in.; (Celica) 64.6 in.; (Supra) 65.0 in.; (Corona) 65.2 in.; (Cressida) 66.5 in. **Front Tread:** (Corolla) 52.2 in.; (Tercel) 52.4 in.; (Starlet) 50.8 in.; (Celica) 53.1 in.; (Supra) 53.7 in.; (Corona) 53.7 in.; (Cressida) 54.7 in. **Rear Tread:** (Corolla) 52.6 in.; (Tercel) 51.8 in.; (Starlet) 50.2 in.; (Celica) 53.7 in.; (Supra) 53.7 in.; (Corona) 53.7 in.; (Cressida) 54.5 in.

1981 Toyota Celica Sunchaser convertible.

ADDITIONAL MODELS: Toyota's 4WD Land Cruiser remained available.
Manufacturer: Toyota Motor Co. Ltd., Toyota City, Japan.
Distributor: Toyota Motor Sales U.S.A. Inc., Torrance, California.

1984-90 TOYOTA

1985 Toyota MR2.

COROLLA — FOUR — After residing firmly in the best-seller role for several years, the Corolla turned to front-wheel-drive. A Corolla Sport edition, however, retained the rear-drive layout as late as 1987. Both carried a standard 1.6-liter (97-cid) overhead-cam four-cylinder engine, similar to that used in the former Corolla but now mounted transversely up front. An optional twin-cam edition arrived later. Early Corollas also could be ordered with a diesel engine. By 1987, some Corollas were being produced in California rather than Japan. By 1990, two fuel-injected twin-cam 1.6-liter engines were used, delivering 102 or 130 horsepower. Later sedans were available with four-wheel-drive.

TERCEL — FOUR — The front-drive Tercel continued in the form of its 1983 restyle, into 1986. Then came an aero restyle that included a sloping nose, halogen headlamps, raked windshield, and lower beltine. A new overhead-cam engine had three valves per cylinder and a variable-venturi carburetor, and was rated 76 horsepower. Some models kept the prior engine, with only 62 bhp.

CELICA — FOUR — Restyled for 1982, the rear-drive Celica remained in the lineup through 1985, then switched to front-drive. A new 2.0-liter (122-cid) overhead-cam engine developed 97 horsepower. Dual-overhead-cam versions developed 115 or 135 horsepower, while a turbo introduced for 1988 reached all the way to 190 bhp. A convertible joined the coupe and hatchback for the 1987 model year.
Celica got a luscious restyling for 1990, with elegant curves replacing the former sharper-edged look. Base models switched from a 115-horsepower, 2.0-liter engine to a twin-cam, 16-valve 1.6-liter four that developed 103 horsepower. GT and GT-S editions gained a 2.2-liter four with 130-bhp rating. A turbocharged four also was available, delivering 200 horsepower.

CAMRY — FOUR — Introduced as a 1983.5 model, Camry served as Toyota's front-drive successor to the long-lived rear-drive Corona. A four-door sedan and five-door liftback were available, powered by a 2.0-liter overhead-cam four-cylinder engine, producing 92 to 95 horsepower. A turbodiesel also was offered, in 1.8- or 2.0-liter displacement, but never became popular. Wheelbase was 102.4 inches, and the sedans measured 175.6 inches long overall.
Camry enjoyed a restyling for 1987, along the lines of the luxurious Cressida. Wheelbase remained the same, but the car gained in overall length and weight. A new five-door station wagon replaced the former liftback body. Engine displacement was unchanged, but the new version had dual overhead camshafts and 16 valves, which added 20 horsepower. Five-speed manual gearboxes and four-speed automatics were offered. An All Trac sedan with permanent four-wheel-drive arrived for 1988, as did a V-6 engine option. Late sedans were built in Kentucky rather than Japan.

1989 Toyota Cressida.

CRESSIDA — SIX — For one more year, Cressida carried on in the form it had adopted in 1981. Aero restyling for 1985 added only a little to dimensions, and did not alter appearance drastically except for the European-style headlamps and a new front spoiler. Rack-and-pinion steering was added, too. Electronically-controlled overdrive automatic transmissions could have dual-mode operation: Normal or Power Shift. All-new styling arrived for 1989, with less of a straight-edged appearance and slightly larger dimensions. A 3.0-liter six-cylinder (24-valve) engine replaced the former 2.8 liter unit, delivering 190 horsepower.

1990 Toyota Celica GT-S coupe.

1990 Lexus LS 400 four-door sedan.

1990 Lexus ES 250 four-door sedan.

MR2 — FOUR — Toyota finally introduced a full-fledged two-seat sports car, with a mid-engine configuration. Evolved from a prototype coded SV-3, the MR2 debuted in Japan in mid-1984 and arrived in the U.S. in February 1985, riding a 91.3-inch wheelbase. An-

gular styling differed considerably from most sports cars and semi-sports cars. People tended to either love it or hate it. The transverse-mounted twin-cam four-cylinder engine and transaxle came from the front-drive Corolla Sport, but were installed behind the seats in the MR2. The 1587-cd (97-cid) four was rated 112 horsepower at 6600 rpm initially, with 97 pound-feet of torque. That rose to 115 bhp and 100 pound-feet for 1988. Single-cam engines were used in base Japanese versions. Either a five-speed manual gearbox or four-speed automatic was available. MacPherson struts/coil springs with an anti-roll bar made up the front suspension, with struts and trailing arms at the rear. Rack-and-pinion steering was installed. Standard equipment included such goodies as an AM/FM stereo radio, tilt steering, and power mirrors. An aero body kit with decklid spoiler and rocker-panel skirting became available for 1986. Also on the option list were leather upholstery, air conditioning, and power windows. A T-top model with removable glass roof panels joined for 1987. Added for 1988 was a supercharged engine that delivered 145 horsepower at 6400 rpm. The blower went into action only on demand, using an electromagnetic clutch and bypass valve.

LEXUS NOTE: For 1990, Toyota introduced a pair of luxury rear-drive sedans from its new Lexus Division. The ES 250 carried a 2.5-liter twin-cam V-6 rated 156 horsepower, while the bigger LS 400 used a 250-bhp, 4.0-liter V-8 engine.

POSTSCRIPT: Biggest news for 1991 was the arrival of a dramatically restyled MR2 mid-engine coupe, which lost its angular look in favor of sumptuous curves. Two twin-cam engines were offered: a 130-bhp, 2.2-liter four, and a turbocharged 2.0-liter with a 200-bhp rating. The supercharged engine was gone. A Celica convertible became available in 1991. Also new for '91 was a restyled version of the long-lived 4WD Land Cruiser, and a curvy new Previa minivan.

TRIUMPH

Bicycles came first for the Triumph operation in Great Britain, starting in 1887. Those led to motorcycles and then to a three-wheeled motorcar, in 1903. Not until 1923, however, did Triumph turn to a four-wheel vehicle, powered by a 1.4-liter four-cylinder engine with four-speed gearbox. A 1.9-liter model followed in 1925; and a 2.2-liter, two years later. None of these quite took the nation by storm. Triumph's first real success came with the Super Seven of 1928, which carried a much smaller (747-cc) engine, soon enlarged to 832-cc dimensions as the Super Eight. A supercharged sports edition was offered briefly, too, along with a line of family-style sedans.

A name change in 1930 transformed the Triumph Cycle Co. Ltd. into Triumph Motor Co. Ltd. Six-cylinder power arrived in 1931 with the Scorpion, while a Coventry-Climax engine went into the Super Nine a year later. Saloons (sedans) of that era featured pillarless door construction. Triumph Glorias of the mid-1930s were the sporty members of the lineup, with 1.1- to 1.5-liter four-cylinder engines and 1.5- or 2.0-liter sixes. Overhead-valve Triumph-built engines replaced the Coventry-Climax units. A Dolomite series replaced the Gloria line for the late 1930s, offered with a 1.8-liter four or 2.0-liter six. Dolomite roadsters were particularly handsome.

Triumph became a subsidiary of the Standard Motor Co. after World War II, as a result of receivership just before the war broke out. The name Standard-Triumph Motor Co. appeared on sales literature, although the Triumph Motor Co. designation hung on into the 1960s and '70s. Because of the ownership change, postwar Triumphs retained little connection to the Triumphs of the prewar era, but were based instead on Standard components.

Traditional razor-edge styling was the main characteristic of the early postwar saloon. No less striking in appearance was the 1800 roadster, which also used the 1.8-liter, overhead-valve four-cylinder engine created for Jaguar, developing 65 horsepower. Two extra passengers could squeeze into the bustle seat out back, which had its own windshield. Standard Vanguard engines went into 1949 models. Then, in 1950, came a smaller razor-edge two-door saloon known as the Mayflower, on an 84-inch wheelbase with 1247-cc L-head engine. The larger saloon, renamed Renown, lasted until 1955.

Now Triumph was ready to make its name in the sports-car field. Triumph had experimented with an aero-styled sports car in 1950 that featured retracting headlamps and hydraulic doodads. That led to a second prototype, using

the Mayflower's coil-spring front suspension. The production TR2 roadster was ready in 1953, with sharply cutdown doors and a deeply-inset grille opening that gave a unique appearance that tended to prompt a love-it-or-hate-it response. Under the hood was a 2.0-liter version of the Vanguard engine, developing 90 horsepower. A TR2 could top 100 mph, and proved capable in competition as well as popular in the marketplace—even more so outside Britain.

Its TR3 successor added front disc brakes in 1956. A TR3A follow-up for 1958 added outside door and trunk handles and a new full-width grille. Triumph engines also went into other sports cars of the day, including Morgan, Doretti, and Peerless. Only sports cars were produced until 1959, when a small Herald sedan joined the lineup, with styling by Michelotti and four-wheel independent suspension. Triumph became part of Leyland Motors in 1961, and a six-cylinder engine went into the Herald-derived Vitesse.

Triumph introduced the restyled TR4 for 1962, with a 2.1-liter engine and rack-and-pinion steering. Also new was a different sort of sports car, the Spitfire, which used Herald mechanical components including an 1147-cc engine and had independent rear suspension. Spitfires evolved into II, III and IV versions through the 1960s. A GT6 coupe was similar in construction to the Spitfire roadster, but carried a 2.0-liter six-cylinder engine.

Independent rear suspension was part of the change in the larger sports car, to TR4A designation in 1965. By then, a 2000 sedan with 2.0-liter engine also was available. A TR5 follow-up for 1968 had a fuel-injected 2498-cc engine rather than the familiar Vanguard unit. American customers got a TR250 version instead, with a carbureted engine. Then came the TR6 in 1969. New for 1970 was the the Triumph Stag 2+2 luxury convertible (with built-in rollbar), packing a 3.0-liter overhead-cam V-8 beneath its bonnet.

A Toledo two-door sedan replaced the Herald for 1971, and the Dolomite name was revived in 1972, though seldom seen in the U.S. Spitfires remained in production through the 1970s, available in the U.S. into 1981. A wedge-shaped, unibodied TR7 coupe replaced the TR6 for 1976. A five-speed gearbox became available in 1977. Only the U.S. market ordinarily received examples of the final Triumph model, the TR8 convertible with a 3.5-liter Rover V-8 engine. After 1981, the Triumph name remained only on a Honda-based sedan known in Britain as the Acclaim. Yet another of the famed British-built sports cars was gone for good.

TR Model Designation Note: Early sales literature generally used periods in the sports car's model designation: e.g., "T.R.2." Many U.S. publications placed a hyphen within the model name (TR-2), but later Triumph promotional material omitted both the periods and the hyphen.

1946-48 TRIUMPH

1800 SERIES — FOUR — In the spring of 1946, Triumph unleashed two distinctive, memorably-styled models to the postwar marketplace: a razor-edged Town & Country saloon (sedan), and a dramatic roadster. The saloon wore a four-door "Six" body with light alloy panels and a knife-edge profile reminiscent of Rolls-Royces and other luxury British motorcars of the mid-1930s. Long front pontoon fenders extended far past the tall, angled vertical-bar grille. So did the majestic, separately-mounted headlamps. Small parking lights sat atop each front fender. An enclosed rear license plate holder contained two lights. Front doors were rear-hinged ("suicide" style).

Five or six passengers rode on bench-type front and rear seats upholstered in "furniture hide," each with a center folding armrest. Front doors were fitted with pull handles, window winders and pockets; rear doors with window winders and pockets. Pull straps were installed for rear passengers, and the car held a parcel shelf behind the rear seat. No foot wells were used. Front doors contained hinged, adjustable no-draft vents. All windows had Triplex toughened glass. Two glove lockers decorated the dashboard, and a sunvisor was standard. So was a roof light with integral switch. A concealed blind was controlled by the driver.

Beneath the Triumph bonnet was a 1776-cc, overhead-valve four-cylinder engine with 7.5:1 compression and a Solex "economy" downdraft carburetor. A Borg & Beck single dry-plate clutch sent power to the four-speed manual gearbox, which had a column gearshift lever. Independent front suspension used a single transverse multi-blade laminated leaf spring. At the rear were semi-elliptic leaf springs. Marles cam and twin-roller steering was installed, as were Girling "hydrastatic" (hydraulic) brakes. The 1800's tubular frame used 3.5" diameter tubes for side and crossmembers, plus deep box sections. Windtone horns sat under the hood. Standard colors were: Black with beige upholstery, Dark Metallic Grey with grey upholstery, or Maroon with red upholstery. The 1800's tool kit contained a tool roll, "Bevelift" jack, starting handle, grease gun, and hand tire pump.

Also released was the low-slung 1800 Roadster, which contained a front bench seat for three, with a folding center armrest, plus the last "dickey" (rumble) seat installed on a regular production automobile. Triumph described the setup as two occasional seats that folded forward into a recess behind the front seats, with access from the rear of the car. The car's soft top folded down completely behind the front seat, and the rumble-seat passengers even had their own fold-up windshield. Climbing in and out of that outside back seat wasn't an easy matter, however. Styling of the rear end was the work of Arthur Ballard, while Frank Callaby earned credit for the 1800's front end design. Roll-up windows were installed for the front passengers. Twin outside horns sat below the headlamps, to the rear of the front bumper. Standard colors were Black with beige upholstery and a black or fawn top; Dark Metallic Grey with blue upholstery and a black or grey top; or Maroon with red upholstery and a black or fawn top.

1946-'47 Triumph 1800 sports roadster.

I.D. DATA: Serial number is on side of firewall, under the hood. Engine number is on a boss on the side of the block. Serial number prefix: (saloon) TD1; (rds) TRD1.

Model	Body Type & Seating	Engine Type/CID	P.O.E. Price	Weight (lbs.)	Prod. Total
1800	4-dr Saloon-5/6P	I4/107	N/A	2702	N/A
1800	2-dr Rds-3/5P	I4/107	N/A	2380	Note 1

Note 1: A total of 2,501 Triumph 1800 roadsters were produced from 1946-48 (about 750 for export).

ENGINE DATA: BASE FOUR: Inline, overhead-valve four-cylinder. Chromium iron block. **Displacement:** 107 cu. in. (1776 cc). **Bore & Stroke:** 2.87 x 4.17 in. (73 x 106 mm). **Compression Ratio:** 6.7:1 (initially announced as 7.5:1). **Brake Horsepower:** 65 at 4500 rpm. **Torque:** 92 lbs.-ft. at 2000 rpm. Three main bearings. Solid valve lifters. One Solex carburetor. 12-volt electrical system.

CHASSIS DATA: Wheelbase: (saloon) 108 in.; (rds) 100 in. **Overall Length:** (saloon) 176 in.; (rds) 168.5 in. **Height:** (saloon) 63.5 in.; (rds) 56 in. **Width:** (saloon) 63.5 in.; (rds) 65 in. **Front Tread:** 49.75 in. **Rear Tread:** 54.75 in. **Wheel Type:** steel disc. **Standard Tires:** 5.75x16.

TECHNICAL: Layout: front-engine, rear-drive. **Transmission:** four-speed manual (column lever). Overall saloon gear ratios: (1st/rev) 19.18:1; (2nd) 11.8:1; (3rd) 7.06:1; (4th) 4.86:1. Overall roadster gear ratios: (1st/rev) 18.04:1; (2nd) 11.1:1; (3rd) 6.64:1; (4th) 4.57:1. **Standard Final Drive Ratio:** (saloon) 4.86:1; (rds) 4.57:1. **Steering:** Marles cam and twin roller. **Suspension (front):** independent; transverse leaf spring. **Suspension (rear):** rigid axle with semi-elliptic leaf springs. **Brakes:** hydraulic, front/rear drum. **Body Construction:** separate body with light alloy panels over ash wood framework, on ladder-type tubular steel frame.

PERFORMANCE: Top Speed: (saloon) 80 mph claimed; (rds) 84 mph claimed. **Acceleration (0-60 mph):** (saloon) N/A (0-50 mph in 16 sec. claimed); (rds) about 34.4 sec. (0-50 mph in 15 sec. claimed).

PRODUCTION/SALES: Approximately 31 Triumphs were sold in the U.S. during 1948.

Manufacturer: The Triumph Motor Co. Ltd. (subsidiary of The Standard Motor Co. Ltd.), Canley, Coventry, England.

1949 TRIUMPH

2000 — FOUR — Triumph's 1800 series evolved into the 2000 saloon and roadster, by virtue of a larger (Standard Vanguard) engine. The 2088-cc (128-cid) overhead-valve four developed 68 horsepower (3 more than the 1800). Instead of a four-speed gearbox, the 2000 used a three-speed, but fully synchronized. Column shift continued. Front suspension got a big change, to wishbones with coil springs and an anti-roll bar. The roadster got the larger engine first, but lasted only a single season. Saloons switched from 1800 to 2000 designation a little later in the model year, and evolved into the 2000 Renown series.

I.D. DATA: Serial number is on side of firewall, under the hood. Engine number is on a boss on the side of the block. Serial number prefix: (saloon) TAD1; (rds) TRA1.

Model	Body Type & Seating	Engine Type/CID	P.O.E. Price	Weight (lbs.)	Prod. Total
2000	4-dr Saloon-5/6P	I4/128	2950	2660	N/A
2000	2-dr Rds-3/5P	I4/128	2950	2352	Note 1

Note 1: A total of 2,000 Triumph 2000 roadsters were produced in 1948-49 (about 184 for export).

ENGINE DATA: BASE FOUR: Inline, overhead-valve four-cylinder (Standard Vanguard). Chromium iron block. **Displacement:** 128 cu. in. (2088 cc). **Bore & Stroke:** 3.35 x 3.62 in. (85 x 92 mm). **Compression Ratio:** 6.7:1. **Brake Horsepower:** 68 at 4200 rpm. **Torque:** 108 lbs.-ft. at 2000 rpm. Solid valve lifters. One Solex carburetor. 12-volt electrical system.

CHASSIS DATA: Wheelbase: (saloon) 108 in.; (rds) 100 in. **Overall Length:** (saloon) 178 in.; (rds) 168.5 in. **Width:** (saloon) 64 in.; (rds) 65 in. **Rear Tread:** 54 in. **Wheel Type:** steel disc. **Standard Tires:** 5.75x16.

TECHNICAL: Layout: front-engine, rear-drive. **Transmission:** three-speed manual (column lever). **Standard Final Drive Ratio:** (saloon) 4.86:1; (rds) 4.57:1. **Steering:** Marles cam and twin roller. **Suspension (front):** wishbones with coil springs and anti-roll bar. **Suspension (rear):** rigid axle with semi-elliptic leaf springs. **Brakes:** hydraulic, front/rear drum. **Body Construction:** separate body with light alloy panels over ash wood framework, on ladder-type tubular steel frame.

PRODUCTION/SALES: Approximately 11 Triumphs were sold in the U.S. during 1949.

Manufacturer: The Triumph Motor Co. Ltd. (subsidiary of The Standard Motor Co. Ltd.), Canley, Coventry, England.

HISTORY: Motor Trend described usage of the roadster's rumble seat in 1949, explaining that the folding seats were normally in stowed position. When swung backward, the forward section of the "turtleback" lifted forward to create a "windbreaker" for the two lucky (or unlucky, depending on the weather) passengers.

1950-53 TRIUMPH

1950 Triumph Mayflower.

MAYFLOWER — FOUR — A smaller razor-edged saloon debuted late in 1949, for the 1950 model year. Wheelbase was 84 inches, and instead of the usual overhead-valve engine, the Mayflower adopted a 1247-cc L-head powerplant that developed 38 horsepower. Instead of separate headlamps, as on the Renown, the Mayflower's were built into bulges in the fender tops. The bright, tall grille displayed a pattern of thin vertical bars with thick surround moldings. Doors were front-hinged. Mayflower's steel body used unitary construction. The trunk lid was bottom-hinged to form a platform. Disc wheels wore chromed nave plates. Front suspension was independent, with coil springs. A drophead (convertible) coupe also was produced.

2000 RENOWN — FOUR — The 2000 roadster was gone, but the saloon carried on under the "Renown" model designation. "Furniture hide" upholstery was standard on the "divan" seats with folding center armrests. Laycock de Normanville overdrive was optional, starting in mid-1950. A limousine with glass division window joined the original saloon by 1952, but lasted only a single season. Its radio was controlled by rear passengers. Saloon wheelbase grew from 108 to 111 inches, starting in 1952.

I.D. DATA: Serial number is on side of firewall, under the hood. Engine number is on a boss on the side of the block, at exhaust manifold, below the oil filter (Mayflower), or behind the coil (Renown). Starting serial number: (1950 Mayflower) TT1DL; (1952 Mayflower, U.S.) TT25600DL; (1952 Renown, U.S.) TDB-1000; (Renown limo) prefix TDC.

Model	Body Type & Seating	Engine Type/CID	P.O.E. Price	Weight (lbs.)	Prod. Total
MAYFLOWER					
	2-dr Saloon-5P	I4/76	1750	1960	N/A
	2-dr Dhd Coupe	I4/76	N/A	N/A	N/A
RENOWN					
2000	4-dr Saloon-5/6P	I4/128	3150	2600	N/A
2000	4-dr Limo-5/6P	I4/128	3400	2750	N/A

ENGINE DATA: BASE FOUR (Mayflower): Inline, L-head four-cylinder. Chromium iron block. **Displacement:** 76 cu. in. (1247 cc). **Bore & Stroke:** 2.48 x 3.94 in. (63 x 100 mm). **Compression Ratio:** 6.7:1. **Brake Horsepower:** 38 at 4200 rpm. **Torque:** 58 lbs.-ft. at 2000 rpm. Three main bearings. Solid valve lifters. One Solex carburetor. 12-volt electrical system.

BASE FOUR (Renown): Inline, overhead-valve four-cylinder. Chromium iron block. **Displacement:** 128 cu. in. (2088 cc). **Bore & Stroke:** 3.35 x 3.62 in. (85 x 92 mm). **Compression Ratio:** 6.7:1. **Brake Horsepower:** 68 at 4200 rpm. **Torque:** 108 lbs.-ft. at 2000 rpm. Three main bearings. Solid valve lifters. One Solex carburetor. 12-volt electrical system.

1950 Triumph TRX.

CHASSIS DATA: Wheelbase: (Mayflower) 84 in.; (early Renown) 108 in.; (later Renown, limo) 111 in. **Overall Length:** (Mayflower) 154 in.; (early Renown) 178 in.; (later Renown, limo) 181 in. **Height:** (Mayflower) 62 in.; (Renown) 62 in. **Width:** (Mayflower) 62 in.; (Renown) 64 in. **Max.Front Tread:** (Mayflower) 49 in.; (Renown) 54 in. **Wheel Type:** steel disc. **Standard Tires:** (Mayflower) 5.50x15; (Renown) 5.75x16.

TECHNICAL: Layout: front-engine, rear-drive. **Transmission:** three-speed manual (column lever); overdrive optional on Renown. **Steering:** (Mayflower) cam and lever; (Renown) cam and roller. **Suspension (front):** wishbones with coil springs and anti-roll bar. **Suspension (rear):** rigid axle with semi-elliptic leaf springs. **Brakes:** hydraulic, front/rear drum. **Body Construction:** (Mayflower) steel unibody; (Renown) separate body and frame (light alloy body paneling).

PERFORMANCE: Top Speed: (Mayflower) 65 mph claimed. **Acceleration (0-60 mph):** (Mayflower) N/A (0-50 mph in 23 sec. claimed).

PRODUCTION/SALES: Approximately 18 Triumphs were sold in the U.S. during 1950, followed by 10 in 1951, at least 105 (as many as 291) in 1952, and 278 in 1953.

Manufacturer: The Triumph Motor Co. Ltd. (subsidiary of The Standard Motor Co. Ltd.), Coventry, England.

Distributor: Fergus Motors Inc., New York City.

HISTORY: A sales brochure described the Mayflower saloon as "a light car of elegant British styling and unusually handsome appearance." On a larger scale, the "knife-edge coachwork" of the Renown "gives it an air of distinction for town or city use," as well as "sparkling performance."

Saloons weren't quite enough, however. Triumph's craving for a true sports car grew stronger after Sir John Black, the company head, failed in his attempt to purchase the Morgan company. Triumph began experiments with an aero-styled TRX sports car in 1950, which featured retracting headlamps and a selection of hydraulic gadgets. A second 20TS prototype borrowed the coil-spring front suspension from the Mayflower, and carried a less-potent version of the 1991-cc engine that would wind up in the TR2 roadster. That one appeared at the London Motor Show in October 1952, wearing an exposed spare tire and what many viewed as an unattractive rear end. Major reworking of the 20TS (TR1) concept, plus tweaking of the engine to 90 bhp, resulted in the production TR2 that debuted late in 1953. See next listing for full details.

1954-55 TRIUMPH

1954 Triumph TR 2 sports roadster.

TR2 — FOUR — At last, Triumph was ready with the first of its postwar sports cars, leading off a TR series that would last until the end of the nameplate in 1981. Few sports cars, or cars of any sort, were as easy to identify as the TR2 roadster, with its deeply-recessed grille opening that contained an eggcrate pattern far within. Cutdown doors, sans outside handles, were another styling feature. Flowing fenderlines extended across the doors. Headlamps were semi-built-in, and wheel openings were fully rounded. A roomy trunk was part of the pleasant package, marred only by a rather rough ride. Inside, two large dials faced the driver, with supplementary instruments in the center. Under the hood, the 1991-cc overhead-valve four-cylinder engine with twin SU carburetors developed 90 horsepower and 117 pound-feet of torque, sending it to a four-speed gearbox.

Suspension consisted of coil springs up front and semi-elliptic leaf springs at the rear. Later in the model run, center-lock wire wheels became optional. So did a seldom-seen lift-off hardtop and an overdrive transmission. Doors also were shortened slightly, in response to complaints of difficulty exiting when the car was parked next to a low curb. An optional suitcase fit precisely into the luggage compartment, which was quite small. Inside was a grab bar for the passenger, and holes were drilled for small racing shields. Top speeds of 103 mph or more were reported.

I.D. DATA: Serial number is on right side of the firewall, under the hood. Engine number is on left side of block, behind coil mounting. Serial number range: TS1 to TS8636.

Model	Body Type & Seating	Engine Type/CID	P.O.E. Price	Weight (lbs.)	Prod. Total
TR2	2-dr Rds-2P	I4/121	2448	1960	Note 1
TR2	2-dr HT Cpe-2P	I4/121	2695	N/A	Note 1

Note 1: Approximately 8,636 Triumph TR2s were produced over the full model run, from 1953-55 (5,521 for export).

Weight Note: Figure shown is shipping weight.

ENGINE DATA: BASE FOUR: Inline, overhead-valve four-cylinder. Cast iron block. **Displacement:** 121.5 cu. in. (1991 cc). **Bore & Stroke:** 3.27 x 3.62 in. (83 x 92 mm). **Compression Ratio:** 8.5:1. **Brake Horsepower:** 90 at 4800 rpm. **Torque:** 117 lbs.-ft. at 3000 rpm. Three main bearings. Solid valve lifters. Two SU carburetors.

CHASSIS DATA: Wheelbase: 88 in. **Overall Length:** 151 in. **Height:** 50 in. **Width:** 55.5 in. **Front Tread:** 45 in. **Rear Tread:** 45.5 in. **Wheel Type:** disc (wire optional). **Standard Tires:** 5.50x15.

TECHNICAL: Layout: front-engine, rear-drive. **Transmission:** four-speed manual (overdrive optional). Gear ratios: (1st) 3.38:1; (2nd) 2.00:1; (3rd) 1.325:1; (4th) 1.00:1. **Standard Final Drive Ratio:** 3.7:1. **Steering:** cam and lever. **Suspension (front):** unequal-length A-arms with coil springs. **Suspension (rear):** rigid axle with semi-elliptic leaf springs. **Brakes:** hydraulic, front/rear drum. **Body Construction:** steel body on steel frame.

MAJOR OPTIONS: Overdrive ($154). Radio ($99). Heater ($46). Tonneau cover ($32). Wire wheels ($99). Windwings ($23). Special suitcase ($45).

PERFORMANCE: Top Speed: 103-104 mph. **Acceleration (0-60 mph):** 11.9-13.7 sec. (0-50 mph in 7.5 sec. claimed) **Acceleration (quarter-mile):** 19.6 sec. (70 mph).

PRODUCTION/SALES: Approximately 952 Triumphs were sold in the U.S. during 1954.

Manufacturer: The Triumph Motor Co. Ltd. (subsidiary of The Standard Motor Co. Ltd.), Coventry, England.

Distributor: Fergus Motors, New York City; and Standard-Triumph Motor Co., New York and Los Angeles.

HISTORY: Production of the TR2 ran from August 1953 to October 1955. Founding of the Standard-Triumph Motor Co., a new U.S. company, was performed by Sir John Black, the company's head. *Motor Trend* tried out the first TR2 to reach the coast: a white roadster with rosy upholstery, and red top and side curtains. The view from the driver's seat reminded them of the Crosley Hotshot. Early TR2 ads promised "more performance per dollar than any other car in the world," claiming 0-50 mph acceleration in 7.5 seconds. "You're as young as you feel at the wheel of a T.R.2," they continued, "the car that let's you drive, and doesn't drive you!" Ads also promoted the speeds timed by the Royal Auto Club of Belgium: 108 mph in touring trim, and 124 mph in speed trim. A TR2 won the British Royal Automobile Club rally in March 1954. The next-generated TR3 debuted in autumn 1955; see next listing for details.

1956-57 TRIUMPH

1957 Triumph TR3 Ex-works Team Car. (Coys of Kensington)

TR3 — FOUR — Although the TR3's grille opening was shaped similar to that used for the TR2, front-end appearance changed considerably. This version's eggcrate pattern had much larger "holes" and was not recessed. The pattern consisted of six vertical bars ahead of seven horizontal bars. Headlamps again sat almost "bugeye" style, bulging above the front fenders. Engine displacement was the same 1991 cc as before, but modified intake ports and larger-choke SU carburetors boosted horsepower by 5. Because of added weight, however, performance and economy suffered slightly.

Early engines used a "Le Mans" cylinder head, which was changed during the production to a "high-port" design that added 5 more horsepower. Starting in autumn 1956, Girling front disc brakes were installed. The back of the passenger seat folded forward for access to rear space. While the TR2 was strictly a two-seater, the TR3 could have an "occasional" rear seat, which offered barely enough space for even a tiny person to squeeze in. Wire wheels also were optional, as was a detachable hardtop. TR3 body colors were: Pearl White, Signal Red, Black, Salvador Blue, British Racing Green, Sunset Red, and Beige. Soft tops came in black or fawn; side curtains in black, fawn or white. Leather upholstery came in a selection of nine colors.

I.D. DATA: Serial number is on right side of the firewall, under the hood. Engine number is on left side of block, behind coil mounting. Serial number range: TS8636 to TS13045 with drum brakes; TS13046 to TS22013 with front disc brakes.

Model	Body Type & Seating	Engine Type/CID	P.O.E. Price	Weight (lbs.)	Prod. Total
TR3	2-dr Rds-2P	I4/121	2625	2100	Note 1
TR3	2-dr HT Cpe-2P	I4/121	2790	N/A	Note 1

Note 1: As many as 16,801 Triumph TR3s were produced over the full model run, from 1955-57 (15,561 for export).

Price Note: Figures shown were valid in 1957. Initial price for the roadster was $2595.

ENGINE DATA: BASE FOUR: Inline, overhead-valve four-cylinder. Cast iron block. **Displacement:** 121.5 cu. in. (1991 cc). **Bore & Stroke:** 3.27 x 3.62 in. (83 x 92 mm). **Compression Ratio:** 8.5:1. **Brake Horsepower:** 95 at 4800 rpm (later, 100 at 5000 rpm). **Torque:** 117 lbs.-ft. at 3000 rpm. Three main bearings. Solid valve lifters. Two SU carburetors.

CHASSIS DATA: Wheelbase: 88 in. **Overall Length:** 151 in. **Height:** 50 in. **Width:** 55.5 in. **Front Tread:** 45 in. **Rear Tread:** 45.5 in. **Wheel Type:** disc (wire optional). **Standard Tires:** 5.50x15.

TECHNICAL: Layout: front-engine, rear-drive. **Transmission:** four-speed manual (2/3/4 synchro). Gear ratios: (1st) 3.38:1; (2nd) 2.00:1; (3rd) 1.325:1; (4th) 1.00:1. Overdrive available. **Standard Final Drive Ratio:** 3.7:1. **Steering:** cam and lever. **Suspension (front):** unequal-length A-arms with coil springs. **Suspension (rear):** rigid axle with semi-elliptic leaf springs. **Brakes:** hydraulic, front/rear drum (front disc, rear drum starting in October 1956). **Body Construction:** steel body on steel frame.

MAJOR OPTIONS: Heater ($50). Radio ($106). Hardtop with sliding windows. Soft top kit for hardtop ($99). Aero screen racing windshields ($31). Short front undershields. Rear fender skirts: disc wheels only ($31). Center-lock wire wheels: painted ($100); chromed ($198). Overdrive ($154). Occasional seat: either Vynide or leather ($60). Tonneau cover ($35). Adjustable (telescopic) steering wheel ($23). Two-speed wipers. Fitted suitcase for trunk ($46). Competition carburetor-jet needles. Aluminum engine sump ($23). Alfin brake drums ($140). Competition front springs ($5.75). Competition rear shocks ($5.75). Dunlop Road Speed tires.

PERFORMANCE: Top Speed: 102-107 mph (110 mph claimed for 100-bhp). **Acceleration (0-60 mph):** 12.5-13.2 sec. (as little as 9.2 sec. reported in test). **Acceleration (quarter-mile):** (100-bhp) 18.9 sec. (74 mph) (one test reported 16.9 sec. and 81.9 mph). **Fuel Mileage:** 26-35 mpg claimed.

Manufacturer: The Triumph Motor Co. Ltd. (subsidiary of The Standard Motor Co. Ltd.), Coventry, England.

Distributor: Standard-Triumph Motor Co., New York City.

HISTORY: Production of the original TR3 began in October 1955 and continued until September 1956; then front disc brakes were installed for the remainder of the production run, up to October 1957. "How to drive a fast bargain" was the theme for a U.S. ad for the TR3 in 1956, quoting a price of $2599. Top speed of 110 mph was claimed for the 100-bhp engine, with 0-50 mph acceleration in 8 seconds and fuel mileage up to 30-35 mpg. A TR3, it said, "combines sports car performance with family convenience." A TR3 could be purchased in France (by Americans) for $1925. The TR3A was announced in September 1957 and available early in 1958; see next listing for details.

1958-61 TRIUMPH

1960 Triumph TR3A. (William Siuru Jr.)

TR3A — FOUR — Still based on the original design, the next generation of the Triumph roadster adopted a much wider grille, with parking lights incorporated into its eggcrate pattern. Some called this the "wide mouth" version to separate it from the former "small mouth" (or the TR2's "deep mouth") front end. Outside door handles were new this time, along with a locking trunk handle. Headlamps no longer protruded as much. Under the hood was the same 1991-cc engine used in the final TR3, developing 100 bhp and 117 pound-feet. A four-speed gearbox was standard; overdrive optional. TR3A colors included Signal Red, Pearl White, Silverstone Grey, Sebring White, Powder Blue, Pale Yellow, British Racing Green, Black, and Pearl Grey. Top and side curtains came in black, fawn or white.

I.D. DATA: Serial number is on right side of the firewall, under the hood. Engine number is on left side of block, behind coil mounting. Serial number range: TS22014 to TS82346.

Model	Body Type & Seating	Engine Type/CID	P.O.E. Price	Weight (lbs.)	Prod. Total
TR3A	2-dr Rds-2P	I4/121	2675	2016	Note 1
TR3A	2-dr HT Cpe-2P	I4/121	2835	N/A	Note 1

Note 1: Approximately 58,236 Triumph TR3As were produced over the full model run, from 1957-61 (some sources give a lower total: namely 58,097, including the TR3B).

Price Note: Figures shown were valid in 1958-60.

ENGINE DATA: BASE FOUR: Inline, overhead-valve four-cylinder. Cast iron block. **Displacement:** 121.5 cu. in. (1991 cc). **Bore & Stroke:** 3.27 x 3.62 in. (83 x 92 mm). **Compression Ratio:** 8.5:1. **Brake Horsepower:** 100 at 5000 rpm. **Torque:** 117 lbs.-ft. at 3000 rpm. Three main bearings. Solid valve lifters. Two SU carburetors.

Note: Starting in 1959, some TR3A models came with a larger (2138-cc) engine.

CHASSIS DATA: Wheelbase: 88 in. **Overall Length:** 151 in. **Height:** 50 in. **Width:** 55.5 in. **Front Tread:** 45 in. **Rear Tread:** 45.5 in. **Wheel Type:** disc (wire optional). **Standard Tires:** 5.50x15.

TECHNICAL: Layout: front-engine, rear-drive. **Transmission:** four-speed manual (2/3/4 synchro); overdrive available. **Standard Final Drive Ratio:** 3.7:1. **Steering:** cam and lever. **Suspension (front):** unequal-length A-arms with coil springs. **Suspension (rear):** rigid axle with semi-elliptic leaf springs. **Brakes:** front disc, rear drum. **Body Construction:** steel body on steel frame.

MAJOR OPTIONS: Similar to 1956-57.

PERFORMANCE: Top Speed: about 102 mph. **Acceleration (0-60 mph):** about 12.5 sec.

PRODUCTION/SALES: Approximately 16,245 Triumphs were sold in the U.S. during 1958, followed by 22,922 in 1959, 17,720 in 1960, and 11,683 in 1961.

ADDITIONAL MODELS: By 1958, a Triumph TR10 sedan was available solely for the American market, on an 84-inch wheelbase and priced at $1899. An Estate Wagon sold for $1899. The 948-cc engine developed 40 horsepower at 5000 rpm. Torque was 50 lbs.-ft. at 2700 rpm. Ads promoted it as "the only auto at this price with no-clutch push-button shift," adding that its engine had TR3 sports car engineering. Top speed up to 78 mph was claimed, with fuel mileage to 40 mpg. Knock-down rear seats gave 30 cubic feet of storage space.

After the TR10 came the Triumph Herald series, available in the U.S. for the 1960 model year. A two-door sedan sold for $1849; a coupe for $2149; and a convertible cost $2229. Wheelbase was 91.5 inches. Heralds were powered by a 948-cc (57.8-cid) four-cylinder engine that developed 40 horsepower (50 bhp with twin SU carburetors in the coupe and convertible). *Motor Trend* described the Herald convertible as "a unique combination of the practical and the sporty." A Herald convertible could accelerate to 60 mph in 23.8 seconds.

Manufacturer: The Triumph Motor Co. Ltd. (subsidiary of The Standard Motor Co. Ltd.), Coventry, England.

Distributor: Standard-Triumph Motor Co., New York City.

HISTORY: Production of the TR3A began in September 1957 and lasted until October 1961. Production of the TR4 began in August 1961. A TR3B follow-up was available during 1962, for U.S. consumption only, marketed alongside the TR4; see next listing for details on both models. By 1959, there were more than 700 Triumph dealers in the U.S. Standard-Triumph suffered financial ills in 1961, and became part of British Leyland.

1962-66 TRIUMPH

1965 Triumph Herald convertible. (William Siuru Jr.)

SPITFIRE — Mk I — FOUR — Just as MG had its Midget and Austin-Healey its Sprite, Triumph had a smaller sports car available for sale in late 1962. Based on the Triumph Herald chassis, the Spitfire sold more copies than its two British rivals combined. Though conceived by 1960, production did not get underway until after the takeover of Triumph by the Leyland organizatoin. Giovanni Michelotti of Italy was credited with the design, while the name came from the famed fighter plane of World War II. Up front was a small split grille, consisting of two side-by-side rectangles. Headlamps were partly recessed; doors just slightly cutdown. Suspension was the same fully-independent design used in the Herald, but atop a new backbone-style chassis with a shorter (83-inch) wheelbase than the Herald. Welded monocoque (unibody) construction was employed, and the hood/fenders tilted upward as a unit for excellent access to the engine bay. Inside that bay was a modified Herald 1147-cc (70-cid) overhead-valve four, rated 63 horsepower at 5750 rpm. A four-speed gearbox was installed, with overdrive optional. Center-lock wire wheels became available in 1963.

SPITFIRE — Mk II — FOUR — The next edition of the smaller sports car, introduced at the end of 1964, gained 4 horsepower and a vinyl-covered dashboard, and carpeting replaced the former rubber mats. Three different tuning kits could be ordered. The basic (Interim) kit included a Solex downdraft carburetor with modified manifolds, good for 70 horsepower. Stage I stepped up the power; and Stage III went all the way with a pair of Weber carbs, higher-lift cam, and exhaust headers. Few of the latter were sold.

TR3B — FOUR — Because Triumph's importer and dealers in the U.S. were concerned that the new TR4 would not sell well, they requested a special extension of the TR3 design for an additional year. Thus, the TR3B was produced only for sale in America, during 1962. Early examples were identical to the TR3A; later ones were similar in appearance but carried the TR4's larger engine and its new all-synchro gearbox.

TR4 — FOUR — Triumph's next-generation "full-size" sports car was totally restyled, with the assistance of Giovanni Michelotti. Chassis details weren't much different from the TR3A, except for the adoption of rack and pinion steering, but the body had a much different look: longer, lower, wider, more square and contemporary, with straight-through fenderlines and a wider stance. In fact, tread dimensions grew by some 3 inches. A wide horizontal-bar grille was slightly recessed, incorporating headlamps which sat below hood humps that formed small dead lids. Wraparound bumpers were installed at both ends. The windshield was larger than before, and slightly curved. Wind-up windows were a "first" for Triumph roadsters. So was the TR4's face-level ventilation

system. Another curious feature arrived on the optional hardtop. Its center section could be lifted out, and replaced by a canvas top. Under the hood was a 2138-cc (130-cid) engine, as installed in final examples of the TR3B, developing 105 horsepower via 9.0:1 compression. The smaller (1991-cc) engine remained available, however, for use in 2.0-liter class racing. Standard TR4 colors were: Spa White, Signal Red, Black, Powder Blue, or British Racing Green. Soft tops came only in black or white. Upholstery could be black, red or blue, keyed to the body color.

TR4A — FOUR — Modest modifications were made to the TR4's engine, which boosted top speed a bit. The main change from the TR4, however, was adoption of independent rear suspension, using semi-trailing arms and coil springs. Some examples were sold with the old (rigid-axle) rear end.

1965 Triumph Herald station wagon. (Elliott Kahn)

I.D. DATA: Serial number is on right side of the firewall, under the hood. Engine number is on left side of block, behind coil mounting. Serial number range: (Spitfire Mk I) FC-1-L up; (Spitfire Mk II) FC50001L up; (TR3B w/1991-cc) TSF1 to TSF830; (TR3B w/2138-cc) TCF1 to TCF2804; (TR4) CT1 to CT40304; (TR4A) CTC50001 to CTC78684 (except those with rigid rear axle had "CT" serial numbers).

Model	Body Type & Seating	Engine Type/CID	P.O.E. Price	Weight (lbs.)	Prod. Total
SPITFIRE (1963-64)					
Mk I	2-dr Rds-2P	I4/70	2199	1474	Note 1
SPITFIRE (1965-66)					
Mk II	2-dr Rds-2P	I4/70	2155	1474	Note 2
Mk II	2-dr HT Cpe-2P	I4/70	2299	1474	Note 2
TR3B (1962 only)					
TR3B	2-dr Rds-2P	I4/121	2675	2016	Note 3
TR3B	2-dr Rds-2P	I4/121	2835	2016	Note 3
TR4(1962-64)					
TR4	2-dr Rds-2P	I4/130	2849	2072	Note 4
TR4	2-dr HT Cpe-2P	I4/130	2999	2072	Note 4
TR4A (1965-66)					
TR4A	2-dr Rds-2P	I4/130	2840	2072	Note 5
TR4A	2-dr HT Cpe-2P	I4/130	2987	2072	Note 5

Note 1: Approximately 45,753 Triumph Spitfire Mk Is were produced in 1962-64.

Note 2: Approximately 37,409 Triumph Spitfire Mk IIs were produced from 1964-67.

Note 3: Approximately 3,331 Triumph TR3Bs were produced in 1962.

Note 4: Approximately 40,253 Triumph TR4s were produced over the full model run, from 1961-64.

Note 5: Approximately 28,465 Triumph TR4As were produced over the full model run, from 1965-67.

Price Note: Figures shown for Spitfire Mk I, TR3B and TR4 were valid in 1962; for Spitfire Mk II and TR4A, in 1966.

ENGINE DATA: BASE FOUR (Spitfire): Inline, overhead-valve four-cylinder. Cast iron block. **Displacement:** 70 cu. in. (1147 cc). **Bore & Stroke:** 2.73 x 2.99 in. (69.3 x 76 mm). **Compression Ratio:** 8.5:1. **Brake Horsepower:** (Mk I) 63 at 5750 rpm; (Mk II) 67 at 6000 rpm. **Torque:** 67 lbs.-ft. at 3500/3750 rpm. Three main bearings. Solid valve lifters. Two SU carburetors.

BASE FOUR (early TR3B); OPTIONAL (TR4): Inline, overhead-valve four-cylinder. Cast iron block. **Displacement:** 121.5 cu. in. (1991 cc). **Bore & Stroke:** 3.27 x 3.62 in. (83 x 92 mm). **Compression Ratio:** 8.5:1. **Brake Horsepower:** 100 at 5000 rpm. **Torque:** 117 lbs.-ft. at 3000 rpm. Three main bearings. Solid valve lifters. Two SU carburetors.

BASE FOUR (late TR3B, TR4): Inline, overhead-valve four-cylinder. Cast iron block. **Displacement:** 130.4 cu. in. (2138 cc). **Bore & Stroke:** 3.39 x 3.62 in. (86 x 92 mm). **Compression Ratio:** 9.0:1. **Brake Horsepower:** 100 at 4600 rpm (105 at 4750 rpm in U.S.). **Torque:** 127 lbs.-ft. at 3350 rpm. Three main bearings. Solid valve lifters. Two SU carburetors.

BASE FOUR (TR4A): Same as TR4, except — **Brake Horsepower:** 104 at 4700 rpm (105 at 4150 rpm in U.S.). **Torque:** 132 lbs.-ft. at 3350 rpm.

CHASSIS DATA: Wheelbase: (Spitfire) 83 in.; (TR) 88 in. **Overall Length:** (Spitfire) 145 in.; (TR3) 151 in.; (TR4) 156 in. **Height:** (Spitfire) 47.5 in.; (TR4) 50 in. **Width:** (Spitfire) 57 in.; (TR3) 55.5 in.; (TR4) 57.5 in. **Front Tread:** 49 in. **Rear Tread:** 48 in. **Wheel Type:** disc (wire optional). **Standard Tires:** (Spitfire) 5.20x13; (TR4) 5.90x15.

TECHNICAL: Layout: front-engine, rear-drive. **Transmission:** four-speed manual; overdrive available. **Steering:** rack and pinion. **Suspension (front):** unequal-length A-arms with coil springs. **Suspension (rear):** (Spitfire) swing axles with radius arms and transverse leaf spring; (TR4) rigid axle with semi-elliptic leaf springs; (TR4A) independent with semi-trailing links and coil springs. **Brakes:** front disc, rear drum. **Body Construction:** steel body on steel frame.

PERFORMANCE: Top Speed: (Spitfire) about 92 mph. **Acceleration (0-60 mph):** (Spitfire) 15.5-16.5 sec.; (TR4) 11.5 sec. **Acceleration (quarter-mile):** (TR4) 18.2 sec.

PRODUCTION/SALES: Approximately 15,967 Triumphs were sold in the U.S. during 1962, followed by 20,117 in 1963, 21,214 in 1964, 20,347 in 1965, and 17,184 in 1966.

ADDITIONAL MODELS: A larger (1147-cc) engine went into the Herald, which soon changed its name to the Triumph 1200, offered again in coupe, convertible and two-door sedan body styles. This engine developed 43 horsepower at 4500 rpm. Prices in 1962 ranged from $1649 to $1999. A Sports Six convertible was available in mid-1962, using the 1200's body shell with a different nose, grille, headlamp setup, and bumper dividers. As the name suggests, a six-cylinder engine was installed, with 1596-cc displacement and 70-bhp rating. This model was known as the Vitesse in the home market, and had fully independent suspension and front disc brakes, plus rack-and-pinion steering. A 2000 sedan entered the U.S. market for the 1966 model year, with a larger (2.0-liter) six-cylinder engine under its hood.

Manufacturer: Triumph Motor Company Ltd., Coventry, England (part of British Leyland).

Distributor: Standard-Triumph Motor Co., New York City.

HISTORY: Production of the TR3B (first series) began in March 1962 and ended in September of that year; the second series, with larger engine, started in May 1962 and lasted into October. Production of the TR4 ran from August 1961 to January 1965, followed by the TR4A into August 1967. Spitfire Mk I was on sale in autumn 1962, continuing until December 1964. Spitfire Mk II followed, into 1967.

1967-68 TRIUMPH

SPITFIRE — Mk II — FOUR — Production of the Spitfire Mk II continued into 1967.

SPITFIRE — Mk III — FOUR — The next Spitfire edition debuted early in 1967, with a larger (1296-cc) engine that had been used in the front-drive 1300 sedan, rated 75 horsepower. Front disc brakes and the clutch were toughened to handle the extra strength. Styling was similar to the prior edition, except for the addition of a thick wraparound bumper directly ahead of the grille. Thus, parking/signal lights wound up below the bumper. Rear quarter-bumpers were installed as before, but modified in shape. The Spitfire's folding soft top now was permanently attached and easier to erect, and the dashboard added a touch of walnut veneer. Starting in 1969, Spitfires destined for the U.S. got a revised dashboard, with instruments mounted directly ahead of the driver (formerly in the center of the dash). Production continued until the end of 1970.

GT6 — SIX — A six-cylinder companion to the Spitfire arrived late in 1966, on a chassis that differed little from the Mk II roadster. Instead of an open two-seater, however, the GT6 came in closed fastback coupe form. Under its hood was the 1998-cc six that also powered 2.0-liter Triumph sedans. With 95 horsepower on tap, working through Triumph's new all-synchro four-speed gearbox, a GT6 could edge past 100 mph and accelerate to 60 mph in the 12-second neighborhood. Overdrive was optional, as on most Triumphs. Clean styling was similar to the Spitfire, but the fastback top and large hatch glass gave the GT6 a distinct personality.

TR4A — FOUR — Production of the TR4A roadster continued into August 1967. See previous listing for details.

TR250/TR5 PI — SIX — Adding more power to the TR roadster was accomplished by adding two more cylinders. Europeans were treated to a TR5 PI model (PI stood for port fuel injection by Lucas), with 150 horsepower at hand. American customers got a less-potent TR250 with a carbureted version of the 2.5-liter engine. Needless to say, performance differed wildly between the two. Appearance in either case was similar to the TR4A, except that the grille lost its small vertical center bar, leaving only a pattern of full-width horizontal bars. Standard steel wheels came with covers intended to look like "mags," but many of the new convertibles wore optional center-lock wire wheels instead. American TR250 hoods displayed a set of racing stripes. Radial tires now were standard. Production lasted less than two years, ceasing before the end of 1968.

I.D. DATA: Serial number is on right side of the firewall, under the hood. Engine number is on left side of block. Starting serial number: (Spitfire Mk III) FD7796; (1968 GT6) KC6540; (TR250 conv) CK1L; (TR250 HT cpe) CD1L.

Model	Body Type & Seating	Engine Type/CID	P.O.E. Price	Weight (lbs.)	Prod. Total
SPITFIRE (1967)					
Mk II	2-dr Conv Cpe-2P	I4/70	2199	1474	Note 1
Mk II	2-dr HT Cpe-2P	I4/70	2343	1474	Note 1
SPITFIRE (1968)					
Mk III	2-dr Conv Cpe-2P	I4/79	2235	1586	Note 2
Mk III	2-dr HT Cpe-2P	I4/79	2385	1586	Note 2
GT6					
Mk I	2-dr Fbk Cpe-2P	I6/122	2895	1900	Note 3
TR4A (1967)					
TR4A	2-dr Conv Cpe-2P	I4/130	2899	2003	Note 4
TR4A	2-dr HT Cpe-2P	I4/130	3046	2003	Note 4
TR250 (1968)					
TR250	2-dr Conv Cpe-2P	I6/152	3175	2165	Note 5
TR250	2-dr HT Cpe-2P	I6/152	3175	2165	Note 5

Note 1: Approximately 37,409 Triumph Spitfire Mk IIs were produced from 1964-67.

Note 2: Approximately 65,320 Triumph Spitfire Mk IIIs were produced from 1967-70.

Note 3: Approximately 15,818 Triumph GT6 coupes (Mk I) were produced over the full model run, from 1966-68.

Note 4: Approximately 28,465 Triumph TR4As were produced over the full model run, from 1965-67.

Note 5: Approximately 8,484 Triumph TR250s were produced in 1967-68.

Price Note: Figures shown for Spitfire Mk II and TR4A were valid in 1967; for Spitfire Mk III, GT6 and TR250, in 1968.

ENGINE DATA: BASE FOUR (Spitfire Mk II): Inline, overhead-valve four-cylinder. Cast iron block and head. **Displacement:** 70 cu. in. (1147 cc). **Bore & Stroke:** 2.73 x 2.99 in. (69.3 x 76 mm). **Compression Ratio:** 8.5:1. **Brake Horsepower:** 67 at 6000 rpm. **Torque:** 67 lbs.-ft. at 3750 rpm. Three main bearings. Solid valve lifters. Two SU carburetors.

BASE FOUR (Spitfire Mk III): Inline, overhead-valve four-cylinder. Cast iron block and head. **Displacement:** 79.1 cu. in. (1296 cc). **Bore & Stroke:** 2.90 x 2.99 in. (73.7 x 76 mm). **Compression Ratio:** 9.0:1. **Brake Horsepower:** 75 at 6000 rpm. **Torque:** 75 lbs.-ft. at 4000 rpm. Three main bearings. Solid valve lifters. Two SU carburetors.

BASE FOUR (TR4A): Inline, overhead-valve four-cylinder. Cast iron block. **Displacement:** 130.4 cu. in. (2138 cc). **Bore & Stroke:** 3.39 x 3.62 in. (86 x 92 mm). **Compression Ratio:** 9.0:1. **Brake Horsepower:** 104 at 4700 rpm (105 at 4150 rpm in U.S.). **Torque:** 132 lbs.-ft. at 3350 rpm. Three main bearings. Solid valve lifters. Two SU carburetors.

BASE SIX (GT6): Inline, overhead-valve six-cylinder. Cast iron block and head. **Displacement:** 121.9 cu. in. (1998 cc). **Bore & Stroke:** 2.94 x 2.99 in. (74.7 x 76 mm). **Compression Ratio:** 9.5:1. **Brake Horsepower:** 95 at 5000 rpm. **Torque:** 117 lbs.-ft. at 3000 rpm. Four main bearings. Solid valve lifters. Two Stromberg carburetors.

BASE SIX (TR250): Inline, overhead-valve six-cylinder. Cast iron block and head. **Displacement:** 152.4 cu. in. (2498 cc). **Bore & Stroke:** 2.94 x 2.99 in. (74.7 x 76 mm). **Compression Ratio:** 8.5:1. **Brake Horsepower:** 104 (111 SAE) at 4500 rpm. **Torque:** 143 (152 SAE) lbs.-ft. at 3000 rpm. Four main bearings. Solid valve lifters. Zenith-Two Stromberg carburetors.

CHASSIS DATA: Wheelbase: (Spitfire III/GT6) 83 in.; (TR4A/TR250) 88 in. **Overall Length:** (Spitfire III) 147 in.; (GT6) 145 in.; (TR4A/TR250) 153.6 in. **Height:** (Spitfire) 47.5 in.; (GT6) 47 in.; (TR4A/TR250) 50 in. **Width:** (Spitfire) 57 in.; (TR4A/TR250) 58 in. **Front Tread:** (Spitfire/GT6) 49 in.; (TR4A/TR250) 49.25 in. **Rear Tread:** (Spitfire/GT6) 48 in.; (TR4A/TR250) 48.75 in. **Wheel Type:** disc (wire optional). **Standard Tires:** (Spitfire) 5.20x13; (GT6) 155x13; (TR4A) 6.95x15; (TR250) 185HR15.

TECHNICAL: Layout: front-engine, rear-drive. **Transmission:** four-speed manual; overdrive available. **Steering:** rack and pinion. **Suspension (front):** unequal-length A-arms with coil springs. **Suspension (rear):** (Spitfire) swing axles with radius arms and transverse leaf spring; (TR4A/TR250) independent with semi-trailing arms and coil springs. **Brakes:** front disc, rear drum. **Body Construction:** steel body on steel frame.

PERFORMANCE: Top Speed: (Spitfire III) about 95 mph; (GT6) 106 mph; (TR250) about 107 mph. **Acceleration (0-60 mph):** (Spitfire III) about 14.0 sec.; (GT6) 12.0-12.3 sec.; (TR250) about 10.6 sec.

PRODUCTION/SALES: Approximately 15,806 Triumphs were sold in the U.S. during 1967, followed by 18,600 in 1968.

ADDITIONAL MODELS: For the 1967 model year, Triumph marketed the 1200 sedan and convertible in the U.S., as well as the six-cylinder 2000 sedan. In 1968, only the sports cars were available.

Manufacturer: Triumph Motor Company Ltd., Coventry, England (part of British Leyland).

1969-74 TRIUMPH

1972 Triumph Stag. (William Siuru Jr.)

SPITFIRE — Mk III — FOUR — Production of the third-generation Spitfire continued through 1970.

SPITFIRE — Mk IV/1500 — FOUR — Another generation of Triumph's small open two-seater debuted in 1970. While retaining its backbone chassis and a number of body panels, the Spitfire gained a fresh look that included single-unit front fenders (formerly in two pieces) and a wider grille opening, plus a reshaped chopped tail, on the order of the TR6. U.S. models wore black bumpers. Most noteworthy of the chassis modifications was the installation of a revised independent rear suspension, replacing the familiar swing-axle setup with a configuration that allowed the transverse leaf spring to pivot. An all-synchro four-speed gearbox was installed, as in the GT6 coupe. American Spitfires initially used a carryover 1296-cc engine, rated 58 horsepower. For 1973, displacement grew to 1493 cc and the name changed to Spitfire 1500. At the same time, rear track grew an extra two inches, reclining seats became standard, and the black bumpers added gigantic guards along with a low front spoiler. After many years of availability, wire wheels departed from the option list. Although the Herald sedan on which the Spitfire had been based was gone, and the related GT6 coupe departed after 1973, Spitfire hung on until August 1980.

GT6+/GT6 Mk II — SIX — Introduced in fall 1968, the second-generation GT6 fastback coupe adopted a completely different form of independent rear suspension, to help quell criticisms of touchy handling with the original Spitfire-based swing axles. The transverse leaf spring now functioned as a set of upper wishbones, accompanied by jointed half-shafts and lower A-arms. Engine displacement remained at 1998 cc (121.9-cid), but modifications that included a new cylinder head and revised camshaft profile boosted power to 104 bhp in European trim. Emissions controls in the U.S., on the other hand, limited output to 95 horsepower in a model known as the GT6+ rather than Mk II. Front-end appearance changed, by adopting a high bumper right ahead of the grille, just like the Spitfire. Mag-type wheel covers now were standard. New air exhaust grilles on the long C-pillars eased interior ventilation.

GT6 — Mk III — SIX — Restyling of the Spitfire for 1971 also applied to the GT6 coupe. This time, both European and U.S. models took the same Mk III designation. Appearance changes included smoother bumpers, slightly flared wheel openings, recessed door handles, rear quarter windows that reached farther back, and a reprofiled tail end. Overdrive could now be selected at the gearshift lever (formerly via a switch on the dashboard). Horsepower ratings of U.S. models declined through the early 1970s, dropping to 79 bhp in 1972-73, but part of the loss was due to the shift to SAE net figures from the former gross horsepower ratings. Production came to a halt before the 1974 model year.

TR6 — SIX — The TR250 (and European TR5 PI) had served as interim models, awaiting the debut of the next "real" Triumph open sports car. That debut came at the beginning of 1969, with a restyled TR6. Styling at the center of the body was similar to the prior series, but the front and rear changed considerably. Changes included a flatter hood, additional front overhang, wider blackout grille with horizontal bars and center insignia, and repositioning of headlamps all the way out on the fenders. At the rear, the stylists tacked on Kamm-type chopped-off tail. The optional hardtop was now one-piece, rather than in two sections as before. Except for the addition of a front anti-roll bar, little was new beneath the surface. Like the TR250/TR5 PI, however, the TR6 came in two flavors: fuel injected for European consumption, carbureted for Americans, the latter with considerably less power. Only a few changes arrived during the early 1970s: altered transmission ratios in mid-1971, a lip-style front spoiler in 1973, and black bumper guards in 1974 to meet U.S. standards. Production continued into mid-1976, even after the debut of the TR7.

STAG — V-8 — Starting in the spring of 1971, another sort of Triumph became available in the U.S. Styled by Giovanni Michelotti (no stranger to Triumph design), the Stag was a grand touring machine and the first Triumph to carry a V-8 engine. Offered in convertible form with a built-in roll bar, the Stag also came with a detachable hardtop. The 2997-cd (183-cid) V-8 developed 145 horsepower. Wheelbase was 100 inches. Stags had a full-width horizontal-bar grille that encompassed quad round headlamps. Importation continued into 1973.

1973 Triumph Stag. (William Siuru Jr.)

I.D. DATA: Serial number is on right side of firewall, under the hood; on plate adjacent to driver's door striker plate; or on left side of dashboard, near the windshield. Engine number is stamped on left of block. Starting serial number: (1970 Spitfire Mk III) FDU75000; (1971 Spitfire) FK1; (1972 Spitfire) FK25001; (1973 Spitfire 1500) FM1V; (1970 GT6+) KC75000; (1971 GT6 Mk III) KF1; (1972 GT6 Mk III) KF100001; (1973 GT6 Mk III) KF200001; (1969 TR6) CC25000; (1970 TR6) CC50000; (1971 TR6) CC58298; (1972 TR6) CC75001; (1973 TR6) CF1.

Model	Body Type & Seating	Engine Type/CID	P.O.E. Price	Weight (lbs.)	Prod. Total
SPITFIRE (1969-70)					
Mk III	2-dr Conv Cpe-2P	I4/79	2295	1568	Note 1
SPITFIRE (1971-72)					
Mk IV	2-dr Conv Cpe-2P	I4/79	2649	1620	Note 2
SPITFIRE (1973-74)					
1500	2-dr Conv Cpe-2P	I4/91	2995	1710	Note 3
GT6+ (1969-70)					
GT6+	2-dr Fbk Cpe-2P	I6/122	2995	1792	Note 4
GT6 (1971-73)					
Mk III	2-dr Fbk Cpe-2P	I6/122	3374	1936	Note 5
TR6 (1969-74)					
TR6	2-dr Conv Cpe-2P	I6/152	3275	2156	Note 6
STAG (1971-73)					
	2-dr HT Cpe-2+2P	V8/183	5805	2807	N/A
	2-dr Conv Cpe-2+2P	V8/183	N/A	N/A	N/A

Note 1: Approximately 65,320 Triumph Spitfire Mk IIIs were produced from 1967-70.

Note 2: Approximately 70,021 Triumph Spitfire Mk IVs were produced from 1970-74.

Note 3: Approximately 95,829 Triumph Spitfire 1500s were produced from 1974-80.

Note 4: Approximately 12,066 Triumph GT6+ (and Mk II) coupes were produced over the full model run, from 1968-70.

Note 5: Approximately 13,042 Triumph GT6 Mk III coupes were produced over the full model run, from 1971-73.

Note 6: Approximately 94,619 Triumph TR6s were produced over the full model run, from 1969-76.

Price Note: Figures shown for Spitfire Mk III and TR6 were valid in 1969; for GT6+ in 1970; Spitfire Mk IV and GT6 Mk III in 1971; Stag in 1972; Spitfire 1500 in 1973.

ENGINE DATA: BASE FOUR (Spitfire Mk III): Inline, overhead-valve four-cylinder. Cast iron block and head. **Displacement:** 79.1 cu. in. (1296 cc). **Bore & Stroke:** 2.90 x 2.99 in. (73.7 x 76 mm). **Compression Ratio:** 9.0:1. **Brake Horsepower:** 63/68 at 5500/6000 rpm. **Torque:** 73 lbs.-ft. at 3000 rpm. Three main bearings. Solid valve lifters. Two carburetors.

BASE FOUR (1971 Spitfire Mk IV): Same as 1296-cc four above, except — **Compression Ratio:** 9.0:1. **Brake Horsepower:** 58 at 5200 rpm. **Torque:** 72 lbs.-ft. at 3000 rpm. Two Zenith-Stromberg carburetors.

BASE FOUR (1972 Spitfire Mk IV): Same as 1296-cc four above, except — **Compression Ratio:** 7.0:1. **Brake Horsepower:** 48 at 5500 rpm. **Torque:** 60.8 lbs.-ft. at 2900 rpm.

BASE FOUR (1973 Spitfire 1500): Inline, overhead-valve four-cylinder. Cast iron block and head. **Displacement:** 91.1 cu. in. (1493 cc). **Bore & Stroke:** 2.90 x 3.44 in. (73.7 x 87 mm). **Compression Ratio:** 7.5:1. **Brake Horsepower:** 57 at 5500/6000 rpm. **Torque:** 73 lbs.-ft. at 3000 rpm. Solid valve lifters. Two Zenith-Stromberg carburetors.

BASE SIX (GT6+): Inline, overhead-valve six-cylinder. Cast iron block and head. **Displacement:** 121.9 cu. in. (1998 cc). **Bore & Stroke:** 2.94 x 2.99 in. (74.7 x 76 mm). **Compression Ratio:** 9.25:1. **Brake Horsepower:** 95 at 4700 rpm. **Torque:** 117 lbs.-ft. at 3400 rpm. Four main bearings. Solid valve lifters. Two Zenith-Stromberg carburetors.

BASE SIX (GT6 Mk III): Same as 1998-cc six above, except — **Compression Ratio:** 8.0:1. **Brake Horsepower:** 79 at 4900 rpm. **Torque:** 97 lbs.-ft. at 2900 rpm.

BASE SIX (1969-71 TR6): Inline, overhead-valve six-cylinder. Cast iron block and head. **Displacement:** 152.4 cu. in. (2498 cc). **Bore & Stroke:** 2.94 x 2.99 in. (74.7 x 76 mm). **Compression Ratio:** 8.6:1. **Brake Horsepower:** 104 at 4500 rpm. **Torque:** 142 lbs.-ft. at 3000 rpm. Four main bearings. Solid valve lifters. Zenith Two Stromberg carburetors.

BASE SIX (1972-73 TR6): Same as 2498-cc six above, except — **Compression Ratio:** 7.75:1. **Brake Horsepower:** 106 at 4900 rpm. **Torque:** 133 lbs.-ft. at 3000 rpm.

BASE V-8 (Stag): Overhead-valve "vee" type eight-cylinder. **Displacement:** 182.9 cu. in. (2997 cc). **Bore & Stroke:** 3.39 x 2.54 in. (86 x 64.5 mm). **Compression Ratio:** 8.8:1. **Brake Horsepower:** 145 at 5500 rpm. **Torque:** 170 lbs.-ft. at 3500 rpm. Two carburetors.

CHASSIS DATA: Wheelbase: (Spitfire/GT6) 83 in.; (TR6) 88 in.; (Stag) 100 in. **Overall Length:** (Spitfire/GT6) 147-149 in.; (TR6) 155 in.; (Stag) 173.7 in. **Height:** (Spitfire) 47.5 in.; (GT6) 47 in.; (TR6) 50 in.; (Stag) 49.5 in. **Width:** (Spitfire/GT6) 57 in.; (TR6) 58 in.; (Stag) 63.5 in. **Front Tread:** (Spitfire/GT6) 49 in.; (TR6) 50.25 in.; (Stag) 52.5 in. **Rear Tread:** (Spitfire) 48 in.; (GT6) 49 in.; (TR6) 49.75 in.; (Stag) 52.9 in.

TECHNICAL: Layout: front-engine, rear-drive. **Transmission:** four-speed manual; overdrive available. **Steering:** rack and pinion. **Suspension (front):** unequal-length A-arms with coil springs. **Suspension (rear):** (Spitfire III) swing axles with radius arms and transverse leaf spring; (Spitfire IV) swing axles with radius arms and pivoting transverse leaf spring; (GT6) double-jointed half-shafts with lower A-arms and transverse leaf springs; (TR6) rigid axle with semi-trailing arms and coil springs. **Brakes:** front disc, rear drum. **Body Construction:** steel body on steel frame.

PRODUCTION/SALES: Approximately 17,112 Triumphs were sold in the U.S. during 1969, followed by 14,561 in 1970, 20,563 in 1971, 22,827 in 1972, 21,438 in 1973, and 18,396 in 1974.

Manufacturer: Triumph Motor Company Ltd., Coventry, England (part of British Leyland).

Distributor: British Leyland Motors Inc., Leonia, New Jersey.

1975-79 TRIUMPH

SPITFIRE — 1500 — FOUR — Production of Triumph's smaller two-seater continued until August 1980, powered by the 1493-cc engine. An improved version of that engine arrived in 1977, along with a race-type steering wheel.

TR6 — SIX — Production of the TR6 continued into mid-1976, and it was marketed alongside the TR7 for a time.

TR7 — FOUR — Not only styling, but also the powertrain, underwent a major change in the transition from TR6 to TR7. Triumph's Italian-styled open two-seater with a separate frame and fully independent suspension faded away. This one was a closed coupe that featured unibody construction and a rigid rear axle, as well as a four-cylinder engine instead of the TR6's six. Styling of the wedge-profiled coupe was accomplished in Britain, at the British Leyland facility. Under the hood went a 1998-cc overhead-cam four, also used in the Triumph Dolomite sedan. Three transmissions were offered: standard four-speed, optional five-speed manual, or a three-speed Borg-Warner automatic (built in Britain). MacPherson struts made up the front suspension. Wider tires were installed for 1978, along with a new front air dam. A convertible version arrived in 1979, with various structural modifications to enhance rigidity, including a brace behind the seats, across the cowl and firewall, and at chassis rear.

I.D. DATA: Triumph's serial number is on driver's door post. Prefix denotes model and/or whether it is a U.S. version. Suffix may indicate transmission type, left-hand drive, or (1977-79) model type. Starting serial number: (1975 Spitfire) FM28001U; (1976 Spitfire) FM40001U; (1975 TR6) CF35000U; (1976 TR6) CF50001U; (1975 TR7) ACL1U; (1976 TR7) ACL10001U; (1977 Spitfire) FM60000U; (1977 TR7) ACW07001U; (1978 Spitfire) FM70001; (1978 TR7) ACW40000U; (1979 Spitfire) 90001U; (1979 TR7) 100001U.

Model	Body Type & Seating	Engine Type/CID	P.O.E. Price	Weight (lbs.)	Prod. Total
SPITFIRE					
1500	2-dr Conv Cpe-2P	I4/91	3745	1828	Note 1
TR6					
TR6	2-dr Conv Cpe-2P	I6/152	5295	2280	Note 2
TR7					
TR7	2-dr Coupe-2P	I4/122	5100	2241	Note 3

Note 1: Approximately 95,829 Triumph Spitfire 1500s were produced from 1974-80.

Note 2: Approximately 94,619 Triumph TR6s were produced over the full model run, from 1969-76.

Note 3: Approximately 112,368 Triumph TR7s were produced over the full model run, from 1975-81.

Price Note: Figures shown were valid in 1975. Prices in 1979 were $5795 for the Spitfire, $7695 for the TR7 coupe, and $8395 for the new TR7 convertible.

ENGINE DATA: BASE FOUR (Spitfire 1500): Inline, overhead-valve four-cylinder. Cast iron block and head. **Displacement:** 91.1 cu. in. (1493 cc). **Bore & Stroke:** 2.90 x 3.44 in. (73.7 x 87 mm). **Compression Ratio:** 7.5:1. **Brake Horsepower:** 52.5/57 at 5000 rpm. **Torque:** 68.8/71 lbs.-ft. at 2500/3000 rpm. Three main bearings. Solid valve lifters. One Zenith-Stromberg carburetor.

BASE SIX (TR6): Inline, overhead-valve six-cylinder. Cast iron block and head. **Displacement:** 152.4 cu. in. (2498 cc). **Bore & Stroke:** 2.94 x 2.99 in. (74.7 x 76 mm). **Compression Ratio:** 7.5:1. **Brake Horsepower:** 101 at 4900 rpm. **Torque:** 128 lbs.-ft. at 3000 rpm. Four main bearings. Solid valve lifters. Two Zenith-Stromberg carburetors.

BASE FOUR (TR7): Inline, overhead-cam four-cylinder. Cast iron block and light alloy head. **Displacement:** 121.9 cu. in. (1998 cc). **Bore & Stroke:** 3.56 x 3.07 in. (90 x 78 mm). **Compression Ratio:** 8.0:1. **Brake Horsepower:** 85.5/90 at 5000 rpm. **Torque:** 102.5/105 lbs.-ft. at 3000/3250 rpm. Five main bearings. Two Stromberg carburetors.

Engine Note: Specifications above are for U.S.-spec models.

CHASSIS DATA: Wheelbase: (Spitfire) 83 in.; (TR6) 88 in.; (TR7) 85 in. **Overall Length:** (Spitfire) 156.3 in.; (TR6) 162.1 in.; (TR7) 164.5 in. **Height:** (Spitfire) 45.6 in.; (TR6) 50 in.; (TR7) 49.9 in. **Width:** (Spitfire) 58.5 in.; (TR6) 58 in.; (TR7) 66.2 in. **Front Tread:** (Spitfire) 49 in.; (TR6) 50.3 in.; (TR7) 55.5 in. **Rear Tread:** (Spitfire) 50 in.; (TR6) 49.8 in.; (TR7) 55.3 in.

TECHNICAL: Layout: front-engine, rear-drive. **Transmission:** four-speed manual; overdrive available on Spitfire/TR6; five-speed manual or three-speed automatic optional on TR7. **Steering:** rack and pinion. **Suspension (front):** (Spitfire/TR6) unequal-length A-arms with coil springs and anti-roll bar; (TR7) MacPherson struts with coil springs and anti-roll bar. **Suspension (rear):** (Spitfire) swing axles with radius arms and pivoting transverse leaf spring; (TR6) rigid axle with semi-trailing arms and coil springs; (TR7) rigid axle with radius arms, trailing arms, coil springs and anti-roll bar. **Brakes:** front disc, rear drum. **Body Construction:** steel body on steel frame except (TR7) steel unibody.

PRODUCTION/SALES: Approximately 22,803 Triumphs were sold in the U.S. during 1975, followed by 28,238 in 1976, 29,258 in 1977, 16,447 in 1978, and 12,733 in 1979.

Manufacturer: BL Ltd. (Jaguar Rover Triumph Ltd.), Coventry, England.

Distributor: British Leyland Motors Inc., Leonia, New Jersey.

HISTORY: "The shape of things to come" was Triumph's theme for the TR7 coupe, offering "the bold wedge line of the great international sports-racers." TR7 production took place at a new plant near Liverpool, which turned out to be subject to frequent labor disputes and strikes. In 1978, manufacture moved to another plant at Coventry; and later yet, to Solihull. Just over 200 early TR8 coupes with V-8 engines arrived in the U.S. during 1978-79, for evaluation purposes, before that model made its official debut for the 1980 model year.

1980-81 TRIUMPH

1980 Triumph TR8 convertible. (William Siuru Jr.)

SPITFIRE — 1500 — FOUR — Production of Triumph's smaller two-seater continued until August 1980, still powered by the 1493-cc engine.

TR7 — FOUR — Production of the four-cylinder wedge-shaped coupe and convertible continued until October 1981.

TR8 — V-8 — In a last-ditch attempt to recapture lost sales, especially in the U.S., Triumph slipped Rover's all-aluminum 3528-cc (215-cid) V-8 engine into the TR7 body. That engine had long before seen life under the hoods of early 1960s GM compacts, and found its way into a number of British automobiles after Rover purchased the tooling. Both a coupe and convertible were offered. Appearance was similar to the TR7, except for a bulge in the hood to accommodate the V-8 engine. With dual carburetors, the V-8 developed 133 horsepower in U.S. trim; Bosch L-Jetronic fuel injection, required in California and installed on all TR8s for 1981, added 4 more bhp. Either a five-speed or three-speed automatic transmission was available. Power rack-and-pinion steering was standard, as were cast alloy wheels, tinted glass, AM/FM stereo, and metallic paint. Air conditioning was the only option.

I.D. DATA: Triumph's serial number is on driver's door post or atop the instrument panel. Starting serial number: (1980 Spitfire) TFVDW2AT000001; (1980 TR7) TPV()J8AT200001; (1980 TR8) TPVDV8AT200001.

Model	Body Type & Seating	Engine Type/CID	P.O.E. Price	Weight (lbs.)	Prod. Total
SPITFIRE					
1500	2-dr Conv Cpe-2P	I4/91	7365	1887	Note 1
TR7					
TR7	2-dr Coupe-2P	I4/122	8465	2487	Note 2
TR7	2-dr Conv Cpe-2P	I4/122	9235	2505	Note 2
TR8					
TR8	2-dr Coupe-2P	V8/215	11150	2650	Note 3
TR8	2-dr Conv Cpe-2P	V8/215	11900	2677	Note 3

Note 1: Approximately 95,829 Triumph Spitfire 1500s were produced from 1974-80.
Note 2: Approximately 112,368 Triumph TR7s were produced over the full model run, from 1975-81.
Note 3: Approximately 2,497 Triumph TR8s (including 2,308 U.S.-spec models) were produced in 1980-81.

ENGINE DATA: BASE FOUR (Spitfire 1500): Inline, overhead-valve four-cylinder. Cast iron block and head. **Displacement:** 91.1 cu. in. (1493 cc). **Bore & Stroke:** 2.90 x 3.44 in. (73.7 x 87 mm). **Compression Ratio:** 7.5:1. **Brake Horsepower:** 52.5 at 5000 rpm. **Torque:** 69 lbs.-ft. at 2500 rpm. Three main bearings. Solid valve lifters. One carburetor.
BASE FOUR (TR7): Inline, overhead-cam four-cylinder. Cast iron block and light alloy head. **Displacement:** 121.9 cu. in. (1998 cc). **Bore & Stroke:** 3.56 x 3.07 in. (90 x 78 mm). **Compression Ratio:** 8.0:1. **Brake Horsepower:** 88.5 at 5250 rpm. **Torque:** 100 lbs.-ft. at 2500 rpm. Five main bearings.
BASE V-8 (1980 TR8): Overhead-valve, "vee" type eight-cylinder (Rover). **Displacement:** 215 cu. in. (3528 cc). **Bore & Stroke:** 3.50 x 2.80 in. (89 x 71 mm). **Compression Ratio:** 8.1:1. **Brake Horsepower:** 133 at 5000 rpm. **Torque:** 174 lbs.-ft. at 3000 rpm. Hydraulic valve lifters. Two Stromberg carburetors.
BASE V-8 (1981 TR8): Same as 3528-cc V-8 above, except with Bosch L-Jetronic fuel injection — **Brake Horsepower:** 137 at 5000 rpm.

CHASSIS DATA: Wheelbase: (Spitfire) 83 in.; (TR7/TR8) 85 in. **Overall Length:** (Spitfire) 157.5 in.; (TR7/TR8) 165.4 in. **Height:** (Spitfire) 45.6 in.; (TR7/TR8) 49.5 in. **Width:** (Spitfire) 58.5 in.; (TR7/TR8) 66.2 in. **Front Tread:** (Spitfire) 49 in.; (TR7/TR8) 55.5 in. **Rear Tread:** (Spitfire) 50 in.; (TR7/TR8) 55.3 in.

TECHNICAL: Layout: front-engine, rear-drive. **Transmission:** (Spitfire) four-speed manual, overdrive optional; (TR7/TR8), five-speed manual, three-speed automatic optional. **Steering:** rack and pinion. **Suspension (front):** (Spitfire) unequal-length A-arms with coil springs and anti-roll bar; (TR7/TR8) MacPherson struts with coil springs and anti-roll bar. **Suspension (rear):** (Spitfire) swing axles with radius arms and pivoting transverse leaf spring; (TR8) rigid axle with lower trailing arms, angled upper arms, coil springs and anti-roll bar. **Brakes:** front disc, rear drum. **Body Construction:** (Spitfire) steel body on steel frame; (TR7/TR8) steel unibody.

PRODUCTION/SALES: Approximately 14,939 Triumphs were sold in the U.S. during 1980, dropping to 9,768 in 1981.
Manufacturer: BL Ltd. (Jaguar Rover Triumph Ltd.), Coventry, England.
Distributor: British Leyland Motors Inc., Leonia, New Jersey.

HISTORY: By October 1981, Triumph production came to a permanent halt.

TURNER

Turner Sports Cars, founded in 1949 by British racing driver and engine builder John H. Turner, focused first on engines. He entered the competition car business as early as 1951 in Britain, producing a handful of 96-inch wheelbase sports models powered by MG, Ford Zephyr, Vauxhall and Lea-Francis engines. Early in the 1950s, Turner also produced a midget-sized (500 cc, or 30.5 cid) Formula III engine with twin overhead camshafts that delivered half its weight in horsepower, peaking at some 9,500 rpm. Each air-cooled cylinder was deeply finned, and the head water-cooled. Four Amal-type carburetors were used.

A smaller, lightweight model 803 roadster with fiberglass body debuted by 1955, capable of more than 80-mph speeds with its ordinary 803-cc Austin A30 engine. When Austin moved up to a 948-cc four-cylinder engine for its A35 model in 1956, Turner also adopted the larger powerplant, raising horsepower to 34 (then 40) and top speed close to 90 mph. Quite a few of the handcrafted sports cars went to U.S. customers. The next Turner model, carrying a 1098-cc Coventry Climax four-cylinder engine, went on sale in export form before being offered to British enthusiasts by 1960. It was aimed at racing rather than road use, and British race victories attracted both export and home-market customers to the Turner selection. By that time, too, Turner developed a new Alexander model (tuned by Alexander Engineering), urging 80 bhp out of its twin-carb, 948-cc BMC engine with high-compression head. Production was limited to about 10 cars per month. In 1962, Turner announced a prototype fiberglass-bodied GT coupe, its first with a solid top. The production coupe, of which fewer than ten were built, was powered by a Ford 122E engine of 1499-cc displacement. That same engine powered the last of the Turners, the open 1500. During 1963, production began to ease to a halt, though Turner Sprints continued to be sold (and listed in American directories) as late as 1966. Most Turners were exported, and home-market sales were often in kit form rather than fully assembled cars.

1951-58 TURNER

Early roadsters, weighing in around 1,400 pounds, rode a 96-inch wheelbase and 5.25x16 tires. Beneath their bonnets, British race fans could order a selection of powerplants: MG or Lea-Francis fours, as well as Vauxhall's Wyvern or Velox. The 803 model, introduced in 1955, was more standardized, with an Austin 803-cc four-cylinder engine of 7.2:1 compression rated at 30 bhp. Wheelbase shrunk to 80.5 inches, and the car measured only 138 inches overall, and 54 inches wide. The lightweight body amounted to only about 1,200 pounds, with coil springs at the front and a torsion-bar rear suspension. The 803 carried 5.25x15 tires instead of the 16-inchers of earlier models.

Engine size grew to 948 cc in 1956, and compression to 8.3:1, for the Turner 950. The overhead-valve powerplant produced 34 horsepower with a Zenith carburetor, or up to 40 with SU carburetion. Price in the U.S. was near $2000. A second series, introduced in 1958, boosted output to 43 bhp with twin carbs.

1959-63 TURNER

1959 Turner.

950 — FOUR — "Easy to drive--easy to look at--easy to keep." Such was the slogan used by Turner for its roadster series in the late 1950s. *Motor Trend* wasn't so sure about the "easy to look at" portion of the claim, or about the fact that the center bow of the soft top rode against the driver's head, but otherwise praised the tiny two-seater as "a real goer." A semicircular opening with flat base characterized the Turner roadster's cast aluminum grille, which contained an eggcrate (square crosshatch) pattern. Slightly protruding round headlamps stood directly above round parking lights at the ends of the front panel. The basic 948-cc Austin A35 four-cylinder engine in the 950 Sports Series II produced 43 horsepower, with a four-speed gearbox sending power to the rear wheels. Turners were intended to mix street operation with the prospect of Class H production racing.

SPR60 — FOUR — The modified 950 version reached 60 bhp. Both the base model and the SPR60 were offered for sale in the U.S. Appearance was the same as the basic model, but the engine got a compression boost (from the usual 8.3:1 up to 9.5:1) and a more radical camshaft, as well as an exhaust header and heavy-duty cadmium-bronze bearing inserts. Front brake drums enlarged from 7 to 8 inches in diameter for 1959, but rear drums remained at 7 inches. Either bolt-on disc or Dunlop wire wheels were available. Leather upholstery was standard. So was a telescopic adjustment for the multiple spring-spoke steering wheel. The leatherette-covered dashboard held a 6-inch (120-mph) speedometer and matching 8000-rpm tachometer, along with gauges for oil pressure, fuel level, battery current, and water temperature. Side curtains were included with the folding soft top, which contained wedge-shaped side windows.

COVENTRY CLIMAX I/III — FOUR — In Stage I form, the 1098-cc overhead-cam Coventry Climax engine developed 75 bhp at 6000 RPM. The Stage III version reached 90 bhp with higher compression. Upon request, customers could get rear coil springs (surrounding the telescopic shocks) in place of the usual rear torsion bars. A Stage II version was developed, but not put into production.

I.D. DATA: Serial and engine number is on the left side of the firewall, under the hood.

950

Model	Body Type & Seating	Engine Type/CID	P.O.E. Price	Weight (lbs.)	Prod. Total
Sports	2-dr Rds-2P	I4/58	2245	1175	Note 1
SPR60	2-dr Rds-2P	I4/58	2635	1288	Note 1
COVENTRY CLIMAX					
I	2-dr Rds-2P	I4/67	3170	1396	Note 1
III	2-dr Rds-2P	I4/67	3370	1396	Note 1

Note 1: A total of about 600 Turner Sports models were produced.

Price Note: Base price for the basic 950 Sports was $2345 on the West Coast. By 1962, prices ranged from $2345 to $3570.

ENGINE DATA: BASE FOUR (950): Inline, overhead-valve four-cylinder. Cast iron block and head. **Displacement:** 57.8 cu. in. (948 cc). **Bore & Stroke:** 2.478 x 3.00 in. (62.9 x 76.2 mm). **Compression Ratio:** 8.3:1. **Brake Horsepower:** 43 at 4000 rpm. Three main bearings. Solid valve lifters. Two SU sidedraft carburetors. 12-volt electrical system.

BASE FOUR (SPR60): Same as above, except — **Compression Ratio:** 9.5:1. **Brake Horsepower:** 60 at 6500 rpm. Two SU carburetors.

BASE FOUR (Coventry Climax Stage I): Inline, overhead-cam four-cylinder. Cast iron block. **Displacement:** 67 cu. in. (1098 cc). **Bore & Stroke:** 2.85 x 2.62 in. (72.4 x 66.6 mm). **Compression Ratio:** 9.8:1. **Brake Horsepower:** 75 at 6000 rpm. Solid valve lifters. Two SU sidedraft carburetors.

BASE FOUR (Coventry Climax Stage III): Same as above, except — **Compression Ratio:** 10.5:1. **Brake Horsepower:** 90 at 6900 rpm.

CHASSIS DATA: Wheelbase: 80.5 in. **Overall Length:** 138 in. **Height:** 45 in. **Width:** 54 in. **Front Tread:** 45.5 in. **Rear Tread:** 44.75 in. **Wheel Type:** bolt-on steel disc or Dunlop wire. **Standard Tires:** 5.20x15 or 5.60x13.

TECHNICAL: Layout: front-engine, rear-drive. **Transmission:** four-speed manual (synchro 2nd/3rd/4th). **Overall SPR60 gear ratios:** (1st) 16.51:1; (2nd) 10.8:1; (3rd) 6.42:1; (4th) 4.55:1. **Standard Final Drive Ratio:** 4.55:1. **Steering:** rack and pinion. **Suspension (front):** pressed steel wishbones with coil springs. **Suspension (rear):** solid axle with trailing links and short transverse torsion bars (coil springs available). **Brakes:** hydraulic, front/rear drum. **Body Construction:** fiberglass body on T-shaped tubular frame; main members of 3-inch diameter, 16-gauge steel tubing, with welded sheet steel subframe. **Fuel Tank:** 6.9 gallon (U.S.).

MAJOR OPTIONS: Alexander cross-flow cylinder head. Girling front disc brakes. Center-lock wire wheels (13- or 15-inch). Many other performance options were available.

PERFORMANCE: Top Speed: (950) 80 mph (estimated); (SPR60) 80 mph (indicated); (Climax) near 99 mph. **Acceleration (0-60 mph):** (950) 21.3 seconds; (SPR60) 17.5 sec.; (Climax Stage I) 12.4 seconds. **Acceleration (quarter-mile):** (950) 21.8 seconds (61 mph). **Fuel Mileage:** (950) 25-32 mpg.

Manufacturer: Turner Sports Cars (Wolverhampton) Ltd., Pendeford Airport, Wolverhampton, England.

Distributor: Tri-City Sports Cars, Massillon, Ohio; Nemet Imported Cars, Jamaica, New York.

HISTORY: In 1957, a Turner won its class at the Six-Hour Sam Collier Memorial Trophy race in Florida, taking second place the next year. In 1958, Turners won the Team Challenge Trophy, taking first and second place in the 1100-cc class, at the *Autosport* Series Production Sports Car Championship in Britain. 1960 models were introduced in the U.S. on August 1, 1959.

1964-66 TURNER

950/CLIMAX — FOUR — Some earlier models with 948-cc and Coventry Climax 1098-cc engines were sold after 1963, but production focused on the GT/1500 Sprint series. See previous listing for details on earlier models.

SPRINT (1500) — FOUR — American directories listed the Super Sprint and Super Sprint Speciale roadster as late as 1966, the latter offered only with right-hand drive. These were comparable to the 1500 series in Britain, produced in limited numbers and powered by a 1499-cc Ford 122E engine. Wheelbase was longer than the earlier Turners, and the larger cars rode 5.60x13 tires rather than the original 15-inch rubber. Coil springs were used at front and rear. The Super Sprint was offered for $2789 in the U.S., the Speciale for $3389.

I.D. DATA: Serial and engine number is on the left side of the firewall, under the hood.

Model SPRINT	Body Type & Seating	Engine Type/CID	P.O.E. Price	Weight (lbs.)	Prod. Total
Super	2-dr Rds-2P	I4/91	2789	1232	Note 1
Speciale	2-dr Rds-2P	I4/91	3389	1232	Note 1

Note 1: A total of about 600 Turner Sports models were produced.

Weight Note: Figures shown are approximate.

ENGINE DATA: BASE FOUR: Inline, overhead-valve four-cylinder (Ford 122E). Cast iron block. **Displacement:** 91.4 cu. in. (1499 cc). **Bore & Stroke:** 3.19 x 2.86 in. (80.96 x 72.7 mm). **Compression Ratio:** 9.5:1. **Brake Horsepower:** 85 at 5500 rpm. Five main bearings. Solid valve lifters. Two SU carburetors. 12-volt electrical system.

CHASSIS DATA: Wheelbase: 82 in. **Overall Length:** 138 in. **Height:** 46 in. **Front Tread:** 45.5 in. **Rear Tread:** 43.15 in. **Standard Tires:** 5.60x13.

Note: British sources indicate that the 1500 series, powered by the Ford 122E engine, had a longer wheelbase (87 inches) and measured 154 inches overall.

TECHNICAL: Similar to 1959-63, but with coil springs front and rear.

Manufacturer/Distributor: Same as 1959-63.

HISTORY: By 1966, the *Car and Driver* Yearbook reported that Ford-powered Turners were battling the Czechoslovakian-built Skoda for 68th place in U.S. imported-car registrations, being sold mainly via classified ads from service stations. The Yearbook dubbed the tiny but sure-footed Turners "unholy terrors in SCCA production-car racing."

TVR

TVR started small and, unlike most British marques of the past, has managed to hang on into the modern era. Trevor Wilkinson started it all in 1947 by building a modification of an Alvis Firebird with light-alloy two-seat body, naming his creation TVR (a shortening of his first name). By 1949, TVR Engineering was producing tubular chassis that were used in local race events. Soon, he was selling kit cars (and fully assembled models) from headquarters at Blackpool, England. Following the appearance of a fiberglass-bodied one-off in 1954, the scene shifted to America. A replica of that first example wound up in the hands of dealer Ray Saidel, who promptly ordered half a dozen chassis from England. Those were marketed in the U.S. under the Jomar name, distributed from Manchester, New Hampshire. The idea was for aluminum sports-racing bodies to be produced in New Hampshire; chassis and fiberglass bodies in Britain. By 1957-58, Jomars were ready for the road (and race courses) in the U.S.

At around the same time, the first British-built TVR, a Mk I Grantura, was available for sale. The model name stemmed from Grantura Plastic, owned by Bernard Williams, who joined with Wilkinson in 1956. Offered either fully assembled or in kit form, the TVRs wore fiberglass bodies over a tubular backbone chassis; and like the Jomar, they were designed to accept a variety of engines and suspensions. Early models came with a choice of su-

perchaged Ford 100E, or an 1098-cc Coventry Climax four-cylinder engine. Both the Jomar and TVR used fully independent suspension with transverse torsion bars. Styling was notable for what *The Complete Catalogue of British Cars* described as a "generally chunky appearance," with minimal front and rear overhang. That basic profile continued with subsequent models.

Modified Mk II and IIA Granturas arrived in 1959, followed by a Mk III during 1962. Emergence of the MGB brought a change in available engine, and the designation Mk III 1800. Financial troubles ran rampant in the early 1960s, leading to three stages of corporate reorganization.

Meanwhile, after three MGA-powered Granturas ran at Sebring, an American, Jack Griffith (who'd served as a mechanic for one of those race cars) succeeded in stuffing a Ford Cobra V-8 into a Grantura. After seeing the result, TVR accepted Griffith's proposal to blend American horsepower with the TVR body/chassis. By 1964, the first Griffiths were on sale in the U.S.; and the next year, also sold in Britain (though on a limited scale). Granturas disappeared by 1967, replaced by a new Vixen series of similar appearance, and a V-6/V-8 Tuscan series. TVR production continued through the 1970s with the M-Series, which evolved into the Taimar. Then, in 1980, a new wedge-shaped Tasmin series emerged. By 1990, the company was still producing sports cars with a V-6 powered S2 convertible.

1957-58 JOMAR (TVR)

Development of the Jomar (British/U.S.) and TVR (all-British) began in 1954, and by 1957-58 examples of both were available. Early in 1958, the first 10 Jomars were shipped to the U.S. Wearing fiberglass bodies atop a tubular chassis, the Jomar came with a choice of three engines: an L-head 71-cid four from the Ford 100E, a supercharged version of the Ford, and a 67-cid Coventry Climax four. Sports-racing models with aluminum bodies were produced in New Hampshire, on chassis supplied by TVR Engineering.

Jomars rode an 84-inch wheelbase and used transverse torsion bars for both the front and rear suspension. Girling hydraulic brakes were installed. Ford-engined models came with a Ford three-speed gearbox (close-ratio gearing available). A Shorrock supercharger was optional. Coventry Climax engines came with an MG four-speed gearbox. The entire front end lifted for access to the engine and chassis components. *Sportscar Quarterly* reported in 1958 that the basic Jomar coupe with disc wheels cost $2950 in the U.S.; GT coupe with supercharged engine and Dunlop racing tires on center-lock wire wheels, $3495; Climax Coupe with wire wheels and Al-fin brake drums, $4195. Sports-racing models with Coventry Climax engine came to $3995 (with fiberglass body), or $4595 (aluminum body). Jomars were distributed by Saidel Sports Racing Cars of Manchester, New Hampshire.

1957-59 TVR

GRANTURA — Mk I — FOUR — The stubby profile of the fastback two-seat coupe was thought by some to resemble that of a Lotus Elite. A fiberglass body rode a tubular backbone chassis with 84-inch wheelbase, and was available either assembled or in kit form. Styling was similar to the Jomar marketed in the U.S. Recessed headlamps sat in lower nacelles. Small parking lights went slightly inboard and below, alongside the very low, small, wide oval grille opening. Two engines were available: an 1172-cc, L-head four from the Ford 100E, offered with supercharger; and the famed 1098-cc Coventry Climax four. Four-wheel independent suspension consisted of transverse torsion bars and trailing links at both ends. Though hard riding, the lightweight TVRs soon became known for their superior handling and roadholding abilities.

I.D. DATA: Starting serial number: (MG engine) 7B.

Model	Body Type & Seating	Engine Type/CID	P.O.E. Price	Weight (lbs.)	Prod. Total
GRANTURA					
Mk I	2-dr Fbk Cpe-2P	I4/71	N/A	1455	Note 1

Note 1: A total of 100 Mark I Granturas were built by 1960.

ENGINE DATA: BASE FOUR: Inline, L-head four-cylinder. Cast iron block. **Displacement:** 71.5 cu. in. (1172 cc). **Bore & Stroke:** 2.50 x 3.64 in. (63.5 x 92.5 mm). **Compression Ratio:** 7.0:1. **Brake Horsepower:** 36. Solid valve lifters. Solex carburetor.

616

OPTIONAL FOUR: Inline, overhead-cam four-cylinder. Cast iron block. **Displacement:** 67 cu. in. (1098 cc). **Bore & Stroke:** 2.85 x 2.62 in. (72.4 x 66.6 mm). **Compression Ratio:** 9.8:1. **Brake Horsepower:** 85 at 7000 rpm. Solid valve lifters. Two SU carburetors.

CHASSIS DATA: Wheelbase: 84 in. **Overall Length:** 138 in. **Width:** 64 in. Max. **Tread:** 52 in. **Standard Tires:** 5.00x15.

TECHNICAL: Layout: front-engine, rear-drive. **Transmission:** (Ford) three-speed manual; (Coventry) four-speed manual. **Suspension (front):** trailing links with transverse torsion bars. **Suspension (rear):** trailing links with transverse torsion bars. **Brakes:** hydraulic. **Body Construction:** fiberglass body on tubular backbone chassis.

Manufacturer: TVR Engineering Ltd.; then Layton Sports Cars Ltd; Blackpool, England.

HISTORY: The first TVR coupe was shown at the 1957 New York Auto Show. By 1959, the original TVR firm had changed hands and become Layton Sports Cars Ltd.

1960-61 TVR

GRANTURA — Mk II/IIA — FOUR — Modifications were modest for the Mk II and IIA versions, which were now available with two different engines: a 1588-cc BMC (MG) four, rated 80 horsepower; or 1216-cc, 83-horsepower four. In addition to full model changes (Mk II, III, etc.), TVR made improvements to the coupe as needed.

I.D. DATA: Not available.

Model	Body Type & Seating	Engine Type/CID	P.O.E. Price	Weight (lbs.)	Prod. Total
II	2-dr Fbk Cpe-2P	I4/97	N/A	1482	Note 1
IIA	2-dr Fbk Cpe-2P	I4/97	N/A	1482	Note 1

Note 1: A total of 400 Mark II/IIA Granturas were built from 1959 to 1962.

ENGINE DATA: BASE FOUR: Inline, overhead-valve four-cylinder (BMC). Cast iron block and head. **Displacement:** 97 cu. in. (1588 cc). **Bore & Stroke:** 2.96 x 3.50 in. (75.3 x 88.9 mm). **Compression Ratio:** 8.3:1. **Brake Horsepower:** 80 at 5600 rpm. Three main bearings. Solid valve lifters. Two SU carburetors.

OPTIONAL FOUR: Inline, overhead-cam four-cylinder. **Displacement:** 74.2 cu. in. (1216 cc). **Bore & Stroke:** 3.00 x 2.62 in. (76.2 x 66.7 mm). **Compression Ratio:** 10.0:1. **Brake Horsepower:** 83 at 6000 rpm. Solid valve lifters. Two SU carburetors.

CHASSIS DATA: Wheelbase: 84 in. **Overall Length:** 138 in. **Width:** 64 in. Max. **Tread:** 52 in. **Standard Tires:** 5.00x15 or 5.60x15.

TECHNICAL: Layout: front-engine, rear-drive. **Transmission:** four-speed manual. **Standard Final Drive Ratio:** 4.1:, 4.7:1 or 5.1:1. **Suspension (front):** trailing links with transverse torsion bars. **Suspension (rear):** trailing links with transverse torsion bars. **Brakes:** hydraulic. **Body Construction:** fiberglass body on tubular backbone chassis.

PERFORMANCE: Top Speed: (1216-cc) 101 mph. **Acceleration (quarter-mile):** (1216-cc) 18.3 sec.

Manufacturer: Layton Sports Cars Ltd., Blackpool, England.

1962-63 TVR

1962 TVR Grantura.

GRANTURA — Mk III — FOUR — An MGA 1622-cc four-cylinder engine powered the next version of the TVR coupe, which had front disc brakes. Coil-spring fully-independent suspension (from Triumph Herald) on all four wheels replaced the former transverse torsion bars. As before, the Grantura rode a multi-tube chassis (but stiffer this time) and had rack-and-pinion steering, with what TVR described as a "sumptuous sound-insulated interior." Wheelbase grew slightly, to 85.5 inches, but overall length remained the same as before. Standard body colors were: British Racing Green, Pippin Red, Cirrus White, Charcoal Grey, Ambassador Blue, Signal Red, Riviera Blue, Imperial Crimson, Lichen Green, Powder Blue, Sunburst Yellow, Opalescent Silver Blue, Opalescent Silver Grey, and Opalescent Bronze. Upholstery (standard vynide) came in Cherry Red, Steel Grey, Forest Green, Saxe Blue, or Finnish Black. Competition-type bucket seats were standard, with the driver's seat adjustable. Doors held wind-up windows. The dashboard held a tachometer, trip odometer, and gauges for oil pressure, ammeter, water temperature, and fuel. The MG engine also was available with two Weber carburetors and an alloy cylinder head.

GRANTURA — Mk III 1800 — FOUR — A larger (1798-cc) version of the MG engine was installed for the next edition, introduced in 1963. By this time, Granturas had a larger back window and the familiar chopped-look tail.

I.D. DATA: Starting serial number: (Grantura Mk III) 18-001.

Model	Body Type & Seating	Engine Type/CID	P.O.E. Price	Weight (lbs.)	Prod. Total
Mk III	2-dr Fbk Cpe-2P	I4/99	N/A	1435	90
Mk III 1800	2-dr Fbk Cpe-2P	I4/110	N/A	N/A	Note 1

Note 1: A total of 206 Grantura 1800s were built (Mk III/IV).

Price Note: Grantura Mk III price in Britain was 862 pounds (Sterling) with disc wheels (plus purchase tax); or 888 pounds (Sterling) with wire wheels.

1963 TVR Grantura Mark III.

ENGINE DATA: BASE FOUR (Grantura Mk III): Inline, overhead-valve four-cylinder (MGA). Cast iron block and head. **Displacement:** 99.1 cu. in. (1622 cc). **Bore & Stroke:** 3.00 x 3.50 in. (76.2 x 88.9 mm). **Compression Ratio:** 9.5:1. **Brake Horsepower:** 90 at 5500 rpm. Three main bearings. Solid valve lifters. Two SU carburetors.

OPTIONAL FOUR (Grantura Mk III): Same as above, except — Cast iron block and light-alloy HRG head. **Compression Ratio:** 9.0:1. **Brake Horsepower:** 108 at 6000 rpm. **Torque:** 109 lbs.-ft. at 4500 rpm. Two Weber carburetors.

BASE FOUR (Grantura Mk III 1800): Inline, overhead-valve four-cylinder. Cast iron block and head. **Displacement:** 109.7 cu. in. (1798 cc). **Bore & Stroke:** 3.16 x 3.50 in. (80.3 x 88.9 mm). **Compression Ratio:** 8.8:1. **Brake Horsepower:** 95 at 5500 rpm. Three main bearings. Solid valve lifters. Two SU carburetors.

CHASSIS DATA: Wheelbase: 85.5 in. **Overall Length:** 138 in. **Height:** 48 in. **Width:** 64 in. **Front Tread:** 51 in. **Rear Tread:** 52 in. **Wheel Type:** pressed steel disc. **Standard Tires:** Dunlop 5.60x15.

TECHNICAL: Layout: front-engine, rear-drive. **Transmission:** four-speed manual. **Steering:** rack and pinion. **Suspension (front):** unequal-length wishbones and coil springs. **Suspension (rear):** unequal-length wishbones and coil springs. **Brakes:** Girling front disc, rear drum. **Body Construction:** fiberglass body on multi-tube chassis. **Fuel Tank:** 12 gallon (U.S.).

MAJOR OPTIONS: Wire wheels. Leather upholstery.

PERFORMANCE: Top Speed: (Mk III 1800) 107 mph. **Acceleration (quarter-mile):** (Mk III 1800) 18 seconds.

Manufacturer: Layton Sports Cars Ltd.; then Grantura Engineering Ltd.; Blackpool, England.

HISTORY: Mark III production began in September 1962, some months after announcement. *The Motor* (in Britain) said the Mark III's "deceptively good road holding, allows the T.V.R. to cover cross-country journeys remarkably quickly." *Autocar* described it as "A car for the person who drives for the sheer fun of it," one that was "extremely comfortable" and "eminently controllable." The TVR firm changed hands again in 1962, to become Grantura Engineering Ltd. Trevor Wilkinson, whose name continued to adorn the sports cars he'd created, left the firm in 1962. The British/American Griffith debuted in 1963; see next listing for details.

1964-66 TVR

1965 TVR Griffith. (William Siuru Jr.)

GRANTURA — Mk IV 1800S — FOUR — The final version of the Grantura coupe, introduced in 1966, was powered by the 1798-cc four-cylinder engine, now rated 88 horsepower. It was replaced by the Vixen in 1967.

GRIFFITH — 200 — V-8 — TVR's Griffith (introduced in 1963) qualifies as a semi-import, with its British-built body and U.S.-manufactured engine. Bodies were completed in Britain and shipped, sans engine, to America for installation of a 289-cid Ford V-8 engine and transmission at Griffith Motors. The small-block V-8 came with either 195 horsepower or, in high-performance tune, rated 271 bhp, either one hooked to Ford's own four-speed manual gearbox. Wire wheels were stronger than before, with wider rims. Blending stunning performance with excellent handling, Griffiths also rode hard. They had a tight cockpit and miniature luggage space, with no trunk lid. Griffiths also suffered overheating and quality-control problems, especially at first.

GRIFFITH — 400 — V-8 — Introduced at the April 1964 New York Auto Show, the modified Griffith looked identical to the Grantura Mark III 1800, except for their hood bulge, now sporting a sharply cutoff tail and massive wraparound back window. At the cowl was an open horizontal air vent on cowl. The protruding nose held a fairly wide but low grille opening, which contained small parking lights at its ends. Headlamps sat in recessed lower nacelles. Small horizontal bumperettes stood at each side of the front end. TVR coupes had no rear quarter windows, but doors contained vent wings. Some of the earlier mechanical and quality-control problems had been corrected, with the installation of a larger radiator, plus Kenlowe thermostatically-controlled fans. Large round trisection taillamps came from the Ford Consul. Soon, TVR was sending five cars per week to Griffith in the U.S., without engine.

I.D. DATA: Starting serial number: (Grantura 1800S) 18-001; (Griffith 200) 200-001; (Griffith 400) 400-001 or 200/GB/5001.

Model	Body Type & Seating	Engine Type/CID	P.O.E. Price	Weight (lbs.)	Prod. Total
GRANTURA					
Mk IV 1800S	2-dr Fbk Cpe-2P	I4/110	N/A	1938	Note 1
GRIFFITH					
200	2-dr Fbk Cpe-2P	V8/289	3893	1905	Note 2
400	2-dr Fbk Cpe-2P	V8/289	4895	1905	Note 2

Note 1: A total of 206 Grantura 1800s were built (Mk III/IV).

Note 2: Approximately 300 Griffiths were produced (200 and 400).

ENGINE DATA: BASE FOUR (Grantura Mk IV 1800S): Inline, overhead-valve four-cylinder. Cast iron block and head. **Displacement:** 109.7 cu. in. (1798 cc). **Bore & Stroke:** 3.16 x 3.50 in. (80.3 x 88.9 mm). **Compression Ratio:** 8.8:1. **Brake Horsepower:** 88 at 5400 rpm. Three main bearings. Solid valve lifters. Two SU carburetors.

BASE V-8 (Griffith): Overhead-valve V-8 (Ford). Cast iron block and head. **Displacement:** 289 cu. in. (4727 cc). **Bore & Stroke:** 4.00 x 2.87 in. (101.6 x 72.9 mm). **Compression Ratio:** 9.0:1. **Brake Horsepower:** 195 at 4400 rpm. **Torque:** 282 lbs.-ft. at 2400 rpm. Five main bearings. Holley carburetor.

Note: High-performance version of the 289-cid V-8 produced 271 horsepower at 6500 rpm, and 314 lbs.-ft. at 3400 rpm.

CHASSIS DATA: Wheelbase: 85.5 in. **Overall Length:** (Grantura Mk IV 1800) 141.5 in.; (Griffith) 138 in. **Width:** (Grantura Mk IV 1800) 65.5 in.; (Griffith) 64 in. **Front Tread:** (Griffith) 52.5 in. **Rear Tread:** (Griffith) 53.5 in. **Wheel Type:** pressed steel disc. **Standard Tires:** (Grantura) 165x15; (Griffith) 185x15.

TECHNICAL: Layout: front-engine, rear-drive. **Transmission:** four-speed manual. **Standard Final Drive Ratio:** (Grantura) 3.91:1; (Griffith) 3.89:1. **Steering:** rack and pinion. **Suspension (front):** unequal-length wishbones and coil springs. **Suspension (rear):** unequal-length wishbones and coil springs **Brakes:** Girling front disc, rear drum. **Body Construction:** fiberglass body on multi-tube chassis.

MAJOR OPTIONS: Wire wheels (Grantura). Leather upholstery (Grantura).

PERFORMANCE: Top Speed: (Grantura Mk IV 1800) near 108 mph; (Griffith) estimates ranged from 125 to 155 mph. **Acceleration (0-60 mph):** (Griffith) 5.7 seconds. **Acceleration (quarter-mile):** (Grantura Mk IV 1800) 18 sec.; (Griffith) 15 seconds.

Manufacturer: TVR Cars Ltd.; then TVR Engineering Ltd.; Blackpool, England. Distributor: Griffith Motors Inc., New York.

HISTORY: In addition to quality problems, a lengthy dock strike harmed Griffith sales in the U.S. Another name change came in 1964, to TVR Cars Ltd., but that lasted only a year. After liquidation in 1965, TVR was acquired by Martin Lilley (a TVR dealer) and Arthur Lilley (his father), reorganized as TVR Engineering Ltd. Production of the Mk IV began in fall 1966. Subsequent models followed up on the original theme, starting with the Vixen, which debuted in 1967.

1967-71 TVR

VIXEN — S1/S2/S3 — FOUR — For the home market, TVR's replacement for the Grantura series carried a four-cylinder Cortina engine, with smaller displacement than before: just 1599 cc.

TUSCAN — V-6/V-8 — The next high-performance evolution of the Grantura/Griffith still wore a fiberglass body on a tubular steel chassis, with all-independent suspension. The first 28 examples, on the short (85-inch) wheelbase chassis, again used Ford's 289-cid V-8 engine. A total of 24 were said to be sold in the U.S., distributed by Gerry Sagerman. Some had the 195-bhp Ford 289; others the 271-bhp edition. The next two dozen examples rode a longer (90-inch) wheelbase, and differed in styling with a tail that was less abruptly stubby. They used different taillamps (from the Cortina Mk II) and a restyled hood, and half went to the U.S. in 1967-68. A total of 21 "wide-body" SE V-8 models then were built, after announcement at the 1968 New York Auto Show, shaped similar to the later M-series. Finally, starting in October 1969, a total of 101 Tuscans were powered by Ford's "Essex" 3.0-liter V-6. The last V-8 models carried a larger V-8 engine. Exempt from U.S. safety standards because of TVR's low production, the coupes had to be modified to meet emissions requirements. Tuscans had fancier interiors than their predecessors, including a polished wood dashboard. Styling features included an open-up vertical air vent on the lower cowl, and a horizontal opening on the upper cowl covered by two thin horizontal bars. Large wraparound taillamps were used, and the hood displayed a bulge. Otherwise, appearance was similar to the former Griffith.

I.D. DATA: Serial numbers are on a vertical plate on the left side of the cowl, under the hood. Serial number range: (Vixen S1) VX117; (Vixen S2) LVX1234/F to 1736/4; (Vixen S3) LVX1737/4 to 2239/4. Starting serial number: (Tuscan) 200-011.

Model	Body Type & Seating	Engine Type/CID	P.O.E. Price	Weight (lbs.)	Prod. Total
VIXEN					
S1	2-dr Fbk Cpe-2P	I4/97	N/A	N/A	N/A
S2	2-dr Fbk Cpe-2P	I4/97	N/A	1650	N/A
S3	2-dr Fbk Cpe-2P	I4/97	N/A	1650	N/A

Model	Body Type & Seating	Engine Type/CID	P.O.E. Price	Weight (lbs.)	Prod. Total
TUSCAN					
	2-dr Fbk Cpe-2P	V6/183	N/A	2052	101
	2-dr Fbk Cpe-2P	V8/289	N/A	N/A	28
SE	2-dr Fbk Cpe-2P	V8/289	6250	2308	24
	2-dr Fbk Cpe-2P	V8/302	N/A	2165	N/A

ENGINE DATA: BASE FOUR (Vixen): Inline, overhead-valve four-cylinder (Ford Cortina). Cast iron block and head. **Displacement:** 97.5 cu. in. (1599 cc). **Bore & Stroke:** 3.19 x 3.06 in. (81 x 77.6 mm). **Compression Ratio:** 9.0:1 or 9.2:1. **Brake Horsepower:** 86-90 at 5400/5500 rpm. Five main bearings. Solid valve lifters. Weber carburetor.

BASE V-6 (Tuscan): Overhead-valve V-6 (Ford "Essex"). Cast iron block and head. **Displacement:** 183 cu. in. (2994 cc). **Bore & Stroke:** 3.69 x 2.85 in. (93.7 x 72.4 mm). **Compression Ratio:** 8.9:1. **Brake Horsepower:** 136 at 4750 rpm. **Torque:** 173 lbs.-ft. at 3000 rpm. Four main bearings. Weber carburetor.

BASE V-8 (Tuscan V-8/SE): Overhead-valve V-8 (Ford). Cast iron block and head. **Displacement:** 289 cu. in. (4727 cc). **Bore & Stroke:** 4.00 x 2.87 in. (101.6 x 72.9 mm). **Compression Ratio:** 9.0:1. **Brake Horsepower:** 195 at 4400 rpm. **Torque:** 282 lbs.-ft. at 2400 rpm. Five main bearings. Holley four-barrel carburetor.

Note: High-performance version of the 289-cid V-8 produced 271 horsepower at 6500 rpm, and 314 lbs.-ft. at 3400 rpm. A 302-cid (4949-cc) V-8 was used for the final Tuscans, producing 220 bhp.

CHASSIS DATA: Wheelbase: (Vixen S1, early Tuscan) 85.5 in.; (Vixen S2/S3, Tuscan) 90.0 in. **Overall Length:** 138 or 145 in. **Height:** 48 in. **Width:** 64 in. **Max. Tread:** 53-54 in. **Standard Tires:** (Vixen) 165x15; (Tuscan) 185x15.

TECHNICAL: Layout: front-engine, rear-drive. **Transmission:** four-speed manual (overdrive optional). **Standard Final Drive Ratio:** (Vixen) 3.91:1 or 3.89:1; (Tuscan V-6) 3.54:1; (Tuscan SE) 3.67:1. **Steering:** rack and pinion. **Suspension (front):** unequal-length wishbones and coil springs. **Suspension (rear):** unequal-length wishbones and coil springs. **Brakes:** front disc, rear drum. **Body Construction:** fiberglass body on multitube chassis.

PERFORMANCE: Top Speed: (Vixen) 106-109 mph; (Tuscan V-6) 125 mph; (Tuscan V-8/SE) 155 mph. **Acceleration (0-60 mph):** (Tuscan) 5.7 to 8.3 seconds. **Acceleration (quarter-mile):** (Vixen) 17-18 sec.; (Tuscan V-6) 16.3 sec.; (Tuscan SE) 14.1 seconds. **Fuel Mileage:** (Tuscan V-6) about 28 mpg.

Manufacturer: TVR Engineering Ltd., Blackpool, England.

1972-76 TVR

Circa 1973 TVR with Cobra V-8.

2500/2500M/3000M — SIX/V-6 — Built on the same longer (90-inch wheelbase) as the former Tuscan, the M-series was targeted at U.S. customers. Under the hood was a 2.5-liter inline six, from the Triumph TR6, but European buyers could also get a Ford "Essex" 3.0-liter V-6. A space-frame chassis made up of small-diameter tubing (square and round) with a central backbone replaced the former tubular steel platform, but bodies were still made of fiberglass. As before, the coupes were designed to take various engines and no trunk lid was installed. Appearance was similar to the earlier "widebody" Tuscan V-8 SE, with a longer nose and tail than the Vixen/Griffith. The cowl vent was split into two sections, one atop the other, with thin horizontal bars. No lower cowl vent was used. Amber and clear park/signal lights stood at the ends of the unadorned grille opening. Twin air vents went into hood sides, above the wheel openings. Doors contained vent wings. At the rear were wraparound red/amber/clear taillamps. Quarter bumpers were installed. Some Turbo models had huge 'Turbo' lettering on the bodyside. An initial (1971) model called, simply, 2500, was essentially a V-6 Tuscan with American-spec TR6 engine. A total of 289 were built, plus 96 copies of another variant that put the old body on M-Series chassis.

1300/1600M — FOUR — Two four-cylinder models appeared after the demise of the Vixen. The 1300 series used a 1.3-liter overhead-valve Triumph Spitfire four-cylinder engine. The 1600M turned to Ford's "crossflow" 1.6-liter "Kent" four.

I.D. DATA: Chassis and engine numbers are on a plate in the center of the cowl, along with a paint code.

Model	Body Type & Seating	Engine Type/CID	P.O.E. Price	Weight (lbs.)	Prod. Total
2500	2-dr Cpe-2P	I6/152	N/A	1960	385
2500M	2-dr Cpe-2P	I6/152	Note 1	1960	947
3000M	2-dr Cpe-2P	V6/183	N/A	2165	654
1300	2-dr Cpe-2P	I4/79	N/A	1765	Note 2
1600M	2-dr CPE-2P	I4/98	N/A	N/A	Note 2

Note 1: Price in U.S. was $5450 in 1973, rising to $8888 by 1976.

Note 2: Total TVR production peaked at 421 units in 1974, followed by only 132 in 1975, as a result of a fire in the factory. A total of 333 TVRs were produced in 1976. **Production Note:** A total of 63 turbocharged 3000M/Taimar models were built.

1974 TVR 2500M.

ENGINE DATA: BASE FOUR (1300): Inline, overhead-valve four-cylinder. **Displacement:** 79 cu. in. (1296 cc). **Bore & Stroke:** 2.90 x 2.99 in. (73.7 x 76 mm). **Compression Ratio:** 9.0:1. **Brake Horsepower:** 83 at 6000 rpm. Solid valve lifters. Two SU carburetors.

BASE FOUR (1600M): Inline, overhead-valve four-cylinder (Ford). Cast iron block and head. **Displacement:** 97.6 cu. in. (1599 cc). **Bore & Stroke:** 3.19 x 3.06 in. (81 x 77.6 mm). **Compression Ratio:** 9.0:1. **Brake Horsepower:** 86 (DIN) at 5500 rpm. **Torque:** 92 lbs.-ft. (DIN) at 4000 rpm. Five main bearings. Solid valve lifters. Weber two-barrel carburetor.

BASE SIX (2500/2500M): Inline, overhead-valve six-cylinder (Triumph TR6). Cast iron block and head. **Displacement:** 152.4 cu. in. (2498 cc). **Bore & Stroke:** 2.94 x 3.74 in. (74.7 x 95 mm). **Compression Ratio:** 8.5:1. **Brake Horsepower:** 106 at 4950 rpm. **Torque:** 133 lbs.-ft. at 3000 rpm. Four main bearings. Solid valve lifters. Two SU carburetors.

BASE V-6 (3000M): Overhead-valve V-6 (Ford "Essex"). Cast iron block and head. **Displacement:** 183 cu. in. (2994 cc). **Bore & Stroke:** 3.69 x 2.85 in. (93.7 x 72.4 mm). **Compression Ratio:** 8.9:1. **Brake Horsepower:** 142 (SAE) at 5000 rpm. **Torque:** 172 lbs.-ft. at 3000 rpm. Four main bearings. Weber carburetor.

Note: A turbocharged version of the V-6 produced 230 bhp (DIN) at 5500 rpm, and 273 lbs.-ft. of torque at 3500 rpm.

Circa 1975 TVR 3000M. (Elliott Kahn)

CHASSIS DATA: Wheelbase: 90.0 in. **Overall Length:** (1300/2500) 145 in.; (2500M) 160 in.; (3000M) 154 in. **Height:** 48 in. **Width:** 64 in. **Front Tread:** (2500/3000) 53.75 in. **Rear Tread:** (2500/3000) 53.75 in. **Standard Tires:** 165x15 exc. (3000M) 185x14.

TECHNICAL: Layout: front-engine, rear-drive. **Transmission:** four-speed manual (overdrive optional). **Standard Final Drive Ratio:** 3.45:1 or 3.89:1. **Steering:** rack and pinion. **Suspension (front):** unequal-length wishbones and coil springs. **Suspension (rear):** unequal-length wishbones and coil springs. **Brakes:** front disc, rear drum. **Body Construction:** fiberglass body on space-frame chassis.

PERFORMANCE: Top Speed: (1300) 104 mph; (2500) about 110 mph; (3000M) 127 mph (U.S. 3000M) near 115 mph; (turbo) 140 mph. **Acceleration (0-60 mph):** 5.8 (turbo) to 9.3 seconds. **Acceleration (quarter-mile):** (2500) 18 sec.; (3000M) 16.2 seconds.

Manufacturer: TVR Engineering Ltd., Blackpool, England. **Distributor:** TVR Cars of America Ltd., Huntington, New York.

HISTORY: Production of the 2500M halted in 1977 because the TR6 engine had been cancelled some time earlier, cutting off the supply. The 3000M was offered through 1979. Some turbochargers were added by private tuners rather than the TVR company.

1977-79 TVR

2500M/3000M — SIX/V-6 — Production of the 2500M continued into 1977, the 3000M into 1979. See previous listing for details.

TAIMAR — V-6 — Late in 1976, styling of the 3000M changed from a fastback coupe to a hatchback. What was the large wraparound back window now served as a hatch. Along with that came a name change, to Taimar. Then, in 1978, a convertible (roadster) with removable side curtains and a trunk lid joined the Taimar coupe. Whether sold in Britain or the U.S., Taimars contained the British Ford 3.0-liter V-6 engine, because the cars were exempted from U.S. emissions requirements. Taillamps were repositioned, and flush-fit bumpers were new. Gas struts supported the raised tailgate (hatch). Standard Taimar equipment included 185HR14 tires on alloy wheels, sunroof, leather upholstery, and power windows.

I.D. DATA: Similar to 1972-76.

Model	Body Type & Seating	Engine Type/CID	P.O.E. Price	Weight (lbs.)	Prod. Total
Taimar	2-dr Hatch-2P	V6/183	15900	2335	395
Taimar	2-dr Rds-2P	V6/183	N/A	2335	258

Production Note: A total of 63 turbocharged 3000M/Taimar models were built.

ENGINE DATA: BASE V-6: Overhead-valve V-6 (Ford "Essex"). Cast iron block and head. **Displacement:** 183 cu. in. (2994 cc). **Bore & Stroke:** 3.69 x 2.85 in. (93.7 x 72.4 mm). **Compression Ratio:** 8.9:1. **Brake Horsepower:** 142 (SAE) at 5000 rpm. **Torque:** 172 lbs.-ft. at 3000 rpm. Four main bearings. Weber carburetor.

Note: A turbocharged version of the V-6 produced 230 bhp (DIN) at 5500 rpm, and 273 lbs.-ft. of torque at 3500 rpm.

CHASSIS DATA: Wheelbase: 90.0 in. **Overall Length:** 155 in. **Height:** 47 in. **Width:** 64 in. **Front Tread:** 53.8 in. **Rear Tread:** 53.8 in. **Standard Tires:** 185HR14.

TECHNICAL: Layout: front-engine, rear-drive. **Transmission:** four-speed manual (overdrive optional). **Steering:** rack and pinion. **Suspension (front):** unequal-length wishbones and coil springs with anti-roll bar. **Suspension (rear):** unequal-length wishbones and coil springs. **Brakes:** front disc, rear drum. **Body Construction:** fiberglass body on space-frame chassis.

PERFORMANCE: Top Speed: 130 + mph; (turbo) 145 mph. **Acceleration (0-60 mph):** 7.5 sec.; (turbo) 5.9 seconds.

Manufacturer: TVR Engineering Ltd., Blackpool, England.

Distributor: TVR Cars of America Ltd., Huntington, New York.

HISTORY: Debut of the Taimar coupe took place at the 1976 London Motor Show.

1980-89 TVR

1987 TVR convertible.

TASMIN/280i — V-6 — A dramatic new wedge-shaped series replaced the former M-Series and Taimar, powered by either Rover or Ford engines. A convertible, coupe, and 2+2 coupe body was available, with manual or automatic transmission. Examples sold in the U.S. (mostly convertibles) had a German Ford 2.8-liter V-6. A 2.9-liter V-6 replaced that powerplant in 1987. A lower-priced version also was available, powered by a Ford 2.0-liter four-cylinder engine; but few were sold. All rode a 94-inch wheelbase and used the same "space frame" as the M-Series/Taimar, with square and round small-diameter tubes. Suspension and steering also were similar to the former versions, but four-wheel disc brakes were new. Bodies again were made of fiberglass. A long, squared-off nose and hidden headlamps stood ahead of a very long hood. That gave the Tasmin a lengthy front overhang, but short at the rear. Because wheelbase was the same on all models, back seats were tight in the 2+2. Convertibles had a fold-down Targa-style bar. An AM/FM stereo radio with cassette player was standard. Tasmin upholstery came in suede velours and ambla. The passenger sunvisor held a vanity mirror, and doors contained ashtrays. Power windows were standard.

350i/390SE/420SEAC — V-8 — Later in the 1980s, other engines were installed, including a turbocharged V-6. In 1983, a V-8 edition appeared, with a Rover 3.5-liter engine (based on the early 1960s Buick design), producing up to 190 bhp. By 1984, the V-6 Tasmin was called 280i; and the V-8 became 350i. A 3.9-liter V-8 also were produced in the mid-1980s. Then came the debut of the 420SEAC (Special Equipment Aramad Composite), powered by a 300-bhp, 4.2-liter V-8 and capable of more than 150 mph. It used lightweight Kelvar body materials.

I.D. DATA: An identification plate on the right inner fender contains the chassis and engine numbers, and body code.

Model	Body Type & Seating	Engine Type/CID	P.O.E. Price	Weight (lbs.)	Prod. Total
Tasmin 280i	2-dr Coupe-2P	V6/170	Note 1	2348	Note 2
Tasmin 280i	2-dr Conv-2P	V6/170	Note 1	2335	Note 2
Tasmin 280i	2-dr Coupe-2 + 2P	V6/170	Note 1	2536	Note 2
350i	2-dr Conv-2P	V8/215	Note 3	N/A	Note 2
390SE	2-dr Coupe-2P	V8/238	N/A	N/A	Note 2
390SE	2-dr Conv-2P	V8/238	N/A	N/A	Note 2
420SEAC	2-dr Coupe-2P	V8/258	Note 4	N/A	Note 2

Note 1: Tasmin 280i prices in Britain ranged from 13,254 to 15,500 pounds (Sterling) in 1984.

Note 2: TVR production reached a low of 121 units in 1982, rising to 472 in 1985.

Note 3: Price of the 350i convertible in Britain was 14,800 pounds (Sterling) in 1984.

Note 4: Price of the 420SEAC was about $45,000 in Britain.

Model Note: Tasmin 200 coupes and convertibles also were available, powered by a 1993-cc four-cylinder engine; only 61 were sold.

ENGINE DATA: BASE V-6 (Tasmin/280i): Overhead-valve, 60-degree V-6 (German Ford). Cast iron block and head. **Displacement:** 170.4 cu. in. (2792 cc). **Bore & Stroke:** 3.66 x 2.07 in. (93.0 x 68.5 mm). **Compression Ratio:** 9.2:1. **Brake Horsepower:** 160 (DIN) at 5700 rpm; U.S. version, 145 bhp (SAE). **Torque:** 162 lbs.-ft. (DIN) at 4300 rpm; U.S. version, 150 lbs.-ft. (SAE). Four main bearings. Bosch K-Jetronic fuel injection.

BASE V-8 (350i): Overhead-valve V-8 (Rover). Light alloy block and head. **Displacement:** 215.2 cu. in. (3528 cc). **Bore & Stroke:** 3.50 x 2.80 in. (88.8 x 71 mm). **Compression Ratio:** 9.8:1. **Brake Horsepower:** 190 (DIN) at 5300 rpm. **Torque:** 220 lbs.-ft. (DIN) at 4000 rpm. Five main bearings. Hydraulic valve lifters. Fuel injection.

BASE V-8 (390SE): Overhead-valve V-8 (Rover). **Displacement:** 238.3 cu. in. (3905 cc). **Brake Horsepower:** 275 (DIN) at 5500 rpm. **Torque:** 270 lbs.-ft. (DIN) at 3500 rpm.

BASE V-8 (420SEAC): Overhead-valve V-8 (Rover). **Displacement:** 258 cu. in. (4228 cc). **Brake Horsepower:** 300 (DIN) at 5500 rpm. **Torque:** 290 lbs.-ft. (DIN) at 4500 rpm.

CHASSIS DATA: Wheelbase: 94.0 in. **Overall Length:** 158 in.; (2+2) 161 in. **Height:** 47 in. **Width:** 68 in. **Front Tread:** 56.5 in. **Rear Tread:** 56.7 in. **Wheel Type:** (Tasmin) cast alloy. **Standard Tires:** (Tasmin) 205/60VR14; (350i) 205/60VR15.

TECHNICAL: Layout: front-engine, rear-drive. **Transmission:** four- or five-speed manual, or three-speed automatic. Tasmin four-speed gear ratios: (1st) 3.16:1; (2nd) 1.94:1; (3rd) 1.41:1; (4th) 1.00:1. **Standard Final Drive Ratio:** 3.07:1. **Steering:** rack and pinion (power assist optional). **Suspension (front):** unequal-length wishbones, coil springs and anti-roll bar. **Suspension (rear):** lateral links, trailing arms and coil springs. **Brakes:** front/rear disc. **Body Construction:** fiberglass body on space-frame chassis.

PERFORMANCE: Top Speed: 108 mph or more; (Tasmin) 133 mph claimed; (U.S. Tasmin) 125 mph; (350i) 135-140 mph; (390SE) 150 mph; (420SEAC) 150+ mpg. **Acceleration (0-60 mph):** 5.6 to 11.8 seconds; (Tasmin) 7.5 seconds claimed; (390SE) 5.0-5.5 seconds. **Acceleration (quarter-mile):** (Tasmin) 16 seconds claimed. **Fuel Mileage:** (Tasmin) 24-30 mpg claimed.

Manufacturer: TVR Engineering Ltd., Blackpool, England.

Distributor: TVR North America Ltd., Scarborough, Ontario, Canada.

HISTORY: The hatchback coupe debuted in January 1980, after appearance at the Brussels Motor Show; followed by the convertible and 2+2 late that year. The 350i first appeared in August 1983, declared to have "more appeal than a Ferrari" by CAR magazine. At the October 1984 Motor Show in Birmingham, England came the debut of the bigger (3.9-liter) V-8 engine. No TVRs were sold in the U.S. in the early 1980s, but sales resumed by 1983. By 1982, the company had changed hands again, with Peter Wheeler taking over from Martin Lilley.

1990 TVR Speed Eight. (William Siuru Jr.)

POSTSCRIPT: By 1990, yet another model was available in North America, the S2, powered by a fuel-injected 2933-cc V-6 engine rated 168 bhp (DIN) at 6000 rpm. The convertible top was designed to run either fully open, fully closed, or targa-style. The S2 could reach 98 mph in a quarter-mile run, with a top speed of 140 mph. Prices began at $48,280.

VAUXHALL

Boats, not automobiles, were among the first products from the Vauxhall Iron Works at London, England. Not until 1903 did the first Vauxhall motorcars leave the plant, in the form of a chain-drive runabout with horizontally-mounted single-cylinder engine and two forward speeds (no reverse). A year later, a steering wheel replaced the original tiller, a reverse gear was added, and Vauxhalls also were available with three-cylinder engines. A move from London to the city of Luton came in 1905, a year in which Vauxhall made its first stab at competition, sending an entrant to the Tourist Trophy race. By 1906, a four-cylinder Vauxhall with T-head engine was offered, displaying the fluted radiator that became a virtual Vauxhall trademark. Pomeroy was responsible for the design of the L-head four-cylinder model that won the 2,000-Mile Trial in 1908. A rounded-nose sports model with 3-liter engine fared well at the Prince Henry trials race in Germany, in 1910. Those cars carried the Prince Henry name, becoming one of the best-known Vauxhall models. In the period just prior to World War I, Vauxhall also marketed six-cylinder automobiles.

After the Armistice, Vauxhall resumed civilian production with the D-type and the sporty E-type 30/98, both of which had debuted before the war. The latter car, in fact, had won many competition trophies. A smaller M-type 14/40 with 2.3-liter engine came in 1922, with three forward speeds instead of the usual four; but that changed in 1925. An overhead-valve engine became available for the 30/98 in 1922, guaranteed to be capable of 100 mph. That car was produced until 1928. Financial ills in the mid-1920s led to a purchase of the Vauxhall organization by General Motors.

An S-type model with 3.9-liter sleeve-valve six-cylinder engine debuted in 1926. For its final year in the lineup, the 14/40 could get a Wilson preselector transmission—an option offered by a number of British automakers in the late 1920s and early '30s.

General Motors' influence was felt in the 20/60 six-cylinder R-type introduced for 1928, which had more of an American look than prior Vauxhalls. Not long after the start of the Depression, in 1931, Vauxhall came out with a low-cost Cadet that had a 2-liter (2048-cc) six-cylinder engine. Synchromesh was added to the Cadet's gearbox a year later—a "first" in the British auto industry. Additional smaller models known as "light sixes" arrived in 1933, joining their larger mates. Small Vauxhalls adopted GM's "knee action" independent front suspension in 1935.

Exposed radiators faded away after 1936, as was the case with many makes at that time, fronted instead by separate grillework with attached headlamps. A unibodied Vauxhall Ten sedan with 1.2-liter engine debuted in 1938, but the coupe version had a separate body. The Ten was the first mass-produced British car with a unibody. Other Vauxhalls adopted unit construction just before World War II began.

After the war, a few Vauxhalls were made with separate bodies and chassis, but only for export. All others were unibodied. The early postwar lineup included a Ten, Twelve and Fourteen, all carried over from 1940. Vauxhall's first new postwar creations were the Wyvern and Velox, on the same body but powered by a 1442-cc four-cylinder engine or a 2275-cc six, respectively. Each of these models was restyled in 1951, to a full-width body in the modern mode but without dramatic mechanical change. All-new short-stroke engines were installed in 1952. Then, for 1955, a posh six-cylinder model called the Cresta was introduced.

A new and wholly modern Victor replaced the Wyvern in 1957. Styling had distinct American overtones, including a wraparound windshield, and this was indeed the first Vauxhall to make a significant stab at the American market. Power came from a 1507-cc overhead-valve engine, with three-speed manual gearbox. Vauxhall Victors were marketed by Pontiac dealers in the U.S.

Six-cylinder models adopted similar styling a year later. Overdrive became available in 1959, followed by an automatic transmission. Not until 1962 did vestiges of the traditional radiator "fluting" disappear from Vauxhall front ends. Victor styling changed considerably by that time, and engine output grew to 56 horsepower. A variant with twin carburetors and 71-horsepower rating, known as the VX 4/90, carried front disc brakes. Velox and Cresta models added the front discs in 1963, as part of their restyling.

Vauxhall introduced a smaller Viva for 1964, based upon the German-built Opel Kadett with a 1057-cc engine. Victors moved up to 1.6-liter displacement for 1965, and sixes reached 3.3 liters. By then, Victors no longer were ordinarily imported into the U.S., though the make remained strong elsewhere in the world market.

Elsewhere in the world, a posh edition of the Cresta, called Viscount, arrived in 1966 with an automatic transmission and vinyl top. Then came an all-new Victor with a choice of two overhead-cam four-cylinder engines: 1599-cc (FD series) and 1975-cc (Victor 2000). Each had a four-speed gearbox, four-wheel coil springs, and rack-and-pinion steering. Also appearing was a sporty Ventora sedan, followed by a Viva GT that blended the small body with a 2.0-liter Victor engine.

Vauxhall's Firenza coupe arrived in 1971, powered by either a Viva or Victor engine. Vivas with bigger engines adopted the Magnum designation by 1974, while a short-lived Firenza coupe with 131-horsepower engine and five-speed gearbox added a jolt of performance to the Vauxhall name. Just as the T-car Chevette was introduced in the U.S. market, a Vauxhall version arrived in Britain, using the Viva's engine. A Rallye Chevette carried a twin-cam engine that churned out 132 horsepower. Other Vauxhalls of the 1970s and '80s were based on German Opel designs, or even built in Germany. Long before then, the Vauxhall name had faded away from American memories.

1946-56 VAUXHALL

Vauxhall's revived Ten, Twelve and Fourteen saloons (sedans) differed little from their prewar predecessors. The Ten had a 1203-cc overhead-valve four-cylinder engine, and rode a 97.8-inch wheelbase. The Twelve had a larger bore and 1442-cc displacement, for a few extra horsepower (35 versus 31.5 for the Ten). Wheelbase was the same as the Ten. Largest of the lot was the Fourteen, with a 105-inch wheelbase and 1781-cc six-cylinder engine, which developed 47.5 horsepower. The Ten was produced in 1946-47, while its mates lasted into 1948.

Appearance of the new Wyvern and Velox, introduced in 1948, differed considerably from those carryover models. Each had built-in headlamps and a fairly wide horizontal-bar grille, with semi-modern styling. A 1442-cc four-cylinder engine went into the Wyvern, similar to that used in the former Twelve but rated 33 horsepower at 3600 rpm. The Velox saloon carried a six-cylinder engine that displaced 2275 cc and developed 54 horsepower at 3300 rpm. Both models rode a 97.8-inch wheelbase and measured 164.5 inches long overall. Torsion bars were used for the front suspensions, with semi-elliptic leaf springs at the rear. A Wyvern could travel about 62 mph, while the Velox six was capable of 74 mph.

Both the Wyvern and Velox enjoyed a major restyled in 1951, with full-width bodies. Engine ratings rose slightly (to 35 and 55 horsepower), and front coil springs replaced the former torsion bars. Wheelbase of the new models was 103 inches, and each measured 170.5 inches long. Styling was more square, with a crossbar-shaped grille pattern made up of thick moldings. Fifteen-inch tires replaced the former 16-inch rubber.

A year later, each model got a new short-stroke engine. Bore/stroke dimensions were identical for the four- and six-cylinder versions: 79.4-inch bore and 76.2-inch stroke, for 1507 and 2262 cc (respectively). The four-cylinder Wyvern engine developed 40 horsepower on 6.4:1 compression, or close to 48 bhp with 7.3:1 compression. Velox sixes likewise came in two flavors: 64 bhp on 6.4:1 compression, or 67.5 bhp using 7.7:1 compression. As before, each engine used a Zenith carburetor. A re-engined Wyvern could come close to 72 mph, while a Velox might be able to hit 80 mph. Added for 1955 was a luxury edition of the Velox, called the Cresta.

1957-59 VAUXHALL

1958 Vauxhall Cresta four-door sedan.

VICTOR — SUPER — FOUR — Squarish in profile, the new Vauxhall aimed at international sales and carried a 1507-cc overhead-valve four-cylinder engine (as in the latest Wyvern). Output was 55 horsepower, on 7.8:1 compression. Wheelbase was 98 inches, or 5 inches shorter than the Wyvern. Victors, according to the sales literature, offered full circle vision with a panoramic windshield and rear window, and a new low glass line. The all-synchromesh three-speed gearbox had a column-mounted shift lever. A hydraulic-assisted clutch was standard. A new "flat-ride" suspension system consisted of coil springs up front and semi-elliptic leaf springs at the rear. The rectangular grille had a very tight mesh pattern. Vertical parking lights were built into the surround molding at the outer ends of that grille, and stood above projectile-shaped bumper guards.

Two models were produced, but the luxury "Super" edition was the one exported to the U.S. The Super came in a choice of eight colors, versus five for the base model. Supers had armrests on each door, a rear ashtray, two-spoke steering wheel with horn ring, automatic courtesy-light switches, dual sunvisors, and a twin-tone horn. Additional chromed trim also was used in the Super, including windshield and window surround moldings, taillamp bezels, and flashing on rear fenders and doors. Exhaust gases exited via a pipe that passed through a "porthole" in the rear bumper. Rear-door badges declared the 'Super' model name in white, while 'Victor' identification went on the front fenders. An upper bodyside trim strip began near the headlamps and extended into the rear door. A lower trim strip started near the termination point of the upper strip, extending all the way to the rear end. Parallel trim moldings decorated the hood.

Standard body colors for the Super were Gypsy Red, Harvest Yellow, Horizon Blue, Empress Blue, Charcoal Grey, Laurel Green, Shantung Beige, and Black. Two upholstery styles were offered, each a two-tone fabric. Early literature issued in Europe described the Victor as a four-passenger car, but American ads declared it to be a five-seater. A station wagon also became available in the car's first season in the American market.

1959 Vauxhall Victor Super station wagon.

I.D. DATA: Serial number is on right side of firewall, under the hood. Starting serial number: (sedan) FD-1001; (wagon) FW-1001. Engine number is on right side of block. Starting engine number: F4-2001.

Model	Body Type & Seating	Engine Type/CID	P.O.E. Price	Weight (lbs.)	Prod. Total
FD	4-dr Sedan-4/5P	I4/92	1988	2150	Note 1
FW	4-dr Sta Wag-4/5P	I4/92	2400	2280	Note 1

Note 1: Approximately 91,500 Vauxhalls (all models) were produced in 1957 (up from 66,000 in 1956), followed by 120,000 in 1958.

Note: Price was $74 higher in Great Lakes region and $197 higher on West Coast.

1959 Vauxhall Victor Super four-door sedan.

ENGINE DATA: BASE FOUR: Inline, overhead-valve four-cylinder. **Displacement:** 92 cu. in. (1507 cc). **Bore & Stroke:** 3.125 x 3.00 in. (79.4 x 76.2 mm). **Compression Ratio:** 7.8:1. **Brake Horsepower:** 54.8 at 4200 rpm. **Torque:** 85 lbs.-ft. at 2400 rpm. Four main bearings. Solid valve lifters. One Zenith carburetor.

CHASSIS DATA: Wheelbase: 98 in. **Overall Length:** 166.5 in. **Height:** 58 in. **Width:** 62 in. **Front Tread:** 50 in. **Rear Tread:** 50 in. **Standard Tires:** (sed) 5.60x13; (wag) 5.90x13.

TECHNICAL: Layout: front-engine, rear-drive. **Transmission:** three-speed manual (column lever, all-synchro). **Gear ratios:** (1st) 3.186:1; (2nd) 1.653:1; (3rd) 1.00:1; (rev) 3.05:1. **Standard Final Drive Ratio:** (sed) 4.125:1; (wag) 4.625:1. **Steering:** recirculating ball. **Suspension (front):** transverse control arms with coil springs. **Suspension (rear):** rigid axle with semi-elliptic leaf springs. **Brakes:** hydraulic, front/rear drum. **Body Construction:** steel unibody.

PERFORMANCE: Top Speed: 72-74 mph. **Acceleration (0-60 mph):** 31 sec. **Acceleration (quarter-mile):** 26.3 sec. (56 mph). **Fuel Mileage:** about 28-31 mpg.

ADDITIONAL MODELS: Vauxhall also continued to produce the Velox six-cylinder sedan with its 2262-cc engine, and the posh Cresta version. By this time, the engine developed 82.5 horsepower using 7.8:1 compression. Only the Victor was ordinarily exported to the U.S. market.

Manufacturer: Vauxhall Motors Ltd., Luton, Bedfordshire, England.

Distributor: Pontiac Motor Division, General Motors Corp., Pontiac, Michigan.

HISTORY: "Reaching out into the future for their inspiration," said early literature for the new model, "Vauxhall designers have created the Victor." The new Victor was introduced to the American market in September 1957, though it arrived elsewhere in the world earlier in the year. Literature for this Vauxhall model was distributed at the Detroit auto show in January 1958. American ads promised "British craftsmanship and distinction...with more of the features Americans want." The original Victor design continued into early 1959, when it was replaced by the Series 2; see next listing for details.

1960-61 VAUXHALL

VICTOR — SERIES 2 (SUPER) — FOUR — Introduced during 1959, the second-series Victor adopted a wider rectangular grille (tight mesh pattern, as before) with small round projectile-shaped parking lights at its outer ends. A revised, wide wing-style emblem went on the hood front, which now contained only a single molding. Bumpers and taillamps also were new. 'Victor' block lettering went on the lower front fender, between the headlamp and wheel opening, while 'Super' lettering (slightly angled) decorated the upper rear fenders. The chrome bodyside molding at the beltline extended only halfway onto the car's rear quarter panel. Mechanical changes were minimal, continuing the 1507-cc engine with its 55-bhp rating. Deluxe equipment, according to literature issued at the London auto show, included a choice of six single-color and four two-color body finishes; special wheel embellishers and hubcap badges; individual front seats; leather upholstery; and pile carpets. Series 2 sales brochures also targeted United States forces stationed in Europe, noting that the Victor complied with U.S. state requirements except that sealed beam headlamps could be installed after returning home, by a Pontiac dealer.

Minor styling changes for 1961 included the addition of 'Vauxhall' lettering above a horizontal-bar grille, and a new round emblem at the grille center. A chrome bodyside molding extended the full length of the beltline, with 'Victor' lettering above the front wheel opening, 'Vauxhall' at the hood front, and 'Super' atop the rear fenders.

I.D. DATA: Serial number is on right side of firewall, under the hood. Engine number is on right side of block.

Model	Body Type & Seating	Engine Type/CID	P.O.E. Price	Weight (lbs.)	Prod. Total
FD	4-dr Sedan-4/5P	I4/92	1988	2150	Note 1
FW	4-dr Sta Wag-4/5P	I4/92	2400	2280	Note 1

Note 1: Approximately 145,000 Vauxhalls (all models) were produced in 1960, dropping to 85,000 in 1961.

ENGINE DATA: BASE FOUR: Inline, overhead-valve four-cylinder. **Displacement:** 92 cu. in. (1507 cc). **Bore & Stroke:** 3.125 x 3.00 in. (79.4 x 76.2 mm). **Compression Ratio:** 7.8:1. **Brake Horsepower:** 54.8 at 4200 rpm. **Torque:** 85 lbs.-ft. at 2400 rpm. Four main bearings. Solid valve lifters. One Zenith carburetor.

CHASSIS DATA: Wheelbase: 98 in. **Overall Length:** 168 in. **Height:** 58 in. **Width:** 63.5 in. **Front Tread:** 50 in. **Rear Tread:** 50 in. **Standard Tires:** (sed) 5.60x13; (wag) 5.90x13.

TECHNICAL: Layout: front-engine, rear-drive. **Transmission:** three-speed (column lever, all-synchro). Gear ratios: (1st) 3.186:1; (2nd) 1.653:1; (3rd) 1.00:1; (rev) 3.05:1. **Standard Final Drive Ratio:** (sed) 4.125:1; (wag) 4.625:1. **Steering:** recirculating ball. **Suspension (front):** transverse control arms with coil springs. **Suspension (rear):** rigid axle with semi-elliptic leaf springs. **Brakes:** hydraulic, front/rear drum. **Body Construction:** steel unibody.

PERFORMANCE: Similar to 1957-58.

ADDITIONAL MODELS: Vauxhall introduced revised Velox and Cresta models in 1960, with a larger (2651-cc) six-cylinder engine but the same 105-inch wheelbase as their late 1950s predecessors.

Manufacturer: Vauxhall Motors Ltd., Luton, Bedfordshire, England.

Distributor: Pontiac Motor Division, General Motors Corp., Pontiac, Michigan.

HISTORY: Vauxhall's 1960 models were introduced to the U.S. market on October 1, 1959.

1962 VAUXHALL

VICTOR — FB SUPER — FOUR — Total restyling came for the 1962 model year. Wheelbase grew 2 inches, overall length by more than 5 inches. A soft sculpture line ran from the headlamp along the upper fender and bodyside reaching downward at the rear, at the outer end of the taillamp assembly, which consisted of horizontal oval amber lenses. Wheel openings also displayed a softer appearance, and headlamps no longer sat beneath hoods. The Victor's horizontal grille was considerably taller than before, made up of horizontal bars with a vertical center emblem. Headlamps now were enclosed within the grille, rather than mounted above. Horizontal hexagonal parking lights sat below the headlamps. 'Vauxhall' block lettering now ran almost the full width of the hood's nose. Rocker panels extended slightly outward from the door panels. 'A' pillars angled rearward to create an inverted 'V' shape for the front vent wings. Under the hood, the 1507-cc engine developed slightly more horsepower via higher compression. In addition to the standard column-shift three-speed, a four-speed floor-shift gearbox became optional.

I.D. DATA: Serial number is stamped on a plate attached to left front door hinge pillar post. Starting serial number: FBD-1001. Engine number is on right side of block.

Model	Body Type & Seating	Engine Type/CID	P.O.E. Price	Weight (lbs.)	Prod. Total
FBD	4-dr Sedan-4/5P	I4/92	2138	2023	Note 1
FBW	4-dr Sta Wag-4/5P	I4/92	2322	2123	Note 1

Note 1: Approximately 145,000 Vauxhalls (all models) were produced in 1960, dropping to 85,000 in 1961.

ENGINE DATA: BASE FOUR: Inline, overhead-valve four-cylinder. **Displacement:** 92 cu. in. (1507 cc). **Bore & Stroke:** 3.125 x 3.00 in. (79.4 x 76.2 mm). **Compression Ratio:** 8.1:1. **Brake Horsepower:** 56.3 at 4600 rpm. **Torque:** 85.6 lbs.-ft. at 2200 rpm. Four main bearings. Solid valve lifters. One Zenith carburetor.

CHASSIS DATA: Wheelbase: 100 in. **Overall Length:** 173.2 in. **Height:** 55.5 in. **Width:** 64 in. **Front Tread:** 50.8 in. **Rear Tread:** 51.1 in. **Standard Tires:** (sed) 5.60x13; (wag) 5.90x13.

TECHNICAL: Layout: front-engine, rear-drive. **Transmission:** three-speed manual (column lever); four-speed (floor lever) optional. **Steering:** recirculating ball. **Suspension (front):** transverse control arms with coil springs. **Suspension (rear):** rigid axle with semi-elliptic leaf springs. **Brakes:** hydraulic, front/rear drum. **Body Construction:** steel unibody.

Manufacturer: Vauxhall Motors Ltd., Luton, Bedfordshire, England.

Distributor: Pontiac Motor Division, General Motors Corp., Pontiac, Michigan.

POSTSCRIPT: This was the final year for official importation of the Victor (or any Vauxhall model) into the U.S., partly because Pontiac was focusing on its new compact Tempest. Sales of leftovers continued into 1963. Vauxhall remained a potent contender in the European marketplace, offering a broad selection of continued and new models, but never again resumed exports to the U.S.

VESPA

Even though the internationally popular Italian Vespa motorscooter of the 1950s remains well remembered today, not everyone recalls the French-built minicar of the same name. For several years, that tiny sunroofed two-door made a stab at the American market. The Piaggio company had a history dating back to 1884, and had become an aircraft manufacturer by the time of the First World War. Three decades later, after World War II, production turned to scooters. By 1955, according to *Motor Trend,* the Vespa scooter was particularly commonplace in Spain, "the latest

in the Spanish way of life." With a top speed of 45 mph from its one-cylinder engine, and gas mileage approaching 125 mpg, it was a sensible alternative in countries with high fuel (and automobile) prices. Still, since the $423 price tag was more than the average Spaniard earned in a year, the scooter became more of a toy for the well-to-do than a means of transport for the working class.

Introduced in 1957, the tiny two-seat motorcar found a willing audience in quite a few countries, including the U.S. Development was said to have taken six years, by the same team that produced the scooter. While the scooter had been produced in Italy (as well as in Britain and France) by the Piaggio firm, the minicar was actually built in France, though by the same company. One reason: the manufacturer didn't want to try and compete with the little Fiat 500 in Italy.

With a two-cylinder, air-cooled two-stroke engine, the Vespa was capable of traveling about 56 mph. For the U.S. market, it had one major virtue: a low price tag. The $1080 base price was considerably lower than the $1545 charged for a Volkswagen of that day. Even though a rather impressive number were sold in America, the experiment didn't quite succeed; and by 1961, Piaggio was back in the motorscooter and moped business.

1958-61 VESPA

1960 Vespa convertible. (William Siuru Jr.)

400 — TWO — The tiny two-seater that *Motor Trend* called a "well-engineered miniature" was ready for open-air motoring, with a standard plastic folding sunroof. Unibodied in structure, short and stubby in appearance, the Vespa was powered by a rear-mounted, air-cooled two-stroke engine, displacing 24 cubic inches. Independent four-wheel suspension included a swinging-style rear axle and deep coil springs at each wheel. Rack-and-pinion steering was used, and at the rear was a three-speed synchromesh transmission. Seating was provided for only two, but a space behind the seats could hold either luggage or small children. A spare tire fit below the passenger seat. A fake front grille (phony because the engine was in back) made up of two horizontal trim strips removed for access to the battery and brake master cylinder. Doors were hinged at the rear, with handles at the front ("suicide" style). The stubby cockpit had no rear quarter windows or vent wings. Small round parking lights sat below hooded headlamps. Electric windshield wipers were standard.

I.D. DATA: Not available.

Model	Body Type & Seating	Engine Type/CID	P.O.E. Price	Weight (lbs.)	Prod. Total
400	2-dr Conv-2P	I2/24	1080	850	Note 1

Note 1: Approximately 514 Vespas were sold in the U.S. during 1959 and 1,138 in 1960.

Body Note: Vespa was actually a two-door sedan with a sunroof, not a true convertible.

ENGINE DATA: BASE TWO: Inline, two-stroke two-cylinder (air cooled). **Displacement:** 24.5 cu. in. (393 cc). **Bore & Stroke:** 2.40 x 2.40 in. (63 x 63 mm). **Compression Ratio:** 6.4:1. **Brake Horsepower:** 20 at 4600 rpm.

1960 Vespa 400 two-door.

CHASSIS DATA: Wheelbase: 66.7 in. **Overall Length:** 112 in. **Height:** 49 in. **Width:** 50 in. **Front Tread:** 43.3 in. **Rear Tread:** 43.3 in. **Wheel Type:** disc. **Standard Tires:** 4.40x10.

TECHNICAL: Layout: rear-engine, rear-drive. **Transmission:** three-speed manual (floor lever). **Standard Final Drive Ratio:** 6.4:1. **Steering:** rack and pinion. **Suspension (front):** independent; deep-coil springs. **Suspension (rear):** independent; swing axle and deep-coil springs. **Brakes:** hydraulic, front/rear drum. **Body Construction:** steel unibody. **Fuel Tank:** 5 gallons.

PERFORMANCE: Top Speed: about 56 mph. **Fuel Mileage:** 60 mpg (claimed).

Manufacturer: Ateliers de Constructions de Motos et Accessoires (A.C.M.E.), Fourchamboult, Nievre, France.

Distributor: Boston Vespa Co., Boston, Massachusetts.

HISTORY: The four-wheeled Vespa appeared at the Paris (France) auto show in October 1957. Production halted in 1961, but the company remained in business through the 1980s.

VOLKSWAGEN

No single car model, with the exception of Ford's Model T, has played such a major role in changing automotive history as the Volkswagen "Beetle." More than any other make, the German-built Volkswagen paved the way for the import invasion of the 1950s and '60s, which in turn affected the types of cars turned out by Detroit for years. Without question, the "people's car" (the direct translation of *Volkswagen)* that brought motoring to postwar Germans and other Europeans had no less significant an impact when the first examples began to arrive on American shores, starting in 1949. Such a feat is all the more amazing when viewed against the backdrop of history, since the first production Volkswagens emerged so soon after Germany had begun its painful recovery from the ashes of war, and had been conceived as part of Hitler's plan for a Nazi-led future.

Volkswagen history began prior to Hitler's takeover of power with the formation, late in 1930, of a new company: Dr.-Ing. h.c. Ferdinand Porsche GmbH. Porsche's start-up staff included body designer Erwin Komenda and air-cooled engine expert Joseph Kales, as well as his son Ferry. Porsche saw the creation of small cars as a challenge. Over the prior decade, he'd worked on such early attempts as the Sascha (for Austro-Daimler).

Early in the new engineering firm's history came Project 12, which evolved into the Beetle. Most of the car's basic elements were selected early. Designers chose a rear-mounted engine, partly because it eliminated the need for a long driveshaft. To go the rear-engine route without impairing safe weight distribution, however, such an engine would have to be light in weight. Thus, aluminum and magnesium castings found their way into the concept. Air cooling meant no radiator would be needed, and owners need not worry about coolant freeze-ups. Finally, the horizontally-opposed cylinder configuration allowed a

short crankshaft and would mate neatly with the proposed rear transaxle. Instead of a separate body and frame, the car would have a platform-type chassis with a central backbone and integral floorpan. Torsion bars were the choice for a front suspension, and swing axles for the rear.

Rather than pursuing this small-car project further at the time, Porsche took on other work for such companies as Wanderer and Zundapp, including development of prototypes for a Zundapp *Volksauto* (which also translates to "people's car"), powered by a five-cylinder radial engine. After Zundapp nixed that project in 1932, Porsche established a connection with NSU to develop yet another set of prototypes, which evolved from the Project 12 design with a flat-four engine.

By this time, in 1933, Adolf Hitler had recently risen to power and made the first announcement of his desire to create not only the *Autobahnen* (high-speed highway network), but also a "people's car" for the ordinary working-man's family. As outlined by automotive historian Dan R. Post, Hitler wanted a car that could travel at 100-kph (62-mph) speeds, deliver fuel mileage of 33 mpg, demand minimal repair and maintenance, contain space for four or five occupants, and have an air-cooled engine (partly because so few people had garages in Germany). Porsche eventually was chosen for the job, in part because of his prior design work on Auto Union racing cars. His first estimates of such a car's final cost proved too expensive for Hitler's plan, but in 1934 Porsche got a go-ahead regardless. So Porsche proceeded with evolution of the Zundapp/NSU ideas, to create what would be called the "VW Series 3."

Late in 1936, the final prototypes were ready, with body design generally credited to Erwin Komenda, and the German automaker's association undertook extensive testing. By 1937, it was determined that a separate government company would be needed to complete development and enter into production. Later that year, 30 prototypes were prepared (with the assistance of Daimler-Benz), known as the Series 30, and road-tested by Nazi storm troopers. Dr. Porsche twice visited the U.S. and met with auto-industry leaders, including Henry Ford. He also sought engineers of German ancestry to come back and help set up the factory. Work began on the plant at Wolfsburg in mid-1938, with the first cars scheduled to emerge late the following year. Meanwhile, Porsche people kept refining the car's design, until it finally emerged as Series 38, ready for production and destined to become an automotive icon over the next four decades. Initially sold as the KdF-Wagen *(Kraft durch Freude,* which means "Strength through Joy," and was the name of a sponsoring Nazi group), the car quickly adopted the Volkswagen nickname that had been hung onto it for several years. Both 704- and 984-cc air-cooled engines were installed.

Early examples weren't to be sold by ordinary means, but via a stamp-purchase plan. In theory, a worker would purchase stamps each week; and when his stamp "card" was full, he'd be the owner of a Volkswagen. World War II intervened with that notion, before civilian production ever really got started. Years later, however, quite a few Germans presented their collections of saved-up stamps; and in 1961, Volkswagen allowed those people a certain credit toward a new car, or a stated amount of cash.

During World War II, Volkswagens were manufactured for military use, with larger (1131-cc) engines. A Jeep-like Kubelwagen also was produced. Actual passenger-car production began after the war, early in 1946, as the Wolfsburg plant wound up in the British-occupied zone of the country. Most of the initial models went to British forces. Heinz Nordhoff took over international distribution in 1947, presiding over the car's development into a 1950s phenomenon. Two years later, the British departed from the operation, returning the company to German control.

Just as American owners of British-built sports cars in the 1950s shared a camaraderie, so too did early VW owners feel a kinship, often expressed by waves and horn toots. A succession of improvements—some significant, others not—arrived through the 1950s and '60s, often promoted in advertisements. For that reason, tracing the evolution of the Beetle is far easier than is researching comparable changes for other imported makes. A convertible became available in 1949, actually built by the Karmann coachbuilding firm. A synchronized gearbox (except for first gear) arrived on 1952 models. The original split back window was replaced by a single oval pane the next year. A bigger (1192-cc) engine replaced the original 1131-cc unit for 1954, boosting horsepower to 36. Horsepower wasn't increased again until 1961; and again in 1966, when the engine grew to 1285-cc (nomimally 1300) displacement. A year later, another enlargement sent it to 1493-cc (as the 1500). Then, in 1970, came a final increase to 1585-cc size (as the 1600). Early in 1972, the model set a production record for a single model, topping even the long-lived Model T Ford. Beetle sedans were exported to the U.S. until 1977, while the convertible lasted two years longer. Even though manufacture came to a halt in Germany, Beetles remained in production elsewhere in the world into the 1980s, and were especially popular in Mexico.

Meanwhile, Volkswagen had expanded its lineup on a regular basis. As early as 1949, the boxy Transporter (Microbus) became available, using regular Beetle mechanical components, which eventual evolved into Camper buses. In the 1960s, VW buses would become a "trademark" of the burgeoning counterculture, popular among "hippies" for their combination of economy and practicality—and the ease with which their slab sides could be adorned with decals and decorations.

Karmann-Ghia designed a stylish 2+2 coupe based upon the Beetle chassis, first offered in 1956. A cabriolet (convertible) joined two years later. A much different form of sedan, the Type 3 (1500), debuted in Europe in 1961, rear-engined like its mates but with a squarish body and larger (1493-cc) powerplant. Two years later, it was the 1500S with even more power; then the 1600TL, with a 1.6-liter engine. Both fastback sedans and squareback wagons were produced.

By 1968, both the Beetle and the 1600 could get an early form of automatic shift. A Type 411 came next, in 1969, taking advantage of unibody construction and with MacPherson struts up front. Fuel injection became available on some models in 1970. Also new was the open-air Jeep-like Type 181, which became known as "The Thing" when it debuted on the American market for 1973.

Volkswagen began turning away from rear-mounted, air-cooled engines as early as 1971, offering a variant of the Audi/NSU model with an inline four-cylinder engine. That happened because VW had taken over NSU in 1969, just as it had obtained Audi earlier. The first front-engined Dashers arrived in America for 1974, Rabbits a year later, along with the sporty Scirocco coupe (styled by Giugiaro). By 1978, Rabbits were being manufactured in the U.S. (at New Stanton, Pennsylvania), though that venture wouldn't last through the 1980s. The Rabbit led to Golf and Jetta models of the 1980s, marketed along with a Rabbit-based Cabriolet (one of the few convertibles to survive in the U.S. marketplace of that time). Diesel engines also were part of the picture.

Later in the 1980s, a Brazilian-built Fox debuted. For 1990, the lineup included a Corrado sports car and a new Passat sedan and station wagon. Evolutions of the long-lived Transporter still remained available, too, after a succession of changes. Long before that time, though, the original Beetle and its variants were largely forgotten, though many still mourned its passing. In the Beetle's heyday, some people loved it, others hated it; while most who owned one or more seemed to experience a unique love/hate relationship unlike that connected to any other automobile.

Model Name Note: Although the "Beetle" nickname soon became common among American owners, as did the term "Bug," such designations never were used by the company as official names. The Beetle was sometimes referred to as Type I, whereas the Transporter (Microbus) was Type II.

Model Year Note: Not until 1955 did the Volkswagen company recognize official model years, but improvements occurred on a regular basis—and eventually were promoted in full-page advertisements intended to demonstrate VW's commitment to ongoing change. Not all of the changes outlined below necessarily took place at the start of the stated model year, but may have appeared later in that season.

Transporter (Microbus) Note: Through 1967, Transporters had two hinged side doors, and are referred to in this Catalog as four-door wagons. Restyling in 1968 replaced the hinged doors with a single sliding door for passenger entry; thus, later models are referred to as three-door station wagons.

1946-48 VOLKSWAGEN

1948 Volkswagen Beetle two-door sedan.

TYPE 11 (BEETLE) — FLAT FOUR — Few people who were alive at the time of the Beetle's rise to prominence need to be reminded of its appearance. Many described the two-door sedan with its rounded profile as an "ugly duckling," a fact that Volkswagen would later capitalize upon rather than attempt to dispute. As everyone would eventually realize, that shape was destined to change little over the next three decades, even though Volkswagen promoted its continuous sequence of mechanical and detail improvements.

Early engines were rated 24 horsepower, which grew to 25 bhp by 1947, and 30 bhp the next year. An unsynchronized four-speed gearbox meant plenty of double-clutching was required to change gears, especially when downshifting. Next to the gearshift lever was the manual choke button.

Early VW models had a split-oval rear window, with a rather thick pillar between the tiny panes. American cars had abandoned running boards before World War II, but VWs kept them—though they weren't the kind that anyone could stand on. A notch below the rear bumper permitted insertion of a hand crank. Early examples wore nipple-shaped chrome hubcaps. The gas tank sat under the hood, which meant the hood had to be raised with each fillup. Lighted turn-signal semaphores were activated by a switch on the dashboard. Also on the dashboard sat a pair of gloveboxes, neither of which contained a door. No gas gauge would be installed until 1962, but when the driver noticed evidence that fuel might be running out, he could reach down to the firewall and turn a tap to open the reserve tank, which held an extra gallon or so. Lack of body insulation contributed to noisy running, a trait that actually helped endear early VWs to their owners.

I.D. DATA: Serial number is on a plate on the front hood center, at back of spare tire; and stamped on chassis backbone, under rear seat. Engine number is stamped on the generator support, on the crankcase.

Model	Body Type & Seating	Engine Type/CID	P.O.E. Price	Weight (lbs.)	Prod. Total
11	2-dr Sedan-4P	H4/69	N/A	1600	Note 1

Note 1: A total of 9,931 Volkswagens were produced in 1946, followed by 8,940 in 1947 and 19,127 in 1948.

ENGINE DATA: BASE FOUR: Horizontally opposed, overhead-valve four-cylinder (air cooled). Light alloy block; cast-iron cylinders. **Displacement:** 69.0 cu. in. (1131 cc). **Bore & Stroke:** 2.95 x 2.52 in. (75 x 64 mm). **Compression Ratio:** 5.8:1. **Brake Horsepower:** 24 at 3000 rpm. Solid valve lifters. Downdraft carburetor. 6-volt electrical system.

Note: Engine output rose to 25 bhp in 1947, and 30 bhp (SAE) in 1948. However, many U.S. sources published the German rating of 25 bhp through 1953.

CHASSIS DATA: Wheelbase: 94.5 in. **Overall Length:** 160 in. **Height:** 61.0 in. **Width:** 60.5 in. **Front Tread:** 51.0 in. **Rear Tread:** 49.2 in. **Standard Tires:** 5.00x16.

TECHNICAL: Layout: rear-engine, rear-drive. **Transmission:** four-speed manual (unsynchronized). Gear ratios: (1st) 3.60:1; (2nd) 2.07:1; (3rd) 1.25:1; (4th) 0.80:1; (rev) 6.60:1. **Standard Final Drive Ratio:** 4.43:1. **Steering:** worm and cap nut. **Suspension (front):** kingpins with transverse torsion bars and upper/lower trailing arms. **Suspension (rear):** swing axles with trailing arms and torsion bars. **Brakes:** mechanical, front/rear drum. **Body Construction:** steel unibody on stamped steel floorpan. **Fuel Tank:** 8.8 gallon.
Manufacturer: Volkswagenwerk GmbH, Wolfsburg, West Germany.

1949-50 VOLKSWAGEN

1949 Volkswagen Beetle two-door sedan.

1100 (BEETLE) — FLAT FOUR — An under-dashboard pull cable replaced the former locking-handle hood release on the 1949 model, and a Solex carburetor became standard for the engine. A redesigned instrument panel contained a single gauge, positioned ahead of the driver. Volkswagens no longer had a hole for a crank handle, and lacked license-plate identification on the rear deck. Standard and Deluxe versions were sold in the U.S. A two-door convertible based on the sedan, noteworthy for its unusually bulky top (when folded), also became available at this time. *Motor Trend* observed that a VW was capable of 34 mpg and could easily hit 60 mph, and had independent suspension on all four wheels.

For the 1950 model year, hydraulic brakes replaced the original mechanical system, a sunroof became available, the interior contained ashtrays on the dashboard and the right rear quarter panel, the engine added a heat-riser, and the car's heater became quieter as a result of the addition of duct mufflers. A thermostatically-controlled throttle ring provided automatic air cooling.

TRANSPORTER — FLAT FOUR — In addition to the original two-door sedan and new two-door convertible, a boxy Transporter bus (later called Microbus) became available in 1949. Transporters carried the same engine used in the sedan, mounted at the rear, and quickly found their own legion of devoted fans.

1950 Volkswagen Beetle two-door cabriolet.

I.D. DATA: Serial number is on a plate on the front hood center, at back of spare tire; and stamped on chassis tunnel (backbone), under the rear seat. Engine number is stamped on the generator support, on the crankcase. Serial number range: (1949) 91922 to 138554; (1950) 138555 to 220471.

Model	Body Type & Seating	Engine Type/CID	P.O.E. Price	Weight (lbs.)	Prod. Total
1100 STANDARD					
	2-dr Sedan-4P	H4/69	1280	1600	Note 1
1100 DELUXE					
	2-dr Sedan-4P	H4/69	1480	1600	Note 1
Sunroof	2-dr Sedan-4P	H4/69	1550	1600	Note 1
	2-dr Conv Sed-4P	H4/69	1997	1600	Note 1
TRANSPORTER					
Standard	4-dr Sta Wag-8P	H4/69	N/A	N/A	Note 2
DeLuxe	4-dr Sta Wag-8P	H4/69	N/A	N/A	Note 2

Note 1: A total of 46,646 Volkswagen passenger cars were produced in 1949, followed by 82,399 in 1950.

Note 2: A total of 1,141 Transporters were produced in 1950.

ENGINE DATA: BASE FOUR: Horizontally opposed, overhead-valve four-cylinder (air cooled). Light alloy block, heads and finned cylinders; cast iron cylinder liners. **Displacement:** 69.0 cu. in. (1131 cc). **Bore & Stroke:** 2.95 x 2.52 in. (75 x 64 mm). **Compression Ratio:** 5.8:1. **Brake Horsepower:** 30 (SAE) at 3300 rpm. Solid valve lifters. Solex carburetor. 6-volt electrical system.

Note: Some U.S. sources published the German engine rating as low as 24.5 bhp.

CHASSIS DATA: Wheelbase: 94.5 in. **Overall Length:** (sed) 160 in. **Height:** (sed) 61.0 in. **Width:** (sed) 60.5 in. **Front Tread:** (sed) 51.0 in. **Rear Tread:** (sed) 49.2 in. **Standard Tires:** (sed) 5.00x16.

TECHNICAL: Layout: rear-engine, rear-drive. **Transmission:** four-speed manual. **Standard Final Drive Ratio:** (sed) 4.43:1. **Steering:** worm and cap nut. **Suspension (front):** kingpins with transverse torsion bars and upper/lower trailing arms. **Suspension (rear):** swing axles with trailing arms and torsion bars. **Brakes:** (1949) mechanical, front/rear drum; (1950) hydraulic, front/rear drum. **Body Construction:** steel unibody on stamped steel floorpan. **Fuel Tank:** 8.8 gallon.

PERFORMANCE: Top Speed: 60+ mph. **Fuel Mileage:** about 34 mpg.

PRODUCTION/SALES: A total of two Volkswagens were sold in the U.S. during 1949, followed by 270 in 1950.

Manufacturer: Volkswagenwerk GmbH, Wolfsburg, West Germany.

Distributor: Hoffman Motor Car Co., New York City.

HISTORY: Even non-enthusiasts may be aware that only two Volkswagens arrived for sale in the U.S. during the car's first year as an import—a fact later mentioned frequently in ads, as VWs grew more popular. "Roadability is said to be phenomenal for a light sedan," advised *Motor Trend* in late 1950, and the car was said to be rapidly becoming an "outstanding success." By that time, the magazine said that "several hundred" had been sold in the New York area.

1951 VOLKSWAGEN

1951 Volkswagen Beetle two-door sedans.

1100 (BEETLE) — FLAT FOUR — For this year only, kick-panel vents were added to the interior. Also new was a chrome windshield molding, as well as a Wolfsburg hood crest (above the handle). As before, Standard and DeLuxe versions of both the Beetle and Transporter were offered.

TRANSPORTER — FLAT FOUR — Production of the boxy station wagon (Microbus) continued with little change, using the same drivetrain layout as the sedan.

I.D. DATA: Serial number is on a plate on the front hood center, at back of spare tire; and stamped on chassis tunnel (backbone), under the rear seat. Engine number is stamped on the generator support, on the crankcase. Chassis number range: 220472 to 313829.

Model	Body Type & Seating	Engine Type/CID	P.O.E. Price	Weight (lbs.)	Prod. Total
1100 STANDARD					
	2-dr Sedan-4P	H4/69	1295	1600	Note 1
1100 DELUXE					
	2-dr Sedan-4P	H4/69	1480	1600	Note 1
Sunroof	2-dr Sedan-4P	H4/69	1550	1600	Note 1
	2-dr Conv Sed-4P	H4/69	2296	1600	Note 1
TRANSPORTER					
Standard	4-dr Sta Wag-8P	H4/69	2058	2100	Note 2
DeLuxe	4-dr Sta Wag-8P	H4/69	2195	2100	Note 2

Note 1: A total of 93,534 Volkswagen passenger cars were produced in 1951.

Note 2: A total of 3,074 Transporters were produced in 1951.

ENGINE DATA: BASE FOUR: Horizontally opposed, overhead-valve four-cylinder (air cooled). Light alloy block, heads and finned cylinders; cast iron cylinder liners. **Displacement:** 69.0 cu. in. (1131 cc). **Bore & Stroke:** 2.95 x 2.52 in. (75 x 64 mm). **Compression Ratio:** 5.8:1. **Brake Horsepower:** 30 (SAE) at 3300 rpm. Solid valve lifters. Solex carburetor. 6-volt electrical system.

Note: Some U.S. sources published the German engine rating as low as 24.5 bhp.

CHASSIS DATA: Wheelbase: 94.5 in. **Overall Length:** (sed) 160 in. **Height:** (sed) 61.0 in. **Width:** (sed) 60.5 in. **Front Tread:** (sed) 51.0 in. **Rear Tread:** (sed) 49.2 in. **Standard Tires:** 5.00x16.

TECHNICAL: Layout: rear-engine, rear-drive. **Transmission:** four-speed manual. **Standard Final Drive Ratio:** (sed) 4.43:1. **Steering:** worm and cap nut. **Suspension (front):** kingpins with transverse torsion bars and upper/lower trailing arms. **Suspension (rear):** swing axles with trailing arms and torsion bars. **Brakes:** hydraulic, front/rear drum. **Body Construction:** steel body welded to floorpan with tubular center section.

PERFORMANCE: Top Speed: 60 + mph. **Fuel Mileage:** up to 34 mpg.

PRODUCTION/SALES: A total of 550 Volkswagens were sold in the U.S. during 1951.

Manufacturer: Volkswagenwerk GmbH, Wolfsburg, West Germany.

Distributor: Hoffman Motor Car Co., New York City.

1952 VOLKSWAGEN

1100 (BEETLE) — FLAT FOUR — A number of changes hit the 1952 models. All forward gears except first now had synchromesh. Dual combination tail/stop lights were installed, replacing the former single fender lamp and deck stoplight. A T-type decklid handle replaced the earlier loop-style handle. Tires switched to 5.60x15 size. Inside, a rotary heater knob replaced the former pull-type; the turn-signal switch moved from the dashboard to alongside the steering wheel; and only one-third as many turns were needed to crank the windows up or down.

TRANSPORTER — FLAT FOUR — Production of the boxy rear-engined Transporter (Microbus) station wagon continued with little change.

I.D. DATA: Serial number is on a plate on the front hood center, at back of spare tire; and stamped on chassis tunnel (backbone), under the rear seat. Engine number is stamped on the generator support, on the crankcase. Chassis number range: 313830 to 428156.

Model	Body Type & Seating	Engine Type/CID	P.O.E. Price	Weight (lbs.)	Prod. Total
1100 STANDARD	2-dr Sedan-4P	H4/69	1395	1600	Note 1
1100 DELUXE	2-dr Sedan-4P	H4/69	1595	1600	Note 1
Sunroof	2-dr Sedan-4P	H4/69	1667	1600	Note 1
	2-dr Conv Sed-4P	H4/69	2395	1700	Note 1
TRANSPORTER					
Standard	4-dr Sta Wag-8P	H4/69	1995	2100	Note 2
DeLuxe	4-dr Sta Wag-8P	H4/69	2169	2140	Note 2

Note 1: A total of 114,348 Volkswagens were produced in 1952.

Note 2: A total of 5,194 Transporters were produced in 1952.

ENGINE DATA: BASE FOUR: Horizontally opposed, overhead-valve four-cylinder (air cooled). Light alloy block, heads and finned cylinders; cast iron cylinder liners. **Displacement:** 69.0 cu. in. (1131 cc). **Bore & Stroke:** 2.95 x 2.52 in. (75 x 64 mm). **Compression Ratio:** 5.8:1. **Brake Horsepower:** 30 (SAE) at 3300 rpm. Four main bearings. Solid valve lifters. Solex carburetor. 6-volt electrical system.

Note: Some U.S. sources published the German engine rating as low as 24.5 bhp.

CHASSIS DATA: Wheelbase: 94.5 in. **Overall Length:** (sed) 160 in. **Height:** (sed) 61.0 in. **Width:** (sed) 60.5 in. **Front Tread:** (sed) 51.0 in. **Rear Tread:** (sed) 49.2 in. **Standard Tires:** (sed) 5.60x15.

TECHNICAL: Layout: rear-engine, rear-drive. **Transmission:** four-speed manual. **Standard Final Drive Ratio:** (sed) 4.43:1. **Steering:** worm and cap nut. **Suspension (front):** kingpins with transverse torsion bars and upper/lower trailing arms. **Suspension (rear):** swing axles with trailing arms and torsion bars. **Brakes:** hydraulic, front/rear drum. **Body Construction:** steel body welded to floorpan with tubular center section.

PERFORMANCE: Top Speed: up to 65 mph. **Fuel Mileage:** up to 34 mpg.

PRODUCTION/SALES: A total of 601 Volkswagens were sold in the U.S. during 1952.

Manufacturer: Volkswagenwerk GmbH, Wolfsburg, West Germany.

Distributor: Hoffman Motor Car Co., New York City.

1953 VOLKSWAGEN

1100 (BEETLE) — FLAT FOUR — Volkswagen's original split rear window was replaced by a single oval pane for 1953. Vent-window handles added a lock button, and the brake-fluid reservoir moved from the master cylinder to behind the spare tire.

TRANSPORTER — FLAT FOUR — Production of boxy rear-engined Transporter (Microbus) station wagon continued with little change.

I.D. DATA: Serial number is on a plate on the front hood center, at back of spare tire; and stamped on chassis tunnel (backbone), under the rear seat. Engine number is stamped on the generator support, on the crankcase. Serial number range: (sedan) 428157 to 575414.

Model	Body Type & Seating	Engine Type/CID	P.O.E. Price	Weight (lbs.)	Prod. Total
1100 STANDARD	2-dr Sedan-4P	H4/69	N/A	N/A	Note 1

Model	Body Type & Seating	Engine Type/CID	P.O.E. Price	Weight (lbs.)	Prod. Total
1100 DELUXE	2-dr Sedan-4P	H4/69	1595	1540	Note 1
Sunroof	2-dr Sedan-4P	H4/69	1675	1540	Note 1
	2-dr Conv Sed-4P	H4/69	2350	1790	Note 1
TRANSPORTER					
Standard	4-dr Sta Wag-8P	H4/69	N/A	N/A	Note 2
DeLuxe	4-dr Sta Wag-8P	H4/69	N/A	N/A	Note 2

Note 1: A total of 151,323 Volkswagens were produced in 1953.

Note 2: A total of 5,375 Transporters were produced in 1953.

1953 Volkswagen Beetle two-door sedan.

ENGINE DATA: BASE FOUR: Horizontally opposed, overhead-valve four-cylinder (air cooled). Light alloy block, heads and finned cylinders; cast iron cylinder liners. **Displacement:** 69.0 cu. in. (1131 cc). **Bore & Stroke:** 2.95 x 2.52 in. (75 x 64 mm). **Compression Ratio:** 5.8:1. **Brake Horsepower:** 30 (SAE) at 3300 rpm. Four main bearings. Solid valve lifters. Solex carburetor. 6-volt electrical system.

Note: Some U.S. sources published the German engine rating as low as 24.5 bhp.

CHASSIS DATA: Wheelbase: 94.5 in. **Overall Length:** (sed) 160 in. **Height:** (sed) 61.0 in. **Width:** (sed) 60.5 in. **Front Tread:** (sed) 50.8 in. **Rear Tread:** (sed) 49.2 in. **Standard Tires:** (sed) 5.60x15.

TECHNICAL: Layout: rear-engine, rear-drive. **Transmission:** four-speed manual. **Standard Final Drive Ratio:** (sed) 4.43:1. **Steering:** worm and cap nut. **Suspension (front):** kingpins with transverse torsion bars and upper/lower trailing arms. **Suspension (rear):** swing axles with trailing arms and torsion bars. **Brakes:** hydraulic, front/rear drum. **Body Construction:** steel body welded to floorpan with tubular center section.

PERFORMANCE: Top Speed: 66 mph. **Acceleration (0-60 mph):** 42.1 sec. **Fuel Mileage:** 22-28 mpg average.

PRODUCTION/SALES: A total of 1,237 Volkswagens were sold in the U.S. during 1953.

Manufacturer: Volkswagenwerk GmbH, Wolfsburg, West Germany.

Distributor: Hoffman Motor Car Co., New York City.

HISTORY: "Handling qualities are exceptional," declared *Motor Trend* of the Beetle in 1953. "You can break the rear end loose, but only if you work at it" and "interior trim is as good as in some cars costing an additional $1000."

1954 VOLKSWAGEN

1954 Volkswagen Beetle two-door sedan.

1200 (BEETLE) — FLAT FOUR — Displacement of the flat-four engine grew from 1131 to 1192 cc this year, and compression rose from 5.8:1 to 6.6:1, boosting output from 30 to 36 horsepower. An oil-bath air cleaner replaced the former felt-element filter. Taillamp housings no longer had a top window. A key-type starter replaced the earlier pushbutton starter, and a three-way dome light was installed. Engines no longer required a break-in period.

TRANSPORTER — FLAT FOUR — Production of the rear-engined Transporter (Microbus) station wagon continued with little change, except for the adoption of the larger engine.

I.D. DATA: Serial number is on a plate on the front hood center, at back of spare tire; and stamped on chassis tunnel (backbone), under the rear seat. Engine number is stamped on the generator support, on the crankcase. Serial number range: (sedan) 575415 to 722934.

Model	Body Type & Seating	Engine Type/CID	P.O.E. Price	Weight (lbs.)	Prod. Total
1200 STANDARD					
	2-dr Sedan-4P	H4/73	N/A	N/A	Note 1
1200 DELUXE					
	2-dr Sedan-4P	H4/73	1595	1540	Note 1
Sunroof	2-dr Sedan-4P	H4/73	1675	1540	Note 1
	2-dr Conv Sed-4P	H4/73	2350	1790	Note 1
TRANSPORTER					
Standard	4-dr Sta Wag-8P	H4/73	N/A	N/A	Note 2
DeLuxe	4-dr Sta Wag-8P	H4/73	N/A	N/A	Note 2

Note 1: A total of 202,174 Volkswagens were produced in 1954.
Note 2: A total of 7,630 Transporters were produced in 1954.

ENGINE DATA: BASE FOUR: Horizontally opposed, overhead-valve four-cylinder (air cooled). Light alloy block, heads and finned cylinders; cast iron cylinder liners. **Displacement:** 72.7 cu. in. (1192 cc). **Bore & Stroke:** 3.03 x 2.52 in. (77 x 64 mm). **Compression Ratio:** 6.6:1. **Brake Horsepower:** 36 (SAE) at 3700 rpm. Four main bearings. Solid valve lifters. Solex downdraft carburetor. 6-volt electrical system.

CHASSIS DATA: Wheelbase: 94.5 in. **Overall Length:** (sed) 160.2 in. **Height:** (sed) 59.1 in. **Width:** (sed) 60.6 in. **Front Tread:** (sed) 50.8 in. **Rear Tread:** (sed) 49.2 in. **Standard Tires:** (sed) 5.60x15.

TECHNICAL: Layout: rear-engine, rear-drive. **Transmission:** four-speed manual. **Standard Final Drive Ratio:** (sed) 4.4:1. **Steering:** worm and cap nut. **Suspension (front):** kingpins with transverse torsion bars and upper/lower trailing arms. **Suspension (rear):** swing axles with trailing arms and torsion bars. **Brakes:** hydraulic, front/rear drum. **Body Construction:** steel body welded to floorpan with tubular center section.

PRODUCTION/SALES: A total of 6,344 Volkswagens were sold in the U.S. during 1954.
Manufacturer: Volkswagenwerk GmbH, Wolfsburg, West Germany.
Distributor: Hoffman Motor Car Co., New York City.

1955 VOLKSWAGEN

1200 (BEETLE) — FLAT FOUR — This was a year of minimal change, except for the fact that fender-mounted turn-signal flashers replaced the original mechanical semaphore units.

TRANSPORTER — FLAT FOUR — Only a single Kombi station wagon was listed as available in the Transporter series for 1955.

I.D. DATA: Serial number is on a plate on the front hood center, at back of spare tire; and stamped on chassis tunnel (backbone), under the rear seat. Engine number is stamped on the generator support, on the crankcase. Chassis number range: 722935 to 929745.

Model	Body Type & Seating	Engine Type/CID	P.O.E. Price	Weight (lbs.)	Prod. Total
1200 DELUXE					
	2-dr Sedan-4P	H4/73	1495	1609	Note 1
Sunroof	2-dr Sedan-4P	H4/73	1575	1690	Note 1
	2-dr Conv Sed-4P	H4/73	1995	1764	Note 1
TRANSPORTER					
Kombi	4-dr Sta Wag-8P	H4/73	N/A	2127	Note 2

Note 1: A total of 279,986 Volkswagens were produced in 1955.
Note 2: A total of 10,152 Transporters were produced in 1955.

ENGINE DATA: BASE FOUR: Horizontally opposed, overhead-valve four-cylinder (air cooled). Light alloy block, heads and finned cylinders; cast iron cylinder liners. **Displacement:** 72.7 cu. in. (1192 cc). **Bore & Stroke:** 3.03 x 2.52 in. (77 x 64 mm). **Compression Ratio:** 6.6:1. **Brake Horsepower:** 36 (SAE) at 3700 rpm. Four main bearings. Solid valve lifters. Solex downdraft carburetor. 6-volt electrical system.

CHASSIS DATA: Wheelbase: 94.5 in. **Overall Length:** (sed) 160.2 in.; (wag) 165 in. **Height:** (sed) 59.1 in. **Width:** (sed) 60.6 in.; (wag) 67.9 in. **Front Tread:** (sed) 50.8 in. **Rear Tread:** (sed) 49.2 in. **Standard Tires:** (sed) 5.60x15; (wag) 6.40x15.

TECHNICAL: Layout: rear-engine, rear-drive. **Transmission:** four-speed manual. **Standard Final Drive Ratio:** (sed) 4.4:1. **Steering:** worm and cap nut. **Suspension (front):** kingpins with transverse torsion bars and upper/lower trailing arms. **Suspension (rear):** swing axles with trailing arms and torsion bars. **Brakes:** hydraulic, front/rear drum. **Body Construction:** steel body welded to floorpan with tubular center section.

PRODUCTION/SALES: A total of 28,907 Volkswagens were sold in the U.S. during 1955.
Manufacturer: Volkswagenwerk GmbH, Wolfsburg, West Germany.
Distributor: Hoffman Motor Car Co., New York City.

1956 VOLKSWAGEN

1956 Volkswagen Beetle two-door cabriolet.

1200 (BEETLE) — FLAT FOUR — Bumper overriders (guards) and dual chromed tailpipes were new this year. Taillamps sat two inches higher on the rear fenders, and the gas tank was redesigned to permit greater luggage space under the hood. Front seatbacks now could be adjusted, and faced a new steering wheel with a lower (off-center) horizontal spoke. Sunroofs now were made of nylon instead of cloth. The heater knob was moved forward from its former location in back of front seats.

KARMANN-GHIA — FLAT FOUR — This was the first year for the stylish Karmann-Ghia coupe, which blended the mechanical components and structure of the Beetle with a handsome Italian-designed 2 + 2 coupe body. Body manufacture was performed by Karmann, the firm that also turned out VW convertibles. The driving position was lower than in a sedan, described by *Motor Trend* as "more like Porsche." The shapely body had a sculpted line leading from the lower door, upward and along the rear quarter panel. Rear quarter windows were installed, along with curved door windows. Either cloth or leatherette upholstery was available. Controls were similar to those of the sedan, but not identical.

TRANSPORTER — FLAT FOUR — In the Transporter series, the Kombi differed from the Microbus in that the latter had windows around its entire body, as well as skylights above the side windows. A Kamper kit was available, which converted an ordinary VW bus into a vehicle that could sleep a small family and included ample storage and a pop-up top.

I.D. DATA: Serial number is on a plate on the front hood center, at back of spare tire; and stamped on chassis tunnel (backbone), under the rear seat. Engine number is stamped on the generator support, on the crankcase. Chassis number range: 929746 to 1246618.

Model	Body Type & Seating	Engine Type/CID	P.O.E. Price	Weight (lbs.)	Prod. Total
1200 DELUXE					
	2-dr Sedan-4P	H4/73	1495	1609	Note 1
Sunroof	2-dr Sedan-4P	H4/73	1575	1690	Note 1
	2-dr Conv Sed-4P	H4/73	1995	1764	Note 1
KARMANN-GHIA					
1200	2-dr Coupe-2 + 2P	H4/73	2395	1720	Note 1
TRANSPORTER					
Kombi	4-dr Sta Wag-8P	H4/73	N/A	2127	Note 2
Microbus	4-dr Sta Wag-8P	H4/73	N/A	2447	Note 2

Note 1: A total of 333,190 Volkswagens were produced in 1956.
Note 2: A total of 11,798 Transporters were produced in 1956.

ENGINE DATA: BASE FOUR: Horizontally opposed, overhead-valve four-cylinder (air cooled). Light alloy block, heads and finned cylinders; cast iron cylinder liners. **Displacement:** 72.7 cu. in. (1192 cc). **Bore & Stroke:** 3.03 x 2.52 in. (77 x 64 mm). **Compression Ratio:** 6.6:1. **Brake Horsepower:** 36 (SAE) at 3700 rpm. Four main bearings. Solid valve lifters. Solex 28 PCI downdraft carburetor. 6-volt electrical system.

CHASSIS DATA: Wheelbase: 94.5 in. **Overall Length:** (sed) 160.2 in.; (Karmann) 163 in.; (wag) 165 in. **Height:** (sed) 59.1 in. **Width:** (sed) 60.6 in.; (Karmann) 64.4 in.; (wag) 67.9 in. **Front Tread:** (sed) 50.8 in. **Rear Tread:** (sed) 49.2 in. **Standard Tires:** (sed/Karmann) 5.60x15; (wag) 6.40x15.

TECHNICAL: Layout: rear-engine, rear-drive. **Transmission:** four-speed manual. **Gear ratios:** (1st) 3.60:1; (2nd) 1.88:1; (3rd) 1.23:1; (4th) 0.82:1; (rev) 4.63:1. **Standard Final Drive Ratio:** (sed) 4.4:1. **Steering:** worm and nut. **Suspension (front):** kingpins with transverse torsion bars and upper/lower trailing arms. **Suspension (rear):** swing axles with trailing arms and torsion bars. **Brakes:** hydraulic, front/rear drum. **Body Construction:** steel body welded to floorpan with tubular center section.

PERFORMANCE: Top Speed: (sed) 68 mph claimed; (Karmann) "over 70" mph claimed. **Fuel Mileage:** 32 mpg claimed.

PRODUCTION/SALES: A total of 50,011 Volkswagens were sold in the U.S. during 1956.
Manufacturer: Volkswagenwerk GmbH, Wolfsburg, West Germany.
Distributor: Hoffman Motor Car Co., New York City.

HISTORY: "On a lonely stretch," declared *Motor Trend* of their test coupe, the "Ghia's high-speed behavior proved impeccable," as a result of the car's weight and streamlining.

1957 VOLKSWAGEN

1957 Volkswagen Beetle two-door sedan.

1200 (BEETLE) — FLAT FOUR — Tubeless tires were installed for the first time. Each door added an adjustable striker, and the front heater outlets moved toward the rear, within a foot of the doors, to improve heat distribution.

KARMANN-GHIA — FLAT FOUR — Production of the 2 + 2 sport coupe continued with little change, except as noted above for the Beetle.

TRANSPORTER — FLAT FOUR — Standard and DeLuxe editions of the Microbus were offered at this time, along with the Kombi, which had fewer windows. A Camper bus also was available, fitted with such extras as a folding table and fold-out beds.

I.D. DATA: Serial number is on a plate on the front hood center, at back of spare tire; and stamped on chassis tunnel (backbone), under the rear seat. Engine number is stamped on the generator support, on the crankcase. Serial number range: (sedan and Karmann-Ghia) 1246619 to 1600439; (Transporter) 191842 up.

Model	Body Type & Seating	Engine Type/CID	P.O.E. Price	Weight (lbs.)	Prod. Total
1200 DELUXE					
	2-dr Sedan-4P	H4/73	1495	1609	Note 1
Sunroof	2-dr Sedan-4P	H4/73	1575	1609	Note 1
	2-dr Conv Sed-4P	H4/73	1995	1764	Note 1
KARMANN-GHIA					
1200	2-dr Coupe-2 + 2P	H4/73	2395	1720	Note 1
TRANSPORTER					
Kombi	4-dr Sta Wagon	H4/73	1995	2127	Note 2
Microbus	4-dr Sta Wag-8P	H4/73	2095	2447	Note 2
DeL Micro	4-dr Sta Wag-8P	H4/73	2235	2447	Note 2
Camper	4-dr Sta Wagon	H4/73	2712	N/A	Note 2

Note 1: A total of 380,561 Volkswagens were produced in 1957.

Note 2: A total of 20,711 Transporters were produced in 1957.

ENGINE DATA: BASE FOUR: Horizontally opposed, overhead-valve four-cylinder (air cooled). Light alloy block, heads and finned cylinders; cast iron cylinder liners. **Displacement:** 72.7 cu. in. (1192 cc). **Bore & Stroke:** 3.03 x 2.52 in. (77 x 64 mm). **Compression Ratio:** 6.6:1. **Brake Horsepower:** 36 (SAE) at 3700 rpm. Four main bearings. Solid valve lifters. Solex 28 PCI downdraft carburetor. 6-volt electrical system.

CHASSIS DATA: Wheelbase: 94.5 in. **Overall Length:** (sed) 160.2 in.; (Karmann) 163 in.; (wag) 165 in. **Height:** (sed) 59.1 in. **Width:** (sed) 60.6 in.; (Karmann) 64.4 in.; (wag) 67.9 in. **Front Tread:** (sed) 50.8 in. **Rear Tread:** (sed) 49.2 in. **Standard Tires:** (sed/Karmann) 5.60x15; (wag) 6.40x15.

TECHNICAL: Layout: rear-engine, rear-drive. **Transmission:** four-speed manual. **Gear ratios:** (1st) 3.60:1; (2nd) 1.88:1; (3rd) 1.23:1; (4th) 0.82:1; (rev) 4.63:1. **Standard Final Drive Ratio:** (sed) 4.4:1. **Steering:** worm and nut. **Suspension (front):** kingpins with transverse torsion bars and upper/lower trailing arms. **Suspension (rear):** swing axles with trailing arms and torsion bars. **Brakes:** hydraulic, front/rear drum. **Body Construction:** steel body welded to floorpan with tubular center section.

PERFORMANCE: Top Speed: 68 mph claimed. **Fuel Mileage:** 32 mpg claimed.

PRODUCTION/SALES: A total of 64,242 Volkswagens were sold in the U.S. during 1957.

Manufacturer: Volkswagenwerk GmbH, Wolfsburg, West Germany.

Distributor: Hoffman Motor Car Co., New York City; Competition Motors, Hollywood, California.

1958-59 VOLKSWAGEN

1200 (BEETLE) — FLAT FOUR — New 1958 Beetles were easy to spot, as the back window grew larger and assumed a rectangular shape, instead of the former small oval. The windshield was larger, too. Front turn-signal indicators moved atop the fenders. Inside, a flat gas pedal replaced the former roller-style pedal and the radio grille now faced the driver. Brakes grew wider for 1958.

Changes weren't so easy to see for 1959, as the chassis added some reinforcement. Other improvements were made to the clutch (stronger springs) and fanbelt.

KARMANN-GHIA — FLAT FOUR — The Karmann-Ghia line added a cabriolet (convertible) for 1958, as well as reinforced bumpers.

TRANSPORTER — FLAT FOUR — Production of the three station-wagon versions continued with little change. A sunroof was included on the deluxe Microbus.

1958 Volkswagen 1200 Beetle two-door sedan.

I.D. DATA: Serial number is on a plate on the front hood center, at back of spare tire; and stamped on chassis tunnel (backbone), under the rear seat. Engine number is stamped on the generator support, on the crankcase. Chassis number range: (1958) 1600440 to 2007615; (1959) 2007616 to 2528667.

Model	Body Type & Seating	Engine Type/CID	P.O.E. Price	Weight (lbs.)	Prod. Total
1200 DELUXE					
113	2-dr Sedan-4P	H4/73	1545	1609	Note 1
117	2-dr Sunroof Sed-4P	H4/73	1625	1609	Note 1
151	2-dr Conv Sed-4P	H4/73	2045	1764	Note 1
1200 KARMANN-GHIA					
143	2-dr Spt Cpe-2 + 2P	H4/73	2445	1720	Note 1
141	2-dr Conv Cpe-2 + 2P	H4/73	2725	1786	Note 1
TRANSPORTER					
Kombi	4-dr Sta Wagon	H4/73	1955	2127	Note 2
Microbus	4-dr Sta Wagon	H4/73	2120	2447	Note 2
DeL Micro	4-dr Sta Wagon	H4/73	2576	2447	Note 2
DeL Camper	4-dr Sta Wagon	H4/73	2737	N/A	Note 2

Note 1: A total of 451,526 Volkswagens were produced in 1958, followed by 575,407 in 1959.

Note 2: A total of 23,841 Transporters were produced in 1958, followed by 29,184 in 1959.

ENGINE DATA: BASE FOUR: Horizontally opposed, overhead-valve four-cylinder (air cooled). Light alloy block, heads and finned cylinders; cast iron cylinder liners. **Displacement:** 72.7 cu. in. (1192 cc). **Bore & Stroke:** 3.03 x 2.52 in. (77 x 64 mm). **Compression Ratio:** 6.6:1. **Brake Horsepower:** 36 (SAE) at 3700 rpm. **Torque:** 56 lbs.-ft. at 2000 rpm. Four main bearings. Solid valve lifters. Solex downdraft carburetor. 6-volt electrical system.

CHASSIS DATA: Wheelbase: 94.5 in. **Overall Length:** (sed) 160.2 in.; (Karmann) 163 in.; (Microbus) 165-166 in. **Height:** (sed) 59.1 in.; (Karmann) 52.2 in. **Width:** (sed) 60.6 in.; (Karmann) 64.4 in.; (Microbus) 67.9-68.9 in. **Front Tread:** (sed/Karmann) 51.4 in. **Rear Tread:** (sed/Karmann) 49.2 in. **Standard Tires:** (sed/Karmann) 5.60x15; (Microbus) 6.40x15.

TECHNICAL: Layout: rear-engine, rear-drive. **Transmission:** four-speed manual. **Standard Final Drive Ratio:** (sed/Karmann) 4.43:1. **Steering:** worm and nut. **Suspension (front):** kingpins with transverse torsion bars and upper/lower trailing arms. **Suspension (rear):** swing axles with trailing arms and torsion bars. **Brakes:** hydraulic, front/rear drum. **Body Construction:** steel body welded to floorpan with tubular center section.

PERFORMANCE: Similar to 1957.

PRODUCTION/SALES: A total of 78,588 Volkswagens were sold in the U.S. during 1958, followed by 120,442 in 1959.

Manufacturer: Volkswagenwerk GmbH, Wolfsburg, West Germany.

1960 VOLKSWAGEN

1200 (BEETLE) — FLAT FOUR — Pushbutton grab-type door handles replaced the former pull-type this year. Inside, padded sunvisors were installed (formerly transparent plastic), plastic headlining replaced the earlier mouse hair fabric, a dished-style steering wheel was added, and seatbacks were contoured. An anti-sway bar was added to improve cornering, plus a steering damper for better handling. Generator output grew from 160 to 180 watts. The front-seat passenger now had a footrest.

KARMANN-GHIA — FLAT FOUR — Production of the sporty coupe and convertible continued, with some of the changes noted above.

TRANSPORTER — FLAT FOUR — Production of the boxy station-wagon (bus) series continued without major change.

I.D. DATA: Serial number is on a plate on the front hood center, at back of spare tire; and stamped on chassis tunnel (backbone), under the rear seat. Engine number is stamped on the generator support, on the crankcase. Serial number range: (sedan/Karmann-Ghia) 2528668 to 3192506; (Transporter) 491002.

Model	Body Type & Seating	Engine Type/CID	P.O.E. Price	Weight (lbs.)	Prod. Total
1200 DELUXE					
113	2-dr Sedan-4P	H4/73	1565	1609	Note 1
117	2-dr Sunroof Sed-4P	H4/73	1655	1609	Note 1
151	2-dr Conv Sed-4P	H4/73	2055	1764	Note 1

Model	Body Type & Seating	Engine Type/CID	P.O.E. Price	Weight (lbs.)	Prod. Total
1200 KARMANN-GHIA					
143	2-dr Spt Cpe-2 + 2P	H4/73	2430	1720	Note 1
141	2-dr Conv Cpe-2 + 2P	H4/73	2695	1786	Note 1
TRANSPORTER					
Kombi	4-dr Sta Wagon	H4/73	1995	2127	Note 2
	4-dr Sta Wagon	H4/73	2245	2447	Note 2
DeLuxe	4-dr Sta Wagon	H4/73	2495	2447	Note 2
Camper	4-dr Sta Wagon	H4/73	2886	N/A	Note 2

Note 1: A total of 725,939 Volkswagens were produced in 1960.
Note 2: A total of 30,350 Transporters were produced in 1960.

ENGINE DATA: BASE FOUR: Horizontally opposed, overhead-valve four-cylinder (air cooled). Light alloy block, heads and finned cylinders; cast iron cylinder liners. **Displacement:** 72.7 cu. in. (1192 cc). **Bore & Stroke:** 3.03 x 2.52 in. (77 x 64 mm). **Compression Ratio:** 6.6:1. **Brake Horsepower:** 36 (SAE) at 3700 rpm. Four main bearings. Solid valve lifters. Solex downdraft carburetor. 6-volt electrical system.

CHASSIS DATA: Wheelbase: 94.5 in. **Overall Length:** (sed) 160.2 in.; (Karmann) 163 in.; (Microbus) 165-166 in. **Height:** (sed) 59.1 in.; (Karmann) 52.2 in. **Width:** (sed) 60.6 in.; (Karmann) 64.4 in.; (Microbus) 67.9-68.9 in. **Front Tread:** (sed/Karmann) 51.4 in. **Rear Tread:** (sed/Karmann) 49.2 in. **Standard Tires:** (sed/Karmann) 5.60x15; (Microbus) 6.40x15.

TECHNICAL: Layout: rear-engine, rear-drive. **Transmission:** four-speed manual. **Standard Final Drive Ratio:** (sed/Karmann) 3.61:1. **Steering:** worm and nut. **Suspension (front):** kingpins with transverse torsion bars and upper/lower trailing arms. **Suspension (rear):** swing axles with trailing arms and torsion bars. **Brakes:** hydraulic, front/rear drum. **Body Construction:** steel body welded to floorpan with tubular center section.

PERFORMANCE: Top Speed: (sed) 68 mph; (Karmann) 72 mph. **Fuel Mileage:** about 32 mpg.

PRODUCTION/SALES: A total of 159,995 Volkswagens were sold in the U.S. during 1960.

Manufacturer: Volkswagenwerk GmbH, Wolfsburg, West Germany.
Distributor: Volkswagen of America Inc., Englewood Cliffs, New Jersey.

1961 VOLKSWAGEN

1961 Volkswagen 1500/1500S two-door sedan.

1200 (BEETLE) — FLAT FOUR — Engine output got a boost from 36 to 40 horsepower for 1961, and the four-speed gearbox added synchronization in low gear. The engine added an automatic choke, and a transparent brake-fluid reservoir was easier to check. A passenger grab handle and sunvisor were installed. So was a pump-type windshield washer. A flatter gas tank increased luggage space. Side marker lights and a non-repeating starter switch also were new. Key slots in doors were now horizontal (formerly vertical).

KARMANN-GHIA — FLAT FOUR — The more potent engine also went into the stylish sport coupe and convertible for 1961.

TRANSPORTER — FLAT FOUR — Microbuses got a horsepower boost along with the Beetle sedans.

I.D. DATA: Serial number is on a plate behind the spare tire; and on the frame tunnel, under the back seat. Engine number is stamped on the generator support, on the crank-case. Serial number range: (sedan/Karmann-Ghia) 3192507 to 4010994; (Transporter) 623734 to 802426.

Model	Body Type & Seating	Engine Type/CID	P.O.E. Price	Weight (lbs.)	Prod. Total
1200 DELUXE					
113	2-dr Sedan-4P	H4/73	1565	1631	Note 1
117	2-dr Sunroof Sed-4P	H4/73	1655	1631	Note 1
151	2-dr Conv Sed-4P	H4/73	2055	1764	Note 1
1200 KARMANN-GHIA					
143	2-dr Coupe-2 + 2P	H4/73	2430	1786	Note 1
141	2-dr Conv Cpe-2 + 2P	H4/73	2695	1786	Note 1
TRANSPORTER					
231	4-dr Kombi	H4/73	1995	2161	Note 2
221	4-dr Sta Wagon	H4/73	2245	2315	Note 2
241/M130	4-dr DeL Wagon	H4/73	2495	2315	Note 2
Camper	4-dr Sta Wagon	H4/73	2973	N/A	Note 2

Note 1: A total of 807,488 Volkswagen passenger cars were produced in 1961.
Note 2: A total of 33,506 Transporters were produced in 1961.

ENGINE DATA: BASE FOUR: Horizontally opposed, overhead-valve four-cylinder (air cooled). Light alloy block, heads and finned cylinders; cast iron cylinder liners. **Displacement:** 72.7 cu. in. (1192 cc). **Bore & Stroke:** 3.03 x 2.52 in. (77 x 64 mm). **Compression Ratio:** 7.0:1. **Brake Horsepower:** 40 at 3900 rpm. **Torque:** 64.4 lbs.-ft. at 2400 rpm. Four main bearings. Solid valve lifters. Solex single-barrel carburetor. 6-volt electrical system.

CHASSIS DATA: Wheelbase: 94.5 in. **Overall Length:** (sed) 160.6 in.; (Karmann) 163 in.; (wagon) 168.9 in. **Height:** (sed) 59.1 in.; (Karmann) 52.4 in. **Width:** (sed) 60.6 in.; (Karmann) 64.4 in.; (wagon) 68.9 in. **Front Tread:** (sed/Karmann) 51.4 in. **Rear Tread:** (sed/Karmann) 50.7 in. **Standard Tires:** (sed/Karmann) 5.60x15; (wagon) 6.40x15.

TECHNICAL: Layout: rear-engine, rear-drive. **Transmission:** four-speed manual. **Steering:** worm and sector. **Suspension (front):** kingpins with transverse torsion bars and upper/lower trailing arms. **Suspension (rear):** swing axles with trailing arms and torsion bar. **Brakes:** hydraulic, front/rear drum. **Body Construction:** unitized; steel body welded to floorpan.

PERFORMANCE: Top Speed: (sed) 70 mph (cruising). **Acceleration (0-60 mph):** (sed) 22 sec. **Fuel Mileage:** (sed) 28-32 mpg.

PRODUCTION/SALES: A total of 177,308 Volkswagens were sold in the U.S. during 1961.

ADDITIONAL MODELS: Volkswagen also marketed panel and pickup truck versions of the Transporter in the U.S.

Manufacturer: Volkswagenwerk AG, Wolfsburg, West Germany.

Distributor: Volkswagen of America Inc., Englewood Cliffs, New Jersey.

HISTORY: Volkswagen advised that the new 1961 model had 27 different changes, though some were undeniably minor. Production of the new Type 3 (also called 1500) began during 1961, but that car would not become readily available in the U.S. market until the 1966 model year. Through the 1960s, Type 3 Karmann-Ghias were produced, which differed in appearance from the familiar coupes and convertibles, but they were not sold in America.

1962 VOLKSWAGEN

1962 Volkswagen Beetle two-door sedan.

1200 (BEETLE) — FLAT FOUR — Taillamps grew larger for 1962 and a conventional fuel gauge was installed, replacing the original tap lever for a reserve tank. The hood now was spring-loaded. Three-point seatbelt mountings and sliding covers for the heater outlets were added this year. Also new: a compressed-air windshield washer. Steering was now worm-and-sector, replacing the former worm-and-roller unit, and tie-rod ends were permanently lubricated.

KARMANN-GHIA — FLAT FOUR — Production of VW's sport coupe and convertible continued without major change, except for the modifications noted above.

TRANSPORTER — FLAT FOUR — Microbuses and related station wagons remained available with the same powertrain as other Volkswagens.

I.D. DATA: Serial number is on a plate behind the spare tire; and on the frame tunnel, under the back seat. Engine number is stamped on the generator support, on the crank-case. Serial number range: (sedan/Karmann-Ghia) 4010995 to 4846835; (Transporter) 802427 to 971550.

Model	Body Type & Seating	Engine Type/CID	P.O.E. Price	Weight (lbs.)	Prod. Total
1200 DELUXE					
113	2-dr Sedan-4P	H4/73	1595	1565	Note 1
117	2-dr Sunroof Sed-4P	H4/73	1685	1565	Note 1
151	2-dr Conv Sed-4P	H4/73	2095	1698	Note 1
1200 KARMANN-GHIA					
143	2-dr Coupe-2 + 2P	H4/73	2295	1742	Note 1
141	2-dr Conv Cpe-2 + 2P	H4/73	2495	1742	Note 1
TRANSPORTER					
231	4-dr Kombi	H4/73	1995	2095	Note 2
221	4-dr Sta Wagon	H4/73	2275	2414	Note 2
241/M130	4-dr DeL Wagon	H4/73	2655	2414	Note 2
Camper	4-dr Sta Wagon	H4/73	2982	2547	Note 2

Note 1: A total of 925,747 Volkswagen passenger cars were produced in 1962.
Note 2: A total of 41,179 Transporters were produced in 1962.

ENGINE DATA: BASE FOUR: Horizontally opposed, overhead-valve four-cylinder (air cooled). Light alloy block, heads and finned cylinders; cast iron cylinder liners. **Displacement:** 72.7 cu. in. (1192 cc). **Bore & Stroke:** 3.03 x 2.52 in. (77 x 64 mm). **Compression Ratio:** 7.0:1. **Brake Horsepower:** 40 at 3900 rpm. **Torque:** 64.4 lbs.-ft. at 2400 rpm. Four main bearings. Solid valve lifters. Solex single-barrel carburetor. 6-volt electrical system.

CHASSIS DATA: Wheelbase: 94.5 in. **Overall Length:** (sed) 160.2 in.; (Karmann) 163 in.; (wagon) 168.9 in. **Height:** (sed) 59.1 in.; (Karmann) 52.4 in. **Width:** (sed) 60.6 in.; (Karmann) 64.4 in.; (wagon) 68.9 in.; (DeL wagon) 70.9 in. **Front Tread:** (sed/Karmann) 51.4 in. **Rear Tread:** (sed/Karmann) 50.7 in. **Standard Tires:** (sed/Karmann) 5.60x15; (wagon) 6.40x15.

TECHNICAL: Layout: rear-engine, rear-drive. **Transmission:** four-speed manual. **Steering:** worm and sector. **Suspension (front):** kingpins with transverse torsion bars and upper/lower trailing arms. **Suspension (rear):** swing axles with trailing arms and torsion bar. **Brakes:** hydraulic, front/rear drum. **Body Construction:** unitized; steel body welded to floorpan.

PERFORMANCE: Top Speed: (sed) 72 mph (cruising); (Karmann) 75 mph. **Acceleration (0-60 mph):** (sed) 22 sec. **Fuel Mileage:** (sed) 28-32 mpg.

PRODUCTION/SALES: A total of 192,570 Volkswagens were sold in the U.S. during 1962.

Manufacturer: Volkswagenwerk AG, Wolfsburg, West Germany.

Distributor: Volkswagen of America Inc., Englewood Cliffs, New Jersey.

1963 VOLKSWAGEN

1200 (BEETLE) — FLAT FOUR — Appearance changes included the deletion of the Wolfsburg crest that had decorated VW hoods since 1951. The sunroof handle now folded flush, the headliner was made of leatherette, and the car's floorboard added foam insulation. Fresh-air heating also was new, and window guides were now made of nylon for longer life.

KARMANN-GHIA — FLAT FOUR — Production of VW's sport coupe and convertible continued without major change, except for the modifications noted above.

TRANSPORTER — FLAT FOUR — Larger round front turn-signal indicators were installed on Microbuses, beginning in 1963. A fresh-air heating system also became available. Microbuses could get an optional "1500" engine starting this year, which would become standard by the 1965 model year.

I.D. DATA: Serial number is on a plate behind the spare tire; and on the frame tunnel, under the back seat. Engine number is stamped on the generator support, on the crankcase. Serial number range: (sedan) 4846836 to 5677118; (conv) 4765156 up; (Karmann cpe) 4763000 up; (Karmann conv) 4763007 up; (Transporter) 971551 up.

Model	Body Type & Seating	Engine Type/CID	P.O.E. Price	Weight (lbs.)	Prod. Total
1200 DELUXE					
113	2-dr Sedan-4P	H4/73	1595	1565	Note 1
117	2-dr Sunroof Sed-4P	H4/73	1685	1565	Note 1
151	2-dr Conv Sed-4P	H4/73	2095	1698	Note 1
1200 KARMANN-GHIA					
143	2-dr Coupe-2 + 2P	H4/73	2295	1742	Note 1
141	2-dr Conv Cpe-2 + 2P	H4/73	2495	1742	Note 1
TRANSPORTER					
231	4-dr Kombi	H4/73	1995	2095	Note 2
221	4-dr Sta Wagon	H4/73	2275	2414	Note 2
241/M130	4-dr DeL Wagon	H4/73	2655	2414	Note 2

Note 1: A total of 891,521 Volkswagen passenger cars were produced in 1963.

Note 2: A total of 45,960 Transporters were produced in 1963.

ENGINE DATA: BASE FOUR: Horizontally opposed, overhead-valve four-cylinder (air cooled). Light alloy block, heads and finned cylinders; cast iron cylinder liners. **Displacement:** 72.7 cu. in. (1192 cc). **Bore & Stroke:** 3.03 x 2.52 in. (77 x 64 mm). **Compression Ratio:** 7.0:1. **Brake Horsepower:** 40 at 3900 rpm. **Torque:** 64.4 lbs.-ft. at 2400 rpm. Four main bearings. Solid valve lifters. Solex single-barrel carburetor. 6-volt electrical system. **OPTIONAL FOUR (Transporter):** Same as above, except — **Displacement:** 91.1 cu. in. (1493 cc). **Bore & Stroke:** 3.27 x 2.72 in. (83 x 69 mm). **Compression Ratio:** 7.8:1. **Brake Horsepower:** 50 at 3900 rpm.

CHASSIS DATA: Wheelbase: 94.5 in. **Overall Length:** (sed) 160.2 in.; (Karmann) 163 in.; (wagon) 168.9 in. **Height:** (sed) 59.1 in.; (Karmann) 52.4 in. **Width:** (sed) 60.6 in.; (Karmann) 64.4 in.; (wagon) 68.9 in.; (DeL wagon) 70.9 in. **Front Tread:** (sed/Karmann) 51.4 in. **Rear Tread:** (sed/Karmann) 50.7 in. **Standard Tires:** (sed/Karmann) 5.60x15; (wagon) 6.40x15.

TECHNICAL: Layout: rear-engine, rear-drive. **Transmission:** four-speed manual. **Steering:** worm and sector. **Suspension (front):** kingpins with transverse torsion bars and upper/lower trailing arms. **Suspension (rear):** swing axles with trailing arms and torsion bar. **Brakes:** hydraulic, front/rear drum. **Body Construction:** unitized; steel body welded to floorpan.

PERFORMANCE: Top Speed: (sed) 72 mph (cruising); (Karmann) 75 mph. **Acceleration (0-60 mph):** (sed) 22 sec. **Fuel Mileage:** (sed) 28-32 mpg.

PRODUCTION/SALES: A total of 240,143 Volkswagens were sold in the U.S. during 1963.

Manufacturer: Volkswagenwerk AG, Wolfsburg, West Germany.

Distributor: Volkswagen of America Inc., Englewood Cliffs, New Jersey.

1964 VOLKSWAGEN

1200 (BEETLE) — FLAT FOUR — Perforated vinyl upholstery replaced the former non-porous leatherette material for 1964, and a sliding steel sunroof (with crank) replaced the familiar fold-back fabric unit. The rear license-plate light grew larger, and dual thumb buttons replaced the horn half-ring. Standard colors for 1964 were: Panama Beige, Bahama Blue, Sea Blue, Java Green, Black, Pearl White, Anthracite, and Ruby Red.

KARMANN-GHIA — FLAT FOUR — Production of VW's sport coupe and convertible continued without major change, except for the modifications noted above. After the start of the model year, the license plate grew larger.

TRANSPORTER — FLAT FOUR — Microbus production continued without major change, again with the option of a larger engine.

I.D. DATA: Serial number is on a plate behind the spare tire; and on the frame tunnel, under the back seat. Engine number is stamped on the generator support, on the crankcase. Serial number range: (sedan) 5677119 to 6502399; (Transporter) 1144303 up.

Model	Body Type & Seating	Engine Type/CID	P.O.E. Price	Weight (lbs.)	Prod. Total
1200 DELUXE					
113	2-dr Sedan-4P	H4/73	1595	1609	Note 1
117	2-dr Sunroof Sed-4P	H4/73	1685	1609	Note 1
151	2-dr Conv Sed-4P	H4/73	2095	1720	Note 1
1200 KARMANN-GHIA					
143	2-dr Coupe-2 + 2P	H4/73	2295	1742	Note 1
141	2-dr Conv Cpe-2 + 2P	H4/73	2495	1742	Note 1
TRANSPORTER					
2313	4-dr Kombi	H4/73	2140	2282	Note 2
2213	4-dr Sta Wagon	H4/73	2385	2469	Note 2
2413/M130	4-dr DeL Wagon	H4/73	2605	2469	Note 2

Note 1: A total of 1,034,797 Volkswagen passenger cars were produced in 1964.

Note 2: A total of 54,146 Transporters were produced in 1964.

ENGINE DATA: BASE FOUR: Horizontally opposed, overhead-valve four-cylinder (air cooled). Light alloy block, heads and finned cylinders; cast iron cylinder liners. **Displacement:** 72.7 cu. in. (1192 cc). **Bore & Stroke:** 3.03 x 2.52 in. (77 x 64 mm). **Compression Ratio:** 7.0:1. **Brake Horsepower:** 40 at 3900 rpm. **Torque:** 64.4 lbs.-ft. at 2400 rpm. Four main bearings. Solid valve lifters. Solex single-barrel carburetor. 6-volt electrical system. **OPTIONAL FOUR (Transporter):** Same as above, except — **Displacement:** 91.1 cu. in. (1493 cc). **Bore & Stroke:** 3.27 x 2.72 in. (83 x 69 mm). **Compression Ratio:** 7.8:1. **Brake Horsepower:** 50 at 3900 rpm.

CHASSIS DATA: Wheelbase: 94.5 in. **Overall Length:** (sed) 160.6 in.; (Karmann) 163 in.; (wagon) 168.9 in. **Height:** (sed) 59.1 in.; (Karmann) 52.4 in. **Width:** (sed) 60.6 in.; (Karmann) 64.4 in.; (wagon) 68.9 in.; (DeL wagon) 70.9 in. **Front Tread:** (sed/Karmann) 51.4 in. **Rear Tread:** (sed/Karmann) 50.7 in. **Standard Tires:** (sed/Karmann) 5.60x15.

TECHNICAL: Layout: rear-engine, rear-drive. **Transmission:** four-speed manual. **Steering:** worm and sector. **Suspension (front):** kingpins with transverse torsion bars and upper/lower trailing arms. **Suspension (rear):** swing axles with trailing arms and torsion bar. **Brakes:** hydraulic, front/rear drum. **Body Construction:** unitized; steel body welded to floorpan.

PERFORMANCE: Top Speed: (sed) 72 mph (cruising); (Karmann) 75 mph. **Acceleration (0-60 mph):** (sed) 22 sec. **Fuel Mileage:** (sed) 28-32 mpg.

PRODUCTION/SALES: A total of 307,173 Volkswagens were sold in the U.S. during 1964.

Manufacturer: Volkswagenwerk AG, Wolfsburg, West Germany.

Distributor: Volkswagen of America Inc., Englewood Cliffs, New Jersey.

1965 VOLKSWAGEN

1965 Volkswagen Beetle two-door sedan.

1200 (BEETLE) — FLAT FOUR — Windows and the windshield grew larger for 1965, giving 15 percent more glass area, and a pushbutton replaced the former T-type handle on the engine lid. Front seatbacks now were slightly thinner and contoured, while rear seat folded almost flat. Twin levers operated the heater, which delivered greater heating volume as four thermostically-controlled flaps at the fan housing replaced the former throttle ring. This allowed heated air to flow immediately after the engine was started. Pivoting sunvisors also were installed. Windshield-wiper blades were longer, operated by a more powerful motor, and "parked" on the left side (formerly on the right). The brake system also was improved.

KARMANN-GHIA — FLAT FOUR — Production of VW's sport coupe and convertible continued without major change, except for the modifications noted above.

TRANSPORTER — FLAT FOUR — Microbus production continued without major change, except that the formerly-optional "1500" engine was now standard.

I.D. DATA: Serial number is on a plate behind the spare tire; and on the frame tunnel, under the back seat. A new numbering system using nine-digit numbers began with the 1965 models. The first two digits indicate the model; the next digit identifies the model year; and the final six digits form the sequential production number. Engine number is stamped on the generator support, on the crankcase. Serial number range: (sedan) 11-5000001 to 11-5979202; (Karmann) 14-5000001 up; (Transporter) 2()-5000001 up.

Model	Body Type & Seating	Engine Type/CID	P.O.E. Price	Weight (lbs.)	Prod. Total
1200 (BEETLE)					
113	2-dr Sedan-4P	H4/73	1563	1609	Note 1
117	2-dr Sunroof Sed-4P	H4/73	1653	1609	Note 1
151	2-dr Conv Sed-4P	H4/73	2053	1720	Note 1
1200 KARMANN-GHIA					
143	2-dr Coupe-2 + 2P	H4/73	2250	1742	Note 1
141	2-dr Conv Cpe-2 + 2P	H4/73	2445	1742	Note 1
TRANSPORTER					
23121	4-dr Kombi	H4/91	2135	2282	Note 2
2212	4-dr Sta Wagon	H4/91	2321	2436	Note 2
2412	4-dr DeL Wagon	H4/91	2577	2469	Note 2

Note 1: A total of 1,174,687 Volkswagen passenger cars were produced in 1965.
Note 2: A total of 50,400 Transporters were produced in 1965.

1965 Volkswagen Karmann-Ghia Type 3.

ENGINE DATA: BASE FOUR: Horizontally opposed, overhead-valve four-cylinder (air cooled). Light alloy block, heads and finned cylinders; cast iron cylinder liners. **Displacement:** 72.7 cu. in. (1192 cc). **Bore & Stroke:** 3.03 x 2.52 in. (77 x 64 mm). **Compression Ratio:** 7.0:1. **Brake Horsepower:** 40 at 3900 rpm. **Torque:** 64.4 lbs.-ft. at 2400 rpm. Four main bearings. Solid valve lifters. Solex single-barrel carburetor. 6-volt electrical system.
BASE FOUR (Transporter): Same as above, except — **Displacement:** 91.1 cu. in. (1493 cc). **Bore & Stroke:** 3.27 x 2.72 in. (83 x 69 mm). **Compression Ratio:** 7.8:1. **Brake Horsepower:** 50 at 3900 rpm.

CHASSIS DATA: Wheelbase: 94.5 in. **Overall Length:** (sed) 160.6 in.; (Karmann) 163 in.; (wagon) 168.9 in. **Height:** (sed) 59.1 in.; (Karmann) 52.4 in. **Width:** (sed) 60.6 in.; (Karmann) 64.4 in.; (wagon) 68.9 in.; (DeL wagon) 70.9 in. **Front Tread:** (sed/Karmann) 51.4 in. **Rear Tread:** (sed/Karmann) 50.7 in. **Standard Tires:** 5.60x15.
TECHNICAL: Layout: rear-engine, rear-drive. **Transmission:** four-speed manual. **Steering:** worm and sector. **Suspension (front):** kingpins with transverse torsion bars and upper/lower trailing arms. **Suspension (rear):** swing axles with trailing arms and torsion bar. **Brakes:** hydraulic, front/rear drum. **Body Construction:** unitized; steel body welded to floorpan.
PERFORMANCE: Similar to 1964.
PRODUCTION/SALES: A total of 371,222 Volkswagens were sold in the U.S. during 1965 (including tourist deliveries).
Manufacturer: Volkswagenwerk AG, Wolfsburg, West Germany.
Distributor: Volkswagen of America Inc., Englewood Cliffs, New Jersey.

1966 VOLKSWAGEN

1966 Volkswagen Beetle 1300 cabriolet.

1300 (BEETLE) — FLAT FOUR — A horsepower boost from 40 to 50 was the major change for 1966, as the engine grew to 1285-cc displacement. That change brought a '1300' emblem on the decklid. Wheels now contained vent slots and flat hubcaps. Inside, the half horn-ring that had been deleted two years earlier was reinstated, front backrests added safety latches, the headlight dimmer now was mounted on the steering column, and the dashboard held a central defroster outlet.

KARMANN-GHIA — FLAT FOUR — Production of VW's sport coupe and convertible continued with the larger engine described above.

TRANSPORTER — FLAT FOUR — Microbus production continued with a boost to 53 horsepower.

1600 — FLAT FOUR — An all-new Volkswagen, evolved from the European Type 3, came in two-door fastback or squareback form, with a 1585-cc horizontally-opposed engine that developed 65 horsepower. Appearance was completely different from the Beetle or Karmann-Ghia, but similar to the "1500" that had been marketed elsewhere in the world (and occasionally brought into the U.S.). The fastback had long rear quarter windows, a sharply-slanted back window, and vertical taillamps at rear fender tips. The squareback's rear window was almost vertical, similar to a station wagon.

I.D. DATA: Serial number is on a plate behind the spare tire; and on the frame tunnel, under the back seat. The first two digits indicate the model; the next digit identifies the model year; and the final digits form the sequential production number. Engine number is stamped on the generator support, on the crankcase. Serial number range: (sedan/conv) 116-000001 to 116-1021298; (Karmann) 146-000001 up; (1600 fastback) 316-000001; (1600 squareback) 366-000001; (Transporter) 2(6-000001 up.

Model	Body Type & Seating	Engine Type/CID	P.O.E. Price	Weight (lbs.)	Prod. Total
1300 (BEETLE)					
113	2-dr Sedan-4P	H4/78	1585	1653	Note 1
117	2-dr Sunroof Sed-4P	H4/78	1675	1653	Note 1
151	2-dr Conv Sed-4P	H4/78	2075	1742	Note 1
1300 KARMANN-GHIA					
143	2-dr Coupe-2 + 2P	H4/78	2250	1764	Note 1
141	2-dr Conv Cpe-2 + 2P	H4/78	2445	1764	Note 1
1600 (FASTBACK/SQUAREBACK)					
311	2-dr Fbk Sed-4P	H4/97	2140	1962	Note 1
361	2-dr Sqbk Sed-4P	H4/97	2295	2029	Note 1
TRANSPORTER					
23121	4-dr Kombi	H4/91	2135	2282	Note 2
2212	4-dr Sta Wagon	H4/91	2321	2436	Note 2
2412	4-dr DeL Wagon	H4/91	2577	2469	Note 2

Note 1: A total of 1,168,146 Volkswagen passenger cars were produced in 1966.
Note 2: A total of 49,557 Transporters were produced in 1966.

1966 Volkswagen Karmann-Ghia cabriolet.

ENGINE DATA: BASE FOUR (1300): Horizontally opposed, overhead-valve four-cylinder (air cooled). Light alloy block, heads and finned cylinders; cast iron cylinder liners. **Displacement:** 78.4 cu. in. (1285 cc). **Bore & Stroke:** 3.03 x 2.72 in. (77 x 69 mm). **Compression Ratio:** 7.3:1. **Brake Horsepower:** 50 at 4600 rpm. **Torque:** 69 lbs.-ft. at 2600 rpm. Four main bearings. Solid valve lifters. Solex single-barrel carburetor. 6-volt electrical system.
BASE FOUR (Transporter): Same as above, except — **Displacement:** 91.1 cu. in. (1493 cc). **Bore & Stroke:** 3.27 x 2.72 in. (83 x 69 mm). **Compression Ratio:** 7.8:1. **Brake Horsepower:** 53 at 4200 rpm.
BASE FOUR (1600): Same as above, except — **Displacement:** 96.7 cu. in. (1585 cc). **Bore & Stroke:** 3.36 x 2.72 in. (85 x 69 mm). **Compression Ratio:** 7.7:1. **Brake Horsepower:** 65 at 4600 rpm. **Torque:** 87 lbs.-ft. at 2800 rpm.

CHASSIS DATA: Wheelbase: 94.5 in. **Overall Length:** (1300 sed) 160.2 in.; (Karmann) 163 in.; (1600) 166.3 in.; (wagon) 168.9 in. **Height:** (1300 sed) 59.1 in.; (Karmann) 52.4 in.; (1600) 58.1 in. **Width:** (1300 sed) 60.6 in.; (Karmann) 64.3 in.; (1600) 63.2 in.; (wagon) 68.9 in.; (DeL wagon) 70.9 in. **Front Tread:** (1300 sed/Karmann) 51.4 in.; (1600) 51.6 in. **Rear Tread:** (1300 sed/Karmann) 51.2 in.; (1600) 53 in. **Standard Tires:** (1300 sed/Karmann) 5.60x15; (1600) 6.00x15.

TECHNICAL: Layout: rear-engine, rear-drive. **Transmission:** four-speed manual. **Steering:** worm and sector. **Suspension (front):** transverse torsion bars with upper/lower trailing arms. **Suspension (rear):** swing axles with trailing arms and torsion bars. **Brakes:** (1300) hydraulic, front/rear drum; (1600) front disc, rear drum. **Body Construction:** unitized with backbone platform; steel body welded to floorpan.

PERFORMANCE: Top Speed: (1300) 82 mph; (Transporter) 72 mph. **Fuel Mileage:** (1300) about 25 mpg; (Transporter) about 23 mpg.

PRODUCTION/SALES: A total of 427,694 Volkswagens were sold in the U.S. during 1966 (including tourist deliveries).
Manufacturer: Volkswagenwerk AG, Wolfsburg, West Germany.
Distributor: Volkswagen of America Inc., Englewood Cliffs, New Jersey.

1967 VOLKSWAGEN

1967 Volkswagen Beetle 1500 two-door sedan.

1500 (BEETLE) — FLAT FOUR — Still another engine enlargement sent horsepower from 50 to 53. Glass headlamp covers no longer were installed, and parking lamps were part of the turn signals. Backup lights were added for 1967, and 'Volkswagen' script went on the decklid, which now held the license plate vertically. Locking door buttons were installed, as was a dual brake system. The electrical system was now 12-volt, after two decades of 6-volt operation. Two-speed windshield wipers were installed.

KARMANN-GHIA — FLAT FOUR — Production of VW's sport coupe and convertible continued, with the larger "1500" engine described above. Seat backrests now locked in position when the door was closed.

1600 — FLAT FOUR — Production of the fastback and squareback sedans, introduced to the U.S. for 1966, continued without major change. These two models used a different form of horizontally-opposed engine than the Beetle, sometimes referred to as a "suitcase" engine because of its overall shape. Each body style was available with or without a sunroof.

TRANSPORTER — FLAT FOUR — Microbus production continued with minimal change.

I.D. DATA: Serial number is on a plate behind the spare tire; and on the frame tunnel, under the back seat. 1600 serial number is on a plate in front luggage compartment, ahead of the spare tire. Transporter serial number is on right side of engine-compartment floor. The first two digits indicate the model; the next digit identifies the model year; and the final digits form the sequential production number. Engine number is stamped on the generator support, on the crankcase. Starting serial number: (1500 sedan/conv) 117-000001; (1600) 317-000001; (Transporter) 217-000001 up.

Model	Body Type & Seating	Engine Type/CID	P.O.E. Price	Weight (lbs.)	Prod. Total
1500 (BEETLE)					
113	2-dr Sedan-4P	H4/91	1639	1698	Note 1
117	2-dr Sunroof Sed-4P	H4/91	1729	1698	Note 1
151	2-dr Conv Sed-4P	H4/91	2075	1786	Note 1
1500 KARMANN-GHIA					
143	2-dr Coupe-2+2P	H4/91	2250	1786	Note 1
141	2-dr Conv Cpe-2+2P	H4/91	2445	1786	Note 1
1600 (FASTBACK/SQUAREBACK)					
311	2-dr Fbk Sed-4P	H4/97	2148	1962	Note 1
313 Sunroof	2-dr Fbk Sed-4P	H4/97	2273	1962	Note 1
361	2-dr Sqbk Sed-4P	H4/97	2295	2029	Note 1
363 Sunroof	2-dr Sqbk Sed-4P	H4/97	2420	2029	Note 1
TRANSPORTER					
2312/	4-dr Kombi	H4/91	2150	2283	Note 2
2212/2812	4-dr Sta Wagon	H4/91	2337	2436	Note 2
2412/2512	4-dr DeL Wagon	H4/91	2597	2469	Note 2
23129	4-dr Campmobile	H4/91	2667	N/A	Note 2

Note 1: A total of 921,013 Volkswagen passenger cars (all models) were produced in 1967.

Note 2: A total of 31,016 Transporters were produced in 1967.

ENGINE DATA: BASE FOUR (1500, Transporter): Horizontally opposed, overhead-valve four-cylinder (air cooled). Light alloy block, heads and finned cylinders; cast iron cylinder liners. Displacement: 91.1 cu. in. (1493 cc). Bore & Stroke: 3.27 x 2.72 in. (83 x 69 mm). Compression Ratio: 7.5:1. Brake Horsepower: 53 at 4200 rpm. Torque: 78 lbs.-ft. at 2600 rpm. Four main bearings. Solid valve lifters. Single-barrel carburetor. 12-volt electrical system.

BASE FOUR (1600): Same as above, except — Displacement: 96.7 cu. in. (1585 cc). Bore & Stroke: 3.36 x 2.72 in. (85 x 69 mm). Compression Ratio: 7.7:1. Brake Horsepower: 65 at 4600 rpm. Torque: 87 lbs.-ft. at 2800 rpm.

CHASSIS DATA: Wheelbase: 94.5 in. **Overall Length:** (1500 sed) 160.6 in.; (Karmann) 163 in.; (1600) 166.3 in.; (wagon) 168.9 in.; (DeL wagon) 169.3 in. **Height:** (1500 sed) 59.1 in.; (Karmann) 52.4 in.; (1600) 58.1 in. **Width:** (1500 sed) 60.6 in.; (Karmann) 64.3 in.; (1600) 63.2 in.; (wagon) 68.9 in.; (DeL wagon) 70.9 in. **Front Tread:** (1500 sed) 53.4 in.; (Karmann) 53.1 in.; (1600) 51.6 in. **Rear Tread:** (1500 sed/Karmann) 51.2 in.; (1600) 53 in. **Standard Tires:** (1500 sed/Karmann) 5.60x15; (1600) 6.00x15.

TECHNICAL: Layout: rear-engine, rear-drive. **Transmission:** four-speed manual. **Steering:** worm and sector. **Suspension (front):** transverse torsion bars with upper/lower trailing arms. **Suspension (rear):** swing axles with trailing arms and torsion bars. **Brakes:** (1500) hydraulic, front/rear drum; (1600) front disc, rear drum. **Body Construction:** unitized with backbone platform; steel body welded to floorpan.

PERFORMANCE: Top Speed: (1500) 82 mph; (Transporter) 72 mph. **Fuel Mileage:** (1500) about 25 mpg; (Transporter) about 23 mpg.

PRODUCTION/SALES: A total of 454,801 Volkswagens were sold in the U.S. during 1967 (including tourist deliveries).

Manufacturer: Volkswagenwerk AG, Wolfsburg, West Germany.

Distributor: Volkswagen of America Inc., Englewood Cliffs, New Jersey.

1968 VOLKSWAGEN

1968 Volkswagen Beetle two-door sedan.

1500 (BEETLE) — FLAT FOUR — Changes for 1968 included a switch to single-bar (one-piece) bumpers without overriders, which shortened overall length. Other revisions included larger taillamps with integrated backup lights, an external gas filler with spring-loaded door, and flatter door handles with trigger release. The rear decklid was bulged slightly. The car now had a cowl air inlet, and the hood release moved to the outside. A collapsible steering column became standard, while Automatic Stick Shift became optional. That semi-automatic unit could be shifted from low to driving range without using the clutch, simply by moving the gearshift lever. "Sarcophagus" seatbacks were now used, with integrated head restraints. A certification sticker on the door post advised that the car met federal safety standards.

KARMANN-GHIA — FLAT FOUR — Production of VW's sport coupe and convertible continued with changes noted above, and with the addition of front disc brakes.

1600 — FLAT FOUR — Production of the fastback and squareback sedans continued without major change, except that the fuel filler door went on the right front fender and the engine added electronic fuel injection. An automatic transmission became available during 1968.

TRANSPORTER — FLAT FOUR — Microbuses and Campmobiles were restyled for 1968, taking on an appearance closer to American vans, with a sliding-type side door. They also gained a larger "1600" engine.

I.D. DATA: Serial number is on a plate behind the spare tire; and on the frame tunnel, under the back seat. 1600 serial number is in the front luggage compartment, beside the hood lock. Transporter serial number is on right side of engine-compartment floor. The first two digits indicate the model; the next digit identifies the model year; and the final digits form the sequential production number. Engine number is stamped on the generator support, on the crankcase. Serial number range: (1500 sedan/conv) 118-000001 to 119-1016098; (Karmann-Ghia) 148-000001 up; (1600 fastback) 348-000001 up; (1600 squareback) 368-000001 up; (Transporter wgn) 218-000001 up; (Kombi) 238-000001 up.

Model	Body Type & Seating	Engine Type/CID	P.O.E. Price	Weight (lbs.)	Prod. Total
1500 (BEETLE)					
1131	2-dr Sedan-4P	H4/91	1699	1742	Note 1
1171	2-dr Sunroof Sed-4P	H4/91	1789	1742	Note 1
1511	2-dr Conv Sed-4P	H4/91	2099	1852	Note 1
1500 KARMANN-GHIA					
1431	2-dr Coupe-2+2P	H4/91	2254	1852	Note 1
1411	2-dr Conv Cpe-2+2P	H4/91	2449	1852	Note 1
1600 (FASTBACK/SQUAREBACK)					
3111	2-dr Fbk Sed-4P	H4/97	2179	2050	Note 1
3131 Sunrf	2-dr Fbk Sed-4P	H4/97	2299	2050	Note 1
3611	2-dr Sqbk Sed-4P	H4/97	2349	2050	Note 1
3631 Sunrf	2-dr Sqbk Sed-4P	H4/97	2469	2050	Note 1
TRANSPORTER					
23101	3-dr Kombi	H4/97	2269	2535	Note 2
2211	3-dr Sta Wagon	H4/97	2499	2634	Note 2
23129	3-dr Campmobile	H4/97	2765	N/A	Note 2

Note 1: A total of 1,191,854 Volkswagen passenger cars (all models) were produced in 1968.

Note 2: A total of 64,411 Transporters were produced in 1968.

ENGINE DATA: BASE FOUR (1500): Horizontally opposed, overhead-valve four-cylinder (air cooled). Light alloy block, heads and finned cylinders; cast iron cylinder liners. Displacement: 91.1 cu. in. (1493 cc). Bore & Stroke: 3.27 x 2.72 in. (83 x 69 mm). Compression Ratio: 7.5:1. Brake Horsepower: 53 at 4200 rpm. Torque: 78 lbs.-ft. at 2600 rpm. Four main bearings. Solid valve lifters. Single-barrel carburetor. 12-volt electrical system.

BASE FOUR (1600): Same as above, except — Displacement: 96.7 cu. in. (1585 cc). Bore & Stroke: 3.36 x 2.72 in. (85 x 69 mm). Compression Ratio: 7.7:1. Brake Horsepower: 65 at 4600 rpm. Torque: 87 lbs.-ft. at 2800 rpm. Electronic fuel injection.

CHASSIS DATA: Wheelbase: 94.5 in. **Overall Length:** (1500 sed) 158.7 in.; (Karmann) 163 in.; (1600) 166.3 in.; (wagon) 174.0 in. **Height:** (1500 sed) 59.1 in.; (Karmann) 52.4 in.; (1600) 58.1 in. **Width:** (1500 sed) 61.0 in.; (Karmann) 64.3 in.; (1600) 63.2 in.; (wagon) 69.5 in. **Front Tread:** (1500 sed) 51.6 in.; (Karmann) 51.8 in.; (1600) 51.6 in. **Rear Tread:** (1500 sed/Karmann) 53.1 in.; (1600) 53 in. **Standard Tires:** (1500 sed/Karmann) 5.60x15; (1600) 6.00x15; (wagon) 7.00x14.

TECHNICAL: Layout: rear-engine, rear-drive. **Transmission:** four-speed manual (automatic available on 1600). **Steering:** worm and sector. **Suspension (front):** transverse torsion bars with upper/lower trailing arms. **Suspension (rear):** swing axles with trailing arms and torsion bars. **Brakes:** (1500) hydraulic, front/rear drum; (Karmann-Ghia, 1600) front disc, rear drum. **Body Construction:** unitized with backbone platform; steel body welded to floorpan.

PERFORMANCE: Top Speed: (1500) 82 mph; (Transporter) 72 mph. **Fuel Mileage:** (1500) about 25 mpg; (Transporter) about 23 mpg.

PRODUCTION/SALES: A total of 582,009 Volkswagens were sold in the U.S. during 1968 (including tourist deliveries).

Manufacturer: Volkswagenwerk AG, Wolfsburg, West Germany.

Distributor: Volkswagen of America Inc., Englewood Cliffs, New Jersey.

1969 VOLKSWAGEN

1969 Volkswagen Beetle two-door sedan.

1500 (BEETLE) — FLAT FOUR — For the first time, the Beetle had truly independent rear suspension, with a double-jointed rear axle and semi-trailing arms instead of the customary swing axles. After moving to the outside a year earlier, the hood release now went inside the glovebox. Warm-air outlets at the door bases moved to the rear. An electric rear-window defogger/defroster was installed, as were an inside fuel-door release, a steering-wheel, and day/night mirror. Later in the year, the odometer added readings in tenths of a mile.

KARMANN-GHIA — FLAT FOUR — Production of VW's sport coupe and convertible continued with changes noted above.

1600 — FLAT FOUR — Production of the fastback and squareback sedans continued without major change, with either manual shift or an automatic transmission available. The 1.6-liter horizontally-opposed engine used fuel injection.

TRANSPORTER — FLAT FOUR — Restyled for 1968, VW's Microbuses and Campmobiles continued without major change this year.

1969 Volkswagen Karmann-Ghia.

I.D. DATA: Serial number is on the upper left of the dashboard, near the windshield. 1600 serial number is in front luggage compartment, beside the hood lock. Transporter serial number is on right side of engine-compartment floor. The first two digits indicate the model; the next digit identifies the model year; and the final digits form the sequential production number. Engine number is stamped on the generator support, on the crankcase. Serial number range: (1500 sedan/conv) 119-000001 to 119-1093704; (Karmann-Ghia) 149-000001 up; (1600 fastback) 319-000001 up; (1600 squareback) 369-000001 up; (Kombi) 239-000001 up; (wagon) 229-000001 up.

Model	Body Type & Seating	Engine Type/CID	P.O.E. Price	Weight (lbs.)	Prod. Total
1500 (BEETLE)					
1131	2-dr Sedan-4P	H4/91	1799	1742	Note 1
1171	2-dr Sunroof Sed-4P	H4/91	1889	1742	Note 1
1511	2-dr Conv Sed-4P	H4/91	2209	1852	Note 1
1500 KARMANN-GHIA					
1431	2-dr Coupe-2 + 2P	H4/91	2365	1852	Note 1
1411	2-dr Conv Cpe-2 + 2P	H4/91	2575	1852	Note 1

Model	Body Type & Seating	Engine Type/CID	P.O.E. Price	Weight (lbs.)	Prod. Total
1600 (FASTBACK/SQUAREBACK)					
3111	2-dr Fbk Sed-4P	H4/97	2295	2050	Note 1
3131 Sunrf	2-dr Fbk Sed-4P	H4/97	2415	2050	Note 1
3611	2-dr Sqbk Sed-4P	H4/97	2470	2050	Note 1
3631 Sunrf	2-dr Sqbk Sed-4P	H4/97	2590	2050	Note 1
TRANSPORTER					
23101	3-dr Kombi	H4/97	2414	2469	Note 2
2211	3-dr Sta Wag-7P	H4/97	2650	2634	Note 2
2215	3-dr Sta Wag-9P	H4/97	2672	2634	Note 2
23109	3-dr Campmobile	H4/97	2850	N/A	Note 2

Note 1: A total of 1,241,580 Volkswagen passenger cars (all models) were produced in 1969.

Note 2: A total of 64,411 Transporters were produced in 1969.

ENGINE DATA: BASE FOUR (1500): Horizontally opposed, overhead-valve four-cylinder (air cooled). Light alloy block, heads and finned cylinders; cast iron cylinder liners. **Displacement:** 91.1 cu. in. (1493 cc). **Bore & Stroke:** 3.27 x 2.72 in. (83 x 69 mm). **Compression Ratio:** 7.5:1. **Brake Horsepower:** 53 at 4200 rpm. **Torque:** 78 lbs.-ft. at 2600 rpm. Four main bearings. Solid valve lifters. Single-barrel carburetor. 12-volt electrical system.

BASE FOUR (1600): Same as above, except — **Displacement:** 96.7 cu. in. (1585 cc). **Bore & Stroke:** 3.36 x 2.72 in. (85 x 69 mm). **Compression Ratio:** 7.7:1. **Brake Horsepower:** 65 at 4600 rpm. **Torque:** 87 lbs.-ft. at 2800 rpm. Fuel injection.

CHASSIS DATA: Wheelbase: 94.5 in. **Overall Length:** (1500 sed) 158.7 in.; (Karmann) 163 in.; (1600) 166.3 in.; (wagon) 174.0 in. **Height:** (1500 sed) 59.1 in.; (Karmann) 52.4 in.; (1600) 57.9 in. **Width:** (1500 sed) 61.0 in.; (Karmann) 64.3 in.; (1600) 63.2 in.; (wagon) 69.5 in. **Front Tread:** (1500 sed) 51.6 in.; (Karmann) 51.8 in.; (1600) 51.6 in. **Rear Tread:** (1500 sed/Karmann) 53.3 in.; (1600) 53 in. **Standard Tires:** (1500 sed/Karmann) 5.60x15; (1600) 6.00x15; (wagon) 7.00x14.

TECHNICAL: Layout: rear-engine, rear-drive. **Transmission:** four-speed manual (automatic available on 1600). **Steering:** worm and sector. **Suspension (front):** transverse torsion bars with upper/lower trailing arms. **Suspension (rear):** independent with semi-trailing arms and torsion bars. **Brakes:** (1500) hydraulic, front/rear drum; (Karmann-Ghia, 1600) front disc, rear drum. **Body Construction:** unitized with backbone platform; steel body welded to floorpan.

PERFORMANCE: Top Speed: (1500) 82 mph; (Transporter) 72 mph. **Fuel Mileage:** (1500) about 25 mpg; (Transporter) about 23 mpg.

PRODUCTION/SALES: A total of 566,356 Volkswagens were sold in the U.S. during 1969 (including tourist deliveries).

Manufacturer: Volkswagenwerk AG, Wolfsburg, West Germany.

Distributor: Volkswagen of America Inc., Englewood Cliffs, New Jersey.

1970 VOLKSWAGEN

1500 (BEETLE) — FLAT FOUR — Displacement grew to 1585 cc for 1970, with a horsepower boost from 53 to 57. Despite the increase to 1.6 liters, the Beetle was still commonly referred to as a "1500" sedan. Front turn signals grew larger and were combined with the side marker lights. The engine lid added air-intake slots (introduced earlier on the convertible), and reflectors went on the rear bumper and taillamp housings. Head restraints were standard this year, and the glovebox added a lock. Remote-control knobs for the warm air outlets were dropped. A buzzer now went off when the door was opened, if the key was in the ignition. Volkswagen's diagnosis and maintenance program was introduced this year.

KARMANN-GHIA — FLAT FOUR — Production of VW's sport coupe and convertible continued with changes noted above.

1600 — FLAT FOUR — Production of the fastback and squareback sedans continued without major change. A three-speed automatic transmission was available.

TRANSPORTER — FLAT FOUR — Restyled for 1968, VW's Microbuses and Campmobiles continued without major change.

I.D. DATA: Serial number is on the upper left of the dashboard, near the windshield. Fastback/squareback serial number is in front luggage compartment, beside the hood lock. Transporter serial number is on right side of engine-compartment floor. A 10-symbol identification number was now used. The first two digits indicate the model; the next digit identifies the model year; and the final seven digits form the sequential production number. Engine number is stamped on the generator support, on the crankcase. Starting serial number: (Beetle) 1102000001; (Karmann-Ghia) 1402000001; (1600 fastback) 3102000001; (1600 squareback) 3602000001; (Kombi) 2302000001; (wagon) 2202000001.

Model	Body Type & Seating	Engine Type/CID	P.O.E. Price	Weight (lbs.)	Prod. Total
1500 (BEETLE)					
113	2-dr Sedan-4P	H4/97	1839	1807	Note 1
117	2-dr Sunroof Sed-4P	H4/97	1929	1807	Note 1
151	2-dr Conv Sed-4P	H4/97	2249	N/A	Note 1
KARMANN-GHIA					
143	2-dr Coupe-2 + 2P	H4/97	2399	1978	Note 1
141	2-dr Conv Cpe-2 + 2P	H4/97	2609	1918	Note 1
1600 (FASTBACK/SQUAREBACK)					
311	2-dr Fbk Sed-4P	H4/97	2339	2226	Note 1
313 Sunroof	2-dr Fbk Sed-4P	H4/97	2459	2226	Note 1
361	2-dr Sqbk Sed-4P	H4/97	2499	2282	Note 1
363 Sunroof	2-dr Sqbk Sed-4P	H4/97	2619	2282	Note 1
TRANSPORTER					
23101	3-dr Kombi	H4/97	2495	2665	Note 2
2211	3-dr Sta Wag-7P	H4/97	2750	2743	Note 2
2215	3-dr Sta Wag-9P	H4/97	2772	N/A	Note 2
23109	3-dr Campmobile	H4/97	3077	2921	Note 2

Note 1: A total of 1,193,853 Volkswagen passenger cars (all models) were produced in 1970.

Note 2: A total of 71,729 Transporters were produced in 1970.

ENGINE DATA: BASE FOUR (Beetle, Karmann-Ghia): Horizontally opposed, overhead-valve four-cylinder (air cooled). Light alloy block, heads and finned cylinders; cast iron cylinder liners. **Displacement:** 96.7 cu. in. (1585 cc). **Bore & Stroke:** 3.36 x 2.72 in. (85 x 69 mm). **Compression Ratio:** 7.5:1. **Brake Horsepower:** 57 at 4400 rpm. **Torque:** 81.7 lbs.-ft. at 3000 rpm. Four main bearings. Solid valve lifters. Single-barrel carburetor. 12-volt electrical system.

BASE FOUR (1600): Same as above, except — **Compression Ratio:** 7.7:1. **Brake Horsepower:** 65 at 4600 rpm. **Torque:** 86.8 lbs.-ft. at 2800 rpm. Fuel injection.

CHASSIS DATA: Wheelbase: 94.5 in. **Overall Length:** (Beetle) 158.7 in.; (Karmann) 163 in.; (1600) 170.9 in.; (wagon) 174.0 in. **Height:** (Beetle) 59.1 in.; (Karmann) 52.4 in.; (1600) 57.9 in. **Width:** (Beetle) 61.0 in.; (Karmann) 64.3 in.; (1600) 63.2 in.; (wagon) 69.5 in. **Front Tread:** (Beetle) 51.6 in.; (Karmann) 51.6 in.; (1600) 51.6 in. **Rear Tread:** (Beetle/Karmann) 53.3 in.; (1600) 53 in. **Standard Tires:** (Beetle/Karmann) 5.60x15; (1600) 6.00x15; (wagon) 7.00x14.

TECHNICAL: Layout: rear-engine, rear-drive. **Transmission:** four-speed manual (automatic available on fastback/squareback). **Steering:** worm and sector. **Suspension (front):** transverse torsion bars with upper/lower trailing arms. **Suspension (rear):** independent with semi-trailing arms and torsion bars. **Brakes:** (Beetle) hydraulic, front/rear drum; (Karmann-Ghia, 1600) front disc, rear drum. **Body Construction:** unitized with backbone platform; steel body welded to floorpan.

PERFORMANCE: Top Speed: (sedans) 82 mph; (Transporter) 72 mph. **Fuel Mileage:** about 25-26 mpg.

PRODUCTION/SALES: A total of 582,573 Volkswagens were sold in the U.S. during 1970 (including tourist deliveries).
Manufacturer: Volkswagenwerk AG, Wolfsburg, West Germany.
Distributor: Volkswagen of America Inc., Englewood Cliffs, New Jersey.

1971-72 VOLKSWAGEN

1971 Volkswagen Beetle two-door sedan.

BEETLE/SUPER BEETLE — FLAT FOUR — A Super Beetle debuted for 1971, with coil-spring front suspension and a bigger trunk. Volkswagen promoted the fact that the car had 89 improvements, including a boost to 60 horsepower. New flow-through vent ports went behind the side windows. The Super Beetle had chrome trim around its side windows and a modified front-lid shape. The front tread dimension grew wider, and turning radius was smaller. Computer-analysis plugs were installed in models built during the second half of the 1971 model year.

Changes for 1972 were modest, including installation of an energy-absorbing safety steering wheel and inertia-reel seatbelts. The rear window grew larger, and a hinged parcel shelf covered the luggage well.

KARMANN-GHIA — FLAT FOUR — Production of VW's sport coupe and convertible continued with changes noted above.

SQUAREBACK/TYPE 3 (1600) — FLAT FOUR — Production of the squareback sedan and the fastback sedan (now named Type 3) continued without major change.

411 — TYPE 4 — FLAT FOUR — Marketed elsewhere in the world since the 1969 model year, the Type 4 now was available in the U.S. Two body styles were offered: a three-door hatchback and four-door sedan. A three-door station wagon was added for 1972. The rear-mounted 1679-cc horizontally-opposed engine developed 85 horsepower.

TRANSPORTER — FLAT FOUR — VW's Microbuses and Campmobiles continued without major change, except the the amber side safety light was now oblong in shape, and positioned farther forward.

1971 Volkswagen 181 Thing.

I.D. DATA: Serial number is on the upper left of the dashboard, visible through the windshield. Beetle/Karmann-Ghia serial number may also be behind the spare tire; fastback/squareback, adjacent to the hood lock under the front hood; Transporters, stamped on right engine-cover plate. A 10-symbol identification number was used. The first two digits indicate the model; the next digit identifies the model year; and the final seven digits form the sequential production number. Engine number is stamped on the generator support, on the crankcase. Starting serial number (1971 models): (Beetle) 1112000001; (conv) 1512000001; (Karmann-Ghia) 1412000001; (1600 squareback) 3612000001; (Type 3) 31120000001; (411 squareback 3-dr) 4612000001; (411 4-dr sedan) 42120000001; (Kombi/Campmobile) 2312000001; (wagon) 2212000001.

Model	Body Type & Seating	Engine Type/CID	P.O.E. Price	Weight (lbs.)	Prod. Total
BEETLE					
1111	2-dr Sedan-4P	H4/97	1845	1786	Note 1
1131 Super	2-dr Sedan-4P	H4/97	1985	1874	Note 1
1171	2-dr Sunroof Sed-4P	H4/97	2075	1874	Note 1
1511	2-dr Conv Sed-4P	H4/97	2399	1896	Note 1
KARMANN-GHIA					
1431	2-dr Coupe-2+2P	H4/97	2575	1874	Note 1
1411	2-dr Conv Cpe-2+2P	H4/97	2750	1896	Note 1
1600 (SQUAREBACK)					
3611	2-dr Sqbk Sed-4P	H4/97	2599	2161	Note 1
3631 Sunrf	2-dr Sqbk Sed-4P	H4/97	2719	N/A	Note 1
TYPE 3 (FASTBACK)					
3111	2-dr Fbk Sed-4P	H4/97	2450	2117	Note 1
3131 Sunrf	2-dr Fbk Sed-4P	H4/97	2570	N/A	Note 1
411 (TYPE 4)					
4613	3-dr Hatch-5P	H4/102	2999	2381	Note 1
4213	4-dr Sedan-5P	H4/102	2999	2315	Note 1
TRANSPORTER					
2311	3-dr Kombi	H4/97	2720	2623	Note 2
2211	3-dr Sta Wag-7P	H4/97	2795	2778	Note 2
2215	3-dr Sta Wag-9P	H4/97	3100	N/A	Note 2
23109	3-dr Campmobile	H4/97	3440	2535	Note 2

Note 1: A total of 1,284,928 Volkswagen passenger cars (all models) were produced in 1971, followed by 1,082,098 in 1972.

Note 2: A total of 74,852 Transporters were produced in 1971, followed by 66,400 in 1972.

Price Note: Figures shown were valid in 1971. Prices in 1972 ranged from $1999 for the basic Beetle to $3099 for the Karmann-Ghia convertible and $3838 for the Campmobile. The 411 station wagon added for 1972 sold for $3299.

1972 Volkswagen two-door sedan.

ENGINE DATA: BASE FOUR (Beetle, Karmann-Ghia, Transporter): Horizontally opposed, overhead-valve four-cylinder (air cooled). **Displacement:** 96.7 cu. in. (1585 cc). **Bore & Stroke:** 3.36 x 2.72 in. (85 x 69 mm). **Compression Ratio:** 7.5:1. **Brake Horsepower:** 60 at 4400 rpm. **Torque:** 81.7 lbs.-ft. at 3000 rpm. Four main bearings. Solid valve lifters. Single-barrel carburetor. 12-volt electrical system.

BASE FOUR (1600 Squareback, Type 3 Fastback): Same as above, except — **Compression Ratio:** 7.7:1. **Brake Horsepower:** 65 at 4600 rpm. **Torque:** 86.8 lbs.-ft. at 2800 rpm. Fuel injection.

BASE FOUR (411 Type 4): Horizontally opposed, overhead-valve four-cylinder (air cooled). **Displacement:** 102.5 cu. in. (1679 cc). **Bore & Stroke:** 3.54 x 2.60 in. (90 x 66 mm). **Compression Ratio:** 8.2:1. **Brake Horsepower:** 85 at 5000 rpm. **Torque:** 99.4 lbs.-ft. at 3500 rpm. Four main bearings. Solid valve lifters. Bosch fuel injection.

1972 Volkswagen Karmann-Ghia coupe.

CHASSIS DATA: Wheelbase: 94.5 in. except (Super Beetle) 95.3 in.; (411) 98.4 in. Overall Length: (Beetle) 158.6 in.; (Super Beetle) 161.8 in.; (Karmann) 163 in.; (Type 3/Squareback) 170.9 in.; (411) 179.2 in.; (wagon) 174.0 in. Height: (Beetle) 59.1 in.; (Karmann) 52 in.; (Type 3/Squareback) 57.9 in.; (411) 58.5 in.; (wagon) 76.4 in. Width: (Beetle) 61.0 in.; (Super Beetle) 62.4 in.; (Karmann) 64.3 in.; (Type 3/Squareback) 63.2 in.; (wagon) 69.5 in. Front Tread: (Beetle) 51.6 in.; (Super Beetle) 54.3 in.; (Karmann) 51.6 in.; (Type 3/Squareback) 51.6 in.; (411) 54.7 in.; (wagon) 54.6 in. Rear Tread: (Beetle/Karmann) 53.3 in.; (Type 3/Squareback) 53 in.; (411) 52.8 in.; (wagon) 56.6 in. Standard Tires: (Beetle/Karmann) 5.60x15; (Type 3/Squareback) 6.00x15; (411 3-dr) 165SR15; (411 4-dr) 155SR15; (wagon) 7.00x14.

TECHNICAL: Layout: rear-engine, rear-drive. Transmission: four-speed manual; automatic available. Steering: (Beetle, 1600) worm and roller; (411) recirculating ball. Suspension (front): (Beetle) transverse torsion bars with upper/lower trailing arms; (Super Beetle, 411) MacPherson struts with coil springs. Suspension (rear): (Beetle, Type 3/Squareback) independent with semi-trailing arms and torsion bars; (411) semi-trailing arms with coil springs. Brakes: (Beetle) front/rear drum; (Karmann-Ghia, Type 3/Squareback, 411) front disc, rear drum.

PRODUCTION/SALES: A total of 532,904 Volkswagens were sold in the U.S. during 1971, followed by 491,742 in 1972 (including tourist deliveries).

Manufacturer: Volkswagenwerk AG, Wolfsburg, West Germany.

Distributor: Volkswagen of America Inc., Englewood Cliffs, New Jersey.

1973 VOLKSWAGEN

1973 Volkswagen Super Beetle two-door sedan.

BEETLE/SUPER BEETLE — FLAT FOUR — VW's Super Beetle had a bigger windshield and improved flow-through ventilation, while all Beetles had black windshield-wiper arms. Larger taillamps were installed, along with 5-mph bumpers. Front seats could be adjusted 77 ways. Improved intake-air preheating was intended to deliver quicker starts in cold weather.

KARMANN-GHIA — FLAT FOUR — Production of VW's sport coupe and convertible continued with changes noted above.

SQUAREBACK/TYPE 3 — FLAT FOUR — This would be the final year for the rear-engined squareback sedan and Type 3 fastback sedan.

412 — TYPE 4 — FLAT FOUR — Model 412 replaced the former 411 this year in the Type 4 series, offered in two- and four-door sedan body styles, as well as a station wagon. The horizontally-opposed engine was rated 76 horsepower (SAE net).

TRANSPORTER — FLAT FOUR — An automatic transmission now was available in VW's Microbuses and Campmobiles. Front amber safety lights moved to a higher position. The new 102.5-cid engine developed 63 horsepower (SAE net).

I.D. DATA: Volkswagen's 10-symbol serial number is on the upper left of the dashboard, visible through the windshield. The first two digits indicate the model; the next digit identifies the model year; and the final seven digits form the sequential production number. Starting serial number: (Beetle) 1132000001; (Super Beetle) 1332000001; (conv) 1532000001; (Karmann-Ghia) 1432000001; (Squareback) 3632000001; (Type 3) 31320000001; (412 2-dr) 4132000001; (412 4-dr sedan) 42320000001; (Kombi/Campmobile) 2332000001; (wagon) 2232000001.

Model	Body Type & Seating	Engine Type/CID	P.O.E. Price	Weight (lbs.)	Prod. Total
BEETLE					
1111	2-dr Sedan-4P	H4/97	2299	1742	Note 1
1131 Super	2-dr Sedan-4P	H4/97	2499	1911	Note 1
1511	2-dr Conv Sed-4P	H4/97	3050	1979	Note 1
KARMANN-GHIA					
1431	2-dr Coupe-2 + 2P	H4/97	3050	1853	Note 1
1411	2-dr Conv Cpe-2 + 2P	H4/97	3450	1853	Note 1
SQUAREBACK					
3611	2-dr Sqbk Sed-4P	H4/97	2995	2217	Note 1
TYPE 3 (FASTBACK)					
3111	2-dr Fbk Sed-4P	H4/97	2795	2161	Note 1
3101	2-dr Fbk Sed-4P	H4/97	2650	2161	Note 1
412 (TYPE 4)					
4111	2-dr Sedan-5P	H4/102	3299	2300	Note 1
4213	4-dr Sedan-5P	H4/102	3599	2345	Note 1
4613	2-dr Sta Wag-5P	H4/102	3699	N/A	Note 1
TRANSPORTER					
2301	3-dr Kombi	H4/102	3500	2759	Note 2
2211	3-dr Sta Wag-7P	H4/102	3799	2946	Note 2
2231	3-dr Sta Wag-9P	H4/102	3850	N/A	Note 2
2391	3-dr Campmobile	H4/102	4449	3105	Note 2

Note 1: A total of 1,128,784 Volkswagen passenger cars (all models) were produced in 1973.

Note 2: A total of 58,442 Transporters were produced in 1973.

1973 Volkswagen Thing.

ENGINE DATA: BASE FOUR (Beetle, Karmann-Ghia): Horizontally opposed, overhead-valve four-cylinder (air cooled). Displacement: 96.7 cu. in. (1585 cc). Bore & Stroke: 3.36 x 2.72 in. (85 x 69 mm). Compression Ratio: 7.3:1. Brake Horsepower: 46 (SAE net) at 4000 rpm. Torque: 72 lbs.-ft. at 2800 rpm. Four main bearings. Solid valve lifters. Single-barrel carburetor. 12-volt electrical system.

BASE FOUR (Squareback, Type 3 Fastback): Same as above, except — Compression Ratio: 7.3:1. Brake Horsepower: 52 (SAE net) at 4000 rpm. Torque: 77 lbs.-ft. at 2200 rpm. Fuel injection.

BASE FOUR (412 Type 4): Horizontally opposed, overhead-valve four-cylinder (air cooled). Displacement: 102.5 cu. in. (1679 cc). Bore & Stroke: 3.54 x 2.60 in. (90 x 66 mm). Compression Ratio: 8.2:1. Brake Horsepower: 76 at 4900 rpm. Torque: 95 lbs.-ft. at 2700 rpm. Four main bearings. Solid valve lifters. Bosch fuel injection.

CHASSIS DATA: Wheelbase: 94.5 in. except (Super Beetle) 95.3 in.; (412) 98.4 in. Overall Length: (Beetle) 159.8 in.; (Super Beetle) 163 in.; (Karmann) 165 in.; (Type 3) 170.8 in.; (Squareback) 172 in.; (412) 180.4 in.; (wagon) 177.4 in. Height: (Beetle) 59.1 in.; (Karmann) 52 in.; (Type 3/Squareback) 57.9 in.; (412) 58.1 in.; (wagon) 76.4 in. Width: (Beetle) 61.0 in.; (Super Beetle) 62.4 in.; (Karmann) 64.3 in.; (Type 3/Squareback) 63.2 in.; (wagon) 67.7 in. Front Tread: (Beetle) 52.1 in.; (Super Beetle) 54.6 in.; (Karmann) 52.7 in.; (Type 3/Squareback) 53.1 in.; (412) 54.2 in.; (wagon) 54.6 in. Rear Tread: (Beetle) 53.6 in.; (Karmann) 52.7 in.; (Type 3/Squareback) 53.1 in.; (412) 53.1 in.; (wagon) 56.6 in. Standard Tires: (Beetle/Karmann) 6.00x15L; (Type 3/Squareback) 6.00x15L; (412) 165SR15; (wagon) 185R14C.

TECHNICAL: Layout: rear-engine, rear-drive. Transmission: four-speed manual; automatic available. Suspension (front): (Beetle) transverse torsion bars with upper/lower trailing arms; (Super Beetle, 412) MacPherson struts with coil springs. Suspension (rear): (Beetle, Type 3/Squareback) independent with semi-trailing arms and torsion bars; (412) semi-trailing arms with coil springs. Brakes: (Beetle) front/rear drum; (Karmann-Ghia, Type 3/Squareback, 412) front disc, rear drum.

ADDITIONAL MODELS: Introduced this year was "The Thing" (model 181), an open Jeep-like vehicle with folding top, derived from the Type 82 Kubelwagen of World War II. Introduced elsewhere in the world during 1969, the "Thing" became available in the U.S. for 1973, after production moved to a Volkswagen factory in Mexico. Power came from the same rear-mounted engine used in the Beetle, rated 46 (SAE net) horsepower. The car's spare tire was under the tall front hood. Doors could be removed, and the windshield folded flat. It would remain available into 1975.

PRODUCTION/SALES: A total of 480,602 Volkswagens were sold in the U.S. during 1973 (including tourist deliveries).

Manufacturer: Volkswagenwerk AG, Wolfsburg, West Germany.

Distributor: Volkswagen of America Inc., Englewood Cliffs, New Jersey.

HISTORY: In 1973, Volkswagen's Beetle surpassed the production total set long before by the Model T Ford.

1974 VOLKSWAGEN

1974 Volkswagen Sun Bug.

DASHER — FOUR — After nearly three decades on the market, the concept of a rear-mounted air-cooled engine was starting to fade away. So Volkswagen introduced the Dasher to the U.S. market as its first front-engine automobile—water cooled at that. The conventional inline 1471-cc four-cylinder engine developed 75 horsepower. Dashers came in two- and four-door hatchback sedan form, or as a station wagon.

BEETLE/SUPER BEETLE — FLAT FOUR — Energy-absorbing bumpers were new this year, as were the Beetle's wheels and a seatbelt-ignition interlock system. Headrests were smaller. This was the final year for the "Super Beetle."

KARMANN-GHIA — FLAT FOUR — This was the final year for the stylish Karmann-Ghia sport coupe and convertible.

412 — TYPE 4 — FLAT FOUR — This was the final season for the Type 4 series. A larger (109.5-cid) engine went into the four-door sedan and station wagon.

TRANSPORTER — FLAT FOUR — A larger engine went into the Kombi and station wagons this year.

I.D. DATA: Volkswagen's 10-symbol serial number is on the upper left of the dashboard, visible through the windshield. The first two digits indicate the model; the next digit identifies the model year; and the final seven digits form the sequential production number. Starting serial number: (Beetle) 1142000001; (Super Beetle) 1342000001; (conv) 1542000001; (Karmann-Ghia) 1442000001; (412 2-dr) 4142000001; (412 4-dr sedan) 42420000001; (412 wagon) 46420000001; (Dasher sed) 3242000001; (Dasher wag) 33420000001; (Kombi) 2342000001; (wagon) 2242000001.

Model	Body Type & Seating	Engine Type/CID	P.O.E. Price	Weight (lbs.)	Prod. Total
DASHER					
3441	4-dr Hatch-4/5P	I4/90	4110	N/A	Note 1
3241	2-dr Hatch-4/5P	I4/90	N/A	N/A	Note 1
3641	4-dr Sta Wag-4/5P	I4/90	4295	N/A	Note 1
BEETLE					
1111	2-dr Sedan-4P	H4/97	2625	1831	Note 1
1131 Super	2-dr Sedan-4P	H4/97	2849	1955	Note 1
1511	2-dr Conv Sed-4P	H4/97	3475	2043	Note 1
KARMANN-GHIA					
1431	2-dr Coupe-2 + 2P	H4/97	3475	1919	Note 1
1411	2-dr Conv Cpe-2 + 2P	H4/97	3935	1919	Note 1
412 (TYPE 4)					
4111	2-dr Sedan-5P	H4/102	3775	2322	Note 1
4213	4-dr Sedan-5P	H4/110	4100	2365	Note 1
4613	2-dr Sta Wag-5P	H4/110	4200	2411	Note 1
TRANSPORTER					
2301	3-dr Kombi	H4/110	4000	2946	Note 2
2211	3-dr Sta Wag-7P	H4/110	4350	2946	Note 2
	3-dr Sta Wag-9P	H4/110	4400	N/A	Note 2
	3-dr Campmobile	H4/110	5274	N/A	Note 2

Note 1: A total of 955,355 Volkswagen passenger cars (all models) were produced in 1974.

Note 2: A total of 38,700 Transporters were produced in 1974.

1974 Volkswagen 181 Thing.

ENGINE DATA: BASE FOUR (Dasher): Inline, overhead-valve four-cylinder (water cooled). **Displacement:** 89.7 cu. in. (1471 cc). **Bore & Stroke:** 3.01 x 3.15 in. (76.5 x 80 mm). **Compression Ratio:** 8.5:1. **Brake Horsepower:** 75 at 5800 rpm. **Torque:** 81 lbs.-ft. at 4000 rpm. Solid valve lifters.

BASE FOUR (Beetle, Karmann-Ghia): Horizontally opposed, overhead-valve four-cylinder (air cooled). **Displacement:** 96.7 cu. in. (1585 cc). **Bore & Stroke:** 3.36 x 2.72 in. (85 x 69 mm). **Compression Ratio:** 7.3:1. **Brake Horsepower:** 46 at 4000 rpm. **Torque:** 72 lbs.-ft. at 2800 rpm. Four main bearings. Solid valve lifters. Single carburetor.

BASE FOUR (412 two-door): Horizontally opposed, overhead-valve four-cylinder (air cooled). **Displacement:** 102.5 cu. in. (1679 cc). **Bore & Stroke:** 3.54 x 2.60 in. (90 x 66 mm). **Compression Ratio:** 8.2:1. **Brake Horsepower:** 76 at 4900 rpm. **Torque:** 95 lbs.-ft. at 2700 rpm. Four main bearings. Solid valve lifters. Bosch fuel injection.

BASE FOUR (412 four-door, wagon): Horizontally opposed, overhead-valve four-cylinder (air cooled). **Displacement:** 109.5 cu. in. (1795 cc). **Bore & Stroke:** 3.66 x 2.59 in. (93 x 66 mm). **Compression Ratio:** 7.3:1. **Brake Horsepower:** 72 at 4800 rpm. **Torque:** 91 lbs.-ft. at 3000 rpm. Four main bearings. Solid valve lifters.

BASE FOUR (Transporter): Same as 1795-cc flat four above, except — **Brake Horsepower:** 65 at 4200 rpm.

CHASSIS DATA: Wheelbase: 94.5 in. except (Super Beetle) 95.3 in.; (Dasher) 97.2 in.; (412) 98.4 in. **Overall Length:** (Beetle) 163.4 in.; (Super Beetle) 164.8 in.; (Karmann) 165.8 in.; (Dasher) 172.8 in.; (412) 183.7 in.; (wagon) 179.0 in. **Height:** (Beetle) 59.1 in.; (Karmann) 52 in.; (412) 58.1 in.; (wagon) 76.4 in. **Width:** (Beetle) 61.0 in.; (Super Beetle) 62.4 in.; (Karmann) 64.3 in.; (Dasher) 63 in.; (wagon) 69.3 in. **Front Tread:** (Beetle) 51.5 in.; (Super Beetle) 54.9 in.; (Karmann) 51.7 in.; (412) 54.6 in.; (wagon) 54.9 in. **Rear Tread:** (Beetle) 53.1 in.; (Karmann) 53.1 in.; (Dasher) 52.6 in.; (412) 53.2 in.; (wagon) 57.3 in. **Standard Tires:** (Beetle/Karmann) 6.00x15L; (Dasher) 155SR13; (412) 155SR15; (wagon) 185R14C.

TECHNICAL: Layout: rear-engine, rear-drive except (Dasher) front-engine, front-drive. **Transmission:** four-speed manual; automatic available. **Suspension (front):** (Beetle) transverse torsion bars with upper/lower trailing arms; (Super Beetle, 412) MacPherson struts with coil springs. **Suspension (rear):** (Beetle) independent with semi-trailing arms and torsion bars; (412) semi-trailing arms with coil springs.

PRODUCTION/SALES: A total of 336,257 Volkswagens were sold in the U.S. during 1974 (including tourist deliveries).
Manufacturer: Volkswagenwerk AG, Wolfsburg, West Germany.
Distributor: Volkswagen of America Inc., Englewood Cliffs, New Jersey.

1975-77 VOLKSWAGEN

1977 Volkswagen Dasher station wagon.

DASHER — FOUR — Production of the front-engined, front-wheel-drive Volkswagen, introduced for 1974, continued into 1975 with little change. For 1976, a larger (1588-cc) engine replaced the original 1471-cc unit.

RABBIT — FOUR — A transverse-mounted 1471-cc engine went into the new front-drive Rabbit, as opposed to the longitudinal engine in the Dasher. Some Rabbits had all-drum brakes, but by 1976 front discs were standard. After one year with a 1471-cc engine, the Rabbit adopted a larger (1588-cc) four. A year later, that engine added fuel injection and the Rabbit added more standard equipment. Deluxe and Custom models added open-up vent windows. After 1977, the Rabbit would also be built in the U.S. A diesel engine became available in 1977.

SCIROCCO — FOUR — Following the demise of the Karmann-Ghia, Volkswagen needed another sporty model and found it in the Scirocco hatchback coupe, named for a North African wind. "German sportscar, Italian style" was the slogan. Like the Rabbit and Dasher, this one was front-wheel drive. After one year with a 1471-cc engine, the Scirocco adopted a larger (1588-cc) four. Styling features included quad road headlamps and a short tail. Standard equipment by 1977 included tinted glass, styled wheels, a clock, reclining bucket seats, and a rear defogger.

BEETLE — FLAT FOUR — Electronic fuel injection became standard in Beetles for 1975. Sporty wheels went on the Beetle for 1976, in what would be its final year in the U.S. market, in sedan form. A rear-window defogger was installed.

TRANSPORTER — FLAT FOUR — Electronic fuel injection was now standard in the boxy station wagon's rear engine. A 1970-cc engine went into Transporters for 1976, developing 67 horsepower, to replace the former 1795-cc powerplant. Starting in 1976, Transporters had an exposed fuel filler cap.

I.D. DATA: Volkswagen's 10-symbol serial number is on the upper left of the dashboard, visible through the windshield. The first two digits indicate the model; the next digit identifies the model year; and the final seven digits form the sequential production number.

Model	Body Type & Seating	Engine Type/CID	P.O.E. Price	Weight (lbs.)	Prod. Total
DASHER					
3241	2-dr Hatch-4/5P	I4/90	4510	1995	Note 1
3441	4-dr Hatch-4/5P	I4/90	4650	2050	Note 1
3643	4-dr Sta Wag-4/5P	I4/90	4875	2105	Note 1
RABBIT					
1701	2-dr Hatch-4/5P	I4/90	3330	1757	Note 1
1721 Cust	2-dr Hatch-4/5P	I4/90	3660	1797	Note 1
1741 Cust	4-dr Hatch-4/5P	I4/90	3800	1827	Note 1
1761 DeL	2-dr Hatch-4/5P	I4/90	3890	1817	Note 1
1781 DeL	4-dr Hatch-4/5P	I4/90	4030	1847	Note 1
SCIROCCO					
5311	2-dr Coupe-4P	I4/90	4949	1847	Note 1
BEETLE					
1101	2-dr Sedan-4P	H4/97	2999	1831	Note 1
1111	2-dr Sedan-4P	H4/97	3295	1831	Note 1
1511	2-dr Conv Sed-4P	H4/97	3595	1955	Note 1
TRANSPORTER (TYPE II)					
2301	3-dr Kombi	H4/110	4750	2825	Note 2
2211	3-dr Sta Wag-7P	H4/110	5100	2946	Note 2
2231	3-dr Sta Wag-9P	H4/110	5150	2946	Note 2
2391	3-dr Campmobile	H4/110	6174	2719	Note 2

Note 1: A total of 904,005 Volkswagen passenger cars (all models) were produced in 1975, rising to 1,061,940 in 1976 and 1,123,575 in 1977.

Note 2: A total of 29,082 Transporters were produced in 1975, rising to 31,390 in 1976 and 38,068 in 1977.

Price Note: Figures shown were valid in 1975. Only the basic Beetle was available after 1975, priced at $3499 in 1976 and $3699 in 1977. The Beetle convertible rose to $4545 in 1976 and $4799 in 1977. The Scirocco coupe rose to $4995 in 1976 and $5295 in 1977.

ENGINE DATA: BASE FOUR (1975 Dasher, Rabbit, Scirocco): Inline, overhead-cam four-cylinder (water cooled). **Displacement:** 89.7 cu. in. (1471 cc). **Bore & Stroke:** 3.01 x 3.15 in. (76.5 x 80 mm). **Compression Ratio:** 8.2:1. **Brake Horsepower:** 70 at 5800 rpm. **Torque:** 81 lbs.-ft. at 3500 rpm. Solid valve lifters. Two-barrel carburetor.

BASE FOUR (1976 Rabbit, Scirocco): Inline, overhead-cam four-cylinder (water cooled). Cast iron block and aluminum alloy head. **Displacement:** 97.0 cu. in. (1588 cc). **Bore & Stroke:** 3.13 x 3.15 in. (79.5 x 80 mm). **Compression Ratio:** 8.2:1. **Brake Horsepower:** 71 at 5600 rpm. **Torque:** 82 lbs.-ft. at 3300 rpm. Five main bearings. Solid valve lifters. Zenith two-barrel carburetor.

BASE FOUR (1976-77 Dasher, 1977 Rabbit/Scirocco): Same as 1588-cc four above, except with CIS fuel injection — **Brake Horsepower:** 78 at 5500 rpm.

Note: Starting in 1977, a 1471-cc diesel engine became available in Rabbits.

BASE FOUR (Beetle): Horizontally opposed, overhead-valve four-cylinder (air cooled). **Displacement:** 96.7 cu. in. (1585 cc). **Bore & Stroke:** 3.36 x 2.72 in. (85 x 69 mm). **Compression Ratio:** 7.3:1. **Brake Horsepower:** 48 at 4200 rpm. **Torque:** 73.1 lbs.-ft. at 2800 rpm. Four main bearings. Solid valve lifters. Electronic fuel injection.

BASE FOUR (1975 Transporter): Horizontally opposed, overhead-valve four-cylinder (air cooled). **Displacement:** 109.5 cu. in. (1795 cc). **Bore & Stroke:** 3.66 x 2.59 in. (93 x 66 mm). **Compression Ratio:** 7.3:1. **Brake Horsepower:** 67 at 4400 rpm. **Torque:** 90 lbs.-ft. at 2400 rpm. Four main bearings. Solid valve lifters. Electronic fuel injection.

BASE FOUR (1976-77 Transporter): Horizontally opposed, overhead-valve four-cylinder (air cooled). **Displacement:** 120.2 cu. in. (1970 cc). **Bore & Stroke:** 3.70 x 2.80 in. (94 x 71 mm). **Compression Ratio:** 7.3:1. **Brake Horsepower:** 67 at 4200 rpm. **Torque:** 101 lbs.-ft. at 3000 rpm. Four main bearings. Solid valve lifters. Electronic fuel injection.

1977 Volkswagen Beetle two-door sedan.

CHASSIS DATA: Wheelbase: 94.5 in. except (Dasher) 97.2 in. **Overall Length:** (Beetle) 163.4 in.; (Dasher) 172.8 in.; (Rabbit) 155.3 in.; (Scirocco) 155.7 in.; (wagon) 179.0 in. **Height:** (Beetle) 59.1 in.; (Dasher) 53.5 in.; (Rabbit) 55.5 in.; (Scirocco) 51.5 in.; (wagon) 77 in. **Width:** (Beetle) 61.0 in.; (Dasher) 63 in.; (Rabbit) 63.4 in.; (Scirocco) 64 in.; (wagon) 69.3 in. **Front Tread:** (Beetle) 51.5 in.; (Dasher) 52.7 in.; (Rabbit) 54.7 in.; (Scirocco) 54.7 in.; (wagon) 54.9 in. **Rear Tread:** (Beetle) 53.1 in.; (Dasher) 52.5 in.; (Rabbit) 53.1 in.; (Scirocco) 53.1 in.; (wagon) 57.3 in. **Standard Tires:** (Beetle) 5.60x15; (Dasher) 155SR13; (Rabbit) 145x13; (Scirocco) 175/70SR13; (wagon) 185R14C.

TECHNICAL: Layout: (Beetle/Transporter) rear-engine, rear-drive; (Dasher /Rabbit /Scirocco) front-engine, front-drive. **Transmission:** four-speed manual; automatic available. **Steering:** (Beetle/Transporter) worm and roller; (others) rack and pinion. **Suspension (front):** MacPherson struts with coil springs. **Suspension (rear):** (Beetle) semi-trailing arms with torsion bars; (Rabbit/Scirocco) independent stabilizer axle with struts and coil springs; (Dasher) torsion crank axle with Panhard rod and coil springs. **Brakes:** (Beetle) front/rear drum; (others) front disc, rear drum.

PERFORMANCE: Top Speed: (Dasher) 100 mph claimed; (Rabbit) 93 mph claimed; (Scirocco) 103 mph claimed (100 mph with automatic).

PRODUCTION/SALES: A total of 268,751 Volkswagens were sold in the U.S. during 1975, followed by 203,234 in 1976 and 262,932 in 1977 (including tourist deliveries). **Manufacturer:** Volkswagenwerk AG, Wolfsburg, West Germany. **Distributor:** Volkswagen of America Inc., Englewood Cliffs, New Jersey.

1978-79 VOLKSWAGEN

1978 Volkswagen Rabbit L two-door.

DASHER — FOUR — Quad round headlamps replaced the former single round units on VW's first front-drive model, initially introduced for 1974. Combined with a new grille and hoodline, that gave the car a fresh look, somewhat akin to the new Audi 5000. Large amber safety lights were installed at front fender tips, with wraparound taillamps at the rear, as well as polyurethane-coated bumpers. As before, the Dasher came as a two-door hatchback, four-door sedan, or four-door station wagon. Trim was upgraded at this time, and ride quality softened. Seats were upholstered in velour. A diesel engine became available in 1979 Dashers.

RABBIT — FOUR — A smaller (1457-cc) engine went into the Rabbit for 1978, and the radiator was enlarged. Otherwise, production continued with little change except for additional chrome. Starting in 1978, Rabbits also were produced in America. German-built Rabbits kept their round headlamps, while those that hailed from Pennsylvania switched to rectangular headlamps. A "Champagne Edition" introduced in mid-1978 included silver-green or rose metallic paint, with crushed velour upholstery. A five-speed manual gearbox became available by 1979. The diesel-engined Rabbit, rated 48 horsepower, earned an EPA rating of 53 mpg (highway) and 40 mpg (city), and was built only in Germany.

1978 Volkswagen Scirocco coupe.

SCIROCCO — FOUR — A smaller (1457-cc) engine was installed in 1978 Sciroccos, but the 1588-cc four returned by the 1979 model year. A new polyurethane-coated front bumper extended back to the front wheel openings, and new black metal moldings went around the side windows. The Scirocco grille was restyled, and a woodgrained instrument panel added. A Limited Edition Scirocco offered in 1978 included body striping and a spoiler. The 1979 model added a bright molding surrounding the grille. By then, either a four- or five-speed manual gearbox was available. A three-speed automatic also was optional, as before.

BEETLE — FLAT FOUR — Only the Beetle convertible remained in the U.S. market after 1977, following nearly three decades in which it had become one of the biggest phenomena in automotive history. *Car and Driver* declared that the top-down Beetle "can be one of the world's finest convertibles." Though "terribly slow...the flat-out driving style required to keep it moving compensates for a lot of flaws." With so "few weaknesses" remaining, they added, it should be regarded "as an institution rather than an automobile." Only a four-speed manual gearbox was available.

TRANSPORTER — FLAT FOUR — Production of the Microbus series continued without major change, powered by a 2.0-liter horizontally-opposed rear-mounted engine. EPA mileage ratings by 1978 were 18 mpg (city) and 25 mpg (highway) with manual shift, dropping to 16/22 with automatic.

I.D. DATA: Volkswagen's 10-symbol serial number is on the upper left of the dashboard, visible through the windshield. The first two digits indicate the model; the next digit identifies the model year; and the final seven digits form the sequential production number.

Model	Body Type & Seating	Engine Type/CID	P.O.E. Price	Weight (lbs.)	Prod. Total
DASHER					
3241	2-dr Hatch-4/5P	I4/97	5975	2085	Note 1
3441	4-dr Hatch-4/5P	I4/97	6075	2140	Note 1
3641	4-dr Sta Wag-4/5P	I4/97	6375	2181	Note 1
RABBIT					
1701	2-dr Hatch-4/5P	I4/89	4220	1777	Note 1
1721 Cust	2-dr Hatch-4/5P	I4/89	4699	1900	Note 1
1741 Cust	4-dr Hatch-4/5P	I4/89	4839	1955	Note 1
1761 DeL	2-dr Hatch-4/5P	I4/89	5060	1900	Note 1
1781 DeL	4-dr Hatch-4/5P	I4/89	5200	1955	Note 1
SCIROCCO					
5311	2-dr Coupe-4P	I4/89	6095	1888	Note 1
BEETLE (TYPE I)					
1511	2-dr Conv Sed-4P	H4/97	5695	2059	Note 1
TRANSPORTER (TYPE II)					
2321	3-dr Kombi	H4/120	6185	2831	Note 2
2211	3-dr Sta Wag-7P	H4/120	6445	2952	Note 2
2231	3-dr Sta Wag-9P	I4/120	6495	2952	Note 2
2391	3-dr Campmobile	H4/120	6145	2724	Note 2

Note 1: A total of 1,177,106 Volkswagen passenger cars (all models) were produced in 1978, followed by 1,156,455 in 1979.

Note 2: A total of 34,331 Transporters were produced in 1978, dropping to 22,384 in 1979.

Price Note: Figures shown were valid in 1978. Price of the Beetle convertible rose to $6800 in 1979, its final year on the U.S. market. The Scirocco coupe rose to $7090 in 1979.

ENGINE DATA: BASE FOUR (Rabbit, 1978 Scirocco): Inline, overhead-cam four-cylinder (water cooled). Cast iron block and aluminum alloy head. **Displacement:** 88.9 cu. in. (1457 cc). **Bore & Stroke:** 3.13 x 2.89 in. (79.5 x 73.4 mm). **Compression Ratio:** 8.0:1. **Brake Horsepower:** 71 at 5800 rpm. **Torque:** 73 lbs.-ft. at 3500 rpm. Five main bearings. Solid valve lifters. Fuel injection.

Note: A 1471-cc diesel engine, rated 48 horsepower at 5000 rpm, also was available in Rabbits. Gasoline-engine horsepower ratings were lower in California.

BASE FOUR (Dasher, 1979 Scirocco): Inline, overhead-cam four-cylinder (water cooled). Cast iron block and aluminum alloy head. **Displacement:** 97.0 cu. in. (1588 cc). **Bore & Stroke:** 3.13 x 3.15 in. (79.5 x 80 mm). **Compression Ratio:** 8.0:1. **Brake Horsepower:** 78 at 5500 rpm. **Torque:** 84 lbs.-ft. at 3200 rpm. Five main bearings. Solid valve lifters. CIS fuel injection.

BASE FOUR (Beetle): Horizontally opposed, overhead-valve four-cylinder (air cooled). **Displacement:** 96.7 cu. in. (1585 cc). **Bore & Stroke:** 3.36 x 2.72 in. (85 x 69 mm). **Compression Ratio:** 7.3:1. **Brake Horsepower:** 48 at 4200 rpm. **Torque:** 73.1 lbs.-ft. at 2800 rpm. Four main bearings. Solid valve lifters. Electronic fuel injection.

BASE FOUR (Transporter): Horizontally opposed, overhead-valve four-cylinder (air cooled). **Displacement:** 120.2 cu. in. (1970 cc). **Bore & Stroke:** 3.70 x 2.80 in. (94 x 71 mm). **Compression Ratio:** 7.3:1. **Brake Horsepower:** 67 at 4200 rpm. **Torque:** 101 lbs.-ft. at 3000 rpm. Four main bearings. Solid valve lifters. Electronic fuel injection.

CHASSIS DATA: Wheelbase: 94.5 in. except (Rabbit) 94.4 in.; (Dasher) 96.7 in.; (Dasher diesel) 97.2 in. **Overall Length:** (Beetle) 164.8 in.; (Dasher) 172.4 in.; (Rabbit) 155.3 in.; (Scirocco) 155.7 in.; (wagon) 179.0 in. **Height:** (Beetle) 59.1 in.; (Dasher) 53.5 in.; (Rabbit) 55.5 in.; (Scirocco) 51.5 in.; (wagon) 77 in. **Width:** (Beetle) 62.4 in.; (Dasher) 63.0 in.; (Rabbit) 63.4 in.; (Scirocco) 63.9 in.; (wagon) 69.3 in. **Front Tread:** (Beetle) 54.9 in.; (Dasher) 52.7 in.; (Rabbit) 54.7 in.; (Scirocco) 54.7 in.; (wagon) 54.9 in. **Rear Tread:** (Beetle) 54.7 in.; (Dasher) 52.5 in.; (Rabbit) 53.5 in.; (Scirocco) 53.5 in.; (wagon) 57.3 in. **Standard Tires:** (Beetle) 165SR15; (Dasher) 155SR13; (Rabbit) 145x13; (Rabbit dsl) 155SR13; (Scirocco) 175/70SR13; (wagon) 185R14C.

TECHNICAL: Layout: (Beetle/Transporter) rear-engine, rear-drive; (Dasher /Rabbit /Scirocco) front-engine, front-drive. **Transmission:** four-speed manual; three-speed automatic available on FWD models; five-speed manual available in 1979. **Suspension (front):** MacPherson struts with coil springs. **Suspension (rear):** (Beetle) semi-trailing arms with torsion bars; (Dasher) rigid axle with Panhard rod and coil springs; (Rabbit/Scirocco) independent with trailing arms and coil springs. **Brakes:** (Beetle) front/rear drum; (Dasher/Rabbit/Scirocco) front disc, rear drum.

PRODUCTION/SALES: A total of 219,414 Volkswagens were sold in the U.S. during 1978, followed by 129,779 in 1979 (including tourist deliveries but not including domestically-built Rabbits).

Manufacturer: Volkswagenwerk AG, Wolfsburg, West Germany.

Distributor: Volkswagen of America Inc., Englewood Cliffs, New Jersey.

HISTORY: Difficulty in meeting emissions standards contributed to the demise of the Beetle, as did certain safety problems.

1980-81 VOLKSWAGEN

1980 Volkswagen Rabbit LS four-door.

DASHER — FOUR — Little change was evident for 1980, and only diesel-engined Dashers were offered for the 1981 model year.

RABBIT — FOUR — With the Beetle-based convertible gone, Volkswagen needed a ragtop—and created one with the Rabbit cabriolet. This new convertible had a Targa-style roll bar, but was otherwise strictly an open car. A carbureted version of the Rabbit's 1457-cc engine replaced the fuel-injected edition as standard, but a larger (1588-cc) fuel-injected four was optional. So was the diesel engine. Rabbits enjoyed a facelift for 1981, including a new front end similar to that used in the Scirocco, with wraparound parking/marker lights and a thicker bumper. Inside was a new dashboard. Larger gasoline and diesel engines were installed for the 1981 model year.

JETTA — FOUR — Another front-drive Volkswagen debuted in 1980, powered by a 1588-cc fuel-injected four-cylinder engine and offered as a two-door or four-door sedan. Ranking as a more plush version of the Rabbit, the Jetta rode a similar-size wheelbase but measured a foot longer overall. Like the Rabbit, Jetta got a larger (1.7-liter) gasoline engines for 1981, as well as diesel option.

SCIROCCO — FOUR — Production of the sporty coupe continued with minimal change, with a 1588-cc engine under the hood. Europeans could get a turbo Scirocco, but that wasn't ready for America. A larger (1.7-liter) engine became standard in 1981.

VANAGON — FLAT FOUR — Though still rear-engined, the VW Microbus series was restyled for 1980: longer, wider, and cleaner look than its predecessor. Rather than Transporter, the new series adopted the Vanagon designation.

I.D. DATA: Volkswagen's 10-symbol serial number is on the upper left of the dashboard, visible through the windshield. The first two digits indicate the model; the next digit identifies the model year; and the final seven digits form the sequential production number. A 17-symbol Vehicle Identification Number went into use for 1981.

Model	Body Type & Seating	Engine Type/CID	P.O.E. Price	Weight (lbs.)	Prod. Total
DASHER					
3214	2-dr Hatch-4/5P	I4/97	7970	2085	Note 1
3234	4-dr Hatch-4/5P	I4/97	8190	2140	Note 1
3314	4-dr Sta Wag-4/5P	I4/97	8470	2181	Note 1
RABBIT					
1751	2-dr Hatch-4/5P	I4/89	5215	1750	Note 1
1752 Cust	2-dr Hatch-4/5P	I4/89	5695	1781	Note 1
1772 Cust	4-dr Hatch-4/5P	I4/89	5890	1845	Note 1
1753 DeL	2-dr Hatch-4/5P	I4/89	6095	1821	Note 1
1773 DeL	4-dr Hatch-4/5P	I4/89	6290	1844	Note 1
1555	2-dr Conv-4P	I4/97	9340	2126	Note 1
JETTA					
1614	2-dr Sedan-5P	I4/97	7650	1946	Note 1
1634	4-dr Sedan-5P	I4/97	7870	2001	Note 1
SCIROCCO					
5315	2-dr Coupe-4P	I4/97	8130	1888	Note 1
5315	2-dr S Cpe-4P	I4/97	8860	1933	Note 1

638

Model	Body Type & Seating	Engine Type/CID	P.O.E. Price	Weight (lbs.)	Prod. Total
VANAGON (TRANSPORTER TYPE II)					
2535	3-dr Kombi	H4/120	9540	2976	Note 2
2554	3-dr Sta Wag-7P	H4/120	9900	3075	Note 2
2555	3-dr Sta Wag-9P	H4/120	9950	3075	Note 2
2539	3-dr Campmobile	H4/120	9540	3427	Note 2

Note 1: A total of 1,064,534 Volkswagen passenger cars (all models) were produced in 1980, followed by 981,471 in 1981.

Note 2: A total of 28,673 Vanagons were produced in 1980, dropping to 25,083 in 1981.

Price Note: Figures shown were valid in 1980.

ENGINE DATA: BASE FOUR (1980 Rabbit): Inline, overhead-cam four-cylinder (water cooled). Cast iron block and aluminum alloy head. **Displacement:** 88.9 cu. in. (1457 cc). **Bore & Stroke:** 3.13 x 2.89 in. (79.5 x 73.4 mm). **Compression Ratio:** 8.0:1. **Brake Horsepower:** 62 at 5400 rpm. **Torque:** 76.6 lbs.-ft. at 3000 rpm. Five main bearings. Solid valve lifters. One single-barrel carburetor.

BASE FOUR (1980 Dasher, Rabbit conv, Jetta, Scirocco); OPTIONAL (Rabbit): Inline, overhead-valve four-cylinder (water cooled). Cast iron block and aluminum alloy head. **Displacement:** 97.0 cu. in. (1588 cc). **Bore & Stroke:** 3.13 x 3.15 in. (79.5 x 80 mm). **Compression Ratio:** 8.2:1. **Brake Horsepower:** 76 at 5500 rpm. **Torque:** 82.7 lbs.-ft. at 3200 rpm. Five main bearings. Solid valve lifters. Fuel injection.

BASE FOUR (1981 Rabbit, Jetta, Scirocco): Inline, overhead-cam four-cylinder (water cooled). Cast iron block and aluminum alloy head. **Displacement:** 105 cu. in. (1715 cc). **Bore & Stroke:** 3.13 x 3.40 in. (79.5 x 86.4 mm). **Compression Ratio:** 8.2:1. **Brake Horsepower:** 74 at 5000 rpm. **Torque:** 89.6 lbs.-ft. at 3000 rpm. Five main bearings. Solid valve lifters. Fuel injection.

Note: A 1471-cc diesel engine, rated 48 horsepower at 5000 rpm, was available in 1980 Rabbits and Dashers (enlarged to 1588-cc for 1981).

BASE FOUR (Vanagon): Horizontally opposed, overhead-valve four-cylinder (air cooled). **Displacement:** 120.2 cu. in. (1970 cc). **Bore & Stroke:** 3.70 x 2.80 in. (94 x 71 mm). **Compression Ratio:** 7.3:1. **Brake Horsepower:** 67 at 4200 rpm. **Torque:** 101 lbs.-ft. at 3000 rpm. Four main bearings. Solid valve lifters. Electronic fuel injection.

CHASSIS DATA: Wheelbase: (Rabbit/Scirocco) 94.5 in.; (Jetta) 94.4 in.; (Dasher) 97.2 in.; (Vanagon) 96.8 in. **Overall Length:** (Dasher) 173.1 in.; (Rabbit) 155.3 in.; (Jetta) 167.8 in.; (Scirocco) 155.7 in.; (wagon) 179.0 in. **Height:** (Dasher) 53.5 in.; (Rabbit) 55.5 in.; (Rabbit conv) 55.6 in.; (Jetta) 55.5 in.; (Scirocco) 51.5 in.; (wagon) 77 in. **Width:** (Dasher) 63.6 in.; (Rabbit/Jetta) 63.4 in.; (Scirocco) 63.9 in.; (wagon) 69.3 in. **Front Tread:** (Dasher) 52.7 in.; (Rabbit/Jetta) 54.7 in.; (Scirocco) 54.7 in.; (wagon) 54.9 in. **Rear Tread:** (Dasher) 53.1 in.; (Rabbit/Jetta) 53.5 in.; (Scirocco) 53.5 in.; (wagon) 57.3 in. **Standard Tires:** (Dasher) 155SR13; (Rabbit) 155x13; (Rabbit conv) 175SR13; (Jetta) 175/70SR13; (Scirocco) 175/70SR13; (wagon) 185R14C.

TECHNICAL: Layout: front-engine, front-drive except (Vanagon) rear-engine, rear-drive. **Transmission:** four-speed or five-speed manual; three-speed automatic available. **Suspension (front):** MacPherson struts with coil springs. **Suspension (rear):** (Dasher) rigid axle with Panhard rod and coil springs; (Rabbit/Jetta/Scirocco) independent with trailing arms and coil springs. **Brakes:** front disc, rear drum.

PRODUCTION/SALES: A total of 90,952 Volkswagens were sold in the U.S. during 1980, followed by 82,173 in 1981 (not including domestically-built Rabbits).

ADDITIONAL MODELS: Volkswagen also introduced a small front-drive pickup truck at this time, to take the place of the Transporter-based pickups and vans that had been offered all along.

Manufacturer: Volkswagenwerk AG, Wolfsburg, West Germany.

Distributor: Volkswagen of America Inc., Englewood Cliffs, New Jersey.

1982 VOLKSWAGEN

1982 Volkswagen Jetta two-door sedan.

RABBIT — FOUR — Production of the front-drive Rabbit (and Rabbit-based convertible) continued with little change, powered by the 105-cid engine introduced in 1981. Standard Rabbit equipment included a four- or five-speed manual gearbox (automatic available), power brakes, bright body moldings, reclining front seats, tinted glass, and clock. LS added opening front vent windows, dual remote mirrors, full wheel covers, intermittent wipers, woodgrain instrument panel applique, and lighter. The Rabbit convertible included a floor console, integral roll bar, passenger vanity mirror, lockable gas cap, dual-tone horn, digital clock, padded steering wheel, and carpeted lower door panels.

JETTA — FOUR — Production of the Jetta sedans, similar to Rabbit but more luxurious, continued with minimal change. Standard equipment included a five-speed manual gearbox (automatic optional), power brakes, electric rear defroster, dual remote mirrors, AM/FM stereo radio, intermittent wipers, tinted glass, floor console, padded steering wheel, and woodgrain instrument panel applique.

1982 Volkswagen Quantum coupe.

QUANTUM — FOUR — Volkswagen's replacement for the Dasher rode a 100.4-inch wheelbase and was powered by a 1715-cc (105-cid) engine. Three body styles were offered: fastback (hatchback) coupe, four-door sedan, and four-door station wagon. Standard equipment included a five-speed manual gearbox (three-speed automatic optional), electric rear-window defroster, quartz clock, reclining front bucket seats, tinted glass, dual remote-control mirrors, and light alloy wheels. A GL option added cruise control, power door locks, electric remote mirrors, a lighted visor vanity mirror, and power windows.

SCIROCCO — FOUR — Mechanical details changed little, but the sporty Scirocco coupe wore an all-new, more rounded body created to reduce air drag. Wheelbase remained the same, but the car grew in overall length, which added space to the rear-seat area and luggage compartment. Expanded window area included a deeper back window, which curved downward to reach the hatchback door. A small under-the-bumper lip spoiler was installed up front. Standard equipment included power brakes, electric rear defroster, tinted glass, remote driver's mirror, AM/FM stereo radio with cassette player, reclining front bucket seats with height adjuster, front/rear spoilers, and a four-spoke sport steering wheel. A GL option package included power windows, power remote mirrors, and a power antenna.

VANAGON — FLAT FOUR — Production of the Microbus descendants continued without major change.

I.D. DATA: Volkswagen's 17-digit Vehicle Identification Number is on the upper left of the dashboard, visible through the windshield. Symbols 1-3 indicate country, make and vehicle type ('WVW' = Volkswagen in Germany). Symbol four identifies the body style, five the engine, six the restraint system. Symbols 7-8 identify the model ('15' = Rabbit conv.; '17' = Rabbit; '16' = Jetta; '53' = Scirocco; '32' = Quantum; '33' = Quantum wagon). Next is a check digit. Symbol 10 denotes the model year ('C' = 1982); symbol 11, the assembly plant. The six final digits form the sequential serial number, starting with 000001.

Model	Body Type & Seating	Engine Type/CID	P.O.E. Price	Weight (lbs.)	Prod. Total
RABBIT					
	2-dr Hatch-4/5P	I4/105	5990	1805	Note 1
L	2-dr Hatch-4/5P	I4/105	6615	1858	Note 1
L	4-dr Hatch-4/5P	I4/105	6825	1915	Note 1
LS	2-dr Hatch-4/5P	I4/105	7065	1920	Note 1
LS	4-dr Hatch-4/5P	I4/105	7275	1964	Note 1
S	2-dr Hatch-4/5P	I4/105	7305	1920	Note 1
15	2-dr Conv-4P	I4/105	10595	2126	Note 1
JETTA					
	2-dr Sedan-5P	I4/105	8375	1946	Note 1
	4-dr Sedan-5P	I4/105	8595	2001	Note 1
QUANTUM					
	2-dr Coupe-5P	I4/105	10770	2389	Note 1
	4-dr Sedan-5P	I4/105	11070	2140	Note 1
	4-dr Sta Wag-5P	I4/105	11470	2455	Note 1
SCIROCCO					
	2-dr Coupe-4P	I4/105	10150	1933	Note 1
VANAGON					
L	3-dr Sta Wagon	H4/120	10860	3075	Note 2
	3-dr Campmobile	H4/120	14900	3475	Note 2

Note 1: A total of 974,140 Volkswagen passenger cars (all models) were produced in 1982.

Note 2: A total of 24,203 Vanagons were produced in 1982.

ENGINE DATA: BASE FOUR (Rabbit, Jetta, Scirocco, Quantum): Inline, overhead-cam four-cylinder (water cooled). Cast iron block and aluminum alloy head. **Displacement:** 105 cu. in. (1715 cc). **Bore & Stroke:** 3.13 x 3.40 in. (79.5 x 86.4 mm). **Compression Ratio:** 8.2:1. **Brake Horsepower:** 74 at 5000 rpm. **Torque:** 89.6 lbs.-ft. at 3000 rpm. Five main bearings. Solid valve lifters. Fuel injection.

Note: A 1.6-liter diesel engine, rated 52 horsepower at 4800 rpm (72 lbs.-ft. at 3000 rpm), was available in Rabbits and Jettas.

BASE FOUR (Vanagon): Horizontally opposed, overhead-valve four-cylinder (air cooled). **Displacement:** 120.2 cu. in. (1970 cc). **Bore & Stroke:** 3.70 x 2.80 in. (94 x 71 mm). **Compression Ratio:** 7.3:1. **Brake Horsepower:** 67 at 4200 rpm. **Torque:** 101 lbs.-ft. at 3000 rpm. Four main bearings. Solid valve lifters. Electronic fuel injection.

CHASSIS DATA: Wheelbase: (Rabbit/Jetta/Scirocco) 94.5 in.; (Quantum) 100.4 in.; (Vanagon) 96.9 in. **Overall Length:** (Rabbit) 155.3 in.; (Jetta) 167.8 in.; (Quantum cpe) 178.2 in.; (Quantum sed) 180.2 in.; (Quantum wag) 183.1 in.; (Scirocco) 165.7 in.; (Vanagon) 179.9 in. **Height:** (Rabbit/Jetta) 55.5 in.; (Quantum) 55.1 in.; (Scirocco) 51.4 in.; (Vanagon) 77.2 in. **Width:** (Rabbit/Jetta) 63.4 in.; (Quantum) 66.9 in.; (Scirocco) 64.0 in.; (Vanagon) 72.6 in. **Front Tread:** (Rabbit/Jetta/Scirocco) 54.7 in.; (Quantum) 55.7 in.; (Vanagon) 61.8 in. **Rear Tread:** (Rabbit/Jetta) 53.1 in.; (Quantum) 56.0 in.; (Scirocco) 53.5 in.; (Vanagon) 61.8 in.

TECHNICAL: Layout: front-engine, front-drive except (Vanagon) rear-engine, rear-drive. **Transmission:** four-speed or five-speed manual; three-speed automatic available. **Steering:** rack and pinion. **Suspension (rear):** (Rabbit) beam axle with coil springs; (Jetta) beam axle with coil springs and anti-roll bar; (Quantum) beam twist axle with anti-roll function and coil springs; (Scirocco) beam axle with anti-roll function, trailing arms, coil springs and anti-roll bar. **Brakes:** front disc, rear drum.

MAJOR OPTIONS: Air conditioning. Electric rear defroster (Rabbit). Leatherette upholstery (Rabbit L/LS, Quantum wagon). AM/FM radio (Rabbit). AM/FM stereo (Rabbit). AM/FM stereo w/cassette player (Rabbit/Jetta/Quantum). Metallic paint. Sunroof (Scirocco). Electric sunroof (Quantum). Alloy wheels (Quantum). Rear wiper/washer (Scirocco).

PRODUCTION/SALES: A total of 67,350 imported Volkswagens were sold in the U.S. during 1982.

Manufacturer: Volkswagenwerk AG, Wolfsburg, West Germany; and Volkswagen of America Inc. (plant in Pennsylvania).

Distributor: Volkswagen of America Inc.

HISTORY: Rabbit sales fell by almost 50 percent in the 1982 model year.

1983 VOLKSWAGEN

1983 Volkswagen Rabbit GTI.

RABBIT — FOUR — A new sporty GTI two-door hatchback carried an enlarged (1.8-liter) version of the fuel-injected 1.7-liter four, which was now standard in the Rabbit LS/GL. Standard GTI equipment included a close-ratio five-speed manual gearbox, wider wheels/tires, black body trim, flared wheel wells, sport steering and front seats, special instruments, and a tuned exhaust system. A carbureted version of the 1.7-liter four powered the Rabbit L. Rabbits could also have a 1.6-liter diesel four, or a new turbocharged diesel. Standard equipment was similar to 1982.

JETTA — FOUR — Two- and four-door notchback sedans came with the same 1.7-liter (105-cid) fuel-injected engine as the upper Rabbit models. Diesel and turbodiesel engines were available. Standard equipment was similar to 1982.

QUANTUM — FOUR — Little change was evident in the fastback coupe, sedan and wagon, except for an additional engine choice: a turbodiesel four. Base engine remained the 1.7-liter four with fuel injection, hooked to a five-speed manual gearbox. Three-speed automatic was optional. Turbodiesel models could have an "E-Mode" transmission with special economy position, which employed a form of freewheeling (disconnecting the engine whenever the gas pedal was released). An Audi five-cylinder engine became available at mid-year; see next listing for details.

SCIROCCO — FOUR — VW's sporty coupe continued with no significant change, riding a Rabbit/Jetta chassis and powered by the 1.7-liter fuel-injected four. Standard equipment was similar to 1982. Scirocco bodies were built by Karmann.

I.D. DATA: Volkswagen's 17-digit Vehicle Identification Number is on the upper left of the dashboard, visible through the windshield. Symbols 1-3 indicate country, make and vehicle type ('WVW' = Volkswagen in Germany). Symbol four identifies the body style, six the restraint system. Symbols 7-8 identify the model ('15' = Rabbit conv.; '17' = Rabbit; '16' = Jetta; '53' = Scirocco; '32' = Quantum; '33' = Quantum wagon). Next is a check digit. Symbol 10 denotes the model year ('D' = 1983); symbol 11, the assembly plant. The six final digits form the sequential serial number, starting with 000001.

Model	Body Type & Seating	Engine Type/CID	P.O.E. Price	Weight (lbs.)	Prod. Total
RABBIT					
L	2-dr Hatch-4P	I4/105	6415	1845	Note 1
L	4-dr Hatch-4P	I4/105	6625	1880	Note 1
LS	2-dr Hatch-4P	I4/105	6890	1850	Note 1
LS	4-dr Hatch-4P	I4/105	7100	1885	Note 1
GL	2-dr Hatch-4P	I4/105	7490	1966	Note 1
GL	4-dr Hatch-4P	I4/105	7700	2010	Note 1
GTI	2-dr Hatch-4P	I4/109	7990	1918	Note 1
	2-dr Conv-4P	I4/105	10595	2101	Note 1
JETTA					
	2-dr Sedan-4P	I4/105	7990	2072	Note 1
	4-dr Sedan-4P	I4/105	8210	2127	Note 1
QUANTUM					
	2-dr Coupe-5P	I4/105	10770	2389	Note 1
	4-dr Sedan-5P	I4/105	11280	2140	Note 1
	5-dr Wagon-4P	I4/105	11680	2455	Note 1
SCIROCCO					
	2-dr Coupe-4P	I4/105	10150	2079	Note 1

Note 1: A total of 77,009 imported Volkswagens were sold in the U.S. during 1983.

Engine Note: Diesel engines were available in Rabbit/Jetta models.

ENGINE DATA: BASE FOUR (Rabbit L): Inline, overhead-cam four-cylinder. Cast iron block and light alloy head. **Displacement:** 105 cu. in. (1715 cc). **Bore & Stroke:** 3.13 x 3.40 (79.5 x 86.4 mm). **Compression Ratio:** 8.0:1. **Brake Horsepower:** 65 at 5000 rpm. **Torque:** 88 lbs.-ft. at 2800 rpm. Five main bearings. Two-barrel carburetor.

BASE FOUR (Rabbit LS/GL, Jetta, Quantum, Scirocco): Same as above, but with fuel injection — **Brake Horsepower:** 74 at 5000 rpm. **Torque:** 90 lbs.-ft. at 3000 rpm.

BASE FOUR (Rabbit GTI, late Scirocco): Inline, overhead-cam four-cylinder. Cast iron block and light alloy head. **Displacement:** 109 cu. in. (1786 cc). **Bore & Stroke:** 3.19 x 3.40 (81 x 86.4 mm). **Compression Ratio:** 8.5:1. **Brake Horsepower:** 90 at 5500 rpm. **Torque:** 100 lbs.-ft. at 3000 rpm. Five main bearings. Fuel injection.

DIESEL FOUR (Rabbit, Jetta): Inline, overhead-cam four-cylinder. Cast iron block and light alloy head. **Displacement:** 97 cu. in. (1588 cc). **Bore & Stroke:** 3.01 x 3.40 (76.5 x 86.4 mm). **Compression Ratio:** 23.0:1. **Brake Horsepower:** 52 at 4800 rpm. **Torque:** 72 lbs.-ft. at 2000 rpm. Five main bearings. Fuel injection.

TURBODIESEL FOUR (Rabbit, Jetta, Quantum): Same as diesel above, but turbocharged — **Brake Horsepower:** 68 at 4500 rpm. **Torque:** 98 lbs.-ft. at 2800 rpm.

1983 Volkswagen five-cylinder Quantum GL5.

CHASSIS DATA: Wheelbase: (Rabbit/Jetta/Scirocco) 94.5 in.; (Quantum) 100.4 in. **Overall Length:** (Rabbit) 155.3 in.; (Jetta) 167.8 in.; (Quantum cpe) 178.2 in.; (Quantum sed) 180.2 in.; (Quantum wag) 183.1 in.; (Scirocco) 165.7 in. **Height:** (Rabbit/Jetta) 55.5 in.; (Quantum) 55.1 in.; (Scirocco) 51.4 in. **Width:** (Rabbit/Jetta) 63.4 in.; (Quantum) 66.9 in.; (Scirocco) 64.0 in. **Front Tread:** (Rabbit/Jetta/Scirocco) 54.7 in.; (Quantum) 55.7 in. **Rear Tread:** (Rabbit/Jetta) 53.1 in.; (Quantum) 56.0 in.; (Scirocco) 53.5 in.

TECHNICAL: Layout: front-engine, front-drive. **Transmission:** (Rabbit) four- or five-speed manual; (others) five-speed manual. Three-speed automatic available. **Steering:** rack and pinion. **Suspension (front):** (Rabbit/Jetta/Scirocco) MacPherson struts with lower control arms and coil springs; (Quantum) MacPherson struts with lower control arms, coil springs and anti-roll bar. **Suspension (rear):** (Rabbit) beam axle with coil springs; (Jetta) beam axle with coil springs and anti-roll bar; (Quantum) beam twist axle with anti-roll function and coil springs; (Scirocco) beam axle with anti-roll function, trailing arms, coil springs and anti-roll bar. **Brakes:** front disc, rear drum. **Body Construction:** steel unibody. Fuel Tank: (Rabbit) 10.0 gal.; (Jetta/Scirocco) 10.6 gal.; (Quantum) 15.8 gal.

MAJOR OPTIONS: Similar to 1982.

ADDITIONAL MODELS: Volkswagen also continued to produce the Vanagon station wagon and Campmobile, as well as a line of pickup trucks (including a Sportruck). A water-cooled engine became standard during the 1983 model year; see next listing for details.

Manufacturer: Volkswagenwerk AG, Wolfsburg, West Germany; and Volkswagen of America Inc. (plant in Pennsylvania).

Distributor: Volkswagen of America Inc., Troy, Michigan.

HISTORY: Volkswagen's 1983 models were introduced in the U.S. in October 1982. Rabbits were made in the U.S., Jettas and other models in Germany.

1984 VOLKSWAGEN

RABBIT — FOUR — Apart from a reshuffling of the model lineup, little was new in the Rabbit line. The LS series was dropped. Rabbit GLs used the carbureted 1.7-liter engine, while the convertible carried the 1.8-liter engine as in the high-performance GTI hatchback.

JETTA — FOUR — Not much was new in the Jetta sedans. Base models could have a standard 1.6-liter diesel engine, while the GL came with a standard 1.7-liter gas engine. A turbodiesel also was available. A high-performance GLI used the same engine as the Rabbit GTI.

QUANTUM — FIVE — Only a four-door sedan and a station wagon were available in the Quantum series, with five-cylinder Audi engine and five-speed gearbox. A 1.6-liter turbodiesel and three-speed automatic were optional.

SCIROCCO — FOUR — A 1.8-liter engine had become standard in Sciroccos during the 1983 model year, along with a close-ratio five-speed gearbox.

I.D. DATA: Volkswagen's 17-digit Vehicle Identification Number is on the upper left of the dashboard, visible through the windshield. Symbols 1-3 indicate country, make and vehicle type ('WVW' = Volkswagen in Germany). Symbol four identifies the body style, five the engine, six the restraint system. Symbols 7-8 identify the model ('15' = Rabbit conv; '17' = Rabbit; '16' = Jetta; '53' = Scirocco; '32' = Quantum sed; '33' = Quantum wagon). Next is a check digit. Symbol 10 denotes the model year ('E' = 1984); symbol 11, the assembly plant. The six final digits form the sequential serial number, starting with 000001.

Model	Body Type & Seating	Engine Type/CID	P.O.E. Price	Weight (lbs.)	Prod. Total
RABBIT					
L	2-dr Hatch-4P	I4/105	6530	1834	Note 1
L	4-dr Hatch-4P	I4/105	6740	1878	Note 1
GL	4-dr Hatch-4P	I4/105	7130	1945	Note 1
GTI	2-dr Hatch-4P	I4/109	8350	1950	Note 1
	2-dr Conv-4P	I4/109	10980	2145	Note 1

Model	Body Type & Seating	Engine Type/CID	P.O.E. Price	Weight (lbs.)	Prod. Total
JETTA					
	2-dr Sedan-4P	I4/105	7630	1998	Note 1
	4-dr Sedan-4P	I4/105	7850	2048	Note 1
GL	4-dr Sedan-4P	I4/105	8210	2053	Note 1
GLI	4-dr Sedan-4P	I4/109	8690	2064	Note 1
QUANTUM					
GL	4-dr Sedan-5P	I5/131	12980	2516	Note 1
GL	5-dr Wagon-4P	I5/131	13780	2604	Note 1
SCIROCCO					
	2-dr Coupe-4P	I4/109	10870	2070	Note 1

Note 1: A total of 103,479 imported Volkswagens were sold in the U.S. during 1984.

Engine Note: Diesel engines were available in Rabbit/Jetta models; Turbodiesel in Rabbit, Jetta and Quantum.

ENGINE DATA: BASE FOUR (Rabbit L): Inline, overhead-cam four-cylinder. Cast iron block and light alloy head. **Displacement:** 105 cu. in. (1715 cc). **Bore & Stroke:** 3.13 x 3.40 (79.5 x 86.4 mm). **Compression Ratio:** 8.2:1. **Brake Horsepower:** 65 at 5000 rpm. **Torque:** 88 lbs.-ft. at 2800 rpm. Five main bearings. Two-barrel carburetor.

BASE FOUR (Rabbit GL, Jetta): Same as above, but with fuel injection — **Brake Horsepower:** 74 at 5000 rpm. **Torque:** 90 lbs.-ft. at 3000 rpm.

BASE FOUR (Rabbit GTI, convertible, Jetta GLI, Scirocco): Inline, overhead-cam four-cylinder. Cast iron block and light alloy head. **Displacement:** 109 cu. in. (1786 cc). **Bore & Stroke:** 3.19 x 3.40 (81 x 86.4 mm). **Compression Ratio:** 8.5:1. **Brake Horsepower:** 90 at 5500 rpm. **Torque:** 100 lbs.-ft. at 3000 rpm. Five main bearings. Multi-point fuel injection.

DIESEL FOUR (Rabbit, Jetta): Inline, overhead-cam four-cylinder. Cast iron block and light alloy head. **Displacement:** 97 cu. in. (1588 cc). **Bore & Stroke:** 3.01 x 3.40 (76.5 x 86.4 mm). **Compression Ratio:** 23.0:1. **Brake Horsepower:** 52 at 4800 rpm. **Torque:** 72 lbs.-ft. at 2000 rpm. Five main bearings. Fuel injection.

TURBODIESEL FOUR (Rabbit, Jetta, Quantum): Same as diesel above, but turbocharged — **Brake Horsepower:** 68 at 4500 rpm. **Torque:** 98 lbs.-ft. at 2800 rpm.

BASE FIVE (Quantum): Inline, overhead-cam five-cylinder. Cast iron block and light alloy head. **Displacement:** 131 cu. in. (2144 cc). **Bore & Stroke:** 3.13 x 3.40 (79.5 x 86.4 mm). **Compression Ratio:** 8.2:1. **Brake Horsepower:** 100 at 5100 rpm. **Torque:** 112 lbs.-ft. at 3000 rpm. Six main bearings. Multi-point fuel injection.

CHASSIS DATA: Wheelbase: (Rabbit/Jetta/Scirocco) 94.5 in.; (Quantum) 100.4 in. **Overall Length:** (Rabbit) 155.3 in.; (Rabbit conv) 159.3 in.; (Jetta) 167.8 in.; (Quantum sed) 180.2 in.; (Quantum wag) 183.1 in.; (Scirocco) 165.7 in. **Height:** (Rabbit/Jetta) 55.5 in.; (Rabbit conv) 55.6 in.; (Quantum) 55.1 in.; (Scirocco) 51.4 in. **Width:** (Rabbit/Jetta) 63.4 in.; (Rabbit conv) 64.2 in.; (Quantum) 66.9 in.; (Scirocco) 64.0 in. **Front Tread:** (Rabbit/Jetta/Scirocco) 54.7 in.; (Quantum) 55.7 in. **Rear Tread:** (Rabbit/Jetta) 53.1 in.; (Quantum) 56.0 in.; (Scirocco) 53.5 in.

TECHNICAL: Layout: front-engine, front-drive. **Transmission:** (Rabbit) four- or five-speed manual; (others) five-speed manual. Three-speed automatic available. **Steering:** rack and pinion. **Suspension (front):** (Rabbit/Jetta) MacPherson struts with lower control arms and coil springs; (Rabbit GTI/Jetta GLI/conv, Quantum, Scirocco) MacPherson struts with lower control arms, coil springs and anti-roll bar. **Suspension (rear):** (Rabbit/Jetta/Scirocco) beam axle with coil springs and anti-roll bar; (Quantum) beam axle with trailing arms and coil springs, anti-roll bar on wagon. **Brakes:** front disc, rear drum. **Body Construction:** steel unibody. **Fuel Tank:** (Rabbit) 10.0 gal.; (Jetta/Scirocco) 10.6 gal.; (Quantum) 15.8 gal.

MAJOR OPTIONS: RABBIT OPTIONS: Air cond. ($650) exc. conv ($700). Cruise control ($180) exc. conv ($200). Power steering ($220) exc. conv ($265). Sliding sunroof ($300). Rear wiper/washer ($130). Leatherette upholstery ($80). AM/FM radio ($165). AM/FM stereo ($260). AM/FM stereo w/cassette ($365). Electronic-tuning AM/FM stereo w/cassette ($575). Sport seats: conv ($220). Metallic paint ($140). Alloy wheels ($220) exc. conv ($280).

JETTA OPTIONS: Air cond. ($700). Power steering ($265). AM/FM stereo w/cassette ($565). Sport pkg.: 2-dr ($290). Sliding sunroof ($315). Cruise control ($200). Leatherette interior ($80).

QUANTUM OPTIONS: Leatherette interior: wag ($80). Electric sunroof ($575). Alloy wheels ($340). Metallic paint ($140).

SCIROCCO OPTIONS: Air cond. ($700). Power steering ($265). Slide/tilt sunroof ($445). Cruise control ($200). Leather interior trim ($695). Power windows/antenna ($490).

Manufacturer: Volkswagenwerk AG, Wolfsburg, West Germany; and Volkswagen of America Inc. (plant in Pennsylvania).

Distributor: Volkswagen of America Inc., Troy, Michigan.

ADDITIONAL MODELS: Volkswagen also continued to produce the Vanagon station wagon and Camper bus. A new water-cooled horizontally-opposed 1.9-liter (117-cid) engine was installed in mid-1983, replacing the familiar air-cooled flat four. The engine had multi-point fuel injection and developed 82 horsepower at 4800 rpm, with 105 pound-feet of torque at 2600 rpm, using 8.6:1 compression. Vanagons came in three price levels: L, GL, and Camper (with pop-up top). Installation of the water-cooled engine allowed Volkswagen to add a second heater under the back seat. Either a four-speed manual gearbox or three-speed automatic was available.

HISTORY: Volkswagen's 1984 models were introduced in the U.S. in October 1983. Rabbits were made in the U.S., Jettas and other models in Germany.

1985-86 VOLKSWAGEN

CABRIOLET — FOUR — Only the convertible remained of Volkswagen's initial Rabbit design, now called Cabriolet. A 1.8-liter engine provided the propulsion, rated at 90 horsepower.

GOLF/JETTA — FOUR — Restyling of the Rabbit resulted in the new Golf series (a name formerly used elsewhere in the world) and a revised Jetta. Larger dimensions caused the EPA to reclassify them as compacts, rather than subcompacts, and they ranked as full five-passenger vehicles. Wheelbase was almost three inches longer than before, and tread dimensions were wider. The front suspension was revised, and a new torsion beam axle was similar to the one used in the Quantum. The Golf came in two- and four-door hatchback form, while Jettas remained notchback sedans. Under the hood was a modified version of the 1.8-liter engine, developing 85 horsepower.

QUANTUM — FOUR/FIVE — Audi's 2.1-liter five-cylinder engine no longer was available, but a 2.2-liter version became standard on the sedan. Wagons used a 1.8-liter four. Otherwise, production continued with little change. For 1986, the wagon was dropped, leaving only the GL sedan with its Audi five-cylinder engine.

SCIROCCO — FOUR — Little was new for VW's sporty coupe except for the addition of black bumpers and a larger rear spoiler, the latter included with the Wolfsburg Limited Edition model.

1985 Volkswagen 50th anniversary Beetle.

I.D. DATA: Volkswagen's 17-digit Vehicle Identification Number is on the upper left of the dashboard, visible through the windshield. Symbols 1-3 indicate country, make and vehicle type ('WVW' = Volkswagen in Germany). Symbol four identifies the body style, five the engine, six the restraint system. Symbols 7-8 identify the model ('15' = Cabriolet; '16' = Jetta; '17' = Golf; '53' = Scirocco; '32' = Quantum sed; '33' = Quantum wagon). Next is a check digit. Symbol 10 denotes the model year ('F' = 1985; 'G' = 1986); symbol 11, the assembly plant. The six final digits form the sequential serial number, starting with 000001.

Model	Body Type & Seating	Engine Type/CID	P.O.E. Price	Weight (lbs.)	Prod. Total
CABRIOLET					
	2-dr Conv-4P	I4/109	11595	2254	Note 1
GOLF					
	2-dr Hatch-5P	I4/109	6990	2150	Note 1
	4-dr Hatch-5P	I4/109	7200	2150	Note 1
GTI	2-dr Hatch-5P	I4/109	8990	2196	Note 1
JETTA					
	2-dr Sedan-5P	I4/109	7975	2275	Note 1
	4-dr Sedan-5P	I4/109	8195	2252	Note 1
GL	4-dr Sedan-5P	I4/109	8495	2252	Note 1
GLI	4-dr Sedan-5P	I4/109	9995	2252	Note 1
QUANTUM					
GL	4-dr Sedan-5P	I5/136	13295	2661	Note 1
	5-dr Sta Wag-4P	I4/109	11570	2563	Note 1
SCIROCCO					
	2-dr Coupe-4P	I4/109	9980	2181	Note 1

Note 1: A total of 140,505 imported Volkswagens were sold in the U.S. during 1985, followed by 143,319 in 1986.

Price Note: Figures shown were valid in 1985.

1985 Volkswagen Jetta GLI.

ENGINE DATA: BASE FOUR (Cabriolet, Golf, Jetta, Quantum wagon, Scirocco): Inline, overhead-cam four-cylinder. Cast iron block and light alloy head. **Displacement:** 109 cu. in. (1786 cc). **Bore & Stroke:** 3.19 x 3.40 (81 x 86.4 mm). **Compression Ratio:** 8.5:1 (Quantum, 9.0:1). **Brake Horsepower:** (Golf/Jetta) 85 at 5250 rpm; (Quantum) 88 at 5500 rpm; (Cabriolet/Scirocco) 90 at 5550 rpm. **Torque:** (Golf/Jetta) 98 lbs.-ft. at 3000 rpm; (Quantum) 96 at 3250 rpm; (Cabriolet/Scirocco) 100 at 3000 rpm. Five main bearings. Multi-point fuel injection.
DIESEL FOUR (Golf, Jetta): Inline, overhead-cam four-cylinder. Cast iron block and light alloy head. **Displacement:** 97 cu. in. (1588 cc). **Bore & Stroke:** 3.01 x 3.40 (76.5 x 86.4 mm). **Compression Ratio:** 23.0:1. **Brake Horsepower:** 52 at 4800 rpm. **Torque:** 71 lbs.-ft. at 2000 rpm. Five main bearings. Fuel injection.
TURBODIESEL FOUR (Golf, Jetta GL, Quantum): Same as diesel above, but turbocharged — **Brake Horsepower:** 68 at 4500 rpm. **Torque:** 98 lbs.-ft. at 2500 rpm.
BASE FIVE (Quantum sedan): Inline, overhead-cam five-cylinder. Cast iron block and light alloy head. **Displacement:** 136 cu. in. (2229 cc). **Bore & Stroke:** 3.19 x 3.40 (81 x 86.4 mm). **Compression Ratio:** 8.5:1. **Brake Horsepower:** 110 at 5500 rpm. **Torque:** 126 lbs.-ft. at 3000 rpm. Six main bearings. Multi-point fuel injection.

CHASSIS DATA: Wheelbase: (Golf/Jetta) 97.3 in.; (Cabr/Scirocco) 94.5 in.; (Quantum) 100.4 in. **Overall Length:** (Golf) 158.0 in.; (Jetta) 171.7 in.; (Cabr) 159.3 in.; (Quantum sed) 180.2 in.; (Quantum wag) 183.1 in.; (Scirocco) 165.7 in. **Height:** (Golf/Jetta) 55.7 in.; (Cabr) 55.6 in.; (Quantum) 55.1 in.; (Scirocco) 51.4 in. **Width:** (Golf/Jetta) 65.5 in.; (Cabr) 64.2 in.; (Quantum) 66.9 in.; (Scirocco) 64.0 in. **Front Tread:** (Golf/Jetta) 56.3 in.; (Cabr) 54.7 in.; (Quantum) 55.7 in.; (Scirocco) 54.7 in. **Rear Tread:** (Golf/Jetta) 56.0 in.; (Cabr) 53.5 in.; (Quantum) 56.0 in.; (Scirocco) 53.5 in.

1986½ Volkswagen Wolfsburg Limited Edition Jetta.

TECHNICAL: Layout: front-engine, front-drive. **Transmission:** five-speed manual; three-speed automatic available. **Steering:** rack and pinion. **Suspension (front):** MacPherson struts with coil springs. **Suspension (rear):** (Golf/Jetta/Cabr/Quantum) torsion beam axle with trailing arms and coil springs; (Scirocco) torsion beam axle with coil springs. **Brakes:** front disc, rear drum. **Body Construction:** steel unibody.

ADDITIONAL MODELS: Volkswagen also continued to produce the Vanagon station wagon and Camper bus, with additional standard equipment for 1985. This equipment was similar to that included in the Wolfsburg Limited Edition option package, which became available during the 1984 model year. The GL could get a "Weekender" option with a rear bench seat that turned into a double bed. A 1.9-liter (117-cid) engine again provided the power. For 1986, Volkswagen introduced an automatic four-wheel-drive version of the Vanagon, called the Syncro, and engines grew to 2.1-liter displacement and 95 horsepower.

Manufacturer: Volkswagenwerk AG, Wolfsburg, West Germany; and Volkswagen of America Inc. (plant in Pennsylvania).

Distributor: Volkswagen of America Inc., Troy, Michigan.

1987-89 VOLKSWAGEN

1987 Volkswagen Golf GL hatchback sedan.

FOX — FOUR — Another front-drive Volkswagen emerged for 1987, built not in Germany or the U.S. but in Brazil. The subcompact came as a two-door sedan, four-door sedan, or two-door station wagon. Under the hood was VW's familiar 1.8-liter engine, developing 81 horsepower. Only a four-speed manual transmission was available in early models, but a five-speed arrived for 1989.

CABRIOLET — FOUR — Little change was evident in VW's convertible, based on the old Rabbit chassis.

GOLF/JETTA — FOUR — Production of the hatchback Golf and notchback Jetta continued with little change, except that the 16-valve engine from the Scirocco 16V became available in the GTI/GLI editions, developing 123 bhp. GT versions adopted the 102-bhp engine. Horsepowers rose in 1988. Anti-lock braking became optional for 1989 on top models.

QUANTUM — FIVE — A four-wheel-drive (Syncro) wagon debuted during the 1986 model year, and continued along with the 2WD sedan with little change. Both models used an Audi five-cylinder engine, and dropped out after the 1988 model year.

SCIROCCO — FOUR — A stronger engine was installed in the 16V edition of Volkswagen's sport coupe, rated 123 horsepower with a 16-valve configuration. Base Sciroccos retained the 90-bhp engine. The Scirocco remained available into 1988, but then was dropped.

I.D. DATA: Volkswagen's 17-digit Vehicle Identification Number is on the upper left of the dashboard, visible through the windshield. Breakdown is similar to 1985-86.

Model	Body Type & Seating	Engine Type/CID	P.O.E. Price	Weight (lbs.)	Prod. Total
FOX					
	2-dr Sedan-4P	I4/109	5690	2150	Note 1
GL	4-dr Sedan-4P	I4/109	6490	2190	Note 1
GL	2-dr Sta Wag-4P	I4/109	6590	2190	Note 1

Model	Body Type & Seating	Engine Type/CID	P.O.E. Price	Weight (lbs.)	Prod. Total
CABRIOLET					
	2-dr Conv-4P	I4/109	13250	2254	Note 1
GOLF					
GL	2-dr Hatch-5P	I4/109	8190	2137	Note 1
GL	4-dr Hatch-5P	I4/109	8400	N/A	Note 1
GT	2-dr Hatch-5P	I4/109	9675	2137	Note 1
GT	4-dr Hatch-5P	I4/109	9885	2310	Note 1
GTI	2-dr Hatch-5P	I4/109	10325	2203	Note 1
GTI/16V	2-dr Hatch-5P	I4/109	12240	N/A	Note 1
JETTA					
	2-dr Sedan-5P	I4/109	9290	2275	Note 1
	4-dr Sedan-5P	I4/109	9510	2330	Note 1
GL	4-dr Sedan-5P	I4/109	9990	2330	Note 1
GLI	4-dr Sedan-5P	I4/109	11690	2348	Note 1
GLI/16V	4-dr Sedan-5P	I4/109	13725	N/A	Note 1
QUANTUM					
GL	4-dr Sedan-5P	I5/136	14985	2661	Note 1
	5-dr Sta Wag-5P	I5/136	13450	2745	Note 1
Syncro	5-dr Sta Wag-5P	I5/136	16645	2976	Note 1
SCIROCCO					
	2-dr Coupe-4P	I4/109	10680	2221	Note 1
16V	2-dr Coupe-4P	I4/109	12980	2287	Note 1

Note 1: A total of 130,641 imported Volkswagens were sold in the U.S. in 1987, followed by 128,503 in 1988, and 129,705 in 1989.

Price Note: Figures shown were valid in 1987.

1988 Volkswagen Cabriolet.

ENGINE DATA: BASE FOUR (Fox, Cabriolet, Golf, Jetta, Scirocco): Inline, overhead-cam four-cylinder. Cast iron block and light alloy head. **Displacement:** 109 cu. in. (1786 cc). **Bore & Stroke:** 3.19 x 3.40 (81 x 86.4 mm). **Compression Ratio:** (Fox) 9.0:1; (Golf/Jetta) 8.5:1; **Brake Horsepower:** (Fox) 81 at 5500 rpm; (Golf/Jetta) 85 at 5250 rpm; (Cabriolet/Scirocco) 90 at 5550 rpm. **Torque:** (Fox) 93 lbs.-ft. at 3250 rpm; (Golf/Jetta) 98 lbs.-ft. at 3000 rpm; (Cabriolet/Scirocco) 100 at 3000 rpm. Five main bearings. Multi-point fuel injection.

Note: Horsepower rose to 100 on base Golf/Jetta for 1988.

OPTIONAL FOUR (Golf GTI, Jetta GLI): Same as above, except — **Compression Ratio:** 10.0:1. **Brake Horsepower:** 102 at 5250 rpm (rose to 105 bhp in 1988). **Torque:** 110 lbs.-ft. at 3250 rpm.

BASE FOUR (Golf GTI 16V, Jetta GLI 16V, Scirocco 16V): Inline, overhead-cam four-cylinder (16-valve). Cast iron block and light alloy head. **Displacement:** 109 cu. in. (1786 cc). **Bore & Stroke:** 3.19 x 3.40 (81 x 86.4 mm). **Compression Ratio:** 10.0:1. **Brake Horsepower:** 123 at 5800 rpm. **Torque:** 120 lbs.-ft. at 4250 rpm. Five main bearings. Multi-point fuel injection.

DIESEL FOUR (Golf, Jetta): Inline, overhead-cam four-cylinder. Cast iron block and light alloy head. **Displacement:** 97 cu. in. (1588 cc). **Bore & Stroke:** 3.01 x 3.40 (76.5 x 86.4 mm). **Compression Ratio:** 23.0:1. **Brake Horsepower:** 52 at 4800 rpm. **Torque:** 71 lbs.-ft. at 2000 rpm. Five main bearings. Fuel injection.

BASE FIVE (Quantum): Inline, overhead-cam five-cylinder. Cast iron block and light alloy head. **Displacement:** 136 cu. in. (2229 cc). **Bore & Stroke:** 3.19 x 3.40 (81 x 86.4 mm). **Compression Ratio:** 8.5:1. **Brake Horsepower:** 110/115 at 5500 rpm. **Torque:** 122/126 lbs.-ft. at 3000 rpm. Six main bearings. Multi-point fuel injection.

1988 Volkswagen Scirocco 16V.

1988 Volkswagen Fox GL station wagon.

CHASSIS DATA: Wheelbase: (Fox) 92.8 in.; (Golf/Jetta) 97.3 in.; (Cabr/Scirocco) 94.5 in.; (Quantum) 100.4 in. **Overall Length:** (Fox) 163.4 in.; (Golf) 158.0 in.; (Jetta) 171.7 in.; (Cabr) 159.3 in.; (Quantum sed) 180.2 in.; (Quantum wag) 183.1 in.; (Scirocco) 165.7 in. **Height:** (Fox) 53.7-54.3 in.; (Golf/Jetta) 55.7 in.; (Cabr) 55.6 in.; (Quantum) 55.1 in.; (Quantum Syncro) 60.9 in.; (Scirocco) 51.4 in. **Width:** (Fox) 63.0-63.9 in.; (Golf/Jetta) 65.5 in.; (Cabr) 64.2 in.; (Quantum) 66.7-66.9 in.; (Scirocco) 64.0 in.

TECHNICAL: Layout: front-engine, front-drive. **Transmission:** five-speed manual except (Fox) four-speed; three-speed automatic available. **Steering:** rack and pinion. **Suspension (front):** MacPherson struts with coil springs. **Suspension (rear):** (Golf/Jetta/Cabr/Quantum) torsion beam axle with trailing arms and coil springs; (Scirocco) torsion beam axle with coil springs. **Brakes:** front disc, rear drum except (Scirocco 16V) front/rear disc. **Body Construction:** steel unibody.

ADDITIONAL MODELS: Volkswagen also continued to produce the Vanagon station wagon and Camper bus, with two- or four-wheel drive. The Vanagon GL added a second sliding side door for 1987.

Manufacturer: Volkswagenwerk AG, Wolfsburg, West Germany or Volkswagen of America Inc., Pennsylvania (Fox built in Brazil).

Distributor: Volkswagen of America Inc., Troy, Michigan.

1990 VOLKSWAGEN

1990 Volkswagen Corrado sports car.

1990 Volkswagen Passat GL.

1990 Volkswagen Fox GL station wagon.

1990 Volkswagen Cabriolet Boutique.

A driver's airbag became standard in the Cabriolet for 1990, but not in other VW models. A larger, more potent (131-bhp) 2.0-liter engine went into the Golf GTI 16V and Jetta GLI 16V. Otherwise, each of those models—and the Vanagon—continued without major change.

VW's new Passat sedan and station wagon arrived during the 1990 model year, powered by a 2.0-liter engine, to replace the Quantum. With 10.8:1 compression, the engine developed 134 horsepower at 5800 rpm, and produced 133 pound-feet of torque. Both models had a 103.3-inch wheelbase.

Also introduced for 1990 was a supercharged Corrado hatchback coupe, promoted as VW's "first full-blooded sports car." The four-seat, front-drive coupe carried a "G-Charger" engine (so called because the supercharger was G-shaped) that developed 158 horsepower at 5600 rpm. Only a five-speed manual gearbox was available. Four-wheel disc brakes were standard, with anti-locking optional. Corrado also had an automatic "active" rear spoiler that rose at speeds above 45 mph to reduce lift, then retracted when speed fell below 12 mph. Price was $17,900, and the Corrado rode a 97.3-inch wheelbase.

VOLGA

Serving as a successor of sorts to the postwar Pobeda (also listed in this Catalog), the Volga M-21 debuted in 1955, produced at Zavod Imieni Molotova in the city of Gorky, Soviet Union. For a few years, both the old-style Pobeda and more modern Volga were built at the Gorky plant; but from 1959 on, production was limited to the Volga.

The four-door sedan was powered by a 2.5-liter, overhead-valve four-cylinder engine that had five main bearings. Horsepower ratings over the years started at 70-75, but later reached as much as 97 bhp. The car's front seat could fold down to become a bed. In addition to the sedan, Volga built an M-22G station wagon as well as an ambulance. Sedans often turned up as taxis. An automatic transmission was offered for a time early on, but did not prove successful. Features included pedal-operated lubrication of 16 chassis points. Early models were equipped

with an electric heater, clock, and multi-band radio. Styling highlights included a solid, wide grille that contained a series of side-by-side vertical slots, with parking lights sitting low at the tips of high-crowned fenders. Overall, the Volga's profile had a forward-angled look. Top speed was about 80 mph. Price in the Soviet Union in 1955 was estimated at $4,000.

Volga literature was distributed at the London show in October 1959, explaining that a Volga had received the "Grand Prix" award at the Universal and International Exhibition at Brussels in 1958. By this time, the M-21K had an 80-bhp version of the 2445-cc engine, with 7.5:1 compression and equal bore/stroke dimensions (3.62 inches). The three-speed gearbox had a column-mounted lever, and was synchronized in second and third. Coil springs were used for the front suspension, with semi-elliptic leaf springs at the rear. A worm-type steering gear contained a double roller. Wheelbase was 106 inches, and the car measured 190 inches overall and stood 64 inches high, weighing 3,000 pounds (dry). The four-door sedan held five passengers and had a curved windshield and back window. Tires were 6.70x15 size, on pressed disc wheels. Top speed was claimed to be 84 mph. Later in the 1960s, the car was known as the Volga Gaz 21.

A restyled Volga 24 emerged in 1968, with a longer (110-inch) wheelbase but a lower body that stood 58.7 inches tall. By that time, the engine was rated 110 horsepower and produced 138 pound-feet of torque, and worked into a four-speed gearbox. Volga production continued through the 1970s and into the '80s, when a 3102 sedan and station wagon with 2.5-liter gas engine (or 2.3-liter Indenor diesel) were the standard models.

VOLVO

Founded in 1926, the Volvo company of Gothenburg, Sweden introduced its first production automobile in April of 1927. Assar Gabrielsson, who headed the business end of the venture, had worked since 1916 for Svenska Kullager-fabriken (SKF), a ball-bearing manufacturer. After seeing the first prototype, designed under the direction of Gustaf Larson, SKF provided some financial backing for the new automobile firm. Guarantees of credit from SKF were sufficient to allow an initial run of a thousand cars, half of them open models. Even the company's name had a tie to SKF. In Latin, Volvo means "I roll," a reference to the well-known Swedish ball bearings.

Volvo's first car was the P.4, with a 1.9-liter four-cylinder engine that developed 28 horsepower. Contrary to initial plans, more than three times as many PV4 four-door sedans were built than open OV4 models, as the latter did not enjoy stunning sales in the frigid Swedish climate. A six-cylinder PV650 model debuted in 1929, with a 3010-cc engine. Through the 1930s, that engine grew to 3266- and 3670-cc displacement. These early Volvos displayed lines similar to various American models of the time. Volvo built its first all-metal car in 1934. The streamlined PV36 Carioca sedan bore a striking resemblance to the Chrysler Airflow. Considered ahead of its time (like the Airflow), the Carioca also had a relatively high price tag for those Depression years. Only about 500 were produced.

A new sedan, the PV60, was ready for production when World War II broke out. Because of its neutral status, Swe-

den continued to manufacture automobiles through the war years, but was nonetheless restrained by material shortages.

A five-passenger, 90-bhp model, the PV60 went into serious production right after the war and was manufactured until 1950. During the war, however, Volvo had elected to focus on smaller cars as soon as possible and built several prototypes. Thus came the PV444, a unibodied five-seat sedan (though registered as a four-passenger model) that carried a 1414-cc overhead-valve engine, and went on sale in 1947. A substantial proportion of the new Volvos went for export. Official importation of PV444s into the U.S. began in 1956, and enthusiasts pointed out the close resemblance between the profile of the Volvo and that of the 1946-48 Ford two-door sedan—similar in shape, though not in size.

Volvo also produced several dozen examples of a fiberglass-bodied two-seat sports car in 1956, known as the P1900 and styled in America by the Glaspar company; but the time wasn't ripe for entry into that market.

Evolution turned the PV444 into a PV544, with a 1.6-liter Sport engine rated 85 horsepower. A four-speed gearbox became available in 1958, to replace the initial three-speed unit. Volvo also turned to a four-door sedan, the 122 series, marketed alongside the original two-doors. By 1966, that model became the third best-selling imported sedan in the U.S. market.

A more successful entry into the sports-car field came in 1961, with the P1800 coupe, based on a prototype shown two years earlier. Running gear was similar to the ordinary 122S sedan, but styling was a blend of two Italian companies: Ghia and Frua. P1800 bodies were assembled not in Sweden but by Jensen, in England, from kits provided by the Pressed Steel company. These two-seaters were capable of top speeds beyond 110 mph, with their 115-bhp engines. During 1964, P1800 production moved to Sweden and lasted for another decade, evolving by 1972 into an 1800ES sports estate wagon variant with fuel-injected engine (not unlike the British Reliant, also listed in this Catalog).

Another new model debuted for 1968: the 140-series sedan, with a 1.8-liter engine. Drivetrain components were similar to the 122S, but the new body was created with a growing focus on safety. Engineering details included a reinforced passenger compartment, telescopic steering column, and dual-circuit all-disc brakes. A 145S station wagon appeared within the year, replacing the 122S wagon. In 1969, the 140 series edged aside the former 122 line.

Engines grew in displacement in 1969, to 2 liters. A six-cylinder Volvo 164 also became available. Bosch fuel injection was standard on all Volvo models by 1972. Volvo's evolutionary 240 series arrived by 1975, and soon turned to a 2.1-liter overhead-cam engine. Six-cylinder models adopted the PRV (Peugeot-Renault-Volvo) 2.7-liter V-6 engine, while the option of diesel power arrived as the 1970s ended.

Like the comparable Swedish-built and German-built BMW, Volvo became a "yuppie" favorite in the 1980s, partly because of its safety orientation. Turbochargers became available early in the 1980s, as did a top-rung 760GLE with a restyled body, automatic transmission, and automatic leveling. Later in the 1980s, the 240/260 series changed into DL/GL designations, with the 740 and 760 ranking as luxury-oriented models. Also added was a 780 coupe with styling by Bertone, which debuted in 1985 and sold in tiny numbers.

1944-55 VOLVO

1954 Volvo PV444 two-door sedan.

PV444 — FOUR — Volvo's memorable unibodied fastback two-door sedan debuted in Sweden during World War II (Sweden maintaining neutrality during that conflict). At an exhibition in Stockholm in 1944, the PV444 was shown alongside the prewar-styled PV60. Its B4B overhead-valve 1414-cc engine developed 40 horsepower, hooked to a three-speed gearbox. Production was delayed, however, largely because of a strike in 1945. Thus, the first production models did not emerge until 1947. Early models were painted black, with mechanical turn-signal indicators mounted in the door pillars and wraparound taillamps. A B series debuted in 1950; a C edition a year later. By the start of 1952, a total of 25,000 PV444s had been built. Improvements came with each edition, as did the availability of various colors. A Duett station wagon, based on the PV444, arrived during the summer of 1953. By the mid-1950s, Volvo was ready to send its sedan across the Atlantic.

PRODUCTION/SALES: A total of 6,525 Volvos were produced in 1946 (before the PV444 model began), of which 2,632 were exported; 9,758 were produced in 1947 (2,747 exported); 10,998 were produced in 1948 (2,103 exported); 13,495 produced in 1949 (2,182 exported); 18,747 produced in 1950 (3,553 exported); 23,258 produced in 1951 (5,031 exported); 19,695 produced in 1952 (4,761 exported); and 26,510 produced in 1953 (4,069 exported).

1956-58 VOLVO

1956 Volvo 445 cabriolet. (William Siuru Jr.)

PV444/PV445 — FOUR — At the time of its emergence into the American import-car marketplace, this original Volvo PV series had a two-piece windshield, and a grille with a loose mesh pattern. Later models switched to a tight-mesh grille pattern. Tiny round parking lights sat below and outboard of the headlights, and the hood displayed a hood ornament. Small round taillamps stood at the ends of the fenders, with auxiliary lights higher up. In overall profile, the PV-series often was compared to the side view of a 1946-48 Ford two-door sedan, albeit on a smaller scale. The Volvo produced for U.S. consumption was actually a modified version of the Swedish-market PV444, with a more powerful engine, an extra bumper, and American-style directional indicators. Two engines were available: initially a 70-horsepower four, then later an optional 85-horsepower four, the latter with larger bore and higher compression. Displacement of the smaller B14A engine was 1414 cc (87 cid); the larger B16B engine was 1580 cc (97

cid). A radiator blind was standard. A three-speed gearbox was used, with a long, angled floor-mounted lever (in the style of prewar American cars). Front suspension consisted of wishbones and coil springs, while the rigid axle rear had coil springs and radius arms.

Volvos were built with a welded, all-steel integral body and chassis, and could convert into a sleeper. Though capable of seating five people, the car was registered as a four-passenger. Twin sunvisors were standard. Claimed top speed of the basic U.S. model was more than 80 mph; but in California road races, production sedans were clocked at 98 mph. A four-speed gearbox became optional in 1958.

Volvo's Duet station wagon, displayed at the New York Auto Show in April 1956, had a different front-end appearance with a horizontal-bar grille and two-tone paint (second color around the window frames). This was similar to the front-end appearance of earlier models. With two optional seats, the five-seater could transform into a seven-passenger vehicle. A roof rack also was optional.

1957 Volvo PV444. (William Siuru Jr.)

I.D. DATA: Serial number plate is on right side of firewall, under the hood. Engine number is on left side of block, behind fuel pump. Serial number range (1958 models): 151123 to 185000.

Model	Body Type & Seating	Engine Type/CID	P.O.E. Price	Weight (lbs.)	Prod. Total
PV444	2-dr Sedan-4/5P	I4/87	2170	2140	Note 1
PV444	2-dr Sedan-4/5P	I4/97	2239	2140	Note 1
PV445	2-dr Sta Wag-5P	I4/87	2345	2368	Note 1
PV445	2-dr Sta Wag-5P	I4/97	2490	2450	Note 1

Note 1: A total of 31,260 Volvos were produced in 1956, followed by 41,488 in 1957, and 53,360 in 1958.

Price Note: Prices shown were valid in 1957. Initial announced price in the U.S. with 70-bhp engine was $1995. Prices in 1958 were $2239 for the sedan and $2490 for the station wagon.

ENGINE DATA: BASE FOUR: Inline, overhead-valve four-cylinder (B14A). Cast iron block. **Displacement:** 86.65 cu. in. (1414 cc). **Bore & Stroke:** 2.96 x 3.15 in. (75 x 80 mm). **Compression Ratio:** 7.8:1. **Brake Horsepower:** 70 at 5500 rpm. **Torque:** 75.9 lbs.-ft. at 3000 rpm. Three main bearings. Solid valve lifters. Two SU carburetors. 6-volt electrical system.

Note: Basic B4B engine used elsewhere in the world was rated 51 bhp at 4500 rpm and 72.5 lbs.-ft. at 2500 rpm, with 7.3:1 compression.

OPTIONAL FOUR (B16B): Same as above, except — **Displacement:** 97 cu. in. (1580 cc). **Bore & Stroke:** 3.125 x 3.15 in. (79.4 x 80 mm). **Compression Ratio:** 8.2:1. **Brake Horsepower:** 85 at 5500 rpm. **Torque:** 87 lbs.-ft. at 3500 rpm.

CHASSIS DATA: Wheelbase: 102.5 in. **Overall Length:** (sed) 177 in.; (wag) 173.25 in. **Height:** (sed) 61.5 in.; (wag) 66 in. **Width:** (sed) 62.5 in.; (wag) 63 in. **Front Tread:** 51 in. **Rear Tread:** (sed) 51.5 in.; (wag) 52 in. **Wheel Type:** steel disc. **Standard Tires:** (sed) 5.90x15; (wag) 6.00x15.

TECHNICAL: Layout: front-engine, rear-drive. **Transmission:** three-speed manual (floor lever). Gear ratios: (1st) 3.23:1; (2nd) 1.62:1; (3rd) 1.00:1; (rev) 2.92:1. Four-speed manual optional in 1958. **Standard Final Drive Ratio:** 4.56:1. **Steering:** roller sector and worm. **Suspension (front):** wishbones with coil springs. **Suspension (rear):** rigid axle with radius arms, track rod and coil springs. **Brakes:** hydraulic, front/rear drum. **Body Construction:** steel unibody. **Fuel Tank:** 9.5 gallon (U.S.).

MAJOR OPTIONS: Four-speed transmission.

PERFORMANCE: Top Speed: (70-bhp) 90 mph; 80+ mph claimed initially (later 95 mph). **Acceleration (0-60 mph):** (PV444 w/4-spd) 13.5 sec.; (PV444 w/3-spd) 16.3 sec. **Acceleration (quarter-mile):** (PV444 w/4-spd) 19.5 sec. (71.5 mph); (PV444 w/3-spd) 20.3 sec. (67.6 mph). **Fuel Mileage:** 35 mpg claimed (wagon, 30-35 mpg); under 24 mpg average in road test.

PRODUCTION/SALES: Approximately 12,000 Volvos were sold in the U.S. during 1957.

ADDITIONAL MODELS: During 1955-56, Volvo also produced a striking two-door Sport convertible sports car (also known as the P1900), with an entirely different appearance that included a deeply recessed crosshatch grille. The sports car was a hand-tooled two-passenger model with plastic body and tubular frame, capable of over 100 mph. Production was limited, and Volvo announced that only about 300 were to be made during 1956. As it turned out, only 67 were built. Nevertheless, *Motor Trend* in 1956 claimed that Volvo's reputation stemmed from the fine looks of its plastic-bodied sports two-seater. The sports car carried a 70-bhp engine with two SU carburetors, a higher-compression head, oversize valves, and special manifold. That Sport engine would also be used in sedans destined for the U.S. market. Wheelbase of the Sport was 94.5 inches, and it measured 144 inches overall. An example appeared at the New York Auto Show in April 1956.

Manufacturer: AB Volvo (Aktiebolaget Volvo), Gothenburg, Sweden.

Distributor: Aktiebolaget Volvo, Detroit, Michigan; Richard D. Harris Auto Imports Inc., Studio City, California; then Volvo Distributing Co., Englewood Cliffs, New Jersey.

HISTORY: Importation of Volvos officially began early in 1956. Volvo's 444 appeared at the New York Auto Show in May 1956, billed as "a Swedish car—the leader in its class." At that show, Volvo announced a European delivery plan with the following prices (FOB Gothenburg): $1395 with a 51-bhp engine, or $1495 with 70 bhp. A Duet station wagon sold for $1595 in Sweden. Early on, Volvos gained a reputation for longevity. Many were claimed to run 125,000 miles before a major overhaul, and enjoyed low repair costs.

Volvo announced a 120-series four-door sedan in Sweden during 1956, named "Amazon" in Scandinavia. Styling features included a split grille and curved pontoon fenders. The 120-series would not arrive in the U.S. until the 1960 model year, as the 122S sedan.

1959 VOLVO

PV544 — FOUR — Volvo's evolution of the PV444 displayed the same profile but underwent a number of significant changes. A larger windshield was in one-piece rather than split, slightly curved, with slimmer pillars. The rear windows grew wider and deeper, the taillamps larger. Volvo's rectangular grille opening contained a tight crosshatch pattern. Inside was a roomier rear seat, a new padded instrument panel, and thermometer-type speedometer. More powerful brakes demanded lower pedal pressure, and the hand brake lever went between the front seats. Turn signals and the steering system were new, as were nozzles for the windshield washer. A suspended vibration-free gas pedal was installed. In addition to new color and upholstery combinations, Volvos offered safety belt attachments for the rear seat.

Under the hood, the 85-bhp Sport (B16B), 97-cid engine now was standard in U.S. models. A four-speed manual gearbox replaced the earlier three-speed as standard, with the latter optional. Both used the long floor-mounted gearshift lever, different from most European cars that used a short indirect gearshift control.

PV445 — FOUR — Availability of the earlier station wagon continued with little change.

I.D. DATA: Serial number plate is on right side of firewall, under the hood. Engine number is on left side of block, behind fuel pump. Starting serial number: 185001.

Model	Body Type & Seating	Engine Type/CID	P.O.E. Price	Weight (lbs.)	Prod. Total
PV544	2-dr Sedan-4/5P	I4/97	2330	2140	Note 1
PV445	2-dr Sta Wag-5P	I4/97	2490	2450	Note 1

Note 1: A total of 71,712 Volvos were produced in 1959.

Model Note: The PV444 sedan remained available early in the year, priced at $2290.

ENGINE DATA: BASE FOUR (PV544): Inline, overhead-valve four-cylinder (B16B Sport). Cast iron block. **Displacement:** 97 cu. in. (1580 cc). **Bore & Stroke:** 3.125 x 3.15 in. (79.4 x 80 mm). **Compression Ratio:** 8.2:1. **Brake Horsepower:** 85 at 5500 rpm. **Torque:** 87 lbs.-ft. at 3500 rpm. Three main bearings. Solid valve lifters. Two SU horizontal carburetors. 6-volt electrical system.

CHASSIS DATA: Wheelbase: 102.5 in. **Overall Length:** (sed) 177 in.; (wag) 173.25 in. **Height:** (sed) 61.5 in.; (wag) 66 in. **Width:** (sed) 62.5 in.; (wag) 63 in. **Front Tread:** 51 in. **Rear Tread:** (sed) 51.8 in.; (wag) 52 in. **Wheel Type:** steel disc. **Standard Tires:** (sed) 5.90x15; (wag) 6.00x15.

Dimension Note: Initial announced height for the PV544 was 60.25 inches.

TECHNICAL: Layout: front-engine, rear-drive. **Transmission:** four-speed manual (floor lever); three-speed optional. **Standard Final Drive Ratio:** 4.56:1. **Steering:** hourglass worm and sector. **Suspension (front):** control arms with coil springs. **Suspension (rear):** rigid axle with radius arms, track rod and coil springs. **Brakes:** hydraulic, front/rear drum. **Body Construction:** welded steel unibody. **Fuel Tank:** 9.5 gallon (U.S.).

MAJOR OPTIONS: Three-speed transmission.

PERFORMANCE: Top Speed: (PV544) 95+ mph. **Fuel Mileage:** (PV544) 25-35 mpg.

PRODUCTION/SALES: Approximately 18,468 Volvos were sold in the U.S. during 1959.

Manufacturer: AB Volvo, Gothenburg, Sweden.

Distributor: Volvo Distributing Inc., Englewood Cliffs, New Jersey.

HISTORY: Volvo's PV544 was introduced to the U.S. market in April 1959. According to *Foreign Cars Illustrated and Auto Sport* magazine, in the late 1950s about 15 Volvo bolt-on "little LeMans" kits were exported to the U.S., then "sold to customers likely to use them to best advantage, and fortified with the parts listings necessary to make them legal for competition." The four-door 122S debuted late in 1959; see next listing for details.

1960 VOLVO

PV544 — FOUR — Production of Volvo's old-style two-door sedan continued with little change, again powered by the B16B Sport engine. A four-speed gearbox was standard.

PV445 — FOUR — Volvo's station wagon remained available in the U.S. for another year.

122S — FOUR — Introduced earlier in Europe, the four-door Volvo arrived in the U.S. late in 1959, for the 1960 model year, bearing little resemblance to the two-door PV544. This was a notchback design, not a rounded fastback. Instead of a single-unit rectangular grille as in the PV544, the 122S had a split grille with tight crosshatch pattern in each side-by-side segment, plus a thick horizontal divider bar. Rectangular park/signal lights stood below and outboard of the single round headlamps. Bodysides now flowed in a continuous line, as opposed to the separate-fender profile used for the PV544. Under the hood was the same B16B Sport engine used in the current PV544, developing 85 horsepower. A four-speed, fully synchronized gearbox was standard. Also standard were whitewall tires, a padded dashboard, dual padded sunvisors, two-speed wipers, a heater and radiator blind.

I.D. DATA: Serial number plate is on right side of firewall, under the hood. Engine number is on left side of block, behind fuel pump. Starting serial number: (PV544) 232786; (122S) 28167.

Model	Body Type & Seating	Engine Type/CID	P.O.E. Price	Weight (lbs.)	Prod. Total
PV544	2-dr Sedan-4/5P	I4/97	2330	2140	Note 1
PV445	2-dr Sta Wag-5P	I4/97	N/A	2450	Note 1
122S					
122S	4-dr Sedan-4/5P	I4/97	2795	2400	Note 1

Note 1: A total of 72,378 Volvos were produced in 1960.

ENGINE DATA: BASE FOUR (PV544, 122S): Inline, overhead-valve four-cylinder (B16B Sport). Cast iron block. **Displacement:** 97 cu. in. (1580 cc). **Bore & Stroke:** 3.125 x 3.15 in. (79.4 x 80 mm). **Compression Ratio:** 8.2:1. **Brake Horsepower:** 85 at 5500 rpm. **Torque:** 87 lbs.-ft. at 3500 rpm. Three main bearings. Solid valve lifters. Two SU horizontal carburetors. 6-volt electrical system.

CHASSIS DATA: Wheelbase: (PV544) 102.5 in.; (122S) 102.4 in. Overall Length: (PV544) 177 in.; (PV445 wag) 173.25 in.; (122S) 175.2 in. Height: (PV544) 61.5 in.; (PV445 wag) 66 in.; (122S) 59.5 in. Width: (PV544) 62.5 in.; (PV445 wag) 63 in.; (122S) 63.8 in. Front Tread: (PV544) 51.8 in.; (122S) 51.8 in. Rear Tread: (PV544/122S) 51.8 in.; (PV445 wag) 52 in. Wheel Type: steel disc. Standard Tires: (PV544/122S) 5.90x15.

TECHNICAL: Layout: front-engine, rear-drive. Transmission: four-speed manual (floor lever); three-speed available on PV544. Steering: (PV544) hourglass worm and sector; (122S) cam and roller. Suspension (front): (PV544) control arms with coil springs; (122S) coil springs with drag links. Suspension (rear): rigid axle with radius arms, track rod and coil springs. Brakes: hydraulic, front/rear drum. Body Construction: welded steel unibody.

PERFORMANCE: Top Speed: (PV544) 95 + mph; (122S) 92-94 mph. Acceleration (0-60 mph): (122S) 16.2 sec. Acceleration (quarter-mile): (122S) 20 sec. (66 mph).

PRODUCTION/SALES: Approximately 13,926 Volvos were sold in the U.S. during 1960.

Manufacturer: AB Volvo, Gothenburg, Sweden.

Distributor: Volvo Import Inc., Englewood Cliffs, New Jersey.

HISTORY: In his book *Wonderful World of the Automobile*, Ken Purdy stated that "Volvo is probably the fastest of all the small cars...among the most rugged, and it can honestly claim the most efficient passenger-car engine currently made: it produces more horse-power per cubic inch of size than any American-built engine."

1961 VOLVO

1961 Volvo 545 Duet station wagon.

PV544 — FOUR — Production of Volvo's old-style two-door sedan, with B16B (85-bhp) engine, continued with little change other than new contoured front bucket seats and a reworked four-speed gearbox. Special and Special Deluxe models carried a detuned engine with lower compression and a single carbureted, rated at only 60 bhp.

122S — FOUR — Production of the four-door Volvo continued with little change.

P1800 — FOUR — Although few people in America had ever seen the fiberglass sports car built by Volvo in limited numbers during the mid-1950s, the new P1800 two-seat coupe was destined to garner far more attention. Styling features included a protruding oval grille with crosshatch pattern, round parking lights below the headlamps (just above the bumper), and tiny rear quarter windows. Distinctive bodyside moldings began just to the rear of each headlamp, sweeping upward at the rear of the door. Taillamps sat below moderately finned rear fenders. Identifying script went on the C-pillar. Under the hood went an enlarged version of the four-cylinder engine used in the PV544/122S, displacing 1778 cc (108.5 cid) and developing 100 horsepower. That engine would enter PV544 and 122S compartments a year later. An all-synchro four-speed gearbox (with overdrive) was standard. The coupe contained a tiny back seat, which served more as a shelf than a space for passengers. Front disc brakes were installed.

I.D. DATA: Serial number plate is on right side of firewall, under the hood. Engine number is on left side of block, behind fuel pump. Starting serial number: (PV544) 244000; (122S) 29000.

Model	Body Type & Seating	Engine Type/CID	P.O.E. Price	Weight (lbs.)	Prod. Total
PV544					
Special	2-dr Sedan-4/5P	I4/97	1895	2140	Note 1
Spec DeL	2-dr Sedan-4/5P	I4/97	1995	2450	Note 1
	2-dr Sedan-4/5P	I4/97	2195	2140	Note 1
122S					
122S	4-dr Sedan-4/5P	I4/97	2495	2400	Note 1
P1800					
P1800	2-dr Spt Cpe-2P	I4/109	N/A	2480	Note 2

Note 1: A total of 71,719 Volvos (all models) were produced in 1961.

Note 2: Approximately 6,000 P1800 Volvos were produced from 1961-64.

ENGINE DATA: BASE FOUR (PV544, 122S): Inline, overhead-valve four-cylinder (B16B Sport). Cast iron block. Displacement: 97 cu. in. (1580 cc). Bore & Stroke: 3.125 x 3.15 in. (79.4 x 80 mm). Compression Ratio: 8.2:1. Brake Horsepower: 85 at 5500 rpm. Torque: 87 lbs.-ft. at 3500 rpm. Three main bearings. Solid valve lifters. Two SU horizontal carburetors. 6-volt electrical system.

BASE FOUR (PV544 Special/Special Deluxe): Same as 1588-cc four above, but with single Zenith carburetor — Compression Ratio: 7.4:1. Brake Horsepower: 60 at 4500 rpm. Torque: 82 lbs.-ft. at 2500 rpm.

BASE FOUR (P1800): Inline, overhead-valve four-cylinder (B18B). Cast iron block. Displacement: 108.5 cu. in. (1778 cc). Bore & Stroke: 3.31 x 3.15 in. (84 x 80 mm). Compression Ratio: 9.5:1. Brake Horsepower: 100 at 5500 rpm. Torque: 108 lbs.-ft. at 4000 rpm. Five main bearings. Solid valve lifters. Two SU horizontal carburetors. 6-volt electrical system.

CHASSIS DATA: Wheelbase: (PV544) 102.5 in.; (122S) 102.4 in.; (P1800) 96.5 in. Overall Length: (PV544) 177 in.; (122S) 175.2 in.; (P1800) 173 in. Height: (PV544) 61.5 in.; (122S) 59.5 in.; (P1800) 51 in. Width: (PV544) 62.5 in.; (122S) 63.8 in.; (P1800) 67 in. Front Tread: (PV544) 51 in.; (122S) 51.8 in.; (P1800) 52 in. Rear Tread: (PV544/122S) 51.8 in.; (P1800) 52 in. Wheel Type: steel disc. Standard Tires: 5.90x15.

TECHNICAL: Layout: front-engine, rear-drive. Transmission: four-speed manual (floor lever); three-speed manual available on PV544. Steering: (PV544) hourglass worm and sector; (122S/P1800) cam and roller. Suspension (front): (PV544) control arms with coil springs; (122S) coil springs with drag links; (P1800) upper/lower A-arms with coil springs and anti-roll bar. Suspension (rear): (PV544/122S) rigid axle with radius arms, track rod and coil springs; (P1800) rigid axle with Panhard rod and coil springs. Brakes: (PV544/122S) front/rear drum; (P1800) front disc, rear drum. Body Construction: welded steel unibody.

PERFORMANCE: Top Speed: (122S) 90 mph; (P1800) 105-107 mph. Acceleration (0-60 mph): (PV544) 13.4 sec.; (PV544 Special DeL) 18.1 sec.; (122S) 16.5 sec.; (P1800) 12.4-13.9 sec. Acceleration (quarter-mile): (122S) 20.4 sec. (66.3 mph); (P1800) 18 sec. (72 mph).

PRODUCTION/SALES: Approximately 12,787 Volvos were sold in the U.S. during 1961.

Manufacturer: AB Volvo, Gothenburg, Sweden.

Distributor: Volvo Import Inc., Englewood Cliffs, New Jersey.

HISTORY: Photos of the two-seat Volvo had appeared in Europe as early as spring 1959, when the developing car was called Volvo Sport (same name as the earlier fiberglass model). Although introduced at the New York Auto Show in April 1961, the P1800 did not become readily available until the 1962 model year. Ads early in 1961 repeated comments made by the *The New York World-Telegram and Sun*, to the effect that "the P-1800 has that $15,000 hand-crafted look about it...Many styling experts have exalted it to the Valhalla of great auto styles." Tooling for the P1800's new unibody was developed by the Pressed Steel company in Britain, with early assembly handled by Jensen (also in Britain). Not until late 1964 would manufacture move to Sweden. Performance of the two-seater lagged behind its distinctive styling, though ride and handling scored well. Volvo's image got a boost when Simon Templar (actor Roger Moore) regularly slipped behind the wheel of one of the two-seaters on the TV series, *The Saint*.

1962-63 VOLVO

1963 Volvo PV544 B-18 two-door sedan. (Christie's)

PV544 — FOUR — Volvo's old-style two-door sedan gained a larger engine for 1962. The B18D four-cylinder engine displaced 1778 cc (108.5 cid), and developed 90 horsepower. This was essentially a detuned version of the engine used in the P1800 coupe. A 12-volt electrical system replaced the former 6-volt setup.

122S — FOUR — Like the PV544, Volvo's four-door sedan adopted the larger engine and 12-volt electrical system. The grille area was enlarged to enhance cooling. A two-door sedan and a station wagon joined the original four-door sedan at this time.

P1800 — FOUR — Little change was evident in the Volvo two-seat coupe, introduced during 1961 but not readily available at dealerships until the latter portion of the 1962 model year. See previous listing for details.

I.D. DATA: Serial number plate is on right side of firewall, under the hood. Engine number is on left side of block, behind fuel pump. Starting serial number: (PV544) 244000; (122S) 29000.

Model	Body Type & Seating	Engine Type/CID	P.O.E. Price	Weight (lbs.)	Prod. Total
PV544					
	2-dr Sedan-4/5P	I4/109	2295	2105	Note 1
122S					
122S	2-dr Sedan-4/5P	I4/109	2495	2250	Note 1
122S	4-dr Sedan-4/5P	I4/109	2595	2295	Note 1
122S	4-dr Sta Wag-4/5P	I4/109	2495	2625	Note 1
P1800					
P1800	2-dr Spt Cpe-2P	I4/109	3995	2215	Note 2

Note 1: A total of 79,933 Volvos (all models) were produced in 1962, followed by 89,759 in 1963 (plus 13,814 vans and wagons).

Note 2: Approximately 6,000 P1800 Volvos were produced from 1961-64.

Price Note: Figures shown were valid in 1962.

ENGINE DATA: BASE FOUR (PV544, 122S): Inline, overhead-valve four-cylinder (B18D). Cast iron block. Displacement: 108.5 cu. in. (1778 cc). Bore & Stroke: 3.31 x 3.15 in. (84 x 80 mm). Compression Ratio: 8.5:1. Brake Horsepower: 90 at 5000 rpm. Torque: 105 lbs.-ft. at 3500 rpm. Five main bearings. Solid valve lifters. Two SU horizontal carburetors. 12-volt electrical system.

Note: Some PV544 and 122S models were sold in 1962 with the earlier (smaller) 97-cid engine.
BASE FOUR (P1800): Same as 1778-cc four above, except code B18B — **Compression Ratio:** 9.5:1. **Brake Horsepower:** 100 at 5500 rpm. **Torque:** 108 lbs.-ft. at 4000 rpm.

1963 Volvo P220 station wagon. (William Siuru Jr.)

CHASSIS DATA: Wheelbase: (PV544/122S) 102.4 in.; (P1800) 96.5 in. **Overall Length:** (PV544) 175 in.; (122S) 175-175.2 in.; (P1800) 173 in. **Height:** (PV544) 61.5 in.; (122S) 59.25-59.5 in.; (P1800) 51 in. **Width:** (PV544) 62.5 in.; (122S) 63.8 in.; (P1800) 67 in. **Front Tread:** (PV544) 51 in.; (122S) 51.8 in.; (P1800) 52 in. **Rear Tread:** (PV544/122S) 51.8 in.; (P1800) 52 in. **Wheel Type:** steel disc. **Standard Tires:** 5.90x15.
TECHNICAL: Layout: front-engine, rear-drive. **Transmission:** four-speed manual (floor lever). **Steering:** (PV544) hourglass worm and sector; (122S/P1800) cam and roller. **Suspension (front):** (PV544) control arms with coil springs; (122S) coil springs with drag links; (P1800) upper/lower A-arms with coil springs and anti-roll bar. **Suspension (rear):** (PV544/122S) rigid axle with radius arms, track rod and coil springs; (P1800) rigid axle with Panhard rod and coil springs. **Brakes:** (PV544/122S) front/rear drum; (P1800) front disc, rear drum. **Body Construction:** welded steel unibody.
PERFORMANCE: Top Speed: (122S) about 100 mph; (P1800) 105-107 mph. **Acceleration (0-60 mph):** (122S) 14.6 sec.; (P1800) 13.6-13.9 sec. **Acceleration (quarter-mile):** (122S) 19.9 sec.; (P1800) 19 sec. (70.5 mph).
PRODUCTION/SALES: Approximately 13,157 Volvos were sold in the U.S. during 1962, followed by 14,188 in 1963.
Manufacturer: AB Volvo, Gothenburg, Sweden.
Distributor: Volvo Distributing Inc., Englewood Cliffs, New Jersey; then Volvo Inc., Rockleigh, New Jersey.

1964-67 VOLVO

1964 Volvo PV544. (William Siuru Jr.)

PV544 — FOUR — In its final form, the parking lights on Volvo's old-style fastback two-door sedan moved farther out from the headlamps. Otherwise, appearance was similar to prior models, still with separate fenders rather than an integrated line. A single horizontal chrome molding crossed each fender, just above the wheel opening. 'VOLVO' block letters again were evident across the nose, with '544' numerals on the hood, above the fenders. At the upper left of the grille was 'B18' script to identify the 90-bhp engine. For 1965, the chrome bar above the front bumper was dropped, a '544' designation was inset in an emblem to the rear of the hood, and a round Volvo emblem replaced the 'B18' grille identification. Final year of official availability was 1965, but some leftovers were sold as '66 models.

Note: By this time, some Volvo literature omitted the "PV" prefix and described the model as, simply, "544."
122S — FOUR — Little change was evident on the more modern two- and four-door sedan and station wagon, again powered by a 90-bhp engine. Front disc brakes now were standard. 'Volvo 122S' lettering was evident on front fenders, just ahead of the door hinge. An automatic transmission became available by 1965. In addition to changes in emblems for that year, the bar above the front bumper was dropped and the grille sections adopted a slim divider instead of the former heavy bar. Engine horsepower and compression rose for the 1966 model year.
1800S — FOUR — The original P1800 two-seat coupe evolved into the 1800S in 1964. Changes were relatively minor, including a modified, less dramatic oval crosshatch (open-mesh) grille and slight easing of the upsweep on the bodyside chrome strip, which ran along the upper rear fenders into the modestly rounded tailfins. Engine output rose to 108 horsepower and 110 pound-feet of torque. Volvo's sport coupe featured a sharply slanted windshield and back window, thin wraparound back bumper, and a wedge-shaped emblem on the nose. Widely-spaced 'VOLVO' letters decorated the rear deck. Overdrive became optional for 1965, and the bumper was now straight instead of upward-curved at its center. Engine output rose again for the 1966 model year, to 115 bhp.

1965 Volvo PV544 two-door sedan.

I.D. DATA: Serial number plate is on right side of firewall, under the hood. Engine number is on left side of block, behind fuel pump. Starting serial number: (1964 PV544) 369000; (1964 122S 2-dr) 11600; (1964 122S 4-dr) 112000; (1964 122S wag) 4000; (1964 1800S) 6001; (1965 PV544) 406643; (1965 122S 2-dr) 57555; (1965 122S 4-dr) 150532; (1965 122S wag) 11756; (1965 1800S) 9247; (1966 122S 2-dr) 108243; (1966 122S 4-dr) 176814; (1966 122S wag) 22217; (1966 1800S) 13679; (1967 122S 2-dr) 172249; (1967 122S 4-dr) 206143; (1967 122S wag) 35303; (1967 1800S) 18253.

Model	Body Type & Seating	Engine Type/CID	P.O.E. Price	Weight (lbs.)	Prod. Total
PV544					
	2-dr Sedan-4/5P	I4/109	2330	2055	Note 1
122S					
122S	2-dr Sedan-4/5P	I4/109	2530	2195	Note 1
122S	4-dr Sedan-4/5P	I4/109	2630	2260	Note 1
122S	4-dr Sta Wag-4/5P	I4/109	2845	2475	Note 1
1800S					
1800S	2-dr Spt Cpe-2P	I4/109	3920	2320	Note 2

Note 1: A total of 96,150 Volvos (all models) were produced in 1964, followed by 111,827 in 1965, 108,120 in 1966, and 145,447 in 1967. (1964-66 figures do not include vans and wagons.)
Note 2: Approximately 23,993 type 1800S Volvos were produced from 1964-68.
Price Note: Figures shown were valid in 1965.
Weight Note: Figures shown are unladen weights.

1965 Volvo 1800S. (William Siuru Jr.)

ENGINE DATA: BASE FOUR (1964-65 PV544, 122S): Inline, overhead-valve four-cylinder (B18D). Cast iron block. **Displacement:** 108.5 cu. in. (1778 cc). **Bore & Stroke:** 3.31 x 3.15 in. (84 x 80 mm). **Compression Ratio:** 8.5:1. **Brake Horsepower:** 90 at 5000 rpm. **Torque:** 105 lbs.-ft. at 3500 rpm. Five main bearings. Solid valve lifters. Two SU horizontal carburetors. 12-volt electrical system.

BASE FOUR (1966-67 122S): Same as 1778-cc four above, except — **Compression Ratio:** 8.7:1. **Brake Horsepower:** 95 at 5400 rpm. **Torque:** 107 lbs.-ft. at 3500 rpm.

BASE FOUR (1964-65 1800S): Same as 1778-cc four above, except — **Compression Ratio:** 10.0:1. **Brake Horsepower:** 108 at 5800 rpm. **Torque:** 110 lbs.-ft. at 4000 rpm.

BASE FOUR (1966-67 1800S): Same as 1778-cc four above, except — **Brake Horsepower:** 115 at 6800 rpm. **Torque:** 112 lbs.-ft. at 4000 rpm.

CHASSIS DATA: Wheelbase: (PV544/122S) 102.4 in.; (1800S) 96.5 in. **Overall Length:** (PV544/122S) 175.3 in.; (122S wag) 176.5 in.; (1800S) 173.3 in. **Height:** (PV544) 61.5 in.; (122S) 59.25 in.; (122S wag) 60.25 in.; (1800S) 50.5 in. **Width:** (PV544) 62.5 in.; (122S) 63.8 in.; (1800S) 67 in. **Front Tread:** (PV544) 51 in.; (122S/1800S) 51.8 in. **Rear Tread:** 51.8 in. **Wheel Type:** steel disc. **Standard Tires:** (PV544/122S) 6.00x15; (122S wag) 6.40x15; (1800S) 165x15.

TECHNICAL: Layout: front-engine, rear-drive. **Transmission:** four-speed manual (floor lever). PV544/1800S gear ratios: (1st) 3.13:1; (2nd) 1.99:1; (3rd) 1.36:1; (4th) 1.00:1; (rev) 3.25:1. Overdrive optional on 1800S in 1965. Borg-Warner automatic optional on 122S in 1965. **Standard Final Drive Ratio:** (PV544) 4.56:1; (1800S) 4.1:1. **Steering:** (PV544) hourglass worm and sector; (122S/1800S) cam and roller. **Suspension (front):** upper/lower A-arms with coil springs and anti-roll bar. **Suspension (rear):** rigid axle with support arms, torque rods, track rod and coil springs. **Brakes:** (PV544) front/rear drum; (122S/1800S) front disc, rear drum. **Body Construction:** welded steel unibody.

PERFORMANCE: Top Speed: (122S) 100 mph; (144S) 103 mph; (1800S) 107-112 mph. **Acceleration (0-60 mph):** (122S) 14.9 sec.; (144S) 12.2 sec.; (1800S w/108-bhp) 11.2 sec. **Acceleration (quarter-mile):** (144S) 18.3-19.6 sec. (74-76 mph).

PRODUCTION/SALES: Approximately 17,326 Volvos were sold in the U.S. during 1964, followed by 18,115 in 1965, 25,155 in 1966, and 34,396 in 1967.

Manufacturer: AB Volvo, Gothenburg, Sweden.

Distributor: Volvo Inc., Rockleigh, New Jersey.

HISTORY: Starting late in 1964, production of the P1800 moved to Sweden and the car changed name to 1800S. During this era, Volvos were advertised as "The car that lasts for 11 years in Sweden."

1968-69 VOLVO

1969 Volvo 144 four-door sedan.

122S — FOUR — Only the two-door sedan and station wagon remained of the 122S series, and only the two-door lasted through 1968.

140 SERIES (142S/144S/145S) — FOUR — All-new styling highlighted this new series, which displayed a more squarish profile with sharper edges than the 122S. A single bright grille insert was made up of horizontal strips with vertical dividers, and a thicker center divider. Single round headlamps were mounted at the end of the grille. Construction features included energy-absorbing body sections, built-in head restraint, safety-rim wheels, and a relief valve for rear-brake pressure. Odometers now registered all the way to a million miles. Reclining front seats were standard. Under the hood at first was the same 109-cid engine used in the 1800S coupe, developing 115 horsepower. Then, for 1969, displacement grew to 121.2 cid (1986 cc), with a 118-bhp rating. Four-wheel disc brakes then became standard, and a 'B20' emblem (to identify the engine) went on the grille.

1800S — FOUR — Production of the 1800S continued as before, but a larger engine was installed in final models. That 121.2-cid (1986-cc) four developed 118 horsepower and 123 pound-feet of torque.

I.D. DATA: Serial number plate is on right side of firewall, under the hood. Engine number is on left side of block, behind fuel pump. A new numbering system began for 1968. Starting serial number: (1968 122S 2-dr) 133441262715; (1968 122S wag) 223441056880; (1968 142S) 1423441000001; (1968 144S) 1423441000001; (1968 1800S) 183451024100; (1969 142S) 1423441052900; (1969 144S) 1443441089800; (1969 1800S) 183451028300.

Model	Body Type & Seating	Engine Type/CID	P.O.E. Price	Weight (lbs.)	Prod. Total
122S	2-dr Sedan-4/5P	I4/109	2775	2360	Note 1
122S	4-dr Sta Wag-4/5P	I4/109	3090	2640	Note 1
140 SERIES					
142S	2-dr Sedan-5P	I4/109	2995	2520	Note 1
144S	4-dr Sedan-5P	I4/109	3090	2600	Note 1
145S	4-dr Sta Wag-5P	I4/109	N/A	N/A	Note 1
1800S					
1800S	2-dr Spt Cpe-2P	I4/109	4115	2460	Note 2

648

Note 1: A total of 170,746 Volvos (all models) were produced in 1968, followed by 181,668 in 1969.

Note 2: Approximately 23,993 type 1800S Volvos were produced from 1964-68.

Price Note: Figures shown were valid in 1968.

1969 Volvo 145 station wagon.

ENGINE DATA: BASE FOUR (122S, 140 series, 1968 1800S): Inline, overhead-valve four-cylinder (B18). Cast iron block. **Displacement:** 108.5 cu. in. (1778 cc). **Bore & Stroke:** 3.31 x 3.15 in. (84 x 80 mm). **Compression Ratio:** 10.0:1. **Brake Horsepower:** 115 at 6000 rpm. **Torque:** 112 lbs.-ft. at 4000 rpm. Five main bearings. Solid valve lifters. Two SU horizontal carburetors. 12-volt electrical system.

BASE FOUR (1969 140 series, 1800S): Inline, overhead-valve four-cylinder (B20B). Cast iron block. **Displacement:** 121.2 cu. in. (1986 cc). **Bore & Stroke:** 3.50 x 3.15 in. (89 x 80 mm). **Compression Ratio:** 9.5:1. **Brake Horsepower:** 118 at 5800 rpm. **Torque:** 123 lbs.-ft. at 3500 rpm. Five main bearings. Solid valve lifters. Two Zenith-Stromberg horizontal carburetors. 12-volt electrical system.

CHASSIS DATA: Wheelbase: (122S) 102.4 in.; (140 series) 102.4 in.; (1800S) 96.5 in. **Overall Length:** (122S) 175 in.; (140 series) 182.7 in.; (1800S) 173.3 in. **Height:** (122S) 59.3 in.; (142S/144S) 56.7 in.; (145S) 57.0 in.; (1800S) 50.5 in. **Width:** (122S) 65.7 in.; (140 series) 68.1 in.; (1800S) 67 in. **Front Tread:** (122S/1800S) 51.8 in.; (140 series) 53.1 in. **Rear Tread:** (122S/1800S) 51.8 in.; (140 series) 53.1 in. **Standard Tires:** 165x15.

TECHNICAL: Layout: front-engine, rear-drive. **Transmission:** four-speed manual (floor lever). Overdrive optional on 1800S. Automatic optional on 122S and 140 series. **Steering:** cam and roller. **Suspension (front):** upper/lower A-arms with coil springs and anti-roll bar. **Suspension (rear):** rigid axle with trailing arms, Panhard rod and coil springs. **Brakes:** front disc, rear drum (front/rear disc in 1969). **Body Construction:** steel unibody.

PERFORMANCE: Top Speed: (122S) 100 mph; (1800S) up to 112 mph. **Acceleration (0-60 mph):** (122S) 14.9 sec.; (1800S) about 13.9 sec.

PRODUCTION/SALES: Approximately 38,826 Volvos were sold in the U.S. during 1968, followed by 36,146 in 1969.

Manufacturer: AB Volvo, Gothenburg, Sweden.

Distributor: Volvo Inc., Rockleigh, New Jersey.

1969 Volvo 164 four-door sedan.

HISTORY: A six-cylinder Volvo 164 four-door sedan debuted in 1969, with a 182-cid inline engine and $3995 price tag. See next listing for details.

1970-74 VOLVO

140 SERIES (142S/144S/145S) — FOUR — Production of the three body styles continued into 1970 with little change. Then came a restyling that gave the car an even squarer profile, and added a diagonal stripe with Volvo insignia to the grille. Still another grille revision came for 1974.

164S — SIX — Volvo installed a six-cylinder engine into the basic 140-series bodyshell to create the 164S series. The 2978-cc (182-cid) six developed 145 horsepower in its initial form. Early examples of the 164S had a different look from the 140 series, largely because of their tall rounded rectangular grille, made up of thin vertical bars with a narrow diagonal trim bar and insignia. The 140 series wore a wider, lower grille. A lower grille was installed on 1973 models, but still not as wide as the 140's because the 164S had large round auxiliary grilles between the center grille and the headlamps.

1800E — FOUR — A more potent version of the 1986-cc engine with Bosch fuel injection went into the final version of Volvo's two-seat sport coupe. This one had a blacked-out grille, small exhaust grids at the rear, and five-spoke cast alloy wheels. A sturdier gearbox, developed for the new 164S sedan, also was installed in the 1800E coupe. Production continued only into 1971.

1972 Volvo P1800ES sport wagon.

1800ES — FOUR — Before the sport coupe faded away, Volvo turned out an intriguing squareback "coupe/wagon" variant, along the lines of the Reliant Scimitar produced in Britain (also listed in this Catalog). Each was conceived independently, however. Styling features included long rear quarter windows, sharply slanted C-pillars, and a frameless glass hatch. The rear backrest folded down to create a long storage space inside. A Borg-Warner three-speed automatic transmission now was optional, but a four-speed manual (with overdrive) remained standard. For U.S. distribution, compression dropped to 8.7:1 and a 112-bhp rating. Production came to halt in mid-1973.

I.D. DATA: Serial number plate is on left windshield post or (1800E) left door post. Starting serial number: (1970 142S) 142-112400; (1970 144S) 144-138700; (1970 145S) 145-30900; (1970 164S) 164-12200; (1970 1800E) 1800E-30000; (1971 1800E) 184353032800; (1972 1800E) 037550; (1972 1800ES) 000001.

Model	Body Type & Seating	Engine Type/CID	P.O.E. Price	Weight (lbs.)	Prod. Total
140 SERIES					
142S	2-dr Sedan-5P	I4/121	3020	2487	Note 1
144S	4-dr Sedan-5P	I4/121	3120	2542	Note 1
145S	4-dr Sta Wag-5P	I4/121	3420	2659	Note 1
164S					
164S	4-dr Sedan-5P	I6/182	3995	2844	Note 1
1800E					
1800E	2-dr Spt Cpe-2P	I4/121	N/A	2456	Note 2
1800ES					
1800ES	2-dr Spt Wag-4P	I4/121	5150	2614	Note 3

Note 1: A total of 204,991 Volvos (all models) were produced in 1970, followed by 214,438 in 1971, 233,965 in 1972, 252,036 in 1973, and 234,189 in 1974.
Note 2: Approximately 9,414 type 1800E Volvos were produced from 1969-71.
Note 3: Approximately 8,078 type 1800ES Volvos were produced from 1971-73.
Price Note: Figures shown were valid in 1970, except (1800ES) 1972.

1972 Volvo 1800E coupe and 1973 Volvo 1800ES sport wagon. (William Siuru Jr.)

ENGINE DATA: BASE FOUR (140 series): Inline, overhead-valve four-cylinder (B20B). Cast iron block. Displacement: 121.2 cu. in. (1986 cc). Bore & Stroke: 3.50 x 3.15 in. (89 x 80 mm). Compression Ratio: 9.5:1. Brake Horsepower: 118 at 5800 rpm. Torque: 123 lbs.-ft. at 3500 rpm. Five main bearings. Solid valve lifters. Two Zenith-Stromberg horizontal carburetors. 12-volt electrical system.

BASE FOUR (1800E): Same as 1986-cc four above, except — Compression Ratio: 10.5:1. Brake Horsepower: 130 at 6000 rpm. Torque: 130 lbs.-ft. at 3500 rpm. Bosch fuel injection.

BASE SIX (164S): Inline, overhead-valve six-cylinder. Displacement: 182 cu. in. (2978 cc). Bore & Stroke: 3.50 x 3.15 in. (89 x 80 mm). Compression Ratio: 9.3:1. Brake Horsepower: 145 at 5500 rpm. Torque: 163 lbs.-ft. at 3000 rpm. Seven main bearings. Solid valve lifters. 12-volt electrical system.

Note: Engine specifications above were valid in 1970. From 1972, all Volvo engines were fuel-injected.

CHASSIS DATA: Wheelbase: (140 series) 102.4 in.; (164S) 106.3 in.; (1800E) 96.5 in. **Overall Length:** (140 series) 182.7 in.; (164S) 185.6 in.; (1800E) 173.3 in. **Height:** (140 series) 56.7 in.; (164S) 56.7 in.; (1800E) 50.5 in. **Width:** (140 series) 68.3 in.; (164S) 68.3 in.; (1800E) 67 in. **Front Tread:** (140 series) 53.1 in.; (164S) 53.1 in.; (1800E) 51.7 in. **Rear Tread:** (140 series) 53.1 in.; (164S) 53.1 in.; (1800E) 51.7 in. **Standard Tires:** (140 series, 164S) 6.85x15; (1800E) 165x15.

TECHNICAL: Layout: front-engine, rear-drive. **Transmission:** four-speed manual (floor lever); overdrive on 1800E; three-speed automatic optional. **Steering:** cam and roller. **Suspension (front):** upper/lower A-arms with coil springs and anti-roll bar. **Suspension (rear):** rigid axle with trailing arms, Panhard rod and coil springs. **Brakes:** front/rear disc. **Body Construction:** steel unibody.

PERFORMANCE: Top Speed: (early 164S) 109 mph; (1800E) 115 mph; (1800ES) up to 115 mph. **Acceleration (0-60 mph):** (early 164S) 9.6 sec.; (1800E) 10.1 sec.; (1800ES) 9.7-11.3 sec.

PRODUCTION/SALES: Approximately 44,513 Volvos were sold in the U.S. during 1970, followed by 48,222 in 1971, 57,772 in 1972, 60,761 in 1973, and 53,043 in 1974.
Manufacturer: AB Volvo, Gothenburg, Sweden.
Distributor: Volvo Inc., Rockleigh, New Jersey.

1975-82 VOLVO

1979 Volvo 262C coupe.

240 SERIES — FOUR — Evolutionary rather than revolutionary, the 240-series arrived on the U.S. market for the 1975 model year. Like the prior 140 series, it came in two- and four-door sedan form, along with a station wagon. Styling was even boxier, setting the tone for Volvos into the 1980s, though with a slightly angled-back front end. A carryover 1986-cc (121-cid) engine provided the power for 1975 models; but that grew to 2127-cc (130-cid) displacement by 1976. All models got a revised front-end look for 1978, along with improved "orthopedic" seats. A turbocharged engine became available for the 1981 model year.

A sporty 242GT two-door introduced for 1978 came with a tuned handling suspension that included front and rear sway bars, plus foglamps, alloy wheels, paint stripes, a front air dam, and padded sport steering wheel. A diesel engine became available for the 1980 model year.

260 SERIES — V-6 — A 163-cid overhead-cam V-6 engine went into the 260 series, introduced to the U.S. for the 1976 model year. Styling was nearly identical to the 240 series. A larger V-6 engine (174-cid) was installed in this model, starting in 1980.

A posh 262C coupe, essentially hand built by Bertone, debuted for 1978 with a $15,000 price tag and intended for limited production. Luxury features included hand-stitched black Italian leather, and elm veneer door trim. Early examples came only in silver with a black vinyl roof and matching interior. Later coupes could have a gold body with brown interior. In 1979, a GLE "Executive" option package for the 260 series included velour seats, automatic transmission, mag wheels, sunroof, and four-speed stereo.

Note: Availability of the 164S sedan continued into 1975 only, with a 130-bhp version of the 182-cid inline six-cylinder engine; see previous listing for details.
Model Number Note: Starting with the 1980 model year, model designations changed from 242, 262, 264, etc., to DL, GL, and GLE.

1980 Volvo 345 GL four-door sedan.

I.D. DATA: Serial number is on left windshield pillar or (1981-up) atop the instrument panel, visible through the windshield.

Model	Body Type & Seating	Engine Type/CID	P.O.E. Price	Weight (lbs.)	Prod. Total
240 SERIES					
242	2-dr Sedan-5P	I4/130	6295	2901	Note 1
244	4-dr Sedan-5P	I4/130	6595	2938	Note 1
245	4-dr Sta Wag-5P	I4/130	7495	3163	Note 1
260 SERIES					
262GL	2-dr Sedan-5P	V6/163	9595	3085	Note 1
264	4-dr Sedan-5P	V6/163	8450	3092	Note 1
264GL	4-dr Sedan-5P	V6/163	9895	3114	Note 1
265	4-dr Sta Wag-5P	V6/163	9495	3265	Note 1

Note 1: A total of 225,388 Volvos (all models) were produced in 1975, followed by 221,199 in 1976, 158,885 in 1977, 181,740 in 1978, 212,782 in 1979, 169,566 in 1980, 191,869 in 1981, and 211,236 in 1982.

Price Note: Figures shown were valid in 1976.

ENGINE DATA: BASE FOUR (1975 240 series): Inline, overhead-valve four-cylinder. Cast iron block. **Displacement:** 121.2 cu. in. (1986 cc). **Bore & Stroke:** 3.50 x 3.15 in. (89 x 80 mm). **Compression Ratio:** 8.7:1. **Brake Horsepower:** 98 at 6000 rpm. **Torque:** 110 lbs.-ft. at 3500 rpm. Five main bearings. Solid valve lifters. Fuel injection.

BASE FOUR (1976-up 240 series): Inline, overhead-cam four-cylinder. **Displacement:** 130 cu. in. (2127 cc). **Bore & Stroke:** 3.62 x 3.15 in. (92 x 80 mm). **Compression Ratio:** 8.7:1. **Brake Horsepower:** 98 at 6000 rpm. **Torque:** 110 lbs.-ft. at 3500 rpm. Five main bearings. Solid valve lifters. Fuel injection.

Note: Horsepower rating of 2127-cc four was 102 at 5200 in 1976 (on 8.5:1 compression), and 107 at 5250 rpm in 1980 (via 9.3:1 compression).

TURBO FOUR (optional 1981-82): Same as 2127-cc four above, but with turbocharger — **Compression Ratio:** 7.5:1. **Brake Horsepower:** 127 at 5400 rpm. **Torque:** 150 lbs.-ft. at 3750 rpm.

BASE V-6 (1976-79 260 series): 90-degree, overhead-cam "vee" type six-cylinder. **Displacement:** 162.6 cu. in. (2664 cc). **Bore & Stroke:** 3.46 x 2.87 in. (88 x 73 mm). **Compression Ratio:** 8.2:1. **Brake Horsepower:** 125 at 5500 rpm. **Torque:** 150 lbs.-ft. at 2750 rpm. Four main bearings. Solid valve lifters. Fuel injection.

BASE V-6 (1980-82 260 series): 90-degree, overhead-cam "vee" type six-cylinder. **Displacement:** 174 cu. in. (2849 cc). **Bore & Stroke:** 3.58 x 2.87 in. (91 x 73 mm). **Compression Ratio:** 8.8:1. **Brake Horsepower:** 130 at 5500 rpm. **Torque:** 153 lbs.-ft. at 2750 rpm. Seven main bearings. Solid valve lifters. Fuel injection.

DIESEL SIX (optional 1980, 1982): Inline, overhead-cam six-cylinder (Volkswagen/Audi). **Displacement:** 145 cu. in. (2377 cc). **Bore & Stroke:** 3.01 x 3.40 in. (76 x 86 mm). **Compression Ratio:** 23.5:1. **Brake Horsepower:** 78 at 4800 rpm. **Torque:** 102 lbs.-ft. at 3000 rpm. Fuel injection.

Note: Though officially available in 1980, no diesels were sold in the U.S. because of difficulty meeting EPA emissions standards.

CHASSIS DATA: Wheelbase: 104.0 in. **Overall Length:** 192.5 in. **Height:** (sed) 56.5 in.; (wag) 57.5 in. **Width:** 67.1 in. **Front Tread:** 55.9 in. **Rear Tread:** 53.1 in.

TECHNICAL: Layout: front-engine, rear-drive. **Transmission:** four-speed manual; three-speed automatic optional. **Steering:** rack and pinion. **Suspension (front):** MacPherson struts with coil springs and anti-roll bar. **Suspension (rear):** rigid axle with Panhard rod, coil springs and anti-roll bar. **Brakes:** front/rear disc. **Body Construction:** steel unibody.

PRODUCTION/SALES: Approximately 60,338 Volvos were sold in the U.S. during 1975, followed by 43,887 in 1976, 46,790 in 1977, 50,880 in 1978, 56,602 in 1979, 56,999 in 1980, 64,477 in 1981, and 72,375 in 1982.

Manufacturer: AB Volvo, Gothenburg, Sweden.

Distributor: Volvo Inc., Rockleigh, New Jersey.

HISTORY: As the decade rolled on, Volvo focused more on luxury, rather than solely on safety and utility. When it debuted in 1977, for instance, the 265GL was called "the world's most expensive station wagon," with a price tag of $9995.

1985 Volvo 740 GLE four-door sedan.

740/760 SERIES — FOUR/V-6 — Riding a longer wheelbase than the former 260 series, the 760 GLE debuted for 1983 with the same light-alloy 2.8-liter V-6 engine (or an optional inline turbodiesel), hooked to a four-speed overdrive automatic transmission. A turbocharged 2.3-liter four joined in 1984, when both 740 GLE and 760 GLE models were offered. A year later came a new 740 series, powered by a 2.3-liter four (as in the 240 series) or a turbocharged edition of that overhead-cam engine. A station wagon joined the original sedan during 1985. Anti-lock braking became standard on the 760 sedan for 1987; the 740 a year later. During the 1989 model year, a more potent 16-valve engine became standard on the 740 GLE. All 1990 models included a driver's airbag. For 1988, Volvo's 760 models switched from a rear axle to multi-link independent rear suspension.

1986 Volvo 780 two-door sedan.

1988 Volvo 240 GL station wagon.

1983-90 VOLVO

1984 Volvo Deluxe DL four-door sedan.

240 SERIES (DL/GL) — FOUR/DIESEL SIX — Production of the four-cylinder Volvos continued with successive improvements but little overall change, except for the adoption of a larger (2.3-liter) engine. The six-cylinder 260 GLE of the early 1980s was replaced by the new 760 GLE, on a longer wheelbase. A six-cylinder diesel engine was available into 1985, as was a turbocharged four. An intercooler soon was added to the turbo, boosting engine output from its initial 131-bhp rating up to 162 bhp. Starting in 1986, the 240 designation returned, after several years of identification as DL and GL models. All 1990 models added a driver's airbag.

I.D. DATA: Serial number is atop the instrument panel, visible through the windshield.

Model	Body Type & Seating	Engine Type/CID	P.O.E. Price	Weight (lbs.)	Prod. Total
DL/GL (240) SERIES					
DL	4-dr Sedan-5P	I4/141	12940	2917	Note 1
DL	4-dr Sta Wag-5P	I4/141	13415	3042	Note 1
GL	2-dr Sedan-5P	I4/141	15985	2939	Note 1
GL	4-dr Sta Wag-5P	I4/141	16515	3042	Note 1
GLT Turbo	4-dr Sedan-5P	I4/130	12940	3045	Note 1
GLT Turbo	4-dr Sta Wag-5P	I4/130	13415	3157	Note 1
740 SERIES					
GLE	4-dr Sedan-5P	I4/141	16845	2952	Note 1
GLE	4-dr Sta Wag-5P	I4/141	19360	3078	Note 1
GLE TD	4-dr Sedan-5P	I6/145	19015	3095	Note 1
GLE TD	4-dr Sta Wag-5P	I6/145	20760	3245	Note 1
Turbo	4-dr Sedan-5P	I4/141	20130	3049	Note 1
Turbo	4-dr Sta Wag-5P	I4/141	21340	3185	Note 1
760 SERIES					
GLE	4-dr Sedan-5P	V6/174	21485	3012	Note 1
Turbo GLE	4-dr Sedan-5P	I4/141	22625	3062	Note 1
Turbo	4-dr Sedan-5P	I4/141	23440	3185	Note 1
TD GLE	4-dr Sedan-5P	I6/145	22470	3217	Note 1
TD	4-dr Sta Wag-5P	I6/145	23660	3262	Note 1

Note 1: Approximately 88,857 Volvos were sold in the U.S. during 1983, followed by 99,541 in 1984, 104,267 in 1985, 113,267 in 1986, 106,539 in 1987, 98,497 in 1988, 102,620 in 1989, and 89,894 in 1990.

Price Note: Figures shown were valid in 1985.

1988 Volvo 740 Turbo four-door sedan.

1989 Volvo 780 Turbo two-door sedan.

ENGINE DATA: BASE FOUR (240 series, 740 series): Inline, overhead-cam four-cylinder. **Displacement:** 141 cu. in. (2316 cc). **Bore & Stroke:** 3.78 x 3.15 in. (96 x 80 mm). **Compression Ratio:** 9.5:1. **Brake Horsepower:** 111 at 5400 rpm. **Torque:** 136 lbs.-ft. at 2750 rpm. Five main bearings. Solid valve lifters. Fuel injection.

TURBO FOUR (optional 1984-86 740/760 series): Same as 2316-cc four above, but with turbocharger — **Compression Ratio:** 8.7:1. **Brake Horsepower:** 157 at 5300 rpm. **Torque:** 185 lbs.-ft. at 2900 rpm.

BASE FOUR (1989-90 740 GLE): Inline, dual-overhead-cam four-cylinder (16-valve). **Displacement:** 141 cu. in. (2316 cc). **Bore & Stroke:** 3.78 x 3.15 in. (96 x 80 mm). **Compression Ratio:** 10.0:1. **Brake Horsepower:** 153 at 5700 rpm. **Torque:** 150 lbs.-ft. at 4450 rpm. Five main bearings. Solid valve lifters. Fuel injection.

TURBO FOUR (optional 1983-85 240 series): Inline, overhead-cam four-cylinder. **Displacement:** 130 cu. in. (2127 cc). **Bore & Stroke:** 3.62 x 3.15 in. (92 x 80 mm). **Compression Ratio:** 7.5:1. **Brake Horsepower:** 162 at 5100 rpm. **Torque:** 181 lbs.-ft. at 3900 rpm. Five main bearings. Solid valve lifters. Fuel injection.

BASE V-6 (760 series): 90-degree, overhead-cam "vee" type six-cylinder. **Displacement:** 174 cu. in. (2849 cc). **Bore & Stroke:** 3.58 x 2.87 in. (91 x 73 mm). **Compression Ratio:** 8.8:1. **Brake Horsepower:** 134 at 5500 rpm. **Torque:** 159 lbs.-ft. at 2750 rpm. Seven main bearings. Solid valve lifters. Fuel injection.

DIESEL SIX (optional 1983-85 240): Inline, overhead-cam six-cylinder (Volkswagen/Audi). **Displacement:** 145 cu. in. (2377 cc). **Bore & Stroke:** 3.01 x 3.40 in. (76 x 86 mm). **Compression Ratio:** 23.0:1. **Brake Horsepower:** 80 at 4800 rpm. **Torque:** 103 lbs.-ft. at 2800 rpm. Fuel injection.

TURBODIESEL SIX (optional 1983-86 760): Same as 2377-cc diesel above, but with turbocharger — **Brake Horsepower:** 106 at 4800 rpm. **Torque:** 140 lbs.-ft. at 2400 rpm.

Engine Note: Specifications above were valid in 1985, except as noted.

CHASSIS DATA: Wheelbase: (240) 104.3 in.; (760 GLE) 109.1 in. **Overall Length:** (240) 188.5 in.; (760 GLE) 188.4 in. **Height:** (240 sed) 56.2 in.; (240 wag) 57.5 in.; (760 GLE) 55.5 in. **Width:** (240) 67.3 in.; (760 GLE) 68.9 in. **Front Tread:** (240) 56.3 in.; (760 GLE) 57.5 in. **Rear Tread:** (240) 53.5 in.; (760 GLE) 57.5 in.

1990 Volvo 240 station wagon.

TECHNICAL: Layout: front-engine, rear-drive. **Transmission:** (240) four-speed manual, or optional three- or four-speed automatic; (760 GLE) four-speed automatic or (some models) four-speed manual. **Steering:** rack and pinion. **Suspension (front):** MacPherson struts with coil springs and anti-roll bar. **Suspension (rear):** rigid axle with Panhard rod, coil springs and anti-roll bar (self-leveling on 760 GLE); except (1988-90 760) multi-link independent. **Brakes:** front/rear disc. **Body Construction:** steel unibody.

ADDITIONAL MODELS: A limited-production 780 luxury coupe, styled and built by Bertone, debuted in 1987. A year later, it gained the multi-link independent rear suspension installed in the 760 series. Power came from the same 2.8-liter V-6 engine used in the 760 GLE, with a four-speed automatic transmission.

Manufacturer: AB Volvo, Gothenburg, Sweden.

Distributor: Volvo North America Corp., Rockleigh, New Jersey.

POSTSCRIPT: For 1991, Volvo introduced a new 940 series, which was similar to the former 760 series but with additional features, a taller rear deck, and sloping back window. The Bertone coupe remained available in 1991, but dropped its former 780 designation.

WARTBURG

Production of the Wartburg at Eisenach, Germany began in 1899, nearly half a decade before Germany was split into East and West. That first single-cylinder, four-stroke Wartburg had a 15-mph top speed and was a product of Fahrzeugfabrik Eisenach, founded in December 1896. The two-seater had its engine at the rear axle, below the driver's seat. An air-cooled version also was produced, with chain drive and tiller steering. By 1899, racing Wartburgs capable of 36-mph speeds appeared at Berlin's international motor vehicle exhibition. In 1902, a more powerful Wartburg racer with 22-horsepower four-cylidner engine reached 72 mph in an international race at Frankfort-on-Main.

"Dixi" motorcars entered production in 1904 and would make Wartburg's reputation over the next three decades. Early models had four-cylinder engines producing anywhere from 8.5 to 32 horsepower. Each had a front-mounted engine and rigid rear axle with leaf springs. In 1906, gate-style gearboxes replaced the original "in series" (progressive) layout. Changes were modest over the next 21 years. Six international racing victories came in 1907, while the company's new trucks earned an award for fuel economy. The most potent Dixis of all arrived in 1925-26, with 3.5-liter six-cylinder engines rated 60 horsepower. Still, the little four-cylinder Dixi with its 750-cc engine was the one people remembered, bearing the slogan "the inside is larger than the outside."

A slightly larger engine (800 cc) powered the car that evolved from the Dixi in 1932, which went under the BMW name. Six-cylinder engines followed, with displacements of 1200, 1500 and 1900 cc. Most notable of all was the 328 race car with its two-liter six and triple carburetors. A 328 won the last Mille Miglia race in 1940. The factory was nearly destroyed during World War II.

Production resumed after the war, by October 1946, with the model 321. Supplementing that two-liter automobile was an R 35/3 motorcycle, with shaft drive and 350-cc four-stroke engine. Next came the 340-1 four-door sedan, starting in October 1949, with two-liter six-cylinder engine and torsion-bar suspension. A streamlined IFA F9 sedan with front-wheel drive and three-cylinder engine emerged in 1953. Displacing 900 cc, the two-stroke engine produced 28 horsepower. Production of those vehicles under the Wartburg name began in 1955. In 1956, a 1.5-liter AWE race car with twin-cam six-cylinder engine produced 135 horsepower, good enough for speeds topping 135 mph.

In the mid-1950s, few would have imagined that an East German automobile world make a stab at the American market. But by 1958, Wartburg was doing exactly that--an effort that persisted into the early 1960s before the car faded away from the imported-car lists, having attracted only a modest number of fans. In 1962, the Wartburg gained a 1000-cc version of the two-stroke engine, with 45-horsepower output. Production continued through the 1960s with a restyled Knight line, but by 1965 the experiment with U.S. imports had fizzled.

1956-58 WARTBURG

1958 Wartburg convertible.

311 — THREE — Successor to the IFA/F9 (East Germany's version of the DKW), the front-drive Wartburg was longer in wheelbase and overall, but carried the same two-stroke, water-cooled engine. Ignition was supplied by three coils (one per cylinder). The 900-cc (55-cid) three-cylinder engine produced 37 horsepower. A column lever controlled the four-speed manual transmission, with overdrive that could be locked out. Features included one-shot central lubricaton. Inside were piano-key controls, like those in the Ford Taunus 17M. Both the trunk and gas-filler lock released from inside the car. The station wagons rear side windows reached up into the roof for an "observation car" effect. As in most German models, the convertible's top bulged upward considerably when down. Rarest of the lot may be the Bellevue hardtop version of the roadster, with its roof transparent up front and fold-down at the rear.

I.D. DATA: Not available.

Model	Body Type & Seating	Engine Type/CID	P.O.E. Price	Weight (lbs.)	Prod. Total
311	4-dr Sedan-4/5P	I3/55	1686	2120	Note 1
311	2-dr Spt Rds	I3/55	N/A	N/A	Note 1
311	4-dr Sta Wag-4/5P	I3/55	N/A	N/A	Note 1

Note 1: Approximately 140 Wartburgs were sold in the U.S. in 1958.
Price Note: Figure shown was effective in 1958, when Wartburgs became available in the U.S.

ENGINE DATA: BASE THREE: Inline three-cylinder (two-stroke). **Displacement:** 55 cu. in. (900 cc). **Bore & Stroke:** 2.75 x 3.07 in. (70 x 78 mm). **Compression Ratio:** 6.8:1. **Brake Horsepower:** 37 at 4000 rpm. **Torque:** 60 lbs.-ft. at 2200 rpm. One horizontal carburetor. 6-volt electrical system (three ignition coils).

CHASSIS DATA: Wheelbase: 96.5 in. **Overall Length:** 169 in. **Height:** 58 in. **Width:** 62 in. **Front Tread:** 47 in. **Rear Tread:** 49.5 in. **Standard Tires:** 6.40x15.

TECHNICAL: Layout: front-engine, front-drive. **Transmission:** four-speed manual with overdrive and freewheeling; column lever. **Standard Final Drive Ratio:** 4.78:1. **Steering:** rack and pinion. **Suspension (front):** independent; transverse leaf spring with wishbones. **Suspension (rear):** rigid (live) axle with transverse leaf spring. **Brakes:** hydraulic, front/rear drum. **Body Construction:** steel unibody.

PERFORMANCE: Top Speed: 70 mph. **Acceleration (0-60 mph):** 26 seconds. **Fuel Mileage:** 25-30 mpg.
Manufacturer: Veb Automobilwerk, Eisenach, East Germany.
Distributor: Wartburg of America Inc., Brooklyn, New York.

HISTORY: Elsewhere in the East German auto industry, the new Trabant was being produced, with a plastic body over a tin/steel structure. Its air-cooled two-stroke engine produced 18 horsepower, for mileage of 39 mpg. Little known in the U.S. for decades, the Trabant received considerable publicity in 1990 when the Berlin Wall finally fell and many of the little two-strokes chugged their way into West Berlin.

1959-62 WARTBURG

WARTBURG — THREE — On sale in the U.S., these East German cars were "tailor-made for you," according to the sales brochure, offering "extraordinary roominess" and "homely comfort." Seven Wartburg models were available this year, including a Standard four-door Limousine (sedan), DeLuxe four-door sedan, two-door station wagon, four-door (camping) station wagon, five-passenger convertible and coupe, and a two-door sport coupe. Mechanical details and appearance were the same as 1958. Most models had a wide grille made up of three horizontal bars, but the two-seat coupe's grille displayed a crosshatch pattern. Round parking lights sat below the headlamps. Under the hood was a three-cylinder, two-stroke engine with 55-cid displacement and only seven horsepower, producing 37 horsepower. The four-speed manual transmission freewheeled in all forward speeds and was described by the company as "semi-automatic." Standard equipment included a heater/defroster; automatic lighting for hood, trunk and interior; cigar lighter; carpeting; turn signals; backup lights; front and rear ashtrays; safety door locks; central lubrication system; and provision for a radio. Adjustable front seats that folded into beds were available for many models. Wagons had rear side windows that wrapped into the roof and a standard sunroof, with fold-down front seats.

I.D. DATA: Not available.

Model	Body Type & Seating	Engine Type/CID	P.O.E. Price	Weight (lbs.)	Prod. Total
Standard	4-dr Sedan-5P	I3/55	1688	2120	Note 1
Deluxe	4-dr Sedan-5P	I3/55	1799	N/A	Note 1
	2-dr Sta Wag-5P	I3/55	1898	N/A	Note 1
	4-dr Camp Wag-5P	I3/55	2085	N/A	Note 1
	2-dr Coupe-5P	I3/55	2199	N/A	Note 1
	2-dr Conv-5P	I3/55	2099	2225	Note 1
	2-dr Spt Rds-2P	I3/55	2799	N/A	Note 1

Note 1: As many as 403 Wartburgs were sold in the U.S. in 1959, and 240 in 1960.

Price Note: A sunroof added $90 to the sedan's price.

ENGINE DATA: BASE THREE: Inline three-cylinder (two-stroke). Displacement: 55 cu. in. (900 cc). Bore & Stroke: 2.75 x 3.07 in. (70 x 78 mm). Compression Ratio: 6.8:1 (later, 7.3:1 or 7.5:1). Brake Horsepower: 37 at 4000 rpm (later, 40/43 bhp). Torque: up to 61.7 lbs.-ft. at 2200 rpm. One BHF H 362/5 carburetor. 6-volt electrical system (three ignition coils).

CHASSIS DATA: Wheelbase: 96.5 in. Overall Length: 169.3 in. Height: 57 in. Width: 62 in. Front Tread: 46.8 in. Rear Tread: 49.6 in. Wheel Type: drop-base five-nut disc. Standard Tires: 5.90x15 or 6.40x15.

TECHNICAL: Layout: front-engine, front-drive. Transmission: four-speed manual with freewheeling (3rd/4th synchro); column lever. Steering: rack and pinion. Suspension (front): independent; laminated transverse spring. Suspension (rear): rigid axle with high-suspended transverse springs. Brakes: hydraulic, front/rear drum. Body Construction: steel unibody on box-type frame. Fuel Tank: 10 gallon.

PERFORMANCE: Top Speed: 70 mph (80 mph claimed). Acceleration (0-60 mph): 26-34 seconds. Fuel Mileage: 27-34 mpg (35-40 mpg claimed).

Manufacturer: Veb Automobilwerk, Eisenach, East Germany.

Distributor: Wartburg of America Inc., Brooklyn, New York.

HISTORY: News releases in the U.S. described the Wartburg as "built to traditional standards by the skilled craftsmen of one of the major automobile manufacturers...in business since 1898. It wasn't brought over until the makers felt that the Wartburg was ready for America...and that America was ready for the Wartburg. " Promotional material promised that customers would receive "an entirely new motoring sensation" from "the low-priced car that makes driving a pleasureful experience in whirling city traffic, or on the broad white ribbon of highway. Wartburg was also described as "the automobile with fingertip control" because of its adjustable fold-down front seats. Ads in 1960 promised buyers three technical benefits: "Never change oil for the life of the engine" (completely self-lubricating); "Never grind valves;" and "Never grease it" (because of central lubrication system).

1963-66 WARTBURG

1966 Wartburg 1000 Deluxe. (William Siuru Jr.)

1000 — THREE — Engine size grew to 991 cubic centimers during 1962, as a result of increase in the bore dimension. Wartburg promoted the 1000 series for its "outstanding rallye qualities," and added two new station wagons for 1964. Under the hood was a three-cylinder two-stroke engine, displacing 991 cc and producing 50 (SAE) horsepower at 4200 rpm. Torque amounted to 71 pounds-feet at 2200 rpm. The four-speed gearbox was synchronized in the upper three gears and freewheeled in all four. The transverse leaf-spring suspension included double-acting telescopic shock absorbers, and rack-and-pinion steering was used. Elastic suspension of the exhaust system was intended to reduce vibration and noise inside the car. Space was provided for five people. At the rear was a large locking trunk. The four-door sedan had two ventipanes, as well as wind-up windows in each door. Front seats were separately adjustable.

Standard equipment included armrests, ashtrays, door pockets, glovebox, a shelf behind the rear seat, clothes peg, automatic lighting of trunk and underhood, windshield washer, twin padded sunvisors (makeup mirror on the passenger side), and a heater. Anchorage was provided for three-point safety belts. Body features included side moldings, hubcaps, and headlamp anti-dazzle rings. A sliding steel sunroof was optional. Models included a five-passenger standard and DeLuxe four-door sedan, a two/three-seat coupe, and a five-door camping sedan. New this year were two three-door station wagons, standard and DeLuxe, each carrying five passengers. Wagons wore 6.40x15 tires and a 5.67:1 axle ratio. The DeLuxe sedan included a leatherette/cloth interior, foam rubber cushions, folding front backrests, and a transistor radio. Wartburg's coupe had a two-tone finish and an interior of two-tone leatherette.

I.D. DATA: Not available.

Model	Body Type & Seating	Engine Type/CID	P.O.E. Price	Weight (lbs.)	Prod. Total
Standard	4-dr Sedan-5P	I3/60	N/A	2057	N/A
Deluxe	4-dr Sedan-5P	I3/60	N/A	N/A	N/A
	2-dr Coupe-2/3P	I3/60	N/A	2101	N/A
	5-dr Camp Sed-5P	I3/60	N/A	N/A	N/A
Standard	3-dr Sta Wag-5P	I3/60	N/A	N/A	N/A
DeLuxe	3-dr Sta Wag-5P	I3/60	N/A	N/A	N/A

ENGINE DATA: BASE THREE: Inline three-cylinder (two-stroke). Cast iron block and light alloy head. Displacement: 60.5 cu. in. (991 cc). Bore & Stroke: 2.89 x 3.07 in. (73.5 x 78 mm). Compression Ratio: 7.3:1 to 7.5:1. Brake Horsepower: 50 (SAE) at 4200 rpm. Torque: 71 lbs.-ft. (DIN) at 2200 rpm. Four main bearings. Otto carburetor. 6-volt electrical system.

CHASSIS DATA: Wheelbase: 96.5 in. Overall Length: (cpe) 165.7 in.; (sed) 169.3 in. Height: 57 in. Width: 62 in. Front Tread: 46.8 in. Rear Tread: 49.6 in. Standard Tires: 5.90x15 except (wagon) 6.40x15.

TECHNICAL: Layout: front-engine, front-drive. Transmission: four-speed manual with freewheeling (2nd/3rd/4th synchro); column lever. Standard Final Drive Ratio: 4.857:1 except (wagon) 5.67:1; later sedan/coupe, 4.429:1. Steering: rack and pinion. Suspension (front): independent; transverse leaf springs with lower wishbones. Suspension (rear): rigid axle with high transverse leaf spring. Brakes: hydraulic, front/rear drum. Body Construction: steel unibody on box-type frame.

PERFORMANCE: Top Speed: 77 mph claimed; (coupe) 83 mph. Fuel Mileage: 27 mpg.

Manufacturer: Veb Automobilwerk, Eisenach, East Germany.

Distributor: Wartburg of America Inc., Brooklyn, New York.

POSTSCRIPT: Distribution of the Wartburg in the U.S. ceased in the early Sixties, though it continued on sale elsewhere in the world. Late in the 1960s, for instance, the restyled Knight series of sedans and station wagons was sold in Britain. "Whether (Wartburg) would have succeeded eventually if the cold war had not heated up we'll never know," said the Small Car Guide published by Mechanix Illustrated in 1962. "Probably not, though, since it attracted few buyers in this country from the first."

WOLSELEY

Not many automakers made a transition from machines that shear sheep to machines that travel the highways. A three-wheeler was the first vehicle created by the Wolseley Sheep Shearing Machine Company of Birmingham, England, under the direction of Herbert Austin—who would later become known for motorcars under his own name. Completed in 1896, this prototype was followed three years later by a four-wheeled vehicle with a horizontally-mounted single-cylinder engine. That one formed the basis for the first production Wolseley, which had belt/chain drive and tiller steering. A steering wheel arrived in 1901, along with straight chain drive. By then, two- and four-cylinder engines also were available. A top speed of 52 mph was claimed for the 5.2-liter four-cylinder model of 1902. Wolseley even offered a short-lived three-cylinder automobile.

Austin resigned from the company in 1905, to form the firm that would bear his own name. By 1906 Wolseley had turned to a model with vertical four-cylinder engine of 3.3-liter displacement, designed by J.D. Siddeley. Some Wolseleys had shaft drive, others chain, while displacements reached as high as 15.7 liters. Thermo-syphon cooling arrived in 1907, as did the first six-cylinder engine. By 1908, L-head engines were customary; and a year later, the last chain drive Wolseley was produced.

After half a dozen years of marketing under the Wolseley-Siddeley name, the suffix was dropped in 1911. By the time World War I erupted, Wolseleys were available with four- and six-cylinder engines, and had electric lighting and detachable wire wheels. Six-cylinder models used compressed-air starters until 1919.

During the war, Wolseley manufactured Hispano-Suiza V-8 aircraft engines. Most early postwar models had overhead-cam engines with detachable cylinder heads, except for a 3.9-liter L-head six. Both small and large models made the lineup, with engines as large as 6.9 liters. Sporting Wolseleys with aluminum bodies were among the models issued during the 1920s, with 1.3- and 2.6-liter engines. The company even offered a model Seven with a flat two-cylinder engine, from 1922-25.

Bankruptcy in 1927 led to a takeover by Sir William Morris (also known as Lord Nuffield). Over the next decade, then, Wolseleys used a number of components from the Morris and MG models that were part of the Nuffield organization. A new 2.0-liter overhead-cam engine went into the Silent 6, introduced in 1927 with a four-speed transmission. A straight eight was available by 1928. A year later, one export model had an all-steel body.

Wolseley's low-budget six-cylinder Hornet debuted in 1930, similar to the four-cylinder Morris Minor of that time. Also available was a Viper, with a larger (2025-cc) six. Wolseleys built from 1933 onward had a lighted radiator badge, while synchromesh arrived a year after that. So did a new Nine with a 1018-cc engine. Like other British automakers, Wolseley offered a preselector transmission in 1935, as a new Wasp replaced the Nine and the Hornet adopted a bigger engine. A Hornet Special offered in 1935-36 carried a 50-bhp engine and was said to be capable of 80-mph speeds.

By 1937, the overhead-cam engines were gone, replaced by overhead-valve units. As World War II erupted, Wolseley offered a broad range of models, all the way up to a Model 25 with a 3485-cc engine that developed at least 105 horsepower. Scotland Yard, the famed British police force, adopted Wolseley Eighteens by this time, with their 2321-cc engines.

Peacetime in 1945 brought a smaller selection of Wolseleys, including an Eight with a 918-cc four-cylinder engine. Two new unibodied models debuted in 1949, as the company moved from Birmingham to Cowley, Oxford: a 4/50 with 1476-cc overhead-cam four-cylinder engine, and a 6/80 with a 2215-cc six-cylinder version. Front suspensions turned to coil springs with the arrival of the 4/44 model in 1953, replacing the earlier torsion-bar setup. The 4/44 was powered by a detuned variant of the 1250-cc engine used in the MG T-series.

A merger of Austin and the Nuffield organization led by 1955 to the model 6/90, with a 2639-cc overhead-valve six. An automatic transmission soon became available for that model, which was similar to Riley's Pathfinder. Next, in 1958, came a 1500 sedan with 1489-cc four-cylinder engine, on a short (86-inch) wheelbase. Among other technical features, the 1500 had rack-and-pinion steering and a close-ratio four-speed manual gearbox. All subsequent Wolseley models were little more than luxury variants of Austin and Morris automobiles. The Wolseley name lasted into 1975, but "real" Wolseleys had expired long before. An occasional early Wolseley wound up on American soil, either when new or secondhand, but the later, less interesting models tend to be rarer yet in the U.S.

1945-48 WOLSELEY

One new model, the Eight sedan, became available in 1946 with a 918-cc overhead-valve engine that developed 33 horsepower. Wheelbase was 89 inches, and the car measured 145 inches overall. Tires were 4.50x17 size.

All other Wolseleys introduced in the early postwar period were carryovers from 1938-39, each with an overhead-valve engine. The Ten had a 1140-cc four, delivering 40 horsepower, and rode a 90-inch wheelbase. The Twelve's engine displaced 1548 cc, and its wheelbase was longer (98 inches). Next up was the Fourteen, with an 1818-cc six-cylinder engine rated 55 horsepower using twin SU carburetors, and a 104.5-inch wheelbase. A Wolseley Eighteen was powered by six cylinders that displaced 2321 cc, for an 85-bhp rating. Topping the list: the model 25 limousine, with a 3485-cc six that developed 105 bhp, atop a wheelbase of 141 inches.

1949-52 WOLSELEY

4/50 (FOUR-FIFTY) — FOUR — More contemporary styling was used for the two new models introduced for 1949, including headlamps built into the fenders. The tall, rather narrow grille consisted of thin vertical bars. Beneath the bonnet of the four-door saloon (sedan) was a 1476-cc four-cylinder overhead-cam engine that developed 51 horsepower. Wheelbase was 102 inches.

6/80 (SIX-EIGHTY) — SIX — Appearance of the 6/80 was similar to the 4/50, but it carried a 2215-cc six-cylinder engine. Bore and stroke dimensions were the same on both engines. Wheelbase of this larger model was 110 inches.

I.D. DATA: Chassis serial number is stamped on a plate on the side of the firewall. Engine number is on the right side of the crankcase.

Model	Body Type & Seating	Engine Type/CID	P.O.E. Price	Weight (lbs.)	Prod. Total
4/50	4-dr Saloon	I4/90	N/A	2575	N/A
6/80	4-dr Saloon	I6/135	N/A	2690	N/A

ENGINE DATA: BASE FOUR (4/50): Inline, overhead-cam four-cylinder. **Displacement:** 90 cu. in. (1476 cc). **Bore & Stroke:** 2.89 x 3.42 in. (73.5 x 87 mm). **Compression Ratio:** 7.0:1. **Brake Horsepower:** 51 at 4400 rpm. Solid valve lifters. One SU carburetor.
BASE SIX (6/80): Inline, overhead-cam six-cylinder. **Displacement:** 135 cu. in. (2215 cc). **Bore & Stroke:** 2.89 x 3.42 in. (73.5 x 87 mm). **Compression Ratio:** 7.0:1. **Brake Horsepower:** 72 at 4600 rpm. Solid valve lifters. Two SU carburetors.

CHASSIS DATA: Wheelbase: (4/50) 102 in.; (6/80) 110 in. **Overall Length:** (4/50) 170 in.; (6/80) 177 in. **Width:** 66 in. **Max. Tread:** 54 in. **Standard Tires:** (4/50) 5.50x15; (6/80) 6.00x15.

TECHNICAL: Layout: front-engine, rear-drive. **Transmission:** four-speed manual. **Standard Final Drive Ratio:** (4/50) 4.55:1; (6/80) 4.1:1. **Suspension (front):** torsion bars. **Suspension (rear):** rigid axle with semi-elliptic leaf springs. **Brakes:** hydraulic, front/rear drum. **Body Construction:** steel unibody.

PERFORMANCE: Top Speed: (4/50) 78 mph; (6/80) 81 mph. **Acceleration (quarter-mile):** (4/50) 24.3 sec.; (6/80) 23.8 sec.
Manufacturer: Wolseley Motors Ltd., Cowley, Oxford, England (formerly at Birmingham, England).

HISTORY: Production of the 4/50 halted at the beginning of 1953, by which time the 4/44 had been introduced.

1953-54 WOLSELEY

4/44 (FOUR-FORTY FOUR) — FOUR — This was the first of the lighter-weight Wolseleys, using unibody construction but not much different in appearance from the former 4/50. A detuned version of the 1250-cc overhead-valve four that powered MG's T-series was installed in the next Wolseley saloon. Output was 46 horsepower, and the car's wheelbase was 102 inches (same as the former 4/50). Coil springs replaced torsion bars in the front suspension. Doors had pushbutton handles that formed a continuous line with the window-frame strip, and the car had a flush-fitting gas filler cover with pushbutton release. Interiors held polished wood garnish rails and leather upholstery. Standard body colors were metallic grey with grey trim, metallic green with green trim, and black with brown or maroon trim.

6/80 (SIX-EIGHTY) — SIX — Production of the 6/80 lasted through the 1954 model year; see previous listing for additional details.

I.D. DATA: Chassis serial number is stamped on a plate on the side of the firewall (6/80), or at its center (4/44). Engine number is on the right side of the crankcase.

Model	Body Type & Seating	Engine Type/CID	P.O.E. Price	Weight (lbs.)	Prod. Total
4/44	4-dr Saloon-4/5P	I4/76	N/A	2435	N/A
6/80	4-dr Saloon-5/6P	I6/135	N/A	2690	N/A

ENGINE DATA: BASE FOUR (4/44): Inline, overhead-valve four-cylinder. **Displacement:** 76.3 cu. in. (1250 cc). **Bore & Stroke:** 2.62 x 3.54 in. (66.5 x 90 mm). **Compression Ratio:** 7.3:1. **Brake Horsepower:** 46 at 4800 rpm. Three main bearings. Solid valve lifters. One SU carburetor.
BASE SIX (6/80): Inline, overhead-cam six-cylinder. **Displacement:** 135 cu. in. (2215 cc). **Bore & Stroke:** 2.89 x 3.42 in. (73.5 x 87 mm). **Compression Ratio:** 7.0:1. **Brake Horsepower:** 72 at 4600 rpm. Solid valve lifters. Two SU carburetors.

CHASSIS DATA: Wheelbase: (4/44) 102 in.; (6/80) 110 in. **Overall Length:** (4/44) 173 in.; (6/80) 177 in. **Width:** (4/44) 61 in.; (6/80) 66 in. **Max. Tread:** (4/44) 51 in.; (6/80) 54 in. **Standard Tires:** (4/44) 5.50x15; (6/80) 6.00x15.

TECHNICAL: Layout: front-engine, rear-drive. **Transmission:** four-speed manual (column lever). **Standard Final Drive Ratio:** (4/44) 5.125:1; (6/80) 4.1:1. **Steering:** (4/44) rack and pinion; (6/80) cam gear. **Suspension (front):** (4/44) wishbones with coil springs; (6/80) wishbones with torsion bars. **Suspension (rear):** rigid axle with semi-elliptic leaf springs and anti-sway bar. **Brakes:** hydraulic, front/rear drum. **Body Construction:** steel unibody.

PERFORMANCE: Top Speed: (4/44) near 73 mph; (6/80) 81 mph. **Acceleration (quarter-mile):** (4/44) 24.2 sec.; (6/80) 23.8 sec.
Manufacturer: Wolseley Motors Ltd., Cowley, Oxford, England.

1955-57 WOLSELEY

4/44 (FOUR-FORTY FOUR) — FOUR — Production of the 4/44 continued into mid-1956, when it was replaced by the 15/50. The car's "craftsman made" facia panel had its instruments in the center, with provision for a "His Master's Voice" radio. A one-piece bowed windshield was used, and bodies got eight coats of paint. Styling features included an illuminated radiator nameplate, and narrow roof guttering for reduction of wind noise.

15/50 (FIFTEEN-FIFTY) — FOUR — A new Wolseley arrived for 1956, with a 1489-cc four-cylinder engine under its hood. This was the Austin (BMC) B-series engine. A spear-like bodyside trim strip extended only part of the body's length. Up front was an angled vertical-bar grille. Small park/signal lights stood immediately below the headlamps.

6/90 (SIX-NINETY) — SERIES I/II — SIX — Introduced prior to the 15/50, this Wolseley arrived as a result of the merger between the Austin and Nuffield organizations, and carried a 2639-cc overhead-valve six-cylinder engine that was claimed to "represent remarkable advances in B.M.C. engine design." Using twin SU carburetors and 7.3:1 compression, that engine developed 95 horsepower. Series II, introduced in 1956, rose slightly to 97 bhp. Standard equipment included a windshield washer, polished wood garnish rail, and provision for a "His Master's Voice" radio. The gearshift and headlight dimmer were on the car's telescopic steering column. Standard body colors were Mist Grey with grey or maroon upholstery, Connaught Green with grey upholstery, Black with brown or maroon upholstery, or Maroon with maroon upholstery. Left-hand-drive models had flashing turn signals.

I.D. DATA: Chassis serial number is stamped on a plate on the side of the firewall (6/90), or at its center (4/44). Engine number is on the right side of the crankcase or (6/90) on the side of the block, next to the oil dipstick.

Model	Body Type & Seating	Engine Type/CID	P.O.E. Price	Weight (lbs.)	Prod. Total
4/44	4-dr Saloon-4/5P	I4/76	N/A	2435	N/A
15/50	4-dr Saloon-4/5P	I4/91	N/A	2465	N/A
6/90	4-dr Saloon-5/6P	I6/161	N/A	3360	N/A

ENGINE DATA: BASE FOUR (4/44): Inline, overhead-valve four-cylinder. **Displacement:** 76.3 cu. in. (1250 cc). **Bore & Stroke:** 2.62 x 3.54 in. (66.5 x 90 mm). **Compression Ratio:** 7.3:1. **Brake Horsepower:** 46 at 4800 rpm. Three main bearings. Solid valve lifters. One SU carburetor.
BASE FOUR (15/50): Inline, overhead-valve four-cylinder. **Displacement:** 90.8 cu. in. (1489 cc). **Bore & Stroke:** 2.87 x 3.50 in. (73 x 88.9 mm). **Compression Ratio:** 7.2:1. **Brake Horsepower:** 50 at 4200 rpm. Solid valve lifters. One SU carburetor. **Note:** A higher-powered version of the 1489-cc four developed 55 horsepower at 4500 rpm, using 8.3:1 compression.
BASE SIX (6/90): Inline, overhead-valve six-cylinder. **Displacement:** 161 cu. in. (2639 cc). **Bore & Stroke:** 3.13 x 3.50 in. (79.4 x 88.9 mm). **Compression Ratio:** 7.3:1. **Brake Horsepower:** 95/97 at 4500 rpm. Solid valve lifters. Two SU carburetors.

CHASSIS DATA: Wheelbase: (4/44) 102 in.; (15/50) 102 in.; (6/90) 113.5 in. **Overall Length:** (4/44) 173 in.; (15/50) 173 in.; (6/90) 188 in. **Width:** (4/44) 61 in.; (15/50) 61 in.; (6/90) 67 in. **Max. Tread:** (4/44) 51 in.; (15/50) 51 in.; (6/90) 51.8 in. **Standard Tires:** (4/44) 5.50x15; (15/50) 5.60x15; (6/90) 6.00x15.

TECHNICAL: Layout: front-engine, rear-drive. **Transmission:** four-speed manual (column lever). **Standard Final Drive Ratio:** (4/44) 5.125:1; (15/50) 4.875:1; (6/90) 4.1:1. **Steering:** (4/44, 15/50) rack and pinion; (6/90) cam and lever. **Suspension (front):** (4/44, 15/50) wishbones with coil springs; (6/90) wishbones with torsion bars. **Suspension (rear):** (4/44, 15/50) rigid axle with semi-elliptic leaf springs; (6/90) rigid axle with coil springs, radius arms and anti-sway bar. **Brakes:** hydraulic, front/rear drum. **Body Construction:** steel unibody.

PERFORMANCE: Top Speed: (4/44) near 73 mph; (15/50) near 78 mph; (6/90) 96 mph. **Acceleration (quarter-mile):** (4/44) 24.2 sec.; (15/50) 23.9 sec.; (6/90) 20.7 sec.
Manufacturer: Wolseley Motors Ltd., Cowley, Oxford, England.

HISTORY: Literature distributed at the Paris show in October 1955 advised that a 4/44 was intended for "those with an eye for beauty...and an inherent appreciation of genuine craftsmanship." Sales literature also promised that "the distinctively beautiful 6-90 is Wolseley's latest creation for the connoisseurs among car users who naturally prefer Wolseley."

1958-65 WOLSELEY

15/60 (FIFTEEN-SIXTY) — FOUR — A new 1489-cc overhead-valve engine went into the replacement for the 15/50, which had a much squarer profile than its rounded predecessor. The body was styled by Farina. Production continued into 1961.

1500 — FOUR — Company literature claimed the new small 1500 as "the most sensational Wolseley ever," describing the sedan as "a compact, high performance car with the traditional Wolseley luxury." Under the hood was the same engine that went into the 15/60, but with lower compression (7.2:1) and horsepower (50). Wheelbase was 86 inches, versus 99.25 inches for the 15/60, as this was essentially the same platform used for the Morris Minor. Rack-and-pinion steering was installed, along with a close-ratio four-speed manual gearbox.

6/90 — SERIES III — SIX — Output from the 2639-cc engine rose to 101 horsepower for the third version of Wolseley's six-cylinder model, produced from 1957-59.

I.D. DATA: Chassis serial number is stamped on a plate on the firewall, under the hood. Engine number is on the right side of the block or (6/90) on the side of the block, next to the oil dipstick.

Model	Body Type & Seating	Engine Type/CID	P.O.E. Price	Weight (lbs.)	Prod. Total
1500	4-dr Saloon-4/5P	I4/91	N/A	1990	N/A
15/60	4-dr Saloon-4/5P	I4/91	N/A	2465	N/A
6/90	4-dr Saloon-5/6P	I6/161	N/A	3360	N/A

ENGINE DATA: BASE FOUR (1500, 15/60): Inline, overhead-valve four-cylinder. **Displacement:** 90.8 cu. in. (1489 cc). **Bore & Stroke:** 2.87 x 3.50 in. (73 x 88.9 mm). **Compression Ratio:** (1500) 7.2:1; (15/60) 8.3:1. **Brake Horsepower:** (1500) 50 at 4200 rpm; (15/60) 55 at 4400 rpm. Solid valve lifters. One SU carburetor.
BASE SIX (6/90): Inline, overhead-valve six-cylinder. **Displacement:** 161 cu. in. (2639 cc). **Bore & Stroke:** 3.13 x 3.50 in. (79.4 x 88.9 mm). **Compression Ratio:** 8.3:1. **Brake Horsepower:** 101 at 4500 rpm. Solid valve lifters. Two SU carburetors.

CHASSIS DATA: Wheelbase: (1500) 86 in.; (15/60) 99.25 in.; (6/90) 113.5 in. **Overall Length:** (1500) 152 in.; (15/60) 178 in.; (6/90) 188 in. **Width:** (1500) 60.5 in.; (15/60) 63.5 in.; (6/90) 67 in. **Max. Tread:** (1500) 50.8 in.; (15/60) 49.8 in.; (6/90) 51.8 in. **Standard Tires:** (1500) 5.00x14; (15/60) 5.90x14; (6/90) 6.00x15.

TECHNICAL: Layout: front-engine, rear-drive. **Transmission:** four-speed manual. **Standard Final Drive Ratio:** (1500) 3.73:1; (15/60) 4.55:1; (6/90) 4.1:1. **Steering:** (1500, 15/60) rack and pinion; (6/90) cam and lever. **Suspension (front):** (1500, 6/90) torsion bars; (15/60) wishbones with coil springs. **Suspension (rear):** (1500, 15/60) rigid axle with semi-elliptic leaf springs; (6/90) rigid axle with coil springs, radius arms and anti-sway bar. **Brakes:** hydraulic, front/rear drum. **Body Construction:** steel unibody.
Manufacturer: Wolseley Motors Ltd., Cowley, Oxford, England.

Wolseley 6/110.

HISTORY: The little 1500, produced from 1958 to 1965, ranked as the last "true" Wolseley, though the nameplate lasted into 1975. Later models were little more than posh versions of Austin and Morris automobiles. A 6/99 saloon arrived in 1959, with a 2912-cc six-cylinder engine that developed 117 horsepower. That was followed by a 6/110, which added 3 bhp, and remained available as late as 1968. Wolseley's 16/60 saloon debuted in 1961 with a 1622-cc four, and continued in the lineup for a decade.

Also produced through the 1960s decade was the front-drive Hornet series, based upon the Austin Mini and powered by an 848-cc four-cylinder engine, riding a short (80.25-inch) wheelbase. Displacement grew to 998 cc in 1963, for the Second Series. Other late Wolseleys were variants of the BMC 1100, 1300 and 1800 series, topped by a 2200 saloon with 2227-cc overhead-cam engine that arrived in 1972.

YUGO

Although the low-budget Yugo did not arrive in the U.S. market until the 1986 model year, its Yugoslavian manufacturer—Crvena Zastava, which means red flag—began to produce automobiles in 1954. In fact, it originated a full century earlier, as a manufacturer of agricultural implements.

The first Zastava cars were variants of the Fiat 1400 and 1900. Next came Yugoslavian versions of the Fiat 600, which remained in production long after that model ceased to exist in Italy. Through the 1960s, Zastava turned out a further succession of Fiat-based automobiles, evolved from the 1100, 1300, 1500, 124 and 125. Zastava's version of the front-drive Fiat 128, introduced in 1971 and known as the 101, had a restyled rear panel and later became available as a hatchback, a body style that had not been issued in Italy.

By 1981, the old Fiat 600 was still coming out of the Zastava plant, but so was a three-door hatchback Yugo 45, related to the Fiat 127 but different in appearance. In addition to examples with a 903-cc engine, the company turned out 1.1-liter enlargements, and an optional 1.3-liter four-cylinder engine.

Critics tended to scoff at the Yugo not long after it went on sale in the U.S. for the 1986 model year, imported by Malcolm Bricklin and priced at an amazingly low $3990. Some branded it more a toy than an automobile, and smugly pointed out a series of flaws. As it happened, many of the criticisms were valid, and the Yugo's image suffered from the start. Owners began to complain about a large number of mechanical ills. The insurance industry faulted the car's crash resistance, which didn't help either.

Bankruptcy of the American importing firm in early 1989 threatened to remove Yugo from the U.S. market, but the little car clung to life. No 1989 models at all were imported, but a revived Yugo with fuel-injected engine arrived for 1990. So too did a Cabrio (convertible), priced twice as high as the hatchback. Even after sales slumped badly in 1990, and Peugeot and Sterling departed the American marketplace in mid-1991, the reorganized Yugo operation still had ambitious plans for the future.

CHASSIS DATA: Wheelbase: 84.6 in. **Overall Length:** 139.0 in. **Height:** 54.7 in. **Width:** 60.7 in. **Front Tread:** 51.5 in. **Rear Tread:** 51.7 in. **Standard Tires:** 145x13.

TECHNICAL: Layout: front-engine, front-drive. **Transmission:** four-speed manual. **Standard Final Drive Ratio:** 3.76:1. **Steering:** rack and pinion. **Suspension (front):** MacPherson struts with coil springs and stabilizer bar. **Suspension (rear):** independent with struts and transverse leaf spring. **Brakes:** front disc, rear drum. **Body Construction:** steel unibody.

Manufacturer: Zavodi Crvena Zastava, Kragujevac, Yugoslavia.

Distributor: Malcolm Bricklin; then Yugo America Inc. (part of Global Motors Inc.), Upper Saddle River, New Jersey.

HISTORY: Soon after the announcement that the Yugo was about to arrive, East-coast customers stormed the 90 dealers in droves. People plunked down deposits even before seeing the car, much less driving one. By the time 1,500 cars had arrived, dealers had orders for five times that amount. Nevertheless, first-year sales fell well below initial predictions, though they rose in the second season. A sportier GVX model with larger engine was expected in 1987, but did not arrive until midway through the 1988 model year.

1988-89 YUGO

GV SERIES — FOUR — A modest price increase sent the basic Yugo nearly $200 above the $4000 mark (still mighty cheap, even for a subcompact), while an upgraded GVL sold for $300 more, and a "limited edition" GVS had a $4699 list price. The GVL's seats differed from those on the basic GV, and the GVS contained velour upholstery as well as stereo radio with cassette player. Even farther up the scale, a sportier GVX arrived during the 1988 model year, with a larger (1.3-liter) engine and more power, plus a five-speed gearbox. The GVX also had a front air dam, aero body trim components, and foglamps.

I.D. DATA: Yugo's 17-symbol Vehicle Identification Number is atop the instrument panel on the driver's side, visible through the windshield.

Model	Body Type & Seating	Engine Type/CID	P.O.E. Price	Weight (lbs.)	Prod. Total
GV	3-dr Hatch Sed-4P	I4/68	4199	1832	Note 1
GVL	3-dr Hatch Sed-4P	I4/68	4499	1832	Note 1
GVS	3-dr Hatch Sed-4P	I4/68	4699	1832	Note 1
GVX	3-dr Hatch Sed-4P	I4/79	5699	N/A	Note 1

Note 1: A total of 31,545 Yugos were sold in the U.S. during 1988, followed by 10,576 in 1989.

ENGINE DATA: BASE FOUR (GV/GVL/GVS): Inline, overhead-cam four-cylinder. **Displacement:** 68 cu. in. (1116 cc). **Bore & Stroke:** 3.15 x 2.18 in. (80 x 55 mm). **Compression Ratio:** 9.2:1. **Brake Horsepower:** 52 at 5000 rpm. **Torque:** 52 lbs.-ft. at 4600 rpm. Two-barrel carburetor.

BASE FOUR (GVX): Inline, overhead-cam four-cylinder. **Displacement:** 79.3 cu. in. (1301 cc). **Bore & Stroke:** 3.40 x 2.18 in. (86 x 55 mm). **Compression Ratio:** 9.1:1. **Brake Horsepower:** 61 at 5000 rpm. **Torque:** 68 lbs.-ft. at 4000 rpm. Two-barrel carburetor.

CHASSIS DATA: Wheelbase: 84.6 in. **Overall Length:** 139.0 in. **Height:** 54.7 in. **Width:** 60.7 in. **Front Tread:** 51.5 in. **Rear Tread:** 51.7 in. **Standard Tires:** 145SR13 except (GVX) 155/70SR13.

TECHNICAL: Layout: front-engine, front-drive. **Transmission:** four-speed manual except (GVX) five-speed. **Standard Final Drive Ratio:** 3.76:1. **Steering:** rack and pinion. **Suspension (front):** MacPherson struts with coil springs and stabilizer bar. **Suspension (rear):** independent with struts and transverse leaf spring. **Brakes:** front disc, rear drum. **Body Construction:** steel unibody.

Manufacturer: Zavodi Crvena Zastava, Kragujevac, Yugoslavia.

Distributor: Yugo America Inc. (part of Global Motors Inc.), Upper Saddle River, New Jersey.

HISTORY: A GVC convertible (at a considerably higher price) was expected, but before that model could arrive, Yugo America underwent Chapter 11 bankruptcy in January 1989. For that reason, no 1989 models entered the U.S. market, but the company continued to sell leftover 1988s, with the base price of the GV raised to $4349.

1986-87 YUGO

GV — FOUR — During the summer of 1985, the Yugo went on sale as the cheapest car sold in the U.S. market. At 139 inches overall, it was also the shortest car sold in America. Styling was performed by the Zastava organization, but the chassis was based on the Fiat 128, which had been marketed during the 1970s. A 1.1-liter overhead-cam four-cylinder engine was rated 55 horsepower, hooked to a four-speed manual gearbox. Only one body style was offered: a three-door hatchback sedan. (As with most subcompacts, that designation meant two passenger doors, with the hatch ranking as the third door). Standard equipment included fabric upholstery, reclining front seats, fold-down rear seats, rear wiper/washer, front vent wings, open-up rear quarter windows, and bodyside moldings.

I.D. DATA: Yugo's 17-symbol Vehicle Identification Number is atop the instrument panel on the driver's side, visible through the windshield.

Model	Body Type & Seating	Engine Type/CID	P.O.E. Price	Weight (lbs.)	Prod. Total
GV	3-dr Hatch Sed-4P	I4/68	3990	1832	Note 1

Note 1: A total of 35,959 Yugos were sold in the U.S. during 1986, followed by 48,812 in 1987.

Price Note: Figure shown was valid at the Yugo's introduction in 1986 and continued in 1987.

ENGINE DATA: BASE FOUR: Inline, overhead-cam four-cylinder. **Displacement:** 68 cu. in. (1116 cc). **Bore & Stroke:** 3.15 x 2.18 in. (80 x 55 mm). **Compression Ratio:** 9.2:1. **Brake Horsepower:** 55 at 6000 rpm. **Torque:** 52 lbs.-ft. at 4600 rpm. Two-barrel carburetor.

1990 YUGO

1990 Yugo convertible.

1990 Yugo hatchback sedan.

GV PLUS — FOUR — Reorganization brought Yugo America back to life, but the company still faced a major struggle to recapture its lost image. In addition to the basic hatchback, Yugo finally introduced the long-promised Cabrio (convertible) later in the model year, with a sticker price double that of a hatchback. Both models were now powered by a 1.3-liter four-cylinder engine, with fuel injection in the hatchback but a two-barrel carburetor in the convertible. The convertible included a power top and heated glass rear window.

I.D. DATA: Yugo's 17-symbol Vehicle Identification Number is atop the instrument panel on the driver's side, visible through the windshield.

Model	Body Type & Seating	Engine Type/CID	P.O.E. Price	Weight (lbs.)	Prod. Total
GV Plus	3-dr Hatch Sed-4P	I4/79	4435	1870	Note 1
Cabrio	2-dr Conv-4P	I4/79	8990	1947	Note 1

Note 1: A total of 6,359 Yugos were sold in the U.S. during 1990.

ENGINE DATA: BASE FOUR (GV Plus): Inline, overhead-cam four-cylinder. **Displacement:** 79.3 cu. in. (1301 cc). **Bore & Stroke:** 3.40 x 2.18 in. (86 x 55 mm). **Compression Ratio:** 9.1:1. **Brake Horsepower:** 67 at 5500 rpm. **Torque:** 74 lbs.-ft. at 3750 rpm. Five main bearings. Multi-point fuel injection.

BASE FOUR (Cabrio): Same as above, but with Carter-Weber two-barrel carburetor — **Brake Horsepower:** 61 at 5800 rpm. **Torque:** 68 lbs.-ft. at 4000 rpm.

CHASSIS DATA: Wheelbase: 84.6 in. **Overall Length:** 139.0 in. **Height:** (sed) 54.1 in.; (conv) 55.2 in. **Width:** 60.7 in. **Front Tread:** 51.8 in. **Rear Tread:** 52.0 in.

TECHNICAL: Layout: front-engine, front-drive. **Transmission:** five-speed manual. **Steering:** rack and pinion. **Suspension (front):** MacPherson struts with coil springs and stabilizer bar. **Suspension (rear):** independent with struts and transverse leaf spring. **Brakes:** front disc, rear drum. **Body Construction:** steel unibody.

Manufacturer: Zavodi Crvena Zastava, Kragujevac, Yugoslavia.

Distributor: Yugo America Inc., Upper Saddle River, New Jersey.

POSTSCRIPT: Following its bankruptcy, Yugo of America became a subsidiary of the parent company in Yugoslavia rather than a separate organization. Sales slipped to a minimal level in 1990, but the company continued to hang on into the early 1990s.

ZIM/ZIS/ZIL

In the years following World War II, Americans often scoffed at the full-size automobiles produced in the Soviet Union, noting their obvious similarities to American-built cars. Less well known is the fact that at least one of those Soviet automobiles was indeed a copy—but a copy made using body dies obtained legally in America. Others were produced without such a direct connection.

Soviet literature on vintage cars noted that the first Russian automobile was produced as early as 1896, at St. Petersburg. Zis was the first of the major limousines, produced in the Soviet Union from 1936 to 1956 by Zavod Imieni Stalini (an older plant recently renamed for Joseph Stalin), at Moscow. The first Zis, known as the model 101, looked similar to various full-size American sedans of the late prewar era. Its 5.6-liter, 90-horsepower overhead-valve engine was said to be based on, or at least strongly influenced by, Buick's straight-eight. Semi-elliptic leaf springs were used all around. The 101 had separately-mounted headlamps, a horizontal-bar grille, side-mounts—and an undeniable GM appearance. Each car was custom-built, on order from government agencies, and limited to use by top-ranked government officials or other prominent personages. *Life* magazine estimated at the time that each one cost some $75,000 to build. Around the time that World War II erupted, the original limo was replaced by a Model 102, offered in both open and closed body styles.

After the war, production resumed with a Model 110, which looked similar to the big 1941 Packard 180, with its narrow vertical-bar grille. This shouldn't have been a surprise, since Russian agents had purchased body dies from the Briggs coachbuilding company in the U.S., after Packard had decided not to continue production of that model. Power for the Model 110 came from a 140-horsepower L-head straight eight, also influenced by Packard, with three-speed gearbox. Power windows were standard, as were folding jump seats. Top speed was estimated at 87 to 90 mph, which was rather swift for a car on a 148-inch wheelbase that weighed more than 5,600 pounds. Gas mileage was estimated at 10 mpg.

Some 110s were produced as convertible sedans and ambulances, and even used as taxis. Open models had a power top. A sliding glass screen separated passengers from the chauffeur.

In 1956, the plant that had produced the Zis was renamed in honor of Ivan A. Likhachev, its former director and minister of roads. Subsequent vehicles were known by the Zil name, starting with the Model 111 that debuted in 1959. This limousine, too, was clearly influenced by American Packards—but logically enough, by mid-1950s models rather than the earlier body style, and was not as close a copy. Under the hood was a 220-horsepower V-8, hooked to an automatic transmission with pushbutton gear selection (like the units popular in various American models of the time). Like their predecessors, Zils were made available mainly to government officials.

A new Model 111-G debuted in 1963, with styling ties to General Motors models, since Packard had departed the scene years earlier. Power now came from a 6.0-liter V-8 that developed 230 horsepower. Another restyling came in

1970 for the Model 114, featuring a razor-edged upper body. By then, air conditioning and four-wheel disc brakes were standard and the engine grew to 7.0-liter displacement. A shorter five-passenger Model 117 limo also was produced. So was a seven-seat Model 4104 with a 7.7-liter V-8, which remained in production into the 1980s.

Another Soviet automobile with a similar name, the Zim, was produced at Gorky from 1949-57, by Zavod Imiene Molotova. A luxury sedan like its Zis counterpart, the Zim was considered a cut below in status, suitable for second-ranked officials. By 1954, however, according to *Motor Trend,* the Zim went on sale to the general public at a price of about $10,000, and export models could be obtained for around $2500.

Instead of a straight eight or V-8, the Zim had a 212-cid L-head six-cylinder engine, capable of 94 horsepower. A fluid coupling transmitted power from the three-speed gearbox. The typical bustleback Zim had a large-hole checkerboard grille and looked vaguely akin to Cadillacs and Buicks of the late 1940s, with a few styling elements that resembled Chrysler products. The customary wheelbase was 126 inches. Styling was credited to the same team that developed the smaller Pobeda, and the car had seating for six. In addition to the closed sedans and limos, a small number of Zim four-door convertibles were built. Top speed was 78 mph, and a Zim weighed about 3,960 pounds. Acceleration to 60 mph took about 27 seconds. Gas mileage was estimated at about 15 mpg.

An occasional example of one of these three big Soviet limousines managed to reach American shores, typically winding up on display in a museum. One Zis Model 110 was brought home early in the Korean War by General Walton Walker, and sold to Trend Inc., which displayed the huge car at the Motorama of 1951, and then sent it on a tour of the country.

Note: Zil, Zim and Zis models were sometimes identified in capital letters, as ZIL, ZIM and ZIS, since their names were acronyms. In some cases, too, the model number was included as part of the name, separated by a hyphen (e.g., ZIS-110).

1945 Zis 110 limousine.

1945-'46 Zis-110 Conveyor at Moscow Auto Works. (Novosti)

1957 Zis-110 V.

1949 Zis 115-S used by Josef Stalin during the last four years of his life. Windshield and window glass is all more than three inches thick.

1954 Zis 112 hardtop (prototype).

ZUNDAPP

More of a curiosity than a notable motorcar, the odd little Zundapp Janus came from a major German manufacturer of motorcycles. The company had been founded at Nuremberg in 1917, to produce munitions; but elected to depart from that business after the end of World War I. The first motorcycle emerged in 1921, selling at a low price.

Early in the 1930s, as motorcycle sales were sagging, the company had made a quick stab at production of an automobile. Designed by Dr. Ferdinand Porsche, then at work on a German "people's car," this creation had a five-cylinder radial engine, but it never got beyond the construction of a trio of prototypes. By that time, the motorcycle trade was looking better, so Zundapp returned to its primary interest, and later to aircraft engines.

A quarter-century later, after a decade of postwar concentration on motorcycles and light machinery, the completely different Janus went into actual production. Named for the Roman god who faced in two directions, the Janus had seats that did likewise: the driver and one passenger faced forward, while two additional passengers faced to the rear. Dornier, an airplane manufacturer, was responsible for the design. Approximately 6,900 were built before Zundapp again abandoned the car business and returned to motorcycles.

1956-58 ZUNDAPP

JANUS 250 — ONE — A four-passenger vehicle, the Janus contained seats that faced away from each other (back to back), with entry doors at the front and rear that "give easy and unhindered access." This "unusual but extremely practical seating and spacing arrangement...is ideal," declared company literature, because "symmetrically placed seats are all within the wheel base." Power came from a 245-cc single-cylinder, two-stroke engine that evolved from the company's motorcycle work, and was positioned between the two bench-type seats. Those seats could fold down to create sleeping space for two. A four-speed gearbox was standard, with a gate-type hand lever for gear-shifting and rear-wheel drive. Swing axles with coil springs made up the independent rear suspension. With its nearly-symmetrical angled front and rear ends, the Janus looked just about the same whether travelling forward or backward. Standard equipment included an optical gear indicator, ivory-color steering wheel, inside and outside mirrors, and front and rear vents on both sides. Adriatic Blue was the sole standard body color offered.

I.D. DATA: Chassis serial number is on a plate on the firewall. Engine number is stamped on the block.

1958 Zundapp Janus.

Model	Body Type & Seating	Engine Type/CID	P.O.E. Price	Weight (lbs.)	Prod. Total
JANUS					
250	2-dr Sedan-4P	H1/15	N/A	926	Note 1

Note 1: Approximately 6,900 Janus models were produced from 1956-58.

ENGINE DATA: BASE ONE: Horizontal single-cylinder (two-stroke). **Displacement:** 15 cu. in. (245 cc). **Bore & Stroke:** 2.64 x 2.76 in. (67 x 70 mm). **Compression Ratio:** 6.7:1. **Brake Horsepower:** 14 at 5000 rpm. **Torque:** 14.9 lbs.-ft. at 4800 rpm. Solex carburetor.

CHASSIS DATA: Wheelbase: 71.65 in. **Overall Length:** 113.8 in. **Height:** 53.1 in. **Width:** 53.5 in. **Front Tread:** 45.3 in. **Rear Tread:** 46.5 in. **Standard Tires:** 4.40x12.

TECHNICAL: Layout: central-engine, rear-drive. **Transmission:** four-speed manual. Gear ratios: (1st) 4.16:1; (2nd) 2.10:1; (3rd) 1.33:1; (4th) 1.11:1; (rev) 3.975:1. **Standard Final Drive Ratio:** 2.69:1. **Steering:** worm and nut. **Suspension (front):** trailing links with coil springs. **Suspension (rear):** swing axle with coil springs. **Brakes:** hydraulic, front/rear drum. **Body Construction:** steel unibody.

MAJOR OPTIONS: Sunroof. Heater. Two-tone paint. Chrome bumpers. Chrome hubcaps. Sunvisors (front and rear). Luggage net.

PERFORMANCE: Top Speed: 50 mph claimed. **Fuel Mileage:** 64 mpg (British gallons) claimed at 25 mph, 52 mpg at 37 mph.
Manufacturer: Zundapp-Werke GmbH, Nuremberg, Munich, West Germany.

HISTORY: "Economical to run, pleasant to look at and balanced in its dimensions the JANUS is the ideal vehicle for the whole family." That was the claim of Zundapp sales literature issued at the London Auto Show in October 1957. "Campers are enthusiastic, as with only two movements it is possible to turn the seats into level foam rubber upholstered sleeping accommodations for two." Sales literature also promoted the car's "air litres," which meant that it had a large cubic volume of air in the interior for "freedom of movement and breathing."

VEHICLE CONDITION SCALE

Excellent

1) EXCELLENT: Restored to current maximum professional standards of quality in every area, or perfect original with components operating and appearing as new; a 95-plus point show vehicle that is not driven.

Fine

2) FINE: Well-restored, or a combination of superior restoration and excellent original. Also, an *extremely* well-maintained original showing very minimal wear.

Very Good

3) VERY GOOD: Completely operable original or "older restoration" showing wear. Also, a good amateur restoration, all presentable and serviceable inside and out. Plus, combinations of well-done restoration and good operable components or a partially restored vehicle with all parts necessary to complete and/or valuable NOS parts.

Good

4) GOOD: A driveable vehicle needing no or only minor work to be functional. Also, a deteriorated restoration or a very poor amateur restoration. All components may need restoration to be "excellent," but the vehicle is mostly useable "as is."

Restorable

5) RESTORABLE: Needs *complete* restoration of body, chassis and interior. May or may not be running, but isn't weathered, wrecked or stripped to the point of being useful only for parts.

Parts Car

6) PARTS VEHICLE: May or may not be running, but is weathered, wrecked and/or stripped to the point of being useful primarily for parts.

HOW TO USE THE IMPORTED CAR PRICE GUIDE

On the following pages is a **collector car value guide.** The value of an old car is a "ballpark" estimate at best. The estimates contained here are based upon national and regional data compiled by the editors of *Old Cars Weekly* and *Old Cars Price Guide*, as well as foreign car expert William Siuru Jr. of Colorado Springs, Colo.

These data include actual auction bids and prices at collector car auctions and sales, classified and display advertising of such vehicles, verified reports of private sales and input from experts.

Value estimates are listed for cars in six different states of condition. These conditions (1-6) are illustrated and explained in the **VEHICLE CONDITION SCALE** on the following pages. Values are for complete vehicles, not parts cars, except as noted. Modified car values are not included, but can be estimated by figuring the cost of restoring to original condition and adjusting the figures shown here.

Appearing below is a sample price table listing that illustrates the following elements:

A. MAKE: The make (or marque) appears in large, bold-faced type at the beginning of each value section.

B. DESCRIPTION: The extreme left-hand column indicates vehicle year, model name, body type, engine configuration and, in some cases, wheelbase.

C. CONDITION CODE: The six columns to the right are headed by the numbers 1 to 6, which correspond to the conditions described in the **VEHICLE CONDITION SCALE** in this book.

D. VALUE: The value estimates, in dollars, appear below their respective condition codes and across from the vehicle descriptions.

A. MAKE ——— **MERCEDES-BENZ**

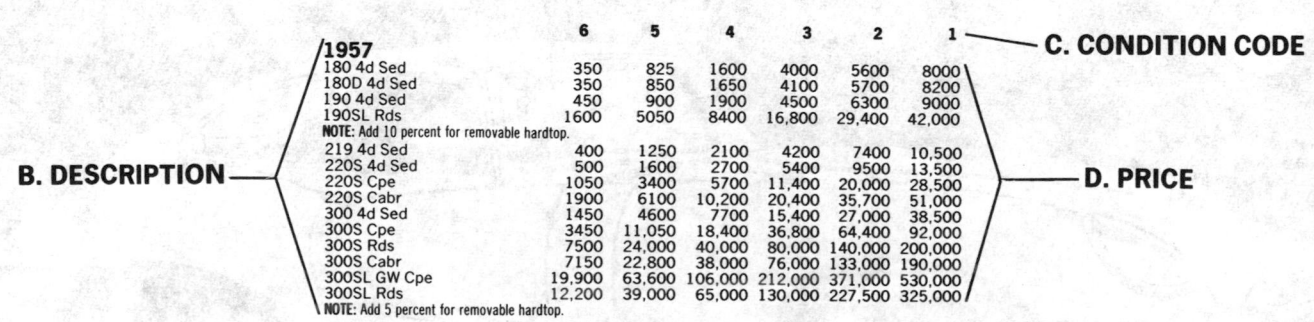

1957	6	5	4	3	2	1
180 4d Sed	350	825	1600	4000	5600	8000
180D 4d Sed	350	850	1650	4100	5700	8200
190 4d Sed	450	900	1900	4500	6300	9000
190SL Rds	1600	5050	8400	16,800	29,400	42,000
NOTE: Add 10 percent for removable hardtop.						
219 4d Sed	400	1250	2100	4200	7400	10,500
220S 4d Sed	500	1600	2700	5400	9500	13,500
220S Cpe	1050	3400	5700	11,400	20,000	28,500
220S Cabr	1900	6100	10,200	20,400	35,700	51,000
300 4d Sed	1450	4600	7700	15,400	27,000	38,500
300S Cpe	3450	11,050	18,400	36,800	64,400	92,000
300S Rds	7500	24,000	40,000	80,000	140,000	200,000
300S Cabr	7150	22,800	38,000	76,000	133,000	190,000
300SL GW Cpe	19,900	63,600	106,000	212,000	371,000	530,000
300SL Rds	12,200	39,000	65,000	130,000	227,500	325,000
NOTE: Add 5 percent for removable hardtop.						

C. CONDITION CODE

B. DESCRIPTION

D. PRICE

AC

1947-52
Two-Litre - (6-cyl) - (117" wb) - (various bodies)

	6	5	4	3	2	1
2d DHC	800	2500	4200	8400	14,700	21,000
4d Saloon	600	1900	3200	6400	11,200	16,000

1953-54
Ace - (6-cyl) - (90" wb)

2d Rds	900	2900	4800	9600	16,800	24,000

1955-56
Ace - (6-cyl) - (90" wb)

2d Rds	900	2900	4800	9600	16,800	24,000

Aceca - (6-cyl) - (90" wb)

2d FBk Cpe	650	2050	3400	6800	11,900	17,000

1957
Ace - (6-cyl) - (90" wb)

2d Rds	900	2900	4800	9600	16,800	24,000

Aceca - (6-cyl) - (90" wb)

2d FBk Cpe	650	2050	3400	6800	11,900	17,000

1958
Ace - (6-cyl) - (90" wb)

2d Rds	900	2900	4800	9600	16,800	24,000

Aceca - (6-cyl) - (90" wb)

2d FBk Cpe	650	2050	3400	6800	11,900	17,000

1959
Ace - (6-cyl) - (90" wb)

2d Rds	900	2900	4800	9600	16,800	24,000

Aceca - (6-cyl) - (90" wb)

2d FBk Cpe	650	2050	3400	6800	11,900	17,000

1960
Ace - (6-cyl) - (90" wb)

2d Rds	900	2900	4800	9600	16,800	24,000

Aceca - (6-cyl) - (90" wb)

2d FBk Cpe	650	2050	3400	6800	11,900	17,000

1961
Ace - (6-cyl) - (90" wb)

2d Rds	900	2900	4800	9600	16,800	24,000

Aceca - (6-cyl) - (90" wb)

2d FBk Cpe	650	2050	3400	6800	11,900	17,000

1962
Ace - (6-cyl) - (90" wb)

2d Rds	1000	3100	5200	10,400	18,200	26,000

Aceca - (6-cyl) - (90" wb)

2d FBk Cpe	700	2300	3800	7600	13,300	19,000

Ford/AC Shelby Cobra - (260/289 V-8) - (90" wb)

2d Rds	4350	13,900	23,200	46,400	81,200	116,000

1963
Ace - (6-cyl) - (90" wb)

2d Rds	1000	3100	5200	10,400	18,200	26,000

Aceca - (6-cyl) - (90" wb)

2d FBk Cpe	700	2300	3800	7600	13,300	19,000

Ford/AC Shelby Cobra Mark II - (289 V-8) - (90" wb)

2d Rds	4500	14,400	24,000	48,000	84,000	120,000

NOTE: Add 20 percent for 1956-63 Ace or Aceca with Bristol engine.

1964
Ace - (6-cyl) - (90" wb)

2d Rds	1000	3100	5200	10,400	18,200	26,000

Aceca - (6-cyl) - (90" wb)

2d FBk Cpe	700	2300	3800	7600	13,300	19,000

Ford/AC Shelby Cobra Mark II - (289 V-8) - (90" wb)

2d Rds	4500	14,400	24,000	48,000	84,000	120,000

1965
Ford/AC Shelby Cobra Mark II - (289 V-8) - (90" wb)

2d Rds	4500	14,400	24,000	48,000	84,000	120,000

Ford/AC Shelby Cobra Mark III - (427-428 V-8) - (90" wb)

2d Rds	9750	31,200	52,000	104,000	182,000	260,000

Ford/AC 428 - (428 V-8) - (96" wb)

2d Conv	1150	3600	6000	12,000	21,000	30,000
2d Cpe	750	2400	4000	8000	14,000	20,000

Shelby Cobra Mark III - (427 SC V-8) - (90" wb)

2d Rds	value not estimable

NOTE: Approxiamtely 26 made.

Shelby Cobra Daytona

2d Cpe	value not estimable

NOTE: 6 made.

1966
Ford/AC Shelby Cobra Mark III - (427/428 V-8) - (90" wb)

2d Rds	9750	31,200	52,000	104,000	182,000	260,000

Ford/AC 289 - (289 V-8) - (90" wb)

2d Rds	1300	4200	7000	14,000	24,500	35,000

Ford/AC 428 - (428 V-8) - (96" wb)

2d Conv	1450	4550	7600	15,200	26,600	38,000
2d Cpe	950	3000	5000	10,000	17,500	25,000

1967
Ford/AC Shelby Cobra Mark III (427/428 V-8) - (90" wb)

2d Rds	9750	31,200	52,000	104,000	182,000	260,000

Ford/AC 289 - (289 V-8) - (90" wb)

2d Rds	1500	4800	8000	16,000	28,000	40,000

Ford/AC 428 - (428 V-8) - (96" wb)

2d Conv	1450	4550	7600	15,200	26,600	38,000
2d Cpe	950	3000	5000	10,000	17,500	25,000

1968
Ford/AC Shelby Cobra Mark III 427/428 V-8) - (90" wb)

	6	5	4	3	2	1
2d Rds	9750	31,200	52,000	104,000	182,000	260,000

Ford/AC 289 - (289 V-8) - (90" wb)

2d Rds	1500	4800	8000	16,000	28,000	40,000

Ford/AC 428 - (428 V-8) - (96" wb)

2d Conv	1300	4200	7000	14,000	24,500	35,000
2d Cpe	950	3000	5000	10,000	17,500	25,000

1969-73
Ford/AC 428 - (428 V-8) - (96" wb)

2d Conv	1200	3850	6400	12,800	22,400	32,000
2d Cpe	900	2900	4800	9600	16,800	24,000

ACURA

1986
Integra

3d HBk RS	200	500	1100	1900	3500	5000
5d HBk RS	200	550	1150	2100	3800	5400
3d HBk LS	200	600	1200	2200	3850	5500
5d HBk LS	200	650	1250	2400	4200	6000

Legend

4d Sed	400	1200	2000	4000	7000	10,000

1987
Integra

3d HBk RS	200	650	1250	2400	4200	6000
5d HBk RS	200	675	1300	2500	4350	6200
3d HBk LS	350	700	1350	2800	4550	6500
5d HBk LS	350	750	1450	3300	4900	7000

Legend

4d Sed	500	1550	2600	5200	9100	13,000
2d Cpe	550	1700	2800	5600	9800	14,000

1988
Integra

3d HBk RS	350	750	1450	3300	4900	7000
5d HBk RS	350	750	1450	3300	4900	7000
3d HBk LS	350	825	1600	4000	5600	8000
5d HBk LS	350	875	1700	4250	5900	8500
3d HBk SE	450	900	1900	4500	6300	9000

Legend

4d Sed	550	1800	3000	6000	10,500	15,000
2d Cpe	600	1900	3200	6400	11,200	16,000

1989
Integra

3d HBk RS	400	1300	2200	4400	7700	11,000
5d HBk RS	450	1450	2400	4800	8400	12,000
3d HBk LS	450	1450	2400	4800	8400	12,000
5d HBk LS	450	1500	2500	5000	8800	12,500

Legend

4d Sed	750	2450	4100	8200	14,400	20,500
2d Cpe	850	2650	4400	8800	15,400	22,000

ALFA-ROMEO

1946-1953
6C-2500 Series
(6-cyl) - (118" wb) - (106" SS) - (2443cc)

3P Spt Cpe	650	2050	3400	6800	11,900	17,000
3P Sup Spt Cpe	950	3000	5000	10,000	17,500	25,000
Spt Cbr	800	2500	4200	8400	14,700	21,000
Sup Spt Cabr	1150	3700	6200	12,400	21,700	31,000
Freccia d'Oro Cpe	800	2500	4200	8400	14,700	21,000
Spt Sed	650	2050	3400	6800	11,900	17,000

1950
1900 - (4-cyl) - (98.5" wb) - (1884cc)

4d Berlina Sed	400	1300	2200	4400	7700	11,000

1951
1900 - (4-cyl) - (98.5" wb) - (1884cc)

4d Berlina Sed	400	1300	2200	4400	7700	11,000
Sprint Cpe	600	1900	3200	6400	11,200	16,000

1952
1900 - (4-cyl) - (98.5" wb) - (1884cc)

4d Berlina Sed	400	1300	2200	4400	7700	11,000
T.I. 4d Sed	500	1550	2600	5200	9100	13,000
Sprint Cpe	600	1900	3200	6400	11,200	16,000
Sup Sprint Cpe	700	2300	3800	7600	13,300	19,000
Cabr	800	2500	4200	8400	14,700	21,000

1953
1900 - (4-cyl) - (98.5" wb) - (1884cc)

4d Berlina Sed	400	1300	2200	4400	7700	11,000

1900 - (4-cyl) - (98.5" wb) - (1975cc)

T.I. 4d Sup Sed	500	1550	2600	5200	9100	13,000
Sup Sprint Cpe	700	2300	3800	7600	13,300	19,000

1954
1900 - (4-cyl) - (98.5" wb) - (1884cc)

4d Berlina Sed	400	1300	2200	4400	7700	11,000

1900 - (4-cyl) - (98.5" wb) - (1975cc)	6	5	4	3	2	1
T.I. 4d Sup Sed	500	1550	2600	5200	9100	13,000
Sup Sprint Cpe	750	2400	4000	8000	14,000	20,000
(4-cyl) - (93.7" wb) - (1290cc)						
Giulietta Sprint Cpe	450	1450	2400	4800	8400	12,000
1955						
1900 - (4-cyl) - (98.5" wb) - (1975cc)						
T.I. 4d Sup Sed	500	1550	2600	5200	9100	13,000
Sup Sprint Cpe	750	2400	4000	8000	14,000	20,000
Giulietta						
(4-cyl) - (93.7" wb) - (88.6" wb Spider) - (1290cc)						
4d Berlina Sed	450	900	1900	4500	6300	9000
Sprint Cpe	450	1450	2400	4800	8400	12,000
Spider Conv	550	1800	3000	6000	10,500	15,000
1956						
1900 - (4-cyl) - (98.5" wb) - (1975cc)						
Sup Sprint Cpe	750	2400	4000	8000	14,000	20,000
Giulietta						
(4-cyl) - (93.7" wb) - (88.6" wb Spider) - (1290cc)						
4d Berlina Sed	450	900	1900	4500	6300	9000
Sprint Cpe	450	1450	2400	4800	8400	12,000
Sprint Veloce Cpe	400	1300	2200	4400	7700	11,000
Spider Conv	550	1750	2900	5800	10,200	14,500
Spider Veloce Conv	600	1850	3100	6200	10,900	15,500
1957						
Giulietta						
Spider Rds	550	1700	2800	5600	9800	14,000
Sup Spider Rds	550	1800	3000	6000	10,500	15,000
Sprint Cpe	450	1500	2500	5000	8800	12,500
Veloce Cpe	600	1850	3100	6200	10,900	15,500
1900 Sup Sprint Cpe	650	2050	3400	6800	11,900	17,000
1958						
Giulietta						
Spider Rds	550	1700	2800	5600	9800	14,000
Sup Spider Rds	550	1800	3000	6000	10,500	15,000
Sprint Cpe	450	1500	2500	5000	8800	12,500
Veloce Cpe	600	1850	3100	6200	10,900	15,500
1900 Sup Sprint Cpe	650	2050	3400	6800	11,900	17,000
1959						
Giulietta						
Spider Rds	550	1700	2800	5600	9800	14,000
Sup Spider Rds	550	1800	3000	6000	10,500	15,000
Sprint Cpe	450	1450	2400	4800	8400	12,000
Veloce Cpe	550	1800	3000	6000	10,500	15,000
2000 4d Sed	450	1450	2400	4800	8400	12,000
2000 Rds	850	2650	4400	8800	15,400	22,000
1960						
Giulietta						
Spider Rds	500	1550	2600	5200	9100	13,000
Sup Spider Rds	550	1700	2800	5600	9800	14,000
Sprint Cpe	450	1500	2500	5000	8800	12,500
Sprint Veloce	550	1800	3000	6000	10,500	15,000
2000 4d Sed	450	1450	2400	4800	8400	12,000
2000 Rds	850	2650	4400	8800	15,400	22,000
1961						
Giulietta						
Spider Conv	500	1550	2600	5200	9100	13,000
Veloce Conv	700	2300	3800	7600	13,300	19,000
Sprint Cpe	450	1450	2400	4800	8400	12,000
Sprint Veloce Cpe	550	1700	2800	5600	9800	14,000
2000 Spider Conv	800	2500	4200	8400	14,700	21,000
1962						
Giulietta						
Spider Conv	500	1550	2600	5200	9100	13,000
Sprint Cpe	450	1450	2400	4800	8400	12,000
Spider Veloce Conv	700	2300	3800	7600	13,300	19,000
Sprint Veloce Cpe	550	1700	2800	5600	9800	14,000
2000 Spider Conv	800	2500	4200	8400	14,700	21,000
1963						
Giulietta						
Spider Conv	450	1450	2400	4800	8400	12,000
Sprint Cpe	350	875	1700	4250	5900	8500
Sprint Veloce	400	1300	2200	4400	7700	11,000
Giulia						
Spider Conv	450	1450	2400	4800	8400	12,000
Sprint Cpe	450	950	2100	4750	6650	9500
2600 Spider Conv	550	1700	2800	5600	9800	14,000
2600 Spider Cpe	800	2500	4200	8400	14,700	21,000
1964						
Giulia						
T.I. 4d Sed	200	650	1200	2300	4100	5800
Spider Conv	400	1250	2100	4200	7400	10,500
Sprint Cpe	350	875	1700	4250	5900	8500
2600 Cpe	500	1600	2700	5400	9500	13,500
2600 Conv	750	2450	4100	8200	14,400	20,500
1965						
Giulia						
T.I. 4d Sed	200	600	1200	2300	4000	5700
Sprint GT Cpe	350	850	1650	4100	5700	8200
Sprint Spl Cpe	350	850	1650	4150	5800	8300
Spider Conv	400	1200	2000	4000	7000	10,000
Spider Veloce Conv	450	1450	2400	4800	8400	12,000
2600 Sprint Cpe	500	1550	2600	5200	9100	13,000
2600 Spider Conv	750	2400	4000	8000	14,000	20,000
1966						
T.I. 4d Sed	200	600	1200	2200	3850	5500
Sprint GT Cpe	350	825	1600	4000	5600	8000
Sprint Spl Cpe	350	875	1700	4250	5900	8500
Spider Conv	400	1200	2000	4000	7000	10,000
Spider Veloce Conv	450	1450	2400	4800	8400	12,000
2600 Sprint Cpe	500	1550	2600	5200	9100	13,000
2600 Spider Conv	750	2400	4000	8000	14,000	20,000
1967						
4d Sup Sed	200	600	1200	2200	3850	5500
1600 Dueto Rds	400	1200	2000	4000	7000	10,000
Veloce GT Cpe (2 plus 2)	350	700	1350	2800	4550	6500
T.I. 4d Sed	200	600	1200	2200	3850	5500
Sprint Spl Cpe	350	875	1700	4250	5900	8500
2600 Sprint Cpe	500	1550	2600	5200	9100	13,000
2600 Spider Conv	750	2400	4000	8000	14,000	20,000
1968						
4d Berlina Sed	200	550	1150	2000	3600	5200
Veloce GT Cpe (2 plus 2)	350	700	1350	2800	4550	6500
Spider Veloce	350	875	1700	4250	5900	8500

1969	6	5	4	3	2	1
4d Berlina Sed	200	500	1100	1900	3500	5000
Veloce GT Cpe (2 plus 2)	200	650	1250	2400	4200	6000
Spider Veloce	350	825	1600	4000	5600	8000
1970						
4d Berlina Sed	150	450	1050	1750	3250	4700
Veloce GT Cpe	200	600	1200	2300	4000	5700
Spider Veloce	350	825	1600	4000	5600	8000
1971						
4d Berlina Sed	150	400	1000	1650	3150	4500
Veloce GT Cpe	200	600	1200	2200	3850	5500
Spider Veloce	350	825	1600	4000	5600	8000
1972						
4d Berlina Sed	150	400	1000	1650	3150	4500
Veloce GT Cpe	200	600	1200	2200	3850	5500
Spider Veloce	350	825	1600	4000	5600	8000
1973						
4d Berlina Sed	150	400	1000	1650	3150	4500
Veloce GT Cpe	200	600	1200	2200	3850	5500
Spider Veloce	350	825	1600	4000	5600	8000
1974						
4d Berlina Sed	150	400	1000	1650	3150	4500
Veloce GT Cpe	200	600	1200	2200	3850	5500
Spider Veloce	350	825	1600	4000	5600	8000
1975						
Alfetta Sed	150	350	950	1450	3000	4200
Alfetta GT Cpe	200	550	1150	2100	3800	5400
Spider Veloce	350	825	1600	4000	5600	8000
1976						
Alfetta Spt Sed	150	350	950	1450	3000	4200
Alfetta GT Cpe	200	550	1150	2100	3800	5400
Spider Veloce	350	825	1600	4000	5600	8000
1977						
4d Spt Sed	150	350	950	1350	2800	4000
Sprint Veloce Cpe	200	500	1100	1900	3500	5000
Spider Veloce	350	825	1600	4000	5600	8000
1978						
4d Spt Sed	150	350	950	1350	2800	4000
Sprint Veloce Cpe	200	500	1100	1900	3500	5000
Spider Veloce	350	875	1700	4250	5900	8500
1979						
4d Spt Sed	150	350	950	1350	2800	4000
Sprint Veloce Cpe	200	500	1100	1900	3500	5000
Spider Veloce	150	350	950	1350	2800	4000
1980						
Spider Veloce	400	1250	2100	4200	7400	10,500
1981						
Cpe (2 plus 2)	350	700	1350	2900	4600	6600
Spider Veloce	400	1250	2100	4200	7400	10,500
1982						
Cpe	350	700	1350	2800	4550	6500
Spider Veloce	400	1300	2200	4400	7700	11,000
1983						
GTV6 Cpe	350	875	1700	4350	6050	8700
Spider Veloce	400	1300	2200	4400	7700	11,000
1984						
GTV6 Cpe	450	900	1800	4450	6250	8900
Spider Veloce	450	1450	2400	4800	8400	12,000
1985						
GTV6 Cpe	350	775	1500	3750	5250	7500
Graduate Conv	450	1450	2400	4800	8400	12,000
Spider Veloce	500	1550	2600	5200	9100	13,000
1986						
GTV6 Cpe	350	800	1550	3900	5450	7800
Quadrifoglio	450	1450	2400	4800	8400	12,000
Graduate Conv	450	900	1900	4500	6300	9000
Spider Veloce	400	1250	2100	4200	7400	10,500
1987						
4d Milano Silver	350	825	1600	4000	5600	8000
Quadrifoglio	400	1300	2200	4400	7700	11,000
Graduate Conv	400	1200	2000	4000	7000	10,000
Spider Veloce	400	1300	2200	4400	7700	11,000
1988						
4d Milano Gold	400	1300	2200	4400	7700	11,000
4d Milano Plat	450	1450	2400	4800	8400	12,000
4d Milano Verde	500	1550	2600	5200	9100	13,000
Quadrifoglio	550	1700	2800	5600	9800	14,000
Graduate Conv	400	1300	2200	4400	7700	11,000
Spider Veloce	500	1550	2600	5200	9100	13,000
1989						
4d Milano Gold	500	1550	2600	5200	9100	13,000
4d Milano Plat	550	1800	3000	6000	10,500	15,000
4d Milano 3.0	600	1900	3200	6400	11,200	16,000
Quadrifoglio	650	2050	3400	6800	11,900	17,000
Graduate Conv	550	1700	2800	5600	9800	14,000
Spider Veloce	600	1900	3200	6400	11,200	16,000

ALLARD

1946-49						
J1 - (V-8) - (100" wb)						
2d Rds	3000	9600	16,000	32,000	56,000	80,000
K1 - (V-8) - (106" wb)						
2d Rds	3250	10,300	17,200	34,400	60,200	86,000
L - (V-8) - (112" wb)						
2d Tr	2050	6600	11,000	22,000	38,500	55,000
M - (V-8) - (112" wb)						
2d DHC	2150	6850	11,400	22,800	39,900	57,000
1950-51						
J2 - (V-8) - (100" wb)						
2d Rds	2250	7200	12,000	24,000	42,000	60,000
K2 - (V-8) - (106" wb)						
2d Rds	2350	7450	12,400	24,800	43,400	62,000
2d Spt Sed	1900	6000	10,000	20,000	35,000	50,000
L - (V-8) - (112" wb)						
2d Tr	2050	6600	11,000	22,000	38,500	55,000
M - (V-8) - (112" wb)						
2d DHC	2150	6850	11,400	22,800	39,900	57,000

1952-54

K3 - (V-8) - (100" wb)

	6	5	4	3	2	1
2d Rds	2250	7200	12,000	24,000	42,000	60,000
J2X - (V-8) - (100" wb)						
2d Rds	2850	9100	15,200	30,400	53,200	76,000
2d LeMans Rds	2650	8400	14,000	28,000	49,000	70,000
JR - (V-8) - (96" wb)						
2d Rds	3000	9600	16,000	32,000	56,000	80,000
Monte Carlo/Safari - (V-8) - (112" wb)						
2d M.C. Sed	1500	4800	8000	16,000	28,000	40,000
2d Safari Wag	1900	6000	10,000	20,000	35,000	50,000
Palm Beach - (4-cyl) - (96" wb)						
2d Rds	1800	5750	9600	19,200	33,600	48,000
Palm Beach - (6-cyl) - (96" wb)						
2d Rds	2050	6600	11,000	22,000	38,500	55,000

1955-59

Palm Beach - (4-cyl) - (96" wb)

	6	5	4	3	2	1
2d Rds	1800	5750	9600	19,200	33,600	48,000
Palm Beach - (6-cyl) - (96" wb)						
2d Rds	2050	6600	11,000	22,000	38,500	55,000

AMPHICAR

1961
(4-cyl) - (83" wb) - (43 hp)

	6	5	4	3	2	1
2d Conv	750	2400	4000	8000	14,000	20,000

1962
(4-cyl) - (83" wb) - (43 hp)

	6	5	4	3	2	1
2d Conv	750	2400	4000	8000	14,000	20,000

1963
(4-cyl) - (83" wb) - (43 hp)

	6	5	4	3	2	1
2d Conv	750	2400	4000	8000	14,000	20,000

1964
(4-cyl) - (83" wb) - (43 hp)

	6	5	4	3	2	1
2d Conv	750	2400	4000	8000	14,000	20,000

1965
(4-cyl) - (83" wb) - (43 hp)

	6	5	4	3	2	1
2d Conv	750	2400	4000	8000	14,000	20,000

1966
(4-cyl) - (83" wb) - (43 hp)

	6	5	4	3	2	1
2d Conv	750	2400	4000	8000	14,000	20,000

1967-68
(4-cyl) - (83" wb) - (43 hp)

	6	5	4	3	2	1
2d Conv	750	2400	4000	8000	14,000	20,000

ASTON-MARTIN

(Saloon - two door coupe)

1949 Borgward 2 door sedan

1948-1950
DBI - (4-cyl) - (108" wb) - (1970cc)

	6	5	4	3	2	1
2S Rds (14 made)				value not estimable		

1950-1953
DB2 - (6-cyl) - (99" wb) - (2580cc)

	6	5	4	3	2	1
Saloon	1900	6000	10,000	20,000	35,000	50,000
DHC	3400	10,800	18,000	36,000	63,000	90,000
Graber DHC (3 made)				value not estimable		

1951-1953
DB3 - (6-cyl) - (93" wb) - (2580/2922cc)

	6	5	4	3	2	1
Racer (10 made)				value not estimable		

1953-1955
DB2/4 - (6-cyl) - (99" wb) - (2580/2922cc)

	6	5	4	3	2	1
Saloon	1700	5400	9000	18,000	31,500	45,000
DHC	3250	10,300	17,200	34,400	60,200	86,000
DHC by Graber	3600	11,500	19,200	38,400	67,200	96,000
Rds by Touring (2 made)				value not estimable		

1953-1956
DB3S - (6-cyl) - (87" wb) - (2922cc)

	6	5	4	3	2	1
Racer				value not estimable		
Cpe	2850	9100	15,200	30,400	53,200	76,000

1955-1957
DB2/4 Mark II - (6-cyl) - (99" wb) - (2922cc)

	6	5	4	3	2	1
Saloon	950	3000	5000	10,000	17,500	25,000
DHC	1700	5400	9000	18,000	31,500	45,000
FHC	1050	3350	5600	11,200	19,600	28,000
Spider by Touring (12 made)				value not estimable		

1957-1959
DB Mark III - (6-cyl) - (99" wb) - (2922cc)

	6	5	4	3	2	1
Saloon	950	3000	5000	10,000	17,500	25,000
DHC	1700	5400	9000	18,000	31,500	45,000
FHC	1050	3350	5600	11,200	19,600	28,000

1956-1960
DBR - (6-cyl) - (90" wb) - (2493/2992/4164cc)

	6	5	4	3	2	1
Racer (14 made)				value not estimable		

1958-1960
Series 1
DB4 - (6-cyl) - (98" wb) - (3670cc)

	6	5	4	3	2	1
Saloon	1200	3850	6400	12,800	22,400	32,000

1960-1961
Series 2
DB4 - (6-cyl) - (98" wb) - (3670cc)

	6	5	4	3	2	1
Saloon	1200	3850	6400	12,800	22,400	32,000

1961
Series 3
DB4 - (6-cyl) - (98" wb) - (3670cc)

	6	5	4	3	2	1
Saloon	1200	3850	6400	12,800	22,400	32,000

1961-1962
Series 4
DB4 - (6-cyl) - (98" wb) - (3670cc)

	6	5	4	3	2	1
Saloon	1200	3850	6400	12,800	22,400	32,000
DHC	2050	6600	11,000	22,000	38,500	55,000

1962-1963
Series 5
DB4 - (6-cyl) - (98" wb) - (3670cc)

	6	5	4	3	2	1
Saloon	1200	3850	6400	12,800	22,400	32,000
DHC	2050	6600	11,000	22,000	38,500	55,000

1959-1963
DB4GT - (6-cyl) - (93" wb) - (3670cc)

	6	5	4	3	2	1
Saloon	3600	11,500	19,200	38,400	67,200	96,000
Cpe by Zagato				value not estimable		
Bertone (1 made)				value not estimable		

1963-1965
DB5 - (6-cyl) - (98" wb) - (3995cc)

	6	5	4	3	2	1
Saloon	1300	4200	7000	14,000	24,500	35,000
DHC	2050	6600	11,000	22,000	38,500	55,000
Radford Shooting Brake (12 made)				value not estimable		
Volante (37 made)				value not estimable		

1965-1969
DB6 - (6-cyl) - (102" wb) - (3995cc)

	6	5	4	3	2	1
Saloon	1350	4300	7200	14,400	25,200	36,000
Radford Shooting Brake (6 made)				value not estimable		
Volante	2500	7900	13,200	26,400	46,200	66,000

1967-1972
(6-cyl) - (103" wb) - (3995cc)

	6	5	4	3	2	1
DBS Saloon	1200	3850	6400	12,800	22,400	32,000
DBSC Saloon (2 made)				value not estimable		

1969-1970
DB6 Mark II - (6-cyl) - (102" wb) - (3995cc)

	6	5	4	3	2	1
Saloon	1300	4100	6800	13,600	23,800	34,000
Volante	2500	7900	13,200	26,400	46,200	66,000

1970-1972
DBSV8 - (V-8) - (103" wb) - (5340cc)

	6	5	4	3	2	1
Saloon	1300	4100	6800	13,600	23,800	34,000
Saloon by Ogle (2 built)				value not estimable		

1972-1973
(6-cyl) - (103" wb) - (3995cc)

	6	5	4	3	2	1
AM Vantage Saloon (70 made)				value not estimable		

Series II
AMV8 - (V-8) - (103" wb) - (5340cc)

	6	5	4	3	2	1
Saloon	1500	4800	8000	16,000	28,000	40,000

1973-1978
Series III
AMV8 - (V-8) - (103" wb) - (5340cc)

	6	5	4	3	2	1
Saloon	1750	5500	9200	18,400	32,200	46,000

1977-1978
AMV8 - (103" wb) - (5340cc)

	6	5	4	3	2	1
Vantage Saloon	2050	6600	11,000	22,000	38,500	55,000

1979
Aston Martin

	6	5	4	3	2	1
2d Vantage Cpe	2150	6850	11,400	22,800	39,900	57,000
2d Volante Conv	3550	11,300	18,800	37,600	65,800	94,000
Lagonda						
4d Saloon	2800	8900	14,800	29,600	51,800	74,000

1980
Aston Martin

	6	5	4	3	2	1
2d Vantage Cpe	2200	7100	11,800	23,600	41,300	59,000
2d Volante Conv	3550	11,300	18,800	37,600	65,800	94,000
Lagonda						
4d Saloon	2800	8900	14,800	29,600	51,800	74,000

1981
Aston Martin

	6	5	4	3	2	1
2d Vantage Cpe	2250	7200	12,000	24,000	42,000	60,000
2d Volante Conv	3550	11,300	18,800	37,600	65,800	94,000
Lagonda						
4d Saloon	2800	8900	14,800	29,600	51,800	74,000

1982
Aston Martin

	6	5	4	3	2	1
2d Vantage Cpe	2400	7700	12,800	25,600	44,800	64,000
2d Volante Conv	3600	11,500	19,200	38,400	67,200	96,000
Lagonda						
4d Saloon	2800	8900	14,800	29,600	51,800	74,000

1983
Aston Martin

	6	5	4	3	2	1
2d Vantage Cpe	2650	8400	14,000	28,000	49,000	70,000
2d Volante Conv	3700	11,750	19,600	39,200	68,600	98,000
Lagonda						
4d Saloon	2850	9100	15,200	30,400	53,200	76,000

1984
Aston Martin - (V-8)

	6	5	4	3	2	1
2d Vantage Cpe	3450	11,050	18,400	36,800	64,400	92,000
2d Volante Conv	3700	11,750	19,600	39,200	68,600	98,000
Lagonda - (V-8)						
4d Saloon	2850	9100	15,200	30,400	53,200	76,000

1985
Aston Martin - (V-8)

	6	5	4	3	2	1
2d Vantage Cpe	3450	11,050	18,400	36,800	64,400	92,000
2d Volante Conv	3700	11,750	19,600	39,200	68,600	98,000
Lagonda - (V-8)						
4d Saloon	2850	9100	15,200	30,400	53,200	76,000

1986
Aston Martin - (V-8)

	6	5	4	3	2	1
2d Vantage Cpe	3550	11,300	18,800	37,600	65,800	94,000
2d Volante Conv	3750	12,000	20,000	40,000	70,000	100,000
Lagonda - (V-8)						
4d Saloon	2950	9350	15,600	31,200	54,600	78,000

1987
Aston Martin - (V-8)

	6	5	4	3	2	1
2d Vantage Cpe	3550	11,300	18,800	37,600	65,800	94,000
2d Volante Conv	3750	12,000	20,000	40,000	70,000	100,000
Lagonda - (V-8)						
4d Saloon	2950	9350	15,600	31,200	54,600	78,000

1988
Aston Martin - (V-8)

	6	5	4	3	2	1
2d Vantage Cpe	3600	11,500	19,200	38,400	67,200	96,000
2d Volante Conv	3850	12,250	20,400	40,800	71,400	102,000
Lagonda - (V-8)						
4d Saloon	3000	9600	16,000	32,000	56,000	80,000

1989
Aston Martin - (V-8)

	6	5	4	3	2	1
2d Vantage Cpe	3750	12,000	20,000	40,000	70,000	100,000
2d Volante Conv	3900	12,500	20,800	41,600	72,800	104,000
Lagonda - (V-8)						
4d Saloon	3100	9850	16,400	32,800	57,400	82,000

AUDI

1970

	6	5	4	3	2	1
Super 90						
2d Sed	200	600	1200	2200	3900	5600
4d Sed	200	600	1200	2300	4000	5700
4d Sta Wag	200	600	1200	2300	4000	5700
100 LS						
2d Sed	200	650	1200	2300	4100	5800
4d Sed	200	650	1250	2400	4150	5900

1971

	6	5	4	3	2	1
Super 90						
2d Sed	200	600	1200	2200	3900	5600
4d Sed	200	600	1200	2300	4000	5700
4d Sta Wag	200	600	1200	2300	4000	5700
100 LS						
2d Sed	200	650	1200	2300	4100	5800
4d Sed	200	650	1250	2400	4150	5900

1972

	6	5	4	3	2	1
Super 90						
2d Sed	200	600	1200	2200	3900	5600
4d Sed	200	600	1200	2300	4000	5700
4d Sta Wag	200	600	1200	2300	4000	5700
100						
2d Sed	200	600	1200	2300	4000	5700
4d Sed	200	650	1200	2300	4100	5800
100 LS						
2d Sed	200	600	1200	2300	4000	5700
4d Sed	200	650	1250	2400	4150	5900
100 GL						
2d Sed	200	650	1250	2400	4150	5900
4d Sed	200	650	1250	2400	4200	6000

1973

	6	5	4	3	2	1
100						
2d Sed	200	600	1200	2200	3900	5600
4d Sed	200	600	1200	2300	4000	5700
100 LS						
2d Sed	200	600	1200	2300	4000	5700
4d Sed	200	650	1200	2300	4100	5800
100 GL						
2d Sed	200	650	1200	2300	4100	5800
4d Sed	200	650	1250	2400	4150	5900
Fox						
2d Sed	150	350	950	1350	2800	4000
4d Sed	150	350	950	1350	2800	4000

1974

	6	5	4	3	2	1
100 LS						
2d Sed	200	600	1200	2200	3900	5600
4d Sed	200	600	1200	2300	4000	5700
Fox						
2d Sed	150	350	950	1350	2800	4000
4d Sed	150	350	950	1350	2800	4000

1975

	6	5	4	3	2	1
100 LS						
2d Sed	200	600	1200	2200	3850	5500
4d Sed	200	600	1200	2200	3900	5600
Fox						
2d Sed	150	350	950	1350	2800	4000
4d Sed	150	350	950	1350	2800	4000
4d Sta Wag	150	350	950	1450	3000	4200

1976

	6	5	4	3	2	1
100 LS						
2d Sed	200	550	1150	2100	3800	5400
4d Sed	200	600	1200	2200	3850	5500
Fox						
2d Sed	150	350	950	1350	2800	4000
4d Sed	150	350	950	1350	2800	4000
4d Sta Wag	150	350	950	1450	3000	4200

1977

	6	5	4	3	2	1
Sedan						
2d	200	550	1150	2100	3700	5300
4d	200	550	1150	2100	3800	5400
Fox						
2d Sed	150	350	950	1350	2800	4000
4d Sed	150	350	950	1350	2800	4000
4d Sta Wag	150	350	950	1450	3000	4200

1978

	6	5	4	3	2	1
5000						
4d Sed	200	550	1150	2100	3800	5400
Fox						
2d Sed	150	350	950	1350	2800	4000
4d Sed	150	350	950	1350	2800	4000
4d Sta Wag	150	350	950	1450	3000	4200

1979

	6	5	4	3	2	1
5000						
4d Sed	200	550	1150	2100	3700	5300
4d Sed S	200	600	1200	2200	3900	5600
Fox						
2d Sed	150	350	950	1350	2800	4000
4d Sed	150	350	950	1350	2800	4000
4d Sta Wag	150	350	950	1450	3000	4200

1980

	6	5	4	3	2	1
5000						
4d Sed	200	550	1150	2000	3600	5200
4d Sed S	200	600	1200	2200	3850	5500
4d Sed (Turbo)	200	650	1250	2400	4200	6000
4000						
2d Sed	200	500	1100	1850	3350	4900
4d Sed	200	500	1100	1900	3500	5000

1981

	6	5	4	3	2	1
5000						
4d Sed	200	500	1100	1900	3500	5000
4d Sed S	200	550	1150	2000	3600	5200
4d Sed (Turbo)	200	600	1200	2200	3850	5500
4000						
2d Sed 4E	150	400	1000	1600	3100	4400
4d Sed 4E	150	400	1000	1650	3150	4500
2d Sed (5 plus 5)	200	500	1100	1850	3350	4900
2d Cpe	200	500	1100	1900	3500	5000

1982

	6	5	4	3	2	1
5000						
4d Sed S	200	500	1100	1900	3500	5000
4d Sed (Turbo)	200	600	1200	2200	3850	5500
4000						
2d Sed	150	400	1000	1650	3150	4500
4d Sed (Diesel)	150	350	950	1350	2800	4000
4d Sed S	150	450	1050	1800	3300	4800
2d Cpe	200	500	1100	1850	3350	4900

1983

	6	5	4	3	2	1
5000						
4d Sed S	200	500	1100	1900	3500	5000
4d Sed (Turbo)	200	600	1200	2200	3850	5500
4d Sed (Turbo Diesel)	150	450	1050	1800	3300	4800
4000						
2d Sed	150	400	1000	1650	3150	4500
4d Sed S	150	450	1050	1800	3300	4800
4d Sed S (Diesel)	150	350	950	1350	2800	4000
2d Cpe	200	500	1100	1850	3350	4900

1984

	6	5	4	3	2	1
5000						
4d Sed S	200	600	1200	2200	3850	5500
4d Sed (Turbo)	200	650	1250	2400	4200	6000
4d Sta Wag S	200	600	1200	2300	4000	5700
4000						
2d Sed S	200	500	1100	1900	3500	5000
4d Sed S	200	550	1150	2000	3600	5200
2d GT Cpe	200	650	1200	2300	4100	5800
4d Sed S Quattro (4WD)	200	650	1250	2400	4200	6000

1985

	6	5	4	3	2	1
5000						
4d Sed S	350	775	1500	3750	5250	7500
4d Sed (Turbo)	350	825	1600	4000	5600	8000
4d Sta Wag S	350	800	1550	3850	5400	7700
4000						
4d Sed S	200	650	1250	2400	4200	6000
2d GT Cpe	350	775	1500	3750	5250	7500
4d Sed S Quattro (4WD)	350	825	1600	4000	5600	8000

1986

	6	5	4	3	2	1
5000						
4d Sed S	350	825	1600	4000	5600	8000
4d Sed CS (Turbo)	450	950	2100	4750	6650	9500
4d Sed CS Quattro (Turbo - 4WD)	400	1300	2200	4400	7700	11,000
4d Sta Wag S	350	875	1700	4250	5900	8500
4d Sta Wag CS Quattro (Turbo - 4WD)	450	1450	2400	4800	8400	12,000
4000						
4d Sed S	350	775	1500	3750	5250	7500
2d GT Cpe	350	875	1700	4250	5900	8500
4d Sed CS Quattro (4WD)	450	900	1900	4500	6300	9000

1987

	6	5	4	3	2	1
5000						
4d Sed S	400	1300	2200	4400	7700	11,000
4d Sed CS (Turbo)	450	1400	2300	4600	8100	11,500
4d Sed CS Quattro (Turbo - 4WD)	500	1600	2700	5400	9500	13,500
4d Sta Wag S	550	1750	2900	5800	10,200	14,500
4d Sta Wag CS Quattro (Turbo - 4WD)	600	1850	3100	6200	10,900	15,500
4000						
4d Sed S	350	875	1700	4250	5900	8500
2d GT Cpe	450	900	1900	4500	6300	9000
4d Sed CS Quattro (4WD)	400	1200	2000	4000	7000	10,000

1988

	6	5	4	3	2	1
5000						
4d Sed S	550	1800	3000	6000	10,500	15,000
4d Sed CS (Turbo)	700	2150	3600	7200	12,600	18,000
4d Sed S Quattro (4WD)	650	2050	3400	6800	11,900	17,000
4d Sed CS Quattro (Turbo - 4WD)	750	2400	4000	8000	14,000	20,000
4d Sta Wag S	500	1550	2600	5200	9100	13,000
4d Sta Wag CS Quattro (Turbo - 4WD)	750	2400	4000	8000	14,000	20,000
80 and 90						
4d Sed 80	500	1550	2600	5200	9100	13,000
4d Sed 90	550	1800	3000	6000	10,500	15,000
4d Sed 80 Quattro (4WD)	600	1850	3100	6200	10,900	15,500
4d Sed 90 Quattro (4WD)	650	2050	3400	6800	11,900	17,000

1989

	6	5	4	3	2	1
80 and 90						
4d Sed 80	600	1900	3200	6400	11,200	16,000
4d Sed 90	700	2150	3600	7200	12,600	18,000
4d Sed 80 (4WD)	700	2200	3700	7400	13,000	18,500
4d Sed 90 (4WD)	750	2400	4000	8000	14,000	20,000
100						
4d Sed E	700	2150	3600	7200	12,600	18,000
4d Sed	750	2400	4000	8000	14,000	20,000
4d Sed Quattro (4WD)	800	2500	4200	8400	14,700	21,000
4d Sta Wag	750	2400	4000	8000	14,000	20,000
200						
4d Sed (Turbo)	850	2650	4400	8800	15,400	22,000
4d Sed Quattro (Turbo - 4WD)	900	2900	4800	9600	16,800	24,000
4d Sta Wag Quattro (Turbo - 4WD)	1050	3350	5600	11,200	19,600	28,000

AUSTIN

1947-48

A40 - (4-cyl) - (92.5" wb) - (40 hp)

	6	5	4	3	2	1
2d Dorset Sed	400	1250	2100	4200	7400	10,500
2d Devon Sed	400	1250	2100	4200	7400	10,500

1949

A40 - (4-cyl) - (92.5" wb) - (40 hp)

	6	5	4	3	2	1
2d Dorset Sed	400	1250	2100	4200	7400	10,500
2d Devon Sed	400	1250	2100	4200	7400	10,500
2d Countryman Wag	400	1300	2200	4400	7700	11,000

A90 Atlantic - (4-cyl) - (96" wb) - (88 hp)

	6	5	4	3	2	1
2d Conv	600	1900	3200	6400	11,200	16,000

A125 Sheerline - (6-cyl) - (119" wb) - (125 hp)

	6	5	4	3	2	1
4d Sed	450	1500	2500	5000	8800	12,500

	6	5	4	3	2	1
1950						
A40 Devon - (4-cyl) - (92.5" wb) - (40 hp)						
4d Mk II Sed	400	1250	2100	4200	7400	10,500
4d DeL Sed	400	1250	2100	4200	7400	10,500
A40 Countryman - (4-cyl) - (92.5" wb) - (40 hp)						
2d Sta Wag	400	1300	2200	4400	7700	11,000
A90 Atlantic - (4-cyl) - (96" wb) - (88 hp)						
2d Conv	600	1900	3200	6400	11,200	16,000
A125 Sheerline - (6-cyl) - (119" wb) - (125 hp)						
4d Sed	450	1500	2500	5000	8800	12,500
1951						
A40 Devon - (4-cyl) - (92.5" wb) - (40 hp)						
4d Mk II Sed	400	1200	2000	4000	7000	10,000
4d DeL Sed	400	1250	2100	4200	7400	10,500
A40 Countryman - (4-cyl) - (92.5" wb) - (40 hp)						
2d Sta Wag	450	1400	2300	4600	8100	11,500
A90 Atlantic - (4-cyl) - (96" wb) - (88 hp)						
2d Conv	600	1900	3200	6400	11,200	16,000
2d Spt Sed	450	1450	2400	4800	8400	12,000
A125 Sheerline - (6-cyl) - (119" wb) - (125 hp)						
4d Sed	450	1500	2500	5000	8800	12,500
1952						
A40 Somerset - (4-cyl) - (92.5" wb) - (42/50 hp)						
2d Conv	500	1550	2600	5200	9100	13,000
2d Spt Conv	500	1600	2700	5400	9500	13,500
4d Sed	450	950	2100	4750	6650	9500
A40 Countryman - (4-cyl) - (92.5" wb) - (42 hp)						
2d Sta Wag	400	1300	2200	4400	7700	11,000
A90 Atlantic - (4-cyl) - (96" wb) - (88 hp)						
2d Spt Sed	400	1300	2200	4400	7700	11,000
A125 Sheerline - (6-cyl) - (119" wb) - (125 hp)						
4d Sed	450	1500	2500	5000	8800	12,500
1953						
A30 "Seven" - (4-cyl) - (79.5" wb) - (30 hp)						
4d Sed	350	825	1600	4000	5600	8000
A40 Somerset - (4-cyl) - (92.5" wb) - (42/50 hp)						
2d Conv	500	1550	2600	5200	9100	13,000
2d Spt Conv	500	1600	2700	5400	9500	13,500
4d Sed	400	1200	2000	4000	7000	10,000
A40 Countryman - (4-cyl) - (92.5" wb) - (42 hp)						
2d Sta Wag	400	1300	2200	4400	7700	11,000
1954						
A30 "Seven" - (4-cyl) - (79.5" wb) - (30 hp)						
2d Sed	350	825	1600	4000	5600	8000
4d Sed	350	825	1600	4000	5600	8000
A40 Somerset - (4-cyl) - (92.5" wb) - (42/50 hp)						
2d Conv	500	1550	2600	5200	9100	13,000
4d Sed	400	1200	2000	4000	7000	10,000
A40 Countryman - (4-cyl) - (92.5" wb) - (42 hp)						
2d Sta Wag	400	1300	2200	4400	7700	11,000
1955						
A50 Cambridge - (4-cyl) - (99" wb) - (50 hp)						
4d Sed	350	875	1700	4250	5900	8500
A90 Westminster - (6-cyl) - (103" wb) - (85 hp)						
4d Sed	450	900	1900	4500	6300	9000
1956						
A50 Cambridge - (4-cyl) - (99" wb) - (50 hp)						
4d Sed	350	875	1700	4250	5900	8500
A90 Westminster - (6-cyl) - (103" wb) - (85 hp)						
4d Sed	450	900	1900	4500	6300	9000
1957						
A35 - (4-cyl) - (79" wb) - (34 hp)						
2d Sed	350	850	1650	4200	5850	8400
A55 Cambridge - (4-cyl) - (99" wb) - (51 hp)						
4d Sed	350	875	1700	4350	6050	8700
A95 Westminster - (6-cyl) - (106" wb) - (92 hp)						
4d Sed	450	925	2000	4600	6400	9200
1958						
A35 - (4-cyl) - (79" wb) - (34 hp)						
2d Sed	350	850	1650	4200	5850	8400
A55 Cambridge - (4-cyl) - (99" wb) - (51 hp)						
4d Sed	350	875	1700	4350	6050	8700
1959						
A35 - (4-cyl) - (79" wb) - (34 hp)						
2d Sed	350	850	1650	4200	5850	8400
A40 - (4-cyl) - (83" wb) - (34 hp)						
2d Std Sed	350	875	1700	4250	5900	8500
2d DeL Sed	350	875	1700	4300	6000	8600
A55 Cambridge - (4-cyl) - (99" wb) - (51 hp)						
4d Sed	350	875	1700	4350	6050	8700
A55 Mark II - (4-cyl) - (99" wb) - (51 hp)						
4d Sed	450	900	1800	4400	6150	8800
1960						
850 Mini - (4-cyl) - (80" wb) - (37 hp)						
2d Sed	350	825	1600	4000	5600	8000
A40 - (4-cyl) - (83" wb) - (34 hp)						
2d Std Sed	350	875	1700	4250	5900	8500
2d DeL Sed	350	875	1700	4300	6000	8600
A55 Mark II - (4-cyl) - (99" wb) - (51 hp)						
4d Sed	450	900	1800	4400	6150	8800
A99 Westminster - (6-cyl) - (108" wb) - (112 hp)						
4d Sed	450	900	1800	4450	6250	8900
1961						
850 Mini - (4-cyl) - (80" wb) - (37 hp)						
2d Sed	350	825	1600	4000	5600	8000
Mini Cooper - (4-cyl) - (80" wb) - (55 hp)						
2d Sed	500	1600	2700	5400	9500	13,500
A40 - (4-cyl) - (83" wb) - (34 hp)						
2d Std Sed	350	875	1700	4250	5900	8500
2d DeL Sed	350	875	1700	4300	6000	8600
2d Std Sta Wag	350	875	1700	4300	6000	8600
2d DeL Sta Wag	350	875	1700	4350	6050	8700
A55 Mark II - (4-cyl) - (99" wb) - (51 hp)						
4d Sed	450	900	1800	4400	6150	8800
A99 Westminster - (6-cyl) - (108" wb) - (112 hp)						
4d Sed	450	900	1800	4450	6250	8900
1962						
850 Mini - (4-cyl) - (80" wb) - (37 hp)						
2d Sed	350	825	1600	4000	5600	8000
Mini Cooper - (4-cyl) - (80" wb) - (55 hp)						
2d Sed	500	1550	2600	5200	9100	13,000
A40 - (4-cyl) - (83" wb) - (34 hp)						
2d Sed	350	875	1700	4250	5900	8500
A55 Mark II - (4-cyl) - (99" wb) - (51 hp)						
4d Sed	350	875	1700	4300	6000	8600
1963						
850 Mini - (4-cyl) - (80" wb) - (37 hp)						
2d Sed	350	825	1600	4000	5600	8000
2d Sta Wag	400	1200	2000	4000	7000	10,000
850 Mini Cooper - (4-cyl) - (80" wb) - (56 hp)						
2d Sed	500	1550	2600	5200	9100	13,000
850 Mini Cooper "S" - (4-cyl) - (80" wb) - (75 hp)						
2d Sed	550	1800	3000	6000	10,500	15,000
A60 - (4-cyl) - (100" wb) - (68 hp)						
4d Sed	350	875	1700	4250	5900	8500
4d Countryman	350	875	1700	4350	6050	8700
1964						
850 Mini - (4-cyl) - (80" wb) - (37 hp)						
2d Sed	350	825	1600	4000	5600	8000
2d Sta Wag	400	1200	2000	4000	7000	10,000
850 Mini Cooper - (4-cyl) - (80" wb) - (56 hp)						
2d Sed	500	1550	2600	5200	9100	13,000
850 Mini Cooper "S" - (4-cyl) - (80" wb) - (75 hp)						
2d Sed	550	1800	3000	6000	10,500	15,000
A60 - (4-cyl) - (100" wb) - (68 hp)						
4d Sed	350	875	1700	4250	5900	8500
4d Countryman	350	875	1700	4350	6050	8700
Mark II Princess - (6-cyl) - (110" wb) - (175 hp)						
4d Sed	450	900	1800	4400	6150	8800
1965						
850 Mini - (4-cyl) - (80" wb) - (34 hp)						
2d Sed	350	825	1600	4000	5600	8000
850 Mini Cooper "S" - (4-cyl) - (80" wb) - (75 hp)						
2d Sed	550	1800	3000	6000	10,500	15,000
Mark II Princess - (6-cyl) - (110" wb) - (175 hp)						
4d Sed	450	900	1800	4400	6150	8800
1966						
850 Mini - (4-cyl) - (80" wb) - (34 hp)						
2d Sed	350	825	1600	4000	5600	8000
850 Mini Cooper "S" - (4-cyl) - (80" wb) - (75 hp)						
2d Sed	550	1800	3000	6000	10,500	15,000
Mark II Princess "R" - (6-cyl) - (110" wb) - (175 hp)						
4d Sed	450	900	1800	4400	6150	8800
1967						
850 Mini Cooper "S" - (4-cyl) - (80" wb) - (75 hp)						
2d Sed	550	1800	3000	6000	10,500	15,000
1968						
850 Mini Cooper "S" - (4-cyl) - (80" wb) - (75 hp)						
2d Sed	600	1850	3100	6200	10,900	15,500
America - (4-cyl) - (93" wb) - (58 hp)						
2d Sed	200	500	1100	1900	3500	5000
1969						
America - (4-cyl) - (93" wb) - (58 hp)						
2d Sed	200	500	1100	1900	3500	5000
1970						
America - (4-cyl) - (93" wb) - (58 hp)						
2d Sed	200	500	1100	1900	3500	5000
1971						
America - (4-cyl) - (93" wb) - (58 hp)						
2d Sed	200	500	1100	1900	3500	5000
1972						
No Austins imported in 1972.						
1973						
Marina - (4-cyl) - (96" wb) - (68 hp)						
2d GT Sed	150	400	1000	1650	3150	4500
4d Sed	150	350	950	1350	2800	4000
1974						
Marina - (4-cyl) - (96" wb) - (68 hp)						
2d GT Sed	150	400	1000	1650	3150	4500
4d Sed	150	350	950	1350	2800	4000
1975						
Marina - (4-cyl) - (96" wb) - (68 hp)						
2d GT Sed	150	400	1000	1650	3150	4500
4d Sed	150	350	950	1350	2800	4000

AUSTIN-HEALEY

	6	5	4	3	2	1
1953-1954						
"100" - (4-cyl) - (90" wb) - (90 hp)						
2d Spt Rds	1000	3100	5200	10,400	18,200	26,000
1955						
"100" - (4-cyl) - (90" wb) - (90 hp)						
2d Spt Rds	1000	3100	5200	10,400	18,200	26,000
"100M" - (4-cyl) - (90" wb) - (110 hp)						
2d Spt Rds	1100	3500	5800	11,600	20,300	29,000
"100S" - (4-cyl) - (90" wb) - (132 hp)						
2d Spt Rds	1150	3700	6200	12,400	21,700	31,000
1956						
"100" - (4-cyl) - (90" wb) - (90 hp)						
2d Spt Rds	1000	3100	5200	10,400	18,200	26,000
2d LeMans Rds	1050	3350	5600	11,200	19,600	28,000
"100M" - (4-cyl) - (90" wb) - (110 hp)						
2d Spt Rds	1100	3500	5800	11,600	20,300	29,000
"100-6" - (6-cyl) - (92" wb) - (102 hp)						
2d Spt Rds	1150	3600	6000	12,000	21,000	30,000
1957						
"100-6" - (6-cyl) - (92" wb) - (102 hp)						
2d Spt Rds	850	2750	4600	9200	16,100	23,000
1958						
"100-6" - (6-cyl) - (92" wb) - (102 hp)						
2d Spt Rds	1000	3100	5200	10,400	18,200	26,000
Sprite Mark I - (4-cyl) - (80" wb) - (43 hp)						
2d Rds	400	1200	2000	4000	7000	10,000
1959						
"100-6" - (6-cyl) - (92" wb) - (102 hp)						
2d Spt Rds	1000	3100	5200	10,400	18,200	26,000
Sprite Mark I - (4-cyl) - (80" wb) - (43 hp)						
2d Rds	400	1300	2200	4400	7700	11,000
"3000" Mark I - (6-cyl) - (92" wb) - (124 hp)						
2d Spt Rds	1050	3350	5600	11,200	19,600	28,000
1960						
"3000" Mark I - (6-cyl) - (92" wb) - (124 hp)						
2d Spt Rds	1050	3350	5600	11,200	19,600	28,000

	6	5	4	3	2	1
Sprite Mark I - (4-cyl) - (80" wb) - (43 hp)						
2d Rds	850	2650	4400	8800	15,400	22,000
1961						
"3000" Mark I - (6-cyl) - (92" wb) - (124 hp)						
2d Spt Rds	1000	3100	5200	10,400	18,200	26,000
"3000" Mark II - (6-cyl) - (92" wb) - (132 hp)						
2d Spt Rds	1000	3250	5400	10,800	18,900	27,000
Sprite Mark I - (4-cyl) - (80" wb) - (43 hp)						
2d Rds	400	1200	2000	4000	7000	10,000
Sprite Mark II - (4-cyl) - (80" wb) - (46 hp)						
2d Rds	350	750	1450	3300	4900	7000
1962						
"3000" Mark II - (6-cyl) - (92" wb) - (132 hp)						
2d Spt Rds	1000	3250	5400	10,800	18,900	27,000
Sprite Mark II - (4-cyl) - (80" wb) - (46 hp)						
2d Rds	350	750	1450	3300	4900	7000
1963						
"3000" Mark II - (6-cyl) - (92" wb) - (132 hp)						
2d Spt Rds	1000	3250	5400	10,800	18,900	27,000
Sprite Mark II - (4-cyl) - (80" wb) - (56 hp)						
2d Rds	350	750	1450	3300	4900	7000
1964						
"3000" Mark II - (6-cyl) - (92" wb) - (132 hp)						
2d Spt Rds	1050	3300	5500	11,000	19,300	27,500
"3000" Mark III - (6-cyl) - (92" wb) - (150 hp)						
2d Spt Rds	1050	3400	5700	11,400	20,000	28,500
Sprite Mark II - (4-cyl) - (80" wb) - (56 hp)						
2d Rds	350	750	1450	3300	4900	7000
Sprite Mark III - (4-cyl) - (80" wb) - (59 hp)						
2d Rds	350	750	1450	3300	4900	7000
1965						
"3000" Mark III - (6-cyl) - (92" wb) - (150 hp)						
2d Spt Rds	1050	3400	5700	11,400	20,000	28,500
Sprite Mark III - (4-cyl) - (80" wb) - (59 hp)						
2d Rds	350	750	1450	3300	4900	7000
1966						
"3000" Mark III - (6-cyl) - (92" wb) - (150 hp)						
2d Spt Rds	1100	3500	5800	11,600	20,300	29,000
Sprite Mark III - (4-cyl) - (80" wb) - (59 hp)						
2d Rds	350	750	1450	3300	4900	7000
1967						
"3000" Mark III - (6-cyl) - (92" wb) - (150 hp)						
2d Spt Rds	1100	3500	5800	11,600	20,300	29,000
Sprite Mark III - (4-cyl) - (80" wb) - (59 hp)						
2d Rds	350	750	1450	3300	4900	7000
1968						
Sprite Mark III - (4-cyl) - (80" wb) - (59 hp)						
2d Rds	350	750	1450	3300	4900	7000
Sprite Mark IV - (4-cyl) - (80" wb) - (62 hp)						
2d Rds	350	750	1450	3300	4900	7000
1969						
Sprite Mark IV - (4-cyl) - (80" wb) - (62 hp)						
2d Rds	350	750	1450	3300	4900	7000
1970						
Sprite Mark IV - (4-cyl) - (80" wb) - (62 hp)						
2d Rds	350	750	1450	3300	4900	7000

BENTLEY

	6	5	4	3	2	1
1946-1951						
(6-cyl) - (120" wb) - (4257cc)						
4d Sed	850	2750	4600	9200	16,100	23,000
1951-1952						
Mark VI - (6-cyl) - (120" wb) - (4566cc)						
Std Steel Saloon	700	2200	3700	7400	13,000	18,500
Abbott						
DHC	2050	6600	11,000	22,000	38,500	55,000
FHC	950	3050	5100	10,200	17,900	25,500
Facel						
FHC	1350	4300	7200	14,400	25,200	36,000
Franay						
Sedanca Cpe	1300	4200	7000	14,000	24,500	35,000
DHC	2250	7200	12,000	24,000	42,000	60,000
Freestone & Webb						
Cpe	1100	3550	5900	11,800	20,700	29,500
Saloon	800	2500	4200	8400	14,700	21,000
Graber						
Cpe	1450	4550	7600	15,200	26,600	38,000
Gurney Nutting						
Sedanca Cpe	1350	4300	7200	14,400	25,200	36,000
Hooper						
Cpe	1450	4700	7800	15,600	27,300	39,000
Saloon	1350	4300	7200	14,400	25,200	36,000
Sedanca Cpe	1550	4900	8200	16,400	28,700	41,000
H.J. Mulliner						
DHC	3250	10,300	17,200	34,400	60,200	86,000
2d Saloon	1100	3500	5800	11,600	20,300	29,000
4d Saloon	950	3000	5000	10,000	17,500	25,000
Park Ward						
DHC	3250	10,300	17,200	34,400	60,200	86,000
Cpe	1150	3700	6200	12,400	21,700	31,000
Saloon	1100	3500	5800	11,600	20,300	29,000
Radford						
Countryman	1150	3700	6200	12,400	21,700	31,000
Windovers						
2d Saloon	1150	3600	6000	12,000	21,000	30,000
Worlaufen						
DHC	1900	6000	10,000	20,000	35,000	50,000
James Young						
Clubman Cpe	1100	3500	5800	11,600	20,300	29,000
Saloon	1000	3100	5200	10,400	18,200	26,000
Spt Saloon	1150	3700	6200	12,400	21,700	31,000
NOTE: Deduct 30 percent for Right-Hand Drive.						
1952-1955						
R Type - (6-cyl) - (120" wb) - (4566cc)						
NOTE: Numbers produced in ( ).						
Std Steel Saloon	800	2500	4200	8400	14,700	21,000
Abbott (16)						
Cont	2500	7900	13,200	26,400	46,200	66,000
DHC	2650	8400	14,000	28,000	49,000	70,000
Frankdale						
Saloon	950	3000	5000	10,000	17,500	25,000
Freestone & Webb (29)						
Saloon	1050	3350	5600	11,200	19,600	28,000
Franay (2)						
Cpe	2150	6850	11,400	22,800	39,900	57,000
Hooper (41)						
2d Saloon	1100	3500	5800	11,600	20,300	29,000
4d Saloon	1000	3250	5400	10,800	18,900	27,000
Sedanca Cpe	1200	3850	6400	12,800	22,400	32,000
Graber (7)						
H.J. Mulliner (67)						
DHC	2500	7900	13,200	26,400	46,200	66,000
Saloon	900	2900	4800	9600	16,800	24,000
Radford (20)						
Countryman	1250	3950	6600	13,200	23,100	33,000
Park Ward (50)						
FHC	1300	4100	6800	13,600	23,800	34,000
DHC	2250	7200	12,000	24,000	42,000	60,000
Saloon	850	2700	4500	9000	15,800	22,500
James Young (69)						
Cpe	1000	3100	5200	10,400	18,200	26,000
Saloon	700	2300	3800	7600	13,300	19,000
Sedanca Cpe	950	3000	5000	10,000	17,500	25,000
R Type Continental						
A-C Series, (6-cyl) - (120" wb) - (4566cc)						
D-E Series - (4887cc)						
Bertone						
Saloon	1350	4300	7200	14,400	25,200	36,000
Farina						
Cpe (1)	6929			Only one made		
Franay (5)	—			value not estimable		
Graber (3)	—			value not estimable		
J.H. Mulliner						
Cpe (193)	1350	4300	7200	14,400	25,200	36,000
Park Ward (6)						
Cpe (2)	950	3000	5000	10,000	17,500	25,000
DHC (4)	2250	7200	12,000	24,000	42,000	60,000
NOTE: Deduct 20 percent for Right-Hand Drive.						
1955-1959						
S1 Type						
(6-cyl) - (123" or 127" wb) - (4887cc)						
Std Steel Saloon	1000	3100	5200	10,400	18,200	26,000
Saloon (LWB - after 1957)	1100	3500	5800	11,600	20,300	29,000
Freestone & Webb						
Saloon	1150	3700	6200	12,400	21,700	31,000
Graber						
DHC	2050	6600	11,000	22,000	38,500	55,000
Hooper						
Saloon	1150	3700	6200	12,400	21,700	31,000
H.J. Mulliner						
Saloon	1350	4300	7200	14,400	25,200	36,000
Limo (5)	1350	4300	7200	14,400	25,200	36,000
Park Ward						
FHC	1750	5500	9200	18,400	32,200	46,000
James Young						
Saloon	1150	3700	6200	12,400	21,700	31,000
S1 Type Continental - (6-cyl) - (123" wb) - (4887cc)						
Franay						
Cpe	1850	5900	9800	19,600	34,300	49,000
Graber						
DHC	3250	10,300	17,200	34,400	60,200	86,000
Hooper						
Saloon (6)	1000	3100	5200	10,400	18,200	26,000
H.J. Mulliner						
Cpe	1000	3100	5200	10,400	18,200	26,000
DHC	1700	5400	9000	18,000	31,500	45,000
Spt Saloon	1350	4300	7200	14,400	25,200	36,000
Flying Spur (after 1957)	1500	4800	8000	16,000	28,000	40,000
Park Ward						
DHC	2050	6600	11,000	22,000	38,500	55,000
Spt Saloon	1550	4900	8200	16,400	28,700	41,000
James Young						
Saloon	850	2700	4500	9000	15,800	22,500
NOTE: Deduct 20 percent for Right-Hand Drive.						
1959-1962						
S2 Type						
(V-8) - (123" or 127" wb) - (6230cc)						
Std Steel Saloon	950	3000	5000	10,000	17,500	25,000
Saloon (LWB)	1100	3500	5800	11,600	20,300	29,000
Franay	1450	4550	7600	15,200	26,600	38,000
Graber	1450	4550	7600	15,200	26,600	38,000
Hooper	1450	4700	7800	15,600	27,300	39,000
H.J. Mulliner						
DHC (15)	3000	9600	16,000	32,000	56,000	80,000
Park Ward						
DHC	1900	6000	10,000	20,000	35,000	50,000
Radford						
Countryman	1350	4300	7200	14,400	25,200	36,000
James Young						
Limo (5)	1350	4300	7200	14,400	25,200	36,000
S2 Type Continental - (V-8) - (123" wb) - (6230cc)						
H.J. Mulliner						
Flying Spur	1900	6100	10,200	20,400	35,700	51,000
Park Ward						
DHC	1900	6000	10,000	20,000	35,000	50,000
James Young						
Saloon	950	3050	5100	10,200	17,900	25,500
NOTE: Deduct 20 percent for Right-Hand Drive.						
1962-1965						
S3 Type						
(V-8) - (123" or 127" wb) - (6230cc)						
Std Steel Saloon	1050	3350	5600	11,200	19,600	28,000
Saloon (LWB)	1350	4250	7100	14,200	24,900	35,500
H.J. Mulliner						
Cpe	1250	4000	6700	13,400	23,500	33,500
DHC	1900	6000	10,000	20,000	35,000	50,000
Park Ward						
Cpe	1750	5500	9200	18,400	32,200	46,000
DHC	2650	8400	14,000	28,000	49,000	70,000
James Young						
Limo (1)	1750	5500	9200	18,400	32,200	46,000

S3 Continental - (V-8) - (123" wb) - (6230cc)
H.J. Mulliner-Park Ward

	6	5	4	3	2	1
Cpe	1400	4500	7500	15,000	26,300	37,500
DHC	2250	7200	12,000	24,000	42,000	60,000
Flying Spur	1900	6100	10,200	20,400	35,700	51,000
James Young						
Cpe	1100	3550	5900	11,800	20,700	29,500
Saloon	1350	4250	7100	14,200	24,900	35,500

NOTE: Add 10 percent for factory sunroof.
Deduct 30 percent for Right-Hand Drive.

1966

2d James Young	1700	5400	9000	18,000	31,500	45,000
2d Park Ward	3750	12,000	20,000	40,000	70,000	100,000

1967

2d James Young	1650	5300	8800	17,600	30,800	44,000
2d Park Ward	2850	9100	15,200	30,400	53,200	76,000
2d Park Ward Conv	3600	11,500	19,200	38,400	67,200	96,000
4d T	850	2650	4400	8800	15,400	22,000

1968

2d Park Ward	2850	9100	15,200	30,400	53,200	76,000
2d Park Ward Conv	3600	11,500	19,200	38,400	67,200	96,000
4d T	850	2650	4400	8800	15,400	22,000

1969

2d Park Ward	2850	9100	15,200	30,400	53,200	76,000
2d Park Ward Conv	3700	11,750	19,600	39,200	68,600	98,000
4d T	850	2750	4600	9200	16,100	23,000

1970

2d Park Ward	2950	9350	15,600	31,200	54,600	78,000
2d Park Ward Conv	3700	11,750	19,600	39,200	68,600	98,000
4d T	900	2900	4800	9600	16,800	24,000

1971

4d T	1050	3350	5600	11,200	19,600	28,000

1972

4d T	1050	3350	5600	11,200	19,600	28,000

1973

4d T	1050	3350	5600	11,200	19,600	28,000

1974

4d T	1100	3500	5800	11,600	20,300	29,000

1975

4d T	1100	3500	5800	11,600	20,300	29,000

1976

4d T	1150	3600	6000	12,000	21,000	30,000

1977

4d T2	1150	3600	6000	12,000	21,000	30,000
2d Corniche	1500	4800	8000	16,000	28,000	40,000
2d Corniche Conv	2050	6600	11,000	22,000	38,500	55,000

1978

4d T2	1200	3850	6400	12,800	22,400	32,000
2d Corniche	1500	4800	8000	16,000	28,000	40,000
2d Corniche Conv	2050	6600	11,000	22,000	38,500	55,000

1979

4d T2	1300	4200	7000	14,000	24,500	35,000
2d Corniche	1600	5050	8400	16,800	29,400	42,000
2d Corniche Conv	2150	6850	11,400	22,800	39,900	57,000

1980

4d T2	1500	4800	8000	16,000	28,000	40,000
4d Mulsanne	1700	5400	9000	18,000	31,500	45,000
2d Corniche	1750	5650	9400	18,800	32,900	47,000
2d Corniche Conv	2250	7200	12,000	24,000	42,000	60,000

1981

4d Mulsanne	1750	5650	9400	18,800	32,900	47,000
2d Corniche Conv	2350	7450	12,400	24,800	43,400	62,000

1982

4d Mulsanne	1900	6000	10,000	20,000	35,000	50,000
2d Corniche Conv	2500	7900	13,200	26,400	46,200	66,000

1983

4d Mulsanne	1950	6250	10,400	20,800	36,400	52,000
2d Corniche Conv	2550	8150	13,600	27,200	47,600	68,000

BMW

1952

(6-cyl) - (111.6" wb) - (1917cc)						
501 4d Sed	400	1250	2100	4200	7400	10,500

1953

(6-cyl) - (111.6" wb) - (1971cc)						
501 4d Sed	400	1250	2100	4200	7400	10,500

1954

(6-cyl) - (111.6" wb) - (1971cc)						
501 4d Sed	450	900	1900	4500	6300	9000
501A 4d Sed	450	900	1900	4500	6300	9000
501B 4d Sed	450	900	1900	4500	6300	9000
(V-8) - (111.6" wb) - (2580cc)						
502/2.6 4d Sed	500	1600	2700	5400	9500	13,500

1955

Isetta - (1-cyl) - (59.1" wb) - (250cc)						
250 1d Std Sed	150	350	950	1350	2800	4000
250 1d DeL Sed	150	350	950	1450	3000	4200
(6-cyl) - (111.6" wb) - (1971cc)						
501A 4d Sed	450	900	1900	4500	6300	9000
501B 4d Sed	450	900	1900	4500	6300	9000
(6-cyl) - (111.6" wb) - (2077cc)						
501/3 4d Sed	450	1400	2300	4600	8100	11,500
(V-8) - (111.6" wb) - (2580cc)						
501 4d Sed	500	1600	2700	5400	9500	13,500
502/2.6 4d Sed	550	1750	2900	5800	10,200	14,500
(V-8) - (111.6" wb) - (3168cc)						
502/3.2 4d Sed	450	1500	2500	5000	8800	12,500

1956

Isetta - (1-cyl) - (59.1" wb) - (250cc)						
250 1d Std Sed	150	350	950	1350	2800	4000
250 1d DeL Sed	150	350	950	1450	3000	4200
(6-cyl) - (111.6" wb) - (2077cc)						
501/3 4d Sed	450	900	1900	4500	6300	9000
(V-8) - (111.6" wb) - (2580cc)						
501 4d Sed	450	1400	2300	4600	8100	11,500
502/2.6 4d Sed	450	1400	2300	4600	8100	11,500
(V-8) - (111.6" wb) - (3168cc)						
	6	**5**	**4**	**3**	**2**	**1**
502/3.2 4d Sed	500	1600	2700	5400	9500	13,500
503 Cpe	1150	3600	6000	12,000	21,000	30,000
503 Conv	1500	4800	8000	16,000	28,000	40,000
(V-8) - (97.6" wb) - (3168cc)						
507 Rds	4500	14,400	24,000	48,000	84,000	120,000

1957

Isetta - (1-cyl) - (59.1" wb) - (300cc)						
300 1d Std Sed	200	500	1100	1900	3500	5000
300 1d DeL Sed	200	500	1100	1900	3500	5000
(2-cyl) - (66.9" wb) - (582cc)						
600 2d Sed	200	500	1100	1900	3500	5000
(6-cyl) - (111.6" wb) - (2077cc)						
501/3 4d Sed	450	900	1900	4500	6300	9000
(V-8) - (111.6" wb) - (2580cc)						
501 4d Sed	450	1400	2300	4600	8100	11,500
502/2.6 4d Sed	450	1400	2300	4600	8100	11,500
(V-8) - (111.6" wb) - (3168cc)						
502/3.2 4d Sed	450	1500	2500	5000	8800	12,500
502/3.2 Sup 4d Sed	500	1600	2700	5400	9500	13,500
503 Cpe	1150	3600	6000	12,000	21,000	30,000
503 Conv	1500	4800	8000	16,000	28,000	40,000
(V-8) - (97.6" wb) - (3168cc)						
507 Rds	5650	18,000	30,000	60,000	105,000	150,000

1958

Isetta - (1-cyl) - (59.1" wb) - (300cc)						
300 1d Std Sed	200	500	1100	1900	3500	5000
300 1d DeL Sed	200	500	1100	1900	3500	5000
(2-cyl) - (66.9" wb) - (582cc)						
600 2d Sed	150	350	950	1350	2800	4000
(6-cyl) - (111.6" wb) - (2077cc)						
501/3 4d Sed	450	900	1900	4500	6300	9000
(V-8) - (111.6" wb) - (2580cc)						
501 4d Sed	450	1400	2300	4600	8100	11,500
502/2.6 4d Sed	450	1400	2300	4600	8100	11,500
(V-8) - (111.6" wb) - (3168cc)						
502/3.2 4d Sed	450	1500	2500	5000	8800	12,500
502/3.2 Sup 4d Sed	500	1600	2700	5400	9500	13,500
503 Cpe	1300	4200	7000	14,000	24,500	35,000
503 Conv	1500	4800	8000	16,000	28,000	40,000
(V-8) - (97.6" wb) - (3168cc)						
507 Rds	5650	18,000	30,000	60,000	105,000	150,000

1959

Isetta - (1-cyl) - (59.1" wb) - (300cc)						
300 1d Std Sed	200	500	1100	1900	3500	5000
300 1d DeL Sed	200	500	1100	1900	3500	5000
(2-cyl) - (66.9" wb) - (582cc)						
600 2d Sed	200	500	1100	1900	3500	5000
(2-cyl) - (83.5" wb) - (697cc)						
700 Cpe	200	500	1100	1900	3500	5000
700 2d Sed	150	350	950	1350	2800	4000
(V-8) - (111.6" wb) - (2580cc)						
501 4d Sed	450	1400	2300	4600	8100	11,500
502/2.6 4d Sed	450	1400	2300	4600	8100	11,500
(V-8) - (111.6" wb) - (3168cc)						
502/3.2 4d Sed	450	1500	2500	5000	8800	12,500
502/3.2 Sup 4d Sed	500	1600	2700	5400	9500	13,500
503 Cpe	1150	3600	6000	12,000	21,000	30,000
503 Conv	1500	4800	8000	16,000	28,000	40,000
(V-8) - (97.6" wb) - (3168cc)						
507 Rds	4750	15,100	25,200	50,400	88,200	126,000

1960

Isetta - (1-cyl) - (59.1" wb) - (300cc)						
300 1d Std Sed	200	500	1100	1900	3500	5000
300 1d DeL Sed	200	500	1100	1900	3500	5000
(2-cyl) - (66.9" wb) - (582cc)						
600 2d Sed	200	500	1100	1900	3500	5000
(2-cyl) - (83.5" wb) - (697cc)						
700 Cpe	200	500	1100	1900	3500	5000
700 2d Sed	150	350	950	1350	2800	4000
(V-8) - (111.6" wb) - (2580cc)						
501 4d Sed	450	1400	2300	4600	8100	11,500
502/2.6 4d Sed	450	1400	2300	4600	8100	11,500
(V-8) - (111.6" wb) - (3168cc)						
502/3.2 4d Sed	400	1250	2100	4200	7400	10,500
502/3.2 Sup 4d Sed	500	1600	2700	5400	9500	13,500

1961

Isetta - (1-cyl) - (59.1" wb) - (300cc)						
300 1d Std Sed	200	500	1100	1900	3500	5000
300 1d DeL Sed	200	500	1100	1900	3500	5000
(2-cyl) - (83.5" wb) - (697cc)						
700 Cpe	200	500	1100	1900	3500	5000
700 2d Sed	150	350	950	1350	2800	4000
700 Luxus 2d Sed	150	400	1000	1650	3150	4500
(V-8) - (111.6" wb) - (2580cc)						
501 4d Sed	450	1400	2300	4600	8100	11,500
502/2.6 4d Sed	450	1400	2300	4600	8100	11,500
2600 4d Sed	450	1400	2300	4600	8100	11,500
2600L 4d Sed	450	1400	2300	4600	8100	11,500
(V-8) - (111.6" wb) - (3168cc)						
502/3.2 4d Sed	450	1400	2300	4600	8100	11,500
502/3.2 Sup 4d Sed	450	1500	2500	5000	8800	12,500
3200L 4d Sed	450	1400	2300	4600	8100	11,500
3200S 4d Sed	450	1500	2500	5000	8800	12,500

1962

Isetta - (1-cyl) - (59.1" wb) - (300cc)						
300 1d Std Sed	200	500	1100	1900	3500	5000
300 1d DeL Sed	200	500	1100	1900	3500	5000
(2-cyl) - (83.5" wb) - (697cc)						
700 Cpe	200	500	1100	1900	3500	5000
700CS Cpe	200	550	1150	2000	3600	5200
700 2d Sed	150	350	950	1350	2800	4000
(2-cyl) - (89.8" wb) - (697cc)						
700LS Luxus 2d Sed	150	350	950	1450	3000	4200
(4-cyl) - (100.4" wb) - (1499cc)						
1500 4d Sed	200	650	1250	2400	4200	6000
(V-8) - (111.6" wb) - (2580cc)						
2600 4d Sed	400	1200	2000	4000	7000	10,000
2600L 4d Sed	400	1200	2000	4000	7000	10,000
(V-8) - (111.6" wb) - (3168cc)						
3200L 4d Sed	400	1250	2100	4200	7400	10,500
3200S 4d Sed	450	1400	2300	4600	8100	11,500
3200CS Cpe	950	3000	5000	10,000	17,500	25,000

1963

	6	5	4	3	2	1
(2-cyl) - (83.5" wb) - (697cc)						
700 Cpe	200	550	1150	2000	3600	5200
700 2d Sed	150	350	950	1350	2800	4000
700CS Spt Cpe	200	600	1200	2300	4000	5700
700 Spt Conv	500	1550	2600	5200	9100	13,000
(2-cyl) - (89.8" wb) - (697cc)						
700LS Luxus 2d Sed	150	350	950	1450	3000	4200
(4-cyl) - (100.4" wb) - (1499cc)						
1500 4d Sed	200	650	1250	2400	4200	6000
(4-cyl) - (100.4" wb) - (1773cc)						
1800 4d Sed	350	750	1450	3300	4900	7000
(6-cyl) - (111.6" wb) - (2580cc)						
2600L 4d Sed	450	950	2100	4750	6650	9500
(V-8) - (111.6" wb) - (3680cc)						
3200S 4d Sed	450	1450	2400	4800	8400	12,000
3200CS Cpe	950	3000	5000	10,000	17,500	25,000

1964

	6	5	4	3	2	1
(2-cyl) - (83.5" wb) - (697cc)						
700 Cpe	200	550	1150	2000	3600	5200
700 2d Sed	150	350	950	1350	2800	4000
700CS Cpe	200	600	1200	2300	4000	5700
700CS Conv	500	1550	2600	5200	9100	13,000
(2-cyl) - (89.8" wb) - (697cc)						
700LS Luxus Cpe	200	675	1300	2500	4350	6200
700LS Luxus 2d Sed	150	400	1000	1650	3150	4500
(4-cyl) - (100.4" wb) - (1499cc)						
1500 4d Sed	200	650	1250	2400	4200	6000
(4-cyl) - (100.4" wb) - (1573cc)						
1600 4d Sed	350	700	1350	2800	4550	6500
(4-cyl) - (100.4" wb) - (1773cc)						
1800 4d Sed	350	750	1450	3300	4900	7000
1800ti 4d Sed	350	775	1500	3750	5250	7500
1800ti/SA 4d Sed	350	775	1500	3750	5250	7500
(6-cyl) - (111.6" wb) - (2580cc)						
2600L 4d Sed	450	900	1900	4500	6300	9000
(V-8) - (111.6" wb) - (3168cc)						
3200CS Cpe	950	3000	5000	10,000	17,500	25,000

1965

	6	5	4	3	2	1
(2-cyl) - (89.8" wb) - (697cc)						
700LS Luxus Cpe	200	675	1300	2500	4350	6200
700LS Luxus 2d Sed	150	400	1000	1650	3150	4500
(4-cyl) - (100.4" wb) - (1573cc)						
1600 4d Sed	350	700	1350	2800	4550	6500
(4-cyl) - (100.4" wb) - (1773cc)						
1800 4d Sed	350	825	1600	4000	5600	8000
1800ti 4d Sed	350	875	1700	4250	5900	8500
1800ti/SA 4d Sed	350	875	1700	4250	5900	8500
(4-cyl) - (100.4" wb) - (1990cc)						
2000C Cpe	750	2400	4000	8000	14,000	20,000
2000CS Cpe	850	2650	4400	8800	15,400	22,000
(V-8) - (111.4" wb) - (3168cc)						
3200CS Cpe	950	3000	5000	10,000	17,500	25,000

1966

	6	5	4	3	2	1
(4-cyl) - (98.4" wb) - (1573cc)						
1600-2 2d Sed	400	1200	2000	4000	7000	10,000
(4-cyl) - (100.4" wb) - (1573cc)						
1600 4d Sed	350	700	1350	2800	4550	6500
(4-cyl) - (100.4" wb) - (1773cc)						
1800 4d Sed	350	750	1450	3300	4900	7000
1800ti 4d Sed	350	800	1550	3850	5400	7700
(4-cyl) - (100.4" wb) - (1990cc)						
2000 4d Sed	350	750	1450	3500	5050	7200
2000ti 4d Sed	350	875	1700	4250	5900	8500
2000tilux 4d Sed	400	1200	2000	4000	7000	10,000
2000C Cpe	850	2650	4400	8800	15,400	22,000
2000CS Cpe	950	3000	5000	10,000	17,500	25,000

1967

	6	5	4	3	2	1
(4-cyl) - (98.4" wb) - (1573cc)						
1602 2d Sed	400	1200	2000	4000	7000	10,000
1600ti 2d Sed	450	1450	2400	4800	8400	12,000
(4-cyl) - (91.3" wb) - (1573cc)						
Glas 1600GT Cpe	550	1800	3000	6000	10,500	15,000
(4-cyl) - (100.4" wb) - (1773cc)						
1800 4d Sed	350	750	1450	3300	4900	7000
(4-cyl) - (100.4" wb) - (1990cc)						
2000 4d Sed	350	750	1450	3500	5050	7200
2000ti 4d Sed	350	875	1700	4250	5900	8500
2000tilux 4d Sed	400	1200	2000	4000	7000	10,000
2000C Cpe	850	2650	4400	8800	15,400	22,000
2000CS Cpe	950	3000	5000	10,000	17,500	25,000
(V-8) - (98.4" wb) - (2982cc)						
Glas 3000 Cpe	950	3000	5000	10,000	17,500	25,000

1968

	6	5	4	3	2	1
(4-cyl) - (98.4" wb) - (1573cc)						
1600 2d Sed	400	1200	2000	4000	7000	10,000
1600 Cabr	600	1900	3200	6400	11,200	16,000
(4-cyl) - (91.3" wb) - (1573cc)						
Glas 1600 GT Cpe	550	1800	3000	6000	10,500	15,000
(4-cyl) - (100.4" wb) - (1773cc)						
1800 4d Sed	350	750	1450	3300	4900	7000
(4-cyl) - (100.4" wb) - (1766cc)						
1800 4d Sed	350	750	1450	3500	5050	7200
(4-cyl) - (98.4" wb) - (1990cc)						
2002 2d Sed	400	1250	2100	4200	7400	10,500
2002ti 2d Sed	500	1550	2600	5200	9100	13,000
(4-cyl) - (100.4" wb) - (1990cc)						
2000 4d Sed	350	750	1450	3300	4900	7000
2000ti 4d Sed	350	775	1500	3750	5250	7500
2000tilux 4d Sed	350	875	1700	4250	5900	8500
2000C Cpe	850	2650	4400	8800	15,400	22,000
2000CS Cpe	950	3000	5000	10,000	17,500	25,000
(6-cyl) - (106" wb) - (2494cc)						
2500 4d Sed	350	775	1500	3750	5250	7500
(6-cyl) - (109.9" wb) - (2788cc)						
2800 4d Sed	350	875	1700	4250	5900	8500
(6-cyl) - (103.3" wb) - (2788cc)						
2800CS Cpe	750	2400	4000	8000	14,000	20,000
(V-8) - (98.4" wb) - (2982cc)						
Glas 3000 Cpe	950	3000	5000	10,000	17,500	25,000

1969

	6	5	4	3	2	1
(4-cyl) - (98.4" wb) - (1573cc)						
1600 2d Sed	450	900	1900	4500	6300	9000
1600 Cabr	650	2050	3400	6800	11,900	17,000
(4-cyl) - (100.4" wb) - (1766cc)						
1800 4d Sed	350	750	1450	3300	4900	7000
(4-cyl) - (98.4" wb) - (1990cc)						
2002 2d Sed	400	1250	2100	4200	7400	10,500
2002ti 2d Sed	500	1550	2600	5200	9100	13,000
(4-cyl) - (100.4" wb) - (1990cc)						
2000tilux 4d Sed	450	900	1900	4500	6300	9000
2000C Cpe	850	2650	4400	8800	15,400	22,000
2000CS Cpe	950	3000	5000	10,000	17,500	25,000
(6-cyl) - (106" wb) - (2494cc)						
2500 4d Sed	350	750	1450	3300	4900	7000
(6-cyl) - (106" wb) - (2788cc)						
2800 4d Sed	350	775	1500	3750	5250	7500
(6-cyl) - (103.3" wb) - (2788cc)						
2800CSA Cpe	700	2150	3600	7200	12,600	18,000
2800CS Cpe	750	2400	4000	8000	14,000	20,000

1970

	6	5	4	3	2	1
(4-cyl) - (98.4" wb) - (1573cc)						
1600 2d Sed	400	1200	2000	4000	7000	10,000
1600 Cabr	700	2150	3600	7200	12,600	18,000
(4-cyl) - (100.4" wb) - (1766cc)						
1800 4d Sed	350	750	1450	3300	4900	7000
(4-cyl) - (98.4" wb) - (1990cc)						
2002 2d Sed	450	900	1900	4500	6300	9000
(4-cyl) - (100.4" wb) - (1990cc)						
2000tilux 4d Sed	350	875	1700	4250	5900	8500
2000tii 4d Sed	450	900	1900	4500	6300	9000
(6-cyl) - (106" wb) - (2494cc)						
2500 4d Sed	350	775	1500	3750	5250	7500
(6-cyl) - (106" wb) - (2788cc)						
2800 4d Sed	350	875	1700	4250	5900	8500
(6-cyl) - (103.3" wb) - (2788cc)						
2800CSA	700	2150	3600	7200	12,600	18,000
2800CS Cpe	750	2400	4000	8000	14,000	20,000
3.0CS Cpe	750	2400	4000	8000	14,000	20,000
3.0CSi Cpe	1000	3250	5400	10,800	18,900	27,000
3.0CSL Cpe	1500	4800	8000	16,000	28,000	40,000
(6-cyl) - (103.3" wb) - (3003cc)						
3.0CSL Cpe	2250	7200	12,000	24,000	42,000	60,000

1971

	6	5	4	3	2	1
(4-cyl) - (98.4" wb) - (1573cc)						
1600 2d Sed	400	1200	2000	4000	7000	10,000
1600 Tr	400	1200	2000	4000	7000	10,000
1600 Cabr	700	2300	3800	7600	13,300	19,000
(4-cyl) - (100.4" wb) - (1766cc)						
1800 4d Sed	350	750	1450	3300	4900	7000
(4-cyl) - (98.4" wb) - (1990cc)						
2002 2d Sed	450	900	1900	4500	6300	9000
2002 Cabr	850	2650	4400	8800	15,400	22,000
2002 Targa	600	1900	3200	6400	11,200	16,000
2000 Tr	450	900	1900	4500	6300	9000
2002ti 2d Sed	400	1300	2200	4400	7700	11,000
(4-cyl) - (100.4" wb) - (1990cc)						
2000tii 4d Sed	400	1200	2000	4000	7000	10,000
(6-cyl) - (106" wb) - (2494cc)						
2500 4d Sed	350	750	1450	3300	4900	7000
(6-cyl) - (106" wb) - (2788cc)						
2800 4d Sed	350	775	1500	3750	5250	7500
Bavaria 4d Sed	350	775	1500	3750	5250	7500
(6-cyl) - (106" wb) - (2985cc)						
3.0S 4d Sed	350	875	1700	4250	5900	8500
Bavaria 4d Sed	350	875	1700	4250	5900	8500
(6-cyl) - (103.3" wb) - (2788cc)						
2800CSA Cpe	550	1800	3000	6000	10,500	15,000
2800CS Cpe	750	2400	4000	8000	14,000	20,000
(6-cyl) - (103.3" wb) - (2788cc)						
3.0CSA Cpe	950	3000	5000	10,000	17,500	25,000
3.0CS Cpe	1000	3250	5400	10,800	18,900	27,000
3.0CSi Cpe	1150	3600	6000	12,000	21,000	30,000
3.0CSL Cpe	1500	4800	8000	16,000	28,000	40,000

1972

	6	5	4	3	2	1
(4-cyl) - (100.4" wb) - (1766cc)						
1800 4d Sed	350	750	1450	3300	4900	7000
(4-cyl) - (100.4" wb) - (1990cc)						
2000tii 4d Sed	450	900	1900	4500	6300	9000
(4-cyl) - (98.4" wb) - (1990cc)						
2002 2d Sed	450	900	1900	4500	6300	9000
2002 Targa	600	1900	3200	6400	11,200	16,000
2000 Tr	450	900	1900	4500	6300	9000
2002ti 2d Sed	450	950	2100	4750	6650	9500
2002tii 2d Sed	400	1300	2200	4400	7700	11,000
2002tii Tr	450	1450	2400	4800	8400	12,000
(6-cyl) - (106" wb) - (2788cc)						
2800 4d Sed	350	775	1500	3750	5250	7500
Bavaria 4d Sed	350	775	1500	3750	5250	7500
(6-cyl) - (106" wb) - (2985cc)						
3.0S 4d Sed	350	875	1700	4250	5900	8500
Bavaria	350	875	1700	4250	5900	8500
(6-cyl) - (103.3" wb) - (2985cc)						
3.0CSA Cpe	700	2150	3600	7200	12,600	18,000

1973

	6	5	4	3	2	1
(4-cyl) - (98.4" wb) - (1990cc)						
2002 2d Sed	450	900	1900	4500	6300	9000
2000 Targa	600	1900	3200	6400	11,200	16,000
2002ti 2d Sed	450	950	2100	4750	6650	9500
2002tii 2d Sed	400	1300	2200	4400	7700	11,000
2002tii Tr	450	1450	2400	4800	8400	12,000
2002 (Turbo)	950	3000	5000	10,000	17,500	25,000
(6-cyl) - (106" wb) - (2788cc)						
2800 4d Sed	350	775	1500	3750	5250	7500
Bavaria 4d Sed	350	775	1500	3750	5250	7500
(6-cyl) - (106" wb) - (2985cc)						
3.0S 4d Sed	350	875	1700	4250	5900	8500
Bavaria 4d Sed	350	875	1700	4250	5900	8500
(6-cyl) - (103.3" wb) - (2985cc)						
3.0CSA Cpe	700	2150	3600	7200	12,600	18,000
3.0CS Cpe	850	2650	4400	8800	15,400	22,000
3.0CSi Cpe	950	3000	5000	10,000	17,500	25,000
(6-cyl) - (103.3" wb) - (3003cc)						
3.0CSL Cpe	2250	7200	12,000	24,000	42,000	60,000
(6-cyl) - (103.3" wb) - (3153cc)						
3.0CSL	3000	9600	16,000	32,000	56,000	80,000

1974

	6	5	4	3	2	1
(4-cyl) - (98.4" wb) - (1990cc)						
2002 2d Sed	450	900	1900	4500	6300	9000
2002 Targa	600	1900	3200	6400	11,200	16,000
2000 Tr	450	900	1900	4500	6300	9000
2002ti 2d Sed	450	950	2100	4750	6650	9500
2002tii 2d Sed	400	1300	2200	4400	7700	11,000

	6	5	4	3	2	1
2002tii Tr	450	1450	2400	4800	8400	12,000
2002 (Turbo)	950	3000	5000	10,000	17,500	25,000
(6-cyl) - (106" wb) - (2788cc)						
2800 4d Sed	350	775	1500	3750	5250	7500
Bavaria 4d Sed	350	775	1500	3750	5250	7500
(6-cyl) - (106" wb) - (2985cc)						
3.0S 4d Sed	350	875	1700	4250	5900	8500
Bavaria 4d Sed	350	875	1700	4250	5900	8500
(6-cyl) - (103.3" wb) - (2985cc)						
3.0CSA Cpe	700	2150	3600	7200	12,600	18,000
3.0CS Cpe	850	2650	4400	8800	15,400	22,000
3.0CSi Cpe	950	3000	5000	10,000	17,500	25,000
(6-cyl) - (103.3" wb) - (3153cc)						
3.0CSL Cpe	3000	9600	16,000	32,000	56,000	80,000
(6-cyl) - (103" wb) - (2985cc)						
530i 4d Sed	350	875	1700	4250	5900	8500
1975						
(4-cyl) - (98.4" wb) - (1990cc)						
2002 2d Sed	450	950	2100	4750	6650	9500
2002 Targa	600	1900	3200	6400	11,200	16,000
2002ti 2d Sed	400	1300	2200	4400	7700	11,000
2002 Turbo	950	3000	5000	10,000	17,500	25,000
(4-cyl) - (100.9" wb) - (1990cc)						
320i 2d Sed	350	750	1450	3300	4900	7000
(6-cyl) - (106" wb) - (2788cc)						
2800 4d Sed	350	775	1500	3750	5250	7500
Bavaria	350	775	1500	3750	5250	7500
(6-cyl) - (106" wb) - (2985cc)						
3.0S 4d Sed	450	900	1900	4500	6300	9000
Bavaria	450	900	1900	4500	6300	9000
(6-cyl) - (103.3" wb) - (2985cc)						
3.0CSA Cpe	700	2150	3600	7200	12,600	18,000
3.0CS Cpe	850	2650	4400	8800	15,400	22,000
3.0CSi Cpe	950	3000	5000	10,000	17,500	25,000
(6-cyl) - (103.3" wb) - (3153cc)						
3.0CSL Cpe	3000	9600	16,000	32,000	56,000	80,000
(6-cyl) - (103" wb) - (2985cc)						
530i 4d Sed	450	900	1900	4500	6300	9000
1976						
(4-cyl) - (100.9" wb) - (1990cc)						
2002 2d Sed	350	775	1500	3700	5200	7400
320i 2d Sed	350	775	1500	3750	5250	7500
(6-cyl) - (106" wb) - (2788cc)						
2800 4d Sed	350	775	1500	3750	5250	7500
Bavaria	350	775	1500	3750	5250	7500
(6-cyl) - (106" wb) - (2985cc)						
3.0Si 4d Sed	450	950	2100	4750	6650	9500
Bavaria	450	950	2100	4750	6650	9500
(6-cyl) - (103" wb) - (2985cc)						
530i 4d Sed	450	950	2100	4750	6650	9500
(6-cyl) - (103.4" wb) - (2985cc)						
630CS Cpe	750	2400	4000	8000	14,000	20,000
1977						
(4-cyl) - (100.9" wb) - (1990cc)						
320i 2d Sed	350	875	1700	4250	5900	8500
(6-cyl) - (106" wb) - (2788cc)						
2800 4d Sed	350	875	1700	4250	5900	8500
Bavaria	350	875	1700	4250	5900	8500
(6-cyl) - (106" wb) - (2985cc)						
3.0S 4d Sed	450	950	2100	4750	6650	9500
Bavaria	450	950	2100	4750	6650	9500
(6-cyl) - (103.4" wb) - (2985cc)						
530i 4d Sed	450	950	2100	4750	6650	9500
630CS Cpe	750	2400	4000	8000	14,000	20,000
630CSi Cpe	850	2650	4400	8800	15,400	22,000
(6-cyl) - (103.4" wb) - (3210cc)						
633CSi Cpe	950	3000	5000	10,000	17,500	25,000
1978						
(4-cyl) - (100.9" wb) - (2563cc)						
320i 2d Sed	450	900	1900	4500	6300	9000
(6-cyl) - (103" wb) - (2788cc)						
528i 4d Sed	400	1300	2200	4400	7700	11,000
(6-cyl) - (103.4" wb) - (2985cc)						
630CS Cpe	750	2400	4000	8000	14,000	20,000
630CSi Cpe	850	2650	4400	8800	15,400	22,000
(6-cyl) - (103.4" wb) - (3210cc)						
633CSi Cpe	950	3000	5000	10,000	17,500	25,000
(6-cyl) - (110" wb) - (2788cc)						
733i 4d Sed	700	2150	3600	7200	12,600	18,000
1979						
320i 2d Sed	450	950	2100	4750	6650	9500
528i 4d Sed	500	1550	2600	5200	9100	13,000
733i 4d Sed	750	2400	4000	8000	14,000	20,000
633Si 2d Cpe	950	3000	5000	10,000	17,500	25,000
M1 Cpe	7500	24,000	40,000	80,000	140,000	200,000
1980						
320i 2d Sed	400	1250	2100	4200	7400	10,500
528i 4d Sed	500	1550	2600	5200	9100	13,000
733i 4d Sed	750	2400	4000	8000	14,000	20,000
633CSi 2d Cpe	950	3050	5100	10,200	17,900	25,500
M1 Cpe	7500	24,000	40,000	80,000	140,000	200,000
1981						
320i 2d Sed	450	1400	2300	4600	8100	11,600
528i 4d Sed	550	1750	2900	5800	10,200	14,500
733i 4d Sed	850	2650	4400	8800	15,400	22,000
633CSi 2d Cpe	1050	3300	5500	11,000	19,300	27,500
1982						
320i 2d Sed	450	1450	2400	4800	8400	12,000
528E 4d Sed	550	1800	3000	6000	10,500	15,000
733i 4d Sed	850	2750	4600	9200	16,100	23,000
633CSi 2d Cpe	1050	3400	5700	11,400	20,000	28,500
1983						
320i 2d Sed	400	1250	2100	4200	7400	10,500
528E 4d Sed	500	1550	2600	5200	9100	13,000
533i 4d Sed	600	1900	3200	6400	11,200	16,000
733i 4d Sed	900	2900	4800	9600	16,800	24,000
633CSi 2d Cpe	1100	3500	5800	11,600	20,300	29,000
1984						
318i 2d Sed	400	1200	2000	4000	7000	10,000
325e 2d Sed	450	1400	2300	4600	8100	11,500
528e 4d Sed	550	1700	2800	5600	9800	14,000
533i 4d Sed	650	2050	3400	6800	11,900	17,000
733i 4d Sed	950	3000	5000	10,000	17,500	25,000
633CSi Cpe	1150	3600	6000	12,000	21,000	30,000

1985	6	5	4	3	2	1
318i 2d Sed	550	1700	2800	5600	9800	14,000
318i 4d Sed	550	1700	2800	5600	9800	14,000
325e 2d Sed	550	1800	3000	6000	10,500	15,000
325e 4d Sed	550	1800	3000	6000	10,500	15,000
528e 4d Sed	700	2200	3700	7400	13,000	18,500
535i 4d Sed	750	2400	4000	8000	14,000	20,000
524td 4d Sed	900	2900	4800	9600	16,800	24,000
735i 4d Sed	1100	3500	5800	11,600	20,300	29,000
635CSi Cpe	1250	3950	6600	13,200	23,100	33,000
1986						
325 2d Sed	550	1800	3000	6000	10,500	15,000
325 4d Sed	550	1800	3000	6000	10,500	15,000
325es 2d Sed	600	1900	3200	6400	11,200	16,000
325e 4d Sed	600	1900	3200	6400	11,200	16,000
524td 4d Sed	550	1800	3000	6000	10,500	15,000
528e 4d Sed	650	2100	3500	7000	12,300	17,500
535i 4d Sed	750	2450	4100	8200	14,400	20,500
735i 4d Sed	900	2800	4700	9400	16,500	23,500
L7 4d Sed	900	2950	4900	9800	17,200	24,500
635CSi Cpe	1100	3500	5800	11,600	20,300	29,000
1987						
325 2d Sed	700	2150	3600	7200	12,600	18,000
325 4d Sed	700	2150	3600	7200	12,600	18,000
325es 2d Sed	700	2300	3800	7600	13,300	19,000
325es 4d Sed	700	2300	3800	7600	13,300	19,000
325is 2d Sed	800	2500	4200	8400	14,700	21,000
325i 4d Sed	750	2400	4000	8000	14,000	20,000
325i Conv	1000	3100	5200	10,400	18,200	26,000
528e 4d Sed	750	2400	4000	8000	14,000	20,000
535i 4d Sed	850	2750	4600	9200	16,100	23,000
535is 4d Sed	900	2800	4700	9400	16,500	23,500
735i 4d Sed	1050	3400	5700	11,400	20,000	28,500
L7 4d Sed	1100	3500	5800	11,600	20,300	29,000
635CSi Cpe	1200	3800	6300	12,600	22,100	31,500
L6 Cpe	1200	3850	6400	12,800	22,400	32,000
MG Cpe	1400	4450	7400	14,800	25,900	37,000
1988						
325 2d Sed	750	2450	4100	8200	14,400	20,500
325 4d Sed	750	2450	4100	8200	14,400	20,500
325is 2d Sed	900	2900	4800	9600	16,800	24,000
325i 4d Sed	850	2750	4600	9200	16,100	23,000
325i Conv	1100	3500	5800	11,600	20,300	29,000
325ix (4WD)	950	3000	5000	10,000	17,500	25,000
M3 2d Sed	1000	3250	5400	10,800	18,900	27,000
528e 4d Sed	900	2900	4800	9600	16,800	24,000
535i 4d Sed	1050	3300	5500	11,000	19,300	27,500
535is 4d Sed	1050	3350	5600	11,200	19,600	28,000
M5 4d Sed	1250	3950	6600	13,200	23,100	33,000
735i 4d Sed	1400	4450	7400	14,800	25,900	37,000
750iL 4d Sed	2000	6350	10,600	21,200	37,100	53,000
635CSi Cpe	1350	4400	7300	14,600	25,600	36,500
M6 Cpe	1600	5150	8600	17,200	30,100	43,000
1989						
325i 2d Sed	900	2900	4800	9600	16,800	24,000
325i 4d Sed	900	2900	4800	9600	16,800	24,000
325is 2d Sed	1000	3100	5200	10,400	18,200	26,000
325i Conv	1200	3850	6400	12,800	22,400	32,000
325ix 2d Sed (4WD)	1050	3350	5600	11,200	19,600	28,000
325ix 4d Sed (4WD)	1050	3350	5600	11,200	19,600	28,000
M3 2d Sed	1150	3700	6200	12,400	21,700	31,000
525i 4d Sed	1200	3850	6400	12,800	22,400	32,000
535i 4d Sed	1400	4500	7500	15,000	26,300	37,500
735i 4d Sed	1750	5500	9200	18,400	32,200	46,000
735iL 4d Sed	1900	6000	10,000	20,000	35,000	50,000
750iL 4d Sed	2200	7100	11,800	23,600	41,300	59,000
635CSi Cpe	1500	4800	8000	16,000	28,000	40,000

BORGWARD

	6	5	4	3	2	1
1949-53						
Hansa 1500 - (4-cyl) - (96" wb)						
2d Sed	200	600	1200	2200	3850	5500
2d Conv	350	700	1350	2800	4550	6500
Hansa 1800 - (4-cyl) - (102" wb)						
4d Sed	200	600	1200	2200	3900	5600
Hansa 2400 - (4-cyl) - (102" wb or 111" wb)						
4d Sed	200	600	1200	2300	4000	5700
1954-55						
Isabella - (4-cyl) - (102" wb)						
2d Sed	200	600	1200	2200	3850	5500
Hansa 1500 - (4-cyl) - (96" wb)						
2d Sed	200	600	1200	2200	3900	5600
2d Conv	200	675	1300	2500	4350	6200
Hansa 1800 - (4-cyl) - (102" wb)						
4d Sed	200	600	1200	2200	3900	5600
Hansa 2400 - (4-cyl) - (102" or 111" wb)						
4d Sed	200	600	1200	2300	4000	5700
1956						
Isabella - (4-cyl) - (102" wb)						
2d Sed	200	600	1200	2300	4000	5700
2d TS Sed	200	650	1200	2300	4100	5800
2d Sta Wag	200	600	1200	2300	4000	5700
2d Cabr	350	825	1600	4000	5600	8000
1957						
Isabella - (4-cyl) - (102" wb)						
2d Sed	200	600	1200	2300	4000	5700
2d Sta Wag	200	600	1200	2300	4000	5700
2d TS Sed	200	650	1200	2300	4100	5800
2d TS Conv Cpe	350	825	1600	4000	5600	8000
2d TS Spt Cpe	350	750	1450	3300	4900	7000
1958						
Isabella - (4-cyl) - 102" wb)						
2d Sed	200	600	1200	2300	4000	5700
2d Sta Wag	200	600	1200	2300	4000	5700
2d TS Sed	200	650	1200	2300	4100	5800
2d TS Spt Cpe	350	750	1450	3300	4900	7000

1959
Isabella - (4-cyl) - (102" wb)

	6	5	4	3	2	1
2d Sed	200	600	1200	2300	4000	5700
2d SR Sed	200	650	1200	2300	4100	5800
2d Combi Wag	200	650	1200	2300	4100	5800
2d TS Spt Sed	200	650	1200	2300	4100	5800
2d TS DeL Sed	200	650	1250	2400	4150	5900
2d TS Spt Cpe	350	750	1450	3300	4900	7000

1960
Isabella - (4-cyl) - (102" wb)

2d Sed	200	600	1200	2300	4000	5700
2d SR Sed	200	650	1200	2300	4100	5800
2d Combi Wag	200	650	1200	2300	4100	5800
2d TS Spt Sed	200	650	1200	2300	4100	5800
2d TS DeL Sed	200	650	1250	2400	4150	5900
2d TS Spt Cpe	350	750	1450	3300	4900	7000

1961
Isabella - (4-cyl) - (102" wb)

2d Sed	200	650	1200	2300	4100	5800

DAIHATSU

1988

2d HBk CLS	150	400	1000	1650	3150	4500
2d HBk CLX	200	500	1100	1850	3350	4900
2d HBk CSX	200	600	1200	2200	3850	5500

1989

2d HBk CES	200	600	1200	2200	3850	5500
2d HBk CLS	200	650	1250	2400	4150	5900
2d HBk CLX	350	700	1350	2800	4550	6500

DATSUN

1960
Fairlady Roadster
(4-cyl) - (87.4" wb) - (1189cc)

SPL 212	350	825	1600	4000	5600	8000

1961-1962
Fairlady Roadster
(4-cyl) - (86.6" wb) - (1189cc)

SPL 213	350	825	1600	4000	5600	8000

1963-1965
1500 - (4-cyl) - (89.8" wb) - (1488cc)

Rds SPL 310	350	825	1600	4000	5600	8000

1966
1600 - (4-cyl) - (89.8" wb) - (1595cc)

Rds SPL 311	350	825	1600	4000	5600	8000

1967
1600 - Roadster
(4-cyl) - (89.8" wb) - (1595cc)

SPL 311 (Early Model)	350	825	1600	4000	5600	8000

2000 - Roadster

SRL 311 (Late Model)	450	900	1900	4500	6300	9000

1968
(4-cyl) - (95.3" wb) - (1595cc)

4d Sed 510	200	500	1100	1900	3500	5000

1600 - (4-cyl) - (89.8" wb) - (1595cc)

Rds SPL 311	350	825	1600	4000	5600	8000

2000 - (4-cyl) - (89.8" wb) - (1982cc)

Rds SRL 311	450	900	1900	4500	6300	9000

1969
(4-cyl) - (95.3" wb) - (1595cc)

2d Sed 510	200	500	1100	1900	3500	5000
4d Sed 510	150	350	950	1350	2800	4000

1600 - (4-cyl) - (89.8" wb) - (1595cc)

Rds SPL 311	350	825	1600	4000	5600	8000

2000 - (4-cyl) - (89.8" wb) - (1982cc)

Rds SRL 311	450	900	1900	4500	6300	9000

1970
(4-cyl) - (95.3" wb) - (1595cc)

2d Sed 510	200	500	1100	1900	3500	5000
4d Sed 510	150	350	950	1350	2800	4000

1600 - (4-cyl) - (89.8" wb) - (1595cc)

Rds SPL 311	350	825	1600	4000	5600	8000

2000 - (4-cyl) - (89.8" wb) - (1982cc)

Rds SRL 311	450	900	1900	4500	6300	9000

240Z - (6-cyl) - (90.7" wb) - (2393cc)

2d Cpe	400	1200	2000	4000	7000	10,000

1971
(4-cyl) - (95.3" wb) - (1595cc)

2d Sed 510	200	500	1100	1900	3500	5000
4d Sed 510	150	350	950	1350	2800	4000

240Z - (6-cyl) - (90.7" wb) - (2393cc)

2d Cpe	400	1200	2000	4000	7000	10,000

1972
(4-cyl) - (95.3" wb) - (1595cc)

2d Sed 510	200	500	1100	1900	3500	5000
4d Sed 510	150	350	950	1350	2800	4000

240Z - (6-cyl) - (90.7" wb) - (2393cc)

2d Cpe	400	1200	2000	4000	7000	10,000

1973
(4-cyl) - (95.3" wb) - (1595cc)

2d Sed 510	200	500	1100	1900	3500	5000

240Z - (6-cyl) - (90.7" wb) - (2393cc)

2d Cpe	400	1200	2000	4000	7000	10,000

1974
260Z - (6-cyl) - (90.7" wb) - (2565cc)

2d Cpe	350	700	1350	2800	4550	6500

260Z - (6-cyl) - (102.6" wb) - (2565cc)

2d Cpe (2 plus 2)	350	725	1400	3000	4700	6700

1975
260Z - (6-cyl) - (90.7" wb) - (2565cc)

2d Cpe	350	775	1500	3750	5250	7500

260Z - (6-cyl) - (102.6" wb) - (2565cc)

2d Cpe (2 plus 2)	350	800	1550	3850	5400	7700

280Z - (6-cyl) - (90.7" wb) - (2753cc)

	6	5	4	3	2	1
2d Cpe	350	825	1600	4000	5600	8000

280Z - (6-cyl) - (102.6" wb) - (2753cc)

2d Cpe (2 plus 2)	350	825	1600	4000	5600	8000

1976
280Z - (6-cyl) - (90.7" wb) - (2753cc)

2d Cpe	350	875	1700	4250	5900	8500

280Z - (6-cyl) - (102.6" wb) - (2753cc)

2d Cpe (2 plus 2)	350	875	1700	4350	6050	8700

1977
(6-cyl) - (104.3" wb) - (2393cc)

4d Sed 810	100	175	525	1050	2100	3000

280Z - (6-cyl) - (90.7" wb) - (2753cc)

2d Cpe	350	875	1700	4250	5900	8500

280Z - (6-cyl) - (102.6" wb) - (2753cc)

2d Cpe (2 plus 2)	350	875	1700	4350	6050	8700

DATSUN/NISSAN

1978
200SX - (4-cyl) - (92.1" wb) - (1952cc)

Cpe	150	300	900	1250	2650	3800

280Z - (6-cyl) - (90.7" wb) - (149 hp)

Cpe	350	875	1700	4250	5900	8500
Cpe (2 plus 2)	350	875	1700	4350	6050	8700

1979
200SX - (4-cyl) - (92.1" wb) - (1952cc)

Cpe	150	300	900	1250	2650	3800

280ZX - (4-cyl) - (92.1" wb) - (1952cc)

Cpe	350	875	1700	4250	5900	8500
Cpe (2 plus 2)	350	875	1700	4300	6000	8600

1980
280ZX

Cpe	350	850	1650	4100	5700	8200
Cpe (2 plus 2)	350	850	1650	4200	5850	8400

1981
280ZX

Cpe	350	850	1650	4100	5700	8200
Cpe GL (2 plus 2)	350	850	1650	4200	5850	8400
Cpe GL (Turbo)	350	875	1700	4300	6000	8600

1982
280ZX

Cpe	350	825	1600	4050	5650	8100
Cpe (2 plus 2)	350	850	1650	4150	5800	8300
Cpe (Turbo)	350	875	1700	4250	5900	8500
Cpe (2 plus 2 - Turbo)	350	875	1700	4300	6000	8600

1983
280ZX

Cpe	350	825	1600	4000	5600	8000
Cpe (2 plus 2)	350	850	1650	4100	5700	8200
Cpe (Turbo)	350	850	1650	4200	5850	8400
Cpe (2 plus 2 - Turbo)	350	875	1700	4250	5900	8500

1984
Sentra (FWD)

2d Sed	100	150	450	1000	1750	2500
2d Sed DeL	100	150	450	1000	1750	2500
4d Sed DeL	100	150	450	1000	1800	2600
4d Wag DeL	100	175	525	1050	1950	2800
2d HBk XE	100	175	525	1050	2100	3000
2d Sed XE	100	175	525	1050	1950	2800
4d Sed XE	100	175	525	1050	2050	2900
4d Wag XE	125	200	600	1100	2200	3100

Pulsar (FWD)

Cpe	125	200	600	1100	2200	3100

Stanza (FWD)

2d HBk XE	100	175	525	1050	2100	3000
4d HBk XE	125	200	600	1100	2200	3100
4d Sed GL	125	250	750	1150	2400	3400

200 SX

2d HdTp DeL	150	350	950	1350	2800	4000
2d HBk DeL	150	300	900	1350	2700	3900
2d HdTp XE	150	350	950	1450	3000	4200
2d HBk XE	150	350	950	1450	2900	4100

Maxima

4d Sed	150	400	1000	1650	3150	4500
4d Sta Wag	150	450	1050	1700	3200	4600

300 ZX

2d Cpe GL	200	675	1300	2500	4300	6100
2d Cpe GL (2 plus 2)	200	675	1300	2500	4350	6200
2d Cpe GL (Turbo)	350	700	1350	2800	4550	6500

1985
Sentra (FWD)

2d Sed	100	150	450	1000	1750	2500
2d Sed DeL	100	175	525	1050	2050	2900
4d Sed DeL	100	175	525	1050	2100	3000
4d Sta Wag DeL	125	200	600	1100	2250	3200
2d Sed (Diesel)	125	250	750	1150	2400	3400
2d Sed XE	125	200	600	1100	2250	3200
4d Sed XE	125	200	600	1100	2300	3300
4d Sta Wag XE	125	250	750	1150	2450	3500
2d HBk XE	125	250	750	1150	2400	3400
2d HBk SE	125	250	750	1150	2500	3600

Pulsar (FWD)

2d Cpe	125	250	750	1150	2500	3600

Stanza (FWD)

4d HBk XE	150	400	1000	1600	3100	4400
4d NBk GL	150	450	1050	1750	3250	4700
2d NBk GL	200	500	1100	1900	3500	5000
2d NBk XE	200	550	1150	2100	3700	5300
2d HBk DeL	200	550	1150	2000	3600	5200
2d HBk XE	200	600	1200	2200	3850	5500
2d HBk (Turbo)	200	600	1200	2300	4000	5700

Maxima (FWD)

4d Sed SE	350	725	1400	3000	4700	6700
4d Sed GL	350	725	1400	3100	4800	6800
4d Sta Wag GL	350	725	1400	3100	4800	6800

300 ZX

Cpe	350	800	1550	3900	5450	7800
Cpe (2 plus 2)	350	825	1600	3950	5500	7900
Cpe (Turbo)	350	850	1650	4150	5800	8300

NISSAN

	6	5	4	3	2	1
1986						
Sentra (FWD)						
2d Sed	125	250	750	1150	2450	3500
2d Sed DeL	150	300	900	1250	2600	3700
4d Sed DeL	150	300	900	1250	2650	3800
4d Sta Wag DeL	150	350	950	1350	2800	4000
2d Sed (Diesel)	125	200	600	1100	2200	3100
2d Sed XE	150	350	950	1350	2800	4000
4d Sed XE	150	350	950	1450	2900	4100
4d Sta Wag XE	150	400	1000	1550	3050	4300
2d HBk XE	150	350	950	1450	2900	4100
2d HBk SE	150	400	1000	1600	3100	4400
Pulsar (FWD)						
2d Cpe	150	400	1000	1650	3150	4500
Stanza (FWD)						
4d Sed GL	200	500	1100	1950	3600	5100
4d Sta Wag XE	200	550	1150	2000	3600	5200
4d Sta Wag XE (4WD)	200	650	1250	2400	4150	5900
200 SX						
2d Sed E	200	650	1200	2300	4100	5800
2d Sed XE	200	675	1300	2500	4350	6200
2d HBk E	200	650	1250	2400	4150	5900
2d HBk XE	200	675	1300	2600	4400	6300
2d HBk (Turbo)	350	700	1350	2900	4600	6600
Maxima (FWD)						
4d Sed SE	350	825	1600	4000	5600	8000
4d Sed GL	350	825	1600	4050	5650	8100
4d Sta Wag GL	350	850	1650	4100	5700	8200
300 ZX						
Cpe	450	950	2100	4750	6650	9500
Cpe (2 plus 2)	450	975	2200	4850	6800	9700
Cpe (Turbo)	400	1200	2050	4100	7100	10,200
1987						
Sentra (FWD)						
2d Sed	150	350	950	1450	3000	4200
2d Sed E	200	500	1100	1900	3500	5000
4d Sed E	200	500	1100	1950	3600	5100
2d HBk E	200	500	1100	1900	3500	5000
4d Sta Wag	200	550	1150	2100	3700	5300
2d Sed XE	200	550	1150	2100	3700	5300
4d Sed XE	200	550	1150	2100	3800	5400
2d HBk XE	200	550	1150	2100	3700	5300
4d Sta Wag XE	200	600	1200	2300	4000	5700
4d Sta Wag (4WD)	200	675	1300	2600	4400	6300
4d Sed GXE	200	650	1200	2300	4100	5800
4d Sta Wag GXE	200	650	1250	2400	4200	6000
Cpe XE	200	650	1200	2300	4100	5800
Cpe SE	200	675	1300	2500	4350	6200
Pulsar (FWD)						
Cpe XE	350	750	1450	3500	5050	7200
Cpe SE (16V)	350	800	1550	3850	5400	7700
Stanza (FWD)						
4d Sed E	350	725	1400	3200	4850	6900
4d Sed GXE	350	775	1500	3700	5200	7400
4d HBk XE	350	750	1450	3500	5050	7200
4d Sta Wag XE	350	775	1500	3700	5200	7400
4d Sta Wag XE (4WD)	350	825	1600	4000	5600	8000
200 SX						
2d Sed XE	350	750	1450	3400	5000	7100
2d HBk XE	350	750	1450	3500	5050	7200
2d HBk (6-cyl)	350	850	1650	4150	5800	8300
Maxima (FWD)						
4d Sed SE	450	975	2300	4900	6850	9800
4d Sed GXE	450	975	2200	4850	6800	9700
4d Sta Wag GXE	400	1200	2000	4000	7000	10,000
300 ZX						
Cpe GS	550	1700	2800	5600	9800	14,000
Cpe GS (2 plus 2)	550	1750	2900	5800	10,200	14,500
Cpe (Turbo)	550	1800	3000	6000	10,500	15,000
1988						
Sentra (FWD)						
2d Sed	150	450	1050	1750	3250	4700
2d Sed E	200	600	1200	2300	4000	5700
4d Sed E	200	650	1250	2400	4200	6000
2d HBk E	200	600	1200	2300	4000	5700
4d Sta Wag E	200	675	1300	2600	4400	6300
2d Sed XE	200	675	1300	2500	4300	6100
4d Sed XE	350	700	1350	2700	4500	6400
4d Sta Wag XE	350	725	1400	3000	4700	6700
4d Sta Wag XE (4WD)	350	775	1500	3700	5200	7400
4d Sed GXE	350	725	1400	3100	4800	6800
Cpe XE	350	725	1400	3000	4700	6700
Cpe SE	350	750	1450	3500	5050	7200
Pulsar (FWD)						
Cpe XE	450	900	1800	4400	6150	8800
Cpe SE (16V)	450	925	2000	4600	6400	9200
Stanza (FWD)						
4d Sed E	350	850	1650	4100	5700	8200
4d Sed GXE	450	900	1900	4500	6300	9000
4d Sta Wag XE	350	875	1700	4350	6050	8700
4d Sta Wag XE (4WD)	450	950	2100	4700	6600	9400
200 SX						
2d Sed XE	350	875	1700	4350	6050	8700
2d HBk XE	450	900	1800	4450	6250	8900
2d HBk SE (6-cyl)	400	1200	2000	4000	7000	10,000
Maxima (FWD)						
4d Sed SE	450	1450	2400	4800	8500	12,100
4d Sed GXE	450	1450	2400	4800	8400	12,000
4d Sta Wag GXE	450	1500	2500	5000	8800	12,500
300 ZX						
Cpe GS	550	1700	2800	5600	9800	14,000
Cpe GS (2 plus 2)	550	1750	2900	5800	10,200	14,500
Cpe (Turbo)	600	1850	3100	6200	10,900	15,500
1989						
Sentra (FWD)						
2d Sed	200	650	1250	2400	4200	6000
2d Sed E	350	750	1450	3300	4900	7000
4d Sed E	350	775	1500	3700	5200	7400
4d Sta Wag E	350	800	1550	3850	5400	7700
2d Sed XE	350	800	1550	3800	5300	7600
4d Sed XE	350	825	1600	3950	5500	7900
4d Sta Wag XE	350	850	1650	4100	5700	8200
4d Sta Wag XE (4WD)	450	900	1800	4450	6250	8900
Cpe XE	350	875	1700	4250	5900	8500
Cpe SE	450	900	1800	4450	6250	8900
Pulsar (FWD)						
Cpe XE	400	1200	2050	4100	7100	10,200
Cpe SE (16V)	400	1300	2150	4300	7600	10,800
Stanza (FWD)						
4d Sed E	400	1200	2050	4100	7100	10,200
4d Sed GXE	400	1300	2200	4400	7700	11,000
240 SX						
2d Sed XE	450	1500	2450	4900	8600	12,300
2d HBk SE	450	1500	2500	5000	8700	12,400
Maxima (FWD)						
4d Sed SE	600	1900	3150	6300	11,100	15,800
4d Sed GXE	600	1850	3100	6200	10,800	15,400
300 ZX						
Cpe GS	650	2100	3500	7000	12,200	17,400
Cpe GS (2 plus 2)	650	2100	3500	7000	12,300	17,500
Cpe (Turbo)	700	2200	3700	7400	12,900	18,400

DE TOMASO

	6	5	4	3	2	1
1967-1971						
(V-8) - (98.4" wb) - (302 cid)						
Mangusta 2d Cpe	2150	6850	11,400	22,800	39,900	57,000
1971-1974						
(V-8) - (99" wb) - (351 cid)						
Pantera 2d Cpe	2050	6600	11,000	22,000	38,500	55,000
1975-1978						
(V-8) - (99" wb) - (351 cid)						
Pantera 2d Cpe	2050	6500	10,800	21,600	37,800	54,000

NOTE: After 1974 the Pantera was not "officially" available in the U.S. Add 5 percent for GTS models.

FACEL VEGA

	6	5	4	3	2	1
1954						
FV - (V-8) - (103" wb)						
2d HdTp Cpe	900	2900	4800	9600	16,800	24,000
1955						
FV - (V-8) - (103" wb)						
2d HdTp Cpe	850	2750	4600	9200	16,100	23,000
1956						
FVS - (V-8) - (103" wb)						
2d HdTp Cpe	850	2750	4600	9200	16,100	23,000
Excellence - (V-8) - (122" wb)						
4d HdTp Sed	700	2300	3800	7600	13,300	19,000
1957						
FVS - (V-8) - (103" wb)						
2d HdTp Cpe	850	2650	4400	8800	15,400	22,000
Excellence - (V-8) - (122" wb)						
4d HdTp Sed	700	2300	3800	7600	13,300	19,000
1958						
FVS - (V-8) - (105" wb)						
2d HdTp Cpe	850	2650	4400	8800	15,400	22,000
Excellence - (V-8) - (122" wb)						
4d HdTp Sed	700	2300	3800	7600	13,300	19,000
1959						
HK500 - (V-8) - (105" wb)						
2d HdTp Cpe	850	2650	4400	8800	15,400	22,000
Excellence - (V-8) - (125" wb)						
4d HdTp Sed	700	2300	3800	7600	13,300	19,000
1960						
Facellia - (4-cyl) - (96" wb)						
2d Cpe	850	2650	4400	8800	15,400	22,000
2d Conv	1100	3500	5800	11,600	20,300	29,000
HK500 - (V-8) - (105" wb)						
2d HdTp Cpe	900	2900	4800	9600	16,800	24,000
Excellence - (V-8) - (125" wb)						
4d HdTp Sed	700	2300	3800	7600	13,300	19,000
1961						
Facellia - (4-cyl) - (96" wb)						
2d Cpe	850	2650	4400	8800	15,400	22,000
2d Conv	1100	3500	5800	11,600	20,300	29,000
HK500 - (V-8) - (105" wb)						
2d HdTp Cpe	900	2900	4800	9600	16,800	24,000
Excellence - (V-8) - (125" wb)						
4d HdTp Sed	700	2300	3800	7600	13,300	19,000
1962						
Facellia - (4-cyl) - (96" wb)						
2d Cpe	850	2650	4400	8800	15,400	22,000
2d Conv	1100	3500	5800	11,600	20,300	29,000
Facel II - (V-8) - (105" wb)						
2d HdTp Cpe	900	2900	4800	9600	16,800	24,000
Excellence - (V-8) - (125" wb)						
4d HdTp Sed	700	2300	3800	7600	13,300	19,000
1963						
Facellia - (4-cyl) - (96" wb)						
2d Cpe	850	2650	4400	8800	15,400	22,000
2d Conv	1100	3500	5800	11,600	20,300	29,000
Facel II - (V-8) - (105" wb)						
2d HdTp Cpe	950	3000	5000	10,000	17,500	25,000
Facel III - (4-cyl) - (97" wb)						
2d HdTp Cpe	850	2650	4400	8800	15,400	22,000
Facel 6 - (6-cyl) - (97" wb)						
2d HdTp Cpe	850	2750	4600	9200	16,100	23,000
Excellence - (V-8) - (125" wb)						
4d HdTp Sed	700	2300	3800	7600	13,300	19,000
1964-65						
Facellia - (4-cyl) - (96" wb)						
2d Cpe	850	2650	4400	8800	15,400	22,000
2d Conv	1100	3500	5800	11,600	20,300	29,000
Facel II - (V-8) - (105" wb)						
2d HdTp Cpe	950	3000	5000	10,000	17,500	25,000
Facel III - (4-cyl) - (97" wb)						
2d HdTp Cpe	850	2650	4400	8800	15,400	22,000
Facel 6 - (6-cyl) - (97" wb)						
2d HdTp Cpe	850	2750	4600	9200	16,100	23,000

FIAT

1947-52
(4-cyl) - (78.75" wb) - (570cc)

	6	5	4	3	2	1
500 2d Sed	350	825	1600	4000	5600	8000

(4-cyl) - (95.4" wb) - (1089cc)

| 1100B 4d Sed | 200 | 500 | 1100 | 1900 | 3500 | 5000 |
| 1100BL 4d Sed | 200 | 500 | 1100 | 1900 | 3500 | 5000 |

(4-cyl) - (95.25" wb) - (1089cc)

| 1100E 4d Sed | 200 | 650 | 1250 | 2400 | 4200 | 6000 |

(4-cyl) - (106" wb) - (1089cc)

1100EL 4d Sed	200	650	1250	2400	4200	6000
1100S 2d Spt Cpe	400	1200	2000	4000	7000	10,000
1100ES 2d Spt Cpe	400	1200	2000	4000	7000	10,000

(4-cyl) - (104.2" wb) - (1395cc)

| 1400 4d Sed | 200 | 600 | 1200 | 2200 | 3850 | 5500 |
| 1400 2d Cabr | 450 | 1450 | 2400 | 4800 | 8400 | 12,000 |

(6-cyl) - (110" wb) - (1493cc)

| 1500 4d Sed | 200 | 600 | 1200 | 2200 | 3850 | 5500 |
| 2d Conv Cpe | 450 | 1450 | 2400 | 4800 | 8400 | 12,000 |

1953-56
500 - (4-cyl) - (78.75" wb) - (570cc)

| 2d Sed | 350 | 825 | 1600 | 4000 | 5600 | 8000 |
| 2d Sta Wag | 450 | 900 | 1900 | 4500 | 6300 | 9000 |

600 - (4-cyl) - (78.75" wb) - (633cc)

| 2d Sed | 200 | 500 | 1100 | 1900 | 3500 | 5000 |
| 2d Conv (S/R) | 200 | 600 | 1200 | 2200 | 3850 | 5500 |

600 Multipla - (4-cyl) - (78.75" wb) - (633cc)

| 4d Sta Wag | 200 | 650 | 1250 | 2400 | 4200 | 6000 |

1100 - (4-cyl) - (92.1" wb) - (1089cc)

103 4d Sed	200	500	1100	1900	3500	5000
103E 4d Sed	200	500	1100	1900	3500	5000
103E TV 4d Sed	200	550	1150	2000	3600	5200
103E 4d Sta Wag	200	600	1200	2200	3850	5500
103F TV 2d Spt Rds	550	1800	3000	6000	10,500	15,000

1400 - (4-cyl) - (104.2" wb) - (1395cc)

| 4d Sed | 200 | 600 | 1200 | 2200 | 3850 | 5500 |
| 2d Cabr | 450 | 1450 | 2400 | 4800 | 8400 | 12,000 |

1900 - (4-cyl) - (104" wb) - (1901cc)

| 4d Sed | 200 | 600 | 1200 | 2200 | 3850 | 5500 |

8V - (V-8) - (94.5" wb) - (1996cc)

| 2d Cpe | 950 | 3000 | 5000 | 10,000 | 17,500 | 25,000 |

1957
500 - (2-cyl) - (72.4" wb) - (479cc)

| 2d Sed | 350 | 750 | 1450 | 3300 | 4900 | 7000 |

600 - (4-cyl) - (78.75" wb) - (633cc)

| 2d Sed | 200 | 500 | 1100 | 1900 | 3500 | 5000 |
| 2d Conv (S/R) | 200 | 600 | 1200 | 2200 | 3850 | 5500 |

600 Multipla - (4-cyl) - (78.75" wb) - (633cc)

| 4d Sta Wag (4/5P) | 200 | 650 | 1250 | 2400 | 4200 | 6000 |
| 4d Sta Wag (6P) | 200 | 650 | 1250 | 2400 | 4200 | 6000 |

1100 - (4-cyl) - (92.1" wb) - (1089cc)

| 4d Sed | 200 | 500 | 1100 | 1900 | 3500 | 5000 |
| 4d Sta Wag | 200 | 600 | 1200 | 2200 | 3850 | 5500 |

1100 TV - (4-cyl) - (92.1" wb) - (1089cc)

| 4d Sed | 200 | 650 | 1200 | 2300 | 4100 | 5800 |
| 2d Conv | 450 | 1450 | 2400 | 4800 | 8400 | 12,000 |

1958
500 - (2-cyl) - (72.4" wb) - (479cc)

| 2d Sed | 150 | 350 | 950 | 1350 | 2800 | 4000 |

600 - (4-cyl) - (78.75" wb) - (633cc)

| 2d Sed | 200 | 500 | 1100 | 1900 | 3500 | 5000 |
| 2d Conv (S/R) | 200 | 600 | 1200 | 2200 | 3850 | 5500 |

600 Multipla - (4-cyl) - (78.75" wb) - (633cc)

| 4d Sta Wag (4/5P) | 200 | 650 | 1250 | 2400 | 4200 | 6000 |
| 4d Sta Wag (6P) | 200 | 650 | 1250 | 2400 | 4200 | 6000 |

1100 - (4-cyl) - (92.1" wb) - (1089cc)

| 4d Sed | 200 | 600 | 1200 | 2200 | 3850 | 5500 |
| 4d Familiare Sta Wag | 200 | 650 | 1200 | 2300 | 4100 | 5800 |

1100 TV - (4-cyl) - (92.1" wb) - (1089cc)

| 4d Sed | 200 | 600 | 1200 | 2200 | 3850 | 5500 |
| 2d Conv | 450 | 1450 | 2400 | 4800 | 8400 | 12,000 |

1200 Gran Luce - (4-cyl) - (92.1" wb) - (1221cc)

| 4d Sed | 200 | 500 | 1100 | 1900 | 3500 | 5000 |
| TV, 2d Conv | 450 | 1450 | 2400 | 4800 | 8400 | 12,000 |

1959
500 - (2-cyl) - (72.4" wb) - (479cc)

2d Sed	150	350	950	1350	2800	4000
2d Bianchina Cpe	200	500	1100	1900	3500	5000
2d Jolly Sed	200	650	1250	2400	4200	6000

500 Sport - (2-cyl) - (72.4" wb) - (499cc)

| 2d Sed | 150 | 400 | 1000 | 1650 | 3150 | 4500 |
| 2d Bianchina Cpe | 200 | 600 | 1200 | 2200 | 3850 | 5500 |

600 - (4-cyl) - (78.75" wb) - (633cc)

| 2d Sed | 200 | 500 | 1100 | 1900 | 3500 | 5000 |
| 2d Sed (S/R) | 200 | 600 | 1200 | 2200 | 3850 | 5500 |

600 Multipla - (4-cyl) - (78.75" wb) - (633cc)

| 4d Sta Wag (4/5P) | 200 | 650 | 1250 | 2400 | 4200 | 6000 |
| 4d Sta Wag (6P) | 200 | 650 | 1250 | 2400 | 4200 | 6000 |

1100 - (4-cyl) - (92.1" wb) - (1089cc)

| 4d Sed | 200 | 500 | 1100 | 1900 | 3500 | 5000 |
| 4d Sta Wag | 200 | 600 | 1200 | 2200 | 3850 | 5500 |

1200 - (4-cyl) - (92.1" wb) - (1221cc)

| 4d Sed | 200 | 500 | 1100 | 1900 | 3500 | 5000 |
| 2d Spider Conv | 400 | 1300 | 2200 | 4400 | 7700 | 11,000 |

1500, 1500S - (4-cyl) - (92.1" wb) - (1491cc)

| 2d Spider Conv | 450 | 1500 | 2500 | 5000 | 8800 | 12,500 |

1960
500 - (2-cyl) - (72.4" wb) - (479cc)

2d Sed	150	350	950	1350	2800	4000
2d Bianchina Cpe	200	500	1100	1900	3500	5000
2d Jolly Sed	200	650	1250	2400	4200	6000

500 Sport - (2-cyl) - (72.4" wb) - (499cc)

| 2d Sed | 150 | 400 | 1000 | 1650 | 3150 | 4500 |
| 2d Bianchina Cpe | 200 | 600 | 1200 | 2200 | 3850 | 5500 |

600 - (4-cyl) - (78.75" wb) - (633cc)

2d Sed	200	500	1100	1900	3500	5000
2d Sed (S/R)	200	600	1200	2200	3850	5500
2d Jolly Sed	200	650	1250	2400	4200	6000

600 Multipla - (4-cyl) - (78.75" wb) - (633cc)

| 4d Sta Wag (4/5P) | 200 | 650 | 1250 | 2400 | 4200 | 6000 |
| 4d Sta Wag (6P) | 200 | 650 | 1250 | 2400 | 4200 | 6000 |

1100 - (4-cyl) - (92.1" wb) - (1089cc)

	6	5	4	3	2	1
4d Sed	200	500	1100	1900	3500	5000
4d DeL Sed	200	550	1150	2000	3600	5200
4d Sta Wag	200	600	1200	2200	3850	5500

1200 - (4-cyl) - (92.1" wb) - (1221cc)

| 4d Sed | 200 | 500 | 1100 | 1900 | 3500 | 5000 |
| 2d Spider Conv | 450 | 1500 | 2500 | 5000 | 8800 | 12,500 |

1500, 1500S - (4-cyl) - (92.1" wb) - (1491cc)

| 2d Spider Conv | 500 | 1600 | 2700 | 5400 | 9500 | 13,500 |

2100 - (6-cyl) - (104.3" wb) - (2054cc)

| 4d Sed | 200 | 600 | 1200 | 2200 | 3850 | 5500 |
| 4d Sta Wag | 200 | 600 | 1200 | 2200 | 3850 | 5500 |

1961
500 - (2-cyl) - (72.4" wb) - (479cc)

| Bianchina DeL Cpe | 200 | 600 | 1200 | 2200 | 3850 | 5500 |
| 2d Jolly Sed | 200 | 650 | 1250 | 2400 | 4200 | 6000 |

500 Sport - (2-cyl) - (72.4" wb) - (499cc)

| 2d Sed | 150 | 400 | 1000 | 1650 | 3150 | 4500 |
| 2d Bianchina Cpe | 200 | 650 | 1200 | 2300 | 4100 | 5800 |

600 - (4-cyl) - (78.75" wb) - (633cc)

2d Sed	200	500	1100	1900	3500	5000
2d Sed (S/R)	200	600	1200	2200	3850	5500
2d Jolly Sed	350	700	1350	2800	4550	6500

600 Multipla - (4-cyl) - (78.75" wb) - (633cc)

| 4d Sta Wag (4/5P) | 200 | 650 | 1250 | 2400 | 4200 | 6000 |
| 4d Sta Wag (6P) | 200 | 650 | 1250 | 2400 | 4200 | 6000 |

1100 - (4-cyl) - (92.1" wb) - (1089cc)

4d Sed	200	500	1100	1900	3500	5000
4d DeL Sed	200	550	1150	2000	3600	5200
4d Sta Wag	200	600	1200	2200	3850	5500

1200 - (4-cyl) - (92.1" wb) - (1225cc)

| 4d Sed | 200 | 500 | 1100 | 1900 | 3500 | 5000 |
| 2d Spider Conv | 400 | 1300 | 2200 | 4400 | 7700 | 11,000 |

1500, 1500S - (4-cyl) - (92.1" wb) - (1491cc)

| Spider Conv | 450 | 1500 | 2500 | 5000 | 8800 | 12,500 |

2100 - (6-cyl) - (104.3" wb) - (2054cc)

| 4d Sed | 200 | 500 | 1100 | 1900 | 3500 | 5000 |
| 4d Sta Wag | 200 | 600 | 1200 | 2200 | 3850 | 5500 |

1962
600D - (4-cyl) - (78.75" wb) - (767cc)

| 2d Sed | 200 | 500 | 1100 | 1900 | 3500 | 5000 |

1100 - (4-cyl) - (92.1" wb) - (1089cc)

| 4d Export Sed | 200 | 500 | 1100 | 1900 | 3500 | 5000 |
| 4d Spl Sed | 200 | 550 | 1150 | 2000 | 3600 | 5200 |

1200 Spider - (4-cyl) - (92.1" wb) - (1221cc)

| 2d Conv | 400 | 1300 | 2200 | 4400 | 7700 | 11,000 |

1963
600D - (4-cyl) - (78.5" wb) - (767cc)

| 2d Sed | 200 | 500 | 1100 | 1900 | 3500 | 5000 |

1100 Special - (4-cyl) - (92.1" wb) - (1089cc)

| 4d Sed | 200 | 500 | 1100 | 1900 | 3500 | 5000 |

1100D - (4-cyl) - (92.1" wb) - (1221cc)

| 4d Sed | 200 | 500 | 1100 | 1900 | 3500 | 5000 |

1200 Spider - (4-cyl) - (92.1" wb) - (1221cc)

| 2d Conv | 400 | 1300 | 2200 | 4400 | 7700 | 11,000 |

1964
600D - (4-cyl) - (78.5" wb) - (767cc)

| 2d Sed | 200 | 500 | 1100 | 1900 | 3500 | 5000 |

1100D - (4-cyl) - (92.1" wb) - (1221cc)

| 4d Sed | 200 | 600 | 1200 | 2200 | 3850 | 5500 |

1500 Spider - (4-cyl) - (92.1" wb) - (1481cc)

| 2d Conv | 450 | 1400 | 2300 | 4600 | 8100 | 11,500 |

1965
600D - (4-cyl) - (78.5" wb) - (767cc)

| 2d Sed | 200 | 500 | 1100 | 1900 | 3500 | 5000 |

1100D - (4-cyl) - (92.1" wb) - (1221cc)

| 4d Sed | 200 | 500 | 1100 | 1900 | 3500 | 5000 |
| 4d Sta Wag | 200 | 600 | 1200 | 2200 | 3850 | 5500 |

1500 Spider - (4-cyl) - (92.1" wb) - (1481cc)

| 2d Conv | 450 | 1400 | 2300 | 4600 | 8100 | 11,500 |

1966
600D - (4-cyl) - (78.5" wb) - (767cc)

| 2d Sed | 200 | 500 | 1100 | 1900 | 3500 | 5000 |

1100D - (4-cyl) - (92.1" wb) - (1221cc)

| 4d Sed | 200 | 500 | 1100 | 1900 | 3500 | 5000 |
| 4d Sta Wag | 200 | 600 | 1200 | 2200 | 3850 | 5500 |

1500 Spider - (4-cyl) - (92.1" wb) - (1481cc)

| 2d Conv | 450 | 1400 | 2300 | 4600 | 8100 | 11,500 |

1967
600D - (4-cyl) - (78.7" wb) - (767cc)

| 2d Sed | 200 | 500 | 1100 | 1900 | 3500 | 5000 |

850 - (4-cyl) - (79.8" wb) - (843cc)

| FBk Cpe 2 plus 2 | 200 | 500 | 1100 | 1900 | 3500 | 5000 |
| 2d Spider Conv | 350 | 775 | 1500 | 3750 | 5250 | 7500 |

124 - (4-cyl) - (95.3" wb) - (1197cc)

| 4d Sed | 150 | 350 | 950 | 1350 | 2800 | 4000 |
| 4d Sta Wag | 150 | 400 | 1000 | 1550 | 3050 | 4300 |

1100R - (4-cyl) - (92.2" wb) - (1089cc)

| 4d Sed | 200 | 500 | 1100 | 1900 | 3500 | 5000 |
| 4d Sta Wag | 200 | 600 | 1200 | 2200 | 3850 | 5500 |

1500 Spider - (4-cyl) - (92.1" wb) - (1481cc)

| 2d Conv | 450 | 1400 | 2300 | 4600 | 8100 | 11,500 |

1968
850 - (4-cyl) - (79.8" wb) - (817cc)

2d Sed	150	350	950	1350	2800	4000
2d FBk Cpe	200	500	1100	1900	3500	5000
2d Spider Conv	350	700	1350	2800	4550	6500

124 - (4-cyl) - (95.3" wb) - (1197cc)

| 4d Sed | 150 | 350 | 950 | 1350 | 2800 | 4000 |
| 4d Sta Wag | 150 | 350 | 950 | 1350 | 2800 | 4000 |

124 - (4-cyl) - (95.3" wb) - (1438cc)

| 2d Spt Cpe | 350 | 700 | 1350 | 2800 | 4550 | 6500 |

124 Spider - (4-cyl) - (89.8" wb) - (1438cc)

| 2d Conv | 350 | 775 | 1500 | 3750 | 5250 | 7500 |

1969
850 - (4-cyl) - (79.8" wb) - (817cc)

2d Sed	150	350	950	1350	2800	4000
2d FBk Cpe 2 plus 2	200	500	1100	1900	3500	5000
2d Spider Conv	350	700	1350	2800	4550	6500

124 - (4-cyl) - (95.3" wb) - (1197cc)

| 4d Sed | 150 | 350 | 950 | 1350 | 2800 | 4000 |
| 4d Sta Wag | 150 | 350 | 950 | 1350 | 2800 | 4000 |

124 - (4-cyl) - (95.3" wb) - (1438cc)

| 2d Spt Cpe | 350 | 700 | 1350 | 2800 | 4550 | 6500 |

124 Spider - (4-cyl) - (89.8" wb) - (1438cc)

| 2d Conv | 350 | 775 | 1500 | 3750 | 5250 | 7500 |

1970

	6	5	4	3	2	1
850 - (4-cyl) - (79.8" wb) - (817cc)						
2d Sed	150	350	950	1350	2800	4000
850 - (4-cyl) - (79.8" wb) - (903cc)						
Spt FBk Cpe 2 plus 2	200	600	1200	2200	3850	5500
Racer 2d HdTp Cpe	200	650	1200	2300	4100	5800
850 Spider - (4-cyl) - (79.8" wb) - (903cc)						
2d Conv	350	700	1350	2800	4550	6500
124 - (4-cyl) - (95.3" wb) - (1438cc)						
4d Spl Sed	150	350	950	1350	2800	4000
4d Spl Sta Wag	150	350	950	1350	2800	4000
2d Spt Cpe	350	700	1350	2800	4550	6500
124 Spider - (4-cyl) - (89.8" wb) - (1438cc)						
2d Conv	350	775	1500	3750	5250	7500

1971

	6	5	4	3	2	1
850 - (4-cyl) - (79.8" wb) - (817cc)						
2d Sed	150	350	950	1350	2800	4000
850 - (4-cyl) - (79.8" wb) - (903cc)						
2d FBk Cpe, 2 plus 2	200	500	1100	1900	3500	5000
Racer, 2d HdTp Cpe	200	650	1200	2300	4100	5800
850 Spider - (4-cyl) - (79.8" wb) - (903cc)						
2d Conv	350	700	1350	2800	4550	6500
124 - (4-cyl) - (95.3" wb) - (1438cc)						
4d Spl Sed	150	350	950	1350	2800	4000
4d Spl Sta Wag	150	350	950	1350	2800	4000
2d Spt Cpe	350	700	1350	2800	4550	6500
124 Spider - (4-cyl) - (89.8" wb) - (1438cc)						
2d Conv	350	775	1500	3750	5250	7500

NOTE: The 124 coupe and convertible could be ordered with the larger 1.6 liter engine (1608cc).

1972

	6	5	4	3	2	1
850 Spider - (4-cyl) - (79.8" wb) - (903cc)						
2d Conv	350	700	1350	2800	4550	6500
128 - (4-cyl) - (96.4" wb) - (1116cc) - (FWD)						
2d Sed	125	250	750	1150	2450	3500
4d Sed	125	250	750	1150	2450	3500
2d Sta Wag	125	250	750	1150	2450	3500
124 - (4-cyl) - (95.3" wb) - (1438cc)						
4d Spl Sed	150	350	950	1350	2800	4000
4d Sta Wag	150	350	950	1350	2800	4000
124 - (4-cyl) - (95.3" wb) - (1608cc)						
2d Spt Cpe	350	700	1350	2800	4550	6500
124 Spider - (4-cyl) - (89.8" wb) - (1608cc)						
2d Conv	350	775	1500	3750	5250	7500

1973

	6	5	4	3	2	1
850 Spider - (4-cyl) - (79.8" wb) - (903cc)						
2d Conv	350	700	1350	2800	4550	6500
128 - (4-cyl) - (96.4" wb) - (1116cc) - (FWD)						
2d Sed	125	250	750	1150	2450	3500
4d Sed	125	250	750	1150	2450	3500
2d Sta Wag	125	250	750	1150	2450	3500
128 - (4-cyl) - (87.5" wb) - (1290cc) - (FWD)						
SL 1300 2d Cpe	150	300	900	1250	2650	3800
124 - (4-cyl) - (95.3" wb) - (1438cc)						
4d Spl Sed	150	350	950	1350	2800	4000
4d Sta Wag	150	350	950	1350	2800	4000
124 - (4-cyl) - (95.3" wb) - (1608cc)						
2d Spt Cpe	350	700	1350	2800	4550	6500
124 Spider - (4-cyl) - (89.8" wb) - (1608cc)						
2d Conv	350	775	1500	3750	5250	7500

1974

	6	5	4	3	2	1
128 - (4-cyl) - (96.4" wb) - (1290cc) - (FWD)						
2d Sed	125	250	750	1150	2450	3500
4d Sed	125	250	750	1150	2450	3500
2d Sta Wag	125	250	750	1150	2450	3500
128 - (4-cyl) - (87.5" wb) - (1290cc) - (FWD)						
SL 2d Cpe	150	300	900	1250	2650	3800
X1/9 - (4-cyl) - (86.7" wb) - (1290cc)						
2d Targa Cpe	200	500	1100	1900	3500	5000
124 - (4-cyl) - (95.3" wb) - (1593cc)						
4d Spl Sed	150	350	950	1350	2800	4000
4d Sta Wag	150	350	950	1350	2800	4000
124 - (4-cyl) - (95.3" wb) - (1756cc)						
2d Spt Cpe	150	350	950	1350	2800	4000
124 Spider - (4-cyl) - (89.8" wb) - (1756cc)						
2d Conv	350	775	1500	3750	5250	7500

1975

	6	5	4	3	2	1
128 - (4-cyl) - (96.4" wb) - (1290cc) - (FWD)						
2d Sed	125	250	750	1150	2450	3500
4d Sed	125	250	750	1150	2450	3500
2d Sta Wag	125	250	750	1150	2450	3500
128 - (4-cyl) - (87.5" wb) - (1290cc)						
SL 2d Cpe	150	300	900	1250	2650	3800
X1/9 - (4-cyl) - (86.7" wb) - (1290cc)						
2d Targa Cpe	200	500	1100	1900	3500	5000
131 - (4-cyl) - (98" wb) - (1756cc)						
2d Sed	125	250	750	1150	2450	3500
4d Sed	125	250	750	1150	2450	3500
4d Sta Wag	150	300	900	1250	2650	3800
124 - (4-cyl) - (95.3" wb) - (1756cc)						
2d Spt Cpe	350	700	1350	2800	4550	6500
124 Spider - (4-cyl) - (89.7" wb) - (1756cc)						
2d Conv	350	775	1500	3750	5250	7500

1976

	6	5	4	3	2	1
128 - (4-cyl) - (96.4" wb) - (1290cc) - (FWD)						
2d Sed	125	250	750	1150	2450	3500
2d Cus Sed	125	250	750	1150	2450	3500
4d Cus Sed	125	250	750	1150	2450	3500
2d Sta Wag	125	250	750	1150	2450	3500
128 Sport - (4-cyl) - (87.5" wb) - (1290cc) - (FWD)						
3P HBk Cpe	150	300	900	1250	2650	3800
X1/9 - (4-cyl) - (86.7" wb) - (1290cc)						
AS Targa Cpe	200	500	1100	1900	3500	5000
131 - (4-cyl) - (98" wb) - (1756cc)						
A3 2d Sed	125	250	750	1150	2450	3500
A3 4d Sed	125	250	750	1150	2450	3500
AF2 4d Sta Wag	125	250	750	1150	2450	3500
124 Sport Spider - (4-cyl) - (89.7" wb) - (1756cc)						
CS 2d Conv	350	775	1500	3750	5250	7500

1977

	6	5	4	3	2	1
128 - (4-cyl) - (96.4" wb) - (1290cc) - (FWD)						
2d Sed	125	250	750	1150	2450	3500
2d Cus Sed	125	250	750	1150	2450	3500
4d Cus Sed	125	250	750	1150	2450	3500
2d Sta Wag	125	250	750	1150	2450	3500
128 - (4-cyl) - (87.5" wb) - (1290cc) - (FWD)						
3P Cus HBk Cpe	150	300	900	1250	2650	3800
X1/9 - (4-cyl) - (86.7" wb) - (1290cc)						
AS Targa Cpe	200	500	1100	1900	3500	5000
131 - (4-cyl) - (98" wb) - (1756cc)						
A3 2d Sed	125	250	750	1150	2450	3500
A3 4d Sed	125	250	750	1150	2450	3500
AF2 4d Sta Wag	125	250	750	1150	2450	3500
124 Sport Spider - (4-cyl) - (89.7" wb) - (1756cc)						
CS 2d Conv	350	775	1500	3750	5250	7500

1978

	6	5	4	3	2	1
128 - (4-cyl) - (96.4" wb) - (1290cc) - (FWD)						
A1 2d Sed	125	250	750	1150	2450	3500
A1 4d Sed	125	250	750	1150	2450	3500
128 - (4-cyl) - (87.5" wb) - (1290cc) - (FWD)						
AC Spt HBk	150	300	900	1250	2650	3800
X1/9 - (4-cyl) - (86.7" wb) - (1290cc)						
AS Targa Cpe	200	500	1100	1900	3500	5000
131 - (4-cyl) - (98" wb) - (1756cc)						
A 2d Sed	125	250	750	1150	2450	3500
A 4d Sed	125	250	750	1150	2450	3500
AF 4d Sta Wag	125	250	750	1150	2450	3500
Brava - (4-cyl) - (98" wb) - (1756cc)						
2d Sed	125	250	750	1150	2450	3500
2d Sup Sed	125	250	750	1150	2450	3500
4d Sup Sed	125	250	750	1150	2450	3500
4d Sup Sta Wag	125	250	750	1150	2450	3500
Spider 124 - (4-cyl) - (89.7" wb) - (1756cc)						
2d Conv	350	775	1500	3750	5250	7500
X1/9						
AS Targa Cpe	350	700	1350	2800	4550	6500

NOTE: At mid-year the Brava series and Spider contained the new twin cam 2.0 liter four, (1995cc).

1979

	6	5	4	3	2	1
128A1 - (4-cyl) - (96.4" wb) - (1290cc) - (FWD)						
2d Sed	125	250	750	1150	2450	3500
4d Sed	125	250	750	1150	2450	3500
128AC - (4-cyl) - (87.5" wb) - (1290cc) - (FWD)						
2d Spt HBk	150	300	900	1250	2650	3800
X1/9 - (4-cyl) - (86.7" wb) - (1498cc)						
AS Targa Cpe	200	500	1100	1900	3500	5000
Strada 138A - (96.4" wb) - (1498cc) - (FWD)						
2d HBk	125	250	750	1150	2450	3500
2d Cus HBk	125	250	750	1150	2450	3500
4d Cus HBk	125	250	750	1150	2450	3500
Brava 131 - (4-cyl) - (98" wb) - (1995cc)						
A4 2d Sed	125	250	750	1150	2450	3500
A4 4d Sed	125	250	750	1150	2450	3500
AF 4d Sta Wag	125	250	750	1150	2450	3500
Spider 2000 - (4-cyl) - (89.7" wb) - (1995cc)						
2d Conv	350	825	1600	4000	5600	8000
X1/9						
AS Targa Cpe	350	700	1350	2800	4550	6500

1980

	6	5	4	3	2	1
Strada 138 - (4-cyl) - (96.4" wb) - (1498cc) - (FWD)						
2d HBk	125	250	750	1150	2450	3500
2d Cus HBk	125	250	750	1150	2450	3500
4d Cus HBk	125	250	750	1150	2450	3500
X1/9 - (4-cyl) - (86.7" wb) - (1498cc)						
128 Targa Cpe	200	500	1100	1900	3500	5000
Brava 131 - (4-cyl) - (98" wb) - (1995cc)						
2d Sed	125	250	750	1150	2450	3500
4d Sed	125	250	750	1150	2450	3500
Spider 2000 - (4-cyl) - (89.7" wb) - (1995cc)						
124 2d Conv	350	825	1600	4000	5600	8000

NOTE The Brava series and the Spider 2000 were also available with fuel injection in 1980.

1981

	6	5	4	3	2	1
Strada 138 - (4-cyl) - (96.4" wb) - (1498cc) - (FWD)						
2d HBk	125	250	750	1150	2450	3500
2d Cus HBk	125	250	750	1150	2450	3500
4d Cus HBk	125	250	750	1150	2450	3500
X1/9 - (4-cyl) - (86.7" wb) - (1498cc)						
128 Targa Cpe	200	500	1100	1900	3500	5000
Brava 131 - (4-cyl) - (98" wb) - (1995cc)						
2d Sed	125	250	750	1150	2450	3500
4d Sed	125	250	750	1150	2450	3500
Spider 2000 - (4-cyl) - (89.7" wb) - (1995cc)						
124 2d Conv	350	825	1600	4000	5600	8000
124 2d Turbo Conv	350	875	1700	4250	5900	8500

1982

	6	5	4	3	2	1
Strada - (4-cyl) - (96.4" wb) - (1498cc) - (FWD)						
DD 2d HBk	125	250	750	1150	2450	3500
DD 2d Cus HBk	125	250	750	1150	2450	3500
DE Cus 4d HBk	125	250	750	1150	2450	3500
X1/9 - (4-cyl) - (86.7" wb) - (1498cc)						
BS Targa Cpe	200	500	1100	1900	3500	5000
Spider 2000 - (4-cyl) - (89.7" wb) - (1995cc)						
AS 2d Conv	350	825	1600	4000	5600	8000
2d Turbo Conv	350	875	1700	4250	5900	8500

1983

	6	5	4	3	2	1
X1/9 - (4-cyl) - (86.7" wb) - (1498cc)						
BS Targa Cpe	200	500	1100	1900	3500	5000
Spider 2000 - (4-cyl) - (89.7" wb) - (1995cc)						
AS 2d Conv	350	825	1600	4000	5600	8000
2d Turbo Conv	350	875	1700	4250	5900	8500

NOTE: The Spider 2000 convertible was produced under the Pininfarina nameplate during 1984-85. The X1/9 Targa coupe was produced under the Bertone nameplate during 1984-90.

FORD - BRITISH

1948

	6	5	4	3	2	1
Anglia - (4-cyl) - (90" wb)						
2d Sed	350	825	1600	4000	5600	8000
Prefect - (4-cyl) - (94" wb)						
4d Sed	350	775	1500	3750	5250	7500

1949

	6	5	4	3	2	1
Anglia - (4-cyl) - (90" wb)						
2d Sed	350	825	1600	4000	5600	8000
Prefect - (4-cyl) - (94" wb)						
4d Sed	350	775	1500	3750	5250	7500

1950

	6	5	4	3	2	1
Anglia - (4-cyl) - (90" wb)						
2d Sed	350	825	1600	4000	5600	8000
Prefect - (4-cyl) - (94" wb)						
4d Sed	350	775	1500	3750	5250	7500

1951

	6	5	4	3	2	1
Anglia - (4-cyl) - (90" wb)						
2d Sed	200	550	1150	2000	3600	5200
Prefect - (4-cyl) - (90" wb)						
4d Sed	200	500	1100	1950	3600	5100
Consul - (4-cyl) - (100" wb)						
4d Sed	200	550	1150	2000	3600	5200

1952

Anglia - (4-cyl) - (90" wb)						
2d Sed	200	550	1150	2000	3600	5200
Prefect - (4-cyl) - (94" wb)						
4d Sed	200	500	1100	1950	3600	5100
Consul - (4-cyl) - (100" wb)						
4d Sed	200	550	1150	2000	3600	5200
Zephyr - (6-cyl) - (104" wb)						
4d Sed	200	600	1200	2200	3850	5500

1953

Anglia - (4-cyl) - (90" wb)						
2d Sed	200	550	1150	2000	3600	5200
Prefect - (4-cyl) - (94" wb)						
4d Sed	200	500	1100	1950	3600	5100
Consul - (4-cyl) - (100" wb)						
4d Sed	200	550	1150	2000	3600	5200
Zephyr - (6-cyl) - (104" wb)						
4d Sed	200	600	1200	2200	3850	5500

1954

Anglia - (4-cyl) - (87" wb)						
2d Sed	200	550	1150	2000	3600	5200
Prefect - (4-cyl) - (87" wb)						
4d Sed	200	500	1100	1950	3600	5100
Consul - (4-cyl) - (100" wb)						
4d Sed	200	550	1150	2000	3600	5200
Zephyr - (6-cyl) - (104" wb)						
4d Sed	200	600	1200	2200	3850	5500

1955

Anglia - (4-cyl) - (87" wb)						
2d Sed	200	550	1150	2000	3600	5200
Prefect - (4-cyl) - (87" wb)						
4d Sed	200	500	1100	1950	3600	5100
Consul - (4-cyl) - (100" wb)						
4d Sed	200	550	1150	2100	3800	5400
2d Conv	350	825	1600	4000	5600	8000
Zephyr - (6-cyl) - (104" wb)						
4d Sed	200	600	1200	2200	3850	5500
Zodiac - (6-cyl) - (104" wb)						
4d Sed	200	600	1200	2200	3900	5600
2d Conv	350	825	1600	4000	5600	8000

1956

Anglia - (4-cyl) - (87" wb)						
2d Sed	200	550	1150	2000	3600	5200
Prefect - (4-cyl) - (87" wb)						
4d Sed	200	500	1100	1950	3600	5100
Escort/Squire - (4-cyl) - (87" wb)						
2d Sta Wag	200	550	1150	2100	3800	5400
Consul - (4-cyl) - (100" wb)						
4d Sed	200	550	1150	2100	3800	5400
2d Conv	350	825	1600	4000	5600	8000
Zephyr - (6-cyl) - (104" wb)						
4d Sed	200	600	1200	2200	3850	5500
2d Conv	350	825	1600	4000	5600	8000
Zodiac - (6-cyl) - (104" wb)						
4d Sed	200	600	1200	2200	3900	5600

1957

Anglia - (4-cyl) - (87" wb)						
2d Sed	200	550	1150	2000	3600	5200
Prefect - (4-cyl) - (87" wb)						
4d Sed	200	500	1100	1950	3600	5100
Escort/Squire - (4-cyl) - (87" wb)						
2d Sta Wag	200	550	1150	2100	3800	5400
Consul - (4-cyl) - (104" wb)						
4d Sed	200	550	1150	2100	3800	5400
2d Conv	350	825	1600	4000	5600	8000
Zephyr - (6-cyl) - (107" wb)						
4d Sed	200	600	1200	2200	3850	5500
2d Conv	350	825	1600	4000	5600	8000
Zodiac - (6-cyl) - (107" wb)						
4d Sed	200	600	1200	2200	3900	5600
2d Conv	350	875	1700	4250	5900	8500

1958

Anglia - (4-cyl) - (87" wb)						
2d Sed	200	550	1150	2000	3600	5200
2d DeL Sed	200	550	1150	2100	3700	5300
Prefect - (4-cyl) - (87" wb)						
4d Sed	200	550	1150	2000	3600	5200
Escort/Squire - (4-cyl) - (87" wb)						
2d Sta Wag	200	550	1150	2100	3800	5400
Consul - (4-cyl) - (104" wb)						
4d Sed	200	550	1150	2100	3800	5400
2d Conv	350	825	1600	4000	5600	8000
Zephyr - (6-cyl) - (107" wb)						
4d Sed	200	600	1200	2200	3850	5500
2d Conv	350	825	1600	4000	5600	8000
Zodiac - (6-cyl) - (107" wb)						
4d Sed	200	600	1200	2200	3900	5600
2d Conv	350	875	1700	4250	5900	8500

1959

Anglia - (4-cyl) - (87" wb)						
2d DeL Sed	200	550	1150	2000	3600	5200
Prefect - (4-cyl) - (87" wb)						
4d Sed	200	550	1100	1950	3600	5100
Escort/Squire - (4-cyl) - (87" wb)						
2d Sta Wag	200	550	1150	2100	3800	5400
Consul - (4-cyl) - (104" wb)						
4d Sed	200	550	1150	2100	3800	5400
2d Conv	350	825	1600	4000	5600	8000
4d Sta Wag	200	600	1200	2200	3850	5500
Zephyr - (6-cyl) - (107" wb)						
4d Sed	200	600	1200	2200	3850	5500
2d Conv	350	825	1600	4000	5600	8000
4d Sta Wag	200	600	1200	2200	3900	5600
Zodiac - (6-cyl) - (107" wb)						
4d Sed	200	600	1200	2200	3900	5600
2d Conv	350	825	1600	4000	5600	8000
4d Sta Wag	200	600	1200	2300	4000	5700

1960

	6	5	4	3	2	1
Anglia - (4-cyl) - (90" wb)						
2d Sed	150	350	950	1450	2900	4100
Prefect - (4-cyl) - (90" wb)						
4d Sed	150	350	950	1350	2800	4000
Escort/Squire - (4-cyl) - (87" wb)						
2d Sta Wag	200	550	1150	2100	3800	5400
Consul - (4-cyl) - (104" wb)						
4d Sed	200	550	1150	2100	3800	5400
2d Conv	350	750	1450	3300	4900	7000
Zephyr - (6-cyl) - (107" wb)						
4d Sed	200	600	1200	2200	3850	5500
2d Conv	350	750	1450	3500	5050	7200
Zodiac - (6-cyl) - (107" wb)						
4d Sed	200	600	1200	2200	3900	5600
2d Conv	350	775	1500	3750	5250	7500

1961

Anglia - (4-cyl) - (90" wb)						
2d Sed	150	350	950	1450	2900	4100
Prefect - (4-cyl) - (90" wb)						
4d Sed	150	350	950	1350	2800	4000
Escort - (4-cyl) - (87" wb)						
2d Sta Wag	200	550	1150	2100	3800	5400
Consul - (4-cyl) - (104" wb)						
4d Sed	200	550	1150	2100	3800	5400
2d Conv	350	825	1600	4000	5600	8000
Zephyr - (6-cyl) - (107" wb)						
4d Sed	200	600	1200	2200	3850	5500
2d Conv	350	825	1600	4000	5600	8000
Zodiac - (6-cyl) - (107" wb)						
4d Sed	200	600	1200	2200	3900	5600
2d Conv	350	875	1700	4250	5900	8500

1962

Anglia - (4-cyl) - (90" wb)						
2d Sed	150	350	950	1450	2900	4100
2d DeL Sed	150	350	950	1450	3000	4200
2d Sta Wag	150	350	950	1450	3000	4200
Consul 315 - (4-cyl) - (99" wb)						
2d Sed	150	400	1000	1550	3050	4300
4d DeL Sed	150	400	1000	1600	3100	4400
Consul Capri - (4-cyl) - (99" wb)						
2d HdTp Cpe	200	600	1200	2200	3850	5500

1963

Anglia - (4-cyl) - (90" wb)						
2d Sed	150	350	950	1450	2900	4100
2d DeL Sed	150	350	950	1450	3000	4200
2d Sta Wag	150	350	950	1450	3000	4200
Consul 315 - (4-cyl) - (99" wb)						
2d Sed	150	400	1000	1550	3050	4300
4d DeL Sed	150	400	1000	1600	3100	4400
Capri - (4-cyl) - (99" wb)						
2d HdTp Cpe	200	600	1200	2200	3850	5500
Cortina - (4-cyl) - (98" wb)						
2d DeL Sed	150	350	950	1450	3000	4200
4d DeL Sed	150	400	1000	1550	3050	4300
4d Sta Wag	150	400	1000	1550	3050	4300
Zephyr - (6-cyl) - (107" wb)						
4d Sed	150	400	1000	1600	3100	4400
Zodiac - (6-cyl) - (107" wb)						
4d Sed	150	400	1000	1650	3150	4500

1964

Anglia - (4-cyl) - (90" wb)						
2d Sed	150	350	950	1450	2900	4100
2d DeL Sed	150	350	950	1450	3000	4200
2d Sta Wag	150	350	950	1450	3000	4200
Consul 315 - (4-cyl) - (99" wb)						
2d Sed	150	400	1000	1550	3050	4300
4d DeL Sed	150	400	1000	1600	3100	4400
Consul Capri - (4-cyl) - (99" wb)						
2d Cpe	200	600	1200	2200	3850	5500
2d GT Cpe	200	600	1200	2200	3850	5500
Cortina - (4-cyl) - (98" wb)						
2d GT Sed	150	450	1050	1700	3200	4600
2d DeL Sed	150	400	1000	1650	3150	4500
4d DeL Sed	150	400	1000	1600	3100	4400
4d Sta Wag	150	400	1000	1600	3100	4400
Zodiac - (6-cyl) - (107" wb)						
4d Sed	150	400	1000	1650	3150	4500

1965

Anglia - (4-cyl) - (90" wb)						
2d DeL Sed	150	350	950	1450	3000	4200
Capri - (4-cyl) - (99" wb)						
2d Cpe	150	400	1000	1550	3050	4300
2d GT Cpe	150	400	1000	1600	3100	4400
Cortina - (4-cyl) - (98" wb)						
2d GT Sed	200	500	1100	1900	3500	5000
2d Sed	150	350	950	1450	3000	4200
4d Sed	150	350	950	1450	2900	4100
4d Sta Wag	150	350	950	1450	3000	4200

1966

Anglia 1200 - (4-cyl) - (90" wb)						
2d DeL Sed	150	350	950	1450	3000	4200
Cortina 1500 - (4-cyl) - (98" wb)						
2d GT Sed	200	500	1100	1900	3500	5000
2d Sed	150	350	950	1450	3000	4200
4d Sed	150	400	1000	1550	3050	4300
4d Sta Wag	150	400	1000	1600	3100	4400
Cortina Lotus - (4-cyl) - (98" wb)	400	1200	2000	4000	7000	10,000

1967

Anglia 113E - (4-cyl) - (90" wb)						
2d DeL Sed	150	350	950	1450	3000	4200
Cortina 116E - (4-cyl) - (98" wb)						
2d GT Sed	150	400	1000	1550	3050	4300
2d Sed	150	350	950	1450	3000	4200
4d Sed	150	400	1000	1550	3050	4300
4d Sta Wag	150	400	1000	1600	3100	4400

1968

Cortina - (4-cyl) - (98" wb)						
2d Sed	150	400	1000	1550	3050	4300
4d Sed	150	400	1000	1600	3100	4400
2d GT Sed	150	400	1000	1650	3150	4500
4d GT Sed	150	400	1000	1650	3150	4500
4d Sta Wag	150	400	1000	1650	3150	4500

1969
Cortina - (4-cyl) - (98" wb)

	6	5	4	3	2	1
2d Sed	150	400	1000	1550	3050	4300
4d Sed	150	400	1000	1600	3100	4400
2d GT Sed	150	450	1050	1700	3200	4600
4d GT Sed	150	450	1050	1700	3200	4600
2d DeL Sed	150	400	1000	1650	3150	4500
4d DeL Sed	150	400	1000	1650	3150	4500
4d Sta Wag	150	450	1050	1700	3200	4600

1970
Cortina - (4-cyl) - (98" wb)

	6	5	4	3	2	1
2d Sed	150	400	1000	1550	3050	4300
4d Sed	150	400	1000	1600	3100	4400
2d GT Sed	150	450	1050	1700	3200	4600
4d GT Sed	150	450	1050	1700	3200	4600
2d DeL Sed	150	400	1000	1650	3150	4500
4d DeL Sed	150	400	1000	1650	3150	4500
4d Sta Wag	150	450	1050	1700	3200	4600

FORD-CAPRI

1969-70
1600 - (4-cyl) - (100.8" wb) - (1599cc)

	6	5	4	3	2	1
2d Spt Cpe	150	400	1000	1650	3150	4500

1971
1600 - (4-cyl) - (100.8" wb) - (1599 cc)

2d Spt Cpe	200	500	1100	1900	3500	5000

2000 - (4-cyl) - (100.8" wb) - (1993cc)

2d Spt Cpe	200	600	1200	2200	3850	5500

1972
1600 - (4-cyl) - (100.8" wb) - (1599cc)

2d Spt Cpe	150	400	1000	1650	3150	4500

2000 - (4-cyl) - (100.8" wb) - (1993cc)

2d Spt Cpe	200	500	1100	1900	3500	5000

2600 - (V-6) - (100.8" wb) - (2548 cc)

2d Spt Cpe	200	600	1200	2200	3850	5500

1973
2000 - (4-cyl) - (100.8" wb) - (1993cc)

2d Spt Cpe	200	500	1100	1900	3500	5000

2600 - (V-6) - (100.8" wb) - (2548 cc)

2d Spt Cpe	200	600	1200	2200	3850	5500

1974
2000 - (4-cyl) - (100.8" wb) - (1993cc)

2d Spt Cpe	200	500	1100	1900	3500	5000

2800 - (V-6) - (100.8" wb) - (2792cc)

2d Spt Cpe	200	600	1200	2200	3850	5500

CAPRI II

1975-76
2300 - (4-cyl) - (100.9" wb) - (2300cc)

2d HBk Cpe	200	500	1100	1900	3500	5000
2d Ghia Cpe	200	600	1200	2200	3850	5500
2d "S" Cpe	200	600	1200	2200	3850	5500

2800 - (V-6) - (100.9" wb) - (2795cc)

2d HBk Cpe	200	500	1100	1900	3500	5000

NOTE: No Capri's were imported for the 75 model year. Late in the year came the Capri II (intended as a '76 model).

1977-78
2300 - (4-cyl) - (100.9" wb) - (2300cc)

2d HBk Cpe	200	500	1100	1900	3500	5000
2d Ghia Cpe	200	600	1200	2200	3850	5500

2800 - (V-6) - (100.9" wb) - (2795cc)

2d HBk Cpe	200	600	1200	2200	3850	5500

NOTE: 1977 was the final model year for Capri II. They were not imported after 1977.

GEO

1989
Metro

2d HBk	200	600	1200	2200	3900	5600
2d HBk LSi	200	675	1300	2500	4300	6100
4d Sed LSi	200	675	1300	2500	4350	6200
Prizm						
4d Sed	350	850	1650	4100	5700	8200
5d HBk	350	850	1650	4150	5800	8300
Spectrum						
2d HBk	350	700	1350	2900	4600	6600
4d Sed	350	725	1400	3100	4800	6800
Tracker (4WD)						
Wag HdTp	400	1250	2100	4200	7400	10,500
Wag Soft-top	400	1200	2000	4000	7000	10,000

HILLMAN

1948
Minx - (4-cyl) - (92" wb)

4d Sed	200	500	1100	1900	3500	5000
2d Conv	350	775	1500	3750	5250	7500
4d Est Wag	200	600	1200	2200	3850	5500

1949
Minx - (4-cyl) - (93" wb)

4d Sed	200	500	1100	1900	3500	5000
2d Conv	350	775	1500	3750	5250	7500
4d Est Wag	200	600	1200	2200	3850	5500

1950
Minx - (4-cyl) - (93" wb)

4d Sed	200	500	1100	1900	3500	5000
2d Conv	350	775	1500	3750	5250	7500
4d Est Wag	200	600	1200	2200	3850	5500

1951
Minx Mark IV - (4-cyl) - (93" wb)

	6	5	4	3	2	1
4d Sed	200	500	1100	1900	3500	5000
2d Conv	350	775	1500	3750	5250	7500
4d Est Wag	200	600	1200	2200	3850	5500

1952
Minx Mark IV - (4-cyl) - (93" wb)

4d Sed	200	500	1100	1900	3500	5000
2d Conv	350	775	1500	3750	5250	7500
4d Est Wag	200	600	1200	2200	3850	5500

Minx Mark V - (4-cyl) - (93" wb)

4d Sed	200	500	1100	1900	3500	5000
2d Conv	350	800	1550	3800	5300	7600
4d Est Wag	100	175	525	1050	2100	3000

1953
Minx Mark VI - (4-cyl) - (93" wb)

4d Sed	200	500	1100	1900	3500	5000
2d HdTp	200	650	1250	2400	4200	6000
2d Conv	350	800	1550	3850	5400	7700
4d Est Wag	200	600	1200	2200	3850	5500

1954
Minx Mark VII - (4-cyl) - (93" wb)

4d Sed	200	500	1100	1900	3500	5000
2d HdTp	200	650	1250	2400	4200	6000
2d Conv	350	800	1550	3850	5400	7700
4d Est Wag	200	600	1200	2200	3850	5500

1955
Husky - (4-cyl) - (84" wb)

2d Sta Wag	200	500	1100	1900	3500	5000

Minx Mark VIII - (4-cyl) - (93" wb)

4d Sed	200	500	1100	1900	3500	5000
2d HdTp Cpe	200	650	1250	2400	4200	6000
2d Conv	350	800	1550	3850	5400	7700
4d Est Wag	200	600	1200	2200	3850	5500

1956
Husky - (4-cyl) - (84" wb)

2d Sta Wag	200	500	1100	1900	3500	5000

Minx Mark VIII - (4-cyl) - (93" wb)

4d Sed	200	600	1200	2200	3850	5500
2d HdTp Cpe	200	650	1250	2400	4200	6000
2d Conv	350	800	1550	3850	5400	7700
4d Est Wag	200	600	1200	2200	3850	5500

1957
Husky - (4-cyl) - (84" wb)

2d Sta Wag	200	500	1100	1900	3500	5000

New Minx - (4-cyl) - (96" wb)

4d Sed	200	500	1100	1900	3500	5000
2d Conv	350	775	1500	3700	5200	7400
4d Est Wag	200	600	1200	2200	3850	5500

1958
Husky - (4-cyl) - (84" wb)

2d Sta Wag	200	500	1100	1900	3500	5000

Husky - (2nd Series) - (4-cyl) - (86" wb)

2d Sta Wag	200	500	1100	1900	3500	5000

Minx - (4-cyl) - (96" wb)

4d Spl Sed	200	500	1100	1900	3500	5000
4d DeL Sed	200	600	1200	2200	3850	5500
2d Conv	350	775	1500	3700	5200	7400
4d Est Wag	350	700	1350	2700	4500	6400

1959
Husky - (4-cyl) - (86" wb)

2d Sta Wag	200	500	1100	1900	3500	5000

Minx Series II - (4-cyl) - (96" wb)

4d Spl Sed	200	600	1200	2200	3850	5500
4d DeL Sed	200	600	1200	2200	3850	5500
2d Conv	350	775	1500	3700	5200	7400
4d Est Wag	200	600	1200	2200	3850	5500

1960
Husky - (4-cyl) - (86" wb)

2d Sta Wag	200	500	1100	1900	3500	5000

Minx Series IIIA - (4-cyl) - (96" wb)

4d Spl Sed	200	600	1200	2200	3850	5500
4d DeL Sed	200	600	1200	2200	3850	5500
2d Conv	350	775	1500	3750	5250	7500
4d Est Wag	200	600	1200	2200	3850	5500

1961
Husky - (4-cyl) - (86" wb)

2d Sta Wag	200	500	1100	1900	3500	5000

Minx Series IIIA - (4-cyl) - (96" wb)

4d Spl Sed	200	600	1200	2200	3850	5500
4d DeL Sed	200	600	1200	2200	3850	5500
2d Conv	350	775	1500	3750	5250	7500
4d Est Wag	200	600	1200	2200	3850	5500

1962
Husky - (4-cyl) - (86" wb)

2d Sta Wag	200	500	1100	1900	3500	5000

Minx Series 1600 - (4-cyl) - (96" wb)

4d Sed	200	500	1100	1900	3500	5000
2d Conv	350	750	1450	3300	4900	7000
4d Est Wag	200	600	1200	2200	3850	5500

Super Minx - (4-cyl) - (101" wb)

4d Sed	200	600	1200	2200	3850	5500

1963
Husky II - (4-cyl) - (86" wb)

2d Sta Wag	200	500	1100	1900	3500	5000

Minx Series 1600 - (4-cyl) - (96" wb)

4d Sed	200	500	1100	1900	3500	5000

Super Minx Mark I - (4-cyl) - (101" wb)

4d Sed	200	500	1100	1900	3500	5000
2d Conv	350	750	1450	3300	4900	7000
4d Est Wag	200	500	1100	1900	3500	5000

Super Minx Mark II - (4-cyl) - (101" wb)

4d Sed	350	825	1600	4000	5600	8000
2d Conv	350	750	1450	3500	5050	7200
4d Est Wag	200	500	1100	1900	3500	5000

1964
Husky - (4-cyl) - (86" wb)

2d Sta Wag	200	500	1100	1900	3500	5000

Minx Series 1600 Mark V - (4-cyl) - (96" wb)

4d Sed	200	500	1100	1900	3500	5000

Super Minx Mark II - (4-cyl) - (101" wb)

4d Sed	200	500	1100	1900	3500	5000
2d Conv	350	750	1450	3400	5000	7100
4d Est Wag	200	500	1100	1900	3500	5000

1965

Husky - (4-cyl) - (86" wb)

	6	5	4	3	2	1
2d Sta Wag	200	500	1100	1900	3500	5000
Super Minx Mark II - (4-cyl) - (101" wb)						
4d Sed	200	500	1100	1900	3500	5000
4d Est Wag	200	500	1100	1900	3500	5000

1966

Husky - (4-cyl) - (86" wb)

	6	5	4	3	2	1
2d Sta Wag	200	500	1100	1900	3500	5000
Super Minx Mark III - (4-cyl) - (101" wb)						
4d Sed	200	500	1100	1900	3500	5000
4d Est Wag	200	500	1100	1900	3500	5000

1967

Husky - (4-cyl) - (86" wb)

	6	5	4	3	2	1
2d Sta Wag	200	500	1100	1900	3500	5000

HONDA

1980

	6	5	4	3	2	1
Civic 1300						
3d HBk	150	350	950	1350	2800	4000
3d DX	150	350	950	1350	2800	4000
Civic 1500						
3d HBk	150	350	950	1350	2800	4000
3d HBk DX	150	350	950	1450	2900	4100
3d HBk GL	150	350	950	1450	3000	4200
5d Sta Wag	150	350	950	1450	2900	4100
Accord						
3d HBk	150	400	1000	1650	3150	4500
4d Sed	200	500	1100	1900	3500	5000
3d HBk LX	200	500	1100	1900	3500	5000
Prelude						
2d Cpe	200	600	1200	2300	4000	5700

1981

	6	5	4	3	2	1
Civic 1300						
3d HBk	150	350	950	1350	2800	4000
3d HBK DX	150	350	950	1450	2900	4100
Civic 1500						
3d HBk DX	150	350	950	1350	2800	4000
3d HBk GL	150	350	950	1350	2800	4000
4d Sed	150	350	950	1450	2900	4100
4d Sta Wag	150	350	950	1450	2900	4100
Accord						
3d HBk	200	500	1100	1900	3500	5000
4d Sed	200	500	1100	1900	3500	5000
3d HBk LX	200	500	1100	1950	3600	5100
4d Sed SE	200	500	1100	1950	3600	5100
Prelude						
2d Cpe	200	650	1250	2400	4200	6000

1982

	6	5	4	3	2	1
Civic 1300						
3d HBk	150	350	950	1350	2800	4000
3d HBk FE	150	350	950	1350	2800	4000
Civic 1500						
3d HBk DX	150	350	950	1450	2900	4100
3d HBk GL	150	350	950	1450	3000	4200
4d Sed	150	400	1000	1550	3050	4300
4d Sta Wag	150	350	950	1450	2900	4100
Accord						
3d HBk	100	175	525	1050	2100	3000
4d Sed	200	500	1100	1950	3600	5100
3d HBk LX	200	550	1150	2000	3600	5200
Prelude						
2d Cpe	200	675	1300	2500	4350	6200

1983

	6	5	4	3	2	1
Civic 1300						
3d HBk	150	350	950	1350	2800	4000
3d HBk FE	150	350	950	1350	2800	4000
Civic 1500						
3d HBk DX	150	350	950	1450	2900	4100
3d HBk S	150	350	950	1450	3000	4200
4d Sed	150	400	1000	1550	3050	4300
4d Sta Wag	150	350	950	1450	2900	4100
Accord						
3d HBk	200	500	1100	1900	3500	5000
3d HBk LX	200	500	1100	1950	3600	5100
4d Sed	200	550	1150	2000	3600	5200
Prelude						
2d Cpe	200	675	1300	2600	4400	6300

1984

	6	5	4	3	2	1
Civic 1300						
2d Cpe CRX	150	350	950	1350	2800	4000
3d HBk	150	350	950	1350	2800	4000
Civic 1500						
2d Cpe CRX	200	500	1100	1900	3500	5000
3d HBk DX	150	350	950	1350	2800	4000
3d HBk S	150	350	950	1350	2800	4000
4d Sed	150	350	950	1450	3000	4200
4d Sta Wag	150	350	950	1450	3000	4200
Accord						
3d HBk	200	500	1100	1950	3600	5100
3d HBk LX	200	550	1150	2000	3600	5200
4d Sed	200	550	1150	2100	3700	5300
4d Sed LX	200	600	1200	2200	3850	5500
Prelude						
2d Cpe	350	750	1450	3300	4900	7000

1985

	6	5	4	3	2	1
Civic 1300						
3d HBk	150	350	950	1350	2800	4000
Civic 1500						
2d Cpe CRX HF	200	600	1200	2200	3850	5500
2d Cpe CRX	200	600	1200	2300	4000	5700
2d Cpe CRX Si	200	650	1250	2400	4200	6000
3d HBk DX	200	500	1100	1900	3500	5000
3d HBk S	100	175	525	1050	2100	3000
4d Sed	125	200	600	1100	2200	3100
4d Sta Wag	100	175	525	1050	2100	3000
4d Sta Wag (4WD)	125	250	750	1150	2450	3500

Accord (1985, continued)

	6	5	4	3	2	1
3d HBk	200	650	1250	2400	4200	6000
3d HBk LX	350	700	1350	2800	4550	6500
4d Sed LX	350	700	1350	2900	4600	6600
4d Sed LX	350	725	1400	3100	4800	6800
4d Sed SEi	350	775	1500	3750	5250	7500
Prelude						
2d Cpe	350	775	1500	3750	5250	7500
2d Cpe Si	350	850	1650	4150	5800	8300

1986

	6	5	4	3	2	1
Civic						
3d HBk	150	350	950	1450	3000	4200
3d HBk DX	150	450	1050	1750	3250	4700
3d HBk Si	200	550	1150	2100	3800	5400
4d Sed	200	600	1200	2200	3850	5500
4d Sta Wag	200	500	1100	1900	3500	5000
4d Sta Wag (4WD)	200	600	1200	2200	3900	5600
Civic CRX						
2d Cpe HF	200	550	1150	2000	3600	5200
2d Cpe Si	200	650	1250	2400	4200	6000
2d Cpe	200	600	1200	2200	3850	5500
Accord						
3d HBk DX	350	700	1350	2900	4600	6600
3d HBk LXi	350	825	1600	4000	5600	8000
4d Sed DX	350	775	1500	3750	5250	7500
4d Sed LX	350	825	1600	4000	5600	8000
4d Sed LXi	450	900	1800	4450	6250	8900
Prelude						
2d Cpe	450	900	1800	4400	6150	8800
2d Cpe Si	450	975	2200	4850	6800	9700

1987

	6	5	4	3	2	1
Civic						
3d HBk	200	600	1200	2200	3850	5500
3d HBk DX	200	675	1300	2500	4300	6100
3d HBk Si	350	725	1400	3100	4800	6800
4d Sed	350	750	1450	3300	4900	7000
4d Sta Wag	350	700	1350	2700	4500	6400
4d Sta Wag (4WD)	350	750	1450	3400	5000	7100
Civic CRX						
2d Cpe HF	350	700	1350	2900	4600	6600
2d Cpe	350	725	1400	3200	4850	6900
2d Cpe Si	350	775	1500	3750	5250	7500
Accord						
3d HBk DX	350	825	1600	4000	5600	8000
3d HBk LXi	450	950	2100	4700	6600	9400
4d Sed DX	450	975	2200	4850	6800	9700
4d Sed LX	450	950	2100	4750	6650	9500
4d Sed LXi	400	1250	2100	4200	7400	10,500
Prelude						
2d Cpe	400	1200	2000	4000	7000	10,000
2d Cpe Si	400	1300	2200	4400	7700	11,000

1988

	6	5	4	3	2	1
Civic						
3d HBk	350	700	1350	2800	4550	6500
3d HBk DX	350	775	1500	3700	5200	7400
4d Sed DX	350	850	1650	4100	5700	8200
4d Sed LX	450	900	1800	4400	6150	8800
4d Sta Wag	350	800	1550	3900	5450	7800
4d Sta Wag (4WD)	350	875	1700	4250	5900	8500
Civic CRX						
2d Cpe HF	350	825	1600	4000	5600	8000
2d Cpe Si	450	900	1900	4500	6300	9000
2d Cpe	350	850	1650	4150	5800	8300
Accord						
3d HBk DX	450	925	1900	4550	6350	9100
3d HBk LXi	400	1300	2200	4400	7600	10,900
2d Cpe DX	450	975	2300	4950	6900	9900
2d Cpe LXi	450	1400	2300	4600	8100	11,500
4d Sed DX	400	1200	2000	4000	7100	10,100
4d Sed LX	400	1300	2150	4300	7600	10,800
4d Sed LXi	450	1500	2500	5000	8700	12,400
Prelude						
2d Cpe S	450	1450	2400	4800	8400	12,000
2d Cpe Si	500	1600	2700	5400	9500	13,500
2d Cpe Si (4WD)	550	1700	2800	5600	9800	14,000

1989

	6	5	4	3	2	1
Civic						
3d HBk	350	775	1500	3600	5100	7300
3d HBk DX	350	850	1650	4150	5800	8300
3d HBk Si	450	925	1900	4550	6350	9100
4d Sed DX	450	925	2000	4650	6500	9300
4d Sed LX	450	975	2300	4950	6900	9900
4d Sta Wag	450	900	1900	4500	6300	9000
4d Sta Wag (4WD)	450	975	2300	4900	6850	9800
Civic CRX						
2d Cpe HF	450	900	1900	4500	6300	9000
2d Cpe	450	950	2100	4750	6650	9500
2d Cpe Si	400	1250	2100	4200	7400	10,500
Accord						
3d HBk DX	400	1300	2150	4300	7500	10,700
3d HBk LXi	500	1550	2550	5100	9000	12,800
2d Cpe DX	450	1400	2300	4600	8100	11,600
2d Cpe LXi	500	1650	2750	5500	9700	13,800
4d Sed DX	450	1400	2350	4700	8300	11,800
4d Sed LX	500	1550	2600	5200	9100	13,000
4d Sed LXi	550	1800	2950	5900	10,400	14,800
2d Cpe SEi	550	1800	2950	5900	10,400	14,800
4d Sed SEi	600	1850	3100	6200	10,900	15,500
Prelude						
2d Cpe S	450	1450	2400	4800	8400	12,000
2d Cpe Si	500	1600	2650	5300	9300	13,300
2d Cpe Si (4WD)	500	1650	2750	5500	9700	13,800

ISUZU

1961-65

Bellel 2000 - (4-cyl) - (99.6" wb) - (1991cc)

	6	5	4	3	2	1
Diesel 4d Sed	150	350	950	1350	2800	4000
Diesel 4d Sta Wag	150	350	950	1350	2800	4000

NOTE: An optional diesel engine (DL200) was available.

1966-80

NOTE: See detailed listings.

1981-82

I-Mark, (Gasoline) - (4-cyl) - (94.3" wb) - (1817cc)	6	5	4	3	2	1
AT77B 2d DeL Cpe	125	250	750	1150	2450	3500
AT69B 4d DeL Sed	125	250	750	1150	2450	3500
AT77B 2d LS Cpe	125	250	750	1150	2450	3500
I-Mark, (Diesel) - (4-cyl) - (94.3" wb) - (1817cc)						
AT77P 2d Cpe	100	175	525	1050	2100	3000
AT77P 2d DeL Cpe	100	175	525	1050	2100	3000
AT69P 4d DeL Sed	100	175	525	1050	2100	3000
AT77P 2d LS Cpe	100	175	525	1050	2100	3000

1983-85

I-Mark, (Gasoline) - (4-cyl) - (94.3" wb) - (1817cc)						
T77 2d DeL Cpe	150	350	950	1350	2800	4000
T69 4d DeL Sed	150	350	950	1350	2800	4000
T77 2d LS Cpe	150	350	950	1350	2800	4000
T69 4d LS Sed	150	350	950	1350	2800	4000
I-Mark, (Diesel) - (4-cyl) - (94.3" wb) - (1817cc)						
T77 2d Cpe	150	350	950	1350	2800	4000
Impulse - (4-cyl) - (96" wb) - (1949cc)						
2d Spt Cpe	200	650	1250	2400	4200	6000

JAGUAR

1946-1948

3-5 Litre - (6-cyl) - (120" wb) - (125 hp)						
Conv Cpe	2500	7900	13,200	26,400	46,200	66,000
Saloon	1150	3700	6200	12,400	21,700	31,000

1949

Mark V - (6-cyl) - (120" wb) - (125 hp)						
Conv Cpe	2500	7900	13,200	26,400	46,200	66,000
Saloon	1150	3700	6200	12,400	21,700	31,000

1950

Mark V - (6-cyl) - (120" wb) - (160 hp)						
Saloon	1150	3600	6000	12,000	21,000	30,000
Conv Cpe	2500	7900	13,200	26,400	46,200	66,000
XK-120 - (6-cyl) - (102" wb) - (160 hp)						
Rds	2700	8650	14,400	28,800	50,400	72,000

NOTE: Some X-120 models delivered early as 1949 models, use 1950 prices.

1951

Mark VII - (6-cyl) - (120" wb) - (160 hp)						
Saloon	850	2650	4400	8800	15,400	22,000
XK-120 - (6-cyl) - (102" wb) - (160 hp)						
Rds	2500	7900	13,200	26,400	46,200	66,000
Cpe	1750	5650	9400	18,800	32,900	47,000

1952

Mark VII - (twin-cam) - (6-cyl) - (120" wb) - (160 hp)						
Std Sed	850	2650	4400	8800	15,400	22,000
Del Sed	850	2750	4600	9200	16,100	23,000
XK-120S - (modified) - (102" wb) - (160 hp)						
Rds	2700	8650	14,400	28,800	50,400	72,000
Cpe	1950	6250	10,400	20,800	36,400	52,000
XK-120 - (6-cyl) - (102" wb) - (160 hp)						
Rds	2500	7900	13,200	26,400	46,200	66,000
Cpe	1750	5650	9400	18,800	32,900	47,000

1953

Mark VII - (6-cyl) - (120" wb) - (160 hp)						
Std Sed	850	2650	4400	8800	15,400	22,000
XK-120S - (6-cyl) - (102" wb) - (160 hp)						
Rds	2700	8650	14,400	28,800	50,400	72,000
Cpe	1900	6100	10,200	20,400	35,700	51,000
Conv	2200	6950	11,600	23,200	40,600	58,000
XK-120 - (6-cyl) - (102" wb) - (160 hp)						
Rds	2500	7900	13,200	26,400	46,200	66,000
Cpe	1750	5650	9400	18,800	32,900	47,000
Conv	1950	6250	10,400	20,800	36,400	52,000

1954

Mark VII - (6-cyl) - (120" wb) - (160 hp)						
Sed	1000	3100	5200	10,400	18,200	26,000
XK-120S - (modified) - (6-cyl) - (102" wb)						
Rds	2700	8650	14,400	28,800	50,400	72,000
Cpe	1900	6100	10,200	20,400	35,700	51,000
Conv	2200	6950	11,600	23,200	40,600	58,000
XK-120 - (6-cyl) - (102" wb) - (160 hp)						
Rds	2500	7900	13,200	26,400	46,200	66,000
Cpe	1750	5650	9400	18,800	32,900	47,000
Conv	1950	6250	10,400	20,800	36,400	52,000

1955

Mark VII M - (6-cyl) - (120" wb) - (190 hp)						
Saloon	850	2750	4600	9200	16,100	23,000
XK-140 - (6-cyl) - (102" wb) - (190 hp)						
Cpe	1600	5050	8400	16,800	29,400	42,000
Rds	2350	7450	12,400	24,800	43,400	62,000
Conv	1950	6250	10,400	20,800	36,400	52,000
XK-140M - (6-cyl) - (102" wb) - (190 hp)						
Cpe	1750	5650	9400	18,800	32,900	47,000
Rds	2650	8400	14,000	28,000	49,000	70,000
Conv	2400	7700	12,800	25,600	44,800	64,000
XK-140MC - (6-cyl) - (102" wb) - (210 hp)						
Cpe	1950	6250	10,400	20,800	36,400	52,000
Rds	2850	9100	15,200	30,400	53,200	76,000
Conv	2650	8400	14,000	28,000	49,000	70,000

1956

Mark VII M - (6-cyl) - (120" wb) - (190 hp)						
Saloon	850	2650	4400	8800	15,400	22,000
XK-140 - (6-cyl) - (102" wb) - (190 hp)						
Cpe	1600	5050	8400	16,800	29,400	42,000
Rds	2350	7450	12,400	24,800	43,400	62,000
Conv	1950	6250	10,400	20,800	36,400	52,000
XK-140M - (6-cyl) - (102" wb) - (190 hp)						
Cpe	1750	5650	9400	18,800	32,900	47,000
Rds	2650	8400	14,000	28,000	49,000	70,000
Conv	2400	7700	12,800	25,600	44,800	64,000
XK-140MC - (6-cyl) - (102" wb) - (210 hp)						
Cpe	1950	6250	10,400	20,800	36,400	52,000
Rds	2850	9100	15,200	30,400	53,200	76,000
Conv	2650	8400	14,000	28,000	49,000	70,000
2.4 Litre - (6-cyl) - (108" wb) - (112 hp)						
Sed	800	2500	4200	8400	14,700	21,000
3.4 Litre - (6-cyl) - (108" wb) - (210 hp)						
Sed	850	2650	4400	8800	15,400	22,000

Mark VIII - (6-cyl) - (120" wb) - (210 hp)	6	5	4	3	2	1
Lux Sed	950	3000	5000	10,000	17,500	25,000

NOTE: 3.4 Litre available 1957 only; Mark VIII luxury sedan available 1957 only.

1957

Mark VIII - (6-cyl) - (102" wb) - (210 hp)						
Saloon	800	2500	4200	8400	14,700	21,000
XK-140						
Cpe	1600	5050	8400	16,800	29,400	42,000
Rds	2350	7450	12,400	24,800	43,400	62,000
Conv	1950	6250	10,400	20,800	36,400	52,000
XK-150 - (6-cyl) - (102" wb) - (190 hp)						
Cpe	1250	3950	6600	13,200	23,100	33,000
Rds	1950	6250	10,400	20,800	36,400	52,000
2.4 Litre - (6-cyl) - (108" wb) - (112 hp)						
Sed	700	2200	3700	7400	13,000	18,500
3.4 Litre - (6-cyl) - (108" wb) - (210 hp)						
Sed	800	2600	4300	8600	15,100	21,500

1958

3.4 Litre - (6-cyl) - (108" wb) - (210 hp)						
Sed	750	2450	4100	8200	14,400	20,500
XK-150 - (6-cyl) - (120" wb) - (190 hp)						
Cpe	1250	3950	6600	13,200	23,100	33,000
Rds	1950	6250	10,400	20,800	36,400	52,000
Conv	1750	5650	9400	18,800	32,900	47,000
XK-150S - (6-cyl) - (102" wb) - (250 hp)						
Rds	2550	8150	13,600	27,200	47,600	68,000
Mark VIII - (6-cyl) - (120" wb) - (210 hp)						
Saloon	700	2200	3700	7400	13,000	18,500

1959-60

XK-150 - (6-cyl) - (102" wb) - (210 hp)						
Cpe	1250	3950	6600	13,200	23,100	33,000
Rds	2000	6350	10,600	21,200	37,100	53,000
Conv	1750	5650	9400	18,800	32,900	47,000
XK-150SE - (6-cyl) - (102" wb) - (210 hp)						
Cpe	1450	4550	7600	15,200	26,600	38,000
Rds	2400	7700	12,800	25,600	44,800	64,000
Conv	2000	6350	10,600	21,200	37,100	53,000
XK-150S - (6-cyl) - (102" wb) - (250 hp)						
Rds	2550	8150	13,600	27,200	47,600	68,000
3.4 Litre - (6-cyl) - (108" wb) - (210 hp)						
Sed	750	2350	3900	7800	13,700	19,500
Mark IX - (6-cyl) - (120" wb) - (220 hp)						
Sed	900	2900	4800	9600	16,800	24,000

1961

XK-150 - (6-cyl) - (102" wb) - (210 hp)						
Cpe	1300	4100	6800	13,600	23,800	34,000
Conv	1800	5750	9600	19,200	33,600	48,000
XKE - (6-cyl) - (96" wb) - (265 hp)						
Rds	2550	8150	13,600	27,200	47,600	68,000
Cpe	1800	5750	9600	19,200	33,600	48,000
3.4 Litre - (6-cyl) - (108" wb) - (265 hp)						
Sed	750	2450	4100	8200	14,400	20,500
Mark IX - (6-cyl) - (120" wb) - (265 hp)						
Sed	850	2750	4600	9200	16,100	23,000

1962

XKE - (6-cyl) - (96" wb) - (265 hp)						
Rds	2550	8150	13,600	27,200	47,600	68,000
Cpe	1800	5750	9600	19,200	33,600	48,000
Mark II 3.4 Litre - (6-cyl) - (108" wb) - (265 hp)						
Sed	750	2450	4100	8200	14,400	20,500
Mark X - (6-cyl) - (120" wb) - (265 hp)						
Sed	850	2750	4600	9200	16,100	23,000

1963

XKE - (6-cyl) - (96" wb) - (265 hp)						
Rds	2700	8650	14,400	28,800	50,400	72,000
Cpe	1900	6000	10,000	20,000	35,000	50,000
Mark II - 3.8 Litre - (6-cyl) - (108" wb) - (265 hp)						
Sed	750	2450	4100	8200	14,400	20,500
Mark X - (6-cyl) - (120" wb) - (265 hp)						
Sed	850	2750	4600	9200	16,100	23,000

1964

XKE - (6-cyl) - (96" wb) - (265 hp)						
Rds	2700	8650	14,400	28,800	50,400	72,000
Cpe	1950	6250	10,400	20,800	36,400	52,000
Mark II - 3.8 Litre - (6-cyl) - (108" wb) - (265 hp)						
4d Sed	750	2450	4100	8200	14,400	20,500
Mark X - (6-cyl) - (120" wb) - (265 hp)						
4d Sed	850	2750	4600	9200	16,100	23,000

1965

XKE - 4.2 Litre - (6-cyl) - (96" wb) - (265 hp)						
Rds	2700	8650	14,400	28,800	50,400	72,000
Cpe	1950	6250	10,400	20,800	36,400	52,000
4d Sed	750	2450	4100	8200	14,400	20,500
3.8 Litre						
4d Sed	750	2400	4000	8000	14,000	20,000
Mk II Sed	750	2450	4100	8200	14,400	20,500

1966

XKE - 4.2 Litre - (6-cyl) - (96" wb) - (265 hp)						
Rds	2950	9350	15,600	31,200	54,600	78,000
Cpe	2100	6700	11,200	22,400	39,200	56,000
4d Sed	700	2200	3700	7400	13,000	18,500
Mark II - 3.8 Litre						
4d Sed	750	2400	4000	8000	14,000	20,000
4d Sed S	800	2500	4200	8400	14,700	21,000

1967

XKE - 4.2 Litre - (6-cyl) - (96" wb) - (265 hp)						
Rds	2950	9350	15,600	31,200	54,600	78,000
Cpe	2100	6700	11,200	22,400	39,200	56,000
Cpe (2 plus 2)	1650	5300	8800	17,600	30,800	44,000
Model 340 - (6-cyl) - (108" wb) - (225 hp)						
4d Sed	700	2300	3800	7600	13,300	19,000
Model 420 - (6-cyl) - (108" wb) - (255 hp)						
4d Sed	700	2300	3800	7600	13,300	19,000
Model 420 G - (6-cyl) - (107" wb) - (245 hp)						
4d Sed	750	2400	4000	8000	14,000	20,000

1968

Model XKE - 4.2 Litre - (96" wb) - (245 hp)						
Rds	2550	8150	13,600	27,200	47,600	68,000
Cpe	1950	6250	10,400	20,800	36,400	52,000
Cpe (2 plus 2)	1600	5050	8400	16,800	29,400	42,000

	6	5	4	3	2	1
1969						
Model XKE - (96" wb) - (246 hp)						
Rds	2550	8150	13,600	27,200	47,600	68,000
Cpe	1950	6250	10,400	20,800	36,400	52,000
Cpe (2 plus 2)	1600	5050	8400	16,800	29,400	42,000
Model XJ - (96" wb) - (246 hp)						
4d Sed	950	3000	5000	10,000	17,500	25,000
1970						
Model XKE - (96" wb) - (246 hp)						
Rds	2550	8150	13,600	27,200	47,600	68,000
Cpe	1950	6250	10,400	20,800	36,400	52,000
Cpe (2 plus 2)	1600	5150	8600	17,200	30,100	43,000
Model XJ - (96" wb) - (246 hp)						
4d Sed	700	2200	3700	7400	13,000	18,500
1971						
Model XKE - (96" wb) - (246 hp)						
Rds	2550	8150	13,600	27,200	47,600	68,000
Cpe	1950	6250	10,400	20,800	36,400	52,000
Cpe (2 plus 2) (V-12)	1950	6250	10,400	20,800	36,400	52,000
Conv (V-12)	3000	9600	16,000	32,000	56,000	80,000
Model XJ - (96" wb) - (246 hp)						
4d Sed	650	2100	3500	7000	12,300	17,500
1972						
Model XKE - (V-12) - (105" wb) - (272 hp)						
Rds	3000	9600	16,000	32,000	56,000	80,000
Cpe (2 plus 2)	1900	6000	10,000	20,000	35,000	50,000
Model XJ6 - (108.9" wb) - (186 hp)						
4d Sed	600	2000	3300	6600	11,600	16,500
1973						
Model XKE - (V-12) - (105" wb) - (272 hp)						
Rds	3000	9600	16,000	32,000	56,000	80,000
Cpe (2 plus 2)	1900	6000	10,000	20,000	35,000	50,000
Model XJ - (108.9" wb) - (186 hp)						
4d XJ6	600	1900	3200	6400	11,200	16,000
4d XJ12	850	2650	4400	8800	15,400	22,000
1974						
Model XKE - (V-12) - (105" wb) - (272 hp)						
Rds	3000	9600	16,000	32,000	56,000	80,000
Model XJ						
4d XJ6	600	2000	3300	6600	11,600	16,500
4d XJ6 (LWB)	650	2100	3500	7000	12,300	17,500
4d XJ12L	900	2800	4700	9400	16,500	23,500
1975						
Model XJ6						
Cpe C	900	2800	4700	9400	16,500	23,500
4d Sed L	650	2050	3400	6800	11,900	17,000
Model XJ12						
Cpe C	950	3050	5100	10,200	17,900	25,500
4d Sed L	700	2300	3800	7600	13,300	19,000
1976						
Model XJ6						
Cpe C	900	2950	4900	9800	17,200	24,500
4d Sed L	650	2050	3400	6800	11,900	17,000
Model XJ12						
Cpe C	1050	3300	5500	11,000	19,300	27,500
4d Sed L	700	2300	3800	7600	13,300	19,000
Model XJS						
Cpe (2 plus 2)	850	2750	4600	9200	16,100	23,000
1977						
Model XJ6						
Cpe C	1000	3250	5400	10,800	18,900	27,000
4d Sed L	650	2050	3400	6800	11,900	17,000
Model XJ12L						
4d Sed	700	2300	3800	7600	13,300	19,000
Model XJS						
GT Cpe (2 plus 2)	850	2750	4600	9200	16,100	23,000
1978						
Model XJ6L						
4d Sed	700	2150	3600	7200	12,600	18,000
Model XJ12L						
4d Sed	850	2650	4400	8800	15,400	22,000
Model XJS						
Cpe	900	2900	4800	9600	16,800	24,000
1979						
Model XJ6						
4d Sed	700	2150	3600	7200	12,600	18,000
4d Sed Series III	700	2300	3800	7600	13,300	19,000
Model XJ12						
4d Sed	850	2650	4400	8800	15,400	22,000
Model XJS						
Cpe	1000	3100	5200	10,400	18,200	26,000
1980						
4d Sed XJ6	700	2300	3800	7600	13,300	19,000
2d Cpe XJS (2 plus 2)	900	2900	4800	9600	16,800	24,000
1981						
Model XJ6						
4d Sed	700	2300	3800	7600	13,300	19,000
Model XJS						
2d Cpe	950	3000	5000	10,000	17,500	25,000
1982						
Model XJ6						
4d Sed	800	2500	4200	8400	14,700	21,000
4d Sed Vanden Plas	900	2900	4800	9600	16,800	24,000
Model XJS						
2d Cpe	1100	3500	5800	11,600	20,300	29,000
1983						
Model XJ6						
4d Sed	800	2500	4200	8400	14,700	21,000
4d Sed Vanden Plas	900	2900	4800	9600	16,800	24,000
Model XJS						
2d Cpe	1100	3500	5800	11,600	20,300	29,000
1984						
Model XJ6						
4d Sed	700	2300	3800	7600	13,300	19,000
4d Sed Van Plas	850	2650	4400	8800	15,400	22,000
Model XJS						
2d Cpe	1000	3250	5400	10,800	18,900	27,000
1985						
Model XJ6						
4d Sed	750	2400	4000	8000	14,000	20,000
4d Sed Van Plas	850	2750	4600	9200	16,100	23,000
Model XJS						
2d Cpe	1050	3350	5600	11,200	19,600	28,000
1986						
Model XJ6						
4d Sed	800	2500	4200	8400	14,700	21,000
4d Sed Van Plas	900	2900	4800	9600	16,800	24,000
Model XJS						
2d Cpe	1100	3500	5800	11,600	20,300	29,000
1987						
Model XJ6						
4d Sed	900	2900	4800	9600	16,800	24,000
4d Sed Van Plas	1000	3250	5400	10,800	18,900	27,000
Model XJS						
2d Cpe	1200	3850	6400	12,800	22,400	32,000
2d Cpe Cabrio	1350	4300	7200	14,400	25,200	36,000
1988						
Model XJ6						
4d Sed	1050	3350	5600	11,200	19,600	28,000
4d Sed Van Plas	1150	3700	6200	12,400	21,700	31,000
Model XJS						
2d Cpe	1300	4200	7000	14,000	24,500	35,000
2d Cpe Cabrio	1550	4900	8200	16,400	28,700	41,000
2d Conv	1750	5500	9200	18,400	32,200	46,000
1989						
Model XJ6						
4d Sed	1450	4550	7600	15,200	26,600	38,000
4d Sed Van Plas	1550	4900	8200	16,400	28,700	41,000
Model XJS						
2d Cpe	1650	5300	8800	17,600	30,800	44,000
2d Conv	1900	6100	10,200	20,400	35,700	51,000

LAMBORGHINI

	6	5	4	3	2	1
1964-1966						
350/400 GT - (V-12) - (99.5" wb) - (3464/3929cc)						
Cpe	3750	12,000	20,000	40,000	70,000	100,000
1966-1968						
400 GT - (V-12) - (99.5" wb) - (3929cc)						
Cpe (2 plus 2)	3600	11,500	19,200	38,400	67,200	96,000
1966-1969						
P400 Miura - (V-12) - (97.5" wb) - (3929cc)						
Cpe	4500	14,400	24,000	48,000	84,000	120,000
1969-1971						
P400 Miura S - (V-12) - (97.7" wb) - (3929cc)						
Cpe	4500	14,400	24,000	48,000	84,000	120,000
1971-1972						
P400 Miura SV - (V-12) - (97.7" wb) - (3929cc)						
Cpe	4600	14,650	24,400	48,800	85,400	122,000
1968-1978						
Espada - (V-12) - (99.5" wb) - (3929cc)						
Cpe (2 plus 2)	3600	11,500	19,200	38,400	67,200	96,000
1968-1969						
400 GT Isiero, Isiero S - (V-12) - (99.5" wb) - (3929cc)						
Cpe (2 plus 2)	3250	10,300	17,200	34,400	60,200	86,000
1970-1973						
400 GT Jarama - (V-12) - (92.8" wb) - (3929cc)						
Cpe (2 plus 2)	3250	10,300	17,200	34,400	60,200	86,000
1973-1976						
400 GTS Jarama - (V-12) - (92.8" wb) - (3929cc)						
Cpe (2 plus 2)	3300	10,550	17,600	35,200	61,600	88,000
1972-1976						
P250 Urraco - (V-8) - (95.5" wb) - (2462cc)						
Cpe (2 plus 2)	3300	10,550	17,600	35,200	61,600	88,000
1975-1977						
P200 Urraco - (V-8) - (95.5" wb) - (1994cc)						
Cpe (2 plus 2)	3300	10,550	17,600	35,200	61,600	88,000
1976-1978						
Silhouette - (V-8) - (95.5" wb) - (2995.8cc)						
Targa Conv	3750	12,000	20,000	40,000	70,000	100,000
1975-1979						
P300 Urraco - (V-8) - (95.5" wb) - (2995.8cc)						
Cpe (2 plus 2)	3400	10,800	18,000	36,000	63,000	90,000
1973-1978						
LP400 Countach - (V-12) - (95.5" wb) - (3929cc)						
Cpe	4900	15,600	26,000	52,000	91,000	130,000
1978-Present						
LP400S Countach - (V-12) - (95.5" wb) - (3929cc)						
Cpe	5250	16,800	28,000	56,000	98,000	140,000
1982-Present						
LP5000 Countach - (V-12) - (95.5" wb) - (4754cc)						
Cpe	6000	19,200	32,000	64,000	112,000	160,000
P350 Jalpa - (V-8) - (95.5" wb) - (3485cc)						
Targa Conv	4000	12,700	21,200	42,400	74,200	106,000

MASERATI

	6	5	4	3	2	1
1946-50						
A6/1500 - (6-cyl) - (100.4" wb) - (1488cc)						
2d Cpe 2 plus 2	1150	3600	6000	12,000	21,000	30,000
2d Cabr	1900	6000	10,000	20,000	35,000	50,000
1951-53						
A6G - (6-cyl) - (100.4" wb) - (1954cc)						
2d Cpe 2 plus 2	950	3000	5000	10,000	17,500	25,000
2d Cabr 2 plus 2	1700	5400	9000	18,000	31,500	45,000
1954-56						
A6G - (6-cyl) - (100.4" wb) - (1954cc)						
2d Cpe 2 plus 2	1150	3600	6000	12,000	21,000	30,000
2d Cabr 2 plus 2	1700	5400	9000	18,000	31,500	45,000
A6G/2000 - (6-cyl) - (100.4" wb) - (1985cc)						
2d Cpe 2 plus 2	950	3000	5000	10,000	17,500	25,000
2d Cabr 2 plus 2	950	3000	5000	10,000	17,500	25,000
1957-61						
A6G/2000/C - (6-cyl) - (100.4" wb) - (1985cc)						
Allemano Cpe 2 plus 2	1300	4200	7000	14,000	24,500	35,000
Frua Cabr 2 plus 2	1150	3600	6000	12,000	21,000	30,000
Frua 2d Cpe	1300	4200	7000	14,000	24,500	35,000
Zagato Cpe 2 plus 2	1500	4800	8000	16,000	28,000	40,000

	6	5	4	3	2	1
3500 GT - (6-cyl) - (102.3" wb) - (3485cc)						
2d Cpe	850	2650	4400	8800	15,400	22,000
3500 GT Spider (6-cyl) - (98.4" wb) - (3485cc)						
2d Rds	1500	4800	8000	16,000	28,000	40,000
1962						
3500 GTI - (6-cyl) - (102.3" wb) - (3485cc)						
2d Cpe 2 plus 2	750	2400	4000	8000	14,000	20,000
3500 GTI - (6-cyl) - (98.4" wb) - (3485cc)						
Spider 2d Rds	1500	4800	8000	16,000	28,000	40,000
Sebring - (6-cyl) - (98.4" wb) - (3485cc)						
2d Cpe 2 plus 2	950	3000	5000	10,000	17,500	25,000
1963-64						
3500 GTI - (6-cyl) - (102.3" wb) - (3485cc)						
2d Cpe 2 plus 2	850	2650	4400	8800	15,400	22,000
Spider 2d Conv	1450	4700	7800	15,600	27,300	39,000
Sebring - (6-cyl) - (102.3" wb) Early 3485cc, Later 3694cc						
2d Cpe 2 plus 2	950	3000	5000	10,000	17,500	25,000
Mistral - (6-cyl) - (94.5" wb) Early 3485cc, Later 3694cc						
2d Cpe	850	2750	4600	9200	16,100	23,000
Spider 2d Conv	1550	4900	8200	16,400	28,700	41,000
Quattroporte - (V-8) - (108.3" wb) - (4136cc)						
4d Sed	550	1800	3000	6000	10,500	15,000
1965-66						
Sebring II - (6-cyl) - (102.3" wb) - (3694cc)						
2d Cpe 2 plus 2	1050	3300	5500	11,000	19,300	27,500
Mistral - (6-cyl) - (94.5" wb) - (3694cc)						
2d Cpe	850	2650	4400	8800	15,400	22,000
Spider 2d Conv	1500	4800	8000	16,000	28,000	40,000
NOTE: Optional Six engine (4014cc) available in Sebring & Mistral models.						
Mexico - (V-8) - (103.9" wb) - (4136cc)						
2d Cpe	850	2650	4400	8800	15,400	22,000
Quattroporte - (V-8) - (108.3" wb) - (4136cc)						
4200 4d Sed	550	1800	3000	6000	10,500	15,000
1967-68						
Mistral - (6-cyl) - (94.5" wb) - (3694cc)						
2d Cpe	850	2650	4400	8800	15,400	22,000
Spider 2d Conv	1500	4800	8000	16,000	28,000	40,000
Ghibli - (V-8) - (100.4" wb) - (4719cc)						
4700 2d Cpe	1500	4800	8000	16,000	28,000	40,000
Mexico - (V-8) - (103.9" wb) - (4136cc-4719cc)						
4200 2d Cpe	750	2400	4000	8000	14,000	20,000
4700 2d Cpe	750	2400	4000	8000	14,000	20,000
Quattroporte - (V-8) - (108.3" wb) - (4136cc-4719cc)						
4200 4d Sed	550	1800	3000	6000	10,500	15,000
4700 4d Sed	550	1800	3000	6000	10,500	15,000
1969-70						
Mistral - (6-cyl) - (94.5" wb) - (3694cc)						
2d Cpe	850	2650	4400	8800	15,400	22,000
Spider 2d Conv	1500	4800	8000	16,000	28,000	40,000
Ghibli - (V-8) - (100.4" wb) - (4719cc)						
2d Cpe	850	2650	4400	8800	15,400	22,000
Spider 2d Conv	1500	4800	8000	16,000	28,000	40,000
Indy - (V-8) - (102.5" wb) - (4136cc)						
2d Cpe 2 plus 2	750	2400	4000	8000	14,000	20,000
Quattroporte - (V-8) - (108.3" wb) - (4719cc)						
4d Sed	550	1800	3000	6000	10,500	15,000
1971-73						
Merak - (V-6) - (102.3" wb) - (2965cc)						
2d Cpe 2 plus 2	750	2400	4000	8000	14,000	20,000
Bora - (V-8) - (102.3" wb) - (4719cc)						
2d Cpe	1050	3300	5500	11,000	19,300	27,500
Ghibli - (V-8) - (100.4" wb) - (4930cc)						
2d Cpe	1500	4800	8000	16,000	28,000	40,000
Spider 2d Conv	2250	7200	12,000	24,000	42,000	60,000
Indy - (V-8) - (102.5" wb) - (4136cc)						
2d Cpe 2 plus 2	750	2400	4000	8000	14,000	20,000
1974-76						
Merak - (V-6) - (102.3" wb) - (2965cc)						
2d Cpe 2 plus 2	750	2400	4000	8000	14,000	20,000
Bora - (V-8) - (102.3" wb) - (4930cc)						
2d Cpe	1300	4200	7000	14,000	24,500	35,000
Indy - (V-8) - (102.5" wb) - (4930cc)						
2d Cpe	750	2400	4000	8000	14,000	20,000
Khamsin - (V-8) - (100.3" wb) - (4930cc)						
1977-83						
Merak SS - (102.3" wb) - (2965cc)						
2d Cpe 2 plus 2	750	2400	4000	8000	14,000	20,000
Bora - (V-8) - (102.3" wb) - (4930cc)						
2d Cpe	1500	4800	8000	16,000	28,000	40,000
Khamsin - (V-8) - (100.3" wb) - (4930cc)						
2d Cpe 2 plus 2	1400	4500	7500	15,000	26,300	37,500
Kyalami - (V-8) - (102.4" wb) - (4930cc)						
2d Cpe 2 plus 2	550	1800	3000	6000	10,500	15,000
1984-88						
Biturbo - (V-6) - (99" wb) - (1996cc)						
2d Cpe	400	1200	2000	4000	7000	10,000
E 2d Cpe	400	1300	2200	4400	7700	11,000
Biturbo - (V-6) - (94.5" wb) - (2491cc)						
Spider 2d Conv	550	1800	3000	6000	10,500	15,000
425 4d Sed	350	875	1700	4250	5900	8500
Quattroporte - (V-8) - (110.2" wb) - (4930cc)						
4d Sed	550	1800	3000	6000	10,500	15,000

MAZDA

	6	5	4	3	2	1
1970-71						
Conventional Engine						
1200 - (4-cyl) - (88.9" wb) - (1169cc)						
2d Sed	125	250	750	1150	2450	3500
2d Cpe	125	250	750	1150	2450	3500
2d Sta Wag	125	250	750	1150	2450	3500
616 - (4-cyl) - (97" wb) - (1587cc)						
2d Cpe	125	250	750	1150	2450	3500
4d Sed	125	250	750	1150	2450	3500
1800 - (4-cyl) - (98.4" wb) - (1769cc)						
4d Sed	125	250	750	1150	2450	3500
4d Sta Wag	125	250	750	1150	2450	3500
Wankel Rotary Engine						
R100 - (88.9" wb) - (1146cc)						
2d Spt Cpe 2 plus 2	150	350	950	1350	2800	4000
RX-2 - (97" wb) - (1146cc)						
2d Cpe	150	350	950	1350	2800	4000
4d Sed	125	250	750	1150	2450	3500
1972						
Conventional Engine						
808 - (4-cyl) - (91" wb) - (1587cc)						
2d Cpe	125	250	750	1150	2450	3500
4d Sed	125	250	750	1150	2450	3500
4d Sta Wag	125	250	750	1150	2450	3500
618 - (4-cyl) - (97" wb) - (1796cc)						
2d Cpe	125	250	750	1150	2450	3500
4d Sed	125	250	750	1150	2450	3500
Wankel Rotary Engine						
R100 - (88.9" wb) - (1146cc)						
2d Cpe 2 plus 2	125	250	750	1150	2450	3500
RX-2 - (97" wb) - (1146cc)						
2d Cpe	150	350	950	1350	2800	4000
4d Sed	125	250	750	1150	2450	3500
RX-3 - (91" wb) - (1146cc)						
2d Cpe	150	350	950	1350	2800	4000
4d Sed	125	250	750	1150	2450	3500
4d Sta Wag	125	250	750	1150	2450	3500
1973						
Conventional Engine						
808 - (4-cyl) - (91" wb) - (1587cc)						
2d Cpe	125	250	750	1150	2450	3500
4d Sed	125	250	750	1150	2450	3500
4d Sta Wag	125	250	750	1150	2450	3500
Wankel Rotary Engine						
RX-2 - (97" wb) - (1146cc)						
2d Cpe	150	350	950	1350	2800	4000
4d Sed	125	250	750	1150	2450	3500
RX-3 - (162" wb) - (1146cc)						
2d Cpe	150	350	950	1350	2800	4000
4d Sed	125	250	750	1150	2450	3500
RX-3 - (163" wb) - (1146cc)						
4d Sta Wag	125	250	750	1150	2450	3500
1974						
Conventional Engine						
808 - (4-cyl) - (91" wb) - (1587cc)						
2d Cpe	150	350	950	1350	2800	4000
4d Sta Wag	125	250	750	1150	2450	3500
Wankel Rotary Engine						
RX-2 - (97" wb) - (1146cc)						
2d Cpe	150	350	950	1350	2800	4000
4d Sed	125	250	750	1150	2450	3500
RX-3 - (91" wb) - (1146cc)						
2d Cpe	150	350	950	1350	2800	4000
4d Sta Wag	125	250	750	1150	2450	3500
RX-4 - (99" wb) - (1308cc)						
2d HdTp Cpe	150	350	950	1350	2800	4000
4d Sed	125	250	750	1150	2450	3500
4d Sta Wag	125	250	750	1150	2450	3500
1975						
Conventional Engine						
808 - (4-cyl) - (91" wb) - (1587cc)						
2d Cpe	125	250	750	1150	2450	3500
4d Sta Wag	125	250	750	1150	2450	3500
Wankel Rotary Engine						
RX-3 - (91" wb) - (1146cc)						
2d Cpe	150	350	950	1350	2800	4000
4d Sta Wag	125	250	750	1150	2450	3500
RX-4 - (99" wb) - (1308cc)						
2d HdTp Cpe	150	350	950	1350	2800	4000
4d Sed	125	250	750	1150	2450	3500
4d Sta Wag	125	250	750	1150	2450	3500
1976						
Conventional Engine						
Mizer 808-1300 - (4-cyl) - (91" wb) - (1272cc)						
2d Cpe	125	250	750	1150	2450	3500
4d Sed	125	250	750	1150	2450	3500
4d Sta Wag	125	250	750	1150	2450	3500
808-1600 - (4-cyl) - (91" wb) - (1587cc)						
2d Cpe	125	250	750	1150	2450	3500
4d Sed	125	250	750	1150	2450	3500
4d Sta Wag	125	250	750	1150	2450	3500
Wankel Rotary Engine						
RX-3 - (91" wb) - (1146cc)						
2d Cpe	150	350	950	1350	2800	4000
4d Sta Wag	125	250	750	1150	2450	3500
RX-4 - (99" wb) - (1308cc)						
2d HdTp Cpe	150	350	950	1350	2800	4000
4d Sed	125	250	750	1150	2450	3500
4d Sta Wag	125	250	750	1150	2450	3500
Cosmo 2d HdTp Cpe	200	650	1250	2400	4200	6000
1977						
Mizer - (4-cyl) - (1272cc)						
2d Cpe	125	250	750	1150	2450	3500
4d Sed	125	250	750	1150	2450	3500
4d Sta Wag	125	250	750	1150	2450	3500
GLC - (4-cyl) - (91.1" wb) - (1272cc)						
2d HBk	125	250	750	1150	2450	3500
2d DeL HBk	125	250	750	1150	2450	3500
808 - (4-cyl) - (91" wb) - (1587cc)						
2d Cpe	125	250	750	1150	2450	3500
4d Sed	125	250	750	1150	2450	3500
4d Sta Wag	125	250	750	1150	2450	3500
Wankel Rotary Engine						
RX-3SP - (91" wb) - (1146cc)						
2d Cpe	150	350	950	1350	2800	4000
RX-4 - (99" wb) - (1308cc)						
4d Sed	125	250	750	1150	2450	3500
4d Sta Wag	125	250	750	1150	2450	3500
Cosmo 2d HdTp Cpe	125	250	750	1150	2450	3500
1978						
GLC - (4-cyl) - (91.1" wb) - (1272cc)						
2d HBk	125	250	750	1150	2450	3500
2d DeL HBk	125	250	750	1150	2450	3500
2d Spt HBk	125	250	750	1150	2450	3500
4d DeL HBk	125	250	750	1150	2450	3500
Wankel Rotary Engine						
RX-3SP - (91" wb) - (1146cc)						
2d Cpe	150	350	950	1350	2800	4000
RX-4 - (99" wb) - (1308cc)						
4d Sed	125	250	750	1150	2450	3500
4d Sta Wag	125	250	750	1150	2450	3500
Cosmo 2d Cpe	200	650	1250	2400	4200	6000

1979
GLC - (4-cyl) - (91" wb) - (1415cc)

	6	5	4	3	2	1
2d HBk	125	250	750	1150	2450	3500
2d DeL HBk	125	250	750	1150	2450	3500
2d Spt HBk	125	250	750	1150	2450	3500
4d DeL HBk	125	250	750	1150	2450	3500
4d Sta Wag	125	250	750	1150	2450	3500
4d DeL Sta Wag	125	250	750	1150	2450	3500

626 - (4-cyl) - (98.8" wb) - (1970cc)

2d Spt Cpe	150	350	950	1350	2800	4000
4d Spt Sed	125	250	750	1150	2450	3500

Wankel Rotary Engine
RX-7 - (95.3" wb) - (1146cc)

S 2d Cpe	350	700	1350	2800	4550	6500
GS 2d Cpe	350	750	1450	3300	4900	7000

1980
GLC - (4-cyl) - (91" wb) - (1415cc)

2d HBk	150	350	950	1350	2800	4000
2d Cus HBk	150	350	950	1350	2800	4000
2d Spt HBk	150	350	950	1450	3000	4200
4d Cus HBk	150	350	950	1450	3000	4200
4d Cus Sta Wag	150	350	950	1450	3000	4200

626 - (4-cyl) - (98.8" wb) - (1970cc)

2d Spt Cpe	150	400	1000	1650	3150	4500
4d Spt Sed	150	350	950	1350	2800	4000

Wankel Rotary Engine
RX-7 - (95.3" wb) - (1146cc)

S 2d Cpe	350	700	1350	2800	4550	6500
GS 2d Cpe	350	750	1450	3300	4900	7000

1981
GLC - (4-cyl) - (93.1" wb) - (1490cc)

2d HBk	150	350	950	1350	2800	4000
2d Cus HBk	150	350	950	1350	2800	4000
4d Cus HBk	150	350	950	1350	2800	4000
4d Cus Sed	150	350	950	1350	2800	4000
2d Cus L HBk	150	350	950	1350	2800	4000
4d Cus L Sed	150	350	950	1350	2800	4000
2d Spt HBk	150	350	950	1350	2800	4000

GLC - (4-cyl) - (91" wb) - (1490cc)

4d Sta Wag	150	350	950	1350	2800	4000

626 - (4-cyl) - (98.8" wb) - (1970cc)

2d Spt Cpe	150	400	1000	1650	3150	4500
4d Spt Sed	150	350	950	1350	2800	4000
2d Lux Spt Cpe	150	450	1050	1750	3250	4700
4d Lux Spt Sed	150	400	1000	1600	3100	4400

Wankel Rotary Engine
RX-7 - (95.3" wb) - (1146cc)

S 2d Cpe	350	700	1350	2800	4550	6500
GS 2d Cpe	350	750	1450	3300	4900	7000
GSL 2d Cpe	350	775	1500	3750	5250	7500

1982
GLC - (4-cyl) - (93.1" wb) - (1490cc)

2d HBk	150	400	1000	1650	3150	4500
2d Cus HBk	150	400	1000	1650	3150	4500
4d Cus Sed	150	400	1000	1650	3150	4500
2d Cus L HBk	150	400	1000	1650	3150	4500
4d Cus L Sed	150	400	1000	1650	3150	4500
2d Spt HBk	150	400	1000	1650	3150	4500

GLC - (4-cyl) - (91" wb) - (1490cc)

4d Cus Sta Wag	150	350	950	1350	2800	4000

626 - (4-cyl) - (98.8" wb) - (1970cc)

2d Spt Cpe	150	450	1050	1700	3200	4600
4d Spt Sed	150	350	950	1450	3000	4200
2d Lux Spt Cpe	150	450	1050	1750	3250	4700
4d Lux Spt Sed	150	400	1000	1550	3050	4300

Wankel Rotary Engine
RX-7 - (95.3" wb) - (1146cc)

S 2d Cpe	350	750	1450	3300	4900	7000
GS 2d Cpe	350	775	1500	3750	5250	7500
GSL 2d Cpe	350	800	1550	3900	5450	7800

1983
GLC - (4-cyl) - (93.1" wb) - (1490cc)

2d HBk	150	400	1000	1650	3150	4500
2d Cus HBk	150	400	1000	1650	3150	4500
4d Cus Sed	150	400	1000	1650	3150	4500
2d Cus L HBk	150	400	1000	1650	3150	4500
4d Cus L Sed	150	400	1000	1650	3150	4500
2d Spt HBk	150	400	1000	1650	3150	4500
4d Sed	150	450	1050	1700	3200	4600

GLC - (4-cyl) - (93.1" wb) - (1490cc)

4d Cus Sta Wag	150	450	1050	1700	3200	4600

626 - (4-cyl) - (98.8" wb) - (1998cc)

2d Spt Cpe	200	500	1100	1900	3500	5000
4d Spt Sed	150	400	1000	1650	3150	4500
2d Lux Spt Cpe	200	550	1150	2100	3700	5300
4d Lux Spt Sed	150	450	1050	1800	3300	4800
4d Lux HBk	200	550	1150	2000	3600	5200

Wankel Rotary Engine
RX-7 - (95.3" wb) - (1146cc)

S 2d Cpe	350	750	1450	3300	4900	7000
GS 2d Cpe	350	775	1500	3750	5250	7500

1984-85
GLC - (4-cyl) - (93.1" wb) - (1490cc)

2d HBk	200	500	1100	1900	3500	5000
2d DeL HBk	200	500	1100	1900	3500	5000
4d DeL Sed	200	500	1100	1900	3500	5000
2d Lux HBk	200	500	1100	1900	3500	5000
4d Lux Sed	200	500	1100	1900	3500	5000

626 - (4-cyl) - (98.8" wb) - (1998cc)

2d DeL Cpe	200	600	1200	2200	3850	5500
4d DeL Sed	200	500	1100	1900	3500	5000
2d Lux Cpe	200	650	1200	2300	4100	5800
4d Lux Sed	200	550	1150	2100	3700	5300
4d Tr HBk	200	550	1150	2100	3700	5300

Wankel Rotary Engine
RX-7 - (95.3" wb) - (1146cc)

S 2d Cpe	350	775	1500	3750	5250	7500
GS 2d Cpe	350	825	1600	4000	5600	8000
GSL 2d Cpe	350	875	1700	4250	5900	8500

RX-7 - (95.3" wb) - (1308cc)

GSL-SE 2d Cpe	350	825	1600	4000	5600	8000

MERCEDES-BENZ

1951

	6	5	4	3	2	1
Sed	450	1500	2500	5000	8800	12,500

1952

300 Clb Cpe	3600	11,500	19,200	38,400	67,200	96,000
220 Cabr	2050	6600	11,000	22,000	38,500	55,000
300 Cabr	5800	18,600	31,000	62,000	108,500	155,000
300 Rds	6200	19,800	33,000	66,000	115,500	165,000
300 Sed	1350	4250	7100	14,200	24,900	35,500
300S Cpe	2700	8650	14,400	28,800	50,400	72,000

1953

180 Sed	450	1400	2300	4600	8100	11,500
300 Conv Sed	4800	15,350	25,600	51,200	89,600	128,000
300 Cabr	5800	18,600	31,000	62,000	108,500	155,000
300 Rds	6200	19,800	33,000	66,000	115,500	165,000
300 Cpe	3600	11,500	19,200	38,400	67,200	96,000
220 Cabr	2050	6600	11,000	22,000	38,500	55,000

1954

220 A Cabr	2050	6600	11,000	22,000	38,500	55,000
300 B Conv-Sed	4800	15,350	25,600	51,200	89,600	128,000
300S Cabr	5800	18,600	31,000	62,000	108,500	155,000
300S Rds	6200	19,800	33,000	66,000	115,500	165,000
300S Cpe	3600	11,500	19,200	38,400	67,200	96,000
300SL GW	18,750	60,000	100,000	200,000	350,000	500,000
300 B Saloon	1500	4850	8100	16,200	28,400	40,500

1955

190SL Rds	1600	5050	8400	16,800	29,400	42,000

NOTE: Add 10 percent for removable hardtop.

300SL GW	18,750	60,000	100,000	200,000	350,000	500,000
300SC Cpe	4800	15,350	25,600	51,200	89,600	128,000
300SC Rds	9400	30,000	50,000	100,000	175,000	250,000
300SC Cabr	6750	21,600	36,000	72,000	126,000	180,000
300 Sed	1900	6100	10,200	20,400	35,700	51,000
300 Conv Sed	6550	21,000	35,000	70,000	122,500	175,000

1956

180 4d Sed	350	825	1600	4000	5600	8000
180D 4d Sed	350	825	1600	4000	5600	8000
190 4d Sed	450	900	1900	4500	6300	9000
190SL Rds	1600	5050	8400	16,800	29,400	42,000

NOTE: Add 10 percent for removable hardtop.

219 4d Sed	450	1500	2500	5000	8800	12,500
220S 4d Sed	600	1850	3100	6200	10,900	15,500
220S Cpe	950	3050	5100	10,200	17,900	25,500
220S Cabr	1900	6100	10,200	20,400	35,700	51,000
300 4d Sed	1350	4250	7100	14,200	24,900	35,500
300S Cpe	4800	15,350	25,600	51,200	89,600	128,000
300S Cabr	6750	21,600	36,000	72,000	126,000	180,000
300S Rds	9400	30,000	50,000	100,000	175,000	250,000
300SL GW Cpe	19,700	63,000	105,000	210,000	367,500	525,000

1957

180 4d Sed	350	825	1600	4000	5600	8000
180D 4d Sed	350	850	1650	4100	5700	8200
190 4d Sed	450	900	1900	4500	6300	9000
190SL Rds	1600	5050	8400	16,800	29,400	42,000

NOTE: Add 10 percent for removable hardtop.

219 4d Sed	400	1250	2100	4200	7400	10,500
220S 4d Sed	500	1600	2700	5400	9500	13,500
220S Cpe	1050	3400	5700	11,400	20,000	28,500
220S Cabr	1900	6100	10,200	20,400	35,700	51,000
300 4d Sed	1450	4600	7700	15,400	27,000	38,500
300S Cpe	3450	11,050	18,400	36,800	64,400	92,000
300S Rds	7500	24,000	40,000	80,000	140,000	200,000
300S Cabr	7150	22,800	38,000	76,000	133,000	190,000
300SL GW Cpe	19,900	63,600	106,000	212,000	371,000	530,000
300SL Rds	12,200	39,000	65,000	130,000	227,500	325,000

NOTE: Add 5 percent for removable hardtop.

1958

180a 4d Sed	350	825	1600	4000	5600	8000
180D 4d Sed	350	850	1650	4100	5700	8200
190 4d Sed	450	900	1900	4500	6300	9000
190SL Rds	1600	5050	8400	16,800	29,400	42,000

NOTE: Add 10 percent for removable hardtop.

219 4d Sed	400	1250	2100	4200	7400	10,500
220S 4d Sed	500	1600	2700	5400	9500	13,500
220S Cpe	900	2800	4700	9400	16,500	23,500
220S Cabr	1900	6100	10,200	20,400	35,700	51,000
220SE Cpe	1100	3550	5900	11,800	20,700	29,500
220SE Cabr	1750	5500	9200	18,400	32,200	46,000
300D 4d Sed	1200	3900	6500	13,000	22,800	32,500
300SL Rds	12,200	39,000	65,000	130,000	227,500	325,000

NOTE: Add 5 percent for removable hardtop.

1959-60

180a 4d Sed	350	775	1500	3750	5250	7500
180D 4d Sed	350	825	1600	4000	5600	8000
190 4d Sed	450	900	1900	4500	6300	9000
190SL Rds	1600	5050	8400	16,800	29,400	42,000

NOTE: Add 10 percent for removable hardtop.

219 4d Sed	400	1250	2100	4200	7400	10,500
220S 4d Sed	500	1600	2700	5400	9500	13,500
220S Cpe	900	2800	4700	9400	16,500	23,500
220S Cabr	1900	6100	10,200	20,400	35,700	51,000
220SE Cpe	1100	3550	5900	11,800	20,700	29,500
220SE Cabr	2000	6350	10,600	21,200	37,100	53,000
300 4d HdTp	1900	6100	10,200	20,400	35,700	51,000
300SL Rds	12,200	39,000	65,000	130,000	227,500	325,000

NOTE: Add 5 percent for removable hardtop.

1960
Fin Body

180 4d Sed	350	700	1350	2800	4550	6500
180D 4d Sed	350	775	1500	3750	5250	7500
190 4d Sed	350	750	1450	3300	4900	7000
190D 4d Sed	350	825	1600	4000	5600	8000
190SL Rds	1600	5050	8400	16,800	29,400	42,000
220 4d Sed	450	1500	2500	5000	8800	12,500
220S 4d Sed	550	1750	2900	5800	10,200	14,500
220SE 4d Sed	600	1850	3100	6200	10,900	15,500
220SE Cpe	950	3050	5100	10,200	17,900	25,500
220SE Cabr	1900	6100	10,200	20,400	35,700	51,000
220SEb Cpe	1150	3650	6100	12,200	21,400	30,500
220SEb Cabr	1750	5500	9200	18,400	32,200	46,000
300 4d HdTp	1900	6100	10,200	20,400	35,700	51,000
300 4d Cabr	4750	15,100	25,200	50,400	88,200	126,000
300SL Rds	12,200	39,000	65,000	130,000	227,500	325,000

NOTE: Add 5 percent for removable hardtop.

1961

	6	5	4	3	2	1
180 4d Sed	200	650	1250	2400	4200	6000
180D 4d Sed	350	750	1450	3300	4900	7000
190 4d Sed	350	700	1350	2800	4550	6500
190D 4d Sed	350	825	1600	4000	5600	8000
190SL Rds	1600	5050	8400	16,800	29,400	42,000
220 4d Sed	450	1500	2500	5000	8800	12,500
220S 4d Sed	550	1750	2900	5800	10,200	14,500
220SE 4d Sed	600	2000	3300	6600	11,600	16,500
220SE Cpe	750	2450	4100	8200	14,400	20,500
220SE Cabr	1850	5900	9800	19,600	34,300	49,000
220SEb Cpe	1050	3400	5700	11,400	20,000	28,500
220SEb Cabr	1650	5300	8800	17,600	30,800	44,000
300 4d HdTp	1900	6100	10,200	20,400	35,700	51,000
300 4d Cabr	4750	15,100	25,200	50,400	88,200	126,000
300SL Rds	12,200	39,000	65,000	130,000	227,500	325,000

NOTE: Add 5 percent for removable hardtop.

1962

	6	5	4	3	2	1
180c 4d Sed	200	600	1200	2200	3850	5500
180Dc 4d Sed	350	700	1350	2800	4550	6500
190c 4d Sed	200	650	1250	2400	4200	6000
190Dc 4d Sed	350	750	1450	3300	4900	7000
190SL Rds	1600	5050	8400	16,800	29,400	42,000

NOTE: Add 10 percent for removable hardtop.

	6	5	4	3	2	1
220 4d Sed	400	1200	2000	4000	7000	10,000
220S 4d Sed	450	1400	2300	4600	8100	11,500
220SE 4d Sed	500	1600	2700	5400	9500	13,500
220SEb Cpe	850	2700	4500	9000	15,800	22,500
220SEb Cabr	1850	5900	9800	19,600	34,300	49,000
300 4d HdTp	1900	6100	10,200	20,400	35,700	51,000
300 4d Cabr	4750	15,100	25,200	50,400	88,200	126,000
300SL Rds	12,200	39,000	65,000	130,000	227,500	325,000

NOTE: Add 5 percent for removable hardtop.

1963

	6	5	4	3	2	1
180Dc 4d Sed	350	700	1350	2800	4550	6500
190c 4d Sed	200	650	1250	2400	4200	6000
190Dc 4d Sed	350	750	1450	3300	4900	7000
190SL Rds	1600	5050	8400	16,800	29,400	42,000

NOTE: Add 10 percent for removable hardtop.

	6	5	4	3	2	1
220 4d Sed	400	1200	2000	4000	7000	10,000
220S 4d Sed	400	1300	2200	4400	7700	11,000
220SE 4d Sed	450	1500	2500	5000	8800	12,500
220SEb Cpe	750	2450	4100	8200	14,400	20,500
220SEb Cabr	1850	5900	9800	19,600	34,300	49,000
300SE 4d Sed	1050	3400	5700	11,400	20,000	28,500
300SE Cpe	1350	4250	7100	14,200	24,900	35,500
300SE Cabr	3400	10,800	18,000	36,000	63,000	90,000
300 4d HdTp	1350	4250	7100	14,200	24,900	35,500
300SL Rds	12,200	39,000	65,000	130,000	227,500	325,000

NOTE: Add 5 percent for removable hardtop.

1964

	6	5	4	3	2	1
190c 4d Sed	200	600	1200	2200	3850	5500
190Dc 4d Sed	350	700	1350	2800	4550	6500
220 4d Sed	400	1200	2000	4000	7000	10,000
220S 4d Sed	400	1300	2200	4400	7700	11,000
220SE 4d Sed	500	1550	2600	5200	9100	13,000
220SEb Cpe	700	2200	3700	7400	13,000	18,500
220SEb Cabr	1600	5150	8600	17,200	30,100	43,000
230SL Cpe/Rds	1050	3350	5600	11,200	19,600	28,000
300SE 4d Sed	650	2100	3500	7000	12,300	17,500
300SE 4d Sed (112)	750	2450	4100	8200	14,400	20,500
300SE Cpe	1300	4200	7000	14,000	24,500	35,000
300SE Cabr	3400	10,800	18,000	36,000	63,000	90,000

1965

	6	5	4	3	2	1
190c 4d Sed	200	600	1200	2200	3850	5500
190Dc 4d Sed	350	700	1350	2800	4550	6500
220b 4d Sed	400	1200	2000	4000	7000	10,000
220Sb 4d Sed	400	1300	2200	4400	7700	11,000
220SEb 4d Sed	500	1550	2600	5200	9100	13,000
220SEb Cpe	600	1850	3100	6200	10,900	15,500
220SEb Cabr	1650	5300	8800	17,600	30,800	44,000
230SL Cpe/Rds	1050	3350	5600	11,200	19,600	28,000
250SE Cpe	650	2100	3500	7000	12,300	17,500
250SE Cabr	1700	5400	9000	18,000	31,500	45,000
300SE 4d Sed	550	1750	2900	5800	10,200	14,500
300SEL 4d Sed	600	2000	3300	6600	11,600	16,500
300SE Cpe	750	2450	4100	8200	14,400	20,500
300SE Cabr	3400	10,800	18,000	36,000	63,000	90,000
600 4d Sed	1500	4850	8100	16,200	28,400	40,500
600 Limo	2100	6700	11,200	22,400	39,200	56,000

1966

	6	5	4	3	2	1
200 4d Sed	200	600	1200	2200	3850	5500
200D 4d Sed	350	700	1350	2800	4550	6500
230 4d Sed	200	650	1250	2400	4200	6000
230S 4d Sed	200	675	1300	2500	4350	6200
230SL Cpe/Rds	1050	3350	5600	11,200	19,600	28,000
250SE Cpe	650	2100	3500	7000	12,300	17,500
250SE Cabr	1700	5400	9000	18,000	31,500	45,000
250S 4d Sed	350	700	1350	2800	4550	6500
250SE 4d Sed	350	750	1450	3300	4900	7000
300SE Cpe	750	2450	4100	8200	14,400	20,500
300SE Cabr	2700	8650	14,400	28,800	50,400	72,000
600 4d Sed	1500	4850	8100	16,200	28,400	40,500
600 Limo	2100	6700	11,200	22,400	39,200	56,000

1967

	6	5	4	3	2	1
200 4d Sed	200	600	1200	2200	3850	5500
200D 4d Sed	350	700	1350	2800	4550	6500
230 4d Sed	200	650	1250	2400	4200	6000
230S 4d Sed	200	675	1300	2500	4350	6200
230SL Cpe/Rds	1050	3350	5600	11,200	19,600	28,000
250S 4d Sed	350	700	1350	2800	4550	6500
250SE 4d Sed	350	750	1450	3300	4900	7000
250SE Cpe	650	2100	3500	7000	12,300	17,500
250SE Cabr	1200	3900	6500	13,000	22,800	32,500
250SL Cpe/Rds	1150	3650	6100	12,200	21,400	30,500
280SE Cpe	750	2400	4000	8000	14,000	20,000
280SE Cabr	1900	6000	10,000	20,000	35,000	50,000
300SE Cpe	950	3000	5000	10,000	17,500	25,000
300SE Cabr	2700	8650	14,400	28,800	50,400	72,000
300SE 4d Sed	750	2350	3900	7800	13,700	19,500
300SEL 4d Sed	850	2700	4500	9000	15,800	22,500
600 4d Sed	1500	4850	8100	16,200	28,400	40,500
600 Limo	2100	6700	11,200	22,400	39,200	56,000

1968

	6	5	4	3	2	1
220/8 4d Sed	200	600	1200	2200	3850	5500
220D/8 4d Sed	350	700	1350	2800	4550	6500
230/8 4d Sed	200	650	1250	2400	4200	6000
250/8 4d Sed	350	700	1350	2900	4600	6600
280/8 4d Sed	350	700	1350	2800	4550	6500
280SE/8 4d Sed	350	750	1450	3300	4900	7000
280SEL/8 4d Sed	350	775	1500	3750	5250	7500
280SE Cpe	750	2400	4000	8000	14,000	20,000
280SE Cabr	2050	6600	11,000	22,000	38,500	55,000
280SL Cpe/Rds	1450	4600	7700	15,400	27,000	38,500
300SEL/8 4d Sed	950	3050	5100	10,200	17,900	25,500
600 4d Sed	1500	4850	8100	16,200	28,400	40,500
600 Limo	2100	6700	11,200	22,400	39,200	56,000

1969

	6	5	4	3	2	1
220/8 4d Sed	200	600	1200	2200	3850	5500
220D/8 4d Sed	350	700	1350	2800	4550	6500
230/8 4d Sed	200	650	1250	2400	4200	6000
250/8 4d Sed	200	675	1300	2500	4350	6200
280S/8 4d Sed	350	700	1350	2800	4550	6500
280SE/8 4d Sed	350	750	1450	3300	4900	7000
280SEL/8 4d Sed	350	775	1500	3750	5250	7500
280SE Cpe	850	2650	4400	8800	15,400	22,000
280SE Cabr	2050	6600	11,000	22,000	38,500	55,000
280SL Cpe/Rds	1450	4600	7700	15,400	27,000	38,500
300SEL/8 4d Sed	700	2200	3700	7400	13,000	18,500
300SEL/8 4d Sed	850	2700	4500	9000	15,800	22,500
600 4d Sed	1500	4850	8100	16,200	28,400	40,500
600 Limo	2100	6700	11,200	22,400	39,200	56,000

1970

	6	5	4	3	2	1
220/8 4d Sed	200	600	1200	2200	3850	5500
220D/8 4d Sed	350	700	1350	2800	4550	6500
250/8 4d Sed	200	675	1300	2500	4350	6200
250C/8 Cpe	350	825	1600	4000	5600	8000
280S/8 4d Sed	350	700	1350	2800	4550	6500
280SE/8 4d Sed	350	750	1450	3300	4900	7000
280SEL/8 4d Sed	350	775	1500	3750	5250	7500
280SE Cpe	1050	3350	5600	11,200	19,600	28,000
280SE Cabr	2650	8400	14,000	28,000	49,000	70,000
280SL Cpe/Rds	1500	4850	8100	16,200	28,400	40,500
300SEL/8 4d Sed	700	2200	3700	7400	13,000	18,500
600 4d Sed	1500	4850	8100	16,200	28,400	40,500
600 Limo	2100	6700	11,200	22,400	39,200	56,000

1971

	6	5	4	3	2	1
220/8 4d Sed	200	600	1200	2200	3850	5500
220D/8 4d Sed	350	700	1350	2800	4550	6500
250/8 4d Sed	200	650	1250	2400	4200	6000
250C/8 Cpe	350	825	1600	4000	5600	8000
280S/8 4d Sed	200	650	1250	2400	4200	6000
280SE/8 4d Sed	350	700	1350	2800	4550	6500
280SEL/8 4d Sed	350	750	1450	3300	4900	7000
280SE 3.5 Cpe	1150	3600	6000	12,000	21,000	30,000
280SE 3.5 Cabr	3400	10,800	18,000	36,000	63,000	90,000
280SL Cpe/Rds	1500	4850	8100	16,200	28,400	40,500
300SEL/8 4d Sed	750	2350	3900	7800	13,700	19,500
600 4d Sed	1500	4850	8100	16,200	28,400	40,500
600 4d Limo	2250	7200	12,000	24,000	42,000	60,000

1972

	6	5	4	3	2	1
220/8 4d Sed	200	600	1200	2200	3850	5500
220D/8 4d Sed	350	700	1350	2800	4550	6500
250/8 4d Sed	200	650	1250	2400	4200	6000
250C/8 Cpe	450	900	1900	4500	6300	9000
280SE 4d Sed	350	875	1700	4250	5900	8500
280SE 3.5 Cpe	650	2100	3500	7000	12,300	17,500
280SE 3.5 Cabr	1700	5400	9000	18,000	31,500	45,000
280SEL 4d Sed	350	875	1700	4250	5900	8500
300SEL 4d Sed	750	2450	4100	8200	14,400	20,500
350SL Cpe/Rds	1500	4850	8100	16,200	28,400	40,500
600 4d Sed	1500	4850	8100	16,200	28,400	40,500
600 Limo	2250	7200	12,000	24,000	42,000	60,000

1973

	6	5	4	3	2	1
220 4d Sed	200	650	1250	2400	4200	6000
220D 4d Sed	350	750	1450	3300	4900	7000
280 4d Sed	350	750	1450	3500	5050	7200
280C Cpe	400	1250	2100	4200	7400	10,500
280SE 4d Sed	350	875	1700	4350	6050	8700
280SEL 4d Sed	450	900	1800	4450	6250	8900
300SEL 4d Sed	850	2700	4500	9000	15,800	22,500
450SE 4d Sed	450	1500	2500	5000	8800	12,500
450SEL 4d Sed	550	1750	2900	5800	10,200	14,500
450SL Cpe/Rds	1500	4850	8100	16,200	28,400	40,500
450SLC Cpe	1150	3650	6100	12,200	21,400	30,500

1974

	6	5	4	3	2	1
230 4d Sed	350	700	1350	2800	4550	6500
240D 4d Sed	350	825	1600	4000	5600	8000
280 4d Sed	350	775	1500	3750	5250	7500
280C Cpe	450	950	2100	4750	6650	9500
450SE 4d Sed	550	1750	2900	5800	10,200	14,500
450SEL 4d Sed	650	2050	3400	6800	11,900	17,000
450SL Cpe/Rds	1500	4850	8100	16,200	28,400	40,500
450SLC Cpe	1150	3650	6100	12,200	21,400	30,500

1975

	6	5	4	3	2	1
230 4d Sed	350	775	1500	3750	5250	7500
240D 4d Sed	450	1400	2300	4600	8100	11,500
300D 4d Sed	400	1200	2000	4000	7000	10,000
280 4d Sed	350	875	1700	4250	5900	8500
280C Cpe	400	1200	2000	4000	7000	10,000
280S 4d Sed	400	1300	2200	4400	7700	11,000
450SE 4d Sed	500	1600	2700	5400	9500	13,500
450SEL 4d Sed	600	1850	3100	6200	10,900	15,500
450SL Cpe/Rds	1500	4850	8100	16,200	28,400	40,500
450SLC Cpe	1150	3650	6100	12,200	21,400	30,500

1976

	6	5	4	3	2	1
230 4d Sed	450	900	1900	4500	6300	9000
240D 4d Sed	400	1200	2000	4000	7000	10,000
300D 4d Sed	450	1400	2300	4600	8100	11,500
280 4d Sed	450	950	2100	4700	6600	9400
280C Cpe	550	1750	2900	5800	10,200	14,500
280S 4d Sed	450	1500	2500	5000	8800	12,500
450SE 4d Sed	600	1900	3200	6400	11,200	16,000
450SEL 4d Sed	650	2100	3500	7000	12,300	17,500
450SL Cpe/Rds	1500	4850	8100	16,200	28,400	40,500
450SLC Cpe	1150	3650	6100	12,200	21,400	30,500

	6	5	4	3	2	1
1977						
230 4d Sed	450	950	2100	4750	6650	9500
240D 4d Sed	400	1250	2100	4200	7400	10,500
300D 4d Sed	550	1750	2900	5800	10,200	14,500
280E 4d Sed	450	1400	2300	4600	8100	11,500
280SE 4d Sed	600	1850	3100	6200	10,900	15,500
450SEL 4d Sed	750	2450	4100	8200	14,400	20,500
450SL Cpe/Rds	1500	4850	8100	16,200	28,400	40,500
450SLC Cpe	1150	3650	6100	12,200	21,400	30,500
1978						
230 4d Sed	450	975	2300	4900	6850	9800
240D 4d Sed	400	1200	2000	4000	7000	10,000
300D 4d Sed	450	1450	2400	4800	8400	12,000
300CD Cpe	500	1600	2700	5400	9500	13,500
300SD 4d Sed	550	1800	3000	6000	10,500	15,000
280E 4d Sed	450	1500	2500	5000	8800	12,500
280CE Cpe	600	2000	3300	6600	11,600	16,500
280SE 4d Sed	600	2000	3300	6600	11,600	16,500
450SEL 4d Sed	800	2600	4300	8600	15,100	21,500
450SL Cpe/Rds	1500	4850	8100	16,200	28,400	40,500
450SLC Cpe	1200	3900	6500	13,000	22,800	32,500
6.9L 4d Sed	1150	3650	6100	12,200	21,400	30,500
1979						
240D 4d Sed	450	900	1900	4500	6300	9000
300D 4d Sed	400	1200	2000	4000	7000	10,000
300CD Cpe	550	1750	2900	5800	10,200	14,500
300TD SW	550	1800	3000	6000	10,500	15,000
300SD 4d Sed	550	1800	3000	6000	10,500	15,000
280E 4d Sed	500	1600	2700	5400	9500	13,500
280CE Cpe	600	2000	3300	6600	11,600	16,500
280SE 4d Sed	650	2100	3500	7000	12,300	17,500
450SEL 4d Sed	850	2700	4500	9000	15,800	22,500
450SL Cpe/Rds	1500	4850	8100	16,200	28,400	40,500
450SLC Cpe	1200	3900	6500	13,000	22,800	32,500
6.9L 4d Sed	1200	3900	6500	13,000	22,800	32,500
1980						
240D 4d Sed	450	900	1900	4500	6300	9000
300D 4d Sed	450	1450	2400	4800	8400	12,000
300CD 2d Cpe	600	1900	3200	6400	11,200	16,000
300TD 4d Sta Wag	550	1750	2900	5800	10,200	14,500
300SD 4d Sed	700	2150	3600	7200	12,600	18,000
280E 4d Sed	650	2050	3400	6800	11,900	17,000
280CE 2d Cpe	700	2150	3600	7200	12,600	18,000
280SE 4d Sed	650	2100	3500	7000	12,300	17,500
450SEL 4d Sed	700	2300	3800	7600	13,300	19,000
450SL 2d Conv	1600	5050	8400	16,800	29,400	42,000
450SLC 2d Cpe	1200	3850	6400	12,800	22,400	32,000
1981						
240D 4d Sed	400	1200	2000	4000	7000	10,000
300D 4d Sed	500	1550	2600	5200	9100	13,000
300CD 2d Cpe	600	1900	3200	6400	11,200	16,000
300 TD-T 4d Sta Wag	550	1750	2900	5800	10,200	14,500
300SD 4d Sed	700	2150	3600	7200	12,600	18,000
280E 4d Sed	650	2100	3500	7000	12,300	17,500
280CE 2d Cpe	700	2200	3700	7400	13,000	18,500
280SEL 4d Sed	950	3000	5000	10,000	17,500	25,000
380SL 2d Conv	1650	5300	8800	17,600	30,800	44,000
380SLC 2d Cpe	1300	4100	6800	13,600	23,800	34,000
1982						
240D 4d Sed	400	1200	2000	4000	7000	10,000
300D-T 4d Sed	450	1450	2400	4800	8400	12,000
300CD-T 2d Cpe	600	2000	3300	6600	11,600	16,500
300TD-T 4d Sta Wag	550	1750	2900	5800	10,200	14,500
300SD 4d Sed	700	2150	3600	7200	12,600	18,000
280SEL 4d Sed	950	3000	5000	10,000	17,500	25,000
380SL 2d Conv	1700	5400	9000	18,000	31,500	45,000
380SEC 2d Cpe	1300	4200	7000	14,000	24,500	35,000
1983						
240D 4d Sed	400	1200	2000	4000	7000	10,000
300D-T 4d Sed	500	1550	2600	5200	9100	13,000
300CD-T 2d Cpe	600	2000	3300	6600	11,600	16,500
300TD-T 4d Sta Wag	550	1750	2900	5800	10,200	14,500
300SD 4d Sed	700	2200	3700	7400	13,000	18,500
300SEL 4d Sed	1000	3100	5200	10,400	18,200	26,000
380SL 2d Conv	1750	5500	9200	18,400	32,200	46,000
380SEC 2d Cpe	1350	4300	7200	14,400	25,200	36,000
1984						
190E 4d Sed	400	1300	2200	4400	7700	11,000
190D 4d Sed	400	1200	2000	4000	7000	10,000
300D-T 4d Sed	500	1600	2700	5400	9500	13,500
300CD-T 2d Cpe	550	1800	3000	6000	10,500	15,000
300TD-T 4d Sta Wag	550	1800	3000	6000	10,500	15,000
300SD 4d Sed	850	2650	4400	8800	15,400	22,000
500SEL 4d Sed	1000	3250	5400	10,800	18,900	27,000
500SEC 2d Cpe	1150	3700	6200	12,400	21,700	31,000
380SE 4d Sed	900	2900	4800	9600	16,800	24,000
380SL 2d Conv	1150	3700	6200	12,400	21,700	31,000
1985						
190E 4d Sed	450	1450	2400	4800	8400	12,000
190D 4d Sed	400	1250	2100	4200	7400	10,500
300D-T 4d Sed	550	1750	2900	5800	10,200	14,500
300 2d Cpe	600	1900	3200	6400	11,200	16,000
300TD-T 4d Sta Wag	600	1900	3200	6400	11,200	16,000
300SD 4d Sed	900	2900	4800	9600	16,800	24,000
380SE 4d Sed	1000	3100	5200	10,400	18,200	26,000
380SL 2d Conv	1250	3950	6600	13,200	23,100	33,000
500SEL 4d Sed	1100	3500	5800	11,600	20,300	29,000
500SEC 2d Cpe	1200	3900	6500	13,000	22,800	32,500
1986						
190E 4d Sed	650	2100	3500	7000	12,300	17,500
190D 4d Sed	600	1900	3200	6400	11,200	16,000
190E 4d Sed (16V)	950	3000	5000	10,000	17,500	25,000
300E 4d Sed	1000	3250	5400	10,800	18,900	27,000
300SDL 4d Sed	1150	3700	6200	12,400	21,700	31,000
420SEL 4d Sed	1200	3850	6400	12,800	22,400	32,000
560SEL 4d Sed	1450	4700	7800	15,600	27,300	39,000
560SEC 2d Cpe	1700	5400	9000	18,000	31,500	45,000
560SL 2d Conv	1600	5150	8600	17,200	30,100	43,000

	6	5	4	3	2	1
1987						
190E 4d Sed	850	2700	4500	9000	15,800	22,500
190D 4d Sed	800	2500	4200	8400	14,700	21,000
190D-T 4d Sed	850	2650	4400	8800	15,400	22,000
190E 4d 2.6 Sed	1000	3100	5200	10,400	18,200	26,000
190E 4d Sed (16V)	1100	3500	5800	11,600	20,300	29,000
260E 4d Sed	1000	3250	5400	10,800	18,900	27,000
300E 4d Sed	1150	3600	6000	12,000	21,000	30,000
300D-T 4d Sed	1050	3350	5600	11,200	19,600	28,000
300TD-T 4d Sta Wag	1150	3700	6200	12,400	21,700	31,000
300SDL-T 4d Sed	1350	4300	7200	14,400	25,200	36,000
420SEL 4d Sed	1450	4700	7800	15,600	27,300	39,000
560SEL 4d Sed	1700	5400	9000	18,000	31,500	45,000
560SEC 2d Sed	1950	6250	10,400	20,800	36,400	52,000
560SL 2d Conv	1750	5650	9400	18,800	32,900	47,000
1988						
190E 4d Sed	900	2900	4800	9600	16,800	24,000
190D 4d Sed	850	2650	4400	8800	15,400	22,000
190D-T 4d Sed	850	2750	4600	9200	16,100	23,000
190E 4d 2.6 Sed	1050	3400	5700	11,400	20,000	28,500
190E 4d Sed (16V)	1150	3700	6200	12,400	21,700	31,000
260E 4d Sed	1100	3500	5800	11,600	20,300	29,000
300E 4d Sed	1200	3850	6400	12,800	22,400	32,000
300CE 2d Cpe	1550	4900	8200	16,400	28,700	41,000
300TE 4d Sta Wag	1150	3600	6000	12,000	21,000	30,000
300SE 4d Sed	1450	4700	7800	15,600	27,300	39,000
300SEL 4d Sed	1600	5150	8600	17,200	30,100	43,000
420SEL 4d Sed	1750	5500	9200	18,400	32,200	46,000
560SEL 4d Sed	1850	5900	9800	19,600	34,300	49,000
560SEC 2d Cpe	2050	6500	10,800	21,600	37,800	54,000
560SL 2d Conv	1850	5900	9800	19,600	34,300	49,000
1989						
190D 4d Sed	1000	3250	5400	10,800	18,900	27,000
190E 4d 2.6 Sed	1150	3600	6000	12,000	21,000	30,000
260E 4d Sed	1300	4200	7000	14,000	24,500	35,000
300E 4d Sed	1500	4800	8000	16,000	28,000	40,000
300CE 2d Cpe	1750	5650	9400	18,800	32,900	47,000
300TE 4d Sta Wag	1600	5050	8400	16,800	29,400	42,000
300SE 4d Sed	1650	5300	8800	17,600	30,800	44,000
300SEL 4d Sed	1750	5650	9400	18,800	32,900	47,000
420SEL 4d Sed	1900	6000	10,000	20,000	35,000	50,000
560SEL 4d Sed	2150	6850	11,400	22,800	39,900	57,000
560SEC 2d Cpe	2400	7700	12,800	25,600	44,800	64,000
560SL 2d Conv	2200	6950	11,600	23,200	40,600	58,000

MERKUR

1985						
HBk XR4Ti	200	500	1100	1900	3500	5000
1986						
HBk XR4Ti	200	650	1250	2400	4200	6000
1987						
HBk XR4Ti	350	825	1600	4000	5600	8000
1988						
HBk XR4Ti	400	1250	2100	4200	7400	10,500
HBk Scorpio	450	1500	2500	5000	8800	12,500
1989						
HBk XR4Ti	550	1700	2800	5600	9800	14,000
HBk Scorpio	650	2100	3500	7000	12,300	17,500

METROPOLITAN (Nash & Hudson)

1954-55						
541 - (4-cyl) - (85" wb) - (1200cc)						
2d Conv	350	825	1600	4000	5600	8000
542 - (4-cyl) - (85" wb) - (1200cc)						
2d HdTp Cpe	200	650	1250	2400	4200	6000
1956-62						
Nash/Hudson/American Motors						
1500 - (4-cyl) - (85" wb) - (1489cc)						
561 2d Conv	350	825	1600	4000	5600	8000
562 2d Hdtp Cpe	200	650	1250	2400	4200	6000

MG

1947-48						
MG-TC - (4-cyl) - (94" wb)						
Rds	950	3000	5000	10,000	17,500	25,000
1949						
MG-TC (4-cyl) - (94" wb)						
Rds	950	3000	5000	10,000	17,500	25,000
1950						
MG-TD - (4-cyl) - (94" wb) - (54.4 hp)						
Rds	850	2650	4400	8800	15,400	22,000
1951						
MG-TD - (4-cyl) - (94" wb) - (54.4 hp)						
Rds	850	2650	4400	8800	15,400	22,000
Mark II - (4-cyl) - (94" wb) - (54.4 hp)						
Rds	900	2900	4800	9600	16,800	24,000
1952						
MG-TD - (4-cyl) - (94" wb) - (54.4 hp)						
Rds	850	2650	4400	8800	15,400	22,000
Mark II - (4-cyl) - (94" wb) - (62 hp)						
Rds	900	2900	4800	9600	16,800	24,000
1953						
MG-TD - (4-cyl) - (94" wb) - (54.4 hp)						
Rds	850	2750	4600	9200	16,100	23,000
MG-TDC - (4-cyl) - (94" wb) - (62 hp)						
Rds	900	2900	4800	9600	16,800	24,000
1954						
MG-TF - (4-cyl) - (94" wb) - (57 hp)						
Rds	850	2650	4400	8800	15,400	22,000
1955						
MG-TF - (4-cyl) - (94" wb) - (68 hp)						
Rds	850	2650	4400	8800	15,400	22,000

1956
MG-"A" - (4-cyl) - (94" wb) - (68 hp)

	6	5	4	3	2	1
1500 Rds	600	1900	3200	6400	11,200	16,000

1957
MG-"A" - (4-cyl) - (94" wb) - (68 hp)

	6	5	4	3	2	1
1500 Rds	600	1900	3200	6400	11,200	16,000

1958
MG-"A" - (4-cyl) - (94" wb) - (72 hp)

	6	5	4	3	2	1
1500 Cpe	650	2050	3400	6800	11,900	17,000
1500 Rds	600	1900	3200	6400	11,200	16,000

1959-60
MG-"A" - (4-cyl) - (94" wb) - (72 hp)

	6	5	4	3	2	1
1600 Rds	600	1900	3200	6400	11,200	16,000
1600 Cpe	650	2050	3400	6800	11,900	17,000

MG-"A", Twin-Cam - (4-cyl) - (94" wb) - (107 hp)

	6	5	4	3	2	1
Rds	600	1900	3200	6400	11,200	16,000
Cpe	650	2050	3400	6800	11,900	17,000

1961
MG-"A" - (4-cyl) - (94" wb) - (79 hp)

	6	5	4	3	2	1
1600 Rds	550	1800	3000	6000	10,500	15,000
1600 Cpe	600	1850	3100	6200	10,900	15,500
1600 Mk II Rds	600	1900	3200	6400	11,200	16,000
1600 Mk II Cpe	650	2050	3400	6800	11,900	17,000

1962
MG-Midget - (4-cyl) - (80" wb) - (50 hp)

	6	5	4	3	2	1
Rds	350	700	1350	2800	4550	6500

MG-"A" - (4-cyl) - (94" wb) - (90 hp)

	6	5	4	3	2	1
1600 Mk II Rds	550	1800	3000	6000	10,500	15,000
1600 Mk II Cpe	650	2050	3400	6800	11,900	17,000

NOTE: Add 40 percent for 1600 Mark II Deluxe.

1963
MG-Midget - (4-cyl) - (80" wb) - (56 hp)

	6	5	4	3	2	1
Rds	350	750	1450	3300	4900	7000

MG-B - (4-cyl) - (91" wb) - (95 hp)

	6	5	4	3	2	1
Rds	450	900	1900	4500	6300	9000

1964
MG-Midget - (4-cyl) - (80" wb) - (56 hp)

	6	5	4	3	2	1
Rds	350	750	1450	3300	4900	7000

MG-B - (4-cyl) - (91" wb) - (95 hp)

	6	5	4	3	2	1
Rds	450	900	1900	4500	6300	9000

1965
MG-Midget Mark II - (4-cyl) - (80" wb) - (59 hp)

	6	5	4	3	2	1
Rds	350	750	1450	3300	4900	7000

MG-B - (4-cyl) - (91" wb) - (95 hp)

	6	5	4	3	2	1
Rds	450	900	1900	4500	6300	9000

1966
MG-Midget Mark III - (4-cyl) - (80" wb) - (59 hp)

	6	5	4	3	2	1
Rds	350	750	1450	3300	4900	7000

MG-B - (4-cyl) - (91" wb) - (95 hp)

	6	5	4	3	2	1
Rds	350	825	1600	4000	5600	8000

1100 Sport - (4-cyl) - (93.5" wb) - (58 hp)

	6	5	4	3	2	1
2d Sed	150	350	950	1350	2800	4000
4d Sed	150	350	950	1350	2800	4000

1967
MG Midget Mark III - (4-cyl) - (80" wb) - (59 hp)

	6	5	4	3	2	1
Rds	350	750	1450	3300	4900	7000

MGB - (4-cyl) - (91" wb) - (98 hp)

	6	5	4	3	2	1
Rds	350	825	1600	4000	5600	8000
GT Cpe	350	875	1700	4250	5900	8500

1100 Sport - (4-cyl) - (93.5" wb) - (58 hp)

	6	5	4	3	2	1
2d Sed	150	350	950	1350	2800	4000
4d Sed	150	350	950	1350	2800	4000

1968
MG Midget - (4-cyl) - (80" wb) - (65 hp)

	6	5	4	3	2	1
Rds	350	825	1600	4000	5600	8000

MGB - (4-cyl) - (91" wb) - (98 hp)

	6	5	4	3	2	1
Conv	350	850	1650	4100	5700	8200
Cpe GT	350	825	1600	4000	5600	8000

1969
MG Midget Mark III - (4-cyl) - (80" wb) - (65 hp)

	6	5	4	3	2	1
Rds	350	825	1600	4000	5600	8000

MGB/GT, Mark II - (4-cyl) - (91" wb) - (98 hp)

	6	5	4	3	2	1
Cpe	350	850	1650	4100	5700	8200
Rds 'B'	350	850	1650	4150	5800	8300

MG-C - (6-cyl) - (91" wb) - (145 hp)

	6	5	4	3	2	1
Rds	450	900	1900	4500	6300	9000
Cpe GT	350	825	1600	4000	5600	8000

1970
MG Midget - (4-cyl) - (80" wb) - (65 hp)

	6	5	4	3	2	1
Rds	350	750	1450	3300	4900	7000

MGB-MGB/GT - (4-cyl) - (91" wb) - (78.5 hp)

	6	5	4	3	2	1
Rds	350	825	1600	4050	5650	8100
Cpe GT	350	800	1550	3900	5450	7800

NOTE: Add 10 percent for wire wheels.
Add 5 percent for overdrive.

1971
MG Midget - (4-cyl) - (80" wb) - (65 hp)

	6	5	4	3	2	1
Rds	350	750	1450	3300	4900	7000

MGB-MBG/GT - (4-cyl) - (91" wb) - (78.5 hp)

	6	5	4	3	2	1
Rds	350	825	1600	4050	5650	8100
Cpe GT	350	800	1550	3900	5450	7800

NOTE: Add 10 percent for wire wheels.
Add 5 percent for overdrive.

1972
MG Midget - (4-cyl) - (80" wb) - (54.5 hp)

	6	5	4	3	2	1
Conv	350	750	1450	3300	4900	7000

MGB-MGB/GT - (4-cyl) - (91" wb) - (78.5 hp)

	6	5	4	3	2	1
Conv	350	850	1650	4100	5700	8200
Cpe GT	350	800	1550	3900	5450	7800

NOTE: Add 10 percent for wire wheels.
Add 5 percent for overdrive.

1973
MG Midget - (4-cyl) - (80" wb) - (54.5 hp)

	6	5	4	3	2	1
Conv	350	750	1450	3300	4900	7000

MGB-MGB/GT - (4-cyl) - (91" wb) - (78.5 hp)

	6	5	4	3	2	1
Conv	350	850	1650	4100	5700	8200
Cpe GT	350	800	1550	3900	5450	7800

NOTE: Add 10 percent for wire wheels.
Add 5 percent for overdrive.

1974
MG Midget - (4-cyl) - (80" wb) - (54.5 hp)

	6	5	4	3	2	1
Conv	350	750	1450	3400	5000	7100

MG-B - (4-cyl) - (91" wb) - (78.5 hp)

	6	5	4	3	2	1
Conv	350	850	1650	4150	5800	8300
Cpe GT	350	825	1600	4000	5600	8000

Interim MG-B - (4-cyl) - (91.125" wb) - (62.9 hp)

	6	5	4	3	2	1
Conv	350	775	1500	3750	5250	7500
Cpe GT	350	750	1450	3400	5000	7100

NOTE: Add 10 percent for wire wheels.
Add 5 percent for overdrive.

1975
MG Midget - (4-cyl) - (80" wb) - (50 hp)

	6	5	4	3	2	1
Conv	200	650	1250	2400	4200	6000

MGB - (4-cyl) - (91.125" wb) - (62.9 hp)

	6	5	4	3	2	1
Conv	350	750	1450	3300	4900	7000

NOTE: Add 10 percent for wire wheels.
Add 5 percent for overdrive.

1976
MG Midget - (4-cyl) - (80" wb) - (50 hp)

	6	5	4	3	2	1
Conv	350	700	1350	2700	4500	6400

MGB - (4-cyl) - (91.13" wb) - (62.5 hp)

	6	5	4	3	2	1
Conv	350	750	1450	3500	5050	7200

NOTE: Add 10 percent for wire wheels.
Add 5 percent for overdrive.

1977
MG Midget - (4-cyl) - (80" wb) - (50 hp)

	6	5	4	3	2	1
Conv	350	700	1350	2800	4550	6500

MGB - (4-cyl) - (91.13" wb) - (62.5 hp)

	6	5	4	3	2	1
Conv	350	775	1500	3750	5250	7500

NOTE: Add 10 percent for wire wheels.
Add 5 percent for overdrive.

1978

	6	5	4	3	2	1
Conv B	350	775	1500	3750	5250	7500
Conv Midget	350	700	1350	2800	4550	6500

1979

	6	5	4	3	2	1
Conv B	350	775	1500	3750	5250	7500
Conv Midget	350	700	1350	2800	4550	6500

1980

	6	5	4	3	2	1
Conv B	350	800	1550	3800	5300	7600

MITSUBISHI

1982-83
Cordia - (4-cyl) - (96.3" wb) - (1795cc) - (FWD)

	6	5	4	3	2	1
2d HBk	125	200	600	1100	2300	3300
L 2d HBk	125	250	750	1150	2400	3400
LS 2d HBk	150	350	950	1350	2800	4000

Tredia - (4-cyl) - (96.3" wb) - (1795cc) - (FWD)

	6	5	4	3	2	1
4d Sed	100	175	525	1050	2100	3000
L 4d Sed	125	200	600	1100	2300	3300
LS 4d Sed	125	250	750	1150	2450	3500

Starion - (4-cyl) - (95.9" wb) - (2555cc)

	6	5	4	3	2	1
2d Cpe 2 plus 2	150	350	950	1450	3000	4200
LS 2d Cpe 2 plus 2	200	500	1100	1900	3500	5000

1984
Cordia - (4-cyl) - (96.3" wb) - (1997cc) - (FWD)

	6	5	4	3	2	1
2d HBk	150	350	950	1450	3000	4200
L 2d HBk	150	450	1050	1700	3200	4600
LS 2d HBk	150	450	1050	1750	3250	4700

Cordia - (4-cyl) - (96.3" wb) - (1795cc) - (FWD)

	6	5	4	3	2	1
2d HBk Turbo	200	500	1100	1900	3500	5000

Tredia - (4-cyl) - (96.3" wb) - (1997cc) - (FWD)

	6	5	4	3	2	1
4d Sed	150	300	900	1250	2600	3700
L 4d Sed	150	300	900	1250	2650	3800
LS 4d Sed	150	350	950	1350	2800	4000

Tredia - (4-cyl) - (96.3" wb) - (1795cc) - (FWD)

	6	5	4	3	2	1
4d Sed Turbo	150	350	950	1450	3000	4200

Starion - (4-cyl) - (95.9" wb) - (2555cc)

	6	5	4	3	2	1
LS Cpe 2 plus 2	200	650	1250	2400	4200	6000
LE Cpe 2 plus 2	350	700	1350	2800	4550	6500
ES Cpe 2 plus 2	350	725	1400	3000	4700	6700

1985-86
Mirage - (4-cyl) - (93.7" wb) - (1468cc) - (FWD)

	6	5	4	3	2	1
2d HBk	150	350	950	1350	2800	4000
L 2d HBk	150	350	950	1450	3000	4200
LS 2d HBk	150	400	1000	1650	3150	4500

Mirage - (4-cyl) - (93.7" wb) - (1597cc) - (FWD)

	6	5	4	3	2	1
2d HBk Turbo	200	500	1100	1900	3500	5000

Cordia - (4-cyl) - (96.3" wb) - (1997cc) - (FWD)

	6	5	4	3	2	1
L 2d HBk	200	650	1250	2400	4200	6000

Cordia - (4-cyl) - (96.3" wb) - (1795cc) - (FWD)

	6	5	4	3	2	1
2d HBk Turbo	200	675	1300	2500	4350	6200

Tredia - (4-cyl) - (96.3" wb) - (1997cc) - (FWD)

	6	5	4	3	2	1
4d Sed	150	350	950	1350	2800	4000
L 4d Sed	150	400	1000	1650	3150	4500

Tredia - (4-cyl) - (96.3" wb) - (1795cc) - (FWD)

	6	5	4	3	2	1
4d Sed Turbo	200	500	1100	1900	3500	5000

Galant - (4-cyl) - (102.4" wb) - (2350cc) - (FWD)

	6	5	4	3	2	1
4d Sed	350	750	1450	3300	4900	7000

Starion 2 plus 2 - (4-cyl) - (95.9" wb) - (2555cc)

	6	5	4	3	2	1
LS 2d Cpe	350	750	1450	3300	4900	7000
LE 2d Cpe	350	750	1450	3400	5000	7100
ES 2d Cpe	350	775	1500	3600	5100	7300
ESI 2d Cpe	350	775	1500	3700	5200	7400
ESI-R 2d Cpe	350	775	1500	3750	5250	7500

MORGAN

1945-50
4/4, Series I - (4-cyl) - (92" wb) - (1267cc)

	6	5	4	3	2	1
2d Rds	600	1900	3200	6400	11,200	16,000
2d Rds 2 plus 2	550	1800	3000	6000	10,500	15,000
2d DHC	700	2150	3600	7200	12,600	18,000

1951-54
Plus Four I - (4-cyl) - (96" wb) - (2088cc)

	6	5	4	3	2	1
2d Rds	550	1700	2800	5600	9800	14,000
2d Rds 2 plus 2	500	1600	2700	5400	9500	13,500
2d DHC	600	1900	3200	6400	11,200	16,000
2d DHC 2 plus 2	600	2000	3300	6600	11,600	16,500

	6	5	4	3	2	1
1955-62						
Plus Four I (1954-1962)						
(4-cyl) - (96" wb) - (1991cc)						
2d Rds	500	1550	2600	5200	9100	13,000
2d Rds 2 plus 2	450	1500	2500	5000	8800	12,500
2d DHC	600	1900	3200	6400	11,200	16,000
Plus Four Super Sports						
(4-cyl) - (96" wb) - (2138cc)						
2d Rds	600	1900	3200	6400	11,200	16,000
4/4 II (1955-59)						
(L-head) - (4-cyl) - (96" wb) - (1172cc)						
2d Rds	500	1600	2700	5400	9500	13,500
4/4 III (1960-61)						
(4-cyl) - (96" wb) - (997cc)						
2d Rds	450	1500	2500	5000	8800	12,500
4/4 IV (1961-63)						
(4-cyl) - (96" wb) - (1340cc)						
2d Rds	500	1600	2700	5400	9500	13,500
1963-67						
Plus Four (1962-68)						
(4-cyl) - (96" wb) - (2138cc)						
2d Rds	550	1700	2800	5600	9800	14,000
2d Rds 2 plus 2	550	1750	2900	5800	10,200	14,500
2d DHC	650	2050	3400	6800	11,900	17,000
2d Sup Spt Rds	600	1850	3100	6200	10,900	15,500
Plus Four Plus (1963-66)						
(4-cyl) - (96" wb) - (2138cc)						
2d Cpe	value not estimable					
4/4 Series IV (1962-63)						
(4-cyl) - (96" wb) - (1340cc)						
2d Rds	550	1700	2800	5600	9800	14,000
4/4 Series V (1963-68)						
(4-cyl) - (96" wb) - (1498cc)						
2d Rds	550	1750	2900	5800	10,200	14,500
1968-69						
Plus Four (1962-68)						
(4-cyl) - (96" wb) - (2138cc)						
2d Rds	550	1800	3000	6000	10,500	15,000
2d Rds 2 plus 2	550	1750	2900	5800	10,200	14,500
2d DHC	650	2050	3400	6800	11,900	17,000
2d Sup Spt Rds	600	1850	3100	6200	10,900	15,500
Plus 8 - (V-8) - (98" wb) - (3528cc)						
2d Rds	600	1900	3200	6400	11,200	16,000
4/4 Series V (1963-68)						
(4-cyl) - (96" wb) - (1498cc)						
2d Rds	550	1800	3000	6000	10,500	15,000
4/4 1600 - (4-cyl) - (96" wb) - (1599cc)						
2d Rds	600	1850	3100	6200	10,900	15,500
2d Rds 2 plus 2	550	1800	3000	6000	10,500	15,000
1970-90						
Plus 8 (1972-90)						
(V-8) - (98" wb) - (3528cc)						
2d Rds	600	1900	3200	6400	11,200	16,000
4/4 1600 (1970-81)						
(4-cyl) - (96" wb) - (1599cc)						
2d Rds	600	1850	3100	6200	10,900	15,500
2d Rds 2 plus 2	550	1800	3000	6000	10,500	15,000
4/4 1600 (1982-87)						
(4-cyl) - (96" wb) - (1596cc)						
2d Rds	750	2400	4000	8000	14,000	20,000
2d Rds 2 plus 2	750	2350	3900	7800	13,700	19,500

MORRIS

	6	5	4	3	2	1
1946-48						
Eight Series - (4-cyl) - (89" wb) - (918cc)						
2d Sed	350	825	1600	4000	5600	8000
4d Sed	350	750	1450	3300	4900	7000
2d Rds	400	1200	2000	4000	7000	10,000
Ten Series - (4-cyl) - (1140cc)						
4d Sed	350	750	1450	3300	4900	7000
1949						
Minor MM - (4-cyl) - (86" wb) - (918.6cc)						
2d Sed	350	750	1450	3300	4900	7000
2d Conv	400	1200	2000	4000	7000	10,000
Oxford MO - (4-cyl) - (97" wb) - (1476cc)						
4d Sed	350	750	1450	3300	4900	7000
1950						
Minor MM - (4-cyl) - (86" wb) - (918.6cc)						
2d Sed	350	750	1450	3300	4900	7000
2d Conv	400	1200	2000	4000	7000	10,000
Oxford MO - (4-cyl) - (97" wb) - (1476cc)						
4d Sed	350	750	1450	3300	4900	7000
1951						
Minor MM - (4-cyl) - (86" wb) - (918.6cc)						
2d Sed	350	750	1450	3300	4900	7000
2d Conv	400	1200	2000	4000	7000	10,000
4d Sed	350	750	1450	3300	4900	7000
Oxford MO - (4-cyl) - (97" wb) - (1476cc)						
4d Sed	350	750	1450	3300	4900	7000
1952						
Minor MM - (4-cyl) - (86" wb) - (918.6cc)						
2d Sed	350	750	1450	3300	4900	7000
2d Conv	400	1200	2000	4000	7000	10,000
4d Sed	350	750	1450	3300	4900	7000
Oxford MO - (4-cyl) - (97" wb) - (1476cc)						
4d Sed	350	750	1450	3300	4900	7000
1953						
Minor II - (4-cyl) - (86" wb) - (803cc)						
2d Sed	350	750	1450	3300	4900	7000
4d Sed	350	750	1450	3300	4900	7000
2d Conv	400	1200	2000	4000	7000	10,000
Oxford MO - (4-cyl) - (97" wb) - (1476cc)						
4d Sed	350	750	1450	3300	4900	7000
4d Sta Wag	450	1450	2400	4800	8400	12,000
1954						
Minor II - (4-cyl) - (86" wb) - (803cc)						
2d Sed	350	750	1450	3300	4900	7000
4d Sed	350	750	1450	3300	4900	7000
2d Tr Conv	400	1200	2000	4000	7000	10,000
2d Sta Wag	450	1450	2400	4800	8400	12,000

	6	5	4	3	2	1
Oxford MO - (4-cyl) - (97" wb) - (1476cc)						
4d Sed	350	750	1450	3300	4900	7000
4d Sta Wag	400	1200	2000	4000	7000	10,000
1955-56						
Minor II - (4-cyl) - (86" wb) - (803cc)						
2d Sed	350	750	1450	3300	4900	7000
4d Sed	350	750	1450	3300	4900	7000
2d Conv	400	1200	2000	4000	7000	10,000
2d Sta Wag	450	1450	2400	4800	8400	12,000
1957-59						
Minor 1000 - (4-cyl) - (86" wb) - (948cc)						
2d Sed	350	750	1450	3300	4900	7000
4d Sed	350	750	1450	3300	4900	7000
2d Conv	400	1200	2000	4000	7000	10,000
2d Sta Wag	450	1450	2400	4800	8400	12,000
1960-62						
Minor 1000 - (4-cyl) - (86" wb) - (997cc)						
2d Sed	350	750	1450	3300	4900	7000
2d DeL Sed	350	775	1500	3750	5250	7500
4d Sed	350	750	1450	3300	4900	7000
4d DeL Sed	350	775	1500	3750	5250	7500
2d Conv	400	1200	2000	4000	7000	10,000
2d DeL Conv	400	1250	2100	4200	7400	10,500
2d Sta Wag	450	1450	2400	4800	8400	12,000
2d DeL Sta Wag	450	1500	2500	5000	8800	12,500
Mini-Minor - (4-cyl) - (80" wb) - (997cc) - (FWD)						
850 2d Sed	350	750	1450	3300	4900	7000
850 2d Sta Wag	450	900	1900	4500	6300	9000
Oxford V - (4-cyl) - (99.2" wb) - (1489cc)						
4d Sed	350	750	1450	3300	4900	7000
1963-71						
Minor 1000 - (4-cyl) - (86" wb) - (1098cc)						
2d Sed	350	750	1450	3300	4900	7000
2d Conv	400	1200	2000	4000	7000	10,000
2d Sta Wag	450	1450	2400	4800	8400	12,000
2d DeL Wag	450	1500	2500	5000	8800	12,500
Mini-Minor 850 Cooper						
(4-cyl) - (80" wb) - (848cc) - (FWD)						
2d Sed	350	750	1450	3300	4900	7000
2d Sta Wag	450	900	1900	4500	6300	9000

NOTE: The Mini-Minor Mark II 1000 (1967-69) contained a 998cc engine. The Mini-Minor Cooper a 997cc until 1964; 998cc thru 1964-65. The 1071 "S" a 1071cc; the 970 "S" a 970cc; the 1275 "S" a 1275cc. Add 50 percent for Mini-Minor Coopers.

NASH-HEALEY

	6	5	4	3	2	1
1951						
Series 25 - (6-cyl) - (102" wb) - (3847cc)						
162 2d Spt Rds	950	3000	5000	10,000	17,500	25,000
1952						
Series 25 - (6-cyl) - (102" wb) - (3847cc-4140cc)						
262 2d Spt Rds	950	3000	5000	10,000	17,500	25,000
1953-54						
Series 25 - (6-cyl) - (102" wb) - (4140cc)						
362 2d Spt Conv	950	3000	5000	10,000	17,500	25,000
LeMans - (6-cyl) - (102" wb) - (4140cc)						
367 2d HdTp Cpe	750	2400	4000	8000	14,000	20,000

OPEL

	6	5	4	3	2	1
1947-52						
Olympia - (4-cyl) - (94.3" wb) - (1488cc)						
2d Sed	200	500	1100	1900	3500	5000
Kapitan - (6-cyl) - (106.1" wb) - (2473cc)						
4d Sed	200	500	1100	1900	3500	5000
1953-57						
Olympia Rekord - (4-cyl) - (97.9" wb) - (1488cc)						
2d Sed	150	350	950	1350	2800	4000
Caravan - (4-cyl)						
2d Sta Wag	150	350	950	1350	2800	4000
Kapitan - (6-cyl) - (108.3" wb) - (2473cc)						
4d Sed	150	350	950	1350	2800	4000
1958-59						
Olympia Rekord 28 - (4-cyl) - (100.4" wb) - (1488cc)						
2d Sed	150	350	950	1350	2800	4000
Caravan 29 - (4-cyl) - (100.4" wb)						
2d Sta Wag	150	350	950	1350	2800	4000
1960						
Olympic Rekord 28 - (4-cyl) - (100.4" wb) - (1488cc)						
2d Sed	150	350	950	1350	2800	4000
Caravan 29 - (4-cyl) - (100.4" wb)						
2d Sta Wag	150	350	950	1350	2800	4000
1961-62						
Olympic Rekord 11 - (4-cyl) - (100" wb) - (1680cc)						
2d Sed	150	350	950	1350	2800	4000
Caravan 14 - (4-cyl) - (1680cc)						
2d Sta Wag	150	350	950	1350	2800	4000
1964-65						
Kadett - (4-cyl) - (91.5" wb) - (987cc)						
31 2d Sed	150	350	950	1350	2800	4000
32 2d Spt Cpe	150	350	950	1350	2800	4000
34 2d Sta Wag	150	350	950	1350	2800	4000
1966-67						
Kadett - (4-cyl) - (95.1" wb) - (1077cc)						
31 2d Sed	150	350	950	1350	2800	4000
32 2d Spt Cpe	150	350	950	1350	2800	4000
38 2d DeL Sed	150	350	950	1450	3000	4200
37 4d DeL Sed	150	350	950	1450	3000	4200
39 2d DeL Sta Wag	150	350	950	1450	3000	4200
Rallye - (4-cyl) - (95.1" wb) - (1077cc)						
32 2d Spt Cpe	150	400	1000	1650	3150	4500
1968						
Kadett - (4-cyl) - (95.1" wb) - (1077cc)						
31 2d Sed	150	350	950	1450	3000	4200
39 2d Sta Wag	150	350	950	1350	2800	4000
Rallye - (4-cyl) - (95.1" wb) - (1491cc)						
92 2d Spt Cpe	150	400	1000	1650	3150	4500

Sport Series - (4-cyl) - (95.1" wb) - (1491cc)

	6	5	4	3	2	1
91 2d Spt Sed	150	350	950	1350	2800	4000
99 2d LS Cpe	150	350	950	1350	2800	4000
95 2d DeL Spt Cpe	150	350	950	1350	2800	4000

NOTE: Two larger engines were optional in 1968. The 4-cyl., 1491cc engine that was standard in the Rallye Cpe and the even larger 4-cyl., 1897cc.

1969
Kadett - (4-cyl) - (95.1" wb) - (1077cc)

	6	5	4	3	2	1
31 2d Sed	150	350	950	1350	2800	4000
39 2d Sta Wag	150	350	950	1350	2800	4000

Rallye/Sport Series - (4-cyl) - (95.1" wb) - (1077cc)

	6	5	4	3	2	1
92 Rallye Spe Cpe	150	400	1000	1650	3150	4500
91 2d Spt Sed	150	350	950	1350	2800	4000
95 DeL Spt Cpe	150	350	950	1350	2800	4000

GT - (4-cyl) - (95.7" wb) - (1077cc)

	6	5	4	3	2	1
2d Cpe	350	750	1450	3300	4900	7000

NOTE: Optional, 4-cyl, 1897cc engine.

1970
Kadett - (4-cyl) - (95.1" wb) - (1077cc)

	6	5	4	3	2	1
31 2d Sed	150	350	950	1350	2800	4000
39 2d Sta Wag	150	350	950	1350	2800	4000

Rallye/Sport (FB) Series - (4-cyl) - (95.1" wb) - (1077cc)

	6	5	4	3	2	1
92 Rallye Spt Cpe	150	350	950	1450	3000	4200
91 2d Spt Sed	150	350	950	1350	2800	4000
95 DeL Spt Cpe	350	750	1450	3300	4900	7000

GT - (4-cyl) - (95.7" wb) - (1077cc)

	6	5	4	3	2	1
93 2d Cpe	150	350	950	1350	2800	4000

1971-72
Kadett - (4-cyl) - (95.1" wb) - (1077cc)

	6	5	4	3	2	1
31 2d Sed	150	350	950	1350	2800	4000
31D DeL 2d Sed	150	350	950	1350	2800	4000
36 4d Sed	150	350	950	1350	2800	4000
36D DeL 4d Sed	150	350	950	1350	2800	4000
39 DeL 2d Sta Wag	150	350	950	1350	2800	

1900 Series - (4-cyl) - (95.7" wb) - (1897cc)

	6	5	4	3	2	1
51 2d Sed	150	350	950	1350	2800	4000
53 4d Sed	150	350	950	1350	2800	4000
54 2d Sta Wag	150	350	950	1450	2900	4100
57 2d Spt Cpe	150	350	950	1450	3000	4200
57R 2d Rallye Cpe	350	750	1450	3300	4900	7000

GT - (4-cyl) - (95.7" wb) - (1897cc)

	6	5	4	3	2	1
77 2d Cpe	150	350	950	1350	2800	4000

1973
1900 Series - (4-cyl) - (95.7" wb) - (1897cc)

	6	5	4	3	2	1
51 2d Sed	150	350	950	1350	2800	4000
53 4d Sed	150	350	950	1350	2800	4000
54 2d Sta Wag	150	350	950	1350	2800	4000

Manta 57 - (4-cyl) - (95.7" wb) - (1897cc)

	6	5	4	3	2	1
2d Spt Cpe	200	500	1100	1900	3500	5000
Luxus 2d Spt Cpe	150	350	950	1350	2800	4000
R 2d Rallye Cpe	150	350	950	1350	2800	4000

GT - (4-cyl) - (95.7" wb) - (1897cc)

	6	5	4	3	2	1
77 2d Cpe	350	750	1450	3300	4900	7000

1974-75
1900 - (4-cyl) - (95.7" wb) - (1897cc)

	6	5	4	3	2	1
51 2d Sed	150	350	950	1350	2800	4000
54 2d Sta Wag	150	350	950	1450	2900	4100

Manta 57 - (95.7" wb) - (1897cc)

	6	5	4	3	2	1
2d Spt Cpe	200	500	1100	1900	3500	5000
Luxus Spt Cpe	150	350	950	1350	2800	4000
R, 2d Rallye Cpe	150	400	1000	1650	3150	4500

NOTE: FI was available in 1975.

1976-79
Opel Isuzu (1976 models)
(4-cyl) - (94.3" wb) - (1817cc)

	6	5	4	3	2	1
77 2d Cpe	125	250	750	1150	2450	3500
2d DeL Cpe	125	250	750	1150	2450	3500

Opel Isuzu (1979 models)
(4-cyl) - (94.3" wb) - (1817cc)

	6	5	4	3	2	1
T77 2d Cpe	125	250	750	1150	2450	3500
Y77 2d DeL Cpe	125	250	750	1150	2450	3500
Y69 4d DeL Sed	125	250	750	1150	2450	3500
W77 2d Spt Cpe	125	250	750	1150	2450	3500

PEUGEOT

1945-48
202 - (4-cyl) - (1133cc)

	6	5	4	3	2	1
Sed	200	600	1200	2200	3850	5500

1949-54
203 - (4-cyl) - (102 or 110" wb) - (1290cc)

	6	5	4	3	2	1
4d Sed	200	600	1200	2200	3850	5500
4d Family Limo	200	500	1100	1900	3500	5000
2d Cabr	400	1200	2000	4000	7000	10,000
4d Conv	450	1450	2400	4800	8400	12,000

1955-57
203 (minimal changes)
403 - (4-cyl) - (105" wb) - (1468cc)

	6	5	4	3	2	1
4d Sed	200	600	1200	2200	3850	5500
4d Sta Wag	200	500	1100	1900	3500	5000
2d Conv Cpe	450	1450	2400	4800	8400	12,000

403L - (4-cyl) - (114" wb) - (1468cc)

	6	5	4	3	2	1
4d Family Sed	150	400	1000	1650	3150	4500

1958-59
403 - (4-cyl) - (105" wb) - (1468cc)

	6	5	4	3	2	1
4d Sed	150	400	1000	1650	3150	4500
L 4d Family Sed	200	600	1200	2200	3850	5500
4d Sta Wag	350	825	1600	4000	5600	8000
2d Conv Cpe	450	1450	2400	4800	8400	12,000

1960
403 - (4-cyl) - (105" wb) - (1468cc)

	6	5	4	3	2	1
4d Sed	150	400	1000	1650	3150	4500

403 - (4-cyl) - (116" wb) - (1468cc)

	6	5	4	3	2	1
4d Sta Wag	200	500	1100	1900	3500	5000

1961-62
403 - (4-cyl) - (105" wb) - (1468cc)

	6	5	4	3	2	1
4d Sed	150	400	1000	1650	3150	4500

403 - (4-cyl) - (116" wb) - (1468cc)

	6	5	4	3	2	1
4d Sta Wag	150	400	1000	1650	3150	4500

404 - (4-cyl) - (104.3" wb) - (1618cc)

	6	5	4	3	2	1
4d Sed	150	400	1000	1650	3150	4500

1963-64
403 - (4-cyl) - (105" wb) - (1468cc)

	6	5	4	3	2	1
4d Sed	150	400	1000	1650	3150	4500

404 - (4-cyl) - (104.3" wb) - (1618cc)

	6	5	4	3	2	1
4d Sed	150	400	1000	1650	3150	4500
4d Sta Wag	200	500	1100	1900	3500	5000

1965-67
403 - (4-cyl) - (105" wb) - (1468cc)

	6	5	4	3	2	1
4d Sed	150	400	1000	1650	3150	4500

404 - (4-cyl) - (104.3" wb) - (1618cc)

	6	5	4	3	2	1
4d Sed	150	350	950	1350	2800	4000

404 - (4-cyl) - (111.8" wb) - (1618cc)

	6	5	4	3	2	1
4d Sed	150	400	1000	1650	3150	4500

1968-69
404 - (4-cyl) - (104.3" wb) - (1618cc)

	6	5	4	3	2	1
4d Sed	150	350	950	1350	2800	4000

404 - (4-cyl) - (111.8" wb) - (1618cc)

	6	5	4	3	2	1
4d Sta Wag	150	400	1000	1650	3150	4500

NOTE: Convertibles were available on a special order basis.

1970
404 - (4-cyl) - (111.8" wb) - (1796cc)

	6	5	4	3	2	1
4d Sta Wag	150	350	950	1350	2800	4000

504 - (4-cyl) - (108" wb) - (1796cc)

	6	5	4	3	2	1
4d Sed	150	350	950	1350	2800	4000

1971-72
304 - (4-cyl) - (101.9" wb) - (1288cc)

	6	5	4	3	2	1
4d Sed	150	350	950	1350	2800	4000
4d Sta Wag	150	400	1000	1650	3150	4500

504 - (4-cyl) - (108" wb) - (1971cc)

	6	5	4	3	2	1
4d Sed	150	350	950	1350	2800	4000
4d Sta Wag	150	400	1000	1650	3150	4500

1973-76
504 (1973 models)
(4-cyl) - (1971cc)

	6	5	4	3	2	1
4d Sed	150	350	950	1350	2800	4000
4d Sta Wag	150	400	1000	1650	3150	4500

504 (1974 models)
(4-cyl) - (1971cc)

	6	5	4	3	2	1
4d Sed	150	350	950	1350	2800	4000
4d Sta Wag	150	400	1000	1650	3150	4500

Diesel - (2111cc)

	6	5	4	3	2	1
4d Sed	150	350	950	1350	2800	4000
4d Sta Wag	150	400	1000	1650	3150	4500

504 (1975 models)
(4-cyl) - (1971cc)

	6	5	4	3	2	1
4d Sed	150	350	950	1350	2800	4000
4d Sta Wag	150	400	1000	1650	3150	4500

Diesel - (2111cc)

	6	5	4	3	2	1
4d Sed	150	350	950	1350	2800	4000
4d Sta Wag	150	400	1000	1650	3150	4500

504 (1976 models)
(4-cyl) - (1971cc)

	6	5	4	3	2	1
GL 4d Sed	150	350	950	1350	2800	4000
SL 4d Sed	150	350	950	1350	2800	4000
4d Sta Wag	150	400	1000	1650	3150	4500

Diesel - (2111cc)

	6	5	4	3	2	1
4d Sed	150	350	950	1350	2800	4000
4d Sta Wag	150	400	1000	1650	3150	4500

NOTE: The sedans had a 108" wb. The station wagons had a 114" wb.

1977-79
504 (1977 models)
(4-cyl) - (1971cc)

	6	5	4	3	2	1
SL 4d Sed	150	350	950	1350	2800	4000
4d Sta Wag	150	400	1000	1650	3150	4500

Diesel - (2304cc)

	6	5	4	3	2	1
4d Sed	150	350	950	1350	2800	4000
4d Sta Wag	150	400	1000	1650	3150	4500

604 (1977 models)
(V-6) - (110.2" wb) - (2664cc)

	6	5	4	3	2	1
4d Sed	150	350	950	1350	2800	4000

NOTE: 504 sedans - 108" wb, 504 wagons - 114" wb.

1980-81
505/504 (1980 models)
(4-cyl) - (107.9" wb) - (1971cc)

	6	5	4	3	2	1
4d Sed	150	400	1000	1650	3150	4500

Diesel - (2304cc)

	6	5	4	3	2	1
505 4d Sed	150	400	1000	1650	3150	4500
504 4d Sta Wag	200	500	1100	1900	3500	5000

505 Turbodiesel (1981 models)

	6	5	4	3	2	1
D 4d Sed	150	400	1000	1650	3150	4500

604 (1980 models)
(V-6) - (110.2" wb) - (2849cc)

	6	5	4	3	2	1
SL 4d Sed	150	400	1000	1650	3150	4500

1982
505 - (4-cyl) - (107.9" wb) - (1971cc)

	6	5	4	3	2	1
4d Sed	200	500	1100	1900	3500	5000
S 4d Sed	200	500	1100	1900	3500	5000
STI 4d Sed	200	550	1150	2100	3700	5300

Diesel - (2304cc)

	6	5	4	3	2	1
505 4d Sed	150	350	950	1350	2800	4000
504 4d Sta Wag	150	400	1000	1550	3050	4300

505/604 Turbodiesel - (2304cc)

	6	5	4	3	2	1
505 4d Sed	150	400	1000	1550	3050	4300
505S 4d Sed	150	400	1000	1550	3050	4300
604TD 4d Sed	150	400	1000	1650	3150	4500

1983
505/504

	6	5	4	3	2	1
505 4d Sed	200	500	1100	1900	3500	5000
505S 4d Sed	200	500	1100	1900	3500	5000
505 STI 4d Sed	200	500	1100	1900	3500	5000
505 Dsl 4d Sed	150	350	950	1350	2800	4000
504 Dsl Sta Wag	150	400	1000	1650	3150	4500

505/604 Turbodiesel

	6	5	4	3	2	1
505 4d Sed	200	500	1100	1900	3500	5000
505 S 4d Sed	200	500	1100	1900	3500	5000
604 4d Sed	200	500	1100	1900	3500	5000

1984
505 Series

	6	5	4	3	2	1
GL 4d Sed	200	600	1200	2200	3850	5500
S 4d Sed	200	600	1200	2200	3850	5500
STI 4d Sed	200	600	1200	2200	3850	5500
GL 4d Sta Wag	200	650	1250	2400	4200	6000
S 4d Sta Wag	200	650	1250	2400	4200	6000

	6	5	4	3	2	1
505/604 Turbodiesel						
GL 4d Sed	200	500	1100	1900	3500	5000
S 4d Sed	200	500	1100	1900	3500	5000
STI 4d Sed	200	500	1100	1900	3500	5000
GL 4d Sta Wag	200	600	1200	2200	3850	5500
S 4d Sta Wag	200	600	1200	2200	3850	5500
604 4d Sed	200	600	1200	2200	3850	5500
1985						
505						
GL 4d Sed	200	650	1250	2400	4200	6000
S 4d Sed	200	650	1250	2400	4200	6000
STI 4d Sed	200	650	1250	2400	4200	6000
Turbo 4d Sed	200	675	1300	2600	4400	6300
GL 4d Sta Wag	200	675	1300	2600	4400	6300
S 4d Sta Wag	200	675	1300	2600	4400	6300
505 Turbodiesel						
GL 4d Sed	200	600	1200	2200	3850	5500
S 4d Sed	200	600	1200	2200	3850	5500
STI 4d Sed	200	500	1100	1900	3500	5000
GL 4d Sta Wag	200	650	1250	2400	4200	6000
S 4d Sta Wag	200	650	1250	2400	4200	6000

PORSCHE

	6	5	4	3	2	1
1950						
Model 356 - (40 hp) - (1100cc)						
Cpe	1450	4550	7600	15,200	26,600	38,000
1951						
Model 356 - (40 hp) - (1100cc)						
Cpe	900	2900	4800	9600	16,800	24,000
Cabr	1000	3100	5200	10,400	18,200	26,000
1952						
Model 356 - (40 hp) - (1100cc)						
Cpe	900	2900	4800	9600	16,800	24,000
Cabr	1000	3100	5200	10,400	18,200	26,000
1953						
Model 356 - (40 hp)						
Cpe	900	2900	4800	9600	16,800	24,000
Cabr	1000	3100	5200	10,400	18,200	26,000
1954						
Model 356, 1.5 litre - (55 hp)						
Cpe	900	2900	4800	9600	16,800	24,000
Cabr	1000	3100	5200	10,400	18,200	26,000
Model 356, Super 1.5 litre						
Cpe	1050	3350	5600	11,200	19,600	28,000
Cabr	1250	3950	6600	13,200	23,100	33,000
1955						
Model 356 - (4-cyl) - (55 hp)						
Spds	1700	5400	9000	18,000	31,500	45,000
Cpe	900	2900	4800	9600	16,800	24,000
Cabr	1000	3100	5200	10,400	18,200	26,000
Model 356, Super 1.5 litre - (70 hp)						
Spds	1900	6000	10,000	20,000	35,000	50,000
Cpe	950	3000	5000	10,000	17,500	25,000
Cabr	1050	3350	5600	11,200	19,600	28,000
1956						
Model 356A, Standard 1.6 litre - (60 hp)						
Spds	1700	5400	9000	18,000	31,500	45,000
Cpe	900	2900	4800	9600	16,800	24,000
Cabr	1000	3100	5200	10,400	18,200	26,000
Model 356A, Super 1.6 litre - (75 hp)						
Spds	1900	6000	10,000	20,000	35,000	50,000
Cpe	950	3000	5000	10,000	17,500	25,000
Cabr	1050	3350	5600	11,200	19,600	28,000
Model 356A, Carrera, 1.5 litre - (100 hp)						
Spds	2250	7200	12,000	24,000	42,000	60,000
Cpe	1400	4450	7400	14,800	25,900	37,000
Cabr	1500	4800	8000	16,000	28,000	40,000
1957						
Model 356A, Standard 1.6 litre - (60 hp)						
Spds	1700	5400	9000	18,000	31,500	45,000
Cpe	900	2900	4800	9600	16,800	24,000
Cabr	1000	3100	5200	10,400	18,200	26,000
Model 356A, Super 1.6 litre - (70 hp)						
Spds	1900	6000	10,000	20,000	35,000	50,000
Cpe	950	3000	5000	10,000	17,500	25,000
Cabr	1050	3350	5600	11,200	19,600	28,000
Model 356A, Carrera, 1.5 litre - (100 hp)						
Spds	2250	7200	12,000	24,000	42,000	60,000
Cpe	1400	4450	7400	14,800	25,900	37,000
Cabr	1500	4800	8000	16,000	28,000	40,000
1958						
Model 356A, Standard 1.6 litre - (60 hp)						
Spds	1700	5400	9000	18,000	31,500	45,000
Cpe	900	2900	4800	9600	16,800	24,000
Cabr	1000	3100	5200	10,400	18,200	26,000
HdTp	1000	3100	5200	10,400	18,200	26,000
Model 356A, Super 1.6 litre - (75 hp)						
Spds	1900	6000	10,000	20,000	35,000	50,000
Cpe	950	3000	5000	10,000	17,500	25,000
Cabr	1050	3350	5600	11,200	19,600	28,000
HdTp	1050	3350	5600	11,200	19,600	28,000
Model 356A, Carrera, 1.5 litre - (100 hp)						
Spds	2250	7200	12,000	24,000	42,000	60,000
Cpe	1400	4450	7400	14,800	25,900	37,000
Cabr	1450	4550	7600	15,200	26,600	38,000
HdTp	1450	4550	7600	15,200	26,600	38,000
1959						
Model 356A, Standard - (60 hp)						
Cpe	900	2900	4800	9600	16,800	24,000
Cpe/HdTp	1050	3350	5600	11,200	19,600	28,000
Conv D	1000	3250	5400	10,800	18,900	27,000
Cabr	1050	3350	5600	11,200	19,600	28,000
Model 356A, Super - (75 hp)						
Cpe	1000	3250	5400	10,800	18,900	27,000
Cpe/HdTp	1150	3600	6000	12,000	21,000	30,000
Conv D	1100	3500	5800	11,600	20,300	29,000
Cabr	1150	3600	6000	12,000	21,000	30,000
Model 356A, Carrera, 1.6 litre - (105 hp)						
Cpe	1350	4300	7200	14,400	25,200	36,000
Cpe/HdTp	1450	4700	7800	15,600	27,300	39,000
Cabr	1750	5500	9200	18,400	32,200	46,000

	6	5	4	3	2	1
1960						
Model 356B, Standard 1.6 litre - (60 hp)						
Cpe	900	2900	4800	9600	16,800	24,000
Rds	1000	3250	5400	10,800	18,900	27,000
Cabr	1100	3500	5800	11,600	20,300	29,000
HdTp	1100	3500	5800	11,600	20,300	29,000
Model 356B, Super 1.6 litre - (75 hp)						
Cpe	950	3000	5000	10,000	17,500	25,000
Rds	1000	3250	5400	10,800	18,900	27,000
Cabr	1050	3350	5600	11,200	19,600	28,000
HdTp	1050	3350	5600	11,200	19,600	28,000
Model 356B, Super 90, 1.6 litre - (90 hp)						
Cpe	1000	3250	5400	10,800	18,900	27,000
Rds	1100	3500	5800	11,600	20,300	29,000
Cabr	1150	3700	6200	12,400	21,700	31,000
HdTp	1150	3700	6200	12,400	21,700	31,000
1961						
Model 356B, Standard 1.6 litre - (60 hp)						
Cpe	900	2900	4800	9600	16,800	24,000
Rds	1050	3350	5600	11,200	19,600	28,000
Cabr	1100	3500	5800	11,600	20,300	29,000
HdTp	1100	3500	5800	11,600	20,300	29,000
Model 356B, Super 90, 1.6 litre - (90 hp)						
Cpe	1000	3250	5400	10,800	18,900	27,000
Rds	1100	3500	5800	11,600	20,300	29,000
Cabr	1150	3700	6200	12,400	21,700	31,000
HdTp	1150	3700	6200	12,400	21,700	31,000
Model 356B, Carrera, 2.0 litre - (130 hp)						
Cpe	1500	4800	8000	16,000	28,000	40,000
Rds	1600	5050	8400	16,800	29,400	42,000
Cabr	1800	5750	9600	19,200	33,600	48,000
1962						
Model 356B, Standard 1.6 litre - (60 hp)						
Cpe	900	2900	4800	9600	16,800	24,000
HdTp	1100	3500	5800	11,600	20,300	29,000
Model 356C - (4-cyl) - (95 hp)						
Cpe SC	950	3000	5000	10,000	17,500	25,000
Rds	1000	3250	5400	10,800	18,900	27,000
Cabr SC	1100	3500	5800	11,600	20,300	29,000
Cabr	1100	3500	5800	11,600	20,300	29,000
Model 356B, Super 90, 1.6 litre - (90 hp)						
Cpe	1000	3250	5400	10,800	18,900	27,000
Rds	1100	3500	5800	11,600	20,300	29,000
Cabr	1150	3700	6200	12,400	21,700	31,000
HdTp	1150	3700	6200	12,400	21,700	31,000
Model 356B, Carrera 2, 2.0 litre - (130 hp)						
Cpe	1450	4700	7800	15,600	27,300	39,000
Rds	1600	5050	8400	16,800	29,400	42,000
Cabr	1750	5650	9400	18,800	32,900	47,000
1963						
Model 356C, Standard 1.6 litre - (75 hp)						
Cpe	850	2750	4600	9200	16,100	23,000
Cabr	1000	3100	5200	10,400	18,200	26,000
Model 356C, SC, 1.6 litre - (95 hp)						
Cpe	900	2900	4800	9600	16,800	24,000
Cabr	1000	3250	5400	10,800	18,900	27,000
Model 356C, Carrera 2, 2.0 litre - (130 hp)						
Cpe	1450	4700	7800	15,600	27,300	39,000
Cabr	1750	5650	9400	18,800	32,900	47,000
1964						
Model 356C, Standard 1.6 litre - (75 hp)						
Cpe	850	2750	4600	9200	16,100	23,000
Cabr	1000	3100	5200	10,400	18,200	26,000
Model 356C, SC, 1.6 litre - (95 hp)						
Cpe	900	2900	4800	9600	16,800	24,000
Cabr	1000	3250	5400	10,800	18,900	27,000
Model 356C, Carrera 2, 2.0 litre - (130 hp)						
Cpe	1450	4700	7800	15,600	27,300	39,000
Cabr	1750	5650	9400	18,800	32,900	47,000
1965						
Model 356C, 1.6 litre - (75 hp)						
Cpe	850	2750	4600	9200	16,100	23,000
Cabr	1000	3250	5400	10,800	18,900	27,000
Model 356SC, 1.6 litre - (95 hp)						
Cpe	900	2900	4800	9600	16,800	24,000
Cabr	1050	3350	5600	11,200	19,600	28,000
1966						
Model 912 - (4-cyl) - (90 hp)						
Cpe	600	1900	3200	6400	11,200	16,000
Model 911 - (6-cyl) - (130 hp)						
Cpe	700	2300	3800	7600	13,300	19,000
1967						
Model 912 - (4-cyl) - (90 hp)						
Cpe	450	1450	2400	4800	8400	12,000
Targa	550	1800	3000	6000	10,500	15,000
Model 911 - (6-cyl) - (110 hp)						
Cpe	700	2300	3800	7600	13,300	19,000
Targa	750	2400	4000	8000	14,000	20,000
Model 911S - (6-cyl) - (160 hp)						
Cpe	900	2900	4800	9600	16,800	24,000
Targa	1000	3100	5200	10,400	18,200	26,000
1968						
Model 912 - (4-cyl) - (90 hp)						
Cpe	450	1450	2400	4800	8400	12,000
Targa	550	1800	3000	6000	10,500	15,000
Model 911 - (6-cyl) - (130 hp)						
Cpe	700	2300	3800	7600	13,300	19,000
Targa	750	2400	4000	8000	14,000	20,000
Model 911L - (6-cyl) - (130 hp)						
Cpe	1050	3350	5600	11,200	19,600	28,000
Targa	800	2500	4200	8400	14,700	21,000
1969						
Model 912 - (4-cyl) - (90 hp)						
Cpe	450	1450	2400	4800	8400	12,000
Targa	550	1800	3000	6000	10,500	15,000
Model 911T - (6-cyl) - (110 hp)						
Cpe	700	2150	3600	7200	12,600	18,000
Targa	700	2300	3800	7600	13,300	19,000
Model 911E - (6-cyl) - (140 hp)						
Cpe	700	2300	3800	7600	13,300	19,000
Targa	750	2400	4000	8000	14,000	20,000
Model 911S - (6-cyl) - (170 hp)						
Cpe	850	2750	4600	9200	16,100	23,000
Targa	1000	3250	5400	10,800	18,900	27,000

	6	5	4	3	2	1
1970						
Model 914, 1.7 litre - (4-cyl) - (80 hp)						
Cpe/Targa	400	1200	2000	4000	7000	10,000
Model 914/6, 2.0 litre - (6-cyl) - (110 hp)						
Cpe/Targa	550	1800	3000	6000	10,500	15,000
Model 911T - (6-cyl) - (125 hp)						
Cpe	650	2050	3400	6800	11,900	17,000
Targa	700	2150	3600	7200	12,600	18,000
Model 911E - (6-cyl) - (155 hp)						
Cpe	700	2150	3600	7200	12,600	18,000
Targa	700	2300	3800	7600	13,300	19,000
Model 911S - (6-cyl) - (180 hp)						
Cpe	850	2750	4600	9200	16,100	23,000
Targa	1000	3250	5400	10,800	18,900	27,000
1971						
Model 914, 1.7 litre - (4-cyl) - (80 hp)						
Cpe/Targa	400	1200	2000	4000	7000	10,000
Model 914/6, 2 litre - (6-cyl) - (110 hp)						
Cpe/Targa	550	1800	3000	6000	10,500	15,000
Model 911T - (6-cyl) - (125 hp)						
Cpe	650	2050	3400	6800	11,900	17,000
Targa	700	2150	3600	7200	12,600	18,000
Model 911E - (6-cyl) - (155 hp)						
Cpe	700	2150	3600	7200	12,600	18,000
Targa	700	2300	3800	7600	13,300	19,000
Model 911S - (6-cyl) - (180 hp)						
Cpe	900	2900	4800	9600	16,800	24,000
Targa	1050	3350	5600	11,200	19,600	28,000
1972						
Model 914, 1.7 litre - (4-cyl) - (80 hp)						
Cpe/Targa	400	1200	2000	4000	7000	10,000
Model 911T - (6-cyl) - (130 hp)						
Cpe	700	2150	3600	7200	12,600	18,000
Targa	700	2300	3800	7600	13,300	19,000
Model 911E - (6-cyl) - (165 hp)						
Cpe	700	2300	3800	7600	13,300	19,000
Targa	750	2400	4000	8000	14,000	20,000
Model 911S - (6-cyl) - (190 hp)						
Cpe	900	2900	4800	9600	16,800	24,000
Targa	1050	3350	5600	11,200	19,600	28,000
1973						
Model 914, 1.8 litre - (4-cyl) - (76 hp)						
Cpe/Targa	400	1200	2000	4000	7000	10,000
Model 914, 2 litre - (4-cyl) - (95 hp)						
Cpe/Targa	450	1450	2400	4800	8400	12,000
Model 911T - (6-cyl) - (140 hp)						
Cpe	700	2150	3600	7200	12,600	18,000
Targa	700	2300	3800	7600	13,300	19,000
Model 911E - (6-cyl) - (165 hp)						
Cpe	700	2300	3800	7600	13,300	19,000
Targa	750	2400	4000	8000	14,000	20,000
Model 911S - (6-cyl) - (190 hp)						
Cpe	900	2900	4800	9600	16,800	24,000
Targa	1050	3350	5600	11,200	19,600	28,000
1974						
Model 914, 1.8 litre - (4-cyl) - (76 hp)						
Cpe/Targa	400	1200	2000	4000	7000	10,000
Model 914, 2 litre - (4-cyl) - (95 hp)						
Cpe/Targa	450	1450	2400	4800	8400	12,000
Model 911 - (6-cyl) - (150 hp)						
Cpe	700	2300	3800	7600	13,300	19,000
Targa	750	2400	4000	8000	14,000	20,000
Model 911S - (6-cyl) - (175 hp)						
Cpe	900	2900	4800	9600	16,800	24,000
Targa	1050	3350	5600	11,200	19,600	28,000
Model 911, Carrera - (6-cyl) (175 hp)						
Cpe	1150	3700	6200	12,400	21,700	31,000
Targa	1250	3950	6600	13,200	23,100	33,000
NOTE: Add 10 percent for RS. Add 20 percent for RSR.						
1975						
Model 914, 1.8 litre - (4-cyl) - (76 hp)						
Cpe/Targa	400	1200	2000	4000	7000	10,000
Model 914, 2 litre - (4-cyl) - (95 hp)						
Cpe/Targa	400	1300	2200	4400	7700	11,000
Model 911, 2 litre - (6-cyl) - (150 hp)						
Cpe	700	2300	3800	7600	13,300	19,000
Targa	750	2400	4000	8000	14,000	20,000
Model 911S - (6-cyl) - (175 hp)						
Cpe	900	2900	4800	9600	16,800	24,000
Targa	1050	3350	5600	11,200	19,600	28,000
Model 911, Carrera - (6-cyl) - (210 hp)						
Cpe	1200	3850	6400	12,800	22,400	32,000
Targa	1300	4200	7000	14,000	24,500	35,000
1976						
Model 914, 2 litre - (4-cyl) - (95 hp)						
Cpe/Targa	400	1300	2200	4400	7700	11,000
Model 912E - (4-cyl) - (90 hp)						
Cpe	650	2050	3400	6800	11,900	17,000
Model 911S - (6-cyl) - (165 hp)						
Cpe	950	3000	5000	10,000	17,500	25,000
Targa	1100	3500	5800	11,600	20,300	29,000
Model 930, Turbo & T. Carrera						
Cpe	1950	6250	10,400	20,800	36,400	52,000
1977						
Model 924 - (4-cyl) - (95 hp)						
Cpe	400	1200	2000	4000	7000	10,000
Model 911SC - (6-cyl) - (165 hp)						
Cpe	950	3000	5000	10,000	17,500	25,000
Targa	1050	3350	5600	11,200	19,600	28,000
Model 930 Turbo - (6-cyl) - (245 hp)						
Cpe	1950	6250	10,400	20,800	36,400	52,000
1978						
Model 924						
Cpe	400	1200	2000	4000	7000	10,000
Model 911SC						
Cpe	950	3000	5000	10,000	17,500	25,000
Cpe Targa	1050	3350	5600	11,200	19,600	28,000
Model 928						
Cpe	1250	3950	6600	13,200	23,100	33,000
Model 930						
Cpe	1950	6250	10,400	20,800	36,400	52,000
1979						
Model 924						
Cpe	500	1550	2600	5200	9100	13,000
Model 911SC						
Cpe	1000	3100	5200	10,400	18,200	26,000
Targa	1100	3500	5800	11,600	20,300	29,000
Model 928						
Cpe	1200	3850	6400	12,800	22,400	32,000
1980						
Model 924						
Cpe	400	1300	2200	4400	7700	11,000
Cpe (Turbo)	500	1550	2600	5200	9100	13,000
Model 911SC						
Cpe	1000	3250	5400	10,800	18,900	27,000
Cpe Targa	1100	3500	5800	11,600	20,300	29,000
Model 928						
Cpe	1150	3600	6000	12,000	21,000	30,000
1981						
Model 924						
Cpe	400	1200	2000	4000	7000	10,000
Cpe (Turbo)	450	1450	2400	4800	8400	12,000
Model 911SC						
Cpe	1000	3100	5200	10,400	18,200	26,000
Cpe Targa	1050	3350	5600	11,200	19,600	28,000
Model 928						
Cpe	1150	3600	6000	12,000	21,000	30,000
1982						
Model 924						
Cpe	400	1200	2000	4000	7000	10,000
Cpe (Turbo)	400	1300	2200	4400	7700	11,000
Model 911SC						
Cpe	950	3000	5000	10,000	17,500	25,000
Cpe Targa	1000	3250	5400	10,800	18,900	27,000
Model 928						
Cpe	1100	3500	5800	11,600	20,300	29,000
1983						
Model 944						
Cpe	450	950	2100	4700	6600	9400
Model 911SC						
Cpe	400	1200	2000	4000	7000	10,000
Cpe Targa	900	2950	4900	9800	17,200	24,500
Conv	1000	3200	5300	10,600	18,600	26,500
Model 928						
Cpe	1100	3500	5800	11,600	20,300	29,000
1984						
Model 944						
2d Cpe	500	1550	2600	5200	9100	13,000
Model 911						
2d Cpe	550	1800	3000	6000	10,500	15,000
2d Cpe Targa	1200	3850	6400	12,800	22,400	32,000
2d Conv	1350	4300	7200	14,400	25,200	36,000
Model 928S						
2d Cpe	1550	4900	8200	16,400	28,700	41,000
1985						
Model 944						
2d Cpe	550	1700	2800	5600	9800	14,000
Model 911						
2d Cpe (Turbo)	700	2150	3600	7200	12,600	18,000
2d Cpe Targa	1300	4100	6800	13,600	23,800	34,000
2d Cpe Conv	1450	4550	7600	15,200	26,600	38,000
Model 928S						
2d Cpe	1600	5150	8600	17,200	30,100	43,000
1986						
Model 944						
2d Cpe	550	1800	3000	6000	10,500	15,000
2d Cpe (Turbo)	750	2400	4000	8000	14,000	20,000
Model 911						
2d Cpe Carrera	1300	4200	7000	14,000	24,500	35,000
2d Cpe Targa	1350	4300	7200	14,400	25,200	36,000
2d Cpe Conv	1500	4800	8000	16,000	28,000	40,000
Model 928S						
2d Cpe	1700	5400	9000	18,000	31,500	45,000
1987						
Model 924S						
2d Cpe	600	1900	3200	6400	11,200	16,000
Model 944						
2d Cpe	850	2650	4400	8800	15,400	22,000
2d S Cpe	850	2750	4600	9200	16,100	23,000
2d Cpe (Turbo)	1000	3100	5200	10,400	18,200	26,000
Model 911						
2d Cpe Carrera	1450	4550	7600	15,200	26,600	38,000
2d Cpe Targa	1450	4700	7800	15,600	27,300	39,000
2d Cpe Conv	1600	5150	8600	17,200	30,100	43,000
Model 928S4						
2d Cpe	1850	5900	9800	19,600	34,300	49,000
1988						
Model 924S						
2d Cpe	750	2400	4000	8000	14,000	20,000
Model 944						
2d Cpe	1000	3100	5200	10,400	18,200	26,000
2d S Cpe	1000	3250	5400	10,800	18,900	27,000
2d Cpe (Turbo)	1150	3600	6000	12,000	21,000	30,000
Model 911						
2d Cpe Carrera	1550	4900	8200	16,400	28,700	41,000
2d Cpe Targa	1600	5050	8400	16,800	29,400	42,000
2d Cpe Conv	1750	5500	9200	18,400	32,200	46,000
Model 928S4						
2d Cpe	1950	6250	10,400	20,800	36,400	52,000
1989						
Model 944						
2d Cpe	1150	3700	6200	12,400	21,700	31,000
2d Cpe (Turbo)	1450	4550	7600	15,200	26,600	38,000
2d S2 Cpe	1300	4200	7000	14,000	24,500	35,000
2d S2 Conv	2250	7200	12,000	24,000	42,000	60,000
Model 911						
2d Carrera	1800	5750	9600	19,200	33,600	48,000
2d Targa	1850	5900	9800	19,600	34,300	49,000
2d Conv	2050	6600	11,000	22,000	38,500	55,000
Model 928						
2d Cpe	2500	7900	13,200	26,400	46,200	66,000

RENAULT

1946-48						
Juvaquatre - (4-cyl) - (760cc)						
4CV - (4-cyl) - (83" wb) - (760cc)						
4d Sed	350	750	1450	3300	4900	7000

	6	5	4	3	2	1
1949						
4CV - (4-cyl) - (83" wb) - (760cc)						
Std 4d Sed	350	750	1450	3300	4900	7000
Grande Luxe 4d Sed	350	750	1450	3300	4900	7000
1950						
4CV - (4-cyl) - (83" wb) - (760cc)						
Grande Luxe 4d Sed	350	750	1450	3300	4900	7000
1951						
4CV (Sliding Windows)						
(4-cyl) - (83" wb) - (747cc)						
R-1060 4d Sed	350	750	1450	3300	4900	7000
4CV Luxe (Rolldown Windows)						
R-1062 4d Sed	350	750	1450	3300	4900	7000
4CV Super Grande Luxe (Rolldown Windows)						
R-1062 4d Sed	350	750	1450	3300	4900	7000
R-1062 4d Conv	350	775	1500	3750	5250	7500
1952						
4CV Luxe - (4-cyl) - (83" wb) - (747cc)						
R-1062 4d Sed	350	750	1450	3300	4900	7000
4CV Super Grande Luxe						
R-1062 4d Sed	350	750	1450	3300	4900	7000
R-1062 4d Conv	350	775	1500	3750	5250	7500
NOTE: All models had roll-up windows.						
1953-54						
4CV Luxe (Sport Line)						
(4-cyl) - (83" wb) - (747cc)						
R-1062 4d Sed	350	750	1450	3300	4900	7000
4CV Super Grande Luxe (Sport Line)						
(4-cyl) - (83" wb) - (747cc)						
R-1062 4d Conv	350	775	1500	3750	5250	7500
Fregate - (4-cyl) - (110.25" wb) - (1997cc)						
R-1100 4d Sed	200	500	1100	1900	3500	5000
1955-56						
4CV Luxe (Sport Line)						
(4-cyl) - (82.7" wb) - (747cc)						
R-1062 4d Sed	350	750	1450	3300	4900	7000
4CV Super Grande Luxe						
(4-cyl) - (82.7" wb) - (747cc)						
R-1062 4d Conv	350	775	1500	3750	5250	7500
1957-59						
4CV (Sport Line)						
(4-cyl) - (82.7" wb) - (747cc)						
R-1062 4d Sed	350	750	1450	3300	4900	7000
Dauphine - (4-cyl) - (89" wb) - (845cc)						
R-1090 4d Sed	150	400	1000	1650	3150	4500
1960-62						
4CV (1960-61)						
(4-cyl) - (83" wb) - (747cc)						
R-1062 4d Sed	350	750	1450	3300	4900	7000
4d Sed S/R	350	750	1450	3300	4900	7000
Dauphine - (4-cyl) - (89" wb) - (845cc)						
R-1090 4d Sed	150	400	1000	1650	3150	4500
4d Sed S/R	150	400	1000	1650	3150	4500
Gordini (1961-62)						
(4-cyl) - (89" wb) - (845cc)						
R-1091A 4d Spt Sed	200	500	1100	1900	3500	5000
Caravella R-1092 - (4-cyl) - (89" wb) - (845cc)						
2d Conv	350	750	1450	3300	4900	7000
2d Cpe	350	750	1450	3300	4900	7000
2d HdTp Conv	350	750	1450	3300	4900	7000
1963-66						
Dauphine - (4-cyl) - (89" wb) - (845cc)						
R-1090 4d Sed	150	400	1000	1650	3150	4500
Caravella S, 1963 - (4-cyl) - (89" wb) - (956cc)						
R-1133 2d Conv	350	750	1450	3300	4900	7000
R-1131 2d Cpe	350	750	1450	3300	4900	7000
2d HdTp Cpe	350	750	1450	3300	4900	7000
Caravella 1964-66 - (4-cyl) - (89" wb)						
R-1133 2d Conv	350	750	1450	3300	4900	7000
R-1131 2d Cpe	350	750	1450	3300	4900	7000
R8 - (4-cyl) - (89" wb) - (956cc)						
R-1130 4d Sed	125	250	750	1150	2450	3500
R8 1100, 1964-66 - (4-cyl) - (89" wb) - (1108cc)						
R-1132 4d Sed	125	250	750	1150	2450	3500
R8 Gordini, 1965-66 - (4-cyl) - (89" wb)						
R-1134 4d Sed	150	400	1000	1650	3150	4500
1967-68						
10, R-10 - (4-cyl) - (89" wb) - (1108cc)						
R-1190 4d Sed	125	250	750	1150	2450	3500
1969-70						
10, 1969 R-10 - (4-cyl) - (89" wb) - (1108cc)						
R-1190 4d Sed	125	250	750	1150	2450	3500
10, 1970 R-10 - (4-cyl) - (89" wb) - (1289cc)						
4d Sed	150	350	950	1350	2800	4000
16, 1970 R-16 - (4-cyl) - (105.8" wb) - (1565cc) - (FWD)						
R-1152 4d Sed Wag	150	350	950	1350	2800	4000
1971-75						
R-10, 1971 only - (4-cyl) - (89" wb) - (1289cc)						
4d Sed	125	250	750	1150	2450	3500
R-12, 1972-up - (4-cyl) - (96" wb) - (1565cc) - (FWD)						
4d Sed	150	350	950	1350	2800	4000
4d Sta Wag	150	350	950	1350	2800	4000
R-15, 1972-up - (4-cyl) - (96" wb) - (1647cc) - (FWD)						
2d Cpe	150	350	950	1350	2800	4000
R-16, 1971-72 only - (4-cyl) - (105.8" wb) - (1565cc) - (FWD)						
4d Sed	150	350	950	1350	2800	4000
R-17, 1972-up - (4-cyl) - (96" wb) - (1565cc-1647cc) - (FWD)						
2d Spt Cpe	200	500	1100	1900	3500	5000
1976-80						
R-5, 1976 - (4-cyl) - (94.6-95.8" wb) - (1289cc) - (FWD)						
R-5TL 2d HBk	150	350	950	1350	2800	4000
R-5GTL 2d HBk	150	350	950	1350	2800	4000
LeCar, 1977-up - (4-cyl) - (1289cc-1397cc) - (FWD)						
TL 2d HBk	150	350	950	1350	2800	4000
GTL 2d HBk	150	350	950	1350	2800	4000
R-12, 1976-77 only - (4-cyl) - (96" wb) - (1647cc) - (FWD)						
TL 4d Sed	125	250	750	1150	2450	3500
GTL 4d Sed	125	250	750	1150	2450	3500
R-12 4d Sta Wag	150	300	900	1250	2650	3800
R-15, 1976 only - (4-cyl) - (96" wb) - (1647cc) - (FWD)						
TL 2d Cpe	125	250	750	1150	2450	3500
R-17 - (4-cyl) - (96" wb) - (1647cc) - (FWD)						
TL 2d Cpe/Conv	200	500	1100	1900	3500	5000
Gordini 2d Cpe/Conv	200	600	1200	2200	3850	5500

	6	5	4	3	2	1
1981						
LeCar - (4-cyl) - (95.2" wb) - (1397cc) - (FWD)						
2d HBk	150	350	950	1350	2800	4000
DeL 2d HBk	150	350	950	1350	2800	4000
DeL 4d HBk	150	350	950	1350	2800	4000
18i - (4-cyl) - (96.1" wb) - (1647cc) - (FWD)						
4d Sed	150	350	950	1350	2800	4000
4d Sta Wag	150	350	950	1350	2800	4000
DeL 4d Sed	150	350	950	1350	2800	4000
DeL 4d Sta Wag	150	350	950	1350	2800	4000
1982						
LeCar - (4-cyl) - (95.2" wb) - (1397cc) - (FWD)						
2d HBk	150	350	950	1350	2800	4000
DeL 2d HBk	150	350	950	1350	2800	4000
DeL 4d HBk	150	350	950	1350	2800	4000
Fuego - (4-cyl) - (96.1" wb) - (1647cc) - (FWD)						
2d Cpe	200	500	1100	1900	3500	5000
18i - (4-cyl) - (96.1" wb) - (1647cc) - (FWD)						
4d Sed	150	350	950	1350	2800	4000
4d Sta Wag	150	350	950	1350	2800	4000
DeL 4d Sed	150	350	950	1350	2800	4000
DeL 4d Sta Wag	150	350	950	1350	2800	4000
1983						
LeCar - (4-cyl) - (95.2" wb) - (1397cc) - (FWD)						
2d HBk	150	350	950	1350	2800	4000
DeL 2d HBk	150	350	950	1350	2800	4000
DeL 4d HBk	150	350	950	1350	2800	4000
Fuego - (4-cyl) - (96.1" wb) - (1647cc) - (FWD)						
2d Cpe	200	500	1100	1900	3500	5000
Fuego Turbo - (4-cyl) - (96.1" wb) - (1565cc) - (FWD)						
2d Cpe	200	600	1200	2200	3850	5500
18i - (4-cyl) - (96.1" wb) - (1647cc) - (FWD)						
DeL 4d Sed	150	350	950	1350	2800	4000
DeL 4d Sta Wag	150	350	950	1350	2800	4000
1984						
Fuego - (4-cyl) - (96.1" wb) - (2165cc) - (FWD)						
2d Cpe	200	500	1100	1900	3500	5000
Fuego Turbo - (4-cyl) - (96.1" wb) - (1565cc) - (FWD)						
2d Cpe	200	600	1200	2200	3850	5500
Sportwagon - (4-cyl) - (96.1" wb) - (2165cc) - (FWD)						
4d Sta Wag	150	350	950	1350	2800	4000
1985						
Fuego - (4-cyl) - (96.1" wb) - (2165cc) - (FWD)						
2d Cpe	200	600	1200	2200	3850	5500
Sportwagon - (4-cyl) - (96.1" wb) - (2165cc) - (FWD)						
4d Sta Wag	150	350	950	1350	2800	4000

ROLLS-ROYCE

1947-1951						
Silver Wraith-(6-cyl)-(127" or 133" wb-1951)-(4257cc)						
Freestone & Webb						
Cpe	1900	6100	10,200	20,400	35,700	51,000
Limo	1400	4450	7400	14,800	25,900	37,000
Saloon	1150	3700	6200	12,400	21,700	31,000
Spt Saloon	1250	3950	6600	13,200	23,100	33,000
Hooper						
DHC	2950	9350	15,600	31,200	54,600	78,000
Treviot	1400	4450	7400	14,800	25,900	37,000
Treviot II	1400	4500	7500	15,000	26,300	37,500
Treviot III	1450	4550	7600	15,200	26,600	38,000
H.J. Mulliner						
Sedanca DeV	2550	8150	13,600	27,200	47,600	68,000
Tr Limo	1450	4550	7600	15,200	26,600	38,000
Park Ward						
Saloon	1100	3500	5800	11,600	20,300	29,000
James Young						
Limo	1350	4300	7200	14,400	25,200	36,000
Saloon	1150	3700	6200	12,400	21,700	31,000
1949-1951						
Silver Dawn - (6-cyl) - (120" wb) - (4257cc)						
Std Steel Saloon	1150	3700	6200	12,400	21,700	31,000
Farina						
Spl Saloon	1900	6100	10,200	20,400	35,700	51,000
Freestone & Webb						
Saloon	1350	4300	7200	14,400	25,200	36,000
Park Ward						
DHC	2100	6700	11,200	22,400	39,200	56,000
FHC	1550	4900	8200	16,400	28,700	41,000
1950-1956						
Phantom IV - (8-cyl) - (145" wb) - (5675cc)						
Park Ward Limo	5800	18,600	31,000	62,000	108,500	155,000
1951-1952						
Silver Wraith - (6-cyl) - (127" wb) - (4566cc)						
Freestone & Webb						
Cpe	1350	4300	7200	14,400	25,200	36,000
1951-1955						
Silver Wraith - (6-cyl) - (133" wb) - (4566cc)						
Freestone & Webb						
Spt Saloon	1300	4200	7000	14,000	24,500	35,000
Hooper						
Tr Limo	1200	3850	6400	12,800	22,400	32,000
H.J. Mulliner						
Tr Limo	1300	4200	7000	14,000	24,500	35,000
Park Ward						
Limo	1300	4100	6800	13,600	23,800	34,000
1951-1955						
Silver Dawn - (6-cyl) - (120" wb) - (4566cc)						
Std Steel Saloon	1250	3950	6600	13,200	23,100	33,000
Park Ward						
DHC	2100	6700	11,200	22,400	39,200	56,000
1955-1959						
Silver Cloud - (6-cyl) - (123" or 127" wb - 1957) - (4887cc)						
Std Steel Saloon	1100	3500	5800	11,600	20,300	29,000
H.J. Mulliner						
DHC	2950	9350	15,600	31,200	54,600	78,000
Park Ward						
Saloon (LWB)	1150	3700	6200	12,400	21,700	31,000
James Young						
Saloon	1750	5500	9200	18,400	32,200	46,000

NOTE: Deduct 20 percent for Right-Hand Drive.

1955-1959
Silver Wraith - (6-cyl) - (133" wb) - (4887cc)

	6	5	4	3	2	1
Hooper						
Limo (LWB)	1450	4550	7600	15,200	26,600	38,000
Saloon	1350	4300	7200	14,400	25,200	36,000
H.J. Mulliner						
Tr Limo	1550	4900	8200	16,400	28,700	41,000
Park Ward						
Limo	1300	4100	6800	13,600	23,800	34,000
Saloon	1200	3850	6400	12,800	22,400	32,000

NOTE: Deduct 20 percent for Right-Hand Drive.

1959-1962
Silver Cloud II - (V-8) - (123" or 127" wb - after 1960) - (6230cc)

	6	5	4	3	2	1
Std Steel Saloon	1150	3600	6000	12,000	21,000	30,000
H.J. Mulliner						
DHC	3850	12,250	20,400	40,800	71,400	102,000
Radford						
Countryman	1550	4900	8200	16,400	28,700	41,000
James Young						
Limo (LWB)	1900	6100	10,200	20,400	35,700	51,000

NOTE: Deduct 20 percent for Right-Hand Drive.

1960-1968
Phantom V - (V-8) - (144" wb) - (6230cc)

	6	5	4	3	2	1
H.J. Mulliner-Park Ward						
Landaulette	5800	18,600	31,000	62,000	108,500	155,000
Limo	2350	7450	12,400	24,800	43,400	62,000
Park Ward						
Limo	1750	5500	9200	18,400	32,200	46,000
James Young						
Limo	2700	8650	14,400	28,800	50,400	72,000
Sedanca DeV	5800	18,600	31,000	62,000	108,500	155,000

NOTE: Deduct 20 percent for Right-Hand Drive.

1962-1966
Silver Cloud III - (V-8) - (123" or 127" wb) - (6230cc)

	6	5	4	3	2	1
Std Steel Saloon	1150	3700	6200	12,400	21,700	31,000
H.J. Mulliner						
2d Saloon	1150	3600	6000	12,000	21,000	30,000
DHC	4800	15,350	25,600	51,200	89,600	128,000
Flying Spur	2950	9350	15,600	31,200	54,600	78,000

NOTE: Deduct 20 percent for Right-Hand Drive.

	6	5	4	3	2	1
James Young						
4d Spt Saloon	1000	3100	5200	10,400	18,200	26,000
Cpe	1350	4300	7200	14,400	25,200	36,000
Tr Limo (SWB)	2100	6700	11,200	22,400	39,200	56,000
Tr Limo (LWB)	2550	8150	13,600	27,200	47,600	68,000
Park Ward						
DHC	1900	6100	10,200	20,400	35,700	51,000
Limo (LWB)	2100	6700	11,200	22,400	39,200	56,000

NOTE: Deduct 20 percent for Right-Hand Drive.

1965-1969
Silver Shadow - (V-8) - (119.5" or 123.5" wb) - (6230cc)

	6	5	4	3	2	1
Std Steel Saloon	1000	3100	5200	10,400	18,200	26,000
Saloon (LWB)	1100	3500	5800	11,600	20,300	29,000
Mulliner-Park Ward						
2d Saloon	1150	3700	6200	12,400	21,700	31,000
DHC	1300	4100	6800	13,600	23,800	34,000
James Young						
2d Saloon	1150	3700	6200	12,400	21,700	31,000

NOTE: Deduct 20 percent for Right-Hand Drive.

1968-1977
Phantom VI - (V-8) - (145" wb) - (6230cc)

	6	5	4	3	2	1
Lan	3300	10,550	17,600	35,200	61,600	88,000
Limo	2950	9350	15,600	31,200	54,600	78,000
Mulliner-Park Ward						
Laudaulette	6750	21,600	36,000	72,000	126,000	180,000

NOTE: Deduct 20 percent for Right-Hand Drive.

1970-1976
Silver Shadow - (V-8) - (119.5" or 123.5" wb) - (6750cc)

	6	5	4	3	2	1
Std Steel Saloon	1500	4750	7900	15,800	27,700	39,500
Saloon (LWB)	1650	5300	8800	17,600	30,800	44,000
Mulliner-Park Ward						
2d Saloon	1900	6100	10,200	20,400	35,700	51,000
DHC	2350	7450	12,400	24,800	43,400	62,000

NOTE: Deduct 20 percent for Right-Hand Drive.

1971-1977
Corniche - (V-8) - (119" wb) - (6750cc)

	6	5	4	3	2	1
2d Saloon	2100	6700	11,200	22,400	39,200	56,000
Conv	2800	8900	14,800	29,600	51,800	74,000

NOTE: Deduct 20 percent for Right-Hand Drive.

1975-1978
(V-8) - (108.5" wb) - (6750cc)

	6	5	4	3	2	1
Camarque	1750	5500	9200	18,400	32,200	46,000

NOTE: Deduct 20 percent for Right-Hand Drive.

1977-1978
(V-8) - (120" wb) - (6750cc)

	6	5	4	3	2	1
Silver Shadow II	1500	4850	8100	16,200	28,400	40,500
(V-8) - (123.5" wb) - (6750cc)						
Silver Wraith II	1700	5400	9000	18,000	31,500	45,000

NOTE: Add 10 percent for factory sunroof.
NOTE: Deduct 20 percent for Right-Hand Drive.

1979

	6	5	4	3	2	1
4d Silver Spirit	2350	7450	12,400	24,800	43,400	62,000
4d Silver Spur	2550	8150	13,600	27,200	47,600	68,000
2d Corniche Conv	3150	10,100	16,800	33,600	58,800	84,000
2d Camargue	2400	7700	12,800	25,600	44,800	64,000
4d Phantom VI	6550	21,000	35,000	70,000	122,500	175,000
4d Silver Shadow	2250	7200	12,000	24,000	42,000	60,000
4d Silver Wraith	2350	7450	12,400	24,800	43,400	62,000

1980

	6	5	4	3	2	1
4d Silver Spirit	2350	7450	12,400	24,800	43,400	62,000
4d Silver Spur	2550	8150	13,600	27,200	47,600	68,000
2d Corniche Conv	3150	10,100	16,800	33,600	58,800	84,000
2d Camarque	2400	7700	12,800	25,600	44,800	64,000
4d Phantom VI	6550	21,000	35,000	70,000	122,500	175,000
4d Silver Shadow	2250	7200	12,000	24,000	42,000	60,000
4d Silver Wraith	2350	7450	12,400	24,800	43,400	62,000

1981

	6	5	4	3	2	1
4d Silver Spirit	2350	7450	12,400	24,800	43,400	62,000
4d Silver Spur	2550	8150	13,600	27,200	47,600	68,000
2d Corniche Conv	3150	10,100	16,800	33,600	58,800	84,000
2d Camarque	2400	7700	12,800	25,600	44,800	64,000
4d Phantom VI	6550	21,000	35,000	70,000	122,500	175,000

1982

	6	5	4	3	2	1
4d Silver Spirit	2350	7450	12,400	24,800	43,400	62,000
4d Silver Spur	2550	8150	13,600	27,200	47,600	68,000
2d Corniche Conv	3250	10,300	17,200	34,400	60,200	86,000
2d Camarque	2500	7900	13,200	26,400	46,200	66,000
4d Phantom VI	6550	21,000	35,000	70,000	122,500	175,000

1983

	6	5	4	3	2	1
4d Silver Spirit	2350	7450	12,400	24,800	43,400	62,000
4d Silver Spur	2550	8150	13,600	27,200	47,600	68,000
2d Corniche Conv	3250	10,300	17,200	34,400	60,200	86,000
2d Camarque	2500	7900	13,200	26,400	46,200	66,000
4d Phantom VI	6550	21,000	35,000	70,000	122,500	175,000

SAAB

1950-1952
(2-cyl) - (97.2" wb) - (764cc)

	6	5	4	3	2	1
92 2d Sed	200	650	1250	2400	4200	6000

1953-1955
(2-cyl) - (97.2" wb) - (764cc)

	6	5	4	3	2	1
92B 2d Sed	200	650	1250	2400	4200	6000

1956-1957
(3-cyl) - (98" wb) - (748cc)

	6	5	4	3	2	1
93 2d Sed	200	500	1100	1900	3500	5000

1958
(3-cyl) - (98" wb) - (748cc)

	6	5	4	3	2	1
93B 2d Sed	200	500	1100	1900	3500	5000
GT 750 2d Sed	200	600	1200	2200	3850	5500

1959
(3-cyl) - (98" wb) - (748cc)

	6	5	4	3	2	1
93B 2d Sed	200	500	1100	1900	3500	5000
GT 750 2d Sed	200	600	1200	2200	3850	5500
(3-cyl) - (98" wb) - (841cc)						
95 2d Sta Wag	200	550	1150	2100	3700	5300

1960
(3-cyl) - (98" wb) - (748cc)

	6	5	4	3	2	1
93F 2d Sed	200	500	1100	1900	3500	5000
GT 750 2d Sed	200	550	1150	2100	3700	5300
(3-cyl) - (98" wb) - (841cc)						
96 2d Sed	150	350	950	1350	2800	4000
95 2d Sta Wag	150	400	1000	1650	3150	4500

1961
(3-cyl) - (98" wb) - (748cc)

	6	5	4	3	2	1
GT 750 2d Sed	200	650	1250	2400	4200	6000
(3-cyl) - (98" wb) - (841cc)						
96 2d Sed	150	350	950	1350	2800	4000
95 2d Sta Wag	150	400	1000	1650	3150	4500

1962
(3-cyl) - (98" wb) - (748cc)

	6	5	4	3	2	1
GT 750 2d Sed	200	650	1250	2400	4200	6000
(3-cyl) - (98" wb) - (841cc)						
96 2d Sed	150	350	950	1350	2800	4000
95 2d Sta Wag	150	400	1000	1650	3150	4500
2d Spt Sed	200	500	1100	1900	3500	5000

1963
(3-cyl) - (98" wb) - (841cc)

	6	5	4	3	2	1
96 2d Sed	150	350	950	1350	2800	4000
95 2d Sta Wag	150	400	1000	1650	3150	4500
850 Spt/GT 2d Sed	200	600	1200	2200	3850	5500

1964
(3-cyl) - (98" wb) - (841cc)

	6	5	4	3	2	1
96 2d Sed	150	350	950	1350	2800	4000
95 2d Sta Wag	150	400	1000	1650	3150	4500
850 Spt/Monte Carlo 2d Sed	200	600	1200	2200	3850	5500

1965
(3-cyl) - (98" wb) - (841cc)

	6	5	4	3	2	1
96 2d Sed	150	350	950	1350	2800	4000
95 2d Sta Wag	150	400	1000	1650	3150	4500
850 Spt/Monte Carlo 2d Sed	200	600	1200	2200	3850	5500

1966
(3-cyl) - (98" wb) - (841cc)

	6	5	4	3	2	1
96 2d Sed	150	400	1000	1650	3150	4500
96 Spl 2d Sed	150	400	1000	1650	3150	4500
95 2d Sta Wag	150	400	1000	1650	3150	4500
850 Monte Carlo 2d Sed	200	600	1200	2200	3850	5500
(3-cyl) - (84.6" wb) - (841cc)						
Sonett II	350	750	1450	3300	4900	7000

1967
(3-cyl) - (98" wb) - (841cc)

	6	5	4	3	2	1
96 Shrike 2d Sed	150	350	950	1350	2800	4000
95 2d Sta Wag	150	350	950	1350	2800	4000
850 Monte Carlo 2d Sed	150	400	1000	1650	3150	4500
(3-cyl) - (84.6" wb) - (841cc)						
Sonett II	350	750	1450	3300	4900	7000
(V-4) - (98" wb) - (1498cc)						
96 2d Sed	150	350	950	1350	2800	4000
95 2d Sta Wag	150	400	1000	1650	3150	4500
Monte Carlo 2d Sed	200	600	1200	2200	3850	5500
(V-4) - (84.6" wb) - (1498cc)						
Sonett	350	750	1450	3300	4900	7000

1968
(3-cyl) - (98" wb) - (841cc) - (816cc Shrike)

	6	5	4	3	2	1
96 Shrike 2d Sed	150	350	950	1350	2800	4000
96 2d Sed	150	350	950	1450	2900	4100
95 Shrike 2d Sta Wag	150	350	950	1350	2800	4000
95 2d Sta Wag	150	350	950	1450	2900	4100
(V-4) - (98" wb) - (1498cc)						
96 2d Sed	150	350	950	1350	2800	4000
96 DeL 2d Sed	150	350	950	1350	2800	4000
95 2d Sta Wag	150	350	950	1350	2800	4000
95 C 2d Sta Wag	150	400	1000	1650	3150	4500
Monte Carlo 2d Sed	200	600	1200	2200	3850	5500
(V-4) - (84.6" wb) - (1498cc)						
Sonett	350	750	1450	3300	4900	7000

1969
(V-4) - (98" wb) - (1498cc)

	6	5	4	3	2	1
96 2d Sed	150	350	950	1350	2800	4000
96 DeL 2d Sed	150	350	950	1350	2800	4000
95 2d Sta Wag	150	400	1000	1650	3150	4500

	6	5	4	3	2	1
(V-4) - (84.6" wb) - (1498cc)						
Sonett	350	750	1450	3300	4900	7000
(4-cyl) - (97.4" wb) - (1709cc)						
99 2d Sed	150	350	950	1350	2800	4000
1970						
(V-4) - (98" wb) - (1498cc)						
96 2d Sed	150	350	950	1350	2800	4000
95 2d Sta Wag	150	400	1000	1650	3150	4500
(V-4) - (84.6" wb)						
Sonett III	350	775	1500	3750	5250	7500
(4-cyl) - (97.4" wb) - (1709cc)						
99 2d Sed	150	350	950	1350	2800	4000
99 4d Sed	150	350	950	1350	2800	4000
1971						
(V-4) - (98" wb) - (1698cc)						
96 2d Sed	150	350	950	1350	2800	4000
95 2d Sta Wag	150	400	1000	1650	3150	4500
(V-4) - (84.6" wb) - (1698cc)						
Sonett III	350	775	1500	3750	5250	7500
(4-cyl) - (97.4" wb) - (1709cc)						
99 2d Sed	150	350	950	1350	2800	4000
99 4d Sed	150	400	1000	1650	3150	4500
1972						
(V-4) - (98" wb) - (1698cc)						
96 2d Sed	150	350	950	1350	2800	4000
95 2d Sta Wag	150	400	1000	1650	3150	4500
(V-4) - (84.6" wb) - (1698cc)						
Sonett III	350	775	1500	3750	5250	7500
(4-cyl) - (97.4" wb) - (1850/1985cc)						
99 2d Sed	150	350	950	1350	2800	4000
99EMS 2d Sed	150	400	1000	1650	3150	4500
99 4d Sed	150	350	950	1350	2800	4000
1973						
(V-4) - (98" wb) - (1698cc)						
96	150	350	950	1350	2800	4000
95 2d Sta Wag	150	400	1000	1650	3150	4500
(V-4) - (84.6" wb) - (1698cc)						
Sonett III	350	775	1500	3750	5250	7500
(4-cyl) - (97.4" wb) - (1850/1985cc)						
99X7 2d Sed	150	350	950	1350	2800	4000
99L 2d Sed	150	350	950	1350	2800	4000
99L 4d Sed	150	350	950	1350	2800	4000
99EMS 2d Sed	150	400	1000	1650	3150	4500
1974						
(V-4) - (98" wb) - (1698cc)						
96 2d Sed	150	350	950	1350	2800	4000
95 2d Sta Wag	150	400	1000	1650	3150	4500
(V-4) - (84.6" wb) - (1698cc)						
Sonett III	200	675	1300	2600	4400	6300
(4-cyl) - (97.4" wb) - (1985cc)						
99X7 2d Sed	150	350	950	1350	2800	4000
99L 2d Sed	150	350	950	1350	2800	4000
99L 4d Sed	150	350	950	1350	2800	4000
99L 3d Combi Cpe	150	350	950	1350	2800	4000
99EMS 2d Sed	150	400	1000	1550	3050	4300
1975						
(V-4) - (98" wb) - (1498cc)						
96 2d Sed	150	350	950	1350	2800	4000
95 2d Sta Wag	150	400	1000	1650	3150	4500
(4-cyl) - (97.4" wb) - (1985cc)						
99 2d Sed	150	350	950	1350	2800	4000
99L 2d Sed	150	400	1000	1650	3150	4500
99L 4d Sed	150	400	1000	1650	3150	4500
99L 3d Combi Cpe	150	400	1000	1650	3150	4500
99EMS 2d Sed	200	500	1100	1900	3500	5000
1976						
(4-cyl) - (97.4" wb) - (1985cc)						
99L 2d Sed	150	350	950	1350	2800	4000
99GL 2d Sed	150	400	1000	1650	3150	4500
99GL 4d Sed	150	400	1000	1650	3150	4500
99GL 3d Combi Cpe	150	400	1000	1650	3150	4500
99GL 5d Combi Cpe	150	400	1000	1650	3150	4500
99EMS 2d Sed	200	500	1100	1900	3500	5000
99GLE 4d Sed	150	450	1050	1800	3300	4800
1977						
(4-cyl) - (97.4" wb) - (1985cc)						
99L 2d Sed	150	350	950	1350	2800	4000
99GL 2d Sed	150	400	1000	1650	3150	4500
99GL 4d Sed	150	400	1000	1650	3150	4500
99GL 3d Combi Cpe	150	400	1000	1650	3150	4500
99GL 5d Combi Cpe	150	400	1000	1650	3150	4500
99EMS 2d Sed	200	500	1100	1900	3500	5000
99GLE 4d Sed	150	400	1000	1650	3150	4500
1978						
(4-cyl) - (97.4" wb) - (1985cc)						
99L 2d Sed	150	350	950	1350	2800	4000
99L 4d Sed	150	350	950	1350	2800	4000
99L 3d Combi Cpe	150	400	1000	1650	3150	4500
99GL 2d Sed	150	350	950	1350	2800	4000
99GL 4d Sed	150	350	950	1350	2800	4000
99GL 3d Combi Cpe	150	400	1000	1650	3150	4500
99GL 5d Combi Cpe	150	400	1000	1650	3150	4500
99EMS 2d Sed	150	400	1000	1650	3150	4500
99EMS 3d Combi Cpe	150	450	1050	1750	3250	4700
99GLE 5d Combi Cpe	150	450	1050	1750	3250	4700
99 3d Combi Cpe (Turbo)	200	550	1150	2000	3600	5200
1979						
99GL 2d Sed	200	500	1100	1900	3500	5000
900GL 2d HBk	200	500	1100	1900	3500	5000
900GLE 4d HBk	200	600	1200	2200	3850	5500
900EMS 2d HBk	200	650	1250	2400	4200	6000
900 2d HBk (Turbo)	200	650	1250	2400	4200	6000
900 4d HBk (Turbo)	200	650	1250	2400	4200	6000
1980						
99GL 2d Sed	200	500	1100	1900	3500	5000
900GLI 2d HBk	200	600	1200	2200	3850	5500
900GLE 4d HBk	200	600	1200	2200	3850	5500
900EMS 2d HBk	200	600	1200	2300	4000	5700
900 2d HBk (Turbo)	200	650	1250	2400	4200	6000
900 4d HBk (Turbo)	200	650	1250	2400	4200	6000

1981	6	5	4	3	2	1
900 2d HBk	200	500	1100	1900	3500	5000
900S 2d HBk	200	600	1200	2200	3850	5500
900S 4d Sed	200	600	1200	2200	3850	5500
900 2d HBk (Turbo)	200	650	1250	2400	4200	6000
900 4d HBk (Turbo)	200	650	1250	2400	4200	6000
1982						
900 2d HBk	200	500	1100	1900	3500	5000
900 4d Sed	200	600	1200	2200	3850	5500
900S 2d HBk	200	600	1200	2200	3850	5500
900S 4d Sed	200	600	1200	2200	3850	5500
900 2d HBk (Turbo)	200	650	1250	2400	4200	6000
900 4d Sed (Turbo)	200	650	1250	2400	4200	6000
1983						
900 2d HBk	200	500	1100	1900	3500	5000
900 4d Sed	200	600	1200	2200	3850	5500
900S 2d HBk	200	600	1200	2200	3850	5500
900S 4d Sed	200	600	1200	2200	3850	5500
900 2d HBk (Turbo)	200	650	1250	2400	4200	6000
900 4d Sed (Turbo)	200	650	1250	2400	4200	6000
1984						
900 2d HBk	200	600	1200	2200	3850	5500
900 4d Sed	200	650	1250	2400	4200	6000
900S 2d HBk	350	775	1500	3750	5250	7500
900S 4d Sed	350	825	1600	4000	5600	8000
900 2d HBk (Turbo)	450	900	1900	4500	6300	9000
900 4d Sed (Turbo)	400	1300	2200	4400	7700	11,000
1985						
900 2d HBk	350	700	1350	2800	4550	6500
900 4d Sed	350	750	1450	3300	4900	7000
900S 2d HBk	350	875	1700	4250	5900	8500
900S 4d Sed	450	900	1900	4500	6300	9000
900 2d HBk (Turbo)	400	1200	2000	4000	7000	10,000
900 4d HBk (Turbo)	450	1450	2400	4800	8400	12,000
1986						
900 2d HBk	350	775	1500	3750	5250	7500
900 4d Sed	350	825	1600	4000	5600	8000
900S 2d Sed	450	900	1900	4500	6300	9000
900S 2d HBk	450	950	2100	4750	6650	9500
900S 4d Sed	400	1200	2000	4000	7000	10,000
900 2d HBk (Turbo)	400	1300	2200	4400	7700	11,000
9000 4d HBk (Turbo)	500	1550	2600	5200	9100	13,000
1987						
900 2d HBk	400	1250	2100	4200	7400	10,500
900 4d Sed	400	1300	2200	4400	7700	11,000
900S 2d HBk	450	1450	2400	4800	8400	12,000
900S 4d Sed	450	1500	2500	5000	8800	12,500
900 2d HBk (Turbo)	550	1700	2800	5600	9800	14,000
900 2d Conv (Turbo)	850	2650	4400	8800	15,400	22,000
900S 4d HBk	500	1550	2600	5200	9100	13,000
9000 4d HBk (Turbo)	600	1900	3200	6400	11,200	16,000
1988						
900 4d Sed	450	1400	2300	4600	8100	11,500
900 2d HBk	400	1300	2200	4400	7700	11,000
900S 2d HBk	500	1550	2600	5200	9100	13,000
900S 4d Sed	500	1600	2700	5400	9500	13,500
900 2d HBk (Turbo)	600	1900	3200	6400	11,200	16,000
900 2d Conv (Turbo)	950	3000	5000	10,000	17,500	25,000
900S 4d HBk	700	2150	3600	7200	12,600	18,000
9000 4d HBk (Turbo)	750	2400	4000	8000	14,000	20,000
1989						
2d HBk (16V)	550	1750	2900	5800	10,200	14,500
4d Sed (16V)	550	1800	3000	6000	10,500	15,000
2d HBk (S/16V)	650	2050	3400	6800	11,900	17,000
4d Sed (S/16V)	650	2100	3500	7000	12,300	17,500
4d HBk (S/16V)	850	2650	4400	8800	15,400	22,000
2d HBk (Turbo)	750	2400	4000	8000	14,000	20,000
4d Sed (Turbo)	750	2450	4100	8200	14,400	20,500
2d Conv (Turbo)	1050	3350	5600	11,200	19,600	28,000
4d HBk (Turbo)	950	3000	5000	10,000	17,500	25,000
4d Sed (Turbo CP)	1000	3100	5200	10,400	18,200	26,000

SIMCA

1946-50	6	5	4	3	2	1
Series 5 - (4-cyl) - (79" wb) - (570cc)						
2d Cpe	350	825	1600	4000	5600	8000
Series 6 - (4-cyl) - (79" wb) - (570cc)						
2d Cpe	350	825	1600	4000	5600	8000
Series 8, 1000 - (4-cyl) - (95" wb) - (1089cc)						
4d Sed	350	775	1500	3750	5250	7500
2d Bus Cpe	350	825	1600	4000	5600	8000
2d Conv Cpe	400	1200	2000	4000	7000	10,000
Series 8, 1200 - (4-cyl) - (95" wb) - (1221cc)						
4d Sed	350	775	1500	3750	5250	7500
2d Bus Cpe	350	825	1600	4000	5600	8000
2d Conv Cpe	400	1200	2000	4000	7000	10,000
Series 8 - (4-cyl) - (95" wb) - (1221cc)						
2d Spt Rds	450	1500	2500	5000	8800	12,500
1951-55						
Series 8 - (4-cyl) - (95" wb) - (1221cc)						
2d Spt Rds	450	1500	2500	5000	8800	12,500
2d Spt Cpe	400	1200	2000	4000	7000	10,000
Aronde 9 - (4-cyl) - (96" wb) - (1221cc)						
2d Sed	350	775	1500	3750	5250	7500
4d Sed	150	400	1000	1650	3150	4500
2d Sta Wag	200	500	1100	1900	3500	5000
2d HdTp Cpe	200	650	1250	2400	4200	6000
1956-58						
Aronde 1300 - (4-cyl) - (96.2" wb) - (1290cc)						
4d DeL Sed	150	350	950	1350	2800	4000
4d Elysee Sed	150	400	1000	1550	3050	4300
2d Plein Ciel Sed	150	400	1000	1650	3150	4500
Grand Large HdTp Cpe	200	650	1250	2400	4200	6000
Chatelaine Sta Wag	200	500	1100	1900	3500	5000
Oceane 2d Conv	400	1200	2000	4000	7000	10,000
Vedette (V-8) - (106" wb) - (2351cc)						
Versailles Sed	200	500	1100	1900	3500	5000

1959-61
Aronde - (4-cyl) - (96.3" wb) - (1290cc)

	6	5	4	3	2	1
4d DeL Sed	150	350	950	1350	2800	4000
Sup DeL Sed	150	400	1000	1550	3050	4300
Elysee 4d Sed	150	400	1000	1650	3150	4500
Montlhery Sed	150	450	1050	1750	3250	4700
Grand Large HdTp Cpe	200	650	1250	2400	4200	6000
Plain Ciel HdTp Cpe	200	650	1250	2400	4200	6000
Chatelaine Sta Wag	200	500	1100	1900	3500	5000
Oceane 2d Conv	400	1200	2000	4000	7000	10,000

Aronde (Second Series 1959)
(4-cyl) - (96.3" wb) - (1290cc)

Elysee 4d Sed	150	350	950	1350	2800	4000
Montlhery Sed	150	400	1000	1550	3050	4300
Grand Large HdTp Cpe	200	650	1250	2400	4200	6000
Monaco HdTp Cpe	200	650	1250	2400	4200	6000
Etoile 4d Sed	150	400	1000	1550	3050	4300

Vedette Beaulieu - (V-8) - (106" wb) - (2351cc)

4d Sed	200	500	1100	1900	3500	5000

Ariane - (106" wb) - (2351cc)

Four 4d Sed	150	350	950	1350	2800	4000
V-8 4d Sed	200	500	1100	1900	3500	5000

1962-68
Series 5 - (4-cyl) - (96.3" wb) - (1290cc)

4d Sed	150	350	950	1350	2800	4000

Series 1000 - (4-cyl) - (87.3" wb) - (944cc)

4d Sed	150	350	950	1350	2800	4000

Bertone 1000 - (4-cyl) - (87.7" wb) - (944cc)

2d Cpe	200	500	1100	1900	3500	5000

1969-71
Series 1118 - (4-cyl) - (87.4" wb) - (1118cc)

GL 4d Sed	150	350	950	1350	2800	4000
GLS 4d Sed	150	350	950	1350	2800	4000

Series 1204 - (4-cyl) - (99.2" wb) - (1204cc)

LS 2d Sed	150	350	950	1350	2800	4000
GLS 2d Sed	150	350	950	1350	2800	4000
GLS 4d Sed	150	350	950	1350	2800	4000
GLS 2d Sta Wag	150	400	1000	1550	3050	4300
GLS 4d Sta Wag	150	400	1000	1550	3050	4300

SUBARU

1958-70
360 - (2-cyl) - (70.9" wb) - (356cc)

	6	5	4	3	2	1
2d Cpe	125	250	750	1150	2450	3500
2d Cus Cpe	150	300	900	1250	2600	3700

NOTE: Imports began in the late 60's.

1971
FF-1 Star - (4-cyl) - (95.2" wb) - (1088cc)

1100 2d Sed	125	250	750	1150	2450	3500
1100 4d Sed	125	250	750	1150	2450	3500
1100 4d Sta Wag	150	300	900	1250	2600	3700

1972
1300 - (4-cyl) - (95.3" wb) - (1267cc)

A15L 2d Sed	125	250	750	1150	2450	3500
A15L 4d Sed	125	250	750	1150	2450	3500
A44L 4d Sta Wag	150	300	900	1250	2600	3700

1300 - (4-cyl) - (96.6" wb) - (1267cc)

GL 2d Cpe	150	350	950	1350	2800	4000

1973-76
1400 - (4-cyl) - (96.7" wb) - (1361cc)

DL 2d Sed	125	250	750	1150	2450	3500
DL 4d Sed	125	250	750	1150	2450	3500
DL 4d Sta Wag	150	300	900	1250	2600	3700
GL 2d Cpe	150	350	950	1350	2800	4000

NOTE: A 4WD Station Wagon was available in 1975 with a 96.1" wb.

1977-79
1600 - (4-cyl) - (96.7" wb) - (1595cc)

STD 2d Sed	125	250	750	1150	2450	3500
DL 2d Sed	125	250	750	1150	2450	3500
DL 4d Sed	125	250	750	1150	2450	3500
DL 2d Cpe	150	300	900	1250	2600	3700
GF 2d HdTp Cpe	150	350	950	1350	2800	4000
DL 4d Sta Wag	150	300	900	1250	2600	3700

1600 - (4-cyl) - (96.1" wb) - (1595cc)

DL 4WD Sta Wag	150	400	1000	1650	3150	4500

1980-84
1600/1800 Series - (4-cyl) - (1595cc)

STD 2d HBk	125	250	750	1150	2450	3500
STD 2d HBk, 4WD	150	350	950	1350	2800	4000
DL 2d HBk	125	250	750	1150	2450	3500
DL 2d HBk, 4WD	150	350	950	1350	2800	4000
DL 4d Sed	125	250	750	1150	2450	3500
DL 2d HdTp Cpe	150	350	950	1350	2800	4000
DL 4d Sta Wag	125	250	750	1150	2450	3500
DL Sta Wag, 4WD	150	400	1000	1650	3150	4500
GL 4d Sed	125	250	750	1150	2450	3500
GL 4d Sta Wag	150	350	950	1350	2800	4000
GL Sta Wag, 4WD	150	400	1000	1650	3150	4500
GLF HdTp Cpe	150	350	950	1350	2800	4000

NOTE: Optional 4-cyl., 1781cc engine also available.

1985-86
STD/DL/GL

STD 2d HBk	150	350	950	1350	2800	4000
DL 4d Sed	150	400	1000	1650	3150	4500
DL 4d Sta Wag	200	500	1100	1900	3500	5000
GL 2d HBk	150	350	950	1450	3000	4200
GL HBk, 4WD	200	500	1100	1900	3500	5000
GL 4d Sed	150	350	950	1450	3000	4200
GL 4d Sed, 4WD	200	500	1100	1900	3500	5000
GL 4d Sta Wag	150	400	1000	1650	3150	4500
GL Sta Wag, 4WD	200	600	1200	2200	3850	5500

Turbo RX/GL

RX 4d Sed, 4WD	200	600	1200	2200	3850	5500
GL 4d Sed, 4WD	200	600	1200	2200	3850	5500

XT

DL 2d Cpe	200	500	1100	1900	3500	5000
GL 2d Cpe	200	550	1150	2000	3600	5200
Turbo 2d Cpe, 4WD	200	650	1250	2400	4200	6000

SUNBEAM

1948-1957
Sunbeam-Talbot 90
(4-cyl) - (97.5" wb) - (2267cc)

	6	5	4	3	2	1
4d Sed	350	750	1450	3300	4900	7000
DHC	400	1200	2000	4000	7000	10,000

1948-1951
Sunbeam-Talbot 90
(4-cyl) - (97.5" wb) - (1944cc)

4d Sed	350	750	1450	3300	4900	7000
DHC	400	1200	2000	4000	7000	10,000

1953-1955
Sunbeam Alpine
(4-cyl) - (97.5" wb) - (2267cc)

Rds	350	825	1600	4000	5600	8000

1956-1958
Sunbeam Rapier Series I
(4-cyl) - (96" wb) - (1390cc)

2d HdTp	150	350	950	1350	2800	4000
Conv	200	600	1200	2200	3850	5500

1959-1961
Sunbeam Rapier Series II/III
(4-cyl) - (96" wb) - (1494cc)

2d HdTp	150	350	950	1350	2800	4000
Conv	200	600	1200	2200	3850	5500

1962-1965
Sunbeam Rapier Series III/IV
(4-cyl) - (96" wb) - (1592cc)

2d HdTp	150	350	950	1350	2800	4000
Conv	200	600	1200	2200	3850	5500

1966-1967
Sunbeam Rapier Series V
(4-cyl) - (96" wb) - (1725cc)

2d HdTp	150	350	950	1350	2800	4000
Conv	200	600	1200	2200	3850	5500

1960
Sunbeam Alpine Series I
(4-cyl) - (86" wb) - (1494cc)

Conv	350	750	1450	3300	4900	7000

1961
Sunbeam Alpine Series II
(4-cyl) - (86" wb) - (1592cc)

Conv	350	750	1450	3300	4900	7000

1962
Sunbeam Alpine Series II
(4-cyl) - (86" wb) - (1592cc)

Conv	350	775	1500	3750	5250	7500

Sunbeam Herrington LeMans

Cpe	400	1200	2000	4000	7000	10,000

1963
Sunbeam Alpine Series II/III
(4-cyl) - (86" wb) - (1592cc)

Conv	350	775	1500	3750	5250	7500
Conv GT	350	750	1450	3300	4900	7000

Sunbeam Herrington LeMans

Cpe	400	1200	2000	4000	7000	10,000

1964
Sunbeam Alpine Series III/IV
(4-cyl) - (86" wb) - (1592cc)

Conv	350	775	1500	3750	5250	7500
Conv GT	350	750	1450	3300	4900	7000

Sunbeam Venezia by Superleggera

Cpe	400	1200	2000	4000	7000	10,000

Sunbeam Tiger Series I
(V-8) - (86" wb) - (260 cid)

Conv	700	2300	3800	7600	13,300	19,000

1965
Sunbeam Alpine Series IV
(4-cyl) - (86" wb) - (1592cc)

Conv	350	775	1500	3750	5250	7500

Sunbeam Venezia by Superleggera

Cpe	400	1200	2000	4000	7000	10,000

Sunbeam Tiger Series I
(V-8) - (86" wb) - (260 cid)

Conv	700	2300	3800	7600	13,300	19,000

1966
Sunbeam Alpine Series V
(4-cyl) - (86" wb) - (1725cc)

Conv	350	775	1500	3750	5250	7500

Sunbeam Tiger Series I/IA
(V-8) - (86" wb) - (260 cid)

Conv	750	2400	4000	8000	14,000	20,000

1967-1968
Sunbeam Alpine Series V
(4-cyl) - (86" wb) - (1725cc)

Conv	350	775	1500	3750	5250	7500

Sunbeam Tiger Series II
(V-8) - (86" wb) - (289 cid)

Conv	800	2500	4200	8400	14,700	21,000

1969-1970
Sunbeam Alpine
(4-cyl) - (98.5" wb) - (1725cc)

FBk HdTp	150	350	950	1350	2800	4000
FBk HdTp GT	150	400	1000	1650	3150	4500

SUZUKI

1986
Samurai (4WD)

Util HdTp	150	400	1000	1650	3150	4500
Util Conv	200	500	1100	1900	3500	5000

1987
Samurai (4WD)

Util HdTp	200	500	1100	1900	3500	5000
Util Conv	200	600	1200	2200	3850	5500

1988
Samurai (4WD)

	6	5	4	3	2	1
Utl HdTp	200	600	1200	2200	3850	5500
Utl Conv	200	650	1250	2400	4200	6000

1989
Swift FWD

	6	5	4	3	2	1
GTi 2d HBk	350	700	1350	2800	4550	6500
GLX 4d HBk	200	650	1250	2400	4200	6000

Samurai (4WD)

	6	5	4	3	2	1
Utl	350	700	1350	2700	4500	6400
Conv	350	700	1350	2900	4600	6600

Sidekick (4WD)

	6	5	4	3	2	1
JA Utl Conv	350	825	1600	4000	5600	8000
JX Utl HdTp	400	1200	2000	4000	7000	10,000
JX Utl Conv	450	900	1900	4500	6300	9000

TOYOTA (TOYOPET)

1958-60
Crown - (4-cyl) - (99.6" wb) - (1453cc)

	6	5	4	3	2	1
RSL 4d Sed	150	350	950	1350	2800	4000

1961-66
Tiara - (4-cyl) - (94.5" wb) - (1453cc)

	6	5	4	3	2	1
4d Sed	150	350	950	1350	2800	4000

Crown - (4-cyl) - (99.6" wb) - (1879cc)

	6	5	4	3	2	1
4d Cus Sed	150	350	950	1450	3000	4200
4d Cus Sta Wag	150	350	950	1450	3000	4200

TOYOTA

1967-68
Corona - (4-cyl) - (95.3" wb) - (1879cc)

	6	5	4	3	2	1
4d Sed	150	350	950	1350	2800	4000
2d HdTp Cpe	150	400	1000	1650	3150	4500

Crown - (6-cyl) - (105.9" wb) - (2254cc)

	6	5	4	3	2	1
4d Sed	150	350	950	1350	2800	4000
4d Sta Wag	150	350	950	1450	3000	4200

2000 GT - (6-cyl) - (91.7" wb) - (1988cc)

	6	5	4	3	2	1
2d FBk Cpe	950	3000	5000	10,000	17,500	25,000

1969-70
Corolla, 1969 - (4-cyl) - (90" wb) - (1079cc)
1970 - (4-cyl) - (90" wb) - (1166cc)

	6	5	4	3	2	1
2d Sed	125	250	750	1150	2450	3500
2d FBk Cpe	150	300	900	1250	2650	3800
2d Sta Wag	150	300	900	1250	2650	3800

Corona - (4-cyl) - (95.3" wb) - (1879cc)

	6	5	4	3	2	1
4d Sed	125	250	750	1150	2450	3500
2d HdTp Cpe	150	350	950	1350	2800	4000

Corona Mark II - (4-cyl) - (98.8" wb) - (1859cc)

	6	5	4	3	2	1
4d Sed	150	350	950	1350	2800	4000
2d HdTp Cpe	150	400	1000	1550	3050	4300
4d Sta Wag	150	400	1000	1550	3050	4300

Crown - (6-cyl) - (105.9" wb) - (2254cc)

	6	5	4	3	2	1
4d Sed	150	350	950	1350	2800	4000
4d Sta Wag	150	400	1000	1650	3150	4500

1971-77
Corolla 1200 - (4-cyl) - (91.9" wb) - (1166cc)

	6	5	4	3	2	1
2d Sed	125	250	750	1150	2450	3500
2d Cpe	125	250	750	1150	2450	3500
2d Sta Wag	150	300	900	1250	2650	3800

Corolla 1600 - (4-cyl) - (91.9" wb) - (1588cc)

	6	5	4	3	2	1
2d Sed	125	250	750	1150	2450	3500
4d Sed	125	250	750	1150	2450	3500
2d Cpe	150	300	900	1250	2650	3800
2d Sta Wag	150	300	900	1250	2650	3800

Celica, 1971-74 - (4-cyl) - (1967cc)
1975-77 - (2189cc)

	6	5	4	3	2	1
2d Cpe	200	500	1100	1900	3500	5000

Corona - (4-cyl) - (95.7" wb) - (1859cc)

	6	5	4	3	2	1
4d Sed	150	350	950	1350	2800	4000
2d HdTp Cpe	150	400	1000	1650	3150	4500

Corona Mark II - (4-cyl) - (98.8" wb) - (1859cc)

	6	5	4	3	2	1
4d Sed	150	350	950	1350	2800	4000
2d HdTp Cpe	150	400	1000	1650	3150	4500
4d Sta Wag	150	400	1000	1650	3150	4500

Crown, 1971 only - (6-cyl) - (105.9" wb) - (2254cc)

	6	5	4	3	2	1
4d Sed	150	350	950	1350	2800	4000
4d Sta Wag	150	400	1000	1650	3150	4500

1978-83
Corolla - (4-cyl) - (94.5" wb) - (1770cc)

	6	5	4	3	2	1
2d Sed	125	250	750	1150	2450	3500
DeL 2d Sed	125	250	750	1150	2450	3500
DeL 4d Sed	125	250	750	1150	2450	3500
DeL Sta Wag	125	250	750	1150	2450	3500
DeL HdTp Cpe	150	300	900	1250	2650	3800
SR5 2d HdTp Cpe	150	350	950	1350	2800	4000
DeL 3d LBk	125	250	750	1150	2450	3500
DeL 2d Spt Cpe	150	300	900	1250	2650	3800
SR5 3d LBk	150	350	950	1350	2800	4000
SR5 2d Spt Cpe	150	350	950	1350	2800	4000

Tercel - (4-cyl) - (98.4" wb) - (1452cc)

	6	5	4	3	2	1
2d Sed	150	350	950	1350	2800	4000
DeL 2d Sed	150	350	950	1350	2800	4000
4d Sed	150	350	950	1350	2800	4000
DeL 3d LBk	150	350	950	1350	2800	4000
SR5 3d LBk	150	400	1000	1650	3150	4500

Starlet - (4-cyl) - (90.6" wb) - (1290cc)

	6	5	4	3	2	1
3d LBk	150	350	950	1350	2800	4000

Celica - (4-cyl) - (98.4" wb) - (2366cc)

	6	5	4	3	2	1
ST 2d Spt Cpe	200	600	1200	2200	3850	5500
GT 2d Spt Cpe	200	600	1200	2200	3900	5600
GT 3d LBk	200	600	1200	2300	4000	5700

Celica Supra - (6-cyl) - (103.5" wb) - (2759cc)

	6	5	4	3	2	1
GT 2d Spt Cpe	350	700	1350	2800	4550	6500

Corona - (4-cyl) - (99.4" wb) - (2366cc)

	6	5	4	3	2	1
DeL 4d Sed	150	350	950	1350	2800	4000
DeL 5d Sta Wag	150	400	1000	1650	3150	4500
LE 4d Sed	150	350	950	1350	2800	4000
LE 5d LBk	150	400	1000	1650	3150	4500

Cressida - (6-cyl) - (104.1" wb) - (2759cc)

	6	5	4	3	2	1
Lux 4d Sed	150	350	950	1350	2800	4000
Lux 4d Sta Wag	150	400	1000	1650	3150	4500

NOTE: Specifications in this section are for 1981 models only. Prices are averages for the 1980-1981 model years.

TRIUMPH

1946-48
1800 - (4-cyl) - (108" wb) - (63 hp)

	6	5	4	3	2	1
T&C Saloon	400	1200	2000	4000	7000	10,000

1800 - (4-cyl) - (100" wb) - (63 hp)

	6	5	4	3	2	1
Rds	950	3000	5000	10,000	17,500	25,000

1949
1800 - (4-cyl) - (108" wb) - (63 hp)

	6	5	4	3	2	1
T&C Saloon	400	1200	2000	4000	7000	10,000

2000 - (4-cyl) - (108" wb) - (68 hp)

	6	5	4	3	2	1
Saloon	400	1200	2000	4000	7000	10,000

2000 Renown - (4-cyl) - (108" wb) - (68 hp)

	6	5	4	3	2	1
Saloon	400	1200	2000	4000	7000	10,000

Mayflower - (4-cyl) - (84" wb) - (38 hp)

	6	5	4	3	2	1
Saloon	350	775	1500	3750	5250	7500

2000 - (4-cyl) - (100" wb) - (68 hp)

	6	5	4	3	2	1
Rds	950	3000	5000	10,000	17,500	25,000

1950
2000 Renown - (4-cyl) - (108" wb) - (68 hp)

	6	5	4	3	2	1
Saloon	400	1200	2000	4000	7000	10,000

Mayflower - (4-cyl) - (84" wb) - (38 hp)

	6	5	4	3	2	1
Saloon	350	775	1500	3750	5250	7500
Conv	550	1800	3000	6000	10,500	15,000

TRX (New Rds Prototype) - (4-cyl) - (94" wb) - (71 hp)

	6	5	4	3	2	1
Rds			value inestimable			

NOTE: Car was offered but none were ever delivered.

1951
2000 Renown - (4-cyl) - (108" wb) - (68 hp)

	6	5	4	3	2	1
Saloon	400	1200	2000	4000	7000	10,000

2000 - (4-cyl) - (111" wb) - (68 hp)

	6	5	4	3	2	1
Limo	450	1450	2400	4800	8400	12,000

Mayflower - (4-cyl) - (84" wb) - (38 hp)

	6	5	4	3	2	1
Saloon	350	775	1500	3750	5250	7500

1952
2000 - (4-cyl) - (111" wb) - (68 hp)

	6	5	4	3	2	1
Limo	450	1450	2400	4800	8400	12,000

Mayflower - (4-cyl) - (84" wb) - (38 hp)

	6	5	4	3	2	1
Saloon	350	775	1500	3750	5250	7500

20TS (prototype) - (4-cyl) - (130" wb) - (75 hp)

	6	5	4	3	2	1
TR-1 Rds			value inestimable			

NOTE: Only one prototype built.

2000 Renown - (4-cyl) - (111" wb) - (68 hp)

	6	5	4	3	2	1
Saloon	400	1200	2000	4000	7000	10,000

1953
2000 Renown - (4-cyl) - (108" wb) - (68 hp)

	6	5	4	3	2	1
Saloon	400	1200	2000	4000	7000	10,000

2000 - (4-cyl) - (111" wb) - (68 hp)

	6	5	4	3	2	1
Limo	450	1450	2400	4800	8400	12,000

Mayflower - (4-cyl) - (84" wb) - (38 hp)

	6	5	4	3	2	1
Saloon	350	775	1500	3750	5250	7500

TR-2 - (4-cyl) - (88" wb) - (90 hp)

	6	5	4	3	2	1
Rds	550	1800	3000	6000	10,500	15,000

1954
2000 Renown - (4-cyl) - (108" wb) - (68 hp)

	6	5	4	3	2	1
Saloon	400	1200	2000	4000	7000	10,000

TR-2 - (4-cyl) - (88" wb) - (90 hp)

	6	5	4	3	2	1
Rds	550	1800	3000	6000	10,500	15,000

1955
TR-2 - (4-cyl) - (88" wb) - (90 hp)

	6	5	4	3	2	1
Rds	400	1200	2000	4000	7000	10,000

TR-3 - (4-cyl) - (88" wb) - (95 hp)

	6	5	4	3	2	1
Rds	550	1800	3000	6000	10,500	15,000

1956
TR-3 - (4-cyl) - (88" wb) - (95 hp)

	6	5	4	3	2	1
Rds	550	1800	3000	6000	10,500	15,000
HdTp Rds	600	1900	3200	6400	11,200	16,000

1957
TR-3 - (4-cyl) - (88" wb) - (100 hp)

	6	5	4	3	2	1
Rds	550	1800	3000	6000	10,500	15,000
HdTp Rds	600	1900	3200	6400	11,200	16,000

TR-10 - (4-cyl) - (84" wb) - (40 hp)

	6	5	4	3	2	1
Saloon	200	650	1250	2400	4200	6000

1958
TR-3 - (4-cyl) - (88" wb) - (100 hp)

	6	5	4	3	2	1
Rds	550	1800	3000	6000	10,500	15,000
HdTp Rds	600	1900	3200	6400	11,200	16,000

TR-10 - (4-cyl) - (84" wb) - (40 hp)

	6	5	4	3	2	1
Saloon	200	650	1250	2400	4200	6000
Sta Wag	200	650	1250	2400	4200	6000

1959
(NOTE: All cars registered after 9-15-58 are 1959 models).
TR-3 - (4-cyl) - (88" wb) - (100 hp)

	6	5	4	3	2	1
Rds	550	1800	3000	6000	10,500	15,000
HdTp Rds	600	1900	3200	6400	11,200	16,000

TR-10 - (4-cyl) - (84" wb) - (40 hp)

	6	5	4	3	2	1
Saloon	200	650	1250	2400	4200	6000
Sta Wag	200	650	1250	2400	4200	6000

1960
Herald - (4-cyl) - (84" wb) - (40 hp)

	6	5	4	3	2	1
Sed	200	500	1100	1900	3500	5000
Cpe	200	500	1100	1900	3500	5000
Conv	350	750	1450	3300	4900	7000
Sta Wag	200	500	1100	1900	3500	5000

TR-3 - (4-cyl) - (88" wb) - (100 hp)

	6	5	4	3	2	1
Rds	550	1800	3000	6000	10,500	15,000
HdTp Rds	600	1900	3200	6400	11,200	16,000

1961
(NOTE: All cars registered after 9-15-60 are 1961 models).
Herald - (4-cyl) - (91.5" wb) - (40 hp)

	6	5	4	3	2	1
Sed	200	500	1100	1900	3500	5000
Cpe	200	500	1100	1900	3500	5000
Conv	350	750	1450	3300	4900	7000
Sta Wag	200	500	1100	1900	3500	5000

TR-3 - (4-cyl) - (88" wb) - (100 hp)

	6	5	4	3	2	1
Rds	550	1800	3000	6000	10,500	15,000
HdTp Rds	600	1900	3200	6400	11,200	16,000

1962

	6	5	4	3	2	1
Herald - (4-cyl) - (91.5" wb) - (40 hp)						
Sed	200	500	1100	1900	3500	5000
Cpe	200	500	1100	1900	3500	5000
Conv	350	750	1450	3300	4900	7000
TR-3 - (4-cyl) - (88" wb) - (100 hp)						
Rds	550	1800	3000	6000	10,500	15,000
HdTp Rds	600	1900	3200	6400	11,200	16,000
TR-4 - (4-cyl) - (88" wb) - (105 hp)						
Rds	450	1450	2400	4800	8400	12,000
HdTp Rds	500	1550	2600	5200	9100	13,000
Spitfire - (4-cyl) - (83" wb) - (100 hp)						
Conv	350	775	1500	3750	5250	7500

1963

	6	5	4	3	2	1
TR-3 - (4-cyl) - (88" wb) - (100 hp)						
Rds	550	1800	3000	6000	10,500	15,000
HdTp Rds	600	1900	3200	6400	11,200	16,000
TR-4 - (4-cyl) - (88" wb) - (105 hp)						
Conv	400	1300	2200	4400	7700	11,000
HdTp	450	1450	2400	4800	8400	12,000
Four - (4-cyl) - (91.5" wb) - (40 hp)						
Sed	150	350	950	1350	2800	4000
Conv	150	450	1050	1800	3300	4800
Spitfire - (4-cyl) - (83" wb) - (100 hp)						
Spt Conv	350	775	1500	3750	5250	7500
Six - (6-cyl) - (91.5" wb) - (70 hp)						
Spt Conv	350	825	1600	4000	5600	8000

1964

	6	5	4	3	2	1
TR-4 - (4-cyl) - (88" wb) - (105 hp)						
HdTp Cpe	400	1300	2200	4400	7700	11,000
Conv	450	1450	2400	4800	8400	12,000

1965

	6	5	4	3	2	1
TR-4 - (4-cyl) - (88" wb) - (105 hp)						
HdTp Cpe	400	1300	2200	4400	7700	11,000
Conv	450	1450	2400	4800	8400	12,000
Spitfire Mark II - (4-cyl) - (83" wb) - (100 hp)						
Conv	350	750	1450	3300	4900	7000

1966

	6	5	4	3	2	1
TR-4 - (4-cyl) - (88" wb) - (105 hp)						
Conv	400	1300	2200	4400	7700	11,000
HdTp Cpe	450	1450	2400	4800	8400	12,000
2000 - (6-cyl) - (106" wb) - (90 hp)						
Sed	150	350	950	1450	2900	4100
Spitfire Mark II - (4-cyl) - (83" wb) - (100 hp)						
Conv	350	775	1500	3750	5250	7500

1967

	6	5	4	3	2	1
TR-4A - (4-cyl) - (88" wb) - (105 hp)						
HdTp Cpe	400	1300	2200	4400	7700	11,000
Conv	450	1450	2400	4800	8400	12,000
2000						
Sed	150	350	950	1350	2800	4000
Spitfire Mark II - (4-cyl) - (83" wb) - (68 hp)						
HdTp Cpe	350	775	1500	3750	5250	7500
Conv	350	750	1450	3300	4900	7000
1200 Sport						
Sed	150	450	1050	1750	3250	4700
Conv	200	600	1200	2200	3850	5500

1968

	6	5	4	3	2	1
TR-250 - (6-cyl) - (88" wb) - (104 hp)						
Conv	350	875	1700	4250	5900	8500
Spitfire Mark III - (4-cyl) - (83" wb) - (68 hp)						
Conv	350	775	1500	3750	5250	7500
GT-6 Plus - (6-cyl) - (83" wb) - (95 hp)						
Cpe	350	750	1450	3300	4900	7000

NOTE: Add 10 percent for wire wheels.
Add 10 percent for factory hardtop.
Add 5 percent for overdrive.

1969

	6	5	4	3	2	1
TR-6 - (6-cyl) - (88" wb) - (104 hp)						
Conv	350	875	1700	4250	5900	8500
Spitfire Mark III - (4-cyl) - (83" wb) - (68 hp)						
Conv	350	775	1500	3750	5250	7500
GT-6 Plus - (6-cyl) - (83" wb) - (95 hp)						
Cpe	350	750	1450	3300	4900	7000

NOTE: Add 10 percent for wire wheels.
Add 10 percent for factory hardtop.
Add 5 percent for overdrive.

1970

	6	5	4	3	2	1
TR-6 - (6-cyl) - (88" wb) - (104 hp)						
Conv	350	825	1600	4000	5600	8000
Spitfire Mark III - (4-cyl) - (83" wb) - (68 hp)						
Conv	200	650	1250	2400	4200	6000
GT-6 Plus - (6-cyl) - (83" wb) - (95 hp)						
Cpe	350	750	1450	3300	4900	7000
Stag - (8-cyl) - (100" wb) - (145 hp)						
Conv	400	1250	2100	4200	7400	10,500

NOTE: Add 10 percent for wire wheels.
Add 10 percent for factory hardtop.
Add 5 percent for overdrive

1971

	6	5	4	3	2	1
TR-6 - (6-cyl) - (88" wb) - (104 hp)						
Conv	350	825	1600	4050	5650	8100
Spitfire Mark IV - (4-cyl) - (83" wb) - (58 hp)						
Conv	200	600	1200	2200	3850	5500
GT-6 Mark III - (6-cyl) - (83" wb) - (90 hp)						
Cpe	350	750	1450	3300	4900	7000
Stag - (8-cyl) - (100" wb) - (145 hp)						
Conv	450	950	2100	4750	6650	9500

NOTE: Add 10 percent for wire wheels.
Add 10 percent for factory hardtop.
Add 5 percent for overdrive.

1972

	6	5	4	3	2	1
TR-6 - (6-cyl) - (88" wb) - (106 hp)						
Conv	350	825	1600	4000	5600	8000
Spitfire Mark IV - (4-cyl) - (83" wb) - (48 hp)						
Conv	200	600	1200	2200	3850	5500
GT-6 Mark III - (6-cyl) - (83" wb) - (79 hp)						
Cpe	350	750	1450	3300	4900	7000
Stag - (8-cyl) - (100" wb) - (127 hp)						
Conv	450	950	2100	4750	6650	9500

NOTE: Add 10 percent for wire wheels.
Add 10 percent for factory hardtop.
Add 5 percent for overdrive.

1973

	6	5	4	3	2	1
TR-6 - (6-cyl) - (88" wb) - (106 hp)						
Conv	350	825	1600	4000	5600	8000
Spitfire Mark IV - (4-cyl) - (83" wb) - (57 hp)						
Conv	200	600	1200	2200	3850	5500
GT-6 Mark III - (6-cyl) - (83" wb) - (79 hp)						
Cpe	350	750	1450	3300	4900	7000
Stag - (8-cyl) - (100" wb) - (127 hp)						
Conv	450	975	2300	4950	6900	9900

NOTE: Add 10 percent for wire wheels.
Add 10 percent for factory hardtop.
Add 5 percent for overdrive.

1974

	6	5	4	3	2	1
TR-6 - (6-cyl) - (88" wb) - (106 hp)						
Conv	350	825	1600	4000	5600	8000
Spitfire Mark IV - (4-cyl) - (83" wb) - (57 hp)						
Conv	200	600	1200	2200	3850	5500

NOTE: Add 10 percent for factory hardtop.
Add 5 percent for overdrive.

1975

	6	5	4	3	2	1
TR-6 - (6-cyl) - (88" wb) - (106 hp)						
Conv	350	825	1600	4000	5600	8000
TR-7 - (4-cyl) - (85" wb) - (92 hp)						
Cpe	200	650	1250	2400	4200	6000
Spitfire 1500 - (4-cyl) - (83" wb) - (57 hp)						
Conv	350	700	1350	2800	4550	6500

NOTE: Add 10 percent for factory hardtop.
Add 5 percent for overdrive.

1976

	6	5	4	3	2	1
TR-6 - (6-cyl) - (88" wb) - (106 hp)						
Conv	350	875	1700	4250	5900	8500
TR-7 - (4-cyl) - (85" wb) - (92 hp)						
Cpe	200	650	1250	2400	4200	6000
Spitfire 1500 - (4-cyl) - (83" wb) - (57 hp)						
Conv	200	650	1250	2400	4200	6000

NOTE: Add 10 percent for factory hardtop.
Add 5 percent for overdrive.

1977

	6	5	4	3	2	1
TR-7 - (4-cyl) - (85" wb) - (92 hp)						
Cpe	200	600	1200	2200	3850	5500
Spitfire 1500 - (4-cyl) - (83" wb) - (57 hp)						
Conv	200	650	1250	2400	4200	6000

NOTE: Add 10 percent for factory hardtop.
Add 5 percent for overdrive.

1978

	6	5	4	3	2	1
TR-7 - (4-cyl) - (85" wb) - (92 hp)						
Cpe	200	600	1200	2200	3850	5500
TR-8 - (8-cyl) - (85" wb) - (133 hp)						
(About 150 prototypes in USA)						
Cpe	550	1800	3000	6000	10,500	15,000
Spitfire 1500 - (4-cyl) - (83" wb) - (57 hp)						
Conv	200	650	1250	2400	4200	6000

NOTE: Add 10 percent for factory hardtop.
Add 5 percent for overdrive.

1979

	6	5	4	3	2	1
TR-7 - (4-cyl) - (85" wb) - (86 hp)						
Conv	350	750	1450	3300	4900	7000
Cpe	200	650	1250	2400	4200	6000
Spitfire 1500 - (4-cyl) - (83" wb) - (53 hp)						
Conv	350	700	1350	2800	4550	6500

NOTE: Add 10 percent for factory hardtop.
Add 5 percent for overdrive.

1980

	6	5	4	3	2	1
TR-7 - (4-cyl) - (85" wb) - (86 hp)						
Conv	350	725	1400	3200	4850	6900
Spider Conv	350	800	1550	3800	5300	7600
Cpe	200	675	1300	2600	4400	6300
TR-8 - (8-cyl) - (85" wb) - (133 hp)						
Conv	750	2400	4000	8000	14,000	20,000
Cpe	550	1800	3000	6000	10,500	15,000
Spitfire 1500 - (4-cyl) - (83" wb) - (57 hp)						
Conv	350	775	1500	3700	5200	7400

NOTE: Add 10 percent for factory hardtop.
Add 5 percent for overdrive.

1981

	6	5	4	3	2	1
TR-7 - (4-cyl) - (85" wb) - (89 hp)						
Conv	350	825	1600	3950	5500	7900
TR-8 - (8-cyl) - (85" wb) - (148 hp)						
Conv	750	2400	4000	8000	14,000	20,000

VAUXHALL

1946-56

	6	5	4	3	2	1
Ten - (4-cyl) - (97.8" wb) - (1203cc)						
Saloon	200	650	1250	2400	4200	6000
Twelve - (4-cyl) - (97.8" wb) - (1442cc)						
Saloon	350	750	1450	3300	4900	7000
Fourteen - (6-cyl) - (105" wb) - (1781cc)						
Saloon	350	825	1600	4000	5600	8000
Wyvern, 1948 - (97.8" wb) - (1442cc)						
1951 - (103" wb)						
Saloon	350	825	1600	4000	5600	8000
Velox, 1948 - (6-cyl) - (97.8" wb) - (2275cc)						
1951 - (103" wb)						
Saloon	350	875	1700	4250	5900	8500

1957-59

	6	5	4	3	2	1
Victor Super - (4-cyl) - (98" wb) - (1507cc)						
FD 4d Sed	200	500	1100	1900	3500	5000
FW 4d Sta Wag	200	600	1200	2200	3850	5500

1960-61

	6	5	4	3	2	1
Victor Super - (4-cyl) - (98" wb) - (1507cc)						
Series 2						
FD 4d Sed	150	350	950	1350	2800	4000
FW 4d Sta Wag	150	350	950	1450	3000	4200

1962

	6	5	4	3	2	1
Victor FB Super - (4-cyl) - (100" wb) - (1507cc)						
FBD 4d Sed	150	350	950	1350	2800	4000
FBW 4d Sta Wag	150	350	950	1450	3000	4200

VOLKSWAGEN

1945
Standard - (4-cyl) - (94.5" wb) - (25 hp)

	6	5	4	3	2	1
2d Sed	600	1850	3100	6200	10,800	15,400

1946
Standard - (4-cyl) - (94.5" wb) - (25 hp)

	6	5	4	3	2	1
2d Sed	450	1500	2500	5000	8700	12,400

1947-1948
(4-cyl) - (94.5" wb) - (25 hp)

	6	5	4	3	2	1
Std	400	1250	2100	4200	7300	10,400
Export	450	1350	2300	4600	8000	11,400

1949
Standard - (4-cyl) - (94.5" wb) - (25 hp)

	6	5	4	3	2	1
2d Sed	450	975	2300	4950	6900	9900

DeLuxe - (4-cyl) - (94.5" wb) - (10 hp)

	6	5	4	3	2	1
2d Sed	400	1250	2100	4200	7300	10,400
Conv	600	1850	3100	6200	10,800	15,400
Heb Conv	750	2400	4000	8000	14,000	20,000

NOTE: Only 700 Hebmuller Cabriolet convertibles were built during 1949-1950. Add 10 percent for sunroof.

1950
DeLuxe - (4-cyl) - (94.5" wb) - (25 hp)

	6	5	4	3	2	1
2d Sed	400	1250	2100	4200	7300	10,400
Conv	600	1850	3100	6200	10,800	15,400
Heb Conv	750	2400	4000	8000	14,000	20,000

NOTE: Add 10 percent for sunroof.

1951-1952
(Serial Nos. 170000-Up)
DeLuxe - (4-cyl) - (94.5" wb) - (25 hp)

	6	5	4	3	2	1
2d Sed	450	900	1900	4500	6300	9000
Conv	500	1550	2600	5200	9100	13,000

NOTE: Add 10 percent for sunroof.

1952-1953
(Serial Nos. 1-0264198-Up)
DeLuxe - (4-cyl) - (94.5" wb) - (25 hp)

	6	5	4	3	2	1
2d Sed	450	900	1800	4400	6150	8800
Conv	450	1350	2300	4600	8000	11,400

NOTE: Add 10 percent for sunroof.

1953
(Serial Nos. later than March 1953)
DeLuxe - (4-cyl) - (94.5" wb) - (25 hp)

	6	5	4	3	2	1
2d Sed	350	850	1650	4200	5850	8400
Conv	400	1250	2100	4200	7300	10,400

NOTE: Add 10 percent for sunroof.

1954
DeLuxe - (4-cyl) - (94.5" wb) - (36 hp)

	6	5	4	3	2	1
2d Sed	350	850	1650	4200	5850	8400
Conv	450	975	2300	4950	6900	9900

NOTE: Add 10 percent for sunroof.

1955
DeLuxe - (4-cyl) - (94.5" wb) - (36 hp)

	6	5	4	3	2	1
2d Sed	350	850	1650	4200	5850	8400
Conv	450	975	2300	4950	6900	9900

NOTE: Add 10 percent for sunroof.

1956
DeLuxe - (4-cyl) - (94.5" wb) - (36 hp)

	6	5	4	3	2	1
2d Sed	350	850	1650	4200	5850	8400
Conv	450	975	2300	4950	6900	9900

NOTE: Add 10 percent for sunroof.

Karmann-Ghia - (4-cyl) - (94.5" wb) - (36 hp)

	6	5	4	3	2	1
Cpe	450	900	1900	4500	6300	9000

1957
Beetle - (4-cyl) - (94.5" wb) - (36 hp)

	6	5	4	3	2	1
2d Sed	350	850	1650	4200	5850	8400
Conv	450	950	2100	4700	6600	9400

NOTE: Add 10 percent for sunroof.

Karmann-Ghia - (4-cyl) - (94.5" wb) - (36 hp)

	6	5	4	3	2	1
Cpe	450	900	1900	4500	6300	9000

1958
Beetle - (4-cyl) - (94.5" wb) - (36 hp)

	6	5	4	3	2	1
2d DeL Sed	350	825	1600	3950	5500	7900
Conv	450	950	2100	4700	6600	9400

Karmann-Ghia - (4-cyl) - (94.5" wb) - (36 hp)

	6	5	4	3	2	1
Cpe	450	900	1900	4500	6300	9000
Conv	400	1300	2200	4400	7700	11,000

1959
Beetle - (4-cyl) - (94.5" wb) - (36 hp)

	6	5	4	3	2	1
2d Sed	350	775	1500	3700	5200	7400
Conv	450	900	1900	4500	6300	9000

NOTE: Add 10 percent for sunroof.

Karmann-Ghia - (4-cyl) - (94.5" wb) - (36 hp)

	6	5	4	3	2	1
Cpe	450	900	1900	4500	6300	9000
Conv	400	1300	2200	4400	7700	11,000

1960
Beetle - (4-cyl) - (94.5" wb) - (36 hp)

	6	5	4	3	2	1
2d DeL Sed	350	775	1500	3700	5200	7400
Conv	450	900	1900	4500	6300	9000

NOTE: Add 10 percent for sunroof.

Karmann-Ghia - (4-cyl) - (94.5" wb) - (36 hp)

	6	5	4	3	2	1
Cpe	450	900	1900	4500	6300	9000
Conv	400	1300	2200	4400	7700	11,000

1961
Beetle - (4-cyl) - (94.5" wb) - (40 hp)

	6	5	4	3	2	1
2d DeL Sed	350	750	1450	3300	4900	7000
Conv	450	900	1900	4500	6300	9000

NOTE: Add 10 percent for sunroof.

Karmann-Ghia - (4-cyl) - (94.5" wb) - (40 hp)

	6	5	4	3	2	1
Cpe	450	900	1900	4500	6300	9000
Conv	400	1300	2200	4400	7700	11,000

1962
Beetle - (4-cyl) - (94.5" wb) - (40 hp)

	6	5	4	3	2	1
2d DeL Sed	350	700	1350	2800	4550	6500
Conv	450	900	1900	4500	6300	9000

NOTE: Add 10 percent for sunroof.

Karmann-Ghia - (4-cyl) - (94.5" wb) - (40 hp)

	6	5	4	3	2	1
Cpe	350	875	1700	4250	5900	8500
Conv	400	1250	2100	4200	7400	10,500

1963
Beetle - (4-cyl) - (94.5" wb) - (40 hp)

	6	5	4	3	2	1
2d DeL Sed	350	700	1350	2800	4550	6500
Conv	450	900	1900	4500	6300	9000

NOTE: Add 10 percent for sunroof.

Karmann-Ghia - (4-cyl) - (94.5" wb) - (40 hp)

	6	5	4	3	2	1
Cpe	350	875	1700	4250	5900	8500
Conv	400	1250	2100	4200	7400	10,500

1964
Beetle - (4-cyl) - (94.5" wb) - (40 hp)

	6	5	4	3	2	1
2d DeL Sed	200	650	1250	2400	4200	6000
Conv	350	875	1700	4250	5900	8500

NOTE: Add 10 percent for sunroof.

Karmann-Ghia - (4-cyl) - (94.5" wb) - (40 hp)

	6	5	4	3	2	1
Cpe	400	1200	2000	4000	7000	10,000
Conv	400	1200	2000	4000	7000	10,000

1965
Beetle - (4-cyl) - (94.5" wb) - (40 hp)

	6	5	4	3	2	1
2d DeL Sed	200	650	1250	2400	4200	6000
Conv	350	875	1700	4250	5900	8500

NOTE: Add 10 percent for sunroof.

Karmann-Ghia - (4-cyl) - (94.5" wb) - (40 hp)

	6	5	4	3	2	1
Cpe	350	825	1600	4000	5600	8000
Conv	450	950	2100	4750	6650	9500

1966
Beetle - (53 hp)

	6	5	4	3	2	1
2d DeL Sed	200	650	1250	2400	4200	6000
Conv	350	875	1700	4250	5900	8500

NOTE: Add 10 percent for sunroof.

Karmann Ghia - (53 hp)

	6	5	4	3	2	1
Cpe	350	825	1600	4000	5600	8000
Conv	450	900	1900	4500	6300	9000

1600 Series - (65 hp)

	6	5	4	3	2	1
2d Sed FBk	150	300	900	1250	2600	3700
2d Sed SqBk	150	300	900	1250	2650	3800

NOTE: Add 10 percent for sunroof.

1967
Beetle - (53 hp)

	6	5	4	3	2	1
2d DeL Sed	200	650	1250	2400	4200	6000
2d SR DeL Sed	350	700	1350	2800	4550	6500
Conv	350	875	1700	4250	5900	8500

NOTE: Add 10 percent for sunroof.

Karmann Ghia - (53 hp)

	6	5	4	3	2	1
Cpe	350	825	1600	4000	5600	8000
Conv	450	950	2100	4750	6650	9500

1600 Series - (65 hp)

	6	5	4	3	2	1
2d Sed FBk	150	400	1000	1600	3100	4400
2d Sed SqBk	150	450	1050	1700	3200	4600

NOTE: Add 10 percent for sunroof.

1968
Beetle - (53 hp)

	6	5	4	3	2	1
2d Sed	200	650	1250	2400	4200	6000
Conv	350	875	1700	4250	5900	8500

NOTE: Add 10 percent for sunroof.

Karmann Ghia - (53 hp)

	6	5	4	3	2	1
Cpe	350	825	1600	4000	5600	8000
Conv	450	950	2100	4750	6650	9500

1600 Series - (65 hp)

	6	5	4	3	2	1
2d Sed FBk	150	400	1000	1600	3100	4400
2d Sed SqBk	150	450	1050	1700	3200	4600

NOTE: Add 10 percent for sunroof.

1969
Beetle - (53 hp)

	6	5	4	3	2	1
2d Sed	200	650	1250	2400	4200	6000
Conv	350	875	1700	4250	5900	8500

NOTE: Add 10 percent for sunroof.

Karmann Ghia - (53 hp)

	6	5	4	3	2	1
Cpe	350	700	1350	2800	4550	6500
Conv	450	900	1900	4500	6300	9000

1600 Series - (65 hp)

	6	5	4	3	2	1
2d Sed FBk	125	250	750	1150	2500	3600
2d Sed SqBk	150	300	900	1250	2600	3700

NOTE: Add 10 percent for sunroof.

1970
Beetle - (60 hp)

	6	5	4	3	2	1
2d Sed	200	600	1200	2200	3850	5500
Conv	350	875	1700	4250	5900	8500

NOTE: Add 10 percent for sunroof.

Karmann Ghia - (60 hp)

	6	5	4	3	2	1
Cpe	200	650	1250	2400	4200	6000
Conv	450	900	1900	4500	6300	9000

1600 Series - (65 hp)

	6	5	4	3	2	1
2d Sed FBk	125	250	750	1150	2500	3600
2d Sed SqBk	150	300	900	1250	2600	3700

NOTE: Add 10 percent for sunroof.

1971
Beetle - (60 hp)

	6	5	4	3	2	1
2d Sed	200	600	1200	2200	3850	5500
2d Sup Sed	200	600	1200	2200	3850	5500
Conv	350	875	1700	4250	5900	8500

NOTE: Add 10 percent for sunroof.

Karmann Ghia

	6	5	4	3	2	1
Cpe	200	650	1250	2400	4200	6000
Conv	450	900	1900	4500	6300	9000

Type 3, Square Back or 411

	6	5	4	3	2	1
2d Sed SqBk	125	250	750	1150	2400	3400
3d Sed 411	125	250	750	1150	2450	3500
4d Sed 411	125	250	750	1150	2450	3500
2d Sed Type 3	125	250	750	1150	2400	3400

1972
Beetle - (60 hp)

	6	5	4	3	2	1
2d Sed	200	600	1200	2200	3850	5500
2d Sup Sed	200	600	1200	2200	3850	5500
Conv	350	875	1700	4250	5900	8500

NOTE: Add 10 percent for sunroof.

Karmann Ghia

	6	5	4	3	2	1
Cpe	200	650	1250	2400	4200	6000
Conv	450	900	1900	4500	6300	9000

Type 3, Square Back or 411

	6	5	4	3	2	1
2d Sed	125	250	750	1150	2400	3400
2d Sed Type 3	125	250	750	1150	2400	3400
2d Sed 411	125	250	750	1150	2450	3500
4d Sed AT 411	125	250	750	1150	2450	3500
3d Wag 411	125	250	750	1150	2450	3500

NOTE: Add 10 percent for sunroof.

1973
Beetle - (46 hp)

	6	5	4	3	2	1
2d Sed	200	550	1150	2000	3600	5200
2d Sup Sed	200	550	1150	2000	3600	5200
Conv	200	550	1150	2000	3600	5200
Karmann Ghia						
Cpe	200	650	1250	2400	4200	6000
Conv	450	900	1900	4500	6300	9000
Type 3, Square Back or 412						
2d Sed SqBk	125	250	750	1150	2400	3400
2d Sed Type 3	125	250	750	1150	2400	3400
2d Sed 412	125	250	750	1150	2450	3500
4d Sed 412	125	250	750	1150	2450	3500
3d Sed 412	125	250	750	1150	2450	3500
Thing Conv	200	500	1100	1850	3350	4900

1974
Beetle

	6	5	4	3	2	1
2d Sed	200	500	1100	1900	3500	5000
2d Sup Sed	200	500	1100	1900	3500	5000
2d Sun Bug Sed	200	550	1150	2000	3600	5200
Conv	350	825	1600	4000	5600	8000
Karmann Ghia						
Cpe	200	650	1250	2400	4200	6000
Conv	450	900	1900	4500	6300	9000
Thing						
Conv	200	600	1200	2200	3850	5500
Dasher						
2d Sed	125	200	600	1100	2250	3200
4d Sed	125	250	750	1150	2400	3400
4d Wag	150	300	900	1250	2600	3700
412						
2d Sed	125	200	600	1100	2250	3200
4d Sed	125	200	600	1100	2250	3200
3d Sed	125	200	600	1100	2250	3200

1975
Beetle

	6	5	4	3	2	1
2d Sed	200	500	1100	1900	3500	5000
2d Sup Sed	200	500	1100	1900	3500	5000
Conv	350	825	1600	4000	5600	8000
Rabbit (FWD)						
2d Cus Sed	125	200	600	1100	2200	3100
4d Cus Sed	125	200	600	1100	2250	3200
NOTE: Add 5 percent for DeLuxe.						
Dasher						
2d Sed	125	200	600	1100	2200	3100
4d Sed	125	200	600	1100	2300	3300
HBk	125	250	750	1150	2400	3400
4d Wag	125	250	750	1150	2500	3600
Scirocco (FWD)						
Cpe	150	400	1000	1600	3100	4400

1976
Beetle

	6	5	4	3	2	1
2d Sed	200	500	1100	1900	3500	5000
Conv	350	825	1600	4000	5600	8000
Rabbit (FWD)						
2d Sed	125	200	600	1100	2200	3100
2d Cus Sed	125	200	600	1100	2250	3200
4d Cus Sed	125	200	600	1100	2250	3200
NOTE: Add 10 percent for DeLuxe.						
Dasher						
2d Sed	125	200	600	1100	2250	3200
4d Sed	125	250	750	1150	2400	3400
4d Sta Wag	150	300	900	1250	2600	3700
Scirocco (FWD)						
Cpe	150	450	1050	1800	3300	4800

1977
Beetle

	6	5	4	3	2	1
2d Sed	200	500	1100	1900	3500	5000
Conv	350	825	1600	4000	5600	8000
Rabbit (FWD)						
2d Sed	125	200	600	1100	2200	3100
2d Cus Sed	125	200	600	1100	2250	3200
4d Cus Sed	125	200	600	1100	2250	3200
NOTE: Add 10 percent for DeLuxe.						
Dasher						
2d Sed	125	200	600	1100	2250	3200
4d Sed	125	250	750	1150	2400	3400
4d Sta Wag	150	300	900	1250	2600	3700
Scirocco (FWD)						
Cpe	200	500	1100	1850	3350	4900

1978
Beetle

	6	5	4	3	2	1
2d Conv	400	1200	2000	4000	7000	10,000
Rabbit (FWD)						
2d Sed	100	175	525	1050	2100	3000
2d Cus Sed	125	200	600	1100	2200	3100
4d Cus Sed	125	200	600	1100	2200	3100
2d DeL Sed	125	200	600	1100	2250	3200
4d DeL Sed	125	200	600	1100	2250	3200
Dasher						
2d	125	250	750	1150	2450	3500
4d	125	250	750	1150	2450	3500
Dasher						
4d Sta Wag	125	250	750	1150	2500	3600
Scirocco (FWD)						
2d Cpe	150	350	950	1350	2800	4000

1979
Beetle

	6	5	4	3	2	1
2d Conv	400	1200	2000	4000	7000	10,000
Rabbit (FWD)						
2d Sed	100	175	525	1050	2100	3000
2d Cus Sed	125	200	600	1100	2200	3100
4d Cus Sed	125	200	600	1100	2200	3100
2d DeL Sed	125	200	600	1100	2250	3200
4d DeL Sed	125	200	600	1100	2250	3200
Dasher						
2d HBk	125	250	750	1150	2450	3500
4d HBk	125	250	750	1150	2450	3500
4d Sta Wag	125	250	750	1150	2500	3600
Scirocco (FWD)						
2d Cpe	150	350	950	1350	2800	4000

1980
Rabbit (FWD)

	6	5	4	3	2	1
2d Conv	350	700	1350	2700	4500	6400
2d Cus Sed	100	175	525	1050	2100	3000
4d Cus Sed	100	175	525	1050	2100	3000
2d DeL Sed	125	200	600	1100	2200	3100
4d DeL Sed	125	200	600	1100	2200	3100
Jetta (FWD)						
2d	125	250	750	1150	2400	3400
4d	125	250	750	1150	2400	3400
Dasher						
2d	125	200	600	1100	2300	3300
4d	125	200	600	1100	2300	3300
4d Sta Wag	125	250	750	1150	2400	3400
Scirocco (FWD)						
2d Cpe	125	250	750	1150	2500	3600
2d Cpe S	150	300	900	1250	2650	3800

1981
Rabbit (FWD)

	6	5	4	3	2	1
2d Conv	200	675	1300	2600	4400	6300
2d	100	175	525	1050	2050	2900
2d L	100	175	525	1050	2100	3000
4d L	100	175	525	1050	2100	3000
2d LS	125	200	600	1100	2200	3100
4d LS	125	200	600	1100	2200	3100
2d S	125	200	600	1100	2250	3200
Jetta (FWD)						
2d	125	250	750	1150	2400	3400
4d	125	250	750	1150	2400	3400
Dasher						
4d	125	200	600	1100	2250	3200
Scirocco (FWD)						
2d Cpe	125	250	750	1150	2500	3600
2d S Cpe	150	300	900	1250	2600	3700

1982
Rabbit (FWD)

	6	5	4	3	2	1
2d Conv	200	675	1300	2500	4300	6100
2d	100	175	525	1050	2050	2900
2d L	100	175	525	1050	2100	3000
4d L	100	175	525	1050	2100	3000
2d LS	125	200	600	1100	2200	3100
4d LS	125	200	600	1100	2200	3100
2d S	125	200	600	1100	2250	3200
Jetta (FWD)						
2d	125	200	600	1100	2300	3300
4d	125	200	600	1100	2300	3300
Scirocco (FWD)						
2d Cpe	150	300	900	1250	2600	3700
Quantum (FWD)						
2d Cpe	150	350	950	1350	2800	4000
4d	150	350	950	1350	2800	4000
4d Sta Wag	150	350	950	1450	2900	4100

1983
Rabbit (FWD)

	6	5	4	3	2	1
2d Conv	200	675	1300	2500	4350	6200
2d L	100	175	525	1050	1950	2800
4d L	100	175	525	1050	1950	2800
2d LS	100	175	525	1050	2050	2900
4d LS	100	175	525	1050	2050	2900
2d GL	100	175	525	1050	2100	3000
4d GL	100	175	525	1050	2100	3000
2d GTi	125	250	750	1150	2450	3500
Jetta (FWD)						
2d	125	250	750	1150	2400	3400
4d	125	250	750	1150	2400	3400
Scirocco (FWD)						
2d Cpe	150	350	950	1450	2900	4100
Quantum (FWD)						
2d Cpe	150	350	950	1450	2900	4100
4d	150	350	950	1450	2900	4100
4d Sta Wag	150	350	950	1450	3000	4200

1984
Rabbit (FWD)

	6	5	4	3	2	1
2d Conv	350	725	1400	3100	4800	6800
2d L HBk	100	175	525	1050	2100	3000
4d L HBk	125	200	600	1100	2200	3100
4d GL HBk	125	250	750	1150	2450	3500
2d GTi HBk	150	350	950	1350	2800	4000
Jetta (FWD)						
2d Sed	150	300	900	1250	2650	3800
4d Sed	150	300	900	1350	2700	3900
4d GL Sed	150	350	950	1350	2800	4000
4d GLi Sed	150	350	950	1450	3000	4200
Scirocco (FWD)						
2d Cpe	150	350	950	1350	2800	4000
Quantum (FWD)						
4d GL Sed	150	300	900	1250	2650	3800
4d GL Sta Wag	150	300	900	1250	2600	3700

1985
Cabriolet (FWD)

	6	5	4	3	2	1
2d Conv	350	825	1600	4000	5600	8000
Golf (FWD)						
2d HBk	150	350	950	1350	2800	4000
4d HBk	150	350	950	1450	3000	4200
2d GTi HBk	200	600	1200	2200	3850	5500
Jetta (FWD)						
2d Sed	150	400	1000	1650	3150	4500
4d Sed	150	450	1050	1750	3250	4700
4d GL Sed	200	500	1100	1850	3350	4900
4d GLi Sed	200	600	1200	2200	3850	5500
Scirocco (FWD)						
2d Cpe	200	650	1250	2400	4200	6000
2d Cpe (16V)	350	750	1450	3300	4900	7000
Quantum (FWD)						
4d GL Sed	350	700	1350	2800	4550	6500
4d Sta Wag	200	675	1300	2500	4350	6200
4d Sta Wag (4WD)	350	750	1450	3300	4900	7000

1986
Cabriolet (FWD)

	6	5	4	3	2	1
2d Conv	350	875	1700	4250	5900	8500
Golf (FWD)						
2d HBk	150	400	1000	1650	3150	4500
4d HBk	150	450	1050	1750	3250	4700
2d GTi HBk	200	650	1250	2400	4200	6000

Jetta (FWD)

	6	5	4	3	2	1
2d Sed	200	500	1100	1900	3500	5000
4d Sed	200	500	1100	1950	3600	5100
4d GL Sed	200	600	1200	2200	3850	5500
4d GLi Sed	350	700	1350	2800	4550	6500
Scirocco (FWD)						
2d Cpe	200	675	1300	2500	4350	6200
2d Cpe (16V)	350	750	1450	3300	4900	7000
Quantum (FWD)						
4d GL Sed	350	700	1350	2800	4550	6500
4d Sta Wag	200	650	1250	2400	4200	6000
4d Sta Wag (4WD)	350	700	1350	2900	4600	6600

1987
Fox (FWD)

	6	5	4	3	2	1
2d Sed	150	400	1000	1650	3150	4500
4d GL Sed	200	500	1100	1900	3500	5000
2d GL Sta Wag	200	500	1100	1900	3500	5000
Cabriolet (4WD)						
2d Conv	400	1200	2000	4000	7000	10,000
Golf (FWD)						
2d GL HBk	200	600	1200	2200	3850	5500
4d HBk	200	600	1200	2300	4000	5700
2d GT HBk	350	700	1350	2800	4550	6500
4d GT HBk	350	725	1400	3000	4700	6700
2d GTi HBk	350	750	1450	3300	4900	7000
2d GTi HBk (16V)	350	825	1600	4000	5600	8000
Jetta (FWD)						
2d Sed	350	700	1350	2800	4550	6500
4d Sed	350	700	1350	2900	4600	6600
4d GL Sed	350	750	1450	3300	4900	7000
4d GLi Sed	350	800	1550	3900	5450	7800
4d GLi Sed (16V)	350	875	1700	4250	5900	8500
Scirocco (FWD)						
2d Cpe	350	825	1600	4000	5600	8000
2d Cpe (16V)	450	900	1900	4500	6300	9000
Quantum (FWD)						
4d GL Sed	350	875	1700	4250	5900	8500
4d Sta Wag	350	825	1600	4000	5600	8000
4d Sta Wag (4WD)	350	875	1700	4300	6000	8600

1988
Fox (FWD)

	6	5	4	3	2	1
2d Sed	200	600	1200	2200	3850	5500
4d GL Sed	200	650	1250	2400	4200	6000
2d GL Sta Wag	200	675	1300	2500	4350	6200
Cabriolet (FWD)						
2d Conv	500	1550	2600	5200	9100	13,000
Golf (FWD)						
2d HBk	350	700	1350	2800	4550	6500
2d GL HBk	350	750	1450	3300	4900	7000
4d GL HBk	350	750	1450	3400	5000	7100
2d GTi HBk (16V)	400	1300	2200	4400	7700	11,000
Jetta (FWD)						
2d Sed	450	900	1900	4500	6300	9000
4d Sed	450	950	2100	4750	6650	9500
4d GL Sed	400	1300	2200	4400	7700	11,000
4d Carat Sed	450	1450	2400	4800	8400	12,000
4d GLi Sed (16V)	450	1500	2500	5000	8800	12,500

1989
Fox (FWD)

	6	5	4	3	2	1
2d Sed	350	750	1450	3300	4900	7000
2d GL Sed	350	775	1500	3750	5250	7500
4d GL Sed	350	800	1550	3850	5400	7700
4d GL Sta Wag	350	800	1550	3850	5400	7700
2d GLS Sed	350	800	1550	3900	5450	7800
4d GLS Sed	350	825	1600	4050	5650	8100
Cabriolet (FWD)						
2d Conv	550	1800	3000	6000	10,500	15,000
Golf (FWD)						
2d HBk	350	825	1600	4000	5600	8000
2d GL HBk	350	875	1700	4250	5900	8500
4d GL HBk	350	875	1700	4300	6000	8600
2d GTi HBk (16V)	450	1450	2400	4800	8400	12,000
Jetta (FWD)						
2d Sed	400	1250	2100	4200	7400	10,500
4d Sed	400	1300	2200	4400	7700	11,000
4d GL Sed	500	1550	2600	5200	9100	13,000
4d Carat Sed	550	1700	2800	5600	9800	14,000
4d GLi Sed (16V)	550	1750	2900	5800	10,200	14,500

VOLVO

1944-1950
PV444 - (4-cyl) - (102.4" wb) - (1414cc)

		5	4	3	2	1
2d Sed	350	750	1450	3500	5050	7200

1951
PV444 - (4-cyl) - (102.4" wb) - (1414cc)

		5	4	3	2	1
2d Sed	350	750	1450	3300	4900	7000

1952
PV444 - (4-cyl) - (104.4" wb) - (1414cc)

		5	4	3	2	1
2d Sed	350	750	1450	3300	4900	7000

1953
PV444 - (4-cyl) - (102.4" wb) - (1414cc)

		5	4	3	2	1
2d Sed	350	750	1450	3300	4900	7000

1954
(4-cyl) - (102.4" wb) - (1414cc)

		5	4	3	2	1
PV444 2d Sed	350	750	1450	3300	4900	7000
PV445 2d Sta Wag	400	1200	2000	4000	7000	10,000

1955
(4-cyl) - (102.4" wb) - (1414cc)

		5	4	3	2	1
PV444 2d Sed	350	750	1450	3300	4900	7000
PV445 2d Sta Wag	400	1200	2000	4000	7000	10,000

1956
(4-cyl) - (102.4" wb) - (1414cc)

		5	4	3	2	1
PV444 2d Sed	350	750	1450	3300	4900	7000
PV445 2d Sta Wag	400	1200	2000	4000	7000	10,000

1957
(4-cyl) - (102.4" wb) - (1414cc)

		5	4	3	2	1
PV444 2d Sed	350	750	1450	3300	4900	7000
PV445 2d Sta Wag	400	1200	2000	4000	7000	10,000

(4-cyl) - (104.4" wb) - (1583cc)
(4-cyl) - (94.5" wb) - (1414cc)

		5	4	3	2	1
P1900 Conv	550	1800	3000	6000	10,500	15,000

1958
(4-cyl) - (102.4" wb) - (1583cc)

	6	5	4	3	2	1
PV544 2d Sed	350	750	1450	3300	4900	7000
PV445 2d Sta Wag	400	1200	2000	4000	7000	10,000

1959
(4-cyl) - (102.4" wb) - (1583cc)

	6	5	4	3	2	1
PV544 2d Sed	350	775	1500	3750	5250	7500
PV445 2d Sta Wag	400	1200	2000	4000	7000	10,000
122S 4d Sed	200	500	1100	1900	3500	5000

1960
(4-cyl) - (102.4" wb) - (1583cc)

	6	5	4	3	2	1
PV544 2d Sed	350	750	1450	3300	4900	7000
PV445 2d Sta Wag	400	1200	2000	4000	7000	10,000
122S 4d Sed	150	400	1000	1650	3150	4500

1961
(4-cyl) - (102.4" wb) - (1583cc)

	6	5	4	3	2	1
PV544 2d Sed	350	750	1450	3300	4900	7000
P210 2d Sta Wag	400	1200	2000	4000	7000	10,000
122S 4d Sed	150	400	1000	1650	3150	4500
P1800 - (4-cyl) - (96.5" wb) - (1778cc)						
Cpe	450	900	1900	4500	6300	9000

1962
P210 - (4-cyl) - (102.4" wb) - (1583cc)

	6	5	4	3	2	1
2d Sta Wag	400	1200	2000	4000	7000	10,000
PV544 - (4-cyl) - (102.4" wb) - (1778cc)						
2d Sed	350	750	1450	3300	4900	7000
122S - (4-cyl) - (102.4" wb) - (1778cc)						
2d Sed	150	400	1000	1550	3050	4300
4d Sed	150	350	950	1350	2800	4000
4d Sta Wag	150	450	1050	1750	3250	4700
P1800 - (4-cyl) - (96.5" wb) - (1778cc)						
Cpe	450	900	1900	4500	6300	9000

1963
(4-cyl) - (102.4" wb) - (1778cc)

	6	5	4	3	2	1
PV544 2d Sed	350	750	1450	3300	4900	7000
210 2d Sta Wag	450	900	1900	4500	6300	9000
P122S - (4-cyl) - (102.4" wb) - (1778cc)						
2d Sed	150	350	950	1450	2900	4100
4d Sed	150	300	900	1250	2600	3700
4d Sta Wag	150	450	1050	1700	3200	4600
1800S - (4-cyl) - (96.5" wb) - (1778cc)						
Cpe	450	900	1900	4500	6300	9000

1964
(4-cyl) - (102.4" wb) - (1778cc)

	6	5	4	3	2	1
PV544 2d Sed	350	750	1450	3300	4900	7000
P210 2d Sta Wag	400	1200	2000	4000	7000	10,000
122S - (4-cyl) - (102.4" wb) - (1778cc)						
2d Sed	150	350	950	1350	2800	4000
4d Sed	150	300	900	1250	2600	3700
4d Sta Wag	150	400	1000	1650	3150	4500
1800S - (4-cyl) - (96.5" wb) - (1778cc)						
Cpe	450	900	1900	4500	6300	9000

1965
(4-cyl) - (102.4" wb) - (1778cc)

	6	5	4	3	2	1
PV544 2d Sed	350	750	1450	3300	4900	7000
P210 Sta Wag	400	1200	2000	4000	7000	10,000
122S - (4-cyl) - (102.4" wb) - (1778cc)						
2d Sed	150	350	950	1450	3000	4200
4d Sed	150	300	900	1250	2600	3700
4d Sta Wag	150	450	1050	1700	3200	4600
1800S - (4-cyl) - (96.5" wb) - (1778cc)						
Cpe	450	900	1900	4500	6300	9000

1966
210S - (4-cyl) - (102.4" wb) - (1778cc)

	6	5	4	3	2	1
2d Sta Wag	400	1200	2000	4000	7000	10,000
122S - (4-cyl) - (102.4" wb) - (1778cc)						
2d Sed	150	350	950	1350	2800	4000
4d Sed	150	300	900	1250	2600	3700
4d Sta Wag	150	400	1000	1650	3150	4500
1800S - (4-cyl) - (96.5" wb) - (1778cc)						
Cpe	450	900	1900	4500	6300	9000

1967
P210 - (4-cyl) - (102.4" wb) - (1778cc)

	6	5	4	3	2	1
2d Sta Wag	400	1200	2000	4000	7000	10,000
122S - (4-cyl) - (102.4" wb) - (1778cc)						
2d Sed	150	350	950	1350	2800	4000
4d Sed	125	250	750	1150	2450	3500
4d Sta Wag	150	400	1000	1650	3150	4500
(4-cyl) - (96.5" wb) - (1778cc)						
123 GT	200	650	1250	2400	4200	6000
1800S Cpe	450	900	1900	4500	6300	9000

1968
122S - (4-cyl) - (102.4" wb) - (1778cc)

	6	5	4	3	2	1
2d Sed	150	350	950	1350	2800	4000
4d Sta Wag	150	400	1000	1650	3150	4500
(4-cyl) - (102.4" wb) - (1778cc)						
123 GT	200	650	1250	2400	4200	6000
142S 2d Sed	150	300	900	1250	2600	3700
144 4d Sed	150	300	900	1250	2600	3700
1800S - (4-cyl) - (96.5" wb) - (1778cc)						
Cpe	450	900	1900	4500	6300	9000

1969
(4-cyl) - (102.4" wb) - (1986cc)

	6	5	4	3	2	1
142S 2d Sed	150	300	900	1250	2600	3700
144S 4d Sed	150	300	900	1250	2600	3700
145S 4d Sta Wag	150	300	900	1250	2650	3800
1800S - (4-cyl) - (96.5" wb) - (1986cc)						
Cpe	450	900	1900	4500	6300	9000

1970
(4-cyl) - (102.4" wb) - (1986cc)

	6	5	4	3	2	1
142 2d Sed	150	300	900	1350	2700	3900
144 4d Sed	150	300	900	1350	2700	3900
145 4d Sta Wag	150	350	950	1450	2900	4100
1800E - (4-cyl) - (96.5" wb) - (1986cc)						
Cpe	450	950	2100	4750	6650	9500
164 - (6-cyl) - (106.3" wb) - (2978cc)						
4d Sed	150	300	900	1250	2650	3800

1971
(4-cyl) - (103.2" wb) - (1986cc)

	6	5	4	3	2	1
142 2d Sed	150	350	950	1350	2800	4000
144 4d Sed	150	350	950	1350	2800	4000
145 4d Sta Wag	150	350	950	1450	3000	4200
1800E - (4-cyl) - (96.5" wb) - (1986cc)						
Cpe	400	1200	2000	4000	7000	10,000

164 - (6-cyl) - (107" wb) - (2978cc)	6	5	4	3	2	1
4d Sed	150	300	900	1350	2700	3900
1972						
(4-cyl) - (103.2" wb) - (1986cc)						
142 2d Sed	150	350	950	1450	3000	4200
144 4d Sed	150	350	950	1450	3000	4200
145 4d Sta Wag	150	400	1000	1650	3150	4500
(4-cyl) - (96.5" wb) - (1986cc)						
1800E Cpe	400	1200	2000	4000	7000	10,000
1800ES Spt Wag	400	1250	2100	4200	7400	10,500
164 - (6-cyl) - (107" wb) - (2978cc)						
4d Sed	150	350	950	1450	2900	4100
1973						
(4-cyl) - (103.2" wb) - (1986cc)						
142 2d Sed	150	400	1000	1650	3150	4500
144 4d Sed	150	400	1000	1650	3150	4500
145 4d Sta Wag	150	450	1050	1750	3250	4700
1800ES - (4-cyl) - (96.5" wb) - (1986cc)						
Spt Wag	400	1300	2200	4400	7700	11,000
164E - (6-cyl) - (107" wb) - (2978cc)						
4d Sed	150	400	1000	1650	3150	4500
1974						
(4-cyl) - (103.2" wb) - (1986cc)						
142 2d Sed	150	450	1050	1700	3200	4600
144 4d Sed	150	450	1050	1700	3200	4600
145 4d Sta Wag	150	450	1050	1800	3300	4800
142GL 2d Sed	150	450	1050	1750	3250	4700
144GL 4d Sed	150	450	1050	1750	3250	4700
164E - (6-cyl) - (107" wb) - (2978cc)						
4d Sed	150	450	1050	1750	3250	4700
1975						
(4-cyl) - (103.9" wb) - (2127cc)						
242 2d Sed	150	450	1050	1750	3250	4700
244 4d Sed	150	450	1050	1750	3250	4700
245 4d Sta Wag	200	500	1100	1900	3500	5000
242GL 2d Sed	200	500	1100	1850	3350	4900
244GL 4d Sed	200	500	1100	1850	3350	4900
164 - (6-cyl) - (107" wb) - (2978cc)						
4d Sed	200	500	1100	1850	3350	4900
1976						
(4-cyl) - (103.9" wb) - (2127cc)						
242 2d Sed	200	500	1100	1900	3500	5000
244 4d Sed	200	500	1100	1900	3500	5000
245 4d Sta Wag	200	550	1150	2100	3700	5300
(6-cyl) - (103.9" wb) - (2664cc)						
262GL 2d Sed	200	550	1150	2100	3700	5300
264 4d Sed	200	550	1150	2100	3700	5300
265 4d Sta Wag	200	600	1200	2200	3900	5600
264GL 4d Sed	200	600	1200	2200	3850	5500
1977						
(4-cyl) - (103.9" wb) - (2127cc)						
242 2d Sed	200	600	1200	2200	3850	5500
244 4d Sed	200	600	1200	2200	3850	5500
245 4d Sta Wag	200	650	1250	2400	4150	5900
(6-cyl) - (103.9" wb) - (2664cc)						
264GL 4d Sed	200	650	1200	2300	4100	5800
265GL 4d Sta Wag	200	650	1250	2400	4200	6000
262C 2d Cpe	400	1200	2000	4000	7000	10,000
1978						
244 4d	150	450	1050	1750	3250	4700
242GT 2d	150	450	1050	1800	3300	4800
242 2d	200	500	1100	1850	3350	4900
245 4d Sta Wag	200	500	1100	1900	3500	5000
264GL 4d	200	500	1100	1850	3350	4900
265GL 4d Sta Wag	200	500	1100	1950	3600	5100
262C 2d	400	1200	2000	4000	7000	10,000
1979						
242DL 2d	150	450	1050	1800	3300	4800
242GT 2d	200	500	1100	1850	3350	4900
244DL 4d	200	500	1100	1850	3350	4900
245DL 4d Sta Wag	200	500	1100	1900	3500	5000
245GL 4d	200	500	1100	1900	3500	5000
265GL 4d Sta Wag	200	500	1100	1950	3600	5100
262C 2d Cpe	400	1250	2100	4200	7400	10,500
1980						
DL						
2d	150	350	950	1450	3000	4200
GT 2d	150	400	1000	1600	3100	4400
4d	150	400	1000	1600	3100	4400
4d Sta Wag	150	450	1050	1750	3250	4700
GL						
4d	150	450	1050	1750	3250	4700
GLE						
4d	150	450	1050	1800	3300	4800
4d Sta Wag	200	500	1100	1850	3350	4900
2d Cpe Bertone	400	1200	2000	4000	7100	10,100
1981						
DL						
2d	150	350	950	1450	3000	4200
4d	150	400	1000	1600	3100	4400
4d Sta Wag	150	450	1050	1750	3250	4700
GL						
2d	150	400	1000	1650	3150	4500
4d	150	400	1000	1650	3150	4500
GLT						
2d	150	400	1000	1650	3150	4500
4d Sta Wag	150	450	1050	1800	3300	4800
2d (Turbo)	200	500	1100	1850	3350	4900
4d (Turbo)	200	500	1100	1850	3350	4900
GLE						
4d	200	500	1100	1900	3500	5000
Bertone						
2d Cpe	400	1250	2100	4200	7400	10,500
1982						
DL						
2d	150	350	950	1450	3000	4200
4d	150	350	950	1450	3000	4200
4d Sta Wag	150	400	1000	1550	3050	4300
GL						
4d	150	400	1000	1550	3050	4300
4d Sta Wag	150	400	1000	1600	3100	4400
GLT						
2d	150	400	1000	1550	3050	4300
2d (Turbo)	150	450	1050	1700	3200	4600
4d (Turbo)	150	450	1050	1700	3200	4600
4d Sta Wag (Turbo)	150	450	1050	1750	3250	4700

GLE	6	5	4	3	2	1
4d	150	450	1050	1750	3250	4700
1983						
DL						
2d	150	350	950	1450	3000	4200
4d	150	350	950	1450	3000	4200
4d Sta Wag	150	400	1000	1550	3050	4300
GL						
4d	150	400	1000	1550	3050	4300
4d Sta Wag	150	400	1000	1600	3100	4400
GLT (Turbo)						
2d	150	400	1000	1550	3050	4300
4d	150	450	1050	1700	3200	4600
4d Sta Wag	150	450	1050	1750	3250	4700
760 GLE						
4d	150	450	1050	1750	3250	4700
4d (Turbo Diesel)	150	450	1050	1750	3250	4700
1984						
DL						
2d Sed	200	500	1100	1900	3500	5000
4d Sed	200	650	1250	2400	4200	6000
4d Sta Wag	350	750	1450	3300	4900	7000
GL						
4d Sed	350	775	1500	3750	5250	7500
4d Sta Wag	350	825	1600	4000	5600	8000
GLT (Turbo)						
2d Sed	450	900	1900	4500	6300	9000
4d Sed	450	950	2100	4750	6650	9500
4d Sta Wag	400	1200	2000	4000	7000	10,000
760 GLE						
4d Sed	400	1300	2200	4400	7700	11,000
4d Sed (Turbo)	450	1400	2300	4600	8100	11,500
4d Sed (Turbo Diesel)	400	1200	2000	4000	7000	10,000
1985						
DL						
4d Sed	350	875	1700	4250	5900	8500
4d Sta Wag	450	950	2100	4750	6650	9500
GL						
4d Sed	450	950	2100	4750	6650	9500
4d Sta Wag	400	1250	2100	4200	7400	10,500
GLT (Turbo)						
4d Sed	450	1450	2400	4800	8400	12,000
4d Sta Wag	500	1550	2600	5200	9100	13,000
740						
4d Sed	400	1300	2200	4400	7700	11,000
4d Sta Wag	450	1450	2400	4800	8400	12,000
4d Sed (Turbo Diesel)	400	1200	2000	4000	7000	10,000
4d Sta Wag (Turbo Diesel)	400	1300	2200	4400	7700	11,000
4d Sed (Turbo)	500	1550	2600	5200	9100	13,000
4d Sta Wag (Turbo)	550	1700	2800	5600	9800	14,000
760 GLE						
4d Sed	550	1700	2800	5600	9800	14,000
4d Sed (Turbo)	600	1900	3200	6400	11,200	16,000
4d Sta Wag (Turbo)	650	2050	3400	6800	11,900	17,000
760 (Turbo Diesel)						
4d Sed	400	1300	2200	4400	7700	11,000
4d Sta Wag	450	1450	2400	4800	8400	12,000
1986						
DL						
4d Sed	400	1200	2000	4000	7000	10,000
4d Sta Wag	400	1300	2200	4400	7700	11,000
GL						
4d Sed	400	1300	2200	4400	7700	11,000
4d Sta Wag	450	1450	2400	4800	8400	12,000
740						
4d Sed	500	1550	2600	5200	9100	13,000
4d Sta Wag	550	1700	2800	5600	9800	14,000
4d Sed (Turbo Diesel)	400	1300	2200	4400	7700	11,000
4d Sta Wag (Turbo Diesel)	450	1450	2400	4800	8400	12,000
4d Sed (Turbo)	550	1700	2800	5600	9800	14,000
4d Sta Wag (Turbo)	550	1800	3000	6000	10,500	15,000
760 GLE						
4d Sed	550	1800	3000	6000	10,500	15,000
4d Sed (Turbo)	600	1900	3200	6400	11,200	16,000
760						
4d Sta Wag (Turbo)	650	2050	3400	6800	11,900	17,000
1987						
DL						
4d Sed	450	1450	2400	4800	8400	12,000
4d Sta Wag	500	1550	2600	5200	9100	13,000
GL						
4d Sed	500	1550	2600	5200	9100	13,000
4d Sta Wag	550	1700	2800	5600	9800	14,000
740 GLE						
4d Sed	550	1700	2800	5600	9800	14,000
4d Sta Wag	550	1800	3000	6000	10,500	15,000
4d Sed (Turbo)	600	1900	3200	6400	11,200	16,000
4d Sta Wag (Turbo)	650	2050	3400	6800	11,900	17,000
760 GLE						
4d Sed (Turbo)	700	2150	3600	7200	12,600	18,000
4d Sta Wag (Turbo)	700	2300	3800	7600	13,300	19,000
780 GLE						
2d Cpe	900	2900	4800	9600	16,800	24,000
1988						
DL						
4d Sed	550	1700	2800	5600	9800	14,000
4d Sta Wag	550	1800	3000	6000	10,500	15,000
GL						
4d Sed	600	1900	3200	6400	11,200	16,000
4d Sta Wag	650	2050	3400	6800	11,900	17,000
740 GLE						
4d Sed	650	2050	3400	6800	11,900	17,000
4d Sta Wag	700	2150	3600	7200	12,600	18,000
4d Sed (Turbo)	850	2650	4400	8800	15,400	22,000
4d Sta Wag (Turbo)	850	2750	4600	9200	16,100	23,000
760 GLE						
4d Sed	900	2900	4800	9600	16,800	24,000
4d Sed (Turbo)	950	3000	5000	10,000	17,500	25,000
4d Sta Wag (Turbo)	1000	3100	5200	10,400	18,200	26,000
780 GLE						
2d Cpe	1050	3350	5600	11,200	19,600	28,000
1989						
DL						
4d Sed	600	1900	3200	6400	11,200	16,000
4d Sta Wag	650	2050	3400	6800	11,900	17,000

GL	6	5	4	3	2	1
4d Sed	650	2050	3400	6800	11,900	17,000
4d Sta Wag	700	2150	3600	7200	12,600	18,000
740 GL						
4d	700	2300	3800	7600	13,300	19,000
4d Sta Wag	750	2400	4000	8000	14,000	20,000
740 GLE						
4d Sed (16V)	850	2650	4400	8800	15,400	22,000
4d Sta Wag (16V)	850	2750	4600	9200	16,100	23,000
740 (Turbo)						
4d Sed	900	2900	4800	9600	16,800	24,000
4d Sta Wag	950	3000	5000	10,000	17,500	25,000
760 GLE						
4d Sed	1000	3100	5200	10,400	18,200	26,000
4d Sed (Turbo)	1000	3250	5400	10,800	18,900	27,000
4d Sta Wag (Turbo)	1050	3350	5600	11,200	19,600	28,000

780	6	5	4	3	2	1
2d Cpe	1150	3700	6200	12,400	21,700	31,000
2d Cpe (Turbo)	1300	4200	7000	14,000	24,500	35,000

YUGO

	6	5	4	3	2	1
1986						
2d HBk GV	100	150	450	1000	1750	2500
1987						
2d HBk GV	100	150	450	1000	1750	2500
1988						
2d HBk GV	100	150	450	1000	1750	2500
2d HBk GVL	100	150	450	1000	1800	2600

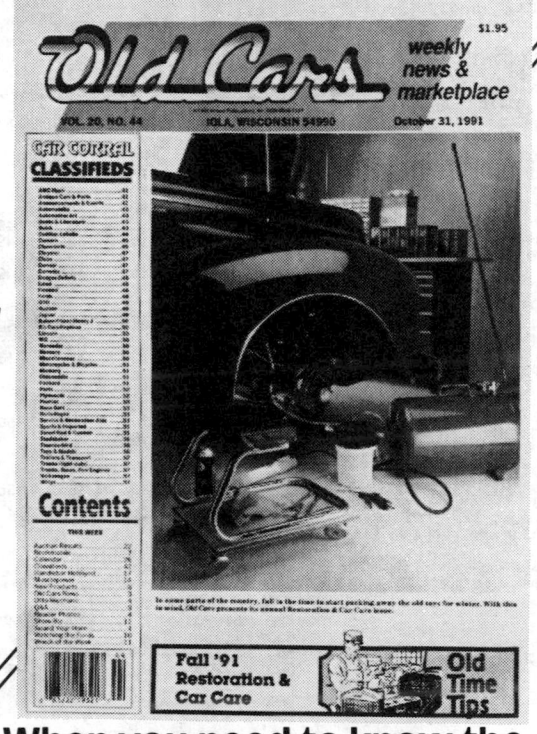
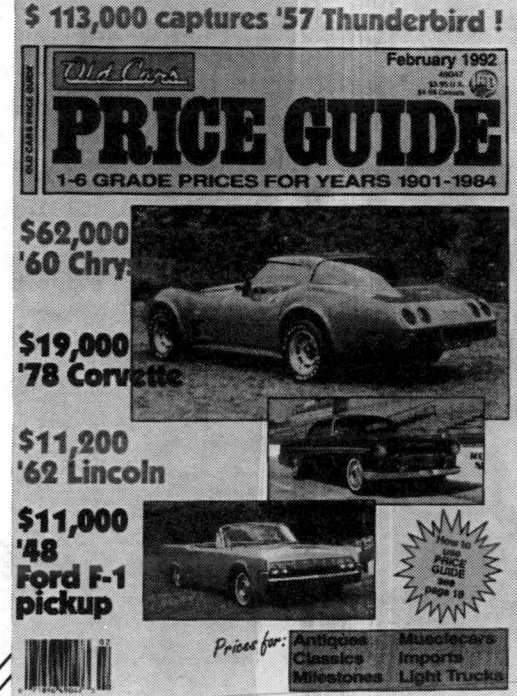